# THE WORLD OF LEARNING
1981-82

# THE WORLD OF LEARNING 1981-82

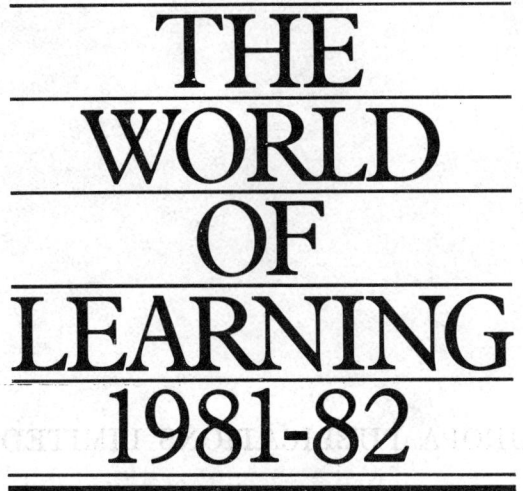

## 32nd Edition

### VOLUME TWO

### ROMANIA–ZIMBABWE

### INDEX

**EUROPA PUBLICATIONS LIMITED**

EUROPA PUBLICATIONS LIMITED 18 BEDFORD SQUARE LONDON WC1B 3JN

© EUROPA **PUBLICATIONS LIMITED** 1981

*All rights reserved*

Library of Congress Catalog Card Number 47-30172

*JAPAN*
Maruzen Co. Ltd., Tokyo

*INDIA*
UBS Publishers' Distributors Pvt. Ltd., P.O.B. 1882, 5 Ansari Road, Daryaganj, Delhi 6

*AUSTRALIA AND NEW ZEALAND*
James Bennett (Collaroy) Pty. Ltd., Collaroy, N.S.W., Australia

**British Library Cataloguing in Publication Data**
The World of Learning 1981-82: thirty-second edition
1. Learned institutions and societies—Directories
060           AS2
ISBN 0-905118-70-7
ISSN 0084-2117

Printed and bound in England by
Staples Printers Rochester Limited
at The Stanhope Press.

# FOREWORD

We have once again tried to ensure that we include the latest possible information concerning entries in THE WORLD OF LEARNING. Every year a folder containing the previous year's proof is sent to each entry; continuous research in the world press and educational journals, as well as contact with official sources all over the world, supplements this method of revision. We welcome information and suggestions from users of the book, concerning either existing entries or possible new material.

We are always grateful to those individuals and organizations who help us to bring our information up to date with their prompt replies. We particularly emphasize the necessity for revised entries to be returned to us without delay, since important material may otherwise be held over until a later edition. Only by maintaining a strict timetable can the regular production of such a large work as THE WORLD OF LEARNING be assured.

In co-operation with IFLA we invite all institutions in the book to indicate by the sign † those of their periodical publications which are available for exchange. We ask readers who are interested in the exchange of publications to communicate directly with the institution concerned, and not with us.

We should like to point out that in the sections on Universities and Colleges our classification usually follows the practice of the country concerned. This in no way implies any official evaluation on our part. We suggest that readers who are interested in the matter of equivalences of institutions, degrees or diplomas, should correspond directly with the institution concerned, or with the national or international bodies set up for this purpose.

November 1981

# CONTENTS
## VOLUME TWO

| | Page | | Page |
|---|---|---|---|
| ROMANIA | 1115 | UNION OF SOVIET SOCIALIST REPUBLICS | 1313 |
| RWANDA | 1141 | UNITED ARAB EMIRATES | 1391 |
| SAUDI ARABIA | 1142 | UNITED KINGDOM | 1392 |
| SENEGAL | 1145 |   Northern Ireland | 1554 |
| SIERRA LEONE | 1148 | UNITED KINGDOM OVERSEAS | 1558 |
| SINGAPORE | 1150 |   Bermuda | 1558 |
| SOLOMON ISLANDS | 1152 |   Gibraltar | 1558 |
| SOMALIA | 1153 |   Hong Kong | 1559 |
| SOUTH AFRICA | 1154 | UNITED STATES OF AMERICA | 1562 |
| SPAIN | 1185 | UNITED STATES OF AMERICA EXTERNAL TERRITORIES | 1936 |
| SRI LANKA | 1224 | UPPER VOLTA | 1937 |
| SUDAN | 1229 | URUGUAY | 1938 |
| SURINAME | 1231 | VATICAN CITY STATE | 1942 |
| SWAZILAND | 1232 | VENEZUELA | 1949 |
| SWEDEN | 1233 | VIET-NAM | 1962 |
| SWITZERLAND | 1253 | WESTERN SAMOA | 1964 |
| SYRIA | 1277 | YEMEN ARAB REPUBLIC | 1965 |
| TAIWAN (*see* China (Taiwan)) | | YEMEN, PEOPLE'S DEMOCRATIC REPUBLIC | 1965 |
| TANZANIA | 1280 | YUGOSLAVIA | 1966 |
| THAILAND | 1283 | ZAIRE | 1995 |
| TOGO | 1292 | ZAMBIA | 1997 |
| TRINIDAD AND TOBAGO | 1293 | ZIMBABWE | 2000 |
| TUNISIA | 1295 | INDEX TO VOLS. I AND II | 2005 |
| TURKEY | 1298 | | |
| UGANDA | 1311 | | |

# ABBREVIATIONS

| | |
|---|---|
| A.A. | Associate in Arts |
| A.A.A.S. | American Association for the Advancement of Science |
| A.A.S.A. | Associate of Australian Society of Accountants |
| A.A.U.Q. | Associate in Accountancy, University of Queensland |
| A.B. | Bachelor of Arts |
| A.B.S.M. | Associate of the Bendigo School of Mines |
| A.C.A. | Associate of the Institute of Chartered Accountants |
| Acad. | Academy; Academician |
| A.C.I.I. | Associate of the Chartered Insurance Institute |
| A.C.I.S. | Associate of the Chartered Institute of Secretaries |
| A.C.L.S. | American Council of Learned Societies |
| A.C.T. | Australian Capital Territory |
| Admin. | Administrative, Administration |
| Agr. de D. | Agrégé de Droit |
| Agr. de M. | Agrégé de Médecine |
| Agr. de Sc. | Agrégé de Science |
| Agr. des L. | Agrégé des Lettres |
| A.I.A. | Associate of the Institute of Actuaries; American Institute of Architects |
| A.I.B. | Associate of the Institute of Bankers |
| A.I.C.E. | Associate of the Institution of Civil Engineers |
| A.I.C.E.A. | Association of Industrial and Commercial Executive Accountants |
| A.I.Ch.E. | American Institute of Chemical Engineers |
| A.I.C.T.A. | Associate of the Imperial College of Tropical Agriculture |
| A.I.I.S. | Associate of the Irish Institute of Secretaries |
| A.I.L. | Associate of the Institute of Linguists |
| A.I.M. | Associate of the Institution of Metallurgists |
| A.I.M.T.A. | Associate of the Institute of Municipal Treasurers and Accountants |
| A.Inst.C.E. | Associate of the Institution of Civil Engineers |
| A.K.C. | Associate of King's College (London) |
| A.L.A. | Associate of the Library Association |
| Ala. | Alabama |
| A.L.S. | Associate of the Linnaean Society |
| A.M. | Master of Arts |
| A.M.A. | Associate of the Museums Association |
| A.M.I.C.E. | Associate Member of the Institution of Civil Engineers |
| A.M.I.E.E. | Associate Member of the Institution of Electrical Engineers |
| A.M.I.E.R.E. | Associate Member of the Institute of Electronic and Radio Engineers |
| A.M.I.Mech.E. | Associate Member of the Institution of Mechanical Engineers |
| A.M.I.Struct.E. | Associate Member of the Institution of Structural Engineers |
| A.M.T.P.I. | Associate of Town Planning Institute |
| A.O. | Order of Australia |
| A.P. | Andhra Pradesh |
| Apdo. | Apartado (Post Office Box) |
| A.R.A. | Associate of the Royal Academy |
| A.R.A.M. | Associate of the Royal Academy of Music |
| A.R.C.A. | Associate of the Royal College of Art |
| A.R.C.M. | Associate of the Royal College of Music |
| A.R.C.O. | Associate of the Royal College of Organists |
| A.R.C.S. | Associate of the Royal College of Science |
| A.R.E. | Associate of the Royal Society of Painter Etchers |
| A.R.I.B.A. | Associate of the Royal Institute of British Architects |
| A.R.I.C.S. | Associate of the Royal Institution of Chartered Surveyors |
| Ariz. | Arizona |
| Ark. | Arkansas |
| A.R.P.S. | Associate of the Royal Photographic Society |
| A.R.S.A. | Associate of the Royal Scottish Academy; Associate of the Royal Society of Arts |
| A.R.W.S. | Associate of the Royal Society of Painters in Water Colours |
| A.S.C.E. | American Society of Civil Engineers |
| A.S.E. | Engineer Associate of The Society of Engineers |
| A.S.M.E. | American Society of Mechanical Engineers |
| Asscn. | Association |
| Assoc. | Associate |
| Asst. | Assistant |
| A.S.T.C. | Associate of the Sydney Technical College |
| Atty. | Attorney |
| A.T.I. | Associate of the Textile Institute |
| Avv. | Avvocato (Italian) |
| B.A. | Bachelor of Arts |
| B.Agr. | Bachelor of Agriculture |
| B.A.(Ed.) | Bachelor of Arts in Education |
| B.A.O. | Bachelor of Obstetrics |
| Bar.-at-Law | Barrister-at-Law |
| B.Arch. | Bachelor of Architecture |
| B.A.S. | Bachelor in Agricultural Science |
| B.A.Sc. | Bachelor of Applied Science |
| B.B.A. | Bachelor of Business Administration |
| B.C.E. | Bachelor of Civil Engineering |
| B.Ch., B.Chir. | Bachelor of Surgery |
| B.Chem.E. | Bachelor of Chemical Engineering |
| B.C.L. | Bachelor of Civil Law; Bachelor of Canon Law |
| B.Com(m). | Bachelor of Commerce |
| B.C.S. (and B.Com.Sc.) | Bachelor of Commercial Sciences |
| B.D. | Bachelor of Divinity |
| B.D.S. | Bachelor of Dental Surgery |
| B.E. | Bachelor of Engineering; Bachelor of Education |
| B.Ec. | Bachelor of Economics |
| B.Ed. | Bachelor of Education |
| B.E.E. | Bachelor of Electrical Engineering |
| B.Eng. | Bachelor of Engineering |
| B.Eng.A. | Bachelor of Agricultural Engineering |
| B.E.Sc. | Bachelor of Engineering Science |
| B.F.A. | Bachelor of Fine Arts |
| B.F(or). | Bachelor of Forestry |
| B.I.D. | Bachelor of Industrial Design |
| B.Lit(t). | Bachelor of Letters |
| B.LL. | Bachelor of Laws |
| B.L.S. | Bachelor of Library Science |
| Blvd. | Boulevard |
| B.M. | Bachelor of Medicine |
| B.M.A. | British Medical Association |

# ABBREVIATIONS

| | | |
|---|---|---|
| B.M.E. | .. | Bachelor of Mining Engineering |
| B.Mus. | .. | Bachelor of Music |
| B.N. | .. | Bachelor of Nursing |
| B.Paed. (or Pd.) | .. | Bachelor of Pedagogy |
| B.P.E. | .. | Bachelor of Physical Education |
| B.Phar. | .. | Baccalauréat en Pharmacie |
| B.Pharm. | .. | Bachelor of Pharmacy |
| B.Phil. | .. | Bachelor of Philosophy |
| Br. | .. | Branch |
| Bro. | .. | Brother |
| B.S. | .. | Bachelor of Science; Bachelor of Surgery |
| B.S.A. | .. | Bachelor of Scientific Agriculture |
| B.Sc. | .. | Bachelor of Science |
| B.Sc.Agr. | .. | Bachelor of Science in Agriculture |
| B.Sc.C.E. | .. | Bachelor of Science in Civil Engineering |
| B.S.C. | .. | Bachelor of Science in Commerce |
| B.Sc.Com. | .. | Bachelor of Commercial Science |
| B.Sc.(Econ.) | .. | Bachelor of Science in Economics |
| B.Sc.(Eng.) | .. | Bachelor of Science in Engineering |
| B.Sc.F. | .. | Bachelor of Science in Forestry |
| B.S. in H.E. | .. | Bachelor of Science in Home Economics |
| B.Sc.(M.E.) | .. | Bachelor of Science in Mechanical Engineering |
| B.Sc.Met. | .. | Bachelor of Science in Metallurgy |
| B.Sc.Pharm. | .. | Bachelor of Science in Pharmacy |
| B.S.D. | .. | Bachelor of Didactic Science; Bachelor of Science in Dentistry |
| Bt. | .. | Baronet |
| B.Theol. | .. | Bachelor of Theology |
| B.V. Sc. | .. | Bachelor of Veterinary Science |
| c. | .. | circa (approximately) |
| C.A. | .. | Chartered Accountant |
| CAE | .. | College of Advanced Education |
| Calif. | .. | California |
| Cantab. | .. | Of Cambridge University |
| C.B. | .. | Companion of the Order of the Bath |
| C.B.E. | .. | Commander of the Order of the British Empire |
| C.C. | .. | Companion of the Order of Canada |
| C.Chem. | .. | Chartered Chemist |
| C.E. | .. | Civil Engineer |
| CEA | .. | Commissariat à l'Energie Atomique |
| C.Eng. | .. | Chartered Engineer |
| C.G.A. | .. | Certified General Accountant |
| C.G.I.A. | .. | City and Guilds Insignia Award |
| C.H. | .. | Companion of Honour |
| Chair. | .. | Chairman |
| Ch.B. | .. | Bachelor of Surgery |
| Ch.M. | .. | Master of Surgery |
| C.I.E. | .. | Companion of the Order of the Indian Empire |
| C.I.E.E. | .. | Companion of the Institution of Electrical Engineers |
| C.J. | .. | Compagnie de Jésus |
| C.M. | .. | Master in Surgery |
| C.M.G. | .. | Companion of the Order of St. Michael and St. George |
| C.N.A.A. | .. | Council for National Academic Awards |
| CNRS | .. | Centre National de la Recherche Scientifique |
| Co. | .. | Company; County |
| Colo. | .. | Colorado |
| Cmdr. | .. | Commander |
| Comm. | .. | Commission |
| Commr. | .. | Commissioner |
| Comp. T.I. | .. | Companion of the Textile Institute |
| Conf. | .. | Conference |
| Conn. | .. | Connecticut |
| Corpn. | .. | Corporation |
| Corresp. | .. | Correspondent, Corresponding |
| C.P.A. | .. | Certified Public Accountant; Chartered Patent Agent |
| C.P.H. | .. | Certificate of Public Health |
| Cr. | .. | Contador |
| C.S.I. | .. | Companion of the Order of the Star of India |
| CSIRO | .. | Commonwealth Scientific and Industrial Research Organization |
| C.S.S.F. | .. | Confédération des Sociétés Scientifiques Françaises |
| C.St.J. | .. | Commander of the Order of St. John of Jerusalem |
| Cttee. | .. | Committee |
| C.V.O. | .. | Commander of the Royal Victorian Order |
| D.Agr. | .. | Doctor of Agriculture |
| D.Arch. | .. | Doctor of Architecture |
| D.B. | .. | Bachelor of Divinity |
| D.B.A. | .. | Doctor of Business Administration |
| D.B.E. | .. | Dame Commander of the Order of the British Empire |
| D.C. | .. | District of Columbia |
| D.C.L. | .. | Doctor of Civil Law |
| D.C.M. | .. | Distinguished Conduct Medal |
| D.Cn.L. | .. | Doctor of Canon Law |
| D.C.S. | .. | Doctor of Commercial Science |
| D.C.T. | .. | Doctor of Christian Theology |
| D.D. | .. | Doctor of Divinity |
| D.D.C. | .. | Doctorat en droit canonique |
| D. de l'U. | .. | Docteur de l'Université |
| D.D.S. | .. | Doctor of Dental Surgery |
| D.Econ. | .. | Doctor of Economics |
| D.Ed. | .. | Doctor of Education |
| Del. | .. | Delegate, delegation; Delaware |
| D. en D. | .. | Docteur en Droit |
| D.Eng. | .. | Doctor of Engineering |
| Dept. | .. | Department |
| D. ès L. | .. | Docteur ès lettres |
| D. ès Sc. | .. | Docteur ès sciences |
| D.F. | .. | Doctor of Forestry; Distrito Federal |
| D.F.A. | .. | Doctor of Fine Arts |
| D.F.C. | .. | Distinguished Flying Cross |
| D.H.L. | .. | Doctor of Hebrew Literature |
| D.Hy. | .. | Doctor of Hygiene |
| Dir. | .. | Director |
| D. Iur. Utr. | | Doctor of both Civil and Canon Law |
| Div. | .. | Division |
| D.L. | .. | Doctor of Laws |
| D.Lett. | .. | Doctorat ès lettres |
| D.Lit(t). | .. | Doctor of Letters; Doctor of Literature |
| D.Litt.S. | .. | Doctor of Sacred Letters |
| D.L.S. | .. | Doctor of Library Science |
| D.M. | .. | Doctor of Medicine |
| D.M.A. | .. | Doctor of Musical Arts |
| D.Math.Sc. | | Doctor of Mathematical Science |
| D.Math.Stats. | | Doctor of Mathematical Statistics |
| D.M.D. | .. | Doctor of Medical Dentistry |
| D.Met. | .. | Doctor of Metallurgy |
| D.Mus. | .. | Doctor of Music |
| D.Oph. | .. | Doctor of Ophthalmology |
| Dott. | .. | Dottore (Italian) |
| Dott.L. | .. | Dottore in Lettere |
| D.Paed. | .. | Doctor of Paediatrics |
| D.Phil. | .. | Doctor of Philosophy |
| D.Phil.Nat. | | Doctor of Natural Philosophy |
| Dr. Ing. | .. | Doctor of Engineering |
| Dr. Jur. | .. | Doctor of Laws |
| Dr. Med. | .. | Doctor of Medicine |
| Dr.Med.Dent. | | Doctor of Dentistry |
| Dr.Med.Vet. | | Doctor of Veterinary Medicine |
| Dr. Oec. | .. | Doctor of Commerce |
| Dr. Phar. | .. | Doctor of Pharmacy |
| Dr.rer.Hort. | | Doctor of Horticulture |
| Dr.rer.Nat. | | Doctor of Natural Science |
| Dr.rer.Pol. | | Doctor of Political Science |
| Dr. Theol. | .. | Doctor of Theology |

x

## ABBREVIATIONS

| | |
|---|---|
| Drs... | Doctorandus (term used in The Netherlands to denote a doctor's degree) |
| D.S.A. | Doctor of Scientific Agriculture |
| D.S.C. | Distinguished Service Cross |
| D.Sc. | Doctor of Science |
| D.Sc.A. | Doctor of Applied Science |
| D.Sc.Agr. | Doctor of Science in Agriculture |
| D.Sc.Pol. | Doctor of Political Sciences |
| D.Soc.Sc. | Doctor of Social Sciences |
| D.S.I.R. | Department of Scientific and Industrial Research |
| D.S.M. | Distinguished Service Medal |
| D.S.O. | Distinguished Service Order |
| D.S.T. | Doctor of Sacred Theology |
| D.S.W. | Doctor of Social Work |
| D.Tech. | Doctor in Technology |
| D.Theol. | Doctor of Theology |
| D.T.M.&H. | Diploma in Tropical Medicine and Hygiene |
| D.U.(P.) | Docteur de l'Université (de Paris) |
| D.V.M. | Doctor of Veterinary Medicine |
| D.V.S. (Sc.) | Doctor of Veterinary Science |
| ECOSOC | Economic and Social Council (UN) |
| ECSC | European Coal and Steel Community |
| EEC | European Economic Community |
| ESCAP | Economic and Social Commission for Asia and the Pacific |
| E.D. | Doctor of Engineering (U.S.A.) |
| Ed.B. | Bachelor of Education |
| Ed.D. | Doctor of Education |
| Edn. | Edition |
| Ed.M. | Master of Education |
| E.E. | Doctor of Electrical Engineering |
| Est... | Established |
| E.T.H. | Eidgenössische Technische Hochschule |
| Exec. | Executive |
| f. | founded |
| F.A.A. | Fellow of the Australian Academy of Science |
| F.A.A.A.S. | Fellow of the American Association for the Advancement of Science |
| F.A.C.C.A | Fellow of the Association of Certified and Corporate Accountants |
| F.A.C.D. | Fellow of the American College of Dentistry |
| F.A.C.D.S. | Fellow of the Australian College of Dental Surgeons |
| F.A.C.M.A. | Fellow of the Australian College of Medical Administrators |
| F.A.C.P. | Fellow of American College of Physicians |
| F.A.C.S. | Fellow of the American College of Surgeons |
| F.A.H.A. | Fellow of the Australian Academy of the Humanities |
| F.A.I. | Fellow of the Chartered Auctioneers' and Estate Agents' Institute |
| F.A.I.A. | Fellow of the American Institute of Architects |
| F.A.I.A.S. | Fellow of the Australian Institute of Agricultural Sciences |
| F.A.I.M. | Fellow of the Australian Institute of Management |
| F.A.I.P. | Fellow of the Australian Institute of Physics |
| FAO | Food and Agriculture Organization |
| F.A.S.A. | Fellow of the Australian Society of Arts |
| F.A.S.E. | Fellow of the Antiquarian Society, Edinburgh |
| F.A.S.S.A. | Fellow of the Academy of the Social Sciences in Australia |
| F.B.A. | Fellow of the British Academy |
| F.B.A.A. | Fellow of the British Association of Accountants and Auditors |
| F.B.I.M. | Fellow of the British Institute of Management |
| F.B.I.S. | Fellow of the British Interplanetary Society |
| F.B.Ps.S. | Fellow of the British Psychological Society |
| F.C.A. | Fellow of the Institute of Chartered Accountants |
| F.C.I.C. | Fellow of the Chemical Institute of Canada |
| F.C.I.I. | Fellow of the Chartered Insurance Institute |
| F.C.I.S. | Fellow of the Chartered Institute of Secretaries |
| F.C.I.T. | Fellow of the Chartered Institute of Transport |
| F.C.R.A. | Fellow of the College of Radiologists of Australasia |
| F.C.T. | Federal Capital Territory |
| F.C.W.A. | Fellow of the Chartered Institute of Cost and Works Accountants |
| F.D.S.R.C.S. | Fellow of the Royal College of Surgeons in Dental Surgery |
| F.E. | Fuels Engineer |
| Fed. | Federation, Federal |
| F.E.I.S. | Fellow of the Educational Institute of Scotland |
| F.F.A.R.C.S. | Fellow of the Faculty of Anaesthetics, Royal College of Surgeons |
| F.F.D.R.C.S.I. | Fellow of the Faculty of Dentistry, Royal College of Surgeons in Ireland |
| F.F.R. | Fellow of the Faculty of Radiologists |
| F.G.A. | Fellow of the Gemmological Association |
| F.G.S. | Fellow of the Geological Society |
| F.I.A. | Fellow of the Institute of Actuaries |
| F.I.A.L. | Fellow of the International Institute of Arts and Letters |
| F.I.B. | Fellow of the Institute of Bankers |
| F.I.Biol. | Fellow of the Institute of Biology |
| F.I.C.D. | Fellow of the Institute of Canadian Dentists |
| F.I.C.E.A. | Fellow of Industrial and Commercial Executive Accountants |
| F.I.C.S. | Fellow of the International College of Surgeons |
| F.I.E.Aust. | Fellow of the Institute of Engineers of Australia |
| F.I.E.R.E. | Fellow of the Institution of Electronic and Radio Engineers |
| F.I.I.S. | Fellow of the Irish Institute of Secretaries |
| F.I.L. | Fellow of the Institute of Linguists |
| Fil. Dr. | Doctor of Philology |
| F.I.Inf.Sc. | Fellow of the Institute of Information Scientists |
| F.I.M. | Fellow of the Institution of Metallurgists |
| F.I.Mech.E. | Fellow of the Institution of Mechanical Engineers |
| F.I.Min.E. | Fellow of the Institution of Mining Engineers |
| F.I.M.L.T. | Fellow of the Institute of Medical Laboratory Technology |
| F.Inst.E. | Fellow of the Institute of Energy |
| F.Inst.P. | Fellow of the Institute of Physics |
| F.Inst.Pet. | Fellow of the Institute of Petroleum |
| F.I.R.E. | Fellow of the Institution of Radio Engineers |
| F.I.R.E.E. | Fellow of the Institution of Radio and Electronics Engineers (Australia) |
| F.J.I. | Fellow of the Institute of Journalists |
| F.K.C. | Fellow of King's College (London) |
| Fla... | Florida |
| F.L.A. | Fellow of the Library Association |
| F.L.A.A. | Fellow of the Library Association of Australia |
| F.L.S. | Fellow of the Linnaean Society |

# ABBREVIATIONS

| | | |
|---|---|---|
| F.M.A. | .. | Fellow of the Museums Association |
| F.N.A. | .. | Fellow of the National Academy of Sciences (India) |
| F.N.Z.I.C. | .. | Fellow of the New Zealand Institute of Chemists |
| F.Ph.S. | .. | Fellow of the Philosophical Society of England |
| F.Phys.S. | .. | Fellow of the Physical Society |
| F.P.R.I. | .. | Fellow of the Plastics and Rubber Institute |
| F.R.A.C.I. | .. | Fellow of the Royal Australian Chemical Institute |
| F.R.A.C.P. | .. | Fellow of the Royal Australasian College of Physicians |
| F.R.A.C.S. | .. | Fellow of the Royal Australasian College of Surgeons |
| F.R.Ae.S. | .. | Fellow of the Royal Aeronautical Society |
| F.R.A.H.S. | .. | Fellow of the Royal Australian Historical Society |
| F.R.A.I. | .. | Fellow of the Royal Anthropological Institute |
| F.R.A.I.A. | .. | Fellow of the Royal Australian Institute of Architects |
| F.R.A.I.C. | .. | Fellow of the Architectural Institute of Canada |
| F.R.A.M. | .. | Fellow of the Royal Academy of Music |
| F.R.A.S. | .. | Fellow of the Royal Astronomical Society; Fellow of the Royal Asiatic Society |
| F.R.B.S. | .. | Fellow of the Royal Society of British Sculptors |
| F.R.C.M. | .. | Fellow of the Royal College of Music |
| F.R.C.O. | .. | Fellow of the Royal College of Organists |
| F.R.C.O.G. | .. | Fellow of the Royal College of Obstetricians and Gynaecologists |
| F.R.C.P.A. | .. | Fellow of the Royal College of Pathologists of Australasia |
| F.R.C.P.(C.) | .. | Fellow of the Royal College of Physicians of Canada |
| F.R.C.P.ED. | .. | Fellow of the Royal College of Physicians of Edinburgh |
| F.R.C.P.I. | .. | Fellow of the Royal College of Physicians of Ireland |
| F.R.C.S.(C.) | .. | Fellow of the Royal College of Surgeons of Canada |
| F.R.C.S.ED. | .. | Fellow of the Royal College of Surgeons of Edinburgh |
| F.R.C.V.S. | .. | Fellow of the Royal College of Veterinary Surgeons |
| F.R.E.S. | .. | Fellow of the Royal Entomological Society of London |
| F.R.Econ.S. | .. | Fellow of the Royal Economic Society |
| F.R.G.S. | .. | Fellow of the Royal Geographical Society |
| F.R.Hist.S. | .. | Fellow of the Royal Historical Society |
| F.R.Hort.S. | .. | Fellow of the Royal Horticultural Society |
| F.R.I.B.A. | .. | Fellow of the Royal Institute of British Architects |
| F.R.I.C.S. | .. | Fellow of the Royal Institution of Chartered Surveyors |
| F.R.I.Z. | .. | Fellow of the Royal Institute of Zoologists |
| F.R.Met.Soc. | .. | Fellow of the Royal Meteorological Society |
| F.R.P.S. | .. | Fellow of the Royal Photographic Society |
| F.R.S. | .. | Fellow of the Royal Society |
| F.R.S.A. | .. | Fellow of the Royal Society of Arts |
| F.R.San.I. | .. | Fellow of the Royal Sanitary Institute |
| F.R.S.C. | .. | Fellow of the Royal Society of Canada; Fellow of the Royal Society of Chemistry |
| F.R.S.E. | .. | Fellow of the Royal Society of Edinburgh |
| F.R.S.G.S. | .. | Fellow of the Royal Scottish Geographical Society |
| F.R.S.H. | .. | Fellow of the Royal Society of Health |
| F.R.S.L. | .. | Fellow of the Royal Society of Literature |
| F.R.S.S. | .. | Fellow of the Royal Statistical Society |
| F.R.S.S.Af. | .. | Fellow of the Royal Society of South Africa |
| F.R.S.T.M. | .. | Fellow of the Royal Society of Tropical Medicine and Hygiene |
| F.S.A. | .. | Fellow of the Society of Antiquaries |
| F.S.A.(Scot.) | | Fellow of the Society of Antiquaries of Scotland |
| F.S.A.L.A. | .. | Fellow of the South African Library Association |
| F.S.B.E. | .. | Fellow of the Society for British Entomology |
| F.S.E. | .. | Fellow of The Society of Engineers |
| F.S.S. | .. | Fellow of the Statistical Society |
| F.T.C.D. | .. | Fellow of Trinity College, Dublin |
| F.T.C.L. | .. | Fellow of Trinity College of Music, London |
| F.T.I. | .. | Fellow of the Textile Institute |
| F.Z.S. | .. | Fellow of the Zoological Society |
| Ga. | .. | Georgia |
| G.B.E. | .. | Knight (or Dame) Grand Cross of the Order of the British Empire |
| G.C.B. | .. | Knight Grand Cross of the Order of the Bath |
| G.C.I.E. | .. | Knight Grand Commander of the Indian Empire |
| G.C.M.G. | .. | Knight Grand Cross of the Order of St. Michael and St. George |
| G.C.S.I. | .. | Knight Grand Commander of the Star of India |
| G.C.V.O. | .. | Knight Grand Cross of the Royal Victorian Order |
| Gen. | .. | General |
| Gov. | .. | Governor |
| Govt. | .. | Government |
| h.c. | .. | honoris causa |
| H.Q. | .. | Headquarters |
| H.E. | .. | His Eminence; His Excellency |
| H.M. | .. | His (or Her) Majesty |
| H.M.S.O. | .. | His (or Her) Majesty's Stationery Office |
| H.N.D. | .. | Higher National Diploma |
| Hon. | .. | Honourable; Honorary |
| Ia. | .. | Iowa |
| IAEA | .. | International Atomic Energy Agency |
| IAU | .. | International Astronomical Union |
| IBE | .. | International Bureau of Education |
| I.C.E. | .. | Institute of Civil Engineers |
| ICPHS | .. | International Council for Philosophy and Humanistic Studies |
| I.C.S. | .. | Indian Civil Service |
| ICSU | .. | International Council of Scientific Unions |
| Ida. | .. | Idaho |
| IFAN | .. | Institut Fondamental d'Afrique Noire |
| IFLA | .. | International Federation of Library Associations and Institutions |
| IGU | .. | International Geographical Union |
| Ill. | .. | Illinois |
| ILO | .. | International Labour Organization |
| IMS | .. | India Medical Service |
| IMU | .. | International Mathematical Union |
| Inc. | .. | Incorporated |
| Ind. | .. | Indiana; Independent |
| I.N.R.A. | .. | Institut National de la Recherche Agronomique |
| Int. | .. | International |
| ISME | .. | International Society for Music Education |
| I.S.O. | .. | Companion of the Imperial Service Order |
| IUB | .. | International Union of Biochemistry |
| IUBS | .. | International Union of Biological Sciences |
| IUCr | .. | International Union of Crystallography |
| IUGG | .. | International Union of Geodesy and Geophysics |
| IUGS | .. | International Union of Geological Sciences |
| IUHPS | .. | International Union of the History and Philosophy of Science |

## ABBREVIATIONS

| | | |
|---|---|---|
| IUIS | .. | International Union of Immunological Societies |
| IUNS | .. | International Union of Nutritional Sciences |
| IUPAB | .. | International Union of Pure and Applied Biophysics |
| IUPAC | .. | International Union of Pure and Applied Chemistry |
| IUPAP | .. | International Union of Pure and Applied Physics |
| IUPHAR | .. | International Union of Pharmacology |
| IUPS | .. | International Union of Physiological Sciences |
| IUTAM | .. | International Union of Theoretical and Applied Mechanics |
| J.C.B. | .. | Juris Canonici Bachelor (Bachelor of Canon Law) |
| J.C.D. | .. | Juris Canonici Doctor (Doctor of Canon Law) |
| J.C.L. | .. | Juris Canonici Lector (Reader of Canon Law) |
| J.D. | .. | Doctor of Jurisprudence |
| J.P. | .. | Justice of the Peace |
| Jl. | .. | Jalan (Indonesia, Malaysia) |
| J.S.D. | .. | Doctor of Juristic Science |
| J.U.D(r). | .. | Juris utriusque Doctor (Doctor of both Civil and Canon Law) |
| Ju.D. | .. | Doctor of Law |
| Kan. | .. | Kansas |
| K.B.E. | .. | Knight Commander of the Order of the British Empire |
| K.C.B. | .. | Knight Commander of the Order of the Bath |
| K.C.I.E. | .. | Knight Commander of the Order of the Indian Empire |
| K.C.M.G. | .. | Knight Commander of the Order of St. Michael and St. George |
| K.C.S.I. | .. | Knight Commander of the Star of India |
| K.C.V.O. | .. | Knight Commander of the Royal Victorian Order |
| K.G. | .. | Knight of the Order of the Garter |
| K.P. | .. | Knight of the Order of St. Patrick |
| K.St.J. | .. | Knight of the Order of St. John of Jerusalem |
| K.T. | .. | Knight of the Order of the Thistle |
| Kt. | .. | Knight |
| Ky. | .. | Kentucky |
| La. | .. | Louisiana |
| L.C.L. | .. | Licentiate of Canon Law |
| L.D.S. | .. | Licentiate in Dental Surgery |
| L. ès L. | .. | Licencié ès lettres |
| L. ès Sc. | .. | Licencié ès sciences |
| L.H.D. | .. | Literarum Humaniorum Doctor (Doctor of Letters) |
| Lic. Droit et Sc. Pol. | .. | Licencié en Droit et Sciences Politiques |
| Lic.Med. | .. | Licentiate in Medicine |
| L.I.M. | .. | Licentiate of the Institution of Metallurgists |
| Litt.D. | .. | Doctor of Letters |
| LL.B. | .. | Bachelor of Laws |
| LL.D. | .. | Doctor of Laws |
| L.Lett. | .. | Licentiate of Letters |
| LL.L. | .. | Licentiate of Laws |
| LL.M. | .. | Master of Laws |
| L.M. | .. | Licentiate of Medicine or Midwifery |
| L.M.S. | .. | Licentiate in Medicine and Surgery |
| L.M.S.S.A. | .. | Licentiate in Medicine and Surgery of the Society of Apothecaries |
| L.Mus. | .. | Licentiate in Music |
| L.Ph. | .. | Licentiate of Philosophy |
| L.R.C.P. | .. | Licentiate of the Royal College of Physicians |
| L.R.C.S. | .. | Licentiate of the Royal College of Surgeons |
| L.R.P.S. | .. | Licentiate of the Royal Photographic Society |
| L.S. | .. | Library Science |
| L.S.A. | .. | Licentiate of Science in Agriculture |
| L.S.T. | .. | Licentiate in Sacred Theology |
| Lt. | .. | Lieutenant |
| L.Th. | .. | Licentiate or Master of Theology |
| M.A. | .. | Master of Arts |
| M.A.C.E. | .. | Member of the Australian College of Education |
| M.A.C.V.S. | .. | Member of the Australian College of Veterinary Surgeons |
| M.Agr. | .. | Master of Agriculture |
| M.A.L.S. | .. | Master of Arts in Library Science |
| Man. | .. | Manager, Managing; Manitoba |
| M.A.O. | .. | Master of Obstetrics |
| M.Arch. | .. | Master in Architecture |
| M.A.Sc. | .. | Master of Applied Science |
| M.A.S.C.E. | .. | Member of the Australian Society of Civil Engineers |
| Mass. | .. | Massachusetts |
| M.B. | .. | Bachelor of Medicine |
| M.B.A. | .. | Master of Business Administration |
| M.B.E. | .. | Member of the Order of the British Empire |
| M.B.I.M. | .. | Member of the British Institute of Management |
| M.C. | .. | Military Cross |
| M.C.D. | .. | Master of Civic Design |
| M.C.E. | .. | Master of Civil Engineering |
| M.Ch. | .. | Master of Surgery |
| M.Ch.D. | .. | Master of Dental Surgery |
| M.Ch.E. | .. | Master of Chemical Engineering |
| M.C.I.T. | .. | Member of the Chartered Institute of Transport |
| M.C.L. | .. | Master of Civil Law |
| M.Com(m). | .. | Master of Commerce |
| M.C.P. | .. | Master of City Planning |
| M.C.S. | .. | Master of Commercial Science |
| Md. | .. | Maryland |
| M.D. | .. | Doctor of Medicine |
| M.D.S. | .. | Master of Dental Surgery |
| M.E. | .. | Mechanical Engineer; Master of Education; Master of Engineering; Military Engineer; Mining Engineer |
| Me. | .. | Maine |
| M.Econ. | .. | Master of Economics |
| M.Ed. | .. | Master of Education |
| M.E.E. | .. | Master of Electrical Engineering |
| M.E.I.C. | .. | Member of the Engineering Institute of Canada |
| Mem(s). | .. | Member(s) |
| M.Aus.I.M.M. | .. | Member of the Australasian Institute of Mining and Metallurgy |
| M.Eng. | .. | Master of Engineering |
| M.F. | .. | Master of Forestry |
| M.F.A. | .. | Master of Fine Arts |
| Mgr. | .. | Monseigneur; Monsignor; Magister (Master's degree) |
| M.H.A. | .. | Member of the House of Assembly |
| M.H.R. | .. | Member of the House of Representatives |
| M.I.Biol. | .. | Member of the Institute of Biology |
| M.I.C.E. | .. | Member of the Institution of Civil Engineers |
| M.I.Chem.E. | .. | Member of the Institution of Chemical Engineers |
| Mich. | .. | Michigan |
| M.I.E.A. | .. | Member of the Institution of Engineers of Australia |
| M.I.E.E. | .. | Member of the Institution of Electrical Engineers |
| M.I.E.R.E. | .. | Member of the Institution of Electronic and Radio Engineers |

## ABBREVIATIONS

| | | |
|---|---|---|
| M.I.L. | .. | Member of the Institute of Linguists |
| Mil. | .. | Military |
| M.I.Mar.E. | .. | Member of the Institute of Marine Engineers |
| M.I.Mech.E. | .. | Member of the Institution of Mechanical Engineers |
| M.I.Min.E. | .. | Member of the Institution of Mining Engineers |
| M.I.M.M. | .. | Member of the Institution of Mining and Metallurgy |
| Minn. | .. | Minnesota |
| Miss. | .. | Mississippi |
| M.I.P.E. | .. | Member of the Institution of Production Engineers |
| M.I.P.M. | .. | Member of the Institute of Personnel Management |
| M.I.Struct.E. | .. | Member of the Institution of Structural Engineers |
| M.I.T. | .. | Massachusetts Institute of Technology |
| M.I.W.E. | .. | Member of the Institute of Water Engineers |
| M.L. | .. | Master of Laws |
| M.L.A. | .. | Member of the Legislative Assembly; Master of Landscape Architecture |
| M.L.C. | .. | Member of the Legislative Council |
| M.Litt. | .. | Master of Letters |
| M.L.S. | .. | Master of Library Science |
| M.M.S.A. | .. | Master of Midwifery of the Society of Apothecaries |
| M.Mus. | .. | Master of Music |
| Mo. | .. | Missouri |
| Mont. | .. | Montana |
| M.P. | .. | Member of Parliament |
| M.P.H. | .. | Master of Public Health |
| M.Ph. | .. | Master of Philosophy |
| M.R.A.I.C. | .. | Member of the Royal Architectural Institute of Canada |
| M.R.A.S. | .. | Member of the Royal Asiatic Society |
| M.R.C.Path. | .. | Member of the Royal College of Pathologists |
| M.R.C.P.ED. | .. | Member of the Royal College of Physicians of Edinburgh |
| M.R.C.S.ED. | .. | Member of the Royal College of Surgeons of Edinburgh |
| M.R.C.V.S. | .. | Member of the Royal College of Veterinary Surgeons |
| M.R.I. | .. | Member of the Royal Institution |
| M.R.I.A. | .. | Member of the Royal Irish Academy |
| M.R.S.A. | .. | Member of the Royal Society of Arts |
| M.R.S.A.E. | .. | Member of Royal Society of Agricultural Engineers |
| M.R.C.S. | .. | Member of the Royal Society of Chemistry |
| M.R.S.L. | .. | Member of the Royal Society of Literature; Member of the Order of the Republic of Sierra Leone |
| M.S. | .. | Master of Science; Master of Surgery |
| M.S.A. | .. | Master of Scientific Agriculture |
| M.Sc. | .. | Master of Science |
| M.Sc.A. | .. | Master of Applied Science |
| M.Sc.Agr. | .. | Master of Science in Agriculture |
| M.Sc.(Chem. Tech.) | .. | Master of Science in Chemical Technology |
| M.Sc.D. | .. | Master of Science in Dentistry |
| M.Sc.F. | .. | Master of Science in Forestry |
| M.Sc.(Med.) | .. | Master of Science in Medicine |
| M.Sc.N. | .. | Master of Science in Nursing |
| M.Sc.Tech. | .. | Master of Science in Technology |
| M.S.D. | .. | Doctor of Medieval Studies |
| M.S.E. | .. | Member of The Society of Engineers |
| M.S.L. | .. | Licentiate of Medieval Studies |
| M.S.P. | .. | Master of Science in Pharmacy |
| M.Soc.Sc. | .. | Master of Social Science |
| M.S.W. | .. | Master of Social Work |
| M.Th. | .. | Master of Theology |
| M.T.P.I. | .. | Member of the Town Planning Institute |
| Mus.Bac. or B. | | Bachelor of Music |
| Mus.Doc. or D. | | Doctor of Music |
| Mus.M. | .. | Master of Music |
| M.V.O. | .. | Member of the Royal Victorian Order |
| M.V.Sc. | .. | Master of Veterinary Science |
| NASA | .. | National Aeronautics and Space Administration |
| N.B. | .. | New Brunswick |
| N.C. | .. | North Carolina |
| N.D. | .. | North Dakota |
| N.D.D. | .. | National Diploma in Dairying |
| Neb. | .. | Nebraska |
| Nev. | .. | Nevada |
| N.H. | .. | New Hampshire |
| N.J. | .. | New Jersey |
| N.M. | .. | New Mexico |
| N.S. | .. | Nova Scotia |
| N.S.W. | .. | New South Wales |
| N.U.I. | .. | National University of Ireland |
| N.Y. | .. | New York |
| N.Z. | .. | New Zealand |
| O. | .. | Ohio |
| OAS | .. | Organization of American States |
| O.B.E. | .. | Officer of the Order of the British Empire |
| OECD | .. | Organization for Economic Co-operation and Development |
| O.F.M. | .. | Order of Friars Minor |
| O.F.S. | .. | Orange Free State |
| Okla. | .. | Oklahoma |
| O.M. | .. | Member of the Order of Merit |
| O.M.I. | .. | Oblate of Mary Immaculate |
| On. | .. | Onorevole (Italian) |
| O.N.D. | .. | Ordinary National Diploma |
| Ont. | .. | Ontario |
| O.P. | .. | Order of Preachers (Dominicans) |
| Ore. | .. | Oregon |
| ORSTOM | .. | Office de la Recherche Scientifique et Technique Outre-Mer |
| O.S.B. | .. | Order of St. Benedict |
| O. St. J. | .. | Officer of (the Order of) St. John of Jerusalem |
| OStR. | .. | Oberstudienrat |
| Oxon. | .. | Of Oxford University |
| Pa. | .. | Pennsylvania |
| P.C. | .. | Privy Councillor |
| Pd.B. | .. | Bachelor of Pedagogy |
| Pd.D. | .. | Doctor of Pedagogy |
| Pd.M. | .. | Master of Pedagogy |
| P.E. | .. | Petroleum Engineer |
| P.E.I. | .. | Prince Edward Island |
| P.E.N. | .. | Poets, Playwrights, Essayists, Editors and Novelists (Club) |
| P.Eng. | .. | Member of The Society of Professional Engineers Ltd. |
| Ph.B. | .. | Bachelor of Philosophy |
| Ph.D. | .. | Doctor of Philosophy |
| Ph.G. | .. | Graduate in Pharmacy |
| Ph.L. | .. | Licentiate in Philosophy |
| Ph.M. | .. | Master of Philosophy |
| P.M.B. | .. | Private Mail Bag |
| P.O.B. | .. | Post Office Box |
| P.Q. | .. | Province of Quebec |
| P.R.A. | .. | President of the Royal Academy |
| Pres. | .. | President |
| P.R.I. | .. | President of the Royal Institute of Painters in Water Colours |
| P.R.I.B.A. | .. | President of the Royal Institute of British Architects |
| Prof. | .. | Professor |
| P.R.S. | .. | President of the Royal Society |

xiv

## ABBREVIATIONS

| | | | | |
|---|---|---|---|---|
| P.R.S.A. | President of the Royal Scottish Academy | Sec. | Secretary | |
| Publ(s). | Publication(s) | S.J. | Society of Jesus | |
| | | S.J.D. | Doctor of Juristic Science | |
| Q.C. | Queen's Counsel | S.M. | Master of Science | |
| q.v. | quod vide (which see) | S.R.R. | Socialist Republic of Romania | |
| | | S.S.R. | Soviet Socialist Republic | |
| R.A. | Royal Academy; Royal Academician | S.T.B. | Bachelor of Sacred Theology | |
| R.A.C.P. | Royal Australasian College of Physicians | S.T.D. | Doctor of Sacred Theology | |
| R.A.C.S. | Royal Australasian College of Surgeons | S.Th.L. | Sacrae Theologiae Lector (Reader or Professor of Sacred Theology) | |
| R.A.F. | Royal Air Force | S.T.M. | Master of Sacred Theology | |
| R.A.M. | Royal Academy of Music | Supt. | Superintendent | |
| R.A.S. | Royal Astronomical (or Asiatic) Society | | | |
| R.B.A. | Royal Society of British Artists | T.D. | (Territorial) Efficiency Decoration; Tealta Dáil (Member of the Dail) | |
| R.C.A. | Member of the Royal Cambrian Academy; Member of the Royal Canadian Academy | Tenn. | Tennessee | |
| R.C.M. | Royal College of Music | Tex. | Texas | |
| R.C.S. | Royal College of Surgeons | Th.A. | Associate in Theology | |
| Rep. | Representative; Represented | Th.B. | Bachelor of Theology | |
| retd. | retired | Th.D. | Doctor of Theology | |
| Rev. | Reverend | Th.M. | Master of Theology | |
| R.G.S. | Royal Geographical Society | | | |
| R.Hist.S. | Royal Historical Society | | | |
| R.I. | Rhode Island; Royal Institute of Painters in Water Colours; Royal Institution | U.G.C. | University Grants Committee | |
| | | U.K. | United Kingdom | |
| R.I.A. | Royal Irish Academy; Registered Industrial and Cost Accountant | UN | United Nations | |
| | | UNDP | United Nations Development Programme | |
| R.I.B.A. | Royal Institute of British Architects | UNESCO | United Nations Educational, Scientific and Cultural Organization | |
| R.I.C.S. | Royal Institution of Chartered Surveyors | | | |
| R.M.P.A. | Royal Medico-Psychological Association | UNICEF | United Nations International Children's Emergency Fund | |
| R.N. | Royal Navy | | | |
| R.O.I. | Royal Institute of Oil Painters | Univ. | University | |
| R.P. | Member of the Royal Society of Portrait Painters | UNRWA | United Nations Relief and Works Agency | |
| | | U.P. | Uttar Pradesh (United Provinces) | |
| R.S.A. | Royal Scottish Academy; Royal Society of Arts | URSI | Union Radio-Scientifique Internationale | |
| | | U.S.A. | United States of America | |
| R.S.C. | Royal Society of Canada | U.S.S.R. | Union of Soviet Socialist Republics | |
| R.S.F.S.R. | Russian Soviet Federative Socialist Republic | | | |
| | | Va. | Virginia | |
| R.S.W. | Royal Scottish Society of Painters in Water Colours | V.C. | Victoria Cross | |
| | | Vols. | Volumes | |
| Rt. Hon. | Right Honourable | Vt. | Vermont | |
| Rt. Rev. | Right Reverend | | | |
| R.W.S. | Royal Society of Painters in Water Colours | W.A. | Western Australia | |
| | | Wash. | Washington (State) | |
| S.A. | South Africa(n) | W.E.A. | Workers' Educational Association | |
| S.C. | South Carolina; Senior Counsel (Republic of Ireland) | Wis. | Wisconsin | |
| | | W. Va. | West Virginia | |
| Sc.B. | Bachelor of Science | Wyo. | Wyoming | |
| Sc.D. | Doctor of Science | | | |
| S.C.D. | Doctor of Commercial Science | † | indicates a periodical title available for exchange | |
| S.Dak. | South Dakota | | | |
| S.D.I. | Selective Dissemination of Information | | | |

# ROMANIA

Population 22,300,000

## ACADEMIES

**Academia Republicii Socialiste România** (*Academy of the Socialist Republic of Romania*): Bucharest, Calea Victoriei 125; f. 1948, as a result of the re-organization of the Academia Română, formerly the Societatea Literară Română, f. 1866.
*President:* GHEORGHE MIHOC.
*Secretary:* GEORGE CIUCU.
Library: *see* Libraries.

### PRESIDIUM OF THE ACADEMY
CRISTOFOR SIMIONESCU, ŞERBAN ŢIŢEICA, ION ANTON (*Vice-Presidents*); GEORGE CIUCU (*Secretary*); V. PREDA (*Chairman of the Cluj-Napoca Branch*); PETRE JITARIU (*Chairman of the Iaşi Branch*); CAIUS IACOB (*Chairman of the Section of Mathematics*); THEODOR IONESCU (*Chairman of the Section of Physics*); EMILIAN BRATU (*Chairman of the Section of Chemistry*); ELIE CARAFOLI (*Chairman of the Section of Technical Sciences*); NICOLAE SĂLĂGEANU (*Chairman of the Section of Biology*); GRIGORE OBREJANU (*Chairman of the Section of Agriculture and Forestry*); SABBA ŞTEFĂNESCU (*Chairman of the Section of Geology, Geophysics and Geography*); ŞTEFAN MILCU (*Chairman of the Section of Medical Sciences*); MANEA MĂNESCU (*Chairman of the Section of Economics and Sociological Sciences*); C. IONESCU-GULIAN (*Chairman of the Section of Philosophical, Psychological and Juridical Sciences*); ŞTEFAN PASCU (*Chairman of the Section of History*); ALEXANDRU GRAUR (*Chairman of the Section of Philology, Literature and Arts*).

### I. Section of Mathematics:
FULL MEMBERS:
IACOB, C.
MARINESCU, GH.
MIHOC, GH.
ONICESCU, O.
TEODORESCU, N.

CORRESPONDING MEMBERS:
CIUCU, G.
CRISTESCU, R.
DRÂMBĂ, C.

### II. Section of Physics:
FULL MEMBERS:
IONESCU, TH. V.
ŢIŢEICA, Ş.
URSU, I.

CORRESPONDING MEMBERS:
CORCIOVEI, A.
GRIGOROVICI, R.
MERCEA, V.
NOVACU, V.
POPESCU, I.-I.

### III. Section of Chemistry:
FULL MEMBERS:
BRATU, E.
CEAUŞESCU, ELENA
CIORĂNESCU-NENIŢESCU, ECATERINA
MURGULESCU, I.
SIMIONESCU, CR.

CORRESPONDING MEMBERS:
BALABAN, AL.
BODEA, C.
FLORESCU, M.
IONESCU, T. D.
MACAROVICI, C.
OSTROGOVICH, G.
SAHINI, V.-EM.
SPACU, P.-G.
SUCIU, GH.-C.
ZUGRĂVESCU, I.

### IV. Section of Technical Sciences:
FULL MEMBERS:
ANTON, I.
AVRAMESCU, A.
BĂLAN, ŞT.
CARAFOLI, E.
DUMITRESCU, D.
MATEESCU, D.
RĂDULEŢ, R.
VOINEA, R.

CORRESPONDING MEMBERS:
ANTONIU, I.
ARAMĂ, C.
AVRAM, C.
BUZDUGAN, GH.
CARTIANU, GH.
DIMO, P.
DINCULESCU, C.
DRĂGĂNESCU, M.
GÂDEA, SUZANA
MARINESCU, M.
PATRAULEA, N.
PENESCU, C.
SĂLĂGEAN, T.-L.

### V. Section of Biology:
FULL MEMBERS:
CODREANU, R.
JITARIU, P.
MACOVSCHI, E.
PORA, E.
PREDA, V.
SĂLĂGEANU, N.

CORRESPONDING MEMBERS:
BĂCESCU, M.
BOTNARIUC, N.
IONESCU, M.
NECRASOV, OLGA
RADU, V.
RUDESCU, L.

### VI. Section of Agriculture and Forestry:
FULL MEMBERS:
CEAPOIU, N.
GIOSAN, N.
OBREJANU, GR.
RĂDULESCU, E.
VASILIU, A.

CORRESPONDING MEMBERS:
CHIRIŢĂ, C.
DAVIDESCU, D.
GHEŢIE, V.
MOŢOC, M.
MUNTEAN, S.
NEGRUŢIU, E.
POPOVICI, I.
PRIADCENCU, AL.
STAICU, I.
VELICAN, V.

### VII. Section of Geology, Geophysics and Geography:
FULL MEMBERS:
FILIPESCU, M.
GIUŞCĂ, D.
MURGEANU, GH.
PETRULIAN, N.
ŞTEFĂNESCU, S.

CORRESPONDING MEMBERS:
BOTEZATU, R.
CONSTANTINESCU, L.
NOVICI, V.
MORARIU, T.

### VIII. Section of Medical Sciences:
FULL MEMBERS:
ASLAN, ANA
FĂGĂRĂŞANU, I.
KREINDLER, A.
MÂRZA, V.
MILCU, ST.-M.

CORRESPONDING MEMBERS:

Anastasatu, C.
Arseni, C.
Brînzeu, P.
Cajal, N.
Menkeş, B.
Olănescu, Gh.

Pavel, I.
Popescu, V.
Soru, Eugenia
Vancea, P.
Voiculescu, M.

IX. *Section of Economics and Sociological Sciences:*

FULL MEMBERS:

Bîrlădeanu, Al.
Malinschi, V.

Mănescu, M.
Voitec, Şt.

CORRESPONDING MEMBERS:

Biji, M.
Constantinescu, N.
Dobrescu, Em.
Moldovan, R.
Murgescu, C.

Postolache, T.
Rachmuth, I.
Stahl, H.
Zaharescu, B.

X. *Section of Philosophical, Psychological and Juridical Sciences:*

FULL MEMBERS:

Ionaşcu, T.
Ionescu-Gulian, C.

Maurer, I. Gh.
Pavelcu, V.

CORRESPONDING MEMBERS:

Barasch, E.
Bârsănescu, Şt.
Bugnariu, T.
Ceterchi, I.

Gall, E.
Maliţa, M.
Roşca, Al.
Stanciu, S.

XI. *Section of History:*

FULL MEMBERS:

Condurachi, E.
Pascu, Şt.

Prodan, D.

CORRESPONDING MEMBERS:

Pippidi, D.

Ştefănescu, Şt.

XII. *Section of Philology, Literature and Arts:*

FULL MEMBERS:

Beniuc, M.
Bogza, G.
Cioculescu, Ş.
Coteanu, I.
Graur, Al.

Iordan, I.
Jalea, I.
Jebeleanu, E.
Rosetti, Al.
Vătăşianu, V.

CORRESPONDING MEMBERS:

Baba, C.
Balaci, Al.
Barbu, E.
Caragea, B.
Cazacu, B.
Dumitreşcu-Busulenga, Zoe
Gheorghiu, M.

Ivănescu, Gh.
Livescu, J.
Macrea, D.
Meliusz, I.
Mihăescu, H.
Popovici, T.
Teodorescu, V.

Branches and Scientific Departments

*Filiala Cluj-Napoca* (Cluj-Napoca Branch): Cluj, Str. Republicii 9; Pres. Acad. V. Preda.

*Filiala Iaşi* (Iaşi Branch): Iaşi, Str. Universităţii 16; Pres. Acad. Petre Jitariu.

*Baza de Cercetări Timişoara* (Timişoara Department of Scientific Research): Str. Mihai Viteazul 24; Dir. Acad. Dan Mateescu.

*Baza de cercetări Tg. Mureş* (Tg. Mureş Department of Scientific Research): Str. Universităţii 38; Dir. Prof. Mihail Gündisch.

Publishing House

**Editura Academiei** (*Publishing House of the Academy*): 71021 Bucharest, Calea Victoriei 125; f. 1948; publishes works in the various fields of study of the Academy and 66 journals (37 in foreign languages); Dir. Constantin Busuioceanu.

Publications†: *Studii şi cercetări matematice* (Studies and Research in Mathematics); *Revue Roumaine de mathematiques pures et appliquees*; *L'Analyse numérique et la théorie de l'approximation*; *Mathematica—Revue d'analyse numérique et de théorie de l'approximation—Mathematica*; *Studii şi cercetări de fizică* (Studies and Research in Physics); *Revue Roumaine de physique*; *Revue Roumaine de chimie*; *Cellulose Chemistry and Technology*; *Studii şi cercetări de mecanică aplicată* (Studies and Research in Applied Mechanics); *Revue Roumaine des sciences techniques: Série de mécanique appliquée*; *Revue Roumaine des sciences techniques: Série électrotechnique et énergétique*; *Studii şi cercetări de biochimie* (Studies and Research in Biochemistry); *Revue roumaine de biochimie*; *Studii şi cercetări de biologie: Seria biologie vegetală; Seria biologie animală* (Studies and Research in Biology: Series of Vegetal Biology; Series of Animal Biology); *Revue Roumaine de biologie: Série de biologie végétale; Série de biologie animale*; *Studii şi cercetări de antropologie* (Studies and Research in Anthropology); *Annuaire Roumain d'Anthropologie*; *Ocrotirea naturii şi a mediului înconjurător* (The Protection of Nature and of the Environment); *Travaux de l'Institut de spéléologie "Emille Racovitza"*; *Studii şi cercetări de geologie, geofizică şi geografie* (Studies and Research in Geology, Geophysics and Geography, 3 series); *Revue Roumaine de géologie, géophysique et géographie* (3 series); *Studii si cercetări lingvistice* (Studies and Research in Linguistics); *Revue Roumaine de Linguistique*; *Cahiers de linguistique théorique et appliquée*; *Cercetări de lingvistică—Cluj-Napoca* (Linguistic Researches—Cluj-Napoca); *Limba română* (The Romanian Language); *Nyelv- és Irodalomtudományi Közlemények*; *Revista de etnografie şi folclor* (Journal of Ethnography and Folklore).

---

**Academia de Ştiinţe Agricole şi Silvice** (*Academy of Agricultural and Forest Sciences*): Bucharest, Bd. Mărăşti 61; f. 1969.

Presidium:

Nicolae Giosan (*President*); Grigore Obrejanu, Ion Moldovan (*Vice-Presidents*); Mircea Moţoc; Ana Hulea; Emil Negruţiu; Emil Negulescu; Mircea Oprean; Constantin Pîntea; Nicolae Ştefan; Savu Timaru; Ion Ceauşescu; Dumitru Teaci; Alexandru Covor; Vasile Otopeleanu; Tiberiu Mureşan; Alexandru Lazăr; Ion Puia; Ştefan Romoşan; Marius Popescu; Dragoş Toma; Nichifor Ceapoiu; Ovidiu Ppoescu; Stelian Dinescu; Smarand Duică.

I. *Plants Culture Section:*

Honorary Member:

Safta, I. S.

Members:

Anghel, G.
Bîlteanu, G.
Ceapoiu, N.
Coculescu, G.
Giosan, N.
Hulea, Ana
Hulpoi, N.
Mureşan, T.

Priadcencu, A.
Rădulescu, E.
Sluşanschi, H.
Staicu, I.
Valuţă, G.
Vasiliu, A.
Velican, V.

Corresponding Members:

Bălan, C.
Berindei, M.
Capisizu, M.
Covor, A.
Cristea, M.
Dorneanu, A.
Hamar, M.
Lazany, A.

Lăpuşan, A.
Popa, F.
Popovici, I.
Puia, I.
Tomoroga, P.
Vineş, G.
Vlaicu, E.

II. *Horticulture Section:*

Honorary Members:

Ionescu, T.
Juncu, V.

Radu, I.

## MEMBERS:
MARTIN, T.
OPREAN, M.
SONEA, V.
ȘTEFAN, N.
TEODORESCU, S

### CORRESPONDING MEMBERS:
ANDRONICESCU, D.
BAICU, T.
BANIȚĂ, P.
CEAUȘESCU, I.
COTEA, V.
DAVIDOIU, I.
IONIȚĂ, C.
MĂNESCU, B.
MODORAN, I.
NEAGU, M.
OȘLOBEANU, M.
SĂVESCU, A.
SOCIU, S.
SUTA, VICTORIA
VASILESCU, I.

*III. Zootechnics and Veterinary Science Section:*

HONORARY MEMBER:
BĂICOIANU, C.

MEMBERS:
BĂIA, G.
GHEȚIE, V.
NEGRUȚIU, E.
POPOVICI, I.
STAMATIN, N.
VLĂDUȚIU, O.

CORRESPONDING MEMBERS:
MOLDOVAN, I.
NEGRUȚIU, T.
OȚEL, V.
SILVAȘ, E.
TEMIȘAN, V.
TÎRLEA, S.

*IV. Silviculture Section:*

MEMBER:
NEGULESCU, E.

CORRESPONDING MEMBERS:
COSTIN, E.
LUPE, I.
MILESCU, I.
RUCĂREANU, N.

*V. Pedology, Land Improvement, Water Economy and Mechanization Section:*

HONORARY MEMBERS:
MIRICĂ, G.
PÎNTEA, C.

MEMBERS:
BOTZAN, M.
CHIRIȚĂ, C.
DAVIDESCU, D.
DRĂGAN, G.
MOȚOC, M.
OBREJANU, G.
TOMA, O.

CORRESPONDING MEMBERS:
FLOREA, N.
NAGHY, M.
NICOLAU, C.
RĂUȚĂ, C.
SÎRBU, E.

*VI. Agrarian Economy Section:*

HONORARY MEMBER:
CORNĂȚEANU, N.

MEMBERS:
MICULESCU, A.
ȘCHIOPU, B.
STANCU, M.

CORRESPONDING MEMBERS:
DIMENY, A.
DUMITRU, D.
GIB, C.
HATMANU, L.

## RESEARCH INSTITUTES ATTACHED TO THE ACADEMY OF AGRICULTURAL AND FOREST SCIENCES

**Institutul de Cercetări pentru Apicultură** (*Research Institute for Beekeeping*): Bucharest, Bd. Ficusului nr. 42, S.1.; f. 1974; 26 mems.; library of 9,000 vols.; Dir. Eng. AUREL MĂLAIU; publ. *Apicultura* (monthly).

**Institutul de Cercetări pentru Cereale și Plante Tehnice** (*Research Institute for Cereals and Industrial Crops*): Fundulea, jud. Călărași; f. 1957; 336 mems.; library of 9,238 vols.; Dir. Prof. Dr. doc. NICHIFOR CEAPOIU; publs. *Analele, Probleme de genetică teoretică și aplicată* (every 2 months), *Probleme de agrofitotehnie teoretică și aplicată, Probleme de protecția plantelor* (quarterly).

**Institutul de Cercetări pentru Creșterea Taurinelor** (*Cattle Research Institute*): 8113 Com. Corbeanca, jud. Ilfov; f. 1970; research in genetics and cytogenetics, physiology, animal nutrition, biochemistry, beef and milk production, histology, cattle improvement, feeding, behaviour and reproduction, management, technological design; 65 mems.; library of 11,000 vols.; Dir. Eng. Dr. STELIAN DINESCU; publ. *Taurine—Scientific Works*† (annually).

**Institutul de Cercetări Pomicole** (*Research Institute for Fruit Growing*): 0312 Pitești-Mărăcineni, Jud. Argeș; f. 1977; 272 staff; library of 10,350 vols.; Dir. Dr. Ing. P. PARNIA; publ. *Annual Reports*†.

**Institutul de Cercetare și Producție a Cartofului** (*Potato Research and Production Institute*): 2200 Brașov, Str. Fundăturii 2; f. 1977; potato breeding, seed production, cropping technology, protection, storage and processing; 53 staff; library of 7,684 vols.; Dir. Dr. doc.ing. MATEI BERINDEI; publ. *Anale (Lucrări științifice*†).

**Institutul de Economie Agrară** (*Research Institute for Agrarian Economy*): Bucharest, Bd. Mărăști 61; f. 1967; 42 mems.; library of 2,600 vols.; Dir. DUMITRU DUMITRU.

**Institutul de Cercetări pentru Chimie și Industrie Alimentară** (*Research Institute for Chemistry and Food Industry*): Bucharest, Str. Gîrlei 1; f. 1950; 240 mems.; library of 10,000 vols.; Dir. Dr. Eng. OVIDIU POPESCU; publ. *Lucrări științifice* (annually).

**Institutul de Cercetări și Inginerie Tehnologica pentru Irigații și Drenaj** (*Research and Engineering Institute for Irrigation and Drainage*): Băneasa-Giurgiu 8384; f. 1933; library of 3,100 vols., 60 periodicals; Dir. Dr. Ing. GH. HÎNCU; publs. *Studies and Research in Irrigation and Drainage* (annually).

**Institutul de Cercetări pentru Legumicultură și Floricultură** (*Research Institute for Vegetable and Flower Growing*): 8268 Vidra, jud. Giurgiu; f. 1967; library of 14,000 vols.; Dir. Dr.-Eng. GHEORGHE VÎLCEANU; publ. *Annual Report*†.

**Institutul de Cercetare, Proiectare și Inginerie Tehnologică pentru Mecanizarea Agriculturii** (*Research, Design and Technological Engineering Institute for Agricultural Mechanization*): 71592 Bucharest, Bd. Ion Ionescu de la Brad 6, Sectorul 1; f. 1952; 1,300 mems.; library of 38,000 vols.; Dir. Ing. PETRESCU ALEXANDRU; publ. *Lucrări științifice*† (Scientific Works, annual, with abstracts in English, French, German and Russian).

**Institutul de Cercetări pentru Nutritia Animală** (*Research Institute for Animal Nutrition*): Balotești, jud. Ilfov; f. 1970; Dir. Ing. C. DAMIAN.

**Institutul de Cercetări pentru Pedologie și Agrochimie** (*Research Institute for Soil Science and Agrochemistry*): 73111 Bucharest, Bd. Mărăști 61; f. 1969; 272 mems.; library of 9,000 vols.; Dir. Ing. CORNELIU RĂUȚĂ; publ. *Anale*† (annual).

**Institutul de Cercetări pentru Protecția Plantelor** (*Research Institute for Plant Protection*): 71592 Bucharest, Bd. Ion Ionescu de la Brad 8; f. 1967; plant virology, bacteriology and mycology, entomology, rodents and pesticides; 215 mems.; library of 6,045 vols.; Dir. Dr. TUDOREL BAICU; publs. *Analele*† (annual), *Pesticide Tests*†.

**Institutul de Cercetări pentru Viticultură și Vinificație** (*Research Institute for Wine Growing and Wine Making*): 2040 Valea Călugărească, jud. Prahova; f. 1967; 173 mems.; library of 11,850 vols.; Man. Dr. Ing. L. MIHALACHE; publ. *Anale*†.

**Institutul de Cercetări și Amenajări Silvice** (*Forest Research and Design Institute*): Bucharest, 128 Șoseaua Ștefănești, Sector 2; f. 1933; 130 staff; library of 12,000 vols.; Dir. Eng. G. BUMBU; publs. *Anale, Revista pădurarilor* (every 2 months).

**Institutul de Cercetări și Proiectări "Delta Dunării"** (*Danube Delta Research and Design Institute*): 8800 Tulcea, Str. Alex. Sahia 2; f. 1970; pisciculture, agriculture, forestry, research into natural resources of the Danube Delta; 75 staff; library of 30,000 vols.; Dir. Eng. ALEXANDRU VOLCOV.

**Institutul de Cercetări și Proiectări pentru Gospodărirea Apelor** (*Research and Design Institute for Water Resources Engineering*): Bucharest, Spl. Independenței 294; f. 1971; 580 mems.; library of 5,000 vols.; Dir. Dr. Eng. FLORIN IORGULESCU.

**Institutul de Cercetări și Proiectări pentru Valorificarea și Industrializarea Legumelor și Fructelor (ICPVILF)** (*Research and Design Institute for Marketing and Processing Fruit and Vegetables*): 75162 Bucharest, Str. Lînăriei 93, P.O.B. 93; f. 1967; 160 staff; library of 8,000 vols.; Dir. Dr. Eng. ION RĂDULESCU; publ. *Lucrări științifice ICPVILF* (annually).

**Institutul de Cercetări Veterinare și Biopreparate "Pasteur"** (*"Pasteur" Institute for Veterinary Research and Biological Products*): Bucharest, Șoseaua Giulești 333; f. 1909; veterinary research and production of biological preparations for veterinary use; 143 mems.; library of 15,000 vols.; Dir. Dr. VALENTIN POPOVICI; publs. *Archiva Veterinaria*† (2 a year), *Lucrările ICVB Pasteur-Bucharest*† (annual).

**Institutul de Geodezie, Fotogrametrie, Cartografie și Organizarea Teritoriului** (*Institute for Geodesy, Photogrammetry, Cartography, and Land Management*): 78334 Bucharest, Bd. Expoziției 1 A, sector 1; f. 1958; 1,000 staff; library of 4,457 vols.; Dir. Dr. Eng. NICOLAE ZEGHERU.

**Oficiul de Informare Documentară pentru Agricultură și Industrie Alimentară** (*Office of Documentary Information for Agriculture and the Food Industry*): Bucharest, Bd. Mărăști 61; f. 1965; library of 50,000 vols.; Dir. I. DAVIDOVICI.

**Stațiunea Centrală de Cercetări pentru Cultivarea Plantelor de Nisipuri** (*Central Research Station for Plant Cultivation of the Sands*): 1185 Dăbuleni, jud. Dolj; f. 1959; 26 mems.; library of 12,432 vols.; Dir. Dr. Eng. PETRE BANIȚĂ.

**Stațiunea Centrală de Cercetări Avicole** (*Central Research Station for Poultry*): Corbeanca, Jud. Ilfov; Dir. Dr. M. ȘTEFĂNESCU.

**Stațiunea Centrală de Cercetări pentru Creșterea Ovinelor** (*Central Research Station for Sheep Breeding*): Constanța (Palas), jud. Constanța; f. 1970; Dir. Dr. ȘTEFAN MOISE.

**Stațiunea Centrală de Cercetări pentru Cresterea Porcinelor** (*Central Research Station for Pig Breeding*): Periș, Jud. Ilfov; Dir. Dr. Eng. ION ARIȘANU.

**Stațiunea Centrală de Cercetări pentru Combaterea Eroziunii Solului** (*Central Research Station for Soil Erosion Control*): Perieni, jud. Vaslui; Dir. Ing. GH. STOIAN.

**Stațiunea Centrală de Cercetări pentru Ameliorares Solurilor Săraturate** (*Central Research Station for Saline Soils Improvement*): Brăila, jud. Brăila; Dir. Eng. EMIL BĂLĂUȚĂ.

**Stațiunea Centrală de Cercetări pentru Cultura Pajiștilor** (*Central Grasslands Research Station*): 2200 Brașov-Măgurele, str. Cucului 5; f. 1969; grassland-research; 25 mems.; library of 5,000 vols.; Dir. Dr. MIRCEA POP; publ. *Lucrări științifice*† (annually).

**Stațiunea Centrală de Cercetări pentru Cultura și Industrializarea Tutunului** (*Central Research Station for Tobacco Growing and Industrialization*): Bucharest, Str. Gîrlei nr. 1; f. 1974; 100 mems.; Dir. Dr. Eng. EUGEN IOAN.

**Stațiunea de Cercetări pentru Piscicultură** (*Research Station for Fishbreeding*): Nucet, jud. Dîmbovița; f. 1940; 140 mems.; library of 26,000 vols.; Dir. Eng. C. ENE.

**Stațiunea de Cercetări pentru Plante Medicinale și Aromatice** (*Research Station for Medicinal and Aromatic Plants*): Fundulea, jud. Talomița; f. 1975; 11 mems.; Dir. dr. Eng. EMIL PĂUN.

**Stațiunea de Cercetări pentru Sericicultură** (*Research Station for Sericiculture*): Bucharest, Șos. București-Ploiești nr. 69, Sector 1; f. 1906; library of 16,000 vols.; Dir. Eng. ION LOGOFETICI; publ. *Sericiculture* (quarterly).

**Stațiuni de Cercetări Agricole** (*Agricultural Research Stations*): at Albota, jud. Argeș; Caracal, jud. Olt; Dobrogea, jud. Constanța; Livada, jud. Satu Mare; Lovrin, jud. Timiș; Podu Iloaiei, jud. Iași; Oradea, jud. Bihor; Simnic, jud. Dolj; Suceava, jud. Suceava; Turda, jud. Cluj; Mărculești, jud. Călărași; Teleorman, jud. Teleorman.

**Stațiuni de Cercetări Legumicole** (*Vegetable Research Stations*): Aradul Nou, jud. Arad; Bacău, jud. Bacău; Buzău, jud. Buzău; Ișalnița, jud. Dolj; Almaj, jud. Dolj; T. Vladimirescu, jud. Brăila; Iernut, jud. Mureș.

**Stațiuni de Cercetare și Producție Pomicolă** (*Fruit Growing Research and Production Stations*): at Baia Mare, jud. Maramureș; Bistrița, jud. Bistrița-Năsăud; Caransebeș, jud. Caraș-Severin; Fălticeni, jud. Suceava; Geoagiu, jud. Hunedoara; Tîrgu Jiu, jud. Gorj; Voinești, jud. Dîmbovița; Dolj, jud. Dolj; Iași, jud. Iași; Mehedinți, jud. Mehedinți; Mureș, jud. Mureș; Prahova, jud. Prahova; Sibiu, jud. Sibiu; Vîlcea, jud. Vîlcea; Ștefănești-Argeș, jud. Argeș; Băneasa-București, Ilfov; Bihor, jud. Bihor; Buzău, jud. Bihor; Cluj-Napoca, jud. Cluj; Lipova, jud. Arad; Srejești, jud. Olt; Zalău, jud. Sălaj; Viile, jud. Satu Mare; Bacău, jud. Bacău.

**Stațiuni de Cercetări Viticole** (*Vine-Growing and Wine-Making Research Stations*): at Blaj, jud. Alba; Bujoru, jud. Galați; Drăgășani, jud. Vîlcea; Greaca, jud. Giurgiu; Iași, jud. Iași; Miniș, jud. Arad; Murfatler, jud. Constanța; Odobești, jud. Vrancea; Ștefănești, jud. Argeș; Pietroasele, jud. Buzău.

**Stațiuni de Cercetări pentru Cultura Cartofului** (*Potato Research and Production Stations*): Tg. Secuiesc, jud. Covasna; Mărșani, jud. Dolj; Tg. Jiu, jud. Gorj; Miercures Ciuc, jud. Harghits; Tulcea, jud. Tulcea

**Stațiuni de Cercetări Zootehnice** (*Research Stations for Animal Breeding*): at Bonțida, jud. Cluj; Secuieni-Roman, jud. Neamț; Tg. Mureș, jud. Mureș; Maramureș, jud. Maramureș; Popăuți, jud. Botoșani; Rușețu, jud. Buzău.

**Stațiuni de Cercetări și Amenajări Silvice** (*Sylvicultural and Design Research Stations*): at Hemeiuș, jud. Bacău; Focșani, jud. Vrancea; Roman, jud. Neamț; Cîmpuling, jud. Suceava; Cornetu, jud. Giurgiu; Craiova, jud. Dolj; Tulcea, jud. Tulcea; Bărăgan, jud. Călărași; Pitești, jud. Argeș; Mihăiești, jud. Argeș; Caransebeș, jud. Caraș-Severin; Pădurea Verde, jud. Timiș; Brașov, jud. Brașov; Tg. Mureș, jud. Mureș; Simeria, jud. Hunedoara; Orades, jud. Bihor; Cluj-Napoca, jud. Cluj; Bistrița, jud. Bistrița-Năsăud; Sinaia, jud. Prahova.

---

**Academia de Științe Medicale** (*Academy of Medical Sciences*): 79173 Bucharest, Bd. 1 Mai 11; f. 1969; publ. *Annals*†.

PRESIDIUM:

*President:* (vacant).
*Vice-Presidents:* Prof. STEFAN MILCU; Prof. IOAN MORARU; Prof. RADU PĂUN; Prof. LUDOVIC CSÖGÖR.
*General Secretary:* Prof. EMIL MĂGUREANU.
*Members:* Prof. PIUS BRÎNZEU; Prof. NICOLAE CAJAL; Prof. MIHAI DUCA; Prof. PETRE IONESCU-STOIAN; Prof. MARCELA PITIȘ; Prof. VASILE MÂRZA; Prof. VALERIAN POPESCU; Prof. VASILE SĂBĂDEANU.

## ACADEMIES

*I. Section of Biology:*
President: Prof. ŞTEFAN MILCU.
Scientific Secretary: C. I. TRUIA, M.D.

MEMBERS:

BACIU, I.
MENKEŞ, B.
MÂRZA, V.
MORARU, I.
SORU, E.

CORRESPONDING MEMBERS:

GEORGESCU, L.
MAROŞ, T.
OPRIŞIU, C.
POPESCU, A.
REPCIUC, E.

*II. Section of Clinical Medicine:*
President: Prof. RADU PĂUN.
Scientific Secretary: BOGDAN CUPCEANCU, M.D.

MEMBERS:

ANASTASATU, C.
ARSENI, C.
BALŞ, M.
BRÎNZEU, P.
CSÖGÖR, L.
DOCZY, P.
FĂGĂRĂŞANU, I.
HĂRĂGUŞ, S.
JUVARA, I.
KREINDLER, A.
MILCU, ŞT.
NANA, A.
NEGOIŢĂ, C.
OLĂNESCU, G.
PĂCURARIU, I.
PĂUN, R.
PITIŞ, M.
POPESCU, V.
SĂBĂDEANU, V.
VOICULESCU, M.
VOICULESCU, V.

CORRESPONDING MEMBERS:

ALESSANDRESCU, D.
BĂDĂRĂU, G.
BARBU, R.
BURLUI, D.
CINCA, I.
COSTĂCHEL, O.
DUMA, D.
MAREŞ, E.
POP D. POPA, I.
POPOVICI, O.
PREDESCU, V.
PRIŞCU, R.
PUŞKAŞ, G.
SOFLETEA, A.
VANCEA, P.

*III. Section of Prophylactic Medicine:*
President: Prof. NICOLAE CAJAL.
Scientific Secretary: CONSTANTIN NAGHIU, M.D.

MEMBERS:

CAJAL, N.
DUCA, M.
MESROBEANU, I.

CORRESPONDING MEMBER:

PORTOCALĂ, R.

*IV. Section of Pharmaceutical Research:*
President: Prof. PETRE IONESCU-STOIAN.
Scientific Secretary: ELENA AITEANU, PH.D.

MEMBER:

STOIAN-IONESCU, P.

HONORARY MEMBERS:

ASLAN. ANA
GOIA, I.
PAVEL, I.

### RESEARCH INSTITUTES ATTACHED TO THE ACADEMY OF MEDICAL SCIENCES

**Centrul de Cercetări Medicale** (*Medical Research Centre*): 4300 Tîrgu-Mureş, Str. Gh. Marinescu nr. 40; f. 1956; experimental and clinical research into tissue and organ transplantation, immune response, cardiovascular diseases and athero-sclerosis; library of 12,000 vols.; Dir. Prof. ZENO BARBU.

**Centrul de Igienă şi Sănătate Publică** (*Centre of Hygiene and Public Health*): 1900 Timişoara, Bd. V. Babeş 16; f. 1946; environmental pollution (air, water, soil and food); industrial hygiene; epidemiology, pathogenesis and laboratory diagnosis of certain infectious and non-infectious diseases; experimental research in the field of embryology and teratology; library of 15,890 vols.; Dir. Prof. LEONIDA GEORGESCU; publ. *Morphologie et Embryologie* (series of *Revue Roumaine de Morphologie, d'Embryologie et de Physiologie* (quarterly).

**Centrul National de Fono-Audiologie şi Chirurgie Funcţională O.R.L.** (*National Centre for Phono-Audiology and ENT Surgery*): 76231 Bucharest, Mihai Cioranu 21; f. 1972; library of 2,000 vols.; Dir. Prof. DORIN HOCIOTA.

**Institutul de Endocrinologie "C. I. Parhon"** (*"C. I. Parhon" Institute of Endocrinology*): 79660 Bucharest, Bul. Aviatorilor 34-36; f. 1946; 113 mems.; a complex clinico-experimental unit; university teaching centre; library of 59,675 vols.; Dir. Prof. MARCELLA PITIŞ; publ. *Endocrinologie*† (series of *Revue roumaine de Médecine*, quarterly).

**Institutul de Fiziologie Normală şi Patologică "D. Danielopolu"** (*"D. Danielopolu" Institute of Normal and Pathological Physiology*): 79645 Bucharest, Bd. 1 Mai 11; f. 1949; graduate and postgraduate teaching; experimental and clinical physiology, patho-physiology of digestion and circulation; 55 mems.; library of 82,764 vols.; Dir. Prof. P. GROZA; publ. *Physiologie* (series of *Revue Roumaine de Morphologie, d'Embryologie et de Physiologie*†, quarterly).

**Institutul de Igienă şi Sănătate Publică** (*Institute of Hygiene and Public Health*): 79636 Bucharest, Str. Dr. Leonte 1-3; f. 1927; graduate and postgraduate teaching; library of 35,300 books and separate medical history library of 40,000 vols.; Dir. Dr. M. ALDEA; publ. *Studies and Research in Hygiene and Public Health*†.

**Institutul de Igienă şi Sănătate Publică** (*Institute of Hygiene and Public Health*): 3400 Cluj-Napoca, Str. Pasteur 6; f. 1930; environmental hygiene, occupational health, school hygiene, sanitary statistics, radiobiology, epidemiology, virology, clinical research; 84 mems.; library of 28,954 vols.; Dir. (vacant).

**Institutul de Medecină Internă "Nicolae Gh. Lupu"** (*"Nicolae Gh. Lupu" Institute of Internal Medicine*): Bucharest, Sos. Stefan cel Mare 19-21; f. 1949; university teaching centre; library of 58,000 vols.; Dir. Prof. S. PURICE; publ. *Médecine Interne* (series of *Revue Roumaine de Médecine*†, quarterly).

**Institutul Cantacuzino:** 70.100 Bucharest 1, Spl. Independenţei 103, c.p.l.-525; f. 1921; research in the field of microbiology and parasitology; studies in epidemiology; manufacture and control of sera and vaccines; teaching centre for university and post-graduate medical education; library of 80,000 vols.; Dir. Prof. V. BÎLBÎE; publ. *Archives Roumaines de Pathologie Expérimentale et de Microbiologie*† (in French and English, quarterly).

**Institutul de Neurologie şi Psihiatrie** (*Institute of Neurology and Psychiatry*): 79644 Bucharest, Şos. Berceni 10-12; f. 1950; library of 7,957 vols.; university teaching centre; Dir. Prof. V. VOICULESCU; publ. *Neurologie et Psychiatrie* (series of *Revue Roumaine de Médecine*, quarterly).

**Institutul Oncologic** (*Institute of Oncology*): 79645 Bucharest, Bd. 1 Mai 11, Sector 1, P.O.B. 1005; f. 1949; experimental and clinical oncology and radiobiology, chemotherapy and immunotherapy; teaching centre for postgraduate education; 503 mems.; library of 41,144 vols.; Dir. Prof. AL. TRESTIOREANU; publ. *Oncologia*† (quarterly).

**Institutul "V. Babeş"** (*"V. Babeş" Institute*): 79630 Bucharest, Spl. Independenţei 99-101; f. 1887; genetics, immunology, pathology and ultra-structure; library of 20,000 vols.; university and postgraduate teaching; Dir. Prof. IOAN MORARU.

**Institutul de Igienă şi Sănătate Publică** (*Institute of Hygiene and Public Health*): 6600 Iaşi, Str. Dr. V. Babeş 14; f. 1930; environmental hygiene and pollution; working conditions in industry; experiments with pesticides, etc.; library of 35,912 vols.; Dir. V. RUGINĂ; publ. *Morphologie et Embryologie* (series of *Revue Roumaine de Morphologie, d'Embryologie et de Physiologie*, quarterly).

**Institutul de Virusologie "St. S. Nicolau"** (*"St. S. Nicolau" Institute of Virology*): 79650 Bucharest, Şos. Mihai

Bravu 283-285; f. 1949; basic and applied virological research and teaching centre for university and postgraduate education, WHO Virus Collaborating Centre; 200 staff; library of 3,500 vols.; Dir. Prof. NICOLAE CAJAL; publ. *Virologie—série de la Revue Roumaine de Médecine*† (quarterly).

**Institutul pentru Controlul de Stat al Medicamentului și Cercetări Farmaceutice** (*Institute of State Control of Medicament and Pharmaceutical Research*): Bucharest, Str. Aviator Sănătescu 48; f. 1929; research on drugs; graduate and postgraduate teaching; Dir. Prof. CORNELIU BALOESCU; publ. *Drug Monitoring* (quarterly).

---

**Academia de Științe Sociale și Politice** (*Academy of Social and Political Sciences*): Bucharest, Str. Onești 11; f. 1970; 97 full mems., 82 corresponding mems.; publs. a total of 40 reviews, bulletins, annuals, etc.

*Honorary President:* NICOLAE CEAUȘESCU.

PRESIDIUM:

*President:* MINHEA GHEORGHIU.

*Vice-Presidents:* ION CETERCHI; ZOE DUMITRESCU-BUȘULENGA; ROMAN MOLDOVAN; STEFAN VOICU.

*Presidents of Sections:* ALEXANDRU BÎRLĂDEANU (Economic Sciences); DUMITRU GHIȘE (Philosophy and Logic); STEFAN STEFĂNESCU (History and Archaeology); JANOȘ DEMETER (Juridical Sciences); VALTER ROMAN (Political Sciences); ALEXANDRU ROȘCA (Psychology and Pedagogy); HENRI H. STAHL (Sociology); ION FRUNZETTI (Theory and History of Arts and Literature).

*Members:* TUDOR BUGNARIU; EMILIAN DOBRESCU, ERNEST GALL; CAROL GÖLLNER; CONSTANTIN IONESCU-GULIAN; MIRCEA MALIȚA; MIRCEA PETRESCU-DÎMBOVIȚA; ION POPESCU-PUȚURI.

*I. Section of Economic Sciences:*

MEMBERS:

BIJI, M.
BÎRLĂDEANU, A.
CONSTANTINESCU, N.
DESMIREANU, I.
DOBRESCU, E.
DOLGU, G.
FLORESCU, M.
HUTIRA, E.
LEVENTE, M.

MALINSCHI, V.
MOLDOVAN, R.
MURGESCU, C.
NEGUCIOIU, A.
POSTOLACHE, T.
RACHMUTH, I.
RĂDULESCU, G.
RAUSSER, V.
ZAHARESCU, B.

CORRESPONDING MEMBERS:

ALBU, A.
APOSTOL, G.
AXENCIUC, V.
BADRUS, G.
CREȚOIU, G.
DEMETRESCU, M.

MĂLCOMETE, P.
NICOLAE-VĂLEANU, I.
ROMÂNU, I.
STĂNESCU, N.
TODOSIA, M.
VACAREL, G. I.

*II. Section of Philosophy and Logic:*

MEMBERS:

APOSTOL, P.
BANU, I.
BREAZU, M.
BUGNARIU, T.
GHIȘE, D.
IONESCU-GULIAN, C.

KALLOS, N.
POSESCU, A.
TĂNASE, A.
VLAD, C.
WALD, H.

CORRESPONDING MEMBERS:

BELLU, N.
BORGEANU, C.
BOTEZATU, P.
CORNEA, I.
ENESCU, G.
FLORIAN, R.

GEORGESCU, S.
MARE, C.
MIHĂILESCU, E.
PANTAZI, R.
PETRE, C.

*III. Section of History and Archaeology:*

MEMBERS:

BERCIU, D.
CIOHODARU, C.
CONDURACHI, E.

GEORGESCU, V.
GÖLLNER, C.
JAKO, S.

PASCU, S.
PETRESCU-DÎMBOVIȚA, M.
PIPPIDI, D.
POPESCU-PUȚURI, I.

PRODAN, D.
ȘTEFĂNEESCU, S.
TUDOR, D.
VULPE, R.

CORRESPONDING MEMBERS:

ARDELEANU, I.
BANTEA, E.
BODOR, A.
CÎNDEA, V.
DEAC, A.
DEMENY, L.
DUȚU, A.
GEORGESCU, T.
HOREDT, K.

HUREZEANU, D.
LOGHIN, A.
LUPU, N.
MUREȘAN, C.
POPESCU, D.
RUSU, I.
STĂNESCU, E.
SZEKELY, Z.
ZAHARIA, G.

*IV. Section of Juridical Sciences:*

MEMBERS:

BARASCH, E.
CETERCHI, I.
DEMETER, I.
DRĂGANU, T.
GEAMĂNU, G.
IONAȘCU, A.
IONAȘCU, T.

LEPĂDĂTESCU, M.
MAURER, I.-GH.
STĂTESCU, C.
STOENESCU, I.
TAKACS, L.
VÎNTU, I.

CORRESPONDING MEMBERS:

HANGA, V.
JACOTĂ, M.
MAZILU, D.

STEGĂROIU, C.
TATOMIR, N.
TEODORU, G.

*V. Section of Political Sciences:*

MEMBERS:

FAZEKAS, I.
ILIESCU, I.
MĂNESCU, C.
NICULESCU, P.
RĂDULESCU, I.

RĂUTU, L.
ROMAN, V.
VOICU, ȘT.
VOITEC, ȘT.

CORRESPONDING MEMBERS:

ANTAL, A.
BREITENHOFFER, A.
CORBU, N.
IGNAT, N.
IONESCU, A.
MARȚIAN, D.

MITEA, C.
NICHITA, V.
RUS, V.
TELESCU, M.
TRĂSNEA, O.

*VI. Section of Psychology and Pedagogy:*

MEMBERS:

BÎRSĂNESCU, S.
CHIRCEV, A.
PAVELCU, V.

ROȘCA, A.
STOIAN, S.
TODORAN, D.

CORRESPONDING MEMBERS:

COSMOVICI, P.-A.
DANCSULY, A.
POP, T.

SALADE, D.
VĂIDEANU, G.

*VII. Section of Sociology:*

MEMBERS:

BĂDINA, O.
GALL, E.
IONESCU, C.
MALIȚA, M.

MĂNESCU, M.
NICUȚĂ, C.
POPESCU, D.
STAHL, H.

CORRESPONDING MEMBERS:

ALBERT, F.
BĂRBAT, A.
MARICA, EM. G.

MATEI, I.
MIHU, A.

*VIII. Section for the Theory and History of Arts and Literature:*

MEMBERS:

BALACI, A.
BALOGH, E.
CAPESIUS, B.
CIOCULESCU, Ș.
CIOPRAGA, C.
CROHMĂLNICEANU, O.
DUMITRESCU-BUȘULENGA, Z.
FRUNZETTI, I.
GHEORGHIU, M.

GEORGESCU, P.
IVAȘCU, G.
MACOVESCU, G.
POPESCU, M.
PIRU, AL.
RUSU, L.
TODUȚĂ, S.
VĂTĂȘIANU, V.
VANCEA, Z.

CORRESPONDING MEMBERS:

Achiței, G.
Bălan, I.-D.
Chițimia, I.
Hajdu, G.
Haulică, D.
Ianoși, I.
Lascu, N.
Milicescu, E.
Micu, D.
Pascu, G.
Râpeanu, V.
Stoffel, E.
Tomescu, V.
Zaciu, M.

## RESEARCH INSTITUTES ATTACHED TO THE ACADEMY OF SOCIAL AND POLITICAL SCIENCES

**Centrul de Cercetări Sociologice** (*Centre for Sociological Research*): Bucharest, Str. Negustori 9; f. 1965; library of 2,500 vols.; Dir. Dr. I. Drăgan; publ. *Revue Roumaine des Sciences Sociales—Série de Sociologie, Viitorul Social* (quarterly).

**Centrul de Științe Sociale** (*Centre for Social Sciences*): Cluj-Napoca, Str. B. Nagy Antal 2; f. 1969; Dir. Prof. I. Gliga.

**Centrul de Științe Sociale** (*Centre for Social Sciences*): Craiova, Str. Calea Unirii 79; f. 1965; 30 mems.; library of 300,000 vols.; Dir. Ion Pătroiu; publ. *Arhivele Olteniei* (annually).

**Centrul de Științe Sociale** (*Centre for Social Sciences*): 6600 Iași, Str. Codrescu 2; f. 1969; 28 staff; Dir. Ionel Hagiu.

**Centrul de Științe Sociale** (*Centre for Social Sciences*): Sibiu, Str. Octombrie Roșu 2; f. 1970; linguistics, history, history of literature, sociology; library of 5,000 vols.; Dir. Dr. Ion Vesa; publ. *Forschungen zur Volks- und Landeskunde* (2 a year).

**Centrul de Științe Sociale** (*Centre for Social Sciences*): Tîrgu-Mureș, Str. Bolyai 17; f. 1957; research in philosophy, social and political sciences, history and history of literature, folklore and art; library of 175,000 vols.; Dir. Prof. Dr. V. Rus.

**Centrul de Științe Sociale** (*Centre for Social Sciences*), Timișoara, Bd. V. Pirvan 4; f. 1970; philosophy, economy, law, history, pedagogy, social psychology; 9 mems.; library of 1,040 vols.; Dir. Prof. Dr. I. Iliescu.

**Comisia de Istorie a Economiei și a Gîndirii Economice** (*Commission on Economic History and Theory*): Bucharest, Calea Victoriei 125; f. 1970; Pres. (vacant).

**Comitetul Național pentru Literatură Comparată** (*National Committee for Comparative Literature*): Bucharest, Str. Onești 11; f. 1970; 22 mems.; Pres. Prof. Dr. Zoe Dumitrescu-Bușulenga; Sec. Dr. Alexandru Duțu; publ. *Synthesis*† (annual).

**Institutul de Arheologie** (*Institute of Archaeology*): Bucharest, Str. I. C. Frimu 11; f. 1956; Dir. Prof. D. M. Pippidi; publ. *Dacia-Revue d'Archéologie et d'Histoire Ancienne* (annual), *Studii și cercetări de istorie veche* (quarterly), *Studii și cercetări de numismatică* (annual), *Materiale și cercetări arheologice* (annual).

**Institutul de Cercetări Economice** (*Institute of Economic Research*): Bucharest, Calea Dorobanți 11-25; f. 1953; Deputy Dir. I. Totu; publ. *Revista Economică* (weekly), *Revue Roumaine des Sciences Sociales—série de Problèmes Économiques* (2 a year).

**Institutul de Cercetări Juridice** (*Institute of Juridical Research*): Bucharest, Bul. Gh. Gheorghiu-Dej 33-35; f. 1954; Dir. Prof. Dr. Doc. Constantin Stătescu; publs. *Studii și cercetări juridice* (quarterly), *Revue Roumaine des Sciences Sociales—Série de Sciences juridiques* (2 a year).

**Institutul de Cercetări Pedagogice și Psihologice** (*Institute of Educational and Psychological Research*): Bucharest, Str. Sfinții Apostoli 14; f. 1975; Dir. Dr. Virgiliu Radulian; publs. *Revista de Psihologie* (quarterly), *Revue Roumaine des Sciences Sociales—Série de Psychologie*† (bi-annual), *Revista de Pedagogie* (monthly).

**Institutul de Filozofie** (*Institute of Philosophy*): Bucharest, Bd. Ilie Pintilie 6; f. 1948; Dir. Prof. Dr. I. Tudosescu; publs. *Revista de Filosofie* (monthly), *Revue roumaine de Philosophie et Logique—Série de Philosophie* (quarterly).

**Institutul de Istorie Artei** (*Institute of the History of Art*): Bucharest, Calea Victoriei 196; f. 1949; research in fine arts, folk art, theatre, music and cinematography; library of 47,000 vols., 200,000 negatives, 110,000 photographs; Dir. Prof. V. Drăguț; publs.† *Studii și cercetări de istoria artei—Revue Roumaine d'Histoire de l'Art* (annual, with 2 series, on fine arts and on theatre, music and cinema).

**Institutul de Istorie "Nicolae Iorga"** (*"Nicolae Iorga" Institute of History*): Bucharest, Bul. Aviatorilor 1; f. 1936; 60 mems.; library of 140,000 vols.; Dir. Prof. Dr. Stefan Stefănescu; publs. *Studii și materiale de istorie medie*† (annual), *Studii și materiale de istorie contemporană*† (annual), *Studii și materiale de istorie modernă*† (annual).

**Institutul de Istorie și Arheologie** (*Institute of History and Archaeology*): Cluj-Napoca, Str. Napoca 11; f. 1920; library of 40,000 vols.; Dir. Acad. Stefan Pascu; publ. *Anuarul*.

**Institutul de Istorie și Arheologie "A. D. Xenopol"** (*"A. D. Xenopol" Institute of History and Archaeology*): Iași, str. Karl Marx 15A; f. 1941; Romanian and world history; 35 mems.; library of 52,000 vols.; Dir. Prof. M. Petrescu-Dîmbovița; publs. *Anuarul*†, *Arheologia Moldovei*† (every 2-3 years).

**Institutul de Istorie și Teorie Literară "George Călinescu"** (*"George Călinescu" Institute of Literary History and Theory*): Bucharest, Bd. Republicii 73; f. 1949; 42 mems.; library of 11,000 vols.; Dir. Prof. Dr. Zoe Dumitrescu-Bușulenga; publ. *Revista de Istorie și Teorie Literară* (quarterly).

**Institutul de Științe Politice și de Studiere a Problemei Naționale** (*Institute of Political Science and Study of National Policy*): Bucharest. Bd. Armata Poporului 1-3; f. 1971; scientific research on problems of political parties, state, international relations; library of 800,000 vols.; Dir. Prof. C. Vlad; publs. *Viitorul Social*†, *Analele Academiei "Stefan Gheorghiu"*†, occasional papers.

**Institutul de Studii Sud-Est Europene** (*Institute for South-East European Studies*): Bucharest, Str. I. C. Frimu 9; f. 1963; social sciences; library of 10,000 vols.; Dir. (vacant); publ. *Revue des études sud-est européennes*† (quarterly).

**Oficiul de Informare Documentare in Științele Sociale și Politice** (*Office of Information and Documentation in Social and Poliitcal Sciences*): Bucharest, Bd. Republicii 17; f. 1970; Dir. M. Ioanid; publs. *Romanian Scientific Abstracts* (2 a year).

## LEARNED SOCIETIES

**Asociația Cineaștilor din R.S.R.** (*Cinema Workers' Association of the S.R.R.*): Bucharest, Bd. Gh. Gheorghiu-Dej 65; f. 1963; 902 mems.; Pres. I. Popescu Gopo; Vice-Pres. I. Grigorescu, M. Mureșan.

**Asociația de Drept Internațional si Relații Internaționale din R.S.R.** (*Association of International Law and International Relations of S.R.R.*): Bucharest, Șos. Kiseleff 47; f. 1966; to investigate international law, the history of international relations and diplomacy of Romania, and to examine foreign policy problems today; 430 mems.; library of 4,000 vols.; Pres. Prof. TRAIAN IONASCO; Sec.-Gen. Dr. NICOLAE ECOBESCU; Scientific Dir. NICOLAE FOTINO; publ. *Revue roumaine d'etudes internationales*†.

**Asociaţia Filateliştilor din R.S.R.** (*Philatelists' Association of the S.R.R.*): Bucharest, Str. Boteanu 6; f. 1958; 66,000 mems.; Pres. Dr. APOSTOL TURBATU; publ. *Filatelia*† (monthly).

**Asociaţia Juriştilor din R.S.R.** (*Jurists' Association of the S.R.R.*): Bucharest, Bd. G-ral Magheru 22; f. 1949; 14,000 mems.; Pres. Prof. Dr. C. STĂTESCU; publ. *Revista Română de Drept* (monthly).

**Asociaţia Oamenilor de Artă din Instituţiile Teatrale şi Muzicale** (*Theatre and Performing Artists' Association*): Bucharest, Bd. Schitu Măgureanu; f. 1957; 9,467 mems.; Pres. D. COCEA.

**Asociaţia Oamenilor de Ştiinţa din R.S.R.** (*Scientists' Association of the S.R.R.*): Bucharest, Bd. Ana Ipătescu 29; f. 1956; Pres. (vacant); Gen. Sec. C. PENESCU.

**Asociaţia Psihologilor din R.S.R.** (*Asscn. of Psychologists of the S.R.R.*): Bucharest, Str. Frumoasă 26; f. 1964; Pres. Prof. AL. ROSCA.

**Asociaţia Română de Ştiinţe Politice** (*Romanian Association of Political Sciences*): Bucharest, Sos. Kiseleff 47; f. 1968; 357 mems.; Pres. G. MACOVESCU; Gen. Sec. I. CETERCHI; publ. *Viitorul social*.

**British Council:** British Embassy, 24 Strada Jules Michelet, Bucharest; library of 3,878 vols., 14 periodicals; Cultural Attaché M. B. L. NIGHTINGALE.

**Comitetul Naţional al Geologilor din R.S.R.** (*National Council of Geologists of the S.R.R.*): Bucharest, Str. Mendeleev 36; f. 1962; Pres. D. RĂDULESCU; Vice-Pres. V. IANOVICI.

**Comitetul Naţional al Istoricilor din România** (*National Committee for Historical Sciences of the S.R.R.*): 71261 Bucharest, Bd. Aviatorilor 1; f. 1955; 29 mems.; Hon. Pres. Acad. ŞTEFAN PASCU; Deputy Pres. ŞTEFAN ŞTEFĂNESCU; Sec. DAN BERINDEI.

**Consiliul Naţional al Inginerilor şi Tehnicienilor din R.S.R.** (*National Council of Engineers and Technicians of the S.R.R.*): Bucharest, Calea Victoriei 118; f. 1881, reorganized 1962; 243 mems.; library of 27,000 vols.; Pres. I. TRIPŞA; Gen. Sec. I. C. URSU.

**Consiliul Ziariştilor din Uniunea Sindicatelor din Presă, Poligrafie şi Edituri** (*Journalists' Union of the S.R.R.*): Bucharest, Piata Scînteii 1; 27 mems.; Pres. OCTAVIAN PALER; publ. *Presa noastră* (Our Press).

**P.E.N Club:** Casa Scriitorilor Mihail Sadoveanu, Bucharest, Calea Victoriei 115; Vice-Pres. EUGEN JEBELEANU, HORIA LOVINESCU.

**Societatea de Ştiinţe Biologice din R.S.R.** (*Society of Biological Sciences of the S.R.R.*): Bucharest, Bd. Schitu Măgureanu 9; f. 1949; 3,500 mems.; library of 5,800 vols.; Chair. NICOLAE SĂLĂGEANU; Sec. Gen. I. POPESCU.

**Societatea de Ştiinţe Filologice din R.S.R.** (*Society of Philological Sciences of the S.R.R.*): Bucharest, Str. Spiru Haret 12; f. 1949; language, literature, folklore and ethnography, methodology; 9 brs.; 12,000 mems.; Chair. Prof. BORIS CAZACU; Sec.-Gen. Prof. ION HANGIU; publs. *Limbă şi literatură*† (quarterly), *Studii de literatură universală*† ( annually), *Limbile moderne în şcoală*† (2 a year, summaries in foreign languages), *Limbă şi literatură romană* (quarterly).

**Societatea de Ştiinţe Fizice şi Chimice din R.S.R.** (*Society of Physical and Chemical Sciences of the S.R.R.*): Bucharest, Str. Spiru Haret 12; f. 1964; 8,000 mems.; Pres. Prof. Dr. TH. IONESCU; Gen. Sec. Prof. N. MARTALOGU; publs. *Revista de Fizică şi Chimie*† (monthly).

**Societatea de Ştiinţe Geografice din R.S.R.** (*Society of Geographical Sciences of the S.R.R.*): Bucharest, Bd. Bălcescui 1875; 5,000 mems.; library of 3,800 vols.; Chair. I. SANDRU; Gen. Sec. I. ILIE; publs. *Terra, Bulletin*.

**Societatea de Ştiinţe Geologice din R.S.R.** (*Society of Geological Sciences of the S.R.R.*): Bucharest, Str. Berzei 46; f. 1930, reorganized 1968; 850 mems.; Pres. G. MURCEANU; Gen. Sec. V. LĂZĂRESCU.

**Societatea de Ştiinţe Istorice din R.S.R.** (*Society of Historical Sciences of the S.R.R.*): Bucharest, Bd. Republicii 13; f. 1949; 4,000 mems.; Chair. (vacant); Sec.-Gen. Prof. ION DRAGOMIRESCU; publ. *Studii şi articole de istorie* (2 a year).

**Societatea de Ştiinţe Matematice din R.S.R.** (*Society of Mathematical Sciences of the S.R.R.*): 79547 Bucharest, Str. Academiei 14; f. 1949; 5,000 mems.; Pres. Acad. N. TEODORESCU; publs. *Bulletin Mathématique, Gazeta Matematica* (series A and B), *Matematikai Lapok* (Cluj-Napoca).

**Societatea Naţională Română pentru Ştiinţa Solului** (*Romanian National Society for Soil Research*): Bucharest, Bv. Mărăşti 61; f. 1961; soil science development and the study of practical problems concerning the use and fertility increase of soils; 600 mems.; library of 2,000 vols.; Pres. Acad. Prof. Dr. G. OBREJANU; Sec.-Gen. Dr. D. TEACI.

**Societatea Numismatică Română** (*Romanian Numismatic Society*): 71111 Bucharest, Bd. Ana Ipătescu 21, Sect. 1; f. 1903; coins, medals, seals, decorations, banknotes, insignia, etc.; 1,500 mems.; library of 5,600 vols.; brs. in Arad, Bacău, Braşov, Caracal, Cluj-Napoca, Craiova, Iaşi, Petroşani, Reşita, Sibiu, Suceava, Tîrgu-Mureş, Timişoara; Pres. Acad. EMIL CONDURACHI; Sec.-Gen. AURICĂ SMARANDA; publ. *Buletinul*† (annually).

**Societatea Română de Lingvistică** (*Romanian Society of Linguistics*): Bucharest, Calea Victoriei 194; f. 1970; Pres. Prof. EMANUEL VASILIU; Sec. L.TEBAN.

**Uniunea Arhitecţilor din R.S.R.** (*Architects' Union of the S.R.R.*): 70109 Bucharest, Str. Academiei 18-20; f. 1952; affiliated to the Int. Union of Architects; 2,700 mems.; library of 13,000 vols.; Pres. Dr. CEZAR LĂZĂRESCU; publ. *Arhitectura* (bi-monthly).

**Uniunea Artiştilor Plastici din R.S.R.** (*Artists' Union of the S.R.R.*): Bucharest, Str. Nicolae Iorga 42; f. 1950; 1,650 mems.; library of c. 15,000 vols.; Hon. Pres. Acad. I. JALEA; Pres. I. IRIMESCU; publ. *Arta*† (monthly).

**Uniunea Compozitorilor din R.S.R.** (*Composers' Union of the S.R.R.*): Bucharest I, Str. Constantin Esarcu 2; f. 1920, reorganized 1949; 330 mems.; library of 55,350 vols.; Pres. PETRE BRĂNCUŞI; publ. *Muzica* (monthly).

**Uniunea Scriitorilor din R.S.R.** (*Writers' Union of the S.R.R.*): Bucharest, Calea Victoriei 115; f. 1949; Pres. GEORGE MACOVESCU; publs. *România Literară*†, *Luceafărul*†, *Viaţa Românească*†, *Secolul 20*†, *Steaua*†, *Convorbiri literare*†, *Orizont*†, *Vatra, Utunk*†, *Igaz Szó*†, *Neue Literatur*†, *Knijevni Jivot*†.

**Uniunea Societăţilor de Ştiinţe Medicale din R.S.R.** (*Union of Societies of Medical Sciences of the S.R.R.*): Bucharest, Str. Progresului 10; f. 1877; Pres. Prof. MARIN VOICULESCU; Exec. Sec. Prof. EMANOIL POPESCU; publ. *Viaţa Medicală* (monthly).

AFFILIATED SOCIETIES:

**Society of Anaesthesiology and Intensive Care:** f. 1973; Pres. Dr. ZOREL FILIPESCU; Sec. Dr. RADU SIMIONESCU.

**Society of Cardiology:** f. 1947; Pres. Prof. MIHAI ANTON; Sec. POMPILIU POPESCU.

**Society of Dermatology:** f. 1928; Pres. Dr. AL. DIMITRESCU; Sec. Prof. P. VULCAN; publ. *Dermato-Venerologia* (quarterly).

**Society of Endocrinology:** f. 1918; Pres. Acad. ȘTEFAN MILCU; Sec. Dr. C. TAȘCĂ.

**Society of Forensic Medicine:** f. 1973; Pres. Prof. MOISE TERBANCEA; Sec. Assoc. Prof. VLADIMIR BELIS.

**Society of Gastro-Enterology:** f. 1959; Pres. Prof. L. BERINDEI (acting); Sec. Dr. BENEDICT GHEORGHESCU.

**Society of General Medicine:** f. 1961; Pres. Prof. GH. PANAITESCU; Secs. Dr. M. RĂDULESCU, Dr. MIRCEA ANGELESCU.

**Society of Gerontology:** f. 1956; Pres. Prof. ANA ASLAN; Sec. Dr. LIDIA HARTIA.

**Society of Histochemistry and Cytochemistry:** f. 1964, Pres. Prof. V. PREDA; Sec. Prof. D. ONICESCU.

**Society of the History of Medicine and Pharmacy:** f. 1929; Pres. Prof. Dr. B. DUȚESCU; Sec. Dr. N. MARCU.

**Society of Hygiene and Public Health:** f. 1949; Pres. Prof. Dr. P. MANU; Sec. Dr. T. NICULESCU; publ. *Igiena* (quarterly).

**Society of Infectious Diseases, Parasitology and Epidemiology:** f. 1955; Pres. Prof. MARIN VOICULESCU; Sec. Prof. Dr. LUDOVIC PĂUN; publs. *Bacteriologia, Virusologia, Parazitologia, Epidemiologia* (quarterly).

**Society of Internal Medicine:** f. 1919; Pres. Prof. I. BRUCKNER; Sec. Dr. RUDOLF GEIB; publ. *Medicina Interna* (every 2 months).

**Society of the Middle Sanitary Staff:** f. 1949; Pres. GABRIELA BOCEC-STOIAN; Secs. LIVIA OGLEJAN, GH. RAICU; publ. *Viața Medicală* (monthly).

**Society of Military Medicine and Pharmacy:** f. 1900; Pres. Gen. Dr. ALEX. GR. POPESCU; Sec. Col. Dr. AUREL NICOLAU; publ. *Revista Sanitară Militară* (quarterly).

**Society of Neurology and Neurosurgery:** f. 1918; Pres. Prof. VLAD VOICULESCU; Sec. Dr. I. STAMATOIU; publs. *Neurologia, Psihiatria, Neurochirurgia* (quarterly).

**Society of Normal and Pathological Morphology:** f. 1900; Pres. Acad. V. MÂRZA; Sec. Dr. AL. ESKENASY.

**Society of Obstetrics and Gynaecology:** f. 1900; Pres. Prof. Dr. PANAIT SÎRBU; Sec. Dr. GH. TEODORU; publ. *Obstetrica și Ginecologia* (quarterly).

**Society of Oncology:** f. 1928; Pres. Prof. A. TRESTIOREANU; Sec. Dr. I. POPP; publ. *Oncologie* (quarterly).

**Society of Ophthalmology:** f. 1922; Pres. Prof. Dr. M. DAVID; Sec. Prof. MIRCEA OLTEANU; publ. *Oftalmologia* (quarterly).

**Society of Orthopaedics and Traumatology:** f. 1935; Pres. Prof. AUREL DENISCHI; Sec. Dr. OLEG MEDREA.

**Society of Oto-Rhino-Laryngology:** f. 1908; Pres. Prof. D. HOCIOTĂ; Sec. R. CĂLĂRAȘU; publ. *Oto-Rino-Laringologie* (quarterly).

**Society of Paediatrics:** f. 1925; Pres. Prof. RĂSVAN PRIȘCU; Sec. Dr. T. POPESCU; publ. *Pediatrie* (quarterly).

**Society of Pharmacy:** f. 1880; Pres. Prof. P. IONESCU-STOIAN; Sec. Prof. I. CIULEI; publ. *Farmacia* (quarterly).

**Society of Pneumology and Phthisiology:** f. 1930; Pres. Prof. C. ANASTASATU; Sec. Dr. EUGENIA ALBULESCU; publ. *Pneumo-ftiziologie* (quarterly).

**Society of Physical Medicine, Balneoclimatology and Medical Rehabilitation:** f. 1922; Pres. Prof. TR. DINCULESCU; Sec. Dr. G. GEORGESCU.

**Society of Physiology:** f. 1949; Pres. Prof. P. GROZA; Sec. Prof. Dr. ELVIRA MIULESCU.

**Society of Psychiatry:** f. 1918; Pres. Prof. V. PREDESCU; Sec. Dr. ȘT. MILEA.

**Society of Radiology, Radiobiology and Nuclear Medicine:** f. 1924; Pres. Prof. I. BÂRZU; Sec. Dr. I. TUDOSIU; publ. *Radiologie* (quarterly).

**Society of Sports Medicine:** f. 1932; Pres. Prof. A. DEMETER; Sec. Dr. I. DRĂGAN.

**Society of Stomatology:** f. 1938; Pres. Prof. LUCIAN ENE; Sec. Prof. C. BURLIBAȘA; publ. *Stomatologie* (quarterly).

**Society of Surgery:** f. 1898; Pres. Prof. D. BURLUI; Sec. Dr. ULPIU MATESCU; publ. *Chirurgie* (every 2 months).

## RESEARCH INSTITUTES AND DOCUMENTATION CENTRES

*(see also under Academies of the S.R.R.)*

**Centrul de Cercetări Biologice Cluj-Napoca** (*Biological Research Centre*): 3400 Cluj-Napoca, Str. Republicii 48; f. 1958; controlled by the Ministry of Education; library of 8,300 vols., 8,059 periodicals; Dir. Prof. Dr. V. PREDA.

**Centrul de Cercetări Biologice Iași** (*Biological Research Centre*): 6600 Iași, Calea 23 August 20A; f. 1970; controlled by the Ministry of Education; 210 staff; library of 41,000 vols.; Dir. Prof. Dr. Doc. C.C. ZOLYNEAK.

**Centrul de Fizică Tehnică Iași** (*Technical Physics Centre*): Iași, Splai Bahlui 47; f. 1951; research in magnetism and metal physics; library of 44,500 vols.; Dir. Dr. NICOLAE REZLESCU.

**Centrul de Studii și Cercetări de Istorie și Teorie Militară** (*Centre for Studies and Research in Military History and Theory*): Bucharest, Calea 13 Septembrie 16-18, sector 6; f. 1969; research on Romania's military history and problems of military doctrine and theory; Dir. Maj.-Gen. E. BANTEA.

**Institutul Central de Chimie, Oficiul de Informare Documentară pentru Industria Chimică** (*Central Institute of Chemistry, Office for Documentary Information on the Chemical Industry*): Calea Plevnei 139, 77131 Bucharest; f. 1956; disseminates national and foreign documentation; central library of 70,000 vols.; Dir. Eng. MAIA RUXANDA BAYER; publs. *Revista de Chimie*† *Journal of Chemistry* (monthly), *Materiale Plastice*† (Plastics, quarterly).

**Institutul de Cercetare și Proiectare pentru Sistematizare Locuințe și Gospodărie Comunală** (*Institute of Research and Design for Physical Planning, Housing and Municipal Engineering*): Bucharest, Str. Snagov 53-55; f. 1949; research and standard building design for territory, buildings, sewerage, water supply, sanitation, communal management; Dir. Eng. ADRIAN ALEXANDRESCU; publ. *ISLGC—"b.d.i."* (Bulletin of Documentation and Information).

**Institutul Național de Informare și Documentare** (*National Institute for Information and Documentation*): 70074 Bucharest, Str. Cosmonauților 27-29, Sector 1; f. 1949; furnishes management with documentary information; promotes the use of modern equipment for automatic data processing in the area of documentary information; provides translations; assists production, research, design and educational organizations; library: see Libraries; Dir. Eng. GH. ANGHEL; publs. *Abstracts of Romanian Scientific and Technical Literature*† (in English, French, Russian and Romanian, 2 a year),

*Probleme de informare și documentare†* (Information and Documentation Problems, in English and Romanian, quarterly).

**Institutul de Cercetări Științifice pentru Protecția Muncii** (*Scientific Research Institute for Labour Safety*): Bucharest, Str. Gral. Budișteanu 15, sector 1; f. 1951; fundamental and applied studies and research in labour safety; library of 15,000 vols. and journals; Dir. Eng. V. CARACUDOVICI.

**Institutul de Studii Istorice și Social-Politice de pe lîngă Comitetul Central al Partidului Comunist Român** (*Institute of Historical, Social and Political Studies of the Central Committee of the Romanian Communist Party*): Bucharest, Str. Ministerului 4; f. 1951; research on the history of the working class, of the democratic and revolutionary movement in Romania; history of the Romanian Communist Party, of other parties and working class revolutionary organizations; Dir. I. POPESCU-PUȚURI; publs. *Anale de istorie†* (every 2 months), the collection *Biblioteca de istorie†*, the collection *Evocări* (both published jointly with Editura politică), *Magazin Istoric†* (monthly).

**Institutul de Planificare și Prognoză** (*Planning and Forecasting Institute*): Bucharest, Calea Victoriei 152; f. 1970; elaboration of studies and forecasts intended to indicate alternatives for the long-term development of the national economy, perfecting of methods and techniques in planning; Dir. C. CALUIANU; Sec. T. MELINTE; publs. *Conjunctura economiei mondiale* (annually), *Piața internațională* (daily).

**Institutul Central de Fizică** (*Central Institute of Physics*): Bucharest-Măgurele 76900, Sect. 6, P.O.B. 5206; f. 1956; library of 300,000 vols.; Dir. Gen. Dr. M. IVAȘCU; publs. *Studii și Cercetări de Fizică†*, *Revue Roumaine de Physique†*, *ICEFIZ-Preprints†*, *Conference Proceedings†*.

**Institutul de Economie Mondială** (*Institute of World Economy*): Bucharest, Bd. Republicii 12; f. 1967; international market research, marketing studies, forecasting of world economy and international trade; up-to-date information supplied to economic organizations for foreign trade; library of 11,000 vols. and 216 periodicals; Dir. Acad. C. MURGESCU; publs. *Conjunctura economiei mondiale* (annually), *Evoluția prețurilor internaționale* (2 a year), *Piața internațională* (daily).

**Institutul de Medicină Legală "Prof. Dr. Mina Minovici"** (*"Prof. Dr. Mina Minovici" Medico-Legal Institute*): Bucharest, Str. Căuzași 7-9; f. 1892; forensic medicine and criminology; library of 25,000 vols. and 36 periodicals; Dir. Prof. Dr. M. TERBANCEA; publ. *Problems of Forensic Medicine and Criminalistics*.

**Institutul de Cercetări Etnologice și Dialectologice** (*Institute of Ethnological and Dialectological Research*): Bucharest, Str. Nikos Beloiannis 25; f. 1949; 182 mems.; research in folk culture; library of 43,000 vols.; Dir. I. ILIȘIU; publs. *Revista de etnografie și folclor†* (2 a year).

**Institutul de Geologie și Geofizică** (*Institute of Geology and Geophysics*): Bucharest, Str. Caransebeș 1; f. 1906; reorganized 1960, 1974; controlled by the Ministry of Mining, Petroleum and Geology; museum and library of 180,000 vols.; Dir. IOSIF BERCIA; publs. *Mémoires* (annually), *Anuarul†*, *Comptes Rendus des séances†* (5 a year), *Studii tehnice și economice†* (Technical and Economic Papers†, irregular).

**Institutul de Meteorologie și Hidrologie** (*Institute of Meteorology and Hydrology*): Bucharest, Șos. București-Ploiești 97; f. 1884; Dir. N. CIOVICĂ; publs. include: daily weather reports, *Studii și Cercetări†* (in 2 parts: Meteorology, Hydrology, 1 vol. annually), *Meteorology and Hydrology Journal†* (2 a year), *Bibliografia hidrologică—Hydrological Bibliography†* (annually), *Bibliografia meteorologică—Meteorological bibliography†* (annually).

**Institutul Național de Metrologie** (*National Institute of Metrology*): Bucharest, Șos. Vitan-Bîrzești 11, sector 4; f. 1951; Dir. I. ISCRULESCU; publ. *Metrologia aplicatu†* (quarterly).

**Institutul Central de Perfecționare a Personalului Didactică** (*Central Institute for the Inservice Training of Teachers*): Bucharest, Șos. Panduri 90; f. 1952; post-graduate courses for general and secondary school teachers; 337 mems.; library of 242,400 books; Rector V. RADULIAN.

**Institutul Român de Cercetări Marine** (*Romanian Institute of Marine Research*): Constanța, Bd. Lenin 300, C.P. 53; f. 1970; oceanography, marine biology, fishing; 90 scientific staff; library of 18,000 books and periodicals; Dir. Eng. CONSTANTIN TOMESCU; publ. *Cercetări marine* (bi-annual).

**Institutul Român pentru Relațiile Culturale cu Străinătatea** (*Romanian Institute for Cultural Relations with Foreign Countries*): R79495 Bucharest, Str. M. Eminescu 8; Sec. IOAN BOTAR.

**Laboratorul de Cercetări Masini Hidraulice, Timișoara** (*Laboratory of Hydraulic Machine Research*): 1900 Timișoara, Bd. Mihai Viteazul 1; f. 1929; library of 1,400 vols., 20 collections of periodicals; Dir. Acad. I. ANTON; publ. *Buletinul†*.

**Muzeul, Herbarul și Grădina botanică** (*Institute of Botany*): Cluj-Napoca University, Str. Republicii 42, Cluj-Napoca; f. 1920; Dir. Prof. Dr. ONORIU RAȚIU; publs. *Contribuții botanice*, *Flora Romaniae Exsiccata*, *Delectus seminum*.

**Oficiul de Informare Documentară pentru Construcții, Arhitectură și Sistematizare** (*Documentation and Information Office for Building, Architecture and Town Planning*): Bucharest, Bulevardul 1848 10; f. 1957; prepares and disseminates documentary materials; library of 56,120 vols. and 350 current periodicals; exhibitions of the building industry; Dir. AURELIA DOBRESCU; publs. *Construcții†*, *Architectura†*.

**Oficiul de informare documentară pentru energetică** (*Energy Information and Documentation Office*): 74568 Bucharest, Bd. Energeticienilor 8, Sector 3; f. 1966; library of 19,000 vols.; Dir. M. DAVID; publs. *Energetică†* (monthly) and several information works.

**Oficiul de Informare documentară pentru Învățămînt** (*Office of Documentary Information in Education*): Bucharest, Str. Frumoasă 26; f. 1961; information and documentation on teaching and educational management; information for specialists abroad on scientific research and information science problems; Head CONSTANTIN MĂTUȘOIU; publs. include: *Educație-învățămînt* (6 a year), *Studii și cercetări de documentare* (quarterly).

# LIBRARIES

## BUCHAREST

**Arhivele Statului** (*State Archives*): Bucharest, Bd. Gheorghe Gheorghiu-Dej 29; f. 1831; 221,500 medieval documents, 22,000 seals, 4,585 manuscripts, 14,000 plans and maps; documentary libraries; Gen. Dir. IONEL GAL; publ. *Revista Arhivelor* (quarterly).

**Biblioteca Academiei Republicii Socialiste România:** Bucharest, Calea Victoriei 125; f. 1867; 7,760,000 items; legal national deposit for all Romanian and UN publs.; special collections include Romanian, Greek, Slavonic, Oriental and Latin manuscripts, maps, engravings, old Romanian, Slavonic and Greek documents, medals and coins; co-ordinating National Exchange centre; publs. of all Academies; Dir. Prof. VICTOR SAHINI; publs. *Studii și Cercetări de Bibliologie*, *Cărți Străine intrate în Bibliotecile din România* (4 series, monthly),

*Cărți recent intrate în bibliotecă* (monthly), bibliographies.

**Biblioteca Centrală: Academia de Studii Economice:** Bucharest, Str. Piața M. Romană 6, Sector 1; f. 1913; 1,823,407 vols.; special collection in economic sciences; Chief Librarian PETRE MAREȘ.

**Biblioteca Centrală a Academiei de Științe Agricole și Silvice** (*Central Library of the Academy of Agricultural and Forestry Sciences*): Bucharest, Bul. Mărăști 61; f. 1928; 91,550 books, 7,140 periodicals; publs. *Bibliografia agricolă curentă română* (quarterly), *Noutăți documentare F.A.O.* (monthly), *Cărți străine intrate în bibliotecile din România—seria Agricultură* (monthly).

**Biblioteca Centrală a Institutului Agronomic "Nicolae Bălcescu"** (*Central Library of the "Nicolae Bălcescu" Agronomic Institute*): Bucharest, Bd. Mărăști 59; f. 1948; 437,000 vols. on agronomy, horticulture, animal husbandry, land reclamation; Dir. TEODORA COCIU.

**Biblioteca Centrală de Stat** (*Central State Library*): Bucharest, Str. Ion Ghica 4; f. 1955; 7,733,045 vols. and periodicals; important collections of MSS., old and rare books, musical scores, photographs, maps, prints and drawings; acts as Copyright Deposit, establishing statistics of national production of books and other materials, as Centre of Bibliographical Information, with the following functions: Centre of National current bibliographies; Centre of the union catalogues; Centre of bibliographical research; Centralized cataloguing; Research centre for librarianship and book pathology and restoration; Documentation centre in cultural policy; lifelong education; theatre; music; fine arts; literature; museum, historical and art monuments; cultural establishments and amateur art movement; publishing activity; Centre of methodological guidance which carries out sociological researches concerning the place of the library in the society and in the sociology of reading; it concerns with library organization and methodology of book dissemination; National exchange centre, National centre for the distribution of duplicates; Dir. Prof. ANGELA POPESCU-BRĂDICENI; publs. *Bibliografia Republicii Socialiste România* (10 series, quarterly), *Catalogul colectiv al cărților străine intrate în bibliotecile din România*, *Repertoriul periodicelor străine intrate în bibliotecile din România* (annually), *Repertoriul periodicelor străine de drept intrate în bibliotecile din R.S.R.*, *Cărți străine intrate în bibliotecile din România* (15 series), *Buletin de informare în bibliologie*, *Revista de referate in bibliologie* (quarterly); *Buletin de informare documentare în cultură* (9 series); *Repertoriul colectiv al bibliografiilor republicate; Probleme de patologie a cărții*, etc.

**Biblioteca Centrală Medicală** (*Central Medical Library*): Bucharest, Splaiul Independenței 48; f. 1951; c. 500,000 vols.; publs. *Medical Bibliographical Bulletin*, *Current Union Catalogue of Foreign Books: Medicine*, *Information Médicale Roumaine*, etc.

**Biblioteca Centrală Pedagogică:** Bucharest, Str. Zalomit 12; f. 1880; 285,000 vols.; Dir. ALFRED LAUTERMAN; publs. *L'Enseignement et la pédagogie en Roumanie*† (annually), *Colecția Modernizarea învățămîntului* (c. 2 a year), *Bibliographia pedagogica*†.

**Biblioteca Centrală Universitară** (*Central University Library*): 70119 Bucharest, Str. Onești 1; f. 1895; reorganized 1948; 2,400,000 vols., incorporating a central library (f. 1891) and 26 branch, institute and student hostel libraries; Dir. Prof. ION STOICA; publs. *Cărți străine intrate în bibliotecile din România: Seria Educație Învățămînt* (Foreign Books Acquired by the S.R.R. Libraries: Education, Teaching series, quarterly), *Din sumarul periodicelor străine: Filosofie, Științe sociale, Istorie* (Selected summary of foreign periodicals: Social Sciences, Philosophy, History,

every 2 months), *Drept* (Law, monthly), guide books and bibliographical researches.

**Biblioteca Comitetului de Stat al Planificării** (*Library of the State Committee of Planning*): Bucharest, Calea Victoriei nr. 152; 80,000 vols. mainly on economic sciences, politics, natural sciences.

**Biblioteca Conservatorului de muzică "Ciprian Porumbescu":** Bucharest, Str. Știrbei Vodă 33; f. 1864, reorganized 1948; 201,090 musical works, including 46,003 vols., 124,973 scores, 11,437 recordings, 7,760 tapes, c. 9,240 periodicals, 1,677 rarities, scores and MSS.; Dir. IENCIU VERONA.

**Biblioteca Documentară a Direcției Generale a Arhivelor Statului** (*Documentary Library of the Central Office of State Archives*): Bucharest, Bd. Gheorghe Gheorghiu-Dej 29; f. 1862; 115,000 vols.

**Biblioteca Documentară de Istorie a Medicinei** (*Documentary Library of the History of Medicine*): Bucharest, Str. Dr. Leonte 1-3; f. 1953; 36,000 books, 1,100 periodicals, 3,500 MSS. and documents, 5,200 museum pieces, medals, etc.; comprehensive collection of ancient medical books; Dir. Prof. MARIOARA GEORGESCU; publs. *Iconografia medicală românească*, *Studii și cercetări de istoria medicinei*.

**Biblioteca Institutului National de Informare și Documentare** (*Library of the National Institute for Information and Documentation*): I.N.I.D., 70074 Bucharest, Str. Cosmonauților 27-29, Sectoi 1; f. 1949; c. 150,000 books, 6,000 periodicals.

**Biblioteca Institutului de Arte Plastice "N. Grigorescu"** (*Library of the "N. Grigorescu" Institute of Fine Arts*): Bucharest, Cal. Victoriei 196; f. 1864; 336,528 books and periodicals, slides and photos; Dir. CEZARA MUCENIC; publs. *Studii și cercetări de istoria artei*†, *Revue Romaine de l'Histoire de l'Art*, etc.

**Biblioteca Institutului Medico-Farmaceutic** (*Library of the Medical and Pharmaceutical Institute*): Bucharest, Bd. Dr. Petru Groza 8; f. 1857; central library and 118 branches; 790,491 books and 9,300 periodicals; Dir. Prof. SILVICĂ PETRE.

**Biblioteca Institutului Politehnic "Gheorge Gheorghiu-Dej" București:** Bucharest, Calea Griviței 132; f. 1868; 1,250,000 books and periodicals; Dir. VORONCA LIVIU; publ. *Buletinul*†.

**Biblioteca Municipală "Mihail Sadoveanu":** Bucharest 1, Str. Nikos Beloiannis 4; f. 1935; 1,335,234 vols.; Dir. A. HOAJĂ; publ. *Bibliografia municipiului București* (2 a year).

PROVINCIAL LIBRARIES
(in alphabetical order by town)

**Biblioteca Batthyaneum:** Alba Iulia, Str. Bibliotecii 1; f. 1794; 61,747 vols.; collection of MSS. dating from the 8th century; 569 incunabula, documents, rare books; important mineralogical and numismatic collection; astronomy observatory of 18th century; Dir. CHRISTINA BICĂ.

**Biblioteca Județeană Arad:** Arad, Piața George Enescu 1; f. 1888; 306,237 books, Romanian and foreign periodicals; rare and ancient books about history of Romanian people; Dir. I. MIHAILOVICI.

**Biblioteca Județeană Bacău:** Bacău, B-dul 6 Martie 1; f. 1950; 237,541 vols. and periodicals; Dir. R. STOIAN.

**Biblioteca Județeană Brașov:** Brașov, Bd. Gh. Gheorghiu-Dej 35; f. 1926; 389,728 vols., including MSS. and ancient Romanian books; recordings, albums, maps; Dir. MARIA LAMBUCĂ.

**Biblioteca Centrală a Universitatii din Brașov** (*University of Brașov Library*): 2200 Brașov, Bd. Gheorghe Gheorghiu-Dej 9; f. 1948; 520,000 vols. mainly on technological, forestry, wood industry, chemistry, physics, mathematics, informatics, economic and political subjects; Dir. Dr. Eng. AUREL NEGRUȚIU; publ. *Buletin de informare științifică* (quarterly).

**Biblioteca Centrală Universitară Cluj-Napoca:** 3400 Cluj-Napoca, Str. Clinicilor 2; f. 1872; 3,261,519 vols.; depts of old Romanian prints, art, archaeology, maps, MSS. incunabula and music; Dir. Prof. C. NEGULESCU; publs. *Bibliographical Indexes*.

**Biblioteca Filialei Cluj-Napoca a Academiei Republicii Socialiste România** (*The Library of the Cluj-Napoca Branch of the Academy of the R.S.R.*): Cluj-Napoca, Str. M. Kogălniceanu 12-14; f. 1950; 600,000 books and periodicals from the field of the humanities and science; old and rare books; 170 incunabula; special collections include Romanian, Latin, Hungarian, Slavonic MSS.; 10,000 vols. orientalia; 2,000,000 documents; Dir. Acad. Prof. ȘTEFAN PASCU.

**Biblioteca Documentară "Timotei Cipariu"** (*"Timotei Cipariu" Documentary Library*): Blaj, Str. Armata Roșie 2; f. 1754; c. 25,000 vols. in humanities, sciences, rare and ancient books about history of the Romanian people, including Romanian and foreign periodicals, microfilms.

**Biblioteca Documentară Năsăud** (*The Năsăud Documentary Library*): Năsăud, Republicii 41; f. 1931; c. 50,000 vols.

**Biblioteca Institutului Medico-Farmaceutic:** Cluj-Napoca, Piața Libertății 10; f. 1775; 274,406 books and periodicals; 48 brs.; Dir. I. CONDOR; publ. *Clujul Medical*† (quarterly).

**Biblioteca Institutului Politehnic:** Cluj-Napoca, Str. Emil Isac 15; f. 1884, reorganized 1948; 495,000 books, periodicals, standards, microfilms; mainly on mechanical, electrotechnical and building subjects; Dir. V. NICHIFOR; publ. *Buletinul științific*† (annually).

**Biblioteca Județeană Cluj-Napoca:** Cluj-Napoca, Piața Ștefan cel Mare 1; f. 1950; 280,355 vols. and periodicals; Dir. V. TURDEANU.

**Biblioteca Județeană Constanța:** Constanța, Str. Muzeelor 23; f. 1931; 339,789 Romanian and foreign vols. and publications; Dir. D. CONSTANTIN-ZAMFIR; publ. *Bibliografia Dobrogei* (annually).

**Biblioteca Centrală Universitară** Craiova, Str. Al. I. Cuza 13; f. 1966; 650,000 vols.; Dir. EUGENIA TATOMIRESCU

**Biblioteca Județeană Dolj:** Craiova, Str. M. Kogălniceanu 9; f. 1908; 300,000 vols. including MSS., 16th- and 17th-century rare and ancient books; Dir. Prof. TUDOR NEDELCEA.

**Biblioteca Județeană Mehedinți:** Drobeta-Turnu Severin, B-dul Republicii 2; f. 1921; 142,542 vols., rare and ancient books; Dir. V. PÎRVĂNESCU.

**Biblioteca Județeană "Duiliu Zamfirescu":** Focșani, Str. M. Kogălniceanu 12; f. 1910 by Putna Student's Circle; 122,000 vols.; Dir. Prof. VICTOR RENEA.

**Biblioteca Centrală Universitară Galați:** 6200 Galați, Bul. Republicii 47; f. 1951; 365,306 vols. mainly on technology, shipbuilding, chemistry, food industry, fishing; Dir. MARGARETA TARABAS.

**Biblioteca Județeană "V. A. Urechia":** Galați, Str. Mihai Bravu 16; f. 1890; 458,634 vols., 3,629 prints and designs, 1,467 MSS., 600 maps, 11 incunabula, 407 documents, 375 microfilms and 3,802 records; Dir. N. OPREA.

**Biblioteca Centrală Universitară "M. Eminescu":** Iași, Str. Păcurari 4; f. 1640; 2,175,000 vols. and c. 1,260 Romanian MSS., especially Byzantine, Greek and Romanian; Dir. Dr. MIHAI BORDEIANU.

**Biblioteca Institutului Medico-Farmaceutic:** Iași, Str. Vasile Alecsandri 7; f. 1884; central library with 75 brs.; 310,000 vols.; Dir. MIHAI LIȚU; publ. *Buletin Bibliografic*† (monthly).

**Biblioteca Institutului Politehnic Iași:** Iași, Str. 23 August 11; f. 1937; 559,145 books. microfilms, standards, 5,260 periodicals; Dir. G. MEDVIGHI.

**Biblioteca Județeană "Gh-Asachi":** Iași, Str. Palat. 1; f. 1920; destroyed during World War II and re-established 1950; 400,000 vols., periodicals and microfilms; 6,500 records; Dir. Prof. CONSTANTIN GÎLEA; publs. *Bibliographical Bulletin* (monthly), *Regional Bibliography*, catalogues.

**Biblioteca Județeană Bihor:** 3700 Oradea, Piața Victoriei 3; f. 1950; 417,258 vols. and periodicals, MSS., maps; Dir. TRAIAN BLAJOVICI.

**Biblioteca Județeană Argeș:** Pitești, Str. Victoriei 8; f. 1950; 212,784 vols. and periodicals; Dir. S. VOINESCU.

**Biblioteca Județeană "N. Iorga" Ploiești:** Ploiești, Str. N. C. Krupskaia 1; f. 1921; 215,094 vols. and periodicals; Dir. G. MAXÎN.

**Biblioteca Județeană "Astra" Sibiu:** Sibiu, Str. Gh. Barițiu 5; f. 1861; 568,241 books and periodicals; valuable collections of old Romanian books and periodicals; 6,500 documents and MSS.; 5,700 iconographies; Dir. Prof. IOAN HOLHOȘ.

**Biblioteca Muzeului Brukenthal:** Sibiu, Piața Republicii 4; f. by Samuel de Brukenthal (1721-1803), Governor of Transylvania; 260,401 vols., mainly scientific books, among them 382 incunabula, and MSS., maps, recordings; is now the property of the State; Dir. Dr. C. IRIMIE.

**Biblioteca Județeană Suceava:** Suceava, Str. V. I. Lenin 4; f. 1920; 208,000 vols. and periodicals; Dir. LIDIA ANDRIESCU.

**Biblioteca Centrală Universitară:** 1900 Timișoara, Bv. V. Pârvan 4; f. 1948; 472,275 books and 68,000 periodicals; Dir. T. KNEZEVIĆ.

**Biblioteca Județeană Timiș:** Timișoara, Piata Libertății 3; f. 1904; 517,333 books, periodicals and MSS.; Dir. M. IANCULESCU.

**Biblioteca Județeană Mureș:** Tîrgu-Mureș, Str. Enescu 2; f. 1913; 732,741 vols., 5,000 periodicals; Dir. IULIAN MOLDOVEAN.

**Biblioteca Teleki-Bolyai:** Tîrgu Mureș, Str. Bolyai 17; f. 1802 by the Chancellor Sàmuel Teleki; 200,000 vols.; natural and social science works and representative books of the 16th, 17th, 18th and 19th centuries, including incunabula and MSS.; Dir. ROMEO POJAN.

## MUSEUMS AND ART GALLERIES
### BUCHAREST

**Colecția "Ion Minulescu":** Bucharest, Bd. Gh. Marinescu 1; collection of the poet Ion Minulescu and his wife, the writer Claudia Millian.

**Muzeul de Artă Plastică "Fr. Storck și C. Cuțescu Storck":** Bucharest, Str. Vasile Alecsandri 16; sculptures by Karl and Frederic Storck and paintings by Cecilia Cuțescu-Storck (wife of Frederic), and their own collections; Curator ALINA ȘERBU.

**Muzeul Theodor Aman:** Bucharest, Str. C. A. Rosetti 8; f. 1908; paintings by Theodor Aman; Curator VASILE BORILĂ.

**Muzeul de Artă al R.S.R.:** Bucharest, Str. Știrbei Vodă 1; f. 1950; national museum attached to the Council of Culture and Socialist Education; consists of five sections: (i) the National Gallery containing national, old Romanian, modern and contemporary works of art; (ii) the Universal Gallery, containing paintings, sculptures, European decorative arts and Oriental art; (iii) Graphic art and prints; (iv) Restoration; (v) Public Relations and Documentation; Dir. Prof. Dr. ALEXANDRU CEBUC; publ. *Studii Muzeale*†.

**Muzeul de artă brîncovenească:** Com. Mogoșoaia, Ilfov District, Str. Donca Simo 18; f. 1957; collections of old Romanian art.

**Muzeul de Artă Feudală D. Minovici:** Bucharest, Str. Dr. N. Minovici 3; foreign decorative art collections; Curator GH. MINOVICI.

**Muzeul colecțiilor de artă:** Bucharest, Calea Victoriei 113; f. 1978; Romanian and foreign fine arts.

**Muzeul de Istorie a Municipiului București** (*Historical Museum of Bucharest*): Bucharest, Bd. 1848 2; f. 1921, reorganized 1959; collections representing the most important moments in the history of the capital, documents, works of art, etc.; library of 45,000 vols.; Dir. Prof. P. DACHE; publ. *București Materiale de istorie și muzeografie, vol. I-X* (Bucharest Historical and Museological Works, vol. I-X); affiliated museums:

**Muzeul Curtea Veche:** Str. 30 Decembrie 25-31; f. 1972; first royal residential palace in Bucharest.

**Muzeul Științelor Experimentale-Observatorul Astronomic Popular:** Bd. Ana Ipătescu 21.

**Muzeul de Istorie a Partidului Comunist, a Mișcării Revoluționare și Democratice din România** (*Museum of the History of the Communist Party, of the Revolutionary and Democratic Movement in Romania*): Bucharest. Șos. Kiseleff 3; f. 1948; library of 20,000 vols.; Dir. N. CIOROIU.

**Muzeul de Istorie al R.S.R.** (*National History Museum of the S.R.R.*): Bucharest, Calea Victoriei 12; f. 1968; attached to the Council of Culture and Socialist Education; history of the Romanian people, with collections of archaeology, documents, costumes, coins, lapidarium and treasury of gold objects; library of 45,000 vols.; Dir. Prof. Dr. FLORIAN GEORGESCU; publs. *Muzeul Național†, Cercetări arheologice, Cercetări numismatice, Cercetări istorice* (annually).

**Muzeul de Istorie Naturală "Grigore Antipa":** 71268 Bucharest, Soseaua Kiseleff 1; f. 1834; ecology, zoology, oceanography, palaeontology; library of 26,703 vols., 12,944 periodicals; Dir. Dr. MIHAI C. BACESCU; publ. *Travaux†* (annually).

**Muzeul Literaturii Române:** Bucharest, Str. Fundației 4; f. 1957; history of Romanian literature; library of 30,000 vols. and 15,000 manuscripts and photographs; Dir. A. OPREA; publ. *Manuscriptum* (quarterly review).

**Muzeul Militar Central** (*Central Military Museum*): Bucharest 76111, Str. Izvor 137; f. 1923; the evolution of weapons and fortifications; displays of documents, photographs, weapons, costumes, medals; Dir. Gen. C. ANTIP; publs. Studies and materials of museography and military history.

**Muzeul Satului și de Artă Populară** (*Village and Folk Art Museum*): 71321 Bucharest, Șos. Kiseleff 28-30; f. 1936 and 1874; an ethnographic open-air museum, containing exhibits of folk art, including architecture, interiors of country dwelling houses, with farm buildings, technical machinery, etc., representing village life from 17th to 20th centuries, total of about 85,000 pieces; Dir. (vacant); publ. *Studii și cercetări de etnografie și artă populară*.

**Muzeul Sporturilor:** Bucharest, Bd. Muncii 37-39; f. 1971; Dir. N. POSTOLACHE.

**Muzeul Teatrului Național** (*National Theatre Museum*): Bucharest, Bd. Bălcescu 1; f. 1942; history of the Romanian theatre; library of 10,000 vols.; Dir. (vacant).

**Muzeul Tehnic "Prof. Ing. Dimitrie Leonida"** (*Technical Museum "Prof. Ing. Dimitrie Leonida"*): 75206 Bucharest, str. Candiano Popescu 2; f. 1909; sections of mechanics, electricity, chemistry, nuclear energy, mining, oil industry, energetics, illuminations engineering, cinematography, telecommunications, calculating machines, hydraulics, air- and spacecraft, printing and typewriters, power engines and cars, electrical engineering; library of 20,000 vols.; Dir. Dipl. Ing. NICOLAE DIACONESCU; publ. *Yearbook†*.

## PROVINCIAL MUSEUMS
(in alphabetical order by town)

**Muzeul de Istorie Aiud:** Aiud, Piața Republicii 24, jud. Alba; f. 1796; archaeology of the primitive commune, the Dacian-Roman period and the pre-feudal period; library of 1,146 vols.; Dir. LIDIA CHIȚU.

**Muzeul de Științele Naturii Aiud** (*Natural Sciences Museum*): Aiud, Str. 11 Iunie 1; f. 1796; plants, mineralogica collections, petrography, palaeontology, entomology, birds and animals; Curator Prof. LÖRINCZ LADISLAU.

**Muzeul Unirii:** Alba Julia, Str. Mihai Viteazul 12-14; f. 1887; exhibits relating to Romanian Union from early times to the present; folk art; library of 38,000 vols.; Dir. Dr. GH. ANGHEL; publ. *Apulum-Acta Musei Apulensis* (annual).

**Muzeul Județean de Istorie** (*County History Museum*): Alexandria, Str. Dunării 188, jud. Teleorman; f. 1951; archaeology, history, numismatics, ethnography; Dir. ECATERINA ANGELESCU.

**Muzeul Județean Arad** (*Arad District Museum*): Arad, Piața Enescu 1; f. 1892; archaeological and ethnographical exhibits relating to the Arad region; classical and contemporary Romanian art; European paintings of 17th-20th centuries; decorative arts; exhibits of the 1848 Revolution in Transylvania; Dir. NICOLAE ROȘUȚ; publ. *Ziridava* (irregular).

**Muzeul Județean de Istorie și Artă:** Bacău, Str. Karl Marx 23; f. 1959; exhibits illustrating history, art, archaeology, ethnography, literature; library of 6,000 vols.; Dir. I. MITREA; publ. *Carpica* (annually).

**Muzeul de Științele Naturii** (*Natural Sciences Museum*) Bacău, Str. Karl Marx 2; f. 1959; herbarium and zoological collection; library of 8,000 vols.; Dir. (vacant); publ. *Studii și Comunicări* (annual review).

**Muzeul Județean Maramureș** (*Maramureș District Museum*): 4800 Baia Mare, Str. Bicazului 1-3, jud. Maramureș; f. 1899; history, ethnography, modern and contemporary Romanian art, mineralogy; library of 12,000 vols.; Dir. VALERIU ACHIM; publ. *Marmația†* (annually).

**Muzeul Județean Bistrița-Năsăud** (*Bistrița-Năsăud District Museum*): Bistrița, Str. Dornei 5; f. 1950; archaeology, history, ethnography, natural sciences; Dir. IOAN MARINESCU.

**Muzeul din Blaj:** Blaj, Str. Armata Roșie 2; f. 1939; documents on the Transylvanian School; Dir. C. TATAI.

**Muzeul Județean Botoșani** (*Botoșani District Museum*): Botoșani, Unirii 13; f. 1955; collections of archaeology, history, ethnography, fine arts; a memorial house "Nicolae Iorga", the Memorial Exhibition "1907 Peasants' Rising" in the village of Flămînzi, a memorial house "Mihai Eminescu" in the village of Ipotești; library of 8,070 vols.; Dir. M. BUCĂTARU; publ. *Hierasus†*.

**Muzeul din Brăila:** Brăila, Piața Lenin 3; f. 1950; archaeology, history, fine arts, ethnography, natural sciences; Dir. FLORIAN ANASTASIU.

**Muzeul Cetății Bran** (*Bran Walled City Museum*): Bran, Str. Principală 460, jud. Brașov; f. 1957; history, ethnography and feudal art; Dir. I. PRAHOVEANU.

**Muzeul, Biblioteca și arhiva istorică a primei școli românești din Scheii Brașovului:** Brașov, Piața Unirii 1; f. 1961; historical museum in building of first Romanian school (15th century); ancient books and documents; Romanian, Slavonic and Greek MSS.; medieval and ecclesiastical art; Dir. Dr. VASILE OLTEANU.

**Muzeul Județean Brașov** (*Brașov District Museum*): Brașov, Piața 23 August 30; f. 1908; archaeology, numismatics, history, ethnography and folk art; library of 15,500 vols., archives; Dir. TITUS HAIDEU; publ. *Cumidava†* (Yearbook).

**Muzeul Județean de Istorie** (*County History Museum*): Buzău, Str. Unirii 149, Buzău county; f. 1951; archaeology, history, folk art and fine arts; Dir. M. CONSTANTINESCU; publ. *Museos* (annually).

**Muzeul Județean Călărași** (*Călărași District Museum*): Călărași, Str. Progresului 90; f. 1951; history and archaeology; Dir. ION VLĂDILĂ.

**Muzeul memorial B. P. Hasdeu:** Cîmpina (Județul Prahova), Str. 23 August 199; f. 1965; Curator GH. OPREA.

**Muzeul "N. Grigorescu":** Cîmpina, Str. 23 August 170; Curator Ș. DUMITRESCU.

**Muzeul Artei Lemnului:** Cîmpulung Moldovenesc, Str. Pictor Grigorescu 1, jud. Suceava; f. 1936; ornamental wooden objects; Dir. M. ZAHARCIUC.

**Muzeul Zoologic:** 3400 Cluj-Napoca, Str. Clinicilor 5-7; f. 1859; herpetology, entomology; Dirs. Dr. L. DUȘA, Dr. M. DRAGOȘ, S. F. DAN; publ. *Studia†*.

**Muzeul Etnografic al Transilvaniei:** Cluj-Napoca, Str. 30 Decembrie 21; f. 1922; over 53,000 exhibits, with special emphasis on Transylvanian traditional occupations; also section on primitive peoples; library and valuable collection of archives; the Ethnographical Park (f. 1929), the first open-air museum in Romania, is a special section of the Ethnographic Museum and displays the larger exhibits; Dir. TIBERIU GRAUR; publ. *Anuarul Muzeului etnografic al Transilvaniei†*.

**Muzeul de Artă:** Cluj-Napoca, 30 Piața Libertății; f. 1951; collections of Romanian and foreign art (paintings, sculptures, drawings, decorative art) from 16th to 20th centuries; houses of some of the most important collections of the country; library of 2,800 vols.; Dir. ALEXANDRA RUS.

**Muzeul de Istorie al Transilvaniei:** Cluj-Napoca, Str. Emil Isac 2; f. 1859 (reorganized in 1963); archaeology, ancient, medieval and modern Transylvanian history; library of 12,868 vols.; Dir. H. DAICOVICIU; publ. *Acta Musei Napocensis* (annually), monographs, guides.

**Muzeul de Istorie Națională și Arheologie din Constanța:** 8700 Constanța, Piața Ovidiu 12; f. 1879; exhibits relating to the prehistory, modern history and archaeology of the region; collections of neolithic vessels and coins; library of 20,000 vols.; Dir. Dr. A. RĂDULESCU; publ. *Pontica†* (annually).

**Complexul Muzeal de Științe ale Naturii:** Constanța, Bd. 16 Februarie 1; f. 1958; Dir. MARCEL STANCIU.

**Muzeul de Artă Constanța:** Constanța, Str. Muzeelor 12; f. 1961; modern and contemporary Romanian art; 4,500 exhibits; library of 3,800 vols.; Dir. FLORICA POSPAI CRUCERU.

**Muzeul Marinei Române** (*Romanian Maritime Museum*): Constanța, Str. Traian 53; f. 1969; submarine archaeology, history of Romanian navy and merchant fleet, documents, maritime paintings; Dir. N. PETRESCU.

**Muzeul de Artă din Craiova:** Craiova, Calea Unirii 15; f. 1908, reorganized 1954; Romanian and world art; library of 3,500 vols.; Dir. Dr. P. REZEANU.

**Muzeul Olteniei** (*Oltenia Museum*): Craiova, Str. Maxim Gorki 44; f. 1915; history, ethnography and natural sciences; library of 7,737 vols.; Dir. Dr. L. DEACONU; publ. *Oltenia! Studii și comunicări†*.

**Muzeul Județean Hunedoara-Deva** (*Hunedoara District Museum*): Deva, Str. Dr. Petra Groza 39; f. 1882; archaeology, history and natural sciences; library of 33,000 vols.; Dir. I. LAZĂR; publ. *Sargeția†*.

**Muzeul Județean de Istorie și Etnografie din Focșani:** Focșani, Str. Karl Marx 1, jud. Vrancea; f. 1951; archaeology and ethnography; Dir. G. CARCADIA.

**Muzeul de Științele Naturii** (*Natural Science Museum*): Focșani, Str. Republicii 79; f. 1948; Dir. MIHAI MIHALCIUC.

**Muzeul de Artă Contemporană Românească:** Galați, Str. Republicii 141; f. 1956; Dir. NICOLAE ITU.

**Muzeul Județean de Istorie Galați:** Galați, Str. Al. I. Cuza 80; f. 1939; archaeology, history and ethnography; library of 7,750 vols.; Dir. ANETA ANGHEL; publ. *Danubius*.

**Muzeul de Științele Naturii** (*Natural Science Museum*): Galați, Str. Științei 115; flora and fauna of the region; f. 1956; Dir. ILEANA RADU.

**Muzeul de Istorie Gherla:** Gherla, Str. Avram Iancu 7, jud. Cluj; f. 1881; history, archaeology, ethnography, numismatics, iconography, heraldry; library of 5,500 vols.; Dir. IOAN CHIFOR.

**Complexul Muzeal Golești:** Golești, jud. Argeș; f. 1939; history, memorial, pedagogical and folk art departments, open-air department of fruit and wine growing; library of 8,115 vols.; Dir. Dr. VASILE NOVAC; publ. *Museum*.

**Muzeul Județean Harghita** (*Harghita District Museum*): Miercurea Ciuc, Str. Gh. Doja 2, jud. Harghita; f. 1950; archaeology, history, numismatics, ethnography; Dir. IANOȘ PÁLL; publ. *Comunicări* (annually).

**Complexul Muzeistic Iași:** Iași, Palatul Culturii, Str. Palatului 1; Dir. I. ARHIP; affiliated museums:

   **Muzeul Etnografic al Moldovei:** Iași, Str. Palatului 1; f. 1943; folk art, ethnography.

   **Muzeul de Artă din Iași:** Iași, Str. Palatului 1; extensive collection of Romanian art, particularly Moldavian (19th and 20th century); collection of classical foreign paintings.

   **Muzeul de Istorie a Moldovei** (*Moldavian History Museum*): Iași, Palatul Culturii, Str. Palatului 1; f. 1916; archaeology and history.

   **Muzeul de Literatură a Moldovei:** Iași, Str. I. C. Frimu 4; f. 1971.

   **Muzeul memorial Bojdeuca Ion Creangă** (*Memorial Museum of Ion Creangă*): Iași, Str. Simion Bărnuțiu 4; f. 1918; memorial house to life and works of writer Ion Creangă.

   **Muzeul Politehnic** (*Technical Museum*): Iași, Palatul Culturii, Str. Palatului 1; f. 1961.

   **Muzeul Teatrului:** Iași, Str. Vasile Alecsandri 3; f. 1976; Dir. (vacant).

   **Muzeul Unirii** (*Museum of the Union*): Iași, Str. Lăpușneanu 14; f. 1955; dedicated to period of creating and maintaining Union of Romanian lands.

**Muzeul de Istorie, Etnografie și Artă** (*Museum of History, Ethnography and Arts*): Lugoj, Nicolaie Bălcescu 2, Timiș county; f. 1905; archaeology, history, ethnography, fine arts; Dir. GH. RUSU.

**Muzeul de Arheologie din Mangalia:** Mangalia, Calea Constanței 26; f. 1925; Graeco-Roman finds from Old Callatis; Dirs. ELENA BÎRLĂDEANU, VALERIU GEORGESCU.

**Muzeul Țării Crișurilor:** Oradea, Str. Stadionului 2; f. 1872, reorganized 1971; history, art, ethnography and natural science; library of 15,200 vols.; Dir. SEVER DUMITRAȘCU; publ. *Crisia†*, *Biharea†*, *Nymphaea†*.

**Muzeul Mineritului** (*Mining Museum*): Petroșani, Str. N. Bălcescu 21; f. 1961; history of mining in the Jiu Valley; Dir. PLATON GEORGHE.

**Muzeul Județean de Istorie Piatra Neamț** (*Piatra Neamț District History Museum*): Piatra Neamț, jud. Neamț; f. 1934; archaeology and contemporary Romanian art;

Dir. ST. Cucoș; publs. *Memoria Antiquitatis*† (annual), *Bibliotheca Memoria Antiquitatis*†.

**Muzeul de Științele Naturii:** Piatra-Neamț, Str. V. I. Lenin 26; f. 1960; herbarium, palaeontology, zoology; Dir. MIHAI CIOBANU; publ. *Studii și comunicări*.

**Muzeul Județean Argeș** (*Argeș District Museum*): Pitești, str. Horia, Cloșca și Crișan 44, jud. Argeș; f. 1956; history, modern and contemporary art, natural sciences specializing in ecology and nature conservation; library of 11,000 vols.; Dir. RADU STANCU; publ. *Studii și comunicări*† (Studies and Reports).

**Muzeul de Artă Ploiești:** Ploiești, Bd. Gheorghiu-Dej 1; f. 1929; collections of the classical and contemporary plastic art of Romania; Dir. RUXANDRA IONESCU.

**Muzeul de Științele Naturii** (*Natural Science Museum*): Ploiești, Str. Krupskaia 1; f. 1956; Dir. ZOE APOSTOLACHE-STOICESCU; publ. *Comunicări și referate*.

**Muzeul Județean de Istorie Prahova** (*Prahova District History Museum*): Ploiești, Str. Teatrului 10; f. 1955; archaeology, history, numismatics, ethnography; Dir. V. TEODORESCU; publ. *Studii și comunicări* (annually).

**Muzeul Petrolului** (*Petroleum Museum*): Ploiești, Str. Dr. Bagdasar 8; f. 1961; exhibits relating to the history and development of petroleum research, extraction and refining in Romania and of the Romanian petrochemical industries; Curator ION STEFĂNESCU.

**Muzeul Etnografic Rădăuți:** Rădăuți, Str. Bogdan Vodă 2, jud. Suceava; f. 1920; earthenware, costumes, furniture; Dir. H. DRAGOȘ.

**Muzeul Etnografic Reghin** (*Reghin Ethnographic Museum*): 4225 Reghin, Str. Vînătorilor 51, Mureș county; f. 1960; trades, peasant industries, transport, peasant textiles, everyday costume and folk art; library of 3,500 vols; Dir. ANTON BADEA.

**Muzeul Județean Caraș Severin:** Reșița, Str. Vălingului 23; f. 1950; archaeology, ethnography, contemporary Romanian art; Dir. I. UZUM; publ. *Banatica*.

**Muzeul de Istorie din Roman:** Roman, Str. Cuza Vodă 33; f. 1957; archaeology, ethnography and art; Dir. V. URSACHE.

**Muzeul de Științele Naturii:** Roman, Str. Proletariatului 4; f. 1956; Dir. Dr. C. TĂRĂBUȚĂ.

**Muzeul Arheologic "Ulpia Traiana Sarmizegetusa":** Sarmizegetusa, jud. Hunedoara; f. 1924; Curator E. NEMEȘ.

**Muzeul Județean de Istorie Satu Mare:** 3900 Satu Mare, Piața Libertății 21; f. 1891; history, archaeology, ethnography, folk art and paintings by Aurel Popp; library of 14,000 vols.; Dir. DORU RADOSAV; publs. *Studii și comunicări*†, monographs, catalogues.

**Muzeul din Sebeș:** Sebeș, Str. 8 mai 4, jud. Alba; f. 1951; natural sciences, history, art, African ethnography.

**Muzeul Județean Covasna** (*Covasna District Museum*): Sf. Gheorghe, Str. 16 Februarie 10; f. 1879; local archaeological, ethnographical and natural history exhibits; modern Romanian art; Dir. Dr. Z. SZEKELY; publ. *Aluta*.

**Muzeul Brukenthal:** Sibiu, Piața Republicii 4; f. 1817; archaeology, history, ethnography, European paintings 15th-18th centuries; library of 249,780 vols.; Dir. C. IRIMIE; publs. *Cibinum, Studii și Comunicări*.

**Muzeul de Istorie Naturală din Sibiu:** Sibiu, Str. Cetății 1; f. 1849; zoology, botany, paleontology, mineralogy, petrology, universal fauna and flora; affiliated to Muzeul Brukenthal; library of 60,000 vols.; publ. *Studii și Comunicări de Stiințe Naturale*†.

**Muzeul Maramureșean:** Sighetul Marmației, Str. Bogdan Vodă 2; ethnography and folk art from Maramureș; Dir. M. DĂNCUȘ.

**Muzeul de Istorie Sighișoara:** Sighișoara, Str. Turnului 1; f. 1899; exhibits relating to the history of Sighișoara and region; Dir. I. MOSORA.

**Muzeul Peleș** (*Pelesh Museum*): Sinaia, Str. Peleș 2; collection of world decorative art; Dir. Prof. DAN POPA

**Muzeul Județean Suceava:** Suceava, Str. Ștefan cel Mare 33; f. 1900; folk art, local history, natural history, Romanian fine arts; Romanian folk art of the Suceava district; library of 82,000 vols.; Dir. Dr. OCTAV MONORANU; publs. *Suceava—Anuarul Muzeului județean*† (History and Natural Sciences sections).

**Muzeul Banatului** (*Museum of the Banate*): Timișoara, Piața Huniade 1; f. 1872; archaeology, natural sciences, ethnography, Romanian and foreign art; Dir. MIHAI FĂTU; publ. *Tibiscum* (annually).

**Muzeul Județean Dîmbovița** (*Dîmbovița District Museum*): Tîrgoviște, Str. Muzeului 4; f. 1940; archaeology, ethnography and fine arts; Dir. M. OPROIU; publ. *Vallachica*. Affiliated museums:

**Muzeul Tiparului și Cărții Vechi Românești** (*Printing and Old Romanian Book Museum*): Tîrgoviște, Str. Justiției 3-5, jud. Dîmbovița; f. 1967.

**Muzeul Scriitorilor Tîrgovișteni** (*Museum of the Writers of Tîrgoviște*): Tîrgoviște, Str. Justiției 3-5, jud. Dîmbovița; f. 1967.

**Muzeul Județean Gorj** (*Gorj District Museum*): Tîrgu-Jiu, Str. Tudor Vladimirescu 73, jud. Gorj; f. 1894; history, ethnography and folk art; open-air museum of Gorj region; Dir. ELENA UDRIȘTE.

**Muzeul de Artă din Tîrgu-Mureș:** Tîrgu-Mureș, Piața Eroilor Sovietici 1; f. 1913; two galleries of Hungarian art of the 19th and 20th centuries and Romanian contemporary art; Dir. GH. OLARIU.

**Muzeul Județean din Tîrgu-Mureș:** Tîrgu-Mureș, Str. Horea 24; f. 1893; archaeology, ethnography, natural history; DIR. VALERIU LAZAR; publ. *Marisia* (annually).

**Muzeul Deltei Dunării** (*Danube Delta Museum*): Tulcea, Str. Gloriei 4; f. 1949; sections of natural sciences (with aquarium), history and archaeology (with open-air archaeological parks), art (modern, medieval and oriental), ethnography (with a preserved "in situ" farm); library of 14,000 vols.; Dir. GAVRILĂ SIMION; publ. *Peuce* (periodical).

**Muzeul "Portile de Fier"** (*"Iron Gates" Museum*): Drobeta Turnu Severin, Str. Independenței 2; f. 1912; natural history, ethnography, archaeology and Roman ruins; Dir. M. DAVIDESCU; publ. *Drobeta* (annually).

**Muzeul de Istorie Turda:** Turda, Str. B. P. Hașdeu 2; f. 1951; history and ethnography; Curator CLAUDIA LUCA.

**Muzeul Județean Vilcea:** Rîmnicu-Vilcea, Str. Argeș 29; f. 1921; collections of history, art, ethnography; Dir. HORIA NESTORESCU-BĂLCEȘTI.

## UNIVERSITIES

**UNIVERSITATEA BUCUREŞTI**
BUCHAREST,
BULEVARDUL GH. GHEORGHIU DEJ 64
Telephone: 16. 01. 87.
Founded 1864.

*Rector:* Prof. Dr. I. Ioviţ Popescu.
*Pro-Rectors:* I. Anghel, D. Chiţoran, S. Ghimpu, N. Boboc.
*Registrar:* El. Ivan.
*Librarian:* I. Stoica.
Library: *see* Libraries.
Number of teachers: 947.
Number of students: 9,164.
Publications: *Analele Universităţii din Bucureşti, Acta horti botanicae bucurestiensis.*

### Deans:

*Faculty of History and Philosophy:* Prof. Dr. Şt. Ştefănescu.
*Faculty of Romanian Language and Literature:* Prof. Dr. I. Coteanu.
*Faculty of Foreign Languages:* Prof. Dr. Paul Miclău.
*Faculty of Law:* Prof. Const. Stătescu.
*Faculty of Mathematics:* Prof. Dr. Cabiria Andreian.
*Faculty of Physics:* Conf. Dr. C. Plăviţu.
*Faculty of Biology:* Prof. Dr. Gh. Zarnea.
*Faculty of Geology and Geography:* Prof. Dr. G. Cioflica.

### Professors:

*Faculty of History and Philosophy:*
Apostol, P., Marxist Philosophy
Bărbulescu, D., Pedagogy
Boboc, A., History of Philosophy
Bogdan, A., Psychology
Bulborea, I., History of Economic Doctrines
Cazacu, A., Sociology
Cazan, G. H., History of Philosophy
Cazan, Gh., World History
Cerghit, I., Pedagogy
Ciachir, I., World History
Cîrţîna, I., Romanian History
Condurachi, E., Ancient World History
Constantinescu, M., Logic
Constantinescu, V., Sociology
Corbu, C., Romanian History
Creţoiu, Gh., Political Economy
Cristescu, I., Political Economy
Cruceru, S., Pedagogy
Curticăpeanu, V., Romanian History
Diamandescu, S., Political Economy
Dobrin, T., History of Pedagogy
Drăgan, I., Sociology
Drăghici, I., Marxist Philosophy
Enescu, Gh., Logic
Florian, M., Theory of Knowledge
Florian, R., Scientific Socialism
Georgescu, S., Epistemology and Methods in Science, Marxist Philosophy
Georgescu, T., Romanian History
Gheorghiu, I., Romanian History
Ghimeş, G., Scientific Socialism
Giurgea, M., Pedagogy
Golu, M., Psychology
Golu, P., Psychology
Ianoşi, I., Aesthetics
Ionescu, Gh., Medical Psychology
Ioniţă, Gh., History of the RCP Workers Movement
Lupu, N., World History
Maftei, E., Psychology
Manolescu, R., World History
Niculescu, H., Political Economy
Petric, A., Romanian History
Pop, T., Pedagogy
Popescu, P., Psychology
Pufan, C., Defectology
Pufan, P., Work Psychology
Radu, I., Pedagogy
Stanciu, L., Pedagogy
Sîrbu, C., Political Economy
Stoica, S., Ethics
Stroia, Gh., Aesthetics
Şafran, O., Pedagogy
Ştefănescu, St., Medieval Romanian History
Totu, I., Political Economy
Tudosescu, I., Marxist Philosophy
Valentin, A., Marxist Philosophy
Vladu, M., Romanian History
Vlăduţescu, G., History of Philosophy
Zamfir, Z., World History

*Faculty of Romanian Language and Literature:*
Bălan, I. D., History of Romanian Literature
Brâncuşi, Gr., Contemporary Romanian Language
Bulgăr, Gh., Romanian Language
Buşulenga, Zoe, History of World Literature
Cahn, M., History of Romanian Contemporary Literature
Cazimir, St., History of Romanian Literature
Cornea, P. L., History of Romanian Literature
Coteanu, I., Contemporary Romanian Language
Diaconescu, I., Contemporary Romanian Language
Diaconescu, P., History of Romanian Language
Ghiţă, F., History of Romanian Literature
Grigorescu, D., Comparative Literature
Hanţă, A., History of Romanian Literature
Hristea, T., Contemporary Romanian Language
Iosifescu, S., Theory of Literature
Marcea, P., History of Romanian Literature
Marioţeanu, M., Dialectology
Micu, D., History of Romanian Literature
Muntean, G., History of Romanian Literature
Munteanu, R., History of Comparative World Literature
Niculescu, F., History of Romanian Grammar
Oană, I., History of Romanian Literature
Onu, L., History of Romanian Language
Păcurariu, D., Modern Romanian Literature
Piru, Al., Old Romanian Literature
Romalo, V., Contemporary Romanian Language
Rotariu, I., History of Romanian Literature
Simion, E., Contemporary Romanian Literature
Vasiliu, E., Contemporary Romanian Language

*Faculty of Foreign Languages:*
Anghelescu, N., Arab Languages
Balaci, A., History of Italian Literature
Barborică, C., Slovak Language
Bercescu, Sorina, French Literature
Chiţoran, D., English Language
Cizek, E., History of Latin Literature
Colomei, A., French Language
Cristea, Teodora, Contemporary French Language
Dobroiu, E., Latin Language and Literature
Drimba, V., Turkish Language
Dumitriu, G., English Literature
Dumitrescu, M., Russian Language
Fischer, I., Greek and Latin Language
Fodor, E., Russian Language and Literature
Gămulescu, D., Serbo-Croat Language
Goga, Ecaterina, Romance Linguistics
Ion, Angela, French Literature
Isbăşescu, M., German Language
Jivcovici, M., Serbo-Croatian Language and Literature
Kovacs, A., Russian and Soviet Literature
Lăzărescu, G., Contemporary Italian Language
Linţă, E., Comparative Grammar of Slavonic Languages
Lipatti, V., History of French Literature
Miclău, P., French Stylistics
Mihăilă, Gh., Old Slavonic Languages
Murăreţ, I., History of French Language
Nicolescu, A., English Language
Niculescu, Al., Romance Literature
Oiţă, I., Russian Language
Pandelescu, Silvia, French Literature
Petrică, I., Polish Language and Literature
Slave, Elena, Linguistics
Ştef, Felicia, Greek Grammar
Şoptereanu, V., Russian and Soviet Literature
Vascenco, V., Russian Language
Vrabie, E., Russian Language
Wald, Lucia, Comparative Grammar

*Faculty of Law:*
Bulai, C., Penal Law
Cărpenaru, S., Civil Law
Ceterchi, I., Theory of State and Law
Deak, F., Civil Law
Filipescu, I., Family Law
Ghimpu, Sanda, Labour Law
Gilescu, Gh., Financial Law
Gogeanu, P., Theory of State
Luburici, M., Theory of State Law
Moca, Gh., International Law
Negoiţă, Al., Administrative Law
Pop, A., Economic Law
Popescu, T., International Law
Stătescu, C., Civil Law
Volonciu, N., Penal Law
Zilberstein, S., Civil Law

*Faculty of Mathematics:*
Andreian, C., Variable Functions
Boboc, N., Mathematical Analysis
Ciucu, G., Calculus of Probabilities
Colojoară, I., Mathematical Analysis
Cristescu, N., Plasticity
Cristescu, R., Functional Analysis
Cuculescu, I., Calculus of Probabilities
Dincă, Gh., Computers
Dragoş, L., Magneto-hydrodynamics
Galbură, G. Gh., Algebra
**Halanay, A., Differential Equations**
Iacob, C., Mechanics of Fluids
Ion, D. I., Algebra

JURCHESCU, M., Mathematical Analysis
LIVOVSCHI, L., Informatics
MALIŢA, M., Mathematical Programming
MARCUS, S., Mathematical Analysis
MARINESCU, G., Higher Mathematics
MIHĂILĂ, I., Astronomy
POPOVICI, C., Intomatics
RADU, N., Algebra
RUDEANU, S., Informatics
SÂMBOAN, G., Mathematical Statistics
TELEMAN, C., Geometry
TEODORESCU, I., Geometry
TEODORESCU, P., Elasticity
VĂDUVA, I., Informatics
VAIDA, D., Informatics

*Faculty of Physics:*
BEȘLIU, C., Nuclear Physics
BRĂTESCU, G., Optics
CIOBANU, G., Thermodynamics
CIOBOTARU, D., Plasma Physics
CONSTANTINESCU, C., Solid State Physics
DIMA, I., Semiconductor Physics
GHEORGHE, V., Electronics and Biophysics
GRECU, V., Nuclear and Atomic Physics
IOVA, I., Spectroscopy
LEVAI, ȘT., Nuclear Spectroscopy
MIHUL, A., High-energy Physics
MÎNZATU, J., Nuclear Spectroscopy
MUSCALU, ȘT., Nuclear Physics
PÂRVAN, R., Electronics
PETREA, I., Polymer Physics
PLĂVIŢU, C., Molecular Physics and Heat
POPESCU, I., Mathematics
POPESCU, I. I., Plasma Physics
SPÎNULESCU, I., Electronics
TRUŢIA, A., Spectroscopy
TURBATU, S., Mathematics
TURCU, G., Biochemistry
URSU, I., Nuclear and Atomic Physics
VREJOIU, C., Electrodynamics

*Faculty of Biology:*
ANDREI, M., Plant Biology
ANGHEL, I., Microbial Genetics
ATANASIU, L., Plant Physiology
BOLDOR, O., Plant Physiology
BOTNARIUC, N., General Biology
CEAUȘESCU, I., Animal Physiology
CHENZBRAUN, EUGENIA, Animal Physiology
CHIRIAC, ELENA, Parasitology
DUMITRU, I., Biochemistry
ELIADE, E., Phytopathology
IONESCU-VARO, M., Cell Biology
IVAN, D., Geobotany
LĂCĂTUȘU, MATILDA, Entomology
MIȘCALENCU, D., Comparative Anatomy
NEȘTORESCU, EMILIA, Microbiology
PAPADOPOL, M., Hydrobiology
PETREA, V., Plant Physiology
PICOȘ, C., Animal Physiology
POPESCU, I., Plant Physiology
RAICU, P., Genetics, Plant and Animal Improvement
SĂNDULESCU, N., Agrophytotechnics
ȘERBĂNESCU, G., Plant Anatomy
STRUNGARU, GR., Animal Physiology
TEODORESCU, MARIA, Cytology
ZARNEA, GH., General Microbiology

*Faculty of Geology and Geography:*
AIRINEI, ST., Geophysics
ALMĂȘAN, B., Technological Geology
BOMBOE, P., Engineering Geology
BOTEZATU, R., Geology and Geophysics
CALOIANU, N., Economic Geography
CHIŢU, MARIA, Geography of Economic Resources
CIOFLICĂ, G., Prospection and Exploitation of Ore Deposits
CUCU, V., Population Geography
DOBRA, GH., Working of Deposits
DOROBANŢU, M., Mechanics of Geology
DRAGU, GH., Ethnography
FLOREA, M., Geomechanics
GHEORGHE, AL., Hydrogeology
HANGANU, E., Palaeontology
HARNAJ, V., Hydraulics
ILIE, I., Geomorphology
LĂZĂRESCU, V., General Geology
MANOLIU, E., Palaeontology
MURGU, M., Mechanics of Deposits
MUTIHAC, V., Romanian Geology
NAUM, T., Geography of Romania
NĂSTASE, A., Cartography and Topography
NEAGU, T., Micropalaeontology
PANĂ, I., Petrography
PANAITE, L., Economic-Geographical Research Methods
PAUCĂ, M., Geophysical Machinery
PAULIUC, S., Structural Geology
PELIN, M., Geology
PIȘOTĂ, I., General Physical Geography
POPOVICI, I., Regional Economic Geography
POSEA, G., General Geomorphology
PREDA, I., Geology
RĂDULESCU, D., Petrography of Sediment Rocks
RADO, G., Palaeontology
ROȘU, AL., Geography of Romania
SANDU, D., Coal Deposits
STĂNESCU, V., Geology of Oil Deposits
STIOPOL, V., Geochemistry, Crystallography
TĂTARÎM, N., Historical Geology
TUDOR, M., Geology of Romania
VELCEA, I., Geography of Agriculture
VELCEA, V., Applied Geography

## UNIVERSITATEA "BABEȘ-BOLYAI"
CLUJ-NAPOCA,
STR. M. KOGALNICEANU 1
Telephone: 22619, 16100.
Telex: 31330.
Founded 1919.

Languages of instruction: Romanian, Hungarian; Academic year: September to July (two semesters).

*Rector:* Prof. Dr. I. VLAD.
*Pro-Rectors:* Prof. dr. I. HAIDUC, Prof. dr. J. KOVACS, Prof. dr. I. RUS.
*Secretary-General:* C. IUREȘ.
*Librarian:* C. NEGULESCU.

Library: *see* Libraries.
Number of teachers: 889.
Number of students: 9,394.

Publications: *Studia Universitatis "Babeș-Bolyai"†, Studia Index Alphabeticus†, Contribuții Botanice†, Anuarul Universităţii†, Echinox†.*

### DEANS:
*Faculty of Mathematics:* A. PAL.
*Faculty of Physics:* V. MERCEA.
*Faculty of Chemistry:* Z. ANDREI.
*Faculty of Biology and Geography:* ȘT. KISS.
*Faculty of History and Philosophy:* C. MUREȘAN.
*Faculty of Philology:* O. ȘCHIAU.
*Faculty of Law:* G. BOBOȘ.
*Faculty of Economic Sciences:* R. CRIȘAN.

### PROFESSORS:
*Faculty of Mathematics:*
GROZE, S., Informatics
IONESCU, D. V., Differential and Integral Equations
KALIK, C., Equations
MARUSCIAC, I., Approximations Theory
MOCANU, P., Complex Analysis
MUNTEANU, I., Mathematical Analysis
PÁL, A., Astronomy and Celestial Mechanics
PIC, G., Algebra
POPOVICIU, E., Mathematical Analysis
RADO, F., Geometry and Algebra
RUS, A. I., Differential Equations
STANCU, D., Numerical Analysis

*Faculty of Physics:*
BODI, A., Electronics
DRĂGANU, M., Theoretical Physics
GÁBOS, Z., Theory of Elementary Particles
KOCH, FR., Atomic and Nuclear Physics
LÁSZLÓ, T., Electronics
MERCEA, V., Atomic and Nuclear Physics
NICULA, A., Electricity and Magnetism
POP, I., Mechanics
TĂTARU, E., Radiophysics
TINTEA, H., Optics

*Faculty of Chemistry:*
ALMĂȘI, N., Stereo- and Photochemistry
CĂDARIU, I., Physical Chemistry
CHIFU, E., Colloidal Chemistry
CRIȘAN, I. A., Analytical Chemistry
FĂRCĂȘANU, I., Organic Chemistry
HAIDUC, I., Inorganic and Metal-organic Chemistry
IONESCU, M., Organic Chemistry
KEKEDY, L., Analytical Chemistry
LITEANU, C., Analytical Chemistry
LITERAT, L., Technology of Building Materials
MACAROVICI, C., Inorganic Chemistry
MARCU, G., Inorganic Chemistry
ONICIU, L., Physical Chemistry
POP, A., Technological Chemistry

*Faculty of Biology and Geography:*
BERINDEI, I., Geography
BUTA, I., Hydrology
CEUCA, TR., Vertebrate Zoology
CLICHICI, O., Geology
CSŰRÖS, ST., Botany
GHIȘA, E., Systematic Botany
GYURKO, ST., Zoology
HODIȘAN, I., Plant Anatomy
MATIC, Z., Invertebrate Zoology
MÉSZÁROS, N., Geology
MORARIU, T., Geomorphology
MUREȘAN, I., Mineralogy
PERSECĂ, T., General Biology
POP, I., Systematic Botany
PORA, A. E., Physiology and Biology
RADU, V., Invertebrate Zoology
RAŢIU, I., Phytocenology
ROȘCA, I. D., Physiology
SAVU, A., Geography of Romania
SĂNDULACHE, A., Cartography and Topography
STOICOVICIU, E., Geology
UJVÁRI, I., Oceanography

*Faculty of History and Philosophy:*
BODOR, A., Ancient History
CHIRCEV, A., Child Psychology
DAICOVICIU, H., Ancient History of Romania
DANCSULY, A., Pedagogics
DRONDOE, GR., History of Philosophy
GÁLL, E., Ethics and Aesthetics
GÁLL, I., Contemporary Political Doctrines
GÁLL, T., Pedagogics
HĂGAN, T., Political Science
IRIMIE, I., Sociology
ISAC, D., History of Ancient Philosophy
JAKÓ, S., Auxiliary Historical Sciences
KALLÓS, N., Philosophy
KOVÁCS, J., History of South-East Europe
LASCU, N., Ancient World History

Mare, C., Philosophy
Mihu, A., Anthropology
Mureșan, C., World History
Pascu, S., Romanian Medieval History
Pop, Tr., History of Philosophy
Radu, I., Psychology
Roșca, A., General Psychology
Roth, I., Dialectic and Historical Materialism
Salade, D., General and Experimental Pedagogics
Surdu, B., Contemporary History of Romania
Teodor, P., Medieval History of Romania
Tomuța, G., Contemporary Political Doctrines
Vătășianu, V., History of Art

*Faculty of Philology:*
Antal, A., Hungarian Literature
Câmpeanu, E., Stylistics
Dumitrașcu, P., History of Romanian Literary Language
Gálffy, M., Hungarian Language
Gheorghe, I., History of French Literature
Pamfil, V., Historical Grammar
Pătruț, I., Comparative Grammar of Slavonic Languages
Pervain, I., History of Romanian Literature
Pop, D., Literary Folklore
Rusu, L., World Literature
Scridon, G., History of Modern Romanian Literature
Szabó, Gy., Theory of Literature and Comparative Literature
Szabó, T. A., Hungarian Language, Historical Grammar
Szabó, Z., History of Hungarian Literary Language
Szigeti, I., History of Old Hungarian Language
Todoran, R., Dialectology
Vlad, I., Theory of Literature
Zaciu, M., History of Romanian Contemporary Literature

*Faculty of Law:*
Albu, I., Law of Family
Basarab, M., Criminal Law
Câmpeanu, V., Labour Law
Demeter, I., Theory of Law
Drăganu, T., State Law
Gliga, I., Financial Law
Hanga, V., Roman Law
Ionașcu, A., Civil Law
Lupan, E., Cooperative Legislation
Porumb, G., Civil Law
Takács, L., International Public Law

*Faculty of Economic Sciences:*
Benke, Al., Agrarian Economy
Berenyi, A., Political Economy
Crișan, R., Organization and Planification
Dani, E., Applied Mathematics
Diculescu, V., History of National Economy
Giurgiu, A., Finance
Jura, E., Agrarian Economics
Mleșnița, V., Agrarian Technology
Negucioiu, A., Political Economy
Olah, C., Political Economy

Attached Institutes:
*Institutul de Matematică:* Str. Republicii 37; Dir. Prof. Dr. Á. Pál.
*Institutul de Lingvistică și Istorie Literară:* Str. E. Racoviță 21; Dir. O. Schiau.
*Institutul de Istorie și Arheologie:* Str. Napoca 11; Dir. Acad. Prof. Dr. doc. Ș. Pascu.

*Centrul de Științe Sociale:* Str. Budai Nagy Antal 2; Dir. Conf. Dr. G. Boboș.
*Centrul Teritorial de Cercetări Economice:* Piața Ștefan Cel Mare 1; Dir. Prof. Dr. Ing. R. Crișan.

## UNIVERSITATEA DIN BRAȘOV
2200 BRAȘOV,
BD. GH. GHEORGHIU-DEJ 29
Telephone: 41580.

Founded 1971 by merger of Polytechnical and Pedagogical Institutes of Brașov.

State control; Language of instruction: Romanian; Academic year: September to June.

*Rector:* Prof. Dr. Eng. Florea Dudiță.
*Pro-Rectors:* Profs. Vasile Câmpian, Mircea Ivan, Filofteia Negruțiu.
*Registrar:* Valentina Rusu.
*Library Director:* Dr. Eng. Aurel Negruțiu.
Library: see Libraries.
Number of teachers: 797.
Number of students: 10,445.

Publication: *Buletinul Universității din Brașov.*

Deans:
*Faculty of Mechanics:* Dr. Eng. Gheorghe Bobescu.
*Faculty of Mechanical Engineering Technology:* Dr. Eng. Constantin Rădulescu.
*Faculty of Forestry:* Dr. Victor Stănescu.
*Faculty of Wood Technology:* Dr. Eng. Ștefan Alexandru.
*Faculty of Mathematics:* Dr. Constantin Marinescu.

Professors:
*Faculty of Mechanical Engineering Technology:*
Alexandru, P., Mechanisms
Baraș, V., Materials Technology
Bednar, H., Chemistry and Physics
Bednar, V., Chemistry and Physics
Boangiu, Gh., Machine Tools and Aggregates
Boncoi, G., Automatic Machine Tools
Chiș, E., Chemistry
Curtu, I., Strength of Materials
Deutsch, I., Strength of Materials
Diaconescu, C., Physical Training and Sports
Drăghici, G., Machine Engineering Technology
Drăghici, I., Machine Parts
Dudiță, F., Mechanisms
Gavrilă, I., Physics
Goia, I., Strength of Materials
Iliescu, C., Technology of Cold-pressing
Ința, I., Physics
Ivan, M., Machine Tools and Dimensional Control
Jakab, E., Materials Technology
Jula, A., Machine Elements
Maniu, A., Equipment for Plastic Flow
Munteanu, G., Physics
Obaciu, G., Electric Drive and Machine Tools
Popescu, I., Technical Measurement and Tolerance

Rădulescu, C., Machine Elements and Mechanisms
Rusan, G., Machine Tool Hydraulics
Secară, C., Metal Cutting, Tool Design
Silianu, E., Machine Elements and Mechanisms Theory
Sofonea, L., Physics
Tudoran, P., Study of Metals
Tureac, I., Machines for Processing by Deformation
Vaida, A., Design of Machine Tools
Vulcu, V., Casting Technology

*Faculty of Mechanics:*
Abăitâncei, D., Automobile Engines
Benche, L., Mechanics and Strength of Materials
Benche, V., Fluid Mechanics
Bobescu, Gh., Auto-vehicle engines
Cîmpian, V., Automobiles
Cruțu, Gh., Computers for Data Processing
Dâmboiu, E., Electrical Mechanics
Deliu, Gh., Theoretical Mechanics
Fokt, L., Political Economy
Hoffmann, V., Heat Engineering
Ionescu, E., Tractors and Automobiles
Leftner, C., Political Economy
Lupu, I., Political Economy
Mărgineau, I., Power Plant Systems and Power Supplies
Marinescu, R., French Language
Matlac, I., Electrical Apparatus
Moșu, N., Theoretical Mechanics
Nagy, T., Transport
Nastasoiu, S., Turbomachines and Hydraulic Drives for Automobiles
Nicolaide, A., Electrical Machines
Olariu, V., Theoretical Mechanics
Oprei, I., Organization and Management
Popescu, S., Agricultural Equipment
Radu, Gh., Automobile Engines
Saal, C., Electromechanical Drives
Sălăjan, C., Transport
Seitz, N., Electrical Equipment
Sima, P., Theoretical Mechanics
Soare, I., Automobile Repair
Sova, V., Heat Engineering
Szabo, W., Electric and Electronic Measurements
Tănase, V., Automobile Repair
Todicescu, A., Fluid Mechanics
Topa, I., Electrical Mechanics
Untaru, M., Motor Cars
Veștemeanu, N., Heat Engineering and Equipment

*Faculty of Forestry:*
Bereziuc, R., Forest Roads
Boș, N., Forest Photogrammetry
Chiru, V., Forest Machinery
Ciortuz, I., Forest Improvement
Corlățeanu, S., Forest Products
Costea, C., Forestry and Business Management
Damian, I., Afforestation
Florescu, I., Silviculture
Furnică, H., Forest Exploitation and Wood Production
Gătej, P., Forest Management
Ionașcu, Gh., Forest Equipment
Marcu, M., Forest Meteorology and Climatology
Marcu, O., Forest Phytopathology
Mihai, Gh., Pedology and Forest Stations
Munteanu, Șt., Torrent Correction
Negruțiu, A., Hunting and Pisciculture
Negruțiu, F., Open Spaces
Parascan, D., Botany and Plant Physiology
Popovici, T., Dendrometry
Rusu, A., Topography
Stănescu, V., Dendrology
Tudor, I., Forest Protection

*Faculty of Wood Technology:*
 ALEXANDRU, ȘT., Automatization of Technological Processes
 BARBA, V., Economics of Enterprises
 BUJDOIU, N., Philosophy
 COTTA, N., Design and Protection of Industrial Wood Products
 DOGARU, V., Basics of Mechanical Wood Processing
 DULDNER, M., Industrial Pedagogy
 ISTRATE, V., Technology of Particle Board Production
 NĂSTASE, V., Furniture Production and Design
 RADU, A., Wood Processing Machinery
 ȚĂRAN, N., Forestry Equipment Use
 TUDOR, E., Machinery for Transport and Lifting

*Faculty of Mathematics:*
 ATANASIU, C., Linear Algebra, Analytical Geometry and Programming
 BADEA, CL., Mathematical Analysis
 MARINESCU, C., Differential Equations with Partial Derivatives
 ORMAN, G., Measure Theory
 POPESCU, E., Mathematical Analysis and Special Mathematics
 SIMIONESCU, C., Geometry

## UNIVERSITATEA DIN CRAIOVA
STR. "AL.I.CUZA" 13,
CRAIOVA, JUD. DOLJ.
Telephone: Centrale 10711.

Founded 1966.

State control; Academic year: September to June.

*Rector:* Prof. Dr. Eng. SILVIU PUȘCAȘU.
*Vice-Rectors:* I. DOGARU, G. ȘOROP, MARIA MARGARETA BOROȘ.
*Secretary-General and Archivist:* I. OANCĂ.
*Librarian:* E. TATOMIRESCU.

Library: see Libraries.
Number of teachers: 651.
Number of students: 10,200.

Publications: *University Records* (annually) in five series: *Philology, History and Geography; Social and Economic Sciences; Mathematics, Physics and Chemistry; Electronics and Mechanics; Agricultural and Biological Sciences.*

DEANS AND HEADS OF FACULTIES:
*Faculty of Natural Sciences:* A. DINCĂ.
*Faculty of Philology:* C. DIACONU.
*Faculty of Economic Sciences:* C. BĂRBĂCIORU.
*Faculty of Medicine:* P. GEORGESCU.
*Faculty of Electrical Engineering:* C. AMBROZIE.
*Faculty of Mechanics:* E. CERNĂIANU.
*Faculty of Agriculture:* N. MARIN.
*Faculty of Horticulture:* F. ENE.

PROFESSORS:
*Faculty of Natural Sciences:*
 AVRAMESCU, C., Mathematical Analysis
 BOROȘ, M. M., Technological Chemistry
 BRAD, I., Biochemistry
 DINCĂ, AL., Algebra and Linear Programme
 DOBRESCU, E., Functional Analysis
 DRĂGHICESCU, D., Mechanics, Astronomy
 GĂNESCU, I., Analytical Chemistry
 GHERMAN, O., Atomic and Nuclear Physics
 HAMBURG, A. P., Mathematical Analysis
 IONESCU, V., Mathematics Applied in Economics
 KESSLER, P. G., Mathematical Analysis
 LEONTE, A., Calculus of Probability
 MUREȘAN, V., Organic and Analytical Chemistry
 RAILEANU, M., Inorganic Chemistry
 SCONDAC, I., Technology of Industrial Products
 STAVRE, P., Mathematics Applied to Economics
 TUDOR, M., Physics and Meteorology
 ULIU, F., Physical Electronics
 VRACIU, G., Algebra

*Faculty of Philology:*
 BEȘTELIU, M., History of Modern Romanian Literature
 BOLOCAN, GH., Old Slavonic, Russian Language
 CĂLIN, I., Contemporary History
 CHIȚU, C., Regional Physical Geography
 DONAT, L., Latin
 DUMITRESCU, I., Education
 ILIESCU, M., Romance Linguistics
 NEGRESCU, M., Romance Linguistics
 NICOLA, T., Philosophy
 OLANESCU, C., French Grammar
 PĂTRAȘCU, I., Italian
 PETRIȘOR, M., Romanian Dialectology
 SORESCU, G., History of Romanian Literature
 SCHIOPIU, A., World Economic Geography
 STOICA, D., Education
 STOICA, M., Education
 TOROPU, O., History of Romania
 TRĂISTARU, E., Scientific Socialism
 TRĂISTARU, I., History of Old Romanian Literature
 TUGUI, P., History of Romanian Literature

*Faculty of Economic Sciences:*
 BĂBEANU, M., Political Economy
 BĂRBĂCIORU, C., Political Economy
 BĂRBĂCIORU, V., Elements of Accountancy
 BOTEA, C., Political Economy
 BRÎNZAN, A., General and Agricultural Accountancy
 CIȚU, D., Farm Organization
 DOGARU, I., Law
 GEORGESCU, P., Theoretical and Economic Statistics
 MAREȘ, I., Bookkeeping
 MARIN, E., Political Economy
 MĂNOIU, I., Problems of Modern Agriculture
 NEGULESCU, C., Industrial Organization
 ONCESCU, V., Political Economy
 ROȘCA, C., Ergonomics
 TĂNASE, G., Industrial Economics
 TOPALĂ, S., Direction, Organization and Planning of Economic Units
 TRĂISTARU-CLUJ, I., Political Economy

*Faculty of Medicine:*
 BĂDĂNOIU, AL., Dermatology
 BOGDAN, F., Histology
 BUȘU, I., Surgery
 CERNEA, M., Obstetrics and Gynaecology
 CERNEA, P., Ophthalmology
 CHITA, O., Biology
 CREȚU, S., Paediatrics
 DRĂGOI, G., Anatomy
 GEORGESCU, P., Urology
 NEGOMIREANU, T., Infectious Diseases and Epidemiology
 NEȘTIANU, V., Physiology
 OBREJA, S., Stomatology
 PARHON, I., Clinic, Obstetrics and Gynaecology
 POPESCU, I., Internal Medicine
 ROȘCA, T., Internal Medicine
 STOICA, I., Neurology
 TĂNĂSESCU, D., Biochemistry
 VOICU, V., Pharmacology
 VOICULESCU, C., Microbiology, Parasitology, Virology

*Faculty of Electrical Engineering:*
 AMBROZIE, C., Electric and Magnetic Measures
 BADEA, M., Basic Electrical Engineering
 BELEA, C., Theory of Automatic Systems
 CÎMPEANU, A., Special Electronic Machinery
 DEGERATU, P., Automatization
 ENE, A., Mechanical Design and Descriptive Geometry
 IVĂNESCU, M., Discrete Industrial Automation
 MARIN, C., Automatic Regulators
 PUȘCAȘU, S., Basic Electrical Engineering
 SAVIUC, V., Electrical Machinery
 VINTILĂ, N., Theory and Application of Electrical Machinery

*Faculty of Mechanics:*
 BUCULEI, I. M., Fluid Mechanics and Hydraulic Machinery
 CERNĂIANU, E., Resistance of Materials
 PETRESCU, G., Mechanics and Resistance of Materials
 POPESCU, I., Mechanisms
 SONTEA, S., Technology

*Faculty of Agriculture:*
 BADEA, E., Animal Husbandry
 BARBU, C., Economy of Socialist Agriculture
 CAMALESA, N., Animal Husbandry
 CIOBANU, F., Phytotechnics
 HAȚEGAN, I., Farm Organization
 MARIN, N., Agrochemistry
 MATEI, I., Phytotechnics
 MINULESCU, P., Horticultural Machinery
 NEDELCU, P., Plant Physiology and General Microbiology
 NEGREA, I., Agro-Phyto-Technology
 PAUN, M., Botany
 PAVEL, C., Pasture Production and Conservation
 POP, L., Agro-Phyto-Technics
 POPESCU, C. I., Irrigated Crop Cultivation
 POPESCU, N. I., Plant Improvement
 SOROP, GR., Pedology

*Faculty of Horticulture:*
 BĂLASA, M., Forced Crops and Vegetables
 BANIȚĂ, P., Special Viticulture
 BOBÎRNAC, B., Entomology
 COLEȘ, N., Genetics
 COMEȘ, I., Phyto-pathology
 ENE, F., Plant Improvement
 MILIȚIU, I., Pomiculture and Horticulture
 OPREAN, M., Viticulture
 POPESCU, M., Pomiculture and Intensive Cultivation of Fruit Trees
 TEODORESCU, ȘT., Vinification
 SORESCU, C., Vertebrate Zoology

## UNIVERSITATEA DIN GALAȚI
6200 GALAȚI, BD. REPUBLICII NR. 47

Telephone: 1.36.02.

Founded 1948, University status 1974.

State control; Academic year: September to July.

ROMANIA

*Rector:* FLORIA OPREA.
*Pro-Rectors:* MIHAI HONORIUS TEODORESCU, DUMITRIU RĂILEANU.
*Secretary:* GR. RĂCARIU.
*Librarian:* M. TARABAȘ.

Number of teachers: 442.
Number of students: 5,498.

Publication: *Bulletin.*

### DEANS:

*Faculty of Food Technology and Fisheries:* MIRCEA LEONTE.
*Faculty of Mechanics:* DUMITRU CALUIANU.
*Faculty of Education:* DUMITRU VRABIE.

### PROFESSORS:

*Faculty of Food Technology and Fisheries:*
ADAM, A., Fishing Materials, Mechanization in Pisciculture
BACALBAȘA, N., Fishing Technology
BANU, C., Meat Technology
BEȘCHEA, M., Organic Chemistry and Biochemistry
BOGATU, D., Ichthyopathology
BULANCEA, M., Oenology
CONSTANTINESCU, F., Building Materials, Civilian, Industrial and Agricultural Buildings
COSTIN, G. M., Milk Technology
CULACHE, D., Technology of Sugar Production
GIURCĂ, V., Baking Technology
LEONTE, M., Organic Chemistry
MORARU, N., Bread-making
PANĂ, N., Microbiology, Oenology
RAUȚĂ, M., Hydrology and Oceanography
SEGAL, B., Technology of Preserving Fruit and Vegetables
SEGAL, R., Biochemistry and Bases of Feeding
TATRU, V., Sugar Products Industry
TOFAN, I., Cereals and Flour Preservation
TUDOSE, C., Physics
VASILESCU, G., Hydrobiology, Aquatic Exploitation, Biological Non-piscatorial Resources
VASU, S., Biochemistry
VELICAN, N., Physics

*Faculty of Mechanics:*
AILOAIE, G., Electrical and Electrotechnical Engineering
ALEXANDRU, C., Naval Equipment and Machinery
BEȘCHEA, R., Elements of Mechanical Engineering
CALUIANU, D., Electrical Engineering and Electrical Machines
CĂRBUNARU, A., Thermotechnics and Combustion Engines
CĂRUNTU, M., Mathematical Analysis and Special Mathematics
CEANGĂ, E., Electrotechnics and Automation
CIUCA, C., Study of Metals, Physical Metallurgy
CONSTANT, E., Machine Tool Design, Equipment and Welded Constructions
CREȚULESCU, C., Metallurgical Chemistry
CRUCERU, C., Electrical Engineering
CRUDU, I., Machine Parts
DRUGESCU, E., Physical Metallurgy and Heat Treatments
DUMITRESCU, T., Metallurgical Processes
EPUREANU, A., Machine Building Technology
GOCIU, GH., Heat Transmission

IONIȚĂ, I., Ship-Deck Equipment and Hydraulic Drive
IOSIFESCU, C., Refrigeration Techniques
JISCANU, M., Machine Parts
MARIAN, E., Ship Dynamics
MATULEA, I., Mechanics, Vibrations
MITOȘERIU, C., Machine Tools and Aggregates
MODIGA, M., Ship Structure
MÜLLER, A., Mechanical Engineering
OANCEA, N., Cutting and Surface Generation
OLARU, E., Mathematical Analysis and Special Mathematics
OPREA, F., Theory af Metallurgical Process-extracting Metallurgy
ORĂNESCU, A., Theory of Mechanism and Machines
POPESCU, S., Physical Chemistry
POPOVICI, O., Shipbuilding
RAILEANU, D., Welding
SGRUMALĂ, M., Shipbuilding Technology
STAN, ST., Naval Electrical Installations
STOIAN, L., Technology of Metals
STOICESCU, L., Material Resistance
TEODORESCU, M., Machine Building Technology
TIRU, E., Tool-cutting Design
VAGU, P., Economy and Production Organization
VASILESCU, A., Hydromechanics

*Faculty of Education:*
APOSTU, D., Institutional Organization and Management
BALAIS, F., Physical Education and Sport
BREZEANU, I., Folklore Studies
MANOLESCU, G., Theory of Physical Education, Sports Training
MIHALY, E., Scientific Socialism
PANȚIRU, P., Political Economy
ȘIPOȘ, F., Institutional Organization and Management
SÎRBU, D., Handball
SÎRBU, I., Political Economy
STANCIU, D., Sport
TURLAN, V., Romanian Language
VAGU, P., Production Economics
VRABIE, D., Psychology and Education

## UNIVERSITATEA "AL. I. CUZA" DIN IAȘI

IAȘI, CALEA 23 AUGUST, 11
Telephone: 40967.
Founded 1860.

Academic year: September to June.

*Rector:* Prof. Dr. VIOREL BARBU.
*Pro-Rectors:* Prof. Dr. I. HAGIU, Prof. Dr. V. ARVINTE, Conf. Dr. E. PUHA.
*Registrar:* OCTAVIAN DAVIDEANU.
*Librarian:* Dr. M. BORDEIANU.

Number of teachers: 557.
Number of students: 6,577.

Publication: *Analele Universității "Al. I. Cuza" din Iași†.*

### DEANS:

*Faculty of Mathematics:* Conf. Dr. CĂLIN-PETRU IGNAT.
*Faculty of Physics:* Conf. Dr. CONSTANTIN POPUSOI.
*Faculty of Biology, Geography and Geology:* Prof. Dr. ION DONISA.
*Faculty of Law:* Conf. Dr. STEFAN RAUSCHI.
*Faculty of Philology:* Conf. Dr. SILVIA BUTUREANU.

*Faculty of History and Philosophy:* Conf. Dr. VASILE CRISTIAN.
*Faculty of Economic Sciences:* Prof. Dr. ENE MARIN.

### PROFESSORS:

*Faculty of Mathematics:*
BARBU, V., Differential Equations
BORȘ, C., Mathematics
CAZACU, C., Computer Science
CÎMPAN, FL., History of Mathematics
COSTINESCU, O., Topology
CREANGĂ, I., Algebra
CRUCEANU, V., Geometry
GHEORGHIEV, G., Differential Geometry
GHEORGHIU, N., Mathematical Analysis
HAIMOVICI, A., Physico-Mathematical Equations
LUCHIAN, T., Algebra
MIRON, R., Differential Geometry
NEGOESCU, N., Mathematical Analysis
PETROVANU, D., Mathematics
POPA, I., Mathematical Analysis
RADU, A., Theoretical Mechanics

*Faculty of Physics:*
BURSUC, I., Molecular Physics
GOTTLIEB, I., Theoretical Physics
IONITA, I., Nuclear Physics
MIHUL, C., Optics
SANDU, D., Electronic Devices and Circuits
SANDULOVICIU, M., Plasma Physics
SOROHAN, M., Molecular Physics
TUTOVAN, V., Electricity and Magnetism

*Faculty of Biology, Geography and Geology:*
ALEXA, E., Physiology and Biology
BĂCĂOANU, V., Geomorphology
BUDEANU, E., General Chemistry
BURDUJA, C., Botany
CĂRĂUSU, S. Hydrobiology
CONSTANTINEANU, M., Zoology
DUMITRESCU, R., Mineralogy and Petrography
DONISĂ, L., Geomorphology
ERHAN, V., Mineralogy, Petrography
GUGIUMAN, I., Meteorology, Climatology
HARJOABA, I., Geography
HASSAN, G., Vertebrate Zoology
IONESI, L., Geology
JEANRENAUD, P., Geology
JITARIU, P., Physiology and Biology
LEOCOV, M., Agrophytotechnology
MARTINIUC, C., Geomorphology
NECRASOV, OLGA, Anthropology
OBREJA, A., Geography
ȘANDRU, I., Economic Geography of the S.R.R.
SFICLEA, V., Topographic Geography of the S.R.R.
SÎRCU, I., Physical Geography of the S.R.R.
SOLOMON, L., Vertebrate Zoology
TOMA, C., Plant Anatomy
TOPALĂ, N., General Microbiology
VANCEA, S., Invertebrate Zoology
ZOLYNEAK, C., Genetic Biology

*Faculty of Philology:*
ANDRIESCU, A., Romanian Literature
ARVINTE, V., Romanian Language
CIOPRAGA, C., Romanian Literature
CUCIUREANU, ST., Romanian Language
GIOSU, S., Romanian Language
ISTRATE, G., Romanian Language
IVĂNESCU, G., Romance Language
LĂUDAT, I., Ancient Romanian Literature
PERETZ, H., German Literature
PLATON, M., Romanian Literature
POPA, N. I., French Literature
STOLERIU, V., Contemporary French Literature
VRACIU, A., Russian Language

1134

**Faculty of History and Philosophy:**
BÎRSĂNESCU, S., Pedagogics
BOLD, E., Romanian Modern History
BORCEA, P., Biology
BOTEZATU, P., Logic
CERNICHEVICI, S., General Theory of Education (Pedagogy)
CIHODARU, C., Romanian Medieval History
COPTIL, L., Scientific Socialism
COSMOVICI, A., Psychology
DAVIDSOHN, I., History of Philosophy
DUMITRESCU, P., History of Philosophy
DUMITRIU, C., Pedagogics
GRĂMADĂ, I., World Medieval History
GRIGORAS, I., Ethics
HAGIU, I., Scientific Socialism
LOGHIN, A., Romanian History
NATANSOHN, I., Sociology
PAVELCU, V., Psychology
PETRESCU-DÎMBOVIȚA, M., Romanian History
PLATON, GH., Romanian Modern History
RAVEICA, T., History of Modern Philosophy
TEODORESCU, S., Psychology
VĂIDEANU, G., Pedagogy

**Faculty of Law:**
BENDITER, I., Constitutional Law
BRAUNSTEIN, B., Penal Law
IAVORSCHI, I., Labour Law
JACOTĂ, M., Roman Law
LOGHIN, O., Penal Law
NEGRU, V., Civil Law
TAȚOMIR, N., International Public Law
THEODORU, G., Penal Law

**Faculty of Economic Sciences:**
BÂRBAT, A., Statistics
MARIN, E., Political Economy
NICULICIOIU, C., Political Economy
RUSU, D., Book-Keeping Theory
SECRIERU, C., World Agricultural Economy and Politics
TĂTARU, A., Economic Statistics
TODOSIA, M., History of Economic Theory
TURLIUC, V., Money and Banking

ATTACHED INSTITUTES:
**Astronomical Observatory:** Iași, Aleea M. Sadoveanu 5.
**"A. D. Xenopol" Institute of History and Archaeology:** Iași, Str. K. Marx 17.
**Botanical Garden:** Iași Str. Dumbrava Roșie 7-9.
**Computing Centre:** Iași, Str. Berthelot 16.
**Economic Research Centre:** Iași, Str. General Berthelot 16.
**Institute of Mathematics:** Iași, Calea 23 August 11.
**Natural History Museum:** Iași, Str. Stefan Gheorghiu 9.
**Research Centre of Linguistics, Literary History and Folklore:** Iași, Str. Codrescu 2.
**Research Centre of Social Sciences:** Iași, Str. Codrescu 2.

## UNIVERSITATEA DIN TIMIȘOARA
TIMIȘOARA, V. PÂRVAN 4
Telephone: 1.28.05.

Founded 1962.

State control; Academic year: September to June.

*Rector:* C. POPA.
*Pro-Rectors:* P. ONIȚA, O. BIRĂU.
*Librarian:* T. KNEZEVIĆ.

Library: see Libraries.
Number of teachers: 375.
Number of students: 4,550.

Publications: *Analele Universității din Timișoara—științe matematice, științe fizice-chimice, științe filologice, științe sociale.*

DEANS:
*Faculty of Philology:* V. ȘERBAN.
*Faculty of Economic Studies:* M. EPURAN.
*Faculty of Natural Sciences:* E. BOROȘ.

PROFESSORS:
*Faculty of Philology:*
BOCIORT, I. G., Literary Criticism
HEINRICH, A., Russian Language
MUNTEANU, ST., General Linguistics
ȘERBAN, V., Romanian Language
TODORAN, E., History of Romanian Literature
TOHĂNEANU, GH., Romanian Language
VINTILESCU, V., History of Romanian Literature

*Faculty of Economic Sciences:*
CORNEA, I., Philosophy
CRĂCIUNESCU, V., Construction of Electric Machinery
ILIESCU, I., Philosophy
LUCA, I., Scientific Socialism
ONIȚA, P., Political Economy
ȘCHIOPESCU, V., Economy
TCACIUC, M., Accountancy

*Faculty of Natural Sciences:*
ARDELEANU, V., Geography
BOROȘ, E., Algebra and Operational Research
CIUHANDU, GH., Organic Chemistry
PAPUC, D. I., Geometry
POPA, C., Mathematical Analyses
REGHIȘ, M., Differential Equations
ZĂGĂNESCU, M., Quantum Mechanics and Quantum Theory of Solids

ATTACHED RESEARCH INSTITUTES:
Social Sciences Centre.
Economic Research Centre.
Electronic Computer Bureau.

# TECHNOLOGICAL UNIVERSITIES

## INSTITUTUL POLITEHNIC "GH. GHEORGHIU-DEJ"
BUCHAREST,
SPLAIUL INDEPENDENȚEI 313
Telephone: 37.20.55.
Telex: 10490 pibuh r.

Founded 1819.

Academic year: September to June (two semesters).

*Rector:* Prof. Dr. Eng. VOICU TACHE.
*Vice-Rectors:* Prof. Dr. Eng. RODICA VELCU, Prof. Dr. Eng. C. BĂLĂ, Prof. Dr. Eng. AL. DĂNESCU, Prof. Dr. Eng. I. M. POPESCU.
*Chief Administrative Officer:* N. DIMA.
*Librarian:* L. VORONCA.

Library: see Libraries.
Number of teachers: 1,517.
Number of students: 27,351.

Publication: *Buletinul Institutului Politehnic "Gheorghe Gheorghiu-Dej".*

DEANS:
*Faculty of Electrical Engineering:* A. ȚUGULEA.
*Faculty of Power Engineering:* I. IORDĂNESCU.
*Faculty of Mechanical Engineering:* A. MANOLE.
*Faculty of Agricultural Engineering:* P. BABICIU.
*Faculty of Automation:* S. FLOREA.
*Faculty of Electronics and Telecommunications:* ADELAIDA MATEESCU.
*Faculty of Machine-Building Technology:* AL. RĂDULESCU.
*Faculty of Transport Engineering:* AL. NEAGU.
*Faculty of Aircraft Engineering:* C. BERBENTE.
*Faculty of Metallurgy:* SILVIA VACU.
*National Institute of Chemistry:*
*Faculty of Chemical Technology:* S. ROȘCA.
*Faculty of Equipment and Chemical Process Engineering:* GHEORGHIȚA JINESCU.

PROFESSORS:
*Common Courses:*
ACHIM, I., Philosophy
ATANASIU, M., Mechanics
BĂDILĂ, N., Political Economy
BIR, H., Political Economy
BLUMENFELD, M., Strength of Materials
BOGDAN, R., Theory of Mechanisms
BOIANGIU, D., Mechanics
BUGA, M., Strength of Materials
BUZDUGAN, G., Strength of Materials
CARABULEA, A., Industrial Management
CARAGHEORGHE, E., Mechanics
CLEJA, A., Scientific Socialism
COROI, M., Special Mathematics
CREȚU, T., Physics
CUCUREZEANU, I., Physics
DĂNESCU, AL., Technical Thermodynamics
DIACON, AL., Hydro-electric Power
FLOREA, J., Fluid Mechanics
GRĂDISTEANU, I., Political Economy
HOMOȘ, T., Industrial Management
IONIȚĂ, P., Political Economy
MANEA, F., Fundamental Electrical Engineering
MOCANU, C., Fundamental Electrical Engineering
MOISIL, GH., Physics
MONCEA, J., Descriptive Geometry and Drawing
MOȚOC, C., Physics
OLARU, V., Algebra, Mathematical Analysis
PANĂ, T., Strength of Materials
PAVELESCU, D., Machine Elements
PELECUDI, C., Theory of Mechanisms
POPA, C., Philosophy

Popescu, I., Physics
Prahoveanu, E., Political Economy
Preda, M., Fundamental Electrical Engineering
Radcenco, V., Technical Thermodynamics
Rădoi, M., Mechanics
Rădulescu, Gh., Machine Elements
Rebușapcă, D., Political Economy
Roșculeț, M., Algebra, Mathematical Analysis
Roman, V., Scientific Socialism
Rusu, O., Strength of Materials
Sonea, P., Fundamental Electrical Engineering
Stănciou, Iu., Industrial Management
Șerbănescu, I., Scientific Socialism
Stănășilă, O., Algebra, Mathematical Analysis
Timotin, Al., Fundamental Electrical Engineering
Tugulea, Al., Fundamental Electrical Engineering
Voiculescu, D., Mechanics
Voinea, R., Mechanics

*Specialized Courses:*
*A. Electrical Engineering:*
*Faculty of Electrical Engineering:*
Bălă, C., Electrical Machines
Fransua, A., Electrical Machines
Hortopan, G., Theory and Design of Electrical Apparatus
Ifrim, A., Electrical Machines

*Faculty of Automation:*
Călin, S., Automation
Florea, S., Automation
Ionescu, V., Automation
Lăzăroiu, F., Automation
Petrescu, A., Computers
Petrescu, M., Computers
Tertișco, M., Automation

*Faculty of Electronics and Telecommunications:*
Barbu, E., Telephone, Telegraphy
Cătuneanu, V., Electronic Technology and Reliability
Corlăteanu, V., Electronic Technology and Reliability
Drăgănescu, M., Electronic Devices Circuits
Mateescu, A., Telephone, Telegraphy
Nicolau, E., Radiocommunications
Postelnicu, P., Telephone, Telegraphy
Rulea, G., Radiocommunications
Săvescu, M., Radiocommunications
Spătaru, A., Theory of Information Transmission
Theodorescu, I., Industrial Electronics
Vasiliu, Cr., Telephone, Telegraphy

*B. Power Engineering:*
*Faculty of Power Engineering:*
Arie, A., Electric Networks
Carabogdan, I. Gh., Electric Power Plants
Cristescu, D., High Voltage Technique
Dănilă, N., Electric Power Plants
Diacon, Al., Hydroelectric Power
Drăgan, G., Electric Networks
Iacobescu, G., Electric Networks
Iordănescu, I., Electrical Networks
Potolea, E., Electric Networks

*C. Mechanical Engineering*
*Faculty of Mechanical Engineering:*
Apostolescu, N., Internal Combustion Engines
Aramă, C., Internal Combustion Engines
Demian, T., Fine Mechanics
Diaconescu, Gh., Fine Mechanics
Dodoc, P., Optical Apparata
Grunwald, B., Car Engines

Postelnicescu, M., Boilers and Steam Gas Turbines
Seleșteanu, A., Boilers and Steam Gas Turbines

*Faculty of Machine Building Technology:*
Ciocîrdia, C., Machine Building Technology
Drimer, D., Metal Technology and Welding
Enache, S., Machine Tools and Tools
Gavrilaș, I., Machine Building Technology
Gheghea, I., Machine Tools
Miclosi, V., Metal Technology and Welding
Oprean, A., Machine Tools and Tools
Rădulescu, Al., Machine Building Technology
Tabără, V., Machine Tools and Tools
Tache, V., Machine Building Technology
Zgură, Gh., Technology of Materials

*Faculty of Transport Engineering:*
Condacse, N., Rolling Stock
Frîncu, P., Railway Transport
Nancu, Al., Railway Transport
Popa, A., Rolling Stock

*Faculty of Agricultural Engineering:*
Segărceanu, M., Agricultural Machines

*Faculty of Aircraft Engineering:*
Constantinescu, V. N., Aircraft Engineering
Guță, C., Aircraft Engineering
Niță, M., Aircraft Engineering
Petre, A., Aircraft Engineering
Pimsner, V., Aircraft Engineering
Racoveanu, N., Aircraft Engineering

*D. Metallurgical Engineering:*
*Faculty of Metallurgical Engineering:*
Adrian, M., Iron and Steel Metallurgy
Buzilă, S., Foundry
Dragomir, I., Iron and Steel Metallurgy
Dulămiță, T., Heat Treatment and Metal Studies
Gâdea, Suzana, Physical Metallurgy
Geru, N., Physical Metallurgy
Ienciu, M., Metallurgy of Non-Ferrous Metals
Murguleț, N., Metallurgical Aggregates and Technical Equipment
Oprea, F., Metallurgy of Non-Ferrous Metals
Oprescu, I., Iron and Steel Metallurgy
Petrescu, M., Physical Metallurgy
Petrescu, N., Metallurgy of Non-Ferrous Metals
Popescu, N., Physical Metallurgy and Metal Studies
Popescu, V., Forge-Foundry
Protopopescu, M., Physical and Metal Studies
Sofroni, L., Forge-Foundry
Tripșa, I., Iron and Steel Metallurgy
Vacu, Silvia, Iron and Steel Metallurgy

*E. Chemical Engineering:*
*National Institute of Chemistry:*
*Faculty of Chemical Technology:*
Angelescu, E., Inorganic Chemical Technology
Avram, M., Chemistry and Inorganic Technology
Balaban, Al., Chemistry and Inorganic Technology
Balță, P., Silicate and Oxide Compound Chemistry
Bărbulescu, N., Physical Chemistry
Bejan, C., Inorganic Chemistry
Brezeanu, M., Chemistry and Inorganic Technology

Constantinescu, I., Inorganic Chemical Technology
Cornea, F., Chemistry and Inorganic Technology
Croitoru, V., Analytical Chemistry
Dimonie, M., Polymer Technology
Dinescu, R., Silicate and Oxide Compound Chemistry
Gheorghiu, C., Chemistry and Inorganic Technology
Luca, C., Analytical Chemistry
Negoiu, D., Chemistry and Inorganic Technology
Nicolescu, I., Chemistry and Inorganic Technology
Panait, C., Chemistry and Inorganic Technology
Pincovschi, E., Chemistry and Inorganic Technology
Teodorescu, G., Chemistry and Inorganic Technology
Teoreanu, I., Silicate and Oxide Compound Chemistry

*Faculty of Equipment and Chemical Process Engineering:*
Albert, F., Chemistry and Electrochemical Technology
Danciu, E., Techniques and Apparata
Firoiu, C., Physical Chemistry and Electrochemical Technology
Floarea, O., Chemical Engineering
Georgescu, I., Chemistry and Electrochemical Technology
Landauer, O., Physical Chemistry and Electrochemical Technology
Mihail, R., Chemical Engineering
Oncescu, T., Physical Chemistry and Electrochemical Technology
Radovici, O., Physical Chemistry and Electrochemical Technology
Sahini, V., Physical Chemistry and Electrochemical Technology
Segal, E., Physical Chemistry and Electrochemical Technology
Smigelschi, O., Chemical Engineering
Sternberg, S., Physical Chemistry and Electrochemical Technology
Vîlcu, R., Physical Chemistry and Electrochemical Technology

Attached Research Units
*Biotechnology:* Dr. M. D. Nicu.
*Materials Testing:* Prof. Dr. Eng. Gh. Buzdugan.
*Electric Power Plants:* Prof. Dr. Eng. I. Carabogdan.
*Electric Networks:* Prof. Dr. Eng. G. Drăgan.
*Metallurgy:* Prof. Dr. Eng. S. Vacu.
*Chemical Technology and Corrosion Prevention:* Dr. Eng. R. Avram.
*Hydraulics:* Prof. Dr. Eng. A. Diacon.
*Computer Centre:* Prof. Dr. Eng. M. Petrescu.

## INSTITUTUL POLITEHNIC CLUJ-NAPOCA

CLUJ, STR. EMIL ISAC 15

Telephone: 25640-25699.

Founded 1948.

Academic year: September to June.

*Rector:* Dr. Eng. Attila Pálfalvi.
*Pro-Rectors:* Dr. Eng. I. Dragan, Dr. Eng. Al Cătărig, Dr. Eng. D. Comsa.
*Registrar:* T. Nilas.
*Librarian:* V. Nichifor.

Library of 459,000 vols.
Number of teachers: 644.
Number of students: 8,663.

Publications: *Scientific Bulletin of the Cluj Polytechnic Institute* (annual).

### DEANS:

*Faculty of Mechanics:* Dr. Eng. GH. PETRICEAN.
*Faculty of Construction:* Dr. Eng. G. BÂRSAN.
*Faculty of Electrical Engineering:* Dr. Eng. A. KELEMEN.

### PROFESSORS:

**Faculty of Mechanics:**
ALB, TH., Descriptive Geometry and Design
ALBU, A., Tool Mechanics
BATAGA, N., Heat Engines, Testing, Agricultural Machinery, Driving
BOGDAN, M., Factory Equipment and Transportation, Machine Components
CHIRILA, A., Thermo-Technics and Thermal Equipment in Farming
CHISIU, A., Machine Components
CODREANU, C., Physics
COLAN, H., Metal Technology
DEACU, L., Machine Tools, Bases of Cutting and Generation of Surfaces
DOMȘA, A., Machine Tools and Metal-Working
DRAGAN, I., Technology of Plastics Deformation
IONUȚ, V., Technology of Metal Working
LĂZĂRESCU, I., Theory of Metal-Cutting and Tool Design
MAROS, D., Theory of Mechanisms
MATEI, G., Machine Tools, Tolerance and Technical Gaugeing, Metallurgy, Mechanics
MOLDOVAN, V., Tools for Plastics Deformation
NIAC, G., Physical Chemistry
NICOLAE, V., Metal Technology
PÁLFALVI, A., Metal Technology
PĂSTRAV, I., Strength of Materials
PAVEL, G., Tolerance and Gaugeing, Technical Control
PETRICEANU, G., Technology of Machine Construction
POPA, B., Thermo-Technics and Thermal Machines
POPESCU, P., Theoretical Mechanics
RIPIANU, A., Theoretical Mechanics
SAGYEBO, F., Tooling Design
SZEKELY, E., Theory of Mechanisms and Organs of Machines
ZIRBO, G., Foundry and Moulding Technology
ZUBAC, V., Foundry Equipment

**Faculty of Construction:**
BÂRSAN, G., Mechanics, Statics, Stability and Dynamics, Seismic Engineering
BEIU, A., Technology of Construction
BOTA, O., Reinforced Concrete Construction
CĂTĂRIG, A., Statics, Stability and Dynamics, Optimal Calculus of Structures
GOBESZ, F., Statistics, Stability and Dynamics
IANCĂU, V., Geometrical Representation
ILLE, V., Strength of Materials, Elasticity Plasticity
JUNCAN, N., Metal Constructions
LAZAR, I., Building Equipment
MARUSCEAC, D., Agricultural and Transport Construction
MIHĂILESCU, M., Reinforced Concrete Constructions
ONEȚ, T., Reinforced Concrete
POP, V., Geotechnics and Foundations
TERTEA, I., Reinforced and Prestressed Concrete

**Faculty of Electrical Engineering:**
COLOȘI, T., Industrial Electronics and Automatics
COMȘA, D., Industrial Energetics, Electrothermics
COȚIU, A., Analysis
DANCEA, I., Computer Programming, Data Processing
HĂNGĂNUȚ, M., Automatics
IONESCU, GH., Linear Algebra and Analytical Geometry
KELEMEN, A., Electric Drive
MOINA, I., Physical Training
PATACHI, N., Electrotechnics, Electrical Measurements
SIMION, E., Basic Electrical Engineering

## INSTITUTUL POLITEHNIC "GHEORGHE ASACHI"
IAȘI, CALEA 23 AUGUST, 22
Telephone: 13577.
Founded 1912.

State control; Academic year: September to September.

*Rector:* Prof. Dr. Ing. MIHAI GAFIȚANU.
*Pro-Rectors:* Prof. Dr. Ing. TUDOR SILION, Prof. Dr. GHEORGHE CHIRIȚĂ, Prof. Dr. Ing. NICOLAE GAVRILAȘ, Prof. Dr. Ing. CAMELUȚA BELDIE.
*Registrar:* V. STANCIU.
*Librarian:* GEORGETA MEDVIGHI.

Library: see Libraries.
Number of teachers: 1,270.
**Number of students:** 16,774.
Publication: *Bulletin* (2 a year).

### DEANS:

*Faculty of Chemical Technology:* S. OPREA.
*Faculty of Civil Engineering:* V. FOCȘA.
*Faculty of Electrical Engineering:* I. BEJAN.
*Faculty of Hydrology:* M. PATRAȘ.
*Faculty of Textile Technology and Chemistry:* D. LIUȚE.
*Faculty of Mechanical Engineering:* V. BELOUSOV.

### PROFESSORS:

*Faculty of Chemical Technology:*
ABABI, V., General Technology
ASANDEI, N., Macromolecular Chemistry and Man-made Fibres
BELDIE, C., Chemical Thermodynamics
BOLD, A., Analytical Chemistry
BUDEANU, C., Organic Chemistry
CALISTRU, C., Technology of Inorganic Substances
CALU, N., Inorganic Chemistry
COMANIȚA, E., Heterocyclic Chemistry
CORLĂȚEANU, E., Agrochemistry
CRISTIAN, GH., Organic Chemistry
CRUCEANU, M., Industrial Technology
CURIEVICI, I., Automation, Chemical Technology
DIACONESCU, V., Pulp and Paper Technology
DRUȚA, I., Organic Chemistry
DUCA, AL., Analytic Chemistry
DUMITRESCU, S., Polymer Physics
DUMITRU, S., Special Organic Chemistry
FIȘEL, S., Analytical Chemistry
GHIRVU, C., Structural and Quantum Chemistry
GOLGOȚIU, T., Inorganic Chemistry
GRIGORIU, T., Equipment for Inorganic Technology
HANCU, I., Pollution
HURDUC, N., Physical Chemistry of Macromolecules
IFRIM, S., General Chemistry
IVAȘCAN, ST., Corrosion and Electrochemical Industries
LEONTE, C., Organic Chemistry
LEONTE, C., Technology of Inorganic Substances
LIXANDRU, T., Organic Chemistry
MACOVEI, V., Physical Chemistry
MOCANU, R., Analytical Chemistry
NACU, AL., Analytical Chemistry
OBROCEA, P., Pulp and Paper Technology
ONISCU, C., Technology of Synthetic and Biosynthetic Drugs
OPREA, CL., Mecanochemistry of Polymers
OPREA, S., Chemical Organic Technology
PETROVANU, M., Organic Chemistry
PETROVANU, O., General Chemistry
PETROVANU, S., Organic Chemistry
POPA, A., General Technology
POPPEL, E., Rheology and Equipment in Paper Technology
RANG, A., Inorganic Chemistry
ROȘCA, I., Inorganic Chemistry
ROZMARIN, GH., Wood Chemistry
RUCINSCHI, E., Organic Synthesis
RUSU, M., Organic Chemistry
SIMIONESCU, C., Macromolecular Chemistry
TUDOSE, R., Equipment for Macromolecular Compounds Industry
TUTOVEANU, M., Organic Chemistry
UNGUREANU, ST., Automation
VASILIU, R., Electrochemistry
VICOL, O., Inorganic Chemistry

*Faculty of Civil Engineering:*
AMARIEI, C., Statics, Plastic Design
ANTON, C., Railways
BENCHEA, N., Wood and Steel Bridges
BOGHIAN, V., Industrial Engineering
BOȚI, M., Soil Mechanics and Foundations
CAPATU, CH., Bridges
CEPAREANU, R., Sociology
CIONGRADI, I., Dynamics
CIORNEI, AL., Buildings
COROBCEANU, S., Foundations
COSMULESCU, P., Steel Constructions
DIACONU, M., Resistance of Metals
DUMITRAȘ, A., Structural Mechanics
FOCȘA, V., Building Theory and Physics
GROLL, L., Building Materials
HUMĂ, D., Philosophy
JEANRENAUD, A., Social Sciences
JERCA, ST., Structural Mechanics
JOFA, C., Social Science
MIHUL, A., Building Technology
NEGOIȚĂ, AL., Seismic Engineering
NOUR, S., Foundations
ORLOVSCHI, N., Statics
PICHIU, D., Philosophy
PORUMBESCU, M., History of Architecture
PORUMBESCU, N., Architecture
PRECUPAN, D., Strength of Materials
RADU, A., Building Technology
RAILEANU, P., Building Foundations
SALINIUC, Z., Roads and Highways
SERBESCU, C., Steel Constructions
SILION, T., Foundations
STRAT, L., Structural Mechanics
TRELEA, A., Construction Technology
TURCU, N., Philosophy
UNGUREANU, N., Strength of Materials
VEREȘ, A., Buildings
VULPE, A., Statics
ZAROJAN, H., Highways

*Faculty of Electrical Engineering:*
ALEXA, D., Microwave Engineering
ALEXANDRESCU, V., Power Systems
ANTONESCU, M., Telecommunications
ANTONIU, M., Electric and Electronic Measurements
BABEI, N., Electrical and Electronic Measurement
BALABAN, E., Electrical Drives
BĂRBULESCU, D., **Electrical and Magnetic Measures**
BEJAN, I., Control Systems
BERGMAN, I., Electrical Machines
BOȚAN, N., **Electro-Mechanical Controls**
CANTEMIR, L., Electric Traction, Uses of Electric Energy
CIUBOTARU, C., Physics
CREȚU, M., Electric and Electronic Measurements
CUTU, L., Mathematics
FILIPIUC, I., Electrical Machines
GAVRILAȘ, N., High-Tension Technology
GIOSAN, T., Power Systems
HANGANU, E., Electroenergetics
HUȚANU, C., Uses of Electric Energy
IVAS, D., Power Systems
LEONTE, P., Electrical Equipment
LUCA, E., Physics
MAXIM, GH., Electronics
MELINTE, S., Physics
MITREA, S., Fundamentals of Electrical Engineering
MUNTEANU, V., Electronics
OLAH, I., Uses of Electric Energy
POEATA, AL., **Electric Energy**
POEATA, N., Digital and Analogue Computers
POPESCU, I., Fundamentals of Electrical Engineering
POPOVICI, A., Electrical Machines
PREDA, L., Electrical Equipment of Power Plants
REUS, N., Electronics
ROSMAN, H., Fundamentals of Electrical Engineering
SAVIN, GH., Fundamentals of Electrical Engineering
SEBASTIAN, L., Control Systems
ȚIȚARU, I., Uses of Electric Energy
TURIC, L., Industrial Electronics
VALACHI, A., Digital and Analogue Computers
VASILIU, A., Physics
ZET, G., Physics

*Faculty of Hydrology:*
BALOIU, V., Erosion and Regulation of Water Courses
BÎRSAN, E., Erosion and Regulation of Water Courses
BLIDARU, E., Hydraulics
BLIDARU, V., Irrigation and Drainage
BRAIER, A., Mechanics of Vibration
CISMARU, C., Irrigation and Drainage
CLIMESCU, A., Algebra and Related Fields
CORDUNEANU, A., Algebra and Related Fields
DIMA, M., Sanitary Engineering
ENESCU, I., Algebra and Related Fields
GAVRILOV, GH., Erosion and Regulation of Water Courses
GHEORGHIU, E., Amelioration Pedology
GRADINARU, N., Algebra and Related Fields
GUȘTIUC, L., Amelioration Pedology
OPREA, A., Algebra and Related Fields
PATRAS, M., Reinforced Concrete
POPESCU, D., General Agriculture
RUSCIOR, ST., Algebra and Related Fields
SERBAN, D., Mechanization of Reclamation Works
TALPALARU, P., Mathematics
VAMANU, E., Mathematics
ZAVATI, V., Hydraulics

*Faculty of Textile Technology and Chemistry:*
ADUMITRACESEI, I., Political Economy
BUTNARU, R., Chemistry and Technology of Tanning Materials
CHINCIU, D., Management and Organization of Textile Industry
CHIRIȚA, A., Chemistry and Technology of Tanning Materials
COCIU, V., Basis of Technology of Leather Products
COJOCARU, N., Spinning Technology
DIMA, A., Economy and Organization of Chemical Industry
DUMA, D., Footwear Design
FLOREA, E., Economy and Organization of Chemical Industry
FORST, T., Dyeing and Textile Printing
HAGIU, E., Knitted Fabric Structures
HANGANU, V., Machine Parts, Elements of Spinning Machine Design
LIUȚE, D., Preparatory Weaving Processes
MACARIE, G., Political Economy
MÂLCOMETE, O., Chemistry and Physics of Textile Fibres
MÂLCOMETE, P., **Political Economy**
MARCHIȘ, A., **Structure and Designing of Fabrics**
MARCHIȘ, O., Weaving
MATEESCU, M., Advanced Weft Knitting
MEDRIHAN, G., Political Economy
NICOLAE, M., Economy and Organization
NIȚA, I., Political Economy
NETEA, M., **Technology of Wool-spinning**
POPA, E., **Economy and Organization of Chemical Industry**
PREDA, C., Nonconventional Textile Structures
REICHER, F., Weaving Machine Design
RUSU, C., Management and Organization of Textile Industry
VALU, F., Equipment in Textile Chemical Industry
VLAD, I., **Textile Fibres**

*Faculty of Mechanical Engineering:*
AILINCAI, GH., Materials Technology
BAUSIC, V., **Resistance of Materials**
BELOUSOV, V., Cutting Tools
BENDESCU, I., Thermotechnics and Heat Engines
BRAIER, AL., Mechanics
CIOBANU, C., Hydraulics
CIOCHINA, C., Technology of Materials
CIUBOTARU, C., Agricultural Engineering
COMAN, GH., Machine Building Technology
COZMINCA, M., Machine Tools
GAFIȚANU, M., Machine Vibrations and Acoustics
GAIGINSCHI, R., Mechanics
GOJINETCHI, N., Devices
HOPULELE, I., Technology of Thermal Treatments
HORBANIUC, D., Resistance of Materials
ILIESCU, GH., Machine Parts
IRIMICIUC, N., Mechanics
LINDE, CR., Agricultural Machines
MALUREANU, I., Technology of Metals
MANGERON, D., Theoretical Mechanics
MATEI, P., **Hydraulics and Hydraulic Machines**
MERTICARU, V., Machine Dynamics
MOCANU, D., **Resistance of Materials**
NECULAIASA, V., Agricultural Machines
PERETZ, D., Thermotechnics
PICOȘ, C., **Technology of** Machine Building
PLAHTEANU, B., Machine Tools
PRUTEANU, O., Machine Building Technology
RAILEANU, A., Technical Control
RENER, A., Theory and Design of Machine Tools
URSESCU, D., Gas and Steam Turbines
ZETU, D., Machine Tools
ZUGRAVEL, M., Internal Combustion Engines

## INSTITUTUL POLITEHNIC "TRAIAN VUIA" TIMIȘOARA
TIMIȘOARA,
BUL. 30 DECEMBRIE 2
Telephone: 3.47.13.
Founded 1920.

State control; Academic year: September to June.

*Rector:* I. DE SABATA.
*Pro-Rectors:* H. THEIL, T. DORDEA, O. CRIȘAN, S. ANGHEL.
*Librarian:* I. GHIȘE.

Number of teachers: 1,061.
Number of students: 14,795.

Publication: *Buletinul Științific* (Scientific Bulletin, half-yearly).

### DEANS:
*Faculty of Mechanical Engineering:* F. KOVACS.
*Faculty of Electrical Engineering:* T. MUREȘAN.
*Faculty of Civil Engineering:* T. NICOARĂ.
*Faculty of Chemical Engineering:* D. BECHERESCU.
*Faculty of Agricultural Mechanics:* I. NIȚĂ.

### PROFESSORS:
*Faculty of Mechanical Engineering:*
ANTON, I., **Hydraulic Turbines and Turbo-Transmissions**
BERINDEAN, V., **Theory of Internal Combustion Engines**
BOLEANȚU, L., Strength of Materials
BRÎNDEU, L., Mechanics
CREȚA, G., Steam Turbines
DODON, E., Machine Tools
DREUCEAN, A., Machine Tools and Dimension Control
GHEORGHIU, N., Machine Parts
GROȘANU, I., Mechanics
GYULAI, F., Pumps, Ventilators, Compressors
HAJDU, I., **Strength of Materials**
HOANCĂ, V., Traction Heat Engines
KOVACS, F., **Mechanical Theory and Machine Dynamics**
NANU, A., **Technology of Materials**
PERJU, D., Mechanisms
PREDA, I., Hydroelectric Power Stations and Pumping Stations
ROSINGER, S., Designing of Stamps and Oil-blocks
SĂLĂGEAN, T., Fusion Welding Technology
SILAȘ, G., Theoretical Mechanics
SULEA, P., Wagons and Brakes
THEIL, H., **Heat Engineering**
TRUȘCULESCU, M., Study of Metals
UNGUREANU, C., Steam Boilers

*Faculty of Electrical Engineering:*
BABUȚIA, I., Industrial Electronics
BOGOEVICI, N., Basics of Electrotechnics
BORNEAS, M., Physics
BUDIȘAN, N., **Automation and Telecontrol**

CRIȘAN, O., Energy Systems
CRSTICI, B., Special Mathematics
DE SABATA, C., Physics
DE SABATA, I., Basis of Electrotechnics
DORDEA, T., Electrical Machines
FRÄNKEL, D., Basics of Electro-Technics
GHEORGHIU, O., Special Mathematics
HEINRICH, I., Electrical Parts of Power Stations
HELLER, A., Electrical Engineering and Machinery
MUNTEANU, A., Physics
MUREȘAN, T., Electronic Circuits
NEGRU, V., High Voltage Engineering
NOVAC, I., Electrical Machines
POLICEC, A., Medical Electronic Devices
POP, E., Electrical and Magnetic Measurements
POP, V., Systems for Digital Data Processing
ROGOJAN, A., Digital Computers
ROTHENSTEIN, B., Physics
SERACIN, E., Electro-Mechanical Drive and Equipment
SIMOIU, C., Physics
SORA, C., Basis of Electro-Technics
SUCIU, I., Electrical Machines
VĂZDĂUȚEANU, V., Utilization of Electricity

*Faculty of Civil Engineering:*
BÂLĂ, M., Hydraulic Engineering
BOTA, V. Concrete Bridges
CREȚU, G., Hydrology and Water Economy
DAN, E., Water Course Regulations
FILIMON, I., Reinforced Concrete
FLEȘERIU, I., Metal Bridges
GUȚESCU, D., Topography
JURA, I., Water Supplies
MATEESCU, D., Metallic Constructions
MIHĂESCU, Prestressed Reinforced Concrete
MÎRSU, O., Reinforced Concrete
MUNTEANU, I., Statics, Stability and Dynamics of Construction
NOCOARĂ, L., Road Design and Construction
PĂUNESCU, M., Geotechnics and Foundations
RAFIROIU, M., Production Organization and Control

*Faculty of Chemical Engineering:*
BECHERESCU, D., Furnaces and Drying Plants for Silicates Industry
BLAGA, A., Organic Technology
BUCUR, C., Medical Gymnastics
COCHECI, V. Chemical Technology
DRĂGOI, I., Cement Chemistry
FACSKO, GH., Electro-Chemistry and Corrosion
GROPȘIAN, Z., Operations and Equipment in Chemical Industry
MANOVICIU, I., Macromolecular Products and Physical Chemistry
RĂDOI, I., Electrochemistry and Corrosion
TRIBUNESCU, P., Physical Chemistry

*Faculty of Agricultural Mechanics:*
CĂPROIU, S., Agricultural Machines
SANDRU, A., Use of Agricultural Machinery and Labour Protection
TECUȘAN, N., Tractors and Automobiles

## OTHER INSTITUTES OF HIGHER EDUCATION

**Academia de Studii Economice:** Bucharest, Piața Romană 6; f. 1913; faculties of economics of production, planning and economic cybernetics, accounting and agricultural economics, foreign trade; 684 teachers, 12,042 students; library of 779,591 vols.; includes the Centre of Economic Computation and Economic Cybernetics; Rector Prof. Dr. VĂDUVA ILIE; publ. *Studies and Research in Economic Computation and Economic Cybernetics* (quarterly, in Romanian and English).

**Conservatorul "George Dima":** 3400 Cluj-Napoca, Str. 23 August 25; f. 1819, reorganized 1919; faculties of instrumental music and singing, musical composition and musicology; 98 teachers, 411 students; library of 118,315 vols.; Rector Prof. Dr. RODICA POP; publ. *Lucrări de Muzicologie* (Musicological Works, annual).

**Conservatorul "George Enescu":** Iași, Str. Cuza Vodă 29; f. 1860, renamed 1960; faculties of music and plastic arts; 78 teachers, 261 students; library of 80,000 vols.; Rector Prof. Dr. M. COZMEI; Librarian ANA DUMITRESCU.

**Conservatorul de Muzică "Ciprian Porumbescu":** Bucharest, Str. Stirbei Vodă Nr. 33; f. 1864; faculties of instruments and singing, pedagogy and musical composition, musicology; 145 teachers, 500 students; library of 201,090 vols.; Rector NICOLAE CALINOIU.

**Institutul Agronomic "N. Balcescu":** Bucharest, Bul. Mărăști 59; f. 1852; faculties of agriculture, horticulture, animal husbandry, veterinary medicine, land reclamation and improvement; 349 teachers, 3,537 students; library of 436,000 vols.; Rector T. MUREȘAN; publ. *Lucrări Științifice* (annual).

**Institutul Agronomic "Dr. Petru Groza":** 3400 Cluj-Napoca, Str. Mănăștur 3; f. 1869; faculties of agriculture, horticulture, veterinary medicine and animal husbandry; 201 teachers; 2,200 students; library of 183,231 vols.; Rector Prof. I. PUIA, PH.D., SC.D.; Pro-Rector Prof. Z. NAGY, D.SC.AGR.; publ. Buletinul†.

**Institutul Agronomic "Ion Ionescu de la Brad":** Iași, Aleea M. Sadoveanu 3; f. 1908; faculties of agriculture, horticulture, animal breeding and veterinary medicine; 198 teachers; 2,200 students; 151,000 vols. in library; Rector Prof. C. TEȘU; publ. *Lucrări Științifice*† (3 a year).

**Institutul Agronomic Timișoara:** Timișoara, Calea Aradului 119; f. 1945; faculties of agronomy, veterinary medicine and animal husbandry; 151 teachers, 1,627 students; library of 243,120 vols.; Rector Prof. Dr. DUVLEA ILIE; publ. *Lucrări Științifice* (Series Agronomy, Veterinary Medicine and Animal Husbandry†) (annually).

**Institutul de Arhitectură "Ion Mincu":** Bucharest, Str. Academiei 18-20; f. 1897; Architecture and Town Planning; 124 teachers, 1,400 students; library of 166,500 vols.; Rector Prof. Arch. Dr. CORNEL DUMITRESCU; publ. *Studii și proiecte* (Studies and Designs).

**Institutul de Arte Plastice "Ion Andreescu"** (*Institute of Fine and Decorative Art "Ion Andreescu"*): Cluj-Napoca, Sq. Libertății 31; f. 1950; departments of Fine Arts (painting, sculpture, print-making), Decorative Arts (textiles, ceramics, glass, metal, interior design); 52 teachers, 195 students; library of 51,887 vols.; Rector L. FESZT; publ. termly bibliographical bulletin.

**Institutul de Arte Plastice "N. Grigorescu":** Bucharest, Str. Gl. Budișteanu 19; f. 1864; departments of Fine Arts, Decorative Arts; 91 teachers, 478 students; library of 357,837 vols.; Rector Dr. VASILE DRĂGUT.

**Institutul de Artă Teatrală și Cinematografică "I. L. Caragiale":** Bucharest, Bul. N. Bălcescu 2; f. 1864; 84 teachers, 150 students; the library contains 68,814 vols.; Rector Prof. Univ. OCTAVIAN COTESCU.

**Institutul de Construcții** (*Institute of Civil Engineering*): Bucharest, Bul. Republicii 176; f. 1948; faculties of civil, industrial and agricultural engineering; railways, roads, bridges and geodesy; hydraulics; building installations and construction equipment; 625 teachers, 7,500 students; library of 500,000 vols.; Rector CONSTANTIN IAMANDI; publ. *Scientific Bulletin*† (quarterly).

**Institutul de Educație Fizică și Sport** (*Institute of Physical Education and Sport*): 76102 Bucharest, Str. Maior Ene 12; f. 1922; teacher training; 76 teachers, 750 students; library of 154,000 vols.; Rector IOAN KUNST-GHERMANESCU; Dean ELENA FIREA.

**Institutul de Medicină:** Timișoara, Piața 23 August 2; f. 1945; faculties of general medicine, paediatrics, stomatology; 301 teachers, 3,275 students; library of 190,000 vols.; Rector Prof. Dr. GHEORGHE BĂCANU; publ. *Timișoara Medicala* (quarterly).

**Institutul de Medicină și Farmacie:** Bucharest, Str. Dionisie Lupu 37; f. 1857; faculties of general medicine, stomatology, pharmacy, paediatrics; postgraduate medical school; 1,860 teachers, 7,917 students; Rector LEONIDA GHERASIM; publs. *Anuarul* (Annual), *Învățămîntul Medical și Farmaceutic* (Medical and Pharmaceutical Education).

**Institutul de Medicină și Farmacie:** Cluj-Napoca, Str. 1 Mai 13; f. 1948; faculties of general medicine, paediatrics, dentistry and pharmacy; 655 teachers (64 professors), 5,220 students; library of 281,036 vols.; Rector I. BACIU; publs. *Clujul Medical†* (Medical Cluj, quarterly), *Anuarul.*

**Institutul de Medicină și Farmacie:** Iași, Str. Universității 16; f. 1879; faculties of general medicine (with a section on paediatrics), stomatology and pharmacy; 408 teachers, 3,600 students; Rector Prof. Dr. LORICA GAVRILIȚA.

**Institutul de Medicină și Farmacie:** Tîrgu-Mureș, Str. Gheorghe Marinescu 38; f. 1945; faculties of medicine (including general medicine and paediatrics), stomatology, pharmacy; 306 teachers, 1,720 students; library of 225,000 vols.; Rector LÁSZLÓ IOAN; publ. *Revista Medicală* (twice a year).

**Institutul de Mine Petroșani** (*Mining Institute Petroșani*): 2675 Petroșani, Str. Institutului 20; f. 1948; 224 teachers, 3,704 students; library of 300,161 vols.; Rector Prof. Dr. Ing. FODOR DUMITRU.

**Institutul de Petrol și Gaze:** 2000 Ploiești, Bulevardul București 39; f. 1948; faculties of oil and gas drilling and exploitation, technological equipment, oil processing technology, petro-chemistry; post-graduate training courses (UNESCO); 322 teachers, 5,100 students; library of 350,000 vols.; Rector Prof. Dr. Eng. D. SĂNDULESCU; publ. *Buletinul†.*

**Institutul de Teatru "Szentgyörgyi István":** Tîrgu-Mureș, Str. Köteleg Samuel 6; f. 1948; 32 teachers, 59 students; Rector ANDREI CSORBA.

**Academia "Stefan Gheorghiu" pentru Pregatirea și Perfectionarea Cadrelor de Conducere** (*"Stefan Gheorghiu" Academy for Management Training*): Bucharest, Bd. Armata Poporului Nr. 1-3; f. 1945; consists of Institute for Training Cadres in the Problems of Social-Political Management; Central Institute for the Training of Senior Cadres in Economy and State Administration; Faculty of Journalism; Central School for Training Trade Union Cadres; Central School for Training Cadres of The Union of Communist Youth; Centres for the Higher Training of Party, of Senior Cadres in Economy and State Administration, of Personnel in the Field of Foreign Relations; Institute for Political Sciences and for Studying the National Problem; International CEPECA Centre for Training and Perfecting Senior Cadres in Economic Enterprises and State Administration in the Developing Countries; library of 350,000 vols.

*Rector and President of Council:* LEONTE RAUTU.

*Scientific Secretary:* I. FLOREA.

Publications: *Analele Academiei "Stefan Gheorghiu"* (2 a year), *CEPECA Review* (2 a year, in Romanian), *CEPECA Management Training Review* (2 a year, in English).

# RWANDA
Population 4,819,000

## RESEARCH INSTITUTES

**Institut des Sciences Agronomiques du Rwanda (I.S.A.R.):** B.P. 138, Butare; f. 1932; 950 personnel; six centres; library of 2,000 vols.; Gen. Man. FAUSTIN IYAMUREMYE; publs. Annual Report†, Technical Letters†. Includes the following branches:

*Rubona:* laboratories (chemistry, technology, phytopathology), environmental studies, phytotechnics (living plants, cash crops: coffee, tobacco), zootechnics.

*Songa:* zootechnics (cattle, sheep, poultry).

*Rwerere:* high altitude cultures (wheat, peas, potato).

*Karama:* phytotechnics (living plants, irrigation), zootechnics (cattle, goats).

*Ruhande:* forestry.

*Tamira:* high altitude cultures (pyrethrum).

**Service Géologique du Rwanda:** Ministère des Ressources Naturelles, des Mines et des Carrières, B.P. 413, Kigali; f. 1962; geological services to the Government and private industry; to prepare a geological map of Rwanda; prospecting; library of 6,000 vols.; Dir. J. ZIGIRABABILI; publ. *Bulletin du Service Géologique* (annually).

## UNIVERSITY

### UNIVERSITÉ NATIONALE DU RWANDA
B.P. 117, BUTARE

Telephone: 271/2/3.

Founded 1963.

Language of instruction: French; State control; Academic year: October to July (three terms).

*Rector:* VENANT NTABOMAVURA.
*Vice-Rector:* DISMAS GASHEGU.
*Secretary-General:* SPIRIDION SHYIRAMBERE.
*Chief Librarian:* EMMANUEL SERUGENDO.

Library of 65,000 vols.
Number of teachers: 115.
Number of students: 683.

Publication: *Etudes Rwandaises* (termly).

DEANS:

*Faculty of Letters:* JEAN LUC RONDREUX.
*Faculty of Medicine:* Dr. JOHN GAHUNGU NEWPORT.
*Faculty of Sciences:* ANDRÉ TURCOTTE.
*Faculty of Social and Economic Sciences:* JEAN DUCHARME.
*Faculty of Law:* Prof. V. WIEME.

AFFILIATED INSTITUTES:

**Centre Universitaire de Recherche sur la Pharmacopée et la Médecine Traditionnelle:** B.P. 52, Butare; interfaculty, multi-disciplinary research.

**Institut National de Recherche Scientifique:** P.O.B. 80, Butare; f. 1947 as the Institut pour la Recherche Scientifique en Afrique Centrale; undertakes basic research in anthropology, economics, geophysics, and in animal, vegetable and mineral resources; library of 3,000 vols.; 2 stations at Uinka and Mimuli; Dir. and Prof. of Botany PAUL DEUSE; Prof. of Linguistics ANDRÉ COUPEZ; Prof. of Social Anthropology MARCEL D'HERTEFELT; Prof. of Nutrition H. VIS; publ. *Publications de l'Institut*.

**Ecole Supérieure des Sciences Infirmières:** B.P. 118, Butare; f. 1969; 40 students; Dir. THÉRÈSE ZALLONI.

## COLLEGES

**Ecole Technique Officielle Don Bosco:** B.P. 80, Kigali; f. 1956.

**Institut Africain et Mauricien de Statistique et d'Economie Appliquée:** B.P. 1109, Kigali; f. 1975 by the OCAM states; 3-year diploma course; 10 staff, 75 students; library of 3,500 vols.; Dir. BENOÎT NTIGULIRWA.

# SAUDI ARABIA
## Population 8,112,000

## LEARNED SOCIETIES AND RESEARCH INSTITUTES

**Arab Bureau of Education for the Gulf States:** P.O.B. 3908, Riyadh; f. 1975 to co-ordinate all aspects of education in the member states (U.A.E., Bahrain, Kuwait, Saudi Arabia, Iraq, Oman, Qatar), to create joint education centres and organizations, and to co-ordinate the efforts of the member states in the field of science; includes the Arab Gulf University Project to plan the establishment of a university in Bahrain; 80 staff; library of 10,000 vols.; Dir. Dr. MOHAMMAD AHMED RASHEED. Affiliates:

**Arab Center for Educational Research:** Kuwait (q.v.).

**British Council:** P.O.B. 2701, off Washem St., Mura'aba, Riyadh; libraries: see Libraries; Rep. M. R. W. DEXTER, O.B.E.; P.O.B. 3424, Jeddah; Regional Dir. J. A. D. MCGRATH.

**Bureau de Recherches Géologiques et Minières:** P.O.B. 1492, Jeddah. (See main entry under France.)

**Higher Council for Promotion of Arts and Letters:** Riyadh; Dir.-Gen. ABDULLAH BEN ABDULAZIZ IDRIS.

**Industrial Studies and Development Centre:** P.O.B. 1267, Riyadh; f. 1967; research and studies on the preparation of industrial policy, guidance for the establishment of new industries, implementation of research projects; provides technical assistance to industry: advice on equipment, plant operation, management, marketing, etc.; films and documentaries on industry in Saudi Arabia and abroad; 98 specialist staff; library of 7,500 vols., 100 journals, 200 films; Dir.-Gen. RIDA M. ABBAR; publs. *Alam Elsenaa*† (2 a year), *Elnashrah Elsenaya*† (every 2 months), annual reports†, specialized booklets for industry†, research studies†, *Guide to Industrial Investment in Saudi Arabia*.

**King Abdulaziz Research Centre:** P.O.B. 2945, Riyadh; f. 1972 in memory of the late king; historical, geographical, literary and cultural material; library of 7,000 vols.; also the private library of the late king (2,000 vols.); historical archive including documents in various languages, especially Turkish and English; King Abdul Aziz Memorial Hall shows events in the late king's life, especially his military battles; Sec.-Gen. TAMI IBN HUDAYF AL-BUQMI; publ. quarterly cultural magazine.

**Society of Esaff Alkhairia:** Mecca; f. 1946; Pres. H.E. Sheikh MUHAMMAD SAROUR AL-SABBAN; Hon. Sec. Sheikh AHMED SIBAI.

**U.S. International Communication Agency:** c/o U.S. Embassy, Jeddah; library of 4,000 vols.

**World Centre for Islamic Education:** P.O.B. 1034, Mecca; f. 1980 by the Organization of the Islamic Conference; aims to promote Islamic values in education by training teachers and producing textbooks written on Islamic precepts; governing body of 15 mems. incl. representatives from the four regions of the Organization of the Islamic Conference: South Asia, Middle Region, the Arab World, the rest of Africa; Dir.-Gen. Dr. SYED ALI ASHRAF (Pakistan); publ. *News and Views* (every 2 months).

## LIBRARIES

**Abbas Kattan Library:** Mecca; 7,800 vols., 200 MSS.

**Arif Hikmat Library:** Medina; 1,500 vols., 4,500 MSS.

**British Council Library:** P.O.B. 2701, Off Washem St., Mura'aba, Riyadh; f. 1970; 7,948 vols., 58 periodicals; Librarian M. ABDULLAH.

**Dar al Kutub al-Wataniya:** King Faisal Street, Riyadh; f. 1963; run by the Ministry of Education; model public library with children's and reference sections and periodicals department; 36,935 vols. in Arabic, English and French, 150 MSS.; Dir. ABDUR RAHMAN AL SARRA.

**Educational Library:** General Directorate of Broadcasting, Press and Publications, Jeddah.

**Institute of Public Administration Library:** P.O.B. 205, Riyadh; f. 1962; 76,506 vols. in Arabic and English; Dir. MOSTAFA M. SADHAN; publ. *Library Journal* (Arabic, 3 a year).

**Library of Alharam:** Mecca; 6,000 vols.

**Islamic University Library:** Medina Munawarah; consists of a central library and three college libraries (law, theology and secondary institute); total number of vols. 30,000.

**Madrasat Ahl Al Hadith Library:** Mecca.

**Medina Awkaf Libraries:**
*Aref Hikmet Library:* 6,000 vols., 5,000 MSS.
*Mahmoudia Library:* 3,600 vols., 3,220 MSS.
*Medina General Library:* 10,000 vols., 3,500 MSS.
*Holy Quran Library:* 2,000 Quran MSS.
General Supervisor and Librarian: SAID ELDERBY.

**National Library:** Riyadh; f. 1968; 16,000 vols.; Gen Dir. TAMI H. EL BOKOMI.

**University of Riyadh Libraries:** P.O.B. 2454, Riyadh; f. 1957; central library and 12 branches; 557,756 vols., 4,340 periodicals, 8,997 MSS.; Dean Dr. A. S. AL-HELABI; publs. *Accession List* (quarterly), *Abstracts of Periodicals*, *Union List of Periodicals* (annually), *Union List of Books*, *MSS Catalogue* (irregular), *Analytical Indexes of R.U. Council's Resolutions* (annually), *Bibliographies* (irregular), scientific publications, directories, guides, etc.

**The Saudi Library:** Riyadh; 14,800 vols., 200 MSS.

There are 35 other public libraries.

## MUSEUMS

**Department of Antiquities and Museums:** P.O.B. 3734, Riyadh; Dir. Gen. Dr. ABDULLAH H. MASRY. Responsible for:

**Museum of Archaeology and Ethnography:** Riyadh; f. 1978; exhibits from Stone Age, the "Age of Trade", and "After the Revelation" (rise and spread of Islam).

Six local museums near the main archaeological sites are to open shortly, and there are plans for the establishment of a national museum and five regional museums.

# UNIVERSITIES

## UNIVERSITY OF RIYADH

P.O.B. 2454, RIYADH
Telephone: 4769345.
Telex: 201019 R UNIV SJ.
Founded 1957.

Languages of instruction: Arabic and English; State control; Academic year: October to June.

*Chancellor:* H.E. The Minister of Higher Education.
*President:* Dr. MANSOUR AL-TARKI.
*Vice-Presidents:* Dr. SALEH ABDUL RAHMAN AL-ATHEL (Academic Studies), Dr. HAMOUD ABDUL AZIZ AL-BADR (Financial and Administrative Affairs).
*Registrar:* Dr. SALEH MUHAMMAD AL OGLA.
*Librarian:* Dr. ABDULLAZIZ SALEH AL-HALABI.
*Student Affairs:* Dr. MUHAMMAD ALI ESSA.

Library: see Libraries.
Number of teachers: 1,644.
Number of students: 15,066.
Publications: *Annual Report*†, various faculty bulletins†.

### DEANS:

*Faculty of Arts:* Dr. ALI BAKR JAD.
*Faculty of Science:* Dr. ABDULLAH AL-KADHI AL-MOHAMMADI.
*Faculty of Administrative Sciences:* Dr. HUSSEIN MOHD ALWI.
*Faculty of Pharmacy:* Dr. ABDULLAH A. AL-BADAR.
*Faculty of Agriculture:* Dr. NABIL YEHIA ABDULLAH.
*Faculty of Education:* Dr. ABDUL REHMAN.
*Faculty of Engineering:* Dr. MOHD. ABDUL AZIZ AL EL-SHEIKH.
*Faculty of Medicine:* Dr. HASSAN ABDULLAH KAMIL.
*Faculty of Dentistry:* Dr. AMIN ABDULLAH SIRAJ.
*Faculty of Allied Medical Sciences:* Dr. IBRAHIM AL SOWAIGH.
*Faculty of Education in Abha:* Dr. MAZYAD IBRAHIM AL-MAZYAD.
*Women's Academic Studies Centre:* Dr. IBRAHIM AL HAZMY.

## ISLAMIC UNIVERSITY OF IMAM MUHAMMAD IBN SAUD

P.O.B. 5701, RIYADH
Telephone: 51597-25335.
Telex: 201166 UNIVER
Founded 1953, University status 1974.

State control; Language of instruction: Arabic; Academic year: September to May.

*Rector:* Dr. ABDULLAH IBN ABDULMOHSIN AL-TURKI.
*Vice-Rectors:* Dr. ABDULAZIZ IBN ABDURRAHMAN AL-SAID; Sheikh MUHAMMAD IBN ABDULLAH AL-AJLAN.
*Secretary-General:* Dr. ABDULLAH IBN YUSEF AL-SHIBL.
*Administrative Director-General:* Sheikh ABDULLAH IBN SAAD AL-SAAD.
*Registrar:* SALEH IBN SAUD AL-ALI.
*Librarian:* Dr. ZAHER AWAD AL-ALMAI.

Number of teachers: 619.
Number of students: 5,910.

(Affiliated with the University are 48 intermediate- and secondary-level schools distributed throughout the country, and 3 schools abroad; number of teachers: 780; number of students: 15,235.)

Publications: *The Statistical Book, University Guide, Message of the Muslim Student, Magazine of the High Institute of Islamic Dawa* (Propagation of Islam) and faculty magazines and guides.

### DEANS AND DIRECTORS:

*Higher Judiciary Institute:* Dr. SALEH IBN FAWZAN AL-ABDALLAH.
*Higher Institute of Islamic Dawa:* Sheikh SAUD IBN ABDULLAH AL-BISHR (acting).
*Faculty of Law:* Sheikh ABDULAZIZ IBN ZAID AL-ROUMI.
*Faculty of Arabic:* Sheikh NASSER IBN ABDULLAH AL-TUREIM.
*Faculty of Fundamentals of Religion:* Sheikh ABDUL-KARIM IBN MUHAMMAD ALLAHEM.
*Faculty of Social Sciences:* Sheikh MUHAMMAD IBN ABDULLAH ARAFA.
*Faculty of Law and Arabic (Qassim):* Dr. SAHEH IBN ABDULAZIZ AL-MANSOUR.
*Faculty of Law and Arabic (in the South):* Sheikh ABDULLAH IBN ABDULAZIZ AL-MUSLEH.

## ISLAMIC UNIVERSITY

P.O.B. 170, MEDINA
Founded 1961

*Chancellor:* The Minister of Higher Education.
*Vice-Rector:* ABDUL MUHSIN BEN HAMAD AL-ABBAD.

Number of teachers: 85.
Number of students: 1,055.
Faculties of law, Arabic and arts, Koranic studies.

## KING ABDULAZIZ UNIVERSITY

P.O.B. 1540, JEDDAH
Telephone: 6879033.
Founded 1967.

State control; Languages of instruction: Arabic and English; Academic year: September to June.

*Chancellor:* H.E. The Minister of Higher Education.
*President:* Dr. ABDULLAH OMAR NASSEEF.
*Dean of Libraries:* Dr. IBRAHIM ALAWI.

Library (Jeddah Campus) contains 225,000 vols., periodicals, MSS, 50,000 other items.
Library (Mecca Campus) contains 40,000 vols., 400 periodicals.
Number of teachers: 992.
Number of students: 14,609.

Publications: *Akhbar-al-Jameah* (University News, monthly), *Al-Likaa Al-Jamei* (monthly), *Al-Manar* (monthly).

### DEANS:

*Faculty of Arts and Humanities:* Dr. HAMAD AL-ARINAN.
*Faculty of Economics and Administration:* Dr. GHAZI OBEID MEDANI.
*Faculty of Science:* Dr. AHMAD MOHAMMAD ASHI.
*Faculty of Marine Sciences:* Dr. ABDUL KADIR BUHAIRY.
*Faculty of Earth Sciences:* Dr. AHMAD NASSER ba-SAHEL.
*Faculty of Engineering:* Dr. MOHAMMAD MOHAMMAD OMAR JAMJOOM.
*Faculty of Medicine and Allied Sciences:* Dr. FOUAD MOSTAFA ZAHRANI.
*Faculty of Meteorology and Environmental Studies:* Dr. FAWAZ ABDUL SATTAR AL-ALAMI.
*Faculty of Education (Medina):* Dr. ISMAEEL ZAFIR.

SAUDI ARABIA

ATTACHED INSTITUTE:

**Research and Development Centre:** P.O.B. 9031, Jeddah; f. 1975; part of Faculty of Economics and Administration; 9 staff; library of 5,000 vols.; Dir. Dr. AHMED A. AL-SABAB; publ. *Economics & Administration†* (3 a year).

### KING FAISAL UNIVERSITY
P.O.B. 1982, DAMMAM

Founded 1975.

*Vice-Chancellor:* MOH. SAID ABDUL RAHMAN AL-QAHTANI, PH.D. (acting).

Faculties of agriculture and food sciences, architecture, medicine.

Number of teachers: 99.
Number of students: 350.

### THE UNIVERSITY OF PETROLEUM AND MINERALS
DHAHRAN

Telephone: Dhahran 860-2000.

Founded 1963, University status 1975.

State control with semi-autonomous operation under a Board of the University; Languages of instruction: English (for technical subjects) and Arabic; Academic year: September to June.

*Chair. of Board of Trustees:* H.E. SHEIKH HASSAN IBN ABDULLAH AL-SHEIKH, Minister of Higher Education.
*Rector:* Dr. BAKR ABDULLAH BAKR.
*Vice-Rectors:* Dr. ABDEL AZIZ AL-GWAIZ, Dr. FAHD H. AL-DAKHIL.
*Secretary-General:* Dr. SALEH A. BAKHREBAH.
*Registrar:* NORMAN KEITH HESTER.
*Librarian:* Dr. SALEH ASHOUR.

Number of teachers: 602.
Number of students: 3,200.

Publications: *Arabian Journal for Science and Engineering†* (2 a year), *ELI Monthly†* (English Language Institute), *DPC Bulletin†* (Data Processing centre monthly), *Library Scene†* (quarterly), *Faculty News Bulletin* (weekly), annual handbook, academic bulletins, student publications, etc.

DEANS:
*Science:* Dr. ALI A. AL-DAFFA.
*Engineering Science:* Dr. YOUSSEF O. AL-RASHID.
*Industrial Management:* Dr. ALI D. JOHANY.
*Graduate School:* Dr. REDA A. AL-THIGA.
*Faculty and Personnel:* Dr. ABDUL RAHMAN AL-SAID.
*Environmental Design:* Ds. ZAMIL A. R. MOKRIN.

### UMM EL-QURAH UNIVERSITY
MECCA

Founded 1979 from existing faculties of King Abdulaziz University.

DEANS:
*Faculty of Sharia and Islamic Studies:* Dr. ULIAN EL-HAZMY.
*Faculty of Education:* Dr. MANSOUR ABU-LABAN.

## INSTITUTES OF HIGHER EDUCATION

**English Language Teaching Institute:** P.O.B. 2701, Riyadh; f. 1969 by Ministry of Education and directed by the British Council; library of 8,000 vols. available to teachers and scholars of the English language; Dir. of Studies JAMES H. COLEMAN.

**Institute of Public Administration:** P.O.B. 205, Riyadh; f. 1961; conducts training courses for government employees; researches into and offers advice on administrative problems; Dir. MOHAMMED A. AL-TAWAIL; publ. *I.P.A. Journal* (3 a year, in Arabic).

**Jeddah Health Institute:** Jeddah; provides basic medical training; similar Institutes at Riyadh and Hofouf.

**King Abdulaziz Military Academy:** Riyadh; f. 1955; courses given in modern languages, including English, French and Hebrew, science and military subjects.

**Madrasat Ahl Al Hadith:** Mecca; f. 1933; the College provides instruction in the Hadith, Koran, Fiqh, Tawheed and other Islamic religious studies; Principal Sheikh MUHAMMAD ABDUL RAZZAQ; Sec. MUHAMMAD OMAR ABDULHADI.

**Saudi Arabian Institute for Higher Education:** Mecca; f. 1962; courses in education, engineering, English, mathematics and physics; 125 students.

**School of Applied Arts:** Medina; f. 1955; *c.* 300 students.

**Technical Institute:** Riyadh; f. 1964; 1,000 students.

# SENEGAL
Population 5,518,000

## LEARNED SOCIETIES

**Alliance Française:** B.P. 1777, Dakar.

**American Cultural Center:** Dakar Building, Place de l'Indépendance, Dakar; f. 1958; 3,000 mems.; library of 5,000 vols. on American culture, history, politics, general reference works, African literature; Librarian Mme LOUISE DIAW; publs. *Panorama* (twice weekly).

**Association africaine pour l'avancement des sciences et techniques:** Dakar; Pres. H. NOGBE-NLEND (Univ. of Yaoundé); Sec.-Gen. M. EDWARDS (Nigeria).

**British Council:** rue du Dr. Guillet, B.P. 6025, Dakar; Rep. J. P. JACKSON.

**British Senegalese Institute:** rue du 18 juin, B.P. 35, Dakar; f. 1967; built as part of British technical aid and financed by the Senegalese Govt.; English Language Teaching and Resource Centre for Ministry of Higher Education; library of 8,000 vols.; 1,000 students; Dir. H. BREWER.

**Bureau Régional de l'Unesco pour l'Education en Afrique/Unesco Regional Office for Education in Africa:** B.P. 3311, 12 ave. Roume, Dakar; f. 1970; 43 member states; 3 sections: educational planning and administration; educational content and programming; literacy, adult education and rural development; also a Multi Media Centre (13,000 vols. and documents, 270 periodicals, 350 microfiches, 305 microfilms) and Co-ordinating Unit of the Network of Educational Innovations for Development in Africa (NEIDA); activities also in the field of natural sciences, social sciences, culture and communication; Dir. BABA AKHIB HAIDARA; publs. *Liste trimestrielle des nouvelles acquisitions*, *Rapports trimestrielles d'activités*, *EducAfrica*† (2 a year), studies, reports, etc.

**Institut Géographique National (Agence de Dakar):** 7 rue Jean Mermoz, B.P. 4016, Dakar; f. 1945; relations with the governments of Senegal, The Gambia, Guinea Bissau, Mauritania and Cape Verde Islands; cartography of these States; Chief M. DURIEUX.

## RESEARCH INSTITUTES

**Bureau de Recherches Géologiques et Minières:** B.P. 268, Dakar; also directs research in Mali and Mauritania; Dir. M. DELAFOSSE.

**Centre de Recherches et de Documentation du Sénégal (C.R.D.S.):** B.P. 382, Saint-Louis; f. 1943 as Centre IFAN-Senegal; 19 mems.; library of 20,000 vols.; Dir. MOHAMED FADEL DIA; Librarian LAURENT GOMIS.

**Centre Régional de Recherche et de Documentation pour le Développement Culturel (CREDEC)** (*Regional Research and Documentation Centre for Cultural Development*): 13 ave. Bourguiba, P.O.B. 01, Dakar; part of African Cultural Institute (see under International); Dir. Dr. E. O. ADRONTI (acting); publ. *CREDEC Journal*† (quarterly).

**Centre Technique Forestier Tropical:** Division des Recherches Piscicoles, Résidence Faidherbe; B.P. 28, Richard-Toll; f. 1966; fishery research; Dir. C. REIZER.

**Institut d'Hygiène Sociale:** ave. Blaise-Diagne, Dakar.

**Institut de Recherches pour les Huiles et Oléagineux:** Bambey; brs. at Louga and Darou.

**Institut Fondamental d'Afrique Noire (IFAN):** Université de Dakar, B.P. 206, Dakar; f. 1936, reconstituted 1959; scientific and humanistic studies on Black Africa; library and museums (*see* below); Dir. Prof. AMAR SAMB; publs. *Bulletin de l'I.F.A.N.*, Série A—Sciences Naturelles, Série B—Sciences Humaines, *Notes Africaines* (quarterly), *Mémoires de l'I.F.A.N.*, *Initiations et Etudes Africianes*, *Instructions Sommaires*, *Catalogues et Documents*, etc.

**Institut Pasteur:** B.P. 220, Dakar; f. 1896; medical research; library of 1,126 vols., 54 periodicals; Dir. Dr. J. P. DIGOUTTE; publ. *Annual Report*.

**Institut Sénégalais de Recherches Agricoles (ISRA):** B.P. 3120, Dakar; f. 1974; research in all fields of agriculture, forestry and pisciculture; Dir. Gen. Dr. P. IBRAHIMA THIONGANE.

Controls the following:

**Centre National de Recherches Agronomiques (CNRA):** B.P. 41, Bambey; f. 1921; applied agricultural research; 45 research mems.; library of 6,700 vols.; stations at Louga and Tivaouane; Dir. MAHAWA MBODJ; publs. *Rapport de synthèse*†, *Annuaire analytique des travaux de l'IRAT au Sénégal* (each annually).

**Laboratoire National de L'Elevage et de Recherches Vétérinaires (LNERV):** B.P. 2057, Dakar; f. 1935; six departments; library of 12,000 vols.; Dir. A. K. DIALLO.

**Centre National de Recherches Forestières (CNRF):** B.P. 2312, Dakar-Hann; f. 1935; forestry research; Dir. OLIVIER HAMEL.

**Centre de Recherches Océanographiques de Dakar-Thiaroye (CRODT):** B.P. 2241, Dakar; f. 1956; for the study of oceanographic physics and biology; 67 scientists; 450 vols. and 74 periodicals in library; Dir. A. FONTANA.

**Centre de Recherches Zootechniques de Dahra-Djoloff:** Dahra-Djoloff; f. 1950; amelioration of local bovine and ovine breeds, rearing and cross-breeding; Dir. Dr. MAMADOU MBAYE.

**Centre de Recherches Zootechniques de Kolda:** Kolda; f. 1972; amelioration of local bovine and ovine breeds; fodder cultivation; Dir. Dr. EL HADJ GUEYE.

**Centre de Recherches Rizicoles de Djibelor (CRR):** B.P. 34, Ziguinchor; f. 1967; station at Séfa; rice cultivation and improvement of varieties, growing techniques; Dir. MOCTAR TOURE.

**Centre de Recherches Agricoles de Richard-Toll (CRA):** B.P. 29, Richard-Toll; f. 1942; annexes: Jardin d'Essais (St. Louis), Fanaye, Guédé and Ndiol; irrigation systems in the Senegal river valley; Dir. MAMADOU KHOUMA.

**Secteur Centre Sud-Kaolack (SCS):** B.P. 199, Kaolack; f. 1979; stations at Nioro du Rip, Suithiou Malème and Darou; cultivation systems under rain in central-southern and east Senegal, cotton research; Dir. MADICKE NIANG.

**Centre pour le Développement de l'Horticulture (CDH):** B.P. 2619, Dakar; f. 1972; market garden research; Dir. FRANÇOIS FAYE.

**Office de la Recherche Scientifique et Technique Outre-Mer Centre ORSTOM de Dakar:** Route des Pères Maristes, B.P. 1386, Dakar; soil biology, pedology, medical entomology, hydrology, geology, nematology, demography, economics, zoology, botany, agronomy, geography, sociology, nutrition; library; Dir. B. DALMAYRAC. (*See* main entry under France.)

**Office de la Recherche Scientifique et Technique Outre-Mer (ORSTOM) Station Ecologique de Richard-Toll:** B.P. 20, Richard-Toll; ecology, ornithology; Dir. Dr. G. MOREL.

**Office de la Recherche Scientifique et Technique Outre-Mer, Station Géophysique:** B.P. 50, M'Bour; magnetism, seismology, meteorology, magneto-telluric and geomagnetic prospecting.

**Organisme de Recherches sur l'Alimentation et la Nutrition Africaines (ORANA):** 39 Avenue Pasteur, B.P. 2089, Dakar; f. 1956; research on African foods and nutritional values, investigations, documentation, teaching; 30 mems.; Dir. Dr. A. M. N'DIAYE.

## LIBRARIES

**Archives de Sénégal:** Immeuble administratif, Av. Roume, Dakar; f. 1913; 21,276 vols., 1,064 periodicals; Dir. SALIOU MBAYE; publ. *Rapport annuel*.

**Bibliothèque de l'Alliance Française:** 10 rue Colbert, B.P. 1777, Dakar; f. 1948; 10,000 vols.; Librarian M. CAUSSADE.

**Bibliothèque de l'Institut Fondamental d'Afrique Noire:** B.P. 206, Dakar; f. 1938; research in social and natural sciences; 60,404 vols., 7,224 brochures, 4,022 collections of periodicals, 1,600 microfilms, 2,566 maps, 32,000 photographs, 2,100 slides, 12,200 files of documents; Librarian Mme. NDEYE TOUGA DIALLO.

**Bibliothèque Universitaire Centrale de Dakar:** B.P. 2006, Dakar; f. 1952; Law, Humanities, Medicine, Pharmacy, Veterinary Science, Sciences; 273,418 vols., 12,736 pamphlets, 5,000 periodicals; Dir. T. NDIAYE.

## MUSEUMS

**Musées de l'Institut Fondamental d'Afrique Noire:** B.P. 206, Dakar.

**Musée d'Art Africain de Dakar:** f. 1936; ethnography and African art; Curator B. THIAM.

**Musée Historique:** Gorée; Curator COUMBA NDOFFÉNE DIOUF.

**Musée de la Mer:** Gorée; f. 1959; sea sciences, oceanography, fishing; Curator CHEIKH NIANG.

## UNIVERSITIES

### UNIVERSITÉ DE DAKAR
(University of Dakar)
DAKAR-FANN

Telephone: 25-05-30.

Telex: 262.

Founded 1949, University 1957.

State control; Language of instruction: French; Academic year: November to June.

*Rector and President:* SEYDOU MADANI SY.
*Vice-President:* ALASSANE NDAW.
*Secretary-General:* MAHADY DIALLO.

*Librarian:* THEODORE NDIAYE.
Library: *see* Libraries.
Number of teachers: 602.
Number of students: 11,677.

Publications (periodical): *Annuaire, Annales Africaines* (annual), *Annales de la Faculté des Sciences* (annual), *Bulletin et Mémoires de la Faculté de Médecine et de Pharmacie* (annual).

DEANS:
*Faculty of Law and Economics:* IBRAHIMA FALL.
*Faculty of Medicine and Pharmacy:* IBRAHIMA MAR DIOP.
*Faculty of Sciences:* SOULEYMANE NIANG.
*Faculty of Arts and Humanities:* ALASSANE NDAW.

DIRECTORS:
*Institut Fondamental d'Afrique Noire:* see under Research Institutes.
*Institut Universitaire de Technologie:* ANDRÉ KERGREIS.
*Ecole Normale Supérieure:* IBA DER THIAM.

ATTACHED RESEARCH INSTITUTES:

**Centre de Linguistique Appliquée de Dakar (CLAD):** Dir. A. BALDE.

**Centre de Recherches, d'Etudes et de Documentation sur les Institutions et la Législation Africaines (CREDILA):** Dir. ABDEL KADER BOYE.

**Centre de Recherches Biologiques sur la Lèpre:** Dir. YVETTE PARES.

**Centre de Recherches Economiques appliquées (CREA):** Dir. MAKHTAR DIOUF.

**Centre de Recherches psychopathologiques:** Dir. BABACAR DIOP.

**Centre d'Etudes des Sciences et Techniques de l'Information:** f. 1965; offers Diploma courses in journalism; Dir. BABACAR SINÉ.

**Centre d'Etudes et de Recherches sur les Energies renouvelables "Henri Masson":** Dir. DJIBRIL FALL.

**Centre des Hautes Etudes Afro-Ibéro-Américaines:** concerned with all matters relating to Africa and Latin America in the fields of Law, Science and the Arts; Dir. Mme. GOUDIARD.

**Ecole des Bibliothécaires, Archivistes et Documentalistes:** Faculty of Arts and Social Sciences, B.P. 3252, Dakar; f. 1963, attained present status as university institute 1967; provides a two-year librarianship course, giving priority to students from French-speaking countries in Africa; Dir. A. BOUSSO.

**Institut de Français pour les Etudiants étrangers:** Dir. GENEVIÈVE NDIAYE.

**Institut de Mathématiques appliquées "Souleymane Fall":** Dir. D. S. THIAM.

**Institut de Médecine Tropicale Appliquée:** Dir. BIRAM DIOP.

**Institut de Pédiatrie Sociale:** Dir. GABRIEL SENGHOR.

**Institut de Recherches sur l'Enseignement de la Mathématique, de la Physique et de la Technologie:** Dir. SOULEYMANE NIANG.

**nstitut des Sciences de l'Environnement:** Dir. Mme. ROY.

**Institut d'Odontologie et de Stomatologie:** Dir. ANDRÉ SCHVARTZ (acting).

**nstitut de Technologie nucléaire appliquée:** Dir. (vacant).

### UNIVERSITÉ DES MUTANTS
RUE DE HESSE, GORÉE

Telephone: 22-00-83.

Founded 1978.

State control; Language of instruction: French; Academic year: 2 terms of 3 months.

*President:* IBA DER THIAM.
*Vice-President:* STANISLAS SPERO ADOTEVI.
*Secretary-General:* PATHÉ GUEYE.
*Librarian:* MAMADOU DIOP.

Number of teachers: 13.
Number of students: 30 a term.

## COLLEGES

**Ecole Inter-Etats des Sciences et Médecine Vétérinaires:** representing 14 French-speaking African countries; Dir. Prof. A. L. NDIAYE.

**Ecole Nationale d'Administration du Sénégal:** B.P. 5209, Dakar; f. 1959; Dir. A. N'DENE N'DIAYE.

**Ecole Polytechnique de Thiès:** B.P. 10, Thiès; f. 1973; attached to the Ministry of the Armed Forces; 4-year diploma courses in engineering.
*Commandant:* SIDY BOUYA NDIAYE.
*General Secretary:* JEAN DE VARENNES.

*Librarian:* OUMAR CHÉRIF DIAGNE.
Library of 20,000 vols.
Number of teachers: 21 full-time, 20 part-time.
Number of students: 175.

HEADS OF DEPARTMENTS:

*Core Curriculum:* PIERRE RICHARD.
*Civil Engineering:* SAMI BOULOS.
*Mechanical Engineering:* PIERRE BRUN.

**Institut Africain de Développement Economique et de Planification:** rue 18 Juin, Dakar; administered by the UN; trains specialists and officials of African government services responsible for economic development and planning, conducts research in order to prepare the teaching material and documentation required for the organization of seminars, conferences and courses; offers fellowships to enable young Africans holding a "D.E.S." or M.A. and having some working experience to follow a six-month research training course; Dir. ESSAM MONTASSER.

# SIERRA LEONE
Population 3,111,000

## LEARNED SOCIETIES AND RESEARCH INSTITUTES

**British Council:** Tower Hill, P.O.B. 124, Freetown; library of 5,800 vols., 182 periodicals; Rep. B. T. CHADWICK; Librarian Mrs. M. BANGURA MANA.

**Geological Survey Division:** Ministry of Mines, Lands and Labour, New England, Freetown; f. 1918; to locate mineral deposits and to advise on all matters relating to the earth; library of 16,000 vols. including periodicals; Dir. A. H. GABISI; publs. *Annual Report, Bulletin, Short Papers* (all annually).

**Historical Society of Sierra Leone:** c/o Dept. of History, Fourah Bay College, University of Sierra Leone, Freetown; f. 1975; 30 mems.; Pres. G. S. ANTHONY; Sec. Dr. A. J. G. WYSE; publ. *Journal* (2 a year).

**Institute of African Studies:** c/o University of Sierra Leone, Fourah Bay College, Freetown; f. 1962; undertakes research in sociology and culture of Sierra Leone; Dir. Dr. C. MAGBAILY FYLE; publ. *Africana Research Bulletin* (3 a year).

**Institute of Marine Biology and Oceanography:** Fourah Bay College, University of Sierra Leone, Freetown; f. 1966; research and training in oceanography, marine algae and plankton, fishery biology and management, aquaculture and pollution of estuaries; Dir. Prof. D. E. B. CHAYTOR; publ. *Annual Bulletin*.

**Sierra Leone Library Association:** c/o Sierra Leone Library Board, P.O.B. 326, Freetown; f. 1970; 45 mems.; Pres. G. E. DILLSWORTH; Sec. F. THORPE; publs. *Sierra Leone Library Journal*†, directories of libraries and information services†.

**Sierra Leone Science Association:** c/o Dept. of Physics, Fourah Bay College, University of Sierra Leone, Freetown; Hon. Pres. Dr. E. R. T. AWUNOR-RENNER; Hon. Sec. Dr. H. G. MORGAN.

**U.S. International Communication Agency:** 8 Walpole St., Freetown; American cultural centre.

## LIBRARIES AND MUSEUMS

**Fourah Bay College Library:** University of Sierra Leone, Freetown; f. 1827; 113,500 vols., 552 current periodicals; Librarian Mrs. G. M. JUSU-SHERIFF, B.A., M.S., F.L.A.

**Public Archives of Sierra Leone:** c/o Fourah Bay College Library, P.M.B. 87, Freetown; Hon. Archivist C. MAGBAILY FYLE.

**Sierra Leone Library Board:** P.O.B. 326, Freetown; f. 1961; aims to provide a national library service; 156,357 vols., 100 periodical titles; libraries at Freetown, Bo, Magburaka, Makeni, Pujehun, Kailahun, Kenema, Kono, Bonthe, Mattru, Bumbuna, Kissy; Chief Librarian Mrs. G. E. DILLSWORTH; publ. *Annual Report, Sierra Leone Publications* (annually).

**Sierra Leone National Museum:** Cotton Tree Building, P.O.B. 908, Freetown; historical, ethnographical and archaeological collection; Curator DOROTHY A. VAN AMSTERDAM-CUMMINGS.

## UNIVERSITY AND COLLEGES

### UNIVERSITY OF SIERRA LEONE
PRIVATE MAIL BAG, FREETOWN

Established 1967 and incorporating Fourah Bay College and Njala University College; inaugurated February 1969.

State control; Language of instruction: English; Academic year: October to June.

*Chancellor:* H.E. SIAKA P. STEVENS, G.C.R.S.L., G.C.M.G., President of the Republic of Sierra Leone.

*Pro-Chancellor:* A. B. M. KAMARA, LL.M.

*Vice-Chancellor:* Dr. A. T. PORTER, M.A., PH.D., M.R.S.A.

*Pro-Vice Chancellor:* Prof. E. D. JONES, M.A., PH.D., M.R.S.L.

*Secretary:* T. J. TUCKER, B.A., B.ED.

Publication: *Calendar and Prospectus* (annually).

### Fourah Bay College
P.O.B. 87, FREETOWN
Telephone: Freetown 27260.

Founded by the Church Missionary Society in 1827, it was affiliated to the University of Durham in 1876 and became a constituent college of the University of Sierra Leone in 1966.

Language of instruction: English; Academic year: October to June.

*Principal:* Prof. E. D. JONES, M.A., PH.D., M.R.S.L.

*Registrar:* I. S. A. COLE, M.A. (acting).

*Librarian:* GLADYS M. E. SHERIFF, B.A., M.SC., F.L.A.

Library: see Libraries.

Number of teachers: 149.
Number of students: 1,349.

Publications: *Principal's Annual Report, Sierra Leone Studies, Sierra Leone Bulletin of Religion, Fourah Bay College Library Annual Report*.

DEANS:

*Faculty of Economics and Social Studies:* H. M. JOKO SMART, LL.M., PH.D.
*Faculty of Arts:* C. P. FORAY, B.A.
*Faculty of Pure and Applied Science:* Prof. E. R. T. AWUNOR-RENNER, M.SC., PH.D.
*Faculty of Engineering:* B. B. IBRAHIM, M.SC. (acting).

PROFESSORS:

*Faculty of Economics and Social Studies:*
INDARATNA, A. D. V. DES, M.COMM., Economics
OLU-WILLIAMS, A. E., O.B.E., L.R.C.P., L.R.C.S., F.R.C.S., O.R., Community Health

UNIVERSITY AND COLLEGES — SIERRA LEONE

TUBOKU-METZGER, F. C., LL.M., Law

*Faculty of Arts:*
FASHOLE-LUKE, Rev. E. W., PH.D., Theology
JONES, E. D., M.A., PH.D., F.R.S.A., M.R.S.L., English
LECINA, R. L., M. ÈS L., Modern Languages
PALMER, E. J. T., PH.D., English
SMART, N. D. J., M.A., Education

*Faculty of Pure and Applied Science:*
BOWEN, R., PH.D., Geology
CHAYTOR, D. E. B., B.SC., PH.D., Marine Biology and Oceanography
COLE, N. H. A., M.SC., PH.D., F.L..S, Botany
FORDE, E. R. A., PH.D., Geography
JONAH, D. A., PH.D., Mathematics
SINGH, N., PH.D., Botany
TAYLOR-SMITH, R. E. K., PH.D., F.R.S.C., F.R.S.A., Chemistry
WILLIAMS, E. J. A., B.SC., PH.D., Mathematics
WILLIAMS, M. O., M.A., PH.D., Zoology
WRIGHT, E. H., B.SC., PH.D., F.R.S.C., Chemistry

*Faculty of Engineering:*
DEAN, J. S., M.A., PH.D., C.ENG., F.I.MECH.E., F.I.PROD.E., Mechanical Engineering
GARBER, N. J., M.SC., PH.D., C.ENG., M.I.CE., M.A.SC.E., Civil Engineering
IBRAHIM, B. B., M.SC., Civil Engineering
KANU, A. H., M.SC., C.ENG., F.I.E.E., A.M.I.E.R.E.
MORETON, P. L., PH.D., C.ENG., M.I.E.E., Electrical Engineering
THOMAS, M. E. K., PH D., C.ENG., M.I.C.E., Civil Engineering

## Njala University College

PRIVATE MAIL BAG, FREETOWN
Telephone: 08.
Founded 1963.
State control; Language of instruction: English; Academic year: October to July.

*Principal:* Prof. JOHN A. KAMARA, D.T.V.M., M.R.C.V.S.

*Senior Assistant Registrar:* G. B. GOBA, M.A., B.SC.

*Librarian:* A. N. T. DEEN, B.SC. (acting).

Number of teachers: 114.
Number of students: 920.

Publications: *University Calendar, College Prospectus* (every 2 years), *Gazette* (annually), *College Newsletter* (monthly).

DEANS:

*Education:* E. T. BANGURA, M.S., PH.D.
*Agriculture:* N. G. KUYEMBEH, M.SC. AGRIC.ENG., M.A.S.A.E., M.I.AGRIC.E.

PROFESSORS:

*Faculty of Agriculture:*
KAMARA, J. A., Animal Science
TAYLOR, W. E., Agronomy

*Faculty of Education:*
CHHONKAR, M. S., Physics
WHITE, P. T., Biological Sciences
WILLIAMS, H. J., Chemistry

ATTACHED INSTITUTE:

**Institute of Education:** Private Mail Bag, Tower Hill, Freetown; Dir. T. J. L. FORDE, M.A.; Sec. V. O. YOUNGE, B.A.

---

**Milton Margai Teachers College:** Goderich, nr. Freetown; f. 1960; trains secondary school teachers.

Library of 20,000 vols.
Number of teachers: 58.
Number of students: 548.

*Principal:* USMAN S. A. KAGBO, B.A., M.ED.

*Vice-Principal:* G. S. ANTHONY, B.A.

*Registrar:* A. G. CARTER, B.A.

**Technical Institute:** Congo Cross, Freetown; City and Guilds Craft and Technical Courses and Commercial Education; Principal T. C. F. A. DAVIES.

**Technical Institute:** Kenema; vocational courses.

# SINGAPORE
Population 2,362,000

## ACADEMY

**Singapore National Academy of Science:** 1st Floor, Singapore Science Centre Building, off Jurong Town Hall Rd., Singapore 2260; established to promote the advancement of science and technology and to represent the founder/affiliate members of the Academy.
*President:* Prof. ANG KOK PENG.
*Secretary:* Dr. R. S. BHATHAL.
Constituent bodies:
  Institute of Physics, Singapore.
  Science Teachers Association of Singapore.
  Singapore Institute of Biology.
  Singapore Mathematical Society.
  Singapore National Institute of Chemistry.
  Singapore Association for the Advancement of Science.
  Singapore Institute of Statistics.

## LEARNED SOCIETIES AND RESEARCH INSTITUTES

**Academy of Medicine, Singapore:** Medical Centre, 4A College Rd., Singapore 0316; f. 1957; professional corporate body of medical and dental specialists; also involved in the postgraduate training of doctors; Master Prof. LIM PIN; Exec. Sec. Miss Y. L. LAM; publ. *Annals*† (quarterly).

**Alliance Française:** 4 Draycott Park, Singapore 1025; f. 1949; French language teaching and culture; 500 mems., 2,000 language students; library of 10,000 vols.; Pres. Tan Sri Dr. RUNME SHAW; Dir. ROLAND R. DRIVON; publ. *Lien*†.

**American Library Resource Center:** American Embassy, 30 Hill St., Singapore 0617; f. 1950; conducts exhibitions; resources library of 6,300 vols., 170 periodicals, VTRs, microfilm, microfiche.

**Botanic Gardens:** Parks and Recreation Dept., Cluny Rd., Singapore 1025; f. 1859; botanical and horticultural research with particular reference to South-East Asia; Commissioner, Parks and Recreation Dept., WONG YEW KUAN, M.A., M.S.I.BIOL.; Curator of Herbarium Miss CHANG KIAW LAN, PH.D.; library of 15,000 vols.; Librarian JOHAN ABDUL RAHMAN; publs. *The Gardens' Bulletin, Singapore*† (2 a year), and horticultural works.

**British Council:** Singapore Rubber House, Collyer Quay, Singapore 0104; Rep. Dr. J. L. MUNBY; library of 12,100 vols., 144 periodicals; Librarian R. S. DAVIES, A.L.A.

**British Institute in South-East Asia:** B-5 2nd floor, International Building, Orchard Rd., Singapore 0923; f. 1976; sponsored by the British Academy, London, for the promotion of South-East Asian studies, especially history, archaeology and cultural anthropology; library of 1,000 vols.; Chair. of Cttee. of Management Prof. J. G. D. CLARK, C.B.E.; Dir. Dr. J. F. H. VILLIERS; publ. *South-East Asian Studies Newsletter* (quarterly).

**China Society, The:** 190 Keng Lee Rd., Singapore 11; f. 1948 to promote Chinese culture and to introduce Chinese culture to the non-Chinese; 250 mems.; Pres. LEE SIOW MONG; publ. *Annual of China Society*.

**Institute of Physics, Singapore:** c/o Dept. of Physics, National University of Singapore, Kent Ridge, Singapore 0511; f. 1973 to promote study of and research in physics in Singapore; organizes conferences, talks, seminars, exhibitions, visits to industrial and commercial establishments and educational tours abroad; encourages study of physics in schools; 153 mems.; Pres. Prof. LIM YUNG KUO; Vice-Pres. Dr. KOH CHOR JIN; Hon. Sec. Dr. LUA KIM TENG; publ. *Bulletin*† (quarterly).

**Institute of Southeast Asian Studies:** Heng Mui Keng Terrace, Pasir Panjang, Singapore 0511; f. 1968 to undertake research on South-East Asia, especially problems of development, modernization, political and social change; library of 38,630 vols.; Dir. Prof. KERNIAL S. SANDHU; Exec. Sec. S. L. PANG; Librarian P. LIM PHUI HUEN; publs. *Contemporary Southeast Asia* (quarterly), *Southeast Asian Affairs* (annually).

**Library Association of Singapore:** c/o National Library, Stamford Rd., Singapore 0617; f. 1955; 339 mems.; Pres. Miss WEE JOO GIM; Hon. Sec. Mrs. NORISAH MANSOR; publs. *Singapore Libraries* (annually), *LAS Newsletter* (quarterly).

**Regional Institute of Higher Education and Development (RIHED):** 15 Grange Rd., Singapore 0923; f. 1970 to facilitate co-operation between universities and governments in S.E. Asia, and to enhance the contributions of higher education to the social and economic development of the region; holds seminars and conferences; conducts research; provides advisory and clearinghouse services; library of 8,000 vols.; Dir. VISWANATHAN SELVARATNAM; Documentation Officer Miss VIMALA NAMBIAR; publs. *Bulletin*, monographs, research papers, occasional reports, conference, seminar and workshop proceedings.

**Science Council of Singapore:** Singapore Science Centre Bldg., Science Centre Rd., Singapore 2260; f. 1967 to advise the Minister for Science and Technology on scientific and technological research and development in Singapore; the effective training and utilization of scientific and technological manpower in Singapore, the establishment of official relations with other scientific organizations; 17 council mems.; Chair. Dr. ANG HOW GHEE; Sec. Mrs. SIEW WENG HIN; publs. *Annual Report*†, occasional papers, educational publications.

**Singapore Association for the Advancement of Science:** 1st floor, Singapore Science Centre Bldg., off Jurong Town Hall Rd., Singapore 2260; f. 1976 for the dissemination of science and technology; Pres. Prof. ANG KOK PENG; Sec. Dr. R. S. BHATHAL.

**Singapore Institute of Architects:** 393A–397A, Block 23, Outram Park, Singapore 0316; f. 1923; 557 mems.; Pres. EDWIN S. H. CHOO; Hon. Sec. MOK YEW FUN; publs. *SIAJ* (6 a year), *SIA Year Book*.

**Singapore Institute of International Affairs:** c/o Dept. of Political Science, University of Singapore, Bukit Timah Rd., Singapore 10.

**Singapore Medical Association:** 4A College Rd., Singapore 0316; f. 1959; 1,545 mems.; library of 448 vols.; Pres. Dr. Low Lip Ping; Hon. Sec. Dr. Goh Lee Gan; publs. *Singapore Medical Journal†, SMA Newsletter.*

**Vocational and Industrial Training Board (VITB):** Vocational Drive, Singapore 0513; Chair. Dr. Ahmad Mattar; Dir. Lim Jit Poh; publs. *VITB News†* (fortnightly), *Tomorrow's Workforce* (monthly).

## LIBRARIES AND ARCHIVES

**National Archives and Records Centre:** 17-18 Lewin Terrace, Singapore 0617; f. 1979; library of 4,783 vols., 3,081 metres of archival holdings, 3,938 maps, 20,166 photographs, 80,459 building plans; Dir. Mrs. Lily Tan; publ. *Annual Report.*

**National Library:** Stamford Rd., Singapore 0617; f. 1823; formerly Raffles Library and Raffles National Library, a department of the Government of Singapore providing reference and lending library facilities for the Republic; 1,352,276 vols., 53.1 per cent of the collection in English; growing collections of Chinese, Malay and Tamil books; official repository for publications received under the Printers and Publishers Act, United Nations publications and selected publications of its specialized agencies; five branch libraries (in addition to the main library) and a mobile library service for rural areas; national centre of bibliographical information and national exchange centre; Dir. Mrs. Hedwig Anuar; publs. *Annual Report†, Singapore Periodicals Index†* (annually), *Books about Singapore†* (every 2 years), *Checklist of Southeast Asian Serials†, Singapore National Bibliography†* (annually), *Catalogue of music records†, Union Catalogue of scientific and technical serials†*, other occasional bibliographies.

**National University of Singapore Library:** Kent Ridge, Singapore 0511; central library 596,365 vols., medical library 103,119 vols., law library 74,475 vols., Chinese library 286,045 vols.; Chief Librarian Mrs. Peggy Wai Chee Hochstadt, M.A.; publs. *Library Handbook, Serials Checklist, Monthly Accessions List, Catalogue of the Singapore/Malaysia Collection.*

## MUSEUM

**National Museum:** Stamford Rd., Singapore 0617; formerly Raffles Museum; f. 1849; ethnology, history and art of Singapore and surrounding region; houses the National Museum Art Gallery (f. 1976) and the Young People's Gallery for students' art and crafts; reference library of 13,000 vols.; Dir. Christopher Hooi; publs. *Heritage* (2 a year), *National Museum Memoirs, National Museum Publications.*

## UNIVERSITY AND COLLEGES

### NATIONAL UNIVERSITY OF SINGAPORE
KENT RIDGE,
SINGAPORE 0511

Telephone: Singapore 7756666.
Telex: 33943 UNISPO RS.

Founded 1980 by merger of former University of Singapore and Nanyang University. (The University of Singapore had its origins in the King Edward VII College of Medicine, Raffles Colleges and the University of Malaya in Singapore.)

Language of instruction: English; State control; Academic year: July to June (two semesters).

*Chancellor:* President of the Republic of Singapore.
*Pro-Chancellors:* E. S. Monteiro, B.B.M., C.B.E., M.D., F.R.C.P., F.R.F.P.S., D.C.H., A. P. Rajah, LL.B.
*Vice-Chancellor:* Lim Pin, M.D., M.A., F.R.C.P.
*Registrar:* Mrs. Y. T. Lu Sinclair, P.P.A., M.A.
*Chief Librarian:* Mrs. P. Hochstadt, M.A.

Number of teachers: 800.
Number of students: 9,500.

#### DEANS:
*Faculty of Accountancy and Business Administration:* Lee Soo Ann, M.A., PH.D.
*Faculty of Architecture and Building:* Bill Lim Biu Pui, PH.D., F.R.A.I.A.
*Faculty of Arts and Social Sciences:* Edwin Thumboo, PH.D.
*Faculty of Dentistry:* E. Tay Mai Hiong, B.D.S., F.D.S.R.C.S., F.I.C.D.
*Faculty of Engineering:* Cham Tao Soon, PH.D.
*Faculty of Law:* Tan Sook Yee, LL.B., B.A.
*Faculty of Medicine:* Edward Tock Peng Chong, PH.D., M.D., F.C.A.P., F.R.C.P.A., P.P.A.
*Faculty of Science:* Koh Lip Lin, PH.D., F.S.N.I.C.

#### DIRECTORS:
*School of Postgraduate Dental Studies:* Lim Kheng Ann, M.D.S., F.D.S.R.C.S., D.D.O.R.C.P.S., F.I.C.D.
*School of Postgraduate Medical Studies:* Wong Hock Boon, P.J.M., M.B., B.S., F.R.C.P.
*School of Management:* Lee Soo Ann, M.A., PH.D.

#### PROFESSORS:
*Faculty of Architecture and Building:*
Lim Biu Pui, Bill, PH.D., Building Science
Rao, K. R., PH.D., Building Science

*Faculty of Arts and Social Sciences:*
Alatas, S. H., D.R., D.R.S., Malay Studies
Lee Soo Ann, M.A., PH.D., Economics and Statistics
Lee Yong Leng, M.A., PH.D., Geography
Lim Chee Then, M.A., PH.D., Chinese Studies
Lim Chong Yah, M.A., D.PHIL., Economics and Statistics
Ooi Jin Bee, M.A., D.PHIL., Geography
Saw Swee Hock, M.A., PH.D., Economics and Statistics
Thumboo, E., PH.D., English Language and Literature
Wong Lin Ken, M.A., PH.D., History

*Faculty of Dentistry:*
Tay Mai Hiong, E., B.D.S., F.D.S.R.C.S., Prosthetic Dentistry

*Faculty of Engineering:*
Choo Seok Cheow, PH.D., Electrical Engineering
Chow Shuh-Twu, M.S., PH.D., Mechanical Engineering
Lee Seng Lip, M.S.E., PH.D., Civil Engineering

*Faculty of Law:*
Jayakumar, S., LL.M., Law
Koh Kheng Lian, Mrs., PH.D., Law
Koh Thong Bee, T., LL.M., Law

*Faculty of Medicine:*
Cheah Jin Seng, M D., M.B., B.S., F.R.A.C.P., Medicine
Phoon Wai-On, M.B., B.S., F.R.F.P.S., F.R.C.P., Social Medicine and Public Health
Ratnam, S. S., M.D., F.R.C.S., Obstetrics and Gynaecology
Shanmugaratnam, K., P.P.A., M.D., PH.D., Pathology
Sinniah, R., M.A., PH.D., M.D., B.A.O., M.R.C., F.R.C.P.I., F.R.C.P.A., Pathology
Tan Kim Leong, M.B.B.S., M.R.C.P., D.C.H., F.I.C.P., F.R.A.C.P., Paediatrics
Tock Peng Chong, P.P.A., M.D., PH.D., F.R.C.P.A., Pathology
Wong Hee Aik, Miss, PH.D., Biochemistry
Wong Hock Boon, P.M.J., M.B., B.S., F.R.C.P., Paediatrics
Wong Poi Kwong, M.B., B.S., F.R.C.P., Medicine
Wong Wai Chow, PH.D., Anatomy
Yeoh Teow Seng, PH.D., Pharmacology
Zaman, V., D.SC., PH.D., M.B.B.S., Microbiology

*Faculty of Science:*
Ang How Ghee, M.SC., PH.D., F.R.S.C., Chemistry
Ang Kok Peng, M.SC., PH.D., F.R.S.C., Chemistry
Huang Hsing Hua, D.SC., F.R.S.C., Chemistry
Rajaratnam, A., M.SC., PH.D., Physics
Rao, A. N., M.SC., PH.D., Botany

TEH HOON HENG, M.SC., PH.D., Mathematics

RESEARCH CENTRES:

**Economic Research Centre:** Kent Ridge, Singapore 0511; Dir. Dr. PANG ENG FONG.

**Chinese Language and Research Centre:** Jurong Campus, Upper Jurong Rd., Singapore 2264; Dir. LOO SHAW CHANG.

### INSTITUTE OF EDUCATION
PATERSON RD., SINGAPORE 0923

Telephone: 7374511.
Founded 1973.

Languages of instruction: English, Chinese, Tamil; Academic year: July to November, January to May.

*Director:* Miss LIM HSIU MEI.
*Registrar:* Mrs. LIN CHOR YEE.
*Librarian:* Mrs. WANG CHEN HSIU CHIN.

Library of 80,000 vols., 325 periodicals.

Number of teachers: 143.
Nubmer of students: 4,332.
Publication: *Prospectus* (annually).

DEANS:

*School of Advanced Studies:* Dr. TAN WEE KIAT.
*School of Creative and Applied Arts:* YAP BOON CHUAN.
*School of Educational Service:* Dr. TAN WEE KIAT.
*School of Language Studies:* HO WAH KAM.
*School of Professional Studies:* Dr. ENG SOO PECK.
*School of Sciences:* CHIN LONG FAY.

### NGEE ANN TECHNICAL COLLEGE
535 CLEMENTI RD., SINGAPORE 2159

Founded 1963.
Language of instruction: English.

*Principal:* KHONG KIT SOON.
*Registrar:* CHEW YONG SOO.
*Librarian:* Mrs. MARGARET KWAN-HO.
*Bursar:* Mrs. FLORENCE CHIA-LAM CHI LAN.

Library of 54,800 vols.
Number of teachers: 220.
Number of students: 3,173.

HEADS OF DEPARTMENTS:

*Mechanical Engineering:* MOHD. MAIRAJUL HODA.
*Shipbuilding and Repair Technology:* Dr. A. K. M. MOAZZEM HUSSAIN.
*Electrical and Electronic Engineering:* CHAN YOKE LOCK.
*Building Services:* CHEAH AH LEE.
*Business Studies:* LIM SEAH ENG.

### SINGAPORE POLYTECHNIC
DOVER RD., SINGAPORE 0513

Telephone: 7751133.
Founded 1954.

State control; Language of instruction: English; Academic year: May to March (three terms).

Offers courses leading to Technician Diploma in Building, Chemical Process Technology, Civil Engineering, Architectural Draughtsmanship, Electrical Engineering, Electronics and Communication Engineering, Land Surveying, Mechanical Engineering, Marine Engineering, Production Engineering, Ship Construction and Structural Engineering and courses to Technician Cert. level in Architectural Draughtsmanship, Aeronautical Maintenance Engineering and Maritime Radio Communications; Pre-Sea Training Course; post-technician courses in Industrial Management, Shipping Management, Plastics Mould Design and Process Plant Engineering Design.

*Chairman:* CHUA CHOR TECK, B.SC. (NAV. ARCH.).
*Principal:* KHOO KAY CHAI, P.P.A., B.E. (Civil), P.ENG., C.ENG., M.I.C.E., F.I.E.S., M.I.E.(M.).
*Registrar:* TEH YAP CHENG (acting).
*Librarian:* Mrs. R. D. YEAP, F.L.A., A.L.A.A.

Number of teachers: 315 full-time, 107 part-time.
Number of students: 5,417 full-time, 3,494 part-time.

Publications: *Prospectus* (annually), *Annual Report, Polynews* (every 2 months).

**Southeast Asian Ministers of Education Organization (SEAMEO) Regional Language Centre (RELC):** 30 Orange Grove Rd., Singapore 1025; f. 1968; aims to improve the teaching of English and other languages in the SEAMEO countries; conducts 6 advanced courses, including M.A. and Ph.D. courses in applied linguistics; research, regional conferences; provides technical services to national programmes; library of *c.* 30,000 vols.; 12 staff and approx. 150 students; Dir. Mrs. TAI YU-LIN; publs. *RELC Journal: A Journal of Language Teaching and Research in South-east Asia* (2 a year), *Newsletter* (quarterly), monograph series, anthology series, seminar reports, etc.

# SOLOMON ISLANDS
Population 221,000

## LIBRARY AND ARCHIVES

**Solomon Islands National Archives:** Ministry of Youth and Cultural Affairs, P.O.B. G.20, Honiara; f. 1979; British Solomon Islands Protectorate records 1900–78, Solomon Islands Government records 1978–; collections of MSS, microfilm, film and sound recordings on Solomon Islands and Western Pacific; Government Archivist R. G. A. CHESTERMAN.

**Solomon Islands National Library:** Ministry of Youth and Cultural Affairs, Honiara; f. 1974; 22,000 vols.; Librarian LENCY WANEATONA.

## MUSEUM

**Solomon Islands National Museum and Cultural Centre:** P.O.B. 313, Honiara; run in conjunction with the Cultural Association of the Solomon Islands; collection began in 1950s, permanent site 1969; research into all aspects of Solomons culture (pre-history, language, oral tradition, music, dance, architecture, etc.); promotes traditional craft, music and dance; Curator HENRY ISA; publs. *Journal, Custom Stories.*

## COLLEGES

**Honiara Technical Institute:** P.O.B. G23, Honiara; f. 1969.
*Principal:* A. W. HATFIELD, DIP.BUS.ADMIN., F.T.C.
*Registrar:* F. IRO.
*Librarian:* D. MAN CHEUNG.

Number of teachers: 35.
Number of students (including part-time): 450.

DEANS:

*Trade School:* A. BRIGGS, B.A., F.T.C. (Engineering Section).
*Marine School:* T. DE M. OGIER, MASTER MARINER F.G.
*Commerce School:* M. R. MORGAN, B.A.ECON.
*Survey School:* G. C. POPE.
*English Section:* G. R. HOOPER.
*Mathematics Section:* C. V. MORGAN, B.SC.
*Science Section:* R. C. MORRIS.

**University of the South Pacific Solomon Islands Centre:** P.O.B. 460, Honiara; f. 1970; library of 2,989 vols.; Dir. HUGH PAIA, B.ED.

# SOMALIA
## (SOMALI DEMOCRATIC REPUBLIC)
### Population 3,354,000

## LEARNED SOCIETIES

**Accademia de la Cultura:** c/o Ministry of Culture, Mogadishu; research on the culture of the country.

**Casa degli Italiani:** Mogadishu; organizes meetings, art exhibitions, etc.

**Egyptian Cultural Center:** Mogadishu.

**Institut Culturel et Social:** Mogadishu.

**Russian Friendship Cultural Center:** Mogadishu.

## RESEARCH INSTITUTES

**Geological Survey Department:** Ministry for Minerals and Water Resources, P.O.B. 744, Mogadishu; library of 500 vols.; Dir. V. N. KOZERENKO.

**Institute for the Preparation of Serums and Vaccines:** Mogadishu.

**Laboratory of Hygiene and Prophylaxy:** Mogadishu; sections in medicine and chemistry.

**Society of Medicine and Tropical Hygiene:** Mogadishu.

**Survey and Mapping Department:** Ministry of Public Works, P.O.B. 24, Mogadishu; f. 1966; the official surveying and mapping department; Dir. MUSA ADAN WADADID.

## LIBRARIES

**Somali Institute of Public Administration Library:** Mogadishu.

**National Library of Higher Education and Culture:** Ministry of Higher Education and Culture, P.O.B. 1182, Mogadishu; f. 1934; 8,000 vols.; Librarian OSMAN GAHIR JAMA.

**Società Dante Alighieri:** Mogadishu; library of books on Italian culture.

## MUSEUM

**National Museum:** Mogadishu; ethnographical, historical and natural science collections.

## UNIVERSITY

### SOMALI NATIONAL UNIVERSITY
P.O.B. 15, MOGADISHU

Telephone: 25035/40042.

Founded 1954; University status 1969.

Languages of instruction: Somali, Arabic, Italian, English.

*President:* Dr. MOHAMED HASSAN MUDEY.
*Vice-President for Academic Affairs:* Dr. MOHAMUD ABDI NUR.
*Registrar:* NUREYN SHEIKH ABRAR.
*Librarian:* Mrs. SIRAD YUSUF ISMAIL.

Number of teachers: 490.
Number of students: 3,700.

DEANS:

*Faculty of Medicine:* ABDULLAHI MOHAMED OMAR.
*Faculty of Agriculture:* ABDULQADIR HASSAN SHIRWAA.
*Faculty of Veterinary Medicine:* MOHAMED GAANNI MOHAMED.
*Faculty of Engineering:* MOHAMED NUR ALIYO.
*Faculty of Geology:* IBRAHIM HERSI AADAN.
*Faculty of Chemistry:* ABDURASAK OSMAN HASSAN.
*Faculty of Education:* MOHAMED ELMI BULLALE.
*Faculty of Law:* Dr. MOHAMED HASSAN MUDEY.
*Faculty of Economics:* IBRAHIM MOHAMED ABDI.

## COLLEGES

**School of Islamic Disciplines:** Mogadishu; includes a faculty of law.

**École Industrielle:** Mogadishu; departments of radio, carpentry, mechanics, electricity, building construction.

**School of Public Health.**

**School of Seamanship and Fishing:** 170 students.

**Technical College:** Burgo; f. 1965; 4-year courses.

**Veterinary College:** Mogadishu; 30 students; 10 teachers; Projects Dir. Dr. J. NEILSEN.

# SOUTH AFRICA
Population 23,771,000

## LEARNED SOCIETIES

### GENERAL

**Royal Society of South Africa:** c/o University of Cape Town, Rondebosch 7700; f. 1877, Royal Charter 1908; 4 honorary and 91 Ordinary Fellows, 300 mems.; publ. *Transactions*†.
*President:* B. WARNER, PH.D., M.A., D.SC., F.R.A.S., F.INST.P.
*Vice-Presidents:* E. S. W. SIMPSON, M.SC., PH.D., C. K. BRAIN, PH.D., D.SC., F.Z.S.
*Hon. Secretary:* A. V. HALL, M.SC., PH.D., F.L.S.
*Hon. Treasurer:* A. O. FULLER, PH.D.

FELLOWS:
*Honorary:*
BOZZOLI, G. R., D.SC.(ENG.).
NABARRO, F. R. N., M.B.E., D.SC., F.R.S.
PAPENFUSS, J. F., PH.D.
WOOLLEY, Sir RICHARD, O.B.E., F.R.S., F.R.A.S., SC.D., M.A.
*Ordinary:*
ADLER, C., M.B., CH.B.
AHRENS, Prof. L. H., M.A., D.SC., F.R.I.C., F.G.S.
ALLANSON, Prof. B. R., M.SC., PH.D.
BALINSKY, Prof. B. I., DR.BIOL.SC.
BATSON, Prof. E., B.SC.(ECON.), F.R.ECON.S.
BEATER, B. E., D.SC.
BIESHEUVEL, S., M.A., PH.D., D.SOC.SC., F.S.A.I.P.
BIGALKE, R. C., DR.PHIL.NAT.
BIGALKE, R. C. H., M.A., PH.D.
BLEKSLEY, Prof. A. E. H., M.SC., D.SC.
BOND, G. W., D.SC.
BOTHWELL, T. H., M.D., D.SC., F.R.C.P.
BRAIN, C. K., PH.D.
BRINK, C. V. D. M., M.SC., D.SC.
BROWN, A. C., D.MUS, M.SC., F.Z.S., PH.D., F.R.E.S.
BURSELL, E., D.SC., PH.D.
CAMPBELL, G. D., M.D., D.SC., F.R.C.P.(E.).
CLARK, J. D., C.B.E., M.A., PH.D., F.S.A., F.R.A.I.
COOKE, H. B. S., M.A., D.SC., F.G.S., F.R.MET.S.
COPENHAGEN, W. J., O.B.E., M.SC., F.R.I.C.
DART, Prof. R. A., M.SC., M.D., CH.M., D.SC.
DAVIS, D. H. S., M.A., D.SC., F.Z.S.
DAY, Prof. J. H. O., D.F.C., B.SC., PH.D., F.L.S.
DU TOIT, Prof. C. A., M.SC., PH.D.
DYER, R. A., D.SC.
EALES, Prof. L., CH.B., M.D., F.R.C.P.
ELSDON-DEW, R., M.B., CH.B., M.D.
EVANS, D. S., M.A., PH.D., F.INST.P., F.R.A.S.
EWER, D. W., M.A., PH.D.
FREED, L. F., M.A., D.PHIL., M.B., CH.B., M.D., D.P.H., D.T.M.&H.
FULLER, A. O., M.SC., PH.D.
GEAR, J. H. S., M.B.B.CH., D.P.H., M.D., D.T.M&H., F.R.C.P.
GEVERS, Prof. W., CH.B., M.A., D.PHIL.
GORDON, Prof. I., M.A., PH.D.
HALES, Prof. A. L., PH.D., M.A., F.R.A.S.
HALL, A. V., M.SC., PH.D., F.L.S.
HARINGTON, J. S., PH.D., D.SC.
HAUGHTON, S. H., D.SC., LL.D., F.R.S., F.G.S., F.G.S.A.
HESSE, A. J., B.SC., PH.D., F.R.E.S.
HEY, D., D.SC.
ISAACSON, L. C., M.D., PH.D., F.R.C.P.(E.).
JACKSON, W. P. U., M.A., M.D.
JENKINS, T., M.D., M.R.C.S., L.R.C.P., D.R.C.O.G.
JOUBERT, J. D. M., PH.D., D.SC., F.I.BIOL.
KENT, L. E., M.SC., PH.D., F.G.S.
KERRICH, Prof. J. E., M.SC., LL.D., F.A.S.A., F.S.A.S.A.
KING, L. C., D.SC., PH.D., F.G.S.
LAWRENCE, R. F., M.A., PH.D.
LOUW, G. N., M.SC., PH.D.
LÜTJEHARMS, Prof. W. J., PHIL.NAT.D.
MALAN, B. D., B.A.
MARLOTH, R. H., B.A., M.SC., PH.D.
MATHIAS, F. C. M., M.A., PH.D., D.SC.
METZ, J., M.D., F.R.C.PATH.
MILLARD, N. A. H., B.SC., PH.D.
NAUDÉ, S. M., M.SC., PH.D., D.SC., LL.D.
PHILLIPS, J. F. V., D.SC., F.R.S.E.
PLUMSTEAD, E. P., D.SC.
RAPSON, W. S., M.SC., D.PHIL., A.R.I.C.
RENNIE, Prof. J. V. L., M.A., PH.D.
RYCROFT, Prof. H. B., M.SC., PH.D., F.L.S.
SCHAMROTH, L., M.D., D.SC., F.R.C.P.
SCHAPERA, Prof. I., M.A., PH.D., D.SC.
SCHELPE, E. A. C. L. E., M.SC., D.PHIL., F.L.S.
SCHRIRE, T., M.A., M.B., CH.B., F.R.C.S., F.C.C.P.
SCOTT, Dr. K. M. F., M.SC., PH.D., F.R.E.S.
SHAPIRO, H. A., M.B., CH.B., PH.D.
SHEAR, M., M.D.S., D.SC., F.O.S.S.A., F.R.C.PATH.
SIMPSON, Prof. E. S. W., M.SC., PH.D.
SLOAN, Prof. A. W., M.D., PH.D., F.R.C.P.
STAZ, J., D.D.S., H.DD., L.D.S., R.C.S.
STOY, R. H., M.A., PH.D., F.R.A.S.
SUMMERS, R. F. H., F.S.A.
TALBOT, Prof. W. J., B.SC.
THORNTON, Prof. D. A., PH.D.
TOBIAS, Prof. P. V., PH.D., D.SC., M.B., B.CH., F.R.A.I., F.L.S.
TWYMAN, Prof. E. S., M.SC., PH.D.
VAN DER WALT, J. P., M.SC., D.SC.TECH.
VAN DER WERFF, T. J., PR.ENG., D.PHIL.
VAN ZINDEREN BAKKER, Prof. E. M., M.SC., PHIL.NAT.D.
VAN ZYL, A., M.SC., PH.D.
VON BONDE, C., M.A., PH.D.
WARNER, B., M.A., PH.D., D.SC.
WARREN, Prof. F. L., PH.D., D.SC., A.R.C.S., D.I.C.
WILLCOX, A. R., F.S.A., F.R.A.I.
WILSON, Prof. MONICA, M.A., PH.D.
WYNDHAM, Prof. C. H., M.B., CH.B.
ZWARENSTEIN, Prof. H. J., M.A., M.SC., PH.D., D.SC.

**Africa Institute of South Africa:** cnr. Hamilton and Belvedere Streets, Arcadia, P.O.B. 630, Pretoria; f. 1960; collection and dissemination of information and research concerning the African continent, especially southern Africa; Dir. Dr. G. M. E. LEISTNER; publs. *Africa Institute Bulletin* (fortnightly), *Africa Insight* (quarterly), *Journal of Contemporary African Studies* (2 a year), *Communications of the Africa Institute, Occasional Papers.*

**Suid-Afrikaanse Akademie vir Wetenskap en Kuns** (*South African Academy of Science and Arts*): Engelenburghuis, Hamilton St., Pretoria; f. 1909; for the advancement of the Afrikaans language, literature, South African art, science and technology; 381 mems., 1,243 assoc. mems.; Chair. Prof. G. BEUKES; Sec. D. J. C. GELDENHUYS; publs. *Tydskrif vir Geesteswetenskappe, Tydskrif vir Natuurwetenskappe, Nuusbrief, Tegnikon* (quarterlies), *Jaarboek.*

### ARCHITECTURE AND TOWN PLANNING

**Institute of S.A. Architects:** 10th Floor, Samro House, 73 Juta St., P.O.B. 31750, Braamfontein 2017, Johannesburg; f. 1927; 2,400 mems.; Sec. M. KNOETZE.

**Simon van der Stel Foundation:** P.O.B. 1743, Pretoria 0001; f. 1959; S.A. National Trust; historic conservation; 4,500 mems.; Chair. Dr. S. MEIRING NAUDÉ; Dir. DEON JOOSTE; publ. *Restorica*† (2 a year).

## The Arts

**Federasie van Afrikaanse Kultuurvereniginge (F.A.K.)** (*Association of Afrikaans Cultural Societies*): P.O.B. 91050, Auckland Park 2006; f. 1929; 4,000 affiliated Afrikaans cultural societies; Chair. Prof. G. G. CILLIE; Sec. Dr. A. M. VAN DEN BERG; publs. *Lectures, Handhaaf* (monthly).

**South African Association of Arts (Western Cape Region):** 35 Church Street, Cape Town 8001; f. 1945 as successor to South Africa Fine Arts Association to encourage arts nationally and internationally; 800 mems. (W. Cape region); National Pres. Prof. G. MULLER BALLOT; Regional Chair. S. RAPPOPORT; publ. *South Africa Arts Calendar* (monthly).

### Bibliography, Library Science and Museology

**South African Institute for Librarianship and Information Science/Suid-Afrikaanse Institut vir Biblioteek en Inligtingwese:** c/o Ferdinand Postma Library, Potchefstroom University, Potchefstroom; f. 1930; 1,663 mems.; Pres. Prof. A. J. VILJOEN, D.PHIL., F.S.A.I.L.I.S.; Hon. Sec. C. J. H. LESSING, M.A.(BIBL.); publs. *South African Libraries/Suid-Afrikaanse Biblioteke* (quarterly), *Newsletter/Nuusbrief* (monthly) and a few irregular publications.

**Southern African Museums Association:** c/o South African Museum, P.O.B. 61, Cape Town; f. 1930; 430 mems.; Hon. Sec. Mrs. E. PAAP; publ. *Samab* (quarterly).

### Economics, Law and Politics

**Economic Society of South Africa:** P.O.B. 929, Pretoria 0001; f. 1925 to promote the thorough discussion of, and research into economic questions, in particular those affecting South Africa; 570 mems.; brs. in Bloemfontein, Cape Town, Eastern Province, Johannesburg, Natal, Pretoria, Stellenbosch and Western Transvaal; Sec. J. P. DREYER; publ. *The South African Journal of Economics* (quarterly).

**Institute of Bankers in South Africa:** P.O.B. 10335, Johannesburg 2000; f. 1904; 19,000 mems.; publ. *South African Banker* (quarterly); Sec.-Gen. P. KRAAK, F.I.B.S.A.

**South Africa Foundation:** P.O.B. 7006, Johannesburg 2000; f. 1959 to promote international understanding of South Africa; 5,000 mems.; Founder Pres. Maj.-Gen. Sir FRANCIS DE GUINGAND, K.B.E., C.B., D.S.O.; Pres. G. W. H. RELLY; Dir.-Gen. J. DE L. SOROUR; publs. *South Africa International†* (independent foreign affairs quarterly), *South Africa Foundation News* (monthly survey), *Briefing Papers* (occasional papers on topical affairs).

**South African Institute of International Affairs:** Jan Smuts House, P.O.B. 31596, Braamfontein, Johannesburg 2017; f. 1934 to facilitate the scientific study of international questions, particularly those affecting Southern Africa; 2,000 mems.; library of 12,000 vols.; Chair. H. F. OPPENHEIMER; Dir.-Gen. JOHN BARRATT; publs. *International Affairs Bulletin†* (3 a year), *Occasional Papers†* (monthly), *Southern Africa Record†* (quarterly).

### History, Geography and Archaeology

**Genealogical Society of South Africa:** P.O.B. 3566, Cape Town 8000; f. 1963; 500 mems.; Chair. C. PAMA; Hon. Sec. W. S. ROBERTSON; publs. *Familia†, Newsletter†* (quarterly).

**Heraldry Society of Southern Africa:** P.O. Box 4839, Cape Town 8000; f. 1953; 150 mems.; Chair. Dr. C. PAMA; Hon. Sec. W. S. ROBERTSON; publ. *Arma†* (quarterly).

**South African Archaeological Society:** P.O.B. 31, Claremont 7735; f. 1945; 1,000 mems.; library of 400 vols., 5,000 periodicals; Sec. Dr. M. HALL; publs. *South African Archaeological Bulletin†* (half yearly), *Goodwin Series†* (irregular), *Monograph Series* (occasional).

**South African Geographical Society:** P.O.B. 31201, Braamfontein 2017, Transvaal; f. 1917; 450 mems.; six lectures a year, quadrennial conference, seminars etc.; Pres. Prof. K. S. O. BEAVON; Hon. Sec. J. HENNING; publs. *South African Geographical Journal†* (bi-annually), *South African Geographical Society Newsletter* (bi-annually), *Landscape Monographs* (irregular).

**Van Riebeeck Society:** c/o South African Library, Cape Town; f. 1918; 1,500 mems.; publishes South African Historical Documents; Chair. Dr. F. R. BRADLOW; Sec. Dr. C. PAMA; publ. 1 volume annually.

### International Cultural Institutes

**British Council:** 170 Pine St., Arcadia, Pretoria 0083; Rep. R. T. L. WATKINS; 91 Parliament St., Cape Town 8001; Regional Dir. A. D. BATES.

**Nederlands Cultuurhistorisch Instituut:** University of Pretoria, Pretoria; f. 1931; offers books and information on Dutch culture, history and art; 250 mems.; library of 32,000 vols., 96 periodicals; Dir. Prof. Dr. P. G. NEL; publ. *Mededelingen* (10 a year), annual report.

### Language and Literature

**Classical Association of South Africa:** f. 1956; 400 mems.; Chair. Prof. D. M. KRIEL; Sec. Prof. S. M. BRUWER, University of Stellenbosch; publs. *Acta Classica†* (annually), *Akroterion* (quarterly).

**English Academy of Southern Africa:** Ballater House, 35 Melle St., Braamfontein, Johannesburg; f. 1961; to stimulate interest in the English language and its literature including the literature of Southern Africa; to promote literacy and maintain standards of English in schools and universities, especially in black education; to ensure the full and free use of English as an official language and defend the rights to free speech and publication; 450 full, 100 assoc. mems.; library specializing in teaching materials; Pres. Prof. E. PEREIRA; publs. *ELTIC Reporter†* (quarterly), *Annual Review*.

**Federasie van Rapportryerskorpse:** P.O.B. 6772, Johannesburg; f. 1961; 486 brs.; 12,500 mems.; Chair. Prof. P. J. GLASE, M.P.; Sec. H. S. HATTINGH.

**South African P.E.N. Centre (Cape):** Apartment C, 2 Scott Rd., Claremont, Cape Town; f. 1960; 70 full and 30 associate mems.; Pres. MARY RENAULT; Sec. ADÈLE NAUDÉ; publ. *Newsletter*.

### Medicine

**Medical Association of South Africa:** P.O.B 20272, Alkantrant 0005; f. 1927; 9,500 mems.; library incorporated into the libraries of all the medical schools in the country; Chair. of Council Prof. J. N. DE KLERK; Sec. Gen. C. E. M. VILJOEN, M.B., CH.B.; publs. *South African Medical Journal* (weekly).

**South African Medical Research Council:** P.O.B. 70, Tygerberg 7505; f. 1969; Pres. Prof. A. J. BRINK; Vice-Pres. Dr. P. D. R. VAN HEERDEN; Sec. G. G. PIENAAR; publ *Annual Report:*

The Council has the following research establishments:

**National Research Institute for Nutritional Diseases:** Dir. Dr. J. E. ROSSOUW.

**Institute for Biostatistics:** Dir. Dr. S. A. FELLINGHAM.

**Institute for Medical Literature:** Dir. Dr. S. F. ROSSOUW.

**Institute for Electron Microscopy:** Dir. Dr. E. D. F. WILLIAMS.

**Research Institute for Diseases in a Tropical Environment:** Dir. Prof. M. G. MOSHAL.

**Tuberculosis Research Institute:** (attached to Univ. of Pretoria); Dir. Dr. H. H. KLEEBERG.

**Bilharzia Field Research Unit:** Dir. Dr. R. J. PITCHFORD.

**Bacterial Genetics Research Unit:** (attached to Univ. of Pretoria); Dir. Prof. J. N. COETZEE.

**Neuro- and Electrophysiology Research Unit:** (attached to Univ. of Pretoria); Dir. Prof. B. J. MEYER.

**Photobiology Research Unit:** (attached to Univ. of Pretoria); Dir. Prof. G. H. FINDLAY.

**Iron and Red Cell Metabolism Research Unit:** Dir. Prof. T. H. BOTHWELL.

**Dental Research Institute:** Dir. Prof. P. E. CLEATON-JONES.

**Research Unit for Transplantation:** Dir. Prof. J. A. MYBURGH.

**Preclinical Diagnostic Chemistry Research Group:** Dir. Prof. S. M. JOUBERT.

**Research Unit for the Design of Catecholaminergic Drugs:** Dir. Prof. J. OFFERMEIER.

**Snail Research Unit:** Dir. Prof. J. A. VAN EEDEN.

**Molecular and Cellullar Cardiology Research Unit:** Dir. Dr. A. J. BESTER.

**Iodine Metabolism Research Unit:** Dir. Prof. A. VAN ZYL.

**Neuro Chemistry Research Group:** Dir. Prof. J. J. TALJAARD.

**Research Group for the Diffuse Obstructive Pulmonary Syndrome:** Dir. Prof. M. A. DE KOCK.

**Clinical Cytology Research Group:** Dir. Prof. W. A. VAN NIEKERK.

**Research Group for Dental Epidemiology:** Dir. Prof. C. W. VAN WYK.

**Ischaemic Heart Disease Research Unit:** Dir. Prof. L. H. OPIE.

**Porphyria Research Group:** Dir. Prof. L. EALES.

**Liver Research Group:** Dirs. Prof. J. TERBLANCHE, Prof. R. KIRSCH.

**Human Biochemistry Research Unit:** Dir. Dr. A. R. P. WALKER.

**Human Ecogenetics Research Unit:** Dir. Prof. T. JENKINS.

**Circulation Research Unit:** Dir. Prof. C. ROSENDORFF.

**Muscle Research Unit:** Dir. Prof. W. GEVERS.

**Biomembrane Research Unit:** Dir. Prof. M. C. BERMAN.

**Research Unit for Human Cellular Immunology:** Dir. Prof. A. R. RABSON.

**Unit for Research in Clinical Psychiatry:** Dir. Prof. L. S. GILLIS.

**Bone Metabolism Research Group:** Dir. Prof. L. SOLOMON.

**Blood Platelet Research Unit:** Dir. Prof. A. DU P. HEYNS.

**Research Unit for Emergent Pathogens:** Dir. Prof. H. J. KOORNHOF.

**Brain Metabolism Research Group:** Dir. Dr. S. KRAMER.

**South African Nutrition Society:** c/o National Research Institute for Nutritional Diseases, P.O.B. 70, Tygerberg 7505; f. 1955; 174 mems.; Pres. Dr. J. P. DU PLESSIS; Chair. Dr. S. J. VAN RENSBURG; Sec. Prof. J. E. ROSSOUW; *Proceedings* publ. in *South African Medical Journal*.

### SCIENCE
#### General

**Associated Scientific and Technical Societies of South Africa:** Kelvin House, 2 Hollard St., Johannesburg; P.O.B. 61019, Marshalltown, 2107 Transvaal; f. 1920; to promote the interests of scientific, professional and technical societies; to advance the knowledge of scientific and technical subjects and to provide secretarial, liaison, meeting and club facilities, etc., for its member societies: *Foundation Societies:* S.A. Inst. of Mechanical Engineers, S.A. Inst. of Mining and Metallurgy, Geological Society of S.A., S.A. Asscn. for the Advancement of Science (Witwatersrand Centre), Inst. of Land Surveyors of the Transvaal, S.A. Inst. of Electrical Engineers, S.A. Chemical Inst.; *Admitted Societies:* S.A. Inst. of Assayers and Analysts, Inst. of Certificated Mechanical and Electrical Engineers (S.A.), S.A. Inst. of Civil Engineers, S.A. Inst. of Chemical Engineers, Mine Ventilation Society of S.A., Inst. of Mine Surveyors of S.A. and S.A. Inst. of Town and Regional Planners, Inst. of Municipal Engineers of S.A., S.A. Society for Quality Control; *Associate Societies:* Royal Society of S.A., Inst. of Metallurgists (S.A. Region), Soil Science Society of Southern Africa, S.A. Mathematical Society, S.A. Inst. of Agricultural Engineers, Zoological Society of S.A., S.A. Inst. for Production Engineering, Textile Inst. (S.A. Sections), The Inst. of Structural Engineers (S.A. Branch), Engineers' Asscn. of S.A., Inst. of Land Surveyors of the O.F.S., S.A. Inst. of Physics, S.A. Inst. of Forestry, S.A. Assn. of Botanists, S.A. Inst. of Marine Engineers and Naval Architects, Inst. of Land Surveyors of Natal, S.A. Veterinary Asscn., S.A. Acoustics Institute, Fed. of Science and Mathematics Teachers Asscn. of S.A., Inst. of Nuclear Engineers (S.A. Branch), Inst. of Energy—S.A. Section; *Affiliated Societies:* Natal Inst. of Engineers, Eastern Province Society of Engineers, Aeronautical Society of S.A.; *Student Societies:* S.A. Federation of University Engineering Students (SAFUES), and University Science Students Asscn. of S.A. (USSASA); Pres. Prof. W. J. VAN BILJON; Man. ERIC BODEN; publ. *Annual Proceedings*.

**South African Association for the Advancement of Science:** c/o CSIR, P.O.B. 395, Pretoria 0001; f. 1902; 747 mems.; Pres. Prof. D. M. JOUBERT; Asst. Gen. Sec. H. P. HOFMEYR; publ. *South African Journal of Science*† (monthly).

#### Biological Sciences

**Botanical Society of South Africa:** Kirstenbosch, Claremont, Cape 7735; f. 1913; 7,400 mems.; aims to promote public interest in the development of the National Botanic Gardens of South Africa at Kirstenbosch and elsewhere and to promote the conservation and cultivation of the indigenous flora of South Africa; Pres. Dr. M. C. BOTHA; Sec. and Treas. Mrs. P. A. COLEY; publ. *Veld and Flora* (quarterly).

**Herpetological Association of Africa:** Port Elizabeth Museum, P.O.B. 13147, Humewood 6013; Sec. W. R. BRANCH; publ. *Journal*.

**South African Biological Society (Suid-Afrikaanse Biologiese Vereniging):** P.O.B. 820, Pretoria; f. 1907; 140 mems.; Pres. Dr. G. K. THERON; Hon. Sec. Mrs. M. W. VAN ROOYER; publ. *Journal* (annually).

**Southern African Ornithological Society:** P.O.B. 87234, Houghton, Johannesburg 2041; f. 1930; 3,000 mems.; Pres. P. A. CLANCEY; Sec. Mrs. J. B. WOLHUTER; publs. *Ostrich*†, *Bokmakierie*† (both quarterly).

**Southern African Wildlife Management Association:** P.O.B. 44189, Linden 2104; f. 1971; publishes original papers and reviews relating to research and management in the broad field of renewable natural resources; 900 mems.; publ. *Scientific Journal*.

**Wildlife Society of Southern Africa:** P.O.B. 44189, Linden 2104; f. 1902; conservation of fauna and flora; 23,000 mems.; publs. *African Wildlife International* (every 2 months), books, regional magazines.

#### Physical Sciences

**Astronomical Society of Southern Africa:** c/o S.A. Astronomical Observatory, P.O.B. 9, Observatory 7935; f.

1922; Pres. S. S. BOOYSEN; Hon. Sec. T. W. RUSSO; 500 mems.; publs. *Notes* (monthly), *Handbook* (annually); local centres at Cape Town, Johannesburg, Bloemfontein, Durban, Pietermaritzburg, Salisbury and Pretoria.

**Geological Society of South Africa:** P.O.B. 61019, Marshalltown, 2107; f. 1895; 1,460 mems.; Hon. Sec. J. J. LE R. CILLIERS; Asst. Secs. The Associated Scientific and Technical Societies of South Africa; publs. include *Quarterly News Bulletin*, *Transactions of the Geological Society of South Africa*†.

**South African Chemical Institute:** Kelvin House, 2 Hollard St., Johannesburg; P.O.B. 61019, Marshalltown, Johannesburg 2107; f. 1912; 1,170 mems.; publs. *South African Journal of Chemistry* (quarterly) and *ChemSa* (monthly).

**South African Institute of Physics:** c/o SUNI, P.O.B. 17, Faure, Cape; f. 1955; 360 mems.; Pres. Dr. D. REITMANN; Sec. Dr. W. R. MCMURRAY; publ. *S.A. Journal of Physics* (quarterly).

RELIGION, SOCIOLOGY AND ANTHROPOLOGY

**South African Bureau of Racial Affairs (SABRA):** P.O.B. 2768, Pretoria; f. 1948; research on race relations; biennial congress; Dir. Dr. C. JOOSTE; publ. *Journal of Racial Affairs* (quarterly).

**South African Institute of Race Relations:** P.O.B. 97, Johannesburg; f. 1929; 4,313 mems., 78 affiliated bodies; translation service of Afrikaans newspaper editorials (to subscribers and members); Pres. Prof. C. J. R. DUGARD; Dir. Dr. F. J. VAN WYK; publs. *Race Relations News*† (monthly), *A Survey of Race Relations in South Africa* (annual), other occasional publs.

TECHNOLOGY

**Institute of Transport** (*Southern Africa Division*): P.O.B. 23853, Joubert Park 2044, Johannesburg; f. 1926; 1,200 mems.; Chair. H. A. LOOTS, F.C.I.T.; Hon. Sec. R. A. FARMAN, F.C.I.T.; publs. *Journal, Transport and Traffic* (monthly).

**Institution of Certificated Mechanical and Electrical Engineers, South Africa:** P.O.B. 61019, Marshalltown, 2107; f. 1911; 1,600 mems.; Secs. The Associated Scientific and Technical Societies of South Africa; publs. *Journal, The Certificated Engineer*.

**South African Institute of Assayers and Analysts:** Kelvin House, 2 Hollard St., P.O.B. 61019, Marshalltown 2107, Transvaal; f. 1919 to uphold the status and interests of the profession of assaying in all its branches; 181 mems.; Pres. J. F. LEATHERBARROW; publ. *Bulletin* (quarterly).

**South African Institute of Electrical Engineers:** P.O.B. 61019, Marshalltown, 2107; f. 1909; 3,500 mems.; Pres. G. A. PARK; Secs. The Associated Scientific and Technical Societies of South Africa; publ. *Transactions*† (monthly).

**South African Institute of Mining and Metallurgy:** Kelvin House, 2 Hollard St., P.O.B. 61019, Marshalltown 2107, Transvaal; f. 1884; 2,186 mems.; Pres. G. Y. NISBET; publ. *Journal*† (monthly), *SAIMM Monograph Series*.

**South African Institution of Civil Engineering:** P.O.B. 61019, Marshalltown 2107, Transvaal; f. 1903; 6,500 mems.; Pres. C. SKEEN; publ. *The Civil Engineer in South Africa* (monthly).

**South African Institution of Mechanical Engineers:** P.O.B. 61019, Marshalltown 2107, Transvaal; f. 1892; 3,000 mems.; Secs. The Associated Scientific and Technical Societies of South Africa; publ. *Journal* (monthly).

# RESEARCH INSTITUTES

(*see* also under Universities)

GENERAL

**Council for Scientific and Industrial Research (CSIR):** Scientia, P.O.B. 395, Pretoria 0001; f. 1945; Pres. Dr. C. F. GARBERS; Deputy Pres. Dr. J. F. KEMP; Vice-Pres. J. P. DE WIT, Dr. G. HEYMANN, Dr. E. N. VAN DEVENTER, Prof. D. H. JACOBSON, Prof. R. R. ARNDT; Sec. J. D. VAN ZYL; mems.: Dr. C. F. GARBERS; (Chair.), Prof. A. J. BRINK, M. T. DE WAAL, D. P. DE VILLIERS, J. W. L. DE VILLIERS, Dr. L. B. KNOLL, Dr. J. G. H. LOUBSER, J. W. SHILLING, Dr. C. VAN DER POL, Prof. H. P. VAN DER SCHIJFF, L. F. RIVE. The Council has attached:

Centre for Scientific and Technical Information, Pretoria; Dir. Dr. R. VAN HOUTEN.

Co-operative Scientific Programmes Group, Pretoria; Gen.-Man. Dr. R. G. NOBLE.

Technical Services Department, Pretoria; Dir. Dr. T. HODGSON.

Information and Research Services, Pretoria; Dir. D. G. KINGWILL.

CSIR Western Cape Regional Office, P.O.B. 288, Bellville 7530.

CSIR Natal Regional Office, P.O.B. 17001, Congella 4013.

CSIR Eastern Cape Regional Office, P.O.B. 1124, Port Elizabeth 6000.

Office of the Scientific Counsellor, Embassy of the Republic of South Africa, Chichester House, 278 High Holborn, London WC1V 7HE, England.

Office of the Scientific Counsellor, Embassy of the Republic of South Africa, 3rd Floor, 2555 M St., N.W., Washington, D.C. 20037, U.S.A.

Office of the Scientific Counsellor, Embassy of thr Republic of South Africa, 5300 Bonn 2, Auf dee Hostert 3, Federal Republic of Germany.

Office of the Scientific Counsellor, Embassy of the Republic of South Africa, 59 Quai d'Orsay, 75007 Paris, France.

**National Chemical Research Laboratory (CSIR):** P.O.B. 395, Pretoria 0001; serves as centre where latest developments in chemical science are brought to bear on problems of national significance; divisions include analytical chemistry, inorganic chemistry, biological chemistry, physical chemistry, a corrosion research division, molecular biochemistry, organic chemistry; Dir. Dr. P. R. ENSLIN.

**Applied Chemistry Unit (CSIR):** P.O.B. 395, Pretoria 0001; undertakes studies into the application of chemistry to various production and engineering problems; research supported by industry; Head Dr. J. P. DE VILLIERS.

**National Physical Research Laboratory (CSIR):** P.O.B. 395, Pretoria 0001; research and development work in response to industrial and national needs; has statutory responsibility for maintaining national standards for the measurement of mass, length, electricity, time, radiation, light, temperature, pressure; has divisions specializing in physical acoustics, optics, crystallography, electron microscopy, geochronology, atmospheric physics, high pressure physics, geophysics, applied spectroscopy, natural isotopes, precise physical measurements, ion bombardment and physics of materials; Dir. Dr. A. STRASHEIM.

**National Research Institute for Mathematical Sciences (CSIR):** P.O.B. 395, Pretoria 0001; research covers various branches of mathematics and their application; participates in development of theory, planning and interpretation of experiments; basic research and services to industry, government and other organizations; divisions: mathematics, computer science, statistics and operations research; Dir. Dr. D. H. JACOBSON.

**National Institute for Aeronautics and Systems Technology (CSIR):** P.O.B. 395, Pretoria 0001; development of multi-disciplinary systems technology and aeronautical research and development; separate divisions for electronic systems, mechanics, aeronautics, and management and technical services; Dir. Dr. T. J. HUGO.

**South African Astronomical Observatory (CSIR):** Headquarters: P.O.B. 9, Observatory 7935, Cape Town; outstation: Sutherland, Cape Province; f. 1972 by a merger of the Royal Cape Observatory and the Republic Observatory in Johannesburg; administered by the CSIR as a national research institute, and financed jointly by the CSIR and the British Science Research Council; equipment includes 1,900-, 1,000-, 750- and 500-mm. reflectors; variety of measuring instruments and computer facilities; staff and visitors engaged in wide variety of astrophysical studies, some topics being variable stars, globular clusters, galactic structure, Magellanic Clouds and other galaxies; also work on minor planets and comets; Dir. Dr. M. W. FEAST.

**National Institute for Telecommunications Research (CSIR):** P.O.B. 3718, Johannesburg 2000; ionospheric research; study of the radiation and propagation of radio waves; monthly forecasts of propagation conditions for high-frequency radio waves; study of lightning and precipitation, by means of radio and radar; development of electromagnetic systems for distance measurement and position fixing; study of advanced techniques in radio and radar; research and development aspects of defence radar and telecommunications; operates a satellite tracking station in co-operation with the French *Centre National d'Etudes Spatiales* (*CNES*); Dir. R. W. VICE.

**Centre for Computing Services (CSIR):** P.O.B. 395, Pretoria 0001; provides CSIR and other research organizations with comprehensive computing services, enhances and maintains computer operating systems, develops and applies methods to measure the performance of large computer systems, and investigates the arrangement of large-scale scientific computing centres and the distribution of computing power; Dir. Dr. E. N. VAN DEVENTER.

**National Institute for Transport and Road Research (CSIR):** P.O.B. 395, Pretoria 0001; research programme aimed primarily at finding practical solutions to problems concerning transportation, road construction and road safety; a transportation branch including groups for transport planning, transport operations, transport systems, traffic engineering, rural transport and transport analysis; a materials and design branch including research groups for soil engineering, treated materials, pavement engineering, maintenance and construction, bridges and concrete pavements; a road safety branch including groups for safety analysis, road users, safety engineering and vehicle safety, a national data bank for roads, a computer services section and a research application and information group; Dir. Dr. S. H. KÜHN.

**National Institute for Water Research (CSIR):** P.O.B. 395, Pretoria 0001; basic and applied research on a contract basis for industries, local authorities, provincial administrations and government departments; research divisions: limnology, water quality, biotechnology, physico-chemical technology, technological application, mineralized waters; regional laboratories in Natal, Orange Free State and the Cape, and also in Namibia (South West Africa); Dir. Dr. G. G. CILLIÉ.

**National Electrical Engineering Research Institute (CSIR):** P.O.B. 395, Pretoria 0001; work covers the various fields of both heavy and light current electrical engineering, particularly automation, e.g., computer technology; solid state electronics, e.g., microcircuit development and applications; application of electronics to instrumentation and measurement, including medical electronics; power electrical engineering, including research on lightning, surges on transmission lines, battery powered vehicles; also divisions for electronic instrumentation, training and information, signal processing; Dir. J. D. N. VAN WYK.

**National Research Institute for Oceanology (CSIR):** P.O.B. 320, Stellenbosch 7600; est. 1974 to take over and merge pre-existing CSIR activities in marine science and technology, and to provide professional, technical and logistic advice, assistance and support to SA and foreign organizations as required for work in the coastal and oceanic areas adjacent to South Africa; research divisions include marine geology and geophysics, marine chemistry and biology, coastal engineering and hydraulics, physical oceanography and technical research and services; runs a national oceanographic data centre and an estuarine research unit; Dir. F. P. ANDERSON.

**National Accelerator Centre:** P.O.B. 320, Stellenbosch 7600; facilities for multi-disciplinary use, for cancer therapy, basic and applied research and production of radioisotopes; work divided between the Accelerator Group and the Pretoria Cyclotron Group; Head Dr. G. HEYMANN.

**National Mechanical Engineering Research Institute (CSIR):** P.O.B. 395, Pretoria 0001; concerned mainly with the development of new ideas and techniques in mechanical engineering, as well as the improvement of machines and materials used in industry; research departments: metal mechanics, strength mechanics, geomechanics, aeromechanics, process mechanics, fluid mechanics, heat mechanics; a mine equipment research unit; Dir. Dr. H. G. DENKHAUS.

**National Building Research Institute (CSIR):** P.O.B. 395, Pretoria 0001; wide research on national problems of the building and construction industry; divisions include architecture; building research application; building services; fire and concrete engineering; environmental engineering; evaluations and performance criteria; geotechnics; inorganic materials; methods and applied economics; organic materials; structural engineering; Dir. Dr. T. L WEBB.

**National Food Research Institute (CSIR):** P.O.B. 395, Pretoria 0001; fundamental and applied research into aspects of food composition, utilization, preservation, packaging and storage, as well as product and process development; research divisions: food chemistry, food technology, biological evaluation, techno-economics, fermentation technology; a microbiology research group and sorghum beer unit; Dir. Dr. L. NOVELLIE.

**National Institute for Personnel Research (CSIR):** P.O.B. 32410, Braamfontein 2017; major fields of research: personnel selection, training, human productivity, occupational psychology; research divisions: management studies, personnel selection and vocational guidance, training studies, psychometrics, test construction, human development, personnel adaptation, neuro-psychology, sensory-motor studies, ergonomics, computer services; Dir. Dr. G. K. NELSON.

**National Timber Research Institute (CSIR):** P.O.B. 395, Pretoria 0001; research into timber engineering, timber economics (including industrial engineering and techno-economic studies), wood processing, pulp and paper; other divisions: composite products, timber harvesting and transport, sawmilling, saw maintenance, wood chemistry, information and liaison services; Dir. Dr. D. L. BOSMAN.

**South African Wool and Textile Research Institute (CSIR):** P.O.B. 1124, Port Elizabeth 6000; research into processing characteristics of wool, mohair, cotton, phormium and other plant fibres; in-depth study of fibre blends, comprehensive services to the textile and clothing industry; research divisions: chemistry, textile dyeing and finishing, topmaking and worsted spinning, scouring, textile physics, statistics, testing services, knitting, weaving and clothing technology, cotton spinning, phorium processing, technical services, publications and information; Dir. Dr. D. W. F. TURPIE.

**Magnetic Observatory (CSIR):** P.O.B. 32, Hermanus 7200; studies of geomagnetism, cosmic rays, the ionosphere; analysis and interpretation of geomagnetic and related time series; library; Head Dr. G. J. KÜHN.

**Chemical Engineering Research Group (CSIR):** P.O.B. 395, Pretoria 0001; studies most aspects of particle technology, particularly solid/liquid separation and related physico-chemical surface phenomena; investigates new chemical processes for converting coal and its products to useful hydro-carbons and develops catalysts for these processes; also investigates problems in the transfer of heat, mass and momentum in areas where design information is insufficient, and develops programmes for computer-aided design in chemical engineering; Head W. G. B. MANDERSLOOT.

**Air Pollution Research Group (CSIR):** P.O.B. 395, Pretoria 0001; studies the chemical and metallic pollutants in city air and the dispersion of pollutants in the atmosphere; conducts long-term surveys of the state of smoke and sulphur dioxide pollution in some cities, studies the potential for pollution dispersion of the atmosphere in regions where industrial development is planned, measures motor vehicle exhaust pollution, co-ordinates research on air pollution in South Africa; research divisions: air pollution physics, air pollution meteorology, air pollution chemistry, monitoring of pollutants; Head Dr. G. P. N. VENTER.

Co-operative industrial research is subsidized through the following autonomous research institutes, registered as non-profitmaking companies and controlled by industrial subscribers:

Fishing Industry Research Institute, Cape Town.
Leather Industries Research Institute, Grahamstown.
Sugar Milling Research Institute, Durban.

Research units, groups and institutes in the following fields (mainly at universities) are supported by way of grants:

Bernard Price Institute for Palaeontological Research, Precambrian Research Unit, Carbohydrate Chemistry Research Unit, Cenozoic and Sedimentological Research Group, Chromatin Research Unit, Cosmic Rays Research Unit, Desert Ecological Research Unit, Flavanoid Chemistry Research Unit, Geochemistry Research Unit, Hydrological Research Unit, Institute for Chromatography, Institute for Environmental Sciences, Institute for Freshwater Studies, Institute for Groundwater Studies, Institute for Geological Research on the Bushveld Complex, Institute for Microstructures, J. L. B. Smith Institute for Ichthyology, Magnetism and Semi-conductor Physics Research Unit, Mammal Research Institute, Percy Fitzpatrick Institute of African Ornithology, Photosynthetic Nitrogen Metabolism Research Unit, Polyene Chemistry Research Unit, Research Group on Solid State Electronics, Solid State Physics Research Group, Southern Universities Nuclear Institute, Tick Research Unit, Uranium Chemistry Research Unit.

Publications†: *CSIR Annual Report, Scientiae* (quarterly), *CSIR—Research for South Africa* (irregular), *CSIR —Organization and Activities* (irregular), *TI—Technical Information for Industry* (monthly), *CSIR Publications* (quarterly), *Calendar of Scientific and Technical Meetings in South Africa* (twice yearly), *Scientific Research Organisations in South Africa* (every 2 years), *Scientific and Technical Societies in South Africa* (every 2 years), *Scientific and Technical Periodicals published in South Africa* (every 2 years); National Institute for Telecommunications Research: *Radio Propagation Predictions for Southern Africa* (monthly), *Monthly Bulletin of Ionospheric Characteristics recorded at Johannesburg and Hermanus*; National Institute for Personnel Research: *Psychologia Africana* (irregular); National Building Research Institute: *NBRI Information Sheets* (every two months); National Institute for Transport and Road Research: *VIA* (2 a year); National Timber Research Unit: *Houtim* (quarterly); National Institute for Water Research: *Water Report* (2 a year); South African Wool and Textile Research Institute: *SAWTRI Bulletin* (quarterly); Magnetic Observatory: *Hermanus Magnetic Bulletin* (monthly), *Hermanus Neutron Monitor Data* (monthly and annually), *Tsumeb Neutron Monitor Data* (annually), *Magnetic Observations at Hermanus, Tsumeb, Hartebeesthoek, Grahamstown, Sanae, Marion* (respectively, annual), *Geomagnetic Secular Variation in Southern Africa* (quinquennially). In addition research reports and other *ad hoc* publications are issued from time to time by various institutes of the CSIR.

### AGRICULTURE AND VETERINARY SCIENCE

**Directorate of Agricultural Research (Pretoria):** Dept. of Agricultural Technical Services, Private Bag X116, Pretoria; cultural research; Sec. Dr. D. W. IMMELMAN; publs. *South African Journal of Agricultural Science:* (i) *Agroplantae* (plant sciences), (ii) *Agroanimalia* (animal sciences), (iii) *Agrochemophysica* (chemical and physical sciences), (iv) *Phytophylactica* (plant protection sciences and microbiology) (all quarterly); *Onderstepoort Journal for Veterinary Research* (bi-annually), *Bothalia* (annually), *Botanical Survey Memoirs* (bi-annually), *Flowering Plants of Southern Africa* (bi-annually), *Flora of Southern Africa* (annually), *Technical Communications* (monthly), *Agricultural Research* (annually), *Entomology Memoirs* (irregular), scientific pamphlets, monthly popular science publications, irregular publications, etc.; the Directorate controls the following specialized and regional research institutes:

**Animal Husbandry and Dairy Research Institute:** Private Bag X2, Irene 1675; f. 1962; performance and progeny testing of and fundamental research on breeding, nutrition and physiology of farm animals; Dir. Dr. J. H. HOFMEYR.

**Botanical Research Institute:** Private Bag X101, Pretoria 0001; botanical surveys, classification of plants and study of morphology, taxonomy and ecology of South African flora; administers the National Herbarium at Pretoria; Dir. Dr. B. DE WINTER.

**Citrus and Subtropical Fruit Research Institute:** Private Bag X11208, Nelspruit; research on citrus and subtropical fruit for the entire Republic; Dir. Dr. J. H. GROBLER.

**Fruit and Food Technology Research Institute:** Private Bag X5013, Stellenbosch 7600; research on deciduous fruit under winter rainfall conditions and food technology research; Dir. Dr. P. G. MARAIS.

**Horticultural Research Institute:** Roodeplaat, Private Bag X293, Pretoria 0001; research on horticulture (deciduous fruits, vegetables and ornamental plants) under summer rainfall conditions; Dir. E. STRYDOM.

**Plant Protection Research Institute:** Private Bag X134, Pretoria 0001; fundamental and applied research on plant pathology, microbiology and taxonomy of insects; economic zoology, toxicology of insecticides and biology and control of insect pests; Dir. Dr. I. H. WIESE.

**Soils and Irrigation Research Institute:** Private Bag X79, Pretoria 0001; classification and mapping of soils; chemical research; analysis of soils, water, rock, plant materials, fertilizers, weedicides, insecticides and fungicides; Dir. Dr. M. C. F. DU PLESSIS.

**Tobacco Research Institute:** Kroondal, Rustenburg 0300; research on culture and technology of tobacco; Dir. Dr. D. J. ROSSOUW.

**Veterinary Research Institute:** Onderstepoort, Pretoria; research on animal diseases (infectious and functional, including disease caused by malnutrition); production of vaccines and remedies; biological evaluation of dips and remedies offered for registration; Dir. Dr. K. E. WEISS.

**Viticultural and Oenological Research Institute:** Nietvoorby, Private Bag X5026, Stellenbosch 7600; Research on viticulture and wine technology; Dir. Dr. J. BURGER.

**Regional Research Institutes:** Transvaal (Private Bag X180, Pretoria 0001), Highveld (Private Bag X804, Potchefstroom 2520), O.F.S. (P.O. Glen, 9360), Karroo (Grootfontein Agricultural College, Private Bag X519, Middleburg C.P. 5900), Natal (Cedara Agricultural College, Private Bag X9059, Pietermaritzburg 3200), Eastern Cape (Dohne Agricultural Research Station, Private Bag X15, Stutterheim 4930); Winter Rainfall (Private Bag X5023, Pretoria 0001); Namibia (South West Africa), Private Bag X13184, Windhoek 9100; Institute for Crops and Pastures (Private Bag X116, Pretoria 0001).

**South African Forestry Research Institute:** P.O.B. 727, Pretoria 0001; f. 1919; headquarters of the Research Branch of the Dept. of Forestry of the Republic of South Africa; research undertaken at the institute and in field stations includes timber technology, silviculture, tree-breeding, conservation, forestry and catchment research; Chief Dir. for Research and Information Dr. H. A. LÜCKHOFF; publs. *Journal*, bulletins, papers, etc.

**South African Society of Dairy Technology:** Dept. of Food Science, University of Pretoria; f. 1967; approx. 700 mems.; Pres. C. E. CHEESMAN; Sec. Prof. S. H. LOMBARD; publ. *South African Journal of Dairy Technology* (quarterly).

### MEDICINE

**College of Medicine of South Africa, The:** 17 Milner Rd., Rondebosch 7700; f. 1954; provides postgraduate examinations in all branches of medicine for all doctors in South Africa; c. 3,000 mems.; small archive and reference library; Pres. Prof. F. GELDENHUYS; Sec. Mrs. B. BOTHMA; publ. *Transactions*† (2 a year).

**Natal Institute of Immunology:** P.O.B. 2356, Durban 4000; f. 1968; (Division of the Natal Blood Transfusion Service); a research institute of the University of Natal; 7 research divisions with interests in clinical immunology, HL-A typing, immune response in primates, cell culture, immunoassay and human genetics; 37 mems.; library of 4,000 vols.; Dir. Prof. PETER BRAIN.

**South African Institute for Medical Research (SAIMR):** Hospital St., Johannesburg; f. 1912; medical research into the causes, treatment and methods of prevention of human diseases, with emphasis on those of particular relevance to Southern Africa; diagnostic pathology services in 62 regional laboratories situated in Johannesburg, Witwatersrand area and the rest of the Transvaal, Northern and Eastern Cape, Orange Free State and Namibia (South West Africa); training of laboratory technologists; teaching of under- and postgraduate students is provided by the School of Pathology, the staff being joint members of SAIMR and the University of the Witwatersrand; organized in four divisions: Research, Diagnostic, Production of Vaccines and Sera, Education; library of 14,000 vols., 520 serial titles, 2,500 reprint titles of staff papers; Chair. of Board of Management P. H. ANDERSON; Dir. Prof. J. METZ; Head of Dept. of Medical Biochemistry Prof. C. ROSENDORFF (acting); Head of Dept. of Haematology Prof. B. A. BRADLOW; Head of Dept. of Anatomical Pathology Prof. C. ISAACSON; Head of Dept. of Microbiology Prof. H. J. KOORNHOF; Head of Dept. of Human Genetics Prof. T. JENKINS; Head of Dept. of Immunology Prof. A. R. RABSON; Head of Dept. of Tropical Pathology and Dept. of Epidemiology Prof. M. ISAACSON; publ. *Annual Report*.

### NATURAL SCIENCES
#### Biological Sciences

**Municipal Botanic Gardens** (*Parks, Recreation and Beaches Department, Durban Corporation*): 70 St. Thomas' Rd., Durban; f. ca. 1849; for the propagation and development of ornamental and useful plants, shrubs, trees, etc., and as a place of instruction in botany, horticulture and the related subjects; Dir. Parks, Recreation and Beaches T. A. LINLEY, F.I P R.A.(S.A.), A.INST. P.R.A. (G.B.); Curator, Durban Botanic Gardens K. J. WYMAN, A.I.P.R.A.(S.A.).

**National Botanic Gardens of South Africa:** Head Office: Kirstenbosch, Newlands, Cape Province; Regional Gardens at Worcester, Betty's Bay, Bloemfontein, Harrismith, Pietermaritzburg, Nelspruit; f. 1913 for scientific and educational purposes; the collection, cultivation, display and study of the indigenous flora of South Africa; the preservation of the native vegetation of Southern Africa; Dir. Prof. H. B. RYCROFT; publ. *Journal of South African Botany*† (quarterly).

**National Zoological Gardens of South Africa:** P.O.B. 754, Pretoria; f. 1899; Dir. Dr. D. J. BRAND, M.SC., PH.D., F.Z.S.; publ. *Zoon*†.

#### Physical Sciences

**Boyden Observatory:** P.O.B. 334, Bloemfontein; f. 1891; now Dept. of Astronomy of the University of the Orange Free State; photoelectric photometry, spectroscopy, interferometry, photography, variable star survey, southern sky patrol; Dir. Prof. A. H. JARRETT.

**Geological Survey of South Africa:** Private Bag X112, Pretoria 0001; f. 1912; applied and fundamental geological research, mapping; staff of 355; library of 6,000 vols. and 48,000 periodicals; Dir. L. N. J. ENGELBRECHT; publs. *Bibliographies*†, *Annals*† (annually), *Bulletins*†, *Memoirs*†, *Sheet Maps and Explanations*†, *Seismological Series*†, *Handbooks*†, *Special Publications*†.

**Leiden Southern Station:** P.O.B. 13, Broederstroom 0240; astronomy; Superintendent D. F. STEVENSON.

**Radio Space Research Station:** P.O.B. 3718, Johannesburg 2000; f. 1961 as part of U.S. Deep Space and Satellite Tracking Networks; operated since 1975 by SA CSIR as Radio Astronomy Observatory (Head Dr. G. D. NICOLSON) and Satellite Remote Sensing Centre (Head W. J. BOTHA); library of about 500 vols. and 30 periodicals.

**South African Atomic Energy Board:** Private Bag X256, Pretoria 0001; f. 1949; activities include Chemistry, Extraction Metallurgy, Geology, Isotopes and Radiation, Life Sciences, Physical Metallurgy, Physics, Process Metallurgy, Reactor Development, Instrumentation and Licensing of nuclear installations, library of 329,040 vols.; Pres. J. W. L. DE VILLIERS; publs. *Annual Report†*, *Nuclear Active†* (every 6 months), *PEL—Reports†*, *PER-Reports†*.

RELIGION, SOCIOLOGY AND ANTHROPOLOGY

**Human Sciences Research Council (HSRC):** Private Bag X41, Pretoria 0001; est. 1969 as a corporate body controlled by a council, consisting of a full-time President and ten other members appointed by the Minister of National Education. The HSRC controls all matters with regard to research and development in the field of human sciences, including the humanities and social sciences. It undertakes, promotes, coordinates (by means of the S.A. Plan for Research in the Human Sciences) and finances research as approved by the Minister of National Education and advises the Minister on research to be undertaken. It also co-operates with persons and authorities in other countries and acts as liaison between the Republic and other countries in connection with research in human sciences. The Council awards bursaries and grants for research, publishes research findings or financially supports the publication thereof, fosters the training of persons for research work and incorporates the following research institutes: Institute for Educational Research, Institute for Manpower Reseach, Institute for Psychological and Psychometric Research, Institute for Sociological, Demographic and Criminological Research, Institute for Statistical Research, Institute for Languages, Literature and Arts, Institute for Communication Research, Institute for Historical Research, Institute for Research Development; Pres. Dr. J. G. GARBERS; Vice-Pres. Dr. A. J. v. ROOY, Dr. P. SMIT and Dr. J. D. VENTER; Sec.-Treas. J. G. G. GRÄBE; publs. *HSRC Annual Report*, *Humanitas*, *Journal for Research in the Human Sciences*, *Research Bulletin* (10 a year), *RSA 2000*, *Contree*, *Research Reports*, *Newsletter* (monthly).

**Institute for the Study of Man in Africa:** Room A16, Old Medical School, Hospital St., Johannesburg 2001; f. 1960 to perpetuate the work of Prof. Raymond A. Dart on the study of man in Africa, past and present, in health and disease; associated with the Museum of Man and serves as a centre of anthropological and medical field work; it functions partly through the auspices of the University of the Witwatersrand; Pres. N. J. PINES.

TECHNOLOGY

**National Institute for Metallurgy:** Private Bag X3015, Randburg 2125; f. 1934; library of 37,000 vols.; research and development work in response to the needs, national and private, of the mineral industry; investigates all aspects of the extraction of metals and minerals from their ores and the physical metallurgy of metallurgical plant; divisions specializing in mineralogy, ore-dressing, process development, instrumentation and control, mineral and process chemistry; sponsors university research groups; Pres. Dr. L. ALBERTS; publs. *Research Reports* (irregular), *Minerals Science and Engineering†* (quarterly), *NIM Research Digest* (quarterly), *Annual Report†*.

**Sea Fisheries Institute:** Private Bag X2, 8012 Rogge Bay; f. 1895; fisheries research and administration, oceanography and marine pollution including oil; 8 research vessels; total research staff 116; library of 3,200 vols., 1,000 periodical titles and about 20,000 pamphlets; Dir. G. H. STANDER; publs. *Annual Reports†*, *Investigational Report†* (irregular), *Fisheries Bulletin†* (irregular).

**South African Bureau of Standards:** Private Bag X191, Dr. Lategan Rd., Groenkloof, Pretoria; f. 1945; 1,100 mems.; draws up national standards, specifications, codes of practice, administers the SABS mark scheme; library of 24,500 vols.; Dir. Gen. G. P. VERSTER; publ. *Bulletin†*.

# LIBRARIES AND ARCHIVES

### Bloemfontein

**Bloemfontein Regional Library/Bloemfonteinse Streekbiblioteek:** P.B. X20606; Regional Librarian H. S. FOURIE.

**Free State Provincial Library Service/Vrystaatse Provinsiale Biblioteekdiens:** P.B. X20606; f. 1948; consists of Central Organization and Regional Libraries at Bloemfontein, Kroonstad and Bethlehem, serving 330 libraries, school libraries and depots; book stock 2,430,663; Dir. G. L. NORDIER, B.A.; publ. *Free State Libraries* (quarterly).

**Public Library:** P.O.B. 1029; f. 1875; Copyright, Legal Deposit, National Drama library, and Public library; 268,201 vols.; Librarian P. J. VAN DER WALT; publ. *Catalogue of the National Drama Library* and supplement.

**University of the Orange Free State Library:** Bloemfontein; f. 1906; the collection includes rare pamphlets and other early South African publications of the Dreyer-Africana Collection; 350,000 vols. (3,300 magazines); Dir. H. DE BRUIN, B.A., H.D.B., M.BIBL.

### Cape Town

**Cape Education Department Library Service:** 14 Queen Victoria St.; f. 1970; Head Miss P. B. EHLERS; comprises:

*Education Department Library:* f. 1895; professional library and reference service for teachers in the Cape Province and officials and research workers in the Cape Education Dept.; 86,000 vols., 300 current periodicals; Head Miss E. M. MALAN; publ. *Catalogue of the Education Library* (every 2 months).

*School Library Service:* f. 1964; model library and advisory service for teacher-librarians; 25,600 vols., 109 current periodicals; Head Mrs. W. A. FERGUSON; publs. *Booklist for high school libraries*, *Booklist for primary school libraries*, *Reference works and periodicals* (all annually), *Subject lists* (irregularly).

**Cape Provincial Library Service:** P.O.B. 2108, Cape Town; f. 1945; consists of Central Library, Cape Town, 18 regional libraries serving 241 affiliated municipal public libraries and 372 library depots in Cape Province; Dir. G. R. MORRIS, B.A., F.S.A.I.L.I.S.; Librarians Miss J. TE GROEN, Mrs. M. B. GERTZ.

**Cape Town City Libraries:** P.O.B. 4728; f. 1952; free municipal public library service; central library and 34 suburban brs., travelling, hospital, old age homes library services; 1,000,000 vols.; Librarian C. H. VERMEULEN; publ. *Annual Report*.

**Library of Parliament:** Parliament House, P.O.B. 18, Cape Town 8000; f. 1857; 200,000 items, including Government documents and the Mendelssohn Library of Africana, which contains 45,000 vols. on Africa, especially South Africa; Librarian J. C. QUINTON.

**Library of the Royal Society of South Africa:** c/o University of Cape Town, Rondebosch 7700; f. 1877; 33,000 vols. of scientific periodicals; Librarian Prof. B. WARNER, PH.D., D.SC., F.R.A.S., F.INST.P.

**South African Library:** Queen Victoria St., Cape Town 8001; f. 1818; contains rare book collections, including Grey, Dessinian and Fairbridge collections, also Africana and Muir Mathematical (periodical) collections, and MSS.; National Reference and Research Library with Legal Deposit privileges; 530,000 vols.; Dir. A. M. LEWIN ROBINSON, B.A., PH.D., F.L.A.; publs. *Quarterly Bulletin†*, *Grey Bibliographies†*, *Reprint Series*.

**University of Cape Town Libraries:** Private Bag, Rondebosch 7700; f. 1829; 793,366 vols., 8,046 current periodicals, 49,281 drawings, plans and illustrations, incl. Architectural Library of 21,867 vols., 239 current periodicals; Education Library of 28,696 vols., 234 current periodicals; Hiddingh Hall Library of 45,301 vols., 49 current periodicals; Institute of Child Health Library of 3,820 vols., 115 current periodicals; Law Library of 22,641 vols. (incl. Van Zyl Collection of Roman Dutch Law), 262 current periodicals; Medical Library of 97,889 vols. (incl. Medical History Collection), 929 current periodicals; Music Library of 11,413 vols. (incl. Music Africana Collection), 83 current periodicals, 42,467 items of printed music, 11,738 records. Special collections incl. African Studies Collection (central and southern Africa); Ballot Collection (18th-century Dutch books); Bowle-Evans Collection (English literary works, 1680-1830); Cape Town Diocesan Library; Crawford Collection (mathematical monographs); Clifford Hall Collection (fore-edge paintings); Duker Collection (Jewish history and culture); Kipling Collection; Lady Mossop Chinese Collection; Royal Society of South Africa library; Silverman Collection (Hebraica); Swellendam Church Library; Western European Cultural History Collection; Willis Collection (naval history). Non-book collections incl. McMillan Collection of South African illustrations; Sibbett Collection of pictorial matter on Rhodes and his contemporaries; MSS. collections of letters and documents of prominent South African literary and public figures, incl. W. G. Ballinger, Dr. W. H. I. Bleek (Bushman and Bantu linguistics and ethnology), Sir Patrick Duncan, H. G. Lawrence, C. Louis Leipoldt, Donald Molteno, Olive Schreiner, Pauline Smith, Sir Walter Stanford, Sir Baldwin Walker (naval history); South African music MSS., incl. W. H. Bell and Erik Chisholm; the F. K. Kendall and Marriott Earle Collection of architectural plans and documents relating to the work of Sir Herbert Baker, 1895-1920; archival material incl. the University Archive and the Leo Marquard Collection (N.U.S.A.S. archive). Librarian: A. S. C. HOOPER, M.S.L.S., P.S.A. I.L.I.S.; publs. *U.C.T. Bibliographical series†*, *Varia series†*.

### Durban

**Durban Municipal Library:** City Hall, P.O.B. 917, Durban; f. 1853; 600,000 vols.; special collections of Africana and Shakespeareana; 8 br. libraries and 10 depot libraries.

**University of Natal Library.**

**Durban Campus:** King George V Ave., Durban 4001; University Librarian F. SCHOLTZ, B.A., F.S.A.I.L.I.S.
*Main Library:* f. 1922; 176,901 vols.; Powell Collection of Early Science and Technology and Webb Collection of works by Black Authors.
*Architectural Branch Library:* f. 1969; 12,404 vols.; Assistant Librarian Miss H. D. SHERWOOD, B.A., P.S.A.I.L.I.S.
*Eleanor Bonnar Music Branch Library:* f. 1971; 3,960 vols.; Assistant Librarian Mrs. J. H. ENGELBRECHT, B.MUS., P.S.A.I.L.I.S.
*G. M. J. Sweeney Law Branch Library:* f. 1972; 12,350 vols.; Librarian Mrs. M. G. MORTON, B.SC., P.S.A.I.L.I.S.
*Killie Campbell Africana Library:* f. 1935; 59,313 items; Librarian Miss J. F. DUGGAN, B.A., P.S.A. I.L.I.S.
*Medical School Branch Library:* f. 1951; 37,016 vols.; Librarian Miss C. B. MAGUIRE, A.L.A., P.S.A.I.L.I.S.
*Science and Engineering Branch Library:* f. 1973; 36,004 vols.; houses Industrial Information Centre (2,319 vols.); Librarian Miss M. M. VAN DER WALT, B.A., P.S.A.I.L.I.S.

**Pietermaritzburg Campus:** see under Pietermaritzburg.

### East London

**East London Municipal Library Service:** Buxton St., P.O.B. 652; f. 1876; 30,000 mems.; 180,000 vols.; Librarian Miss M. H. VAN DEVENTER, F.S.A.I.L.I.S.

### Fort Hare

**University of Fort Hare Library:** P.B. 1322, Alice 5700; f. 1916; 110,000 vols.; contains the Howard Pim Library of Africana; Librarian M. SPRUYT, B.A., LL.DRS., DIP.(LIBR.).

### Grahamstown

**Grahamstown Public Library:** Free Municipal Library; P.O.B. 180; f. 1842; 71,849 vols.; Librarian Miss M. J. HARTZENBERG.

**Rhodes University Library:** Rhodes University, P.O.B. 184, Grahamstown 6140; f. 1904; 260,000 vols.; Cory Library for Historical Research; Librarian G. D. QUINN.

### Johannesburg

**Johannesburg Public Library:** Market Square; f. 1890; 1,439,659 vols.; Librarian Miss L. KENNEDY, B.A., F.S.A.I.L.I.S.; publs. *Annual Report†*, *Index to S.A. Periodicals* (annual), *Municipal Reference Library Bulletin* (monthly), bibliographies (occasional).

**Library of the South African Institute of Race Relations:** P.O.B. 97; f. 1929; 5,685 vols.; valuable archival and documentary material; newspaper clippings from 1930; microfilming service; bibliographies on race relations; photocopy service; Librarian S. R. MOKOBANE.

**University of the Witwatersrand Library:** Private Bag 31550, Braamfontein 2017; f. 1922; 751,495 vols.; two central libraries (undergraduate and research), also Divisional and Constituent Libraries: Architecture, Biological Sciences, Business Administration, Dental, Geology and Mining, Engineering, Geography, Geophysics, International Affairs, Law, Mathematical Sciences, Medical, Nuclear Physics, Palaeontology, Performing Arts, Physical Sciences. Special Collections: Africana, Hebraica and Judaica, Portuguese, Archaeology and Egyptology, Historical and Literary Papers (incl. Church of the Province of South Africa), Early Printed Books; Librarian R. MUSIKER, B.SC., M.A., DIP.LIB., F.S.A.I.L.I.S.

### Kimberley

**Kimberley Public Library:** P.O.B. 627; f. 1882; c. 90,000 vols.; Librarian Mrs. F. VAN NIEKERK, B.A.

### Pietermaritzburg

**Natal Provincial Library Service:** Private Bag X9016; f. 1952; consists of central organization and reference

## LIBRARIES AND ARCHIVES

library at Pietermaritzburg; four regional offices for north coast, south coast, midlands and northern areas, serving 118 public libraries, 117 library depots, 136 school libraries, 34 departmental libraries; 1,447,381 vols.; film lending service with 891 films; gramophone record lending service with 12,692 records; Dir. C. J. FOURIE, M.A.; publ. *Libri Natales*† (monthly).

**Natal Society Public Library:** P.O.B. 415, Pietermaritzburg, Natal; f. 1851; lending, reference and legal deposit library; children's br. library; 232,366 vols.; Librarian Mrs. S. S. WALLIS, M.A.; publ. *Natalia* (annual).

**University of Natal Library, Pietermaritzburg Campus:** P.O.B. 375; f. 1909; 200,000 vols.; Librarian Miss C. VIETZEN.

**Durban Campus:** *see under* Durban.

### Port Elizabeth

**Port Elizabeth City Libraries:** P.O.B. 66; f. 1965; 408,198 vols.; City Librarian DONALD RODGER, B.A., LIB.DIP.

**University of Port Elizabeth Library:** Private Bag X6058, 6000; f. 1964; 235,000 vols., 2,055 current periodicals; Librarian J. C. CRONJÉ, B.A., F.S.A.I.L.I.S.; publs. *Libra*† (annual), *Periodicals and other serial publications received*† (irregular), *List of new accessions*† (monthly).

### Potchefstroom

**Potchefstroom University for Christian Higher Education Libraries:** f. 1921; 475,524 vols., 4,816 current periodicals; Main Library (Ferdinand Postma Library), Library of the Theological School of the Reformed Church in South Africa, Conservatoire of Music Library, Natural Sciences Library, Vaal River Branch Library at Vanderbijlpark, Small Business Advisory Bureau Library; special collections: Carney Africana Collection, Hertzog Law Collection, Collection of the Institute for Research in Children's Literature; Librarian C. J. H. LESSING, M.A., F.S.A.I.L.I.S.; publs. *Union Catalogue of Theses and Dissertations of South African Universities*, *Abstracts of Theses and Dissertations accepted for higher Degrees in the Potchefstroom University*.

### Pretoria

**Central Agricultural Library:** Private Bag 116; f. 1910, 58,950 vols., 1,453 current periodicals; branch libraries in each of the research institutes under the Directorate of Agricultural Research (*q.v.*); Librarian J. A. REYNECKE.

**Council for Scientific and Industrial Research (CSIR) Library:** P.O.B. 395, Pretoria 0001; f. 1945; *c.* 150,000 bound vols., 7,300 serial titles and 22,000 pamphlets; scientific and technical collections; 8 brs.; Librarian Mrs. J. I. SNYMAN, P.S.A.I.L.I.S.; publs. *Periodicals in Southern African Libraries* (on behalf or the National Library Advisory Council).

**Department of National Education Library:** Private Bag X122; special collections: general education, educa- of the handicapped, library science, philology, psychology, domestic science; 87,000 vols., 330 current periodicals, 10,000 S.A. university theses and dissertations; Librarian Mrs. J. REDELINGHUYS.

**Human Sciences Research Council Library:** S.A. Agricultural Union Bldg., Schoeman St., Pretoria, Private Bag X41; f. 1969; *c.* 79,000 vols.; 1,100 current periodicals (titles); loan; reference, current awareness service and retrospective searches for research staff; collection on human and social sciences; Librarian J. FOURIE, B.A.

**State Library:** P.O.B. 397, Pretoria 0001; f. 1887; national and legal depository library, and depository library for U.S. Government and UN publications; 750,000 vols., 6,330 current periodicals; responsible for the Joint Catalogue of Books in South African Libraries; National and Inter-library Loans centre; South Africa book exchange centre; ISBN and ISSN centre for South Africa; Dir. H. J. ASCHENBORN, M.A., PH.D.; publs. *South African National Bibliography*† (quarterly and annual cumulations), *State Library Bibliographies*, *Contributions to Library Science*, *Africana Reprint Series* (all irregular), *Annual Report*, *Union Catalogue of Monographs in South African Libraries* (on microfiche, quarterly), *Bibliography of overseas publications about South Africa*† (2 a year), *Index to South African periodicals* (5 a year on microfiche), *Government Gazette* (on microfiche, quarterly), *Government Gazette Index* (hard copy and microfiche, quarterly), *Microfiche Series* (irregular),

**Transvaal Education Library and Audio-Visual Ancillary Service:** 328 Van der Walt St., Private Bag X290, Pretoria 0001; f. 1951; Dir. Miss C. F. M. VAN WYK; comprises *Education Library:* 170,000 vols., 1,000 periodicals; subject specialization, SDI services according to user profiles, alphabetic subject catalogue, information retrieval system for periodicals (based on EUDISED); publs. *Book Catalogue* (with annual supplement), bibliographies. *Centralized Services to School Media Centres:* Model Media Centre, 50,000 vols.; book selection; evaluation of audio-visual software; catalogue for media centre (incl. hardware); Media-advisers: advisory services, courses for teacher-librarians; publs. *Media Guide* (5 a year), bibliographies for school subjects, *Skoolmediasentrum/School Media Centre* (2 a year). *Audio-Visual Services:* hardware and software information services, technical and professional advisory services to schools, courses in the use of instructional media.

**Transvaal Provincial Library Service:** Private Bag X288, Pretoria 0001; f. 1943; consists of Central Organization and Reference Library at Pretoria and 16 Regional Libraries; entire province served by 214 affiliated public libraries and 314 depots; 4,313,914 vols.; Dir. S. C. J. VAN NIEKERK, B.A., F.S.A.I.L.I.S.; publs. *Book Parade* (quarterly), *Overvaal Musea News* (quarterly).

**University of Pretoria Libraries:** f.1 908; 649,718 vols., pamphlets, Govt. publs., periodicals, etc., 5,801 gramophone records, 19,406 sheet-music; Main Library (Merensky Library), Macfadyen Library, Central Medical Library, Basic Medical Science Library, Music Library, Veterinary Science Library, Agricultural Sciences Library; Special Collections: Africana, Goethe, Jacob de Villiers, J. Roos, J. du Plessis, Brand, Luther, F. van der Merwe; Dir. E. D. GERRYTS, M.A. (BIBL.), D.LITT.ET.PHIL. (BIBL.).

**University of S. Africa, Sanlam Library:** P.O.B. 392, Pretoria; f. 1947; 712,000 vols., 78,000 bound serials, 70,000 items microfilm, audio-visual materials, 6,200 current periodicals; Science Library, Music Library and Law Library specializing in Foreign and Comparative Law; brs. in Cape Town, Durban and Windhoek; Librarian J. WILLEMSE, M.A., T.H.O.D., F.S.A.L.A.; publ. *Mousaion* (irregular).

**Government Archives Service:** Private Bag X236, Union Buildings, Pretoria 0001; Dir. of Archives for the Republic of South Africa J. F. PRELLER; administers the following depots:

*Cape Archives Depot:* Private Bag X9025, Queen Victoria St., Cape Town; Asst. Dir. S. J. SCHOEMAN.

*Transvaal Archives Depot:* Private Bag X236, Union Buildings, Pretoria 0001; Asst. Dir. G. J. RENECKE.

*Central Archives Depot:* Private Bag X236, Union Buildings, Pretoria 0001; Asst. Dir. G. J. RENECKE.

*Orange Free State Archives Depot:* Private Bag X0504, Elizabeth St., Bloemfontein 9300; Chief Archivist J. W. CRONJE.

*Natal Archives Depot:* Private Bag X9012, Pietermaritz St., Pietermaritzburg 3200; Chief Archivist F. NEL.

*Archives Intermediate Depot, Transvaal:* Private Bag X236, Union Buildings, Pretoria 0001 and Heyvries Buildings, Pretorius St., Pretoria 0001; Chief Archivist A. F. DE VILLIERS.

*Archives Intermediate Depot, Cape:* Private Bag X9025, Cape Town 8000; Senior Archivist M. PRINS.

*Record Management Section:* Private Bag X236, Union Buildings, Pretoria; Asst. Dir. D. J. J. SMITH.

*Data Processing Section:* Private Bag X236, Union Buildings, Pretoria 0001; Chief Archivist M. OLIVIER.

*Publications Section:* Private Bag X236, Union Buildings, Pretoria 0001; Chief Archivist D. C. JOUBERT.

The administration of the Director of Archives also embraces the following: Section State Historians (State Historian: Dr. J. H. BREYTENBACH); National Monuments Commission; Heraldry Section (State Herald N. F. HARTMAN); S.A. Defence Force Archives.

### Stellenbosch

**University of Stellenbosch Library:** University of Stellenbosch, Private Bag 5036, Van Ryneveld St.; f. 1900; 554,000 vols., 7,176 current periodicals; 7 brs.; Librarian F. DU PLESSIS, F.S.A.I.L.I.S.; publ. *Annals of the University of Stellenbosch†* (irregular).

## MUSEUMS AND ART GALLERIES

### Bloemfontein

**National Museum:** P.O.B. 266; f. 1877; Institute for Herpetology, Ornithology, Mammalogy, Arachnology, Palaeontology, Archaeology, Local History, Anthropology, Entomology and Ethnology; the unique Florisbad human fossil skull housed here; library of 4,400 vols., 2,600 serial titles; Dir. J. J. OBERHOLZER, M.SC.; publs. *Memoirs†, Navorsinge van die Nasionale Museum†/Researches of the National Museum†, Museum News/Museum Nuus.*

### Cape Town

**Maritime Museum:** The Castle; f. 1971; ship models, maritime Africana oils and prints, uniforms, swords, etc.

**Military Museum:** The Castle; f. 1966; uniforms, swords, military paintings, war medals, pistols, rifles, etc.
(Both museums administered by the Directorate of Military Museums, P.B. X175, Pretoria.)

**Michaelis Collection:** The Old Town House, Greenmarket Square; f. 1917; Dutch and Flemish paintings and graphic art of the 16th-18th centuries; Dir. J. C. HAAK.

**South African Museum:** P.O.B. 61, Cape Town 8000; f. 1825; archaeology, ethnology, zoology, palaeontology, marine biology, entomology; library of c. 7,600 vols. and c. 4,000 periodicals; Dir. Prof. T. H. BARRY; publs. *Annals†, Reports†, Brochures†.*

**South African Cultural History Museum:** P.O.B. 645, Cape Town 8000; f. 1966; decorative arts, archaeology, history; library of 5,884 vols. and pamphlets; Dir. A. P. ROUX.

*Groot Constantia:* Constantia Rd., Wynberg; restored 18th-century manor house displaying period furniture, porcelain, paintings and illustrating country life at the Cape during the 18th and 19th centuries; wine museum in 18th-century wine cellar containing drinking vessels dating from antiquity to the 19th century.

*Bertram House:* Orange Street, Gardens, Cape Town; late Georgian red brick town house illustrating the domestic life of the English during the early 19th century.

*Koopmans de Wet House:* 35 Strand St.; unique specimen of 18th-century Cape Dutch house displaying rare period furniture, silver, glass, china and pictures, and illustrating the conditions of domestic life in South Africa in the 18th and 19th centuries.

*Bo-Kaap Museum:* 71 Wale St.; 19th-century Cape Moslem home.

**William Fehr Collection:** The Castle, Cape Town; f. 1965; antique Cape furniture, silver, copper, glass, and Africana oils (Rust en Vreugd, Buitenkant St.; collection of Africana water colours and prints); Dir. Mrs. E. J. PAAP; publs. *Rust en Vreugd, Treasures at the Castle.*

**South African National Gallery:** Government Ave., P.O.B. 2420; f. 1871; 19th- and 20th-century South African art; 20th-century African art; 16th-20th-century European art; "Touch Gallery" for the blind; library of 5,000 vols.; Dir. Dr. R. H. VAN NIEKERK.

### Durban

**Durban Museum and Art Gallery:** City Hall, Smith St., P.O.B. 4085, Durban 4000; f. 1887; South African fauna, flora, ethnography, archaeology, paintings, graphic art, porcelain, sculptures, local history; Dir. P. A. CLANCEY; publ. *Novitates.*

**Local History Museum:** Old Court House, Aliwal St.; f. 1966; local and Natal historical collections; Dir. P. A. CLANCEY, A.M.A.; Curator of Local History Mrs. D. H. STRUTT, A.M.A.

### East London

**East London Museum:** 319 Oxford St.; f. 1921; research departments and displays of conchology, ichthyology, malacology, ornithology of the Eastern Cape Province, cultural history of the Border region and ethnography of the Southern Nguni tribal group; houses first Coelacanth caught in 1938; educational service; administers Victorian house museum; Chair. Board of Trustees B. W. WATSON; Dir. E. H. BIGALKE; publs. *Cape Provincial Museums Annals†* (jointly with 4 other museums), *Annual Report†.*

### Franschhoek

**Huguenot Memorial Museum:** Lambrechts St., P.O.B. 37, Franschhoek; f. 1967; research into Cape Huguenot history, exhibition of over 400 Huguenot pieces and documents; 450 mems.; Chair. S. THERON; Curator (vacant); publ. *Bulletin of the Huguenot Society of South Africa†.*

### Grahamstown

**Albany Museum:** f. 1855; archaeology, entomology, freshwater ichthyology, freshwater invertebrates, 1820 British Settler history; maintains school service, circulation of display cases throughout eastern Cape Province; Dir. B. C. WILMOT; publ. *Cape Provincial Museums Annals†* (jointly with 4 other museums, irregularly).

## MUSEUMS AND ART GALLERIES — SOUTH AFRICA

### Johannesburg

**Adler Museum of the History of Medicine:** University of the Witwatersrand, P.O.B. 1038, Johannesburg 2000; f. 1962; collection of medical, dental and surgical instruments and equipment; reconstructions of early 20th-century pharmacy, doctor's and dentist's surgeries, African herb shop, 1900 hospital, library of over 8,000 vols. and a rare book collection, others written and autographed by S.A. doctors; photographs, pictures, etc.; Dir./Curator Dr. C. ADLER, D.PHYS.MED., F.R.S.S.AF.; publ. *Bulletin*† (3 a year).

**Africana Museum:** Public Library, Market Square; f. 1935; history and ethnology of Africa south of the Zambezi; Curator Mrs. E. B. NAGELGAST; publs. *Africana Notes and News* (quarterly), *Annual Report*, catalogues of special exhibitions, Frank Connock publications.

**Africana Museum in Progress:** Bree St., Newtown; f. 1979; ethnology, archaeology, toys and dolls.

**Bensusan Museum of Photography:** 17 Empire Rd., Parktown; f. 1969; history of photography, particularly in South Africa.

**Bernberg Museum of Costume:** 1 Duncombe Rd., Forest Town; f. 1973; costumes and accessories dating from c. 1790.

**Geological Museum:** Public Library, Market Square; f. 1890; economic geology especially of Southern Africa, gemmology, mineralogy, physical geology and petrology, South African stratigraphy and archaeology.

**James Hall Museum of Transport:** Pioneers' Park, Rosettenville Rd., La Rochelle, Johannesburg; f. 1964; history of land transport in South Africa (excluding public railways).

**Museum of South African Rock Art:** Zoological Gardens, Jan Smuts Ave.; f. 1969; open air display of rock engravings.

**Municipal Art Gallery:** P.O.B. 23561, Joubert Park 2044; f. 1911; European and South African painting and sculpture, print collection, textiles, Oriental ceramics; library of 2,500 vols.; Dir. PATRICIA A. SENIOR.

### Kimberley

**McGregor Museum:** P.O.B. 316; f. 1907; archaeology and rock art, geology and zoology of N. Cape; Herbarium; ethnological collection housed in Duggan-Cronin Bantu Gallery, f. 1936; Dir. R. LIVERSIDGE; publ. *Cape Provincial Museums Annals*† (jointly with 4 other museums).

**Battlefield Museum:** Magersfontein; f. 1971; Dir. R. LIVERSIDGE.

### King William's Town

**Kaffrarian Museum:** 3 Lower Albert Rd.; f. 1886; contains a large collection of mammals; also collections of Eastern Cape ethnological material and material associated with early European settlement; Dir. DEREK M. COMINS; publs. *Annual Report*, *Cape Provincial Museums Annals*† (jointly with 4 other museums).

**South African Missionary Museum:** Berkeley St.; f. 1972; missionary endeavour in Southern Africa and by South Africans abroad; Curator Rev. ERNEST BEAUD.

### Pietermaritzburg

**Natal Museum:** 237 Loop St.; f. 1904; extensive natural history exhibits, especially the collections of African animals, birds, shells and insects; ethnology; Natal's history; research in Diptera, Arachnida, Mollusca, herpetology, small mammals, archaeology and ethnoarchaeology; library of c. 6,000 vols., 1,600 periodicals, 17,000 pamphlets, special collections; Dir. Dr. B. R. STUCKENBERG; publ. *Annals*†.

**Tatham Art Gallery (Municipal):** City Hall; f. 1903; 19th-century and modern graphic art of the British School; 19th- and early 20th-century British and French painting and sculpture; 20th-century foreign graphics; South African art relating to the collection; English and Lalique glass; Curator LORNA FERGUSON.

### Port Elizabeth

**King George VI Art Gallery:** 1 Park Drive; f. 1956; municipal art museum; major collection of British painting; also South African art, Oriental miniatures, international graphics, Chinese ceramics, historical pictures of early days of Port Elizabeth; reference library of 1,200 vols.; Dir. CLAYTON S. HOLLIDAY, B.A.F.A.

**Port Elizabeth Museum:** (incorporating Snake Park, Oceanarium, Tropical House and Historical Museum); P.O.B. 13147, Humewood 6013; f. 1885, moved 1959; research on marine biology, herpetology, ornithology and local history; library of 20,000 vols.; Museum: whale skeletons, shells and general marine life; fossils, geology, birds and local history; Snake Park: African and worldwide collection of reptiles; Oceanarium: local fish, sharks, sea birds, seals and dolphins; Dir. J. H. WALLACE, PH.D.; Curator Snake Park and Tropical House C. MCCARTNEY; Curator Oceanarium J. SHORT; publs. *Cape Provincial Museums Annals*† (jointly with 4 other museums), *Annual Reports*†.

### Pretoria

**Foundation for Education, Science and Technology:** P.O.B. 1758; f. 1960; art, education, science, history, biography, travel; Man. Dir. Dr. S. MEIRING NAUDÉ; publs. *Lantern* (quarterly), *Spectrum* (quarterly), *Archimedes* (quarterly), *Crux* (quarterly), *Klasgids* (quarterly).

**Military Museum:** Fort Schanskop; f. 1978; old fort built for Transvaal State Artillery in 1867, depicting chronological military history of old South African Republic, 1800–1902; exhibition of Pretoria Regiment.

**National Cultural History and Open-Air Museum:** P.O.B. 3300; f. 1964; comprises Cultural Museum (Boom St.), Voortrekker Monument Museum, Paul Kruger House Museum, Jansen Collection (Struben St.), Willem Prinsloo Agricultural Museum (dist. Pretoria) and Pioneer Open-Air Museum (Silverton); Dir. Dr. BEN CRONJÉ.

**Pretoria Art Museum (Municipal Art Gallery):** Arcadia Park, Arcadia; f. 1964; South African art (with emphasis on art around Pretoria), small collection of European graphic works; some 17th-century Dutch art; Dir. A. J. WERTH; publ. *Bulletin* (quarterly).

**Transvaal Museum:** Paul Kruger St., P.O.B. 413; f. 1893, from 1964 a Natural History museum only; taxonomy, ecology, zoo-geography and evolutionary studies with main emphasis on Southern Africa; mammals, birds, lower vertebrates, palaeontology (incl. mammal-like reptiles and early hominids), Coleoptera, Lepidoptera and archaeology; library of 10,000 vols., and 2,000 Pioneer Open-Air Museum (Silverton); Dir. Dr. BEN CRONJÉ.

### Stellenbosch

**Stellenbosch Museum:** Private Bag X5048; f. 1962; Curator M. J. LE ROUX, M.A.; comprises:

**Grosvenor House:** Drostdy St.; completed 1803; several period rooms containing Cape furniture, Cape silver and other household articles.

**V.O.C. Kruithuis:** The Braak; built 1777; Exhibition of 17th-century cannon and other firearms and weapons; also articles relating to the military history of the town.

**Schreuder House:** Van Ryneveld St.; built 1709; furnished as early Stellenbosch pioneer dwelling.

**Van der Bijl House:** 37 Market St.; original dwelling built c. 1797; period room, pictorial exhibition, administration and Standard Bank Reference Library of 2,000 vols. and 250 microfiche.

**Old Agricultural Hall:** The Avenue; permanent exhibition "The Story of Stellenbosch 1679–1979".

Publ. *Stellenbossiana*† (quarterly).

## UNIVERSITIES

### UNIVERSITY OF CAPE TOWN
PRIVATE BAG,
RONDEBOSCH 7700

Telephone: 694351.

Founded as South African College 1829, established as university 1918.

Language of instruction: English; Academic year: March to December (two terms).

*Chancellor:* H. F. OPPENHEIMER, M.A., D.ECON., LL.D.

*Principal and Vice-Chancellor:* S. J. SAUNDERS, M.D., F.R.C.P., F.C.P.(S.A.).

*Deputy Principals:* ANDREW DONALD CARR, PH.D., F.(S.A.)I.CHEM.E., JOHN V. O. REID, M.A., B.M., B.CH., F.R.C.P.

*Registrar:* L. READ.

*Librarian:* A. S. C. HOOPER, M.SC.

Library: see Libraries.

Number of teachers: 684 full-time, 576 part-time.

Number of students: 11,038.

#### DEANS:

*Faculty of Arts:* Prof. C. DE B. WEBB, M.A.
*Faculty of Science:* Prof. J. S. DE WET, M.A., PH.D.
*Faculty of Engineering:* Prof. V. L. GRANGER, PH.D., F.I.C.E.
*Faculty of Law:* Prof. E. J. WHITAKER, B.A., LL.B., Q.C.
*Faculty of Medicine:* Prof. D. MACKENZIE, M.MED.
*Faculty of Education:* Prof. M. J. ASHLEY, M.ED.
*Faculty of Commerce:* Prof. J. D. SIMPSON, M.B.A., PH.D.
*Faculty of Music:* Prof. B. PRIESTMAN, M.A., D.F.A.
*Faculty of Fine Art and Architecture:* Prof. I. PRINSLOO, M.SC.(T.R.P.), M.I.A., ARCH.S.A., A.I.P.
*Faculty of Social Science:* M. H. VON BROEMBSEN, M.A., PH.D.

#### PROFESSORS:

*Faculty of Arts and Sciences:*
BAUMBACH, L., M.A., Classics
BROOKS, F. D., M.SC., Nuclear Physics
BROWN, A. C., M.SC., PH.D., F.Z.S., Zoology
BRUNDRIT, G. B., PH.D., A.F.I.M.A., Physical Oceanography
CHERRY, R. D., M.SC., PH.D., Physics
CUMPSTY, J. S., M.S., PH.D., Religious Studies
DAVIES, R. J., M.SC., PH.D., Geography
DE CRESPIGNY, A. R. C., PH.D., Political Science
DINGLE, R. V., PH.D., Marine Geoscience
DU RY, C., Cultural History of Western Europe
ELLIS, G. F. R., PH.D., Applied Mathematics
FRAHN, W. E., DIP.PHYS., DR.RER.NAT., Theoretical Physics
GILLHAM, D. G., M.A., PH.D., English
GURZYNSKI, Z. S., B.COM., Economics
HARDIE, K. A., M.SC., PH.D., Mathematics
HOPKINS, S. A., PH.D., Hebrew Studies
HORN, P. R. G., PH.D., German
HOUSEHAM, K. O., M.SC., M.A., Mathematics
IRVING, H. M. N. H., D.PHIL., D.SC., F.R.I.C., Analytical Science
JOUBERT, P., M.SC., PH.D., Geology
KESTING, J. G., M.A., F.S.A.L.A., Librarianship
LEWIS, O. A. M., M.SC., PH.D., Botany
LOUW, G. N., M.SC., PH.D., Zoology
MACGREGOR, K. J., M.SC., Computer Science
MOHR, R., Speech Training and Dramatic Art
NASSIMBENI, L. R., PH.D., Chemical Crystallography
PAAP, A. H. R. E., D.LITT., Classics
PHEIFFER, R. H., M.A., LITT.DRS., PH.D., Afrikaans and Dutch
PROUT, E. G., PH.D., D.SC., Physical Chemistry
REID, A. M., M.SC., PH.D., Geology
RYCROFT, H. B., M.SC., PH.D., F.R.S.S.AF., Botany
SCHELPE, E. A. C. L. E., M.SC., D.PHIL., F.R.S.S.AF., F.L.S., Plant Taxonomy
SHACKLETON, M., M.A., PH.D., French
SIMPSON, E. S. W., M.A., PH.D., Oceanography
STEPHEN, A. M., PH.D., D.PHIL., M.R.I.C., Organic Chemistry
THORNTON, D. A., PH.D., Inorganic Chemistry
TROSKIE, C. G., M.SC., PH.D., Mathematical Statistics
VAN DER MERWE, N. J., PH.D., Archaeology
VON HOLT, C., M.D., Biochemistry
WARNER, B., PH.D., D.SC., Astronomy
WEBB, C. DE B., M.A., F.R.HIST.S., History
WELSH, D. J., M.A., PH.D., Comparative African Government and Law
WEST, M. E., M.A., PH.D., Social Anthropology
WESTPHAL, E. O. J., M.A., PH.D., African Languages
WILSON, F. A. H., M.A., PH.D., Labour Economics
WOODS, D. R., D.PHIL., Microbiology

*Faculty of Engineering:*
ADAMS, L. P., PH.D., F.R.I.C.S., Surveying
BALL, A., PH.D., Metallurgy and Materials Science
BRADLOW, H. S., D.PHIL., Electrical Engineering
DENBIGH, P. N., PH.D., Electrical Engineering
DUTKIEWICZ, R. K., M.SC., PH.D., Mechanical Engineering
ENSLIN, N. C. DE V., M.SC., PH.D., Electrical Engineering
HANSFORD, G. S., M.SC., PH.D., Chemical Engineering
MARAIS, G. VAN R., M.SC., Water Resources and Public Health Engineering
MARTIN, J. B., PH.D., D.SC., Civil Engineering
METCALF, P., M.A., Mechanical Engineering
WILLIAMS, H. S., M.SC., PH.D., F.R.I.C.S., Surveying

*Faculty of Law:*
DEAN, W. H. B., LL.B., Public Law
DE VOS, W., DOC.JUR., LL.D., Roman-Dutch Law
GIBSON, J. T. R., LL.B., Commercial Law
LEEMAN, I., B.A., LL.B., South African Private Law
ZIMMERMAN, R., LL.D., Roman Law

*Faculty of Medicine:*
BARNARD, C. N., M.D., D.SC., PH.D., F.A.C.S., F.A.C.C., Cardiac Surgery
BEIGHTON, M. D., M.R.C.P., D.C.H., Human Genetics
BELONJE, D.V.SC., Physiology
BENATAR, S. R., M.B., CH.B., F.R.C.P., F.F.A.(S.A.), Medicine
BERMAN, M. C., M.MED., PH.D., Chemical Pathology
CREMIN, B. J., M.B., L.R.C.P., Radiodiagnosis
CYWES, S., M.MED., Paediatric Surgery
DALL, G., CH.M., Orthopaedic Surgery
DAVEY, D., M.B., B.S., PH.D., M.R.C.S., L.R.C.P., D.C.R.O.G., M.R.C.O.G., Obstetrics and Gynaecology
DE VILLIERS, J. C., M.D., F.R.C.S., Neurosurgery
DOWDLE, E. B. D., M.D., M.R.C.P., Clinical Science and Immunology
EALES, L., M.D., F.R.C.P., Clinical Medicine
FOLB, P. I., M.D., F.R.C.P., Pharmacology
GEVERS, W., M.A., D.PHIL., Medical Biochemistry
GILLIS L. S., M.D., Psychiatry
HARRISON, G. G., M.D., F.F.A.R.C.S., Anaesthesiology
HARRISON, P., D.N., Nursing
HEESE, H. DE V., M.D., D.C.H., Paediatrics and Child Health
JACKSON, W. P. U., M.A., M.D., F.R.C.P., Medicine
JACOBS, P., M.D., Haematology
KEEN, E. N., M.D., F.R.C.S., Anatomy
KIBEL, M. A., M.B., CH.B., F.R.C.P.(E.), D.C.H.
KOTTLER, R. E., M.MED., Radiology
McKENZIE, D., M.MED., F.R.C.(PATH.), Medical Education
MEYERS, O. L., M.B., CH.B., F.C.P., Rheumatology
MOODIE, J. W., M.D., Clinical Virology
OPIE, L. H., PH.D., M.D., Medicine
SEALY, G. R. H., M.A., M.MED., Radiotherapy
SLOAN, A. W., M.D., PH.D., F.R.F.P.S., M.R.C.P., F.R.S.S.AF., Physiology
SMITH, L. S., M.B., B.CH., D.P.H.D.BACT., M.C.PATH., Forensic Medicine and Toxicology
TERBLANCHE, J., CH.M., F.C.S., F.R.C.S., Surgery
UYS, C. J., M.D., D.CLIN., F.R.C.PATH., Pathology

UNIVERSITIES SOUTH AFRICA

Van Selm, J. L., M.B., CH.B., F.A.S.C., D.O.M.S., Ophthalmology
Watermeyer, G. S., M.B., CH.B., F.C.P.(S.A.), Community Health

*Faculty of Education:*
Ashley, M. J., M.ED., Philosophy of Education
Hart, I. E. J., M.A., M.ED., PH.D., English Education
Heyns, I. de V., PH.D., Psychology of Education
Millar, C. J., M.SC., Adult Education
Young, D. N., M.LITT., Specialized Education

*Faculty of Commerce:*
Hampton, J. D., M.SC., Business Science
Kritzinger, L., C.A.(S.A.), Accounting
Simpson, J. D., M.B.A., PH.D., Graduate School of Business

*Faculty of Music:*
Priestman, B., M.A.

*Faculty of Fine Art and Architecture:*
Dubow, N. E., B.ARCH., M.I.A., A.R.I.B.A., F.R.S.A., Fine Art
Falck, D. A. L., M.U.R.P., A.R.I.B.A., M.I.A., Architecture
Killian, W. F., M.COMM., Building
Prinsloo, I. C., B.ARCH., M.SC.(T.R.P.), Architecture
Rabie, J. W., M.A.Q.S., F.R.I.C.S., Quantity Surveying
Uytenbogaardt, R. S., M.ARCH., M.C.P., M.I.A., Urban and Regional Planning

*Faculty of Social Science:*
Beekman, J. F., O.O.N., LL.D., M.DIV., Public Administration
Du Preez, P. D., M.SC., PH.D., Psychology
Hare, A. P., A.ST., PH.D., Sociology
Helm, Mrs. B., M.SOC.SC., Applied Sociology in Social Work
Saayman, G. S., M.A., PH.D., Psychology

Attached Research Institutes:

**Abe Bailey Centre for Intergroup Studies:** Rondebosch; f. 1968 from funds provided by the Abe Bailey Trust, to promote good relations between the peoples of South Africa; research in race and language group relations; Dir. Prof. H. W. van der Merwe, M.A., PH.D.

**Central Acoustics Laboratory:** f. 1972 to cater for research requirements in acoustics for staff and postgraduate students; Dir. R. New, PH.D.

**Centre for African Studies:** f. 1975 to promote research on man in Africa, to forge academic links with other African countries and to develop U.C.T. as a resource centre for African research; Dir. Prof. M. E. West, PH.D.

**Chamber of Mines Precambrian Research Unit:** f. 1963; attached to the Dept. of Geology to conduct and co-ordinate research on Precambrian rocks; Dir. P. Joubert, M.SC., PH.D.

**Electron Microscope Unit:** provides service for advanced research; Dir. D. Crawford, PH.D.

**Energy Research Unit:** f. 1976; to co-ordinate work on various aspects of energy production; Dir. Prof. R. K. Dutkiewicz, M.SC., PH.D.

**Fishing Industry Research Institute:** Rondebosch; f. 1946; financed by industry, the C.S.I.R. and the Admin. of South West Africa; Dir. Prof. R. J. Nachenius, PH.D.

**Institute of Child Health:** f. 1974 to co-ordinate activities regarding the care of children; Chair. Prof. H. de V. Heese, M.D., F.R.C.P.

**Institute of Criminology:** f. 1977; Dir. Prof. R. G. Nairn, LL.B.

**Institute of Oceanography:** Rondebosch; f. 1963 to co-ordinate activities in branches of marine research; controlled by a Board on which other university institutes and research departments are represented; Dir. Prof. E. S. W. Simpson, M.SC., PH.D.

**Percy Fitzpatrick Institute of African Ornithology:** Rondebosch; affiliated to U.C.T. in 1960 to promote studies in African ornithology and to provide advanced teaching in this field; Dir. W. R. Siegfried, PH.D.

**Professional Communication Unit:** inter-faculty body teaching and researching into principles of effective oral and written communication; Dir. M. L. Fielding, M.A.

**School of Environmental Studies:** f. 1973; teaching and research, mainly at post-graduate level, on an interdisciplinary basis; Dir. Prof. R. F. Fuggle, M.SC., PH.D.

**South African Mining Research Centre for Heart Disease and Organ Transplantation:** f. 1968 with a gift from South African Mining Finance Houses; provides facilities for investigation of heart disease and organ transplantation; Dir. Prof. E. B. D. Dowdle, M.D., F.R.C.P.

**Southern Universities Nuclear Institute:** Faure; f. 1961 by the Universities of Cape Town and Stellenbosch to provide advanced research facilities to university staff and postgraduate students; main research facility is a 5.5 MeV Van de Graaff accelerator with pulsed ion source; Chief Scientist Dr. I. J. Van Heerden.

**Teaching Methods Unit:** f. 1977 to improve quality of teaching and learning by diagnostic analysis of teaching programmes and learning processes and by promoting experimental research; Dir. Prof. J. H. F. Meyer, M.SC., PH.D.

## UNIVERSITY OF DURBAN-WESTVILLE
PRIVATE BAG X54001,
DURBAN 4000
Telephone: 821211.

Founded 1960, for Indian students. (Also open to white students from 1978.)

Language of instruction: English; State control; Academic year: February to December (three terms).

*Chancellor:* Senator O. P. F. Horwood.
*Vice-Chancellor and Rector:* Prof. S. P. Olivier, M.ED., D.PHIL.
*Vice-Rector:* Prof. J. J. C. Greyling, M.A., PH.D.
*Registrar (Administration):* G. E. Heystek.
*Registrar (Academic):* Prof. J. St. E. Pretorius, M.A.
*Librarian:* R. de Wet, M.A.

Number of teachers: 340.
Number of students: 4,890.

Publications: *Journal*† (irregular), *Calendar*† (annual).

Deans:

*Faculty of Arts:* Prof. S. S. Nadvi.
*Faculty of Commerce and Administration:* Prof. J. Buijs.
*Faculty of Education:* Prof. S. R. Maharaj.
*Faculty of Law:* Prof. D. Scott-Macnab.
*Faculty of Science:* Prof. M. A. H. Smout.
*Faculty of Theology:* Prof. C. J. Wethmar.
*Faculty of Engineering:* Prof. R. M. Morris.
*Faculty of Health Sciences:* Prof. A. L. Du Preez.

Professors and Heads of Departments:
*Faculty of Arts:*
Anderson, W. W., Social Work
Bhana, S., History
Brimer, A., English
Bughwan, D., Speech and Drama
Cipolla, G., Classical Languages
Graser, R. R., Criminology
Heiberg, L. R., Afrikaans and Dutch
Jithoo, S., Anthropology
Krishna, P. M., Oriental Studies
Lakhi, C. M., History of Art
Nadvi, S. H. H., Arabic, Urdu and Persian
Nadvi, S. S., Islamic Studies
Oosthuizen, G. C., Science of Religion
Ramfol, C., Psychology
Rauche, G. A., Philosophy
Schoombee, G. F., Sociology
Sitaram, R., Hindi
Verstraete, D. A. J., French
Volschenk, P., Fine Arts
Van der Spuy, H. H., Music
Zangenberg, F., Indian Philosophy

*Faculty of Commerce and Administration:*
Behr, D., Industrial Psychology
Buijs, J., Business Economics
Calitz, F., Statistics
Coetzee, W. A. J., Public Administration
Folscher, G. C. K., Economics
Orpen, R. D., Accounting and Auditing
Reese, K., Business Administration
Venter, J., Business Administration
Viljoen, J. H., Accounting and Auditing

*Faculty of Education:*
Behr, A. L., Education
Cilliers, J. L. le R., Education
Du Toit, S. F., Physical Education
Maharaj, S. R., Education
Nel, B. F., Education

Pienaar, P. T., Education
Ramphal, A., Education

*Faculty of Law:*
Ramsden, W. A., Mercantile Law
Ranchod, B. G., Private Law
Roeleveld, L., Public Law
Scott Macnab, D., Mercantile Law

*Faculty of Science:*
Bharuth-Ram, K., Physics
Burger, F. J., Human Physiology
Engel, D. W., Physics
Frank, G. H., Zoology
Govinden, H. S., Chemistry
Hawtrey, A. O., Biochemistry
Hurt, C. A. R., Chemistry
Laidlaw, M. G. G., Computer Science
Posel, K., Mathematics and Applied Mathematics
Roth, G., Microbiology and Hygiene
Smith, A. L., Zoology
Smit, J. van R., Chemistry
Smout, M. A. H., Geography and Geology
Steinke, T. D., Botany

*Faculty of Theology:*
Krige, W. A., Theology
Wethmar, C. J., Theology

*Faculty of Engineering:*
Bennet, T. H., Civil Engineering
Guthrie, A. M., Engineering
Horn, R. P. S., Engineering
Morris, R. M., Engineering

*Faculty of Health Sciences:*
Du Preez, A. L., Pharmacology
Kane, G. T., Anatomy
Tunley, I. A. P., Medical Rehabilitation
Turnbull, D. K., Optometry
Van Rensburg, J. H. J., Dentistry
Veltman, A. M., Pharmacy

Attached Institutes:

**Cancer Research Institute:** Dir. Dr. J. D. Randeria, M.SC., PH.D.

**Child Guidance and Research Centre:** Dir. Prof. A. L. Behr, M.ED., D.ED.

**Communications Media Research:** Dir. R. W. H. Pope, B.ED.

**Institute for Social and Economic Research:** Dir. Prof. T. J. D. Fair.

## UNIVERSITY OF FORT HARE
PRIVATE BAG X1314,
ALICE 5700, CISKEI

Telephone: Alice 281.

Founded under the name "South African Native College" in 1916 by the United Free Church of Scotland. In 1960 the College was transferred to the Department of Bantu Education to cater specifically for the Xhosa ethnic group. In 1970 the University College received its academic autonomy and became known as the University of Fort Hare.

Language of instruction: English; Academic year: February to November (two terms).

*Chancellor:* Dr. P. E. Rousseau, M.SC., D.SC.

*Vice-Chancellor and Rector:* Prof. J. M. de Wet, M.SC., PH.D.

*Vice-Rector:* A. Coetzee, CAND. THEOL., M.A., D.LITT.

*Chairman of the Council:* Judge G. G. A. Munnik.

*Chairman of Advisory Council:* S. S. Guzana.

*Registrars:* D. J. Jacobs, B.SC., B.A., B.COM. (Finance); P. D. Hartzer, B.A. (Academic).

*Dean of Students:* H. M. Nabe, B.A.

*Librarian:* M. Spruyt, LL.M.

Library: see Libraries.

Number of teachers: 186, including 42 professors.

Number of students: 2,400.

Publications: *Speculum Juris, Fort Hare Papers, The Fort Harian.*

Deans:

*Faculty of Law:* Prof. J. Labuschagne, M.A., LL.M.
*Faculty of Arts:* Prof. E. J. de Jager, D.PHIL.
*Faculty of Education:* Prof. R. P. van Rooyen, D.ED.
*Faculty of Science:* Prof. G. J. J. van Rensburg, PH.D.
*Faculty of Economic Sciences:* Prof. W. C. Botha, D.ADMIN.
*Faculty of Theology:* Prof. J. A. Lamprecht, D.D.
*Faculty of Agriculture:* J. H. E. de Villiers, M.SC.(AGRIC.).

Professors:

Bembridge, T. J., M.SC.AGRIC., Agricultural Extension
Botha, C. E. J., PH.D., Botany
Botha, W. C., D.ADMIN., Industrial Psychology
Brand, J. M., PH.D., Agriculture
Brown, D. L., D.SC., Animal Science
Coetzee, A., M.A., D.LITT., Afrikaans-Nederlands
Coetzee, C. G., M.A., D.PHIL., History
De Jager, E. J., M.A., D.PHIL., African Studies
Du Plessis, J. R., B.A., LL.B., Criminal Law
Du Preez, J. P. A., B.SC., D.ED., Psychology
Eekhout, L., B.SC., Land Surveying
Eksteen, M. C., Political Science
Els, J. M., D.LITT., Classical Languages
Gardner, J. B., B.COM., C.A., Accounting
Giesekke, E. W., PH.D., Chemistry
Gitywa, V. Z., D.LITT. ET PHIL., African Studies
Graven, E. H., PH.D., Agronomy
Groenewald, H. J., M.A., D.PHIL., Communications
Hecht, F., Theology
Hough, M. A., B.A., M.S., Social Work
Human, S. S., C.A., Accountancy
Katiya, N., D.ED., Philosophy and History of Education
Kriel, A. P., M.A., PH.D., Bantu Languages
Kruger, J. H., D.ED., Didactics and Comparative Education
Labuschagne, J., M.A., LL.M., Constitutional Law
Laker, M. C., D.SC., Soil Science
Lamprecht, J. A., Systematic Theology
Marais, E. J., M.A., B.D., D.TH., Philosophy
Marais, J. N., PH.D., Agronomy
Marker, M. E., M.A., M.AG.SC., PH.D., Geography
Pahl, H. W., B.A., B.SC., Bantu Languages

Prins, M. J., D.LITT., Afrikaans/Dutch
Radford, M. D., PR.ENG., B.SC., Agricultural Engineering
Seretlo, J. R., PH.D., Physics
Steenekamp, J. J. A., D.COM., Business Economics
Van den Berg, R. A., M.SC., D.SC., Zoology
Van der Merwe, W. G., M.A., D.LITT.ET PHIL., Psychology
Van Oortmerssen, J., M.A., English
Van Rensburg, G. J. J., PH.D., Mathematics
Van Rooyen, R. P., D.ED., Philosophy and History of Education
Viljoen, G. P., Applied Mathematics and Statistics
Wagener, P. C., M.SC., M.A., Applied Mathematics

## MEDICAL UNIVERSITY OF SOUTHERN AFRICA
P.O. MEDUNSA 0204

Telephone: (012) 58-2844/5/6/7.
Telex: 3-0580 SA.

Founded 1976 to provide training in Medicine (and Supplementary Health Disciplines), Dentistry and Veterinary Science for Black students.

State control; Language of instruction: English; Academic year: January to December (two terms).

*Vice-Chancellor and Rector:* F. P. Retief, D.PHIL., F.R.C.P.(E.), M.D.

*Chairman of the Council:* P. C. Snijman, B.DS., F.D.S.R.C.S., H.DD., R.F.P.S.

*Academic Registrar:* G. J. Loubser, B.A.

*Administrative Registrar:* G. J. de Korte, M.B.A.

*Librarian:* A. D. P. Pienaar, B.A., T.H.E.D.

Number of teachers: 71.
Number of students: 310.

Deans:

*Faculty of Dentistry:* L. T. Taljaard, B.CH.D., D.T.V.G.
*Faculty of Medicine:* T. H. J. Dunston, M.B.B.CH., M.D.
*Faculty of Veterinary Science:* N. C. Owen, M.MED.(VET.), D.V.SC.

Heads of Departments:

*Anaesthesiology:* Prof. J. L. Couper, M.B.CH.B., F.F.A.
*Anatomical Pathology:* Prof. L. Dreyer, M.B.CH.B., M.MED.
*Anatomy:* Prof. C. G. J. le Roux, M.B.CH.B.
*Cardiology:* Prof. A. L. van Gelder, M.B.CH.B., F.C.P.
*Chemical Pathology:* Prof. H. J. Joubert, M.B.CH.B., M.MED.
*Community Health:* Prof. E. Glatthaar, M.B.CH.B., D.P.H., D.I.H.
*Dermatology:* Prof. T. Heyl, M.B.CH.B., M.MED.
*Diagnostic Radiology:* Prof. J. V. Todes, M.B.B.CH., D.M.R.D., R.C.P., R.C.S.
*Dietetics:* Miss M. Olivier, B.SC.
*Family Medicine:* Prof. G. S. Fehrsen, M.B.CH.B., M.F.G.P.

*General Surgery:* Prof. O. E. Hansen, m.b.b.ch., f.r.c.s.e.
*Haemotological Pathology:* Prof. T. H. J. Dunston, m.b.b.ch., m.d.
*Internal Medicine:* Prof. W. J. Bam, m.b.b.ch., m.med.
*Microbiology:* Prof. H. H. Crewe-Brown, m.b.b.ch., d.c.h., f.c.path.
*Neurosurgery:* Prof. M. J. Joubert, m.b.b.ch., f.r.c.s.e., m.sc.
*Obstetrics and Gynaecology:* Prof. E. T. Mongokong, m.b.ch.b., f.c.o.g.
*Occupational Therapy:* Miss A. E. Holsten, b.a.
*Ophthalmology:* Prof. R. C. Stegman, m.b.ch.b., m.med.
*Orthopaedics:* Prof. J. G. A. du Toit, m.b.ch.b., ch.m., f.r.c.s.e.
*Paediatrics and Child Health:* Prof. D. T. Fourie, m.b.ch.b., m.med.
*Pharmacology and Therapeutics:* Prof. P. H. Joubert, m.b.b.ch., f.c.p.(s.a.), m.med.sc.
*Physiology:* Prof. J. Booyens, ph.d., d.sc.
*Physiotherapy:* Mrs. A. A. McFarlane, b.sc.
*Psychiatry:* Prof. J. H. Robbertze, m.b.ch.b., m.a.(psych.), m.d.
*Radiography:* Mrs. A. M. J. Snyman.
*Urology:* Prof. I. P. Maas, m.b.ch.b., m.ch.
*Faculty of Dentistry:*
  *Community Dentistry:* Prof. J. B. du Plessis, b.ch.d., d.t.v.g.

## UNIVERSITY OF NATAL
KING GEORGE V AVENUE, DURBAN
AND P.O.B. 375, PIETERMARITZBURG, NATAL

Telephone: 25-3411 (Durban), 63320 (Pietermaritzburg).

Founded in 1910 as a constituent college of the University of South Africa, achieved independent status under the control of its own Council and Senate in 1949.

Language of instruction: English; Academic year: February to November (two terms)

*Chancellor:* Dr. B. A. Armitage, l.d.s., f.r.c.s.(e.)
*Vice-Chancellor and Principal:* Prof. N. D. Clarence, ph.d.
*Chairman:* L. S. Robinson.
*Vice-Principal (Durban):* Prof. P. de V. Booysen, m.sc.agric., ph.d.
*Vice-Principal (Pietermaritzburg):* Prof. G. D. L. Schreiner, ph.d.
*Registrar:* A. K. B. Skinner.
*Finance Officer:* E. L. Beyers, b.com., a.i.m.t.a.(sa), a.i.co.s., a.i.a.c.(s.a.).
*University Librarian (Durban):* F. Scholtz, b.a.
*University Librarian (Pietermaritzburg):* Colleen Vietzen, m.a.

Libraries: see under Libraries.
Number of staff: 822.

Number of students: 8,958.

Publications: *Natal University News, Theoria, Calendar* (annual), Student newspapers: *Nux* (fortnightly), *Dome* (fortnightly).

### DEANS:
*Faculty of Arts:* Prof. G. J. Trotter, m.a.
*Faculty of Science:* Prof. B. M. Nevin, m.a., ph.d.
*Faculty of Education:* Prof. A. M. Barrett, m.a., m.ed.
*Faculty of Law:* Prof. J. R. L. Milton, ll.m., ph.d.
*Faculty of Commerce:* Prof. T. J. H. Waldeck, m.com., c.a.
*Faculty of Engineering:* Prof. K. Knight, pr.eng., ph.d.
*Faculty of Social Science:* Prof. W. J. Argyle, d.phil.
*Faculty of Agriculture:* Prof. W. J. Stielau, m.sc.agric., ph.d.
*Faculty of Medicine:* Prof. T. L. Sarkin, m.ch., m.d., f.r.c.s., f.r.c.s.ed.

### PROFESSORS:
*Faculty of Agriculture:*
  Allan, P., Horticultural Science
  Behrmann, H. I., Agricultural Economics
  Gous, R. M., Animal Science and Poultry Science
  Lea, J. D., Crop Science
  Lishman, A. W., Animal Science and Poultry Science
  Martin, M. M., Plant Pathology and Microbiology
  Nathanson, K., Crop Science
  Nievwoudt, W. L., Agricultural Economics
  Rijkenberg, F. H. J., Plant Pathology and Microbiology
  Stielau, W. J., Animal Science and Poultry Science
  Tainton, N. M., Pasture Science
  Weyers, W. H., Genetics
  Wolstenholme, B. N., Horticultural Science

*Faculty of Architecture:*
  Biermann, B. E., Architecture
  Boaden, B. G., Quantity Surveying
  Dyke-Wells, D. N., Architecture
  Kahn, M., Town and Regional Planning
  O'Brien, E. J., Building

*Faculty of Arts:*
  Ballantine, C. J., Music
  Benyon, J. O., Historical and Political Studies
  Blondeel, E. E. E., Econonomics
  Botha, T. J. R., Afrikaans and Dutch
  Bredenkamp, V. J., Divinity
  Brückl, O. K. J., German
  Cahill, Audrey F., English
  Clifford-Vaughan, F. M. McA., Political Science
  Conradie, Anna, Philosophy
  Cope, A. T., Zulu languages and literature
  De Wet, B. X., Classics
  Duminy, A. H., History
  Freese, W. F. O., German
  Gardner, C. O., English
  Horton, J. W., History
  Hunnings, G., Philosophy
  Maasdorp, G. G., Economics
  Mornet, C., Library Science
  Nattrass, Jill, Economics

Nienaber, C. J. M., Afrikaans and Dutch
Orton, R., Speech and Drama
Sands, R., English
Scholtz, P. J. H., Speech and Drama
Schoonraad, M. G., Fine Arts and History of Art
Sienaert, E. R., French
Trotter, G. J., Economics
van der Spuy Heyns, J., Economics
Wakerley, Isolina-Colette, French

*Faculty of Commerce:*
  Allan, I. K., Business Administration
  Clulow, D. A., Accountancy
  Reese, K., Business Administration
  Seneque, P. J. C., Accountancy
  Waldeck, T. J. H., Accountancy

*Faculty of Education:*
  Barrett, A. M., Education
  Coetsee, I., Educational Psychology
  Fouché, G. W., Educational Psychology
  Hayward, F. J. D., Education
  Niven, J. McG., Education

*Faculty of Engineering:*
  Bindon, J. P. P., Mechanical Engineering
  Broadhurst, A. D., Electrical Engineering
  Fleming, C. J., Civil Engineering
  Harley, R. G., Electrical Engineering
  Hellawell, R. A., Electrical Engineering
  Jenkins, D. P., Land Surveying
  Judd, M. R., Chemical Engineering
  Katz, Z., Mechanical Engineering
  Knight, K., Civil Engineering
  Meiring, P., Agricultural Engineering
  Nattrass, H. L., Electrical Engineering
  Pegram, G. G. S., Civil Engineering
  Raal, J. D., Chemical Engineering
  Reed, M., Mechanical Engineering
  Roberts, L. W., Mechanical Engineering
  Scogings, D. A., Surveying
  Windsor, J. S., Civil Engineering

*Faculty of Law:*
  Blackman, M. S., Law
  Burchell, E. M., Law
  Lund, J. R., Law
  Mathews, A. S., Law
  Milton, J. R. L., Law
  McLennan, J. S., Law
  McQuoid-Mason, D. J., Law

*Faculty of Medicine:*
  Baker, L. W., Surgery
  Braithwaite, J. L., Anatomy
  Brock-Utne, J. G., Physiology
  Downing, J. W., Anaesthetics
  Engelbrecht, H. E., Radiology
  Fernandes, C. M. C., Oto-rhino-laryngology
  Greig, H. B. W., Haematology
  Jordaan, J. P., Radiology
  Joubert, S. M., Chemical Pathology
  Leary, W. P. P., Experimental and Clinical Pharmacology
  Le Roux, B. T., Thoracic Surgery
  Mitha, A. S., Cardiology
  Moosa, A., Paediatrics and Child Health
  Naude, J. H., Urology
  Nel, J. P., Forensic Medicine
  Pudifin, D. J., Medicine
  Robins-Browne, R., Microbiology
  Rogers, N. M. A., Thoracic Surgery
  Sarkin, T. L., Orthopaedic Surgery
  Seedat, Y. K., Medicine
  Spencer, I. W. F., Community Health
  Welsh, W. H., Ophthalmology
  Wessels, W. H., Psychiatry

*Faculty of Science:*
  Alexander, Anne, Biological Sciences (Animal)

BARRETT, P. J., Physics
BAYLES, J. W., Chemistry and Chemical Technology
BERJAK, PATRICIA, Biological Sciences
BOSMAN, T., Entomology
BREEN, C. M., Botany
DALE, A. I., Mathematical Statistics
DREWES, S. E., Chemistry and Chemical Technology
HAINES, R. J., Chemistry and Chemical Technology
HAWKSWORTH, W. A., Chemistry and Chemical Technology
HEEG, J., Zoology
HELLBERG, M. A., Physics
HUNTER, D. R., Geology and Mineralogy
JACKSON, P. I., Physics
LAING, M. J., Chemistry and Chemical Technology
MACLEAN, G. L., Zoology
MATTHEWS, P. E., Geology and Mineralogy
MEESTER, J. A. J., Zoology
MEIJER, A. R., Mathematics and Applied Mathematics
MCGEE, O. S., Geography
MCKENZIE, J. F., Mathematics and Applied Mathematics
NEVIN, B. M., Mathematics and Applied Mathematics
NOEL, A. R. A., Botany
PIENAAR, R. N., Botany
QUICKE, G. V., Biochemistry
RAAB, R. E., Physics
RAYNER, A. A., Statistics and Biometry
SAGGERSON, E. P., Geology and Mineralogy
SCOURFIELD, M. W. J., Physics
SWART, J. H., Mathematics and Applied Mathematics
TAVENER-SMITH, R., Geology and Mineralogy
TAYLOR, D. A. H., Chemistry and Chemical Technology
THERON, P. A., Psychology
VAN DIJK, D. E., Zoology
VAN STADEN, J., Botany
VERBEEK, A. A., Chemistry and Chemical Technology
WALKER, A. D. M., Physics
WILLIAMS, O., Geography
WILLIAMS-WYNN, D. E. A., Chemistry and Chemical Technology

*Faculty of Social Science:*
ALBINO, R. C., Psychology
ARGYLE, W. J., African Studies
PRESTON-WHYTE, R. A., Geography
SHARRATT, P. A., Psychology
SHAW, FRANCES C., Social Work
WATTS, H. L., Sociology

RESEARCH INSTITUTES:

**Centre for Applied Social Sciences:** Durban; f. 1953.
*Director:* L. SCHLEMMER, B.A.

**Natal Institute of Immunology:** see under Research Institutes.

**Oceanographic Research Institute:** 2 West St., Durban; f. 1959.
*Director:* Prof. A. P. BOWMAKER, PH.D.

**Research Institute for Diseases in a Tropical Environment:** Umbilo Rd., Durban; f. 1948.
*Director:* Prof. M. G. MOSHAL, M.B.CH.B., F.R.C.P., F.A.C.G.

**Sugar Milling Research Institute:** Francois Rd., Durban; f. 1948.
*Director:* Dr. A. B. RAVNÖ, M.SC. (CHEM.), PH.D., D.I.C., M.S.A.I.CH.E.

**Wattle Research Institute:** Scottsville, Pietermaritzburg; f. 1946.
*Director:* J. A. STUBBINGS, B.SC.

**Plasma Physics Research Institute:** University of Natal, Durban; f. 1979.
*Director:* M. A. HELLBERG, PH.D.

**Institute of Natural Resources:** University of Natal, Pietermaritzburg; f. 1980.
*Director:* J. HANKS, M.A., PH.D.


# UNIVERSITY OF THE NORTH
PRIVATE BAG X5090,
PIETERSBURG 0700

Central Telephone: Sovenga 33/34.

Founded 1959 to serve the Tsonga, Sotho, Venda and Tswana peoples.

State control; Languages of instruction: English and Afrikaans; Academic year: February to November (two semesters).

*Chancellor:* Dr. M. J. MADIBA.
*Vice-Chancellor and Rector:* Prof. Dr. P. C. MOKGOKONG, M.A., D.LITT. ET PHIL.
*Registrar (Academic):* Prof. J. C. STEENEKAMP, D.ED., PH.D.
*Registrar (Administrative):* H. J. J. KIRSTEN.
*Librarians:* S. P. MANAKA, M.A.(BIBL.), C. P. BOTHMA, B.SC.

Number of teachers: 167.
Number of students: 2,174.

Publications: *Unikon* (annual), *Series A, B and C* (irregular).

DEANS:

*Faculty of Arts:* Prof. F. J. ENGELBRECHT, M.A., D.PHIL.
*Faculty of Theology:* Prof. J. A. VAN WYK, D.TH.
*Faculty of Education:* Prof. J. A. T. WENTZEL, D.ED.
*Faculty of Mathematics and Natural Sciences:* Prof. A. G. LE ROUX, D.LITT. ET PHIL.
*Faculty of Economics and Administration:* B. P. BOTHA, M.A.
*Faculty of Law:* Prof. P. W. DU PLESSIS, LL.D.
*Dean of Students:* S. P. MANAKA, M.A.

PROFESSORS:

*Faculty of Arts and Philosophy:*
BENADE, J. T., D.LITT., Classical Languages
DE BRUTO, H. F., D.LITT., Afrikaans and Communications Media
ENGELBRECHT, F. J., M.A., Philosophy
GROVÉ, D., M.A., D.LITT. ET PHIL., Sociology and Criminology
HERHOLDT, A. N. J., D.PHIL., Political Science
LE ROUX, A. G., M.A., D.LITT. ET PHIL., Psychology
MALAN, J. S., D.LITT. ET PHIL., Anthropology
MATHIVA, M. E. R., M.A., D.LITT., Venda
MULLER, C. H., PH.D., D.LITT., English
PRETORIUS, J. G., PH.D., History
VAN DER WESTHUIZEN, L., M.A., German

*Faculty of Mathematics and Natural Science:*
DE VILLIERS, P. A., M.SC., PH.D., Chemistry
ELS, W. J., D.SC., Physiology
JANSE VAN VUUREN, D. R., D.SC., Botany
LOMBARD, R. H., D.SC., M.P.S., Pharmaceutics
MORGAN, P. J. K., PH.D., Animal Production
OLIVIER, P. C. DU V., M.SC., PH.D., Mathematical Statistics
OOSTHUIZEN, H. J., M.SC., PH.D., Computer Science
SAAYMAN, J. E., M.SC., PH.D., Zoology and Biology
THERON, J. C., D.SC., Geology

*Faculty of Economics and Administration:*
BOTHA, W. J., D.B.A., S.M.B.A., Business Economics
ROOS, B., M.COMM., Accounting and Auditing

*Faculty of Education:*
HEIBERG, P. J., M.A., Fundamental Education
MOHANOE, P. F., D.ED., Didactics
MPHAHLELE, M. C. J., D.ED., History of Education
VERMEULEN, A., D.ED., Empirical Education
WENTZEL, J. A. T., D.ED., Comparative Education

*Faculty of Theology:*
BOLINK, P., THEOL.CAND., D.TH., Church History, Mission
MALAN, F. S., B.A., B.D., New Testament
SCHEEPERS, J. H., D.TH., Old and New Testament
VAN AS, J. J., TH.DR., Old Testament
VAN DER MERWE, H., M.A., D.D., Dogmatics, Theological Ethics and Practical Theology
VAN NIEKERK, A. S., B.A., B.D., Practical Theology
VAN WYK, J. A., D.TH., Dogmatics, Theological Ethics and Practical Theology

*Faculty of Law:*
CLOETE, P. H., LL.D., African Government and Law
DU PLESSIS, P. W., LL.D., Mercantile Law
VAN DEN HEEVER, J. A., B.IURIS, B.A., LL.B., Criminal Law
VISSER, D. P., B.IURIS., LL.B., Private Law


# UNIVERSITY OF THE ORANGE FREE STATE
P.O.B. 339,
BLOEMFONTEIN, O.F.S.

Telephone: 70711.

Founded 1855. Formerly a Constituent College of the University of South Africa; independent status 1949.

Principal language of instruction: Afrikaans; Academic year: February to November.

*Chancellor:* Prof. B. KOK, M.A., LITT.DOCTS., D.LITT.
*Vice-Chancellor and Rector:* Prof. W. L. MOUTON, M.SC., PH.D.
*Chairman:* J. B. FAURE, B.SC., B.ED.
*Administrative and General Registrar:* H. P. JOHNSON, B.COM.

# UNIVERSITIES  SOUTH AFRICA

*Academic Registrar:* Prof. C. D. ROODE, M.A., D.PHIL.
*Librarian:* H. DE BRUIN, B.A., M.BIBL.
Number of teachers: 405.
Number of students: 8,332.

## DEANS:
*Faculty of Arts:* Prof. C. VAN HEERDEN, M.A., D.LITT.
*Faculty of Science:* Prof. H. J. POTGIETER, PH.D.
*Faculty of Social Science:* Prof. R. A. VILJOEN, M.A., D.PHIL.
*Faculty of Education:* Prof. N. T. VAN LOGGERENBERG, M.ED., D.ED.
*Faculty of Law:* Prof. D. W. MARKEL, LL.D.
*Faculty of Economic and Administrative Science:* Prof. T. G. BORDER, M.COM., D.COM.
*Faculty of Medicine:* Prof. C. F. SLABBER, M.MED., M.D.
*Faculty of Agriculture:* Prof. H. A. KOTZE, D.SC.AGRIC.
*Teachers' College:* Prof. J. A. BOSCH, M.A.

### PROFESSORS:
*Faculty of Arts:*
BRUSSOW, A. V., B.P.E.D., M.ED., Physical Education
DE KOKER, B., D.PHIL., Drama
DRIJEPONDT, H. L. F., D.LITT. ET PHIL., Latin
FOKKER, D. W., M.SC., Librarianship
GILDENHUYS, J. G., M.A., D.LITT., Bantu Language
JOUBERT, J., M.A., D.LITT., Romance Languages
LAUBSCHER, F. DU T., M.A., D.LITT., Hebrew
LOMBARD, J. C., M.A., TH.D., V.U., Biblical Studies
MALAN, C. W., M.A., D.LITT., Afrikaans and Dutch
MARAIS, H. C., M.A., D.PHIL., Communication Science
MARAIS, H. M., M.A., D.PHIL., History
MOLL, J. C., M A., D.PHIL., History
MOSTERT, C. W., M.A., D.LITT., English
MULLER, F. R., M.A., D.LITT., English
NEL, C. J., M.A., D.PHIL., Anthropology
NEL, D. E., M.A., D.LITT. ET PHIL., Geography
OVERDUIN, P. G. J., D.ED., Librarianship
POTGIETER, J. H., D.MUS., U.O.L.M., U.V.L.M., Music
SENEKAL, J. H., M.A., D.LITT., Afrikaans/Dutch
SNYMAN, A. H., M.A., D.LITT., Classical Culture
STRAUSS, D. F. M., M.A., D.PHIL., Philosophy
STRYDOM, L., M.A., D.LITT., Afrikaans Literature
TEURLINCKX, A. A. F., D.PHIL., History and Appreciation of Art
VAN SCHOOR, M. C. E., M.A., M.ED., D.LITT., History
VENTER, C. L., D.MUS., Music
VENTER, J. F., M.A., D.PHIL., Applied Anthropology
VON DELFT, K. U. T., D.LITT., German

*Faculty of Science:*
BOK, L. D. C., M.SC., DR.RER.NAT., Physical and Applied Chemistry
BOTHA, B. J. V., M.A., D.SC., Geology
DE LA ROSA, B., M.SC., DR.SC.T., Pure Mathematics
DE WAAL, D. J., PH.D., Statistics and Finance
ELOFF, J. N., D.SC., Botany
GROBLER, N. J., D.SC., Geology
HEWITT, P. H., PH.D., Entomology
JARRETT, A. H., M.SC., PH.D., Astronomy
KRITZINGER, A., D.SC., Genetics
LATEGAN, P. M., M.SC., D.SC., Microbiology
LE ROUX, P. L., M.SC., PH.D., Biochemistry
MALAN, W. H., B.SC., Q.S., Quantity Surveying
NEL, D. G., D.SC., Statistics
POTGIETER, H. J., M.SC., PH.D., Microbiology
ROODT, L., M.ARCH., L.I.A., S.A.I.T.P., A.R.I.B.A., A.M.I.P.I., Architecture
ROUX, D. G., M.SC., PH.D., Organic Chemistry
SMITH, T. H. C., M.SC., PH.D., Computer Science
VAN PLETZEN, R., D.SC., Zoology
VAN WYK, C. B., M.SC., PH.D., Applied Mathematics
VAN ZYL, F. D. W., PH.D., Architecture
VILJOEN, G., M.SC., D.SC., Mathematics
VILJOEN, P. E., D.SC., Physics
WESSELS, H. L., M.S., Domestic Science

*Faculty of Social Science:*
BOTHA, Dr. D., M.A., D.PHIL., Social Work
COETZEE, J. K., D.PHIL., Sociology
LOOTS, I., M.CUR., Nursing
PRINSLOO, M. J., M.CUR., Nursing
RADEMEYER, G., M.A., D.PHIL., Psychology
SCHOEMAN, W. J., M.A., D.PHIL., Psychology
STRAUSS, J., M.A., D.PHIL., Business Sociology
VAN RENSBURG, H. C. J., M.A., D.PHIL., Sociology
VAN RENSBURG, W. J. J., M.A., Criminology

*Faculty of Education:*
PRETORIUS, J. L., M.ED., D.ED., Educational Psychology
SCHOEMAN, P. G., M.A., D.ED., Education
VAN DER WALT, J. S., D.ED., Educational Psychology
VAN LOGGERENBERG, N. T., B.A., M.ED., D.ED., General Didactics
VERMAAK, D., D.ED., History of Education

*Faculty of Economic and Administrative Science:*
BUYS, L. C., B.COM., Accounting
EKSTEEN, R. B., D.COM., Transport Economics
FOURIE, P. C., M.ADMIN., Public and Municipal Administration
JOUBERT, W. A., D.COM., C.A., Accountancy and Auditing
LANGENHOVEN, H. P., M.A., D.PHIL., Industrial Psychology
LOURENS, J. J., B.COM., B.ED., D.COM., Economics
NORTJE, J. D., D.COM., Business Commerce

*Faculty of Medicine:*
ANDERSON, J. D., M.B., CH.B., M.MED., F.F.R., Radiotherapy
CILLIERS, P. H. K., CH.B., M.MED., Surgery
DU TOIT, P. W., CH.B., M.PRAX., M.MED., Clinical Care
ESTERHUIZEN, A. C., D.SC., Physiology
HARMS, J. H. K., M.MED., Psychiatry
HEYNS, A. DU P., M.B., CH.B., D.T.M. & H., D.M., Haematology
HUGO, J. M., CH.B., M.MED., Anaesthetics
HUNDT, H. K. L., PH.D., Pharmacology
KLEYNHANS, P. H. T., CH.B., M.MED., Internal Medicine
LÖTTER, M. G., Biophysics
MEYER, J. D., M.B., CH.B., M.D., Internal Medicine
MEYER, J. M., M.B., CH.B., M.MED., Thoracic Surgery
MINNAAR, P. C., D.SC., Biophysics
MORRISON, A. G. M., B.A., M.B., CH.B., CH.M., Anatomy
MÜLLER, F. O., M.B., CH.B., Pharmacology
NEL, C. J. C., M.MED., Surgery
ODENDAAL, M. J., M.R.C.O.G., M.D., Obstetrics and Gynaecology
OLINSKY, A., M.B., CH.B., F.C.P., Paediatrics
OLIVIER, J. A., M.B., CH.B., M.MED., Forensic Medicine
PISTORIUS, G. J., M.MED., Primary Medical Care
POTGIETER, F., M.MED., Ophthalmology
POTGIETER, G. M., M.B., CH.B., M.MED., PH.D., Chemical Pathology
POMPE VAN MEERDERVOORT, H. F., M.B., CH.B., M.MED., Orthopædics
RÖHM, G. F., M.MED., Anatomic Pathology
SNOWDOWNE, R. B., CH.B., M.MED., Orthopaedics
STEENKAMP, E. C., M.B., CH.B., M.MED., Diagnostic Radiology
STEYN, A. F., M.MED., Internal Medicine
UNGERER, M. J., B.CH.D., M.B., M.MED., Anaesthesiology
UYS, M., M.B.CH.B., Community Health
VAN DEN ENDE, J., M.MED., Medical Microbiology
VAN DER HEEVER, C. M., M.B.CH.B., F.R.C.S., Neurosurgery
VAN NIEKERK, CH.B., D.C.H.(S.A.), M.D., Paediatrics
VAN VELDEN, D. J. J., M.B., CH.B., M.MED., Anatomic Pathology
VENTER, P. F., M.MED., Obstetrics and Gynaecology
VERSLER, F., CH.B., M.MED., Neurology
VORSLER, A. J., M.CH., Anatomy

*Faculty of Agriculture:*
BLIGNANT, C. S., D.SC., Agricultural Economics
BURGER, R. DU T., M.SC., PH.D., Soil Conservation
DE JAGER, J. M., PH.D., Agricultural Meteorology
HUMAN, J. J., D.SC., Agronomy
KRITZINGER, J. A., M.SC.(AGRIC.), D.SC.(AGRIC.), Sheep and Wool Science
NEL, J. A., M.SC.(AGRIC.), D.SC.(AGRIC.), Sheep and Wool Science
NOVELLO, J. C., D.SC., Dairy Science
OPPERMAN, D. P. J., D.SC.(AGRIC.)
PAUER, G. D. C., M.SC.(AGRIC.), D.SC. (AGRIC.), Plant Pathology
SMITH, A., M.SC.(AGRIC.), PH.D., Animal Husbandry
VAN HEERDEN, D. F. I., M.SC., PH.D., Biometry

*Faculty of Law:*
CILLIERS, C., LL.D., Private Law
CLAASEN, J. Y., B.COM., LL.B., Private Law
DU TOIT, D. C., IUR.DRS., Constitutional Law
DU PLESSIS, J. V., B.A., LL.B., Law
MORKEL, D. W., B.A., LL.B., Process Law
VAN SCHALKWYK, J. H., IUR.DRS., Private Law
WESSELS, Dr. H. A., M.A., LL.B., D.PHIL., Roman Law

ATTACHED INSTITUTES:
**Institute of Environmental Research.**
*Director:* Prof. D. F. TOERJEN, D.SC.AGRIC.

**Institute for Groundwater Studies.**
*Director:* Prof. F. D. I. HODGSON, D.SC.

**Institute of Social and Economic Research.**
*Director:* Prof. W. J. H. VREY, D.PHIL.

**Institute for Contemporary History.**
*Director:* J. C. MOLL, D.PHIL. (acting).

## UNIVERSITY OF PORT ELIZABETH

P.O.B. 1600,
PORT ELIZABETH 6000,
CAPE PROVINCE

Telephone: 5311-928.

Founded 1964.

Languages of instruction: Afrikaans and English; Academic year: February to November (two semesters).

*Chancellor:* A. E. RUPERT, M.SC.
*Vice-Chancellor and Principal:* Prof. S. J. SCHOEMAN, D.PHIL., D.ED.
*Registrar:* J. A. ROBBERTSE, B.SC., M.P.A.
*Librarian:* J. C. CRONJÉ, B.A., F.S.A.I.L.I.S.

Number of teachers: c. 260.
Number of students: c. 3,000.

Publications: *Prospectus, Calendar, Student Diary, U.P.E. Publication Series, U.P.E. Image* (all annually), *U.P.E. Focus, UPPIECAMPUS* (2 a year), *Institute for Planning Research—Research Reports, UPEN* (fortnightly newspaper).

### DEANS:

*Faculty of Arts:* Prof. J. A. VAN AARDE, M.A., D.PHIL., T.H.E.D.
*Faculty of Science:* Prof. T. ERASMUS, D.SC.
*Faculty of Education:* Prof. J. M. A. KOTZÉ, D.ED.
*Faculty of Economic Sciences:* Prof. A. P. J. IMMELMAN, M.A., PH.D., C.A.
*Faculty of Law:* Prof. J. T. DELPORT, LL.D.
*Students:* Prof. C. J. BOTHA, M.A., M.ED., D.LITT., S.T.D.

### DIRECTORS:

*Music Centre:* J. G. DE WET, U.P.L.M., U.T.L.M., F.T.C.L.
*Institute for Planning Research:* J. F. POTGIETER, M.A., D.PHIL.
*Uranium Chemistry Research Unit:* J. G. H. DU PREEZE, D.SC., A.R.S.C.
*Institute for Church Architecture and Church Art:* D. P. KESTING, D.ARCH.
*Institute for the Didactics of Mathematics:* B. R. BUYS, M.A., U.ED.

## POTCHEFSTROOM UNIVERSITY FOR CHRISTIAN HIGHER EDUCATION

POTCHEFSTROOM, TRANSVAAL

Telephone: Potchefstroom 2-2112.

Founded 1869; incorporated in University of South Africa as Constituent College 1921; assumed full university status March 1951.

Principal language of instruction: Afrikaans; Academic year: February to November.

*Chancellor:* Dr. P. W. VORSTER.
*Vice-Chancellor and Principal:* Prof. T. VAN DER WALT, TH.D.
*Vice-Principals:* Prof. J. S. DU PLESSIS, M.A., DLITT., Prof. N. J. SWART, M.COM., PH.D.
*Chairman of the Council:* Rev. A. A. VENTER, B.D.
*President of Convocation:* Prof. S. C. W. DUVENAGE, TH.D., D.LITT. ET PHIL.
*Registrar:* Prof. E. J. SMIT, M.A., D.LITT.
Library: see Libraries.
Number of lecturers: 464, including 128 professors.
Number of students: 6,698.

Publications: *Nuus oor Afrika*† (monthly), *Die Wêreld in Oënskou*† (monthly), *Die P.U.-kaner*† (monthly), *Koers*† (6 a year).

### DEANS:

*Faculty of Arts:* Prof. A. J. VILJOEN, D.PHIL., F.S.A.I.L.I.S.
*Faculty of Science:* Prof. P. H. STOKER, D.SC.
*Faculty of Theology:* Prof. J. J. VAN DER WALT, TH.D.
*Faculty of Education:* Prof. J. J. DE WET, D.ED.
*Faculty of Economic Sciences:* Prof. D. J. L. JACOBS, D.COM.
*Faculty of Law:* Prof. H. N. PRETORIUS, B.A., LL.B.

### PROFESSORS:

*Faculty of Arts:*

BALLOT, G. M., D.PHIL., History of Art
BOTHA, Miss M. E., M.A., D.PHIL., Philosophy and Inter-Disciplinary Philosophy
BOTHA, T., D.LITT., Speech and Drama
CLOETE, T. T., M.A., D.LITT ET PHIL., Afrikaans Linguistics and Theory of Literature, Afrikaans and Dutch
COERTSE, Mrs. E., D.PHIL., Nursing
COETZEE, H. P. A., D.MUS., Music
COETZEE, J. H., M.A., D.PHIL., Ethnology
DE VILLIERS, Mrs. F. M. J., D.ED., Nursing
DE VILLIERS, P. J., B.A., L.R.A.M., A.R.C.M., Music
DU PLESSIS, H. G. W., D.LITT.ET PHIL., Afrikaans and Dutch
DU PLESSIS, M. J. H., M.A., LIC. ES LETTRES, DOCT. ES L., French and Italian
DU PLOOY, F. D., M.A., D.LITT., German
DUVENAGE, B., TH.D., D.PHIL., Inter-Disciplinary Philosophy and Philosophy
ELOFF, D. J., M.A., D.PHIL., Social Work
GOUWS, L. A., M.A., D.PHIL., Psychology
HENNING, J. J., M.A., D.PHIL., Development Administration
KRÜGER, C. J. H., M.A., D.LITT., Bantu Languages
LOHANN, C. A., M.A., D.PHIL., F.S.A.L.A., Library and Information Service
MARITZ, C. J., M.A., D.PHIL., Development Administration

POTGIETER, F. J., M.A., D.PHIL., Town and Regional Planning
PRINSLOO, W. J. DE V., B.ED., M.A., D.LITT., English
SCHUTTE, P. J., M.A., D.PHIL., Library and Information Science
STEENBERG, D. H., M.A., D.LITT., Afrikaans and Dutch
SWANEPOEL, H. F., D.PHIL., Psychology
TALJAARD, J. A. L., M.A., D.PHIL., Philosophy
TÖNSING, L. R., M.A., D.LITT., German
VAN DEN BERGH, G. N., M.A., D.LITT., History
VAN DER ELST, J., M.A., PH.D., Afrikaans and Dutch
VAN DER MERWE, N. T., M.A., DRS.PHIL., Philosophy
VAN DER SCHYFF, P. F., M.A., D.LITT., History
VAN DER WALT, B. J., M.A., D.PHIL., Philosophy
VAN DER WALT, C. P., M.A., D.PHIL., International Politics
VAN DER WALT, J. J. A., M.MUS., D.PHIL., Music
VAN DER WALT, P. D., M.A., D.LITT., Afrikaans and Dutch
VAN DER WATEREN, H., M.A., D.PHIL., Ethnology
VAN DYK, T. A., B.SC., M.A., D.LITT. ET PHIL., Head of Vaal River Branch at Vanderbijlpark
VAN JAARSVELD, P. E., M.A., D.PHIL., Psychology
VAN TONDER, J. J., M.A., D.PHIL., Political Science
VAN WYK, E. M., M.B.CH.B., Psychology
VENTER, J. A., B.ED., M.A., D.LITT., English
VILJOEN, A. J., M.A., D.PHIL., F.S.A.L.A., Library and Information Science
VON S. VENTER, A. J. N., M.A., Fine Arts
WISSING, D. P., M.A., D.LITT., Afrikaans Linguistics and Theory of Literature

*Faculty of Law:*

AUCAMP, P. VAN Z., B.A., LL.B., Mercantile Law
DE BEER, C. R., LL.D., Mercantile Law
JACOBS, S. C., DRS.JURIS., Public Law
OLIVIER, N. J. J., D.JUR., Roman Law
POSTMA, S., B.A., LL.B., D.JUR., Roman Law
PRETORIUS, H. N., B.A., LL.B., Law of Procedure, Evidence and Forensic Medicine
SCOTT, W. E., LL.D., Criminal Law
VAN DER WALT, C. F. C., LL.D., Private Law
VENTER, F., LL.D., Public Law

*Faculty of Science:*

BISSCHOFF, A. A., D.SC., Geology
BOTHA, D. J., D.SC., Botany
DE BEER, Miss H. M., PH.D., Domestic Science
DE BEER, J. F., D.SC., Computer Science
DREYER, A. C., D.SC., Pharmacology
EVERSON, R. C., PH.D., Engineering Chemistry
GEERTSEMA, J. C., M.SC., PH.D., Statistics
GOOSSENS, A. P. G., D.SC., Pharmaceutics
GROBLER, J. J., D.SC., Mathematics and Applied Mathematics
HARMSE, H. J. V. M., M.SC., PH.D., Pedology
HATTINGH, J. M., D.SC., Statistics (Vaal River Branch)
JOOSTE, T. DE W., PH.D., Mathematics and Applied Mathematics
KOELEMAN, H. A., D.SC., Pharmaceutics
LÖTTER, A. P., D.SC., Pharmaceutics
MARAIS, J. F., D.SC., Zoology

UNIVERSITIES                                                                                                                                            SOUTH AFRICA

MARTINS, F. J. C., D.SC., Chemistry
MEYER, M. A. DU T., D.SC., Physics
OFFERMEIER, J., M.SC., PH.D., Pharmacology
PAPENDORF, M. C., M.SC., PH.D., Botany
PRETORIUS, P. J., D.SC., Physiology
REINECKE, C. J., D.SC., Biochemistry
STOKER, P. H., D.SC., Physics
STRYDOM, B. C., M.SC., MATH.D., Mathematics and Applied Mathematics
SWANEPOEL, J. W. H., D.SC., Statistics
TAUTE, W. J., M.SC., F.S.A.I.E.E., Electronics
VAN AARDT, W. J., D.SC., Zoology
VAN DEN BERG, J. A., D.SC., Chemistry
VAN DER WALT, J. J., D.SC., Physiology
VAN EEDEN, D., M.SC., PH.D., Microbiology and Hygiene
VAN EEDEN, J. A., D.SC., Zoology
VAN ELDIK, P., D.SC., Mathematics and Applied Mathematics
VAN ROOYEN, Miss J. M., M.B.CH.B., D.SC., Pharmacology
VAN WYK, D. J., D.SC., Mathematics and Applied Mathematics
VAN WYK, J. J. P., M.SC., PH.D., Botany
VENTER, J. H., M.SC., PH.D., Statistics

*Faculty of Theology:*
BUYS, P. W., TH.D., Apologetics, Ethics
COETZEE, J. C., TH.D., New Testament Exegesis
COETZEE, P. J., M.A., B.D., D.PHIL., Dogmatics
D'ASSONVILLE, V. E., TH.M., PH.D., Church History
FLOOR, L., TH.D., New Testament Exegesis
HELBERG, J. L., M.A., TH.D., Old Testament Exegesis
LION-CACHET, F. N., M.A., TH.D., Old Testament Exegesis
VAN DER LINDE, G. P. L., TH.D., Church Law
VAN DER WALT, I. J., M.A., TH.D., Missionary Science
VAN DER WALT, J. J., TH.D., Pastoral Subjects

*Faculty of Education:*
BARNARD, S. S., B.SC., D.ED., Historical and Comparative Education
CALITZ, L. P., D.ED., Teaching Practice
DE WET, J. J., B.SC., D.ED., Empirical Education
KRUGER, H. B., B.A., D.ED., Guidance and Special Education
PUTTER, W. J., D.P.ED., Physical Education
SCHOLTZ, G. J. L., M.ED., PH.D., Physical Education
STEYN, I. N., D.ED., Guidance and Special Education
STRYDOM, G. L., M.A., PHIL., Physical Education
VAN DER WALT, J. L., D.ED., Theoretical Education

*Faculty of Economic Sciences:*
BARNARD, A. L., D.COM., Industrial and Personnel Psychology
BOSHOFF, C. H., D.COM., Economics
ELS, J. H., D.COM., C.A., Accountancy and Auditing
ERASMUS, D. P., D.COM., Economics
HAVENGA, J. J. D., D.ECON., Business Economics
JACOBS, D. J. L., B.A., D.COM., Business Economics
SCHOEMAN, C. F., M.A., D.PHIL., Industrial and Personnel Psychology
SORGDRAGER, A. J. E., M.COM., D.ECON., A.C.W.A., M.B.I.M., A.I.C.B., Cost and Management Accountancy
SWANEPOEL, H. J., M.COM., Cost and Management Accountancy (Vaal River Branch)

VAN DER MERWE, D. S., D.COM., C.A., Accountancy and Auditing
VAN WYK, L. A., D.COM., Economics
VAN ZIJL, A. S., M.A., D.PHIL., Industrial Sociology
VENTER, W. J., M.COM., D.ECON., Economics
WEBER, H. J., D.COM., Economics (Vaal River Branch)

ATTACHED INSTITUTES:

**Conservatoire of Music.**
*Head:* Prof. J. J. A. VAN DER WALT.

**Bureau for Continuing Education.**
*Director:* H. M. ROBINSON.

**Bureau for Research.**
*Director:* Prof. P. A. J. RYKE.

**Sport Bureau.**
*Executive Chairman and President:* Prof. J. T. CLAASSEN.
*Director:* P. MALAN.

**Bureau for University Education.**
*Director:* Prof. S. J. PRELLER.

**Institute for the Advancement of Calvinism.**
*Director:* Prof. B. J. VAN DER WALT.

**Institute of African and Bantu Studies.**
*Director:* Prof. C. J. MARITZ.

**Institute for Afrikaans Culture and Folklore.**
*Director:* (vacant).

**Institute of Communication Research.**
*Director:* P. G. SNYMAN.

**Centre for International Politics.**
*Director:* Prof. C. P. VAN DER WALT.

**Institute of Linguistic and Literary Research.**
*Director:* (vacant).

**Institute of Regional Planning.**
*Director:* Prof. F. J. POTIGETER.

**Institute for Research in Children's Literature.**
*Director:* Prof. C. A. LOHANN.

**Institute of South African Music.**
*Director:* Prof. H. P. A. COETZEE.

**Institute of South African Politics.**
*Chairman:* Prof. C. P. VAN DER WALT.
*Director:* Prof. J. J. VAN TONDER.

**Institute of Botanic Research.**
*Director:* Prof. J. J. P. VAN WYK.

**Research Unit for Chemical Kinetics.**
*Director:* Prof. J. A. VAN DEN BERG.

**Research Unit for Cosmic Rays.**
*Director:* Prof. P. H. STOKER.

**Research Unit for the Design of Catecholaminergic Drugs (MRC):** *see* under S. A. Medical Research Council.

**Institute of Industrial Pharmacy.**
*Director:* Prof. A. P. LÖTTER.

**Institute for Pedology.**
*Director:* Prof. H. J. v. M. HARMSE.

**Institute of Petrochemical Research.**
*Director:* (vacant).

**Institute of Physical Research.**
*Director:* Prof. M. A. DU T. MEYER.

**Institute of Physiological Research.**
*Director:* Prof. J. J. VAN DER WALT.

**Institute of Psychological and Educational Services and Research.**
*Director:* Prof. P. E. VAN JAARSVELD.

**Snail Research Unit (MRC):** *see* under S.A. Medical Research Council.

**Institute of Zoological Research.**
*Director:* Prof. W. J. VAN AARDT.

**Institute of Administrative Automation.**
*Director:* Prof. A. J. E. SORGDRAGER.

**South African Institute of Co-operatives.**
*Director:* Prof. D. J. L. JACOBS.

**General Bureau of Economic Research.**
*Director:* Prof. D. P. ERASMUS.

**Small Business Advisory Bureau.**
*Director:* Dr. J. G. SMITH.

INSTITUTIONS IN CO-OPERATION WITH THE UNIVERSITY:

**Theological School of the Reformed Church in South Africa.**
*Rector:* Prof. P. J. COETZEE, M.A., B.D., D.PHIL.

**Potchefstroom College of Education.**
*Rector:* (vacant).

## UNIVERSITY OF PRETORIA
BROOKLYN, PRETORIA

Telephone: 43-6051.

Founded as Transvaal University College 1908. Granted Charter as University of Pretoria 1930.

Private control; Language of instruction: Afrikaans; Academic year: February to December (two semesters).

*Chancellor:* The Hon. Dr. H. MULLER, LL.B., M.A., D.LITT.

*Principal and Vice-Chancellor:* Prof. D. M. JOUBERT, PH.D., D.SC.

*Vice-Principals:* Prof. P. OOSTHUIZEN, B.A., LL.B., Prof. H. P. VAN DER SCHIJFF, D.SC.

*Chairman of the Council:* S. M. NAUDE, M.SC., PH.D.

*President of Convocation:* The Hon. Chief Justice F. L. H. RUMPFF, B.A., LL.B.

*Director of Physical Planning and Business Administration:* W. J. COETZEE, M.B.A.

*Head, Academic Administration and Registrar:* A. C. BOTHMA, B.A., LL.B.

*Head, Financial Administration and Registrar:* W. L. KOK, B.COM., A.C.C.S., A.C.I.S.

*Director of Library Service:* Prof. E. D. GERRYTS, D.LITT.ET.PHIL.(BIBL.).

Library, *see* Libraries.

Number of teachers: 2,456.
Number of students: 16,660.

Publications: *Jaarboek* (annually), *Skakelblad* (Link Up, 2 a year), *Tukkie-Werf* (quarterly), *Perdeby* (weekly students' newspaper), *Publikasies van die Universiteit van Pretoria—Nuwe reeks* (Publications of the University of Pretoria—New Series) (I) Research results, etc., periodically, (II) Titles of dissertations (annually), *Ad-Destinatum: Gedenkboek van die Universiteit van Pretoria 1960, Opvoedkundige Studies* (Educational Studies, 3–4 issues annually), *Openbare Fakulteitslesings* (periodically), *Huldigingsbundels* (occasionally), *Trek* (students' magazine, annually).

DEANS:

*Faculty of Arts:* Prof. A. P. GROVE, M.A., D.LITT.
*Faculty of Science:* (vacant).
*Faculty of Agricultural Sciences:* Prof. D. J. J. POTGIETER, PH.D.
*Faculty of Law:* Prof. D. J. JOUBERT, LL.D.
*Faculty of Theology—Dutch Reformed Church of Africa:* Prof. B. J. ENGELBRECHT, TH.DR.
*Faculty of Theology—Dutch Reformed Church:* Prof. J. A. HEYNS, B.PHIL., TH.DRS.
*Faculty of Economic and Political Sciences:* Prof. C. F. NIEUWOUDT, M.A., D.PHIL.
*Faculty of Veterinary Science:* Prof. J. M. W. LE ROUX, DR.MED.VET.
*Faculty of Education:* Prof. F. VAN DER STOEP, D.ED.
*Faculty of Medicine:* Prof. F. G. GELDENHUYS, M.D., D.V.G., F.R.C.O.G., F.I.C.S.
*Faculty of Dentistry:* Prof. P. C. SNIJMAN, B.D.S., R.C.S., H.D.D.
*Faculty of Engineering:* Prof. D. J. SCHOEMAN, PH.D.

PROFESSORS:

*Faculty of Arts:*
BOSHOFF, M. C., M.A.(BIBL.), D.LITT. ET PHIL., Library Science
BOTHA, J. L., M.A., D.PHIL., Physical Education
COERTZE, R. D., M.A., D.PHIL., Ethnology
DREYER, P. S., M.A., D.PHIL., D.D., Philosophy
EKSTEEN, L. C., D.LITT., Afrikaans
ELOFF, J. F., M.A., Archaeology
GROENEWALD, P. S., M.A., D.LITT., Bantu Languages
GROVE, A. P., M.A., D.LITT., Afrikaans
HAY, I. S., M.A., Speech Science and Logopaedics
HERHOLDT, W. VAN DER M., D.PHIL., Psychology
KRIEL, D. M., D.LITT., Latin
LOUW, J. P., M.A., D.LITT., Greek
NEL, P. G., M.A., D.PHIL., History of Afrikaans and Dutch Culture
NILANT, F. G. E., M.A., PH.D., History of Art
ODENDAAL, L. B., M.A., D.LITT., Drama
OOSTHUIZEN, J. S., D.PHIL., Sociology
PAXINOS, S., D.MUS., Music
PEETERS, L. F. H. M. C., PH.D., Romance Languages
ROOS, N. O., D.PHIL., Fine Arts
SMIT, P. J., PH.D., Physical Education
STEYN, D. G., D.PHIL., Criminology
STRYDOM, S., D.LITT., Afrikaans
SWIEGERS, D. J., D.PHIL., Psychology
TITLESTAD, P. J. H., M.A., D.LITT., English
VAN AARDE, A. M., D.LITT., German
VAN JAARSVELD, F. A., M.A., LITT. ET PHIL., History
VAN ROOYEN, I. J. J., D.PHIL., Social Work
VAN WYK, W. C., D.D., Semitic Languages

*Faculty of Science:*
BOSHOFF, E., PH.D., Domestic Science
BOTHA, P. R., M.SC., Architecture
BOTHMA, J. DU P., PH.D., Zoology
BURGER, A. P., B.ARCH., Architecture
BUYS, T. S., D.SC., Chemistry
ELOFF, F. C., M.SC., D.SC., Zoology
FRIEDLAND, E. K. H., D.SC., Physics
GEERTHSEN, J. M. P., D.SC., Genetics
GRÄBE, P. J., D.PHIL., Mathematics
GROBBELAAR, N., M.SC., PH.D., Botany
HATTINGH, P. S., D.LITT. ET PHIL., Geography
HAUPTFLEISCH, A. C., M.B.A., Building Management
HOLM, E., D.SC., Entomology
ROBBERTSE, P. J., D.SC., Botany
SAUER, N., M.SC., PH.D., Applied Mathematics
SCHOEMAN, M. J., DR.SC.T.WET., Mathematics
SKINNER, J. D., M.SC., PH.D., Zoology
SMALL, J. G. C., D.SC., Botany
SNYMAN, C. P., DR.RER.NAT., Geology
VAN DEN HEEVER, R. J., M.SC., PH.D., Computer Science
VAN DER MERWE, J. H., PH.D., Physics
VAN ROOYEN, E., D.SC., Physics
VAN SCHALWYK, A., M.SC., Geology
VILJOEN, J. T. B., B.SC., Quantity Surveying
VON GRUENEWALDT, G., D.SC., Geology
WIECHERS, A., D.SC., PH.D., Chemistry
ZIETSMAN, P. J., M.SC., Mathematics

*Faculty of Agricultural Sciences:*
DUVEL, G. H., D.INST.AGRAR., Agrarian Extension
FÖLSCHER, W. J., PH.D., Soil Technology and Plant Nutrition
GROENEWALD, J. A., M.SC., PH.D., Agricultural Economics
GRUNOW, J. O., D.SC., Plant Production
HOLTZHAUSEN, L. C., D.SC., Horticulture
KOTZE, J. M., D.SC.AGRIC., Microbiology and Plant Pathology
LOMBARD, S. H., M.SC., PH.D., Food Science
MAREE, C., D.SC., Animal Production
NEL, P. C., D.SC., Plant Production
POTGIETER, D. J. J., M.SC., PH.D., Biochemistry
STEYN, P. L., M.SC., PH.D., Microbiology and Plant Pathology

*Faculty of Law:*
ECKARD, C. F., LL.D., Procedure and Evidence
JOUBERT, D. J., LL.D., Roman Dutch Law and International Private Law
LABUSCHAGNE, J. M. T., M.A., D.PHIL., LL.D., Bantu Law
SCOTT, T. J., LL.D., Roman Dutch Law and International Private Law
VAN DER WESTHUIZEN, J. V., LL.D., History of Law, Comparative Law and Philosophy of Law
VAN JAARSVELD, S. R., LL.D., Mercantile Law
VAN ROOYEN, J. C. W., LL.D., Criminal Law
VORSTER, M. P., B.A., LL.B., DRS.IUR., Public Law

*Faculty of Theology (Dutch Reformed Church of Africa):*
DE WET, J. I., D.D., Practical Theology
ENGELBRECHT, B. J., B.D., TH.DR., Dogmatics and Christian Ethics
OBERHOLZER, J. P., M.A., D.D., Old Testament Exegesis and Theology
PELSER, G. M. M., D.D., New Testament Exegesis and Theology
PONT, A. D., M.A., TH.DR., History of Christianity
VAN DER MERWE, P. J., D.D., Philosoph of Religion and Missions

*Faculty of Theology (Dutch Reformed Church):*
BARNARD, A. C., D.PHIL., D.TH., Practical Theology
BOSHOFF, C. W. H., M.A., D.D., Philosophy of Religion and Missions
DE KLERK, J. J., D.PHIL., D.TH., Practical Theology
DU TOIT, A. B., M.A., B.D., TH.D., New Testament Exegesis and Theology
HEYNS, J. A., B.D., TH.DR., D.PHIL., Dogmatics and Christian Ethics
VAN DER WATT, P. B., B.D., D.TH., History of Christianity
VAN ZYL, A. H., M.A., D.D., Old Testament Exegesis and Theology

*Faculty of Economic and Political Sciences:*
BOSHOFF, A. B., D.COM., Business Management
BOTES, P. S., D.ADMIN., Political Science, Public Administration and International Politics
CHURR, E. G., D.B.A., Business Economics
GILDENHUYS, J. S. H., D.PHIL., Political Science, Public Administration and International Politics
LOMBARD, J. A., M.A., PH.D., Economics
MARX, F. W., D.COM., Business Economics
MARX, S., M.B.A., D.COM., Business Economics
NIEUWOUDT, C. F., M.A., D.PHIL., Political Science, Public Administration and International Politics
OLIVIER, G. C., D.PHIL., Political Science, Public Administration and International Politics
PISTORIUS, C. W. I., M.COM., C.A.(S.A.), Business Management
SCHOEMAN, H. S., D.SC., Statistics
SMIT, C. F., D.SC., Statistics
STADLER, J. J., D.COM., Economics
STAPELBERG, N. H., D.COM., Business Management
STEYN, A. G. W., PH.D., Statistics
VAN VUUREN, M. J. C., D.B.A., Business Management
VILJOEN, G. V. N., M.COM., M.B.A., Accounting and Auditing
ZEVENBERGEN, A. P., M.COM., M.B.A., Business Management

*Faculty of Veterinary Science:*
COUBROUGH, R. I., M.V.SC., Genesiology
GROSSKOPF, J. F. W., M.MED.VET., PH.D., Physiology, Pharmacology and Toxicology
HOWELL, P. G., D.V.SC., Infectious Diseases
LITTLEJOHN, A., D.V.SC., Equine Research
OSTERHOFF, D. R., DR.(AGRON.), D.SC., Zootechnics
REINECKE, R. K., D.V.SC., Veterinary Parasitology
STEYN, D. G., D.V.SC., Surgery
TUSTIN, R. C., M.MED.VET.(PATH.), Pathology
VAN DER WALT, K., B.V.SC., Medicine

*Faculty of Education:*
BONDESIO, M. J., D.ED., Historical and Comparative Pedagogics
JOUBERT, C. J., D.ED., Psycho-, Socio-, and Vocational Guidance Pedagogics
LANDMAN, W. A., M.A., D.ED., D.PHIL., Fundamental Pedagogics
LOUW, W. J., D.ED., Didactic Pedagogics and Subject Didactics

POTGIETER, F. J., M.A., D.ED., Historical and Comparative Pedagogics
SONNEKUS, M. C. H., DR.PAED., D.ED., Psycho-, Socio-, and Vocational Guidance Pedagogics
VAN DYK, C. J., D.ED., Didactic Pedagogics and Subject Didactics
VAN NIEKERK, P.A., D.ED., Ortho-Pedagogics

*Faculty of Medicine:*
BODEMER, W., M.MED., Psychiatry
BROWN, J. M. M., D.V.SC., Physiology
COETZEE, J. N., M.D., Medical Microbiology
CRONJÉ, R. E., M.B., B.CH., Paediatrics
DE BRUYN, T. B., M.B., CH.B., Anaesthetics
DE KLERK, A. J., M.MED., Orthopaedics
DE VILLIERS, L. S., M.B., CH.B., B.SC., M.MED., Chemical Pathology
DU PLESSIS, D. J., M.MED., Surgery
EVANS, W. B. D. I., M.B., B.CH., Obstetrics and Gynaecology
FALKSON, G., M.B.CH.B., M.MED., M.D., Cancer Chemotherapy
FINDLAY, G. H., D.SC., M.D., Dermatology
FRANZ, R. C., M.MED., Surgery
GRÄBE, R. P., M.B., CH.B., M.MED., Orthopaedics
HAMERSMA, H., M.B., CH.B., M.D., Oto-rhino-laryngology
HUMAN, G. P., M.B.CH.B., M.MED., Medicine
KOTZÉ, W. J., D.CUR., G.SD., Nursing
LESSING, A. J. P., M.B., CH.B., M.MED., Anaesthetics
LOUBSER, J. D., M.B., CH.B., M.MED., Forensic Medicine
MEYER, B. J., M.B., CH.B., M.D., D.SC., Physiology
MEYER, H., M.MED., Ophthalmology
MIENY, C. J., M.D., M.CH., Surgery
PRINSLOO, J. G., M.D., Paediatrics
PRINSLOO, S. F., M.ED.(RAD-D), Radiodiagnosis
PROZESKY, O. W., M.D., Medical Microbiology
ROSSOUW, D. S., M.MED., Medicine
SANDISON, A. G., M.D., Radiotherapy
SCHMID, E. U., M.B., CH.B., M.MED., Surgery
SIMSON, I. W., M.D., Anatomical Pathology
SOMMERS, DE K., M.B.CH.B., B.CH.D., M.D., Pharmacology
STEVENS, K., M.B., CH.B., M.D., Haematology
SWART, J. G., M.B., CH.B., Oto-rhino-laryngology
THERON, J. J., M.B.CH.B., D.SC., Physiology
VAN DEN BERG, A. D. P., M.B.CH.B., M.PRAX.MED., Family Practice
VAN DER MERWE, J. V., M.MED., Obstetrics and Gynaecology
VAN DER MEYDEN, C. H., M.B.B.CH., Medicine
VAN DER SPUY, J. C., M.B.B.CH., Surgery
VAN DER WALT, C. M., M.MED., Radiodiagnosis
VAN DYK, J. J., M.MED., Cancer Chemotherapy
VAN NIEKERK, I. J. M., M.MED., Anatomy
VAN RENSBURG, A. J., M.SC., M.D., Medical Microbiology
VAN RENSBURG, M. J., M.MED., Surgery
VAN STADEN, D. A., M.PRAX.MED., Family Practice

*Faculty of Dentistry:*
DUVENAGE J. G., M.CH.D., Maxillo-facial and Oral Surgery
LIGTHELM, A. J., M.CH.D., Oral Pathology and Oral Medicine
NEL, J. C., M.CH.D., H.D.D., Endodontics and Occlusal Rehabilitation
POTGIETER, P. J., B.CH.D., M.SC., Prosthetics and Dental Mechanics
PRETORIUS, J. A., M.CH.D., Periodontics
SCHOEMAN, P. J., B.SC., B.D.S., Conservative Dentistry and Oral Pedodontics
SEELIGER, J. E., M.DENT., Maxillo-facial and Oral Surgery
SNYMAN, W. D., M.CH.D., Community Dentistry
ZIETSMAN, S. T., M.CH.D., B.D.S., H.D.D., Orthodontics

*Faculty of Engineering:*
BOTHA, J. P., M.B.A., PH.D., Production Engineering
BROWN, A. N., M.SC.(ENG.), Mining Engineering
DIPPENAAR, R. J., M.SC., PH.D., Material Science and Metallurgical Engineering
FOURIE, F., B.SC.(ENG.), Civil Engineering
GRIMSEHL, U. H. J., B.SC.(ENG.), Chemical Engineering
GROBLER, B. J. G. W., D.SC., Agricultural Engineering
HAARHOFF, P. C., D.SC., D.ENG., Mechanical Engineering
JORDAAN, P. W., M.SC.(ENG.), Civil Engineering
KUHN, G. J., B.SC.(ENG.), Electronic Engineering
LOUW, W. J., M.SC., PH.D., Electronic Engineering
MALHERBE, J. A. G., PH.D., Electronic Engineering
MAREE, N., M.SC., Surveying and Town Planning and Regional Planning
PRETORIUS, W. A., D.SC., M.S., Chemical Engineering
RADEMEYER, P., D.SC., Electronic Engineering
ROOSEBOOM, A., D.SC., D.H.E., Civil Engineering
SAVAGE, P. F., M.SC., Civil Engineering
VAN BILJON, L., D.SC.(ENG.), Electronic Engineering
VAN ROOYEN, G. T., D.SC., M.COMM. (B. & A.), Material Science and Metallurgical Engineering
VISSER, J., B.SC.(ENG.), Mechanical Engineering
VON WILLICH, G. P. R., SC.D., Civil Engineering
WESSELS, N., B.SC.(ENG.), Electrical Engineering

RESEARCH INSTITUTES:

**Bacterial Genetics Research Unit:** Dir. Prof. J. N. COETZEE.

**Institute for the Study of Plural Societies:** Dir. Prof. J. S. OOSTHUIZEN.

**Institute for Chromatography:** Dir. Prof. V. PRETORIUS.

**Mammal Research Institute:** Dir. Prof. J. D. SKINNER.

**Institute for Microstructures (Epitaxy, Thin Layers, Electro-Optics, Mos and other structures):** Dir. Prof. L. VAN BILJON.

**Institute for Geological Research on the Bushveld Complex:** Dir. Prof. G. VON GRUENEWALDT.

**Margaretha Mes Institute for Seed Research:** Dir. Prof. P. J. ROBBERTSE.

**Institute for Strategic Studies:** Dir. Dr. M. HOUGH.

**Child Guidance Institute:** Dir. Prof. M. C. H. SONNEKUS.

**Hans Snyckers Institute for the Study of Disease Phenomena peculiar to Southern Africa:** Dir. Prof. D. A. VAN STADEN.

**Institute for Stomatology and Bone Biology:** Dir. Prof. L. M. JONCK.

**Institute of Cellular Physiology:** Dir. Prof. B. J. MEYER.

**Institute for Missiological Research:** Dir. Dr. J. M. CRONJÉ.

**Sport Research and Training Institute:** Dir. Prof. J. L. BOTHA.

**South African Institute for Agricultural Extension:** Dir. Prof. G. H. DÜVAL.

**Glaxo Institute for Clinical Pharmacology:** Dir. Prof. DE K. SOMMERS.

RESEARCH BUREAUX:
*Bureau for Economic Policy and Analysis:* Dir. Prof. J. J. STADLER.
*Bureau for Financial Analysis:* Dir. Prof. A. P. ZEVENBERGEN.

RESEARCH UNITS AND INSTITUTES OF THE M.R.C.
(See under South African Medical Research Council).

# RAND AFRIKAANS UNIVERSITY
P.O.B. 524, JOHANNESBURG
Telephone: 726-500.

Founded in 1966; the first students were enrolled in 1968.

State control; Language of instruction: Afrikaans; Academic year: January to November.

*Chancellor:* P. J. MEYER, DRS.PHIL. ET LITT.
*Vice-Chancellor and Principal:* Prof. J. P. DE LANGE, M.ED., T.O.D., T.H.O.D.
*Vice-Principals:* (Business Administration) Prof. J. DOOLMAN, M.B.A., D.COM.; (Academic) Prof. G. J. HAUPTFLEISCH, DR.TECH.WET.
*Registrars:* (Financial) H. J. KRUGER, B.ADMIN., B.COMM.; (Academic) W. J. DU PLESSIS, B.A.
*Chief Librarian:* P. AUCAMP, D.PHIL.
Library of 287,703 vols.
Number of teachers: 263.
Number of students: 5,170.

DEANS:
*Faculty of Arts:* Prof. A. F. STEYN.
*Faculty of Economics:* Prof. G. L. DE WET.
*Faculty of Education:* Prof. P. J. MAREE.
*Faculty of Law:* (vacant).
*Faculty of Science:* Prof. D. H. WILD.

PROFESSORS:

ALBERTS, H. L., Experimental and Theoretical Physics
AUGUSTYN, J. C. D., Industrial Psychology
BARRIE, G. N., Public Law
BASSON, C. J., Education
BEYERS, D., Psychology
BLOM, A., Library and Information Science
BREDENKAMP, G. L., Electrical and Electronic Engineering
BROERE, I., Mathematics
DE JAGER, F. J., Public Law
DE KOCK, E. L., Classical Languages
DE KONING, T. L., Communication
DE SWARDT, G. H., Botany
DE VILLIERS, I. J., Accountancy
DE WET, G. L., Economics
DU PLESSIS, P. G. W., Philosophy
DU PLESSIS, P. J, Biblical Studies
DU PLESSIS, P. DE V., Experimental and Theoretical Physics
DU TOIT, H. DE V., Strategic Studies
ENGEL, E. P., History of Art
ENGELBRECHT, A. H. P., Botany
ENGELBRECHT, C. S., Education
FAURE, P. K., Chemistry
FERREIRA, G. V., Education
FERREIRA, J. A., Bantu Languages
FRANCISCO-LA GRANGE, F. H., Social Work
GOUS, S. C., Business Economics
HEIDEMA, J., Mathematics
HENDERSON, W. J., Classical Languages
HENDRICKX, B., Classical Languages
HEYNS, J., Zoology
HOLZAPFEL, C. W., Chemistry
KAPP, P. H., History
KÖHNKE, K. F. H. O., German
KOK, J. C., Education
KRUGER, R. A., Education
LEIGHTON, J. M., English
LEMMER, H. H., Statistics
LOURENS, J. A. J., Experimental and Theoretical Physics
LUTSCH, A. G. K., Electrical and Electronic Engineering
MANS, K., Accountancy
MAREE, P. J., Education
MULLER, E. C. C., Education
NAUDÉ, J. A., Semitic Languages
NEL, F. J., Accountancy
NIEUWENHUIZEN, P. J., Economics
ODENDAL, F. F., Afrikaans and Dutch Philology
OOSTHUIZEN, M. J., Mercantile Law
PAUW, D. A., Classics
PELSER, H. S., Semitic Languages
PIEK, B. J., Sociology
PRINSLOO, M. W., African Law and Development Administration
RADEMEYER, W. F., Business Economics
RAUBENHEIMER, H. G., Chemistry
RAUBENHEIMER, I. VON W., Industrial Psychology
REINECKE, M. F. B., Mercantile Law
ROERING, C., Geology
SCHABORT, J. C., Biochemistry
SCHEEPERS, J. N., Geography
SCHEPERS, J. M., Psychology
SCHOONBEE, H. J., Zoology
SONNEKUS, J. C., Private Law
STEYN, A. F., Sociology
STIELAU, H. I., German
SWANEPOL, J. H., Zoology
SWART, J., Mathematics
SWART, P. L., Electrical and Electronic Engineering
VAN ASWEGEN, H. J., History
VAN BERGE, P. C., Chemistry
VAN BILJON, W. J., Geology
VAN DER MERWE, S. E., Private Law
VAN DER MERWE, S. W. J., Private Law
VAN DER WALT, J. C., Private Law
VAN DER WALT, T., Mathematics
VAN HUYSSTEEN, M. C., Nursing
VAN RENSBURG, F. I. J., Afrikaans and Dutch Literature
VAN WYK, E. B., General Linguistics
VAN WYK, J. D., Electrical and Electronic Engineering
VON SOLMS, S. H., Computer Science
VON STADEN, P. M. S., Bantu Languages
VORSTER, G., Psychology
WIID, A. J. B., Statistics
WIID, D. H., Experimental and Theoretical Physics
WELGEMOED, P. J., Transport Economics
ZASTRAU, H. D. K., Library and Information Science

ATTACHED INSTITUTES:

**Institute for Urban Studies:** Dir. Prof. A. J. G. OOSTHUIZEN.

**Institute for Development Studies:** Dir. Prof. B. J. PIEK.

**Institute for Child and Adult Guidance:** Chair. Prof. T. R. BOTHA.

**Bureau for Higher Education:** Head Prof. F. A. J. MARAIS.

**Institute for Energy Studies:** Chair. Prof. D. J. KOTZÉ.

**Institute for Islamic Studies:** Head Prof. J. A. NAUDÉ.

**Institute for American Studies:** Dir. Prof. P. H. KAPP (acting).


# RHODES UNIVERSITY
(Formerly Rhodes University College)
P.O.B. 94, GRAHAMSTOWN
Telephone: Grahamstown 2023.
Telegraphic Address: Rhodescol

Founded 1904.

Language of instruction: English; Academic year: March to November (four terms).

*Chancellor:* I. MACKENZIE, M.A., LL.D., C.A., D.S.O.
*Chairman of the Council:* N. C. ADDLESON, B.A., LL.B.
*Principal and Vice-Chancellor:* D. S. HENDERSON, M.A., PH.D., F.C.S.S.A.
*Vice-Principal and Pro-Vice-Chancellor:* J. W. BROMMERT, B.SC.
*Registrar:* (vacant).
*Librarian:* G. D. QUINN, M.A.
Library, see Libraries.
Number of teachers: 231, including 50 professors.
Number of students: 2,890.

DEANS:

*Faculty of Arts:* H. J. SCHUTTE, M.SC., DR.MATH.
*Faculty of Science:* E. E. BAART, PH.D., F.R.A.S.
*Faculty of Education:* A. NOBLE, M.ED.
*Faculty of Commerce:* P. VAN DER WATT, M.SC., PH.D.
*Faculty of Divinity:* C. W. COOK, M.A., TH.D.
*Faculty of Law:* R. C. BEUTHIN, B.A., LL.B.
*Faculty of Social Science:* E. HIGGINS, M.A., PH.D.

*Faculty of Pharmaceutical Sciences:* B. POTGIETER, D.SC., D.T.D., M.P.S.

PROFESSORS:

ALLANSON, B. R., M.SC., PH.D., F.R.S.S.AF., Zoology and Entomology
BAART, E. E., PH.D., F.R.A.S., Physics
BEARD, T. V. R., M.A., Political Studies
BEUTHIN, R. C., B.A., LL.B., Law
BLACK, J. K., C.A., Accounting
BRANFORD, W. R. G., M.A., PH.D., Linguistics and English Language
BRINK, A. P., M.A., D.LITT., Afrikaans and Dutch
BUNTING, I. A., M.A., PH.D., Philosophy
BUTLER, F. G., M.A., M.A. (OXON.), D.LITT., English
CATTANEO, J. L., M.A., B.ÈS.L., French
COOK, C. W., M.A., TH.D., Ecclesiastical History
DANIEL J. B. McI., M.A., PH.D., Geography
DAVENPORT, T. R. H., M.A , PH.D., History
DE WET, T., D.SC., Statistics
EALES. H. V., M.SC., PH.D., Geology
FIVAZ, D., M.A., PH.D., African Languages
GAIN, D. B., M.A., PH.D., Classics
GLEDHILL, J. A., M.SC., PH.D., Physics
HIGGINS, E., M.A., PH.D., Sociology
HOLLAND, J. A. B., PH.D., Divinity
KANFER, I., PH.D., Pharmaceutical Sciences
KERR, A. J., LL.M., Law
KRUGER, T. M. D., M.A., D.LITT. ET PHIL., Psychology
LANHAM, L. W., M.A., PH.D., Linguistics and English Language
LETCHER, T. M., M.SC., PH.D., Physical Chemistry
LOCKE, E. E., B.SC., Physical Education
MAYR, R., D.PHIL., L.R.S.M., Music
MITCHELL, W. A., M.SOC.SC., D.PHIL., Social Work
MORAN, V. C., PH.D., F.R.E.S., Entomology
NOBLE, A., M.ED., Education
PAROLIS, H., PH.D., Pharmaceutical Sciences
POTGIETER, B., D.SC., D.T.D., Pharmaceutical Sciences
SARGEANT, R., B.A., Speech and Drama
SCHUTTE, H. J., M.SC., DR.MATH., Pure and Applied Mathematics
SEAGRIEF, S. C., M.SC., PH.D., Botany
SMITH, H. H., M.COM., PH.D., Commerce
STAUDE, G. E., M.COM., M.B.A., Business Administration
STEWART, G. M., Journalism
SUGGIT, J. N., M.A., New Testament Studies
SWITZER, L. E., PH.D., Journalism
TRUU, M. L., PH.D., Economics
TUNMER, R., B.ED., B.A., Education
VAN DER WATT, P., M.SC., PH.D., Statistics
VAN WYK SMITH, M., PH.D., English
WELZ, D. W., M.A., PH.D., German
WHISSON, M. G., PH.D., Anthropology

ATTACHED INSTITUTES:

**Institute for the Study of English in Africa (I.S.E.A.):** f. 1964; Dir. Prof. A. R. W. DE VILLIERS.

**Institute of Social and Economic Research (I.S.E.R.):** f. 1954; Dir. Prof. J. OPLAND.

**Rhodes Institute for Freshwater Studies:** f. 1967; Dir. Prof. B. R. ALLANSON.

**J. L. B. Smith Institute of Ichthyology:** f. 1968; Dir. Assoc. Prof. M. M. SMITH.

**Leather Industries Research Institute:** f. 1941; Dir. Prof. D. R. COOPER.

# UNIVERSITY OF SOUTH AFRICA

P.O.B. 392, PRETORIA
Telephone: 440-3111.

Founded 1873, Royal Charter 1877.

Since 1946 the University has been a correspondence and examining institution, accepting only external students; multi-racial, bilingual Afrikaans and English.

Academic year: February to November.

*Chancellor:* The Hon. Chief Justice of Bophuthatswana, V. G. HIEMSTRA, B.A., LL.B.

*Vice-Chancellor and Principal:* Prof. T. VAN WIJK, M.A.

*Chairman of the Council:* Dr. A. J. KOEN, B.A., B.ED.

*Vice-Principals:* Prof. C. F. CROUSE, M.SC., PH.D. (Planning), Prof. B. S. VAN AS, M.A. (Tuition).

*Registrars:* A. P. SCHUTTE, B.COM. (Finance), D. W. STEYN, M.SC., M.A. (Administration), M. H. STOCKHOFF, B.A. (Academic).

*Librarian:* Prof. J. WILLEMSE, M.A., T.H.E.D., F.S.A.L.A.

Number of teachers: c. 1,076.
Number of students: c. 56,086.

Publications: *Unisa Bulletin†, Unisa News†*, and departmental and technical journals.

### DEANS:

*Faculty of Arts:* Prof. R. S. MEYER, D.LITT. ET PHIL.
*Faculty of Commerce and Administration:* Prof. J. A. CILLIERS, M.COM., C.A.
*Faculty of Education:* Prof. J. C. G. J. VAN VUUREN, M.A., D.ED.
*Faculty of Law:* Prof. W. J. HOSTEN, B.A., LL.B.
*Faculty of Science:* Prof. W. J. A. STEYN, M.SC., PH.D.
*Faculty of Theology:* Prof. I. H. EYBERS, M.A., TH.D., PH.D.

### PROFESSORS:

ALANT, C. J., D.LITT. ET PHIL., Sociology
BARKHUIZEN, B. P., D.EP., Empirical Education
BARNARD, A. H., LL.D., Private Law
BARNARD, C. J., M.A., D.LITT. ET PHIL., History
BAUMBACH, E. M. J., M.A., D.LITT. ET PHIL., African Languages
BEETON, D. R., M.A., D.LITT.ET.PHIL., English
BEKKER, J., M.A., M.BIBL., PH.D., Library Science
BEKKER, P. M., LL.D., Criminal and Procedural Law
BOOYSEN, H., LL.D., Constitutional and International Law
BORNMAN, C. H., D.SC., Computer Science
BOSCH, D. J., TH.D., Church History
BOSMAN, F. J., LL.B., Roman and Comparative Law
BOUCHER, M., M.A., D.LITT. ET PHIL., History
BROWNE, M. W., M.SC., PH.D., Statistics and Operational Research
BURDEN, J. J., D.LITT., Old and New Testament Theology
CILLIERS, H. S., LL.D., C.A., Accountancy
CILLIERS, J. A., M.COM., C.A., Accountancy
CLOETE, M. G. T., M.A., D.PHIL., Criminology
CLUVER, A. D. DE V., D.LITT. ET PHIL., Linguistics
COETZEE, N., D.SC., Computer Science and Information Systems
COPELING, A. J. C., M.SC., PH.D., Mercantile Law
CRONJE, D. S. P., LL.M., Private Law
CRONJE, G. J. DE J., D.COM., Business Economics
CROUSE, C. F., M.SC., PH.D., Mathematical Statistics
DANEEL, M. L., D.TEOL., Church History
DANNENBRING, R. K. W. H., LL.B., DR.JUR., Roman and Comparative Law
DE BRUYN, M., M.A., Social Work
DEIST, F. E., D.LITT., D.TEOL., Old and New Testament Theology
DE KLERK, G. J., M.A., D.LITT. ET PHIL., Afrikaans and Dutch
DE KLERK, W. J., M.A., D.LITT., Afrikaans and Dutch
DÖCKEL, J. A., PH.D., Economics
DREYER, H. J., M.A., B.D., D.LITT. ET PHIL., Semitics
DU PLESSIS, I. J., D.TH., Old and New Testament Theology
DU TOIT, L. M., M.COM., C.A., Auditing
EDWARDS, A. B., LL.B., Roman and Comparative Law
ELS, W. C., M.A., M.ED., D.LITT. ET PHIL., Geography
EYBERS, I. H., M.A., TH.D., PH.D., Old and New Testament Theology
FAUL, M. A., B.COM., B.ED., Accountancy
FIELDELDEY, H., M.SC.(PHYSICS), M.SC. (MATHS), D.SC., Physics
FOUCHE, B., M.A., D.LITT. ET PHIL., Library Science
FOURIE, H. P., M.A., Communication
FOURIE, L. J., B.COM., Economics
GASINSKI, T. Z., PH.D., Russian
GERDES, L. C., D.LITT. ET PHIL., Psychology
GLÜCK, J. J., M.A., D.LITT., Semitics
GRÄSSER, H. S. P., M.SC., PH.D., Mathematics and Applied Mathematics
GROBBELAAR, J. W., M.SC., PH.D., Statistics and Operations Research
GROBBELAAR, W. C., M.CUR., Nursing
HAFFTER, P., D.PHIL., French and Italian
HANEKOM, S. X., D.PHIL., Political Science
HARLEY, G. S., M.ED., Didactics and Comparative Education
HERBST, W., D.COM., Business Economics
HEYNS, A. M., M.SC., PH.D., Chemistry
HOSTEN, W. J., B.A., LL.B., Roman Law and Comparative Law
HOWELL, U. M. M., B.COM., C.A., Auditing
HUGO, L. H., M.A., D.LITT. ET PHIL., English
HUPKES, G. J., D.COM., Business Leadership
JONES, J., M.A., D.PHIL., Economics
JOOSTE, P. G., M.A., D.PHIL., Geography
JORDAAN, W. J., M.A., Psychology
KACHELHOFFER, G. C., B.A., B.COM., LL.D., Mercantile Law
KILIAN, C. J. G., D.ED., Fundamental Education
KLEYNHANS, W. A., M.A., D.PHIL., Political Science
KÖNIG, A. M.A., D.D., Divinity
KOTZE, D. A., D.PHIL., Development Administration
KRIEK, D. J., M.A., D.PHIL., Political Science
LE ROUX, P. A. K., LL.M., Mercantile Law
LIEBENBERG, B. J., DRS.HIST., D.LITT. ET PHIL., History
LOMBARD, D. P., D.LITT. ET PHIL., African Languages
LOMBARD, F., PH.D., Statistics and Operational Research
LOMBARD, A., D.D., Old and New Testament Theology
LOTZ, J. G., B.A., LL.B., Private Law
LOUW, J. A., D.LITT., African Languages
LUBBE, W. J. C., M.A., B.D., D.LITT., D.PHIL., Classics
LUCAS, G. H. G., D.COM., Business Economics
MACNAMARA, M. R. H., M.A., D.LITT., D.PHIL., Philosophy
MALAN, S. I., M.A., D.LITT., Library Science
MARAIS, G., PH.D., Business Leadership
MARITZ, F. A., DRS.SOC., Sociology
MARITZ, N. G., M.SC., PH.D., Business Economics
MAUER, K. F., D.LITT., D.PHIL., Psychology
McGILLIVRAY, G., PH.D., Chemistry
MEYER, R. S., M.A., D.LITT. ET PHIL., Philosophy
MEYER, W. F., D.PHIL., Psychology
MIDDLETON, A. J., B.A., LL.B., Criminal and Procedural Law
MÖLLER, N. J., M.A., D.LITT., D.PHIL., Psychology
MURRAY, C. H. DE C., M.A., D.ED., Ortho-Pedagogics
NAUDE, S. J., LL.D., Mercantile Law
NEETHLING, J., B.A., LL.B., Private Law
NEULAND, E. W., D.B.A., Business Economics
NURNBERGER, L. B., D.THEOL., D.TH., Systematic Theology
OBERHOLZER, M. O., D.ED., T.H.O.D., Fundamental Pedagogics
OOSTHUIZEN, J. D., D.ED., Empirical Education
PAUW, B. A., M.A., B.D., PH.D., Anthropology and Native Law
PELSER, G. P. J., M.SC., M.B.A., Business Leadership
PEREIRA, E., M.A., D.LITT. ET PHIL., English
PIENAAR, W. D., M.A., PH.D., Business Leadership
PIRON, J., LL.D., Business Leadership
PLUG, C., M.A., D.LITT., D.PHIL., Psychology
POTGIETER, W. F., B.COM., D.B.A., Business Economics
PREKEL, H. J., D.SC., M.B.L., Business Leadership
PRETORIUS, E. A. C., D.TH., B.D., Old and New Testament Theology
PRETORIUS, S. J., PH.D., Afrikaans and Dutch
REYNHARDT, E. C., PH.D., Physics
ROBERTS, J. H., M.A., TH.D., Theology
RONCA, I., DR.PHIL., D.LITT. ET PHIL., Classical Languages
SCHMIDT, C. W. H., LL.D., Law
SCHNEIDER, B. A. T., M.A., D.LITT., German
SCHULTZ, D. M., M.SC., PH.D., Statistics and Operations Research
SCHUTTE, C. J. H., DR.MATH.ET.PHYS., Chemistry
SCHUTTE, F. G., D.COM., C.A.(S.A.), Business Leadership
SEARLE, C., M.A., D.PHIL., Nursing
SKAWRAN, K., D.LITT. ET PHIL., History of Art and Fine Arts
SMITH, C. H., B.A., LL.B., Mercantile Law
SNYMAN, C. R., B.A., LL.D., Criminal and Procedural Law
SNYMAN, J. W., M.A., PH.D., African Languages
SPIES, S. B., M.A., PH.D., History
STASSEN, J. C., LL.M., Mercantile Law
STEFFENS, F. E., D.SC., Statistics and Operational Research
STEYN, P. G., D.COM., Business Economics
STEYN, W. J. A., M.SC., PH.D., Chemistry
STONE, B. A., D.ED., Education, Didactics and Comparative Education

Stoop, J. A. A. A., B.D., THEOL.D., Church History
Strauss, S. A., LL.D., Public Law, Criminal and Procedural Law
Swart, S. P. C., M.COM., Economics
Theron, J. S., M.A., D.PHIL., Social Work
Troost, A. P., M.A., D.LITT. ET PHIL., B.ED., Industrial Psychology
Van As, B. S., M.A., Development Administration
Van den Bogaerde, F., D.COM., Economics
Van der Linde, B. S., M.MUS., D.PHIL., Music
Van der Mark, J., M.SC., D.PHIL., Mathematics and Applied Mathematics
Van der Walt, P. J., M.A., D.PHIL., Criminology
Van Heerden, T. J., M.A., D.LITT. ET PHIL., Criminology
Van Niekerk, A. F., M.COM., LL.B., Mercantile Law
Van Reenen, M. J., M.COM., Business Economics
Van Rensburg, A. D. J., B.COM., LL.D., Private Law
Van Rensburg, B. P. J., D.COM., Economics
Van Rooy, C. A., M.A., D.LITT., Classical Languages
Van Rooyen, C. S., D.LITT. ET PHIL., African Languages
Van Rooyen, J. H., LL.B., M.CL., Criminal and Procedural Law
Van Schoor, M. B., D.PHIL., Communication
Van Veijeren, C. F., B.SC., D.B.A., Business Leadership
Van Vuuren, J. C. G. J., M.A., D.ED., Fundamental Education
Van Vuuren, L. M., C.A.(S.A.), A.C.M.A., Applied Accountancy
Van Wyk, D. H., LL.D., Constitutional and International Law
Van Wyk, T., LL.M., Mercantile Law
Van Zyl, M. C., D.PHIL., History
Venter, I. S. J., D.ED., Historical Education
Verwoerd, W. S., PH.D., Physics
Viltoen, T. A., D.ED., Fundamental Pedagogics
Vlok, A., M.A., D.PHIL., Industrial Psychology
Vogel, U. R. D., M.A., DR.PHIL., Classical Languages
Vorster, W. S., D.D., Institute for Theological Research
Vrey, J. D., M.ED., D.ED., Empirical Education
Weyers, J. L., M.COM., D.LITT. ET PHIL., Business Economics
Wiechers, G., M.SC., DRS., D.SC., M.C.S.S.A., Computer Science
Wiechers, M., LL.D., Constitutional and International Law
Wiehahn, G., M.A., D.PHIL., Psychology
Wolvaardt, J. S., D.PHIL., Statistics and Operations Research
Zaaiman, R. B., B.A., Library Science

ATTACHED INSTITUTES:

**Institute for Behavioural Sciences:** Dir. Prof. R. D. Griesel, M.A., D.PHIL.

**Institute for Computer Services:** Dir. Prof. N. Coetzee, D.SC.

**Institute for Criminology:** Dir. Prof. J. van der Westhuizen, D.LITT. ET PHIL.

**Institute for Educational Technology:** Dir. J. M. Smith, B.A.

**Institute of Foreign and Comparative Law:** Dir. Prof. M. Wiechers, LL.D.

**Institute for Labour Relations:** Dir. Prof. D. de Villiers, D.LITT. ET PHIL.

**Bureau of Market Research:** Dir. Prof. P. A. Nel, D.COM.

**Centre for Operations Research and Statistics:** Prof. F. E. Steffens, D.SC.

**Centre for Tax Law:** Head Prof. A. F. van Niekerk, M.COM., LL.B. (acting)

**Institute for Theological Research:** Dir. Prof. W. S. Vorster, M.A., D.D.

**Centre for Transport Economic Research:** Head Prof. W. F. Potgieter, D.B.A.

**Bureau for University Research:** Dir. Prof. H. T. Gous, M.ED., D.PHIL.

# UNIVERSITY OF STELLENBOSCH
STELLENBOSCH, CAPE PROVINCE

Telephone: 77911.
Telegraphic Address: University
Incorporated 1918.
Language of instruction: Afrikaans.
Academic year: February to December (four terms).

*hancellor:* The Hon. B. J. Vorster, LL.B.
*Vice-Chancellor:* Rev. J. S. Gericke, B.A.
*Principal:* Prof. M. J. de Vries, M.SC., DR.RER.NAT.
*Vice-Principal:* Prof. J. W. R. de Villiers, M.SC., PH.D.
*Registrar (Academic):* R. P. Conradie, M.A., M.ED.
*Registrar (Financial):* T. G. D. van Schalkwyk, B.COMM.
*Librarian:* F. du Plessis, B.A., F.S.A.L.A.

Number of teachers: 749.
Number of students: 12,072.

Publications†: *Annals of the University, Calendar, Matieland, Maatskaplike Werk* (Social Work, quarterly), *Opinion Survey Report* (Bureau of Economic Research, quarterly), *Survey of Contemporary Economic Conditions and Prospects* (annually), *Report of the Rector, Campusnews.*

### DEANS:

*Faculty of Arts and Philosophy:* Prof. A. Nel, M.A., D.PHIL.
*Faculty of Science:* Prof. J. A. de Bruyn, M.SC., PH.D.
*Faculty of Education:* Prof. W. L. Nell, D.ED.
*Faculty of Agriculture:* Prof. H. A. Louw, M.SC.AGRIC., PH.D.
*Faculty of Law:* Prof. A. B. de Villiers, B.A., LL.D.
*Faculty of Theology:* Prof. D. W. de Villiers, D.D., TH.DR.
*Faculty of Commerce:* Prof. D. E. W. Schumann, M.COMM., PH.D.
*Faculty of Engineering:* Prof. H. C. Viljoen, M.ENG., PH.D.(ENG.).
*Faculty of Medicine:* Prof. A. J. Brink, M.B., B.CH., M.D., F.R.C.P., F.A.C.C.
*Faculty of Forestry:* Prof. R. C. Bigalke, DR.PHIL. NAT.
*Faculty of Military Science:* Prof. J. v. d. B. Breedt, D.COMM.
*Faculty of Dentistry:* Prof. F. X. Prins, B.SC., M.SEC., B.CH.D., H.D.D., R.F.P.S.

### PROFESSORS:

*Faculty of Arts and Philosophy:*
Barnard, W. S., M.A., D.PHIL., Geography
Behrens, R. H., B.A., B.MUS., Music
Booyens, B., M.A., D.PHIL., Afrikaans Culture and Folklore Studies
Botha, A. G., M.A., M.ED., D.PHIL., Psychology
Botha, R. P., M.A., PH.D., Linguistics
Bowman, L. C., Music
Bruwer, J. M., D.LITT., Classics
Cillie, P. J., B.SC., Journalism
Cilliers, S. P., M.A., D.PHIL., Sociology
Claassen, W. T., D.LITT., Semitics
Combrink, J. G. H., D.LITT., Afrikaans-Nederlands
Conradie, P. J., M.A., D.LITT., Classics
Deacon, H. J., PH.D., Archaeology
Degenaar, J. J., M.A., D.PHIL., Political Philosophy
De Villiers, J. J., M.A., D.PHIL., Social Work
Du Plessis, J. A., M.A., D.LITT., African Languages
Du Toit, A. B., DRS.PHIL., D.PHIL., Political Philosophy
Ehlers, D. L., M.A., D.PHIL., Librarianship
Esterhuyse, W. P., M.A., D.PHIL., Philosophy
Fensham, F. C., M.A., D.D., PH.D., Semitic Languages
Hanekom, C., M.A., D.PHIL., Social Anthropology
Harvey, C. J. D., M.A., English
Jansen, J. P., M.A., D.PHIL., African Studies
Jeppe, W. J. O., M.A., D.PHIL., Development Administration
Joubert, D. D., M.A., D.PHIL., Sociology
Kabat, L. J., M.A., PH.D., Italian
Kotzé, D. J., M.A., D.PHIL., History
Kruger, G. van W., PH.D., Classics
Kussler, H. R., M.A., D.LITT., German
Lategan, B. C., M.A., TH.D., Biblical Studies
Le Roux, M. A., D.PHIL., Psychology
Meiring, E. G., M.A., D.LITT., French
Möller, A. T., M.A., D.PHIL., Psychology
Nel, A., M.A., D.PHIL., Geography
Nel, E. M., D.PHIL., Psychology
Otterman, R. E., M.MUS., D.PHIL., Music
Ponelis, F. A., D.LITT. ET PHIL., Afrikaans and Dutch
Rossouw, H. W., M.A., B.D., TH.DR., Philosophy
Scholtz, H. v. d. M., D.LITT. ET PHIL., Afrikaans and Dutch
Schüler, G. M. K., M.A., D.PHIL., Social Anthropology
Scully, L., M.A., Fine Arts
Swanevelder, G. J., M.A., D.PHIL., Geography
Thompson, J. B., M.A., D.LITT., English
Van Niekerk, H. G., M.A., M.ED., D.PHIL., Psychology
Van Rooyen, J. W., D.PHIL., Psychology
Van Zyl, D. J., M.A., D.PHIL., History
Welch, C. T., B.ARCH., Town and Regional Planning

*Faculty of Science:*
Belonjé, M., D.V.SC., Human and Animal Psychology

BURGER, B. V., D.SC., Chemistry
CRUYWAGEN, J. J., D.SC., Chemistry
DE BRUYN, G. F. C., PH.D., D.PHIL., Mathematics
DE BRUYN, J. A., M.SC., PH.D., Botany
DE WIT, J. L., M.SC., D.SC., Biochemistry
ENGELBRECHT, C. A., PH.D., Physics
ENGELBRECHT, W. J., D.SC., Physical Chemistry
GÖLDNER, S. R. F., M.SC., PH.D., Mathematics
HÄLBICH, I. W., D.SC., Geology
KOEN, J. W., D.SC., Physics
KRITZINGER, S., PH.D., Physics
MALAN, M. E., M.SC., D.SC., Zoology
MARAIS, D. J., M.SC., PH.D., Physics
MURRAY, G. L., B.SC., D.PHIL., Computer Science
NAUDE, W. J., D.SC., Physics
RAUTENBACH, W. L., M.SC., D.SC., Physics
SCHNEIDER, D. F., D.SC., Chemistry
VAN DER MERWE, K. J., DR.RER.NAT., Biochemistry
VAN DER WALT, A. P. J., D.SC., Mathematics
VAN DER WALT, J. J. A., D.SC., DR.SC.AG., Botany
VAN HEERDEN, L. E., PH.D., Domestic Science
VAN NIEKERK, C. H., D.V.S.(SC.), MD.ME.VET., Physiology
VERWOERD, W. J., D.SC., Geology
VISSER, J. H., DR.SC.AG., Botany
WEBB, M., D.SC., Zoology
ZEEMAN, P. B., M.SC., D.SC., Experimental Physics

*Faculty of Medicine:*
BARNARD, P. M., M.B., CH.B., M.D., F.A.C.S., Cardio-Thoracic Surgery
BECKER, W. B., M.B., CH.B., M.MED., M.D., F.R.C.(PATH.), F.C.M.(PATH.), Virology
BESTER, A. J., PH.D., Medical Physiology and Biochemistry
BEYERS, J. A., M.D., M.MED., Radiology
BEZUIDENHOUT, D. J., M.B., CH.B., M.D.(CLIN.), Internal Medicine
BOTHA, D., M.B., CH.B., M.MED., Internal Medicine
BRINK, A. J., M.B., B.CH., M.D., M.R.C.P., D.SC., Internal Medicine
DE GRAAFF, A. S., MED. ARTS DIPL., M.D., Internal Medicine
DE KLERK, H. C., M.B., CH.B., M.D., Medical Microbiology
DE KLERK, J. N., M.B., CH.B., F.R.C.S., Urology
DE KOCK, M. A., M.B.CH.B., M.D., F.R.C.P., Internal Medicine
DU TOIT, C. J., M.MED., M.B.CH.B., D.T.M.N.H., Otolaryngology
DU TOIT, J. P., M.B., CH.B., M.MED., L.K.O.G., Preventative Medicine
ENGELBRECHT, F. M., D.SC., Medical Physiology and Biochemistry
ERASMUS, F. R., M.MED., Anaesthesiology
FOSTER, P.A., M.B., CH.B., F.F.A., R.C.S.I., D.A., Anaesthesiology
HOFMEYR, I. M., B.SC., D.ED., Nursing
KEET, M. P., M.B., CH.B., M.MED.(PAED.), Paediatrics
LOCHNER, J. DE V., D.SC., M.B.CH.B., L.K., Medical Physiology and Biochemistry
LOUW, N. S., M.B., CH.B., M.MED., Preventative Medicine
MALAN, A. D., M.B.CH.B., Anatomy
MALHERBE, W. D. F., M.D., Plastic Surgery
ROSE-INNES, A. P., M.B., CH.B., F.C.S., Neurosurgery
ROSENSTRAUCH, W. J. C. J., M.B., CH.B., M.MED., M.D., Internal Medicine
ROSSOUW, D. J., M.B.CH.B., Radiotherapy Oncology
ROUX, J. T., M.B., CH.B., L.F.PSYCH., D.P.M., Psychiatry
SCHWÄR, T. G., M.D., M.C.PATH., D.P.H., Forensic Medicine
SMIT, B. J., M.B.CH.B., M.MED., Radiotherapy Oncology
STEYTLER, J. G., M.SC., M.B., CH.B., M.MED., M.D., Internal Medicine
TALJAARD, J. J. F., M.D., Chemical Pathology
VAN DER WALT, J. J., M.B., CH.B., M.MED., M.D., Pathology
VAN JAARSVELD, P. P., PH.D., Pharmacology
VAN NIEKERK, W. A., M.B.CH.B., M.MED., M.D., F.R.C.O.G., L.K.O.G., Gynaecology and Obstetrics
VAN ROOYEN, M. M. B., M.B.CH.B., M.MED., Ophthalmology
VAN VUREN, J. P., M.B., CH.B., F.R.C.S., Orthopaedics
VAN ZYL, J. A., B.SC., M.B.CH.B., M.MED., PH.D., Pharmacology
VAN ZYL, J. J. W., M.B.CH.B., M.D., F.R.C.S., Surgery
WASSERMANN, H. P., M.B., CH.B., M.MED.(INT.), M.D., General Internal Medicine
WEBER, H. W., M.D., F.R.C., Pathology
WICHT, C. L., M.B., CH.B., M.MED., M.D., Comprehensive Medicine

*Faculty of Education:*
CAWOOD, J., D.ED., Didactics
DE VRIES, C. G., D.ED., Educational Philosophy
DE WET, P. R., D.ED., Educational Administration
HUMAN, P. G., D.ED., Educational Philosophy
NEL, H. I., M.SC., D.ED.PH., Physical Education
NELL, W. L., D.ED., Educational Administration
STANDER, G., D.ED., Educational Psychology
THIART, B. F., D.SC., Physical Education

*Faculty of Agriculture:*
DE WET, P. J., M.SC.(AGRIC.), PH.D., Sheep and Wool Science
DÜRR, H. J. R., M.SC., D.SC., Entomology
GILIOMEE, J. H., M.SC.(AGRIC.), PH.D., Entomology
HATTINGH, M. J., D.SC., Plant Pathology
HAYES, J. P., M.SC.(AGRIC.), D.SC. (AGRIC.), Poultry Science
KASSIER, W. E., M.SC.(AGRIC.), DR.AGR., Agricultural Economics
KNOX-DAVIES, P. S., B.SC., M.S., PH.D., Plant Pathology
LAUBSCHER, E. W., PH.D., Field Husbandry
LOOS, M. A., M.SC., PH.D., Microbiology and Virology
LOUW, H. A., M.SC.(AGRIC.), PH.D., Microbiology
ORFFER, C. J., M.SC. (AGRIC.), PH.D., Viticulture
PIENAAR, R. DE V., PH.D., Genetics
STRYDOM, D. K., M.SC.(AGRIC.), PH.D., Horticultural Science
THERON, A. A., M.SC., PH.D., Soil Science
THERON, J. G., M.SC., PH.D., Entomology
VAN AARDE, I. M. R., M.SC., PH.D., Biometrics
VAN DER MERWE, F. J., M.SC.(AGRIC.), D.SC.AGRIC., Animal Science
VAN NOORT, G., PH.D., Food Science
VAN WYK, C. J., M.SC.(AGRIC.), PH.D., Viticulture
WEBER, H. W., DR.AGRIC., Soil Science

*Faculty of Law:*
DE VILLIERS, A. B., LL.D.
ERASMUS, H. J., D.LITT. ET D.PHIL., Law
LOUBSER, M. M., D.PHIL.
LUBBE, G. F., B.A., LL.B.
RABIE, M. A., LL.D., Law
SCHWIETERING, K. F. J., B.A., LL.B.
VAN DER MERWE, C. G., B.A., B.CL., LL.D.
VAN WYK, A. H., B.A., LL.B.

*Faculty of Theology:*
BROWN, E., S.T.M., TH.D.
DE VILLIERS, D. W., D.D., TH.DR.
DE VILLIERS, J. L., TH.DR., New Testament
JONKER, W. D., M.A., TH.DR.
MÜLLER, B. A., B.TH., TH.DR.
ODENDAAL, D. H., M.A., DRS.TH., TH.D.
SMITH, N. J., D.D., Missionary Science

*Faculty of Commerce:*
BOUWER, B., D.COMM., Mathematical Statistics
FRANZSEN, D. G., D.PHIL., Economics
HAMMAN, W. D., M.B.A., C.A., C.W.A., Business Management and Administration
LAMBRECHTS, I. J., D.COMM., Business Economics
MATTHEE, J. A., B.COMM., C.T.R., C.A., Accounting
MULLER, H. P., D.COMM., Business Economics
SADIE, J. L., M.COMM., EC.D., Economics
SCHEURKOGEL, A. E., D.COM., Commerce and Transport Economics
SCHOEMAN, A., D.COMM., Mathematical Statistics
SCHUMANN, D. E. W., M.COMM., PH.D., Mathematical Statistics
SMIT, J. VAN Z., D.COMM., LL.B., C.T.R., G.R., Accounting
SMITH, C. A., B.COMM., C.A., Accounting
TERREBLANCHE, S. J., M.A., D.PHIL., Economics
TUSENIUS, R. R., M.B.A., D.COMM., Business Administration
VAN BILJON, I. J., M.A., M.ED., D.PHIL., Industrial Psychology
VAN WYK, R. J., D.COMM., M.B.A., Business Economics

*Faculty of Engineering:*
COETSEE, A., B.SC.ENG., Civil Engineering
DE VILLIERS, J. W. R., PH.D., Applied Mathematics
DREYER, T. P., M.SC., PH.D., Applied Mathematics
DU PLESSIS, J. J., B.SC., B.ING., S.M.(M.I.T.), Electric-Electronic Engineering
DU PREEZ, R. J., M.SC.(ENG.), DR.ING., Civil Engineering
GELDENHUYS, G., M.SC., PH.D., Applied Mathematics
HATTINGH, H. V., B.SC.ENG., D.C.AE., M.B.A., Mechanical Engineering
HIEMSTRA, L. A. V., PH.D., Civil Engineering
HUGO, F., M.SC.ENG., Civil Engineering
KRÖGER, D. G., S.M., SC.D., Mechanical Engineering
LOUW, J. M., SC.D., Civil Engineering
LOUW, N. J., M.SC., DR.ING., Chemical and Metallurgical Engineering
MEIJ, J. T., PH.D., Mechanical Engineering
REINECKE, R., D.B.A., Mechanical Engineering
RELIEF, G. DE F., M.ENG., Civil Engineering
VAN DER MERWE, F. S., PH.D., Electrical and Electronic Engineering
VAN DER WALT, P. W., M.ENG., Electrical and Electronic Engineering

VILJOEN, H. C., M.ENG., PH.D., Electrical and Electronic Engineering

*Faculty of Forestry:*
BIGALKE, R. C., B.SC., DR.PHIL.NAT., Nature Conservation
DONALD, D. G. M., D.SC., Silviculture
GERISCHER, F. R. G., PH.D., Wood Science
VAN LAAR, A., L.IR., D.SC., Forestry
VERMAAS, H. F., D.SC., Wood Science

*Faculty of Military Science:*
BREEDT, J. V.D. B., M.COMM., D.COMM., Economics

*Faculty of Dentistry:*
BREYTENBACH, H. S., PH.D.(ODONT.), Dentistry
DREYER, W. P., H.D.D., PH.D., Oral Medicine and Periodontics
GROTEPASS, F. W., M.CH.D., Maxillo-Facial and Oral Surgery
NAUDE, D. A., CH.D., Restorative Dentistry
NORTJE, C. J., PH.D., Röntgenology
PRINS, F. X., M.SC., B.CH.D., H.D.D., R.F.P.S., Restorative Dentistry
STEYN, C. L., M.CH.D., Orthodontics
THOMAS, C. J. P., H.D.D., Dental Prosthetics
VAN RENSBURG, B. G. J., B.D.S., H.D.D., M.SC.(DENT. SCI.), Oral Biology
VAN WYK, C. W., B.CH.D., PH.D. (ODONT.), F.D.S.R.C.S., Oral Pathology

There are attached institutes for Agricultural Research, Applied Computer Science, Cartographical Analysis, Economic Research, Electronics, Entrepreneurship and Management, Industrial Engineering, Language Teaching, Marxism, Mathematics and Science Education, Planning Research, Polymer Science, Structural Engineering, Transport Economics; also the Nuclear Institute of the Southern Universities (with the University of Cape Town).

## UNIVERSITY OF THE WESTERN CAPE
PRIVATE BAG X17,
BELLVILLE

Telephone: 97-6161.

Founded 1960; for Coloured, Griqua and Malay students. (White, Indian and black students now admitted under special conditions.)

State control; Languages of instruction Afrikaans and English; Academic year: February to December (four terms).

*Chancellor:* Prof. E. THERON, M.A., D.PHIL.
*Vice-Chancellor and Rector:* Prof. R. E. VAN DER ROSS, M.A., D.ED., PH.D.
*Registrar (Academic):* Prof. H. J. PIENAAR, M.SC.
*Registrar (Finance):* J. H. C. STASSEN, B.COMM.
*Librarian:* A. P. S. DE KOCK, B.A. HONS. (LIB.).

Number of teachers: 223.
Number of students: 3,501.

Publications: *Inaugural Addresses,* etc.

DEANS:
*Faculty of Arts and Philosophy:* Prof. J. A. VAN ZYL, M.A., D.PHIL.
*Faculty of Dentistry:* Prof. N. C. OWEN, D.V.SC., M.MED.VET.
*Faculty of Education:* Prof. P. P. KIRSTEIN, M.ED.
*Faculty of Science:* Prof. B. ESTERHUIZEN, PH.D.
*Faculty of Law:* Prof. M. A. BOEHMKE, B.A., LL.B.
*Faculty of Theology:* Prof. J. J. F. DU RAND, M.A., TH.D., D.TH.
*Faculty of Economic and Management Sciences:* Prof. J. P. HAMMAN, B.COMM., C.A.(S.A.).

PROFESSORS:
*Faculty of Arts and Philosophy:*
BROEKMANN, N. C., Psychology
DU PLESSIS, S. I. M., Philosophy
DU TOIT, J. B., Sociology
DUVENHAGE, G. D. J., History
LE ROUX, I. A., Human Ecology
PLÜDDEMANN, U. R. R., German
RIDGE, S. G. M., English
SCHOLTZ, P. L., History
SINCLAIR, A. J. L., Afrikaans
SMITH, P. J., Semitic Languages
SNIJMAN, P. N. J., Latin
SNYMAN, S. A., Social Work
VAN DER WALT, M. J., Linguistics
VAN ZYL, J. A., Geography
VENTER, A. M., Nursing

*Faculty of Science:*
COETZEE, C. J., Chemistry
DELPIERRE, G. R., Chemistry
DU PLESSIS, N. M., Applied Mathematics
ESTERHUIZEN, B., Pharmaceutical Chemistry
KIES, J. D., Computer Science
MCCARTHY, T. J., Pharmaceutics
PIENAAR, K. J., Botany
SADIE, F. G. DU B., Chemistry
SKINNER, J. H., Zoology
VAN SCHALKWYK, T. G. D., Physics
VERMEULEN, J., Mathematics

*Faculty of Dentistry:*
JOHNSON, P. G. W., Dental Prosthetics
LE ROUX, L. C., Medical Microbiology
LOUW, N. P., Conservative Dentistry
MIDDLECOTE, B. D., Pathological Anatomy and Oral Pathology
OWEN, N. C., Physiological Sciences
REDDY, J., Dental Science
VAN DER WESTHUIZEN, C. M., Anatomy and Oral Biology

*Faculty of Education:*
CUPIDO, A. J. J., Fundamental Pedagogy
DE VILLIERS, D. I., Empirical Pedagogy
KIRSTEIN, P. P., Historical Pedagogy
PISTORIUS, P., Sociopedagogy
ROUX, C. J., Didactics and Administration

*Faculty of Economic and Management Sciences:*
HAMMAN, J. P., Accounting
MULLER, A. D., Industrial Psychology
VAN DER MEULEN, J., Business Economics

*Faculty of Law:*
BOEHMKE, M. A., Private Law
KARABUS, A., Comparative Law and International Law
VAN HUYSSTEEN, L. F., Public Law
VISAGIE, G. G., Mercantile Law

*Faculty of Theology:*
BOTHA, C. J., Ecclesiastical History
DURAND, J. J. F., Systematic Theology
ELS, P. J. J. S., Old Testament
HOLZAPFEL, E. H., Practical Theology

ATTACHED INSTITUTES:
**Institute for Social Development:** Dir. P. J. LE ROUX, B.COMM.

**Institute for Child Guidance:** Dir. Prof. W. L. STEENKAMP, M.A., M.ED.

**Institute for Historical Research:** Dir. Prof. J. L. HATTINGH, PH.D.

## UNIVERSITY OF THE WITWATERSRAND, JOHANNESBURG
JAN SMUTS AVE.,
JOHANNESBURG 2001

Telephone: 39-4011.
Telex: 54 22460 SA.

Founded 1922.

State subsidized, but functions under its own charter; Language of instruction: English; Academic year: February to November.

*Chancellor:* B. L. BERNSTEIN, B.A., LL.B.
*Vice-Chancellor and Principal:* Prof. D. J. DU PLESSIS, M.B., CH.B., CH.M., F.R.C.S.
*Deputy Vice-Chancellors:* Prof. K. TOBER, DR.PHIL., Prof. P. D. DYSON, PH.D., Prof. R. W. CHARLTON, B.SC., M.B., B.CH., M.D., F.R.C.P.
*Chairman of the Council:* N. STUTTERHEIM, D.SC.(ENG.), PR.ENG.
*Registrar (Academic and Administrative):* K. W. STANDENMACHER, B.A.
*Registrar (Research):* Col. S. C. SMITH, M.SC., P.ENG., C.ENG., M.I.MECH.E., M.S.A.I.MECH.E., F.I.NUC.E., F.B.I.M.
*Registrar (Staffing and Planning):* E. E. GLOVER, B.A., M.B.A.
*Librarian:* R. MUSIKER, M.A., F.S.A.L.A.
*Director of Performing Arts Centre:* D. HORNER, B.A., F.T.C.L., L.R.A.M.

Library: see Libraries.

Number of teachers: 789 full-time, 276 part-time.
Number of students: 14,165.

Publications: *Calendar, Annual Report†, Build Your Future at Wits.: Information for Prospective Undergraduates†, Palaeontologia Africana†* (all annually), *African Studies, Gazette, English Studies in Africa* (2 a year), *The Reporter†* (fortnightly). Over 300 further Witwatersrand University Press publications are available on exchange by application to the Exchange Section of the University Library.

DEANS:
*Facuoty of Architecture:* Prof. J. G. MULLER, M.A.
*Faculty of Arts:* Prof. B. D. CHEADLE, PH.D.

*Faculty of Business Administration:* Prof. G. F. JACOBS, O.B.E., M.A., D.PHIL.
*Faculty of Commerce:* Prof. J. T. STEELE, M.COM., C.A.(S.A.), F.C.A., M.C.S.S.A.
*Faculty of Dentistry:* Prof. J. F. VAN REENEN, B.D.S.
*Faculty of Engineering:* Prof. H. E. HANRAHAN, PH.D., PR.ENG., A.M.I.E.E., M.S.A.I.E.E.
*Faculty of Education:* Prof. K. S. O. BEAVON, M.SC., PH.D., F.S.A.G.S.
*Faculty of Law:* Prof. LOUISE A. TAGER, LL.M.
*Faculty of Medicine:* Prof. P. V. TOBIAS, PH.D., D.SC., F.R.S.(S.A.), F.L.S., F.R.A.I.
*Faculty of Science:* Prof. J. P. F. SELLSCHOP, M.SC., PH.D., F.INST.P.

PROFESSORS:

*Faculty of Architecture:*
GUEDES, A. D. M., B.ARCH., M.I.S.A.A., Architecture
MULLER, J. G., M.A., M.I.A., A.R.I.B.A., M.S.A.I.T.R.P., Town and Regional Planning
WALKER, C., B.SC., R.Q.S., M.A.Q.S., F.R.I.C.S., Quantity Surveying

*Faculties of Arts and Science:*
ALDRIDGE, M. V., PH.D., Linguistics
ARNHEIM, M. T. W., M.A., PH.D., Classical Civilization
ARON, MYRTLE L., M.A., PH.D., Speech Pathology and Audiology
BARLING, J. I., PH.D., Industrial Psychology
BEAVON, K. S. O., M.SC., PH.D., F.S.A.G.S., Human Geography
BOEYENS, J. C. A., D.SC., Theoretical Chemistry
CHEADLE, B. D., PH.D., English
CLIFFORD, T. N., PH.D., F.G.S., F.G.S.A., Geology
COLE, D. T., M.A., African Languages
CRESSWELL, C. F., M.SC., PH.D., Botany
CRUMP, A., M.F.A., Fine Arts
DOYLE, G. A., M.A., PH.D., Comparative Psychology
GARNETT, H. M., PH.D., Microbiology
GARSON, N. G., M.A., History
GEYSER, A. S., M.A., D.D., M.S.N.T.S., M.N.T.W.S.A., Divinity
GLASSER, L., PH.D., D.I.C., F.R.S.C., M.S.A.CHEM.I., Physical Chemistry
HAMMOND-TOOKE, W. D., M.A., PH.D., Social Anthropology
HARTFORD, G. F., M.A., English
HARTMAN, A. C., M.MUS., U.P.L.M., Music
HORNER, D., B.A., Dramatic Art
HUFFMAN, T. N., M.A., PH.D., Archaeology
KANNEMEYER, J. C., D.LITT., Afrikaans and Nederlands
KADDARI, M. Z., M.A., PH.D., Hebrew Studies
KNOPFMACHER, J. L. P., M.SC., PH.D., Mathematics
KUNERT, D. T., PH.D., International Relations
LEMMER, R. H., D.SC., PH.D., Mathematical Physics
LINDENBERG, E., LITT.DOCTS., PH.D., Afrikaans and Nederlands
LOUBSER, J. H. N., M.SC., D.PHIL., Experimental Physics
MANCHESTER, K. L., M.A., PH.D., Biochemistry
MANN, J. W., M.A., PH.D., Psychology
MASKE, S., M.SC., D.SC., Mining Geology

MASON, R. J., B.COM., B.A., PH.D., African Prehistory
MERRY, B., M.A., PH.D., Italian
MIDGLEY, D. C., PH.D., Hydrological Research
MPHAHLELE, E., PH.D., African Literature
MULLER, C., M.A., R.S.W., M INST.PH., Social Work
MUSIKER, R., M.A., F.S.A.L.A., Librarianship
NABARRO, F. R. N., M.B.E., M.A., D.SC., F.R.S., F.R.S.S.AF., Physics
NETHERSOLE, R., PH.D., Comparative Literature
NICOLAYSEN, L. O., M.SC., PH.D., Geophysics
PATERSON, H. E. H., PH.D., Zoology
PEROLD, G. W., D.SC., DR.SC.TECH., M.S.A.CHEM.I., Organic Chemistry
PRATT, J. M., M.A., D.PHIL., M.S.A. CHEM.I., Inorganic Chemistry
PRETORIUS, D. A., M.SC.(ENG.), PH.D., Exploration Geology
RAATH, M. A., PH.D., Palaeontology
RAIDT, E. M., PH.D., Afrikaans and Nederlands
RESCIGNO, A., L.PHYS., Biomathematics
SCHNEIDER, U. V., M.MUS., PH.D., L.R.U.C.T., L.R.U.C.P., Music
SCHUTTE, A. G., M.A., D.PHIL., Sociology
SEARS, D. B., PH.D., D.SC., D.PHIL., Mathematics
SEARS, M., PH.D., Mathematics
SELLSCHOP, J. P. F., M.SC., PH.D., F.INST.P., F.I.NUC.E., Nuclear Physics
STADLER, A. W., PH.D., Political Studies
STRAKER, G., PH.D., Applied Psychology
SUZMAN, L. J., M.A., Philosophy
TOBER, K., DR.PHIL., German Studies and Comparative Literature
TYSON, P. D., M.SC., PH.D., F.R.MET.S., F.S.A.G.S., Physical Geography
VAN ONSELEN, C., D.PHIL., African Studies
VAN SCHAIK, NANCY W., M.S., PH.D., M.R.S.S.AF., Genetics
WALKER, B. H., M.SC., PH.D., Botany
WHITAKER, MARIE J., M.A., PH.D., French
WOODWARD, A. G., M.A., English
ZERNITZ, P., M.A., DR.PHIL., Sociology

*Faculty of Business Administration:*
ANDREWS, G. S., PH.D., Business Administration
DUFFY, N. M., D.B.L., Management Information Systems
HERSH, M., PH.D., Quantitative Methods
JACOBS, G. F., O.B.E., M.A., D.PHIL., Business Administration
JAMIESON, R. T., PH.D., F.C.S.(S.A.), Production and Project Management
STRUMPFER, D. J. W., M.SC., PH.D., Organizational Behaviour
VAN DER MERWE, A. J., D.COM., Busines, Administration
VAN DER MERWE, SANDRA, M.B.A., D.B.A.S Marketing

*Faculty of Commerce:*
BOTHA, D. J. J., M.COM., EC.DR., Economics
BRITS, R. N., M.COM., PH.D., Business Economics
MACGREGOR, I. H., PH.D., C.A.(S.A.), F.C.A., Accounting
STEELE, J. T., M.COM., C.A.(S.A.), F.C.A., Accounting

*Faculty of Dentistry:*
CLEATON-JONES, P. E., B.D.S., M B., B.CH., PH.D., D.A.(S.A.), Experimental Odontology
HATTINGH, J., M.SC., PH.D., General Physiology

LEMMER, J., B.D.S., H.DIP.DENT., Oral Medicine and Periodontology
LEWIN, A., B.D.S., H.DIP.DENT., Conservative Dentistry
PRESTON, C. B., M.DENT., Orthodontics
RAWDON, B. B., PH.D., General Anatomy
SHEAR, M., M.D.S., D.SC.(DENT.), H.DIP.DENT., F.O.S.(S.A.), F.R.C.PATH., F.R.S.S.AF., Oral Pathology
SLABBERT, J. C. G., M.DENT., T.O.D., Prosthetic Dentistry

*Faculty of Education:*
FREER, D. J., M.PHIL.
WHITE, D. R., D.ED.

*Faculty of Engineering:*
BLIGHT, G. E., M.SC., PH D., D.SC., D.I.C., PR.ENG., F.S.A.I.C.E., M.A.S.C.E., M.A.A.P.T., Construction Materials
BROWN, R. J., D.L.C.(ENG.), Transport Engineering
BRYSON, A. W., PH.D., PR.ENG., M.S.A.I. CH.E., M.S.A.I.M.M., Chemical Engineering
BUDAVARI, S., PH.D., F S.A.I.M.M., Rock Mechanics
BUNT, E. A., M.SC.ENG., PH.D., D.SC.(ENG.), PR.ENG., C.ENG., F.I.MECH.E., F.R.AE.S., F.S.A.I.MECH.E., Fluid Mechanics
GARRETT, G. G., PH.D., M.I.M., Physical and Fabrication Metallurgy
GLASSER, D., PH.D., PR.ENG., D.I.C., F.S.A.I. CHEM.E., Chemical Engineering
HANRAHAN, H. E., PH.D., PR.ENG., A.M.I.E.E., M.S.A.I.E.E., Communications Engineering
HARRIS, W. F., PH.D., Micro-Biomechanics
KEMP, A. R., M.SC.(ENG.), PH.D., PR.ENG., M.S.A.I.C.E., Structural Engineering
KING, R. P., M.SC.(ENG.), PH.D., PR.ENG., M.I.C.E., M.S.A.I.C.E., F.S.A.I.M.M., Metallurgy
KRIGE, D. G., D.SC.(ENG.), Mineral Economics
MARCUS, R. D., M.SC.(ENG.), PH.D., PR.ENG., F.S.A.I.MECH.E., C.ENG., M.I.MECH.E., M.A.S.M.E., Mechanical Engineering
PLEWMAN, R. P., B.SC.(ENG.), M.A., PR.ENG., A.M.A.M.M., F.S.A.I.M.M., Mining Engineering
RALLIS, C. J., PH.D., PR.ENG., C.ENG., F.I.MECH.E., F.E.A.S.A., Mechanical Engineering
REYNDERS, J. P., PH.D., PR.ENG., M.S.A.I.E.E., Electrical Engineering
ROBINSON, F. R. A., PH.D., PR.ENG., F.I.M., F.I.CORR.T., Corrosion Science and Engineering
RODD, M. G., M.SC.(ENG.), PH.D., PR.ENG., C.ENG., M.S.A.I.E.E., M.I.E.E., Electronics
STEPHENSON, D., M.SC.(ENG.), PH.D., PR.ENG., C.ENG , M.S.A.I.C.E., M.I.C.E., M.A.S.C.E., Hydraulic Engineering
STREATHER, R. A., M.A., PH.D., C.ENG., M.R.AE.S., M.AE.S.S.A., M.S.A.I.AE.E., Aeronautical Engineering
VOLCKMAN, O. B., PH.D., PR.ENG., C.ENG., A.R.C.S., F.I.CHEM.E., F.S.A.I. CHEM.E., Chemical Engineering
WALKER, C., B.SC., Quantity Surveying
WATT, I. B., B.SC., Surveying

*Faculty of Law:*
BOBERG, P. Q. R., B.A., LL.D., Law
DUGARD, C. J. R., B.A., LL.D., Law
KAHN, E., B.COM., LL.D., Law
SINCLAIR, JUNE D., B.A., LL.B., Law
TAGER, LOUISE A., LL.M., Law
VAN DER VYVER, J. D., LL.D., Law
WHITING, R. C., M.A., Law
ZEFFERTT, D. T., B.A., LL.B., Law

## SOUTH AFRICA

*Faculty of Medicine:*
ALLAN, J. C., M.B.B.CH., C.H.M., M.D., F.R.C.S., Functional and Applied Anatomy
ANDREW, ANN, M.SC., PH.D., Embryology
BARLOW, J. B., M.D., F.R.C.P., Cardiology
BEATON, G. R., PH.D., Medical Education
BOTHWELL, T. H., M.D., D.SC., F.R.C.P., F.A.C.P., F.R.S.S.AF., Medicine
BRADLOW, B. A., M.D., Haematological Pathology
BREMNER, C. G., CH.M., F.R.C.S., Surgery
CHAPPELL, J. S., M.B.B.CH., F.C.S.(S.A.), Paediatric Surgery
CHARLTON, R. W., M.D., F.R.C.P., Experimental and Clinical Pharmacology
DE MOOR, N. G., M.B.B.CH., D.M.R., Radiation Therapy
FELDMAN, M. B., M.B.B.CH., D.P.M., R.C.P. AND S., F.R.C.P., F.R.C.PSYCH., Psychiatry and Mental Hygiene
FITSCHEN, W. H. E., PH.D., Medical Biochemistry
GEAR, J. S. S., B.SC., M.B., B.CH., D.PHIL., F.C.P.(SA.), Community Medicine
HANSEN, J. D. L., M.D., F.R.C.P., D.C.H., Paediatrics
ISAACSON, C., M.B., B.CH., M.D., F.R.C.PATH., Anatomical Pathology
ISAACSON, MARGARETHA, M.D., Tropical Pathology
JENKINS, T., M.B.B.S., M.D., M.R.C.S., L.R.C.P., D.R.C.O.G., F.R.S.S.AF., Human Genetics
KEW, M. C., M.D., PH.D., F.C.P.(S.A.), F.R.C.P., Medicine
KINSLEY, R. H., M.B.B.CH., F.C.S., Cardio-thoracic Surgery
KOORNHOF, H. J., M.B., M.CH.B., D.C.P., F.R.C.PATH., Microbiological Pathology
LAWSON, H. H., CH.M., D.SC., F.R.C.S., Surgery
LEVIN, J., M.B.B.CH., D.M.R.T., Nuclear Medicine
LEVIN, S. E., M.B., B.CH., F.R.C.P., D.CH.R.C.P. AND S., Paediatric Cardiology
LIPSCHITZ, R., M.B.B.CH., PH.D., F.R.C.S., Neurosurgery
MITCHELL, D., M.SC., PH.D., Physiology
MOYES, D. G., M.B.CH.B., M.R.C.S., L.R.C.P., F.F.R.C.S., Anaesthesia
MYBURGH, J. A., CH.M., F.R.C.S., Surgery
RABSON, A. R., M.B.B.CH., D.C.P., R.C.P., M.R.C.PATH., Immunological Pathology
RIPPEY, J. J., M.B.B.S., D.P.H., D.PATH., R.C.P., R.C.S., M.R.C.P., M.R.C.PATH., Anatomical Pathology
ROSENDORFF, C., B.CH., PH.D., F.R.C.P., Physiology
SCHAMROTH, L., M.D., D.SC., F.R.C.P., F.A.C.C., F.R.S.S.AF., Medicine
SCHEPERS, N. J., M.MED., Forensic Medicine
SCHOUB, B. D., M.MED., M.D., Virology
SEFTEL, H. C., M.B., B.CH., DIP.MED., African Diseases
SOLOMON, L., M.B., CH.B., M.D., F.R.C.S., Orthopaedic Surgery
STEIN, H., M.B., B.CH., D.C.H., R.C.P. AND S., F.R.C.P., Paediatrics
TOBIAS, P. V., PH.D., D.SC., F.R.S.(S.A.), F.L.S., F.R.A.I., Anatomy
VAN BLERK, P. J. P., B.SC., M.B., B.CH., Urology
VAN DONGEN, L. G. R., M.SC., M.D., F.R.C.O.G., F.I.C.S., Obstetrics and Gynaecology
VAN HASSELT, C. H., M.B., B.CH., D.A., R.C.P.S., Anaesthesia
WAGSTAFF, L., M.B., B.CH., D.C.H., D.OBST., R.C.O.G., Community Paediatrics
WILLIAMSON, S. B., M.CUR., D.N., D.A.(S.A.N.C.), Nursing Education
ZWI, S., M.B., B.CH., B.SC., F.R.C.P., Respiratory Medicine

ATTACHED INSTITUTES:

**African Studies Institute.**
*Directors:* Prof. C. VAN ONSELEN, D.PHIL., Prof. E. MPHAHLELE, M.A., PH.D.

**Archaeological Research Unit.**
*Director:* Prof. R. J. MASON, B.COM., B.A., PH.D.

**Bernard Price Institute of Geophysical Research:** f. 1936
*Director:* Prof. L. O. NICOLAYSEN, M.SC., PH.D.

**Bernard Price Institute for Palaeontological Research:** f. 1949.
*Director:* Prof. M. A. RAATH, PH.D.

**Bureau for Mineral Studies.**
*Director:* Dr. A. H. TAUTE, M.S., D.SC.

**Cardiovascular Research Unit.**
*Director:* Prof. J. B. BARLOW, M.D.

**Centre for Applied Legal Studies.**
*Director:* Prof. C. J. R. DUGARD, B.A., LL.D.

**Centre for Continuing Education.**
*Director:* Mrs. P. W. WENTZEL, B.A.

**Circulation Research Unit.**
*Director:* Prof. C. ROSENDORFF, PH.D., M.D., F.R.C.P.

**Computer Centre.**
*Director:* Dr. C. W. WOLHUTER, PH.D.

**Dental Research Institute.**
*Director:* Prof. P. E. CLEATON-JONES, B.D.S., M.B.B.CH., PH.D.

**Economic Geology Research Unit.**
*Director:* Prof. D. A. PRETORIUS, M.SC.(ENG.), PH.D.

**Electron Microscope Unit.**
*Director:* M. J. WITCOMB, M.SC., PH.D.

**Ernest Oppenheimer Institute of Portuguese Studies.**
*Chairman:* Dr. L. A. DE V. LEAL, D.LITT.

**Hydrological Research Unit.**
*Director:* Prof. D. C. MIDGLEY, PH.D., PR.ENG., F.I.C.E., M.A.S.C.E., F.S.A.I.C.E.

**Iron and Red Cell Metabolism Research Unit.**
*Director:* Prof. T. H. BOTHWELL, M.D., D.SC., F.R.C.P., F.A.C.P., F.R.S.S.AF.

**Language Laboratory.**
*Honorary Director:* Prof. EDITH H. RAIDT, M.A., PH.D.

**Materials Handling Research Group.**
*Director:* Prof. R. D. MARCUS, M.SC.(ENG.), PH.D., PR.ENG., F.S.A.I.MECH.E., C.ENG., M.I.MECH.E., M.A.S.M.E.

**Metabolic and Nutrition Research Unit.**
*Director:* Prof. J. D. L. HANSEN, M.D., F.R.C.P., D.C.H.

**Nuclear Physics Research Unit.**
*Director:* Prof. J. P. F. SELLSCHOP, M.SC., PH.D., F.INST.P., F.I.NUC.E.

**Nuffield Lake Kariba Research Station.**
*Chairman:* (vacant).

**Oral and Dental Teaching Hospital.**
*Director:* Prof. J. F. VAN REENEN, B.D.S.

**Photosynthetic Nitrogen Metabolism Unit.**
*Director:* Prof. C. F. CRESSWELL, M.SC., PH.D.

**Planetarium.**
*Director:* T. E. GEARY, F.R.A.S.

**Pre-University School.**
*Director:* Dr. G. C. GERRANS, PH.D.

**Primate Behaviour Research Group.**
*Director:* Prof. G. A. DOYLE, M.A., PH.D.

**Programme for Research in the Field of Music.**
*Director:* Prof. U. V. SCHNEIDER, M.MUS., PH.D., L.R.U.C.T., L.R.U.C.P.

**Solid State Physics Research Unit.**
*Director:* Prof. F. R. N. NABARRO, M.B.E., M.A., D.SC., F.R.S., F.R.S.S.AF.

**Speech and Hearing Clinic.**
*Director:* Prof. MYRTLE ARON, M.A., PH.D.

**Transplantation Research Unit.**
*Director:* Prof. J. A. MYBURGH, M.B., CH.M., F.R.C.S.

## UNIVERSITY OF ZULULAND
PRIVATE BAG,
KWA-DLANGEZWA,
VIA EMPANGENI, NATAL 3880

Telephone: Kwa-Dlangezwa 0351-93611.

Founded 1960 for Zulu and Swazi students. There is an extra-mural division at Umlazi (Durban).

State control; Language of instruction: English; Academic year: February to December.

*Chancellor:* The Honourable MNTWANA M. G. BUTHELEZI, B.A.

*Rector:* Prof. A. C. NKABINDE, M.A., D.LITT.ET PHIL., T.E.D.

*Registrar (Academic Administration):* E. W. REDELINGHUYS, B.A.

*Librarian:* P. MINAAR, B.SC., B.BIBL., U.E.D., M.A.

Number of teachers: 169.
Number of students: 2,535.

DEANS:

*Faculty of Arts:* Prof. H. J. VAN EETVELDT, D.LITT.
*Faculty of Science:* Prof. J. G. J. VISSER, D.SC.
*Faculty of Education:* A. J. VOS, D.ED.

UNIVERSITIES, COLLEGES OF UNIVERSITY STANDING — SOUTH AFRICA

*Faculty of Economic and Political Sciences:* Prof. P. S. JOUBERT, D.PHIL.
*Faculty of Law:* Prof. M. G. ERASMUS, B.A., LL.B.
*Faculty of Theology:* Prof. B. J. ODENDAAL, TH.DR.

PROFESSORS:

*Faculty of Arts:*
BADENHORST, L. H., TH.DR., M.TH., M.A., D.PHIL., Sociology
DE BEER, C. S., M.A., D.PHIL., D.E.A., Philosophy
DE CLERQ, D. P., Anthropology and Development Studies
DU PLESSIS, A. P., M.A., D.LITT. ET PHIL., U.E.D., Sociology
HAASBROEK, D. J. P., M.A., D.PHIL., T.E.D., History
MAKHANYA, E. M., PH.D., Geography
MNGOMA, K. V., Music
VAN DER MERWE, W., M.A., T.E.D., D.PHIL., History
VAN EETVELDT, H. J., D.LITT., Afrikaans
VAN DER WALT, J., M.A., U.E.D., Classics

VAN HUYSSTEEN, J. A., B.A., U.E.D., English
VENTER, W. A., D.PHIL., History
WHITE, J. M., M.A.(LIB.), Library Science

*Faculty of Economic and Political Sciences:*
FOURIE, L. J., M.COM., Economics
JOUBERT, P. S., D.PHIL., Political Science and Public Administration
LEMMER, H. R., M.COM.(B. AND A.), D.B.A., L.V.B., T.H.E.D., A.S.A.I.M., Business Economics
POTGIETER, J. J., D.COM., T.H.E.D., Business Economics
VOGES, R. P., B.COM., C.A., Accountancy and Auditing

*Faculty of Education:*
DUMINY, P. A., M.ED., D.LIT. ET PHIL., Didactics
LUTHULI, P. C., D.ED., B.A., Philosophy of Education
NDABA, E. P., D.ED., Pedagogics
NEL, A., D.ED., Educational Psychology
VOS, A. J., D.ED., History of Education and Comparative Education

*Faculty of Law:*
KEMP, K. J., LL.D.

ERASMUS, M. G., B.A., LL.B., Zulu and Roman Law

*Faculty of Science:*
BOSHOFF, D. N., D.SC., Botany
COETZEE, F., D.SC., Geology
LAMPRECHT, G. J., M.SC., PH.D., Chemistry
SPOELSTRA, B., D.SC., Physics
VAN ROOYEN, D. A., M.SC., U.E.D., Mathematics
VISSER, J. G. J., D.SC., Zoology

*Faculty of Theology:*
FRYER, N. S. L., B.A., B.D., New Testament
MOSTERT, J. P., PH.D., Science of Religion and Science of Mission
ODENDAAL, B. J., TH.DR., Church History

ATTACHED INSTITUTES:

*Institute for Public Service and Vocational Training:* Dir. Prof. J. C. BEKKER, B.A., LL.D.
*Extra-Mural Division:* Umlazi; Dir. Prof. H. J. DREYER, D.LITT. ET PHIL.

## COLLEGES OF UNIVERSITY STANDING

### CAPE TECHNIKON
LONGMARKET ST.,
P.O.B. 652, CAPE TOWN 8000

Telephone: Cape Town 22-1035.

Founded 1923, present name 1979.

Languages of Instruction: English and Afrikaans.

*Director:* Dr. T. C. SHIPPEY, M.ED., PH.D.
*Deputy Director (Humanities):* C. V. D. W. KOTZE, M.A., B.ED., A.I.A.C., A.S.A.I.M.
*Deputy Director (Technical):* S. J. CILLIÉ, B.SC. MECH.ENG., PR.ENG.
*Registrar:* J. VAN ZYL, B.COM.
*Librarian:* A. KERKHAM, B.THEOL.

Library of 20,000 vols.

Number of teachers: 215 full-time, 270 part-time.

Number of students: 2,500 full-time, 3,500 part-time.

Publication: *Development* (annual).

Departments: humanities: art, food and clothing, languages and communication, management and administration, secretarial studies, teacher training (commerce); technical: civil engineering, mechanical engineering, paramedical and biological sciences, physical science and mathematics, technical training.

### M.L. SULTAN TECHNIKON
CENTENARY RD.,
P.O.B. 1334, DURBAN 4000

Founded 1946, essentially for Indian students.

*Rector:* Dr. A. SOLOMON, D.ED.

*Deputy Rector (Technology):* R. P. DE STADLER, B.SC., B.ED.
*Deputy Rector (Humanities):* A. RAMSAMY, B.COMM.
*Registrar and Secretary to Technikon Council:* R. JAGATH.

Number of students: 8,099 (including part-time).

Secondary- and tertiary-level courses in Hotel and Catering School, Commerce, Apprentice School, General Studies, Home Economics, Physical Education, Technology.

Publications: *Technikon Magazine*† (annually), *Brochures of Courses in different Divisions*† (annually), *Annual Report* (annually).

### TECHNIKON NATAL
P.O.B. 953, DURBAN

Telephone: (031) 318711.

Founded 1907, present name 1979.

*President of Council:* Prof. W. E. PHILLIPS, D.SC.ENG., LL.D., M.I.E.E., SNR.M.I.R.E., M.(S.A.)I.E.E.
*Director:* A. PITTENDRIGH, B.SC., B.COM., B.ED.

Library of 25,000 vols.
Number of teachers: 267 full-time, 350 part-time.
Number of students: 8,000.

Publication: *LAMP*† (annually).

Departments of applied science, civil engineering, creative design, education and industrial training, electrical engineering, fine art, food and clothing technology, languages and communication, management and professional education, mechanical engineering, pharmacy, secretarial training.

### PORT ELIZABETH TECHNIKON
PRIVATE BAG 6011,
PORT ELIZABETH

Founded 1925, present name 1979.

*Director:* Dr. D. P. VELDSMAN, D.SC.
*Registrar:* G. J. VAN BLERK.

Number of students: 2,500.

### TECHNIKON PRETORIA
420 CHURCH ST. EAST,
PRETORIA

Telephone: 283811.

Telegraphic Address: Technikol.

Founded 1906, present name 1980.

*Director:* Dr. D. J. J. VAN RENSBURG, PH.D.
*Registrar:* J. R. BOOT, M.COM., F.I.A.C., T.H.E.D.

Number of lecturers: 390 full-time, 200 part-time.

Number of students: 7,980.

Departments of Mechanical, Electrical and Civil Engineering, Biological Sciences, Chemical Sciences, Physical Sciences, Pharmacy, Health Services, Agriculture and Horticulture, Computer Science, Food and Clothing, Mathematics, Management and Administration, Secretarial Studies, Art and Design, Performing Arts, Education, Languages and Communication.

### VAAL TRIANGLE TECHNIKON
PRIVATE BAG X021,
VANDERBIJLPARK,
1900 TRANSVAAL

Telephone: (016) 33-5951/2/3.

Founded 1966, present name 1979.

*Director:* Dr. I. STEYL.
*Registrar:* J. DE W. DU TOIT.
*Deputy Directors:* M. S. L. BOSHOFF (Technology), L. O. PIENAAR (Humanities).

*Librarian:* L. J. HARTZENBERG.

Library of 14,000 vols.

Number of teachers: 102 full-time, 56 part-time.

Number of students: 4,300.

Departments of electrical engineering, mechanical engineering, applied sciences, management and administration, visual arts, food and clothing technology.

### WITWATERSRAND TECHNIKON
ELOFF ST., P.O.B. 3293,
JOHANNESBURG

Founded 1925, present name 1979.

*President:* D. J. MALAN.
*Director:* C. A. J. BORNMAN.
*Registrar:* C. P. SCHOLTZ.

Number of teachers: 272 full-time, 174 part-time.

Number of students: 3,363 full-time, 2,370 part-time.

# BOPHUTHATSWANA

### UNIVERSITY OF BOPHUTHATSWANA
PRIVATE BAG X2046,
MONTSHIWA 8681

Telephone: 449/450.

Founded 1979; in process of formation.

*Chancellor:* Sir ALBERT ROBINSON.
*Rector:* Dr. J. R. KRIEL.
*Registrar:* I. D. GOULD.
*Librarian:* P. J. LOR.

Number of teachers: 30.

Number of students: 170.

HEADS OF SCHOOLS:

*Administration and Management:* Prof. JAN LANGE.

*Education:* Prof. DERYCK N. NUTTALL.

*Law:* Prof. VERLOREN VAN THEMAAT.

# TRANSKEI

### UNIVERSITY OF TRANSKEI
PRIVATE BAG X5092,
UMTATA

Telephone: 2151.

Founded 1977.

State control through University Council; Language of instruction: English.

*Chancellor:* Dr. K. D. MATANZIMA, President.
*Vice-Chancellor:* Prof. B. DE V. VAN DER MERWE.
*Registrar (Administration):* J. DE M. MALAN.
*Registrar (Finance):* S. D. MAJOKWENI.
*Librarian:* J. T. PHEHANE.

Number of teachers: 81.
Number of students: 904.

DEANS:

*Faculty of Arts:* Prof. N. C. MANGANYI.
*Faculty of Natural Sciences:* Prof. W. MÖDINGER.
*Faculty of Economic Sciences:* Prof. W. L. NKUHLU.
*Faculty of Law:* Prof. D. F. L. THOMPSON.
*Faculty of Education:* Prof. J. M. NORUWANA.

PROFESSORS/HEADS OF DEPARTMENTS:

*Faculty of Arts:*
HODGE, N. M., English
JAFTA, D. N., African Languages (Sesotho and Xhosa)
LANDMAN, W. A., Philosophy
MANGANYI, N. C., Psychology
MASHASHA, F. J., History
O'CONNELL, M. C., Anthropology

TÖTEMEYER, G. K. H., Political Science
VAN DYK, T. J., Afrikaans
VERHOEF, P., Geography
VILAKAZI, H. W., Sociology

*Faculty of Natural Sciences:*
DARES, G. E., Physics
DU PREEZ, A. L., Chemistry
MÖDINGER, W., Mathematics
TEW, A. J., Botany

*Faculty of Economic Sciences:*
LANGUAGE, J. M., Business Management
NKUHLU, W. L., Accounting
ROOS, H. W., Public Administration
THOMAS, W. H., Economics

*Faculty of Law:*
THOMPSON, D. F. L.

*Faculty of Education:*
NORUWANA, J. M.

# SPAIN
**Population 37,538,000**

## ACADEMIES

The six official Spanish Academies were reorganized by governmental decree in 1939, when their title of "Real" was restored to them in recognition of their historical origin. This decree ordains their incorporation with the Instituto de España, thus forming a "Senado de la Cultura Española".

Madrid

**Instituto de España:** San Bernardo 49; f. 1939; Pres. FERNANDO CHUECA GOITIA; Sec.-Gen. ANTONIO RUMEU DE ARMAS; publ. *Anuario*.

**Real Academia Española** (*Royal Spanish Academy*): Calle de Felipe IV 4; Tel. 2 39 46 05; f. 1713, Charter granted 1714 by Philip V when various privileges were allowed to the Academy and the Academicians; first in order of precedence among the Royal Academies; library of 53,000 vols.; publs. *Diccionario de la Lengua Española, Gramática de la Lengua Española*, etc.

*President:* DÁMASO ALONSO.
*Permanent Secretary:* ALONSO ZAMORA VICENTE.
*Censor:* PEDRO LAÍN ENTRALGO.
*Librarian:* ALFONSO GARCÍA VALDECASAS.
*Treasurer:* ANTONIO BUERO VALLEJO.

MEMBERS:

ALARCOS LLORACH, EMILIO
ALEIXANDRE, VICENTE
ALONSO, DÁMASO
ALVAR, MANUEL
BOUSOÑO PRIETO, CARLOS
BUERO VALLEJO, ANTONIO
CALVO SOTELO, JOAQUÍN
CELA, CAMILO JOSÉ
COLINO LÓPEZ, ANTONIO
CONDE, CARMEN
DELIBES SETIÉN, MIGUEL
DÍAZ-PLAJA, GUILLERMO
DIEGO CENDOYA, GERARDO
DÍEZ ALEGRÍA, MANUEL
ENRIQUE Y TARANCÓN, CARDINAL VICENTE
FERNÁNDEZ RAMÍREZ, SALVADOR
GARCÍA GÓMEZ, EMILIO
GARCÍA VALDECASAS, ALFONSO
HALCÓN VILLALÓN-DAOIZ, MANUEL
LAÍN ENTRALGO, PEDRO
LAPESA MELGAR, RAFAEL
LÁZARO CARRETER, FERNANDO
LORENZO CRIADO, EMILIO
LUCA DE TENA Y BRUNET, TORCUATO
MARÍAS, JULIÁN
MONTES, EUGENIO
RIQUER, MARTÍN DE
ROSALEZ CAMACHO, LUIS
SÁINZ RODRÍGUEZ, PEDRO
SECO REYMUNDO, MANUEL
TERÁN ALVAREZ, MANUEL
TORRENTE BALLESTER, GONZALO
TOVAR LLORENTE, ANTONIO
ZAMORA VICENTE, ALONSO
ZUNZUNEGUI Y LOREDO, JUAN ANTONIO

Corresponding members: Spanish, 28; Spanish-American, 10; foreign, 36.

**Real Academia de la Historia** (*Royal Academy of History*): León 21, Madrid 14; f. 1738; 2nd in order of precedence among the Royal Academies; library of 350,000 vols., 180,000 MSS; publs. *Memorias, Memorial Histórico, Boletín*, historical works, etc.

*Director:* DIEGO ANGULO IÑIGUEZ.
*Secretary:* DALMIRO DE LA VÁLGOMA Y DÍAZ-VARELA.
*Librarian:* ANTONIO BLANCO FREIJEIRO.

**Real Academia de Bellas Artes de San Fernando** (*San Fernando Royal Academy of Fine Arts*): Calvo Sotelo 20; f. 1744; 3rd in order of precedence among the Royal Academies; publs. *Boletín*; works on Fine Arts; has affiliated museums of paintings and sculpture; library of 22,600 vols., including 127 rare editions and 140 MSS.

*Director:* FEDERICO MORENO TORROBA.
*Secretary:* ENRIQUE PARDO CANALIS.
*Librarian:* JOSÉ SUBIRA PUIG.
*Curator:* FERNANDO LABRADA MARTÍN.

**Real Academia de Ciencias Exactas, Físicas y Naturales** (*Royal Academy of Exact, Physical and Natural Sciences*): Valverde 22 y 24; f. 1847; 4th in order of precedence among the Royal Academies; publs. *Memorias, Revista, Anuario*.

*President:* MANUEL LORA TAMAYO.
*Vice-President:* OBDULIO FERNÁNDEZ RODRÍGUEZ.
*General Secretary:* JOSÉ M. TORROJA MENÉNDEZ.
*Treasurer:* ANTONIO ALMELA SAMPER.
*Librarian:* ANGEL MARTÍN MUNICIO.

*Sección de Ciencias Exactas:*
 *President:* SIXTO RÍOS GARCÍA.
 *Secretary:* BALTASAR RODRÍGUEZ SALINAS.

MEMBERS:

LAFITA BABÍO, FELIPE
DOU MASDEXEXÁS, P. ALBERTO
ANCOCHEA QUEVEDO, GERMÁN
ROMAÑÁ PUJÓ, S.J., ANTONIO
GARCÍA FRIAS, JUAN
MARAVALL CASESNOVES, DARÍO
TORROJA MENÉNDEZ, JOSÉ MA.
GODED ECHEVERRÍA, FEDERICO
MILLÁN BARBANY, GREGORIO
VALDIVIA UREÑA, MANUEL

*Sección de Ciencias Físicas:*
 *President:* JOSÉ GARCÍA SANTESMASES.
 *Secretary:* JESÚS MORCILLO RUBIO.

MEMBERS:

FERNÁNDEZ Y RODRÍGUEZ, OBDULIO
OTERO NAVASCUÉS, JOSÉ MARÍA
LORA TAMAYO, MANUEL
COLINO LÓPEZ, ANTONIO
COSTA NOVELLA, ENRIQUE
SÁNCHEZ DEL RÍO SIERRA, CARLOS
DURÁN MIRANDA, ARMANDO
CALVO CALVO, FELIPE
GALINDO TIXAIRE, ALBERTO

*Sección de Ciencias Naturales:*
 *President:* MIGUEL BENLLOCH MARTÍNEZ.
 *Secretary:* MANUEL ALÍA MEDINA.

MEMBERS:

BUSTINZA LACHIONDO, FLORENCIO
RÍOS GARCÍA, JOSÉ MA.
ALMELA SAMPER, ANTONIO
MARTIN MUNICIO, ANGEL
SÁNCHEZ-MONGE PARELLADA, ENRIQUE
ALVARADO FERNÁNDEZ, SALUSTIO
LOSADA VILLASANTE, MANUEL
GARRIDO MARECA, JULIO
MELÉNDEZ MELÉNDEZ, BERMUDO

*Elected:*
FÚSTER CASAS, JOSÉ M.

Corresponding members: Spanish, 42; foreign, 78.

**Real Academia de Ciencias Morales y Políticas** (*Royal Academy of Moral and Political Sciences*): Casa de los Lujanes, Plaza de la Villa 2; f. 1857; 5th in order of precedence among the Royal Academies; publs. historical and scientific works; library of 53,398 vols., 260 MSS, 300 periodicals.

*President:* Alfonso García Valdecasas.
*Vice-President:* Carlos Ruíz del Castillo.
*Secretary:* Manuel Alonso Olea.
*Librarian:* Antonio Truyol Serra.
*Registrar:* Manuel Díez Alegría.
*Treasurer:* Enrique Fuentes Quintana.

Members:

Alcorta y Echeverría, José I.
Alonso Olea, Manuel
Alvarez, Valentín Andrés
Areilza, José, Conde de Motrico
Campo Urbano, Salustriano
Díez Alegría, Manuel
Díez Del Corral, Luis
Fernández de la Mora, Gonzalo
Fraga Iribarne, Manuel
Fuentes Quintana, Enrique
García Hoz, Víctor
González Alvarez, Angel
González Martín, Cardenal Marcelo.
Jordana de Pozas, Luis
López-Rodó, Laureano
Millán Puelles, Antonio
Navarro, Rubio Mariano
Ollero Gómez, Carlos
Oriol y Urquijo, José María de, Marques de Casa Oriol
Palacios Rodríguez, Leopoldo Eulogio
Perpiñá Rodríguez, Antonio
Quintana, Dr. Primitivo de la
Sánchez Agesta, Luis
Sarda, Juan
Velarde Fuertes, Juan
Viñas Mey, Carmelo

*Elected:*
Fueyo Alvarez, Jesús
Garcia Pelayo, Manuel
González Pérez, Jesús

Corresponding members: Spanish, 20; foreign, 25.

**Real Academia Nacional de Medicina** (*Royal National Academy of Medicine*): Arrieta 12; f. 1732 as a group of famous court physicians, surgeons and pharmacists; present name 1917; 6th in order of precedence among the Royal Academies; 40 mems.; corresponding mems., 93 Spanish, 57 foreign; publs. *Anales, Biblioteca Clásica de la Medicina Española* (17 vols.).

*President:* Benigno Lorenzo Velázquez.
*Vice-President:* José Botella Llusiá.
*Secretary:* Dr. Valentín Matilla Gómez.
*Librarian:* Félix Sanz Sánchez.
*Treasurer:* Agustín Bullón Ramírez.
*Accountant:* Gonzalo Piédrola Gil.

Members:

Alonso Fernández, Francisco
Armijo Valenzuela, Manuel
Bosch Marín, Juan
Botella Lusía, José
Bravo Oliva, José
Bru Villaseca, Luis
Bullón Ramírez, Agustín
Calatrava Páramo, Luis
Casares López, Román
Cifuentes Delatte, Luis
Cortes Gallego, Rafael
Costa Novella, Enrique
De la Fuente Chaos, Alfonso
De la Quintana Lopes, Primitivo
Durán Sacristán, Hipólito
Fernández-Cruz Liñán, Arturo
Fernández y Rodríguez, Obdulio
Fernández-Galiano y Fernández, Dimas
Gallego Fernández, Antonio
García Alfonso, Cristino
García-Conde Gómez, Francisco Javier
García Orcoyen, Jesús
Gilsanz García, Vicente
Gómez Durán, Manuel
Gómez Orbaneja, José
González Gómez, César
Laguna Serrano, Ciriaco
Lain Entralgo, Pedro
López Ibor, Juan José
Lorenzo Velásquez, Benigno
Matilla Gómez, Valentín
Orts Llorca, Francisco
Pérez Llorca, José
Piédrola Gil, Gonzalo
Piga Sánchez-Morate, Bonifacio
Poch Viñals, Rosendo
Rof Carballo, Juan
Sanz Sánchez, Félix
Tamarit Torres, Jorge
Vara López, Rafael

**Real Academia de Jurisprudencia y Legislación** (*Royal Academy of Jurisprudence and Legislation*): Marqués de Cubas 13; f. 1730; 40 mems.

*President:* Antonio Hernández Gil.
*Vice-President:* Raimundo Fernández-Cuesta y Merelo.
*Secretary:* Juan Vallet de Goytisolo.
*Librarian:* Juan Becerril y Anton Miralles.

**Real Academia de Farmacia** (*Royal Academy of Pharmacy*): Farmacia 11, Madrid 4; f. 1589 as Congregación de San Lucas, 1737 as Real Colegio de Farmacéuticos, 1932 as Real Academia de Farmacia; library of 12,000 vols.; 40 mems.; publ. *Anales*† (quarterly).

*Director:* Angel Santos-Ruíz.
*Permanent Secretary:* Manuel Ortega.
*Librarian:* Víctor Villanueva Vadillo.

**Academia de Cirugía de Madrid** (*Madrid Academy of Surgery*): Avenida de José Antonio 34; f. 1931.
*President:* Dr. Tomás Rodríguez de Mata.

**Academia Española de Dermatología y Sifilografía** (*Spanish Academy of Dermatology and Syphilography*): Sandoval 7; f. 1909; 435 mems., 51 hon., 3 corresp.; library of 900 vols.; publ. *Actas Dermosifiliográficas*.

*Honorary Presidents:* Prof. José Gómez Orbaneja, Prof. José Gay Prieto.
*President:* D. José Cabre Piera.
*Vice-Presidents:* Dr. Félix Contreras Dueñas, José Mascaro Ballester.
*Secretary-General:* Ramón Morán López.
*Librarian:* Dr. Juan José Apellaniz Fernández.
*Branches:* Catalonia, Valencia, Biscay-Navarre-Aragon, Eastern Andalusia, Western Andalusia and Canary Islands.

**Academia Médico-Quirúrgica Española** (*Spanish Academy of Medicine and Surgery*): Villanueva 11, Madrid 1; f. 1891; 492 mems.; publ. *Anales*.
*President:* Prof. Eduardo Arias Vallejo.
*Secretary:* Dr. Julio Múñiz González.

**Academia Iberoamericana y Filipina de Historia Postal** (*Spanish-American and Philippine Academy of Postal History*): Palacio de Comunicaciones, Dirección General de Correos y Telecomunicación; f. 1930; publ. *Boletín* (quarterly).

*President:* Aníbal Martín García.
*Secretary-General:* José Jusdado Martín.

Members, 40; hon., 33; foreign, 37.

Barcelona

**Real Academia de Bellas Artes de San Jorge** (*Royal Academy of Fine Arts*): Casa Lonja, Paseo de Isabel II, 2°; f. 1849; library of 1,500 vols.; publs. historical, literary and artistic works.

*President:* Federico Marés Deulovol.
*Secretary-General:* Luis Solé Sabarís.
*Librarian:* Rafael Benet Vancells.

**Real Academia de Ciencias y Artes de Barcelona** (*Barcelona Royal Academy of Science and Arts*): Rambla de los Estudios 115, Barcelona 2; f. 1764; 45 mems.; library of 50,000 vols.; publs. *Nómina, Memorias*†.

*President:* Dr. D. Luis Solé Sabarís.
*Vice-President:* Dr. D. Enrique Ras Oliva.
*Secretary:* Dr. D. Manuel Puigcerver Zanón.
*Librarian:* José Iglesias Fort.

Members:

Augé Farreras, Juan
Barella Miró, Alberto
Bassegoda, Buenaventura
Bassegoda Nonell, Juan
Bolós, Oriol
Brugalla Turmo, Emilio
Buscarons U., Francisco
Caballero, Arturo
Cases, José
Codina Vidal, José Maria
Crusafont P., Miguel
Cumella, Antonio
Español, Francisco
Folch Girona, Joaquin
Font T., José María
Freixa, Enrique
Iglesias F., José
Lafita B., Felipe
Margalef, Ramón
Mir, Jesús
Múñoz Oms, Victoriano
Ollé Pinell, Antonio
Pascual De Sans, Pero
Ponz Piedrafita, Francisco
Prevosti, Antonio
Puigcerver Zanón, Manuel
Ras Oliva, Enrique
Sales Vallés, Francisco
Santomá, Luis
Solé Sabarís, Luis
Vidal L., José Maria
Vives, José Luis

Has affiliated:
**Observatorio Astronómico Meteorológico y Sismico Fabra:** Tibidabo, Barcelona; f. 1905.
*Director:* José María Codina.

**Academia de Buenas Letras de Barcelona** (*Barcelona Academy of Belles Lettres*): Calle Obispo Cassador 3; f. 1729; 36 mems.; publ. *Boletín, Memorias.*
*President:* Martín de Riquer.
*Secretary:* José Alsina Clota.
*Librarian:* Pedro Bohigas Balaguer.

**Acadèmia de Ciències Mèdiques de Catalunya i de Balears** (*Catalonian Academy of Medicine*): Paseo de la Bonanova 47; f. 1878; 5,000 mems.; publs. *Annals de Medicina, Monografies Mèdiques.*
*President:* Oriol Casassas i Simó.
*Secretary:* Joaquim Ramis i Coris.
*Librarian:* Ferran Fernandez i Nogués.

### Bilbao

**Academia de Ciencias Médicas de Bilbao** (*Academy of Medicine*): Lersundi 9-1°, Apdo. 414, Bilbao 10; f. 1895; 1,300 mems.; library of 9,050 vols.
*President:* Dr. Jesús María Garibi Undabarrena.
*Secretary-General:* Dr. Benito de las Heras Niño.
Publication: *Gaceta Médica de Bilbao†* (every month).

**Euskaltzaindia/Real Academia de la Lengua Vasca** (*Academy of the Basque Language*): Arbieto 3-3°; delegations in: Palacio Diputación Foral, San Sebastián; Museo de Navarra, Pamplona; Facultad de Filosofía y Letras, Seminario Diocesano, Vitoria; f. 1919; research into and conservation of the Basque language; 24 mems. and an indeterminate number of honorary and corresponding mems.; library of 15,000 vols. specializing in philology and linguistics, principally of the Basque language.
*President:* Luis Villasante.
*Vice-President:* Jean Haritschelhar.
*Secretary:* José Ma. Satrustegi.
*Vice-Secretary:* José Luis Lizundia.
*Treasurer:* Endrike Knörr.
*Librarian:* Alfonso Irigoyen.
Publication: *Euskera* (2 a year).

### Cádiz

**Real Academia Hispano-Americana** (*Royal Spanish-American Academy*): Plaza de San Francisco 3, Apdo. 16; f. 1910; 29 mems.; publ. *Boletín.*
*Director:* José María Pemán y Pemartín.
*Secretary-General:* Manuel Antonio Rendón y Gómez.

### Córdoba

**Real Academia de Ciencias, Bellas Letras y Nobles Artes** (*Royal Academy of Science, Literature and Fine Arts*): Ambrosio de Morales 9; f. 1810; 35 mems., 35 corresponding mems.; publs. *Boletín* (half- yearly), scientific, historical and literary works.
*Director:* Dr. Rafael Castejón.
*Secretary:* Juan Gómez Crespo.

### La Coruña

**Real Academia Gallega** (*Royal Galician Academy*): Palacio Municipal; f. 1905; 40 mems.; library of 20,000 vols., including valuable collection of books on Galicia; publs. *Boletín, Diccionario Gallego-Castellano.*
*President:* Sebastián Martínez Risco.
*Secretary:* Francisco Vales Villamarín.
*Librarian:* Juan Naya Pérez.

### Málaga

**Real Academia de Bellas Artes de San Telmo** (*Royal Academy of Fine Arts*): f. 1849; 28 mems.
*President:* José Luis Estrada Segalerva.
*Secretaries:* Baltasar Peña Hinojosa, Luis Bono Hernández de Santaolalla.

### Seville

**Real Academia Sevillana de Buenas Letras** (*Seville Royal Academy of Belles Lettres*): Plaza del Museo 8; f 1751; 30 mems., including 2 elected; library of 5,000 vols.; publ. *Boletín de Buenas Letras* (quarterly).
*Director:* Dr. Antonio Cortés Llado.
*Secretary:* Dr. Ildefonso Camacho Baños.
*Librarian:* Dr. Antonio González Meneses Meléndez.

**Real Academia de Bellas Artes de Santa Isabel de Hungría** (*Royal Fine Arts Academy*): Abades 14 (Sevilla 4); f. 1660; 30 mems.; library of 1,327 vols.; publ. *Boletín* (annually).
*President:* José Hernández Díaz.
*Secretary-General:* Antonio de la Banda y Vargas.
*Librarian:* José A. Calderón Quijano.

**Real Academia de Medicina de Sevilla** (*Royal Academy of Medicine of Seville*): Plaza de España; f. 1697; 25 mems.; corresponding mems.: Spanish 100, foreign 50; library of 6,000 vols.
*President:* Dr. Gabriel Sánchez de la Cuesta y Gutiérrez.
*Vice-President:* Dr. Antonio González-Meneses y Meléndez.
*Secretary:* Dr. Lucas Bermudo Fernández.
*Librarian:* Dr. Eloy Domínguez-Rodiño y Domínguez-Adame.

### Toledo

**Real Academia de Bellas Artes y Ciencias Históricas de Toledo** (*Toledo Royal Academy of Fine Arts and Historical Sciences*): Calle Esteban Illán 9; f. 1916; 25 mems., 8 elected mems.; library of 4,000 vols.; publ. *Toletum†.*
*Director:* Dr. D. Rafael Sancho de S. Román.
*Secretary:* Dra. Esperanza Pedraza Ruiz.
*Censor:* Julio Porres Martín-Cleto.
*Librarian:* Dr. J. Carlos Gómez Menor.
*Archaeologist:* Matilde Revuelta Tubino.
*Treasurer:* Dr. José Miranda Calvo.

Members:

Aguado Villalba, José
Carillo Rojas, Luis
Celada Alonso, Antonio B.
García Rodríguez, Emilio
Colomina Torner, Jaime
Goitia Graells, Mariano
Gómez Luengo, José
Gómez-Menor Fuentes, José
Gonzálvez Ruiz, Ramón
Lopez-Fando Rodríguez, Alfonso
Martín Aguado, Máximo
Méndez Aparicio, Julia
Miranda Calvo, José
Palencia Flores, Clemente
Palomino Jimenez, Angel
Payo Subiza, Gonzalo
Pedraza Ruiz, Esperanza
Rivera Recio, Juan F.
Rojas Gomez, Francisco
Santacruz S. de Rojas, Guillermo
Valle Díaz, Félix del

### Valladolid

**Real Academia de Bellas Artes de la Purísima Concepción** (*Royal Academy of Fine Arts*): Calle del Rastro, Casa de Cervantes; f. 1746; 30 mems.
*President:* Dr. Nicomedes Sanz y Ruiz de la Peña.
*Secretary:* Dr. Nemesio Montero Pérez.
Members: 30.

### Zaragoza

**Real Academia de Nobles y Bellas Artes de San Luis** (*Royal Academy of Fine Arts*): Plaza de José Antonio 6; f. 1792; library of 4,517 vols.; composed of 28 Academicians, 84 Spanish and 28 foreign corresponding members and variable number of delegates; comprises 5 sections (architecture, sculpture, painting, music, literature) and 3 permanent committees; publs. *Boletín* (irregularly), catalogues, works.
*President:* Teodoro Ríos Balaguer.
*Secretary-General:* Joaquín Albareda Piazuelo.
*Librarian:* Mariano Burriel Rodrigo.

**Academia de Ciencias Exactas, Físicas, Químicas y Naturales** (*Academy of Exact, Physical, Chemical and Natural Sciences*): Facultad de Ciencias, Ciudad Universitaria; f. 1916; comprises sections on Exact Sciences, Physics and Chemistry, and Natural Sciences; publ. *Revista* (quarterly).

*President:* JUSTINIANO CASAS PELÁEZ.

*Secretary:* ÁNGEL SÁNCHEZ FRANCO.

*Librarian:* JUAN SANCHO DE SAN ROMÁN.

Members 40; corresponding: Spanish 30, foreign 30.

Palma de Mallorca

**Real Academia de Medicina y Cirugía de Palma de Mallorca** (*Royal Academy of Medicine and Surgery*): Morey 20; 19 mems.

*President:* JOSÉ SAMPOL VIDAL.

*Secretary:* SANTIAGO FORTEZA FORTEZA.

# LEARNED SOCIETIES

### AGRICULTURE AND VETERINARY SCIENCE

**Consejo General de Colegios Oficiales de Ingenieros Técnicos Agrícolas de España** (*Council of Agricultural Colleges*): Plaza de Santo Domingo 13-1°-B, Madrid; f. 1949; formerly Asociación Nacional de Peritos Agrícolas, f. 1880; 3,668 mems.; library of 3,668 vols.; Pres. JOSÉ LUIS LINAZA DE LA CRUZ; Sec. CONSTANTINO LAGARON YÁÑEZ; publ. *A.G.* (monthly).

**Institut Agricola Catala de Sant Isidre** (*Catalan Agricultural Institute*): Plaça Sant Josep Oriol 4, Barcelona 2; f. 1851; 10,356 mems.; Pres. IGNACIO DE PUIG Y GIRONA; Sec.-Gen. FERNANDO DE MULLER Y DE DALMASES; publs. *Revista* (quarterly), *Boletín* (monthly), *Calendari del Pagés*† (annually).

**Sociedad Veterinaria de Zootecnia de España** (*Spanish Veterinary Society of Zootechnics*): Facultad de Veterinaria, Ciudad Universitaria, Madrid 3; f. 1945; zootechnical science, animal husbandry, ethology, animal behaviour, animal genetics, economics, animal production; 250 ordinary mems., 3,500 corresp. mems.; library of 5,000 vols.; Pres. Dr. R. DÍAZ MONTILLA; Technical Sec.-Dir. Prof. Dr. C. L. DE CUENCA; publ. *Zootecnia*† (quarterly).

### ARCHITECTURE AND TOWN PLANNING

**Colegio Oficial de Arquitectos de Cataluña** (*College of Architects of Catalonia*): Plaza Nueva 5, Barcelona 2; f. 1931; 2,953 mems.; library of 27,918 vols.; Sec. MIGUEL DONADA GAJA; publ. *Cuadernos de Arquitectura y Urbanismo*.

**Dirección General de Arquitectura y Tecnología de la Edificación** (*Dept. of Architecture and Building Technology*): Plaza de San Juan de la Cruz 1, Madrid 3; f. 1940; restoration and conservation of monuments of historical or artistic value; construction of government buildings; formulating quality control regulations in the building industry; 234 mems.; Dir.-Gen. ANTONIO VALLEJO ACEVEDO; publ. *Normas Tecnológicas de la Edificación* (weekly).

### THE ARTS

**Asociación Española de Pintores y Escultores de España** (*Association of Spanish Artists and Sculptors*): Infantas 30, Madrid 4; f. 1910; Pres. FRANCISCO PRADOS DE LA PLAZA; Perm. Sec. MIGUEL CARRIÓN; annual autumn exhibition in Palacio del Retiro; publ. *Boletín Informativo*.

**Ateneo Barcelonés** (*Barcelona Athenaeum*): Calle Canuda 6, Barcelona; f. 1860; library: see libraries; 2,500 mems.; governed by a Directorate; Pres. IGNACIO AGUSTÍ PEYPOCH; Sec.-Gen. JULIO MANEGAT PÉREZ.

**Ateneo Científico, Literario y Artístico** (*Scientific, Literary and Artistic Athenaeum*): Calle Cifuentes 25, Mahón, Minorca, Balearic Is.; f. 1905; library of 14,000 vols.; 495 mems.; Pres. GUILLERMO DE OLIVES PONS; Secs. CALIXTO MARTÍN NEÉ, MARÍA ESTHER SEBASTIÁN SANDINO; publ. *Revista de Menorca* (quarterly).

**Ateneo Científico y Artístico** (*Scientific, Literary and Artistic Athenaeum*): Calle del Prado 21, Apdo. 272, Madrid 14; f. 1820; 5,000 mems.; library of 500,000 vols.; Pres. FERNANDO CHUECA GÓITIA; Gen. Sec. JOSÉ GERRARDO MANRIQUE DE LARA.

**Comité Nacional Español del Consejo Internacional de la Musica** (*National Cttee. of the International Music Council*): Avenida Reina Victoria 58, Madrid 3.

**Instituto Amatller de Arte Hispánico** (*Institute of Hispanic Art*): Paseo de Gracia 41, Barcelona; f. 1941; library; collection of 500,000 photographs; Dir. Prof. JOSE GUDIOL RICART; Sec. SANTIAGO ALCOLEA-BLANCH.

**Instituto de Arte "Diego Velázquez"**: Duque de Medinaceli 4, Madrid 14; f. 1939; history of Spanish art and history of European art in Spain; 17 mems.; library of 34,465 vols.; Dir. ELISA BERMEJO MARTÍNEZ; publ. *Archivo Español de Arte*† (quarterly).

**Institut del Teatre** (*Theatrical Institute*): Carrer Nou de la Rambla 3, Barcelona 1; f. 1913; exhibitions of scenery, lectures, etc.; library of 125,000 vols.; Dir. HERMANN BONNIN; Sec. XAVIER FÁBREGAS; publs. works on the theatre.

**Real Sociedad Fotográfica Española** (*Royal Spanish Photographic Society*): Calle del Príncipe 16, Madrid 12; f. 1899; 750 mems.; library of 1,500 vols.; Pres. GERARDO VIELBA CALVO; Sec. FERNANDO BEDMAR IZQUIERDO; publ. *Boletín*† (monthly).

**Sociedad de Ciencias, Letras y Artes "El Museo Canario"** (*Scientific, Literary and Art Society*): Dr. Chil 33, Las Palmas, Canary Is.; f. 1879; incorporated in the Consejo Superior de Investigaciones Científicas (q.v.); museum: see Museums; laboratories; important library (40,000 vols), archives and periodicals relating to the history and primitive peoples of the Canary Islands; Pres. JOSÉ M. ALZOLA; Sec. JUAN RODRÍGUEZ DORESTE; publ. *El Museo Canario* (quarterly).

### BIBLIOGRAPHY, LIBRARY SCIENCE AND MUSEOLOGY

**Asociación Amigos de los Museos** (*Friends of the Museums Association*): Palacio de la Virreina, Barcelona; f. 1933; 980 mems., 6 hon., 81 associates, 52 others; Pres. VIZCONDE DE GÜELL; Vice-Pres. GUSTAVO GILI ESTEVE; Sec.-Gen. JOSÉ R. ESPINOS Y PÉREZ-ROSALES; publs. *Historiales*, monographs.

**Asociación Nacional de Bibliotecarios, Archiveros, Arqueólogos y Documentalistas (ANABAD):** Paseo de Recoletos 22, Apdo. 14281, Madrid; f. 1949; 1,000 mems.; groups all specialists working in the country's archive services, libraries, museums and documentation services; includes 3 councils which advise the Ministry of Culture; Pres. MANUEL CARRIÓN GÚTIEZ; Sec. MA. JESUS CUESTA ESCUDERO; publs. *Boletín* and many irregular works.

**Asociación Nacional de Bibliotecarios, Archiveros y Arqueólogos (Delegación de Cataluña y Baleares)** (*National Association of Archivists and Librarians*): Apdo. 1868, Barcelona; Pres. MERCÈ ROSSELL.

**Instituto Bibliográfico Hispánico** (*Spanish Bibliographic Institute*): Calle de Atocha 106, Madrid 12; f. 1970; attached to the Ministry of Culture; legal deposit, national bibliography and bibliographical information; Dir. VICENTE SÁNCHEZ MÚÑOZ; publs. *Bibliografía Española* (monthly), *Indices de Revistas de Bibliotecología*† (3 a year), *Revistas españolas en curso de publicación*† (annually).

### ECONOMICS, LAW AND POLITICS

**Centro de Estudios Constitucionales** (*Centre for Constitutional Studies*): Plaza de la Marina Española 9, Madrid 13; f. 1977, having merged with Instituto de Estudios Políticos; organizes courses, lectures and seminars on political, constitutional and administrative questions; library of 80,000 vols.; Dir. FRANCISCO MURILLO FERROL; Man. DANIEL VILLAGRA BLANCO; publs. *Revista de Estudios Políticos*† (6 a year), *Revista Española de Derecho Constitucional*† (3 a year), *Revista de Estudios Internacionales*† (quarterly), *Revista de Administración Pública* (3 a year)†, *Revista de Política Social*† (quarterly), *Revista de Economía Política*† (3 a year), *Revista de Instituciones Europeas*† (3 a year).

**Colegio de Abogados de Barcelona** (*Barcelona College of Lawyers*): Calle Mallorca 283; f. 1832; 4,138 mems.; library of 120,000 vols.; Dean JOSÉ J. PINTÓ RUIZ; Sec. JOSÉ PI-SUÑER CUBERTA; publs. *Revista Jurídica de Cataluña*†, *Anuario de Sociología y Psicología Jurídicas*.

**Colegio Notarial** (*College of Notaries*): Calle Notariado 4, Barcelona 1; 222 mems.; Pres. CARLOS FERNÁNDEZ-CASTAÑEDA; Sec. ANGEL MARTÍNEZ SARRIÓN.

**Instituto de Estudios de Administración Local** (*Institute for the Study of Local Government*): Santa Engracia 7, Madrid 10; f. 1940; library of 55,000 vols., 1,000 periodicals; Dir. LUIS COSCULLUELA MONTANER; publs. *Revista Estudios Vida Local* (quarterly), *Ciudad y Territorio* (quarterly).

**Instituto Nacional de Estadística** (*National Statistical Office*): Paseo de la Castellana 183, Madrid 16; f. 1945; library of 107,620 vols.; Pres. Dr. AZORÍN; Dir.-Gen. Sr. BALLESTER; publs. *Anuario Estadístico de España, Censos de la Población y de la Vivienda, Boletín Mensual de Estadística, Censo Agrario, Estadística Industrial, Indicadores de conyuntura, Revista "Estadística Española"*, etc.

**Real Sociedad Económica de Amigos del País de Tenerife** (*Royal Economic Society of Friends of Tenerife*): La Laguna de Tenerife, Calle San Agustín 23, Tenerife, Canary Is.; f. 1777; 490 mems.; sections: *Intereses Morales, Intereses Materiales, Intereses Culturales, Intereses Económicos, Prensa y Propaganda*; library of 11,000 vols.; museum; Dir. Marqués de Villanueva del Prado, D. MANUEL DE QUINTANA; publs. works relating to the Canary Islands.

### EDUCATION

**Consejo Nacional de Colegios Oficiales de Doctores y Licenciados en Filosofía y Letras y en Ciencias** (*National Council of Official Colleges of Doctors and Licentiates in Philosophy, Letters and Science*): Bolsa 11, 2°, Madrid 12; f. 1944; 43,100 mems.; Pres. Dr. MARTÍN SANTOS ROMERO; Sec.-Gen. EZEQUIEL PUIG MAESTRO-AMADO; publs. information bulletins of the colleges in Barcelona, Bilbao, Madrid, Seville and Valladolid.

**Fundación Juan March:** Castelló 77, Madrid; f. 1955; awards scholarships and research grants to Spanish professors and scholars in the arts and sciences; organizes cultural, artistic and musical activities; Pres. JUAN MARCH DELGADO; Gen. Dir. JOSÉ LUIS YUSTE GRIJALBA; publs. *Boletín Informativo*† (monthly), *Anales*.

### HISTORY, GEOGRAPHY AND ARCHAEOLOGY

**Comisión Provincial de Monumentos Históricos y Artísticos de Barcelona** (*Barcelona Provincial Commission for the Preservation of Historical and Artistic Monuments*): Calle del Obispo Cassador 3, Plaza de San Justo; f. 1844; Pres. FEDERICO MARÉS DEULOVAL; Sec. PEDRO VOLTES BOU.

**Deutsches Archaeologisches Institut** (*German Archaeological Institute*): Serrano 159, Madrid 16; library of 33,000 vols.; archive of photographs; Dir. Prof. Dr. HERMANFRID SCHUBART; publs. *Madrider Mitteilungen* (annual), *Madrider Forschungen, Madrider Beiträge, Hispania Antiqua, Studien über frühe Tierknochenfunde von der Iberischen Halbinsel*.

**Instituto Arqueológico del Ayuntamiento de Madrid** (*Archaeological Institute of the City of Madrid*): Parque de la Fuente del Berro; conducts research into the archaeology of Madrid and environs; library (6,000 vols.), laboratory and museum; Dir. Dr. ENRIQUE PASTOR MATEOS; Curators SALVADOR QUERO CASTRO, CARMEN PRIEGO FERNÁNDEZ DEL CAMPO; publ. *Anuario de Arqueología Madrileña*.

**Instituto Español de Oceanografía (Ministerio de Transportes y Comunicaciones-Subsecretaría de Pesca y Marina Mercante)** (*Spanish Institute of Oceanography*): Alcalá 27, Madrid 14; f. 1919; comprises Physics, Chemistry, Pollution, Geology, Fishery Biology and Marine Biology sections in Madrid, coastal laboratories at Santander, La Coruña, Vigo, Málaga, San Pedro del Pinatar, Santa Cruz de Tenerife, and Palma de Mallorca; library of 7,000 vols.; research vessels "Cornide de Saavedra" (1,100 tons), "Jafuda Cresques" (35 tons), "Argos" (50 tons), "Naucrates" (100 tons); 121 mems.; Dir.-Gen. MIGUEL OLIVER MASSUTI; publs. *Boletín, Trabajos* (both irregular).

**Instituto Geográfico Nacional** (*National Geographical Institute*): Calle del General Ibáñez de Ibero 3, Madrid 3; f. 1870; 1,200 mems.; library of 20,000 vols.; Dir.-Gen. RODOLFO NÚÑEZ DE LAS CUEVAS; comprises the following sections:

*Geographical, Astronomical and Cadastral Council:* Pres. VICENTE PEÑA GEROMINI.

*National Astronomical Observatory:* Dir. JOSÉ PENSADO IGLESIAS.

*Economic Development Service:* Dir. RAFAEL SABATER GAY.

*National Commission on Astronomy:* Pres. RODOLFO NÚÑEZ DE LAS CUEVAS.

*National Commission for Geodesy and Geophysics:* Pres. RODOLFO NÚÑEZ DE LAS CUEVAS.

*National Commission for Metrology and Metrotechnology:* Pres. RODOLFO NÚÑEZ DE LAS CUEVAS.

*Permanent Commission on Earthquake Resistance:* Pres. RODOLFO NÚÑEZ DE LAS CUEVAS.

Publs.: *Boletín Astronómico, Anuario del Observatorio Astronómico, Anuario de Geomagnetismo, Boletines Sísmicos, Boletín de Teledetección, Boletín Informativo del I.G.C.*

**Instituto Histórico de Marina** (*Naval History Institute*): Montalbán 2, Madrid; f. 1942; associated with the Consejo Superior de Investigaciones Científicas; for library see entry under Museo Naval; Dir. C. N. D. JOSÉ MARÍA ZUMALACÁRREGUI.

**Instituto Municipal de Historia de la Ciudad:** Calle de Santa Lucia 1, Casa del Arcediano, Barcelona; f. 1943; the Institute has taken over and added to the activities of the former Archivo Histórico de la Ciudad; it undertakes historical research on Barcelona, organizes courses, lectures, exhibitions, etc.; library of 125,000 vols.; Archives of Municipal records and local press; Dir. Dr. PEDRO VOLTES; publs. include *Divulgación Histórica de Barcelona, Estudios y Documentos, Cuadernos de Historia Económica de Cataluña*†, etc.

**Real Sociedad Arqueológica Tarraconense** (*Archaeological Society*): Calle Ventallols 1, Apdo. 573, Tarragona; f. 1844; Iberian, Roman and early Christian archaeology; ancient, medieval, modern and contemporary history of Tarragona; 710 mems.; library of 5,000 vols.; Pres. Rafael Gabriel Costa; Sec. Joaquín Parareda Sanz; publ. *Boletín Arqueológico*† (quarterly).

**Real Sociedad Geográfica** (*Royal Geographical Society*): Calle de Valverde 22, Madrid 13; f. 1876; geography and earth sciences; 400 mems.; library of 6,200 vols. and 8,500 booklets; Pres. Dr. José María Torroja Menéndez; Perm. Sec. Dr. Ing. Francisco Vázquez Maure; publ. *Boletín*† (annually).

**Servicio de Investigación Prehistórica de la Excelentísima Diputación Provincial** (*Prehistoric Research Society of the Province of Valencia*): Pl. Manises 4, Valencia 3; f. 1927; palaeolithic, neolithic, Bronze and Iron Ages, Iberian and colonial exhibits, Prehistoric Americana; 9 mems.; specialized library of over 22,000 vols.; Dir. Domingo Fletcher Valls; publs. *La Labor de S.I.P. y su Museo*†, *Trabajos Varios*†, *Archivo de Prehistoria Levantina*†.

**Societat Arqueològica Lul·liana** (*Archaeological Society*): Montesión 29, Palma de Mallorca, Balearic Is.; f. 1880; 300 mems.; library of 20,000 vols.; museum; Pres. Nicolás Morell Cotoner; Sec. Bartolomeu Pastor; publ. *Boletín* (annual).

### International Cultural Institutes

**British Council** (*El Consejo Británico*): Calle Almagro 5, Madrid 4; Rep. S. R. Smith; Calle Amigo 83, Barcelona 6; Reg. Dir. P. A. Harrison.

**British Institute:** Calle Amigo 83, Barcelona 6; f. 1944; provides adult English classes; 1,600 students; library of 16,000 vols.; Dir. P. A. Harrison.

**Casa de Velázquez:** Ciudad Universitaria, Madrid 3; f. 1928; French school for research into all aspects of Iberia; grants senior fellowships to French artists or scholars to work in Spain; 34 mems.; library of 70,000 vols.; Dir. Didier Ozanam; Sec.-Gen. Bernard Vincent; Librarian Odette Bresson; publs. *Mélanges*†, *Publications*, *Recherches en Sciences Sociales*, *Recherches en Archéologie*.

**Centro Iberoamericano de Cooperación** (*Ibero-American Cultural Centre*): Avenida de los Reyes Católicos s/n, Ciudad Universitaria, Madrid 3; f. 1946; promotes cultural understanding between Spain and America by organizing conferences, congresses, cultural exhibitions and exchanges, exchanges between university teachers, help for students; information department and department of technical co-operation; centre for Latin American legal studies; Christopher Columbus Council coordinates activities concerned with the discovery of America; radio, cinema and theatre unit; large library open to students; Spanish Library: see Libraries; Pres. H.R.H. Alfonso de Bourbon-Dampierre, Duque de Cádiz; Dir. Juan Ignacio Tena Ybarra; Sec.-Gen. Carlos Abella; publs. include *Cuadernos Hispanoamericanos* (monthly), *Mundo Hispánico* (monthly).

**Dirección General de Relaciones Culturales** (*Cultural Relations Department*): Ministerio de Asuntos Exteriores, Plaza de la Provincia 1, Madrid 12; f. 1926; exhibitions; exchange of professors and lecturers, scholarships, etc.; Dir.-Gen. Amaro González de Mesa; publs. *Indice Cultural Español* (in English, French and Spanish).

**Instituto Alemán:** Calle Zurbarán 21, Madrid 4; f. 1957; Dir. Eckart Plinke.

**Instituto Alemán:** Avda. José Antonio 591, Barcelona 7; f. 1955; library of 11,800 vols.; Dir. H. P. Hebel.

**Instituto de Estudios Norteamericano** (*American Cultural Institute*): Vía Augusta, P.O.B. 12138, Barcelona 6; f. 1952; cultural programme of lectures, discussions, musical events, art exhibitions, etc.; courses in English language, business management and technology; sponsors the American College of Barcelona; runs an academic counselling service and examinations for students entering U.S. universities; c. 400 mems.; library of c. 8,000 vols.; Pres. Dr. José Ma. Poal; Exec. Dir. John S. Zvereff.

**Instituto Egipcio de Estudios Islámicos** (*Egyptian Institute of Islamic Studies*): Francisco de Asís Méndez Casariego 10, Madrid 2; f. 1950; 6 mems.; library of 11,000 vols.; Dir. Dr. Salah Fadl; Spanish Sec. Dr. Mercedes González Más; publ. *Revista* (annually).

**Institut Français** (*French Institute*): Marqués de la Ensenada 12, Madrid; Dir. A. Bengio; also at Barcelona, Bilbao, San Sebastián, Seville, Valencia, Zaragoza.

**Instituto Hispano-Arabe de Cultura** (*Spanish-Arabic Cultural Institute*): Paseo de Juan XXIII 5, Madrid 3; cultural activities, conferences, humanistic and scientific research, exchanges between university teachers, information dept.; library of 10,000 vols., 500 periodicals; Dir. Francisco Utray Sardá; publs. *Arabismo* (quarterly), *AWRAQ*† (annually).

**Istituto Italiano di Cultura** (*Italian Cultural Institute*): Pasaje Méndez Vigo 5, Barcelona; refounded 1947; library of 9,433 vols.; Dir. Dr. Aldo Penasa.

**Istituto Italiano di Cultura:** Calle Mayor 86, Madrid; library of 18,675 vols.; Dir. Prof. Ottavio Mulas.

### Language and Literature

**Asociación de Escritores y Artistas Españoles** (*Writers' and Artists' Association*): Calle de Leganitos 10, Madrid 13; f. 1872; 645 mems.; library of 3,000 vols.; Pres. Guillermo Díaz-Plaja; Sec. José Gerardo Manrique de Lara.

**Instituto Aula de "Mediterráneo":** Universidad de Valencia; f. 1942; 545 mems.; Dir. Dr. F. Sánchez-Castañer; publ. *Mediterráneo, Unión de Literatura* (quarterly).

**Instituto Nacional del Libro Español (I.N.L.E.)** (*National Institute of Spanish Books*): Santiago Rusiñol 8, Madrid 3; f. 1939; Dir. Alfredo Timermans; publs. *El Libro Español* (monthly), *Catálogo de Libros Infantiles y Juveniles*, *Catálogo de Libros y Material de Enseñanza*, *Catálogo de Libros en Gallego*, *Catálogo de Libros en Catalán*, *Libros Españoles ISBN*, *Quién es quién en las Letras Españolas*, *Guía de Editores y de Libreros*.

**Oficina Internacional de Información y Observación del Español:** Avda. de los Reyes Católicos 4, Madrid 3; f. 1963; Sec.-Gen. Manuel Alvar; publs. *Español Actual*, *Lingüística Española Actual*.

**Seminario de Filología Vasca "Julio de Urquijo"** (*"Julio de Urquijo" Seminary of Basque Philology*): Palacio de la Diputación de Guipúzcoa, San Sebastián; f. 1953 to encourage the use and scientific study of the Basque language; attached to the University of País Vasco, Vitoria; Dir. Luis Michelena; publ. *Anuario*.

**Sociedad General de Autores de España** (*General Society of Spanish Authors*): Fernando VI 4, Apdo. 484, Madrid 4; f. 1932; library of 22,000 vols., relating to the theatre and cinema only; Pres. Federico Moreno-Torroba; Sec.-Gen. Carlos Galiano de Prados; publ. *Boletín* (quarterly).

### Medicine

**Consejo General de Colegios Médicos de España** (*General Council of Medical Colleges*): Villanueva 11, Madrid; f. 1930; 21 mems.; Pres. Alfonso de la Fuente Chaos; publs. *Boletín Formativo e Informativo* (monthly) and *Medicina de España*.

**Consejo General de Colegios Oficiales de Farmacéuticos** (*General Council of Official Colleges of Pharmacists*):

Villanueva 11-4°, Madrid 1; f. 1942; 13,500 mems.; Pres. ERNESTO MARCO CAÑIZARES; publ. *Boletín de Información*.

**Instituto Antituberculosis "Francisco Moragas"** (*Antituberculosis Institute*): Lauria 59, Barcelona 9; f. 1932; library of 7,294 vols., 88 periodical publs.; Dir. Dr. EUDALDO XALABARDER; publ. *Publicaciones del Instituto*† (annually).

**Instituto Español de Hematología y Hemoterapia** (*Institute of Haematology and Haemotherapy*): Gral. Oraá 15, Madrid; f. 1940; Dir. Dr. CARLOS ELÓSEGUI; publ. *Anales*.

**Instituto Llorente** (*Institute of Medicine*): Ferraz 9, Madrid; f. 1894; library of 1,500 vols.; Dir. Dr. GABRIEL MEGÍAS; publs. *Anales*, monographs.

**Instituto Nacional de Medicina y Seguridad del Trabajo** (*National Institute of Medicine and Safety*): Pabellón 8, Facultad de Medicina, Ciudad Universitaria, Madrid 3; Dir. Prof. MANUEL BERMEJILLO MARTÍNEZ.

**Instituto Nacional de Reeducación de Inválidos** (*National Institute for Retraining Physically Handicapped*): Finca de Vista-Alegre, Madrid 25; f. 1922; Dir. Dr. ANSELMO ALVAREZ CUÉ; publs. booklets and films.

**Sociedad Española de Patología Digestiva y de la Nutrición** (*Society of Digestive and Nutritional Diseases*): Almagro 38, Madrid; f. 1933; 800 mems.; Pres. Dr. HELIODORO G. MOGENA; publ. *Revista Española de las Enfermedades del Aparato Digestivo y de la Nutrición*.

**Sociedad Española de Radiología y Electrología Médicas y de Medicina Nuclear** (*Society of Radiology, Electrology and Nuclear Medicine*): Goya 38, 3° piso, Madrid 1; f. 1946; 1,000 mems., 209 founder mems.; Pres. Dr. CÉSAR S. ÁLVAREZ PEDROSA; publ. *Radiología*† (every 2 months).

**Sociedad de Pediatría de Madrid y Región Centro** (*Paediatrics Society of Madrid and the Central Region*): Villanueva 11, Madrid 1; f. 1913; 750 mems.; Pres. Dr. J. A. VELASCO COLLAZO; Sec.-Gen. J. M. APARICIO MEIX; publ. *Boletín* (2 a month).

### NATURAL SCIENCES
#### General

**Asociación Española para el Progreso de las Ciencias** (*Spanish Association for the Advancement of Science*): Calle de Valverde 24, Madrid; f. 1908; Pres. Prof. MANUEL LORA-TAMAYO; Sec. Prof. JOSÉ M. TORROJA; publ. *Las Ciencias* (4 times yearly).

**Sociedad de Ciencias "Aranzadi" Elkartea:** Museo de San Telmo, Plaza de I. Zuloaga, San Sebastián 3; f. 1947; to encourage interest in the various branches of natural science, prehistory and ethnology; 1,944 mems.; Pres. JESÚS ALTUNA; Sec. JOSÉ MIGUEL LARRAÑAGA; publs. *Munibe* (quarterly), *Eusko-Folklore* (annually), *Aranzadiana*.

#### Biological Sciences

**Institut Botànic de Barcelona** (*Botanical Institute*): Parc de Montjuïc, Avinguda dels Muntanyans, Barcelona 4; f. 1917; 16 mems.; library of 12,000 vols.; Dir. Dr. O. DE BOLOS I CAPDEVILA; Dir. Botanic Gardens EUGENI SIERRA I RÁFOLS; publs. *Collectanea Botanica*†, *Treballs*†, etc.

**Patronato de Biología Animal:** Embajadores 68, Madrid 12; f. 1933; library of 5,500 vols.; 300 periodicals; Dir. Dr. ANGEL CAMPANO LÓPEZ; Sec. Dr. RAFAEL DÍAZ MONTILLA; publ. *Revista* (quarterly).

**Real Sociedad Española de Historia Natural** (*Royal Spanish Natural History Society*): Museo Nacional de Ciencias Naturales, Paseo de la Castellana, Madrid 6; Pres. Prof. JOSÉ MA. FÚSTER; Sec. Prof. FRANCISCO HERNÁNDEZ-PACHECO; publ. *Boletín* (quarterly).

#### Mathematics

**Real Sociedad Matemática Española** (*Royal Spanish Mathematical Society*): Serrano 123, Madrid; f. 1911; 450 mems.; Pres. Prof. JOSÉ JAVIER ETAYO MIQUEO; Sec. GONZALO CALERO ROSILLO; publs. *Revista Matemática Hispano-Americana*, *Revista Gaceta Matemática*.

#### Physical Sciences

**Asociación Nacional de Químicos de España** (*National Association of Chemists*): Lagasca 83, 1°, Madrid 6; f. 1945; 9,000 mems.; a member of the international Federation of Mediterranean Associations and of European Federation of Chemical Engineering; Pres. JOSÉ LUIS NEGRO LÓPEZ; Sec. JOAQUÍN COPADO LÓPEZ; publs. *Química e Industria* (monthly), technical and professional works.

**Instituto Nacional de Meteorología** (*National Meteorological Institute*): Ciudad Universitaria, Apdo. 285, Madrid; f. 1887; library of 19,500 vols., 2,000 reports; 511 mems., 4,500 correspondents; Dir. ANGEL GONZÁLEZ RIVERO; 4,500 stations; publs. *Boletín diario, Boletín mensual climatológico, Resúmenes anuales, Calendario Meteorofenológico*.

**Real Sociedad Española de Física y Química** (*Royal Spanish Society of Physics and Chemistry*): Facultad de Ciencias, Ciudad Universitaria, Madrid 3; f. 1903; Pres. CARLOS SÁNCHEZ DEL RÍO Y SIERRA; Sec.-Gen. A. TIEMBLO RAMOS; publ. *Anales* (monthly, in 2 parts: physics, chemistry).

**Sociedad Astronómica de España y América** (*Astronomical Society of Spain and America*): Avda. Diagonal 337, Barcelona 8; f. 1911; 250 mems.; library of 2,800 vols.; lectures, courses, etc.; Acting Pres. Dr. JOSEPH M. CODINA-VIDAL; Sec. ANTONIO PALUZIE-BORRELL; publs. *Urania* (quarterly), *Suplemento de Urania* (twice monthly).

**Unión Nacional de Astronomía y Ciencias Afines** (*National Union of Astronomy and Related Sciences*): Pabellón de Matemáticas, Ciudad Universitaria, Madrid; f. 1946; Sec. Rev. A. ROMAÑA, S.J.; publs. *Urania*† (2 a year), with Soc. Astronómica de España y América), Affiliations: *Observatorio Geofísico de Cartuja* (Granada), *Observatorio de Física Cósmica del Ebro, Observatorio Astronómico de la Univ. de Santiago, Seminario de Astronomía y Geodesia de la Univ. de Madrid*.

### PHILOSOPHY AND PSYCHOLOGY

**Instituto Nacional de Psicología Aplicada y Orientación Profesional** (*National Institute of Applied Psychology and Vocational Guidance*): C. Juan Huarte de San Juan, Ciudad Universitaria, Madrid 3; f. 1927; 86 mems.; library of 9,700 vols.; Dir. RAFAEL GUTIÉRREZ BENITO; Sec. (vacant); publ. *Revista de Psicología General y Aplicada* (6 a year).

### RELIGION, SOCIOLOGY AND ANTHROPOLOGY

**Federación Española de Religiosos de Enseñanza (FERE)** (*Spanish Federation of Religious Teaching*): Conde de Peñalver 45, Apdo. 53,052, Madrid; f. 1957; groups all the centres of elementary, secondary and higher education of the Catholic Church; there are 3,000 centres; library specializing in psychology and pedagogy containing 2,000 vols.; Pres. R.P. AQUILINO BOCOS MERINO; Sec. SANTIAGO MARTÍN JIMÉNEZ; publs. *Educadores* (Teachers' Review) (bi-monthly), *Boletín de la FERE* (monthly).

**Instituto de Estudios Africanos** (*Institute of African Studies*): Castellana 5, Madrid 1; f. 1945; 20 mems.; Dir. EDUARDO BLANCO RODRÍGUEZ; Sec. JOAQUÍN VENTURA BAÑARES; publs. *Africa* (monthly), *Collección Monográfica Africana* (irregular).

**Instituto de Estudios Asturianos** (*Institute of Asturian Studies*): Plaza de Porlier 5, Oviedo; f. 1946; 50 mems.; Dir. Jesús Evaristo Casariego; publs. *Boletín*, related works.

**Institut d'Estudis Catalans** (*Institute of Catalan Studies*): Carrer de París 150, Apartat 1146, Barcelona; f. 1907; first installed in the Palau de la Generalitat, 1932 in the ancient Casa de Convalescència of the Hospital de la Santa Creu, in 1963 in the Palau Dalmases; Pres. Joan Ainaud de Lasarte; Sec.-Gen. R. Aramon i Serra; publs. *Anuari, Memòries de la Secció Històrico-Arqueològica, Arxius de la Secció de Ciencies, Butlletí de Dialectologia Catalana, Estudis Romànics Biblioteca Filològica, Treballs de la Secció de Filosofia i Ciències Socials, Flora i Fauna de Catalunya, Butlletí de la Biblioteca de Catalunya, Publicacions del Departament de Música de la Biblioteca de Catalunya, Estudis d'Història Medieval, Treballs de la Societat Catalana de Biologia*, related works.

Members:

*History and Archaeology Section:*
President: Miquel Coll i Alentorn
Ainaud de Lasarte, Joan
Font i Rius, Josep M.
Giralt, Emili.
Mundó Anscari M.
Rubío, Jordi
Tarradell, Miquel

*Philological Section:*
President: Pere Bohigas
Aramon i Serra, Ramon
Badia i Margarit, A. M.
Bastardas, Joan
Casacuberta, Josep M. de
Coromines, Joan
Foix, J. V.
Moll, Francesc de B.
Sanchis i Guarner, Manuel

Associate:
Carbonell, Jordi

*Science Section:*
President: Enric Casassas
Alsina i Bofill, Josep
Bolòs, Oriol de
Laporte, Josep
Solé i Sabarís, Lluís
Teixidor i Batlle, Josep

*Philosophy and Social Science Section:*
President: Ramon Faus
Colomer, Eusebi
Iglésies, Josep
Noguera de Guzman, Raimon
Sardà i Dexeus, Joan
Trias i Fargas, Ramon
Vila, Pau

Associates:
Gasòliba, Carles A.
Muntaner i Pascual, Josep M.
Triadú, Joan

Corresponding members in Spain, 28; foreign, 56.

Affiliated Societies:
Institució Catalana d'Història Natural.
Societat Catalana de Biologia.
Societat Catalana de Ciències Físiques, Químiques i Matemàtiques.
Societat Catalana de Geografia.
Societat Catalana d'Estudis Històrics.
Societat Catalana d'Estudis Jurídics, Econòmics i Socials.
Societat Catalana d'Estudis Litúrgics.
Societat Catalana de Musicologia.
Biblioteca de Catalunya: library of 400,000 vols.

**Instituto de Estudios Ibéricos y Etnología Valenciana** (*Institute of Iberian Studies and Valencian Ethnology*): Diputación Provincial, Caballeros 2, Valencia; f. 1950; 22 Spanish mems., 5 foreign mems.; Dir. Prof. Dr. Julián San Valero Aparisi; Sec. Prof. José Cano Marqués; publs. *Estudios Ibéricos* (4 vols.), *Etnología Valenciana* (4 vols.).

**Institución "Fernando el Católico" de la Excma. Diputación Provincial:** Palacio Provincial, Plaza de España, Zaragoza; f. 1943; part of C.S.I.C.; Sections: Philology, Literature, Art, Archaeology and Numismatics, Folklore, History, Medicine, Geography, Economic and Social Studies, Exhibitions and Films, Architecture, Culture, Religion, Agricultural Studies, Regional Aragonese Law, Ecology and Environmental Studies, Music for Young People, Ancient Music; Pres. Gaspar Castellano y de Gastón; Dir. Angel Canellas López; Sec. Antonio Serrano Montalvo; Council of 12 representing the Church, University, Municipality, Delegation of Culture, Amigos del País, collaborate in archaeological explorations; library of 50,000 vols.; mems.: 35 ordinary, 11 ex-officio, 35 hon., 69 corresp.; includes the Colegio de Aragón; Dean Luis Jordana de Pozas; 40 mems.; periodical publs. *Archivo de Filología Aragonesa†, Cesaraugusta†, Seminario de Arte Aragonés†, Archivos de Estudios Médicos Aragoneses, Archivos de Estudios Médicos Aragoneses†, Cuadernos de Historia "Jerónimo Zurita"†, Zaragoza†, Cuadernos de Aragón†, Temas aragoneses†, Nueva colección monográfica†, Estudios Pedagógicos†, Geographicalia*.

**Real Sociedad Vascongada de los Amigos del País** (*Royal Society of Friends of the Basque Country*): Museo de San Telmo, San Sebastián; f. 1764, the first of such societies in Spain; 24 mems.; organized Museo de San Telmo and Museo Naval, also Conservatorio Municipal de Música; f. Editorial Guipuzcoana de Ediciones y Publicaciones, Books in Basque and Biblioteca Vascongada de los Amigos del País, collaborated in archaeological exploration of the pre-historic cave dwellings of the district; is the Guipuzcoan Office of the Consejo Superior de Investigaciones Científicas, Madrid (*see* below); Dir. Alvaro del Valle de Lersundi; publs. *Boletín* (quarterly), *Egan* (literary supplement), *Muñibe* (natural sciences supplement), *Boletín de la Confradía Vasca de Gastronomía, Boletín de Estudios Históricos sobre San Sebastián* (annual), *Anuario de Eusko-Folklore Aranzadiana Orria*.

**Sociedad Española de Antropología, Etnografía y Prehistoria** (*Spanish Society of Anthropology, Ethnography and Prehistory*): Apdo. 1014, Madrid; f. 1921; 543 mems.; library 7,050 vols. and 217 journals; Pres. José Luis de Arrese; Vice-Pres. Manuel Maura Salas; Sec. (Life) Dr. Julio Martínez Santa-Olalla; publs. *Actas y Memorias*, related works.

Technology

**Colegio Oficial de Ingenieros Industriales de Cataluña:** Vía Layetana 39; 6,000 mems.; is an association of engineer-graduates of the School of Industrial Engineers of Barcelona; Pres. and Dean Joan Majó Cruzate; Sec. Josep Cornet Colom.

**Junta de Energía Nuclear:** Ciudad Universitaria, Avenida Complutense 22, Madrid 3; f. 1951; controls and directs research and study in all peaceful applications of nuclear energy to national purposes; 2,135 mems.; library of 26,100 vols., 60,000 reports, 256,000 microcards, 653 periodicals; Pres. Jesús Olivares Baque; Vice-Pres. and Gen. Man. Francisco Pascual Martínez; Technical Sec.-Gen. Manuel López Rodríguez; publs.† *Energía Nuclear* (every 2 months), and JEN reports.

**Instituto de la Ingeniería de España** (*Spanish Institute of Engineering*): General Arrando 38, Madrid 4; f. 1905;

20,000 mems.; comprises 9 associations of higher engineers and the *Aula de Ingeniería* (training centre), offering courses, seminars, etc. for post-graduate students; Gen. Sec. Jaime Tornos.

**Sociedad Española de Cerámica y Vidrio** (*Spanish Ceramic and Glass Society*): Carretera de Valencia, Km. 24,300, Arganda del Rey, Madrid; f. 1960; promotes technical progress in ceramic and glass work and disseminates information about manufacture and developments within the field; Gen. Sec. Dr. Juan Espinosa de los Monteros; publ. *Cerámica y Vidrio* (every 2 months).

## RESEARCH INSTITUTES

(*see* also under Universities)

**Consejo Superior de Investigaciones Científicas (C.S.I.C.)** (*Council for Scientific Research*): Headquarters: Serrano 117, Madrid 6; f. 1940; the Council aims to develop, direct and co-ordinate research mainly in the fields of science and technology, through its own research Institutes throughout the country; it also sponsors some university research. The Council has 1,218 research workers and 5,000 technical and auxiliary personnel; it has its own editorial department which has published about 6,200 books and 100 periodicals; library of 197,000 vols.; several specialized libraries.

*President:* Carlos Sánchez del Río.
*Vice-Presidents:* José Luis Cánovas, José Luis Mateo, Emilio Sáez.
*Secretary-General:* Lucio Rafael Soto.

Constituent Institutes:

*Mathematics*
  Instituto de Matemáticas "Jorge Juan": Serrano 123, Madrid 6.
  Seminario Matemático (Universidad de Barcelona): Facultad de Ciencias, Avda. José Antonio 585, Barcelona 7.
  Seminario Matemático (Universidad de Salamanca): Facultad de Ciencias, Salamanca.
  Seminario Matemático (Universidad de Santiago): Facultad de Ciencias, Santiago de Compostela.
  Seminario Matemático (Universidad de Zaragoza): Facultad de Ciencias, Ciudad Universitaria de Aragón, Zaragoza.

*Operative and Statistical Research*
  Instituto de Investigación Operativa y Estadística: Serrano 123, Madrid 6.

*Astronomy*
  Departamento de Mecánica y Astronomía (Universidad Complutense): Facultad de Ciencias, Cátedra de Astronomía, Madrid 3.

*Physics*
  Instituto de Física de Materiales: Serrano 144, Madrid 6.
  Instituto de Física del Estado Sólido: Facultad de Ciencias, Universidad Autónoma "Canto Blanco", Madrid 34.
  Instituto de Estructura de la Materia: Serrano 119, Madrid 6.
  Departamento de Física Fundamental (Universidad de Zaragoza): Facultad de Ciencias, Universidad de Zaragoza.
  Departamento de Física Fundamental (Universidad de Valladolid): Facultad de Ciencias, Universidad de Valladolid.
  Instituto de Física Corpúscular (Universidad de Valencia): Facultad de Ciencias, Paseo del Mar 13, Valencia 10.
  Instituto de Física Teórica: Diagonal 647, Barcelona 18.

*Electricity and Electronics*
  Instituto de Electrónica de Comunicaciones: Serrano 144, Madrid 6.
  Centro de Física Aplicada "Leonardo Torres Quevedo": Serrano 144, Madrid 6.

*Optics*
  Instituto de Optica "Daza de Valdés": Serrano 121, Madrid 6.

*Acoustics*
  Instituto de Acústica: Serrano 144, Madrid 6.

*Automatics and Informatics*
  Instituto de Electricidad: Facultad de Ciencias, Universidad Complutense, Madrid 3.
  Instituto de Automática Industrial: Km. 22, 800 Carretera Madrid-Valencia, Arganda del Rey.
  Instituto de Cibernética: Diagonal 647, 2A planta, Barcelona 14.

*Astrophysics*
  Instituto de Astrofísica de Andalucía: Oficios 16, Apdo. 2. 144, Granada.
  Instituto de Astrofísica de Canarias: Facultad de Ciencias, Universidad de La Laguna (Tenerife).
  Departamento de Física de la Tierra y del Cosmos (Universidad de Barcelona): Facultad de Física, Avda. Generalísimo Franco 647, Barcelona 14.

*Physical Chemistry*
  Instituto de Química Física "Rocasolano": Serrano 119, Madrid 6.
  Departamento de Investigaciones Químicas (Univ. Autónoma de Madrid): Facultad de Ciencias, Canto Blanco, Madrid 34.
  Departamento de Investigaciones Químicas (Universidad de Valladolid): Facultad de Ciencias, Valladolid.

*Inorganic Chemistry*
  Instituto de Química Inorgánica "Elhuyar": Serrano 113, Madrid 6.
  Departamento de Química Analítica (Universidad Complutense): Facultad de Ciencias, Ciudad Universitaria, Madrid 3.
  Departamento de Química Inorgánica (Universidad de Zaragoza): Facultad de Ciencias, Zaragoza.
  Departamento de Química Analítica (Universidad de Murcia): Facultad de Ciencias de Murcia.
  Departamento de Investigaciones Físicas y Químicas de la Universidad de Sevilla: Facultad de Ciencias, Sevilla.
  Departamento de Investigaciones Químicas (Universidad de Granada): Facultad de Ciencias, Granada.

*Organic Chemistry*
  Instituto de Química Orgánica General: Juan de la Cierva 3, Madrid 6.
  Instituto de Productos Naturales Orgánicos de La Laguna: Carretera de la Esperanza 2, La Laguna, Tenerife.
  Instituto de Química Bio-Orgánica de Barcelona: Jorge Girona Salgado s/n, Barcelona 17.
  Departamento de Química Orgánica de Santiago: Universidad de Santiago de Compostela.
  Sección de Productos Naturales: Universidad de Santiago de Compostela.
  Departamento de Química Macromolecular: E.T.S.I.I. Avda. Diagonal 999, Barcelona 14.
  Departamento de Investigaciones Químicas (Universidad de Salamanca): Facultad de Ciencias, Salamanca.

*Centro Nacional de Química Orgánica:* Juan de la Cierva 3, Madrid 6.

**Applied Chemistry**
*Instituto de Catálisis y Petroleoquímica:* Serrano 119, Madrid 6.
*Instituto de Plásticos y Caucho:* Juan de la Cierva 3, Madrid 6.
*Instituto de Carboquímica (Zaragoza):* Plaza del Paraíso 1, Zaragoza 5.
*Instituto de Química Médica:* Juan de la Cierva 3, Madrid 6.

**Other Specialities**
*Instituto Químico de Sarriá (Barcelona):* Instituto Químico de Sarriá s/n, Barcelona 17.
*Departamento de Investigaciones Químicas (Universidad de Santiago):* Facultad de Ciencias, Santiago de Compostela.
*Departamento de Investigaciones Químicas Farmacéuticas (Universidad de Santiago):* Facultad de Farmacia, Santiago de Compostela.

**Geology**
*Instituto de Geología:* Paseo de la Castellana 84, Madrid 6.
*Instituto "Jaime Almera" de Investigaciones Geológicas:* Egipciacas 15, Barcelona 1.
*Departamento de Geología Económica:* Facultad de Ciencias, Universidad Complutense, Madrid 3.
*Departamento de Investigaciones Geológicas (Universidad de Granada):* Facultad de Ciencias, Granada.
*Departamento de Investigaciones Geológicas (Universidad de Oviedo):* Facultad de Ciencias, Oviedo.
*Departamento de Investigaciones Geológicas (Universidad de Salamanca):* Facultad de Ciencias, Salamanca.

**Geophysics**
*Observatorio de Física Cósmica del Ebro:* Roquetas, Tortosa, Tarragona.

**Museum**
*Museo Nacional de Ciencias Naturales:* Paseo Castellana 84, Madrid 6.

**Hydrology**
*Instituto de Hidrología:* Paseo Bajo Virgen del Puerto 3, Madrid 3.

**Chemical and Related Technology**
*Instituto de Tecnología Química y Textil (Barcelona):* Jorge Girona Salgado s/n, Barcelona 17.
*Instituto Nacional del Carbón "Francisco Pintado Fe":* La Coredoria s/n, Oviedo.
*Centro de Investigaciones del Agua:* Km. 22,800 Carretera Madrid-Valencia (Arganda).
*Instituto de Ingeniería Química y Desarrollo de Procesos:* Serrano 117, Madrid 6.
*Centro de Investigación y Desarrollo (Barcelona):* Zona Universitaria de Pedralbes, Barcelona.

**Metallurgy**
*Centro Nacional de Investigaciones Metalúrgicas:* Ciudad Universitaria, Madrid 3.

**Construction**
*Instituto de Cerámica y Vidrio:* Km. 24,300 Carretera Madrid-Valencia (Arganda del Rey).
*Instituto de la Construcción y del Cemento "Eduardo Torroja":* Costillares (Chamartín de la Rosa), Madrid 33.

**Molecular Biology**
*Instituto de Biología del Desarrollo:* Velázquez 144, Madrid 6.
*Instituto de Biología Molecular:* Universidad Autónoma Canto Blanco, Madrid 34.
*Instituto de Bioquímica de Macromoléculas:* Facultad de Ciencias, Universidad Autónoma de Canto Blanco, Madrid 34.
*Instituto de Biofísica y Neurobiología:* San Antonio María Claret 171, Barcelona 13.
*Centro de Biología Molecular "Severo Ochoa":* Universidad Autónoma "Canto Blanco", Madrid 34.

**Cellular Biology**
*Instituto de Biología Celular:* Velázquez 144, Madrid 6.
*Instituto de Investigaciones Citológicas:* Amadeo de Saboya 4, Valencia 10.
*Instituto de Biología:* San Antonio Maria Claret 171, Barcelona 13.
*Centro de Investigaciones Biológicas:* Velázquez 144, Madrid 6.

**Immunology and Microbiology**
*Instituto de Inmunología y Biología Microbiana:* Velázquez 144, Madrid 6.
*Instituto "Jaime Ferrán" de Microbiología:* Joaquín Costa 32, Madrid 6.
*Instituto de Investigaciones Médicas Fundación "Jiménez Díaz":* Avda. Reyes Católicos 2, Madrid 3.

**Anthropology and Genetics**
*Instituto de Genética:* Velázquez 144, Madrid 6.

**Biochemistry**
*Instituto de Enzimología y Patología Molecular:* Universidad Autónoma, Arzobispo Morcillo s/n, Madrid 34.
*Instituto de Microbiología Bioquímica (Salamanca):* Facultad de Ciencias, Salamanca.
*Departamento de Bioquímica:* Facultad de Farmacia, Universidad Complutense, Madrid 3.
*Departamento de Bioquímica:* Facultad de Ciencias Químicas, Universidad Complutense, Madrid 3.
*Departamento de Bioquímica (Sevilla):* Facultad de Ciencias, Universidad de Sevilla.
*Departamento de Bioquímica Clínica:* Avda. Flor de Maig s/n, Cerdanyola, Barcelona.
*Departamento de Bioquímica Oncológica:* Instituto Nacional de Oncología, Ciudad Universitaria, Madrid 3.

**Histology and Anatomy**
*Instituto "Santiago Ramón y Cajal":* Velázquez 144, Madrid 6.
*Departamento de Anatomía:* Facultad de Medicina, Paseo Calvo Sotelo 2, Zaragoza.
*Instituto de Investigaciones "Federico Oloriz Aguilera":* Facultad de Medicina, Universidad de Granada.
*Departamento de Anatomía (Salamanca):* Facultad de Medicina, Fonseca 2, Salamanca.
*Departamento de Anatomía y Patología Médica (Universidad Valencia):* Facultad de Medicina, Paseo del Mar 17, Valencia 10.
*Departamento de Biofísica:* Joaquín Costa 32, Madrid 6.

**Pharmacology**
*Departamento de Farmacología y Terapéutica:* Facultad de Medicina 143, Barcelona 11.
*Departamento de Farmacología Aplicada (Barcelona):* Jorge Girona s/n, Barcelona 17.
*Departamento de Farmacología y Toxicología:* Facultad de Medicina, Universidad Complutense, Madrid 3.
*Instituto de Medicina Experimental:* Facultad de Medicina, Pabellón II, Universidad Complutense, Madrid 3.
*Departamento de Investigaciones Oncológicas:* Maiquez 7, Madrid 9.
*Departamento de Investigaciones Neonatológicas Perinatales:* O'Donnell 55, Madrid 9.
*Instituto de Investigaciones Clínicas:* Facultad de Medicina, Fonseca 2, Salamanca.
*Departamento de Investigaciones Médicas:* Facultad de Medicina, Granada.

*Departamento de Cancerología Experimental:* Hospital Clínico, Ciudad Universitaria, Madrid 3.
*Departamento de Investigaciones Médicas (Universidad de Navarra):* Facultad de Medicina, Universidad de Navarra, Pamplona.
*Departamento de Patología Comparada:* Facultad de Veterinaria, Universidad Complutense, Madrid 3.

Physiology
*Instituto "Gregorio Marañón":* Velázquez 144, Madrid 6.
*Departamento de Bioquímica y Fisiología, Salamanca:* Facultad de Ciencias, Universidad de Salamanca.
*Departamento de Investigaciones Fisiológicas (Universidad de Navarra):* Universidad de Navarra, Pamplona.
*Departamento de Fisiología y Bioquímica (Universidad de Granada):* Facultad de Medicina, Granada.
*Departamento de Fisiopatología de la Reproducción Humana (Universidad Complutense):* Hospital Clínico 5a planta, Madrid 3.
*Departamento de Especialidades Médicas (Granada):* Facultad de Medicina, Granada.

Botany
*Departamento de Fisiopatología Cerebral:* Serrano 57, Madrid.
*Jardín Botánico (Madrid):* Plaza de Murillo 2, Madrid 14.
*Instituto Botánico Municipal (Barcelona):* Avda. de Montañals, Parque de Montjuich, Barcelona 4.

Zoology
*Instituto de Zoología "José de Acosta":* Paseo de la Castellana 84, Madrid 6.
*Instituto Español de Entomología:* Paseo de la Castellana 84, Madrid 6.
*Instituto de Biología Aplicada (Barcelona):* Facultad de Ciencias, Universidad de Barcelona.

Parasitology
*Instituto de Parasitología "López Neyra" (Granada):* Ventanilla 11, Granada.

Experimental Biology Stations
*Estación Biológica de "Doñana" (Sevilla):* Paraguay 1, Sevilla 12.
*Centro Pirenaico de Biología Experimental (Jaca):* Avda. del Regimiento de Galicia s/n, Jaca (Huesca).
*Estación Experimental de Zonas Áridas:* General Segura 1, Almería.
*Estación de Biología Alpina "El Ventorrillo":* Kilómetro 55 de la Carretera Madrid-Segovia.
*Reserva integral del "Coto de Doñana" (Huelva):* Palacio del Coto de Doñana", Almonte (Huelva).
*Centro de Rescate de la Fauna Sahariana (Almería):* Finca "La Hoya", Almería.
*Estación "Cueva del Ojo de Guareña" (Burgos):* D.P.: Museo Ciencias Naturales, Paseo Castellana 84, Madrid 6.
*Finca "El Boalar de Jaca" (Huesca):* D.P.: Cto. Pirenaico de Biología Experimental, Jaca (Huesca).

Oceanography
*Barco oceanográfico "Córnide de Saavedra".*
*Barco oceanográfico "García del Cid".*
*Centro Nacional de Investigaciones Pesqueras:* Paseo Nacional s/n, Barcelona 3.

Marine Biology
*INIP Laboratorio de Barcelona:* Paseo Nacional s/n, Barcelona 3.

Aquiculture
*Estación de Investigaciones Pesqueras de Torre de la Sal:* Castellón.
*Instituto de Investigaciones Pesqueras de Cádiz:* Puerto Pesquero, Cádiz.

*Instituto de Investigaciones Pesqueras de Vigo:* Muelle de Bouzas, Vigo (Pontevedra).

Aquariums
*Acuario de Barcelona:* Paseo Nacional s/n, Barcelona 3.
*Acuario de Planes:* Esplanada del Puerto 15 (Apdo. 15), Blanes, Gerona.

Soils
*Instituto de Edafología y Biología Vegetal:* Serrano 115 bis, Madrid 6.
*Centro de Edafología y Biología Aplicada (Salamanca):* Cordel de Merinas s/n, Salamanca.
*Centro de Edafología y Biología Aplicada del Cuarto:* Cortijo del Cuarto, Bellavista, Sevilla.
*Centro de Edafología y Biología Aplicada (Santa Cruz de Tenerife):* Cabildo Insular, Santa Cruz de Tenerife.
*Sección de Edafología de La Palma:* Cabildo Insular, Tenerife, Isla La Palma.
*Finca "La Higueruela" (Santa Olaya) Toledo:* Serrano 115 bis, Madrid 6 (provisional).
*Finca "Muñobela" (Salamanca):* Cordel de Merinas s/n, Salamanca.
*Finca "Aljarafe"(Sevilla):* Cortijo del Cuarto (Bellavista), Sevilla.

Soils and Plants
*Estación Experimental "Aula Dei" (Zaragoza):* Montañana 177, Zaragoza.
*Centro de Investigaciones Agrícolas (Badajoz):* Virgen de la Soledad 5, Badajoz.
*Departamento de Química Agrícola:* Facultad de Ciencias, Universidad Autónoma, Madrid 34.
*Finca Experimental de "Aula Dei" (Zaragoza):* Montañana 177, Zaragoza.

Plants
*Estación Experimental del "Zaidín" (Granada):* Professor Albareda 1, Granada.
*Centro de Edafología y Biología Aplicada del Segura:* Avda. del 18 de julio 1, Murcia.
*Instituto de Investigaciones Agrobiológicas de Galicia:* Avda. de las Ciencias s/n, Santiago de Compostela.
*Misión Biológica de Galicia (Pontevedra):* Salcedo-Pontevedra.
*Estación Experimental "La Mayora" (Málaga):* Algarrobo-Costa, Málaga.
*Finca "La Matanza" (Murcia):* Avda. 18 de julio 1, Murcia.
*Finca "La Mimbre" (Granada):* Profesor Albareda 1, Granada.
*Finca "Pazo de Gandarón" (Pontevedra):* Avda. Ciencias s/n, Santiago de Compostela.
*Finca "La Mayora" (Málaga):* Algarrobo-Costa, Málaga.

Zoology and Animal Husbandry
*Instituto de Alimentación y Productividad Animal:* Facultad de Veterinaria, Ciudad Universitaria, Madrid 3.
*Estación Agrícola Experimental (León):* Avda. Facultad Veterinaria 25, León.
*Instituto de Economía y Producciones:* Facultad de Veterinaria, Zaragoza.
*Instituto de Zootecnia (Córdoba):* Facultad de Veterinaria, Córdoba.
*Departamento de Cirugía y Reproducción (Zaragoza):* Facultad de Veterinaria, Zaragoza.
*Finca "La Poveda" (Arganda del Rey):* Km. 22.800 de la Carretera Madrid-Valencia.
*Centro de Investigación y Desarrollo (Santander):* Avda. de los Castros s/n, Santander.
*Finca "El Espino" (León):* c/o Avda. Facultad Veterinaria 25, León.

*Pathology*
  Instituto de Investigaciones en Patología de las Colectividades Ganaderas: Facultad de Veterinaria, Zaragoza.
  Instituto de Investigaciones Veterinarias: Facultad de Veterinaria, Universidad Complutense, Madrid 3.

*Food Technology*
  Instituto de la Grasa y sus Derivados (Sevilla): Avda. Padre García Tejero 4, Sevilla 12.
  Instituto de Industrias Cárnicas: Serrano 117, Madrid 6.
  Instituto de Agroquímica y Tecnología de Alimentación Vegetal: Jaime Roig 11, Valencia 10.
  Instituto del Frío: Ciudad Universitaria, Madrid 3.
  Instituto de Fermentaciones Industriales: Juan de la Cierva 3, Madrid 6.
  Planta Piloto Instituto Fermentaciones Industriales (Arganda): Km. 24.400 Carretera Madrid-Valencia.
  Centro Experimental de Arganda del Rey: Km. 24.400 Carretera Madrid-Valencia.

*Nutrition and Bromatology*
  Instituto de Nutrición: Fac. de Farmacia, Cátedra Fisiología Animal, Ciudad Universitaria, Madrid 3.
  Departamento de Investigaciones Bromatológicas: Fac. Farmacia, Universidad Complutense, Madrid 3.

*Prehistory*
  Instituto Español de Prehistoria: Serrano 13, Madrid 1.
  Departamento de Prehistoria y Arqueología: Egipciacas 15, Barcelona 1.
  Servicio de Investigación Prehistórica: Plaza Manises 2, Valencia 3.

*Archaeology*
  Instituto de Arqueología "Rodrigo Caro": Duque de Medinaceli 4, Madrid 14.
  Escuela Española de Historia y Arqueología (Roma): Via di Villa Albani 16, Roma.

*History of Spain*
  Instituto de Historia "Jerónimo Zurita": Duque de Medinaceli 4, Madrid 14.
  Seminario de Historia Moderna: Universidad de Navarra, Pamplona.
  Instituto Histórico de la Marina: Montalbán 2, Madrid 14.
  Centro "Marcelino Menéndez Pelayo": Duque de Medinaceli 4, Madrid 14.

*History of America*
  Instituto de Historia Hispanoamericana "Gonzalo Fernández de Oviedo": Duque de Medinaceli 4, Madrid 14.
  Escuela de Estudios Hispanoamericanos: Alfonso XII 16, Sevilla 2.

*History of Art*
  Instituto de Arte "Diego Velázquez": Duque de Medinaceli 4, Madrid 14.
  Seminario de Estudios de Arte y Arqueología: Facultad de Filosofía y Letras, Universidad de Valladolid.
  Instituto de Musicología (Barcelona): Egipciacas 15, Barcelona 1.

*Genealogy and Heraldry*
  Instituto de Genealogía y Heráldica: Duque de Medinaceil 4, Madrid 14.

*Numismatics*
  Instituto de Numismática "Antonio Agustín": Facultad de Filosofía y Letras, Universidad Complutense, Madrid 3.

*History of Science*
  Instituto de Historia de la Medicina "Arnau de Vilanova": Facultad de Medicina, Universidad Complutense, Madrid 3.

*Hispanic Studies*
  Instituto de Filología Hispánica "Miguel de Cervantes": Duque de Medinaceli 4, Madrid 14.
  Instituto de Filología de Barcelona: Egipciacas 15, Barcelona 1.

*Classics*
  Instituto de Filología Clásica "Antonio de Nebrija": Duque de Medinaceli 4, Madrid 14.
  Colegio Trilingue (Salamanca): Facultad de Filosofía y Letras, Salamanca.
  Institución "Milá y Fontanals": Egipciacas 15, Barcelona 1.

*Hebrew Studies*
  Instituto de Estudios Hebráicos, Sefardies y de Oriente Próximo "Benito Arias Montano": Duque de Medinaceli 4, Madrid 14.

*Arabic Studies*
  Instituto de Estudios Arabes "Miguel Asín": Hortaleza 104, Madrid 4.
  Escuela de Estudios Arabes (Granada): Cuesta del Chapiz 22, Granada.
  Casa del Chapiz (Granada): Cuesta del Chapiz 22, Granada.

*Theology*
  Instituto de Teología "Francisco Suárez": Duque de Medinaceli 4, Madrid 14.

*History of the Spanish Church*
  Instituto de Historia Eclesiástica "P. Enrique Flórez": Serrano 123, Madrid 6.

*Canon Law*
  Instituto de Derecho Canónico "S. Raimundo de Peñafort: Compañía 1, Salamanca.

*Philosophy*
  Instituto de Filosofía "Luis Vives": Serrano 127, Madrid 6.
  Maioricensis Schola Llullística (Palma de Mallorca): Apartado 17, Palma de Mallorca.

*Education*
  Instituto de Pedagogía "San José de Calasanz": Serrano 127, Madrid 6.

*Economics*
  Instituto de Economía "Sancho de Moncada": Duque de Medinaceli 4, Madrid 14.
  Centro de Estudios Económicos y Sociales (Barcelona): Egipciacas 15, Barcelona 1.
  Instituto de Economía Aplicada (Universidad Autónoma): Facultad de Ciencias Económicas y Empresariales, Madrid 34.

*Sociology*
  Instituto de Sociología "Balmes": Duque de Medinaceli 4, Madrid 14.

*Agricultural Socio-Economics*
  Departamento de Economía Agraria: Serrano 113, Madrid 6.

*Geography*
  Instituto de Geografía "Juan Sebastián Elcano": Vitrubio 8, Madrid 6.
  Instituto de Geografía Aplicada: Serrano 115 bis, Madrid 6.
  Instituto de Geografía, Etnografía e Historia: Egipciacas 15, Barcelona 1.
  Departamento de Geografía (Universidad de Salamanca): Facultad de Filosofía y Letras, Salamanca.
  Departamento de Geografía (Universidad de Valladolid): Facultad de Filosofía y Letras, Valladolid.
  Instituto "Alfonso el Magnánimo": Palacio de la Generalidad, Caballeros 2, Valencia 1.

# RESEARCH INSTITUTES

## International Law
Instituto de Derecho Internacional "Francisco de Vitoria": Duque de Medinaceli 4, Madrid 14.
Seminario de Estudios Internacionales "Alvaro Pelayo": Facultad de Derecho, Universidad de Santiago de Compostela.

## Civil Law
Instituto de Derecho Administrativo: Alberto Aguilera 13, Madrid 15.
Instituto Nacional de Estudios Jurídicos: Duque de Medinaceli 6, Madrid 14.

## Regional Law
Ceutro de Estudios de Derecho Aragonés (Zaragoza): Jaime 1 18, Zaragoza.

### REGIONAL STUDIES:

## Galicia
Instituto de Estudios Gallegos "Padre Sarmiento": Franco 1, Santiago de Compostela.
Museo de Pontevedra: Pasantería 12, Pontevedra.

## Asturias
Instituto de Estudios Asturianos: Plaza de Polier 5, Oviedo.

## León
Institución "Fray Bernardino de Sahagún": Edificio Fierro, Reina s/n, León.
Centro de Estudios e Investigaciones "San Isidoro": Plaza de la Regla 6, León.
Centro de Estudios Salmantinos: Palacio de Garci-Grande, Salamanca.
Institución—Casa Museo de Zorrilla: Fray Luis de Granada s/n, Valladolid.
Institución "Tello Téllez de Meneses": Diputación Provincial, Palencia.

## Old Castile
Institución Cultural "Cantabria": Diputación Provincial, Santander.
Institución "Fernán González": Diputación Provincial, Burgos.
Instituto de Estudios Riojanos: Apartado 72, Logroño.
Centro de Estudios Sorianos: Casa de la Cultura, Paseo Doctor Fléming 5, Soria.
Instituto "Diego de Colmenares": Capuchinos Alta 4 y 5, Segovia.
Institución "Gran Duque de Alba": Esteban Domingo 2, Avila.

## Basque Provinces
Real Sociedad Vascongada de Amigos del País: Museo de San Telmo, San Sebastián.
Grupo "Aranzadi" de la Real Sociedad Vascongada de Amigos del País: Museo de San Telmo, San Sebastían.
Junta Cultural de Vizcaya: Paseo de la Diputación, Bilbao.
Consejo de Cultura de la Diputación Foral de Alava: Fray Francisco de Vitoria 8, Vitoria.

## Navarre
Institución "Príncipe de Viana": Diputación Foral de Navarra, Pamplona.

## Aragón
Instituto de Estudios Oscenses: General Franco 16, Huesca.
Instituto de Estudios Pirenaicos (Jaca): Avda. Regimiento de Galicia s/n, Jaca (Huesca).
Institución "Fernando el Católico": Plaza de España 2, Zaragoza.
Instituto de Estudios Turolenses: Biblioteca, Apartado 77, Teruel.

## Catalonia
Instituto de Estudios Ilerdenses: Plaza de la Catedral s/n, Lerida.
Instituto de Estudios Gerundenses: Plaza del Aceite 7, Gerona.
Instituto de Estudios Tarraconenses "Ramón Berenguer IV": Casa de la Cultura, Tarragona.

## Balearic Isles
Instituto de Estudios Baleáricos: Diputación Provincial, Palma Mallorca.
Sociedad Arqueológica Luliana: Monte Sión 29, Palma, Mallorca.
Instituto de Estudios Ibicencos: Vía Púnica 2, Ibiza.

## Valencia
Institución "Alfonso el Magnánimo": Palacio de la Generalidad, Caballeros 2, Valencia 1.
Centro de Cultura Valenciana: Palacio de la Lonja, Valencia 1.
Sociedad Castellonense de Cultura: Mayor 103, Castellón de la Plana.
Instituto de Estudios Alicantinos: Diputación Provincial, Alicante.

## Murcia
Academia "Alfonso X el Sabio: Avda. Alfonso X el Sabio 7, Murcia.

## Extremadura
Instituto de Estudios Extremeños: Plaza de Minayo 1, Badajoz.

## New Castile
Instituto de Estudios Madrileños: Madrid.
Institución "Marqués de Santillana": Plaza Alférez Provisional, Guadalajara.
Instituto Provincial de Investigaciones y Estudios Toledanos: Diputación Provincial, Toledo.
Instituto de Estudios Visigóticos y Mozárabes: Seminario Mayor Diocesano "San Ildefonso", Toledo.
Instituto de Estudios Manchegos: Diputación Provincial, Ciudad Real.

## Andalusia
Instituto de Estudios Onubenses "Padre Marchena": Sor Paula Alzola 8, Huelva.
Instituto de Estudios Gaditanos: Diputación Provincial, Cádiz.
Instituto de Estudios Históricos Jerezanos: Ayuntamiento, Jerez de la Frontera.
Instituto de Estudios Sevillanos "Rey Alfonso X el Sabio": Diputación Provincial, Sevilla.
Academia de Bellas Artes "Santa Isabel de Hungría": Plaza del Museo 9, Sevilla.
Instituto de Estudios Malagueños: Casa del Consulado, Plaza José Antonio, Malaga.
Instituto de Estudios Granadinos: Plaza de Bibataubín s/n, Granada.
Real Academia de Ciencias, Bellas Letras y Nobles Artes: Pedro López 7, Córdoba.
Instituto de Estudios Giennenses: Plaza de San Francisco s/n, Jaen.
Museo Arqueológico de Linares: Calle Pontón, Linares.

## Ceuta
Instituto de Estudios Ceutíes: Ayuntamiento, Ceuta.

## Canary Isles
Instituto de Estudios Canarios: Universidad de La Laguna.
Museo Canario: Dr. Chill 25, Las Palmas de Gran Canaria.

## Data Processing
Centro de Cálculo Electrónico: Serrano 142, Madrid 6.

## SPAIN

*Documentation and Information*
  *Instituto de Información y Documentación en Ciencia y Tecnología:* Joaquín Costa 22, Madrid 6.
  *Instituto de Información y Documentación en Biomedicina:* Paseo al Mar 17, Valencia 10.
  *Instituto de Información en Humanidades y Ciencias Sociales:* Serrano 117, Madrid 6.

*Standardization*
  *Instituto de Racionalización y Normalización:* Serrano 150, Madrid 6.

*Instrumentation*
  *Instituto de Instrumentación Didáctica:* Serrano 144, Madrid 6.

---

**Centro Meteorológico de Baleares** (*Meteorological Station*): Muelle de Poniente-Porto Pi, Apdo. Oficial, Palma de Mallorca, Balearic Is.; f. 1934; library of 600 vols.; Dir. Cosme Gayá Obrador; publ. *Boletín* (monthly).

**Departamento de Perfeccionamiento y Prospección Educativa** (*Teacher Training and Educational Research Departments*): Ciudad Universitaria, Madrid 3; f. 1974; trains staff for the *Institutos de Ciencias de la Educación*; co-ordinates research of the ICEs and carries out its own; 120 staff; Dirs. Serafín Vegas González, Isidoro Alonso Hinojal.

**Departamento Nacional de Protección Vegetal** (*Plant Protection Department*): Puerta de Hierro 1, Carretera de la Coruña km. 7, Apdo. 8.111, Madrid; f. 1888; entomology, plant pathology and virology, weed control, phytotherapeutics; attached to the Instituto Nacional de Investigaciones Agrarias; 35 mems.; Dir. Manuel Arroyo Varela; publ. *Anales de Producción Vegetal*.

**Instituto Cajal** (*Santiago Ramón y Cajal Institute of Neurobiological Research*): Velázquez 144, Madrid 6; f. 1906; 20 mems.; library of 20,000 vols.; Dir. Alfredo Carrato Ibáñez; Sec. Ma. Luisa Bentura Remacha; a Department of the C.S.I.C.; publ. *Trabajos†*.

**Instituto de Estudios Fiscales** (*Institute of Fiscal Studies*): Calle Casado del Alisal 6, Madrid 14; f. 1960; public finance; library of 25,000 vols.; Dir. César Albiñana García-Quintana; Sec.-Gen. Manuel G. Margallo Riaza; publs. *Hacienda Pública Española†* (every 2 months), *Crónica Tributaria†*, *Presupuesto, Gasto Público* (quarterly).

**Instituto Forestal de Investigaciones y Experiencias** (*Institute of Forestry Research*): Puerta de Hierro, Carretera de la Coruña, Km. 7, Apdo. 8111, Madrid 20; f. 1922; library of 20,000 vols.; Dir. Manuel María de Arana Santoyo; Sec.-Gen. Antonio Poveda Fuentes; publs. *Boletín* and *Comunicación*.

**Instituto Geológico y Minero de España** (*Geological and Mining Institute*): Ministry of Industry, Ríos Rosas 23, Madrid 3; f. 1849; library of 42,500 vols.; documentation centre of 20,000 items in microfilm; staff of 400; sections: geology, mining, research, geophysics, subterranean hydrology, data banking, geomathematics, laboratories, museums; Dir. Ricardo M. Echevarría Caballero; Sec. Julio Luquero; publs. *Boletín Geológico Minero†* (every 2 months), *Notas y Communicaciones, Memorias del IGME†*, geological maps.

**Instituto Germano-Español de Investigación** (*German-Spanish Research Institute for History*): Calle Serrano 123, Madrid 6; studies on German-Spanish relations in the 19th century; publ. *Berichte der diplomatischen Vertreter des Wiener Hofes aus Spanien in der Regierungszeit Karls III*.

**Instituto Nacional de Geofísica** (*National Institute of Geophysics*): Serrano 123, Madrid; f. 1941; 17 mems.; Dir. Luis Lozano Calvo; Sec. Manuel Rodríguez Ron; publ. *Revista de Geofísica* (quarterly).

**Instituto Nacional de Investigaciones Agrarias** (*National Institute of Agronomical Research*): Ministerio de Agricultura, José Abascal 56, Madrid 3; f. 1940; library of 11,263 vols.; 1,079 staff; over 200 depts. in more than 10 regional centres; Pres. Ing. de Montes, Mariano Jaquotot Uzuriaga; Sec. Ing. de Montes Antonio Cuesta Areales; publ. *Anales†* (annual).

**Instituto y Observatorio de Marina** (*Naval Institute and Observatory*): San Fernando, Cádiz; f. 1753; positional astronomy, geophysics and satellite geodesy; 26 mems.; library of 22,500 vols., 1,800 maps and plans; Dir. Alberto Orte; collaborates with the British and the American Nautical Almanac Offices, Le Bureau des Longitudes and Das Astronomische Rechen Institut; publs. *Almanaque Náutico* (annual), *Efemérides Astronómicas* (annual,) *Anales, Observaciones Meteorológicas, Magnéticas y Sísmicas, Boletín Rotación de la Tierra, Boletín de Ocultaciones de Estrellas por la Luna*.

**Observatorio Astronómico Nacional** (*National Astronomical Observatory*): Calle de Alfonso XII 3, Madrid; f. 1790; attached to the Instituto Geográfico y Catastral; library of approx. 10,000 vols.; Dir. José Pensado Iglesias; publs. *Anuario†, Boletín Astronómico†*.

**Observatorio de Cartuja** (*Observatory of Cartuja*): Apdo. 32, Granada; f. 1902; 10 mems.; library of 5,000 vols.; Dir. F. J. López Aparicio; publs. *Trabajos Científicos*, Series A, B and C (A, Astronomy; B, Geophysics; C, Meteorologics), *Contribuciones Astronómicas del Observatorio de Cartuja*. High altitude stations in the Sierra Nevada.

**Observatorio del Ebro** (*Ebro Observatory*): Roquetas, Tarragona; f. 1904; library of 16,000 vols., rare works dating from 1499; Dir. Rev. J-O. Cardús, s.j.; Vice-Dir. Rev. E. Galdón, s.j.; Hon.-Dir. Rev. A. Romañá, s.j.; publs.† *Boletín* in five series: (a) Heliophysics; (b) Meteorology; (c) Seismology; (d) Terrestrial Magnetism, Atmospheric Electricity; (e) Ionosphere; publs. *Memorias, Miscelanea*, etc.

**Real Jardín Botánico** (*Royal Botanical Garden*): Claudio Moyano 1, Madrid 7; f. 1755; botanical research; 46 staff; herbarium with 500,000 specimens; library of 10,500 vols., 1,000 periodicals, 11,500 offprints; Dir. Dr. F. de Diego Calonge; Sec. A. Ceballos; publ. *Anales†* (annually).

**Seminario de Astronomía y Geodesia de la Universidad Complutense de Madrid** (*Research Centre of Astronomy and Geodesy of the Complutense University of Madrid*): Ciudad Universitaria; f. 1948; Dir. Prof. J. M. Torroja; publs. *Publicaciones* (irregular).

# LIBRARIES AND ARCHIVES

In Spain Archives and Libraries are run mainly by the state. With rare exceptions all such services are co-ordinated under the General Directorate of Archives and Libraries, which is a section of the Ministry of Education.

## Madrid

**Archivo General de la Administración Civil del Estado:** Ronda Fiscal 1, Alcalá de Henares, Madrid; f. 1969; preserves and makes available for information or scientific research documents on public administration which are no longer of current administrative relevance; 21 mems.; library of 1,500 vols.; Dir. Dra. MARÍA DEL CARMEN PESCADOR DEL HOYO (acting); Sec.-Gen. MA. LUISA CONDE VILLAVERDE.

**Archivo Histórico Nacional** (*National Historical Archives*): Calle Serrano 115; f. 1866; Dir. L. SÁNCHEZ BELDA; Sec. CARMEN GUZMÁN PLÁ; publs. catalogues, indexes, historical documents, private library, 12,920 vols.

**Biblioteca Central de Marina** (*Central Naval Library*): Cuartel General de la Armada, Montalbán 2, Madrid 14; f. 1856; 50,500 vols.; Technical Dir. JUAN B. OLAECHEA.

**Biblioteca Central Militar** (*Army Library*): Calle Mártires de Alcalá 9; f. 1932; 250,000 vols. on military history; rare books, engravings, photographs, maps and plans; Dir. Col. ANTONIO MANZANEDO CERECEDA; publ. *Revista de Historia Militar*.

**Biblioteca Central del Ministerio del Aire** (*Central Library of the Air Ministry*): Romero Robledo 8; f. 1927; reorganized 1942; 32,745 vols. on aeronautics, engineering, meteorology, chemistry, mathematics and military subjects; Dir. PEDRO BARRIO MARTÍN.

**Biblioteca Central del Ministerio de Hacienda** (*Central Library of the Ministry of Finance*): Calle de Alcalá 11: f. 1852; 21,206 vols. on economics, finance and Government legislation; Librarians JOSÉ A. MONTENEGRO GONZÁLEZ, MARÍA MARTÍNEZ APARICIO, JOSÉ MANUEL MATA CASTILLIÓN.

**Biblioteca Ducal de Lerma:** Velásquez 86; 14,500 vols., 600 MSS.; Librarian PEDRO LONGAS.

**Biblioteca del Ministerio de Asuntos Exteriores** (*Library of the Ministry of Foreign Affairs*): Plaza de la Provincia 1; f. 1900; 43,256 vols.; works on history, geography; literature, international law, political and civil law; Dir. MIGUEL SANTIAGO Y RODRÍGUEZ.

**Biblioteca Washington Irving (Centro Cultural de los Estados Unidos):** San Bernardo 107.

**Ministerio de Educación y Ciencia, Gabinete de Documentación, Biblioteca y Archivo** (*Ministry of Education and Science, Library and Archives*): Alcalá 34; f. 1900; 50,000 vols.; Dir. Prof. MARÍA BEGOÑA IBÁÑEZ ORTEGA; publs. *Bibliografías Educativas*, *Boletín Bibliográfico* (monthly), *Boletín de sumarios de revistas* (quarterly).

**Biblioteca del Ministerio de Información y Turismo** (*Library of the Ministry of Information and Tourism*): Avda. del Generalísimo 39, 2°; f. 1942; 28,384 vols., and a newsprint collection of 111,624 vols. and pamphlets, 7,655 magazines; Dir. MARCELINA IÑIGUEZ GALÍNDEZ.

**Biblioteca Nacional** (*National Library*): Paseo de Recoletos 20, Madrid 1; f. 1712 as Royal Library; over 3,000,000 vols., 26,122 vols. of MSS., 3,000 incunabula, 45,000 rare books, prints, music, maps, reviews; Sala de Cervantes; Research Room; deposit library; photographic and recording laboratories; loan service for specialists and students; Dir. HIPÓLITO ESCOLAR SOBRINO; Sec. ROBERTO LITER CURIESES; publs. catalogues, bibliographies.

**Biblioteca de la Escuela Técnica Superior de Ingenieros de Caminos, Canales y Puertos** (*Library of Special School for Road, Canal and Port Engineers*): Ciudad Universitaria, Madrid 3; f. 1799; 70,000 vols.; Dir. ENRIQUE BALAGUER CAMPHUIS; Librarian ALFREDO MENDIZÁBAL ARACAMA.

**Biblioteca de la Escuela Técnica Superior de Ingenieros Industriales** (*Library of the Special School for Industrial Engineers*): Paseo de la Castellana 86; f. 1905; 17,014 vols.; Dir. EMILIO BAUTISTA PAZ; Librarian ELISA PARRA GONZÁLEZ; publ. *Arista* (monthly).

**Biblioteca del Palacio Real** (*Library of the Royal Palace*): Palacio Real; f. 1716; 300,000 vols.; fine collections of MSS, incunabula, music, rare editions dating from the 16th century, engravings and drawings; collections of bookbindings and medals; research library exclusively open to the general public as museum; Hon. Dir. MATILDE LÓPEZ SERRANO; Dir. JUSTA MORENO GARBAYO; publs. historical works, catalogues.

**Biblioteca de la Universidad Complutense de Madrid** (*Complutense University of Madrid Library*): Ciudad Universitaria, Madrid 3; f. 1341; second in importance in Madrid; one of the most complete in Spain; 821,503 vols., 270,000 pamphlets; Dir. FERNANDO HUARTE.

**Biblioteca Hispánica (del Centro Iberoamericano de Cooperación):** approx. 500,000 vols. and 7,000 periodicals; includes library of Spanish and Latin American incunabula, press and periodicals; Dir. JOSÉ IBÁÑEZ CERDÁ; publs. *Sumario Actual de Revistas*†, *Selección de Obras Incorporadas*†.

**British Council Library:** Calle Almagro 5, Madrid 4; f. 1941; 31,209 vols., 122 periodicals; Librarian A. G. A. PICKFORD, M.I.INF.SC.

**Hemeroteca Municipal de Madrid** (*Madrid Library of Spanish and Foreign Periodicals*): Plaza de la Villa 3; f. 1918; over 20,000 titles; the library maintains a microfilm service; Dir. MIGUEL MOLINA CAMPUZANO.

**Servicio de Publicaciones del Ministerio de Trabajo** (*Publication Service of the Ministry of Labour*): Plaza Nuevos Ministerios; library with 80,000 vols. excluding pamphlets and newspapers; publs. *Revista de Trabajo* (quarterly), *Boletín Oficial del Ministerio de Trabajo* (monthly), *Jurisprudencia Social* (twice monthly), etc.

## Barcelona

**Archivo Capitular de la Santa Iglesia Catedral de Barcelona:** Catedral de Barcelona; f. 9th century; documents from 9th to 20th centuries; treatises on Holy Scripture, ecclesiastical history and law; religious and economic history; 200 MSS., c. 200 incunabula and various printed books from the original Biblioteca Capitular; 40,000 documents, 20,000 vols.; Archives Prefect ANGEL FÁBREGA; Archivist JOSEP BAUCELLS.

**Archivo de la Corona de Aragón** (*Royal Archives of Aragon*): Condes de Barcelona 2; f. 9th century; auxiliary library of 11,400 vols.; Dir. FEDERICO UDINA MARTORELL; Sec. RAFAEL CONDE Y DELGADO DE MOLINA; publs. publication on unedited MSS, *Colección de Documentos Inéditos del Archivo de la Corona de Aragón*†, Guides, Catalogues and Indexes.

**Archivo Diocesano** (*Diocesan Archives*): Palacio Episcopal; f. 11th century, registers (1,200) from 1302; Diocesan Archivist Pbro. JOSÉ SANABRE SANROMÁ; publ. *El Archivo Diocesano de Barcelona* (1947).

**Biblioteca de l'Associació de Enginyers Industrials de Catalunya** (*Library of the Association of Industrial Engineers of Catalonia*): Vía Layetana 39; f. 1863;

32,047 vols.; Librarian RAMON PUIGVERT CABANAS; publs. *Ingeniería Textil†*, *Fulls Informatius* (monthly), *Novática†* (every 2 months).

**Biblioteca Balmes** (*Balmes Library*): Durán y Bas 9-11; f. 1923; specializes in church studies; 35,000 vols., 345 periodicals; Dir. FRANSISCO DE P. SOLÁ.

**Biblioteca de Catalunya, Diputación Provincial de Barcelona:** Apdo. 1077, Carmen 47, Barcelona 1; f. 1914; 721,809 vols.; special sections: manuscripts, incunabula; collections: Aguiló, Verdaguer, Bonsoms, Cervantes, Elzeviers, Bibliografía Española de Italia, Kempis, Torres Amat, Catalan theatre; music, etchings, stamps and maps; Dir. ROSALÍA GUILLEUMAS; Sec. MERCÉ ROSSELL; publs. *Catálogo de publicaciones*, *Anuari de la Biblioteca de Catalunya i de las Populars*, exhibition catalogues.

**Biblioteca de la Cámara Oficial de Comercio, Industria y Navegación de Barcelona** (*Library of Chamber of Commerce, Industry and Navigation*): Casa Lonja de Mar, Paseo Isabel II, no. 1, and Calle Ample 11 and 13 (Administration); 89,507 vols.; Sec-Gen. JOSÉ M. CALPE IBARZ; Librarian NURIA SAGALÁ; publs. *Boletín de la Cámara* (monthly), *Noticiario de Comercio Exterior*, *Boletín Estadístico Coyuntural*.

**Biblioteca de la Delegación Provincial de Barcelona de la Organización Nacional de Ciegos** (*Braille Library*): Calle Ample 2, Barcelona 2; f. 1939; 6,670 vols.; loan service.

**Biblioteca del Centro Excursionista de Cataluña** (*Library of the Mountaineering Centre*): Paradís 10; f. 1876; 6,000 mems.; *c.* 20,000 vols., mostly on mountaineering; Librarian-Dir. MODEST MONTLLEÓ; publs. *Muntanya* (every 2 months), *Espeleòleg, Speleon*.

**Biblioteca del Colegio de Abogados de Barcelona** (*Barcelona College of Lawyers' Library*): Mallorca 283; f. 1832; 4,100 mems.; 120,000 items; Dean JUAN FORNER MATAMALA; publ. *Revista Jurídica de Cataluña*, *Anuario de Sociología y Psicología Jurídicas*.

**Biblioteca del Colegio Notarial de Barcelona** (*Library of College of Notaries*): Notariado 4; f. 1862 in present form, though in existence before 1395; 4,900 vols., 49,200 protocols from 13th century; Dean CARLOS FERNÁNDEZ-CASTAÑEDA; Sec. ANGEL MARTÍNEZ SARRIÓN.

**Biblioteca del Collegi de Farmacèutics de la Província de Barcelona** (*Library of Barcelona Province College of Pharmaceutists*): Via Laietana 94; f. 1926, reorg. 1942 and 1970; 12,978 vols.; Dir. ENRIC FUSTER; publs. *Circular Farmacèutica*, *Butlletí Informatiu*.

**Biblioteca del Fomento del Trabajo Nacional** (*Library of Dept. of Trade Development*): Vía Layetana 32 and 34; f. 1889; 69,858 vols.; Librarian EVA FRANQUERO RIBAS; publ. *Horizonte Empresarial* (monthly).

**Biblioteca del Instituto Municipal de Historia de la Ciudad:** Casa del Arcediano, Calle de Santa Lucía 1; 125,000 vols., divided into several sections; general works, books published in Barcelona from the 16th century; the Massana Library, containing works on iconography and the history of costume; other libraries donated by private donors, e.g. Eduardo Toda (British and general books); Dir. Prof. Dr. PEDRO VOLTES.

**Biblioteca del Instituto Nacional del Libro Español (I.N.L.E.)** (*Library of the National Book Institute, Barcelona Office*): Mallorca 274-6; f. 1930; 20,288 vols. on bibliography, copyrights, history and technology of books, printing and allied trades, etc.

**Biblioteca del Seminario de Química de la Universidad de Barcelona:** Facultad de Ciencias Químicas, Diagonal 647, Barcelona 28; f. 1937; 33,600 vols., 1,138 chemical and pharmaceutical periodicals; chemical information and reference library; Dir. Dr. JOSÉ CASTELLS; Chief Librarian ANA MARIA PLANET.

**Biblioteca Universitaria y Provincial:** Gran Via de les Corts Catalanes, Barcelona 7; f. 1847; 400,000 vols., of which more than 5,000 are of the 16th century, 914 incunabula, 2,000 MSS. dating from the 10th century; Dir MA. ANTONIA DE MENA FERNÁNDEZ-ZENDRERA; publs. *Inventario General de Manuscritos, Inventario de Incunables, Boletín de Noticias, Memorias* (irregular).

**British Council Library:** Calle Amigo 83, Barcelona 6; f. 1944; 18,100 vols., 87 periodicals; Librarian ROSA RICART RIBERA.

El Escorial

**Real Biblioteca de San Lorenzo de El Escorial** (*The Escorial Library*): El Escorial; f. 1575; 50,000 vols., 650 incunabula; MSS.: 2,000 Arabic, 2,090 Latin and vernacular, 72 Hebrew, 580 Greek; many rare and unique editions, including complete copy of the *Biblia Poliglota Complutensis* and of the *Biblia Poliglota* of Antwerp on parchment, and *Epítome de Anatomía*, by Vesalius, also on parchment; 10,000 engravings and prints; Dir. P. GREGORIO DE ANDRÉS.

Granada

**Archivo de la Real Chancillería de Granada** (*Archives of the Royal Chancery of Granada*): Plaza del Padre Suárez, 1; f. 1505 by Ferdinand and Isabella; consists of 16,753 boxes of documents, 6,349 MSS., some of which are lawsuits settled by the *Tribunal de la Real Chancillería* from 1490 to 1854; covers the territory south of the Tagus; catalogues covering genealogy, history, institutions, geography; specialized library of 2,180 printed books; also keeps historical records from the Treasury including tax assessments and surveys (16th century) and the land register of the Marqués de la Ensenada (18th century) of the old kingdom of Granada (Almería, Jaén, Málaga and Granada); Dir. MA. PILAR NÚÑEZ ALONSO.

Jerez de la Frontera, Cádiz

**Biblioteca, Archivo y Colección Arqueológica Municipal** (*Town Library and Archaeological Museum*): Plaza de la Asunción 1; library f. 1873, museum 1933; 27,000 vols.; historical series neolithic to Renaissance; important coin collection, Hispanic, Roman, Arab, ancient Spanish; increased by collections of objects recovered from excavations in Asta Regia relating to the Mediterranean Bronze Age I; archives include documents dating from the reconquest of Jerez by Alfonso El Sabio; Dir. MANUEL ESTEVE GUERRERO.

La Coruña

**Archivo Regional de Galicia** (*Regional Archives of Galicia*): f. 1775; comprise a total of 54,770 bundles of documents dating back to 1480, concerning 910,000 disputes and lawsuits relative to the clergy, the nobility and private persons; 19th- and 20th-century documents from the provincial State offices; 9,137 vols. of MSS. covering years 876–1970; library of 7,200 vols. closely related to the archives and of special interest for research; Dir. Dr. ANTONIO GIL MERINO.

Lérida

**Archivo Histórico Provincial:** Casa de Cultura, Plaza San Antonio Ma. Claret s/n; f. 1952; 1,555 vols.; Dir. CRISTINA USON FINKENZELLER.

Perelada (Gerona)

**Biblioteca del Palacio de Perelada** (*The Palace of Perelada Library*): f. 1882 by the Count of Perelada; contains 61,300 vols., 200 incunabula, 20,000 pamphlets and 6 parchments on History and Art; Librarian Don MARTÍN COSTA.

Sabadell

**Archivo Histórico de la Ciudad** (*Historical Archives*): f. 1793; documents date from 1200; MS. of *El Libro de Privilegios y Formularios Notariales*, one dating from the

14th century; collection of local journals and reviews dating from 1853; Dir. ERNEST MATEU VIDAL.

### Santander
**Biblioteca de Menéndez Pelayo** (*Menéndez Pelayo Library*): Rubio 6; comprises: (1) the private library of this writer, 45,000 vols., not to be increased in number, left by him to the town; opened to the public 1915; (2) **Biblioteca Municipal—Biblioteca Pública del Estado** (*Public Library*) housed in an adjacent building; opened to the public 1908; 120,000 vols.; both sections of Menéndez Pelayo Library inaugurated 1923 by Alfonso XIII; Dir. MANUEL REVUELTA SAÑUDO; Sec. VICTORIANO PUNZANO MARTÍNEZ; publ. *Boletín*† (quarterly).

### Seville
**Archivo de la Casa de Medinaceli y Camarasa** (*Medinaceli and Camarasa Archives*): Plaza de Pilatos 1; archives of 9th to 20th centuries; 8,000 files; Archivist JOAQUÍN GONZALES MORENO; publ. *Histórica*.

**Archivo General de Indias** (*Archives of the Indies*): Queipo de Llano 3; f. 1785; over 20,293 vols., 38,903 files; Dir. ROSARIO PARRA CALA; publs. include *Catálogo de Pasajeros a Indias durante los siglos XVI, XVII* and *XVIII, Catálogo de Documentos de la Sección Novena, Archivo General de Indias de Sevilla, Guía del Visitante Madrid 1958*.

**Biblioteca Capitular Colombina:** The Cathedral; f. 1450; 90,500 vols.; Dir. Dr. FRANCISCO ALVAREZ SEISDEDOS.

### Simancas, Valladolid
**Archivo General de Simancas** (*Simancas General Archives*): f. 1540; 68,242 filed documents and 4,979 vols. of documents; library of 9,383vols. on history; Dir. AMANDO REPRESA; publs.*Guía del Investigador, Guía del Visitante* and 28 catalogues (40 vols.).

### Toledo
**Archivo y Biblioteca Capitulares** (*Archives and Library of the Cathedral Chapter*): Catedral de Toledo; the *Archivo Capitular* contains 11,000 documents (mostly medieval) dating from 1086; the library (f. 1398) contains 2,521 MSS,. 1,200 printed books; Dir. RAMÓN GONZÁLVEZ RUIZ (*Canónigo Archivero Bibliotecario*).

### Valencia
**Archivo del Reino de Valencia:** Alameda 22; f. 1419; 67,719 MSS. book (13th to 20th centuries), 28,591 files of MSS., 55,712 charters, deeds, etc., from the 13th century onwards; Dir. DESAMPARADOS PÉREZ PÉREZ.

**British Council Library:** Pascual y Genis 12, Valencia 2; 7,497 vols., 19 periodicals; Librarian M. C. SIRERA.

### Zaragoza (Saragossa)
**Biblioteca Moncayo:** Mayor 62, Jarque; f. 1972; 15,000 vols. by Aragonese authors or on the subject of Aragon; Dir. LUIS MARQUINA MARÍN.

### Palma de Mallorca, Balearic Is.
**Archivo del Reino de Mallorca** (*Historical Archives of Mallorca*): Calle Ramón Llull 3; f. 13th century; archives of c. 33,750 vols., 10,400 documents and c. 22,500 files; library of 5,381 vols.; Dir. ANTONIO MUT CALAFELL.

# MUSEUMS

### Madrid
**Patrimonio Nacional:** Calle de Bailén s/n.; f. 1940 to administer former Crown property; it is responsible for all the Museums situated in Royal Palaces and properties and is governed by an Administrative Council presided over by LUIS CARRERO BLANCO; publs. Guides to all the Museums, *Reales Sitios* (quarterly). Controls the following:

**Palacio Real de Madrid:** special rooms devoted to 16th to 18th century tapestries, clocks, paintings and porcelain from the Royal Palaces and Pharmacy; there is also an Armoury and a Coach Museum and the Library of more than 300,000 volumes is second in importance in Spain and contains many rare books and incunabula; the archives date from the 12th century.

**Palacio Real de Aránjuez:** Aránjuez; former Royal Palace rich in 18th-century art.

**Monasterio de San Lorenzo de El Escorial:** El Escorial; built by Juan de Herrera; contains many famous works by international artists of the 16th century and 18th century from Royal residences.

**Alcázar de Sevilla:** Seville; Royal residence.

**Museo-Monasterio de las Huelgas:** Burgos; founded by Alfonso VIII in the 9th century.

**Museo-Monasterio de Tordesillas:** Valladolid; 14th century.

**Museo de la Encarnación:** Madrid; monastic life in the 16th and 17th centuries.

**Museo de las Descalzas Reales:** Madrid; showing monastic life in the 16th and 17th centuries.

**Palacio de Riofrío:** Segovia; founded in 18th century; notable furniture and paintings of Spanish romantic movement.

**Palacio de la Granja de San Ildefonso:** Segovia; gardens and fountains in imitation of Versailles, tapestry museum.

**Museo de Pedralbes:** Barcelona; 19th-century Royal residence; replicas of modern Royal residences.

**Castillo de Bellver:** Majorca; Royal Palace; small museum of the 18th century.

**Instituto de Valencia de Don Juan** (*Don Juan Institute of Valencia*): Fortuny 43; f. 1916; historical archives, historical and art library of 10,024 vols.; illuminated MS. *Les Statuts de la Toison d'Or* with miniatures; museum of ancient Spanish industrial arts; Pres. D. DIEGO ANGULO IÑÍGUEZ; Dir. BALBINA MARTÍNEZ CAVIRO.

**Museo Arqueológico Nacional** (*National Archaeological Museum*): Serrano 13, Madrid 1; f. 1867; library of 30,200 vols.; medieval MSS. include Huesca Bible of 12th century, Cardeña *Beato* of 12th or 13th century, *Regla de San Benito* and *Calendario* of the Abbey of Las Huelgas de Burgos of 13th century; most notable archaeological library in Spain; very rich collections relating to national prehistory, Iron Age Iberian Art, Egyptian, Cypriot, Greek and Etruscan Antiquities, Roman Spain, medieval and modern times, numismatics, ivory carvings, Spanish pottery, Islamic pottery, brocades, tapestries; Dir. Dr. LUIS CABALLERO ZOREDA; publs. *Trabajos de Prehistoria*†, *Acta Arqueológica Hispana*†, *Monografías, Noticiario Arqueológico Hispánico*†, *Excavaciones Arqueológicas en España*†, etc.

**Museo Cerralbo:** Ventura Rodríguez 17, Madrid 8; f. 1924; the seventeenth Marquis of Cerralbo left his house to the nation as a Museum, together with his collection of paintings, drawings, engravings, porcelain, arms, carpets, coins, furniture; includes paintings by El Greco,

Ribera, Titian, Van Dyck, Tintoretto; 12,000 vols.; Dir. Consuelo Sanz-Pastor Fz. de Piérola; publs. *Guía*†, *Museos y Colecciones de España*, *Catálogo de Dibujos del Museo Cerralbo*.

**Museo Español de Arte Contemporáneo:** Avda. Juan de Herrera, Ciudad Universitaria; f. 1959; Spanish and foreign contemporary art; Dir. Joaquín de la Puente Pérez.

**Museo Nacional de Ciencias Naturales** (*Natural Science Museum*): Paseo de la Castellana 84; f. 1771 as Gabinete de Historia Natural by Carlos III; based on the valuable collections of Pedro Franco Dávila; malacological section noteworthy for rich exhibits from the Americas sent by the Viceroys; Dir. Francisco Hernández-Pacheco.

**Museo del Ejército** (*Army Museum*): Méndez Núñez 1; f. 1804; some 27,000 exhibits; collections of arms, war trophies, flags and tin soldiers; library of 7,000 vols.; Dir. Lieut.-Gen. D. José Angosto Goméz Castrillon; publ. *Guía del Visitante*.

**Museo Nacional de Etnología** (*National Anthropological and Ethnological Museum*): Alfonso XII 68; f. 1875; some 8,000 exhibits and about 1,000 skulls; famous collections form the former Spanish Guinea, the Philippines and South America and a complete collection of Chiu-Chiu mummies from Bolivia; library of 8,000 vols.; Curator Pilar Romero de Tejada; publs. *Catalogues*.

**Museo de Historia Primitiva:** Jorge Juan 51; Dir. Julio Martínez Santa-Olalla; Curator Bernardo Sáez Martín. (See under Seminario de Historia Primitiva.)

**Museo Lázaro Galdiano:** Calle Serrano 122; f. 1951; Italian, Spanish and Flemish Renaissance paintings; Primitives; Golden Age, 18th- and 19th-century Spanish paintings; 17th-century Dutch paintings; English 18th-century collection; collections of ivory, enamels, watches, jewellery, furniture, weapons and armour, oriental and Spanish tapestries and cloth; publ. *"Goya" Revista de Arte*† (every 2 months).

**Museo Municipal de Madrid** (*Madrid Museum*): Calle Fuencarral 78, Madrid 4; f. 1928; portraits, paintings, designs, engravings, plans, silversmiths' work, coins, ceramics, porcelain, paintings by Bayeu and Castillo for the Royal Madrid Looms, theatrical and bullfighting relics, all showing history of Madrid; Dir. Enrique Pastor Mateos.

**Museo Nacional de Artes Decorativas:** Calle Montalbán 12; f. 1912; contains collections of interior decorative arts, especially Spanish of 15th to 19th centuries, including carpets, furniture, leatherwork, jewellery, tapestries, ceramics, glass, porcelain, textiles, etc.; library of 8,000 vols.; Dir. Ma. Dolores Enríquez Arranz.

**Museo Naval** (*Naval Museum*): Montalbán 2, Madrid 14; f. 1843; library of 15,000 vols.; engravings of sea battles; 2,440 vols. of MSS.; some 12,000 original maps of many countries dating from 1600; files containing over 17,800 photographs; Dir. Capt. José María Zumalacárregui.

**Museo del Prado** (*National Museum of Paintings and Sculpture*): Calle de Felipe IV; f. 1819; paintings by Botticelli, Rembrandt, Velázquez, El Greco, Goya, Murillo, Raphael, Bosch, Van der Weyden, Zurbarán, Van Dyck, Tiepolo, Ribalta, Rubens, Titian, Veronese, Tintoretto, Moro, Juanes, Menéndez, Poussin, Ribera, etc.; Classical and Renaissance sculpture; jewels and medals; Dir. Xavier de Salas; publs. Catalogues.

**Museo de Pintura y Salas de Escultura:** Alcalá 13.

**Museo del Pueblo Español** (*Museum of the Spanish People*): Atocha 106; f. 1925; 15,000 exhibits, with special reference to ethnography and historic costume; library of 3,892 vols.; Dir. María Luisa Herrera Escudero; Sub-Dir. María Braña de Diego; publs. Catalogues† and *Conferencia sobre Museos al Aire Libre*†.

**Museo de Reproducciones Artísticas** (*Reproductions of Works of Art*): Ciudad Universitaria; f. 1878; library of 6,464 vols.; 3,219 reproductions of Oriental, Greek, Roman and Hispano-Roman statuary, medieval and Renaissance art, classical and medieval decorative arts; Dir. Ma. José Almagro Gorbea.

**Museo Romántico** (*Museum of the Romantic Period; Vega-Inclán Foundation*): San Mateo 13; paintings, furniture, books and decorations of the Spanish romantic period; Dir. María Elena Gómez-Moreno.

**Museo Sorolla** (*Sorolla Museum*): General Martínez Campos 37; f. 1932; permanent exhibition of some 350 of the artist's works, including drawings, water-colours, portraits, and his own art collections; library of 1,700 vols.; Dir. Francisco Pons-Sorolla y Arnau; Curator Florencio de Santa-Ana y Alvarez Ossorio.

### Barcelona

**Biblioteca y Museo del Instituto del Teatro** (*Library and Museum of the Institute of Theatre*): Calle Nou de la Rambla 3-5; f. 1912; exhibits show the evolution of the theatre, cinema, dance, opera, puppets; scenery, costumes, posters, personal mementoes, etc.; library of 120,000 vols.; Dir. Hermann Bonnin; Curator Irene Peypoch; Chief Librarian Anna Vázquez; publs. *Estudios Escénicos*†, *Monografies de Teatre*, *Teatre Clàssic Universal*.

**Museo de Arte de Cataluña** (*Museum of Ancient Art*): Palacio Nacional, Parc de Montjuïc; f. 1934; collections of Catalan Romanesque and Gothic paintings and sculpture; Renaissance and Baroque paintings; Dir. Juan Ainaud de Lasarte; Curator M. Carmen Farré Sanpera.

**Museo de Cerámica** (*Museum of Ceramics*): Palacio Nacional de Montjuïc; f. 1966; foreign and national collections.

**Museo de Arte Moderno:** Palacio de la Ciudadela; f. 1946; Dir. Juan Barbeta Antones; publs. *Anales y Boletín de los Museos de Barcelona*, catalogues; library of 50,657 vols. on art and history.

**Museo Arqueológico de Barcelona** (*Archaeological Museum*): Parque de Montjuich; f. 1932; collections of prehistoric, Greek, Phoenician, Visigothic and Roman art; library of 40,000 vols.; Dir. E. Ripoll Perello; publs. *Ampurias*†, *Informació Arqueològica* (annually), monographs.

**Museo de Geología** (*Museo Martorell*): Parque de la Ciudadela; f. 1882; Dir. (*Petrography*) Prof. Dr. Alfredo San Miguel Arribas; Curator A. Masriera González.

**Museo de Historia de la Ciudad:** Casa Padellás (14th-century mansion), Royal Chapel and Throne Room ('Tinell') (14th century); f. 1943; Roman and Visigothic sections with remains *in situ*; sculpture, funeral remains, medieval and modern sections, Jewish and Arabic rooms, etc.; Dir. Josep M. Garrut.

**Museo de Zoología:** Parque de la Ciudadela, Barcelona 3, Apdo. 593; f. 1882; Dir. (*Ornithology*) Rosario Nos; Curators O. Escolá Boada, Dr. Joaquim Gosàlbez; publs. *Treballs*†, *Miscelània Zoològica*† (annually).

**Museo Etnológico:** Parc de Montjuïc; f. 1948; African, Asiatic, American, Oceanic and Spanish ethnography; Dir. Augusto Panyella Gómez.

**Museo Marítimo de Barcelona** (*Maritime Museum*): Reales Atarazanas; f. 1941; Dir. José M. Martínez-Hidalgo y Terán.

**Museo de Música:** Bruch 110; f. 1946; valuable collections of antique instruments; Founder Dr. Tomás Carrera Artau; Dir. J. Ricart Matas.

**Museo Picasso:** Calle Montcada 15–17, Barcelona 3; f. 1963; paintings, sculpture, drawings and engravings by Pablo Picasso, 1890–1972, including the series "Las Meninas" and the artist's donation, in 1970, of 940 works of art; Dir. Rosa María Subirana.

**Salmer, Archivo Fotográfico Internacional** (*International Photographic Archives*): Rambla de Cataluña 54–3° 1a, Barcelona 7; f. 1962; collection of art works from every museum in Spain; transparencies on geography, monuments, ethnology, folklore, etc.; art works, etc. from other countries; exclusively in colour; Man. Dirs. Santiago Ortega Alonso, Roberto Castell Esteban, Miguel Castell Esteban.

### Bilbao

**Museo de Bellas Artes:** Parque de Doña Casilda Iturriza; f. 1913; 1,923 exhibits of paintings, sculpture, furniture; famous works by El Greco, Goya, Velázquez, Jordaens, Teniers, Ribera, Gauguin and many others including an important collection of early Spanish paintings and a new building containing contemporary art; Dir. Javier de Bengoechea.

### Burgos

**Museo Arqueológico de Burgos:** Casa de Miranda, Calle de la Calera, No. 25; f. 1871; collections of ivories, enamels, pictures and sculpture; notably an enamel of Christ and the Apostles (7 ft. × 2 ft.), an Arabic ivory case (10th century) from the workshop of Medina Azahara, the statue of Don Juan de Padilla praying, and a 16th-century painting, "Ecce Homo"; Dir. Basilio Osaba y Ruiz de Erenchun; publ. *Anales*.

### Cartagena

**Museo Arqueológico Municipal:** Calle de Canales; f. 1943; important collections of Roman remains found in the area, including mining, submarine, industrial arts exhibits; Dir. Dr. Arq. Pedro A. San Martín Moro; publs. *Publicaciones de la Junta Municipal, Boletín Arqueológico del Sudeste Español, Crónicas de los Congresos Arqueológicos, Artes Industriales Cartageneras*.

### Chipiona, Cadiz

**Museo Misional de Nuestra Señora de Regla:** Colegio de Misioneros Franciscanos; f. 1939; about 600 exhibits of early Roman Christian relics, ancient Egyptian and other North African objects, antique coins, etc.; Dir. R. P. Rector del Colegio.

### Córdoba

**Museo Arqueológico Provincial de Córdoba:** Palacio de Jerónimo Páez; f. 1898; 28,590 archaeological and historical exhibits; library of 4,861 vols.; Dir. Ana María Vicent Zaragoza; publ. "*Córdoba*" (annually).

### Figueras

**Museo Dalí:** f. 1974; Pres. of Board of Trustees Salvador and Gala Dalí; Dir. Salvador Dalí.

### Ibiza

**Museo Arqueológico de Ibiza:** Plaza de la Catedral 3; f. 1907; 5,000 exhibits, almost exclusively Carthaginian; museum has other sections in other buildings; library of 2,675 vols. situated in the Museo del Puig des Molins; Dir. Jorge H. Fernández Gómez; publ. *Trabajos*.

**Museo y Necrópolis del Puig des Molins:** Via Romana; f. 1967; Carthagian and Roman remains from the national monument of Puig des Molins; excavations in Ibiza and Formentera; library of 2,132 vols.; Dir. Jorge H. Fernández Gómez.

### La Escala, Gerona

**Museo Monográfico de Ampurias** (*Ampurias Monographic Museum*): f. 1946; collection of excavations of the Greco-Roman city; Dir. Prof. E. Ripoll-Perelló; Curator M. Llongueras.

### Lérida

**Museo Arqueológico del Instituto de Estudios Ilerdenses:** Antiguo Hospital de Santa María, Avda. Blondel 62; f. 1953; archaeology from prehistoric times; Dirs. Juan-Ramón González Pérez, José-Ignacio Rodríguez Duque, Luis Díez-Coronel Montull; publ. *Separatas de "Ilerda"*†.

**Gabinete Numismático de Lérida:** Diputación Provincial de Lérida; Roman, Iberian, Ibero-Roman, Medieval and Modern exhibits; local collections.

**Museo de la Paherra de la Ciudad de Lérida:** Historical documents and objects belonging to the municipality; archaeological finds of Lérida.

**Museo Diocesano:** Jaime Conquistador 67; medieval sculptures; also sub-section at Rambla de Aragón containing religious paintings, metal work and vestments; Dir. Jesús Tarragona Muray.

**Museo de Arte Moderno "Jaime Morera":** Edificio Roser, Calle Caballeros 15; f. 1917; museum of modern paintings mainly by Catalan artists, including works by Morera, C. Haes and others; Curator Víctor Pérez Pallarés.

### Mérida, Badajoz

**Museo Arqueológico de Mérida** (*Archaeological Museum*): Plaza de Santa Clara 5; f. before 1838, in present form 1929; pre-Roman and Roman, early Christian, Visigothic, Arab; heraldry, etc.; Dir. José Alvarez Sáenz de Buruaga.

### Pontevedra

**Museo de Pontevedra:** Calle de la Pasantería, Apdo. 104; f. 1927, opened 1929; library of 44,000 vols. on literature, art and archaeology of Galicia; pottery and ancient industrial and naval history of Galicia; prehistoric jewellery and jet ornaments; Spanish 15th–20th-century paintings; Dir. José Filgueira Valverde; Sec. Alfredo García Alén; publs. *El Museo de Pontevedra* (annually), *Archivo de Mareantes, Materiales para la Carta Arqueológica de la Provincia de Pontevedra*.

### Sabadell, Barcelona

**Museo de Bellas Artes:** Calle Dr. Puig; Dirs. Alfons Borrell Palazon, Jaume Camps Sans.

**Museo de Historia:** Calle Sant Antoni 13; f. 1931; prehistoric archaeological, numismatic collections, native handicrafts: Iberico-Roman section, and sections on Textiles and Mineralogy; publ. *Arrahona*† (2 a year).

### San Roque, Cádiz

**Museo Histórico de San Roque:** Ayuntamiento, San Roque, Prov. Cádiz; f. 1956; documents of Gibraltar and museum of Carteyan excavations; Dir. D. Rafael Caldela López; Chief of Archaeological Section D. Francisco Prescedo.

### San Sebastián, Guipúzcoa

**Museo Municipal de San Telmo:** housed in an ancient Convent dating from the reign of Charles V; inaug. 1902 by Alfonso XIII; prehistoric, archaeological, anthropological, numismatics; paintings by Vicente López, El Greco, Goya, etc., and moderns; the ancient chapel decorated with 11 famous murals by José María Sert; Museo Vasco, Ethnographical Section, shows the rural life of the Basques; weapons, history of San Sebastián; Dir. Julián Martínez Ruiz; governed by a Junta de Patronato.

**Museo Naval y Aquarium** (*Naval Museum*): Sociedad de Oceanografía de Guipúzcoa, Muelle; f. 1914; models of famous ships, portraits of navigators, local fishing tackle, and aquarium; oceanographic museum and marine laboratory.

### Santander
**Museo de Prehistoria y Arqueología** (*Prehistoric and Archaeological Museum*): Palacio de la Excma. Diputación Provincial; f. 1926; important palaeolithic and bronze collections from the caves of Altamira, Pendo, El Castillo, El Rey, El Juyo, La Chora, La Pasiega, El Piélago; collection relating to the Bronze Age in Spain; Celtic stelae connected with sun worship; Roman collection; Dir. Dr. MIGUEL ANGEL GARCÍA GUINEA; publs. *Cuadernos de Espeleología†, Publicaciones del Patronato de las Cuevas Prehistóricas†*.

### Seville
**Museo Arqueológico Provincial:** Plaza de América (Parque de María Luisa); f. 1880; *c.* 10,000 exhibits; Roman statues, lead coffins; incorporates the municipal collections; treasures of Tarshish; Dir. FERNANDO FERNÁNDEZ GÓMEZ; publs. *Guía, Catálogo de los Retratos Romanos del Museo, Catálogo del Museo Arqueológico de Sevilla, Trajano el Militar*, and various monographs.

### Sitges
**Museo del "Cau Ferrat":** f. 1893; ironwork, glass, painting; incorporated with Museo Maricel in 1967; Dir. FELIO A. VILLARRUBIAS.

### Soria
**Museo Numantino:** Paseo del Espolón 8; f. 1916; prehistoric, ethnological, Roman and medieval archaeological collections, comprising 30,000 objects; library of 5,357 vols.; Dir. JOSÉ LUIS ARGENTE.

### Tarragona
**Museo Arqueológico Provincial** (*Archaeological Museum*); Plaza del Rey; f. 1834; archaeological, historical, local Roman exhibits; Dir. PEDRO-MANUEL BERGES SORIANO; publ. *Boletín Arqueológico*.

**Museo Paleocristiano:** Paseo Independencia 34; f. 1930; objects discovered during excavation of the Roman-Christian necropolis; Dir. PEDRO-MANUEL BERGES SORIANO.

### Toledo
**Casa del Greco: Fundaciones Vega Inclán** (*El Greco's House*): the artist's house, furniture of the period, and a collection of the artist's paintings and those of his followers; 16th-century furniture; Curator MARÍA ELENA GÓMEZ-MORENO.

**Museo del Greco:** El Greco's paintings including portraits of Christ and the Apostles and other 16th- and 17th-century paintings.

**Museo de Santa Cruz de Toledo:** Calle Cervantes 3; f. 1961; Sections of Archaeology and Fine Arts in Hospital de Santa Cruz, f. 1958; section of Moorish art in Taller del Moro; f. 1963; section of Visigothic art in Museo de los Concilios y de la Cultura Visigoda, f. 1969; Museo de Arte Contemporáneo, f. 1973; library of 3,000 vols.; Dir. MATILDE REVUELTA; publs. *Museo de Santa Cruz, Museo Taller del Moro, Museo de los Concilios y de la Cultura Visigoda*.

**Sinagoga del Tránsito:** Jewish synagogue built in the 14th century by Samuel Ha-Levi, treasurer to King Don Pedro I, "The Cruel"; converted into Christian church of Sta. María del Tránsito 1494; national monument; now Sephardic Museum.

### Valencia
**Museo de Bellas Artes** (*Museum of Fine Arts*): Calle de San Pio V 9; housed in an old Palace; f. 1839; more than 1,000 paintings, sculpture and archaeology sections; Dir. FELIPE GARÍN LLOMBART.

**Museo Nacional de Cerámica "González Marti":** Palacio del Marqués de Dos Aguas, Valencia 2; a national museum of ceramics, set in the Palace of the Marquis of Dos Aguas; f. 1947; Dir. FELIPE-VICENTE GARÍN LLOMBART.

### Valladolid
**Casa de Cervantes** (*Cervantes' House*): furniture and possessions of the writer; Dir. N. SANZ Y RUIZ DE LA PEÑA.

**Museo Arqueológico:** Palacio de Fabio Nelli; f. 1879; archaeology and fine art, articles from palaeolithic times to the 18th century; Dir. ELOISA GARCÍA GARCÍA; publs. monographs.

**Museo Nacional de Escultura Policromada:** Cadenas de San Gregorio 1; f. 1933; housed in the old Colegio de San Gregorio, dating from end of 15th century; works by Alonso Berruguete, Juan de Juni, Gregorio Fernández, and others; Dir. Dr. ELOISA GARCÍA DE WATTENBERG.

### Vich, Barcelona
**Museu Arqueològic Artistic Episcopal de Vic** (*Archaeological and Artistic Episcopal Museum*): f. 1891; medieval arts, provincial Romanesque, Gothic precious metalwork, textiles, embroideries, liturgical vestments, forged iron, etc.; Curator M. S. GROS.

### Zamora
**Museo de Zamora:** Palacio del Cordón; f. 1877 and inaugurated 1911 as Museo Provincial de Bellas Artes; housed in 16th-century palace; paintings, sculpture, models, etc.; pictures by Carducci, Madrazo, Padró, Melgosa, Ramón Zaragoza, Acosta, Esquivel, Nani, Van de Parc, Secundo; sculptures by Benlliure, R. Alvarez, Quintin de Torre; photographs and plastic reproductions of historic and artistic monuments of the province; metalwork, ceramics, coins; 18th-century artistic textiles of Sanabria; archaeological exhibits of the 6th–11th centuries; armorial bearings; fossils of the Tertiary Period; Dri. JORGE JUAN FERNÁNDEZ; publ. *Catálogos de Exposiciones†*.

### Zaragoza (Saragossa)
**Museo Provincial de Bellas Artes:** Plaza de los Sitios 6; f. 1880; archaeological; prehistory, Roman, Arab, Gothic, Moorish, Romanesque and Renaissance exhibits; primitive arts and crafts, paintings from 14th to 19th centuries, contemporary Aragonese artists; Dir. Dr. MIGUEL BELTRÁN LLORIS.

### Palma de Mallorca, Balearic Islands
**Museo de Mallorca:** Calle Ramón Llull 3, Palma; f. 1961; Dir. GUILLERMO ROSSELLÓ BORDOY; various sections, including:
Sección Etnológica: Casa Alomar, Calle Mayor 5, Muro.
Seccion Arqueológica: Calle Ramón Llull 3, Palma.
Sección Bellas Artes: Ancient Ayamans Palace, Calle Portella 5, Palma.

### Las Palmas, Canary Islands
**El Museo Canario:** Dr. Chil 25; f. 1879; local archaeology and anthropology, ethnography and natural sciences; library of 40,000 vols.; Pres. JOSÉ M. ALZOLA; publ. *El Museo Canario* (quarterly).

# UNIVERSITIES

## UNIVERSIDAD NACIONAL DE EDUCACIÓN A DISTANCIA
(Open University)
APDO. 50.487,
CIUDAD UNIVERSITARIA,
MADRID 3

Telephone: 4-49-36-00/02/04/08/12.
Telex: 45256 UNED E.
Founded 1972.

State control; Language of instruction: Spanish; Academic year: October to June.

*Rector:* TOMÁS RAMÓN FERNÁNDEZ RODRÍGUEZ.

*Vice-Rectors:* JOSÉ LUIS LORENTE GUARSCH (Research), JOSÉ JAVIER LÓPEZ JACOÍSTE (Academic Affairs), ALBERTO BERCOVITZ RODRÍGUEZ-CANO (Associated Centres), EMILIO LLEDÓ IÑIGO (Permanent Education).

*Chief of Administration:* D. FRANCISCO VELASCO ARMILLAS.

*Secretary-General:* ALFONSO SERRANO GÓMEZ.

Number of teachers: 503.
Number of students: c. 47,800.

### DEANS AND VICE-DEANS:

*Faculty of Law:* MERCEDES VERGEZ SÁNCHEZ.
*Faculty of Philosophy and Letters:* JOSÉ L. FERNÁNDEZ TRESPALACIOS.
*Faculty of Economics and Management Studies:* ENRIQUE FUENTES QUINTANA.
*Faculty of Engineering:* FERMÍN DE LA SIERRA ANDRÉS.
*Faculty of Sciences:* JESÚS MORCILLO RUBIO.
*Foundation Course Faculty:* RAFAEL GIBERT Y SÁNCHEZ DE LA VEGA.

The University has 52 associated centres.

## UNIVERSIDAD DE ALCALÁ DE HENARES
CARRETERA DE BARCELONA, KM. 33,
ALCALÁ DE HENARES

Telephone: 889.04.00.
Telex: 23896.
Founded 1977.

*Rector:* MANUEL MARTEL SAN GIL.

*Vice-Rectors:* SANTIAGO GARCÍA ECHEVARRÍA (Research), ALEJANDRO NIETO GARCÍA (Extension), MANUEL ORTEGA MATA (Academic).

*Administrative Director:* FERNANDO SANTISO DIÉGUEZ.

*Librarian:* JUAN LLOVET VERDUGO.

Number of teachers: 240.
Number of students: 1,689.

### DEANS:
*Faculty of Philosophy and Letters:* BARTOLOMÉ ESCANDELL BONET.
*Faculty of Chemical and Biological Sciences:* ALBERTO PÉREZ DE VARGAS LUQUE.
*Faculty of Pharmacy:* MANUEL ORTEGA MATA.
*Faculty of Law:* ENRIQUE GIMBERNAT ORDEIG.
*Faculty of Economic and Business Sciences:* SANTIAGO GARCÍA ECHEVARRÍA.
*Faculty of Medicine:* OCTAVIO SALMERÓN VIGIL.

### PROFESSORS:
*Faculty of Philosophy and Letters:*
ALMAGRO GORBEA, MARTÍN, Prehistory
DE LA CIERVA Y HOCES, RICARDO, Contemporary World and Spanish History
ENJUTO BERNAL, JORGE, History of Philosophy
ESCANDELL BONET, BARTOLOMÉ, Modern World and Spanish History
HORIA IUCAL, VINTILA, History of Literature
SAYAS ABENGOECHEA, JUAN JOSÉ, Ancient World and Spanish History

*Faculty of Chemical and Biological Sciences:*
BERNALTE MIRALLES, ANTONIO, General Physics
DE MENDOZA SANZ, FRANCISCO, Organic Chemistry
ESTEVE CHUECA, FERNANDO, Botany
FERNÁNDEZ RUIZ, BENJAMÍN, Cytology and Histology
MARTEL SAN GIL, MANUEL, General Geology (Petrography)
MAÑAS DÍAZ, JUSTO, Electricity and Magnetism
PÉREZ DE VARGAS LUQUE, ALBERTO, Applied Mathematics
ROIG MUNTANER, ANTONIO, General Physics
ROMERO GONZÁLEZ, ANGEL, Industrial Chemistry
SABATER GARCÍA, BARTOLOMÉ, Plant Physiology

*Faculty of Pharmacy:*
LUQUE CABRERA, JOSÉ, Biochemistry
NAVARRO RUIZ, ANGEL, Animal Physiology
ORTEGA MATA, MANUEL, Instrument Technology
SELLES FLORES, EUGENIO, Galenic Pharmacy

*Faculty of Law:*
ARCHE DOMINGO, FERNANDO VICENTE, Financial and Taxation Law
DE AZCARRAGA Y BUSTAMENTE, JOSÉ LUIS, International Public Law
DE LA OLIVA SANTOS, ANDRÉS, Procedural Law
ESCUDERO LÓPEZ, JOSÉ ANTONIO, History of Spanish Law
FERRANDO BADIA, JUAN, Political Law
GIMBERNAT ORDEIG, ENRIQUE, Penal Law
GÓMEZ CARBAJO DE VIEDMA, FERNANDO J., Roman Law
GULLÓN BALLESTEROS, ANTONIO, Civil Law
LÓPEZ MARICHAL, JUAN, History of Spanish Constitution
NIETO GARCÍA, ALEJANDRO, Administrative Law
RODRÍGUEZ PANIAGUA, JOSÉ MARÍA, Natural Law and Philosophy of Law
SAGARDOY BENGOECHEA, JUAN ANTONIO, Labour Law
SANTOS DIEZ, JOSÉ LUIS, Canon Law

*Faculty of Economic and Business Sciences:*
ALMANSA PASTOR, JOSÉ MANUEL, Labour Law
ARANDA GALLEGO, JOAQUÍN, Economic and Business Statistics
CAMPOS NORDMAN, RAMIRO, Spanish Economic Foreign Relations
CAPELO MARTÍNEZ, MANUEL, Economic Policy
CASAS SÁNCHEZ, JOSÉ MIGUEL, Economic and Business Statistics
DE VEGA GARCÍA, PEDRO, Theory of State and Constitutional Law
GARCÍA ECHEVARRÍA, SANTIAGO, Company Economic Policy
GARCÍA LÓPEZ, JOSÉ ANTONIO, Public Finance and Fiscal Law
PENA TRAPERO, JESÚS BERNARDO, Econometrics and Statistical Methods
TORTELLA CASARES, GABRIEL, World and Spanish Economy
VIÑAS MARTÍN, ANGEL, Economic Policy

*Faculty of Medicine:*
CUENCA FERNÁNDEZ, EDUARDO, Pharmacology
GÓMEZ PELLICO, LUIS, Human Anatomy
GONZÁLEZ SANTANDER, RAFAEL, Histology and General Embryology
SALMERÓN VIGIL, OCTAVIO, General Pathology and Preliminary Clinical Medicine

## UNIVERSIDAD DE ALICANTE
CARRETERA DE SAN VICENTE, ALICANTE

Founded 1979; in process of formation.

*President of the Preparatory Commission:* ANTONIO GIL OLCINA.

## UNIVERSIDAD DE LAS BALEARES
CALLE MIGUEL DE LOS SANTOS OLIVER 2,
PALMA DE MALLORCA

Founded 1978.

*Rector:* ANTONIO RUIG MUNTANER.
*Administrative Director:* LUIS PIÑA.

Faculties of philosophy and letters, science, law.

## UNIVERSIDAD CENTRAL DE BARCELONA
GRAN VÍA DE LAS CORTES CATALANAS 585, BARCELONA 7

Telephone: 301-42-36, 301-42-90, 318-24-96.
Founded 1430.

State control; Languages of instruction: Castilian and Catalan; Academic year: October to June.

*Rector:* Dr. ANTONIO BADÍA MARGARIT.

*Vice-Rectors:* Dr. ORIOL DE BOLÓS CAPDEVILA (Research), Dr. MIGUEL

Siguán Soler (Planning), Doña Victoria Abellán Honrubia (Administration), Dr. Enrique Casassas Simó (Academic Affairs), Dr. Joaquín Monturiol Pous (Extension), Dr. José Luis Sureda Carrión (Public Relations).
*General Secretary:* Dr. Ramón Valls Plana.
*Registrar:* José Ma. Farrando Boix.
*Librarian:* Rosalía Guilleumas Brosa.

Number of teachers: 2,882 (1,242 part-time).
Number of students: 56,634.

### DEANS:

*Faculty of Philosophy and Education:* Dr. Francisco Gomá Musté.
*Faculty of Law:* Dr. Juan Córdoba Roda.
*Faculty of Medicine:* Dr. Jacinto Corbella Corbella.
*Faculty of Economics and Business Studies:* Dr. Juan Hortalá Arau.
*Faculty of Pharmacy:* Dr. Ricardo Granados Jarque.
*Faculty of Philology:* Dr. Gabriel Oliver Coll.
*Faculty of Geography and History:* Dr. Emilio Giralt Raventós.
*Faculty of Biology:* Dr. Luis Vallmitjana Rovira.
*Faculty of Mathematics:* Dr. Federico Gaeta Maurelo.
*Faculty of Chemistry:* Dr. José Costa López.
*Faculty of Physics:* Dr. Ricardo Marqués Fernández.
*Faculty of Geology:* Dr. Salvador Reguant Serra.
*Faculty of Fine Arts:* Dr. Jaime Coll Puig.
*University School of Business Studies:* Dr. Magín Pont Mestres.

### PROFESSORS:

*Faculty of Philosophy and Education:*
Alcorta Echevarría, José I. de, Ethics and Sociology
Canals Vidal, Francisco, Metaphysics
Gomá Musté, Francisco, History of Philosophy
Lledo Iñigo, Emilio, History of Modern Philosophy
Sanvisens Marfull, Alejandro, General Pedagogy
Siguán Soler, Miguel, Psychology
Valverde Pacheco, José María, Aesthetics

*Faculty of Philology:*
Alsina Clota, José, Greek Philology
Badia Margarit, Antonio Ma., History of Grammar in the Spanish Language
Bastardas Parera, Juan, Latin Philology
Bejarano Sánchez, Virgilio, Latin Philology
Blecua Teijeiro, José Manuel, History of Spanish Language and Literature
Comas Pujol, Antonio, Catalan Language and Literature
Díaz Esteban, Fernando, Hebrew Language and Literature
Marsa Gómez, Francisco, Spanish Grammar
McDermott Goodridge, Doirean, English Language
Oliver Coll, Gabriel, History of Romance Literature
Riquer Morera, Martín de, History of Romance Literature and Commentary on Classical, Modern and Romance Texts
Romano Ventura, David, Italian Language and Literature
Vernet Ginés, Juan, Classical and Modern Arabic Language
Vilanova Andreu, Antonio, History of Spanish Language and Literature

*Faculty of Geography and History:*
Alcolea Gil, Santiago, History of Modern and Contemporary Art
Buendía Muñoz, José Rogelio, History of Ancient and Medieval Art
Cacho Viu, Vicente, Contemporary History
Esteva Fabregat, Claudio, Ethnology
Giralt Raventós, Emilio, Modern Spanish History
Lucena Salmoral, Manuel, American History and History of the Spanish Colonization
Maluquer de Motes Nicolau, Juan, Prehistory
Mateu Ibars, Josefina, Palaeography and Diplomacy
Molas Ribalta, Pedro, Modern Spanish History
Palol Salellas, Pedro, Medieval and Christian Archaeology
Palomeque Torres, Antonio, Modern World History
Riu Riu, Manuel, World History of the Middle Ages
Tarradell Mateu, Miguel, Archaeology, Epigraphy and Numismatics
Vila Valentí, Juan, Geography

*Faculty of Biology:*
Bolos Capdevila, José Oriol de. Phytography and Plant Ecology
Caballero López, Arturo, Plant Anatomy and Physiology, Applied Botany
Gadea Buisán, Enrique, Zoology of Non-arthropod Invertebrates
Herrera Castillón, Emilio, General Physiology
Margalef López, Ramón, Ecology
Nadal Puigdefabregas, Jacinto, Zoology of Vertebrates
Pares Farras, Ramón, Plant Microbiology and Bacteriology
Planas Mestres, José, Animal Physiology
Pons Rosell, José, Anthropology
Prevosti Pelegrín, Antonio, Genetics
Vallmitjana Rovira, Luis, Plant and Animal Histology and Cytology

*Faculty of Mathematics:*
Aguilo Fuster, Rafael, Mathematical Analysis
Auge Farreras, Juan, Mathematical Analysis
Cascante Davila, Joaquín María, Mathematical Analysis
Gaeta Maurelo, Federico, Geometry
Mallol Balmaña, Rafael, Algebra
Sales Valles, Francisco de A., Mathematical Statistics and Calculus of Probability
Simo Torres, Carlos, Numerical Analysis
Teixidor Batlle, José, Analytical Geometry and Topology
Vaquer, Timoner, José, Geometry

*Faculty of Physics:*
Cartujo Estebánez, Pedro, Electronics
Codina Vidal, José María, Electricity and Magnetism
Francisco Moneo, José Ramón de, Optics
Garrido Arilla, Luis, Physical Mathematics
Marqués Fernández, Ricardo, Industrial Physics
Orus Navarro, Juan José, General Astronomy, Topography and Geodesy
Pascual de Sans, Pedro, Theoretical Mechanics
Puigcerver Zanon, Manuel, Physics of the Air
Vidal Llenas, José Ma., Thermology

*Faculty of Chemistry:*
Bozal Fes, Jorge, Biochemistry
Casassas Simó, Enrique, Analytical Chemistry
Castells Guardiola, José, Organic Chemistry
Coronas Ribera, Juan María, Inorganic Chemistry
Costa López, José, Technical Chemistry
Núñez Alvarez, Carlos, Metallurgy
Virgili Vinade, José, Physical Chemistry and Electrochemistry

*Faculty of Geology:*
Crusafont Pairó, Miguel, Palaeontology
Font Altaba, Manuel, Crystallography and Mineralogy
Fontbote Mussolas, José María, Applied Geology
Riba Arderiu, Oriol, Stratigraphy
San Miguel Arribas, Alfredo, Petrology

*Faculty of Law:*
Alonso García, Manuel, Labour Law
Carreras Llansana, Jorge, Procedural Law
Córdoba Roda, Juan, Penal Law
Entrena Cuesta, Rafael, Administrative Law
Fernández-Villavicencio, Francisco, Civil Law
Font Rius, José M., Mercantile Law
Luna Serrano, Agustín, Civil Law
Pérez-Vitoria Moreno, Octavio, Penal Law
Puente Egido, José, International Law
Reina Bernández, Víctor, Canon Law
Serra Domínguez, Manuel, Procedural Law
Sureda Carrión, José L., Political Economy and Public Finance
Vicente-Arche Domingo, Fernando, Financial and Tax Law

*Faculty of Medicine:*
Arandes Adán, Ramón, Pathology and Clinical Surgery
Badell Suriol, Mariano, Physical Therapeutics
Balcells Gorina, Alfonso, General Pathology
Carreras Barnes, José, Biochemistry
Corbella Corbella, Jacinto, Legal Medicine
Cruz Hernández, Manuel, Paediatrics and Child Development
Garcia de Valdecasas Santamaría, Francisco, Pharmacology
Gil-Vernet Vila, José M., Urology
González Fuste, Francisco, Health and Hygiene
González Merlo, Jesús, Obstetrics and Gynaecology
Máscaro Ballester, José María, Medical Surgical Dermatology and Venereology
Nalda Felipe, Miguel Angel, Anaesthesiology and Resuscitation

OBIOLS VIÉ, JUAN, Psychiatry
PERA BLANCO-MORALES, CRISTÓBAL, Clinical Surgery and Pathology
PITA SALORIA, DEMETRIO, Ophthalmology
PUMAROLA BUSQUETS, AGUSTÍN, Microbiology and Parasitology
RIBAS MUJAL, DIEGO, Histology and Pathological Anatomy
ROZMAN BORSTNAR, CIRILO, Pathology and Clinical Medicine
RUANO GIL, DOMINGO, Descriptive Anatomy
TRASSERRA PAREDA, JOSÉ, Oto-rhino-laryngology
VIDAL SIVILLA, SANTIAGO, General and Specialized Physiology

*Faculty of Pharmacy:*
CARDÚS AGUILAR, JOSÉ, Edaphology
GALLEGO BERENGUER, JAIME, Parasitology
GARCÍA FERNÁNDEZ, SERAFÍN, Physical Technics and Applied Physics and Chemistry
GRANADOS JARQUE, RICARDO, Organic Chemistry
IRANZO RUBIO, VICENTE, Applied and Analytical Inorganic Chemistry
POZO OJEDA, ALFONSO DEL, Galenic Pharmacy, Professional Techniques and Comparative Legislation
SAN MARTÍN CASAMADA, RAMÓN, Pharmacology
SEOANE CAMBRA, JUAN ANTONIO, Botany
SERRANO GARCÍA, MANUEL, Plant Physiology
SUÑÉ ARBUSSA, JOSÉ M., History of Pharmacy and Pharmaceutic Legislation
TORRALBA RODRÍGUEZ, ANTONIO, Applied Animal Physiology
TORRE BORONAT, MA. DEL CARMEN DE LA, Applied Chemical Analysis and Bromatology

*Faculty of Economic Science and Business Studies:*
ARDERIU GRAS, ENRIQUE, Verification of Accounts
ARTIS ORTUÑO, MANUEL, Econometrics and Statistical Methods
BERINI GIMÉNEZ, JOSÉ, Economic Structures
CONDOMINAS RIBAS, SALVADOR, Political Economy
ESTAPÉ RODRÍGUEZ, FABIÁN, Political Economy
GIL ALUJA, JAIME, Business Economics
GONZÁLEZ CASANOVA, JOSÉ ANTONIO, Theory of Government
HORTALA ARAU, JUAN, Economic Theory
JANÉ SOLÁ, JOSÉ, Political Economy
MIGUEL RODRÍGUEZ, AMANDO DE, Sociology
MUNS ALBUIXENCH, JOAQUÍN, International Economic Organization
PARADA VÁZQUEZ, JOSÉ RAMÓN, Administrative Law
PEDROS ABELLO, ALEJANDRO, Accountancy, Treasury and Public Enterprise Procedures
PIFARRÉ RIERA, MARIO, Theory of Accountancy
POLO SÁNCHEZ, EDUARDO, Mercantile Law
RIBAS MIRANGELS, ENRIQUE, Business Economics
RODRÍGUEZ RODRÍGUEZ, ALFONSO, Financial Mathematics
SIMÓN SEGURA, FRANCISCO, Economic History
TORRE Y DE MIGUEL, JOSÉ-MANUEL DE LA, Economic Theory
TRIAS FARGAS, RAMÓN, Public Taxation and Fiscal Law
VELASCO LARA, RAFAEL, Theory and Mathematics of Insurance
VOLTES BOU, PEDRO, Economic History

AFFILIATED RESEARCH INSTITUTES:
**Instituto de Arqueología y Prehistoria:** Gran Vía de las Cortes Catalanas 585, Barcelona 7; Dir. Dr. JUAN MALUQUER DE MOTES Y NICOLAU.

**Instituto de Ciencias de la Educación:** Gran Vía de las Cortes Catalanas 585, Barcelona 7; Dir. Dr. MIGUEL SIGUÁN SOLER.

**Instituto Tecnológico y Metalúrgico "Emilio Jimeno":** Núcleo Universitario Pedralbes, Facultad de Ciencias, Diagonal s/n., Barcelona 34; Dir. Dr. CARLOS NÚÑEZ ALVAREZ.

**Instituto de Criminología:** Facultad de Derecho, Diagonal s/n., Barcelona 34; Dirs. Dr. OCTAVIO PÉREZ-VITORIA MORENO, Dr. JUAN CÓRDOBA RODA.

## UNIVERSIDAD AUTÓNOMA DE BARCELONA

CAMPUS UNIVERSITARIO, BELLATERRA (BARCELONA)

Telephone: 692-00-00.
Telex: 52.040.
Founded 1968.

Independent control; Academic year: September to June; Languages of instruction: Spanish and Catalan.

*Rector:* ANTONIO SERRA RAMONEDA.
*Registrar:* ALBERT BUSQUETS BLAY.
*Librarian:* MANUEL MUNDÓ MARCET.
Number of teachers: 1,500.
Number of students: 21,539.
Publications: *Administración Pública*, *Anuario*, faculty and department bulletins and catalogues, documents, papers.

DEANS:
*Faculty of Letters:* JOSEP FONTANA LÁZARO.
*Faculty of Medicine:* FRANCISCO GONZÁLES SASTRE.
*Faculty of Economics:* JOSEP MA. VEGARA CARRIÓ.
*Faculty of Science:* JULIÀ CUFÍ SOBREGRAU.
*Faculty of Law:* LLUIS PUIG I FERRIOL.
*Faculty of Information Science:* NAZARIO GONZALEZ.

AFFILIATED INSTITUTES:
**Instituto de Biologia Fundamental:** Casa de Convalecencia del Hospital de la Santa Cruz y San Pablo, Avda. San Antonio María Claret 171.

**Instituto de Bioquimica Clínica:** Calle Roberto Bassas 1.

**Instituto de Ciencias de la Educación:** Campus Universitario.

## UNIVERSIDAD DE BILBAO*

APDO 1397, SIMÓN BOLÍVAR 1, BILBAO 10

Telephone: 312170, 315390.
Founded 1968.
State control.

*Rector:* JUSTO PASTOR RUPÉREZ.
*Secretary-General:* JOSÉ MA. AIZPITARTE PALACIOS.
*Librarian:* MARÍA FERNANDA IGLESIAS LESTEIRO.
Number of teachers: 642.
Number of students: 10,300.

DEANS:
*Faculty of Science:* JUSTO MAÑAS DÍAZ.
*Faculty of Medicine:* JOSÉ MARÍA RIVERA POMAR.
*Faculty of Economics and Business:* FERNANDO DE LA PUENTE Y FDEZ. DE ULLIVARRI.
*Technical High School of Industrial Engineering:* JOAQUÍN MARÍA DE AGUINAGA TORRANO.

* No reply received to our questionnaire this year.

## UNIVERSIDAD DE CÁDIZ

PLAZA DE FRAGELA S/N, APDO. 190, CÁDIZ

Telephone: (34-56) 222604.
Founded 1979; in process of formation.

*Rector:* FELIPE GARRIDO GARCÍA.
*Administrative Director:* MANUEL SUPERVIELLE MARZAN.

## UNIVERSIDAD PONTIFICIA "COMILLAS"

(Pontifical University "Comillas")

MADRID 34

Telephone: 734-39-50.

Founded by Pope Leo XIII, classes commencing at Comillas in 1892. The right to confer Degrees was granted in 1904. Moved to Madrid in 1960. Private control (Society of Jesus); Academic year: October to June.

*Grand Chancellor:* M.R.P. PEDRO ARRUPE, S.J.
*Rector:* R.P. URBANO VALERO, S.J.
*Vice-Rectors:* Prof. AUGUSTO HORTAL, S.J., Prof. RAFAEL SANZ DE DIEGO, S.J.
*Librarians:* ALEJANDRO BARCENILLA, JULIÁN IBÁÑEZ.
*Secretary-General:* RICARDO LOBATO GARCÍA.

Number of teachers: 351.
Number of students: 4,725.
Library of 235,000 vols.
Publications: *Miscelánea Comillas* (2 a year), *Estudios eclesiásticos*, *Pensamiento* (quarterly).

DEANS:
*Faculty of Theology:* Prof. FEDERICO PASTOR.

*Faculty of Canon Law:* Prof. LUIS VELA SÁNCHEZ, S.J.
*Faculty of Philosophy and Letters:* Prof. JUAN MANUEL COBO SUERO.
*Faculty of Law:* Prof. ESTANISLAO JUST.
*Higher Technical School of Industrial Engineering:* Prof. JUAN R. SALAZAR-SIMPSON.
*University School of Industrial Technical Engineering:* Prof. JUAN SALAZAR-SIMPSON.

Institutes of business administration and management, matrimonial law and modern languages.

There are other Theological and Philosophical Faculties in Spain conferring degrees, which are partly associated with the Pontifical Universities, as follows:

**Facultades S. Francisco de Borja:** Sant Cugat del Vallés, Barcelona; Jesuit College for the Province of Catalonia; f. 1864; Tel. 674-11-50. Since 1967 the Faculty of Theology has formed part of the Faculty of Theology of Barcelona, and is open to non-Jesuit students.

*Chancellor:* Dr. NARCISO JUBANY, Cardinal Archbishop of Barcelona.
*Vice-Chancellor:* R.P. IGNACIO SALVAT, S.J.
*Rector:* R.P. PEDRO RIBAS, S.J.
*Registrar:* P. JOSÉ MA. ROCAFIGUERA, S.J.
*Librarian:* P. ANTONIO BORRÁS, S.J.

Number of teachers: 41.
Number of students: 182.

Publications: *Pensamiento, Estudios Eclesiásticos, Manresa, Selecciones de Teología, Studia Papyrologica, Selecciones de Libros.*

DEANS:

*Dean of Theology:* P. ORIOL TUÑÍ, S.J.
*Dean of Philosophy:* P. EUSEBIO COLOMER, S.J.

PROFESSORS:

*Faculty of Theology:*
ABEL, FRANCISCO, Bioethics
ALBERDI, RAMÓN, Ecclesiastical History
ALDAZÁBAL, JOSÉ, Sacramental Theology
ALEGRE, XAVIER, New Testament Scripture
BARTINA, SEBASTIÁN, Old Testament Scripture
BAYÉS, GABRIEL, Liturgy
BENITEZ, JOSÉ MA., Ecclesiastical History
BORRÁS, ANTONIO, Ecclesiastical History, Christian Archaeology
BOADA, JOSÉ, Fundamental Theology
CAMPS, GUIU, Old Testament Scripture
CASAL, FERMIN, Fundamental Theology
CODINA, VÍCTOR, Dogmatic Theology
COLL, JOSÉ MARIA, Dogmatic Theology
CUYÁS, MANUEL, Moral Theology
ESCUDÉ, JORGE, Moral Theology
FONDEVILA, JOSÉ MA., Dogmatic Theology
FONT, JORGE, Moral Theology and Psychopathology
GONZÁLEZ FAUS, JOSÉ I., Dogmatic Theology
MANRESA, FERNANDO, Fundamental Theology
MILLAS, EDUARDO, Dogmatic Theology
MILLAS, JOSÉ MA., Fundamental Theology
MÚÑOZ, RAFAEL, Fundamental Theology
O'CALLAGHAN, JOSÉ, Greek Biblical and Papyrology
RECOLONS, LUIS, Sociology of Religion
RIUDOR IGNACIO, Fundamental Theology
RICART, IGNACIO, New Testament Scripture
SALVAT, IGNACIO, Moral Theology, Canon Law
SIVATTE, RAFAEL DE, Old Testament Scripture
TORTRAS, ANTONIO, Sacramental Theology
TUÑÍ, ORIOL, New Testament Scripture
VALL, HÉCTOR, Ecumenical Theology
VERGÉS, SALVADOR, Dogmatic Theology
VIVES, JOSÉ, Dogmatic Theology and Patrology

*Faculty of Philosophy:*
ACORDAGOICOECHEA, JUAN PEDRO, Metaphysics
ARAGÓ, JOAQUÍN, Psychology
AVESANI, GIUSEPPE, Metaphysics
COLOMER, EUSEBIO, History of Philosophy
GARCÍA-DONCEL, MANUEL, Cosmology
GOMIS, ANTONIO, Experimental Psychology
MIRALLES, JOSÉ, History of Political Systems
PEGUEROLES, JUAN, History of Philosophy
ROIG, JUAN, Ontology
SUÑER, PEDRO, Ethics and Natural Law

ATTACHED DEPARTMENT:

**Departamento de Papirología:** Dir. P. JOSÉ O'CALLAGHAN.

**Facultad de Teología:** Apdo. 2002, Granada; f. 1939.

*Grand Chancellor:* M. R. P. PEDRO ARRUPE, S.J.
*Vice-Grand Chancellor:* R.P. LUIS MARÍA ALVAREZ-OSSORIO, S.J.
*Rector:* R.P. MATIAS GARCÍA GÓMEZ.
*Vice-Rector:* (vacant).
*Secretary:* ALBERTO GARCÍA TORRES, S.J.
*Board of Administration:* ELADIO CAMPE MARTÍN, S.J.
*Librarians:* GABRIEL VERD, AUGUSTO SEGOVIA.

Library: 200,000 vols.

Number of professors: 40.
Number of students: 427.

Publications: *Archivo Teológico Granadino (Anuario de Teología Postridentina)*† (quarterly), *Biblioteca Teológica Granadina*† (collection of textbooks and theses), *Centro de Cultura Religiosa Superior* and *Cuadernos de Teología* (textbooks), *Proyección*†; in collaboration with other Spanish Jesuit reviews: *Estudios Eclesiásticos, Manresa, Razón y Fe.*

PROFESSORS:

BARÓN, ENRIQUE, Dogmatic Theology
CASTILLO SÁNCHEZ, JOSÉ M., Dogmatic Theology
CAMACHO LARAÑA, ILDEFONSO, Moral Theology
CASTÓN BOYER, PEDRO, Sociology
COLLANTES LOZANO, JUSTO, Dogmatic Theology
CONTRERAS MOLINA, FRANCISCO, Scripture
CRIADO RODRÍGUEZ CARRETERO, RAFAEL, Scripture
CUESTA LEIVA, MANUEL, Dogmatic Theology
DOMÍNGUEZ MORANO, CARLOS, Psychology
ESQUIVIAS FRANCO, JUAN, Biblical Hebrew
ESTRADA DÍAZ, JUAN, Dogmatic Theology
FRANCO HERNÁNDEZ, RICARDO, Dogmatic Theology
GARCÍA GÓMEZ, MATIAS, Pastoral Theology
GÓMEZ MARTÍNEZ, MANUEL, Moral Theology
GRANADO BELLIDO, CARMELO, Patrology
JIMÉNEZ ORTÍZ, ANTONIO, Fundamental Theology
LÓPEZ AZPITARTE, EDUARDO, Moral Theology
LÓPEZ CUADRADO ELEUTERIO, C.M.F., Philosophy
MOORE CANDELERA, EDUARDO, Moral Theology
MÚÑOZ, ISIDRO, History of Philosophy
NAVAS GUTIÉRREZ, ANTONIO, Ecclesiastical History
OLIVARES, ESTANISLAO, Canon Law
ORGE RAMÍREZ, MANUEL, Scripture
PEINADO MÚÑOZ, MIGUEL, Scripture
POZO, CANDIDO, Dogmatic Theology
RAMOS, MANUEL, Pastoral Theology and Liturgy
RODRÍGUEZ CARMONA, ANTONIO, Scripture
RODRÍGUEZ MOLERO, FRANCISCO X., Scripture
SEGOVIA, AUGUSTO, Dogmatic Theology, History of Dogma
SICRE DÍAZ, JOSÉ LUIS, Scripture
SOTOMAYOR MURO, MANUEL DE, Ecclesiastical History, Christian Archaeology
TORRES FERNÁNDEZ, ANTONIO, Biblical Theology
VÍLCHEZ LÍNDEZ, JOSÉ, Dogmatic Theology, Scripture

ATTACHED INSTITUTES:

*Centro Colaborador de Málaga:* Santa María 20, Málaga 15.
*Centro Estudios Teológicos:* Paseo de María Cristina, Seville; Rector VALERIANO GARCÍA MARTÍN.

## UNIVERSIDAD DE CÓRDOBA

CALLE ALFONSO XIII No. 17, CÓRDOBA

Telephone: 22-19-05.

Founded 1972.

State control; Language of instruction: Spanish; Academic year: October to June.

*Rector:* ALBERTO LOSADA VILLASANTE.

UNIVERSITIES                                                                                                                                             SPAIN

*Vice-Rectors:* AMADOR JOVER MOYANO, RODRIGO POZO LORA, JOSÉ ANDRÉS DE MOLINA REDONDO.
*Registrar:* ANTONIO RODERO FRANGANILLO.
*Librarian:* MANUEL IGLESIAS.
  Number of teachers: 800.
  Number of students: 10,000.

DEANS:

*Faculty of Veterinary Science:* DIEGO JORDANO BAREA.
*Faculty of Medicine:* RAFAEL MARTÍNEZ SIERRA.
*Faculty of Science:* MIGUEL VALCARCEL CASES.
*Faculty of Philosophy and Letters:* JOSÉ MA. CUENCA TORIBIO.
*Higher Technical School for Agricultural Engineers:* MANUEL GARCÍA NIETO.
*University School of Technical Mining Engineering:* RAFAEL HERNANDO LUNA.
*University School of Technical Industrial Engineering:* CARLOS MARTÍNEZ MARTÍNEZ.
*Education:* FRANCISCO MARTÍN LÓPEZ.
*University School of Nursing:* RAFAEL MARTÍNEZ SIERRA.
*University College of Business Studies:* PEDRO CALDENTEY ALBERT.

DIRECTORS:

*Institute of Animal Husbandry:* DIEGO JORDANO BAREA.
*Institute of Sociology and Rural Studies:* FELISA DELGADO CEÑA.
*Institute of Andalusian History.*

## UNIVERSIDAD DE DEUSTO
AVDA. DEL. DR. MORCILLO S/N, APARTADO 1, BILBAO 7
Telephone: 4-45-31-00.
Founded 1886.

Private control, directed by the Jesuits; Language of instruction: Spanish; Academic year: October to June.

*Chancellor:* R.P. PEDRO ARRUPE, S.J.
*Vice-Chancellor:* R.P. JUAN PLAZAOLA, S.J.
*Rector:* R.P. DIONISIO ARANZADI, S.J.
*Secretary-General:* R.P. JOSÉ ANTONIO ALDECOA ZARRABEITIA, S.J.
*Librarian:* R.P. JOSÉ I. ARESTI, S.J.
  Number of teachers: 517.
  Number of students: 7,912.

  Publications: *Estudios de Deusto* (2 a year), *Boletín de Estudios Económicos* (3 a year), *Letras de Deusto*† (2 a year).

DEANS:

*Faculty of Law:* RICARDO DE ANGEL.
*Faculty of Philosophy and Letters:* R.P. LUIS REIZÁBAL, S.J.
*Faculty of Theology:* R.P. ISIDRO MA. SANS, S.J.
*Faculty of Political Sciences and Sociology:* R.P. ROMÁN GÁRATE, S.J.
*Faculty of Philosophy and Education:* JUAN MARÍA ISASI.

*Faculty of Economics and Business Studies:* R.P. JOSÉ MARÍA OSTOLAZA, S.J.
*Faculty of Informatics:* JUAN LUIS GUTIÉRREZ.

DIRECTORS:

*Institute of Education:* R.P. MARIANO IBAR, S.J.
*Institute of Christian Living and Faith:* R.P. LUIS ERDOZAIN, S.J.
*Institute of Languages:* WINFRIED ARNOLD.
*School of Legal Practice:* R.P. JESÚS MARÍA DÍAZ DE ACEBEDO, S.J.
*"Bilbao Consulate" Institute of Maritime Law and Economics:* IGNACIO ARTAZA.
*School of Tourism and Secretarial Studies:* LUIS RAMOS.
*Department of Biscayan Studies:* ANDRÉS MAÑARICÚA.
*Institute of Higher Education in Religious Studies:* R.P. JESÚS TERÁN, S.J.
*International Institute of Business Management:* Hermanos Aguirre 2, Apdo. 153, Bilbao 7; ANTONIO FREIJE.
*School of Administration:* Hermanos Aguirre 2, Apdo. 153, Bilbao 7; R.P. ANTONIO COLINAS, S.J.
*Institute of European Studies:* f. 1979; Dir. Dr. JUAN FRANCISCO SANTACOLOMA.

## UNIVERSIDAD DE EXTREMADURA
AVDA. DE ELVAS S/N, BADAJOZ and CALLE PIZARRO 8, CACERES
Telephone: 924-238800 (Badajoz), 927-211655 (Caceres).
Founded 1973.

State control; Language of instruction: Spanish; Academic year: October to September.

*Rector:* ANDRÉS CHORDI CORBO.
*Vice-Rectors:* MANUEL ROMÁN CEBA (Academic Affairs); JUAN JOSÉ SAYAS ABENGOCHEA (Extension); LUIS GARCÍC-SANCHO MARTÍN (Research).
*Secretary-General:* JOSÉ LUIS MASOT FERNÁNDEZ.
  Number of teachers: 485.
  Number of students: 7,500.

  Publications: *NORBA (Anuario de Estudios de Geografía, Arte e Historia)*†, *Anuario de Estudios Filológicos*†, *Guia de la Universidad*†.

DEANS:

*Faculty of Sciences (Badajoz):* MANUEL GÓMEZ GUILLÉN.
*Faculty of Medicine (Badajoz):* MÁXIMO BARTOLOMÉ RODRÍGUEZ.
*Faculty of Philosophy and Letters (Caceres):* RICARDO SENABRE SEMPERE.
*Faculty of Law (Caceres):* LUIS MORELL OCAÑA.

PROFESSORS:

*Faculty of Sciences:*
  ARENAS ROSADO, JUAN FRANCISCO, Physical Chemistry
  CEBA, MANUEL ROMÁN, Analytical Chemistry
  CHORDI CORBO, ANDRÉS, Microbiology
  FUGAROLAS VILLAMARÍN, ANTONIO, Mathematical Analysis
  GÓMEZ GUILLÉN, MANUEL, Organic Chemistry
  RAMOS FERNÁNDEZ, FELICÍSIMO, Mechanics and Thermology
  SOTELO SANCHO, JOSÉ LUIS, Technical Chemistry
  VALENZUELA CALAHORRO, CRISTÓBAL, Inorganic Chemistry

*Faculty of Medicine:*
  BARTOLOMÉ RODRÍGUEZ, MÁXIMO, Pharmacology
  GARCÍA-SANCHO MARTÍN, LUIS, Pathology and Clinical Surgery
  PARILLA SÁNCHEZ, ROBERTO, Physiology
  PORTUGAL ALVAREZ, JOSÉ DE, Pathology and Clinical Medicine
  SILLERO REPULLO, ANTONIO, Biochemistry

*Faculty of Law:*
  IGLESIAS FERREIROS, AQUILINO, History of Spanish Law
  MORELL OCAÑA, LUIS, Administrative Law

*Faculty of Philosophy and Letters:*
  ROZAS LÓPEZ, JUAN MANUEL, Spanish Literature
  SAYAS ABENGOCHEA, JUAN JOSÉ, World and Spanish Ancient History
  SENABRE SEMPERE, RICARDO, General Grammar and Literary Criticism

## UNIVERSIDAD DE GRANADA
PLAZA DE LA UNIVERSIDAD GRANADA
Telephone: 27-84-00/04/08/12.

Founded 1526, established 1532, charter granted 1531.

Private control; Language of instruction: Spanish; Academic year: October to May.

*Rector:* ANTONIO GALLEGO MORELL.
*Vice-Rectors:* JOSÉ ANTONIO SAINZ CANTERO, DOMINGO SÁNCHEZ-MESA MARTÍN, JESÚS BIEL GAYÉ, RAFAEL LUZÓN CUESTA.
*Secretary-General:* FERMÍN CAMACHO EVANGELISTA.
*Librarian:* JERÓNIMO MARTÍNEZ GONZÁLEZ.

  University Library: c. 78,600 vols., 35 incunabula, 14th-century MS. *Historia Natural de Alberto Magno*; Faculty libraries: 183,995 volumes.

  Number of teachers: 1,460.
  Number of students: c. 32,000.

  Publications include: *Misceldnea de Estudios Arabes y Hebraicos*, *Anales del Desarrollo*, *Anales de la cátedra Francisco Suárez*, *Ars Pharmacéutica*.

DEANS:

*Faculty of Science:* GERARDO PARDO SÁNCHEZ.
*Faculty of Pharmacy:* FERMÍN SÁNCHEZ DE MEDINA CONTRERAS.

Faculty of Philosophy: ANGEL SÁENZ-BADILLOS PÉREZ.
Faculty of Medicine: IGNACIO ARCELUZ IMAZ.
Faculty of Law: JOSÉ CAZORLA PÉREZ.
Institute of Education: Dr. ASUNCIÓN LINARES RODRÍGUEZ.

### AFFILIATED SCHOOLS AND INSTITUTIONS:
**Escuela de Estudios Arabes** (School of Arabic Studies).
Director: P. DARIO CABANELAS.

**Instituto Federico Olóriz, Sección de Anatomía** (Anatomy Section of the Federico Olóriz Institute).
Director: Dr. GUIRAO PÉREZ.

**Instituto López Neyra de Parasitología** (Institute of Parasitology).
Director: Dr. GUEVARA POZO.

**Estación Experimental del Zaidín** (Experimental Station).
Director: Dr. LACHICA GARRIDO.

**Cátedra Francisco Suárez** (Courses in Philosophy of Law and Sacred Theology).
Director: Dr. NICOLÁS MARÍA LÓPEZ CALERA.

## UNIVERSIDAD DE LA LAGUNA
LA LAGUNA, TENERIFE, CANARY ISLANDS
Telephone: 25811920.
Founded 1701.
State control; Language of instruction: Spanish.

Rector: (vacant).
Vice-Rectors: Dr. FRANCISCO RUBIO ROYO (Academic), Dr. MANUEL MEDINA ORTEGA (Las Palmas Campus), Dr. FRANCISCO SÁNCHEZ MARTÍNEZ (Research), Dr. JOSÉ BUENO GÓMEZ (University Extension).
Registrar: DOMINGO PÉREZ CALERO.
Librarian: D. EMILIO JEREZ FRÍAS.
Number of teachers: 648.
Number of students: 14,630.
Publications: Revista de Historia (quarterly), Anales de la Facultad de Ciencias, Anales de la Universidad de a Laguna, Biblioteca Filológica.

### DEANS:
Faculty of Law: Dr. MANUEL MORÓN PALOMINO.
Faculty of Sciences: Dr. TELESFORO BRAVO EXPÓSITO.
Faculty of Philosophy and Letters: Dr. SEBASTIÁN DE LA NUEZ CABALLERO.
Faculty of Medicine: Dr. JAVIER PARACHE HERNÁNDEZ.
Faculty of Pharmacy: Dr. ANTONIO CEREZO GALÁN.
Faculty of Economics and Business Studies: Dr. GUMERSINDO TRUJILLO FERNÁNDEZ.
School of Industrial Engineering: Dr. ROBERTO MORENO DÍAZ.
School of Architecture: Dr. JAIME LÓPEZ DE ASIAÍN.

## UNIVERSIDAD DE LEÓN
CAMPUS UNIVERSITARIA LA PALOMERA, LEÓN
Telephone: 204412.
Founded 1979.
Rector: JOSÉ LUIS SOTILLO RAMOS.
Vice-Rectors: EDUARDO CADENAS BERGUA (Research), DIEGO SANTIAGO LAGUNA (University Extension), ANDRÉS SUÁREZ SUÁREZ (Academic and Professional).
Administrative Officer: D. EDUARDO VIJIL MAESO.
Number of teachers: 28.
Number of students: 6,075.
Publications: Anales de la Facultad de Veterinaria, Cuadernos del Colegio Universitario.

### DEANS:
Faculty of Veterinary Medicine: JUSTINO BURGOS GONZÁLEZ.
Faculty of Biology: JOSÉ MARIA LOSA QUINTANA.
Faculty of Law: ALFONSO PRIETO PRIETO.
Faculty of Philosophy and Letters: ELOY BENITO RUANO.
School of Professional Training: MANUELA MARTÍN SÁNCHEZ.
School of Business Studies: ISIDORO GARCÍA MARTINEZ.
School of Mining Engineering: FRANCISCO MARTINEZ REBOLLO.
School of Industrial Engineering: FRANCISCO MARTINEZ REBOLLO (acting).
School of Agricultural Engineering: RAFAEL COS JARLHING.

## UNIVERSIDAD COMPLUTENSE DE MADRID
CIUDAD UNIVERSITARIA, MADRID 3
Telephone: 243-06-63.
Founded 1508. Campus at Alcala de Linares.
Rector: Prof. BUSTELO.
Vice-Rectors: Dr. ANTONIO GALLEGO FERNÁNDEZ, Dr. JOSÉ ALCINA FRANCH, LUIS GUTIÉRREZ JODRA, GASPAR GONZÁLEZ GONZÁLEZ, PABLO LUCAS VERDÚ.
Administrator-General: LORENZO RODRÍGUEZ DURÁNTEZ.
Secretary-General: Dr. JOSÉ MARÍA LOZANO IRUESTE.
Librarian: FERNANDO HUARTE MORTON.
Number of teachers: 4,570.
Number of students: 96,503.
Library: second in importance in Madrid; 600,000 volumes, 208,000 pamphlets; comprises the libraries of the different Faculties and Institutes.
Publications: Resúmenes de Revistas Médicas, Boletin de la Biblioteca Universitaria, Revista de la Universidad Complutense.

### DEANS:
Faculty of Fine Arts: Dr. JOAQUÍN GURRUCHAGA FERNÁNDEZ.
Faculty of Philosophy and Education: Dr. SERGIO RÁBADE ROMEO.
Faculty of Geography and History: Dra. MARÍA RUIZ TRAPERO.
Faculty of Philology: Dr. ANTONIO RUIZ DE ELVIRA PRIETO.
Faculty of Biology: Dr. CARLOS VICENTE CÓRDOBA.
Faculty of Mathematics: Dr. BALDOMERO RUBIO SEGOVIA (acting).
Faculty of Physics: Dr. ANTONIO FERNÁNDEZ-RAÑADA Y MENÉNDEZ DE LUARCA.
Faculty of Chemistry: Dr. MATEO DÍAZ PEÑA.
Faculty of Geology: Dr. CARMEN VIRGILI RODÓN.
Faculty of Law: Dr. LUIS RODRÍGUEZ RAMOS (acting).
Faculty of Medicine: Dr. ALBERTO ORIOL BOSCH.
Faculty of Pharmacy: Dr. ANTONIO DOADRIO LÓPEZ.
Faculty of Psychology: Dr. JESÚS AMÓN HORTELANO (acting).
Faculty of Veterinary Medicine: Dr. RAFAEL MARTÍN ROLDÁN.
Faculty of Economics and Management: Dr. ANDRÉS FERNÁNDEZ DÍAZ (acting).
Faculty of Political Science and Sociology: Dr. SALUSTIANO DEL CAMPO URBANO.
Faculty of Information Science: Dr. ANTONIO LARA GARCÍA.

### PROFESSORS:
Faculty of Philosophy and Education:
CALVO SERER, R., History of Spanish Philosophy
GALINO CARRILLO, A., History of Education
GARCIA-HOZ, V., Experimental Education
GONZALEZ ALVAREZ, A., Metaphysics
MARKET GARCIA, O., History of Philosophy
MILLAN PUELLES, A., Metaphysics
PACIOS LOPEZ, A., Didactics
PALACIOS RODRIGUEZ, L., Logic
PINILLOS DIAZ, J. L., Psychology
RABADE ROMEO, S., Metaphysics
ROMERO MARIN, A., General Education
SANCHEZ DE MUNIAIN Y GIL, J. M., Aesthetics
SAUMELLS PANADES, R., Natural Philosophy
TODOLI DUQUE, J., Ethics and Sociology

Faculty of Geography and History:
ALCINA FRANCH, J., American Archaeology
ALMAGRO BOSCH, M., Prehistory
ALVAREZ RUBIANO, P., Modern History
AZCARATE RISTORI, J. M., History of Art
BALLESTEROS GAIBROIS, M., American History
BLANCO FREIJEIRO, A., Archaeology
BLAZQUEZ MARTINEZ, J. M., Spanish History
BONET CORREA, A., History of Art
BOSQUE MAUREL, J., Geography
CASAS TORRES, J. M., Geography
CEPEDA ADAN, J., Spanish History
CESPEDES DEL CASTILLO, G., History of Geographical Discoveries
DELGADO MARTIN, J., American History
GARCÍA-GALLO DE DIEGO, A., History of Indian Law
GONZALEZ GONZALEZ, J., Spanish History

Hera Perez-Cuesta, A. de la, History of the American Church
Hernandez-Perera, J., History of Art
Jover Zamora, J. M., Contemporary History
Marco-Dorta, E., History of Hispano-American Art
Marin Martinez, T., Palaeography
Montero Diaz, S., Ancient History
Moxo y Ortiz de Villajos, S., Spanish History
Palacio Atard, V., Spanish History
Rodriguez Casado, V., Modern History
Romeu de Armas, A., Spanish History
Ruiz-Trapero, M., Epigraphy and Numismatics

*Faculty of Philology:*
Alvar Lopez, M., Spanish Language
Arce Fernandez, J., Italian Language and Literature
Balbin Lucas, R. de, General Grammar
Diaz Macho, A., Hebrew Language and Literature
Fontan Perez, A., Latin Philology
Garcia Calvo, A., Latin Philology
Gil Fernandez, L., Greek Philology
Juretschke Meyer, H., German Literature
Lapesa Melgar, R., Spanish History
Lopez Estrada, F., Spanish Literature
Lorenzo Criado, E., German Philology
Marine Bigorra, S., Latin Philology
Perez Castro, F., Hebrew Language and Literature
Poyan Diaz, D., French Language and Literature
Pujals Fontrodona, E., English Language and Literature
Rodriguez Adrados, F., Greek Philology
Rubio Fernandez, L., Latin Philology
Ruiperez Sanchez, M., Greek Philology
Ruiz de Elvira Prieto, A., Latin Philology
Sanchez-Castañer y Mena, F., Latin American Literature
Sanchez Lasso de la Vega, J., Greek Philology
Simon Diaz, J., Bibliography
Teres Sadaba, E., Arabic Literature
Vallvé Bermejo, J., Arabic
Yndurain Hernandez, F., Spanish Literature and Language
Zamora Vicente, A., Latin

*Faculty of Mathematics:*
Abellanas Cebollero, P., Geometry
Ancochea Quevedo, G., Geometry
Arregui Fernandez, J., Algebra
Botella Raduan, F., Topology
Etayo Miqueo, J. J., Geometry
Lines Escardo, E., Mathematical Analysis
Rios Garcia, S., Statistics
Rodriguez-Salinas Palero, B., Mathematical Analysis
Torroja Menendez, J. M., Astronomy

*Faculty of Physics:*
Aguilar Peris, J., Thermal Physics
Bru Villaseca, L., Theoretical Physics
Catala de Alemany, J., Physics of the Atmosphere
Dominguez Ruiz-Aguirre, R., Physics
Duran Miranda, A., Optics
Fernández-Rañada y Fernández-Luarca, A., Theoretical Physics
Galindo Tixaire, A., Theoretical Physics
Rodriguez-Vidal, M., Electricity
Sanchez del Rio y Sierra, C., Nuclear Physics

*Faculty of Chemistry:*
Calvo Calvo, F. A., Metallurgy
Costa Novella, E., Technical Chemistry
Diaz-Peña, M., Physical Chemistry
Gutierrez-Jodra, L., Industrial Chemistry
Gutierrez Rios, E., Inorganic Chemistry
Morcillo Rubio, J., Spectrography
Perez Alvarez-Ossorio, R., Chemistry
Soto Camara, J. L., Organic Chemistry
Voan-Ortuño, A., Industrial Chemistry

*Faculty of Geology:*
Alustrue Castillo, E., Geology
Alia Medina, M., Geography
Amoros Portoles, J. L., Crystallography
Fuster Casas, J. M., Petrology
Melendez y Melendez, B., Palaeontology
Virgili Rodon, C., Stratigraphy

*Faculty of Biology:*
Alvarado Ballester, Zoology
Bellot Rodriguez, F., Botany
Bernis Madrazo, F., Zoology
Carrato Ibañez, A., Histology
Fernandez-Galiano Fernandez, A., Botany
Fernandez-Galiano Fernandez, D., Bacteriology
Fraile Ovejero, A., Animal Physiology
Lacadena Calero, J. R., Genetics
Martin-Municio, A., Physiological Chemistry
Peris Torres, S. V., Zoology
Valls Medina, A., Anthropology
Vicente Córdoba, C., Plant Physiology

*Faculty of Law:*
Aguilar Navarro, M., International Law
Albaladejo Garcia, M., Civil Law
Alonso-Olea, M., Labour Law
Barbero Santos, M., Penal Law
Bayon Chacon, G., Labour Law
Beltran de Heredia y Castaño, J., Civil Law
Beltran Flores, L., Political Economy
Cossio y Corral, A. de, Civil Law
Diez de Velasco Vallejo, M., International Law
Elias de Tejada Spínola, F., Natural Law and Philosophy of Law
Fenech Navarro, M., Procedural Law
Fernandez-Galiano Fernandez, Philosophy of Law
Fernandez-Miranda Hevia, T., Public Law
Ferrer Sama, A., Penal Law
Galan Gutierrez, E., Philosophy of Law
Garcia de Enterria y Martinez-Carande, E., Administrative Law
Garcia-Gallo de Diego, A., Spanish Law
Gilbert y Sanchez de la Vega, R., Spanish Law
Giron Tena, J., Commercial Law
Guasp Delgado, J., Procedural Law
Hernandez-Gil, A., Civil Law
Hernandez-Tejero Jorge, F., Roman Law
Iglesias Santos, J., Roman Law
Lopez-Rodo, L., Administrative Law
Lopez Vilas, R., Civil Law
Maldonado y Fernandez del Torco, J., Canon Law
Manzano y Manzano, J., History of Spanish Law
Martin Martinez, I., Canon Law
Naharro Mora, J. M., Political Economy
Prados-Arrarte, J., Political Economy
Rodriguez-Devesa, J. M., Penal Law
Ruiz-Gimenez Cortes, J., Philosophy of Law
Sainz Martinez de Bujanda, F., Financial Law
Sanchez-Agesta, L., Public Law
Sebastian Herrador, M., Public Finance
Verdera Tuels, E., Mercantile Law
Villar-Palaso, J. L., Administrative Law

*Faculty of Medicine:*
Alonso Fernández, F., Psychiatry
Armijo Valenzuela, M., Hydrology
Botella Llusia, J., Obstetrics and Gynaecology
Bravo Oliva, J., Microbiology
Bullon Ramirez, A., Anatomy
Cabre Piera, J., Dermatology
Calatrava Paramo, L., Stomatology
Casado de Frias, E., Paediatrics
Duran Sacristan, H., Surgery
Elio Membrado, F. J., Anaesthesiology
Espinos Perez, D., Pathology
Fernandez Cruz, A., Pathology
Fuente Chaos, A. de la, Surgery
Gallego Fernandez, A., Physiology
Garcia de Jalon Hueto, P., Chemical Pharmacy
Garcia Sanchez, J., Ophthalmology
Gil Gayarre, M., Physical Therapeutics
Gilsanz Garvia, V., Pathology
Gomez Oliveros, L., Anatomy
Gomez Orbaneja, J., Dermatology
Lain Entralgo, P., History of Medicine
Lopez Viejo, A., Stomatology
Lucas Tomas, M., Stomatology
Moreno Gonzalez, J. P., Stomatology
Oriol Bosch, A., Endocrinology
Piga Sanchez Morate, B., Forensic Medicine
Poch Viñals, R., Oto-Rhino-Laryngology
Rio de las Heras, F. del, Stomatology
Rodríguez Candela, J. L., General Pathology
Sol Fernandez, J. R. del, Obstetrics and Gynaecology
Tamarit Torres, J., Physiology
Usón Calvo, A., Urology
Zamorano Sanabra, L., Histology

*Faculty of Pharmacy:*
Barcelo Coll, J., Vegetal Physiology
Cadorniga Carro, P., Pharmacy
Casares Lopez, Bromatology
Doadrio Lopez, A., Inorganic Chemistry
Folch Jou, G., History of Pharmacy
Gaston de Iriarte, E., Microbiology
Gomez-Serranillos Fernandez, M., Pharmacy
Gonzalez-Castro, J., Parasitology
Gonzalez Trigo, G., Organic Chemistry
Hoyos de Castro, A., Pedology
Otero Aenlle, E., Physics
Rivas Martinez, S., Botany
Santos Ruiz, A., Biochemistry
Varela Mosquera, G., Animal Physiology

*Faculty of Veterinary Medicine:*
Carda Aparici, P., Pathology
Cuenca y Gonzalez-Ocampo, C. L. de, Genetics
Gallego Garcia, E., Histology
Gonzalez Gonzalez, G., Phthisiology
Illera Martin, M., Physiology
Lopez Lorenzo, P., Food Biochemistry
Martin Roldan, R., Anatomy
Perez Perez, F., Surgery
Ruiz Amil, M., Biochemistry
Sans Perez, B., Bromatology
Sanz Sanchez, F., Pharmacology
Sanchez Botija, C.
Suarez Fernandez, G., Microbiology

*Faculty of Economics and Management:*
Alcaide Inchausti, A., Econometrics
Anes Alvarez, G., Economic History
Berlanga Barba, M., Business Economics

Borrajo Dacruz, E., Labour Law
Bourkaib Broussain, J., Prices Insurance Law
Campo Urbano, S. del, Sociology
Cotorruelo Sendagorta, A., Economic Policy
Echevarria Gangoiti, J. M., Economic Theory
Fernandez-Pirla, J. M., Business Economics
Figueroa Martinez, E. de, Economic Policy
Fuentes Quintana, E., Public Finance
Gil-Pelaez, L., Mathematics of Financial Operations
Irastorza Revuelta, J., Economic Policy
Lopez-Moreno, M. J., Business Economics
Lozano Irueste, J. M., Spanish Public Finance
Martinez Cortiña, R., Economic Structures
Nieto de Alba, U., Mathematical Theory of Insurance
Rivero Romero, J., Business Accountancy
Rojo Duque, L. A., Economic Theory
Schwartz Giron, P., History of Economic Doctrines
Segura Sanchez, J., Economic Theory
Suarez Suarez, A. S., Business Economics
Varela Parache, M., International Economic Organization
Vegas Perez, A., Statistics
Velarde Fuertes, J., Economic Structures

*Faculty of Political Sciences:*
Borrajo Dacruz, E., Labour Law
Calle Saiz, R., Public Finance and Monetary Policy
Campo Urbano, S. del, Sociology
Diez-Nicolas, J., Human Ecology
Diez del Corral Pedruzo, L., History of Political Ideas and Forms
Espin Canovas, D., Civil Law
Fraga Iribarne, M., Theory of the State
Fueyo Alvarez, J. F., Political Theory
Garcia-Trevijano Fos, J. A., Administrative Law
Garrido Falla, F., Administrative Law
Gimenez y Martinez de Carvajal, J., Public Ecclesiastical Law
Gonzalez-Seara, L., Sociology
Lacruz Berdejo, J. L., Civil Law
Maravall Casesnoves, J. A., History of Spanish Political Thought
Martin Lopez, E., Sociology of Communication
Ollero Gomez, C., Theory of the State
Pérez Prendes, M., History of Political Institutions
Rodriguez Rodriguez, F., Social Policy
Truyol Serra, A., International Law

*Faculty of Information Sciences:*
Castillo Castillo, J., Sociology
Perez de Armiñan, G., Political Economy
Seco Serrano, C., History of Spain
Varela Iglesias, J. L., Literature

## UNIVERSIDAD AUTÓNOMA DE MADRID
CIUDAD UNIVERSITARIA,
CANTO BLANCO,
MADRID 34

Telephone: 734-01-00.

Founded 1968.

Language of instruction: Spanish.

*Rector:* Pedro Martínez Montávez.
*Registrar:* Emilio de Castro Gracia.
*Secretary-General:* Rodrigo Bercovitz y Rodríguez-Cano.
*Librarian:* Vicente Llorca Zaragoza.

The library contains 80,000 vols.

Number of teachers: 1,176.
Number of students: c. 24,000.

### DEANS:
*Faculty of Medicine:* José Perianes Carro.
*Faculty of Economics:* Eduardo Bueno Campos.
*Faculty of Philosophy and Letters:* Carlos París Amador.
*Faculty of Science:* José Ignacio Fernández Alonso.
*Faculty of Law:* Luis Enrique de la Villa.

## UNIVERSIDAD DE MÁLAGA
EL EJIDO, MÁLAGA

Telephone: 25-50-54.

Telex: 77173.

Founded 1972.

State control; Language of instruction: Spanish; Academic year: October to July.

*Rector:* Prof. Antonio Pérez de la Cruz Blanco.
*Vice-Rectors:* José Castilla Gonzalo (Academic Affairs), José María Otero Moreno (Research).
*Administrative Officer:* Marcelino Sánchez Pérez.
*Secretary-General:* Ignacio Pérez de Vargas Ferroni.

Library of 89,468 vols., 1,399 periodicals.

Number of teachers: 648.
Number of students: 10,287.

Publications: *Cuadernos de Ciencias Económicas y Empresariales*† (2 a year), *Revista de Estudios Regionales*† (2 a year), *Analecta Malacitana*† (2 a year), *Baética*† (2 a year).

### DEANS:
*Economic and Business Sciences:* Dr Francisco Mochón Morcillo.
*Medicine:* Prof. D. Felipe Sánchez de la Cuesta y Alcarcón.
*Science:* Dra. Aurora Rodríguez García.
*Philosophy and Letters:* Dr. Cristobal Cuevas García.
*University School of Business Studies:* Luís Cabra Fernández.
*University School of Teacher Training:* Manuel del Campo y del Campo.
*University School of Industrial Engineering:* José María Alonso Pedreira.

### PROFESSORS:
*Faculty of Economic and Business Sciences:*
Argandoña Ramís, Antonio, Economic Theory
Cabrera Bazán, José, Labour Law
Cuadra Echaide, Ignacio de, Company Law
Cuadrado Roura, Juan Ramón, Political Economy
Durán Herrera, Juan José, Company Law
García Barbancho, Alfonso, Econometrics and Statistical Methods
Ortiz Díaz, José, Administrative Law
Otero Moreno, José María, Econometrics and Statistical Methods
Pérez de la Cruz Blanco, Antonio, Mercantile Law
Requena Rodríguez, José María, Company Accountancy and Costing Statistics

*Faculty of Medicine:*
Calbo Torrecillas, Francisco, Microbiology and Parasitology
Castilla Gonzalo, José, Forensic Medicine
Morell Ocaña, Miguel, Physiology
Sánchez de la Cuesta y Alarcón, Felipe, Pharmacology
Smith Agreda, José María, Descriptive and Topographic Anatomy and Anatomical Techniques

*Faculty of Philosophy and Letters:*
Abad Nebot, Francisco, General Grammar and Literary Criticism
Cuevas García, Cristóbal, Spanish Literature
García de la Fuente, Olegario, Latin Philology
García Manrique, Eusebio, Geography

*Faculty of Sciences:*
Castillo Abanades, Florencio del, Mathematical Analysis
González Donoso, José María, Palaeontology
Hernando Huelmo, José María, Physical Chemistry
Marín Girón, Fernando, Animal and Plant Cytology and Histology
Rodríguez García, Aurora, Inorganic Chemistry

*University School of Business Studies:*
Bueno Temprano, Benjamín, Economic Structure
Cabra Fernández, Luis, Basic Commercial Products
Saez de Ibarra y Oraá, Miguel, Law
Sanz Jiménez, León, Expression Techniques
Serrano Moreno, María Luisa, Arabic

*University School of Teacher Training:*
Campo del Campo, Manuel del, Music
Carmen del Pozo Rincón, María del, Spanish Language and Literature
Cerezuela Navarro, Florencio, Natural Sciences
Martín Arenas, Salvador, Physics and Chemistry
Río Sánchez-Bethencourt, Alvaro del, Pedagogy
Rivera Sánchez, María Josefa, Geography and History
Vela Díaz, Rafael, Spanish Language and Literature
Verdú Aparicio, Pío Augusto, Drawing

*University School of Industrial Engineering:*
Aldenueva Salguero, Valentín, Mathematics I
Alonso Pedreira, José María, Mechanics I
Alvarez Quirós, Luís, Physics
Cristófol Alvarez, José, Electricity II
López Larrotcha, Rafael, Mechanics III

MORENTE DEL POZO, JOSÉ MARÍA, Design I
PIÑEIRO BARRAIRO, JOSÉ MIGUEL, Mathematics II
PORTILLO FRANQUELO, PEDRO, Design II
SÁNCHEZ-APELLANÍZ VALDERRAMA, MIGUEL, Company Organization and Economics

## UNIVERSIDAD DE MURCIA
SANTO CRISTO 1, MURCIA

Telephone: 249200.

Telex: 67058.

Founded 1915.

State control; language of instruction Spanish; Academic year: October-June.

*Rector:* Dr. JOSÉ ANTONIO LOZANO TERUEL.

*Vice-Rectors:* Dr. ANTONIO REMIRO BROTONS (Academic), Dr. JUAN TORRES FONTES (Research), Dr. JOSÉ MARÍA MORALES MESEGUER (Extension).

*Secretary-General:* Dr. ANTONIO BÓDALO SANTOYO.

*Director:* AUGUSTO PARDO GRANADOS.

*Librarian:* Doña CARMEN FERNÁNDEZ VILLAMIL.

Library: f. 1916; 80,000 vols.

Number of teachers: 800.
Number of students: 14,000.

Publications: *Anales* (quarterly), and *Monteagudo*.

### DEANS:
*Faculty of Philosophy and Letters:* Dr. FRANCISCO LÓPEZ BERMÚDEZ.
*Faculty of Law:* Dr. JUAN BAUTISTA MARTÍN QUERALT.
*Faculty of Science:* Dr. ANTONIO SOLER ANDRÉS.
*Faculty of Medicine:* Dr. FRANCISCO RODRÍGUEZ LÓPEZ.

### DIRECTORS OF DEPARTMENTS:
*Faculty of Philosophy and Letters:*
BAQUERO GOYANES, M., Spanish Literature
DE LA PLAZA SANTIAGO, F. J., History of Art
GARCÍA BERRIO, A., Spanish Linguistics
GARCÍA LÓPEZ, J., Logic
GARCÍA MARTÍNEZ, A., History of Philosophy
GONZÁLEZ BLANCO, A., Ancient History
LUCENA SALMORAL, M., Modern and Contemporary History
MOYA DEL BANO, F., Latin Language and Literature
MUÑOZ AMILIBIA, A. M., Archaeology
MUÑOZ CORTES, M., History of Grammar
PLANS SANZ DE BREMOND, P., Geography
ROLDÁN PÉREZ, A., General Linguistics and Literary Criticism
RUBIO GARCÍA, L., Romance Philology
TORRES FONTES, J., Medieval History
VÁSQUEZ RODRÍGUEZ, J. M., Ethics and Sociology

*Faculty of Law:*
BURILLO LOSHUERTOS, J., Roman Law
FERNÁNDEZ-CARVAJAL GONZÁLEZ, R., Political Law
GACTO FERNÁNDEZ, E., History of Law
HURTADO BAUTISTA, M., Natural Law and Philosophy of Law
JIMÉNEZ CONDE, F., Procedural Law
LANDROVE DÍAZ, G., Penal Law
LÓPEZ ALARCÓN, M., Canon Law
MARTÍNEZ-USEROS USEROS, E., Administrative Law
MONTOYA MELGAR, A., Labour Law
RAGA GIL, J. T., Political Economy and Public Finance
REMIRO BROTONS, A., International Public and Private Law
ROCA JUAN, J., Civil Law

*Faculty of Science:*
ALÍAS PÉREZ, L. J., Geology
CHICOTE OLAYA, M. T., Inorganic Chemistry
FERNÁNDEZ VINAS, J. A., Mathematical Analysis
MARTÍN RODRÍGUEZ, E., Physics
NAVARRO BLAYA, S., Agricultural Chemistry
SABATER GARCÍA, F., Biology
SÁNCHEZ-PEDRENO MARTÍNEZ, C., Analytical Chemistry
SERNA SERNA, A., Physical Chemistry
SOLER ANDRÉS, A., Technical Chemistry
ZOROA TEROL, P., Probability

*Faculty of Medicine:*
ABAD MARTÍNEZ, L., Obstetrics and Gynaecology
BARCIA SALORIO, D., Psychiatry
BRUGGER AUBÁN, A., Pharmacology
CARMENA RODRÍGUEZ, R., Medical and Clinical Pathology
DOMENECH RATTÓ, G., Human Anatomy
HERNÁNDEZ CALVO, F., Histology and Embryology
LOZANO TERUEL, J. A., Biochemistry
MARSET CAMPOS, P., History of Medicine
MERINO SÁNCHEZ, J., General Pathology
ORTUÑO PACHECO, G., Pathological Anatomy
PARRAS GUIJOSA, L., Biostatistics
PARRILLA PARICIO, P., Surgical and Clinical Pathology
QUESADA PÉREZ, T., General and Special Physiology
RODRÍGUEZ LÓPEZ, F., Paediatrics
SPREKELSEN GASSÓ, C., Oto-rhino-laryngology

## UNIVERSIDAD DE NAVARRA
CIUDAD UNIVERSITARIA, PAMPLONA

Telephone: 34-48-252700.

Founded 1952.

Private control; Language of instruction: Spanish; Academic year: October to June.

*Chancellor:* ALVARO DEL PORTILLO.
*Vice-Chancellor:* FLORENCIO SÁNCHEZ BELLA.
*Rector:* ALFONSO NIETO TAMARGO.
*Vice-Rectors:* FRANCISCO PONZ, ISMAEL SÁNCHEZ BELLA.
*Financial Affairs:* VICENTE PICÓ.
*General Secretary:* JAIME NUBIOLA AGUILAR.
*Manager:* EDUARDO GUERRERO PÉREZ.
*Librarian:* ANGEL MARTÍN DUQUE.

Number of teachers: 736.
Number of students: 7,733.

Publications: *Revista de Medicina, Ius Canonicum, Nuestro Tiempo, Scripta Theologica, Redacción, Anuario Filosófico, Anuario de Derecho Internacional, Persona y Derecho.*

### DEANS:
*Faculty of Law:* JAVIER HERVADA.
*Faculty of Arts:* ANGEL MARTÍN DUQUE.
*Faculty of Journalism:* CARLOS SORIA.
*Faculty of Medicine:* GONZALO HERRANZ.
*Faculty of Canon Law:* AMADEO DE FUENMAYOR.
*Faculty of Pharmacy:* JESÚS LARRALDE.
*Faculty of Science:* JESÚS JAIME VÁZQUEZ.
*Faculty of Theology:* JOSÉ LUIS ILLANES.
*Higher Technical School of Industrial Engineering:* JOSÉ MARÍA BASTERO.
*Higher Technical School of Architecture:* LEOPOLDO GIL.
*Graduate School of Business Administration:* JUAN ANTONIO PÉREZ.

### DIRECTORS OF AFFILIATED SCHOOLS AND INSTITUTES:
*School of Technical Engineering:* JOSÉ MA. MONTES ANDÍA.
*School of Laboratory Technicians:* SALVADOR VALDÉS.
*Institute of Liberal Arts:* LUKA BRAJNOVIC.
*Institute of Church History:* JOSÉ ORLANDIS.
*Institute of Modern Languages:* JOSÉ DAWID.
*Institute of Administration:* MA. ESTHER DEL VAL DE DIEGO.
*Institute of Education:* DAVID ISAACS.
**Institute of Spanish Language and Culture:** JESÚS CAÑEDO.
*School of Nursing:* PURIFICACIÓN DE CASTRO.

### ATTACHED INSTITUTES:
**Instituto Martín Azpilcueta:** Biblioteca de Humanidades; Dir. PEDRO LOMBARDÍA.

**Centro de Cálculo:** Urdaneta 7, San Sebastián; Dir. F. P. MOLLER.

**Centro de Investigaciones Técnicas de Guipúzcoa:** Av. de Tolosa, Ibaeta, San Sebastián; Dir. FRANCISCO TEGERIZO.

**Escuela Profesional de Medicina Interna:** Facultad de Medicina; Dir. EDUARDO ORTIZ DE LANDÁZURI.

**Laboratorio de Edificación:** Escuela Técnica Superior de Arquitectura; Dir. JAVIER LAHUERTA.

**Clínica Universitaria:** Universidad de Navarra; Dir. (vacant).

**Centro de Estudios de Ecología Urbana:** Dir. MANUEL FERRER.

**Centro de Estudios sobre la Responsibilidad de la Iniciativa Privada:** Dir. ALEJANDRO LLANO.

## UNIVERSIDAD DE OVIEDO

CALLE SAN FRANCISCO 1, OVIEDO

Telephone: 21-98-85.

**Founded 1608.**

Language of instruction: Spanish; State control; Academic year: October to June.

*Rector:* Dr. Teodoro López-Cuesta Egocheaga.
*Vice-Rectors:* Dr. Emilio Anadón Frutos, Dr. Carlos Bertrand Bertrand, Dr. Miguel Abad Gavín.
*Secretary-General:* Dr. Francisco Sosa Wagner.
*Librarian:* Dra. Herminia Rodríguez Balbín.

The library contains 192,000 vols.
**Number of teachers:** 1,090.
**Number of students:** 20,065.

**Publications:** *Revista de Ciencias, Archivum, Speleon, Monografías del Instituto Jurídico, Anales de la Facultad de Veterinaria, Boletín del Centro de Estudios del siglo XVIII.*

### DEANS:

*Faculty of Law:* Dr. Armando J. Torrent Ruiz.
*Faculty of Philosophy and Letters:* Dr. Eloy Benito Ruano.
*Faculty of Science:* Dr. José Coca Prados.
*Faculty of Veterinary Medicine:* Dr. José Luis Sotillo Ramos.
*Faculty of Medicine:* Dr. Antonio Pérez Casas.
*Faculty of Economics:* Dr. Luis Carlón Sánchez.
*Faculty of Biology:* Dr. Eduardo Cadenas Bergúa.
*Higher Technical School of Mining:* Dr. Luis Fernández Velasco.

## UNIVERSIDAD PAIS VASCO
(Basque University)

CAMPUS DE LEJONA, LEJONA (VIZCAYA)

Founded 1979; in process of formation.

*Administrative Director:* José Ma. Aizpitarte Palacios.
*Secretary-General:* José Ma. Rivera Pomar.

## UNIVERSIDAD PONTIFICIA DE SALAMANCA

CALLE COMPAÑÍA 1, APDO. 541, SALAMANCA

Telephone: 218316 and 212260.

Founded 1134 as the Ecclesiastical School of Salamanca Cathedral; named a University by Alfonso IX of León in 1219. The University had ceased to function by the end of the 18th century, but was restored to its former activities in 1940 by Pope Pius XII. Private control; Language of instruction: Spanish; Academic year: October to June.

*Grand Chancellor:* H.E. Vicente Enrique y Tarancón, Archbishop of Madrid.
*Rector:* Excmo. Juan Luis Acebal Luján.
*Administrative Officers:* Vicente de Lorenzo y Rodríguez, P. Luis Rodríguez Martínez.
*General Secretary:* Dr. Román Sánchez Chamoso.
*Director of Library:* Dr. Enrique Llamas Martínez.

The library contains 80,000 vols. and numerous MSS.

Number of teachers: 112.
Number of students: 1,776.

Publications: *Salmanticensis†, Helmántica†, Boletín de Información†, Cuadernos Salmantinos de Filosofía†, Diálogo Ecuménico†, Colectanea de Jurisprudencia Canónica†,* and many religious, philosophical and other works.

### DEANS:

*Faculty of Theology:* Dr. Ricardo Blázquez Pérez.
*Faculty of Canon Law:* Dr. Juan Sánchez y Sánchez.
*Faculty of Philosophy:* Dr. Saturnino Alvarez Turienzo.
*Faculty of Trilingual Biblical Philology:* Dr. José Oroz Reta.
*Faculty of Education:* Dr. Juan A. Cabezas Sandoval.
*Faculty of Psychology:* Dr. Gerardo Pastor Ramos.
*Faculty of Political and Social Sciences:* Dr. Manuel Capelo Martínez.

### PROFESSORS:

*Faculty of Theology:*
Blázquez Pérez, R., Ecclesiology
Castro Cubella, C., Phenomenology and History of Religion
Fernández Ramos, F., Scripture
García Cordero, M., Old Testament Exegesis
Garijo Guembe, M., Ecumenical Theology
González Hernández, O., Christology
Martín Hernández, F., Church History
Pérez Rodríguez, G., Scripture
Pikaza Ibarrondo, J., Phenomenology of Religion
Sánchez Vaquero, J., Ecumenism
Tellechea Idígoras, J. I., Church History
Trevijano Echeverria, R., Patrology

*Faculty of Canon Law:*
Acebal Luján, J. L., Procedural Law
Echeverría y Mart. de Marigorta, L., Reconciliation Law
García y García, A., Canon Law
Jiménez Urresti, T., Fundamental Canon Law
Manzanares Marijuán, J., Constitutional Law
Sánchez y Sánchez, J., Constitutional Law

*Faculty of Philosophy:*
Alvarez Turienzo, S., Ethics
Arranz Rodrigo, M., Natural Philosophy
Aubach Guiu, M. T., World History
Muñoz Delgado, V., Logic
Pérez de Laborda, A., History of Science
Pintor Ramos, A., History of Modern Philosophy
Rivera de Ventosa, E., History of Ancient Philosophy

*Faculty of Trilingual Biblical Philology:*
Carrete Parrondo, C., Hebrew Language and Literature
Guillén Cabañero, J., Latin Language and Literature (Patristics)
Oroz Reta, J., Hispano-Latin Language and Literature
Ortega Carmona, A., Greek Language and Literature
Panyagua R., E., History of Art

*Faculty of Education:*
Alcalde Gómez, J., Evolutionary Psychology
Cabezas Sandoval, J. A., General Psychology
Fernández Pellitero, M., Biological Sciences
Mencia de la Fuente, E., Ecology
Sans Vila, J., Theology of Education
Schramm Martín, C., Statistics
Sopeña Alcorlo, A., Professional Orientation

*Faculty of Psychology:*
Basabe Barcala, J., General Psychopathology
González González, J. A., Psychophysiology
Málaga Guerrero, J., Psychopathology of Human Communications
Pastor Ramos, G., Social Psychology
Rodrigues Isidoro, J., Psychometrics and Psychodiagnostics
Sánchez Granjel, L., History of Medicine

*Faculty of Political and Social Sciences:*
Buceta Facorro, L., Social Psychology
Campo Urbano, S., Social Structure
Capelo Martínez, M., Economic Policy
González Estefani, J. M., History of Ideas and Political Systems
Pereña Vicente, L., Social Ethics
Valverde Mucientes, C., Theology of Social Reality

### AFFILIATED INSTITUTES:

*Higher Institute of Pastoral Studies:* Paseo Juan XXIII 3, Madrid 3; Dir. Luis Maldonado Arenas.

*"Pius X" Higher Institute of Catechetical Studies:* Marqués de Mondejar 32, Madrid 28; Dir. José María Martínez Beltrán.

*Theological Institute of the Religious Life:* Colmenar Viejo, Madrid; Dir. Jesús Alvarez Gómez.

*San Esteban Theological Institute:* Plaza Concilio de Trento 4, Salamanca; Dir. Rafael Larrañeta Olleta.

*Higher Institute of Philosophy:* Plaza de San Pablo 4, Valladolid; Dir. José Antonio Lobo Alonso.

*"Luis Vives" Professional University Schools:* Avda. de los Maristas 7, Salamanca; Dir. Arturo Rodríguez de la Torre.

*Higher Centre of Theological Studies:* Seminario Metropolitano, Oviedo; Dir. Angel Fernández Llano.

*Institute of Ecclesiastical Studies of the Church in Galicia:* Plaza Immaculada 5, Santiago de Compostela; Dir. Carlos García Cortes.

*"Mater Ecclesiae" Theological Institute:* PP. Franciscanos, Plaza Andrés Hibernón 4, Murcia; Dir. Isidoro Rodríguez.

## UNIVERSIDAD DE SALAMANCA
PATIO DE ESCUELAS 1, APDO. 20, SALAMANCA

Telephone: 21-36-05, 21-68-00-03-04.

**Founded 1218 by Alfonso IX of León and reorganized 1254 by Alfonso X of Castile.**

*Rector:* D. Pedro Amat Muñoz.
*Vice-Rectors:* D. Feliciano Pérez Varas (Extension); D. Alfonso Domínguez-Gil Hurlé (Research); D. Manuel Peláez del Rosal (Graduation).
*Secretary:* D. Juan Alberto Izquierdo de la Torre.
*Administrator:* Benigno I. González Díez.
*Librarian:* Teresa Santander Rodríguez.

Library: *c.* 190,000 vols. and MSS.; the Faculty libraries have an additional 50,500 vols.

Number of teachers: 580.
Number of students: 16,000.

Publications: *Cuadernos de la Cátedra Miguel de Unamuno* (Faculty of Philosophy and Letters), *Zephyrus* (Archaeology), *Cuadernos de Historia de la Medicina Española* (Faculty of Medicine).

Deans:
*Faculty of Philology:* Antonio López Eire.
*Faculty of Geography and History:* Angel de Cabo Alonso.
*Faculty of Philosophy and Education:* José Gimeno Sacristán (acting).
*Faculty of Sciences:* Pedro Luis García Pérez.
*Faculty of Chemistry:* Joaquín de Pascual Teresa.
*Faculty of Biology:* Gregorio Nicolás Rodrigo.
*Faculty of Law:* Alfredo Calonge Matellanes.
*Faculty of Medicine:* Alberto Gómez Alonso.
*Faculty of Pharmacy:* Abel Mariné Font (acting).

Professors:
*Faculty of Philology:*
Bustos Tovar, Eugenio de, History of the Spanish Language
Castresana Udaeta, Ricardo, Latin Philology
Codoñer Merino, Carmen, Latin Philology
Cortés Vázquez, Luis, French Philology
Coy Ferrer, Francisco Javier, English Philology
Fernández Murga, Félix, Italian

García de la Concha, Víctor, History of Spanish Language and Literature
Hoz Bravo, Javier de, Greek Philology
López Eire, Antonio, Greek Philology and Literature
Llorente Maldonado, Antonio, Grammar and Literary Criticism
Navarro González, Alberto, History of Spanish Language and Literature
Pensado Tomé, José Luis, Romance Philology
Peréz Varas, Feliciano, German
Villar Liébana, Francisco, Indoeuropean Linguistics

*Faculty of Philosophy and Education:*
Cencillo Ramírez, Luis, Anthropology
Escolano Benito, Agustín, Introduction to Educational Science
Romano Pérez, Eugenia, Psychology

*Faculty of Geography and History:*
Caamaño Martínez, Jesús Ma., History of Art
Cabo Alonso, Angel de, Geography
Fernández Alvarez, Modern History
Gómez Molleda, Dolores, Contemporary World and Spanish History
Jordá Cerdá, Francisco, Archaeology, Epigraphy and Numismatics
Martín Rodríguez, José L., Medieval History
Vigil Pascual, Marcelo, Ancient World and Spanish History

*Faculty of Science:*
Agapito Serrano, Juan A. de, Electricity and Magnetism
Aldaya Vaverde, Florencio, Physical Geography
Arribas Moreno, Antonio, Geology
Barcala Herrero, José, Optics
Boya Balet, Luis J., Mathematical Physics
Corrales Zarauza, Immaculada, Stratigraphy
García de Figuerola, Luis C., Petrology
García Loygorri Urzaiz, Cristóbal, Algebra and Topology
García Pérez, Pedro L., Analytical Geometry
Garmendia Iraundegui, José, Physics
Ortega Aramburu, Joaquín Ma., Mathematical Analysis
Porta Vernet, Jaime de, Palaeontology
Sancho Guimerá, Juan B., Descriptive Geometry

*Faculty of Biology:*
Cabezas Fernández del Campo, José A., Biochemistry
Casaseca Mena, Bartolomé, Botany
Fuente Freire, José A. de la, Zoology
Nicolás Rodrigo, Gregorio, Plant Physiology
Rodríguez Villanueva, Julio, Microbiology

*Faculty of Chemistry:*
Alvarez González, José R., Technical Chemistry
Bañares Muñoz, Miguel A., Inorganic Chemistry
Hernández Méndez, Jesús, Analytical Chemistry
Herráez Zarza, Miguel A., Physical Chemistry
Pascual Teresa, Joaquín de, Organic Chemistry and Biochemistry

*Faculty of Law:*
Alonso Pérez, Mariano, Civil Law
Begué Cantón, Gloria, Political Economy and Public Finance

Beltrán de Heredia y Onis, Pablo, Civil Law
Calonge Matellanes, Alfredo, Roman Law
Delgado Pinto, José, Natural Law and Philosophy of Law
Echeverría, Lamberto de, Canon Law
González García, Eusebio, Financial and Tax Law
Martín Valverde, Antonio, Labour Law
Ortego Costales, José, Penal Law
Peláez del Rosal, Manuel, Procedural Law
Ramírez de Arellano Marcos, Vicente, International Law
Rivero Yrsen, Enrique, Administrative Law
Rojo Fernández, Angel J., Mercantile Law
Tomás y Valiente, Francisco de, History of Law
Vega García, Pedro de, Political Law

*Faculty of Medicine:*
Amat Muñoz, Pedro, Anatomy
Armijo Moreno, Miguel, Dermatology
Barahona Hortelano, José Ma., Ophthalmology
Bullón Sopelana, Agustín, Pathological Anatomy
Cañizo Suárez, Casimiro del, Otorhino-laryngology
Castro del Pozo, Sisinio de, General Pathology
Fernández Molina y Cañas, Antonio, Physiology
García Hernández, Angel, Obstetrics and Gynaecology
García Rodríguez, José Angel, Microbiology
Ledesma Jimeno, Matias, Psychiatry
Montero Gómez, Juan, Urology
Moya Pueyo, Vicente, Forensic Medicine
Portugal Alvarez, José de, Pathology and Clinical Medicine
Salazar Alonso-Villalobos, Valentín, Paediatrics and Puericulture
Sánchez Granjel, Luis, History of Medicine
Soler Ripoll, Jóse, Physical Therapeutics

*Faculty of Pharmacy:*
Domínguez-Gil Hurlé, Alfonso, Galenic Pharmacy
Giral González, Francisco, Organic Chemistry
Mariné Font, Abel, Bromatology and Toxicology
San Román del Barrio, Luis, Pharmacognosy and Pharmacodynamics

## UNIVERSIDAD DE SANTANDER
AVDA. DE LOS CASTROS S/N, SANTANDER

Telephone: 21-81-61, 21-99-61.

Telex: 35861 educi e.

**Founded 1972.**

State control; Language of instruction: Spanish; Academic year: October to June.

*Rector:* José Miguel Ortiz Melón.
*Vice-Rectors:* Alfredo Páez Balaca, Antolín Mellado Pollo, Miguel Rebolledo Sanz.
*Secretary-General:* José Luis Romero Palanco.

## SPAIN

*Librarian:* Juan Pablo Fusi Aizpurua.

Number of teachers: 503.
Number of students: 5,471.

Publication: *Memoria de la Universidad*† (annually).

### Deans:

*Higher Technical School of Road, Canal and Port Engineers:* Angel Uriarte González.
*Faculty of Science:* Salvador Bracho del Pino.
*Faculty of Medicine:* Juan José Jordá Catala.
*Faculty of Philosophy:* Ramón Teja Casuso.

### Professors:

*Faculty of Philosophy:*
García de Cortazar y Ruiz de Aguirre, J. A., Medieval History
Teja Casuso, R., Ancient, World and Spanish History

*Higher Technical School of Road, Canal and Port Engineers:*
Arenas, Juan José, Bridges
Castillo Ron, E., Mathematics III
García Diez de Villegas, J. M., Railways
Gómez-Laá, Guillermo, Applied Geology
González de Posada, F., Basic Physics of Technology
Izquierdo de Bartolome, R., Transport Economy and Co-ordination
Liria, José, Hydraulic Engineering
Losada Rodríguez, M. A., Ports
Páez, Alfredo, Reinforced and Prestressed Concrete
Quince Salas, R., Draughtsmanship
Sagaseta Millán, C., Geotechnology and Foundations
Samartín Quiroga, Avelino, Theory of Structures
Uriarte González, Angel, Economics

*Faculty of Science:*
Bracho Del Pino, Salvador, Electronics
Cendrero Uceda, A., Petrology
Lobo Hidalgo, M., Mathematical Analysis III
Onieva Aleixandre, V. M., Mathematical Analysis II
Santos, E., Atomic and Nuclear Physics
Villar García, E., General Physics
Mellado Pollo, A., Microbiology and Parasitology

*Faculty of Medicine:*
Flórez Beledo, Jesús, Pharmacology
Ojeda Sahagún, José Luis, Human Anatomy
Ortiz, Miguel, Biochemistry and General Physiology

### University Institutes:

*Escuela Universitaria del Profesorado de Educación General Básica:* Cisneros 74, Santander; Dir. Francisco Ruiloba Palazuelos.
*Escuela Universitaria de Ingeniería Técnica Industrial:* Sevilla 6, Santander; Dir. Antonio Acebes Chamorro.
*Escuela Universitaria de Ingeniería Técnica Minera:* Avda. de Oviedo s/n, Torrelavega; Dir. Miguel Remón Otí.
*Escuela Universitaria de Estudios Empresariales:* Avda. de los Castros s/n, Apdo. 231, Santander; Dir. Manuel Rodríguez Rodríguez.
*Escuela Universitaria de Formación del Profesorado de Educación General Básica "Sagrados Corazones":* Calle Sierrapando 470, Torrelavega, Santander; Dir. José Manuel Iglesias Gil.
*Escuela Universitaria de Enfermería "Casa Salud Valdecilla":* Avda. de Valdevilla s/n; Dir. José Ramón Berrazueta Fernández.

## UNIVERSIDAD DE SANTIAGO DE COMPOSTELA

PLAZA ESPAÑA, PALACIO DE SAN GERÓNIMO S/N, SANTIAGO DE COMPOSTELA

Telephone: (9) 58 38 00.

Founded 1501.

State control; Language of instruction: Spanish.

*Rector:* José María David Suárez Núñez.
*Vice-Rectors:* Agustín Fernández Albor, Manuel Díaz y Díaz.
*Secretary-General:* Gonzalo Vázquez Gómez.
*Administrator:* Dositeo Rodríguez Rodríguez.
*Librarian:* Daría Vilariño Pintos.

General Library: 100,000 volumes, over 100 incunabula, prayer book of Fernando I of Castile (11th century); other special libraries in the faculties.

Number of teachers: 975.
Number of students: 26,000.

Publications: *Trabajos Compostelanos de Biología, Memoria, Verba, Anuario Gallego de Filología, Anejos de la revista Verba, Cursos y Congresos de la Universidad de Santiago de Compostela, Monografías, Acta Científica Compostelana.*

### Deans:

*Faculty of Philosophy and Education:* Gonzálo Vásquez Gómez.
*Faculty of Law:* José A. Souto Paz.
*Faculty of Science:* Guillermo Rodríguez-Izqierdo Gavala.
*Faculty of Medicine:* Ramón Varela Núñez.
*Faculty of Pharmacy:* Francisco Guitián Ojea.
*Faculty of Economic and Business Science:* Luis Suárez-Llanos Gómez.
*Faculty of Philology:* Constantino García González.
*Faculty of Geography and History:* Ramón Otero Túñez.

University professional schools in La Coruña, Vigo, El Ferrol and Lugo.

## UNIVERSIDAD DE SEVILLA

CALLE DE SAN FERNANDO 4, SEVILLE

Telephone: 218600 (954).
Telex: 72161.
Founded 1502.

State control; Academic year: October to July.

*Rector:* Dr. Francisco González García.
*Vice-Rectors:* Dr. J. L. Justo Alpañés; Dr. J. Collantes de Terán; Dr. A. Valls Sánchez de Puerta.
*Administrator:* Lcdo. Manuel Pérez González.
*General Secretary:* Dr. A. Pérez Moreno.
*Librarian:* Lcda. Rocío Caracuel Moyano.
*Director, Publications and Scientific Interchange:* Dr. José Martínez Gijón.

Number of teachers: 1,553.
Number of students: 32,451.

Publication: *Anales de la Universidad Hispalense* (annually).

### Deans:

*Faculty of Geography and History:* Dr. Emilio Gómez Piñol.
*Faculty of Philology:* Dr. Vidal Lamíquiz Ibáñez.
*Faculty of Philosophy and Education:* Dr. Jesús Arellano Catalan.
*Faculty of Law:* Dr. Miguel Rodríguez-Piñero y Bravo-Ferrer.
*Faculty of Medicine:* Dr. Raimundo Goberna Ortiz.
*Faculty of Biology:* Dr. Julio Pérez Silva.
*Faculty of Physics:* Dr. Antón Civit Breu.
*Faculty of Mathematics:* Dr. Rafael Infante Macias.
*Faculty of Chemistry:* Dr. Juan Manuel Martínez Moreno.
*Faculty of Pharmacy:* Dr. J. Rubia Pacheco.
*Faculty of Economics (Business Administration Branch):* Dr. Guillermo J. Jiménez Sánchez.
*School of Architecture:* Dr. Pablo Arias García.
*School of Engineering:* Dr. Miguel Bermejo Herrero.
*Faculty of Fine Arts:* Dr. Juan Cordero Ruíz.
*Institute of Education:* Dr. Rafael Márquez Delgado.

### Professors:

*Faculty of Geography and History:*
Banda y Vargas, Antonio de la, History of Art
Benito Arranz, Juan, Geography
Calderón Quijano, José, American History
Cano García, Gabriel, Geography
Comellas García Llera, José-L., Contemporary History
Gil Munilla, Octavio, Modern Universal History
Gómez Piñol, Emilio, History of Spanish-American Art

González Jiménez, Manuel, Spanish and World Medieval History
Guerrero Lovillo, José, History of Art
Jiménez N., Alfredo, American Prehistory and Archaeology
Morales Padrón, Francisco, History of Geographical Discoveries and Geography of America
Navarro García, Luis, American History
Núñez Contreras, Luis, Spanish Palaeography
Pellicer Catalan, Manuel, Archaeology, Epigraphy and Numismatics
Presedo Velo, Francisco, Spanish Ancient History

*Faculty of Philology:*
Collantes de Teran y Collantes de Teran, Juan, History of Spanish-American Literature
Díaz-Regañón López, José Ma., Greek Language and Literature
Díaz Tejera, Alberto, Greek
García Tortosa, Francisco, English Language and Literature
Garnica Silva, Antonio, English Language
Gil Fernández, Juan, Latin Philology
Lamiquiz Ibañez, Vidal, Historic Spanish Grammar
Urrutia Gómez, Jorge, Spanish Language and Literature
Vázquez Ruíz, José, Arab Language and Literature
Yllera Fernández, Ma. Alicia, French Language

*Faculty of Philosophy and Education:*
Arellano Catalan, Jesús, Philosophy
Peñalver Simo, Patricio, Anthropology

*Faculty of Law:*
Aparici Díaz, José, Roman Law
Bernárdez Cantón, Alberto, Canon Law
Carrillo Salcedo, Manuel Fr., Administrative Law
Clavero Arévalo, Manuel, Administrative Law
García Añoveros, Jaime, Economics and Financial Law
Gutiérrez-Alviz Armario, Faustino, Law of Procedure
Jordano Barea, Juan, Civil Law
Lojendio e Irure, Ignacio Ma., Political Law
López y López, Angel Ma., Civil Law
Martínez Gijón, José, History of Spanish Law
Navarrete Urieta, José M., Penal Law
Olivencia Ruíz, M., Mercantile Law
Pérez Luño, Antonio E., Natural Law
Rodríguez-Piñero y Bravo-Ferrer, Miguel, Labour Law
Sánchez Appellaniz y Valderrama, Francisco, Private International Law

*Faculty of Biology:*
Cerda Olmedo, Enrique, Genetics
García Novo, Francisco, Ecology
López Campos, José Luis, Cytology
Losada Villasante, Manuel, Physiological Chemistry
Pablos y Casanova, Fernando de, Zoology
Pérez Silva, Julio, Microbiology
Valdes Castrillón, Benito, Botany

*Faculty of Physics:*
Civit Breu, Antón, Electricity and Magnetism
Madurga Lacalle, Gonzalo, Nuclear Physics
Márquez Delgado, Rafael, General Physics
Rubia Pacheco, Juan de la, Statistical Mechanics
Zamora Carranza, Manuel, Thermology

*Faculty of Mathematics:*
Castro Brzezicki, Antonio, Mathematics
Echarte Reula, Francisco J., Geometry
Infante Macias, Rafael, Mathematical Statistics
Valle Sánchez, Antonio, Mathematical Analysis

*Faculty of Chemistry:*
Bertrán Rusca, Juan, Physical Chemistry
Coy Ill, Ramón, Crystallography and Geology
González García, Francisco, Inorganic Chemistry
Martínez Moreno, Juan M., Chemical Engineering
Pereda Marín, Juan, Industrial Chemistry
Pino Pérez, Francisco, Analytical Chemistry

*Faculty of Medicine:*
Aznar Reig, Antonio, Pathology and Clinical Medicine
Bedoya González, José, Gynaecology and Obstetrics
Frontela Carreras, Forensic Medicine
Galera Davidson, Hugo, Histology
García Díaz, Sebastián, Clinical and Surgical Pathology
Garrido Peralta, Miguel, Pathology and Clinical Medicine
Genís Gálvez, José M., Anatomy
Giner Ubago, José, Psychiatry
Goberna Ortiz, Raimundo, Biochemistry
Jiménez-Castellanos y Calvo Rubio, Juan, Clinical and Medical Anatomy
Mir Jordano, Diego, Physiology and Biochemistry
Ocaña Sierra, Juan, Dermatology
Perea Pérez, Evelio J., Microbiology
Piñero Carrión, Antonio, Ophthalmology
Rodríguez Adrados, Felipe, Oto-Rhino-Laryngology
Romero Velasco, Enrique, General Pathology

*Faculty of Pharmacy:*
Adzet Porredón, Tomás, Pharmacognosy and Pharmacodynamics
Alcudia González, Felipe, Organic Chemistry
Faulí Trillo, Claudio, Galenic Pharmacy
Trillo de Leyva, José M., Inorganic Chemistry

*Faculty of Economics (Business Administration Branch):*
García Barbancho, Alfonso, Econometrics and Statistical Methods
Jiménez Sánchez, Guillermo, Mercantile Law
Lebón Fernández, Camilo, Economics
Ortigueira Bouzada, Manuel, Business Administration
Sáez Torrecilla, Angel, Accountancy Theory

*Faculty of Fine Arts:*
Arquillo Torres, Francisco, Restoration
Berriobeña Elorza, Ignacio, Printing
Borras Verdera, Francisco, Drawing moving figures from Nature
Cordero Ruíz, Juan, Perspective Geometric Drawing
García del Moral y Garrido, Amalio, Classic Techniques of Drawing
García Gómez, Francisco, Ornamental Drawing
García Ruíz, José Antonio, Techniques of Painting
Gavira Alba, Antonio, Preparation of Clay Modelling
Gutiérrez Fernández, Miguel, Landscape Drawing
Jiménez Serrano, Carmen, Clay Modelling and Composition
Maireles Vela, Francisco, Preparation of Colours
Pérez Aguilera, Miguel, Drawing from Nature
Rio Llabona, Armando del, Colouring and Composition
Romero Escassi, José, Artistic Anatomy
Sancho Corbacho, Antonio, History of Design

*School of Architecture:*
Arias García, Pablo, Urban Planning
Balbuena Cavallini, Fernando, Mathematics
Donaire Rodríguez, Alberto, Composition
Espejo y Pérez de la Concha, Enrique, Legislation and Assessment
García de Castro Márquez, Emilio, Design
García Diéguez, Rafael, Construction
García Valcarce, Antonio, Construction
Gómez de Terreros Sánchez, Aurelio, Construction Materials
Hervás Burgos, Pablo, Physics
Justo Alpañes, José Luis, Soil Mechanics and Foundations
López de Asiaín Martín, Jaime, Composition
López Palanco, Rafael, Structure
Manzanares Japón, José L., Structure
Manzano Martos, Rafael, History of Architecture
Recasens-Mendez Queipo de Llano, Luis, Design

*School of Engineering:*
Aguilar Clavijo, Manuel, Siderurgy
Barrero y Ripoll, Antonio, Mechanics
Bermejo Herrero, Miguel, Technical Drawing
Cos Castillo, Manuel Alejandro de, Project
Domínguez Abascal, Jaime, Mechanism and Machines Theory
Gracia Manarillo, Ignacio, Chemistry
Hernández Iglesias, Feliciano, Economics
Lozano Campoy, José, Physics
Martín Pérez, Antonio, Chemistry
Morales Palomino, Sisenando C., Industrial Construction
Ranninger Rodríguez, Carlos, Metallurgy
Ruiz Hernández, Valeriano, Thermodynamics
Salvador Martínez, Luis, Chemistry Technology

## UNIVERSIDAD DE VALENCIA
NAVE 2, VALENCIA 3
Telephone: 32-173-80.

Founded 1500

*Rector:* Joaquín Colomer Sala.
*Vice-Rectors:* José A. Gómez Segade, José Viña Giner, Pedro Pérez

Puchal, Angel Ma. Villar del Fresno.
*Administrative Officer:* Francisco Egea Bombarelli.
*Secretary:* Jesús Rodríguez Marín.
*Librarian:* Pilar Gómez.

The University Library contains 216,204 vols. and 2,432 MSS. Libraries are also attached to each faculty.

Number of teachers: 1,070.
Number of students: 24,257.

Publication: *Memoria Anual.*

DEANS:

*Faculty of Geography and History:* Julián San Valero Aparisi.
*Faculty of Philosophy and Education:* Fernando Montero Moliner.
*Faculty of Law:* Antonio Mostaza Rodríguez.
*Faculty of Mathematical Sciences:* Lorenzo Ferrer Figueras.
*Faculty of Medicine:* Francisco Gomar Guarner.
*Faculty of Economics:* Ángel Orti Lahoz.
*Faculty of Pharmacy:* Enrique Hernandez Giménez.
*Faculty of Philology:* Angel R. Fernández González.
*Faculty of Physical Sciences:* Mariano Aguilar Rico.
*Faculty of Biology:* José L. Mensua Fernández.
*Faculty of Chemistry:* Francisco Bosch Reig.

PROFESSORS:

*Faculty of Geography and History:*
Lamagro Gorbea, Martín, Archaeology, Epigraphy and Numismatics
Pérez Puchal, Pedro, Geography
Rosello Verger, Vicente María, Geography
San Valero Aparisi, Julián, Prehistory and World History
Sebastián López, Santiago, History of Art
Tusell Gómez, Javier, Contemporary World and Spanish History

*Faculty of Philology:*
Fernández González, Angel R., Spanish Language and Literature and World Literature

*Faculty of Philosophy and Education:*
Carpintero Capell, H., Psychology
Garrido Giménez, M., Logic
Gutiérrez Zuluaga, Ma. Isabel, History of Education
Marín Ibáñez, R., General Education
Montero Moliner, Fernando, History of Philosophy
Pelechano Barberá, Vicente, Psychology
Secadas Marcos, F., Psychology

*Faculty of Law:*
Almansa Pastor, José Manuel, Labour Law
Boquera Oliver, José María, Administrative Law
Broseta Pont, Manuel, Commercial Law
Cobo del Rosal, Manuel, Penal Law
Ferreiro Lapatza, José J., Financial and Taxation Law
García González, Juan, History of Spanish Law
Gitrama González, Manuel, Civil Law
Lalaguna Domínguez, Enrique, Civil Law
Miaja de la Muela, Adolfo, International Public and Private Law
Montero Aroca, Juan, Procedural Law
Mostaza Rodríguez, Antonio, Canon Law
Sevilla Andrés, Diego, Political Law
Valiño del Rio, Emilio, Roman Law

*Faculty of Science:*
Aguilar Rico, Mariano, Material Structure and Optics
Beltrán Martínez, José, Inorganic Chemistry
Bosch Reig, Francisco, Analytical Chemistry
Docavo Alberti, Ignacio, Zoology
Escardino Benlloch, Agustín, Technical Chemistry
Ferrer Figueras, Lorenzo, Mathematics
Gandia Gomar, Vicente, Termology
Gutiérrez Cabria, Segundo, Statistics and Calculus of Probability
Lloret Sebastián, José Luis, Electricity and Magnetism
Mansanet Mansanet, José, Botany
Martínez Naveira, Antonio, Geometry
Mensua Fernández, J. L., Genetics
Núñez Cachazo, Antonio, Animal Physiology
Pérez Monasor, Francisco, Algebra
Senent Pérez, Fernando, Theoretical Experimental Physics
Seoane Bardanca, Eliseo, Organic Chemistry
Sesma Bienzobas, Javier, Mathematical Physics
Valdivia Ureña, Manuel, Mathematical Analysis
Villar del Fresno, Ángel, Pharmacognosy and Pharmacodynamics

*Faculty of Medicine:*
Báguena Candela, Rafael, Genetics
Belloch Zimmermann, Vicente, Therapeutics
Carbonell Antolí, Carlos, Surgical and Clinical Pathology
Carmena Villarta, Miguel, Pathology
Carreras Matas, Marcelo, Ophthalmology
Colomer Sala, Joaquín, Paediatrics and Puericulture
Esplugues Requena, Juan, Pharmacology
García-Conde Gómez, Francisco Javier, Pathology and Clinical Medicine
Gisbert Calabuig, Juan Antonio, Forensic Medicine
Gomar Guarner, Francisco, Surgical and Clinical Pathology
Llombart Bosch, Antonio, Histology, Embryology and Pathological Anatomy
López Piñero, José Ma., Medical History
Marco Clemente, Jaime, Oto-Rhino-Laryngology
Rojo Sierra, Miguel, Psychiatry
Smith Agreda, Victor, Anatomy
Valdes Ruiz, Manuel, Pathology
Viña Giner, José María, Physiology, Biochemistry

*Faculty of Economics and Business Studies:*
Campos Nodmann, Ramiro, Comparative Economic Structures and Institutes
Ferrando Badia, Juan, State and Constitutional Law
Gómez Segade, J. A., Mercantile Law
González y Catala, Vicente T., Mathematics of Financial Transactions
Orti Lahoz, Ángel, Economic Theory
Sánchez Ayuso, Manuel, Politico-economics
Santamaria Pastor, Juan A., Administrative Law
Tortella Casares, Gabriel, Spanish and World Economic History
Vela Pastor, Manuel, Accounting Theory

## UNIVERSIDAD DE VALLADOLID

VALLADOLID 8
Telephone: 29.94.99.

Founded 1346.

*Rector:* Dr. Alfonso Candau Parias.
*Vice-Rectors:* Dr. Juan Ayala Montoro, Dr. Olegario Ortiz Manchado, Dr. Juán José Martín González.
*Administrative Officer:* Nicolás García Díez.
*Secretary:* Dr. José Luis de los Mozos y de los Mozos.
*Librarian:* Dra. Nieves Alonso-Cortes.

The library contains 134,000 volumes
Number of students: 5,345 men, 2,082 women.

DEANS:

*Faculty of Law:* Dr. Carlos de Miguel y Alonso.
*Faculty of Science:* Dr. José Manuel Aroca Hernández-Ros.
*Faculty of Philosophy and Letters:* Dr. Alberto Balil Illana.
*Faculty of Medicine:* Dr. Antonio Rodríguez Torres.
*Faculty of Political, Economic and Commercial Sciences:* Dr. Julio García Villalón.

PROFESSORS:

*Faculty of Law:*
Azcarraga y Bustamante, J., International Law
Baena del Alcázar, M., Administrative Law
Brufau Prats, J., Philosophy of Law
Duque Domínguez, Justino, Commercial Law
García Villarejo, Avelino, Economy and Public Finance
Guilarte Zapatero, Vicente, Civil Law
López Pina, A., Political Law
Martínez Díez, G., History of Law
Miguel y Alonso, C., Judicial Procedure
Mozos de los Mozos, J. L. de los, Civil Law
Prieto Prieto, A., Canon Law
Torio López, Angel, Criminal Law
Torrent Ruiz, A., Roman Law

*Faculty of Science:*
Alberola Figueroa, A., Organic Chemistry
Aleixandre Campos, Vicente, Industrial Physics
Aroca Hernández-Ros, J. M., Geometry
Ayala Montoro, J., Electrical Physics
Casanova, Colás José, Physics
Gutiérrez Suárez, Juan J., Mathematical Analysis

MARTÍN DÍAZ, M., Statistics
MARTÍNEZ SALAS, JOSÉ, Mathematics
MATO VÁZQUEZ, F., Technical Chemistry
QUINTANILLA MONTÓN, M., Optics
RECIO PASCUAL, J. M., Biology
RIERA GONZÁLEZ, VÍCTOR, Inorganic Chemistry
SENENT PÉREZ, SALVADOR, Electro-Chemistry

*Faculty of Medicine:*
ALVAREZ QUIÑONES CARAVIAS, PEDRO, Dermatology
BELMONTE GONZÁLEZ, NICOLÁS, Ophthalmology
BELMONTE MARTÍNEZ, CARLOS, Physiology
BELTRÁN DE HEREDIA ONÍS, JOSÉ MA., Surgical Pathology
CARDESA GARCÍA, ANTONIO, Anatomical Pathology
CONDE LÓPEZ, VALENTÍN, Psychiatry
GÓMEZ BOSQUE, PEDRO, Anatomy
GONZÁLEZ PÉREZ, M., Oto-Rhino-Laryngology
HERREROS FERNÁNDEZ, B., Physiology
LOPEZ LARA, F., Physical Therapeutics
MARAÑÓN CABELLO, A., Medical Pathology
NAVARRO CLEMENTE, JOSÉ, Obstetrics and Gynaecology
ORTIZ MANCHADO, OLEGARIO, Medical Pathology
RIERA PALMERO, J., History of Medicine
RODRÍGUEZ TORRES, ANTONIO, Hygiene
SÁNCHEZ S. VILLARES, ERNESTO, Paediatrics
VELASCO ALONSO, RAMÓN, General Pathology
VELASCO MARTÍN, A., Pharmacology

*Faculty of Philosophy and Letters:*
BALIL ILLANA, ALBERTO, Archaeology
BRAVO LOZANO, MILLÁN, Latin
CANDAU PARIAS, ALFONSO, Theory of Knowledge
ENCISO RECIO, LUIS MIGUEL, Modern World History
FRADEJAS LEBRERO JOSÉ, Spanish Language and Literature
GARCÍA FERNÁNDEZ, JESÚS, Geography
HERNÁNDEZ RODRÍGUEZ, F., French Language
MARCOS MARÍN, F., Spanish History
MARTÍN GONZÁLEZ, JUAN JOSÉ, History of Art
MONTENEGRO DUQUE, ANGEL, Ancient and Medieval Spanish History
MOZOS Y MOCHA, S., General Grammar
RAMOS PÉREZ, D., American History
RUIZ ASENCIO, JOSÉ M., Palaeography and Diplomatics
VALDEÓN BARUQUE, J., Ancient and Medieval History

*Faculty of Political, Economic and Commercial Sciences:*
GARCÍA VILLALÓN, J., Business Mathematics
RAMOS, CERVERO R., Theory of Accountancy
RODRÍGUEZ ARTIGAS, F., Mercantile Law
TOÑA BASAURI, IGNACIO, Economics of Management

*Faculty of Law (San Sebastian):*
BERISTAIN IPIÑA, A., Criminal Law
CALVO ORTEGA, R., Public Finance
DORAL GARCÍA, JOSÉ ANTONIO, Civil Law
FERNÁNDEZ RODRÍGUEZ, T., Administrative Law
GARCÍA, CANTERO GABRIEL, Civil Law
GUILARTE ZAPATERO, V., Civil Law
GUTIÉRREZ ALVIZ, F., Procedural Law
MONTALVO CORREA, J., Labour Law

MORENO QUESADA, B., Civil Law
SALCEDO IZU, JOAQUÍN, History of Law
SAMPER, POLO, F., Roman Law

ATTACHED INSTITUTE:
**Instituto Vasco de Criminología** (*Basque Institute of Criminology*): Facultad de Derecho, San Sebastian; f. 1978; 230 mems.; library of 6,000 vols., 40 periodicals; Dir. Dr. ANTONIO BERISTAIN.

## UNIVERSIDAD DE ZARAGOZA
PLAZA SAN FRANCISCO,
CIUDAD UNIVERSITARIA,
ZARAGOZA

Telephone: 35-41-00.

Telex: 58064.

Founded in 1533 by the Emperor Carlos V.

State control; Language of instruction: Spanish; Academic year: October to May.

*Rector:* FEDERICO LÓPEZ MATEOS.
*Vice-Rectors:* JULIÁN SANZ ESPONERA, ISAIAS ZARAZAGA BURILLO, VICENTE BIELZA DE ORY, MANUEL RAMÍREZ JIMÉNEZ.
*Registrar:* GUILLERMO R. ROMEO Y AZNAR.
*Secretary-General:* JOSÉ BERMEJO VERA.
*Director of Publications Office:* ANTONIO UBIETO ARIETA.

The library contains 600,000 vols.

Number of teachers: 1,077.
Number of students: 17,049.

Publications: *Temas, Archivos de la Facultad de Medicina, Anales de la Facultad de Veterinaria, Guía, Boletín Informativo.*

DEANS:

*Faculty of Philosophy and Letters:* Dr. ANTONIO BELTRÁN MARTÍNEZ.
*Faculty of Law:* JUAN RIVERO LAMAS.
*Faculty of Science:* JOSÉ MARÍA SAVIRÓN DE CIDÓN.
*Faculty of Medicine:* MANUEL BUENO SÁNCHEZ.
*Faculty of Veterinary Science:* JOSÉ ANTONIO BASCUAS ASTA.
*Faculty of Economics and Business Studies:* ANTONIO AZNAR GRASA.
*Higher School of Industrial Engineering:* FCO. JAVIER CASTANY VALERY.

PROFESSORS:

*Faculty of Philosophy and Letters:*
BELTRÁN MARTÍNEZ, ANTONIO, Archaeology, Epigraphy and Numismatics
BIELZA DE ORY, VICENTE, Geography
BUESA OLIVIER, TOMÁS, Spanish Language
CANELLAS LÓPEZ, ANGEL, Palaeography
CARRERAS ARES, JUAN JOSÉ, Contemporary General and Spanish History
CORONA BARATECH, CARLOS, Contemporary World History
CORRIENTE CÓRDOBA, FEDERICO, Arabic Language and Literature
GARCÍA MORENO, LUIS AGUSTÍN, Ancient General and Spanish History

HIGUERAS ARNAL, ANTONIO, Geography
LOMBA FUENTES, JOAQUÍN, History of Philosophy
MIRALBES BEDHA, MA. ROSARIO, Geography
MONGE CASO, TADEO FÉLIX, Spanish Grammar and Literary Criticism
PÉREZ GALLEGO, CANDIDO, English
RODÓN BINUÉ, EULALIA, Latin Language and Literature
ROMERO TOBAR, LEONARDO, Spanish Literature
SOLANO COSTA, FERNANDO, Modern Spanish History
TORRALBA SORIANO, FEDERICO, History of Art
UBIETA ARTETA, ANTONIO, Ancient and Medieval Spanish History and Prehistory

*Faculty of Law:*
CALVO OTERO, JUAN, Canon Law
CEREZO MIR, JOSÉ, Criminal Law
FERNÁNDEZ FLORES, JOSÉ LUIS, International Law
GARCÍA AMIGO, MANUEL, Civil Law
GARCÍA CANTERO, GABRIEL, Civil Law
GIL CREMADES, J. J., Philosophy of Law
MARTÍN-BALLESTRO COSTEA, LUIS, Civil Law
MARTÍN-RETORTILLO B. L., Administrative Law
MURGA GENER, J. L., Roman Law
PALAO TABOADA, CARLOS, Economics
PÉREZ GORDO, ALFONSO, Procedural Law
RAMÍREZ JIMÉNEZ, M., Political Law
RIVERO LAMAS, JUAN, Labour Law
SANTOS MARTÍNEZ, VICENTE, Mercantile Law

*Faculty of Science:*
ARRESE SERRANO, FÉLIX, Crystallography, Mineralogy and Mineral Technology
AZNAREZ ALDUAN, JOSÉ L., Analytical Chemistry
CORELLA TUDANCA, JOSÉ, Technical Chemistry
CASAS PELAEZ, JUSTINIANO, Optics
CID PALACIOS, RAFAEL, Astronomy
DEL MORAL GAMIZ, AGUSTÍN, Electricity and Magnetism
GARAY DE PABLO, JOSÉ, Mathematical Analysis
GUTIÉRREZ LOSA, CELSO, Physical Chemistry and Electrochemistry
LÓPEZ MATEOS, FEDERICO, Industrial Chemistry
MARTÍNEZ GIL, JAVIER, Physical Geography
MELÉNDEZ ANDREU, E., Organic Chemistry and Biochemistry
MIRACLE SOLE, S., Theoretical Physics
MORALES VILLASEVIL, ANGEL, Atomic and Nuclear Physics
NÚÑEZ-LAGOS ROGLA, R., Mechanical Calculus
PLANS SANZ DE BREMOND, ANTONIO, Analytical Geometry and Topography
QUINTANILLA MONTÓN, MANUEL, General Physics
RAMOS SALAVERT, ISIDORO, Electronics
RODRÍGUEZ-VIDAD, RAFAEL, Mathematical Analysis, Algebra
SÁNCHEZ CELA, VICENTE ERNESTO, Petrology
SANCHO SAN ROMÁN, J., Project and Descriptive Geometry
SAVIRÓN CIDÓN, JOSÉ M., Mechanics and Thermology
SESMA BENZOBAS, JAVIER, Mathematical Physics
TORRES IGLESIAS, MIGUEL, Algebra
USÓN LACAL, RAFAEL, Inorganic Chemistry

Vigil Vázquez, Angel-luis, Mathematical Analysis
Viviente Mateu, José L., Differential Geometry

*Faculty of Medicine:*
Balaguer Periguell, Emilio, History of Medicine
Bueno Sánchez, Manuel, Paediatrics
Bueno Gómez, José, Pathology and Clinical Medicine
Carapeto Márquez de Prado, José, Dermatology and Venerology
Escolar García, José, Anatomy
Fairén Guillén, Manuel, Oto-rhino-laryngology
González González, Manuel, Pathology and Clinical Surgery
Guillén Martínez, Gabriel, General Pathology
Jiménez González, Luis, Anatomy
Lozano Mantecón, Ricardo, Pathology and Clinical Surgery
Marín Gorriz, Francisco, Radiology and Physical Medicine
Martinez Hernandez, Heraclio, Obstetrics and Gynaecology

Pié Jorda, Andrés, Physiology
Piñeiro Bustamente, Antonio, Ophthalmology
Romero Aguirre, Francisco, Urology
Sanz Esponera, Julián, Histology
Seva Díaz, Antonio, Psychiatry

*Faculty of Veterinary Science:*
Ballesteros Moreno, Emilio, Pharmacology
Bascuas Asta, José Antonio, Histology and Pathological Anatomy
Herrera Marteache, Antonio, Bromatology and Microbiology of Foodstuffs
López Lorenzo, Pascual, Meat, Milk and Fish Industries
Martín Martín, Eloy, Surgery and Reproduction
Murillo Ferrol, Narciso, L., Descriptive Anatomy
Ocaña García, Manuel, Agriculture and Agrarian Economics
Sainz y Sainz Pardo, Jesús, Physiology

Sánchez Franco, Angel, Parasitology and Infectious Diseases
Vera y Vega, Alfonso, Animal Products
Zarazaga Burillo, Isaias, Genetics

*Faculty of Economics and Business Studies:*
Aznar Grasa, Antonio, Econometric and Statistical Methods
Cruz Roche, Ignacio, Company Economics
Fernández Arupe, Josefa E., Economic Policy
Pablo López, Andres de, Mathematics of Financial Operations

*Higher School of Industrial Engineering:*
Camarena Badia, V., Mathematics
Castany Valeri, F. J., Cinematics and Dynamics of Machines
Correas Dobato, J. M., Mathematics

There are attached University Schools and Colleges in other towns.

## POLYTECHNICS

### UNIVERSIDAD POLITÉCNICA DE BARCELONA

AVDA. GREGORIO MARAÑÓN S/N, BARCELONA 34

Telephone: 249-3804/3/2.

Founded 1971.

Autonomous control under Ministry of Universities and Research; Languages of instruction: Spanish and Catalan; Academic year: October to June.

*Rector:* Gabriel A. Ferraté Pascual.

*Vice-Rectors:* Pedro Ramón Moliner, Enrique Ras Oliva, Manuel Martí Recober, Alberto Corominas Subías, Juan Llaverías Sanmarti, José Ma. Valeri Ferret.

*Administrative Director:* Francisco Javier Puig Rovira.

Libraries: each constituent school has a library attached.

Number of teachers: 1,622.
Number of students: 16,491.

Publications: *Guía del estudiante, Boletín U.P B.*

Constituent Schools:

**Escuela Técnica Superior de Arquitectura:** Dir. Oriol Bohigas Guardiola.

**Escuela Técnica Superior de Ingenieros Industriales de Barcelona:** Dir. Jaime Blasco Font de Rubinat.

**Escuela Técnica Superior de Ingenieros Industriales de Tarrasa:** Dir. Luis Virto Albert.

**Escuela Técnica Superior de Ingenieros de Telecomunicación:** Dir. Jesús Galván Ruiz.

**Escuela Técnica Superior de Ingenieros de Caminos, Canales y Puertos:** Dir. Eduardo Alonso Pérez de Agreda.

**Escuela Universitaria de Arquitectura Técnica:** Dir. Eugenio Llopart Coll.

**Escuela Universitaria de Ingeniería Técnica Industrial de Tarrasa:** Dir. Fernando González Lagunas.

**Escuela Universitaria de Ingeniería Técnica Industrial de Villanueva y Geltrú:** Dir. Juan Majó Torrent.

**Escuela Universitaria de Ingeniería Técnica Agrícola de Lérida:** Dir. Juan Antonio Martín Sánchez.

**Escuela Universitaria Politécnica de Gerona:** Dir. José Arnau Figuerola.

**Escuela Universitaria Politécnica de Manresa:** Dir. Juan E. Segarra Hernández.

**Escuela Universitaria de Optica de Tarrasa:** Dir. Fernando González Lagunas.

**Escuela Técnica Superior de Ingenieros Agrónomos de Lérida:** Dir. Juan Antonio Martín Sánchez.

**Escuela Técnica Superior de Arquitectura del Vallés:** Dir. Carlos Fochs Alvarez.

**Facultad de Informática:** Dir. Manuel Martí Recober.

Attached Institutes:

**Instituto de Ingeniería Cibernética:** Diagonal 647, Barcelona 28; Dir. Luis Basañez Villaluenga (acting).

**Instituto de Investigación Textil y Cooperación Industrial:** Colon 11, Tarrasa; Dir. José Cegarra Sánchez.

**Instituto de Ciencias de la Educación:** Diagonal 647, Barcelona 28; Dir. Fernando Puerta Sales.

**Instituto de Petrolquimia Aplicada:** Diagonal 647, Barcelona 28; Dir. Jaime Blasco Font de Rubinat.

**Instituto de Investigación Aplicada al Automóvil:** Diagonal 647, Barcelona 28; Dir. Victor de Buen Lozano.

**Instituto de Técnicas Energéticas:** Diagonal 647, Barcelona 28; Dir. Javier Ortega Arranburu.

### UNIVERSIDAD POLITÉCNICA DE LAS PALMAS

CASA COLÓN/HERRERÍA 1, LAS PALMAS, CANARY ISLANDS

Telephone: 31.23.73.

Founded 1980.

*Rector:* Javier de Cárdenas y Chávarri.

*Vice-Rectors:* Sergio Pérez Parrilla, Julio Melian Pérez-Marín, Juan Pulido Castro.

Number of teachers: 350.
Number of students: 2,100.

Deans:

*Higher Technical School of Architecture:* Simón Marchán Fiz.

*Higher Technical School of Industrial Engineers:* Alvaro Gómez Sabucedo.

*University Polytechnic School:* Rafael Estevez Reyes.

*University School of Agricultural Engineers:* Ciro Casanova Bento.

*University School of Technical Architecture:* Melchor Ruiz-Benítez de Lugo y Zaráte.

## UNIVERSIDAD POLITÉCNICA DE MADRID

CEA BERMÚDEZ 14,
MADRID 3
Telephone: 254-02-27.
Founded 1971.

State control; Language of instruction: Spanish; Academic year: October to July.

*Rector:* Dr. Rafael Portaencasa Baeza.
*Vice-Rectors:* D. Carlos Benito Hernández, D. Juan del Campo Aguilera, D. Luis de Mazarredo Beutel.
*Registrar:* Manuel Balgañón Moreno.
*Secretary-General:* D. Jesús Langreo y Langreo.

There is a library attached to each constituent school of the University.

Number of teachers: c. 2,800.
Number of students: 33,000.

CONSTITUENT SCHOOLS:

**Escuela Técnica Superior de Ingenieros Aeronáuticos:** Ciudad Universitaria; Dir. Juan de Burgos Román.

**Escuela Técnica Superior de Arquitectura:** Juan de Herrera 4; Dir. Juan del Corro Gutiérrez.

**Escuela Técnica Superior de Ingenieros Agrónomos:** Ciudad Universitaria; Dir. Joaquín Miranda de Onís.

**Escuela Técnica Superior de Ingenieros de Caminos, Canales y Puertos:** Ciudad Universitaria; Dir. Enrique Balaguer Camphuí.

**Escuela Técnica Superior de Ingenieros Industriales:** Gutiérrez Abascal 2; Dir. Emilio Bautista Paz.

**Escuela Técnica Superior de Ingenieros de Minas:** Ríos Rosas 21; Dir. Emilio Llorente Gómez.

**Escuela Técnica Superior de Ingenieros de Montes:** Ciudad Universitaria; Dir. Ignacio Claver Torrente.

**Escuela Técnica Superior de Ingenieros Navales:** Ciudad Universitaria; Dir. José M. de los Ríos Claramunt.

**Escuela Técnica Superior de Ingenieros de Telecomunicación:** Ciudad Universitaria; Dir. Narciso García Redondo.

**Escuela Universitaria de Ingeniería Técnica Aeronáutica:** Ciudad Universitaria; Dir. Jacinto Alonso Las Peñas.

**Escuela Universitaria de Arquitectura Técnica:** Ciudad Universitaria; Dir. Ricardo Bielsa Padilla.

**Escuela Universitaria de Ingeniería Técnica Agrícola:** Ciudad Universitaria; Dir. Fernando Ruiz García.

**Escuela Universitaria de Ingeniería Técnica Agrícola de Ciudad Real:** Ciudad Real; Dir. Eduardo Iriarte Burgos.

**Escuela Universitaria de Ingeniería Técnica Forestal:** Ciudad Universitaria; Dir. Pio Alfonso Pita Carpenter.

**Escuela Universitaria de Ingeniería Técnica Industrial:** Ronda de Valencia 3, Madrid 5; Dir. Higinio Gascón Sánchez Cerrudo.

**Escuela Universitaria Politécnica:** Almadén, Ciudad Real; Dir. Luis Juan Mateo López.

**Escuela Universitaria de Ingeniería Técnica de Obras Publicas:** Alfonso XII 5, Madrid 7; Dir. Emilio Sicilia Ródenas.

**Escuela Universitaria de Ingeniería Técnica de Telecomunicación:** Ciudad Universitaria; Dir. Mario Meléndez Rolla.

**Escuela Universitaria de Ingeniería Técnica de Topografía:** Gral. Ibáñez de Ibero 3, Madrid 3; Dir. Nicolás Serramo Colmenarejo.

**Escuela Universitaria de Informática:** Carretera de Valencia km. 7, Madrid 31; Dir. Rafael Portaencasa Baeza.

## UNIVERSIDAD POLITÉCNICA DE VALENCIA

CAMPUS DEL CAMINO DE VERA, APDO. 2012, VALENCIA 15
Telephone: 369-67-00.
Founded 1968.

State control; Languages of instruction: Spanish, English, French and German; Academic year: September to July.

*Rector:* Prof. Dr. Saturnino de la Plaza Pérez.
*Vice-Rector:* Prof. Dr. Ing. José Juárez Mateos.
*Administrative Director:* D. Germán Marco Ponce.
*Secretary-General:* Fernando Romero Saura.
*Librarian:* (vacant).

Number of teachers: c. 500.
Number of students: c. 6,000.

CONSTITUENT SCHOOLS:

**Escuela Técnica Superior de Ingenieros Agrónomos:** Paseo del Mar 21, Valencia 10; Dir. D. Saturnino de la Plaza Pérez.

**Escuela Técnica Superior de Arquitectura:** Plaza de Galicia 4, Valencia 10; Dir. (vacant).

**Escuela Técnica Superior de Ingenieros de Caminos, Canales y Puertos:** Campus del Camino de Vera, Valencia 11; Dir. D. Vicente Delgado de Molina y Juliá.

**Escuela Técnica Superior de Ingenieros Industriales:** Campus del Camino de Vera, Valencia 11; Dir. D. José Luis Manglano de Mas.

**Escuela Universitaria de Ingeniería Técnica Agrícola:** Paseo al Mar 19, Valencia 10; Dir. D. Vicente Puertas Bonilla.

**Escuela Universitaria de Ingeniería Técnica Industrial:** Paseo Calvo Sotelo 1, Alcoy (Alicante); Dir. D. Octavio Candela Carbonell.

**Escuela Universitaria de Ingeniería Técnica Industrial:** Av. José Antonio 46, Valencia 5; Dir. D. Vicente Tortosa La-Casta.

**Escuela Universitaria de Ingeniería Técnica de Obras Públicas:** San Vicente del Raspeig (Alicante); Dir. D. Sergio Campos Ferrera.

**Escuela Universitaria de Arquitectura Técnica:** Campus del Camino de Vera, Valencia 11; Dir. D. Luis Ortiz Berrocal.

## TECHNICAL UNIVERSITIES

**Centro de Enseñanzas Integradas (Universidad Laboral) de Alcalá de Henares:** Campo del Angel, Madrid; f. 1966; c. 1,800 students; Rector Dr. José Ma. Azáceta y García de Albéniz; Administrative Sec. Francisco Carmona Galisteo.

**Centro de Enseñanzas Integradas (Universidad Laboral) de Eibar:** Avda. de Bilbao 29, Eibar; f. 1968; 78 professors, 1,200 students; library of 10,000 vols.; Dir. José Ignacio Borinaga López; Administrator Francisco Riesco Galache; Sec. Itziar Aseguiuolaza Badiola; publs. *Abots Berriak, Orain* (University Revues), *Boletín Informativo* (fortnightly), *Memoria de Actividades* (annually).

**Centro de Enseñanzas Integradas (Universidad Laboral) de la Coruña:** Aptdo. de Correos 736, La Coruña; f. 1964; nautical and fishery studies; technical and industrial training; 850 internal students, 700 external students; library of 15,000 vols.; Rector Martín Díaz González; Dir. of Studies Domiciano García Martín; publ. *Memoria General de Actividades*.

**Centro de Enseñanzas Integradas (Universidad Laboral) de Zaragoza:** Apdo. de Correos 619, Zaragoza; f. 1967;

*c.* 1,620 female students; library of 15,000 vols.; Dir. José Antonio Perales Anton; Administrator Jesús Gómez de la Guerra; publ. *Memoria anual de actividades del Centro.*

**Centro de Enseñanzas Integradas (Universidad Laboral) "Francisco Franco":** Apdo. de Correos 119, Carretera de Salou s/n., Tarragona; f. 1956; private control; 325 staff, 1,975 students; library of 27,077 vols.; Rector Victoriano Martín Urquizu; Gen. Sec. Juan Noguera y Salort.

**Centro de Enseñanzas Integradas (Universidad Laboral) "José Antonio Girón":** Girón, Asturias; f. 1955; 330 staff, 2,000 students; library of 40,000 vols.; Rector Viliulfo Díaz Pérez; Administrative Sec. Julio Fanjul Calleja; publs. *La Torre de la Universidad Laboral.*

**Centro de Enseñanzas Integradas (Universidad Laboral) de Sevilla:** Carretera de Utrera, Sevilla; f. 1956; 1,600 students; library of 12,000 vols.; Rector Manuel Yoldi Delgado; Head of Studies José Olivero Troncoso; publs. academic theses and scientific research reports.

**Centro de Enseñanzas Integradas (Universidad Laboral) Onésimo Redondo de Córdoba:** Carretera de Madrid-Cádiz s/n., Córdoba; f. 1956; 70 professors, 1,584 students; library of 8,543 vols.; Rector Fr. Santiago Pirallo Prieto, o.p.; Sec. Enrique Pozón Lobato; Registrar Fr. Santiago Guerrero Contreras, o.p.; Librarian Juan Sanjurjo y San Millán; publ. *Memorias de actividades del curso académico†*

## COLLEGES

### ESCUELA SUPERIOR DE ADMINISTRACIÓN Y DIRECCIÓN DE EMPRESAS (ESADE)
AVENIDA DE PEDRALBES 60-62, BARCELONA 34

Telephone: 203-78-00.

Founded 1958; B.A. and M.A. courses in Business Administration and Management Development.

*Director-General:* Xavier Adroer.
*Registrar and Secretary-General:* Carlos Tomas.
*Dean:* Lluis M. Pugés.
*Librarian:* Antoni M. Güell.

Library of 21,500 vols.
Number of teachers: 220.
Number of students: 2,400.

Publications: *Colección ESADE* (30 vols).

DIRECTORS:
*Social Sciences:* Joan Travé.
*Law:* Antonio Marzal.
*Marketing Management:* Alfonso Durán Pich.
*Finance Management:* Christià Sala.
*Personnel Management:* Samuel Husenman.
*Economics:* Pere Puig.
*Production Management:* Pere Batallé.
*Business Policy:* Francesc Vilahur.
*Data Processing:* Josep Rucabado.
*Quantitative Methods:* Eduard Bonet.

Affiliated Research Institute:
**Instituto de Estudios Laborales** (*Institute of Labour Relations*).

### ESTUDIOS UNIVERSITARIOS Y TÉCNICOS DE GUIPÚZCOA
PASEO DEL URUMEA, MUNDAIZ, SAN SEBASTIÁN

Telephone: (943) 273100.

Founded 1956.
Private control.

*Rector:* Dr. José Antonio Obieta, s.j.
*Secretary-General:* Carlos Machimbarrena, s.j.
*Librarian:* Marichu Petrirena.

Library of 35,200 vols.
Number of teachers: 150.
Number of students: 2,502.

Publications: *Estudios Empresariales, Mundáiz.*

*Faculty of Philosophy and Letters.*
*Faculty of Business Administration.*
*School of Tourism.*
*School of Theology.*
*School of Languages.*

**Institut d'Estudis Europeus:** Via Laietana 32, Barcelona 3; f. 1951; studies and information in political, economic, cultural, scientific and judicial aspects of modern Europe; participates in conferences on European themes throughout Spain; Spanish branch of the European University; Pres. J. Prat Ballester; Dir. Prof. E. Sunyer Coma; publs. various.

### REAL COLEGIO UNIVERSITARIO "MARÍA CRISTINA"
SAN LORENZO DEL ESCORIAL, MADRID

Telephone: (91) 896.0101.

Founded 1892. Private university of the Augustinian Fathers.

*Rector:* Gabriel del Estal Gutiérrez.
*Vice-Rector:* Agustín Alonso Rodríguez.
*Secretary:* Fidel Rodríguez Diez.
*Dean of the Faculty of Law:* Avelino Folgado Fernández.
*Dean of the Faculty of Economics:* Octavio Una Juárez.
*Librarian:* Avelino Folgado Fernández.

Library of 185,000 vols.
Number of teachers: *c.* 50.
Number of students: *c.* 450.

Publications: *Anuario Jurídico Escurialense†* (annually), *La Ciudad de Dios†* (3 a year), *Nueva Etapa†* (annually).

### UNIVERSIDAD INTERNACIONAL MENÉNDEZ PELAYO
PALACIO DE LA MAGDALENA, SANTANDER

Telephone: 27-26-50.

Founded 1948.

Offers summer courses to Spanish and foreign students and grants fellowships for scientific research.

*Rector:* Dr. Raúl Morodo.
*Vice-Rectors:* Dr. Pablo Lucas Verdú, Dr. Angel Viñas Martín.
*Director of Courses for Foreigners:* Dr. Manuel Medina Ortega.
*Secretary-General:* Dr. Francisco Bobillo de la Peña.
*Administrator-General:* Juan Carlos Beneyto.

Library of 15,200 vols.
Number of teachers: 700.
Number of students: 6,000.

There are campuses in Toledo, Pontevedra, Sitges, La Laguna, and Rome (Italy).

#### TECHNOLOGY

**Escuela Superior de Técnica Empresarial Agrícola** (*Higher School of Agricultural Management*): Escritor Castilla Aguayo 4, Apdo. 439, Córdoba; f. 1963; five-year undergraduate and postgraduate courses; research institute; school of languages; extension courses in farm management; farm management consultancy services; 51 professors; library of 8,000 vols.; Dir. Jaime Loring Miró; Sec. Alfonso López Caballero.

**Escuela Técnica Superior de Ingenieros Industriales** (*School of Industrial Engineering*): Alberto Aguilera 23, Madrid 15; f. 1908; number of teachers 103, number of students 398; library of 14,435 vols.; Dir. Luis Tomás Sánchez del Río y Sierra, s.j.

**Instituto Químico de Sarriá** (*Sarriá Institute of Chemistry*): Calle del Instituto Químico de Sarriá s/n., Barcelona 17; f. 1916; number of teachers 78, number of students

489; library of 27,414 vols.; publs. *Afinidad*† (every 2 months), *I.Q.S.*† (annually).

*Director:* Dr. MIGUEL MONTAGUT BUSCÁS, S.J.
*Secretary:* Dr. SEBASTIÁN JULIA ARECHAGA.
*Librarian:* Prof. RAFAEL QUERALT TEIXIDÓ, S.J.

*Directors of Teaching and Research Departments:*
Analytical Chemistry: Dr. LUIS VICTORI COMPANYS.
*Organic Chemistry:* Dr. JUAN J. BONET SUGRAÑES.
*Physics:* Dr. LUIS CONDAL BOSCH.
*Chemical Engineering:* Dr. ALBERTO BARRERA BERRO, S.J.
*Computer Centre:* Dr. JOSEP M. RIERA ANGUERA.

### MILITARY SCIENCE
**Escuela de Estado Mayor** (*Military Staff School*): Santa Cruz de Marcenado 25, Madrid 8; f. 1842; number of lecturers 52; number of students 189; library of 117,866 vols.; Dir. Brig.-Gen. JESÚS GONZÁLEZ DEL YERRO MARTÍNEZ.

### SOCIAL STUDIES
**Cátedra "Ramiro de Maeztu":** Avenida de los Reyes Católicos, Ciudad Universitaria, Madrid; attached to the Instituto de Cultura Hispánica (*q.v.*); f. 1947; courses on "Contemporary Man" under various aspects (literature, art, economics, medicine, politics, philosophy, etc.), with special relation to the study of Spain and the Hispanic countries; Dir. TOMÁS SALINAS.

## SCHOOLS OF ART, ARCHITECTURE AND MUSIC

### Madrid

**Escuela de Arte Dramático** (*School of Dramatic Art*): Calle del Pez 38; Dir. FERNANDO FERNÁNDEZ DE CÓRDOBA.

**Escuela Nacional de Artes Gráficas** (*Madrid School of Graphic Arts*): Calle Jesús Maestro, Madrid 3; f. 1911; library of 3,200 vols.
*Director:* LUIS GIMENO SOLDEVILLA.
*Vice-Director:* JOSÉ LÓPEZ MARTÍNEZ.
*Director of Studies:* ANGEL MACEDO JIMÉNEZ.

Number of teachers: 30.
Number of students: 450.
Publication: *Grafinsa*.

**Escuela Superior de Bellas Artes de Madrid** (*Madrid Higher School of Fine Arts*): Calle de El Greco, Ciudad Universitaria, Madrid 3; f. 1845; 29 teachers. 400 students; library of 3,681 vols.; Dir. ANTONIO FERNÁNDEZ CURRO; Sec. GUILLERMO VARGAS RUIZ.

**Escuela Superior de Musica Sagrada y de Pedagogia Musical** (*Higher School of Sacred Music and Music Teaching*): Víctor Pradera 65 bis, Madrid 8; f. 1925; 600 students; Dir. LUIS ELIZALDE; publs. *Tesoro Sacro Musical*†, *Melodias*†, etc.

**Real Conservatorio Superior de Música de Madrid** (*Royal Academy of Music*): Plaza de Isabel II; f. 1830; 3,223 registered students and 1,460 free students, 77 teachers; library of 100,000 vols.; Dir. FRANCISCO CALES OTERO; Sec. JULIÁN LÓPEZ GIMENO; publ. *Anuario*.

**Real Escuela Superior de Arte Dramático** (*Royal Higher School of Dramatic Art*): Plaza de Isabel II.

### Málaga

**Conservatorio Profesional de Música y Escuela de Arte Dramático:** number of students 450; Dir. JOSÉ ANDREU NAVARRO.

### Barcelona

**Escuela Superior de Bellas Artes de San Jorge** (*Barcelona School of Fine Arts*): Calle Europa s/n, Ciudad Universitaria, Barcelona 14.

**Conservatorio Superior de Música de Barcelona:** Calle Bruch 112; f. 1885; incorporates the Conservatorio Superior Municipal de Música (formerly the Escuela Municipal de Música) and the Conservatorio de Música del Liceo (formerly Conservatorio del Liceo Isabel II); teaching staff of 35 full-time and 40 part-time; Dir. XAVIER TURULL CREIXELL; Sec. MANUEL SÁEZ FINESTRES.

### Cadiz

**Conservatorio de Música "Manuel de Falla":** Calle del Tinte 1, Edif. de la Escuela de Maestria Industrial; 221 students.

### Córdoba

**Conservatorio Superior de Musica y Escuela de Arte Dramático y Danza** (*Academy of Music and School of Dramatic Art and Dance*): Angel de Saavedra 1; f. 1862; 2,481 students; library of 12,444 vols.; Dir. RAFAEL QUERO CASTRO; Sub-Dir. MIGUEL SALCEDO HIERRO; Sec. TERESA GARCÍA MORENO.

### Murcia

**Conservatorio Superior de Música y Escuela de Arte Dramático:** Plaza Romea; f. 1916; 1,000 students; Dir MANUEL MASSOTTI LITTEL.

### San Sebastián

**Conservatorio Profesional Municipal de Música:** Víctor Pradera 39; f. 1897; 20 teachers; Dir. FRANCISCO ESCUDERO.

### Seville

**Conservatorio Superior de Música y Escuela de Arte Dramático:** Calle Jesús del Gran Poder 49; f. 1935; teaching and training in music and drama; staff of 40; Dir. MARIANO PÉREZ GUTIERREZ; Vice-Dir. JOSÉ MARIA DE MENA CALVO; Sec. LUIS BLANES ARQUES.

**Escuela Superior de Bellas Artes de Santa Isabel de Hungría de Sevilla** (*Seville School of Fine Arts*): Gonzalo Bilbao 7-9; f. 1940; 250 students; Dir. JOSÉ HERNÁNDEZ DÍAZ; Vice-Dir. ANTONIO SANCHO CORBACHO; private specialized library.

**Escuela Técnica Superior de Arquitectura de Sevilla** (*School of Architecture*): Avda. Reina Mercedes s/n; f. 1960; 1,600 students, 120 teachers; library of 9,000 vols.; Dir. ALBERTO DONAIRE RODRÍGUEZ; Sec. EDUARDO MARTÍNEZ ZÚÑIGA.

### Valencia

**Escuela Superior de Bellas Artes de San Carlos** (*Valencia School of Fine Arts*): Calle del Museo 2; f. 1756; library 5,105 vols.; teaching personnel 26; students 300; Dir. DANIEL DE NUEDA LLISIONA; Sec. AMANDO BLANQUER PONSODA.

**Conservatorio Superior de Música y Escuela de Arte Dramático y Danza de Valencia:** Plaza San Esteban 3; f. 1879; 84 teachers, 9,600 students; library of 10,820 vols.; Dir. SALVADOR SEGUÍ PÉREZ; Sec. JOSÉ ROSELL PONS; publ. *Memoria* (annually).

# SRI LANKA
Population 14,471,000

## LEARNED SOCIETIES

**Alliance Française:** 54 Ward Place, Colombo 7; f. 1954; library of 10,000 vols.; Dir. F. GRAVIER; Kandy br. 106 Yatinuwara Vidiya; f. 1968; Jaffna br.: 130 1st Cross St.; f. 1977.

**American Center:** 39 Sir Ernest de Silva Mawatha (Flower Rd.), P.O.B. 1245, Colombo 7.

**Asia Foundation, The:** 3/1A Racecourse Ave., Colombo 7; Rep. FRANK E. DINES.

**British Council:** P.O.B. 753, 190 Galle Rd., Colombo 3; Rep. Dr. V. A. ATKINSON; libraries: see Libraries.

**Buddhist Academy of Ceylon:** 109 Rosmead Place, Colombo.

**Ceylon Gemmologists Association:** 61 Abdul Caffoor Mawatha, Colombo 3; Pres. Prof. K. KULARATNAM.

**Ceylon Geographical Society:** 61 Abdul Caffoor Mawatha, Colombo 3; f. 1938; 100 mems.; Pres. Prof. K. KULARATNAM; Secs. Dr. K. U. SIRINANDA, Dr. W. P. T. SILVA; publ. *The Ceylon Geographer* (annually).

**Ceylon Humanist Society:** 35 Guildford Crescent, Colombo 7; Pres. J. T. RUTNAM; Sec. O. M. DE ALWIS.

**Ceylon Institute of World Affairs:** c/o Mervyn de Silva, 82B Ward Place, Colombo 7; f. 1957; Pres. Maj.-Gen. ANTON MUTTUKUMARU.

**Ceylon Palaeological Society:** 61 Abdul Caffoor Mawatha, Colombo 3; Pres. Prof. K. KULARATNAM.

**Ceylon Society of Arts:** Art Gallery, Ananda Coomarassamy Mawatha, Colombo 7; f. 1887.

**Classical Association of Ceylon, The:** f. 1935; 146 mems.; Pres. E. C. S. PERERA; Hon. Sec. Mrs. N. L. RAJASINGHAM, 8 Selbourne Rd., Colombo 3.

**German Cultural Institute:** 92 Rosmead Place, Colombo 7; f. 1957; Dir. Dr. T. LINDEMANN.

**Maha Bodhi Society of Ceylon:** 130 Maligakande Rd., Maradana, Colombo 10; f. 1891 for propagation of Buddhism throughout the world; 12,000 mems.; Pres. HEMA H. BASNAYAKA, Q.C.; Hon. Sec. LALITH HEWAVITARNE; publs. *Sinhala Bauddhaya* (monthly), *Sinhala Bauddhaya* (Wesak number; annual).

**National Education Society of Ceylon:** Hon. Sec. DOUGLAS WALATARA, Dept. of Education, University of Sri Lanka, Peradeniya; Pres. Dr. T. RANJIT RUBERU.

**Royal Asiatic Society:** 1st Floor, Grandstand Building, Reid Ave., Colombo 7; f. 1845 and incorporated with the Royal Asiatic Society of Great Britain and Ireland; institutes and promotes inquiries into the history, religions, languages, literature, arts, sciences and social conditions of the present and former inhabitants of Ceylon and connected cultures; Pres. Prof. Dr. D. E. HETTIARATCHI, PH.D.; Hon. Secs. P. R. SITTAMPALAM, K. M. W. KURUPPU; library contains one of the largest collections of books on Sri Lanka, and others on Indian and Eastern culture in general; publ. *Journal*.

**Sri Lanka Association for the Advancement of Science:** 120/10 Wijerama Mawatha, Colombo 7; f. 1944 to provide for systematic direction of scientific enquiry in the interests of the country, to promote contact among scientific workers, and to disseminate scientific knowledge, etc.; holds annual session; six sections; 1,400 mems.; Gen. Pres. Dr. O. S. PIERIS; Gen. Secs. D. A. T. A. SENARTHYAPA, Dr. J. ELIEZER; publs. *Proceedings†*, *Vidya Viyapthi*.

**Sri Lanka Library Association:** c/o The Library, University of Colombo premises, Race Course, Reid Ave., Colombo 7; f. 1960; 960 mems.; Pres. FELIX SAMARARATNE; Gen. Sec. Miss ANGELA BASTIAMPILLAI; publ. *Ceylon Library Review†* (annual).

**Sri Lanka Medical Association:** S.L.M.A. House, 6 Wijerama Mawatha, Colombo 7; Pres. Dr. H. B. PERERA; Hon. Gen. Sec. Dr. G. W. KARUNARATNE; publ. *Ceylon Medical Journal*.

**Theosophical Society of Ceylon:** Besant House, 49 Peterson Lane, Colombo 6.

## RESEARCH INSTITUTES

**Agrarian Research and Training Institute:** P.O.B. 1522, 114 Wijerama Mawatha, Colombo 7; f. 1972; research into agrarian structures and the economic, social and institutional aspects of agricultural development; operates training programmes; library: see Libraries; Dir. T. B. SUBASINGHE; publs. *Annual Report*, *News Letter*, *Farmers' Journal* (in Sinhala and Tamil), *Journal of Agrarian Studies*, research studies, occasional publications.

**Central Agricultural Research Institute:** Gannoruwa, Peradeniya; f. 1965; research in agriculture with special reference to rice, vegetables, fruits, minor export crops, subsidiary food crops, floriculture; mushroom production and processing.

**Ceylon Institute of Scientific and Industrial Research:** 363 Bauddhaloka Mawatha, Colombo 7; f. 1955; applied technical research institute working in many fields for industry, government agencies and the public; process research, resource studies, waste material utilization, product testing, standards, calibration and repair of instruments, trouble shooting, technical consultation; industrial extension service; Dir. M. S. WIJERATNE, F.I.R.I., M.PHIL.

Consists of the following depts.:

*Agro-Industries:* Dir. (vacant).
*Applied Physics and Electronics:* Dir. S. GNANALINGAM, PH.D.
*Chemical Technology:* Dir. Mrs. B. MUNASIRI, PH.D.
*Fats and Oils:* Dir. R. C. WIJESUNDERA, PH.D.
*Food Technology:* Dir. K. G. GUNATILEKE, PH.D.
*Industrial Economics Research:* Dir. P. T. NUGAWELA, PH.D.
*Industrial Microbiology:* Dir. P. M. JAYATISSA, PH.D.
*Materials Science and Physico-Mechanical Testing:* Dir. M. H. C. WIJETUNGE, DR.RER.NAT., DIPL.-ING.
*Minerals:* Dir. M. G. M. ISMAIL, M.ENG.
*Natural Products:* Dir. E. R. JANSZ, PH.D.
*Physical Chemistry:* Dir. (vacant).
*Pilot Plant and Design:* Dir. S. A. ABEYSEKERA, PH.D.
*Rubber Technology:* Dir. L. P. MENDIS, PH.D.
*Wood and Cellulose:* Dir. D. DE SILVA, PH.D.

Publs. *Annual Reports†*, *Bulletins†*, *Seminar Proceedings*, *Cisireach†* (newsletter).

**Coconut Research Institute:** Bandirippuwa Estate, Lunuwila; f. 1929; quasi-government research institute serving coconut industry of Sri Lanka; library of 8,500 vols. which also houses the International Coconut Information Centre; Chair. Prof. B. A. ABEYWICKRAMA; Dir. Dr. U. PETHIYAGODA; publs. *Ceylon Coconut Quarterly†, Ceylon Coconut Planters' Review†, Annual Reports†, Bibliographical Series on Coconut†*, newsletters, bulletins and directories.

**Colombo Observatory:** Bauddhaloka Mawatha, Colombo 7; f. 1907; climatological data for Sri Lanka; seismology; time service; astronomical service; radarwind and radiosonde observations for Colombo; admin. headquarters of Sri Lanka Meteorological Service; Dir. K. D. N. DE SILVA; publ. *Report of the Department of Meteorology†* (annually).

**Government Research Departments:**

**Department of Archaeology:** Sir Marcus Fernando Rd., Colombo 7; preservation and excavation of ruins and ancient monuments; Commissioner Dr. R. H. DE SILVA; publs. *Administration Report, Ancient Ceylon* (annually).

**Department of Cultural Affairs:** Dharmapala Mawatha, Colombo 7; preservation of traditional culture; Dir. P. A. ABEYWICKREMA.

**Fisheries Research Station, Department of Fisheries:** P.O.B. 531, Macan Macar Mawatha, Colombo 3; Officer-in-Charge A. S. MENDIS.

**Geological Survey Department:** 48 Sri Jinaratana Rd., Colombo 2; f. 1902; geological mapping, mineral investigation and exploration, mineralogy and metallurgy, engineering geology including water supply investigations, mines inspection and safety of mines, ore dressing and sale of mineral sands; 207 mems.; Dir. D. J. A. C. HAPUARACHCHI; publs. *Annual Report, Memoirs, Mineral Information Series, Economic Bulletins, Professional Papers*.

**Department of Wild Life Conservation:** 29 Gregory's Rd., Colombo 7; f. 1950; Dir. S. D. SAPARAMADU; publs. *Sri Lanka Wild Life, Vana Divi* (monthly), *Wild Life* (annually), *National Parks of Sri Lanka*.

**Fisheries Research Station:** Negombo.

**Central Rice Breeding Station:** Batalagoda, Ibbagamuwa; f. 1952; 5 staff; Principal Officer D. SENADHIRA.

**Economic Research Unit:** Business Intelligence Dept., Bank of Ceylon, Colombo; Business Intelligence Officer S. E. A. JAYAWICKREMA.

**Industrial Development Board of Sri Lanka:** 615 Galle Rd., Katubedda, Moratuwa; f. 1969; promotion, evaluation and development of industries, manufacture of machinery, provision of industrial information and extension facilities; 8 regional offices; library of c. 10,000 vols., 600 periodicals, 2,500 reports; Chair. NAUFEL ABDUL RAHMAN; Dir. Documentation and Publications Division Mrs. I. UNAMBOOWE; publs. *Karmantha*, annual reports, project profiles, current awareness bulletins, bibliographic series, etc.

**Medical Research Institute:** Borella, Colombo; f. 1900; comprising departments of Bacteriology, Biochemistry, Calf Lymph, Entomology, Food and Water, Leptospira, Media, Mycology, Clinical Pathology, Parasitology, Nutrition, Pharmacology, Salmonella, Serology, Vaccines, Virus, Pasteur Chemistry of Natural Products and School of Medical Laboratory Technology; Dir. Dr. K. NITYANANDA; Sec. H. L. WIJESINGHE.

**National Science Council of Sri Lanka:** 47/5 Maitland Place, Colombo 7; f. 1968; advises government on research co-ordination, scientific policy, funds and research and its application in Sri Lanka; initiates and promotes research, liaises with similar overseas bodies and publishes scientific reports; the Sri Lanka Scientific and Technical Information Centre (SLSTIC), the Sri Lanka Social Sciences Research Centre and the "Man and the Biosphere" Programme for Sri Lanka work under the auspices of the Council; library of 3,700 vols.; documentation and publications unit; Sec.-Gen. Dr. R. P. JAYEWARDENE; publs. *Journal†* (2 a year), *Annual Report†, Union Catalogue of Scientific and Technical Books†* (quarterly), *Sri Lanka Science Index†* (quarterly), *Vidurava*.

**Royal Botanic Gardens:** Peradeniya; f. 1821; Supt. D. T. EKANAYAKE.

**Rubber Research Institute of Sri Lanka:** Agalawatta; f. 1910; Colombo office and laboratories: Telawala Rd., Ratmalana, Mt. Lavinia; research and advisory services on rubber planting and manufacture; comprises five research depts., extension dept. and economic research unit, specification unit and estate dept.; about 500 staff; Dir. Dr. O. S. PERIES, PH.D.; Chief Admin. Officer M. N. J. JAYARATNE B.A.; publs. *Annual Report, Annual Review*, quarterly journals, bulletins and advisory circulars.

**Sri Lanka Water Resources Board:** 2 Gregory's Ave., Colombo 7; established 1966; advises the Government on all matters concerning the conservation and utilization of water resources; library of 2,595 vols., 100 periodicals; Chair. Dr. LESLIE HERATH.

**Tea Research Institute of Sri Lanka:** St. Coombs, Talawakelle; f. 1925; tea processing, propagation and pest control techniques, fertilizer economy, plant biochemical and sand culture technology; library of 20,000 vols., 250 periodicals; Dir. R. L. DE SILVA, PH.D., D.I.C. (acting); publs. *Tea Quarterly, Annual Report*.

**Veterinary Research Institute:** Gannoruwa, Peradeniya; concerned with research and investigations into health and production problems of livestock and poultry; Dir. Dr. J. A. DE S. SIRIWARDENE, PH.D.

# LIBRARIES

**Agrarian Research and Training Institute Library:** P.O.B. 1522, 114 Wijerama Mawatha, Colombo 7; f. 1972; 6,000 vols. and 180 periodicals; several hundred reports and reprints; special collection on Sri Lanka; to become part of proposed national centre for agrarian information; Librarian W. RANASINGHE.

**British Council Library:** P.O.B. 753, 154 Galle Rd., Colombo 3; f. 1950; 42,331 vols., 104 periodicals; Librarian Mrs. N. COLONNÉ, M.A.; Branch Library: Dalada, Vidiya, Kandy; f. 1960; 20,829 vols., 41 periodicals; Librarian Mrs. L. M. WIRASINGHA, B.A., A.L.A.

**Ceylon Institute of Scientific and Industrial Research Library:** 363 Bauddhaloka Mawatha, Colombo 7; f. 1955; 20,000 vols., 300 journals; several thousand reports, reprints, standards; information service to scientists, industrialists and engineers; Librarian Miss C. L. M. NETHSINGHA, M.A., A.L.A.; publs. *Current technical literature†* (quarterly), *Bibliographical Series†*, State of the Art surveys on spices and essential oil-bearing plants.

**Colombo National Museum Library:** P.O.B. 854, Colombo 7; f. 1877 (incorporating collection of Government Oriental Library, f. 1870); depository for Sri Lanka publications since 1885; 600,000 items (including 131,224 monographs, 4,500 periodical titles, 3,578 palm leaf MSS. in Sinhala and Sanskrit, Pali, Burmese and Cambodian); Librarian Mrs. C. I. KARUNANAYAKE, B.A.; publs. *Sri Lanka Periodicals Index, NML Acquisitions Bulletin, Periodicals Directory, Bibliographical Series*.

**Department of National Archives:** 7 Reid Avenue, Colombo 7; f. 1902; contains official records of the Dutch Administration from 1640 to 1796, British Administration from 1796 to 1948; official records of Independent Ceylon from 1948 onwards; a few codices of Portuguese Administration prior to 1656 and some documents in French, Sinhalese and Tamil; operates a Presidential Archival Depository and a Reference Service; deals with documents in private possession; is the legal depository for all printed material in the country, effects the registration of printing presses, printed publications, and newspapers; holds copies of books printed after 1885 and newspapers since 1832; Dir. A. DEWARAJA, B.A.; publs. *Administration Report of The National Archives*, *Quarterly Statement of Books printed in Sri Lanka* (quarterly), *Catalogue of Newspapers* (annual).

**Law Library:** Hultsdorp, Colombo 12.

**Public Library:** 18 Sir Marcus Fernando Mawatha, Colombo 7; f. 1925; 11 brs.; one mobile library; 44,204 mems.; library of 177,346 vols., 465 periodical titles; Chief Librarian Mrs. ISHVARI COREA, B.A., DIP.LIB., A.L.A.; publs. *Quarterly Accessions List*, *Programme of Extension Activities* (quarterly), *Administration Report* (annually).

**Sri Lanka National Library Services Board:** Independence Ave., Colombo 7; f. 1970; responsible for the establishment and maintenance of the National Library of Sri Lanka; plans and assists in the organization and development of library services in general, the publication of reading material and audiovisual aids; advises on professional qualifications for library personnel; promotes development of library education and training; Unesco and Sri Lanka deposit library; reference and professional library; book loan collections for schools and public libraries; Chair. M. J. PERERA; Dir./Sec. N. AMARASINGHE; publs. *Ceylon National Bibliography†* (quarterly), *Library News†* (quarterly).

**Tea Research Institute Library:** St. Coombs, Talawakelle; f. 1925; 20,000 vols. and 250 periodicals for reference and loan, including a specialist reference section dealing with tea and allied subjects; Librarian Miss Y. S KANDAMBY, B.A.

**University of Colombo Library:** Colombo 3; f.1967; 125,000 vols.; Librarian Mrs. V. DE SOUZA, B.A., DIP.LIB., A.L.A.; publ. *Ceylon Journal of Medical Science†* (half-yearly).

**University of Peradeniya Library:** Peradeniya; f. 1921; c. 400,000 vols.; Librarian S. MURUGAVERL (acting); publs. *Ceylon Journal of Science†*, *Modern Ceylon Studies†*, *Sri Lanka Journal of Humanities†* (half-yearly).

## MUSEUMS

**National Museums of Sri Lanka:** P.O.B. 854, Albert Crescent, Colombo 7; Dir. Dr. P. H. D. H. DE SILVA, PH.D., F.Z.S., F.A.Z.; publs. *Spolia Zeylanica* (Bulletin of the National Museum of Ceylon) (annual), *Administration Report of the Director of National Museums, Sri Lanka* (annual).

**Colombo National Museum:** Colombo; f. 1877; national collection of art and antiquities, natural sciences and folk culture; Dir. P. H. D. H. DE SILVA, PH.D., F.Z.S., F.A.Z.

**Kandy National Museum:** Kandy; f. 1942; regional museum for the Central Province; Curator H. M. A. B. HERATH.

**Ratnapura National Museum:** Ratnapura; f. 1942; regional museum for the Sabaragamuwa Province; Curator C. KURUPPU.

**Anuradhapura Folk Museum:** Anuradhapura; f. 1971; regional museum for North Central Province.

## UNIVERSITIES

### UNIVERSITY OF COLOMBO
94 CUMARATUNGA MUNIDASA MAWATHA, COLOMBO 3

Telephone: 81835, 84695, 85509.

Telex: University.

Founded 1967, reorganized 1972, present name 1979.

State control; Languages of instruction: Sinhalese, Tamil, English; Academic year: October to September.

*Chancellor:* Dr. P. R. ANTHONIS.
*Vice-Chancellor:* Prof. S. WIJESUNDERA.
*Registrar:* M. D. G. ABEYRATNE.
*Librarian:* M. A. P. SENADHIRA.

Number of teachers: 317.
Number of students: 3,286.

Publication: *Journal of Medical Sciences*.

#### DEANS:
*Faculty of Arts:* Dr. H. A. RATNAYAKE.
*Faculty of Law:* Prof. T. NADARAJA.
**Faculty of Medicine: Prof. S. R. KOTTEGODA.**
*Faculty of Natural Sciences:* Prof. V. R. SAMARANAYAKE.
*Faculty of Education:* Prof. W. A. DE SILVA.

PROFESSORS AND HEADS OF DEPARTMENTS:

*Faculty of Arts:*
ABEYASINGHE, T. B. H., History and Political Science
ARIYAPALA, M. B., Sinhalese
BASTIAMPILLAI, B. E. ST. J., History and Political Science
FONSEKA, H. N. C., Geography
JAYARATNE, W. M., Commerce and Management Studies
JAYASURIYA, G. W., Economics
ROBERTS, G. W., Demographic Training and Research Unit
SATHASIVAM, A., History and Political Science
SILVA, W. P. T., Geography
WEERAMUNDA, A. J,. Sociology
WICKRAMASURIYA, Miss C., English
WIJAYAWARDHANA, G. D., Sinhalese

*Faculty of Education:*
ARAMPATTA, D., Social Science Education
JAYASEKERA, U. D., Humanities Education
MUTHULINGAM, S., Educational Psychology
WANASINGHE, J., Science and Technical Education

*Faculty of Law:*
CHANDRAHASAN, Mrs. A. N. V., Law

*Faculty of Medicine:*
ATTYGALLE, Mrs. D., Pathology
BALASUBRAMANIAM, K., Biochemistry
DISSANAYAKE, S. A. W., Psychiatry
FERNANDO, H. V. J., Forensic Medicine
FONSEKA, Mrs. C. DE, Microbiology
FONSEKA, C. C., Physiology
FONSEKA, T. E. J. DE, Community Medicine
GUNATILLEKE, D. E., Obstetrics and Gynaecology
LIONEL, N. D. W., Pharmacology
NAVARATNE, R. A., Surgery
PANDITHARATNE, P. S. S., Anatomy
RAJAKULENDRAN, Mrs. S., Parasitology
SENEVIRATNE, S. A. W., Physiology
SOYSA, Mrs. P. E., Paediatrics

*Faculty of Natural Sciences:*
ABEYWICKREMA, B. A., Botany
ARUDPRAGASAM, K. D., Zoology
DHARMAWARDENA, K. G., Radio Isotope Centre
EPASINGHE, P. W., Mathematics and Statistical Unit
KANNANGARA, M. L. T., Physics
RAMAKRISHNA, R. S., Chemistry
SENEVIRATNE, Mrs. A. S., Botany

ATTACHED INSTITUTES:

*Institute of Indigenous Medicine:* Rajagiriya, Sri Lanka; Dir. D. M. R. B. DISSANAYAKE.
*Institute of Postgraduate Medicine:* Faculty of Medicine, Kynsey Rd., Colombo 8; Dir. S. A. CABRAL.
*Institute of Workers' Education:* Reid Ave., Colombo 3; Dir. Dr. D. WALATARA.

## UNIVERSITY OF JAFFNA
THIRUNELVELY, JAFFNA
Telephone: 481, 7626.
Founded 1974, present name 1978.
State control; Languages of instruction: Tamil and English.

Chancellor: V. MANICKAVASAGAR.
Vice-Chancellor: Prof. S. VITHIANAN-THAN, M.A., PH.D.
Registrar: K. C. LOGESWARAN, B.A.
Librarian: R. S. THAMBIAH, M.A., M.SC.
  Library of 76,000 vols.
  Number of teachers: 186.
  Number of students: 1,523.
  Publications: Cintanai (quarterly), Sri Lanka Journal of South Asian Studies (annually).

### DEANS:
Faculty of Arts: Prof. K. KAILASA-PATHY, PH.D.
Faculty of Science: Prof. V. THARMARATNAM, PH.D.
Faculty of Medicine: Prof. A. A. HOOVER, PH.D.

### PROFESSORS:
BALASUBRAMANIAM, C. C., Pathology
GANESHALINGAM, V. K., Zoology
HOOVER, A. A., Biochemistry
INDRAPALA, K., History
JEYASINGHAM, W. L., Geography
KUNARATNAM, K., Physics
KURUKKAL, K. K., Hindu Civilization
MAGESWARAN, S., Chemistry
SELLIAH, J. B., Mathematics and Statistics
SIVAGNANASUNDARAM, C., Community Medicine
SIVASURIYA, M., Obstetrics and Gynaecology
SIVATHAMBY, K., Tamil
SREEHARAN, N., Medicine
THARMARATNAM, V., Mathematics and Statistics
THEIVENDRARAJAH, K., Botany

## UNIVERSITY OF KELANIYA
DALUGAMA, KELANIYA
Telephone: 075-391, 397.

Formerly Vidyalankara Pirivena; University status 1959; reorganized 1972 as campus of University of Sri Lanka; present name 1978.

Chancellor: Rev. Dr. WALPOLA RAHULA.
Vice-Chancellor: Prof. TILAK RATNAKARA.
Registrar: W. D. TISSERA (acting).
Librarian: T. G. PIYADASA.
  Number of teachers: 346, including 126 part-time.
  Number of students: 2,651.

### DEANS:
Faculty of Science: Prof. I. BALASOORIYA.
Faculty of Humanities: Prof. S. L. KEKULAWALA.

Faculty of Social Science: Prof. M. P. PERERA.

### PROFESSORS:
ARIYARATNE, J. K. P., PH.D., Chemistry
BALASOORIYA, I., PH.D., Botany
COSTA, H. H., PH.D., Zoology
DAHANAYAKE, C., PH.D., Physics
GUNATILAKA, D. C. R. A., English
JAYASURIYA, M. H. F., PH.D., Sanskrit
JAYAWICKREMA, N. A., PH.D., Pali
KARUNADASA, Y., PH.D., Pali
KULATILAKE, C. R., M.A., Mathematics
LIYANAGAMAGA, A., PH.D., History
MUDIYANSE, N., PH.D., Sinhalese
PERERA, M. P., M.A., PH.D., Geography
WEERASINGHE, S. G. M., M.A., PH.D., Philosophy
WICKREMASURIYA, S. B. P., PH.D., Mathematics

## UNIVERSITY OF MORATUWA
MORATUWA

Founded 1966 as College of Technology; present name 1978.
Languages of instruction: Sinhala, Tamil, English; Academic year: October to September.

Chancellor: Dr. ARTHUR C. CLARKE.
Vice-Chancellor: Prof. C. PATUWATHAVITHANE, PH.D., M.I.E., C.ENG.
Registrar: K. C. F. SILVA, B.A. (acting).
Librarian: S. RUBASINGHAM, B.A., DIP.LIB.
  Number of teachers: 340 (including part-time).
  Number of students: 1,350 full-time, 1,400 part-time.

### DEANS:
Faculty of Engineering: Prof. D. S. WIJEYASEKERA, PH.D.
Faculty of Architecture: Prof. K. R. S. PEIRIS, B.ARCH.

### PROFESSORS AND HEADS OF DEPARTMENTS:
ALWIS, L., B.ARCH., Architecture
DE SILVA, G. T. F., M.SC., Mathematics and Physics
FERNANDO, L. D., PH.D., Textile Technology
FERNANDO, W. L. W., M.SC., Mining and Mineral Processing
GOONEWARDENA, V., B.A., Language and Social Studies
HERATH, K., M.SC., Mechanical Engineering
JAYATILAKE, A. DE S., PH.D., Materials Science
KARUNARATNE, S., M.SC., Electrical Engineering
MENDIS, M. W. J. G., M.SC., Town and Country Planning
SAPARAMADU, A. A. D. D., B.SC., M.ED., Technical Teacher Training
SHIVAPRAKASHAPILLAI, P., PH.D., Electronics and Telecommunications
SILVA, H. D. J., M.SC., Chemical Engineering
SOMASUNDARAM, C. K., PH.D., Marine Engineering
TENNEKOON, C. L. K., PH.D., Chemical Engineering

## UNIVERSITY OF PERADENIYA
UNIVERSITY PARK, PERADENIYA
Telephone: Peradeniya: Private Exchange through Kandy.

Founded 1942 by the incorporation of the Ceylon Medical College (f. 1870) and the Ceylon University College (f. 1921); reorganized 1972, present name 1978.

State control; Languages of instruction: Sinhala, Tamil, English; Academic year: October to September.

Chancellor: VICTOR TENNAKOON.
Vice-Chancellor: Prof. B. L. PANDITHARATNE, B.A., M.SC., PH.D.
Registrar: M. B. ADIKARAM, B.A.
Librarian: S. MURUGAVERL, B.A., DIP.LIB. (acting).
  Number of teachers: 438.
  Number of students: 5,083.

### DEANS:
Faculty of Arts: Prof. C. R. DE SILVA.
Faculty of Science: Prof. H. W. DIAS.
Faculty of Medicine: Prof. R. G. PANABOKKE, M.B.B.S., PH.D.
Faculty of Engineering: Prof. W. P. JAYASAKERA, PH.D.
Faculty of Agriculture: Prof. Y. D. A. SENANAYAKE, PH.D.
Faculty of Veterinary Medicine and Animal Health: Prof. S. T. FERNANDO, PH.D.

### PROFESSORS:
Faculty of Arts:
GOONEWARDENE, K. W., PH.D., History
HALPE, K. A. C. G., PH.D., English
HEWAVITHARANA, B., PH.D., Economics
KODIKARA, S. U., PH.D., Economics
KULASURIYA, S. U., PH.D., Tamil
PANDITHARATNE, B. L., M.A., M.SC., Geography
SILVA, K. M. DE, PH.D., Ceylon History
SILVA, M. W. P. DE, PH.D., Philosophy and Psychology
TILAKASIRI, J., PH.D., Sanskrit

Faculty of Science:
CRUSZ, H., PH.D., B.SC., Zoology
DASSANAYAKE, M. D., PH.D., Botany
DISSANAIKE, G. A., PH.D., Physics
MAHESWARAN, M., PH.D., Mathematics
SULTAN BAWA, M. U. S., PH.D., D.I.C., F.R.I.C., Chemistry
VITHANAGE, P. W., M.SC., PH.D., Geology

Faculty of Medicine:
AMARASEKARA, D. C. P., M.B.B.S., F.R.C.P., Forensic Medicine
APONSO, H. A., M.D., F.R.C.P., Paediatrics
ARSECULARATNE, S. N., D.PHIL., Bacteriology
BARR-KUMARAKULASINGHE, C., M.B., B.S., F.R.C.S., Surgery
BASNAYAKE, V., M.B., B.S., D.PHIL., Physiology
DISSANAYAKE, S. B., F.D.S., R.C.S., L.D.S., B.D., Dental Surgery
FERNANDO, M. A., M.B.B.S., PH.D., Community
JAYATILLEKE, A. D. P., M.B., B.S., PH.D., Anatomy
PANABOKKE, R. G., M.B.B.S., PH.D., Pathology

RODRIGO, M. A. A., M.B.B.S., M.R.C.P., D.P.M., Psychiatry
SILVA, M. L. D. N. K. DE, M.B.B.S., F.R.C.S., M.R.C.O.G., Obstetrics and Gynaecology
TENNAKOON, G. E., PH.D., Pathology
VARAGUNAM, T., M.D., M.R.C.P., Medicine
WICKREMANAYAKE, T. W., M.B.B.S., PH.D., Biochemistry

*Faculty of Engineering:*
AMARATUNGA, A. A. D. M. M., PH.D., Civil Engineering
FERNANDO, W. M. G., M.SC., Electrical Engineering
JAYASEKERA, W. P., PH.D., Electrical Engineering
JAYATILEKE, C. L. V., PH.D., Mechanical Engineering
MAHALINGHAM, S., PH.D., Mechanical Engineering
SAMUEL, T. D. M. A., M.SC., PH.D., Engineering Mathematics
THURAIRAJAH, A., PH.D., Civil Engineering

*Faculty of Agriculture:*
HERATH, H. M. W., M.SC.(AGRIC.), PH.D., Animal Husbandry
JOGARATNAM, T., M.S.A., Agricultural Economics and Farm Management
RAJAGURU, A. S. B., M.SC.(AGRIC.), Animal Husbandry
SENANAYAKE, Y. D. A., M.SC., PH.D., Crop Science
THENABADU, M. W., PH.D., Agricultural Chemistry

*Faculty of Veterinary Medicine and Animal Health:*
FERNANDO, S. T., PH.D., Veterinary Paraclinical Studies
KODITUWAKKU, G. E., PH.D., Veterinary Clinical Studies
WIJEWANTHA, E. A., PH.D., Veterinary Paraclinical Studies

*Postgraduate Institute of Agriculture:*
JOGARATNAM, T. (Director)

### Dumbara Campus
POLGOLLA

*Rector:* Dr. B. K. BASNAYAKE.
*Deputy Registrar:* L. B. MEEKOTUWE.

### UNIVERSITY OF SRI JAYEWARDENEPURA
GANGODAWILA, NUGEGODA
Telephone: 073-2695/6.

Founded 1959; reorganized 1972 as campus of University of Sri Lanka; present name 1978.
Languages of instruction: Sinhalese and English.

*Chancellor:* Dr. E. W. ADIKARAM.
*Vice-Chancellor:* Prof. K. JINADASA PERERA.
*Registrar:* W. P. P. ABEYDEERA.
*Librarian:* W. B. DORAKUMBURA, M.LIB.SC.
Number of teachers: 185.
Number of students: 3,033.

DEANS:
*Faculty of Arts:* Dr. T. B. KANGAHAARACHCHI.
*Faculty of Science:* Dr. P. L. D. WAIDYASEKERA.
*Faculty of Management Studies and Commerce:* G. M. H. WIJEWARDENA.

PROFESSORS:
ALWIS, S. P. DE, Mathematics
BALAGALLE, W., B.A., Sinhala
DAYANANDA, R. A., Statistics
FERNANDO, P. C. B., PH.D., Physics
GNANAWASA, H., Buddhist Studies
KARUNANAYAKE, M. M., Geography
PALIHAWADANA, M., Sanskrit
PERERA, K. J., M.A., PH.D., Languages and Cultural Studies
DE SILVA, K. T., Chemistry
THILAKARATNA, S., M.A., PH.D., Economics
WEERAKOON, A. C. J., PH.D., Biology

### RUHUNA UNIVERSITY COLLEGE
MEDDAWATTE, MATARA
Telephone: 041/2682-4, 2701.
Founded 1978.

State control; Languages of instruction: Sinhala and English; Academic year: October to September.

*Director:* D. A. KOTELAWELE, PH.D.
*Secretary:* B. ABEYSUNDERA, B.A.
Library of 13,000 vols.
Number of teachers: 95.
Number of students: 616.

DEANS:
*Faculty of Science:* Prof. R. H. WIJAYANAYAKE.
*Faculty of Arts:* Prof. G. S. RANAWELLA.
*Faculty of Agriculture:* Dr. S. K. CHARLES.
*Faculty of Medicine:* Prof. T. W. WIKRAMANAYAKE.

HEADS OF DEPARTMENTS:
*Faculty of Agriculture:*
CHARLES, S. K., PH.D., Agricultural Economics
WEERARATNE, C. S., PH.D., Agronomy, Animal Science (acting)

*Faculty of Arts:*
ATAPATTU, D., PH.D., Economics, Geography (acting)
DE SILVA, M. U., PH.D., History
EKANAYAKE, P. B., M.A., Sinhala
WICKRAMASURIYA, Miss C., M.A., English (acting)

*Faculty of Medicine:*
FONSEKA, M. N. T., M.B.B.S., F.R.C.S., M.R.C.O.G., Surgery
HETTIARACHCHI, J., M.B.B.S., M.D., M.R.C.P., Medicine
LAMABADUSURIYA, S. P., PH.D., D.C.H., M.R.C.P., Paediatrics
PERERA, D. J. B., D.PATH., PH.D., Pathology
SAMARAWICKRAMA, G. P., M.SC., PH.D., Community Medicine
SIRISENA, L. A. W., M.B.B.S., M.S., M.R.C.O.G., Obstetrics and Gynaecology
WICKRAMANAYAKE, T. W., PH.D., Biochemistry

*Faculty of Science:*
DE SILVA, S. S., PH.D., Zoology
PEMADASA, M. A., PH.D., Botany
TENNEKONE, K., PH.D., Physics
TILLEKARATNE, K., M.SC., Mathematics
WIJAYANAYAKE, R. H., PH.D., Chemistry

## COLLEGES

### AQUINAS COLLEGE OF HIGHER STUDIES
COLOMBO 8
Founded 1954.

Courses for the external examinations of Universities of Sri Lanka, for the Aquinas Diplomas and Certificates, and for examinations conducted by professional institutions in Sri Lanka and abroad.

*Rector:* Rev. Dr. W. L. A. DON PETER.
*Registrar:* T. M. PERERA.

Faculties of Arts, Science and Law; Institute of Religious Formation; Institute of Technology; School of Agriculture; School of English; c. 1,500 students; library of c. 30,000 vols.; experimental farm at Ragama.

**Ceylon College of Physicians:** 6 Wijerama Mawatha, Colombo 7; f. 1967.
*President:* Prof. N. D. W. LIONEL, M.D., F.R.C.P.

*Joint Hon. Secretaries:* Dr. LAKSHMAN RANASINGHE, M.R.C.P., D.C.H., Dr. D. N. ATUKORALA, M.R.C.P., D.D.M.

**In-Service Training Institute and Central Research Station:** Peradeniya.
*Agricultural Officer (In-Service Training):* S. D. WIJEGOONAWARDENA, B.SC.(AGRIC.).

**Jaffna College:** Vaddukoddai; f. 1823, renamed 1872; provides primary, secondary and external Advanced level examinations of London University and technical courses; agricultural courses at Maruthanamadam.
*Principal:* A. KADIRGAMAR.
*Director Technical Education:* G. D. SOMASUNDARAM.
*Principal, Agriculture:* C. L. DEVASAGAYAM.

ATTACHED INSTITUTE:
**Christian Institute for the Study of Religion and Society:** Christa Seva Ashram, Chunnakam; Dir. Rev. SAM ALFRED.

**School of Agriculture:** Kundasale.
*Principal:* P. O. S. ABEYWARDENE, B.SC.
*Additional Principal:* S. R. ARASASINGHAM, B.SC.AGRIC., M.S.

**Sri Lanka Law College:** 244 Hulftsdorp St., Colombo 12; f.1900; Principal R. K. W. GOONESEKERE.

**Sri Lanka Technical College:** Colombo 10; f. 1893; courses in trades and commerce.
*Principal:* B. P. H. S. MENDIS.
*Registrar:* H. V. S. BREMADASA.
*Librarian:* A. A. WIJERATNE.
Number of students: 4,525.

# SUDAN
Population 16,126,000

## LEARNED SOCIETIES AND RESEARCH INSTITUTES

**Agricultural Research Corporation, Ministry of Agriculture:** P.O.B. 126, Wadi Medani; f. 1918; 130 specialists; includes the following sections: Agronomy and Crop Physiology; Botany and Plant Pathology; Entomology (pest control, etc.); Breeding; Soil Science; Horticultural Research; Statistics and Agricultural Economics; Food Technology; Forestry Research; Fish Research; Wildlife Research; Range and Pasture; 10 regional research stations, 2 commodity stations, 5 specialized centres, testing sites; library: see Libraries; Dir.-Gen. MOHAMED BAKHEIT SAID, PH.D. (acting).

**American Cultural Center:** Qasr Ave., Khartoum; library of 5,000 vols.

**Animal Production Corporation, Research Division:** P.O.B. 624, Khartoum; Dir. of Research Dr. MUHAMMAD EL TAHIR ABDEL RAZIG, DIP.VET.SC., M.SC., PH.D.; Senior Veterinary Research Officer Dr. AMIN MAHMOUD EISA, M.SC.

**Antiquities Service:** P.O.B. 178, Khartoum; f. 1939; Commissioner for Archaeology NAJM ED DIN SHAREEF; library: see Libraries; publs. *Kush* (journal of the Antiquities Service) (annual), occasional papers.

**British Council:** 45 Sharia Gamaa, P.O.B. 1253, Khartoum; Rep. C. K. SMITH, O.B.E.; libraries: see Libraries.

**Centre Culturel Français:** P.O.B. 1568, Khartoum; Dir. JEAN-MICHEL PETTINELLI.

**Educational Documentation and Research Centre:** P.O.B. 2490, Khartoum; f. 1967; 12 mems., library of 20,000 vols.; Dir. NEIMET TOHA SALIH; publs. *Al-Tawitheq El Tarbawi†* (Educational Documentation, quarterly), annual reports and educational researches.

**Forest Research and Education Institute:** P.O.B. 658, Khartoum; f. 1962; Dir. A. A. BAYOUMI.

**Geological Survey Department:** P.O.B. 410, Khartoum; applied research and surveys; library: see Libraries; Dir. ABDEL LATIF WIDATALLA.

**Industrial Consultancy Corporation:** P.O.B. 268, Khartoum; f. 1965 by the Government with assistance from the UN Development Programme; performs tests, investigations, analysis, research and surveys; offers advice and consultation services to industry; Dir. ABDEL RAHMAN ABDEL HALIM.

**Institute of Public Administration:** P.O.B. 1492, Khartoum; f. 1960; a joint undertaking between the UN and the Sudan, to provide practical and academic training for government officials; to conduct studies on current administrative problems and to produce manuals and other documents on administrative operation in the Sudan; library of 5,000 vols.; Dir. EL SUNNI BANAGA; publs. *Sudan Journal of Administration and Development†*, *Occasional papers†*.

**National Council for Research:** P.O.B. 2404, Khartoum; f. 1970; responsible for organization, planning and direction of scientific research within State policy for the realization of economic and social development; four sub-councils: Agricultural Research Council, Economic and Social Research Council, Medical Research Council and Scientific and Technological Research Council; six centres: National Atomic Energy Commission, National Computer Centre, National Commission on the Peaceful Uses of Outer Space (under establishment), National Documentation Centre and Scientific and Technological Potentials Survey Unit; Pres. H. E. WADIE HABASHI; Sec.-Gen. Prof. MOHAMED OSMAN KHIDIR.

**Philosophical Society:** P.O.B. 526, Khartoum; f. 1946; covers many subjects, including archaeology, ethnology, economics, sociology and natural history; publs. *Sudan Notes and Records*, *Proceedings of Annual Conferences*.

**Soviet Cultural Centre:** P.O.B. 359, Khartoum; Library of 9,800 vols.; Dir. Dr. SHOTA GOURGALLASHIVILI.

**Sudan Medical Research Laboratories:** P.O.B. 287, Khartoum; f. 1935; Dir. MAHMOUD ABDEL RAHMAN ZIADA, D.K.S.M., M.C.PATH.

## LIBRARIES

**Agricultural Research Corporation Library:** P.O.B. 126, Wadi Medani; f. 1931; c. 15,000 vols. and pamphlets, 450 periodicals; abstracting, literature searches; Librarian S. A. MOHAMED.

**Antiquities Service Library:** P.O.B. 178, Khartoum; f. 1946; 7,200 vols. excluding periodicals; Librarian AWATIF AMIN BEDAWI.

**Bakht er Ruda Institute of Education Library:** Khartoum; central library, postal library for teachers.

**British Council Library:** 45 Sharia Gamaa, P.O.B. 1253, Khartoum; f. 1963; 13,555 vols., 40 periodicals; Regional Librarian S. ROMAN, M.A., A.L.A.; also at Omdurman: f. 1958; 7,267 vols., 35 periodicals; Wadi Medani: f. 1960; 10,802 vols., 12 periodicals; El Obeid: 6,723 vols., 12 periodicals.

**Central Records Office:** P.O.B. 1914, Khartoum; f. 1953; 5,000,000 documents covering Sudanese history since 1870; library of 12,820 vols.; Dir. Dr. M. I. ABU SALEEM; publ. *Majallatal Wathaiq†* (Archives Magazine).

**Flinders Petrie Library:** Sudan Antiquities Service, P.O.B. 178, Khartoum; f. 1946; number of vols. 6,000.

**Geological Survey Library:** P.O.B. 410, Khartoum; f. 1904; 3,000 vols.; publs. *Annual Report*, *Bulletin*.

**Gezira Research Station Library:** Wadi Medani; 6,500 vols. on agricultural topics.

**Khartoum Polytechnic Library:** P.O.B. 407, Khartoum; f. 1950; 10,000 vols. on technical subjects; Librarian GABIR ABDUL RAHIM.

**Omdurman Central Public Library:** Omdurman; f. 1951; 17,650 vols.

**Sudan Medical Research Laboratories Library:** P.O.B. 287, Khartoum; f. 1904 (as part of Wellcome Tropical Research Laboratories); 7,000 pamphlets, 6,000 vols.

**University of Khartoum Library:** P.O.B. 321, Khartoum; f. 1945; contains 209,000 vols. and receives 4,200 periodicals and journals; includes a special Sudan and African collection; acts as a depository library for UN, FAO, ILO, WHO and UNESCO publications; both are under the general charge of the University Librarian ABDEL RAHMAN EL NASRI.

**Wellcome Chemical Laboratories Library:** Chemical Laboratories, Ministry of Health, P.O.B. 303, Khartoum; f. 1904; Librarian, Government Analyst; 1,600 pamphlets, 2,500 vols.

## MUSEUMS

**Ethnographical Museum:** Khartoum, P.O.B. 178; f. 1956; collection and preservation of ethnographical objects; Curator SAYED MAHDI SATTI SALIH.

**Khalifa's House:** Omdurman.

**Merowe Museum:** Merowe, Northern Province; antiquities and general.

**Sheikan Museum:** El Obeid; archaeological and ethnographic museum.

**Sudan Natural History Museum:** University of Khartoum, P.O.B. 321, Khartoum; f. 1920; transferred from the Ministry of Education to the University of Khartoum, and reorganized 1956; Keeper Dr. FAYSAL T. ABUSHAMA, M.SC., PH.D.; Curator MUHAMMAD A. AL RAYAH.

**Sudan National Museum:** P.O.B. 178, Khartoum; f. 1971; Departments of Antiquities, Ethnology and Sudan Modern History; controls the Ethnographical, Merowe, Sheikan and Khalifa museums; Commissioner for Archaeology SAYED N. M. SHERIF, B.A.; Deputy Commissioner SAYED AKASHA M. ALI, B.SC., A.M.A.; Chief Curator MAHDI SATTI, M.SC.; publs. *Report on the Antiquities Service and Museums, Kush* (annually), occasional papers, museum pamphlets, etc.

## UNIVERSITIES

### UNIVERSITY OF GEZIRA
P.O.B. 20, WADI MEDANI

Founded 1975; in process of formation.
*Vice-Chancellor:* Dr. MOHD. OBEID MUBARAK.

Faculties of agriculture, economics, medicine, science and technology.

### UNIVERSITY OF JUBA
P.O.B. 82, JUBA
Telephone: 2114.

Founded 1975 with financial help from the EEC; first student admission 1977.

State control; Language of instruction: English; Academic year: September to July (two semesters).

*Chancellor:* Major-Gen. P. S. C. GAAFAR MOHAMED NIMERI, President of the Republic.
*Vice-Chancellor:* Dr. ABDEL RAHMAN ABU ZAYD.
*Secretary-General:* MOSES MACAR (acting).
*Librarian:* Mrs. DIANA ROSENBERG.
Number of teachers: 50.
Number of students: 425.
Publications: *Juvarsity* (monthly), *Juvarsity News* (weekly).

DEANS:

*College of Natural Resources and Environmental Studies:* Dr. JOSEPH AWAD MORGAN.
*College of Social and Economic Studies:* Dr. ROBIN MILLS (acting).
*College of Education:* (vacant).
*College of Adult Education and Training:* ERIK VAN DER SLEEN.
*College of Medicine:* (vacant).
*Dean of Students:* MIKAYA LUMORI.

PROFESSORS:

COMHAIRE, J. J., Anthropology
MILLS, R., Manpower

### UNIVERSITY OF KHARTOUM
P.O.B. 321, KHARTOUM
Telephone: 75100.

Founded 1956; formerly University College of Khartoum.

Language of instruction: English (except for departments of Arabic and Sharia Law); Academic year: July to April.

*Chancellor:* THE PRESIDENT OF THE REPUBLIC.
*Vice-Chancellor:* ALI MOHAMED FADL, PH.D.
*Principal:* Ustaz AHMED ISMAIL EL NADIF.
*Personnel Secretary:* Ustaz ELZAIN ALI IBRAHIM, B.A., M.P.A.
*Librarian:* Ustaz ABDEL RAHMAN EL NASRI HAMZA, M.A.
Library: see Libraries.
Number of teachers: 675.
Number of students: 8,777.

DEANS:

*Faculty of Agriculture:* ABDEL GADIR HASSAN KHATTAB.
*Faculty of Arts:* OSMAN SID AHMED ISMAIL.
*Faculty of Education:* MALIK BABIKER BADRI.
*Faculty of Economic and Social Studies:* ALI MOHAMED SULIMAN.
*Faculty of Engineering and Architecture:* AWAD SALIM EL HAKEEM.
*Faculty of Law:* Dr. MOHAMED EL FATIH HAMID.
*Faculty of Medicine:* Prof. SAAD AHMED IBRAHIM.
*Faculty of Pharmacy:* Dr. YAHIA MOHAMED EL KHEIR.
*Faculty of Science:* MAMOUN DAWOUD EL KHALIFA.
*Faculty of Veterinary Science:* Prof. AMIR MOHAMED SALIH MUKHTAR.

*Graduate College:* FAISAL TAG EL DIN ABU SHAMA.
*Institute of African and Asian Studies:* Dir. Dr. YOUSIF FADL HASSAN.
*School of Extra Mural Studies:* Dir. Dr. SID AHMED NUGDALLA.

### CAIRO UNIVERSITY KHARTOUM BRANCH
P.O.B. 1055, KHARTOUM

Founded October 1955, as a branch of Cairo University.

*Vice-Chancellor:* Prof. MUHAMMAD RIFAAT RAMADAN.
*Registrar:* MUHAMMAD SABRY EL SAADI, LL.B.
Number of teachers: c. 80.
Number of students: c. 5,000.

Faculties of Arts, Commerce and Law (evening courses).

ATTACHED INSTITUTE:

**Higher Institute of Statistics:** f. 1969; offers two-year postgraduate course; 10 teachers, 150 students; Dir. A. M. SHAFIE, M.SC., PH.D.

### OMDURMAN ISLAMIC UNIVERSITY
P.O.B. 382, OMDURMAN
Telephone: 54220.

Founded 1912; university status 1965.

State control; Language of instruction: Arabic; Academic year: July to March.

*Chairman of University Council:* Dr O'ON EL SHARIF GASIM.
*Vice-Chancellor:* Prof. MOHAMED AHMED EL-HAG.
*Secretary-General:* EL AMIN MOHAMMED AHMED KIWIRRA.
*Academic Secretary:* AHMED HASSAN IBRAHIM.
*Librarian:* (vacant).
Library of 89,000 vols.
Number of teachers: 192.
Number of students: 1,734.
Publication: *Faculty of Arts Magazine*.

DEANS:

*Faculty of Islamic Studies:* Dr. Mohammed Osman Salih.
*Faculty of Social Studies:* Dr. Yousif Hamid El A'alim.
*Faculty of Arts:* Dr. Hassan Mohammed El Fatih.
*Girls' College:* Dr. M. Hossein A. Abu Sum.
*Dean of Students:* Dr. Abdel Aziz M. Osman.

PROFESSORS:

El Baghir, K. S. M., Philosophy of Education
Khalil, M. E., Arabic Languages
Mukhtar, M. A., Islamic History
Omar, M. S., General International Law

## COLLEGES AND INSTITUTES

(In Khartoum unless otherwise indicated.)

**Ahfad University College for Women:** P.O.B. 167, Omdurman; f. 1966; library of 15,000 vols.; 12 full-time, 12 part-time staff; 280 students; Dir. Yusuf Badri.

**College of Fine and Applied Art:** P.O.B. 407; f. 1946 as Higher School of Arts and Crafts, present status 1971; courses in Graphic Design, Printing and Binding, Calligraphy, Sculpture, Ceramics, Painting, Industrial Design, History of Art, Drawing, General Studies; 23 teachers, 180 students; Dean Ahmed Mohamed Shibrain.

**Institute of Laboratory Technology:** 3-year diploma course; Principal A. A. Akoor.

**Institute of Radiography and Radiotherapy:** P.O.B. 1908; f. 1970; 3-year diploma course; 120 students; Principal A. M. Salih.

**Institute of Survey Technicians:** 3-year diploma course; Principal M. O. Adam.

**Khartoum Nursing College:** P.O.B. 1063; 3-year diploma course; Principal A. M. Osman.

**Khartoum Polytechnic:** P.O.B. 407; f. 1967; incorporates previously existing colleges and institutes; agriculture, commerce, fine arts, engineering.

**School of Hygiene:** P.O.B. 205; 3-year diploma course; Principal S. El Gezoli.

**Forest Rangers College:** P.O.B. 6146; f. 1946; 3-year diploma course; 16 teachers; c. 90 students; library of 4,000 vols.; Principal E. Satti el Mahdi, b.sc.for.; publ. *Sudan Silva†* (quarterly).

# SURINAME
Population 352,041

## LEARNED SOCIETIES AND RESEARCH INSTITUTES

**Centre for Agricultural Research in Suriname:** P.O.B. 1914, Paramaribo; f. 1965; a branch of the University of Suriname; research in tropical agriculture; Dir. Hans Prade; publ. *Celos Bulletins.*

**Geologisch Mijnbouwkundige Dienst** (*Geological Mining Service*): 2-6 Kleine Waterstraat, Paramaribo; Dir. Drs. R. A. Cambridge; 13,102 vols. in library; publs. *Yearbook*, contributions in *Mededelingen*, geological maps.

**Landbouwproefstation** (*Agricultural Experiment Station*): P.O.B. 160, Paramaribo; f. 1903; attached to the Department of Agriculture, Animal Husbandry and Fisheries; library of 28,502 vols., including bound periodicals and pamphlets; Dir. Ir. I. E. Soe Agnie; publs. *Annual Report, Suriname Agriculture* (2 to 3 a year), *Bulletins* (irregular).

**Stichting Cultureel Centrum Suriname** (*Suriname Cultural Centre*): P.O.B. 1241, Paramaribo; f. 1947 to promote and improve cultural activities throughout the country; library of 180,000 vols., 6 branches, 2 book-mobiles; Pres. R. Ritfeld; Librarian Mrs. C. Carrilho-Fazal Alikhan.

**Stichting Planbureau Suriname** (*Suriname Planning Board*): Dr. S. Redmondstraat 118, P.O.B. 172, Paramaribo; Dir. Drs. H. E. Rijsdijk.

**Stichting voor Wetenschappelijk Onderzoek van de Tropen** (**WOTRO**) (*Netherlands Foundation for the Advancement of Tropical Research*): P.O.B. 1914, Paramaribo. (See also under Netherlands).

## MUSEUM

**Stichting Surinaams Museum:** P.O.B. 2306, Paramaribo; f. 1954; library of 4,500 vols.; archaeology, cultural and natural history; Dir. J. Douglas; publ. *Mededelingen†* (quarterly).

## UNIVERSITY

### UNIVERSITEIT VAN SURINAME
(**University of Suriname**)
DR. SOPHIE REDMONDSTRAAT 118, PARAMARIBO

Telephone: 2364.

Founded 1968.

*President:* M. G. de Miranda.
*Registrar:* Drs. Ch. H. Eersel.

Library: in process of formation.
Number of teachers: 34.
Number of students: 550.

DEANS:

*Faculty of Law:* Prof. Dr. L. Th. Waaldijk.
*Faculty of Medicine:* Prof. Dr. F. Jessurun.

# SWAZILAND
**Population 530,000**

## LEARNED SOCIETY

**Swaziland Art Society:** P.O.B. 812, Mbabane; f. 1970; classes, workshops, exhibitions, films, discussions, etc.; 60 mems.; Chair. Mrs. F. BERRANGÉ.

## RESEARCH INSTITUTES

**Lowveld Experiment Station:** P.O.B. 53, Big Bend; f. 1964; agricultural research, dryland crops agronomy, cotton breeding, cotton entomology, horticulture; Chief Officers J. S. WATSON, R. O. S. CLARKE, K. D. SHEPHERD.

**Geological Survey and Mines Department:** P.O.B. 9, Mbabane; f. 1944; activities include the mapping of the territory (published at a scale of 1:25,000 and 1:50,000), the investigation of mineral ocurrences by prospecting, detailed mapping and diamond drilling, mine and quarry inspections, control of explosives and prospecting; 13 mems.; small library; Dir. A. S. DLAMINI; publs. *Annual Reports†, Bulletins†*.

**Malkerns Research Station:** P.O.B. 4, Malkerns; f. 1959; general research on crops, pastures and forestry; 13 research sections; library of 4,000 vols.; Chief Research Officer J. S. WATSON, B.SC.

**Mpisi Cattle Breeding Experimental Station:** Mpisi; to improve indigenous Nguni cattle; to provide multiplication studs of Brahman, Simmentaler and Friesland cattle for beef, milk and cross breeding; Dir. R. A. JOHN; Man. I. A. MORLEY HEWITT.

**Swaziland Sugar Association:** P.O.B. 131, Big Bend; Extension Officer D. E. B. ROGERS.

## LIBRARIES AND ARCHIVES

**Swaziland National Archives:** P.O.B. 946, Mbabane; f. 1970; government records from 1880s to the present; reference library of c. 3,200 vols.; collection of historical photographs, newspapers, maps, coins, stamps; Dir. J. S. DLAMINI.

**Swaziland National Library Service:** P.O.B. 652 and Private Bag, Manzini; f. 1971; operates a public library service throughout the country with branch libraries at Manzini, Nhlangano, Siteki, Mhlume, Pigg's Peak, Malkerns, Big Bend, Bhunya, Tshaneni and school libraries at secondary schools; there is also a mobile library service to Sidvokodvo, Lavumisa, Luve and Siphofaneni; 80,000 vols., 150 periodicals; Dir. B. J. K. KINGSLEY; publs. *Annual Report†, Index to Swaziland Collection†* (occasional), *Accessions List†* (irregular).

## MUSEUM

**Swaziland National Museum:** P.O.B. 100, Lobamba; f. 1972, under the patronage of the Swaziland National Trust Commission; museum with extra-mural functions, giving information about Swazi culture as well as other countries; reference library; Curator THOKO T. GININDZA, M.A.; publs. *Yearbook, Quarterly Reports*.

## UNIVERSITY

### UNIVERSITY COLLEGE OF SWAZILAND
PRIVATE BAG, KWALUSENI

Telephone: 5111/2/3.

Telex: 2087 WD.

Founded 1964 as part of University of Botswana, Lesotho and Swaziland, present name 1976.

Private control; Language of instruction: English; Academic year: August to May.

*Chancellor:* H.M. KING SOBHUZA II, K.B.E.

*Rector:* Prof. S. M. GUMA, M.A., D.LITT. ET PHIL.

*Registrar:* A. B. SHONGWE, B.A.

*Librarian:* A. W. Z. KUZWAYO, M.A.

Number of teachers: 79.
Number of students: 778.

Publications: *Swaziland National Bibliography†* (annually), *Directory of Swaziland Libraries†* (irregular).

#### DEANS:

*Faculty of Agriculture:* G. T. MAGAGULA, PH.D.
*Faculty of Education:* E. B. PUTSOA, M.A.
*Faculty of Humanities:* N. M. B. BHEBE, PH.D.
*Faculty of Social Sciences:* Miss G. N. SIMELANE, M.A.
*Faculty of Science:* C. F. SCHMIDT, PH.D.

#### PROFESSORS:

*Faculty of Agriculture:*
 GODFREY-SAM-AGGREY, W., DR.SC.AGRIC., Crops
*Faculty of Humanities:*
 OBUMSELU, B. E., D.PHIL., English
*Faculty of Social Sciences:*
 HOE, A. M., B.A., Accounting
*Faculty of Science:*
 MAKHUBU, L. P., M.SC., PH.D., Chemistry
 WARD, A. H., PH.D., F.INST.P., M.I.E.E., Physics

# SWEDEN
Population 8,303,000

## FOUNDATION

**Nobelstiftelsen/Nobel Foundation:** Nobel House, Sturegatan 14, 114 36 Stockholm; was established in 1900 in pursuance of the provisions of the will of Alfred Nobel (1833–96), by which the whole of his fortune (more than 30 million Kronor) was bequeathed to a fund, the interest of which should be annually paid out to those who during the preceding year "have conferred the greatest benefit on mankind." The interest is divided into five equal parts, to be allotted as follows: "One part to the person who shall have made the most important discovery or invention in the domain of *physics*; one part to the person who shall have made the most important *chemical* discovery or improvement; one part to the person who shall have made the most important discovery in the domain of *physiology* or *medicine*; one part to the person who shall have produced in the field of *literature* the most distinguished work of an idealistic tendency; and one part to the person who shall have done most to promote the *fraternity of nations*, the abolition or diminution of standing armies, and the formation and propagation of a Peace Congress."

The funds of the Foundation are administered by a Board: Prof. SUNE BERGSTRÖM (Chair.), T. BROWALDH (Deputy Chair.), STIG RAMEL (Exec. Dir.), TORD GANELIUS, L.-E. THUNHOLM, L. GYLLENSTEN; Deputies A. MAGNELI, JAN LINDSTEN.

Prizes are distributed annually (for the first time in 1901) on the festival day of the Foundation, i.e. Dec. 10th, and are awarded by the following:

*Physics:* The Royal Swedish Academy of Sciences.
*Chemistry:* The Royal Swedish Academy of Sciences.
*Medicine:* The Karolinska Institutet.
*Literature:* The Swedish Academy.
*Peace:* The Norwegian Nobel Committee.
*Economics:* The Royal Swedish Academy of Sciences (prize money endowed by the Bank of Sweden).

The advisory body concerned with symposia and other special activities is The Nobel Symposium Committee: Chair. STIG RAMEL (Exec. Dir. of the Foundation); mems. Prof. STIG LUNDQVIST (Chair. Cttee. for Physics), Prof. STIG CLAESSON (Chemistry), Prof. JAN LINDSTEN (Sec. Cttee. for Medicine), LARS GYLLENSTEN (Perm. Sec. of Swedish Acad.), JAKOB SVERDRUP (Dir. Norwegian Nobel Inst.), RAGNAR H:SON BENTZEL (Sec. Cttee. for Economics), NILS-ERIC SVENSSON (Exec. Dir. Bank of Sweden Tercentenary Foundation), ULF VON EULER (mem. Bd. Wallenberg Foundation).

Publs. *Les Prix Nobel* (annually), *Nobelstiftelsens Kalender* (biennially), *Code of Statutes, Nobel Lectures, Publications de l'Institut Nobel Norvégien.*

## ACADEMIES

**Svenska Akademien** (*Swedish Academy*): Källargränd 4, Börshuset, S-111 29 Stockholm; f. by Gustavus III in 1786 on the model of the French Academy; the Academy annually awards the Nobel Prize in Literature and many Swedish prizes; Pres. changed every six months; there are eighteen members; publs. *Svenska Akademiens Handlingar* (annually) and a dictionary of the Swedish language.
*Permanent Secretary:* Prof. LARS GYLLENSTEN.
*Chief Librarian:* ANDERS RYBERG.

**MEMBERS:**

RUDHOLM, STEN
SEGERSTEDT, TORGNY
FORSSELL, LARS
OLSSON, HENRY
SUNDMAN, PER OLOF
GIEROW, KARL RAGNAR
SJÖSTRAND, ÖSTEN
JOHANNISSON, TURE
LÖNNROTH, ERIK
LINDE, ULF
ASPENSTRÖM, WERNER
ÖSTERLING, ANDERS
GYLLENSTEN, LARS
EKMAN, KERSTIN
ESPMARK, KJELL
EDFELT, JOHANNES
LUNDKVIST, ARTUR

**Kungl. Vetenskapsakademien** (*Royal Swedish Academy of Sciences*): Box 50005, S-104 05 Stockholm; f. 1739 by a society among whose members was Carl Linnaeus, for the promotion of mathematics and natural sciences; awards the Nobel prizes for physics, chemistry and economics.
*President:* Prof. ALF JOHNELS.
*Vice-Presidents:* Prof. FRANS E. WICKMAN, Prof. SVEN JOHANSSON, Prof. INGA FISCHER-HJALMARS.
*Secretary-General:* Prof. TORD GANELIUS.

Number of Swedish members: *c.* 250; foreign members *c.* 115.

Publications: *Acta Mathematica, Acta Zoologica, Arkiv för Matematik, Chemica Scripta, Physica Scripta, Zoologica Scripta, Ambio, Documenta.*
Library: see Libraries.

Research institutes: see Research Institutes.

PATRON:
H.M. THE KING.

HONORARY MEMBER:
H.R.H. PRINCE BERTIL.

SWEDISH MEMBERS:
1. *Mathematics*

BEURLING, ARNE
CARLESON, LENNART
GANELIUS, TORD
GRENANDER, ULF
GÅRDING, LARS
HÖRMANDER, LARS
KREISS, HEINZ-OTTO
NAGELL, TRYGGVE
PLEIJEL, ÅKE
ROOS, JAN-ERIK
THOMÉE, VIDAR

2. *Astronomy*

ELVIUS, AINA
ELVIUS, TORD
HOLMBERG, ERIK
HÖGBOM, JAN
LARSSON-LEANDER, GUNNAR
LINDBLAD, PER OLOF
MALMQUIST, GUNNAR
RAMBERG, JÖRAN
SCHALÉN, CARL A. W.
WALLENQUIST, ÅKE
WESTERLUND, BENGT E.
ÖHMAN, YNGVE

### 3. Physics

Bergström, Ingmar
Borelius, Gudmund
von Dardel, Guy
Edlén, Bengt
Ekspong, Gösta
von Friesen, Sten
Grimmeiss, Herrann
Gustafson, Torsten
Hulthén, Lamek
Ingelstam, Erik
Johansson, Sven
Lagerqvist, Albin
Larsson, Karl-Erik
Lehnert, Bo
Linde, Jonas Otto
Lindgren, Ingvar
Lundqvist, Stig
Löwdin, Per-Olov
Minnhagen, Lennart
Nagel, Bengt
Nordling, Carl
Ryde, Nils
Siegbahn, Kai
Sjölander, Alf
Svartholm, Nils
Waller, Ivar
Wilhelmsson, Hans

### 4. Chemistry

Abrahamsson, Sixten
Bergson, Göran
Brändén, Carl-Ivar
Claesson, Stig
Ehrenberg, Anders
Erdtman, Holger
Ernster, Lars
Fischer-Hjalmars, Inga
Forsén, Sture
Fredga, Arne
Fronaeus, Sture
Gronowitz, Salo
Hägg, Gunnar
Lindberg, Bengt
Lindqvist, Ingvar
Magnéli, Arne
Malmström, Bo
Melander, Lars
Myrbäck, Karl
Nilsson, Ragnar
Olovsson, Ivar
Porath, Jerker
Ölander, Arne

### 5. Mineralogy, Geology and Physical Geography

Boström, Kurt
Gavelin, Sven
Hessland, Ivar
Hjelmqvist, Sven
Hjulström, Filip
Hoppe, Gunnar
Lundqvist, Jan
Norin, Erik
Ramberg, Hans
Rapp, Anders
Regnéll, Gerhard
Reyment, Richard
Schytt, Valter
Sundborg, Åke
Thorslund, Per
Welin, Eric
Wickman, Frans E.

### 6. Botany

Björk, Sven
Björn, Lars Olof
Burström, Hans
Ehrenberg, Lars
Fagerlind, Folke
Fries, Nils
Gustafsson, Åke
Hagberg, Arne
Harling, Gunnar
Hedberg, Olov
Hemberg, Torsten
Lundqvist, Arne
Müntzing, Arne
Nannfeldt, John A.
Rodhe, Wilhelm
Ryberg, Måns
Santesson, Rolf
Sjörs, Hugo
Tamm, Carl Olof
Virgin, Hemming
Åberg, Börje

### 7. Zoology

Brinck, Per
Brundin, Lars
Caspersson, Torbjörn
Dahl, Erik
Enemar, Anders
Gustafson, Tryggve
Hörstadius, Sven
Jacobson, Carl-Olof
Jansson, Bengt-Owe
Jarvik, Erik
Johnels, Alf G.
Jägersten, Gösta
Karling, Tor G.
Kihlström, Jan Erik
Kullenberg, Bertil
Levan, Albert
Lindahl, Per Eric
Lindahl-Kiessling, Kerstin
Lindberg, Olov
Lindroth, Arne
Nyholm, Karl-Georg
Olsson, Ragnar
Rasmuson, Marianne
Silen, Lars
Stensiö, Erik
Svärdson, Gunnar
Ørvig, Tor

### 8. Medical Sciences

Ahlström, Carl Gustaf
Andersson, Bengt
Bárány, Ernst
Bergström, Sune
Bernhard, Carl Gustaf
Borell, Ulf
Carlsson, Arvid
Engström, Arne
von Euler, Ulf
Folkow, Björn
Forssman, Hans
Fuxe, Kjell
Gard, Sven
Granit, Ragnar
Grubb, Rune
Gustafsson, Bengt
Holmstedt, Bo
Kahlson, Georg
Klein, Georg
Kugelberg, Eric
Laurell, Carl-Bertil
Lehmann, Jörgen
Leksell, Lars
Lindsten, Jan
Luft, Rolf
Norrby, Erling
Ouchterlony, Örjan
Philipson, Lennart
Reichard, Peter
Samuelsson, Bengt
Theorell, Hugo
Teorell, Torsten
Uvnäs, Börje
Waldenström, Jan
Zetterström, Rolf
Zotterman, Yngve

### 9. Technical Sciences

Ahrbom, Nils
Berndt, Sune
Brohult, Sven
Eklund, Sigvard
Engström, Gunnar
Fant, Gunnar
Gralén, Nils
Gullstrand, Tore
Hast, Nils
Hedén, Carl-Göran
Hult, Jan
Hörmander, Olof
Jacobaeus, Christian
Kiessling, Roland
Lamm, Uno
Liander, Halvard
Malmström, Sven
Odqvist, Folke
Samuelsson, Olof
Sterky, Håkon
Wallman, Henry
Westermark, Torbjörn

### 10. Economics, Statistics and Social Sciences

Bentzel, Ragnar
Carlsson, Gösta
Carlson, Sune
Cramér, Harald
Dahmén, Erik
Husén, Torsten
Hägerstrand, Torsten
Jöreskog, K. G.
Lindbeck, Assar
Lundberg, Erik
Myrdal, Gunnar
Mäler, Karl-Göran
Segerstedt, Torgny
Ståhl, Ingemar
Söderlund, Ernst
Werin, Lars
Westerståhl, Jörgen
Wold, Herman

### 11. Geophysics

Alfvén, Hannes
Block, Lars
Bolin, Bert
Eriksson, Erik
Fredga, Kerstin
Fälthammar, Carl-Gunne
Hultqvist, Bengt
Kullenberg, Börje
Köhler, Hilding
Liljequist, Gösta
Nyberg, Alf
Nybrant, Gunnar
Rydbeck, Olof
Ångström, Anders

### 12. Other Sciences and Distinguished Services to Scientific Research

Browaldh, Tore
Clemedson, Carl-Göran
Edberg, Rolf
Edenman, Ragnar
Ekelöf, Per Olof
Eriksson, Gunnar
Frisk, Hjalmar
Gjerstad, Einar
Gyllensten, Lars
Hambraeus, Gunnar
Hamdahl, Bengt
Hellner, Jan
Jonsson, Inge
Karling, Sten
Lönnroth, Erik
Magnusson, David
Michanek, Ernst
Norberg, Dag
Odelberg, Wilhelm
Ramel, Stig
Selling, Gösta
Säve-Söderbergh, Torgny
Thordeman, Bengt

**Kungl. Vitterhets Historie och Antikvitets Akademien** (*Royal Academy of Letters, History and Antiquities*): Villagatan 3, 114 32 Stockholm; f. 1753 to promote the study of the humanities, history and archaeology; 110 Swedish, 42 foreign mems.; Pres. Prof. Torgny Säve-Söderbergh; Sec. Prof. Örjan Lindberger; publs. *Fornvännen* (journal), *Handlingar* (memoirs), *Arkiv* (archives), *Årsbok* (yearbook), monographs; library and archives: see under Libraries.

**Kungl. Skogs- och Lantbruksakademien** (*Royal Swedish Academy of Agriculture and Forestry*): Drottninggatan 95B, Box 6806, 113 86 Stockholm; f. 1811 to apply science to the development and improvement of agriculture and forestry; Pres. Johan Curman; Perm. Sec. Prof. Olle Johansson; 15 hon., 210 working mems., 75 foreign mems.; 76,000 vols. in library; publs. *Kungl. Skogs- och Lantbruksakademiens Tidskrift* (6 a year), *Acta Agriculturae Scandinavica* (4 a year).

**Kungl. Akademien för de fria Konsterna** (*Royal Academy of Fine Arts*): Fredsgatan 12, Box 16317, 103 26 Stockholm; f. 1735 to promote the development of painting, sculpture, architecture and allied arts; 76 mems., 12 hon. mems.; library of c. 20,000 vols.; Pres. Anders Tengbom; Vice-Pres. Ake Pallarp; Sec. Karin Lindegren; publ. *Meddelanden* (annually).

## ACADEMIES, LEARNED SOCIETIES

**Kungl. Musikaliska Akademien** (*Royal Academy of Music*): Blasieholmstorg 8, 111 48 Stockholm; f. 1771 for the promotion and protection of the art and science of music; approx. 170 mems.; library; Dir. HANS NORDMARK; Sec. HANS ÅSTRAND; publ. *Årsskrift* (year book), etc.

**Kungl. Krigsvetenskapsakademien** (*Royal Swedish Academy of Military Sciences*): Box 80022, S-104 50 Stockholm; f. 1796 to promote military sciences, including civil defence, economic defence and psychological defence; 342 mems.; Pres. GUNNAR THYRESSON; Sec. Brig. HANS ULFHIELM; publ. *Handlingar och Tidskrift* (6 a year)†.

**Ingenjörsvetenskapsakademien** (*Royal Swedish Academy of Engineering Sciences*): Box 5073, S-102 42 Stockholm; f. 1919 to promote engineering sciences through the establishment of new research facilities; acts as a clearing house for scientific information; establishes contacts with foreign research organizations by means of lectures and conferences, trade research organizations and research agreements with East European countries; 460 Swedish mems. (88 foreign or corresponding mems.); Dir. Prof. GUNNAR HAMBRAEUS; publ. *Meddelanden, Rapporter* (irregular bulletins).

**Kungl. Gustav Adolfs Akademien** (*Royal Gustavus Adolphus Academy*): 2 Klostergatan, 753 21 Uppsala; f. 1932; 180 mems. (including honorary); Pres. Prof. STEN CARLSSON; Vice-Pres. Prof. LENNART MOBERG; Sec. Prof. LENNART ELMEVIK; publs. *Saga och Sed, Arv. Journal of Scandinavian Folklore, Ethnologia Scandinavica, Namn och Bygd* (annually), *Acta*.

## LEARNED SOCIETIES

### GENERAL

**Kungl. Humanistiska Vetenskapssamfundet i Uppsala** (*Royal Society of Humanities at Uppsala*): f. 1889 to promote the study of humanities; 70 Swedish, 40 foreign mems.; Pres. Prof. R. ZEITLER; Sec. Prof. L. MOBERG, Fredsgatan 2, 752 24 Uppsala; publs. *Skrifter* (Acta), *Årsbok*† (Yearbook, available for exchange through the University Library, Uppsala (*q.v.*) ).

**Kungl. Vetenskaps- och Vitterhets-Samhället i Göteborg** (*Göteborg Royal Society of Arts and Sciences*): Universitetsbiblioteket, P.O.B. 5096, 402 22 Göteborg; f. 1778; Sec. Prof. E. J. HOLMBERG; publ. *Acta Regiae Societatis Scientiarum et Litterarum Gothoburgensis*† (monographs), *Årsbok*; 157 Swedish and 49 foreign mems.

**Kungl. Vetenskaps-Societeten i Uppsala** (*Royal Society of Sciences of Uppsala*): S:t Larsgatan 1, S-752 20 Uppsala; f. 1710, charter 1728; to promote research principally in mathematics, natural sciences, medicine, Swedish antiquities and topography, by (a) publishing works of scholarship, (b) awarding grants, (c) collecting and making available relevant publications, (d) lectures; mems. in four sections: physics and mathematics (40 national, 40 foreign), natural history and medicine (50 national, 40 foreign), history and archaeology (20 national, 10 foreign), technology and economics (20 national, 10 foreign); library of 600 periodicals; Pres. Prof. GÖSTA H. LILJEQUIST; Sec. Prof. PER OLOF FRÖMAN; publs. *Nova Acta*†, *Årsbok*†.

### ARCHITECTURE AND TOWN PLANNING

**Svenska Arkitekters Riksforbund** (*National Asscn. of Swedish Architects*): Odengatan 3, 114 24 Stockholm; f. 1936; objects are to promote the standing of architects in Sweden and maintain the people's right to a good environment by promoting good architecture and planning; 3,300 mems.; Chair. STURE LJUNGQVIST; Sec.-Gen. MATS BECKMAN; publ. *Arkitekttidningen* (fortnightly).

### THE ARTS

**Föreningen Svensk Form** (*Swedish Society of Industrial Design*): Nybrogatan 7, Box 7404, S-103 91 Stockholm; f. 1845; 6,000 mems.; Dir. BEATE SYDHOFF; Man.-Dir. LENNART LINDKVIST; publ. *Form* (8 a year).

**Föreningen Svenska Tonsättare** (*Society of Swedish Composers*): P.O.B. 5091, Birger Jarlsgatan 6B, S-102 42 Stockholm 5; f. 1918; 118 mems.

**Fylkingen** (*Society of Contemporary Music*): Rindögatan 27, Stockholm.

**Musikaliska Konstföreningen** (*Musical Art Association*): Blasieholmstorg 8, S-111 48, Stockholm; f. 1859 for the publication of Swedish music; Chair. I. MILVEDEN; Sec. G. PERCY.

**Statens kulturråd** (*Swedish National Council for Cultural Affairs*): Box 7843, 103 98 Stockholm; f. 1974 as advisory and investigatory body concerning state grants for cultural purposes; covers theatre, dance, music, literature, public libraries, art, museums and exhibitions.

**Svenska samfundet för musikforskning** (*Swedish Society for Musicology*): Strandvägen 82, 115 27 Stockholm; f. 1919; approx. 550 mems.; Pres. Prof. INGMAR BENGTSSON, Uppsala University; Sec. Fil. kand. ERIK KJELLBERG; publs. *Svensk Tidskrift för Musikforskning* (2 a year), *Monumenta Musicae Svecicae, Musik i Sverige* (jointly with Svenskt musikhistoriskt arkiv).

**Sveriges Allmänna Konstförening** (*Swedish General Art Asscn.*): Stora Nygatan 5, P.O.B. 2151, 103 14 Stockholm 2; f. 1832; approx. 21,000 mems.; Pres. STEN RUDHOLM; Dir. GÖRAN NILSSON; Sec. GUNNAR DALGREN; publ. *Sveriges Allmänna Konstforenings årspublikation*† (Swedish General Art Association's annual publication).

### BIBLIOGRAPHY AND LIBRARY SCIENCE

**Delegationen för vetenskaplig och teknisk informationsförsörjning (DFI)** (*Delegation for Scientific and Technical Information*): Box 43033, S-100 72 Stockholm; f. 1979; planning and co-ordination of activities relating to scientific and technical information provision; research and development in the field of information and documentation and international co-operation; Chair. H. BRYNIELSSON; Sec. B. THOMASSON.

**Svenska Bibliotekariesamfundet** (*Swedish Asscn. of University and Research Libraries*): c/o Birgit Nilsson, Sveriges lantbruksuniversitets bibliotek, Ultunabiblioteket, S-750 07 Uppsala; f. 1921; 810 mems.; Pres. LARS-ERIK SANNER; Sec. BIRGIT NILSSON; publs. *Bibliotekariesamfundet, Meddelar*†.

### ECONOMICS, LAW AND POLITICS

**Centre for the Study of International Relations:** Döbelnsgatan 81, Box 19112, S-104 32 Stockholm 19; f. 1971; studies social sciences, international politics, law and economy; independent of any political party; organizes lectures and conferences, research seminars; library; Chair. H.R.H. SIGVARD BERNADOTTE; Pres. CLÄES PALME; Vice-Pres. and Dir. Dr. FRANÇOIS H. C. HSIEH; Secs. Prof. Dr. JACOB W. F. SUNDBERG, Prof. Dr. LARS HJERNER, Dr. RICHARD K. T. HSIEH; publs. *Review*, CSIR courses and lecture series.

**International Law Association, Swedish Branch:** f. 1922; Pres. HANS BLIX; Hon. Sec. KLAS G. KLEBERG, P.O.B. 7448, 103 91 Stockholm.

**Nationalekonomiska Föreningen** (*National Economics Society*): Box 16067, 103 22 Stockholm 16; f. 1877; study of economics; about 1,200 mems.; Chair. Lars Werin; Sec. Jan Herin; publ. *Ekonomisk Debatt* (8 a year).

**Utrikespolitiska Institutet** (*Swedish Institute of International Affairs*): L. Nygatan 23, S-111 28 Stockholm; f. 1938; object: to improve public understanding of current international affairs; research dept., library of c. 20,000 vols., 400 periodicals; Pres. Yngve Möller; Man. Dir. Dr. Åke Sparring; publs. *Världspolitikens dagsfrågor, Internationella studier, UfBlick, Länder i fickformat, World Press Archives*, research reports, monograph series, etc.

### EDUCATION

**Svenska Institutet** (*The Swedish Institute*): Box 7434, S-103 91 Stockholm; f. 1945; object: to promote cultural, scientific and educational exchanges with countries abroad and spread knowledge of Swedish life by means of information work; administers scholarships and grants for study or research in Sweden; Pres. Birgit Rodhe; Dir. Göran Löfdahl.

### HISTORY, GEOGRAPHY AND ARCHAEOLOGY

**Kartografiska Sällskapet** (*The Swedish Cartographic Society*): c/o Statens Lantmäteriverk, 801 12 Gävle; f. 1908; 680 mems.; Pres. Sven-Eric Lindqvist; Sec. Lars Ottoson; publ. *Sveriges Kartläggning* (mapping of Sweden).

**Svenska Museiföreningen** (*Swedish Museums Society*): Nordiska Museet, 115 21 Stockholm; f. 1906; society for Swedish museums and members of staff; debates, etc., concerning scientific and practical problems of museums; 900 mems. and 70 institutional mems.; Pres. Iréne Westlund; Sec. Bo Sylvan; publ. *Svenska Museer* (quarterly).

**Svenska Sällskapet för Antropologi och Geografi** (*Swedish Society for Anthropology and Geography*): Naturgeografiska Institutionen, Stockholms Universitet, P.O.B. 6801, 113 86 Stockholm; f. 1880; aims: to forward the development of anthropology and geography in Sweden, to communicate with foreign societies with the same objectives, and to support investigations into anthropology and geography; 1,100 mems.; library of 10,000 vols.; Pres. Jan Lundqvist; Sec. Ann-Catherine Ulfstedt; publs. *Geografiska Annaler, Ymer, Atlas of Sweden*.

### INTERNATIONAL CULTURAL INSTITUTES

**American Center:** Sveavägen 118, S-113 50 Stockholm; library of 7,500 vols.; reference service; specialized programmes about the U.S.A.

**British Centre:** Grevturegatan 11A, Box 5507, 114 85 Stockholm; f. 1954 to spread knowledge of the English language and Britain; employs 55 British teachers of English in provincial towns throughout the country; Controller-Gen. Anne-Marie Lundberg.

**British Council:** c/o The British Embassy, Skarpögatan 6, S-115 27 Stockholm; f. 1941; Rep. R. Adlam, o.b.e.

**Centre Français:** Grevturegatan 9, 114 46 Stockholm; f. 1947; object: to further knowledge of the French language in Sweden; employs 30 French teachers in provincial towns; Dir. Marcel Bouvier.

**Dag Hammarskjöld Foundation:** Dag Hammarskjöld Centre, Ovre Slottsgatan 2, 752 20 Uppsala; f. 1962; set up to organize seminars and conferences for nationals of developing countries on the economic and social problems of these countries; Exec. Dir. Sven Hamrell; publ. *Development Dialogue* (2 a year).

**Deutsches Zentrum:** Nordenskiöldsgaten 20, Gothenburg-SV; Dir. Dr. A. Nägel.

**Goethe Institut Stockholm—Kulturinstitut der Bundesrepublik Deutschland:** Linnégatan 76, 115 23 Stockholm; Dir. G. Coenen.

**Ibero-American Institute:** University of Gothenburg, Lundgrensgatan 7, 412 56 Gothenburg; f. 1939; information, research, courses; library of 40,000 vols.; Dir. Dr. Per Rosengren; publ. regular cultural series, monographs†.

**Institut Français:** Grevgatan 36-38, 114 53 Stockholm; f. 1937 to encourage cultural relations between France and Sweden; library of 20,000 vols.; Dir. François-Noël Simoneau.

**Istituto Italiano di Cultura "C. M. Lerici":** Gärdesgatan 14, 115 27 Stockholm; f. 1941; 1,000 mems.; library of 16,000 vols.; Dir. Profa. Lucia Pallavicini; publ. *Kulturella Nyheter* (quarterly).

**Sverige-Amerika Stiftelsen** (*The Sweden-America Foundation*): Grevturegatan 14, 114 46 Stockholm; f. 1919 to increase understanding between Sweden and the United States and, since 1950, Canada; awards fellowships for Swedes to study in the United States and Canada and advises students from those countries about studies in Sweden; Chair. Axel Iveroth; Dir. Suzanne Bonnier; publs. *Resor och Studier i U.S.A., Travel, Study and Research in Sweden*.

### LANGUAGE AND LITERATURE

**Pennklubben** (*Swedish PEN Centre*): Norstedt och Söner, Tryckerig 2, Stockholm 2; f. 1922; 400 mems.; Pres. Thomas von Vegesack; Sec. Britt Arenander.

**Samfundet de Nio** (*Nine Swedish Authors' Society*): c/o Anders Öhman, Smålandsgatan 14, 111 46 Stockholm; f. 1913; Pres. Astrid Lindgren (novelist); Sec. Anders R. Öhman (lawyer); mems. Knut Ahnlund (professor), Karl Vennberg (poet and essayist), Inge Jonsson (professor), Kerstin Ekman, Ulla Isaksson, Birgitta Trotzig, Gunnel Vallqvist (novelists); publ. *Svensk Litteraturtidskrift* (quarterly).

**Sveriges Författarförbund** (*Swedish Union of Writers*): Box 5252, Grev Turegatan 29, 5 tr, 102 45 Stockholm; f. 1893 to protect the intellectual and economic interests of authors and translators; c. 2,000 mems.; Pres. Jan Gehlin; Sec. Sonja Thunborg; publ. *Författaren*.

### MEDICINE

**Scandinavian Society of Forensic Odontology:** Dept. of Forensic Odontology, Faculty of Odontology, Fack, S-141 04 Huddinge; f. 1961; 40 mems.; to expand co-operation with the forensic, dental and medical world and with national and international police and other agencies; Chair. Dr. Gunnar Johanson; Sec. Dr. Tore Solheim.

**Socialstyrelsen** (*National Board of Health and Welfare*): S-106 30 Stockholm; public health, medical and social services administration; f. 1663; Dir.-Gen. Barbro Westerholm, m.d.; publs. *Allmän Hälso-och Sjukvård* (Official Statistics: Public Health in Sweden), annual report on the state of public health, *Cancer Incidence in Sweden* (Report of the Board's Cancer Registry), *Socialnytt* (monthly bulletin), etc.

**Svenska Läkaresällskapet** (*Swedish Society of Medical Sciences*): Box 558, S-101 27 Stockholm; f. 1807; c. 10,000 mems.; Pres. Prof. Lars O. Thorén, m.d.; Sec. Hans O. Hallander, m.d.; publ. *Svenska Läkaresällskapets Handlingar Hygiea*†.

### NATURAL SCIENCES

**Geologiska Föreningen** (*Geological Society*): P.O.B. 670, 75128 Uppsala; f. 1871; 850 mems.; Pres. Hans Ramberg; Sec. Fil. Lic. S. Schager; Editor Bengt Lindqvist; publ. *Geologiska Foreningens i Stockholm Förhandlingar* (*GFF*) (quarterly).

**Kungl. Fysiografiska Sällskapet i Lund** (*Royal Physiographical Society of Lund*): Inorganic Chemistry 1, Chemical Centre, 220 07 Lund; f. 1772; science and medicine; 281 mems., 78 foreign correspondents; Pres. Prof. Lennart Stigmark; Sec. Prof. Sten Ahrland; publ. *Årsbok* (annually).

LEARNED SOCIETIES, RESEARCH INSTITUTES

**Kungl. Vetenskaps-Societeten** (*Royal Society of Sciences at Uppsala*): St. Larsgatan 1, S-752 20 Uppsala; f. 1710; 130 mems., 100 foreign corresps.; Pres. Prof. GUNNAR ÅGREN; Sec. Prof. AKE WALLENQUIST; Libr. Fil. Kand. GUN KARLBERG; publs. *Nova Acta Regiae Societatis Scientiarum Upsaliensis*†, *Kungl. Vetenskaps Societetens Årsbok* (annually).

**Lunds Matematiska Sällskap** (*Lund Mathematical Society*): Matematiska Institutionen, Lund; f. 1923; 106 mems.; Sec. and Treas. PEIK GUSTAFSSON.

**Matematiska Föreningen, Universitetet, Uppsala** (*Mathematical Society*): Department of Mathematics, Uppsala University, Thunbergsvägen 3, S-752 38 Uppsala; f. 1853; 50 mems.; Sec. LARS HÖGLUND.

**Statistiska Föreningen** (*Statistical Society*): Statistiska centralbyrån, S-11581 Stockholm; f. 1901; forms a link between practising statisticians and laymen interested in statistics, and by means of lectures, discussions and reports contributes to the analysis of problems in this field of science; 500 mems.; Pres. KURT HUGOSSON; Sec. ANDERS RICKARDSSON.

**Svenska fysikersamfundet** (*Swedish Physical Society*) Dept. of Physics, Lund Institute of Technology P.O.B. 725, S-220 07 Lund; f. 1920; 850 mems.; Chair. Prof. INGVAR LINDGREN; Sec. Dr. WILLY PERSSON; publ. *Kosmos*.

**Svenska Geofysiska Föreningen** (*Swedish Geophysical Society*): Swedish Meteorological and Hydrological Institute, P.O.B. 923, S-60119 Norrköping; f. 1920; 180 mems.; Pres. INGEMAR LARSSON; Sec. LARS E. OLSSON; publ. *Tellus*.

**Svenska Matematikersamfundet** (*Swedish Mathematical Society*): Dept. of Mathematics, Univ. of Stockholm, P.O.B. 6701, 113 85 Stockholm; f. 1950; 400 mems.; Chair. Prof. JAN-ERIK ROOS; Sec. ANDERS BJÖRNER; publ. *Nordisk Matematisk Tidskrift*, *Mathematica Scandinavica* (with other Scandinavian Mathematical Societies).

**Svenska Naturskyddsföreningen** (*The Swedish Society for the Conservation of Nature*): Kungsholms strand 125, S-11234 Stockholm; f. 1909; mem. of IUCN; 70,000 mems.; Exec. Dir. MATS SEGNESTAM; Sec. BO OLSSON; publs. *Sveriges Natur* (bi-monthly) and a yearbook.

**Wenner-Gren Center Foundation for Scientific Research (WGC):** Sveavägen 166, S-113 46 Stockholm; f. 1962; residence and meeting place for foreign and visiting scientists; Pres. of the Board Prof. HUGO THEORELL, N.P.; Sec. Prof. YNGVE ZOTTERMAN; publs. *The Wenner-Gren Center International Symposium Series*, *Wenner-Gren Center Svenska Symposier*.

TECHNOLOGY

**Svenska Konsulterande Ingenjörers Förening** (*Swedish Association of Consulting Engineers*): Kungsholmstorg 1, Box 22076, S-104 22 Stockholm; f. 1910; 950 mems.; Pres. LARS ROMARE; Man. Dir. RAGNAR WIDEGREN.

**Sveriges Civilingenjörsförbund (CF-STF)** (*The Swedish Association of Graduate Engineers*): Malmskillnads gatan 48A, Box 1419, S-111 84 Stockholm; f. 1861 present name 1974; 30,000 mems.; Pres. JAN OLOF CARLSSON; Man. Dir. PER-ERIK OLSON; publs. *Civilingenjören* (10 a year), *Ny Teknik*, *Teknisk Tidskrift* (weekly).

## RESEARCH INSTITUTES
(*see* also under Universities)

AGRICULTURE AND VETERINARY SCIENCE

**Jordbrukstekniska Institutet** (*Swedish Institute of Agricultural Engineering*): Ultuna, S-750 07 Uppsala; f. 1945; library of 3,000 vols.; Dir. SVEN-UNO SKARP, M.SC.AGR.; publ. *Meddelanden*† (bulletins on the various investigations) at irregular intervals.

**Skogs- och jordbrukets forskningsråd** (*Council for Forestry and Agricultural Research*): Drottninggatan 95B, Box 6806, 113 86 Stockholm; f. 1945 as the Swedish Agricultural Research Council, re-named 1981 ; to promote scientific research in agriculture and forestry; 11 mems., 10 personal deputies; Pres. Governor RAGNAR EDENMAN; Sec. Prof. OLLE JOHANSSON.

**Statens veterinärmedicinska anstalt** (*National Veterinary Institute*): S-750 07 Uppsala; f. 1911 (reorganized 1944 and 1977); research, diagnostic work, preparation of sera and vaccines, consultative work concerning control and prophylaxis of animal diseases: consists of eight departments: Bacteriological, Virological, Pathological, Parasitological, Chemical, Epizootiological, Consultative and Production as well as an Economic Division; library of 10,000 vols.; Dir. H.-J. HANSEN, V.M.D.; Admin. Dir. L. EHRENGREN; Librarian G. MARTENIUS ERNE; 55 scientific staff, 210 technicians and other employees; publ. *Collected Papers of the National Veterinary Institute*† (issued bi-annually).

**Svenska Träforskningsinstitutet** (*Swedish Forest Products Research Laboratory*): 53-71 Drottning Kristinas väg, S-114 86 Stockholm; f. 1944; carries out research on forest products, their development and use; trains scientists and engineers; approx. 350 mems.; depts. for chemistry, physics, wood products, fibre building board, pulp technology, paper technology, general analysis; Man. Dir. Prof. LENNART STOCKMAN; publ. *Meddelanden från Svenska Träforskningsinstitutet*.

ARCHAEOLOGY

**Riksantikvarieämbetets Gotlandsundersökningar** (*Gotland-Research Institute of the Central Office of Antiquities*): Strandgatan 10, S-621 56 Visby; f. 1970; anthropology, particularly prehistory and the middle ages; experimental archaeology and technical development; Dir. Dr. ERIK NYLÉN; Head of Medieval Dept. WALDEMAR FALCK; publs. *Annual Proceedings*†, *Research Reports*†.

ARCHITECTURE AND TOWN PLANNING

**Nordiska Institutet för samhällsplanering** (*Nordic Institute for Studies in Urban and Regional Planning*): Skeppsholmen, S-111 49 Stockholm; f. 1968; mem. countries Denmark, Finland, Iceland, Norway, Sweden; provides an advanced course for planners and undertakes research and research education; Chair. of Board LENNART HOLM; Dir. PER ANDERSSON; publs. *Årsrapport*† (annual), *Rapporter*†, *Grupparbeten*†.

ECONOMICS, LAW AND POLITICS

**Ekonomiska Forskningsinstitutet vid Handelshögskolan i Stockholm** (*The Economic Research Institute at the Stockholm School of Economics*): see under Handelshögskolan i Stockholm.

**Industriens Utredningsinstitut** (*The Industrial Institute for Economic and Social Research*): Grevgatan 34, S-114 53 Stockholm; f. 1939; research into economic and social conditions relevant to Swedish industrial development; 20 research fellows; Dir. GUNNAR ELIASSON, D.ECON.; Sec. BO CARLSSON; publs. books, research reports, working papers; English summaries of most publications available.

**Latinamerika-institutet** (*Institute of Latin American Studies*): Odengatan 61, P.O.B. 6909, 102 39 Stockholm; f. 1951, reorganized 1969 and 1977; library of 28,000 vols.; social science research, information, seminars, courses; Dir. WEINE KARLSSON; Librarian BRITT JOHANSSON; publs. monographs†, *Latinoamericana*†, documents.

**Nordiska samfundet för Latinamerika-forskning** (*Scandinavian Association for Research on Latin America*): c/o Latinamerika-institutet, P.O.B. 6909, 102 39 Stockholm; to promote research, publications, conferences and seminars on Latin America in the Nordic countries; publs. *Ibero-Americana*,† *Scandinavian Studies on Latin America*†.

**Nordiska Afrikainstitutet** (*The Scandinavian Institute of African Studies*): P.O.B. 2126, S-750 02 Uppsala; f. 1962; documentation and research centre for current African affairs, library, publication work, lectures, seminars and courses; library of 26,000 vols., 800 periodicals; Dir. CARL GÖSTA WIDSTRAND; Librarian Mrs. B. FAHLANDER; Secs. K. E. ERICSON, THOMAS RIDAEUS; publs. *Annual seminar Proceedings*†, *Research Reports*†, *Africana*†, *Newsletter*†.

### MEDICINE

**Medicinska forskningsrådet** (*Medical Research Council*): Box 6713, 113 85 Stockholm; f. 1945, reorganized 1977; established under the Ministry of Education and Public Instruction to administer funds provided annually by the Swedish Parliament for the promotion of scientific research in medicine; 10 mems.; Chair. BENGT PETRI; Sec. Prof. HENRY DANIELSSON, M.D.

**Statens Livsmedelsverk** (*The National Food Administration*): S-751 26 Uppsala; f. 1972; highest supervising agency in Sweden for foodstuffs and handling of foodstuffs in accordance with the Food Act; 230 mems.; library of about 10,000 vols.; Dir.-Gen. A. ENGSTRÖM; publs. *Vår Föda*† (research report), *Livsmedelsverkets författningar*† (The National Food Administration's Announcements), various papers in scientific journals in the fields of Food Hygiene and Human Nutrition.

### NATURAL SCIENCE

**Abisko naturvetenskapliga station** (*Abisko Natural Science Research Station*): 980 24 Abisko; belongs to Royal Swedish Academy of Sciences; research mainly on sub-arctic mountain ecology; Dir. Prof. MATS SONESSON.

**Beijerinstitutet** (*International Institute for Energy and Human Ecology*): Box 50005, 104 05 Stockholm; f. 1977; belongs to the Royal Swedish Academy of Sciences; research on long-term issues of international importance concerned with man's use of energy and its impact on the environment; Dir. Prof. GORDON T. GOODMAN.

**Bergianska stiftelsen** (*Bergius Foundation*): Box 50017, 104 05 Stockholm; f. 1976; belongs to the Royal Swedish Academy of Sciences; botanical and horticultural research; Dir. Prof. BERGIANUS MÅNS RYBERG.

**Forskningsinstitutet för Atomfysik** (*Physics Research Institute*): Roslagsvägen 100, S-104 05 Stockholm 50; f. 1937 as Nobel Institute of Physics, present name 1964; research in nuclear, atomic, molecular and surface physics; accelerator, electronics, nuclear chemistry and nuclear theory divisions; computer section; library of 10,000 vols.; Dir. Prof. INGMAR BERGSTRÖM; publs. *Annual Report.*

**Forskningsstationen för astrofysik på La Palma** (*Astrophysical Research Station at La Palma*): c/o Stockholms observatorium, 133 00 Saltsjöbaden; f. 1951, reorganized 1978; solar research; works in co-operation with Danish, British and Spanish observatories in La Palma; Dir. Prof. ARNE WYLLER.

**Kristinebergs marinbiologiska station** (*Kristineberg Marine Biological Station*): 450 34 Fiskebäckskil; f. 1877; belongs to the Royal Swedish Academy of Sciences; marine ecology and physiological research on marine animals and plants; Dir. Prof. JARL-OVE STRÖMBERG.

**Makarna Mittag-Lefflers Matematiska Stiftelse** (*Mittag-Leffler Institute*): Auravägen 17, S-182 62 Djursholm; f. 1916; research institute to promote pure mathematics; belongs to Swedish Academy of Science; about 20 mems.; library of 40,000 vols.; Dir. LENNART CARLESON; publs. *Acta Mathematica, Arkiv för Matematik.*

**Naturvetenskapliga forskningsrådet** (*Swedish Natural Science Research Council*): Box 6711, 113 85 Stockholm; f. 1977 by amalgamation of *Statens naturvetenskapliga forskningsråd* (f. 1946) and *Statens råd för atomforskning* (f. 1945); objects are to promote basic research in natural sciences in Sweden and internationally through CERN, CEBM, EMBL, ESO, NORDITA and EISCAT; offers grants to scientists and scientific institutions; 11 mems.; Pres. Gov. MATS LEMNE; Sec. Prof. INGVAR LINDQVIST; publs. *Svensk naturvetenskap* (yearbook), *Annual Report.*

**Statistiska Centralbyran** (*National Central Bureau of Statistics*): Karlavägen 100, Stockholm; postal address: S-11581 Stockholm; f. 1858; Dir.-Gen. Dr. LENNART NILSSON; seven departments: three are subject-matter depts. for special statistical branches, and four functional depts.; publs. include *Statistical Abstract of Sweden, Statistical Review, Monthly Digest of Swedish Statistics*; library: see Libraries.

**Stockholms Observatorium** (*Stockholm Observatory*): S-133 00 Saltsjöbaden; f. 1753; Dir. Prof. P. O. LINDBLAD.

**Sveriges Geologiska Undersökning** (*Geological Survey of Sweden*): S-751 28 Uppsala; f. 1858; Government institute for scientific and practical research on the geology of Sweden; 772 mems.; library with 2,200 metres vols.; Dir. GUNNAR RIBRANT; publs. geological maps with details†, memoirs†.

### SOCIAL SCIENCES

**Humanistisk-samhällsvetenskapliga forskningsrådet** (*Swedish Council for Research in the Humanities and Social Sciences*): Sveavägen 166, S-113 46 Stockholm; f. 1977 as a fusion of Swedish Humanistic Research Council and Swedish Council for Social Science Research; 11 mems.; Chair. Prof. ERIK LÖNNROTH; Sec. Prof. PÄR-ERIK BACK.

### TECHNOLOGY

**Cement och Betonginstitutet** (*Swedish Cement and Concrete Research Institute*): Fack, S-100 44 Stockholm 70; f. 1941; conducts research into and acts as a consultancy for engineering materials based on cement and concrete and allied materials; library of 7,000 vols.; Dir. Prof. SVEN G. BERGSTRÖM; Librarian Miss TUULA OJALA; publs. *CBI rapporter/reports*†, *CBI forskning/research*†, *CBI rekommendationer/recommendations*†.

**Flygtekniska Försöksanstalten, FFA** (*The Aeronautical Research Institute of Sweden*): Ranhammarsvägen 12, Box 11021, S-161 11 Bromma; f. 1940; 250 mems.; Dir-Gen. SVEN-OLOF OLIN; Heads of Aerodynamics Dept. G. DROUGGE, G. ERIKSSON; Chief of Structures Dept. S. LUNDGREN; Heads of Engineering Dept. C. NELANDER, L. DANIELSSON; Admin. Head B. SEDIN; Librarian Mrs. G. LARSSON; publ. *FFA Meddelanden*† (Reports).

**Institutet för metallforskning** (*Swedish Institute for Metals Research*): Drottning Kristinas väg 48, S-11428 Stockholm; f. 1919, reorganized 1943 and 1962; research activities include the use of methods for chemical analyses of steels and other metallic materials, examination of the relationship between microstructures and their mechanical properties and of the influence of non-metallic inclusions on the mechanical and chemical properties of metals; equipment in use includes electron-microscopes up to 1000 kV, a scanning electron microscope image analyser, X-ray diffraction equipment, three MTS universal hydraulic testing machines, a computer-controlled multiple rig of 10 machines for fatigue testing, a creep laboratory, X-ray fluorescence spectrometer, IDES optical spectrometer, automated electron probe microanalyser, atomic absorption instruments and furnaces for study of solidification phenomena; 2,000 monographs and 120 periodicals; Pres. Prof. RUNE LAGNEBORG; publ. *Annual Report.*

**Marintekniska institutet, SSPA** (*Swedish Maritime Research Centre, SSPA*): P.O.B. 24001, S-400 22 Göteborg 24; f. 1940; testing and research work; library of 4,900 vols. (incl. library of Stiftelsen Svensk Skeppsforskning (Swedish Ship Research Foundation); Dir.-Gen. Dr. HANS LINDGREN; publ. *Meddelanden*† (in English or English summary).

**Statens Geotekniska Institut** (*Swedish Geotechnical Institute*): 581 01 Linköping; f. 1944; staff of 75; research, information and consulting work in soil mechanics and foundation engineering; computerized library retrieval system; Dir. J. HARTLÉN; publ. *Report*†.

**Statens Provningsanstalt** (*National Swedish Testing Institute*): P.O.B. 857, S-501 15 Borås; f. 1920 (Testing Institute of the Royal Institute of Technology, 1896–1920); object is to carry out, on behalf of government institutions and private firms, impartial expert tests of raw products and manufactured articles, to investigate and report on their mechanical, physical and chemical properties and their commercial utilization, to test precious metals and to inspect weights and measures; c. 500 mems.; library of c. 15,000 vols.; Dir.-Gen. HENRIC BILDT; publs. *Tekniska rapporter* (technical reports), *Provningsmetoder* (testing methods), *Författningar, Godkännandelista.*

**Statens råd för byggnadsforskning** (*Swedish Council for Building Research*): St. Göransgatan 66, 112 33 Stockholm; f. 1960; aim is to promote and finance research in building and town planning ; 15 mems.; Pres. Prof. LENNART HOLM; Dir. INGRID ÅRLIN; publs. *Rapporter* (Reports), *Summaries, Synopses, Documents* (in English).

**Styrelsen för teknisk utveckling** (*National Swedish Board for Technical Development*): Liljeholmsvägen 32, P.O.B. 43200, S-100 72 Stockholm.

**Svenska Livsmedelsinstitutet (SIK)** (*Swedish Food Institute*): Box 5401, 402 29 Gothenburg; f. 1946; technological and scientific research on processing, preservation and storage of food, its manufacturing, packaging, distribution and consumption; documentation; education; service to Swedish and foreign food industries; staff of 95; library of 20,000 vols.; Dir. Prof. NILS BENGTSSON; publs. *SIK-Publikation, SIK-Rapport.*

**Svenska Textilforskningsinstitutet** (*Swedish Institute for Textile Research*): P.O.B. 5402, S-402 29 Göteborg; f. 1943; technical and scientific research on textile products, materials and processes; library of 5,000 vols.; Dir. Prof. JOEL LINDBERG.

# LIBRARIES AND ARCHIVES

## PRINCIPAL PUBLIC LIBRARIES

**Borås stadsbibliotek** (*City Library and County Library of Älvsborgs län*): Box 856, S-501 15 Borås; f. 1860; 477,100 vols.; Chief Librarian INGEMAR KALÉN.

**Eskilstuna stadsbibliotek** (*City Library and County Library of Södermanlands län*): Kriebsensg. 4, 632 20 Eskilstuna; f. 1925; 558,413 vols.; Chief Librarian GUNNEL WORTZELIUS.

**Gävle stadsbibliotek** (*City Library and County Library of Gävleborgs län*): S. Strandgatan 6, Box 801, 801 30 Gävle; f. 1907; 445,000 vols.; Chief Librarian WESTER WESTESON.

**Göteborgs stadsbibliotek** (*City Library and County Library of Göteborgs och Bohus län*): Götaplatsen, Gothenburg; f. 1861; 1,000,000 vols.; Chief Librarian SIGURD MÖHLENBROCK.

**Halmstads stadsbibliotek** (*City Library and County Library of Hallands län*): Fredsgatan 2, Halmstad; f. 1922; 400,000 vols.; Chief Librarian BARBRO FORSBERG.

**Jämtlands läns bibliotek** (*City Library of Östersund and County Library of Jämtlands län*): Rådhusgatan 25, 83100 Östersund; f. 1833; 380,000 vols.; Chief Librarian SIGRID THOMSON.

**Jönköpings stadsbibliotek** (*City Library and County Library of Jönköpings län*): Slottsgatan 2, 552 40 Jönköping; f. 1916; 600,000 vols.; Chief Librarian GUNVOR ERIKSSON.

**Kalmar stadsbibliotek** (*City Library and County Library of Kalmar län*): Slottsvägen 1, 392 33 Kalmar; f. 1922; 327,000 vols.; Chief Librarian RUNE ARNLING.

**Landsbiblioteket i Växjö** (*City and County Library, Kronobergs län*): Västra Esplanaden 7B, Växjö; f. 1954; 350,000 vols.; Chief Librarian OLLE WINGBORG.

**Luleå stadsbibliotek** (*City Library and County Library of Norrbottens län*): Kyrkogatan 15, 95100 Luleå; f. 1903; 220,000 vols.; special collection of Finnish Literature; Chief Librarian EVA VIIRMAN.

**Malmö stadsbibliotek** (*City Library, County Library of Malmöhus län and Loan Centre for South Sweden*): Regementsgatan 3, 21142 Malmö; f. 1905; 1,134,346 vols.; Chief Librarian BENGT HOLMSTRÖM; publs. annual acquisitions catalogue, *Litteratur om Skåne* (Bibliography of Scania 1974–).

**Norrköpings stadsbibliotek** (*Norrköping City Library*): Box 2062, 600 08 Norrköping; f. 1913; 275,400 vols.

**Örebro stadsbibliotek** (*City Library and County Library of Örebro län*): Box 60. 701 02 Örebro; f. 1862; 610,000 vols.; Chief Librarian EVA VIIRMAN.

**Stifts- och landsbiblioteket i Linköping** (*State County Library, Östergötlands län*): Box 3085, 580 03 Linköping 3; f. 1926; 670,000 vols.; Chief Librarian BIRGIT VAN ERK.

**Stifts- och landsbiblioteket i Skara** (*State County and City Library of Skaraborgs län*): Biblioteksgatan, Skara; f. 1938; 330,000 vols.; Chief Librarian ARNE STRÄNG.

**Stockholms stadsbibliotek** (*City Library of Stockholm*): Box 6502, 113 83 Stockholm; f. 1927; 1,882,329 vols.; Chief Librarian ULF DITTMER; publ. *Katalog över nyförvärv* (annual).

**Umeå stadsbibliotek** (*City Library and County Library of Västerbottens län*): Box 712, S-901 10 Umeå; f. 1903; 450,000 vols.; Chief Librarian GUSTAV LUNDBLAD.

**Uppsala stadsbibliotek** (*City Library and County Library of Uppsala län*): Box 643, 751 27 Uppsala 1; f. 1906; 655,450 vols.; Chief Librarian ESTRID LARSSON.

**Västerås stadsbibliotek** (*City and County Library of Västmanlands län*): Box 717, S-721 20 Västerås; f. 1952; 600,000 vols.; Chief Librarian JAN NILSSON.

## OTHER LIBRARIES
### STOCKHOLM

**Riksarkivet** (*The National Record Office*): Fyrverkarbacken 13-17, Box 34 104, 100 26 Stockholm; f. 1618; National

Archivist Prof. SVEN LUNDKVIST; publ. *Meddelanden från Svenska riksarkivet.*

**Handelshögskolans Bibliotek** (*Library of the Stockholm School of Economics*): Box 6501, S-113 83 Stockholm; f 1909; 193,000 vols.; economic and administrative subjects; Librarian BIRGITTA JANSON; publ. *List Econ.* (irregular).

**Karolinska Institutets Bibliotek och Informationscentral** (*Karolinska Institute Library and Medical Information Centre*): Box 60201, S-104 01 Stockholm; f. 1810; 232,000 vols., 212,000 theses, 2,700 current periodicals, 875 MSS. on medicine; centre for computerized information and documentation services and Nordic MEDLARS centre; affiliated library at Huddinge Hospital, branch library at the Faculty of Odontology; Chief Librarian HANS BAUDE; publs. *List bio-med* (biomedical serials in Scandinavian libraries), list of new acquisitions (every 2 months), *KIB-Rapport* (irregular).

**Krigsarkivet** (*Military Archives*): Fack, S-104 50 Stockholm; f. 1805; documents and maps from military authorities and regiments; Chief Keeper Dr. ALF ÅBERG.

**Kungl. Biblioteket** (*Royal Library*): Box 5039, S-102 4 1 Stockholm; f. early 17th century; 2 million vols.; National Library of Sweden with the most complete collection of Swedish printed books in the world; foreign holdings in humanities and social sciences; important collections of Old Swedish and Icelandic MSS.; special collections include incunabula, elzeviers, maps, portraits, heraldry, Japanese collection of A. E. Nordenskiöld; Dir. Dr. LARS TYNELL; publs. *Accesionskatalog* (since 1886), listing foreign books acquired by Swedish research libraries (annual), *Svensk bokförteckning* (National Bibliography), *Acta.*

**Kungl. Musikaliska akademiens bibliotek** (*Library of the Royal Swedish Academy of Music*): Box 16326, 103 26 Stockholm; f. 1771; about 50,000 books on music, 300,000 scores of music, 22,500 MSS. and about 10,000 letters; the library is especially rich in 18th-century music; Chief Librarian ANDERS LÖNN; publs. *Urvalsförteckning över nyförvärv* (List of Acquisitions), *Publikationer utgivna av Kungl. Musikaliska akademiens bibliotek* (Publications of the Library of the Royal Swedish Academy of Music).

**Kungl. Tekniska Högskolans Bibliotek** (*Royal Institute of Technology Library*): Valhallavägen 81, S-100 44 Stockholm 70; f. 1826; centre for computerized information and documentation services in science and technology; 12,000 metres shelving, 5,000 periodicals; Chief Librarian STEPHAN SCHWARZ; publs. *Students' Guide*†, *Curricula*†, *Catalogue of the Royal Institute of Technology*†, *List Tech* (list of foreign periodicals and serials in Swedish libraries in technological fields)†, Report series *Stockholm Papers in Library and Information Science*†, *Stockholm Papers in History and Philosophy of Technology*†.

**Kungl. Vitterhets Historie och Antikvitetsakademiens Bibliotek** (*Library of the Royal Academy of Letters, History and Antiquities*): P.O.B. 5405, Storgatan 41, S-114 84 Stockholm; f. 1786; 150,000 vols.; open to the public; Chief Librarian Dr. ANDERS HEDVALL.

**Riksdagsbiblioteket** (*Parliamentary Library*): S-100 12 Stockholm 46; f. 1851; central administrative library intended to serve the Riksdag and the administrative services; 500,000 vols.; chiefly devoted to law, political science, administration and social science; Chief Librarian LENNART GRÖNBERG; publs. *Årsberättelse* (Annual Report), *Sveriges statliga publikationer: årsbibliografi* (Swedish government publications: annual bibliography).

**Stadsarkivet i Stockholm** (*Stockholm City Archives*): Kungsklippan 6, Box 22 063, S-104 22 Stockholm; f. 1930; documents from local authorities and the municipal government of Stockholm; archives on urban history of Stockholm; c. 110,000 vols.; 46,000 shelfmetres; City Archivist Dr. ROLF VALLERÖ; publs. *Studier och handlingar rörande Stockholms historia*† (irregular), *Stockholms arkivnämd och stadsarkiv. Årsberättelse*† (annually), *Stockholms tänkeböcker från år 1592*† (irregular).

**Statens Psykologisk-Pedagogiska Bibliotek** (*National Library for Psychology and Education*): Hagagatan 23 A, Stockholm; P.O.B. 23099, S-104 35 Stockholm 23; f. 1885; 200,000 vols.; Librarian ELIN EKMAN.

**Statistiska centralbyråns bibliotek** (*Library of the National Central Bureau of Statistics*): S-11581 Stockholm; f. 1858; incorporating since 1972 the libraries of the National Boards of Building and Planning, Education, and Health and Welfare; c. 5,000 periodicals as well as statistics both official and international; Chief Librarian M. LINDMARK.

**Svenska Akademiens Nobelbibliotek** (*Nobel Library of the Swedish Academy*): Börshuset, Källargränd 4, 111 29 Stockholm; f. 1901: 175,000 vols.; Librarian ANDERS RYBERG.

**Svenskt musikhistoriskt arkiv** (*Swedish Music History Archive*): Box 16326, 103 26 Stockholm; f. 1965; Director Dr. A. HELMER; a documentation centre for music bibliography and for research on musical sources and musical life in Sweden; publs. *Bulletin* (periodical), series *Musik i Sverige* (jointly with the Swedish Society for Musicology).

**Sveriges Radio Bibliotek och Arkiv** (*Libraries and Archives of the Swedish Broadcasting Corporation*): 105 10 Stockholm; f. 1925; documents relating to Swedish broadcasting and television.

**Stockholm universitets bibliotek med Kungl. Vetenskapsakademiens Bibliotek** (*Stockholm University Library with the Library of the Royal Academy of Sciences*): S-106 91 Stockholm; 1,400,000 vols.; in 1978 incorporated: **Kungl. Vetenskapsakademiens Bibliotek** (*Library of the Royal Academy of Sciences*): Box 50 001, S-104 05 Stockholm; f. 1739; 600,000 vols., chiefly devoted to natural sciences, 10,500 MSS., including the valuable Bergius and Swedenborg collections; open to the public; Head Librarian Dr. WILHELM ODELBERG.

**Utrikesdepartementet** (*Library of The Royal Swedish Ministry of Foreign Affairs*): P.O.B. 16121, S-103 23 Stockholm; works on modern history and politics, law, international law, economy and statistics; not open to the public; Deputy Head of Division STAFFAN RUNESTAM.

### GOTHENBURG

**Chalmers Tekniska Högskolas Bibliotek** (*Chalmers University of Technology Library*): 412 96 Gothenburg 5; f. 1829; 280,000 vols.; Chief Librarian SVEN WESTBERG.

**Göteborgs Universitetsbibliotek** (*Gothenburg University Library*): Central Library, P.O.B. 5096, S-402 22 Göteborg 5; Bio-Medical Library, P.O.B. 33 031, S-400 33 Göteborg; Botanical Library, Carl Skottsbergs gata 22, S-413 19 Göteborg; Economics Library, Vasagatan 3, S-411 24 Göteborg; Mölndal Library, P.O.B. 1010, S-431 26 Mölndal; f. 1861; 1,400,000 vols., 500,000 pamphlets; Chief Librarian P. HALLBERG; publs. *Acta*†, *Acta Universitatis Gothoburgensis*† (monographs), *New Literature on Women*† (bibliography).

### LINKÖPING

**Linköpings universitetsbibliotek** (*Linköping University Library*): S-581 83 Linköping; f. 1969; 200,000 vols.; Chief Librarian K. MARKLUND; publ. *Publikation*†.

### LUND

**Lund University Library:** Box 1010, S-221 03 Lund; f. 1671; deposit and international lending library; main library (humanities and social sciences) 2,100,000 vols., c. 13,000 MSS.; the Bibliotheca Gripenhielmiana (6,000 vols. 16th and 17th century prints); library 2 (medicine, science and technology) 900,000 vols.; library 3 (textbooks) 17,000 vols.; library 4 (newspapers) 240,000 vols., 16,000 reels of microfilm; Chief Librarian BJÖRN TELL; publ. *Skrifter utgivna*.

### NYKÖPING

**Studsvik Energiteknik AB Library:** S-611 82 Nyköping; f. 1947; energy research and technology; 50,000 vols., 650,000 reports (c. 500,000 on microfilm), 1,400 periodicals; publ. *Studsvik Reports†*.

### UMEÅ

**Umeå Universitetsbibliotek** (*University Library of Umeå*): Box 718, S-901 10 Umeå; f. 1964; 400,000 vols.; Chief Librarian K. SNELLMAN.

### UPPSALA

**Sveriges lantbruksuniversitets bibliotek** (*Library of the Swedish University of Agricultural Sciences*): S-750 07 Uppsala 7; f. 1932; 8,000 shelf-metres including those in branch libraries: Alnarp Library, Garpenberg Library, Skara Veterinary Library, Forestry Library (Umeå); Dir. LARS-ERIK SANNER.

**Uppsala University Library:** Box 510, 751 20 Uppsala; f. 1620; over 2,000,000 vols. (including more than 2,500 incunabula and over 700,000 foreign dissertations); 32,000 MSS., including the famous *Codex argenteus*, the "Silver Bible" of the 6th century, a translation of the Gospels into the Gothic language, Swedish and Icelandic medieval MSS., the Bibliotheca Walleriana (medical books), a collection of old music books and MSS, a collection of old maps, engravings and drawings, including the *Carta Marina* of 1539 by Olaus Magnus (earliest accurate map of Scandinavia); Librarian THOMAS TOTTIE; publs. include *Acta Universitatis Upsaliensis†*, *Acta Bibliothecae R. Universitatis Upsaliensis†*, *Bibliotheca Ekmaniana†*, *Årsberättelse†* (Annual Report), etc.

## MUSEUMS AND ART GALLERIES

### STOCKHOLM

**Armémuseum** (*Army Museum*): Riddargatan 13, P.O.B. 14095, S-10 441 Stockholm; f. 1879; c. 50,000 exhibits, 15th-20th century; library with 30,000 vols.; open daily; Dir. Dr. BENGT M. HOLMQUIST; Curators ARNE DANIELSSON, ULF G. HJORTH-ANDERSÉN, BENGT HERMANSSON; publs. *Meddelanden*.

**Etnografiska Museet** (*Ethnographical Museum of Sweden*): S-115 27 Stockholm; f. 1880; collection of 150,000 artefacts from Africa, America, Asia, Australia and the Pacific; the Museum also houses the *Sven Hedin Foundation*; Dir. KARL ERIK LARSSON; publs. *Ethnos†* (quarterly), *Klotet* (quarterly), Monograph Series.

**Livrustkammaren, Skoklosters Slott och Hallwylska Museet** (*Royal Armoury, Skokloster Castle and Hallwyl Museum*): Slottsbacken 3, 111 30 Stockholm; Dir. KERSTI HOLMQUIST.

*Livrustkammaren:* Slottsbacken 3, 111 30 Stockholm; f. 1628; housed in south wing of Royal Palace; historical collections dating from mid 16th century; Swedish royal arms, costumes, jewels, coaches, etc.; Dir. KERSTI HOLMQUIST; Curators GUDRUN EKSTRAND, NILS DREJHOLT; publ. *Livrustkammaren*.

*Skoklosters Slott:* 198 00 Bålsta; baroque castle built 1654 by Count C. G. Wrangel; contains mainly 17th-century furniture, paintings, applied art and armour; library; Dir. ARNE LOSMAN; Curator KARIN SKERI; publ. *Skokloster Studies*.

*Hallwylska Museet:* Hamngatan 4, 111 47 Stockholm; f. c. 1900; private residence of Hallwyl family; collection of furniture, paintings, applied art, etc.; Dir. EVA HELENA CASSEL-PHIL.

**Musikmuseet:** Sibyllegatan 2, 11451 Stockholm; f. 1899; over 4,000 exhibits including European art and folk instruments, also non-European instruments; archives and library; Dir. G. LARSSON.

**Nationalmuseum:** 103 24 Stockholm; f. 1792; 6,450 paintings, icons and miniatures, 3,850 sculptures, incl. antiquities, 194,000 drawings and prints, 28,000 numbers of applied art, library with 165,000 vols. and 620,000 clippings; also administers collections of several royal castles with 7,170 works of art; Supt. P. BJURSTRÖM; Heads of Depts.: Paintings and Sculptures P. GRATE; Prints and Drawings B. MAGNUSSON; Applied Art Mrs. H. DAHLBÄCK-LUTTEMAN; Lending Dept. Mrs. A.-S. TOPELIUS; Education N. G. HÖKBY; Royal Castles Collection ULF G. JOHNSSON; publs. *Bulletin* (with annual report)†, *Year Book* and catalogues.

**Moderna Museet** (*Contemporary Art Museum*): Skeppsholmen, Box 16382, 103 27 Stockholm 16; f. 1958; 3,700 paintings and sculptures; also administers Photographic Museum, f. 1971; 400,000 photographs; Dir. OLLE GRANATH.

**Naturhistoriska Riksmuseet** (*Swedish Museum of Natural History*): S-104 05 Stockholm; f. 1819; Museum Department (exhibitions and administration): Dir. K. ENGSTROM; Research Department: Head: Prof. A. G. JOHNELS; Heads of Sections: Vertebrate, Prof. A. G. JOHNELS; Entomology, Prof. E. SYLVÉN; Invertebrate, Prof. L. ORRHAGE; Palaeozoology, Prof. T. ØRVIG; Phanerogamic Botany, Prof. B. NORDENSTAM; Cryptogamic Botany, Prof. R. SANTESSON; Palaeobotany, Prof. A. BRITTA LUNDBLAD; Mineralogy, Prof. E. WELIN; publ. *Fauna och flora* (popular biology magazine).

**Nordiska Museet:** S-115 21 Stockholm, Djurgårdsvägen 6-16; f. 1873; ethnological and industrial art collections; c. 1,500,000 exhibits; library of 300,000 vols.; Dir. SUNE ZACHRISSON; Keeper of Trade, Industry and Crafts JONAS BERG; Keeper of Buildings, Household and Furnishing ELISABET STAVENOW-HIDEMARK; Keeper of Textiles INGRID BERGMAN; Keeper of Cultural Field Research MÁTYÁS SZABÓ; Head of Education and Public Relations SKANS TORSTEN NILSSON; Institute of Folk Life Research Prof. ÅKE DAUN; Chief Librarian JAN-ÖJVIND SWAHN; publs. *Acta Lapponica†*, *Fataburen†* (year book), *Nordiska museets handlingar†*, *Svenskt liv och arbete†*, books on industrial art and architecture, ethnology and folklore.

**Östasiatiska Museet** (*Museum of Far Eastern Antiquities*): Skeppsholmen, Box 16381, S-103 27 Stockholm; f. 1959; art section containing mainly Chinese paintings, sculptures and ceramics; archaeological section containing pottery and bronze objects; Japanese, Korean and Indian art; Dir. Dr. JAN WIRGIN; Curator P. O. LEIJON; publ. *Bulletin†* (annually).

**Riksantikvarieämbetet och Statens historiska museer** (*The Central Board for Antiquities and National Historical Museums*): Box 5405, S-114 84 Stockholm; f. 1630, refounded 1847; consists of the following:

*Riksantikvarieämbetet* (Central Board of National Antiquities): supervises historic monuments, registers them, conducts excavations and research; Dir.-Gen. ROLAND PÅLSSON; publs. *Årsbok* (annually), *Kulturminnesvård* (every 2 months), *Rapport* (continuously), *ICO Iconographic Post* (quarterly).

**Statens historiska museum** (*Museum of National Antiquities*): Dir. OLOV ISAKSSON; publ. *Historiska Nyheter* (continuously).

**Kungl. Myntkabinettet statens museum för mynt medalj och penninghistoria** (*Royal Coin Cabinet National Museum of Monetary History*): Dir. ULLA WESTERMARK; publs. *Sylloge Nummorum Graecorum†*, *Catalogue of Coins from the Viking Age found in Sweden†*, *Numismatica Stockholmiensia†*.

**Medelhavsmuseet** (*Museum of Mediterranean and Near Eastern Antiquities*): Dir. CARL-GUSTAF STYRENIUS; publs. *Bulletin* (annually), *Memoir*.

**Tekniska institutionen** (*Institute of Technology*): central conservation and analysis laboratory for archaeological finds, stone, wood, textiles, leather, ceramics and photographic documentation; Dir. LARS BARKMAN.

**Antikvarisk-topografiska arkivet** (*Antiquarian Topographical Archives*): P.O.B. 5405, 114 84 Stockholm; f. 1786 (1666); archives of the Collegium Antiquitatum and the Royal Archives of Antiquities (1666–1786), archives and collections of the Royal Academy of Letters, History and Antiquities, and of the Central Board for Antiquities (1786–1975) and National Historical Museums, archives of the office of monuments (1918–67) of the National Board of Public Buildings; 1,100 million vols., etc.; 90,000 maps and drawings; 1,000,000 negatives and photographs; open to the public; Head Dr. STEFAN ÖSTERGREN.

**Kungl. Vitterhets Historie och Antikvitets Akademien Bibliotek** (*Library of the Royal Academy of Letters, History and Antiquities*): see under Libraries.

**Skansen:** S-115 21 Stockholm; f. 1891; ancient buildings, zoological garden; Dir. NILS ERIK BAEHRENDTZ; Keeper of Buildings ARNE BIÖRNSTAD; Keeper of Natural History PER OLOF PALM; publs. daily programmes, guides, etc.

**Statens sjöhistoriska museum** (*National Maritime Museum*): Wasavarvet, S-11527 Stockholm; f. 1938; the oldest part of the Royal Naval Section originates from the Royal Chambers in 1752; collections give a view of Swedish naval and merchant history, vessels of the past and of today; c. 40,000 vols.; Dir. PER LUNDSTRÖM; publ. *Sjöhistorisk årsbok†*.

**Wasavarvet** (*Warship Wasa Museum*): f. 1962; the oldest fully identified and salvaged ship in the world; lost 1628, raised 1961; Curator LARS-ÅKE KVARNING.

**Stockholms Stadsmuseum** (*City Museum*): Ryssgården, Slussen, Stockholm; f. 1932; c. 48,000 items including the "Lohe treasure", naive 19th-century paintings of Josabeth Sjöberg and armed 15th-century vessel; over 1,000,000 photographs, 2,000 paintings, 30,000 drawings, sketches and engravings; Dir. BJÖRN HALLERDT; Curator Archives, Library, Collections and Preservation Bo WINGREN; Curator Building and Archaeological Dept. JONAS FERENIUS; Curator Museums Dept. HANS EKLUND; publs. *Stadsvandringar†* (year book), *Annual Report*, catalogues.

**Tekniska Museet** (*National Museum of Science and Technology*): Museivägen 7, 115 27 Stockholm; f. 1924; 35,000 old machines, models, tools, etc.; Telemuseum: telegraphy, telephony; 700 metres of archives; library of 37,000 vols.; open daily; Dir. ERIC DYRING; publ. *Daedalus†* (year book).

## GOTHENBURG

**Göteborgs Konstmuseum** (*Gothenburg Art Gallery*): Götaplatsen, S-412 56 Göteborg; f. 1861; European paintings, sculpture, prints and drawings from 1500, special collections of French art from 1820 onwards and Scandinavian art; art library; Dir. KARL-GUSTAF HEDÉN.

**Göteborgs Museer** (*Museums of the City of Gothenburg*): f. 1861; Chair. of Trustees Prof. LARS ÅGREN; publs. *Annual Reports* and special series from various museums; comprises the following:

**Archaeological Museum:** Skärgårdsgatan 4; Dir. Dr. LILI KAELAS.

**Ethnographical Museum:** N. Hamngaten 12; Dir. Dr. KJELL ZETTERSTRÖM.

**Historical Museum:** N. Hamngaten 12; Dir. Dr. ALLAN T. NILSON.

**Museum of Fine Arts:** Götaplatsen; Dir. Dr. KARL-GUSTAV HEDEN.

**Museum of Natural History:** Slottsskogen; Dir. Dr. BENGT HUBEN-DICK.

**Röhss Museum of Arts and Crafts:** Vasagatan 37-39; Dir. JAN BRUNIUS.

**Theatre Museum:** Berzeliigaten; Dir. ÅKE PETTERSSON.

**Military Museum "Kronan":** attached to Historical Museum; Curator Capt. H. WARFVINGE.

**Sjöfartsmuseet** (*The Maritime Museum and Aquarium*): Karl Johansgatan 1-3, S-414 59 Göteborg; f. 1913 by the Nautical Society of Gothenburg; illustrates Swedish maritime history, as exemplified by the work of the Royal Navy, Merchant Navy, Fishing Fleets and yachtsmen; includes an open-air museum; the collection includes models, marine paintings, portraits, drawings, maps and a library of 14,000 books and prints; Dir. Commdr. GÖRAN SUNDSTRÖM; publ. *Unda Maris†* (year book).

## LUND

**Kulturhistoriska Museet** (*Cultural History Museum*): Box 1095, 221 04 Lund; f. 1882; ethnography, cultural history, medieval archaeology; open-air museum, town and country houses; applied arts (ceramics, textiles, archaeological finds from medieval Lund); Östarp, old farm with inn, 30 km. from Lund; library of 35,000 vols.; Dir. Dr. EVA NORDENSON; publ. *Kulturen†* (yearbook).

## MARIEFRED

**The Swedish National Portrait Gallery:** Gripsholm Castle, S-150 30 Mariefred; f. c. 1550; Curator ULF G. JOHNSSON (National Museum, Stockholm 16).

## UPPSALA

**Upplandsmuseet** (*Upplands Museum*): Box 2076, 750 02 Uppsala; f. 1959; provincial cultural history; Curator OLA EHN; publ. *Uppland*.

# UNIVERSITIES

## UNIVERSITETS- OCH HÖGSKOLEÄMBETET
(National Swedish Board of Universities and Colleges)
DROTTNINGGATAN 95A,
P.O.B. 45501, S-104 30 STOCKHOLM
Telephone: 08/24 85 60.

Government Agency in charge of management of the Swedish higher education system.

*Chancellor*: CARL-GUSTAF ANDRÉN.
*Deputy Chancellor*: ERLAND RINGBORG.
*Head of Information*: ERNST ERIK EHNMARK.

## CHALMERS TEKNISKA HÖGSKOLA
(Chalmers University of Technology)
S-412 96 GOTHENBURG
Telephone: (031) 81 01 00.
Telex: 2369 Chalbib S.

Founded 1829.

State control; Academic year: September to June.

*Rector*: Prof. S. OLVING.
*Vice-Rector*: Prof. R. MAGNUSSON.
*Chief Administrative Officer*: F. HJALMERS.
*Chief Librarian*: S. WESTBERG.
Library: see Libraries.

Number of teachers: 300, including 91 professors.

Number of students: 6,000 (incl. 500 postgraduate).

Publications: *Annual Report, Catalogue of Courses, Departmental Reports, Handbooks*.

### DEANS:

*Faculty Dean*: Prof. A. SAMUELSSON.
*School of Mathematics*: Prof. V. THOMÉE.
*School of Physics*: Prof. P. MYERS.
*School of Mechanical Engineering*: Prof. E. NILSSON.
*School of Electrical Engineering*: Prof. B. STENBORG.
*School of Civil Engineering*: Prof. Y. HAMMARLUND.
*School of Chemical Engineering*: Prof. P. FLODIN.
*School of Architecture*: Prof. W. KIESSLING.

### PROFESSORS:

*School of Mathematics*:
 FRIBERG, J., Mathematics
 JACOBINSKI, H., Mathematics
 JAGERS, P., Mathematical Statistics
 JOHNSON, C., Applied Mathematics
 THOMÉE, V., Mathematics

*School of Physics*:
 ALMÉN, O., Physics
 ANDERSSON, G., Physics
 ANDERSSON, S., Physics
 LINDGREN, I., Physics
 LUNDÉN, A., Physics
 LUNDQVIST, B., Mathematical Physics
 LUNDQVIST, S., Mathematical Physics
 MYERS, P., Solid State Physics
 NILSSON, J., Mathematical Physics
 SJÖLANDER, A., Statistical Physics
 SJÖSTRAND, N. G., Nuclear Physics

*School of Mechanical Engineering*:
 ALDMAN, B., Traffic Safety
 BOHLIN, H., Industrial Organization
 COLLIN, L., Combustion Engines
 EDBERG, B., Textile Technology
 FALKEMO, C., Ship Hydromechanics
 FISCHMEISTER, H., Engineering Metals
 HOLMBERG, B., Mechanics
 HULT, J., Strength of Materials
 JACOBSSON, B., Machine Design
 KUBÁT, J., Polymeric Materials
 LANGE, H., Marine Engineering
 McHUGH, B., Nuclear Engineering
 NILSSON, E., Turbomachines
 NORDSTRÖM, L., Steam Engineering
 OLSSON, E., Applied Thermodynamics and Fluid Dynamics
 SJÖSTEDT, L., Transport and Logistics
 SVENNERUD, A., Shipbuilding
 ÅKESSON, B., Strength of Materials

*School of Electrical Engineering*:
 BOLINDER, F., Circuit Theory
 BOOTH, R. S., Electron Physics
 CEGRELL, T., Electronic Systems Engineering
 ENG, S., Electrical Measurement Technique
 HÖGLUND, B., Electron Physics
 KRISTIANSSON, L., Information Theory
 MAGNUSSON, R., Applied Electronics
 OLSSON, T., Medical Electronics
 OLVING, S., Electron Physics, Vacuum and Gas Electron Physics
 QVARNSTRÖM, B., Control Engineering
 STEMME, E., Computer Technique
 STENBORG, B., Applied Electrical Engineering
 WALLMARK, T., Electron Physics, Solid State Electron Physics
 WILHELMSSON, H., Electromagnetic Field Theory
 THORBORG, K., Power Electronics

*School of Civil Engineering*:
 ABEL, E., Building Services Engineering
 BALMÉR, P., Water Supply and Sewerage Engineering
 ERIKSSON, K. G., Geology and Mineralogy
 HAMMARLUND, Y., Building Economics and Organization
 HANSBO, S., Geotecnnical Engineering
 KIHLMAN, T., Building Acoustics
 LARSSON, L.-E., Building Technology
 LOSBERG, A., Structural Engineering, Concrete Constructions
 MALINOWSKI, R., Science of Building Materials
 NILSSON, L. E., Highway Engineering
 SAMUELSSON, A., Structural Mechanics
 SJÖBERG, A., Hydraulics

*School of Chemical Engineering*:
 FLODIN, P., Polymer Technology
 HEDSTRÖM, B., Chemical Engineering Equipment
 NILSSON, M., Organic Chemistry
 NORDEN, B., Physical Chemistry
 OTTERSTEDT, J.-E., Engineering Chemistry
 RYDBERG, J., Nuclear Chemistry
 SCHÖÖN, N. H., Chemical Reaction Engineering
 SIMONSSON, R., Engineering Chemistry
 VANNERBERG, N.-G., Inorganic Chemistry

*School of Architecture*:
 BJÖRKMAN, A., Basic Design and Sketching, Painting and Sculpture
 CORNELL, E., Architectural History and Theory (Humanities)
 GUNNARSSON, O., Town Planning
 KIESSLING, W., Building Construction
 KÄRRHOLM, G., Building Construction
 NORDENSTRÖM, H., Planning and Design Methods
 OLIVEGREN, J., Architecture
 ÅGREN, L., Architecture

ATTACHED INSTITUTE:
**Onsala Space Observatory:** 439 00 Onsala; Dir. Prof. B. RÖNNÄNG.

## GÖTEBORGS UNIVERSITET
(Gothenburg University)
VASAPARKEN,
411 24 GOTHENBURG
Telephone: 031 810400.

Founded 1891, became state university 1954.

Academic year: September to June.

*Rector*: Prof. G. LUNDGREN.
*Vice-Rector*: Prof. S. ALLÉN.
*Chief Administrative Officer*: L. HJ. GURMUND.
*Librarian*: P. HALLBERG.

Library: see Libraries.

Number of professors: 140.
Number of students: 22,000.

### DEANS:

*Faculty of Arts*: Prof. A. ELLEGÅRD.
 *Historical-Philosophical Section*: Prof. J. WEIBULL.
 *Language Section*: Prof. A. ELLEGÅRD.
*Faculty of Social Sciences*: Prof. B. RUNBLAD.
*Faculty of Natural Sciences*: Prof. B. MALMSTRÖM.
 *Chemical Section*: Prof. T. VÄNNGÅRD.
 *Biological-Geographical Section*: Prof. A. ENEMAR.
*Faculty of Medicine*: Prof. P. LUNDIN.
*Faculty of Dentistry*: Prof. J. LINDHE.

### PROFESSORS:

*Faculty of Arts*:
 *Historical-Philosophical Section*:
  EK, S., Ethnology
  HALLBERG, P., History of Literature
  HOLMBERG, Å., History
  JOHANSEN, A., Archaeology
  LIEDMAN, S.-E., History of Ideas and Learning
  LING, J., Musicology
  SEGELBERG, I., Philosophy
  TÖRNEBOHM, H., Theory of Science
  WADELL, M.-B., History of Art
  WEIBULL, J., History
  ÅSTRÖM, P., Ancient Culture and Civilization

*Language Section:*
ALLÉN, S., Computational Linguistics
BENSON, S., Northern Languages
ELLEGÅRD, A., English
FABRICIUS, C., Greek
FRIDH, Å., Latin
FRYKMAN, E., English
JACOBSSON, G., Slavonic Languages
LIEBERT, G., Sanskrit and Comparative Philology
PALVA, H., Arabic
VON PROSCHWITZ, G., Romance Languages
ÅSDAHL HOLMBERG, M., German

*Faculty of Social Sciences:*
AIJMER, G., Social Anthropology
BERGENDAHL, G., Business Finance
BUBENKO, JANIS, Computer Science
DAHLSTRÖM, E., Sociology
GODLUND, S., Human Geography
GOLDBERG, W., Business Finance
GRÖNFORS, K., Naval Law
HERLITZ, L., Economic History
HÄRNQVIST, K., Pedagogy
JÖNSSON, S., Business Finance
KLEVMARKEN, A., Statistics
LARSSON, K., Comparative Physiological Psychology
LAULAJAINEN, R., Economic Geography
LYBECK, J., Economics
MARTON, F., Pedagogy
RUBENOWITZ, S., Applied Psychology
RUNDBLAD, B., Sociology
SANDSTRÖM, J., Commercial Law
SJÖBERG, L., Psychology
STUKÁT, K.-G., Pedagogy
SWEDNER, H., Social Work
WESTERSTÅHL, J., Political Science
WICKSTRÖM, B., Business Finance

*Faculty of Natural Sciences:*
  *Mathematical-Physical Section:*
ERIKSSON, K.-E., Theoretical Physics
HANNER, O., Mathematics

  *Chemical Section:*
ANIANSSON, G., Physical Chemistry
DYRSSEN, D., Analytical Chemistry
LUNDGREN, G., Inorganic Chemistry
MALMSTRÖM, B., Biochemistry
MELANDER, L., Organic Chemistry
VÄNNGÅRD, T., Biophysics

  *Biological-Geographical Section:*
ENEMAR, A., Zoology
FÄNGE, R., Zoophysiology
GUNDERSEN, K., Marine Microbiology
HARLING, G., Systematic Botany
JAASUND, E., Marine Botany
LEVAN, G., Genetics
RUDBERG, S., Physical Geography
VIRGIN, H., Plant Physiology
WENDELBO, P., Botany (Systematics and Phytogeography)

*Faculty of Medicine:*
AHRÉN, K., Physiology
ANDERSSON, S., Physiology
ANGERVALL, L., Pathology
BERTHOLD, C.-H., Anatomy
BJÖRK, L., X-Ray Diagnostics
BJÖRNTORP, P., Medicine
BRATTGÅRD, S.-O., Handicap Research
BRÅNEMARK, P.-I., Anatomy
BUCHT, H., Medicine, especially Nephrology
CARLSSON, A., Pharmacology
CARLSTEN, A., Clinical Physiology
EKHOLM, R., Anatomy
ENERBÄCK, L., Pathology
FOLKOW, B., Physiology
GOTTFRIES, C.-G., Psychiatry
HAGBERG, B., Paediatrics
HALLBERG, L., Medicine
HALLÉN, O., Oto-rhino-laryngology
HAMBERGER, A., Histology
HANSON, L.-Å., Clinical Immunology
HEDBERG, H., Rheumatology
HEDLUND, P., Infectious Diseases
HYDÉN, H., Histology
HÖÖK, O., Medical Rehabilitation
ISAKSSON, B., Clinical Nutrition
IWARSON, S., Infectious Diseases
JOHANSSON, B., Plastic Surgery
KARLBERG, P., Paediatrics
KOCK, N., Surgery
LAGERKVIST, U., Medical and Physiological Chemistry
LIND, A., Bacteriology
LINDAHL, T., Medical and Physiological Chemistry
LINDEGÅRD, B., Social Medicine
LINDGREN, S., Neurosurgery
LINDSTEDT, G., Clinical Chemistry
LINDSTEDT, S., Clinical Chemistry
LINNÉR, E., Ophthalmology
LUNDBERG, A., Physiology
LUNDIN, P. M., Pathology
NACHEMSON, A., Orthopaedic Surgery
NILSSON, N. J., Clinical Physiology
NOTTER, G., Radio-Therapeutics
OTTOSSON, J. O., Psychiatry
PETERSÉN, I., Clinical Neurophysiology
RÖCKERT, H., Histology
RYLANDER, R., Hygiene
SKÖLDBORN, H., Medical Radiophysics
SOURANDER, P., Pathology
STEG, G., Neurology
STENER, B., Orthopaedic Surgery
SVANBORG, A., Geriatric and Long-Term Care Medicine
SVENNERHOLM, L., Neurochemistry
SWANBECK, G., Dermatology and Venereal Diseases
WIQVIST, N., Obstetrics and Gynaecology
ZETTERGREN, L., Pathology
ÅKESSON, H. O., Psychiatry

*Faculty of Odontology:*
CARLSSON, G., Stomatognathic Physiology
ENGSTRÖM, B., Endodontics
HÄGGENDAL, J., Pharmacology
HEDEGÅRD, B., Prosthetics
HEYDEN, G., Oral Pathology
HOLLENDER, L., Oral Roentgendiagnosis
KRASSE, B., Cariology
LINDHE, J., Periodontology
MAGNUSSON, B., Pedodontics
MÖLLER, Å., Oral Microbiology
THILANDER, B., Orthodontics
THILANDER, H., Oral Surgery

# HÖGSKOLAN I KARLSTAD

BOX 9501, 650 09 KARLSTAD
Telephone: 054-13 00 20.

Founded 1967 as Universitetsfilialen, present name 1977.

State control; Academic year: September to June.

*Rector:* LENNART ANDERSSON.
*Vice-Rector:* OLA BRUNSTRÖM.
*Head of Administration:* BENGT NYLANDER.
*Chief Librarian:* BARBRO MARIN.
Library of 90,000 vols.
Number of teachers: 150.
Number of students: 3,500.
Publication: *Information från högskolan i Karlstadt* (monthly).

### HEADS OF SECTORS:

*Technology:* TRYGGVE BERGEK.
*Administration, Economics and Social Science:* INGEMAR ADOLFSSON.
*Cultural and Information Education:* STEN BLOMBERG.
*Teacher Training:*
  *Nursery School Training:* JOHAN HAESERT.
  *Primary and Middle School Teacher Training:* TORBJÖRN WIKLUND.
  *Upper School Teacher Training:* BRITA WERNER.
  *Recreation Instructor Training:* ALF SUNDIN.

### HEADS OF DEPARTMENTS:

ADOLFSSON, I., Mathematics and Statistics
ALWALL, G., Education and Psychology
BODLAND-JOHNSON, K., Arts and Crafts
BRUN, O., Music
CANNERHEIM, M., Educational Methods
COOPER, M., Modern Languages
KÄLLGREN, K.-G., Economics
LUNDBERG, B., Social Sciences
NILSSON, J., Swedish
OLDBERG, B., Natural Sciences

# KUNGLIGA TEKNISKA HÖGSKOLAN
(Royal Institute of Technology)

S-100 44 STOCKHOLM
Telephone: 08-7870000.
Telegraphic Address: "Technology".
Founded 1827.

State university; Academic year: September to June.

*President:* Prof. G. BRODIN.
*Vice-President:* Prof. G. SOHLENIUS.
*Chief Administrative Officer:* J. NYGREN.
*Chief Librarian:* S. SCHWARZ.

Library: see Libraries.

Number of teachers: 1,500, including 106 professors.

Number of students: 7,500.

Publications: *Catalogue*, *Study Handbook* (annual).

### DEANS:

*Faculty:* Prof. S. BERNDT.
*School of Physics:* Prof. N. ÅSLUND.
*School of Mechanical Engineering:* Asst. Prof. S. LUNDGREN.
*School of Aeronautics:* Prof. F. HJELTE.
*School of Electrical Engineering:* Prof. L. H. ZETTERBERG.
*School of Civil Engineering:* Prof. O. ANDERSSON.
*School of Chemical Engineering:* Prof. F. SETTERWALL.
*School of Mining and Metallurgy:* Prof. J. O. EDSTRÖM.
*School of Architecture:* Prof. H. RYD.
*School of Surveying:* Prof. E. CARLEGRIM.

### PROFESSORS:

*School of Physics:*
BIEDERMANN, K., Physics
BOHLIN, T., Automatic Control
BRULIN, O., Mechanics
DAHLQUIST, G., Numerical Analysis and Computing Science
ERMAN, P., Physics
GRIMVALL, G., Theoretical Physics

# UNIVERSITIES

HELLSTEN, U., Mathematics
HJALMARS, S., Mechanics
HULDT, L., Physics
INGELSTAM, L., Mathematics
KJELLBERG, B., Mathematics
LANDAHL, M. Mechanics
LARSSON, K.-E., Reactor Physics
NAGEL, B., Mathematical Physics
OLSSON, P.-O., Mathematical Physics
ROSÉN, B., Mathematical Statistics
SHAPIRO, H., Mathematics
THULIN, S., Applied Physics
ÅSLUND, N., Physics
ÅSTRÖM, H. U., Solid State Physics

*School of Mechanical Engineering:*
BECKER, K., Nuclear Reactor Engineering
BLOMBERG, F., Machine Design
DANIELSSON, A., Industrial Economics and Management
GADEFELT, G., Technical Acoustics
HEDGRAN, A., Nuclear Security
NORÉN, A., Fluid Technology
NORÉN-BRANDEL, T., Welding Technology
PETERSON, F., Heating and Ventilating
PIERRE, B., Applied Thermodynamics and Refrigeration
SAARMAN, E., Wood Technology and Processing
SCHNITTGER, J., Machine Elements
SÖDERBERG, O., Thermal Engineering
SOHLENIUS, G., Machine Tools
STENEROTH, E., Naval Architecture
ÅBERG, U., Industrial Ergonomics

*School of Aeronautics:*
ANDERSSON, B. J., Hydromechanics
BERNDT, S., Gas Dynamics
CARLSSON, J., Strength of Materials and Solid Mechanics
HJELTE, F., Aeronautics
STORÅKERS, B., Strength of Materials

*School of Electrical Engineering:*
EKBERG, S., Telecommunication Networks and Systems
FÄLTHAMMAR, C.-G., Plasma Physics
FANT, G., Speech Communication
HELLGREN, G., Applied Electronics
HERLOFSON, N., Electron Physics
LEHNERT, B., Plasma Physics and Fusion Research
RUSCK, S., Electric Power Systems Engineering
SUNDBERG, J., Music Acoustics
THORELLI, L.-E., Computer Systems
TÖRÖK, V., Electrical Power Conversion
ZETTERBERG, L.-H., Telecommunication Theory
ÅSTRÖM, E., Electromagnetic Theory

*School of Civil Engineering:*
ANDERSSON, O., Highway Engineering
BJÖRKMAN, B., Traffic and Transport Engineering
BROMS, B., Soil and Rock Mechanics
CEDERWALL, K., Hydraulics
HÖGLUND, I., Building Technology
KINNUNEN, S., Building Statics
LORENTSEN, M., Structural Engineering and Bridge Building
RAHM, H. G., Building Economics and Organization
SAHLIN, S., Building Statics
ÖDEEN, K., Building Materials

*School of Chemical Engineering:*
ALLANDER, C., Heat Technology
GATENBECK, S., Biochemistry
GRENTHE, I., Inorganic Chemistry
HARTLER, N., Cellulose Technology
INGMAN, F., Analytical Chemistry
LINDSTRÖM, O., Chemical Technology
NERETNIEKS, I., Chemical Engineering
NORIN, T., Organic Chemistry
NORMAN, B., Paper Technology
RÅNBY, B., Polymer Technology
SETTERWALL, F., Transport Phenomena
SJÖBERG, K., Chemical Technology
WESTERMARK, T., Nuclear Chemistry
WETTERMARK, G., Physical Chemistry
WRANGLÉN, G., Applied Electro-Chemistry and Corrosion Science

*School of Mining and Metallurgy:*
BERGSTRÖM, Y., Physical Metallurgy
COLLIN, R., Heat and Furnace Technology
EDSTRÖM, J. O., Production Technology, Mining and Steel Industry
FREDRIKSSON, H., Casting of Metals
HILLERT, M., Physical Metallurgy
HUML, P., Metal Working
STAFFANSSON, L.-I., Theoretical Metallurgy
TORSELL, K., Applied Extractive Metallurgy

*School of Architecture:*
DERGALIN, I., Town Planning
HIDEMARK, B., Architecture Building Design
JOHNSON, A., Building Construction
RYD, H., Forms
SILOW, S., Architecture
THIBERG, S., Building Function Analysis
WÅHLSTRÖM, O., Methods of Projection

*School of Surveying:*
BJERHAMMAR, A., Geodesy
CARLEGRIM, E., Real Estate Economics
KNUTSSON, G., Land Improvement and Drainage
LARSSON, G., Real Estate Planning
TORLEGÅRD, K., Photogrammetry

## UNIVERSITETET I LINKÖPING
**(Linköping University)**
581 83 LINKÖPING
Telephone: 013/11-17-00.

Founded 1970.

*Rector:* Prof. H. MEIJER.
*Vice-Rector:* Prof. B. G. A. PERSSON.
*Head of Administration:* P. ALMEFELT
*Chief Librarian:* K. MARKLUND.

Library: see Libraries.

Number of teachers: 650, including 46 professors.

Number of students: 7,500.

### DEANS:
*Faculty of Technology:* Prof. S. ERLANDER.
*Faculty of Medicine:* Prof. N. H. ARESKOG.
*Faculty of Arts and Sciences:* S. HELLSTRÖM.

### PROFESSORS:
*Faculty of Technology:*
BJÖRCK, Å., Numerical Analysis
BRANDES, O., Industrial Marketing
DAHLSTRAND, S., Structural Engineering
DANIELSSON, P.-E., Computer Technology
ERICSON, T., Data Transmission
ERICSSON, T., Constructional Materials
ERLANDER, S., Optimization
FJÄLLBRANT, T., Applied Electronics
GRUBBSTRÖM, R. W., Production Engineering
INGEMARSSON, I., Information Theory
JUNG, L., Control Engineering
KARLSSON, B., Applied Energy Research

SWEDEN

LAWSON, H. W., Telecommunications
LUNDSTRÖM, I., Applied Physics
MÖLLER, E., Measurement Technology
OLSSON, O., Hydraulics and Pneumatics
PERSSON, B. G. A., Mechanics of Materials
SANDEWALL, E., Computer Science
SANDKULL, B., Industrial Organization
WANDEL, S., Transportation Systems
WIDMAN, K.-O., Applied Mathematics
WIGERTZ, O., Medical Engineering (Medical Information Processing)
ÖBERG, Å., Medical Engineering (Instrumentation)

*Faculty of Medicine:*
ALMQVIST, S., Internal Medicine
ARESKOG, N.-H., Clinical Physiology
ASCHAN, G., Oto-Rhino-Laryngology
AXELSSON, O., Occupational Medicine
BERGMAN, S., Clinical Bacteriology
BERTLER, Å., Clinical Pharmacology
BJURULF, P., Preventive and Social Medicine
CARLSSON, C., Radiology
EDEBO, L., Bacteriology
EDHOLM, P., X-Ray Diagnostics
D'ELIA, G., Psychiatry
GROTH, O., Dermatology and Venereal Diseases
GRÖNTOFT, O., Pathology
KJESSLER, B., Obstetrics and Gynaecology
LARSSON, Y., Paediatrics
LEWIS, D., Clinical Research
LILJEDAHL, S.-O., Surgery
LINDAHL, O., Orthopaedic Surgery
LINK, H., Neurology
LUNDHOLM, L., Pharmacology
LÖFSTRÖM, B., Anaesthesiology
NILSSON, S.-E., Ophthalmiatrics
NORDENSKJÖLD, B., Oncology
SÖRBO, B., Clinical Chemistry
WIGERTZ, O., Medical Engineering (Medical Information Processing)
WRETMARK, G., Psychiatry
ÖBERG, Å., Medical Engineering (Instrumentation)

*Faculty of Arts and Sciences:*
MALMQUIST, E., Education
MEIJER, H., Political Science
WERDELIN, I., Education

## HÖGSKOLAN I LULEÅ
**(University of Luleå)**
S-951-87 LULEÅ
Telephone: 0920-910 00.
Telex: 80447 Luh S.

Founded 1971.

State control; Language of instruction: Swedish.

*President:* TORBJÖRN HEDBERG.
*Vice-President:* ABIEL OLDGREN.
*Chief Administrative Officer:* DANIEL ENQUIST.
*Dean of Technical Faculty:* ERIC FORSSBERG.
*University Librarian:* TORBJÖRN SÖDERHOLM.

Number of teachers: 300.
Number of students: 2,500.

Publications: *Research Reports, Technical Reports.*

### PROFESSORS:
*Department of Civil Engineering:*
BRINCK, C. E., Highway Engineering

CEDERWALL, K., Structural Engineering
GRENNBERG, T., Construction Management
PUSCH, R., Soil Mechanics

*Department of Materials Technology:*
EASTERLING, K., Materials Science
KÄLLSTRÖM, K., Metal Working

*Department of Mechanical Engineering:*
GRINNDAL, L., Transportation and Materials Handling
JACOBSON, B., Machine Elements
LESSER, M., Fluid Mechanics and Acoustics
LUNDBERG, B., Solid Mechanics
NILSON, C.-G., Machine Design
SCHMIDTBAUER, B., Industrial Electronics

*Department of Minerals and Prospecting:*
BOSTRÖM, K., Economic Geology
FORSSBERG, E., Mineral Processing
PARASNIS, D., Applied Geophysics

*Department of Mining Engineering:*
ALMGREN, G., Mining and Rock Excavation
GRANHOLM, S., Mining Equipment Engineering
STEPHANSSON, O., Rock Mechanics

*Department of Urban Planning and Development:*
BENGTSSON, L., Water Resources Engineering

*Department of Work Sciences:*
DAHLIN, T., Industrial Ergonomics
KARLSSON, L.-E., Social Psychology of Labour
OMSÉN, A., Product Planning
ÖSTBERG, O., Technical Psychology


## LUNDS UNIVERSITET
(University of Lund)

P.O.B. 1703, S-221 01 LUND
Telephone: 10-70-00.

**Founded 1668.**

Language of instruction: Swedish; State control; Academic year: September to May (two semesters).

*Chancellor:* C.-G. ANDRÉN.
*Rector:* Prof. N. STJERNQVIST.
*Vice-Rector:* Prof. P. E. PERSSON.
*Head of Administration:* S. HAMMAR.
*Chief Librarian:* BJÖRN TELL.

Library: see Libraries.

Number of teachers: 1,900, including 260 professors.

Number of students: c. 20,000.

Publication: *LUM* (20 a year).

### DEANS:

*Faculty of Theology:* Prof. B. HÄGGLUND.
*Faculty of Law:* Prof. K. Å. MODÉER.
*Faculty of Medicine:* Prof. H. WESTLING.
*Faculty of Humanities:* Prof. B. SIGURD.
Prof. B. BERG (Philologic Section).
Prof. B. STJERNQVIST (Historic-Philosophic Section).
*Faculty of Political and Social Sciences:* Prof. O. WÄRNERYD.

*Faculty of Mathematics and Natural Sciences:* Prof. L. EBERSON.
Prof. B. E. Y. SVENSSON (Mathematics Section).
Prof. L. I. ELDING (Chemical Section).
Prof. N. MALMER (Biological-Geographical Section).
*Faculty of Odontology:* Asst. Prof. B. ÖWALL.
*Faculty of Technology:* Prof. S. BORGLIN.
I. BRINCK (School of Technical Physics).
L. GRAHM (School of Electrical Engineering).
Prof. H. AHLMANN (School of Mechanical Engineering).
Prof. G. LINDHAGEN (School of Civil Engineering).
Prof. B. KRANTZ (School of Architecture).
Prof. S. FORSÉN (School of Chemical Engineering).

### PROFESSORS:

*Faculty of Theology:*
BROHED, I., Ecclesiastical History
GERHARDSSON, B., New Testament Exegesis
GUSTAFSSON, G., Sociology of Religion
HARTMAN, S., History and Psychology of Religions
HEMBERG, J., Ethics
HÄGGLUND, B., History of Christian Doctrine
LYTTKENS, H., Philosophy of Religion
LÖVESTAM, E., Early Christian Literature
METTINGER, T., Old Testament Exegesis
PERSSON, P. E., Systematic Theology

*Faculty of Law:*
BOLDING, P. O., Judicial Procedure
CERVIN, U., Civil Law
CHRISTENSEN, A., Civil Law
EDLUND, S., Labour Law
ELWING, C. M., Judicial Procedure
ENGLUND, G., Financial Law
GORTON, L., Civil Law
LAVIN, R., Public Law
MODÉER, K. Å., History of Law
PECZENIK, A., Central Jurisprudence
PÅLSSON, L., International Law
ROOS, C. M., Civil Law
STRÖMBERG, H., Public Law
WALLÉN, P.-E., Criminal Law

*Faculty of Medicine:*
ANDERSSON, K.-E., Clinical Pharmacology
BAUER, G., Orthopaedic Surgery
BENGMARK, S., Surgery
BENGTSSON, U., Nephrology
BERG, N., Pathology
BERGENTZ, S.-E., Experimental Surgery
BERGLUND, K., Rheumatology
BERLIN, M., Hygiene
BOIJSEN, E., X-Ray Diagnostics
BORGSTRÖM, B., Medical and Physiological Chemistry
EDMAN, P., Pharmacology
EHINGER, B., Ophthalmology
EKHOLM, J. T., Anatomy
EMMELIN, N., Physiology
ENEROTH, C.-M., Oto-Rhino-Laryngology
FALCK, B., Histology
FALKMER, S., General Pathology and Pathological Anatomy
FORSBERG, J.-G., Anatomy
FORSGREN, A., Clinical Bacteriology
GARDELL, S., Medical Chemistry
GRUBB, R., Bacteriology
GUSTAFSON, A., Medicine
HAGNELL, O., Psychiatry
HOOD, B., Practical Medicine
HULTH, A. G., Orthopaedic Surgery
HÖKFELT, B. M., Endocrinology
JOHANSSON, B., Physiology
JONSSON, N., Pathology
KAIJ, L., Psychiatry
KILLANDER, D., Oncology
KJELLEN, L., Virology
KULLANDER, S., Obstetrics and Gynaecology
KÄLLÉN, B., Embryology
LAGERSTEDT, S., Histology
LAURELL, A.-B., Immunology
LAURELL, C.-B., Clinical Chemistry
LINDELL, S.-E., Clinical Physiology
LINDQVIST, B., Paediatrics
MELLANDER, J. S., Physiology
MORITZ, U. E., Physiotherapy
MÜLLER, R., Neurology
MÖLLER, H., Dermatology and Venerology
NILSSON, E., Anaesthesiology
NORDBRING, F. E. S., Infectious Diseases
NORDEN, Å., Community Medicine
NYMAN, E., Psychiatry
OLIN, T., X-ray Diagnostics
OSCARSSON, O., Physiology
OWMAN, CH., Histology
PANDOLFI, M., Ophthalmology
PERSSON, B., Medical Radio Physics
RORSMAN, H., Dermatology and Venereal Diseases
RÄIHÄ, N. C. R., Paediatrics
SIMONSSON, B., Pulmonary Diseases
SJÖGREN, H. A., Tumour Immunology
STENRAM, U., General Pathology and Pathological Anatomy
STERNBY, N., Pathology
SUNDIN, T., Urology
THESLEFF, S., Pharmacology
THULIN, C.-A., Neurosurgery
VOIGT, G., Forensic Medicine
WESTLING, H., Clinical Physiology
ZEDERFELDT, B., Surgery
ÅSTEDT, B., Obstetrics and Gynaecology
ÖCKERMAN, P. A., Clinical Chemistry
ÖHMAN, R. L., Psychiatry

*Faculty of Humanities:*
BERGH, B., Latin Language and Literature
BJÖRCK, S., History of Literature with Poetics
BRINGÉUS, N.-A., Folklore
CINTHIO, E., Medieval Archaeology
DUROVIC, L., Slavonic Languages
EJDER, B., Swedish Language
GIEROW, P. G., Classical Archaeology and Ancient History
GÅRDING, E. M., Phonetics
HALLDÉN, S., Theoretical Philosophy
HERMERÉN, G., Practical Philosophy
HOLM, G., Scandinavian Philology
HOLM, I., History of Literature, Drama
ODÉN, B., History
REUTERSVÄRD, O., Art and Art Theory
ROSENGREN, I., German Language
RUDBERG, S., Greek Language and Literature
RYSTAD, G., History
SANDSTRÖM, S., Art History, especially Contemporary Art and Environment
SCHAAR, C., English Literature
SIGURD, B., General Linguistics
SÖDERGÅRD, Ö., Romance Languages
STJERNQVIST, B., Archaeology
SVARTVIK, J., English Language
VINGE, L., Literature
VITESTAM, G., Semitic Languages

*Faculty of Political and Social Sciences:*
ADLERCREUTZ, A., Commercial Law
BJERKE, B., Business Administration

# UNIVERSITIES
SWEDEN

Bjerstedt, Å., Pedagogics
Bondeson, U., Sociology of Law
Frank, O., Statistics
Hägerstrand, T., Geography
Höglund, B., Economics
Israel, J., Sociology
Jörberg, L., Economic History
Kihlstedt, C., Business Administration
Klingberg, G., Pedagogics
Kragh, U., Applied Psychology
Lindell, E., Pedagogics
Peterson, H. F., Political Science
Smith, G., Psychology
Stjernquist, N. N., Political Science
Ståhl, I., Economics
Södersten, B., International Economics
Thalberg, B., Economics
Törnqvist, G., Economic Geography
Wikström, S., Business Administration
Wärneryd, O., Social Geography

*Faculty of Mathematics and Natural Sciences:*
Albertsson, P. Å., Biochemistry
Ardeberg, A., Astronomy
Berglund, B., Quaternary Geology
Berglund, S., Physics
Björk, S., Limnology
Björn, L. O., Botany
Brinck, P., Zoology
Dahl, E., Zoology
von Dardel, G., Physics
Eberson, L. E., Organic Chemistry
Edström, A., Zoophysiology
Elofsson, R. G. I., Structural Zoology
Forkman, B., Physics
Fredga, K., Genetics
Fröberg, C.-E., Numerical Analysis
Fronæus, S., Chemistry
Gårding, L., Mathematics
Gorbatschev, R., Geology and Mineralogy
Gronowitz, S., Chemistry
Hedin, L., Theoretical Physics
Hörmander, L., Mathematics
Johansson, G., Chemistry
Landin, B. O., Entomology
Larsson-Leander, G., Astronomy
Lindman, B., Chemistry
Lundqvist, A., Genetics
Malmer, N., Plant Ecology
Martinsson, I., Atomic Physics
Nilsson, N., Mathematics
Rapp, A., Geography
Runemark, H., Botany
Ryde, H., Cosmic and Subatomic Physics
Sandström, J., Organic Chemistry
Sonesson, M., Plant Ecology
Svensson, B. E. Y., Theoretical Physics
Weibull, C., Microbiology

*Faculty of Odontology:*
Ahlgren, J., Orthodontics
Bratthall, D., Cariology
Edwardsson, S., Oral Microbiology
Glantz, P.-O., Prosthetics
Granath, L.-E., Pedodontics
Larsson, Å., Oral Pathology
Mannerberg, F., Cariology
Omnell, K. Å., Oral Radiology
Rosengren, E., Pharmacology
Wallenius, K., Oral Surgery
Östlund, S., Dental Technology

*Faculty of Technology:*
Adamson, B., Building Science
Ahlmann, H., Industrial Management
Asp, N.-G. L., Chemistry of Foodstuffs
Asplund, H., Architecture
Aurivillius, B., Inorganic Chemistry
Bjerle, G. I., Chemical Technology
Bjerninger, S., Transport Engineering
Blom, G., Mathematical Statistics

Borglin, S., Heat and Power Engineering
Broberg, B., Solid Mechanics
Brundell, P.-O., Electromagnetic Theory
Dahlqvist, A., Industrial Nutritional Science
Einarsson, G., Telecommunication Theory
Floberg, L., Machine Elements
Fénors, S., Physical Chemistry
Forsén, K. S., Physical Chemistry
Grimmeiss, H., Solid State Physics
Hallström, B., Food Engineering
Hertz, H., Electrical Measurements
Hillerborg, A., Building materials
Hulten, B., Town Planning
Jensen, L. H., Installations
Jernqvist, Å., Chemical Engineering
Johansson, S., Nuclear Physics
Krantz, B., Building Function Theory
Kullberg, G., Production and Materials Engineering
Kvarnström, L., Architecture
Larsson, K., Food Technology
Lind, K. G., Electronics
Lindblad, C. S. G., Architecture
Lindh, G., Water Resources Engineering
Lindhagen, G., Traffic Planning and Engineering
Lundin, S. T., Chemical Technology
Löfgren, L., Automata and General Systems Sciences
Molin, N., Technical Microbiology
Mosbach, H. K., Biochemistry
Neretnieks, I. E. A., Chemical Engineering
Nevander, L.-E., Building Technology
Peetre, J., Mathematics
Peterss, H. B., Architecture
Pettersson, O., Structural Mechanics and Concrete Construction
Samuelson, S., Architecture
Smith, B., Technical Analytical Chemistry
Sundström, J., Machine Design
Svanberg, S. R., Physics
Thafvelin, H., Theoretical and Applied Aesthetics
Tyllered, G., Mechanical Theory of Heat and Fluid Mechanics
Törnell, E. B., Chemical Technology
Uhlhorn, U., Mechanics
Wallin, S., Construction Management and Industrial Engineering
Wallström, B., Telecommunication Systems
Wickberg, B., Organic Chemistry
Wimmerstedt, R. V., Chemical Engineering
Åström, K. J., Automatic Control
Åström, K., Town Planning
Östberg, G., Engineering Materials
Östlund, L., Structural Engineering

## HÖGSKOLAN I ÖREBRO
### (University of Örebro)
BOX 923, S-701 30 ÖREBRO
Telephone: 019/14 01 00.

Founded 1967.

State control; Academic year: September to June.

*Vice-Chancellor:* Stefan Björklund.
*Deputy Vice-Chancellor:* Sven-Ola Lindeberg.
*Chief Administrative Officer:* Åke Berglund.
*Librarian:* Margareta Hjelm.

Library of 60,000 vols.

Number of teachers: c. 190.
Number of students: c. 5,000.

Deans of Departments:
*Business Administration:* Sune Jansson.
*Data Analysis:* Hans Hedén.
*Economics:* Walter Stervander.
*Humanities:* Lars Gustafsson.
*Law:* Anders Stening.
*Mathematics and Natural Sciences:* Göte Nordlander.
*Modern Languages:* Jan Henrik Granberg.
*Planning and Human Geography:* Margareta Hassbring.
*Politics and Public Administration:* Bo Jonsson.
*Psychology and Education:* Bo Edvardsson.
*Social Work:* Lars-Ebbe Hansson.
*Sociology:* Bernt Johansson.
*Sports and Physical Training:* Lennart Mattsson.
*Trainee Administration Unit:* Harriet Björkquist.
*Training of Kindergarten Teachers and Leisure Organizers:* Benny Lawin.
*Training of Music Teachers:* Göran Strandberg.

## STOCKHOLMS UNIVERSITET
### (University of Stockholm)
UNIVERSITETSVÄGEN 10,
S-10691 STOCKHOLM
Telephone: 16 20 00.

Telex: Univer s.

Founded 1877, became State University 1960.

State control; Language of instruction: Swedish; Academic year: September to June.

*President:* Prof. S. Helmfrid.
*Vice-President:* Prof. H. Thornstedt.
*Head of Administration:* R. Lindquist.

Library: see Libraries.

Number of teachers: 950, including 120 professors.

Number of students: 30,000.

Publications: *Katalog*†  (annually), *Acta Universitatis Stockholmiensis*†.

Deans:
*Faculty of Law:* Prof. H. Thornstedt.
*Faculty of Humanities:*
 *History-Philosophy Section:* Prof. I. Jonsson.
 *Language Section:* Prof. G. Holmér.
*Faculty of Social Sciences:* Prof. O. Ruin.
*Faculty of Natural Sciences:*
 *Mathematics-Physics Section:* Prof. G. Ekspong.
 *Chemistry Section:* Prof. P. Kirkegaard.
 *Biology-Geography Section:* Prof. V. Shytt.

Professors:
*Faculty of Law:*
Almgren, G., Civil Law

ANNERS, E., History of Law
BERNITZ, U., Civil Law, Consumer Protection Law and Market Law
HELLNER, J., Insurance Law
HJERNER, L., International Law
HOFLUND, O., Criminal Law
JACOBSSON, U., Judicial Procedure
LARSSON, S., Judicial Procedure
LODIN, S.-O., Financial Law
RAGNEMALM, H., Public Law
RAMBERG, J., Civil Law
SIGEMAN, T., Civil Law, with emphasis on Labour Law
SUNDBERG, J., General Jurisprudence
SVERI, K., General Criminal Law
THORNSTEDT, H., Criminal Law
VAHLÉN, L., Civil Law
WERIN, L., Political Economy
WESTERBERG, O., Public Law

*Faculty of Humanities:*

*History-Philosophy Section:*
BEREFELT, G., Scandinavian and Comparative Art History
BERGQVIST, B., Ancient Culture and Civilization
ESPMARK, K., Literary History with Poetics
FURHAMMAR, L., Film Science
GRAM HOLMSTRÖM, K., Theatre Science
HAMMARSTRÖM, I., History
HULTKRANTZ, Å., History of Religions
JONSSON, I., General and Comparative Literature
MALMER, M., North-European Archaeology
OFSTAD, H., Moral Philosophy
PRAWITZ, D., Theoretical Philosophy
REHNBERG, M., Scandinavian and Comparative Ethnology
REUTERSWÄRD, P., Art History and Art Theory
RUNEBY, N., History of Ideas
SCHÜCK, H., History

*Language Section:*
AMER, A., Arabic Language
BJÖRK, L., English Language
CHO, S., Japanese Language
DAHL, Ö., General Linguistics
GEIJERSTAM, R. AF, Romance Languages with emphasis on Ibero Romance Languages
HOLMÉR, G., Romance Languages, with emphasis on the French language
HORMIA, O., Finnish Language and Culture
LIENHARD, S., Indology
LJUNG, M., English Language
MALMQVIST, G., Sinology, with emphasis on the modern Chinese Language
NILSSON, N. Å., Slavonic Languages, with emphasis on Russian Language and Literature
RUKE-DRAVINA, V., Baltic Languages
SJÖBERG, A., Slavonic Languages
STOLT, B., German Language
ÖBERG, J., Latin

*Faculty of Social Sciences:*
ADAMSON, R., Economic History
ANDRÉN, N., Political Science
BERGLIND, H., Social Work
BOHM, P., Political Economy
BRUUN, K., Sociology of Alcoholic Behaviour
DALENIUS, T., Statistics
EDFELDT, Å., Pedagogics
GARDELL, B., Working Life Psychology
GOLDMAN, K., Political Sciences
HANNERZ, U., Social Anthropology
HELMFRID, S., Human and Economic Geography
HUSÉN, T., International Pedagogics
JANSON, C.-G., Sociology
JONSSON, C.-O., Psychology

KRAGH, B., Political Economy, with emphasis on Business Cycle Research
KÜHLHORN, E., Social Work (especially Care of Drug Addicts)
LINDBECK, A., International Economics
MAGNUSSON, D., Psychology
MALMQUIST, S., Statistics
PAULSSON-FRENCKNER, T. B., Business Administration
PERSSON, L., Business Administration
RUIN, O., Political Science
SIVEN, C.-H., Political Economy
TRANKELL, A., Pedagogics

*Faculty of Natural Sciences:*
*Mathematics-Physics Section:*
BAHR, B. VON, Insurance and Mathematical Statistics
BJÖRK, J.-E., Mathematics
BOLIN, B., Meteorology
ELVIUS, A., Astronomy
ERLANDSSON, G., Electronics
EKSPONG, G., Physics
FISCHER-HJALMARS, I., Theoretical Physics
GERHOLM, T.-R., Physics
LAGERQVIST, A., Physics
LAURENT, B., Physics
LECH, C., Mathematics
LINDBLAD, P. O., Astronomy
ROHDE, H., Chemical Meteorology
ROOS, J. E., Mathematics
SINNERSTAD, U., Astronomy

*Chemistry Section:*
BALTSCHEFFSKY, H., Biochemistry and Bioenergetics
ERNSTER, L., Biochemistry
KIERKEGAARD, P., Structural Chemistry
KIHLBORG, L., Inorganic Chemistry
LINDBERG, B., Organic Chemistry
WENNERSTRÖM, H., Physical Chemistry
WIDMARK, G., Analytical Chemistry

*Biology-Geography Section:*
ACKEFORS, H., Ecological Zoology
BERGGREN, W., General and Historical Geology
BOMAN, H., Microbiology
BOSTRÖM, K., Mineralogy, Petrology and Geochemistry
EHRENBERG, A., Biophysics
EHRENBERG, L., Radiation Biology
ELIASSON, L., Physiological Botany
GUSTAFSON, T., Animal Physiology
JANSSON, B.-O., Marine Ecology
LINDBERG, U., Zoological Cell Biology
LUNDQVIST, J., Quaternary Geology
LÜNING, K. G., Genetics
OHLSSON, R., Zoology
PERLMANN, P., Immunobiology
RADESÄTER, T., Ethology
RAMEL, C., Toxicological Genetics
WALLES, B., Morphological Botany
WASTENSSON, L., Remote Sensing
ØSTREM, G., Physical Geography

AFFILIATED INSTITUTES:

*Askö-laboratoriet* (Askö Laboratory, Institute of Marine Ecology): Rådmansg. 70A, P.O.B. 6801, 113 86 Stockholm; Dir. Prof. BENGT-OWE JANSSON.

*Bergianska botaniska trädgården* (Bergius Botanic Gardens): P.O.B. 50017, 104 05 Stockholm; Dir. Prof. MÅNS RYBERG.

*Centrum för barnkulturforskning* (Centre for the Study of Childhood Culture): Universitetsv. 10D, 106 91 Stockholm; Dir. Prof. GUNNAR BEREFELT.

*Centrum för japan-studier* (Centre for Japanese Studies): Universitetsv. 10, 106 91 Stockholm; Exec. Sec. JONAS ENGBERG.

*Centrum för masskommunikationsforskning* (Centre for Mass Communication Research): Universitetsv. 10A, 106 91 Stockholm; Dir. KJELL NOWAK.

*IES/Stockholm University Institute for English-Speaking Students:* Universitetsv. 10, 106 91 Stockholm; Dir. Prof. NILS ANDRÉN.

*Institutet för internationell ekonomi* (Institute for International Economic Studies): Universitetsv. 10A, 106 91 Stockholm; Dir. Prof. ASSAR LINDBECK.

*Latinamerika-institutet* (Institute of Latin American Studies): Odeng. 61, Box 6909, 102 39 Stockholm; Dir. WEINE KARLSSON.

*Swedish Language Courses:* Dir. ELIZABETH NYLUND.

# SVERIGES LANTBRUKSUNIVERSITET
(Swedish University of Agricultural Sciences)

S-750 07 UPPSALA
Telephone: (018) 10-20-00.

Founded 1977 by amalgamation of the former *Lantbrukshögskolan, Skogshögskolan,* and *Veterinärhögskolan.*

Rector: L. HJELM, AGR.D.
Vice-Rector: C. G. SCHMITERLÖW, M.D., VET.M.D.
Chief of Administration: G. OSCARSSON.
Director of Library: L.-E. SANNER, FIL.L.

Library: see Libraries.

Number of teachers: 277, including 62 professors.

Number of students: c. 2,500.

Publications: *Swedish Journal of Agricultural Research, Aktuellt från Lantbruksuniversitetet, Studia Forestalia Suecica†, Rapporter* (Reports); College of Veterinary Medicine: *Collected Papers, Catalogue, List of Publicaions, Students' Handbook* (annually).

DEANS:

*Faculty of Agriculture:* Prof. U. RENBORG.

*Faculty of Forestry:* Prof. G. VON SEGEBADEN.

*Faculty of Veterinary Medicine:* Prof. I. MÅNSSON.

PROFESSORS:
(some professors serve in more than one faculty)

*Faculty of Agriculture:*
CARLSSON, C. M., Horticultural Economics
CLAESSON, C. O., Animal Husbandry
ERIKSSON, S. S., Animal Nutrition
FERNQVIST, I. B., Pomology
FOLKESSON, L.-G., Agricultural Marketing
FRIBERG, P.-Å., Landscape Architecture
HAGBERG, N. A., Genetics and Plant Breeding

Haraldson, L. Å., Farm Mechanization
Heinonen, R., Soil Management
Henriksson, R. A., Farm Buildings
Hjelm, K. G. L., Agricultural Economics
Håkansson, A., Agricultural Hydrotechnics
Jansson, S. L. H., Soil Fertility
Knutsson, P.-G. K., Animal Physiology
Kristoffersen, T., Ornamental Gardening
Larsson, P. R., Plant Husbandry
Lindqvist, F. I., Inorganic Chemistry
Mac Key, J. F., Plant Breeding
Norén, A. B., Microbiology
Odén, N. F. S., Pedology
Ottosson, K. L., Vegetable Growing
Pettersson, J. G. P., Applied Entomology
Renborg, U. B., Agricultural Economics
Rönningen, K., Animal Breeding
Skage, O. R., Overhead Planning
Steen, E. V., Environment Research and Ecology
Stenlid, G., Plant Physiology
Theander, O., Organic Chemistry and Biochemistry
Umaerus, V. R., Plant Pathology
Östergren, S. G., Genetics

*Faculty of Forestry:*
Ahlén, T. I., Forest Vertebrate Ecology
Andersson, S.-O., Forest Yield Research
Bäckström, P. O., Reforestation
Eidmann, H. H. T., Forest Entomology
Jonsson, B., Forest Management
Lindgren, D. G., Forest Genetics
von Malmborg, G., Forest Economics
Matérn, B., Forest Biometry
von Segebaden, G. O. U., Forest Survey
Sirén, G., Reforestation
Staaf, A., Operational Efficiency I
Sundberg, U., Operational Efficiency II
Tamm, C. O., Forest Ecology
Troedsson, T., Forest Soils
Unestam, T. K.-G., Forest Mycology and Microbial Ecology

*Faculty of Veterinary Medicine:*
Bengtsson, S. G., Animal Hygiene
Dinter, Z., Virology
Einarsson, S. G., Obstetrics and Gynaecology
Ekesbo, A. G. I., Animal Hygiene
Ekman, L. G., Clinical Chemistry
Funkqvist, B. D. E., Surgery
Holtenius, P. H., Medicine for Ruminants
Lindahl, U. P. F., Medical and Physiological Chemistry
Månsson, I. M., Bacteriology and Epizootology
Nilsson, K. G. A., Pathology
Nilsson, T. E., Food Hygiene
Persson, S. G. B., Medicine
Plöen, L., Anatomy and Histology
Ronéus, O., Parasitology
Schmiterlöw, C. G., Pharmacology

## UMEÅ UNIVERSITET
**(Umeå University)**

S-901 87 UMEÅ

Telephone: 090/16 50 00.

Founded 1963.

*Rector:* Prof. L. Beckman, ph.d.
*Vice-Rector:* Prof. U. Zackrisson, ph.d.
*Head of Administration:* L. O. Mårdell, ll.b.

*Chief Librarian:* K. Snellman, ph.l.

Library: see Libraries.

Number of teachers: c. 400, including 95 professors.

Number of students: c. 8,500.

### Deans

*Faculty of Humanities:* Prof. Evert Baudou.
*Faculty of Social Sciences:* Prof. Ulf Olsson.
*Faculty of Medicine:* Prof. Sven Dahlgren.
*Faculty of Odontology:* Prof. Bo Bergman.
*Faculty of Mathematics and Natural Sciences:* Prof. Arne Claesson.

### Professors

*Faculty of Humanities:*
Baudou, E., Archaeology
Dahlstedt, K.-H., General Linguistics
Danell, K. J., French
Edman, M., Philosophy of Science and Humanities
Elert, C.-Ch., Phonetics
Fries, S., Scandinavian Languages
Nordström, F., Arts
von Platen, M., Literary History
Seppänen, A., English
Sköld, T., Finnish Language
Åkerman, S., History

*Faculty of Social Sciences:*
Andersson, Å., Regional Economics
Back, P.-E., Political Science
Bergström, S. S., Applied Psychology
Bylund, E., Geography
Börjesson, B., Social Work
Grosskopf, G., Law
Henrysson, S., Pedagogics
Karlsson, G., Sociology
Lundin, R., Business Administration and Economics
Nilsson, L.-G., Psychology
Olsson, U., Economic History
Puu, T., Economics
Zackrisson, U., Statistics

*Faculty of Medicine:*
Beckman, L., Medical Genetics
Bergman, F., Pathology
Bjersing, L., Pathology
Bloom, G., Histology
Bohman, M., Child Psychiatry
Boquist, L., Pathology
Coutinho, A., Immunology
Dahlgren, B., Surgery
Diamant. H., Oto-Rhino-Laryngology
Ekstedt, J., Neurology
Fugl-Meyer, A., Physical Medicine and Rehabilitation
Halldén, U., Ophthalmology
Hassler, O., Pathology
Helander, H., Anatomy
Hollunger, G., Pharmacology
Holm, S., Clinical Bacteriology
Jacobsson, L., Clinical Chemistry
Jacobsson, L., Psychiatry
Joelsson, I., Obstetrics and Gynaecology
Kellerth, J.-O., Anatomy
Landgren, S., Physiology
Larsson, L.-G., Oncology
Lidén, S., Dermatology and Venereology
Linderholm, H., Clinical Physiology
Littbrand, B., Oncology
Norderg, N., Hygiene
Normark, S., Medical Microbiology
Norrby, R., Infectious Diseases
Odeblad, E., Biochemistry
Olivecrona, T., Medical Chemistry
Paul, K.-G., Medical Chemistry

Perris, C., Psychiatry
Saltzman, G. F., X-ray Diagnostics
Steen, B., Geriatrics
Täljedal, I.-B., Histology
Vallbo, Å., Physiology
Wadell, G., Urology
Wahlqvist, L., Urology
Wahlström, G., Pharmacology
Wester, P. O., Medicine

*Faculty of Odontology:*
Bergenholtz, A., Periodontology
Bergman, B., Prosthetics
Bergman, M., Dental Technology
Carlsson, J., Oral Microbiology
Ericson, Th., Cariology
Gustafson, G., Oral Histopathology
Oreland, L., Pharmacology
Persson, M., Orthodontics
Rosenquist, J., Dental Surgery
Welander, U., Dental Diagnostic Radiology

*Faculty of Mathematics and Natural Sciences:*
Björk, G., Microbiology
Bäckström, G., Physics
Cedergren, A., Analytical Chemistry
Claesson, A., Theoretical Physics
Eliasson, L., Physiological Botany
Ericsson, L., Ecological Botany
Hagner, M., Forest Production
Hultqvist, B., Physics of Near Space
Ingri, N., Inorganic Chemistry
Kinell, P.-O., Physical Chemistry
Kulldorff, G., Mathematical Statistics
Lindskog, S., Biochemistry
Løvtrup, S., Zoophysiology
Müller, K., Ecological Zoology
Rappe, C., Organic Chemistry
Rasmuson, B., Genetics
Rasmuson, M., Genetics
Ruhe, A., Information Processing
Stenflo, L., Theoretical Plasma Physics
Wallin, H., Mathematics

## UPPSALA UNIVERSITET
**(University of Uppsala)**

P.O.B. 256, 751 05 UPPSALA

Telephone: 018/155400.

Founded 1477.

Academic year: September to May.

*Chancellor:* C.-G. Andrén.
*Rector:* Prof. M. H:son Holmdahl, m.d.
*Vice-Rector:* Prof. S. F. Strömholm, ll.d.
*Chief of Administration:* G. Wijkman, m.d.
*Chief Librarian:* T. Tottie.

Library: see Libraries.

Number of teachers: 1,200, including 200 professors.

Number of students: 18,000.

### Deans

*Faculty of Theology:* Prof. E. T. Källstad.
*Faculty of Law:* Prof. A. L. G. Agell.
*Faculty of Medicine:* Prof. J. Sjöquist.
*Faculty of Arts:* Prof. L. Carlsson.
  *Historical-Philosophical Division:* Prof. L. Bergström.
  *Linguistic Division:* Prof. N. L. Carlsson.
*Faculty of Social Science:* Prof. G. Arpi.

*Faculty of Science:* Prof. D. C.-O. JACOBSON.
  *Mathematical-Physical Division:* Prof. O. BECKMAN.
  *Biology and Earth Science Division:* Prof. B. COLLINI.
  *Chemical Division:* Prof. O. I. G. OLOVSSON.
*Faculty of Pharmacy:* Prof. H. DANIELSSON.

PROFESSORS:
*Faculty of Theology:*
  ANDRÉN, Å., Practical Theology
  BERGMAN, J., History of Religions
  GUSTAFSSON, G., Sociology of Religion
  HALLENCREUTZ, C. F., Missiology
  HARTMAN, L., Exegesis
  HOF, H. B., Philosophy of Religions
  HOLTE. K. R., Ethics and Philosophy of Religion
  JEFFNER, B. A. G., Theological and Ideological Studies
  KÄLLSTAD, E. T., Psychology of Religion
  MONTGOMERY, I., Church History
  RINGGREN, H., Exegesis

*Faculty of Law:*
  AGELL, A. L. G., Private Law
  BOMAN, J. R., Judicial Procedure
  BRAMSTÅNG, N. Å. G., Public Law
  GRAHL-MADSEN, A., International Law
  HILLERT, S., Private Law
  HÅSTAD, T., Private Law
  INGER, G. J. A., Legal History
  LINDBLOM, P.-H., Judicial Procedure
  MATTSSON, N., Taxation
  NELSON, A., Penal Law
  NYMAN, O., Public Law
  OHLIN, G., Economics
  SALDEEN, Å., Private Law
  STRÖMHOLM, S., Jurisprudence

*Faculty of Medicine:*
  ANDÉN, N.-E., Pharmacology
  ARTURSON, G., Burn Research
  BERGGREN, L., Ophthalmology
  BILL, A., Physiology
  BOHM. E., Neurosurgery
  BOSTRÖM, J. H., Medicine
  DAHLHAMN, T., Hygiene
  DIDERHOLM, H., Virology
  ENGSTRÖM, L., Medical Chemistry
  ERICSSON, J., Pathology
  FRISK, M., Child Psychiatry
  GAMSTORP, I., Paediatric Neurology
  GUNNE, L.-M., Psychiatry
  HAGBARTH, K. E., Clinical Neurophysiology
  HAKELIUS, L., Plastic Surgery
  HAMBRAEUS, L., Nutrition
  HELLMAN, B. O. A., Anatomy
  HOFVANDER, Y., International Child Health
  HOLMDAHL, M., Anaesthesiology
  JAKOBSON, P. A., Oncology
  JOHANSSON, E. D. B., Obstetrics and Gynaecology
  JUHLIN, A. L. A., Dermato-Venereology
  LAURELL, G., Clinical Bacteriology
  LAURENT, T. C., Medical Chemistry
  LODIN, H. W., X-Ray Diagnosis
  LUNDBERG, P. O. M., Neurology
  NILSSON, K., Cell Pathology
  NILSSON, O., Anatomy
  OLERUD, S., Orthopaedic Surgery
  OLSSON, Y., Neuropathology
  PETERSON, P. A., Cell Research
  PONTÉN, J., Pathology
  ROOS, B.-E., Psychiatry
  ROOTH, G., Perinatal Medicine
  SALDEEN, T., Forensic Medicine
  SJÖLIN, S., Paediatrics
  SJÖQUIST, J., Medical Chemistry
  STAHLE, J., Oto-rhino-laryngology
  STRÖM, G. O. F., Clinical Physiology
  SÖDERBERG, U., Psychiatric Neurophysiology
  THORÉN, L., Surgery
  ULFENDAHL, H., Physiology
  VERDIER, C.-H. A. O. DE, Clinical Chemistry
  WERNER, I., Geriatrics
  WESTRIN, C.-G., Social Medicine
  WIGZELL, H. L. R., Immunology
  WISTRAND, P., Pharmacology
  ÖBRINK, K. J., Physiology

*Faculty of Arts:*
  *I. Historical-Philosophical Division:*
  ALMGREN, B. O., Archaeology of Northern Europe
  ANDRAE, C.-G., History
  BENGTSSON, L. I., Musicology
  BERGSTRÖM, L. O., Practical Philosophy
  CARLSSON, S. C. O., History
  ELLENIUS, A. M., Art
  ERIKSSON, G., History of Science and Ideas
  FURULAND, L. G. A., Literature
  HOLTHOER, R., Egyptology
  JACOBSON-WIDDING, H. A., Cultural Anthropology
  KANGER, S., Theoretical Philosophy
  LINDERS, T., Ancient Culture and Society
  ROOTH, A. B., European Ethnology
  SHARPE, E., History of Religions
  STENSTRÖM, T. O., Literature
  TORSTENDAHL, R., History

  *II. Linguistic Division:*
  ANDERSSON, K. T. G., Scandinavian Languages
  BATTAIL, J.-F., French Language and Literature
  CARLSSON, N. L., Romance Languages
  ELMEVIK, L., Scandinavian Languages
  FRYCKSTEDT, O. W., American Literature
  GUSTAVSSON, S. A., Slavic Languages
  HERMODSSON, L. F. H., German Language
  HÅKANSON, L. Å., Latin Language
  MOBERG, L. A., Scandinavian Languages
  PALM, J. W. J., Greek Language and Literature
  RUNDGREN, G. F., Semitic Languages
  RYDÉN, L., Byzantine Studies
  SIMONSSON, N., Sanskrit and Comparative Indo-European Philology
  SÖDERLIND, J., English Language
  SORELIUS, E. G., English Language and Literature
  WICKMAN, B. N. V., Finno-Ugric Languages
  WIDMARK, G. M., Swedish Language
  ÖHMAN, S. E. G., Phonetics

*Faculty of Social Sciences:*
  AHLSTRÖM, K.-G., Education
  ARPI, G., Cultural Geography
  BENTZEL, R. H., Economics
  BERGLUND, G., Education and Educational Psychology
  BJÖRKMAN, M., Psychology
  BRATTEMO, C.-E., Psychology
  BREHMER, B., Psychology
  CHRISTOFFERSSON, A., Statistics
  DAHLLÖF, U. S., Education
  ELVANDER, N., Political Science
  GOUDE, G., Psychology
  GUSTAFSSON, B., Economic History
  HIMMELSTRAND, J. W. I., Sociology
  JÖRESKOG, K. G., Statistics
  LEWIN, L., Political Science
  LINDSKOG, B., Social Anthropology
  LYTTKENS, E., Statistics
  MATTSSON, L.-G., Business Economics
  OHLIN, G., Economics
  RAMSTRÖM, D., Business Economics
  TÄRNLUND, S.-Å., Information Processing
  WALLIN, E., Education
  ÅDAHL, A., Eastern European Research

*Faculty of Science:*
  *I. Mathematical-Physical Division:*
  BECKMAN, O., Solid State Physics
  BOSTRÖM, R., Geocosmic Physics
  CARLESON, L. A. E., Mathematics
  DAHLBERG, B., Mathematics
  DOMAR, E. Y., Mathematics
  ESSEEN, C.-G. H., Mathematical Statistics
  FISCHER, H. C. P., Solid Mechanics
  FRÖMAN, P. O., Theoretical Physics
  GOSCINSKI, O., Quantum Chemistry
  GUSTAFSSON, B., Numerical Analysis
  JOHANSSON, K. E. A., Nuclear Physics
  KARLSON, E. T., Electromagnetic Theory
  KARLSSON, T. E., Physics
  KISELMAN, C. O., Mathematics
  KULLANDER, S., High Energy Physics
  LODÉN, L.-O., Astronomy
  LÖWDIN, P.-O., Quantum Chemistry
  LUNDQUIST, S. A. S., Electricity with High Voltage Research
  NORDLING, C. L. A., Nuclear and Molecular Physics
  OJA, T., Astronomy
  SIEGBAHN, K. N. B., Physics
  TOVE, P.-A., Electronics
  VINGSBO, O., Material Science
  WESTERLUND, B. E., Astronomy

  *II. Chemical Division:*
  AHLBERG, P., Physical Organic Chemistry
  BERGSON, G., Organic Chemistry
  CLAESSON, S. M., Physical Chemistry
  HJERTEN, W. E. S., Biochemistry
  LIMINGA, R., Inorganic Chemistry
  NYGÅRD, B. A. V., Analytical Chemistry
  OLOVSSON, O. I. G., Inorganic Chemistry
  PORATH, L. O., Biochemistry
  ROOS, P. F. G., Biochemistry
  RUNDQVIST, S., Inorganic Chemistry

  *III. Biology and Earth Science Division:*
  COLLINI, B. H. E., Mineralogy
  DAHL, C., Entomology
  ERIKSSON, E., Hydrology
  ERIKSSON, T., Physiological Botany
  FORSBERG, C., Limnology
  FREDGA, K., Genetics
  HEDBERG, K. O., Systematical Botany
  HÖGSTRÖM, U., Meteorology
  JACOBSON, D. C. O., Morphology, Zoology
  KIHLMAN, B., Biochemical Cytogenetics
  KIHLSTRÖM, J.-E., Ecotoxicology
  KOARK, H., Ore Geology
  KURLAND, C. G., Molecular Biology
  KÖNIGSSON, L.-K. A., Quaternary Geology
  LARSSON, H. B., Physical Biology
  LINDAHL-KIESSLING, KERSTIN M., Zoophysiology
  VAN DER MAAREL, E., Ecological Botany
  MARCSTRÖM, V., Population Dynamics
  MARTINSSON, A., Palaeobiology
  NORRMAN, J. O., Physical Geography
  PEJLER, B., Limnology
  PHILIPSON, C. L., Microbiology
  RAMBERG, H., Mineralogy
  REYMENT, R. A., Historical Geology
  STRANDBERG, R., Molecular Biology
  SUNDBORG, Å. O. F., Physical Geography
  ULFSTRAND, S., Ecological Zoology

*Faculty of Pharmacy:*
  DAHLBOM, J. R., Organic Pharmaceutical Chemistry

DANIELSSON, B., Organic Pharmaceutical Chemistry
DANIELSSON, H., Pharmaceutical Biochemistry
LUNDGREN, P., Galenic Pharmacy
PAALZOW, L., Biopharmacy
SANDBERG, F., Pharmacognosy
SCHILL, G., Analytical Pharmaceutical Chemistry
SKÖLD, O., Pharmaceutical Microbiology
SUNDELÖF, L.-O., Inorganic and Physical Chemistry
TERENIUS, L., Pharmaceutical Pharmacology
ULLBERG, S., Toxicology

## HÖGSKOLAN I VÄXJÖ
(Växjö University College)
P.O.B. 5035, 350 05 VÄXJÖ
Telephone: 0470/81 000.

Founded 1967 as a branch of Lund University; independent status 1977.

Academic year: September to June.
*Rector:* Prof. HANS WIESLANDER.
*Registrar:* LARS WRÅÅK.
*Chief Librarian:* FREDRIK LIEPE.

Library of 80,000 vols.
Number of teachers: 200.
Number of students: 2,500.

Publications: *Acta Wexionensia*, series including: *Växjö Social Studies†, Växjo Migration Studies†, Economy and Labour Market†.*

HEADS OF DEPARTMENTS:
*Behavioural Science:* D. STURESSON.
*Economics and Administration:* I. SJÖGERÅS.
*Mathematics, Statistics and Computer Science:* A. TENGSTRAND.
*Educational Methods:* LARS WIGER.
*Swedish and Fine Arts:* A. LINDVÅG.
*Physical Education:* S. FRENNBERG.
*Social Sciences and History:* L.-O. LARSSON.
*Science:* A. JOHANSSON.
*Modern Languages:* S. KLINTBORG.

PROFESSORS:
ANDERSSON, S., French
APELKRANS, M., Information Processing/Computer Science
BJÖRKLUND, I., Music
BOOK, T., Geography
CARLBERG, L., Fine Arts
CARLSSON, B., Education
DAHMSTRÖM, P., Statistics
FRENNBERG, S., Physical Education
JANSSON, A., Education
JOHANNISSON, B., Business Administration
JOHANSSON, A., Physics
HYLTÉN-CAVALLIUS, B., Biology
LARSSON, L.-O., History
JOHANSSON, E., German
JÖNSSON, F., Scandinavian Languages
LINDBLAD, K.-E., English
LINDEÅS, B., Religious Knowledge
LINDVÅG, A., Scandinavian Languages
MULLAERT, Å., Sociology
MÖLLER, T., Educational Methods
NIKLASSON, H., Economics
RING, H., Administration
SELTÉN, B., English
SJÖLAND, S., Chemistry
STRAND, S.-E., Public Health
SWÄRD, S.-O., History
SÖDERSTRÖM, U., Mathematics
TENGSTRAND, A., Mathematics
WIESELGRAN, A.-M., Scandinavian Languages
WIESLANDER, H., Political Science
WINDAHL, S., Information Techniques

## OTHER INSTITUTES OF UNIVERSITY STANDING

GENERAL:
**Högskolan i Borås** (*Borås University College*): P.O.B. 55 067, 500 05 Borås; f. 1977 after reorganization.

*Rector:* NILS-BERTIL FAXÉN.
*Secretary:* ULF BOHMAN.
*Librarian:* KERSTIN QUENTZER.

Library of 50,000 vols.
Number of teachers: 115.
Number of students: 1,675 (full- and part-time).

DEANS:
*Swedish National Institute of Librarianship:* KERSTIN QUENTZER.
*Pre-School Teacher Training Institute:* KERSTIN THORBURN.

ART:
**Konstfackskolan** (*Swedish State College of Arts and Design*): P.O.B. 27 116, Valhallavägen 191, 102 52 Stockholm 27; f. 1844.

*Principal:* GUNILLA LAGERBIELKE.
*Headmaster of the Training College for Art Teachers:* GERT NORDSTRÖM.

Number of teachers: 135.
Number of students: 650.

**Konsthögskolan** (*College of Fine Arts*): Fredsgatan 12, Box 16 317, 103 26, Stockholm; f. 1735.

*Principal:* SVEN LJUNGBERG.
*Vice-Principal:* PER OLOV ULTVEDT.
*Secretary:* BJÖRN BERGMAN.
*Librarian:* B. LARSSON.

Number of students: 245.

Publications: *Konsthögskolans Timplan, Konsthögskolan Elevkatalog.*

PROFESSORS:
BEJEMARK, K. G., Sculpture
BERGMARK, T., Theory of Modern Art
HALLSTRÖM, B. H., Artistic Materials and Conservation
JANSSON, A., Painting
KÅKS, O., Painting
LINDAHL, G., History of Swedish Architecture, Comparative Architectural History
PALLARP, Å., Painting
SJÖSTROM, JOHN, Architecture
STENQVIST, N. G., Graphic Arts and Design
VIKSTEN, H., Painting
ÖSTMAR, T., Drawing

ECONOMICS:
**Handelshögskolan i Stockholm** (*Stockholm School of Economics*): Box 6501, 113 83 Stockholm; Tel. 08/736 01 20; f. 1909; Private.

*Rector:* Prof. P.-J. ELIAESON.
*Director of Administration:* R. LINNÉ.
*Librarian:* B. JANSON.

Library: *see* Libraries.

Number of teachers: 87, including 12 professors.
Number of students: 1,224.

PROFESSORS:
ALEXANDERSSON, G., International Economic Geography
BURENSTAM LINDER, S., International Economics
CLAESON, C.-FR., Economic Geography
DAHMÉN, E., Economics, Economic and Social History
JOHANSSON, S.-E., Business Administration
JUNGENFELT, K.-G., Economics
KARNELL, G., Legal Science
KRISTENSSON, F., Business Administration
MÄLER, K.-G., Economics
NÄSLUND, B., Business Administration
PERSSON, S., Economic Information Processing
RUIST, E. H., Statistics and Economics
SJÖSTRAND, S.-E., Business Administration
STYMNE, B., Organizational Theory
WÄRNERYD, K.-E., Economic Psychology

AFFILIATED INSTITUTE:
**Ekonomiska Forskningsinstitutet vid Handelshögskolan i Stockholm** (*The Economic Research Institute at the Stockholm School of Economics*): Sveavägen 65, Stockholm; f. 1929; scientific research in management science and economics; 80 research fellows; Dir. Prof. WÄRNERYD; publs. *EFI News*, reports, working papers.

MEDICINE:
**Karolinska Institutet:** Solnavägen 1, P.O.B. 60400, 104 01 Stockholm; Tel. 34-05-60; f. 1810.

*Rector:* B. PERNOW.
*Vice-Rector:* A. G. LJUNGQVIST.
*Head of Administration:* MARGARETA ALMLING.
*Librarian:* H. BAUDE.

Library: *see* Libraries.

Number of teachers: 750, including 136 professors.
Number of students: 3,667.

Publications: *Computerized Publication Register* (information on all publs. issued by the Institute), *Curriculum, Students' Handbook.*

DEANS:
*Faculty of Medicine:* Prof. B. I. SAMUELSSON.

*Faculty of Odontology:* Prof. L. EDWALL.

PROFESSORS:
*Faculty of Medicine:*
ALLANDER, E., Social Medicine
ANDERSSON, K. L., Urology
BARR, B. O., Clinical Audiology
BENGTSSON, E. I., Infectious Diseases
BERGMAN, H. O. M., Psychology of Alcoholism
BERGSTRAND, A. F., Pathology

Bertani, G., Microbiological Genetics
Birke, G., Medicine
Biörck, C. G. W., Medicine
Björk, V. O., Thoracic Surgery
Blomstrand, R. L., Clinical Chemistry
Blombäck, G. E. B., Coagulation Research
Borell, U. S. M., Obstetrics and Gynaecology
Broberger, C. G. O., Paediatrics
Bygdeman, M. A., Obstetrics and Gynaecology
Böttiger, L. E. J., Medicine
Brodin, H., Physiotherapy
Brody, S. S., Obstetrics and Gynaecology
Carlson, L. A. F., Medicine
Celada, F., Immunology
Drettner, O. B., Oto-Rhino-Laryngology
Edström, J. E., Histology
Einhorn, J., Radiotherapy
Ekblom, B. T., Exercise Physiology
Eklund, A. G., Epidemiology
Elfvin, L.-G., Anatomy
Engfeldt, B. O., Pathology
Engström, A. V., Medical Physics
von Euler-Chelpin, C. L. U., Brain Research
Frankenhauser, V. M., Psychology
Franksson, L. E. C., Surgery
Friberg, L. T., Hygiene
Fuxe, K. G., Histology
Granholm, L. G., Neurosurgery
Grant, N. G., Anatomy
Greitz, T. V. B., Neuroradiology
Grillner, S. E., Exercise Physiology
Gullberg, K. R., Medicine (Rheumatology)
Gustafsson, B. E., Germ-Free Research
Gustafsson, J.-Å., Medical Nutrition
Hall, K., Endocrinology
Hallberg, D. K., Surgery
Hanngren, S. Å. G., Medicine-Pulmonary Medicine
Hedén, C.-G., Bacteriology
Holm, O. G., Clinical Immunology
Holme, T. E. B., Bacteriology
Holmstedt, B. R., Toxicology
Hultman, E. H., Clinical Chemistry
Hökfelt, T. G. M., Histology with Cell Biology
Ideström, C.-M., Clinical Alcohol and Narcotic Research
Ivemark, B. I., Paediatric Pathology
Jacobson, N. B., Medical Technology
Jansson, B. I., Psychiatry
Johansson, S. G. O., Clinical Immunology
Klein, E., Tumour-Biology
Klein, G., Tumour-Biology
Kristensen, S. K., Pathology (Neuropathology)
Lagerlöf, B. A. M., Pathology
Lidberg, L. G., Social and Forensic Psychiatry
Lindblom, U. F., Neurology
Lindsten, J. E., Medical Genetics
Lindström, B., Medical Physics and Statistics
Ljungqvist, A. G., Pathology
Löw, H. E., Experimental Endocrinology
Moberger, J. G. V., Tumour Pathology
Mutt, V., Biochemistry
Möller, L. G., Immunobiology
Nordenström, B. E. W., Diagnostic Radiology
Norlander, O. P., Anaesthesiology
Norman, A. J., Clinical Chemistry
Norrby, E. J. C., Virus Research
Nylander, I., Child and Youth Psychiatry
Nylander, P. G., Surgery
Olsson, P. I., Experimental Surgery
Orrenius, S. G., Forensic Medicine
Ottoson, D. H. R., Physiology
Pernow, B. B., Clinical Physiology
Piscator, E. M., Hygiene
Reichard, P. A., Biochemistry
Révész, L., Tumour Biology
Ringertz, N. R., Medical Cell Genetics
Rosell, B. S., Pharmacology
Rudhe, U.-G., Diagnostic Radiology
Samuelsson, B. J., Medical and Physiological Chemistry
Sedvall, C. G., Psychiatry
Sevastikoglou, J., Orthopaedic Surgery
Sjöqvist, F. G. F., Clinical Pharmacology
Sjövall, J. B., Medical Chemistry
Stjärne, P. L., Physiology
Svanström, L. O. E., Social Medicine
Tengroth, B. M., Ophthalmology
Thomasson, B. H., Paediatric Surgery
Thorell, B. G., Pathology
Thyresson, N., Dermatology and Venereology
Tribukait, B., Medical Radiobiology
Tunevall, T. G., Clinical Bacteriology
Ungersted, C. U., Neuropsychopharmacology
Wahren, J., Clinical Physiology
Walstam, R. Radiophysics
Wersäll, J. O., Oto-Rhino-Laryngology
Wettenberg, C. L. E., Psychiatry
Widén, J. O. L., Clinical Neurophysiology
Winberg, J., Paediatrics
Zetterberg, A. H. D., Pathology, Tumour Cytology
Zetterberg, R. O. F., Paediatrics
Zetterström-Karpe, T. B., Ophthalmology
Åstrand, K. P.-O., Exercise Physiology
Änggård, E. E., Experimental Alcohol and Narcotics Research

*Faculty of Odontology* (Tandläkarhögskolan i Stockholm):
Edwall, L. G. A., Endodontics
Ericsson, S. G., Stomatognathic Physiology
Frostell, G., Cariology
Hammarström, L. E., Oral Pathology
Henrikson, C. O., Dental Roentgenology
Koch, S. G. M., Pedodontics
Linder-Aronson, S. Y., Orthodontics
Lockowandt, P. L. O., Dental Technology
Nord, C.-E., Oral Microbiology
Nordenram, F. Å., Oral Surgery
Söder, P.-Ö., Periodontology
Söremark, R., Prosthetics

Music:

**Musikhögskolan i Göteborg:** Dicksonsg. 10, 41256 Gothenburg; f. 1971.

*President:* Gunnar Sjöström.
*Dean:* Gösta Ohlin.
*Librarian:* Charlotta Ström.

Number of teachers: 135.
Number of students: 330.

**Musikhögskolan i Malmö:** Fridhemsvägen 2, S-217 74 Malmö; f. 1971.

*Rector:* Bengt Hall.

Number of teachers: 115.
Number of students: 280.

**Musikhögskolan i Stockholm** (*State Academy of Music, Stockholm*): Valhallavägen 103-109, 115 31 Stockholm; f. 1771.

*Principal:* Prof. I. Gabrielsson.
*Directors of Studies:* Bengt Holmstrand, Per-Olov Hjerpe.

Number of teachers: 175, including 3 professors.

Number of students: 500.

**Valands Konsthögskola:** Box 9004, S-400 70 Gothenburg; f. 1865; affiliated to Gothenburg University.

*President:* Georg Suttner.
*Secretary:* Ulla Ugolini.

Number of professors: 9.
Number of students: 60.

Physical Education:

**Gymnastik- och Idrottshögskolan** (*Physical Education Institute*): Box 923, 70130, Örebro; f. 1966; library of 3,500 vols.; 20 teachers, 200 students; Rector Lennart Mattsson.

**Gymnastik- och Idrottshögskolan i Stockholm** (*College of Physical Education in Stockholm*): Lidingövägen 1, S-114 33 Stockholm; f. 1813; library of 13,000 vols.; 50 teachers, 250 students; Rector Stina Ljunggren.

# SWITZERLAND
Population 6,314,000

## LEARNED SOCIETIES

### Agriculture and Veterinary Science

**Fédération des Sociétés d'Agriculture de la Suisse Romande:** Ave. des Jordils 3, Case postale, CH-1000 Lausanne 6; f. 1881; 28,000 mems.; library of 200 vols.; Sec. D. GROSCLAUDE; publs. *Revue suisse de viticulture, d'arboriculture et d'horticulture* (6 a year), *Revue suisse d'agriculture* (6 a year).

**Gesellschaft Schweizerischer Landwirte/Société Suisse des Agriculteurs** (*Swiss Agricultural Society*): ETH-Zentrum, 8092 Zürich; f. 1885; 1,100 mems.; Pres. H. HUI; Sec. Dr. G. BRUNNER; publ. *Schweizerische Landwirtschaftliche Monatshefte*.

**Gesellschaft Schweizerischer Tierärzte/Société des Vétérinaires Suisses:** Elfenstrasse 18, 3000 Bern 16; f. 1813; 1,200 mems.; Pres. Dr. E. HUBER; Sec.-Gen. H. DE GENDRE; publs. *Schweizer Archiv für Tierheilkunde* (monthly), *G.S.T. Bulletin SVS* (monthly).

### Architecture and Town Planning

**Bund Schweizer Architekten (BSA)/Fédération des Architectes Suisses (FAS):** Keltenstr. 45, 8044 Zürich; 438 mems.; Pres. C. PAILLARD; publs. *Werk, Bauen und Wohnen*.

**Schweizer Heimatschutz** (*Swiss National Trust*): Postfach, 8032 Zürich; Pres. Councillor R. C. SCHULE; publs. *Heimatschutz* (French and German, every 2 months).

**Société Suisse des Ingénieurs et des Architectes:** Selnaustrasse 16, 8039 Zürich; f. 1837; 7,400 mems.; Pres. A. COGLIATTI; Gen. Sec. Dr. U. ZÜRCHER; publs. *Schweizerische Bauzeitung, Bulletin technique de la Suisse romande, Rivista tecnica della Svizzera italiana*.

### The Arts

**Arbeitsgemeinschaft Schweizer Grafiker:** Weinbergstrasse 11, 8001 Zürich; f. 1972; 520 mems.; Pres. WILLY GÖTTIN; publ. *ASG Information* (4–6 a year).

**Fondation Hindemith:** c/o M. M. Décombaz, 40 rue du Simplon, 1800 Vevey; f. 1968 to promote and cultivate music, in particular contemporary music; to maintain the musical and literary heritage of Paul Hindemith; to encourage research in the field of music and diffusion of research results; archives in Hindemith Institute, Untermainkai 14, 6 Frankfurt, Fed. Rep. of Germany; Pres. Dr. ARNO VOLK (Mainz); Vice-Pres. Dr. K. H. SCHOBER (Washington); publs. *Hindemith General Original Edition, Les Annales Hindemith, Frankfurter Studien*.

**Gesellschaft für Schweizerische Kunstgeschichte:** Willadingweg 27, 3006 Bern; f. 1880; 12,000 mems.; Pres. LUCIE BURCKHARDT; publs. *Die Kunstdenkmäler der Schweiz†, Schweiz. Kunstführer, Mitteilungsblatt "Unsere Kunstdenkmäler†, Beiträge zur Kunstgeschichte der Schweiz†, Kunstführer durch die Schweiz*.

**Gesellschaft Schweizerischer Maler, Bildhauer und Architekten/Société des Peintres, Sculpteurs et Architectes Suisses:** Kirchplatz 9, 4132 Muttenz; f. 1865; 1,600 active mems.; Pres. NIKI PIAZZOLI; Vice-Pres PETER HÄCHLER; Sec. ESTHER BRUNNER-BUCHSER; publs. *Schweizer Kunst, Art Suisse, Arte Svizzera*.

**Kunstverein St. Gallen:** Katharinengasse 11, CH-9000 St. Gallen; f. 1827; 2,100 mems.; Pres. H. MÜLLER; Sec. CH. KALTHOFF.

**Schweizerische Musikforschende Gesellschaft:** 23 Sonnenweg, Basel; f. 1916; 540 mems.; Pres. Prof. ERNST LICHTENHAHN; Sec. Dr. VICTOR RAVIZZA; publs. *Schweiz Musikdenkmäler, Publikation der SMG Serie II, Schweiz Beiträge zur Musikwissenschaft†, Jahrbuch†* (annually).

**Schweizerischer Kunstverein/Société Suisse des Beaux-Arts/Società Svizzera di Belle Arti:** c/o Dr. Guido Baumgartner, Hauptstr. 28, 4126 Bettingen BS; f. 1806; acts as the umbrella organization for 25 member sections; aims to promote and protect the interests of artists and art lovers on a federal level; Pres. GUIDO BAUMGARTNER; Sec. HEINI WIDMER; publ. *Bulletin†* (monthly).

**Schweizerischer Musikerverband:** Elisabethenstrasse 2, 4051 Basel; f. 1914; an organization of Swiss professional musicians; branches in 10 localities; 1,622 mems.; Pres. H. HEUSI; Sec. Dr. P. KUSTER; publ. *Schweizer Musikerblatt* (monthly).

**Schweizer Musikrat/Conseil Suisse de la Musique:** P.O.B. 2054, CH 4001 Basel; f. 1964; mem. of the CIM of UNESCO; membership of various musical organizations; Pres. LANCE TSCHANNEN; Sec. ELISABETH KÜNG; publ. *Guide for Musical Studies in Switzerland*.

**Schweizerischer Tonkünstlerverein/Association des Musiciens Suisses:** Ave. du Grammont 11 bis, 1000 Lausanne 13; f. 1900; 710 mems.; Pres. Prof. KLAUS HUBER; Sec. Dr. DOMINIQUE CREUX; publs. *Revue Musicale Suisse* (bi-monthly), *Tendances et Réalisations*.

**Schweizerischer Werkbund:** Weinbergstrasse 11, 8001 Zürich; f. 1913; 800 mems.; Pres. DANIEL REIST; publ. *Werk-archithese* (monthly).

**Schweizerisches Institut für Kunstwissenschaft/Institut Suisse pour l'Etude de l'Art:** Waldmannstrasse 6-8, 8001 Zürich; f. 1951; registration of Swiss works of art—studies in art and technology; 2,000 mems.; library of 25,000 books, 35,000 reproductions; Pres. Dr. HANS LACHER; Dir. Dr. HANS A. LÜTHY; Archives and Library, Dr. HANSJÖRG HEUSSER; Conservation and Restoration, EMIL BOSSHARD; Publications, Dr. GEORG GERMANN; publs. *Jahresbericht, Jahrbuch*, catalogues of Swiss artists and collections, Technological Reports, etc.

**Société Suisse de Pédagogie Musicale:** Forchstrasse 376, 8008 Zürich; f. 1893; 3,180 mems.; Pres. J. ROMAN WIDMER; Sec. HANNA BRANDENBERGER; publs. *Feuillets suisses de pédagogie musicale, Bulletin mensuel SSPM, Agenda du musicien*.

### Bibliography, Library Science and Museology

**Schweizerische Bibliophilen-Gesellschaft/Société Suisse des Bibliophiles:** 43 Voltastr., 8044 Zürich; f. 1921; 700 mems.; Pres. Dr. CONRAD ULRICH; publs. *Stultifera Navis 44-57, Librarium 58-* (three times a year).

**Schweizerische Gesellschaft für die Rechte der Urheber musikalischer Werke (SUISA)** (*Swiss Society for Rights of Authors of Musical Works*): 82 Bellariastrasse, 8038

Zürich; f. 1942; 4,900 mems.; Pres. Hermann Haller; Dir. Dr. U. Uchtenhagen; publ. *Schweizerische Musikzeitung* (bi-monthly).

**Schweizerische Vereinigung für Dokumentation/Association Suisse de Documentation:** c/o BID PTT, 3030 Bern; f. 1939; collaboration and representation of Swiss documentation in national and international spheres; consultation on documental problems; training of documentalists; 500 mems. (individual and collective); Pres. Dr. F. Köver; Sec. W. Bruderer; publ. *Nachrichten VSB/SVD* (6 a year).

**Verband der Museen der Schweiz/Association des Musées Suisses:** Postfach 8023, Zürich; f. 1966; association of Swiss museums, zoological and botanical gardens and cultural institutions to represent their interests; forms a link between Swiss museums and ICOM (*q.v.*); organizes annual conference and work sessions on conservation, restoration and other related topics; 280 mems.; Pres. Dr. Gerhard Baer; Sec. Dr. Jenny Schneider; publ. *Bulletin* (2 a year).

**Vereinigung Schweizerischer Archivare** (*Association of Swiss Archivists*): Archivstr. 24, 3003 Bern; f. 1922; lectures, discussions, etc., concerning archive work; 170 mems.; Pres. Dr. Walter Lendi; publ. *Mitteilungen*.

**Vereinigung Schweizerischer Bibliothekare** (*Association of Swiss Librarians*): Hallwylstrasse 15, CH-3003 Bern; f. 1897; 1,152 mems.; Pres. Dr. Fredy Gröbli; Sec. Dr. W. Treichler; publ. *Nachrichten* (six a year).

### Economics, Law and Politics

**Association Suisse de Science Politique** (*Swiss Political Science Association*): Institut de sociologie et de science politique, Université de Neuchâtel, Pierre-à-Mazel 7, 2000 Neuchâtel; f. 1959; 500 mems.; Pres. Prof. Ernest Weibel; Exec. Sec. Philippe Oertlé; publs. *Annuaire Suisse de Science Politique* (annually), *Année Politique Suisse* (annually).

**Bundesamt für Statistik/Office Fédéral de la Statistique** (*Federal Bureau of Statistics*): Hallwystrasse 15, 3003 Bern; f. 1862; for production and publications of statistics; Dir. Jean-Jaques Senglet, ph.d.; publs. *Statistical Yearbook*, other statistical and economics publications.

**Gottlieb Duttweiler Institute for Economic and Social Studies:** Langhaldenstrasse, 8803 Rüschlikon/Zürich; f. 1946; independent, but part of the Green Meadow Foundation; library of 5,000 vols. and 500 periodicals; Pres. Rudolf Suter; Dir. Dr. Christian Lutz; publs. *gdi-information*, occasional publications.

**Schweizerische Gesellschaft für Aussenpolitik/Association Suisse de Politique Etrangère:** Stapferhaus, Schloss, 5600 Lenzburg; f. 1968; 360 mems.; Pres. Amb. Felix Schnyder; Sec. B. Tholen.

**Schweizerische Vereinigung für Internationales Recht/Société Suisse de Droit International:** P.O.B. 690, 8027 Zürich; f. 1914; 277 mems.; Pres. Prof. Dr. L. Wildhaber; Sec. Dr. P. M. Gutzwiller; publ. *Swiss Yearbook for International Law*.

**Schweizerischer Anwaltsverband** (*Swiss Bar Association*): Lavaterstr. 83, 8027 Zürich; f. 1898; 2,900 mems.; Pres. Me. André Nardin; Sec. Dr. Max P. Oesch; publ. *Bulletin*.

**Schweizerischer Juristenverein/Société suisse des juristes:** Beatusstr. 28, 3006 Bern; f. 1861; 2,800 mems.; Pres. Fritz Gygi.

**Schweizerischer Notaren-Verband/Fédération des Notaires de Suisse:** Via G.B. Pioda 12, 6900 Lugano; f. 1920; 1,300 mems.; Pres. Avv. dott. Mario Pozzi; Sec. Brenno Brunoni.

**Zentrale für Wirtschaftsdokumentation** (*Economic Documentation Centre*): 8032 Zürich, Apollostrasse 2; f. 1910; attached to the University of Zurich; large world-wide collection of annual reports and accounts of the main companies; daily newspapers, magazines and statistical material available.

### Education

**Centre Suisse de Documentation en Matière d'Enseignement et d'Education** (*Swiss Documentation Centre for Educational Matters*): Palais Wilson, 1211 Geneva 14; f. 1962; to inform Swiss and foreign services on questions concerning teaching and education in Switzerland; the centre is the secretariat of the Swiss Conference of Cantonal Directors of Education; publs. *Bibliographie pédagogique suisse†*, *Bulletin*, *Politique de l'éducation* (annual), *Bulletin d'information de la CDIP*.

**Institut Romand de Recherches et de Documentation Pédagogiques:** Faubourg de l'Hôpital 43-45, CH-2000 Neuchâtel; f. 1969; co-ordination of documentation and research for French-speaking Switzerland, research in educational methods, organization and administration; 18 mems.; library of 13,500 vols.; Pres. J. Cavidini; Dir. J. A. Tschoumy; publs. *Coordination*, *Liste des acquisitions*, reports, textbooks.

**Schweizerische Hochschulkonferenz/Conférence Universitaire Suisse:** Wildhainweg 21, 3012 Bern; f. 1969; co-ordination of Swiss universities and institutes of higher education; 29 mems. representing cantons, polytechnics, National Union of Students, etc.; Pres. M. Cottier; Sec.-Gen. R. Deppeler; publs. *Rapport annuel*, articles in *Politique de la science* (4–6 times annually).

**Schweizerische Zentralstelle für Hochschulwesen/Office Central Universitaire Suisse** (*Central Office of the Swiss Universities*): Sophienstrasse 2, 8032 Zürich; f. 1920; information service on Swiss and foreign universities, university teacher and student exchange, secretariat of the Conference of Swiss University Rectors and of the Federal Committee for Scholarships to Foreign Students; Sec. Prof. Dr. Andreas Miller.

**Vereinigung Schweizerischer Hochschuldozenten/Association suisse des professeurs d'université:** Sophienstrasse 2, 8032 Zürich; 1,450 mems.; Pres. Prof. Dr. L. Leuba; Sec. Prof. Dr. Andreas Miller.

### History, Geography and Archaeology

**Allgemeine Geschichtforschende Gesellschaft der Schweiz/Société Générale Suisse d'Histoire:** Stadt- und Universitätsbibliothek, Münstergasse 61, CH-3000 Bern 7; f. 1841; 1,025 mems.; Pres. Dr. A. Staehelin; publs. *Schweizerische Zeitschrift für Geschichte†*, *Bulletin AGGS*, *Quellen zur Schweizergeschichte*.

**Antiquarische Gesellschaft:** Predigerplatz 33, 8001 Zürich; f. 1832; 560 mems.; Pres. Dr. H. Meyer; publs. *Mitteilungen der Antiquar, Gesellschaft†*, *Urkundenbuch der Stadt und Landschaft Zürich*.

**Geographisch-Ethnographische Gesellschaft Zürich:** Geographisches Institut Universität Zürich, Postfach, 8033 Zürich; f. 1889; 510 mems.; Pres. Prof. Dr. H. Haefner; Sec. A. Schaeppi; publs. *Mitteilungen 1899–1945*, *Geographica Helvetica†*.

**Geographisch-Ethnologische Gesellschaft Basel:** Klingelbergstrasse 16, CH-4056 Basel; f. 1923; 625 mems.; Pres. Dr. Chr. Kaufmann; Sec. Dr. W. Leimgruber; publs. *Regio Basiliensis†* (6-monthly), *Basler Beiträge zur Geographie†*, *Basler Beiträge zur Ethnologie†* (irregular), *Basler Beiträge zur Physiogeographie†* (irregular).

**Geographische Gesellschaft Bern:** Hallerstr. 12, 3012 Bern; f. 1873; 560 mems.; Pres. Dr. K. Aerni; Sec. Dr. H. Wanner; publs. *Jahrbuch†*, *Beihefte zum Jahrbuch†* (irregularly), *Berner Geographische Mitteilungen†* (annually).

**Historisch-Antiquarischer Verein Heiden:** 9410 Heiden; f. 1874; concerned with the maintenance and preservation of fabrics, furniture, armour, coins, etc., of historical interest; Pres. RUDOLF ROHNER.

**Historische und Antiquarische Gesellschaft zu Basel:** Universitätsbibliothek, Schönbeinstrasse 20, Basel; f. 1836; 750 mems.; library contains 20,000 vols.; Pres. Dr. CHRISTOPH JUNGCK; publ. *Basler Zeitschrift für Geschichte und Altertumskunde*†.

**Historischer Verein des Kantons Bern:** Stadt- und Universitäts-bibliothek, Münstergasse 61, CH-3000 Bern 7; f. 1847; Pres. Prof. Dr. H. MICHEL; publs. *Archiv des Historischen Vereins*†, *Berner Zeitschrift für Geschichte und Heimatkunde*†.

**Opera Svizzera dei Monumenti d'Arte:** (Ticino office) Casa del Negromante, Via Borghese 14, 6600 Locarno; f. 1963; to gather and publish material on the Ticino area; 10,000 mems.; Pres. F. CACCIA; Dir. V. GILARDONI; publ. *Archivo Storico Ticinese, Arte e monumenti della Lombardia prealpina, Die Kunstdenkmäler der Schweiz: Ticino, Ticinensia*.

**Schweizerische Gesellschaft für Kartographie:** c/o Institut für Kartographie, ETH-Hönggerberg, 8093 Zürich; f. 1969; educational publications and courses; 192 mems.; Pres. K. FICKER; Sec. CH. HOINKES.

**Schweizerische Gesellschaft für Ur- und Frühgeschichte:** Rheinsprung 20, CH-4000 Basel; 3,000 mems.

**Schweizerische Heraldische Gesellschaft/Société suisse d'Héraldique:** Lützelmattstrasse 4, CH-6006 Lucerne; f. 1891; 550 mems.; Pres. JOSEPH M. GALLIKER; Sec. LOUIS MÜHLEMANN; publs. *Annuaire* (Yearbook), *Archivum Heraldicum* (2 a year).

**Schweizerische Numismatische Gesellschaft/Société suisse de numismatique:** Stadt- und Universitätsbibliothek, Münstergasse 61, CH-3000 Bern 7; 743 mems.; Pres. H.-U. GEIGER; Sec. E. TOBLER; publs. *Schweizer Münzblätter, Gazette suisse de numismatique*†, *Schweizerische Numismatische Rundschau, Revue suisse de numismatique*†, *Schweizer Münzkatalog*†.

**Schweizerische Vereinigung für Altertumswissenschaft/ Association suisse pour l'étude de l'antiquité:** Klass.-Phil. Seminar, Florhofgasse 11, 8001 Zürich; f. 1943; 121 mems.; Pres. Prof. WALTER BURKERT; Sec. Prof. PIERRE DUCREY.

**Società Storica Locarnese:** Casa del Negromante, Via Borghese 14, 6600 Locarno; f. 1955; collection and conservation of documents relating to the history of the Locarno area, organizes exhibitions and lectures; 100 mems.; Pres. Prof. V. GILARDONI; Sec. M. BACILIERI.

**Société de Géographie de Genève:** Palais de l'Athénée, Geneva; f. 1858; 200 mems.; publ. *Le Globe*.

**Société d'Histoire et d'Archéologie:** c/o Bibliothèque Publique et Universitaire, Geneva; f. 1838; 400 mems.; library contains 10,000 vols.; 1,000 MSS.; Pres. JEAN-ETIENNE GENEQUAND; Sec. LEÏLA EL-WAKIL; publs. *Bulletin* (annual), *Mémoires et Documents*.

**Société d'Histoire de la Suisse Romande:** Bibliothèque Universitaire, Palais de Rumine, Lausanne; f. 1837; 330 mems.; Library: see Bibliothèque Cantonale et Universitaire de Lausanne; Pres. PAUL ROUSSET; publs. *Mémoires, Documents*.

**Société vaudoise d'histoire et d'archéologie:** Archives Cantonales, 47 rue du Maupas, 1004 Lausanne; f. 1902; 961 mems.; Pres. L. HUBLER; publ. *Revue Historique vaudoise* (annual).

**Vereinigung der Freunde antiker Kunst/Association des amis de l'art antique:** Archäologisches Seminar der Universität, Schönbeinstr. 20, CH-4056 Basel; f. 1956; 750 mems.; Pres. Prof. Dr. ROLF A. STUCKY; publ. *Antike Kunst* (2 a year).

### INTERNATIONAL CULTURAL INSTITUTES

**Dänisches Institut für Information und kulturellen Austausch:** Gotthardstrasse 21, 8002 Zürich; branch of Det Danske Selskab, Copenhagen; Dir. GUNNER GOESKJÆR.

**Schweizerische Akademische Gesellschaft der Anglisten/ Société suisse d'études anglaises:** Beaux-Arts 10, Neuchâtel; f. 1947; 44 mems.; Pres. Prof. GEORGES DENIS ZIMMERMANN; publ. *English Studies in Swiss Universities* (annually).

**Schweizerische Gesellschaft für Asienkunde/Société suisse d'études asiatiques:** Sekretariat, Ostasiatisches Seminar, Universität, Mühlegasse 21, 8001 Zürich; f. 1947; 200 mems.; Pres. R. P. KRAMERS; publs. *Asiatische Studien/ Etudes Asiatiques* (twice yearly).

**Schweizerische Gesellschaft für Skandinavische Studien:** Deutsches Seminar der Universität Zürich, Abteilung für Nordische Philologie, Pestalozzistrasse 50, 8032 Zürich; f. 1961; 180 mems.; Pres. Prof. Dr. H.-P. NAUMANN; Sec. Dr. J. GLAUSER; publ. *Beiträge zur nordischen Philologie*† (vol. XI).

**Société suisse des Américanistes/Schweizerische Amerikanisten-Gesellschaft:** 65-67 blvd. Carl-Vogt, 1205 Geneva; f. 1949; 150 mems.; Pres. ANDRÉ JEANNERET; Sec.-Gen. RENÉ FUERST; publ. *Bulletin*† (annual).

**Swiss–American Society for Cultural Relations:** c/o Credit Suisse, P.O.B. 590, 8021 Zürich; f. 1940; lectures and activities concerned with Swiss-American relations; 200 mems.; Pres. Dr. E. K. STÄMPFLI; Sec. H. L. DAVATZ.

### LANGUAGE AND LITERATURE

**Collegium Romanicum:** rue Léon-Michaud 1, 1400 Yverdon; f. 1947; study of Romance languages and literature; 146 mems.; Pres. A. STÄUBLE; Sec. J.-J. MARCHAND; publs. *Vox Romanica*† (annually), *Romanica Helvetica*.

**Deutsch-Schweizerisches P.E.N.-Zentrum:** Regensdorferstr. 179, CH-8049 Zürich; f. 1932, present name 1979; 152 mems.; Pres. OTTO STEIGER; Sec. ANDREAS LÜTHI; publ. *Annals*.

**Gesellschaft für deutsche Sprache und Literatur in Zürich:** Deutsches Seminar der Universität Zürich, Postfach 147, CH-8028 Zürich; f. 1894; 242 mems.; Pres. Prof. Dr. H. WYSLING; Sec. Dr. J. ETZENSPERGER.

**Institut et Musée Voltaire:** rue des Délices 25, 1203 Geneva; f. 1952; library of 20,000 vols. and MSS; Curator CHARLES WIRZ.

**P.E.N. Club de Suisse Romande:** 4 rue du Mont-de-Sion, CH-1206 Geneva; f. 1951; defends freedom of expression; 78 mems.; Pres. RAYMOND TSCHUMI; Sec. JULIETTE MONNIN-HORNUNG.

**Schweizerische Schillerstiftung/Fondation Schiller Suisse:** Im Ring 2, 8126 Zumikon; f. 1905; 500 mems.; Pres. Dr. FRITZ LEUTWILER; Vice-Pres. Mme. YVETTE Z'GRAGGEN; publ. *Jahresbericht*.

**Schweizerische Sprachwissenschaftliche Gesellschaft/ Société suisse de linguistique:** 2000 Neuchâtel, Evole 31; f. 1947; 105 mems.; Pres. Prof. CLAUDE SANDOZ; Sec. ALEX LEUKART; publ. *Cahiers Ferdinand de Saussure* (annually).

**Schweizerischer Schriftsteller-Verband** (Society of Swiss Writers): 25 Kirchgasse, 8001 Zürich; f. 1912; 540 mems.; Pres. MOUSSE BOULANGER; Sec. OTTO BÖNI; publ. *Welt im Wort/Voix des lettres* (2 a year).

**Società Retorumantscha:** Rohanstrasse 5, 7000 Coire/ Grisons; f. 1885; conservation and research into the Romansh language; approx. 600 mems.; Pres. Dr. GION DEPLAZES; publ. *Annalas*.

### MEDICINE

**Académie Suisse des Sciences Médicales/Schweizerische Akademie der Medizinischen Wissenschaften:** 13 Petersplatz, 4051 Basel; f. 1943; 57 mems.; Pres. Prof. Dr.

A. Cerletti; Sec.-Gen. Prof. Dr. J. Girard; publ. *Bulletin*†.

**Schweizerische Gesellschaft für Chirurgie/Société Suisse de Chirurgie:** Spital Limmattal, 8952 Schlieren/Zürich; f. 1915; 670 mems.; Pres. Prof. A. Cuendet; Sec. Prof. H. Schwarz; publ. *Helvetica chirurgica acta*.

**Schweizerische Gesellschaft für Geschichte der Medizin und der Naturwissenschaften/Société Suisse d'Histoire de la Médecine et des Sciences Naturelles:** 8006 Zürich, Rämistr. 71; f. 1921; 280 mems.; Sec. Dr. Med. A. Gubser; publs. *Gesnerus* (quarterly), *Veröffentlichungen der SGGMN* (individual monographs).

**Schweizerische Gesellschaft für Innere Medizin/Société Suisse de Médecine Interne:** c/o Secretary, Prof. F. Nager, Chefarzt Med. Klinik, Kantonsspital, 6004 Luzern; f. 1932; 1,036 mems.; Pres. Prof. B. Courvoisier; publs. reports of meetings, etc.

**Schweizerische Gesellschaft für Orthopädie/Société Suisse d'Orthopédie:** f. 1942; professional organization for orthopaedic surgeons which promotes specialization in orthopaedics and safeguards professional interests; c. 250 mems.; Pres. PD Dr. med. Hans Christoph Meuli; Sec. Dr. Hansbeat Burch, Hôpital cantonal, 1700 Fribourg; publs. *Bulletin d'information* (3 a year), report of annual congress.

**Schweizerische Neurologische Gesellschaft:** Neurologische Klinik, Kantonsspital, 4031 Basel; f. 1908; 228 mems.; Pres. Prof. G. Gauthier; Sec. Prof. H. E. Kaeser; publ. *Schweizer Archiv für Neurologie*.

**Schweizerischer Apotheker-Verein/Société Suisse de Pharmacie:** Marktgasse 52, 3011 Bern; f. 1843; 3,000 mems.; Secs. Dr. J. Bider, Dr. J. Metzger, Dr. H. Bartlome; publs. *Schweizerische Apothekerzeitung*†, *Pharmaceutica Acta Helvetiae*†, *Index Nominum*.

### Natural Sciences
#### General

**Institut National Genevois:** Promenade du Pin 1, 1204 Geneva; f. 1853; 600 mems.; Pres. P. Pittard; Sec.-Gen. F. Strub; consists of Natural Science and Mathematics Section (Pres. Jacques Deferne), Moral and Political Sciences Section (Pres. P. Pittard), Archaeology and History Section (Pres. vacant), Literary Section (Pres. vacant), Industry and Agriculture Section (Pres. M. Herzig), Fine Arts Section (Pres. vacant), Astronomy Section (Pres. M. Keller); publs. *Mémoires* and *Bulletin*.

**Naturforschende Gesellschaft in Basel:** Universitätsbibliothek, Basel; f. 1817; 597 mems.; library contains 60,557 vols.; Pres. Dr. W. Wehrli; Sec. Dr. H. Meindl; publ. *Verhandlungen* (2 a year).

**Naturforschende Gesellschaft in Bern:** Stadt- und Universitätsbibliothek, Münstergasse 61, CH-3000 Bern 7; f. 1786; 472 mems.; publ. *Mitteilungen*†.

**Naturforschende Gesellschaft in Zürich:** 113 Kilchbergstrasse, 8038 Zürich; f. 1746; 1,200 mems.; Editor Prof. Dr. E. A. Thomas; publs. *Neujahrsblatt*†, *Vierteljahrsschrift*† (quarterly).

**Naturforschende Gesellschaft Schaffhausen:** Ungarbuhlstrasse 34, CH-8200 Schaffhausen; f. 1822; furtherance of interest and research in natural science and spread of nature conservation; 470 mems.; library of about 3,000 vols.; Pres. Dr. H. Hubscher; Sec. Ing. H. Lustenberger; publs. *Mitteilungen*, *Neujahrsblätter*, pamphlets on nature conservation.

**Naturwissenschaftliche Gesellschaft Winterthur:** CH-8400 Winterthur, Bachtelstrasse 6; f. 1884; 270 mems.; Pres. Prof. Lutz Ibscher; publ. *Mitteilungen*† (every 3 years).

**Schweizerische Naturforschende Gesellschaft/Société Helvétique des Sciences naturelles:** Hirschengraben 11, Postfach 2535, CH-3001 Bern; f. 1815; library: see Stadtbibliothek, Bern; mems.: 21 honorary, 9 institutions, 58 societies; Pres. Prof. Dr. E. Niggli; Sec.-Gen. Dr. B. Sitter; publs. *Jahrbuch*, *Denkschriften*†, *Berichte der SNG zur Kernergie*, *Bulletin*.

**Schweizerische Stiftung für Alpine Forschungen** (Swiss Foundation for Alpine Research): Binzstrasse 17, 8045 Zürich; f. 1939; Pres. Ernst Feuz; Sec. Dr. F. H. Schwarzenbach; publs. *The Mountain World*, *Berge der Welt*, etc.

**Schweizerischer Nationalfonds zur Förderung der Wissenschaftlichen Forschung/Fonds national suisse de la recherche scientifique** (Swiss National Science Foundation): Wildhainweg 20, Bern; f. 1952 for the encouragement of research in the social, legal, economic, natural and medical sciences, humanities and technology; has a Council of Foundation, on which the Government, the universities and other cultural institutions are represented, and a National Research Council, consisting of scientists; Pres. Council of Foundation Prof. Heinrich Zollinger; Pres. National Research Council Prof. Alfred Pletscher; Sec.-Gen. Dr. P. Fricker.

**Società ticinese di scienze naturali:** c/o Biblioteca cantonale, viale Cattaneo, CH-6900 Lugano; f. 1903; promotion of scientific research; 220 mems.; Pres. Prof. P. L. Zanon; Sec. Prof. Paolo Amman; publ. *Bollettino*† (annually).

**Société de Physique et d'Histoire Naturelle:** Museum d'histoire naturelle, route de Malagnou, Geneva; f. 1790; 135 mems.; Pres. G. Bocquet; Sec. Jacques Deferne; publs. *Archives des sciences*, *Comptes-Rendus* (3 numbers per year).

**Société Vaudoise des Sciences Naturelles:** Palais de Rumine, 1005 Lausanne; f. 1815; 560 mems.; 1,000 periodicals in the library reading-room; see also Bibliothèque Cantonale et Universitaire de Lausanne; Sec. Mme Harris; publs. *Bulletin*, *Mémoires*†.

**Schweizerischer Wissenschaftsrat/Conseil Suisse de la Science:** Wildhainweg 9, 3001 Bern; f. 1965 to co-ordinate and examine national policy on science and research and aid its implementation; 24 mems.; library of 1,500 vols., 150 periodical titles; Pres. Prof. Gerhard Huber; Gen. Sec. André Vifian.

#### Biological Sciences

**Bernische Botanische Gesellschaft:** Altenbergrain 21, 3013 Bern; f. 1918; 250 mems.; Pres. Dr. O. Hegg; Sec. Dr. B. Ammann; publ. *Sitzungsberichte*† (annually).

**Schweizerische Botanische Gesellschaft:** Institut für Spezielle Botanik der Eidgenössischen Technischen Hochschule, Universitätstrasse 2, CH-8092 Zürich; f. 1890; 600 mems.; publ. *Berichte*.

**Schweizerische Entomologische Gesellschaft:** ETH-Zentrum, Zürich; f. 1858; 350 mems.; library of 18,058 vols.; Pres. Prof. Dr. G. Lampel; Sec. Dr. E. Günthart; publs. *Mitteilungen*†, *Insecta Helvetica* (*Fauna*, *Catalogus*); Library and Exchange Agency: Library of the Swiss Federal Institute of Technology, Leonhardstrasse 33, 8092 Zürich.

#### Mathematics

**Schweizerische Mathematische Gesellschaft/Société Mathématique Suisse:** Universität Bern, Mathematik Statistik, Sidlerstr. 5, CH-3012 Bern; f. 1910; 365 mems.; Pres. P. Gabriel; Sec. H. Carnal; publs. *Commentarii Mathematici Helvetici*† (quarterly), *Elemente der Mathematik*† (6 a year).

#### Physical Sciences

**Physikalische Gesellschaft Zürich:** Schönberggasse 9, 8001 Zürich; f. 1887; 530 mems; Pres. Dr. M. Brüllmann; Sec. Dr. P. F. Meier.

**Schweizerische Astronomische Gesellschaft/Société Astronomique de Suisse:** Hirtenhofstrasse 9, CH-6005 Lucerne; f. 1939; 3,100 mems.; Pres. Prof. Dr. Rinaldo Roggero; Sec. Andreas Tarnutzer; publ. *Orion* (bi-monthly).

**Schweizerische Chemische Gesellschaft/Société Suisse de Chimie:** Ciba-Geigy Ltd., CH-4002 Basel; f. 1901; 1,800 mems.; Pres. Dr. K. Heusler; Sec. Dr. O. Rohr; publ. *Helvetica Chimica Acta*.

**Schweizerische Geologische Gesellschaft/Société Géologique Suisse:** c/o Schweizerische Geologische Kommission, Birmannsgasse 8, CH-4055 Basel; f. 1882; 1,947 mems.; promotes geology from a general viewpoint; regular annual meetings; Pres. Prof. R. Trümpy; publ. *Eclogae geologicae Helvetiae* (3 a year).

**Schweizerische Meteorologische Anstalt:** Krähbühlstr. 58, 8044 Zürich; f. 1880; 200 mems.; meteorological services; library of 35,000 vols.; Dir. G. Simmen; publs. *Annalen†* (annual), *Veröffentlichungen†* (irregular).

**Schweizerische Paläontologische Gesellschaft/Société Paléontologique Suisse:** Naturhistorisches Museum, Basel; f. 1921; 207 mems.; Sec. and Treas. Dr. H. Schaefer; publ. *Bericht*.

**Schweizerische Physikalische Gesellschaft/Société Suisse de Physique:** 1,220 mems.; Pres. Prof. P. Dinichert, 2 rue A.-L. Breguet, 2001 Neuchâtel; Sec. Dr. Ingo Sick; publ. *Helvetica Physica Acta*.

Philosophy and Psychology

**Schweizerische Gesellschaft für Psychologie und ihre Anwendungen/Société Suisse de Psychologie et de Psychologie appliquée:** Postfach 197, 3000 Bern 7; f. 1943; 406 mems.; Pres. Prof. Dr. F. Stoll; publs. *Psychologie, Bulletin der Schweizer Psychologen/Bulletin Suisse des Psychologues*.

**Schweizerische Philosophische Gesellschaft/Société suisse de philosophie:** Ave. J. Crosnier 4, 1206 Geneva; f. 1940; 675 mems.; Pres. Prof. J.-P. Leyvraz; Sec. Dr. A. Gräser; publs. *Studia philosophica* (annual), *Supplementa* (irregular).

**Schweizerische Stiftung für Angewandte Psychologie/Fondation Suisse pour la psychologie appliquée:** Turnerstr. 1, ETH-Zentrum, CH-8092 Zurich; f. 1927; 150 mems.; Pres. H. Fischer; Sec. E. Marazzi.

**Schweizerischer Berufsverband für Angewandte Psychologie/Association professionnelle suisse de psychologie appliquée:** Hedwigstr. 3, Postfach, 8032 Zürich; f. 1952; 300 mems.; Pres. Dr. Peter Müri; Sec. Ruth Anderegg.

Religion, Sociology and Anthropology

**Betriebspädagogisches Institut** (*Institute of Organizational Pedagogy*): Arnold Böcklinstr. 25, CH-4011 Basel; f. 1961; for consultation and training of managers and staff mems. in human and organizational integration, in problems of organizational development and group dynamics, communication and encounter training, etc.; international co-operation with group of 6 free consultants and trainers in Europe dealing with industrial, welfare, administrative and educational organizations; Dir. Drs. W. Brokerhof.

**Pro Helvetia:** Hirschengraben 22, CH-8001 Zürich; f. 1949; public foundation under the supervision of the Swiss Federal Council to maintain and promote Switzerland's spiritual and cultural heritage and to foster cultural relations with foreign countries. In addition to sending printed material for foreign enquirers, it organizes exhibitions, concerts, lectures and theatrical performances abroad; the Swiss Federal Council appoints the President and the 25 mems. of the board of the Foundation; Pres. Roland Ruffieux; Dir. Luc Boissonnas.

**Schweizerische Geisteswissenschaftliche Gesellschaft/Société Suisse des Sciences Humaines** (*Swiss Society of Humanities and Social Sciences*): C.P. 2535, Hirschengraben 11, 3001 Bern; f. 1946; 36 mem. socs.; Pres. Prof. Dr. Thomas Gelzer; Sec.-Gen. Dr. Beat Sitter.

**Schweizerische Gesellschaft für Soziologie/Société Suisse de Sociologie:** E. E. S. P., Case 152, 1000 Lausanne 24; f. 1955; 400 mems.; Pres. Walo Hutmacher; Sec. J.-P. Fragnière; publs. *Bulletin* (5 or 6 a year), *Revue Suisse de Sociologie* (3 a year).

**Schweizerische Gesellschaft für Volkskunde/Société suisse des traditions populaires:** St. Alban-Vorstadt 56, 4006 Basel; f. 1896; 1,850 mems.; Pres. Dr. Theo Gantner; Sec. Dr. W. Escher; publs. *Schweizerisches Archiv für Volkskunde* (quarterly), *Schweizer Volkskunde* (6 vols.), *Folklore suisse/Folklore svizzero* (4 vols.).

**Schweizerische Theologische Gesellschaft/Société suisse de Théologie:** Postfach 2323, 3001 Bern; f. 1965; 278 mems.; Pres. Prof. H. D. Altendorf; Sec. Dr. Chr. Müller.

**Schweizerische Trachtenvereinigung/Fédération Nationale des Costumes Suisses:** Schipfe 30/32, 8023 Zürich Postfach; f. 1926; folk dance records and descriptions; 20,000 mems.; Pres. Dr. E. Dettwiler; publ. *Heimatleben* (French edition: *Costumes et Coutumes*) (3 a year).

**Schweizerischer Protestantischer Volksbund:** Rosengartenstrasse 1A, 8037 Zürich; f. 1924; 12,000 mems.; Pres. Prof. August Bänziger; Sec. Rev. Fritz Johner.

**Verband Jüdischer Lehrer und Kantoren der Schweiz** (*Society of Jewish teachers and cantors in Switzerland*): Brandschenkesteig 12, 8002 Zürich; f. 1926; 60 mems.; Pres. Erich Hausmann; Sec. Isaac Heiselbeck; publ. *Bulletin*.

Technology

**Schweizerische Gesellschaft für Feintechnik/Association Suisse de Microtechnique:** c/o VSM, Kirchenweg 4, 8032 Zürich; f. 1962; 93 mems.; Pres. H. Vonarburg; Sec. K. Eckstein; publ. *Bulletin†* (annually).

**Schweizerischer Technischer Verband** (*Association of Engineers and Architects*): Weinbergstrasse 41, 8006 Zürich, STV-Haus; f. 1905; 16,000 mems.; Pres. W. Gysin; Sec. H. A. Hafner; publ. *Schweizerische Technische Zeitschrift*.

**Schweizerischer Verband der Ingenieur-Agronomen und der Lebensmittelingenieure/Association suisse des ingénieurs agronomes et des ingénieurs en technologie alimentaire:** Länggasse, 3052 Zollikofen, Bern; f. 1901; 1,500 mems.; Pres. D. Grosclaude; Sec. E. Matter; publ. *Bulletin* (quarterly).

**Verband Schweizerischer Abwasserfachleute** (*Association of Sewage Engineers*): Grütlistr. 44, 8027 Zürich; f. 1944; 977 mems., 1,513 reps.; Pres. C. von der Weid.

**Verband Schweizerischer Vermessungstechniker** (*Association of Swiss Surveyors*): 1815 Baugy-Montreux, Riant Val; f. 1929; 1,110 mems.; Pres. F. Loosli; Sec. Alfred Heuggeler; publ. *Vermessung-Mensuration* (9 a year).

# RESEARCH INSTITUTES
(*see* also under Universities)

### Agriculture

**Division de l'Agriculture:** Ministry of Public Economy, Mattenhofstr. 5, 3003 Bern; Dir. Jean-Claude Piot; Deputy Dir. for Agricultural Research Prof. Dr. J. von Ah. The centre for federal agricultural research, which is carried out by the following *Stations Agronomiques Fédérales:*

**Station Fédérale de Recherches Agronomiques de Zürich-Reckenholz:** 8046 Zürich-Reckenholz; Dir. Dr. A. Brönnimann.

**Station Fédérale de Recherches Agronomiques de Changins:** Château de Changins, 1260 Nyon; Dir. Dr. Alexandre Vez.

**Station Fédérale de Recherches en Chimie Agricole et sur l'Hygiène de l'Environnement:** 3097 Liebefeld-Bern; Dir. Dr. Ernest Bovay.

**Station Fédérale de Recherches Laitières de Liebefeld-Bern:** 3097 Liebefeld-Bern; Dir. Prof. Dr. Bernard Blanc.

**Station Fédérale de Recherches en Arboriculture, Viticulture et Horticulture de Wädenswil:** 8820 Wädenswil; Dir. Prof. Dr. R. Fritzsche.

**Station Fédérale de Recherches sur la Production animale de Grangeneuve:** 1725 Posieux; Dir. Dr. Heinrich Schneeberger.

**Station Fédérale de Recherches d'Economie d'entreprise et de génie rural de Tänikon:** 8355 Tänikon b. Aadorf; Dir. Dr. Paul Faessler.

### Economics, Law and Politics

**Institut Suisse de recherche sur les Pays de l'Est** (*Swiss Eastern Institute*): CH-3000 Bern 6, Jubiläumsstr. 41; f. 1959; study and information on the development of Communist countries; Dir. Peter Sager; Admin. Dir. Peter Dolder; publs. *Zeitbild*† (fortnightly), *Etudes Politiques*† (10 a year), *Swiss Press Review*† (fortnightly, also in French and Spanish), *Informationsdienst, Wirtschaftsdienst, SOI-Bilanz* (monthly).

**Schweizerisches Institut für Auslandforschung** (*Swiss Institute of International Studies*): Münstergasse 9, 8001 Zürich; Dir. Dr. Daniel Frei; publ. *Sozialwissenschaftliche Studien* (annually).

### Medicine

**Institut für Immunologie:** Grenzacherstrasse 487, CH-4058 Basel; f. 1970; 55 mems.; library of 1,700 monographs and 101 journals; Dir. Prof. N. K. Jerne; publ. *Annual Report*.

**Institut Sérothérapique et Vaccinal Suisse:** 79 Rehhagstrasse, Bern; f. 1898; Pres. E. Cardinaux.

**Institut suisse de recherches expérimentales sur le cancer/ Schweizerisches Institut für Experimentelle Krebsforschung** (*Swiss Institute for Experimental Cancer Research*): Av. des Boveresses, 1066 Epalinges s. Lausanne; f. 1964; 120 mems.; library of 7,000 vols., 160 periodicals; Pres. J.-J. Cevey; Dir. Prof. B. Hirt; Sec.-Gen. A. Zagnoli.

**Schweizerisches Tropeninstitut (STI):** Socinstrasse 57, 4051 Basel; f. 1943; library of 3,313 vols.; Dir. Prof. T. A. Freyvogel; publ. *Acta Tropica*.

### Natural Sciences
#### General

**Amt für Wissenschaft und Forschung des Eidgenössischen Departement des Innern/Office de la science et de la recherche du Département fédéral de l'intérieur:** Postfach 2732, 3001 Bern; f. 1969; prepares policy decisions for education and science and executes scientific policy; co-ordinates activities of Federal bodies concerned with research and education; supports universities and other institutes of higher education and advises on grants; encourages research and is responsible for atomic and space research; with other Departments deals with international scientific affairs; undertakes documentation and information services on science and research nationally and internationally; library for own use only; Dir. Prof. Urs Hochstrasser; publ. *Politique de la Science* (five issues yearly).

**Botanische Institute und Botanischer Garten/Instituts et Jardin Botaniques de l'Université:** Altenbergrain 21, 3013 Bern; f. 1862; research is carried out in the following institutes:

**Pflanzenphysiologisches Institut:** Dir. Prof. Dr. K. H. Erismann.

**Systematisch-Geobotanisches Institut:** Dir. Prof. Dr. G. Lang.

**Commission pour l'Encouragement des Recherches Scientifiques:** Wildhainweg 20, Postfach 2338, CH-3001 Bern; f. 1944; promotes applied research; 14 mems.; Pres. Dr. Waldemar Jucker; Sec. Dr. Peter Kuentz; publ. *Annual Report*† (German and French).

**Conservatoire et Jardin botaniques de la Ville de Genève:** C.P. 60, CH-1292 Chambésy; systematic botany, taxonomy, floristics, ecology, phytogeography; 70 mems. including 10 scientific mems.; library of 132,000 vols.; Dir. Prof. Gilbert Bocquet; publs. *Candollea, Boissiera, Index Seminum*.

**Institut für Allgemeine Mikrobiologie:** Bühlstr. 24, 3012 Bern.

**Jungfraujoch and Gornergrat Scientific Stations:** Secretariat, Sidlerstrasse 5, 3012 Bern; f. 1930; high-altitude research in astronomy, astrophysics, botany, geology, glaciology, hydrology, medicine, meteorology, physics and zoology; international foundation by scientific organizations of Austria, Belgium, France, Germany, Great Britain, Italy, Netherlands, Switzerland; Pres. Prof. H. Debrunner; publ. *Review on Activity*.

#### Physical Sciences

**Astrophysical Observatory:** Arosa-Tschuggen; f. 1939; Dir. Prof. Dr. J. O. Stenflo.

**Eidgenössisches Institut für Schnee- und Lawinenforschung** (*Swiss Federal Institute for Snow and Avalanche Research*): 7260 Wesisfluhjoch/Davos; f. 1942; physics and mechanics of snow and snow pack, avalanche formation and mechanics, protective structures, snow and avalanche effects on forests, and an avalanche warning service; 32 mems.; library of 2,000 vols.; Dir. Prof. Dr. C. Jaccard; publs. *Winterbericht* (annual), *Interne Berichte und Gutachten, Mitteilungen, Sonderdrucke*.

**Institut für Astronomie:** ETH-Zentrum, 8092 Zürich; f. 1864; 21 mems.; astrophysics, particularly solar physics; Dir. Prof. J. O. Stenflo.

**Observatoire:** Geneva, CH-1290 Sauverny/Ge; f. 1772; astrophysics, galactic structure, photometry, space research; 90 staff; library of 3,500 vols., 500 periodicals; Dir. Prof. M. Golay; publ. *Observatoire de Genève*†.

**Observatoire Cantonal:** Neuchâtel; f. 1858; library contains 100,000 vols.; astronomical time service; chronometry department; Dir. J. Bonanomi; publs. time service bulletins, annual reports.

**Specola Solare Ticinese:** 6605 Locarno-Monti; f. 1957; Dir. S. Cortesi.

### Technology

**Institut für nichtnumerische Informationsverarbeitung** (*Institute of Non-Numerical Information Processing*): Thalerstr. 8, Postfach 500, 9400 Rorschach SG; f. 1976; computational linguistics, machine translation, terminology data banks, information systems and networks, automatic documentation, library automation; computer chess, computer art, computers and law; artificial intelligence, consulting services, contract research; Dir. Herbert E. Bruderer.

## LIBRARIES AND ARCHIVES

### Basel

**Allgemeine Bibliotheken der Gesellschaft für das Gute und Gemeinnützige:** Rümelinsplatz 6, Gerbergasse 24, 4051 Basel; f. 1807; 8 br. libraries; 100,000 vols.; Dir. Peter Marti.

**Archiv für Schweizerische Kunstgeschichte:** Munzgässlein 16; Dir. Dr. François Maurer-Kuhn.

**Bibliothek des Museums fur Völkerkunde:** Pf. 1048, Augustinergasse 2; 30,000 vols. on ethnography of the world; Librarian Mrs. Elisabeth Idris.

**Medizinhistorische Bibliothek:** Klingelbergstr. 23, 4031 Basel; f. 1964; 9,000 vols.; Dir. Prof. Dr. H. Buess.

**Öffentliche Bibliothek der Universität Basel** (*Public University Library*): 20 Schönbeinstrasse; f. 1460; 2,300,000 vols.; scientific works, special collections of MSS., incunabula, maps, portraits; Pres. of Library Commission Dr. Paul Huber; Chief Librarian Dr. F. Gröbli; publs. *Bericht über die Verwaltung der Öffentlichen Bibliothek der Universität Basel†* (annually), *Jahresverzeichnis der Schweizerischen Hochschulschriften*, *Die mittelalterlichen Handschriften der Universitätsbibliothek Basel*, *Die Matrikel der Universität Basel*, *Die Amerbachkorrespondenz*.

**Schweizerisches Wirtschaftsarchiv/Archives Economiques Suisses:** Kollegienhaus der Universität, Petersgraben, Basel; f. 1910; over 650,000 vols., including business reports, periodicals, statistical publications, reports on social institutions and international conferences, professional societies and law and economics; 1,000,000 newspaper cuttings; the library is open to the public; Dir. Dr. C. Mentha.

**Staatsarchiv Basel-Stadt:** Martinsgasse 2, CH-4001 Basel; 20,000 vols.; Dir. Prof. Dr. A. Staehelin; publs. *Jahresberichte*, *Quellen und Forschungen zur Basler Geschichte*.

### Bern

**Bibliothek des Konservatoriums für Musik:** 36 Kramgasse, 3011 Bern; f. 1917; library of c. 25,000 books; Pres. Annamarie Zinsli.

**Bibliothèque Nationale Suisse/Schweizerische Landesbibliothek:** 15 Hallwylstrasse; f. 1895; contains all publications issued in Switzerland and foreign publications if by Swiss authors or if concerning Switzerland; 1,500,000 vols., 200,000 engravings and photos, 20,000 maps, 20,000 posters; Swiss union catalogue; Dir. Dr. F. G. Maier; Vice-Dir. Dr. R. Luck; publs. *Le Livre suisse*, *Répertoire du livre suisse 1948-80*, *Répertoire des périodiques suisses* (5-yearly issues), *Répertoire des périodiques étrangers reçus par les bibliothèques suisses*, 6th edition 1981, *Bibliographia scientiae naturalis Helvetica*, *Bibliographie de l'histoire suisse*, *Bibliographie des publications officielles suisses*.

**Burgerbibliothek Bern/Bibliothèque de la Bourgeoisie de Berne:** Münstergasse 63, CH-3000 Bern 7; f. 1951; 700 metres of historical MSS., of which 50 metres medieval MSS.; Curators Dr. H. A. Haeberli, Dr. Ch. von Steiger.

**Eidgenössische Parlaments- und Zentralbibliothek** (*Library of the Parliament and Federal Administration*): Bundeshaus West, 3003 Bern; f. 1849; 85,000 vols.; open to the public for reference only; Dir. Roland R. Wiedmer.

**Pharmazeutische Zentralbibliothek:** 10 Sahlistrasse, 3012 Bern; f. 1919; pharmacy; 6,000 vols., 750 periodicals; Dir. K. Humbel.

**Schweizerische Volksbibliothek/Bibliothèque pour tous:** Hallerstrasse 58, 3000 Bern 26; f. 1920; c. 250,000 vols., 8 brs.; Dir. T. Murk.

**Schweizerisches Bundesarchiv:** 24 Archivstr., CH-3003 Bern; f. 1798; Dir. Dr. Osacr Gauye.

**Staatsarchiv des Kantons Bern:** 4 Falkenplatz, 3012 Bern; contains the archives of the Canton of Bern; Archivist Fritz Häusler; publ. *Das Staatsarchiv des Kantons Bern*.

**Stadt- und Universitätsbibliothek:** 61 Münstergasse, CH-3000 Bern 7; f. 1528; 1,100,000 vols.; Chief Librarian Prof. Dr. H. Michel.

### Fribourg

**Bibliothèque Cantonale et Universitaire/Kantons- und Universitätsbibliothek:** 16 rue St-Michel, 1701 Fribourg; f. 1848; 1,000,000 vols.; Dir. G. Delabays.

### Geneva

**Archives d'Etat:** 1 rue de l'Hôtel de Ville, Geneva; 6 mems.; material on history of Geneva; Archivist Miss C. Santschi; Research Dir. Louis Binz.

**Bibliothèque d'Art et d'Archéologie** (annexe of Musée d'Art et d'Histoire): 5 Promenade du Pin, 1204 Geneva; 100,000 vols., 100,000 slides, 2,750 periodicals; Librarian J. P. Dubouloz.

**Bibliothèque des Nations Unies** (*United Nations Library*): Palais des Nations, 1211 Geneva 10; f. 1919; 850,000 vols.; Librarian Heinz Waldner; publs. *Monthly Bibliography, Pt. I—Books, Official Documents†, Pt. II—Selected Articles†, Catalogue of Periodicals†*.

**Bibliothèque Publique et Universitaire de Genève:** Promenade des Bastions, Geneva; f. 1562; 1,600,000 vols. and pamphlets, 23,000 maps, 45,000 engravings, 400 painted portraits, 15,000 MSS.; Dir. Dr. Paul Chaix.

**Bibliothèques Municipales:** 16 place de la Madeleine, 1204 Geneva; f. 1931; adult libraries 133,278 vols., children's libraries 44,064 vols., school libraries 43,572 vols.; Chief Librarian Miss Roberte Pipy.

**International Labour Office Library:** 1211 Geneva 22; f. 1929; 500,000 vols. and pamphlets, 12,000 periodicals (including annuals and official gazettes); open to the public on special request; computerized data base (LABORDOC), containing abstracts of all items catalogued since 1965, available for on-line searching world-wide through the facilities of System Development Corpn., Santa Monica (U.S.A.); Official-incharge K. Wild; publs. *International Labour Documentation†* (monthly), *Directory of information resources in the ILO, ILO Thesaurus: labour, employment and training terminology, Library Catalogue, Index to ILO Publications, Register of Periodicals*.

### Grand Saint-Bernard

**Bibliothèque de L'Hospice du Grand Saint-Bernard:** 1920 Martigny, Canton de Valais (library of Austin Canons monastery, f. 1050); works on botany and numismatics, ancient MSS. and maps; over 30,000 vols. and many thousands of brochures.

### Graubünden

**Staatsarchiv Graubünden:** CH-7001 Chur, Reichsgasse, Archivgebäude; f. 1803; Archivist Dr. S. MARGADANT.

### Lausanne

**Bibliothèque Cantonale et Universitaire de Lausanne:** Palais de Rumine, 1005 Lausanne; f. 1537; libraries of the "Société vaudoise des sciences naturelles" and the "Société d'histoire de la Suisse romande"; 700,000 vols., 150 incunabula; the library is open to the public; Dir. JEAN-PIERRE CLAVEL; publs. *Liste des acquisitions récentes, Catalogues des fonds de manuscrits, Catalogue des manuscrits musicaux, Rapport annuel.*

**Bibliothèque et Centre de documentation de la Faculté de Médecine:** Centre Hospitalier Universitaire Vaudois, 1011 Lausanne; f. 1968; 4,000 vols., 600 periodicals; Librarian Mrs. V. BOHANES.

**Bibliothèque Municipale de la Ville de Lausanne:** 1003 Lausanne, 9 place Chauderon; Dir. SUZANNE GRIN-PINGEON.

### Lucerne

**Staatsarchiv des Kantons Luzern:** Bahnhofstrasse 18, CH-6003 Luzern; f. 1803; local history; 6 mems.; 15,000 vols.; Archivist Dr. F. GLAUSER; publs. *Jahresbericht des Staatsarchivs Luzern, Luzerner Historische Veröffentlichungen* (irregular).

**Zentralbibliothek Luzern:** Sempacherstrasse 10, CH-6002 Lucerne; 500,000 vols., 2,500 MSS., 110,000 engravings, photos and maps; Dir. Dr. A. SCHACHER.

### Lugano

**Biblioteca Cantonale: Lugano, Ticino:** Viale C. Cattaneo 6, 6900 Lugano; f. 1852; 200,000 vols.; only public library of Italian culture in Switzerland, incorporates *Liberia Patria*, special collection of "Ticinensia", 20,000 vols.; Dir. Dott. A. SOLDINI.

### Neuchâtel

**Archives de l'Etat:** Le Château, 2001 Neuchâtel; f. 1898; maintains a historical library and an administrative library; Archivist JEAN COURVOISIER.

**Bibliothèque des Pasteurs:** 3 Collégiale, 2000 Neuchâtel; f. 1538; theological; 60,000 vols., 17,000 pamphlets; Librarian RENÉ PÉTER-CONTESSE.

**Bibliothèque Publique de la Ville:** 3 place Numa-Droz; f 1788; 500,000 vols., including vols. of periodicals, an Encyclopaedia Library, Swiss theses, many reviews received mostly by exchange; MSS. of J.-J. Rousseau (works and correspondence) and Mme de Charrière; archives of Société typographique de Neuchâtel; Dir. J. RYCHNER; publs. *Bulletin des acquisitions récentes†, Bibliothèques et musées†, Musée neuchâtelois,†* and bulletins of chronometry†, geography†, and natural sciences†.

### St. Gallen

**Kantonsbibliothek:** Regierungsgebäude; Dir. Dr. W. LENDI.

**Kantonsbibliothek Vadiana:** Notkerstrasse 22, CH-9000 St. Gallen; f. 1551; 400,000 vols.; the library is open to the public; Dir. Prof. Dr. PETER WEGELIN.

**Stifts-Bibliothek St. Gallen:** Klosterhof 6; library of former Benedictine Abbey of St. Gall; f. about 720 A.D.; important collection of manuscripts and incunabula, some dating from Irish period; 100,000 vols.; Dir. Prof. Dr. JOHANNES DUFT.

### Solothurn

**Zentralbibliothek:** 39 Bielstr., 4500 Solothurn; f. 1763 as town library; 300,000 vols., 2,000 MSS.; the library is open to the public; Dir. Dr. HANS SIGRIST; publs. *Jahresbericht, Veröffentlichungen.*

### Winterthur

**Stadtbibliothek:** 52 Museumstr., 8400 Winterthur; f. 1660; 600,000 items; special collections of local history, numismatics, music, African languages and literature; open to the public; Dir. Dr. PETER SULZER; publ. *Neujahrsblatt†* (annually).

### Zürich

**ETH-Bibliothek** (*Library of the Swiss Federal Institute of Technology*): Rämistrasse 101, CH-8092 Zürich; f. 1855; 2,900,000 vols. and docs. (9,000 current periodicals, 18,500 current serials, 1,000,000 reports, 120,000 maps, 100,000 docs. on history of science); university library specializing in science and technology; affiliated libraries: Geological Inst. Library, Architecture and Civil Engineering Library; service for microfilms and photostats; Dir. Dr. J.-P. SYDLER; publs. *Catalogues on microfiches* (monthly in COM), printed catalogue of periodicals holdings, *Theses†.*

**Kunstgewerbemuseum der Stadt Zürich, Bibliothek:** Zürich, Ausstellungsstr. 60, Postfach, 8031 Zürich; f. 1875; 40,000 vols.; Librarian Dr. JÜRG ETZENSPERGER.

**Schweizerisches Sozialarchiv:** Neumarkt 28, 8001 Zürich; f. 1906; Swiss centre of social documentation; 80,000 vols. and over 300,000 brochures, pamphlets, etc.; 1,300 current newspapers and reviews in the lecture hall; newspaper cuttings; the library is open to the public; Librarian Dr. M. TUCEK.

**Staatsarchiv des Kantons Zürich:** 33 Predigerplatz, 8001 Zürich; f. 1837; contains the archives of the canton of Zürich and a specialized library (local publications and collections of statutes; 22,000 vols. and numerous pamphlets); Dir. Dr. U. HELFENSTEIN.

**Zentralbibliothek Zürich:** Zähringerplatz 6, 8025 Zürich; f. 1914; city, cantonal and university library, incorporating also the libraries of Naturforschende Gesellschaft in Zürich, Antiquarische Gesellschaft in Zürich, Geographisch-Ethnographische Gesellschaft Zürich, Schweizerischer Alpenclub, Allgemeine Musikgesellschaft Zürich, Bibliotheca Fennica, etc. About 1,800,000 vols., 20,000 MSS. and autographs, 1,500 incunabula, 150,000 maps, and special collections of graphic arts (160,000 items), records and cassettes (18,000 items), genealogy, heraldry. Service for photostats, xerocopies, microfilms; Dir. HANS BAER.

## MUSEUMS AND ART GALLERIES

### Aarau
**Aargauer Kunsthaus:** Aargauer-Platz, 5000 Aarau; f. 1860; Swiss painting and sculpture from 1750 to the present day; considerable collection of paintings by Caspar Wolf (1735-1783), the first painter of the Alps, and by the landscape painter, Adolf Staebli, and by Auberjonois, Brühlmann, Amiet, G. Giacometti, Hodler, Meyer-Amden, Louis Soutter, Vallotton; Dir. Prof. HEINY WIDMER.

### Avenches
**Musée Romain Avenches:** CH-1580 Avenches; f. 1824; excavations of Aventicum; 950 mems.; library of 3,000 vols.; Pres. Prof. J.-P. VOUGA; Sec. Prof. Dr. H. BOEGLI; publ. *Bulletin de l'Association Pro Aventico*† (annual).

### Basel
**Antikenmuseum Basel und Sammlung Ludwig:** St. Albangraben 5, 4051 Basel; f. 1961; collections of Greek art (2,500-100 B.C.), Italian art (1,000 B.C.-300 A.D.) and Etruscan art; Dir. Prof. Dr. E. BERGER.

**Gewerbemuseum Basel:** Spalenvorstadt 2; f. 1878; applied art, collections, exhibitions, Dir. GUSTAV KYBURZ; Curator Dr. ALEX CIZINSKY.

**Historisches Museum:** Verwaltung, Steinenberg 4; f. 1856; 3 brs. containing collection of objects from prehistoric times to 17th century, civic culture of Basel in 18th and 19th centuries and collection of old musical instruments; Dir. Dr. HANS LANZ; publ. *Jahresberichte*.

**Kunstmuseum Basel (Öffentliche Kunstsammlung):** St. Albangraben 16, CH-4010 Basel; f. 1662; pictures from 15th century to present day, notably by Witz, Holbein and contemporary painters; collection includes Grünewald, Greco, Rembrandt, 16th-and 17th-century Netherlandish painting, Cézanne, Gauguin and Van Gogh; large collection of cubist art; sculptures by Rodin and 20th-century artists; American art since 1945; Dept. of prints and drawings with old Upper Rhine, German and Swiss masters; library of 100,000 vols.; Dir. Dr. FRANZ MEYER; Curators Dr. PAUL BOERLIN, Dr. DIETER KOEPPLIN; Librarian NIKOLAUS MEIER.

**Museum für Völkerkunde und Schweizerisches Museum für Volkskunde Basel:** Pf. 1048, Augustinergasse 2; f. 1892; ethnographical collections from all parts of the world, especially from Oceania, Indonesia, South America and Europe; library of 30,000 vols.; Dir. Dr. G. BAER; publs. *Annual Report*†, *Basler Beiträge zur Ethnologie*†, and guides†.

### Bern
**Bernisches Historisches Museum:** Helvetiaplatz 5, 3000 Bern 6; f. 1881; Pre- and Early History, Applied Arts, Coin Collections, Ethnology, Folklore; Dirs. R. L. WYSS, H. MATILE; publ. *Jahrbuch*†.

**Kantonales Amt für Wirtschafts- und Kulturausstellungen—Gewerbemuseum und Gewerbebibliothek** (*Industrial Museum*): Zeughausgasse 2, 3011 Bern; f. 1869; Dir. MAX WERREN.

**Kunstmuseum:** 12 Hodlerstrasse, Bern 3011; f. 1879, and enlarged 1936; 1,200 mems.; contains Italian paintings from 14th to 16th centuries, works by Swiss masters from 15th to 19th centuries and modern works by Hodler and other Swiss, French and German masters; Paul Klee foundation; Hermann and Margrit Rupf foundation, including paintings by Picasso, Braque, Léger, Gris and Kandinsky; Adolf Wölfli Foundation; paintings, reliefs, water-colours, gouache paintings and illustrations by Sophie Taeuber-Arp; the graphic art collection contains over 20,000 drawings and engravings; c. 25,000 vols.; Dir. Dr. H. WAGNER; publ. *Berner Kunstmitteilungen*† (8 a year).

**Naturhistorisches Museum:** 15 Bernastrasse, Bern; f. 1832; collection includes 220 dioramas of Swiss mammals and birds, big game (especially African), Swiss fish, amphibians and reptiles, minerals of the Swiss Alps, Alpine fossils, insects, vertebrates, molluscs; Dir. Prof. Dr. W. HUBER; Curator of Zoology Dept. Dr. P. LÜPS; Curator of Entomology Dept. Dr. H. D. VOLKART; Curator of Mineralogy and Geology Dept. Prof. Dr. H. A. STALDER; publ. *Jahrbuch*.

### Biel
**Museum Schwab:** Biel/Bienne; f. 1865; contains prehistoric exhibits, especially of the lake-dwelling culture, the New Stone Age, the Bronze Age, and the second Iron Age; also a collection of the Roman period (Petinesca); Dir. Dr. MARCUS BOURQUIN.

### Chur
**Bündner Kunstmuseum:** Postplatz, 7000 Chur.; f. 1900; contains works by Swiss artists, principally Segantini, Hodler, Alberto, Augusto and Giovanni Giacometti, E. L. Kirchner and Angelica Kauffmann; Dir. H. HARTMANN.

### Fribourg
**Musée d'art et d'histoire:** rue Pierre-Aeby 227, CH-1700 Fribourg; f. 1823; housed in Hotel Ratzé (16th century); antiques, furniture, stained glass, sculpture, portraits, Roman, Burgundian and prehistoric collections; Swiss painting and sculpture of the Middle Ages, and 16th and 17th centuries collection of the Duchess of Castiglione-Colonna; collection of prints; Curator MICHEL TERRAPON; Deputy Curator YVONNE LEHNHERR; publs. *Rapport annuel*, exhibition catalogues.

### Geneva
**Collections Baur:** 8 rue Munier Romilly, Geneva; f. 1944, opened to public 1964; ceramics and works of art from China and Japan; Pres. GUSTAVE MARTIN; Curator PIERRE F. SCHNEEBERGER; publ. *Bulletin des Collections Baur*.

**Musée d'Art et d'Histoire:** rue Charles Galland, Geneva; f. 1910; works by Swiss painters, Italian, French, German and Flemish Primitives, special collection of paintings by Hodler; modern art; historical section devoted to history and archaeology of Geneva and district, and Classical, Egyptian, Near Eastern and Byzantine archaeology, European sculpture and decorative arts, and numismatic collection; library of 95,000 vols.; Dir. C. LAPAIRE; publs. *Genava* (annually), *Les Musées de Genève* (monthly).

Attached Museums:

**Musée Ariana:** ave. de la Paix, Geneva; f. 1884; European and Eastern ceramics; Curator MARIE THÉRÈSE COULLERY.

**Musée d'Histoire des Sciences:** 128 rue de Lausanne, CH-1202 Geneva; f. 1964; library of 10,000 vols.; Curator MARGARIDA ARCHINARD.

**Musée d'Instruments Anciens de Musique:** 23 rue Lefort, Geneva 1206; f. 1960; Curators FRITZ ERNST, Miss ELISA-ISOLDE CLERC.

**Musée de l'Horlogerie:** route de Malagnou, Geneva; f. 1972; European clock and watchmaking; enamels and miniatures, 1600-1900; Curator FABIENNE STURM.

**Cabinet des estampes:** 5 Promenade du Pin, Geneva; f. 1952; ancient and modern prints; Curator RAINER M. MASON.

**Musée d'Ethnographie de la Ville de Genève:** 65-67 Boulevard Carl Vogt, Geneva; f. 1901; contains exhibits from

Africa, Asia, Americas, Australia and Oceania, collection of musical instruments and of popular pottery; library of 8,000 vols.; also houses the Société Suisse des Américanistes; Dir. Dr. Louis Necker; Curators Jean Eracle (Asia), Dr. Claude Savary (Africa), Daniel Schoepf (Americas), Dr. Bernard Crettaz (Europe); publs. *Bulletin*† (annual) and *Bulletin de la Société suisse des Américanistes*†.

**Muséum d'Histoire Naturelle:** Route de Malagnou, 1211 Geneva 6; f. 1820; 140 mems.; departments of mammalogy and ornithology, herpetology and ichthyology, invertebrates, arthropods and insects, entomology, geology and palaeontology of invertebrates, mineralogy and petrography, palaeontology of vertebrates; library of 120,000 vols.; Dir. Prof. Dr. V. Aellen; Admin. Sec. R. Descombes; Librarians C. Favarger, T. Dénes; publs. *Catalogue des Invertébrés de la Suisse*, *Catalogue Illustré de la collection Lamarck* (Fossils), *Revue Suisse de Zoologie* (quarterly).

### 8750 Glarus

**Kunsthaus Glarus:** Glarus; f. 1870; works by modern Swiss artists; pictures and sculptures; Curator Fritz Brunner.

### Heiden

**Dunant-Museum:** 9410 Heiden; f. 1962; objects, documents, etc., pertaining to the life and works of Henry Dunant, founder of the Red Cross, who spent the last years of his life in Heiden; Dir. J. Haug.

### 2300 La Chaux-de-Fonds

**Musée des Beaux-Arts:** 33 rue des Musées; f. 1864; comprises paintings and sculpture by Swiss artists, particularly of the Neuchâtel district, and modern European painting, sculpture and tapestries; Dir. Paul Seylaz; publs. Catalogues†.

**Musée International d'Horlogerie:** 29 rue des Musées, C.P. 331, 2301 La Chaux-de-Fonds; f. 1902; artistic and technical collections of watches, clocks, instruments and objects connected with the measurement of time; a modern carillon; specialist library of 2,000 vols.; Curator André Curtit.

### Lausanne

**Musée Cantonal des Beaux-Arts:** Palais de Rumine, 1005 Lausanne; f. 1841 by the painter Marc-Louis Arlaud; collection of works by artists from the canton of Vaud; also works by other Swiss artists, and artists of other European countries, international exhibitions; Dir. Dr. René Berger.

**Musée Historique de l'Ancien Evêché:** 2 place de la Cathédrale, CH-1005 Lausanne; f. 1898; archaeological and historical collection; Curator Jaques Bonnard.

### 6853 Ligornetto

**Museo Vela:** Ligornetto; f. 1897 by the Vela family, whose works comprise the basis of the collection, which also includes paintings from old and modern Italian schools (19th century), sketches and drawings; Curator Giuseppe Casanova.

### 6600 Locarno

**Castello Visconti:** f. 1970; 14th-century fortress housing Jean Arp collection of modern art; works by Alexander Calder, Van Doesburg, Arp, Hans Richter, etc.

### Lucerne

**Historisches Museum:** Kornmarkt 1, Lucerne; f. 1873; Curator Dr. Gottfried Boesch.

**Kunstmuseum:** Robert-Zündstr. 1, 6002 Lucerne; f. 1872; Swiss art from ancient times to 20th century, with special collection of contemporary works; exhibitions of modern art; Curator Martin Kunz, lic.phil.

**Richard Wagner-Museum:** 6012 Lucerne-Tribschen; f. 1933; home of Richard Wagner from 1866 to 1872; contains original scores of *Siegfried-Idyll*, *Schusterlied* (*Meistersinger*), etchings, paintings, busts and the Erard grand piano which accompanied Wagner throughout Europe; also collection of 200 old musical instruments; Pres. of Museum Commission Dr. H. R. Meyer; publs. *Katalog* (German, French and English), *Tribschener Blätter* (annual).

**Verkehrshaus der Schweiz** (*Swiss Transport Museum*): Lidostrasse 5, 6006 Lucerne; f. 1942; Europe's largest transport museum; land, water and air, telecommunications and tourism; unique vehicles, engines, working models, diagrams, photographs; transportation archives; headquarters of the Swiss Transport Research Association; Planetarium Longines (Switzerland's only planetarium); Dir. Dr. Arnold Kappler.

**Hans-Erni-Museum:** paintings, lithographs and other artefacts by the artist.

### 6900 Lugano

**Museo Civico di Belle Arti:** Villa Ciani, Lugano; f. 1893 by Antonio Caccia; works by artists of the Ticino from 17th to 20th centuries, and by French and Italian artists including Tintoretto, Henri Rousseau, Matisse.

### Neuchâtel

**Musée d'Art et d'Histoire:** Quai Léopold Robert, 2000 Neuchâtel; f. 1885; pictures, drawings, prints and sculptures by local and other Swiss artists; French 18th- and 19th-century works (Courbet, Corot, and others); French Impressionists; furniture, coins and medals; an exceptional collection of 18th-century automata by Jaquet-Droz; Curators P. von Allmen (fine arts), Jean-Pierre Jelmini (history and decorative arts).

**Musée d'Ethnographie:** 4 St. Nicolas, 2006 Neuchâtel; f. 1795; North Africa, Sahara, Angola, Bhutan; non-European musical instruments; library of *c.* 5,000 vols., 175 periodicals; *c.* 100 records of non-European music, catalogues of Tuareg music and folk songs; Curator Jacques Hainard (acting); publ. *Rapport annuel des Musées et Bibliothèques*†.

**Musée d'Histoire Naturelle:** Terreaux 14, Neuchâtel; f. 1835; Curator Christophe Dufour.

### Olten

**Kunstmuseum:** Kirchgasse 8, 4600 Olten; f. 1845; drawings and paintings by Martin Disteli; paintings, drawings and sculptures by Swiss artists; library of 500 vols.; Curator Paul Meier.

### St. Gallen

**Historisches Museum:** Museumstrasse 50, CH-9000 St. Gallen; f. 1877; collection of arms, banners, porcelain, painted glass, coins, ancient chambers, ancient stoves; Curator Dr. Louis Specker; ethnological collection, Curator Rudolf Hanhart.

**Industrie- und Gewerbemuseum mit Textil- und Modeschule:** Vadianstr. 2, 9000 St. Gallen; f. 1878; lace, embroideries, Jacquard woven and printed fabrics of seven centuries; Coptic fabrics; period and modern textiles; library of 14,000 vols.

**Kunstmuseum:** Museumstr. 50, and Kirchhoferhaus, Museumstrasse 27, St. Gallen 1; f. 1877; works by 19th- and 20th-century Swiss, French and German painters, with special collection devoted to the art of Eastern Switzerland; Dir. Rudolf Hanhart.

**Museum für Völkerkunde:** Museumstrasse 50, St. Gallen; Curator Rudolf Hanhart.

**Museum Kirchhoferhaus:** Museumstrasse 27; local and historical exhibits; also houses temporarily the most important collections from the *Kunst-Museum*; French paintings by Corot, Pissarro, Sisley, Monet and others; works by German artists, including Koch, Kirchner,

## MUSEUMS AND ART GALLERIES, SWITZERLAND

Feuernach and Spitzweg; representative collection of 19th-century Swiss painting.

**Naturhistorisches Museum St. Gallen:** Rosenbergstr. 89, CH-9000 St. Gallen; f. 1870; Curator ROLAND MÜLLER (acting); publ. *Jahrbuch naturwissenschaftliche Gesellschaft*.

### Schaffhausen

**Museum zu Allerheiligen:** Klosterplatz, Schaffhausen; f. 1928; prehistory, history and art of the Canton of Schaffhausen and district; Dir. Dr. MAX FREIVOGEL; publ. *Jahresbericht*.

### Solothurn

**Kunstmuseum Solothurn:** Werkhofstr. 30, 4500 Solothurn; f. 1902; works by Swiss and foreign artists from early 15th century onwards, including Hans Holbein the younger, Ribera, Hodler, J. R. Byss, Buchser, Frölicher; paintings, sculptures, drawings, water-colours and engravings; Curator ANDRÉ KAMBER.

### Vevey

**Musée Jenisch:** Vevey; f. 1897; paintings and sculpture by Swiss and foreign artists, including Bocion, Courbet, Canaletto; large summer exhibitions; natural science collections of fauna, minerals, birds, shells, etc.; collection illustrating the folklore and history of the district.

**Le Château:** historical museum depicting old Vevey.

### Winterthur

**Collection Oskar Reinhart "am Römerholz":** Haldenstr. 95, 8400 Winterthur; f. 1958; public art gallery; library of 1,300 vols.; Pres. Prof. Dr. H.-P. LANDOLT; Curator Dr. LISBETH STÄHELIN.

**Kunstmuseum:** Museumstrasse 52, Winterthur; f. 1864; Swiss painting and sculpture from 18th century to present day; French, Italian and German painting and sculpture of 19th and 20th centuries, including Monet, Picasso, Gris, Léger, Klee, Arp, Kandinsky, Renoir, Bonnard, Maillol, Van Gogh, Rodin, Brancusi, Morandi, Giacometti, de Staël, etc.; drawings and prints; administered by Kunstverein Winterthur; 1,500 mems.; Pres. Dr. H. HUBER; Curator Dr. RUDOLF KOELLA; Sec. E. BIRRER; publs. *Jahresbericht des Kunstvereins Winterthur*, collection and exhibition catalogues.

### Zürich

**Botanischer Garten und Museum der Universität Zürich:** Zollikerstr. 107, 8008 Zürich; f. 1836; world-wide herbarium, especially of African and New Caledonian Flora; library of c. 50,000 vols.; Dir. Prof. Dr. C. D. K. COOK; publ. *Mitteilungen*†.

**Graphische Sammlung der Eidgenössischen Technischen Hochschule:** Rämistr. 101, 8092 Zürich; f. 1867; over 100,000 examples of the graphic art of all periods and schools, with special reference to the development of graphic art in Switzerland; Curator LEO ZIHLER; publs. catalogues covering the work of individual artists and the exhibitions.

**Kunstgewerbemuseum der Stadt Zürich, Museum für Gestaltung:** Ausstellungsstr. 60, Postfach, CH-8031 Zürich; f. 1875; architecture, applied arts, industrial design, visual communication; graphic art collection, poster collection; public library of 40,000 vols.; Dir. Dr. HANSJÖRG BUDLIGER; affiliated museum:

**Museum Bellerive:** Höschgasse 3, Postfach, CH-8034 Zürich; Curator Dr. SIGRID BARTEN.

**Kunsthaus:** 1 Heimplatz, Zürich; f. 1787; chiefly 19th- and 20th-century paintings and sculptures by Swiss and foreign artists; early German masters; French impressionists; extensive collection covering all branches of graphic art from 15th century onwards; library of 45,000 vols.; Dir. Dr. FELIX BAUMANN.

**Museum Rietberg:** Gablerstrasse 15, 8002 Zürich; f. 1952; permanent collection: Asiatic art, art of the Americas, Africa and Oceania, Chinese bronzes, Egyptian textiles; E. von der Heydt collection and others; Dir. Dr. E. FISCHER.

**Paläontologisches Institut und Museum der Universität:** Künstlergasse 16, CH-8006 Zürich; f. 1956; Triassic reptiles and fishes, Triassic and Jurassic invertebrates, Tertiary mammals; library of 4,000 vols., 21,500 publs.; Dir. Prof. Dr. H. RIEBER.

**Schweizerisches Landesmuseum/Musée National Suisse:** Museumstrasse 2, CH-8023 Zürich; f. 1898; exhibits illustrate the history and development of culture in Switzerland from prehistoric times to the 20th century; library of 75,000 vols. and 950 periodicals; Dir. Dr. HUGO SCHNEIDER; publs. *Zeitschrift für schweizerische Archäologie und Kunstgeschichte*† (quarterly), *Jahresbericht*† (annually).

**Zoologisches Museum der Universität:** Künstlergasse 16, 8006 Zürich; f. 1837; research in systematics, taxonomy, and population biology; exhibitions of birds, molluscs and mammals of the world and Swiss fauna; public slide shows and films; library of 7,000 vols.; Dir. Prof. H. BURLA; publs. *Jahresbericht*† (annually), *list of publications*† (c. 2 a year).

## UNIVERSITIES

### UNIVERSITÄT BASEL

PETERSPLATZ 1, CH-4051 BASEL

Telephone: 25.73.73.
Founded 1460.
Language of instruction: German; Academic year: October to March, April to July.

*Rector:* Prof. J. M. LOCHMAN.
*Pro-Rector:* Prof. F. VISCHER.
*Rector-Designate:* (vacant).
*Secretary:* H. Joss.
*Librarian:* Dr. F. GRÖBLI.

Number of teachers: 680.
Number of students: 5,700.

#### DEANS:

*Faculty of Theology:* Prof. M. BARTH.
*Faculty of Jurisprudence:* Prof. K. SPIRO.
*Faculty of Medicine:* Prof B. HERZOG.
*Faculty of Philosophy and History:* Prof. E. KOLB.
*Faculty of Science:* Prof. J. N. JANSONIUS.

#### PROFESSORS:

*Faculty of Theology:*
BARTH, M., New Testament
JENNI, E., Old Testament
LOCHMAN, J. M., Systematic Theology
NEIDHART, W., Practical Theology
OTT, H., Systematic Theology
REICKE, B., New Testament Studies
SCHMIDT, M. A., Ecclesiastical History, Dogmatics
SEYBOLD, K., Old Testament

*Faculty of Law:*
EICHENBERGER, K., Public Law
FUCHS, J.-G., Roman Law
HAGEMANN, H. R., History of Law
KLEIN, F. E., Civil Law, Comparative Law
KRAUSS, D., Penal Law
SIMONINS, P., Civil Law
SPIRO, K., Civil Law, History of Law
STRATENWERTH, G., Penal Law
VISCHER, F., Civil Law
WILDHABER, L., Public Law

*Faculty of Medicine:*
ALLGÖWER, M., Surgery
BATTEGAY, R., Psychiatry
DETTLI, L., Internal Medicine
DUBACH, U. C., Internal Medicine
GLOOR, B., Ophthalmology
GRATZL, O., Neurosurgery
HARTWEG, H., Medical Radiology
HERZOG, B., Paediatrics
HÖSLI, L., Physiology
KAESER, H. E., Neurology
KÄSER, O., Gynaecology and Obstetrics

KIELHOLZ, P., Psychiatry
LAVER, M., Anaesthetics
LÖFFLER, H., Bacteriology, Immunology and Epidemiology
LUDWIG, K. S., Anatomy, Histology, Embryology
MORSCHER, E., Orthopaedics
PFALTZ, C. R., Oto-Rhino-Laryngology
RUTISHAUSER, G., Urology
SASSE, D., Anatomy
SCHUPPLI, R., Dermatology and Venereal Diseases
STALDER, G., Paediatrics
STAUFFACHER, W., Internal Medicine
WALTER, P., Chemical Physiology

*Faculty of Philosophy and History:*
ALLERTON, D. J., English Philology
BANDLE, O., Northern Philology
BERGER, L. R., Early History
BERNHOLZ, P., Political Economics
BOMBACH, G., Political Economics
BONALUMI, G., Italian Philology
BORNER, S., Political Economics
BRENK, B., History of Art
COLÓN, G., Iberoromance Philology
DELZ, J., Latin
ENGLER, B., English Philology
FREY, R. L., Political Economics
GRAUS, F., Medieval History
GUGGISBERG, H. R., Swiss and Modern History
GUTH, H., Statistics
HILL, W., Economic Aspects of Enterprise
HORNUNG, E., Egyptology
KOLB, E., Old English and Icelandic Philology
KOPP, R., Romance Philology
LANDOLT, H. P., Modern History of Art
LÖFFLER, H., German Philology
MATTMULLER, M., Swiss and Modern History
MEIER, F., Islamic Studies
OESCH, H., Musicology
PESTALOZZI, K., German Philology
PIEPER, A., Philosophy
RUPP, H., German Philology
SALMONY, H., Philosophy
SCHUSTER, M., Ethnology
STEINER, G., Psychology
STERN, G., German Philology
STUCKY, R., Classical Archaeology
THIERGEN, P., Slavonic Philology
TRAPPE, P., Sociology
TRÜMPY, H., Folklore
VON UNGERN-STERNBERG, J., Ancient History

*Faculty of Science:*
ALDER, K., Physics
ARBER, W., Molecular Microbiology
BACKENSTOSS, G., Physics of Nuclear Structures
BALLI, H., Dyestuff Chemistry
BAUMGARTNER, E., Physics
BURGER, M. M., Biochemistry
DE ROBERTIS, C., Cell Biology
ENGEL, J., Biophysical Chemistry
FALLAB, S., Modern Structural Chemistry
FRANKLIN, R. M., Virology
FREY, M., Mineralogy and Petrography
GALLUSSER, W. A., Geography
GEHRING, W. J., Philosophy of Development and Genetics
GERSON, F., Physical Chemistry
GÜNTHERODT, H. J., Experimental Physics
GROB, C., Organic Chemistry
HABICHT, W., Mathematics
HEILBRONNER, E., Physical Chemistry
HUBER, H., Mathematics
JANSONIUS, J. N., Structure determination of Biopolymers
KELLENBERGER, E., Microbiology

KIRSCHNER, K., Biophysical Chemistry
KRAFT, H., Mathematics
LAUBSCHER, H. P., Geology and Palaeontology
LESER, H., Physical Geography
LINDE, H. H. A., Pharmaceutical Chemistry
ROWELL, C. H. F., Zoology
SCHATZ, G., Biochemistry
SCHWARZ, G., Biophysical Chemistry
STINGELIN, W., Zoology and Morphology
TAMM, CH., Organic Chemistry
TAMMANN, G. A., Astronomy
THOMAS, H., Physics
ZOLLER, H., Botany

## UNIVERSITÄT BERN
HOCHSCHULSTRASSE 4,
3012 BERN
Telephone: 031/65 81 11.
Founded 1834.
(incorporating the Theological School, founded 1528).
Language of instruction: German.

*Rector:* Prof. Dr. R. FANKHAUSER.
*Pro-Rector:* Prof. Dr. A. SCHROEDER.
*Secretary:* Dr. P. MURNER.
*Chief Librarian:* Prof. Dr. H. MICHEL.

Number of teachers: 661, including 208 professors.
Number of students: 7,014.

### DEANS:
*Faculty of Evangelical Theology:* Prof. Dr. M. A. KLOPFENSTEIN.
*Faculty of Old Catholic Theology:* Prof. Dr. H. ALDENHOVEN.
*Faculty of Jurisprudence and Economics:* Prof. Dr. J. KRIEHAUS.
*Faculty of Medicine:* Prof. Dr. B. ROOS.
*Faculty of Veterinary Science:* Prof. Dr. F. STECK.
*Faculty of Philosophy and History:* Prof. Dr. A. ESCH.
*Faculty of Pure Science:* Prof. Dr. R. SCHUMACHER.

### PROFESSORS:
*Faculty of Evangelical Theology:*
KLOPFENSTEIN, M. A., Protestant Theology
LINDT, A., History of Religion
LINK, CH., Dogma and History of Philosophy
LUZ, U., New Testament
MÜLLER, T., Homilectics
RINGELING, H., Ethics and Psychology
SCHINDLER, A., History of the Church and Dogma
WEGENAST, K., Catechetics

*Faculty of Old Catholic Theology:*
ALDENHOVEN, H., Systematic Theology and Liturgy
STALDER, K., New Testament Exegesis, Homilectics, Catechetics

*Faculty of Jurisprudence and Economics:*
ARZT, G., Penal Law, Procedure and Criminology
BÄR, R., Swiss Civil Law, International Civil and Commercial Law
BÄUMLIN, R., Constitutional, Administrative and Church Law

BIERI, H. G., Theoretical Economics and Finance
BRUNNER, C., Econometrics
BUCHER, E., Private Law
CARONI, P., Swiss and German Law
GRUNER, E., Social History and Political Analysis
GYGI, F., Administrative Law
HESS, W., Applied Economics
KAUFMANN, H., Roman, Comparative and International Private Law
KUMMER, M., Commercial Law
MÜLLER, J. P., Constitutional, Administrative and Civil Law
MÜLLER, W., Business Administration
NIEHANS, J., Political Economy
POPP, W., Operations Research
RUEGG, W., Sociology
SALADIN, P., Constitutional and Administrative Law
TLACH, P., Business Administration
TUCHTFELDT, E., Practical Economy
WALDER, H., Penal Law
WIEGAND, W., Private Law

*Faculty of Medicine:*
ABELIN, T., Social and Preventive Medicine
AEBI, H., Biochemistry
BERCHTOLD, R., Internal Surgery
BERGER, MAX, Obstetrics and Gynaecology
BETTEX, M., Child Surgery
BICKEL, H., Pharmacology
BÖKER, W., Psychiatry
BUCHER, U., Internal Medicine
CIOMPI, L., Psychiatry
CLERC, TH., Analytical Chemistry
COTTIER, H., Pathology and Anatomy
ECKMANN, L., Surgery
FLEISCH, H. A., Pathology
FUCHS, W., Medicinal Radiology
GEERING, A. H., Dentistry
GERBER, N., Rheumatology and Physical Therapy
GURTNER, H. P., Internal Medicine
HEIM, E., Psychiatry
HODLER, J., Internal Medicine
HUBER, P., Radiology
JACHERTZ, D., Hygiene and Bacteriology
KREBS, A., Dermatology and Venereal Diseases
LÄUPPI, E., Forensic Medicine
LÜSCHER, E. F., Biochemistry
MÜLLER, P., Physiology
NEIGER, M., Oto-Rhino-Laryngology
NORNES, H., Neurosurgery
NIESEL, PETER, Ophthalmology
PAULI, H., Internal Medicine
PREISIG, R., Clinical Pharmacology
REUBI, F., Internal Medicine
REUTER, H., Pharmacology
RIVA, G., Clinical Propaedontics
ROOS, B., Pathology
ROSSI, E., Children's Diseases
SCHENK, R., Anatomy
SCHERRER, M., Internal Medicine
SCHINDLER, R., Experimental Pathology
SCHROEDER, A., Dental Conservation, Histology and Pathology of Teeth
SENN, A., Thorax Surgery
SOLIVA, M., History of Ancient Pharmacology
STEINEGGER, E., Pharmacology
STRAUB, W., Internal Medicine
STUDER, H., Internal Medicine
TSCHIRREN, B., Anaesthetics
VAN DER ZYPEN, E., Anatomy
VERAGUTH, P. C., Medicinal Radiology
VON WARTBURG, J.-P., Biochemistry
WECK, A. DE, Clinical Immunology
WEIBEL, E., Anatomy, Histology and Cytology
WEIDMANN, S., Physiology
ZINGG, E., Urology

*Faculty of Veterinary Medicine:*
FANKHAUSER, R., Neuropathology of Domestic Animals
FEY, H., Bacteriology, Serology and Parasitology
FREUDIGER, U., Pathology
GERBER, H., Diseases of Domestic Animals
LUGINBÜHL, H., Veterinary Pathology
MOSIMANN, W., Anatomy, Embryology and Histology
NICOLET, J., Microbiology
SCHATZMANN, H.-J., Pharmacology
STECK, F., Microbiology, Virology

*Faculty of Philosophy and Letters:*
AEBLI, H., Psychology
BANDI, H.-G., Prehistory and Palaeontology
BEER, ELLEN, History of Medieval Art
BLICKLE, P., Modern History
BÜRGEL, J.-C., Islamic Studies
CONTI, P., Italian Language and Literature
VON CRANACH, M., Psychology
DONZÉ, R., French Philology
ESCH, A., Medieval History
FOPPA, NIKOLAUS, Psychology
FRICKER, R., English Language and Literature
GELZER, T., Classical Philology
GIGON, O., Classical Philology and Latin
GLATTHARD, P., Dialect and Folklore of (German) Switzerland
GRAESER, A., Philosophy
GRAWE, K., (Clinical) Psychology
HEINIMANN, S., Romance Philology
HERKOMMER, H., Philology (German)
HERZIG, H., Ancient History
HOFER, W., Modern History
HÜTTINGER, E., History of Art
IM HOF, U., Swiss History
JÁNOSKA, GEORG, Philosophy
JUCKER, H., Classical Archaeology
KUNZE, S., Music
LANG, A., Psychology
LÜTHI, H. J., Modern German Language and Literature
MARSCHALL, W., Ethnology
MESMER, BEATRIX, History
MOJON, L., Medieval History of Art
DE NORA, E. G. G., Spanish Language and Literature
REDARD, G., Indo-Germanic Studies, with special attention to Classical Languages
RUSTERHOLZ, P., Modern German Literature
SANDERS, W., German Language
UTZ, HANS, English Language and Literature
WALZER, P., Romance Philology, Modern French Language and Literature
WEISSKOPF, T., Philosophy
WILDBOLZ, R., Modern German Language and Literature

*Faculty of Science:*
ALLEMANN, F., Geology
ARM, H., Organic Chemistry
BEBIE, H., Physics (Theoretical)
BRAUN, R., Microbiology
CARNAL, H., Theory of Appearances
DANIEL, K., Mathematical Statistics
DEBRUNNER, H., Mathematics
DEBRUNNER, H. E., Physics (Cosmic Rays)
EBERHARDT, P., Experimental Physics
ERISMANN, K., Botany
GEISS, J., Experimental Physics
GROSJEAN, G., Geography
VON GUNTEN, H.-R., Radiochemistry
HAHN, B., Experimental and High Energy Physics
JÄGER, EMILIE, Experimental Mineralogy and Petrography
LANG, G., Systematic Botany and Geobotany
LEUPOLD, U., Microbiology and General Biology
LEUTWYLER, H., Theoretical Physics
LUDI, A., Inorganic Chemistry
LÜSCHER, E. F., Biochemistry
MESSERLI, B., Geography
MEY, HJ., Computer Science
NABHOLZ, W., Geology
NEF, W., Higher Mathematics
NEUENSCHWANDER, M., Organic Chemistry
NIGGLI, E., Mineralogy and Petrography
NOWACKI, W., Crystallography
OESCHGER, H., Experimental Physics
PETERS, TJ., Mineralogy and Petrography
RÄTZ, J., Mathematics
REIMANN, M., Mathematics
RIEDWYL, H., Applied Statistics
SCHANDA, E., Applied Physics
SCHEFFOLD, R., Organic Chemistry
SCHINDLER, P., Inorganic Chemistry
SCHMIDT, E., Physical Chemistry
SCHUMACHER, E., Inorganic Chemistry
TSCHANZ, B., Zoology
TSCHUMI, P., Zoology
WEBER, R., Zoology
WILD, P., Astronomy
WILKER, P., Mathematics
ZAHLER, P., Biochemistry

## UNIVERSITÉ DE FRIBOURG
1700 FRIBOURG
Telephone: 037/21-91-11.
Founded 1889.

Languages of instruction: French and German; State control.

*Rector:* Prof. B. SCHNYDER.
*Vice-Rectors:* Profs. CH. CARON, P. LADNER, B. TRÉMEL.
*Administrator:* H. E. BRÜLHART.
*Librarian:* G. DELABAYS.

The library contains over 1,000,000 vols.

Number of teachers: 228.
Number of students: 3,998.

DEANS:

*Faculty of Theology:* Prof. E. CORECCO.
*Faculty of Law, Economics and Social Sciences:* Prof. L. CARLEN.
*Faculty of Letters:* Prof. G. KÜNG.
*Faculty of Sciences:* Prof. A. ANTILLE.

FULL PROFESSORS:

*Faculty of Theology:*
BARTHÉLEMY, J.-D., Old Testament Exegesis
BAUMGARTNER, J., Liturgy
BRANTSCHEN, L., Dogmatic Theology
CORECCO, E., Canon Law
FRIEDLI, R., Missiology and Science of Religions
HÖFFE, O., Political Philosophy
KEEL, O., Old Testament
MIETH, D., Moral Theology
NICOLAS, J.-H., Dogmatic Theology
O'NEILL, C. E., Dogmatic Theology
PHILIPPE, MARIE-DOMINIQUE, Philosophy
PINTO DE OLIVEIRA, C. J., Moral Theology
SCHÜEPP, G., Pastoral Theology
SIEGWART, J., Ecclesiastical History
STIRNIMANN, H., Fundamental Theology
TREMEL, B., New Testament
VAN DAMME, D., Patrology
VITALINI, S., Dogmatic Theology

*Faculty of Law, Economics and Social Sciences:*
ABELE, H., Economics
BALESTRA, P., Econometrics
BILLETER, E. P., Statistics, Automation, Operations Research
BLÜMLE, E. B., Marketing
CARLEN, L., History of Law
CLERC, F., Criminal Law and Canon Law
DARBELLAY, J.-J., Public Law, Administrative Law, Philosophy of Law
DICKE, C. D., Public Law
DUFOUR, A., History of Law
EPPLER, R., Economics
FLECK, F., Economic Theory
FLEINER, T., General and Swiss Public Law
GAUCH, P., Civil Procedural Law
GAUDARD, G., International Commerce, Regional Economics
KIRSCH, G., Science of Finance
KOHLAS, J., Operations Research
KLEINEWEFERS, H., Political Economy
KÜHN, R., Business Economy
LUCCHINI, R., Sociology
MACHERET, A., General Administrative Law
OVERBECK, A., Private International Law
PASQUIER, J., Marketing
SCHMITT, B., Economic Theory
SCHNYDER, B., Private Law
TERCIER, P., Private Law
VALARCHÉ, J.-M., Economics
WITTMANN, W., Theoretical Economics and Finance
WUBBE, F., Roman Law

*Faculty of Letters:*
AEBERLIN, U., Therapeutic Pedagogy
AGAZZI, E., Philosophy
ALTERMATT, U., Swiss History
BÜRGEL, C., Islamology
CAPOL, M., Applied Psychology
FLAMMER, A., Psychology
GIRAUD, Y., French Literature
HOEFFE, O., Social Philosophy
HUBER, H., Ethnology
KAHIL, L., Classical Archaeology
KÜNG, G., Philosophy
LADNER, P., Science of History
MENICHETTI, A., Romanistic Philology
MORTIMER, A., English
MÜLLER, K., Classical Philology
PERREZ, M., Education
PFAFF, C., General Medieval History
PIÉRART, M., Latin
POZZI, G., Italian Literature
PUELMA, M., Classical Philology
RAAB, H., Modern History
ROUDAUT, J., French Literature
RUFFIEUX, R., General Modern History
SCHMID, A. A., History of Art
SEEBOLD, E., German Philology
STUDER, E., German Philology
SUGRANYES DE FRANCH, R., Iberian Literatures
TAGLIAVINI, L., History of Music
ZAWADSKI, T., Ancient History
ZELLER, H., Modern German Literature

*Faculty of Sciences:*
ANTILLE, A., Mathematics
CARON, C., Geology
CONTI, G., Histology
EMMENEGGER, F. P., Inorganic Chemistry
HAAB, P., Physiology
HANSEN, H.-J., Organic Chemistry
HOLMANN, H., Mathematics
HOURIET, A., Theoretical Physics
HUBER, O., Experimental Physics
KLEISLI, H., Mathematics

MEIER, H., Botany
NICKEL, E., Mineralogy and Petrography
PIVETEAU, J.-L., Geography
PORTMANN, P., Physiological Chemistry
SCHMID, J., Mathematics
SCHOWING, J., Zoology
TOBLER, H., Zoology
WIESENDANGER, M., Physiology
VON ZELEWSKY, A., Inorganic Chemistry

ASSOCIATED INSTITUTES:

**Institute of Pastoral Theology:** Dirs. Prof. SCHÜEPP, J.-M. PASQUIER.

**Institute of Moral Theology:** Dir. F. COMPAGNONI.

**Institute for Missions and the Study of Religions:** Dir. R. FRIEDLI.

**Institute for Ecumenical Studies:** Dir. H. STIRNIMANN.

**Institute of Ecclesiastical Law:** Dir. L. CARLEN.

**Institute for Automation and Operations Research:** Dir. J. KOHLAS.

**Institute of Economic and Social Sciences:** Dir. F. H. FLECK.

**Institute for Journalism:** Dir. F. FLECK.

**Institute of Pedagogy:** Dir. Prof. M. PERREZ.

**Institute of Therapeutic Pedagogy and Social Work:** Dir. U. AEBERLIN.

**Institute for East European Studies:** Dir. G. KÜNG.

**Institute for Practical French:** Sec. M. HATEM.

**Institute for Practical German:** Dir. G. SCHNEIDER.

**Institute for Practical English:** Dir. Prof. A. MORTIMER.

**International Institute of Social and Political Sciences:** Dir. O. HÖFFE.

**Institute of Medieval Studies:** Dirs. P. LADNER, A. SCHMID, C. PFAFF.

**Institute of Psychology:** Dir. A. FLAMMER.

**Institute for Cardio-Angiological Research:** Dir. Y. F. LIARD.

**Institute of Physical Education and Sport:** Dir. (vacant).


## UNIVERSITÉ DE GENÈVE
3 PLACE DE L'UNIVERSITÉ,
1211 GENEVA 4

Telephone: (022) 20-93-33.

Founded 1559.

Language of instruction: French.

*Rector:* Prof. JUSTIN THORENS.
*Registrars:* B. DUCRET, C. BOSSY.
*Librarian:* P. CHAIX.

Library: see Libraries.

Number of teachers: 1,992, including 542 professors.
Number of students: 9,863.

Publications: *Programme, Guide, Catalogue, Dies Academicus.*

DEANS:

*Faculty of Science:* Prof. H. GREPPIN.
*Faculty of Letters:* Prof. M. BURGER.
*Faculty of Economics and Social Science:* P. GUICHONNET.
*Faculty of Law:* B. KNAPP.
*Faculty of Medicine:* A. CRUCHAUD.
*Faculty of Protestant Theology:* Prof. O. FATIO.
*Faculty of Psychology and Educational Sciences:* Prof. E. BAYER.

PROFESSORS:

*Faculty of Science:*
BARGETZI, J.-P., Biochemistry
BÉNÉ, G., Hertzian Spectroscopy
BILL, H., Physical Chemistry
BOUVIER, P. B., Astrophysics
BUCHS, A., Mass Spectrometry
BURI, P., Galenic Pharmacy
CARO, L., Biology
CHESSEX, R., Mineralogy, Petrography
CRIPPA, M., Animal Biology
DELALOYE, M., Mineralogy
DESHUSSES, J., Biochemistry
DUCLOZ, C., Geology and Paleontology
ENZ, C., Theoretical Physics
EPSTEIN, R., Biology
EXTERMANN, P., Nuclear Physics
FISCHBERG, M., General Zoology
FISCHER, O., Physics
FRÖLICHER, A., Higher Calculus
FULPIUS, B., Biochemistry
GALLAY, A., Anthropology
GATTO, R., Theoretical Physics
GIOVANNINI, B., Solid State Physics
GLOOR, H., Genetics
GOLAY, M., Astronomy
GREPPIN, H., Botany
GUENIN, M., Theoretical Physics
HAEFLIGER, A., Linear Algebra and Topology
HAERDI, W., Mineral Chemistry
DE HALLER, G., Animal Biology
HARMS, J., Electronic Calculus
HEER, E., Experimental Nuclear Physics
HUGGEL, H., Comparative Anatomy and Physiology
ILLMENSEE, K., Animal Biology
IMHOF, J.-P., Mathematics
JAFFE, F., Mineralogy
JANJIC, D., Chemical Physics
JEANQUARTIER, P., Mathematics
JEFFORD, CH., Organic Chemistry
JØRGENSEN, CH., Chemical Physics
KAPÉTANIDIS, I., Pharmacognosy
KERVAIRE, M., Mathematics
LACROIX, R., Rational Mechanics
LÄMMLI, U., Biochemistry, Biology
LEVRAT, B., Interfaculty Electronic Computing
LUCKEN, A., Chemistry
MAEDER, D., Electronics
MARTIN, M., Nuclear Physics
MARTINET, L., Astronomy
MERMOD, R., Experimental Nuclear Physics
MIÈGE, Systematic Botany
MILLER, J., Biology
MOESCHLER, P., Anthropology
MULLER, EDITH, Astronomy
MULLER, E., Experimental Physics
OPPOLZER, W., Organic Chemistry
PARTHÉ, E., Structural Crystallography
PETER, M., General Physics
PIRON, C., Theoretical Physics
RUEGG, H., Theoretical Physics
RUFENER, F., Astronomy
SAUTER, M., Anthropology, Palaeontology
SIERRO, J., Physics of Condensed Matter
SPAHR, P. F., Genetical Biochemistry
STEIN, E., Biochemistry
STEINIG, J., Mathematics
STREIT, F., Mathematics
TISSIERES, A., Biology
TRONCHET, J., Pharmaceutical Chemistry
TURIAN, G., Botany
VUAGNAT, M., Mineralogy, Petrography, Prospecting
WANNER, G., Mathematics
WEBER, C., Mathematics
WEIL, R., Biology

*Faculty of Letters:*
BACZKO, B., History of Thought
BESSET, M., Contemporary History of Art
BINZ, L., National History
BLAIR, J., American Literature
BOESCHENSTEIN, B., German Literature
BOLENS, L., Medieval History
BOUVERESSE, J., Analytical Philosophy
BOUVIER, B., Modern Greek
BURCKHARDT, A., Modern History
BURGER, M., Romance Philology
BUTOR, M., Modern French Literature
DÄLLENBACH, L., Modern French Literature
DEUCHLER, F., History of Art
DÖRIG, J., Classical Archaeology
DRAGONETTI, R., Medieval Romance Languages and Literature
ESTREICHER, Z., Musicology
FAVEZ, J.-C., Contemporary History
GAGNEBIN, B., Research Techniques
GEITH, K.-E., Medieval German
GIOVANNINI, A., History of Antiquity
GORNI, G., Medieval Italian
HARI, R., Egyptology
HEINEMANN, R., Japanese
HURST, A., Classical Greek
JARGY, S., Muslim and Arab Civilization
JEANNERET, M., History of French Literature
KASSER, R., Coptic
KOLDE, G., German Linguistics and Stylistics
LOPEZ-MOLINA, L., Spanish Language and Literature
DE MURALT, A., Philosophy of Middle Ages
MYSROWICZ, L., Contemporary History
NIVAT, G., Russian Literature and Civilization
OSSOLA, C., Modern Italian
PASCHOUD, F., Latin Literature
POLLETTA, G., Modern English Literature and Civilization
PRIETO, L., General Linguistics
PY, A., French Literature
REVERDIN, O., Greek Language and Literature
ROETHLISBERGER, M., History of Modern Art
ROULET, G.-E., French Linguistics
RUDHARDT, J., History of Ancient Religions
STAROBINSKI, J., History of Ideas and French Literature
STEINER, G., Comparative Literature
TAYLOR, P. B., Medieval English

*Faculty of Economics and Social Science:*
BAILLY, A., Geography
BAIROCH, P., Economic History
BALESTRA, P., Econometry
BENDER, A., Industrial Organization
BOURQUIN, G., Advanced Accounting and Business Law
BURGENMEIER, B., Political Economy
CARLEVARO, F., Econometry
COTTIER, A., Accounting
COURBON, J.-C., Computer Science applied to Business
CUENDET, G., Industrial Organization
DE LAUBIER, P., Sociology

FONTELA, E., Econometry
GIROD, R., Sociology
GRANDVILLE, O. DE LA, Political Economy
GUICHONNET, P., Human Geography
KELLERHALS, J., Sociology
KERR, H., Political Sciences
LALIVE D'EPINAY, C., Sociology
LEONARD, M., Computer Science applied to Business
L'HUILLIER, J., Political Economy
L'HUILLIER, L., Contract Law and Transport Law
MENTHA, G., Industrial Organization
MODOUX, G., Industrial Organization
PERRENOUD, A., Economic History
PIUZ, A.-M., Economic History
RAFFESTIN, C., Geography
ROIG, C., Political Science
SCHELLHORN, J.-P., Statistics
SIDJANSKI, D., Political Sciences
TRICOT, C., Statistics
TSCHOPP, P., Political Economy
URIO, P., Political Science
WEBER, L., Political Economy
ZIEGLER, J., Sociology

Faculty of Law:
AUER, A., Constitutional Law
BAUER, H., Swiss Civil Law
CONDORELLI, C., Public International Law
DALLÈVES, L., Swiss Commercial Law
DOMINICE, C., Public International Law
DUFOUR, A., History of Institutions and Law
GRAVEN, PH., Penal Law
HABSCHEID, W., German Civil Law and Civil Procedure
HANISCH, H., German Civil Law
HIRSCH, A., Commercial Law
JUNOD, CH.-A., General Administrative Law
KNAPP, B., Administrative Law
LALIVE, P., Private International Law
MALINERNI, G., Constitutional Law, Introduction to the Science of Law
MORAND, C.-A., Constitutional Law
OBERSON, R., Fiscal Law
PERRET, F., Patents, Swiss Civil Law
PERRIN, J.-F., Introduction to the Science of Law, Sociology of Law
PETITPIERRE, G., Swiss Civil Law
RENS, I., History of Political Doctrines
REYMOND, J.-A., Commercial and Fiscal Law
ROBERT, C. N., Penal Law, Criminology
SCHMIDLIN, B., Roman Law
SCHONLE, H., Contracts
STAUDER, J., German Commercial Law
THORENS, J., Civil Law

Faculty of Medicine:
ABRAHAM, G., Psychiatry
BARTHOLINI, G., Psychiatry
BAUD, C. A., Morphology
BAUMANN, F., Physiology
BAUME, L., Dentistry
BEGUIN, F., Gynaecology and Obstetrics
BERNEY, J., Neurosurgery
BERNHEIM, J., Legal Medicine
CALAME, A., Surgery
CERRETELLI, P., Physiology
CHANTRAINE, A., Physical Medicine and Rehabilitation
CHATELANAT, F., Pathology
CIMASONI, G., Dentistry
CONSTANTINIDIS, J., Psychiatry
COURVOISIER, B., Medicine
CRUCHAUD, A., Medicine
CUENDET, A., Paediatrics
DIATKINE, R., Psychiatry
DONATH, A., Nuclear Medicine
DREIFUSS, J. J., Physiology
DUNANT, Y., Pharmacology
ENGEL, E., Medical Genetics

FABRE, J., Medicine
FAIDUTTI, R., Cardiology
FALLET, G.-H., Physical Medicine and Rehabilitation
FERRIER, P., Paediatrics
FIORE-DONNO, G., Dentistry
GABBIANI, G., Pathology
GARRONE, S., Psychiatry
GAUTHIER, G., Neurology
GEMPERLE, M., Anaesthesiology
GIRARDIER, L., Physiology
GRABER, P., Surgery
HAHN, CH., Cardiology
HAYNAL, A, Psychiatry
HERRMANN W., Gynaecology and Obstetrics
HOLZ, J., Dental Medicine
HUMAIR, L., Medicine
HUNZIKER, N., Dermatology
JATON, J. C., Medical Biochemistry
JEANNERET, O., Social and Preventive Medicine
JEANRENAUD, B., Medical Research
JOHO, J. P., Dentistry
JUNOD, J.-P., Geriatrics
KAPANCI, Y., Pathology
KOLAKOFSKY, D., Microbiology
KRAUER, F., Gynaecology and Obstetrics
LAGIER, R., Pathology
LAMBERT, G., Social and Preventive Medicine
LAMBERT, P. H., Medicine
LAUGIER, P., Dermatology
LESKI, M., Medicine
LOIZEAU, E., Medicine
MACH, B., Microbiology
MEGEVAND, A., Paediatrics
MEGEVAND, R., Surgery
MEYER, J. M., Dentistry
MIESCHER, P. A., Medicine
MONTANDON, P., Oto-rhino-laryngology
MULLER, A., Medicine
NAEF, A., Surgery
NALLY, J.-N., Dentistry
OFFORD, R., Medical Biochemistry
ORCI, L., Morphology
PASINI, W., Psychiatry
PAUNIER, J.-P., Radiology
PAUNIER, L., Paediatrics
PERRELET, A., Morphology
PERRELET, L., Dentistry
POMETTA, D., Medicine
RENOLD, A., Clinical Biochemistry
REY, P., Social Medicine
RIOTTON, G., Pathology
ROHNER, A., Surgery
ROTH, A., Ophthalmology
RUTISHAUSER, W., Cardiology
SCHERRER, J. R., Informatics
SIZONENKO, P. A., Paediatrics
SPIRGI, M., Dentistry
STRAUB, R., Pharmacology
TAILLARD, W., Surgery
TIMMIS, N., Medical Biochemistry
TISSOT, R., Psychiatry
VAEY, H., Neurosurgery
VALLOTTON, Clinical Investigation
VAN DER LOOS, H., Morphology
VASSALLI, P., Pathology
VISCHER, TH., Physical Medicine and Rehabilitation
WALDVOGEL, F., Microbiology
WERNER, A., Neuro-Surgery
WETTSTEIN, P., Radiology
WILDI, E., Pathology

Faculty of Protestant Theology:
BOVON, F., New Testament Exegesis
CHAPPUIS, J.-M., Practical Theology
FATIO, O., History
FRAENKEL, P., History
MARTIN-ACHARD, R., Old Testament Exegesis

MOREL, B., Apologetics
WIDMER, G., Dogmatics

School of Architecture:
BRIVIO, P., History of Contemporary Architecture
CARLONI, T., General Architecture and Project II
DAGHINI, G., Theory and Problems of Land
GILLIARD, D., Analysis and Planning of Living Conditions
GOLINELLI, P., Structures
HOLY, J.-C., Geometry and Mathematics
INSOLERA, I., Theory and History of Town Planning
LUDI, J. C., Architecture and Communication
MECHKAT, C., Methods of Production of Buildings
MERMINOD, P., Construction
MORENO, P., Analysis of Construction and Alternative Technologies
REVERDIN, R., Analysis of Environment and Landscape

Faculty of Psychology and Educational Sciences:

Section of Psychology:
BANG, V., Educational Psychology and Psychological Methodology
BULLINGER, A., Role of the Sensory Motor in Cognitive Activities
CELLERIER, G., Genetic Epistemology, Models of the Experimental Simulation of Behaviour
DOISE, W., Social Psychology
DE LANNOY, J., Introduction to Psychology, Experimental Psychology
ETIENNE, A., Ethology
INHELDER, B., Genetic and Experimental Psychology, Educational Psychology
MOUNOUD, P., Psychology of Personality Development
MUNARI, A., Educational Psychology in the School
SCHMID-KITSIKIS, E., Clinical Psychology
SINCLAIR, H., Psycholinguistics, Psychopathology of Language
STUCKI, J.-D., Neuropsychology, Introduction to Child Psychopathology, Motor Development and its Pathologies
VONECHE, J., Child and Adolescent Psychology
WERMUS, H., Introduction to Logic, Formal Logic

Section of Educational Sciences:
ALLAL, L., Pedagogical Evaluation
BAYER, E., Research Techniques in Education
BRONCKART, J.-P., Introduction to Language Theories
DENIS, M., Psycho-pedagogy
DENIS-PRINZHORN, M., Psycho-pedagogy
DOMINICE, P., Adult Education
FURTER, P., Planning and Development of Training Programmes
GIORDAN, A., Psycho-pedagogy in Sciences
HAMELINE, D., Philosophy
HUBERMAN, M., General Pedagogy
MASSARENTI, L., Introduction to Experimental Pedagogy
RIEBEN, L., Education and Development of Children

OTHER INSTITUTES, ASSOCIATE COLLEGES, AND SCHOOLS:

**École de Traduction et d'Interprétation:** trains translators and interpreters in 7 languages; Dir. A. F. WILLIAMS.

## SWITZERLAND

**École de langue et civilisations françaises:** Dir. G. MEID.

**École d'Education Physique et de Sport:** Dir. Prof. O. JEANNERET.

**Institut Universitaire de Hautes Etudes Internationales** (*Graduate Institute of International Studies*): 132 rue de Lausanne; f. 1927; a research and teaching institution studying international questions from the juridical, political and economic viewpoints.

*Director:* Dr. CH. DOMINICE.

**Institut Universitaire d'Etudes du Développement:** 24 rue Rothschild, 1202 Geneva; f. 1960; African history, Middle Eastern and Latin American studies, international relations, Switzerland–Third World economic relations.

*Director:* J. FORSTER.

**Institut Universitaire d'Etudes Européennes:** 122 rue de Lausanne, 1211 Geneva 21; f. 1963; teaching and research in the fields of history of ideas, economics, political science, regionalism, law.

*Director:* H. SCHWAMM.

**Centre Universitaire d'Etudes Oecuméniques** (*Graduate School of Ecumenical Studies*): Château de Bossey, Céligny; Dir. K. H. HERTZ.

**Centre d'Etudes Industrielles:** 4 Chemin de Conches, Geneva; f. 1946; a postgraduate school of international industrial administration.

*Director:* B. HAWRYLYSHYN.
*Secretary-General:* M. DAETWYLER.
*Librarian:* Miss T. SEILER.


## UNIVERSITÉ DE LAUSANNE
PLACE DE LA CATHÉDRALE 4,
CASE POSTALE 611,
1000 LAUSANNE 17

Telephone: 021/220031.

Telex: 25110.

Founded 1537.

Language of instruction: French; Academic year: October to July.

*Rector:* Prof. CL. BRIDEL.

*Vice-Rectors:* Prof. J. B. DUPONT, Prof. W. STAUFFACHER, Prof. R. WOODTLI.

*Administrative Director:* CHR. PILLOUD.

*Librarian:* J. P. CLAVEL.

Library: see Libraries.
Number of teachers: 435.
Number of students: 4,000.

Publications: *Cahiers de la Faculté de Théologie, Publications de la Faculté des Lettres. Bulletin de l'Institut de Géologie, Uni Lausanne†*, also essays and documents on the history of the University.

### DEANS:
*Faculty of Theology:* Prof. K. BLASER.
*Faculty of Jurisprudence:* Prof. F. DESSEMONTET.
*Faculty of Medicine:* Prof. J. L. RIVIER.
*Faculty of Letters:* Prof. P. DUCREY.
*Faculty of Science:* Prof. M. BURLET.
*Faculty of Social and Political Science:* Prof. L. BRIDEL.
*School of Higher Commercial Studies:* Prof. CH. IFFLAND.
*School of Pharmacy:* Prof. J. C. ETTER.

### PROFESSORS:
*Faculty of Theology:*
AMSLER, S., Old Testament
BLASER, K., Dogmatics
BRIDEL, CL., Practical Theology
GISEL, P., History of Modern and Contemporary Theology
KELLER, C., Old Testament
PETER, E., History of the Church
RUMPF, L., Ethics
SENFT, C., New Testament
ZOSS, W., Practical Theology

*Faculty of Law:*
DESSEMONTET, FR., Commercial Law
DUTOIT, B., Comparative Civil Law
FLATTET, G., French Civil Law
GAUTHIER, J., Penal Law
GILLIARD, F., Commercial Law
GILLIERON, P., Law of Bankruptcy and Debt
GRISEL, E., General Constitutional Law
HOFSTETTER, J., Roman Law
MATHYER, J., Forensic Science
MERCIER, P., European Law
MOOR, P., General Administrative Law
PERRIN, G., International Law
PIOTET, P., Civil Law
POUDRET, J.-F., History of Law
SCHALLER, F., Political Economy
STURM, F., German Civil Law
VIRET, B., Social Legislation
VOYAME, J., Law of Intellectual Property
WURLOD, M., Fiscal Law

*Faculty of Medicine:*
BACHMANN, F., Haematology
BONIFAS, V., Microbiology
BOSSART, H., Gynaecology, Obstetrics
BRON, CL., Biochemistry
BUCHER, O., Embryology, Histology
BURNER, M., Psychiatry
CANDARDJIS, G., Radiology
DELACHAUX, A., Social and Preventative Medicine
DELACRÉTAZ, J., Dermatology
DOLIVO, M., Physiology
DRAGON, V., Radiotherapy
FAVEZ, G., Pneumology
FREEMAN, J., Anaesthesiology
GAILLOUD, C., Ophthalmology
GARDIOL, D., Pathological Anatomy
GAUTIER, E., Paediatrics
GENTON, N., Child Surgery
GUJER, H. R., Forensic Medicine
HENNY, R., Paedopsychiatry
HOFSTETTER, J.-R., Polyclinic Medicine
ISLIKER, H., Biochemistry
JÉQUIER, E., Physiology
KARAMATA, D., Microbiology
LIVIO, J.-J., Orthopaedics, Traumatology
MAGNENAT, P., Clinical Medicine
MAUEL, J., Biochemistry
MOSIMANN, R., Surgery
MULLER, C., Psychiatry
PERRET, CL., Physiopathology
PETERS, G., Pharmacology
REGLI, F., Neurology
RIBEAUPIERRE, F. DE, Physiology
SAEGESSER, F., Clinical Surgery
SAUDAN, Y., Physiology
SAVARY, M., Oto-Rhino-Laryngology
SCHNEIDER, P.-B., Psychiatry
VAN DER LOOS, H., Anatomy
ZANDER, E., Neuro-Surgery

*Faculty of Letters:*
BERARD, C., Archaeology
BRIDEL, L., Geography
CASTELNUOVO, E., History of Art
CHRISTOFF, D., Philosophy
DENTAN, M., French Literature
DUBOIS, A., Modern History
DUCREY, P., Ancient History
GIDDEY, E., English Language and Literature
GSTEIGER, M., Comparative Literature
HART-NIBBRIG, C., German Language and Literature
JEQUIER, F., General Contemporary History
JUNOD, PH., History of Art
KEMBALL, R., Russian
KIRBY, I., English Philology
LARA, A., Spanish Language and Literature
LASSERRE, F., Greek Language and Literature
LENSCHEN, W., German Philology
MAHMOUDIAN, M., General Linguistics
MAY, J., Buddhist Philosophy and Philology
MOLNAR, M., General Contemporary History
PAPINI, G., Italian Philology
PAUNIER, D., Roman Provincial Archaeology
PIGUET, J.-C., Philosophy
RACINE, J. B., Geography
REICHLER, C., French Language and Literature
RIEGER, D., Medieval French Language and Literature
SANDOZ, C., Historical Linguistics and Comparative Grammar
SCHMID, P., Latin Language and Literature
SCHROETER, J., American Literature
SEYLAZ, J. L., French Language and Literature
STÄUBLE, A., Italian Language and Literature
STAUFFACHER, W., German Language and Literature
TRIPET, A., French Language and Literature
VOELKE, A., Philosophy
ZIMMERMANN, H., Sanskrit

*Faculty of Science and School of Pharmacy:*
AYRTON, S., Mineralogy
BOECHAT, J., Numbers Theory and Differential Geometry
BRUNISHOLZ, G., Special Mineral Chemistry
BURLET, O., Mathematics
BURRI, M., Geology, Palaeontology
CLÉMENÇON, H., Cryptogamy
DAHN, H., Organic Chemistry
DELESSERT, A., Mathematics
DERIGHETTI, A., Algebra
ERDÖS, P., Theoretical Physics
ESCHER, A., Geology
ETTER, J.-C., Pharmacy
FESCHOTTE, P., General Mineral and Analytical Chemistry
GAILLOUD, M., Nuclear Physics
HAUCK, B., Astronomy
HIRT, B., Biochemistry
HUGUENIN, R., Physics
JÉQUIER, E., General Physiology
JOSEPH, C., Nuclear Physics
KESSELRING, U., Pharmaceutical Analysis
LOEFFEL, J.-J., Theoretical Physics
MASSON, H., Geology and Palaeontology
MAUMARY, S., Mathematics

1268

MERBACH, A., Mineral and Analytical Chemistry
METHÉE, P.-D., Mathematics and Analysis
MEYER DE STADELHOFEN, C., Geophysics and Technical Petrography
OJANGUREN, M., Algebra
PILET, P.-E., Vegetal Physiology
PONCET, J., Mathematics and Analysis
RINDERER, L., Physics
RIVIER, D., Experimental Physics
ROTHEN, F., General Physics
ROULET, R., Mineral and Analytical Chemistry
SCHLOSSER, M., Chemistry
SCHWARZENBACH, D., Original Chemistry
STECK, A., Mineralogy, Radio-Cristallography
STEINEMANN, S., Physics of Metal
TESTA, B., Pharmaceutical Chemistry
VILLARET, P., Botany
VOGEL, P., Animal Zoology and Ecology
VOGEL, P., Organic Chemistry
WAHLI, W., Animal Biology
WANDERS, G., Quantum Physics
WIDMER, F., Plant Physiology
WOODTLI, R., Mineralogy
WYLER, H., Organic Chemistry
ZRYD, J. P., Plant Physiology

*Faculty of Social and Political Sciences and School of Higher Commercial Studies:*

AGUET, J.-P., History of Political Doctrines
AMSLER, M.-H., Actuarial Mathematics
BERTHOUD, G., Social and Cultural Anthropology
BONZON, P., Informatics
BORSCHBERG, E., Economics
BRACK, J., Fiscal Law
BRIDEL, L., Geography
BUSINO, G., General Sociology
CHUARD, P., Financial Mathematics, Technique of Insurance
DESCHAMPS, J. CL., Psychosociology
DOLIVO, M., Psychopathology of Neurosystems
DROZ, R., General Psychology
DUPONT, J. B., Psychology
GAILLARD, F., Psychology
GAUDARD, G., Foreign Exchange
GENDRE, F., Applied Psychology
GILLIAND, P., Social Research and Planning
GOETSCHIN, P., Economics
GONVERS, J. P., Technical Research in Social Sciences
HORT, M., Actuarial Mathematics
IFFLAND, C., National Economy
JACOT, S.-P., Management Production
JEANNET, M., Social Psychology
LAMBELET, J. CHR., Economics
LARA, B., Operational Research
LASSERRE, A., 19th- and 20th-Century History
LENOIR-DEGOUMOIS, V., Social Politics
LEONARD, F., Sales Management and Marketing
LERESCHE, G., Mathematics
LEVY, R., General Sociology
LOB, M., Practical Guidance
MASNATA, F., Political Science
MATTEI, A., Economics
MIKDASHI, Z., Banking and Petroleum Economics
MONNIER, L., Political Sciences
PALMADE, G., General Education
PELET, P.-L., Diplomatic History
PROBST, A.-R., Informatics
RACINE, J. B., Geography
REYMOND, C., Introduction to Law Studies
RIEBEN, H., National Economy and European Problems
RUFFIEUX, R., Political Science
RUSCONI, B., Introduction to Law
SCHWARTZ, J.-J., Public Finance
DE SENARCLENS, P., International Relations in the 20th century
VOELIN, C., Child Psychology
WILLENER, A., Sociology of Mass Communications

## UNIVERSITÉ DE NEUCHÂTEL
2000 NEUCHÂTEL
Telephone: 038/253851.
Founded 1909.
Language of instruction: French.

*Rector:* Prof. E. JEANNET.
*Vice-Rectors:* Prof. D. GUINAND, Prof. A. SCHNEIDER.
*Secretary-General:* M. VUITHIER.

Number of teachers: 200.
Number of students: 1,900.

Publications: *Recueils, Annales, Informations.*

DEANS:
*Faculty of Letters:* Prof. A. GENDRE.
*Faculty of Science:* Prof. A. AESCHLIMANN.
*Faculty of Jurisprudence and Economics:* J.-P. GERN.
*Faculty of Theology:* Prof. J. ZUMSTEIN.

FULL PROFESSORS:

*Faculty of Letters:*
ALLEMAND, A., French Language and Literature
BLASER, R.-H., German Language and Literature
BOREL, J.-P., Spanish Language and Literature
BRUNNER, F., History of Philosophy
CENTLIVRES, P., Ethnology
CHIFFELLE, F., Geography
ECKARD, G., Medieval French Language and Literature
EGLOFF, M., Archaeology
EIGELDINGER, M., French Language and Literature
FASANI, R., Italian Language and Literature
GASSIER, P., History of Art
GENDRE, A., French Literature
GRIZE, J.-B., Logic, History and Philosophy of Science
LICHTENHAHN, E., Musicology
LÜDI, G., Linguistics
MARGUERAT, P., Modern History
MARZYS, Z., History of French Language
MATTHEY, F., English Language and Literature
MULLER, PH., General Philosophy, Psychology
PERRET-CLERMONT, A.-N., Psychology
ROULET, LS. ED., Swiss and General History
SCHEURER, R., Medieval History
SCHNEIDER, A., Latin Language and Literature
SPOERRI, W., Greek Language and Literature
THOMPSON, P., French Language and Literature
TREHEUX, J., Archaeology and Ancient History
ZELLWEGER, R., German Language
ZIMMERMANN, G.-D., English Language and Literature

*Faculty of Science:*
AESCHLIMANN, A., Animal Biology
AMIET, J.-P., Theoretical Physics
ARAGNO, H., Bacteriology
BADER, R., Mathematics
BANDERET, P., Mathematics
BECK, H., Theoretical Physics
BERNAUER, K., Inorganic and Analytical Chemistry
BURGER, A., Hydrogeology
DAENDLIKER, R., Optics
DIEHL, P.-A., Zoology
DINICHERT, P., Experimental Physics
ERARD, P.-J., Information Science
FAVARGER, C., Botanical Biology
FISCHER, G., Physics
FORM, W., Metallurgy
HUGUENIN, P., Theoretical Physics
JACCARD, C., Physics
JACOT-GUILLARMOD, A., Organic Chemistry
JEANNET, E., Physics
KÜBLER, B., Mineralogy, Petrography
MARTINOLI, P., Physics
MARTY, W., Inorganic and Analytical Chemistry
MATTHEY, W., Ecology
MERMOD, C., Zoology
PELLANDINI, F., Electronics
PERSOZ, F., Petrography
REMANE, J., Palaeontology
RICHARD, J.-L., Ecology
ROBERT, A., Mathematics
ROSSEL, J., Experimental Physics
SCHAER, J.-P., Geology
SHAH, A., Electronics
SIEGENTHALER, P.-A., Vegetal Physiology
SIGRIST, F., Mathematics
SÖRENSEN, W., Mathematics
STOECKLI, F., Physical Chemistry
STUTZ, E., Biochemistry
SUTER, U., Mathematics
TABACCHI, R., Organic Chemistry
ZANGGER, C., Nuclear Physics

*Faculty of Jurisprudence and Economics:*
AUBERT, J.-F., Constitutional Law
BOIS, P., Administrative Law
BOLLE, P.-H., Penal and Elementary Law
CANNATA, C.-A., History of Law
CURCHOD, F., Property Law
ERARD, M., Sociology
ERBÉ, R., Political Economics
GERN, J.-P., History of Economics
GROSSEN, J.-M., Civil Law
GUINAND, J., Civil Law
HAAG, D., Financial Economics
JEANRENAUD, C., Public Economics
JEANPRETRE, R., Law of Obligation
JUVET, J.-L., International Economics
KNOEPFLER, F., International Law
LEJEUNE, M., Economic Statistics
MAILLAT, D., Political Economics
MEHLING, J., Commercial and Industrial Economy
MONNIER, J., International Law
PAPALOÏZOS, A., Psychology
ROUSSON, M., Psychology
RUEDIN, R., Commercial Law
STROHMEIER, A., Information Science
WEIBEL, E., Political Science

*Faculty of Theology:*
BARTHEL, P., Modern Church History
LEUBA, J.-L., Systematic Theology
DE PURY, A., Old Testament
RORDORF, W., Medieval Church History
ZUMSTEIN, New Testament

ASSOCIATE INSTITUTE:
**Seminary of Modern French for Foreigners:** number of professors, 10; number of students, 150.
*Director:* A. ALLEMAND.

## UNIVERSITÄT ZÜRICH
RÄMISTRASSE 71, 8006 ZÜRICH
Telephone: 257-11-11.
Founded 1833.
Language of instruction: German.

*Rector:* Prof. G. HILTY.
*Secretary:* Dr. F. ZÜSLI-NISCOSI.
The library contains 1,650,000 vols.
Number of teachers: 1,565.
Number of students: 14,055.

### DEANS:
*Faculty of Theology:* Prof. TH. STROHM.
*Faculty of Law and Politics:* Prof. G. HAUSER.
*Faculty of Medicine:* Prof. H. HARTMANN.
*Faculty of Veterinary Medicine:* Prof. K. ŽEROBIN.
*Faculty of Philosophy—I:* Prof. ST. SONDEREGGER.
*Faculty of Philosophy—II:* Prof. K. STREBEL.

### PROFESSORS:

*Faculty of Theology:*
ALTENDORF, H. D., History of Dogma, Patristics
BERNET, W., Psychology of Religion
BÜSSER, F., Ecclesiastical History
GEISSER, H., Systematic Theology
LEUENBERGER, R., Practical Theology
MOSTERT, W., Systematic Theology
SCHMID, H. H., Old Testament and History of Religions
SCHULZ, S., New Testament
STECK, O. H., Old Testament
STOLZ, F., History and Science of Religions
STROHM, TH., Systematic Theology and Social Ethics
WEDER, H., New Testament

*Faculty of Law and Politics and Economics:*
ALLEMANN, H., Practical National Economics
BAUKNECHT, K., Electronic Data Processing (Informatics)
BOHLEY, P., Statistics and Finance
FORSTMOSER, P., Trade Law
FREY, B. S., Theory and Practice of Social Economics
GARBERS, H., Econometry and Mathematical Statistics
HÄFELIN, U., State and Administrative Law, Constitutional History
HALLER, W., State and Administrative Law
HÄSSIG, K., Operations Research
HAUSER, G., Theory and Practice of Social Economics
HAUSER, J. A., Political and Demographic Economics, Development Politics
HAUSER, M., Theory and Practice of Social Economics
HAUSER, R., Criminal Law, Criminal Case Law and Bankruptcy Law
HEGNAUER, C., Swiss Civil Law
HEINI, A., Swiss and International Civil Law
KALL, P., Operations Research and Mathematical Methods of Economics
KELLER, M., Civil Code, Obligatory and Private Insurance Law, International Private Law
KILGUS, E., Vocational Training
KOELZ, A., Administrative Law
KOENIG, P., Mathematics for Economists
KRULIS-RANDA, J., Training in Economics
LINDER, W., Swiss Economics and Special Economic Politics
MEIER-HAYOZ, A., Theoretical and Practical Social Economics
MUELLER, G., State and Administrative Law
NEF, H., Philosophical, State and Administrative Law
NOLL, P., Criminal Law, Law Instruction
PETER, H., Roman Law, Swiss Civil Law
REHBERG, J., Criminal Law
REHBINDER, M., Labour Law, Sociology of Law, Press Law
RIEMER, H. M., Swiss Civil Law
RITZMANN, F., Theory and Practice of Social Economics
RÜHLI, E., Management Training
SCHELBERT-SYFRIG, Mrs. H., Theory and Practice of Social Economics
SCHINDLER, D., Law of Nations, State Administration and European Law
SCHNEIDER, H., Theoretical and Practical Social Economics
SCHLUEP, W. R., Swiss and European Private and Economic Law
SCHOTT, C. D., History of Swiss and German Law
SIEGENTHALER, H. J., Political Economics and Economic History
SOLIVA, C., History of German and Swiss Private Law
STARK, E., Civil and Commercial Law
WALDER-BOHNER, H. U., Civil Case Law, Bankruptcy Law, Swiss Civil Law
WEILENMANN, P., Business Accounting and Training of Commercial Instructors
WEIMAR, P., Roman and Civil Law
ZUPPINGER, F., Financial and Revenue Law

*Faculty of Medicine:*
AKERT, K., Neurology and Anatomy
AMMANN, R., Medical Gastroenterology
ANGST, J., Psychiatry
ANLIKER, M., Biomedicine
BAUMGARTNER, G., Neurology
BINSWANGER, U., Internal Medicine, Nephrology
BINZ, H., Immunology
BOLLINGER, A., Angiology
BORBÉLY, A. A., Psycho-Pharmacology
BRUNNER, U. V., Special Surgery, Lymphology, Phlebology
BUFF, H.-U., Surgery
BÜHLMANN, A., Pathological Physiology
CHRISTEN, PH., Biochemistry
CORBOZ, R., Psychiatry for Children and Juveniles
CUÉNOD, M., Neurology and Anatomy
DUC, G., Neonatology
EBERLE, H., Traumatology
ERNST, K., Clinical Psychiatry
FISCH, U., Oto-Rhino-Laryngology
FISCHER, J. A., Calcium Metabolism and Assimilation in Orthopaedics
FRICK, P., Internal Medicine-Haematology
FRITZ-NIGGLI, Mrs. H., X-ray Biology
FROESCH, E., Biochemical Pathophysiology
GITZELMANN, R., Paediatrics
V. GRAEVENITZ, A., Medical Microbiology
GUTTE, B., Biochemistry
HARTMANN, H., Legal Medicine
HEDINGER, CH., Pathology
HERZKA, H., Psychopathology of Infants and Children
HITZIG, W., Paediatrics
HORST, W., Radio Therapy, Nuclear Medicine
HOSSLI, G., Anaesthetics
HUCH, A., Gynaecology
HUMBEL, R., Biochemistry
HUNSPERGER, R., Physiology, Neurology
ISLER, W., Paediatric Neurology
KÄGI, J., Biochemistry
KAYSER, F., Medical Microbiology
KELLER, P. J., Gynaecology, especially Patho-Physiology of Reproduction
KIND, H., Psychotherapy
KLÖTI, R., Ophthalmology
KOELBING, H. M., History of Medicine
KOLLER, E. A., Physiology
KRAYENBUEHL, H.P., Internal Medicine, Cardiology
KUBIK, S., Anatomy
LABHART, A., Pathological Physiology
LANGEMANN, H., Pharmacology
LARGIADER, F., Transplantation Surgery
LICHTENSTEIGER, W., Neuro-Pharmacology
LINDENMANN, J., Immunology and Virology
MARTZ, G., Clinical Oncology
MAYOR, G., Urology
MEYER, U. A., Clinical Pharmacology
MURER, H., Physiology
NIEMEYER, G., Ophthalmology and Neurophysiology
PRADER, ANDREA, Paediatrics
PRECHT, W., Neurology and Anatomy
RAMSEIER, H., Immunology
RICKENBACHER, J., Anatomy
RICKHAM, P. P., Children's Surgery
RÜTTNER, J., Pathology
SCHÄR, M., Social and Preventive Medicine
SCHARFETTER, CH., Clinical Psychiatry, Psychopathology
SCHAUB, M. C., Biochemical Pharmacology
SCHMID, W., Medical Genetics
SCHNYDER, U. W., Dermatology and Venereology
SCHREIBER, A., Orthopaedics
SCHREINER, W., Gynaecology
SENNING, Å., Surgery
SIEGENTHALER, W., Internal Medicine
STAUFFER, U. G., Children's Surgery
THEILER, K., Anatomy
TURINA, M., Experimental and Clinical Cardiac Surgery
UCHTENHAGEN, A., Social Psychiatry
VONDERSCHMITT, D. J., Clinical Chemistry
WAGENHAEUSER, F., Rheumatology and Physical Therapy
WASER, P. G., Pharmacology
WELLAUER, J., Roentgenology
WILLI, J., Psychiatry and Medical Psychology
WITMER, R., Ophthalmology
YAŞARGIL, G. M., Physiology
YAŞARGIL, M. G., Neuro-Surgery
ZBINDEN, G., Toxicology
ZENKER, W., Anatomy
ZINKERNAGEL, R. M., Experimental Pathology

*Dental Institute:*
GUGGENHEIM, B., Oral Microbiology and General Immunology
MARTHALER, TH., Preventive Dentistry
MUEHLEMANN, H., Histology of the Mouth
OBWEGESER, H., Dental Surgery
PALLA, S., Dental Prosthesis
SCHAERER, P., Crowns and Bridges
SCHROEDER, H. E., Oral Structural Biology
STOECKLI, P. W., Maxillary Surgery and Children's Dentistry

*Faculty of Veterinary Medicine:*
BERCHTOLD, M., Obstetrics
BERTSCHINGER, H.-U., Bacteriology

ECKERT, J., Parasitology
FREWEIN, J., Anatomy
JENNY, E., Pharmacology
JUCKER, H., Animal Nutrition
KUENZLE, C. C., Veterinary Biochemistry
MÜLLER, A., Veterinary Surgery
STUENZI, H., Pathology, Pathological Anatomy, Pathological Histology
SUTER, P., Internal Medicine of Domestic Animals
WYLER, R., Virology
ZEROBIN, K., Biology of Reproduction

*Faculty of Philosophy—I:*
VON ALBERTINI, R., Modern History
BANDLE, O., Nordic Philology
BERRUTO, G., Romance Philology, Italian Language
BESOMI, O., History of Italian Literature
BINDER, W., Modern German History
BISCHOF, N., Biomathematical Psychology
BITTERLI, U., Modern History and European Human History
BOEHLER, M., Modern German Literature
BORNSCHIER, V., Economic Sociology
BRANG, P., Slavic Philology
BRAUN, R., General and Swiss Modern History
BRINKER, H., History of East Asian Art
BUCHER, E., Modern and Swiss History
BURGER, H., German Philology
BURKERT, W., Classical Greek Philology
EBNETER, TH., Applied Linguistics
FRANCILLON, R., History of French Literature from the Renaissance to the Present
FREI, D., Political Science and International Relations
FREI, P., Ancient History
FREY, H.-J., French Literature
FRIES, U., English Philology
GENINASCA, J., History of French Literature
GOEHRKE, C., East European History
GRISSEMANN, H., Special Psychological Pedagogics
GUNTERT, G., Romance Literature
HAAS, A., German Literature until 1700
HAEFELE, H., Latin Philology
HAGER, F.-P., Historical and Systematic Pedagogy
HEESE, G., Special Pedagogics
HEINTZ, P., Sociology
HENKING, K., Ethnology
HERZOG, U., German Literature to 1700
HILTY, G., Romance Philology
HOFFMANN-NOWOTNY, H.-J., Sociology
HOLZHEY, H., History of Philosophy
HUGHES, P., English and American Literature
ISLER, H. P., Archaeology
JUNG, M. R., History of French and Provençal Literature
KAPLONY, P. G., Egyptology
KELLER, H., General Didactics of Intermediate School Teaching
KELLER, L., History of French Literature
KLOETI, U., Political Science, Domestic Policy
KRAMERS, R., Sinology
LEISI, E., English Philology and Medieval Literature
LOEFFLER, L. G., General Ethnology
LUEBBE, H., Philosophy and Political Theory
LÜTOLF, M., Musicology
MAIER, F. G., Ancient History
v. MATT, P., German Literature since 1700
MAURER, E., History of Art
MEYER, R., Philosophy
MOSER, U., Psychology
NÄNNY, M., English and American Literature
NAUMANN, H.-P., Nordic Philology
OUWEHAND, C., Japanology
PETTER, H., History of English and American Literature
PEYER, H. C., General Economic and Social History, Swiss History
PRIMAS, Mrs. M., Primeval History
REINERT, B., Egyptology, Semitic and Islamic Philology
REINLE, A., History of Medieval Art
SABLONIER, R., Medieval History
SAXER, U., Journalism, Sociology of Art
SCHAUFELBERGER, W., General and Swiss War History
SCHELLER, M., General Philological Science
SCHENDA, R., European Folk Literature
SCHMID, H., Romanic Philology
SCHMIDTCHEN, G., Social Psychology and Sociology
SCHMUGGE, L., Medieval History
SCHOBINGER, J.-P., Philosophy
SENNHAUSER, H. R., Medieval Art
SITTA, H., German Language
SONDEREGGER, S., German Philology
STADLER, P., Modern History
STOLL, F., Practical Industrial and Professional Psychology
STRAUCH, Mrs. I., Clinical Psychology
TAROT, R., History of German Literature
TRÄNKLE, H., Classical Philology
TUGGENER, H., Social Pedagogics
VON USLAR, D., Theoretical Psychology
WEBER, W., Literary Criticism
WIDMER, K., Pedagogy, Pedagogic Psychology
WOODTLI, O., Theory of Intermediate School Teaching
WÜEST, J.-TH., Gallo-Romanic Philology
WYSLING, H., German Literature
ZETT, R., Slavic Philology

*Faculty of Philosophy—II:*
AMANN, P., Mathematics, especially for Natural Scientists
AMMETER, J. H., Inorganic Chemistry
BACHOFFEN, R., General Botany
BAUKNECHT, K., Informatics (Electronic Data Processing)
BIEGERT, J., Anthropology
BILLETER, M. A., Molecular Biology
BIRNSTIEL, M., Molecular Biology
BOLLI, H. M., Geology
BRASSEL, K., Geography
BRINKMANN, D., Experimental Physics
BRUN, E., Experimental Physics
BURLA, H., Zoology and Ecology
CHEN, P. C., Experimental Zoology
CHRISTEN, PH., Biochemistry
COOK, C. D. K., Systematic Botany
DREIDING, A., Organic Chemistry
ENDRESS, P. K., Systematic Botany
ENGFER, R., Experimental Physics
EUGSTER, C., Organic Chemistry
FISCHER, H., Physical Chemistry
FURRER, G., Geography
GABRIEL, P., Mathematics
GROSS, H., Mathematics
GRÜNENFELDER, M., Petrography
GUENTER, J. R., Inorganic Chemistry
GUTTE, B., Biochemistry
HAEFNER, H., Geography
HESS, P., Mathematics
HESSE, M., Organic Chemistry
HOHL, H. R., General Botany, especially Electro-microscopy
HUBER, J. R., Physical Chemistry
HUMBEL, R., Biochemistry
JARCHOW, M., Mathematics
KÄGI, J., Biochemistry
KARRER, G., Mathematics
KELLER, H., Mathematics
KRAMER, C. U., Systematic Botany
KUMMER, H., Zoology
KÜNDIG, W., Experimental Physics
LEEMANN, A., Geography
MEIER, W., Crystallography and Crystal Chemistry
MEYER, Mrs. V., Experimental Physics
MÜLLER, S., Geophysics
NAGASAWA, M., Theory of Probability
NIGGLI, A., Crystal Structure Research
NOETHIGER, R., Genetics
OSWALD, H. R., Inorganic Chemistry
PARISH, R., General Botany
VON PHILIPSBORN, W., Organic Chemistry
RAMSAY, J. G., Geology
RASCHE, G., Theoretical Physics
RAST, Mrs. D., General Botany
RIEBER, H. P., Palaeontology
ROHWEDER, O., Systematic Botany
SCHAFFNER, W., Molecular Biology
SCHARF, G., Theoretical Physics
SCHWARZ, H. R., Numerical Mathematics
STENFLO, J. O., Astronomy
STORRER, H. H., Mathematics
STRASSEN, V., Practical Mathematics
STRAUMANN, N., Theoretical Physics
STREBEL, K., Mathematics
TARDENT, P., Zoology
THELLUNG, A., Theoretical Physics
THOMAS, E., Hydro-biology
THOMPSON, A. B., Petrology
TROMMSDORFF, V., Petrography
TRUOEL, P., Experimental Physics
TRÜMPY, R., Stratigraphy
VISCONTINI, M., Organic Chemistry
WAGNIÈRE, G., Physical Chemistry
WALDMEIER, M., Astronomy
WALDNER, F., Experimental Physics
WANNER, H., General Botany
WEHNER, R., Zoological Physiology
WEISSMANN, CH., Molecular Biology
ZISWILER, V., Zoology

## TECHNICAL UNIVERSITIES

### ÉCOLE POLYTECHNIQUE FÉDÉRALE DE LAUSANNE
33 AVENUE DE COUR,
1007 LAUSANNE
Telephone: 021/47.11.11.

Founded 1853; present status 1969.
Language of instruction: French; State Federal control; Academic year: October to July.

*President:* Prof. BERNARD VITTOZ.
*Vice-President:* Prof. ROLAND CROTTAZ.
*Administrative Director:* P. IMMER.
*Secretary-General:* P.-F. PITTET.
*Library Director:* T. TANZER.

Library of 200,000 vols.
Number of teachers: 126.
Number of students: 2,100.

Publications: *General Prospectus†, Annual Report†*.

HEADS OF DEPARTMENTS:
*Department of Civil Engineering:* Prof. R. FAVRE.
*Department of Agricultural Engineering and Surveying:* Prof. J. C. PIGUET.
*Department of Mechanical Engineering:* Prof. P. SUTER.
*Department of Electrical Engineering:* Prof. J.-D. NICOUD.
*Department of Physics:* Prof. ROLAND FIVAZ.
*Department of Chemistry:* Prof. P. LERCH.
*Department of Mathematics:* Prof. D. DE WERRA.
*Department of Materials:* Prof. A. MOCELLIN.
*Department of Architecture:* Prof. A. DECOPPET.

PROFESSORS:
*Department of Civil Engineering:*
BADOUX, J.-C., Dir., Institute of Steel Structures
BAUMGARTNER, J.-P., Institute of Transportation
BOVY, P., Institute of Transportation
BRUSCHIN, J., Hydraulic Laboratory
BURCKHARDT, M., Architecture
CROTTAZ, R., Roads and Tunnels
DESCOEUDRES, F., Dir., Geotechnical Laboratory
FAVRE, R., Structural Engineering
FREY, FR., Statistics and Materials Resistance
GABUS, J., Dir., Institute of Geology
GARDEL, A., Dir., Institute of Energy Production
GENTON, D., Dir., Institute of Transportation
GRAF, W.-H., Dir., Hydraulic Laboratory
JIROUSEK, J., Statics and Material Resistance
LAFITTE, R., Institute of Energy Production
NATTERER, J., Wood Construction
PERRET, F.-L., Management
PFLUG, L., Dir., Optical Stress Analysis Laboratory
RECORDON, E., Geotechnical Laboratory
SARLOS, G., Institute of Energy Production
SINNIGER, R., Geotechnical Laboratory
STUCKY, J.-P., Waterfall and Irrigation
WALTHER, R., Institute of Structural Engineering

*Department of Agricultural Engineering and Surveying:*
DERRON, G., Law
HOWALD, P., Dir., Institute of Geodesy and Surveying
JACQUET, A., Dir., Institute of Geodesy and Surveying
KOLBL, O., Institute of Photogrammetry
MAYSTRE, Y., Dir., Institute of Environmental Engineering
MISEREZ, A., Dir., Institute of Geodesy and Surveying
PERINGER, P., Biological Engineering
PIGUET, J.-C., Reinforced Concrete and Steel Structures
REGAMEY, P., Institute of Agricultural Engineering

*Department of Mechanical Engineering:*
BOREL, L., Dir., Institute of Thermodynamics and Aerodynamics
BURCKHARDT, C., Dir., Institute of Microtechnics
GIANOLA, J.-C., Institute of Thermodynamics
HENRY, P., Institute of Hydraulic Machinery
MOCAFICO, U., Institute of Hydraulic Machinery
PEDRO, M. DEL, Applied Mechanics
PRUVOT, F., Machine Tool Engineering
ROCH, A., Dir., Institute of Automatic Control
RUSCONI, B., Industrial Law
RYHMING, I., Fluid Mechanics
SPINNLER, G., Engineering Design and Projects of Machine Elements
SUTER, P., Dir., Institute of Thermal Engineering

*Department of Electrical Engineering:*
BUEHLER, H., Dir., Industrial Electronics Laboratory
CHATELAIN, J., Dir., Electrical Machines Laboratory
COULON, F. DE, Signal Processing Laboratory
DESSOULAVY, R., Dir., Electronics Laboratory
FONTOLLIET, P.-G., Dir., Telecommunications Laboratory
GARDIOL, F., Dir., Electromagnetism and Microwaves Laboratory
GERMOND, A., Installations Laboratory
JUFER, M., Dir., Electromechanics Laboratory
MANGE, D., Dir., Switching Circuits Laboratory
MORF, J.-J., Dir., Installations Laboratory
NEIRYNCK, J., Circuit and System Theory
NICOUD, J.-D., Dir., Mini- and Microcomputer Laboratory
ROBERT, PH., Electrical Measurement
ROSSI, M., Electromagnetism and Microwaves Laboratory

*Department of Physics:*
BENOIT, W., Nuclear Engineering Laboratory
BOREL, J.-P., Dir., Experimental Physics Laboratory
BUTTET, J., Experimental Physics Laboratory
CHATELAIN, A., Experimental Physics Laboratory
CHOQUARD, P., Dir., Theoretical Physics Laboratory
CORNAZ, P., Experimental Physics Laboratory
FAIST, A., Theoretical Physics Laboratory
FIVAZ, R., Applied Physics Laboratory
GRUBER, C., Theoretical Physics Laboratory
MARTIN, J., Nuclear Engineering Laboratory
MOOSER, E., Dir., Applied Physics Laboratory
QUATTROPANI, A., Theoretical Physics Laboratory
SCHNEEBERGER, J.-P., Dir., Nuclear Engineering Laboratory

*Department of Chemistry:*
GAUMANN, T., Dir., Institute of Physical Chemistry
GRAETZEL, M., Institute of Physical Chemistry
JAVET, P., Institute of Chemical Engineering I
KOVATS, E., Institute of Technical Chemistry
LERCH, P., Dir., Institute of Electrochemistry and Radiochemistry
PLATTNER, E., Institute of Chemical Engineering I
RENKEN, A., Institute of Chemical Engineering III
VON STOCKAR, U., Institute of Chemical Engineering II

*Department of Mathematics:*
ANDRE, M.
ARBENZ, K.
BOBILLIER, P. A.
CAIROLI, R.
CHATTERJI, S.
CORAY, G.
DESCLOUX, J.
LIEBLING, T.
MATZINGER, H.
NUESCH, P.
RAPIN, C.
RUEGG, A.-F.
DE SIEBENTHAL, J.
STUART, C.-A.
DE WERRA, D.
ZWAHLEN, B.

*Department of Materials:*
CHENE, J.-J., Soldering Metallurgy
KAUSCH, H.-H., Dir., Polymer Laboratory
KURZ, W., General Metallurgy
LANDOLT, D., Chemical Metallurgy and Dir., Institute of Metals and Machines
MOCELLIN, A., Ceramics
PASCHOUD, J., Metallurgy Laboratory
WITTMANN, F., Stone Laboratory

*Department of Architecture:*
AUBRY, F., Architecture
BARMAN, J., Modelling
BASSAND, M., Sociology
BEERLI, C., History of Architecture
BEZENCON, P., Drawing
CSILLAGHY, J., Dir., Built Environmental Research Institute
DECOPPET, A., Professional Organization
FORETAY, P., Architecture
FUEG, F., Architecture
GALANTAY, E., Urban Design
HUBER, J.-W., Industrial Architecture
LAMUNIERE, J.-M., Architecture
PETIGNAT, P., Steel Structures
TSCHUMI, A., Architecture

Van Bogaert, G., Construction
Veuve, L., Regional Planning
Von Meiss, P., Dir. Architectural Experimentation Laboratory
Wasserfallen, C., Regional Planning

Interdisciplinary Units:

**Interdepartmental Institute of Metallurgy, Electron Microscopy:** Dir. Prof. W. Benoit.

**Interdepartmental Institute of Micro-Electronics:** Dir. Prof. M. Ilegems.

**Plasma Physics Research Institute:** Dirs. Prof. F. Troyon, Prof. E. Weibel.

**Pedagogy and Didactics:** Dir. Prof. M. Goldschmid.

**Computer Centre:** Dir. P. Santschi.

**Special Mathematics:** Dirs. Prof. P. Kindler, Prof. M. Ziegenhagen.

## EIDGENÖSSISCHE TECHNISCHE HOCHSCHULE ZÜRICH
(Swiss Federal Institute of Technology)
RÄMISTRASSE 101,
8092 ZÜRICH
Telephone: (01) 256-22-11.

Telegraphic Address:
Polytechnikum Zurich

Founded 1855

Language of instruction: German (some basic lectures are given in French); Federal State control; Academic year: October to July (two semesters).

*President:* Prof. H. Ursprung.
*Rector:* Prof. H. Grob.
*Administrative Director:* Dr. E. Freitag.
*Secretary-General:* Dr. H. Denzler.
*Director of the Library:* Dr. J.-P. Sydler.

Library: see Libraries.
Graphic Art Collection: see Museums.
Number of teachers: 758.
Number of students: 6,494.

Publications: *Program of the SFIT* (bi-annual), *ETH Bulletin* (five times a year).

Deans:

*School of Architecture:* Prof. H. Spieker.
*School of Civil Engineering:* Prof. D. Vischer.
*School of Mechanical Engineering:* Prof. H. Thomann.
*School of Electrical Engineering:* Prof. H. Baggenstos.
*School of Chemistry:* Prof. L. M. Venanzi.
*School of Pharmacy:* Prof. P. Speiser.
*School of Forestry:* Prof. V. Kuonen.
*School of Agriculture:* Prof. L. Le Roy.
*School of Rural Engineering and Surveying:* Prof. H. Flury.
*School of Mathematics and Physics:* Prof. J.-P. Blaser.
*School of Natural Science:* Prof. G. Semenza.

*School of Military Science:* Dir. A. Stutz.
*Courses of Physical Education:* H. Keller.
*Humanities Section:* Prof. J.-F. Bergier.

Full Professors:

*School of Architecture:*
Camenzind, A., Architecture
Corboz, A., History of Town Construction
Gunten, H., von, Statics and Constructions
Hauri, H. H., Statics and Constructions
Henz, A., Architecture and Planning
Hoesli, H. B., Architecture
Huber, B., Architecture and Planning
Hugi, H. R., Statics and Constructions
Jaray, W., Architecture
Jenny, P., Drawing and Painting
Kramel, H. E., Architecture and Construction
Kunz, H., Architecture and Construction Planning
Mörsch, G., Preservation of Old Monuments and Sites
Oswald, F., Architecture
Ronner, H., Architecture and Construction
Schaal, R., Construction
Schnebli, D., Architecture
Spieker, H., Architecture
Vogt, A. M., History of Art

*School of Civil Engineering:*
Bachmann, H., Concrete Constructions
Balduzzi. F., Soil Mechanics
Brändli, H., Traffic Engineering
Dietrich, K., Traffic Engineering
Dracos, Th., Hydraulics
Dubas, P., Statics and Steel Construction
Grob, H., Road and Railway Construction, Tunnelling, incl. Rock Mechanics
Hidber, C., Traffic Planning
Huder, J., Soil Engineering and Soil Mechanics
Lang, H.-J., Soil Engineering and Soil Mechanics
Lendi, M., Law
Maurer, J., Methods of Planning
Menn, Ch., Statics and Construction
Pozzi, A., Construction Management
Rotach, M., Traffic Engineering
Stradal, O., Construction Management
Thürlimann, B., Structural Engineering
Trüeb, E., Water Supplies
Vischer, D., Hydraulics

*School of Mechanical Engineering:*
Anliker, M., Biomedical Technology
Berchtold, M., Thermodynamics and Internal Combustion Engines
Böhni, H., Chemical Engineering
Brauchli, H., Mechanics
Buck, A., Chemical Engineering, Refrigeration and Cryogenics
Chaix, B., Fluid Technology
Epprecht, W., Technology of Industrial Materials
Erismann, Th., Material Testing
Fornallaz. P., Light Engineering
Geering, H. P., Control Engineering
Hälg, W., Reactor Engineering
Krause, H. W., Textile Engineering
Matthias, E., Machine Tools and Production Engineering
Ott, H. H., Elements of Machine Construction
Reissner, J., Metallic Raw Materials
Rösli, A., Material Testing
Rott, N., Fluid Mechanics
Sayir, M., Mechanics

Schumann, W., Mechanics—in French
Schürch, H. U., Lightweight Design
Schweitzer, G., Mechanics
Speidel, M., Physics and Metallurgy
Steiner, M., Engineering Measurements and Automatic Control
Thomann, H. H., Fluid Mechanics
Traupel, W., Thermal Turbo Machines
Trepp, Ch., Chemical Engineering
Wehrli, M., Mechanics
Widmer, F., Chemical Engineering

*School of Electrical Engineering:*
Baggenstoss, H., Electrotechnics
Epprecht, G., Electrotechnology and High Frequency Technics
Glavitsch, H., Electric Power Systems
Guggenbühl, W., Electronic Switches
Kern, H., Design Elements for Mechanical and Electrical Engineering
Kübler, O., Image Science
Leuthold, H., Electrical Economy and Power Plants
Leuthold, P., Telecommunications
Mansour, M., Automatics
Massey, J. L., Digital Information
Melchior, H., Electronics
Moschytz, G., Telecommunications
Reichert, K., Energy Conversion
Schaufelberger, W., Automatics
Zaengel, W., High Voltage Engineering
Zwicky, R., Industrial Electronics and Measurement Technology

*School of Chemistry:*
Anderegg, G., Inorganic Chemistry
Arigoni, D., Special Organic Chemistry
Bauder, A., Physical Chemistry
Bourne, J. R., Chemical Engineering
Carafoli, E., Biochemistry
Dressler, K., Molecular Spectroscopy
Dunitz, J. D., Chemical Crystallography
Ernst, R., Physical Chemistry
Eschenmoser, A., Special Organic Chemistry
Geier, G., Inorganic Chemistry
Günthard, H. H., Physical Chemistry
Gut, R., Inorganic Chemistry
Hartland, S., Chemical Engineering
Ibl, N., Chemical Engineering
Jeger, O., Organic Chemistry
Luisi, P. L., Macromolecular Chemistry
Meissner, J., Polymer Physics
Oth, J., Chemistry
Pino, P., Molecular Chemistry
Primas, H., Physical Chemistry
Richarz, W., Chemical Engineering
Rippin, D., Chemical Engineering
Rys, P., Colour and Textile Chemistry
Schneider, W., Inorganic Chemistry
Schwyzer. R., Molecular Biology
Seebach, D., Chemistry
Semenza, G., Biochemistry
Simon, W., Chemistry
Venanzi, M. L., Inorganic Chemistry
Wild, H., Physical Chemistry
Winterhalter, K. H., Biochemistry
Zollinger, H., Chemistry of Textiles and Dyes
Zuber, H., Molecular Biology

*School of Pharmacy:*
Perlia, X., Pharmaceutics
Speiser, P. P., Composition and Preparation of Drugs
Sticher, O., Pharmacognosy
Waser, P. G., Pharmacology
Weder, H. G., Pharmaceutical Chemistry

*School of Forestry:*
Bittig, B., Forestry
Bosshard, H. H., Wood Technology
Kuonen, V., Forestry Engineering
Kurt, A., Forestry
Marcet, E., Forestry

Richard, F., Soils Physics
Schütz, J.-P., Forestry

*School of Agriculture:*
Bach, R., Soil Science
Bachmann, M., Dairy Technology
Emch, F., Food Processing
Ettlinger, L., Microbiology
Fiechter, A., Microbiology
Heusser, H., Animal Hygiene
Huetter, R., Microbiology
Keller, E., Plant Breeding
Künzi, N., Animal Husbandry
Landis, J., Animal Husbandry
Leisinger, Th., Microbiology
Le Roy, H. L., Biometrics
Neukom, J., Agricultural Chemistry
Nösberger, J., Crop Production
Oertli, J., Plant Nutrition
Onigkeit, D., Agricultural Management
Puhan, Z., Dairy Technology
Schmidt-Lorenz, W., Food Technology
Schürch, A., Animal Nutrition
Solms, J., Chemical Agricultural Technology
Sticher, H., Soil Chemistry
Stranzinger, G., Livestock Breeding
Vallat, J., Agricultural Management

*School of Rural Engineering and Surveying:*
Chaperon, F., Geodesy
Conzett, R., Geodesy
Flury, U., Rural Engineering
Grubinger, H., Rural Engineering, Land and Water Use
Kahle, H.-G., Geodesy
Matthias, N., Geodesy
Schmid, H., Photogrammetry
Schmid, W., Rural Engineering
Schneider, J., Statics and Concrete Constructions
Spiess, E., Cartography

*School of Mathematics and Physics:*
Anderheggen, E., Computer Sciences
Baltensperger, W., Theoretical Physics
Baumgartner, W., Technical Physics
Blaser, J.-P., Physics
Blatter, Ch., Mathematics
Bühlmann, H., Mathematics
Chandrasekharan, K., Mathematics
Constantinescu, C., Mathematics
Dütsch, H. U., Physics of Atmosphere
Eckmann, B., Mathematics
Engeler, E., Computer Sciences
Föllmer, H., Mathematics
Gerber, H. J., Experimental Physics
Graenicher, H., Experimental Physics
Hampel, F., Statistics
Heinrich, F., Experimental Physics
Henrici, P., Mathematics
Hepp, K., Theoretical Physics
Hersch, J., Mathematics—in French
Hofer, H., Experimental High-Energy Physics
Huber, A., Mathematics
Hunziker, W., Theoretical Physics
Jeger, M., Mathematics
Jost, R., Theoretical Physics
Kalman, R. E., Mathematics
Känzig, W., Experimental Physics
Kneubühl, F., Experimental Physics
Knus, M., Mathematics
Kostorz, G., Physics
Lang, J., Experimental Physics
Läuchli, H., Mathematics
Läuchli, P., Computer Sciences
Leisi, H. J., Experimetal Physics
Marti, J., Applied Mathematics
Meier, K., Mathematics
Mislin, G., Mathematics
Moser, J., Mathematics
Nievergelt, J., Computer Science
Olsen, J. L., Experimental Physics
Osterwalder, K., Mathematics
Rössler, M., Operations Research
Schmid, Ch., Theoretical Physics
Siegmann, H.-Ch., Physics
Specker, E., Mathematics
Stammbach, U., Mathematics
Stenflo, J. O., Astronomy
Stiefel, E., Applied Mathematics
Telegdi, V., Physics
Voss, K., Mathematics
Wachter, P., Experimental Physics
Weinberg, F., Operations Research
Wirth, N., Computer Sciences
Zehnder, C. A., Computer Science

*School of Natural Science:*
Ambühl, H., Hydrobiology
Benz, G., Entomology
Bolli, H. M., Geology
Braun, R., Utilization of Waste
Delucchi, V., Entomology
Eppenberger, H. M., Biology
Grandjean, E., Hygiene
Grunenfelder, M., Petrography
Hamer, G., Applied Microbiology
Hess, H., Special Botany
Hsu, K. J., Geology
Kern, H., Special Botany
Koller, Th., Biology
Landolt, E., Geobotany
Lowrie, W., Geophysics
Lukosz, W., Optics
Matile, Ph., Plant Physiology
Meier, W. M., Structure of Crystals
Moor, H., Botany
Mühlethaler, K., Electronic Microscopy
Müller, E., Botany
Müller, F., Geography
Müller, S., Geophysics
Niggli, A., Structure of Crystals
Ramsay, J. G., Geology
Rieber, H., Palaeontology
Ruch, F., Botany, Cytology
Schlatter, Ch., Toxicology
Signer, P., Cosmography
Steiger, R. H., Isotope Geology
Steiner, D., Quantitative Geography
Stumm, M., Hydrobiology
Thompson, A. B., Petrology
Trommsdorff, V., Petrography
Trümpy, R., Geology
Weibel, M., Geochemistry
Würgler, F., Zoology
Wüthrich, K., Biophysics

*Department of General Studies (Philosophy, Literature, Social Sciences and Economics):*
Angehrn, O., Accountancy, Management Economics
Bättig, K., Behavioural Sciences
Bergier, J. F., History
Brem, E., Industrial Organization
Büchel, A., Industrial Organization
Delhees, K. H., Psychology
Feyerabend, P., Philosophy of Science
Fischer, H., Didactic Art and Experimental Psychology
Friedrich, H.-P., Law
Fritsch, B., Economics
Huber, G., Philosophy and Pedagogy
Isella, D., Italian Language and Literature
Jagmetti, R. L., Law
Kempf, R., French Literature
Muschg, A., German Language and Literature
Ris, R., German Language and Literature
Tobler, H. W., History
Ulich, E., Applied and Industrial Psychology
Vickers, B., English Language and Literature
Würgler, H., Economics

Affiliated Institutes:

**Eidgenössische Materialprüfungs- und Versuchsanstalt für Industrie, Bauwesen und Gewerbe** (*Federal Institute for Testing Material and Research*): 8600 Dübendorf, nr. Zürich, and Unterstrasse 11, 9001 St. Gallen.

*Directors:* Prof. Th. Erismann (Pres.), Dr. P. Fink.

**Eidgenössische Anstalt für das forstliche Versuchswesen** (*Federal Forest Experiment Station*): 8903 Birmensdorf, nr. Zürich.

*Director:* Dr. W. Bosshard.

**Eidgenössische Anstalt für Wasserversorgung, Abwasserreinigung und Gewässerschutz** (*Federal Institute for Water Supply, Sewage Purification and Water Pollution Control*): 8600 Dübendorf.

*Director:* Prof. Dr. W. Stumm.

**Eidgenössisches Institut für Reaktorforschung** (*Federal Institute for Reactor Research*): 5303 Würenlingen (Aargau).

*Director:* Prof. H. Gränicher.

**Schweizerisches Institut für Nuklearforschung** (*Swiss Institute for Nuclear Research*): 5234 Villigen (Aargau).

*Director:* Prof. Dr. J. P. Blaser.

## COLLEGES

### HOCHSCHULE ST. GALLEN FÜR WIRTSCHAFTS- UND SOZIALWISSENSCHAFTEN
(St. Gallen Graduate School of Economics, Business and Public Administration)
DUFOURSTR. 50,
9000 ST. GALLEN
Telephone: 071/23 31 35.
Founded 1899.

State control; Language of instruction: German; Academic year: April to March.

*Rector:* Prof. Dr. A. MEIER.

*Vice-Rectors:* Prof. Dr. A. RIKLIN, Prof. Dr. C. KASPAR.

*Administrative Director:* W. AEBERLI.

*Librarian:* R. BISCHOFF.

Number of teachers: 189.

Number of students: 1,999.

Publications: *Vorlesungsverzeichnis* (2 a year), *Studienpläne, Prüfungsvorschriften, Studentenführer, Rektoratsbericht* (annually), *HGS-Information* (quarterly), *St. Galler Hochschulnachrichten* (2 a year), *Broschüre öffentliche Vorlesungen* (2 a year), *Bibliotheksführer, Forschungsdokumentation* (annually), *Aulavorträge.*

HEADS OF DEPARTMENTS:

*Department of Business Administration:* Prof. Dr. E. SOOM.

*Department of Economics:* Prof. Dr. B. SCHIPS.

*Department of Jurisprudence:* Prof. Dr. R. ZÄCH.

*Department of Technology and Natural Sciences:* Prof. Dr. P. FINK.

*Department of Cultural Sciences:* Prof. Dr. A. WILDERMUTH.

PROFESSORS:

ANDEREGG, J., German Language and Literature
BALTENSPERGER, E., Economics
BAUMER, J.-M., Development Policy
BINSWANGER, H. CH., Economics
BRAUCHLIN, E., Business Administration
BRIDEL, Y., French Language and Literature
BUGMANN, E., Economic Geography
CAGIANUT, F., Public Law, Tax Law
DACHLER, P., Psychology
DOPFER, K., Foreign Trade and Development Theory
DRUEY, J. N., Civil and Commercial Law
DUBS, R., Economics
FINK, P., Technology
FISCHER, G., Economics
FONTANA, P., Italian Language and Literature
HALLER, M., Insurance and Business Administration, Risk Management
HANGARTNER, Y., Public Law
HAUG, H., Public Law, Law of Nations
HAUSER, H., Foreign Trade Theory and Policy
HÖHN, E., Public Law, Law of Taxes
INGOLD, F. P., Russian Language and Literature
KASPAR, C., Tourism and Transport Economy
KNESCHAUREK, F., Economics and Statistics
KOLLER, A., Civil Law, Economic, Social and European Law
KRAMER, E., Civil and Commercial Law
KÜNG, E., Economics
LATTMANN, C., Business Administration
LEUENBERGER, T., Modern History
LOEFFEL, H., Mathematics, Statistics
LUTZ, B., Finance Administration
MEIER, A., Economics
MILLER, A., Sociology
NIEVERGELT, E., Information Processing
NYDEGGER, A., Applied Economics and Statistics
OESTERLE, H., Information Processing
PEDRAZZINI, M. M., Civil and Commercial Law
PÜMPIN, C., Business Administration
REETZ, N., Economics
RIKLIN, A., Political Science
SCHIPS, B., Economics
SCHMID, H., Economics
SCHUSTER, L., Banking
SIEBENMANN, G., Spanish and Portuguese Language and Literature
SIEGWART, H., Business Administration
SIK, O., Economic Planning
SOLIVA, C., History of Law
SOOM, E., Operations Research
STAERKLE, R., Business Administration
STÄHLY, P., Operations Research
STIER, W., Empirical Social Research and Applied Statistics
TIMMERMANN, M., Business Administration
TRECHSEL, ST., Criminal Law and Criminal Case Law
TSCHUMI, R., English Language and Literature
ULRICH, H., Business Administration
WEINHOLD, H., Business Administration
WILDERMUTH, A., Philosophy
ZÄCH, R., Civil Law
ZÜND, A., Trusteeship and Auditing

ATTACHED INSTITUTES:

**Swiss Institute for International Economics, Regional Science and Market Research:** Dufourstr. 48, 9000 Saint-Gallen; Dir. Prof. Dr. GEORGES FISCHER.

**Swiss Institute of Courses in Public Administration:** Bodanstr. 4; 9000 Saint-Gallen; Dir. Prof. Dr. YVO HANGARTNER.

**Swiss Research Institute of Small Business:** Dufourstr. 48, 9000 Saint-Gallen; Dir. Dr. HANS JOBST PLEITNER.

**Institute of Insurance Economics:** Dufourstr. 48, 9000 Saint-Gallen; Dir. Prof. Dr. MATTHIAS HALLER.

**Institute of Business Administration:** Dufourstr. 48, 9000 Saint-Gallen; Dir. Prof. Dr. EMIL BRAUCHLIN.

**Institute for Economics Research:** Dufourstr. 48, 9000 Saint-Gallen; Dir. Prof. Dr. HANS CHRISTOPH BINSWANGER.

**Institute for Latin-American Research and for Development Co-operation:** Varnbüelstr. 14, 9000 Saint-Gallen; Dir. Prof. Dr. JEAN-MAX BAUMER.

**Institute of European and International Economic and Social Law:** Bodanstr. 4, 9000 Saint-Gallen; Prof. Dr. ARNOLD KOLLER.

**Institute for Tourism and Transport Economy:** Varnbüelstr. 19, 9000 Saint-Gallen; Dir. Prof. Dr. CLAUDE KASPAR.

**Institute for Agricultural Policy and Law:** Bodanstr. 8, 9000 Saint-Gallen; Dir. Prof. Dr. ERNST JAGGI.

**Institute of Public Finance and Fiscal Law:** Varnbüelstr. 19, 9000 Saint-Gallen; Dir. Prof. Dr. ERNST HÖHN.

**Research Institute for Marketing and Distribution:** Bodanstr. 8, 9000 Saint-Gallen; Dir. Prof. Dr. HEINZ WEINHOLD.

**Institute for Banking:** Bodanstr. 6, 9000 Saint-Gallen; Dir. Prof. Dr. LEO SCHUSTER.

**Institute for the Teaching of Economics:** Guisantr. 9, 9000 Saint-Gallen; Dir. Prof. Dr. ROLF DUBS.

**Institute for Operations Research:** Bodanstr. 6, 9000 Saint-Gallen; Dir. Prof. Dr. PAUL STÄHLY.

---

**Institut pour l'Etude des Méthodes de Direction de l'Entreprise (I.M.E.D.E.)** (*Management Development Institute*): 23 Chemin de Bellerive, CH-1007 Lausanne; f. 1957; one-year M.B.A. course; 19-week course for middle managers; 3-week seminar for senior executives; 3-week seminar and modular seminars for operating managers; and various short-term general management courses.

*Dean:* DEREK F. ABELL.

*Director of Administration:* O. RITZ.

*Registrar for Admissions:* C. DE DOMPIERRE.

*Librarian:* S. FARMANFARMA.

Number of teachers: 20 full-time professors.

Number of students: limited (selective enrolment).

**Textil- und Modeschule:** Vadianstrasse 2, 9000 St. Gallen; f. 1878; school of textile design, lace and embroidery, fashion-designing for textile prints and woven jacquards, and general training for textile industry; attached

to Industrie- und Gewerbemuseum (*q.v.*); 8 teachers; about 100 students; library of 14,000 vols.
Director: A. KÜHNE.

**C. G. Jung-Institut Zürich:** Hornweg 28, CH-8700 Küsnacht; f. 1948; private teaching and research institute for analytical psychology as conceived by C. G. Jung; clinical and professional training programme leading to a Diploma; courses of instruction and seminars in German and English for qualified auditors; special training in child-psychotherapy (for German-speaking students); counselling centre; international picture archive and library.

President: H. BARZ.
Secretary of Studies: P. SCHELLENBAUM, LIC.THEOL.
Publication: *Studies from the C. G. Jung Institute*.
Number of teachers: 30.
Number of students: 340.

## SCHOOLS OF ART AND MUSIC

### ART

**Ecoles d'art de Genève:** 9 Bd. Helvétique, 1205 Geneva; Dir. M. MICHEL RAPPO.

   **Ecole supérieure d'art visuel:** 9 Bd. Helvétique; f. 1748; painting, sculpture, etching, audio-visual depts.

   **Ecole des arts décoratifs:** 15 Bd. James-Fazy; f. 1876; industrial art, interior design, jewellery, ceramics, graphic art.

**Ecole Cantonale des Beaux-Arts et d'Art appliqué:** Ave. de l'Elysée 4, 1006 Lausanne; f. 1821; departments of fine arts, general artistic studies (teaching), graphic design, industrial design; 25 teachers, 120 students; Dean L. PREBANDIER; Dir. J. MONNIER.

### MUSIC

**Académie de Musique:** Geneva; f. 1886.

**Conservatoire et Académie de Musique:** 1700 Fribourg, rue Pierre Aeby 228A; Dir. J.-M. HAYOZ.

**Conservatoire de Musique:** Place Neuve, Geneva; f. 1835; all branches of music, dramatic art and classical ballet; organizes a yearly International Competition for musical performers which attracts young virtuosi of all countries; summer masters courses every two years; 100 teachers, 400 full-time students; Dir. CLAUDE VIALA; Librarian JACQUES HORNEFFER; publ. *Bulletin* (monthly).

**Conservatoire de Musique:** 6 rue du Midi, Lausanne; f. 1861 under the auspices of the State and of the City of Lausanne; 1,300 students; Dir. MICHEL ROCHAT.

**Conservatoire de Musique:** Neuchâtel, Faubourg Hôpital 106; Dir. R. BOSS.

**Konservatorium für Musik in Bern:** Kramgasse 36, Bern; f. 1858; 160 teachers; library of 20,000 vols.; Pres. B. DÄHLER; Dir. U. FRAUCHIGER.

**Konservatorium und Musikhochschule Zürich:** Florhofgasse 6, Zürich 1; f. 1876; controlled by the public authorities; professional school, providing comprehensive musical courses for teachers, performers, conductors, composers, leading to State diplomas; department for children and amateurs; about 150 teachers and more than 3,000 pupils and students; library of *c*. 9,000 vols.; Dir. HANS ULRICH LEHMANN; publ. *Der Bindebogen* (4–5 a year).

**Musik-Akademie der Stadt Basel:** Basel, Leonhardsstrasse 4-6; f. 1867; Number of teachers: 210; Number of students: Musikschule 2,300, Konservatorium and Orchesterschule 340, Schola Cantorum Basiliensis 540, Total 3,180; Dir. Prof. Dr. FRIEDHELM DÖHL.

**Musikakademie Zürich:** Florastrasse 52, CH-8008 Zürich; f. 1891; 40 teachers, 200 full-time students, 550 part-time students; library of 3,000 vols.; Pres. Dr. R. MEYER; Dir. H. U. LEHMANN.

**Musikschule und Konservatorium Winterthur:** Tössertobelstr. 1, CH-8400 Winterthur; f. 1873; 120 teachers, 2,500 students; Dir. WILLI GOHL.

# SYRIA
**Population 8,347,000**

## LEARNED SOCIETIES AND RESEARCH INSTITUTES

**Arab Academy of Damascus:** P.O.B. 327, Damascus; f. 1919; research in Arab-Islamic history; studies in Arabic language and literature and Arabic scientific, technical and cultural terminology; publs. important works of Arab-Islamic heritage; library of 15,000 vols., 1,500 MSS.; Pres. Dr. HUSSNI SABAH; publ. *Majallat Majmaa al-Lughah al-Arabiyyah bi-Dimashq* (Review, quarterly).

Members:

Prof. SHAFIK JABRI
Dr. HIKMAT HASHIM
Dr. KAMIL AYAD
Dr. ADNAN AL-KHATIB
Dr. SHUKRI FAISSAL
Prof. MUHAMMAD AL-MUBARAK
Dr. AMJAD TRABULSI
Prof. WAJIH SAMMAN
Prof. ADBUL-HADI HASHIM
Dr. MICHEL KHOURY
Dr. SHAKIR FAHAM
Dr. M. HAYTHAM KHAYAT
Dr. ABDUL-KARIM YAFI
Prof. A. RATIB NAFFAKH

**Arab Center for the Studies of Arid Zones and Dry Lands (ACSAD):** P.O.B. 2440, Damascus; f. 1971 by the Arab League; studies problems of management conservation and development of agricultural resources, including water, soil, plant and animal resources; emphasis on resources survey and assessment, causes of degradation and desertification, processes of conservation and development, economic evaluation and social implications, proper management through appropriate technologies, technical training, processing and dissemination of pertinent scientific and technical knowledge and information; c. 300 staff, library of 500 vols., 150 periodicals, 5,000 references; Dir.-Gen. Dr. MOHAMED EL-KHASH; publs. annual reports of divisions, technical reports, scientific papers.

**British Council:** Meydani Bldg., Abdul Moneim Riyadh St., West Malki, Damascus; library of 3,624 vols., 47 periodicals; Rep. E. M. MARSDEN.

**Centro Cultural Hispánico:** P.O.B. 224, Damascus; f. 1957; 210 mems.; Spanish-language teaching, conferences, excursions, etc.; library of 5,000 vols.; Dir. EMILIO PÉREZ ACOSTA.

**Institut Français d'Etudes Arabes:** B.P. 344, Damascus; f. 1922; library of 38,000 vols., 350 periodicals; Arabic language, Islamic history, archaeology and geography, Syrian and Middle Eastern economy and society; 22 mems.; Dir. GEORGES BOHAS; Exec. Sec. BERNARD BOTIVEAU; Scientific Sec. JEAN-PAUL PASCUAL; Scientific Librarian JÉRÔME LENTIN; publs. *Bulletin d'Etudes Orientales*† (annually), monographs, translations, and Arabic texts.

**Office de la Recherche Scientifique et Technique Outre-Mer (ORSTOM):** Mission auprès de l'ACSAD, P.O.B. 2440, Damascus; pedology; Dir. P. BILLAUX. (See main entry under France.)

## LIBRARIES

**Al Maktabah Al Wataniah** (*National Library*): Bab El-Faradj, Aleppo; f. 1924; Librarian YOUNIS ROSHDI.

**Al Zahiriah** (*National Library*): Bab el Barid, Damascus; f. 1880, attached to the Arab Academy 1919; national public library; main subjects are Islamic religion and history, Arabic literature, sciences; 85,000 vols., 13,000 MSS., 56,000 periodicals, microfilms of MSS.; dept. of photography; Librarian Mrs. SAMA EL MAHASSINI; publ. *Bulletin* (quarterly).

**Dar al-Kutub al-Wataniah** (*National Library*): Homs.

**National Library of Latakia:** Latakia; f. 1944; 12,000 vols.; Dir. MOHAMAD ALI NTAYFI.

**University of Damascus Library:** Damascus; f. 1919; 150,000 vols.; 1,400 scientific, literary and specialized journals and magazines; Librarian THABET JARI; publs. *Conférences Générales* (annual), *Statistic Collection* (annual).

## MUSEUMS

**Adnan Malki Museum:** Damascus.

**Agricultural Museum:** Damascus.

**Aleppo National Museum:** Aleppo; archaeology; f. 1960.

**Bosra Museum:** Bosra; traditional arts and crafts.

**Deir ez-Zor Museum:** Deir ez-Zor; f. 1974; archaeology; library of 1,000 vols.; Dir. ASSAD MAHMOUD; publ. *Les Annales Archéologiques de Syrie*.

**Hama Museum:** Hama; f. 1956; history and folklore.

**Homs Museum:** Homs-Dar-Al-Thakafa; f. 1974; archaeology, folk and modern art; Curator MAJED EL-MOUSSLI.

**Military Museum:** Damascus.

**Museum of Arabic Epigraphy:** Damascus; f. 1974; Dir. FAYEZ HOMSI.

**National Museum:** Syrian University St., Damascus 4; f. 1919; Sections: Prehistory; Ancient Oriental; Greek, Roman and Byzantine; Arab and Islamic; Modern Art; of special interest is the reconstruction of the Palmyrene Hypogeum of Yarhai (2nd century A.D.), of the Dura Synagogue (3rd century A.D.), of the Umayyad Qasr El-Hair El-Gharbi (8th century A.D.) and of the Damascus Hall (18th century A.D.); houses the Directorate-General of Antiquities and Museums, established by decree in 1947 to conserve Syrian antiquities and to supervise the archaeological museums and the excavations; Dir. Dr. AFIF BAHNASSI; publ. *Les Annales Archéologiques Arabes Syriennes*.

**Palmyra Museum:** Palmyra; f. 1961; archaeological and Syrian desert folklore.

**Popular Traditions Museum:** Qasr el-Azem; Curator CHAFIC IMAM.

**Sweida Museum:** Sweida.

**Tartus Museum:** Tartus; Islamic history.

# UNIVERSITIES

## AL-BAATH UNIVERSITY
P.O.B. 77, HOMS
Telephone: 31440.
Founded 1979.

State control; Language of instruction: Arabic; Academic year begins Sept.
*President:* Dr. ABDUL MAJID CHEIKH HUSSEIN.
*Vice-President:* Dr. GEORGES SHAHOUD.
*Administrative Officer:* SOROUR ABDULLAH.
*Librarian:* Miss AHLAM RAHIMEH.

Library of 6,000 vols.
Number of teachers: 50.
Number of students: 4,050.

### DEANS:

*Faculty of Chemical and Petroleum Engineering:* Dr. MOHAMED ALI SHAAR.
*Faculty of Veterinary Science:* Dr. ABDUL RAZAK SAMIR.
*Faculty of Sciences:* Dr. MOHAMMED SOLIMAN.
*Faculty of Literature:* Dr. AHMED DOUHMAN.
*Faculty of Civil Engineering:* Dr. NADIM SOLIMAN.
*Intermediate Institute of Engineering:* Dr. MOHAMMED HAKMI.

## UNIVERSITY OF ALEPPO
ALEPPO
Telephone: 24660, 24661, 25902.
Telex: ALUNIV 31018 Sy.
Founded 1960.

State control; Languages of instruction: Arabic, French and English; Academic year: October to June.
*Rector:* Dr. MOHAMMAD ALI HOURIEH.
*Vice-Rectors:* Dr. KHALED MAGHOUT (Academic Affairs), Dr. GAZI AL HARIRI (Administrative and Student Affairs).
*Chief Administrator and Secretary:* MOHAMMAD IMAM.
*Registrar:* MAHMUD ELWANI.
*Librarian:* Mrs. SAWSAN MAHDALI.

Number of teachers: 280.
Number of students: 30,205.

### DEANS:

*Faculty of Engineering:* Dr. D. AZOUZ.
*Faculty of Agriculture:* Dr. J. IBRAHIM.
*Faculty of Letters:* Dr. O. DAKKAK.
*Faculty of Medicine:* Dr. B. NASSIF.
*Faculty of Sciences:* Dr. A. H. HADDAD.
*Faculty of Economics and Commerce:* Dr. H. KHAWAJKIA.
*Faculty of Dentistry:* (vacant).

### PROFESSORS:

*Faculty of Engineering:*
AL HASSAN, A. Y., Mechanical Engineering
DIA, T. D., Thermodynamic Engineering
HOURBILI, A. M., Architectural Design
ISSA, F., Public Works, Soil Mechanics
ILIYAS, G., Concrete Construction
JAZMATI, S., Topographical Engineering
KAYALI, M. A., Electronic Engineering
KAZAN, M. N., Thermodynamic Engineering
KHAYATA, M. N., Power Distribution
KOUJA, B. D., Mechanical Engineering
MARTINI, M. W., Urban Architecture
MANSOUR, M., Electrical Engineering

*Faculty of Agriculture:*
AL HARIRI, G., Insects
EL ABIDEEN, N., Lands
HOURIEH, M. A., Organic Chemistry
NAHAL, I., Forestry

*Faculty of Letters:*
DAKKAK, O., Arabic Literature
KABAWA, F. D., Arabic Literature

*Faculty of Medicine:*
AL AKTAA, A. R., Paediatrics
BARAKAT, M., General Surgery
CHIHADE, A., K. Dermatology
DAYEH, S., Orthopaedic Surgery
EL KATEB, B., General and Thoracic Surgery
HAMMANII, A. R., Gynaecology and Obstetrics

*Faculty of Sciences:*
ABDEL MOUHTI, M., Inorganic Chemistry
ABOU BAKER, M., Organic Chemistry (Petroleum)
EL AMIR, Z., Fluid Mechanics
HAMZEH, H. K., Plant Physiology
KHATIB, A., Algebra
MAGHOUT, K., Operations Research
MAKKI, M. B., Physics
RUSTOM, M., Chemistry
SAMAAN, M., Physical Chemistry

*Faculty of Economics and Commerce:*
KHAWAJKIA, H., Economy and Commerce
NAIRABI, M., Economic Sciences and Finance

### ATTACHED INSTITUTES:

**Agricultural Research Centre:** Meselmieh, Aleppo.
**Institute for the History of Arabic Science:** Dir. Prof. A. Y. AL HASSAN.
**Intermediate Institute for Agriculture:** Dir. ZIAD KAYALI.
**Intermediate Institute for Commerce:** Dir. Dr. IBRAHIM SHEIKH BANDAR.
**Intermediate Institute for Engineering:** Dir. Dr. ARAM KARBOUJIAN.
**Intermediate Institute for Medicine:** Dir. Dr. ABOUD ZIYADEH.
**School of Nursing:** Dir. Dr. JAWAD SAOUD.

## UNIVERSITY OF DAMASCUS
DAMASCUS
Telephone: 115103-5, 228623.
Founded 1923.

State control; Language of instruction: Arabic; Academic year: September to June.
*President:* Dr. MOUSTAFA HADDAD.
*Vice-President:* Dr. AS'AD LUTFI.
*General Secretary:* M. FAROUK ABOU AL SHAMAT.
*Registrar:* WALID HARIRI.
*Librarian:* THABIT JARI.

Number of teachers: 955.
Number of students: 56,259.
Publications: *The University Catalogue, Faculty Catalogues, Statistical Collections.*

### DEANS:

*Faculty of Agriculture:* Dr. HAMED MUSOKAR.
*Faculty of Commerce:* Dr. AKRAM SHAKRA.
*Faculty of Dentistry:* Dr. ADNAN MASSASSATI.
*Faculty of Engineering:* Dr. IBRAHIM HOLA.
*Faculty of Mechanical and Electrical Engineering:* Dr. FUAD AZAR.
*Faculty of Fine Arts:* MAHMOUD HAMAD.
*Faculty of Islamic Law:* ABDUL-RAHMAN SABOUNI.
*Faculty of Law:* Dr. ABDULLA TULBA.
*Faculty of Letters:* Dr. IHSAN NUSS.
*Faculty of Medicine:* Dr. MOUNIR BITAR.
*Faculty of Pedagogy:* Dr. GABRIEL BUSHARA.
*Faculty of Pharmacy:* Dr. ABDUL-GHANI MAEL-BARED.
*Faculty of Science:* Dr. GHADIR ZAIZAFOUN.

### PROFESSORS:

*Faculty of Agriculture:*
AHDALI, L., Natural Sciences
AWA, U., Agricultural Science
BAZERBASHI, Dr. A., Field Products
HADAD, CH., Dairy Technology
HAFFAR, Dr. S., Plant Physiology
KATANA, H., Agricultural Sciences
MASSRI, S., Industrial Science
ODEH, Dr. K., Food Chemistry
USTWANI, A., Agricultural Sciences
WAZZAN, Dr. S., Agricultural Economics

*Faculty of Commerce:*
BAKJANI, S., Actuarial Studies
DAHMAN, Dr. F., Political Economy
HASHEM, Dr. H., Business Administration
HAYDAR, Dr. N., Applied Statistics
IMADI, M., Planning and Economics
MURAD, Dr. A., Applied Statistics
SAKKA, Dr. H., Accounting
SATTI, Dr. T., General Administration

*Faculty of Dentistry:*
ANBARI, N., Basic Dental Sciences
DIAB, M., Periodontics
HAKIM, M. A., Prosthodontics
HAMMOUDEH, M. W., Dental Sciences
HAWWASH, F., Oral Pathology
KHURDAJI, M. N., Periodontics
MASSASSATI, Dr. A., Prosthodontics
SHABAN, I., Oral Surgery
TULAIMATT, A., Dental Medicine

*Faculty of Education:*
AKEL, Dr. F., Psychology
LUTFI, A., Education
RIFAII, N., Mental and Experimental Education

*Faculty of Engineering:*
FARRA, N., Architecture
HOLA, I., Civil Engineering
HUSRI, A., Modern Physics

KADDOURA, Dr. A.-R., Physics
RIFAII, Dr. N.-D., Irrigation

*Faculty of Mechanical and Electrical Engineering:*
ASHHAB, M., Technological Engineering
MUHASEB, A., Physics
YOUSEFF, A., Electronics

*Faculty of Fine Arts:*
CHOURA, N., Painting
HAMMAD, M., Fine Arts

*Faculty of Islamic Law:*
ATER, N., Islamic Law
DURAYNI, F., Jurisprudence
FAYDALLAH, Dr. M. F., Jurisprudence
KHATTIB, M. O., Islamic Sciences
RAMADAN, M. S., Jurisprudence
SABOUNI, A., Islamic Jurisprudence
SALEH, M. A., Islamic Law
ZUHAYLI, Dr. W., Jurisprudence

*Faculty of Law:*
ABDEEN, A., Civil Law
BARAKAT, Z., General Law
BASHOUR, I., General Law
GHALI, Dr. K., Constitutional Law
HAKIM, Dr. J., Commercial Law
JARRAH, SH., Private Law
SOIR, Dr. W.-D., Civil and Commercial Law

*Faculty of Letters:*
ABDEL-SALAM, A., Geography
ABDULLAH, Dr. A., English
AKEL, Dr. N., History of Arabic and Islamic Nation
ASHTAR, Dr. A.-K.
AWWA, Dr. A., Islamic Philosophy
BADIR, Dr. A., History
DAYE, M. R., Arabic Literature
DIRKAWI, Dr. A. A., Philosophy and Social Studies
FAHHAM, Dr. SH., Arabic
FARIS, M. KH., History
HAMIDEH, Dr. A.-R., Regional Geography
HANA, G., Philosophy
KASSIM, Dr. B., Metaphysical Philosophy
KHAIR, S., Geography
KHOURY, Dr. M., English Literature
MALEH, GH., English Literature
MUAYAD AZEM, M. S., Philosophy
MUBARAK, Dr. M., Arabic Sciences
MUSSA-BASHA, O., Arabic Literature
NUSS, Dr. I., Pre-Islamic and Islamic Literature
RAFEK, Dr. A.-K., History
RIFAII, Dr. B.-D., French Literature
SABBAGH, L., History
SAFADI, H., History
SHABAN, F., English Literature
SUMHOURI, Z., English Language
TARABEN, Dr. A., Modern History
YAFI, A., Sociology

*Faculty of Medicine:*
ABBASS, A., Oto-rhino-laryngology
ABED, Dr. B., Anaesthesiology
ANBARI, A., Ophthalmology
ANBARI, Dr. R., Paediatrics
ASSWAD, M., Surgery
ATASSI, Dr. J., Psychiatry
ATTAR, Dr. A., Urological Surgery
BABA, Dr. CH., Physiology
BADOURA, Dr. S., Paediatrics
BITAR, Dr. M., Experimental Physiology
DADDAD, M., Diseases of Digestive Tract
DARWISH, Dr. Z., Forensic Medicine
DASHASH, M. D., Industrial Medicine
FAR'OAN, Dr. S., Gynaecology
HAFFAR, B., Parasitology
HAKKI, Dr. I., Gynaecology and Obstetrics
HAKKI, Dr. Z., General Surgery
HAKKIM, Dr. S.-D., Bacteriology
HAMOUDEH, B., Medicine
JABI, Dr. K. W., Histology
JALLAD, Dr. M., Dermatology and Venereal Diseases
KAHHALEH, Dr. R., Physical Medicine
KHATIB, Dr. A.-KH., Anatomy
KHIAMI, M. M., Internal Medicine
KOTOB, Dr. N., Biochemistry
MAHASSIN, Dr. M., Surgery
MAHAYNI, Dr. A., Pharmacology
MAHAYNI, Dr. M., General Surgery
MOURADI, Dr. T., Pathology
MOURAIDEN, Dr. M., Surgery
OTHMAN, Dr. S.-D., Oto-Rhino-Laryngology
RIZIK, Dr. M., Internal Medicine
RUSTUM, S., Surgery
SABBAGH, Dr. F., Psychiatry and Neurology
SAKKA-AMINI, Dr. M., Radiology
SHAMI, M., Surgery
SHAN, T., Chest Diseases
TAKRITI, Dr. A., Bacteriology
TARABISHI, Dr. S., General Surgery
TOGOSE, Dr. N., Surgery

*Faculty of Pharmacy:*
BABA, Dr. Z., Pharmaceutics
DAKKAK, Dr. M., Analytical Chemistry
DALLOOL, Dr. M., Pharmaceutical Chemistry
HAWARI, Dr. M., Pharmaceutical Chemistry
KHAWAM, N., Pharmacology
MAHMALJI, Dr. R., Pharmaceutical Chemistry
MANSOUR, Z., Pharmacology
MOUNAJED, H., Pharmacology
MUNAJED, D., Analytical Chemistry

*Faculty of Sciences:*
ABOU-HARB, Dr. M., Zoology
ABOU KHARMA, D., Botanic Physiology
ABU-SHAHIN, I., Radio and Electronics
AHMAD, KH., Astronomy
AHMAD, Dr. S., Algebra and Statistics
ASSWAD, A., Nuclear Reaction
BAGHDADI, W., Biology
BAIRAKDAR, Dr. N., Vertebrates
BARKOUDA, Dr. Y., Botany
BEIRAKDAR, H., Chemistry
DAABOUL, M., Applied Mathematics
HADAD, I., Solid State Physics
HADDAD, Dr. M., Morphology and Microbiology
HAJ-SAIID, Dr. A., Inorganic Chemistry
HAKKI, Dr. W., Inorganic Chemistry
HAMWI, A., Natural Sciences
HAZZI, Dr. B., Botany
HAMU-LEILA, M., Nuclear Reaction
HOMSI, I., Mathematics
IJEL, F., Geology
ISSA, M., Natural Sciences
JAZAIRY, M., Nuclear Reaction
KASSAM, T., Electrical Engineering
KHATIB, Dr. A., Taxonomy of Angiosperms
JAZAIRY, Dr. S., Organic Chemistry
KALLAWI, Physical Chemistry
KANJO, A., Mathematics
KHIAMI, I., Analytical Chemistry
KHOURY, I., Physical Chemistry
KHOURY, Dr. Y., Geology
KNEISH, H., Nuclear Reaction
KUDSI, M. W., Mathematics
KOTTEB, Dr. Z., Animal Physiology
MANSSOUR, Dr. A.-H., Physical Chemistry
MO'TI, M., Geology
MUKAKE, M., Physical Engineering
RISK, Dr. H., Zoology
ROMANOS, J., Physics
SHAHEED, Dr. W., Atomic Physics
SAMMAN, Dr. A., General Physics
SEIADA, M. G., Geology
SHAKHASHIRO, M., Chemistry
SWEIDAN, Dr. A., Pure Mathematics
TARBADAR, Dr. T., Light
TINTAWI, Dr. A.-GH., Pure Mathematics
ZEISAFOON, GH., Physical Chemistry

## TICHREEN UNIVERSITY
(University of October)
LATTAKIA
Telephone: 12104.

Founded 1971 as University of Lattakia; present name 1977.

Language of instruction: Arabic; Academic year: October to June.

*President:* S. YASSIN.
*Vice-President:* I. JANO.
*Secretary:* M. M. GANEM.
*Librarian:* M. ABDLLAH AL HOCHI.

Number of teachers: 50.
Number of students: 4,695.

DEANS:

*Faculty of Sciences:* Dr. HASSAN ISMAIL.
*Faculty of Agriculture:* ADNAN BALEH.
*Faculty of Arts:* (vacant).
*Faculty of Engineering:* Dr. KHALED HALLAJ.
*Faculty of Medicine:* Dr. ABOU OBEID.

## COLLEGES

**Aleppo Institute of Music:** f. 1955; departments of Eastern and Western music.

**Damascus Oriental Institute of Music:** f. 1950; departments of Eastern and Western music; aims to revive Arab music and preserve Syrian folk dances and tunes.

**Higher Industrial School:** Damascus; f. 1964; mechanical and electrical engineering; 120 students.

**Damascus Institute of Technology:** Airport Motorway, P.O.B. 86; f. 1963; mechanical, production, automobile, electrical engineering, heating and ventilation; library of 6,000 vols.; Dean F. NASSER.

**Institute of Electrical Engineering and Electronics:** f. 1974 with aid from Fed. Repub. of Germany.

**Institute of Technical Training:** Damascus; f. 1978 with aid from Fed. Repub. of Germany; 2-year courses.

# TANZANIA
Population 17,982,000

## LEARNED SOCIETIES

**Alliance Française:** P.O.B. 2566, Dar es Salaam; f. 1961; 50 mems., 850 students; library of 1,500 vols.; Dir. PIERRE TISSOT.

**British Council:** Independence Ave., P.O.B. 9100, Dar es Salaam; Rep. E. C. PUGH.

**East African Literature Bureau, Tanzania:** P.O.B. 1408, Dar es Salaam; f. 1948; Dir. N. L. M. SEMPIRA; Senior Book Production Officer N. SHERALY.

**Goethe-Institut:** P.O.B. 9510, Dar es Salaam; f. 1962; German classes, library and cultural programme.

**Historical Association of Tanzania:** P.O.B. 35032, Dar es Salaam; f. 1966; 2,000 mems.; Chair. G. P. MPANGALA; Sec. Mrs. B. OMARI; publ. *Tanzania Zamani†*, seasonal pamphlets.

**Tanzania Library Association:** P.O.B. 2645, Dar es Salaam; f. 1965 as a branch of the East African Library Association, reorganized 1972 as an independent body; 200 mems.; Chair. F. K. TAWETE; Sec. J. J. MASSAWE; publs. *Someni* (2 a year), *Matukio* (Newsletter, irregular).

**Tanzania Society:** Box 511, Dar es Salaam; f. 1936; a non-profit society catering for the geographical, ethnological, historical, and general scientific interests of Tanzania; c. 1,200 mems.; publ. *Tanzania Notes and Records†* (bi-annually).

## RESEARCH INSTITUTES

**Animal Production Research and Training Institute:** Private Bag, Mpwapwa, Dodoma; f. 1905; certificate and diploma courses in breeding and nutrition of livestock; library of 500 vols., 25 periodicals; Dir. A. M. MACHA; publs. *Annual Report†*, *Progressive Stockman†* (quarterly).

**East African Institute of Malaria and Vector-borne Diseases:** P.O.B. 4, Amani, Tanga; f. 1949; investigation into human vector-borne diseases, especially malaria, filariasis, plague and onchocersiasis; Dir. Dr. S. TEMU (acting); publ. *Annual Report†*, occasional research publs.†.

**East African Institute for Medical Research:** P.O.B. 162, Mwanza; f. 1949; investigations into various tropical diseases with emphasis on bilharziasis, and hookworm in East Africa; Dir. Dr. V. M. EYAKUZE; publ. *Annual Report*.

**Forest Division Headquarters:** P.O.B. 426, Dar es Salaam; forest surveying, mapping, industrial development, economics, management and education; library of 2,500 vols.; Dir. E. M. MNZAVA.

**Geology and Mines Division:** Ministry of Water, Energy and Minerals, P.O.B. 903, Dodoma; f. 1925; regional mapping, mineral exploration and assessment; supporting laboratory facilities; library of 3,300 text books, 1,700 bound vols.; reprints and maps; Principal Geologist D. J. CHAO; publs.† *Bulletins*, *Memoirs*, *Annual Reports*, *Records of the Geological Survey of Tanzania*, *Reprints*, *Geological Maps*.

**Institute of Kiswahili Research:** P.O.B. 35110, Dar es Salaam; f. 1970; initiates fundamental research and co-operates with Governments and other public authorities and organizations; promotes the standardization of orthography and the development of language generally; preparing new standard dictionary; Dir. A. M. KHAMISI, M.PHIL.; publs. *Kiswahili†*, *Mulika* (2 a year), Supplements.

**Silviculture Research Institute:** P.O.B. 95, Lushoto; f. 1951; 40 staff; library of 1,800 vols.; Officer-in-Charge L. NSHUBEMUKI; publs. *Technical Notes†*, *Tanzania Silviculture Research Notes†* (quarterly).

**Sisal Research Station (Mlingano):** Ministry of Agriculture, Tanzania, Private Bag, Ngomeni, Tanga; f. 1935; research on cultivation of sisal and other crops; Dir. J. SAMKI.

**Tanzania National Scientific Research Council:** P.O.B. 4302, Dar es Salaam; f. 1968; advises the government on all aspects of research; executive functions: co-ordinates all research in the country, promotes documentation and dissemination of information on research, collaborates with other research organizations; library of 3,000 vols.; Chair. Prof. A. C. MASCARENHAS; Dir.-Gen. Prof. H. Y. KAYUMBO.

**Tropical Pesticides Research Institute:** P.O.B. 3024, Arusha; f. 1962; research into tropical pests, including medical and veterinary carriers of disease, insect pests and weeds in agricultural crops; Dir. Dr. M. E. MATERU; publ. *Annual Report*.

## LIBRARIES

**Agricultural Department Library:** P.O.B. 159, Zanzibar; agriculture in general; 1,100 vols., 50 periodicals.

**American Center Library—U.S. International Communication Agency:** P.O.B. 9170, Dar es Salaam; f. 1959 as USIS Library; 5,500 vols.; Dir. G. K. NAGRI.

**British Council Library:** P.O.B. 9100, Dar es Salaam; f. 1952; 13,863 vols., 79 periodicals; Librarian Miss O. FERNANDES.

**Ladha Maghji Indian Public Library:** P.O.B. 70, Mwanza; 3,000 vols.; Librarian C. B. VYAS.

**Museum Library:** P.O.B. 116, Zanzibar; free public lending service; 3,000 vols. and 41 periodicals.

**National Archives:** India/Chusi St., P.O.B. 2006, Dar es Salaam; f. 1963; German and British Colonial archives, post-independence archives; Dir. M. H. NASSOR; publs. *Annual Report*, *Guide to Archives*.

**Tanzania Information Services Library:** Dar es Salaam; reference books on Tanzania, journalism, photography, social sciences, geography and history; newspapers and periodicals.

**Tanzania Library Service:** P.O.B. 9283, Dar es Salaam; f. 1964; operates the following services:

    **National Central Library:** Dar es Salaam; Documentation Services, Dar es Salaam; public libraries in Arusha, Bukoba, Iringa, Kahama, Korogwe, Mbeya, Morogoro, Moshi, Mwanza, Mtwara, Njombe, Shinyanga, Tabora and Tanga; rural library extension service in five regions; book box exchange service; school library service including mobile service; postal library service; certificate training course; book publishing and translation programme; total stock: 1,000,000 vols.; Dir. E. E. KAUNGAMNO, B.A., M.L.S.

**University of Dar es Salaam Library:** P.O.B. 35092, Dar es Salaam; f. 1961; legal deposit library; 350,000 vols.; Chief Librarian M. K. S. MVAA.

**Zanzibar Government Archives:** P.O.B. 116, Zanzibar; history and administration; 3,500 vols.; Archivist SAIS HILAL EL-BAULY.

## MUSEUMS

**National Museum of Tanzania:** P.O.B. 511, Dar es Salaam; f. 1937 as King George V Memorial Museum, name changed 1963; ethnography, archaeology and history; houses the *Zinjanthropus* skull and other material from Olduvai Gorge and other Stone Age sites; also houses reference library; village museum and mobile museum for Education Service; branch museum of political history at Arusha; Dir. Dr. F. T. MASAO; publs. *Annual Report*†, occasional papers†.

**Zanzibar Government Museum:** P.O.B. 116, Zanzibar; local collection, items relating to exploration in East Africa; library; Archivist and Curator SAIS HILAL EL-BAULY.

## UNIVERSITY AND COLLEGES

### UNIVERSITY OF DAR ES SALAAM
P.O.B. 35091, DAR ES SALAAM
Telephone: 49192.

Founded 1961; University status 1970; Unesco-aided.

Language of Instruction: English; Academic year: July to May (four terms).

*Chancellor:* President JULIUS K. NYERERE, M.A.

*Vice-Chancellor:* N. A. KUHANGA, M.A.

*Chief Academic Officer:* Prof. I. N. KIMAMBO, M.A., PH.D.

*Chief Administrative Officer:* M. J. KINUNDA, B.SC., M.A.

Library: see Libraries.
Number of teachers: 793.
Number of students: 2,678.

Publications: *Calendar, Prospectus, Research Bulletin, Annual Report.*

#### DEANS:

*Faculty of Law:* Prof. G. M. FIMBO, LL.M.
*Faculty of Arts and Social Sciences:* Prof. G. R. V. MMARI, M.A., PH.D.
*Faculty of Science:* A. M. NIKUNDIWE, M.SC., PH.D.
*Faculty of Medicine:* Prof. A. S. MWANKEMWA, M.B., CH.B.
*Faculty of Agriculture, Forestry and Veterinary Science:* A. B. LWOGA, PH.D.
*Faculty of Engineering:* Prof. A. S. MAWENYA, M.SC., PH.D.
*Faculty of Commerce and Management:* Prof. K. L. EDWARDS, M.B.A.

#### PROFESSORS AND HEADS OF DEPARTMENT:

AGH, A., Institute of Development Studies (Prof.)
BAPAT, P., Electrical Engineering (Prof.)
CHOWDHURY, M. S., Soil Science (Prof.)
DARKOH, M. B. K., Geography (Prof.)
DESHPANDE, B. G., Geology (Prof.)
FOOTE, R. J., Rural Economy (Prof.)
HAQ, A., Food Science
HAULI, J. G., Psychiatry
HAVE, H., Agricultural Engineering and Land Science
HIGHAM, ST. C., Foreign Languages and Linguistics
HIZA, P. F., Surgery
INNS, F., Agricultural Engineering (Prof.)
JENGO, E., Art, Music and Theatre
KAMENJU, G., Literature
KAMUZORA, H. L., Biochemistry
KANYWANYI, J. L., Law
KARASHANI, J. T., Anatomy and Histology
KATEGILE, J. A., Animal Science
KILAMA, W. L., Parasitology, Entomology
KIMAMBO, I. N., History (Prof.)
KIMATI, V. P., Child Health
KITUNDU, P. A., Traditional Medicine
KLEM, G. S., Forestry (Prof.)
KOMBO, C. L., Veterinary Science
KUMAR, U., Law (Prof.)
LEMA, R. A., Haematology
LWAKABAMBA, S. B., Mechanical Engineering
MABELE, R. B., Economic Research Bureau
MAGANGA, C., Kiswahili
MAKENE, W. J., Medicine (Prof.)
MALIMA, K., Economics (Prof.)
MASCARENHAS, A. C., Bureau of Resource Assessment and Land Use Planning
MASENGE, M. W. P., Mathematics
MASSAWE, A. E. J., Medicine
MLAY, W. F. L., Geography
MMARI, G. R. V., Education (Prof.)
MONYO, J. H., Crop Science
MORIS, J., Agricultural Education and Extension (Prof.)
MSANGI, A. S., Zoology and Marine Biology (Prof.)
MSHIGENI, K. E., Botany
MSUYA, E. A., Rural Economy
MSUYA, P. M., Biochemistry (Prof.)
MTIMAVALYE, L. A. R., Gynaecology
MUSHI, S. S., Political Science
MUTOKA, C. K., Clinical Chemistry
MWALUKO, G. M. P., Pharmacology
NDAALIO, G., Chemistry
NHONOLI, A. M., Medicine
NIELINGER, H., Electrical Engineering (Prof.)
NKOMA, J. S., Physics
NTAMILA, M. S., Chemistry (Prof.)
OMARI, C. K., Sociology
PARKER, N. A., Civil Engineering
PHILIP, P. J., Surgery
POCS, T., Crop Science (Prof.)
PRASAD, G. S., Geology
PRASAD, J., Statistics
RWEYAMAMU, A. H., Political Science
RYALL, P. C., Civil Engineering (Prof.)
SALEH, M. I., Management and Administration
SARUNGI, P. M., Orthopaedics and Traumatology
SCHILLER, E. J., Hydrology
SHABA, J. K., Pathology
SHARMA, S. K., Ophthalmology
SHERIFF, M. A., History
SHIJA, J. K., Surgery
SWAHNEY, A. N., Microbiology and Immunology (Prof.)
TAKULIA, H. D., Behavioural Sciences
TANDON, Y., Political Science (Prof.)
TUCKER, R., Veterinary Science (Prof.)
URIYO, P. A., Agricultural Chemistry and Soil Science
VITTA, P. B., Physics (Prof.)
YORK, P., Pharmacy

#### ATTACHED INSTITUTES

**Institute of Development Studies:** P.O.B. 35169, Dar es Salaam; Dir. Prof. J. H. J. MAEDA, M.PHIL., PH.D.

**Institute of Kiswahili Research:** see Research Institutes.

**Institute of Marine Sciences:** P.O.B. 668, Zanzibar; f. 1950 as East African Marine Fisheries Research Organization; postgraduate studies and research; Dir. Prof. A. S. MSANGI, B.SC., PH.D.

---

**College of Business Education:** P.O.B. 1968, Dar es Salaam; f. 1965; 36 teachers; 1,050 students; Dir. T. F. MBANGULLA, M.A.

**College of National Education:** P.O.B. 533, Korogwe, Tanga Region; 121 students; Principal F. D. NTEMO.

## TANZANIA

**Dar es Salaam Technical College:** P.O.B. 9182, Dar es Salaam; f. 1956; 125 staff; 1,000 students.

**Eastern and Southern African Management Institute:** P.O.B. 3030, Arusha; f. 1974, reconstituted 1980 to serve Angola, Botswana, Comoros, Djibouti, Ethiopia, Kenya, Lesotho, Malawi, Mauritius, Mozambique, Somalia, Sudan, Swaziland, Seychelles, Tanzania, Uganda, Zambia, Zimbabwe; library of 5,000 vols., 7,000 pamphlets; 16 consultants and advisers; in-service training, postgraduate diploma course; Dir. Prof. J. J. OKUMU, M.A., PH.D.; publs. occasional papers, conference proceedings.

**Kivukoni College:** P.O.B. 9193, Dar es Salaam; f. 1961; residential courses for adults in Politics, Economics, History, Sociology, Public Administration and Industrial Relations; controlled by the Central Committee of TANU and subsidized by the Tanzanian Government; Principal P. J. MHAIKI; 150 students; publ. *Mbioni* (monthly).

**Usambara Trade School:** Lushoto; f. 1961; 70 students.

# THAILAND

Population 46,455,000

## LEARNED SOCIETIES AND RESEARCH INSTITUTES

**Alliance Française de Bangkok:** 29 Sathon Tai Rd., Bangkok 12; f. 1912; French language and culture; 500 mems.; 1,200 students attending language courses; library of 10,000 vols.; cinema, concerts and exhibitions; Dir./Sec.-Gen. EMILE MANTICA; publ. *Bulletin mensuel*†.

**Applied Scientific Research Corporation of Thailand:** 199 Phahonyothin Rd., Bangkok; operates as principal research agency of Government under Act of Parliament of 1963.
*Governor and Chairman:* WADANYU NATHALANG.
*Expert Consultants:* Dr. SANGA SUBHASRI, KRIT SOMBATSIRI, BANCHA LUMSUM, SOMPORN PUNYAGUPTA.
Administers the following:
*Industrial Research Department:* Dir. Dr. MALEE SUNDHAGUL.
*Agricultural Research Department:* Dir. PRAPANDH BOONKLINDAJORN.
*Project Research Department:* Dir. NITASNA PICHITAKUL.
*Economic Research Department:* Dir. Dr. LUMDUAN MAPRASERT.
*Building Research Department:* Dir. PONGPUN VORASUNTHAROSOTH.
*Testing and Standard Department:* Dir. SIRI NANDHASRI.
*Environmental and Ecological Department:* Dir. Dr. SERMPOL RATASUK.
*Thai National Documentation Department:* see below.

**Asia Foundation:** P.O.B. 1910, Bangkok 5; one of 12 branches of the main organization in the U.S.A. (*q.v.*); to assist local institutions and organizations concerned with educational and socio-economic development; Rep. WILLIAM D. EVANS.

**British Council:** 428 Rama I Rd., Siam Square 2, Bangkok 5; library: see Libraries; Rep. Miss A. B. LAMBERT, O.B.E.

**Buddhist Research Centre:** Wat Benchamabopitr, Bangkok; f. 1961; sponsored by Department of Religious Affairs, Ministry of Education; publ. *Pali-Thai-English Dictionary*, vol. 1.

**Department of Mineral Resources:** Ministry of Industry, Rama VI Rd., Bangkok; geological mapping, mineral prospecting, mining, mineral dressing and metallurgical research; Dir.-Gen. Dr. PRABHAS CHAKKAPHAK.

**Department of Science:** Rama VI St., Bangkok 4; f. 1891; research in food technology, industrial fermentation, pulp and paper raw materials, chemical engineering processes, air and water pollution control, industrial standards and specifications, testing and analysis services; staff of 503; library: see Libraries; Dir.-Gen. Dr. PRAPRIT NA NAGARA; publs. *Annual Report, Bulletin* (monthly and every 4 months).

**Fisheries Technology Section:** Division of Research and Investigation, Dept. of Fisheries, Ministry of Agriculture and Co-operatives, Bangkok; f. 1954; fish handling, processing and utilization; Head of Section Mrs. BANG-ORN SAISITHI.

**Forest Products Research Division:** Royal Forest Dept., Ministry of Agriculture and Co-operatives, 61 Paholyothin Rd., Bangkhen, Bangkok 9; f. 1935; timber and forest products utilization and research; staff of 124; Dir. of Division KASSPA AGANIDAD; library of 12,000 vols.

**Goethe-Institut** (*German Cultural Institute*): 102/1 Phra Athit Rd., Bangkok; f. 1960; cultural activities and language courses; library of *c.* 10,000 vols.; Dir. Dr. KLAUS NEUSER.

**Marine Biology Centre:** Marine Fisheries Division, 89/1 Sapanpla, Yanawa, Bangkok 12; f. 1968; research and the training of marine biologists; Dir. DEB MENASWETA.

**Medical Association of Thailand:** 3 Silom St., Bangkok; f. 1921; 3,057 mems.; Pres. Prof. Dr. SONGKRANT NIYOMSEN, M.D., DR.MED.; Hon. Sec. Prof. Dr. SANONG UNAKOL; publ. *Journal*.

**Office of the Atomic Energy Commission for Peace:** Srirubsook Rd., Bangkhen, Bangkok 9; f. 1961; staff of 180; Sec.-Gen. Dr. SVASTI SRISUKH; library of 6,100 vols., 280 periodicals; publ. *Thai AEC 1-76*.

**Royal Institute:** Thanon Na Phra That, Bangkok 2; f. 1933 for the investigation and encouragement of all branches of knowledge, the exchange of knowledge and for advice to the Government; 91 mems.; 10,250 vols.; Pres. Prof. Dr. SERM VINICCHAYAKUL; Vice-Pres. Dr. BOONBHRUGSA CHATAMRA; Sec.-Gen. Prof. Dr. CHAI MUKTABHANT; publs. *Saranukrom Thai* (monthly instalments), *Journal of the Royal Institute*.

**Rubber Research Centre:** Hat Yai, Songkhla, Dept. of Agriculture, Ministry of Agriculture, Bangkok.

**Science Society of Thailand:** Library Building, Faculty of Science, Chulalongkorn University, Phya Thai Rd., Bangkok; f. 1948; aims to encourage education and investigation in all branches of science; *c.* 2,000 mems.; Pres. Dr. KAMCHORN MANUNAPICHU; Sec.-Gen. Dr. PRACHOTE PLENGVIDHYA; Librarian Miss MANEE CHANDAVIMOL; publs. *Journal* (quarterly), *Science* (monthly).

**Siam Society** (formerly the Thailand Society): 131 Soi Asoke, Sukhumvit 21, P.O.B. 65, Bangkok; f. 1904; under royal patronage; *c.* 1,500 mems.; for the investigation and encouragement of art, science and literature of Thailand and neighbouring countries; Pres. M. R. PATANACHAI JAYANT; Hon. Sec. Dr. CHITRIYA TINGSABADH; library of 25,000 vols.; publs. *Journals, Index to the Journal, Natural History Bulletins*.

**Thai Library Association:** c/o National Library, Ta-Vasukri, Bangkok 3; f. 1954; 1,524 mems.; Pres. R. INTARAKUMHANG; Sec. N. PUAKPONG; publs. *T.L.A. Bulletin, The World of Books*.

**Thai-Bhara Cultural Lodge** (f. 1940) and **Swami Satyananda Puri Foundation Library** (f. 1942): 136/1 Siriphongs Rd., Bangkok; 450 mems.; the Swami Satyananda Foundation Library contains 5,500 vols.; Hon. Pres. Phya AUMAN RAJADHON; Hon. Sec. Pandit RAGHUNATH SHARMA; classes conducted in Sanskrit, English,

Hindi, Thai, and on comparative Indio-Siamic topics, comparative philosophy and religion, exegesis of Hindu scriptures.

**Unesco Regional Office for Education in Asia and Oceania:** C.P.O.B. 1425, Bangkok; f. 1961; a base for supporting and planning operational action for the development and reform of education in this area; carries out regional projects in support of national programmes and provides advisory services to the member states in Asia and Oceania; stimulates educational innovations relevant to developmental needs by inter-country co-operation and by the network of associated national centres and development groups; library of 65,000 documents; clearing house service collects information on education in Asia and makes this available to governments, institutions and educational workers; attached are the clearing house service for population education and resource material units for the Asian Centre of Educational Innovation for Development; also office of Regional Advisers for Social Sciences and Culture; 35 staff; Dir. RAJA ROY SINGH; publs. *Bulletin*† (annual), *Education in Asia*† (reviews, reports and notes, 2 a year), *Statistical Review of Education, ACEID Newsletter, Population Education Newsletter, Educational Building Reports and Digests, List of Publications*, staff papers, reports, instructional materials, etc.

## LIBRARIES AND ARCHIVES

**Asian Institute of Technology Library and Regional Documentation Centre:** P.O.B. 2754, Bangkok; 110,000 vols., 900 periodicals; four information centres in: geotechnical engineering, ferrocement, renewable energy resources, environmental sanitation; Dir. JACQUES VALS, PH.D.

**British Council Library:** 428 Rama I Rd., Bangkok 5; f. 1953; 27,357 vols., 75 periodicals; Librarian J. D. ARMSTRONG.

**Chulalongkorn University Library:** Phya Thai Rd., Bangkok 5; f. 1910; 180,000 vols.; Librarian Mrs. KNID TANTAVIRAT, M.S.L.S.; publs. *Academic Resources Journal, Union Catalogue*.

**Library of the Department of Science:** Rama VI St., Bangkok 4; f. 1918; c. 150,000 vols.; Senior Librarian Miss TWEELAK BOONKONG, B.SC.

**Main Library, Kasetsart University:** Bangkok 9; f. 1943; 83,000 vols.; Librarian Miss DARUNA SOMBOONKUN, M.A., M.L.S.; publ. *Kasetsart Journal*† (irregular); *Proceedings of the National Conference on Agricultural and Biological Science* (irregular).

**National Archives Division:** Fine Arts Department, Samsen Rd., Bangkok 3; f. 1952; 4,783 reference books, 58 periodicals, 113,104 dossiers of public and personal records; also maps, photos, tape recordings, etc.; Dir. Mrs. CHOOSRI SWASDISONGKRAM; publ. *Silpákon* (bi-monthly).

**National Library:** Samsen Rd., Bangkok 3; f. 1905; 896,671 vols., 184,075 MSS., 2,367 periodicals; deposit library; controls International Serials Data System (ISDS—Thailand), International Serials Data System Regional Center for Southeast Asia (ISDS-SEA) and National Libraries and Documentation Center of Southeast Asia Consortium (NLDC-SEA, Thailand); Chief Librarian Mrs. KULLASAP GESMANKIT; publs. *National Bibliography, ISDS-SEA Bulletin*.

**Neilson Hays Library:** 195 Suriwongse Rd., Bangkok; f. 1869; Pres. Lady JENNIFER HOLT; Librarian Mom Rajwongse NAPACHARI SIRISINHA.

**Siriraj Medical Library:** Dhonburi, Bangkok 7; 85,000 vols.; Librarian U. DHUTIYABHODHI, B.A., M.S.

**Sri Nakharinwirot University Library:** Bangkok; f. 1954; 95,217 vols.; member ASHAIL; audio-visual centre; Head Librarian Dr. SOONTHORN KAEWLAI; brs. in Bang Saen, Patoom Wan, Pitsanuloke, Mahasarakam, Songkla, Pra Nakorn; publs. *Education in Thailand—a bibliography, Games in the Classroom*.

**Thai National Documentation Department:** 196 Phahonyothin Rd., Bang Khen, Bangkok 9; f. 1961; documentation services to science and technology; Dir. Mrs. CHALERMVARN-CHOOSUP.

**Thammasat University Library:** Bangkok 2; f. 1933; social sciences and humanities; 360,810 vols., 1,303 periodicals; Librarian Mrs. PHAKAIVAN CHIAMCHAROEN.

**United Nations Economic and Social Commission for Asia and the Pacific Library:** United Nations Bldg., Rajdamnern Ave., Bangkok 2; Librarian ALLAN F. WINDSOR.

**U.S. International Communication Agency Library:** 9 Sadaw Rd., Amphur Muang, Songkla; information on U.S.A.

## MUSEUM

**National Museum:** Na Phra-dhart Rd., Bangkok 2; f. 1926; prehistoric artefacts, bronze and stone sculptures, costumes, textiles, ancient weapons, coins, wood-carvings, ceramics, royal regalia, theatrical masks and dresses, marionettes, shadow-play figures, funeral chariots, illustrated books, musical instruments; Dir. Mrs. CHIRA CHONGKOL; publs. *Guide to the National Museum, Official Guide to Ayutthaya and Bang Pa-in, Guide to Old Sukhothai, Thai Cultural Series*, etc.

## UNIVERSITIES AND TECHNICAL INSTITUTES

### ASIAN INSTITUTE OF TECHNOLOGY

P.O.B. 2754, BANGKOK

Telephone: 5168311/21/31.

Founded 1959.

Independent graduate school, open to graduates from all Asian countries; 2-term (8 months) course leading to Diploma; 5-term (20 months) course leading to a Master's degree; further 2 years leading to Doctor's degree; language of instruction: English.

*President:* ROBERT B. BANKS, PH.D.

*Vice-President for Academic Affairs:* M. NAWAZ SHARIF, PH.D.

*Vice-President for Development:* RICARDO P. PAMA, PH.D.

*Vice-President for Administration:* K. R. LONG, B.A.

*Academic Secretary:* F. J. STEPHENS, B.A., B.ECON.

Library: see Libraries.

Number of teachers: 70.
Number of students: 600.

Publications: *Prospectus, Catalog, Research Summary* (annual), *Review* (quarterly).

CHAIRMEN OF DIVISIONS:

ANGEL, S., PH.D., Human Settlements Development
HOSKING, R. J., PH.D., Computer Applications
JONES, J. H., M.S., Geotechnical and Transportation Engineering
KARASUDHI, P., PH.D., Structural Engineering and Construction
SAUNIER, G. Y., PH.D., Energy Technology

UNIVERSITIES AND TECHNICAL INSTITUTES                                                                                                THAILAND

SINGH, G., PH.D., Agricultural and Food Engineering
THANH, N. C., PH.D., Environmental Engineering
VAN OUDHEUSDEN, D. L., M.S., PH.D., Industrial Engineering and Management
VONGVISESSOMJAI, S., M.E., D.ENG., Water Resources Engineering

DIRECTORS:

*Continuing Education Center:* Dr. N. C. AUSTRIACO.
*English Language Centre:* Dr. M. J. MURPHY.
*Library and Regional Documentation Center:* Dr. J. VALLS.
*Regional Computer Center:* Dr. J. A. KEARNS.

## CHIANG MAI UNIVERSITY
CHIANG MAI
Telephone: 221699, 221688.
Founded 1964.

Languages of instruction: Thai and English; State control; Academic year in two semesters.

*Chancellor:* B. MARTIN, M.D.
*Rector:* T. KANGWANPONGSE, M.D.
*Vice-Rectors:* C. ORALRATMANEE, PH.D., K. SWASDIO, M.D., P. WORAURAI, PH.D., P. THITASUT, M.SC., M.D.
*Registrar:* Mrs. S. MEESIRI, M.ED.
*Librarian:* Mrs. S. SUCHINDA, M.S.

Number of teachers: 1,259.
Number of students: 9,573.

Publications: *University Announcement, Chiang Mai Wechasarn, Chiang Mai University Review, Nakorn Chiang Mai Hospital Gazette, General Information, Nursing Newsletter, University Catalogue, Bulletin, Faculties Gazettes.*

DEANS:

*Faculty of Humanities:* R. CHIRANUKROM.
*Faculty of Social Sciences:* R. SIRIMATAYA, B.A.
*Faculty of Science:* U. SRIYOTHA, SC.D.
*Faculty of Medicine:* A. SRISUKRI, M.D.
*Faculty of Agriculture:* D. TIYAWALEE, PH.D.
*Faculty of Education:* C. KREGMATUKORN, M.ED.
*Faculty of Engineering:* S. YOTABOOTR, M.S.
*Faculty of Nursing:* P. SWASDIRAKSA, M.S.
*Faculty of Dentistry:* P. KOTRAJARUS, M.S.
*Faculty of Pharmacy:* S. PANYARAJUN, PH.D.
*Faculty of Technical Medicine:* C. SAENG-UDOM, M.D.
*Graduate School:* P. CHIOWANICH, PH.D.

HEADS OF DEPARTMENTS:

*Faculty of Humanities:*
ARPAKORN, R., PH.D., History
DEJCHAI, S., M.ED., Psychology
LIKHITANONTA, PH.D., Thai
LUMPAOPONG, P., D.U., Modern Languages
PANTUPRAYOON, P., M.ED., Human Relations
SALADYRNANT, T., M.A., Library Science
SUPAKA, Y., M.A., Mass Communication
TIYAPORN, W., M.A., English

*Faculty of Social Sciences:*
KEAWINGKEO, S., M.A., Political Science
PANDEE, P., M.SC., Geography
PREMCHIT, S., M.A., Sociology and Anthropology
RUANGPHONG, C., M.A., Accounting and Business Administration
SHUSUWAN, T., M.A.I., Economics

*Faculty of Science:*
EHMSRITONG, S., M.S., Mathematics
KLUNKLIN, G., PH.D., Chemistry
SOKCHOTIRATANA, M., M.SC., Biology
SUPRIYASILP, V., PH.D., Statistics
TANTISUKIT, C., M.SC., Geology
TUNKASIRI, T., PH.D., Physics

*Faculty of Medicine:*
BALANKURA, O., F.I.C.S., Surgery
DAMRONGSAK, D., Paediatrics
DISYAVANISH, C., M.A., Psychiatry
DUANGRATANA, S., D.O.M.S., Ophthalmology
MENAKANIT, W., M.D., Parasitology
NA-BANGXANG, H., M.P.H., Community Medicine
PHORNPIBOUL, B., M.S., Biochemistry
RATANASIRI, T., Orthopaedics
RUCKPHAUPANT, K., M.D., Otolaryngology
SATAPANAKUL, C., M.D., M.P.H., Medicine
SILPISORNKOSOL, S., M.S., Obstetrics and Gynaecology
SIVASOMBOON, C., M.SC., Pathology
SRISUKRI, S., M.D., Forensic Medicine
TEJA-INTR, M., F.A.C.A., Physiology
TEJASEN, P., M.D., Pharmacology
TEJASEN, T., PH.D., Anatomy

*Faculty of Agriculture:*
HENGSAWAD, V., M.S., Entomology
JONGLAEKHA, N., M.S., Plant Pathology
LAKAWATHANA, S., M.S., Agricultural Economics
POSRI, S., B.A., Animal Husbandry
SENTHONG, C., M.S., Agronomy
SUTHASUPA, P., PH.D., Agricultural Extension
TONGSIRI, N., PH.D., Food Science and Technology
WIVATVONGVANA, M., M.S., Horticulture
WIVATVONGVANA, P., PH.D., Soil Science and Conservation

*Faculty of Education:*
BHAHMNAK, S., M.A., Practical Arts Education
CHAISORN, P., M.ED., Evaluation and Education Research
CHEUNCHOB, S., M.ED., Elementary Education
EAOCHARAERN, A., B.ED., Physical Education
HIRANRAS, R., M.A., Foundation of Education
MARKACHAN, T., M.A., Education Extension
PARAMORRATUD, W., M.A., Secondary Education
SRICHANDON, B., M.ED., Educational Administration
SUDAPRASERT, P., M.ED., Education Technology

*Faculty of Engineering:*
KANTAPANIT, K., M.ELEC., Electrical Engineering
KASEMSET, C., D.ENG., Civil Engineering
TANGTRAKOL, K., M.ENG., Mechanical Engineering

*Faculty of Nursing:*
BOONKLA, P., M.ED., Nursing Administration
DISAYABURTA, S., M.D., Psychiatric Nursing
LIMCHITTI, K., B.S., Fundamentals of Nursing
LIMTRACOOL, P., B.S., Public Health Nursing
TACHAYAPONG, U., B.S., Midwifery, Maternity and Child Care
TOWATTANA, K., M.S., Medical Nursing

*Faculty of Dentistry:*
AKRACHINORAS, A., PH.DENT., Community and Paedodontic Dentistry
ANANTASANT, T., D.D.S., Dental Roentgenology
APISARIYAKUL, S., D.D.S., Orthodontics
KOTRAJARUS, P., M.S., Prosthetic Dentistry
LIMKOOL, P., M.D.S., Restorative Dentistry
METHA, D., D.M.D., Oral Surgery
SRISUWAN, S., D.D.S., Odontology and Oral Pathology

*Faculty of Pharmacy:*
CHUAMANOCHAN, P., B.PHARM., Pharmaceutics
JAREARNSUPAPONG, P., M.ACC., Pharmacy
LIMPITI, D., M.SC., Pharmaceutics
TIAMRAJ, T., B.PHARM., Manufacturing Pharmacy
TUNSHEVAVONG, C., B.PHARM., Biopharmaceutics
VEJAPIKUL, S., B.PHARM., Pharmacognosy

*Faculty of Technical Medicine:*
CHAIYARASAMEE, S., M.T., Clinical Microscopy
HAESUNG-CHARERN, U., PH.D., Clinical Chemistry
MAKONKAWKEYOON, S., PH.D., Clinical Immunology
SUWANKRUGHASN, N., Clinical Microbiology
UKOSKIT, K., M.S., Radiology

ATTACHED RESEARCH INSTITUTES:

**Tribal Research Centre.**

**Lanna Thai Social Sciences Research Centre.**

**Regional Centre of Mineral Resources Region 3.**

**Industrial Economics Centre of Northern Thailand.**

**Anaemia and Malnutrition Research Centre.**

**Multiple Cropping Project.**

## CHULALONGKORN UNIVERSITY
PHYATHAI RD., BANGKOK 5
Telephone: 251-1181-7.
Founded 1917.

State control; Language of instruction: Thai; Academic year: June to March.

*Chancellor:* Prof. BOONROD BINDHSON.
*Rector:* Prof. KASEM SUWANAGUL.
*Vice-Rector for Administrative Affairs:* Asst. Prof. A. NAMATRA.
*Vice-Rector for Academic Affairs:* Assoc. Prof. M. VEERABURUS.

Vice-Rector for Planning and Development: Prof. T. VAJRABHAYA.
Vice-Rector for Property Management: Asst. Prof. P. VEJJAJIVA.
Vice-Rector for Student Affairs: Asst. Prof. S. BUNBONGKARN.
Registrar: Asst. Prof. C. ISRANGKUL.
Librarian: Asst. Prof. K. TANTAVIRATANA.
Library: see Libraries.
Number of teachers: 2,193.
Number of students: 12,443 undergraduate, 3,351 postgraduate.
Publications†: *University Newsletter* (weekly), *"Pra Keaw" Students' Handbook* (annually), *Data on Freshmen Entering Chulalongkorn University*, *Annual Report*, *Research Journal* (annually), *Fact Book* (annually).

### DEANS:

Faculty of Arts: Prof. K. SATHIRATHAI.
Faculty of Science: Prof. V. HAYODOM.
Faculty of Architecture: Assoc. Prof. M. L. P. MALAKUL.
Faculty of Commerce and Accountancy: Prof. S. EKAHITANONDA.
Faculty of Political Science: Prof. K. TONGDHAMACHART.
Faculty of Economics: Assoc. Prof. C. NARTSUPHA.
Faculty of Education: Prof. A. SUCHARITAKUL.
Faculty of Engineering: Assoc. Prof. C. BOONYUBOL.
Faculty of Medicine: Prof. S. VANIKEITI.
Faculty of Veterinary Science: Assoc. Prof. P. BODHIPAKSHA.
Faculty of Dentistry: Prof. S. CHAMNANNIDIADHA.
Faculty of Communications Arts: Asst. Prof. PARAMA SATAWEDIN.
Faculty of Law: Asst. Prof. PRASIT KOWILAIKOOL.
Faculty of Pharmaceutical Science: Asst. Prof. B. SAISORN.
Graduate School: Assoc. Prof. SUPRADIT BUNNAG.

### HEADS OF DEPARTMENTS:

Faculty of Arts:
History: TITIMA PHITAKSPRAIWAN.
Geography: CHATCHAI PONGPRAYOON.
Thai: VACHAREE RAMYANANDA.
English: CHITSOMANAS SIWADIT.
Western Languages: TASANEE NAGAVAJARA.
Eastern Languages: PRAPIN MANOMAIVIBOOL.
Philosophy: SUNTHORN NA-RANGSI.
Library Science: M. L. JOY NANDHIVAJRIN.
Dramatic Arts: SODSAI PANTOOMKOMOL.
Linguistics: VICHIN PANUPONG.
Faculty of Science:
Chemistry: PIRAWAN PHANTUMNAVIN.
Physics: WIJIT SENGHAPHAN.
Mathematics: M. R. PAKPONGSNID SNIDVONGS.
Chemical Technology: PRASOM STHAPITANONDA.
Biology: PUTTIPONGSE VARAVUDHI.
Botany: PRADISTHA INTARAKOSIT.
Geology: NOPADON MUANGNOICHAROEN.
General Science: SAKDA SIRIPANT.
Biochemistry: KRAISRI APHORNRATANA.
Microbiology: NALINE NILUBOL.
Material Science: LEK UTTAMASILL.
Marine Science: TWESUKDI PIYAKARNCHANA.
Faculty of Architecture:
Architecture: CHALERM SOOTCHJARIT.
Fine and Applied Arts: WICHIT CHARERNBHAK.
Urban Planning: KIAT CHIVAKUL.
Landscape: DECHA BOONKHAM.
Faculty of Commerce and Accountancy:
Accounting: PHENKAE SNIDVONGS.
Commerce: NARASRI VAIVANIJKUL.
Statistics: SUCHADA KIRANANDANA.
Banking and Finance: SANGVORN PANYADILOK.
Marketing: PREEYA VORNKHOPORN.
Faculty of Political Science:
Government: JAROON SOOPHARB.
International Relations: KHIEN THEERAVIT.
Sociology and Anthropology: SUNYA SUNYAWIWAT.
Public Administration: ROONGRIT SYAMANANDA.
Faculty of Economics:
Economic Theory: SUTHY PRASARTSET.
Economic Development: SUPACHAI MANUSPHAIBOOL.
International Economics: PRAPANT SVETANANT.
Monetary Economics and Public Finance: PAIROJ VONGVIPANOND.
Quantitative Economics: VIRABONGSA RAMANGKURA.
Faculty of Education:
Education Foundation: RATANA TUNGASVADI.
Educational Research: SOMWANG PITIYANUWAT.
Elementary Education: SUMON AMORNVIVAT.
Secondary Education: THERACHAI BURANAJOTI.
Physical Education: VOROSAK PIENCHOB.
Educational Administration: NOPPONGS BUYAJITRADULYA.
Psychology: YOTHIN SANSANAYUDH.
Audio-visual Education: SUPORN SUWANASAI.
Nursing Education: NEPHARATANA BHLAPIBUL.
Art Education: VIRAJ PICHAYAPAIBOON.
Higher Education: PAITOON SINLARAT.
Faculty of Engineering:
Civil Engineering: SANAN CHAROENPHAO.
Electrical Engineering: PRAMOTH UHAVAITHAYA.
Mechanical Engineering: TAVEE LERTPANYAVIT.
Industrial Engineering: VIJIT TANTASUTH.
Mining Engineering and Mining Geology: CHADAP PADMASUTA.
Sanitary Engineering: SUTCHAI CHAMPA.
Metallurgical Engineering: MANOO VEERABURUS.
Chemical Engineering: SUTHAM VANICHSENI.
Survey Engineering: WICHA JIWALAI.
Computer Engineering: SUYUT SATAYAPRAKORB.
Nuclear Technology: SUWAN SANGPETCH.
Faculty of Medicine:
Anatomy: SUCHIN UNGTHAVORN.
Physiology: SUTHIP VARDHANABAEDYA.
Biochemistry: C. PERMSUK PECHYAPAISIT.
Pharmacology: PAIROJNA SIRIVONGS.
Pathology: PRAYOON SUKONTHAMAN.
Laboratory Medicine: CHAMNONG BHUMIPUDKI.
Microbiology: DILOK YEMBUTRA.
Parasitology: KAMPOL PECHARANOND.
Forensic Medicine: CHAVIT ROONGRUANGRATANA.
Medicine: YACHAI NA SONGKLA.
Preventive and Social Medicine: SUKSA BHAMORNSATHIT.
Psychiatry: PHAICHIT SUTTHIWAN.
Surgery: KASEM JITPATIMA.
Orthopaedics and Rehabilitation Medicine: SAMAK BUKKANASEM.
Anaesthesiology: PLERNSRI CHARUWORN.
Obstetrics and Gynaecology: BANPOT BOONSIRI.
Radiology: SILLAWAT ARTHACHINDA.
Paediatrics: SRISAKUL CHARUCHINDA.
Ophthalmology: KOBCHAI PROMMINDAROJ.
Otolaryngology: KOSOL LEKHAVAT.
Faculty of Veterinary Science:
Veterinary Anatomy: PAYATTRA TANTILIPIKARA.
Veterinary Pathology: PICHOH ARJSONGKOON.
Veterinary Physiology: AYUS PICHAICHARNARONG.
Veterinary Pharmacology: DANIS DAVITIYANANDA.
Veterinary Surgery: PRANEE TUNTIVANICH.
Veterinary Medicine: M. L. AKANEE NAWARAT.
Animal Husbandry: SUCHIN JALAYANAKUPTA.
Obstetrics, Gynaecology and Reproduction: PEERASAK CHANTARAPRATEEP.
Faculty of Dentistry:
Anatomy: SANGIEM LIMBASUTA.
Physiology: TIRASAKDI THAVORNTHON.
Biochemistry: NANDHIKA CHAVALIT.
Microbiology: KALYANI AMATYAKUL.
Oral Pathology: CHUMLONG KITTIVEJ.
Pharmacology: SOMSRI RASMIDATTA.
Operative Dentistry: KHUN ARUNEE KAJAKORN.

*Prosthodontics:* TERB CHARUDILAKA.
*Orthodontics:* SUPA RATANARUANG.
*Oral Surgery:* CHUACHOTE HANGSASUTA.
*Radiology:* BUBPA WISES.
*Pedodontics:* AMPUT INTARAPRASONG.
*Oral Medicine:* PUNNI SOONSAWASDI.
*Community Dentistry:* PENSRI SITTHISOMWONG.
*Periodontology:* VARAPORN BUATONGSRI.
*Dental Hospital:* JERA SUSILVORN.
*Occlusion:* SOMNUK POONSAPAYA.

*Faculty of Communication Arts:*
  *Public Relations:* THANAVADEE BOONLUE.
  *Mass Communications:* JOOMPOL RODCOMDEE.
  *Journalism:* CHUKANYA TEERAVANIJ.
  *Speech and Drama:* CHUMNONG VIBULSRI.

*Faculty of Law:*
  *Civil and Commercial Law:* CHAIYOS HEMARAJATA.
  *Procedural and Court Organization Law:* MOORATA WATANACHEEVAKUL.
  *International Law:* CHUTA KULABUSAYA.
  *Administrative Law and Jurisprudence:* PITOON KUNGSOMBOON.
  *Criminal Law and Criminology:* PRASIT KOWILAIKOOL.

*Faculty of Pharmaceutical Science:*
  *Pharmaceutical Chemistry:* PHENSRI THONGNOPNUA.
  *Pharmacology:* USANA HONGVAREEWATANA.
  *Pharmacy:* PRANOM PHOTIYANONT.
  *Pharmacognosy:* DHAVADEE PONGLUX.
  *Pharmaceutical Botany:* PAYOM TANTIVATANA.
  *Manufacturing Pharmacy:* PREEYA ATMIYANAN.
  *Biochemistry:* PRACHOTE PLENGVIDHYA.
  *Microbiology:* PISAWAT DUTIYAPODHI.
  *Physiology:* SAMLEE JAIDEE.
  *Food Chemistry:* M. L. PRANOD CHUMSAENG.

### DIRECTORS:

*Institute of Social Research:* Assoc. Prof. W. WONGHANCYAO.
*Institute of Health Research:* Assoc. Prof. N. DUSITSIN.
*Institute of Environmental Research:* Prof. S. SETAMANIT.
*Institute of Population Studies:* Assoc. Prof. N. DEBAVALYA.
*Language Institute:* Prof. T. KRISHNAMARA.
*Computer Service Center:* Asst. Prof. S. TAYANYONG.

## KASETSART UNIVERSITY
BANGKHEN, BANGKOK 9
Telephone: 5790113.
Founded 1943.

Languages of instruction: Thai (undergraduate), Thai and English (graduate); State control; Dates of academic year: June to March (two semesters).

*Rector:* P. INGKASUWAN, PH.D.
*Vice-Rector for Academic Affairs:* K. CHUTIMA, PH.D.
*Vice-Rector for Business Affairs:* C. PRICHANANDA, PH.D.
*Vice-Rector for Student Affairs:* B. KALAYANAMITR, M.D.
*Vice-Rector for Kamphaengsaen Campus:* A. CHANTANAO, PH.D. (acting).
*Registrar:* V. SUKKIJ, PH.D.
*Librarian:* Miss DARUNA SOMBOONKUN, M.A., M.L.S.
*Library: see* Libraries.

Number of teachers: 1,199.
Number of students: 8,252 undergraduates, 1,551 graduates.

Publications: *Animal Production* (quarterly), *Kasetsart News* (monthly), *The Kasetsart Journal* (irregular), *Kasetsart Research Reports* (yearly), *Kasetsart Technical Bulletin* (irregular).

### DEANS:

*Faculty of Agriculture:* AROON CHANTANAO, PH.D.
*Faculty of Agricultural Industry:* TASANEE SORASUCHART, M.S.
*Faculty of Fisheries:* MEK BOONBRAHM, M.S.
*Faculty of Forestry:* SOMSAK SUKHVONG, PH.D.
*Faculty of Science and Arts:* SOOKPRACHA VACHANONDA, PH.D.
*Faculty of Engineering:* BOONSOM SUWACHIRAT, M.ENG.
*Faculty of Economics and Business Administration:* SOPIN TONGPAN, PH.D.
*Faculty of Social Sciences:* RADOM SETTEETON, PH.D.
*Faculty of Veterinary Science:* PIBUL CHAYANANT, M.S.
*Faculty of Education:* RUNG JENJIT.
*Graduate School:* Prof. BANJERD KHATIKARN, PH.D.
*Institute of Food Research and Product Development:* Prof. AMARA BHUMIRATANA, M.S.
*Office of Extension and Training:* PORN SUWANVAJOKKASIKIJ, M.S.
*Institute of Research and Development:* KAMPHOL ADULAVIDHAYA, PH.D.
*Dean of Women:* Ms. LAMOM BUSPAVANICH, M.S.
*National Corn and Sorghum Research Centre:* ASCHAN SUKTHAMRONG, PH.D.
*National Swine Research and Training Centre:* SUCHEEP RATARASARN, PH.D.
*Highland Agriculture:* PAVIN PUNSRI, M.S.

### PROFESSORS:

AREEKUL, S., PH.D., Entomology
BHUMIRATANA, A., M.S., Food Science
BURANAMANAS, P., M.S., Veterinary Medicine
CHANDRAPAURAYA, C., B.S., Home Economics
CHUTIMA, K., PH.D., Chemistry
DISSAMARN, R., D.V.M., Veterinary Pathology
HAMBANANDA, P., B.S.F., Forestry
INGKASUWAN, P., PH.D., Poultry Husbandry
KANTASEWI, N., PH.D., Social Science
KASETSUWAN, S., PH.D., Poultry Husbandry
KHATIKARN, B., PH.D., Horticulture
PUNSRI, P., M.S., Pomology
RATARASARN, S., PH.D., Animal Husbandry
SAGARIK, R., B.S., Orchidology
SUJINDA, P., M.S., Cooperatives
VACHAROTHAYAN, S., PH.D., Soil Science
VEJJAJIVA, C., M.A., Mathematics

## KHON KAEN UNIVERSITY
KHON KAEN
Telephone: 236199.
Founded 1966.

State control; Language of instruction: Thai; Academic year: June to March (two semesters), summer session April-May.

*Rector:* Prof. Dr. KAWEE TUNGSUBUTRA, M.D.
*Vice-Rector for Academic Affairs:* Prof. Dr. TERD CHAROENWATANA.
*Vice-Rector for Administration:* Prof. KHEMKHANG SITATHANI.
*Vice-Rector for Student Affairs:* Prof. VANCHAI VATANASAPT, M.D.
*Vice-Rector for Planning and Development:* Prof. Dr. KASEM PRABRIPUTALOONG.

*Librarian:* APHAI PRAKOBPOL.

Library of 93,517 vols.

Number of teachers: 759.
Number of students: 4,297.

Publications: *Khon Kaen Agriculture Journal*†, *Khon Kaen University Health Science Centre Bulletin*†, *K.K.U. Nursing Journal*† (every 2 months), *K.K.U. Engineering*† (quarterly), *Khon Kaen University Science Journal* (3 a year).

### DEANS:

*Faculty of Agriculture:* Prof. KAVI CHUTIKUL, M.S., PH.D.
*Faculty of Education:* Prof. Dr. TEERA RUNCHAROEN.
*Faculty of Engineering:* Prof. RANGSRI NANTASARN.
*Faculty of Medicine:* Prof. Dr. NETRACHALEO SANPITAK, M.D.
*Faculty of Nursing:* Prof. KALAYA PATANASRI.
*Faculty of Science:* Prof. Dr. PADKI THANAURACHORN.
*Faculty of Humanities and Social Sciences:* Prof. CHINDA PODIMUANG.
*Faculty of Associated Medical Science:* Prof. Dr. PISIT SANPITAK, M.D.
*Faculty of Public Health:* Prof. Dr. SOMBAT CHAYABEJARA, M.D.
*Faculty of Dentistry:* Prof. Dr. ISRA YUKTANANDANA.
*Graduate School:* Prof. Dr. SUCHAT CHANTIP, PH.D.

THAILAND

## KING MONGKUT'S INSTITUTE OF TECHNOLOGY

SRIAYUTTHAYA RD., BANGKOK

Telephone: 281-4210, 282-5780.

Founded 1971, combining Thonburi Technical Institute, Northern Bangkok Technical Institute and Nonthaburi Telecommunication Institute.

*Rector:* Prof. BOONYASAK JAIJONGKIT, M.S.

### Thonburi Campus

SUKSWAS 48, BANGMOD, RASBURANA, BANGKOK 14

Telephone: 462-5719.

Founded 1960 as Thonburi Technical Institute.

*Vice-Rector:* PIBOOL HUNGSPREUGS, PH.D.
*Registrar:* Mrs. APAKORN PADUNGSATTAYAWONG, B.A.
*Librarian:* Mrs. AIM-ORN SRINILTA, B.ED., M.S.L.S.

Library of 43,831 vols.
Number of teachers: 180.
Number of students: 1,864.

DEANS AND HEADS OF DEPARTMENTS:
*Faculty of Engineering:* HARIS SUTABUTR, PH.D.
 Civil Engineering Department: NARA KHOMNAMOOL, PH.D.
 Electrical Engineering Department: SAWASD TANTARATANA, PH.D.
 Mechanical Engineering: DECH BUDECHAREONTONG, PH.D.
 Production Engineering: ATTHAKORN GLANKWAMDEE, PH.D.
 Chemical Engineering: SAKARINDR BHUMIRATANA, PH.D.
*Faculty of Industrial Education and Science:* VITTHI BHANTHUMNAVIN, PH.D.
 Industrial Education Department: PAIROAT TIRANATHANAGUL, M.SC.
 Languages and Social Sciences Department: Mrs. NANTHA GOHWONG, M.A.
 Chemistry: Mrs. CLOCHAI PUNYASINGH, M.SC.
 Mathematics: Miss PRUNGCHUN WONG-WISES, DR.RER.NAT.
 Physics: PICHET LIMSUWAN, PH.D.
*School of Energy of Materials:* PRIDA WIBULSWAS, A.C.C.I., D.I.C., PH.D.

### North Bangkok Campus

PRACHARAJ 1 RD., NORTH BANGKOK

Telephone: 585-2111-5.

Founded 1959.

*Vice-Rector:* SOMCHOB CHAIYAVEJ.
*Registrar:* Mrs. PATTAYA YINGWATANA.
*Librarian:* Mrs. SUREE IAMSURIYASIN.

Library of 20,000 vols.
Number of teachers: 270.
Number of students: 3,200.

DEANS AND HEADS OF DEPARTMENT:
*Faculty of Engineering:* SUTHI AKSORNKITTI.
 Mechanical Engineering: TEERACHOON MUANGNAPOH.
 Electrical Engineering: SUVALAI GLANKWAMDEE.
 Material Handling Technology: RUNG ANGURAHITA.
 Production Technology: SATAPON KEOVIMOL.
 Industrial Electrical Technology: TEERAYUTH KUHANONT.
*Faculty of Technical Education and Science:* CHANA KASIPAR.
 Teacher Training in Mechanical Technology: CHAMNONG PUMKUM.
 Teacher Training in Electrical Technology: BHAISAL HOONKEO.
 Science: TANAKARN BHATRAKARN.
 Mathematics: Mrs. UTOMPORN PHALAVONK.
 Language and Social Sciences: Mrs. RAMPAISRI SUVANASANG.
*College of Industrial Technology:* SAMRERNG RUSMIVISVA.
 Mechanical Technology: DUMRONG CHAITEERANUWATANASIRI.
 Electrical Technology: SAMRERNG RUSMIVISVA.
 Civil Construction and Woodwork Technology: PRAKIT LIMTRAKOAL.
 Applied Science and Social Science: PAIROTH PONGSAVEE.
 Industrial Production Training Centre: YUKOL JULUPAI.

### Chaokhun Taharn Ladkrabang Campus

LADKRABANG, EAST BANGKOK

Telephone: 5250160-2.

Founded 1960.

*Vice-Rector:* PRASOM RANSIROCHANA.
*Registrar:* Mrs. WANIDA DHUPATEMIYA.
*Librarian:* Miss SUREE BUHMGAMONKOL.

Library of 35,000 vols.
Number of teachers: 198.
Number of students: 2,007.

DEANS AND HEADS OF DEPARTMENT:
*Faculty of Engineering:* KOSOL PETCHSUWAN.
 Telecommunication Engineering: MANOON SUKASAEM.
 Electrical Engineering: NITAS KRISANAJINDA.
 Industrial Technology: PRAKIT TANHTISANONT.
 Electronics: PAIRASH TASCHAYAPONG.
 Computer and Control Engineering: YOTIN PRAEMPRANEERAT.
*Faculty of Architecture:* PERADES CHAKRABANDHU.
 Architecture: PERADES CHAKRABANDHU.
 Interior Architecture: PRALONG PHIRANONT.
 Industrial Arts: KHONGDES HOONPADUNGRAT.
 Construction Technology: DANG RIENSUWAN.
*Faculty of Industrial Education and Science:* BOONSONG SIWAMOGSATHAM.
 Industrial Education: Mrs. PREEYAPORN WONGANUTROHD.
 Mathematics and Science: WICHEIN SRISUAKAM.
 Languages and Social Science: Miss RAPEE SOMAPHUTE.
*Faculty of Agricultural Technology:* SUPACHAI RATANOPAS.
 Agricultural Techniques: SANONG NILPETCH.
 Plant Production Technology: Mrs. SRIPRAPHAI CHUENSRI.
 Animal Production Technology: PATHOM LOAWHAKASET.
 Agricultural Business: BANLENG SRIBHATANANOTHAI.
 Agricultural Industry: Mrs. RATIPORN HARUENKIT.
 Agricultural Engineering: AMNUAY PANNGA.

## MAHIDOL UNIVERSITY*

PRANNOCK RD., BANGKOK 7

Telephone: 466-1300-9.

Telegraphic Address: Siriraj Hospital, Thailand.

*Rector:* K. CHARTIKAVANIJ, M.R.C.S., L.R.C.P., D.T.M., F.A.C.S.
*Librarian:* U. DHUTIYABHODI, M.A., M.S.

Library: see Libraries.
Number of teachers: c. 900.
Number of students: c. 4,320.

Publications: *University Announcement, Siriraj Hospital Gazette.*

DEANS:
*Faculty of Medicine and Siriraj Hospital:* V. VEERANUVAT.
*Faculty of Dentistry:* I. YUKTANAND.
*Faculty of Pharmacy:* P. HUTANGKUL.
*Faculty of Public Health:* T. MUENGMAN.
*Faculty of Medical Technology:* P. THONGCHAROEN.
*Faculty of Medicine, Ramathibodi Hospital:* R. BURI.
*Faculty of Tropical Medicine:* C. HARINASUTA.
*Faculty of Science:* P. PREMPREE.
*Faculty of Social Sciences and Humanities:* J. OSATHANONDH.
*Faculty of Environmental and Resource Studies:* N. TUNTAWIROON.

* No reply received to our questionnaire this year.

## PRINCE OF SONGKLA UNIVERSITY

HAAD-YAI, SONGKLA

Telephone: 244877 (Haad-Yai), 349111 (Pattani).

Founded 1964; campuses at Pattani and Haad-Yai.

State control; Language of instruction: Thai; Academic year: June to March (two semesters).

*President of University Council:* Hon. OSOT KOSIN.

Rector: Dr. TONGCHAN HONGLADAROM.
Vice-Rectors: Dr. NAKSITE COOVATHANACHAI (Haad-Yai Campus), PANN YUANLAIE (Pattani Campus), Dr. VIMOLYUT VARNASWANG (Planning and Development), Dr. CHAMNARN PRATOOMSINDH (Educational Affairs).
Librarians: WISIT CHINTAWONG (Haad-Yai Campus), Miss SOMBOON LIMCHAROENCHAT (Pattani Campus).
Number of teachers: 853.
Number of students: 4,085.
Publication: University News.

### Haad-Yai Campus

DEANS AND HEADS OF DEPARTMENT:
Faculty of Engineering: CHULLAPHONK CHULLABODHI.
  Civil Engineering: VACHARA THONGCHAROEN.
  Chemical Engineering: PAIBOON INNACHITRA.
  Electrical Engineering: OPAS CHUTATAPE.
  Industrial Engineering: SUPACHOK WIRIYACOSOL.
  Mechanical Engineering: WITAYA CHONGCHAREON.
  Mining and Metallurgical Engineering: BOONSOM SIRIBUMRUNGSUKA.
Faculty of Science: BOONBHRUGSA CHATAMRA.
  Anatomy: KASEM GAEW-IM.
  Mathematics: BANCHERD ARIGULCHAI.
  Chemistry: SUMPUN WONGNAWA.
  Microbiology: Mrs. PANEE PUANGRASSAMI.
  Biology: SUNTHORN SOTTIBUNDHU.
  Biochemistry: RAPIPORN SOTTIBUNDHU.
  Physics: CHAIVITYA SILAWATSHANANAI.
  Foreign Languages: Miss KRITSRI SAMABUDDHI.
  Pharmacology: Mrs. SAREEYA SRISINTORN.
  Physiology: CHAMNONG SUPATRAVIWAT.
Faculty of Medicine: ATIREK NA THALANG.
  Internal Medicine: NOPARATANA PREMASATHIAN.
  Pathology: MALIDA PORNPATKUL.
  Ophthalmology and Otolaryngology: NIMIT RATANAMART.
  Paediatrics: PANTIPYA SANGUANCHUA.
  Orthopaedic Surgery and Physical Medicine: ART ARTHORNTHURASOOK.
  Radiology: CHONDEE SUKTHOMYA.
  Obstetrics and Gynaecology: VICHA SATHONPANICH.
  Anaesthesiology: AMARA PANICH.
  Psychiatry: KAVI SUVARNAKICH.
  Surgery: DICLOK PREMASATHIAN.
  University Hospital: THAWEE DHANATRAKUL.

Faculty of Management Science: CHAVALIT SIRIPIROM.
  Business Administration: MANAT CHAISAWAT.
  Public Administration: SOMBOON CHAIYAPRESITHI.
  Liberal Arts: Miss RAPEEPUN SUWANNATACHOTE.
Faculty of Natural Resources: SUJIN JINAYON.
  Plant Science: PAISAN LAOSUWAN.
  Animal Science: WORAWIT WANICHAPICHART.
  Agro-Industry: PAIBOON THAMMARUTWASIK.
  Agricultural Development: PUNJAPOL BOONCHOO.
Faculty of Pharmacy: SUNALINEE NIKROTHANONTA.
Faculty of Nursing: Miss TONGBAI POONYANUNT.

### Pattani Campus

DEANS AND HEADS OF DEPARTMENT:
Faculty of Education: (vacant).
  Physical Education: PRACHA REUCHUTTAKUL.
  Home Economics: Mrs. WATTANA PRATOOMSINDH.
  Education: PREEMON NAKARIN.
  General Science: BOONTHAM NITHIUTHAI.
  Demonstration School: WIRAT BOONYASOMBAT.
Faculties of Humanities and Sciences: MANOH YUDEN.
  Western Languages: PAITOON BUNNJAWEHT.
  Social Sciences: Mrs. CHAVEEWAN WANAPRASERT.
  Library Science: PARMOTE KRAMUT.
  Thai and Eastern Languages: SOMPRACH AMMAPUNT.
  Philosophy and Culture: KAMBULA SIRIMUNIDA.
Graduate School: (vacant).

ATTACHED INSTITUTE:
**Phuket Community College:** Dir. VICHIT CHANDHRAKUL.


## RAMKHAMHAENG UNIVERSITY
HUAMARK, BANGAPI, BANGKOK 24
Founded 1971.

State control; Academic year: June to March (two semesters), summer session April–May; run on open university system.
Rector: Prof. Dr. SAKDI PASUKNIRANT.
Vice-Rector for Administrative Affairs: Prof. PAIBOOL SUWANAPOSRI.
Vice-Rector for Planning and Development: Prof. Dr. UDOM WAROTAMASIKKHADIT.
Vice-Rector for Academic Affairs: Prof. Mrs. CHINTANA YOSSUNDARA.
Vice-Rector for Student Affairs: Dr. PEERAPAN PALUSUK.

Registrar: SUMON MONGKHA.
Librarian: AMPORN PANSRI.
Number of teachers: 744.
Number of students: 141,925.
Publications: three journals, one weekly bulletin.

DEANS:
Faculty of Business Administration: VISARN TENGAMNUAY.
Faculty of Economics: Dr. THAMNOON SOPARATANA.
Faculty of Education: Dr. APIROM NANAKORN.
Faculty of Humanities: Dr. PAT NOISAENGSRI.
Faculty of Law: VAREE NASKUL.
Faculty of Political Science: SUKHUM NUANSAKUL.
Faculty of Science: SAMORNVADEE FACKPOLNGAM.

HEADS OF DEPARTMENTS:
Business Administration:
  General Administration: PHANEE PRASERTVONG.
  Money and Banking: VILAIVAN THONGPRAYOON.
  Marketing: BANYAT CHULANAPAN.
  Accounting: VISARN TENGAMNUAY.
  Advertising and Public Relations: CHUTHA THIANTHAI.
  Industrial Services: PAIBOON SUWANAPHOSRI.

Economics:
  Economic Theory: CHURI TAPANANONTA.
  Industrial Economics: KRIT PHURISINSIT.
  Monetary Economics: PANYA UDOMRATI.
  Public Finance: SOMCHINTANA SIVALEE.
  International Economics: VIRAT THANESUAN.
  Development Economics: BUNKIT WONGWAIKITPAISARN.
  Economic History: SAMPINPONG CHATRAKOM.
  Quantitative Analysis: BOMSOM SIRISOPANA.
  Agricultural Economics: BANLUE KAMVACHIRAPITAKSA.
  Human Resources Economics: CHINTANA PORNPILAIPAN.

Education:
  Physical Education: CHARIN THANIRAT.
  Curriculum and Teaching: SANGVIAN SRITKUL.
  Education Foundation: Mrs. RUENGSRI SRITHONG.
  Testing and Research: ANEK PIANANUKULBUTARA.
  Geography: Miss VANASIRI DECHAKUPTA.
  Psychology: SIRIVAN SARANAT.
  Audio-Visual Education: RUAMSAKDI KAEWPLANG.
  Demonstration School: WATANA KURUSAWADI.

*Humanities:*
  *English and Linguistics:* Dr. WITAYA NAATONG.
  *Thai and Oriental Languages:* NOMNIJ VONGSUTHITHAM.
  *History:* KHANATHIP KHANTHAPIN.
  *Library Science:* NONTHANA PUEGPONG.
  *Western Languages:* SONGSRI SRIJANTHARAPAN.
  *Philosophy:* SUWAN PETCHNIL.
  *Sociology and Anthropology:* Mrs. REUDEEMON SRISUPAN.

*Law:*
  *Public Law:* Dr. SIRIVAT SUPORNPAIBUL.
  *Civil Law:* KAMTHORN KAMPRASERT.
  *Commercial Law:* SAMRIT RATANADARA.
  *International Law:* PRAKOB PRAPANNETIVUTHI.
  *Legal Procedure:* RANGSAN SAENGSUK.
  *Jurisprudence:* DECHA SIRICHAROEN.

*Political Science:*
  *Government:* ASADANG PANIKKABUT.
  *Political and International Relations:* THANASRIT SATAVETHIN.
  *Public Administration:* CHALIDA SORNMANI.

*Science:*
  *Mathematics:* SUDYONG TOPRASERT.
  *Statistics:* SUTHICHAI NGOWSIRI.
  *Chemistry:* Mrs. RAMPAI PIYAMANAKUL.
  *Physics:* SANIT CHAIYATHASANA.
  *Biology:* MONTRI PETCHTHONGKHAM.

## SILPAKORN UNIVERSITY
NA-PHRALAN RD., BANGKOK

Telephone: 2217760.

Founded 1943.

Language of instruction: Thai; State control; Academic year: June to March.

*Rector:* M. R. TONGYAI TONGYAI.
*Vice-Rectors:* Dr. PRAGOB KUNARAK (Academic Affairs and Development Planning); PRASONG EIAM-ANANT (Administration); VIVAT CHANTARAPORNCHAI (Sanamchan Palace Campus); LIKIT KANCHANAPORN (Student Affairs).

Number of teachers: 378.
Number of students: 2,705.
Publication: *Journal* (2 a year).

### Thapra Palace Campus
BANGKOK

*Registrar:* SOMJAI NIMLEK.
*Librarian:* PREPREM CHATIYANONDA.

DEANS AND HEADS OF DEPARTMENT:
*Faculty of Painting, Sculpture and Graphic Arts:* PRAYAT PONGDAM.
  *Painting:* ITHIPOL THANGCHALOK.
  *Sculpture:* NONTHIVATH CHANDHANAPALIN.
  *Graphic Arts:* TUAN TRIRAPICHIT.
  *Thai Arts:* CHALOOD NIMSAMER.

*Faculty of Architecture:* ORNSIRI PANIN.
  *Architecture:* ANUVIT CHARERNSUPKUL.
  *Related Arts and Architecture:* VANIDA PHUNGSOONDARA.
  *Architectural Technology:* SMARDHA PUNYARATABANDHA.
  *Urban Design and Planning:* KAMTHORN KULACHOL.

*Faculty of Archaeology:* KHAISRI SRIAROON.
  *Archaeology:* Dr. PHASOOK INDRAWOOTH.
  *Art History:* PIBUL SUPAKITVILAKAGARN.
  *Anthropology:* POOT VERAPRASERT.
  *Oriental Languages:* SENI WILAWAN.
  *Western Languages:* WARUNWAN APICHATABUTRA.

*Faculty of Decorative Arts:* ANECK VIRAVEJBHISAI.
  *Interior Design:* CHARK SIRIPANICH.
  *Visual Communication Design:* NIPON PARITAKOMOL.
  *Product Design:* VISIT SIRISAMPAN.
  *Applied Art Studies:* VIRA JOTHAPRASERT.

### Sanamchan Palace Campus
NAKHON PATHOM

*Registrar:* Mrs. PRANEE TO-ADITHEP.
*Librarian:* Mrs. MALINEE SRIPISUTH.

DEANS AND HEADS OF DEPARTMENT:
*Faculty of Arts:* Dr. MANU WALYAPECHRA.
  *Thai:* Dr. KUSUMA RAKSAMANI.
  *English:* Mrs. PATCHANEE SANKABURANURUK.
  *French:* Dr. PENSIRI CHAROENPOTE.
  *German:* Miss NARUMON NGAOSUWAN.
  *History:* Miss CHUSIRI CHAMORAMARN.
  *Geography:* PRAYOON DARSRI.

*Faculty of Education:* Dr. YENCHAI LAOHAVANICH.
  *Educational Administration and Supervision:* Dr. METHI PILANTHANANON.
  *Foundations of Education:* THONGPLEU CHOMCHEUN.
  *Psychology and Guidance:* LIKIT KANCHANAPORN.
  *Curriculum and Methodology:* Dr. CHACH THAOCHALEE.

*Faculty of Science:* Dr. PRADON CHATIKAVANIJ.
  *Mathematics:* Mrs. VAREE KAROT.
  *Biology:* Miss BENCHAR SANGVARA.
  *Chemistry:* Dr. SOMKAIT THADANITI.
  *Physics:* BURI SRICHAN.

*Graduate School:* M. C. SUBHADRADIS DISKUL.

## SRI NAKHARINWIROT UNIVERSITY
PRASARN MIT RD., SUKHUMWIT 23, BANGKOK 11

Telephone: 3912583, 3911039, 3911430, 3911143.

Founded 1954, University status 1974.

State control; Academic year: June to October, November to February, March to May.

*President:* Dr. NIBONDH SASITHORN.
*Vice-Presidents:* Dr. SONGSAK SRIKALASIN (Academic Affairs), Dr. PRASAT LAKSILA (Administrative Affairs), Dr. PRASERT WITAVARAT (Planning and Development), Dr. VICHITR SINSIRI (Student Affairs), Dr. BOON-EARN MILINTASUT (Pathum Wan Campus), Dr. THAWEE HOMCHONG (Bangsean Campus), Dr. PHANAS HANNAKIN (Pitsanulok Campus), Dr. CHATRI MUNGNAPO (Maha Sarakham Campus), Dr. PREECHA DHUNMA (Bang Khen Campus), Dr. NAT INDRAPANA (Palasuksa Campus), SERMSAK VISALAPORN (Songkla Campus).
*Registrar:* LERT CHOONAKA.
*Library:* see Libraries.

Number of teachers: 1,352 (all campuses).
Number of students: 11,503 fulltime, 12,446 evening.

Publications: *News* (monthly), *Graduate School Periodical* (termly), *Thesis Abstracts Series* (annually), faculty and campus periodicals, etc.

DEANS:
*Graduate School:* Dr. KANDA NATHALANG.
*Faculty of Education:* Dr. AREE SANHACHAWEE.
*Faculty of Social Sciences:* Dr. PRASAT LAKSILA.
*Faculty of Sciences:* Dr. PRAYONG PONGTHONGCHAROEN.
*Faculty of Physical Education:* SAMRUAN RATANAJARN.
*Faculty of Humanities:* Mrs. PRANEE THANACHANAN.

DIRECTORS:
*Behavioural Science Research Institute:* Dr. CHANCHA SUVANNATHAT.
*Educational and Psychological Test Bureau:* Dr. SOMBOON CHITRAPONG.
*Bangkok College of Nursing:* Mrs. CHAICHERD APICHARTBUT.

## SUKHOTHAI THAMMATHIRAT OPEN UNIVERSITY
SRI AYUDHYA RD., BANGKOK 4

Telephone: 2814816/21/33.

Founded 1978.

*Rector:* Prof. Dr. WICHIT SRISA-AN.

*Vice-Rector for Academic Affairs:* Dr. IAM CHAYA-NGAM.
*Vice-Rector for Planning and Development:* Dr. TONG-IN WANGSOTORN.
*Registrar:* Dr. WINAI RUNGSINAN.
*Librarian:* SOMPIT CUSRIPITUCK.

Library of 5,049 vols.

Number of teachers: 344.
Number of students: 81,969.

CHAIRMEN:

*School of Liberal Arts:* Dr. IAM CHAYA-NGAM.
*School of Educational Studies:* Dr. SUPON SRIPAHOL.
*School of Management Science:* Dr. KITI TAYAKKANONTA, M.D.
*School of Law:* Dr. SRIRACHA CHAROENPANIJ.
*School of Economics:* Dr. NARONGSAKDI THANAVIBULCHAI.

**THAMMASAT UNIVERSITY**
2 PRACHAND RD.,
BANGKOK 2
Telephone: 221-6111.
Founded 1933.

State control; Language of instruction: Thai; Academic year: June to March (two semesters), Summer Session April to May.

*Rector:* Prof. PRAPASNA AUYCHAI.
*Vice-Rector:* TAWON POTHONG.
*Vice-Rector for Academic Affairs:* Prof. AROON RAJATANAVIN.
*Vice-Rector for Administration:* MONTREE BORISUTDHI.
*Vice-Rector for Planning and Development:* Dr. PICHAI CHARNSUPHARINDR.
*Vice-Rector for Student Affairs:* CHOOSAKDI TIENGTRONG.
*Librarian:* Mrs. PHAKAIVAN CHIAMCHAROEN.

Library: *see* Libraries.

Number of teachers: 537.

Number of students: 10,844.

Publications: *Journal of Political Science, Thammasat University Journal, Thammasat Law Journal, Journal of Business Administration, Faculty Bulletin, Journalism.*

DEANS:

*Faculty of Law:* Dr. PAISITH PIPATANAKUL.
*Faculty of Commerce and Accountancy:* Prof. NONGYAO CHAISERI.
*Faculty of Economics:* Prof. MEDHI KRONGKAEW.
*Faculty of Political Science:* SHAT KITHAM.
*Faculty of Social Administration:* NUTHACHAI TANTISUK.
*Faculty of Liberal Arts:* Prof. MONGKOL SEIHASOPHON.
*Faculty of Journalism and Mass Communication:* BOONLERT SUPADHILOKE.

DIRECTORS:

*Department of Sociology and Anthropology:* CHAMRIENG BHAVICHITRA.
*English Language Center:* SAMUT SENCHAOWANICH.
*Graduate Volunteer Center:* CHALERMSRI DHAMMABUTR.
*Thai Khadi Research Institute:* M. R. AKIN RABIBHADANA.

## COLLEGES AND INSTITUTES

### AGRICULTURE

**Ayuthaya Agricultural College:** Ayuthaya.

**Bang Phra Agricultural College:** Bang Phra, Cholburi; f. 1957; teacher training; 8,000 vols.; Dir. Dr. SURAPHOL SANGUANSRI.

**Maejo Institute of Agricultural Technology (MIAT):** Maejo, Chiangmai; f. 1934; degree courses in agricultural technology, field crop technology (tobacco), poultry technology, horticultural technology (ornamental plants) and agricultural business administration; Rector Prof. VIPATA BOONSRI WANGSAI; Dir. APICHAI RATANAWARAHA.

**Nakorn Sithammarat Agricultural College:** Tungsong, Nakorn Sithammarat.

**Surin Agricultural College:** Surin.

### ECONOMICS AND ADMINISTRATION

**National Institute of Development Administration:** Klong Chan, Bangkapi, Bangkok 24; consists of four graduate schools (Public Administration, Business Administration, Development Economics, Applied Statistics), four centres (Research Center, Training Center, Library and Information Center, Computer Center) and English Language Program; 500 staff members; library of 102,970 vols.; Rector Prof. Dr. TITAYA SUVANAJATA.

### TECHNOLOGY

**Institute of Technology and Vocational Education, Bangkok Campus:** 2 Linchee Rd., Tungmahamek, Bangkok 12; f.1952; 2- to 5- year certificate and diploma courses in mechanics, metal technology, building construction, electrical power, electronics, surveying, industrial technical training, arts, photography, printing, furniture making, textile technology, chemical technology, textile and clothing, food and nutrition, home economics, travel industry, management, business administration, secretarial science, accounting, marketing, vocational teacher education; 370 teachers; 5,259 students; library of 44,500 vols.; Rector Prof. SWATH TSCHEIKUNA; Dir. NAKORN SRIVICHARN; publs. *Newsletter* (monthly), *Mahamek Bulletin* (quarterly).

**Institute of Technology and Vocational Education, Tak Campus:** Tak; library of c. 2,000 vols.; 115 teachers; 2,045 students; Dir. PANYA YAWIRAT; Registrar Mrs. KANYANEE TANGTRAKUL; Librarian Miss SUTTHINEE KETPHASUK.

**Northeastern Technical Institute:** Suranarai Rd., Korat; f. 1956; 218 teachers; 2,402 students; library of 30,000 vols.; 5-year diploma courses; Dir. E. SUNTORNPONG (acting); publ. *Gijagam Technic.*

**Northern Technical Institute:** Huay Kaew Rd., Chiangmai; f. 1957; library of 50,777 vols.; 2–3-year diploma courses; Dir. C. SUWATHEE.

**Southern Technical Institute:** Songkla.

**Thai-German Technical Institute:** 150 Srichundra Rd., Khonkaen; f. 1964; 2- and 3-year courses; 499 students; library of 4,114 vols.; Dir. Dr. V. KAMUDAMAS; publ. *TGTK Periodical* (10 times a year).

# TOGO
Population 2,472,000

## LEARNED SOCIETIES AND RESEARCH INSTITUTES

**Alliance Française:** Lomé; f. 1947.

**American Cultural Center:** B.P. 852, Lomé; reading room, library of 5,000 vols.; cultural activities; Dir. DAVID G. SMITH.

**Association togolaise d'échanges culturelles avec l'étranger** (*Togolese Association for cultural exchanges with foreign countries*): Lomé; Pres. SANVI DE TOVE (President of the Legislative Assembly); Sec. M. ADOSSAMA (Director of Cabinet of the Ministry of Economic Affairs).

**Association togolaise pour le développement de la documentation, des bibliothèques, archives et musée:** s/c Bibliothèque de l'Université de Bénin, B.P. 1515, Lomé; f. 1959; promotes research in the field of documentation and library science; participates in the education of adults and young people; holds conferences, etc.; 60 mems.; Pres. KOFFI ATTIGNON; Sec.-Gen. EKOUE AMAH.

**Goethe-Institut:** B.P. 914, Lomé; f. 1961; cultural exchange; library of 5,000 vols.; Dir. HANS G. SALLMANN.

**Institut de Recherches Agronomiques Tropicales et des Cultures Vivrières (IRAT):** B.P. 1163, Lomé; Dir. M. MARQUETTE. (*See* main entry under France.)

**Institut de Recherches du Coton et des Textiles Exotiques:** B.P. 3300, Lomé; station at Anie-Mono; f. 1948; Dir. M. COÛTEAUX; publs. *Rapports annuels Coton et Fibres Tropicales*. (*See* main entry under France.)

**Institut National de la Recherche Scientifique:** B.P. 2240, Lomé; f. 1965; co-ordination and initiation of national scientific research; 12 permanent staff; library of 5,000 vols.; Dir.-Gen. KOUNOUTCHO SOSSAH; publ. *Etudes Togolaises* (quarterly).

**Institut Togolais des Sciences Humaines:** B.P. 1002, Lomé; f. 1960; a Service de Documentation Générale was created in 1937, to carry out documentation in museums, archives and scientific collections for the advancement of knowledge and study of problems of interest to the territory and to stimulate and assist works relating to varied local activities. This service was taken over by the Institut Français d'Afrique Noire (IFAN) in 1945, and includes publication of scientific reports, organisation of exhibitions, courses and conferences, care of ancient monuments and historic sites, encouragement of indigenous artists and craftsmen, the application of rules concerning excavations and the export of ethnographic objects or indigenous works of art, and protection of fauna and flora. The local centre of IFAN in Togo is the Institut Togolais des Sciences Humaines-Bibliothèque Nationale (INTSHU-BN), and includes departments of anthropology, archaeology, prehistory, history, ethnography, human geography, linguistics, sociology; Dir. KWAOVI GABRIEL JOHNSON.

**Office de la Recherche Scientifique et Technique Outre-Mer:** B.P. 375, Lomé; f. 1949; geology, pedology, geography, sociology, hydrology, geophysics, demography; library; Dir. J. F. VIZIER (*see* main entry under France).

**Service des Mines du Togo:** Lomé.

## LIBRARIES

**Bibliothèque Nationale:** B.P. 1002, Lomé; German and French archives; 7,000 vols.; Dir. ROGER KANAO BEKOUTARE.

**Bibliothèque du Ministère de l'Intérieur:** Lomé; Librarian KWAOVI GABRIEL JOHNSON.

## MUSEUM

**Musée National:** Dept. of Cultural Affairs, Lomé; f. 1975, in process of formation.

## UNIVERSITY

### UNIVERSITÉ DU BÉNIN
B.P. 1515, LOMÉ
Telephone: 3027, 3500.

Founded 1965 as a College: university status 1970; includes all the institutions of higher education in the country.
Language of instruction: French; Academic year: September to July (three terms).

*Rector:* Prof. A. G. JOHNSON.
*Vice-Rector:* Prof. PAKAÏ NABEDE.
*Secretary-General:* A. BAKPESSI.
*Librarian:* E. E. AMAH.
Library of 5,000 vols.
Number of teachers: 456.
Number of students: 3,700.
Publications: *Livrets de l'Etudiant, Annales*† (*Lettres, Sciences, Médecine*).

#### DEANS:
*School of Letters:* A. AKAKPO.
*School of Sciences:* K. KEKEH.
*Higher School of Administration and Law:* W. YAGLA.
*Higher School of Economics and Business Management:* T. GOGUE.
*Higher School of Industrial Engineering:* K. ADOTEVI-AKUE.
*School of Medicine:* K. KEKEH.
*Higher School of Agriculture:* Y. AMEGEE.
*Medical Training School:* Dr. K. NATHANIELS.
*National Institute of Education:* M. GNININVI.
*Higher Institute of Journalism.*

---

**Centre de Formation Professionnelle Agricole de Tove:** B.P. 401, Kpalime; f. 1901; 21 teachers, 230 students; library of 3,500 vols.; Dir. S. N. KANKARTI; Sec.-Gen. I. KUEVI.

**Ecole Africaine et Mauricienne d'Architecture et d'Urbanisme:** B.P. 2067, Lomé; f. 1975; specialist courses in architecture and town planning; in-service courses for trained architects; c. 30 staff; 105 students; Dir. MICHEL GBÉYÉRÉ SOPI.

**Ecole Nationale d'Administration:** ave. de la Libération, Lomé; f. 1958; provides training for Togolese civil servants; approx. 50 students; library of over 1,000 vols.; Dir. FOUSSÉNI MAMA; Sec.-Gen. NICOLAS ADJETEY.

**Technical College:** Sokodé; apprentice training.

# TRINIDAD AND TOBAGO
### Population 1,156,000

## LEARNED SOCIETIES AND RESEARCH INSTITUTES

**Agricultural Society of Trinidad and Tobago:** 17-19 Edward St., Port-of-Spain; f. 1894; 528 mems.; Pres. IAN F. MCDONALD; Sec. LEO C. NANTON; publ. *Journal* (quarterly).

**American Center:** 2B Marli St., Port of Spain.

**Commonwealth Institute of Biological Control:** Gordon St., Curepe; f. 1946; biological control of noxious pests and weeds; 15 mems.; library of 5,000 vols., 20,000 separates on entomology; also operates stations in India, Pakistan, Switzerland, U.K., Kenya and sub-stations in Ghana, Malaysia and Mexico; Dir. Dr. F. D. BENNETT; publs. *Communications, Parasite Catalogue, Biocontrol News and Information.*

**Historical Society of Trinidad and Tobago:** 20 Henry St., Port-of-Spain; Pres. E. E. WILLIAMS; Hon. Sec. and Treas. E. JOHNSON.

**Library Association of Trinidad and Tobago:** P.O.B. 1177, Port of Spain; f. 1960; Pres. YVONNE BOBB, B.A., B.L.S.; Sec. Miss ANN BECKLES, B.A.; publ. *Bulletin of the Library Association of Trinidad and Tobago.*

**Pharmaceutical Society of Trinidad and Tobago:** 80 Charlotte St., Port-of-Spain; f. 1899; 300 mems.; Pres. (vacant); Hon. Sec. W. E. WILLIAMS.

**Sugar Technologists' Association of Trinidad and Tobago:** 80 Abercromby St., P.O.B. 230, Port-of-Spain; f. 1967; to promote technical discussion and research and publish information of interest to the sugar industry; 272 mems.; Pres. G. H. MAINGOT; Sec. M. Y. KHAN; publ. *Proceedings.*

**Theosophical Society of Trinidad:** Eastern Main Rd., Guaico; Organizing Sec. L. R. KHILLAWAN.

**Tobago District Agricultural Society:** Scarborough; Pres. Capt. R. H. HARROWER; Sec. Miss S. A. DAVIES.

**Trinidad and Tobago Law Society:** 28 St. Vincent St., Port-of-Spain; f. 1897; 80 mems.; Pres. O. J. WILSON; Hon. Sec. Senator the Hon. M. T. I. JULIEN, C.M.; publ. *Annual Report.*

**Trinidad Art Society:** Art Centre, French St., Port-of-Spain; f. 1945; 520 mems.; Pres. DENIS MAHABIR; Hon. Sec. ROBERT ALLFREY.

**Trinidad Music Association:** Bishop Anstey High School, Abercromby St., Port-of-Spain; f. 1941; 102 mems.; Pres. Mrs. ROBERT JOHNSTONE, C.B.E.; Hon. Sec. Mrs. VELMA JARDINE.

## LIBRARIES AND MUSEUM

**Carnegie Free Library:** 19-21 St. James St., San Fernando; f. 1919; 61,000 vols.; functions as regional headquarters for Central Library rural services in the south of Trinidad; Chair. The MAYOR OF SAN FERNANDO; Librarian SALLY-ANN MONTSERIN.

**Central Library of Trinidad and Tobago:** P.O.B. 547, Port-of-Spain; f. 1945; a division of the Ministry of Education and Culture; 429,000 vols.; public library with special West Indian Reference Collection; Dir. Mrs. L. C. HUTCHINSON, F.L.A.; publ. *Trinidad and Tobago National Bibliography.*

**National Archives:** The Government Archivist, P.O.B. 763, 105 St. Vincent St., Port-of-Spain; f. 1960; government and private archives; microfilm copies of Trinidad and Tobago records in other countries; Dir. ENOS SEWLAL; publ. *Select Documents.*

**Trinidad Public Library:** Knox St., Port-of-Spain; f. 1851; 68,000 vols.; Librarian Miss S. W. LEWSEY, A.L.A.

**University of the West Indies Library:** St. Augustine; f. 1926; 173,112 vols., 7,180 serials, 59,071 pamphlets, 417,978 unbound serial parts; Librarian Mrs. A. T. JORDAN, A.L.A., M.S., D.L.S., A.R.C.M. (*see also* under Jamaica).

**National Museum and Art Gallery:** 117 Frederick St., Port-of-Spain; f. 1962; fine arts, natural history, archaeology, history; Dir. (of Culture) PATRICK CHU JOON (acting); publs. occasional papers on Folk Arts, History, etc.

# UNIVERSITY

## UNIVERSITY OF THE WEST INDIES
### ST. AUGUSTINE, TRINIDAD
### Telephone: 662-7171.

Founded 1946 by the Governments of the Caribbean Commonwealth Territories with the co-operation of the British Government. It was sited at Mona, Jamaica, which became the first campus. The St. Augustine campus was the second, founded in 1960 by a merger with the former Imperial College of Tropical Agriculture; the third campus was opened in 1963 at Cave Hill, Barbados. The University serves Jamaica, Trinidad and Tobago, Barbados and the Commonwealth Territories in the Caribbean.

Autonomous control; Language of instruction: English; Academic year: October to June.

*Chancellor:* Sir ALLEN MONTGOMERY LEWIS, G.C.M.G., Q.C., LL.B.

*Vice-Chancellor:* A. Z. PRESTON, J.P., LL.B., F.C.A., F.C.I.S., F.R.ECON.S.

*Pro-Vice-Chancellors at St. Augustine:* L. E. S. BRAITHWAITE, B.A., Prof. G. M. RICHARDS, M.SC., PH.D.

*Secretary of St. Augustine:* H. McE. GIBSON, B.A., F.C.I.S.

*Librarian at St. Augustine:* ALMA T. JORDAN, M.S., A.L.A., B.A., D.L.S., A.R.C.M.

Number of teachers: 272.
Number of students: 2,923.

Publications: *Handbook of Caribbean International Relations, Social Studies Journal, Mathematics Journal* (2 a year), *Concept Learning in Social Studies* (quarterly), *Working Papers on Caribbean Society* (occasional).

### DEANS:
*Faculty of Agriculture:* Prof. L. WILSON, M.SC., PH.D.
*Faculty of Engineering:* Prof. I. D. C. IMBERT, M.E., PH.D., M.A.S.C.E.

### VICE-DEANS:
*Faculty of Arts and General Studies:* B. SAMAROO, M.A., PH.D.
*Faculty of Social Sciences:* G. DRAPER, M.B.A.
*Faculty of Natural Sciences:* Prof. W. CHAN, PH.D.
*School of Education:* E. H. GIFT, M.ED., PH.D.

### PROFESSORS:
AHMAD, N., Soil Sciences
BARTHOLOMEW, C. F., Medicine
BEAUBRUN, M., Psychiatry
BOURNE, C., Economics
BRUCE, P. N., Petroleum Engineering
CHAN, W. R., Chemistry
IMBERT, I. D. C., Construction Engineering
JULIEN, K. S., Electrical Engineering
KENNY, J. S., Biological Sciences
KING, ST. C., Electronics and Instrumentation
LAURENCE, K. O., History
MAHADEVA, K., Production Engineering
McFARLANE, H., Chemical Pathology
NIGAM, R., Accounting
PHELPS, H. O., Civil Engineering
RAMASASTRY, A., Industrial Management
RICHARDS, G. M., Chemical Engineering
ROOPNARINESINGH, S., Obstetrics and Gynaecology
SAMMY, G. M., Food Technology
SATCUNANATHAN, S., Mechanical Engineering
SAUNDERS, R. M., Physics
SHARMA, B., Mathematics
SPENCE, J. A., Botany
WILLIAMS, H. E., Livestock Science
WILSON, L. A., Crop Science

### ATTACHED INSTITUTES:
**Caribbean Agricultural Research and Development Institute:** Exec. Dir. J. BURGASSE, B.COM., M.A. (Field units in Barbados and Jamaica.)

**Institute of Social and Economic Research:** Assoc. Dir. J. HAREWOOD, B.SC.

**Institute of International Relations:** Dir. B. INCE, M.A., PH.D. (acting).

# TUNISIA
Population 6,218,000

## LEARNED SOCIETIES

**Association Tunisienne de Bibliothécaires, Documentalistes et Archivistes:** B.P. 575, Tunis; f. 1966; publ. *Quarterly Bulletin*.

**British Council:** c/o British Embassy, 5 place de la Victoire, Tunis; library of 11,316 vols., 80 periodicals; Rep. W. D. BROWN.

**Centre de Documentation Nationale:** Ministry of Information, 2 rue d'Alger, Tunis; f. 1966; Dir. MOHAMED DABBAB; publ. *Documentation Tunisienne, Revue "Tunisie Actualités", Bulletin d'Information*.

**Comité Culturel National:** 105 avenue de la Liberté, Tunis; central body co-ordinating national and international cultural activities, sponsored by the Ministry of Culture and by foreign embassies; Regional and Local Cultural Committees throughout the country; Pres. LAMINE CHABBI.

**Comité National des Musées:** Musée National du Bardo; f. 1961; Pres. Mme NAYLA ATTYA; publ. *Les musées de Tunisie*.

**Deutsches Kulturinstitut:** 17 ave. de France, Tunis; Dir. Dr. H. P. ADOLF.

**Institut National d'Archéologie et d'Art:** 4 place du Château, Tunis; f. 1957; 48 mems.; library of 10,000 vols.; archaeology, museography, ethnography; Dir. A. BESCHAOUCH; publs. *Africa†, Notes et Documents†, Cahiers des Arts et Traditions Populaires†, Bibliothèque Archéologique†, Etudes Hispano-Andalouses*.

Comprises the following five departments:

**Centre de la Recherche Archéologique et Historique:** Sec.-Gen. Mme HARBI-RIAHI.

**Conservation du Patrimoine Archéologique et Historique:** Sec.-Gen. M. DAOULATLI.

**Commission des Musées Archéologiques et Historiques:** Sec.-Gen. M. ENNAÏFER.

**Centre des Arts et Traditions Populaires:** administers museums of art and ethnography at Sfax and Jerba; Sec.-Gen. Mme S. SETHOM.

**Centre des Etudes Hispano-Andalouses:** Dir. M. ZBISS.

**Institut des Belles Lettres Arabes:** 12 rue Jamâa el Haoua, 1008 Tunis Bab Menara; f. 1930; cultural centre; library of Tunisian studies (25,000 vols.); Dir. J. FONTAINE; publs. *IBLA†* (2 a year), various studies on Tunisian, Arab and Islamic studies.

**Istituto Italiano di Cultura:** 35 ave. de la Liberté, Tunis; f. 1962; Dir. Prof. RAIMONDO PIZZUTO; library of 4,000 vols.

**Organisation de la Ligue Arabe pour l'Education, la Culture et la Science/Arab League Educational, Cultural and Scientific Organization (ALECSO):** B.P. 1120, Tunis; f. 1970 for the development of education, culture and sciences in Arab countries; mems.: 20 Arab countries; library of 3,000 vols.; Dir. Gen. D. MOHEDDINE SABER; publs. *Revue Arabe de l'Education†, Revue Arabe d'Etude Pédagogique†, Revue d'Information et Documentation†, Bulletin†, Statistique de l'Education†* (annually), *Annuaire Culturel†*.

**Union Nationale des Arts Plastiques:** Musée du Belvédère, Tunis.

**Union des Ecrivains Tunisiens:** Maison de la Culture Ahmed Khiereddine, B.P. 18, Tunis; f. 1970; 100 mems.; Pres. MOHAMED MZALI; Sec. Gen. BECHIR BEN SLAMA.

## RESEARCH INSTITUTES

**Centre de Recherches pour l'Utilisation de l'Eau Salée en Irrigation:** Route de Soukra, B.P. 10, Ariana; f. 1963; agronomy, irrigation, etc.

**Institut Artoing:** Tunis; veterinary research.

**Institut de Recherches Scientifiques et Techniques:** Tunis-Carthage; f. 1966; Dir. T. BEN MENA.

**Institut National de la Recherche Agronomique de Tunisie:** Ariana; f. 1914 as the Service Botanique et Agronomique de Tunisie; library of 6,000 vols., 1,200 periodicals; Dir. M. STA'M'RAD; publs. *Annales*, and miscellaneous reprints: *Documents techniques*.

**Institut National de Recherches Forestières de Tunisie:** B.P.2, Ariana; f. 1967 under present title; research in all aspects of forestry; 152 staff, of whom 42 are research workers; Documentation Centre comprises 2,100 vols. and 2,400 documents; Dir. H. HAMZA; Gen. Sec. M. DAHMAN; publs. *Bulletin d'Information†* (2 or 3 a year), *Annales†, Notes Techniques†*.

**Institut National de Recherches Vétérinaires:** Tunis; centre for veterinary research.

**Institut National des Sciences de l'Education:** 17 rue Fénelon, Tunis; f. 1968; 20 staff; conducts research into oral methods of teaching French and Arabic, the training of primary school teachers, teaching techniques; medico-psycho-pedagogical centre; closed circuit TV; Dir. ABDELMEJID ATTIA; publs. *Revue*, pedagogical documents.

**Institut National Scientifique et Technique d'Océanographie et de Pêche:** Salammbô; f. 1924; fisheries research; library of 1,720 vols., 1,407 periodicals; Dir. Dr. M. HADJ ALI SALEM; publ. *Bulletin†*.

**Institut Pasteur:** 13 place Pasteur, 1002 Tunis Belvédère; f. 1906; library of 4,500 vols.; scientific staff of 16; Dir. Dr. AMOR CHADLI; publ. *Archives de l'Institut Pasteur de Tunis* (quarterly).

**Office de la Recherche Scientifique et Technique Outre-Mer: Mission ORSTOM auprès du Ministère de l'Agriculture:** 18 rue Charles Nicolle, 1002 Tunis Belvédère; f. 1958; pedology, hydrology, geology, geomorphology, hydrobiology, climatology, agronomy, geography, economics, demography; library; Dir. R. LEFÈVRE. (*See* main entry under France.)

**Service Géologique:** 95 ave. Mohamed V, Tunis; f. 1921; geological map-making; staff of 27; library of 1,200 vols., 500 periodicals; Dir. T. LAJMI; publs. *Annales des Mines et de la Géologie†, Notes du service géologique†*.

## LIBRARIES

**Archives Nationales:** Présidence de la République, place du Gouvernement, Tunis; 19th-century MSS. in Arabic, Turkish, French, Italian and English.

TUNISIA

**Bibliothèque Nationale:** B.P. 42, 20 Souk-el-Attarine, Tunis; f. 1885; 500,000 vols. in 12 languages; 8,000 periodicals; 25,000 Arabic and Oriental MSS.; depository of books published in Tunisia or written by Tunisians; documentation and information dept.; Curator EZZEDINE GUELLOUZ; publs. *Bibliographie Nationale*† (quarterly), *Informations Bibliographiques*†, *Catalogue général des Manuscrits*† (3 a year), occasional bibliographies on Tunisian subjects†.

**Bibliothèques Publiques:** Head Office: 10 rue de Russie, Tunis; f. 1965; 806,326 vols. in 54 public libraries throughout the country, notably at Béja, Bizerta, Gabès, Gaisa, Jendouba, Kairouan, Kasserine, Le Kef, Medenine, Monastir, Nabeul, Sfax, Sousse, Siliana and Mahdia; 39 children's libraries, 100 local and community libraries and 15 mobile libraries; Dir. BACHIR EL FANI; publs. *Statistics of public libraries*, *Répertoire*, *Bulletin* (annually).

## MUSEUMS

**Musée National du Bardo:** Le Bardo, Tunis; f. 1888; contains prehistoric collections, relics of Punic, Greek and Roman art, and ancient and modern Islamic arts largest collection in the world of Roman mosaics; Dir. ENNAIFER MONGI; publs. *La Civilisation Tunisienne à Travers la Mosaïque*, *Corpus des Mosaïques Antiques de Tunisie*, *La Cité d'Althiburos*, and occasional publications.

Other Museums under the control of the *Direction des Musées Nationaux*:

**Musée Archéologique de Sfax:** Sfax.
**Musée d'Art Islamique du Ribat:** Monastir.
**Musée Archéologique de Sousse (Kasbah):** Sousse.
**Musée de Village de Moknine.**
**Musée Archéologique:** Carthage.
**Musée Antiquarium:** Utique; Punic and Roman.
**Musée Archéologique d'El Jem:** Thysdrus.
**Musée d'Art Islamique:** Kairouan.
**Musée d'Enfidaville.**
**Musée Archéologique de Mactar:** Punic and Roman.

**Musée National de Carthage:** f. 1964; Dir. ABDELMAJID ENNABLI.

Controls the following:
*Parc des Thermes d'Antonin:* f. 1953.
*Parc des Villas Romaines de l'Odeon.*
*Basilique de Saint Cyprien.*
*Tophet de Salammbô.*
*Parc Archéologique de Carthage.*
*Conservation du Site de Carthage:* Ave. de la Republique, Carthage; administers the excavation, restoration, preservation and display of Carthaginian monuments and sites; also the *Centre d'Etudes et de Documentation Archéologique*, f. 1978; publ. *Bulletin CEDAC Carthage*† (1 or 2 a year).

## UNIVERSITY

### UNIVERSITÉ DE TUNIS
94 BOULEVARD DU 9 AVRIL 1938, TUNIS
Telephone: 261-414, 260-389.

Founded 1960, incorporating existing higher education institutions.

Languages of instruction: Arabic, French; Academic year, October to June (2 semesters).

Number of teachers: c. 1,600 full-time, 3,000 part-time.
Number of students: 29,640.

Publications: *Cahiers de Tunisie*† (each semester), *Annales de l'Université de Tunis*† (annually).

WORLD OF LEARNING

CONSTITUENT INSTITUTIONS:

*Faculty of Mathematics, Physics and Natural Sciences:* Dean ALI EL HILI.
*Faculty of Letters and Human Sciences:* Dean MOHAMED ABDESSALEM.
*Faculty of Law, Political and Economic Sciences:* Dean MONDHER GARGOURI.
*"Ez Zitouna" Faculty of Theology and Religious Science:* Dean CHEDLY ENNAIFER.
*Faculty of Medicine:* Dean HASSOUNA BEN AYED.
*Faculty of Medicine (Sousse):* 65 rue Dr. Moreau, Sousse; Dean SOUAD LYAGOUBI.
*Faculty of Pharmacy (Monastir):* Dean MAHMOUD YACOUB.
*Faculty of Dentistry (Monastir):* Dean MAHMOUD YACOUB.
*Faculty of Science and Technology (Monastir):* Dean KHELIFA HARZALLAH.
*Faculty of Economics and Business Administration (Sfax)* rue Habib Maazoun, Sfax; Dean ABDELLATIF KHEMAKHEM.
*Faculty of Medicine (Sfax):* Dean ABDELHAFIDH SELLAMI.
*Faculty of Science and Technology (Sfax):* Dean RADHOUANE ELLOUZE.

**Institut des Hautes Etudes Commerciales:** Carthage-Présidence; f. 1942; 32 teachers, 788 students; Dir. RIDHA FERCHIOU.

**Institut Bourguiba des Langues Vivantes:** 47 ave. de la Liberté, Tunis; f. 1961; classes for adults in English, Arabic, French, German, Spanish, Russian; 660 students; library of 20,000 vols.; Dir. MOHAMED MAAMOURI; brs. in Bizerte, Gafsa, Sfax, Sousse.

**Institut Supérieur de Gestion des Entreprises:** 1 ave. de France, Tunis; f. 1969; library of 1,400 vols.; 843 students; Dir. MAHMOUD TRIKKI.

**Institut de Presse et des Sciences de l'Information:** Montfleury, Tunis; 375 students; Dir. MONSEF CHANOUFI.

**Ecole Normale Supérieure:** Le Bardo; 100 teachers, 855 students; Dir. AMMAR MAHJOUBI.

**Ecole Normale Supérieure de l'Enseignement Technique:** 5 ave. Taha Hussein, Tunis; 89 teachers; 744 students; Dir. MOHAMED ANNABI.

**Ecole Nationale d'Ingénieurs de Tunis:** Campus Universitaire; 127 teachers; 1,151 students; Dir. AHMED MARRAKCHI.

**Ecole Nationale d'Ingénieurs:** Gabès; f. 1975; 50 teachers; 338 students; Dir. BELGACEM BACCAR.

**Institut Supérieur Technique de Gabès:** Dir. MOHAMED CHEHATA.

ATTACHED RESEARCH INSTITUTES:

**Centre d'Etudes et de Recherche Economiques et Sociales:** 23 rue d'Espagne, Tunis; 25 staff; Dir. ABDELWAHEB BOUHDIBA.

**Institut de Recherche Scientifique et Technique:** Campus Universitaire, Tunis; 13 staff; Dir. AHMED BOURAOUI.

**Centre Inter-Régional d'Informatique et d'Automatique "El Khawarezmi":** Campus Universitaire, Tunis; Dir. MOHAMED AMARA.

## OTHER INSTITUTIONS OF HIGHER EDUCATION

**Centre d'Art Dramatique (Etudes Théâtrales):** Hammamet; f. 1965; theatrical techniques, history and sociology of the theatre.

**Conservatoire National de Musique, de Danse et d'Arts Populaires:** 20 ave. de Paris, Tunis.

**Ecole Nationale d'Administration:** 24 ave. du Docteur Calmette, Mutuelleville, Tunis; f. 1949; reorganized 1964; postgraduate courses; 1,050 students; library of 42,000 vols.; Dir. MOHAMED ALI SLIM; publs. *Servir Cahiers, Études et Documents, Manuels.*

**Ecole Nationale de Médecine Vétérinaire:** Medjez El Bab; 5-year postgraduate courses; 297 students.

**Ecole des Postes et des Télécommunications:** 12 rue de l'Angleterre, Tunis; f. 1967; 2- and 4-year postgraduate courses; 495 students.

**Ecole de l'Aviation Civile et de la Météorologie:** Tunis; f. 1957; 2- and 4-year postgraduate courses; 12 teachers; 150 students.

**Ecole Nationale de la Statistique:** Tunis.

**Institut d'Economie Quantitative Ali-Bach-Hamba:** 2 rue Benghazi, Tunis; f. 1964; quantitative studies, methodological research in planning and documentation, social and economic fields; 23 staff; Dir. Gen. NOURI ZORGATI.

**Institut National Agronomique de Tunisie:** 43 ave. Charles Nicolle, Tunis; f. 1898; postgraduate courses; 63 teachers, 351 students; library of 8,000 vols., 300 periodicals; Dir. K. BELKHODJA; Librarian MOHAMED BEN MOUSSA; publ. *Bulletin†.*

**Institut National de Nutrition et de Technologie Alimentaire:** 11 rue Aristide Briand Bab Saadoun, Tunis; f. 1969; applied and clinical nutrition, research, food technology, control of medicines and cosmetics; 250 staff and consultants, 200 students; library of 2,500 vols.; Dir. Prof. ZOUHAIR KALLAL; publ. *Nutrition Appliquée†* (every 2 months).

**Institut National de Service Social:** Tunis; 144 students; 2-year diploma courses.

**Institut Technologique d'Art, d'Architecture et d'Urbanisme de Tunis:** Route de l'Armée Nationale, Tunis; f. 1973 from Ecole des Beaux Arts de Tunis; architecture and town planning, and fine arts section; 600 students; Dir. Prof. M. L. BOUGUERRA.

# TURKEY
Population 45,217,000

## LEARNED SOCIETIES

**British Council:** c/o British Embassy, 50-52 Güniz Sok., Kavaklidere, Ankara; Counsellor for British Council and Cultural Affairs J. J. BARNETT; Books Officer Miss M. S. JACK; and Office of the Consul for British Council and Cultural Affairs, Kat 2, Ege Han, 22-24 Cumhuriyet Caddesi, Elmadag, Istanbul; Consul W. B. HUDSON; Libraries: see Libraries.

**Centro di Studi Italiani in Turchia:** Adakale Sok. 68, Ankara; Dir. Dr. M. ELDEM; Istanbul Centre: Mesrutiyet Caddesi 161, Tepebaşı, Istanbul; Dir. Prof. GIUSEPPE MANICA.

**Österreichisches Kulturinstitut Istanbul:** Istanbul-Tesvikiye, Belvedere Apt. 101/2, P.K. 6; Dir. Prof. Dr. J. E. KASPER.

**P.E.N. Yazarlar Derneği** (*P.E.N.—Turkish Centre*): Cağaloğlu Yokuşu 40, Istanbul; f. 1951; 70 mems.; Pres. YAŞAR NABI NAYIR.

**Türk Biyoloji Derneği** (*Turkish Biological Society*): P.K. 144, Sirkeci-Istanbul; f. 1949; 240 mems.; Pres. Prof. Dr. H. DEMIRIZ; to promote biological research and to organize lectures, congresses and training courses on biology and nature study; publ. *Turk Biyoloji Dergisi* (*Acta Biologica Turcica*) (three issues a year).

**Türk Cerrahi Cemiyeti** (*Turkish Surgical Society*): Etibba Odası, Cağaloğlu, Istanbul; f. 1931.

**Türk Dil Kurumu** (*Turkish Linguistic Society*): 217 Atatürk Bulevar, Ankara; f. 1932; 541 mems.; library of 25,000 vols.; Pres. Prof. Dr. SERAFETTIN TURAN; Sec.-Gen. CAHIT KÜLEBI; publs. *Türk Dili* (monthly), *Türk Dili Araştırmaları Yilliği-Belleten* (annually).

**Türk Eczacıları Birliği** (*Turkish Pharmaceutical Association*): 26 Ortaklar Han, Cağaloğlu, Istanbul; publ. *Türk Eczacıları Birligi Mecmuası* (bi-monthly).

**Türk Halk Bilgisi Derneği** (*Turkish Folklore Society*): Çemberlitaş, Atik Ali Paşa Medresi 43, Istanbul; f. 1946; Pres. S. Y. ATAMAN; Sec. IHSAN HİNÇER.

**Türk Hukuk Kurumu** (*Turkish Law Association*): Yenişehir, Adakale Sokak, No. 28, Ankara; f. 1934; publs. *La Turquie* (Vie Juridique des Peuples, Paris), *Türk Hukuk Lûgati* (Turkish Law Dictionary).

**Türk Mikrobiyoloji Cemiyeti** (*Turkish Microbiological Society*): P.K. 57, Beyazit, Istanbul; f. 1931; Pres. Prof. SADETTIN YARAR; Sec. Gen. Prof. Dr. ÖZDEM ANĞ; publ. *Türk Mikrobiyoloji Cemiyeti Dergisi*† (Journal of Turkish Microbiological Society) (quarterly).

**Türk Nöro-Psikiyatri Derneği** (*Turkish Neuro-Psychiatric Society*): Psikiyatri Kliniği, Çapa/Istanbul; f. 1914; 620 mems.; monthly meetings to discuss aspects of neuro-psychiatry; National Congress every year; Hon. Pres. Prof. Dr. İHSAN SÜKRÜ AKSEL; Pres. Prof. BURHANETTIN NOYAN; Sec.-Gen. Dr. İMADETTIN AKKÖK; publ. *Nöro-Psikiyatri Arşivi* (Archives of Neuro-Psychiatry) (quarterly).

**Türk Ortopedi ve Travmatoloji Derneği** (*Turkish Orthopaedic and Traumatology Society*): Çapa/Istanbul; f. 1939; 370 mems.; library of 2,500 vols.; Pres. Prof. Dr. M. A. GÖKSAN; Sec.-Gen. Dr. M. J. KOKİNO; publ. *Acta Orthopaedica et Traumatologica Turcica*† (quarterly).

**Türk Oto-Rino-Larengoloji Cemiyeti** (*Turkish Oto-Rhino-Laryngological Society*): c/o Çapa Kulak Bogaz, Burun Kliniği, Istanbul.

**Türk Sırfı ve Tatbikl Matematik Derneği** (*Turkish Society of Pure and Applied Mathematics*): Dedeefendi Caddesi 8, Şehzadebaşı, Istanbul; f. 1948; development of mathematics among young people; 100 mems.; Pres. Prof. CAHIT ARF.

**Türk Tarih Kurumu** (*Turkish Historical Society*): Kizilay Sok. 1, Ankara; f. 1931; 41 mems.; library of 150,000 vols.; Pres. Ord. Prof. ENVER ZIYA KARAL; Gen. Dir. ULUĞ İĞDEMİR; Librarian MİHİN EREN LUGAL; publs. *Belleten* (quarterly), *Belgeler* (twice a year).

**Türk Tibbi Elektro Radyografi Cemiyeti** (*Turkish Electro-Radiographical Society*): Etibba Odası, Cağaloğlu, Istanbul; f. 1924.

**Türk Tıb Cemiyeti** (*Turkish Medical Society*): Tabib Odasi, Cağaloğlu, Kizilay Cad. 6, St. 1, Istanbul; f. 1856; 312 mems.; Pres. Dr. KAZIM İSMAİL GÜRKAN; Sec. Dr. ASIL MUKBİL ATAKAM; publs. *Turk Tıp Cemiyeti Mecmuası*, *Anadolu Klinigi* (Turkish Medical Journal).

**Türk Tıp Tarihi Kurumu** (*Turkish Medical History Society*): Tıp Tarihi Enstitüsü, Istanbul University, Istanbul; f. 1938; 48 mems.; library of 70,000 vols.; Dirs. Prof. BEDI N. ŞEHSUVAROĞLU, M.D., Prof. FERIDUN FRIK, M.D.

**Türk Tüberküloz Cemiyeti** (*Turkish Tuberculosis Society*): Selime Hatun. Sağlik Sokak, Taksim, Istanbul; f. 1937

**Türk Üniversite Rektörleri Konseyi** (*Council of Turkish University Rectors*): Hacettepe University, Ankara; rectors of all Turkish universities, with former rectors; promotes co-operation between universities; Pres. Prof. Dr. İHSAN DOĞRAMACI; Sec.-Gen. Dr. İLHAN KUM.

**Türk Uroloji Dernegi** (*Turkish Urological Society*): c/o Dr. Cafer Yildiran, Urological Clinic, Haseki Hospital, Aksaray, Istanbul; f. 1933; 150 mems.; Pres. Dr. CAFER YILDIRAN; Gen. Sec. Dr. SEDAT TELLALOĞLU; publs. *Türk Uroloji Dergisi*† (Turkish Journal of Urology, quarterly).

**Türk Veteriner Hekimleri Dernegi** (*Turkish Veterinary Medicine Association*): Saglik Sokak 21-3, Yenisehir, Ankara; f. 1930.

**Türkiye Akil Sağliği Derneği** (*Turkish Society of Mental Hygiene*): Psikiyatri Kliniği, Çapa-Istanbul; f. 1930; 186 mems.; mem. of many international and world federations; Pres. Prof. Dr. SELIM ÖZAYDIN; Sec.-Gen. Prof. Dr. METIN ÖZEK.

**Türkiye Jeoloji Kurumu** (*Turkish Geological Society*): Posta Kutusu 464-Kizilay, Ankara; f. 1946; 1,410 mems.; library of 12,000 vols.; Pres. TAHIR ÖNGÜR; publs. *Türkiye Kurum Bülteni*† (2 a year), *Yeryuvarive Insan* (quarterly), *Tuytek Bülteni* (every 2 months).

**Türkiye Kimya Cemiyeti** (*The Chemical Society of Turkey*): Harbiye, Halaskârgazi Caddesi No. 53, Uzay Apt. D.8, P.O.B. 829, Istanbul; f. 1919; 970 mems.; Pres. Prof. Dr. ALI RIZA BERKEM; Vice-Pres. Chem. Eng. HADI

TAMER; Sec. Chem. Eng. Ç. TURHAN ÖZALP; Treas. Chem. Eng. ERDEM TARGUL; publ. *Kimya ve Sanayi* (Chemistry and Industry).

**Yeni Felsefe Cemiyeti** (*The New Philosophical Society*): Işık Lisesi, Nişantaşı, Istanbul; f. 1943.

# RESEARCH INSTITUTES
(see also under Universities)

**Ankara Nükleer Araştırma ve Eğitim Merkezi** (*Ankara Nuclear Research and Training Centre*): Beşevler, Ankara; f. 1967; attached to the Turkish Atomic Energy Commission; nuclear analysis and radioisotope applications for industry, applied and basic research in physics, chemistry, electronics and agriculture; 180 staff; library, including collection of 20,000 technical reports, 62 vols. of journals; Dir. Prof. Dr. NAMIK K. ARAS; publ. *Technical Journal*† (3 a year).

**Araştırma Fen Heyeti Müdürlüğü** (*Directorate of Materials and Research*): Yücetepe, Ankara; f. 1948; attached to the General Directorate of Turkish Highways; road materials testing and geotechnical investigations; 60 staff; library of 2,371 vols.; Dir. Dr. HIKMET ÇAVUŞOĞLU; publ. *Research Bulletin*†.

**British Institute of Archaeology at Ankara:** Tahran Caddesi 24, Kavaklidere, Ankara; f. 1947 with the object of furthering archaeological research by British and Commonwealth students or scholars in Turkey; London Office: c/o The British Academy, Burlington House, W1; library of 15,000 vols.; Pres. Prof. SETON LLOYD, C.B.E., M.A., F.B.A., F.S.A., A.R.I.B.A.; Dir. D. H. FRENCH; publ. *Anatolian Studies*† (annually).

**Çay Araştırma Enstitüsü** (*Tea Research Institute*): Rize; f. 1958; attached to the Turkish Tea Board; 68 mems.; library of 950 vols.; Dir. HIZIR NURIK.

**Çocuk Sağlığı Enstitüsü** (*Institute of Child Health*): Hacettepe University, Ankara; f. 1958; library incorporated in main University Library; Dir Dr İ. DOĞRAMACI.

**Coğrafya Enstitüsü** (*Geographical Institute*): Mǔsküle sok. Vefa, Istanbul; f. 1933; 22 mems.; library of 10,661 vols.; Dir. Prof. Dr. AJUN KURTER; publ. *Coğrafya Enstitüsü Dergisi, Review*† (once or twice a year).

**Deprem Araştırma Enstitüsü** (*Earthquake Research Institute*): Yüksel Caddesi No. 7/B, Yenişehir, Ankara; f. 1969; 106 staff; attached to the Ministry of Reconstruction and Resettlement; establishment, operation and maintenance of nationwide strong ground motion recorder network; earthquake prediction; preparation of codes and regulations for earthquake resistant design and construction; research on earthquake hazard minimization; education and information of the public; Pres. OKTAY ERGÜNAY; publ. *Bulletin*† (quarterly).

**Deutsches Archäologisches Institut:** Siraselvi 123, Istanbul-Taksim; f. 1929; research into archaeology in Turkey from pre-history to Byzantium; library of 50,000 vols.; Dir. Prof. Dr.-Ing. WOLFGANG MÜLLER-WIENER; publ. *Istanbuler Mitteilungen des D.A.I.* (annually), *Istanbuler Forschungen*.

**Devlet Sulşleri Araştırma Dairesi** (*Research Division, Turkish State Hydraulic Works*): Ankara; f. 1958; research and laboratory work on hydraulic engineering, soil mechanics, construction materials and concrete, chemistry, isotopes for hydrology; *in situ* research on water works; 355 staff; library; Dir. Dr. F. ŞENTÜRK; publs. *DSI Teknik Bülteni*†, *DSI Teknik Bülteni Özel Savı*† (original papers, some in foreign languages).

**Gıda, Tarım ve Hayvancılık Bakanlığı Bölge Zirai Mücadele Araştırma Enstitüsü** (*Ministry of Food, Agriculture and Animal Husbandry, Plant Protection Research Institute*): Kalaba, Ankara; f. 1934; responsible for licensing all agricultural chemicals to be used for plant protection; 12 depts. dealing with disease and pests attacking the various types of crops, plants and vegetables; 43 technical staff; library of 3,050 vols.; Dir. A. ULVİ KILIÇ; publ. *Bitki Koruma Bülteni* (Plant Protection Bulletin, English, French or German summary, quarterly).

**Hollanda Tarih ve Arkeoloji Enstitüsü** (*Netherlands Historical and Archaeological Institute*): Istiklâl Cad. 393, Beyoğlu, Istanbul; f. 1958; library of 12,500 vols.; Pres. J. G. BEELAERTS; Dir. J. J. ROODENBERG; Sec. T. SMIT-ÖKTEM; publs. *Publications, Anatolica*.

**Institut Français d'Etudes Anatoliennes d'Istanbul:** Palais de France, Istanbul-Beyoğlu, Istanbul; f. 1930; library of c. 6,000 vols.; 3 mems.; Dir. GEORGES LE RIDER; publ. *Bibliothèque de l'Institut Français d'Etudes Anatoliennes d'Istanbul*.

**Kavak ve Hızlı Gelişen Orman Ağaçları Araştırma Enstitüsü** (*Poplar and Fast Growing Forest Trees Research Institute*): P.K. 44, İzmit; f. 1962; attached to the Ministry of Forestry; reafforestation, introduction of new forest tree species, increase of wood production, research in popular and eucalyptus cultivation; 50 staff; library of 3,000 vols.; Dir. M. ALI SEMİZOĞLU; publ. *Annual Bulletin*†.

**Maden Tetkik ve Arama Enstitüsü (M.T.A.)** (*Mineral Research and Exploration Institute*): İsmet İnönü Bulvarı, Ankara; f. 1935; conducts the Geological Survey of Turkey and evaluates mineral resources; library: see Libraries; Dir.-Gen. Dr. SADRETTİN ALPAN; publs. *Bulletin*, Monographs, annual reports and maps.

**Marmara Scientific and Industrial Research Institute:** P.O.B. 21, Gebze-Kocaeli and P.O.B. 141 Kadıköy-İstanbul; f. 1972; research on basic and applied sciences, and industrial research; staff of 520; library of 40,000 vols., 850 periodicals; Dir. Prof. LÜTFULLAH ULUKAN; publs. Research reports.

**Milletlerarası Şark Tetkikleri Cemiyeti** (*International Society for Oriental Research*): Türkiyat Enstitüsü, Bayezit, Istanbul; f. 1947; Pres. Prof. FUAD KÖPRÜLÜ.

**Türk Kültürünü Araştırma Enstitüsü** (*Turkish Cultural Research Institute*): P.K. 14, Çankaya, Ankara; f. 1961; scholarly research into all aspects of Turkish culture; Dir. Dr. AHMET TEMİR; publs. *Türk Kültürü* (monthly), *Cultura Turcica* (half-yearly), *Türk Kültürü Araştırmaları* (half-yearly).

**Türkiye Bilimsel ve Teknik Araştırma Kurumu** (*Scientific and Technical Research Council of Turkey*): Atatürk Boulevard 221, Kavaklidere/Ankara; f. 1963; 223 staff mems.; library of 10,000 vols., 759 periodicals; government body which promotes and co-ordinates research activities in pure and applied sciences; mems. of Scientific Board: Prof. Dr. RATIP BERKER (Pres.), Prof. Dr. İ. AKIF KANSU (Vice-Pres.), Prof. Dr. TEVFIK KARABAĞ (Sec.-Gen.), Prof. Dr. NAMIK AKSOYCAN, Prof. Dr. METIN BARA, Prof. Dr. SADIK KAKAÇ, Prof. Dr. HAKKI ORANÇ, Prof. Dr. HAKKI ÖGELMAN, Prof. Dr. EMIN ULUSOY; publs. science congress and conference proceedings, research projects reports, *Science and Technique* (monthly), *Doğa* (monthly), *Information Profiles*† (irregularly), *Current Titles in Turkish Science*† (Turkish and English, quarterly), *National and International Meetings on Science and Technology*† (English, quarterly), *Turkish Dissertation Index*† (Turkish and English, annually), subject bibliographies.

**Zirai Mücadele İlâç ve Aletleri Enstitüsü** (*Plant Protection Chemicals and Equipment Institute*): P.K. 49, Yenimahalle/Ankara; f. 1957; attached to the Ministry of

Agriculture; research and surveys on all matters concerning the use of pesticides; 35 staff; library of 930 vols., 43 periodicals; Dir. KEMÂL KUNTER.

## LIBRARIES

**Ankara University Library:** the main library has 70,050 vols.; there are also separate faculty libraries, with a total of over 395,000 vols.; Dir. ZEKERİYA ERDAL.

**Atıf Efendi Library:** Istanbul; f. 1741; 7,000 vols., 2,800 MSS.

**Beyazıt Devlet Kütüphanesi** (*Beyazit State Library*): İmaret Sok. 18, Beyazit, Istanbul; f. 1882; legal deposit library; 461,000 vols. in various languages, 11,098 MSS., 32,500 photographs, 14,641 periodicals; Dir. HASAN DUMAN.

**Boğaziçi University Library:** Bebek, P.K. 2, Istanbul; f. 1863; 175,000 vols. in English and other languages, including a special collection of over 27,000 vols. on the Near East; Librarian NURTEN ÇAKIR.

**British Council Libraries:** 50-52 Güniz Sok., Kavaklidere, Ankara; f. 1942; 13,118 vols., 72 periodicals; Librarian Mrs. S. ASLAN; Istanbul: Kat 2, Ege Han, 22-24 Cumhuriyet Caddesi, Elmadag, Istanbul; f. 1942; 15,725 vols., 65 periodicals; Librarian Miss I. SALTIKGİL.

**Damat Ibrahim Paşa Library:** Nevsehir; f. 1727; 5,500 vols., 600 MSS.

**Ecumenical Patriarchate Library:** Istanbul; foundation dates from beginning of Patriarchate, reorganization 1890; 25,000 vols. in main library, and 1,500 MSS.; 45,000 vols. in branch library at Orthodox Seminary of Heybeliada; dir. by Rev. PANAĞHIOTIS THEODORIDIS, under the jurisdiction of the Holy Synod.

**Gedik Ahmed Paşa Library:** Afyon; f. 1785; 21,000 vols.

**General Library of İzmir:** Milli Kütüphane Caddesi, No. 39, İzmir; f. 1912; 68,317 vols. in Turkish, 17,807 vols. in European languages, 10,500 vols. in Oriental scripts, largely Turkish; over 1,500 MSS.; dir. by the Ministry of Education; Chief Officer KEMAL ÖZERTEM.

**Grand National Assembly Library:** Grand National Assembly Palace, Ankara; f. 1920; 78,500 vols. in Turkish, 93,000 vols. in European languages, 1,000 vols. in Arabic and Persian, 500 MSS.; Dir. MELİH EGE; Librarian S. NAZMI COSKUNLAR.

**Halil Hamit Paşa Library:** Isparta; f. 1783; 20,200 vols., over 850 MSS.; Dir. MAHMUT KAYICI.

**Halil Nuri Bey Library:** Bor; f. 1932; 12,000 vols., nearly 500 MSS. in Persian, Arabic and Turkish.

**Halkevi Library:** Ankara; f. 1935; 20,000 vols.

**Hisar Salepçioglu Library:** Izmir; f. 1775; 7,000 vols., over 900 MSS.

**Hüsrev Paşa Library:** Eyup; f. 1839; public library; 13,468 vols., over 300 MSS., 562 periodicals; Dir. ŞÜKRÜ YAMAN.

**Il Halk Kütüphanesi** (*Provincial Public Library*): Balikeşir; f. 1901; 828 MSS. in Turkish, Arabic and Persian, 29,970 vols. in Turkish, Arabic and English, 2,101 in other languages, 1,276 periodicals; Dir. NECDET ELAL.

**Institute of Education Library:** Ministry of Education, Ankara; f. 1926; 1,400 vols. in Turkish, 6,000 vols. in European languages.

**Institute of Turkology Library:** Istanbul University, Bayezit; f. 1924; over 20,000 vols. relating to Turkish language, literature, history and culture.

**İstanbul Belediyesi Kütüphane ve Müzeleri** (*Municipal Libraries and Museums of Istanbul*): Head Office: Bayezit Meydanı, İstanbul; Dir. O. GÖK; administers 2 libraries and 5 museums (see under Museums).

**Belediye Kütüphanesi** (*Municipal Library*): Bayezit Meydanı, İstanbul; f. 1939; 155,412 vols., 6,543 MSS. in Turkish, Arabic, Persian and other languages; foremost library for Turkish newspaper collections since 19th century (21,200 vols.).

**F.K. Gökay Library:** Türbedar Sok., Çemberlitaş. Istanbul; 7,500 vols. in different languages.

**Atatürk Library:** Mete Cad., Taksim, Istanbul; f. 1980; in process of formation; reference and student reading library.

**Istanbul Technical University Library:** Gumussuyu Cad. 87, Beyoglu; f. 1795; central library: c. 28,000 vols., faculty libraries: c. 26,000 vols.; Librarian NURTEN ATALIK.

**Istanbul University Central Library:** Istanbul-Beyazit; f. 1925; the main university library contains 275,000 vols. and 18,600 MSS.; in addition, each faculty possesses its own specialized library; Dir. Mrs. LEMAN SENALP; publ. *Bibliography of the Publications of Istanbul University*.

**Köprülü Library:** Istanbul; f. 1677; 3,000 vols., 2,775 MSS., of which 193 are from early Ottoman presses, and 42 handwritten works over 1,000 years old.

**Library of National Defence:** Ankara; f. 1877; 8,678 vols. in Turkish, 5,820 vols. in other languages; State-governed.

**Mehmet Paşa Library:** Darende; f. 1776; 4,000 vols., 800 MSS.

**Middle East Technical University Library:** İsmet İnönü Bulvari, Ankara; f. 1956; maintains custody of the university's recording, microfilm and projection equipment; 252,000 vols.; 2,253 periodicals received mainly in English; Dir. Miss FURUZAN OLŞEN; publ. *Abstracts of Graduate Theses*.

**Millet Kütüphanesi** (*Public Library*): Fatih, Istanbul; f. 1916; 33,980 vols., 8,844 MSS.

**Milli Kütüphane** (*National Library*): Yenişehir, Ankara; f. 1946; 596,697 vols., 5,184 current periodicals, 119,000 vols. periodicals, 4,720 MSS. in Turkish, Arabic and Persian and 9,324 microfilms; provides facilities for artistic and scientific research; Gen. Dir. MÜJGÂN CUNBUR; publs.† *Türkiye Bibliyografyası* (Turkish National Bibliography), *Türkiye Makaleler Bibliyografyası* (Bibliography of articles in Turkish Periodicals, quarterly), *T.C. Devlet Yayınları Bibliyografyası* (Bibliography of Turkish State Publs., monthly), numerous other bibliographies concerning famous persons, catalogues, etc.

**Mineral Research and Exploration Institute Library:** İsmet İnönü Bulvarı, Ankara; f. 1935; 95,000 vols. in various languages; Librarian SEVİM ÖZERTAN; publs. *Bulletin*, monographs, annual reports and maps (in Turkish and English).

**Murat Molla Library:** Istanbul; f. 1775; 4,000 vols., 5,000 MSS.

**Nuruosmaniye Library:** Istanbul; f. 1755; 6,000 vols., 5,000 MSS.

**Public Library:** Ankara; f. 1922; 21,000 vols. in Turkish, 10,200 vols. in European languages, over 1,200 MSS. in Arabic and Persian.

**Public Library:** Konya; f. 1947; 20,000 vols., over 6,000 MSS.

**Ragib Paşa Library:** Istanbul; f. 1762; 4,958 vols., 2,200 MSS.

**Selimiye Library:** Selimiye Kütüphanesi, Edirne; f. 1575; 33,071 vols. (including 3,117 MSS. and 3,894 vols. in Arabic); Librarian Mrs. ÖZLEM AĞIRGAN.

**Süleymaniye Library:** Istanbul; f. 1557; 99,917 vols. and c. 70,000 MSS. in Turkish, Uyghur, Arabic and Persian;

122 different collections including those from Ayasofya and Fatih; MS. restoration service; Dir. MUAMMER ÜLKER.

**Tekelioğlu Library:** Antalya; f. 1924; 5,000 vols., nearly 2,000 MSS. in Persian, Arabic and Turkish.

**Ulucami Library:** Bursa; f. 1787; 8,000 vols., over 1,300 MSS.

**Yegen Mehmet Paşa Library:** Akseki; f. 1926; 6,000 vols.

There are 165 public libraries throughout Turkey.

# MUSEUMS

**Adana Bölge Müzesi** (*Adana Regional Museum*): Adana; f. 1926; depts. of archaeology and ethnography; conference hall, laboratories, library and administrative sections; over 18,000 items from the Neolithic to Roman and Byzantine periods; unique statue of a god made from natural crystal dating from Hittite Empire.

**Amasya Müzesi:** Amasya; f. 1926, moved 1961 to the Gök Medrese Mosque; archaeological finds from the early Bronze Age to Ottoman period; includes mummies dating from the Imperial period.

**Anadolu Medeniyetleri Müzesi** (*Museum of Anatolian Civilizations*): Ankara; f. 1923; exhibits cover the Palaeolithic, Neolithic, Chalcolithic, Early Bronze Age, Hittite, Phrygian and Urartian periods. Hittite reliefs from Alaca, Carchemish, Sakçagözü and Aslantepe and Ankara regions. Collections represent excavations at Karain, Çatal Höyük, Hacılar, Can Hasan, Alacahöyük, Ahlatıbel, Karaz, Alişar, Karaoğlan, Karayavşan, Oymaağaç-Merzifon, Beycesultan, Kültepe, Acemhöyük, İnandik, Boğazköy, Eskiyapar, Patnos, Adilcevaz, Uşak-Ikiztepe, Pazarli, Gordion, Altıntepe, with special sections for cuneiform tablets and coins; library of 5,699 vols.; Dir. RECAİ TEMİZER.

**Anıt-Kabir Muzesi** (*Ataturk's Mausoleum and Museum*): Ankara; f. 1953; Ataturk's official and civil possessions: documents, medals, plaques, albums, etc.; library of 3,113 vols.

**Antalya Bölge Müzesi** (*Antalya Regional Museum*): Antalya; f. 1923; natural history, pre-history, ethnography.

**Âsiyan Museum:** next to Boğaziçi (Bosphorus) University, Bebek, İstanbul; home of Turkish poet and artist T. Fikret.

**Atatürk's Revolution Museum:** Halâskârgazi Caddesi, Sişli, İstanbul; f. 1942; Dir. SEYFİ AKYIL.

**Ayasofya (Saint Sophia) Museum:** Sultan Ahmet, Istanbul; f. 1934; the Museum is housed in the Byzantine Basilica; built by Justinian and dedicated in A.D. 537, it was a church until 1453, after which it became a mosque; in 1935 it was made a state museum; contains Byzantine and Turkish antiquities; Dir. SABAHATTİN TÜRKOĞLU; publ. *The Annual of St. Sophia*. The Director of the Museum of St. Sophia is under the Department of Cultural Affairs, and is in charge of the following Byzantine monuments:

Kariye Church of St. Saviour in Khora.

Fethiye Church of the Virgin Pammakaristos.

Imrahor, Church of the St. John Stoudion.

Church of St. Irene.

Tekfursarayı, Palace of Constantine Porphyrogenitos.

Mosaic Museum.

**Aydın Müzesi:** Aydın; f. 1959; archaeology, ethnography, historical coins.

**Belediye Müzesi** (*Municipal Museum*): Bozdoğan Kemeri yanı, Saraçhanebaşı, Istanbul; f. 1939; folklore and literary collections; Dir. OSMAN GÖK.

**Bodrum Sualtı Arkeoloji Müzesi** (*Bodrum Museum of Underwater Archaeology*): f. 1964 in the castle of Bodrum built in 15th century by the Knights of St. John from Rhodes; finds from land and underwater, including eight ships.

**Büyük Millet Meclisi Müzesi** (*First Grand National Assembly Museum*): Ulus Square, Ankara; the first parliament met in the building in 1920; the republic was announced here; the museum was opened in 1961 when the parliament moved to a new building.

**Bursa Arkeoloji Müzesi:** Bursa; f. 1904; coins, pre-historic finds, stone, ceramics, glass, metal work; art gallery.

**Bursa Türk ve İslâm Eserleri Müzesi** (*Bursa Turkish and Islamic Art Museum*): Bursa; f. 1974 in the Yeşil Medrese which was built by the Ottoman Emperor Çelebi Mehmet; items from 14th century to late Ottoman period: candlesticks, MSS., gilded books, inscriptions, mother-of-pearl and ivory drawers, embroidery, guns, knives; art gallery of the Ottoman period.

**Efes Müzesi Müdürlüğü** (*Ephesus Museum*): Selsuk-Izmir; f. 1939; contains works of art (mostly statues and reliefs) excavated from Ephesus; 2,550 vols.; publ. *Efes Müzesi Yılligı*† (annual).

**Eskişehir Arkeoloji Müzesi:** Akarbaşı, Eskişehir; f. 1935; plant and animal fossils; pre-history (ceramics, idols, stone and bone objects); the walls are decorated with the late Roman mosaics found in excavations at Doryleum.

**Ethnographical Museum:** Ankara; f. 1927; specimens of Turkish and Islamic art, archives and Islamic numismatics; library of 3,500 vols.; Dir. ENİSE YENER.

**Gordion Museum:** Polatlı, Ankara; f. 1965 in a new building built over the Great Tumulus of the Phrygian king Midas; archaeological items found during excavations at Gordion (now Yassıhöyük).

**Hatay Museum:** Gündüz Cad. No. 1, Antakya, Hatay; f. 1934; collection of mosaics from Roman Antioch, also finds from Al-Mina, Atchana, Çatal Hüyük, Judeidah and Tainat excavations; Dir. VAHİT MESTÇIOĞLU.

**Istanbul Arkeoloji Müzeleri** (*Archaeological Museums of Istanbul*): Sultanahmet, Istanbul; f. 1846; first collection of antiquities started by Field-Marshal Fethi Ahmed Paşa in 1846; includes Archaeological, Mosaic and Ancient Orient museums, with Sumerian, Akkadian, Hittite, Assyrian, Egyptian, Urartu, Greek, Roman and Byzantine works of art and a library of 60,000 vols.; Dir. ALTAN AKAT; publ. *Annual*†.

**Istanbul Deniz Müzesi** (*Istanbul Naval Museum*): Beşiktaş-Istanbul; f. 1897; exhibits from the Istanbul Arsenal of the Ottoman Empire; important collection of historical caiques; library of 13,000 vols., 15,000 archive files (Ottoman Enpire period); Dir. Capt. HALÛK ÖZDENİZ.

**İzmir Arkeoloji Müzesi:** Kültür Park, İzmir; f. 1927; works from the Archaic, Classical and Hellenistic periods of the Ionian civilization.

**Karikatür Müzesi** (*Cartoon Museum*): Tepebası, Istanbul.

**Konya Museums:** Konya; 1. Mevlâna: founded in Mevlâna Turbe—Seljuk, Ottoman and Turkish collections, clothing, carpets, coins, library; 2. Classical Museum: founded in new classical museum—collections of Neolithic, early Bronze Age, Hittite, Phrygian, Greek, Roman and Byzantine monuments; 3. Turkish Ceramics Museum: founded in Karatay Medresseh—contains ceramics of the 13th–18th century; 4. Seljuk Museum: founded in İnce Minare—contains stone and wooden works of the Seljuk period; 5. Sirçali Medresseh

—Sarcophagus and inscription, collections of Seljuk and Ottoman period; 6. Atatürk Museum—collection of documents and objects connected with Atatürk, also Konya clothing and other ethnographic exhibits; Dir. of Museums VAHIT MESCIOĞLU.

**Pergamon Museum:** Bergama; houses the historical relics discovered as the result of excavations conducted at Pergamon; Dir. OSMAN BAYATLI.

**Resim ve Heykel Müzesi** (*Museum of Painting and Sculpture*): Beşiktaş, Istanbul; f. 1937.

**Side Müzesi:** Manoivgat-Antalya, Side; f. 1962; museum is located in a Late Roman bath; statues and busts of Roman gods, goddesses and emperors; library of 985 vols.; Dir. ORHAN ATVUR.

**Tanzimat Müzesi** (*Museum of the 1839 Turkish Revolution*): Yıldız Park, Beşiktaş, Istanbul.

**Topkapı Palace Museum:** Istanbul; palace built by Muhammad II; collections of Turkish armour, cloth, embroidery, tiles, glass and porcelain, copper- and silver-ware, treasure, paintings, miniatures, illuminated manuscripts, royal coaches, collections of Sèvres and Bohemian crystal and porcelain, clocks, important collection of Chinese and Japanese porcelain amassed by the Sultans, selection of Islamic relics (coat of the Prophet, etc.), Seals of the Sultans, collection of manuscripts, private collections of Kenan Ozbel, Halil Edhem Arda, and Sami Özgiritli, Ottoman tent; 18,000 MSS. in the library and 23,225 archive documents; Audience Hall, Council Hall of Viziers, Baghdad and Revan Köşks, Harem; Dir. KEMAL ÇIĞ.

**Truva Müzesi** (*Troy Museum*): Çanakkale; at the entrance to the ruins of Troy in Çanakkale is a small museum exhibiting pottery, figurines, statues, glass objects.

**Türk ve Islam Eserleri Müzesi** (*Museum of Turkish and Islamic Art*): Süleymaniye, Istanbul; f. 1914; fine collection of Turkish and Islamic rugs, illuminated MSS., sculpture in stone and stucco, woodcarvings, metalwork and ceramics, all gathered from Turkish mosques and tombs; Dir. CAN KERAMETLİ.

**Turkish Natural History Museum:** Ankara; f. 1968 by the Institute of Mineral Research.

**Türkiye Askeri Müzesi** (*Museum of the Janissaries*): Istanbul; f. 1726; military uniforms, weapons and trophies from the earliest times; Dir. Col. AEVKI ŞSLAN.

**Van Müzesi:** Van; f. 1947; archaeological finds from the Urartu Civilization.

# UNIVERSITIES

## ANADOLU ÜNİVERSİTESİ
### (Anatolian University)
ESKIŞEHIR

Founded 1973.

*Rector:* SERVET BILIR.

Number of teachers: c. 40.
Number of students: c. 200.

## ANKARA ÜNİVERSİTESİ
### (University of Ankara)
TANDOGAN MEYDANI, ANKARA

Telephone: 23 32 45.

Founded 1946.

State control; Language of instruction: Turkish; Academic year: October to June.

*Rector:* Prof. Dr. TÜRKAN AKYOL.
*Vice-Rectors:* Prof. Dr. ADNAN GURIZ, Prof. Dr. SÂTI BARAN.
*General Secretary:* CAHİDE ÇETİN.
*Librarian:* SADİYE YILDAM.

Number of teachers: c. 2,200.
Number of students: c. 26,000.

Publications: *Ankara Üniversitesi Yıllığı* (Annals of the University), and faculty and research institute publications.

DEANS:

*Faculty of Letters:* Prof. Dr. YAŞAR YÜCEL.
*Faculty of Pharmacy:* Prof. Dr. GAZANFER BİNGÖL.
*Faculty of Education:* Prof. Dr. ZIYA BURSALIOĞLU.
*Faculty of Science:* Prof. Dr. ARAL OLCAY.
*Faculty of Law:* Prof. Dr. TURGUT AKINTÜRK.
*Faculty of Divinity:* Prof. Dr. HİKMET TANYU.
*Faculty of Political Science:* Prof. Dr. CEVAT GERAY.
*Faculty of Medicine:* Prof. Dr. CELÂL SUNGUR.
*Faculty of Veterinary Science:* Prof. Dr. HÜSEYIN SAİM KENDİR.
*Faculty of Agriculture:* Prof. Dr. TURAN GÜNEŞ.
*Faculty of Medicine (in Antalya):* Prof. Dr. RÜKNETTIN TANALP.
*Faculty of Dentistry:* Prof. Dr. BEDİİ KÜÇÜKÜÇERLER.

PROFESSORS:

*Faculty of Letters:*
AKINCI, G., Modern Turkish Literature
AKURGAL, E., Classical Archaeology and Contemporary Anatolian Archaeology
ALP, Dr. S., Hittitology
ANBARCIOĞLU, Dr. M., Persian Language and Literature
ARIKAN, M., Spanish Language and Literature
ARIK, Dr. O., History of Art
AYTAÇ, K., Pedagogy
BALKAN, Dr. K., Sumerology
BAŞARAN, F., Psychology
BAŞTAV, S., Hungarian Studies
BOSTANCI, Dr. E., Palaeoanthropology
ERDENTUĞ, N. Ethnology
EREN, H., Turkish Language
ERSOY, O., Library Science
FAUQ, H., Urdu and Pakistan Research
GÜLER, Ş., Sociology
GÜRSOY, Dr. C., Political Geography
IŞIK, K., Arabic Language and Literature
IZBIRAK, Dr. R., Physical Geography and Geology
KAYMAZ, N., History of Turkish Republic and Revolution
KAYNAK, İ., Russian Language and Literature
KINAL, F., Ancient History
KÖYMEN, M. A., General Turkish History
KÜYEL, Dr. M., History of Philosophy
MAZIOĞLU, H., Classical Turkish Literature
ÖNCEL, S., Italian Language and Literature
ÖNEN, Y., German Language and Literature
OZERDIM, Dr. M., Sinology
Özgüç, Dr. T., Protohistory and Near-Eastern Archaeology
SAATÇIOĞLU, A., Physical Anthropology
ŞAHINBAŞ, Dr. I., American Literature
SARIGÖLLÜ, S., Latin
SAYILI, Dr. A., Philosophy
ŞENER, S., Theatre
SİNANOĞLU, Dr. S., Classical Greek
SÜMER, F., History
TEKELİ, S., Systematic Philosophy
TUNCEL, Dr. B., French Language and Literature
TURAN, S., Contemporary History
YÜCEL, Y., Modern History

*Faculty of Pharmacy:*
ALTINKURT, Dr. O., Pharmacology
AYRAL, N., Medicinal Science
BİNGÖL, G., Biochemistry
İZGÜ, E., Pharmaceutical Technology
NOYANALPAN, N., Pharmaceutical Chemistry
OLCAY, A., Analytical Chemistry
TANKER, Dr. M., Pharmacognosy and Pharmaceutical Botany
VURAL, N., Toxicology
YUMUTURUĞ, S., Hygiene and Health Services

*Faculty of Education:*
ADEM, M., Economics and Planning of Education
AKHUN, I., Statistics and Educational Research
AKYÜZ, K., Educational Fine Arts
BURSALIOĞLU, Z., Administration and Supervision of Education
ÇAGLAR, D., Special Education

Doğan, H., Technical Education
Geçtan, E., Educational Psychology
Geray, C., Adult Education
Güriz, A., Educational Philosophy
Koçer, H. A., Social and Historical Background of Education
Varış, F., Curriculum and Instruction

**Faculty of Science:**
Akman, Y., Systematic Botany
Arslan, Dr. N., Botany
Ayan, M., Mineralogy
Aybar, Dr. S., Physical Chemistry
Erk, S., Geology
Gündüz, Dr. T., Analytical Chemistry
Hacisalihoğlu, H., Algebra and Geometry
Küçükekşi, S., General Zoology
Mursaloğu, B., Systematic Zoology
Nasuhoğlu, R., Physics
Olcay, Dr. A., Industrial Chemistry
Süray, Dr. S., Applied Mathematics
Tüfekçioğlu, Z., Astronomy
Tüzün, Dr. C., General Chemistry
Uluçay, Dr. C., Theory of Functions
Yurtsever, Dr. B., Mathematical Analysis

**Faculty of Law:**
Akipek, Dr. İ., Public International Law
Ayiter, K., Roman Law
Bilge, Dr. N., Court Procedures
Bozer, Dr. A., Commercial Law
Düren, A., Administrative Law
Fişek, H., Private International Law
Gürsoy, K., Civil Law
Işık, R., Labour Law and Social Security
Kapani, M., Public Law
Keyman, S., Penal Law and Court Procedures
Öncel, M., Public Finance
Özbudun, E., Constitutional Law
Topçuoğlu, Dr. H., Philosophy and Sociology of Law
Üçok, Dr. C., History of Turkish Law
Zarakoğlu, Dr. A., Economics

**Faculty of Medicine:**
Akkaynak, S., Chest Diseases and Tuberculosis
Ari, Dr. N., Physiotherapy and Rehabilitation
Arinci, K., Anatomy
Avman, Dr. N., Neurosurgery
Baykan, N., Public Medicine
Berk, Dr. U., Radiology
Berkmen, S., Oto-Rhino-Laryngology
Bulay, O., Pathology
Demirağ, Dr. B., Paediatrics
Deniz, E., Medical Biology
Duraman, Dr. A., Orthopaedics and Traumatology
Ekmen, H., Microbiology and Parasitology
Erkoçak, A., Histology and Embryology
Gerçel, R., Urology
Güner, Z., Medicinal Physics
Güvener, A., Neurology
Kandemir, E., Obstetrics and Gynaecology
Kaymakçalan, Dr. S., Pharmacology
Koçaş, H., Physiotherapy
Koloğlu, M., Endocrinology and Metabolic Disorders
Oktay, S., Cardiology
Onul, Dr. B., Infectious Diseases
Örgen, C., Ophthalmology
Öztürel, Dr. A., Medicinal Jurisprudence
Paykoç, Dr. R., Anaesthesiology
Paykoç, Dr. Z., Gastroenterology
Sökmen, Dr. C., Internal Diseases
Tat, Dr. L., Dermatology and Syphilis
Torunoğlu, M., Physiopathology

Ünsal, Dr. G., Psychiatry
Yalav, E., Cardiovascular and Pulmonary Surgery
Yavuzer, S., Physiology
Yaycioğlu, A., General Surgery
Yumuturuğ, S., Hygiene, Preventive Medicine and Statistics
Yurtaslani, Z., Biochemistry and Chemistry

**Faculty of Veterinary Science:**
Akkiliç, M., Nutrients and Animal Nutrition
Akman, Dr. S., Pharmacology and Toxicology
Altan, Dr. Y., Internal Disease
Anteplioğlu, H., Surgery
Arda, M., Bacteriology and Epidemiology
Aritürk, Dr. E., Animal Husbandry
Aslanbey, D., Orthopaedics and Traumatology
Baran, Dr. S., Pathology
Bölükbasi, F., Physiology
Büyükpamukçu, M., Pathological Anatomy
Dinçer, F., History of Veterinary Science
Doğaneli, Z., Obstetrics and Gynaecology
Erençin, Z., Marine Products and Game
Ersoy, Dr. E., Biochemistry
Gültekin, M., Anatomy
Güralp, Dr. N., Parasitology and Helminthology
Gürtürk Dr., S., Virology
Hasa, Dr. O., Histology
Kendir, H. S., Statistics and Planning
Sayin, F., Protozoology and Medicinal Arthropodology
Seving, A., Breeding
Tolgay, Dr. Z., Nutrition Control and Technology

**Faculty of Agriculture:**
Açil, Dr. F., Agricultural Economy and Farm Management
Akpinar, C., Poultry
Akyildiz, R., Nutrients and Animal Nutrition
Altinbaş, E., Fibre Technology and Handicrafts
Atay, D., Fisheries
Aydeniz, A., Radiophysiology and Soil Fertility
Ayfer, M., Fruit Growing
Bakir, O., Forage Crops and Pastures
Cemeroğlu, B., Agricultural Power Machinery
Doğuş, Dr. R., Agricultural Machinery and Implements
Düzgüneş, Z., Entomology
Eker, M., Animal Husbandry
Fidan, Y., Viticulture and Vegetable Crops
Göçüş, Dr. K., Meat and Leather Technology
Hizalan, Dr. E., Soil Science
İlisulu, K., Industrial Crops
İren, S., Phytopathology
Kacar, B., Plant Nutrition
Kaptan, N., Dairy Technology
Kesici, T., Agricultural Genetics and Statistics
Köşker, Dr. O., Agricultural Microbiology
Öztan, Y., Landscape Architecture
Pamir, H., Fermentation Technology
Şahinkaya, R., Home Economics
Sönmez, N., Agricultural Engineering
Tosun, Dr. O., Plant Breeding
Yavuzcan, G., Agricultural Power Machinery

**Faculty of Political Science:**
Alkan, T., Political Behaviour

Aydin, V., Business Economics and Accounting
Bulutay, Dr. T., Statistics and Econometrics
Daver, Dr. B., Political Theories
Demir, A., Economic Policy
Gölcüklü, Dr. F., Criminal Law
Gönlübol, Dr. M., International Relations
Gözübüyük, Dr. Ş. P., Administration
Gürsoy, B., Finance
Mihçioğlu, Dr. C. A., Public Administration
Mimaroğlu, Dr. S. K., Commercial Law
Ozankaya, Ö., Sociology
Öztrak, I., Civil Law
Pazarci, H., Public International Law
Reisoğlu, Dr. S., Civil Law
Sander, O., Political History
Savci, B., Constitutional Law
Serin, N., International Economics and Development
Talas, Dr. C., Social Policy and Labour Law
Timur, T., Turkish Politics
Türkay, O., Economic Theory
Unat, Dr. I., Private International Law
Yalçin, A., History of Economics and Economic Thought
Yavuz, F., Urbanology

**Faculty of Divinity:**
Armaner, N., Religious Psychology
Atay, H., Theology
Çağatay, N., Islamic History and Law
Cerrahoğlu, I., Interpretation
Coşan, E., Turkish Islamic Literature
Cubukçu, Dr. İ. A., Islamic Philosophy
Figlali, E. R., History of Islamic Sects
Karamağali, H., History of Turkish Islamic Art
Kocyiğit, T., Maxims
Öner, N., Logic and Philosophy
Şener, A., Islamic Law
Sunar, C., History of Theosophy
Tanyu, H., History of Religion
Taplamacioğlu, Dr. M., Sociology of Religion
Yurdaydin, H., History of Islamic Institutions

**Faculty of Medicine in Antalya:**
Akkartal, B., Anaesthesiology and Reanimation
Aksu, A., Biochemistry and Chemistry
Akyokuş, A., Physiotherapy and Reanimation
Akyol, T., Cardiology
Altinel, E., Orthopaedics and Traumatology
Arcasoy, A., Paediatrics
Arinci, K., Anatomy
Ayhan, I. H., Pharmacology
Bacaci, K., Pathology
Baykan, N., Forensic Medicine
Berk, U., Radiology
Büyükberker, C., Psychiatry
Çuhruk, Ç., Oth-Rhino-Laryngology
Deniz, E., Medical Biology
Emüler, U., Ophthalmology
Ersöz, A., Cardiovascular Surgery
Göker, Z., Medical Physics
Gürses, H., Chest Diseases and Tuberculosis
Güvener, A., Neurology
Kandilci, S., Infections
Müftüoğlu, Y. Z., Urology
Mutlu, G., Microbiology and Parasitology
Şardaş, O. S., Internal Diseases
Saveren, M., Neurosurgery
Tanalp, R., Physiology
Tat, L., Dermatology and Venereal Diseases
Torunoğlu, K., Physiopathology
Tunali, İ., Medicinal Jurisprudence

TÜZÜNER, A., General Surgery
UZUNALİMOĞLU, A., Endocrinology and Metabolic Disorders
UZUNALİMOĞLU, Ö., Gastroenterology
YAVUZ, H., Obstetrics and Gynaecology
YAZGAN, S., Histology and Embryology
YUMUTURUĞ, S., Hygiene, Preventive Medicine and Statistics

Faculty of Dentistry:
ALTAY, G., Hygiene and Preventive Medicine, Microbiology
AKÇA, S., Oral and Dental Surgery
BACACI, K., Pathology
BALOŞ, K., Periodontics
BAŞARAN, B., Therapy
GÜNAY, N., Orthodontics
KARATEKE, Prosthetics
KÜÇÜKÜÇERLER, B., Pedodontics
TİMLİOĞLU, Ö., Pharmacology, Histology and Embryology
YÜKSEL, M., Genetics

## ATATÜRK ÜNİVERSİTESİ*
(Atatürk University)
ERZURUM

Telephone: 1209.

Founded 1957.

State control; Language of instruction: Turkish.

Rector: Prof. Dr. H. ERTUĞRUL.
Chief Administrative Officer: ORHAN SUNER.
Librarian: MUSTAFA KOCA.
Library of 126,000 vols.
Number of teachers and assistants: 587.
Number of students: 7,985.

Publications: Ziraat Fakültesi Dergisi, Tıp Fakültesi Dergisi, Edebiyat Fakültesi Dergisi, İşletme Fakültesi Dergisi.

DEANS:
Faculty of Agriculture: Prof. Dr. ALİ İŞTAR.
Faculty of Medicine: Prof. Dr. YAŞAR KUYUCU.
Faculty of Science: Prof. Dr. SUAVİ YALVAÇ.
Faculty of Letters: Prof. Dr. HÜSEYİN SESLİ.
Faculty of Business Administration: Prof. Dr. ORHAN TÜRKOOĞAN.
Faculty of Dentistry: Prof. Dr. MÜNİP YEĞİN.
Faculty of Theology: Prof. Dr. AHMET KURT.

ATTACHED INSTITUTES:
**College of Basic Sciences and Foreign Languages:** Dir. Prof. Dr. TEVFİK TARKAN.
**Kürk Hayvanları Enstitüsü** (Institute of Fur-Animals and Handicraft).
**School of Nursing:** Dir. Prof. Dr. İBRAHİM AYKAÇ.

* No reply received to our questionnaire this year.

## BOĞAZİÇİ ÜNİVERSİTESİ
(University of the Bosphorus)
P.K. 2, BEBEK, ISTANBUL

Telephone: 65 34 00.
Telex: 26411.

Founded 1863; formerly the American Colleges in Istanbul.

State control; Language of instruction: English; Academic year: October to June.

Rector: SEMİH TEZCAN.
Vice-Rector: DEMİR DEMİRGİL.
Secretary-General: ORHAN OREL.
Registrar: ECE DİNÇSOY.
Librarian: NURTEN ÇAKIR.

Number of teachers: 392.
Number of students: 3,651.

Publication: Boğaziçi University Journal (annually).

DEANS:
Faculty of Engineering: VEDAT YERLİCİ.
Faculty of Arts and Sciences: ERDAL İNÖNÜ.
Faculty of Administrative Sciences: ÖZER ERTUNA.

HEADS OF DEPARTMENTS:
Faculty of Engineering:
ENGİNOL, TURAN, Nuclear Engineering
KAVRAKOĞLU, İBRAHİM, Industrial Engineering
NOYAN, TURGUT, Chemical Engineering
TANYOLAÇ, NECMİ, Electrical Engineering
TEZEL, AKIN, Mechanical Engineering
YALÇIN, ŞAHAP, Civil Engineering

Faculty of Arts and Sciences:
ENÜSTÜN, VEDAT, Chemistry
İZ, FAHİR, Literature
KORTEL, FİKRET, Mathematics
KURAN, ABDULLAH, Humanities
OĞUZKAN, TURHAN, Education
SAYDAM, TUNCAY, Computer Science
SEVGEN, ALPAR, Physics
STODOLSKY, MARVİN, Biology

Faculty of Administrative Sciences:
KÂĞITÇIBAŞI, CİĞDEM, Social Sciences
SİLİER, OYA, Economics
UMAN, NURİ, Management

## BURSA ÜNİVERSİTESİ
NALBANTOĞLU CAD. TAŞKAPI SOK. KENT İŞHANI, BURSA

Telephone: 26870, 26871, 26877.
Telex: BURN-TR 32225.

Founded 1975; Independent; Language of instruction: Turkish.

Rector: Prof. Dr. NİHAT BALKIR.
Secretary-General: AYDIN GÜRSOY.
Librarian: HANDAN SÖNMEZ.

Library of 1,200 vols.
Number of teachers: 276.
Number of students: 2,167.

Publications: Faculty of Medicine Journal, Faculty of Economics and Social Sciences Journal.

DEANS:
Faculty of Medicine: Prof. Dr. FİKRET KARACA.
Faculty of Economics and Social Sciences: Prof. Dr. NURHAN AKÇAYLI.
Faculty of Mechanical Engineering: Prof. Dr. MUSTAFA KÖSEOĞLU.

Faculty of Electrical Engineering: Prof. HASAN ÖNAL.
Faculty of Veterinary Medicine: Prof. Dr. CEMAL NADİ AYTUĞ.
Faculty of Agriculture: Prof. Dr. M. RIFAT OKUYAN.
Institute of Foreign Languages: Prof. Dr. ÖZTÜRK TEKELİ (Dir.).

## ÇUKUROVA ÜNİVERSİTESİ
BALCALI CAMPUSU, ADANA

Telephone: 20373.
Telex: 62369.

Founded 1973.

State control; Language of instruction: Turkish; Academic year: September to July.

Rector: Prof. Dr. MİTHAT ÖZSAN.
Vice-Rectors: Prof. Dr. ŞEFİK YEŞİLSOY, Prof. Dr. ALİ GÜRÇAY.
Secretary-General: A. ADNAN TİBET.
Librarian: SEVGİ KIRAL.

Number of teachers: 114.
Number of students: 1,500.

DEANS:
Faculty of Agriculture: Prof. Dr. ERCAN TEZER.
Faculty of Medicine: Prof. Dr. FARUK L. ÖZER.
Faculty of Basic Sciences: Prof. Dr. AHMET ACAR.
Faculty of Engineering: Prof. Dr. ERHAN KIRAL.
Faculty of Administrative Sciences: Prof. Dr. MUHSİN YILMAZ.

PROFESSORS:
Faculty of Agriculture:
ALTAN, TÜRKER, Landscape Architecture
ATAKİŞİ, İBRAHİM, Field Crops
ÇINAR, AHMET, Plant Protection
ERKAN, ONUR, Agricultural Economy
GÖKÇE, KEMAL, Food Science and Technology
KAŞKA, NURETTİN, Horticultural Science
ÖZBEK, HÜSEYİN, Soil Science
ÖZCAN, LÜTFİ, Animal Science
TEKİNEL, OSMAN, Agriculture, Irrigation and Engineering
TEZER, ERCAN, Agriculture Mechanization

Faculty of Medicine:
AKAN, EROL, Microbiology
AKOĞUZ, HALE, Anaesthesiology
AKSUNGUR, LÜTFULLAH, Dermatology
AKTAN, FETHİ, Medical Biology
ARIDOĞAN, NİHAT, Obstetrics and Gynaecology
BAYSAL, FİRUZ, Pharmacology
BAYTOK, GÜRBÜZ, Orthopaedics
BAYTOK, VİLDAN, Neurology
BELLİ, VEDAT, Legal Medicine
BİLGİN, İLTER, General Surgery
BİRAND, AHMET, Cardiology
ÇOLAKOĞLU, SALİH, Internal Medicine, Gastroenterology
DERE, FAHRİ, Anatomy
GÜR, AYFER, Paediatric Nephrology
GÜRÇAY, ALİ, Internal Medicine, Nephrology
KABULİ, GIYASEDDİN, Thoracic Surgery
KÜMİ, METİN, Paediatric Haematology

UNIVERSITIES    TURKEY

Olcay, Işık, Paediatric Surgery
Özer, Faruk, Internal Medicine and Haematology
Özgünen, Tuncay, Physiology
Özmen, Ertuğrul, Plastic Surgery
Özşahinoğlu, Can, Otolaryngology
Slem, Gülhan, Ophthalmology
Tanyaş, Yılmaz, Neurosurgery
Tuncer, Ahmet, Public Health
Türkyılmaz, Ruhi, Urology
Ünal, Mehmet, Psychiatry
Yüksel, Arif Hikmet, Pathology
Yüreğir, Güneş, Biochemistry

*Faculty of Basic Sciences:*
Acar, Ahmet, Geology
Kunç, Şeref, Chemistry
Ögelman, Hakkı, Physics
Soran, Haluk, Biology
Ünlü, Yusuf, Mathematics

*Faculty of Engineering:*
Kıral, Erhan, Mechanical and Constructional Engineering

*Faculty of Administrative Sciences:*
Pekel, Erdoğan, Economics
Slem, Gülhan, Social Sciences
Yılmaz, Muhsin, Management

Attached Institutes:
*School of Foreign Languages:* Dir. Tekinel Osman.
*Institute of Librarianship:* Dir. Kıral Erhan.

## CUMHURIYET ÜNİVERSİTESİ
(Republic University)
SİVAS

Telephone: 22-12.

Founded 1973.

State control; Language of instruction: Turkish.

*Rector:* Prof. Dr. Muvaffak Akman.
*Registrar:* Kenan Baştuji.
*Librarian:* Sevin İlgün.

Number of teachers: 54.
Number of students: 109.

Deans:
*Faculty of Medicine:* Prof. Dr. Doğan Remzi.
*Faculty of Sciences and Social Sciences:* Prof. Dr. Mihri Mimioğlu.

## DİYARBAKIR ÜNİVERSİTESİ
(Diyarbakır University)
DİYARBAKIR

Telephone: 3586/7, 3863.

Founded 1966 as branch of Ankara University, independent 1973.

State control; Academic year: October to June.

*Rector:* Prof. Dr. Hasib Kurtpınar.
*General Secretary:* Çetin Aydın.
*Librarian:* Zahit Kızgın.

Number of teachers: 309.
Number of students: 1,409.

Publications: *University Annual*†, *Medical Faculty Journal*†, *Faculty of Science Annual*† (quarterly).

Deans:
*Faculty of Medicine:* Prof. Dr. Asım Duman.
*Faculty of Science:* Prof. Dr. Haseyin Apan (acting).
*Faculty of Dentistry:* Prof. Dr. Yılmaz Tiğin.
*Faculty of Agriculture:* Prof. Dr. Hüseyin Apan.

Professors:
*Faculty of Medicine:*
Aykaç, İ., Histology
Balci, K., Chest Diseases
Başaran, N., Genetics
Bilgin, F., Biology
Bingöl, R., Microbiology
Çobanoğlu, N., Internal Diseases
Erman, O., Gynaecology
Göral, S., Internal Diseases
İlçayto, R., Pathology
Kurtpınar, H., Microbiology and Parasitology
Özdemir, C., Neurology
Yazıcıoğlu, S., Chest Diseases

*Faculty of Science:*
Apan, H., Genetics
Baran, A., Physics
Bilgin, F., Systematic Zoology
Domaniç, F., Physics
Dönmez, A., Mathematics
Elçi, S., Stomatology
Erk, Ç., Organic Chemistry
Gülsün, Z., Physics
Gündüz, T., Analytical Chemistry
Kurtpınar, H., Helminthology
Tözün, C., General Chemistry
Yalçıner, A., Physics
Yılmaz, A., Physics

*Faculty of Dentistry:*
Başaran, B., Therapy
Yavuzyılmaz, H., Prosthesis

*Faculty of Agriculture:*
Apan, H., Horticulture
Baysal, İ., Field Crops
Çakır, A., Animal Science
Demiralay, İ., Soil Science
Güleryüz, M., Fruit Crops
Karakaplan, S., Soil Science
Özer, Z., Phytopathology
Sağlam, T., Soil Science
Uluata, A. R., Agricultural Engineering

Attached Institutes:
**Institute of Medical History:** Dir. Prof. Dr. Şerif Kürkçüoğlu.
**College of Health:** Dir. Prof. Dr. Nedim Çobanoğlu.

## EGE ÜNİVERSİTESİ
(Aegean University)
BORNOVA, İZMİR

Telephone: 180110.

Founded 1955.

State control; Language of instruction: Turkish; Academic year: October to June.

*Rector:* Prof. Dr. İbrahim Karaca.
*Vice-Rectors:* Prof. Dr. Metin Şengonca, Prof. Dr. Cengiz Pınar.
*General Secretary:* N. Aşıkhan.
*Registrar:* Abdürrahim Incekara.
*Librarian:* Maide Unlu.

Number of teachers and assistants: 1,369.
Number of students: 20,000.

Publications: *Tıp Fakültesi Mecmuası, Ziraat Fakültesi Dergisi, Fen Dergisi, Iktisadi ve Ticari Bilimler Fakültesi Dergisi, Aegean Medical Journal,* and faculty publications.

Deans:
*Faculty of Medicine:* Prof. Dr. Baha Taneli.
*Faculty of Medicine (at Izmir):* Prof. Dr. Hamit Ozgönul.
*Faculty of Dentistry:* Prof. Dr. Oğuz Manas.
*Faculty of Pharmacy:* Prof. Dr. Necmettin Zeybek.
*Faculty of Agriculture:* Prof. Dr. Mustafa Harmancıoğlu.
*Faculty of Food Science:* Prof. Dr. Erdal Saygın.
*Faculty of Science:* Prof. Dr. Abdullah Kızılırmak.
*Faculty of Civil Engineering:* Prof. Dr. Turhan Acatay.
*Faculty of Mechanics:* Prof. Dr. Gazanfer Harzadın.
*Faculty of Textile Sciences:* Prof. Dr. İbrahim Aksöz.
*Faculty of Chemistry:* Prof. Dr. Burhan Pekin.
*Faculty of Earth Science:* Prof. Dr. Erol İzdar.
*Faculty of Economics:* Prof. Dr. Fikret Sönmez.
*Faculty of Law:* Prof. Muhittin Alam.
*Faculty of Fine Arts:* Prof. Rauf Beyru.
*Faculty of Social Sciences:* Prof. Dr. Şefik Uysal.

Attached Institutes:
**Nuclear Research and Education Institute:** Dir. Prof. Mehmet Ali Özcel.
**Genetics Institute:** Dir. Prof. İbrahim Demir.
**Medical and Agricultural Drugs Research Institute:** Dir. (vacant).
**Labour Relations Institute:** Dir. Prof. İliter Akat.
**International Economic Relations:** Dir. Prof. Dr. Kutlu Yaşar Zoral.

(*See* also under Colleges.)

## FIRAT ÜNİVERSİTESİ
(Euphrates University)
ELAZIG

Founded 1975; in process of formation.

Number of teachers: 60.
Number of students: 580.

Faculties of arts, sciences and veterinary medicine.

## HACETTEPE ÜNİVERSİTESİ
HACETTEPE PARKİ, ANKARA

Telephone: 11-94-42.

Founded 1206 in Kayseri; Chartered 1967.

State control; Language of instruction: Turkish; Academic year: September to June.

*Rector:* Prof. SÜLEYMAN SAĞLAM.
*Vice-Rectors:* Prof. DINCER ÜLKÜ, GÜROL ATAMAN.
*Secretary-General:* ATILLA KONAÇ.
*Registrar:* MÜCELLA MERDOL.
*Librarians:* YILDIZ ÇAKIN (Haceteppe Campus); AYŞEN ATLIOĞLU (Beytepe Campus).

Central library of 75,000 vols., medical library of 25,000 vols.

Number of teachers: 1,819.
Number of students: 15,906.

Publications: *Hacettepe Tip/Cerrahi Bülteni*† (quarterly), and annual faculty bulletins.

### DEANS:

*Faculty of Graduate Studies:* ULKÜ DINCER.
*Faculty of Medicine:* AKGÜN HIÇSONMEZ.
*Faculty of Sciences:* NIHAT ŞIŞLI.
*Faculty of Engineering:* Prof. ACAR ISIN.
*Faculty of Chemistry:* TÜRKAN BALKIŞ.
*Faculty of Social and Administrative Sciences:* EMEL DOĞRAMACI.
*Faculty of Dentistry:* AYTEKIN BILGE.
*Faculty of Pharmacy:* ENIS OSKAY.
*Faculty of Graduate Medicine and Health Sciences:* DOĞAN TANER.

### PROFESSORS:

*Faculties of Medicine:*
AKKAYA, S., Dermatology
AKMAN, M., Microbiology
ALPAY, M., Obstetrics and Gynaecology
ALTAY, Ç., Paediatrics
ANDAÇ, O., Physiology
AYTAN, N., Internal Medicine (Cardiology)
AYTEK, M., Ophthalmology
BARIŞ, İ., Internal Medicine
BEKDIK, Ç., Nuclear Medicine
BERKEL, A. I., Paediatrics
BERTAN, M., Community Medicine
BERTAN, V., Neurosurgery
BILGIN, N., Surgery
BILGINTURAN, A. N., Paediatrics
BOR, N., Experimental Surgery
BOZER, Y., Surgery
ÇAĞLAR, M., Paediatrics
ÇEVIK, N., Paediatrics
ÇILIV, G., Biochemistry
ÇORUH, M., Paediatrics
DEMIR, Ö., Anaesthesiology
DOĞRAMACI, İ., Paediatrics
DORA, F. T., Neurology
ERBENGI, A., Neurosurgery
ERBENGI, G., Nuclear Medicine
ERDOĞAN, M., Obstetrics and Gynaecology
ERTUĞRUL, A., Paediatrics
FIRAT, D., Internal Medicine
FIRAT, T., Ophthalmology
GÖĞÜŞ, T., Orthopaedics
GÖKSEL, H. H., Surgery
GÖKŞIN, E., Obstetrics and Gynaecology
GÜLMEZOĞLU, E., Microbiology
GÜNALP, A., Biology
GÜRÇAY, O., Neurosurgery
GÜRSU, K. G., Paediatric Surgery
HERSEK, E., Surgery
HIÇSÖNMEZ, A., Paediatric Surgery
HIÇSÖNMEZ, G., Paediatrics

KALABAY, O., Neurosurgery
KALAYOĞLU, M., Paediatrics
KARACADAĞ, S., Internal Medicine
KARAMEHMETOĞLU, A., Internal Medicine (Cardiology)
KARAMEHMETOĞLU, M., Anaesthesiology
KARAN, D., Psychiatry
KARATAY, S., Anatomy
KAYA, S., Ear, Nose and Throat Surgery
KAYAALP, O., Pharmacology
KENANOĞLU, A., Radiology
KERSE, İ., Histology and Embryology
KIŞNIŞÇI, H., Obstetrics and Gynaecology
KÖKSAL, M., Pathology
KÖKSAL, O., Community Medicine
KUTKAM, T., Pathology
MÜFTÜ, Y., Paediatrics
ÖNOL, B., Pathology
ORAL, I., Community Medicine
ORHON, A., Psychiatry
ÖRS, U., Histology and Embryology
ÖZEN, E., Pathology
ÖZKARAGÖZ, K., Paediatrics
ÖZKER, R., Physiotherapy and Rehabilitation
ÖZSOYLU, S., Paediatrics
ÖZTÜRK, M. O., Psychiatry
PEKIN, S., Obstetrics and Gynaecology
PIRNAR, T., Radiology
REMZI, D., Urology
RENDA, Y., Paediatrics
SAATÇI, Ü., Paediatrics
SAĞIROĞLU, N., Obstetrics and Gynaecology
SAĞLAM, S., Neurosurgery
SANAÇ, Y., Surgery
SANCAK, B., Anatomy
SARAÇLAR, M., Paediatrics
SARAÇLAR, Y., Paediatrics
SARIBAŞ, O., Neurosurgery
SAVAŞIR, Y., Psychiatry
SAY, B., Paediatrics
ŞENER, A. N., Radiology
SEZER, V., Paediatrics
TANER, D., Anatomy
TELATAR, E. F., Internal Medicine
TELATAR, H., Internal Medicine
TINAZTEPE, B., Pathology
TINAZTEPE, K., Paediatrics
TOKGÖZOĞLU, N., Orthopaedics
TUNCALI, M. T., Paediatrics
TUNÇBILEK, E., Paediatrics
TUNCER, M., Paediatrics
TÜZMEN, S. B., Ophthalmology
UĞURLU, N., Paediatrics
ÜSTAY, K., Obstetrics and Gynaecology
UYSAL, H., Histology and Embryology
YALAZ, K., Paediatrics
YÖRÜKOĞLU, A., Psychiatry
ZILELI, L., Psychiatry
ZILELI, T., Neurology

*Faculty of Dentistry:*
AYTAN, S.
BILGE, A.
NORAS, Y.
TOKMAN, C.
USMEN, E.

*Faculty of Engineering:*
ATAMAN, G., Geology
BAYSAL, O., Earth Sciences
IŞIN, A., Physics
KÖKSOY, M., Geology
ÜLKÜ, D., Physics

*Faculty of Health Sciences:*
ARI, A. B., Microbiology
AYTAÇ, A., Surgery
BILIR, S., Paediatrics
FIŞEK, N., Microbiology
GÖÇMEN, A., Paediatrics
KOCAÇITAK, D., Chest Diseases
PAYZA, N., Biochemistry

*Faculty of Pharmacy:*
OSKAY, E.

*Faculty of Social and Administrative Sciences:*
ARICI, H., Psychology
BAYMUR, F., Education
ÇAYCI, A., History
DOĞRAMACI, E., English Language and Literature
ELÇIN, S., Turkish Language and Literature
ERTÜRK, S., Education
GÜVENÇ, B., Social Anthropology
KURAN, E., History
NIRUN, N., Sociology
OKYAR, O. F., Economics
TEKIN, T., Turkish Language and Literature
TURGUT, M. F., Education

*Faculty of Sciences:*
IKEDA, G., Mathematics
KUTSAL, A., Statistics
MIMIOĞLU, M., Biology
NOVAN, A.
ŞIŞLI, N., Biology

*Faculty of Chemistry:*
ALPAUT, O.
BALKIŞ, T.
ŞENVAR, C.

*School of Health Technology:*
BAYSAL, A.

## İNÖNÜ ÜNİVERSİTESİ
### MALATYA

Founded 1975; in process of formation.

Number of teachers: *c.* 30.
Number of students: 100.

Faculty of sciences (depts. of chemistry, mathematics and physics).

## İSTANBUL ÜNİVERSİTESİ
### (Istanbul University)
### BEYAZIT, ISTANBUL

Telephone: 22 42 00.

Founded 15th century, reorganized 1933 and 1946. State university; Language of instruction: Turkish; Academic year: November to February, March to July.

*Rector:* Prof. Dr. CEMI DEMIROGLU.
*Vice-Rectors:* Prof. Dr. ERGIN NOMER, Prof. Dr. EROL DÜREN.
*Secretary-General:* Mrs. NILÜFER KASAPOĞLU.
*Librarian:* Mrs. LEMAN ŞENALP.

Number of teachers and assistants: 804.
Number of students: *c.* 33,000.

### DEANS:

*Faculty of Letters:* Prof. Dr. OKTAY AKŞIT.
*Faculty of Science:* Prof. Dr. LÜTFÜ BIRAN.
*Faculty of Law:* Prof. Dr. İLHAN AKIN.
*Faculty of Economics:* Prof. Dr. ESAT ÇAM.

*Faculty of Forestry:* Prof. Dr. BURHAN AYTUĞ.
*Faculty of Medicine:* Prof. Dr. GÜNGÖR ERTEM.
*Faculty of Pharmacy:* Prof. Dr. TURHAN BAYTOP.
*Faculty of Dentistry:* Prof. Dr. YILMAZ MANISALI.
*Faculty of Medicine at Cerrahpaşa:* Prof. Dr. CEMI DEMIROĞLU.
*Faculty of Medicine at Edirne:* Prof. Dr. SUAT VURAL.
*Faculty of Chemistry:* Prof. Dr. FIKRET BAYKUT.
*Faculty of Business Administration:* Prof. Dr. MUZAFFER BEŞE.
*School of Foreign Languages:* Prof. Dr. LÜFTI GÜÇER.

ATTACHED INSTITUTE:
**Turkiyat Enstitüsü** (*Institute of Turcology*): f. 1924; carries out research and publishes material on Turkish language, literature, history and culture; library of 20,000 vols.; Dir. Dr. M. CAVID BAYSUN.

## İSTANBUL TEKNİK ÜNİVERSİTESİ
(Istanbul Technical University)
389 TAKŞİM, TAŞKIŞLA, ISTANBUL
Telephone: 43 31 00-30.
**Founded 1773.**

Independent; Language of instruction: Turkish; Academic year: September to June.

*Rector:* Prof. Dr. KEMAL KAFALI.
*Vice-Rectors:* Prof. Dr. FUAT YAVUZ BOR, Prof. Dr. TEOMAN DORUK.
*Secretary-General:* OSMAN ÇAKIR.
*Librarian:* NURTEN ATALIK.
Library: see Libraries.
**Number of teachers and assistants:** 911.
**Number of students:** 9,787.

Publications: *Bulletin*† (2 a year), *Magazine*† (every 2 months), *News*† (monthly), *Catalogue*† (biennially).

DEANS:
*Faculty of Civil Engineering:* Prof. Dr. GÜNGÖR EVREN.
*Faculty of Mining Engineering:* Prof. Dr. AYTIN GÖKTEKIN.
*Faculty of Electrical Engineering:* Prof. ZIYAETTIN SÜDER.
*Faculty of Architecture:* Prof. Dr. AHMET KESKIN.
*Faculty of Mechanical Engineering:* Prof. AZIZ ERGIN.
*Faculty of Chemical Engineering:* Prof. Dr. ÖZER BEKÂROĞLU.
*Faculty of Engineering and Architecture:* Prof. VAHIT KUMBASAR.
*Faculty of Basic Sciences:* Prof. CEVDET KOÇAK.
*Faculty of Naval Architecture and Ocean Engineering:* Prof. Dr. REŞAT BAYKAL.
*Faculty of Metallurgy:* Prof. Dr. VELI AYTEKIN.

*Faculty of Management Engineering:* Prof. Dr. ZEYYAT HATIPOĞLU.
*Faculty of Architecture (at Maçka):* Prof. ORHAN SAFA.
*Faculty of Electrical Engineering (at Maçka):* Prof. Dr. MUZAFFER ÖZKAYA.
*Faculty of Civil Engineering (at Maçka):* Prof. REMZI ÜLKER.
*Faculty of Mechanical Engineering (at Maçka):* Prof. Dr. YAŞAR ÖZEMIR.

ATTACHED INSTITUTES:
*Institute of Computer Science:* Dir. Prof. Dr. MUZAFFER İPEK.
*Institute of Nuclear Energy:* Prof. NEJAT AYBERS.
*School of Foreign Languages.*

## KARADENİZ TEKNİK ÜNİVERSİTESİ
(Black Sea Technical University)
TRABZON
Telephone: 11 02-53/57-25 27.
Telex: 83111 Ktü tr.
**Founded 1963.**

State control; Language of instruction: Turkish; Academic year: December to June.

*Rector:* Prof. ERDEM AKSOY.
*Vice-Rectors:* Prof. Dr. ERGÜN BAYAR, Prof. Dr. NURAN ÖZALP.
*General Secretary:* TURGUT SEYMEN SEKBEN.
*Librarian:* ÜLKÜ ÖZEN.
**Number of teachers and assistants:** 303.
**Number of students:** 3,480.

Publications: *KTÜ Dergisi* (Bulletin), *Mimarlık Bülteni* (Architectural Bulletin), *TBF Dergisi* (Basic Sciences Bulletin), *YBF Dergisi* (Earth Sciences Bulletin), *OF Dergisi* (Forestry Bulletin).

DEANS:
*Faculty of Basic Sciences:* Prof. Dr. YAVUZ GÜNDÜZALP.
*Faculty of Civil Engineering and Architecture:* Prof. ÖZGÖNÜL AKSOY.
*Faculty of Mechanical and Electrical Engineering:* Prof. Dr. METIN YILMAZ GÜRLEYIK.
*Faculty of Earth Sciences:* Prof. Dr. MUZAFFER ŞERBETÇI.
*Faculty of Forestry:* Prof. Dr. HÜSAMETTIN PEKER.
*Faculty of Medicine and Health Sciences:* Prof. Dr. ŞEVKET UĞURLU.

PROFESSORS:
*Faculty of Basic Sciences:*
BAYAR, ERGÜN, Mathematics
GÜNDÜZALP, YAVUZ, Mathematics
OĞUZER, TURGUT, Physics
ÖZALP, NURAN, Physics
UYANIK, GÜVEN, Chemistry

*Faculty of Civil Engineering and Architecture:*
AKSOY, ERDEM, Architecture

AKSOY, ÖZGÖNÜL, Architecture
ILGAZ, TURAN, Architecture

*Faculty of Mechanical and Electrical Engineering:*
GÜRLEYIK, METIN YILMAZ, Mechanical Engineering

*Faculty of Forestry:*
PEKER, HÜSAMETTIN, Forestry Engineering

*Faculty of Earth Sciences:*
ÖZBENLI, ERDOĞAN, Geodesy
ŞERBETÇI, MUZAFFER, Geodesy

DIRECTORS:
*Computing Centre:* Doç. Dr. BURHAN SOYKAN.
*Institute of Machine Sciences:* Prof. Dr. ERDOĞAN ÖZBENLI.

## KAYSERİ ÜNİVERSİTESİ
P.K. 275, KAYSERİ
Telephone: 21813/4/5.

Founded 1978; State control; Language of instruction: Turkish; Academic year: November to June.

*Chancellor:* Prof. Dr. HUSEYIN SIPAHIOĞLU, M.D.
*Rector:* Prof. YAŞAR YEŞILKAYA, M.D.
*Vice-Rector:* Prof. ABDURRAHMAN ÇAYCI.
*Registrar:* KÄYA ERDEM.
*Librarian:* BECAHAT ELKOVAN.
**Number of teachers:** 201.
**Number of students:** 551.

Publication: *Gevher Nesibe Medical School Journal.*

DEANS:
*Gevher Nesibe Faculty of Medicine:* Prof. A. HULÜSI KÖKER, M.D.
*Faculty of Business Administration and Management:* Prof. ABDURRAHMAN ÇAYCI.

PROFESSORS:
ARICI, H., Psychology
BAYKAL, E., Ophthalmology
ÇAYCI, A., History
ERTÜRK, S., Education
FAZLI, S. A., Microbiology
KÖKER, A. H., Internal Medicine
ÖZER, U., Chemistry
SIPAHIOĞLU, H., Internal Medicine
YEŞILKAYA, Y., General Surgery

ATTACHED INSTITUTES:
*Gevher Nesibe Medical Faculty Hospital for Education and Medical Practice:* Dir. ALI UYAR.
*Institute of Science:* Dir. Prof. ULVIYE ÖZER.
*School of Nursing:* Dir. Prof. A. HULÜSI KÖKER, M.D.

## ORTA DOĞU TEKNİK ÜNİVERSİTESİ
(Middle East Technical University)
İSMET İNÖNÜ BULVARI, ANKARA
Telephone: 23 71 00.
Telex: ODTK-tr 42761.

Founded 1956. Campuses at Gaziantep (sciences, applied chemistry, mechanical and electrical engineering) and İçel (marine science).

State control; Language of instruction: English; Academic year: October to July (two semesters).

*President:* Prof. Dr. MEHMET KICIMAN.
*Vice-President:* Prof. Dr. ALTAY BİRAND.
*Librarian:* F. OLŞEN.

Library: see Libraries.
Number of teachers and assistants: 1,214 (Ankara Campus), 116 (Gaziantep Campus).
Number of students: 11,289 (Ankara Campus), 545 (Gaziantep Campus).

Publications: *METU Journal of Pure and Applied Sciences*† (3 a year), *METU Studies in Development*† (quarterly), *METU Journal of Faculty of Architecture*† (2 a year).

### DEANS:
*Faculty of Administrative Sciences:* Prof. Dr. Ö. YAGIZ.
*Faculty of Architecture:* Assoc. Prof. Dr. M. PULTAR.
*Faculty of Engineering:* Prof. Dr. M. DORUK.
*Faculty of Arts and Sciences:* Prof. Dr. T. TERZİOĞLU.
*Graduate School:* Assoc. Prof. Dr. P. GÜLKAN.
*Student Affairs:* Prof. Dr. E. KARAESMEN.
*Gaziantep Campus:* Prof. Dr. S. DEMOKAN.

### PROFESSORS:
*Faculty of Administrative Sciences:*
DİCLE, A., Management
DİCLE, Ü., Management
PAYASLIOĞLU, A., Political Science and Public Administration

*Faculty of Architecture:*
BİLGÜTAY, A., Architecture
ERDER, C., Restoration
KORTAN, E., Architecture
TANKUT, G., City and Regional Planning
TAŞPINAR, A., Architecture
TEKELİ, İ., City and Regional Planning

*Faculty of Arts and Sciences:*
ARAS, N. K., Chemistry
BALKAS, T., Marine Science
CELASUN, M., Operational Research and Statistics
DOĞRUSÖZ, H., Operational Research and Statistics
ERYURT, D. E., Astrophysics
GRUNBERG, T., Humanities
KURAT, Y. T., Humanities
ÖKTEM, I. F., Physics
ÖZİNÖNÜ, A. K., Education
PAMUK, H. O., Chemistry
TARHAN, O., Chemistry
TERZİOĞLU, T., Mathematics
TOLUN, P., Physics
YALÇIN, C., Physics
YILDIRIM, C., Humanities

*Faculty of Engineering:*
AKTAŞ, Z., Computer Engineering
ANKARA, A., Metallurgical Engineering
ATAMAN, T., Mining and Petroleum Engineering
BENGİ, H., Electrical Engineering
BİRAND, A., Civil Engineering
ÇIRAY, C., Civil Engineering
DOĞAN, Z., Mining and Petroleum Engineering
DORUK, M., Metallurgical Engineering
ERDOĞAN, T., Civil Engineering
ERSOY, E., Civil Engineering
GÖĞÜŞ, Y., Mechanical Engineering
KAFTANOĞLU, B., Mechanical Engineering
KAKAÇ, S., Mechanical Engineering
KARAHAN, E., Engineering Science
KICIMAN, M., Civil Engineering
NORMAN, T., Geological Engineering
OĞURTANI, T., Metallurgical Engineering
ORAL, Ö., Electrical Engineering
ORDEMİR, İ., Civil Engineering
RUMELİ, A., Electrical Engineering
SARYAL, N., Mechanical Engineering
SELAMOĞLU, S., Mechanical Engineering
SİNMAN, S., Electrical Engineering
SOMER, T., Chemical Engineering
TİMUÇİN, M., Metallurgical Engineering
TOKAY, M., Geological Engineering
TOKER, C., Electrical Engineering
TÜRELİ, A., Electrical Engineering
ÜÇER, A. S., Mechanical Engineering
WASTİ, T., Civil Engineering
YAŞAR, K., Civil Engineering

### ATTACHED RESEARCH INSTITUTES:
*Business and Management Systems Research Institute:* Dir. Asst. Prof. Dr. HALİL ÇOPUR.
*System Sciences Research Institute:* Dir. Asst. Prof. Dr. YAŞAR YEŞİLÇAY.
*Environmental Research Institute:* Dir. Asst. Prof. Dr. METE ENUYSAL.
*Earthquake Engineering Research Institute:* Dir. Assoc. Prof. Dr. MUSTAFA ERDİK.
*Polymer Chemistry Research Institute:* Dir. Assoc. Prof. Dr. GÜNERİ AKOVALI.
*Marine Research Institute:* Dir. Prof. Dr. TURGUT BALKAŞ.
*Thermal Environment and Thermal Operations Research Institute:* Dir. Assoc. Prof. Dr. ALİ DURMAZ.
*Coastal and Harbor Engineering Research Institute:* Dir. Asst. Prof. Dr. AYŞEN ERGİN.
*Informatics Research Institute:* Dir. Prof. Dr. ZİYA AKTAŞ.
*Machine Design and Manufacturing Research Institute:* Dir. Prof. Dr. BİLGİN KAFTANOĞLU.
*Aerodynamics and Electromechanics Research Institute:* Dir. Assoc. Prof. Dr. ORHAN KURAL.
*Economic and Social Research Institute:* Dir. SELİM İLKİN.
*Mining and Petroleum Engineering Research Institute:* Dir. Asst. Prof. Dr. GÜNHAN PAŞAMEHMETOĞLU.
*Water Resources Research Institute:* Dir. Asst. Prof. Dr. OSMAN AKAN.
*Transportation Research Institute:* Dir. Asst. Prof. Dr. ÖZDEMİR AKYILMAZ.
*Metallurgy Research Institute:* Dir. Prof. Dr. ALPAY ANKARA.
*Geology and Geophysics Research Institute:* Dir. Prof. Dr. MELİH TOKAY.
*Soil Mechanics Research Institute:* Dir. Asst. Prof. Dr. UFUK ERGUN.

## SELÇUK ÜNİVERSİTESİ
MERAM YENİ YOL, KONYA

Telephone: 18510.
Founded 1975.

State control; Language of instruction: Turkish; Academic year: November to May (2 terms).

*Rector:* Prof. Dr. NEŞ'ET ÇAĞATAY.
*Secretary General:* OSMAN SIVILOĞLU.
*Librarian:* D. HASAN YÜĞRÜK.

Number of teachers: 156.
Number of students: 2,054.

### DEANS:
*Faculty of Letters:* YUSUF BOYSAL.
*Faculty of Science:* FİKRET KURTMAN.

### PROFESSORS AND HEADS OF DEPARTMENTS:
*Faculty of Letters:*
ARIK, OLUŞ, Archaeology and History of Arts
ARIK, RÜÇHAN, Archaeology and History of Arts
AYTÜR, NEJLÂ, English Language and Literature
AYTÜR, ÜNAL, English Language and Literature
BALKAN, KEMAL, Archaeology and History of Arts
BAYBURTLUOĞLU, CEVDET, Archaeology and History of Arts
BOYSAL, YUSUF, Archaeology and History of Arts
ÇAĞATAY, NEŞ'ET, History
EREN, HASAN, Turkish Language and Literature
GÖKER, CEMİL, French Language and Literature
MAZIOĞLU, HASİBE, Turkish Language and Literature
SELEN, NEVİN, German Language and Literature
SEVİM, ALİ, History
UZMEN, ENGİN, English Language and Literature
YÜCEL, YAŞAR, History

*Faculty of Science:*
ÇETİK, RIZA, Botany
KURTMAN, FİKRET, Zoology, Geology
OLCAY, ARAL, Chemical Engineering
ORUÇ, MAİDE, Mathematics
YALÇIN, CENGİZ, Physical Engineering

## 19 MAYIS ÜNİVERSİTESİ
(19th May University)
LİSE CADDESİ 6, SAMSUN

Telephone: 17746.
Founded 1975.

*Rector:* Prof. Dr. AYKUT ERBENGİ.

Library of 7,500 vols.
Number of teachers: 48.
Number of students: 381.

### HEADS OF SCHOOLS:
*Medical School:* Prof. Dr. MUHSİN SARAÇLAR.
*School of Basic Sciences and Engineering:* Prof. Dr. ALÂETTİN KUTSAL.
*College of Agriculture:* Prof. Dr. FAHRETTİN TOSUN.

# COLLEGES AND INSTITUTES OF HIGHER EDUCATION

## EGE ÜNİVERSİTESİ MÜHENDİSLİK BİLİMLERİ FAKÜLTESİ MÜHENDİSLİK VE MİMARLIK YÜKSEK OKULU
(Aegean University Faculty and School of Engineering and Architecture)

BUCA CAMİ SOKAK 2, İZMİR

Founded 1963.

Day school (five-year course) and evening school (five-year course), offering a B.S. degree.

*President:* Dr. AHMET SAMSUNLU.
*Vice-President:* NİHAT YALIN.
*Secretary-General:* MUSTAFA BERAK.

The library contains 4,000 vols.
Number of teaching staff: 175.

HEADS OF DEPARTMENTS:
*Architecture:* Prof. Dr. DOĞAN TUNA.
*Mechanical Engineering:* Dr. ERKAN DOKUMACI.
*Civil Engineering:* Assoc. Prof. Dr. İZAK KAYA.
*Chemical Engineering:* Prof. Dr. GÜRBÜZ ATAGÜNDÜZ.

## ESKİŞEHİR İKTİSADÎ VE TİCARÎ İLİMLER AKADEMİSİ
(Eskişehir Academy of Economic and Commercial Sciences)

ESKİŞEHİR

Telephone: 17780.

Founded 1958.

*President:* Prof. Dr. YILMAZ BÜYÜKERŞEN.
*Vice-Presidents:* Prof. Dr. KAMİL MUTLUER, Prof. Dr. SEMİH BÜKER, Doç. Dr. FAZIL TEKİN, Doç. Dr. BİROL TENEKECİOĞLU.

The library contains 39,000 vols.
Number of teachers: 168.
Number of students: 4,730.

Publication: *Dergisi* (Journal, 2 a year).

CONSTITUENT SCHOOLS AND INSTITUTES:

**Sağlık Bilimleri Fakültesi** (*Faculty of Medical Sciences*): f. 1968; 325 students; Dean Prof. Dr. FAHRETTİN ÇİÇEKDAĞ.

**Kütahya Yönetim Bilimleri Fakültesi** (*Kütahya Faculty of Administrative Sciences*): f. 1974; 838 students; Dean Prof. Dr. MUSA ŞENEL.

**Afyon Mali Bilimler Fakültesi** (*Afyon Faculty of Financial Sciences*): f. 1974; 569 students; Dean Prof. Dr. AYKUT HEREKMEN.

**İşletme Fakültesi** (*Faculty of Business Administration*): f. 1958; 1,191 students; Dean Prof. Dr. ERCAN GÜVEN.

**Ekonomi Fakültesi** (*Faculty of Economics*): f. 1958; 993 students; Dean Prof. Dr. HALİL DİRİMTEKİN.

**TV ile Öğretim ve Eğitim Fakültesi** (*Faculty of Communication Sciences*): f. 1977; 88 students; Dean Prof. Dr. İNAL CEM AŞKUN; publ. *Kurgu* (2 a year).

**Endüstri Bilimleri Fakültesi** (*Faculty of Industrial Sciences*): f. 1977; 726 students; Dean Prof. Dr. DOĞAN BAYAR.

**Yabancı Diller Enstitüsü** (*Institute of Foreign Languages*): Dir. Doç. Dr. CÜNEYT BİNATLI.

**Avrupa Ekonomik Topluluğu Enstitüsü** (*European Economic Community Institute*): Dir. Prof. Dr. AKAR ÖCAL.

**Pazarlama Enstitüsü** (*Institute of Marketing*): Dir. Prof. Dr. DOĞAN BAYAR.

**Zirai İktisat Enstitüsü** (*Institute of Agricultural Economics*): Dir. Prof. Dr. İHSAN ERKUL.

**Kültürel Çalışmalar ve Çevre Eğitimi Enstitüsü** (*Institute of Cultural Studies and Community Development*): Dir. Prof. Dr. İNAL CEM AŞKUN.

**Türkiye Ekonomisini Araştırma Enstitüsü** (*Institute of Research on Turkish Economy*): Dir. Prof. Dr. HALİL DİRİMTEKİN.

## İSTANBUL İKTİSADÎ VE TİCARÎ İLİMLER AKADEMİSİ
(Istanbul Academy of Economic and Commercial Sciences)

SULTANAHMET, ISTANBUL

Founded 1883, reorganized to university level 1971.

*President:* Prof. ORHAN OĞUZ.
*Vice-Presidents:* Prof. Y. ADNAN SUNER, Prof. Dr. E. ZEYTİNOĞLU.
*Secretary-General:* ALTAN KİTAPÇI.
*Registrar:* YÜKSEL BÜYÜKKAYRA.
*Librarian:* AYTEN KORAN.

Number of teachers: 72.
Number of students: Academy 6,000, Colleges 14,625.

Publication: *Iktisadi ve Ticari Ilimler Dergisi* (occasional).

CONSTITUENT COLLEGES:

**Siyasal Bilimler Yüksek Okulu** (*School of Political Science*): Halaskargazi Caddesi 236, Sisli, Istanbul; 61 teachers, 155 students; Dir. Prof. Dr. KIVANÇ ERTOP.

**İşletmecilik Yüksek Okulu** (*School of Business Administration*): Dir. Prof. REŞAT KAYNAR.

**Maliye ve Muhasebe Yüksek Okulu** (*School of Public Finance and Accounting*): Dir. Prof. FİKRET ÖCAL.

**İktisat ve Ticaret Yüksek Okulu** (*School of Economics and Commerce*): Dir. Prof. Dr. SADRETTİN TOSBİ.

**Gazetecilik Halkla İlişkiler Yüksek Okulu** (*School of Journalism and Public Relations*): Dir. Prof. Dr. KENAN ERKURAL.

**Diş Hekimliği Yüksek Okulu** (*School of Dentistry*): Dir. Prof. Dr. SUAT İSMAİL GÜRKAN.

**Eczacılık Yüksek Okulu** (*School of Pharmacy*): Dir. Prof. Dr. FAHİR SANEL.

## İSTANBUL DEVLET MÜHENDİSLİK VE MİMARLIK AKADEMİSİ
(Istanbul State Academy of Engineering and Architecture)

YILDIZ, ISTANBUL

Telephone: 610220.

Founded 1911.

*President:* SUHA TONER.
*Vice-Presidents:* RIFKI ASLAN, NECDET DEMİR, AYSEL UGAN, SELVA ÜNAL, YAHYA KARSLIĞİL.
*Registrar:* MEHMET ALİ SARI.
*Librarian:* HULYA ALBAYRAK.

Library of 45,000 vols.
Number of teachers: 531.
Number of students: 15,000.

Publication: *Periodical* (monthly).

DEANS:
*Civil Engineering:* HÜSEYİN CELASUN.
*Mechanical Engineering:* ŞERAFETTİN OYDAŞIK.
*Electrical Engineering:* KENAN SÜER.
*Architecture:* MARUF ÖNAL.
*Geodesy:* BURHAN TANSUĞ.
*Basic Sciences:* AHMET KARADENİZ.

ATTACHED ENGINEERING FACULTIES:

*Galatasaray Faculty of Engineering:* Okmeydanı, Istanbul; Pres. HÜSEYİN NURAL.

*Işık Faculty of Engineering:* Ayazağa, Istanbul; Pres. REMZİ GÜLGÜN.

*Kadıköy Faculty of Engineering and Architecture:* Acıbadem Kadıköy, Istanbul; Pres. ORHAN ŞİPER.

*Vatan Faculty of Engineering:* Vatan Caddesi, Istanbul; Pres. MUZAFFER SAĞIŞMAN.

## YÜKSEK DENİZCİLİK OKULU
(Higher School of Navigation)

ORTAKÖY, İSTANBUL

Founded 1909; controlled by the Ministry of Communication.

*Director:* NEJAT ODMAN.

Number of teachers: 72.
Number of students: 560.

Four-year university-level courses in navigation, ship engineering, business and communication.

## YÜKSEK İSLÂM ENSTITÜSÜ
### (Higher Institute of the Islam Faith)
BAĞLARBAŞI, ISTANBUL

Founded 1959.

The library contains 10,000 vols.

*Dean:* Dr. ALI ÖZEK.

*Assistant Deans:* Dr. HASAN KÜÇUK, KEMAL TURAN, ZIYA KAZICI, MUSTAFA GÖL.

The purpose of the institute is to provide four years of higher education, at the university level, to graduates of the İmam-Hatip schools, which give a seven-year course and were founded for the education of men of religion and preachers in mosques. Graduate theologians are employed as teachers in the İmam-Hatip schools and in other schools of secondary education level, as officials and müftüs, and preachers in the Department of Religion.

## YÜKSEK İSLÂM ENSTITÜSÜ
### (Higher Institute of the Islam Faith)
KONYA

Founded 1962; State control.

*Director:* VELI ERTAN.

## Zonguldak Maden Teknik Okulu
*(Technical School of Mining):* Zonguldak.

# SCHOOLS OF ART AND MUSIC

**İstanbul Devlet Güzel Sanatlar Akademisi** (*Istanbul State Academy of Fine Arts*): Fındıklı, Istanbul; f. 1883; five-year courses leading to equivalent of a masters degree; faculties of Architecture, Painting, Sculpture, Decorative Arts; 160 teachers, 1,100 students; library of 20,000 vols.; Pres. Prof. ORHAN SHAHILER; Gen. Sec. YÜCEL GÜROCAK; publs. *Akademi Dergisi, Türk Sanat Tarihi Araştırmaları* (Research of Turkish Historical Art).

HEADS OF DEPARTMENTS:
*Architecture:* Prof. ASIM MUTLU.
*Painting:* Prof. NEŞET GÜNAL.
*Sculpture:* Prof. HÜSEYIN GEZER
*Decorative Arts:* Prof. DOĞAN AKSEL.
*Fine Arts Museum:* SABRI BERKEL.
*Turkish Art Historical Institute:* Prof. KERIM SILIVRILI (Director).
*Film Institute:* SAMI ŞEKEROĞLU (Director).
*Institute for Town Planning Research:* Prof. MEHMET ALI HANDAN.
*Institute for Industrial Design, Research and Communication.*
*Institute for Architectural Surveying and Restoration.*

ATTACHED SCHOOLS:
**Mimarlık Y. Okulu** (*School of Architecture*): library of 5,000 vols.; 126 teachers; 1,302 students.

**Uygulamalı Endüstri Sanatlar Y. Okulu** (*School of Applied Industrial Arts*): library of 1,500 vols.; 92 teachers; 631 students.

**Concervatoire municipal** (*Istanbul Municipal Conservatoire*): Çemberlitaş, Istanbul; f. 1923; internal and extra-mural sections.
*Director:* NEDİM OTYAM.
*Members of the Artistic Council:* ÖZEN VEZIROĞLU (Piano), MERAL YAPALI (Violin), NECDET YILDIRIM (Trumpet), SELMA BERK (Voice).

The library contains 18,000 vols.
Number of teachers: 60.
Number of students: 821 external, 90 internal.

**İzmir State Conservatoire:** İzmir; f. 1951.

**State Conservatoire:** Ankara; f. 1936; music, including opera and ballet, and drama; 150 teachers, 400 students; Dir. ALI ÇERÇIOĞLU.

# UGANDA
**Population 12,600,000**

## LEARNED SOCIETIES

**Association for Teacher Education in Africa:** Makerere University, Kampala; f. 1970.

**Inter-University Council for East Africa:** P.O.B. 7110, Kampala; f. 1970 under the East African Community, now autonomous; aims to facilitate contact and co-operation between the universities of Makerere, Dar es Salaam and Nairobi, and to provide a forum for discussion on academic matters, and to maintain comparable academic standards; Exec. Sec. E. K. KIGOZI; publ. *Report* (annually).

**Uganda Library Association:** P.O.B. 5894, Kampala; f. 1972; 110 mems.; Chair. P. BIRUNGI; Sec. J. N. KIYIMBA; publ. *Ugandan Libraries*†.

**Uganda Society:** P.O.B. 4980, Kampala; f. 1933; premises in the Uganda Museum Education Building, Kira Rd., Kampala; membership open to persons of all races and institutions, to promote interest in literary, historic, scientific and general cultural matters, discovering and recording facts about the country, arranging lectures and establishing contacts; reference library and lending library 6,000 vols. and periodicals; publ. *The Uganda Journal*.

## RESEARCH INSTITUTES

**Animal Health Research Centre:** P.O.B. 24, Entebbe; f. 1926; research and field work in animal diseases, husbandry and nutrition; herbarium; library of 13,500 vols.; Dir. Veterinary Research Services Dr. G. CORRY; Librarian H. R. KIBOOLE; publs. *Research Index*† (irregular), *Research Bulletin*† (irregular), *Annual Report*†.

**Child Malnutrition Unit:** Medical Research Council, Mulago Hospital, P.O.B. 7051, Kampala; Dir. Dr. R. G. WHITEHEAD. (*See* also under Medical Research Council, U.K..)

**Cotton Research Station (Namulonge):** (*Cotton Research Corporation*): P.O.B. 7084, Kampala; pure and applied aspects of cotton culture and technology, library of 4,000 vols.

**Geological Survey and Mines Department:** P.O.B. 9, Entebbe; f. 1919; library of 22,900 vols.; Commissioner C. E. TAMALE-SSALI, B.SC., D.I.C., A.I.M.M., F.G.S.

**Government Chemist Department:** P.O.B. 2174, Kampala; forensic chemical examination, bacteriological examination of foods and water, chemical analysis of water, food and drugs, identification and assay of drugs, general chemical analysis of soils and ores.

**Kawanda Agricultural Research Station:** P.O.B. 7065, Kampala; f. 1937; soil and agricultural research; soil and plant chemistry, plant breeding, plant pathology, crop agronomy, entomology, nematology, biometrics, weed science, seed technology, horticulture; herbarium, soil samples and collection of insects; open to visitors by invitation and appointment; library of c. 11,000 vols.; Dir. of Research Dr. Z. M. NYIIRA; publ. *Annual Report of Investigations*.

**Makerere Institute of Social Research:** P.O.B. 16022, Kampala; f. 1950; conducts independent research into social, political and economic problems of East Africa; 8 Research Fellows, University staff in Departments of Economics, Political Science, Rural Economy and Extension, Sociology, Social Work and Social Administration; library of 8,000 vols., 300 current periodicals and extensive pamphlets, etc.; Chair. Dr. B. TURYA-HIKAYO-RUGYEMA, PH.D.; Sec. P. B. MPINGA; Librarian B. NSAMBA; publs. *East African Studies* (irregularly), *East Africa Linguistic Studies* (occasional), working papers, USSC Conference papers (triennial), *Policy Abstracts and Research Newsletter*, library catalogues.

## LIBRARIES

**Cabinet Office Library:** P.O.B. 5, Entebbe; f. 1920; for government officials and for research workers; 1,404 vols.; publ. *Catalogue*.

**Cotton Research Corpn. Library:** P.O.B. 7084, Kampala; specialized library for research students.

**Makerere University Library Service:** P.O.B. 16002, Kampala; f. 1940; comprises Main Library functioning as National Reference Library, with five sub-libraries for the faculties of medicine (functioning as National Library of Medicine), technology, education, social science research and farm management; main library of over 400,000 vols., over 240,000 periodicals, special collections of East Africa, Uganda legal deposit, and private archives; Librarian J. MUGASHA, B.SC., M.S.L.A.; publs. incl. *East African Studies*†, *Mawazo*†, *Makerere Law Journal*†, *Makerere Political Review*†, etc.

**Makerere University, Albert Cook Library:** Makerere Medical School, P.O.B. 7072, Kampala; f. 1946; c. 16,449 vols., 234 periodicals, covering all medical subjects, especially East African and tropical medicine; Librarian L. SSENNYONJO, B.A.; publs. *East African Medical Bibliography* (every 2 months), *Library Bulletin and Accessions List* (irregularly), *Annual Report*.

**Public Libraries Board:** Buganda Rd., P.O.B. 4262, Kampala; f. 1964 to establish, equip, manage and maintain libraries in Uganda; 20 branch libraries, book box and postal services are administered; library of 110,000 vols., 200 serial titles; Dir. P. BIRUNGI; publs. *Quarterly Accessions*†, *Annual Report*†.

**The Secretariat Library:** The Secretariat, P.O.B. 5, Kampala; intended to be a comprehensive collection concerning Uganda, also has main works on East Africa, Africa and the British Commonwealth; available to students at the discretion of the Chief Secretary.

## MUSEUMS

**Entebbe Botanic Gardens:** P.O.B. 40, Entebbe; f. 1898; native and exotic plants, training in horticulture, sales of horticultural produce; Curator J. J. ASEGA; publ. *Index Seminum*† (annual).

**Forest Department Library and Herbarium:** Forest Office, P.O.B. 31, Entebbe; f. 1904; 11,000 specimens; specialized library open to students by special arrangement with the Chief Forest Officer.

**Forestry Research Centre and Museum:** P.O.B. 1752, Kampala; f. 1952; collection of Uganda timbers; entomology section; preservation, seasoning and woodworking tests; logging, milling and building research; small specialized library.

**Game and Fisheries Museum, Zoo, Aquarium and Library:** P.O.B. 4, Entebbe; collections of heads of game animals, reptiles, fish and butterflies, hunting and fishing implements and weapons; library of approx. 1,100 vols.; Chief Game Warden JOHN BUSHARA; Chief Fisheries Officer ALOYSIUS BIRIBONWOHA.

**Geological Survey Museum and Library:** P.O.B. 9, Entebbe; about 37,500 specimens of rocks and minerals; library of over 9,850 vols. and 3,850 periodicals.

**Uganda Museum:** 5-7 Kira Rd., P.O.B. 365, Kampala; f. 1908; natural history, geology, ethnology, archaeology, palaeontology; science and industry pavilion; special collection of African musical instruments; centre for archaeological research in Uganda; library of 3,200 vols.; Curator A. WANZAMA; publ. occasional papers, *Annual Report*.

**Regional Museums:** at Soroti and Kabale.

**National Park Museums:** at Mweya in Rwenzori National Park and at Paraa and Chobe in Kabalega National Park.

# UNIVERSITY AND COLLEGES

## MAKERERE UNIVERSITY
P.O.B. 7062, KAMPALA

Telephone: 42471.

Founded as technical school 1922, became University College 1949, attained University Status 1970.

Language of instruction: English; Academic year: July to March (three terms).

*Chancellor:* H.E. The President of Uganda.
*Vice-Chancellor:* Prof. A. WANDIRA, M.A.
*Secretary:* DAVID SENTONGO, B.A., M.SC. (acting).
*Academic Registrar:* BERNARD ONYANGO, M.A.
*Librarian:* J. MUGASHA, B.SC., M.S.L.A.

Number of teachers: c. 500.
Number of students: c. 4,760.

### DEANS:
*Faculty of Arts:* Dr. A. BYARUHANGA-AKIIKI.
*Faculty of Social Sciences:* A. R. NSIBAMBI.
*Faculty of Agriculture and Forestry:* Prof. JOHN MUGERWA.
*Faculty of Science:* Prof. A. LUTALO-BOSA.
*Faculty of Education:* Dr. J. B. BIGALA.
*Faculty of Medicine:* Prof. R. OWOR.
*Faculty of Law:* Dr. K. MUKUBUYA.
*Faculty of Veterinary Science:* Prof. F. I. B. KAYANJA.
*Faculty of Technology:* Dr. E. LUGUJJO.

### ATTACHED INSTITUTES AND SCHOOLS:

**Centre for Continuing Education:** f. 1953, reorganized into three divisions: Extra Mural Department, Correspondence Courses and Mass Media Division, Adult Studies Centre (one-year post-secondary school courses); shorter courses are also arranged both at the Centre and up-country; Dir. J. KWESIGA (acting).

**East African School of Librarianship:** f. 1963 to train librarians for all parts of East Africa; 2-year course leads to Diploma in Librarianship; also 1-year postgraduate course; Dir. S. A. H. ABIDI, M.A., M.LIB.SC.

**Institute of Statistics and Applied Economics:** a joint enterprise of the Government of Uganda and the United Nations Development Programme; 3-year degree courses; Dir. Dr. S. TULYA-MUHIKA, PH.D.

**Makerere Institute of Social Research:** *see* under Research Institutes.

**Margaret Trowell School of Fine Art:** diploma and degree courses at both undergraduate and graduate levels; Head F. X. NNAGGENDA (acting).

**National Institute of Education:** f. 1964; corporate body representing the Ministry of Education, Teacher Training Colleges of Uganda, Makerere University Faculty of Education; co-ordinates and encourages teacher training, promotes educational research, gives information and advice on new methods and materials, organizes in-service training and one-year advanced diploma courses for teachers; Dir. S. W. SERUGGA, M.SC.ED.; Librarian Mrs. M. O. MUTIBWA, B.A.; publs. *Journal*, *Newsletter*.

## UGANDA TECHNICAL COLLEGE
P.O.B. 7273, KAMPALA

Telephone: 65211.

Founded 1954; formerly Kampala Technical Institute.

*Principal:* N. B. BALYAMUJURA, M.A.S.E.E., M.I.E.E.E., A.M.U.I.M.
*Vice-Principal:* C. NTAMBI, H.N.D., A.I.B.C.C., F.I.E.T.U.
*Registrar:* J. B. KISUULE, LL.M.
*Senior Librarian:* R. NGANWA, A.L.A.

Number of teachers: 104.
Number of students: 1,000.

### HEADS OF DEPARTMENTS:
*Civil Engineering and Building:* C. NTAMBI.
*Electrical Engineering:* J. W. B. EFATA, B.SC.
*Mechanical Engineering:* G. KOOSI, M.SC.
*Science and Mathematics:* E. M. K. NGALOMBI, B.SC.
*Technical Teacher Training:* G. IGABA.
*English and Liberal Studies Section:* N. W. KAJUBI, B.A.
*Industrial Ceramics Section:* L. MUTEBI.

# UNION OF SOVIET SOCIALIST REPUBLICS

Population 264,486,000

## ACADEMIES AND RESEARCH INSTITUTES

*Most learned societies and research institutes in the U.S.S.R. are attached to the relevant academies and ministries.*

### ACADEMY OF SCIENCES OF THE U.S.S.R.
LENINSKY PROSPEKT 14, MOSCOW V-71

Founded 1725

The Academy is directly subordinate to the Council of Ministers of the U.S.S.R. Following the reorganization of the Academy in 1963, its position as the leading Soviet Academy of Sciences was strengthened, and it was also made the chief co-ordinating body for scientific research in the Soviet Union. The Academy directs the work of over 260 scientific institutions, including scientific councils, commissions, museums, research stations, laboratories, naval institutes and observatories. There are 11 scientific societies under the Academy's jurisdiction.

Presidium:

*President:* A. P. Alexandrov.

*Vice-Presidents:* P. N. Fedoseyev, Y. A. Ovchinnikov, A. A. Logunov, A. P. Vinogradov.

*Academic Secretary:* G. K. Skryabin.

*Academician-Secretaries:* N. N. Bogolyubov, A. M. Prokhorov, M. A. Markov, M. A. Styrikovich, A. N. Nesmeyanov, N. M. Zhavoronkov, A. A. Bayev, E. M. Kreps, Y. V. Peyve, V. I. Smirnov, L. M. Brekhovskikh, B. A. Rybakov, F. V. Konstantinov, N. P. Fedorenko, M. B. Khrapchenko.

*Chairman of the Presidium of Scientific Centre of the Urals:* S. V. Vonsovsky.

*Chairman of the Presidium of Far East Scientific Centre:* A. P. Kapitsa.

*Academicians:* A. P. Alexandrov, V. A. Ambartsumyan, N. G. Basov, P. L. Kapitsa, N. I. Mushkhelishvili, B. E. Paton, N. A. Pilyugin, P. N. Pospelov, A. M. Rumyantsev, A. S. Sadykov, N. N. Semenov, A. A. Trofimuk, V. M. Tuchkevich, I. N. Vekua.

Academicians:

Aganbegyan, A. G., Economics
Ageyev, N. V., Physical Chemistry of Inorganic Materials
Alexandrov, A. D., Mathematics
Alexandrov, A. P., Physics
Alexandrov, P. S., Mathematics
Alexeyev, M. P., Russian and West European Literature
Alferov, Z. I., Physics
Alimarin, I. P., Analytical Chemistry
Ambartsumyan, V. A., Astronomy
Arbatov, G. A., Economics
Arbuzov, B. A., Organic Chemistry
Artobolevsky, I. I., Mechanics
Avduevsky, V. S., Mechanics
Bayev, A. A., Molecular Biology
Barmin, V. P., Mechanics
Basov, N. G., Experimental and Theoretical Physics
Beloded, I. K., Languages of the U.S.S.R. peoples
Belotserkovsky, O. M., Mechanics
Belov, A. F., Metallurgy
Belov, N. V., Geochemistry, Crystallochemistry, Structural Mineralogy
Belyayev, D. K., Genetics
Belyayev, S. T., Nuclear Physics
Blokhin, N. N., Physiology
Bochvar, A. A., Metallurgy
Bogolyubov, N. N., Mathematics
Boreskov, G. K., Chemistry
Borkovsky, V. I., Russian Language
Borovic-Romanov, A. S., Physics and Astronomy
Braunstein, A. E., Biochemistry
Brekhovskikh, L. M., Oceanology
Bruyevich, N. G., Mechanics
Bunkin, B. V., Radio Technology
Bushmin, A. S., Literature
Chaylakhyan, M. K., Plant Physiology
Chazov, E. I., Physiology
Chekmarev, A. P., Metallurgy
Chelomey, V. N., Mechanics
Cherenkov, P. A., High Energy Physics
Cherepnin, L. V., History of the U.S.S.R.
Chernigovsky, V. N., Physiology
Chukhrov, F. V., Geology and Geochemistry
Devyatkov, N. D., Electronics
Devyatikh, G. G., Inorganic Chemistry
Dikushin, V. I., Mechanical Engineering
Dolgoplosk, B. A., Chemistry of Macromolecular Compounds
Dollezhal, N. A., Energy
Dorodnitsyn, A. A., Geophysics
Drotsenidze, G. S., Mineralogy and Petrography
Druzhinin, M. M., History of the U.S.S.R.
Dubinin, M. M., Chemistry
Dubinin, N. P., Genetics
Efimov, A. N., Economics
Egorov, A. G., Philosophy
Emanuel, N. M., Physical Chemistry
Engelhardt, V. A., Biochemistry and Molecular Biology
Fedorenko, N. P., Economics
Fedorov, E. K., Applied Geophysics
Fedoseyev, P. N., Philosophy
Flerov, G. N., Nuclear Physics
Fokin, A. V., Chemistry
Frank, G. M., Biophysics
Frank, I. M., Nuclear Physics
Frumkin, A. N., Physical Chemistry
Gaponov-Grekhov, A. V., Physics
Gazenko, O. G., Physiology and Medicine
Gerasimov, I. P., Geography
Gilyarov, M. S., Zoology
Ginzburg, V. L., Experimental and Theoretical Physics
Glushko, V. P., Thermal Engineering
Glushkov, V. M., Mathematics and Computer Mathematics
Grushin, P. D., Mechanics
Gvishiany, D. M., Philosophy and Law
Ilyichev, L. F., Philosophy
Ilyushin, S. V., Aviation
Imshenetsky, A. A., Microbiology
Inozemtsev, N. N., Economics
Isanin, N. N., Ship-building
Ishlinsky, A. Y., Automation and Mechanics

Kabachnik, M. I., Organic Chemistry
Kabanov, V. A., Molecular Chemistry
Kadomtsev, B. B., Physics
Kalesnik, S. V., Geography
Kantorovich, L. V., Mathematics and Economics
Kapitza, P. L., Physics
Kedrov, B. M., Philosophy
Khachaturov, T. S., Economics
Khariton, Y. B., Physics
Khoklov, R. V., Quantitative Electronics
Khristianovich, S. A., Mechanics
Kikoin, I. K., Physics
Kim, M. P., History of the U.S.S.R.
Kirillin, V. A., Energy
Kishkin, S. T., Metallurgy
Knunyantz, I. L., Organic Chemistry
Kobzarev, Y. B., Radiotechnics
Kocheshkov, K. A., Organic Chemistry
Kochetkov, N. K., Chemistry
Kochina, P. Y., Mechanics and Hydrodynamics
Kolmogorov, A. N., Mathematics
Kolosov, M. N., Biochemistry
Kolotyrkin, Y. M., Physical Chemistry
Kondratyev, V. N., Physical Chemistry
Kononov, A. N., Linguistics
Konstantinov, F. V., Philosophy
Koptyug, V. A., Organic Chemistry
Korostovtsev, M. A., History of Non-Soviet East
Korzhinsky, D. S., Petrogeny
Kostenko, M. P., Power Engineering
Kostyuk, P. G., Physiology
Kosygin, Y. A., Geology and Geography
Kotelnikov, V. A., Radioastronomy
Krasovsky, N. N., Physics
Kreps, E. M., Physiology and Biochemistry
Krylov, A. P., Mining and Geology
Kurdyumov, G. V., Metal Physics
Kursanov, A. L., Plant Physiology and Biochemistry
Kutateladze, S. S., Energy
Kuznetsov, N. D., Mechanical Engineering
Kuznetsov, V. A., Geology and Geography
Kuznetsov, V. I., Automation
Kuznetsov, Y. A., Geology

Lavrenko, E. M., Botany
Leonov, L. M., History of Literature
Liefshitz, E. M., Physics
Likhachev, D. S., Russian Literature
Linnik, V. P., Physics
Livanov, M. N., Physiology
Logunov, A. A., Nuclear Physics
Lysenko, T. D., Genetics and Agrobiology
Lyulka, A. M., Power Engineering

Magnitsky, V. A., Geophysics
Makarevsky, A. I., Aviation
Marchuk, G. I., Physics of the Atmosphere
Mardzhanishvili, K. K., Mathematics
Markov, K. K., Geography
Markov, M. A., Nuclear Physics
Melentyev, L. A., Energy
Melnikov, N. P., Mechanics and Control Processes
Menner, V. V., Geology and Geophysics
Migdal, A. B., Nuclear Physics
Mikhaylov, A. A., Astronomy
Mikulin, A. A., Internal Combustion Engines
Minachev, K. M., Organic Chemistry
Mintz, I. I., History
Mishin, V. P., Mechanics
Mishustin, E. N., Microbiology
Mitin, M. B., Philosophy
Mushkelishvili, N. I., Mathematics

Nalivkin, D. V., Geology and Palaeontology
Narochnitsky, A. L., History
Nechkina, M. V., History of the U.S.S.R.
Negin, E. A., Mechanics
Nekrasov, N. N., Economics
Nikolayev, A. V., Chemistry
Nikolayev, G. A., Physical and Inorganic Chemistry
Nikolsky, B. P., Physical Chemistry
Nikolsky, S. M., Mathematics
Novoselova, A. V., Chemistry
Novozhilov, V. V., Mechanics

Obraztsov, I. F., Aviation
Obreimov, I. V., Optics

Obukhov, A. M., Atmospheric Physics
Okladnikov, A. P., History
Ovchinnikov, Y. A., Chemistry

Paton, B. E., Metallurgy and Technology of Metals
Petrov, G. I., Mechanics
Petrovsky, B. V., Physiology and Medicine
Petryanov-Sokolov, I. V., Physical Chemistry
Peyve, A. V., Geology and Geophysics
Peyve, Y. V., Agrochemistry
Pilyugin, N. A., Automation
Piotrovsky, B. B., History
Ponomarev, B. N., History of the Soviet Union Communist Party
Pontekorvo, B. M., Nuclear Physics
Pontryagin, L. S., Mathematics
Popkov, V. I., Energy
Postovski, I. Y., Chemistry
Primakov, E. M., Economics
Prokhorov, A. M., Physics
Prokhorov, Y. V., Mathematics

Rabotnov, Y. N., Mechanics
Razuvayev, G. A., Organic Chemistry
Remeslo, V. N., Plant Biology
Reutov, O. A., Organic Chemistry
Rumyantsev, A. M., Economics
Rybakov, B. A., Archaeology and History of the U.S.S.R.
Rykalin, N. N., Metallurgy

Sadovsky, M. A., Geology and Geophysics
Sadovsky, V. D., Metallurgy
Sadykov, A. S., Organic Chemistry
Sagdeyev, R. Z., Physics
Sakharov, A. D., Physics
Sedov, L. I., Mechanics
Semenikhin, V. S., Mechanics
Semenov, N. N., Chemical Physics
Sergeyev, E. M., Hydrogeology
Severin, S. E., Biochemistry
Severny, A. B., Astronomy and Radioastronomy
Shafarevich, I. R., Mathematics
Shchukin, A. N., Radiotechnics
Sheyndlin, A. E., Energy
Shilo, N. A., Mining
Sholokhov, M. A., Literature
Shuleykin, V. V., Marine Physics
Shults, M. M., Physical Chemistry
Shvarts, S. S., Zoology
Sidorenko, A. V., Geology and Geophysics
Skobeltsyn, D. V., Physics
Skrinsky, A. N., High Energy Physics
Skryabin, G. K., Medical, Technical Biochemistry
Smirnov, V. I., Geology
Sobolev, S. L., Mathematics
Sobolev, V. S., Geology and Geography
Sochava, V. B., Geography
Sokolov, B. S., Geology
Sokolov, V. E., Zoology
Spirin, A. S., Molecular Biology
Spitsyn, V. I., Inorganic Chemistry
Strakhov, N. M., Geology and Lithology
Struminsky, V. V., Mechanics
Styrikovich, M. A., Energy

Takhtadzhyan, A. L., Botany
Tananayev, I. V., Inorganic Chemistry
Tikhonov, A. N., Mathematics
Trapeznikov, V. A., Automation
Trofimuk, A. A., Geology
Tselikov, A. I., Processing of Materials
Tuchkevich, V. M., Semiconductors

Vekua, I. N., Mathematics
Velikhov, E. P., Plasma Physics
Vernov, S. N., High Energy Physics
Vinogradov, A. P., Analytical Chemistry and Geochemistry
Vinogradov, I. M., Mathematics
Vladimirov, V. S., Mathematics
Volfkovich, S. I., Chemical Technology and Inorganic Chemistry
Vonsovsky, S. V., Magnetism
Voronov, A. A., Control Theory
Vorozhtsov, N. N., Chemistry
Vul, B. M., Physics and Astronomy

## ACADEMY OF SCIENCES — UNION OF SOVIET SOCIALIST REPUBLICS

Yakovlev, A. S., Aircraft Design
Yanenko, N. N., Mechanics
Yanshin, A. L., Geology and Geography
Zababakhin, E. I., Physics
Zaslavskaya, T. I., Economics
Zavoysky, E. K., Physics
Zeldovich, Y. B., Physics
Zhavoronkov, N. M., Inorganic Chemistry
Zhukov, A. B., Biology
Zhukov, B. P., Chemistry
Zhurkov, S. N., Physics

### Corresponding Members:

Abdulayev, G. M., Physics
Abrikosov, A. A., Physics
Afanasyev, V. G., Philosophy
Agoshkov, M. I., Mining
Aksenenok, G. A., Law
Alekin, O. A., Hydrochemistry
Alexandrov, K. S., Physics
Alexeyev, A. S., Geophysics
Alexeyevsky, N. E., Physics
Alexovsky, V. B., Physical Chemistry
Amirkhanov, K. Y., Physics
Andriyashev, A. P., Zoology
Asimov, M. S., Philosophy
Asratyan, E. A., Physiology
Avanesov, R. I., Linguistics
Avrorin, V. A., Linguistics
Avsyuk, G. A., Hydrogeology
Babaev, Y. N., Nuclear Physics
Bagdasaryan, K. S., Chemistry
Bakhrakh, L. D., Radio Physics
Baldin, A. M., Nuclear Physics
Barkhudarov, S. G., Linguistics
Barkov, L. M., Physics
Bashkirov, A. N., Chemistry
Bazanov, V. G., Literature
Bekhtereva, N. P., Physiology
Belchikov, N. F., Russian Literature
Beletskaya, I. P., Chemistry
Belousov, V. V., Geology
Belyakov, R. A., Mechanical Engineering
Berdnikov, G. P., Literary Criticism
Berezin, I. V., Chemistry
Bergelson, L. D., Chemistry
Bezrukov, P. L., Oceanology
Bitsadze, A. V., Mathematics
Blagoy, D. D., Russian Literature
Blinova, E. N., Geophysics
Bogolyubov, M. N., Linguistics
Bogomolov, A. F., Radio Physics
Bogomolov, O. T., Economics
Bogorodsky, V. V., Oceanology
Boky, G. B., Physical Chemistry
Bolotin, V. V., Mechanics
Bolshakov, K. A., Chemistry
Bolshev, L. N., Mathematics
Borisevich, N. A., Optics
Borovkov, A. A., Mathematics
Bromley, Y. V., History
Budagov, R. A., Linguistics
Budyko, M. I., Geophysics
Bukin, V. N., Biochemistry
Bulanzhe, Y. D., Geology and Geophysics
Bulashevich, Y. P., Geophysics
Bunich, P. G., Economics
Bushuyev, K. D., Mechanics
Buslayev, Y. A., Chemistry
Buslenko, N. P., Mathematics
Butenko, R. G., Biology
Byushgens, G. S., Mechanics
Chagin, B. A., Philosophy
Chepikov, K. R., Geology of Oil
Cherny, G. G., Mechanics
Chersky, N. V., Mechanics
Chertok, B. E., Control Systems
Chibisov, K. V., Photochemistry
Chinakal, N. A., Mining and Metallurgy
Chkhikvadze, V. M., Law
Chmutov, K. V., Physical Chemistry
Chudakov, A. E., Nuclear Physics
Chufarov, G. I., Physical Chemistry
Chukhanov, Z. F., Power Engineering

Danilov, S. N., Organic Chemistry
Delone, B. N., Mathematics
Denisiuk, Y. N., Optics
Deryagin, B. V., Physical Chemistry
Desnitskaya, A. V., Literature
Dzhelepov, B. S., Physics
Dzhelepov, V. P., Nuclear Physics
Dzyaloshinsky, I. E., Physics

Eichfeld, I. G., Botany
Elyakov, G. B., Chemistry
Elyutin, V. P., Metallurgy
Emelyanov, I. Y., Atomic Energy
Emelyanov, S. V., Automation
Emelyanov, V. S., Metallurgy
Eneyev, T. M., Mechanics
Enikolopov, N. S., Chemistry
Ershov, A. P., Mathematics
Ershov, Y. L., Mathematics
Evstratov, V. F., Chemistry

Faddeyev, D. K., Mathematics
Fedorenko, N. T., Chinese Literature
Fedorov, A. A., Botany
Fedorov, A. A., Biology
Fedotov, S. A., Geology
Fedynsky, V. V., Geophysics
Feofilov, P. P., Physics
Feoktistov, L. P., Nuclear Physics
Feynberg, E. L., Nuclear Physics
Filin, F. P., Linguistics
Florensov, N. A., Geology
Fomin, V. V., Technological Chemistry
Fotiady, E. E., Geology and Geophysics
Fradkin, E. S., Nuclear Physics
Freidlina, R. K., Chemistry
Frish, S. E., Spectroscopy

Gagarinsky, Y. V., Inorganic Chemistry
Galaziy, G. T., Biology
Galin, L. A., Mechanics
Gatovsky, L. M., Economics
Gavrilov, M. A., Automation
Geld, P. V., Inorganic Chemistry
Gelfand, I. M., Mathematics
Georgiev, G. P., Biochemistry
Gerasimov, Y. I., Physical Chemistry
Gershuni, G. V., Physiology
Glebov, I. A., Energy in Mechanical Engineering
Goldansky, V. I., Physical Chemistry
Gonchar, A. A., Mathematics
Gorbunov, G. I., Geology
Gorkov, L. P., Physics
Govorun, N. N., Computer Mathematics
Gribov, V. N., Nuclear Physics
Grigolyuk, E. I., Mechanics
Grinberg, G. A., Mathematical Physics
Grosul, Y. S., History of the U.S.S.R.
Gurevich, I. I., Nuclear Physics
Gutyrya, V. S., Technology of Oil

Ievlev, V. M., Energy
Ilyushin, A. A., Mechanics
Iovchuk, M. T., History of Philosophy
Ivanov, S. N., Geology
Ivanov, V. E., Chemistry
Ivanov, V. K., Mathematics
Izrael, Y. A., Physics of the Atmosphere

Kafarov, V. V., Chemical Technology
Kagan, Y. M., Physics
Kapitza, A. P., Geomorphology
Karakeyev, K. K., History
Karamyan, A. I., Physiology
Karavayev, N. M., Chemistry and Technology of Fuel
Kargapolov, M. I., Mathematics
Karpachev, S. V., Chemistry
Kazansky, V. B., Physical Chemistry
Kazarnovsky, I. A., Chemistry
Keldysh, L. V., Physics
Kerimov, D. A., Law
Khain, V. E., Geology
Khalatnikov, I. M., Physics
Khesin-Lurye, R. B., Biochemistry, Enzymology
Khimich, G. L., Mechanical Engineering
Khitarov, N. I., Geochemistry
Khokhlov, A. S., Chemistry of Biopolymers

Khomentovsky, A. S., Geology
Khrenov, K. K., Metal Welding
Kisunko, G. V., Radiotechnics
Knorre, D. G., Chemistry
Kolesnikov, B. P., Biology
Kolosov, N. G., Histology
Kondratyev, K. Y., Physics
Kontrimavichus, V. L., Biology
Korshak, V. V., Chemistry
Kostenko, M. V., Energy
Koton, M. M., Chemistry
Kovalchenko, I. D., History of the U.S.S.R.
Kovalev, N. N., Mechanics
Kovalsky, A. A., Chemistry
Kovda, V. A., Soil Science
Kozlov, G. A., Economics
Kozlov, V. Y., Mathematics
Kozyrev, B. M., Physics
Krasniy, L. I., Geology
Krasnovsky, A. A., Biochemistry
Krasovsky, A. A., Control Theory
Krat, V. A., Astronomy
Kratts, K. O., Mineralogy and Petrogeny
Kretovich, V. L., Biochemistry
Kropotkin, P. N., Geology and Geophysics
Krushanov, A. I., History
Krushinsky, L. V., General Biology
Kruus, K. K., History
Kruzhilin, G. N., Thermotechnics
Kruzhkov, V. S., Philosophy
Kudryavtsev, V. N., Law
Kukin, D. M., History
Kunaev, A. M., Chemistry
Kunin, V. N., Hydrogeology
Kurbatov, L. N., Technical Physics
Kursanov, D. N., Organic Chemistry
Kuzin, A. M., Radiobiology
Kuznetsov, S. I., Microbiology

Laskorin, B. N., Chemistry
Lavrentyev, M. M., Mathematics
Lavrov, S. S., Automatic Control
Lazarev, V. N., History of Art
Leontiev, A. F., Mathematics
Levich, V. G., Physical Chemistry
Levkoev, I. I., Technical Chemistry
Lidorenko, N. S., Electrical Engineering
Lifshitz, E. M., Physics
Lisitsyn, A. P., Geophysics
Lobashev, V. M., Nuclear Physics
Lomidze, G. I., History of Literature
Luchitsky, I. V., Geophysics
Lupanov, O. B., Mathematics
Lurie, A. I., Mechanics
Lyusternik, L. A., Mathematics

Makarov, I. M., Control Processes
Makeyev, V. P., Mechanics
Malinin, A. K., Mechanics
Malmeister, A. K., Mechanics
Malyusov, V. A., Chemistry
Mamaev, B. P., Chemistry
Markov, A. A., Mathematics
Markov, D. F., Literature
Matulis, Y. Y., Physical Chemistry
Maximov, A. A., History of Science
Meisel, M. N., Microbiology
Melnikov, O. A., Astronomy
Melnikov, P. I., Geophysics
Menshov, D. E., Mathematics
Mergelyan, S. N., Mathematics
Meshcheryakov, M. G., Physics
Migulin, V. V., Physics
Mikhailov, B. M., Chemistry
Mikulinsky, S. R., Philosophy
Mileykovsky, A. G., Economics
Mirchink, M. F., Geology of Oil
Mishchenko, E. F., Control Processes
Molchanov, A. A., Botany
Molin, Y. N., Chemistry
Molodensky, M. S., Physics
Monin, A. S., Oceanology
Moyseyev, N. N., Mechanics
Muratov, M. V., Geology
Mustel, E. R., Astronomy and Astrophysics

Nalivkin, V. D., Geology

Nametkin, N. S., Organic Chemistry
Naumov, A. A., Physics
Nekrasov, B. V., Chemistry
Nesmeyanov, A. N., Radiochemistry
Nesterikhin, Y. E., Physics
Neunilov, B. A., Biology
Nichiporovich, A. A., Biophysics
Nikolsky, G. V., Ichthyology
Novikov, I. I., Thermotechnics
Novikov, S. P., Mathematics
Novikov, S. S., Chemistry

Odintsov, M. M., Mining
Okhotsimsky, D. E., Mechanics
Okun, L. B., Nuclear Physics
Oderogge, D. A., Linguistics
Omelyanovksy, M. E., Philosophy
Osipyan, Y. A., Physics
Ovchinnikov, L. N., Mining
Ovsyannikov, L. V., Mechanics
Oyzerman, T. I., Philosophy

Pariysky, N. N., Geophysics
Pashkov, A. I., Political Economics
Pavlov, I. M., Metallurgy
Petrov, A. A., Organic Chemistry
Petrov, A. P., Transport
Petrov, G. N., Energy
Petrov, V. V., Control Systems
Piruzyan, L. A., Physiology, Medical Biophysics
Pistolkors, A. A., Radio Engineering
Plate, N. A., Chemistry
Plotnikov, K. N., Economics
Pogorelov, A. V., Mathematics
Polikanov, S. M., Nuclear Physics
Polyakov, Y. A., History
Popov, E. P., Automation
Popyrin, L. S., Energy
Poray-Koshits, M. A., Inorganic Chemistry
Pospelov, G. S., Automation
Prokofyev, M. A., Chemistry of Biopolymers
Prokoshkin, Y. D., Nuclear Physics
Pudovik, A. N., Organic Chemistry
Pugachev, V. S., Automation
Puzyrev, N. N., Geophysics
Pyavchenko, N. I., Biology

Rabinovich, I. M., Construction Materials
Radkevich, E. A., Geology
Rafikov, S. R., Chemistry
Rakitin, Y. V., Plant Physiology
Raushenbach, B. V., Automation
Ravdonikas, V. I., Archaeology and History
Razin, N. V., Energetics
Rebane, K., Physics
Reimerz, F. E., Biology
Reizov, B. G., Literature
Reshetnikov, F. G., Physical Chemistry
Riznichenko, Y. V., Geophysics
Romankov, P. G., Chemical Technology
Ronov, A. B., Geochemistry
Roytbak, A. I., Physiology
Rumyantsev, V.V., Mechanics
Rutkevich, M. N., Philosophy
Ryabushkin, T. V., Economics
Ryazansky, M. S., Radiotechnics
Rytov, S. M., Radiotechnics
Ryzhikov, K. M., Helminthology
Ryzhkov, V. L., Botany
Rzhanov, A. V., Radio Electronics
Rzhevsky, V. V., Mining

Saks, V. N., Geology and Geography
Samarsky, A. A., Computer Mathematics
Samsonov, A. M., History
Savarensky, E. F., Geology and Geophysics
Savitsky, E. M., Processing of Materials
Serebrennikov, B. A., Linguistics
Shalnikov, A. I., Physics
Shanidze, A. G., Linguistics
Sharvin, Y. V., Physics
Shatalin, S. S., Economics
Shirkov, D. V., Physics
Shirshov, A. I., Mathematics
Shklovsky, I. S., Radio Astronomy
Shlyk, A. A., Plant Physiology
Shpak, B. S., Chemistry

## ACADEMY OF SCIENCES UNION OF SOVIET SOCIALIST REPUBLICS

Shostakovsky, M. F., Chemistry
Shur, Y. S., Physics
Shvetsov, P. F., Geology
Sidorov, A. A., History of Art
Sidorov, V. A., Nuclear Physics
Siforov, V. I., Radio Engineering
Skulachev, V. P., Biochemistry
Sladkovsky, M. I., Economics
Slinko, M. G., Chemistry
Smolensky, G. A., Physics
Sobolev, V. V., Astronomy
Sokolov, A. V., Agrochemistry
Sokolovsky, V. V., Mechanics
Solodovnikov, V. G., Economics
Solonenko, V. P., Geophysics
Soloukhin, R. I., Mechanics
Solovjev, S. L., Seismology of the Sea-bed
Sorokin, G. M., Economics
Spirkin, A. G., Philosophy
Spivak, P. E., Nuclear Physics
Spivakovsky, A. O., Mining
Stepanov, G. V., Linguistics
Stepanov, V. E., Physics
Stepanyan, T. A., Philosophy
Strogovich, M. S., Law
Subbotin, V. I., Physics
Svetovidov, A. N., Ichthyology
Svishchev, G. P., Mechanical Engineering
Talroze, V. L., Physical Chemistry
Tatarinov, L. P., General Biology
Tatarinov, P. M., Geology
Tauson, L. V., Geochemistry
Terskov, I. A., Biophysics
Tikhomirov, V. V., Radio Engineering
Tikhvinsky, S. L., History
Timofeyev, L. I., Russian Literature
Timofeyev, P. V., Radio Engineering
Timofeyev, T. T., Economics
Tolstov, S. P., History
Torgov, T. V., Chemistry
Tretyakov, P. N., History
Troitsky, V. S., Astronomy
Troshin, A. S., Cytology
Trubachev, O. N., Linguistics
Trukhanovsky, V. G., History
Trutnev, Y. A., Nuclear Physics
Tsvetkov, V. N., Chemistry
Tsypkin, Y. Z., Control Processes
Tsytovich, N. A., Geology
Tugarinov, A. I., Geochemistry
Tumanov, A. T., Inorganic Chemistry
Tumanov, I. I., Plant Physiology
Turpaev, T. M., Physiology

Ugolev, A. M., Physiology and Medicine

Vainshtein, B. K., Physics
Vainshtein, L. A., Radiophysics
Valiev, K. H., Technical Physics
Vanichev, A. P., Energy
Varentsov, M. I., Oil Geology
Vasilyev, O. F., Mechanics
Vasoyevich, N. B., Oil Geology
Vatolin, N. A., Metallurgy
Vdovenko, V. M., Radiochemistry
Velikanov, D. P., Transport
Vinogradov, V. A., Economics
Vladimirsky, V. V., Physics
Volkenstein, M. V., Chemistry
Volobuyev, P. V., History of the U.S.S.R.
Volobuyev, V. R., Soil Science and Agrochemistry
Voronin, L. G., Physiology
Voronkov, M. G., Chemistry
Vorovich, I. I., Mechanics
Voytsekhovsky, B. V., Mechanics

Yablonsky, S. V., Computer Mathematics
Yagodin, G. A., Chemical Engineering
Yanin, V. L., History
Yartseva, V. N., Linguistics

Zaimovsky, A. S., Metallurgy
Zatsepin, G. T., Experimental Nuclear Physics
Zefirov, A. P., Metallurgy
Zharikov, V. A., Mineralogy
Zhdanov, Y. A., Chemistry
Zheltukhin, N. A., Mechanics
Zhilin, P. A., History of the U.S.S.R.
Zhimerin, D. G., Energy
Zhirmunsky, A. V., Marine Biology
Zhukov, M. F., Energy
Zolotov, E. V., Computer Mathematics
Zolotov, Y. A., Analytical Chemistry
Zorev, N. N., Mechanical Engineering
Zuyev, V. E., Physics
Zverev, M. S., Astronomy

### Foreign Members of the U.S.S.R. Academy of Sciences

Akabori, S. (Japan), Biochemistry
Alfvén, H. (Sweden), Physics
Amaldi, E. (Italy), Physics
Bacq, Z. M. (Belgium), Biology
Balevsky, A. T. (Bulgaria), Mechanics
Blaškovič, D. (Czechoslovakia), Virology
de Broglie, L. (France), Physics
Bronk, D. W. (U.S.A.), Biology
Chan Day Ngia (Viet-Nam), Mechanics
Cornu, A. (France), Philosophy
Dirac, P. (U.K.), Physics
Dresch, J. (France), Geography
Ganovsky, S. T. (Bulgaria), Philosophy
Groszkowski, J. (Poland), Physics
Hartke, W. (German Democratic Republic), History
Jabłónski, H. (Poland), History
Kaya, S. (Japan), Physics
Khorana, H. G. (U.S.A.), Chemistry
Klare, H. (G.D.R.), Chemistry
Kozhešník, J. (Czechoslovakia), Mathematics and Mechanics
Krystanov, L. K. (Bulgaria), Geophysics
Kuratowski, K. (Poland), Mathematics
Leray, J. (France), Mathematics
Li Syn Gi (Korean Democratic Republic), Chemistry
Mark, H. F. (U.S.A.), Chemistry
Mothes, K. (German Democratic Republic), Medicine
Murgulescu, G. I. (Romania), Chemistry
Natta, G. (Italy), Chemistry
Neel, L. (France), Physics
Ochoa, S. (U.S.A.), Biochemistry
Oort, J. H. (Netherlands), Astronomy
Pauling, L. (U.S.A.), Chemistry
Pavlov, T. D. (Bulgaria), History, Literature, Philosophy
Pek Nam Un (Korean Democratic Republic), History
Prelog, V. (Switzerland), Chemistry
Rienäcker, G. (German Democratic Republic), Chemistry
Robinson, R. (U.K.), Chemistry
Ružička, L. (Switzerland), Chemistry
Ryle, Sir Martin (U.K.), Radio Astronomy
Salam, A. (Pakistan), Nuclear Physics
Savić, P. (Yugoslavia), Physical Chemistry
Seaborg, G. T. (U.S.A.), Nuclear Physics
Shirendev, B. (Mongolia), History
Siegbahn, M. (Sweden), Physics
Šiška, K. (Czechoslovakia), Surgery
Steinbeck, M. (German Democratic Republic), Physics
Stensjö, E. (Sweden), Palaeontology
Szent-Györgyi, A. (U.S.A.), Biochemistry
Szőkefalvi-Nagy, B. (Hungary), Mathematics
Taylor, Sir James (U.K.), Mechanics
Thiessen, P. A. (German Democratic Republic), Chenistry
Tițeica, G. S. (Romania), Physics
Tomonaga, S. (Japan), Physics
Yukawa, H. (Japan), Physics

## SECTIONS OF THE ACADEMY OF SCIENCES AND THEIR DEPARTMENTS

The Academy is divided into the following sections (each comprising a number of departments) and a Siberian department.

I. Section of Physical-Technical and Mathematical Sciences with Departments: (1) Mathematics, (2) General Physics and Astronomy, (3) Nuclear Physics, (4) Physical Technical Problems of Energy, (5) Mechanics and Control Processes.

II. Section of Chemistry and Biological Sciences with Departments: (1) General and Technological Chemistry, (2) Physical Chemistry and Technology of Inorganic Materials, (3) Biochemistry, Biophysics and Chemistry of Physiologically Active Compounds, (4) Physiology, (5) General Biology.

III. Section of Earth Sciences with Departments: (1) Geology, Geophysics and Geochemistry, (2) Oceanology, Atmospheric Physics and Geography.

IV. Section of Social Sciences with Departments: (1) History, (2) Philosophy and Law, (3) Economics, (4) Literature and Language.

V. Siberian Department.

**I. Section of Physical-Technical and Mathematical Sciences:** Leninsky prospekt 14, Moscow.
*Chairman:* Acad. A. A. LOGUNOV.

ATTACHED TO THE SECTION:

**National Committee of Soviet Physicists:** Chair. Acad. A. M. PROKHOROV.

**Department of Mathematics:** Moscow, Leninsky prospekt 14.
*Academician-Secretary:* Acad. N. N. BOGOLYUBOV.

ATTACHED TO THE DEPARTMENT:

**V. A. Steklov Institute of Mathematics:** 117333 Moscow, Ul. Vavilova 42; Dir. Acad. I. M. VINOGRADOV.

**Institute of Applied Mathematics (Order of Lenin):** Moscow, Miuskaya pl. 4; Dir. (vacant).

**Computing Centre:** Moscow, Ul. Vavilova 40; Dir. Acad. A. A. DORODNITSYN.

**National Committee of Soviet Mathematicians:** Moscow, Ul. Vavilova 42; Chair. Acad. I. M. VINOGRADOV.

**Department of General Physics and Astronomy:** Moscow, Leninsky prospekt 14.
*Academician-Secretary:* A. M. PROKHOROV.

ATTACHED TO THE DEPARTMENT:

**Institute of Terrestrial Magnetism, Radio Research and the Ionosphere:** Akademgorodok, Podolsky raion, Mosk. oblast; Dir. V. V. MIGULIN.

**Institute of Space Research:** Moscow, Profsoyuznaya 88; Dir. Acad. R. Z. SAGDEYEV.

**Institute of Crystallography (Order of the Red Banner of Labour):** Moscow, Leninsky prospekt 59; Dir. B. K. VAINSHTEIN.

**Institute of Radio Engineering and Electronics (Order of the Red Banner of Labour):** Moscow, Prospekt K. Marxa 18; branch in Saratov; Dir. Acad. V. A. KOTELNIKOV.

**Institute of Theoretical Astronomy:** Leningrad, nab. Kutuzova 10; Dir. G. A. CHEBOTAREV.

**Institute of High Pressure Physics (Order of the Red Banner of Labour):** P.O.B. Akademgorodok, Podolsky raion, Mosk. oblast; Dir. Acad. L. F. VERESHAGIN.

**Institute of Solid State Physics:** Moscow, Ul. Radio 23/29; Dir. Y. A. OSIPYAN.

**S. I. Vavilov Institute of Physical Problems (Order of the Red Banner of Labour):** Moscow, Vorobyevskoe chaussée 2; Dir. Acad. P. L. KAPITSA.

**L. D. Landau Institute of Theoretical Physics:** Moscow, Vorobyevskoye shosse 2; Dir. I. M. KHALATNIKOV.

**Acad. A. F. Joffe Institute of Physics and Technology (Order of Lenin):** Leningrad, Politekhnicheskaya ul. 26; Dir. Acad. V. M. TUCHKEVICH.

**P. N. Lebedev Physical Institute (Order of Lenin):** Moscow, Leninsky prospekt 53; Dir. Acad. N. G. BASOV. (Branch in Kuybyshev.)

**Institute of Spectroscopy:** Akademgorodok, Podolsky raion, Mosk. oblast; Dir. S. L. MANDELSHTAM.

**Central Astronomical Observatory:** Leningrad, Pulkovo; Dir. V. A. KRAT.

**Crimean Astro-Physical Observatory:** Crimea, P.O.B. Nauchny Observatory; Dir. A. B. SEVERNY.

**Acoustics Institute:** Moscow, Ul. Shvernika 4; Dir. N. A. GRUBNIK.

**Institute of Precision Mechanics and Computing Technology:** Moscow, Leninsky prospekt 51; Dir. Dr. V. S. BURTSEV.

**Institute of Radio Technology:** Moscow, Ul. 8 Marta 10-12; Dir. B. P. MURIN.

**Institute of Radiophysical Research (Order of the Red Banner of Labour):** Gorky, Ul. Lyadova 25/14; Dir. Dr. G. G. GETMANTSEV.

**Soviet National Committee of the International Scientific Radio Union:** Moscow, Pr. Marxa 18; Chair. V. V. MIGULIN.

**All-Union Astronomical and Geodesical Society:** Moscow, a/y 918; Pres. D. Y. MARTYNOV.

**Department of Nuclear Physics:** Moscow, Leninsky prospekt 14.
*Academician-Secretary:* M. A. MARKOV.

ATTACHED TO THE DEPARTMENT:

**Institute of Nuclear Research:** Moscow, Profsoyuznaya 7a; Dir. Dr. S. K. ESIN.

**B.P. Konstantinov Leningrad Institute of Nuclear Physics:** Gatchina, Leningrad oblast; Dir. Dr. O. I. SUMBAYEV.

**Department of Physical Technical Problems of Energy:** Moscow, Leninsky prospekt 14.
*Academician-Secretary:* Acad. M. A. STYRIKOVICH.

ATTACHED TO THE DEPARTMENT:

**Institute of High Temperatures:** Moscow, Korovinskoye shosse; Dir. Acad. A. E. SHEYNDLIN.

**National Committee on Thermal and Mass Exchange:** Moscow, Krasnokazarmennaya 17a; Chair. Acad. M. A. STYRIKOVICH.

**Department of Mechanics and Control Processes:** Moscow, Leninsky prospekt 14.
*Academician-Secretary:* (vacant).

ATTACHED TO THE DEPARTMENT:

**Institute of Operating Problems (Automatic and Telemechanic) (Order of Lenin):** Moscow, Profsoyuznaya 81; Dir. Acad. V. A. TRAPEZNIKOV.

**Institute of Problems of Mechanics:** Moscow, Leningradsky prospekt 7; Dir. Acad. A. Y. ISHLINSKY.

**Institute of Information Transmission:** Moscow, Aviomotornaya 8a; Dir. V. I. SIFOROV.

ACADEMY OF SCIENCES — UNION OF SOVIET SOCIALIST REPUBLICS

**U.S.S.R. National Committee on Automatic Control:** Moscow, Profsoyuznaya 81; Chair. Acad. V. A. TRAPEZNIKOV.

**U.S.S.R. National Committee on Theoretical and Applied Mechanics:** Moscow, Leningradsky pr. 7; Chair. Acad. N. I. MUSKHELISHVILI.

**II. Section of Chemical, Technological and Biochemical Sciences:** Moscow V-71, Leninsky prospekt 14.
*Chairman:* Acad. Y. A. OVCHINNIKOV.

ATTACHED TO THE SECTION:

**National Committee of Soviet Chemists:** Moscow, Vorobyevskoye shosse 2b; Chair. Acad. N. M. EMANUEL.

**Department of General and Technical Chemistry:** Moscow V-71, Leninsky prospekt 14.
*Academician-Secretary:* Acad. A. N. NESMEYANOV.

ATTACHED TO THE DEPARTMENT:

**Institute of Macro-Molecular Compounds:** Leningrad, Bolshoy prospekt 31; Dir. M. M. KOTON.

**A. V. Topchiev Institute of Oil Chemical Synthesis:** Moscow, Leninsky pr. 29; Dir. N. S. NAMETKIN.

**N. D. Zelinsky Institute of Organic Chemistry:** Moscow, Leninsky pr. 47; Dir. N. K. KOCHETKOV.

**Institute of Physical Chemistry (Order of the Red Banner of Labour):** Moscow, Leninsky pr. 31; Dir. Acad. V. I. SPITSYN.

**Institute of Chemistry:** Gorky, Pochtamt, ul. Tropinina 49; Dir. Acad. G. A. RAZUVAYEV.

**Institute of Chemical Physics (Order of Lenin):** Moscow, Vorobyevskoe chaussée 2b; Dir. Acad. N. N. SEMENOV.

**Institute of Electro-Chemistry:** Moscow, Leninsky prospekt 31; Dir. Acad. A. N. FRUMKIN.

**Institute of Elementary Organic Compounds (Order of Lenin):** Moscow, Ul. Vavilova 28; Dir. Acad. A. N. NESMEYANOV.

**Department of Physical Chemistry and Technology of Inorganic Materials:** Moscow V-71, Leninsky prospekt 14.
*Academician-Secretary:* Acad. N. M. ZHAVORONKOV.

ATTACHED TO THE DEPARTMENT:

**A. A. Baikov Institute of Metallurgy:** Moscow, Leninsky prospekt 49; Dir. E. M. SAVITSKY.

**N. S. Kurnakov Institute of General and Inorganic Chemistry (Order of Lenin):** Moscow, Leninsky prospekt 31; Dir. Acad. N. M. ZHAVORONKOV.

**I. V. Grebenshchikov Institute of Chemistry of Silicates (Order of the Red Banner of Labour):** Leningrad, Naberezhnaya Makarova 2; Dir. Acad. M. M. SHULTS.

**U.S.S.R. National Committee on Welding:** Moscow, Leninsky pr. 49; Chair. Acad. N. N. RYKALIN.

**Department of Biochemistry, Biophysics and Physiological Chemistry:** Moscow V-71, Leninsky prospekt 14.
*Academician-Secretary:* Acad. A. A. BAYEV.

ATTACHED TO THE DEPARTMENT:

**A. N. Bakh Institute of Biochemistry (Order of Lenin):** Moscow, Leninsky prospekt 33; Dir. (vacant).

**Institute of Microbiology:** Moscow, Profsoyuznaya 7; Dir. Acad. A. A. IMSHENETSKY.

**Institute of Molecular Biology:** Moscow, Ul. Vavilova 32; Dir. Acad. V. A. ENGELHARDT.

**K. A. Timiryazev Institute of Plant Physiology (Order of the Red Banner of Labour):** Moscow, Botanicheskaya 35; Dir. Acad. A. L. KURSANOV.

**M. M. Shemyakin Institute of Bio-organic Chemistry:** Moscow, Ul. Vavilova 32; Dir. Acad. Y. A. OVCHINNIKOV.

**Institute of Cytology:** Leningrad, Prospekt Maklina 2; Dir. A. S. TROSHIN.

**Council of Scientific Centre of Biological Research of the U.S.S.R. Academy of Sciences:** Moscow region, Serpukhovsky raion, Pushchino; Chair. Dr. G. R. IVANITSKY.

**Institute of Agrochemistry and Soil Science:** Moscow region, Serpukhovsky raion, Pushchino; Dir. V. A. KOVDA.

**Institute of Protein:** Moscow region, Serpukhovsky raion, Pushchino; Dir. Acad. A. S. SPIRIN.

**Institute of Biological Physics:** Moscow region, Serpukhovsky raion, Pushchino; Dir. Acad. G. M. FRANK.

**Institute of Biochemistry and Physiology of Microorganisms:** Moscow Region, Serpukhovsky raion, Pushchino; Dir. Acad. G. K. SKRYABIN.

**Institute of Photosynthesis:** Moscow region, Serpukhovsky raion, Pushchino; Dir. Dr. V. B. EVSTIGNEYEV.

**National Committee of Soviet Biochemists:** Moscow, Leninsky pr. 33; Chair. Acad. A. I. OPARIN.

**All-Union Biochemical Society:** Moscow, Ul. Vavilova 34; Pres. Acad. S. E. SEVERIN.

**All-Union Microbiological Society:** Moscow, Profsoyuznaya 7; Pres. Prof. M. N. MEISEL.

**All-Union Soil Science Society:** Moscow, Pyzhevsky per. 7; Pres. V. A. KOVDA.

**Department of Physiology:** Moscow, Leninsky prospekt 14.
*Academician-Secretary:* Acad. E. M. KREPS.

ATTACHED TO THE DEPARTMENT:

**Institute of Higher Nervous Activity and Neurophysiology:** Moscow, Ul. Butlerova 5a; Dir. E. A. ASRATYAN.

**I. P. Pavlov Institute of Physiology (Order of the Red Banner of Labour):** Leningrad, nab. Makarova 6; Dir. Acad. V. N. CHERNIGOVSKY.

**I. M. Sechenov Institute of Evolutionary Physiology and Biochemistry:** Leningrad K-223, Prospekt M. Toreza 52; Dir. Dr. V. A. GOVYRIN.

**Soviet National Committee of the International Brain Research Organization:** Moscow, Ul. Fersmana 11; Chair. Acad. P. G. KOSTYUK.

**Commission for Multilateral Co-operation of Academies of Sciences of Socialist Countries "Neurophysiology and Higher Nervous Activity" (Intermozg):** Moscow, Ul. Butlerova 5a; Chair. E. A. ASRATYAN.

**I. P. Pavlov All-Union Physiological Society:** Moscow, Ul. Gertsena 6; Chair. L. G. VORONIN.

**Department of General Biology:** Moscow, Leninsky prospekt 14.

ATTACHED TO THE DEPARTMENT:

**Institute of Water Conservation Biology:** p/o Borok, Yaroslavskaya region; Dir. Dr. N. V. BUTORIN.

**V. L. Komarov Botanical Institute (Order of the Red Banner of Labour):** Leningrad, Ul. Prof. Popova 2; Dir. A. A. FEDOROV.

**Institute of General Genetics:** Moscow, Profsoyuznaya ul. 7; Dir. Acad. N. P. DUBININ.

**Zoological Institute:** Leningrad, Universitetskaya nab. 1; Dir. Cand. D. A. SKARLATA.

**Institute of Developmental Biology:** Moscow V-133, Ul. Vavilova 26; Dir. T. M. Turpayev.

**Paleontological Institute:** Moscow, Leninsky pr. 33; Dir. L. P. Tatarinov.

**A. N. Severtsov Institute of Evolutionary Morphology and Animal Ecology:** Moscow, Leninsky pr. 33; Dir. Acad. V. E. Sokolov.

**Botanical Garden:** Moscow, Botanicheskaya ul. 4; Dir. Acad. N. V. Tsitsin.

**National Committee of Soviet Biologists:** Moscow, Leninsky pr. 33; Chair. Acad. M. S. Gilyarov.

**Soviet National Committee on the International Biological Programme:** Moscow, Leninsky pr. 14; Chair. Acad. M. S. Gilyarov.

**All-Union Botanical Society:** Leningrad, Ul. Prof. Popova 2; Pres. Acad. A. L. Takhtadzan.

**All-Union Society of Geneticists and Breeders:** Moscow, Ul. Fersmana 11; Pres. Dr. N. V. Turbin.

**All-Union Society of Helminthologists:** Moscow, B. Cheremushkinskaya 28; Pres. Acad. V. S. Ershov.

**All-Union Hydrobiological Society:** Moscow, Leninsky pr. 37; Pres. Dr. G. G. Vinberg.

**All-Union Society of Protozoologists:** Leningrad, Pr. Maklina 32; Pres. Y. I. Polyansky.

**All-Union Society of Mammalogists:** Moscow, Leninsky pr. 33; Pres. Acad. V. E. Sokolov.

**All-Union Entomological Society;** Leningrad, Universitetskaya nab. 1; Pres. Acad. M. S. Gilyarov.

**III. Section of Earth Sciences:** Moscow, Leninsky prospekt 14.
*Chairman:* Acad. A. P. Vinogradov.

ATTACHED TO THE SECTION:

**Interdepartmental Geophysical Committee:** Moscow, Molodezhnaya ul. 3; Chair. V. V. Belousov.

**Interdepartmental Commission on the Study of Antarctica:** Moscow, Vavilova 44; Chair. G. A. Avsyuk.

**U.S.S.R. Geographical Society:** Leningrad, per Grivtsova 10; Pres. Acad. S. V. Kalesnik.

**All-Union Mineralogical Society:** Leningrad, V.O., 21 Liniya 2; Pres. P. M. Tatarinov.

**National Committee of Soviet Geologists:** Moscow, Pyzhevsky per 7; Chair. Acad. G. S. Dzotsenidze.

**National Committee of Soviet Geographers:** Moscow, Staromonetny per 29; Chair. Acad. I. P. Gerasimov.

**Department of Geology, Geophysics and Geochemistry:** Moscow, Leninsky prospekt 14.
*Academician-Secretary:* V. I. Smirnov.

ATTACHED TO THE DEPARTMENT:

**Institute of Geology (Order of the Red Banner of Lenin):** Moscow, Pyzhevsky per 7; Dir. Acad. A. V. Peyve.

**Institute of Geology and Precambrian Geochronology:** Leningrad, nab. Makarova 2; Dir. K. O. Kratts.

**Institute of the Geology of Ore Deposits, Petrography, Mineralogy and Geochemistry:** Moscow, Staromonetny per. 35; Dir. F. V. Chukhrov.

**O. Y. Schmidt Institute of Earth Physics:** Moscow, B. Gruzinskaya ul. 10; Dir. Acad. M. A. Sadovsky.

**A. E. Fersman Mineralogical Museum:** Moscow, Leninsky pr. 18; Dir. Dr. G. P. Barsanov.

**V. I. Vernadsky Institute of Geochemistry and Analytical Chemistry (Order of Lenin):** Moscow, Vorobyevskoye shosse 47a; Dir. Acad. A. P. Vinogradov.

**All-Union Scientific Research Institute of Economics of Mineralogical Raw Materials and Prospecting:** Moscow, Ul. Volodarskogo 38; Dir. Dr. E. A. Kozlovsky.

**A. A. Skochinsky Institute of Mining:** Moscow region, Lyubertsy 4; Dir. Dr. A. V. Dokukin.

**Institute of Geology and Exploitation of Mineral Fuels:** Moscow, Ul. Fersmana 50; Dir. Dr. N. A. Eremenko.

**Institute of Mineralogy, Geochemistry and Crystallochemistry of Rare Elements:** Moscow, Sadonicheskaya nab. 71; Dir. L. N. Ovchinnikov.

**Committee on Petrography:** Moscow, Staromonetny per. 35; Chair. Acad. V. S. Sobolev.

**Inter-departmental Committee on Stratigraphy:** Leningrad, Sredny pr. 74; Chair. Acad. B. S. Sokolov.

**Inter-departmental Committee on Tectonics:** Moscow, Pyzhevsky per. 7; Chair. M. V. Muratov.

**All-Union Palaeontological Society:** Leningrad, Sredny pr. 74; Pres. Acad. B. S. Sokolov.

**Department of Oceanology, Atmospheric Physics and Geography:** Moscow, Leninsky prospekt 14.
*Academician-Secretary:* Acad. L. M. Brekhovskikh.

ATTACHED TO THE DEPARTMENT:

**Institute of Water Problems:** Moscow, Sadovaya-Chernogryazkaya 13/3; Dir. V. N. Kunin.

**Institute of Geography:** Moscow, Staromonetny per. 29; Dir. Acad. I. P. Gerasimov.

**Institute of Oceanology:** Moscow, Letnaya ul. 1; Dir. A. S. Monin.

**Institute of Atmospheric Physics:** Moscow, Pyzhevsky per. 3; Dir. Acad. A. M. Obukhov.

**Institute of Lake Conservation:** Leningrad, Petrovskaya nab. 4; Dir. Acad. S. V. Kalesnik.

**IV. Section of Social Sciences:** Moscow, Leninsky prospekt 14.
*Chairman:* Acad. P. N. Fedoseyev.

ATTACHED TO THE SECTION:

**Social Science Scientific Information Institute:** Moscow, Ul. Krasikova 28/45; f. 1969; Dir. Acad. V. A. Vinogradov.

**Commission on National Problems:** Moscow, Ul. Dm. Ulyanova 19; Chair. Acad. E. M. Zhukov.

**Soviet Sociological Association:** Moscow, Novochere. mushkinskaya 46; Chair. M. N. Rutkevich.

**Department of History:** Moscow, Ul. Dm. Ulyanova 19.
*Academician-Secretary:* Acad. B. A. Rybakov.

ATTACHED TO THE DEPARTMENT:

**Institute of Archaeology (Order of the Red Banner of Labour):** Moscow, Ul. Dm. Ulyanova 19; Dir. Acad. B. A. Rybakov.

**Institute of Oriental Studies:** Moscow, Armyansky per. 2; Dir. (vacant).

**Institute of World History:** Moscow, Ul. Dm. Ulyanova 19.

**Institute of History of the U.S.S.R.:** Moscow, Ul. Dm. Ulyanova 19; branch at Leningrad; Dir. Acad. A. L. Narochnitsky.

**Institute of Slavonic and Balkan Studies:** Moscow, Trubnikovsky per 30a; Dir. D. F. Markov.

**N. N. Miklukho-Maklay Institute of Ethnography:** Moscow, Ul. Dm. Ulyanova 19; Dir. Y. V. Bromley.

**Archives of the U.S.S.R. Academy of Sciences:** Moscow, Leninsky pr. 14; Dir. B. V. Levshin.

**National Committee of Soviet Historians:** Moscow, Ul. Dm. Ulyanova 19.

**Russian Palestine Society:** Moscow, Volkhonka 14; Chair. S. L. Tikhvinsky.

## ACADEMY OF SCIENCES — UNION OF SOVIET SOCIALIST REPUBLICS

**Department of Philosophy and Law:** Ul. Frunze 10, Moscow.
*Academician-Secretary:* Acad. F V. Konstantinov.
ATTACHED TO THE DEPARTMENT:
**Institute of State and Law:** Moscow, Ul. Frunze 10; Dir. V. N. Kudryavtsev.
**Institute of History of Natural Science and Engineering:** Moscow, Staropansky per. 1/5; Dir. S. R. Mikulinsky.
**Institute of Philosophy:** Moscow, Volkhonka 14; Dir. Dr. B. S. Ukraintsev.
**Institute of International Labour Movements:** Moscow, Kolpachny per. 9a; Dir. T. T. Timofeyev.
**Institute of Psychology:** Moscow, Ul. Vavilova 37-a; Dir. B. F. Lomov.
**Institute of Sociological Research:** Moscow, Novocheremushkinskaya 46; Dir. M. N. Rutkevich.
**Soviet Association of International Law:** Moscow, Ul. Frunze 10; Chair. Prof. G. I. Tunkin.
**Soviet Association of Political (State) Sciences:** Moscow, Ul. Frunze 10; Pres. Dr. G. K. Shakhnazarov.
**Soviet National Association of History and Philosophy of Natural Science and Engineering:** Moscow, Staropansky per. 1/5; Chair. Acad. B. M. Kedrov.
**Philosophy Society of the U.S.S.R.:** Moscow, Kolpachny per. 9a; Pres. Acad. F. V. Konstantinov.

**Department of Economics:** 2nd Yaroslavskaya ul. 3, Moscow.
*Academician-Secretary:* Acad. N. P. Fedorenko.
ATTACHED TO THE DEPARTMENT:
**Africa Institute:** Moscow, Starokonyshenny per. 16; Dir. A. Gromyko.
**Latin America Institute:** Moscow, B. Ordynka 21; Dir. Dr. V. V. Volsky.
**Institute of World Economics and International Relations:** Moscow, Yaroslavskaya 13; Dir. Acad. N. N. Inozemtsev.
**Institute of Economics:** Moscow, Volkhonka 14; Dir. Dr. E. I. Kapustin.
**Institute of Economics of the World Socialist System:** Novochermushkinskaya 46; Dir. Prof. O. T. Bogomolov.
**Far East Institute:** Moscow, Ul. Krzhizhanovskogo 14; Dir. Prof. M. I. Sladkovsky.
**Central Economic Mathematical Institute:** Moscow, Ul. Vavilova 44; Dir. Acad. N. P. Fedorenko.
**Institute of U.S.A. and Canada Studies:** Moscow, Khlebny per. 2/3; Dir. Acad. G. A. Arbatov.
**Institute of Social Economic Problems:** Leningrad, Chaikovskogo 1; Dir. Dr. G. N. Cherkasov.
**All-Union Scientific Research Institute of Cybernetics:** Moscow, Orlikov per. 1/11; Dir. Dr. V. V. Miloserdov.
**Association of Soviet Economic Scientific Institutions:** Moscow, Ul. Vavilova 44; Chair. Acad. T. S. Khachaturov.

**Department of Literature and Language:** Moscow, Volkhonka 18/2.
*Academician-Secretary:* Acad. M. B. Khrapchenko.
ATTACHED TO THE DEPARTMENT:
**A. M. Gorky Institute of World Literature:** Moscow, Ul. Vorovskogo 25a; Dir. Dr. V. R. Shcherbina (acting).
**Institute of Russian Literature (Pushkin House):** Leningrad. nab. Makarova 4; Dir. Dr. F. Y. Priima (acting).
**Institute of Russian Language:** Moscow, Volkhonka 18/2; Dir. F. P. Filin.
**Institute of Linguistic Studies:** Moscow, Ul. Marxa i Engelsa 1/14; Dir. V. N. Yartseva.
**Soviet Committee of Finno-Ugric Philologists:** Moscow, Ul. Marxa-Engelsa 1/14; Tallin, Ul. Sakala 3; Chair. P. A. Ariste.
**Soviet Committee of Turkish Philologists:** Moscow, Ul. Marxa-Engelsa 1/14; Chair. Acad. A. N. Kononov.
**Soviet Committee of Slavonic Philologists:** Moscow, Volkhonka 18/2; Chair. Acad. M. P. Alexeyev.

V. **Siberian Department:** Prospekt Nauky 17, Novosibirsk.
ATTACHED TO THE DEPARTMENT:
**Institute of Automation and Electrical Measurements:** Novosibirsk, Universitetsky pr. 1; Dir. Y. Y. Nesterikhin.
**Institute of Biology:** Novosibirsk, ul. 11; Dir. Dr. A. I. Cherepanov.
**Institute of Chemistry and Chemical Technology:** Krasnoyarsk.
**Computing Centre:** Novosibirsk, pr. Nauky 6; Dir. G. I. Marchuk.
**Computing Centre:** Krasnoyarsk, pr. Mira 53; Dir. Dr. V. G. Dulov (acting).
**Institute of Geography of Siberia and the Far East:** Irkutsk, Kievskaya 1; Dir. Acad. V. B. Sochava.
**Institute of Geology and Geophysics:** Novosibirsk, Universitetsky pr. 3; Dir. Acad. A. A. Trofimuk.
**Institute of Geochemistry:** Irkutsk, Ul. Favorskogo 1a; Dir. L. V. Tauson.
**Institute of Hydrodynamics:** Novosibirsk, Pr. Nauky 15.
**Institute of Mining:** Novosibirsk, Krasniy prospekt 54; Dir. E. I. Shemyakin.
**Institute of the Earth's Crust:** Irkutsk, Ul. Lermontova 128; Dir. M. M. Odintsov.
**Siberian Institute of Terrestrial Magnetism, the Ionosphere, and Radio Wave Propagation:** Irkutsk, Ul. Lermontova 16; Dir. V. E. Stepanov.
**Institute of History, Philology and Philosophy:** Novosibirsk, pr. Nauky 17; Dir. Acad. A. P. Okladnikov.
**Institute of Catalysis (Order of the Red Banner of Labour):** Novosibirsk, pr. Nauky 15; Dir. Acad. G. K. Boreskov.
**V. N. Sukachev Institute of Forestry and Timber:** Krasnoyarsk, Akademgorodok; Dir. Acad. A. B. Zhukov.
**Institute of Limnology:** Irkutsk region, pos. Listvenichnoye; Dir. G. I. Galazy.
**Institute of Mathematics:** Novosibirsk, Universitetsky pr. 4; Dir. Acad. S. L. Sobolev.
**Institute of Inorganic Chemistry:** Novosibirsk, pr. Nauky 3; Dir. Acad. A. V. Nikolayev.
**Institute of Northern Mining:** Yakutsk.
**Institute of Optics of the Atmosphere:** Tomsk, Ul. Gertsena 8; Dir. V. E. Zuyev.
**Institute of Organic Chemistry:** Novosibirsk, Akademgorodok; Dir. Acad. N. N. Vorozhtsev.
**Irkutsk Institute of Organic Chemistry:** Irkutsk, Ul. Favorskogo 1; Dir. M. G. Voronkov.
**Institute of Permafrost (Order of the Red Banner of Labour):** Yakutsk, Merzlotovedenie; Dir. P. I. Melnikov.
**Institute of Soil Science and Agrochemistry:** Novosibirsk, Sovietskaya 18; Dir. R. V. Kovalev.
**Institute of Theoretical and Applied Mechanics:** Novosibirsk, Akademgorodok; Dir. R. I. Soloukhin.

**Institute of Thermophysics:** Novosibirsk, pr. Nauky 1; Dir. S. S. KUTATELADZE.

**L. V Kirensky Institute of Physics:** Krasnoyarsk, Akademgorodok; Dir. I. A. TERSKOV.

**Institute of Semiconductor Physics:** Novosibirsk, pr. Nauky 13; Dir. A. V. RZHANOV.

**Institute of the Physical and Chemical Foundations of Mineral Processing:** Novosibirsk, ul. Dzerzhinskogo 18; Dir. A. T. LOGVINENKO.

**Siberian Institute of Plant Physiology and Biochemistry:** Irkutsk 33, a/y 1243; Dir. F. E. REIMERS.

**Institute of Chemical Kinetics and Combustion:** Novosibisrk, Institutskaya 3; Dir. Y. N. MOLIN.

**Institute of Oil Chemistry:** Tomsk, Kooperativny per. 5; Dir. Dr. Y. C. KRYAZHEV.

**Institute of Cytology and Genetics:** Novosibirsk, Universitetsky pr. 2; Dir. Acad. D. K. BELYAYEV.

**Central Siberian Botanical Garden:** Novosibirsk, Zolotodolinskaya 101; Dir. Prof. I. F. TARAN.

**Institute of the Economics and Organization of Industrial Production:** Novosibirsk, pr. Nauky 17; Dir. Acad. A. G. AGANBEGYAN.

**Siberian Energy Institute:** Irkutsk, Ul. Lermontova 130; Dir. Y. N. RUDENKO.

**Institute of Nuclear Physics:** Novosibirsk, pr. Nauky 11; Dir. Acad. G. I. BUDKER.

SCIENTIFIC CENTRES OF THE ACADEMY:

**Far Eastern Scientific Centre:** Vladivostok, Leninskaya 50; Chair. Acad. N. A. SHILO.

*Institutions of the Centre:*

**Institute of Automation and Control Processes with Computer Centre:** Vladivostok, Ul. Sukhanova 5-a; Dir. A. A. VORONOV.

**Far Eastern Institute of Geology:** Vladivostok, pr. 100-letia; Dir. Dr. V. G. MOISEENKO.

**Institute of Biology and Soil Science:** Vladivostok, pr. 100-letia; Dir. Dr. R. K. SALYAEV.

**Institute of Ocean Economics.**

**Pacific Ocean Institute of Bio-organic Chemistry:** Vladivostok; Dir. Prof. G. B. ELYAKOV.

**Pacific Ocean Institute:** Vladivostok, pr. 100-letia; Dir. V. I. ILYICHEV.

**Institute of Sea Biology:** Vladivostok, pr. 100-letia;. Dir. A. V. ZHIRMUNSKY.

**Institute of Chemistry:** Vladivostok, pr. 100-letia; Dir. Y. V. GAGARINSKY.

**Institute of Foreign Countries.**

**Institute of History, Archaeology, Ethnography of the Far Eastern Nations:** Vladivostok, Leninskaya 50, Dir. A. I. KRUSHANOV.

**Institute of Mining.**

**Institute of Pacific Ocean Geography:** Vladivostok; Ul. Uborevicha 17; Dir. A. P. KAPITSA.

**Institute of Tectonic and Geophysics:** Khabarovsk, Ul. Serysheva 22; Dir. Acad. Y. A. KOSYGIN.

**Khabarovsk Complex Research Institute:** Khabarovsk, Ul. Kim Yu Chena 65; Dir. M. N. BABUSHKIN (acting).

**North-Eastern Complex Scientific Research Institute:** Magadan, Portovaya 16; Dir. Acad. N. A. SHILO.

**Institute of Biological Problems of the North:** Magadan, Ul. K. Marxa 24; Dir. V. L. KONTRIMAVICHUS.

**Institute of Solar and Terrestrial Communications.**

**Institute of Vulcanology (Order of the Red Banner of Labour):** Petropavlovsk-Kamchatsky, Karaginskaya 56/4; Dir. S. A. FEDOTOV.

**Sakhalin Complex Scientific Research Institute:** Sakhalin Region, Novo-Alexandrovsk; Dir. S. L. SOLOVYEV.

**Saratov Scientific Centre:** Saratov; f. 1980; in process of formation.

**Institute of Biochemistry, Plant and Micro-organism Physiology.**

**Institute of Socio-Economic Problems of the Development of the Agrarian-Industrial Complex.**

**Urals Scientific Centre:** Sverdlovsk region, Ul. Pervomaiskaya 91; Chair of the Presidium Acad. S. V. VONSOVSKY.

*Institutions of the Centre:*

**Institute of Mechanics and Mathematics:** Sverdlovsk Region, Ul. Kovalevshoi 16; Dir. Acad. N. N. KRASOVSKY.

**Institute of Metal Physics:** Sverdlovsk Region, Ul. Kovalevskoi 18; Dir. M. N. MIKHEEV.

**Institute of Chemistry:** Sverdlovsk region, Pervomaiskaya 91; Dir. G. V. SHVEIKIN.

**Institute of Electrochemistry:** Sverdlovsk region, Ul. S. Kovalevskoi 20; Dir. S. V. KARPACHEY.

**Institute of Metallurgy:** Sverdlovsk region, Ul. S. Kovalevskoi 20; Dir. N. A. VATOLIN.

**Institute of Plant and Animal Ecology:** Sverdlovsk region, Ul. S. Kovalevskoy 16; Dir. S. S. SCHWARTZ.

**Acad. A. N. Zavaritsskovo Institute of Geology and Geochemistry:** Sverdlovsk region, Pochtovy per. 7; Dir. S. N. IVANOV.

**Institute of Geophysics:** Sverdlovsk region, Pervomaiskaya 91; Dir. Y. P. BULASHEVICH.

**Institute of Economics:** Sverdlovsk, Pervomaiskaya 91; Dir. M. A. SERGEYEV.

**V. I. Lenin Ilmen State Reservation:** Chelyabinsk Region, Miass; Dir. V. A. KOROTEEV.

BRANCHES OF THE ACADEMY OF SCIENCES OF THE U.S.S.R.:

**Bashkir Branch:** 450025 GSP-99 Ufa 25, Ul. Marxa 6; Chair. of the Presidium S. R. RAFIKOV.

*Institutions of the Branch:*

**Institute of Chemistry:** 450054 Ufa 25, pr. Oktyabrya 71; Dir. S. R. RAFIKOV.

**Institute of Biology:** 450054 Ufa, 25, pr. Oktyabrya 69; Dir. Dr. V. K. GRIFANOV.

**Institute of Geology:** 450054 Ufa 25, Ul. K. Marxa 16/2; Dir. Prof. Dr. M. A. KAMALETDINOV (acting).

**Institute of History, Language and Literature:** 450054 Ufa 25, Oktyabrya 71; Dir. K. S. SAIRANOV.

**Daghestan Branch:** 367596 Makhachkala 25, Ul. Gadzhieva 45; Chair. of the Presidium K. I. AMIRKHANOV.

*Institutions of the Branch:*

**Institute of Geology:** 367596 Makhachkala 3, Ul. Gadzhieva 45; Dir. K. S. MAGATAYEV.

**Institute of History, Language and Literature:** 367596 Makhachkala 3, Ul. Gadzhieva 45; Dir. Cand. G. G. GAMZATOV.

**Institute of Physics:** 367003 Makhachkala 3, 1 gorodok neftyanikov 10; Dir. KH. I AMIRKHANOV.

**Karelian Branch:** 185610 Petrozavodsk, Pushkinskaya ul. 11; Chair. of the Presidium Prof. N. I. PYAVCHENKO.

*Institutions of the Branch:*

**Institute of Geology:** Dir. V. A. SOKOLOV.

**Institute of Forestry:** Dir. V. I. ERMAKOV.

**Institute of Biology:** Dir. S. N. DROZDOV.

**Institute of Linguistics, Literature and History:** Dir. M. N. VLASOVA.

ACADEMY OF SCIENCES — UNION OF SOVIET SOCIALIST REPUBLICS

**Kazan Branch:** 420111 Kazan III, Ul. Lobachevskogo 2/31; Chair. of Presidium M. M. ZARIPOV.

*Institutions of the Branch:*

**Kazan Physical Technical Institute:** 420029 Kazan, Ul. Sibirsky trakt 10/7; Dir. Dr. M. M. ZARIPOV.

**A. E. Arbuzov Institute of Organic and Physical Chemistry:** 420083 Kazan, Ul. Ak. Arbuzova 8; Dir. A. N. PUDOVIK.

**Kazan Institute of Biology:** 420111 Kazan, Ul. Lobachevskogo 2/31; Dir. Dr. A. I. TARCHEVSKY.

**G. Ibragimov Institute of Language, Literature and History:** 420111 Kazan, Ul. Lobachevskogo 2/31; Dir. Dr. M. K. MUKHARYAMOV.

**S. M. Kirov Kola Branch:** 184200 Murmansk Region, P.O. Apatity, Ul. Fersmana 14; Chair. of the Presidium G. I. GORBUNOV.

*Institutions of the Branch:*

**Institute of Geology:** Dir. I. V. BELKOV.

**Institute of Chemistry and Technology of Rare Elements and Minerals:** Dir. Cand. V. I. BELOKOSKOV (acting).

**Polar Institute of Geophysics:** Dir. S. I. ISAEV.

**Mining and Metallurgical Institute:** Dir. I. A. TURCHANINOV.

**Polar Alpine Botanical Garden:** Dir. T. A. KOZUPEYEVA.

**Murmansk Marine Biological Institute:** Dir. Cand. I. B. TOKIN.

**Komi Branch:** 167610 Syktyvkar GSP, Ul. Kommunisticheskaya 24, Komi A.S.S.R.; Chair. of the Presidium V. P. PODOPLELOV.

*Institutions of the Branch:*

**Institute of Geology:** Dir. M. V. FISHMAN.

**Institute of Biology:** Dir. I. V. ZABOYEVA.

**Institute of Linguistics, Literature and History:** Dir. N. N. ROCHEV.

INSTITUTIONS ATTACHED TO THE PRESIDIUM OF THE ACADEMY OF SCIENCES OF THE U.S.S.R.

Council on Co-ordination of Scientific Activities of Academies of the Union Republics: Leninsky prospekt 14, Moscow; Chair. Acad. A. P. ALEXANDROV.

Publishing Council: Leninsky prospekt 13, Moscow; Chair. (vacant).

Scientific Council on Exhibitions of the U.S.S.R. and Union Republic's Academies of Science: Ul. Vavilova 30/6, Moscow; Chair. N. V. MELNIKOV.

Permanent Scientific Exhibition: Moscow: Dir. V. V. BAZYKIN.

International Centre for Scientific and Technical Information: *see* under Research Institutes.

Scientific Council on Cybernetics: Ul. Vavilova 40, Moscow; Chair. Acad. A. I. BERG.

Scientific Council on Philosophy of Contemporary Natural History: Ul. Volkhonka 14, Moscow; Chair. Acad. P. N. FEDOSEYEV.

Scientific Council on Techniques in Production and Processing of Metals: Ul. Gorkogo 69, Kiev; Chair. Acad. B. E. PATON.

Commission on Space Exploration: Ul. Vavilova 32, Moscow; Chair. (vacant).

Council on Scientific Instrument-making: Vorobyevskoe chaussée 2-b, Moscow; Chair. V. L. TALROZE.

Council on Museums: Ul. D. Ulyanova 19, Moscow; Chair. Acad. B. A. RYBAKOV.

Soviet National Committee of the Pacific Ocean Scientific Association: Ul. Vavilova 44, Moscow; Chair. Acad. B. G. GAFUROV.

Council on International Collaboration on Space (Intercosmos): Leninsky prospekt 14, Moscow; Chair. Acad. B. N. PETROV.

Council on Libraries: Leninsky prospekt 14, Moscow; Chair. Acad. P. N. FEDOSEYEV.

Publishing House "Nauka" (Science): Podsosensky per. 21, Moscow; Dir. G. D. KOMEOV.

All-Union Institute for Designing of Scientific Buildings: Maronovsky per. 26, Moscow; Dir. B. A. SAVELYEV.

Moscow House of Scientists: Ul. Kropotkina 16, Moscow; Dir. L. N. VINOGRADOVA.

Leningrad A. M. Gorky House of Scientists: Dvortsovaya nab. 26, Leningrad; Dir. O. M. NIKANDROV.

PRINCIPAL PERIODICALS PUBLISHED BY THE ACADEMY OF SCIENCES OF THE U.S.S.R.:

Izvestia Akademii Nauk S.S.S.R. (*Bulletin of the U.S.S.R. Academy of Sciences*): consists of 14 subject series.

Akusticheskii Zhurnal (*Acoustics Journal*): quarterly.

Astronomicheskii Zhurnal (*Astronomy Journal*): 6 times yearly.

Avtomatika i Telemekhanika (*Automation and Telemechanics*): monthly.

Azia i Afrika (*Asia and Africa*): monthly.

Biofizika (*Biophysics*).

Biokhimia (*Biochemistry*): 6 times yearly.

Botanicheskii Zhurnal (*Journal of Botany*).

Doklady Akademii Nauk S.S.S.R. (*Proceedings of the Academy*): three times a month.

Fiziko-Tekhnicheskie Problemy Razrabotki Poleznykh Iskopaemykh (*Physical and Technical Problems of Mineral Exploitation*).

Fiziologicheskii Zhurnal S.S.S.R. im. Sechenova (*Sechenov Physiological Journal*): monthly.

Geografiya i Prirodnye Resursy (*Geography and Natural Resources*).

Geologiya i Geofizika (*Geology and Geophysics*).

Istoria S.S.S.R. (*U.S.S.R. History*): 6 times yearly.

Izvestia Sibirskogo Otdeleniya Academii Nauk S.S.S.R. (*Bulletin of the Siberian Branch of the U.S.S.R. Academy of Sciences*): monthly.

Kolloidny Zhurnal (*Colloids Journal*): 6 times yearly.

Matematicheskii Sbornik (*Mathematical Collection*).

Mikrobiologia (*Microbiology*): 6 times yearly.

Mirovaya Ekonomika i Mezhdunarodnie Otnosheniya (*World Economics and International Relations*).

Nauka v S.S.S.R. (*Science in the U.S.S.R.*): fortnightly, in Russian and English.

Radiobiologia (*Radiobiology*): 6 times yearly.

Sovyetskoe Gosudarstvo i Pravo (*Soviet State and Law*).

Teoreticheskie Osnovy Khimicheskoi Tekhnologii (*Theoretical Foundations of Chemical Technology*).

Vestnik Akademii Nauk S.S.S.R. (*Journal of the U.S.S.R. Academy of Sciences*): monthly.

Voprosy Ekonomiki (*Economic Questions*): monthly.

Voprosy Filosofii (*Questions of Philosophy*): 6 times yearly.

Voprosy Ikhtiologii (*Questions of Ichthyology*): quarterly.

Voprosy Istorii (*Questions of History*): monthly.

Voprosy Istorii Yestestvoznaniya i Tekhniki (*History of Natural Sciences and Technology*): quarterly.

Voprosy Literatury (*Problems of Literature*).

Voprosy Yazykoznania (*Questions of Linguistics*): 6 times yearly.

Yadernaya Fizika (*Nuclear Physics*).

Zemlya i Vselennaya (*Earth and Universe*).

Zhurnal Analiticheskoi Khimii (*Journal of Analytical Chemistry*): 6 times yearly.

Zhurnal Eksperimentalnoi i Teoreticheskoi Fiziki (*Journal of Experimental and Theoretical Physics*): monthly.

Zhurnal Fizicheskoi Khimii (*Journal of Physical Chemistry*): monthly.

Zhurnal Nauchnoi i prikladnoi fotografii i kinematografii (*Journal of Scientific and Applied Photography and Cinematography*).

Zhurnal Neorganicheskoi Khimii (*Journal of Inorganic Chemistry*).
Zhurnal Obshchei Biologii (*Journal of General Biology*): 6 times yearly.
Zhurnal Obshchei Khimii (*Journal of General Chemistry*): monthly.
Zhurnal Organicheskoi Khimii (*Journal of Organic Chemistry*).
Zhurnal Prikladnoi Khimii (*Journal of Applied Chemistry*): monthly.
Zhurnal Strukturnoi Khimii (*Journal of Structural Chemistry*).
Zhurnal Tekhnicheskoi Fiziki (*Journal of Technical Physics*): monthly.
Zhurnal Vychislityelnoi Matematiki i Matematicheskoi Fiziki (*Journal of Calculating Mathematics and Mathematical Physics*): 6 times yearly.
Zhurnal Vysshoi Nervoi Deyatelnosti im. Pavlova (*Pavlov Journal of Higher Nervous Activity*): bi-monthly.
Zoologicheskii Zhurnal (*Zoological Journal*): monthly.
(*Numerous other publications are also available.*)

## ACADEMIES OF SCIENCES OF THE UNION REPUBLICS

**Council on Co-ordination of Scientific Activities of Academies of the Union Republics:** Leninsky prospekt 14, Moscow.
*Chairman:* Acad. A. P. ALEXANDROV.
*Vice-Chairman:* Acad. V. A. KOTELNIKOV.
*Learned Secretaries:* V. V. BELOUSOV and N. S. PSHIRKOV.

**Armenian S.S.R. Academy of Sciences:** Presidium: Ul. Barekamutyan 24, Erevan; Pres. V. A. AMBARTSUMYAN; Vice-Presidents A. R. YOANNISYAN, S. A. AMBARTSUMYAN; Academician-Secretary S. A. BAKUNTS; Learned Secretary G. A. AVETISYAN; 43 members, 44 corresponding members.

ATTACHED TO THE PRESIDIUM:
Council on Co-ordination of Scientific Activities of Research and Higher Educational Institutions in the Armenian S.S.R.: Chair. Acad. V. A. AMBARTSUMYAN.
Council on the History of Natural Sciences and Technology: Chair. Prof. G. B. PETROSYAN.
Council on Conservation and Restoration of Cultural Monuments: Chair. B. N. ARAKELYAN.
Council on Conservation of Nature: Chair. Prof. K. P. MIRIMANYAN.
Council on Problems of Machine-Building: Erevan 19; Chair. Acad. M. V. KASIYAN.
Council on Cybernetics: Erevan 44, Ul. Gastello 1; Chair. Acad. R. R. VARSHAMOV.
Council on Co-ordination of Economy: Erevan 19, Ul. Barekamutyan 24; Chair. Acad. T. P. AGAYAN.
Council on Semiconductors: Erevan 19, Ul. Barekamutyan 24; Chair. G. M. AVAKYANTS.
Armenian Geographical Society: Chair. Prof. A. D. BAGDASARYAN.
Armenian Physiological Society: Chair. S. K. KARAPETYAN.
Armenian Botanical Society: Chair. V. O. KAZARYAN.
Armenian Biochemical Society; Chair. G. K. BUNATYAN.
Armenian Genetic Society: Chair. Prof. A. A. RUHKYAN.
Section on Technology of Engineering: Erevan 1, Tumanyan 17; Chair. A. M. MARDJANYAN.

*Department of Physical and Mathematical Sciences:* Academician-Secretary G. M. GAZIBYAN; Learned Secretary A. A. NERSESYAN.

ATTACHED TO THE DEPARTMENT:
Institute of Mathematics: Ul. Barekamutyan 24-b, Erevan; Dir. M. M. DZHERBASHYAN.
Byurakan Astro-Physical Observatory: Ashtarak District, Byurakan; Dir. Acad. V. A. AMBARTSUMYAN.
Institute of Radio-Physics and Electronics: Ashtarak; Dir. E. G. MIRZABEKYAN.
Computing Centre: Ul. Gastello 1, Erevan; Dir. Prof. S. N. MERGELYAN.
Institute of Physics: Ul. Ashtarak 2, Erevan; Dir. M. L. TER-MIKAELYAN.
Byurakan Optical and Mechanical Laboratory: Ashtarak District, Byurakan; Dir. G. S. MINASYAN.

*Department of Chemical Sciences:* Academician-Secretary A. B. NALBANDYAN; Acting Learned Secretary E. R. GRIGORYAN.

ATTACHED TO THE DEPARTMENT:
Institute of Fine Organic Chemistry: Erevan 14, Prospekt Azatunyan 26; Dir. S. A. VARTANYAN.
Institute of Biochemistry: Ul. Gastello 5/1, Erevan. Dir. G. K. BUNATYAN.
Institute of Organic Chemistry: Ul. Charentsa 17. Erevan; Dir. Prof. S. G. MATSOYAN.
Institute of Chemical Physics: Ul. Moskovyan 22, Erevan; Dir. Acad. A. M. NALBANDYAN.
Institute of General and Inorganic Chemistry: Ul. Fioletova 10, Erevan; Dir. Acad. M. G. MANVELYAN;

*Department of Earth Sciences:* Academician-Secretary I. G. MAGAKYAN; Learned Secretary L. A. GRIGORYAN.

ATTACHED TO THE DEPARTMENT:
Institute of Geology: Ul. Barekamutyan 24-a, Erevan; Dir. A. T. ASLANYAN.
Institute of Geophysics and Engineering Seismology: Ul. Leningradyan 9, Leninakan; Dir. S. V. BADALYAN.

*Department of Biological Sciences:* Academician-Secretary V. O. KAZDRYAN; Learned Secretary T. G. CHUBARYAN.

ATTACHED TO THE DEPARTMENT:
Institute of Botany: Avan, Erevan; Dir. V. O. KAZARYAN.
Institute of Zoology: Ul. Gastello 7, Erevan; Dir. S. M. SARKISSIAN.
Institute of Microbiology: Ul. Charentsa 19, Erevan; Dir. E. G. AFRIKYAN.
L. Orbaeli Institute of Physiology: Ul. Bratyev Orbeli 3, Erevan; Dir. V. V. FANARDJIAN.
Institute of Agro-Chemical Problems and Hydroponics: Ul. Noragyukh 108, Erevan; Dir. G. S. DAVTYAN.
Institute of Experimental Biology: Ul. Nersisyan 7, Erevan; Dir. J. J. HAKOPIAN.
Sevan Hydrobiological Station: Ul. Kirova 192, Sevan; Dir. R. H. OGANESSYAN.
Central Biological Station: Abovyansky Rayon, Arzni; Dir. E. P. AKOPYAN.

*Department of Social Sciences:* Academician-Secretary T. P. AGAYAN; Learned Secretary K. V. SEHBOSYAN.

ATTACHED TO THE DEPARTMENT:
Institute of History: Ul. Abovyana 15, Erevan; Dir. G. A. GALOYAN.
Institute of Archaeology and Ethnography: Ul. Abovyana 68, Erevan; Dir. B. N. ARAKELYAN.
P. Acharyan Institute of Linguistics: Ul. Abovyana 15, Erevan; Dir. G. B. DJAUKYAN.
M. A. Abegyan Institute of Literature: Ul. Karmir-Banaki 15, Erevan; Dir. V. S. NALBANDYAN.
Institute of Economics: Ul. Abovyana 15, Erevan; Dir. A. A. ARAKELYAN.

Institute of Arts: Ul. Abovyana 15, Erevan; Dir. R. V. Zaryan.

Institute of Oriental Studies: Erevan 1, Ul. Abovyana 15; Dir. G. K. Sarkisyan.

Institute of Philosophy and Law: Ul. Spandargana 44, Erevan; Dir. Y. J. Khachikian.

*Publishing House:* Ul. Abovyana 15, Erevan; Dir. S. G. Gevorkyan.

*Commission on International Scientific Contacts:* Ul. Barekamutyan 24, Erevan; Chair. A. R. Yoannisyan.

Periodical Publications of the Armenian Academy of Sciences:

Doklady Akademii Nauk Armyanskoi S.S.R. (*Reports of the Armenian S.S.R. Academy of Sciences*); Izvestiya Akademii Nauk Armyanskoi S.S.R. (*Bulletins of the Armenian S.S.R. Academy of Sciences*): Mathematics, Mechanics, Physics, Engineering Sciences, Earth Sciences; Khimicheskii Zhurnal Armenii (*Chemical Journal of Armenia*); Biologicheskii Zhurnal Armenii (*Biological Journal of Armenia*); Vestnik Obshchestvennykh Nauk (*Herald of Social Sciences*); Zhurnal Experimentalnoi Kilinicheskoi Meditsiny (*Journal of Experimental and Clinical Medicine*); Istoriko-Filologichesky Zhurnal (*Historical and Philological Journal*); Soobshcheniya Byurakanskoi Observatorii (*Reports of the Byurakan Astrophysical Observatory*).

**Azerbaijan S.S.R. Academy of Sciences:** Presidium: Ul. Kommunisticheskaya 10, Baku; Pres. G. M. Abdullaev; Vice-Presidents M. A. Topchibashev, M. A. M. Dadashzade; Academician-Secretary M. A. Kashkay; Learned Secretary D. A. Kasimov; 56 members, 41 corresponding members.

Attached to the Presidium:

Council on Co-ordination of Scientific Research: Chair. Acad. G. M. Abdullaev.

Scientific Council on the History and Theory of Science: Chair. Prof. I. R. Selimkhanov.

Scientific Council on Complex Problems (Cybernetics): Baku 1, Ul. Kommunisticheskaya 10; Chair. B. A. Azimov.

Council on Exploitation of Scientific Equipment: Baku 1, Kommunisticheskaya 10; Chair. V. Y. Akhundov.

Council on Conservation and Restoration of Cultural Monuments: Chair. M. A. Useinov.

*Department of Physical-Engineering and Mathematical Sciences:* Academician-Secretary A. I. Guseynov; Learned Secretary R. A. Eganov.

Attached to the Department:

Institute of Physics: Prospekt Narimanova 33, Baku; Dir. Acad. G. M. Abdullaev.

Institute of Mathematics and Mechanics: Ul. Ketskhoveli, Kvartal 553, Baku; Dir. Z. I. Khalilov.

Institute of Cybernetics: Ul. Ketskhoveli, Kvartal 553, Baku; Acting Dir. D. E. Allakhverdiev.

Shemakha Astro-Physical Observatory: Shemakha, Pos. Mamedalieva, Ul. Sverdlova 75, Baku; Dir G. F. Sultanov.

Azerbaijan Physical Society: Baku 122, Prospekt Narimanova 33; Chair. Acad. G. M. Abdullaev.

Azerbaijan Mathematics Society: Baku 1, Ul. Kommunisticheskaya 10; Chair. M. A. Dzhavadov.

*Department of Chemical Sciences:* Acting Academician-Secretary S. D. Mekhtiev; Learned Secretary E. T. Suleimanova.

Attached to the Department:

Y. G. Mamedaliev Institute of Oil Processes: 31, Telnova 30, Baku; Dir. V. S. Aliev.

Institute of Inorganic and Physical Chemistry: Prospekt Narimanova 29, Baku; Dir. Z. G. Zulfugarov.

Institute of Chemical Additives: Ul. Telnova 30, Baku; Dir. A. M. Kuliev.

Institute of Theoretical Problems of Chemical Technology: Prospekt Narimanova 27, Baku; Dir. M. F. Nagiev.

Azerbaijan Section of All-Union Chemical Society: Baku, Ul. Telnova 30; Chair. V. S. Aliev.

*Department of Earth Sciences:* Academician-Secretary S. A. Azizbekov; Learned Secretary G. G. Akhmedov.

Attached to the Department:

I. M. Gubkin Institute of Geology: Ul. Nizamy 67, Baku; Dir. Y. N. Alikhanov.

Institute of Problems of Deep Oil and Gas Deposits: Ul. Krilova 5, Baku; Dir. M. T. Babasov.

Institute of Geography: Ul. Narimanova 31, Baku; Dir. G. A. Aliev.

Institute for the Study of Natural Resources from Space: collates information from space and on the ground in environmental studies and protection.

Commission on the Caspian Sea: Ul. Narimanova 31, Baku; Acting Chair. K. K. Gyul.

Commission on Mountain Mud Flows: Ul. Narimanova 31, Baku; Chair. S. G. Rustamov.

Commission on Mining: Baku, Ul. Nizami 67; Chair. A. D. Sultanov.

Geographical Society of the Azerbaijan S.S.R.: Chair. Prof. K. K. Gyul.

Paleontological Society: Chair. K. A. Alizade.

Mineralogical Society: Chair. M. A. Kashkai.

*Department of Biological Sciences:* Academician-Secretary V. R. Volobuev; Learned Secretary S. M. Eyubov.

Attached to the Department:

V. L. Komarov Institute of Botany: Patamdartskoe chaussée 40, Baku; Dir. M. G. Abutalybov.

Institute of Zoology: 6 Khrebtovaya ul. 5, Baku; Dir M. A. Musaev.

Institute of Soil Science and Agrochemistry: Ul. Krilvao 5, Baku; Dir. G. M. Guseynov.

Institute of Genetics and Selection: Kommunisticheskaya 5, Baku; Dir. I. D. Mustafaev.

Botanical Garden: Patamdartskoye shosse 40, Baku; Dir. U. M. Agamirov.

Society of Physiologists and Pharmacologists: Chair. G. G. Gasanov.

Helminthological Society: Chair. S. M. Asadov.

Society of Soil Scientists: Chair. D. M. Guseinov.

Azerbaijan Biochemical Society: Chair. A. A. Gasanov.

Azerbaijan Genetics and Selection Society: Chair. I. K. Abdullayev.

Institute of Physiology: Ul. Sharif-Zade 3, Baku.

Commission on Nature Conservation: Kommunisticheskaya ul. 10, Baku; Chair. G. A. Aliev.

Section of Microbiology: Baku, Prospekt Narimanova 31; Dir. N. A. Mekhtieva.

*Department of Social Sciences:* Academician-Secretary A. S. Sumbat-Zade; Learned Secretary N. A. Akhmedov.

Attached to the Department:

Institute of History: Ul. Mamedalievna 3, Baku; Dir. Prof. A. S. Sumbat-Zade.

Nizami Museum of Literature and Linguistics: Kommunisticheskaya 33, Baku; Dir. Prof. B. A. Nabiev.

Institute of Economics: Prospekt Narimanova 31, Baku; Dir. A. A. Makhmudov.

Institute of Peoples of the Near and Middle East: Prospekt Narimanova 31, Baku; Dir. G. M. Arasly.

Institute of Linguistics: Pr. Narimanova 31, Baku; Dir. M. S. SHIRALIYEV.

Institute of Philosophy and Law: Pr. Narimanova 31, Baku; Dir. Prof. F. K. KOCHARLY.

Institute of Architecture and Arts: Pr. Narimanova 31, Baku; Dir. M. A. USEINOV.

Nizami Institute of Literature: Baku, Prospekt Narimanova 31; Dir. M. A. GULI-ZADE.

Azerbaijan Museum of History: Ul. Malygina 4, Baku; Dir. Prof. P. A. AZIZBEKOVA.

Republican Archives of Manuscripts: Ul. Kommunisticheskaya 10, Baku; Dir. M. S. SULTANOV.

Terminological Committee: Ul. Kommunisticheskaya 10, Baku; Chair. M. A. M. DADASHZADE.

Publishing House: Prospekt Narimanova 27, Baku; Dir. A. R. KHANBABAEV.

Commission on International Scientific Contacts: Ul. Kommunisticheskaya 10, Baku; Chair. M. F. NAGYEV.

PERIODICAL PUBLICATIONS OF THE AZERBAIJAN ACADEMY OF SCIENCES:

Azerbaijanski Khimicheskii Zhurnal (*Azerbaijan Chemical Journal*); Doklady Akademii Nauk Azerbaijanskoy S.S.R. (*Reports of the Azerbaijan S.S.R. Academy of Sciences*); Izvestiya Akademii Nauk Azerbaijanskoy S.S.R. (*Bulletins of the Azerbaijan S.S.R. Academy of Sciences*): Physical Engineering and Mathematics, Geological-Geographical Sciences and Oil, Biology Series, History, Philosophy and Law, Linguistics, Literature and Art, Economic Sciences.

**Byelorussian S.S.R. Academy of Sciences:** f. 1929; Presidium: Leninsky prospekt 66, Minsk; President N. A. BORISEVICH; Vice-Presidents K. K. ATRAKHOVICH, V. A. BIELI, A. S. DMITRIEV, A. S. MAHNACH; Chief Learned Secretary L. I. KISELEVSKI; 57 members, 77 corresponding members.

*Department of Physical and Mathematical Sciences:* Academician-Secretary F. I. FEDOROV; Learned Secretary W. I. KUVSHINOV.

ATTACHED TO THE DEPARTMENT:

Institute of Physics: Leninsky prospekt 70, Minsk; Dir. B. I. STEPANOV.

Institute of Mathematics: Ul. Tipografskaya II, Minsk; Dir. V. P. PLATONOV.

Institute of Solid State and Semiconductor Physics: Ul. Podlesnaya 27, Minsk; Dir. B. B. BOJKO.

Branch of Institute of Physics: Mogilev, Ul. Belynickoho-Biruli 11; Dir. A. M. GONCHARENKO.

Branch of Institute of Mathematics: Gomel, Ul. Kirova 32a; Vice-Dir. S. A. CHUNIHIN.

Branch of Institute of Solid State and Semiconductor Physics: Vitebsk, Ul. Laso 113a; Dir. V. V. KLUBOVICH.

Institute of Electronics: Minsk, Ul. Kolasa, 68/2; Dir. V. A. PILIPOVICH.

*Department of Physical and Engineering Sciences:* Academician-Secretary P. I. JASHTSHERICYN; Learned Secretary V. K. JAROSHEVICH.

ATTACHED TO THE DEPARTMENT:

Institute of Heat and Mass Exchange: Ul. Podlesnaya 15, Minsk; Dir. R. I. SOLOUCHIN.

Physical-Engineering Institute: Ul. Žodzinskaya 4, Minsk; Dir. V. N. CHACHIN.

Institute of Nuclear Energy: Sosny Settlement, Minsk; Dir. V. B. NESTERENKO.

Institute of Engineering Cybernetics: Ul. Surganova 6, Minsk; Dir. O. I. SEMENKOV.

Institute of Metallopolymer Systems of Mechanics: Gomel, Ul. Kirova 32-a; Dir. V. A. BELY.

Institute of Reliability of Machines: Minsk, Ul. Akademicheskaya 12; Dir. O. V. BERESTNEV.

Institute of Applied Physics: Minsk, Ul. Akademicheskaya 16; Dir. N. N. ZACEPIN.

*Department of Chemical and Geological Sciences:* Academician-Secretary N. I. MITSKEVICH; Learned Secretary N. I. PLYUSHCHEVSKY.

ATTACHED TO THE DEPARTMENT:

Institute of Physical-Organic Chemistry: Ul. Surganova 13, Minsk; Dir. A. I. TROCHIMEC.

Institute of General and Inorganic Chemistry: Surganova 9, Minsk; Dir. V. S. KOMAROV.

Institute of Bio-organic Chemistry: Leninsky prospekt 68, Minsk; Dir. A. A. ACHREM.

Institute of Peat: Staroborisovskiy tract 10; Dir. I. I. LISHTVAH.

Institute of Geochemistry and Geophysics: Minsk, Leninsky prospect 68; Dir. R. G. GARECKY.

*Department of Biological Sciences:* Academician-Secretary L. M. SUSHCHENIA; Learned Secretary E. G. MELNIKOV.

ATTACHED TO THE DEPARTMENT:

Institute of Experimental Botany: Ul. Akademicheskaya 27, Minsk; Dir. V. I. PARFENOV.

Institute of Physiology: Ul. Akademicheskaya 28, Minsk; Dir. I. A. BULYGIN.

Institute of Genetics and Cytology: Ul. Akademicheskaya 27, Minsk; Dir. L. V. KHOTYLEVA.

Botanical Garden: Ul. Surganova 2a, Minsk; Dir. E. A. SIDOROVICH.

Institute of Photobiology: Ul. Akademicheskaya 27, Minsk; Dir. A. A. SHLYK.

Institute of Zoology and Parasitology: Ul. Akademicheskaya 27, Minsk; Chair. L. M. SUSHCHENIA.

Section of Gerontology: Ul. Žodinskaya 2, Minsk; Chair. G. G. GACKO.

Institute of Microbiology: Ul. Žodinskaya 2, Minsk; Dir. A. G. LOBANOK.

Branch of Metabolism Regulation: Grodno, Bulvar Leninskoho komsomola 50; Chair. Y. M. OSTROVSKY.

*Department of Social Sciences:* Academician-Secretary N. V. BIRYLLO; Learned Secretary V. V. AGIEVICH.

ATTACHED TO THE DEPARTMENT:

Institute of Philosophy and Law: Ul. Akademicheskaya 25, Minsk; Dir. E. M. BABOSOV.

Institute of History: Ul. Surganova 1 korpus 2, Minsk; Dir. P. T. PETRIKOV.

Institute of Economics: Ul. Surganova 1 korpus 2, Minsk; Dir. V. I. DRITS.

Yanka Kupala Institute of Literature: Ul. Surganova 1, korpus 2, Minsk; Dir. I. Y. NAYMENKO.

Yakub Kolas Institute of Linguistics: Ul. Akademicheskaya 25, Minsk; Dir. M. R. SUDNIK.

Institute of Art, Ethnography and Folklore: Ul. Surganova 1 korpus 2, Minsk; Dir. S. V. MARCELEV.

*Publishing House:* Leninsky prospekt 68, Minsk; Dir. F. I. SAVITSKI.

PERIODICAL PUBLICATIONS OF THE BYELORUSSIAN ACADEMY OF SCIENCES:

Doklady Akademii Nauk Byelorusskoi S.S.R. (*Reports of the Byelorussian S.S.R. Academy of Sciences*); Izvestiya Akademii Nauk Byelorusskoi S.S.R. (*Bulletins of the Byelorussian S.S.R. Academy of Sciences*): Physical Engineering, Biology, Social Sciences, Physical Mathematics, Chemistry, Energetics, Agriculture; Differentsialnye Uravneniya (*Differential Equations*); Zhurnal Prikladnoi Spektroskopii (*Journal of Applied Spectroscopy*); Inzhenerno-Fizichesky Zhurnal (*Engineering and Physical Journal*).

**Estonian S.S.R. Academy of Sciences:** Presidium; Kohtu 6, Tallinn 200103; Pres. K. REBANE; Vice-Presidents V. MAAMÄGI, I. ÖPIK; Chief Learned Secretary A. KÖÖRNA; 20 members, 24 corresponding members; Scientific Library: see under Libraries.

*Department of Physical, Mathematical and Technical Sciences:* Academician-Secretary E. LIPPMAA; Learned Secretary S. G. PIMENOVA.

ATTACHED TO THE DEPARTMENT:

Institute of Astrophysics and Atmospheric Physics/W. Struve Astrophysical Observatory: Tartu 202444, Tõravere; Dir. V. UNT.

Institute of Cybernetics: Lenini puiestee 10, Tallinn 200104; Dir. H. ABEN.

Institute of Thermal and Electrical Physics: Paldiski maantee 1, Tallinn 200105; Dir. L. E. VAIK.

Institute of Physics: Riia 181, Tartu 202400; Dir. H. OIGLANE.

Institute of Chemical and Biological Physics: Dir. ENDEL LIPPMAA.

*Department of Chemical, Geological and Biological Sciences:* Academician-Secretary E. PARMASTO; Learned Secretary M. MAYER.

ATTACHED TO THE DEPARTMENT:

Institute of Chemistry: Akadeemia tee 15, Tallinn 200026; Dir. O. EISEN.

Institute of Experimental Biology: Harju rajoon, Harku 203051; Dir. O. Y. PRIILINN.

Institute of Geology: Estonia puiestee 7, Tallinn 200101; Dir. L. KALJO.

Institute of Zoology and Botany: Vanemuise 21, Tartu 202400; Dir. K. PAAVER.

Society of Naturalists: Hariduse 3, Tartu 202400; Chair. K. KALAMEES.

Botanical Garden: Kloostrimetsa tee 44, Tallinn 200019; Dir. J. MARTIN.

Commission on Nature Conservation: Vanemuise 21, Tartu 202400; Chair. E. KUMARI.

Baltic Commission on Examination of Bird Migration: Vanemuise 21, Tartu 202400; Chair. E. KUMARI.

*Department of Social Science:* Academician-Secretary J. KAHK; Learned Secretary T. KÄBIN.

ATTACHED TO THE DEPARTMENT:

Institute of Economics: Estonia puiestee 7, Tallinn 200101; Dir. V. TARMISTO.

Institute of History: Estonia puiestee 7, Tallinn 200101; Dir. K. SIILIVASK.

Institute of Linguistics and Literature: Sakala 3, Tallinn 200105; Dir. E. SOGEL.

Fr. R. Kreutzwald Literature Museum: Vanemuise 42, Tartu 202400; Dir. E. ERTIS.

Society of the Estonian Language: Sakala 3, Tallinn 200105; Chair. A. KASK.

Estonian Geographical Society: Sakala 3, Tallinn 200105; Chair. V. TARMISTO.

Commission on Regional Studies: Estonia puiestee 7, Tallinn 200101; Chair. V. TARMISTO.

PERIODICAL PUBLICATIONS OF THE ESTONIAN ACADEMY OF SCIENCES:

Eesti NSV Teaduste Akadeemia Toimetised (Bulletins of the Estonian S.S.R. Academy of Sciences): Physics, Mathematics, Chemistry, Geology, Biological Sciences, Social Sciences; Keel ja Kirjandus (Language and Literature—in Estonian); Eesti Loodus (Nature of Estonia—in Estonian); Sovetskoe Finno-Ugrovedenie (Soviet Finno-Ugrian Studies).

**Georgian S.S.R. Academy of Sciences:** Presidium: Ul. Dzerzhinskogo 8, Tbilisi; Pres. I. N. VEKUA; Vice-Presidents E. K. KHARADZE, S. V. DURMISHIDZE, I. V. ABASHIDZE; Academician-Secretary N. A. LANDIA; 60 mems., 44 corresponding mems.

ATTACHED TO THE PRESIDIUM:

S. N. Djanashiya State Museum of Georgia: Ul. Ketskhovely 10, Tbilisi; Dir. N. G. CHERKEZISHVILI.

Council on the Preservation of Cultural Monuments: Chair. I. V. ABASHIDZE.

Georgian Commission on Archaeology: Chair. I. V. ABASHIDZE.

Council on the History of Natural Sciences and Technology: Chair. R. R. DVALI.

Commission on Nature Conservation: Chair. V. Z. GULISASHVILI.

Commission on Speleology: Acting Chair. K. V. DJAVRISHVILI.

Commission on Instillation of Science Achievements in National Economy: Tbilisi, Ul. Dzerzhinskogo 8; Chair. A. A. DZIDZIGURI.

Commission on Exhibitions: Tbilisi, Ul. Dzerzhinskogo 8; Chair. R. R. DVALI.

Commission on Scientific Information: Tbilisi, Ul. Dzerzhinskogo 8; Chair. V. I. GOMELAURI.

Commission on International Scientific Contacts: Tbilisi, Ul. Dzerzhinskogo 8; Chair. R. R. DVALI.

Institute of Palaeobiology: Tbilisi, Potochnaya 4-a; Dir. L. SH. DAVITASHVILI.

*Department of Mathematics and Physics:* Academician-Secretary V. D. KUPRADZE; Learned Secretary K. F. TSITSKISHVILI.

ATTACHED TO THE DEPARTMENT:

Tbilisi A. M. Razmadze Mathematical Institute: Ul. Dzerzhinskogo 8, Tbilisi; Dir. N. I. MUSKHELISHVILI.

Computing Centre: Ul. Akurskaya 8, Tbilisi; Dir. D. A. KVESELAVA.

Institute of Physics: Ul. Guramishvili 6, Tbilisi; Dir. E. L. ANDRONIKASHVILI.

Abastumani Astrophysical Observatory: Adigeni District, Abastumani, Kanobili Mountain; Dir. E. K. KHARADZE.

*Department of Earth Sciences:* Academician-Secretary F. F. DAVITAYA; Learned Secretary G. S. SHENGELAIA.

ATTACHED TO THE DEPARTMENT:

Geological Institute: Ul. Z. Rukhadze 1, Tbilisi; Dir. P. D. GAMKRELIDZE.

Vakhushti Institute of Geography: Ul. Z. Rukhadze 1, Tbilisi; Dir. F. F. DAVITAYA.

Institute of Geophysics: Ul. Z. Rukhadze 1, Tbilisi; Dir. A. V. BUKHNIKASHVILI.

Georgian Geological Society: Chair. A. I. DJANELIDZE.

Georgian Geographical Society: Chair. F. F. DAVITAYA.

Georgian Commission on Clay Studies: Chair. (vacant).

*Department of Applied Mechanics and Control Processes:* Academician-Secretary V. V. MAKHALDIANI; Acting Learned Secretary V. I. LEKISHVILI.

ATTACHED TO THE DEPARTMENT:

Institute of Cybernetics: Ul. Chitadze 6, Tbilisi; Dir. V. V. CHAVCHANIDZE.

Institute of Control Systems: Ul. Pekinskaya 32, Tbilisi; Dir. G. L. KHARATISHVILI.

Institute of Constructional Mechanics and Seismic Resistance: Ul. Z. Rukhadze 1, Tbilisi; Dir. K. S. ZAVRIEV.

G. A. Tsulukidze Institute of Mining Mechanics: Ul. Paliashvili 87, Tbilisi; Dir. I. I. ZURABISHVILI.

Institute of Mechanics of Machines: Ul. Z. Rukhadze 1, Tbilisi; Dir. R. R. DVALI.

*Department of Chemistry and Chemical Technology:* Academician-Secretary G. V. TSITSISHVILI; Acting Learned Secretary M. K. KURDEVANIDZE.

ATTACHED TO THE DEPARTMENT:

P. G. Melikishvili Institute of Physical and Organic Chemistry: Ul. Kamo 14, Tbilisi; Dir. G. V. TSITSISHVILI.

Institute of Inorganic Chemistry and Electrical Chemistry: Ul. Z. Rukhadze 1, Tbilisi; Dir. N. A. LANDIA.

Institute of Pharmaceutical Chemistry: Ul. Perovskoy 22, Tbilisi; Dir. V. S. ASATIANI.

Institute of Metallurgy: Ul. Pavlova 15, Tbilisi; Dir. F. N. TAVADZE.

*Department of Biology:* Academician-Secretary M. N. SABASHVILI; Acting Learned Secretary K. S. RAKVIASHVILI.

ATTACHED TO THE DEPARTMENT:

Institute of Paleobiology: Ul. Potochnaya 4-a, Tbilisi; Dir. L. S. DAVITASHVILI.

Institute of Botany: Kodjorskoe chaussée, Tbilisi; Dir. N. N. KETSKHOVELI.

Botanical Garden: Ul. Botanicheskaya 1, Tbilisi; Dir. M. A. GOGOLISHVILI.

Sukhumi Botanical Garden: Ul. Chavchavadze 18, Sukhumi; Dir. G. G. AIBA.

Batumi Botanical Garden: Makhinjauri, Batumi; Dir. N. M. SHARASHIDZE.

Institute of Zoology: I. Chavchavadze prospekt 31, Tbilisi; Dir. B. E. KURASHVILI.

Institute of Physiology: Voenno-Grusinskaya Doroga 62, Tbilisi; Acting Dir. A. N. BAKURADZE.

A. N. Natishvili Institute of Experimental Morphology: Ul. Kamo 51, Tbilisi; Dir. N. A. DZHAVAKHISHVILI.

Institute of Plant Biochemistry: Dir. S. V. DURMISHIDZE.

Committee on Co-ordinating Studies in Malignant Tumours: Plekhanov prospekt 60, Tbilisi; Chair. V. K. ZHGHENTY.

Georgian Society of Patho-Anatomists: Chair. V. K. ZHGENTI.

Georgian Society of Physiologists: Chair. I. S. BERITASHVILI.

Georgian Society of Helminthologists: Chair. Prof. B. E. KURASHVILI.

Georgian Zoological Society: Chair. Prof. A. G. DZHANASHVILI.

Georgian Botanical Society: Chair. N. N. KETSKHOVELI.
Georgian Biochemical Society: Chair. V. S. ASATIANI.

Institute of Biochemistry of Plants: Tbilisi, Voenno-Gruzinskaya Doroga, 10th kilometre; Dir. S. V. DURMISHIDZE.

Commission on the Study of Cancer Tumours: Tbilisi, Prospekt Plekhanova 60; Chair. V. K. ZHGENTI.

*Department of Social Sciences:* Academician-Secretary A. S. PRANGISHVILI; Learned Secretary L. I. LAZARASHVILI.

ATTACHED TO THE DEPARTMENT:

Institute of Linguistics: Ul. Dzerzhinskogo 8, Tbilisi; Dir. V. N. PANCHVIDZE.

Shota Rustaveli Institute of History of Georgian Literature: Ul. Lenina 5, Tbilisi; Dir. A. G. BARAMIDZE.

K. S. Kekelidze Institute of Manuscripts: Ul. Z. Rukhadze 5, Tbilisi; Dir. E. P. METREVELI.

I. A. Dzhavakhishvili Institute of History, Archaeology and Ethnography: Ul. Dzerzhinskogo 8, Tbilisi; Dir. G. A. MELIKISHVILI.

Institute of History of the Georgian Arts: Ul. Ketskhoveli 10, Tbilisi; Dir. G. N. CHUBINASHVILI.

Institute of Oriental Studies: Ul. Tskhakaya 10, Tbilisi; Dir. G. V. TSERETELI.

Institute of Philosophy: Prospekt Rustaveli 29, Tbilisi; Dir. N. Z. CHAVCHAVADZE.

D. N. Uznadze Institute of Psychology: Ul. Dzhavakhishvili 1, Tbilisi; Dir. A. S. PRANGISHVILI.

Institute of Economy and Law: Ul. Makharadze 14, Tbilisi; Dir. P. V. GUGUSHVILI.

Abkhazian D. I. Gulia Institute of Linguistics, Literature and History: Ul. Rustaveli 28, Sukhumi; Dir. G. A. DZIDZIRIA.

Southern-Ossetian Research Institute: Dom Sovetov, Tskhinivali; Dir. Z. P. TSKHOVREBOV.

Batumi Research Institute: Ul. Ninoshvili 23, Batumi; Dir. A. K. INAISHVILI.

Georgian Society for History, Archaeology, Ethnography and Folklore: Chair. G. S. CHITAYA.

Georgian Society of Psychologists: Chair. R. G. NATADZE.

PERIODICAL PUBLICATIONS OF THE GEORGIAN ACADEMY OF SCIENCES:

Bulletin of the Academy (monthly, in Georgian, abstracts in Russian and English); Matsne (*Herald of the Department of Social Sciences*, monthly); Metsnierba da Technika (monthly).

**Kazakh S.S.R. Academy of Sciences:** Presidium: Ul. Shevchenko 28, Alma-Ata 480021; Pres. A. M. KUNAEV; Vice-Presidents D. V. SOKOLSKY, A. N. NUSUPBEKOV, SH. IBRAGIMOV; Academician-Secretary Z. S. ERZHANOV; 53 members, 75 corresponding members.

ATTACHED TO THE PRESIDIUM:

Council for Study of Productive Forces: Chair. I. L. KIM.

Central Library: Dir. N. B. AKHMEDOVA.

Editorial-Publishing Council: Chair. Z. S. ERZHANOV.

Publishing House "Nauka": Dir. B. JA. NINBURG.

*Department of Physical-Mathematical Sciences:* Academician-Secretary O. A. ZHAUTYKOV; Learned Secretary R. D. NURMAMBETOVA.

ATTACHED TO THE DEPARTMENT:

Institute of Nuclear Physics: Nauchny Gorodok, Alma-Ata; branch in Shevchenko; Dir. S. S. IBRAGIMOV.

Institute of High Energy Physics: Nauchny Gorodok, Alma-Ata; Dir. Z. S. TAKIBAEV.

Institute of Mathematics and Mechanics: Ul. Vinogradova 34, Alma-Ata; Dir. T. I. AMANOV.

Astrophysical Institute: 68, Alma-Ata; Dir. T. B. OMAROV.

Section of the Ionosphere: Kamenskoe plato, Alma-Ata; Dir. M. P. RUDINA.

*Department of Earth Sciences:* Learned Secretary P. O. SUVOROVA.

ATTACHED TO THE DEPARTMENT:

K. I. Satpaev Institute of Geological Sciences: Ul. Kalinina 69-a, Alma-Ata; branch in Karaganda; Dir. A. A. ABDULLIN.

Institute of Mining: Ul. Varlamova 57, Alma-Ata; branch in Karaganda; Dir. V. G. BEREZA.

Institute of Hydrogeology and Hydrophysics: Ul. Krasina 94, Alma-Ata; branch in Karaganda; Dir. U. M. AKHMEDSAFIN.

Section of Geography: Ul. Kalinina 69-a, Alma-Ata; Dir. G. A. TOKMAGAMBETOV.

*Department of Chemical-Technological Sciences:* Academician-Secretary B. A. ZHUBANOV; Learned Secretary T. P. MODESTOVA.

ATTACHED TO THE DEPARTMENT:

Institute of Metallurgy and Ore-Dressing: Ul. Shevchenko 29/33, Alma-Ata; Dir. A. M. KUNAEV.

Institute of Chemical Sciences: Ul. Krasina 106, Alma-Ata; Dir. B. A. ZHUBANOV.

Institute of Organic Catalysis and Electro-chemistry: Ul. K. Marxa 142, Alma-Ata; Dir. D. V. SOKOLSKY.

Chemical-Metallurgical Institute: Sovetskii Prospekt 11-a, Karaganda; Dir. D. N. ABISHEV.

Institute of Petroleum Chemistry and Natural Salts: Ul. Osipenko 47, Guryev; branch in Shevchenko; Dir. N. K. NADIREV.

*Department of Biological Sciences:* Academician-Secretary T. B. DARKANBAEV; Learned Secretary N. N. VORONINA.

ATTACHED TO THE DEPARTMENT:

Institute of Soil Science: P.O. 32, Akademgorodok, Alma-Ata; Dir. V. M. BOROVSKY.

Institute of Botany: Ul. Kirova 103, Alma-Ata; Dir. G. Z. BIYASHEV.

Institute of Zoology: Post Office 65, Alma-Ata; Dir. E. V. GVOZDEV.

Institute of Microbiology: Ul. Kirova 103, Alma-Ata; Dir. A. N. ILYALETDINOV.

Institute of Physiology: P.O. 32, Akademgorodok, Alma-Ata; Dir. N. U. BAZANOVA.

Institute of Experimental Biology: Prospekt Abaya 38, Alma-Ata; Dir. F. M. MUKHAMEDGALIEV.

Botanical Garden: P.O. 70, Alma-Ata; Dir. I. O. BAYTULIN (acting).

*Department of Social Sciences:* Academician-Secretary S. K. KENESBAEV; Learned Secretary S. A. SUNDETOV.

ATTACHED TO THE DEPARTMENT:

Institute of Linguistics: Ul. Shevchenko 28, Alma-Ata; Dir. S. K. KENESBAYEV.

M. O. Auezov Institute of Literature and Arts: Ul. Shevchenko 28, Alma-Ata; Dir. A. S. SHARIPOV.

C. C. Valikhanov Institute of History, Archaeology and Ethnography: Ul. Shevchenko 28, Alma-Ata; Dir. A. N. NUSUPBEKOV.

Institute of Philosophy and Law: Ul. Pushkina 111/113 Alma-Ata; Dir. ZH. A. ABDILDIN.

Institute of Economics: Ul. Pushkina 111/113, Alma Ata; branch in Karaganda; Dir. T. A. ASHIMBAEV.

PERIODICAL PUBLICATION OF THE KAZAKH ACADEMY OF SCIENCES:

Vestnik Akademii Nauk Kazakhskoi S.S.R. (*Herald of the Kazakh S.S.R. Academy of Sciences*); Izvestiya Akademii Nauk Kazakhskoi S.S.R. (Series: physics and mathematics, geology, chemistry, biology, social science).

**Kirghiz S.S.R. Academy of Sciences:** Presidium: 265-a Leninsky Prospekt, Frunze; Pres. Acad. M. IMANALYEV; Vice-Pres. O. D. ALIMOV, A. M. MAMYTOV, S. T. TABYSHALIEV; Chief Learned Secretary R. E. SADYKOV; 27 members, 19 corresponding members.

ATTACHED TO THE PRESIDIUM:

Commission on Terminology: Chair. S. T. TABYSHALIEV.

Kirghiz Branch of the U.S.S.R. Society of Soil Scientists: Chair. A. M. MAMYTOV.

Kirghiz Geographical Society: Chair. S U. UMURZAKOV.

Kirghiz Branch of the U.S.S.R. Mineralogical Society: Chair. I. K. DAVLETOV.

Kirghiz Branch of the U.S.S.R. Biochemical Society: Chair. V. G. YAKOVLEV.

Kirghiz Entomological Society: Chair. R. V. GREBENUK.

Kirghiz Branch of the U.S.S.R. Genetics and Selection Society: Chair. R. E. SADYKOV.

Kirghiz Branch of the Soviet National Association for the History of Natural Sciences and Technology: Chair. O. D. ALIMOV.

Kirghiz Branch of the U.S.S.R. Microbiological Society: Chair. E. H. NIGMATULLIN.

Kirghiz Department of All-Union Botanical Garden: Frunze, 265-a Leninsky Prospekt; Chair. L. I. POPOVA.

Kirghiz Department of All-Union Society of Helminthology; Chair. M. M. TOKOBAYEV.

*Department of Physical-Engineering and Mathematical Sciences:* Chair. O. D. ALIMOV.

ATTACHED TO THE DEPARTMENT:

Institute of Physics and Mathematics: 265-a Leninsky Prospekt, Frunze; Dir. ZH. ZH. ZHEENBAEV.

Institute of Physics and Mechanics of Rocks: Ul. Kommunisticheskaya 98, Frunze; Dir. I. T. AITMATOV.

Institute of Automation: 265-a Leninsky-Prospekt, Frunze; Dir. E. E. MAKOVSKY.

Institute of Geology: Bulvar Dzerzhinskogo 30, Frunze; Dir. F. T. KASHIRIN.

Tyan-Shan Physical-Geographical Station: Pokrovka Village, Dzhety-Oguz District; Dir. B. O. OROZGOZHOEV.

*Department of Chemical-Technological and Biological Sciences:* Chair. A. M. MAMYTOV; Learned Secretary Z. B. POPOVA.

ATTACHED TO THE DEPARTMENT:

Institute of Inorganic and Physical Chemistry: 265-a Leninsky Prospekt, Frunze; Dir. B. I. IMANAKUNOV.

Institute of Organic Chemistry: 267 Leninsky Prospekt, Frunze; Dir. V. A. AFANASJEV.

Institute of Biochemistry and Physiology: 265-a Leninsky Prospekt, Frunze; Dir. V. G. YAKOVLEV.

Institute of Biology: 265-a Leninsky Prospekt, Frunze; Dir. M. M. TOKOBAEV.

Botanical Garden: Ul. Kommunisticheskaya 98, Frunze; Dir. A. K. AKCHMATOV.

Biological Station: Issyk-Kul Lake, Cholpon-Ata; Dir. A. U. KONURBAEV.

Kirghiz Southern Forest Station: Dzhalal-Abad; Dir. A. I. UZOLIN.

*Department of Social Sciences:* Chair. S. T. Tabyshaliev.

ATTACHED TO THE DEPARTMENT:

Institute of History: 265-a Leninsky Prospekt, Frunze; Dir. A. K. Kanimentov.

Institute of Linguistics and Literature: 265-a Leninsky Prospekt, Frunze; Dir. A Sadykov.

Institute of Economics: 265-a Leninsky Prospekt, Frunze; Dir. A. M. Moldokulov.

Institute of Philosophy and Law; 265-a Leninsky Prospekt, Frunze; Dir. A. A. Altmyshbaev.

*Department of General Turc and Dungan Studies:* 265-a Leninsky Prospekt, Frunze; Dir. M. Sushanlo.

*Publishing House "Ilim" (Science):* 265-a Leninsky Prospekt, Frunze; Dir. S. S. Tchernov.

PERIODICAL PUBLICATION OF THE KIRGHIZ ACADEMY OF SCIENCE:

Izvestiya Akademii Nauk Kirghizskoi S.S.R. (*Bulletins of the Kirghiz S.S.R. Academy of Sciences*).

**Latvian S.S.R. Academy of Sciences:** Presidium: Ul. Turgeneva 19, Riga; Pres. A. K. Malmeisters; Vice-Pres. E. A. Jakubaitis, A. A. Drizul; Chief Learned Secretary V. P. Samson; 25 members, 30 corresponding members.

ATTACHED TO THE PRESIDIUM:

Latvian Association for the History of Natural Sciences and Technology: Chair. V. P. Samson.

Commission on Science Equipment: Riga, Ul. Aizkraukles 23; Chair. Y. M. Tarnopolsky.

Scientific Council on Exhibitions: Riga, Ul. Akademiyas 27; Chair. A. F. Krogeris.

Council on Libraries: Riga, Ul. Turgeneva 19; Chair. J. P. Stradin.

Council on Cybernetics: Riga, Ul. Turgeneva 19; Chair. E. A. Jakubaytis.

*Department of Physical and Engineering Sciences:* Academician-Secretary J. A. Mikhailov; Learned Secretary M. P. Zakis.

ATTACHED TO THE DEPARTMENT:

Institute of Physics: Salaspils, Riga District; Dir. J. A. Mikhailov.

Institute of Electronics and Computing Equipment: Ul. Akademiyas 14, Riga; Dir. E. A. Jakubaytis.

Institute of Energy: Ul. Aizkraukles 21, Riga; Dir. A. F. Krogeris.

Institute of Mechanics of Polymer Compounds: Ul. Aizkraukles 23, Riga; Dir. V. A. Latishenko.

Radio-Astrophysical Observatory: Ul. Turgeneva 19, Riga; Acting Dir. A. E. Balklav.

*Department of Chemical and Biological Sciences:* Academician-Secretary B. A. Purin; Learned Secretary M. A. Aleksandrova.

ATTACHED TO THE DEPARTMENT:

Institute of Inorganic Chemistry: Ul. Meistaru 10, Riga; Dir. B. A. Purin.

Institute of Organic Synthesis: Ul. Aizkraukles 21, Riga; Dir. G. I. Chipens.

Institute of Wood Chemistry: Ul. Akademijas 27, Riga; Dir. V. P. Karlivan.

Institute of Biology: Ul. Miera 3, Salaspils, Riga District; Dir. G. P. Andrushaitis.

Institute of Microbiology: Ul. Kleysti, Riga; Dir. R. A. Kukain.

Botanical Garden: P.O. Salaspils, Riga District; Dir. V. K. Ozoliņš.

Latvian Department of All-Union Botanical Society: Ul. Miera 3, Salaspils, Riga District; Chair. L. V. Tabaka.

Latvian Department of All-Union Biochemistry Society: Riga, Ul. Aizkraukles 21; Chair. E. J. Gren.

Latvian Department of All-Union Entomological Society: Riga, Ul. Fricha Gaylya 10; Chair. Z. D. Spuris.

Latvian Department of All-Union N. I. Vavilov Society of Genetics and Selection: Ul. Miera 3, Salaspils, Riga District; Chair. V. J. Dishler.

Latvian Department of All-Union I. P. Pavlov Physiological Society: Riga, Ul. Altonavas 4; Chair. A. A. Krauklis.

*Department of Social Sciences:* Academician-Secretary V. A. Shteinberg; Learned Secretary B. J. Pudels.

ATTACHED TO THE DEPARTMENT:

Institute of Economics: Ul. Turgeneva 19, Riga; Dir. I. Ch. Kirtovsky.

Institute of History: Ul. Turgeneva 19, Riga; Dir. V. A. Shteinberg.

Institute of Language and Literature: Ul. Turgeneva 19, Riga; Dir. J. J. Kalnin.

Terminological Commission: Ul. Krishjana Barona 4, Riga; Chair. J. J. Kalnin.

"Zinatne" Publishing House: Ul. Turgeneva 19, Riga; Dir. M. M. Belyuk.

PERIODICAL PUBLICATIONS OF THE LATVIAN ACADEMY OF SCIENCES:

Izvestiya Akademii Nauk Latviyskoi S.S.R. (*Bulletins of the Latvian S.S.R. Academy of Sciences*): Chemical Sciences, Physical and Engineering Sciences; Mekhanika Polimerov (*Mechanics of Polymers*); Magnitnaya Gidrodinamika (*Magnetic Hydrodynamics*); Khimiya Geterotsiklicheskikh Soedinenii (*Chemistry of Heterocyclic Compounds*).

**Lithuanian S.S.R. Academy of Sciences:** Presidium: Lenino prospektas 3, Vilnius; Pres. J. Matulis; Vice-Pres. A. A. Žukauskas, J. K. Požela; Chief Learned Secretary K. A. Meškauskas; 19 members, 25 corresponding members.

ATTACHED TO THE PRESIDIUM:

Council for Co-ordination of Natural and Social Sciences: Chair. J. Matulis.

Central Library: K. Požełos 2/8, Vilnius; Dir. J. Marcinkevičius.

*Department of Physical, Technical and Mathematical Sciences:* Academician-Secretary P. P. Brazdžiūnas Learned Secretary S. F. Raškovskis.

ATTACHED TO THE DEPARTMENT:

Institute of Physics and Mathematics: K. Požełos 54, Vilnius; Dir. V. A. Statulevičius.

Institute of Physical and Technical Problems of Energetics: Metalo 4, Kaunas; Dir. V. I. Dauknys.

Institute of Semiconductor Physics: K. Požełos 52, Vilnius; Dir. J. Požela.

*Department of Chemical and Biological Sciences:* Academician-Secretary L. Kairiúkštis; Learned Secretary A. Y. Palioniene.

ATTACHED TO THE DEPARTMENT:

Institute of Chemistry and Chemical Technology: K. Požełos 48, Vilnius; Dir. J. Matulis.

Institute of Botany: Turistu 47, Vilnius; Dir. K. K. Jankevičius.

Institute of Biochemistry: K. Požełos 48, Vilnius; Dir. L. Rasteikiene.

Institute of Zoology and Parasitology: K. Požėlos 54, Vilnius; Dir. A. ZAJANČKAUSKAS; attached Dept. of Geography; Head K. BIELIUKAS.

Botanical Garden: Botanikos 3, Kaunas; Dir. A. R. BUDRIŪNAS.

*Department of Social Sciences:* Academician-Secretary V. Y. NIUNKA; Learned Secretary P. A. DIČIUS.

ATTACHED TO THE DEPARTMENT:

Institute of Economics: K. Požėlos 52, Vilnius; Dir. K. A. MEŠKAUSKAS.

Institute of History: Kostiuškos 30, Vilnius; Dir. B. VAITKEVIČIUS. (Department of Philosophy, Law and Sociology attached to the Institute; Head. A. A. GAIDIS.)

Institute of Lithuanian Language and Literature: Antakalnio 3, Vilnius; Dir. K. P. KORSAKAS.

PERIODICAL PUBLICATIONS OF THE LITHUANIAN ACADEMY OF SCIENCES:

Lietuvos T.S.R. M.A. Darbai. (*Proceedings of the Lithuanian S.S.R. Academy of Sciences*); Series A (*Social Sciences*); Series B (*Chemistry, Engineering, Geography*); Series C (*Biological Sciences*).

**Moldavian S.S.R. Academy of Sciences:** Presidium: Prospekt Lenina 1, Kishinev; Pres. Y. S. GROSUL; Vice-President B. R. LAZARENKO; Chief Learned Secretary T. I. MALINOWSKI; 17 members, 21 corresponding members.

ATTACHED TO THE PRESIDIUM:

Commission on the History of Science Technology: Chair. Y. S. GROSUL.

Commission on Nature Conservation: Chair. V. N. VERINA.

*Department of Physical-Engineering and Mathematical Sciences:* Academician-Secretary V. A. ANDRUNAKIEVICH; Learned Secretary I. A. DYAKON.

ATTACHED TO THE DEPARTMENT:

Institute of Mathematics and Computing Centre: Ul. Akademicheskaya 3, Kishinev; Dir. V. A. ANDRUNAKIEVICH.

Institute of Applied Physics: Ul. Akademicheskaya 5, Kishinev; Dir. B. R. LAZARENKO.

Institute of Geophysics and Geology: Kishinev; Dir. A.V. DRUMYA.

Section of Energy Cybernetics: Ul. Akademicheskaya 5, Kishinev; Dir. G. V. CHALY.

Section of Geography: Leninsky prospekt 1, Kishinev; Dir. V. E. PROKA.

Seismic Station: Kostuzhenskoe chaussée 62, Kishinev; Dir. A. V. DRUMYA.

*Department of Biological and Chemical Sciences:* Academician-Secretary I. S. POPOUSHOY; Learned Secretary G. T. BALMOUSCH.

ATTACHED TO THE DEPARTMENT:

Institute of Chemistry: Ul. Akademicheskaya 3, Kishinev; Dir. P. F. VLAD.

Institute of Zoology: Prospekt Lenina 1, Kishinev; Dir. F. I. FURDUI.

Institute of Plant Physiology and Biochemistry: Ul. Akademicheskaya 3, Kishinev; Dir. K. V. MORARU.

Botanical Garden: Kishinev 277032, Ul. Lesnaja 18; Dir. A. A. CHEBOTARU.

Section of Plant Genetics: Ul. Akademicheskaya 3, Kishinev; Dir. V. N. LYSIKOV.

Section of Microbiology: Prospekt Lenina 1, Kishinev; Dir. V. V. KOTELEV.

Section of Palaeontology and Stratigraphy: Ul. Berzarina 10, Kishinev; Dir. K. N. NEGODAEV-NIKONOV.

Complex Experimental Station (Collective Farm "Vyatsa Noue", Orgeev District): Akademicheskaya ul. 13, Kishinev; Dir. I. E. BUKHAR.

Moldavian Department of All-Union Botanical Society: Kishinev 28, Akademicheskaya 3; Chair. T. S. GEIDEMAN.

Moldavian Department D. I. Mendeleyev Chemistry Society: Kishinev, Akademicheskaya 3; Chair. D. P. POPA.

Moldavian Department of All-Union Hydrobiological Society: Kishinev, Akademicheskaya 5; Chair. M. F. JAROSHENKO.

Moldavian Department of All-Union Society of Genetics: Kishinev, Akademicheskaya 3; Acad. A. D. SIMINEL.

Moldavian Department of All-Union Entomological Society: Kishinev, Akademicheskaya 5; Chair. B. V. VERESHCHAGIN.

Moldavian Geographical Society: Kishinev, Prospekt Lenina 1; Chair. A. T. LEVADNUK.

*Department of Social Sciences:* Academician-Secretary A. M. LAZAREV; Learned Secretary T. F. TSCHELAK.

ATTACHED TO THE DEPARTMENT:

Institute of History: Prospekt Lenina 1, Kishinev; Dir. B. K. VIZER.

Institute of Economics: Prospekt Lenina 1, Kishinev; Dir. N. P. FROLOV.

Institute of Language and Literature: Prospekt Lenina, Kishinev; Chair. S. S. CHIBOTARY.

Society for the Protection of Culture: Prospekt Lenina 1, Kishinev; Chair. S. S. CHIBOTARY.

A. S. Pushkin Memorial Committee: Chair. I. K. VARTICHAN.

Department of Philosophy and Law: Kishinev, Prospekt Lenina 1; Chair. D. T. URSUL.

Department of Ethnography and Art: Kishinev, Prospekt Lenina 1; Chair. V. S. ZELENCHUK.

Department of Science Information: Kishinev, Prospekt Lenina 1; Chair. E. E. CHERTAN.

Department of Philosophy: Kishinev, Prospekt Lenina 1; Chair. V. N. ERMURATSKY.

Department of Foreign Languages: Kishinev, Prospekt Lenina 1; Chair. D. V. BEDEREU.

*Committee on International Scientific Contacts:* Chair. T. I. MALINOWSKI.

PERIODICAL PUBLICATIONS OF THE MOLDAVIAN ACADEMY OF SCIENCES:

Izvestiya Akademii Nauk Moldavskoi S.S.R. (*Bulletins of the Moldavian S.S.R. Academy of Sciences*); Elektronnaya Obrabotka Materialov (*Electronic Processing of Materials*); Limba shi Literatura Moldavenyaske (*Moldavian Language and Literature*).

**Tajik S.S.R. Academy of Sciences:** Presidium: Dushanbe; Pres. M. S. ASIMOV; Vice-Pres. A. S. MAKSUMOV; Chief Learned Secretary P. M. SOLOZHENKIN; 22 members, 19 corresponding members.

*Department of Physical-Engineering and Chemical Sciences:* Academician-Secretary R. B. BARATOV; Learned Secretary A. N. BELOV.

UNION OF SOVIET SOCIALIST REPUBLICS

ATTACHED TO THE DEPARTMENT:

S. U. Umarov Physical-Engineering Institute: 8-km., Ordzhonikidzeabadskoe chaussée, Dushanbe; Dir. A. A. ADKHAMOV.

Institute of Astrophysics: Ul. Sviridenko 22, Dushanbe; Dir. O. V. DOBROVOLSKY.

Institute of Seismic Resistant Construction and Seismology; Ul. Ayni 121, Dushanbe; Dir. S. K. NEGMATULLAYEV.

Institute of Chemistry: Ul. Ayni 44, Dushanbe; Dir. I. U. NUMANOV.

Institute of Geology: Dir. R. B. BARATOV.

Tajik Branch of the D. I. Mendeleyev All-Union Chemical Society: Chair. R. B. BARATOV.

Tajik Branch of the All-Union Mineralogical Society: Chair. R. B. BARATOV.

Tajik Branch of the All-Union Paleontological Society: Chair. V. M. REIMAN.

Tajik Geographical Society: Chair. A. P. NEDZVETSKY.

Tajik Branch of the All-Union Biochemical Society: Chair. I. D. MANSUROVA.

Dushanbe Branch of the All-Union Astronomical and Geodesical Society: Chair. A. M. BAKHAREV.

Institute of Mathematics: Dushanbe, Ordzhonikidzebadskoe chaussée; Chair. A. D. DZHURAEV.

*Department of Biological Sciences:* Academician-Secretary M. N. NARZIKULOV; Learned Secretary G. P. SHMELEV.

ATTACHED TO THE DEPARTMENT:

Institute of Plant Physiology and Biophysics: Botanicheskaya ul. 17, Dushanbe; Dir. Y. S. NASYROV.

Institute of Botany: Ul. Lakhuti 6, Dushanbe; Dir. P. N. OVCHINNIKOV.

Academician E. N. Pavlovsky Institute of Zoology and Parasitology: Post Office 70, Dushanbe; Dir. I. A. ABDUSALYAMOV.

Institute of Gastro-Enterology: Dir. K. K. MANSUROV.

Tajik Branch of the All-Union Entomological Society: Chair. M. N. NARZIKULOV.

Pamir Station: Gorno-Badakhshan Autonomous Region, Khorog; Chair. K. Y. YUSUFBEKOV.

*Department of Social Sciences:* Academician-Secretary N. A. MASUMI; Learned Secretary K. E. VASILEV.

ATTACHED TO THE DEPARTMENT:

Donish Institute of History: Prospekt Lenina 33, Dushanbe; Dir. B. I. ISKANDAROV.

Rudaki Institute of Language and Literature: Prospekt Lenina 21, Dushanbe; Dir. N. A. MASUMI.

Institute of Economics: Prospekt Lenina 37, Dushanbe; Dir. R. K. RAKHIMOV.

Section of Philosophy: Prospekt Lenina 33, Dushanbe; Dir. G. A. ASHUROV.

Section of Oriental Studies and Ancient Scriptures: Ul. Parvin 8, Dushanbe; Dir. A. M. MIRZOEV.

*Editorial Board:* Dushanbe 33; Chair. M. S. ASIMOV.

*Publishing House:* Ul. Aym 121, Dushanbe; Dir. M. BABAEV.

PERIODICAL PUBLICATIONS OF THE TAJIK ACADEMY OF SCIENCES:

Doklady Akademii Nauk Tadzhikskoi S.S.R. (*Reports of the Tajik S.S.R. Academy of Sciences*); Izvestiya Akademii Nauk Tadzhikskoi S.S.R. (*Bulletins of the Tajik Academy of Sciences*): Physical-Engineering and Chemical Sciences, Biological Sciences, Social Sciences.

WORLD OF LEARNING

**Turkmen S.S.R. Academy of Sciences:** Presidium: Ul. Gogolya 15, Ashkhabad; Pres. A. G. BABAEV; Vice-Presidents I. S. RABOCHEV, A. A. BERDYEV; Chief Learned Secretary O. N. MAMEDNIYAZOV; 24 members, 21 corresponding members.

ATTACHED TO THE PRESIDIUM:

Turkmen Branch of the All-Union Geographical Society: Chair. A. G. BABAEV.

Turkmen Branch of the All-Union Botanical Society: Chair. S. I. KOGAN.

Turkmen Branch of the All-Union Entomological Society: Chair. A. N. LUPPOVA.

Commission on Nature Conservation: Chair. A. O. TASHLIEV.

Commission on the History of Natural Sciences and Technology: Chair. S. R. SERGIENKO.

Commission on the Orthography and Terminology of the Turkmen Language: Chair. P. A. AZIMOV.

Council on Co-ordination of Science Investigations: Chair. P. A. AZUMOV.

Turkmen Department of All-Union Department of Soil Science: Chair. M. P. ARANBAEV.

Turkmen Department of Protozoologists: Chair. Z. B. KORNIENKO.

*Department of Physical-Engineering and Chemical Sciences:* Acting Academician-Secretary A. A. BERDIEV; Learned Secretary A. V. LEZHNEVA.

ATTACHED TO THE DEPARTMENT:

Physical-Engineering Institute: Ul. Gogolya 15, Ashkhabad; Dir. A. KHANBERDYEV.

Institute of Chemistry: Sad Keshi, Ashkhabad; Dir. A. M. NIYAZOV.

Institute of Earth and Atmospheric Physics: Ul-Gogolya 16, Ashkhabad; Dir. O. A. ODEKOV.

Institute of Geology.

*Department of Biological Sciences:* Acting Academician-Secretary F. F. SULTANOV; Learned Secretary N. B. POLESIKA.

ATTACHED TO THE DEPARTMENT:

Institute of Botany; Prospekt Svobody 77, Ashkhabad; Dir. K. MURADOV.

Institute of Zoology: Ul. Engelsa 6, Ashkhabad; Dir. A. O. TASHLIEV.

Institute of Regional Medicine: Dir. A. K. BABAYEVA.

Botanical Garden: Ul. Timiryazeva 17, Ashkhabad; Dir. N. MURATGELDYEV.

Desert Institute: Ashkhabad, sad Keshi; Dir. N. S. ORLOVSKY.

Scientific Council on Biological Reconstruction of Animals: Chair. A. O. TASHLIEV.

Scientific Council on Studying of Deserts of Middle Asia and Kazakhstan: Chair. N. T. NECHAEVA.

*Department of Social Sciences:* Acting Academician-Secretary A. S. SAPAROV; Learned Secretary V. N. FILYUSHINA.

ATTACHED TO THE DEPARTMENT:

S. Batyrov Institute of History: Ul. Gogolya 15, Ashkhabad; Dir. A. KARRIYEV.

Makhtumkuli Institute of Linguistics and Literature: Ul. Gogolya 15, Ashkhabad; Dir. B. CHARIYAROV.

Institute of Economics: Ul. Gogolya 15, Ashkhabad; Dir. D. A. ALLADOTOV.

Southern Turkmen Complex Archaeological Expedition: Ul. Gogolya 15, Ashkhabad; Dir. M. E. MASSON.

Section of Philosophy and Law: Chair. G. O. MURADOVA.

PERIODICAL PUBLICATIONS OF THE TURKMEN ACADEMY OF SCIENCES:

Izvestiya Akademii Nauk Turkmenskoi S.S.R. (*Bulletins of the Turkmen S.S.R. Academy of Sciences*): Physical-Engineering and Chemical Sciences, Biological Sciences, Social Sciences.

**Ukrainian S.S.R. Academy of Sciences:** Presidium: Ul. Vladimirskaya 54, Kiev; f. 1919; Pres. B. E. PATON; Vice-Presidents G. S. PISARENKO, V. I. TREFILOV, V. M. GLUSHKOV, K. M. SYTNIK, I. K. BELODED; Chief Scientific Secretary I. K. POHODNYA; 119 members, 171 corresponding members.

*Section of Physical-Engineering and Mathematical Sciences:* Ul. Vladimirskaya 54, Kiev; Chair. V. I. TREFILOV; Scientific Secretary V. D. NOVIKOV.

ATTACHED TO THE SECTION:

*Department of Mathematics, Mechanics and Cybernetics:* Academician-Secretary Y. A. MITROPOLSKY; Scientific Secretary A. A. MARTYNJUK.

ATTACHED TO THE DEPARTMENT:

Institute of Mathematics: Ul. Repina 3, Kiev; Dir. Y. A. MITROPOLSKY.

Institute of Hydromechanics: Ul. Zhelyabova 8/4, Kiev; Dir. A. Y. OLEYNIK.

Institute of Cybernetics: Prospekt 40-Letiia Octiabria 142/144, Kiev; Dir. V. M. GLUSHKOV.

Institute of Mechanics: Ul. Nesterova 3, Kiev; Dir. A. N. GOUZ.

Institute of Applied Mechanics and Mathematics: Ul. Nauchnaya 3b, Lvov; Dir. Y. S. PIDSTRYGACH.

Institute of Strength Problems: Ul. Timiryazevskaya 2, Kiev; Dir. G. S. PISARENKO.

Institute of Mechanics of Geological Engineering: Ul. Simferopolskaya 2a, Dnepropetrovsk; Dir. V. N. POTURAEV.

Institute of Applied Mathematics and Mechanics: Ul. Universitetskaya 77, Donetsk; Dir. I. V. SKRYPNIK.

*Department of Physics and Astronomy:* Academician-Secretary V. N. GRIDNEV; Scientific Secretary T. K. YATSENKO.

ATTACHED TO THE DEPARTMENT:

Institute of Physics: Prospekt Nauky 144, Kiev; Dir. M. T. SHPAK.

Institute of Physics of Metals: Prospekt Vernadskogo 36, Kiev; Dir. V. N. GRIDNEV.

Institute of Semiconductor Physics: Prospekt Nauky 115, Kiev; Dir. O. V. SNITKO.

Physical-Engineering Institute: Ul. Akademicheskaya 1, Kharkov; Dir. V. E. IVANOV.

**Physical-Engineering Institute of Low Temperatures:** Lenin prospekt 47, Kharkov; Dir. B. I. VERKIN.

Institute of Radio Physics and Electronics: Ul. Akademika Proskury 12, Kharkov; Dir. V. P. SHESTOPALOV.

Donetsk Physical Engineering Institute: Ul. R. Luxembourg 72, Donetsk; Dir. A. A. GALKIN.

Institute of Theoretical Physics: Ul. Metrologicheskaya 14b, Kiev; Dir. A. S. DAVYDOV.

Institute of Nuclear Research: Prospekt Nauky 119, Kiev; Dir. O. F. NEMETS.

Chief Astronomical Observatory: Goloseyevo, Kiev; Dir. Y. S. YATSKIV.

*Department of Physical-Engineering Problems of Materials:* Academician-Secretary I. N. FEDORCHENKO; Scientific Secretary A. I. KOSTIUK.

ATTACHED TO THE DEPARTMENT:

E. O. Paton Institute of Electrical Welding (Order of Lenin and Order of the Red Banner of Labour): Ul. Bozhenko 11, Kiev; Dir. B. E. PATON.

Institute of Problems of Materials (Order of the Red Banner of Labour): Ul. Krzhizhanovskogo 3, Akademgorodok, Kiev; Dir. V. I. TREFILOV.

Institute of Foundry Problems: Prospekt Vernadskogo 34/1, Akademgorodok, Kiev; Dir. V. A. EFIMOV.

Physical-Mechanical Institute: Ul. Nauchnaya 5, Lvov; Dir. V. V. PANASJUK.

Institute of Superhard Materials: Ul. Avtozavodskaya 2, Kiev; f. 1961; library of 125,000 vols.; Dir. N. V. NOVIKOV.

*Department of Physical-Engineering Problems of Energy:* Academician-Secretary G. E. PUHOV; Scientific Secretary E. E. ANTONOV.

ATTACHED TO THE DEPARTMENT:

Institute of Electrical Dynamics: Brest-Litovsky Prospekt 102, Kiev; Dir. A. K. SHIDLOVSKY.

Institute of Engineering Thermal Physics: Ul. Zhelyabova 2a, Kiev; Dir. O. A. GERASHCHENKO.

Institute of Problems of Engineering: Ul. Oljminskogo 14, Kharkov; Dir. V. N. PODGORNY.

*Department of Earth Problems:* Academician-Secretary N. P. SHCHERBAK; Scientific Secretary V. M. PALIY.

ATTACHED TO THE DEPARTMENT:

Institute of Geology: Ul. Chkalova 55b, Kiev; Dir. E. F. SHNIUKOV.

Institute of Geophysics: Prospekt Akademika Palladina 32, Kiev; Dir. A. V. CHEKUNOV.

Poltava Gravimetric Observatory: Ul. Myasoedova 27/29, Poltava; Dir. N. I. PANCHENKO.

Institute of Geology and Geochemistry of Combustible Minerals: Ul. Nauchnaya 3a, Lvov; Dir. G. N. DOLENKO.

Institute of Geochemistry and Physics of Minerals: Prospekt Akademika Palladina 34, Kiev; Dir. N. P. SHCHERBAK.

**Marine Hydrophysical Institute:** Ul. Lenina 28, Sevastopol; Dir. B. A. NELEPO.

*Section of Chemical-Technological and Biological Sciences:* Chair. F. S. BABICHEV; Scientific Secretary O. F. DEMBNOVETSKY.

ATTACHED TO THE SECTION:

*Department of Chemistry and Chemical Technology:* Academician-Secretary V. P. KUHAR; Scientific Secretary K. E. MAKHORIN.

ATTACHED TO THE DEPARTMENT:

Institute of Physical Chemistry: Chernomorskaya Rd. 86, Odessa; Dir. A. V. BOGATSKY.

Institute of Colloidal Chemistry and Chemistry of Water: Boulvar Akademika Vernadskogo 42, Kiev; Dir. A. N. PILIPENKO.

Institute of General and Inorganic Chemistry: Prospekt Akademika Palladina 32/34, Kiev; Dir. A. V. GORODISKY.

**Institute of Organic Chemistry:** Ul. Murmanskaya 5, Kiev; Dir. A. V. KIRSANOV.

**Institute of Macromolecular Chemistry:** Darnitsa, Kharkovskoye shosse 48, Kiev; Dir. Y. S. LIPATOV.

L. V. Pisarzhevsky Institute of Physical Chemistry (Order of the Red Banner of Labour): Prospekt Nauki 31, Kiev; Dir. K. B. YATSIMIRSKY.

Institute of Gas: Ul. Parhomenko 39, Kiev; Dir. V. F. KOPYTOV.

Institute of Physical-Organic Chemistry and Coal Chemistry: Ul. R. Luxembourg 70, Donetsk; Dir. L. M. LITVINENKO.

*Department of General Biology:* Academician-Secretary A. M. GRODZINSKY; Scientific Secretary I. G. EMELYANOV.

ATTACHED TO THE DEPARTMENT:

V. M. G. Kholodny Institute of Botany: Ul. Repina 2, Kiev; Dir. K. M. SYTNIK.

Ukrainian State Steppe Reservation: Donetsk Region, Khomutovo Village, Novoazov District; Dir. A. P. GENOV.

Central Botanical Garden: Ul. Timiryazevskaya 1, Kiev; Dir. A. N. GRODZINSKY.

Institute of Zoology: Ul. Lenina 15, Kiev; Dir. V. A. TOPACHEVSKY.

Institute of Hydrobiology: Ul. Vladimirskaya 44, Kiev; Dir. V. D. ROMANENKO.

Institute of Plant Physiology: Ul. Vasilkovskaya 31/17, Kiev; Dir. D. M. GRODZINSKY.

Institute of Biology of Southern Seas (Order of the Red Banner of Labour): Nahimova prospekt 2, Sevastopol; Dir. V. E. ZAIKA.

Botanical Gardens: Prospekt Illicha 110, Donetsk; Dir. E. M. KONDRATYUK.

Lvov Science Museum: Ul. Teatralnaya 18, Lvov; Dir. M. I. SERGIENKO.

*Department of Biochemistry, Physiology and Theoretical Medicine:* Academician-Secretary P. G. BOGACH; Scientific Secretary D. M. FEDORIAK.

ATTACHED TO THE DEPARTMENT:

O. V. Palladin Institute of Biochemistry (Order of the Red Banner of Labour): Ul. Leontovicha 9, Kiev; Dir. V. K. LISHKO.

A. A. Bogomolets Institute of Physiology: Ul. Bogomoltsa 4, Kiev; Dir. P. G. KOSTYUK.

D. K. Zabolotny Institute of Microbiology and Virology (Order of the Red Banner of Labour): Ul. Akademika Zabolotnogo 26, Kiev; Dir. D. V. V. SMIRNOV.

Institute of Molecular Biology and Genetics: Ul. Zabolotnogo 24, Kiev; Dir. G. H. MATSUKA.

Institute of Problems of Oncology: Ul. Vasilkovskaya 45, Kiev; Dir. V. G. PINCHUK.

Institute of Problems of Criobiology and Criomedicine: Ul. Pereyaslovskaya 23, Kharkov; Dir. N. S. PUSHKAR.

*Section of Social Sciences:* Chair. I. I. LUKINOV; Scientific Secretary S. I. PIROZHKOV.

ATTACHED TO THE SECTION:

*Department of Economics:* Academician-Secretary I. I. LUKINOV; Scientific Secretary A. B. SEMENKO.

ATTACHED TO THE DEPARTMENT:

Institute of Economics: Ul. P. Myrnogo 26, Kiev; Dir. I. I. LUKINOV.

Institute of Industrial Economics: Ul. Universitetskaga 77, Donetsk; Dir. G. CHUMACHENKO.

Institute of Social and Economic Problems of Foreign Countries: Ul. P. Myrnogo 26, Kiev; Dir. A. N. SHLEPAKOV.

*Department of History, Philosophy and Law:* Academician-Secretary B. M. BABIY; Scientific Secretary I. I. LADYVIR.

ATTACHED TO THE DEPARTMENT:

Institute of History: Ul. Kirova 4, Kiev; Dir. Y. Y. KONDUFOR.

Institute of Archaeology: Ul. Vydubetskaya 40, Kiev; Dir. I. I. ARTEMENKO.

Institute of Philosophy: Ul. Geroyev Revolutsii 4, Kiev; Dir. V. I. SHINKARUK.

Institute of State and Law: Ul. Geroyev Revolutsii 4, Kiev; Dir. B. M. BABIY.

Institute of Social Sciences: Ul. Sovetskaya 24, Lvov; Dir. V. P. CHUGAYOV.

*Department of Language, Literature and Art:* Academician-Secretary V. M. RUSANOVSKY; Scientific Secretary V. N. FOMENKO.

ATTACHED TO THE DEPARTMENT:

T. G. Shevchenko Institute of Literature: Ul. Kirova 4, Kiev; Dir. I. A. DZEVERIN.

A. A. Potebnya Institute of Linguistics: Ul. Kirova 4, Kiev; Dir. I. K. BELODED.

M. F. Rylsky Institute of Art, Folklore and Ethnography: Ul. Kirova 4, Kiev; Dir. S. D. ZUBKOV.

State Museum of Ethnography and Art Handicraft: Prospekt Lenina 15, Lvov; Dir. Y. G. GOSHKO.

Central Library: Ul. Vladimirskaya 62, Kiev; Dir. B. P. KOVALEVSKY.

*Publishing House "Naukova Dumka" (Scientific Thought):* Ul. Repina 3, Kiev; Dir. Y. A. KHRAMOV.

PERIODICAL PUBLICATIONS OF THE UKRAINIAN S.S.R. ACADEMY OF SCIENCES:

Dopovidi Akademii Nauk Ukrainskoi S.S.R. (*Reports of the Ukrainian S.S.R. Academy of Sciences, Series A and B; A—Physico-mathematical and technical sciences; B—geology, biophysics, chemistry and biology*); Geologichnyi Zhurnal (*Geological Journal*); Ukrainskii Khimicheskii Zhurnal (*Ukrainian Chemical Journal*); Teoreticheskaya i Eksperimentalnaya Khimiya (*Theoretical and Experimental Chemistry*); Ukrainskii Botanicheskii Zhurnal (*Ukrainian Botanical Journal*); Gidrobiologicheskii Zhurnal (*Hydriobiological Journal*); Ukrainskii Biokhimicheskii Zhurnal (*Ukrainian Biochemical Journal*); Fiziologicheskii Zhurnal (*Physiological Journal*); Mikrobiologicheskii Zhurnal (*Microbiological Journal*); Ekonomika Sovetskoi Ukrainy (*Economy of the Soviet Ukraine*); Radyanske Pravo (*Soviet Law*); Ukrainskii Istorichnii Zhurnal (*Ukrainian History Journal*); Radyanske Literaturoznavsto (*Soviet Literature Studies*); Narodna Tvorchist ta Etnografiya (*Peoples' Works and Ethnography*); Avtomatika (*Automation*); Kibernetika (*Cybernetics*); Prikladnaya Mekhanika (*Applied Mechanics*); Problemy Prochnosti (*Problems of Strength*); Ukrainskii Matematicheskii Zhurnal (*Ukrainian Mathematical Journal*); Ukrainskii Fizicheskii Zhurnal (*Ukrainian Journal of Physics*); Avtomaticheskaya Svarka (*Welding Journal*); Poroshkovaya Metallurgia (*Powder Metallurgy*); Fiziko-khimicheskaya Mekhanika Materialov (*Physical and Chemical Mechanics of Materials*); Neyrofiziologiya (*Neurophysiology*); Fiziologia i Biozkimiya Kulturnih Rastenii (*Physiology and Biochemistry of Cultivated Plants*); Vestnik Zoologii (*Zoological Reports*); Citologiya i Genetika (*Cytology and Genetics*); Filosofska Dumka (*Philosophical Thought*); Movoznavstvo (*Linguistics*); Visnyk Akademii Nauk Ukrainskoi S.S.R. (*Reports, Scientific and Organizational Problems*); Phisika nizhih temperatur (*Low Temperature Physics*); Upravljayushchiye sistemy i mashiny (*Management Control Systems and Computers*); Khimichesnaya Tehnologiya (*Chemical Technology*); Sinteticheskiye Almazy (*Synthetic Diamonds*).

**Uzbek S.S.R. Academy of Sciences:** Presidium: Ul. Kuibysheva 15, Tashkent; Pres. A. S. SADYKOV; Vice-Presidents S. N. RYZHOV, I. M. MUMINOV, S. K. SIRAJDINOV; Chief Learned Secretary M. K. NURMUKHAMEDOV; 48 members, 56 corresponding members.

*Department of Physical-Mathematical Sciences:* Academician-Secretary U. A. ARIFOV.

ATTACHED TO THE DEPARTMENT:

S. V. Starodubtsev Physical-Engineering Institute: Ul. Observatorskaya 85, Tashkent; Dir. S. A. AZIMOV.

Institute of Nuclear Physics: Tashkent Region, Ulugbek Settlement, Ordjonikidze District; Dir. U. GULYAMOV.

Astronomical Institute: Ul. Astronomicheskaya 33, Tashkent; Dir. V. P. SHCHEGLOV.

V. I. Romanovsky Institute of Mathematics: Astronomichesky tup. 11, Tashkent; Dir. M. S. SALAKHITDINOV.

Institute of Electronics: Ul. Observatorskaya 85, Tashkent; Dir. U. A. ARIFOV.

Institute of Cybernetics and Computing Centre: Ul. Volodarskogo 26, Tashkent; Dir. V. K. KABULOV.

*Department of Mechanics and Control Processes:* Academician-Secretary V. K. KABULOV.

Institute of Mechanics and Seismic Resistance of Constructions: Ul. Akademgorodok 26, Tashkent; Acting Dir. T. R. RASHIDOV.

Uzbek Institute of Energy and Electrification: Tashkent, Akademgorodok; Dir. Z. M. SALIKHOV.

*Department of Earth Sciences:* Academician-Secretary A. M. AKRAMKHODJAYEV; Learned Secretary D. M. SURGUTANOVA.

ATTACHED TO THE DEPARTMENT:

K. M. Abdullaev Institute of Geology and Geophysics: Ul. A. K. Sulaimanovoy 33, Tashkent; Dir. I. K. KHAMRABAEV.

Institute of Seismology: Ul. Observatorskaya 85; Dir. G. MAVLYANOV.

Hydro-Geological Society "Tukan": Tashkent, Ul. Morozova 64.

Institute of Geology, Oil and Gas Deposits: Tashkent, Ul. Rustaveli 114; Dir. A. M. AKRAMKHODZHAEV.

*Department of Chemical-Technological Sciences:* Academician-Secretary M. N. NABIEV.

ATTACHED TO THE DEPARTMENT:

Institute of Chemistry: Akademgorodok, Ul. Cherdantseva 19, Tashkent; Dir. K. S. AKHEMEDOV.

Institute of Botanical Chemistry: Akademgorodok, Ul. Cherdantseva 19, Tashkent; Dir. S. Y. YUNUSOV.

*Department of Biological Sciences:* Tashkent, Ul. Gogolya 70; Academician-Secretary S. K. YULDASHEV.

ATTACHED TO THE DEPARTMENT:

Institute of Experimental Plant Biology: Lunacharskoe chaussée, Akademgorodok, Tashkent Region; Dir. A. A. ABDULLAEV.

Institute of Botany: Lunacharskoe chaussée, Akademgorodok, Tashkent Region; Dir. D. K. SAIDOV.

Institute of Zoology and Parasitology: Ul. Sovietskaya 34, Tashkent; Dir. M. A. SULTANOV.

Botanical Garden: Ul. Abidovoiy 272, Tashkent; Dir. F. N. RUSANOV.

Section of Microbiology: Lunacharskoe chaussée, Akademgorodok, Tashkent; Dir. A. M. MUZAFAROV.

Institute of Biochemistry: Taskhent Region, Ulukbek; Dir. D. K. Khamidov.

Institute of Physiology: Tashkent, Zhukovski per. 47; Dir. Z. I. TURSUNOV.

*Department of Philosophy, Economics and Law:* Tashkent, Ul. Gogolya 70; Academician-Secretary O. B. DZHAMALOV.

ATTACHED TO THE DEPARTMENT:

Institute of Economics: Tashkent, Ul. Gogolya 70; Dir. I. I. ISKANDEROV.

*Department of History, Linguistics and Literature:* Tashkent, Ul. Gogolya 70; Academician-Secretary M. K. NURMYKHAMEDOV.

ATTACHED TO THE DEPARTMENT:

Institute of History: Tashkent, Ul. Gogolya; Dir. M. A. AKHUNOVA.

Institute of Archaeology: Samarkand, Ul. Engelsa 56; Dir. A. ASKAROV.

A. S. Pushkin Institute of Literature and Linguistics: Tashkent, Ul. Gogolya 70; Dir. S. S. SHAARDURAKHMANOV.

Navoi Literature Museum: Tashkent, Ul. Navoi 55; Dir. K. SULEIMANOV.

Museum of History of the Uzbek People: Tashkent, Ul. Kuybysheva 15; Dir. N. S. SADYKOVA.

Complex Institute of Natural Sciences: Nukus, Ul. Gorkogo 179-a; Dir. M. TADZHITDINOV.

PERIODICAL PUBLICATIONS OF THE UZBEK ACADEMY OF SCIENCES:

Doklady Akademii Nauk Uzbekskoi S.S.R. (*Reports of the Uzbek S.S.R. Academy of Sciences*); Uzbekskii Biologicheskii Zhurnal (*Uzbek Biological Journal*); Uzbekskii Geologicheskii Zhurnal (*Uzbek Geological Journal*); Uzbekskii Khimicheskii Zhurnal (*Uzbek Chemical Journal*); Obshchestvennie Nauk v Uzbekistane (*Social Sciences in Uzbekistan*); Izvestiya Akademii Nauk Uzbekskoi S.S.R. (*Bulletins of the Uzbek S.S.R. Academy of Sciences*): Physical and Mathematical Sciences, Engineering Sciences; Geliotekhnica (*Helio Engineering*); Khimiya Prirodnykh Soedinenii (*Chemistry of Natural Compounds*); Uzbek Tili va Adabieti (*Uzbek Language and Literature—in Uzbek*); Fan va Turmush (*Life and Science—in Uzbek*).

## OTHER ACADEMIES

### ALL-UNION V.I. LENIN ACADEMY OF AGRICULTURAL SCIENCES

BOLSHOI KHARITONEVSKY PER. 21,
B-78 MOSCOW 107078
Founded 1929.

The Academy supervises 27 research institutes and many regional experimental and selection stations, laboratories, dendraria and arboreta.

*President:* P. P. VAVILOV.
*Vice-Presidents:* A. A. SOZINOV, I. S. SHATILOV, V. D. PANNIKOV, L. K. ERNST.
*Academician-Secretary of the Department of Plant Production and Selection:* A. V. PUKHALSKY (acting).
*Academician-Secretary of the Department of Arable Farming and the Use of Agricultural Chemicals:* N. P. PANOV.
*Academician-Secretary of the Department of Plant Protection:* Y. N. FADEYEV.

*Academician-Secretary of the Veterinary Department:* V. P. SHISHKOV.
*Academician-Secretary of the Department of Livestock Production:* A. P. KALASHNIKOV.
*Academician-Secretary of the Department of Mechanization and Electrification of Agriculture:* G. M. BUZENKOV (acting).
*Academician-Secretary of the Department of Hydraulic Engineering and Land Reclamation:* B. B. SHUMAKOV.
*Academician-Secretary of the Department of Forestry and Forest Reclamation:* V. N. VINOGRADOV.
*Academician-Secretary of the Department of Economics and Management of Agricultural Production:* A. A. NIKONOV.
*Chief Learned Secretary of the Presidium:* P. I. SUSDIKO.

### MEMBERS:

ALEXANDROV, N. P., Economics
ALIYEV, G. A., Zootechnics
ALPATYEV, A. V., Vegetable Breeding and Seed Production
ALSMIK, P. I., Potato Breeding
ANDREYEV, N. G., Meadow Management
ANUCHIN, N. P., Forestry
ARTAMONOV, K. F., Hydro-engineering
BALAYEV, L. G., Hydro-engineering
BARANOV, P. A., Agrochemistry
BARAYEV, A. I., Arable Farming
BELENKY, N. G., Animal Physiology and Biochemistry
BOGDANOV, G. A., Livestock Management
BREZHNEV, D. D., Plant Growing
BUDIN, K. Z., Plant Growing
BUDZKO, I. A., Electrification of Agricultural Production
BUKASOV, S. M., Potato Selection
BUZANOV, I. F., Plant Physiology
BUZENKOV, G. M., Mechanization in Farming
CHEREKAYEV, A. V., Livestock Production
DANILENKO, I. A., Animal Husbandry
DMITROCHENKO, A. P., Livestock Nutrition
DOLGUSHIN, D. A., Agrobiology, Crop Selection
DUNIN, M. S., Phytopathology
EICHFELD, I. G., Plant Growing
ERNST, L. K., Livestock Management
FADEYEV, Y. N., Phytopathology
GALEYEV, G. S., Seed Cultivation
GARKAVY, P. F., Selection, Genetics
GLADENKO, I. N., Pharmacology
GLUSHCHENKO, I. E., Plant Genetics, Selection
GONCHAROV, P. L., Plant Production and Breeding
GORIN, V. T., Livestock Management
GREBEN, L. K., Livestock Management
IMAMALIYEV, A., Agrochemistry
KALASHNIKOV, A. P., Animal Nutrition
KARPENKO, A. N., Mechanization in Farming
KASHTANOV, A. N., Arable Farming
KAZMIN, G. T., Plant Growing, Selection
KHADZHINOV, M. I., Plant Selection
KHOKHLOV, I. M., Mechanization of Agriculture
KIRICHENKO, F. G., Cereals Selection
KONAREV, V. G., Plant Production
KORNEYEV, N. A., Radiobiology
KOSHKIN, L. N., Mechanization
KOVALENKO, Y. R., Veterinary Microbiology
KUBYSHEV, V. A., Agricultural Machinery Construction
KUVATOV, R. Y., Agricultural Economics and Management
KULAKOVSKAYA, T. N., Agrochemistry
KYASHKOV, V. M., Mechanization in Farming
LADAN, P. E., Zootechnics
LIKHACHEV, N. V., Veterinary Microbiology, Virology
LISTOV, P. N., Electrification
LOBANOV, P. P., Agricultural Economics
LOZA, G. M., Economics and Production
LUCHINSKY, N. D., Agricultural Machinery
LUKINOV, I. I., Agricultural Economics
MALTSEV, T. S., Arable Farming
MAMYTOV, A. M., Soil Science
MELEKHOV, I. S., Forestry
METREVELY, V. I., Electrification in Farming
MILOVANOV, V. K., Animal Breeding Biology
MIRAKHMEDOV, S., Cotton Breeding
MIRTSKHULAVA, T. E., Hydro-engineering

MOZGOV, I. E., Pharmacology
MUKHAMEDGALIEV, F. M., Zootechnics
MUROMTSEV, G. S., Plant Physiology, Microbiology
NEUNYLOV, B. A., Agrochemistry and Rice Production
NIKOLAYEV, A. I., Sheep Breeding
NIKONOV, A. A., Agricultural Economics and Production
OLSHANSKY, M. A., Agrobiology and Plant Selection
PANNIKOV, V. D., Agrochemistry
POLYAKOV, A. A., Veterinary Hygiene
PRISHCHEP, L. G., Farm Electrification
PUKHALSKY, A. V., Grain Selection
RABOCHEV, I. S., Land Reclamation
REMESLO, V. N., Plant Selection
ROSTOVTSEV, N. F., Zootechnics
RUDAKOV, G. M., Mechanization in Farming
RUKHKYAN, A. A., Genetics
RUNCHEV, M. S., Mechanization in Farming
SABLIKOV, M. V., Theory of Agricultural Machines
SERGEYEV, S. S., Statistics
SEVERNEV, M. M., Mechanization in Farming
SHATILOV, I. S., Agronomy
SHEVCHENKO, A. S., Plant Growing
SHISHKOV, V. P., Veterinary Pathology
SHMANENKOV, N. A., Animal Biochemistry
SHUMAKOV, B. A., Irrigation
SINYUKOV, M. I., Agricultural Economics and Management
SKOROPANOV, S. G., Agronomy
SMETNEV, S. I., Poultry Breeding
SOBOLEV, S. S., Pedology, Land Cultivation
SOKOL, P. F., Plant Production
SOKOLOV, B. P., Maize Selection
SOLNTSEV, K. M., Farm Animal Nutrition
SOZINOV, A. A., Crop Breeding
SUSIDKO, P. I., Entomology
SVIRIDOV, A. A., Epizoology
TIKHONOV, V. A., Agricultural Economics
TSITSIN, N. V., Botany, Selection
TURBIN, N. V., Plant Genetics
URBAN, V. P., Epizootiology
VANAG, Y. F., Economics and Management of Agricultural Production
VARUNTSYAN, I. S., Agrobiology, Cotton Selection
VASILENKO, I. F., Agricultural Machinery
VASILENKO, P. M., Agricultural Machinery
VAVILOV, P. P., Plant Production
VINOGRADOV, V. N., Forestry
VLASYUK, P. A., Agrophysiology, Agrochemistry, Pedology
VOLODARSKY, N. I., Plant Production
VSYAKIKH, A. S., Livestock Management
YEGOROV, V. V., Soil Science
YULDASHEV, S. K., Plant Physiology
ZYKOV, Y. D., Arable Farming and Use of Agricultural Chemicals

### CORRESPONDING MEMBERS:

ABUGALIEV, I., Genetics
AFENDULOV, K. P., Agronomy, Agrochemistry, Plant Physiology
AGABEILY, A. A., Livestock Management
AKMALKHANOV, S., Livestock Management
ALBENSKY, A. V., Forestry Melioration
ALESHIN, E. P., Rice
ALIMUKHAMEDOV, S., Agronomy
ALSHINBAYEV, M. R., Mechanization in Farming
ARKHANGELSKY, N. N., Entomology
ATABEKOV, I. G., Molecular Biology
BOBROV, L. G., Agronomy, Horticulture
BOYEV, V. R., Economy
BONDARENKO, N. F., Soil Physics, Hydroengineering
BONDARENKO, N. V., Entomology
BUDBITIS, A. I., Agronomy
BUKSHTYNOV, A. D., Forestry
BULAVAS, I. I., Cereals Selection
BUZILOV, Y. T., Agricultural Production Management
CHAMUKHA, M. D., Livestock Management
CHERKASHCHENKO, I. I., Livestock Management
DMITRIYEV, N. G., Farm Animal Reproduction
DOLGILEVICH, M. I., Forest Soil Science, Soil Conservation, Agricultural Forest Reclamation
DOLGOV, I. A., Mechanization
DOROFEYEV, V. F., Plant Breeding
DRUZHININ, N. I., Hydrology

## ACADEMIES — UNION OF SOVIET SOCIALIST REPUBLICS

DZHALILOV, K. M., Economics and Management of Agricultural Production
EISNER, F. F., Zootechnics
FILEV, D. S., Plant Growing
GADZHIYEV, Y. G., Helminthology
GEORGIYEVSKY, V. I., Physiology and Biochemistry of Farm Animals
GORSHENIN, K. P., Pedology
GRIGORIEV, N. G., Livestock Management and Animal Biochemistry
GROM-MAZNICHEVSKY, L. I., Mechanization
KALINENKO, I. G., Cereal Breeding
KALININA, I. P., Fruit Breeding and Seed Production
KAZIMIROV, N. I., Forestry
KHLEBUTIN, E. B., Economics of Socialist and World Agriculture
KHYDAIKULIYEV, A., Agronomy
KLEIMENOV, N. I., Livestock Nutrition
KLETSKY, L. M., Management of Agricultural Production
KLIMASHEVSKY, E. L., Plant Physiology
KNIGA, M. I., Dairy Farming
KONDRATIEV, R. B., Plant Production
KONKIN, Y. A., Management and Maintenance of Agricultural Machinery
KORENKOV, D. A., Agrochemistry
KOTOV, V. T., Epizootology
KOVALSKY, V. V., Biochemistry
KOZLOVSKY, V. G., Zootechnics
KRAMAROV, V. S., Mechanization
KRASNOV, V. S., Mechanization in Animal Husbandry
KRASOTA, V. F., Livestock Breeding
KULESKO, I. I., Epizootology
KURILOV, N. V., Animal Physiology
KUZMENKO, M. V., Agronomy, Selection
LAZAUSKAS, J. V., Plant Breeding
LISTOPAD, G. E., Mechanization of Agriculture
LUPASHKY, M. F., Plant Growing
MAKSUMOV, A. N., Agriculture
MALINOVSKY, B. N., Plant Selection
MANNANOV, N. M., Cotton Production
MARTYNENKO, I. I., Electrification of Agriculture
MEDEUBEKOV, K. I., Zootechnics
MELNICHENKO, A. N., Darwinism, Ecology, Apiculture
MILASHCHENKO, N. Z., Arable Farming
MILOSERDOV, V. V., Agricultural Economics
MINEYEV, V. G., Agrochemistry
MIRZAYEV, M. M., Agronomy
MOISEYEV, M. I., Economics of Agriculture
MOSHKOV, B. S., Plant Physiology
MOZHIN, V. P., Planning
MUKHAMEDOV, A. M., Hydrotechnics
MUKHAMEDZHANOV, S. M., Hydrogeology and Land Reclamation
MURASHKO, A. I., Hydraulics
MUSIIKO, A. S., Agrobiology
MUSTAKIMOV, R. G., Non-infectious diseases
NAZARENKO, V. I., World Agriculture
NAZIROV, N. N., Physiology and Radiobiology
NERPIN, S. V., Pedology
NESTEROV, Y. S., Biology and Fruit Crops Breeding
NETTEVICH, E. D., Selection and Seed Production of Grain Crops
NOVIKOV, Y. F., Mechanization in Farming
NOVOZHILOV, K. V., Entomotoxicology
ONUFRIYEV, V. P., Virology
ORLOV, I. V., Helminthology
OZOLIN, G. P., Forestry
PALFY, F. Y., Physiology and Biochemistry
PANOV, N. P., Soil Science, Agrochemistry
PAVLOVSKY, E. S., Forest Reclamation
PERESYPKIN, V. F., Plant Pathology and Immunity
POGORELY, L. V., Mechanization in Farming
PUCHKOV, Y. M., Plant Breeding
POGOSYAN, S. A., Viticulture Selection
RASHIDOV, N., Mechanization in Farming
RAZUMOV, V. I., Plant Physiology
ROCHEV, P. A., Zootechnics
ROMANENKO, I. N., Agricultural Economy
RUNOV, B. A., Electrification in Farming
RYZHOV, S. N., Cotton Growing, Soil Science
SIDOROV, M. I., Arable Farming
SHIPILOV, V. S., Obstetrics and Gynaecology
SHKHVATSABAYA, G. Y., Mechanization of Agriculture
SOBKO, A. A., Agronomy
SUBBOTOVICH, A. S., Viticulture
SYURIN, V. N., Virology
SYROYECHKOVSKY, E. E., Animal Ecology
TARAKANOV, G. I., Biology of Vegetables, Vegetable Production under Glass
TSAMUTALI, A. S., Agricultural Economics and Management
TULUPNIKOV, A. I., Economics and Management of Production
TYUTYUNNIKOV, A. I., Agronomy and Field Management
VALDMAN, E.-A. K., Veterinary Science
VARENITSA, E. T., Selection, Plant Growing
VERNIGOR, V. A., Livestock Management
YARNYKH, V. S., Microbiology
YURCHISHIN, V. V., Statistics and Economic Analysis
ZABRODIN, V. A., Epizoology
ZININ, T. G., Mechanization in Cotton Growing
ZVEREVA, G. B., Veterinary Science

### FOREIGN CORRESPONDING MEMBERS:

ÅKERBERG, E. H. (Sweden)
ALEXANDER, D. E. (U.S.A.)
BAKR, M. A. (Egypt)
BARREIRO, F. D. (Cuba)
BLAXTER, K. L. (U.K.)
BORLAUG, N. (Mexico)
BOROEVICH, S. C. (Yugoslavia)
BRATANOV, K. (Bulgaria)
BUSTARRET, J. (France)
CLAUSEN, H. (Denmark)
COOKE, G. W. (U.K.)
DASKALOV, K. (Bulgaria)
DAVIDESCU, D. (Romania)
DE VILMORIN, R. (France)
DE WIT, C. (Netherlands)
DOBZHANSKY, B. (Poland)
FOWDEN, L. (U.K.)
FROIER, K. (Sweden)
JIOSAN, N. (Romania)
KIHARA, H. (Japan)
KLECZKA, A. (Czechoslovakia)
KUDRNA, K. (Czechoslovakia)
LANG, G. (Hungary)
LO DSUN-LO (China, People's Republic)
MAGLIANI, C. (Italy)
NAWROCKI, S. (Poland)
OBREJANU, G. (Romania)
OGG, W. G. (U.K.)
PAL, B. P. (India)
PIENIANZEK, S. A. (Poland)
RAJKI, S. (Hungary)
ROTE, K. (German Democratic Republic)
RÜBENSAM, E. (German Democratic Republic)
SAVICH, R. (Yugoslavia)
SHEBESKY, L. H. J. (Canada)
SOMOS, A. (Hungary)
STOEV, K. D. (Bulgaria)
STUBBE, H. (German Democratic Republic)
SWAMINATHAN, M. S. (India)
SWENTOHOWESKY, B. (Poland)
TAMASI, I. (Hungary)
TOYVGO, T. (Mongolia)
TRIFUNOVICH, V. (Yugoslavia)
TZIN SHAN-BAO (China, People's Republic)
UY DA-FU (China, People's Republic)
VÖRINEN, J. E. (Finland)
VRTJAK, O. J. (Czechoslovakia)
WATSON, I. A. (Australia)
WITTWER, C. H. (U.S.A.)

### REGIONAL DEPARTMENTS

*Southern Department:* 46 Ul. Lenina, 30-Kiev 252000; Chair. G. A. BOGDANOV.

*Siberian Department:* Nauchny gorodok, Novosibirsk 633128; Chair. A. N. KASHTANOV.

*Non-Black Soil Zone of the R.S.F.S.R. Department:* 32 Sovetsky bulvar, Pushkin, Leningrad 190000; Chair. V. M. KRYAZHKOV.

*Western Department:* 96 Ul. Knorina, 49-Minsk 220049; Sec. M. M. SEVERNEV.

*Eastern Department:* 1 Ul. Mira, 91-Alma Ata 480091; Chair. K. U. MEDEUBEKOV (acting).

*Transcaucasian Department:* 14 Ul. Chelyuskintsev, 12-Tbilisi 380012; Sec. I. M. KHOKHLOV.

*Central Asian Department:* 1 Ul. Abduly Tukayeva, Tashkent 700000; Chair. S. K. YULDASHEV.

## RESEARCH INSTITUTES

*Department of Plant Production and Breeding:*

**N. I. Vavilov All-Union Research Institute of Plant Industry:** 44 Ul. Hertsena, Tsentr, Leningrad 190000; Dir. Acad. V. F. DOROFEYEV.

**All-Union Plant Breeding and Genetics Institute:** 3 Ovidiopolskaya Doroga, B-36, Odessa 270036; Dir. L. K. SECHNYAK.

**Mironovsky Research Institute of Wheat Breeding and Seed Production:** P/O Mironovka, Kievskaya oblast 256816; Dir. Acad. V. N. REMESLO.

**All-Union Maize Research Institute:** 14 Ul. Dzerzhinskogo, 27-Dnepropetrovsk 320027; Dir. V. S. TSIKOV.

**All-Union Legumes and Pulse Crops Research Institute:** P/O Streletskoye, Orel 303112; Dir. N. M. CHEKALIN.

**V. S. Pustovoit All-Union Oil-Bearing Crops Research Institute:** 17 Ul. Filatova, 38-Krasnodar 350038; Dir. N. I. DVORYADKIN.

**All-Union Rice Research Institute:** Pos. Belozerny, Dinskoi rayon, Krasnodarsky krai 353204; Dir. E. P. ALYOSHIN.

**All-Union Research Institute of Applied Molecular Biology and Genetics:** 23 Ul. Vucheticha, A-206, Moscow 125206; Dir. Acad. N. V. TOURBIN.

**State Nikitsky Botanical Gardens** Yalta 334267, Crimea; Dir. E. F. MOLCHANOV.

**I. V. Michurin Central Laboratory of Genetics:** Michurinsk 393740, Tambovskaya oblast; Dir. G. A. KURSAKOV.

*Department of Arable Farming and Use of Agricultural Chemicals:*

**D. N. Pryanishnikov All-Union Research Institute of Fertilizers and Agropedology:** 31 Ul. Pryanishnikova, A-8 Moscow 125008; Dir. V. G. MINEYEV.

**V. V. Dokuchaev Institute of Soil Science:** 7 Pyzhevsky per., Zh-17 Moscow 109017; Dir. V. V. YEGOROV.

**All-Union Research Institute of Grain Farming:** P/O Shortandy, Shortandinsky rayon 474070, Tselinogradskaya oblast; Dir. Acad. A. I. BARAYEV.

**Agrophysical Research Institute:** 14 Grazhdansky prospekt, K-220 Leningrad 194220; Dir. I. B. USKOV.

**All-Union Research Institute of Agricultural Microbiology:** 3 Shosse Podbelskogo, Pushkin, Leningrad 188620; Dir. O. A. BERESTETSKY.

**All-Union Research Institute of Soil Erosion Control:** 70-b Ul. Karla Marksa, 4-Koursk 305004; Dir. D. E. VANIN.

*Department of Plant Protection:*

**All-Union Research Institute of Plant Protection:** 3 Shosse Podbelskogo, Pushkin, Leningrad 188620; Dir. K. V. NOVOZHILOV.

**All-Union Research Institute of Biological Methods of Plant Protection:** 7 Poltavskoye shosse, 31-Kishinev 277031; Dir. V. T. VOINYAK (acting).

*Department of Livestock Production:*

**All-Union Research Institute of Animal Husbandry:** Pos. Dubrovitsy, Podolsky rayon, Moskovskaya oblast 142012; Dir. Acad. K. M. SOLNTSEV.

**All-Union Research Institute of Farm Animal Physiology and Biochemistry:** Borovsk 249010, Kaluzhskaya oblast; Dir. Acad. V. I. GEORGIYEVSKY.

**All-Union Research Institute of Livestock Breeding and Genetics:** 55-a Moskovskoye shosse, Pushkin, Leningrad 188620; Dir. M. M. LEBEDEV.

*Department of Veterinary Science:*

**All-Union Institute of Experimental Veterinary Science:** Kuzminki, Zh-472 Moscow 109472; Dir. Acad. G. F. KOROMYSLOV.

**K. I. Skryabin All-Union Institute of Helminthology:** 28 B. Cheremushkinskaya, M-259 Moscow 117259; Dir. Acad. V. S. YERSHOV.

**All-Union Research Institute of Veterinary Entomology and Arachnology:** 2 Ul. Institutskaya, 16-Tumen 625016; Dir. V. Z. YAMOV.

*Department of Mechanization and Electrification in Farming:*

**All-Union Research Institute for Mechanization of Agriculture:** 5, 1st Institutski, Zh-389 Moscow 109389; Dir. Acad. G. M. BUZENKOV.

**All-Union Research Institute for Electrification of Agriculture:** 2 1st Veshnyakovsky pr., Zh-456 Moscow 109456; Dir. Acad. V. I. SYROVATKA.

**Central Research, Design and Technological Institute of Mechanization and Electrification of Livestock Production in the Southern Zone of the U.S.S.R.:** Ostrov Khortitsa, 17-Zaporozhye 330017; Dir. Y. F. NOVIKOV.

*Department of Forestry and Agricultural Forest Reclamation:*

**All-Union Research Institute of Agricultural Forest Reclamation:** 39 Krasnopresnenskaya ul., 62-Volgograd 400062; Dir. G. P. OZOLIN.

*Department of Economics and Management of Agricultural Production:*

**All-Union Research Institute of Economics in Agriculture:** 35 Khoroshevskoye Shosse, Block 3, Moscow 123007; Dir. G. A. DOLGOSHEI.

*Department of Hydraulic Engineering and Land Reclamation:* Sec. B. B. SHUMAKOV.

PERIODICALS PUBLISHED BY THE ACADEMY:
*Vestnik selskokhozyaistvennoy nauki* (Agricultural Science News), *Doklady* (Proceedings), etc.

## ACADEMY OF ARTS OF THE U.S.S.R.
ULITSA KROPOTKINSKAYO 21, MOSCOW
Founded 1947.

The Academy developed from the older Russian Academy of Arts, founded in St. Petersburg in 1757. It comprises departments of painting, sculpture, graphic art, and decorative art; it has councils for the awarding of degrees, research in art education, art history and aesthetics, publishing, museums and decorative art and design.

*President:* N. V. TOMSKY.
*Vice-Presidents:* V. S. KEMENOV, F. P. RESHETNIKOV.
*Chief Learned Secretary:* P. M. SYSOEV.
*Members of the Presidium:* A. M. GRITZAJ, E. A. KIBRIK, D. A. SHMARINOV, F. V. RESHETNIKOV, V. S. KEMENOV, N. V. TOMSKY, M. K. ANIKUSHIN, D. A. NALBANDYAN, A. P. KIBALNIKOV, K. I. ROZDESTVENSKY, N. Y. TOMSKY.
*Academician-Secretary of the Department of Decorative Arts:* K. I. ROZDESTVENSKY.
*Academician-Secretary of the Department of Painting:* A. N. GRITZAJ.
*Academician-Secretary of the Department of Graphic Art:* D. A. SHMARINOV.

## ACADEMIES — UNION OF SOVIET SOCIALIST REPUBLICS

**MEMBERS:**

ALPATOV, M. V., Art Criticism
ANIKUSHIN, M. K., Sculpture
AZGUR, Z. I., Sculpture
BABURIN, M. F., Sculpture
BORODAI, V. S., Painting
BOZHYI, M. M., Painting
DZHAPARIDZE, U. M., Painting
EFIMOV, B. E., Graphic Art
GRIGORIEV, S. A., Painting
GRITSAY, A. M., Painting
KALNYNSH, E. F., Painting
KEMENOV, V. S., Art Criticism
KERBEL, L. E., Sculpture
KHANDZHYAN, G. S., Painting, Graphic Art
KIBALNIKOV, A. P., Sculpture
KIBRIK, E. A., Graphic Art
KORZHEV, G. M., Painting
KRYLOV, P. N., Painting, Graphic Art
KUGACH, Y. P., Painting
KUPRIYANOV, M. V., Painting, Graphic Art
KUZMINSKIS, I. M., Graphic Art
LEBEDEV, A. K., Art Criticism
LIFSHITS, M. A., Art Criticism
MOCHALSKY, D. K., Painting
MOISEENKO, E. E., Painting
MYLNIKOV, A. A., Painting
NALBANDYAN, D. A., Painting
NEPRINTSEV, Y. M., Painting
NISSKY, G. G., Painting
OKAS, E. K., Graphic Art
ORESHNIKOV, V. M., Painting
PINCHUK, V. B., Sculpture
PONOMAREV, N. A., Graphic Art
RESHETNIKOV, F. P., Painting
ROMADIN, N. M., Painting
SABSAY, P. V., Sculpture
SALACHOV, T. T., Painting
SHMARINOV, D. A., Graphic Art
SOKOLOV, N. A., Painting, Graphic Art
SYSOYEV, P. M., Art Criticism
TKACHEV, A., Painting
TKACHEV, S., Painting
TOMSKY, N. V., Sculpture
TOPURIDZEZ, V. B., Sculpture
TSIGAL, V., Sculpture
UGAROV, B., Painting
VEIMARN, B., Art Criticism
VIRSALADZE, S., Stage Design
YABLONSKAYA, T. N., Painting
ZARIN, I., Painting

**CORRESPONDING MEMBERS:**

ABDULLAYEV, M. G., Painting
AITIEV, F. A., Painting
AKHMEDOV, R. A., Painting
BARTENEV, I. A., Art Criticism
BOGDANOV, M. A., Stage Design
BOGDESKO, I. T., Graphic Art
BONDARENKO, P. I., Sculpture
BRIEDIS, A. Y., Sculpture
BRODSKAYA, L. I., Painting
BUKOVSKY, L. V., Sculpture
CHUBARYAN, G. G., Sculpture
DEKHTEREV, B. A., Graphic Art
DEREGUS, M. G., Painting, Graphic Art
DUBINOVSKY, L. I., Sculpture
EINMANN, E. Y., Graphic Art
ELDAROV, O. G., Sculpture
EPIPHANOV, G. D., Graphic Art
FILATCHEV, O., Painting
FOMIN, P., Painting
GAPONENKO, T. G., Painting
GOLOVNITSKY, L., Sculpture
GONCHAROV, A. D., Graphic Art
GORODETZKY, V. M., Decorative Arts
GRIGORASHCHENKO, L. P., Painting, Graphic Art
ILTNER, E. K., Painting
IVANOV, V., Painting
JOKUBONIS, G. H., Sculpture
KLYCHEV, I., Painting
KOBULADZE, S. S., Painting, Graphic Art
KOKORIN, A. V., Graphic Art
KOMOV, O. K., Sculpture
KONSTANTINOV, F. D., Graphic Art
KUZMIN, N. V., Graphic Art
LANGINEN, L. F., Sculpture
LAPIN, A. G., Painting
LEBEDEV, P. I., Art Criticism
LEONOV, P. V., Decorative Art
LEVITIN, A. P., Painting
LIBEROV, A. N., Painting
LOKCHOVININ, Y., Sculpture
LOPUKHOV, A. M., Painting
MAMEDOV, T. G., Sculpture
MERABISHVILY, K. M., Sculpture
MINAEV, V. N., Graphic Art
NECHITAILO, V. K., Painting
NERODA, G. V., Sculpture
OSIPOV, A. N., Painting
PAVLOVSKY, B. V., Art Criticism
PLENKIN, B. A., Sculpture
ROZHDESTVENSKY, K. I., Decorative Art
RUKAVISHNIKOV, J., Sculpture
RYABININ, N. L., Sculpture
RYAUZOV, B Y., Painting
SAMSONOV, M. A., Painting
SAVITSKY, M. A., Painting
SEREBRYANY, I. A., Painting
SHATALIN, V., Painting
SHCERBAKOV, B., Paintng
SHUSHKANOV, D., Appliied Art
SIDOROV, V., Painting
SOIJFERTIS, V. V., Graphic Art
SOKOLOVA, N. I., Art Criticism
STAMOV, V. G., Sculpture
SVESHNIKOV, D. K., Painting
TELZHANOV, K. T., Painting
TOTIBADZE, G. K.
TSIPLAKOV, V. G., Painting
VANSLOV, V. V., Art Criticism
VARES, I., Art Criticism
VASILYEV, A. P., Stage Design
VEREJSKY, O. G., Graphic Art
VETROGONSKY, V. A., Graphic Art
YAKUPOV, H., Painting
ZAGONEK, V. F., Painting
ZAITSEV, E. A., Painting
ZARDARYAN, O. M., Painting
ZHILINSKY, D., Painting
ZVERKOV, E. I., Painting

### INSTITUTES AND OTHER ESTABLISHMENTS

**Research Institute on Theory and History of Fine Arts:** Moscow, Ul. Kropotkina 21; Dir. A. K. LEBEDEV, M.SC.

**Moscow State Art Institute:** see under Educational Institutes.

**Leningrad I. E. Repin Institute of Arts:** see under Educational Institutes.

**Research Museum:** Leningrad, Universitetskaya nab. 17; laboratories and bronze-casting studios; Dir. L. F. YABLOCHKINA.

## ACADEMY OF MEDICAL SCIENCES OF THE U.S.S.R.

UL. SOLYANKA 14, MOSCOW 109801

Founded 1944.

*President:* N. N. BLOKHIN.

*Vice-Presidents:* A. M. CHERNUKH, D.SC., A. S. PAVLOV, D.SC., S. S. DEBOV, D.SC.

*General Secretary:* G. I. SIDORENKO, D.SC.

*Members of the Presidium:* M. N. VOLKOV, D.SC., Orthopaedics, Traumatology; E. I. CHAZOV, D.SC., Therapy; V. I. TOTYAKOV, D.SC., Virology; A. P. ROMODANOV, D.SC., Neurosurgery; K. V. BUNIN, D.SC., Infectious Diseases; A. P. KOLESOV, D.SC., Surgery.

*Academician-Secretary of the Department of Clinical Medicine:* N. A. PREOBRAZHENSKY, D.SC., Oto-Rhino-Laryngology.

*Academician-Secretary of the Department of Medical and Biological Sciences:* N. A. YUDAEV, Biochemistry.

*Academician-Secretary of the Department of Hygiene, Microbiology and Epidemiology:* O. G. ANDZHAPARIDZE, D.SC., Virology.

*Chairman of the Siberian Department:* V. P. KAZNACHEYEV, D.SC., Therapy.

MEMBERS:

ADO, A. D., Pathological Physiology
ANDZHAPARIDZE, O. G., Virology
ANICHKOV, S. V., Pharmacology
AVTSYN, A. P., Pathological Anatomy
BARANOV, V. G., Endocrinology
BAROYAN, O. V., Epidemiology
BEKHTEREVA, N. P., Physiology
BELYAKOV, V. D., Epidemiology
BILIBIN, A. F., Infectious Diseases
BISYARINA, V. P., Paediatrics
BLOKHIN, N. N., Oncology, Surgery
BOCHKOV, N. P., Medical Genetics
BOGOLEPOV, N. K., Neuropathology
BOGUSH, L. K., Surgery of Lung Tuberculosis
BRAUNSTEIN, A. E., Biochemistry
BUNIN, K. V. Infectious Diseases
BURAKOVSKY, V. I., Cardiac Surgery
BURGASOV, P. N., Epidemiology
CHACHAVA, K. V., Obstetrics and Gynaecology
CHAZOV, E. I., Therapy
CHEBOTAREV, D. F., Therapy
CHERNIGOVSKY, V. N., Physiology
CHERNUKH, A. M., Pathological Physiology
CHUMAKOV, M. P., Virology
DEBOV, S. S., Biochemistry
ENGELHARDT, V. A., Biochemistry
FYDOROV, N. A., Pathological Physiology
GAUZE, G. F., Microbiology
GOLIKOV, S. N., Pathological Physiology
GOREV, N. N., Pathological Physiology
GORIZONTOV, P. D., Pathological Physiology
GROMASHEVSKY, L. V., Epidemiology
ILYIN, L. A., Radiation Hygiene
IOFFE, V. I., Microbiology
IVANOV, I. I., Biochemistry
IVANOV-SMOLENSKY, A. G., Pathological Physiology
KANEP, V. V., Social Hygiene and Health Administration
KARPOV, S. P., Microbiology, Epidemiology
KAZANCHEYEV, V. P., Therapy
KLIMOV, A. N., Biochemistry
KOLESNIKOV, I. S., Surgery
KOLESOV, A. P., Surgery
KOMAROV, F. I., Therapy
KOMAKHIDZE, M. E., Surgery
KOROLEV, B. A., Surgery
KOSYAKOV, P. N., Immunology
KOVANOV, V. V., Operational Surgery, Topographical Anatomy
KRASNOV, M. M., Ophthalmology
KRAYEVSKY, N. A., Pathological Anatomy
KROTKOV, F. G., Hygiene
KULAGIN, V. K., Pathological Physiology
KUPRIYANOV, V. V., Anatomy
KUZIN, M. I., Surgery
LAPIN, B. A., Comparative Pathology
LETAVET, A. A., Hygiene
LOPATKIN, N. A., Urology
LOPUKHIN, Y. M., Experimental Surgery
MALAYA, L. T., Therapy
MALINOVSKY, N. N., Surgery
MASHKOVSKY, M. D., Pharmacology
MEDVEDJ, L. I., Industrial Hygiene in Agricultural Production
MESHALKIN, E. N., Cardiac and Vascular Surgery
MINKH, A. A., Hygiene
MOROZOV, G. V., Psychiatry
NEGOVSKY, V. A., Pathological Physiology
NISEVICH, N. I., Paediatrics
OREKHOVICH, V. N., Biochemistry
PAVLOV, A. S., Radiology
PETROV, R. V., Immunogenetics
PETROVSKY, B. V., Surgery
POKROVSKY, A. A., Biochemistry
PREOBRAZHENSKY, N. A., Oto-Rhino-Laryngology
PUCHKOVSKAYA, N. A., Ophthalmology
ROMODANOV, A. P., Neurosurgery
RUSSINOV, V. S., Physiology
RYBAKOV, A. I., Stomatology
SARADJISHVILI, P. M., Neuropathology
SAVELYEV, V. S., Surgery
SAVITSKY, N. N., Therapy, Toxicology
SEREBROV, A. I., Oncology, Gynaecology
SEVERIN, S. E., Biochemistry
SHABAD, L. M., Experimental Oncology, Pathological Anatomy
SHMIDT, E. V., Neuropathology
SIDORENKO, G. I., General and Municipal Hygiene
SIROTININ, N. N., Pathological Physiology
SMIRNOV, E. I., Public Health Administration
SMOLYANNIKOV, A. V., Pathological Anatomy
SMORODINTSEV, A. A., Virology
SNEZHNEVSKY, A. V., Psychiatry
SOLDATOV, I. B., Oto-rhino-laryngology
SOLOVYEV, M. N., Epidemiology
SOLOVYEV, V. D., Virology
STRUCHKOV, V. I., Surgery
STRUKOV, A. I., Pathological Anatomy
STUDENIKIN, M. Y., Paediatrics
TAREYEV, E. M., Therapy
TIMOFEYEVSKY, A. D., Pathological Physiology, Experimental Oncology
TOPCHIBASHEV, M. A., Surgery
TOROPTSEV, I. V., Pathological Anatomy
TRAPEZNIKOV, N. N., Oncology
UGLOV, F. G., Surgery
VASILENKO, V. K., Therapy
VERSHILOVA, P. A., Microbiology
VESELKIN, P. N., Pathological Physiology
VOLKOV, M. V., Traumatology, Orthopaedics
VOTYAKOV, V. I., Virology
VYGODCHIKOV, G. V., Microbiology
YABLOKOV, D. D., Therapy
YANUSHKEVICHUS, Z. I., Therapy
YUDAEV, N. A., Biochemistry
ZAKUSOV, V. V., Pharmacology
ZEDGENIDZE, G. A., Roentgenology, Radiology
ZHDANOV, V. M., Virology
ZHUKOV-VEREZHNIKOV, N. N., Immunology, Microbiology
ZURABISHVILI, A. D., Psychiatry

CORRESPONDING MEMBERS:

ABIDOV, A. A., Immunology
ADRIANOV, O. S., Physiology
ALEXSANDROV, N. N., Oncology
AMOSOV, N. M., Surgery
ANTONOV, I. P., Neuropathology
ASHMARIN, I. P., Molecular Biology
ASKERKHANOV, R. P., Surgery
BADALYAN, L. O., Neuropathology
BAIROV, G. A., Children's Surgery
BELENKOV, N. Y., Physiology
BELYAYEV, I. I., Hygiene
BEREZIN, I. F., Surgery
BEREZOV, T. T., Biochemistry
BLOKINA, I. N., Microbiology
BOCHKOV, N. P., Medical Genetics
BOGDANOV, I. L., Infectious Diseases
BOGOVSKY, P. A., Experimental Oncology
BOLDYREV, T. E., Epidemiology
BONDAR, Z. A., Therapy
BREDIKIS, Y. Y., Surgery
CHAGIN, K. P., Parasitology
CHERKINSKY, S. N., Hygiene
DANILENKO, M. V., Surgery
DAVIDENKOVA, E. F., Medical Genetics
DEMIN, A. A., Therapy
DOLETSKY, S. Y., Surgery
DOMARADSKY, I. V., Microbiology
DROZDOV, S. G., Epidemiology of Viral Infections
DZAGUROV, S. G., Microbiology
DZHAVAD-ZADF-MIR-MAMED-DZHAVADOGLY, Urology
EROSHEVSKY, T. I. Ophthalmology
GASILIN, V. S., Therapy
GAVRILOV, O. K., Haematology and Blood Transfusion
GEORGIU, N. K., Paediatrics
GRITZIUK, A. I., Therapy
ISAKOV, Y. E., Paediatrics
ISHAKI, Y. B., Oto-rhino-laryngology
ISLAMBEKOV, R. K., Endocrinology
IVANOV, N. G., Hygiene
IVANOV, N. R., Paediatrics
KABANOV, B. D., Stomatology
KALNBERZ, V. K., Traumatology
KALYUZHNY, D. N., Municipal Hygiene
KARAKULOV, I. K., Epidemiology
KASATKIN, N. I., Physiology

Khakimova, S. K., Obstetrics, Gynaecology
Khananashvily, M. M., Physiology
Kharkevich, D. A., Pharmacology and Toxicology
Khechinashvili, S. N., Oto-Rhino-Laryngology
Khromov-Borisov, N. V., Chemistry of Medicine
Kibyakov, A. V., Physiology
Kipshidze, Paediatrics
Knorre, A. G., Embryology
Kochergin, I. G., Surgery
Kochetkov, N. K., Chemistry of Medicine
Kolosov, N. G., Neurohistology
Konovalov, A. N., Neurosurgery
Korzh, A. A., Orthopaedics and Traumatology
Krasnov, M. M., Ophthalmology
Kryzanovsky, G. N., Pathological Physiology
Kundiyev, Y. I., Hygiene and Occupational Diseases
Lisitsyn, Y. P., Social Hygiene and Health Administration
Likhachev, A. G., Oto-Rhino-Laryngology
Ljvov, D. K., Virology
Loginov, A. S., Therapy
Lukyanova, E. M., Paediatrics
Marshak, M. E., Physiology
Maruashvili, G. M., Parasitology, Tropical Medicine
Maxumov, D. N., Radiology
Mayevsky, M. M., Microbiology
Mazaev, P. N., Roentgenology
Megrabyan, A. A., Psychiatry
Merkulov, I. I., Ophthalmology
Mirrakhimov, M. M., Therapy
Misyuk, N. S., Neurology
Moroz, B. B., Radiation Pathophysiology
Morozov, V. M., Psychiatry
Moshkov, V. N., Curative Exercises
Moshkovsky, S. D., Parasitology, Epidemiology
Musabaev, I. K., Infectious Diseases
Namazova, A. A., Paediatrics
Nasonova, V. A., Rheumatology
Navashin, S. M., Antibiotics
Neifakh, S. A., Biochemistry
Nesterov, A. P., Ophthalmology
Nikiforov, V. N., Infectious Diseases
Nosov, S. D., Paediatrics
Novikov, Y. I., Obstetrics, Gynaecology
Obrosov, A. N., Physiotherapy
Ogarkov, V. I., Microbiology
Olsufyev, N. G., Microbiology, Parasitology
Ostroverkhov, G. Ye., Topographical Anatomy
Pankov, Y. A., Experimental Endocrinology
Pershin, G. N., Pharmacology, Chemotherapy
Peterson, B. E., Oncology
Petrov, B. D., History of Medicine
Petrov, V. I., Surgery
Pokrovsky, E. I., Infectious Diseases
Portugalov, V. V., Histochemistry
Prokofyeva-Belgovskaya, A. A., Experimental Genetics
Pytel, A. Y., Urology
Rokhlin, D. G., Roentgenology, Radiology
Romantzev, E. F., Biochemistry
Ryabov, G. A., Anaesthesiology and Reanimation
Saarma, J. M., Psychiatry
Samoilov, A. Y., Ophthalmology
Samsonov, M. A., Curative Nutrition
Sapin, M. R., Anatomy
Sarkisov, D. S., Pathological Anatomy
Savelieva, G. M., Obstetrics and Gynaecology
Sedov, K. R., Therapy
Serenko, A. F., Social Hygiene
Sergievsky, M. V., Physiology
Shabanov, A. M., Surgery
Shakhbazyan, G. K., Hygiene
Shamsiyev, S. S., Paediatrics
Shandala, M. G., General and Municipal Hygiene
Shaposhnikov, O. K., Dermatovenerology
Shapot, V. S., Biochemistry
Sharmanov, T. S., Food Hygiene
Shchelkunov, S. I., Histology
Shchelovanov, N. M., Physiology
Shebanov, F. V., Phthisiology
Shitskova, A. P., General and Municipal Hygiene
Shkhvatsabaya, I. K., Cardiology
Shmidt, A. A., Biochemistry
Shubladze, Antonina K., Virology
Shumakov, V. I., Transplantation
Shuvalova, E. P., Infectious Diseases
Smagin, V. G., Therapy
Sobakin, M. A., Physiology
Solovyev, G. M., Surgery
Speranskaya, E. N., Endocrinology
Strelin, G. S., Embriology, Histology
Sudakov, K. V., Physiology
Tabolin, V. A., Paediatrics
Talyzin, F. F., Biology, Parasitology
Tarasenko, Natalia Yu., Hygiene
Tentsova, A. I., Biopharmacy
Tereshin, I. M., Antibiotics
Timoshenko, L. V., Obstetrics and Gynaecology
Tkachenko, B. I., Physiology
Udintsev, G. N., Therapy
Umidova, Z. I., Therapy
Valdman, A. V., Pharmacology
Vantsiyan, E. N., Surgery
Vartanyan, M. E., Pathological Physiology
Vasiljev, N. V., Microbiology
Velichkovsky, B. T., Industrial Hygiene and Occupational Diseases
Vihert, A. M., Pathological Anatomy
Vinogradov, N. A., Public Health Administration
Volkova, O. V., Embryology
Vorobjov, E. I., Radiation Hygiene
Vorontsova, E. I., Hygiene
Voroshilova, M. K., Virology
Zaiko, N. N., Pathological Physiology
Zakhidov, A. Z., Hygiene
Zavodskaya, I. S., Pharmacology
Zazybin, N. I., Histology, Embryology
Zbarsky, I. B., Biochemistry
Zharikov, N. M., Psychiatry

Foreign Members:

Babics, A. (Hungary), Urology
Baumann, R. (German Democratic Republic), Therapy
Brecelij, B. (Yugoslavia), Surgery, Orthopaedics, Traumatology
Candau, M. G (Brazil), Organization of Health
DeBakey, M. (U.S.A.), Surgery
Eckhardt, S. (Hungary), Oncology
Hrbek, J. (Czechoslovakia), Neurology
Huan, Tsya-Sy (People's Republic of China), Surgery
Icic, D. (Yugoslavia), Immunology
Khanolkar, V. R. (India), Pathological Anatomy
Kraatz, H. (German Democratic Republic), Obstetrics Gynaecology
Kurylowicz, W. (Poland), Microbiology
Lepine, P. (France), Virology
Lwoff, A. (France), Virology
Lynen, F. (Federal Repub. of Germany), Biochemistry
Presno Albarran, J. A. (Cuba), Surgery
Puchlev, A. (Bulgaria), Therapy
Raska, K. (Czechoslovakia), Microbiology, Epidemiology
Rosen, S. (U.S.A.), Oto-Rhino-Laryngology
Rowiński, K. (Poland), Paediatrics
Siska, K. (Czechoslovakia), Surgery
Stary, O. (Czechoslovakia), Neurology
Slivinsky, M. (Poland), Surgery
Taslo, A. T. (Bulgaria), Therapy
Ton That Tung (Vietnam), Surgery
Valle, R. (Mexico), Orthopaedics

## RESEARCH INSTITUTES

**Department of Hygiene, Microbiology and Epidemiology:**

**All-Union Scientific Research Institute for the Investigation of New Antibiotics:** Moscow 119021, Pirogovskaya 11; Dir. G. F. Gauze.

**A. N. Sysin Institute of General and Municipal Hygiene:** Moscow 119883, Pogodinskaya ul. 10; Dir. G. I. Sidorenko.

**Institute of Industrial Hygiene and Occupational Diseases:** Moscow 105275, Budionovsky proezd 31, Dir. N. F. Izmerov.

**Institute of Nutrition:** Moscow 109240, Ustyinsky proezd 2/14; br. at Alma-Ata; Dir. V. A. Shaternikov.

**Institute of Poliomyelitis and Virus Encephalitis:** Moskovskaya oblast, Kievskoye chaussée, 27 Kilometr; Dir. S. G. Drozdov.

**D. I. Ivanovsky Institute of Virology:** Moscow 123098, Ul. Gamalei 16; Dir. V. M. Zhdanov, d.sc.

**N. F. Gamalei Institute of Epidemiology and Microbiology:** Moscow 123098, Ul. Gamalei 18; Dir. O. B. BAROYAN, D.SC.

**Institute of Immunology:** Moscow.

**Laboratory of Experimental Immunobiology:** Moscow 125315, Baltiyskaya ul. 8; Dir. N. N. ZHUKOV-VEREZHNIKOV.

**Department of Clinical Medicine:**

**All-Union Cardiological Research Centre:** Moscow 103142, Petroverigsky per. 10; Dir. E. I. CHAZOV.

**Cancer Research Centre:** Moscow 115164, Kashirskoye chaussée; Dir. N. N. BLOKHIN.

**Institute of Gerontology:** Kiev 252114, Vishgorodskaya ul. 67; Dir. D. F. CHEBOTAREV.

**Institute of Neurology:** Moscow 123367, Volokolamskoye chaussée 80; Dir. E. V. SHMIDT.

**Acad. N. N. Burdenko Institute of Neurosurgery:** Moscow 125047, Ul. Fadeyeva 5; Dir. A. N. KONOVALOV.

**Institute of Obstetrics and Gynaecology:** Leningrad 199164, Liniya Mendeleyeva 3; Dir. Y. I. NOVIKOV.

**Institute of Paediatrics:** Moscow 117296, Lomonosovsky prospekt 2/40; Dir. M. Y. STUDENIKIN.

**Institute of Psychiatry:** Moscow 113152, Zagorodnoye chaussée 2; Dir. A. V. SNEZHNEVSKY, D.SC.

**Institute of Medical Radiology:** Kaluga oblast, Obninsk, Ul. Koroleva 14; Dir. E. A. ZHERBIN.

**Institute of Rheumatism:** Moscow 103031, Petrovka 25; Dir. V. A. NASONOVA, D.SC.

**A. V. Vishnevsky Institute of Surgery:** Moscow 113093, Bolshaya Serpukhovskaya 27; Dir. M. I. KUZIN.

**A. L. Myasnikov Institute of Cardiology:** Moscow 103142, Petroverigsky per. 10; Dir. I. K. SHKHVATSABAYA, D.SC.

**Acad. Bakulev Institute of Cardiac and Vascular Surgery:** Moscow 117049, Leninsky prospekt 8; Dir. V. I. BURAKOVSKY.

**Laboratory of Transplantation of Organs and Tissues:** Moscow 129028, Boljshoi Nikolovorobinsky per. 7; Head V. V. KOVANOV.

**Department of Medical and Biological Sciences:**

**Scientific Research Laboratory of Allergology:** Moscow 117071, Leninsky prospekt 10; Dir. A. D. ADO, D.SC.

**Institute of Medical Genetics:** Moscow 115478, Kashirskoye chaussée 6-a; Dir. N. P. BOCHKOV.

**Institute of Brain Research:** Moscow 107120, Per. Obukha 5; Dir. O. S. ADRIANOV.

**Institute of Biological and Medical Chemistry:** Moscow 119117, Pogodinskaya 10; Dir. V. N. OREKHOVICH, D.SC.

**Institute of Experimental Medicine:** Leningrad, Ul. Acad. Pavlov 12; Dir. N. P. BEKHTEREVA.

**Institute of Experimental Endocrinology and Hormone Chemistry:** Moscow 117036, Ul. D. Ulyanova 11; Dir. N. A. JUDAEV.

**Institute of Human Morphology:** Moscow 117469, Ul. Tsyuryupy 3; Dir. A. P. AVTSYN, D.SC.

**Institute of Experimental Pathology and Therapy:** Sukhumi, Gora Trapetsiya, P.O. 66; Dir. B. A. LAPIN, D.SC.

**Institute of Pharmacology:** Moscow 125315, Baltiskaya ul. 8; Dir. V. V. ZAKUSOV, D.SC.

**Institute of General Pathology and Pathological Physiology:** Moscow 125315, Baltiyskaya ul. 8; Dir. A. M. CHERNUKH.

**Institute of Normal Physiology:** Moscow 103009, Karl-Marx prospect 18; Dir. K. V. SUDAKOV.

**Laboratory of Experimental Biological Models:** Moskovskaya oblast, P.O. Yurlovo; Dir. V. A. DUSHKIN.

**Laboratory of Experimental Physiology on Re-animation:** Moscow 104012, Ul. 25 Oktyabrya, 9; Dir. V.A. NEGOVSKY, D.SC.

**Laboratory of Enzymology:** Moscow 123242, Sadovo-Kudrinskaya ul. 3; Head S. S. DEBOV.

**Siberian Department:**

**Institute of Clinical and Experimental Medicine:** 630091 Novosibirsk, Ul. Yadrintsovskaya 14; Dir. Prof. V. P. KAZNACHEYEV.

**Institute of Physiology:** 630090 Novosibirsk, Ul. Zolotodolinskaya 101; Dir. M. A. SOBAKIN.

**Institute of Medical Problems of the North:** 660022 Krasnoyarsk, Ul. Partisana Zhelezniaka 1b; Dir. K. V. OREHOV.

**Institute of Complex Problems of Hygiene and Professional Diseases:** 654059 Novokuznetsk, Ul. Kutuzova 23; Dir. V. V. BESSONENKO.

**Department of International Scientific Relations of the Presidium:** Moscow 109801, Ul. Solyanka 14; Head S. S. DEBOV.

PERIODICAL PUBLISHED BY THE ACADEMY:
*Vestnik Akademii Meditsinskikh Nauk S.S.S.R.* (Herald of the U.S.S.R. Academy of Medical Sciences).

## ACADEMY OF PEDAGOGICAL SCIENCES OF THE U.S.S.R.

BOLSHAYA POLYANKA 58, 113095 MOSCOW M-95
Founded 1943.

The Academy is the leading scientific pedagogical institution in the U.S.S.R., bringing together the most prominent specialists in this field. The functions of the Academy are as follows: the scientific elaboration of general and special pedagogical problems, the history of pedagogics, aesthetic education, the theory and practice of physical training, psychology, defectology, curricular guides on methods in general educational schools, adult education, the planning of scientific work in pedagogics, co-ordination of activity of all the research institutions of the Soviet Union and training of scientific personnel in above mentioned subjects, school equipment and technical aids in education, the promotion of educational development in the country and dissemination of pedagogical knowledge among the people.

The Academy studies the theoretical problems of modern pedagogics, participates in the preparation of regulations concerning basic types of schools, recommendations on school networks and the elaboration of new curricula and projects.

*President:* Prof. V. N. STOLETOV.

*Vice-Presidents:* Prof. M. I. KONDAKOV, Prof. A. G. KHRIPKOVA, Prof. Y. K. BABANSKY.

*Chief Scientific Secretary:* Prof. I. F. PROTCHENKO.

*Academician Secretaries:* Prof. I. D. ZVEREV, Prof. A. A. BODALEV, Prof. S. Y. BATYSHEV, Prof. Y. K. BABANSKY.

*Members of the Presidium:* V. A. BURAVIKHIN, G. N. DZHIBLADZE, A. V. ZAPOROZHETS, V. V. IVASHIN, S. R. RADZHABOV, M. P. KASHIN, A. I. PISKUNOV, N. D. YARMACHENKO.

Library of 1,125,000 vols. including periodicals.

MEMBERS:

ARSENYEV, A. M., Pedagogics
BABANSKY, Y. K., Pedagogics
BATYSHEV, S. Y., Professional and Technical Education
BLAGOY, D. D., Literature
BODALYEV, A. A., Psychology
BUTSKUS, P. F., Chemistry
DANILOV, A. I., History
DAVYDOV, V. V., Psychology

## ACADEMIES

DZHIBLADZE, G. N., Philology
EPSTEIN, D. A., Chemistry
FABRIKANT, V. A., Physics
FRIEDENFELDS, I. J., Linguistics
GERASIMOV, S. A., Art Education
IRKAYEV, M. I., History
IVANOVICH, K. A., Pedagogics
IVASHIN, N. V., Literature
IZMAILOV, A. E., Pedagogics
KABALEVSKY, D. B., Art Education
KHRIPKOVA, A. G., Biology
KIRICHENKO, N. P., History
KOLMOGOROV, A. N., Mathematics
KOSTYUK, G. S., Psychology
KURBANOV, A. A., Philology
KUZIN, N. P., History
LIIMETS, H. I., Pedagogics
LORDKIPANIDZE, D. O., Pedagogics
MAKHMUTOV, M. I., Pedagogics
MAZURKEVICH, A. R., Philology
MEKHTI-ZADE, M. M. O., Pedagogics
MIKHALKOV, S. V., Literature
MONOSZON, E. I., Pedagogics
NAROROCHITSKY, A. L., History
NECHKINA, M. V., History
PETROVSKY, A. V., Psychology
PIDTYCHENKO, M. M., Pedagogics
PISKUNOV, A. I., Pedagogics
PROKOFYEV, M. A., Chemistry
PROTCHENKO, I. F., Philology
RADZHABOV, S. R., Pedagogics
SHANSKY, N. M., Philology
SHAPOVALENKO, S. G., Chemistry
STOLETOV, V. N., Pedagogics
TEKUCHEV, A. V., Russian Language
UDOVICHENKO, P. P., Geography
ZAPOROZHETZ, A. V., Psychology
ZUBOV, V. G., Physics
ZVERYEV, I. D., Biology

### CORRESPONDING MEMBERS:

ALEXEYEV, A. N., Pedagogics
ANTROPOVA, M. V., Physiology of Growth
ASKAROVA, M. A., Philology
ATUTOV, P. R., Professional and Technical Education
AZIZOV, A. A., Philology
BALTABAYEV, M. R., Pedagogics
BELOUSOV, V. D., Mathematics
BOBORYKIN, A. D., Political Economy
BOLTYANSKY, V. G., Mathematics
BROVIKOV, I. S., Mathematics
BURAVIKHIN, V. A., Physics
CHEPELYEV, V. I., Pedagogics
DARINSKY, A. V., Geography
DEMIDENKO, V. K., History
DUDNIKOV, A. V., Russian Language and Literature
DUMCHENKO, N. I., Professional and Technical Education
DZHILELYEV, M. A., Professional and Technical Education
ELKONIN, D. B., Psychology
FEDOSOV, I. A., History
FILONOV, T. N., Communist Education
GORESLAVSKY, S. I., Pedagogics
HENKEL, P. A., Botany
ILENKO, S. G., Russian Language
KALNBERZINA, A. M., Literature
KASHIN, M. P., Didactics
KHAMRAYEV, M. K., Physics
KHARLAMOV, I. F., Pedagogics
KINKULKIN, A. T., History
KIRABAYEV, S. S., Philology
KLIMOV, E. A., Psychology of Work
KOLESOVA, D. V., Physiology of High Nervous Activity
KOLTSOVA, M. A., Physiology of Higher Nervous Activity
KONDAKOV, M. I., Pedagogics
KONDRATENKOV, A. E., Pedagogics
KOOP, A. V., Pedagogics
KOSTOMAROV, V. G., Philology
KOZHEVNIKOV, E. M., Pedagogics

## UNION OF SOVIET SOCIALIST REPUBLICS

KOZHUKHOV, Y. V., History
KULAGIN, Y. A., Specialized Pedagogics
KUZMINA, N. V., Professional and Technical Education
LAZARUK, M. A., Specialized Pedagogics
LOMOV, B. F., Psychology
LVOV, B. R., Science Teaching Methods
MALKOVA, Z. A., Pedagogics
MATUSHKIN, S. E., Professional and Technical Education
MENCHINSKAYA, N. A., Psychology
MIROLYUBOV, A. A., Methods
MOSKALSKAYA, O. I., Philology
NATADZE, R. G., Psychology
NESTERENKO, A. D., Biology
OBIDOV, I. O., History
ONUSHKIN, V. G., Economics
PERYSHKIN, A. V., Physics
PINT, A. O., Pedagogics
PODDYAKOV, W. W., Psychology
PROSKURYAKOV, V. A., Professional and Technical Education
RAKHMANOV, I. V., Philology and Language
RAYATSKAS, V. I., Pedagogics
RAZUMOVSKY, V. G., Physics
SEMBAYEV, A. I., Pedagogics
SHAKHMAYEV, N. M., Didactics
SHARAPOV, G. V., Didactics
SHCHERBINA, V. R., Philology
SHCHUKIN, E. D., Physics
SHCHUKINA, G. I., Pedagogics
SHVARTSBURD, S. I., Mathematics
SKATKIN, M. N., Pedagogics
SOLOVYEV, A. I., Geography
SUNTSOV, N. S., Political Economy
TALYZINA, N. F., Psychology
TSVETKOV, L. A., Chemistry
USOVA, A. B., Physics
VERCHENKO, I. Y., Mathematics
VERZILIN, N. M., Biology
VISHNYAKOV, A. C., Pedagogics
VLASOVA, T. A., Specialized Pedagogics
VOITKO, V. I., Psychology
VOROBYEV, A. A., Physics
VORONIN, L. G., Physiology of Higher Nervous Activity
VORONTSOV-VELYAMINOV, B. A., Astronomy
YARMACHENKO, N. D., Pedagogics
ZINCHENKO, V. P., Psychology
ZVORYKIN, B. S., Physics

### RESEARCH INSTITUTES

**Scientific Research Institute of General Pedagogics:** Moscow, Ul. Pavla Korchagina 7; Dir. Z. A. MALKOVA.

**Scientific Research Institute of General Educational Problems:** Moscow, Pogodinskaya 8; Dir. G. N. FILONOV.

**Scientific Research Institute of Educational Methodology and Standards:** Moscow, Ul. Makarenko 5/16; Dir. M. P. KASHIN.

**Scientific Research Institute of General and Educational Psychology:** Moscow, Prospekt Marksa 20; Dir. Prof. V. V. DAVYDOV.

**Scientific Research Institute of Child and Pre-Adult Physiology:** Moscow, Pogodinskaya ul 8; Dir. A. G. KHRIPKOVA.

**Scientific Research Institute of Pre-School Education:** Moscow, Klimentovsky pereulok 1; Dir. Prof. A. V. ZAPOROZHETS.

**Scientific Research Institute of School Equipment and Technical Aids in Education:** Moscow, Pogodinskaya 8; Dir. Prof. S. G. SHAPOVALENKO.

**Scientific Research Institute of Art Education:** Moscow, Proezd Vladimirova 4; Dir. Prof. B. T. LIKHACHEV.

**Scientific Research Institute of Labour Education and Vocational Studies:** Moscow, Pogodinskaya ul. 8; Dir. N. P. SEMYKIN.

**Scientific Research Institute of Russian Language Instruction in National Schools:** Moscow, Pogodinskaya ul. 8; Dir. Prof. N. M. SHANSKY.

**Scientific Research Institute of Defectology:** Moscow, Pogodinskaya ul. 8; Dir. T. A. VLASOVA.

**Scientific Research Institute of General Adult Education:** Leningrad, Naberezhnaya Kutuzova 8; Dir. Prof. V. G. ONUSHKIN.

**Scientific Research Institute of Professional and Technical Education:** Kazan, Ul. Lenina 10; Dir. Prof. M. I. MAKHMUTOV.

PERIODICALS PUBLISHED BY THE ACADEMY:
*Sovietskaya Pedagogika*† (Soviet Pedagogics): monthly.
*Voprosy Psikhologii*† (Problems of Psychology): monthly.
*Semya i Shkola*† (Family and School): monthly.
*Defektologiya*† (Defective): every 2 months.

## LEARNED SOCIETIES

**All-Union Council of Scientific and Engineering Societies:** Moscow, Ul. Krzhizhanovscogo 20/30.
*Chairman:* A. Y. TSHLINSKY.
*Vice-Chairman:* V. G. SILUYANOV.
*Vice-President:* H. H. GRITSENKO.
*Learned Secretary:* V. F. ORANZHEREYEVA.

The Council unites and co-ordinates the activities of the following 21 scientific and engineering societies in different industries:

**Scientific and Engineering Society of Agriculture:** Moscow, Ul. Kirova 13; Chair. G. V. GULYAEV, D.SC.

**Scientific and Engineering Society of the Building Industry:** Moscow, Karetny ryad 10/8; Chair. T. T. TSEHENKO.

**D. I. Mendeleyev All-Union Chemical Society:** Moscow, Krivokolenny per. 12; Chair. Acad. S. I. VOLFKOVICH, D.SC.

**Scientific and Engineering Society of Ferrous Metallurgy:** Moscow, 2 Baumanskaya ul. 9/23; Chair. V. V. LEMPUTSKY.

**Scientific and Engineering Society of Flour-Grinding and Peeling Industries and Elevator Economy:** Moscow, Chistie prudy 12-a; Chair. Y. V. SHILKIN.

**Scientific and Engineering Society of the Food Industry:** Moscow, Kuznetsky most 19; Chair. L. Y. AUERMAN, D.SC.

**Scientific and Engineering Society of the Instrument Building Industry:** Moscow, pr. K. Marxa 17; Chair. V. V. KAZIBSKY.

**Scientific and Engineering Society of Light Industry:** Moscow, Ul. Vavilova 69; Chair. V. A. USENKO.

**Scientific and Engineering Society of the Machine Building Industry:** Moscow, Bolshoy Cherkassky per. 7; Chair. V. S. VASILIEV.

**Scientific and Engineering Society of Mining:** Moscow, Karetny ryad 10/18; Chair. KUZNETSOV.

**Scientific and Engineering Society of Municipal Economy and Motor Transport:** Moscow, Ul. Kuibysheva 4; Chair. K. K. KLOPOTOV.

**Scientific and Engineering Society of Non-Ferrous Metallurgy:** Moscow, Astrakhansky per. 1/15, Chair. V. V. BORODOJ.

**Scientific and Engineering Society of the Oil and Gas Industry:** Moscow, Ul. Kuibysheva 3/8; Chair. Y. V. ZAJTZEV.

**Scientific and Engineering Society of the Paper and Wood-Working Industry:** Moscow, Ul. 25 Oktyabrya, 8/1; Chair. N. N. CHISTYAKOV.

**Scientific and Engineering Society of Power Industry:** Leningrad, Stremyannaya ul. 10; Chair. Corr. Mem. N. N. KOVALEV.

**Scientific and Engineering Society of the Printing Industry and Publishing Houses:** Moscow, Volkov per. 7/9; Chair. A. P. RYBIN.

**A.S. Popov Scientific and Engineering Society of Radio Engineering and Electrical Communications:** Moscow, Ul. Herzena 10; Chair. Corr. Mem. V. I. SIFOROV, D.SC.

**Scientific and Engineering Society of the Railways:** Moscow, Ul. K. Marxa 11; Chair. A. T. GOLOVATY.

**A.N. Krylov Scientific and Engineering Society of the Shipbuilding Industry:** Leningrad, Ul. Dzerzhinskogo 10; Chair. P. P. PUSTYNTSEV.

**Scientific and Engineering Society of the Timber Industry and Forestry:** Moscow, Proezd Vladimirova 6; Chair. K. J. VORONITSYN.

**Scientific and Engineering Society of Water Transport:** Moscow, Staropansky per. 3; Chair. G. P. KOSTYLEV.

**Council of the U.S.S.R. Scientific Medical Societies:** Moscow, Rakhmanovsky per. 3.
*Chairman:* K. V. BUNIN.
*Chief Learned Secretary:* M. B. TABAKMAN.

**All-Union Scientific Medical Society of Physicians-Analysts:** Moscow, 2-d Botkinsky per. 5; Chair. A. S. PETROVA, M.SC.; Gen. Sec. R. L. MARTSUTEVSKAYA.

**All-Union Scientific Medical Society of Anatomists, Histologists and Embryologists:** Moscow, Mokhovaya ul. 11; Chair. V. V. KUPZIANOV.

**All-Union Scientific Medical Society of Anatomists-Pathologists:** Moscow, Ul. Shchepkina, 61/2; Chair. N. H. KRZEVSKY; Gen. Sec. G. G. AVTANDILOV.

**All-Union Scientific Medical Society of Cardiologists:** Moscow, Malaya Pirogovskaya ul. 1; Chair. P. E. LUKOMSKY, D.SC.

**All-Union Scientific Medical Society of Endocrinologists:** Moscow, Ul. Dm. Uliyanova 4; Chair. V. G. BARANOV; Gen. Sec. N. T. STARKOVA.

**All-Union Scientific Medical Society of Specialists in Medical Control and Exercise Medicine:** Moscow, Ploshchad Vosstaniya 1/2; Chair. V. N. MOSHKOV, D.SC.; Gen. Sec. H. T. ZHURAULEV.

**All-Union Scientific Medical Society of Forensic Medical Officers:** Moscow, Sadovaya-Triumfalnaya ul. 13; Chair. V. M. SMOLYANINOV, D.SC.; Gen. Sec. M. B. TABAKMAN.

**All-Union Scientific Medical Society of Gerontologists and Geriatrists:** Kiev, Vyshgorodskaya ul. 67; Chair. D. F. CHEBOTAREV, D.SC.

**All-Union Scientific Medical Society of Hygienists:** Moscow, Pogodinskaya ul. 10; Chair. F. G. KROTKOV, D.SC.; Gen. Sec. H. G. SUKHAREV.

**All-Union Scientific Society of History of Medicine:** Moscow, Ul. Obukha 12.

**All-Union I.I. Mechnikov Scientific Medical Society of Microbiologists, Epidemiologists and Infectionists:**

Moscow, Pogodinskaya ul. 6; Chair. V. M. ZHDANOV, D.SC.; Gen. Sec. S. G. DZAGUZOV.

**All-Union Scientific Medical Society of Neuropathologists and Psychiatrists:** Moscow, Ul. Kropotkinskaya 23; Gen. Sec. G. Y. LUKACHER.

**All-Union Scientific Medical Society of Neurosurgeons:** Moscow, Ul. Fadeeva 5; Chair. A. T. AZUTYUNOV; Gen. Sec. F. A. SERBEUKO.

**All-Union Scientific Medical Society of Obstetricians and Gynaecologists:** Moscow, Ul. Yablonskogo 2; Chair. L. S. PERSIANINOV, D.SC.

**All-Union Scientific Medical Society of Oncologists:** Moscow, Botkinsky per. 2; Chair. S. J. SERGEEV; Gen. Sec. V. V. GORODILOVA.

**All-Union Scientific Medical Society of Ophthalmologists:** Moscow, Sadovo-Chernogryazskaya ul. 14/19; Chair. E. S. AVETISEV; Gen. Sec. A. S. GOLDENBERG.

**All-Union Scientific Medical Society of Oto-Rhino-Laryngologists:** Moscow, Olsufyevsky per. 13/15; Chair. N. A. PREOBRAZHENSKY; Gen. Sec. G. F. NAZAROVA.

**All-Union Scientific Medical Society of Pathophysiologists:** Leningrad, Ul. Baltijskaya 8; Chair. A. M. CHERNUKH; Acting Gen. Sec. J. P. TERECHENKO.

**All-Union Scientific Medical Society of Paediatricians:** Moscow, Ustyinsky proezd 1/2; Chair. Y. F. DOMBROVSKAYA, D.SC.; Gen. Sec. L. A. ISAEVA, M.SC.

**All-Union Pharmaceutical Society:** Moscow, 1st Kolobovsky per. 19; Chair. I. A. MURAVYEV, D.SC.; Gen. Sec. V. E. CHICHIRO.

**All-Union Scientific Medical Society of Pharmacologists:** Moscow, Baltiyskaya ul. 8; Chair. V. V. ZAKUSOV, D.SC.; Gen. Sec. K. S. RAEVSKY.

**All-Union Scientific Medical Society of Phthisiologists:** Moscow, Ul. Dostoevskogo 4; Chair. F. V. SHEBANOV, D.SC.; Gen. Sec. T. N. YASHCHENKO, D.SC.

**All-Union Scientific Medical Society of Physical Therapists and Health-Resort Physicians:** Moscow, Kutuzov prospekt 4; Chair. A. N. OBROSOV, D.SC.; Gen. Sec. V. T. OLEPIRENKO.

**All-Union Scientific Medical Society of Roentgenologists and Radiologists:** Moscow, Ul. Solyanka 14; Chair. G. A. ZEDGENIDZE, D.SC.; Gen. Sec. G. F. PALYGA.

**All-Union Scientific Medical Society of Stomatologists:** Moscow, Teply per. 16; Chair. A. I. RYBAKOV; Gen. Sec. T. T. ERNIOLAEV.

**All-Union Scientific Medical Society of Surgeons:** Moscow, Bolshaya Pirogovskaya ul. 2/6; Chair. B. V. PETROVSKY, D.SC.; Gen. Sec. L. T. PERELMAN.

**All-Union Scientific Medical Society of Traumatic Surgeons and Orthopaedists:** Moscow, Novoipatovskaya ul. 8; Chair. M. V. VOLKOV, D.SC.; Gen. Sec. S. T. ZATSEPIN.

**All-Union Scientific Medical Society of Therapists:** Moscow, Ul. Petrovka 25; Chair. A. I. NESTEROV, D.SC.; Gen. Sec. J. E. SPERANSKAYA.

**All-Union Scientific Medical Society of Urological Surgeons:** Moscow, Pirogovskaya ul. 1; Chair. N. A. LOPATKIN; Gen. Sec. A. F. DARENKOV.

**All-Union Scientific Medical Society of Venereologists and Dermatologists:** Moscow, Ul. Korolenko 3; Chair. H. J. STUDNITSKY; Gen. Sec. H. A. KALAMKAYYAN.

---

**British Council:** Cultural Section, British Embassy, Naberezhnaya Marisa Teresa 14, Moscow V-79; Asst. Cultural Attaché T. SANDELL.

**Union of U.S.S.R. Architects:** Moscow, Ul. Shchuseva 3; f. 1932; over 10,000 mems.; First Sec. G. M. ORLOV.

**Union of U.S.S.R. Artists:** Moscow, Gogolevskii bul. 10; f. 1957; 31,000 mems.; publs. *Art, Creation, Artist, Moscow Artist*.

**Union of U.S.S.R. Composers:** Moscow, K-9, Ul. Nezhdanovoi 8/10; f. 1932; 2,061 mems.; First Sec. T. N. KHRENNIKOV; publs. *Soviet Music, Musical Life, Information Bulletin* (in five languages).

**Union of U.S.S.R. Writers:** Ul. Vorovskogo 52, Moscow; f. 1935; over 8,000 mems.; First Sec. G. MARKOV; publs. *Literaturnaya Gazeta* (weekly), *Novymir* (monthly), *Inostrannaya Literatura* (monthly).

**Moscow Society of Naturalists:** Moscow 103009, Prospekt Marxa 20; f. 1805; sections for zoology, botany, geology, hydrobiology, geography, biophysics, palaeontology, histology, experimental morphology and genetics; 3,500 mems.; library of 437,000 vols.; Chair. A. L. JANSHIN; publ. *Biulletin Moskovskogo Obshchestva Ispytateley pryrody* (6 a year).

**A.A. Yablochkina All-Russia Theatrical Society:** Moscow, Ul. Gorkogo 16/2; f. 1877; 30,124 mems.; Chair. M. I. TSAREV.

Two important organizations which, though not learned or professional societies in the strict sense, include some of the outstanding scholars and scientists of the U.S.S.R., are the following adult education organizations:

**AU Society "Znanie":** Moscow, Proezd Serova 4; f. 1947; 3,300,000 mems.; Chair. Acad. N. G. BASOV; publs. *Science and Life* (monthly), etc.

**Union of the Soviet Societies of Friendship and Cultural Relations with Foreign Countries:** Moscow, Prospekt Kalinina 14; f. 1958; unites 77 societies of friendship and cultural relations with other countries; 50,000,000 mems.; Chair. Z. M. KROUGLOVA; publs. *Culture and Life, Moscow News* (weeklies).

# RESEARCH INSTITUTES

AGRICULTURE AND VETERINARY SCIENCE

**AU Flax Research Institute:** Torzhok, Ul. Lunacharskogo 35.

**AU Institute for Nature Protection and Reserves:** Moscow.

**AU Research Institute of Astrakhan Raising:** Uzbek S.S.R., Samarkand, Ul. Karla Marxa 47.

**AU Research Institute of Forestry Reclamation:** Volgograd, Ul. Krasnopresnenskaya 37.

**AU Research Institute of Grain Farming:** 474070 Shortandy 1, Tselinograd region; f. 1956; soil erosion control; 650 staff; library of 57,000 vols.; Dir. A. E. BARAYEV.

**AU Research Institute of Winegrowing and Wine Production:** R.S.F.S.R., Novocherkassk, Arsenalmaya ploshchad 15; Dir. Y. I. POTAPENKO.

**AU Sugar Research Institute:** Kiev; Dir. I. D. GOLOVNIAK.

**AU Research Institute of Tea and Subtropical Plants:** Makharadze, Anaseuli, Georgia; f. 1930; 495 staff; library of 42,493 vols.; Dir. V. DZHAKELI; publ. *Subtropical Cultures* (Russian and Georgian, 6 a year).

**Y. V. Samoylov Research Institute of Fertilizers and Insectofungicides:** Moscow, Leninsky prospekt 55; Dir. V. M. BORISOV.

## Architecture and Town Planning

**Central Research and Design Institute for Dwellings:** Moscow I-434, Dmitrovskoe shosse 9; f. 1962; Dir. B. RUBANENKO.

**V. A. Kucherenko Central Research Institute of Building Constructions:** Moscow, Ul. 2-d Institutskaya 6; Dir. NASONOV.

## The Arts

**Institute of History of Arts:** Moscow 103009, Central Kozitskii per. 5; Dir. YURI BARABASH.

## Economics, Law and Politics

**Moscow State Institute of International Relations:** Moscow, Ul. Metrostroevskaya 53; Dir. A. A. SOLDATOV.

**Research Institute of Marxism-Leninism:** Moscow, 3-d Selskokhozyaistvenny pr. 4.

## Medicine

**AU Antileprosy Research Institute:** Saratov, Ul. Universitetskaya ul. 46; f. 1918; library of 59,000 vols.; Dir. Prof. N. I. NIKOLAYEV; publ. *Problems of Particularly Dangerous Infections* (6 issues a year).

**AU Institute of Medical Polymers:** Moscow, 1-st Streletskii per. 14/21; Dir. V. P. PEREPELKIN.

**AU Research Institute of Gastroenterology:** Moscow, Ul. Pogodinskaya 5; Dir. V. K. VASILENKO.

**AU Research Institute of Pharmaceutical Chemistry:** Moscow, Ul. Zubovskaya 7; Dir. K. Y. NOVITSKY.

**AU Research Institute of Pharmaceutical Plants:** Moscow region, platf. Bittsa; Dir. P. T. KONDRATENKO.

**AU Toxicological Institute:** Leningrad, Ul. Kazachya 1; Dir. N. S. GOLIKOV.

**Central Apothecary Research Institute:** Moscow, Ul. Krasikova 20; Dir. A. I. TENTSOVA.

**Central Research Institute of Epidemiology:** Moscow, Ul. Svobody 3-a; Dir. A. SUMAROKOV.

**I. Dzhordania Research Institute of Physiology and Pathology of Woman:** Georgian S.S.R., Tbilisi; Dir. D. R. TSITSISHVILI.

**Institute of Medical Biological Problems:** Moscow region, Pushchino-na-Oke; Dir. V. V. PARIN.

**I. E. Martsinovsky Institute of Medical Parasitology and Tropical Medicine:** Moscow, Ul. Pirogovskaya 20; f. 1920; Dir. C. P. CHAGIN.

**A. L. Polenov Neurosurgery Research Institute:** Leningrad, Ul. Mayakovskogo 12; Dir. V. M. UGRYUMOV.

**Moscow Research Institute of Psychiatry:** Moscow, Ul. Poteshnaya 3; Dir. D. D. FEDOTOV.

**Research Institute of Forensic Medicine:** Moscow, Ul. Sadovaya-Triumfalnaya 13; Dir. Prof. V. I. PROZOROVSKY.

**Serbsky Central Scientific Research Institute of Forensic Psychiatry:** Moscow, Kropotkinsky per. 23; library of 41,000 vols.; Dir. Prof. G. V. MOROZOV; publs. *Problemi Sudebnoi Psikhiatrii, Praktika Sudebno-Psikhiatricheskoy Expertisi*.

**State Research Institute of Eye Diseases:** Moscow K-64, Ul. Sadovaya-Chernogryazskaya 14/19; library of 21,950 vols. and 27,322 periodicals; Dir. K. TRUTNEVA.

**State Research Institute of Vitaminology:** Moscow, Novyye Cheremushki, kv. 35; Dir. M. I. SMIRNOV.

## Natural Sciences

**AU Geological Oil Prospecting Research Institute:** Moscow E-275, Shosse Entuziastov 124; f. 1953; library of 30,000 vols.; Dir. S. P. MAKSIMOV; publ. *Trudy*† (Proceedings).

**AU Geological Research Institute:** Vasilyevsky ostrov, Sredny pros. 726, Leningrad.

**AU Research Institute of Chemical Reagents and Substances of High Purity:** Moscow, Bogorodskii val 3; Dir. V. G. BRUDZ.

**AU Research Institute of Submarine Geology and Geophysics (VNIIMORGEO):** 64 Dzirnavu St., Riga 50; publs.† collections of scientific articles, monographs.

**AU Research Institute of Monocrystals:** Ukrainian S.S.R., Kharkov, Prosp. Lenina 60; Dir. V. N. IZVEKOV.

**Arctic and Antarctic Scientific Research Institute:** Fontanka 34, Leningrad D-104; Dir. A. TRESHNIKOV.

**Baikonur Cosmodrome:** c/o U.S.S.R. Academy of Sciences, 14 Leninski prospekt, Moscow.

**Central Aerological Observatory:** Dolgoprudnaya, Moscow Region.

**Central Research Institute for Geodesy, Aerial Photography and Cartography:** Gorokhovsky per. 4, Moscow.

**Institute of Biophysics:** Moscow, Ul. Zhivopisnaya 22; Dir. L. A. ILYIN.

**Institute of Experimental Meteorology:** Obninsk; Dir. M. A. PETROSYANTS.

**Institute of Geology:** Minsk, Leninsky prosp. 66; Dir. V. K. GOLUBTSOV.

**Institute of Neustonology:** Odessa; Dir. Dr. Y. ZAITSER.

**Institute of Stable Isotopes:** Tbilisi, Saburtalo.

**I. V. Kurchatov Institute of Atomic Energy:** Moscow, Ul. Kurchatova 46; Dir. Acad. A. P. ALEXANDROV.

**Middle Asian Research Institute of Natural Gas:** Tashkent, Ul. Mukimi 98; Dir. U. D. MAMADZHANOV.

**Pacific Scientific Research Institute of Fisheries and Oceanography (TINRO):** Vladivostok, Ul. Leninskaya 20; f. 1925; laboratories of commercial ichthyology, cetacea and pinnipeds, oceanography, commercial invertebrates, commercial marine algae, parasitology of marine animals, commercial fisheries, mechanization of fish processing, technology of fish and marine production, economy; branches at Kamchatka, Sakhalin, Amur (Khabarovsk), Magadan; library of 80,000 vols., 11,000 MSS.; museum (*see* Museums); Dir. Prof. Dr. I. V. KIZEVETTER; publ. *Izvestia TINRO* (1-3 times a year).

**Research Institute of Atomic Reactors:** Melekess, Ulyanovsky region, R.S.F.S.R.; Dir. O. KAZACHKOVSKY.

**Research Institute of Basic Chemistry:** Kharkov, Ul. Dzerzhinskogo 25; Dir. F. M. KONDRATYEVICH.

**Research Institute of Introscopy:** Moscow, Ul. B. Cheremushinskaya 91-a; Dir. P. K. OSHCHEPKOV.

**Research Institute of Mathematical Computing Machines:** Erevan, Ul. Komitasa; Dir. F. T. SARKISYAN.

**Stars' City (Soviet Space Training Centre):** c/o U.S.S.R. Academy of Sciences, 14 Leninski prospekt, Moscow.

## Religion, Sociology and Anthropology

**Institute of Scientific Atheism:** 123268 Moscow D-286, Sadovaya-Kudrinskaya 9; f. 1964; 40 mems.; library of 3,000 vols.; Dir. A. F. OKULOV.

## Technology

**International Centre for Scientific and Technical Information:** 15252 Moscow, Ul. Kuusinen 21B; Dir. Prof. A. I. MIHAILOV.

**AU Research Institute of the Cellulose and Paper Industry:** Leningrad, Institutskii per. 5; Dir. PUZYREV.

**AU Research Institute of Electromechanics:** Moscow, Khromny tupik 4; Dir. A. G. IOSIFYAN.

**AU Research Insitute of Geophysical Prospecting Methods:** Moscow, Ul. Chernyshevskogo 22; Dir. M. K. POLSHKOV.

**AU Research Institute of Gold and Rare Metals:** Magadan, Ul. Gagarina 2.

RESEARCH INSTITUTES, ARCHIVES                    UNION OF SOVIET SOCIALIST REPUBLICS

**AU Research Institute of Hydrogeology and Geological Engineering:** Moscow, B. Ordynka 32; Dir. N. I. PLOTNIKOV.

**AU Research Institute of Hydraulic Engineering and Land Reclamation:** Moscow, Ul. Pryanishnikova 19; Dir. I. I. KOVALENKO.

**AU Research Institute of Marine Fishing Industry and Oceanography:** Moscow, Ul. Verchnyaya Krasnoselskaya 17-a; Deputy Dir. P. A. MOISEYEV.

**AU Research Institute of Meat Industry:** Moscow 109029, Ul. Talalikhina 26.

**AU Research Institute of Metallurgical Machine Building:** Moscow, Ul. 1-st Gorodskaya 10; Dir. A. I. TSELIKOV.

**AU Research Institute of Nonferrous Metals:** Kazakh S.S.R., Ust-Kamenogorsk; Dir. L. S. GETSKIN.

**AU Research Institute of Oil Refineries:** Azerbaijan S.S.R., Baku 25, Telnovaya ul.; f. 1929; theoretical and applied research in oil refining and petrochemistry; 1,200 mems.; library of over 80,000 vols.; Dir. VAGAB S. ALIEV; publ. *Transactions* (annual).

**AU Research and Project Institute of Man-made Fibres:** Moscow region, Mytishchi, Ul. Kolontsova 5; Dir. V. SMIRNOV.

**AU Research Institute of Tobacco and Makhorka:** Krasnodar, P. Box 55.

**Central Paper Research Institute:** Moscow region, Pravdinskii, Ul. Pushkina; Dir. K. A. VEINOV.

**Central Research Institute of Automobile Engineering:** Moscow, Ul. Avtomotornaya 2; Dir. A. KHLEBNIKOV.

**Central Research Institute of Nonferrous Metallurgy:** Moscow, Ul. 2-d Baumanovskaya 9/23; Dir. I. GOLIKOV.

**Central Scientific Research and Design Institute of Wood Chemical Industry:** Gorky, Moskovskoe chaussée 85; f. 1932; library of 153,000 vols.; Dir. P. P. POLYAKOV; publ. *Scientific Works* (annual).

**Institute of Complex Transportation Problems:** Moscow, Ul. Nizne-Krasnoselskaya 39; Dir. V. I. PETROV.

**Institute of Control Sciences:** Moscow GSP-312, Profsojuznaja ul. 81; Dir. V. A. TRAPEZNIKOV.

**Institute of Engineering Studies:** Moscow, Ul. Griboedova 4; f. 1938; research into theory of mechanisms, mechanical engineering, strength of materials, friction, wear and lubrication; Dir. (vacant); publs. *Reports, Mashinovedenie* (6 times a year).

**G. M. Krzhizhanovsky Power Engineering Institute:** Moscow, Leninsky prosp. 19; Dir. D. G. ZHIMERIN.

**S. V. Lebedev AU Research Institute of Synthetic Rubber:** Leningrad, Ul. Gapsalskaya 18; Dir. I. V. GARMONOV.

**Middle Asian Research Institute of Silk Industry:** Dzhar-Aryk, Kalinin district, Tashkent region, Uzbek S.S.R.; Dir. M. P. GANIEVA.

**Scientific Research Institute for the Refrigeration Industry:** Moscow 125422, Ul. Kostyakova 12; Dir. V. F. LEBEDEV.

**State Research Institute for Tractors:** Moscow, Ul. Verkhnyaya 34; Dir. V. KARGOPOLOV.

**State Research Institute of the Nitrogen Industry:** Moscow, Ul. Chkalova 50; Dir. N. D. ZAICHKO.

# ARCHIVES

All Union and Autonomous Republics, Territories, Regions, National Districts and all large cities and district centres have their respective state archives, which assemble documents of republican and local importance.

**Central State Archives of the October Revolution and Higher State Bodies:** Moscow, Bolshaya Pirogovskaya ul. 17; documents of higher bodies of the R.S.F.S.R. (1917–23) and the U.S.S.R. (1923–), documents of the trade unions and other public organizations of All-Union importance, documents of the central administration of the political police of Tsarist Russia (19th century–1917); Dir. S. T. PLESHAKOV.

**Central State Archives of the R.S.F.S.R.:** Moscow, Berezhkovskaya nab. 26; documents of higher state bodies of the R.S.F.S.R., courts and procurators' offices, state organizations and institutions at the Republican level, public, scientific and other organizations of the Russian Federation; Dir. F. I. SHARONOV.

---

**Archives of the U.S.S.R. Academy of Sciences:** Moscow, Leninsky prospekt 4; Dir. B. B. LEVSHIN.

**Central State Archives of the Soviet Army:** Moscow, Bolshaya Pirogovskaya ul. 17; documents of military authorities of the R.S.F.S.R. and the U.S.S.R., of the military areas, detachments, units and establishments of the Soviet Army and Frontier Guards (1918–40); Dir. P. M. KEVDIN.

**Central State Archives of Documentary Films and Photographs of the U.S.S.R.:** Moscow Region, Krasnogorsk, Ul. Rechnaya 1; topical films, newsreels and historical material which was not included in finished films, negatives of documentary photographs (1854–); Dir. O. N. TYAGUNOV.

**Central State Archives of the U.S.S.R. National Economy:** Moscow, Bolshaya Pirogovskaya ul. 17; documents of the U.S.S.R. state bodies in charge of management of industries, agriculture, transportation, communication, construction and of central bodies of financing, planning and statistics (1917–); Dir. A. G. FEDOROV.

**Central State Historical Archives of U.S.S.R.:** Leningrad, Naberezhnaya Krasnogo Flota 4; documents of central state bodies of the Russian Empire, state and private banks, railways, industrial, trade and other companies; private collections of prominent political and public figures, etc. (19th century–1917); Dir. I. N. FIRSOV.

**Central State Archives of Ancient Acts:** Moscow, Bolshaya Pirogovskaya ul. 17; annals, charts of grand dukes and independent princes, legal documents of Early Russia (11th–15th centuries), documents of central and local Russian institutions (16th–18th centuries), personal and patrimonial archives of nobility and gentry, archives of church establishments and the largest monasteries of Russia; Dir. M. I. AVTOKRATOVA.

**Central State Literature and Art Archives of the U.S.S.R.:** Moscow, Leningradskoe chaussée 50; f. 1941; documents of prominent Russian and Soviet writers, composers, artists, theatrical and cinema workers; documents of state and public organizations concerned with the arts (mid-18th century–present day); Dir. N. B. VOLKOVA; publ. *Vstrechi s proshlim* (irregular).

**Central State Military Historical Archives of the U.S.S.R.:** Moscow, 2nd Baumanskaya ul. 3; f. 1819; documents of central and district military administrations and establishments of the Russian Army, private collections of prominent generals, military leaders and historians (end 17th century–1918); Dir. I. G. TISHIN.

**Central State Archives of the U.S.S.R. Navy:** Leningrad, Ul. Kchalturina 36; documents of central institutions of the Russian pre-revolutionary and Soviet Navy and prominent naval officers (17th century–1940); Dir. I. N. SOLOVYEV.

**A. M. Gorky Archives:** Moscow, Ulitsa Vorovskogo 25A.

# LIBRARIES

In the U.S.S.R., there are 360,000 libraries, including 130,000 public libraries, 60,000 scientific, technical and other specialized libraries, 170,000 school libraries and 7,400 children's libraries. The national library is the V. I. Lenin State Library of the U.S.S.R. in Moscow. Each of the Union Republics and each of the Autonomous Republics has at least one large public library in its principal town. Remote areas are served by travelling libraries.

The All-Union Book Chamber prepares bibliographical descriptions of all books and magazine articles published in the U.S.S.R. and abroad and distributes these materials to all libraries of the country.

### Central Libraries of the Soviet Union

**State V. I. Lenin Library of the U.S.S.R.:** 3 Prospect Kalinina, 101000 Moscow; f. 1862 as the Rumyantsev Library, reorganized in 1925; 28,216,000 books, periodicals and serials; complete files of newspapers in all the 91 languages of the Soviet Union and 156 foreign languages; 345,000 MSS.; 625 archival collections; Department of Rare Books includes incunabula, Aldines, palaeotypes, Elzevirs, specimens of earliest Slavonic printing, rare editions of Russian secular works, etc.; acts as enquiry, loan and reference centre throughout the U.S.S.R., as international book exchange centre and state national book depository, as information centre on culture and arts (f. 1972), as leading research institution in library science, bibliography and history of printing, and as methodological library centre; Dir. Prof. N. M. Sikorsky, D.Phil.; publs. *Trudy* (Proceedings), *Zapiski otdela rukopisej* (Memoirs of the Manuscript Division), *Sovetskoje bibliotekovedenie* (Soviet Library Science), *Sovetskoje bibliotekovedenie i bibliografia za rubezhom* (Soviet Library Science and Bibliography Abroad), etc.

**All-Union Geological Library:** Leningrad 199026, Sredny pr. 72b; f. 1882; scientific and technical literature; over 1,000,000 books, monographs, periodicals and special maps; Dir. L. P. Tiukina; publ. *Geologicheskaya literatura S.S.S.R.* (Geological Literature of the U.S.S.R.) (annually).

**All-Union Patent and Technical Library:** 121857 Moscow, Berezhkovskaya nab. 24; f. 1896; the only Soviet library which receives Soviet and all foreign patents; 64,000,000 patent descriptions; Dir. A. N. Morozov.

**All-Union State Library of Foreign Literature:** 109240 Moscow, Ulyanovskaya 1; f. 1921; 4,138,442 vols. in 132 foreign languages; exchange arrangements with 1,401 libraries, publishing houses and universities in 85 countries; Dir. L. A. Gvishiani.

**State Central Library for the Blind:** Moscow 113054, Valovaya ul. 29/33; f. 1954; 359,000 vols.; acts as loan centre for special libraries throughout the R.S.F.S.R.; Dir. D. S. Zarkov; publ. *Life of the Blind in the U.S.S.R. and Abroad* (monthly).

**State Central Polytechnic Library:** Moscow, Politeknichesky proezd 2; f. 1964; 3,000,000 vols. including periodicals; Dir. N. G. Reynberg.

**State Central Scientific Medical Library:** Moscow, Ul. Krasikova; f. 1919; over 3 million vols. including scientific journals; Dir. Cand. Med.Sc. N. A. Yakunin.

**State Central Theatrical Library:** 103009 Moscow, Pushkinskaya ul. 8/1; f. 1922; 150,000 vols. on theatrical subjects, 70,000 theatrical magazines, 107,469 illustrations and prints, 632,965 filed cuttings and rare editions of Russian plays of the 18th and 19th centuries; Dir. L. A. Bykovskaya.

**State Public Historical Library of the R.S.F.S.R.:** 101839 Moscow, Starosadsky per. 9; f. 1938; 2,852,000 vols., including 30,000 in the Department of Rare Historical Books; Dir. K. P. Kuranzeva.

**State Public Scientific and Technical Library:** 103031 Moscow, Kuznetsky most 12; f. 1958; 10,000,000 books, periodicals and documents; special collections of industrial firms' catalogues, scientific translations, etc.; coordinates bibliographical activities of 20,000 technical libraries in U.S.S.R.; international computer system for registering periodicals; Dir. J. I. Tyshkevich.

**State M.E. Saltykov-Shchedrin Public Library:** Leningrad D-69, Sadovaya ul. 18; f. 1795; 21,500,000 vols., including a large collection of incunabula and MSS.; Dir. L. A. Shilov.

### State Libraries of the Union Republics

**A. F. Myasnikian State Public Library of the Armenian S.S.R.:** 375009 Erevan, Ul. Teryana 72; f. 1921; over 6,400,000 vols.; Dir. A. M. Tirabyan.

**M. F. Akhundov State Public Library of the Azerbaijan S.S.R.:** 370601 Baku, Ul. Khagani 29; f. 1923; 3,122,000 vols. including 2,320 periodicals; Dir. K. A. Suleyman-Zade.

**V. I. Lenin State Public Library of the Byelorussian S.S.R.:** 220636 Minsk, Krasnoarmejskaya ul. 9; f. 1922; over 6,000,000 vols.; Dir. E. N. Cygankov; publs. *Letopis Druku B.S.S.R.*, *Novyja Knigi B.S.S.R.* (both monthly).

**F. R. Kreutzwald State Public Library of the Estonian S.S.R.:** 200103 Tallinn, Raamatukogu pl. 1; f. 1940; over 3,018,000 vols. incl. periodicals; Dir. R. Koppelmann; publ. *Nõukogude Eesti raamatukogundus†*.

**K. Marx State Public Library of the Georgian S.S.R.:** 380007 Tbilisi, Ul. Ketskhoveli 5; f. 1946; 8,000,000 vols.; Dir. A. K. Kavkasidze.

**A. S. Pushkin State Public Library of the Kazakh S.S.R.:** 480021 Alma-Ata, Prospekt Abaya 14; f. 1931; over 3,458,700 vols.; Dir. N. K. Dauletova.

**N. G. Chernyshevsky State Public Library of the Kirghiz S.S.R.:** 720873 Frunze, Ul. Ogonbaeva 242; over 3,514,700 vols.; Dir. A. S. Sagimbaeva.

**Vilis Lācis State Library of the Latvian S.S.R.:** 266437 Riga, Ul. Kr. Barona 14; f. 1919; public scientific library; 4,466,858 vols. including periodicals; Dir. A. A. Deglava; publs. *Vila Lāča Latvijas PSR Valsts Bibliotēka, Bibliogrāfija, Latviesu Zinatne un Literatura, Raksti†* (Latvian and Russian) (irregular).

**National Library of the Lithuanian S.S.R.:** 232635 Vilnius, Lenin pr. 51; f. 1919; 2,813,700 vols.; Dir. Jonas Baltušis; publ. *Biblioteku Darbas* (monthly).

**N. K. Krupskaya State Public Library of the Moldavian S.S.R.:** Kishinev 277612, Kievskaya ul. 78-a; f. 1832; national library and principal depository of the Moldavian S.S.R.; largest collection of material on Moldavia; exchange arrangements with libraries and scientific institutions abroad; over 3,000,000 vols.; Dir. P. T. Ganenko.

**Firdousi State Public Library of the Tajik S.S.R.:** 734711 Dushanbe, Lenina pr. 34; 2,528,700 vols.; Dir. N. Babajanova.

**K. Marx State Public Library of the Turkmen S.S.R.:** 744000 Ashkhabad, Pl. Karl Marx; f. 1895; 3,491,300 vols.; Dir. D. N. Seitniyazov.

**State Public Library of the Ukrainian S.S.R.:** 252001 Kiev, Ul. Kirova 1; f. 1866; collection of Ukrainian national books, scientific research centre, international book exchange; 2,051,000 vols.; Dir. V. S. Balich; publ. *Kalendar znamennikh ta pamyatnikh dat* (4 times a year).

# LIBRARIES — UNION OF SOVIET SOCIALIST REPUBLICS

**Alisher Navoi State Public Library of the Uzbek S.S.R.:** 700000 Tashkent, Alleya Narodov 5; f. 1870; 4,157,500 vols.; Dir. D. TAJIEVA.

### LIBRARIES OF THE ACADEMIES OF SCIENCES

**Library of the U.S.S.R. Academy of Sciences:** Leningrad, Birzhevaya linia 1; f. 1714; 12,789,000 vols.; collections of MSS., incunabula and rare books; acts as enquiry, loan and reference centre for the network of 136 libraries in the Academy's departments and institutes; Dir. Prof. D. V. TER-AVANESYAN.

**Institute for Scientific Information on the Social Sciences of the U.S.S.R. Academy of Sciences:** Moscow 117418, Ul. Krasikova 28/45; f. 1969; sections on philosophy, history, economics, scientific communism theory, law, science of sciences, linguistics, theory of literature; 7,491,000 vols.; Dir. V. A. VINOGRADOV.

**State Public Scientific and Technical Library of the Siberian Department of the U.S.S.R. Academy of Sciences:** Novosibirsk-200, Ul. Voskhod 15; f. 1959; 9,974,000 vols.; acts as enquiry, loan, research and co-ordinating centre for 64 Academy institutes located in Siberia and the Far East; Dir. N. S. KARTASHOV.

---

**Central Library of the Academy of Sciences of the Armenian S.S.R.:** 375000 Erevan, Ul. B. Musyana 24; 2,200,000 vols.; Dir. G. N. OVNAN.

**Central Library of the Academy of Sciences of the Azerbaijan S.S.R.:** 370073 Baku, Prospekt Narimanova 31; about 1,276,000 vols.; Dir. M. M. GASANOVA.

**J. Kolas Central Library of the Academy of Sciences of the Byelorussian S.S.R.:** 220000 Minsk, Leninsky pr. 66; f. 1925; 1,589,000 vols.; Dir. M. P. STRIZHONOK.

**Central Library of the Academy of Sciences of the Estonian S.S.R.:** 200104 Tallinn, Lenin puiestee 10; 2,891,272 vols.; Dir. F. KAUBA.

**Central Library of the Academy of Sciences of the Georgian S.S.R.:** 380093 Tbilisi, Ul. Zoi Rukladze 1; 2,279,000 vols.; Dir. S. A. KHADUY.

**Central Library of the Academy of Sciences of the Kazakh S.S.R.:** Alma-Ata 480591, Ul. Shevchenko 28; over 2,455,000 vols.; Dir. N. B. AKHMEDOVA.

**Central Library of the Academy of Sciences of the Kirghiz S.S.R.:** 720071 Frunze, 265-a Leninsky Prospekt; f. 1954; 815,444 vols.; Dir. (vacant).

**Central Library of the Academy of Sciences of the Latvian S.S.R.:** 226000 Riga, Kommunalnaya 4; f. 1524; the oldest library in the U.S.S.R.; 2,174,600 vols., including many MSS., incunabula and rare books; Dir. E. M. ARAIS.

**Central Library of the Academy of Sciences of the Lithuanian S.S.R.:** 232000 Vilnius, Ul. K. Pozhelos 2/8; 1,617,000 vols.; Dir. J. I. MARCINKEVIČIUS.

**Central Library of the Academy of Sciences of the Moldavian S.S.R.:** 277612 Kishinev, pr. Lenin 1; f. 1947; 768,000 vols.; Dir. N. K. SANALATH.

**Central Library of the Academy of Sciences of the Tajik S.S.R.:** 734025 Dushanbe, Pr. Lenina 33; f. 1933; over 500,000 vols.; Dir. Z. M. SHEVCHENKO.

**Central Library of the Academy of Sciences of the Turkmen S.S.R.:** 744000 Ashkhabad, Ul. Gogolya 15; 800,000 vols.; Dir. A. B. YAZBERDYEV.

**Central Library of the Academy of Sciences of the Ukrainian S.S.R.:** 252601 Kiev, Vladimirskaya ul. 62; 7,756,000 vols.; Dir. S. K. GUTJANSKY.

**Central Library of the Academy of Sciences of the Uzbek S.S.R.:** Tashkent, Ul. A. Tukaeva 1; f. 1934; about 1,500,000 vols.; Dir. N. G. UMAROV.

### LIBRARIES OF THE OTHER ACADEMIES

**Central Scientific Agricultural Library of the All-Union Lenin Academy of Agricultural Science:** 3 Korpus V. Orlikov per., B-139, Moscow 107804; f. 1930; centre for bibliographical information on national and foreign agricultural literature, and for scientific and methodological work of agricultural libraries in the U.S.S.R.; 4,000,000 vols., 3,300 periodicals; Dir. A. M. BOCHEVER; publs. *Selskokhozyaistvennaya literatura SSSR*† (monthly), *Selskoye khozyaistvo*† (monthly), *Byulleten*†, *Subject Bibliographic Lists* (15 titles annually), *Bibliographic Information* (weekly).

**Scientific Library of the Academy of Arts of the U.S.S.R.:** 199034 Leningrad, Universitetskaya nab. 17; f. 1764; 352,000 vols. on art, architecture, applied and folk arts, including rare 16th and 17th centuries volumes and a notable collection of 18th century works on architecture; Dir. K. N. ODAR-BOYARSKAYA; Moscow Branch: Moscow, Ul. Kropotkina 21; 35,700 vols.; Dir. E. A. MARINOVA.

**Central Library of the Academy of Medical Sciences:** Moscow, Baltiyskaya ul. 8; f. 1935; 640,000 vols.; acts as an enquiry, loan, research and guide centre for 42 libraries in the institutes and laboratories of the Academy of Medical Sciences; Dir. G. I. BAKHEREVA.

**K. D. Ushinsky State Scientific Library of the Academy of Pedagogical Sciences:** 109017 Moscow, Bolshoi Tolmachevsky per. 3; f. 1925; 2 million units; covers all fields of education and pedagogics; Dir. M. N. MIKHAILOVA (acting).

### FINE ARTS AND MUSEUM LIBRARIES

**Central Music Library:** Leningrad, Ul. Zodchego Rossi 2; contains one of the largest collections in the world of Russian music in MSS., single copies, first editions, etc., 1,500 copies of Russian vaudeville scores, 200 MSS. of ballet scores, and a large collection of opera scores including 1,000 foreign opera; Dir. S. O. BROG.

**Library of the All-Union Museum of A. S. Pushkin:** Leningrad, Naberezhnaya Moyki; f. 1954; 60,000 vols.; Dir. L. P. KUZMINA.

**Library of the Central Museum of the Revolution of the U.S.S.R.:** 103050 Moscow, Ul. Gorkogo 21; f. 1924; 287,000 vols., 515,000 periodicals; Dir. N. G. NOVIKOVA.

**Library of the State Hermitage Museum:** Leningrad, Dvortsovaya nab. 34; f. 1762; over 500,000 vols. on painting, sculpture and all branches of graphic arts throughout the centuries; Dir. MAKAROVA.

**Library of the State Literature Museum:** Moscow, Rozhdestvensky Bulvar 16; f. 1926; collection of 180,000 books, 27,644 periodicals; Russian and foreign works from 16th-20th centuries; letters and autographed works; folklore works; periodical collection; Dir. A. P. SVETLOV.

**Library of the State Museum of Oriental Arts:** 107120 Moscow, Ul. Obukha 16; f. 1918; 50,000 vols.; Dir. V. V. MELNIKOVA; publs. *Scientific reports of the State Museum of Oriental Art*† (annual).

**Library of the State A. S. Pushkin Museum of Fine Arts:** 121019 Moscow, Ul. Volkhonka 12; f. 1898; over 111,000 vols.; Dir. I. V. GORYAEVA.

**Library of the State Theatrical A. Bakhrushin Museum:** 113054 Moscow, Ul. Bakhrushina 32/12; f. 1894; about 63,000 vols. on theatrical art; Dir. E. K. CHIKINA.

**Library of the L. N. Tolstoy State Museum:** Moscow, Kropotkinskaya ul. 11; f. 1911; 120,000 vols.; Dir. A. V. SALOMATIN.

**A. V. Lunarcharsky State Theatrical Library:** Leningrad, Ul. Zodchego Rossi 2; f. 1756; 801,000 vols. of plays and works on theatrical subjects, department of French works with first editions of Corneille, Racine and Molière; department of MSS. and letters by Chekhov, Ostrovsky, Turgenev, Nekrasov; department of stage designs by Bakst, Benoit, etc; department of classical and contemporary fiction; Dir. W. V. PJATKOVA.

**Matenadaran, M. M., Institute of Ancient Armenian Manuscripts:** Erevan, Armenian S.S.R.; f. 1920; the world's oldest and one of the largest repositories of ancient Armenian MSS (5th–18th centuries); 16,000 MSS on many subjects, miniature paintings, also archival documents and works by Greek, Syrian, Persian, Arabic, Latin, Georgian, Ethiopian authors, etc.

**Music Library of the Leningrad Conservatoire:** Leningrad, Teatralnaya ploshchad 3; f. 1862; 63,000 vols., including Russian and foreign works on music and the arts, 125,000 scores including 17th-20th century music by Russian and foreign composers; Dir. E. E. SHVEDE.

**Music Library of the Leningrad State Philharmonic Society:** Leningrad, Ul. Brodskogo 7; f. 1882; over 170,000 scores and books on music, 18,000 engravings, lithographs and paintings of musicians, composers, etc.; over 80,000 newspaper cuttings; Dir. G. L. RETROWSKAJA.

**Scientific Library attached to the State Research Institute of Theatre, Music and Cinematography:** Leningrad, Isakievskaya pl. 5; f. 1912; 232,000 books on theatre, music, cinematography, history of literature, painting, architecture, philosophy, aesthetics; music section contains nearly all Russian musical literature from Glinka to the present day; six brs.; Dir. N. A. BELOZERTSEVA.

**Scientific Library of the State Russian Museum:** Leningrad, Inzhenernaya ul. 4; f. 1918; 70,000 vols. on fine arts, history, philosophy; Dir. V. V. ALEXEYEVA.

**Scientific Library of the State Tretyakov Gallery:** 107017 Moscow, Lavrushinsky per. 10; f. 1899; 210,000 vols.; Dir. A. I. BOLOTOVA.

**Scientific S. I. Taneyev Library of the Moscow P. I. Tchaikovsky State Conservatoire:** 103871 Moscow, Ul. Gerzena 13; f. 1860; Russian and foreign music and books on music; complete files of many Russian and foreign musical periodicals; 1,269,454 vols.; Dir. A. F. CHERKASOVA.

## UNIVERSITY LIBRARIES
(In alphabetical order by university).

**Library of the Altai State University:** 656099 Barnaul, Socialistichesky pr. 68; 159,000 vols.; Dir. V. VORONA.

**Central Library of the Azerbaijan S. M. Kirov State University:** Baku, Ul. Patrice Lumumba 23; 1,700,000 vols.; Dir. K. G. GAZANOV.

**Library of the Bashkir State University:** 450074 Ufa, Ul. Frunze 32; 780,000 vols.; Dir. E. M. KUCHERBAEVA.

**Library of the Byelorussian V. I. Lenin State University:** 220080 Minsk, Universitetsky gorodok; 1,377,000 vols.; Dir. I. V. ORECHOVSKAYA.

**Library of the Checheno-Ingush State University:** 364907 Grozny, Ul. N. Buachidze 34/96; 460,000 vols.; Dir. R. M. NAZARETYANI.

**Scientific Library of the Chernovtsy State University:** Chernovtsy, Ul. Lesy Ukraini 23; over 1,722,000 vols.; Dir. M. I. DEREVOREZ.

**Library of the Chuvash State University:** 428015 Cheboksary, Moskovsky pr. 15; 712,000 vols.; Dir. V. P. MAKAROVA.

**Library of the Daghestan V. I. Lenin State University:** Makhachkala, Ul. Sovetskaya 8; 780,000 vols.; Dir. A. M. SCHAKHSHAEVA.

**Scientific Library of the Dnepropetrovsk State University:** Dnepropetrovsk, Ul. Liebknechta 3-a; 1,200,000 vols.; Dir. N. A. GAIVORONSKAYA.

**Library of the Donetsk State University:** 340055 Donetsk, Ul. Universitetskaya 24; 782,000 vols.; Dir. A. N. KHARCHENKO.

**Scientific Library of the Erevan State University:** 375009 Erevan 49, Ul. Mravyana 1; 1,447,000 vols.; Dir. S. N. ARAKELYAN.

**Central Library of the Far Eastern State University:** 690652 Vladivostok, Okeansky pr. 37/41; 586,000 vols.; Dir. A. G. TRETYAKOVA.

**Central Library of the Gorky N. I. Lobachevsky State University:** 603091 Gorky, Prospekt Gagarina 23; 1,210,470 vols.; Dir. A. I. SAVENKOV.

**Scientific Library of the Irkutsk A. A. Zhdanov University:** 664695 Irkutsk, Gagarina Bulvar 24; 3,200,000 vols.; Dir. V. J. LIBE.

**Library of the Ivanovo State University:** 153377 Ivanovo, Ul. Ermaka 37; 410,000 vols.; Dir. A. N. KRUPPA.

**Library of the Kabardino-Balkar State University:** 360004 Nalchik, Ul. Chernyshevskogo 173; 738,000 vols.; Dir. Z. D. MIGUCHKINA.

**Central Library of the Kazakh S. M. Kirov State University:** 480100 Alma-Ata, Sovetskaya ul. 28; 1,111,000 vols.; Dir. D. O. ORAZBAEVA.

**Library of the Kalinin State University:** 170000 Kalinin, Ul. Sovetskaya 4; 505,800 vols.; Dir. L. T. VOLKOVA.

**Library of the Kaliningrad State University:** 236040 Kaliningrad obl., Ul. Universitetskaya 2; 364,000 vols.; Dir. M. M. PANCHENKO.

**Library of the Kalmuck State University:** Elista, Ul. R. Luxemburg 4; c. 350,000 vols.; Dir. P. A. DOLINA.

**Library of the Karaganda State University:** Karaganda, Ul. Kirova 16; 400,000 vols.; Dir. S. M. ZHERZHISOVA.

**Scientific N. I. Lobachevsky Library of the Kazan V. I. Ulyanov (Lenin) State University:** 420008 Kazan, Ul. Lenina 18; 4,120,000 vols.; Dir. A. S. GURYANOV.

**Library of the Kemerovo State University:** 650043 Kemerovo, Sovetsky pr. 117; 350,000 vols.; Dir. NAGARA.

**Central Scientific Library of the Kharkov A. M. Gorky State University:** Kharkov, Pl. Dzerzhinskogo 4; about 3,000,000 vols.; Dir. M. P. KIRYUKHIN.

**Scientific Library of the Kiev T. G. Shevchenko State University:** 252056 Kiev, Vladimirskaya ul. 58; 2,708,000 vols.; Dir. N. M. NEDOSTUP.

**Library of the Kirghiz State University:** 720024 Frunze, Ul. Frunze 547; 931,500 vols.; Dir. M. A. ASANBAEV.

**Scientific Library of the Kishinev State University:** 277003 Kishinev, Ul. Sadovaya 60; 1,385,000 vols.; Dir. A. M. NOVAK.

**Library of the Komi State University:** 167001 Syktyvkar; 204,000 vols.; Dir. N. F. AKONOVA.

**Library of the Krasnoyarsk State University:** 660049 Krasnoyarsk, Ul. Maerchaka 6, 166,000 vols.; Dir. V. N. TERSKAYA.

**Library of the Kuban State University:** 350751 Krasnodar, Ul. K. Libknechta 149; 950,000 vols.; Dir. O. I. TSCHEBANOVA.

**Library of the Kuibyshev State University:** 443086 Kuibyshev, Ul. Potapova 64/163; 245,000 vols.; Dir. N. I. PARANINA.

**Scientific Library of the Latvian State University "Peter Stuchka":** 226172 Riga, Bulvar Kommunarov 4; 1,900,000 vols.; Dir. S. S. MALINKOVSKAYA; publ. *Zinātniskie raksti*†, *Trudy Botaniceskogo Sada*†, *monographs*†.

**Scientific A. M. Gorky Library of the Leningrad A. A. Zhdanov State University:** Leningrad 199164, Universitetskaya nab. 7/9; f. 1819; 5,100,000 vols.; Dir. K. M. ROMANOVSKAYA.

**Scientific Library of the Lvov Ivan Franko State University:** Lvov, Ul. Dragomanova 5; 2,500,000 vols.; Dir. V. K. POTAICHUK.

**Library of the Mordovian State University:** 430000 Saransk, Bolshevistkaya ul. 68; 927,000 books; Dir. M. G. SHAVARINA.

**Scientific A. M. Gorky Library of the Moscow M. V. Lomonosov State University:** 119808 Moscow, Leninskie Gory; 6,629,000 vols., including periodicals; Dir. N. S. AVALOVA.

**Library of the North-Ossetian State University:** 362000 Orjonikidze, Ul. Vatutina 46; 76,000 vols.; Dir. K. L. KOCHISOV.

**Library of the Novosibirsk State University:** 630090 Novosibirsk, Akademgorodok; 417,000 vols.; Dir. E. A. SLASTNAYA.

**Scientific Library of the Odessa I. I. Mechnikov State University:** Odessa, Ul. Sovetskoy Armii 24; over 2,790,000 vols.; Dir. P. M. BONDARENKO.

**Library of the Omsk State University:** 644077 Omsk, Pr. Mira 55a; 182,000 vols.

**Scientific Library of the People's Friendship "Patrice Lumumba" University:** 117302 Moscow, Ordzonikidze 3; f. 1960; 1,000,000 vols.; Dir. A. N. KRUGLAKOVSKY.

**Central Library of the Perm A. M. Gorky State University (Order of Red Banner of Labour):** 614022 Perm, Ul. Genkelya 7; f. 1968; 1,140,000 vols.; Dir. Z. D. FILINYKH.

**Central Library of the Petrozavodsk University:** 185018 Petrozavodsk, Leninsky pr. 33; 627,000 vols.; Dir. V. S. KLODT.

**Scientific Library of the Rostov State University:** Rostov-on-Don, Pushkinskaya ul. 148; 1,570,000 vols.; Dir. N. K. PAVLOVA.

**Central Library of the Samarkand Alisher Navoi State University:** 703004 Samarkand, Bulvar Gorkogo 15; 1,632,000 vols.; collection of ancient oriental literature; Dir. A. A. ABBASOVA.

**Scientific Library of the Saratov N. G. Chernyshevsky State University:** Saratov, Universitetskaya ul. 42; 2,580,000 vols.; Dir. V. A. ARTISEVICH.

**Library of the Simferopol M. V. Frunze State University:** Simferopol 36, Yaltinskaya ul. 4; 776,000 vols.; Dir. A. E. GOLTS.

**Scientific Library of the Tajik V. I. Lenin State University:** 734016 Dushanbe, Leninsky pr. 17; 640,000 vols.; Dir. V. K. SULEYMANOVA.

**Scientific Library of the Tartu State University:** 202400 Tartu, Toomemägi; 3,400,000 vols.; Dir. L. PEEP.

**Central Library of the Tashkent V. I. Lenin State University:** 700095 Tashkent, Vuzgorodok; 2,460,000 vols.; Dir. S. KHALBAEV.

**Scientific Library of the Tbilisi State University:** 380028 Tbilisi, Ul. I. Chavchavadze 1; 2,851,500 vols.; Dir. S. APAKIDZE.

**Scientific Library of the Tomsk V. V. Kuibyshev State University:** 634010 Tomsk, Leninsky pr. 34-a; 3,320,000 vols.; Dir. M. I. SEREBRYAKOVA.

**Scientific Library of the Turkmen A. M. Gorky State University:** 744014 Ashkhabad, Pr. Lenina 31; about 542,000 vols.; Dir. A. T. VOROBYEVA.

**Library of the Tyumen State University:** 625036 Tyumen, Ul. Volodarskogo 38; 382,000 vols.; Dir. L. P. KRYUKOVA.

**Library of the Udmurt State University:** 426037 Izhevsk, Krasnogvardeysky pr. 71; 402,000 vols.; Dir. K. V. KAREVA.

**Scientific Library of the Urals A. M. Gorky State University:** Sverdlovsk, Ul. Kuibysheva 48-a; 1,000,000 vols.; Dir. T. D. VOROBYEVA.

**Scientific Library of the Uzhgorod State University:** Uzhgorod, Kremlevskaya ul. 9; 1,160,000 vols.; Dir. J. V. SABADOSH.

**Scientific Library of the V. Kapsukas State University of Vilnius:** 232633 Vilnius, Ul. Universiteta 3; f. 1570; 3,500,000 vols.; Dir. J. TORNAU; publs. *Mokslines bibliotekos metraštis†* (Yearbook of the Scientific Library, in Lithuanian, one every two years), *Manuscripta†*.

**Central Library of the Voronezh State University:** 394000 Voronezh, Pr. Revolyutsii 24; 1,470,000 vols.; Dir. S. V. YANU.

**Library of the Yakutsk State University:** 677891 Yakutsk, Leninsky pr. 33; 429,000 vols.; Dir. Z. A. AMMOSOVA.

**Library of the Yaroslavl State University:** 150000 Yaroslavl, Ul. Kirova 8/10; 263,000 vols.; Dir. V. A. DOKTOROVA.

TECHNICAL LIBRARIES:

**Republican Scientific and Technical Library of the Armenian S.S.R.:** 375009 Erevan, Moskovskaya 35; 19,770,000 vols.; Dir. I. S. AKOPYAN.

**Republican Scientific and Technical Library of the Azerbaijan S.S.R.:** 330001 Baku, Ul. G. Gadzhieva 3; 9,000,000 vols.; Dir. G. D. MAMEDOV.

**Republican Scientific and Technical Library of the Byelorussian S.S.R.:** 220676 Minsk, Ul. K. Marxa 10; 1,200,000 vols. (excl. patents); Dir. A. N. ZNARKO.

**Republican Scientific and Technical Library of the Estonian S.S.R.:** Tallinn, Lomonossovi 29; 6,590,000 vols.; Dir. B. USSATENKO.

**G. S. Mikeladze Republican Scientific and Technical Library of the Georgian S.S.R.:** Tbilisi-4, Ul. Dzneladze 27; 10,100,000 vols. (without patents); Dir. R. D. GORGILADZE.

**Republican Scientific and Technical Library of the Kazakh S.S.R.:** 480012 Alma-Ata-12; Ul. Komsomolskaya 73; 9,806,000 vols. (without patents); Dir. V. F. SADYKOVA.

**Republican Scientific and Technical Library of the Kirghiz S.S.R.:** 720302 Frunze, Leninsky pr. 106; 5,817,000 vols. (without patents); Dir. S. I. MAKAROV.

**Republican Scientific and Technical Library of the Latvian S.S.R.:** Riga, Pl. 17 Iyunya 6; 9,000,000 vols. (without patents); Dir. B. E. PAPENDIK.

**Republican Scientific and Technical Library of the Lithuanian S.S.R.:** 232634 Vilnius, Ul. Venuolio 6; 9,936,000 vols.; Dir. S. A. BRADAITIS.

**Republican Scientific and Technical Library of the Moldavian S.S.R.:** Kishinev, Ul. Chernyshevskogo 45; 6,542,000 vols., Dir. A. A. DNESTRYANSKY.

**Republican Scientific and Technical Library of the Tajik S.S.R.:** 734740 Dushanbe, Ul. Aini 14a; 4,700,000 vols. (without patents); Dir. S. D. MASAIDOVA.

**Republican Scientific and Technical Library of the Turkmen S.S.R.:** Ashkhabad, Pr. Svobody 106; 900,000 vols.; Dir. Z. I. CHEREPANOVA.

**State Republican Scientific and Technical Library of the Ukrainian S.S.R.:** 252004 Kiev, Ul. Gorkogo 180; 2,285,000 vols. (without patents); Dir. O. M. SEREGINA.

**Republican Scientific and Technical Library of the Uzbek S.S.R.:** Tashkent, Pr. Lenina 17; 1,200,000 vols. (without patents); Dir. V. I. KUZMINA.

## MUSEUMS AND ART GALLERIES

### ART AND ARCHITECTURE

#### Leningrad

**Leningrad Municipal Museum:** Nab. Krasny Flot 44; f. 1907; contains largest collection of material on the history and practice of city building in the Soviet Union; rare book of 500 drawings of the building of St. Petersburg up to 1836; Dir. L. N. Belova.

**Museum Palaces and Parks in Pavlovsk:** Leningrad region, Pavlovsk, Ul. Revolutsii 20; many examples of Russian garden architecture, sculpture by 18th-century Italian and French masters; paintings; decorations of Russian palaces; Dir. A. J. Zelenova.

**Museum Palaces and Parks in Petrodvoretz:** Petrodvoretz, Leningrad Region; f. 1918; 18th-19th century architecture and landscape gardening; library of 10,000 books; Dir. W. I. Konjukhov.

**Museum Palaces and Parks in Pushkin:** Pushkin, Leningrad Region, Komsomolskaya ul., dom 7; f. 1918; many examples of Russian garden architecture, sculpture by Italian and French masters of the 17th and 18th centuries; Dir. G. E. Beliaev.

**Museum of Sculpture:** Pl. A. Nevskogo 1; largest collection of Russian sculpture, collection and care of documents on architecture and town planning; over 150,000 sheets of architectural drawings; Dir. N. H. Belova.

**State Hermitage Museum:** M. Dvortsovaya naberezhnaya 34; f. 1764 as a court museum; opened to public 1852; richest collection in Soviet Union of the art of prehistoric, ancient Eastern, Graeco-Roman and mediaeval times; preserves over 2,500,000 *objets d'art*, including 40,000 drawings, 500,000 engravings; works by Leonardo de Vinci, Raphael, Titian, Rubens and Rembrandt; collection of coins, weapons and applied art; Dir. B. B. Piotrovsky.

**State Russian Museum:** Inzhenernaya 2; opened as an Art Museum in 1898; 306,000 exhibits of Russian art; largest collection of Russian and Soviet sculpture, drawings and art of the 18th and early 19th centuries; collection of Russian coins and medals and children's drawings; Dir. V. A. Pushkarev.

**Summer Garden and Museum Palace of Peter the Great:** 18th-century architecture and sculpture; Dir. K. M. Egorova.

#### Moscow

**Folk-Art Museum:** Ul. Stanislavskogo 7; f. 1885; three sections devoted to (a) handicrafts connected with peasant daily life; (b) applied arts both ancient and contemporary; (c) experimental decorative applied art; about 30,000 exhibits; under the jurisdiction of the R.S.F.S.R. Council of Industrial Co-operative Societies; Dir. N. N. Ivanova.

**(Andrei) Rublyov Museum of Ancient Russian Art:** Ul. Pryamikova 10; paintings of ancient Moscow; Dir. G. H. Belyaeva-Lorents.

**(A. V.) Shchusev Architectural Museum of the State Committee of Building and Architecture:** Kalininsky prospekt 5; f. 1934; objects: study, collection, care and popularization of historical architecture, outstanding contemporary work, monumental sculpture and painting; collection and care of documents on architecture and town planning; over 70,000 sheets of architectural drawings; over 300,000 negatives and 400,000 photographs of architectural monuments throughout the world; Dir. V. I. Baldin; Deputy Dir. E. B. Purishev; Curator A. N. Lupol; Sec. K. V. Usacheva.

**State Museum of Ceramics (country-seat Kuskovo):** St. Kuskovo; large collection of Russian art, carpets, fabrics, ceramics, etc.; Dir. O. F. Baranova.

**State Museum of Oriental Art:** Ul. Obukha 16; f. 1918; large collection of Middle and Far Eastern art, art of the Soviet Central Asian Republics and Zakavkazie, carpets, fabrics, ceramics, etc.; Dir. V. S. Manin.

**State Pushkin Museum of Fine Arts:** Volkhonka 12; f. 1912; about 500,000 items of ancient Eastern, Graeco-Roman, Byzantine, European and American art; numismatics; library of 110,000 vols.; Dir. I. A. Antonova; publ. *Soobstcheniya* (Information).

**State Tretyakov Gallery:** Lavrushensky per. 10; f. 1856; contains a rich collection of 40,000 Russian icons and works of Russian and Soviet painters, sculptors and graphic artists from the 11th century to modern times; Dir. P. I. Lebedev.

#### State Capitals

**Armenian State Picture Gallery:** Ul. Spandaryana 2, 375010 Erevan, Armenian S.S.R.; f. 1921; 17,000 items of West European, Armenian, Russian and Oriental art; Dir. E. Issapekian.

**Azerbaijan R. Mustafaev State Art Museum:** Ul. Chkalova 9, Baku, Azerbaijan S.S.R.; 7,000 exhibits; Dir. Z. M. Kyazim.

**Byelorussian State Art Museum:** Ul. Lenina 20, Minsk; f. 1939; 14,000 items of Russian, Byelorussian and foreign art; Dir. Elena V. Aladova.

**Estonian State Open Air Museum:** 200016 Tallinn, Rokkaal-Mare, Vabaõhumuuseumi tee 12; 38,000 exhibits including architectural and ethnographical objects of 18th–20th centuries; Dir. L. H. Paiken.

**Georgian State Art Museum:** Ul. Ketskhoveli 1, Tbilisi, Georgian S.S.R.; Dir. S. Y. Amiranishvili.

**Georgian State Museum of Oriental Art:** Tbilisi, Ul. Azizbekova 3; large collection of Georgian art, carpets, fabrics, etc.; Dir. G. M. Gbishiani.

**Georgian State Picture Gallery:** Pr. Rustaveli 11, Tbilisi, Georgian S.S.R.; Dir. M. A. Kipiani.

**Kazakh T. G. Shevchenko State Art Gallery:** Ul. Sovietskaya 22, Alma-Ata, Kazakh S.S.R.; 10,000 exhibits, mainly modern Kazakh artists; Dir. Mrs. Plakhotnaya.

**Kiev State Museum of Ukrainian Art:** Ul. Kirova 6, Kiev, Ukrainian S.S.R.; 11,000 items; chronological exhibition covering eight centuries; icons, portraits, woodcarvings and paintings from the Middle Ages; Dir. V. F. Yatsenko.

**Kiev State Museum of Russian Art:** Ul. Repina 5, Kiev, Ukrainian S.S.R.; 10,000 items; Dir. A. T. Kniukh.

**Kiev State Museum of Western and Oriental Art:** Ul. Repina 15, Kiev, Ukrainian S.S.R.; 16,000 items; Dir. V. F. Ovchinnikov.

**Kiev State Sofiysky Museum:** Kiev, Ul. Vladimirskaya 24; large collection of sculpture; collection and care of documents on architecture; over 100,000 sheets of architectural drawings; Dir. Valentina Achkasova.

**Kirghiz State Museum of Fine Art:** Ul. Pervomaiskaya 90, Frunze, Kirghiz S.S.R.; 4,000 modern items; Dir. K. N. Uzubalieva.

**Latvian State Museum of Foreign Fine Arts:** Pl. Pionerov 3, Riga, Latvian S.S.R.; 15,000 exhibits; Dir. K. G. Andreev.

**Lithuanian State Art Museum:** Ul. Gorkogo 55, Vilnius, Lithuanian S.S.R.; f. 1941; 70,000 items; Lithuanian art and also Italian, Flemish, German, French and English artists from 16th to 19th centuries; Dir. P. Gudinas.

**Lithuanian State Picture Gallery:** Pl. Gediminasa, Vilnius; 12,000 works of Western European and Soviet artists; Dir. V. Pechura.

## MUSEUMS AND ART GALLERIES

**Moldavian State Art Museum:** Ul. Lenina 115, Kishinev, Moldavian S.S.R.; 6,000 exhibits; Dir. M. P. PETRIK.

**State Museum of Latvian and Russian Art:** Gorkogo ul. 10, Riga, Latvian S.S.R.; 42,000 exhibits; Dir. K. G. ANDREEV.

**State Museum Palace of Shirvan-Shakh:** Baku, fortress Zamkovaya Gora 76; large collection of weapons, applied art, decorations of Khan palaces.

**Tallinn State Art Museum:** Kadrioru Palee, Weizenberg[i] 37, Tallinn 200010, Estonian S.S.R.; f. 1919; 28,000 items; Dir. I. TEDER.

**Turkmen State Museum of Fine Art:** Pr. Svobody 84, Ashkhabad, Turkmenian S.S.R.; 7,000 works of Soviet and West European artists; collection of Turkmenian carpets; Dir. N. HODZAMUHAMEDOV.

**Ukrainian Museum of Folk and Decorative Art:** Kiev, Ul. Yanvarskogo Vosstaniya 21; f. 1954; 54,834 exhibits from 16th century onward, including wood carvings, embroideries, weaving, ceramics, national costumes, glass, china; library of 3,180 vols.; Dir. V. G. NAGAI; publ. *Folk Creative Work and Ethnography*.

**Uzbek State Museum of Art:** Ul. Gogolya 101, Tashkent, Uzbek S.S.R.; Dir. S. F. ABDULLAYEV.

### OTHER TOWNS

**Altai State Museum of Applied Arts:** Barnaul, Ul. Sovietskaya 28, R.S.F.S.R.; large collection of wood carvings, ceramics, national costumes, etc.; Dir. A. E. NAJEHAS.

**Alupka Palace Museum:** Alupka, Krymskoi obl.; Dir. A. P. TSARIN.

**Arkhangelsk State Museum of Fine Arts:** Arkhangelsk, Nab. Lenina 79; contains over 25,000 items of ancient North and Western European art; library of 20,000 vols.; Dir. M. V. MITKEVICH.

**Astrakhan State B. M. Kustodiev Gallery:** Astrakhan, Ul. Sverdlova 81; contains a rich collection of works of Russian and Soviet painters, sculptors and graphic artists, etc.

**Baussky Art Museum:** Bausska, Ul. Padomyu 16, Latvian S.S.R.; 8,000 works of Soviet and Western European artists.

**Bryansk State Museum of Soviet Fine Arts:** Bryansk, Ul. Gagarina 19, R.S.F.S.R.; Dir. B. F. FAENKOV.

**Checheno-Ingush Museum of Fine Arts:** Grozny, Pr. Revolutsii 26/36; 5,600 exhibits; Dir. S. S. BRODSKY.

**Chelyabinsk State Picture Gallery:** Chelyabinsk, Ul. Truda 92-a, R.S.F.S.R.; 5,000 items; Dir. I. F. TKACHENKO.

**Chuvash Picture Gallery:** Cheboksary, Ul. R. Luksemburg 13; 7,000 exhibits, mainly modern Russian and Chuvash artists; Dir. L. S. KARANDAEV.

**Daghestan Museum of Fine Arts:** Makhachkala, Ul. Markova 45; 7,000 exhibits.

**Dnepropetrovsk State Art Museum:** Ul. Shevchenko 21, Dnepropetrovsk, Ukrainian S.S.R.

**Donetsk Museum of Art:** Donetsk, Ul. Artema 84, Ukrainian S.S.R.; 3,000 exhibits.

**Erevan Children's Picture Gallery:** Erevan, Ul. Abovian; f. 1970; the first children's art gallery in the Soviet Union; exhibits works of Armenian children as well as those of other nationalities; 100,000 items (drawings, paintings, sculpture, ceramics, etc.); Dir. H. IKITIAN.

**Gorky State Art Museum:** Nab. im. Zhdanova 3, Gorky; 6,500 works of Soviet and Western European artists Dir. B. P. BATURO.

**Irkutsk Museum of Art:** Irkutsk, Ul. K. Marxa 23, R.S.F.S.R.; 2,000 exhibits; Dir. A. D. FATJYASOV.

**Ivanovo Museum of Art:** Ivanovo, Per. Lenina 33, R.S.F S.R.; 3,000 modern items; Dir. I. N. LEBEDEVA.

## UNION OF SOVIET SOCIALIST REPUBLICS

**Kabarda-Balkar Art Museum:** Nalchik, Pr. V. I. Lenina 35; 3,500 exhibits; Dir. I. Z. BATASHOV.

**Kalinin Art Gallery:** Kalinin 170640, Ul. Sovetskaya 3; f. 1937; 3,500 exhibits; Dir. N. F. SUDAROVA.

**Kaluga Museum of Art:** Kaluga, Ul. Lenina 104; 2,700 exhibits; Dir. A. V. KAZAK.

**Karakalpak Art Museum:** Karakalpak A.S.S.R., Nukus, Ul. K. Marxa 2; 1,800 exhibits.

**Karelian Museum of Fine Arts:** Karelian A.S.S.R., Petrozavodsk, Pr. K. Marxa 8; 9,000 items; Dir. M. V. POPOVA.

**Kaunas M. K. Chiurlenis State Art Museum:** Ul. S. Neres 55, Kaunas, Lithuanian S.S.R.; f. 1925; 211,660 items of Lithuanian art and also Russian, French and Italian artists; Dir. P. A. STAUSKAS; additional branches in Kaunas, Druskininkai and Jurbarkas.

**Kharkov State Art Museum:** Sovnarkomovskaya ul. 11, Kharkov, Ukrainian S.S.R.; 8,000 pictures including work by leading Ukrainian and Russian artists; Dir. N. P. ROBOTIAGOV.

**Kirov A. M. Gorky Museum:** Kirov, Ul. K. Marxa 70; 4,000 exhibits; Dir. A. H. NOSKOVA.

**Kolomya State Museum of Folk Art:** Ivanov-Frankivska obl., Teatralnaya ul. 25, Kolomya, Ukrainian S.S.R.

**Komi Art Museum:** Syktyvkar, Ul. Kommunisticheskaya 6; 3,400 exhibits; Dir. F. K. POPOVTSIEVA.

**Komsomolsk-on-Amur Museum of Soviet Fine Arts:** Komsomolsk-on-Amur, Pr. Truda 50; 2,500 exhibits; Dir. V. D. BASHA.

**Kostroma Museum of Fine Arts:** Kostroma, Pr. Mira 5; 2,500 items; Dir. V. Y. IGNATEV.

**Krasnoyarsk Picture Gallery:** Krasnoyarsk, Pr. Krasnoyarskogo 68; contains a large collection of Eastern and Siberian art, carpets, fabrics, etc.; library of 70,000 vols.; Dir. V. I. LOMANOV.

**Kuibyshev Art Museum:** 44301 Kuibyshev 10, Kuibyshev Squ., Palace of Culture; f. 1897; fine arts museum with 11,000 exhibits; library of 7,000 vols.; Dir. ANNETA Y. BASS.

**Kursk Art Gallery:** Kursk, Ul. Sovetskaya 3; 4,800 exhibits; Dir. N. D. VLASOVA.

**Lvov State Museum of Ukrainian Art:** Ul. Dragomanova 42, Lvov, Ukrainian S.S.R.; Dir. G. D. YAKUSHCHENKO.

**Lvov State Picture Gallery:** Ul. Stefanika 3, Lvov, Ukrainian S.S.R.; Dir. B. G. VOZNITSKY.

**Minsk State Art Museum:** Minsk, Ul. Lenina 20; 6,750 exhibits; Dir. E. V. ALADOVA.

**Mordovian Art Gallery:** Saransk, Ul. Sovietskaya 29; 4,000 exhibits.

**Odessa Museum of Western and Eastern Art:** Ul. Pushkinshaya 9, Odessa, Ukrainian S.S.R.; f. 1920; 5,190 exhibits; Dir. I. I. KOZIROD.

**Odessa State Picture Gallery:** Ul. Korolenko 5, Odessa, Ukrainian S.S.R.; 3,300 items; Dir. O. M. KARPENKO.

**Omsk Fine Art Museum:** Omsk, Ul. Lenina 23; 3,780 exhibits; Dir. A. A. GERZON.

**Orenburg Fine Art Museum:** Orenburg, Ul. Pravdy 6; 3,500 items; Dir. L. B. POPOVA.

**Orlovskaya Art Gallery:** Orel, Ul. Saltikova-Schedrina 37; 6,000 exhibits; Dir. N. G. ANTIPOV.

**State Museum of Palekh Art:** Ul. Bakanova 50, selo Palekh, Ivanovsk; 2,500 items of Palekh art; Dir. G. M. MELNIKOV.

**Penza Picture Gallery:** Penza, Ul. Bogdanova 1/6; f. 1898; library of 1,400 vols.; 4,700 exhibits.

**Perm State Art Gallery:** Komsomolsky prospekt 2, Perm.

**Poltava Art Museum:** Poltava, Ul. Dzerdzhiskogo 11; 2,872 exhibits; Curator SASONOV VALERY.

**Rostov Museum of Fine Art:** Rostov-on-Don, Ul. Pushkinskaya 115; 5,780 exhibits; Dir. Y. L. RUDNIZKAYA.

**Ryazan Regional Art Museum:** Ryazan, Kremlin 11; f. 1913; old Russian and Soviet Art; library of 7,500 vols.; Dir. S. M. STEPASHKIN.

**Saratov A. N. Radishchev State Art Museum:** Pl. Radishcheva 39, Saratov; 15,000 exhibits; Dir. V. G. PUGAYEYEV.

**Stavropol Museum of Fine Art:** Stavropol, Ul. Dzerzhinskogo 115; 4,270 exhibits; Dir. N. A. KIRAKOZOVA.

**Sumy State Art Museum:** Ul. Lenina 67, Sumy, Ukrainian S.S.R.; Dir. M. M. KOMAROV.

**Sverdlovsk Picture Gallery:** Sverdlovsk, Ul. Vainera 11; f. 1746; Western European, Russian and Soviet artists and objects from the Kishisk foundries; Dir. E. V. KHAMTSOV.

**Tambov Picture Gallery:** Tambov, Ul. Sovietskaya 59; 3,500 exhibits; Dir. A. K. KULAKOVA.

**Tartu Art Museum:** Tartu, Vallikraavi 14; f. 1940; 10,000 pictures, sculptures and graphic art by Western European, Estonian and Russian artists; Dir. V. TIIK.

**Tatar State Museum of Fine Arts:** Kazan, Ul. K. Marxa 64; large collections of Russian and Soviet paintings.

**Tobolsk Picture Gallery:** Tobolsk, Pl. Krasnaya 2; 1,800 items.

**Tula Art Museum:** Tula, Ul. Engelsa 144; 4,000 exhibits; Dir. S. F. NECHAEVA.

**Tyumen Picture Gallery:** Tyumen, Ul. Republic 29; 9,000 exhibits; Dir. I. S. TERENTJEV.

**Vologda Picture Gallery:** Vologda, Pl. Kremlina 3; 6,500 exhibits; Dir. S. G. IVENSKY.

**Voronezh Art Museum:** Voronezh, Pr. Revolusii 16; 6,900 exhibits; Dir. E. A. REZNIKOVA.

**Yakutsk Museum of Fine Arts:** Yakutsk, Ul. Maxima Ammosova 14; folk art, Western European, Russian and Soviet Art of 17th to 20th centuries; Dir. L. M. GABYSHEV.

## HISTORY AND ETHNOLOGY

### LENINGRAD

**Central Naval Museum:** Leningrad 199164, Pl. Pushkina 4; f. 1709; 174,000 items of relics and other materials from the Russian and Soviet Navies; departments of history of the Russian Navy, history of the Soviet Navy, history of the Navy in the 1941-45 period, history of the Navy in the post-war period; 17,000 vols. in library; Dir. Capt. M. A. FATEEV.

**Military Medical Museum of the U.S.S.R. Ministry of Defence:** Leningrad F-180, Lazaretny per. 2; f. 1942; 125,000 exhibits trace the history of Russian and Soviet military medicine since 14th century; Dir. Col. V. I. MAKAROV.

**Museum of Artillery, Signal Corps and Corps of Engineers:** Park Lenina 7; f. 1702 by Peter the Great; 170,000 items; the present museum traces the history of Russian and Soviet artillery, Corps of Engineers and the Signal Corps; Dir. Col. A. A. BUMAGIN.

**Museum of the History of Religion and Atheism:** 191186 Kazanskaya pl. 2; f. 1932; 150,000 exhibits on religion, sects and denominations, the origin of Christianity and the struggle against religion; includes documents, books, church plate and works of art; Dir. V. N. SHERDAKOV.

**Peter the Great Museum of Anthropology and Ethnography:** Leningrad B-164, Universitetskaya nab. 3; f. 1714; the 340,000 items provide ethnographical, archaeological, and anthropological material on the native peoples of North and South America, Australia, and Oceania, the Near East, Central and Eastern Asia; Asst. Dir. L. M. SABUROVA; publs. *Sbornik Museya Antropologii i Etnografii* (Catalogue of the Museum of Anthropology and Ethnography, irregular), Leningrad Vols. *I–XXV* (1900–1969).

**State Ethnographical Museum of the Peoples of the U.S.S.R.:** Inzhenernaya ul. 4/1; 300,000 exhibits covering 19th century to present day; Dir. D. A. SERGEEV.

**State Museum of the Great October Socialist Revolution:** Ul. Kuibysheva 4; f. 1919; the 310,800 items, which include 204,800 books, show the economic and political background of the Revolution, cover the Civil War and the Second World War and the development of socialism in the U.S.S.R.; Dir. L. A. ULBEYOB.

**State Museum of the History of Leningrad:** Naberezhnaya Krasnogo Flota 44; f. 1918; the museum contains 300,000 exhibits featuring the architecture and history of Leningrad; the museum has a branch at the Peter and Paul Fortress, showing the history and architectural history of St. Petersburg and the history of Soviet cosmonautics; Dir. L. N. BELOVA.

### MOSCOW

**Central Lenin Museum:** Pl. Revolyutsii 2; f. 1936; contains c. 12,500 items including documents, photographs, works of art, and other exhibits relating to Lenin's life and works; Dir. O. S. KRIVOSHEINA.

Annexes of the Central Lenin Museum:
Ulianovsk, Ul. Lva Tolstogo 33.
Leningrad, Ul. Khalturina 5/1.
Kiev, Vladimirskaya ul. 57.
Tbilisi, Pr. Rustaveli 29.
Lvov, Pr. imeni Lenina 20.
Baku, Pr. Neftyanikov 123/a.
Tashkent, Blvd. Lenin 30.

**Central Museum of Aviation and Cosmonautics:** Moscow, Krasnoarmeyskaya 14; f. 1924; to record the national development of aeronautics and astronautics; contains original full-size aircraft, spacecraft, recovered space exploration vehicles, instruments, flight clothing, accessories of technical, historical and biographical interest; library of 12,000 vols.; Learned Sec. I. P. KOSTIENKO.

**Central Museum of the Armed Forces of the U.S.S.R.:** Pl. Communy 2; Dir. V. I. KRASNOV.

**Central Museum of the Revolution of the U.S.S.R. (Order of Lenin):** Ul. Gorkogo 21; f. 1924; 1,000,000 exhibits trace the history of the revolution in Russia, and the history of Soviet society from 1917 to the present; library of 300,000 vols. and 600,000 periodicals; Dir. F. G. KROTOV; publ. *Trudy* (Proceedings).

**M. I. Kalinin State Museum:** Prospekt Marxa 21; f. 1950; the 12,500 exhibits trace the life and work of M. I. Kalinin; Dir. L. I. YUSKOVA.

**Kremlin Museums:** Kremlin; Dir. N. G. NEMIROV.

   **Armoury:** f. 1857; about 80,000 items of applied decorative art from the 12th century onwards.

   **Kremlin Cathedrals:** the cathedrals around the Cathedral Square (Sobornaya ploshchad) include, among others, the following: Cathedral of the Assumption (f. 1479); icons of the 14th–17th centuries; throne of Ivan the Terrible. Cathedral of the Anunciation (f. 1489); iconostasis by leading artists of the 15th century. Archangel Cathedral (1508); tombs of Ivan Kalita and other Russian Grand Dukes and Czars. Rizpolozhensky Cathedral (f. 1485). Cathedral of the Twelve Apostles and Patriarch's Palace; 17th-century items of applied decorative art.

## MUSEUMS AND ART GALLERIES

**Marx-Engels Museum:** Ul. Marxa-Engelsa; f. 1962; 2,000 exhibits descriptive of the lives of Marx and Engels; Dir. N. N. IVANOV.

**Museum of Frontier Guards:** Moscow, Ul. B. Bronnaya 23; 110,000 exhibits featuring the history of Soviet frontier guards.

**Museum of the History and Reconstruction of the City of Moscow:** Novaya pl. 12; f. 1896; Dir. L. A. YASTRZHEMBSKY.

**State Historical Museum:** 1/2 Krasnaya Pl.; f. 1872; the only central historical museum in the U.S.S.R.; 3,812,280 exhibits covering Russian history from prehistory to the present; Dir. K. G. LEVIKIN; Sec. N. PANUKHINA; publs. *Trudi GIM*, *Pamjatnikikulturi GIM* (irregular).

### OTHER TOWNS
(In alphabetical order by town).

**Central State Museum of the Kazakh S.S.R.:** Alma-Ata, Park imeni 28, Panfilovtsev; contains 90,000 exhibits featuring the history, and the climatic and physical conditions of Kazakhstan; Dir. R. K. KOSHAMBEKOVA.

**Arkhangelsk State Museum:** Arkhangelsk, Ul. P. Vinogradova 100; contains 180,000 items featuring the history of the North coast area of the Soviet Union, dating back to ancient times; large collection of sculpture, icons, national costumes; Dir. Y. P. PROKOPIEV.

**Central State Museum of the Turkmen S.S.R.:** Ashkhabad, Ul. Engelsa 90; 200,000 exhibits tracing the history of the Turkmen people, material from excavations of the Stone Age, Mesolithic Age, Neolithic Kurgans, etc.

**Bakhchisarai State Museum of History and Archaeology:** Bakhchisarai, Krymskaya Oblast; f. 1917; contains art collections and architectural monuments; the cave towns are world famous; library of 12,000 vols.; Dir. I. I. CHURILOV; publ. *Sovietskaya arkheologiya*.

**Museum of the History of Azerbaijan of the Azerbaijan S.S.R. Academy of Sciences:** Baku, Ul. Malygina 4; f. 1920; 120,000 exhibits trace the history of the Azerbaijanian people from ancient times; Dir. P. A. AZIZBEKOVA; publ. *Trudy Muzeya Istorii Azerbaijana* (Activities of the Museum of the History of Azerbaijan).

**Borodino State Museum-Preserve of Military History:** Moskovskaya oblast, Mozhaisk, village of Borodino; f. 1903; research into 1812 campaign, the Battle of Borodino and the 1941–45 war; 4,700 exhibits include material on the Battle of Borodino; library of 7,100 vols.; Dir. EVGENI G. SINITSYN; Curator VLADIMIR E. CHISHOV.

**Dneprodzerzhinsk Museum of Town History:** Dneprodzerzhinsk, Ukrainian S.S.R.; 80,000 exhibits, relating to the history of the struggle of the Ukrainian people for their independence; special collections of archaeology; an exhibition devoted to the history of the town.

**Dnepropetrovsk Historical Museum:** Dnepropetrovsk, Ul. K. Marxa 16; 100,000 exhibits tracing the history, economy and culture of Ukrainian people and working class movement.

**Tajik Historical State Museum:** Dushanbe, Ul. Ayni 31; 90,000 items describing the history, culture and art of the peoples of Tajikistan; library of over 200,000 vols.

**State Historical Museum of the Armenian S.S.R.:** Erevan, Pl. Lenina; 160,000 exhibits tracing the history of the Armenian people; Dir. M. S. ASRATYAN.

**State Historical Museum of the Kirghiz S.S.R.:** Frunze, Krasnooktyabrskaya ul. 236; the 20,000 items on display trace the history of Kirghizia from remote times down to the present; Dir. N. M. SEITKAZIEVA.

**Stalin Museum:** Gori, Georgian S.S.R.; reopened 1965; containing exhibits relating to the life and work of Joseph Stalin.

## UNION OF SOVIET SOCIALIST REPUBLICS

**Gorky Historical Museum:** Gorky, Nab. Zhdanova 7; 160,000 exhibits including collections of archaeology, featuring the history of the Central Volga area dating back to ancient times.

**Grodno State Historical Museum:** Grodno, Ul. Zamkovaya 22; 90,000 exhibits feature the history, economy, science, culture and natural history of the Byelorussian S.S.R.

**Kamenets-Podolsk State Historical Museum-Preserve:** Kamenets-Podolsk, Khmelnitskaya Oblast, Ul. K. Marxa 20; extensive collection of exhibits relating to the history of the struggle of the Ukrainian people for their independence; Dir. K. G. MIKOLAIOVICH.

**Kaunas State Historical Museum:** Kaunas, Ul. Donelaitis 64; f. 1921; 127,459 exhibits including special collections of archaeology, numismatics and weaponry and an exhibition devoted to the history of Lithuania; library of 5,510 vols.; Dir. A. Y. KVEDARAS.

**State Museum of the Tatar A.S.S.R.:** Kazan, Ul. Lenina 2; f. 1894; over 500,000 exhibits on the history, life, natural resources, and art of the Tatar A.S.S.R.; library of 5,000 vols.; Dir. V. M. DIAKONOV; publ. *Sbornik nauchnikh rabot* (once every two years).

**Tatar Historical Museum (house of V. I. Lenin):** Kazan, Ul. Ulyanova 58; 10,000 exhibits including documents, photographs, works of art and other exhibits relating to Lenin's life.

**Kerch State Historico-Archaeological Museum:** Kerch, Krymskaya oblast, Ul. Sverdlova 22; material from excavations of the stone age, mesolithic, neolithic, Kurgan, dark ages and mediaeval periods and an exhibition of the history of Kerch from the 19th century; Dir. N. I. LITVINENKO.

**Kharkov State Historical Museum:** Kharkov, Universitetskaya ul. 10; contains 176,000 exhibits on the history of the revolutionary and working class movement; Dir. N. A. VOYEVODIN.

**Khorezm Historical-Revolutionary Museum:** Khiva, Ul. Lermontova 41, Uzbek S.S.R.; 25,000 exhibits relating to the history of the struggle of the Uzbek people for independence.

**Kiev-Pechersky State Historical Museum:** Kiev, Ul. Yanvarskogo Vosstaniya 21; one of the oldest monasteries in the U.S.S.R.; large collection of icons.

**Kiev State Historical Museum:** Kiev, Vladimirskaya 2; the 53,000 exhibits tracing the history, economy and culture of the Ukrainian people from the earliest times; Dir. I. E. DUDNIK.

**Suvorov Museum:** Novogorodskaya Region, Boroviansky district, village of Konchanskoye-Suvorovskoye; the museum features the main periods in the life of A. V. Suvorov; Dir. V. P. MALYSHEVA.

**Kutaissi State Museum of History and Ethnography:** Kutaissi, Ul. Tbilisi 1; 10,000 items provide ethnographical, archaeological and anthropological material on the native peoples of Georgia; large collection, featuring the history and the climatic and physical conditions of Georgia; Dir. M. V. NIKOLISHVILI.

**Latvian Open-Air Ethnographical Museum:** Riga; the 47 wooden structures from all over Latvia collected on the museum grounds demonstrate Latvian art and architecture; Dir. A. N. NESTEROVA.

**Lvov Museum of Ethnology:** Lvov, Pr. Lenina 15; 80,000 items provide ethnographical, archaeological and anthropological material.

**State Museum of Ethnography and Arts and Crafts of the Ukrainian Academy of Sciences:** Lvov, Pr. Lenina 15; f. 1873; 75,500 exhibits; Dir. Dr. Y. G. GOSHKO.

**Lvov Historical Museum:** Lvov, Pl. Rynok 4/6; the 225,000 exhibits trace the history of western Ukraine, from the earliest period to the present time; Dir. A. A. ZHIVAGO.

**Maloyaroslavets Museum of Military History of 1812:** Maloyaroslavets, Moskovskaya ul. 13; Dir. A. E. DMITRIEV.

**Byelorussian State Museum of History of World War II:** Minsk, Pr. Lenina 23; the 100,000 exhibits show aspects of the Soviet Army's history from 1941 to 1945.

**State Museum of the Byelorussian S.S.R.:** Minsk, Ull Marxa 12-k; 206,000 exhibits from primitive communa. society to the present day and local natural history; library of 13,200 vols.; Dir. I. P. ZAGRISHEV.

**Novocherkassk Museum of the History of the Don Cossacks:** Novocherkassk, Ul. Sovetskaya 38; deals with the traditions and exploits of the Don Cossacks; branch at Staro-Cherkassk containing a detailed exhibition on Stepan Razin, the 17th century leader of the peasant liberation movement; Dir. P. I. MOLCHANOV.

**Kara-Kalpak Historical Museum:** Nukus, Ul. Rakhmatova 3; contains material on the part played by the Uzbek people in the October Socialist Revolution, the civil war and the Second World War.

**Odessa Archaeological Museum:** Odessa, Ul. Lastochkina 4; f. 1825; contains about 200,000 items featuring the history of the Northern Black Sea Coast area dating back to ancient times; large collection of coins and medals; Dir. I. T. TCHERNYAKOV.

**Karelian State Museum of Regional History:** Karelian A.S.S.R., Petrozavodsk, Zavodskaya pl. 1; 70,000 exhibits feature the history, economy, science, culture, and natural history of the area; two branches: historical museum of the resort Martsialniye Vody and of petroglyphs at Byelomorsk; Dir. V. IONOVA.

**Kizhi State Historical Museum:** 1 Lenin Square, Petrozavodsk; f. 1961; history, ethnography, early Russian wood architecture; library of 4,000 vols.; Dir. E. EONOVA.

**State Museum of the History of Riga:** Riga, Palasta 4; f. 1773; material on Riga's archaeology, history and navigation; Dir. L. F. BLUMFELD.

**Latvian Historical Museum:** Riga, Pl. Pionerov 3; material on archaeology, history and ethnography; material on the history of religion and atheism; Dir. A. A. BULLITE.

**Latvian S.S.R. Revolution Museum:** Riga, Ul. Smilshu 20; contains material on the part played by the Latvian people in the October Socialist Revolution, the Civil War and the Second World War; Dir. H. Y. LAPINSH.

**P. Stradin Historical-Medical Museum:** Riga, L. Paegles ul. 1, Latvian S.S.R.; f. 1957, opened 1961; contains about 100,000 medical objects, photographs, drawings, etc., illustrating the history of the development of medicine from prehistoric times to the present day; library of 40,000 vols., including 3,000 rare medical books of the 16th to the 20th centuries; Dir. M. S. LEBEDKOVA.

**Roslavl Historical Museum:** Roslavl, Ul. Proletarskaya 63; collection tracing the history, economy and culture of Russian people from the earliest times.

**Ryazan Historico-architectural Museum Reservation:** Ryazan, Kremlin 118; over 108,000 items describing the history, culture and art of the peoples of Russia.

**Museum of Uzbek History, Culture and Arts:** Samarkand, Sovetskaya ul. 51; f. 1874; over 100,000 items describing the history, culture and art of the peoples of Uzbekistan; Dir. N. S. SADYKOVA.

**Khersones Museum of History and Archaeology:** Sevastopol-28; f. c. 1860; includes finds from the excavations of the site of Khersones, a colony of the ancient Greeks; library of 20,000 vols.; Dir. I. A. ANTONOVA.

**Novodevichy Monastery Museum:** Smolensky Cathedral (1524) and other monuments of Russian architecture form the architectural ensemble of the monastery; Russian fine and decorative art (16th–17th centuries); Dir. V. G. VERZHBITSKY.

**Stepano-Kert Museum of History of Nagorno-Karabakhskoy A.O.:** Stepano-Kert, Ul. Gorkogo 4; collection on the history of the Azerbaijan people; material on archaeology and ethnography.

**State Museum of the Abkhasian A.S.S.R.:** Sukhumi, Ul. Lenina 22; f. 1915; 100,000 exhibits trace the history of the Abkhasian people; the museum has an annex at the Novo-Afonsky Monastery; Dir. A. A. ARGUN.

**State Historical Museum of the Estonian S.S.R.:** Tallinn, Pikk 17; f. 1864; 193,000 exhibits trace the history of the Estonian people from ancient times to the present; Dir. P. SILLAOTS.

**Tallinn City Museum:** Tallinn, Vene 17; f. 1937; library of 3,300 vols.; Dir. M. TEDER.

**Museum of Classical Archaeology of the Tartu State University:** Tartu, Ulikooli 18; f. 1802; mainly plaster reproduction of ancient sculpture, gems and coins; a few original vases and original graphic works by Western European authors (15th–19th centuries); library of over 12,000 vols.; Dir. O. UTTER.

**State Ethnographical Museum of the Estonian S.S.R.:** Tartu, N. Burdenko 32; 500,000 exhibits on conditions of work and life of the Estonian and Finno-Ugric people; Dir. A. PETERSON.

**Tashkent Historical Museum of the People of Uzbekistan:** Tashkent, Ul. Kuibysheva 15; 80,000 exhibits on the life of the people of Central Asia, from primitive communal society to the present time.

**State Museum of the History of Georgia:** Tbilisi, Pr. Rustaveli 3; f. 1852; archaeological material on the history and ethnography of Georgia from ancient times to the present; library of over 204,000 vols.; Dir. N. G. CHERKEZISHVILI; publ. *Izvestia* (Bulletin) (annually).

**Tbilisi State Museum of Anthropology and Ethnography:** Tbilisi, Pr. Komsomolsky 11; archaeological material on the history and ethnography of Georgia from ancient times to the present; library of over 150,000 vols.; Dir. A. V. TKESHELASHVILI.

**Tobolsk State Historical Museum:** Tobolsk, Pl. Krasnaya 2; exhibits on the history of the Revolution in Siberia.

**Trakai Historical Museum:** Lithuanian S.S.R., Trakai; f. 1948; the museum has over 20,150 items relating to the history of the city and castle of Trakai and the surrounding areas; Dir. I. V. MISIUNENE.

**Tsessissky State Historical Museum:** Tsessiss, Ul. Pils 9; 60,000 exhibits on every stage of history; special archaeological, numismatic and ethnographical collections.

**Tula Historical Museum:** Tula, Ul. Sovietskaya 68; contains material on the part played by Tula people during the Great October Socialist Revolution.

**Uglich Historical Museum:** Uglich, Kremlin 3; exhibits on the history of the Russian people.

**Vilkovyissky P. I. Bagration Historical Museum:** Vilkovyisk, Ul. Bagrationa 10; aspects of Russian Army history from 1812 to 1814; large collection tracing the history of the Russian Army in the 1812 campaign; library of 10,000 vols.

**Historico-Ethnographic Museum of the Lithuanian S.S.R.:** Vilnius, Ul. Vrublevskio 1; f. 1856; over 150,000 exhibits portray the life of the nation at all stages of its history; special archaeological, numismatic and ethnographical collections; Dir. V. S. ZHILENAS.

**Museum of the Revolution of the Lithuanian S.S.R.:** Vilnius, Ul. K. Pozhelov 32/1; f. 1948; about 70,000 exhibits depicting the revolutionary movement in Lithuania from the end of the 19th century; Dir. A. A. SHVARTSEV.

**State Museum of the Defence of Volgograd:** Volgograd, Ul. Gogolya 10; the 60,000 exhibits feature the defence of the city during the Civil War (1918–20) and the Battle of Stalingrad (1942–43); Dir. G. I. DENISOV.

**Vologodsky Historical Museum:** Vologda, Pl. Kremlin 1; collection of Russian applied art, hand-made lace, and exhibition devoted to the history of the North of the Soviet Union.

**Yaroslavl State Historical Museum:** Yaroslavl, Pl. Podbelskogo 25; over 370,000 exhibits on the history of the Russian people from ancient times to the present; Dir. A. K. MATKEEV.

**History and Art Museum at Zagorsk:** Moscow Region, Zagorsk, the Lavra; f. 1920; the museum consists of most of the buildings of the Trinity-St. Sergius Monastery and includes 60,000 items dealing with the development of Russian art from the 17th century to the present; icons, jewellery, vestments; also secular applied arts; Dir. T. A. POPESKU.

## LITERATURE AND EDUCATION
### LENINGRAD

**Dostoyevsky House-museum:** Leningrad 196002, Kuznechny per. 5; f. 1968; the house where the author lived 1878–81; manuscripts, documentary material, memorial items, library of 5,000 vols.; Dir. B. N. REBALKOY.

**Literary Museum of the Institute of Russian Literature:** (Pushkin House), Nab. Makarova 4; based on the material of the Pushkin Anniversary Exhibition of 1899; contains 95,000 exhibits and over 60,000 items of reference material; seven halls containing permanent exhibitions devoted to Radishchev, Lermontov, Gogol, Dostoyevsky, I. S. Turgenev, and other Russian writers.

**Museum attached to the Institute of Russian Literature of the U.S.S.R. Academy of Sciences:** Ul. Makarova 4; f. 1905 and reorganized 1930; Dir. B. G. BAZANOV.

**N. A. Nekrasov House-Museum:** Liteiny prospekt 36; f. 1946 in flat where poet lived; exhibits illustrating his life.

**Pushkin House-Museum:** Naberezhnaya Moiki 12; in the flat where the poet died; under supervision of the Ministry of Culture of the R.S.F.S.R.; Dir. M. N. PETY.

### MOSCOW

**A. P. Chekhov House-Museum:** Sadovaya-Kudrinskaya 6; f. 1954; flat where the writer lived from 1886–1890; branch of the State Literature Museum.

**F. Dostoyevsky Museum:** Ul. Dostoyevskogo 2; f. 1928; affiliated to the State Literature Museum; exhibits illustrating Dostoyevsky's life, organized in the flat where he lived until sixteen years old; Dr. Y. KOGAN.

**N. V. Gogol House Museum:** Suvorovsky, Bul. 7; exhibits illustrating life and work of Gogol; library, manuscript room.

**A. M. Gorky Memorial Museum:** Moscow 121069, 6/2 Kachalov ul.; f. 1965 in the house where the author lived; contains Gorky's private library of 10,000 vols.; Dir. V. B. KOZMIN.

**A. V. Lunacharsky House Museum:** Ul. Vesnina 9/5, kv. 1; the flat where the writer and the first Minister of Public Education and Art lived from 1924 to 1933.

**N. A. Ostrovsky State Museum:** 14 Ul. Gorkogo; f. 1940 in the writer's former home; Dir. V. P. POPOV.

**A. S. Pushkin Museum:** Ul. Kropotkina 12/2; f. 1957; 77,000 exhibits; library, manuscript room, cinema and lecture hall; ten rooms of permanent exhibitions, with three additional rooms; Dir. A. Z. KREIN.

**State V. V. Mayakovsky Museum:** Serov Lane 3/6; f. 1974 in the building where Mayakovsky lived 1919–30; manuscripts, documentary material, notebooks, memorial items; library and reading room with 76,000 vols., including periodicals; Dir. V. V. MAKAROV.

**State Literature Museum:** Pr. Lenina 64; f. 1934; 750,000 exhibits; the museum is a research and educational centre which collects, studies and publishes material on the history of Russian and Soviet literature; Dir. N. V. SHAKHALOVA.

**Tolstoy Residence Museum:** Ul. Lev Tolstoy 21; rooms arranged as they were when the author lived there; 4,200 exhibits; Dir. A. V. SALOMATIN.

**L. N. Tolstoy State Museum:** 11 Kropotkinskaya ul.; f. 1911; MSS. section contains 170,000 sheets of Tolstoy's writings and nearly 600,000 MSS. and archives material on Tolstoy and his circle; library of 69,500 works by or about Tolstoy; nearly 70,000 newspaper cuttings, and over 42,000 exhibits in the form of painting, sculpture, photographs, etc.; Dir A. V. SALOMATIN.

### OTHER TOWNS
(In alphabetical order by town).

**Alushta S. M. Sergeyev-Tsensky Literary Museum:** Alushta, Ul. Sergeyeva-Tsenskogo 15; the house where the author lived; Dir. T. A. FEFYUZA.

**Stalsky Memorial Museum of Daghestan A.S.S.R.:** Kasumkentsky District, Ashagastal; exhibits on the history of Daghestan literature; library of 20,000 vols.

**Baku Museum of Education:** Baku, Ul. Chkalova 11; exhibits illustrate the work of schools, institutes, universities, colleges; scientific library of over 50,000 vols.

**State Museum of Azerbaijan Literature:** Baku, Ul. Kommunisticheskaya 33; 10,000 exhibits on the history of Azerbaijan literature from ancient times to the present; Dir. G. M. ARSALY.

**V. G. Belinsky State Museum:** Penzenskaya oblast, Belinsky, Ul. Belinskogo 11; f. 1938; 18,000 exhibits on the life and work of the literary critic V. G. Belinsky; Curator ANOKHINA.

**M. Y. Lermontov State Museum:** Penzenskaya oblast, Belinsky District, Lermontovo; f. 1939; 7,000 exhibits on the life and work of M. Y. Lermontov; library of 16,000 books; Dir. V. P. ARZAMASTSEV.

**Chernigov M. M. Kotsyubinsky Literary Museum:** Chernigov, Ul. Kotsyubinskogo 3; f. 1934; 15,000 exhibits on the life and work of Kotsyubinsky; library with 5,000 books; Dir. I. M. KOTSYUBINSKAYA; publs. *Collections*† (every 5 years), Booklets and Guides† (irregular).

**Chernovtsy Y. Fedkovicha Memorial Museum:** Chernovtsy, Ul. Pushkina 17; f. 1945; collection of materials about the life and work of the famous 19th-century Ukrainian writer; 3,500 exhibits, including portraits, photographs, illustrations of works, books, etc.

**State Egishe Charentz Literary and Art Museum:** Erevan, Ul. Spandaryana 2; f. 1954 by merger of Theatre and Literature Museums; exhibits on the history of Armenian literature (14th–19th centuries); also theatrical and musical divisions; library of 25,000 vols.; 600 archives, MSS., photographs, musical instruments, etc.; Dir. S. H. MELEKSETYAN.

**State A. M. Gorky Museum of Literature:** Gorky, Ul. Minina 26; 25,000 exhibits, illustrating the life and work of the writer.

**Kazan State A. M. Gorky Memorial Museum:** Kazan, Ul. Gorky 10; exhibits illustrating Gorky's life in the flat where he lived and wrote.

**Kiev Lesya Ukrainia State Literature Museum:** Kiev, Ul. Saksaganskogo 97; exhibits on the life and work of the Ukrainian poets and artists of the 19th century.

**Kiev T. G. Shevchenko State Museum:** Kiev, Boulevard Shevchenko 12; 21,000 exhibits on the life and work of the Ukrainian poet, artist and revolutionary-democrat, T. G. Shevchenko; Dir. E. P. DOROSHENKO.

**A. M. Gorky Museum:** Kirov, Ul. Lenina 82; material on the life and work of contemporary writers of the Urals and Siberia.

**Kuibyshev A. M. Gorky Memorial Museum:** Kuibyshev, Ul. S. Razina 126; literary museum devoted to the life and work of Gorky; exhibits in the house and furniture which belonged to him.

**A. P. Chekhov Memorial Museum:** Chekhov District, Melikhovo; the house where the writer lived and worked.

**North-Ossetian K. L. Khetagurov Memorial Museum:** Ordzhonikidze, Pr. Mira 12; collection of materials on Caucasian poetry and literature.

**I. S. Turgenev State Museum:** Turgenev Str. 11, Orel 302000; f. 1918; library of 50,000 vols.; Dir. N. M. KIRILLOVSKAYA; the museum has three branches:

*The House-Museum:* f. 1921; Dir. V. B. BORISOV.

*Museum:* Orel, Street of 7th November, 24; f. 1957; devoted to writers born in Orel; Man. I. A. KOSTOMAROVA.

*Museum of N. S. Leskov:* Orel, Ul. Oktjabrskaya 9; f. 1974; Man. R. M. ALEKSINA.

**State Lermontov Literary Memorial Museum:** Lermontov's Cottage, Piatigorsk, Lermontovskaya ul. 4; f. 1912; exhibits feature the life and work of M. Y. Lermontov in the Caucasus; library of 12,000 vols.; Dir. P. E. SELEGEY.

**Poltava State Museum:** Poltava, Ul. Lenina 2; exhibits of materials on the life and work of the Ukrainian writers P. Mirny, E. Kotlyarevsky, V. G. Korolenko, N. V. Gogol; scientific library of over 80,000 vols.; Dir. M. D. ONIPKOV.

**Pushkin State Preserve:** Pskovskaya oblast, Pushkinskiye Gory, Mikhailovskoye P.O.; f. 1922; 10,000 exhibits on the life in exile of the poet; the preserve includes the family lands at Mikhailovskoye, Trigorskoye and Petrovskoye, the ancient towns of Voronich and Savkina Gorka, the Svetororskii monastery and the Uspenskii church containing the grave of Pushkin; Dir. S.S. GEICHENKO.

**All-Union Pushkin Museum:** Pushkin town, Komsomolskaya ul. 1; under supervision of the Ministry of Culture); f. 1938 in Moscow; 45,000 exhibits illustrating the life and work of the poet and his epoque; Dir. M. N. PETY.

Annexes: *Lyceum Museum:* Pushkin town, Komsomolsky st. 1; *Country-House Museum:* Pushkin town, Pushkinsky st. 2.

**J. Rainis Museum of the History of Literature and Arts:** Riga-PDP, 226845 Pionieru lauk 3; f. 1940; compiling, collecting, research, publication and exhibition of materials concerning Latvian literature, theatre, music and cinema; 288,000 exhibits; Dir. M. VERSHANE; Asst. Dir. S. GEIKINA; Curator Z. REISKARTE.

**Chernyishevsky Memorial Museum:** Saratov, Ul. Chernyishevskogo 142; documents about the life and work of the writer.

**State A. N. Radizhchev Memorial Museum:** Saratov, Ul. Radishcheva 39; 29,000 exhibits illustrating the life of the writer.

**T. G. Shevchenko State Memorial Museum:** S. Shevchenko; exhibits illustrating Shevchenko's life; manuscripts, documentary material, etc.

**Sverdlovsk Bazhov Literary Museum:** Sverdlovsk, Pushkinskaya ul. 27; material on the life and work of Mamin-Sibiriak, Bazhov, and contemporary writers of the Urals; Dir. I. I. KULIKOVA.

**A. P. Chekhov Museum:** Taganrog, Ul. Chekhova 69; rooms arranged as they were when Chekhov lived there in his childhood.

**State Literary Museum of Georgia:** Tbilisi, Ul. Djiordjiashivili 8; f. 1929; 150,000 exhibits on the history of Georgian literature (XIX-XX centuries); library of 19,000 vols.; Dir. I. K. KAKABEDZE.

**Leo Tolstoy Museum Estate:** Tulskaya oblast, Shchekinsky District, village of Yasnaya Poliana; f. 1921; 27,695 exhibits in the house and estate belonging to L. N. Tolstoy; literary museum devoted to his life and work; estate with park grounds and forest; Dir. S. J. BUNIN; publ. *Yasnopolyansky Sbornik*.

## NATURAL HISTORY

### LENINGRAD

**Academy of Sciences Museum of Zoology:** Universitetskaya naberezhnaya 1; f. 1832; over 40,000 items describe the origin and evolution of the animal world on earth; Chief D. V. NAUMOV.

**Acad. F. N. Chernyschev Central Scientific Geological and Prospecting Museum:** 199026 Leningrad, Vasilievsky ostrov, Sredny pr. 74; f. 1923, opened 1930; about 1,000,000 geological specimens including examples of mineral deposits from all over the Soviet Union; monographic and paleontological collections; popularization of geological knowledge; Dir. P. N. VARFOLOMEYEV.

**Dokuchayev Central Soil Museum:** Birzhevoi provezd 6; f. 1904; about 5,000 specimens of soil from nearly every soil zone in the world; Dir. Dr. B. F. APARIN.

**Mining Museum of the G. V. Plekhanov Mining Institute:** Vasilievsky ostrov, 21st linia, 2; f. 1773; over 201,000 items on the history of the mining industry in the 19th and early 20th century; collection of precious and imitation stones; Dir. V. D. KOLOMENSKY.

**Museum of the Arctic and the Antarctic:** Ul. Marata 24a; 4,000 exhibits; includes documents and the original equipment of all Soviet expeditions to these areas; Dir. I. YAKIMOVICH.

### Moscow

**D. N. Anuchin Anthropological Institute and Museum:** The Institute of Anthropology, Moscow State University, Prospekt Marxa 18; f. 1879; about 300,000 items; anthropology and archaeology of the Stone Age; collections from outstanding Russian explorers of Africa; Monsterien Man from Teshik-Tash and Staroselyie; Mesolithic burials from the Dnieper Region in the Ukraine; library of 30,000 vols.; Dir. Prof. Dr. V. P. YAKIMOV.

**Fersman Mineralogical Museum of the U.S.S.R. Academy of Sciences:** Moscow V-71, Leninsky pr. 14-16; f. 1716; 117,000 mineral samples from throughout the world; Dir. Prof. G. P. BARSANOV; publ. *New Data about Minerals of the U.S.S.R.* (annual).

**Moscow State University Museum of Zoology:** Ul. Herzena 6; f. 1791; systematics, speciation, zoogeography, faunistic investigations; library of 100,000 vols.; Dir.

Dr. Olga L. Rossolimo; publ. *Proceedings of the Zoological Museum*† (annual).

**Museum of Earth Science of the Moscow State M. V. Lomonosov University:** Moscow B-234, Leninskie Gory; f. 1955; includes material on the origin of the face of the earth, its geospheres, surface landscape sphere, earth crust, climates, waters, soils, plants, animals, economic resources; on the conservation, utilization and reconstruction of nature; complex geological and geographical characteristics of U.S.S.R. territories and of the earth; science-teaching, geological-geographical museum for students of the Geological, Geographical and Biological-Pedological departments of Moscow University; 10,000 vols. in library; Dir. Prof. B. A. Savelyev, D.SC.; publ. *Zhizn' Zemli* (The Life of the Earth, 1 vol. in 1–2 years).

**Museum of the Palaeontological Institute:** Leninsky pr. 16; f. 1936; about 8,300 exhibits featuring fossil specimens of fish, amphibians, reptiles and mammals; Dir. B. A. Treofimov.

**Ordzhonikidze Mineralogical Museum:** Moscow Institute for Geological Prospecting, Pr. Marxa 18; industrial minerals, precious and semi-precious stones; Dir. M. A. Barchanov.

**Pavlov Museum of Geology and Palaeontology:** The Moscow Institute of Geological Prospecting, Pr. Marxa 18; f. 1755; 300,000 exhibits; illustrates various geological processes; palaeontology of invertebrate and vertebrate animals; problems of palaeobotany; Scientific Chief Prof. Dr. M. V. Mouratov.

**State Darwin Museum:** Malaya Pirogovskaya ul. 1; illustrates Darwinism and the theory of evolution; Dir. V. N. Ignatieva.

**K. A. Timiryazev Apartment Museum:** Ul. Granovskogo 2, apart. 29; f. 1942; cultural and historical memorial to K. A. Timiryazev; 7,545 exhibits and archives on his life and work; personal library of 4,871 vols.; Dir. E. V. Polosatova.

**Timiryazev State Museum of Biology:** Malaya Gruzinskaya 15; about 30,000 exhibits trace the origin and evolution of life on earth; Dir. I. V. Abakermova.

### Other Towns
(In alphabetical order by town).

**"Belovezhskaya Pushcha" Museum:** Byelorussian S.S.R., Brestskaya Region, Belovezhskaya Pushcha (Game Preserve); the museum shows the work being done to preserve the almost extinct European Bison, and to acclimatize other animals in this part of Byelorussia; Dir. V. S. Romanov.

**Ilmen Mineral Preserve Museum:** Cheliabinsk Region, Miass 1; f. 1920; the museum shows the mineralogical wealth of the Ilmen Preserve, the grounds of which contain almost all the known minerals; library of 17,000 vols.; Dir. V. G. Spiridonov; publ. *Trudy Ilmenskogo Sapovednika*.

**V. V. Vakhrushev Ural Geological Museum:** Sverdlovsk, Ul. Kuibysheva 30; Dir. N. Korzhov.

**Fisheries Museum of the Pacific Scientific Research Institute of Fisheries and Oceanography:** Primorsky region, Vladivostok, Leninskaya ul. 20; ichthyology, molocology, crustacea and sea mammals, etc.; 11,000 exhibits of flora and fauna of the Pacific Ocean; Dir. A. G. Kaganovsky.

**Meteorological Museum of the Central Geophysical Observatory:** Leningrad region, Vsevolozhsky raion, village of Voyeikovo; Dir. A. A. Vasiliev.

### SCIENCE AND TECHNOLOGY
#### Leningrad

**A. S. Popov Central Museum of Communications:** Ul. Soyuza Sviazi 7; f. 1877; over 4 million items representing the development of all types of communication used in the U.S.S.R.; includes the state postage stamp collection; Dir. B. Sherstniov.

**Industrial Exhibition at the House for Dissemination of Scientific and Technical Propaganda:** All-Union Association "Znanya", Nevsky pr. 58; features the machine-building and the instrument manufacturing industries of Leningrad.

**Leningrad Museum of Railway Transport:** Ul. Sadovaya 50; f. 1813; traces the history of railway transport in Russia; includes unique collection of miniature models of engines and carriages; Dir. G. Zakrevskaya.

#### Moscow

**All-Union Permanent Exhibition of Labour Protection:** Leninsky pr. 10; features the latest labour protection techniques in industry and transport; Dir. Fartunin.

**Pharmaceutical Museum of the Central Drug Research Institute:** Krassikova ul. 20; unique collection of about 6,000 items on the history of pharmacy in the U.S.S.R.; Dir. B. M. Salo.

**Polytechnical Museum:** Novaya pl. 3; f. 1872; about 25,000 exhibits; features history and latest developments in science and technology; belongs to the All-Union Society "Znaniye"; Dir. G. Kozlov.

**K. E. Tsiolkovsky State Museum of the History of Cosmonautics:** Ul. Korolieva 2, Kaluga; f. 1967; contains K. E. Tsiolkovsky's scientific works, history of rocket technique and cosmonautics, large collection of objects relating to astronautics and rocket techniques, including the first experimental rocket launched in 1933, the *Sputniks* and *Luniks*; library of 14,970 vols.; Dir. I. Korochentsev.

**N. E. Zhukovsky Memorial Museum:** Ul. Radio 17; about 25,000 items feature the work of N. E. Zhukovsky, and Soviet contributions to aviation and astronautics; Dir. V. I. Maslov.

#### Other Towns

**Yuri Gagarin Memorial Museum:** G. Gagarin, Ul. Gagarin; f. 1970; exhibits depicting the life and career of Yuri Alexeyevich Gagarin, the first man in space; Dir. Zoya Rogozhina.

### THEATRE AND MUSIC
#### Leningrad

**Museum of the Academic Maly Theatre of Opera and Ballet:** Ploshchad Iskusstv. 1; f. 1935; collection of materials (sketches, posters, etc.) depicting the history of the theatre and its work; Dir. V. Liphart.

**Museum of the Gorky Bolshoi Drama Theatre:** Ul. Fontanka 65.

**Museum of the Kirov Academic Theatre of Opera and Ballet:** Teatralnaya Ploshchad.

**Permanent Exhibition of Musical Instruments:** 5 Isaakievskaya pl.; about 3,000 exhibits, including a large collection of instruments made by the outstanding Russian and foreign craftsmen: Batov, Leman, Nalimov, Krasnoshchiokov, Fiodorov, Amati, Villaume, Tilke and Denner.

**Rimsky-Korsakov House-Museum:** Tikhuin; f. 1944 in flat where composer was born; exhibits illustrating his life and works.

**State Circus Museum:** Ul. Fontanka 3; f. 1928; over 90,000 exhibits of plans, sketches, paintings; library of Russian and foreign works; section on 18th and 19th century circus in Western Europe and on Soviet circus; Dir. A. Z. Levin.

**State Theatrical Museum:** Leningrad 191011, Ostrovski Square 6; f. 1918; over 380,000 exhibits depicting the history of Russian, Soviet and foreign theatre; over

21,000 stage designs, 6,700 prints, 700 sculptures, 206,000 photographs, 15,000 MSS. and documents, 55,000 posters and programmes; library of 500,000 vols.; the museum has two subsidiary branches: *Rimsky-Korsakov Museum:* f. 1971; memorial museum in house where the composer lived; and *F. I. Chaliapin Museum:* f. 1975; museum of history of Russian opera, in former house of Chaliapin; Dir. of State Theatrical Museum I. V. YEVSTIGNEYEVA; publs. *Leningradsky Annuae, Monography of M. Petipa* (annual).

### Moscow

**A. N. Skryabin Museum:** 11 Ul. Vakhtangova; f. 1919, opened in 1922 in flat where the composer lived and died; MSS., letters, Skryabin's personal library and magnetic-tape archive of Skryabin's compositions performed by the author and famous artists; excursions, lectures and concerts; 293 vols. in Skryabin's personal library, 2,515 vols. in scientific library; Dir. SHABORKINA.

**B. V. Shchukin Museum-Room:** Flat 11, Ul. Shchukina 8; contains material he had about him during his lifetime as a great actor at the Vakhtangov Theatre.

**Central A. A. Bakhrushin State Theatrical Museum:** Moscow 113054, 31/12 Ul. Bakhrushina; f. 1894; to collect, house, study and exhibit varied materials on history and theory of theatre; approx. 1,078,989 exhibits; library of 60,000 vols.; archives of original MSS. of Ostrovsky, Lensky, Stanislavsky, etc.; Dir. K. V. VORONKOV.

**Moscow Arts Theatre Museum:** 3A Proezd Khudozhestvenennogo teatra; f. 1922; Dir. P. P. KABANOV.

**K. S. Stanislavsky Flat-Museum:** affiliated to Theatre Museum; f. 1940; deals with Stanislavsky's work and the theatrical career of People's Artist, M. P. Lilina.

**V. I. Nemirovich-Danchenko Flat-museum:** No. 5 Ulitsa Nemirovich-Danchenko; f. 1944; illustrating career of Nemirovich-Danchenko.

**Museum of the State Academic Maly Theatre:** Maly Theatre Building, Sverdlov pl. 1/6; f. 1932, being developed out of 1927 exhibition; illustrates and studies history of the Theatre; Dir. Y. M. STRUTINSKAYA.

**Obraztsov's Central State Puppet Theatre Museum:** Sadovo Samotechnaya ul. 3; f. 1937; over 2,200 exhibits dealing with the history of the puppet theatre; puppet theatres of the Soviet Union and many other countries and the Central Puppet Theatre itself; library of over 4,000 books; Dir. E. KORENBERG.

**Permanent Tchaikovsky Exhibition, in the Tchaikovsky Concert Hall:** Mayakovsky pl. 20; exhibits of the composer's life and works.

**"M. I. Glinka" State Central Museum of Musical Culture:** Georgievsky per. 4; f. 1943; based on the Museum of the Moscow Conservatoire; Sections: archives and MSS.; memoria and illustrative materials; musical instruments; library; records and tape recordings—in all, over 500,000 items; Exhibits: musical instruments of the nations of the U.S.S.R. and other countries; Russian classics and Soviet composers; live music programmes; Dir. E. N. ALEXEYEVA.

**Tchaikovsky House Museum:** Klin; f. 1894; composer's last residence and first Russian musical museum; contains 121,800 documents and museum treasures associated with the life and work of Tchaikovsky and other Russian musicians; *c.* 32,000 vols.; Dir. G. A. SHAMKIN.

**U.S.S.R. State Academic Bolshoi Theatre Museum:** Bolshoi Theatre Building, Sverdlov pl.; f. 1920; objects: documentation of the work of the Bolshoi Theatre, collection of materials and documents on its history and work, study of history of the theatre; Dir. V. I. ZARUBIN.

**U.S.S.R. State Collection of Antique String Instruments:** Herzen ul. 13; f. 1919.

**Vakhtangov Museum-Rocm:** houses relics connected with life and work of Vakhtangov in his former home.

**Vakhtangov Theatre Museum:** history of the Vakhtangov Theatre; Dir. I. L. SERGEEVA.

### Other Towns

**Museum of Theatre and Music of the Estonian S.S.R.:** Müürivahe 12, Tallinn 200001, Estonian S.S.R.; covers the development of theatrical art and music in Estonia; Dir. R. IVALO; publ. *Eesti NSV Teatribibliograafia* (annually).

**Ukrainian State Museum of Theatrical, Musical and Cinematographic Art:** Kiev-15, Sichnevoho Povstanya 21/24; 190,000 exhibits; Dir. V. A. KOZIENKO.

# UNIVERSITIES

## ALTAI STATE UNIVERSITY
656099 BARNAUL, SOCIALISTICESKI PR. 68

Founded 1973.

Faculties of economics, history, law, chemistry and biology, physics and mathematics; evening and extra-mural courses.

## AZERBAIJAN S.M. KIROV STATE UNIVERSITY
BAKU, UL. PATRICE LUMUMBA 23, AZERBAIJAN

Founded 1919.

*Rector:* M. BAGIR-ZADE.
*Pro-Rectors:* Prof. S. N. EGUBOVA, A. Z. ABDULLAEV, Y. Z. MAMEDOV.
*Librarian:* K. G. GAZANOV.

Library of 1,200,000 vols.
Number of teachers: 700.
Number of students: 11,000.

Periodical: *Transactions of the Azerbaizhan S. M. Kirov State University* (8 series).

Faculties of History, Journalism, Philology, Oriental Studies, Law, Library Sciences, Mechanics and Mathematics, Physics, Chemistry, Biology, Geology and Geography; Evening and Extra-Mural Departments.

## BASHKIR STATE UNIVERSITY OF THE FORTIETH ANNIVERSARY OF THE OCTOBER REVOLUTION
UFA, UL. FRUNZE 32, BASHKIR A.S.S.R.

Founded 1957.

*Rector:* S. KH. CHANBARISOV.
*Pro-Rectors:* M. F. GAINULLIN, B. V. AIVAZOV.

Number of teachers: 215.
Number of students: 5,600.

Faculties of history, philology, physics and mathematics, biology, geography, chemistry, foreign languages; evening and extra-mural departments.

UNIVERSITIES

UNION OF SOVIET SOCIALIST REPUBLICS

## BYELORUSSIAN V. I. LENIN STATE UNIVERSITY
MINSK, UNIVERSITETSKY GORODOK, BYELORUSSIA

Founded 1921.

*Rector:* Acad. V. A. BELYI.
*Pro-Rectors:* A. Y. MALYSHEV, V. G. IVASHIN, V. S. BOGDANOV, I. P. CHEPA, N. Y. LEPILO.

Number of teachers: 1,370.
Number of students: 17,600 undergraduate, 1,000 postgraduate.
Publications: *Vestnik* (Journal).
Faculties of history, philology, journalism, law, mathematics, physics, chemistry, biology, geography, radio physics, electronics; evening and extra-mural departments. Research institutes of applied physics, chemistry, social sciences; department of special technical design.

## CHECHENO INGUSH UNIVERSITY
GROZNY, UL. SHERIPOVA 32, CHECHENO INGUSH A.S.S.R.

Founded 1972.

*Rector:* M. P. PAVLOV.

Faculties of Russian language and literature, Chechen language and literature, Ingush language and literature, Romanov-German languages and literature, history, mathematics, physics, chemistry, biology, geography; evening department.

## CHERNOVTSY STATE UNIVERSITY
CHERNOVTSY, UL. KOTSYUBINSKOGO 2, UKRAINE

Founded 1875.

*Rector:* K. A. CHERVINSKY.
*Pro-Rectors:* Prof. V. P. RUBANIC, V. KURILO.
*Librarian:* M. I. DEREVOREZ.

Library of 1,600,000 vols.
Number of teachers: 450.
Number of students: 9,000.
Publication: *Scientific University Annual.*
Faculties of history, foreign languages, general engineering, oriental studies, physics and mathematics, chemistry, biology, geography, philology; extra-mural and evening department.

## CHUVASH I.N. ULYANOV STATE UNIVERSITY
CHEBOKSARY, MOSKOVSKY PROSPECT 15

Founded 1967.

*Rector:* Prof. Dr. S. F. SAIKIN.
*Pro-Rectors:* Prof. S. A. ABRUKOV, A. K. ARAKELYAN.
*Librarian:* O. I. DANILOVA.

Library of 200,000 vols.
Number of teachers: 300.
Number of students: 8,000.
Faculties of History and Philology, Chemistry, Physics and Mathematics, Medicine, Economics, Electrical Engineering, Industrial Electrification; Extra-Mural Faculty; Electronic Computing Centre; Evening and Preparatory departments.

## DAGHESTAN V. I. LENIN STATE UNIVERSITY
MAKHACHKALA, SOVETSKAYA UL. 8, DAGHESTAN A.S.S.R.

Founded 1957.

*Rector:* Prof. A. A. ABILOV.
*Pro-Rectors:* A. A. MAGOMAEV, S. M. GAJIEV.

Number of teachers: 450.
Number of students: 8,000.
Periodical: *Transactions.*
Faculties of history, philology, radio engineering, mathematics, chemical technology, physics, biology, foreign languages, civil engineering; evening and extra-mural departments.

## DNEPROPETROVSK UNIVERSITY OF THE THREE HUNDREDTH ANNIVERSARY OF THE UNION OF RUSSIA AND THE UKRAINE
DNEPROPETROVSK, PROSPEKT GAGARINA 72, UKRAINE

Founded 1918.

*Rector:* Prof. V. I. MOSSAKOVSKY.
*Pro-Rectors:* Prof. Z. S. DONTSOVA, V. I. ONISHCHENKO, N. S. KNIZNY.
*Librarian:* N. A. GAIVORONSKAYA.

Library of 850,000 vols.
Number of teachers: 700.
Number of students: 13,000.
Faculties of history and philology, mechanics and mathematics, physics, chemistry, biology; extra-mural, preparatory and evening departments.

ATTACHED INSTITUTES:

**Institute of Geology.**
**Institute of Hydrobiology.**

## DONETSK STATE UNIVERSITY
DONETSK, UL. UNIVERSITETSKAYA 24, UKRAINE

Founded 1965.

*Rector:* G. A. TIMOSHENKO.
*Pro-Rector:* Prof. A. S. KOSMODEMIANSKY.
*Librarian:* A. N. KHARCHENKO.

Library of 323,000 vols.
Number of students: c. 12,000.
Faculties of economics, philology, physics, mathematics, biology, chemistry, history; evening, extra-mural and preparatory departments.

## EREVAN STATE UNIVERSITY
375049 EREVAN, UL. MROVYANA 1, ARMENIA

Telephone: 524629.

Founded 1920; Languages of instruction: Armenian and Russian; Academic year: September to June.

*Rector:* S. A. AMBARTSUMIAN.
*Vice-Rectors:* G. H. PANOSYAN (Science); L. G. YESAYAN (Education).
*Librarian:* Mrs. A. N. MAKARIAN.

Number of teachers: 791.
Number of students: 7,738.
Publications†: *Scientific Notes* (3 a year), *Herald* (3 a year), *Young Scientific Worker* (2 a year), *Erevan University* (3 a year), *Student's Scientific Notes* (2 a year), etc.

DEANS:

*Faculty of Mechanical-Mathematical Sciences:* R. A. ALEXANDRIAN.
*Faculty of Applied Mathematics:* R. N. TONOYAN.
*Faculty of Physics:* B. Y. TOUMANIAN.
*Faculty of Radiophysics:* Y. L. VARDANIAN.
*Faculty of Chemistry:* S. H. NALCHADZIAN.
*Faculty of Biology:* M. A. DAVTIAN.

*Faculty of Geology:* H. H. SARKISIAN.
*Faculty of Geography:* KH. Y. NAZARIAN.
*Faculty of Philology:* H. KH. BARSEGIAN.
*Faculty of Russian Language and Literature:* Mrs. N. N. SARKISOVA.
*Faculty of Oriental Studies:* Mrs. M. H. COCHAR.
*Faculty of History:* R. L. MOVSESIAN.
*Faculty of Law:* A. S. LALAYAN.

## FAR EASTERN STATE UNIVERSITY
PRIMORIE AREA, VLADIVOSTOK,
UL. SUKHANOVA 8
Founded 1920.

*Rector:* Prof. G. A. UNTELEV.
*Pro-Rectors:* Prof. P. S. DAGEL, A. K. KOROLEV.
*Librarian:* L. F. SHKILYEVA.

Library of 400,000 vols.
Number of professors and lecturers: 400.
Number of students: 7,000.
Periodical: *Transactions of the Far-Eastern State University.*

Faculties of philology, oriental studies, history and law, physics and mathematics, geophysics, chemistry, biology and soil science; evening, preparatory and extra-mural departments.

ATTACHED RESEARCH INSTITUTION:
**Electronic Computer Centre.**

## GOMEL STATE UNIVERSITY
GOMEL, UL. SOVIETSKAYA 108,
BYELORUSSIA
Founded 1969.

*Rector:* V. I. BELY.
*Pro-Rector:* D. A. LEONCHENKO.
*Librarian:* M. A. DRATSEVICH.

Library of 250,000 vols.
Number of teachers: 250.
Number of students: 5,500.

Faculties of History, Philology, Mathematics, Physics, Biology and Soil Science, Geology, Economics, Physical Culture; Extra-Mural Department.

## GORKY N. I. LOBACHEVSKY STATE UNIVERSITY
GORKY, PROSPEKT GAGARINA 23
Founded 1918.

*Rector:* Prof. A. G. UGODCHIKOV.
*Pro-Rectors:* Prof. M. M. KOBRIN, A. I. ODNOSEVTSEV, A. N. BARKHATOV.
*Librarian:* M. N. BOKOV.

Number of teachers: 700.
Number of students: 8,000.
Periodical: *Radiophysics.*

Faculties of history and philology, mechanics and mathematics, physics, computing mathematics and cybernetics, chemistry, biology, industrial economics (evening) and extra-mural departments.

ATTACHED RESEARCH INSTITUTIONS:
**Gorky Research Radiophysical Institute.**
**Physical Engineering Institute.**
**Chemical Institute.**
**Institute of Applied Mathematics and Cybernetics.**
**Botanical Garden.**
**Zoological Museums.**
**Biological Station.**

## GRODNO STATE UNIVERSITY
GRODNO, BYELORUSSIA

Founded 1978; in process of formation. Incorporates the former Grodno Pedagogical Institute, with faculties of history and education; philology, music and singing; physics and mathematics; teacher training.

## IRKUTSK A. A. ZHDANOV STATE UNIVERSITY
IRKUTSK, UL. K. MARX 1, GROSNY
CHECHENO-INGUSH A.S.S.R.
Founded 1918.

*Rector:* Dr. N. F. LOSEV.
*Pro-Rectors:* Prof. A. V. KALABINA, M. A. KORZUN.

Number of professors and lecturers: 500.
Number of students: 9,000.

Periodicals: *Transactions of the Irkutsk State University, Proceedings of the Biological and Geographical Research Institute, Proceedings of the Physical and Chemical Research Institute, Collected Short Scientific Papers.*

Faculties of history, philology, geography, law, physics, mathematics, chemistry, biology and soil science, geology; evening and extra-mural departments; extra-mural law departments in Chita (Ul. Kalinina 56).

ATTACHED RESEARCH INSTITUTIONS:
**Biological and Geographical Research Institute.**
**Physical and Chemical Research Institute.**
**Oil and Coal Products Research Institute.**
**Electronic Computing Centre.**
**Lake Baikal Biological Station.**

## IVANOVO STATE UNIVERSITY
153377 IVANOVO,
UL. ERMAKA 37/7, R.S.F.S.R.
Founded 1974.

Faculties of biology and chemistry, economics, history, law, mathematics, philology, physics; evening and extra-mural courses.

## KABARDA-BALKAR STATE UNIVERSITY
NALCHIK, UL. CHERNYSHEVSKOGO 173,
KABARDA-BALKAR A.S.S.R.
Founded 1957.

*Rector:* Prof. K. N. KEREFOV.
*Pro-Rectors:* B. KH. BALKAROV, G. M. SAPOZHNIKOV.
*Librarian:* E. D. MIGUCHKINA.

Library: 200,000 vols.
Number of teachers: 400.
Number of students: 8,000.

Publication: *Proceedings.*

Faculties of history and philology, medicine, physics and mathematics, agriculture, engineering, chemistry and biology; evening and extra-mural departments.

## KALININ UNIVERSITY
KALININ, UL. URITSKOGO 16/31
Founded 1971.

*Rector:* V. V. KOMIN.
*Pro-Rectors:* A. A. SERGEYEV, V. N. NIKOLSKY.

Number of students: 5,500.

Faculties of mathematics, physics, chemistry, philology, history, law; evening and extra-mural departments.

## KALININGRAD STATE UNIVERSITY
KALININGRAD, R.S.F.S.R.,
UL. UNIVERSITETSKAYA 23
Founded 1967.

*Rector:* Prof. A. A. BORISOV.
*Pro-Rector:* F. P. OKHAPKIN.
*Librarian:* M. M. PANCHENKO.

Library of 250,000 vols.
Number of teachers: 200.
Number of students: 4,000.
Publication: *Proceedings.*

Faculties of Physics and Mathematics, History and Philology and Natural Science, Economics and Law.

## KALMYK STATE UNIVERSITY
ELISTA, UL. PUSHKINA 11
Founded 1970.

*Rector:* N. P. KRASAVCHENKO.
*Pro-Rector:* S. B. BADMAEV.

Faculties of general engineering, philology, physics and mathematics, oriental studies, agronomy, zootechnics; evening and extra-mural departments.

## KARAGANDA UNIVERSITY
KARAGANDA, UL. KIROVA 16,
KAZAKH S.S.R.
Founded 1972.

Faculties of Kazakh language and literature, Russian language and literature, history, mathematics, physics, chemistry, biology; extra-mural law department.

## KAZAKH S. M. KIROV STATE UNIVERSITY
480091 ALMA-ATA, UL. KIROVA 136,
KAZAKH S.S.R.
Founded 1934.

*Rector:* I. A. DZHOLDASBEKOV.
*Pro-Rectors:* Y. A. AUBAKIROV, A. V. CHIGARKIN, D. O. ORAZBAEVA.
*Librarian:* F. I. MEDVEDCHIKOV.

Library of 800,000 vols.
Number of teachers: 739.
Number of students: 10,286.
Periodical: *Proceedings.*

Faculties, of history, philology, philosophy, geography, law, journalism, mechanics and mathematics, physics, chemistry, biology, geology; evening and extra-mural departments.

## KAZAN V. I. LENIN STATE UNIVERSITY
KAZAN, UL. LENINA 18, TATAR A.S.S.R.
Founded 1804.

*Rector:* Prof. M. T. NUZHIN.
*Pro-Rectors:* Prof. SH. T. KHABIBULIN, L. L. TUZOV.
*Librarian:* A. S. GURYANOV.

Number of professors: 700.
Number of students: 10,000.

Faculties of history and philology, law, mechanics and mathematics, physics, chemistry, biology and soil science, geology, geography; evening and extra-mural departments.

ATTACHED RESEARCH INSTITUTIONS:
**N. G. Chebotarev Research Institute of Mathematics and Mechanics.**
**A. M. Butlerov Research Institute of Chemistry.**
**Biological Research Institute.**

## KEMEROVO STATE UNIVERSITY
650043 KEMEROVO,
SOVJETSKY PR. 117, R.S.F.S.R.
Founded 1974.

Faculties of biology, chemistry, economics and law, history, mathematics, philology, physics; extra-mural courses.

## KHARKOV A. M. GORKY STATE UNIVERSITY
KHARKOV, PLOSHCHAD DZERZHIN-SKOGO 4, UKRAINE
Founded 1805.

*Rector:* V. G. KOROTKEVICH.
*Pro-Rectors:* V. I. ASTAKHOV, P. Y. KORZH, I. I. ZALUBOVSKY.

Faculties of history, economics, philology, foreign languages, mechanics and mathematics, physics, radio engineering, chemistry, biology, geography and geology; evening and extra-mural departments; faculty of general science in Gorlovka and Slavyansk.

## KIEV T. G. SHEVCHENKO STATE UNIVERSITY
KIEV, VLADIMIRSKAYA UL. 64,
UKRAINE
Founded 1834.

*Rector:* Dr. M. U. BYELYI.
*Pro-Rectors:* A. T. PILIPENKO, A. Z. ZHMUDSKY.

Library: 1,500,000 vols.
Number of teachers: 120 professors.
Number of students: 20,000.

Publications: *Vestnike Kievskogo Universiteta*, etc.

Faculties of Mechanics and Mathematics, Geography, Physics, Radiophysics, Cybernetics, Chemistry, Biology, Geology, History and Philosophy, Journalism, Law, Philology, International Relations, Economics, Foreign Languages; Evening and Extra-Mural Departments.

Attached Institutes: Physiology of Animals, Astronomical Observatory and two Astronomical Stations, Botanical Garden and two Agro-Biology Stations. Printing and Publishing, Scientific Library, Students' Library, Botanical, Zoological, Geological and Palaeontological Museums, Electronic Computing Centre, Nuclear Centre, Laboratories, etc.

## KIRGHIZ STATE UNIVERSITY
FRUNZE, UL. FRUNZE 547, KIRGHIZ S.S.R.
Founded 1951.

*Rector:* S. T. TABYSHALIYEV.
*Pro-Rectors:* E. DYISHEEV, S. S. PANKOV.

Number of teachers: 550.
Number of students: 12,000.

Faculties of history, law, philology, foreign languages, economics, geography, physics, mathematics and mechanics, biology, chemistry; evening and extra-mural departments.

## KISHINEV V. I. LENIN STATE UNIVERSITY
277003 KISHINEV, UL. SADOVAYA 60,
MOLDAVIAN S.S.R.
Founded 1945.

Languages of instruction: Moldavian and Russian.

*Rector:* B. E. MELNIK.
*Pro-Rectors:* A. Y. SITCHEV, S. A. PANFILOV.
*Librarian:* A. M. NOVAK.

Library of 1,216,000 vols.
Number of teachers: 805.
Number of students: 12,329.
Periodical: *Kishinevsky Universitet* (weekly).

DEANS:
*Faculty of Physics:* A. S. SIRGYI.
*Faculty of Mathematics and Cybernetics:* A. M. STAHYI.
*Faculty of Chemistry:* P. M. KETRUSH.
*Faculty of Biology and Soil Science:* I. I. DEDIU.
*Faculty of Foreign Languages:* S. S. PETROV.
*Faculty of Philology:* K. A. DOBROVOLSKY.
*Faculty of Bibliography:* N. G. BRINZILA.
*Faculty of History:* A. V. REPIDA.
*Faculty of Law:* V. K. VOLCHINSKY.
*Faculty of Economics:* I. I. MOKAN.
*Faculty of Commerce:* P. V. SECRIERU.
*Preparatory Department:* I. N. BURLAKU.
*Preparatory Faculty for Foreign Citizens:* V. G. ISAK.

CORRESPONDENCE COURSES:
*Faculty of History and Law:* P. A. BOYKO.
*Faculty of Philology and Bibliography:* G. V. DODITSA.
*Faculty of Economics:* M. I. MAZUR.

### KRASNOYARSK UNIVERSITY
KRASNOYARSK, UL. MAERCHAKA 6
Founded 1969.

*Rector:* A. I. OROKIN.
*Pro-Rectors:* G. E. BELOUSOV, V. M. BOUSAKHIN.

Faculties of history, philology, philosophy, Russian language and literature, agriculture, physics, mathematics, mechanics, chemistry, biology; evening and extra-mural departments.

### KUBAN STATE UNIVERSITY
350751 KRASNODAR, UL. KARL LIEBKNECHT 149
Founded 1970.

*Rector:* K. A. NOVIKOV.
*Pro-Rectors:* G. P. IVANOV, I. P. MITYUK.

Number of students: 9,800.

Faculties of philology, history, physics, mathematics, biology, chemistry, geography, Russian language and literature, foreign languages and literature (English, French, German), economics, law, graphic art, music; evening and extra-mural departments.

### KUIBYSHEV UNIVERSITY
KUIBYSHEV, UL. POTAPOVA 67/163
Founded 1969.

*Rector:* A. I. MEDVEDEV.
*Pro-Rector:* V. M. GOLOVIN.

Faculties of history, philology, philosophy, physics, mathematics and mechanics, chemistry, biology; preparatory department.

### LATVIAN P. STUCHKA STATE UNIVERSITY
RIGA, BULVAR RAYNISA 19, LATVIAN S.S.R.
Founded 1919.

Languages of instruction; Latvian and Russian; Academic year: September to July.

*Rector:* Prof. Dr. V. O. MILLER.
*Vice-Rectors:* A. J. VARSLAVĀNS, S. K. GRAUSHINIS, M. I. KLEPERE.
*Librarian:* I. I. MALINKOVSKAYA.

Number of teachers: 594.
Number of students: 9,000.
Publications: *Zinatniskie Raksti* (Scientific Transactions), *Latvian Mathematical Annual*.

Faculties of history and philosophy, economics, foreign languages, physics and mathematics, chemistry, biology, geography, law, philology; evening and extra-mural departments.

ATTACHED INSTITUTES:
**Electronic Computing Centre.**
**Four research laboratories.**
**Museum of Zoology.**
**Botanical Garden.**
**Astronomical Observatory.**

### LENINGRAD A. A. ZHDANOV STATE UNIVERSITY (ORDER OF LENIN)
UNIVERSITETSKAYA NAB. 7/9, LENINGRAD B-164
Founded 1819.

Academic year: September to July (two terms).

*Rector:* Prof. G. I. MAKAROV.
*Pro-Rectors:* Prof. N. P. PENKIN, Prof. D. A. KERIMOV.
*Librarian:* K. M. ROMANOVSKAYA.

Number of teachers: 1,700.
Number of students: 20,000.

Publication: *Vestnik Leningradskogeto Universita* (Herald of the Leningrad University).

Faculties of history, economics, applied mathematics, philosophy, psychology, philology, journalism, oriental studies, law, physics, mathematics and mechanics, chemistry, biology and soil science, geology, geography; evening and extra-mural departments.

### LVOV IVAN FRANKO STATE UNIVERSITY
LVOV, UNIVERSITETSKAYA UL. 1, UKRAINE
Language of instruction: Ukrainian.
Academic year: September to June.
Founded 1661.

*Rector:* Prof. H. G. MAXIMOVICH.
*Pro-Rectors:* G. S. DAVYDOVA, E. I. HLADYSHEVSKY, R. V. LUTSIV.
*Librarian:* V. K. POTAICHUK.

Library: 2,000,000 vols.
Number of teachers: 700.
Number of students: 13,000.

Publications: *Vestnik Lvovskogo Universiteta* (Herald of the Lvov University, 12 series), *Inozemna Filologiya* (Foreign Philology), *Ukrainske Literaturoznavstvo* (Ukrainian Literature Studies), *Teoreticheskaya Elektrotekhnika* (Theoretical Electrical Engineering), *Mineralogicheskii Sbornik* (Proceedings on Mineralogy), *Paleontologicheskii Sbornik* (Proceedings on Paleontology).

Faculties of history, philology, journalism, foreign languages, law, economics, physics, mechanics and mathematics, chemistry, biology, geology, geography; evening and extra-mural departments.

ATTACHED INSTITUTE:
**Institute of Social Science.**

### MARI UNIVERSITY
IOSHKAR-OLA, PL. LENINA 1, MARI A.S.S.R.
Founded 1972.

*Rector:* V. I. KOLLA.
*Pro-Rector:* (vacant).

Faculties of Mari language and literature, Russian language and literature, history, mathematics, physics, chemistry, biology, agrochemistry, zootechnics, economy, management of agriculture.

### MORDOVIAN N. P. OGOREV STATE UNIVERSITY
SARANSK, UL. BOLSHEVISTSKAYA 68,
MORDOVIAN A.S.S.R.
Founded 1957.

*Rector:* A. I. SUKHAREV.

Number of students: 4,000.

Faculties of history, philology, foreign languages, geography, medicine, physics and mathematics, chemistry and biology, electrical engineering, civil engineering, mechanization of agriculture, agriculture; evening and extra-mural departments.

### MOSCOW M. V. LOMONOSOV STATE UNIVERSITY
LENINSKIE GORY, MOSCOW V-234
Telephone: 139-27-39.
Founded 1755.

*Rector:* Dr. A. LOGUNOV.
*Pro-Rectors:* Prof. E. M. SERGEYEV, Prof. I. A. KHLYABICH, Prof. I. M. TERNOV, V. I. TROPIN, F. M. VOLKOV.
*Librarian:* NINA AVALOVA.

Number of teachers: 3,700, including 618 professors.
Number of students: 28,833.

Publications: *Vestnik Moskovskogo Universiteta* (10 series, annually), *Bulletin Moskovskogo Obshchestva Ispytatelei Prirody* (2 series), *Russkii Jazyk za Rubezhom*.

#### DEANS:
*Faculty of Mechanics and Mathematics:* Prof. P. M. OGIBALOV.
*Faculty of Computing Mathematics and Cybernetics:* Acad. A. N. TIKHONOV.
*Faculty of Physics:* Prof. V. S. FURSOV.
*Faculty of Chemistry:* Prof. I. V. BEREZIN.
*Faculty of Biology and Soil Science:* Prof. G. V. DOBROVOLSKY.
*Faculty of Geography:* Prof. A. M. RIABCHIKOV.
*Faculty of Geology:* Prof. A. A. BOGDANOV.
*Faculty of History:* Prof. U. S. KUKUSHKIN.
*Faculty of Philosophy:* Prof. M. F. OVSYANNIKOV.
*Faculty of Philology:* Prof. A. G. SOKOLOV.
*Faculty of Law:* Prof. G. V. IVANOV.
*Faculty of Psychology:* Prof. A. N. LEONTYEV.
*Faculty of Economy:* Prof. M. V. SOLODKOV.
*Faculty of Journalism:* Prof. Y. N. ZASURSKY.
*Institute of Oriental Languages:* Prof. A. A. KOVALEV (Rector).
*Faculty for Teachers in Higher Education Institutions:* Doc. I. B. RAKOBOLSKAYA.
*Preparatory Faculty for Foreign Students:* Doc. I. I. POTAPOVA.

#### ATTACHED INSTITUTES:
**Institute of Astronomy.**
**Institute of Mechanics.**
**Institute of Nuclear Studies.**
**Institute of Anthropological Studies.**

### NORTH-OSSETIAN K. L. KHETAGUROV STATE UNIVERSITY
NORTH-OSSETIAN A.S.S.R.,
ORJONIKIDZE, UL. VALUTINA 46
Founded 1969.

*Rector:* A. K. GUDYEV.
*Pro-Rector:* G. J. KRAVCHENKO.

Faculties of physics and mathematics, philology, chemistry, biology, history, foreign languages, law, economics; extra-mural department.

### NOVOSIBIRSK STATE UNIVERSITY
630090 NOVOSIBIRSK, UL. PIROGOVA 2
Telephone: 65-62-44.

Founded 1959; Language of instruction: Russian; Academic year: September to June.

*Rector:* Prof. V. A. KOPTYUG.
*Pro-Rectors:* Prof. N. G. ZAGORUIKO, Dr. A. S. MARCHENKO.
*Registrar:* L. P. PUTRO.
*Librarian:* L. G. TORSHENOVA.

Number of teachers: 550.
Number of students: 5,000.

#### DEANS:
*Faculty of Geology and Geophysics:* Prof. E. E. FOTIADI.
*Faculty of Economics:* Prof. V. K. OZEROV.
*Faculty of Mathematics and Mechanics:* Prof. B. A. ROGOZIN.
*Faculty of Physics:* Prof. S. G. RAUTIAN.
*Faculty of Humanities:* Dr. I. A. MOLETOTOV.
*Faculty of Natural Sciences:* Prof. D. G. KNORRE.

### NUKUS UNIVERSITY
742000 NUKUS, UL. UNIVERSITETSKAYA 1,
UZBEK S.S.R.
Founded 1979.

Faculties of languages, history, economics, sciences, agriculture.

### ODESSA I. I. MECHNIKOV STATE UNIVERSITY
ODESSA, UL. PETRA VELIKOGO 2, UKRAINE
Founded 1865.

*Rector:* Prof. A. V. BOGATSKY.
*Vice-Rectors:* D. I. POLISHCHUK, V. V. FASHCHENKO, G. A. TETERIN, I. E. SEREDA.
*Librarian:* P. M. BONDARENKO.

Number of teachers: 800.
Number of students: 12,000.

Faculties of history, philology, foreign languages, law, mechanics and mathematics, physics, chemistry, biology, geography, geology; evening and extra-mural departments.

#### ATTACHED INSTITUTE:
**Institute of Physics.**

### OMSK STATE UNIVERSITY
644077 OMSK, PR. MIRA 55A, R.S.F.S.R.
Founded 1974.

Faculties of humanities, natural sciences, physics; extra-mural courses.

### PATRICE LUMUMBA PEOPLE'S FRIENDSHIP UNIVERSITY
3 UL. ORDJONIKIDZE, MOSCOW B-302,
117923 GSP
Telephone: 234-00-11.

Founded 1960 to train African, Asian and Latin-American students.

Self-governing; language of instruction: Russian; academic year: September to July.

Vice-Chancellor and Rector: V. F. STANIS.
Pro-Rectors: K. P. STAYEV, YU. N. SOKOLOV, A. E. GOLUBEV, G. U. SHARAPOV.
  Number of teachers: 1,250.
  Number of students: 6,700 from 103 countries.
  Publication: *Drujba* (weekly university newspaper).

DEANS:

*Faculty of History and Philology:* A. N. KOJIN.
*Faculty of Physico-Mathematical and Natural Sciences:* N. S. PROSTAKOV.
*Faculty of Medicine:* D. P. BILIBIN.
*Faculty of Engineering:* V. D. NESMEYANOV.
*Faculty of Economics and Law:* B. P. MOZOLIN.
*Preparatory Faculty:* G. A. FAVSTOV.
*Faculty of Agriculture:* D. V. RULIKOV.

## PERM A. M. GORKY STATE UNIVERSITY
PERM, UL. BUKIREVA 15

Founded 1916.

*Rector:* Prof. V. P. ZHIVOPISTSEV.
*Pro-Rector:* Prof. I. A. PECHERKIN.
*Librarian:* Z. D. FILINYKH.
  Number of teachers: 600.
  Number of students: 12,000.
  Publications: *Uchenie Zapiski Permskogo Gosedarstvennogo Universiteta* (Transactions of the Perm State University), *Izvestiya Estestvennogo Instituta pri Permskom Gosudarstvennom Universitete* (The Journal of Research Institute of Natural Sciences of the Perm State University) (both annually).
  Faculties of History, Philology, Law, Economics, Mechanics and Mathematics, Physics, Chemistry, Biology, Geology, Geography.

ATTACHED RESEARCH INSTITUTIONS:
**Electronic Computing Centre.**
**Institute of Natural Sciences.**
**Institute of Karstology and Speleology.**

## PETROZAVODSK O. V. KUUSINEN STATE UNIVERSITY
PETROZAVODSK, PROSPEKT LENINA 33,
KARELIAN A.S.S.R.

Founded 1940.

*Rector:* V. V. STEPHANIKHIN.
*Pro-Rectors:* Prof. E. A. VESELOV, M. I. SHUMILOV.
*Librarian:* V. S. KLODT.
  Number of teachers: 450.
  Number of students: 7,000.
  Publications: *Uchenie Zapiski Petrozavodskogo Gosudarstvennogo Universiteta imeni O. V. Kuusinena* (Transactions, 11 series), *Trudi Petrozavodskogo Gosudarstvennogo Universiteta im. O. V. Kuusinena* (Works).
  Faculties of history and philology, physics and mathematics, forestry engineering, agriculture, medicine, biology, industrial and civil engineering; evening and extra-mural departments.

## ROSTOV STATE UNIVERSITY
ROSTOV-ON-DON, UL. FRIDRIKHA ENGELSA 105

Founded 1917.

*Rector:* Prof. Y. A. ZHDANOV.
*Pro-Rectors:* V. I. SEDLETSKY, V. P. GRIGORJEV.
  Number of students: 9,600.
  Faculties of philology, philosophy, economics, history, mechanics and mathematics, physics, chemistry, biology and soil science, geology and geography, law; evening and extra-mural departments.

## SAMARKAND ALISHER NAVOI STATE UNIVERSITY
SAMARKAND, BULVAR M. GORKOGO 15,
UZBEK S.S.R.

Founded 1933.

*Rector:* Prof. Acad. A. K. ATAKHODZHAEV.
*Pro-Rectors:* Prof. M. A. RISH, KH. A. ABDULLAEV.
*Librarian:* A. A. ABBASOVA.
  Number of teachers: 600.
  Number of students: 6,500.
  Faculties of history, geography, philology, foreign languages, mechanics and mathematics, physics, chemistry, biology, technology and engineering, Uzbek and Tajik philology; evening and extra-mural departments.

## SARATOV N. G. CHERNYSHEVSKY STATE UNIVERSITY
SARATOV, ASTRAKHANSKAYA UL. 83

Founded 1909.

*Rector:* Prof. V. N. SHEVCHIK.
*Pro-Rectors:* Prof. I. S. KASHKIN, N. P. KUPTSOV.
*Librarian:* V. A. ARTISEVICH.
  Number of teachers: c. 700.
  Number of students: c. 10,000.
  Periodical: *Uchenie zapiski Saratovskogo Gosudarstvennogo Universiteta imeni N. G. Chernyshevskogo* (Transactions).
  Faculties of history, philosophy, mechanics and mathematics, physics, chemistry, biology, geology, geography; evening and extra-mural departments.

## SIMFEROPOL M. V. FRUNZE STATE UNIVERSITY
SIMFEROPOL, UL. YALTINSKAYA 4,
UKRAINE

Founded 1973.

  Number of students: 5,500.
  Faculties of Russian language and literature, Ukrainian language and literature, history, mathematics and computers, physics, geography, biology; evening department.

## SYKTYVKAR STATE UNIVERSITY
SYKTYVKAR, OCTJABRSKY PROSPECT 55,
KOMI A.S.S.R.

Founded 1972.

  Number of students: 3,000.
  Faculties of biology and chemistry, mathematics and physics, history, finance and credit, accounts; evening department.

## TAJIK V. I. LENIN STATE UNIVERSITY
DUSHANBE, PROSPEKT LENINA 17,
TAJIK S.S.R.

Telephone: 22-21-84.

Founded 1948.

Languages of instruction: Tajik and Russian; Academic year: September to July.

*Rector:* Prof. P. B. BABADZHANOV.
*Vice-Rectors:* M. N. NAZARSHOEV (Scientific), V. I. PRIPISNOV (Educational), A. O. ORIPOV (Evening and Extra-Mural Dept.).
*Registrar:* G. S. EGOROVA.
*Librarian:* V. K. SULEYMANOVA.

Number of teachers: 750.
Number of students: c. 6,500 (full-time), 2,225 (evening), 3,576 (extra-mural).

DEANS:

*Faculty of Mechanics and Mathematics:* Prof. D. MURTAZAEV.
*Faculty of Physics:* Prof. S. I. KARIMOV.
*Faculty of Chemistry:* Prof. X. M. YAKUBOV.
*Faculty of Geology:* Prof. A. CH. KHASANOV.
*Faculty of Biology:* Prof. X. M. SAFAROV.
*Faculty of History:* Prof. M. B. BABACHANOV.
*Faculty of Tajik Philology:* Prof. M. D. DAVLJATOV.
*Faculty of Oriental Studies:* Prof. F. N. NADJMONOV.
*Faculty of Russian Language and Literature:* Prof. B. G. ASTACHOV.
*Faculty of Law:* Prof. O. U. USMANOV.
*Faculty of Economics:* Prof. G. B. BOBOSADIKOVA.
*Faculty of Finance:* Prof. X. K. KURBANOV.
*Faculty of English Language:* Prof. A. R. KAMALOVA.

## TARTU STATE UNIVERSITY
TARTU, ÜLIKOOLI 18, ESTONIAN S.S.R.
Founded 1802.

Languages of instruction: Estonian and Russian; Academic year: September to June.

*Rector:* A. KOOP.
*Pro-Rectors:* Prof. U. PALM, Prof. H. METSA, V. HAAMER, Ü. SAAG.
*Scientific Secretary:* I. MAAROOS.
*Librarian:* L. PEEP.

Number of teachers: 690, including 81 professors.
Number of students: 7,200.

Publications: *Transactions of the Tartu State University, Organic Reactivity, Mathematics and the Present Age, Collection of Scientific Transactions.*

DEANS:

*Faculty of History:* A. LIIM.
*Faculty of Philology:* Prof. A. KÜNNAP.
*Faculty of Mathematics:* Prof. U. LUMISTE.
*Faculty of Physics and Chemistry:* Prof. V. PAST.
*Faculty of Biology and Geography:* A. LOOG.
*Faculty of Law:* H. KINGS.
*Faculty of Economics:* V. KRINAL.
*Faculty of Medicine:* Prof. L. ALLIKMETS.
*Faculty of Physical Culture:* Prof. A. VIRU.

## TASHKENT V. I. LENIN STATE UNIVERSITY
TASHKENT 700095, UNIVERSITETSKAYA, VUZGORODOK, UZBEK S.S.R.
Founded 1920.

*Rector:* Acad. M. A. SARYMSAKOV.
*Pro-Rectors:* E. N. KUTSENKO, P. B. AZIZOV, SH. M. SHAMUKHAMEDOV.
*Head of Teaching Department:* A. N. POTEKHIN.
*Library Director:* L. S. YUGAI.

Number of teachers: 1,480.
Number of students: 18,440.

Faculties of history, Uzbek philology, Russian philology, Romance and German philology, oriental studies, journalism, philosophy and economics, law, mathematics, mechanics and applied mathematics, physics, chemistry, biology and soil science, geology, geography.

## TBILISI STATE UNIVERSITY
TBILISI, PROSPEKT CHAVCHAVADZE 1, GEORGIAN S.S.R.
Telephone: 22-96-27.
Founded 1918.

State control; Language of instruction: Georgian, with a Russian section in some faculties; Academic year: September to June.

*Rector:* Prof. David I. CHKHIKVISHVILI.
*Pro-Rectors:* Prof. S. M. DZHORBENADZE, Dr. G. A. CHILASHUILI, Dr. A. KINTSURASHVILI.
*Chief Administrative Officer:* A. I. KHARSHILADZE.
*Librarian:* S. A. APAKIDZE.

Library of 3,000,000 vols.

Number of professors and lecturers: 1,659.
Number of students: 16,000.

Publications: *Tbilisi University* (weekly), *Proceedings of Tbilisi University* (four issues a year, in two series).

DEANS:

*Faculty of Mechanics and Mathematics:* Prof. L. GIGIASHVILI.
*Faculty of Cybernetics and Applied Mathematics:* Dr. R. KORDZADZE.
*Faculty of Physics:* Prof. T. SANADZE.
*Faculty of Chemistry:* Dr. S. MIKADZE.
*Faculty of Geography and Geology:* Dr. N. NACHKEBIA.
*Faculty of Biology:* Prof. B. LOMSADZE.
*Faculty of History:* Prof. A. SURGULADZE.
*Faculty of Philosophy and Psychology:* Prof. G. TEVZADZE.
*Faculty of Philology:* Prof. O. BAKANIDZE.
*Faculty of Western European Languages and Literature:* Dr. I. BACHIASHVILI.
*Faculty of Oriental Studies:* Dr. G. PUTURIDZE.
*Faculty of Economics:* Prof. G. CHANUKVADZE.
*Faculty of Engineering Economics:* Dr. V. GABIDZASHVILI.
*Faculty of Branch Economics:* Dr. N. MESKHI.
*Faculty of Commercial Economics:* Dr. I. MUDZHIRI.
*Faculty of Law:* Dr. V. LORIA.
*Faculty of Fine Arts:* Prof. V. GVAKHARIA.
*University Teachers' Training Faculty:* Dr. A. ISHKHNELI.
*School Teachers' Training Faculty:* Dr. D. DZHIKIA.

ATTACHED INSTITUTES:

**Institute of Applied Mathematics:** Tbilisi, Universitetskaya ul. 2.

**Institute of High Energy Physics.**

## TOMSK V. V. KUIBYSHEV STATE UNIVERSITY
TOMSK, PROSPEKT LENINA 36
Founded 1888.

*Rector:* Prof. A. P. BYCHKOV.
*Pro-Rectors:* E. S. VOROBEICHIKOV, M. P. KORTUSOV.

Library: over 2,500,000 vols.

Number of students: 10,058.

Faculties of history and philology, law, economics, physics, mechanics and mathematics, chemistry, biology and soil science, geology and geography, radiophysics; evening and extra-mural departments.

## TURKMEN A. M. GORKY STATE UNIVERSITY
ASHKHABAD, PROSPEKT LENINA 31, TURKMEN S.S.R.
Founded 1950.

*Rector:* Prof. S. N. MURADOV.
*Pro-Rectors:* G. M. MYALIK-KULIEV, A. A. KURBANOV, T. R. REDZHEPOV.

Number of students: 4,000.

Faculties of philology, foreign languages, history and law, physics and mathematics, biology and geography, economics, physical training; evening and extra-mural departments.

## TYUMEN STATE UNIVERSITY
TYUMEN 3, UL. SEMAKOVA 10

Faculties of history and philology, physics and mathematics, chemistry and biology, economics and geography; extra-mural and preparatory departments.

## UDMURD STATE UNIVERSITY
IZHVSK, KRASNOGEROISKAJA UL. 7, UDMURD A.S.S.R.

Faculties of history, philology, physics and mathematics, biology and chemistry, economics and law, foreign languages, physical training; extra-mural and preparatory departments.

## URALS A. M. GORKY STATE UNIVERSITY
SVERDLOVSK, K-83, PROSPEKT LENINA 51

Founded 1920.

*Rector:* V. A. KUZNETSOV.
*Pro-Rectors:* B. A. SUTIRIN, A. F. GERASIMOV.
*Librarian:* TATIANA DMITRIEVNA VOROBYOVA.

Number of teachers: 425, including 32 professors.
Number of students: 6,000.

Publications: *Uchenie Zapiski Uralskogo Gosudarstvennogo Universiteta* (Scientific Reports of the Urals A. M. Gorky State University, several series), *Matematicheskie Zapiski* (Mathematical Reports, annually in four parts).

DEANS:

*Faculty of Philosophy:* M. N. RUTKEVICH.
*Faculty of History:* P. K. TARASOV.
*Faculty of Philology:* A. S. SUBOTIN.
*Faculty of Mathematics and Mechanics.* Y. M. REPIN.
*Faculty of Physics:* V. N. KONEV.
*Faculty of Chemistry:* V. P. KOCHERGIN.
*Faculty of Biology:* L. A. PODSOSOV.
*Faculty of Journalism:* V. A. CHICHILANOV.
*Department of Extra-Mural Studies:* Dir. P. S. TOMILOV.

## UZHGOROD STATE UNIVERSITY
UZHGOROD, UL. M. GORKOGO 46, UKRAINE

Founded 1945.

*Rector:* D. V. CHEPUR.
*Pro-Rectors:* N. A. LAKUZA, S. M. KISHKO.

Number of students: 4,154.

Faculties of philology, history, physics and mathematics, chemistry, biology, medicine, foreign languages; evening and extra-mural departments.

## VILNIUS V. KAPSUKAS STATE UNIVERSITY
VILNIUS, UNIVERSITETO 3, LITHUANIAN S.S.R.

Founded 1579.

*Rector:* J. KUBILIUS.
*Pro-Rectors:* J. GRIGONIS, B. SUDAVIČIUS, A. VYGONTIENË, P. EIGMINAS.
*Director of the Library:* J. TORNAU.

Number of teachers: 1,094.
Number of students: 16,200.

Publications: *Lithuanian Mathematics, Lithuanian Physics, Baltistica, Problems of the History of the Lithuanian C.P., Problems, Economics, Biology, Geography and Geology, History, Law, Linguistics, Literature, Book Science, Bulletin of Vilnius Observatory, Tarybinis Studentas* (Soviet Student, weekly).

DEANS:

*Faculty of Mathematics:* V. MERKYS.
*Faculty of Physics:* V. KYBARTAS.
*Faculty of Chemistry:* A. LEVINSKAS.
*Faculty of Natural Sciences:* R. TARVYDAS.
*Faculty of Medicine:* S. PAVILONIS.
*Faculty of Philology:* J. PIKČILINGIS.
*Faculty of History:* V. LEŠČIUS.
*Faculty of Industrial Economics:* P. KIUBERIS.
*Faculty of Commercial Economics:* L. BUTKEVIČIUS.
*Faculty of Finance and Discount:* A. ŽILENAS.
*Faculty of Law:* I. NEKROŠIUS.
*Inter-collegiate Faculty* (in Kaunas): V. ČESNAVIČIUS.

RESEARCH INSTITUTES:

Research Section; Semiconductor Physics Laboratory; Laboratory of Molecular Acoustics; Laboratory of Atomic and Molecular Spectroscopy; Laboratory of the Pathology of Digestive Organs; Laboratory of Medicament Synthesis; Department of Experimental Surgery of Cardiac Blood-Vessels; Laboratory of Animal and Plant Growth Stimulators; Botanical Gardens; Observatory.

The University also provides specialized training in various fields of national economy and culture of the country.

## VOLGOGRAD UNIVERSITY
VOLGOGRAD

Founded 1978; in process of formation. First student intake October 1980 (250 students).

Faculties of physics, mathematics, history, Russian, romance languages, Germanic languages.

## VORONEZH STATE UNIVERSITY
VORONEZH, UNIVERSITETSKAYA PLOSHCHAD 1

Founded 1918.

*Rector:* Prof. V. MELESHKO.
*Pro-Rectors:* P. M. GAPONOV, A. A. GLUKHOV.

Number of teachers: 507.
Number of students: 8,000.

Faculties of history, philology, Romance and German philology, economics, law, mathematics and mechanics, physics, chemistry, biology and soil science, geology, geography; evening and extra-mural departments.

## YAKUTSK STATE UNIVERSITY
YAKUTSK, PROSPEKT LENINA 33, YAKUT A.S.S.R.

Founded 1956.

*Rector:* I. G. POPOV.
*Pro-Rectors:* Prof. I. M. BRUNKHAKOV, I. I. KRYLOVA.
*Librarian:* Z. A. AMMOSOVA.

Number of teachers: 400.
Number of students: 6,000.

Faculties of history and philology, physics and mathematics, biology and geography, medicine, engineering and technology, agriculture; evening and extra-mural departments.

## YAROSLAVL UNIVERSITY
YAROSLAVL, UL. SOVIETSKAYA 14

Founded 1971.

*Rector:* M. V. SRETENSKY.
*Pro-Rector:* G. E. SABUROV.

Faculties of physics and mathematics, economics, law, psychology and biology, history; preparatory departments.

## OTHER HIGHER EDUCATIONAL INSTITUTES

### AGRICULTURE

(1) GENERAL AGRICULTURAL INSTITUTES

**All-Union Extra-Mural Agricultural Institute:** Moscow Region, Balashikha 8, Poselok Leonovo; f. 1927; depts.: Agrochemistry and Soil Science. Agronomy, Fruit and Vegetable Growing, Viticulture, Zootechnics, Mechanization, Economics and Management, Irrigation, Electrification; library of 260,000 vols.

**Altai Agricultural Institute:** Barnaul, Krasnoarmeysky prospekt 98; f. 1944; depts.: Agronomy, Veterinary, Mechanization, Economics and Management, Accounting; 340 teachers; 6,500 students; library of 220,000 vols.; Extra-Mural Faculty; Rector E. N. DAVYDOV; publ. *Works of the Altay Agricultural Institute*.

**Armenian Agricultural Institute:** Erevan, Ul. Teryana 74, f. 1930; depts.: Agrochemistry and Soil Science; Agronomy, Fruit and Vegetable Growing, Viticulture, Plant Protection, Wine Making, Technology of Preserving Industry, Mechanization, Irrigation, Economics and Management, Motor Transport; 300 teachers; 5,000 students; library of 240,000 vols.; Extra-Mural Faculty; Rector A. T. TOVMASYAN; publs. *Scientific Works, Collection of Conference Scientific Reports by Young Scientific Workers, Agriculturist*.

**Azerbaijan Agricultural Institute:** Kirovabad, Ul. Azizbekova 222; depts.: Agrochemistry and Soil Science, Agronomy, Fruit and Vegetable Growing, Viticulture; Zootechnics, Veterinary, Silkworm Breeding, Mechanization, Electrification, Economics and Management, Accounting; library of 200,000 vols.; Extra-Mural Faculty; Rector N. A. SAFAROV.

**Bashkir Agricultural Institute:** Ul. 50 Letiya Oktyabrya, Ufa, Bashkir A.S.S.R.; depts.: Agronomy, Zootechnics, Economics, Mechanics; 260 teachers; 5,300 students; library of 150,000 vols.; Extra-Mural Faculty; Rector N. R. BAKHTZIN; publ. *Works of the Bashkir Agricultural Institute*.

**Belotserkovsky Agricultural Institute:** Belaya Tserkov, Kievskaya obl., Pl. Svodoby, 8/1; f. 1920; faculties: Agronomy, Veterinary Science; Zootechnics; Rector Prof. N. S. PALAMAR; publ. *Naychnye Zaniski* (Scientific Notes).

**Blagoveshchensk Agricultural Institute:** Amur Region, Blagoveshchensk, Politekhnicheskaya ul. 86; f. 1950; depts.: Agronomy, Zootechnics, Veterinary, Accounting, Mechanization; library of 160,000 vols.; Extra-Mural Faculty; Rector E. V. BLINNIKOV; publ. *Works of the Blagoveshchensk Agricultural Institute*.

**Buryat Agricultural Institute:** Ulan-Ude, Ul. Pushkina 16; depts.: Agronomy, Zootechnics, Agrochemistry and Soil Science, Veterinary, Economics and Management, Accounting, Mechanization; library of 120,000 vols.; Rector K D. MIRONOV.

**Byelorussian Agricultural Academy:** Gorki, Mogilev District, Byelorussian S.S.R.; f. 1840; faculties of Agronomy, Agrochemistry, Book-keeping, Zootechnics, Economics, Mechanization, Land Exploitation, Hydrology and Amelioration of Operations in Hydrology and Land Reclamation; 520 teachers; 9,900 students; library of 910,000 vols.; Rector Prof. K. M. SOLNTSEV.

**Chuvash Agricultural Institute:** Ul. K. Marxa 29, Cheboksary, Chuvash A.S.S.R.; depts.: Agronomy, Mechanization, Zootechnics; library of 83,000 vols.; Extra-Mural faculty.

**Crimean M. I. Kalinin Agricultural Institute:** Simferopol 30, Vuzgorodok; depts.: Agronomy, Fruit and Vegetable Growing, Viticulture, Economics, Book-keeping; library of 304,450 vols.; Extra-Mural Faculty; Rector A. M. LUKJANCHENKO.

**Daghestan Agricultural Institute:** Ul. M. Gajieva 180, Makhachkala, Daghestan A.S.S.R.; f. 1932; depts.: Zootechnics, Veterinary, Fruit and Vegetable Growing, Accounting; library of 200,000 vols.; Rector M. M. JAMBULATOV; publ. *Works of the Daghestan Agricultural Institute*.

**Dnepropetrovsk Agricultural Institute:** Ul. 40 Letiya Oktyabrya 25, Dnepropetrovsk, Ukrainian S.S.R.; depts.: Agronomy, Mechanization, Economics, Accounting; library of 204,000 vols.; Rector A. T. LYSENKO.

**Don Agricultural Institute:** Rostov Region, Station Persianovka; f. 1916; depts.: Agronomy, Zootechnics, Veterinary; 205 teachers; 3,600 students; library of 210,000 vols.; Rector P. E. LADAN.

**Estonian Agricultural Academy:** Riia 12, Tartu, Estonian S.S.R.; f. 1951; faculties: Veterinary Sciences, Zootechnics, Agronomy, Mechanization, Forestry, Irrigation, Accounting, Economics; 270 teachers, 4,024 students; library of 370,000 vols.; Rector A. F. RUETEL; publ. *Eesti Pollumajanduse Akadeemia Teaduslike Teode Kogumik*.

**Georgian (Order of Red Banner of Labour) Agricultural Institute:** 380031 Tbilisi, 13-km. Voenno-Gruzinskoy Dorogi, Georgian S.S.R.; depts.: Agronomy, Fruit and Vegetable Growing, Viticulture, Mechanization, Electrification, Forestry, Economics and Management, Accounting, Silkworm Breeding, Plant Protection, Wine Making, Preserving Industry; library of 700,000 vols.; Rector I. F. SARISHVILI.

**Georgian Institute of Subtropical Cultivation:** Sukhumi, Kelasuri; depts.: Subtropical Agronomy, Subtropical Cultivation, Mechanization, Preserving Industry; library of 90,000 vols.; Extra-Mural Dept.; Rector I. A. GEORGBERIDZE.

**Gorky Agricultural Institute:** Gorky, 78 Shcherbinki; f. 1918; depts.: Agrochemistry, Agronomy, Zootechnics, Mechanization, Accounting; library of 200,000 vols.; Extra-Mural Faculty; Rector A. I. BARANOV; publ. *Works of the Gorky Agricultural Institute*.

**Gorsky Agricultural Institute:** Orjonikidze, Ul. Kirova 37; depts.: Agronomy, Zootechnics, Mechanization, Economics and Management, Accounting; library of 208,000 vols.; Extra-Mural Faculty.

**Grodno Agricultural Institute:** Byelorussian S.S.R., Grodno, Ul. Tereshkovoj 26; f. 1951; depts.: Agronomy, Zootechnics, Plant Protection; 150 teachers; 3,000 students; library of 150,000 vols.; Extra-Mural Faculty; Rector Y. G. EGOROV.

**Irkutsk Agricultural Institute:** Irkutsk, 38 Pos. Molodezhny; f. 1934; depts.: Agronomy, Plant Protection, Zootechnics, Mechanization, Accounting; 290 teachers; 4,800 students; library of 280,000 vols.; Extra-Mural Faculty; Rector A. N. UGAROV.

**Ivanovo Agricultural Institute:** Ivanovo, Sovetskaya ul. 45; f. 1918; depts.: Agronomy, Zootechnics; library of 112,000 vols.; Extra-Mural Faculty; Rector N. I. BELONOSOV.

**Izhevsk Agricultural Institute:** Udmurd A.S.S.R., Izhevsk, Ul. Kirova 16; depts.: Agronomy, Zootechnics, Mechanization; library of 85,000 vols.; Extra-Mural Faculty.

**Kamenets-Podolsk Agricultural Institute:** Kamenets-Podolsk, Ul. Shevchenko 19; f. 1921; depts.: Agronomy, Zootechnics; library of 220,000 vols.; Extra-Mural Faculty; Rector S. S. SERBIN.

**Kazakh State Agricultural Institute:** Alma-Ata, Prospekt Abaya 8; depts.: Agronomy, Plant Protection, Mechanization, Electrification, Forestry, Economics and Management, Accounting; library of 167,000 vols.; Extra-Mural Faculty; Rector KH. A. ARYSTANBEKOV.

**Kazan A. M. Gorky Agricultural Institute:** Kazan, Ul. Karla Marxa 65; depts.: Agronomy, Mechanization, Economics and Management, Accounting; library of 135,000 vols.; Extra-Mural Faculty; Rector S. A. ILYIN.

**Kharkov V. V. Dokuchaev Agricultural Institute:** 310078 Kharkov, Ul. Artema 44; f. 1816; depts.: Agronomy, Breeding and Seed Production, Plant Protection, Agrochemistry and Soil Science, Land Exploitation, Agricultural Building and Planning of Rural Settlements, Economics and Management, Accounting; 280 teachers, 5,600 students; library of 430,000 vols.; Extra-Mural Faculty; Rector G. F. NAUMOV; publs. *Yearly Scientific Reports on Agronomy and Agricultural Economics and Management*.

**Kherson A. D. Tsuryupa Agricultural Institute:** 325006 Kherson, Rosa Luxembourg 3; f. 1874; faculties of Agronomy, Zootechnics and Hydromelioration; library of 240,500 vols.; extra-mural faculties and postgraduate studies; Rector B. F. BENKOVSKY; publ. *Scientific Reports*.

**Kirghiz Agricultural Institute:** Frunze, Kommunisticheskaya ul. 68-a; f. 1933; depts.: Agronomy, Zootechnics, Mechanization, Irrigation and Land Reclamation; 265 teachers; 4,600 students; library of 184,000 vols.; Extra-Mural Faculty; Rector E. I. ARABAEV.

**Kirov Agricultural Institute:** Kirov, Oktyabrsky prospekt 133; f. 1930; depts.: Agronomy, Zootechnics, Veterinary, Mechanization; library of 270,000 vols.; Extra-Mural Faculty; Rector I. P. MAKAROV.

**Kishinev M. V. Frunze Agricultural Institute:** Kishinev, Sadovaya ul. 111; depts.: Agronomy, Fruit and Vegetable Growing, Viticulture, Zootechnics, Mechanization, Plant Protection, Economics and Management, Accounting; library of 200,000 vols.; Extra-Mural Faculty; Rector G. YA. RUD.

**Kostroma Agricultural Institute:** Kostroma District, State Farm Karavaevo; f. 1949; depts.: Agronomy, Zootechnics, Mechanization, Economics and Management, Accounting; library of 76,000 vols.; Extra-Mural Faculty; Rector R. S. TRIKOZ.

**Krasnoyarsk Agricultural Institute:** Krasnoyarsk, Prospekt Mira 88; f. 1953; depts.: Agronomy, Zootechnics, Mechanization; 210 teachers; 3,600 students; library of 130,000 vols.; Extra-Mural Faculty.

**Kuban Agricultural Institute:** Krasnodar 94, Ul. Kalinina 13; depts.: Agrochemistry and Soil Science, Agronomy, Viticulture, Zootechnics, Mechanization, Economics and Management, Accounting; library of 290,000 vols.; Extra-Mural Faculty; Rector P. F. VARUKHA.

**Kuibyshev Agricultural Institute:** Kuibyshev Region, Kinel; f. 1919; depts.: Agronomy, Zootechnics, Mechanization; 210 teachers; 3,500 students; library of 215,000 vols.; Extra-Mural Faculty; Rector N. S. SHIBRAEV.

**Kurgan Agricultural Institute:** Kurgan, Ul. Kuibysheva 55; f. 1944; depts.: Agronomy, Zootechnics; library of 200,000 vols.; Extra-Mural Department; Rector I. R. KUN.

**Kursk Prof. I Ivanov Agricultural Institute:** 305021 Kursk, Ul. Karla Marxa 70; f. 1956; depts.: Agronomy, Plant Protection, Zootechnics, Mechanization, Economics and Management, Accounting; library of 130,000 vols.; Extra-Mural Faculty; Rector A. A. SYSOEV.

**Latvian Agricultural Academy:** Elgava, Ul. V. 1. Lenina 2; depts.: Agronomy, Zootechnics, Irrigation and Land Reclamation, Forestry, Veterinary, Mechanization, Timber Technology, Public Dietetics, Organization of Land Exploitation, Dairy Technology, Motor Transport, Agricultural Economics; library of 261,000 vols.; Extra-Mural Faculty; Rector O. G. OZEL.

**Leningrad Agricultural Institute:** Leningrad Region, Pushkin, Komsomolskaya ul. 14; f. 1904; depts.: Agrochemistry and Soil Science, Agronomy, Fruit and Vegetable Growing, Viticulture, Plant Protection, Zootechnics, Mechanization, Electrification, Economics and Management, Accounting; 500 teachers; 10,000 students; library of 500,000 vols.; Extra-Mural Faculty.

**Lithuanian Agricultural Academy:** Kaunas, Noreikishkes; f. 1924; depts.: Agronomy, Mechanization, Electrification, Agricultural Machinery, Land Reclamation, Economics and Management, Organization of Land Exploitation, Forestry, Accounting; 290 teachers; 5,200 students; library of 330,000 vols.; Extra-Mural Department; Rector Z. URBONAS; publ. *Transactions of the Lithuanian Agricultural Academy*.

**Lvov Agricultural Institute:** Lvov Region, Nesterov District, Selo Dublyany; f. 1946; depts.: Agronomy, Mechanization, Organization of Land Exploitation, Economics and Management, Accounting; 260 teachers; 6,500 students; library of 150,000 vols.; Extra-Mural Faculty; Rector M. T. GONCHAR; publ. *Transactions of the Lvov Agricultural Institute*.

**Moscow Timiryazev Academy of Agriculture:** Ul. Timiryazevskaya 49, Moscow A-8; f. 1865; seven faculties: Agronomy, Agricultural Chemistry and Soil Science, Stockbreeding, Economy, Horticulture, Agropedagogical, and Extra-Mural; 380 teachers; 31,000 students. Twenty-seven research stations and five experimental and instructional farms are attached to the Academy.

**Novosibirsk Agricultural Institute:** Novosibirsk, Ul. Dobrolyubova 160; depts.: Agronomy, Plant Protection, Mechanization, Economics and Management, Accounting; library of 252,000 vols.; Extra-Mural Faculty; Rector I. I. GUDILIN.

**Odessa Agricultural Institute:** Odessa 39, Ul. Sverdlova 99; depts.: Agronomy, Fruit and Vegetable Growing, Viticulture, Zootechnics, Veterinary, Economics and Management, Accounting; library of 280,000 vols.; Extra-Mural Faculty; Rector I. S. SAMOILENKE.

**Omsk S. M. Kirov Agricultural Institute:** Omsk, Zagorodnyaya Roshcha; depts.: Agrochemistry and Soil Science, Agronomy, Fruit and Vegetable Growing, Viticulture, Zootechnics, Mechanization, Irrigation, Engineering, Geodesy, Meat Technology, Dairy Technology, Economics and Management, Accounting, Grain Processing; library of 300,000 vols.; Extra-Mural Faculty; Rector D. L. SUMTSOV.

**Orenburg A. A. Andreyev Agricultural Institute:** 460200 Orenburg, Ul. Chelyuskintsev 18; f. 1930; depts.: Agronomy, Zootechnics, Veterinary, Mechanization, Economics and Management, Accounting; 280 teachers; 5,000 students; library of 320,000 vols.; Extra-Mural Faculty; Rector V. P. PETROV; publ. *Works*.

**Penza Agricultural Institute:** Penza, 14 Botanicheskaya ul. 10; f. 1951; depts.: Agronomy, Zootechnics,

Mechanization; library of 70,000 vols.; Extra-Mural Faculty; Rector F. A. ZHARKOV.

**Perm Academician D. N. Pryanishnikov Agricultural Institute:** Perm, Kommunisticheskaya ul. 23; f. 1918; depts.: Agrochemistry and Soil Science, Agronomy, Zootechnics, Mechanization, Economics and Management, Accounting; 260 teachers; 4,600 students; library of 320,000 vols.; Extra-Mural Faculty; Rector A. A. EROFEEV.

**Poltava Agricultural Institute:** Poltava, Ul. Skovorody 1/3; depts.: Agronomy, Zootechnics, Economics and Management, Accounting, Pedagogics; library of 93,000 vols.; Extra-Mural Faculty; Rector N. A. DOBROVOLSKY.

**Primorye Agricultural Institute:** Ussuriysk, Prospect Blyukhera 44; depts.: Agronomy, Zootechnics, Mechanization, Irrigation and Land Reclamation, Forestry, Economics and Management, Accounting; library of 72,000 vols.; Extra-Mural Faculty; Rector P. K. SIDORENKO.

**Ryazan Professor P. A. Kostychev Agricultural Institute:** Ryazan, Ul. Lenina 53; depts.: Agronomy, Zootechnics, Mechanization, Economics and Management, Accounting; library of 94,000 vols.; Extra-Mural Faculty; Rector M. I. SALIKOV.

**Samarkand V. V. Kuibyshev Agricultural Institute:** Samarkand, Ul. K. Marxa 77; f. 1929; depts.: Agronomy, Zootechnics, Veterinary; library of 250,000 vols.; Extra-Mural Department.

**Saratov Agricultural Institute:** Saratov, Ploshchad Revolyutsii 1; depts.: Agronomy, Plant Protection, Forestry, Economics and Management, Accounting; library of 314,000 vols.; Extra-Mural Faculty; Rector E. D. MILOVANOV.

**Stavropol Agricultural Institute:** Stavropol, Ul. Mira 347; f. 1933; depts.: Agronomy, Zootechnics, Veterinary, Mechanization, Economics and Management, Accounting; 360 teachers; 2,500 students; library of 362,000 vols.; Extra-Mural Faculty.

**Sverdlovsk Agricultural Institute:** Sverdlovsk 151, Ul. K. Liebknechta 42; depts.: Agronomy, Zootechnics, Veterinary, Mechanization; library of 196,000 vols.; Extra-Mural Faculty; Rector M. P. DORMIDONTOV.

**Tajik Agricultural Institute:** Ministry of Agriculture of the U.S.S.R., Dushanbe, Prospekt V. I. Lenina 146; f. 1931; depts.: Agrochemistry and Soil Science, Agronomy, Plant Protection, Veterinary, Zootechnics, Mechanization, Irrigation and Land Reclamation, Economics and Management, Accounting; Extra-Mural and Qualification Improvement Faculties; 313 teachers; 5,380 students; library of 300,000 vols.; Rector Acad. G. A. ALIEV.

**Tashkent Agricultural Institute:** Tashkent, Obl. p.o. "Institutskoe"; depts.: Agrochemistry and Soil Science, Agronomy, Fruit and Vegetable Growing, Viticulture, Plant Protection, Silkworm Breeding, Economics and Management, Forestry, Accounting; library of 196,000 vols.; Extra-Mural Faculty; Rector A. IMAMALIEV.

**Tselinograd Agricultural Institute:** Tselinograd, Ul. Mira 73, Kazakh S.S.R.; four faculties; 390 teachers; 8,200 students; library of 175,000 vols.; Rector M. A. GENDELMAN.

**Turkmen M. I. Kalinin Agricultural Institute:** Ashkhabad, Ul. 1 Maja 12; depts.: Agrochemistry, Fruit and Vegetable Growing, Viticulture, Veterinary, Zootechnics, Mechanization, Accounting; library of 136,000 vols.; Extra-Mural Faculty; Rector A. K. RUSTAMOV.

**Tyumen Agricultural Institute:** Tyumen, Ul. Respubliki 7; depts.: Agronomy, Zootechnics; library; Extra-Mural Department.

**Ukrainian Agricultural Academy:** Kiev, Goloseyevo; depts.: Agrochemistry and Soil Science, Agronomy, Plant Protection, Mechanization, Electrification, Economics and Management, Forestry, Zootechnics, Veterinary, Accounting; library of 486,000 vols.; Extra-Mural Faculty; Rector V. V. YURCHISHIN.

**Ulyanovsk Agricultural Institute:** Ulyanovsk, Bulvar Novy Venets 1; depts.: Agronomy, Zootechnics, Mechanization, Veterinary; library of 80,000 vols.; Extra-Mural Faculty; V. A. BELOV.

**Uman A. M. Gorky Agricultural Institute:** Charkassy Region, Uman, Dendrological Park "Sofievka"; f. 1844; depts.: Agronomy, Fruit and Vegetable Growing, Viticulture, Pedagogics; 120 teachers; 2,500 students; library of 120,000 vols.; Extra-Mural Faculty; Rector G. J. MUSATOV.

**Velikie Luki Agricultural Institute:** Ploshchad V. I. Lenina 1, Velikie Luki, Pskov Region; f. 1958; depts.: Agronomy, Plant Protection, Mechanization; library of 126,000 vols.; Extra-Mural Faculty; Rector A. K. KUKLIN; Publ. *Works of the Velikie Luki Agricultural School*.

**Volgograd Agricultural Institute:** Volgograd, Institutskaya ul. 8; f. 1944; depts.: Agronomy, Zootechnics, Mechanization, Electrification, Irrigation and Land Reclamation, Accounting; library of 206,000 vols.; Extra-Mural Faculty; Rector G. E. LISTOPAD; publ. *Works of the Volgograd Agricultural Institute*.

**Voronezh Agricultural Institute:** Voronezh, Ul. Michurina 1; f. 1913; depts.: Agrochemistry and Soil Science, Agronomy, Organization of Land Exploitation, Mechanization of Agriculture, Economics and Management, Accounting, Veterinary; 440 teachers; 8,500 students; library of 510,000 vols.; Extra-Mural Faculty; Rector G. V. KORENEV; publ. *Zapisky* (Notes).

**Voroshilovgrad Agricultural Institute:** Voroshilovgrad 8; depts.: Agronomy, Mechanization, Economics, Accounting; Extra-Mural and Preparatory depts.

**West Kazakhstan Agricultural Institute:** Uralsk, Prospekt Lenina 184; f. 1963; depts.: Agronomy, Zootechnics, Mechanization, Economics and Management, Accounting; 150 teachers; 2,700 students; Extra-Mural Faculty; Rector V. K. I. KONNIKOV.

**Zhitomir Agricultural Institute:** Ul. 50-Letiya Oktyabrya 9, Zhitomir, Ukrainian S.S.R.; f. 1922; dept.: Agronomy; Extra-Mural Faculties; 100 teachers; 2,500 students; library of 100,000 vols.; Rector V. S. TCHERNILEVSKI.

(2) AGRICULTURAL ENGINEERING AND ELECTRIFICATION

**Azov-Black Sea Institute of Agricultural Engineering:** Zernograd, Ul. Lenina 21, Rostovsk obl.; library of 192,000 vols.; Rector B. M. TITOV.

**Byelorussian Institute of Agricultural Engineering:** Minsk, Leninsky prospekt 101; depts.: Mechanization, Electrification; library of 175,000 vols.; Extra-Mural Faculty; Rector D. I. GORIN.

**Chelyabinsk Institute of Agricultural Engineering:** Prospekt Lenina 75, Chelyabinsk 22; f. 1920; trains engineers for collective and state farms; 270 teachers; 5,000 students; library of 100,000 vols.; Rector S. E. ULMAN; publ. *Trudy Chimeskh*.

**Kharkov Institute of Agricultural Engineering:** Moskovsky prospekt 45, Kharkov, Ukrainian S.S.R.; f. 1929; library of 150,000 vols.; Extra-Mural Faculty; Rector M. K. EVSEEV.

**Kirovograd Institute of Agricultural Engineering:** Kirovograd, Ordjonikidze Str. 5; f. 1967; faculties: Agricultural Machine Construction, Metallurgy, Technical Science; 200 teachers; 4,500 students; library of 100,000 vols.; Rector F. A. STEPANOV.

**Melitopol Institute of Agricultural Engineering:** B. Khmelnitsky 18, Melitopol, Ukrainian S.S.R.; f. 1932; 210 teachers; 5,100 students; library of 125,000 vols.; Extra-Mural and Engineering Faculties; Rector M. N. EMELYANOV.

**Moscow V. P. Gorjachkin Institute of Agricultural Engineering:** Moscow, A-8, Timirjazev str. 58; f. 1930; faculties: Agricultural Mechanization, Farm Electrification, Agricultural Machine Repairs; library of 350,000 vols.; 225 teachers; 3,000 students; Rector Prof. Dr. L. G. PRISHCHEP.

**Rostov Institute of Agricultural Engineering:** Rostov-on-Don, Ploshchad Gagarina 1; faculties: Agricultural Engineering, Engineering Technology, Instrument Making, Hot Working of Metals, Welding; library of 283,000 vols.; Evening and Extra-Mural Faculties; Rector L. V. KRASNICHENKO.

**Saratov M. I. Kalinin Institute of Agricultural Engineering:** Ul. Sovetskaya 60, Saratov; f. 1932; 200 teachers; 3,500 students; library of 262,000 vols.; Extra-Mural Faculty; Rector D. G. VADIVASOV.

**Tashkent Institute of Agricultural Engineering:** Uchitelskaya 39, Tashkent, Uzbek S.S.R.; depts.: Mechanization, Electrification, Mechanization of Irrigation, Land Exploitation; library of 266,000 vols.; Extra-Mural Faculty; Rector S. P. PULATOV.

(3) LAND IMPROVEMENT

**Djambul Institute of Irrigation, Land Reclamation and Construction:** Djambul, Kommunisticheskaya ul. 91; depts.: Irrigation and Land Reclamation, Riparian Engineering and HydroPower Stations, Mechanization of Irrigation and Land Reclamation, Industrial Construction, Water Supplies and Sewerage; library; Extra-Mural Faculty.

**Moscow Institute of Irrigation and Land Reclamation:** Moscow 8A, Ul. Pryanishnikiva 19; f. 1930; depts.: Irrigation and Land Reclamation, Mechanization of Irrigation and Land Reclamation; Extra-Mural Faculty; Rector N. A. KHABAROVA.

**Moscow Institute of Land Exploitation Engineering:** 103064 Moscow, Ul. Kazakova 15; depts.: Organization of Land Exploitation, Engineering, Geodesy; library of 146,000 vols.; Extra-Mural Faculty; Rector N. D. ILYINSKY.

**Novocherkassk Institute of Engineering Amelioration:** Pushkinskaya 111, Novocherkassk, Rostovsk; f. 1907; depts.: Irrigation and Land Reclamation, Forestry; 250 teachers; 5,100 students; library of 170,000 vols.; Extra-Mural Dept.

**Ukraine Institute of Water Conservation:** 11 Leninskaya ul., Rovno; depts.: Irrigation, Engineering, Hydraulic Engineering, Construction, Textiles; library of 116,000 vols.; Extra-Mural and Engineering Faculties; Rector K. S. SEMENOV.

(4) ZOOTECHNICAL, VETERINARY SCIENCE AND LIVESTOCK BREEDING

**Alma-Ata Zootechnical and Veterinary Institute:** Prospekt Abaya 24, Alma-Ata, Kazakh S.S.R.; f. 1929; depts.: Zootechnic, Veterinary; 310 teachers; 4,900 students; library of 146,000 vols.; Extra-Mural Faculty; Rector M. A. ERMAKOV.

**Erevan Zootechnical and Veterinary Institute:** Ul. Nalbandyana 128, Erevan, Armenian S.S.R.; f. 1928; library of 300,000 vols.; faculties of livestock management, veterinary science, technology of milk and dairy products, engineering technology, economics; extra-mural faculty; c. 200 teachers; c. 2,700 students; Rector O. G. TEROVANOSOVA; publ. *The Works of the Erevan Zooveterinary Institute.*

**Georgian Zootechnical and Veterinary Institute:** Krtsanisi, Tbilisi, Georgian S.S.R.; f. 1932; 105 teachers; 2,250 students; library of 200,000 vols.; Extra-Mural Faculty; Rector V. G. MAMATELASHVILI.

**Kazan N. E. Bauman Veterinary Institute:** Vyetgorodok, 420074 Kazan, Tatar A.S.S.R.; f. 1873; advanced training of veterinary surgeons and zoo-technicians; faculty of advanced study and scientific research; library of 350,000 vols.; Rector Prof. Dr. H. G. GIZATULLIN; publ. *Uchenie Zapiski* (Scientific Notes, 5-6 issues a year).

**Kharkov Zootechnical and Veterinary Institute:** pos. Zoovetinstitut, Kharkov, Ukrainian S.S.R.; library of 320,000 vols.; Extra-Mural Faculty.

**Leningrad Veterinary Institute:** Chernigovskaya 5, Leningrad N-6, R.S.F.S.R.; f. 1919; 140 teachers; 1,340 students; library of 194,000 vols.; Extra-Mural Faculty; Rector G. S. KUZNETSOV; publ. *The Compendium of the Institute Works.*

**Lithuanian Veterinary Academy:** Ul. Adomausko 18, Kaunas 22, Lithuanian S.S.R.; f. 1936; 80 teachers; 1,300 students; library of 105,000 vols.; Extra-Mural Department; Rector I. SHULSKIS.

**Lvov Zootechnical and Veterinary Institute:** Pekarskaya ul. 50, Lvov, Ukrainian S.S.R.; f. 1808; 150 teachers; 3,000 students; library of 215,000 vols.; Extra-Mural Department; Rector S. V. STOJANOVSKY.

**Moscow K. I. Skryabin Veterinary Academy:** Moscow 109472, Ul. Skrabjina 23; f. 1919; faculties: Veterinary Science, Veterinary Biological Science, Zootechnical, Pedagogical, Animal Products; 450 teachers; 5,500 students; library of 600,000 vols.; Rector Prof. V. M. DANILEVSKY.

**Omsk Veterinary Institute:** Oktyabrskaya ul. 92, Omsk; f. 1918; 130 teachers; 3,000 students; library of 184,000 vols.; Extra-Mural Faculty; Rector N. F. BELKOV.

**Saratov Zootechnical and Veterinary Institute:** B. Sadovaya 220, Saratov; f. 1918; 120 teachers; 2,500 students; library of 200,000 vols.; Extra-Mural Faculty; Rector I. I. DEMENTJEV.

**Semipalatinsk Institute of Zootechnics and Veterinary Science:** Ul. Uritskogo 17, Semipalatinsk 50, Kazakh S.S.R.; f. 1951; 180 teachers; 3,000 students; library of 100,000 vols.; Extra-Mural Faculty; Rector U. S. ABDILMANOV.

**Troitsk Veterinary Institute:** Ul. Gargarina 1, Troitsk, Chelyabinsk obl.; f. 1929; library of 110,000 vols.; Extra-Mural Faculty; Rector V. T. LOBANOV.

**Vitebsk Veterinary Institute:** Ul. Dovatora 7/11, Vitebsk, Byelorussian S.S.R.; library of 155,000 vols.; Extra-Mural Faculty; Rector M. S. ZHAKOV.

**Vologda Dairy Institute:** Vologda, Poselok Molochnoe, Prospekt Shmidta 2; f. 1911; depts.: Technology, Zootechnics, Mechanization of Agriculture, Agronomy, Economics; 265 teachers; 4,500 students; library of 240,000 vols.; Extra-Mural Faculty; Rector Prof. SLIVKO; publ. *The Works of the Vologda Dairy Institute.*

## ECONOMICS

### (1) General Economics and Planning

**Alma-Ata Institute of National Economy:** Alma-Ata, Ul. Shevchenko 95; depts.: Industrial and National Planning, Accounting, Finances and Credits; Extra-Mural Departments; Rector N. D. DZAHNDILDIN.

**Azerbaijan Republic D. Buniat-zade Institute of National Economy:** Baku, Kommunisticheskaya 6; f. 1937; faculties: Finance and Statistics, Commerce, Accountancy, Economics and Planning, Industrial Economy; 340 teachers; 8,000 students; library of 125,000 vols.; Rector Prof. Dr. S. R. ASLANOV.

**Byelorussian V. V. Kuibyshev State Institute of National Economy:** Partizansky pr. 24, Minsk, Byelorussian S.S.R.; depts.: Economic Planning, Calculation and Registration; library of 174,000 vols.; Extra-Mural Faculty; Rector F. V. BOROVIK.

**Erevan Institute of National Economy:** Erevan, Armenian S.S.R.; f. 1975; Faculties of Economic Planning, Finance and Statistics, Economic Cybernetics, Science of Commodities; c. 200 teachers; c. 4,000 students; publ. *Economist*.

**Irkutsk Institute of National Economy:** Irkutsk, Ul. Lenina 11; faculties: Finance, Planning, Economics of Industry; library of 236,000 vols.; Evening Faculty; Rector V. P. IVANITSKY.

**Khabarovsk Institute of National Economy:** Khabarovsk 35, Ul. Tikhooceanskaya 136; Planning and Economics, Finance and Economics, Calculation and Registration; 280 teachers; 5,000 students; library of 400,000 vols.; Extra-Mural Faculty.

**Kuibyshev Institute of Planning:** Ul. Sovetskoj Armii 141, Kuibyshev; faculties: Industrial Economics, National Planning; library of 137,000 vols.; Extra-Mural Faculty; Rector A. I. NOSKOV.

**Novosibirsk Institute of National Economy:** Novosibirsk, Kamenskaya 56; f. 1968; faculties of Economics and Accounting; evening and correspondence departments; 4,800 students; library of 250,000 vols.; Rector V. N. SHCHUKIN.

**G. V. Plekhanov Institute of National Economy:** Moscow M-54, per. Stremyanny 28; f. 1907; faculties: General Economics, Industrial Economics, Trade Economics, Finance, Science of Commodities, Technology, Mechanics; 650 teachers; 15,000 students; library of 815,000 vols.; Rector Prof. B. M. MOTCHELOV.

**Rostov-on-Don Institute of National Economy:** Rostov-on-Don, Ul. F. Engelsa 69; f. 1931; faculties: Planning and Economics, Finances and Economics, Calculation and Registration; 260 teachers; 7,200 students; library of 350,000 vols.; Extra-Mural Faculty; Rector G. I. OZEROV.

**Saratov Institute of Economics:** Saratov, Ploshchad Revolyutsii 11; f. 1918; faculties: Industry, Agriculture, Credit and Economics, Calculation and Registration; 160 teachers; 4,000 students; library of 255,000 vols.; Extra-Mural Faculty; Rector K. I. BABAYTSEV.

**Sverdlov Institute of National Economy:** Sverdlovsk L-1, Ul. 8 Marta, 62; f. 1967; faculties: Economics, Planning, Accountancy, Goods Inventory, Mechanics and Technology, Evening course; 300 teachers; 7,500 students; library of 100,000 vols.; Rector L. N. PONOMARYOV.

**Tashkent Institute of National Economy:** Tashkent, Ul. Almazar 183; f. 1931; faculties: Planning and Economics, Finances and Economics; 400 teachers; 11,000 students; library of 300,000 vols.; Extra-Mural Faculty; Rector M. KARIEV.

### (2) Trade

**All-Union Extra-Mural Institute of Soviet Trade:** Chapaevsky per. 16, Moscow; f. 1938; faculties: Trade Economics, Calculation and Registration, Science of Food Stuffs, Science of Commodities; 650 teachers; 32,200 students; library of 1,000,000 vols.; 23 brs.; Rector A. N. RUKOSVYEV.

**Donetsk Institute of Soviet Trade:** Donetsk 50, Ul. Shchorsa 31; faculties: Calculation and Registration, Science of Commodities, Technology; library of 146,000 vols.; Rector F. D. FOSENKO.

**Far Eastern Institute of Soviet Trade:** Vladivostok, Ocean prospekt 19; Trade Economics, Science of Food Stuffs, Science of Commodities; 400 teachers; 10,000 students; library of 220,000 vols.

**Karaganda Co-operative Institute:** 470061 Karaganda, Ul. 40-Letiya Kazakhstan 1; Economic Calculation and Registration, Technology; Extra-Mural Department; branch in Alma-Ata; library of 150,000 vols.

**Kharkov Institute of Food:** Kharkov, Ul. Gudanova 4/10; Economics, Calculation and Registration; library of 200,000 vols.; Evening and Extra-Mural Departments.

**Leningrad F. Engels Institute of Soviet Trade:** Leningrad, Kuznechny per. 9; faculties: Trade Economics, Accounting, Science of Commodities, Engineering; library of 365,100 vols.; Extra-Mural Faculty; Rector K. S. KOROVIN.

**Lvov Institute of Trade Economics:** Lvov, Ul. Chkalova 10; f. 1899; faculties: Economics, Science of Commodities; 240 teachers; 5,000 students; library oi 500,000 vols.; Extra-Mural Faculty; Rector K. I. PIROSHAK.

**Moscow Co-operative Institute:** Moscow Region, 141000 Mytischi, Voloshina ul. 12; f. 1959; faculties: Economics, Science of Commodities; 350 teachers; 16,000 students; library of 575,000 vols.; Rector V. I. KHORIN.

**Novosibirsk Institute of Soviet Co-operative Trade:** Novosibirsk, Prospekt K. Marxa 24; f. 1956; faculties: Economics, Science of Commodities, Technology; 240 teachers; 7,500 students; library of 197,000 vols.; Rector N. N. PROTOPOPOV.

**Samarkand V. V. Kuibyshev Co-operative Institute:** 703000 Samarkand, Kommunisticheskaya ul. 47; f. 1931; faculties: Economics, Science of Commodities, Technology; 210 teachers; 7,000 students; library of 205,718 vols.; Extra-Mural Faculty; branch in Taskhent; Rector M. R. RASVLOV.

### (3) Finance

**All-Union Extra-Mural Finance Institute:** Moscow, Ul. Oleko Dundicha 23; faculties: General Economics, Industrial Economics, Finance and Credits, Calculation and Registration; library of 387,000 vols.; ten brs.

**Kazan V. V. Kuibyshev Finance and Economics Institute:** Kazan, Ul. Butlerova 4; f. 1932; faculties: Finances and Economics, Calculation and Registration; 160 teachers; 4,000 students; library of 200,000 vols.; Extra-Mural Faculty; Rector S. A. LYUSHIN.

**Kiev Institute of National Economy:** Kiev-57, Brest-Litovsky prospekt 98/1; f. 1912; faculties: Planning and Economy, Planning of the Rural Economy, Finance and Economy, Accountancy and Statistics, Supply Economics, Computer Science and data processing; 450 teachers; 10,000 students; library of 500,000 vols.; Pro-Rectors O. BELORUS, O. BOBROFF, Y. PROSHCHAZUK; publs. *Machine Data Processing*, *Problems of Economic Efficiency*.

**Leningrad N. A. Voznesensky Finance and Economics Institute:** 191023 Leningrad, Sadovaya ul.; faculties: Finances and Economics, Planning and Economics,

Calculation and Registration; library of 580,000 vols.; Evening and Extra-Mural Faculties; Rector Y. A. LAVRIKOV.

**Moscow Finance Institute:** Moscow I-164, Ul. Kibalchicha 1; f. 1946; faculties: Finances and Economics, Credits and Economics, Accounting Economics; 200 teachers; 3,000 students; Rector Prof. V. V. SHCHERBAKOV.

**Odessa Institute of National Economy:** Odessa, Ul. Sovetskoy Armii 8; f. 1921; faculties: Credits and Economics, Calculation and Registration; 250 teachers; 7,200 students; library of 238,000 vols.; Rector S. Y. DGORODNIK.

(4) STATISTICS

**Moscow Institute of Economics and Statistics:** Savinsky per. 14, Moscow; faculties: Economics and Statistics, Calculation and Registration; library of 150,000 vols.; Rector M. A. KOROLEV.

## GEOLOGY, METEOROLOGY AND HYDROLOGY

**Leningrad Hydro-Meteorological Institute:** Malo-Okhtensky prospekt 98, Leningrad; f. 1930; library of 243,000 vols.; Extra-Mural Faculty; Rector Y. P. DORONIN; publ. *Proceedings* (2-4 a year).

**Moscow S. Ordjonikidze Institute of Geological Research:** Prospekt Karla Marxa 18, Moscow; faculties: Prospecting, Geophysics, Hydrogeology, Exploitation Methods; library of 128,000 vols.; Rector Prof. D. P. LOBANOV.

**Odessa Hydro-Meteorological Institute:** Ul. Kirova 106, Odessa, Ukrainian S.S.R.; departments: meteorological, agrometeorological, hydrological (hydrology and oceanography), extra-mural; library of 200,000 vols.; Rector E. TERENTIEV.

## GRAPHIC ARTS

**Erevan Institute of Fine Arts and Theatre:** Erevan, Armenian S.S.R.; f. 1944; faculties of fine arts (painting, sculpture, applied and industrial art), theatre (acting, stage directing, musical comedy).

**Estonian S.S.R. State Art Institute:** Tallinn, Tartu maantee 1; f. 1950; depts.: Arts: painting, stage design, sculpture, graphic art, textile and fashion design, leather work, ceramics, glass and metal work; Architecture: industrial design, interior design, architecture; 118 teachers, 505 students; library of 33,460 vols.; Rector Prof. J. VARES.

**Kharkov Institute of Industrial and Applied Arts:** Ul. Krasnoznamyennaya 8, Kharkov, Ukrainian S.S.R.; f. 1927 and renamed 1963; library of 54,000 vols.; Rector M. A. SHAPOSHNIKOV.

**Kiev State Art Institute:** Ul. Smirnova-Lastochkina 20, Kiev, Ukrainian S.S.R.; f. 1917; depts.: Decorative Art, Graphic Art, Architecture, Industrial Draughtsmanship; 100 teachers; 800 students; library of 65,000 vols; Rector V. Z. BORODAY.

**Kirghiz State Institute of Fine Art:** Frunze, Ul. Pavlodarskaya 115; f. 1967; faculties: Piano, Vocal, Orchestra, Theory and Composition, Cultural Studies; 40 teachers; 225 students; library of 11,000 vols.; Rector T. V. MUSURMANKULOV.

**Latvian S.S.R. State Academy of Arts:** Riga, Bulv. Kommunaru 13; f. 1919; depts.: Painting, Sculpture, Graphic Arts, Decorative and Applied Arts, Industrial Art, Textile Art, Pedagogy, History and Theory of Arts, Interior and Furnishings; library of 65,000 vols.; 70 teachers; 450 students; Rector Prof. EDGARS ILTNERS.

**Leningrad I. E. Repin (Order of the Red Banner of Labour) Institute of Arts:** Leningrad V-34, Universitetskaya Naberezhnaya 17; f. 1757; faculties: Painting, Sculpture, Drawing, Architecture, Theory and History of Art; 140 teachers; 1,300 students; library of 300,000 vols.; Rector Prof. V. M. ORESHNIKOV.

**Leningrad V. I. Mukhina Higher Industrial Art School:** Leningrad 192028, Solyanoy per. 13; faculties: Art Finishing of Industrial Constructions, Decorative and Applied Art, Architecture and Interior Design; library of 100,000 vols.; Rector Prof. Y. LUKIN.

**Lithuanian S.S.R. State Arts Institute:** Vilnius, Ul. Tiesos 6; f. 1579; depts.: Art and Mechanical Drawing, Decorative and Applied Arts, Art Finishing, Textiles, History and Theory of Fine Arts, Interior and Furnishing, Industrial Art, Monumental and Decorative Arts; 100 teachers; 550 students; library; Evening and Extra-Mural Departments; Rector VINCENTAS GECHAS.

**Lvov State Institute of Applied and Decorative Art:** Ul. Goncharova 38, Lvov, Ukraine; f. 1947; 75 teachers; 450 students; library of 32,000 vols.; Rector A. P. ZAPASKO.

**Moscow Institute of Architecture:** Ul. Zhdanova 11, Moscow K-31; f. 1866; specialization in architecture, urban planning, architectural restorations, landscaping; 1,500 students; library of 24,000 vols.

**Moscow Higher School of Industrial Art:** Volokolamskoye chaussée 9, 125080 Moscow A-80; f. 1825; refounded 1945; faculties: Industrial Arts, Decorative Arts; 1,300 students; library of 50,000 vols.; Rector Z. N. BYKOV, Vice-Rector G. A. SACHAROV.

**Moscow State Art Institute—Surikov Institute:** Tovarishchesky pereulok 30, Moscow; depts.: Painting, Graphic Arts, Sculpture; library of 43,000 vols.; Dir. N. V. TOMSKY.

**Tbilisi Academy of Arts:** Ul. Griboyedova 22, Tbilisi, Georgian S.S.R.; depts.: Decorative Arts, Applied Arts, Textiles, Architecture, Sculpture.

## INDUSTRY AND PUBLIC WORKS

(1) POLYTECHNICS AND GENERAL INDUSTRIAL INSTITUTES

**All-Union Extra-Mural Polytechnic Institute:** Moscow 278, Ul. Pavla Korchagina 22; f. 1932; faculties: Mining, Oil, Metallurgy, Machine Building, Motor Vehicles, Chemical Technology, Energy, Electronic Physics, Construction, Engineering Economics; three brs.; 968 teachers; 43,000 students; library of 800,000 vols.; Rector Prof. S. K. KANTENIK.

**Altai I. I. Polzunov Polytechnic Institute:** 656099 Barnaul, Pr. Lenina 46; f. 1924; faculties: Mechanical Technology, Machine Building, Chemical Technology, Construction; Extra-Mural Faculty; Rector V. G. RADCHENKO.

**Azerbaijan Polytechnic Institute:** 370122 Baku, Pr. Narimanova 25; faculties: Mechanics, Metallurgy, Automation and Computing Equipment, Electrical Engineering, Technology, Construction, Transport, Irrigation and Soil Reclamation; Extra-Mural Department.

**Byelorussian Polytechnic Institute:** Minsk, Leninsky prospekt 65; f. 1933; faculties: Machine Building, Mechanical Technology, Motor Vehicles and Tractors, Power, Chemical Technology, Construction, Hydraulic Engineering, Peat; Evening and Extra-Mural Faculties; Rector Prof. P. I. YASHCHERITSYN.

**Chelyabinsk Polytechnic Institute:** Chelyabinsk, Prospekt Lenina 76; f. 1943; faculties: Metallurgy, Machine Technology, Motor Vehicles and Tractors, Engines, Instruments and Automation, Power, Instrument Making, Construction; Evening faculties: Machine Technology, Power, Construction; Extra-Mural faculties: Machine Building, Instrument Making; Rector Prof. V. V. MELNIKOV.

**Donetsk (Order of Red Banner of Labour) Polytechnic Institute:** Donetsk, Ul. Artema 58; f. 1921; faculties: Mining, Mining Engineering, Metallurgy, Electrical

EDUCATIONAL INSTITUTES — UNION OF SOVIET SOCIALIST REPUBLICS

Engineering, Chemical Technology, Construction; Rector G. V. MALEEV.

**Erevan K. Marx Polytechnic Institute:** Erevan, Ul. Teryana 105; f. 1930; faculties: Mechanics and Machine-Building, Electrical Engineering, Computer Technology, Cybernetics Technology, Chemical Technology, Mining and Metallurgy, Energetics, Radio Technology, Construction (Civil Engineering and Architecture), Extra-Mural Faculty; library of 650,000 vols.; c. 1,500 teachers; c. 20,000 students; Rector A. M. GASPARYAN.

**Far-Eastern V. V. Kuibyshev Polytechnic Institute:** Vladivostok, Pushkinskaya ul. 10; faculties: Mining, Mechanics, Electrical Engineering, Construction, Ship Building, Evening and Extra-Mural Faculties; Rector M. G. MOROZOV.

**Ferghana Polytechnic Institute, Uzbek S.S.R.:** Ferghana, Kirghili, Ul. Ulugbeka 71; depts.: Electrical Engineering, Machine Technology, Civil Engineering.

**Frunze Polytechnic Institute:** Frunze, Prospekt Mira 66; faculties: Mining and Geology, Mechanics, Technology, Construction, Power; Evening and Extra-Mural Departments.

**Georgian V. I. Lenin (Order of Red Banner of Labour) Polytechnic Institute:** Tbilisi, Ul. Lenina 77; faculties: Mining and Geology, Metallurgy, Mechanics and Machine Building, Power, Automation and Computing Equipment, Chemical and Food Technology, Construction, Light Industry, Transport; Evening and Extra-Mural Faculties; Rector Prof. I. M. BUACHIDZE.

**Gorky A. A. Zhdanov Polytechnic Institute:** Gorky, Ul. K. Minina 24; faculties: Machine Building, Mechanics, Electrical Engineering, Radio Engineering, Metallurgy, Ship Building, Chemical Technology and Silicates; Evening and Extra-Mural Faculties; Rector M. P. TUZOV.

**Irkutsk Polytechnic Institute:** Irkutsk, Ul. Lermontova 83 faculties: Geological Prospecting, Mining, Power, Metallurgy, Chemical Technology, Mechanics, Construction; Evening and Extra-Mural Faculties; Rector Prof. A. A. IGOSHIN.

**Kalinin Polytechnic Institute:** Kalinin, Pervomayskaya naberezhnaya 22; f. 1930; thirteen faculties including Mining, Chemical Technology, Machines and Automation in Industry, Construction and Engineering; library of 350,000 vols.; Evening and Extra-Mural Faculties; Rector Prof. I. F. LARGIN.

**Karaganda Polytechnic Institute:** Karaganda, Bulvar Mira 56; f. 1953; faculties: Mining, Mining Electrical Engineering, Mechanics and Machine Building, Construction; Evening and Extra-Mural Departments; Rector Prof. A. SAGINOV.

**Kaunas Antanas Sniechkus Polytechnic Institute:** Kaunas, Donelaičio 73; f. 1950; faculties: Automation, Chemical Technology, Industrial Economics, Light Industry, Machine Construction, Radio Electronics, Electrical, Mechanical, Civil and Sanitary Engineering, Evening and Extra-Mural depts.; 1,060 teachers; 15,000 students; library of 1,656,000 vols.; Rector Prof. M. MARTYNAITIS.

**Kazakh Polytechnic Institute:** Alma-Ata, Ul. Satpaeva 22; f. 1934; faculties: Geology Prospecting, Mining, Metallurgy, Power, Automation and Computing Equipment, Construction; Extra-Mural Department; Rector A. K. OMAROV.

**Khabarovsk Polytechnic Institute:** Khabarovsk, Ul. Tikhookeanskaya 136; Day, Evening and Extra-Mural Faculties.

**Kharkov V. I. Lenin Polytechnic Institute:** Kharkov, Ul. Frunze 21; f. 1885; faculties: Mechanics and Metallurgy, Machine Building, Power Machine Building, Electrical Machine Building, Automation and Instrument Building, Radio Engineering, Technology of Inorganic Substances, Technology of Organic Substances, Technology of Organic Chemicals, Chemical Machine Building, Transport Machine Building, Physical Engineering; Evening Department, Teachers' Training Department.

**Kiev (Order of Lenin) Polytechnic Institute:** Kiev, Brest-Litovsky prospekt 39; faculties: Mechanical Technology, Mechanics and Machine Building, Mechanics and Instrument Making, Electrical Power, Automation and Electrical Instrument Making, Thermal Power, Chemical Machine Building, Chemical Technology, Radio Engineering, Radio Electronics, Electrical Acoustics; Evening and General Engineering Faculties; Rector B. V. NOVOJILOV.

**Kirov Polytechnic Institute:** Kirov, Ul. Kommuny 36; faculties: Electrical Physics, Electrical Engineering, Machine Building, General Engineering.

**Kishinev Polytechnic Institute:** Kishinev, Ul. Lenina 168; f. 1964; faculties: Economics, Mechanics, Electrical Engineering, Technology, Construction, Electrophysics; Evening and Extra-Mural Departments; library of c. 655,000 vols.; c. 12,000 students; Rector Prof. V. G. ANTOSYAK.

**Komsomolsk-on-Amur Polytechnic Institute:** 681013 Komsomolsk-on-Amur, Prospekt Lenina 27; faculties: Mechanics, Construction.

**Krasnodar Polytechnic Institute:** Krasnodar, Krasnaya ul. 135; faculties: Power, Mechanics and Machine Building, Construction, Chemical Technology, Technology of Food Industry; Evening and Extra-Mural Faculties; Rector Prof. Y. A. RUDAKOV.

**Krasnoyarsk Polytechnic Institute:** Krasnoyarsk, Ul. Kirenskoyo 26; faculties: Machine Building, Motors and Highways, Construction, Power, Radio Engineering; Evening and Extra-Mural Faculties; Rector V. N BORISOV.

**Kuibyshev Polytechnic Institute:** Kuibyshev, Ul. Galaktionovskayo 141; faculties: Mechanics, Oil, Oil Processing, Thermal Power, Electrical Engineering, Automation and Measuring Equipment, Electrical Technology; Evening and Extra-Mural Faculties: Rector I. S. VOLKOV.

**Kursk Polytechnic Institute:** 305538 Kursk, Ul. 50 Oktjabriya 941; faculties: Power, Machine Building, Chemical Technology; Evening Department.

**Kuzbass Polytechnic Institute:** Kemerovo, 26, Ul. Vesennyaya 28; faculties: Mechanics and Metallurgy, Mining, Machine Building, Technology of Inorganic Substances, Transport Machine Building; evening and extra-mural departments.

**Leningrad M. I. Kalinin Polytechnic Institute:** 195251 Leningrad, Politekhnicheskaya ul. 29; f. 1899; faculties: Hydraulic Engineering, Electrical Engineering, Power Machine Building, Mechanics and Machine Building, Physics and Mechanics, Physics and Metallurgy, Industrial Economics, Radio Electronics; Evening and Extra-Mural depts.; Preparatory Faculty for Foreign Students; 1,400 teachers; 16,000 students; library of 2,500,000 vols.; Rector Prof. Dr. K. P. SELEZNEV; publ. *Transactions*.

**Lipetsk Polytechnic Institute:** Lipetsk, Ul. Zegel 1; depts.: Metallurgy, Mechanical Engineering, Construction, Transport; Evening faculty.

**Lvov Polytechnic Institute:** Lvov, Ul. Mira 12, Ukrainian S.S.R.; f. 1844; faculties: Geodesy, Mechanical Technology, Mechanics and Machine Building, Energy, Electrical Engineering, Radio Engineering, Automation, Electrical Physics, Industrial Economics, Chemical Technology, Technology of Organic Materials, Civil and Industrial Construction, General Engineering, Evening and Extra-Mural depts.: Branches in Ivano-Frankovsk, Drogobych, Ternopol; 1,200 teachers; 24,000 students; library of 1,200,000 vols.; Rector Prof. Dr. G. I. DENISENKO; publ. *Journal of the Lvov Polytechnic Institute* (14 series annually).

**North-Western Extra-Mural Polytechnic Institute:** Leningrad, Ul. Khalturina 5; f. 1930; faculties: Power Engineering and Automation, Radio Engineering, Engineering Cybernetics, Instrumentation and Machine Construction, Machine Technology, Chemical Technology and Metallurgy; Evening Dept.; library of 1,544,698 vols.; Rector B. V. SHAMRY; publ. *Proceedings* (3–4 issues a year).

**Novocherkassk Sergo Ordjonikidze Polytechnic Institute:** Novocherkassk, Ul. Prosveshcheniya 132; faculties: Mining and Geology Prospecting, Mechanization and Automation of Mining and Construction, Mechanics, Power, Electrical Engineering, Chemical Technology, Construction; Evening and Extra-Mural Departments; Rector Prof. M. A. FROLOV.

**Odessa Polytechnic Institute:** Odessa, Prosp. Shevchenko 1; f. 1918; faculties: Mechanical Technology, Chemical and General Machine Building, Transport and Elevation Equipment, Thermal Power, Electrical Engineering, Radio Engineering, Automation and Industrial Electronics, Engineering Physics, Chemical Technology; Evening and General Engineering Faculties; Rector K. I. ZABLONSKI.

**Omsk Polytechnic Institute:** Omsk, Pr. Mira 11; faculties: Machine Technology, Hot Working of Metals, Electrical and Radio Engineering; Evening and General Engineering Faculties.

**Orenburg Polytechnic Institute:** Orenburg, Chelyabinskaya 13; faculties: Mechanics, Electrical Engineering; evening and extra-mural departments.

**Penza Polytechnic Institute:** Penza, Krasnaya ul. 40; f. 1943; faculties: Instrument Making, Electrical Engineering, Radio Engineering; Evening and Extra-Mural Faculties; Rector Prof. A. A. STEKLOV.

**Perm Polytechnic Institute:** Perm, Komsomolsky prospekt 29-a; faculties: Mining, Electrical Engineering, Mechanical Technology, Machine Building, Aircraft Engines, Construction, Chemical Technology; Evening Department.

**Riga Polytechnic Institute:** Riga, Ul. Lenina 1; f. 1862; library of 1,400,000 vols.; 1,400 teachers, 14,600 students; faculties: Electrical Engineering, Civil Engineering Economy, Radio Engineering and Communications, Automation and Computing Technique, Mechanical Engineering and Machine Building, Chemistry, Technical Appliances and Automation; Technical Training Faculties in Riga, Liepāja, Daugavpils; Rector Prof. A. R. WEIS; publ. *Scientific Transactions*.

**Saratov Polytechnic Institute:** Saratov, Politechnicheskaya ul. 77; f. 1930; faculties: Machine Building, Engineering, Instrument Making, Energy, Motor Vehicles, Construction, Highways; Evening Department; Rector Prof. A. I. ANDRYUSHCHENKO.

**Stavropol Polytechnic Institute:** Stavropol, Ul. Kominterna 9; depts.: Technology, Mechanical Engineering, Construction Engineering, Economics; Evening, Extra-Mural and Preparatory depts.

**Tajik Polytechnic Institute:** Dushanbe, Prospect Kuibysheva 10-a; faculties: Power, Chemical Technology, Construction; Evening and Extra-Mural Departments.

**Tallinn Polytechnic Institute:** Tallinn, Ehitajate tee 5, Estonian S.S.R.; f. 1936; faculties: Chemistry, Economics, Power Engineering, Electrical Engineering, Civil Engineering, Mechanics; Evening and Extra-Mural Faculties; 624 teachers; 9,620 students; library of 700,000 vols. (Dir. K. KIKAS); Rector Prof. B. TAMM; publs. *Transactions of the Institute, Tallinna Politehnik* (newspaper).

**Tashkent Polytechnic Institute:** Tashkent, Ul. Navoi 13; faculties: Geology and Prospecting, Mining and Metallurgy, Engineering, Power, Physical Engineering, Chemical Technology, Construction; Extra-Mural Department.

**Togliatti Polytechnic Institute:** Togliatti, Byelorussian ul. 14; f. 1967; formerly a branch of the Kuibyshev Polytechnic Institute; faculties: Mechanical Technology, Motor Vehicle Construction, Electrical Engineering, Electronic Computing Centre; Evening and Extra-Mural Faculties; Rector Prof. Dr. A. N. REZNIKOV.

**Tomsk S. M. Kirov (Orders of October Revolution and of Red Banner of Labour) Polytechnic Institute:** Tomsk, Prospekt Lenina 30; f. 1896; faculties: Geological Prospecting, Mechanical Engineering, Thermodynamics, Electrodynamics, Electromechanical Engineering, Chemical Technology, Physical Technology, Electrophysical Engineering, Automatics and Computer Engineering, Industrial Management; Evening and Extra-Mural Faculties; research institutes in Nuclear Physics, Electronic Introscopy, High Voltages; library of 2 m. vols.; Rector Prof. I. I. KALYATSKY.

**Tula Polytechnic Institute:** Tula, Prospekt Lenina 92; f. 1930; faculties: Instrument Making, Engineering, Mechanical Technology, Chemical Machine Building, Automation and Telemechanics, Mining and Metallurgy, Radio Engineering, Construction; Evening and Extra-Mural Faculties; Rector F. V. SEDIKIN.

**Turkmen Polytechnic Institute:** Ashkhabad, Ul. N. Ostrovskogo 47; faculties: Construction, Oil, Machine Technology; Evening and Extra-Mural Faculties.

**Ukrainian Extra-Mural Polytechnic Institute:** Kharkov, Universitetskaya ul. 16; faculties: Metallurgy, Machine Building, Power, Electronic Physics, Chemical Technology, General Engineering.

**Ulyanovsk Polytechnic Institute:** Ulyanovsk, Ul. Tolstogo 50; faculties: Engineering, Radio Engineering; Evening and Extra-Mural Faculties.

**Urals S. M. Kirov Polytechnic Institute:** Sverdlovsk, Vtuzgorodok; f. 1920; faculties: Metallurgy, Technology, Engineering, Electrical Engineering, Thermodynamics, Radio Engineering, Chemical Technology, Construction, Economics, Physical Engineering; Extra-Mural faculties: Engineering, Power, Radio and Engineering, Chemical Technology; Evening Faculties; Rector F. P. ZAOSTROVSKY.

**Vladimir Polytechnic Institute:** 600026 Vladimir, Ul. Gorkogo 87; faculties: Machine Technology, Radio, Instrument Making; Evening and Extra-Mural Faculties; Rector P. A. ANDREEV.

**Volgograd Polytechnic Institute:** Volgograd, Prospekt Lenina 28; f. 1930; faculties: Machine Building, Motor Vehicles and Tractors, Hot Working of Metals, Chemical Technology, Hydro-engineering; Evening and Extra-Mural Faculties; Rector Prof. A. P. KHARDIN.

**Voronezh Polytechnic Institute:** Voronezh, Moskovskii prospekt 14; faculties: Machine Technology, Aviation, Radio Engineering, Electrical Engineering, Physical Engineering, Economical Engineering; Evening and Extra-Mural Faculties; Rector Prof. V. S. POSTNIKOV.

EDUCATIONAL INSTITUTES

(2) MECHANICAL ENGINEERING

**All-Union Extra-Mural Mechanical Engineering Institute:** Moscow 5, Ul. Babaevskaya 3-a; faculties: Complex Mechanization and Automation in Hot Working of Metals, Automation in Machine Building, Instrument Making, Transport and Power Machine Building; library of 250,000 vols.; Rector N. N. SHEVIAKOV.

**All-Union Research Institute of Water Supply, Drainage, Hydro-Engineering Works and Engineering Hydrogeology:** Komsomolsky prosp. 42, Moscow.

**Bryansk Institute of Transport Engineering:** Bryansk, Ul. Institutskaya 16; faculties: Transport Engineering, Engineering Technology; library of 104,000 vols.; Evening and Extra-Mural Faculties; Rector I. V. SHASHIN.

**Izhevsk Mechanical Engineering Institute:** Izhevsk, 9th Podlesnaya ul. 48; faculties: Machine Technology, Mechanical Engineering, Instrument Making; library of 107,000 vols.; Evening and Extra-Mural Faculties; Rector N. V. TALANTOV.

**Kurgan Mechanical Engineering Institute:** Kurgan, Ploshchad Lenina; f. 1959; depts.: Machine Tool Technology, Welding Technology, Motor Transport; 250 teachers; 4,000 students; library of 100,000 vols.; Evening and Extra-Mural Faculties; Rector A. Y. SICHOV.

**Leningrad Institute of Precision Engineering and Optics:** Leningrad, Ul. Sablinskaya 14; faculties: Precision Engineering, Optics, Radio Engineering, Evening and Extra-Mural depts.; 350 teachers; 6,000 students; Rector S. P. MITROFANOV.

**Leningrad (Order of the Red Banner of Labour) Engineering Institute:** Leningrad, 1st Krasnoarmeyskaya ul. 1/21; faculties: Machine Building, Engineering, Instrument Making; library of 405,000 vols.; Evening Faculty; Rector V. A. TETERIN.

**Lugansk Mechanical Engineering Institute:** Lugansk, Ul. Frunze 112; faculties: Engineering Technology, Electrical Machine Building, Automation of Industrial Production; library of 100,000 vols.

**Mogilev Mechanical Engineering Institute:** Mogilev, Ul. Lenina 70; f. 1961; faculties: Engineering, Machine Building; 250 teachers; 4,500 students; library of 37,000 vols.; Evening and Extra-Mural Departments; Rector A. A. BORISOV.

**Moscow Motor Engineering Institute:** Moscow, Bolshaya Semenovskaya ul. 38; faculties: Motor Vehicles and Tractors, Engineering Technology; library of 200,000 vols.; Evening and Extra-Mural Faculties.

**Moscow Institute of Electronic Machine Building:** Moscow, Bolshoi Vuzovskii per. 3/12; faculties: Semiconductors and Electrical Vacuum Machine Building, Automation and Computing Equipment, Radio Engineering; library of 140,000 vols.; Evening and Extra-Mural Faculties; Rector E. V. ARMENCKIJ.

**Moscow N. E. Bauman Technical Institute:** Moscow, 2D Baumanskaya ul. 5; faculties: Automation and Mechanization of Industrial Processes, Power Machine Building, Transport Machine Building, Instrument Making; 1,500 teachers; 15,000 students; Evening and Extra-Mural depts.; Branch in Kaluga; Rector G. A. NIKOLAEV.

**Moscow Machine Tool Engineering Institute:** Moscow, Vadkovsky per. 3-a; faculties: Instrument Making, Machine Tool Engineering, Technology, Automation of Punch Processes; library of 243,000 vols.; Evening and Extra-Mural Faculties; Rector V. A. ARSHINOV.

**Moscow Physical-Engineering Institute:** Moscow, Kashirskoe Chaussée, 1; faculties: Experimental and Theoretical Physics, Physics and Power, Electronic Computors and Automation Equipment; Evening dept.; includes Higher School of Physics to train specialists; 550 teachers; 7,000 students; Rector V. G. KIRRILLOV-UGRYUMOV.

**Sevastopol Institute of Instrument Making:** Sevastopol, Ul. Gogolya 14; faculties: Radio Electronics, Instrument Making Technology and Precision Mechanics, Mechanics, Construction; 550 teachers; 12,000 students; Rector V. T. MALIKOV.

**Yaroslavl Technological Institute:** Moscowski prospect 88, Yaroslavl; faculties: Technology, Engineering; library of 94,000 vols.; Evening and Extra-Mural Faculties.

**Zaporozhye V. Y. Chubar Mechanical Engineering Institute:** Zaporozhye, Ul. Zhukovskogo 64; f. 1930; faculties: Machine Building, Motor Vehicles, Engineering and Metallurgy, Electrical Engineering; 420 teachers; 8,000 students; library of 189,000 vols.; Rector P. K. BELYAKOV.

(3) RADIO AND ELECTRICAL ENGINEERING

**All-Union Extra-Mural Telecommunications Institute:** 123423 Moscow, Ul. Narodnogo Opolcheniya 32; f. 1938; faculties: Radio Communication and Broadcasting, Automatic and Multi-Channel Electrical Communication, Economics; 200 teachers; 10,000 students; library of 233,000 vols.; Rector D. I. ARKADIEV.

**Ivanovo V. I. Lenin Power Institute:** Ivanovo, Rabfakovskaya ul. 34; faculties: Thermodynamics, Industrial Thermodynamics, Electrodynamics, Electrical Engineering; libraries of 128,000 vols.; Evening and Extra-Mural Faculties; Rector A. P. BAZHENOV.

**Kharkov Institute of Radio Electronics:** Kharkov, Per. V. I. Lenina 14; faculties: Automation and Computing, Radio Engineering; evening and extra-mural department; 500 teachers; 8,000 students; library of 200,000 vols.

**Kuibyshev Telecommunications Institute:** 443099 Kuibyshev, Ul. Lva Tolstogo 23; faculties: Radio Communication and Broadcasting, Automatic and Multi-Channel Electrical Communication; library of 52,000 vols.; Evening and Extra-Mural Departments; Rector S. L. SUSLOV.

**Leningrad M. A. Bonch-Bruevich Telecommunications Institute:** 191065 Leningrad, nab. reki Moyki 61; f. 1930; faculties: Radio Engineering, Radio Communication and Broadcasting, Automatic and Multi-Channel Electrical Communication; library of 227,000 vols.; Evening and Extra-Mural Faculties; Rector K. K. MURAVYEV.

**Leningrad V. I. Lenin Institute of Electrical Engineering:** Leningrad, Ul. Prof. Popova 5; faculties: Radio Engineering, Automation and Computing Equipment, Electrification and Automation, Electronic Equipment, Electrical Physics; library of 900,000 vols.; Evening and Extra-Mural Faculties; one br.; Rector A. A. VAVILOV.

**Minsk Institute of Radio Engineering:** Minsk, Podlesnaya ul. 6; faculties: Radio Engineering, Automation and Computing Equipment, Evening and Extra-Mural Faculties; Rector I. S. KOVANOV.

**Moscow Telecommunications Institute:** 111024 Moscow, Aviamotornaya Ul. 8; f. 1921; faculties: Radio Communication and Broadcasting, Automation, Telemechanics and Electronics, Automatic and Multi-Channel Electrical Communication, Economics; 450 teachers; 6,100 students; library of 510,000 vols.; Evening Faculty; Rector V. A. NADEZHDIN.

**Moscow Institute of Physical Engineering:** Moscow Region, Dolgoprudny; faculties: Radio Engineering and Cybernetics, General and Applied Physics, Aerodynamics and Applied Mathematics, Molecular and Chemical Physics, Physical and Quantum Electronics; library of 157,000 vols.; Rector O. M. BELOTSERKOVSKY.

**Moscow Institute of Radio Electronics and Automation:** 105836 Moscow, E.275; library of c. 500,000 vols.; evening and extra-mural depts.

**Moscow Institute of Radio Engineering and Electronics:** Moscow, Krasnokazarmennaya ul. 14; f. 1967; faculties: Power Machine Building, Thermodynamics, Industrial Power, Electrodynamics, Electrical Engineering, Electronic Equipment, Automation and Computing Equipment, Radio Engineering, Electrification and Automation in Industry and Transport; 400 teachers; 12,500 students; library of 500,000 vols.; Evening and Extra-Mural Faculties; Rector N. N. EVTIKHIN.

**Novosibirsk Telecommunications Institute:** 630008 Novosibirsk, Ul. Kirova 86; faculties: Radio Communication and Broadcasting, Automatic and Multi-Channel Electrical Communication, Economics; library of 110,000 vols.; Evening Department and Extra-Mural Faculty; Rector N. V. NAUMOV.

**Novosibirsk Institute of Electrical Engineering:** Novosibirsk, Prospekt Karla Marxa 20; f. 1953; faculties: Radio Engineering, Automation, Mathematical and Computing Designs, Instrument Making, Electrical Engineering, Electrodynamics, Machine Building; Extra-Mural Faculties: Electrical Engineering, Radio Engineering, General Engineering; 850 teachers; 14,000 students; library of 600,000 vols.; Rector G. P. LYSHCHINSKY.

**Odessa Telecommunications Institute:** 270021 Odessa, Ul. Chelyuskintsev 1/3; faculties: Radio Communication and Broadcasting, Automatic and Multi-Channel Electrical Communication; library of 256,000 vols.; Evening Department and Extra-Mural Faculty; Rector B. P. KUTASIN.

**Ryazan V. D. Kalmykov Institute of Radio Engineering:** Ryazan, Ul. Gagarina 59/1; falcuties: Radio Equipment Design, Radio Engineering, Electronics, Automation and Telemechanics, Automatic Control Systems; library of 146,000 vols.; Evening and Extra-Mural Faculties; Rector G. N. PANIKAROVSKIJ.

**Taganrog Institute of Radio Engineering:** Taganrog, Ul. Chekhova 22; faculties: Radio Engineering, Electronics, Automation and Computors; library of 283,000 vols.; Evening and Extra-Mural Faculties; A. V. KALAJAEV.

**Tashkent Telecommunications Institute:** 700000 Tashkent 87, Ul. Engelsa 108; f. 1955; faculties: Radio Communication and Broadcasting, Automatic and Multi-Channel Electrical Communication; 250 teachers; 5,500 students; library of 250,000 vols.; Evening and Extra-Mural Departments; Rector M. I. ASTAKHOV.

**Tomsk Institute of Automatic Control Systems and Radioelectronics:** Tomsk, Prospekt Lenina 40; f. 1962; faculties: Constructive Technology, Radio Engineering, Radio Control, Electronic Equipment; Extra-Mural, evening Faculty; library of 332,000 vols.; Dir. I. P. TCHUCHALIN.

(4) CHEMISTRY, CHEMICAL ENGINEERING AND TECHNOLOGY

**Dnepropetrovsk F. E. Dzerzhinsky Institute of Chemical Technology:** Ul. Gagarina 8, Dnepropetrovsk, Ukrainian S.S.R.; f. 1930; faculties: Inorganic Chemistry, Organic Chemistry, Silicate Technology, Engineering; 360 teachers; 6,300 students; library of 323,000 vols.

**Ivanovo Institute of Chemical Technology:** Ivanovo, Ul. F. Engelsa 7; faculties: Inorganic Chemistry, Technology of Organic Chemistry, Silicates, Engineering; library of 215,000 vols.; Evening and Extra-Mural Departments; Dir. K. H. BELONOGOV.

**Kazakh Chemical Technology Institute:** Chimkent, Kommunistichesky prospekt 5; f. 1943; faculties: Chemical Technology, Silicates, Engineering, Construction, General Engineering; library of 202,000 vols.; Rector S. G. SULEYMANOV.

**Kazan S. M. Kirov Institute of Chemical Technology:** Kazan, Ul. K. Marxa 68: faculties: Technology, Engineering, Oil Processing, Chemical Engineering; library of 295,000 vols.; Evening and Extra-Mural Faculties; Rector P. A. KIRPICHNIKOV.

**Kostroma Technological Institute:** Kostroma, Ul. Dzerzhinskogo 17; f. 1932; faculties: Technology, Forest Engineering, Engineering; library of 187,000 vols.; Evening and Extra-Mural Faculties; Rector N. N. SUSLOV.

**Leningrad Lensoviet Technological Institute:** 198013 Leningrad, Zagorodny pr. 49; faculties: Technology of Inorganic Chemistry, Organic Chemicals, Silicate Technology Engineering, Engineering, Cybernetics, Bioengineering and Physics; library of 412,000 vols; Evening and Extra-Mural Faculties; Rector V. A. PROSKURJAKOV.

**Leningrad Pulp and Paper Technological Institute:** Leningrad, Ul. Ivana Tchernych 4; faculties: Technology, Engineering, Thermodynamics, Economics; library of 450,000 vols.; Evening and Extra-Mural Departments; Rector I.-D. KUGUSHEV.

**D. I. Mendeleyev Institute of Chemical Technology:** Moscow, A-17, Miusskaya Ploshchad 9; faculties: Inorganic Chemical Technology, Organic Chemical Technology, Chemical Technology of Fuel, Silicate Technology, Chemical Engineering, Physical Engineering; Evening dept.; Branch in Novomoskovsk; 650 teachers; 10,000 students; Rector G. A. YAGODIN.

**Moscow M. V. Lomonosov Institute of Fine Chemical Technology:** Moscow, Malaya Pirogovskaya ul. 1; faculties: Electronics Chemistry, Polymer Processing Technology, Organic and Polymer Synthesis; library of 134,000 vols.; Evening and Extra-Mural Faculties; Rector Y. A. BOLSHAKOV.

**Moscow Institute of Chemical Engineering:** Moscow, 66, Ul. K. Marxa 21/4; f. 1920; faculties: Engineering, Organic Processes Engineering, Inorganic Processes Engineering, Technical Cybernetics and Automation of Chemical Production; Evening Dept.; 430 teachers; 6,000 students; library of 415,000 vols.; Rector Prof. D. T. KOKAREV.

**Tambov Institute of Chemical Engineering:** Tambov, Ul. Leningradskaya 1; f. 1965; faculties: Mechanical Sciences, Machine Construction, Automation and Mechanization of Chemical Production, Evening Faculties; Rector V. V. VLASOV.

**Voronezh Technological Institute:** Voronezh, Prospekt Revolyutsii 19; f. 1930; faculties: Technology, Engineering, Chemistry; 450 teachers; 7,700 students; library of 309,000 vols.; Evening and Extra-Mural Departments; Rector B. I. KUSHEV.

(5) MINING AND METALLURGY

**Dneprodzerzhinsk Arsenichev Institute of Metallurgy:** Pr. Pelina 16, Dneprodzerzhinsk, Ukrainian S.S.R.; faculties: Metallurgy, Technology, Engineering; Rector V. L. LOGINOV.

**Dnepropetrovsk Artem Mining Institute:** Prosp. K. Marxa 19, Dnepropetrovsk; faculties: Mining, Prospecting, Machine Building, Electrical Engineering, Construction of Mines; library of 495,000 vols.; Rector A. A. RENGEVICH.

**Dnepropetrovsk (Order of the Red Banner of Labour) Metallurgical Institute:** Dnepropetrovsk, Ul. Gagarina 4; f. 1899; faculties: Metallurgy, Engineering, Chemical Technology, Economics; 500 teachers; 11,500 students; library of 350,000 vols.; Evening and General Engineering Faculties; Rector N. F. ISAENKO.

**Kharkov Institute of Mining Engineering, Automation and Computing Equipment:** Kharkov, Prospekt Lenina 14; faculties: Mining Machine Building, Automation of Production Processes, Radio Engineering; library of 255,000 vols.

**Kommunarsk Institute of Ore Mining and Metallurgy:** Kommunarsk, Prospekt V. I. Lenina 16, Ukrainian S.S.R.; f. 1957; faculties: Mining, Metallurgy, Electrical Machine Building, Construction; library of 105,000 vols.; Rector Y. M. VOEVODIN.

**Krasnoyarsk M. I. Kalinin Institute of Non-Ferrous Metals:** Krasnoyarsk, Vuzovsky per. 3; faculties: Mining, Metallurgy, Technology; library of 191,000 vols.; Evening and Extra-Mural Faculties; Rector B. A. DARYALSKIJ.

**Krivoy Rog Ore Mining Institute:** 324033 Krivoy Rog, Ul. XXII Partseja 11; faculties: Prospecting, Mining, Electrical Engineering, Machine Building, Construction; library of 185,000 vols.; Evening and General Engineering Faculties.

**Leningrad G. V. Plekhanov Mining Institute:** Leningrad V-26, 21 Liniya 2; faculties: Prospecting, Mining, Mine Construction, Geophysics, Mining Electrical Engineering, Economics, Mine Surveying, Metallurgy; library of 1,077,895 vols.; one br.; Rector L. N. KELL.

**Magnitogorsk G. I. Nosov Institute of Ore Mining and Metallurgy:** Magnitogorsk, Prospekt Lenina 38; f. 1932; faculties: Mining, Metallurgy, Automation of Production Processes, Technological and Power, Construction; three Evening and Extra-Mural Faculties; library of 523,000 vols.; Rector Dr. N. I. IVANOV.

**Moscow Evening Institute of Metallurgy:** Moscow, E-250, Lefortovsky Val 26; f. 1931; faculties: Metallurgy, Technology, General Technology; 160 teachers; 209,229 students; library of 54,000 vols.; Rector V. A. KUDRIN.

**Moscow Institute of Steel and Alloys:** Moscow, Leninsky prospekt 6; f. 1918; faculties: Semiconductor Materials and Instruments, Ferrous Metallurgy, Metallurgy of Non-ferrous and Rare Metals, Physics and Physical Chemistry of Metals; 830 teachers; 10,000 students; library of 800,000 vols.; Rector Prof. P. I. POLUKHIN; publs. *Izvestia Visshikh Uchebnikh Zavedenii* (series for ferrous and non-ferrous metallurgy, both monthly).

**Moscow Mining Institute:** Moscow, M-19, Leninsky Prospekt 6; f. 1918; faculties: Mining, Mining Machines, Radio Engineering, Electrification and Automation, Physical Mechanics in Mining; 440 teachers; 6,000 students; library of 540,000 vols.; Evening and Extra-Mural depts.; Rector Prof. Dr. V. V. RZHEVSKY, Corr. Mem. of the U.S.S.R. Academy of Sciences.

**North Caucasian Institute of Ore Mining and Metallurgy:** Orjonikidze, Nikolayeva 44, North-Ossetian A.S.S.R.; faculties: Mining Geology, Electrical Engineering, Metallurgy, Construction; library of 214,000 vols.; Evening and Extra-Mural Faculties; Rector M. I. DURNEV.

**Siberian Sergo Orjonikidze Institute of Metallurgy:** Novokuznetsk, Ul. Kirova 42; faculties: Mining, Metallurgy, Engineering, Technology, Construction; library of 257,000 vols.; Evening Faculty and Extra-Mural Department; Rector Prof. TOLSTOGUZOV.

**Sverdlovsk V. V. Vakhrushev Mining Institute:** Sverdlovsk, Ul. Kuibysheva 30; faculties: Prospecting, Geophysics, Mining, Mining Engineering; library of 385,000 vols.; Evening and Extra Mural Faculties; Rector G. P. SAKOVTSEY.

**Zhdanov Metallurgical Institute:** Ul. Apatova 115, Zhdanov, Ukrainian S.S.R.; f. 1929; faculties: Metallurgy, Technology, Welding, Industrial Energy, Mechanics; library of 540,000 vols.; 350 teachers; 5,500 students; Rector E. A. KASPUTIN.

(6) PETROLEUM AND PEAT

**Azerbaijan M. Azizbekov Institute of Oil and Chemistry:** Baku, Prospekt Lenina 20; faculties: Prospecting, Oil Exploitation, Chemical Technology, Power, Automation of Production, Economics; 900 teachers; 16,000 students; library of 850,000 vols.; Evening and Extra-Mural Departments; Rector I. A. IBRAGIMOV.

**Grozny Oil Institute:** Grozny, Ploshchad Orjonikidze 100; f. 1920; faculties: Prospecting, Oil Deposit Exploration, Oil Processing Technology, Engineering, Construction; 400 teachers; 7,000 students; library of 350,000 vols.; Evening and Extra-Mural Faculties; Rector G. M. SUKHAREV.

**Ivano-Frankovsk Institute of Oil and Gas:** Ivano-Frankovsk, Ul. Lenina 28; f. 1967; 300 teachers; 6,500 students; Rector E. I. SHELEPIN; publ. *Collected Works 'Prospecting and Exploitation of Oil and Gas Deposits'* (quarterly).

**Moscow Academician I. M. Gubkin Institute of Petrochemical and Gas Industries:** Moscow V-296, Leninsky prospekt 65; faculties: Geology, Geophysics and Geochemistry of Oil and Gas Deposits, Mechanical Engineering, Oil and Gas Exploitation, Automation and Computer Technology, Chemical Technology, Industrial Economics, Evening and Extra-Mural departments; brs. in Krasnovodsk, Almetyevsk, Nebit-Dag, Leninogorsk; 850 teachers; 10,700 students; Rector V. N. VINOGRADOV.

**Ufa Oil Institute:** Ufa, Ul. Kosmonavtov 1; faculties: Oil Exploitation, Oil Chemistry, Technology; library of 126,000 vols.; Evening and Extra-Mural Faculties; Rector V. A. BEREZIN.

(7) CIVIL ENGINEERING

**All-Union Extra-Mural Civil Engineering Institute:** Moscow, Ul. Srednyaya Kalitnikovskaya 30; f. 1944; faculties: Construction, Design and Architecture, Technology, Engineering, Road Building, Sanitary Engineering, Municipal Construction and Economy, Economics; 500 teachers; 20,500 students; library of 300,000 vols.; Rector I. G. BUROZDIN.

**Belgorod Civil Engineering Institute:** Belgorod, Ul. Gorkogo 56; faculties: Construction, Engineering, Mechanical Engineering, Sanitary Engineering.

**Brest Civil Engineering Institute:** Brest, 17, Moskovskaja ul. 267; f. 1966; faculties: Architecture, Industrial and Civil Construction, Town Planning, Sanitation; Evening dept.; 150 teachers; 1,900 students; library of 60,000 vols.; Rector I. D. BELOGORTSEV.

**Dnepropetrovsk Civil Engineering Insitute:** Dnepropetrovsk, Ul. Chernyshevskogo 24-A; faculties: Construction, Construction Technology, Engineering; library of 239,000 vols.; Evening and General Engineering Faculties; Rector P. G. REZHICHENKO.

**Gorky V. P. Chkalov Civil Engineering Institute:** Gorky, Ul. Krasnoflotskaya 65; faculties: Construction, Sanitary

Engineering, Hydraulic Engineering; library of 204,000 vols.; Evening and Extra-Mural Faculties; Rector A. S. MEREYEV.

**Kazan Civil Engineering Institute:** Kazan, Ul. Zelenaya 1; faculties: Construction, Constructional Technology; 320 teachers; 6,200 students; library of 213,000 vols.; Evening and General Engineering Faculties; Rector M. I. KULIEV.

**Kharkov Civil Engineering Institute:** Kharkov, Ul. Sumskaya 40; faculties: Construction, Sanitary Engineering; library of 218,000 vols.; Evening and General Engineering Faculties; Rector V. P. SACHKO.

**Kharkov Institute of Municipal Engineers:** Kharkov, Ul. Revolyutsii 12; f. 1930; faculties: Construction, Municipal Electrical Transport, Economics; library of 150,000 vols.; Evening Department; Rector V. BUTENKO.

**Kiev Civil Engineering Institute:** Kiev 37, Vozdukhoflotsky prosp. 99/101; f. 1930; faculties: Architecture, Construction, Constructional Technology, Municipal Construction, Sanitary Engineering and Construction Industry Automation; 530 teachers; 900 students; library of 400,000 vols.; Evening Faculty; Rector I. A. VETROV.

**Kuibyshev A. I. Mikoyan Civil Engineering Institute:** Kuibyshev, Ul. Molodogvardeyskaya 194; f. 1930; faculties: Construction, Sanitary Engineering; 270 teachers; 5,100 students; library of 290,000 vols.; Evening and Extra-Mural Faculties; Rector V. P. KORYAKIN.

**Leningrad Civil Engineering Institute:** Leningrad, Ul. Krasnoarmeyskaya 4; faculties: Construction, Town Building, Sanitary Engineering, Engineering and Motorways; library of 450,000 vols.; Evening and Extra-Mural Faculties; Rector N. A. YAKOVLEУ.

**Moscow V. V. Kuibyshev Civil Engineering Institute:** Moscow, Shlyuzovaya Nab. 8; f. 1921; faculties: Construction, Hydraulic Engineering, Heat and Ventilation, Water and Sewerage, Constructional Technology, Urban Development, Engineering, Evening and Extra-Mural departments; 730 teachers; 9,600 students; library of 800,000 vols.; Rector Prof. N. A. STRELCHUK.

**Novosibirsk V. V. Kuibyshev Civil Engineering Institute:** Novosibirsk, Ul. Leningradskaya 113; faculties: Architecture, Hydraulic Engineering, Construction No. 1, Construction No. 2; library of 278,000 vols.; Evening and Extra-Mural Faculties; Rector K. L. PROVOROV.

**Odessa Civil Engineering Institute:** Odessa, Ul. Didrikhsona 4; faculties: Construction, Hydraulic Engineering, Sanitary Engineering; library of 177,000 vols.; Evening Faculty; Rector P. L. EREMENKO.

**K. D. Pamfilov Academy of Municipal Economy:** Moscow 123373, Volokolamskoe chaussée 116; f. 1931; Departments of Economics, Housing and Municipal Buildings, Automation and Computer Technology, Anti-corrosion Protection of Underground Metal Structures, Public Transport and Roads, Heat Supply and Ventilation, Electricity Supply, Municipal Sanitation, Mechanization, Tree-planting in Towns, Laundry Economy; 4 research institutes (Moscow, Leningrad, Sverdlovsk and Rostov-on-Don); a special designing bureau (Moscow); 3 experimental factories (Moscow and Leningrad); Dir. F. A. SHEVELEVI; Scientific Sec. E. Z. YASIN.

**Penza Civil Engineering Institute:** Penza, Ul. Titora 28; faculties: Construction, Technology, Sanitary Engineering; library of 104,000 vols.; Evening and Extra-Mural Departments; Rector N. A. MANZHOV.

**Poltava Civil Engineering Institute:** Poltava, Prospekt I Maya 24; f. 1930; faculties: Construction, Sanitary Engineering; 200 teachers; 4,100 students; library of 189,000 vols.; Evening Department; Rector I. S. DOTSENKO.

**Rostov-on-Don Civil Engineering Institute:** Rostov-on-Don, Ul. Sozialisticheskaya 162; faculties: Construction, Road Building, Constructional Technology; library of 235,000 vols.; Evening and Extra-Mural Faculties; Rector V. P. ANANIÈV.

**Samarkand Civil Engineering Institute:** Samarkand, Ul. Lyalyazar 64; faculties: Architecture, Industrial and Civil Engineering, Town Planning; evening and extra-mural departments; library of 400,000 vols.

**Tomsk Civil Engineering Institute:** Tomsk, Solyanaya ploshchad 2; f. 1952; faculties: Architecture, Construction, Engineering, Road Building and Technology; Evening and Extra-Mural Departments; 420 teachers; 6,600 students; library of over 400,000 vols.; Rector G. M. ROGOV.

**Tselinograd Civil Engineering Institute:** Tselinograd, Ul. Tsiolkovskogo 2; f. 1964; Faculty of Construction; Evening Department; 140 teachers; 2,700 students; Rector I. A. BAGROV.

**Ust-Kamenogorsk Institute of Construction and Road Building:** Ust-Kamenogorsk, Studenchesky gorodok; f. 1958; faculties: Construction, Road Building, Architecture; 400 teachers; 6,700 students; library of 180,000 vols.; Evening Department; Rector A. K. SIDOROV.

**Vilnius Civil Engineering Institute:** Vilnius 232661, Sauletekio aleja 11, Lithuanian S.S.R.; f. 1969; faculties: Architecture, Construction, Urban Construction, Economic Construction, Mechanical Technology, Automation; library of 437,753 vols.; Rector A. ČYRAS.

**Volgograd Civil Engineering Institute:** Volgograd, Ul. Akademicheskaya 1; f. 1952; faculties: Construction, Sanitary Engineering, Motor Highways; 370 teachers; 7,400 students; library of 225,000 vols.; Evening Faculty and Extra-Mural Department; Rector R. I. TSIGANKOV.

**Voronezh Civil Engineering Institute:** Voronezh, Ul. 20-Letiya Oktyabrya 84; f. 1930; faculties: Engineering, Construction, Sanitary Engineering, Constructional Technology; library of 310,000 vols.; Evening Department and Extra-Mural Faculty; Rector R. S. SHELIAPIN.

(8) TEXTILE AND OTHER LIGHT INDUSTRIES

**All-Union Extra-Mural Institute of the Textile and Light Industries:** Shabolovka 24, Moscow; f. 1932; faculties: Textile Industry, Light Industry, Chemical Technology, Economics; 320 teachers; 13,400 students; library of 290,000 vols.; Rector S. I. OVCHINNIKOV.

**Ivanovo M. V. Frunze Textile Institute:** Ivanovo, Ul. F. Engelsa 21; f. 1930; faculties: Technology, Engineering; 260 teachers; 4,200 students; library of 207,000 vols.; Evening and Extra-Mural Faculty; Rector A. Y. IZMESTYEVA.

**Kiev Technological Institute of Light Industry:** Kiev, Ul. Nemirovicha-Danchenko 2; f. 1930; faculties: Technology of Sewing Industry, Knitted-Wear, Shoe Industry, Chemical Technology, Engineering, Economics; 441 teachers; 8,500 students; library of 700,000 vols.; Extra-Mural department; Evening and General Engineering Faculties; Rector I. E. DEBRIVNY.

**Leningrad S. M. Kirov Institute of Textile and Light Industry:** Leningrad, Ul. Herzena 18; f. 1930; faculties: Technology, Chemical Technology, Engineering, Sewing Industry, Shoe Industry, Industrial Economics, Evening and Extra-Mural departments; 370 teachers;

8,100 students; library of 310,000 vols.; Rector Prof. G. I. AREFYEV.

**Moscow Technological Institute of Light Industry:** Moscow, Ul. Poliny Osipenko 33; faculties: Chemical Technology; Technology, Engineering; library of 180,000 vols., Evening Faculty; branches in Novosibirsk and Podolsk; Rector I. P. STRAKHOV.

**Moscow Textile Institute:** Moscow, Ul. Kalujskaya 1; f. 1919; faculties: Mechanical Technology, Textile Machine Building, Power Engineering, Chemical Technology, Applied Arts, Economics; 450 teachers; 5,500 students; library of 390,000 vols.; Evening and Extra-Mural Faculties (for the improvement of the teaching staff at textile institutes); Rector I. A. MARTYNOV.

**Tashkent Textile Institute:** Tashkent, Ul. Gorbunova 5; f. 1932; faculties: Mechanical Working of Fibre Materials, Technology, Chemistry and Economics; 320 teachers; 6,200 students; library of 227,000 vols.; Evening and Extra-Mural Departments; Rector M. M. MUHAMEDOV.

**Vitebsk Technological Institute of Light Industry:** Vitebsk, Smolenskoe Chaussée 90; f. 1965; faculties: Textile Studies, Textile Technology, Light Industry Studies, Evening and Extra-Mural Faculties; 100 teachers; 1,700 students; Rector S. E. SAVITSKY.

(9) FOOD INDUSTRY

**All-Union Extra-Mural Institute of Food Industry:** Moscow, Ul. Chkalova 73; faculties: Food Production, Technology, Engineering, Fisheries and Fish Processing, Economics, Economics and Management of Storing of Agricultural Products; library of 164,000 vols.; five brs.; Rector G. V. KRUSCHOV.

**Astrakhan Institute of Fish Industry:** Astrakhan, Ul. Tatishcheva 16; faculties: Technology, Fishing, Engineering; library of 115,000 vols.; Evening and Extra-Mural Faculties; Rector A. Z. SHCHERBAKOV.

**Dzhambul Technological Institute of Food and Light Industries:** Dzhambul, Ul. Kommunisticheskaya 58; faculties: Food Technology, Light Industry; Evening and Extra-Mural Departments; Rector H. S. SEITOV.

**Far Eastern Institute of Fish Industry:** Vladivostok, Ul. Leninskaya 25; faculties: Food, Fishing, Engineering, Seamanship; library of 100,000 vols.; Evening and Extra-Mural Faculties; Rector V. P. OLEYNIK.

**Kaliningrad Institute of Fish Industry:** Kaliningrad, Sovetsky prospekt 2; faculties: Fishing, Technology, Ichthyology, Ship Building, Engineering, Economics; library of 295,000 vols.; Evening and Extra-Mural Departments; Rector L. B. EITVID.

**Kiev Technological Institute of Food Industry:** Kiev, Ul. Vladimirskaya 68; faculties: Mechanics, Sugar Technology, Baking, Confectionery and Brewing Technology, Meat and Dairy Industry Technology, Industrial Economics, Thermal-Energetics and Automation of Food Industries; Extra-Mural and Part-Time Departments; library of 236,000 vols.; Evening Department; Rector S. GULY.

**Leningrad Technological Institute of Refrigerating Industry:** Leningrad, Ul. Lomonosova 9; faculties: Refrigeration, Engineering, Technology; library of 272,000 vols.; Evening and Extra-Mural Faculties; Rector M. R. DOROKHIN.

**Moscow Technological Institute of Dairy and Meat Industries:** Moscow, Ul. Talalikhina 33; faculties: Technology, Engineering, Economics, Veterinary and Sanitation; library of 240,000 vols.; Evening and Extra-Mural Faculties; Rector N. P. YANUSHKIN.

**Moscow Technological Institute of Food Industry:** Moscow 125080, Volokolamskoe chaussée 11; faculties: Flour Grinding and Elevators, Food Processing, Engineering, Engineering-Economics; 5,500 students; library of 834,000 vols.; Evening Department; Rector V. V. KRASNIKOV.

**Odessa Technological Institute of Food and Refrigerating Industries:** Odessa, Ul. Petra Velikogo 1–3; f. 1930; faculties: Technology, Engineering, Refrigeration; 400 teachers; 7,500 students; library of 250,000 vols.; Rector V. S. MARTINOVSKY.

(10) TIMBER INDUSTRY

**Arkhangelsk V. V. Kuibyshev Forest Engineering Institute:** Arkhangelsk, Naberezhnaya Lenina 17; f. 1929; faculties: Forest Engineering, Forestry, Forest Machinery, Industrial Thermodynamics, Timber Technology, Industrial and Civil Construction; 400 teachers; 6,600 students; library of 320,000 vols.; Evening and Extra-Mural Faculties; Rector I. M. BOKHOVKIN; publ. *Lesnoy zhurnal* (Forest Journal, six issues a year).

**Byelorussian S. M. Kirov Technological Institute:** Minsk, Ul. Sverdlova 13; f. 1930; faculties: Forest Engineering, Forestry, Timber Engineering, Chemical Technology; 340 teachers; 5,300 students; library of 350,000 vols.; Extra-Mural Department; Rector V. S. VIKHROV.

**Leningrad S. M. Kirov Academy of Wood Technology:** 194018 Leningrad, Institutsky per. 5; f. 1803; faculties: Forestry, Forest Engineering, Forest Machinery, Mechanical Technology of Wood, Chemical Technology of Wood, Economics of Forest Engineering; Evening and Extra-Mural departments; 607 teachers; 12,000 students; library of 1,320,000 vols.; Rector Prof. A. I. KIPRIANOV; publ. *Nautchnye trudy* (3–4 issues a year).

**Lvov Forest Engineering Institute:** Lvov, Ul. Pushkinskaya 103; f. 1945; faculties: Forest Engineering, Forestry, Timber Technology; 270 teachers; 4,700 students; library of 210,000 vols.; Evening and Extra-Mural Faculty; Rector A. I. YATSVK.

**Mari A. M. Gorky Polytechnic Institute:** Mari Autonomous S.S.R., Yoshkar-Ola, Ploshchad Lenina 3; f. 1932 as Povolzhye Forest Engineering Institute; faculties: Mechanics, Timber Engineering, Forest Economy, Evening and Extra-Mural Faculties, Dendrological Garden, Forestry School; Rector A. K. LITOVINSKY; publ. *Trudy Povolzhskogo Lesotechnicheskogo Instituta* (Transactions of the Povolzhye Forest Engineering Institute).

**Moscow Forest Engineering Institute:** Moscow Region, Mytishchi, Poselok Stroitel; faculties: Electronics and Computing Equipment, Mechanization of Wood Working, Mechanization of Wood Plastics, Forestry and Planting in Towns; library of 400,000 vols.; Extra-Mural Faculty; Rector A. H. OBLIVIN.

**Siberian Technological Institute of the Timber Industry:** Krasnoyarsk, Prospekt Mira 82; faculties: Forest Engineering, Forestry, Timber Engineering, Woodworking Technology, Chemical Technology; library of 243,000 vols.; Evening and Extra-Mural Faculties; Rector I. I. TRIBNIKOV.

**Urals Forest Engineering Institute:** Sverdlovsk, Sibirsky Trakt, 5th Kilometre; faculties: Forest Engineering, Forestry, Forest Machinery, Timber Technology, Chemical Technology; library of 370,000 vols.; Extra-Mural Faculty; Rector B. K. KRASNOSENOV.

**Voronezh Forest Engineering Institute:** Voronezh, Ul. Timiryazeva 8; f. 1918; faculties: Forest Engineering, Forestry, Forest Machinery, Timber Technology; 310 teachers; 6,000 students; library of 230,000 vols.; Evening Department and Extra-Mural Faculty; Rector A. D. DUDARYEV.

(11) PRINTING

**Moscow Institute of Printing:** Prianischnikova 2nd, Moscow A-8; faculties: Machine Building, Technology, Economics, Typography; library of 400,000 vols.; Extra-Mural Department.

**Ukrainian Institute of Printing:** Podvalnaya 17, Lvov, Ukrainian S.S.R.; library of 135,000 vols.; Extra-Mural Department.

(12) INSTITUTES FOR ENGINEER-ECONOMISTS

**Kharkov Institute of Engineering and Economics:** Kharkov, Prospekt Lenina 9; f. 1930; faculties: Machine Building, Chemistry, Metallurgy, Mining; 225 teachers; 5,000 students; library of 170,000 vols.; Evening Faculty; Rector K. A. SHTEN.

**Leningrad P. Togliatti Institute of Engineering and Economics:** Leningrad, Ul. Marata 27; faculties: Machine Building, Municipal Economy, Chemistry, Power; library of 220,000 vols.; Evening and Extra-Mural Faculties; Rector I. I. SIGOV.

**Moscow Sergo Orjonikidze Institute of Engineering and Economics:** Moscow, Podsosensky per. 20; faculties: Machine Building, Chemistry and Metallurgy, Power, Motor and Air Transport, Construction and Municipal Economy; library of 280,000 vols.; Evening and Extra-Mural Faculties; Rector O. V. KOZLOVA.

LAND SURVEYING AND CARTOGRAPHY

**Moscow Institute of Engineers for Geodesy, Aerial Photography and Cartography:** Moscow, Gorokhovsky per. 4; faculties: Geodesy, Air Photography and Geodesy, Optics and Mechanics, Cartography; library of 230,000 vols.; Evening Department and Extra-Mural Faculty; Rector V. D. BOLSHAKOV.

**Novosibirsk Institute of Engineers for Geodesy, Aerial Photography and Cartography:** Novosibirsk, Ul. Plakhotnogo 10; faculties: Geodesy, Cartography; library of 100,000 vols.; Extra-Mural Faculty; Rector K. L. PROVOROV.

LANGUAGES

**Alma-Ata Pedagogical Institute of Foreign Languages:** Alma-Ata 12, Ul. Muratbaeva 200; f. 1942; faculties: English, German, French; Rector Dr. D. NURYMBEK.

**Andijan Pedagogical Institute of Languages:** Andijan, Ul. Mira 1; f. 1966; faculties: Russian Language and Literature, Foreign Languages (English, German, French); Rector K. M. ISHANOVICH; publ. *Scientific Proceedings*.

**Azerbaijan M. F. Akhundov Pedagogical Institute of Languages:** Baku, Ul. Lieutenant Shmidta 58; f. 1959; faculties: Russian, English, French and German languages; Evening and Extra-Mural departments; Rector Dr. A. S. ABDULLAJEV; publ. *Scientific Proceedings* (quarterly).

**Valery Bryusov Erevan Institute of Russian and Foreign Languages:** Erevan, Ul. Pravda 11, Armenian S.S.R.; f. 1962; faculties of Russian language and literature, English, French, German; 240 teachers; 2,800 students.

**Maurice Thorez Moscow Institute of Foreign Languages:** Moscow; f. 1930; faculties of English, French, German, translation; in-service training for foreign-language teachers; library of 200,000 vols.; 750 teachers; 5,500 students.

LAW

**All-Union Extra-Mural Law Institute:** Ul. Starokirpitchnaja 13, Moscow B5; library of 210,000 vols.; five brs.

**Kharkov Law Institute:** Ul. Pushkinskaya 77, Kharkov, Ukrainian S.S.R.; library of 256,000 vols.

**Saratov D. I. Kursky Law Institute:** Ul. M. Gorkogo 45, Saratov; library of 195,000 vols.

**Sverdlovsk Law Institute:** Ul. Komsomolskaya 1, Sverdlovsk; f. 1931; 260 teachers; 8,500 students; library of 160,000 vols.; Rector D. D. OSTAPENKO.

LIBRARIANSHIP AND ARCHIVES

**Chelyabinsk State Institute of Culture:** Chelyabinsk, Ul. Ordjonikidze 35; departments: library science, folk music.

**Chimkent State Institute of Culture:** Chimkent, Sovietskaya ul. 33, Kazakh S.S.R.; departments: library science, music and singing.

**Eastern Siberian State Institute of Culture:** Ulan-Ude, Ul. Tereshkovoji 1; library of 91,000 vols.; departments: Library Science, Bibliography; library of 145,000 vols.; Extra-Mural Department; one br.

**Khabarovsk State Institute of Culture:** Khabarovsk, Krasnorechenskaya ul. 112; department: library science.

**Kharkov State Institute of Culture:** Kharkov, Bursatsky Spusk 4, Ukrainian S.S.R.; departments: library science; folk culture.

**Kiev State Institute of Culture:** Kiev, Ul. Chigorina 20, Ukrainian S.S.R.; departments: library science; folk culture.

**Krasnodar State Institute of Culture:** Krasnodar, Shosseinaya ul. 33; departments: library science; folk culture.

**Leningrad N. K. Krupskaya Institute of Culture:** Leningrad D-41, Dvortzovaya naberezhnaya 4; f. 1918; librarianship, cultural and educational work; 625 teachers; 7,212 students; library of 350,000 vols.; Rector Y. Y. ZAZERSKY; publ. *Trudy Instituta* (Proceedings).

**Moscow Institute for Historian-Archivists:** Ul. 25 Oktyabrya 15, Moscow; library of 300,000 vols.; Extra-Mural Department.

LITERATURE

**Moscow Literary Institute of the Union of Soviet Writers:** Tversk. Bd. 25, Moscow; library of 106,000 vols.

MEDICINE

(1) GENERAL MEDICINE

**Aktiubinsk State Medical Institute:** Ul. Lenina 78, Aktiubinsk; library of 62,000 vols.; Evening Department.

**Alma-Ata Medical Institute:** Ul. Komsomolskaya 96, Alma-Ata; departments: General Practice, Paediatrics, Stomatology, Pharmacy; library of 221,000 vols.; Evening and Extra-Mural Departments.

**Altai Medical Institute:** Prospekt V. I. Lenina 40, Barnaul; library of 121,000 vols.; General Practice Dept., Evening Department.

**Andijan Medical Institute:** Prospekt Navoi 239, Andijan, Uzbek S.S.R.; library of 105,000 vols.; Evening Department.

**Arkhangel Medical Institute:** Ul. Vinogradova 51, Arkhangel; departments: General Practice, Stomatology; library of 184,000 vols.; Evening Department; Rector N. P. BYCHIKHIN.

**Astrakhan Medical Institute:** Ul. Mechnikova 20, Astrakhan; f. 1918; library of 281,782 vols.; Evening Department; Rector Prof. U. S. TATAKINOV.

**Azerbaijan N. Narimanov Medical Institute:** Ul. Bakichanova 23, Baku, 22 Azerbaijan S.S.R.; library of 203,000 vols.

**Bashkir 15th Anniversary of the Komsomol Medical Institute:** Ul. Frunze 47, Ufa, Bashkir A.S.S.R.; library of 216,000 vols.

## EDUCATIONAL INSTITUTES

**Blagovestshensk State Medical Institute:** Ul. Gorkogo 93, Blagovestshensk-on-Amur.

**Chelyabinsk State Medical Institute:** Ul. Vorovskogo 64, Chelyabinsk; library of 300,000 vols.; Rector D. A. GLUBOKOV.

**Chernovtsy State Medical Institute:** Teatralnaya pl. 2, Chernovtsy, Ukrainian S.S.R.; library of 174,000 vols.

**Chita State Medical Institute:** Ul. Gorkogo 39A, Chita; library of 160,000 vols.; Rector V. G. KUZMIN.

**Crimean State Medical Institute:** Bd. Lenina 5/7, Simferopol, Ukrainian S.S.R.; library of 118,000 vols.

**Daghestan State Medical Institute:** Ploshchad im. Lenina, Makhachkala, Daghestan A.S.S.R.

**Dnepropetrovsk State Medical Institute:** Ul. Dzerzhinskogo 9, Dnepropetrovsk, Ukrainian S.S.R.; library of 440,000 vols.; Rector Prof. I. I. KRYZHANOVSKY.

**Donetsk A. M. Gorky Medical Institute:** Prospect Iljucha 16, Donetsk, Ukrainian S.S.R.; library of 381,000 vols.

**Erevan State Medical Institute:** Ul. Kirova 2, Erevan 25, Armenian S.S.R.; f. 1922; library of 400,000 vols.; faculties of therapy, paediatrics, sanitation and hygiene, stomatology, pharmacology; c. 400 teachers; c. 3,000 students.

**Gorky S. M. Kirov Medical Institute:** Pl. Minina i Pozharskogo 10/1, Gorky; f. 1920; library of 300,000 vols.; Rector Dr. I. F. MATYUSHIN.

**Grodno State Medical Institute:** Ul. Ozhesho 1, Grodno; Rector D. A. MASLAKOV.

**Irkutsk State Medical Institute:** Ul. Krasnogo Vosstania 1, Irkutsk; f. 1919; Rector Prof. A. I. NIKITIN.

**Ivano-Frankovsk Medical Institute:** Ivano-Frankovsk, Ul. Galitskaya 2; library of 109,000 vols.

**Ivanovo State Medical Institute:** Ul. Engelsa 7, Ivanovo; library of 141,000 vols.

**Izhevsk State Medical Institute:** Revolyutsionnaya 199, Izhevsk, Udmurt A.S.S.R.; library of 200,000 vols.

**Kalinin State Medical Institute:** Ul. Sovietskaya 4, Kalinin; library of 200,000 vols.; Rector R. D. NOVOSELOV.

**Karaganda State Medical Institute:** Ul. Alalikina 7, Karaganda, Kazakh S.S.R.; library of 250,000 vols.; Rector P. M. POSPELOV.

**Kaunas State Medical Institute:** Ul. Mitskevichaus 9, Kaunas, Lithuanian S.S.R.; f. 1951; 352 teachers; library of 530,000 vols.; Rector Prof. Z. I. JANUŠKEVIČIUS.

**Kazan State Medical Institute:** Ul. Butlerova 49, Kazan, Tatar A.S.S.R.; library of 166,000 vols.

**Kemerovo State Medical Institute:** Ul. Nazarova 1, Kemerovo Region; f. 1956; library of 170,000 vols.; Rector A. D. TKACHEV.

**Khabarovsk State Medical Institute:** Ul. K. Marxa 47, Khabarovsk; library of 184,000 vols.

**Kharkov State Medical Institute:** Prospekt Lenina 4, Kharkov, Ukrainian S.S.R.; f. 1921; 400 teachers; 3,600 students; library of 340,000 vols.; Rector B. A. ZADOROZHNY.

**Kiev A. A. Bogomolets Medical Institute:** Bd. Shevchenko 13, Kiev, Ukrainian S.S.R.; library of 400,000 vols.

**Kirghiz State Medical Institute:** Ul. 50 Ut Oktjabrja 92, Frunze, Kirghiz S.S.R.; library of 200,000 vols.; Rector V. A. ISABAEVA.

**Kishinev State Medical Institute:** Pr. Lenina 165, Kishinev, Moldavian S.S.R.; library of 232,000 vols.; publ. *Transactions of Kirghiz State Medical Institute.*

**Krasnoyarsk State Medical Institute:** Ul. Partizana Zheleznyaka 1, Krasnoyarsk; library of 420,000 vols.

## UNION OF SOVIET SOCIALIST REPUBLICS

**Kuban "Red Army" Medical Institute:** Ul. Sedina 4, Krasnodar; library of 350,000 vols.; Rector V. A. LATYSHEV.

**Kuibyshev State Medical Institute:** Ul. Chapaevskaya 89, Kuibyshev; library of 292,000 vols.

**1st Leningrad I. P. Pavlov Medical Institute:** Ul. L. Tolstogo 6/8, Leningrad; library of 563,000 vols.

**Leningrad Institute of Sanitation and Hygiene:** Piskarevsky prospect 17, Leningrad; library of 350,000 vols.; Rector Prof. A. J. IVANOV.

**Leningrad Medical Paediatrics Institute:** Ul. Litovskaya 2, Leningrad; library of 400,000 vols.; Rector Prof. G. A. KAJSARYANTS.

**Lvov State Medical Institute:** Ul. Pekarskaya 69, Lvov, Ukrainian S.S.R.; library of 240,000 vols.

**Minsk State Medical Institute:** Prospekt Lenina 6, Minsk, Byelorussian S.S.R.; library of 230,000 vols.

**1st Moscow Medical Institute:** B. Pirogovskaya 2/6, Moscow; library of 600,000 vols.

**2nd Moscow N. I. Pirogov State Medical Institute:** Moscow, Malaya Pirogovskaya ul. 1; f. 1906; faculties: General Practice, Paediatrics, Medical Biology, Evening dept.; 700 teachers; 7,000 students; Rector Prof. Dr. U. M. LOPUKHIN.

**Moscow Medical Institute of the Health Ministry of the R.S.F.S.R.:** B. Gruzinskaya 10, Moscow.

**North Ossetian Medical Institute:** Pushkinskaya 40, Ordjonikidze, North Ossetian A.S.S.R.; library of 127,000 vols.; Rector M. A. TOTKOV.

**Novosibirsk State Medical Institute:** Krasny pr. 52, Novosibirsk; library of 360,000 vols.; Rector Prof. V. P. KASNAECHEEV.

**Odessa N. I. Pirogov Medical Institute:** Meditsinsky per. 2, Odessa, Ukrainian S.S.R.; library of 433,000 vols.

**Omsk M. I. Kalinin Medical Institute:** Ul. Lenina 12, Omsk; library of 520,000 vols.; Rector Prof. V. P. GOVOROV.

**Orenburg State Medical Institute:** Ul. Sovietskaya 6, Orenburg; library of 160,000 vols.

**Perm State Medical Institute:** Ul. Kommunisticheskaya 26, Perm; library of 300,000 vols.; Rector T. V. IVANOVSKAYA.

**Riga State Medical Institute:** Bulvar Padomyu 12, Riga, Latvian S.S.R.; library of 166,000 vols.

**Rostov State Medical Institute:** Nakhichevansky pr.29a, Rostov-on-Don; f. 1931; library of 340,000 vols.; Rector Prof. U. D. RYZHKOV.

**Ryazan I. P. Pavlov Medical Institute:** Ul. Mayakovskogo 105, Ryazan; library of 213,000 vols.

**Samarkand I. P. Pavlov Medical Institute:** Ul. Jitomirskaya 6, Samarkand, Uzbek S.S.R.; f. 1930; library of 250,000 vols.; Rector U. K. VAKHABOVA.

**Saratov State Medical Institute:** Ul. 20-letya VLKSM 112, Saratov; f. 1909; library of 9,500,000 vols; Rector Prof. N. R. IVANOV.

**Smolensk State Medical Institute:** Ul. Glinki 3, Smolensk; library of 207,000 vols.

**Stavropol Territorial Medical Institute:** Ul. Mira 310, Stavropol-Kavkazsky; f. 1937; library of 175,000 vols.; Rector Prof. V. Y. PERVUSHIN.

**Sverdlovsk State Medical Institute:** Ul. Repina 3, Sverdlovsk; f. 1931; library of 500,000 vols.; Rector V. N. KLIMOV.

**Tajik Ibn-Cina Abu-Ali (Avicenna) State Medical Institute:** Dushanbe, Prospekt Lenina 139, Tajik S.S.R.; f. 1939; library of 128,000 vols.; Rector Prof. Acad. K. T. TADZHIEV.

**Tashkent State Medical Institute:** Ul. K. Marxa 103, Tashkent, Uzbek S.S.R.; f. 1919; library of 470,000 vols.; Rector Prof. K. A. ZUFAKOV.

**Tbilisi State Medical Institute:** Ul. Melikishvili 10, Tbilisi 9, Georgian S.S.R.; f. 1918; 400 staff; 3,500 students; library of 300,000 vols.; Rector P. G. GELBAKHIANI; publ. *Trudy* (Proceedings) (biennially).

**Ternopol State Medical Institute:** Teatralnaya pl. 2, Ternopol, Ukrainian S.S.R.

**Tomsk State Medical Institute:** Moskovsky Tract 2, Tomsk; f. 1888; library of 350,000 vols.; Rector Prof. I. V. TOROPTSEV.

**Turkmen State Medical Institute:** Ul. Shaumyana 58, Ashkhabad, Turkmenian S.S.R.; f. 1932; library of 191,000 vols.; Rector D. N. NEPESOV.

**Tyumen State Medical Institute:** Tyumen, Ul. Odesskaya 58; f. 1963; 280 teachers; 2,500 students.

**Vinnitsa State Medical Institute:** Ul. Pirogova 54, Vinnitsa, Ukrainian S.S.R.; library of 187,000 vols.

**Vitebsk State Medical Institute:** Prospekt Frunze 27, Vitebsk, Byelorussian S.S.R.; library of 145,000 vols

**Vladivostok State Medical Institute:** Ostrjakova prospekt 2, Vladivostok.

**Volgograd State Medical Institute:** Ploshchad Pavshikh Bortsov 1, Volgograd; library of 181,000 vols.

**Voronezh State Medical Institute:** Ul. Studentcheskaya 10, Voronezh; library of 170,000 vols.

**Yaroslavl State Medical Institute:** Ul. Revolutsionnaya 5, Yaroslavl; library of 137,000 vols.

**Zaporozhye State Medical Institute:** Ul. Minskaya 10, Zaporozhye; f. 1965; Rector I. I. TOKARENKO.

(2) PHARMACEUTICS

**Kharkov Pharmaceutical Institute:** Ul. Pushkinskaya 53, Kharkov, Ukrainian S.S.R.; f. 1921; 120 teachers; 1,300 students; library of 52,000 vols.; Rector G. P. PIVNENKO.

**Leningrad Chemical-Pharmaceutical Institute:** Leningrad 197022, Ul. Popova 4/6; f. 1919; 14 mems.; library of 304,000 vols.; Dir. N. V. LESCHEVA.

**Perm Pharmaceutical Institute:** Ul. Lenina 48, Perm; library of 80,000 vols.

**Piatigorsk Pharmaceutical Institute:** Prospekt Kirova 33, Piatigorsk, Stavropolsk; f. 1943; 120 teachers; 1,700 students; library of 56,000 vols.; Rector V. G. BELIKOV.

**Tashkent Pharmaceutical Institute:** Ul. K. Marxa 103, Tashkent, Uzbek S.S.R.; library of 100,000 vols.

(3) STOMATOLOGY

**Moscow Medical Stomatological Institute:** Kalyayevskaya 18, Moscow; f. 1935; library of 113,000 vols.

(4) MOTHER AND CHILD CARE AND DISEASES OF WOMEN AND CHILDREN

**All-Union Research Institute of Obstetrics and Gynaecology:** Moscow G-435, Elansky 2; f. 1944; library of 125,000 vols.; Dir. Acad. Prof. L. S. PERSIANINOV.

**Armenian Gynaecological Institute:** Prosp. Lenina 22, Erevan; f. 1931.

**Azerbaijan Institute of Mother and Child Care:** 7-a Parallelnaya 17, Baku, Azerbaijan S.S.R.

**Byelorussian Maternity and Child Welfare Institute:** Ul. Krasnoarmeyskaya 34, Minsk.

**Gorky Region Institute of Mother and Child Care:** Ul. Semashko 22, Gorky.

**Kazakhstan Maternity and Child Welfare Institute:** Ul. Mnogovodnaya 17, Alma Ata.

**Kharkov Research Institute of Mother and Child Care:** Kharkov, Ukrainian S.S.R.

**Lvov Research Institute of Mother and Child Care:** Ul. Lysenko 31, Lvov, Ukrainian S.S.R.

**Moscow Regional Gynaecological Institute:** Lepeshinsky tupik 3, Moscow.

**Paediatric Research Institute:** Ul. Prof. Popova 9, Leningrad.

**Paediatric Research Institute:** Ul. Kropotkina 37, Moscow.

**Rostov Region Paediatric Research Institute:** Dolomanovsky per. 142, Rostov-on-Don.

**Sverdlovsky Maternity and Child Welfare Institute:** Ul. Repina 1, Sverdlovsk.

**Turner Child Orthopaedics Research Institute:** Lakhtinskaya 10/12, Leningrad.

**Ukrainian Institute of Mother and Child Care:** Vozdukhoflotskoe chaussée 24, Kiev, Ukrainian S.S.R.

(5) TUBERCULOSIS

**Azerbaijan Institute of Tuberculosis:** Prospekt Lenina 83, Baku.

**Byelorussian Institute of Tuberculosis:** Ul. Karla Liebknechta, Minsk.

**I. M. Sechenov Climatotherapy Institute of Tuberculosis:** Ul. Massandrovskaya 42, Yalta.

**Kazakhstan Institute of Tuberculosis:** Ul. Gorodskaya 5, Alma-Ata.

**Kharkov Tuberculosis Research Institute:** Ul. Chernyshevskaya 83, Ukrainian S.S.R.

**Leningrad Institute of Surgical Tuberculosis and Diseases of the Bones and Joints:** Ul. Institutskaya 6, Leningrad.

**Leningrad Institute of Tuberculosis:** Ligovsky pr. 2/4, Leningrad.

**Lithuanian Republican Institute of Tuberculosis:** Vilnius, Ul. Gilioi 8.

**Lvov State Tuberculosis Research Institute:** Ul. Engelsa 22, Lvov, Ukrainian S.S.R.

**Moscow Region Tuberculosis Institute:** Ul. Dostoyevskogo 4, Moscow.

**National Scientific Research Institute of Tuberculosis:** 50 Zacomoldina, Tbilisi, Georgian S.S.R.; f. 1930; library of 24,512 vols.; Dir. O. G. BATIASHVILI, M.D.; publ. Works of members of the Institute.

**Novosibirsk Institute of Tuberculosis:** Ul. Chaplygina 75, Novosibirsk.

**Odessa Tuberculosis Research Institute:** Ul. Belinskogo 11, Odessa, Ukrainian S.S.R.

**Sverdlovsk Tuberculosis Research Institute:** Ul. K. Liebknechta 36, Sverdlovsk.

**Uzbekistan Anti-Tuberculosis Research Institute:** Ul. Madzhlisi 1, Tashkent 86; f. 1932; research work, prophylaxis and treatment; library of 60,000 vols.; Dir. Sh. A. ALIMOV; publs. *Sbornik trudov* (Bulletin of Labour), Reports, *Monographs*.

(6) EPIDEMIOLOGY AND MICROBIOLOGY

**Arkhangel Institute of Epidemiology, Microbiology and Hygiene:** Pr. Ch.-Luchinskogo 32, Arkhangel.

**Ashkhabad Institute of Epidemiology and Hygiene:** Ul. Pervomaiskaya 137, Ashkhabad, Turkmen S.S.R.

**Azerbaijan Institute of Epidemiology, Microbiology and Hygiene:** Ul. Gamalei 23, Baku.

**Byelorussian Institute of Microbiology, Epidemiology and Hygiene:** Ul. Nogina 3, Minsk, Byelorussian S.S.R.

**Central Asian Institute of Microbiology and Virology:** Ul. Kirova 103, Alma-Ata, Kazakh S.S.R.

**Dnepropetrovsk Institute of Epidemiology, Microbiology and Hygiene (Gamaley Institute):** Prospekt Karla Marxa 2, Dnepropetrovsk.

**Gorky Institute of Epidemiology and Microbiology:** Gruzinskaya ul. 44, Gorky.

**Kazan Institute of Epidemiology, Microbiology and Hygiene:** B. Krasnaya ul. 65, Kazan.

**Khabarovsk Institute of Epidemiology and Hygiene:** Ul. Shevchenko 4, Khabarovsk.

**Kirghiz Institute of Epidemiology, Microbiology and Hygiene:** Kirghizskaya 55, Frunze, Kirghiz S.S.R.

**Kuibyshev Institute of Epidemiology, Microbiology and Hygiene:** Chapayevskaya 87, Kuibyshev.

**Leningrad Pasteur Institute of Epidemiology and Microbiology:** Leningrad, Ul. Mira 14; f. 1923; library of 60,000 vols.; Dir. T. V. PERADZE, M.D.; publ. *Proceedings* (1–2 per year).

**Moldavian Institute of Epidemiology, Microbiology and Hygiene:** Kishinev, Ul. Ostrovskogo 13.

**Moscow Mechnikov Institute of Epidemiology, Microbiology and Hygiene:** Ul. Chernyshevskogo 44, Moscow.

**Sverdlovsk Institute of Epidemiology, Microbiology and Hygiene:** Ul. R. Luxemburga 75, Sverdlovsk.

**Ukrainian Institute of Epidemiology, Microbiology and Hygiene:** Ul. S. Razina 4, Kiev, Ukrainian S.S.R.

**Uzhgorod Institute of Epidemiology, Microbiology and Hygiene:** Ul. Grabarya 4, Uzhgorod.

(7) EYE DISEASES

**Azerbaijan Research Institute of Ophthalmology:** 6-ya Kommunisticheskaya ul. 5, Baku.

**Chuvash Eye Diseases Research Institute:** Ul. Sespelya 27, Cheboksary, Chuvash S.S.R.

**Leningrad Institute of Eye Diseases:** Mokhovaya 38, Leningrad.

**Turkmen Eye Diseases Research Institute:** Ul. Soyuznaya 32/2, Ashkhabad, Turkmen S.S.R.

**Ufa Trachoma Institute:** Ul. Pushkinskaya 20, Ufa.

**Ukraine Experimental Institute for Eye Diseases and Tissue Therapy:** Proletarsky Bulvar 49-51, Odessa; Dir. N. A. PUCHKOVSKAYA.

(8) DERMATOLOGY AND VENEREAL DISEASES

**Central Institute of Dermatology and Venereal Diseases:** Ul. Korolenko 3, Moscow.

**Gorky Institute for Skin and Venereal Diseases:** Ul. Kovalikhinskaya 49, Gorky.

**Kazakhstan Skin and Venereal Disease Institute:** Ul. Tsentralnaya 38, Alma-Ata.

**Leningrad Research Institute of Antibiotics:** Ogorodnikov prosp. 23, Leningrad; f. 1956; library of 35,000 vols.; Dir. I. M. TERESHIN.

**Odessa Glavche Research Institute of Dermatology and Venereal Diseases:** Ul. Polevaya 3, Krasnaya slobodka, Odessa, Ukrainian S.S.R.

**Research Institute of Skin and Venereal Diseases:** Tbilisi, ul. Ninoshvili 55; f. 1935; library of 21,300 vols.; Dir. Prof. Dr. L. T. SHETSIRULI; publ. *Trudy* (Proceedings, annual).

**Sverdlovsk Region Institute of Dermatology and Venereal Diseases:** Ul. K. Liebknechta 9, Sverdlovsk.

**Turkmen Skin and Venereal Diseases Institute:** Ul. Pervomaiskaya 77, Ashkhabad.

**Ufa Skin and Venereal Diseases Institute:** Ul. Frunze 43, Ufa.

**Ukraine Skin and Venereal Diseases Institute:** Ul K. Marxa 17, Kharkov.

**Uzbekistan Republic Skin and Venereal Diseases Institute:** Kafanova 104, Tashkent; f. 1932; 45 doctors; library; Dir. N. T. TURSUNOV.

(9) HAEMATOLOGY AND BLOOD TRANSFUSION

**Azerbaijan Blood Transfusion Institute:** Baku, Nagornaya ul. 23.

**Byelorussian Blood Transfusion Institute:** Dolginovsky Trakt 133, Minsk.

**Central Institute of Haematology and Blood Transfusion:** Novozykovsky pr. 4, Moscow; f. 1926; library of 50,000 vols.; publ. *Sovremennie Problemi Hematologii i Perelivaniya Krovi* (monthly).

**Kiev Blood Transfusion Research Institute:** Ul. K. Liebknechta 39, Kiev, Ukrainian S.S.R.

**Leningrad Blood Transfusion Institute:** 2-a Sovetskaya ul. 16, Leningrad.

**Lvov Institute of Blood Transfusion and Emergency Surgery:** Ul. Pushkina 45, Lvov, Ukrainian S.S.R.

**Uzbekistan Blood Transfusion Institute:** Ul. Yaselnaya 51, Tashkent.

(10) ORTHOPAEDICS, TRAUMATOLOGY AND SURGERY

**Azerbaijan Institute of Orthopaedics and Restorative Surgery:** Nagornaya 21, Baku 5.

**K. Bedrosian Erevan Scientific Research Institute of Orthopaedics and Traumatology:** Erevan, Armenian S.S.R.; f. 1945; 6 laboratories, curative physical culture, physiotherapy, etc.

**Central Artificial Limb Research Institute:** 2-y Donskoy pr. 4a, Moscow.

**Central Institute of Traumatology and Orthopaedics:** Ul. Priorova 10, Moscow A-299; f. 1921; eleven clinics; library of over 40,000 vols.; Dir. Prof. M. V. VOLKOV; publ. *Urgent Problems on Traumatology and Orthopaedics* (twice a year).

**Central Scientific Research Institute of Prosthetics and Artificial Limbs:** Moscow 117071, 2 Donskoy pr., dom 6/4; f. 1943; approx. 300 scientific workers; library of 30,000 vols.; Dir. N. I. KONDRASHIN; publ. *Protezirovaniye i protezostroyeniye*† (Prosthetics and Artificial Limbs, bi-annual).

**Donetsk Scientific Research Institute of Traumatology and Orthopaedics:** Ul. Artema 106, Donetsk, Ukrainian S.S.R.

**Georgia Institute of Traumatology and Orthopaedics:** Ul. Kalinina 51, Tbilisi; Dir. B. TSERETELI.

**Gorky Institute of Restorative Surgery, Orthopaedics and Traumatology:** Nab. im. Zhdanova 18, Gorky.

**Irkutsk Institute of Orthopaedics and Traumatology:** Ul. Revoliutsii 1, Irkutsk.

**Kazan State Institute of Orthopaedics and Traumatology:** Ul. Gorkogo 3, Kazan.

**Kharkov M. I. Sitenko Research Institute of Orthopaedics and Traumatology:** Pushkinskaya ul. 80, Kharkov-24, Ukrainian S.S.R.; f. 1907; Dir. A. A. KORZH.

**Kharkov Research Institute of General and Emergency Surgery:** Chernyshevskaya ul. 7/9, Kharkov, Ukrainian S.S.R.

**Kiev Institute of Orthopaedics:** Ul. Vorovskogo 27, Kiev, Ukrainian S.S.R.

**Kiev Research Institute of Neurosurgery:** Kiev, 32 Manuilsky ul.; f. 1950; library of 30,000 vols.; Dir. Acad. Prof. A. P. ROMODANOV; Asst. Dir. Prof. Y. A. ZOZULIA; publ. *Neurosurgery* (annual).

**Leningrad Artificial Limb Research Institute:** Pr. K. Marxa 9/12, Leningrad.

**Leningrad Institute of Traumatology and Orthopaedics:** Park Lenina 5, Leningrad.

**Minsk Institute of Orthopaedics and Restorative Surgery:** Minsk, Ul. Lenina 30, Byelorussian S.S.R.

**Novosibirsk Institute of Orthopaedics and Restorative Surgery:** Ul. Frunze 33, Novosibirsk.

**Saratov Institute of Restorative Surgery, Traumatology and Orthopaedics:** Ul. Chernyshevskogo 148, Saratov.

**Sverdlovsk Institute of Restorative Surgery, Traumatology and Orthopaedics:** Bankovsky per. 7, Sverdlovsk.

**Ukrainian Research Institute of Orthopaedics and Traumatology:** Vorovskogo 27, Kiev, Ukrainian S.S.R.

**Uzbek Institute of Orthopaedics and Traumatology:** Kablukova 5, Tashkent, Uzbek S.S.R.

(11) MALARIA AND PARASITOLOGY

**Azerbaijan Institute of Medical Parasitology and Tropical Medicine:** Baku, Sarainskoe chaussée, 3165 kv.

**R.S.F.S.R. Institute of Medical Parasitology:** Moskovskaya 67, Rostov-on-Don.

**Uzbek Institute of Malaria and Medical Parasitology:** Gospitalnaya Ul. 48, Samarkand, Uzbek S.S.R.

**Virsaladze Institute of Medical Parasitology and Tropical Medicine of the Georgian S.S.R.:** Ul. Plekhanov 139, Tbilisi 64.

(12) VACCINES AND SERA

**Gorky Research Institute of Vaccines and Sera:** Gruzinskaya ul. 44, Gorky.

**L. A. Tarasevich State Research Institute for Standardization and Control of Medical Biological Preparations:** Moscow G-2, Sivtsev-Vrazhek per. 41; f. 1919; 420 staff; library of 16,000 vols.; Dir. Prof. S. G. DZAGUROV; publ. various papers.

**Leningrad Institute of Vaccines and Sera:** Ul. akad. Pavlova 9, Leningrad.

**Moscow Institute of Vaccines and Sera:** Per. Mechnikova 5a, Moscow; Dir. A. KANCHURIN.

**Stavropol Institute of Vaccines and Sera:** Ul. K. Khetagurova 24, Stavropol-Kavkazsky.

(13) RADIOLOGY AND ONCOLOGY

**Azerbaijan Institute of Roentgenology, Radiology and Oncology:** 4-ya Nagornaya ul. 119, Baku.

**Central Institute of Roentgenology and Radiology:** Solyanka 7, Moscow, J28.

**Central Research Insitute of Roentgenology and Radiology:** 188646 Leningrad, Pesochnij-2, Ul. Leningradskaja 70/4; f. 1918; Dir. Prof. Dr. Med. K. B. TIKHONOV.

**Georgian Institute of Roentgenology and Medical Radiology:** Ul. Ordzhonikidze 101, Tbilisi; Dir. G. NAZARISHNILI.

**Kiev Research Institute of Roentgenology and Oncology:** Kiev, Ukrainian S.S.R.

**Lithuanian Research Institute of Oncology:** Vilnius, Polocko str. 2, Lithuanian S.S.R.; Dir. Prof. Dr. A. TELICHENAS.

**P. A. Herzen State Research Institute of Oncology:** Vtoroy Botkinsky pr., Moscow.

**Rostov Institute of Radiology and Oncology:** Voroshilovsky pr. 119, Rostov-on-Don; affiliated to the Cheliabinsk Radiation Hygiene Institute.

**Ukrainian Radiological and Oncological Institute:** Pushkinshaya 82, Kharkov, Ukrainian S.S.R.

**Voronezh Region Radiological and Oncological Institute:** Ul. Kalyayeva 2, Voronezh.

(14) NEUROLOGY AND PSYCHIATRY

**Byelorussian Institute of Neurology, Neuro-surgery and Physiotherapy:** Podlesnaya 5, Minsk.

**Central Sechenov Research Institutes:** Zapadnaya ul. 1, Yalta, Crimea, Ukrainian S.S.R.

**Georgian Institute of Psychiatry:** Elektricheski per. 4, Tbilisi.

**Kharkov Psycho-Neurological Research Institute:** Kharkov, Ukrainian S.S.R.; Dir. O. R. STEPANENKO.

**Turkmen Institute of Neurology and Physiotherapy:** Ul. Soiuznaya 32/2, Ashkhabad.

(15) INDUSTRIAL HYGIENE AND OCCUPATIONAL DISEASES

**All-Union Labour-Protection Research Institute of the Central Council of Trade Unions:** Ul. Furmanova 3, 192187 Leningrad; f. 1927; library of 75,000 vols.; Dir. V. I. FILPOV; publs. Annotations of reports, booklets, information and scientific papers.

**Central Research Institute for Evaluation of Working Capacity and Vocational Assistance to Disabled Persons:** Ul. Ostriakova 3, Moscow A-57; f. 1930; Dir. Prof. Dr. D. I. GRITSKEVICH.

**Donetsk Institute of Industrial Physiology:** 2-a linia 50, Donetsk, Ukrainian S.S.R.

**Georgian Institute of Industrial Hygiene and Occupational Diseases:** Prodolnaia ul. 27, Tbilisi 49.

**Gorky Institute of Industrial Hygiene and Occupational Diseases:** Ul. Semashko 20, Gorky.

**Kharkov Research Institute of Industrial Hygiene and Occupational Diseases:** Kharkov-22, Ul. Trinklera 6, Ukrainian S.S.R.; f. 1923; library of 36,547 vols.; publ. *Bulletin* (once every two years).

**Kiev Institute of Industrial Hygiene and Occupational Diseases:** Ul. Chkalova 33, Kiev, Ukrainian S.S.R.; f. 1928; library of 40,000 vols.; Dir. Prof. J. I. KUNDIEV; publ. *Labour Hygiene*.

**Leningrad Research Institute of Industrial Hygiene and Occupational Diseases:** 2-a Sovetskaya ul. 4, Leningrad.

**Ufa Institute of Hygiene and Occupational Diseases:** Ufa, Pervomayskaya ul. 20a.

**Uzbekistan Institute of Sanitation and Hygiene:** K. Marx 85, Tashkent.

(16) OTHER MEDICAL INSTITUTES

**A. N. Marzeev Scientific Research General and Municipal Hygiene Institute:** Kirova 7, Kiev; f. 1931; controlled

EDUCATIONAL INSTITUTES

by Health Ministry of Ukrainian S.S.R.; research in character, degree and basic laws of effects of environmental factors on the organism; elaboration and argumentation of hygienic standards, experiments on environmental protection; 400 staff; library of 47,000 vols.; Dir. M. G. SHANDALA; publ. *Hygiene of Populated Areas†*.

**Armenian Institute of Spa Treatment and Physiotherapy:** Orbeli St. 41, Erevan 375028; f. 1930; Dir. Prof. G. AGADJANIAN; publ. *Transactions of the Institute*.

**Azerbaijan Institute of Spa Treatment and Physiotherapy:** Balakhanskoe Chaussée 3, Baku.

**Central Institute for Scientific Research in Health Education:** Ul. Kirova 42, Moscow.

**Central Scientific Research Institute of Health Resorts and Physical Therapy:** Moscow 121099, Prospekt Kalinina 50; f. 1920; staff of 577; library of 67,400 vols.; Dir. Prof. V. M. BOGOLUBOV; publ. *Problems of Health Resorts, Physiotherapy and Exercise Therapy* (every 2 months).

**Ersman Health Research Institute:** Pyatnitskaya ul. 1/2, Moscow.

**Institute of Plastic Surgery:** R.S.F.S.R. Ministry of Public Health, Ul. Gorkogo 19, Moscow.

**Kharkov Chemical and Pharmaceutical Research Institute:** Yumovskaya Ul. 7, Kharkov.

**Kharkov Research Institute of Endocrinology and Hormone Chemistry:** Ukrainian S.S.R., Kharkov 2, Ul. Artema 10/12; f. 1919; study of new hormone drugs, treatment of diabetes, thyroid diseases, etc.; library of 52,000 vols.; Dir. V. V. NATAROV.

**Kiev Institute of Nutritional Hygiene:** Ul. Lenina 25, Kiev, Ukrainian S.S.R.

**Leningrad Institute of Oto-Rhino-Laryngology:** Bronnitskaya 9, Leningrad; f. 1930; library of 30,000 vols.; Dir. N.P. PETROV.

**Moscow Municipal Research First Aid Institute:** Kolkhoznaya ploschchad 3, Moscow; f. 1923; library of 30,000 vols.; Dir. Prof. B. D. KOMAROV.

**Omsk Institute of Infectious Diseases:** Omsk, Internatsionalnaya ul. 25.

**Piatigorsk Balneological Institute:** Pr. Kirova 30, Piatigorsk.

**Sochi Health Research Institute:** Sochi, Kurotny prosp. 110.

**N. D. Strazhesko Research Institute of Clinical Medicine:** Ul. Saksaganskogo 75, Kiev GSP-150; f. 1936; cardiovascular diseases; 110 mems.; library of 60,000 vols.; Dir. Prof. A. I. GRITSYUK.

**Sverdlovsk Institute of Physical Curative Methods and Spa Treatment:** Pl. Kommunarov, Sverdlovsk.

**Tomsk Institute of Physiotherapy and Spa Treatment:** Ul. Rosa Luxembourg 1.

**U.S.S.R. Antibiotics Research Institute:** Nagatinskaya ul. 3a, Moscow.

**Uzbekistan Institute of Spa Treatment and Physiotherapy (Semashko Institute):** Labzak 13, Tashkent.

## MUSIC

**Astrakhan State Conservatoire:** Astrakhan, Sovietskaya ul. 28; departments: conducting, orchestral instruments, extra-mural studies.

UNION OF SOVIET SOCIALIST REPUBLICS

**Azerbaijan S.S.R. U. Gajibekov State Conservatoire:** Baku, Ul. Dimitrova 98; f. 1920; piano, orchestral instruments, folk instruments, singing, conducting of chorus, composition; 180 lecturers; 800 students; library of 200,000 vols. and 24,000 scores; Rector A. I. GADZHIEV.

**Byelorussian State Conservatoire:** Internatsionalnaya ul. 30, Minsk, Byelorussian S.S.R.; f. 1932; piano, orchestral and folk instruments, composition, etc.; 150 teachers; 1,100 students; library of 95,060 vols.; Rector V. V. OLOVNIKOV.

**Donetsk Musical-Pedagogical Institute:** Donetsk, Ul. Artena 44, Ukrainian S.S.R.; departments: orchestral instruments, chorus conducting, singing, extra-mural studies.

**Erevan Komitas State Conservatoire:** Erevan, Ul. Sayatnovy 1a; f. 1926; piano, orchestral instruments, singing, conducting of chorus, composition; library of 43,000 vols.

**Far-Eastern Pedagogical Institute of Arts:** Vladivostok, Ul. 1 Maya 3; piano, orchestral instruments, folk instruments, singing, conducting of chorus, acting.

**Gnessiny State Musical and Pedagogical Institute:** Moscow G-69, Ul. Vorovskogo 30/36; f. 1944; piano, orchestral instruments, folk instruments, singing, conducting of chorus, composition, musicology; 310 teachers; 1,246 students; library of 190,000 vols.; Rector V. I. MININ; publs. *Annals*, study books, etc.

**Gorky M. I. Glinka State Conservatoire:** Gorky, Ul. Piskunova 40; f. 1946; piano, orchestral and folk instruments, singing, conducting of chorus, composition, 90 teachers; 700 students; library of 61,000 vols.; Rector G. S. DOMBAYEV.

**Kazakh S.S.R. Kurmangazy State Institute of Arts:** Alma-Ata, Kommunichesky prospekt 90; piano, orchestral and folk instruments, singing, conducting of chorus, drama, composition; library of 56,000 vols.

**Kazan State Conservatoire:** Ul. Boshaya Krasnaya 38, Kazan, Tatar A.S.S.R.; f. 1945; piano, orchestral and folk instruments, voice, chorus training, composition; 120 teachers; 700 students; library of 100,000 vols.; Rector N. G. ZHIGANOV.

**Kharkov State Institute of Arts:** Kharkov, Ploshchad Teveleva 1113; piano, orchestral and folk instruments, singing, chorus training, composition, drama; library of 100,000 vols.

**Kiev P. I. Tchaikovsky Conservatoire:** Kiev, Ul. K. Marxa, 1-3/II; f. 1913; faculties: piano, history and theory, composers, orchestra, conductors and singing; 220 teachers; 950 students; library of 198,403 vols.; Librarian R. P. SABADASH; Rector I. F. LYASHENKO.

**Kishinev G. Musichesku State Conservatoire:** Kishinev, Ul. Sadovaya 87; f. 1940; piano, orchestral and folk instruments, singing, conducting of chorus, composition, drama; 220 teachers; 1,050 students; library of 151,860 vols.; Rector A. K. SUSLOV.

**Latvian S.S.R. Yazep Vitol State Conservatoire:** Riga, Ul. Krishyana Barona 1; f. 1919; piano, orchestral and folk instruments, singing, conducting of chorus, composition, drama, musical comedy; 140 teachers; 520 students; library of 110,000 vols.; Rector Y. A. OZOLIM.

**Leningrad N. A. Rimsky-Korsakov State Conservatoire (Order of Lenin):** Teatralnaya pl. 3, Leningrad; f. 1862; piano, orchestral and folk instruments, singing, operatic, symphonic and choral conducting, composition, opera and ballet stage management; 275 teachers; 1,700 students; library of 227,000 vols.; Rector P. A. SOREBRYAKOV.

**Lithuanian State Conservatoire:** Pr. Lenin 42, Vilnius, Lithuanian S.S.R.; f. 1949; faculties of piano, orchestral, vocal and folk music, and the theory of music; library of 116,579 vols.; 629 students; Rector Prof. J. KARNAVIČIUS; publ. *Menotyra* (Science of Art).

**Lvov M. V. Lysenko State Conservatoire:** Vul. Boyko 5, Lvov, Ukrainian S.S.R.; f. 1903; piano, orchestral and folk instruments, chorus training, composition, singing; 156 teachers; 1,000 students; library of 113,231 vols.; Dir. Z. O. DASHAK.

**Moscow P. I. Tchaikovsky State Conservatoire:** Moscow K-9, Ul. Gerzena 13; f. 1866; faculties: piano, orchestra, theory and composers, singing, choral conducting; 286 teachers; 1,159 students; library of 670,000 vols.; Rector Prof. A. V. SVESHNIKOV, People's Artist of the U.S.S.R.

**Novosibirsk M. I. Glinka State Conservatoire:** Sovetskaya Ul. 31, Novosibirsk 99; f. 1956; piano, orchestral and folk instruments, chorus training, voice, theory and composition; library of 75,000 vols.; Rector Asst. Prof. E. G. GURENKO.

**Odessa A. V. Nezhdanova State Conservatoire:** Odessa, Ul. Ostrovidova 63; f. 1913; piano, orchestral and folk instruments, singing, conducting of chorus; 140 teachers; 680 students; library of 100,000 vols.; Rector V. P. POVZUN.

**Rostov State Institute of Pedagogics and Music:** Rostov-on-Don, Budennovsky pr. 23; f. 1967; faculties: Orchestra, Theory and Composition; 107 teachers; 527 students; library of 80,000 vols.; Rector E. BELODED.

**Saratov L. V. Sobinov State Conservatoire:** Saratov, Prospekt Kirova 1; piano, orchestral and folk instruments, conducting of chorus; library of 52,000 vols.

**Tallinn State Conservatoire:** 200015 Tallinn, Vabaduse pst. 130, Estonian SSR; f. 1919; departments: singing, orchestral instruments, chorus conducting; 134 teachers; 554 students; library of 60,000 vols.; Rector V. A. ALUMYAE.

**Tashkent State Conservatoire:** Pushkinskaya 31, Tashkent, Uzbek S.S.R.; piano, orchestral and folk instruments, voice, operatic, symphonic and choral conducting, composition; library of 92,000 vols.

**Tbilisi V. Sarajishvili State Conservatoire:** Tbilisi, Ul. Griboedova 8; f. 1917; piano, singing, conducting of chorus, composition, conducting of opera and symphony, folk and orchestral instruments, chamber ensembles; 250 teachers; 1,300 students; library of 100,000 vols.; Rector S. F. TSINTSADZE.

**Ufa State Institute of Fine Arts:** Ufa, Ul. Lenina 14, Bashkir, ASSR; departments: orchestral instruments, folk music, chorus conducting, drama production, cinema and film acting, extra-mural studies, singing.

**Urals M. P. Mussorgsky State Conservatoire:** Sverdlovsk Pr. Lenina 26; piano, orchestral and folk instruments, singing, conducting of chorus, composition, musical comedy; library of 83,000 vols.

## SOCIAL SCIENCE

**Academy of Social Sciences:** Moscow, Sadovaya-Kudrinskaya ul. 9; f. 1946; faculties of Philosophy, Scientific Communism, Political Economy, History of the Communist Party of the Soviet Union, Ideology, Social Psychology, Law, Socialist Culture, International Communist Movement, Literary Criticism, Art Criticism and Journalism; 2 research institutes of Soviet Society and Scientific Atheism; library of 2,000,000 vols.; Rector V. MEDVEDYEV.

## THEATRE AND CINEMATOGRAPHY

**All-Union State Institute of Cinematography:** Tretii Selskochosyaistveny proezd 3, Moscow; f. 1919; drama and cinema, production, direction, shooting, screen play and script writing, economics of cinematography; library of 147,000 vols.; 187 teachers; 1,500 students; Rector VITALII JDAN; publs. *Tvorchestvo Molodykh* (Creations of Young Artists), etc.

**Azerbaijan M. A. Aliev Dramatic Institute:** Ul. Karaganova 13, Baku, Azerbaijan S.S.R.

**B. V. Shchukin Drama School attached to the E. B. Vakhtangov State Theatre:** Ul. Vakhtangova 12a, Moscow.

**Byelorussian State Theatrical and Art Institute:** Leninsky prospekt 81, Minsk, Byelorussian S.S.R.; f. 1945; drama and cinema, decorative and applied arts; Rector E. P. GERASIMOVICH.

**Georgian S. Rustaveli State Institute of Dramatic Art:** Pr. S. Rustaveli 17, Tbilisi, Georgian S.S.R.; drama and cinema, musical comedy, stage management; library of 85,000 vols.

**Kiev I. K. Karpenko-Kary State Theatrical Institute:** Kreshchatik 52, Kiev, Ukrainian S.S.R.; drama and cinema, stage management of drama and ballet, film direction; library of 33,000 vols.

**Leningrad Institute of Cinematography:** Ul. Pravdy 13, Leningrad; depts.: Electrical Engineering, Engineering, Chemical Technology; library of 137,000 vols.; Extra-Mural Department.

**Leningrad State Institute of Theatre, Music and Cinematography:** Leningrad, Ul. Mokhovaya 34; f. 1918; drama and cinema, stage management, theatrical equipment and stage painting; 130 teachers; 1,100 students; research department with 52 mems.; library of 204,000 vols.; Rector V. F. SHISHKIN.

**M. S. Shchepkin Drama School attached to the Maly Theatre:** Neglinnaya 6, Moscow.

**State A. V. Lunacharsky Institute of Dramatic Art:** Sobinovsky per. 4, Moscow; drama and cinema, musical comedy, general stage management; library of 111,000 vols.

**Tashkent A. N. Ostrovsky State Theatrical and Art Institute:** Tashkent, Ul. Germana Lopatina 77, Uzbek S.S.R.; f. 1945; drama and cinema, musical comedy, theatrical equipment and stage painting, graphic arts, monumental decorative arts, decorative and applied arts; 120 teachers; 900 students; library of 65,000 vols.; Rector K. A. ABDULAYEV.

**V. I. Nemirovich-Danchenko Studio-School attached to the Moscow Art Theatre:** Pr. Khudozhestvennogo Teatra, 3a Moscow; f. 1948; drama and cinema, theatrical equipment and stage painting; 80 teachers; 300 students; library of 42,000 vols.; Rector V. Z. RADOMYSLENSKY.

## TRANSPORT AND COMMUNICATIONS

### (1) RAILWAYS

**All-Union Extra-Mural Institute of Railway Engineers:** Moscow, Chasovaya Ul. 22/2; faculties: Engineering, Electrical Engineering, Electrification of Railways,

Railway Maintenance, Construction, Economics, General Engineering; library of 250,000 vols.; two brs.; Rector R. I. ROBOL.

**Byelorussian Institute of Railway Engineers:** Gomel, Ul. Kirova 34; faculties: Engineering, Construction, Industrial and Civil Construction; library of 153,000 vols.; Evening and Extra-Mural Faculties; Rector P. A. SYTSKO.

**Dnepropetrovsk Institute of Railway Engineers:** Dnepropetrovsk, ul. Universitetskaya 2; f. 1930; faculties: Engineering, Electrification of Railways, Railway Maintenance, Construction, Computer Technology, Industrial and Civil Construction, Bridges and Tunnels; library of 473,000 vols.; Evening, Extra-Mural and General Engineering Faculties; Rector A. R. YUSHCHENKO.

**Khabarovsk Institute of Railway Engineers:** Khabarovsk, Ul. Serysheva 47; f. 1939; faculties: Engineering, Railway Maintenance, Construction, Industrial and Civil Construction; 300 teachers; 7,500 students; library of 450,000 vols.; Evening and Extra-Mural Faculties.; Rector V. I. DMITRIENKO.

**Kharkov S. M. Kirov Institute of Railway Engineers:** Kharkov, Ploshchad Feuerbacha 7; faculties: Railway Maintenance, Mechanics, Automation, Telemechanics and Communication, Construction, Engineering-Economics; library of 386,000 vols.; Evening, Extra-Mural and General Engineering Faculties; Rector A. P. IGNATIEV.

**Leningrad Academician V. N. Obraztov Institute of Railway Engineers:** Leningrad, Moskovsky prospekt 9; f. 1809; library of 1,200,000 vols.; 700 teachers; faculties: Civil Engineering, Mechanics, Electrical Engineering, Bridge and Tunnel Construction, Railway Operation; Correspondence and Evening departments; Rector E. Y. KRASKOVSKY; publ. *Proceedings.*

**Moscow Institute of Engineers:** Moscow, Ul. Obraztsova 15; faculties: Engineering, Power, Automation and Computing, Electrification of Railways, Maintenance, Construction, Bridges and Tunnels, Economics; library of 865,000 vols.; Evening Faculty; Rector F. P. KOCHNEV.

**Novosibirsk Institute of Railway Engineers:** Novosibirsk, Ul. Dusi Kovalchuk 191; faculties: Railway Maintenance, Construction, Industrial and Civil Construction, Bridges and Tunnels, Road Building Machinery, Economics; library of 394,000 vols.; Evening and Extra-Mural Faculties; Rector N. P. KONDAKOV.

**Omsk Institute of Railway Engineers:** Omsk, Ul. Karla Marxa 35; f. 1930; faculties: Engineering, Electrical Transport, Electrical Engineering; 250 teachers; 5,500 students; library of 270,000 vols.; Extra-Mural Faculty; Rector A. A. SEREGIN.

**Rostov-on-Don Institute of Railway Engineers:** Rostov-on-Don, Ul. Lenina 44; faculties: Power, Railway Maintenance, Road Building Machinery; library of 220,000 vols.; Evening and Extra-Mural Faculties; Rector B. I. DANIN.

**Tashkent Institute of Railway Engineers:** Tashkent, Oboronnaya Ul. 1; f. 1931; faculties: Engineering, Automation and Telemechanics, Railway Maintenance, Construction, Economics; f. 1931; 400 teachers; 12,000 students; library of 500,000 vols.; Evening and Extra-Mural Faculties; Rector M. F. PRASOLOV.

**Urals Electromechanical Institute of Railway Engineering:** Sverdlovsk 79, Ul. Kolmogorova 66; f. 1956; faculties: Electromechanics, Electrical Engineering, Building Maintenance; 320 teachers; 7,500 students; library of 200,000 vols.; Evening and Extra-Mural Faculties; Rector T. V. UTKIN.

(2) WATERWAYS

**Gorky Institute of Water Transport Engineers:** Gorky, Ul. K. Minina 7; faculties: Shipbuilding, Navigation and Maintenance of Water Transport, Marine Engineering; library of 250,000 vols.; Evening Department and Extra-Mural Faculty.

**Kaliningrad Higher School of Marine Engineering:** Kaliningradskaya obl., Ul. Molodezhnaya 6; faculties: navigation, marine engineering, radio engineering; evening and extra-mural departments.

**Leningrad Admiral S. O. Makarov Higher School of Marine Engineering:** Leningrad, Vasilyevsky ostrov, Kosaya Liniya 15-a; faculties: Arctics, Navigation, Marine Engineering, Radio Engineering, Electrical Engineering; library of 140,000 vols.; Extra-Mural Department.

**Leningrad Institute of Water Transport:** Leningrad 198035, Dvinskaya ul. 5/7; f. 1930; library of 600,000 vols.; faculties: Waterways and Ports, Marine Engineering, Shipbuilding, Electrical Engineering, Port Handling and Transport facilities, River-Sea Navigation, Engineering, Economics; Extra-Mural Faculty; Rector V. V. BALANIN.

**Leningrad Shipbuilding Institute:** Leningrad, Ul. Lotsmanskaya 3; f. 1902; faculties: Shipbuilding, Machine Building, Design; library of 355,000 vols.; Evening and Extra-Mural Faculties; one br.; Rector Prof. E. V. TOVSTIKH.

**Murmansk Higher School of Marine Engineering:** Murmansk, Sportivnaya ul. 13/6; f. 1950; faculties: Navigation, Marine Engineering; 140 teachers; 3,000 students; library of 100,000 vols.; Extra-Mural Department; Rector E. I. PORTNOV.

**Nikolaev Admiral S. O. Makarov Shipbuilding Institute:** Nikolaev, Ul. Skorohodova 5; faculties: Shipbuilding, Machine Building; library of 104,000 vols.; Evening and General Engineering Faculties.

**Novosibirsk Institute of Water Transport Engineers:** Novosibirsk, Ul. Shchetinkina 33; f. 1951; faculties: Waterways and Ports, Navigation and Maintenance of Water Transport, Ship Engineers; 200 teachers; 5,000 students; library of 223,000 vols.; Evening Department and Extra-Mural Faculty; A. M. PLATONOV.

**Odessa Higher School of Marine Engineering:** Odessa, Ul. Perekopskoy Pobedy 20; faculties: Navigation, Ship Engineers, Electrical Engineering; library of 135,000 vols.; Extra-Mural Faculty; Rector I. G. SCHLEPCHENKO.

**Odessa Institute of Water Transport Engineers:** Odessa, B-29, Ul. Mechnikova 34; faculties: Hydraulic Engineering, Shipbuilding, Ship Engineers, Maintenance, Engineering; library of 165,000 vols.; Evening and Extra-Mural Faculty.

**Vladivostok Higher School of Marine Engineering:** Vladivostok, Verkhnyaya Portovaya ul. 50-a; faculties: Navigation, Ship Engineers, Electrical Engineering; library of 111,000 vols.; Evening and Extra-Mural Faculty; Rector A. S. FROLOV.

(3) MOTOR TRANSPORT

**Kharkov Motor and Highways Institute:** Kharkov, Ul. Petrobskogo 25; f. 1930; faculties: Road Building, Motor Vehicles, Economics of Engineering, Road-

Building Machinery; library of 360,000 vols.; Evening and Extra-Mural Faculties; 3,000 students; Rector B. V. RESHTNIKOV.

**Kiev Motor Vehicles Institute:** Kiev, Ul. Suvorova 1; f. 1944; faculties: Road Building, Motor Vehicles; 300 teachers; 6,100 students; library of 250,000 vols.; Evening Faculty; Rector E. P. VERIZHENKO.

**Moscow Automobile and Road Construction Institute (MADI):** Moscow A-319, Leningradski Prospekt 64; f. 1930; faculties: Road Building, Bridge Construction, Motor Transport, Airport Construction, Road Building Machinery; Evening and Extra-Mural Faculties; Departments of Advanced and Postgraduate Studies; library of 500,000 vols.; 650 teachers; 8,000 students; Rector Prof. Dr. L. L. AFFANASIEV.; publ. *Scientific Papers of the Moscow Automobile and Road Construction Institute* (irregular).

**Siberian V. V. Kuibyshev Motor and Highways Institute:** Omsk, Prospekt Mira 5; f. 1930; faculties: Road Building, Motor Transport, Road Building Machinery; 320 teachers; 5,000 students; library of 500,000 vols.; Evening and Extra-Mural Faculties; Rector E. V. GNATYUK.

(4) AVIATION

**Kazan A. N. Tupolev Aviation Institute:** 420084 Kazan, Ul. K. Marxa 10; faculties: Aircraft Building, Aircraft Engines, Aircraft Instruments and Automata, Radio Engineering; library of 300,000 vols.; Evening and Extra-Mural Faculty.

**Kharkov Aviation Institute:** 310084 Kharkov, Ul. Shkalova 17; faculties: Aircraft Building, Aircraft Engines, Radio Engineering; library of 222,000 vols.

**Kiev Institute of Civil Aviation:** Kiev, Prospekt Komarova 1; faculties: Engineering, Radio Engineering, Electrical Engineering; library of 182,000 vols.; Extra-Mural Department; Rector N. L. GOLEGO.

**Kuibyshev Aviation Institute:** Kuibyshev, Ul. Molodogvardeyskaya 151; faculties: Aircraft Building, Radio Equipment Design, Aircraft Engines, Aircraft Engine Exploitation, Metal Working by Pressure; library of 167,000 vols.; Evening Faculty and Extra-Mural Department.

**Leningrad (Order of Lenin) Academy of Civil Aviation:** Leningrad, Liteyny prospekt 48; faculty: Exploitation of Air Transport; Rector P. V. KARTAMYSHEV.

**Leningrad Institute of Aircraft Instrumentation:** Leningrad, Ul. Herzena 67; faculties: Aviation Instruments and Automata, Radio Engineering; library of 280,000 vols.; Evening and Extra-Mural Faculties.

**Moscow Institute of Aviation Technology:** Moscow, Petrovka 27; faculties: Aviation Engineering, Aviation Technology, Radio Electronic Equipment; library of 194,000 vols.; Evening Faculty.

**Moscow Sergo Orjonikidze Aviation Institute:** Moscow A-80, Volokolamskoe chaussée 4; faculties: Aircraft Building, Aircraft Engines, Automatic Control of Aircraft, Radio Engineering, Instrument Making and Automation, Economics; library of 909,000 vols.; Evening and Extra-Mural Faculties.

**Riga Institute of Civil Aviation Engineers:** Riga, Ul. Lomonosova 1; faculties: Engineering, Electrical Engineering, Radio Engineering; library of 360,000 vols.; Rector A. I. PUGACHEV.

**Ufa Sergo Orjonikidze Aviation Institute:** Ufa, Ul. K. Marxa 12-b; faculties: Aircraft Engines, Engineering Technology; library of 160,000 vols.; Evening and Extra-Mural Faculties.

# UNITED ARAB EMIRATES
Population 1,063,000

## ABU DHABI

**British Council:** British Embassy, P.O.B. 248; Rep. C. H. MOGFORD.

**Centre for Documentation and Research:** Old Palace, P.O.B. 2380; f. 1968; attached to the Ministry of Foreign Affairs; collects manuscripts, documents, books, maps and articles relevant to the Arabian Gulf and the Arabian peninsula, and carries out research on subjects related to this area; library of 5,000 vols. in Arabic, English and other languages; Dir. MOHAMMAD MORSI ABDULLAH, PH.D.; publ. *Arabian Gulf Research Review* (quarterly).

**Public Library:** P.O.B. 17.

**Archaeological Museum:** Al Ain; archaeological sites at Buraimi and Umm Al Nar island.

### UNITED ARAB EMIRATES UNIVERSITY
AL AIN, P.O.B. 15551
Founded 1974.

State control; Language of instruction: Arabic; Academic year: two semesters.

*Chancellor:* H.E. SAEED ABDULLAH SALMAN.
*Rector:* Prof. Dr. ABDUL AZIZ AL-BASSAM.
*Administrative Secretary:* AHMED ABDULLAH BU HUSSEIN.
*Librarian:* AHMED NASIR AL-NUAIMI.

Library of 28,350 vols.
Number of teachers: *c.* 200.
Number of students: 3,000.

#### DEANS:
*Faculty of Arts:* Prof. Dr. JAMIL SAEED IBRAHIM.
*Faculty of Sciences:* Prof. Dr. MUHAMMED YOUSEF HASSAN.
*Faculty of Management and Political Science:* Prof. Dr. ABDUL HAFEZ EL-KURDY.
*Faculty of Islamic Shariaa and Law:* Prof. Dr. TUAIMAH AL-JURF.
*Faculty of Education:* Prof. Dr. SAYYED M. GHUNAIM.

Faculties of engineering and agriculture are due to open shortly.

#### HEADS OF DEPARTMENT:
*Chemistry:* Prof. Dr. ABDUL QADER AL-SAYYED MANSOUR.
*Physics:* Prof. Dr. JASSIM M. AL HUSSAINI.
*Mathematics:* Prof. Dr. MUHAMMED YOUSEF RIFAII.
*Geology:* Prof. Dr. MUHAMMED YOUSEF HASSAN.
*Zoology:* Prof. Dr. BADRI A. AHMED AL-AANI.
*Geography:* Prof. Dr. YOUSEF ABU AL-HAJAJ IBRAHIM.
*Social Science:* Prof. Dr. AATIF AMIN WASFI.
*Philosophy:* Prof. Dr. YAHYA SADIQ AL-DIJAILI.
*History:* Prof. Dr. ABDUL RAHMAN AL-HAJJI.
*Arabic Language:* Prof. Dr. JAMIL SAEED IBRAHIM.
*Law:* Prof. Dr. OMAR AL-SAEED RAMADAN.
*Islamic Shariaa:* Prof. Dr. ABDUL RAHMAN M. AL-SABOONI.
*Political Science:* Prof. Dr. ALI AHMED ABDUL QADER.
*Education:* Prof. Dr. NAIMAH MUHAMMED EID.

## DUBAI

**British Council:** British Embassy, P.O.B. 65; f. 1970; library of 9,969 vols., 18 periodicals; Dir. J. E. DAWSON; Librarian M. S. ABBAS.

**Dubai Public Library:** P.O.B. 67; 15,000 vols. in Arabic, English and Urdu on all subjects, including reference works.

## RAS AL KHAIMAH

**UNDP/FAO Assisted Project: Water and Soil Investigations for Agricultural Development:** P.O.B. 176, Ras Al Khaimah; f. 1975; run in conjunction with the Ministry of Agriculture and Fisheries; conducts research into irrigation, plant protection, vegetable varieties, fertilizer application rates, etc.; *c.* 40 staff, including 8 experts from FAO; library of 427 vols.; Project Man. M. HAMAD.

# UNITED KINGDOM
Population 55,883,000

## LEARNED SOCIETIES AND PROFESSIONAL ASSOCIATIONS

### General
**THE ROYAL SOCIETY**
6 CARLTON HOUSE TERRACE,
LONDON S.W.1
Telephone: 839-5561.

Founded 1660 for the promotion of natural knowledge. Incorporated by Royal Charter in 1662.

*President:* Sir ANDREW FIELDING HUXLEY, M.A.
*Treasurer and Vice-President:* Sir JOHN MASON, D.SC.
*Biological Secretary and Vice-President:* Sir DAVID PHILLIPS, PH.D.
*Physical Secretary and Vice-President:* Dr. T. M. SUGDEN.
*Foreign Secretary and Vice-President:* Sir MICHAEL STOKER, C.B.E., M.D.
*Executive Secretary:* Dr. R. W. J. KEAY, C.B.E.
*Librarian:* N. H. ROBINSON.
Library: see Libraries.

Publications: *Philosophical Transactions, Proceedings, Year Book, Biographical Memoirs of Fellows, Notes and Records, Bulletins.*

Fellows:
ABRAHAM, EDWARD PENLEY, C.B.E., M.A., D.PHIL., biochemist.
ADAMS, JOHN BERTRAM, C.M.G., physicist.
ADAMS, JOHN FRANK, PH.D., mathematician.
**ADDISON, CYRIL CLIFFORD**, PH.D., D.SC., F.INST.P., F.R.I.C., inorganic chemist.
ADRIAN, Hon. RICHARD HUME, M.A., M.B., B.CHIR., biophysicist
AKHTAR, MUHAMMAD, biochemist.
ALLEN, Sir GEOFFREY, chemist.
ALLEN, JOHN FRANK, M.A., PH.D., physicist.
ALLEN, JOHN ROBERT LAURENCE, geologist.
ALLEN, PERCIVAL, M.A., PH.D., geologist.
**ALLIBONE, THOMAS EDWARD**, C.B.E., D.SC., PH.D., electrical engineer.
**AMOROSO, EMMANUEL CIPRIANO**, C.B.E., B.CH., PH.D., B.A.O., physiologist.
ANDERSON, DONALD THOMAS, PH.D., D.SC., biologist.
ANDERSON, EPHRAIM SAUL, C.B.E., M.D., virologist.
**ANDERSON, JOHN STUART**, PH.D., M.SC., chemist.
ANDREW, SYDNEY PERCY SMITH, chemist.
ANDREWES, Sir CHRISTOPHER (HOWARD), B.SC., M.D., F.R.C.P., pathologist.
ASH, ERIC ALBERT, PH.D., electrical engineer.
ASHBY, OF BRANDON, Baron, ERIC, M.A., D.SC., D.LITT., botanist.
ASHBY, MICHAEL FARRIES, engineer.
**ASHTON, NORMAN HENRY**, D.SC., M.R.C.S., L.R.C.P., F.R.C.P., ophthalmologist and pathologist.
ASKONAS, BRIGITTE ALICE, PH.D., immunologist.
ATIYAH, MICHAEL FRANCIS, PH.D., mathematician.
AUERBACH, CHARLOTTE, PH.D., D.SC., animal geneticist.
BACON, FRANCIS THOMAS, O.B.E., fuel scientist.
BADDILEY, Sir JAMES, PH.D., D.SC., chemist.
**BAGNOLD**, Brigadier RALPH ALGER, O.B.E., M.A., A.M.I.E.E., F.R.G.S., geophysicist.
BAKER, ALAN, mathematician.
BAKER, OF WINDRUSH, Baron, JOHN FLEETWOOD, O.B.E., mechanical engineer.
BAKER, JOHN RANDAL, M.A., PH.D., D.SC., cytologist.
BAKER, PETER FREDERICK, physiologist.
**BAKER, WILSON**, chemist.
BALDWIN, JACK EDWARD, PH.D., chemist.
BAMFORD, **CLEMENT HENRY**, industrial chemist.

BANGHAM, ALEC DOUGLAS, PH.D., biophysicist.
**BARCROFT, HENRY**, M.D., M.R.C.P., physiologist.
BARLOW, HAROLD EVERARD MONTEAGLE, electrical engineer.
BARLOW. HORACE BASIL, physiologist.
BARR, MURRAY LLEWELLYN, anatomist.
BARRER, RICHARD MALING, chemist.
BARRINGTON, ERNEST JAMES WILLIAM, zoologist.
BARTLETT, MAURICE STEVENSON, statistician.
BARTLETT, NEIL, chemist.
BARTON, Sir DEREK (HAROLD RICHARD), chemist.
BASINSKI, ZBIGNIEW STANISLAW, metallurgist.
**BATCHELOR, GEORGE KEITH**, PH.D., mathematician
BATEMAN, LESLIE CLIFFORD, C.M.G., D.SC., chemist.
BATES, Sir DAVID ROBERT, D.SC., M.R.I.A., mathematician.
BATTERSBY, ALAN RUSHTON, chemist.
BAWN, CECIL EDWIN HENRY, C.B.E., PH.D., chemist.
BEALE, EVELYN MARTIN LANSDOWNE, mathematician.
BEALE, GEOFFREY HERBERT, M.B.E., PH.D., geneticist.
BEAMENT, JAMES WILLIAM LONGMAN, SC.D., zoologist.
BELL, GEORGE DOUGLAS HUTTON, C.B.E., PH.D., botanist.
BELL, JOHN STEWART, PH.D., physicist.
BELL, ROBERT EDWARD, nuclear physicist.
**BELL, RONALD PERCY**, M.A., chemist.
BENJAMIN, THOMAS BROOKE, PH.D., physicist.
BERGEL, FRANZ, chemist.
BERRILL, NORMAN JOHN, PH.D., D.SC., zoologist.
BEVERTON, RAYMOND JOHN HEAPHY, C.B.E., M.A., ecologist.
BEYNON, JOHN HERBERT, chemist.
BEYNON, Sir WILLIAM (JOHN GRANVILLE), C.B.E., D.SC., PH.D., physicist.
BIGGS, PETER MARTIN, PH.D., D.SC., zoologist.
BILBY, BRUCE ALEXANDER, PH.D., materials engineer.
BILLINGHAM, RUPERT EVERETT, zoologist.
BINGHAM, JOHN, plant geneticist.
**BINNIE, ALFRED MAURICE**, engineer.
BINNIE, GEOFFREY MORSE, civil engineer.
BIRCH, ARTHUR JOHN, PH.D., M.SC., organic chemist.
BIRCH, BRYAN JOHN, PH.D., mathematician.
BISHOP, ANN, SC.D., chemist.
BISHOP, RICHARD EVELYN DONOHUE, mechanical engineer.
BISHOP, PETER ORLEBAR, M.B., B.S., D.SC., physiologist.
BLACK, Sir JAMES WHYTE, M.B., CH.B., pharmacologist.
BLACKMAN, MOSES, physicist.
BLASCHKO, HERMANN KARL FELIX, M.D., PH.D., pharmacologist.
BLAXTER, Sir KENNETH LYON, D.SC., agriculturist.
**BLEANEY, BREBIS**, C.B.E., M.A., D.PHIL., physicist.
BLIN-STOYLE, ROGER JOHN, theoretical physicist.
BLOW, DAVID MERVYN, PH.D., crystallographer.
BOARDMAN, NORMAN KEITH, PH.D., biochemist.
BODMER, WALTER FRED, PH.D., geneticist.
BOKSENBERG, ALEXANDER, PH.D., astronomer.
BOLTON, JOHN GATENBY, B.A., radio-astronomer.
BOND, GEORGE, botanist.
BONDI, Sir HERMANN, K.C.B., M.A., mathematician.
BONSALL, FRANK FEATHERSTONE, M.A., D.SC., mathematician.
BOON, WILLIAM ROBERT, PH.D., chemist.
BOOTH, ERIC STUART, C.B.E., engineer.
BORN, GUSTAV VICTOR RUDOLF, pharmacologist.
BOTT, MARTIN HAROLD PHILLIPS, M.A., PH.D., geophysicist.
BOWEN, EDWARD GEORGE, C.B.E., PH.D., radio astronomer.
BOWIE, STANLEY HAY UMPHRAY, D.SC., F.R.S.E., F.I.M.M., geochemist.
BOYCOTT, BRIAN BLUNDELL, F.I.BIOL., M.S.E.B., F.Z.S., zoologist and biophysicist.
BOYD, Brig. Sir JOHN (SMITH KNOX), O.B.E., M.D., bacteriologist.
BOYD, ROBERT LEWIS FULLARTON, C.B.E., physicist.
BOYSE, EDWARD ARTHUR, PH.D., biologist.
BRADLEY, DANIEL JOSEPH, physicist (optics).
BRADLEY, DONALD CHARLTON, inorganic chemist.

BRENNER, SYDNEY, D.PHIL., molecular biologist.
**BRIGGS, GEORGE EDWARD, M.A., botanist.**
BRINDLEY, GILES SKEY, M.D., neurophysiologist.
BROADBENT, DONALD ERIC, C.B.E., SC.D., psychologist.
BROADBENT, EDWARD GRANVILLE, aeronautical engineer.
**BROCKHOUSE, BERTRAM NEVILLE, physicist.**
BROOKSBY, JOHN BURNS, C.B.E., veterinarian.
BROWN, GEORGE MALCOLM, M.A., D.PHIL., D.SC., F.R.S.E., F.G.S., geologist.
**BROWN, ROBERT, D.SC., botanist.**
**BROWN, ROBERT HANBURY, radio-astronomer.**
BROWNING, KEITH ANTHONY, PH.D., meteorologist.
BUCKINGHAM, AMYAND DAVID, PH.D., chemist.
**BUDDEN, KENNETH GEORGE, PH.D., physicist.**
BULBRING, EDITH, pharmacologist.
BUNN, CHARLES WILLIAM, D.SC., crystallographer.
BURBIDGE, ELEANOR MARGARET, PH.D., astronomer.
**BURBIDGE, GEOFFREY RONALD, PH.D., astronomer.**
BURCH, CECIL REGINALD, C.B.E., PH.D., physicist.
BURCHAM, WILLIAM ERNEST, M.A., PH.D., physicist.
BURGEN, Sir ARNOLD STANLEY VINCENT, pharmacologist.
BURKE, PHILIP GEORGE, PH.D., M.I.R.A., theoretical physicist.
BURKILL, JOHN CHARLES, SC.D., mathematician.
BURKITT, DENIS PARSONS, C.M.G., D.SC., medical biochemist.
**BURNET, Sir (FRANK) MACFARLANE, O.M., K.B.E., M.D., PH.D., biologist.**
BURNS, BENEDICT DELISLE, M.R.C.S., physiologist.
BURTON, KENNETH, M.A., PH.D., biochemist.
BUTLER, CLIFFORD CHARLES, physicist.
BUTLER, COLIN GASKING, O.B.E., apiarist.

CADOGAN, JOHN IVAN GEORGE, chemist.
CAIRNS, HUGH JOHN FORSTER, PH.D., bacteriologist.
CALLAN, HAROLD GARNET, cytogeneticist.
CALLOW, ROBERT KENNETH, M.A., PH.D., biochemist.
CALNE, ROY YORKE, M.A., F.R.C.S., surgeon.
CAMPBELL, FERGUS WILLIAM, M.A., PH.D., neurophysiologist.
CARRINGTON, ALAN, PH.D., M.A., F.C.S., chemist.
CARTWRIGHT, Dame MARY (LUCY), D.B.E., M.A., D.PH., mathematician.
CASEY, RAYMOND, palaeontologist.
CASSELS, JAMES MACDONALD, physicist.
CASSELS, JOHN WILLIAM SCOTT, PH.D., mathematician.
CATCHESIDE, DAVID GUTHRIE, D.SC., plant cytogeneticist.
CHADWICK, PETER, PH.D., mathematician.
CHALONER, WILLIAM GILBERT, botanist.
CHANDRASEKHAR, SUBRAHMANYAN, M.A., PH.D. astronomer.
CHARNLEY, Sir JOHN, C.B.E., M.B., CH.B., D.SC., F.R.C.S., orthopaedic surgeon.
CHARNOCK, HENRY, oceanographer.
CHATT, JOSEPH, C.B.E., SC.D., chemist.
CHESTERS, JOHN HUGH, O.B.E., D.SC.TECH., metallurgist.
CHIBNALL, ALBERT CHARLES, PH.D., SC.D., biochemist.
CHRISTIAN, JOHN WYRILL, D.PHIL., metallurgist
**CHRISTOPHERSON, Sir DERMAN (GUY), O.B.E., D.PHIL., mechanical engineer.**
CLAPHAM, ARTHUR ROY, C.B.E., botanist.
CLARKE, Sir CYRIL ASTLEY, K.B.E., M.D., SC.D., F.R.C.P., geneticist.
CLARKE, PATRICIA HANNAH, biochemist.
CLEMO, GEORGE ROGER, D.SC., F.R.I.C., chemist.
**COALES, JOHN FLAVELL, C.B.E., M.A., physicist.**
COCHRAN, WILLIAM, PH.D., crystallographer.
**COCKERELL, Sir CHRISTOPHER (SYDNEY), C.B.E., engineer.**
COHEN, SYDNEY, PH.D., M.D., pathologist.
COHN, PAUL MORITZ, mathematician.
COLLAR, ARTHUR RODERICK, C.B.E., aeronautical engineer.
**COOK, ALAN HUGH, D.SC., meteorologist.**
COOK, ARTHUR HERBERT, D.SC., PH.D., F.R.I.C., organic chemist.
**COOK, Sir WILLIAM (RICHARD JOSEPH), KT., C.B., atomic physicist.**
COOKE, GEORGE WILLIAM, C.B.E., PH.D., chemist.
**COOKSON, RICHARD CLIVE, chemist.**
COOMBS, ROBERT ROYSTON AMOS, pathologist.
COOPER, JOHN PHILIP, D.SC., plant physiologist.
COOPER, LESLIE HUGH NORMAN, D.SC., chemist.
COPP, DOUGLAS HAROLD, physiologist.
**CORNER, EDRED JOHN HENRY, M.A., botanist.**
CORNFORTH, Sir JOHN WARCUP, M.SC., D.PHIL., organic chemist.
COSSLETT, VERNON ELLIS, SC.D., electron physicist.
**COTTRELL, Sir ALAN HOWARD, PH.D., D.SC., metallurgist.**
COWLEY, JOHN MAXWELL, physicist.
COWLEY, ROGER ARTHUR, M.A., PH.D., physicist.
**COWLING, THOMAS GEORGE, M.A., D.PH., mathematician.**
COX, DAVID ROXBEE, M.A., PH.D., mathematician.
**COX, Sir (ERNEST) GORDON, K.B.E., T.D., D.SC., F.R.I.C., F.INST.P., chemist.**

COXETER, HAROLD SCOTT MACDONALD, PH.D., mathematician.
CRAIG, DAVID PARKER, chemist.
**CRAIGIE, JOHN HUBERT, S.M., A.B., M.SC., PH.D., D.SC., LL.D., geneticist.**
CRANE, MORLEY BENJAMIN, A.L.S., V.M.H., agriculturist.
CRICK, FRANK HARRY COMPTON, PH.D., biologist.
CRISP, DENNIS JOHN, C.B.E., M.A., PH.D., SC.D., marine biologist.
CROMBIE, LESLIE, D.SC., PH.D., chemist.
CROSS, BARRY ALBERT, M.A., PH.D., SC.D., animal physiologist.
CROSSLAND, BERNARD, mechanical and industrial engineer.
CRUICKSHANK, DURWARD WILLIAM JOHN, chemist.
CRUMPTON, MICHAEL JOSEPH, biochemist.
CULLEN, ALEXANDER LAMB, O.B.E., PH.D., D.SC.(ENG.), electrical engineer.
CURRAN, Sir SAMUEL (CROWE), PH.D., D.SC., physicist.
CURTIS, DAVID RODERICK, M.B., PH.D., F.A.A., neuropharmacologist.
CUSHING, DAVID HENRY, PH.D., marine biologist.

DACIE, Sir JOHN VIVIAN, haematologist.
DAINTON, Sir FREDERICK SYDNEY, M.A., SC.D., F.R.I.C., **physical chemist.**
DALGARNO, ALEXANDER, physicist.
DALITZ, RICHARD HENRY, physicist.
DALZIEL, KEITH, M.A., PH.D., biochemist.
DANCKWERTS, PETER VICTOR, G.C., M.B.E., chemical engineer.
**DANIELLI, JAMES FREDERIC, PH.D., D.SC., zoologist.**
DANIELS, HENRY ELLIS, statistician.
DAVIDSON, JOHN FRANK, SC.D., chemical engineer.
DAVIES, ROBERT ERNEST, biochemist.
DAWES, GEOFFREY SHARMAN, physiologist.
**DEACON, Sir GEORGE (EDWARD RAVEN), C.B.E., D.SC., physicist.**
DE BRUYNE, NORMAN ADRIAN, PH.D., physicist.
DEE, PHILIP IVOR, C.B.E., M.A., physicist.
**DEER, WILLIAM ALEXANDER, mineralogist.**
DE MAYO, PAUL, M.SC., PH.D., D. ES SC., chemist.
**DENBIGH, KENNETH GEORGE, D.SC., chemical engineer.**
DENTON, ERIC JAMES, C.B.E., SC.D., physiologist.
**DEVONS, SAMUEL, M.A., PH.D., physicist.**
**DEWAR, MICHAEL JAMES STEUART, M.A., D.PHIL., chemist.**
**DICKENS, FRANK, M.A., D.SC., PH.D., F.R.I.C., biochemist.**
**DIRAC, PAUL ADRIEN MAURICE, O.M., PH.D., mathematician.**
DITCHBURN, ROBERT WILLIAM, physicist.
DIXEY, Sir FRANK, K.C.M.G., O.B.E., D.SC., geologist.
DIXON, GORDON HENRY, PH.D., biochemist.
**DIXON, MALCOLM, SC.D., biochemist.**
DODD, JAMES MUNRO, PH.D., D.SC., F.R.S.E., zoologist
DOLL, Sir (WILLIAM) RICHARD (SHABOE,) O.B.E., M.D., statistician.
DOMB, CYRIL, M.A., PH.D., theoretical physicist.
**DOWNIE, ALLAN WATT, M.D., CH.B., D.SC., bacteriologist.**
DUNCUMB, PETER, PH.D., physicist.
DUNHAM, Sir KINGSLEY (CHARLES), D.SC., PH.D., SC.D., F.G.S., geologist.
DUNITZ, JACK DAVID, PH.D., crystallographer.
**DYSON, FREEMAN JOHN, B.A., physicist.**
DYSON, JAMES, SC.D., physicist.

EABORN, COLIN, PH.D., D.SC., organic chemist.
ECCLES, Sir JOHN (CAREW), D.PHIL., M.B., B.S., physiologist.
EDWARDS, Sir GEORGE (ROBERT), O.M., C.B.E., aeronautical engineer.
EDWARDS, JOHN HILTON, geneticist.
EDWARDS, Sir SAMUEL FREDERICK, physicist.
EGLINTON, GEOFFREY, geochemist.
ELEY, DANIEL DOUGLAS, O.B.E., physical chemist.
ELLIOT, HARRY, PH.D., physicist.
ELLIOTT, JAMES PHILIP, theoretical physicist.
ELLIOTT, MICHAEL, agriculturist.
ELLIOTT, ROGER JAMES, theoretical physicist.
ELTON, CHARLES SUTHERLAND, M.A., animal ecologist.
**EMELÉUS, HARRY JULIUS, C.B.E., M.A., D.SC., chemist.**
**ENGLEDOW, Sir FRANK (LEONARD), C.M.G., M.A., agriculturist.**
EPSTEIN, MICHAEL ANTHONY, pathologist.
ESHELBY, JOHN DOUGLAS, PH.D., crystallographer.
ESSEN, LOUIS, O.B.E., D.SC., physicist.
EVANS, Sir DAVID GWYNNE, C.B.E., bacteriologist.
EVANS, LLOYD THOMAS, D.SC., industrial scientist.
EVANS, WILLIAM CHARLES, biochemist.
EVERETT, DOUGLAS HUGH, M.B.E., physical chemist.
**EWALD, PAUL PETER, PH.D., physicist.**

FALCON, NORMAN LESLIE, geologist.
FALCONER, DOUGLAS SCOTT, PH.D., SC.D., geneticist.
FARLEY, FRANCIS JAMES MACDONALD, SC.D., physicist.
FATT, PAUL, PH.D., biophysicist.

U.K. (GREAT BRITAIN)　　　　　　　　　　　　　　　　　　　　　　　　　　　　　　　WORLD OF LEARNING

FEILDEN, GEOFFREY BERTRAM ROBERT, C.B.E., engineer.
FELDBERG, WILHELM SIEGMUND, C.B.E., M.A., M.D., physiologist.
FELL, Dame HONOR BRIDGET, PH.D., D.SC., physiologist.
FENNER, FRANK JOHN, M.B.E., M.D., B.S., D.T.M., microbiologist.
FINCHAM, JOHN ROBERT STANLEY, geneticist.
FINNEY, DAVID JOHN, C.B.E., SC.D., statistician.
FINNISTON, Sir HAROLD MONTAGUE, PH.D., metallurgist.
FISHER, MICHEAL ELLIS, statistician and chemist.
FLEMING, Sir CHARLES ALEXANDER, K.B.E., D.SC., palaeontologist.
FLOWERS, Lord, physicist.
FOGG, GORDON ELLIOTT, botanist.
FORD, CHARLES EDMUND, D.SC., geneticist.
FORD, EDMUND BRISCO, D.SC., zoologist.
FORD, Sir HUGH, D.SC.(ENG.), mechanical engineer.
FORREST, JOHN SAMUEL, D.SC., electrical engineer.
FOWDEN, LESLIE, PH.D., plant chemist.
FOWLER, PETER HOWARD, D.SC., physicist.
FRANK, Sir FREDERICK CHARLES, O.B.E., D.PHIL., physicist.
FRANKEL, Sir OTTO (HERZBERG), D.SC., D.AGR., agriculturist.
FREEMAN, RAYMOND, physical chemist.
FRIEDLANDER, FREDERICK GERARD, mathematician.
FRÖHLICH, ALBRECHT, mathematician
FRÖHLICH, HERBERT, D.PHIL., physicist
FRYER, GEOFFREY, D.SC., biologist.
FUCHS, Sir VIVIAN (ERNEST), M.A., PH.D., explorer.
FYFE, WILLIAM SEFTON, geologist.

GALE, ERNEST FREDERICK, SC.D., chemical microbiologist.
GARDNER, RICHARD LAVENHAM, biologist.
GARNHAM, PERCY CYRIL CLAUDE, C.M.G., medical protozoologist.
GARRETT, STEPHEN DENIS, SC.D., mycologist.
GARTON, GEORGE ALAN, PH.D., biochemist.
GARTON, WILLIAM REGINALD STEPHEN, physicist.
GAYDON, ALFRED GORDON, D.SC., chemical engineer.
GAZE, RAYMOND MICHAEL, D.PHIL., biologist.
GEE, GEOFFREY, C.B.E., M.SC., SC.D., chemist.
GELL, PHILIPP GEORGE HOUTHEM, pathologist.
GIBSON, ALAN FRANK, PH.D., laser physicist.
GIBSON, FRANK WILLIAM ERNEST, biochemist.
GIBSON, QUENTIN HOWIESON, biochemist.
GILBERT, GEOFFREY ALAN, M.A., PH.D., SC.D., biochemist.
GILLESPIE, RONALD JAMES, PH.D., D.SC., chemist.
GLYNN, IAN MICHAEL, physiologist.
GODWIN, Sir HARRY, SC.D., botanist.
GOLD, THOMAS, astronomer and radiophysicist.
GOLD, VICTOR, chemist
GOLDSTEIN, SYDNEY, M.A., PH.D., mathematician.
GOLDSTONE, JEFFREY, M.A., PH.D., physicist.
GOODWIN, LEONARD GEORGE, C.M.G., M.B., B.S., B.PHARM., B.SC., zoologist.
GOODWIN, TREVOR WALWORTH, C.B.E., biochemist.
GOWANS, JAMES LEARMONTH, pathologist.
GRACE, MICHAEL ANTHONY, D.PHIL., nuclear physicist.
GRAHAM, ALASTAIR, zoologist.
GRANT, RONALD THOMSON, O.B.E., M.D., M.R.C.P., F.F.P.S., pathologist.
GRAY, EDWARD GEORGE, PH.D., anatomist.
GRAY, Sir JOHN (ARCHIBALD BROWNE), medical biochemist.
GRAY, PETER, M.A., PH.D., SC.D., F.R.I.C., physical chemist.
GREEN, ALBERT EDWARD, M.A., PH.D., SC.D., mathematician.
GREGORY, PHILIP HERRIES, D.SC., mycologist.
GREGORY, RODERIC ALFRED, physiologist.
GRÜNEBURG, HANS, PH.D., M.D., D.SC., geneticist.
GUNNING, BRIAN EDGAR SCOURSE, biologist.
GURDON, JOHN BERTRAND, zoologist.

HAILSHAM OF ST. MARYLEBONE, Baron, of Herstmonceux, QUINTON MCGAREL HOGG, P.C.
HALL, Sir ARNOLD (ALEXANDER), M.A., aeronautical engineer.
HALL, PHILIP, M.A., mathematician.
HALPERN, JACK, PH.D., chemist.
HALSBURY, JOHN ANTHONY HARDING, Earl, metallurgist.
HAMILTON, WILLIAM DONALD, biologist.
HAMMERSLEY, JOHN MICHAEL, M.A., D.SC., mathematician.
HANES, CHARLES SAMUEL, PH.D., agriculturist.
HARDY, Sir ALISTER (CLAVERING), F.L.S., F.R.G.S., F.Z.S., M.A., D.SC., zoologist.
HARISH-CHANDRA, mathematician.
HARLAND, SYDNEY CROSS, D.SC., botanist.
HARLEY, JOHN LAKER, D.PHIL., botanist.
HARPER, JOHN LANDER, M.A., D.PHIL., botanist.
HARRIS, HARRY, biochemist.
HARRIS, HENRY, pathologist.

HARRIS, THOMAS MAXWELL, M.A., PH.D., botanist.
HARRISON, RICHARD JOHN, M.D., anatomist.
HARTLEY, Sir BRIAN SELBY, molecular biologist.
HASZELDINE, ROBERT NEVILLE, chemist.
HATCH, MARSHALL DAVIDSON, botanist.
HAUGHTON, SIDNEY HENRY, D.SC., geologist.
HAWKES, LEONARD, D.SC., geologist.
HAWKING, STEPHEN WILLIAM, PH.D., astronomer.
HAWORTH, LIONEL, O.B.E., aero-engineer.
HAWORTH, ROBERT DOWNS, D.SC., PH.D., F.R.I.C., chemist.
HAWTHORNE, Sir WILLIAM (REDE), C.B.E., M.A., engineer.
HAYDON, DENIS ARTHUR, M.A., biophysicist.
HAYES, WILLIAM, SC.D., bacteriologist.
HAYMAN, WALTER KURT, M.A., SC.D., analyst.
HEATH, OSCAR VICTOR SAYER, D.SC., horticulturist.
HEBB, DONALD OLDING, psychologist.
HEINE, VOLKER, PH.D., theoretical physicist.
HEITLER, WALTER HEINRICH, PH.D., physicist.
HEMS, BENJAMIN ARTHUR, D.SC., organic chemist.
HENDERSON, Sir WILLIAM (MACGREGOR), D.SC., animal virologist.
HERZBERG, GERHARD, C.C., F.R.S.C., physicist.
HESLOP-HARRISON, JOHN, D.SC., PH.D., F.R.S.E., M.R.I.A., F.L.S., botanist.
HEWISH, ANTONY, PH.D., physicist.
HEY, DONALD HOLDROYDE, D.SC., PH.D., F.R.I.C., chemist.
HEY, JAMES STANLEY, M.B.E., D.SC., radio astronomer.
HIDE, RAYMOND, PH.D., F.R.MET.S., F.R.A.S., geophysicist.
HIGMAN, GRAHAM, M.A., PH.D., mathematician.
HILL, Sir AUSTIN (BRADFORD), C.B.E., medical statistician.
HILL, DAVID KEYNES, SC.D., biophysicist.
HILL, DOROTHY, geologist.
HILL, ROBERT, SC.D., biochemist.
HILL, RODNEY, D.SC., mathematician.
HILLS, EDWIN SHERBON, F.A.A., geologist.
HILSUM, CYRIL, physicist.
HIMSWORTH, Sir HAROLD (PERCIVAL), K.C.B., M.D., F.R.C.P., Q.H.P., clinical medicine.
HINDE, ROBERT AUBREY, M.A., SC.D., D.PHIL., biologist.
HINTON OF BANKSIDE, Baron, CHRISTOPHER HINTON, O.M., K.B.E., M.A., M.I.C.E., M.I.MECH.E., M.I.CHEM.E., engineer.
HIRSCH, Sir PETER BERNHARD, PH.D., physicist.
HIRST, JOHN MALCOLM, plant pathologist.
HOARE, CECIL ARTHUR, D.SC., protozoologist.
HODGKIN, Sir ALAN LLOYD, O.M., M.A., physiologist.
HODGKIN, DOROTHY MARY CROWFOOT, M.A., B.SC., PH.D., crystallographer.
HOLLIDAY, ROBIN, PH.D., geneticist.
HOLT, JOHN RILEY, PH.D., physicist.
HOOKER, Sir STANLEY (GEORGE), C.B.E., D.SC., aircraft engineer.
HOPKINS, HAROLD HORACE, D.SC., D. ÈS SC., applied optician.
HOPWOOD, DAVID ALAN, geneticist.
HORLOCK, JOHN HAROLD, M.A., PH.D., SC.D., mechanical engineer.
HORRIDGE, GEORGE ADRIAN, biologist.
HOUGHTON, JOHN THEODORE, physicist.
HOUNSFIELD, GODFREY NEWBOLD, electrical engineer.
HOWARTH, LESLIE, O.B.E., B.SC., M.A., PH.D., applied mathematician.
HOWIE, ARCHIBALD, PH.D., physicist.
HOYLE, Sir FRED, M.A., mathematician.
HUMPHREY, JOHN HERBERT, C.B.E., M.D., immunologist.
HUTCHINSON, Sir JOSEPH (BURTT), C.M.G., SC.D., plant geneticist.
HUTCHISON, Sir (WILLIAM) KENNETH, C.B.E., chemical engineer.
HUXLEY, Sir ANDREW FIELDING, M.A., physiologist.
HUXLEY, HUGH ESMOR, M.B.E., D.SC., PH.D., biophysicist.

IGGO, AINSLEY, D.SC., PH.D., veterinary physiologist.
INGOLD, KEITH USHERWOOD, chemist.
INGRAM, VERNON MARTIN, PH.D., D.SC., biochemist.
IRVING, EDWARD, geophysicist.
ISSIGONIS, Sir ALEC ARNOLD CONSTANTINE, C.B.E., engineer.
IVERSEN, LESLIE LARS, pharmacologist.

JACK, KENNETH HENDERSON, chemist.
JACKSON, DEREK AINSLIE, O.B.E., D.F.C., A.F.C., M.A., D.SC., physicist.
JAMES, IOAN MACKENZIE, D.PHIL., mathematician.
JAMISON, ROBIN RALPH, PH.D., aeronautical engineer.
JARRETT, WILLIAM FLEMING HOGGAN, veterinary pathologist.
JEFFREYS, Sir HAROLD, M.A., D.SC., F.R.A.S., F.R.MET.SOC., geophysicist.
JERNE, NIELS KAJ, immunologist.
JINKS, JOHN LEONARD, geneticist.
JOHNSON, ALAN WOODWORTH, organic chemist.
JOHNSON, BARRY EDWARD, PH.D., mathematician.
JONES, DOUGLAS SAMUEL, M.B.E., mathematician.
JONES, Sir EWART (RAY HERBERT), PH.D., D.SC., chemist.
JONES, FRANCIS EDGAR, M.B.E., PH.D., electrical engineer.

JONES, GEOFFREY MELVILLE, physiologist.
JONES, HARRY, PH.D., mathematician.
JONES, REGINALD VICTOR, C.B., C.B.E., physicist.
JOSEPHSON, BRIAN DAVID, physicist.

**KAPITZA, PETER, PH.D., physicist.**
KASSANIS, BASIL, O.B.E., D.SC., plant pathologist.
KATZ, Sir BERNARD, M.D., PH.D., D.SC., neurophysiologist.
KATRITZKY, ALAN ROY, chemist.
KEARTON, Baron, of Whitchurch, CHRISTOPHER FRANK KEARTON, O.B.E., physicist.
KEKWICK, RALPH AMBROSE, D.SC., biophysicist.
KELLER, ANDREW, polymer scientist.
KELLY, ANTHONY, physical metallurgist.
KEMBALL, CHARLES, chemist.
**KEMMER, NICHOLAS, M.A., PH.D., F.R.S.E., philosopher.**
KENDALL, DAVID GEORGE, statistician.
KENDREW, Sir JOHN COWDERY, C.B.E., PH.D., biologist.
KENNEDY, JOHN STODART, D.SC., insect physiologist.
KENT, Sir PERCY EDWARD, D.SC., PH.D., geologist.
KERENSKY, OLEG ALEXANDER, C.B.E., civil engineer.
KEYNES, RICHARD DARWIN, D.SC., PH.D., physiologist.
KIBBLE, THOMAS WALTER BANNERMAN, theoretical physicist.
KILBURN, TOM, C.B.E., M.A., PH.D., D.SC., F.I.E.E., computer scientist.
**KING, FREDERICK ERNEST, D.SC., chemist.**
KING-HELE, DESMOND GEORGE, scientific officer.
KINGMAN, JOHN FRANK CHARLES, M.A., F.S.S., mathematician and statistician.
KITCHING, JOHN ALWYNE, O.B.E., SC.D., zoologist.
KLUG, AARON, PH.D., biologist.
KNOWLES, JEREMY RANDALL, PH.D., chemist.
KODICEK, EGON HYNEK, C.B.E., M.D., PH.D., biochemist.
KORNBERG, Sir HANS LEO, M.A., D.SC., SC.D., PH.D., biochemist.
KOSTERLITZ, HANS WALTER, M.D., PH.D., D.SC., pharmacologist.
**KREBS, Sir HANS (ADOLF), M.A., M.D., biochemist.**
KREISEL, GEORG, mathematician.
KROHN, PETER LESLIE, endocrinologist.
**KUHN, HEINRICH GERHARD, D.PHIL., physicist.
KURTI, NICHOLAS, D.PHIL., physicist.**

LA COUR, LEONARD FRANCIS, M.B.E., geneticist.
LAL, DEVENDRA, physicist.
LANE, ANTHONY MILNER, D.SC., theoretical physicist.
LANG, ANDREW RICHARD, M.SC., PH.D., physicist.
LAPPERT, MICHAEL FRANZ, chemist.
LAUGHTON, ANTHONY SEYMOUR, oceanographer.
LAWS, RICHARD MAITLAND, mammalian biologist.
LEBLOND, CHARLES PHILIPPE, physiologist.
**LEES, ANTONY DAVID, SC.D., agriculturalist.**
LE FEVRE, RAYMOND JAMES WOOD, PH.D., chemist.
LEGGETT, ANTHONY JAMES, theoretical physicist.
LEHMANN, HERMANN, clinical biochemist.
**LEMIEUX, RAYMOND URGEL, C.C., organic chemist.**
**LEWIS, DAN, PH.D., D.SC., geneticist.**
LEWIS, JACK, M.A., chemist.
**LEWIS, WILFRED BENNETT, C.C., C.B.E., PH.D., physicist.**
LIGGINS, GRAHAM COLLINGWOOD, obstetrician and gynaecological endocrinologist.
LIGHTHILL, Sir (MICHAEL) JAMES, M.SC., mathematician.
LINNANE, ANTHONY WILLIAM, biochemist.
**LIPSON, HENRY SOLOMON, D.SC., M.A., F.INST.P., physicist.**
LISSMANN, HANS WERNER, DR.RER.NAT., mathematician.
LITHERLAND, ALBERT EDWARD, PH.D., physicist.
**LOCKSPEISER, Sir BEN, K.C.B., M.A., M.I.MECH.E., F.R.AE.S., engineer.**
**LONGUET-HIGGINS, HUGH CHRISTOPHER, physical chemist.**
LONGUET-HIGGINS, MICHAEL SELWYN, PH.D., oceanographer.
LOUTIT, JOHN FREEMAN, C.B.E., D.M., radiobiologist.
LOVELL, Sir (ALFRED CHARLES) BERNARD, O.B.E., F.INST.P., physicist.
LOVELOCK, JAMES EPHRAIM, D.SC., applied physicist.
**LOWENSTEIN, OTTO EGON, PH.D., D.PHIL., D.SC., M.I.BIOL., F.R.S.E., zoologist.**
LUCAS, Sir CYRIL EDWARD, C.M.G., D.SC., marine biologist.
LUND, JOHN WALTER GUERRIER, D.SC., biologist.
LYNDEN-BELL, DONALD, M.A., PH.D., astronomer.
LYON, MARY FRANCES, geneticist.
**LYTHGOE, BASIL, organic chemist.**
**LYTTLETON, RAYMOND ARTHUR, M.A., PH.D., mathematician.**

**McCANCE, Sir ANDREW, D.SC., metallurgist.**
**McCANCE, ROBERT ALEXANDER, C.B.E., M.D., experimental medicine.**
McCREA, WILLIAM HUNTER, M.A., PH.D., astronomer.
MACDONALD, IAN GRANT, mathematician.

MACFARLANE, ROBERT GWYN, M.D., haematologist.
McGEE, JAMES DWYER, O.B.E., physicist.
MACINTOSH, FRANK CAMPBELL, M.A., PH.D., physiologist.
MACKANESS, GEORGE BELLAMY, PH.D., immunologist.
MACKENZIE, CHALMERS JACK, C.C., C.M.G., M.C., D.SC., engineer.
McKENZIE, DAN PETER, M.A., PH.D., geophysicist.
McLAREN, ANNE LAURA, D.PHIL., geneticist.
McLAREN, DIGBY JOHNS, geologist.
McMICHAEL, JOHN, M.D., CH.B., F.R.C.P.E., F.R.S.E., cardiologist.
MacMILLAN, JOHN, PH.D., D.SC., organic chemist.
**MACMILLAN, The Rt. Hon. (MAURICE) HAROLD, P.C.**
MADDOCK, Sir IEUAN, C.B., O.B.E., mechanical and electrical engineer.
**MAHLER, KURT, PH.D., D.SC., mathematician.**
MANDELSTAM, JOEL, PH.D., biochemist and microbiologist.
**MANDELSTAM, STANLEY, physicist.**
**MANN, FREDERICK GEORGE, SC.D., D.SC., F.R.I.C., chemist.**
MANN, THADDEUS ROBERT RUDOLPH, C.B.E., M.D., SC.D., biochemist.
MANSFIELD, ERIC HAROLD, mathematician.
MANTON, IRENE, D.SC., botanist.
MARSHALL, NORMAN BERTRAM, zoologist.
MARSHALL, WALTER, PH.D., F.I.M.A., physicist.
MARTIN, ARCHER JOHN PORTER, O.B.E., M.A., PH.D., biochemist.
MARTIN, Sir LESLIE (HAROLD), C.B.E., physicist.
MASON, Sir (BASIL) JOHN, meteorologist.
MASON, RONALD, PH.D., chemist.
MASSEY, Sir HARRIE (STEWART WILSON), M.SC., PH.D., mathematician.
MASSEY, VINCENT, PH.D., biochemist.
MATHER, Sir KENNETH, C.B.E., PH.D., D.SC., geneticist.
**MATTHEWS, Sir BRYAN (HAROLD CABOT), C.B.E., M.A., SC.D., physiologist.**
MATTHEWS, DRUMMOND HOYLE, M.A., PH.D., geologist.
MATTHEWS, LEONARD HARRISON, SC.D., zoologist.
MATTHEWS, PAUL TAUNTON, M.A., PH.D., physicist.
MATTHEWS, PETER BRYAN CONRAD, PH.D., physiologist.
MATTHEWS, RICHARD ELLIS FORD, M.SC., PH.D., microbiologist.
MAY, ROBERT McCREDIE, zoologist.
MAYNEORD, WILLIAM VALENTINE, C.B.E., medical physicist.
MEDAWAR, Sir PETER (BRIAN), C.H., C.B.E., O.M., M.A., D.SC., zoologist.
**MELVILLE, Sir HARRY (WORK), K.C.B., D.SC., chemist.**
MENON, MAMBILLIKALATHIL G. K., physicist.
MENTER, Sir JAMES (WOODHAM), SC.D., engineer.
MERRISON, Sir ALEXANDER WALTER, physicist.
MERTON, PATRICK ANTHONY, physiologist.
MESTEL, LEON, M.SC., PH.D., astronomer.
MILEDI, RICARDO, M.D., biophysicist.
**MILES, Sir (ARNOLD) ASHLEY, C.B.E., pathologist.**
MILLER, JACQUES FRANCIS ALBERT PIERRE, pathologist.
MILLS, BARNARD YARNTON, D.SC., physicist.
MILNE, MALCOLM DAVENPORT, M.D., physiologist.
MILNER, BRENDA, psychologist.
MILSTEIN, CÉSAR, biologist.
MITCHELL, GEORGE FRANCIS, geologist.
MITCHELL, JOHN WESLEY, D.PHIL., physicist.
MITCHELL, JOSEPH STANLEY, C.B.E., M.A., M.B., PH.D., D.M.R., biophysicist.
MITCHELL, PETER DENNIS, PH.D., biologist.
MITCHISON, JOHN MURDOCH, SC.D., zoologist.
**MITCHISON, NICHOLAS AVRION, D.PHIL., biologist.**
**MOLLISON, PATRICK LOUDAN, haematologist.**
MONTEITH, JOHN LENNOX, PH.D., F.INST.P., F.R.MET.S., physicist.
**MOON, PHILIP BURTON, M.A., PH.D., physicist.**
MOORBATH, STEPHEN ERWIN, M.A., D.PHIL., geologist.
MORAN, PATRICK ALFRED PIERCE, M.A., SC.D., D.SC., F.A.A., statistician.
MORGAN, WALTER THOMAS JAMES, C.B.E., PH.D., D.SC., biochemist.
MORROGH, HENTON, C.B.E., metallurgist.
MORTIMER, CLIFFORD HILEY, D.SC. PH.D, limnologist.
MOTT, Sir NEVILL (FRANCIS), M.A., physicist.
MOURANT, ARTHUR ERNEST, D.PHIL., D.M., geneticist.
MUIR, (ISABELLA) HELEN (MARY), M.A., D.PHIL., D.SC., rheumatologist.
MURRAY, KENNETH, molecular biologist.

NABARRO, FRANK REGINALD NUNES, M.B.E., physicist.
**NEEDHAM, Mrs. DOROTHY MARY MOYLE, SC.D., biochemist.
NEEDHAM, JOSEPH, SC.D., M.A., PH.D., biochemist.**
NEUBERGER, ALBERT, C.B.E., PH.D., M.D., biochemist.
NEUMANN, BERNARD HERMANN, D.SC., mathematician.
**NEWMAN, MAXWELL HERMAN ALEXANDER, M.A., mathematician.**
NICHOLSON, ROBIN BUCHANAN, PH.D., chemist.
**NICOL, JOSEPH ARTHUR COLIN, D.SC., zoologist.**

Noble, Denis, physiologist.
Nockolds, Stephen Robert, ph.d., mineralogist.
Norman, Richard Oswald Chandler, m.a., d.sc., organic chemist.
Northcote, Donald Henry, sc.d., biochemist.
Northcott, Douglas Geoffrey, mathematician.
Northumberland, Duke of, Hugh Algernon Percy.
Nutman, Phillip Sadler, ph.d., biologist.
Nye, John Frederick, m.a., ph.d., physicist.

Oatley, Sir Charles (William), o.b.e., m.a., electrical engineer.
Offord, Albert Cyril, d.sc., ph.d., mathematician.
Ogston, Alexander George, b.a., d.phil., biochemist.
Oliphant, Sir Mark (Marcus Laurence Elwin), k.b.e., m.a., ph.d., ll.d., d.sc., f.inst.p., physicist.
Ollis, William David, organic chemist.
Orgel, Leslie Eleazer, d.phil., chemist.
Orowan, Egon, dr.ing., physicist.
Owen, Paul Robert, c.b.e., aviation engineer.
Oxburgh, Ernest Ronald, ph.d., geologist.

Pal, Benjamin Peary, ph.d., agriculturalist.
Page, Frederick William, c.b.e., aeronautical engineer.
Parke, Mary, d.sc., psychologist.
Parkes, Sir Alan (Sterling), c.b.e., m.a., ph.d., d.sc., sc.d., physiologist.
Parsons, Roger, electrochemist.
Partridge, Stanley Miles, zoologist.
Pashley, Donald William, ph.d., physicist.
Pasquill, Frank, ph.d., meteorologist.
Pateman, John Arthur Joseph, m.a., ph.d., geneticist.
Paton, Sir (Thomas) Angus (Lyall), c.m.g., hydroelectrical engineer.
Paton, Sir William Drummond MacDonald, c.b.e., pharmacologist.
Peart, William Stanley, m.d., medical renalogist.
Pease, Rendel Sebastian, m.a., sc.d., atomic physicist.
Peierls, Sir Rudolf (Ernst), c.b.e., m.a., d.sc., d.phil., mathematician.
Penman, Howard Latimer, o.b.e., ph.d., physicist.
Pennell, Montague Mattinson, c.b.e., petroleum engineer.
Penney, William George, Baron, o.m., k.b.e., d.sc., physicist.
Penrose, Roger, mathematician.
Pereira, Helio Gelli, dr.med., virologist.
Pereira, Sir Herbert Charles, d.sc., hydraulic agriculturalist.
Perkins, Donald Hill, physicist.
Perry, Samuel Victor, ph.d., sc.d., biochemist.
Perutz, Max Ferdinand, c.h., c.b.e., ph.d., biophysicist.
Petch, Norman James, ph.d., metallurgist.
Peters, Sir Rudolph (Albert), m.c., m.d., biochemist.
Philip, John Robert, d.sc., ecologist.
Phillips, Charles Garnett, physiologist.
Phillips, David Chilton, molecular biophysicist.
Phillips, Owen Martin, geophysicist.
Pickavance, Thomas Gerald, c.b.e., m.a., ph.d., nuclear physicist.
Pickford, Lillian Mary, d.sc., physiologist.
Pilkington, Sir Alistair (Lionel Alexander Bethune), vitrifactologist.
Pippard, Sir Alfred Brian, ph.d., physicist.
Pirie, Norman Wingate, m.a., biochemist.
Pitt, Sir Harry Raymond, ph.d., mathematician.
Pitt-Rivers, Rosalind Venetia, ph.d., biochemist.
Polani, Paul Emmanuel, m.d., paediatrician.
Polanyi, John Charles, chemist.
Polkinghorne, John Charlton, m.a., ph.d., mathematical physicist.
Pollock, Martin Rivers, biologist.
Pontecorvo, Guido, dr.agr., ph.d., geneticist.
Popják, George Joseph, m.d., radio-pathologist.
Pople, John Anthony, ph.d., physicist.
Popper, Sir Karl Raimund, philosopher.
Porter, Sir George, chemist.
Porter, Helen Kemp, d.sc., physiologist.
Porter, Rodney Robert, ph.d., biochemist.
Posnette, Adrian Frank, ph.d., sc.d., m.a.a.b., f.i.biol., plant pathologist.
Postgate, John Raymond, m.a., d.phil., d.sc., microbiologist.
Powell, Herbert Marcus, m.a., chemical crystallographer.
Powell, Thomas Philip Stroud, m.d., neuroanatomist.
Prescott, James Arthur, c.b.e., soil scientist.
Preston, Reginald Dawson, ph.d., d.sc., f.inst.p., plant biophysicist.
Price, William Charles, physicist.
Priestley, Charles Henry Brian, sc.d., meteorological physicist.

Pringle, John William Sutton, m.b.e., sc.d., zoologist.
Pryce, Maurice Henry Lecorney, m.a., ph.d., physicist.
Pugsley, Sir Alfred (Grenville), o.b.e., m.sc., d.sc., civil engineer.

Quastel, Juda Hirsch, d.sc., biochemist.
Quayle, John Rodney, m.a., ph.d., microbiologist.

Race, Robert Russell, ph.d., m.r.c.s., serologist.
Radda, György Károly, biochemist.
Rado, Richard, ph.d., mathematician.
Rainey, Reginald Charles, ph.d., d.sc., a.r.c.s., d.i.c., f.i.biol.
Ramachandran, Gopalasamudram Narayana, d.sc., ph.d., biophysicist.
Ramsay, Donald Allan, ph.d., molecular physicist.
Ramsay, James Arthur, m.b.e., m.a., ph.d., zoologist.
Ramsay, John Graham, ph.d., geologist.
Randall, Sir John (Turton), d.sc., physicist.
Rang, Humphrey Peter, pharmacologist.
Rao, Calyampudi Radhakrishna, sc.d., statistician.
Raphael, Ralph Alexander, chemist.
Ratcliffe, John Ashworth, c.b., o.b.e., physicist.
Raynor, Geoffrey Vincent, metallurgist.
Reason, Richard Edmund, o.b.e., precision engineer.
Rees, Charles Wayne, ph.d., d.sc., organic chemist.
Rees, David, mathematician.
Rees, Florence Gwendoline, ph.d., d.sc., parasitologist.
Rees, Hubert, d.f.c., d.sc., ph.d., agricultural botanist.
Rees, Martin John, astronomer.
Richards, Owain Westmacott, m.a., d.sc., zoologist.
Richards, Sir Rex Edwards, d.phil., chemist.
Richardson, Frederick Denys, ph.d., d.sc., f.i.m., m.i.m.m., m.i.chem.e., metallurgist.
Richmond, Mark Henry, bacteriologist.
Riley, Ralph, d.sc., botanist.
Rimington, Claude, m.a., ph.d., d.sc., chemical pathologist.
Ringrose, John Robert, m.a., ph.d., mathematician.
Ringwood, Alfred Edward, geochemist.
Rishbeth, John, sc.d., plant pathologist.
Ritchie, Joseph Murdoch, ph.d., d.sc., pharmacologist.
Roberts, Derek Harry, electronic engineer.
Roberts, John Alexander Fraser, c.b.e., m.d., geneticist.
Roberts, Paul Henry, mathematician.
Robertson, Alan, o.b.e., d.sc., animal geneticist.
Robertson, John Monteath, c.b.e., m.a., ph.d., d.sc., chemist.
Robertson, Sir Rutherford (Ness), c.m.g., ph.d., physicist.
Robinson, Stephen Joseph, o.b.e., electrical engineer.
Rochester, George Dixon, physicist.
Rogers, Claude Ambrose, mathematician.
Rooke, Sir Denis Eric, c.b.e., b.sc., gas engineer.
Room, Thomas Gerald, m.a., mathematician.
Rose, Francis Leslie, o.b.e., d.sc., organic chemist.
Rosenbrock, Howard Harry, ph.d., d.sc., control engineer.
Rosenhead, Louis, c.b.e., mathematician.
Roth, Klaus Friedrich, mathematician.
Rotherham, Leonard, c.b.e., d.sc., physicist.
Rothschild, Baron, Nathaniel Mayer Victor Rothschild, g.m., g.b.e., ph.d., sc.d., zoologist.
Rowlinson, John Shipley, b.sc., m.a., d.phil., f.r.i.c., chemist.
Rowson, Lionel Edward Aston, o.b.e., physiologist.
Runcorn, Stanley Keith, physicist.
Russell, Sir Frederick (Stratten), c.b.e., d.sc., d.f.c., b.a., marine biologist.
Ryle, Sir Martin, m.a., physicist, Astronomer Royal.

Salam, Abdus, mathematician.
Salt, George, sc.d., zoologist.
Salton, Milton Robert James, microbiologist.
Sanger, Frederick, c.b.e., ph.d., biochemist.
Sanger, Ruth Ann (Mrs. R. R. Race), ph.d., pathologist.
Saunders, Sir Owen (Alfred), mechanical engineer.
Sawyer, John Stanley, meteorologist.
Schild, Heinz Otto, pharmacologist.
Schneider, William George, ph.d., chemist.
Scott, Alastair Ian, ph.d., chemist.
Seaton, Michael John, physicist.
Series, George William, physicist.
Shackleton, Robert Millner, ph.d., f.g.s., structural geologist.
Shaw, Bernard Leslie, ph.d., chemist.
Sheppard, Norman, chemist.
Shercliff, John Arthur, engineer.
Shoenberg, David, m.b.e., ph.d., physicist.

SHOPPEE, CHARLES WILLIAM, D.PHIL., PH.D., D.SC., F.R.SC., chemist.
SHORT, ROGER VALENTINE, PH.D., SC.D., biologist.
SHORTT, HENRY EDWARD, C.I.E., M.D., CH.D., D.SC., Col. I.M.S. (retd.), parasitologist.
SHOTTON, FREDERICK WILLIAM, M.B.E., geologist.
SIDDIQUI, SALIMUZZAMAN, M.B.E., D.PHIL., organic chemist.
SIMINOVITCH, LOUIS, medical geneticist.
SKEMPTON, ALEC WESTLEY, engineer.
SLATER, EDWARD CHARLES, physiological chemist.
SLATYER, RALPH OWEN, D.SC., F.A.A., biologist.
SMITH, DAVID CECIL, M.A., D.PHIL., botanist.
SMITH, DAVID MACLEISH, D.SC., engineer.
SMITH, ERNEST LESTER, D.SC., biochemist.
SMITH, FRANCIS GRAHAM, M.A., PH.D., F.R.A.S., radio astronomist.
SMITH, Sir (FRANK) EWART, M.A., M.I.MECH.E., M.I.CHEM.E., technologist.
SMITH, HARRY, biologist.
SMITH, HERBERT WILLIAMS, microbiologist.
SMITH, Sir JAMES ERIC, D.SC., PH.D., M.A., SC.D., marine biologist.
SMITH, JOHN DEREK, PH.D., biologist.
SMITH, JOHN MAYNARD, B.A., B.SC., biologist.
SMITH, JOSEPH VICTOR, M.A., PH.D., mineralogist.
SMITH, KENNETH MANLEY, C.B.E., D.SC., PH.D., agricultural entomologist.
SMITH, STANLEY DESMOND, PH.D., D.SC., physicist.
SOUTHWOOD, THOMAS RICHARD EDMUND, PH.D., D.SC., zoologist.
SPEAR, WALTER ERIC, physicist.
SPINKS, ALFRED, C.B.E., PH.D., industrial chemist.
SPRING, FRANK STUART, D.SC., PH.D., D.SC., organic chemist.
STACEY, MAURICE, C.B.E., B.SC., PH.D., D.SC., chemist.
STAFFORD, GODFREY HARRY, physicist.
STANIER, ROGER YATE, PH.D., biologist.
STANLEY, HERBERT MUGGLETON, PH.D., chemist.
STEELE, JOHN HYSLOP, oceanographer.
STEVENS, THOMAS STEVENS, D.PHIL., chemist.
STEWARD, FREDERICK CAMPION, PH.D., DR.SC., botanist.
STEWART, Sir FREDERICK (HENRY), geologist.
STEWART, ROBERT WILLIAM, M.SC., PH.D., oceanologist.
STEWART, WILLIAM DUNCAN PATERSON, PH.D., D.SC., F.I.BIOL., F.R.S.E., biologist.
STEWARTSON, KEITH, mathematician.
STILES, WALTER STANLEY, O.B.E.. D.SC., physicist.
STOCKER, BRUCE ARNOLD DUNBAR, microbiologist.
STOICHEFF, BORIS PETER, M.A., PH.D., physicist.
STOKER, Sir MICHAEL GEORGE PARKE, C.B.E., M.D., pathologist.
STONE, FRANCIS GORDON ALBERT, M.A., PH.D., SC.D., chemist.
STRANG, WILLIAM JOHN, C.B.E., PH.D., C.ENG., F.R.AE.S., aeronautical engineer.
STUART, JOHN TREVOR, PH.D., mathematician.
STUBBLEFIELD, Sir (CYRIL) JAMES, D.SC., PH.D., A.R.C.SC., F.G.S., geologist.
SUCKLING, CHARLES WALTER, PH.D., chemist.
SUGDEN, THEODORE MORRIS, C.B.E., SC.D., chemist.
SUTCLIFFE, REGINALD COCKCROFT. C.B., O.B.E.. meteorologist.
SUTTON, JOHN, geologist.
SUTTON, LESLIE ERNEST, M.A., D.PHIL., chemist.
SWALLOW, JOHN CROSSLEY, PH.D., oceanographer.
SWAMINATHAN, MONKOMBU SAMBASIVAN, PH.D., agriculturist.
SWANN, Sir MICHAEL (MEREDITH), PH.D., zoologist.
SWINNERTON-DYER, HENRY PETER FRANCIS, mathematician.
SYKES, Sir CHARLES, C.B.E., D.SC., metallurgist.
SYNGE, JOHN LIGHTON, M.A., SC.D., F.R.S.C., mathematician.
SYNGE, RICHARD LAURENCE MILLINGTON, B.A., PH.D., biochemist.
SZWARC, MICHAEL, chemist

TABOR, DAVID, SC.D., physicist.
TAIT, JAMES FRANCIS, PH.D., biophysicist.
TAIT, SYLVIA AGNES SOPHIA, biochemist.
TALLING, JOHN FRANCIS, PH.D., freshwater biologist.
TATA, JAMSHED RUSTOM, D. ÈS SC., biochemist.
TAYLOR, EDWIN WILLIAM, PH.D., biophysicist.
TAYLOR, Sir GEORGE, botanist.
TAYLOR, JOHN BRYAN, physicist.
TEMPLE, GEORGE, C.B.E., PH.D., D.SC., mathematician.
THODAY, JOHN MARION, geneticist.
THODE, HENRY GEORGE, C.C., M.B.E., PH.D., chemist and physicist.
THOMAS, JOHN MEURIG, PH.D., D.SC., F.R.I.C., chemist.
THOMPSON, Sir HAROLD (WARRIS), M.A., B.SC., D.PHIL., chemist.
THOMPSON, JOHN GRIGGS, mathematician.
THOMPSON, ROBERT HENRY STEWART, M.A., D.M., D.SC., biochemist.
THORPE. WILLIAM HOMAN, SC.D., entomologist.

THOULESS, DAVID JAMES, physicist.
THRUSH, BRIAN ARTHUR, SC.D., physical chemist.
TINBERGEN, NIKOLAAS, D.PHIL., zoologist.
TODD, of TRUMPINGTON, Baron, ALEXANDER ROBERTUS, O.M., D.SC., D.PHIL., M.A., F.R.I.C., chemist.
TODD, JOHN ARTHUR, PH.D., mathematician.
TOMPKINS, FREDERICK CLIFFORD, D.SC., PH.D., physical chemist.
TOWNSEND, ALBERT ALAN, P.HD., physicist.
TURNER, DAVID WARREN, M.A., PH.D., physical chemist.
TURNER, GRENVILLE, physicist.
TUTIN, WINIFRED ANNE, botanist.
TYRELL, DAVID ARTHUR JOHN, virologist.

UBBELOHDE, ALFRED RENE JOHN PAUL, M.A., D.SC., chemist.
URSELL, FRITZ JOSEPH, mathematician.

VANE, JOHN ROBERT, PH.D., chemist.
VAUGHAN, Dame JANET MARIA, biologist.
VINE, FREDERICK JOHN, PH.D., geologist.
VINEN, WILLIAM FRANK, M.A., PH.D., physicist.
VOGT, MARTHE LOUISE, DR.MED., DR.PHIL., PH.D., M.D., pharmacologist.

WAIN, RALPH LOUIS, C.B.E., D.SC., PH.D., F.R.I.C., agricultural chemist.
WALKER, ARTHUR GEOFFREY, M.A., PH.D., D.SC., F.R.A.S., F.R.S.E., mathematician.
WALKER, DAVID ALAN, biologist.
WALKER, GEORGE PATRICK LEONARD, geologist.
WALL, CHARLES TERENCE CLEGG, mathematician.
WALSH, Sir ALAN, D.SC., chemical physicist.
WARD, JOHN CLIVE, physicist.
WAREING, PHILIP FRANK, botanist.
WARNER, Sir FREDERICK (EDWARD), chemical engineer.
WATERHOUSE, DOUGLAS FREW, C.M.G., D.SC., entomologist.
WATERS, WILLIAM ALEXANDER, SC.D., physical and organic chemist.
WATKINS, WINIFRED MAY. biochemist.
WATSON, JANET VIDA, geologist.
WATT, ALEXANDER STUART, PH.D., ecologist.
WATT, WILLIAM, O.B.E., physical chemist.
WEATHERALL, DAVID JOHN, M.D., F.R.C.P., haematologist.
WEATHERLEY, PAUL EGERTON, M.A., D.PHIL., botanist.
WECK, RICHARD, O.B.E., PH.D., engineer.
WEEDON, BASIL CHARLES LEICESTER, C.B.E., A.R.C.S., PH.D., D.SC., F.R.I.C., organic chemist.
WEISKRANTZ, LAWRENCE, psychologist.
WELFORD, WALTER THOMPSON, physicist.
WELLS, ALAN ARTHUR, PH.D., C.ENG., civil engineer.
WELLS, GEORGE PHILIP, M.A., SC.D., zoologist.
WELSH, HARRY LAMBERT, physicist.
WEST, RICHARD GILBERT, PH.D., botanist.
WESTOLL, THOMAS STANLEY, PH.D., D.SC., geologist.
WETHERELL, ALAN MARMADUKE, nuclear physicist.
WHATLEY, FREDERICK ROBERT, PH.D., botanist.
WHELAN, MICHAEL JOHN, D.PHIL., physicist.
WHIFFEN, DAVID HARDY, D.PHIL., physicist.
WHITE, ERROL IVOR, C.B.E., D.SC., geologist.
WHITE, Sir FREDERICK (WILLIAM GEORGE), K.B.E., physicist.
WHITE, MICHAEL JAMES DENHAM, zoologist.
WHITHAM, GERALD BERESFORD, mathematician.
WHITTAKER, JOHN MACNAUGHTEN, M.A., D.SC., mathematician.
WHITTAM, RONALD, M.A., PH.D., physiologist.
WHITTERIDGE, DAVID, D.M., physiologist.
WHITTINGTON, HARRY BLACKMORE, PH.D., D.SC., F.G.S., palaeontologist and geologist.
WHITTLE, Air Commodore Sir FRANK, K.B.E., C.B., D.SC., M.A., engineer.
WHITTLE, PETER, M.A., mathematician.
WIDDOWSON, ELSIE MAY, SC.D., nutritionist.
WIESNER, KAREL FRANTIŠEK, organic chemist.
WIGGLESWORTH, Sir VINCENT (BRIAN), C.B.E., M.A., bacteriologist.
WILD, JOHN PAUL, radiophysicist.
WILKES, MAURICE VINCENT, M.A., PH.D., mathematician.
WILKIE, DOUGLAS ROBERT, M.D., M.B., B.S., M.R.C.P., physiologist.
WILKINS, MAURICE HUGH FREDERICK, C.B.E., PH.D., biophysicist.
WILKINSON, Sir DENYS HAIGH, PH.D., physicist.
WILKINSON, Sir GEOFFREY, inorganic chemist.
WILKINSON, JAMES HARDY, D.SC., mathematician.
WILLIAMS, ALWYN, geologist.
WILLIAMS, ROBERT JOSEPH PATON, D.PHIL., inorganic chemist.
WILLIAMSON, DAVID THEODORE NELSON, engineer.
WILLMER, EDWARD NEVILL, SC.D., histologist.
WILSON, Sir ALAN (HERRIES), physicist.
WILSON, ARTHUR JAMES COCHRAN, physicist.

WILSON, Sir GRAHAM (SELBY), M.D., medical microbiologist.
WILSON, Rt. Hon. (JAMES) HAROLD, P.C., O.B.E., M.P.
WILSON, JOHN TUZO, O.B.E., geophysicist.
WILSON, ROBERT, C.B.E., PH.D., astronomer.
WITTRICK, WILLIAM HENRY, civil engineer.
WOLFENDALE, ARNOLD WHITTAKER, PH.D., D.SC., F.INST.P., F.R.A.S., physicist.
WOLFSON, Sir ISAAC.
WOLPERT, LEWIS, biologist.
WOOD, ALAN MARSHALL MUIR, civil engineer.
WOOD, RONALD KARSLAKE STARR, PH.D., plant pathologist.
WOODRUFF, Sir MICHAEL (FRANCIS ADDISON), surgeon.
WOODS, STEPHEN ESSLEMONT, PH.D., chemical engineer.
WOOLLEY, Sir RICHARD (VAN DER RIET), K.B.E., M.SC., M.A., SC.D., astronomer.
WYNNE, CHARLES GORRIE, optical designer.
WYNNE-EDWARDS, VERO COPNER, M.A., D.SC., F.R.S.C., F.R.S.E., ecologist.

YATES, FRANK, C.B.E., SC.D., agricultural statistician.
YONGE, Sir (CHARLES) MAURICE, C.B.E., D.SC., zoologist.
YOUNG, ALEC DAVID, O.B.E., M.A., aeronautical engineer.
YOUNG, Sir FRANK GEORGE, M.A., PH.D., D.SC., biochemist.
YOUNG, JOHN ZACHARY, M.A., anatomist.
YOUNG, PIERRE HENRY JOHN, M.SC., aero-engineer.

ZANGWILL, OLIVER, LOUIS, M.A., neuropsychologist.
ZEEMAN, ERIK CHRISTOPHER, M.A., PH.D., mathematician.
ZIENKIEWICZ, OLGIERD CECIL, civil engineer.
ZIMAN, JOHN MICHAEL, physicist.
ZUCKERMAN, Baron, of Burnham Thorpe, SOLLY, O.M., K.C.B., M.A., D.SC., M.R.C.S., L.R.C.P., anatomist.

### FOREIGN MEMBERS:

ALFVÉN, HANNES OLOF GÖSTA (Sweden), physicist.
AMALDI, Prof. EDUARDO (Italy), physicist.
AMBARTSUMIAN, Acad. VIKTOR AMAZASPOVITCH (U.S.S.R.), astronomer.
ANDERSON, PHILIP WARREN (U.S.A.), physicist.
AXELROD, JULIUS (U.S.A.), biochemist.

BARDEEN, Prof. JOHN (U.S.A.), physicist.
BEADLE, Prof. Dr. GEORGE WELLS (U.S.A.), physiologist.
BENZER, Prof. SEYMOUR (U.S.A.), biologist.
BETHE, Prof. HANS ALBRECHT (U.S.A.), nuclear scientist.
BOVET, Prof. DANIELE (Italy), chemist.
BRACHET, Prof. JEAN LOUIS (Belgium), biochemist.
BROGLIE, Prince LOUIS VICTOR PIERRE RAYMOND DE (France), physicist.
BUTENANDT, Prof. ADOLF FRIEDRICH JOHANN (Germany), chemist.

CALVIN, Prof. MELVIN (U.S.A.), chemist.
CARTAN, Prof. HENRI (France), mathematician.
CASIMIR, Dr. HENDRIK BRUGT GERHARD (Netherlands), physicist.
CASPERSSON, TORBJÖRN OSKAR (Sweden), pathologist.
CHANCE, Prof. BRITTON (U.S.A.), biophysicist.
COLE, Dr. KENNETH STEWART (U.S.A.), biophysicist.
CORI, Prof. CARL FERDINAND (U.S.A.), physiologist.
COURRIER, Prof. MARIE JULES CONSTANT ROBERT (France), physiologist.

DULBECCO, Dr. RENATO (Italy), virologist.

EBASHI, Prof. SETSURO (Japan), pharmacologist.
EIGEN, Prof. MANFRED (Fed. Repub. of Germany), chemist.
ENDERS, Prof. JOHN FRANKLIN (U.S.A.), child physician.
VON EULER, Prof. ULF SVANTE (Sweden), physiologist.

FEYNMAN, Prof. RICHARD PHILLIPS (U.S.A.), physicist.
FREUDENBERG, Prof. KARL JOHANN (Germany), chemist.
FREY-WISSLING, Prof. ALBERT (Switzerland), plant physiologist.
FRISCH, Prof. KARL VON (Germany), physiologist.

GELFAND, Prof. IZRAEL MOISEIVICH (U.S.S.R.), mathematician.
GELL-MANN, MURRAY (U.S.A.), physicist.
GILMAN, Prof. HENRY (U.S.A.), chemist.
GRANIT, Prof. RAGNAR ARTHUR (Sweden), physiologist.

HARTLINE, Prof. HALDAN KEFFER (U.S.A.), physicist.
HEIDELBERGER, Prof. MICHAEL (U.S.A.), pathologist.
HITCHINGS, Dr. GEORGE HERBERT (U.S.A.), chemist.
HÖRSTADIUS, Prof. SVEN OTTO (Sweden), zoologist.

JACOB, Prof. FRANÇOIS (France), physiologist.

KATCHALSKI-KATZIR, Prof. EPHRAIM (Israel), biophysicist.
KHORANA, HAR GOBIND (U.S.A.), biochemist.
KISTIAKOWSKY, GEORGE BOGDAN, (U.S.A.), chemist.
KOLMOGOROV, Acad. ANDREI NIKOLAEVICH (U.S.S.R.), mathematician.
KORNBERG, Prof. ARTHUR (U.S.A.), biochemist.

LEDERBERG, JOSHUA (U.S.A.), geneticist.
LEHMANN, Dr. INGE (Denmark), seismologist.
LELOIR, Dr. LUIS FEDERICO (Argentina), biochemist.
LIPMANN, Prof. FRITZ ALBERT (U.S.A.), biochemist.
LORENZ, Prof. KONRAD ZACHARIAS (Germany), zoologist.
LWOFF, Dr. ANDRÉ (France), protozoologist.

MOTHES, Prof. KURT (Germany), plant biochemist.
MULLIKEN, Prof. ROBERT SANDERSON (U.S.A.), chemist.
MUNK, Prof. WALTER HEINRICH (U.S.A.), geophysicist.

NÉEL, Prof. LOUIS EUGÈNE FÉLIX (France), physicist.
NEYMAN, JERZY (U.S.A.), statistician.
NÖRLUND, Prof. NIELS ERIK (Denmark), mathematician.

OCCHIALINI, Prof. GIUSEPPE PAOLO STANISLAO (Italy), physicist.
OCHOA, Prof. SEVERO (U.S.A.), biochemist.
OORT, Prof. JAN HENDRIK (Netherlands), astronomer.

PAULING, Prof. LINUS CARL (U.S.A.), chemist.
PRELOG, Prof. VLADIMIR (Switzerland), chemist.

REICHSTEIN, Prof. TADEUS (Switzerland), organic chemist.

SERRE, JEAN-PIERRE (France), mathematician.
SHAFAREVICH, Acad. I. R. (U.S.S.R.), mathematician.
SIMPSON, Prof. Dr. GEORGE GAYLORD (U.S.A.), palaeontologist.
SONNEBORN, Prof. TRACY MORTON (U.S.A.), zoologist.
SPERRY, Prof. ROGER WOLCOTT (U.S.A.), psychobiologist.
STENSIÖ, Prof. ERIK ANDERSSON (Sweden), palaeozoologist.
SZENTÁGOTHAI, JÁNOS (Hungary), anatomist.

THEORELL, Prof. AXEL HUGO TEODOR (Sweden), chemist.
THIMANN, Prof. KENNETH VIVIAN (U.S.A.), microbiologist.
TOWNES, Prof. CHARLES HARD (U.S.A.), physicist.

VINOGRADOV, Acad. Prof. IVAN MATVEEVICH (U.S.S.R.), mathematician.

WATSON, JAMES DEWEY (U.S.A.), biologist.
WEIL, Prof. ANDRÉ, (U.S.A.), mathematician.
WEINBERG, STEVEN (U.S.A.), physicist.
WIGNER, Prof. EUGENE PAUL (U.S.A.), physicist.
WRIGHT, Prof. SEWALL (U.S.A.), geneticist.
WYCKOFF, Prof. RALPH WALTER GRAYSTONE (U.S.A.), physicist.

ZELDOVICH, Acad. YAKOV BORISSOVITCH (U.S.S.R.), mathematician.

## ROYAL SOCIETY OF EDINBURGH

22, 24 GEORGE STREET, EDINBURGH EH2 2PQ
Telephone: 031-225 6057.

Founded 1783 for the promotion of science and literature.

*President:* Sir KENNETH BLAXTER, F.R.S.
*General Secretary:* Prof. R. M. S. SMELLIE, PH.D., D.SC.
*Treasurer:* Sir JOHN ATWELL.
*Executive Secretary and Librarian:* W. H. RUTHERFORD, F.C.I.S.

Approx. 850 Fellows, 22 British Hon. Fellows, 44 Foreign Hon. Fellows.

Publications: *Proceedings: Section A (Mathematics), Section B (Biological Sciences)†, Communications (Physical Sciences)†, Transactions (Earth Sciences)†, Year Book†.*

### FELLOWS:

ADAM, HENRY MATTHEW, M.B., CH.B., Pharmacologist.
AGLEN, ANTHONY JOHN, C.B., B.A., Agriculturist.
AITCHISON, JOHN, M.A., Statistician.
ALCOCK, LESLIE, M.A., F.S.A., F.R.HIST.S., Archaeologist.

ALDRED, CYRIL, B.A., F.S.A.SCOT., Archaeologist.
ALEXANDER, FRANK, M.R.C.V.S., PH.D., D.SC., Veterinary Surgeon.
ALEXANDER, Sir KENNETH JOHN WILSON, B.SC., Economist.
ALLEN, JACK, D.SC., LL.D., F.I.C.E., Engineer.
ALLEN, JOHN ANTHONY, PH.D., D.SC., Zoologist.
ALLEN, JOHN FRANK, M.A., PH.D., F.R.S., Physicist.
ALSTEAD, STANLEY, C.B.E., M.D., F.R.C.P., F.R.C.P.E., F.R.C.P.G., Pharmacologist.
ANDERSON, DOUGLAS MACDONALD WATT, D.SC., PH.D., F.R.S.C., Chemist.
ANDERSON, FREDERICK WILLIAM, D.SC., Geologist.
ANDERSON, GEORGE WISHART, M.A., D.D., TEOL.D., F.B.A., Theologian.
ANDERSON, JOHN GRAHAM COMRIE, M.A., D.SC., PH.D., F.G.S., Geologist.
ANDERSON, JOHN RUSSELL, B.SC., M.B., CH.B., M.D., M.R.C.P., F.R.C.P.G., Pathologist.
ANDERSON, WILLIAM, M.SC., F.G.S., Geologist.
ANDREASEN, ANTHONY TURNER, M.R.C.S., F.R.C.S.E., F.I.C.S., Surgeon
ANDREW, EDWARD RAYMOND, M.A., PH.D., SC.D., F.INST.P., Physicist.
ANTON, ALEXANDER ELDER, C.B.E., M.A., LL.B., F.B.A., Lawyer.
ARMSTRONG, DAVID GILFORD, M.SC., PH.D., F.R.I.C., Agriculturist.
ARNOTT, Sir (WILLIAM) MELVILLE, M.B., CH.B., B.SC., M.D., F.R.C.P.C., F.R.C.P., F.R.C.P.E., Cardiologist.
ASHCROFT, GEORGE WARBURTON, M.B., CH.B., D.SC., D.R.C.O.G., F.R.C.P.E., D.P.M., M.R.C.PSYCH., Psychiatrist.
ASHTON, PETER SHAW, M.A., PH.D., Botanist.
ASPINALL, GERALD OLIVER, D.SC., PH.D., F.R.I.C., Chemist.
ATKINSON, JAMES ROBERT, M.A., F.INST.P., Engineer.
ATWELL, Sir JOHN WILLIAM, C.B.E., M.SC., LL.D., C.ENG., F.I.MECH.E., Engineer.
AUERBACH, CHARLOTTE, PH.D., D.SC., F.R.S., Geneticist.

BACON, JOHN STANLEY DURRANT, M.A., SC.D., PH.D., Chemist.
BACSICH, PAUL, M.D., D.SC., F.R.C.S.G., F.I.C.S., Embryologist.
BADDILEY, Sir JAMES, PH.D., D.SC., F.R.S., Chemist.
BAIN, ANDREW DAVID, M.A., PH.D., Economist.
BAKER, TERENCE GEORGE, PH.D., D.SC., Physician.
BALERNO OF CURRIE, Baron ALICK, C.B.E., D.L., M.A., D.SC., M.S.A., Geneticist.
BALFOUR, ELIZABETH JEAN, D.SC., Ecologist.
BALL, JOHN MACLEOD, D.PHIL., Mathematician.
BAND, DAVID, M.B., CH.B., F.R.C.S.E., Urologist.
BARNES, MARGARET, D.SC., Marine Biologist.
BARR, LESLIE WILLIAMSON, PH.D., Physicist.
BARROW, GEOFFREY WALLIS STEUART, M.A., D.LITT., F.S.A.SCOT., F.B.A., Historian.
BARTHOLOMEW, JOHN CHRISTOPHER, M.A., Cartographer.
BARTON, Sir DEREK (HAROLD RICHARD), PH.D., D.SC., F.R.S., Chemist.
BATCHELOR, IVOR RALPH CAMPBELL, C.B.E., M.B., CH.B., F.R.C.P.E., F.R.C.PSYCH., D.P.M., Psychiatrist.
BATH, FREDERICK, PH.D., Mathematician.
BAYNE, STEPHEN, B.SC., M.B., CH.B., Biochemist.
BEALE, GOEFFREY HERBERT, M.B.E., PH.D., F.R.S., Geneticist.
BEATTIE, ARTHUR JAMES, M.A., Linguist.
BEATTY, RICHARD ALAN, M.A., PH.D., Geneticist.
BEEVERS, CECIL ARNOLD, D.SC., F.INST.P., Crystallographer.
BEGG, CHARLES MICHAEL MACINTYRE, M.A., PH.D., Zoologist.
BELCH, ALEXANDER ROSS, C.B.E., B.SC., F.B.I.M., Industrialist.
BELL, FRANK, D.SC., F.R.I.C., Chemist.
BELL, GEORGE HOWARD, B.SC., M.D., Physiologist.
BELL, JAMES, PH.D., D.SC., F.R.I.C., Chemist.
BELL, RONALD PERCY, M.A., F.R.S., F.R.I.C., Chemist.
BELLIS, BERTRAM THOMAS, M.A., F.I.M.A., F.R.S.A., Headmaster.
BENTLEY, KENNETH WALTER, PH.D., M.A., F.C.S., Chemist.
BERRY, JOHN, C.B.E., D.L., M.A., PH.D., LL.D., Naturalist.
BERRY, ROBERT JAMES, PH.D., D.SC., Geneticist.
BEVERIDGE, GORDON SMITH GRIEVE, C.ENG., A.R.C.S.T., PH.D., F.I.CHEM.E., Chemical Engineer.
BIJL, DIRK, DR.SC., M.A., Physicist.
BISHOP, GEORGE ROBERT, M.A., D.PHIL., Physicist.
BISHOP, JOHN OLIVER, PH.D., Geneticist.
BLACK, JOHN NICHOLSON, M.A., D.PHIL., D.SC., F.INST.BIOL., Biologist.
BLACK, MATTHEW, M.A., D.LITT., D.D., DR.PHIL., D.THEOL., F.B.A., Theologian.
BLAKE, CHRISTOPHER, M.A., PH.D., Economist.
BLAXTER, JOHN HARRY SAVAGE, M.A., D.SC., Marine Biologist.
BLAXTER, Sir KENNETH LYON, PH.D., D.SC., F.R.S., F.R.S.A., Nutritionist.
BLUCK, BRIAN JOHN, F.G.S., Geologist.
BLYTH, THOMAS SCOTT, D.SC., D. ÈS SC., F.I.M.A., Mathematician.

BODDIE, GEORGE FREDERICK, B.SC., P.P.R.C.V.S., Veterinary Surgeon.
BODDY, KEITH, PH.D., D.SC., Medical Physicist.
BOLTON, WILLIAM, O.B.E., D.SC., F.R.I.C., F.C.S., F.INST.BIOL, Biologist.
BONEY, ARTHUR DONALD, PH.D., D.SC., F.INST.BIOL., F.L.S., Botanist.
BONSALL, FRANK FEATHERSTONE, M.A., D.SC., F.R.S., Mathematician.
BORWEIN, DAVID, PH.D., D.SC., Mathematician.
BOWES, DONALD RALPH, M.SC., PH.D., D.SC., F.G.S., F.G.S.A., D.I.C., Geologist.
BOWIE, STANLEY HAY UMPHRAY, D.SC., F.R.S., F.G.S., M.M.I.M., Geochemist.
BOWMAN, WILLIAM CAMERON, PH.D., D.SC., F.INST.BIOL., M.P.S., Pharmacologist.
BOYD, GEORGE SCOTT, A.H.-W.C., PH.D., A.R.I.C., Biochemist.
BOYD, IAN ALEXANDER, PH.D., M.D., D.SC., M.R.C.P.G., Physiologist.
BOYD, JOHN MORTON, D.SC., PH.D., Naturalist.
BOYNE, ALEXANDER WILLIAM, B.SC., Biochemist.
BRIMACOMBE, JOHN STUART, PH.D., D.SC., F.R.I.C., Chemist.
BROADLEY, JOHN STEWART, PH.D., F.R.I.C., A.I.M., Nuclear Chemist.
BROOK, ALAN JOHN, PH.D., D.SC., Biologist.
BROOK, GEOFFREY BERNARD, D.SC., F.R.C.V.S., Veterinary Surgeon.
BROOKS, CHARLES JOSEPH WILLIAM, PH.D., D.SC., Chemist.
BROOKSBY, JOHN BURNS, C.B.E., PH.D., D.SC., M.R.C.V.S., Veterinary Surgeon.
BROUGH, JAMES, D.SC., Zoologist.
BROWN, ARTHUR FREDERICK, M.A., PH.D., F.I.M., F.INST.P., Physicist.
BROWN, GEORGE MALCOLM, M.A., D.PHIL., Geologist.
BROWN, JEHOIADA JOHN, B.SC., M.B., B.S., F.R.C.P., Physician.
BROWN, LESLIE MAURICE, M.SC., PH.D., Mathematician.
BROWN, PETER EVANS, PH.D., F.G.S., Geologist.
BRUCE, FREDERICK MALLOCH, M.SC., PH.D., M.I.E.E., Electrical Engineer.
BRÜCK, HERMANN ALEXANDER, C.B.E., D.PHIL., PH.D., M.R.I.A., F.R.A.S., Astronomer.
BRYAN, Sir ANDREW MEIKLE, D.SC., LL.D., M.I.MIN.E., Engineer.
BRYDEN, WILLIAM, C.B.E., PH.D., D.SC., Biologist.
BUCHAN, STEVENSON, C.B.E., PH.D., F.G.S., Geologist.
BUCHANAN, JOHN GRANT, M.A., PH.D., SC.D., Chemist.
BURDON, ROY HUNTER, PH.D., Biochemist.
BURGESS, GEOFFREY HAROLD ORCHARD, PH.D., Biochemist.
BURNETT, JOHN HARRISON, M.A., D.PHIL., Botanist.
BURT, DAVID RAITT ROBERTSON, B.SC., F.L.S., Zoologist.
BURTON, WILLIAM KEITH, M.SC., PH.D., Physicist.
BURTT, BRIAN LAURENCE, B.SC., F.L.S., Botanist.
BUTLER, DAVID STANLEY, B.A., F.I.M.A., Mathematician.

CADOGAN, JOHN IVAN GEORGE, PH.D., D.SC., F.R.S., F.R.S.C., Chemist.
CALDER, ALEXANDER, O.B.E., PH.D., N.D.A., Nutritionist.
CALLAN, HAROLD GARNET, M.A., D.SC., F.R.S., Biologist.
CALMAN, KENNETH CHARLES, PH.D., M.D., F.R.C.S., Oncologist.
CAMERON, GEORGE GORDON, PH.D., D.SC., Chemist.
CAMERON, The Hon. Lord, D.S.C., Q.C., D.L., LL.D., M.A., Lawyer.
CAMPBELL, JOHN GORDON, PH.D., F.R.C.V.S., F.R.C.PATH., Veterinary Surgeon.
CAMPBELL, Sir MATTHEW, C.B., M.A., Civil Servant.
CAMPBELL, NEIL, O.B.E., D.SC., PH.D., F.C.S., Chemist.
CAPON, BRIAN, PH.D., Chemist.
CARTER, HAROLD BURNELL, B.V.SC., F.INST.BIOL., Agriculturist.
CARTER, THOMAS CHRISTOPHER, O.B.E., M.A., PH.D., D.SC., Poultry Scientist.
CASSELS, JOHN WILLIAM SCOTT, M.A., F.R.S., Mathematician.
CASSIE, WILLIAM FISHER, C.B.E., PH.D., M.S., F.I.C.E., F.I.STRUCT.E., P.P.INST.H.E., Civil Engineer.
CHALMERS, JAMES GOWANS, B.SC., Biochemist.
CHALMERS, ROBERT ALEXANDER, PH.D., D.SC., F.R.I.C., Chemist.
CHAMBERLAIN, ERIC ALFRED CHARLES, O.B.E., PH.D., A.R.C.S., D.I.C., Chemist.
CHARLTON, THOMAS MALCOLM, B.SC.ENG., M.A., F.I.C.E., Engineer.
CHECKLAND, SYDNEY GEORGE, M.A., M.COM., PH.D., F.B.A., Economist.
CHESTERS, CHARLES GEDDES COULL, M.SC., PH.D., F.L.S., Botanist.
CHILDS, WILLIAM HAROLD JOSEPH, PH.D., D.SC., F.INST.P., F.PHYS.S., Physicist.
CHOUDHURI, HIRAN CHANDRA, M.A., PH.D., Botanist.
CLARK, ARTHUR MELVILLE, K.L.J., M.A., D.PHIL., D.LITT., *Literatum*.
CLARK, ROBERT BERNARD, PH.D., D.SC., F.L.S., F.Z.S., F.INST.BIOL., Zoologist.

CLARK, WILLIAM ANDREW, PH.D., Botanist.
CLERK, Sir JOHN DUTTON, C.B.E., V.R.D., Antiquarian.
CLOW, ARCHIE, M.A., PH.D., D.SC., F.R.S.C., Chemist.
COCHRAN, WILLIAM, PH.D., M.A., F.R.S., Physicist.
COLLINS, MARY, M.A., PH.D., Psychologist.
COLLINS, WILLIAM DEREK, PH.D., D.SC., Mathematician.
COMLINE, ROBERT SEMPLE, M.A., PH.D., M.R.C.V.S., Veterinary Surgeon.
CONNELL, Sir CHARLES GIBSON, B.L., J.P., Solicitor.
CONWAY, ELSIE, PH.D., Botanist.
COOK, ALAN HUGH, M.A., PH.D., SC.D., F.R.S., Physicist.
COOK, JOHN, M.B., CH.M., F.R.C.S.E., Surgeon.
COOK, ROBERT PERCIVAL, D.SC., PH.D., Biochemist.
COOPER, MALCOLM MCGREGOR, B.AGR.SC., B.LITT., Agriculturist.
COPPOCK, JOHN TERENCE, M.A., PH.D., F.B.A., Geographer.
CORMACK, RICHARD MELVILLE, M.A., PH.D., Statistician.
CORMIE, WILLIAM MURRAY, C.B.E., E.R.D., C.ENG., F.I.C.E., F.I.W.E., M.I.E.S., Engineer.
CORNWELL, JOHN FRANCIS, PH.D., A.R.C.S., D.I.C., Physicist.
COSSAR, JAMES, M.A., PH.D., Mathematician.
COULL, ALEXANDER, PH.D., F.I.STRUCT.E., F.I.C.E., F.A.S.C.E., Engineer.
COUPLAND, REX ERNEST, M.D., PH.D., D.SC., Psychiatrist.
COWIE, JOHN MCKENZIE GRANT, PH.D., Chemist.
COWLEY, ROGER ARTHUR, M.A., PH.D., F.R.S., Physicist.
CRACKNELL, ARTHUR PHILIP, M.A., D.PHIL., M.SC., F.INST.P., Physicist.
CRAIG, GORDON YOUNGER, PH.D., F.G.S., Geologist.
CRAIG-BENNETT, ARTHUR LANCELOT, O.B.E., M.A., PH.D., Zoologist.
CRAMOND, WILLIAM ALEXANDER, O.B.E., M.D., D.P.M., Psychologist.
CRAWFORD, LIONEL VIVIAN, PH.D., Biochemist.
CRAWFORD, ROBERT MACGREGOR MARTYN, D.SC., Botanist.
CRICHTON, JOHN ANDREW, M.B.E., M.A., B.SC., Biochemist.
CROSS, ROBERT CRAIGIE, C.B.E., M.A., Logician.
CRUICKSHANK, ARTHUR JAMES OGILVIE, PH.D., F.I.E.E., Electrical Engineer.
CUMMING, Sir RONALD STUART, T.D., Industrialist.
CUNNINGHAM, JOHN MCCANDLISH MURDOCH, PH.D., Agriculturist.
CURLE, SAMUEL NEWBY, M.SC., PH.D., Mathematician.
CURRAN, ROBERT CROWE, M.B., CH.B., M.D., M.R.C.P., Pathologist.
CURRAN, Sir SAMUEL (CROWE), M.A., PH.D., D.SC., F.R.S., Nuclear Physicist.
CURRIE, ALASTAIR ROBERT, B.SC., M.B., CH.B., F.R.C.P.E., F.R.C.P.G., Pathologist.
CURRIE, RONALD IAN, B.SC., F.INST.BIOL., Marine Biologist.
CURTIS, ADAM SEBASTIAN GENEVIEVE, M.A., PH.D., F.INST.BIOL., Biologist.
CUSENS, ANTHONY RALPH, PH.D., C.ENG., F.I.C.E., F.I.STRUCT.E., Civil Engineer.
CUTHBERTSON, Sir DAVID (PATON), C.B.E., M.D., D.SC., LL.D., F.R.C.P.E., Biochemist
CUTTER, ELIZABETH GRAHAM, D.SC., PH.D., Botanist.

DAFT, MELVIN JAMES FRANCIS, PH.D., Botanist.
DAICHES, DAVID, D.LITT., D.PHIL., PH.D., F.R.S.L., *Literatum*.
DAINTY, JACK, M.A., D.SC., Botanist.
DALE, JOHN EGERTON, PH.D., Botanist.
DALLING, Sir THOMAS, M.A., LL.D., D.SC., D.V.M., F.R.C.V.S., Veterinary Surgeon.
DAVIDSON, Sir LEYBOURNE STANLEY PATRICK, B.A., M.D., F.R.C.P., Physician.
DAVIDSON, MAXWELL, PH.D., M.I.MECH.E., Engineer.
DAVIDSON, WILLIAM MACKAY, M.B., CH.B., M.D., Haematologist.
DAVIE, ALEXANDER MUNRO, PH.D., Mathematician.
DAVIE, CEDRIC THORPE, O.B.E., F.R.A.M., LL.D., Musician.
DAVIS, PETER HADLAND, PH.D., F.L.S., Botanist.
DAWSON, IAN MACPHAIL, D.SC., F.R.I.C., Electron Microscopist.
DAWSON, JOHN BARRY, PH.D., D.SC., F.G.S., Geologist.
DEACON, Sir GEORGE (EDWARD RAVEN), C.B.E., D.SC., F.R.S., F.R.MET.S., F.R.A.S., F.R.G.S., Oceanographer.
DEE, PHILIP IVOR, C.B.E., M.A., F.R.S., Physicist.
DICKSON, WILLIAM, M.B., CH.B., T.D., Chemist.
DINGLE, ROBERT BALSON, M.A., PH.D., Physicist.
DOBSON, NORMAN, B.SC., M.R.C.V.S., Veterinary Surgeon.
DODD, JAMES MUNRO, PH.D., F.R.S., Zoologist.
DOIG, ALEXANDER THOM, M.D., F.R.C.P.E., F.R.C.P.G., D.P.H., Physician.
DOLLAR, ARCHIBALD THOMAS JOHN, PH.D., A.K.S., F.G.S., M.I.M.M., Geologist.
DONALDSON, GORDON, M.A., D.LITT., F.B.A., Historian.
DONOVAN, ROBERT JOHN, PH.D., Chemist.
DOVER, Sir KENNETH JAMES, M.A., F.B.A., Classicist.
DOWSON, HENRY RICHARD, PH.D., Mathematician.

DOYLE, WILLIAM PATRICK, PH.D., Chemist.
DRAPER, MORRELL HENRY, O.B.E., M.B., B.S., PH.D., Physician.
DRENNAN, ALEXANDER MURRAY, M.D., F.R.C.P.E., Pathologist.
DREVER, JAMES, M.A., Psychologist.
DREVER, RONALD WILLIAM PREST, M.A., PH.D., Physicist.
DROOP, MICHAEL RICHMOND, D.SC., PH.D., F.INST.BIOL., S.P.S.O., Microbiologist.
DUFF, PETER MCLAREN DONALD, PH.D., F.G.S., Geologist.
DUNBAR, ALEXANDER, PH.D., Industrialist.
DUNBAR NASMITH, JAMES DUNCAN, C.B.E., B.A., D.A., R.I.B.A., P.P.R.I.A.S., Architect.
DUNCAN, ARCHIBALD ALEXANDER MCBETH, M.A., Historian.
DUNCAN, JOHN, M.SC., PH.D., Mathematician.
DUNCAN, WILLIAM BARR MCKINNON, C.B.E., B.SC., LL.D., Industrialist.
DUNHAM, Sir KINGSLEY (CHARLES), PH.D., S.D., D.SC., C.ENG., M.I.M.M., F.G.S., F.R.S., Geologist.
DUNNET, GEORGE MACKENZIE, PH.D., Zoologist.
DURNIN, JOHN VALENTINE GEORGE ANDREW, M.A., M.B., CH.B., D.SC., F.R.C.P.G., Physiologist.
DUTTON, GEOFFREY JOHN FRASER, PH.D., D.SC., Biochemist.

EASON, GEORGE, M.SC., PH.D., Mathematician.
EASTHAM, JOHN FREDERICK, D.SC., PH.D., F.I.E.E., Engineer.
EBSWORTH, EVELYN ALGERNON VALENTINE, PH.D., F.C.S., Chemist.
EDDISON, JAMES ANDREW, M.A., Civil Engineer.
EDEN, ROBERT ARTHUR B.SC. F.G.S., Geologist.
EDGE, WILLIAM LEONARD, M.A., SC.D., Mathematician.
EGGELING, WILLIAM JULIUS, C.B.E., PH.D., Biologist.
EISNER, EDWARD, PH.D., F.INST.P., Physicist.
ELGOOD, LEONARD ALSAGER, O.B.E., M.C., D.L., J.P., C.A., Industrialist.
ELLIOT, GERALD, HENRY, B.A., A.I.C.S., Industrialist.
ELLIOTT, FREDERICK JACOB, M.SC., PH.D., F.R.I.C., Physiologist.
ELPHINSTONE, Sir MAURICE DOUGLAS WARBURTON, M.A., F.F.A., Actuary.
EMERY, ALAN ELGIN HEATHCOTE, M.D., D.SC., PH.D., D.P.M., F.R.C.P.E., M.F.C.M., Geneticist.
EMMETT, WILLIAM GIDLEY, M.A., Educationalist.
ETHERINGTON, IVOR MALCOLM HADDON, B.A., D.SC., Mathematician.
EVANS, HENRY JOHN, PH.D., Geneticist.
EVERETT, DOUGLAS HUGH, M.B.E., M.A., D.PHIL., D.SC., Chemist.
EVERITT, WILLIAM NORRIE, M.A., D.PHIL., Mathematician.

FAIRBAIRN, WILLIAM ALEXANDER, D.SC., Forester.
FALCONER, DOUGLAS SCOTT, PH.D., SC.D., F.R.S., Geneticist.
FARAGO, PETER STEPHEN, PH.D., Physicist.
FARMER, VICTOR COLIN, PH.D., F.R.I.C., Spectrochemist.
FARVIS, WILLIAM EWART JOHN, C.B.E., B.SC., F.I.E.E., Electrical Engineer.
FELLGETT, PETER BERNERS, M.A., PH.D., Physicist.
FENTON, WILFRID DAVID DRYSDALE, C.B.E., B.SC., F.I.E.E., Engineer.
FERGUSON, HUGH, B.SC., N.D.A., N.D.D., Nutritionist.
FERGUSON-SMITH, MALCOLM ANDREW, M.B., CH.B., M.R.C.PATH., F.R.C.P., F.R.C.P.S.G., Geneticist.
FERRIER, ROBERT PATTON, M.SC., PH.D., Physicist.
FEWSON, CHARLES ARTHUR, PH.D., Biochemist.
FINCHAM, JOHN ROBERT STANLEY, PH.D., SC.D., F.R.S., Geneticist.
FINNEY, DAVID JOHN, M.A., SC.D., F.R.S., F.S.S., Statistician.
FINNISTON, Sir HAROLD MONTAGUE, PH.D., D.SC., Industrialist.
FLECK, ADAM, B.SC., M.B., CH.B., PH.D., F.R.I.C., M.R.C.PATH., Biochemist.
FLEMING, WILLIAM LAUNCELOT SCOTT (The Rt Rev. the Dean of Windsor), K.C.V.O., M.A., D.D., M.S., Minister of Religion.
FLETCHER, WILLIAM WHIGHAM, PH.D., F.L.S., Biologist.
FLETT, WILLIAM ROBERTS, B.SC., Geologist.
FLUENDY, MALCOLM ANTHONY DAVID, M.A., D.PHIL., C.CHEM., F.R.S.C., M.INST.P., Chemist.
FOISTER, CHARLES EDWARD, PH.D., Agriculturist.
FORBES, IAN ALEXANDER, PH.D., F.B.I.M., Chemist.
FORFAR, JOHN OLDROYD, M.C., B.SC., M.D., F R.C.P., D.C.H., Paediatrician.
FORREST, ANDREW PATRICK MCEWEN, CH.M., M.D., F.R.C.S.E., F.R.C.S., F.R.C.S.G., Surgeon.
FORREST, HUGH SOMMERVILLE, PH.D., D.SC., Zoologist
FOSTER, ROY, D.PHIL., D.SC., Chemist.
FOTHERGILL, JOHN EDWARD, PH.D., Biochemist.
FRANCIS, EDWARD HOWEL, D.SC., F.G.S., Geologist.
FRASER, Sir IAN, D.S.O., O.B.E., D.L., M.D., M.CH., F.R.C.S.(ENG.)., F.R.C.S.I., Surgeon.
FRASER, Sir JAMES CAMPBELL, B.COM., F.B.I.M., Industrialist.

FRASER, JAMES HENRY, D.SC., PH.D., M.INST.BIOL., Marine Biologist.
FRASER, KENNETH BOYD, M.C., CH.B., M.D., D.SC., Microbiologist.
FRASER, ROBERT, PH.D., Haematologist.
FRAZER, SAMUEL CHERRIE, M.B., CH.B., PH.D., Pathologist.
FREND, WILLIAM HUGH CLIFFORD, T.D., D.PHIL., B.D., M.A., D.D., F.S.A., Theologian.
FULTON, ANGUS ANDERSON, C.B.E., B.SC.ENG., LL.D., P.P.I.C.E., F.I.MECH.E., Engineer.

GANGULI, SANJIBAN, M.A., Educationist.
GARLAND, PETER BRYAN, M.B., CH.B., B.A., PH.D., Biochemist.
GARRY, ROBERT CAMPBELL, O.B.E., M.B., CH.B., D.SC., Physiologist.
GARTON, GEORGE ALAN, PH.D., D.SC., F.R.S., Biochemist.
GASH, NORMAN, B.LITT., M.A., F.R.HIST.S., F.B.A., F.R.S.L., Historian
GAZE, RAYMOND MICHAEL, B.A., D.PHIL., L.R.C.P.E., L.R.C.S.E., F.R.S., Biochemist.
GEDDES, WILLIAM GEORGE NICHOLSON, B.SC., F.I.C.E., F.I.STRUCT.E., C.ENG., Engineer.
GEMMELL, ALAN ROBERTSON, PH.D., M.S., Biologist.
GENTLES, JAMES CLARK, PH.D., Medical Mycologist.
GERARD, ARTHUR GEOFFREY LANGFORD, B.A., M.I.E.E., Engineer.
GIBSON, Sir ALEXANDER, C.B.E., LL.D., MUS.DOC., Musical Conductor.
GIBSON, DAVID TEMPLETON, M.SC., PH.D., D.SC., Chemist.
GIBSON, THOMAS, M.B., CH.B., D.SC., F.R.C.S.E., F.R.C.S.G., Bioengineer.
GIFFORD, CHARLES HENRY PEARSON, M.A., Industrialist.
GILLES, DENIS CYRIL, PH.D., A.R.C.S., D.I.C., F.R.S.A., Computer Scientist.
GILLESPIE, Rev. ALEXANDER MACANDREW, O.B.E., M.D., D.T.M., F.R.C.P.E., F.R.M.S., F.R.G.S., F.S.A.SCOT., F.Z.S., Physician.
GILLESPIE, JOHN SPENCE, M.B., CH.B., PH.D., Pharmacologist.
GILLINGHAM, FRANCIS JOHN, M.B.E., M.B., B.S., F.R.C.S., F.R.C.S.E., F.R.C.P.E., Neurologist.
GIMINGHAM, CHARLES HENRY, PH.D., Botanist.
GINSBORG, BERNARD LIONEL, B.SC., Pharmacologist.
GIRDWOOD, RONALD HAXTON, M.D., PH.D., F.R.C.P.E., F.R.C.P., F.R.C.PATH., Physician.
GLOVER, ROLAND STANLEY, B.SC., F.INST.BIOL., Marine Biologist.
GOLDBERG, ABRAHAM, M.B., CH.B., M.D., D.SC., F.R.C.P.G., F.R.C.P.E., F.R.C.P., Physician.
GORDON, MANFRED, PH.D., D.SC., Chemist.
GOSLING, Sir ARTHUR HULIN, K.B.E., C.B., B.SC.FOR., F.R.I.C.S., Forester.
GOUDIE, ROBERT BARCLAY, M.B., CH.B., M.D., M.R.C.P., F.R.C.P.G., Pathologist.
GOULD, JAMES CAMERON, M.B., CH.B., M.D., D.SC., F.R.C.P.E., F.INST.BIOL., Microbiologist.
GOW, JOHN STOBIE, PH.D., Industrialist.
GOWENLOCK, BRIAN GLOVER, PH.D., D.SC., Chemist.
GRAHAM, DENNIS COULTHARD, PH.D., Agriculturist.
GRAHAM, JAMES DAVID PROVINS, B.SC., M.B., M.D., F.R.C.P.G., Pharmacologist.
GRAHAM, Sir NORMAN WILLIAM, C.B., Educationist.
GRANT, DOUGLAS, Publisher.
GRANT, JAMES KERR, PH.D., F.R.S.C., Biochemist.
GRANT, PATRICK THOMAS, PH.D., F.INST.BIOL., Marine Biologist.
GRASSIE, NORMAN, PH.D., D.SC., F.R.S.C., Chemist.
GREEN, JAMES ALEXANDER, PH.D., Mathematician.
GREENING, JOHN RAYMOND, PH.D., D.SC., F.INST.P., Medical Physicist.
GREENWOOD, CHARLES TREVOR, PH.D., D.SC., F.R.I.C., Chemist.
GREGORY, RICHARD LANGTON, M.A., Psychologist.
GREIG, DAVID CUNNINGHAM, M.A., B.SC., F.G.S., Geologist.
GREIG, JAMES, M.SC., PH.D., M.I.E.E., F.H.-W.C., Electrical Engineer.
GRESSON, RICHARD ARBUTHNOT REYNELL, PH.D., D.SC., M.R.I.A., Zoologist.
GRIEVE, Sir ROBERT, M.A., D.LITT., M.I.C.E., F.R.T.P.I., F.R.I.A.S., Town Planner.
GRIGOR, JAMES, PH.D., A.R.C.S.T., Industrialist.
GUNN, JOHN CURRIE, M.A., Physicist.
GUNSTONE, FRANK DENBY, PH.D., D.SC., F.R.I.C., Chemist.
GUTHRIE, DAVID MALTBY, PH.D., Zoologist.

HADDINGTON, The Rt. Hon. The Earl of, M.C., T.D., D.L., Antiquarian.
HADDOW, Sir (THOMAS) DOUGLAS, M.A., LL.D., Industrialist.
HALE, ARTHUR JAMES, M.B., CH.B., PH.D., D.SC., F.R.C.PATH., F.INST.BIOL., Industrialist.
HALNAN, KEITH EDWARD, M.A., M.D., B.CHIR., F.R.C.R., F.R.C.P.G., F.R.C.P., Radiologist.
HAMILTON, Sir JAMES ARNOT, C.B., B.SC., Educationist.

HAMILTON, JOHN ALEXANDER KING, G.M., D.SC., F.H.-W.C., F.I.C.E., M.I.MECH.E., Civil Engineer.
HAMILTON, RICHARD ALEXANDER, O.B.E., M.A., Meteorologist.
HAMILTON, WILLIAM ALLAN, PH.D., Microbiologist.
HARLAND, SYDNEY CROSS, D.SC., F.R.S., Botanist.
HARLAND, WILLIAM ARTHUR, M.D., PH.D., F.R.C.P.C., F.R.C.P.G., F.R.C.PATH., Forensic Scientist.
HARPER, ALFRED ALEXANDER, M.A., M.B., CH.B., M.D., Physiologist.
HARPER, PHILIP GEORGE, PH.D., Physicist.
HARPER, WALTER FEARN, O.B.E., M.D., PH.D., Anatomist.
HARRIS, PHILLIP, F.R.C.P.E., F.R.C.S.E., F.R.C.S.G., F.R.S.M., Neurosurgeon.
HARRISON, BRYAN DESMOND, PH.D., Virologist.
HARRISON, JOHN HESLOP, D.SC., PH.D., F.R.S., F.L.S., M.R.I.A., Botanist.
HAWTHORN, JOHN, PH.D., F.R.I.C., Nutritionist.
HAXTON, HERBERT ALEXANDER, B.SC., M.B., CH.B., CH.M., M.D., F.R.C.S., Surgeon.
HAY, DENYS, B.A., M.A., D.LITT., F.B.A., Historian.
HAY, ROBERT WALKER, PH.D., Chemist.
HAYES, WILLIAM, B.A., M.B., CH.B., B.A.O., SC.D., D.SC., F.R.S., F.R.C.P.I., D.P.H., Biologist.
HEALD, PETER JOSEPH, D.SC., PH.D., Biochemist.
HEGGIE, JAMES FERGUSON, V.D., M.B., CH.B., B.SC., Pathologist.
HELLIWELL, JOHN BRIAN, PH.D., Mathematician.
HENDERSON, DOUGLAS MACKAY, B.SC., Botanist.
HENDERSON, GEORGE OTTO THOMSON DAWSON, D.SC., PH.D., Oceanographer.
HENDERSON, GEORGE PATRICK, M.A., Philosopher.
HENDERSON, Sir WILLIAM (MACGREGOR), D.SC., F.R.S., F.R.C.V.S., Animal Virologist.
HENDRY, ARNOLD WILLIAM, PH.D., D.SC., F.I.C.E., M.I.STRUCT.E., Civil Engineer.
HEYES, JOHN KENNETH, M.SC., PH.D., F.C.S., Botanist.
HEYWOOD, PHILIP, M.A., D.PHIL., Mathematician.
HIBBERD, GEORGE, PH.D., A.R.C.S.T., M.I.MIN.E., Mining Engineer.
HIGGS, PETER WARE, M.SC., PH.D., Physicist.
HILL, ALEXANDER REID, PH.D., Zoologist.
HILL, Sir IAN GEORGE WILSON, C.B.E., T.D., M.B., CH.B., LL.D., F.R.C.P., Physician.
HILL, WILLIAM GEORGE, Geneticist.
HISLOP, GEORGE STEEDMAN, C.B.E., PH.D., A.R.C.S.T., C.ENG., F.I.MECH.E., F.R.AE.S., F.R.S.A., Engineer.
HOARE, DERRICK ERNEST, M.A., PH.D., Chemist.
HOBSON, PETER NORMAN, PH.D., D.SC., F.R.I.C., Microbiologist.
HOGGAN, HARRY, M.A., ED.B., Broadcaster.
HOLDEN, ALAN VERNON, B.A., P.S.O., Fisheries Biologist.
HOLLIDAY, FREDERICK GEORGE THOMAS, C.B.E., B.SC., Zoologist.
HOLMS, WILLIAM HENRY, PH.D., M.INST.BIOL., Biochemist.
HOME OF THE HIRSEL, Baron, ALEXANDER FREDERICK DOUGLAS-HOME, K.T., P.C., D.L., B.A., Politician.
HOPGOOD, ALARIC MORTIMER, M.SC., PH.D., Geologist.
HOPKINS, CHARLES ADRIAN, PH.D., Parasitologist.
HORN, DAVID BOWES, PH.D., F.R.I.C., F.R.C.PATH., Chemist.
HORSPOOL, WILLIAM MCKIE, PH.D., M.R.I.C., Chemist.
HOWE, GEORGE MELVYN, PH.D., D.SC., Geographer.
HOWIE, JOHN MACKINTOSH, M.A., D.PHIL., Mathematician.
HUGHES, IAN SIMPSON, PH.D., Physicist.
HUNT, OWEN DUKE, B.SC., Zoologist.
HUNTER, Lord, OF NEWINGTON, M.B., CH.B., LL.D., F.R.C.P.E., F.R.C.P., Pharmacologist.
HUTCHINSON, STEPHEN ANGUS, PH.D., T.D., Botanist.
HUTCHISON, JAMES HOLMES, M.B., CH.B., M.D., F.R.C.P.G., F.R.C.P., F.R.C.P.E., Paediatrician.
HUTCHION, THOMAS SHERRET, PH.D., Physicist.
HUTCHISON, WILLIAM MCPHEE, D.SC., PH.D., Parasitologist.
HUTTON, WILLIAM, C.B.E., M.A., LL.B., Solicitor.
HYSLOP, JAMES MORTON, M.A., D.SC., PH.D., Mathematician.

IBALL, JOHN, D.SC., F.INST.P., Chemist.
IGGO, AINSLEY, M.AGR.SC., PH.D., F.R.S., Veterinary Surgeon.
IRVINE, WILLIAM JAMES, B.SC., M.B., CH.B., D.SC., F.R.C.P.E., M.R.C.PATH., Physician.

JACK, DAVID, PH.D., F.P.S., F.R.I.C., Industrialist.
JACKSON, JOHN MEADOWS, PH.D., F.I.M.A., F.R.A.S., Mathematician.
JACKSON, PHILIP, M.SC., C.ENG., F.I.MECH.E., F.I.CHEM.E., Engineer.
JACOBS, PATRICIA ANN, D.SC., Anatomist.
JAEGER, LESLIE GORDON, M.A., PH.D., Engineer.
JAMES, KEITH, PH.D., D.SC., Surgeon.
JARRETT, WILLIAM FLEMING HOGGAN, PH.D., M.R.C.V.S., Pathologist.
JARVIS, PAUL GORDON, PH.D., FIL. DR., Botanist.

Jason, Alfred Charles, ph.d., Physicist.
Jeeves, Malcolm Alexander, m.a., ph.d., f.b.ps.s., f.a.p.s., Psychologist.
Jeffares, Alexander Norman, ph.d., d.phil., f.r.s.a., f.r.s.l., *Literatum.*
Jeffery, Jonathan D'Arden, m.a., d.phil., f.r.s.c., Biochemist.
Jeffrey, Alan, d.sc., ph.d., f.i.m.a., Mathematician.
Jenkins, Arthur Percival, b.sc., f.i.c.e., f.i.p., Chemist.
Johnson, Michael Raymond Walter, ph.d., f.g.s., Geologist.
Johnson, Ralph Hudson, m.a., m.d., d.sc., d.phil., d.m., f.r.c.p.g., Neurosurgeon.
Johnston, John McQueen, c.b.e., m.d., ll.d., f.r.c.s.e., f.r.c.p.e., Physician.
Johnston, Thomas Lothian, ph.d., Economist.
Johnstone, George Scott, b.sc., f.g.s., Geologist.
Jones, Douglas Samuel, m.b.e., m.a., d.sc., f.r.s., Mathematician.
Jones, Reginald Victor, c.b., c.b.e., m.a., d.phil., f.r.s., Physicist.
Jurand, Arthur, ph.d., Teratologist.

Kay, Sir Andrew (Watt), m.d., ch.m., f.r.c.s.e., f.r.c.s.g., f.r.c.s., Surgeon.
Kay, Robin Noel Brunyate, m.a., ph.d., Physiologist.
Keers, Robert Young, m.d., f.r.c.p.e., f.r.c.p.g., Physician.
Keir, Hamish MacDonald, ph.d., f.r.i.c., f.inst.biol., Biochemist.
Kemball, Charles, m.a., sc.d., f.r.i.c., m.r.i.a., f.r.s., Chemist
Kemmer, Nicholas, m.a., ph.d., f.r.s., Physicist.
Kendall, James Tyldesley, m.a., ph.d., f.inst.p., m.i.e.e., f.r.i.c., Industrialist.
Kenedi, Robert Maximillian, ph.d., a.r.c.s.t., f.i.mech.e., m.r.ae.s., Bioengineer.
Kennedy, Walter Phillips, c.st.j., ph.d., f.r.c.p.g., f.r.s.c., Chemist.
Kenny, Anthony John Patrick, f.b.a., d.phil., ph.l., *Literatum.*
Kerr, John Gibson, w.s., f.r.a.s., Solicitor.
Kerr, William Rowan, i.s.o., ph.d., f.r.c.v.s., d.v.s.m., f.r.c.path., Veterinary Surgeon.
Kevan, Douglas Keith McEwan, ph.d., a.i.c.t.a., m.inst.biol., Entomologist.
Kilbey, Brian John, ph.d., d.sc., Geneticist.
King, Basil Charles, ph.d., d.sc., f.g.s., Geologist.
King, John William Beaufoy, m.a., ph.d., f.inst.biol., Biologist.
Kirby, Gordon William, m.a., ph.d., sc.d., f.r.i.c., Chemist.
Knops, Robin John, ph.d., Mathematician.
Knox, John, b.sc., Geologist.
Knox, John Henderson, d.sc., ph.d., Chemist.
Koller, Peo Charles, ph.d., d.sc., Cytogeneticist.
Kosterlitz, Hans Walter, m.d., ph.d., d.sc., f.r.s., Pharmacologist.
Kuper, Charles Goethe, m.a., ph.d., Physicist.

Laing, Ernest William, ph.d., Physicist.
Lamb, John, ph.d., d.sc., m.i.e.e., f.inst.p., Electrical Engineer.
Lambert, John Denholm, ph.d., f.i.m.a., Mathematician.
Lamont, Archibald, m.a., ph.d., f.g.s., Geologist.
Landsberg, Peter Theodore, ph.d., d.sc., f.inst.p., f.i.m.a., Mathematician.
Langmuir, Eric Duncan Grant, m.a., Educationist.
Last, Frederick Thomas, ph.d., d.sc., a.r.c.s., d.i.c., f.inst.biol., Biologist.
Laverack, Michael Stuart, ph.d., m.inst.biol., Marine Biologist.
Lawley, Derrick Norman, m.a., d.sc., Statistician.
Lawrie, Ralston Andrew, d.sc., ph.d., f.r.i.c., f.i.f.s.t., Nutritionist.
Lawrie, Thomas Russell MacLaren, b.sc., Geologist.
Leake, Bernard Elgey, ph.d., d.sc., f.g.s., Geologist.
Learmonth, Catherwood Craig, Administrator.
Leaver, Derek, ph.d., a.r.i.c., Chemist.
Ledermann, Walter, ph.d., d.sc., Mathematician.
Ledingham, Iain McAllan, m.d., Surgeon.
Lees, Howard, ph.d., Microbiologist.
Lenihan, John Mark Anthony, o.b.e., m.sc., ph.d., f.inst.p., m.i.e.e., Physicist.
Lenman, John Andrew Reginald, m.b., ch.b., f.r.c.p.e., Neurologist.
Leslie, Frank Matthews, ph.d., Mathematician.
Lever, Anthony Fairclough, b.sc., m.b., b.s., f.r.c.p., f.r.s.m., Physician.
Lewis, Gething Morgan, m.sc., ph.d., f.inst.p., Physicist.
Lickley, Robert Lang, c.b.e., d.sc., c.eng., f.i.c., f.c.g.l.i., f.r.ae.s., p.p.i.m.e., a.f.a.i.ae.a., Industrialist.

Lister, Harold, ph.d., Glaciologist.
Lloyd, Douglas Mathon Gent, d.sc., f.r.i.c., Chemist.
Lockhart, Robert Douglas, ch.m., m.d., f.s.a.scot., Anatomist.
Long, Albert George, d.sc., ll.d., Palaeobotanist.
Long, Cyril, m.a., d.phil., Biochemist.
Longair, Malcolm Sim, ph.d., Astronomer.
Longuet-Higgins, Hugh Christopher, m.a., d.phil., f.r.s., Psychologist.
Loraine, John Alexander, m.b., ch.b., ph.d., d.sc., f.r.c.p.e., Endocrinologist.
Lord, Reginald Douglas, m.sc., f.s.s., Mathematician.
Love, Phil Prince, b.sc., a.r.c.s.t., f.i.mech.e., Engineer.
Low, James Wotherspoon, ph.d., Zoologist.
Lowe, David Nicoll, o.b.e., m.a., b.sc., Administrator.
Lowenstein, Otto, dr.phil., ph.d., d.sc., f.r.s., Zoologist.
Lucas, Sir Cyril Edward, c.m.g., d.sc., f.r.s., f.inst.biol., Biologist.
Lumsden, George Innes, b.sc., f.g.s., Geologist.
Lumsden, William Hepburn Russell, m.b., ch.b., d.sc., d.t.m. & h., f.r.c.p.e., f.inst.biol., f.r.s.m., Protozoologist.

McAlpine, William Hepburn, Industrialist.
MacBeath, Alexander Murray, m.a., ph.d., Mathematician.
McCall, David, ph.d., f.l.s., Pharmacist.
McCallum, Donald Murdo, b.sc., c.eng., f.i.e.e., Industrialist.
McCombie, Charles William, m.a., ph.d., Physicist.
McCrea, William Hunter, m.a., ph.d., sc.d., f.r.s., f.r.a.s., m.r.i.a., Astronomer.
McDiarmid, Archibald, ph.d., d.sc., m.r.c.v.s., f.r.c.path., Veterinary Surgeon.
MacDonald, Alexander, m.a., m.d., Bacteriologist.
McDonald, Duncan, c.b.e., b.sc., f.h.-w.c., f.i.e.e., s.m.i.e.e.e., Industrialist.
MacDonald, James Alexander, ph.d., d.sc., f.inst.biol., Botanist.
MacDonald, James David, b.sc., f.l.s., f.z.s., f.inst.biol., Zoologist.
McDonald, Peter, ph.d., d.sc., f.r.s.c., Biochemist.
MacDonald, Simon Gavin George, m.a., ph.d., f.inst.p., Physicist.
McDowall, William Crocket, b.a., Industrialist.
MacEwan, Douglas MacLean Clark, m.a., ph.d., f.inst.p., Physicist.
McEwen, Ewen, c.b.e., d.sc., c.eng., f.i.m.e., Industrialist.
MacFarlane, Sir James Wright, ph.d.eng., wh.sc., f.i.e.e., f.i.mech.e., j.p., Engineer.
McGirr, Edward McCombie, c.b.e., b.sc., m.b., ch.b., m.d., f.r.c.p., f.r.c.p.e., f.r.c.p.g., Physician.
MacGregor, Archibald Gordon, m.c., d.sc., f.g.s., Geologist.
MacGregor, Thomas Nicol, m.d., m.r.c.p.e., f.r.c.s.e., f.r.c.o.g., Obstetrician.
McIntosh, Angus, a.m., d.phil., Philologist.
McIntosh, Douglas Haig, m.a., d.sc., Meteorologist.
McIntosh, Douglas Moul, c.b.e., m.a., ph.d., ll.d. f.e.i.s., Educationist.
McIntyre, Alasdair Duncan, d.sc., Marine Biologist.
McIntyre, Donald Bertram, ph.d., d.sc., f.g.s., Geologist.
McIntyre, John, m.a., d.litt., d.d., Cleric.
Mackenzie, Robert Cameron, ph.d., d.sc., f.r.s.c., Chemist.
MacKenzie, William Scott, m.a., ph.d., f.g.s., Geologist.
Mackie, Alexander, d.sc., ph.d., f.r.i.c., Chemist.
Mackie, Andrew George, m.a., ph.d., Mathematician.
MacLagan, Daniel Stewart, d.sc., ph.d., f.r.e.s., Zoologist.
McLaren, Anne, f.r.s., d.phil., Geneticist.
McLean, Thomas Pearson, ph.d., f.inst.p., Physicist.
Macleod, Anna Macgillivray, ph.d., m.inst.biol., Biologist.
McLeod, John Bryce, m.a., d.phil., Mathematician.
Macleod, Norman, ph.d., a.r.c.s., Chemical Engineer.
McManus, John, ph.d., a.r.c.s., d.i.c., Geologist.
McNee, Sir John (William), d.s.o., m.d., d.sc., f.r.c.p., ll.d., Physician.
MacNiven, Angus, m.b., ch.b., f.r.c.p.e., f.r.c.s.g., d.p.m., Physician.
Macpherson, Archibald Ian Stewart, m.b., ch.b., ch.m., f.r.c.s.e., Surgeon.
McVittie, George Cunliffe, o.b.e., m.a., ph.d., f.r.a.s., Astronomer.
McWhirter, Robert, m.b., ch.b., f.r.c.s.e., d.m.r.e., Radiologist.
Maden, Barry Edward Howorth, b.a., m.b., b.chir., ph.d., Biochemist.
Magnusson, Magnus, b.a., Author.
Mair, Alexander, m.b., ch.b., d.p.h., d.i.h., f.r.c.p.e., Physician.
Maitland, Peter S., ph.d., Ecologist.

MALCOLM, JOHN LAURENCE, B.MED.SC., M.B., CH B., Physiologist.
MALLARD, JOHN ROWLAND, PH.D., D.SC., F.INST.P., C.ENG., F.I.E.E., Physicist.
MANNERS, DAVID JOHN, M.A., D.SC., F.R.I.C., Biochemist.
MANNING, AUBREY WILLIAM GEORGE, D.PHIL., Biologist.
MARMION, BARRIE PATRICK, M.D., D.SC., M.R.C.S., L.R.C.P., M.R.C.P.A., F.R.C.P.E., F.R.C.PATH., Bacteriologist.
MARTIN, DANIEL, M.A., PH.D., Mathematician.
MASON, JOHN HUXLEY, F.R.C.V.S., Veterinary Surgeon.
MATTHEW, NORMAN GRAHAM, F.R.A.S., P.P.R.S.S.A., Astronomer.
MATTHEWS, JOHN DRAKE, B.SC.FOR., Forester.
MAULE, JOHN PATRICK, O.B.E., M.A., A.I.C.T.A., Geneticist.
MEARES, PATRICK, M.A., PH.D., D.SC., Chemist.
MEE, ARTHUR JAMES, O.B.E., M.A., B.SC., F.R.I.C., Educationist.
MEGAW, BASIL RICHARDSON STANLEY, B.A., F.S.A., F.M.A., Anthropologist.
MEIDNER, HANS ANTON, PH.D., D.I.C., Biologist.
MEKIE, DAVID ERIC CAMERON, O.B.E., M.B., CH.B., F.R.C.S.E., Surgeon.
MELVILLE, Sir HARRY WORK, K.C.B., PH.D., D.SC., F.R.S., Chemist.
MICHAELSON, SIDNEY, A.R.C.S., B.SC., Computer Scientist.
MICHIE, DONALD, M.A., D.PHIL., Computer Scientist.
MILLAR, ROBERT HANNAY, M.A., PH.D., D.SC., Zoologist.
MILLER, AGNES E., M.A., PH.D., Zoologist.
MILLER, CHRISTINA CRUICKSHANK, PH.D., D.SC., F.H.-W.C., Chemist.
MILLER, RONALD, M.A., PH.D., F.R.G.S., P.R.S.G.S., Geographer.
MILLS, COLIN FREDERICK, M.SC., PH.D., F.R.I.C., Biologist.
MILNE, ALEXANDER, M.A., PH.D., D.SC., F.INST.BIOL., Biologist.
MISSELBROOK, BERTRAM DESMOND, C.B.E., B.A., Industrialist.
MITCHELL, ANDREW RONALD, PH.D., D.SC., Mathematician.
MITCHELL, ROBERT LYELL, PH.D., F.R.I.C., Spectrochemist.
MITCHISON, JOHN MURDOCH, M.A., PH.D., SC.D., F.R.S., Zoologist.
MONTEITH, JOHN LENNOX, D.I.C., PH.D., F.INST.P., F.R.S., Physicist.
MONTGOMERY, GEORGE LIGHTBODY, C.B.E., T.D., PH.D., Pathologist.
MOORHOUSE, ROBERT GORDON, M.A., PH.D., Physicist.
MORGAN, HENRY GEMMELL, B.SC., M.B., CH.B., F.R.C.P.E., F.R.C.P.G., F.R.C.PATH., Pathologist.
MORTON, ALAN GILBERT, PH.D., F.INST.BIOL., Botanist.
MORTON, ANDREW QUEEN, M.A., B.SC., B.D., Minister of Religion.
MULLIGAN, WILLIAM, M.SC., PH.D., Veterinary Physiologist.
MUNN, WALTER DOUGLAS, M.A., D.SC., Mathematician.
MUNRO, HAMISH NISBET, D.SC., M.B., CH.B., Physiologist.
MURCHISON, DUNCAN GEORGE, PH.D., F.G.S., Geologist.
MURRAY, JAMES DICKSON, PH.D., M.A., D.SC., Mathematician.
MUSGRAVE, THEA (Mrs. PETER MARK), B.MUS., Composer.
MYKURA, WALTER, D.SC., F.G.S., Geologist.

NAIRN, RICHARD CHARLES, M.D., PH.D., Pathologist.
NANDY, KASHINATH, M.SC., PH.D., Astronomer.
NASH-WILLIAMS, CRISPIN ST. JOHN ALVAH, M.A., PH.D., Mathematician.
NEVILLE, ADAM MATTHEW, M.C., T.D., D.SC., PH.D., F.I.C.E., F.I.STRUCT.E., F.AM.S.C.E., M.SOC.C.E., F.I.ARB., Engineer.
NEWTH, DAVID RICHMOND, PH.D., Zoologist.
NICOL, THOMAS, M.D., CH.B., D.SC., F.R.C.S., F.R.C.S.E., Anatomist.
NICOLL, GORDON RAMSAY, M.A., B.SC.ENG., C.ENG., M.I.E.E., Electrical Engineer.
NISBET, ANDREW, M.A., Mathematician.
NISBET, STANLEY DONALD, M.A., B.ED., Educationist.
NOBLE, BENJAMIN, M.A., B.SC., A.M.I.E.E., Mathematician.
NOBLE, MARY JESSIE MCDONALD, PH.D., F.INST.BIOL., Biologist.
NOBLE, Sir (THOMAS ALEXANDER) FRASER, M.B.E., M.A., LL.D., Political Economist.
NONHEBEL, DEREK CHARLES, D.PHIL., Chemist.
NORTH, ALASTAIR MACARTHUR, PH.D., D.SC., Chemist.

ODELL, NOEL EWART, PH.D., A.R.S.M., F.G.S., Geologist.
OFFORD, ALBERT CYRIL, D.SC., PH.D., F.R.S., Mathematician
OGG, Sir WILLIAM GAMMIE, M.A., PH.D., Agriculturist.
OGILVIE, ROBERT MAXWELL, M.A., D.LITT., F.B.A., F.S.A., F.S.A.SCOT., Humanitarian.
O'HARA, MICHAEL JOHN, M.A., PH.D., Geologist.
OLIPHANT, WILLIAM DOUGLAS, B.SC., M.I.E.E., F.INST.P., Engineer.
ONG, GUAN BEE, O.B.E., M.B., B.S., F.R.C.S.E., F.R.C.S., F.A.C.S., F.R.A.C.S., Surgeon.
OPPENHEIM, Sir ALEXANDER, O.B.E., M.A., D.SC., PH.D., D.LITT., LL.D., F.W.A., Mathematician.
ORR, JOHN STEWART, D.SC., F.INST.P., Physicist.
OSBORNE, DONALD VERNON, M.A., PH.D., Physicist.
OVENDEN, MICHAEL WILLIAM, PH.D., M.A., Astronomer.
OVERTON, KARL HOWARD, PH.D., D.SC., Chemist.
OWEN, ALAN ERNEST, PH.D., A.R.I.C., F.INST.P., Electrical Engineer.

PACK, DONALD CECIL, C.B.E., M.A., D.SC., Mathematician.
PAGET, GEORGE EDWARD, M.B., B.S., M.D., D.C.H., Toxicologist.
PAINTAL, AUTUR SINGH, PH.D., D.SC., Physician.
PAL, RUDRENDRA KUMAR, D.SC., F.R.C.P.E., F.R.C.S.E., F.N.A., F.A.S., Physiologist.
PARRISH, BASIL BROCKET, B.SC., Marine Biologist.
PARROTT, DELPHINE, PH.D., Immunologist.
PASSMORE, REGINALD, M.A., D.M., Physiologist.
PATEMAN, JOHN ARTHUR JOSEPH, PH.D., M.A., F.R.S., Geneticist.
PATERSON, THOMAS T., B.SC., Economist.
PATTEN, THOMAS DIERY, PH.D., C.ENG., F.I.MECH.E., Mechanical Engineer.
PATTERSON, EDWARD MCWILLIAM, PH.D., Mathematician.
PATTERSON, EDWARD MERVYN, D.SC., M.R.I.A., F.R.S.A., F.G.S., Geologist.
PATTERSON, HENRY DESMOND, D.SC., Statistician.
PAUL, JOHN, M.B., CH.B., PH.D., F.R.C.P.E., F.R.C.P.G., F.R.C.PATH., Physician.
PAUL, WILLIAM, PH.D., Physicist.
PAUSON, PETER LUDWIG, PH.D., F.R.I.C., Chemist.
PAWLEY, GODFREY STEWART, PH.D., Physicist.
PEACOCK, JAMES DOUGLAS, PH.D., Geologist.
PEARCE, ROBERT PENROSE, PH.D., F.R.MET.S., Meteorologist.
PENNINGTON, RONALD JOHN TRUEMAN, D.SC., PH.D., Neurochemist.
PENNY, FRANCIS DAVID, B.SC., C.ENG., M.I.MECH.E., Engineer.
PERCIVAL, (Mrs.) ETHEL ELIZABETH, PH.D., D.SC., Chemist.
PERKINS, PETER GRAHAM, PH.D., D.SC., Chemist.
PERRY, Sir (WALTER) LAING MACDONALD, O.B.E., M.D., D.SC., F.R.C.P.E., Pharmacologist.
PHEMISTER, JAMES, M.A., D.SC., Geologist.
PHEMISTER, THOMAS CRAWFORD, D.SC., PH.D., SC.M., DR.DE L'UNIV., F.G.S., Geologist.
PHILIPSON, Sir ROBIN, A.R.A., H.R.A., R.S.W., D.A., Artist.
PHILLIPS, JOHN FREDERICK VICARS, D.SC., F.R.S.S.AFR., Biologist.
PICHAMUTHU, CHARLES SOLOMON, PH.D., D.SC., F.G.S., Geologist.
PICKFORD, MARY, D.SC., L.R.C.P., M.R.C.S., F.R.S., Physiologist.
PIGGOTT, STUART, DR.LITT.HUM., F.B.A., Archaeologist.
PLENDERLEITH, HAROLD JAMES, C.B.E., M.C., PH.D., LL.D., F.S.A., F.M.A., Conservationist.
POLWARTH, Baron, HENRY ALEXANDER HEPBURNE-SCOTT, T.D., D.L., C.A., LL.D., Industrialist.
PONTECORVO, GUIDO, PH.D., F.R.S., Geneticist.
PORTEOUS, JOHN WARDMAN, PH.D., Biochemist.
POTTER, HAROLD S. A., M.A., D.PHIL., Mathematician.
POWELL, JOHN ALFRED, M.A., D.PHIL., F.I.E.E., F.R.I.M., Industrialist.
PRICE, NORMAN BRIAN, PH.D., Geologist.
PRINGLE, ALEXANDER KERR, B.SC., F.G.S., Geologist.
PRINGLE, DEREK HAIR, PH.D., F.INST.P., Industrialist.
PRINGLE, ROBERT WILLIAM, O.B.E., PH.D., F.INST.P., F.R.S.C., Industrialist.
PROUDFOOT, VINCENT BRUCE, PH.D., Geographer.
PUGH, HUBERT LLOYD DAVID, D.SC., F.INST.P., F.I.M., C.ENG., F.I.M.E., Engineer.
PURSEY, DEREK LINDSAY, PH.D., Physicist.
PYKE, MAGNUS, O.B.E., PH.D., F.R.S.C., Chemist.

RAEBURN, JOHN ROSS, M.S., PH.D., M.A., Agriculturist.
RAISTRICK, BERNARD, PH.D., F.R.I.C., F.I.CHEM.E., Engineer.
RAJAM, RAMAKRISHNA VENKATA, M.B., M.S., Surgeon.
RANDALL, Sir JOHN (TURTON), D.SC., F.INST.P., F.R.S., Biophysicist.
RANKIN, ROBERT ALEXANDER, M.A., PH.D., SC.D., Mathematician.
RAPHAEL, RALPH ALEXANDER, PH.D., D.SC., F.R.S., Chemist.
RAVEN, JOHN ALBERT, PH.D., Botanist.
READ, SELWYN, B.A., Schoolmaster.
REDDISH, VINCENT CARTLEDGE, D.SC., PH.D., Astronomer.
REED, JAMES, B.SC., F.I.C.E., M.I.STRUCT.E., Engineer.
REEVE, ERIC CYRIL RAYNOLD, M.A., D.PHIL., Geneticist.
REID, DAVID HERALD, PH.D., D.SC., Chemist.
REID, JOHN MCARTHUR, M.A., Physicist.
REID, ROBERT LOVELL, PH.D., Agriculturist.
REID, Sir WILLIAM, C.B.E., PH.D., Mining Engineer.
REYNOLDS, DORIS LIVESEY, D.SC., F.G.S., Geologist.
RICHARDS, JOHN CHARLES SHENSTONE, PH.D., M.I.E.E., Physicist.
RICHARDSON, JOHN ALAN, PH.D., M.INST.P., Botanist.
RIDLEY, THOMAS, B.SC., D.I.C., F.I.C.E., M.A.C.E., Engineer.
RILEY, JAMES FREDERICK, M.D., PH.D., D.M.R.T., F.R.C.S.E., Radiotherapist.
RINGROSE, JOHN ROBERT, PH.D., Mathematician.
RITCHIE, ALFRED, O.B.E., PH.D., Marine Biologist.
RITCHIE, ANTHONY ELLIOT, C.B.E., M.A., B.SC., M.D., Physiologist.
RITCHIE, DONALD ANDREW, PH.D., F.INST.BIOL., Geneticist.
RITCHIE, PATRICK DUNBAR, PH.D., F.R.I.C., F.P.R.I., Chemist.

ROACH, GARY FRANCIS, M.SC., PH.D., Mathematician.
ROBB, WILLIAM, N.D.A., Agriculturist.
ROBERTS, EDWARD FREDERICK DENIS, PH.D., Librarian.
ROBERTS, JOHN ALEXANDER FRASER, C.B.E., M.A., M.D., D.SC., F.R.S., F.R.C.P., Physician.
ROBERTS, RONALD JOHN, PH.D., M.R.C.PATH., M.R.C.V.S., M.I.BIOL., Biologist.
ROBERTSON, ALAN, O.B.E., PH.D., D.SC., F.R.S., Geneticist.
ROBERTSON, Sir ALEXANDER, M.A., PH.D., LL.D., Veterinary Surgeon.
ROBERTSON, ALEXANDER PROVAN, M.A., PH.D., F.I.M.A., Mathematician.
ROBERTSON, ANNE STRACHAN, M.A., D.LITT., F.S.A.SCOT., F.S.A., Archaeologist.
ROBERTSON, FORBES WILLIAM, PH.D., D.SC., F.INST.BIOL., Geneticist.
ROBERTSON, HAMISH ALEXANDER, PH.D., F.R.I.C., Agriculturist.
ROBERTSON, JAMES, B.SC., C.ENG., F.I.C.E., Industrialist.
ROBERTSON, JAMES DUNCAN, PH.D., SC.D., F.Z.S., Zoologist.
ROBERTSON, JAMES IAN SUMMERS, B.SC., M.B., B.S., F.R.C.P., Physician.
ROBERTSON, JOHN MONTEATH, C.B.E., M.A., PH.D., D.SC., F.R.I.C., F.INST.P., F.R.S., Chemist.
ROBERTSON, LEWIS FINDLAY, C.B.E., LL.D., Industrialist.
ROBERTSON, NOEL FARNIE, C.B.E., PH.D., M.A., Agriculturist.
ROBERTSON, ROBERT HUGH STANNUS, M.A., F.G.S., F.EUG.S., Mineralogist.
ROBERTSON, STEWART ALEXANDER, PH.D., Mathematician.
ROBERTSON, THOMAS, PH.D., A.H.-W.C., A.M.I.M.M., F.G.S., Geologist.
ROBERTSON, WILLIAM SHEPHERD, C.B.E., B.SC., Industrialist.
ROBSON, JOHN MICHAEL, M.D., D.SC., Pharmacologist.
ROMANES, GEORGE JOHN, B.A., PH.D., M.B., CH.B., Anatomist.
ROOK, JOHN ALLAN FYNES, D.SC., PH.D., F.R.I.C., Nutritionist.
ROPER, JOSEPH ALAN, PH.D., Geneticist.
RORKE, JOHN, PH.D., A.R.T.C., F.I.M.E., Industrialist.
ROSS, ALAN DAWSON, PH.D., F.I.C.E., Civil Engineer.
ROSS, JOHN MUIRHEAD, F.F.A., Actuary.
ROSS, MARION AMELIA SPENCE, M.A., PH.D., Physicist.
ROY, ARCHIBALD EDMISTON, PH.D., F.R.A.S., Astronomer.
RUSHBROOKE, GEORGE STANLEY, PH.D., M.A., Physicist.
RUSHWORTH, FRANCIS ALWYN, PH.D., A.R.C.S., F.INST.P., Physicist.
RUSSELL, DAVID FRANCIS OLIPHANT, C.B.E., M.C., D.L., D.SC., Industrialist.
RUSSELL-HUNTER, WILLIAM DEVIGNE, PH.D., D.SC., M.INST.BIOL., Biologist.
RUTHERFORD, WILLIAM HOOD, F.C.I.S., Chartered Secretary.

SABINE, PETER AUBREY, PH.D., D.SC., A.R.C.S., F.I.M.M., F.R.S.A., Geologist.
SANDS, ARTHUR DAVID, PH.D., Mathematician.
SANG, JAMES HENDERSON, PH.D., Biologist.
SAUNDERS, RICHARD LORRAINE DE CHASTENEY HOLBOURNE, M.D., Anatomist.
SAVILLE, ALAN, B.SC., Marine Biologist.
SAY, MAURICE GEORGE, PH.D., M.I.E.E., Electrical Engineer.
SCARBOROUGH, HAROLD, M.B., CH.B., PH.D., F.R.C.P., Physician.
SCHLAPP, ROBERT, M.A., PH.D., Mathematician.
SCOBIE, JAMES, PH.D., F.INST.P., Physicist.
SCOTHORNE, RAYMOND JOHN, B.SC., M.D., F.R.C.S.G., Anatomist.
SCOTT, ALASTAIR IAN, PH.D., D.SC., F.R.S., Chemist.
SCOTT, GEORGE IAN, C.B.E., M.A., M.B., CH.B., F.R.C.S.E., F.R.C.P.E., Ophthalmologist.
SENIOR, WILLIAM HIRST, C.B., M.SC., Agriculturist.
SHAH, SWARUPCHAND MOHANLAL, M.A., PH.D., D.LITT., Mathematician.
SHARP, DAVID WILLIAM ARTHUR, M.A., PH.D., Chemist.
SHARPE, JOHN WALKER, M.A., F.INST.P., Physicist.
SHARPLES, ALAN, PH.D., Chemist.
SHEPHERD, DAVID MITCHELL, PH.D., F.INST.BIOL., Pharmacologist.
SHERWOOD, JOHN NEIL, PH.D., F.R.I.C., Chemist.
SHEWAN, JAMES MACKAY, PH.D., F.R.I.C., F.INST.BIOL., Biologist.
SHORT, ROGER VALENTINE, PH.D., SC.D., F.R.S., M.R.C.V.S., Biologist.
SILLER, WALTER GEORGE, M.R.C.V.S., PH.D., Veterinary Surgeon.
SILLITTO, RICHARD MALCOLM, B.SC., F.INST.P., Physicist.
SILVER, ROBERT SIMPSON, C.B.E., M.A., PH.D., D.SC., F.INST.P., M.I.MECH.E., M.I.MAR.E., Mechanical Engineer.
SILVEY, SAMUEL DAVID, M.A., PH.D., Statistician.
SIM, GEORGE ANDREW, PH.D., Chemist.
SIMKIN, JULIUS LEONARD, PH.D., Biochemist.
SIMMONDS, NORMAN WILLISON, SC.D., A.I.C.T.A., F.INST.BIOL., Biologist.
SIMPSON, DAVID CUMMING, M.B.E., PH.D., Bioengineer.

SIMPSON, HUGH CAMERON, C.ENG., S.M., SC.D., F.INST.P., F.I.MECH.E., A.M.I.CHEM.E., Engineer.
SIMPSON, JOHN ALEXANDER, M.D., F.R.C.P., F.R.C.P.E., F.R.C.P.G., Neurologist.
SINCLAIR, ALAN MACDONALD, PH.D., Mathematician.
SLACK, HARRY D., PH.D., Zoologist.
SLEEMAN, BRIAN DAVID, PH.D., F.I.M.A., Mathematician.
SMART, JOHN, M.A., PH.D., D.SC., F.R.E.S., Zoologist.
SMELLIE, ROBERT MARTIN STUART, PH.D., D.SC., Biochemist.
SMITH, ALEXANDER MARTIN, O.B.E., PH.D., D.SC., F.R.S.C., F.H.-W.C., Agriculturist.
SMITH, FREDERICK RANDALL, PH.D., F.R.S.C., Chemist.
SMITH, GEORGE, M.B.E., M.D., D.SC., F.R.C.S.E., F.A.C.S., Surgeon.
SMITH, HORACE GEORGE, PH.D., Chemist.
SMITH, JAMES ANDREW BUCHAN, C.B.E., PH.D., D.SC., LL.D., F.R.I.C., Nutritionist.
SMITH, JAMES BOYD, M.A., B.SC., Engineer.
SMITH, JOHN EDWARD, PH.D., D.SC., Microbiologist.
SMITH, RONALD HENRY, PH.D., Biochemist.
SMITH, STANLEY DESMOND, D.SC., PH.D., F.INST.P., SF.R.S., Physicist.
SMITH, THOMAS BROUN, Q.C., M.A., D.C.L., LL.D., F.B.A., Solicitor.
SMITHIES, FRANK, M.A., PH.D., Mathematician.
SMOUT, THOMAS CHRISTOPHER, M.A., PH.D., Historian.
SMYTH, MICHAEL JESSOP, M.A., PH.D., F.R.A.S., Astronomer.
SNEDDON, IAN NAISMITH, O.B.E., M.A., D.SC., Mathematician.
SPEAR, WALTER ERIC, PH.D., D.SC., F.INST.P., Physicist.
SPENCE, DAVID HUGH NEVEN, PH.D., Botanist.
SPENCE, JAMES RAMSAY, O.B.E., B.SC., C.ENG., F.I.MECH.E., M.I.PROD.E., Industrialist.
SPRENT, PETER, PH.D., Mathematician.
STAMP, JOHN TREVOR, C.B.E., D.SC., M.R.C.V.S., Veterinary Surgeon.
STANDLEY, KENNETH JACK, M.A., D.PHIL., Physicist.
STEELE, JOHN HYSLOP, D.SC., F.R.S., Marine Biologist.
STENLAKE, JOHN BEDFORD, PH.D., D.SC., F.P.S., F.R.I.C., F.C.S., Pharmacist.
STEVENS, THOMAS STEVENS, D.PHIL., F.R.S., Chemist.
STEWART, Sir FREDERICK (HENRY), PH.D., F.R.S., F.G.S., Geologist.
STEWART, HAROLD CHARLES, C.B.E., D.L., M.A., M.D., PH.D., F.R.C.P., F.F.A., R.C.S., Pharmacologist.
STEWART, WILLIAM DUNCAN PATERSON, D.SC., PH.D., F.INST.-BIOL., F.R.S., Biologist.
STIBBS, DOUGLAS WALTER NOBLE, M.SC., D.PHIL., F.R.A.S., Astronomer.
STIRLING, JAMES, D.SC., Botanist.
STOKER, MICHAEL GEORGE PARKE, M.A., M.D., F.R.S., Pathologist.
STOWARD, PETER JOHN, M.A., D.PHIL., Anatomist.
STOY, RICHARD HUGH, C.B.E., M.A., PH.D., Astronomer.
STRACHAN, CHARLES, M.A., PH.D., Physicist.
STRACHAN, MICHAEL FRANCIS, M.B.E., M.A., Industrialist.
STRADLING, RICHARD ANTHONY, PH.D., Physicist.
STRONG, JOHN ANDERSON, M.B.E., CH.B., B.A.O., M.A., M.D., F.R.C.P., F.R.C.P.E., Physician.
STUART, ANGUS ERSKINE, M.B., CH.B., PH.D., M.R.C.P.E., M.C.PATH., Pathologist.
STUART, CHARLES ALEXANDER, M.A., D.PHIL., Mathematician.
STURKIE, PAUL DAVID, Environmental Physiologist.
SUBAK-SHARPE, JOHN HERBERT, PH.D., Virologist.
SUTHERLAND, HUGH BROWN, M.SC., M.I.C.E., A.M.I.STRUCT.E., F.G.S., Civil Engineer.
SUTHERLAND, JOHN DERG, C B.E., M.B., CH.B., PH.D., M.R.C.P.E., Physician.
SUTTON, HARRY CALLENDER, M.SC., PH.D., Radiochemist.
SUTTON, RICHARD LIGHTBURN, Jr., M.A., M.D., L.R.C.S.E., L.R.C.P.E., L.R.C.S.G., Dermatologist.
SWANN, Sir MICHAEL (MEREDITH), M.A., PH.D., F.R.S., Zoologist.
SWEET, PETER ALAN, M.A., PH.D., Astronomer.
SWINTON, FINDLAY LEE, PH.D., Chemist.
SWINTON, WILLIAM ELGIN, PH.D., F.L.S., F.G.S., F.A.M., Biologist.
SYMINGTON, THOMAS, B.SC., F.R.I.C., F.R.C.S.G., Pathologist.
SYNGE, RICHARD LAURENCE MILLINGTON, PH.D., F.R.S., F.R.I.C., Chemist.

TANNAHILL, THOMAS RUSSELL, M.A., B.SC., Astronomer.
TAYLOR, CHARLES EDWIN, PH.D., F.INST.BIOL., Biologist.
TAYLOR, CHARLES JAMES, C.B.E., E.D., PH.D., Forester.
TAYLOR, DAVID ERNEST MEGUYER, T.D., M.B., CH.B., F.R.C.S.E., Physiologist
TAYLOR, DUNCAN, PH.D., D.SC., F.R.I.C., Chemist.
TAYLOR, ERIC OPENSHAW, B.SC., F.I.E.E., M.AMER.I.E.E., Electrical Engineer.
TAYLOR, Sir GEORGE, D.SC., LL.D., F.R.S., V.M.H., F.L.S., Botanist.
TAYLOR, HARRY FRANCIS WEST, PH.D., D.SC., Chemist.

TAYLOR OF GRYFE, Baron, THOMAS JOHNSTON, D.L., LL.D., Industrialist.
TEBBLE, NORMAN, D.SC., M.A., F.INST.BIOL., Biologist.
TEDDER, Baron, JOHN MICHAEL, M.A., SC.D., PH.D., F.C.S., Chemist.
TEDFORD, DAVID JOHN, PH.D., A.R.C.S.T., F.I.E.E., F.INST.P., Engineer.
TENNANT, GEORGE, PH.D., Chemist.
TER HAAR, DIRK, D.SC., Physicist.
THOMAS, DAVID BRYNMOR, M.B., B.S., B.SC., F.R.C.PATH., Pathologist.
THOMAS, GORDON ERIC, M.SC., PH.D., Computer Scientist.
THOMAS, HAROLD JAMES, PH.D., Marine Biologist.
THOMPSON, COLIN EDWARD, M.A., Artist.
THOMPSON, IAN MACLAREN, B.SC., M.B., CH.B., F.R.S.C., Anatomist.
THOMSON, ADAM SIMPSON TURNBULL, D.SC., PH.D., A.R.C.S.T., F.I.C.E., F.I.MECH.E., Mechanical Engineer.
THOMSON, DERICK SMITH, M.A., Linguist.
THOMSON, ROBERT, PH.D., C.ENG., A.F.R.AE.S., M.I.MECH.E., Mechanical Engineer.
THOMSON, RONALD HUNTER, PH.D., D.SC., F.R.I.C., Chemist.
THOMSON, SAMUEL JAMES, PH.D., D.SC., F.R.I.C., Chemist.
TIMBURY, MORAG CRICHTON, M.D., PH.D., M.R.C.P., M.R.C.PATH., Bacteriologist.
TIMMS, GEOFFREY, O.B.E., PH.D., Mathematician.
TINSLEY, JOSEPH, PH.D., F.R.I.C., F.C.S., Soil Scientist.
TOLLIN, PATRICK, PH.D., Physicist.
TORRANCE, THOMAS FORSYTH, M.B.E., M.A., D.LITT., D.THEOL., D.D., D.TH., DR.TEOL., Theologian.
TRAPP, GEORGE, M.A., PH.D., B.COM., LL.B., F.L.S., Educationist.
TRIPP, RONALD PEARSON, Palaeontologist.
TRISTRAM, GEORGE ROLAND, PH.D., Biochemist.
TURNBULL, ARCHIE RULE, M.A., Publisher.
TWEED, JOHN, A.R.C.S.T., PH.D., Mathematician.
TWEEDSMUIR OF ELSFIELD, The Lord, JOHN NORMAN STUART BUCHAN, C.B.E., C.D., B.A., LL.D., Explorer.

UPTON, BRIAN GEOFFREY JOHNSON, M.A., D.PHIL., Geologist.
USHERWOOD, PETER NORMAN RUSSELL, PH.D., Zoologist.

VICKERMAN, KEITH, D.SC., PH.D., Zoologist.

WAKELEY, Sir CECIL PEMBREY GREY, Bt., K.B.E., C.B., D.SC., LL.D., Surgeon.
WALKER, ARTHUR GEOFFREY, M.A., PH.D., D.SC., F.R.S., Mathematician.
WALKER, DAVID ARNOLD, O.B.E., M.A., M.ED., PH.D., F.E.I.S., Educationist.
WALKER, DAVID MAXWELL, M.A., PH.D., LL.D., Q.C., F.B.A., Lawyer.
WALKER, PETER MARTIN BRABAZON, PH.D., Biologist.
WALKER, WILLIAM FARQUHAR, M.B., CH.B., CH.M., F.R.C.S.E., F.R.C.S., Surgeon.
WALLACE, DAVID ALEXANDER ROSS, PH.D., Mathematician.
WALLS, ELDRED WRIGHT, M.D., CH.B., B.SC., Anatomist.
WALMSLEY, ROBERT, M.D., Anatomist.
WALSH, EWART GEOFFREY, M.A., M.D., Physiologist.
WALSH, WILLIAM HENRY, M.A., F.B.A., Logician and Metaphysician.
WALTON, EWART KENDALL, PH.D., Geologist.
WARBURTON, GEOFFREY BARRATT, M.A., PH.D., Mechanical Engineer.
WARDLAW, ALASTAIR CONNELL, PH.D., D.SC., Microbiologist.
WARDLAW, CLAUDE WILSON, PH.D., D.SC., F.L.S., Botanist.
WATERSTON, ANDREW RODGER, O.B.E., B.SC., F.R.E.S., Entomologist.
WATERSTON, CHARLES DEWAR, PH.D., F.G.S., F.M.A., Geologist.
WATLING, ROY, PH.D., Botanist.
WATSON, ADAM, PH.D., D.SC., Ecologist.
WATSON, JAMES WREFORD, M.A., PH.D., F.R.S.C., Geographer.
WATSON, JOHN STEVEN, M.A., D.LITT., F.R.HIST.S., Historian.
WATTS, WILLIAM EDWARD, PH.D., D.SC., F.R.I.C., Chemist.
WEATHERLEY, PAUL EGERTON, M.A., D.PHIL., F.R.S., Botanist.
WEBLEY, DONALD MARTIN, M.SC., PH.D., F.INST.BIOL., Biologist.
WEIPERS, Sir WILLIAM (LEE), B.SC., P.P.R.C.V.S., D.V.S.M., Veterinary Surgeon.
WEST, THOMAS SUMMERS, PH.D., D.SC., F.R.I.C., Pedologist.
WEST, WATTIE JESSE, B.A., M.I.AGR.E., Agriculturist.
WESTOLL, THOMAS STANLEY, PH.D., D.SC., F.R.S., F.G.S., Geologist.
WESTWATER, ROBERT, O.B.E., PH.D., C.ENG., F.I.MIN.E., F.I.Q., Engineer.
WHITBY, LIONEL GORDON, M.A., PH.D., M.B., B.CHIR., M.D., F.R.C.P.E., F.R.C.P., F.R.C.PATH., Clinical Chemist.
WHITE, ROBERT GEORGE, D.M., Immunologist.

WHITTAKER, JOHN MACNAUGHTEN, M.A., D.SC., F.R.S., Mathematician.
WHITTERIDGE, DAVID, M.A., D.M., F.R.S., Physiologist.
WIENER, GERALD, PH.D., Genetics.
WIGHT, PETER ALBERT LAING, PH.D., D.V.S.M., M.R.C.PATH., F.R.C.V.S., Veterinary Surgeon.
WIGHTMAN, WILLIAM PERSEHOUSE DELISLE, PH.D., M.SC., Educationist.
WILDY, PETER, M.B., B.CHIR., Pathologist.
WILKIE, JAMES, M.A., Administrator.
WILKINS, MALCOLM BARRETT, PH.D., D.SC., A.K.C., Botanist.
WILLETT, FRANK, M.A., Anthropologist.
WILLIAMS, ALWYN, PH.D., F.R.S., Geologist.
WILLIAMSON, ALAN ROWE, PH.D., Biochemist.
WILLMORE, PATRICK LEVER, M.A., PH.D., Seismologist.
WILSON, CEDRIC WILLIAM MALCOLM, PH.D., M.D., M.A., Pharmacologist.
WILSON, HENRY WALLACE, PH.D., F.INST.P., Physicist.
WILSON, HERBERT REES, PH.D., Physicist.
WILSON, ROBERT BRYDEN, D.SC., Geologist.
WILSON, THOMAS, O.B.E., M.A., PH.D., F.B.A., Economist.
WITTE, WILLIAM, PH.D., D.LITT., Linguist.
WOOD, HAMISH CHRISTOPHER SWAN, PH.D., Chemist.
WOOD-GUSH, DAVID GRAINGER MARCUS, PH.D., Poultry Scientist.
WOODRUFF, Sir MICHAEL (FRANCIS ADDISON), D.SC., M.D., M.S., F.R.C.S., F.R.S., Surgeon.
WOODWARD, FOSTER NEVILLE, C.B.E., PH.D., F.R.I.C., Chemist.
WOOLF, BARNET, M.A., PH.D., Biometrical Geneticist.
WRIGHT, Sir EDWARD MAITLAND, M.A., D.PHIL., Mathematician.
WRIGHT, JOHN DAVID MAITLAND, D.PHIL., Mathematician.
WRIGHT, The Very Rev. RONALD (WILLIAM VERNON) SELBY, C.V.O., T.D., M.A., D.D., F.R.S.A., F.S.A.SCOT., Minister of Religion.
WRIGHT, WILLIAM, PH.D., F.I.C.E., F.I.E.I., Civil Engineer.
WYATT, PETER ARTHUR HARRIS, PH.D., F.C.S., F.R.I.C., Chemist.
WYLLIE, GEORGE ANDREW PARK, PH.D., F.INST.P., Physicist.
WYNNE-EDWARDS, VERO COPNER, C.B.E., M.A., D.SC., F.R.S.C., F.R.S., Biologist.

YARROW, Sir ERIC GRANT, M.B.E., D.L., Industrialist.
YEOMAN, MICHAEL MAGSON, M.SC., PH.D., Botanist.
YONGE, Sir (CHARLES) MAURICE, C.B.E., PH.D., D.SC., F.R.S., Zoologist.
YOUNG, ROGER WILLIAM, M.A., S.TH., Headmaster.

### HONORARY FELLOWS:

H.R.H. Prince PHILIP, Duke of EDINBURGH, K.G., K.T.
H.R.H. Prince CHARLES, Prince of WALES, K.G., G.C.B.

ABETTI, GIORGIO, Astronomer.
ASHBY OF BRANDON, Baron, ERIC, Botanist.
ATKINSON, F. V., Mathematician.

BERGSTRÖM, S., Biochemist.
BLOCH, FELIX, Physicist.
BORLAUG, NORMAN E., Nutritionist.
BRACHET, JEAN, Animal Morphologist.
BRENNER, SYDNEY, F.R.S., Molecular Biologist.
BURNET, Sir (FRANK) MACFARLANE, O.M., K.B.E., F.R.S., Microbiologist.

CALVIN, MELVIN, Chemist.
CARTWRIGHT, Dame MARY (LUCY), D.B.E., F.R.S., Mathematician.
CHIBNALL, ALBERT CHARLES, F.R.S., Biochemist.
COLVILLE, RONALD JOHN BILSLAND, The Rt. Hon. Lord CLYDESMUIR, Industrialist.
CORNER, GEORGE WASHINGTON, Physician.
CRICK, F. H. C., F.R.S., Biologist.

DIRAC, PAUL ADRIEN MAURICE, O.M., F.R.S., Physicist.
DUDEK, A., Geologist.

ENGELHARDT, VLADIMIR ALEKSANDROVITCH, Biologist.
ERINGEN, A. C., Engineer.

FICHERA, GAETANO, Mathematician.
FLORKIN, MARCEL, Biochemist.
FREY WYSSLING, ALBERT, Botanist.

HALMOS, P. R., Mathematician.
HAMBRAEUS, GUNNAR, Engineer.
HARNWELL, G. P., Physicist.
HILDEBRAND, JOEL H., Chemist.
HODGKIN, Sir ALAN, O.M., K.B.E., P.P.R.S., Biophysicist.
HODGKIN, DOROTHY MARY CROWFOOT, O.M., F.R.S., Crystallographer.
HUTT, FREDERICK B., F.S.A.

JEFFREYS, Sir HAROLD, F.R.S., Astronomer.

KREBS, Sir HANS, F.R.S., Biochemist.

U.K. (GREAT BRITAIN)

Kurzweil, Jaroslav, Mathematician.
Lamb, Willis Eugene, Jr., Physicist.
Lehmann, Miss Inge, Seismologist.
Lush, Jay L., Agriculturist.

MacLane, Saunders, Mathematician.
Medawar, Sir Peter, c.b.e., f.r.s., Zoologist.
Mitchell, Peter Dennis, f.r.s., Chemist.

Nolan, Thomas B., Geologist.
Nowacki, Witold, Engineer.

Oort, Jan Hendrik, Astronomer.

Pauling, Linus C., Chemist.
Penney, Baron, William George, o.m., k.b.e., f.r.s., Physicist.
Perutz, Max., c.h., c.b.e., f.r.s., Biologist.
Peters, Sir Rudolph (Albert), Kt., m.c., f.r.c.p., f.r.s., Biochemist.
Pleijel, Ake, Mathematician.
Porter, Rodney Robert, f.r.s., Biochemist.

Sanger, Frederick, c.b.e., Biologist.
Schenck, Gunther O., Organic Chemist.
Seaborg, Glenn Theodore, Chemist.
Selikoff, Irving John, Environmentalist.
Semenov, N. N., Physicist.
Sobolev, Sergei Lvovich, Mathematician.
Stensio, Eric Helge Oswald, Zoologist.
Szent-Gyorgyi, Albert de, Marine Biologist.

Todd of Trumpington, Baron, Alexander Robertus, o.m., f.r.s., Chemist.

Weisskopf, Victor Frederick, Physicist.
Von Weizsacker, Carl Friedrich, Philosopher.
Wright, Sewall, Geneticist.
Wu, (Mrs.) Chien-Shiung, Physicist.

Yukawa, Hideki, Physicist.

## ROYAL ACADEMY OF ARTS IN LONDON
BURLINGTON HOUSE, PICCADILLY, LONDON, W1V 0DS

Telephone: 01-734 9052.

Founded by King George III in 1768.

*President:* Sir Hugh Casson, k.c.v.o., p.r.a.
*Keeper:* Peter Greenham, c.b.e., r.a.
*Treasurer:* Roger de Grey, r.a.
*Secretary:* Sidney C. Hutchison, c.v.o., f.s.a., f.m.a. (to March 1982); Piers Rodgers (from March 1982).
*Comptroller:* Kenneth J. Tanner, m.v.o.

Honorary Retired Academicians:
Frampton, Meredith (1942).

Royal Academicians:
Adams, Norman (1972).
Aldridge, John (1963).
*Bawden, Edward, c.b.e. (1956).
Blackadder, Miss Elizabeth (1976).
Blake, Peter (1981).
Blamey, Norman (1975).
Blow, Miss Sandra (1978).
Bowey, Miss Olwyn (1975).
Bowyer, William (1981).
Bratby, John R. (1971).
Brown, Ralph (1972).
Buhler, Robert (1956).
*Burn, Rodney J. (1962).
Butler, James (1972).

Cadbury-Brown, H. T., o.b.e. (1975).
Casson, Sir Hugh, k.c.v.o. (1970).
Clarke, Geoffrey (1976).
Clatworthy, Robert (1973).
Coker, Peter (1972).
Cooke, Miss Jean (1972).
Cowern, Raymond T. (1968).
Cuming, Frederick (1974).

De Grey, Roger (1969).
Dickson, Miss Jennifer (1976).
Dring, William (1955).
Dunstan, Bernard (1968).

*Eurich, Richard (1953).
*Fitton, James (1954).
Freeth, H. Andrew (1965).
Frink, Miss Elisabeth, c.b.e. (1977).
*Fry, E. Maxwell, c.b.e. (1972).
Gibberd, Sir Frederick, c.b.e. (1969).
*Goldfinger, Ernö (1976).
Gore, Frederick (1972).
Green, Anthony (1977).
Greenham, Peter G., c.b.e. (1960).
*Gwynne-Jones, Allan, d.s.o. (1965).

Harpley, Sydney (1981).
Hayes, Colin (1970).
Hepple, Norman (1961).
*Hermes, Miss Gertrude (1971).
*Hillier, Tristram (1967).

Kneale, Bryan (1974).

Machin, Arnold, o.b.e. (1956).
Manasseh, Leonard (1979).
McFall, David (1963).
Middleditch, Edward (1972).
Moynihan, Rodrigo, c.b.e. (1957).

Paolozzi, Eduardo, c.b.e. (1979).
Philipson, Sir Robin (1981).
*Pitchforth, R. Vivian (1953).
Powell, Sir Philip, o.b.e. (1977).

Roberts-Jones, Ivor, c.b.e. (1973).
Rosoman, Leonard (1969).

*Sanders, Christopher C. (1961).
Sheppard, Sir Richard, c.b.e. (1972).
Soukop, Willi (1969).
Spear, Ruskin (1954).
Swanwick, Miss Betty (1979).

Tindle, David (1979).

Ward, John (1965).
Weight, Carel, c.b.e. (1965).
Williams, Kyffin (1974).
*Wolfe, Edward (1972).

*Senior Academicians.

## ROYAL SCOTTISH ACADEMY
PRINCES STREET, EDINBURGH

Telephone: 031-225-6671

Founded 1826.

*President:* Sir Robin Philipson, p.r.s.a., h.r.a., a.r.a.
*Treasurer:* W. J. L. Baillie, r.s.a.
*Secretary:* H. Anthony Wheeler, o.b.e., r.s.a.
*Librarian:* John Houston, r.s.a.

Honorary Retired Academicians:
Kininmonth, Sir William (1956).
Armour, Mrs. Mary (1958).
Coia, J. A. (1962).
Miller, James (1964).
Johnston, Ninian (1966).
Sutherland, Scott (1970).

Royal Scottish Academicians:
Baillie, W. J. L.
Blackadder, Elizabeth (1972).
Butler, Vincent (1977).
Cameron, G. S. (1971).
Campbell, Alexander (1981).
Collins, Peter (1974).
Crawford, H. A. (1956).
Crosbie, William (1974).
Cumming, James (1970).
Donaldson, David A. (1962).
Fleming, I. (1956).
Glover, John Hardie (1981).
Gordon, Esme (1967).
Houston, John (1972).
Knox, John.

Littlejohn, William (1973).
Lorimer, H. (1957).
McClure, David (1971).
Malcolm, Ellen (1976).
Michie, David (1972).
Morrocco, Alberto (1963).
Patrick, J. McIntosh (1957).
Peploe, Denis (1966).
Philipson, Sir Robin (1962).
Reeves, Philip (1976).
Robertson, R. Ross (1977).
Schotz, B. (1937).
Steedman, Robert R.
Wheeler, H. Anthony (1975).
Whiston, Peter (1977).

BRITISH ACADEMY U.K. (GREAT BRITAIN)

## BRITISH ACADEMY
BURLINGTON HOUSE, PICCADILLY,
LONDON, W1V 0NS
Telephone: 01-734 0457.
Founded 1901.

*President:* Rev. Prof. WILLIAM OWEN CHADWICK, D.D.
*Foreign Secretary:* Prof. E. W. HANDLEY.
*Secretary:* J. P. CARSWELL, C.B., M.A.
*Treasurer:* Prof. P. MATHIAS.

Number of members: 460.

**The Academy is divided into 14 sections.**

Publications: *Proceedings* (annual), *Annual Report, Schweich Lectures on Biblical Archaeology, Monographs.*

FELLOWS:

*Ancient History:*
ANDREWES, Prof. ANTONY, M.B.E., M.A.
BADIAN, Prof. ERNST, M.A., D.PHIL., LITT.D.
BIRLEY, Prof. ERIC, M.B.E., M.A., F.S.A.
Boardman, Prof. JOHN.
Brown, Prof. PETER ROBERT LAMONT, M.A.
Brunt, Prof. PETER ASTBURY, M.A.
Cameron, Prof. AVERIL.
Carson, ROBERT ANDREW GLENDENNING.
Chadwick, Rev. Prof. HENRY, D.D.
Crawford, M. H.
DAUBE, Prof. DAVID, D.C.L., PH.D., DR.JUR.
DE SAINTE-CROIX, GEOFFREY ERNEST MAURICE, M.A., D.LITT.
Dover, Sir KENNETH, M.A.
Finley, Sir MOSES, M.A., PH.D., D.LITT.
FRASER, PETER MARSHALL, M.C., M.A.
Frere, Prof. SHEPPARD SUNDERLAND, C.B.E., M.A.
GRIFFITH, GUY THOMPSON, M.A.
Hammond, Prof. NICHOLAS GEOFFREY LEMPRIÈRE, C.B.E., D.S.O., D.L.
Honoré, Prof. ANTONY MAURICE, D.C.L.
Jeffery, LILIAN HAMILTON, M.A., D.PHIL., F.S.A.
Kraay, Dr. COLIN MACKENNAL
Lewis, DAVID MALCOLM, M.A., P.H.D.
MEIGGS, RUSSELL, M.A.
Millar, Prof. FERGUS GRAHAM BURTHOLME, M.A., D.PHIL.
MOMIGLIANO, Prof. ARNALDO DANTE, D.LITT.
MYRES, JOHN NOWELL LINTON, C.B.E., M.A., LL.D., D.LITT., D.LIT., F.S.A.
Ogilvie, Prof. ROBERT MAXWELL, M.A., D.LITT.
Rivet, Prof. A. L. F.
ROBERTSON, Prof. CHARLES MARTIN, M.A.
SCULLARD, Prof. HOWARD HAYES, M.A., PH.D., F.S.A
SHERWIN-WHITE, ADRIAN NICHOLAS, M.A.
Snodgrass, Prof. ANTHONY McELREA.
Sutherland, CAROL HUMPHREY VIVIAN, C.B.E., M.A., D.LITT., F.S.A.
Syme, Prof. Sir RONALD, O.M., M.A.
Thompson, Prof. EDWARD ARTHUR.
WALBANK, Prof. FRANK WILLIAM, M.A.

*Medieval History:*
BARLOW, Prof. FRANK, M.A., D.PHIL.
BARROW, Prof. GEOFFREY WALLIS STEUART, M.A., B.LITT.
BISHOP, TERENCE ALAN MARTIN, M.A.
Blair, Dr. PETER HUNTER.
BROOKE, Prof. CHRISTOPHER NUGENT LAWRENCE, M.A., F.S A.
Browning, Prof. ROBERT, PH.D.
Cameron, Prof. KENNETH.
CHAPLAIS, PIERRE THÉOPHILE VICTORIEN MARIE, M.A., PH.D.
CHENEY, Prof. CHRISTOPHER ROBERT, M.A.
Chibnall, Dr. MARJORIE.
COLVIN, HOWARD MONTAGU, C.B.E., M.A.
DARBY, Prof. HENRY CLIFFORD, C.B.E., M.A., PH.D., LITT.D.
Davis, Prof. RALPH HENRY CARLESS.
Dickens, Prof. ARTHUR GEOFFREY, C.M.G., M.A., D.LIT., F.S.A.
DOUGLAS, Prof. DAVID CHARLES, M.A.
Du Boulay, Prof. F. R. H.
ELTON, Prof. GEOFFREY RUDOLPH, PH.D., D.LITT.
Grierson, Prof. PHILIP, M.A., F.S.A.
HAY, Prof. DENYS, M.A.
Hilton, Prof. RODNEY HOWARD, B.A., D.PHIL.
Holt, Prof. JAMES CLARKE.
KER, NEIL RIPLEY, C.B.E., B.LITT., M.A.

Lewis, Prof. BERNARD, PH.D.
Loyn, Prof. HENRY ROYSTON.
MAJOR, Miss KATHLEEN, B.LITT.
MANGO, Prof. CYRIL ALEXANDER, M.A., D.UNIV.
Millar, Dr. EDWARD.
MYRES, JOHN NOWELL LINTON, C.B.E., M.A., LL.D., D.LITT., D.LIT., F.S.A.
Nicol, Prof. D. M.
OBOLENSKY, Prof. DIMITRI, M.A., PH.D., F.S.A., F.R.HIST.S.
OFFLER, Prof. H. S., M.A.
Postan, Sir MICHAEL, M.A.
REEVES, Miss MARJORIE, M.A., PH.D., D.LITT
ROSKELL, Prof. JOHN SMITH, M.A., PH.D.
RUBINSTEIN, Prof. NICOLAI.
RUNCIMAN, The Hon. Sir STEVEN, M.A.
SAYLES, Prof. GEORGE OSBORNE, D.LITT.
SMALLEY, Miss BERYL, M.A.
Southern, Sir RICHARD, M.A.
STONES, Prof. EDWARD LIONEL GREGORY.
TAYLOR, ARNOLD JOSEPH, C.B.E., M.A., D.LITT., F.S.A.
TWITCHETT, Prof. DENIS CRISPIN, M.A., PH.D.
ULLMANN, Prof. WALTER, M.A., LITT.D.
Wallace-Hadrill, Prof. JOHN MICHAEL, D.LITT.
WHITELOCK, Prof. DOROTHY, C.B.E., LITT.D., F.S.A.

*Biblical, Theological and Religious Studies:*
ANDERSON, Rev. Prof. GEORGE WISHART, M.A.
BARR, Rev. Prof. JAMES, M.A., D.D.
BARRETT, Rev. Prof. CHARLES KINGSLEY, D.D.
BLACK, Very Rev. Prof. MATTHEW, D.D., D.LITT.
Brock, SEBASTIAN PAUL, M.A., D.PHIL.
BROOKE, Prof. CHRISTOPHER NUGENT LAWRENCE, M.A.
Brown, Prof. PETER ROBERT LAMONT, M.A.
Bruce, Prof. FREDERICK FYFIE, M.A., D.D.
CAIRD, Rev. Prof. GEORGE BRADFORD, M.A., D.PHIL., D.D.
Chadwick, Rev. Prof. HENRY, D.D.
CHADWICK, Rev. Prof. WILLIAM OWEN, D.D.
COPLESTON, Rev. Prof. FREDERICK CHARLES, S.J., M.A., D.PHIL.
DAUBE, Prof. DAVID, D.C.L., PH.D., DR.JUR.
EMERTON, Rev. Prof. JOHN ADNEY.
JOHNSON, Rev. Prof. AUBREY RODWAY, PH.D.
KELLY, Rev. Canon JOHN NORMAN DAVIDSON, D.D
McKane, Prof. W.
MacKinnon, Prof. DONALD MacKENZIE.
Mascall, Rev. ERIC LIONEL, B.A., D.D.
MOULE, The Rev. Prof. CHARLES FRANCIS DIGBY, M.A.
NEILL, The Rt. Rev. STEPHEN CHARLES, M.A.
OBOLENSKY, Prof. DIMITRI, M.A., PH.D., F.S.A., F.R.HIST.S.
RUPP, Rev. Prof. ERNEST GORDON, M.A., D.D.
SEGAL, Prof. JUDAH BENZION, M.C., M.A., D.PHIL.
SMALLEY, Miss BERYL, M.A.
Sparks, Rev. Prof. HEDLEY FREDERICK DAVIS, D.D.
STEAD, Rev. Prof. G. C.
ULLMANN, Prof. WALTER, M.A., LITT.D.
Wiles, Rev. Prof. M. F.
Wilson, Rev. Prof. ROBERT McLACHLAN, M.A., B.D., PH.D.
ZUNTZ, Prof. GÜNTHER, DR.PHIL.

*Oriental and African Studies:*
ALLEN, Prof. WILLIAM SYDNEY, M.A., PH.D.
Bailey, Prof. Sir HAROLD, M.A., D.PHIL.
BARR, Rev. Prof. JAMES, M.A., D.D.
Beasley, Prof. WILLIAM GERALD, C.B.E., PH.D.
Beeston, Prof. ALFRED FELIX LANDON, M.A., D.PHIL.
BLACK, Very Rev. Prof. MATTHEW, D.D., D.LITT.
Boxer, Prof. CHARLES RALPH.
Brock, SEBASTIAN PAUL, M.A., D.PHIL.
Brough, Prof. JOHN, D.LITT.
Burrow, Prof. THOMAS, M.A., PH.D.
Dowsett, Prof. CHARLES JAMES FRANK, M.A., PH.D.
EDWARDS, IORWERTH EIDDON STEPHEN, C.M.G., C.B.E., LITT.D., F.S.A.
GERSHEVITCH, ILYA, PH.D., D.LITT.
Graham, Prof. A. C.
GRAY, BASIL, C.B., C.B.E., M.A.
GURNEY, Prof. OLIVER ROBERT, D.PHIL.
HAMILTON, ROBERT WILLIAM, M.A., F.S.A.
Holt, Prof. P. M., M.A., D.PHIL., D.LITT.
JAMES, THOMAS GARNET HENRY, M.A.
JOHNSON, Rev. Prof. AUBREY RODWAY, PH.D.
LAMBERT, Prof. WILFRED GEORGE, M.A.
LAMBTON, Prof. ANN KATHARINE SWYNFORD, O.B.E., PH.D., D.LIT.
Lewis, Prof. BERNARD, PH.D.
Lewis, Dr. GEOFFREY LEWIS.

1407

Lyons, Prof. John, m.a., ph.d.
McKane, Prof. W.
Needham, Joseph, m.a., sc.d., ph.d., f.r.s.
Palmer, Prof. Frank Robert, m.a.
Picken, Laurence Ernest Rowland, m.a., ph.d., sc.d.
Segal, Prof. Judah Benzion, m.c., m.a., d.phil.
Snellgrove, Prof. David Llewellyn, m.a., ph.d.
Sollberger, Edmond, d.litt.
Turner, Sir Ralph Lilley, m.c., litt.d.
Twitchett, Prof. Denis Crispin, m.a., ph.d.
Ullendorff, Prof. Edward, m.a., d.phil.
Watson, Prof. William, m.a., f.s.a.
Wiseman, Prof. Donald John, o.b.e., m.a., f.s.a.

*Literature and Philology, Classical:*
Allen, Prof. William Sydney, m.a., ph.d.
Andrewes, Prof. Antony, m.b.e., m.a.
Armstrong, Prof. Arthur Hilary, m.a.
Bailey, Prof. David Roy Shackleton, m.a., litt.d.
Barrett, William Spencer, m.a.
Brink, Prof. Charles Oscar, m.a.
Cameron, Prof. A. D. E., m.a.
Chadwick, John, m.a., litt.d.
Dover, Sir Kenneth, m.a.
Handley, Prof. Eric Walter, m.a.
Jeffery, Miss Lilian Hamilton, m.a., d.phil., f.s.a.
Kenney, Prof. Edward John, m.a.
Kirk, Prof. Geoffrey Stephen, d.s.c., m.a.
Kitto, Prof. Humphrey Davy Findley, b.a.
Kneale, Prof. William Calvert, m.a.
Lloyd-Jones, Prof. Peter Hugh Jefferd, m.a.
Lyons, Prof. John, m.a., ph.d.
Minio-Paluello, Lorenzo, d.phil.
Mynors, Sir Roger, m.a.
Nisbet, Prof. Robin George Murdoch, m.a.
Ogilvie, Prof. Robert Maxwell, m.a., d.litt.
Owen, Prof. Gwylim Ellis Lane, m.a., b.phil.
Parsons, Peter John.
Rea, Dr. J. R.
Robertson, Prof. Charles Martin, m.a.
Russell, Donald Andrew Frank Moore, m.a.
Sandbach, Prof. Francis Henry, m.a.
Syme, Prof. Sir Ronald, o.m., m.a.
Trendall, Prof. Arthur Dale, c.m.g., m.a., litt.d., f.s.a.
Turner, Prof. Sir Eric, c.b.e., m.a.
Walbank, Prof. Frank William, m.a.
West, Prof. Martin Litchfield, m.a., d.phil.
Wilson, N. G.
Winnington-Ingram, Prof. Reginald Pepys, m.a.
Winterbottom, Dr. Michael.
Zuntz, Prof. Günther, dr.phil.

*Literature and Philology, Medieval and Modern:*
Austin, Prof. Lloyd James, m.a.
Bruford, Prof. Walter Horace, m.a.
Bullough, Prof. Geoffrey, m.a., f.r.s.l.
Cameron, Prof. Kenneth, ph.d.
Chadwick, John, m.a., litt.d.
Davis, Prof. Norman, m.b.e., m.a.
De Beer, Esmond Samuel, c.b.e., m.a., d.litt., f.s.a., f.r.s.l.
Dionisotti-Casalone, Prof. Carlo, m.a.
Dobson, Prof. Eric John, m.a., d.phil.
Ellmann, Prof. Richard.
Empson, Sir William, m.a.
Forster, Prof. Leonard Wilson, dr.phil.
Fowler, Prof. Alastair David Shaw, d.phil., m.a.
Foxon, David Fairweather.
Gardner, Dame Helen Louise, d.b.e., f.r.s.l., d.litt.
Grayson, Prof. Cecil.
Jackson, Prof. Kenneth Hurlstone, litt.d.
Kane, Prof. George, m.a.
Ker, Neil Ripley, c.b.e., b.litt., m.a.
Kermode, Prof. John Frank, m.a.
Kinsley, Rev. Prof. James, m.a., d.litt., d.phil.
Lascelles, Miss Mary Madge, b.litt.
Legge, Prof. Mary Dominica.
Leigh, Prof. Ralph Alexander, c.b.e., m.a., d.litt.
Lough, Prof. John, m.a., ph.d.
McFarlane, Prof. Ian Dalrimple, m.b.e.
Mango, Prof. Cyril Alexander, m.a., d.univ.
Muir, Prof. Kenneth, m.a.
Oakeshott, Sir Walter, m.a., ll.d., f.s.a.
Oates, John Claud Trewinard, m.a.
Obolensky, Prof. Dimitri, m.a., ph.d., f.s.a., f.r.hist.s.
Palmer, Prof. Frank Robert, m.a.
Parry, Sir Thomas, m.a., d.litt.

Prawer, Prof. S. S.
Quirk, Prof. Charles Randolph, c.b.e., m.a., ph.d., d.lit.
Ricks, Prof. Christopher Bruce, m.a.
Russell, Prof. Peter Edward Lionel, m.a., f.r.hist.s.
Screech, Prof. M. A.
Seznec, Prof. Jean Joseph, m.a.
Shackleton, Prof. Robert, m.a., d.litt., f.s.a.
Smalley, Miss Beryl, m.a.
Stevens, Prof. John Edgar, c.b.e.
Sutherland, Prof. James Runcieman, m.a.
Tate, Prof. R. B.
Tillotson, Prof. Kathleen Mary, m.a., b.litt.
Trapp, Prof. J. B.
Walker, Prof. Daniel Pickering, m.a., d.piil.
Whitelock, Prof. Dorothy, c.b.e., litt.d., f.s.a.
Wilkinson, Prof. Elizabeth Mary, ph.d.
Williams, Prof. John Ellis Caerwyn.

*Philosophy:*
Aaron, Prof. Richard Ithamar, m.a., d.phil.
Ackrill, Prof. J. L.
Anscombe, Prof. Gertrude Elizabeth Margaret, m.a.
Ayer, Prof. Sir Alfred Jules, m.a.
Berlin, Sir Isaiah, o.m., c.b.e., m.a.
Braithwaite, Prof. Richard Bevan, m.a.
Cohen, Laurence Jonathan, m.a.
Copleston, Rev. Prof. Frederick Charles, s.j., m.a., d.phil.
Dummett, Prof. Michael Anthony Eardsley, m.a.
Dworkin, Prof. R. M.
Findlay, Prof. John Niemeyer, m.a., ph.d.
Foot, Mrs. Philippa Ruth, m.a.
Geach, Prof. Peter Thomas, m.a.
Grice, Herbert Paul, m.a.
Hampshire, Sir Stuart, m.a.
Hare, Prof. Richard Mervyn, m.a.
Hart, Prof. Herbert Lionel Adolphus, m.a.
Hesse, Prof. Mary Brenda, m.a., m.sc., ph.d.
Kenny, A. J. P., ph.d., m.a., d.phil.
Kneale, Prof. William Calvert, m.a.
Körner, Prof. Stephan, ph.d.
Lewy, Dr. C.
Lyons, Prof. John, m.a., ph.d.
Mackie, J. L., m.a.
Minio-Paluello, Lorenzo, d.phil.
Owen, Prof. Gwylim Ellis Lane, m.a., b.phil.
Pears, David Francis, m.a.
Popper, Prof. Sir Karl, ph.d., d.lit., f.r.s.
Price, Prof. Henry Habberley, m.a., b.sc.
Quinton, Anthony Meredith, m.a.
Scott, Prof. Dana S., m.a., ph.d.
Sen, Prof. Amartya Kumar.
Strawson, Prof. Sir Peter, m.a.
Taylor, Prof. Charles Margrave.
Walsh, Prof. William Henry, m.a.
Whiteside, Derek Thomas, ph.d.
Wiggins, David.
Williams, Prof. Bernard Arthur Owen, m.a.
Wollheim, Prof. Richard Arthur, m.a.

*Jurisprudence:*
Anderson, Prof. Sir Norman, o.b.e., q.c., m.a., ll.d., d.d.
Anton, Prof. Alexander Elder, c.b.e., m.a., ph.d.
Atiyah, Prof. Patrick Selim.
Brownlie, Prof. Ian.
Daube, Prof. David, d.c.l., ph.d., dr.jur.
Devlin, Rt. Hon. Lord, p.c., m.a.
Dworkin, Prof. Ronald Myles.
Gower, Prof. Laurence Cecil Bartlett, m.b.e., ll.m.
Griffith, Prof. John Aneurin Grey, ll.m.
Hart, Prof. Herbert Lionel Adolphus, m.a.
Honoré, Prof. Anthony Maurice, d.c.l.
Jackson, Prof. Richard Meredith, m.a., ll.d., j.p.
Keeton, Prof. George Williams, ll.d.
Lawson, Prof. Frederick Henry, d.c.l.
Mann, Frederick Alexander, c.b.e., ll.d., dr.jur.
Marshall, Geoffrey, m.a., ph.d.
Megarry, The Rt. Hon. Sir Robert (Edgar), p.c., m.a., ll.d.
Milsom, Prof. Stroud Francis Charles, m.a.
Morris, John Humphrey Carlile, m.a., d.c.l.
Smith, Prof. John Cyril, m.a.
Smith, Sir Thomas, q.c., d.c.l.
Stein, Prof. Peter Gonville, ph.d., m.a.
Street, Prof. Harry, c.b.e., ll.m., ph.d.
Treitel, Prof. Guenter Heinz, b.c.l., m.a.

BRITISH ACADEMY U.K. (GREAT BRITAIN)

ULLMANN, Prof. WALTER.
WADE, Prof. HENRY WILLIAM RAWSON, Q.C., M.A., LL.D., D.C.L.
WALKER, Prof. DAVID MAXWELL, Q.C., PH.D., LL.D.
WEDDERBURN OF CHARLTON, Lord.
WILLIAMS, Prof. GLANVILLE LLEWELYN, LL.D.
YALE, D. E. C.

*Economics and Economic History:*
ALLEN, Prof. GEORGE CYRIL, C.B.E., M.COM., PH.D.
ALLEN, Sir ROY, C.B.E., M.A., D.SC.(ECON.).
BAUER, Prof. PETER THOMAS, M.A.
BLACK, Prof. ROBERT DENIS COLLISON, M.A., PH.D.
BROWN, Prof. ARTHUR JOSEPH, C.B.E.
BROWN, Prof. Sir HENRY PHELPS, M.B.E., M.A.
CAIRNCROSS, Sir ALEC, K.C.M.G.
CARTER, Sir CHARLES, M.A.
CHAMPERNOWNE, Prof. DAVID GAWEN, M.A.
CHECKLAND, Prof. SYDNEY GEORGE, M.A., M.COM., PH.D.
COLEMAN, Prof. DONALD CUTHBERT, B.SC.(ECON.), PH.D.
DEANE, Miss P. M.
GORMAN, Prof. WILLIAM MOORE.
HABAKKUK, Sir (HROTHGAR) JOHN, M.A.
HAHN, Prof. FRANK HORACE, M.A., PH.D.
HAYEK, Prof. FRIEDRICH AUGUST, DR.JUR., DR.SC.POL., D.SC.(ECON.).
HICKS, Sir JOHN, M.A., B.LITT.
HOBSBAWM, Prof. E. J. E.
KAHN, Lord, C.B.E., M.A.
KALDOR, Lord, M.A.
LITTLE, Prof. IAN MALCOLM DAVID, A.F.C., M.A., D.PHIL.
MACDOUGALL, Sir DONALD, C.B.E., M.A.
MATHIAS, Prof. PETER, M.A., F.R.HIST.S.
MATTHEWS, ROBERT CHARLES OLIVER, C.B.E., M.A.
MEADE, Prof. JAMES EDWARD, C.B.
MORISHIMA, Prof. M.
NOVE, Prof. ALEXANDER.
PEACOCK, Prof. ALAN TURNER, D.S.C.
POSTAN, Sir MICHAEL, M.A.
REDDAWAY, Prof. WILLIAM BRIAN, C.B.E., M.A.
ROBBINS, Lord, C.H., C.B., M.A.
ROBINSON, Prof. Sir (EDWARD) AUSTIN (GOSSAGE), C.M.G., O.B.E.
SARGAN, Prof. J. D.
SAYERS, Prof. RICHARD SIDNEY, M.A.
SEN, Prof. AMARTYA KUMAR, M.A., PH.D.
SHACKLE, Prof. GEORGE LENNOX SHARMAN, M.A., PH.D.
SRAFFA, PIERO, M.A.
STONE, Prof. Sir (JOHN) RICHARD (NICHOLAS), C.B.E., M.A.
THIRSK, Dr. IRENE JOAN.
THOMAS, Prof. BRINLEY, C.B.E., PH.D.
WILSON, Prof. CHARLES HENRY, C.B.E., M.A.
WILSON, Prof. THOMAS, O.B.E., M.A., PH.D.
WORSWICK, GEORGE DAVID NORMAN, C.B.E.
YAMEY, Prof. BASIL SELIG, C.B.E., B.COM.

*Archaeology:*
ALLCHIN, Dr. F. R.
ASHMOLE, Prof. BERNARD, C.B.E., M.C., M.A.
BARNETT, RICHARD DAVID, C.B.E., D.LITT., F.S.A.
BIRLEY, Prof. ERIC, M.B.E., M.A., F.S.A.
BLUNT, CHRISTOPHER EVELYN, O.B.E., F.S.A.
BOARDMAN, Prof. JOHN, M.A., F.S.A.
BRUCE-MITFORD, RUPERT LEO SCOTT, M.A., LITT.D.
CARSON, R. A. G.
CATON-THOMPSON, Miss GERTRUDE, LITT.D.
CLARK, Prof. JOHN DESMOND, C.B.E., M.A., PH.D., F.S.A.
CLARK, Prof. JOHN GRAHAME DOUGLAS, C.B.E., PH.D., SC.D., F.S.A.
COLDSTREAM, Prof. JOHN NICOLAS, M.A., F.S.A.
COLES, Prof. JOHN MORTON.
COOK, Prof. JOHN MANUEL, M.A.
COOK, Prof. ROBERT MANUEL, M.A.
CRAWFORD, M. H.
CUNLIFFE, Prof. BARRINGTON WINDSOR.
EDWARDS, Dr. IORWERTH EIDDON STEPHEN, C.M.G., C.B.E.
EVANS, Prof. JOHN DAVIES, M.A., PH.D.
FRASER, PETER MARSHALL, M.C., M.A.
FRERE, Prof. SHEPPARD SUNDERLAND, C.B.E., M.A.
GRAY, BASIL, C.B., C.B.E., M.A.
GRIERSON, Prof. PHILIP, M.A., F.S.A.
HAMILTON, ROBERT WILLIAM, M.A., F.S.A.
HAWKES, Prof. CHARLES FRANCIS CHRISTOPHER, M.A., F.S.A.
HIGGINS, REYNOLD ALLEYNE, M.A., LITT.D., F.S.A.
JAMES, THOMAS GARNET HENRY, M.A.
JEFFERY, Miss LILIAN HAMILTON, M.A., D.PHIL., F.S.A.
JOPE, Prof. EDWARD MARTYN, M.A., B.SC., F.S.A.

KRAAY, Dr. COLIN MACKENNAL.
LEAKEY, Mrs. MARY DOUGLAS.
LLOYD, Prof. SETON HOWARD FREDERICK, C.B.E., M.A., F.S.A.
MELLAART, JAMES.
MOOREY, PETER ROGER STUART, M.A., D.PHIL., F.S.A.
MYRES, JOHN NOWELL LINTON, C.B.E., M.A., LL.D., D.LITT., D.LIT., F.S.A.
OAKLEY, KENNETH PAGE, PH.D., D.SC., F.S.A.
OATES, Prof. EDWARD ERNEST DAVID MICHAEL, M.A., F.S.A.
PIGGOTT, Prof. STUART, C.B.E., B.LITT., F.S.A.
RADFORD, COURTENAY ARTHUR RALEGH, M.A., D.LITT., F.S.A.
RENFREW, Prof. A. C.
ROBERTSON, Prof. CHARLES MARTIN, M.A.
ST. JOSEPH, Prof. JOHN KENNETH SINCLAIR, C.B.E.
SNODGRASS, Prof. ANTHONY McELREA.
SOLLBERGER, EDMOND, D.LITT.
STEWART, Dr. B. H. I. H.
SUTHERLAND, CAROL HUMPHREY VIVIAN, C.B.E., M.A., D.LITT. F.S.A.
TAYLOR, ARNOLD JOSEPH, C.B.E., M.A., D.LITT., F.S.A.
TOYNBEE, Prof. JOCELYN MARY CATHERINE, D.PHIL., F.S.A.
TRENDALL, Prof. ARTHUR DALE, C.M.G., M.A., LITT.D., F.S.A.
WATSON, Prof. WILLIAM, M.A., F.S.A.
WILSON, Dr. D. M.
WISEMAN, Prof. DONALD JOHN, O.B.E., M.A., F.S.A.

*History of Art:*
ABRAHAM, GERALD ERNEST HEAL, C.B.E., M.A.
ARNOLD, Prof. DENIS MIDGLEY, M.A., B.MUS., A.R.C.M.
ASHMOLE, Prof. BERNARD, C.B.E., M.C., M.A.
BAINES, Dr. A. C.
BARRETT, DOUGLAS E.
BECKWITH, JOHN GORDON, M.A., F.S.A.
BOARDMAN, Prof. J.
BUCHTHAL, Prof. HUGO, PH.D.
CLARK, The Lord, O.M., C.H., K.C.B., M.A.
COLVIN, HOWARD MONTAGU, C.B.E., M.A.
DEAN, WINTON BASIL, M.A.
DODWELL, Prof. CHARLES REGINALD, M.A., PH.D., LITT.D., F.S.A.
GERE, JOHN ARTHUR GILES.
GOMBRICH, Prof. Sir ERNST HANS JOSEF, C.B.E., PH.D., F.S.A.
GRAY, BASIL, C.B., C.B.E., M.A.
HALE, Prof. J. R.
HARRISON, Prof. FRANCIS LLEWELLYN, M.A., D.MUS.
HASKELL, Prof. FRANCIS JAMES HERBERT, M.A.
LASKO, Prof. PETER ERIK, C.B.E.
MAHON, JOHN DENIS, C.B.E., M.A.
MANGO, Prof. CYRIL ALEXANDER, M.A., D.UNIV.
MILLAR, Sir OLIVER NICHOLAS, K.C.V.O., F.S.A.
OAKESHOTT, Sir WALTER, M.A., LL.D., F.S.A.
PÄCHT, Prof. OTTO ERNST, D.PHIL.
PARKER, Sir KARL (THEODORE), C.B.E., PH.D.,
PEVSNER, Sir NIKOLAUS, C.B.E., M.A., PH.D., F.S.A.
PICKEN, LAURENCE ERNEST ROWLAND, M.A., PH.D., SC.D.
POPE-HENNESSY, Sir JOHN, C.B.E., F.S.A.
POUNCEY, PHILIP M. R.
ROBBINS, Lord, C.H., C.B.
ROBINSON, B. W.
RUBINSTEIN, Prof. N.
SEZNEC, Prof. JEAN JOSEPH, M.A.
SHEARMAN, Prof. JOHN, PH.D.
STEVENS, Prof. JOHN EDGAR, C.B.E., M.A., PH.D.
SUMMERSON, Sir JOHN, C.B.E., B.A., F.S.A., A.R.I.B.A.
TYSON, Dr. ALAN WALKER.
WATERHOUSE, Prof. Sir ELLIS, C.B.E., M.A., A.M.
WATSON, Sir FRANCIS, K.C.V.O., B.A., F.S.A.
WATSON, Prof. WILLIAM, M.A., F.S.A.
WILSON, Dr. D. M.
ZARNECKI, Prof. GEORGE, C.B.E., M.A., PH.D., F.S.A.

*Social and Political Studies:*
ALLEN, Sir ROY, C.B.E., M.A., D.SC.(ECON.).
BARNES, Prof. J. A.
BELOFF, Lord, M.A.
BERLIN, Sir ISAIAH, O.M., C.B.E., M.A.
BLAKE, Lord, M.A.
BRASS, Prof. WILLIAM, C.B.E.
COHN, Prof. NORMAN.
COPPOCK, Prof. JOHN TERENCE, M.A., PH.D.
DAHRENDORF, Prof. RALF, PH.D., DR.PHIL.
DARBY, Prof. HENRY CLIFFORD, C.B.E., M.A., PH.D., LITT.D.
DORE, Prof. RONALD P.
FIRTH, Sir RAYMOND, PH.D.
FORTES, Prof. MEYER, M.A., PH.D.
GELLNER, Prof. ERNEST ANDRÉ, M.A., PH.D.
GOODY, Prof. JOHN RANKINE, M.A., PH.D., SC.D.

GOTTMANN, Prof. JEAN.
HAJNAL, Prof. JOHN, M.A.
HART, Prof. HERBERT LIONEL ADOLPHUS, M.A.
HAYEK, Prof. FRIEDRICH AUGUST, DR.JUR., DR.SC.POL., D.SC.(ECON.).
JACKSON, Prof. RICHARD MEREDITH, M.A., LL.D., J.P.
KEDOURIE, Prof. ELIE, B.SC.
KENDALL, Sir MAURICE, M.A., SC.D.
KOLAKOWSKI, L.
LASLETT, PETER.
LEACH, Sir EDMUND, M.A., PH.D.
LOCKWOOD, Prof. DAVID, M.A., PH.D.
LYONS, Prof. JOHN, M.A., PH.D.
MACKENZIE, Prof. WILLIAM JAMES MILLAR, C.B.E., M.A., LL.B.
MARSHALL, GEOFFREY, M.A., PH.D.
MATTHEWS, ROBERT CHARLES OLIVER, C.B.E., M.A.
MOSER, Sir CLAUS, K.C.B., C.B.E., B.SC.
NEEDHAM, JOSEPH, M.A., SC.D., PH.D., F.R.S.
NICHOLAS, Prof. HERBERT GEORGE, M.A.
OAKESHOTT, Prof. MICHAEL JOSEPH, M.A.
POPPER, Prof. Sir KARL, PH.D., D.LIT., F.R.S.
POSTAN, Sir MICHAEL, M.A.
RADZINOWICZ, Sir LEON, M.A., LL.D.
RICHARDS, AUDREY ISABEL, C.B.E., M.A., PH.D.
RUNCIMAN, WALTER GARRISON, M.A.
SCHAPERA, Prof. ISAAC, PH.D., D.SC.
SCHAPIRO, Prof. LEONARD BERTTRAM, C.B.E., LL.B.
SEN, Prof. AMARTYA KUMAR.
SETON-WATSON, Prof. GEORGE HUGH NICHOLAS, C.B.E.
SKINNER, Prof. Q. R. D.
WILLIAMS, Prof. BERNARD ARTHUR OWEN, M.A.
WOLLHEIM, Prof. RICHARD ARTHUR, M.A.
WRIGLEY, Dr. E. A.

*Modern History 1500–1800:*
AYLMER, GERALD EDWARD, M.A., D.PHIL.
BERLIN, Sir ISAIAH, O.M., C.B.E., M.A.
BLAKE, Lord, M.A.
BOXER, Prof. CHARLES RALPH, D.LITT.
CARSTEN, Prof. FRANCIS LUDWIG, D.LITT., D.PHIL.
CHRISTIE, Prof. IAN RALPH, M.A., F.R.HIST.S.
COBB, Prof. RICHARD CHARLES, C.B.E., M.A.
COLEMAN, Prof. DONALD CUTHBERT, B.SC.(ECON.), PH.D.
COLVIN, HOWARD MONTAGUE, C.B.E., M.A.
DACRE OF GLANTON, Lord.
DARBY, Prof. HENRY CLIFFORD, C.B.E., M.A., PH.D., LITT.D.
DICKENS, Prof. ARTHUR GEOFFREY, C.M.G., M.A., D.LIT., F.S.A.
DONALDSON, Prof. GORDON, M.A., PH.D., D.LITT.
DOUGLAS, Prof. DAVID CHARLES, M.A.
EHRMAN, JOHN PATRICK WILLIAM, M.A.
ELLIOTT, Prof. JOHN HUXTABLE.
ELTON, Prof. GEOFFREY RUDOLPH, PH.D., LITT.D.
GASH, Prof. NORMAN, M.A.
HABAKKUK, Sir (HROTHGAR) JOHN, M.A.
HALE, Prof. JOHN RIGBY, M.A., F.S.A., F.R.HIST.S.
HALL, Prof. ALFRED RUPERT.
HAMPSON, Prof. N.
HAY, Prof. DENYS, M.A.
HILL, JOHN EDWARD CHRISTOPHER, M.A., D.LITT.
HOSKINS, Prof. WILLIAM GEORGE, C.B.E., M.A., PH.D.
KENYON, Prof. J. P.
McMANNERS, Rev. Prof. JOHN.
PLUMB, Prof. JOHN HAROLD, PH.D., LITT.D., F.S.A.
ROBERTS, Prof. MICHAEL, D.PHIL.
ROSKELL, Prof. JOHN SMITH, M.A., PH.D.
ROWSE, ALFRED LESLIE, D.LITT.
RUBINSTEIN, Prof. NICOLAI.
RUNCIMAN, The Hon. Sir STEVEN, M.A.
RUPP, Rev. Prof. ERNEST GORDON, M.A., D.D.
SAYLES, Prof. GEORGE OSBORNE, D.LITT.
THIRSK, I. JOAN, M.A., PH.D.
THOMAS, KEITH V.
ULLMANN, Prof. WALTER, M.A., LITT.D.
WEDGWOOD, Dame VERONICA, O.M., D.B.E., M.A., F.R.HIST.S.
WHITESIDE, DEREK THOMAS, PH.D.
WILSON, Prof. CHARLES HENRY, C.B.E., M.A.

*Modern History from 1800:*
ALLEN, Prof. GEORGE CYRIL, C.B.E., M.COM., PH.D.
BEASLEY, Prof. WILLIAM GERALD, C.B.E., PH.D.
BELOFF, Lord, M.A.
BLAKE, Lord, M.A.
BRIGGS, Lord.
BROWN, Prof. Sir (ERNEST) HENRY PHELPS, M.B.E., M.A.
BULLOCK, Lord, M.A.
CAIRNCROSS, Sir ALEC KIRKLAND, K.C.M.G.

CARR, ALBERT RAYMOND MAILLARD.
CARR, EDWARD HALLETT, C.B.E., M.A.
CARSTEN, Prof. FRANCIS LUDWIG, D.LITT., D.PHIL.
CHADWICK, Rev. Prof. WILLIAM OWEN, D.D.
COBB, Prof. RICHARD CHARLES, C.B.E., M.A.
COLEMAN, Prof. DONALD CUTHBERT, B.SC.(ECON.), PH.D.
DACRE OF GLANTON, Lord.
EHRMAN, JOHN PATRICK WILLIAM, M.A.
GASH, Prof. NORMAN, M.A.
GOWING, Prof. MARGARET M., C.B.E., M.A.
HABAKKUK, Sir (HROTHGAR) JOHN, M.A.
HANCOCK, Prof. Sir (WILLIAM) KEITH, K.B.E., M.A.
HICKS, Sir JOHN RICHARD, M.A.
HINSLEY, Prof. F. H., O.B.E.
HOBSBAWN, Prof. ERIC JOHN ERNEST, M.A., PH.D.
HOWARD, Prof. MICHAEL ELIOT, C.B.E., M.C., M.A.
JOLL, Prof. JAMES BYSSE, M.A.
KEDOURIE, Prof. ELIE, B.SC.
LEWIS, Prof. BERNARD, PH.D.
LYONS, Prof. FRANCIS STEWART LELAND, M.A., PH.D., LITT.D.
MACK SMITH, DENIS, M.A.
MANSERGH, Prof. PETER NICHOLAS SETON, O.B.E., M.A., D.PHIL., D.LITT., LITT.D.
MATHIAS, Prof. PETER, M.A., F.R.HIST.S.
MATTHEWS, ROBERT CHARLES OLIVER, C.B.E., M.A.
NICHOLAS, Prof. HERBERT GEORGE, M.A.
PERHAM, Dame MARGERY, D.C.M.G., C.B.E., D.LITT.
PLUMB, Prof. JOHN HAROLD, PH.D., LITT.D., F.S.A.
POSTAN, Sir MICHAEL, M.A.
ROSKILL, Capt. STEPHEN WENTWORTH, C.B.E., D.S.C., M.A., LITT.D., R.N. (retd.).
SAYERS, Prof. RICHARD SIDNEY, M.A.
SCHAPIRO, Prof. LEONARD BERTRAM, C.B.E., LL.B.
SETON-WATSON, Prof. GEORGE HUGH NICHOLAS, C.B.E., M.A.
SUTHERLAND, Dame LUCY STUART, D.B.E., M.A., LITT.D.
THOMPSON, Prof. FRANCIS MICHAEL LONGSTRETH.
WILSON, Prof. CHARLES HENRY, C.B.E., M.A.

## ROYAL INSTITUTION OF GREAT BRITAIN
### 21 ALBEMARLE STREET W1X 4BS
Telephone: 01-409-2992.

*President:* H.R.H. The Duke of KENT, G.C.M.G., G.C.V.O.
*Treasurer:* Sir PAUL OSMOND, C.B., M.A.
*Secretary:* Prof. H. J. V. TYRRELL, M.A., D.SC.
*Director:* Prof. Sir GEORGE PORTER, M.A., SC.D., F.R.S.
*Librarian:* Mrs. I. M. McCABE, M.SC., DIP.LIB., M.I.INF.SC.

Founded for the promotion of Science and the extension of useful knowledge; lectures for Members and their guests and for schools; Christmas lectures for children and young people; discussion groups; Davy Faraday Research Laboratory; research on photochemistry.

Library: *see* Libraries.

Number of members: 2,500.

Publications: *Proceedings* (annually), *Royal Institution Library of Science*, various booklets.

### PROFESSORS:
Sir GEORGE PORTER, M.A., SC.D., F.R.S., Fullerian Professor of Chemistry and Director of the Royal Institution and the Davy Faraday Research Laboratory.
D. PHILLIPS, PH.D., F.R.S.C., Wolfson Professor of Natural Philosophy.
RONALD KING, PH.D., F.I.M., F.INST.P., Professor of Physics.
A. HEWISH, F.R.S., Professor of Astronomy.
Prof. Sir DAVID PHILLIPS, F.R.S., Fullerian Professor of Physiology.
Sir PETER MEDAWAR, F.R.S., Professor of Experimental Medicine.
C. A. TAYLOR, D.SC., F.INST.P., Professor of Experimental Physics.
FRANK GREENAWAY, M.A., M.SC., PH.D., F.R.S.C., F.M.A., F.S.A., Reader in History of Science.

### AGRICULTURE AND VETERINARY SCIENCE
**Agricultural Economics Society:** University of Aberdeen, Dept. of Agriculture, School of Agriculture Bldg.,

Aberdeen, AB9 1UD; f. 1926 to promote the study and teaching of history, statistics, economics and sociology, in relation to the agricultural industry and rural communities; approx. 800 mems.; Hon. Sec. J. S. MARSH; Hon. Editor D. I. BATEMAN; publ. *Journal of Agricultural Economics*.

**British Agricultural History Society:** c/o Institute of Agricultural History and Museum of English Rural Life, The University, Whiteknights, Reading, Berks.; f. 1952; 800 mems.; Pres. Prof. W. H. CHALONER; Sec. Dr. J. CHARTRES; publ. *Agricultural History Review* (2 a year).

**British Society of Animal Production:** P.O.B. 47, Winchester, Hants. SO21 1AL; f. 1944; 1,200 mems.; United Kingdom member organization of the European Association for Animal Production; Pres. Prof. W. F. RAYMOND; Sec. C. F. R. SLADE; publ. *Animal Production* (6 a year).

**British Society of Soil Science:** c/o University of Nottingham School of Agriculture, Sutton Bonington, Loughborough, LE12 5RD; f. 1947 to advance the study of the soil itself, and its applications in agriculture, forestry and other fields; 750 mems.; Pres. W. DERMOTT; Hon. Sec. Dr. D. V. CRAWFORD; publ. *Journal of Soil Science* (quarterly).

**British Veterinary Association** (formerly National Veterinary Medical Association of Great Britain and Ireland): 7 Mansfield Street, London, W1M 0AT; f. 1881 to advance the veterinary art by means of publications and conferences, and to forward and protect the interests of mems. of the veterinary profession; c. 8,000 mems.; Pres. Dr. T. E. GIBSON; Sec. P. B. TURNER; publs. *The Veterinary Record* (weekly), *Research in Veterinary Science*, *In Practice* (bi-monthly).

**Commonwealth Forestry Association:** c/o C.F.I., South Parks Rd., Oxford, OX1 3RB; f. 1921; 1,250 mems.; Chair. D. R. JOHNSTON, M.A.; Editor-Sec. C. J. W. PITT, B.SC., M.A., M.I.FOR.; publs. *The Commonwealth Forestry Review* (quarterly), *The Commonwealth Forestry Handbook*.

**Institute of Foresters:** 22 Walker St., Edinburgh EH3 7HR; f. 1925 as Society, became Institute 1973; to maintain and improve standards and professional status of foresters, and to advance, spread and promote the application of all aspects of forestry; 950 mems.; Pres. J. W. DODDS; Sec. M. W. DICK.

**Institution of Agricultural Engineers:** West End Rd., Silsoe, Bedford, MK45 4DU; f. 1938; professional and examining body aiming to advance all those branches of engineering which relate to agriculture; 2,500 mems.; Pres. R. F. NORMAN; Sec. RAY J. FRYETT; publs. *The Agricultural Engineer* (quarterly).

**Royal Agricultural Society of England:** National Agricultural Centre, Stoneleigh, Kenilworth, Warwicks.; f. 1838 (Royal Charter 1840); 20,000 mems.; established National Agricultural Centre at Kenilworth in 1963 to promote advancements in British Agriculture and disseminates information and ideas; organizes annual agricultural show; arranges regular courses, conferences etc.; agricultural history library; Chief Exec. J. D. M. HEARTH.

**Royal College of Veterinary Surgeons:** 32 Belgrave Square, London, SW1X 8QP; f. 1844; the governing body of the veterinary profession in the United Kingdom, which maintains the Statutory Registers and the discipline of the profession and has supervisory functions in relation to veterinary education in the universities; possesses the foremost veterinary library in the U.K., open to veterinary surgeons and *bona fide* scientific workers; Pres. P. G. HIGNETT; Registrar A. R. W. PORTER, M.A.

**Royal Forestry Society of England, Wales and Northern Ireland:** 102 High Street, Tring, Herts., HP23 4AH; f. 1882 as the English Arboricultural Society to advance the knowledge and practice of forestry and arboriculture, and to disseminate knowledge of the sciences on which they are based; 4,000 mems.; library of 1,500 vols.; Pres. Sir MARCUS WORSLEY, Bt., D.L., J.P.; Dir. E. H. M. HARRIS, B.SC.; publ. *Quarterly Journal of Forestry*†.

**Royal Highland and Agricultural Society of Scotland:** Ingliston, Newbridge, Midlothian; f. 1784, inc. by Royal Charter 1787, for the promotion of the science and practice of agriculture in all its branches; 18,000 mems.; library of 6,000 vols.; Pres. Rt. Hon. Lord CLYDESMUIR; Chief Exec. J. D. G. DAVIDSON; publ. *Show Guide and Review of the Royal Highland and Agricultural Society of Scotland*†.

**Royal Horticultural Society:** Exhibition Halls, Library, and Offices, Vincent Square, London, SW1P 2PE; Gardens and School, Wisley, Ripley, Surrey; f. 1804; 80,000 mems.; library of 38,000 vols. (Lindley Library); Pres. The Lord ABERCONWAY, V.M.H.; Sec. J. R. COWELL, M.A.; publs. *The Garden* (monthly), *The Plantsman* (quarterly), *Transactions and Proceedings*, *Wisley Handbooks*, etc.

**Royal Scottish Forestry Society:** 18 Abercromby Place, Edinburgh, EH3 6LB; f. 1854; about 2,100 mems.; Pres. S. F. CARRUTHERS; Sec.-Treas. W. B. C. WALKER; publ. *Scottish Forestry* (quarterly).

**Royal Welsh Agricultural Society:** Llanelwedd, Builth-Wells, Powys LD2 3SY; f. 1904; 7,500 mems.; Chief Exec. J. WIGLEY; publs. annual journals, schedules, etc.

**Society of Dairy Technology:** 172A Ealing Rd., Wembley, Middx., HA0 4QD; f. 1943 for the advancement of dairy technology and for the encouragement of technical education and scientific enquiry in the dairy industry; 3,000 mems.; Pres. F. G. WELDON; Sec. P. H. F. LEE; publ. *Journal* (quarterly).

ARCHITECTURE AND TOWN PLANNING

**Architectural Association (Inc.):** 34–36 Bedford Square, London, WC1B 3ES; f. 1847; 4,000 mems.; library of 23,000 vols., 43,000 classified periodical articles, 60,000 slides; offers facilities for architectural studies; Pres. JOHN PRIZEMAN; Sec. EDOUARD LE MAISTRE; publ. *AA Quarterly*.

**Civic Trust, The:** 17 Carlton House Terrace, London, SW1Y 5AW; f. 1957 to encourage the protection and improvement of the environment; financed mainly by industry; gives advice and support to nearly 1,200 local amenity societies; provides secretariat for Architectural Heritage Fund and Heritage Education Group; Pres. Lord DUNCAN-SANDYS; Dir. M. MIDDLETON, C.B.E.; administered by a board of trustees; publ. *Heritage Outlook*† (every 2 months).

**Commons, Open Spaces and Footpaths Preservation Society:** 25A Bell St., Henley-on-Thames, Oxon RG9 2BA; f. 1865; 2,800 mems.; Chair. Dr. DAVID CLARK, M.P.; publ. *Journal*.

**Council for the Care of Churches** (formerly Council for Places of Worship): 83 London Wall, EC2M 5NA; f. 1921 to maintain the highest standards in the preservation, restoration and alteration of Anglican churches and their contents by making available sound artistic and technical advice; library of 12,000 vols.; Chair. The Archdeacon of Cheltenham; Sec. PETER BURMAN, M.A., F.S.A.; publs. *Journal*† (annual), *Churchyards Handbook*, series on various aspects of caring for churches and their furnishings.

**Council for the Protection of Rural England:** 4 Hobart Place, London, SW1W 0HY; f. 1926; to protect the beauty of the English countryside from disfigurement; to act as an advisory and information centre; 30,000 mems.; Pres. Prof. Sir COLIN BUCHANAN; Dir. ROBIN GROVE-WHITE; publs. *Bulletin, Countryside Campaign* (3 a year), *Annual Report*, leaflets, reports.

**Faculty of Architects and Surveyors:** 15 St. Mary St., Chippenham, Wilts.; f. 1926, Institute of Registered Architects (f. 1933) incorporated 1974; professional association with branches throughout the U.K. and overseas; members' library; Sec. A. D. G. WEBB; publ. *Portico* (quarterly).

**Incorporated Association of Architects and Surveyors:** Jubilee House, Billing Brook Rd., Weston Favell, Northampton NN3 4NW; f. 1925; 4,500 mems.; Pres. H. P. STONE; Hon. Sec. W. J. CLARK; publs. *The Architect and Surveyor* (every 2 months), *Fire Surveyor* (every 2 months).

**London Society:** The City University, Northampton Square, London, EC1V 0HB; f. 1912 to stimulate a wider concern for the beauty of the capital city, the preservation of its charms and the careful consideration of its development; collection of books and manuscripts including journals since 1912, now housed by The City University Library; approx. 400 mems.; Pres. Lord GREENWOOD OF ROSSENDALE; Chair. Exec. Cttee. R. B. C. RYALL; publ. *Journal* (annually).

**National Housing and Town Planning Council Inc.:** Norvin House, Commercial St., London E.1.; est. 1900 as the National Housing Reform Council to secure the abolition of unhealthy and socially undesirable houses; to promote the principle of sound town and country planning; and to disseminate information as to the improvement of the housing conditions of the people and the best standards of planning; Sec. HOWARD SMALL; publ. *The Housing and Planning Review* (quarterly).

**National Trust for Places of Historic Interest or Natural Beauty:** 42 Queen Anne's Gate, London, SW1H 9AS; f. 1895 for the purpose of promoting the permanent preservation of, and public access to, land of natural beauty and buildings of historic interest; list of properties available at above address; 800,000 mems.; Chair. Lord GIBSON; Dir.-Gen. J. D. BOLES; publs. *List of Properties, Annual Report, Newsletters*.

**National Trust for Scotland:** 5 Charlotte Square, Edinburgh, EH2 4DU; f. 1931; promotes the preservation of places of historical or architectural interest or natural beauty in Scotland; 107,000 mems.; Dir. J. C. STORMONTH DARLING, C.B.E., M.C., T.D., W.S.; publs. *Year Book, Newsletter* (3 a year), *Visitors Welcome*†.

**Oxford Preservation Trust:** 10 Turn Again Lane, St. Ebbes, Oxford, OX1 1QL; f. 1927 to combine together Oxford City, University, and County, to work for the beauty of Oxford and its surroundings, particularly planning problems which will affect future development; approx. 1,000 mems.; Chair. Lord WINDLESHAM, C.V.O., P.C.; Sec. F. V. PICKSTOCK, M.A.; publ. *Annual Report*.

**Royal Incorporation of Architects in Scotland:** 15 Rutland Square, Edinburgh; f. 1916 as a professional organization; 2,500 mems.; Pres. A. S. MATHESON; Sec. C. MCKEAN.

**Royal Institute of British Architects:** 66 Portland Place, London, W1N 4AD; f. 1834; 27,100 corporate mems.; Pres. OWEN LUDER; Sec. P. K. HARRISON; publs. *Journal* (monthly), *RIBA Directory of Members* (annual), *Directory of Practices* (annual), *RIBA International Directory of Practices* (annual); library: *see* Libraries.

**Royal Institution of Chartered Surveyors, The:** 12 Great George St., Parliament Square, London, S.W.1; f. 1868 as the Institution of Surveyors, received Royal Charter 1881; proclaimed as a Royal Institution 1946; unified with the Chartered Land Agents' Society and the Chartered Auctioneers' & Estate Agents' Inst. 1970; 54,000 mems.; library of 30,000 vols.; Pres. P. R. V. WATKINS, F.R.I.C.S.; Sec. ROBERT STEEL, C.B.E., B.SC., F.R.I.C.S.; publs. *Chartered Surveyor*† (monthly), *Chartered Quantity Surveyor*† (monthly), *Chartered Land Surveyor/Chartered Minerals Surveyor*† (quarterly), *Library Information Service Weekly Briefing, Abstracts* and *Reviews* (monthly).

**Royal Town Planning Institute:** 26 Portland Place, London, W1N 4BE; f. 1914 to advance the theory and practice of town planning and to promote the interests of those engaged in town planning; 12,500 mems.; library of 12,000 vols.; Pres. JOHN COLLINS; Sec.-Gen. D. R. FRYER; publs. *The Planner*† (every 2 months), *Planner News* (annually).

**Society for the Protection of Ancient Buildings:** 55 Great Ormond St., London, WC1N 3JA; f. 1877 by William Morris. Exists to prevent the unnecessary destruction of old buildings and to advise on their proper repair and treatment; approx. 5,000 mems.; Chair. The Duke of GRAFTON; Sec. DAVID PEARCE; publs. *Annual Report, Newsletter*† (quarterly), technical pamphlets.

**Town and Country Planning Association:** 17 Carlton House Terrace, London, SW1Y 5AS; f. 1899 to campaign for garden cities. Now concerns itself with all aspects of national, regional, town and country planning with emphasis on the decentralization of over-crowded areas and the creation of new towns; holds conferences and study tours; operates environmental education service for schools, planning aid service, Council for Urban Studies Centres; 1,300 mems.; library of 2,000 vols.; Chair. of Exec. MAURICE ASH; Dir. DAVID HALL; publs. *Town and Country Planning* (monthly), *Planning Bulletin* (weekly), *Bulleten of Environmental Education* (monthly), *Planning Bulletin Europe* (every 2 months).

**Victorian Society, The:** 1 Priory Gardens, Bedford Park, London W4 1TT; 1958; aims to preserve the best of Victorian and Edwardian architecture, and to study the art and history of the period; co-operates with the Dept. of the Environment in compiling lists of important buildings of the period; represented at public inquiries on preservation of buildings; 3,500 mems.; Pres. Sir NIKOLAUS PEVSNER; Chair. MICHAEL ROBBINS; Sec. HERMIONE HOBHOUSE; publs. *Annual Reports, Conference Reports*.

### THE ARTS
#### General

**Arts Council of Great Britain:** 105 Piccadilly, London, W1V 0AU; f. 1940 as the Council for the Encouragement of Music and the Arts (C.E.M.A.) and transformed into the Arts Council in 1946 when it was incorporated by Royal Charter; its objects under a new Charter granted in 1967 are to develop and improve the knowledge, understanding and practice of the arts, to increase the accessibility of the arts to the public throughout Great Britain, and to advise and co-operate with Government Depts., local authorities and other bodies concerned with these objects; 20 mems.; Chair. Rt. Hon. KENNETH ROBINSON; Sec.-Gen. Sir ROY SHAW; publs. *Annual Report*, etc.

**Scottish Arts Council:** 19 Charlotte Square, Edinburgh, EH2 4DF; Chair. Lord BALFOUR of BURLEIGH; Dir. TIM MASON.

**Welsh Arts Council:** Holst House, Museum Place, Cardiff, CF1 3NX; Chair. Sir HYWEL EVANS; Dir. A. M. THOMAS.

**Crafts Council:** 12 Waterloo Place, London SW1Y 4AU; f. 1971 as the Crafts Advisory Committee, present name 1979; directly funded by the Office of Arts and Libraries,

Dept. of Education and Science; supports the crafts in England and Wales and promotes the work of the artist craftsman/woman; encourages skills essential to conservation; runs grant and loan schemes, an information service and mounts exhibitions; 25 mems. appointed by the Minister for the Arts; library of 18,000 colour slides; Dir VICTOR MARGRIE; publs. *Crafts* (every 2 months), *News* (quarterly), catalogues.

**Design Council:** The Design Centre, 28 Haymarket, London, SW1Y 4SU; f. 1944 to promote the improvement of design in the products of British industry; permanent exhibition of British goods at The Design Centre; slide loan service of over 25,000 slides: Chair. of Council Sir WILLIAM BARLOW; Dir. KEITH GRANT; publs. *Design* (monthly), *Engineering* (monthly).

**Faculty of Royal Designers for Industry:** Royal Society of Arts, John Adam St., London, WC2N 6EZ; f. 1936 to further the development of design and in particular its application to industrial purposes; number of holders of R.D.I. limited to 100 (68 at present plus 24 Hon.); Pres. Dame DIANA READER HARRIS; Master Prof. HERBERT SPENCER; Sec. CHRISTOPHER LUCAS.

**Institute of Contemporary Arts:** Nash House, The Mall, London, SW1Y 5AH; f. 1948; contemporary cultural centre; organizes exhibitions, lecture series, films, performances, etc.; c. 4,000 mems.; Dir. BILL MCALISTER; Gen. Man. LUKE RANDOLPH; publ. *Monthly Bulletin of Events*.

**National Art-Collections Fund:** 4th Floor, Golden Cross House, 8 Duncannon St., London WC2N 4JF; f. 1903 and incorporated under Royal Charter to secure works of art for the galleries and museums of the U.K. and the British Commonwealth; 12,200 mems.; Chair. The Marquis of NORMANBY, C.B.E.; Sec. Mrs. SHEILA FOLKARD; publ. *Annual Report†*.

**National Society for Art Education:** 7A High St., Corsham, Wilts., SN13 0ES; f. 1888; the recognized professional body for principals, lecturers and teachers employed in colleges and schools of art and other specialist teachers of art and crafts; Gen. Sec. DANIEL GLEESON, A.T.D., A.D.B., F.R.S.A.; publ. *Journal of Art and Design Education* (3 a year).

**Royal Fine Art Commission:** 2 Carlton Gardens, London, SW1Y 5AA; appointed by Royal Warrant, 1924, to inquire into questions of public amenity or artistic importance referred to them from time to time by any of the Departments of State and to report thereon to such Department, and to give advice on similar questions when so requested by public or quasi-public bodies. Further empowered by Royal Warrant, 1933, to call the attention of any Department of State, or appropriate public or quasi-public body, to projects or developments which in the opinion of the Commission may affect amenities of a national or public character, and, in 1946, to call before them such persons as may be likely to afford information and to visit and inspect such places as they may deem expedient; Chair. of Commissioners Sir DERMAN CHRISTOPHERSON; Sec. SHERBAN CANTACUZINO.

**Royal Fine Art Commission for Scotland:** 22 Melville St., Edinburgh, EH3 7NS; f. 1927; advises Government Depts. and local planning authorities on all questions affecting public amenity, especially the conservation and development of the built environment; Sec. CHARLES PROSSER.

**Royal Philatelic Society, London:** 41 Devonshire Place, London, W1N 1PE; f. 1869; 1,300 mems.; Pres. LESLIE S. WHEELER; Sec. J. O. GRIFFITHS; publ. *The London Philatelist* (every 2 months).

**Royal Society of Arts:** 6–8 John Adam St., London, WC2N 6EZ; f. 1754 for the promotion of arts, manufactures and commerce; 11,000 mems.; library of 6,000 vols., 11,000 MSS.; Pres. H.R.H. Prince PHILIP, Duke of EDINBURGH; Chair. IAN HUNTER; Sec. CHRISTOPHER LUCAS; publ. *Journal* (monthly).

**Saltire Society:** Saltire House, 13 Atholl Crescent, Edinburgh, EH3 8HA; branches throughout Scotland, also in London and Cambridge; f. 1936 to conserve and foster the Scottish way of life through education, literature, arts and crafts, and architecture; 1,600 mems.; Pres. Sir KENNETH ALEXANDER; Hon. Sec. IAN G. A. KINNIBURGH; publ. *Scottish Review†* (quarterly).

**Society for Education through Art:** f. 1941 by amalgamation of Art Teachers' Guild and New Society of Art Teachers; seeks to establish an education through art which shall develop the imagination and creative power of the whole rising generation; 500 mems.; Pres. HENRY MOORE, C.H., O.M.; Chair. DEREK POPE; Sec. Mrs. S. BEAUMONT, Bath Academy of Art, Corsham, Wilts., SN13 0DB; publ. *Athene* (bi-annually).

**Society for Renaissance Studies, The:** f. 1967 to further the aims of scholarship in the Renaissance field, including literature, philosophy, art and history; Chair. Prof. D. BAKER-SMITH; Sec. PETER DENLEY, Dept. of History, Westfield College, Kidderpore Ave., London N.W.3.

**Society of Scribes and Illuminators:** c/o 43 Earlham St., London WC2H 9LD; f. 1921; aims to re-establish and perpetuate the tradition of craftsmanship in the production of manuscript books and documents, and to encourage calligraphy: meetings and exhibitions; 80 craft mems., c. 1,100 lay mems.; Hon. Sec. Mrs. S. CAVENDISH; publ. *Newsletter* (3 a year).

**William Morris Society:** Kelmscott House, 26 Upper Mall, London, W.6; f. 1918 (as Kelmscott Fellowship) to stimulate wider appreciation and deepen understanding of the life, work and influence of William Morris and his friends; 1,200 mems.; Hon. Sec. R. S. SMITH; publ. *The Journal*.

### Drama

**British Theatre Association:** (formerly British Drama League) 9 Fitzroy Square, London, W1P 6AE; f. 1919 by Geoffrey Whitworth for the encouragement of the Art of the Theatre, and to promote a right relation between drama and the life of the community; 2,500 mems., affiliated organizations; library: see Libraries; Pres. The Earl of BESSBOROUGH; Chair. CLIFFORD WILLIAMS; Admin. JANE HACKWORTH-YOUNG; publ. *Drama* (quarterly).

**Society for Theatre Research, The:** 17 Kinnerton St., London SW1X 8ED; f. 1948; acts as a clearing house for information concerning the history and technique of the British theatre and encourages research in these subjects; 850 individual and corporate mems.; Pres. Prof. GLYNNE WICKHAM; Chair. JACK READING; Hon. Secs. Miss KATHLEEN BARKER, DEREK FORBES; publs. *Theatre Notebook†* (three a year), an annual publication and occasional pamphlets.

### Fine Arts

**Artists' League of Great Britain:** Bankside Gallery, 48 Hopton St., Blackfriars, London SE1 9JH; f. 1909 to protect, advise and help artists and craftsmen resident in the British Commonwealth who enrol as members; Sec. MALCOLM FRY.

**Contemporary Art Society:** Tate Gallery, Millbank, London S.W.1; f. 1910 to acquire works by living artists for loan or gift to public galleries; 1,500 mems.; Dir. PAULINE VOGELPOEL, M.B.E.

**Federation of British Artists:** 17 Carlton House Terrace, London, S.W.1; Sec Gen. CARL DE WINTER; publ. *Quarterly Magazine*. The Federation administers The Mall Galleries, The Mall, London S.W.1 and holds annual exhibitions, open to all artists, for the following Member Societies:

**National Society of Printers, Sculptors and Printmakers:** f. 1930 to hold an annual exhibition to represent all aspects of art under one roof without prejudice or favour to anyone; 81 mems., 69 assoc. mems.; Pres. KROME BARRATT, R.B.A., V.P.R.O.I.; Sec. CARL DE WINTER; publ. *Catalogue of Exhibitions*.

**New English Art Club:** f. 1886; exhibition held in November, open to all artists; 51 mems., 4 hon. mems.; Hon. Sec. WILLIAM BOWYER, R.A., R.W.S., R.P.; Sec. CARL DE WINTER; publ. *Catalogue of Annual Exhibition*.

**Pastel Society:** 60 mems.; Pres. AUBREY SYKES, P.R.I.; Sec. MAURICE BRADSHAW.

**Royal Institute of Painters in Water Colours:** f. 1831; annual exhibition open to all artists; 61 mems., including 2 hon. retd. mems.; also 1 hon. sculptor mem.; Pres. CHARLES BONE; Sec. CARL DE WINTER; publ. *Catalogue of Exhibition*.

**Royal Institute of Oil Painters:** f. 1883; exhibitions October-November, open to all artists; 53 mems. and 4 hon. retd. mems.; membership limited to 100, exclusive of hon. mems.; Pres. ALAN GOURLEY; Sec. CARL DE WINTER; publ. *Catalogue of Exhibition*.

**Royal Drawing Society:** f. 1888, inc. 1902; holds an annual exhibition (The Children's Royal Academy) to encourage the development of children's creative and imaginative faculties; Pres. JOHN MILLS, F.S.A., F.I.I.C., F.R.S.A.; Sec. L. MILLS.

**Royal Society of British Artists:** 97 mems., 16 assoc. mems., 6 hon. mems.; Pres. PETER GREENHAM, C.B.E., R.A.; Keeper CARL DE WINTER.

**Royal Society of Marine Artists:** 49 mems.; Pres. DAVID COBB, R.O.I.; Sec. MAURICE BRADSHAW.

**Royal Society of Miniature Painters, Sculptors and Gravers:** 55 mems.; 8 hon. and 28 assoc. mems.; Pres. SUZANNE LUCAS; Sec. CARL DE WINTER.

**Royal Society of Portrait Painters:** f. 1891; 41 mems.; mems. limited to 50; annual exhibition; Pres. NORMAN HEPPLE, R.A.; Hon. Sec. GEORGE J. D. BRUCE; Sec. MAURICE BRADSHAW; publ. *Catalogue of Annual Exhibition*.

**Senefelder Group of Artist Lithographers.**

**Society of Aviation Artists.**

**Society of Graphic Artists:** 83 mems.; 5 hon. mems.; Pres. (vacant); Sec. PHILIP HERRIOTT.

**Society of Mural Painters.**

**Society of Portrait Sculptors:** f. 1953 to hold an annual exhibition; 56 mems., 6 hon. mems.; Pres. SHEILA MITCHELL, F.R.B.S.; Sec. M. BRADSHAW.

**Society of Wildlife Artists:** f. 1963; 66 mems.; Pres. KEITH SHACKLETON; Sec. MAURICE BRADSHAW.

**United Society of Artists:** 97 mems., 3 hon. mems., 19 assoc. mems.; Pres. ROBERT HILL; Sec. CARL DE WINTER.

**Oriental Ceramic Society:** 31B Torrington Square, London W.C.1; f. 1921 to increase knowledge and appreciation of Eastern Ceramic and other arts; Pres. Prof. WILLIAM WATSON; Sec. Vice-Adm. Sir JOHN GRAY, K.B.E., C.B.; Hon. Sec. Miss MARGARET MEDLEY.

**Royal Cambrian Academy of Art:** Plas Mawr, Conwy, N. Wales; f. 1882 for the promotion of the arts of painting, engraving, sculpture, architecture, and other forms of art in Wales; 100 mems.; Pres. J. SHORE, A.T.D.; Hon. Sec. JOHN R. WEBSTER; Curator LEONARD H. S. MERCER.

**Royal Society of British Sculptors:** 108 Old Brompton Rd., London, SW7 3RA; f. 1904 for the promotion and advancement of the art of sculpture; 200 mems.; Pres. MICHAEL RIZZELLO, O.B.E.; Sec. MAUREEN O'CONNOR.

**Royal Society of Painters in Water Colours** (*Old Water Colour Society*): Bankside Gallery, 48 Hopton St., Blackfriars, London, SE1 9JH; f. 1804; exhibitions confined to the work of its members are held twice yearly; 50 mems.; 39 assocs.; Pres. ERNEST GREENWOOD, A.R.C.A.; Sec. MALCOLM FRY, M.B.E.

**Royal West of England Academy:** Queen's Rd., Clifton, Bristol, BS8 1PX; f. 1844 to encourage and advance the fine arts in the region covering Bristol and the West of England; to promote the appreciation of the fine arts in the region by exhibitions and occasional lectures and meetings; 125 Academicians and 75 Associate Mems.; small library, mainly exhibition catalogues; Pres. and Chair. of Council BERNARD DUNSTAN, R.A.; Organizing Sec. Miss JEAN MCKINNEY; publs. catalogues of exhibitions.

**Society of Designer Craftsmen:** 24 Rivington St., London EC2A 3DV; f. 1888 by William Morris and others "to establish a standard of integrity in design and workmanship; to educate the public through exhibitions". Now a broader based body concerned also with education, professional practice, promotion and dialogue; 1,000 mems.; Pres. Lord REILLY; Chair. KENNETH CLARK; Sec. JANE BIRKETT.

**Society of Industrial Artists and Designers:** 12 Carlton House Terrace, London, S.W.1; f. 1930, incorporated by Royal Charter 1976; a professional organization of those engaged in design or illustration for publishing, merchandising or publicity, and in the design of goods for production in quantity; 6,500 mems.; Pres. EDWARD POND; Dir. GEOFFREY ADAMS; publs. *The Designer†* (monthly), *Year Book*.

**Society of Miniaturists:** Bankside Gallery, 48 Hopton St., Blackfriars, London, SE1 9JH; f. 1895; 65 mems.; Sec. MALCOLM FRY.

Music

**British Federation of Music Festivals:** Festivals House, 198 Park Lane, Macclesfield, Cheshire SK11 6UD; inc. 1921; headquarters of the Amateur Competitive Festival Movement; incorporates the Music Teachers' Association; organizes summer schools; Patron H.M. The QUEEN; Pres. Sir KNOWLES EDGE; Sec. Mrs. EILEEN CRAINE; publ. *Year Book* (March).

**Composers' Guild of Great Britain:** 10 Stratford Place, London, W1N 9AE; f. 1944 to further the artistic and professional interests of its members; Pres. Sir LENNOX BERKELEY, C.B.E.; Vice-Pres. Sir WILLIAM WALTON, O.M., WILLIAM ALWYN, C.B.E., MALCOLM ARNOLD, C.B.E., EDMUND RUBBRA, C.B.E.; Sec. Miss E. YEOMAN; publ. *Composer*.

**The Dolmetsch Foundation** (an international society for Early Music and Instruments): 14 Chestnut Way, Home Farm Rd., Godalming, Surrey; f. 1928 to encourage research and authentic performance; sponsors annual Haslemere Festival; 900 mems.; Pres. The Hon. Mrs. MAURICE MACMILLAN, D.B.E.; Chair. JOHN C. SUGDEN; Sec. and Editor Mrs. S. M. GODWIN; publs. *The Consort* (annually), *The Bulletin* (2 a year).

**English Folk Dance and Song Society, The:** Cecil Sharp House, 2 Regent's Park Rd., London NW1 7AY; f. 1932 (Folk Song Society 1898, English Folk Dance Society 1911); to collect, study and preserve English folk dances and songs and other folk music and to encourage their performance; 11,000 mems.; library of 9,000 vols. and 4,000 recordings; Dir. S. A. MATTHEWS, M.B.E., T.D.; publs. *Folk Music Journal, English Dance and Song, Folk Directory*, books and records.

**Incorporated Association of Organists:** Regd. Office: 15th Floor, Kennedy Tower, St. Chad's Queensway, Birmingham, B4 6JG; f. 1913 as the National Union of Organists' Associations and inc. 1929; 115 associations, with 8,000 mems. throughout the Commonwealth; aims to improve and advance the knowledge of organ music and teaching methods; administers a Benevolent Fund of organists; Pres. GILLIAN WEIR; Hon. Sec. ROGER BISHTON; publ. *The Organists' Review* (quarterly).

**Incorporated Guild of Church Musicians:** f. 1888; conducts examinations for the Archbishop of Canterbury's Certificate in Church Music; Pres. Sir BERNARD LOVELL, O.B.E., LL.D., D.SC., F.R.S.; Warden The Right Rev. MICHAEL MARSHALL, Bishop of Woolwich; Registrar A. T. PINDER, R.V.M., F.I.G.C.M., F.INST.L.EX., 126 Oxford Rd., Windsor, Berks.

**Incorporated Society of Musicians:** f. 1882; professional association for British musicians (performers, teachers and composers); 6,500 mems.; Pres. RONALD SMITH; Gen. Sec. SUSAN M. ALCOCK, 10 Stratford Place, London, W1N 9AE; publs. *Handbook* (annually), *Music Journal* (3 a year).

**Plainsong and Medieval Music Society:** f. 1888 for the promotion of the study and appreciation of plainsong and medieval music, especially by publication and performance; Pres. Prof. HERBERT HOWELLS, C.B.E.; Sec. S. G. A. KIDDELL, The Church Lodge, Wimborne St. Giles, Wimborne, Dorset.

**Royal Musical Association, The:** c/o British Library, London, WC1B 3DG; f. 1874, inc. 1904, for the investigation and discussion of subjects connected with the art and science of music; 750 mems.; Pres. DENIS ARNOLD; Sec. H. COBBE; publs. *Proceedings*† (annual), *Research Chronicle*† (annually).

**Society for the Promotion of New Music:** 10 Stratford Place, London W1N 9AE; f. 1943; 600 mems.; concert and workshop performances of new music selected from scores submitted by composers resident in Great Britain, composers' week-end seminars; Pres. ELIZABETH MACONCHY, C.B.E.; Vice-Pres. WILLIAM ALWYN, C.B.E., Sir LENNOX BERKELEY, C.B.E., Sir ADRIAN BOULT, C.H., Sir WILLIAM MONTAGU-POLLOCK, K.C.M.B., Dr. EDMUND RUBBRA, C.B.E., Sir MICHAEL TIPPETT, C.H., C.B.E., Sir WILLIAM WALTON, O.M.; founded by FRANCIS CHAGRIN; Admin. RODERICK LAKIN.

### Cinematography and Photography

**British Film Institute:** 127 Charing Cross Rd., London, WC2H 0EA; f. 1933; its aim is to encourage the development of the art of the film and television, to promote their use as a record of contemporary life and to foster their study and public appreciation; among its activities are the upkeep of the National Film Archive (*q.v.*), which also preserves telerecordings, the direction of the National Film Theatre, and the running of an Information Dept., Lecture Service for schools and universities, Film and Book Library, Central Booking Agency; 14,900 mems., 27,200 associates; library of 22,000 vols.; in receipt of annual government grant; Dir. A. SMITH; publs. *Sight and Sound*† (quarterly, illustrated), *Monthly Film Bulletin*†.

**Institute of Incorporated Photographers:** Amwell End, Ware, Herts., SG12 9HN; f. 1901; professional qualifying body; awards the designatory letters F.I.I.P., A.I.I.P. and L.I.I.P.; represents professional photographers and photographic technicians; to improve the quality of photography; to establish recognized examinations and standards of conduct; to safeguard the interests of the public and the profession; c. 4,000 mems.; Sec. B. G. SMALLEY; publs. *The Photographer*† (monthly), *The Register of Members and guide for Buyers of Photography*† (annually).

**Royal Photographic Society of Great Britain:** RPS National Centre of Photography, The Octagon, Milsom St., Bath, BA1 1DN; f. 1853 for the advancement of the science and art of photography; 6,500 mems.; library of 8,000 vols.; Pres. Dr. LESLIE BOWCOCK, M.B., CH.B., A.F.O.M., A.I.M.B.I., A.R.P.S.; Sec. K. R. WARR; publs. *The Photographic Journal* (annually), *The Journal of Photographic Science, Photographic Abstracts* (every 2 months).

**National Centre of Photography:** f. 1981; permanent collection of 20,000 historical photographs.

BIBLIOGRAPHY, LIBRARY SCIENCE AND MUSEOLOGY

**Arlis (Art Libraries Society):** Faculty of Architecture, Art and Design, Hull College of Higher Education, Queen's Gardens, Hull, HU1 3DH; f. 1969; aims to promote art librarianship particularly by acting as a forum for the interchange of information and materials; Chair. PHILIP PACEY, B.A., A.L.A.; Sec. GRAHAM BULLOCK, B.A., A.L.A.; publs. *Art Libraries Journal* (quarterly), *News-sheet* (6 a year).

**Aslib:** 3 Belgrave Square, London, SW1X 8PL; f. 1924; an association of industrial and commercial firms, government departments, research associations and institutions, universities and learned societies in the U.K. and 74 other countries; undertakes research and development in the information field; provides an information service in all subject areas for members including on-line bibliographic searching; maintains an index of translations in science and technology and register of specialist translators; the services of consultants in library management and both computerized and conventional information systems; short courses on all aspects of special librarianship and information work; organizes national and international conferences and meetings; membership of 2,100 organizations; grant-aid by the British Library; Pres. Lord KEARTON; Dir. D. A. LEWIS; publs. *Index to Theses accepted for Higher Degrees in the Universities of Great Britain and Ireland* (2 a year), *The Journal of Documentation* (quarterly), *Aslib Proceedings* (monthly), *Aslib Information* (monthly), *Aslib Book List* (monthly), *Program* (quarterly), *Forthcoming International Scientific and Technical Conferences* (quarterly), handbooks, reports, directories, bibliographies; library: see Libraries.

**Bibliographical Society:** British Academy, Burlington House, London, W1V 0NS; f. 1892; 1,200 mems.; Pres. D. F. FOXON; Joint Hon. Secs. R. J. ROBERTS, Mrs. M. M. FOOT; publs. *The Library* (quarterly), various books on bibliographical subjects.

**Cambridge Bibliographical Society:** University Library, Cambridge; f. 1949; historical bibliography and history of the book trade; 500 mems.; Hon. Treas. W. A. NOBLETT; publs. *Transactions* (annual), *Monographs* (irregular).

**Edinburgh Bibliographical Society:** c/o National Library of Scotland, George IV Bridge, Edinburgh, EH1 1EW; f. 1890 (the oldest bibliographical society in Great Britain) for discussion and elucidation of questions connected with books, printed or manuscript, especially Scottish, the promotion and encouragement of bibliographical studies, the exhibition of rare or remarkable books, and the printing of bibliographical works; c. 210 mems.; Hon. Sec. I. C. CUNNINGHAM, M.A., B.PHIL; publ. *Transactions* (irregular).

**Friends of the National Libraries:** c/o The British Library, Great Russell St., London, WC1B 3DG; f. 1931 to promote the acquisition of printed books and MSS. of historical, literary or archaeological significance for libraries and record offices of national importance; 600 mems.; Chair. Lord KENYON, C.B.E., D.L., J.P., LL.D.; Hon. Sec. J. F. FUGGLES; publ. *Annual Report*.

**Library Association:** 7 Ridgmount St., London, WC1E 7AE; f. 1877; 26,000 mems.; Pres. A. LONGWORTH, F.L.A.; Sec. KEITH LAWREY; publs. include *Library Association Record, Current Technology Index* (monthly), *British Humanities Index, Journal of Librarianship* (quarterlies), *Library and Information Science Abstracts* (bi-monthly), *Radials Bulletin* (2·a year), *Year Book*, books and pamphlets on librarianship and bibliography; library: *see* Libraries.

**Museums Association:** 34 Bloomsbury Way, London, WC1A 2SF; f. 1889 to promote and improve museums and galleries and the training of museum staff; 2,500 mems.; offers various in-service qualifications; Pres. NEIL COSSONS, M.A., F.S.A., F.M.A.; Sec. Miss B. CAPSTICK, O.B.E., M.A.; publs. *Museum Journal* (quarterly), *Museums Bulletin* (monthly), *Museums Yearbook* (annually).

**National Book League:** Book House, 45 East Hill, London, SW18 2QZ; a non-profit-making organization; f. 1944; originally founded in 1925 as The National Book Council to extend the use and enjoyment of books, which is still its aim; provides book lists, Readers' Guides and book information services; organizes meetings, mainly at its London headquarters, and exhibitions all over the country; administers several literary prizes; over 4,000 mems.; reference library containing all children's books published over the past 2 years; library of over 10,000 vols. about books; special collections: Perez collection of British Book Plates, Linder collection of Beatrix Potter; Pres. Lord GOODMAN; Dir. MARTYN GOFF, O.B.E., publ. *Booknews* (quarterly).

**Scottish Library Association:** Dept. of Librarianship, University of Strathclyde, Livingstone Tower, Richmond St., Glasgow, G1 1XH; f. 1908; affiliated to the Library Asscn.; Pres. A. H. HOWSON, A.L.A.; Sec. ROBERT CRAIG, M.A., A.L.A.; publs. *SLA News* (every 2 months), *Annual Conference Proceedings, Triennial Review, Library Resources in Scotland,* etc.

**Standing Commission on Museums and Galleries:** 2 Carlton Gardens, London, SW1Y 5AA; appointed 1931; objects: (1) to advise generally on questions relevant to the most effective development of the National Institutions as a whole, and on any specific questions which may be referred to them from time to time; (2) to promote co-operation between the National Institutions themselves. and between the National and Provincial Institutions; (3) to stimulate the generosity and direct the efforts of those who aspire to become public benefactors; 14 mems.; Chair. Sir ARTHUR DREW, K.C.B., J.P.; Sec. SIMON RIDLEY, M.A., B.D.

**Standing Conference of National and University Libraries (SCONUL):** 102 Euston St., London, NW1 2HA; f. 1950 to promote the work of the national and university libraries; mems.: 75 libraries; Chair. T. H. BOWYER, B.SC.(ECON.), F.L.A.; Sec. A. J. LOVEDAY, M.A., DIP.LIB., A.L.A.

ECONOMICS, LAW AND POLITICS

**Acton Society Trust:** 9 Poland St., London, W.1; f. 1948; charitable research organization concerned with political, economic and social problems; Research Advisers TREVOR SMITH, KRISHAN KUMAR; Hon. Organizer GAENOR AMORY.

**Association of Certified Accountants:** 29 Lincoln's Inn Fields, London, WC2A 3EE; f. 1904; inc. by Royal Charter; 23,000 mems.; Pres. R. A. SPENCER, O.B.E., F.C.C.A.; Sec. R. A. DUDMAN, M.A.; publs. *Certified Accountant* (every 2 months), *List of Members, Students' Newsletter* (monthly), various research publications.

**British Academy of Forensic Sciences:** Department of Forensic Medicine, The London Hospital Medical College, Turner St., London, E1 2AD; f. 1959 to advance forensic science in all its aspects to the benefit of justice and the law; annual meetings; over 500 mems; Sec.-Gen. Prof. J. M. CAMERON, M.D., PH.D., F.R.C.PATH., D.M.J.; publ. *Medicine, Science and the Law* (quarterly).

**British Institute of International and Comparative Law:** Charles Clore House, 17 Russell Square, London, WC1B 5DR; f. 1958 by the amalgamation of the Grotius Society and the Society of Comparative Legislation and International Law; organizes the Commonwealth Legal Advisory Service and research in comparative law, international law, and law of the European Communities; holds conferences, meetings and lectures in international and comparative law; provides information for members on questions of foreign, international, comparative and European Community law; Chair. Lord DENNING; Chair. for public international law section Sir GERALD FITZMAURICE; comparative law, Sir ROBERT MEGARRY, Vice-Chancellor, High Court of Justice; private international law, Lord SCARMAN; Hon. Dir. Prof. K. R. SIMMONDS; publs. *International and Comparative Law Quarterly, Bulletin of Legal Developments* (fortnightly) and other occasional publications on international and comparative law.

**Chartered Insurance Institute:** The Hall, 20 Aldermanbury, London, EC2V 7HY; inc. by Royal Charter 1912 with the object of providing and maintaining a central organization for the promotion of efficiency and progress among insurance employees; primarily an educational and examining body; approx. 50,000 mems.; library of about 15,000 vols.; Sec.-Gen. D. C. McMURDIE, LL.B., F.C.I.I.; Librarian A. LEE, B.A., A.L.A.; publ. *Journal* (3 a year).

**Council of Legal Education:** 4 Gray's Inn Place, London, W.C.1; constituted in 1852 for the purpose of superintending the education and examination of students preparing for call to the Bar at the Inns of Court School of Law; the Council is a committee of the Senate of the Inns of Court and the Bar entrusted with educational duties; teaching staff of 183, including 19 full-time law tutors; Chair. The Hon. Justice GOFF, D.C.L.; Dean C. A. MORRISON, Q.C.; publ. *Calendar* (annually).

**David Davies Memorial Institute of International Studies:** 12 Upper Belgrave St., London, SW1X 8BA; f. 1951 to commemorate and continue the work of Lord Davies (1880–1944), on the means of establishing a viable world order; aims: to advance and promote the development of the science of international relations in the political, economic, legal, social, educational, ecological and other fields, and to carry out and instigate research; works through *ad hoc* groups, seminars, conferences, bringing together experts in the relevant fields; Pres. H.R.H. The Duke of EDINBURGH; Chair. Lord HUNT OF TANWORTH, G.C.B.; Dir. and Editor M. M. SIBTHORP, O.B.E.; publ. *International Relations* (2 a year).

**Economics Association:** 18 Cedar Rd., Sutton, Surrey, SM2 5DF; f. 1948 to promote and extend the study of economics in schools and colleges of further education, to act as a representative body for economics teachers in educational matters and to promote knowledge of and interest in economics among the general public; 3,000 mems.; Pres. Prof. J. PARRY-LEWIS; Chair. R. H. RYBA; Hon. Sec. R. F. R. PHILLIPS, M.A., O.B.E.; publ. *Economics* (quarterly).

**Electoral Reform Society of Great Britain and Ireland Ltd.:** 6 Chancel St., Blackfriars, London, SE1 0UX; f. 1884 to secure an effective vote for every parliamentary and local government elector by the adoption of the single transferable vote form of proportional representation for all elections of representative bodies, and similarly for elections in all voluntary organizations; 1,000 mems.; comprehensive reference library; Chair. GERvase E. N. Tinley; Chief Exec. Seamus Burke; publ. *Representation* (quarterly).

**European Movement, The (British Council):** 1A Whitehall Place, London, S.W.1; f. 1948 to help industrial and commercial companies, banks, trade unions, political parties and professional organizations to keep abreast of developments in the field of European integration and bring their staffs into closer contact with their continental counterparts through various exchanges; Dir. E. Wistrich; publs. *New Europe* (quarterly), *Facts* (monthly), *Women and Europe* (every 2 months), *CEM* (local government quarterly).

**Fabian Society:** 11 Dartmouth St., London, SW1H 9BN; f. 1884 for the furtherance of socialism and the education of the public on socialist lines; 5,000 mems.; Chair. David Lipsey; Gen. Sec. Dianne Hayter; publs. *Fabian News* (monthly), *Fabian Pamphlets* (monthly).

**The Faculty of Actuaries in Scotland:** 23 St. Andrew Sq., Edinburgh, EH2 1AQ; f. 1856; 520 Fellows, 284 students; Sec. W. W. Mair, M.A.; publs. *Transactions, Year Book*.

**Faculty of Advocates:** Advocates Library, Parliament House, Edinburgh, EH1 1RF; f. c. 1532; the sole professional body for Advocates (Barristers) in Scotland; it maintains professional standards, examines Intrants and represents its members; c. 370 mems.; copyright library in respect of Legal works of c. 65,000 Law books associated with National Library of Scotland (*q.v.*); Dean C. K. Davidson, Q.C.; Clerk N. M. P. Morrison; Keeper of the Library J. T. Cameron, Q.C.

**Federal Trust for Education and Research:** 12A Maddox St., London, W1R 9PL; f. 1945 to promote and carry out studies of international relations, in particular issues relating to the European Communities; Dir. Geoffrey Denton.

**Grotian Society, The:** 48 Bedford Square, London, WC1; f. 1960 to promote study and research in the history of international law and relations; Pres. Prof. Clive Parry; Chair. and Sec.-Gen. George K. Goddard; Dir. of Studies Prof. K. R. Simmonds; publ. *Grotian Society Papers* (biennially).

**Hansard Society for Parliamentary Government:** 16 Gower St., London WC1E 6DP; f. 1944, present title 1956; aims to promote parliamentary government in all parts of the world; conducts research work, and educational work in schools; Sec. Maxine Vlieland; publ. *Parliamentary Affairs* (quarterly).

**Institute of Actuaries:** Staple Inn Hall, High Holborn, London, WC1V 7QJ; f. 1848, inc. 1884, for the elevation of the attainments and status of all who are engaged in actuarial pursuits, etc.; approx. 5,675 mems.; library of 10,000 vols.; Pres. A. R. N. Ratcliff, F.I.A.; Hon. Secs. R. D. Corley, B.SC., F.I.A., H. J. Jarvis, F.I.A.; Sec.-Gen. N. J. Page, O.B.E., M.C., F.C.I.S., F.C.C.A., F.S.S.; publs. *Journal* and *Year Book*.

**Institute of Bankers:** 10 Lombard St., London, EC3V 9AS; f. 1879; provides the educational foundation and qualifications for a banking career, information on banking developments to members and awards Associateship (A.I.B.) and Financial Studies Diploma by examination; 110,000 mems.; library of 30,000 vols.; Pres. P. A. Graham, O.B.E.; Sec.-Gen. Geoffrey Dix, O.B.E.; Librarian Paula Jilks; publ. *Journal*† (6 a year).

**Institute of Bankers in Scotland:** 20 Rutland Square, Edinburgh; f. 1875 to improve the qualifications of those engaged in banking, and to raise their status and influence; 10,500 mems.; Sec. B. McKenna, M.SC.; publ. *Scottish Bankers' Magazine* (quarterly).

**Institute of Chartered Accountants in England and Wales:** Chartered Accountants' Hall, Moorgate Place, London, E.C.2; f. 1880 by Royal Charter for the elevation of the profession of public accountants as a whole and the promotion of their efficiency and usefulness; 72,000 mems.; library of 32,000 vols.; Pres. H. B. Singer, T.D., F.C.A.; Sec. J. P. Hough, F.C.A.; Librarian M. F. Bywater; publs. *Accountancy* (monthly), *Accounting and Business Research* (quarterly), *List of Members* (annually).

**Institute of Chartered Accountants of Scotland:** 27 Queen St., Edinburgh, EH2 1LA; f. 1854 to deal with professional matters concerning its members; 10,407 mems.; libraries with 16,178 books; Pres. Sir Ian Morrow, D.UNIV., C.A., F.C.M.A., A.T.I.I., COMP.I.E.E.; Sec. G. R. G. Stewart, M.A., LL.B., W.S.; publs. *Annual Report, Official Directory of Members* (annual), *The Accountant's Magazine* (monthly), various occasional publications.

**Institute of Chartered Secretaries and Administrators:** 16 Park Crescent, London, W1N 4AH; f. 1891 as a professional organization for secretaries of incorporated bodies: over 44,000 mems.; Patron: H.M. The Queen; Pres. E. S. Kirk, F.C.I.S.; Sec. Barry Barker, M.B.E., M.A., F.C.I.S.; Librarian/Information Officer Miss M. Skipp, A.L.A.; publs. *Chartered Secretaries Manual of Company Secretarial Practice Professional Administration* (monthly).

**Institute of Cost and Management Accountants:** 63 Portland Place, London, W1N 4AB; f. 1919 to promote the adoption of scientific methods in cost and management accountancy; and to provide a professional organization; 18,000 mems.; library of 20,000 vols.; Sec. T. B. Degenhardt, M.A., F.C.I.S.; publ. *Management Accounting*.

**Institute of Economic Affairs:** 2 Lord North St., Westminster, London, S.W.1; f. 1955; to improve understanding of economics and its applications to business and public policy; Gen. Dir. Lord Harris; publs. major studies, Research Monographs, IEA Readings, occasional papers, *Journal of Economic Affairs* (quarterly).

**Law Society:** Law Society's Hall, Chancery Lane, London, WC2A 1PL; f. 1825; solicitors' professional association; 36,000 mems.; Sec.-Gen. John Bowron; publ. *Gazette* (weekly); library: see Libraries.

**London and Cambridge Economic Service:** Department of Applied Economics, University of Cambridge, Sidgwick Ave., Cambridge; f. 1923 by economists of London and Cambridge Universities to provide statistical information and current economic assessments; Sec. M. L. Mackie, M.A.; publs. (temporarily suspended) *Bulletin* (half-yearly), occasional booklets containing long-running statistical series.

**Royal Economic Society:** Imperial College of Science and Technology, London, SW7 2AZ; f. 1890; 3,500 mems.; Pres. Prof. P. M. Deane, F.B.A.; Sec.-Gen. Prof. A. Z. Silberston; publ. *Economic Journal* (quarterly).

**Royal Faculty of Procurators in Glasgow, The:** 62 St. George's Place, Glasgow, G2 1BT; inc. long prior to 1668, and by Royal Charter 1796; a legal society; 592 mems.; library of over 30,000 vols.; Dean James Sutherland, C.B.E., LL.B.; Clerk, Treasurer and Fiscal J. G. L. Robinson, B.A., LL.B.; Librarian G. A. Leonard, M.A.

**Royal Institute of International Affairs:** Chatham House, 10 St. James's Square, London, SW1Y 4LE; f. 1920 to facilitate the scientific study of international questions; mems., all categories, approx. 3,000; research programme: studies of broad economic and political trends in international relations and research into foreign policies of individual states; Hon. Pres. Lord Home of the Hirsel, K.T., P.C., Rt. Hon. Lord Noel-Baker, P.C., The Rt. Hon. J. Grimond, P.C., M.P.;

Chair. Lord HARLECH, P.C., K.C.M.G., K.ST.J., D.L.; Dir. DAVID WATT; Dir. of Studies Dr. WILLIAM WALLACE; Admin. Dir. EILEEN MENZIES; affiliated Institutes in many Commonwealth countries; publs. *International Affairs* (quarterly), *The World Today* (monthly), Chatham House Papers (studies on foreign policy issues, 6 or more a year), individual studies; library and press archives library: see Libraries.

**Royal Institute of Public Administration:** 3 Birdcage Walk, London, S.W.1; f. 1922 to promote the study and improve the practice of public administration; many public authorities (including governments) and over 5,000 public officials; library of 12,500 vols., 15,500 pamphlets; Pres. (vacant); Dir.-Gen. WILLIAM PLOWDEN; publs. *Public Administration*, *Public Administration and Development* (quarterly), books and pamphlets.

**Royal Statistical Society:** 25 Enford St., London, W.1; f. 1834; c. 5,000 mems.; Pres. Prof. D. R. COX, PH.D., F.R.S.; Hon. Secs. J. C. GOWER, D. J. BARTHOLOMEW, Mrs. E. J. SNELL; publs. *Journal* (Series A, quarterly), *Journal* (Series B, 3 parts annually), *Applied Statistics* (3 parts annually).

**Selden Society:** c/o Faculty of Laws, Queen Mary College, Mile End Rd., London, E1 4NS; f. 1887; 1,450 mems.; Pres. Sir GODFREY MORLEY, O.B.E., T.D.; Hon. Treas. BRIAN J. PRICHARD; Literary Dirs. D. E. C. YALE, J. H. BAKER; Sec. VICTOR TUNKEL; publs. over 90 vols. on sources and other aspects of English legal history.

**Senate of the Inns of Court and the Bar:** 11 South Square, Gray's Inn, London, WC1R 5EL; f. 1974; acts as governing body for the barristers' profession in England and Wales; Pres. The Rt. Hon. Lord Justice ACKNER; Chair. ANDREW LEGGATT, Q.C.; Vice-Chair. RICHARD SCOTT, Q.C.; Sec. Sir ARTHUR POWER, K.C.B., M.B.E.; publ. *Annual Statement*.

**Stair Society:** 2 St. Giles' St., Edinburgh, EH1 1PU; f. 1934 to encourage the study and advance the knowledge of the history of Scots Law; 600 mems.; Pres. Lord AVONSIDE; Chair. of Council JOHN IMRIE, LL.D.; Sec. G. R. THOMSON, T.D., PH.D.

## EDUCATION

**Advisory Centre for Education (ACE) Ltd.:** 18 Victoria Park Square, London, E2 9PB; f. 1960; aims to provide information on education for parents and others, to encourage close home-school relationships, and to arouse discussion on education issues; Pres. Lord YOUNG OF DARTINGTON; Chair. Dr. ERIC MIDWINTER; publ. *Where* (10 a year), etc.

**British Educational Management and Administration Society:** c/o Dept. of Educational Management and Administration, Moray House College of Education, Holyrood Rd., Edinburgh, EH8 8AQ; f. 1971; to advance the practice of and research into educational administration; to maintain close contact with national and international organizations and to encourage the foundation of local groups; Hon. Pres. Prof. G. BARON; Chair. Prof. M. G. HUGHES; Hon. Sec. Dr. E. A. EWAN; publs. *Educational Administration* (2 a year), *Proceedings of the Annual Conference*.

**Central Bureau for Educational Visits and Exchanges:** Seymour Mews House, Seymour Mews, London W1H 9PE; f. 1948; national information office for all types of educational travel and exchange; Chair. Dame MARGARET MILES, D.B.E., B.A.; Dir. JAMES PLATT, M.A.; publs. *Young Visitors to Britain* (English, French, German, Italian and Spanish editions), *Working Holidays* (annually), *School Travel and Exchange* (2 a year), *Adventure and Discovery* (annually), *Volunteer Work Abroad* (3 a year), *Youth Exchange News* (quarterly).

**City and Guilds of London Institute:** 76 Portland Place, London, W1N 4AA; f. 1878 for the advancement of technical education and the awarding of qualifications to craftsmen and skilled workers in over 300 subjects; over 450,000 candidates a year; Dir.-Gen. HARRY KNUTTON; publs. *Broadsheet* (3 a year), *Report and Accounts* (annually).

**College of Preceptors:** Coppice Row, Theydon Bois, Epping, Essex CM16 7DN; f. 1846, incorporated by Royal Charter 1849; Pres. D. J. JOHNSTON, B.A., F.C.P.; Dean Prof. B. HOLMES, PH.D., F.C.P.; Administrator P. R. DANIELS, B.ED.; provides courses on School Management Studies for Head Teachers and their Deputies and awards qualifications to experienced teachers of Associate, Licentiate (equivalent to university first degree) and Fellow; publs. *Education Today* (termly), *Teachers' Guide* (occasionally), *Your Secondary Modern Schools*.

**Committee of Directors of Polytechnics:** 309 Regent St., London, W1R 7PE; f. 1970 to provide a forum for the discussion of matters of common concern to polytechnics and to contribute to the evolution of policy for the development of this sector of higher education; mems.: directors of the 30 polytechnics in England and Wales, and 2 observer mems. from Scotland and N. Ireland; Chair. R. M. W. RICKETT; Hon. Treas. G. SEABROOKE; Sec. P. L. FLOWERDAY; publs. *Polytechnic Courses Handbook* (annually), *Focus on Polytechnics* (termly), *The Polytechnics: a guide to Full-Time and Sandwich Courses* (annually).

**Committee of Vice-Chancellors and Principals of the Universities of the United Kingdom:** 29 Tavistock Square, London, WC1H 9EZ; established to keep under review the full range of university interests and to speak on behalf of the universities in general in their relations with other fields of education with industry and government; associated bodies serviced from the Committee's secretariat are: the Standing Conference on University Entrance, the University Authorities Panel, the Universities Committee for non-teaching staffs and the Clinical Academic Staff Salaries Committee; Chair. Dr. A. E. SLOMAN, C.B.E., M.A., D.PHIL., D.U.; Sec.-Gen. GEOFFREY CASTON; Exec. Sec. B. H. TAYLOR.

**Commonwealth Secretariat, Education Division:** Marlborough House, Pall Mall, London, SW1Y 5HX; encourages co-operation between Commonwealth countries through conferences, seminars, workshops, publications and the exchange of information; consultants for developing Commonwealth countries and third-country training for their personnel are provided by the Commonwealth Fund for Technical Co-operation; Dir. R. E. O. AKPOFURE; publs. reports, commissioned studies, handbooks on educational topics.

**Council for the Accreditation of Correspondence Colleges:** 27 Marylebone Rd., London, NW1 5JS; f. 1969; independent body grant-aided by the Dept. of Education and Science which nominates the Chairman and 5 members of the Council; only organization in the U.K. officially recognized as responsible for the award of Accreditation to Correspondence Colleges; recognized as a Registered Charity; 35 colleges accredited; Chair. J. BROSGALL, B.SC.

**Council for Education in World Citizenship:** 26 Blackfriars Lane, London, EC4V 6EB; f. 1939; an independent, non-political organization to assist schools and colleges in the teaching of international affairs and promote a more global perspective in curricula; Dir. MARGARET QUASS; publs. *Current Affairs Broadsheet* (6 a year), *World Studies Resource Guide*.

**Council for Educational Technology for the United Kingdom:** 3 Devonshire St., London, W1N 2BA; f. 1973 by the Government; financed by government departments; central organization for promoting the application and development of educational technology, providing advice, co-ordination and a focal point for collection and dissemination of information, initiating development programmes and studies of educational innovations; Dir. G. HUBBARD; publs. *British Journal of Educational Technology* (termly), working papers, occasional papers, training materials, etc. (list on request).

**Council for National Academic Awards:** 344/354 Gray's Inn Rd., London, WC1X 8BP; established by Royal Charter in September 1964 with powers to award degrees, diplomas and other academic awards to persons who have successfully pursued courses of study approved by the Council at educational establishments other than universities or who have successfully carried out research work under the supervision of an educational or research establishment other than a university. In September 1974 the Council merged with the National Council for Diplomas in Art and Design, and in 1976 assumed responsibility for the Diploma in Management Studies. The Council offers the following awards: Certificate, Dip.H.E.; B.A., B.Ed. and B.Sc. as its first degree; M.A., M.Sc., M.Ed. and Diplomas for successful completion of courses of postgraduate and post-experience study; M.Phil. or Ph.D. for successful completion of approved programmes of original work; Pres. H.R.H. The Prince of WALES; Chair. Sir DENIS ROOKE; Chief Officer E. KERR; Sec. B. B. OVERY; publs. *Directory of First Degree and Diploma of Higher Education Courses, Directory of Postgraduate and Post-Experience Courses* (annually), *Annual Report*.

**Educational Institute of Design, Craft and Technology, The:** c/o Gen. Sec., 24 Elm Rd., Kingswood, Bristol, BS15 2ST; f. 1891 to promote education through craft experience, raise standards of craft teaching and safeguard professional interests; the College of Craft Education provides 1–4-year courses for qualified teachers and organizes annual summer schools; c. 2,000 mems.; Gen. Sec. G. DAY, M.I.O.B., F.C.C.ED.; Master of College Lord BUTLER OF SAFFRON WALDEN; Registrar of College J. S. BOUCHER, D.F.M., F.C.C.ED.; publs. *Practical Education, Buyers Guide*, newsletters, special reports.

**Educational Institute of Scotland, The:** 46 Moray Place, Edinburgh, EH3 6BH; f. 1847; to promote sound learning and advance the interests of teachers in Scotland; 48,300 mems.; Pres. Mrs. ROSE GALT, M.A.; Gen. Sec. JOHN POLLOCK, B.SC., F.E.I.S.; publ. *Scottish Educational Journal* (14 per session).

**National Institute of Adult Education (England and Wales):** 19B De Montfort St., Leicester, LE1 7GE; f. 1949 by incorporation of the British Institute of Adult Education and the National Foundation for Adult Education to promote understanding and co-operation between bodies and persons engaged in adult education, to encourage research and training and serve as a centre of information; conferences and meetings; library; develops co-operative relations with foreign and international organizations; both corporate and individual membership; Dir. A. K. STOCK, B.SC., M.ED., A.D.E.; publs. *Adult Education* (quarterly), *Teaching Adults* (2 a year), *Year Book of Adult Education, Residential Short Courses* (2 a year), *Studies in Adult Education* (2 a year), research studies.

**World-wide Education Service of the Parents' National Educational Union Ltd.:** Murray House, Vandon St., London, SW1H 0AJ; f. 1888 as an educational charity; specializes in helping English-speaking expatriates to educate their children themselves; also operates an educational consultancy for companies and organizations and is able to establish and monitor schools on their behalf; Dir. H. BOULTER, M.A.; publ. *WES Journal* (termly).

**University Association for Contemporary European Studies:** King's College London, Strand, London, WC2R 2LS; f. 1968; to bring together academics from different disciplines (law, politics, economics, languages, etc.) with a common interest in West European studies and specifically in European integration; circulates information to mems. about developments in European studies; holds conferences and seminars; research visits to other European countries; documentation on European Studies; 340 individual, 80 corporate mems.; Chair. Prof. S. C. HOLT; Sec. M. SMITH; publs. *Register of Current Research in European Integration, Register of Courses in European Studies in British Universities & Polytechnics* (annually).

**University Grants Committee:** 14 Park Crescent, London, W1N 4DH; f. 1919 to enquire into the financial needs of university education in Great Britain and to advise the Government on the application of any grants made by Parliament towards meeting them; to collect, examine and make available information relating to university education throughout the United Kingdom; and to assist, in consultation with the universities and other bodies concerned, the preparation and execution of such plans for the development of the universities as may from time to time be required in order to ensure that they are fully adequate to national needs; Chair. EDWARD PARKES, SC.D.; Sec. G. F. COCKERILL, C.B.; publs. *Statistics of Education—Universities* (annually), *Annual Survey*.

**Workers' Educational Association:** Temple House, 9 Upper Berkeley St., London, W.1; f. 1903 to stimulate public interest in education and to provide opportunities for adults to pursue liberal studies and to encourage them to render effective service to the community; co-operates with the universities through its twenty-one districts for the provision of classes including tutorial classes based on a three-year period of study; it is recognized by the Dept. of Education and Science as a Responsible Body, and the classes which it provides independently rank for grants from public funds; 175,000 students; Gen. Sec. R. J. JEFFERIES, B.A.; publs. works on adult education.

## Educational Foundations

**Animal Health Trust** (formerly Veterinary Educational Trust): Lanwades Hall, Kennett, Newmarket, Suffolk, CB8 7PN; f. 1942 to raise money for the purpose of advancing the health of all types of animals through improving the facilities for veterinary education, postgraduate specialisation in research and other fields, the establishment and running of research stations, and the provision of a hospital and laboratory diagnosis service behind the veterinary practitioner; two research stations—equine, canine and small animals; Pres. His Grace The Duke of DEVONSHIRE, M.C.; Dir. W. B. SINGLETON, C.B.E., F.R.C.V.S.; Sec. A. V. PAYNE, F.C.I.S.; publ. *Annual Report*, and periodic technical reports.

**Beit Memorial Fellowships for Medical Research:** Sec. Prof. W. G. SPECTOR, Pathology Dept., St. Bartholomew's Hospital, London, E.C.1; f. 1909 to promote the advancement of research in medicine and allied sciences; the fellowships are open to any man or woman, without restriction as to nationality, who has taken a degree in any faculty in any university of the U.K., Her Majesty's Dominions, Protectorates and Mandated Territories, India, Pakistan or the Republic of Ireland, approved by the Trustees; Junior Fellowships, £6,880–£8,515 salary range for 3 years.

**Calouste Gulbenkian Foundation:** 98 Portland Place, London, W1N 4ET; administers grants to education, arts and social welfare for the Gulbenkian Foundation in the area of the United Kingdom and the Commonwealth; Dir. PETER BRINSON, M.A.; publ. *Annual Report*; see also Fundação Calouste Gulbenkian, Lisbon.

**Carnegie Trust for the Universities of Scotland:** The Merchants' Hall, Hanover St., Edinburgh; f. 1901; one-half of the net annual income (at present about £500,000) is applied towards the improvement and expansion of the Universities of Scotland, in the Faculties of Science and Medicine, also for improving and extending the opportunities for scientific study and research, and to increasing the facilities for acquiring a knowledge of History, Economics, English Literature and Modern Languages, and such other subjects cognate to a technical or commercial education as can be brought within the scope of the University curriculum; the other half of the income, or such part thereof as in each year may be found requisite, is devoted to the payment of the whole or part of the ordinary class fees exigible by the Universities from certain qualified students of Scottish birth, extraction, or schooling; any unexpended income from this second purpose being transferable to the first purpose; Sec. and Treas. A. E. RITCHIE, C.B.E., M.D., F.R.S.E.

**Carnegie United Kingdom Trust:** Comely Park House, Dunfermline, Fife; f. 1913; to promote the well-being of the masses of the people of Great Britain and Ireland by "charitable" means: e.g. amateur participation in the arts, particularly for the disabled, neighbourhood mutual help schemes and Heritage Interpretation projects; priority given to national organizations; Sec. GEOFFREY LORD, M.A.; publ. *Annual Report*.

**Cassel Educational Trust:** 21 Hassocks Rd., Hurstpierpoint, Sussex; f. 1919; benefactions to the Women's Colleges at Oxford and Cambridge and to the University of London for the Faculty of Commerce. Periodic grants to Adult Education Institutions and for the promotion of university faculty research abroad; Edwina Mountbatten Grants to Commonwealth students taking courses in U.K.; Chair. Countess MOUNTBATTEN OF BURMA; Sec. DAVID HARDMAN.

**Chadwick Trust:** 13 Grosvenor Place, London, SW1X 7EN; f. 1895 for the promotion of sanitary science and the training of the population therein; Chair. G. M. BINNIE, F.R.S., F.ENG., M.A.

**Ciba Foundation:** 41 Portland Place, London, W1N 4BN; f. 1949; to advance and promote the study of and research in all branches of the sciences of chemistry, medicine and biology, and in particular to promote international co-operation in medical and chemical research; library of 5,000 vols.; Dir., and Sec. to the Exec. Council Dr. DAVID C. EVERED, M.D., F.R.C.P.

**Dartington Hall Trust:** Totnes, Devon TQ9 6JE; includes a progressive co-educational boarding school, incorporating Postern Programme of work experience, College of Arts (Music, Theatre, Art and Design), Adult Education Centre, Pottery Training Workshop, Arts Society, Beaford Centre (North Devon); Chair. M. A. ASH; Sec. G. J. KEENE.

**Educational Foundation for Visual Aids:** National Audio Visual Aids Centre and Film Library, Paxton Place, Gipsy Rd., London SE27 9SR; f. 1948; set up by the Ministry of Education in conjunction with the LEAs for the promotion, production and distribution of audio-visual aids in education; a non-profit making organization which operates as a commercial company offering audio-visual equipment, software, including educational and training films; contract servicing of audio-visual equipment provided nationwide through U.K. network of regional and area centres; training courses in equipment for commercial, industrial and educational institutions; audio and video software production; Dir. G. C. MARCHANT, M.A.

**Gilchrist Educational Trust:** 1 York St., London, W1H 1PZ; the Trust was founded by the will of Dr. John Borthwick Gilchrist (who died in 1841) for the "benefit, advancement and propagation of education and learning in every part of the world as far as circumstances will permit". Trustees: HUMPHREY WHITBREAD, M.A., Lord WOLFENDEN, C.B.E., M.A., Mrs. OLIVE MAGUINNESS, M.SC., D. ÈS SC., Lord GARNER, G.C.M.G., Lord HOLDERNESS; Sec. Miss SINCLAIR SALMON.

**Grocers' Company:** Grocers' Hall, Princes St., London, E.C.2; f. 1345; (1) Laxton School, Oundle, Northants. (founded and endowed as a free grammar school, 1556); the Court of the Company manage and maintain this school for the sons of residents in the town and neighbourhood. (2) Oundle School, Northants.; f. in 1876; (3) Laxton Junior School, opened September 1973; the Court is the Governing Body; Clerk C. P. G. CHAVASSE.

**Gulbenkian Foundation:** see Calouste Gulbenkian Foundation (above).

**Harkness Fellowships of the Commonwealth Fund of New York:** Harkness House, 38 Upper Brook St., London, W1Y 1PE; an American philanthropic foundation est. 1918, supports Harkness Fellowships for study and travel in the United States of America; available to U.K. citizens in all fields of study who have received both secondary and further education wholly or mainly in U.K. Awards are also available to candidates in Australia and New Zealand.

**Leathersellers of the City of London, Worshipful Company of:** 15 St. Helen's Place, London, EC3A 6DQ; First Charter 1444; the Company awards Secular and Theological Exhibitions tenable at Universities in England, open to male undergraduates and graduates in residence at Universities and boys from the Public and recognized Secondary Schools. Candidates must satisfy the Company of their educational attainments and that they are in need of financial aid to complete or proceed to a University Course.

**Leverhulme Trust:** 15–19 New Fetter Lane, London, EC4A 1NR; f. 1932; annual income of about £3,500,000 for fellowships, studentships, etc., for research and education; grants mostly to institutions at home and overseas with charitable status, mainly for specific short-term research projects; a limited number of awards to individuals on the recommendation of a Research Awards Advisory Committee include Fellowships and Grants for senior persons of established position; Emeritus Fellowships for persons retired from universities and similar institutions wishing to complete research; and postgraduate Study Abroad Studentships for advanced study or research in any country other than the U.K. and U.S.A.; Dir. Dr. R. C. TRESS, C.B.E.; Sec. of the Research Awards Advisory Cttee. Miss J. BENNETT; publs. brochure and annual reports.

**Lord Kitchener National Memorial Fund:** Barn Meadow, Great Warley, Brentwood, Essex, CM13 3JR; f. 1916; about 40 scholarships awarded annually to sons of serving or ex-Service personnel of H.M. Forces, tenable at British and Irish universities or approved institutions of university rank, including medical schools, age limit 17–20 at January 1st, or up to 30 for ex-Servicemen. No awards can be made for postgraduate studies; Chair. of Council The Lord Mayor of London; Chair. Exec. Cttee. Air Chief Marshal Sir AUGUSTUS WALKER, G.C.B., C.B.E., D.S.O., A.F.C.; Chair. Scholarship Cttee. DUDLEY G. A. SANDERS, M.A., T.D.; Sec. C. RALPH ALLISON, M.A.

**Nuffield Foundation:** Nuffield Lodge, Regent's Park, London, NW1 4RS. The Nuffield Foundation is the result of the late Lord Nuffield's greatest benefaction. It was established in 1943 as a trust, with a capital valued at

£10,000,000. The four main objects of the Foundation, as stated in the Trust Deed, are: the advancement of health, including the prevention and relief of sickness, particularly by the support of medical teaching and research; the improvement of social well-being, particularly by the furtherance of scientific research; the advancement of education; and the care and comfort of the aged. The policy of the Trustees is to initiate research and experiment, mainly within the fields of Science and Medicine, Social Studies, Ageing, Education, and the Commonwealth overseas; most grants are given to university depts. for the furtherance of research; the Foundation also runs a programme of fellowships and scholarships for the Commonwealth overseas; board of seven Trustees; Chair. Rt. Hon. Lord TREND, G.C.B., C.V.O.; Dir. JAMES CORNFORD.

**Phoenix Trust:** 84 Drayton Gardens, London, SW10 9SD; f. 1959; grants to literature and the arts; Sec. Mrs. JULIA JONES.

**Pilgrim Trust, The:** Fielden House, Little College St., London, S.W.1; f. in 1930 by the late Edward Stephen Harkness of New York to help preserve the national heritage of the United Kingdom of Great Britain and Northern Ireland, and to promote the future well-being of the country and its people; grants are made to charitable or public bodies for charitable purposes only, i.e. for the preservation of: (i) ancient buildings, both ecclesiastical and secular; (ii) art treasures and historical records; and (iii) the countryside, for social welfare and for art and learning; this covers help to libraries, museums and galleries, to theatres and arts centres, to archaeological excavations and for specialist publications of national importance; annual income about £450,000; Sec. ALASTAIR HOYER MILLAR.

**Plunkett Foundation for Co-operative Studies:** 31 St. Giles, Oxford, OX1 3LF; f. 1919; education and training courses for personnel in the U.K. and overseas; research and consultancy projects in agricultural and industrial co-operation for national and international bodies; annual conference in Oxford; information service and library of 28,000 documents; Chair. J. A. E. MORLEY, M.B.E.; Dir. C. E. McKONE; publs. *The Year Book of Agricultural Co-operation*, *Directory of Agricultural Co-operation in the U.K.* (annually), *Agricultural Co-operatives in the U.K.*, *Summary of Statistics* (annually), occasional papers, *Study Series*, *Development Series*, conference papers, research directory, accessions list.

**Rhodes Trust:** Rhodes House, Oxford; f. 1902; the endowment of the Rhodes Scholarships for graduates from the British Commonwealth, South Africa, the United States and Western Germany at Oxford University; Trustees: Sir WILLIAM PATON (Chair.), The Hon. JOHN BARING, Rt. Hon. Lord BLAKE, Sir JOHN HABAKKUK, M. J. HUSSEY, W. G. BARR, Sir ROBERT ARMSTRONG; Sec. Dr. R. A. FLETCHER.

**Rotary International in Great Britain and Ireland:** Sheen Lane House, Sheen Lane, London, SW14 8AF; f. 1914; Rotary Foundation awards are available to carefully selected college graduate and undergraduate students, technical trainees, journalists and teachers of the handicapped from all countries in which Rotary Clubs exist for up to one year of study in universities and technical institutes located in countries other than their own; 60,200 mems. in 1,400 clubs; Sec. JOHN H. JACKSON; publ. *Rotary* (every 2 months).

**Royal Commission for the Exhibition of 1851:** 1 Lowther Gardens, Exhibition Rd., London, SW7 2AA; incorporated by Supplemental Charter as a permanent Commission after winding up the affairs of the Great Exhibition, 1851; its object is the promotion of scientific and artistic education by means of funds derived from its Kensington Estate, purchased with the funds left over from the Exhibition; Pres. H.R.H. The Prince PHILIP, Duke of EDINBURGH; Chair. Board of Management Sir RICHARD WAY, K.C.B., C.B.E.; Chair. Science Scholarships Cttee. Prof. Sir HARRIE MASSEY, F.R.S.; Sec. C. A. H. JAMES.

**Royal Jubilee Trusts:** 8 Buckingham St., London, WC2N 6BU; f. 1935 as King George's Jubilee Trust to advance the physical, mental and spiritual welfare of the younger generation; The Queen's Silver Jubilee Trust f. 1977 to enable and encourage young people to help others in the community; Trustees: The Hon. JOHN BARING, Lord WARDINGTON, The Rt. Hon. The Earl SPENCER, M.V.O., D.L., Sir PETER STUDD; Pres. H.R.H. The Prince of Wales, K.G., K.T., G.C.B.; Dir. HAROLD HAYWOOD, O.B.E.

**Salters' Institute of Industrial Chemistry:** Salters' Hall, 4 Fore St., London, EC2Y 5DE; f. 1918; The Master, Wardens and Court of the Salters' Company; (*a*) Prizes and Scholarships for undergraduates in Chemistry or Chemical Engineering; (*b*) Study Conference for Chemistry Schoolteachers; (*c*) Refresher Courses for Chemistry Teachers; (*d*) Grants to School Chemistry Libraries; (*e*) Grants to School Chemistry Laboratories; (*f*) School Chemistry Prizes.

**Thomson Foundation:** 16th Floor, International Press Centre, Shoe Lane, London, EC4; f. 1963 to provide education and vocational training facilities in the field of mass communications in the developing countries, particularly those countries within the Commonwealth; Chair. J. M. COLTART, LL.D.; Dir. D. G. H. ROWLANDS.

**Wolfson Foundation:** P.O.B. 1BZ, Universal House, 251-56 Tottenham Court Rd., London, W1A 1BZ; f. 1955; promotes education and health in the United Kingdom and Commonwealth with particular reference to scientific and technological education, building facilities for higher education, youth activities, medical research, cancer research, and medical, surgical and nursing services; Pres. Sir ISAAC WOLFSON, Bt., F.R.S., D.C.L.; Chair. of Trustees, Sir LEONARD WOLFSON, LL.D.; Dir. and Sec. Maj.-Gen. A. R. LEAKEY, C.B., D.S.O., M.C.

### HISTORY, GEOGRAPHY AND ARCHAEOLOGY

**Ancient Monuments Society:** St. Andrew-by-the-Wardrobe, Queen Victoria St., London, E.C.4; f. 1924 for the study and conservation of ancient monuments, historic buildings and fine old craftsmanship; 2,000 mems.; Pres. The Rt. Hon. The Marquess of ANGLESEY; Chair. IVOR BULMER-THOMAS, M.A., F.S.A.; Dir. L. M. ANGUS-BUTTERWORTH, M.A., C.ENG., F.I.MECH.E., F.S.A.SCOT.; Sec. M. J. SAUNDERS, M.A.; publ. *Transactions* (annually).

**Association of Contemporary Historians:** c/o Dr. A. POLONSKY (Sec.), London School of Economics and Political Science, Aldwych, London, W.C.2; f. 1967 to promote the study of all aspects of the history of the twentieth century; c. 150 mems.; publ. *Bulletin* (annually).

**Baptist Historical Society, The:** 4 Southampton Row, London, WC1B 4AB; f. 1908 to promote the study of and record the history of the Baptists; assists researchers, and gives advice to Churches on care and preservation of records; library administered jointly with Baptist Union; 530 mems.; Pres. Rev. Dr. B. R. WHITE, M.A., D.PHIL.; Sec. Rev. P. J. WORTLEY, B.A., B.D.; publ. *The Baptist Quarterly*.

**British Archaeological Association:** c/o Hon. Asst. Treasurer and Secretary, 61 Old Park Ridings, Winchmore Hill, N21 2ET; f. 1843; 700 mems.; Pres. Dr. PETER KIDSON, PH.D., M.A., F.S.A.; publ. *Journal* (annual), *Conference Transactions*.

**British Cartographic Society:** 70 Dukes Avenue, Theydon Bois, Epping, Essex, CM16 7HF; f. 1963; 950 mems.;

Pres. I. A. G. KINNIBURGH; Hon. Sec. P. E. SORRELL; publs. *The Cartographic Journal*† (twice yearly), *Automated Cartography*†, *Careers in Cartography*†.

**British Numismatic Society:** Sec. W. SLAYTER, 63 West Way, Edgware, Middx.; f. 1903; 520 mems.; Pres. JOHN BRAND; publ. *British Numismatic Journal* (annually).

**British Records Association:** Master's Court, The Charterhouse, Charterhouse Square, London, EC1M 6AU; f. 1932 for the preservation and use of records (archives), and for the co-ordination of the work of institutions and individuals interested in the subject; 1,000 mems.; conferences; Pres. Rt. Hon. Lord DENNING; publs. *Archives* (2 a year), *Archives and the User* (occasional).

**Cambrian Archaeological Association:** f. 1846; 1,003 mems.; Pres. H. NOEL JERMAN; Gen. Sec. G. L. JONES, Lleifior, Padarn Crescent, Llanbadarn Fawr, Aberystwyth, Dyfed, SY23 3QW; publ. *Archaeologia Cambrensis*.

**Canterbury and York Society:** f. 1904; 228 mems.; Pres. The ARCHBISHOPS OF CANTERBURY and YORK; Sec. Mrs. D. M. OWEN, 35 Whitwell Way, Coton, Cambridge, CB3 7PW; Gen. Editor Prof. Dr. A. K. MCHARDY; publ. *Bishops' Registers*.

**Catholic Record Society:** c/o 114 Mount St., London, W.1; f. 1904; publishes documentary material on Catholic history in England and Wales since the reformation; international membership; Sec. Miss R. RENDEL; publs. occasional volumes of either monograph series or record series; *Journal, Recusant History* (2 a year).

**Challenger Society:** c/o Institute of Oceanographic Sciences, Wormley, nr. Godalming, Surrey; f. 1903 for the promotion of the study of oceanography; about 440 mems.; Hon. Sec. R. I. CURRIE, C.B.E., F.R.S.E.; publs. occasional papers and *The Challenger Society Newsletter*.

**Council for British Archaeology:** 112 Kennington Rd., London, SE11 6RE; f. 1944; for the preservation of ancient monuments and the co-ordination and promotion of archaeological activities in the British Isles; liaises at national level between archaeological societies and government bodies, encourages co-operation between amateur and professional archaeologists, advises on national preservation policy, makes grants for publication of papers; national information centre on British archaeology; 400 institutional mems.; Pres. P. J. FOWLER, M.A., PH.D., F.S.A.; Dir. H. F. CLEERE, PH.D., F.S.A., M.B.I.M.; publs. *British Archaeological Abstracts* (2 a year), *Archaeological Bibliography, Archaeology in Britain* (annually), *Newsletter and Calendar* (monthly), *Research Reports* (occasional), etc.

**Dugdale Society for the Publication of Warwickshire Records:** Shakespeare's Birthplace, Stratford-upon-Avon; f. 1920; 300 mems.; Pres. Sir WILLIAM STRATFORD DUGDALE, Bt., M.C.; Chair. Dr. LEVI FOX, O.B.E., D.L., M.A., F.S.A., F.R.HIST.S., F.R.S.L.; Hon. Sec. Miss P. HALDENBY.

**Ecclesiastical History Society:** c/o The Secretary, Department of History, Birkbeck College, University of London, London, WC1E 7HX; f. 1961; over 500 mems.; aims to further the study of ecclesiastical history and to maintain relations between British ecclesiastical historians and scholars abroad; Pres. Prof. TERENCE RANGER; Sec. Dr. EMMA MASON; publ. *Studies in Church History* (annual), *Subsidia*.

**Economic History Society:** London School of Economics, Houghton St., London, WC2A 2AE; f. 1927 to encourage the teaching and study of economic history; 3,000 mems.; Pres. Prof. M. W. FLINN; Hon. Sec. Prof. T. C. BARKER; publ. *The Economic History Review* (quarterly).

**Egypt Exploration Society:** 3 Doughty Mews, London, WC1N 2PG; f. 1882; Sec. SHIRLEY STRONG; publs. *Excavation Memoirs, Archaeological Survey, Graeco-Roman Memoirs, Texts from Excavations, The Journal of Egyptian Archaeology*, etc.; library: see Libraries.

**English Place-Name Society:** School of English Studies, University of Nottingham, Nottingham, NG7 2RD; f. 1923 for the publication of a yearly volume on the place-names of a county, or part of a county; 650 mems.; Hon. Dir. Prof. K. CAMERON, PH.D., F.B.A.; publ. *Journal* (annually).

**Friends Historical Society:** Friends House, Euston Rd., London, NW1 2BJ; f. 1903; 400 mems.; Sec. EDWARD H. MILLIGAN; publ. *Journal* (annually).

**Geographical Association:** 343 Fulwood Rd., Sheffield, S10 3BP; f. 1893 to further the interests of teachers of geography and the study and teaching of geography generally; approx. 6,600 mems.; library of 17,000 vols.; Pres. Prof. W. R. MEAD; Joint Hon. Secs. B. E. COATES, M. T. WILLIAMS; publs. *Geography* (quarterly), *Teaching Geography* (quarterly), variety of occasional papers and pamphlets.

**German Historical Institute:** 42 Russell Square, London, WC1B 5DA; f. 1976; research in modern and contemporary British and German history; study of international especially, Anglo-German relations; reference library for post-graduate students of 20,000 vols., 120 periodicals; Dir. Prof. Dr. WOLFGANG J. MOMMSEN; Deputy Dr. LOTHAR KETTENACKER.

**Hakluyt Society:** c/o Map Library, British Library, Great Russell St., London, WC1B 3DG; f. 1846; 2,100 mems.; Pres. Prof. GLYNDWR WILLIAMS; Hon. Secs. Prof. E. M. J. CAMPBELL, Dr. T. E. ARMSTRONG; publs. early voyages and travel and other geographical records.

**Harleian Society:** Ardon House, Mill Lane, Godalming, Surrey; f. 1869, inc. 1902, for the transcribing, printing and publishing the Heraldic Visitations of Counties, Parish Registers or any MSS. relating to genealogy, family history and heraldry; c. 300 subscribers; Chair. R. O. DENNYS, M.V.O., O.B.E., F.S.A., Somerset Herald of Arms; Hon. Sec. and Treas. P. LL. GWYNN-JONES, M.A., Bluemantle Poursuivant of Arms.

**Heraldry Society:** 28 Museum St., London, W.C.1; f. 1947 to further the study of heraldry, armory, chivalry, genealogy and kindred subjects; 1,500 mems.; Pres. The Duke of NORFOLK, C.B., C.B.E., M.C.; Sec. Mrs. J. C. G. GEORGE; publ. *The Coat of Arms* (quarterly).

**Historical Association:** 59A Kennington Park Rd., London, SE11 4JH; f. 1906; aims to advance the study and teaching of history at all levels, to increase public interest in all aspects of the subject and to develop it as an essential element in the education of all; 92 branches in the U.K. and Australia, New Zealand, Africa and South Africa; c. 8,500 mems.; extensive up-to-date history textbook collection; Sec. Miss C. M. POVALL, B.A.; publs. *History* (three a year), *Teaching History* (3 a year), *Annual Bulletin of Historical Literature, Helps for Students of History* series, *Appreciations in History* series, *Teaching of History* series.

**Honourable Society of Cymmrodorion:** 118 Newgate St., London, EC1A 7AE; f. 1751; Royal Charter 1951; approx. 1,600 mems.; Patron H.M. THE QUEEN; Pres. Sir THOMAS PARRY, M.A., D.LITT., D.LITT.CELT., LL.D., F.B.A.; Chair. His Honour Judge D. WATKIN POWELL, M.A., Hon. Sec. Mrs. JUNE GRUFFYDD, B.A.; publs. *Transactions*†, Welsh and English versions of *The Dictionary of Welsh Biography*.

**Huguenot Society of London:** c/o Barclays Bank, 1 Pall Mall East, London, SW1Y 5AX; f. 1885; 10 Hon. Fellows, 900 Ordinary Fellows, 9 Junior Fellows, 126 subscribing libraries, 16 societies in correspondence; Pres. J. RANDOLPH VIGNE, M.A.; Hon. Sec. Miss IRENE SCOULOUDI, M.SC.(ECON.), F.S.A., F.R.HIST.S.; publs. *Proceedings, Quarto Series*.

LEARNED SOCIETIES                                                                 U.K. (GREAT BRITAIN)

**Institute of British Geographers:** 1 Kensington Gore, London, SW7 2AR; f. 1933 to hold meetings for the reading and discussion of papers; to publish reports of proceedings and research papers; to promote research in geography, and to act as an association of professional geographers; 1,900 mems.; Pres. Prof. R. S. WATERS; Sec. Dr. J. DOORNKAMP; publs. *Transactions* (quarterly), *Area* (quarterly), *Special Publications*.

**Institute of Heraldic and Genealogical Studies:** Northgate, Canterbury, Kent; f. 1961 for education and research in family history, training and professional qualification; Pres. Major-Gen. The Viscount MONCKTON of BRENCHLEY; Reg. G. M. SWINFIELD; Dir. C. R. HUMPHERY-SMITH; Sec. Mrs. C. J. KELLY; publ. *Family History*.

**Jewish Historical Society of England:** 33 Seymour Place, London, W1H 5AP (Office); Mocatta Library, University College, London; f. 1839; 900 mems.; Pres. Dr. LIONEL KOCHAN; Hon. Sec. A. P. ROSE; publs. *Transactions*, *Miscellanies*, etc.

**London and Middlesex Archaeological Society:** c/o Museum of London, London Wall, London, E.C.2; f. 1855; collects and publishes archaeological and historical information relating to London and Middlesex; 900 mems.; library of 2,000 vols.; Pres. Prof. VALERIE PEARL, M.A., D.PHIL., F.R.HIST.S.; Hon. Sec. JOHN CLARK, M.A., F.S.A., A.M.A.; publ. *Transactions* (annually), *Special Papers* (occasional).

**London Record Society:** f. 1964 to publish the original sources for the history of London and generally to stimulate public interest in archives relating to London; c. 350 mems.; Hon. Sec. HEATHER CREATON, c/o Institute of Historical Research, Senate House, London, WC1E 7HU; publs. *Annual Series* and *Occasional Series*.

**London Topographical Society:** Hamilton's, Kilmersdon, nr. Bath, Somerset; f. 1880; 600 mems.; Patron: H.R.H. The Duke of EDINBURGH, K.G., K.T.; Hon. Sec. S. N. P. MARKS, M.A., F.S.A., R.I.B.A.; publs. *London Topographical Record* (irregular), and maps and views, annually.

**Manchester Geographical Society:** 274 Corn Exchange Buildings, Manchester, M4 3EY; f. 1884 to promote the study of all branches of geographical science; 150 mems.; library of 6,500 vols. (now on permanent loan to the University of Manchester); Pres. Prof. H. B. RODGERS; Sec. Miss E. WHALLEY; publ. *Journal*.

**Maritime Trust:** 16 Ebury St., London, SW1W 0LH; an independent trust f. 1969 to discover, acquire and preserve vessels and things maritime of historic or technical importance and where appropriate arrange for them to be accessible to the public; incorporates the Cutty Sark Society; Historic Ship Collection at St. Katharine's by the Tower, London, E.1; Pres. H.R.H. The Duke of EDINBURGH, K.G., K.T.; Chair. MALDWIN DRUMMOND, D.L., J.P.; Dir. Vice-Admiral Sir PATRICK BAYLY, K.B.E., C.B., D.S.C.

**Monumental Brass Society:** f. 1887 to promote the study of and interest in, better preservation of monumental brasses, and to compile and publish a full and accurate list of all extant and lost brasses, English and foreign; Hon. Sec. W. MENDELSSON, 57 Leeside Cres., London, NW11 0HA; publs. *Transactions*, *Portfolio* (annual), *Bulletin* (3 a year).

**Navy Records Society:** c/o Royal Naval College, Greenwich, London, S.E.10; f. 1893; publishes documents concerning British naval history; 1,000 mems.; Pres. Lord CARRINGTON; Hon. Sec. N. A. M. RODGER.

**Palestine Exploration Fund:** 2 Hinde Mews, Marylebone Lane, London, W1M 5RH; f. 1865; 900 subscribers; to obtain and disseminate non-political information about ancient and modern Syria (Syria, Lebanon, Jordan, Israel); Pres. The Archbishop of CANTERBURY; Hon. Sec. P. J. PARR, M.A.; publ. *Palestine Exploration Quarterly*.

**Prehistoric Society:** c/o Harvest House, 62 London Rd., Reading, RG1 5AS; f. 1908; 2,000 mems.; Pres. Prof. J. M. COLES, M.A., PH.D., F.B.A., F.S.A.; Hon. Sec. R. W. CHAPMAN, M.A., PH.D.; Hon. Editor T. CHAMPION, B.A., D.PHIL., F.S.A.; publ. *Proceedings*.

**Regional Studies Association:** 29 Great James St., London WC1N 3ES; f. 1965; an interdisciplinary group exclusively concerned with regional issues; aims to provide a forum for the exchange of ideas and information on regional problems, to publish the results of regional research, and stimulate studies and research in regional planning and related fields; holds meetings, conferences and seminars; organizes study groups; 12 branches; 600 individual, 200 corporate mems., including government depts., ministries, local authorities, educational institutions, etc.; Chair. DAVID BAYLISS, B.SC.; Hon. Sec. W. I. MORRISON, PH.D.; Exec. Sec. Mrs. GLORIA FRANKEL, B.A.; publs. *Regional Studies*, *Newsletter* (every 2 months), *Built Environment* (quarterly).

**Royal Archaeological Institute:** c/o 304 Addison House, Grove End Rd., London, NW8 9EL; f. 1843; Pres. S. D. T. SPITTLE, O.B.E., M.A., A.R.I.B.A., F.S.A.; Hon. Sec. A. J. CLARK, PH.D., F.S.A.; publ. *Archaeological Journal*.

**Royal Commission on Historical Manuscripts:** Quality House, Quality Court, Chancery Lane, London, WC2A 1HP; f. 1869, reconstituted 1959; locates, reports on, and publishes historical papers of every type outside the Public Records; advises owners and others on their use, preservation and dispersal; co-ordinates activities of all other bodies working in this field; maintains a central *National Register of Archives*, containing over 24,500 indexed reports on MS collections; Sec. B. S. SMITH; publs. over 200 vols.

**Royal Geographical Society:** Kensington Gore, London, SW7 2AR; f. 1830; furtherance of geographical research, teaching, and expeditions; 7,000 mems.; private library of 125,000 vols.; Pres. Prof. MICHAEL WISE, C.B.E., M.C.; Dir. and Sec. Dr. JOHN HEMMING; publs. *Geographical Journal*† (3 a year), *Geographical Magazine* (monthly); public map room; library: see Libraries.

**Royal Historical Society:** University College London, Gower St., WC1E 6BT; f. 1868; library of 12,000 vols.; Pres. Prof. J. C. HOLT, F.B.A.; Exec. Sec. Mrs. J. CHAPMAN; publs. *Transactions*, *Camden Series*, *Guides and Handbook Series*.

**Royal Numismatic Society:** c/o British Museum, London, WC1B 3DG; f. 1836; over 950 mems.; Pres. D. G. SELLWOOD; Secs. M. J. PRICE, D. M. METCALF; publs. *Numismatic Chronicle*, *Coin Hoards* (annual), *Monographs*.

**Royal Scottish Geographical Society:** 10 Randolph Crescent, Edinburgh 3; f. 1884 in order to extend geographical education in Scotland and to maintain contact with Scotsmen abroad and with others interested in the subject; library of 30,000 vols., 60,000 maps, 200 current periodicals; over 3,000 mems.; Pres. Prof. J. WREFORD WATSON, M.A., PH.D., LL.D., F.R.S.C., F.R.S.E., F.R.S.G.S.; Sec. DONALD G. MOIR, F.R.S.G.S.; Hon. Librarian J. T. COPPOCK, M.A., PH.D., F.B.A.; publ. *The Scottish Geographical Magazine* (3 a year).

**Scottish History Society:** Dept. of History, Kings College, Aberdeen, AB9 2UB; f. 1886 for the printing of unpublished documents illustrating the history of Scotland; 774 mems.; Pres. Mrs. R. MITCHISON; Hon. Sec. D. STEVENSON, PH.D.

**Society for Army Historical Research:** c/o National Army Museum, Royal Hospital Rd., London, S.W.3; f. 1921;

over 1,000 mems.; Pres. Gen. Sir DAVID W. FRASER, K.C.B., O.B.E.; Hon. Sec. D. K. SMURTHWAITE, B.A.

**Society for Medieval Archaeology:** c/o University College, Gower St., London, W.C.1; f. 1957 for the study of archaeology of the post-Roman period; 1,800 mems; Pres. J. G. HURST; Sec. J. A. GRAHAM-CAMPBELL; publs. *Medieval Archaeology* (annual), *Monograph Series* (occasional).

**Society for Nautical Research:** c/o National Maritime Museum, Greenwich, London, S.E.10; f. 1910; *c.* 2,100 mems.; Pres. Rear-Admiral E. F. GUERITZ, C.B., O.B.E., D.S.C.; Chair. Dr. HELEN WALLIS; Sec. J. MUNDAY; publ. *The Mariners' Mirror* (quarterly).

**Society for Post-Medieval Archaeology:** f. 1967; 850 mems.; Pres. KENNETH JAMES BARTON; Sec. STEPHEN MOORHOUSE, 27 Moorside Terrace, Drighlington, Bradford, BD11 1HX; publ. *Post-Medieval Archaeology* (annual).

**Society of Antiquaries of London:** Burlington House, London, W1V 0HS; f. 1707; 1,509 Fellows; Pres. Prof. C. N. L. BROOKE; Sec. R. W. LIGHTBOWN; publs. *Archaeologia, The Antiquaries Journal*†; library: *see* Libraries.

**Society of Antiquaries of Scotland:** National Museum of Antiquities, Queen St., Edinburgh EH2 1JD; f. 1780; study of Scottish antiquities and history, particularly by archaeological research; 1,900 mems.; Pres. R. G. CANT; Sec. TREVOR F. WATKINS; publ. *Proceedings* (annual).

**Society of Archivists:** f. 1947; 866 mems.; Pres. Dr. F. HULL, B.A.; Hon. Sec. Mrs. C. M. SHORT, South Yorkshire Record Office, Sheffield, S1 4PL; publ. *Journal* (2 a year).

**Society of Genealogists:** 37 Harrington Gardens, London, SW7 4JX; f. 1911; over 5,000 mems.; library of over 46,000 vols.; Pres. H.R.H. Prince MICHAEL OF KENT; Dir. ANTHONY J. CAMP; publ. *The Genealogists' Magazine* (quarterly).

**United Reformed Church History Society:** 86 Tavistock Place, London WC1H 9RT; f. 1972 to incorporate the Congregational Historical Society (f. 1899) and the Presbyterian Historical Society of England (f. 1913); 600 mems.; library of 7,000 vols.; Hon. Sec. Rev. S. C. ORCHARD, PH.D.; publ. *Journal* (2 a year).

**Wesley Historical Society:** f. 1893 to promote the study of the history and literature of Methodism; 1,000 mems. in U.K. (including N. Ireland); Pres. Rev. A. RAYMOND GEORGE, M.A., B.D.; Gen. Sec. Mrs. E. D. GRAHAM, 34 Spiceland Rd., Birmingham, B31 1NJ; publ. *Proceedings* (3 a year).

**Wiltshire Record Society:** Milestones, Hatchet Close, Hale, Hants., SP6 2NF; to publish the documentary sources for the history of Wiltshire and the means of reference thereto; Pres. Prof. R. B. PUGH; Hon. Sec. Mrs. N. D. STEELE; Hon. Editor Miss J. STEVENSON.

### INTERNATIONAL CULTURAL INSTITUTES

**Anglo-Chinese Educational Institute:** 152 Camden High St., London, NW1; f. 1966; to encourage and promote the study and dissemination of information about all aspects of China and the Chinese people; a Charitable Trust entirely supported by voluntary contributions, and working closely with the Society for Anglo-Chinese Understanding (*q.v.*); makes grants to the Society and other bodies undertaking educational work in relation to China, to promote lectures, conferences, films, educational visits to China, etc.; information centre and specialist library of 1,500 vols.; Sec. ALAN PATERSON; publs. *Modern China* series.

**Austrian Institute:** 28 Rutland Gate, London, SW7 1PQ; f. 1956; agency of the Austrian Ministry of Foreign Affairs, acting also as Cultural Affairs Section of Austrian Embassy in London; promotion of cultural relations between Great Britain and Austria; library of 8,000 vols.; Dir. Dr. WILHELM SCHLAG.

**British Council** (*see page following*).

**Casa do Brasil** (*House of Brazil Foundation*): 49 Lancaster Gate, London, W.2; f. 1960; library of over 10,000 vols.; cultural exchanges; language tuition; Dir. Prof. J. LOURENÇO DA SILVA.

**Commonwealth Institute:** Kensington High St., London, W8 6NQ; aims to foster among the peoples of the Commonwealth a greater knowledge of one another and of the importance of the Commonwealth Association; permanent exhibitions of all Commonwealth countries, open to the public with special provision for visiting parties; wide range of intra- and extra-mural services including talks to schools, and conferences; Library and Resource Centre (100,000 items); Commonwealth Arts Centre (theatre, cinema, art galleries); Dir. JAMES F. PORTER, M.A., B.SC., F.C.P.; publ. *What's On* (monthly).

**Danish Institute:** 3 Doune Terrace, Edinburgh, EH3 6DY; f. 1947 to supply information about Denmark and further cultural co-operation with other countries; summer courses and study tours; library of 1,000 vols.; Danish Rep. KNUD LINDUM-POULSEN, M.A.; publs. *Contact with Denmark, Musical Denmark* (annually).

**English-Speaking Union (of the Commonwealth):** Dartmouth House, 37 Charles St., Berkeley Square, London, W1X 8AB; f. 1918; international voluntary organization which through its educational programme is devoted to the promotion of understanding and friendship; 70,000 mems.; National Committees or Honorary Representatives in Australia, Belgium, Bermuda, Canada, England and Wales, Hong Kong, India, Malta, New Zealand, Nigeria, Pakistan, Scotland, and the U.S.A.; library of 12,000 vols.; Pres. H.R.H. The Prince PHILIP, Duke of EDINBURGH, K.G., K.T., O.M.; Chair. Sir PATRICK DEAN, G.C.M.G.; Dir.-Gen. ALAN LEE WILLIAMS, O.B.E.

**Fédération Britannique des Comités de l'Alliance Française:** 3 Queensberry Place, S. Kensington, London, SW7 2DN; f. 1908; lectures in French, French courses; Sec.-Gen. JEAN-PAUL COUCHOUD.

**Goethe-Institut:** 50 Princes Gate, Exhibition Rd., London SW7 2PH; Dir. GÜNTER COENEN; Dir. of Studies Dr. WERNER WOLF; Programme Dept. MANFRED BROENNER; Librarian CHARLOTTE EZOLD.

**Greek Institute:** 34 Bush Hill Rd., London, N21 2DS; f. 1969 for the promotion of Modern Greek studies through lectures, language and correspondence courses, publications, examinations and cultural activities; Dir. Dr. KYPROS TOFALLIS; publ. *Greek Review*† (quarterly).

**Institut Français du Royaume-Uni:** Queensberry Place, London, SW7 2DT; f. 1913; run in conjunction with the Universities of Paris and Lille; lectures, concerts, films, exhibitions, evening classes; lending library of *c.* 70,000 vols., 250 periodicals; Dir. PATRICK RAFROIDI.

**Institute of Spain:** 102 Eaton Square, London, S.W.1; f. 1946; courses on Spanish language and culture; library of 25,000 vols.; Dir. GUILLERMO BRUGAROLAS.

**Islamic Cultural Centre:** 146 Park Rd., London, N.W.8; f. 1944 to spread Islamic culture and, in particular, to help the growing Muslim community to know more about their religion; library of 10,000 vols., mostly Arabic, also English and Urdu; Dir. Dr. M. A. ZAKI BADAWI; publs. *The Islamic Quarterly, Islamic Literature*.

**Italian Institute:** 39 Belgrave Square, London, SW1X 8NX; f. 1950; principal agent of Italian Government

[*continued on p.* 1426

## THE BRITISH COUNCIL

10 SPRING GARDENS, LONDON, SW1A 2BN

Established November 1934;
incorporated by Royal Charter 1940.

The principal purposes of the British Council are the promotion of a wider knowledge of Britain and the English language abroad and the development of closer cultural relations with other countries. Its estimated expenditure for 1981–82 is £117.9m.

The Council is governed by a board of up to 30 members, six of whom are nominated by Ministers. The Chairman is Sir CHARLES TROUGHTON, C.B.E., M.C., T.D. There are advisory committees for Scotland and Wales, and also advisory committees or panels for the main branches of the Council's work. The Director-General is JOHN BURGH, C.B.

There are offices of the Council in the following Commonwealth countries: Australia, Bangladesh, Botswana, Canada, Cyprus, Ghana, India, Kenya, Malawi, Malaysia, New Zealand, Nigeria, Sierra Leone, Singapore, Sri Lanka, Tanzania, Zambia, Lesotho (with Swaziland), Hong Kong; and in the following foreign countries: Algeria, Argentina, Austria, Bahrain, Qatar and United Arab Emirates, Belgium (with Luxembourg), Brazil, Cameroon, Chile, Colombia, Denmark, Egypt, Ethiopia, Finland, France, Federal Republic of Germany, Greece, Indonesia, Iraq, Israel, Italy, Japan, Jordan, Republic of Korea, Kuwait, Lebanon, Mexico, Morocco, Nepal, Netherlands, Norway, Oman, Pakistan, Peru, Philippines, Poland, Portugal, Saudi Arabia, Senegal (with Mali and Mauritania), South Africa, Spain, Sudan, Sweden, Syria, Thailand, Tunisia, Turkey, Venezuela, Yemen Arab Republic, Yugoslavia, Zimbabwe; the Cultural Attachés at the British Embassies in Burma, China, Czechoslovakia, Hungary, Romania, and the U.S.A., and the Assistant Cultural Attaché at the British Embassy in the Soviet Union are appointed by the British Council.

### ACTIVITIES

Educational work is one of the Council's major tasks. The fields of English language teaching and science have been important for many years; recently the Council has strengthened its activities in such areas as educational technology, distance learning, schools and teacher education, science and mathematics education, non-formal and further and higher education. Assistance and advice is provided in the introduction of new methods, materials and techniques in both the formal and non-formal sectors of education. The emphasis is on the training of teachers and teacher-trainers, and the Council co-operates with overseas governments by maintaining English Language officers overseas and by seconding or recruiting staff for key posts. Further support for English teaching is provided by work in radio and television. There is similar support, on a smaller scale, for science education, and of the lecturers supplied for summer schools and short courses for teachers overseas about a quarter are science and mathematics specialists. In some countries the Council is engaged in direct English teaching, particularly to specialist professional groups, is involved in material preparation, and directs centres for British examinations in English. It recruits educational advisers to Ministries, teachers of English, science and other subjects for schools, colleges and universities. The Council operates a variety of schemes geared to meet the needs of academic interchange with other countries. It also maintains officers in an increasing number of countries to promote liaison with British scientists and to provide information on British science, medicine and technology. It sends overseas specialists in a wide range of subjects to lecture, advise and consult. An English Language Testing Service offered in collaboration with the University of Cambridge Local Examinations Syndicate tests the language proficiency of foreign students seeking admission to British institutions.

In many of these activities the Council co-operates closely with the Overseas Development Administration and other organizations. Support for the overseas activities includes several units within the Education, Medicine and Science Division which meet specific requests from overseas as well as disseminating information through leaflets, other publications and study kits. English language teaching activities are supported by the English Language Division in London, which has a team of specialist advisers, and carries out developmental projects in the teaching and learning of English. TETOC (Technical Education and Training for Overseas Countries) is concerned with the British contribution to technical and agricultural education, industrial training, public administration and management.

The Council aims to promote a wider knowledge and appreciation of British scholarship and achievements in the literary, visual, and performing arts. Writers, actors, dancers and other specialists are invited to perform, lecture or teach overseas; tours by musicians, theatre and dance companies are organized or assisted; fine arts and documentary exhibitions are sent abroad; support is given to literature studies; collections of documentary films are maintained in many overseas offices and in Headquarters the advice of specialist staff is available.

The Council runs or is associated with 125 libraries; as ODA's adviser and agent operates their Books Presentation Programme and the English Language Book Society's Low Priced Books Scheme; promotes the use of British publications overseas by organizing exhibitions of books and periodicals.

The Council provides many services for overseas students in Britain. It arranges programmes of studies for professional people, and gives scholarships and other awards to overseas scholars and research workers to allow them to pursue their studies in Britain. It administers the awards for training in Britain under the technical co-operation programme, and is also responsible for administering in Britain most of the Fellowships schemes of the UN and UN Specialized Agencies. It also administers jointly with the Association of Commonwealth Universities awards offered under the Commonwealth Scholarship and Fellowship Plan. Increasingly, the Council acts as agent for training schemes in Britain financed by overseas governments or international bodies. It finances Youth Exchange programmes with many countries; and it also organizes short courses and summer schools in Britain on a variety of educational and other subjects.

Publications: *British Book News, British Medical Bulletin, Educational Broadcasting International, Science Educational Newsletters, Writers and Their Work, ELT Documents,* a wide variety of bibliographical and other materials relating to the teaching of English and Council work, and various occasional surveys.

*continued from p. 1424]*

for the execution of the Cultural Agreement between Italy and Great Britain; centre for cultural information and exchanges; organizes lectures, concerts, film shows, exhibitions; library of 20,000 vols., and main Italian newspapers and periodicals; Dir. MARIO MONTUORI.

**Maison Française d'Oxford:** Norham Rd., Oxford; f. 1946; attached both to the University of Oxford and the Académie de Paris; cultural and social centre; library of 32,000 vols.; organizes lectures, seminars, exhibitions, concerts and film projections; small residential college for students; Dir. (vacant).

**Polish Cultural Institute:** 34 Portland Place, London, W.1; f. 1946; Dir. Mrs. IRENA GABOR-JATCZAK.

**Queen Elizabeth House:** 21 St. Giles, Oxford; f. 1954 to provide a centre for the study of political, economic, legal, administrative and social matters affecting developing countries and to arrange studies and research, particularly for senior administrators from developing countries; Warden A. D. HAZLEWOOD (*see also under Oxford University*).

**Society for Anglo-Chinese Understanding:** 152 Camden High St., London, NW1 1NE; f. 1965; to promote understanding and friendship between the British and Chinese people by arranging meetings, providing speakers, lectures, film shows, organizing group tours to China; 1,300 mems.; library under administration of Anglo-Chinese Educational Institute; c. 1,500 vols.; Pres. JOSEPH NEEDHAM, F.R.S.; Chair. PETER THEILE; publ. *China Now* (6 a year).

**Society for Cultural Relations with the U.S.S.R.:** 320 Brixton Road, London, SW9 6AB; f. 1924; promotes cultural relations and visits to the U.S.S.R.; information department; speakers on specialist and general subjects; language courses in G.B. and U.S.S.R.; 1,500 mems.; reference library of over 25,000 vols., Soviet periodicals, a variety of visual aids and special arrangements with various universities where many of the Society's Soviet journals etc., are on permanent loan; Chair. S. FORMAN; Sec. J. RUSSELL, B.SC.; publs. *Anglo-Soviet Journal* (3 a year), reading lists, occasional pamphlets, information sheets, quarterly newsletters, etc.

### LANGUAGE AND LITERATURE

**Academi Gymreig** (*Welsh Academy*): 4th Floor, 57 Bute St., Cardiff, CF1 6QP; f. 1959 to promote literature in the Welsh language; 44 mems.; *Welsh Language Section*: Pres. Dr. KATE ROBERTS; Chair. Dr. R. M. JONES; Sec. ANN BEYNON; publs. *Taliesin, Cyfres Cyfieithiadau'r Academi.*

*English Language Section:* f. 1968 to promote Anglo-Welsh literature; 64 mems.; Pres. A. G. PRYS JONES; Chair. G. O. JONES; Sec. SUE HARRIES.

**Association of British Science Writers:** c/o The Royal Institution, 21 Albemarle St., London, W1X 4BS; f. 1947 for the promulgation of science writing; 220 mems.; Pres. Sir HERMANN BONDI, K.C.B., F.R.S.; Chair. BRENDA MADDOX; Sec. PETER COOPER.

**Brontë Society:** The Brontë Parsonage, Haworth, near Keighley, West Yorks.; f. 1893, inc. 1902, to collect and act as guardian of Brontë letters, MSS., and personal belongings which are housed in the Brontë Parsonage Museum, former home of the Brontës and now in the care of the Society; 2,350 mems.; Pres. Lord BOYLE OF HANDSWORTH; Chair. of Council Mrs. D. HENDERSON; Hon. Sec. A. H. PRESTON, 4 Mytholmes Lane, Haworth, Keighley; publ. *Brontë Society Transactions* (annual).

**Charles Lamb Society, The:** 1A Royston Rd., Richmond, Surrey, TW10 6LT; f. 1935; to promote the study of the lives and works of Charles Lamb and his circle and to form a collection of Eliana; library housed in the Guildhall Library, City of London; owns Buttonsnap, Lamb's Hertfordshire cottage; Pres. Prof. JOHN STEVENS, C.B.E.; Hon. Sec. Mrs. M. R. HUXSTEP, M.A.; publ. *The Charles Lamb Bulletin* (quarterly).

**Classical Association:** c/o Dr. JOHN PERCIVAL, Dept. of Classics, University College, P.O.B. 78, Cardiff, CF1 1XL; Mrs. ELYS VARNEY (Joint Secs.); f. 1903; 4,500 mems.; Pres. Sir DAVID HUNT; 31 brs.; publs. *Classical Review, Classical Quarterly, Greece and Rome* (twice a year), *Proceedings*† (annual).

**Dickens Fellowship:** Dickens House, 48 Doughty St., London, WC1N 2LF; f. 1902 to knit together in a common bond of friendship lovers of Charles Dickens, and to assist in the preservation and purchase of buildings and objects associated with Dickens or mentioned in his works; approx. 5,000 mems.; Pres. Prof. SYLVÈRE MONOD; Hon. Sec. ALAN S. WATTS; Hon. Editor ANDREW SANDERS; publ. *The Dickensian* (four-monthly).

**Early English Text Society:** Lady Margaret Hall, Oxford; f. 1864; approx. 1,250 mems.; Hon. Dir. Prof. NORMAN DAVIS, F.B.A.; Exec. Sec. Dr. ANNE HUDSON; texts published annually.

**Edwardian Studies Association:** High Orchard, 125 Markyate Rd., Dagenham, Essex; f. 1975; to encourage related studies of Edwardians—Wells, Gissing, Conrad, Ford, Shaw, Pinero, etc.; publ. *Edwardian Studies*†.

**English Association:** 1 Priory Gardens, London, W4 1TT; f. 1906 to promote the knowledge and appreciation of the English language and of English literature and to uphold the standards of written and spoken English; 2,000 mems.; Chair. Prof. T. S. DORSCH; Pres. Miss RACHEL TRICKETT; Sec. Lt.-Col. R. T. BRAIN; publs. *English* (3 a year), *Essays and Studies, The Year's Work in English Studies.*

**English Speaking Board (International) Ltd.:** 32 Roe Lane, Southport, Merseyside, PR9 9EA; f. 1953; brings together people from educational, professional and industrial spheres who are concerned with oral education as a means of communication; individual and corporate mems. in 34 countries; arranges lectures, courses, etc.; examinations in spoken English for higher education students, certificates and diplomas awarded to teachers, professional speakers; Chair. KLAUS NEUBERG; Pres. CHRISTABEL BURNISTON; publ. *Spoken English* (3 a year).

**Francis Bacon Society Inc., The:** Reg. Office: Canonbury Tower, Islington, London, N.1; f. 1886; to study works and life of Francis Bacon and evidence in respect of the authorship of the plays attributed to Shakespeare; Pres. Commdr. MARTIN PARES; Chair. NOEL FERMOR; publ. *Baconiana* (periodically).

**Hopkins Society:** 114 Mount St., London, W1Y 6AH; f. 1969; to stimulate interest in the poet's life and work, and to enable readers and researchers to keep up with the developments in Hopkins Studies; Pres. Prof. N. H. MACKENZIE; Exec. Chair. Dr. A. THOMAS, S.J.; publs. *Hopkins Research Bulletin, Annual lecture, Annual sermon.*

**Institute of Linguists:** 24A Highbury Grove, London, N5 2EA; f. 1910; professional body for practising linguists; conducts examinations in foreign languages, and in English for speakers of other languages; incorporates Translators' Guild; over 5,000 mems.; library of c. 6,000 vols.; Pres. Sir JOHN PILCHER, G.C.M.G.; Chair. Prof. P. P. NEWMARK; publs. *The Incorporated Linguist* (quarterly), *Translators' Guild Newsletter* (quarterly).

**Institute of Scientific and Technical Communicators Ltd.:** 17 Bluebridge Ave., Brookman's Park, Hatfield, Herts.; f. 1972; professional institute dedicated to the efficient communication of all types of scientific and technical information; aims to establish and maintain professional standards and codes of practice within all branches of scientific and technical communication; 1,500 mems.; Pres. J. D. McINTOSH; Sec. Mrs. EILEEN PARKINSON.

**Johnson Society of London:** f. 1928 to study the life and works of Dr. Johnson and the period in which he lived; Pres. Dr. L. F. POWELL, D.LITT., F.R.S.L., F.L.A.; Hon. Sec. Rev. F. M. HODGESS ROPER, The Manse, Tower Rd., Hindhead, Surrey, GU26 6SU; publ. *The New Rambler* (3 a year).

**Kipling Society:** 18 Northumberland Ave., London, WC2N 5BJ; f. 1927 to honour and extend the influence of the writer and to publish a magazine for Kipling lovers; 900 mems.; Pres. Sir ANGUS WILSON; Hon. Sec. JOHN SHEARMAN; publ. *The Kipling Journal* (quarterly).

**Linguistics Association of Great Britain:** f. 1959 to promote the study of linguistics and provide a forum for discussion and facilities for co-operation in furtherance of this interest in linguistics; annual spring and autumn meetings; 683 mems.; Chair. Dr. N. SMITH; Hon. Sec. Dr. G. J. M. GAZDAR, School of Social Sciences, University of Sussex, Brighton, BN1 9QN; publ. *Journal of Linguistics* (2 a year).

**Malone Society:** f. 1906 for the study of early English drama; Hon. Sec. Miss K. M. LEA, 2 Church St., Beckley, Oxford.

**Modern Language Association:** 24A Highbury Grove, London, N5 2EA; f. 1893 to assist teachers and students of modern languages, and to secure due recognition for modern languages as instruments of general educational and cultural value; incorporates Association of Teachers of German; 3,000 mems.; Hon. Sec. A. SMALLEY; Gen. Sec. Miss E. INGHAM; publs. *Modern Languages* (quarterly), *Treffpunkt* (3 a year).

**Philological Society:** School of Oriental and African Studies, University of London, WC1E 7HP; f. 1842, inc. 1879, to investigate and promote the study and knowledge of the structure, affinities, and history of languages; 695 mems.; Pres. Dr. I. GERSHEVITCH, PH.D.; Secs. Prof. R. H. ROBINS, M.A., D.LIT., J. H. W. PENNEY, M.A., D.PHIL.; publ. *Transactions* (annual).

**Poetry Society:** 21 Earls Court Square, London, SW5 9BY; f. 1909 to promote the study and appreciation of poetry; poetry reading, educational activities; incorporates National Poetry Secretariat; 3,000 mems.; Gen. Sec. BRIAN G. MITCHELL; Education Officer MICHELLE FINK; publs. *The Poetry Review*†, *Newsletter*.

**Royal Society of Literature of the United Kingdom:** 1 Hyde Park Gardens, London, W.2; f. 1823; lectures and poetry readings; 600 fellows and mems.; Pres. Rt Hon. Lord BUTLER, K.G., C.H.; Sec. Mrs. P. M. SCHUTE; publs. *Transactions*, *Report*, Special Editions.

**Shaviana:** High Orchard, 125 Markyate Rd., Dagenham, Essex; f. 1941 to promote a wider interest in and clearer understanding of Bernard Shaw's life and work; Sec. ERIC FORD; publs. *The Shavian*†, *Shavian Tracts*, occasional papers.

**Society for the Promotion of Hellenic Studies:** 31-34 Gordon Square, London, WC1H 0PP; f. 1879; 3,000 mems.; Pres. Prof. P. E. CORBETT; Hon. Sec. Prof. R. P. WINNINGTON-INGRAM, F.B.A.; publ. *Journal of Hellenic Studies* with supplement *Archaeological Reports*; library: see Libraries.

**Society for the Promotion of Roman Studies:** 31-34 Gordon Square, London, WC1H 0PP; f. 1911; 3,493 mems.; Pres. Prof. P. A. BRUNT, F.B.A.; publs. *Journal of Roman Studies*, *Britannia*; library: see Libraries.

**Society for the Study of Medieval Languages and Literature:** f. 1932; Pres. Prof. P. GANZ; Sec. A. V. C. SCHMIDT, Balliol College, Oxford; publs. *Medium Ævum* (2 a year), monographs (occasional).

**Society of Authors:** 84 Drayton Gardens, London, SW10 9SD; f. 1884 to promote and protect the rights of authors in all the media; 3,000 mems.; Pres. Sir VICTOR PRITCHETT, C.B.E., F.R.S.L.; Secs. PHILIPPA MACLEISH, MARK LE FANU; publ. *The Author* (quarterly).

**H. G. Wells Society:** f. 1960 to promote an active interest in and an appreciation of the life, work and thought of H. G. Wells; Sec. C. ROLFE, Dept. of Language and Literature, Polytechnic of North London, Prince of Wales Rd., London, NW5 3LB; publ. *Newsletter*†, *Wellsian*†.

### MEDICINE

**Anatomical Society of Great Britain and Ireland:** f. 1887; c. 600 mems.; Pres. Prof. T. W. GLENISTER, C.B.E., T.D., D.SC., PH.D.; Hon. Sec. Prof. J. D. LEVER, SC.D., M.D.; Programme Sec. Dr. B. A. WOOD, Dept. of Anatomy, Middlesex Hospital Medical School, London, W1P 6DB; publ. *Journal of Anatomy*.

**Apothecaries of London, Worshipful Society of:** Apothecaries' Hall, Black Friars Lane, London, EC4V 6EJ; f. 1617 by King James I; grants a registrable medical qualification (L.M.S.S.A. Lond.), also the post-graduate diplomas in Industrial Health (D.I.H.), in Medical Jurisprudence (D.M.J.), in Venereology (Dip. Ven. S.A.), in History of Medicine (D.H.M.S.A.), Philosophy of Medicine (D.H.P.S.A.), and a certificate for pharmacy technicians; 1,300 mems.; Master Sir RONALD GIBSON, C.B.E., LL.D., M.D., F.R.C.S., F.R.C.G.P.; Clerk Maj. J. C. O'LEARY, M.B.I.M.; Registrar D. H. C. BARRIE.

**Association for the Study of Medical Education:** 150B Perth Rd., Dundee, DD1 4EA; f. 1957 to exchange information and promote research into medical education; over 800 mems.; Pres. Sir JOHN WALTON; Chair. Prof. G. S. KILPATRICK; Gen. Sec. Prof. R. M. HARDEN; publs. *Medical Education* (every 2 months), *Medical Education Booklets*, *Annual Report*.

**Association of Anaesthetists of Great Britain and Ireland:** Room 475/478, Tavistock House South, Tavistock Square, London, WC1H 9LG; f. 1932 to promote the development and study of anaesthetics and their administration and to maintain the high standard of this branch of medicine; 3,600 mems.; Pres. Dr. W. D. WYLIE; Hon. Sec. Dr. JEAN M. HORTON; publ. *Anaesthesia*.

**Association of British Neurologists:** c/o The National Hospital, Queen Sq., London, W.C.1; f. 1933; 190 mems.; Pres. Dr. W. W. GOODDY; Hon. Sec. Prof. P. K. THOMAS.

**Association of Surgeons of Great Britain and Ireland:** at The Royal College of Surgeons, Lincoln's Inn Fields, London, WC2A 3PN; f. 1920 for the advancement of the science and art of surgery; Pres. ANTHONY R. ANSCOMBE, F.R.C.S.; Hon. Sec. JOHN LUMLEY, F.R.C.S.

**British Association for Rheumatology and Rehabilitation:** 41 Eagle St., London, WC1R 4AR; f. 1943 to promote the development of rheumatology, and to develop and promote expertise in rehabilitation; 530 mems.; Pres. Dr. B. E. W. MACE; Hon. Sec. Dr. JEAN R. COLSTON; publ. *Rheumatology and Rehabilitation* (quarterly).

**British College of Ophthalmic Opticians (Optometrists):** 10 Knaresborough Place, London, SW5 0TG; f. 1980 (by The British Optical Association, The Scottish Association of Opticians and The Worshipful Company of Spectacle Makers) for the improvement and conservation of human vision: the advancement for the public benefit of the study of and research into ophthalmic optics and related subjects and the publication of the results thereof; the promotion and improvement for the public benefit of the science and practice of ophthalmic optics; the maintenance for the public benefit of the highest possible standards of professional competence and conduct; 5,750 mems.; library of 10,000 vols.; museum; Pres. P. J. COLE, F.B.C.O., F.B.O.A.HD., D.C.L.P., D.ORTH.; Academic Sec. P. A. SMITH, A.M.C.T., F.B.C.O.; Gen. Sec. T. H. COLLINGRIDGE, M.A.; publs. *Ophthalmic and Physiological Optics*† (3 a year).

**British Dental Association:** 63/64 Wimpole St., London, W1M 8AL; f. 1880 as a professional asscn.; *c.* 13,000 mems.; library of 10,000 vols.; Sec. R. B. ALLEN, B.CH.D., F.D.S.R.C.S.; Librarian Miss M. CLENNETT, B.A., A.L.A.; publ. *British Dental Journal* (twice monthly).

**British Diabetic Association:** 10 Queen Anne St., London, W1M 0BD; f. 1934 to provide an organization for the benefit of and service to diabetics and others interested in diabetes, and to promote the study of the causes thereof and the diffusion of information concerning the same; 70,000 mems.; Chair. of Exec. Council Dr. A. BLOOM, F.R.C.P.; publ. *Balance Newspaper* (every 2 months).

**British Dietetic Association:** Daimler House, 103 Paradise St., Birmingham, B1 2BJ; f. 1936; 1,700 mems.; Chair. Miss E. C. BATEMAN, S.R.D.; Org. Sec. Miss V. JONES; publ. *Journal of Human Nutrition* (6 times a year).

**British Geriatrics Society:** f. 1947 to improve standards of medical care for elderly patients and to encourage research in the problems of old age; over 1,000 mems.; Pres. Prof. A. N. EXTON-SMITH; Hon. Sec. Dr. P. HORROCKS, c/o Bernard Sunley House, 60 Pitcairn Rd., Mitcham, Surrey, CR4 3LL; publ. *Age and Ageing*.

**British Institute of Radiology:** 36 Portland Place, London, W.1; f. 1927; forms a centre for consultation on the medical, physical and biological applications of radiology; Current and Historic Radiological Library; 1,981 mems.; Pres. M. J. DAY, PH.D.; Gen. Sec. Mrs. J. M. ROYSTON; publ. *The British Journal of Radiology*.

**British Institute of Surgical Technologists:** Centre Point, 103 New Oxford St., London, WC1A 1DU; f. 1935; 2,040 mems.; Chair. G. MAURICE DOWN, O.B.E., F.B.I.S.T.; Sec. I. F. SHERWOOD; publ. *Journal* (annual).

**British Medical Association:** Tavistock Square, London, WC1H 9JP; f. 1832; 56,000 mems.; Pres. Sir JOHN WALTON; Chair. of Council ANTHONY GRABHAM; Sec. JOHN HAVARD; Nuffield Library of 90,000 vols.; publs. *British Medical Journal* (weekly), *News Review* (monthly), and numerous journals on specialized medical subjects.

**British Nutrition Foundation:** 15 Belgrave Sq., London, SW1X 8PS; f. 1967; Hon. Pres. Sir DAVID CUTHBERTSON, C.B.E., D.SC., M.D., F.R.C.P.E., F.R.S.E.; Dir.-Gen. Dr. M. R. TURNER, M.SC., PH.D.; Sec. P. M. VICTORY, O.B.E., M.C., F.B.I.M.; publ. *Bulletin*† (four-monthly).

**British Orthopaedic Association:** c/o The Royal College of Surgeons, 35-43 Lincoln's Inn Fields, London, WC2A 3PN; f. 1918; the advancement of the science and art of orthopaedic surgery; 1,600 mems.; Pres. G. P. MITCHELL; Hon. Sec. B. G. ANDREWS; publ. *Journal of Bone and Joint Surgery*.

**British Paediatric Association:** 23 Queen Square, London, WC1N 3AZ; f. 1928 to further the study and promotion of child health and excellence in paediatric practice; 1,521 mems.; Pres. Dr. G. M. KOMROWER; Hon. Sec. Dr. D. R. HARVEY; publs. *Archives of Disease in Childhood* (monthly, with British Medical Association), *Classification of Diseases* Vols. I and II, *Perinatal Supplement*.

**British Pharmacological Society:** c/o Department of Pharmacology, Worsley Medical and Dental Building, University of Leeds, LS2 9JT; f. 1931; 1,412 mems.; Gen. Sec. Prof. A. M. BARRETT; publs. *British Journal of Pharmacology, British Journal of Clinical Pharmacology*.

**British Psychoanalytical Society:** 63 New Cavendish St., London, W.1; f. 1913 for the advancement of psychoanalysis as a science; 380 mems.; library of 11,000 vols.; Pres. (vacant); Hon. Sec. A. B. POLLOCK, M.A.; publs. *The International Journal of Psycho-Analysis* (quarterly), *The International Review of Psychoanalysis* (quarterly).

**British Society for the Study of Orthodontics:** f. 1907; 884 mems.; Pres. R. T. BROADWAY; Sec. I. G. CROSSMAN, Royal Alexander Hospital, Dyke Rd., Brighton, BN1 3JN.

**British Society of Gastroenterology:** Secretariat, Dept. of Surgery, The Rayne Institute, 5 University St., WC1E 6JJ; 1,180 mems.; Pres. Prof. C. G. CLARK; Secs. Dr. G. E. SLADEN (Snr.), R. G. FABER (Jnr.).

**Cancer Research Campaign:** 2 Carlton House Terrace, London, SW1Y 5AR; f. 1923 as British Empire Cancer Campaign for Research with the object of attacking and defeating the disease of cancer in all its forms by research into its causes, distribution, symptoms, pathology and cure; Pres. H.R.H. The Duke of GLOUCESTER; Sec.-Gen. Brig. K. D. GRIBBIN, O.B.E., M.A.; publs. *British Journal of Cancer* (monthly), *Annual Report*.

**Central Council of Physical Recreation:** Francis House, Francis St., London, S.W.1; f. 1935 to formulate and promote measures to improve and develop sport and physical recreation; Pres. H.R.H. The Prince PHILIP, Duke of EDINBURGH, K.G., P.C., K.T., O.M., G.B.E.; Chair. of Exec. Cttee. Mrs. M. A. GLEN HAIG, C.B.E.; Gen. Sec. PETER LAWSON.

  **Sports Council:** 70 Brompton Rd., London, SW3 1EX; established by Royal Charter, 1972; objects are to foster the knowledge and practice of sport and physical recreation among the public at large and the provision of facilities therefor, building upon the work in this field of the Central Council of Physical Recreation and others; 9 autonomous Regional Sports Centres advise the Sports Council and local authorities on regional priorities for sports facilities; Chair. R. E. G. JEEPS; Dir. EMLYN JONES; publ. *Sport and Recreation*† (quarterly).

**Chartered Society of Physiotherapy:** 14 Bedford Row, London, WC1R 4ED; f. 1894, inc. by Royal Charter 1920, to improve the training, education, and professional status of physiotherapists; 26,000 mems.; Pres. Baroness MASHAM OF ILTON; Sec. R. J. S. BRYANT, LL.B., A.C.I.S., F.H.A.; publ. *Physiotherapy* (monthly).

**Chest, Heart and Stroke Association, The:** Tavistock House North, Tavistock Square, London, WC1H 9JE; f. 1899; for the prevention of chest, heart and stroke illnesses, through research, education and rehabilitation; Chair. of Council The Rt. Hon. Lord HILL OF LUTON, M.D.; Dir.-Gen. Air Marshal Sir ERNEST SIDEY, K.B.E., C.B., M.D., F.F.C.M., D.P.H.

**Harveian Society of London:** 11 Chandos St., London, W.1; f. 1831 to promote the advance of medical science; 370 mems.; Pres. KEVIN J. SILKHA; Hon. Sec. DAVID DENISON.

**Health Education Council:** 78 New Oxford St., London, WC1A 1AH; f. 1968; to co-ordinate and develop programmes of health education in England, Wales and Northern Ireland; provides advisory services for statutory, voluntary, industrial and commercial organizations, authorities and teachers, etc. on health education, media and research methodology; resource centre, library and information facilities; Chair. Dr.

Brian Lloyd; Dir.-Gen. Prof. Keith Taylor; publ. *Health Education Journal* (quarterly).

**Heberden Society:** c/o The Arthritis and Rheumatism Council, 41 Eagle St., London, WC1R 4AR; f. 1936; a clinical and scientific society for the advancement of the study of the rheumatic diseases; 700 mems.; Gen. Sec. M. C. G. Andrews, C.B.E.

**Hunterian Society:** f. 1819; 450 mems.; Secs. Georges Jantet, 82 Harley St., London, W1N 1AE; Dr. D. W. Findlay; publ. *Transactions* (every 2 years).

**Institute of Medical Laboratory Sciences:** 12 Queen Anne St., London, W1M 0AU; inc. 1942 to act as a professional body for practitioners of medical laboratory sciences, the Institute awards advanced qualifications in medical laboratory sciences; 16,000 mems.; Pres. D. B. Slade, F.I.M.L.S.; Sec. J. K. Fawcett, F.C.I.S., F.I.M.L.S.; publs. *Medical Laboratory Sciences* (quarterly), *The Gazette* (monthly).

**Listerian Society of King's College Hospital:** King's College Hospital, Denmark Hill, London, S.E.5; f. 1833 as King's College Medical Society; renamed Listerian Society 1912 on the death of Lord Lister.

**Medical Society for the Study of Venereal Diseases:** 11 Chandos St., Cavendish Square, London, W1M 0EB; f. 1922; 650 mems.; Pres. Dr. C. B. S. Schofield; Sec. Dr. J. Barrow; publ. *The British Journal of Venereal Diseases* (6 a year).

**Medical Society of London:** 11 Chandos St., London, W.1; f. 1773; library of 35,000 vols.; Pres. Sir James Watt, K.B.E.; Hon Secs. C. D. M. Drew, R. P. Rosswick.

**Medico-Legal Society:** 71 Lincoln's Inn Fields, London, WC2A 3JF; f. 1901; approx 650 mems.; Pres. Dr. J. Leaky Taylor, M.B., B.S., D.M.J., M.R.C.G.P.; Hon. Sec. James F. Barnes, M.A.; publ. *The Medico-Legal Journal* (quarterly).

**MIND (National Association for Mental Health):** 22 Harley St., London, W1N 2ED; f. 1946 to promote mental health and campaign for the needs of the mentally ill and the mentally handicapped; 1,500 mems., 10,000 local assoc. mems. and 300 affiliated bodies; Pres. The Rt. Hon. Lord Butler, K.G., C.H.; Chair. Lady Bingley; Dir. Tony Smythe; publs. *Mind Out* (monthly), *MIND Information Bulletin* (10 a year), *Mental Health Year Book*, occasional booklets and leaflets.

**Nutrition Society:** Chandos House, 2 Queen Anne St., London, W1M 9LE; f. 1941 to advance the scientific study of nutrition and its application to the maintenance of human and animal health; over 1,000 mems.; Pres. Prof. I. Macdonald, M.D., D.SC., F.I.BIOL.; publs. *Proceedings, British Journal of Nutrition*.

**Ophthalmological Society of the United Kingdom:** at the Royal College of Surgeons, 35–43 Lincoln's Inn Fields, London, WC2A 3PN; f. 1880 for the cultivation and promotion of ophthalmology; approx. 1,500 mems.; Pres. W. S. Foulds; Hon. Secs. T. J. Ffytche, A. M. Hamilton; publ. *Transactions* (4 parts per year).

**Pathological Society of Great Britain and Ireland:** c/o Dept. of Medical Microbiology, University of Sheffield Medical School, Beech Hill Rd., Sheffield, S10 2RX; f. 1906; 1,600 mems.; Secs. Prof. M. G. McEntegart (above address), Prof. A. M. Neville; publs. *Journal of Pathology* and *Journal of Medical Microbiology*.

**Pharmaceutical Society of Great Britain:** 1 Lambeth High St., London, SE17 JN; f. 1841; 1,807 fellows, 29,185 mems.; library of c. 60,000 vols., pamphlets and MSS., c. 500 journals; Pres. Prof. A. H. Beckett, D.SC., PH.D., F.P.S., F.R.S.C.; Sec. and Registrar D. F. Lewis, O.B.E., F.P.S.; publs. *The Pharmaceutical Journal* (weekly), *Journal of Pharmacy and Pharmacology* (monthly), *The Pharmaceutical Society's Calendar* (annual), *Annual Register of Pharmaceutical Chemists, Pharmaceutical Codex, Pharmacy Law and Ethics, Martindale: The Extra Pharmacopoeia, The Pharmaceutical Handbook* (occasional), *Isolation and Identification of Drugs, etc.*, and *British National Formulary* (published jointly with the British Medical Association), *Medicines and Poisons Guide*.

**Royal Association for Disability and Rehabilitation:** 25 Mortimer St., London, W1N 8AB; f. 1977; covers the whole field of rehabilitation; a co-ordinating organization concerned with the environmental problems of disabled people; Chair. His Grace the Duke of Buccleuch; Dir. George Wilson; publs. *Contact* (quarterly), *Bulletin* (monthly).

**Royal College of General Practitioners:** 14 Princes Gate, London, SW7 1PU; f. 1952 to ensure the highest possible standards in general practice; 9,600 mems.; Pres. Dr. J. P. Horder; Hon. Sec. Dr. J. C. Hasler; publ. *Journal* (monthly).

**Royal College of Obstetricians and Gynaecologists:** 27 Sussex Place, Regent's Park, London, NW1 4RG; f. 1929; 2,282 Fellows, 4,121 Mems.; library of 10,000 vols.; Pres. R. M. Feroze, F.R.C.O.G., F.R.C.S.; Sec. D. B. Lloyd, A.C.C.A.; publ. *British Journal of Obstetrics and Gynaecology†* (monthly).

**Royal College of Physicians:** 11 St. Andrew's Place, London, NW1 4LE; f. 1518; membership consists of Fellows, Members and Licentiates; Pres. Sir Douglas Black, M.D., P.R.C.P.; Registrar David A. Pyke, M.D., F.R.C.P.; Sec. G. M. G. Tibbs, M.A.; publ. *Journal*; library: see Libraries.

**Royal College of Physicians and Surgeons of Glasgow:** 234–242 St. Vincent St., Glasgow, G2 5RJ; f. 1599; a medical licensing corporation; 2,500 Mems. and Fellows, incl. Fellows in Dental Surgery; Pres. Douglas H. Clark; Hon. Sec. Dr. Norman MacKay.

**Royal College of Physicians of Edinburgh:** 9 Queen St., Edinburgh, EH2 1JQ; f. 1681; Sec. Dr. C. Mawdsley; library: see Libraries.

**Royal College of Psychiatrists:** 17 Belgrave Square, London, SW1X 8PG; f. 1971 by Charter, previously Royal Medico-Psychological Association, f. 1841 to advance the science and practice of psychiatry and further education therein; special sections for Mental Deficiency, Psychotherapy, Child Psychiatry, Psychiatry of Old Age, Forensic Psychiatry, Social and Community Psychiatry; 4,000 Fellows and mems., 1,100 affiliates; Pres. Prof. Kenneth Rawnsley, P.R.C.PSYCH; Registrar Prof. G. C. Timbury, F.R.C.PSYCH.; publs. *British Journal of Psychiatry* and Special Publications.

**Royal College of Radiologists:** 38 Portland Place, London, W1N 3DG; f. 1939 as the Faculty of Radiologists; practice of radiology; 2,750 mems.; Pres. Dr. J. W. Laws; Registrar Dr. J. O. M. C. Craig; publ. *Clinical Radiology* (every 2 months).

**Royal College of Surgeons of Edinburgh:** Nicolson St., Edinburgh; f. 1505; Pres. Prof. F. John Gillingham, M.B.E., P.R.C.S.ED., F.R.C.S.ENG., F.R.C.P.ED., F.R.S.E.; Hon. Sec. A. C. B. Dean, CH.M., F.R.C.S.ED., F.R.C.S. ENG.; publ. *Journal* (every 2 months).

**Royal College of Surgeons of England:** 35–43 Lincoln's Inn Fields, London, WC2A 3PN; f. 1800; 16,000 Fellows, 26,000 mems., 500 students; incorporates Nuffield College of Surgical Sciences for postgraduate students f. 1957; Pres. Sir Alan Parks, M.D., M.CH., F.R.C.P., F.R.C.S.; Sec. R. S. Johnson-Gilbert, O.B.E., M.A.; publs. *Annals* (every 2 months), *Handbook* (occasional), *Almanack*.

**Royal Institute of Public Health and Hygiene, The:** 28 Portland Place, London, W1N 4DE; f. as R.I.P.H.

U.K. (GREAT BRITAIN)

1886, I.H. 1903, amalgamated 1937; approx. 2,850 mems.; Chief Exec. A. R. HORSHAM, F.C.I.S.; publ. *Health and Hygiene* (quarterly).

**Royal Medical Society:** Students' Centre, Bristo St., Edinburgh, EH8 9AL; f. 1737; 900 mems.; library of 2,000 vols.; Pres. BRIAN W. MONTGOMERY; Sec. SHONA HAMILTON.

**Royal Society of Health:** 13 Grosvenor Place, London, SW1X 7EN; f. 1876 to promote the health of the people; Patron H.M. THE QUEEN; Sec. J. AUDREY ELLISON, B.SC., F.I.F.S.T., F.R.S.H.; publ. *Journal* (every 2 months).

**Royal Society of Medicine:** 1 Wimpole St., London, W1M 8AE; f. 1805; first Royal Charter 1834, supplemental Charter 1907; world-wide membership, over 17,000; library: see Libraries; 34 Sections cover whole field of medicine and surgery; Audio-visual dept. making motion films and stills; Pres. Sir JOHN STALLWORTHY, F.R.C.O.G.; Exec. Dir. R. T. HEWITT, O.B.E., M.A.; publs. *Calendar* (annually), *Annual Report, Journal*† (monthly), *Tropical Doctor* (quarterly), *International Congress and Symposium Series*, occasional papers.

**Royal Society of Tropical Medicine and Hygiene:** Manson House, 26 Portland Place, London, W1N 4EY; f. 1907 for the stimulation of inquiry and research into causes, treatment, and prevention of human and animal diseases in warm climates; 2,617 mems.; Pres. Dr. A. J. DUGGAN; Hon. Secs. R. KILLICK-KENDRICK, D. I. H. SIMPSON; publs. *Transactions* (6 a year), *Year Book*.

**St. John's Hospital Dermatological Society** (incorporating The London Dermatological Society): Lisle St., Leicester Square, London, WC2H 7BJ; meeting at St. John's Hospital for Diseases of the Skin; f. 1911 to promote the knowledge and study of dermatology by showing and discussion of rare and interesting cases; 500 Fellows; Pres. Dr. R. S. WELLS; Hon. Sec. Dr. R. J. HAY; publ. *Clinical and Experimental Dermatology* (6 a year).

**Society for Endocrinology:** 23 Richmond Hill, Bristol, BS8 1EN; f. 1946 to promote the advance of endocrinology by observational, experimental or clinical studies; 1,100 mems., incl. 15 hon. mems.; Chair. J. G. PHILLIPS; Hon. Secs. LESLEY REES, V. H. T. JAMES; publ. *Journal of Endocrinology* (monthly).

**Society of British Neurological Surgeons:** c/o Dept. of Neurological Surgery, Atkinson Morley's Hospital, Copse Hill, Wimbledon, London, SW20 0NE; f. 1926; 370 mems.; Pres. JOHN HANKINSON; Hon. Sec. ALAN RICHARDSON; publ. *Proceedings* (in *Journal of Neurology, Neurosurgery and Psychiatry*).

**Society of Community Medicine, The:** 28 Portland Place, London, W1N 4DE; f. 1856 for the advancement of public health in every branch, and of the knowledge and interests of the public health service; approx. 1,200 mems.; Pres. Dr. D. K. MACTAGGART; Admin. Sec. Miss W. A. WEBB; publ. *Public Health* (bi-monthly).

**Society of Occupational Medicine:** 11 St. Andrew's Place, London, NW1 4LE; f. 1935 as the Association of Industrial Medical Officers; aims to improve the health of people at work and to promote and stimulate research and education in the field of occupational health; 1,600 mems.; Pres. Dr. F. H. TYRER; Hon. Sec. P. G. HARRIES; publ. *Journal* (quarterly).

**Tavistock Institute of Medical Psychology:** Tavistock Centre, Belsize Lane, London, NW3 5BA; f. 1920; promotes the study and practice of psychotherapy and sponsors research and preventive measures in the field of mental health; offers assistance to those undertaking training in psychotherapy at the Tavistock Clinic; Sec. S. G. GRAY, F.C.I.S., F.C.I.I.

WORLD OF LEARNING

NATURAL SCIENCES

General

**Association for Science Education:** College Lane, Hatfield, Herts., AL10 9AA; aims to improve science teaching and to provide a medium of expression for science teachers; 16,850 mems.; Gen. Sec. B. G. ATWOOD; publs. *The School Science Review, Education in Science*.

**British Association for the Advancement of Science:** Fortress House, 23 Savile Row, London, W.1; f. 1831; national institution offering membership to all; aims to promote a more general interest and understanding of the concepts, language, methods, and applications of science; 2,000 mems.; Pres. H.R.H. The Duke of KENT; Gen. Secs. Sir FREDERICK DAINTON, F.R.S., Prof. M. J. FRAZER, Dr. J. G. COLLINGWOOD; publ. *B.A. Spectrum* (quarterly).

**British Society for Social Responsibility in Science:** 9 Poland St., London, W1V 3DG; f. 1969; to stimulate amongst scientists and the public an awareness of the social, political and economic implications and consequences of scientific development; 600 mems.; publs. *Science for People*† (quarterly), *Hazards Bulletin* (every 2 months).

**British Society for the History of Science:** Halfpenny Furze, Mill Lane, Chalfont St. Giles, Bucks., HP8 4NR; f. 1946; 585 mems.; Pres. Dr. ROBERT FOX; publs. *British Journal for the History of Science, Newsletter* (3 a year), monographs in the History of Science.

**British Society for the Philosophy of Science:** f. 1948 to study the logic, the methods, and the philosophy of science, including the social sciences; 520 mems.; Pres. Prof. C. KILMISTER; Sec. G. M. K. HUNT, Social Studies Building, University of Warwick, Coventry, CV4 7AL; publ. *The British Journal for the Philosophy of Science* (quarterly).

**Cambridge Philosophical Society:** Bene't St., Cambridge; f. 1819 to promote scientific enquiry and to facilitate the communication of facts connected with the advancement of science; 1,558 mems.; library of 82,000 vols., mainly periodicals, covering most branches of science, but especially mathematics, physics and general biology; Exec. Sec. Miss J. M. WINTON THOMAS; Librarian Miss E. A. STOW, M.A., A.L.A.; publs. *Mathematical Proceedings*† (6 a year), *Biological Reviews*† (quarterly).

**Council for Environmental Conservation:** Zoological Gardens, Regent's Park, London, NW1 4RY; f. 1969; work in the fields of wildlife, pollution, transport, youth, energy and water; mems.: 33 organizations; Chair. Rt. Hon. Lord CRAIGTON, C.B.E.; publ. *Habitat* (10 a year).

**Field Studies Council:** Preston Montford, Montford Bridge, 'Shrewsbury, SY4 1HW; f. 1943 to provide facilities for every aspect of field work and to set up for this purpose field study and research centres in localities selected for the richness and variety of their ecological features and their geological, geographical, archaeological and artistic interest; ten field centres are at present in operation; approx. 4,500 mems.; Pres. F. GILLIES, B.SC., LL.B.; Chair. I. D. MERCER, B.A.; Dir. C. A. SINKER, O.B.E., M.A.; publs. *Programmes of Courses, Annual Report, Field Studies* (annually).

**Institute of Information Scientists:** 62 London Rd., Reading, Berks., RG1 5AS; f. 1958; 1,800 mems.; Pres. Prof. C. CLEVERDON, F.L.A., F.I.INF.SC.; Sec. J. POPE; publ. *Inform* (quarterly).

**Institution of Environmental Sciences:** 14 Princes Gate, Hyde Park, London, SW7 1PU; f. 1971 for consultation in matters of an environmental nature; aims to promote interdisciplinary studies of the environment, to diffuse information relating to environmental sciences at national and international levels, and to bring together into a corporate professional body all persons throughout the world possessing responsibilities for environmental affairs; 365 individual, 89 collective mems.; Chair. Prof. G. Ashworth, c.b.e.; Sec. Dr. J. F. Potter; Dir. Dr. J. Rose; publs. *Journal of Environmental Education and Information, Newsletter*, occasional publs., pamphlets and monographs.

**London Natural History Society:** f. 1858 for the study of natural history, archaeology and kindred subjects, especially within a radius of 20 miles from St. Paul's Cathedral; library of 3,000 vols.; 1,100 mems.; Sec. J. B. Cresswell, 142 Harborough Rd., London, SW16 2XW; publs. *The London Naturalist, The London Bird Report* (both annual).

**Ray Society:** c/o British Museum (Natural History), Cromwell Rd., London, SW7 5BD; f. 1844 to publish works primarily concerned with the natural history of the British Isles; 370 mems.; 154 vols. published; Pres. D. C. McClintock, t.d., m.a., f.l.s.; Hon. Sec. Dr. G. A. Boxshall.

**Royal Society for Nature Conservation:** The Green, Nettleham, Lincoln, LN2 2NR; f. 1912; inc. by Royal Charter 1916 and 1976, for the collection of information about areas of scientific importance in the United Kingdom; for the establishment of nature reserves; for the education of public opinion on the value of the 42 voluntary Nature Conservation Trusts in Britain with over 137,000 mems.; Pres. J. Christopher Cadbury, c.b.e.; Gen. Sec. Dr. F. H. Perring; publs. annual report, *Natural World* (3 a year).

**Scottish Field Studies Association:** Braefoot, 158 Craigcrook Rd., Edinburgh, EH4 3PP; f. 1945; provides residential facilities for scientific field work and organizes courses at the Association's Kindrogan Field Centre in Perthshire and at other places in Scotland; 400 mems.; Chair. Prof. J. C. Smyth, ph.d., f.i.biol., f.l.s.; publs. *Annual Report*, programmes of courses.

**South-Eastern Union of Scientific Societies:** 53 The Drive, Shoreham-by-Sea, Sussex; f. 1896; unites some 70 natural history and archaeological societies in 12 counties; Pres. Dr. Maurice Burton, f.l.s.; Sec. F. Edwards, f.l.s., f.ph.s.; publ. *South-Eastern Naturalist and Antiquary* (occasional).

### Biological Sciences

**Association for the Study of Animal Behaviour:** f. 1936; 900 mems.; Pres. Prof. A. Manning; Sec. Dr. R. F. Drewett, Dept. of Psychology, University of Durham, DH1 3HP; publ. *Animal Behaviour*.

**Association of Applied Biologists:** f. 1904 to promote the study and advancement of all branches of biology, with special reference to their applied aspects; approx. 1,500 mems.; Pres. Prof. J. K. A. Bleasdale; Hon Sec. D. Gareth Jones, ph.d., d.sc., Dept. of Agricultural Botany, University College of Wales, Aberystwyth, Dyfed, SY23 3DD; publ. *Annals of Applied Biology* (bi-monthly).

**Botanical Society of Edinburgh:** Royal Botanic Garden, Edinburgh; f. 1836; 560 mems. and Fellows; Pres. Prof. R. M. M. Crawford; Hon. Gen. Sec. D. G. Mann, ph.d.; Programme Sec. J. Raven, ph.d.; publs. *Transactions and Proceedings* (annual) and *Contemporary Botanical Thought* (series of lectures), *Newsletter*.

**Botanical Society of the British Isles:** c/o Dept. of Botany British Museum (Natural History), London, SW7 5BD; f. 1836 for study of British native flowering plants and ferns; exhibitions, conferences, field meetings; 2,400 mems.; Hon. Gen. Sec. Mrs. M. Briggs, m.b.e., f.p.s., f.l.s.; publs. *Watsonia* (twice yearly), *Abstracts* (annually), *B.S.B.I. News* (3 a year).

**British Biophysical Society:** c/o The Biochemical Society, 7 Warwick Court, London, WC1R 5DP; f. 1960; 800 mems.; Sec. Dr. G. L. Kellett.

**British Ecological Society:** f. 1913 to promote and foster education and research in the subject of ecology considered as a branch of natural science; over 3,500 mems.; Pres. G. M. Dunnet; Hon. Sec. J. M. Cherrett, Dept. of Applied Zoology, University College of North Wales, Bangor, Gwynedd, LL57 2UW; publs. *Symposium* (annually), *Journal of Ecology* (thrice yearly), *Journal of Animal Ecology* (thrice yearly) and *Journal of Applied Ecology* (thrice yearly).

**British Lichen Society:** Sec. J. R. Laundon, f.m.a., Dept. of Botany, British Museum (Natural History), Cromwell Rd., London, SW7 5BD; f. 1958; 580 mems.; publs. *The Lichenologist* (3 a year), *Bulletin* (2 a year).

**British Mycological Society:** f. 1896; 1,400 mems. and 125 assocs.; Sec. Dr. G. F. Pegg, Dept. of Plant Sciences, Wye College, Ashford, Kent, TN25 5AH; publs. *Transactions* (bi-monthly), *Bulletin* (half-yearly).

**British Ornithologists' Union:** c/o Zoological Society of London, Regent's Park, London, NW1 4RY; f. 1858 for the advancement of the science of ornithology; 1,950 ordinary mems., 15 hon. mems., 30 corresp. mems.; Pres. Stanley Cramp, o.b.e., b.a.; Sec. D. C. Houston, d.phil. (acting); publ. *Ibis* (quarterly).

**British Social Biology Council:** 69 Eccleston Square, London, S.W.1; f. 1935 to promote and encourage the teaching of human biology as a cultural and practical subject, and to preserve and strengthen the family as the basic social unit; Sec. Rajinder Kumar; publ. *Social Biology and Human Affairs* (2 a year).

**British Trust for Ornithology:** Beech Grove, Tring, Herts.; f. 1932 to help bird-watchers of the British Isles by stimulating field research in ornithology and by acting as a clearing centre for information; administers National Bird Ringing Scheme, Nest Records Scheme, Common Birds Census, Estuaries Survey, Moult Enquiry, and enquiries into the status, distribution and habits of British birds; approx. 7,000 mems.; Pres. S. M. Taylor; Dir. Dr. R. J. O'Connor; publs. *Bird Study* (quarterly), *B.T.O. News, Annual Report*, Field Guides, special reports.

**Fauna and Flora Preservation Society, The:** c/o Zoological Society of London, Regent's Park, London, NW1 4RY; f. 1903; an international society working to protect wildlife throughout the world and to save endangered species from extinction; publishes information and news about wildlife conservation throughout the world; c. 3,500 mems.; Pres. Sir Peter Scott; Chair. of Council Lord Craigton; Hon. Sec. David Jones; publ. *Oryx*† (3 a year).

**Freshwater Biological Association:** The Ferry House, Ambleside, Cumbria, LA22 0LP; f. 1929 to promote the investigation of the biology of the animals and plants found in fresh (including brackish) water, and to establish and maintain a laboratory or laboratories equipped with boats and other necessary apparatus for the investigation of freshwater life; 1,900 mems.; library of 60,000 books and reprints and 4,000 vols. of scientific periodicals; River Laboratory at East Stoke, Wareham; Dorset; Pres. Sir Edwin Arrowsmith, k.c.m.c., Chair. of Council Prof. G. E. Fogg, sc.d., f.r.s.; Sec. and Dir. E. D. Le Cren, m.s., m.a., f.i.biol.; publs. *Annual Report*†, *Scientific Publications*†, *Occasional Publications*†.

**Genetical Society:** c/o M.R.C. Clinical and Population Cytogenetics Unit, Western General Hospital, Edinburgh, EH4 2XU; f. 1919; all aspects of genetics and animal and plant breeding; 1,043 mems.; Pres. Prof. J. R. S. Fincham, f.r.s.; Sec. Dr. Ann C. Chandley; publ. *Heredity*.

**Institute of Biology:** 41 Queens Gate, London, S.W.7; f. 1950 to advance the knowledge of biology; 1,100 Fellows, 15,000 mems.; Pres. Prof. J. R. Postgate;

Sec. D. J. B. Copp (from April 1982 P. N. O'Donoghue); publs. *Biologist, Journal of Biological Education.*

**Linnean Society of London:** Burlington House, Piccadilly, London, W1V 0LQ; f. 1788; c. 1,575 Fellows, 50 Foreign Members and 25 Hon Fellows, 40 Associates (under the age of 30) and 20 Student Associates (under the age of 25); Pres. Prof. W. T. Stearn; Secs. Dr. Doris M. Kermack (Zoology), Dr. D. F. Cutler (Botany); Exec. Sec. Miss M. E. Young; publs. *Botanical, Zoological and Biological Journals of the Linnean Society, Synopses of the British Fauna*; possesses the unique collection of Linnaeus's plants and animals (library: see Libraries).

**Malacological Society of London:** c/o Dept. of Science, Bristol Polytechnic, Redland Hill, Bristol, BS6 6UZ; f. 1893 to promote the study of Mollusca; 321 mems.; Pres. E. R. Trueman, D.SC.; publ. *Journal of Molluscan Studies* (3 a year).

**Marine Biological Association of the United Kingdom:** The Laboratory, Citadel Hill, Plymouth; f. 1884 to promote researches leading to the advancement of marine science in all branches of physical, chemical and biological oceanography; the Asscn. receives grants from universities and other public bodies and an annual grant-in-aid from the Natural Environment Research Council; 2,000 mems.; library of 50,000 vols.; Pres. Prof. J. Z. Young, D.SC., F.R.S.; Sec. and Dir. of Laboratory and Editor E. J. Denton, C.B.E., SC.D., F.R.S.; publs. *Journal, Marine Pollution Research Titles* (monthly).

**Physiological Society:** Dept. of Cardiovascular Studies, University of Leeds, Leeds, LS2 9JT (regd. office); f. 1876 to promote the advancement of physiology and facilitate the intercourse of physiologists at home and abroad; 1,323 mems.; Secs. Prof. T. J. Biscoe, Dept. of Physiology, University College, Gower St., London, WC1E 6BT, Dr. C. C. Michel, University Laboratory of Physiology, Parks Rd., Oxford, OX1 3PT; publs. *Journal of Physiology* (monthly), *Quarterly Journal of Experimental Physiology.*

**Royal Entomological Society of London:** 41 Queens Gate, London, SW7 5HU; f. 1833; 1,890 Fellows; library of 16,000 vols.; Pres. Prof. H. F. van Emden; Registrar G. G. Bentley; publs. *Ecological Entomology, Physiological Entomology, Systematic Entomology, Antenna* (quarterly bulletin), *Handbook for the Identification of British Insects* (irregular).

**Royal Society for the Protection of Birds:** The Lodge, Sandy, Bedfordshire SG19 2DL; f. 1889 (inc. 1904) to encourage the better conservation and protection of wild birds; 340,000 mems.; library of c. 5,000 vols.; Pres. E. M. Nicholson, C.B., C.V.O., LL.D.; Chair. D. C. Barber; Dir. Ian Prestt; publs. *Birds* (every 3 months), *Bird Life* (every 2 months), *Annual Report*, and occasional titles.

**Royal Zoological Society of Scotland:** Scottish National Zoological Park, Edinburgh, EH12 6TS; f. 1909, inc. by Royal Charter 1913, for the promotion and study of zoology and animal physiology, investigation and preservation of Scottish wild animal life, the establishment and maintenance of zoological parks or gardens in Scotland, etc.; 6,581 mems.; Pres. The Viscount of Arbuthnott; Dir. Roger J. Wheater; publs. *Annual Report, Illustrated Park Guide.*

**Scottish Marine Biological Association:** Dunstaffnage Marine Research Laboratory, Oban, Argyll, PA34 4AD; f. 1897 for research and education in marine science; 220 mems.; Dir. and Sec. R. I. Currie, C.B.E., B.SC., F.I.BIOL., F.R.S.E.; publs. *Annual Report, Fauna of the Clyde Sea Area†, Collected Reprints†.*

**Selborne Society:** f. 1885 to perpetuate the memory of Gilbert White of Selborne and to promote the study of natural history, especially amongst schoolchildren; 700 mems.; Hon. Sec. A. H. Austin, 10 Sunbeam Cottages, Pollards Wood Rd., Limpsfield, Oxted, Surrey, RH8 0HY; publ. *The Selborne Magazine* (quarterly).

**The Systematics Association:** f. 1937 to study systematics in relation to biology and evolution; Pres. Prof. A. J. Cain, M.A., D.PHIL.; Secs. G. P. Larwood, M.A., PH.D., F.G.S. (Palaeontology), Dept. of Geological Sciences, Durham Univ., Durham, F. A. Bisby, M.A., D.PHIL. (Botany); publs. works on taxonomy and classification.

**Zoological Society of London:** Regent's Park, London, NW1 4RY; f. 1826; 6,900 mems.; Pres. Prof. Lord Zuckerman, O.M., K.C.B., D.SC., F.R.S.; Sec. E. D. Barlow, M.A., M.B., B.CHIR., F.R.C.PSYCH.; publs. *Journal of Zoology†* (3 vols., annually), *Zoological Record* (annually), *International Zoo Yearbook†* (annually), *Nomenclator Zoologicus* (7 vols.), *Symposia†* (irregular), *Transactions†* (irregular). (See also Nuffield Laboratories of Comparative Medicine and Wellcome Laboratories of Comparative Physiology.)

Mathematics

**British Computer Society:** 13 Mansfield St., London, W1M 0BP; f. 1957 to promote knowledge of the development of computing machinery and related techniques, including digital and analogue machines and business and scientific applications; professional qualifications from 1968; 23,500 mems.; joint library with Instn. of Electrical Engineers (q.v.); Sec.-Gen. D. W. Harding; Registrar J. Southall; publs. *Computing* (weekly), *The Computer Journal* (quarterly), *The Computer Bulletin* (quarterly).

**British Society for the History of Mathematics:** provides a forum for all interested in the history and development of mathematics and related disciplines; organizes at least 3 conferences per year; 240 mems.; Pres. Dr. G. Flegg; Sec. Dr. A. J. Crilly, Middlesex Polytechnic, Queensway, Enfield, Middlesex, EN3 4SF.

**Institute of Mathematics and its Applications:** Maitland House, Warrior Square, Southend-on-Sea, Essex; f. 1964 to extend and diffuse knowledge of mathematics and of the applications of mathematics in science, engineering, economics, etc.; to promote education in mathematics; Pres. Dr. Peter Trier, C.B.E.; Sec. and Registrar Norman Clarke; publs. *IMA Journal of Applied Mathematics* (quarterly), *IMA Journal of Numerical Analysis* (quarterly), *Bulletin* (8 a year).

**Institute of Statisticians:** 36 Churchgate St., Bury St. Edmunds, Suffolk, IP33 1RD; f. 1948; professional and examining body; 2,500 mems. of whom 738 are Members and 411 are Fellows; Pres. Prof. Sir Roy Allen, K.B.E., M.A., D.SC.(ECON.), F.B.A.; Hon. Sec. W. Benjamin; publs. *The Statistician* (quarterly), *The Newsletter* (monthly).

**London Mathematical Society:** Burlington House, London, W1V 0NL; f. 1865 for the promotion and extension of mathematical knowledge; approx. 1,500 mems.; Pres. Prof. B. E. Johnson, F.R.S.; Hon. Secs. Dr. P. R. Goodey, Dr. R. A. Bailey; publs. *Journal* (quarterly), *Proceedings* (quarterly), *Bulletin* (6 a year).

Physical Sciences

**Association of Public Analysts:** 30 Russell Square, London, WC1B 5DT; f. 1953 for the furtherance of analytical chemistry in relation to the composition of foodstuffs, fertilizers, animal feeding stuffs, other areas of consumer protection; water, air and land pollution and other environmental matters; 100 mems.; Pres. R. A. Dalley, M.CHEM.A., C.CHEM., F.R.S.C., F.I.F.S.T.; Hon. Sec. J. B. Aldred, M.A., M.CHEM.A., C.CHEM., F.R.S.C., F.I.F.S.T., F.R.S.H.; publ. *Journal* (quarterly).

LEARNED SOCIETIES                                                                                         U.K. (GREAT BRITAIN)

**Biochemical Society, The:** 7 Warwick Court, London, WC1R 5DP; f. 1911 for the advancement of the science of biochemistry; 5,500 mems.; Chair. Prof. S. V. PERRY, F.R.S.; Exec. Sec. A. I. P. HENTON, F.C.I.S., F.I.L.; publs. *The Biochemical Journal* (fortnightly), *The Biochemical Society Transactions*, *Bioscience Reports* (monthly), *Clinical Science* (in conjunction with the Medical Research Society) (monthly), *Essays in Biochemistry* (annually), *Symposia* (annually), *Careers for Biochemists*.

**British Astronomical Association:** Burlington House, London, W1V 0NL; f. 1890; 5,000 mems.; publs. *Journal* and *Handbook*†.

**British Cryogenics Council, The:** c/o Institution of Chemical Engineers, George E. Davis Bldg., 165–171 Railway Terrace, Rugby, CV21 3HQ; f. 1967 to foster and stimulate the development and application of cryogenics in Britain by means of contacts, education and research; 14 mem. socs.; Chair. R. G. SEURLOCK; Hon. Sec. B. A. HANDS; publ. *British Cryogenics Council Newsletter* (quarterly).

**British Horological Institute:** Upton Hall, Upton, Newark, Notts. NG23 5TE; f. 1885 to promote the cultivation of the science of horology; c. 4,800 mems.; Pres. The MASTER OF THE WORSHIPFUL COMPANY OF CLOCKMAKERS; Sec. A. V. WALKER, F.B.H.I.; publ. *The Horological Journal* (monthly).

**British Interplanetary Society:** 27/29 South Lambeth Rd., London, SW8 1SZ; f. 1933 to promote space research and technology by the study of appropriate subjects, e.g. astronomy, rocket technology, electronics, and the dissemination of knowledge thereon; inc. 1945; mem. International Astronautical Federation; branches in U.K. and U.S.A.; 1,000 Fellows, 2,500 mems.; Pres. G. V. E. THOMPSON; Exec. Sec. L. J. CARTER, A.C.I.S.; publs. *Spaceflight* (monthly), *Journal* (monthly).

**British Nuclear Energy Society:** 1-7 Great George St., London, SW1P 3AA; f. 1962 in succession to British Nuclear Energy Conference to provide a forum for discussion, and directed to the broader aspects of nuclear energy, covering engineering and scientific disciplines; 12 constituent institutions; 1,100 mems.; publs. *Nuclear Energy* (6 a year), *Conference Proceedings*.

**Chemical Society:** see Royal Society of Chemistry.

**Geological Society:** Burlington House, Piccadilly, London, W1V 0JU; f. 1807; 5,871 Fellows; Pres. Prof. E. H. FRANCIS; Exec. Sec. R. M. BATEMAN; publs. *Journal*†, *Quarterly Journal of Engineering Geology*†, *Newsletter*, *Special Reports*, *Special Publications*, *Memoirs*, *A. Rep.*, miscellaneous papers; library: see Libraries.

**Geologists' Association:** Burlington House, Piccadilly, London, W1V 0JU; f. 1858 to foster the progress and diffusion of the science of geology and to encourage research and the development of new methods; c. 2,500 mems.; Pres. Prof. ALEC SMITH, PH.D., F.G.S.; Hon. Gen. Sec. W. J. FRENCH, PH.D., F.G.S.; publs. *Proceedings* (quarterly), *Circular* (every 6 weeks).

**Institute of Physics:** 47 Belgrave Square, London, SW1X 8QX; f. 1918, amalgamated with the Physical Society 1960; Chartered 1970; 16,000 mems.; aims to elevate the profession of physicist and to advance and diffuse a knowledge of physics pure and applied; Pres. Sir DENYS WILKINSON, PH.D., SC.D., F.INST.P., F.R.S.; Hon. Sec. E. R. DOBBS, D.SC., PH.D., F.INST.P.; Sec. L. COHEN, PH.D., F.INST.P.; publs. *Reports on Progress in Physics*, *Physics Bulletin*, *Physics in Medicine and Biology*, *Physics in Technology*, *Physics Education*, *Clinical Physics and Physiological Measurement*, *European Journal of Physics*, and *Journal of Physics Series A to G*.

**Institution of Nuclear Engineers:** 1 Penerley Rd., London, SE6 2LQ; f. 1959; 2,000 mems.; Pres. Prof. J. EDWARDS; Sec. Mrs. S. BLACKBURN, B.A., A.L.A.; publ. *The Nuclear Engineer* (every 2 months).

**Mineralogical Society of Great Britain and Ireland:** 41 Queen's Gate, London, SW7 5HR; f. 1876; c. 1,100 mems.; Pres. Prof. W. S. MACKENZIE; Gen. Sec. Dr. D. R. C. KEMPE; publs. *Mineralogical Magazine*, *Mineralogical Abstracts*, *Clay Minerals*, *Mineral Deposits of Europe* and monographs.

**Palaeontographical Society:** c/o Institute of Geological Sciences, Exhibition Rd., South Kensington, London, SW7 2DE; f. 1847 for the illustration and description of British fossils; Pres. Prof. D. T. DONOVAN, D.SC.; Sec. F. G. DIMES, B.SC.; publ. *Annual Volume* (monographs).

**Quekett Microscopical Club:** c/o British Museum (Natural History), Cromwell Rd., London, SW7 5BD; f. 1865 to encourage the study of every branch of microscopical science; 600 mems.; library of c. 1,000 vols.; publ. *Microscopy Q.M.C. Journal*† (2 a year).

**Royal Astronomical Society:** Burlington House, Piccadilly, London, W1V 0NL; f. 1820; granted Royal Charter in 1831; c. 2,800 mems.; Pres. Prof. A. W. WOLFENDALE, F.R.S.; Secs. Prof. R. D. DAVIES, Prof. J. A. JACOBS, Dr. CAROLE JORDAN; publs. *Monthly Notices* (monthly), *Geophysical Journal* (monthly), *Quarterly Journal* (quarterly); library: see Libraries.

**Royal Institute of Chemistry:** see Royal Society of Chemistry.

**Royal Meteorological Society:** James Glaisher House, Grenville Place, Bracknell, Berks., RG12 1BX; f. 1850; 2,700 mems.; library of 1,200 archival books; Pres. P. GOLDSMITH, M.A.; Secs. C. J. READINGS, PH.D., J. A. PYLE, PH.D., J. M. WALKER, M.SC.; publs. *Quarterly Journal*, *Journal of Climatology* (quarterly), *Weather* (monthly).

**Royal Microscopical Society:** 37/38 St. Clements, Oxford, OX4 1AJ; f. 1839 for the promotion of Microscopical Science and its applications; granted Royal Charter in 1866; 2,250 Fellows; Administrator Lt.-Col. P. G. FLEMING; publs. *Journal of Microscopy* (monthly) and *Proceedings* (every 2 months).

**Royal Physical Society of Edinburgh:** c/o Department of Genetics, University of Edinburgh; f. 1771, granted Royal Charter 1788, for the cultivation of the natural and physical sciences; originally covered the whole field of science, but, as other societies. formed, its scope has narrowed to natural history and palaeontology; now mainly concerned with experimental biology and genetics; approx. 160 mems.; Pres. Dr. H. KACSER; publ. *Proceedings* (irregularly).

**Royal Society of Chemistry:** Burlington House, London, W1V 0BN; f. 1980 from unification of the Chemical Society and the Royal Institute of Chemistry (f. 1841 and 1877 respectively); inc. by Royal Charter 1980; over 40,000 mems. (Fellows and Members (designated Chartered Chemists), Licentiates, Graduate Members and Assoc. mems., incl. 1,700 students); United Kingdom Chemical Information Service (UKCIS); library: see Libraries; Pres. Prof. Sir EWART JONES, PH.D., D.SC., C.CHEM., F.R.S.C., F.R.S.; Sec.-Gen. R. D. GUTHRIE, PH.D., D.SC., C.CHEM., F.R.S.C.; Registrar and Sec. for Public Affairs R. E. PARKER, PH.D., C.CHEM., F.R.S.C.; publs. *Chemistry in Britain* (monthly), *Professional Bulletin* (c. 9 a year), *Journal of the Chemical Society* (including Dalton, Faraday and Perkin Transactions and Chemical Communications), *Education in Chemistry*, translations of *Russian Journal of Physical Chemistry*, *Russian Journal of Inorganic Chemistry*, *Russian Chemical Reviews*, series of *Specialist Periodical Reports*.

**Society of Chemical Industry:** 14/15 Belgrave Square, London, SW1X 8PS; f. 1881, Royal Charter 1907;

5,500 mems.; Pres. Lord TODD, O.M., F.R.S.; Gen. Sec. Dr. D. H. SHARP; publs. *Chemistry and Industry* (twice monthly), *Journal of Chemical Technology and Biotechnology* (monthly), *Journal of the Science of Food and Agriculture* (monthly), *Critical Reports on Applied Chemistry*, *Pesticide Science* (every 2 months), *British Polymer Journal* (quarterly).

**Yorkshire Geological Society:** Department of Earth Sciences, The University, Leeds LS2 9JT; f. 1837; 1,200 mems.; library of 5,000 vols.; Pres. Prof. J. W. NEALE, D.SC.; Gen. Sec. J. M. NUNWICK, B.SC.; publ. *Proceedings* (2 a year).

### PHILOSOPHY AND PSYCHOLOGY

**Aristotelian Society:** f. 1880 for the systematic study of philosophy, its historic development and its methods and problems; 650 mems. and 100 subscribing libraries; Hon. Sec. A. A. KASSMAN, 31 West Heath Drive, London, NW11 7QG; publs. *Proceedings* (annual) and *Supplementary Volume* (annual).

**British Psychological Society:** St. Andrews House, 48 Princess Rd. East, Leicester, LE1 7DR; f. 1901; 10,000 mems.; Pres. Prof. D. E. BLACKMAN; Hon. Sec.-Gen. Dr. K. WHELDALL; publs. *Bulletin*, *British Journal of Psychology*, *British Journal of Medical Psychology*, *British Journal of Educational Psychology*, *British Journal of Mathematical & Statistical Psychology*, *British Journal of Social Psychology*, *British Journal of Clinical Psychology*, *Journal of Occupational Psychology*.

**British Society of Aesthetics:** c/o Dept. of Philosophy, Birkbeck College, Malet St., London, W.C.1; f. 1960 to promote study, research and discussion in aesthetics and the growth of artistic taste among the public; 300 mems.; Pres. Prof. Emer. RUTH L. SAW; Sec. BEN MARTIN-HOOGEWERF; publ. *The British Journal of Aesthetics* (quarterly).

**Experimental Psychology Society:** Dept. of Psychology, University of York, Heslington, York, YO1 5DD; f. 1947; to further scientific enquiry within the field of psychology; 325 mems.; Pres. Prof. R. L. GREGORY; Hon. Sec. Dr. E. MACPHAIL; publ. *Quarterly Journal of Experimental Psychology*.

**Leeds Philosophical and Literary Society Ltd.:** City Museum, Leeds, 1; f. 1820 for the advancement of knowledge in all its branches, excepting religion, politics and ethics; 100 mems.; Sec. A. C. CHADWICK; publ. *Proceedings*†.

**Manchester Literary and Philosophical Society:** 55 Brown St., Manchester, M2 2JG; f. 1781 for the advancement of literature and science; 500 mems.; Pres. DAVID G. WILSON; Hon. Secs. Prof. D. S. L. CARDWELL, Dr. B. S. H. RARITY; publ. *Memoirs and Proceedings*† (annually).

**Mind Association:** 108 Cowley Rd., Oxford, OX4 1JF; f. 1900 to publish the journal *Mind* (f. 1876; quarterly), and help organize annual conferences jointly with the Aristotelian Society (*q.v.*); Pres. Prof. G. BIRD; Hon. Sec. D. HOLDCROFT.

**National Institute of Industrial Psychology:** The Mere, Upton Park, Slough, Berks., SL1 2DQ; f. 1921 to ensure the maximum adjustment of the individual to his job by scientific methods of vocational counselling, selection and training, and the promotion of good industrial relations; Sec. J. A. FOX, F.C.I.S., M.I.P.M.

**Philosophical Society of England, The:** f. 1913 to help to spread a knowledge of practical philosophy among the general public; brs. in Scotland and U.S.A.; Pres. Canon A. HOLLOWAY, B.D., M.TH., F.PH.S.; Gen. Sec. Rev. Dr. EDGAR J. FORD, M.A., PH.D., "Epworth", Edwards Rd., Amesbury, Wilts.; publ. *The Philosopher*.

**Royal Institute of Philosophy:** 14 Gordon Square, London, WC1H 0AG; f. 1925; 1,000 mems.; Pres. The Rt. Hon. The Earl of HALSBURY, F.R.S.; Chair. Prof. H. D. LEWIS, M.A., B.LITT., D.D.; Dir. Prof. A. PHILLIPS-GRIFFITHS, B.A., B.PHIL.; Sec. JOAN M. JOYCE; publs. *Philosophy* (quarterly), collection of lectures given in preceding session (annually), *Conference Proceedings* (biennially).

**Royal Philosophical Society of Glasgow:** 6 Hughenden Terrace, Glasgow, W.2.; f. 1802; principal activity: lectures; 300 mems.; Pres. JAMES MCL. FRASER, B.SC., C.ENG., F.I.C.E., F.S.A.(SCOT.); Hon. Sec. J. M. A. LENIHAN, O.B.E., M.SC., PH.D., C.ENG., M.I.E.E., F.INST.P., F.R.S.E.; publ. *The Philosophical Journal* (twice yearly).

**Society for Psychical Research:** 1 Adam and Eve Mews, London, W8 6UG; f. 1882 for the purpose of making an organized and systematic attempt to investigate certain debatable phenomena which are *prima facie* inexplicable on any generally recognized hypothesis; 1,180 mems.; Pres. Prof. A. J. ELLISON; publs. *Proceedings* (irregularly), *Journal* (3 a year), and pamphlets.

**Verulam Institute:** Shopwyke Park, Chichester, Sussex; f. 1971 to promote critical thinking through the study of philosophy; to combat the subordination of the individual to authoritative structures; to reinforce a view of education as an activity formative of the whole personality; holds monthly meetings, public lectures, summer courses; Pres. ALEXANDER THYNN, Viscount WEYMOUTH, M.A.; Dir. A. W. HARRISON-BARBET, M.A., D.PHIL.

**The Victoria Institute or Philosophical Society of Great Britain:** 29 Queen St., London EC4R 1BH; f. 1865; Pres. Sir NORMAN ANDERSON, O.B.E., Q.C., M.A., LL.D., D.D., F.B.A.; Asst. Sec. BRIAN H. T. WELLER; publ. *Faith and Thought* (3 a year).

### RELIGION, SOCIOLOGY AND ANTHROPOLOGY

**African Studies Association of the United Kingdom:** c/o Centre of West African Studies, University of Birmingham, P.O.B. 363, Birmingham 15; f. 1963 to advance academic studies relating to Africa by providing facilities for the interchange of information and ideas; holds inter-disciplinary conferences and symposia; 500 mems.; Hon. Pres. Prof. T. O. RANGER; Hon. Sec. R. A. MAY; publ. *African Research and Documentation* (3 a year).

**Arab Research Centre:** 4th Floor, 1–2 Hanover St., London, WIR 9WB; f. 1979 to promote study of problems and issues in the Arab world; commissions academic papers and holds international symposia; 50 mems.; library of c. 600 vols.; Chair. ABDEL MAJID FARID; Man. EILEEN C. HICK; publ. *Arab Paper* series (10 a year).

**British Society for Middle Eastern Studies:** 68 Woodstock Rd., Oxford, OX2 6JF; f. 1973; to encourage and promote the study in the U.K. of the Middle Eastern cultural region from the end of classical antiquity through the dissemination of information and by the encouragement of co-operation among persons and organizations concerned with the scholarly study of the region; 250 mems.; Pres. Dr. G. L. LEWIS; Sec. Dr. D. HOPWOOD; publ. *Bulletin* (2 a year).

**British Sociological Association, The:** 10 Portugal St., London, WC2A 2HU; f. 1951 to promote interest in sociology, to advance its study and application in Britain, and to encourage contacts between workers in all relevant fields of enquiry; Pres. Prof. M. STACEY; Hon. Gen. Sec. Dr. H. ROBERTS.

**China Society:** 31B Torrington Square, London, WC1E 7JL; f. 1906 to encourage the study of the Chinese language, literature, history, folk-lore, art, etc.; c. 150

## LEARNED SOCIETIES

## U.K. (GREAT BRITAIN)

mems.; Chair. R. BURRELL, D.F.C.; Sec. Vice-Adm. Sir JOHN GRAY, K.B.E., C.B.

**Ecclesiological Society:** St. Ann's Vestry Hall, Carter Lane, London, E.C.4; f. 1839 as The Cambridge Camden Society; object: to study church architecture, furnishings, liturgy and music; 100 mems.; Pres. Very Rev. G. W. O. ADDLESHAW, Dean of Chester; Hon. Sec. Miss M. A. PRICE; publ. occasional papers.

**Eugenics Society:** 69 Eccleston Square, London, SW1V 1PJ; f. 1907 to promote the study of eugenics, genetics, population problems; approx. 400 mems.; 5,000 vols. in library; Pres. Prof. W. H. G. ARMYTAGE; Gen. Sec. Miss EILEEN WALTERS; publs. *Bulletin* (quarterly), *Symposium Proceedings* (annually) and occasional papers.

**Folklore Society:** c/o University College, Gower St., London, WC1E 6BT; f. 1878; about 1,000 mems. and subscribers; library of 11,000 vols.; Pres. Dr. W. M. S. RUSSELL, M.A., D.PHIL.; Hon. Sec. A. ROY VICKERY; publ. *Folklore* (2 a year).

**Hispanic and Luso-Brazilian Council:** Canning House, 2 Belgrave Square, SW1X 8PJ; f. 1943; Librarian M. C. YOUNGER, B.LIB., A.L.A.; library of over 50,000 vols. and over 300 periodicals on Portugal, Spain and Latin America; classes are held in Portuguese and courses are run in Spanish, and a close liaison is maintained with over 1,000 schools, colleges and universities in Great Britain; discussion meetings, lectures, films, recitals, economics seminars, etc., on Latin America, Portugal and Spain; Pres. The Viscount CALDECOTE, D.S.C.; Dir.-Gen. S. M. MACKENZIE, C.B.E., D.S.C.; publs. *British Bulletin of Publications on Latin America, The Caribbean, Portugal and Spain* (six-monthly), *Diamante* (annually).

**Institute of Community Studies:** 18 Victoria Park Square, London, E.2; f. 1954; social research on poverty, deprivation and comparative social policy; housing, urban planning and community; education; Dir. M. YOUNG, M.A., PH.D.

**Institute of Jewish Affairs:** 11 Hertford St., London, W1Y 7DX; f. 1941 New York, transferred to London 1966; to advance education in the field of human relationships with particular reference to the Jewish people and to the causes of racial and religious stress; research into current affairs, international legal problems, cultural issues, sociology of Jews and Jewish communities; library of 15,000 vols.; Pres. The Rt. Hon. Lord GOODMAN, C.H.; Chair. of Research Board The Rt. Hon. Lord LEVER, P.C.; Dir. Dr. S. J. ROTH; publs. *Soviet Jewish Affairs*†, *Christian-Jewish Relations*, *Patterns of Prejudice*†, *Research Reports*.

**Institute of Race Relations:** 247-249 Pentonville Rd., London, N.1.; f. 1958 to promote scientific study and publication on race and racism, and to make information and proposals available on race relations; library of 5,000 books and pamphlets, 900 journals, extensive press cuttings; Dir. A. SIVANANDAN; publ. *Race and Class* (quarterly).

**Maghreb Studies Association:** c/o The Secretary, Keith Sutton, Dept. of Geography, Univ. of Manchester, Oxford Rd., Manchester, M13 9PL; f. 1981 to promote the study of and interest in the Maghreb (North Africa) through lectures, conferences, occasional publs. and co-operation with the current periodical, *The Maghreb Review*; Chair. Prof. ERNEST GELLNER; Sec. KEITH SUTTON.

**Modern Churchmen's Union:** f. 1898 for the advancement of liberal religious thought; 600 mems.; Pres. the Very Rev. E. F. CARPENTER, Dean of Westminster; Chair. Canon A. L. DUNSTAN; Sec. Rev. F. E. COMPTON, The School House, Leysters, Leominster, Herefordshire, HR6 0HB; publ. *The Modern Churchman*† (quarterly).

**National Institute for Social Work:** 5 Tavistock Place, London WC1H 9SS; f. 1961 to advance study, research and experiment in social work; library of c. 15,000 vols.; Pres. Lord SEEBOHM; Chair. PETER M. BARCLAY; Principal DAVID JONES, O.B.E.; Registrar DAVID J. PRATT.

**National Society (Church of England):** Church House, Dean's Yard, Westminster, SW1P 3NZ; f. 1811; promotes religious education in accordance with the principles of the Church of England; Chair. The Bishop of BRISTOL; Gen. Sec. Canon R. M. WADDINGTON.

**Royal African Society:** 18 Northumberland Ave., London, WC2N 5BJ; f. 1901; c. 1,000 mems.; Pres. Rt. Hon. Lord SEEBOHM; Sec. Mrs. LAIMA SPEAKMAN-BROWN; publs. *Journal* (quarterly), *African Affairs*†.

**Royal Anthropological Institute of Great Britain and Ireland:** 56 Queen Anne St., London, W1M 9LA; f. 1843; 2,250 mems.; Pres. Prof. MICHAEL DAY; Dir. JONATHAN BENTHALL; Hon. Sec. Prof. ERIC SUNDERLAND; borrowing rights to library of 70,000 vols.; filmhire library; photographic archive; schools education programme; manages various trust funds; publs. *Man, the journal of the Royal Anthropological Institute*† (quarterly), *Anthropological Index* (quarterly), *Rain*† (bi-monthly), Occasional Papers, etc.

**Royal Asiatic Society of Great Britain and Ireland:** 56 Queen Anne St., London, W1M 9LA; f. 1823 for the study of the history, religions, institutions, customs, languages, literature and art of Asia; approx. 800 mems.; approx. 600 subscribing libraries; branches in various Eastern cities; Pres. Prof. Sir CYRIL PHILIPS, M.A.; Sec. Miss E. V. GIBSON; publs. *Journal* and monographs on Oriental subjects; library: see Libraries.

**Royal Commonwealth Society:** 18 Northumberland Ave., London, WC2N 5BJ; f. 1868; 24,000 mems.; Chair. of Central Council Sir ERIC NORRIS, K.C.M.G.; Sec.-Gen. A. S. H. KEMP, O.B.E.; publ. *Commonwealth* (bi-monthly).

**Royal Society for Asian Affairs:** 42 Devonshire St., London, W.1; f. 1901; 1,400 mems. with knowledge of, and interest in, Central Asia, Middle and Far East; library of about 6,000 vols.; Pres. The Lord GREENHILL OF HARROW, G.C.M.G., O.B.E.; Chair. Sir ARTHUR DE LA MARE, K.C.M.G., K.C.V.O.; Sec. Miss M. FITZSIMONS; publ. *Journal* (3 issues per annum).

**Swedenborg Society, The:** 20-21 Bloomsbury Way, London, WC1A 2TH; f. 1810 for the translation and publication of the writings of Emanuel Swedenborg, Swedish scientist, philosopher and theologian; approx. 1,000 mems.; Pres. PATRICK L. JOHNSON, R.I.B.A.; Sec. Miss MADELINE G. WATERS.

### TECHNOLOGY

**Association of Public Lighting Engineers:** 78 Buckingham Gate, London, SW1E 6PF; f. 1924, inc. 1928, to promote, encourage, and improve the science of efficient public lighting, and to facilitate the exchange of information and ideas on this subject; 1,115 mems.; Pres. B. RUSTON; Sec. Mrs. D. BARNES; publ. *Public Lighting* (quarterly).

**Biological Engineering Society:** c/o Hon. Sec. KEITH COPELAND, Royal College of Surgeons, Lincoln's Inn Fields, London, WC2A 3PN; f. 1960; objective is the collaboration between members of the physical and life sciences, also with industry and government depts., in the application of technology to medicine and biology; affiliated to Int. Fed. for Medical and Biological Engineering and to Council of Engineering Institutions; 600

mems.; Pres. D. W. HILL; publs. *Journal of Biomedical Engineering* (quarterly), *Proceedings of Conferences and Symposia*.

**British Ceramic Society:** Shelton House, Stoke Rd., Shelton, Stoke-on-Trent, Staffs., ST4 2DR; f. 1900 to promote and provide facilities for the advancement of the science of ceramics and its relation to industry, to bring into contact those engaged in ceramic science and industry and to collaborate with other organizations in these objects; 1,000 mems.; extensive library; Asst. Sec. D. E. ASHLEY; publs. *Transactions and Journal†*, *Proceedings†*.

**British Computer Society:** *see* under Mathematics.

**British Institute of Management:** Management House, Parker St., London, WC2B 5PT; f. 1947; the central national body for the study and promotion of good management; mems.: 12,000 companies, 70,000 individuals; library of 68,000 items, 300 periodicals; Dir.-Gen. ROY CLOSE; Sec. MICHAEL KIRK; publs. *Management Review and Digest* (quarterly), *Management Today* (monthly), *Library Bulletin* (every 2 months), surveys, reports, occasional papers, etc.

**British Society of Rheology:** f. 1940; 650 mems.; Pres. Prof. J. R. A. PEARSON; Hon. Sec. Dr. C. J. S. PETRIE, Dept. of Engineering Mathematics, Univ. of Newcastle upon Tyne, Newcastle upon Tyne, NE1 7RU; publs. *Rheology Abstracts*, *Bulletin* (quarterly).

**British Standards Institution:** 2 Park Street, London, W1A 2BS; formed 1901 as Engineering Standards Committee; inc. 1918 as British Engineering Standards Assgn., f. under Royal Charter in 1929 and Supplemental Charter in 1931 when scope was extended and present name adopted; organization for the preparation and promulgation of all national standards for industry, science and technology and for the presentation of the U.K. viewpoint on such standards internationally; over 14,000 subscribing mems.; Chair. of Exec. Board P. T. FLETCHER, C.B.E., F.ENG.; Dir.-Gen. D. G. SPICKERNELL, C.B., C.ENG.; publs. *B.S.I. News* (monthly), *Annual Report*, *British Standards and Codes of Practice*, *Yearbook*.

**Chartered Institute of Building, The:** Englemere, Kings Ride, Ascot, Berks., SL5 8BJ; f. 1834, new name 1980; professional institution for those who are (a) practising building production and engaged in the construction, alteration, maintenance and repair of buildings, (b) teaching building technology and management in educational establishments, (c) engaged in building research, and (d) undergoing training for a career in building production; 28,500 mems.; Pres. ROGER A. BURGESS, B.ARCH., F.C.I.O.B.; Chief Exec. DENNIS A. NEALE, O.B.E., M.C., F.B.I.M.; publs. *Building Technology and Management* (11 a year), *Construction Papers* (3 a year), *Yearbook & Directory of Members*, *List of Building Courses* (annually), occasional papers, etc.

**Chartered Institute of Patent Agents:** Staple Inn Bldgs., High Holborn, London, WC1V 7PZ; f. 1882, chartered 1891; professional and examining body; 1,677 mems., 167 students; Sec. Miss M. E. POOLE, M.A.; publs. *CIPA* (monthly), *Register of Patent Agents* (annually).

**Chartered Institute of Transport:** 80 Portland Place, London, W1N 4DP; f. 1919, inc. by Royal Charter 1926 to promote, encourage, and co-ordinate the study and advancement of the science and art of transport in all its branches, and to provide a source of authoritative views on transport; c. 17,000 mems.; brs. in Australia, Ghana, Hong Kong, Ireland, Malawi, Malaysia, New Zealand, Nigeria, Pakistan, Singapore and South Africa; library of 15,000 vols.; Pres. J. G. DAVIS; Dir.-Gen. Brigadier D. N. LOCKE, O.B.E.; publ. *Transport* (every 2 months).

**Chartered Institution of Building Services:** Delta House 222 Balham High Rd., London, SW12 9BS; f. 1897 for the promotion of the science and practice of such engineering services as are associated with the built environment and industrial processes; incorporates Illuminating Engineering Society (from 1978); 10,000 mems.; Pres. P. A. COLES, M.A., C.ENG., F.C.I.B.S.; Sec. B. A. HODGES, O.B.E., B.A., F.C.I.B.S.; publs. *Building Services* (monthly), *Lighting Research and Technology* (quarterly), *Building Services Engineering Research and Technology* (quarterly), technical guides and codes (irregular).

**Confederation of British Industry:** Centre Point, 103 New Oxford St., London, WC1A 1DU; *Education and Training Committee:* to keep under review policies in the whole field of education and training as they affect industry and commerce and to take any necessary action; Chair. Lord CARR OF HADLEY; Sec. D. STANLEY; *Research and Technology Committee:* to recommend industrial policy relating to research and technology, and to take any necessary action; Chair. Sir AUSTIN E. BIDE; Sec. Dr. R. J. S. GREEN; *Universities, Polytechnics and Industry Joint Committee:* to keep under review matters of common interest and concern and to take any necessary action; Chair. Dr. B. C. L. WEEDON; *Production Committee:* to recommend policy relating to industrial production including relations with Government depts., control of quality, reliability, standards, metric system and industrial design, and to take any necessary action; Chair. I. D. GARDINER; Sec. Miss A. HUMBERSTONE.

**Ergonomics Society:** f. 1949 to provide a common meeting ground for those engaged in the study of psychology, physiology and human anatomy as applied to practical problems; 20 hon. mems., 640 ordinary mems., 53 Associate mems., 155 student mems., 47 affiliated organizations; Chair. Dr. I. D. BROWN; Sec. G. SIMMONDS, 43 The Westerings, Hockley, Essex, SS5 4NY; publs. *Ergonomics*, *Applied Ergonomics*, *Ergonomic Abstracts*, *The Ergonomist*.

**Gemmological Association of Great Britain, Inc.:** Saint Dunstan's House, Carey Lane, London, EC2V 8AB; f. 1931 for promotion of the study of gemmology and the scientific and industrial study of all materials and articles used or dealt in by persons interested in the science of gems; Pres. Sir FRANK CLARINGBULL, PH.D., F.INST.P., F.G.A.; Chair. DAVID J. CALLAGHAN, F.G.A.; Sec. H. J. WHEELER, F.G.A.; publ. *Journal of Gemmology* (quarterly).

**Institute of Ceramics:** Federation House, Station Rd., Stoke-on-Trent, Staffs., ST4 2RT; f. 1955 to promote art and science as applied to the Ceramic Industries, to improve the knowledge of those engaged therein and to facilitate the exchange of information and ideas; 1,250 mems.; Pres. Prof. J. P. ROBERTS; Hon. Sec. R. HARRISON; publ. *Journal* (annually).

**Institute of Energy:** 18 Devonshire St., Portland Place, London. W1N 2AU; f. 1927, Royal Charter 1946, to promote the advancement of energy technology; corporation mem. of Council of Engineering Institutions; 6,000 mems.; publs. *Journal* (quarterly), *Energy World* (monthly), conference proceedings, etc.

**Institute of Food Science and Technology of the United Kingdom:** 105–111 Euston St., London, NW1 2ED; f. 1964 to promote the knowledge, development and application of science and technology of food, the provision of a professional body for food scientists and technologists in the furtherance of their education and training; 2,550 mems.; Pres. E. J. ROLFE; Hon. Sec. R. L.

Stephens; Exec. Sec. H. G. Wild; publs. *The Journal of Food Technology* (every 2 months), *Focus* (quarterly), *The Proceedings of the Institute* (quarterly).

**Institute of Management Services:** 1 Cecil Court, London Rd., Enfield, Middx., EN2 6DD; f. 1941; professional and examining body; 20,000 mems.; library of 3,500 vols. and 225 information folders; Pres. Sir Monty Finniston; Chair. Harold Williams; Dir. and Gen. Sec. E. A. King, f.c.i.s.; publ. *Management Services* (monthly).

**Institute of Marine Engineers:** 76 Mark Lane, London, EC3R 7JN; f. 1889 to promote the scientific development of marine engineering in all its branches; library; technical information service; Pres. J. McNaught; Dir. and Sec. J. Stuart Robinson; publs. *Technical Reports, Marine Engineers Review* (monthly).

**Institute of Measurement and Control:** 20 Peel St., London, W8 7PD; f. 1944 as Society of Instrument Technology; inc. by Royal Charter 1975; to promote the advancement of the science and practice of measurement and control and its application; to co-ordinate and disseminate information and to conduct examinations; 6,220 mems.; Pres. Prof. L. Finkelstein, m.sc., c.eng., m.i.e.e., f.inst.m.c.; Sec. E. Eden, m.a. (Oxon.); publs. *Measurement and Control* (monthly), *Transactions* (quarterly).

**Institute of Petroleum:** 61 New Cavendish St., London, W1M 8AR; f. 1913 to promote, encourage, and co-ordinate the study of petroleum and its allied products, and to accumulate and disseminate information and knowledge relating thereto; 7,000 mems.; library of 15,000 books and 200 journals; Pres. Sir Nevil Macready; Gen. Sec. D. C. Payne; publs. *Petroleum Review* (monthly), *IP Standards for Petroleum and its Products* (annual), *Safety Codes*, etc.

**Institute of Quarrying:** 7 Regent St., Nottingham, NG1 5BY; f. 1917; professional body to provide a professional qualification, to improve science and practice of quarrying and to provide a forum for technical discussion; over 4,000 home and overseas mems.; Dir. B. G. Fish, m.sc., c.eng., f.i.min.e., f.i.m.m.; Sec. R. Oates; publs. *Quarry Management and Products* (monthly), *Register of Members*.

**Institute of Refrigeration:** 76 Mill Lane, Carshalton, Surrey, SM5 2JR; f. 1899 (as the Cold Storage and Ice Association) for the general advancement of refrigeration in all its applications; c. 2,300 mems.; Pres. Prof. G. G. Haselden; Sec. M. J. Horlick; publ. *Proceedings*.

**Institute of Science Technology:** Staple Inn Buildings, South, 335 High Holborn, London, WC1V 7PX; f. 1954 from the Science Technologists' Assen. (f. 1948); professional and qualifying body for laboratory technicians; 4,100 mems.; Pres. Dr. A. Nechvatal, d.sc., m.sc., ph.d.; Hon. Sec. B. C. V. Mitchley, m.i.biol., f.i.s.t.; publ. *Science Technology* (every 2 months).

**Institute of Water Pollution Control, The:** Ledson House, 53 London Rd., Maidstone, Kent ME16 8JH; f. 1901; 2,700 mems.; Pres. G. E. Eden; Exec. Sec. Howard R. Evans; publ. *Water Pollution Control* (5 a year).

**Institution of Chemical Engineers, The:** 165-171 Railway Terrace, Rugby, CV21 3HQ; f. 1922, inc. by Royal Charter to promote the science and practice of chemical engineering, to improve the standards and methods of education therein, and to act as a qualifying body for chemical engineers, etc.; approx. 13,000 mems.; Pres. P. N. Rowe; Gen. Sec. J. T. Evans, ph.d.; publs. *Transactions* (quarterly), and *The Chemical Engineer* (monthly), *Diary* (monthly).

**Institution of Civil Engineers:** 1-7 Great George St., Westminster, London, SW1P 3AA; f. 1818; inc. by Royal Charter in 1828 for the general advancement of mechanical science and more particularly for promoting the acquisition of that species of knowledge which constitutes the profession of a Civil Engineer, being the art of directing the great sources of power in Nature for the use and convenience of man; c. 62,000 corporate and non-corporate mems.; library of 85,000 vols., 22,000 pamphlets; Pres. I. M. Campbell, c.v.o., b.sc.eng., f.eng.; Sec. Robert Campbell; publs. include *Proceedings Part 1: Design and Construction, Part 2: Research and Theory* (each quarterly), *New Civil Engineer* (weekly), *Geotechnique* (quarterly), *Offshore Engineer* (monthly), *International New Civil Engineer* (monthly), *World Water* (6 a year), *ICE Abstracts* (10 a year).

**Institution of Electrical Engineers:** Savoy Place, London, WC2R 0BL; f. in 1871 and inc. by Royal Charter in 1921 to promote the general advancement of electrical science and engineering and their applications, and to facilitate the exchange of information and ideas on those subjects; c. 78,000 mems.; Pres. Sir Francis Tombs, b.sc.(econ.), f.eng., f.i.e.e.; Sec. H. H. W. Losty, f.eng., f.i.e.e.; publs. *Electronics and Power*† (22 issues a year), *Proceedings IEE*† (monthly), *Electronics Record*†, *Control and Science Record*†, *Power Record*† (all quarterly), *Electronics Letters*† (fortnightly), *Science Abstracts*: (a) *Physics Abstracts* (fortnightly), (b) *Electrical and Electronics Abstracts* (monthly), (c) *Computer and Control Abstracts* (monthly), *Current Papers series:* (a) in *Physics* (fortnightly), (b) in *Electrical and Electronics Engineering* (monthly), (c) in *Computers and Control* (monthly), etc.; library: see Libraries.

**Institution of Electronic and Radio Engineers:** 99 Gower St., London, WC1E 6AZ; f. 1925, inc. by Royal Charter 1961, to promote the advancement of the science of radio and electronic engineering and their applications, to facilitate the exchange of information and ideas on these subjects, to conduct examinations in all branches of radio and electronic engineering; 13,065 mems.; Sec. Air Vice-Marshal S. M. Davidson, c.b.e.; publs. *The Radio and Electronic Engineer* (monthly), *The Electronics Engineer* (fortnightly).

**Institution of Electronics:** Pennine House, 78 Shaw Rd., Rochdale, Lancs.; f. 1930, inc. 1935, for the furtherance of the science of electronics and other scientific subjects; over 2,500 mems.; Gen. Sec. W. Birtwistle, m.inst.e.; publ. *Proceedings* (quarterly).

**Institution of Engineering Designers:** Courtleigh, Westbury Leigh, Westbury, Wilts., BA13 3TA; f. 1945 to advance education in engineering, particularly in engineering design and to constitute a body of members qualified to a recognized high standard; 8,000 mems.; Sec. P. J. Booker, m.i.e.d.; publ. *The Engineering Designer* (6 a year).

**Institution of Engineers and Shipbuilders in Scotland:** 183 Bath St., Glasgow, G2 4HT; f. 1857 to facilitate the exchange of information and ideas amongst its mems., and to promote the advancement of the science and practice of engineering and shipbuilding; 1,200 mems.; Pres. B. N. Baxter, ph.d., c.eng.; Sec. W. McLaughlin, m.b.e., c.eng.; publs. *Transactions* (annually), *Year Book and List of Members* (biennial).

**Institution of Fire Engineers:** 148 New Walk, Leicester, LE1 7QB; f. 1918, inc. 1924, to promote, encourage, and improve the science of fire engineering and fire technology; 8,500 home and overseas mems.; Pres. R. A. Haley; Sec. D. S. Ramsey; publ. *The Fire Engineer's Journal*.

**Institution of Gas Engineers:** 17 Grosvenor Crescent, London, SW1X 7ES; f. 1863; Royal Charter 1929, to promote by research, discussion, education or otherwise as may seem to the Institution desirable each and all of the sciences of which knowledge may from time to time be required for the better production, distribution or utilization of gas and of the by-products of its production; 6,000 mems.; library of over 10,000 vols.; Pres. R. EVANS, C.ENG.; publs. *Gas Engineering and Management* (monthly).

**Institution of Highway Engineers:** 3 Lygon Place, London, S.W.1; f. 1930 to promote the furtherance, consideration and discussion of all questions affecting the profession of Highway and Transportation Engineering; 9,000 mems.; Pres. R. J. BRIDLE; Sec. Miss P. A. STEEL; publ. *Monthly Journal*.

**Institution of Mechanical and General Technician Engineers:** 33 Ovington Square, London, SW3 1LJ; f. 1884; as the Vulcanic Society, then as the Junior Institution of Engineers, present name 1976; a qualifying body for T.Eng. (CEI) and Tech. (CEI) registration with the Engineers' Registration Board; to promote education in the field of engineering and allied sciences; lectures, visits to places of technical interest; 4,000 mems.; library of *c*. 5,000 vols.; Pres. Sir CHARLES PRINGLE, K.B.E., F.ENG., F.R.AE.S.; Sec. M. F. LUETCHFORD; publ. *General Engineer*† (monthly).

**Institution of Mechanical Engineers:** 1 Birdcage Walk, London, SW1H 9JJ; f. 1847, inc. by Royal Charter 1930; amalgamated with the Institution of Automobile Engineers and Institution of Locomotive Engineers which form its Automobile Division and Railway Division; 75,000 mems.; library of 155,000 vols.; Pres. DAVID PENNY, F.ENG., F.I.MECH.E.; Sec. ALEX MCKAY, C.B., C.ENG., MEM.A.S.M.E., F.I.MECH.E., F.I.E.E., F.B.I.M.; publs. *Chartered Mechanical Engineer, Mechanical Engineering News* (monthly), *Automotive Engineer, Journal of Mechanical Engineering Science* (every 2 months), *Engineering in Medicine, Journal of Strain Analysis, Proceedings* (quarterly).

**Institution of Metallurgists, The:** Northway House, Whetstone, London, N20 9LW; f. 1945 to bring within one professional body qualified metallurgists engaged in production, research, teaching, consulting work, etc.; to promote the initial qualification, continued education and training of metallurgists; residential courses at least three times a year; *c*. 10,000 mems.; Pres. PETER HOULDCROFT; Registrar-Sec. T. B. MARSDEN, PH.D., C.ENG., F.I.M.; publs. *The Metallurgist and Materials Technologist* (monthly), educational monographs, course proceedings, audio-visual teaching aids and careers literature.

**Institution of Mining and Metallurgy:** 44 Portland Place, London, W1N 4BR; f. 1892 for the advancement of the science and practice of mining, mineral technology, mineral exploitation and mining geology in respect of minerals other than coal, and of metallurgy in respect of metals other than iron; and to afford a means of facilitating the acquisition and preservation of the knowledge which pertains to the professions associated therewith; organizes meetings and conferences worldwide; administers scholarships and fellowships; maintains a specialist library of 50,000 vols., and offers information services; mems. in *c*. 100 countries; Pres. G. R. DAVIS; Sec. M. J. JONES; publs. *IMM Bulletin*†, *Transactions of the Institution of Mining and Metallurgy*† (monthly), *IMM Abstracts*† (every 2 months), special volumes of proceedings of conferences and symposia.

**Institution of Mining Engineers:** Hobart House, Grosvenor Place, London, SW1X 7AE; f. 1889, inc. by Royal Charter 1915, for the advancement of the science of engineering in relation to coal and iron ore mining, and the promotion of the acquisition of the scientific knowledge necessary for the control and direction of mining operations in relation to stratified deposits; approx. 4,000 mems.; Sec. G. R. STRONG; publ. *The Mining Engineer*† (monthly).

**Institution of Municipal Engineers:** 25 Eccleston Square, London, SW1V 1NX; f. 1873, inc. by Royal Charter 1948, to promote the science of engineering and allied subjects as applied to the duties imposed upon and services undertaken by local authorities and other public undertakings for the benefit of the community with the object of securing the highest degree of efficiency; 10,500 mems.; Pres. C. R. ATKINSON, B.SC.(ENG.); Sec. J. R. SPAREY, M.A.; publ. *Chartered Municipal Engineer* (monthly).

**Institution of Plant Engineers:** 138 Buckingham Palace Rd., London, SW1W 9SG; f. 1946: professional body; 8,927 mems.; Pres. S. BENSON, C.ENG., F.INST.E.; Sec. J. K. BENNETT, F.C.I.S., F.R.S.A., F.INST.A.M., F.S.A.E.; publ. *The Plant Engineer*.

**Institution of Production Engineers:** Rochester House, 66 Little Ealing Lane, London, W5 4XX; f. 1921, inc. by Royal Charter 1964, to promote the science and practice of production engineering; *c*. 20,000 mems.; Pres. Dr. ROBERT LICKLEY, C.B.E., F.R.S.E., F.ENG., F.I.PROD.E.; publs. *The Production Engineer* (monthly), *The International Journal of Production Research* (quarterly).

**Institution of Public Health Engineers:** 13 Grosvenor Place, London, SW1X 7EN; f. 1895; 3,400 mems.; Pres. E. W. FLAXMAN, B.SC.; Chair. J. C. CLANCY, O.B.E., B.E.M.; Sec. I. B. MUIRHEAD, B.COM.; publ. *The Public Health Engineer* (quarterly).

**Institution of Structural Engineers:** 11 Upper Belgrave St., London, SW1X 8BH; f. 1908, inc. by Royal Charter 1934, to promote the general advancement of the science and art of structural engineering; library of 8,500 vols.; over 14,000 mems.; Pres. T. N. W. AKROYD, M.SC.TECH., LL.B., C.ENG., F.I.STRUCT.E., M.I.C.E.; Sec. C. D. MORGAN, O.B.E., F.C.I.S.; publs. *The Structural Engineer* (monthly), *Year Book and Directory of Members* and *Technical Reports* (as issued).

**Institution of Water Engineers and Scientists:** 6–8 Sackville St., London, W1X 1DD; f. 1896, inc. 1911, to advance water engineering and science; to promote education, study and research therein and to publish the results for public benefit; *c*. 5,500 mems.; Pres. E. C. REED, O.B.E., D.F.C., F.I.C.E.; Sec. J. P. BANBURY, M.B.E.; publs. *Water Practice Manuals, Journal* (every 2 months).

**Joint Committee for Higher National Certificates and Diplomas in Metallurgy:** The Joint Committee Unit, City and Guilds of London Institute, 46 Britannia St., London, WC1X 9RG; f. 1945; includes representatives of The Metals Society, The Institution of Mining and Metallurgy, The Technician Education Council, The Institution of Metallurgists, Dept. of Education and Science, Ministry of Education of Northern Ireland; administers the award of Higher National Certificates and Higher National Diplomas in Metallurgy (excluding Scotland); Chair. Dr. S. G. COPE; Sec. Miss S. M. ANDREWS.

**Metals Society, The:** 1 Carlton House Terrace, London, SW1Y 5DB; f. 1974 following a merger of The Institute of Metals and the Iron and Steel Institute; Sec. R. B. WOOD, B.A.

**National Society for Clean Air:** 136 North St., Brighton, Sussex; f. in 1899 as Coal Smoke Abatement Society and amalgamated with the Smoke Abatement League of Great Britain in 1929; 1,500 mems., incl. learned societies, local authorities, industrial concerns, etc.; library of 1,000 vols., photographic collection; Pres. Sir DEREK EZRA, M.B.E.; Sec.-Gen. Air Commodore A. C. LANGSTON, C.B.E.; publs. *Clean Air*† (quarterly), *NSCA Members' Handbook, Proceedings of Annual Conferences and Seminars*, reports.

**Newcomen Society for the Study of the History of Engineering and Technology:** Science Museum, South Kensington, London, SW7 2DD; f. 1920 to encourage and foster study of the history of engineering and technology in all parts of the world; c. 1,000 mems.; Hon. Sec. L. R. DAY, M.SC.; Exec. Sec. IAN MCNEIL, M.A.; publs. *Transactions* (annually), *Bulletin* (3 a year).

**Oil and Colour Chemists' Association:** Priory House, 967 Harrow Rd., Wembley, Middx., HA0 2SF; f. 1918 to promote by discussion and scientific investigation the technology of the paint, oil, printing ink, and allied industries; c. 3,000 mems.; Pres. D. J. MORRIS; Dir. and Sec. R. H. HAMBLIN, M.A., F.C.I.S.; publs. *Journal* (monthly), *Introduction to Paint Technology*, *Paint Technology Manuals*, *Annual OCCA Exhibition Guide*, *Monographs*, *UV Polymerization 1+2*.

**Photogrammetric Society, The:** Dept. of Photogrammetry and Surveying, University College, Gower St., London, WC1E 6BT; f. 1952; theory, techniques, instrumentation, applications in surveying, engineering, etc.; 650 mems.; Pres. D. W. PROCTOR; Hon. Sec. O. W. CHEFFINS; publ. *The Photogrammetric Record* (2 a year).

**Plastics and Rubber Institute, The:** 11 Hobart Place, London, SW1W 0HL; f. 1975; amalgamation of the Plastics Institute and the Institution of the Rubber Industry; to advance the standards and methods of education in the fields of plastics, rubber and allied industries and to promote the development of the art, science and technologies of these subjects by facilitating the exchange of information; acts as a qualifying body for plastics and rubber technologists; over 11,000 mems.; Pres. S. GIBBS, C.B.E., F.P.R.I.; Chair. P. W. JACOB, F.P.R.I.; Sec.-Gen. J. N. RATCLIFFE, F.C.I.S.; publs. *Plastics & Rubber International* (every 2 months), *Plastics and Rubber: Processing and Applications* (quarterly), technical monographs, conference proceedings.

**Radio Society of Great Britain:** 35 Doughty St., London WC1N 2AE; f. 1913 to promote interest in the science of radio-communication by amateurs, and to safeguard the interests of those of its members who operate or aspire to operate amateur transmitting stations; c. 30,000 mems.; Gen. Man. D. A. EVANS; publ. *Radio Communication* (monthly).

**Royal Aeronautical Society:** 4 Hamilton Place, London, W1V 0BQ; f. 1886; 13,000 mems.; library of 25,000 vols.; Pres. J. T. STAMPER; Sec. E. M. J. SCHAFFTER, M.A., C.ENG., M.R.AE.S.; publs. *Aeronautical Journal* (monthly), *Aeronautical Quarterly*, *Aerospace* (monthly), *Data Sheets*.

**Royal Institution of Naval Architects, The:** 10 Upper Belgrave St., London, SW1X 8BQ; f. 1860, inc. 1910 and 1960 to promote the improvement of ships; c. 6,600 mems.; Pres. Admiral Sir ANTHONY GRIFFIN, G.C.B.; Sec. P. W. AYLING, B.SC., C.ENG.; publs. *Transactions* (annually), *The Naval Architect* (every 2 months), *Maritime Technology Monographs* (irregular), occasional publications and symposium proceedings.

**Royal Television Society:** Tavistock House East, Tavistock Square, WC1H 9HR; f. 1927 for the furtherance of the arts and sciences of television; over 2,500 mems.; Pres. Sir HUW WHELDON, O.B.E., M.C.; Chair. P. J. SIDEY; publ. *Television* (every 2 months).

**Society of Consulting Marine Engineers and Ship Surveyors:** 6 Lloyds Ave., London, EC3N 3AX; f. 1920 to provide a central organization for consulting engineers, naval architects and ship surveyors, and generally to elevate the status and procure the advancement of the interests of the profession; Pres. P. B. HARRISON; Sec. M. M. CAMPBELL.

**Society of Dyers and Colourists:** Perkin House, P.O.B. 244, Grattan Rd., Bradford, W. Yorks., BD1 2JB; f. 1884 to promote the advancement of the science and technology of colour and colouration; approx. 4,200 mems. and subscribers; Pres. Dr. J. V. BUTCHER, C.CHEM., M.R.S.C., C.COL., F.S.D.C.; Chief Exec. and Gen. Sec. Dr. M. TORDOFF, C.CHEM., F.R.S.C., A.C.I.S.; publs. *Journal of the Society of Dyers and Colourists* (monthly), *Review of Progress in Coloration and Related Topics* (annually), *Colour Index, Additions and Amendments* (quarterly), various textbooks.

**Society of Engineers (Inc.), The:** 21/23 Mossop St., London, SW3 2LW; f. 1854 to promote the science and practice of engineering, etc.; 5,000 mems.; library of 2,000 vols.; Pres. J. A. GARDNER, B.A., F.S.E., P.ENG.; Sec. E. C. BURTON, M.INST.A.M.; publ. *Journal and Transactions*.

**Society of Professional Engineers Ltd.:** 21/23 Mossop St., London, SW3 2LW; f. 1969 to provide a professional register; Pres. V. C. EALEY, M.S.E., P.ENG.; Sec. E. C. BURTON, M.INST.A.M.

**Society of Glass Technology:** "Thornton", 20 Hallam Gate Rd., Sheffield, S10 5BT; f. 1916 to promote the association of persons interested in glass technology; approx. 1,250 mems.; library of 9,000 vols.; Hon. Sec. T. S. BUSBY, B.SC., F.G.S., F.I.CERAM., F.S.G.T.; publs. *Glass Technology*†, *Physics and Chemistry of Glasses*† (bi-monthly).

**Society of Licensed Aircraft Engineers and Technologists:** Grey Tiles, Kingston Hill, Kingston upon Thames, Surrey, KT2 7LW; f. 1944; technical and professional body; 6,500 mems.; Pres. A. G. PARRY, B.SC., C.ENG., M.R.AES., F.S.L.AE.T.; Exec. Dir. J. R. FINNIMORE, M.V.O., C.ENG., F.R.AE.S., F.C.I.T.

**South Wales Institute of Engineers:** Institute Buildings, Park Place, Cardiff, CF1 3UG; f. 1857 for the encouragement and advancement of engineering science and practice; 700 mems.; Pres. Prof. H. K. M. LLOYD, PH.D., F.I.M.; Hon. Sec. T. G. DASH, J.P., C.ENG., F.I.MECH.E., F.I.E.E., F.I.MIN.E.; publ. *Proceedings* (yearly).

**Textile Institute (The):** see under International.

**Welding Institute (The)** (formerly *British Welding Research Association* f. 1945 and *Institute of Welding* f. 1923): Head office and research station: Abington Hall, Cambridge, CB1 6AL; London office: 54 Princes Gate, SW7 2PG; f. 1968 to undertake general and contract research, to advance welding technology in all aspects, to provide consultancy and laboratory services for members, to provide education and training and to improve the professional status and qualification of members; 1,500 research mems.; 5,000 professional mems.; 5,000 vols. in library; specialized information services; Dir.-Gen. A. A. WELLS, F.R.S., F.ENG., PH.D., C.ENG., M.I.MECH.E., F.WELD.I.; publs. *Research Bulletin* (monthly), *Metal Construction* (monthly).

# RESEARCH INSTITUTES

(*see* also under Universities)

### Agriculture and Veterinary Science

**Agricultural Research Council:** 160 Gt. Portland St., London, W1N 6DT; f. by Royal Charter in 1931; under the Secretary of State for Education and Science and the Ministry of Agriculture, Fisheries and Food; Chair. Lord PORCHESTER, K.B.E., D.L.; Sec. Dr. RALPH RILEY, F.R.S.; publs. *Index of Agricultural Research, The Agricultural Research Service, Report of the Agricultural Research Council, Research Briefs.*

The Council controls the following institutes and units:

**Animal Breeding Research Organisation:** King's Buildings, West Mains Rd., Edinburgh, EH9 3JQ; Dir. J. W. B. KING, PH.D.; Sec. A. B. TOTTY, B.A.

**Institute for Research on Animal Diseases:** Compton, Newbury, Berks., RG16 0NN; Dir. Dr. J. M. PAYNE, PH.D.; Sec. D. J. CRAIG, A.C.I.S., D.M.S.

**Institute of Animal Physiology:** Babraham, Cambridge, CB2 4AT; Dir. B. A. CROSS, M.A., PH.D., SC.D.; Sec. B. E. FAULKNER.

**Letcombe Laboratory:** Wantage, Oxfordshire, OX12 9JT; Dir. J. V. LAKE, PH.D.; Sec. E. A. TYRER, D.S.C.

**Poultry Research Centre:** Roslin, Midlothian, EH25 9PS; Dir. D. W. F. SHANNON, PH.D., D.M.S.; Sec. A. I. MENZIES.

**Statistics Group:** Dept. of Applied Biology, Pembroke St., Cambridge, CB2 3DX; under supervision of J. G. ROWELL, M.A.

**Unit of Invertebrate Chemistry and Physiology:** University of Sussex, Falmer, Brighton, Sussex, BN1 9QJ; Hon. Dir. Prof. A. W. JOHNSON, D.SC., SC.D.; Sub-Division: University of Cambridge, Zoology Dept., Downing St., Cambridge, CB2 3EJ; Hon. Assoc. Dir. J. E. TREHERNE, PH.D., SC.D.

**Unit of Nitrogen Fixation:** The Chemical Laboratory, University of Sussex, Falmer, Brighton, Sussex, BN1 9QT; Dir. Prof. J. POSTGATE, F.R.S.; Sec. J. A. DURRANT.

**Unit of Statistics (ARCUS):** Univ. of Edinburgh, James Clerk Maxwell Building, King's Buildings, Mayfield Rd., Edinburgh, EH9 3JZ; Hon. Dir. Prof. D. J. FINNEY, C.B.E., M.A., SC.D., F.R.S., F.R.S.E.; Sec. E. M. HEYBURN.

**Food Research Institute:** Colney Lane, Norwich, NR4 7UA; Dir. R. F. CURTIS, PH.D., D.SC.; Sec. V. H. STANDLEY, D.M.A., M.I.L.G.A.

**Meat Research Institute:** Langford, Nr. Bristol, BS18 7DY; Dir. Prof. A. J. BAILEY, PH.D., SC.D.; Sec. C. A. BLUNT.

**Weed Research Organization:** Begbroke Hill, Sandy Lane, Yarnton, Oxford, OX5 1PF; Dir. J. D. FRYER, C.B.E., M.A.; Sec. B. A. WRIGHT, A.M.B.I.M.

---

**Agricultural Scientific Services:** Department of Agriculture and Fisheries for Scotland, East Craigs, Edinburgh, EH12 8NJ; scientific executive work, associated research and consultation on: seed testing, testing of candidate varieties of crop plants for National Listing and Plant Breeders' Rights, certification of seed and planting stock, production of disease-tested clonal stocks of seed potatoes, statutory aspects of pest and disease control, infestation control in stored products, pesticide usage, pesticide residues, ecology of mammals and birds of actual or potential pest status; Dir. J. M. TODD, B.SC., A.I.C.T.A., F.I.BIOL.

**Agriculture Science Service, Harpenden Laboratory:** Hatching Green, Harpenden, Herts.; f. 1914 as Plant Pathology Laboratory, present name 1979; an integral part of Ministry of Agriculture, Fisheries and Food; advises Ministry on all matters relating to non-indigenous pests and diseases of plants not yet or recently established or subject to control, and on registration of pesticides used in agriculture or forestry including analytical methods, residues, safety and efficiency in use; Officer-in-charge: A. H. STRICKLAND.

**Animal Diseases Research Association:** Moredun Institute, 408 Gilmerton Rd., Edinburgh EH17 7JH; f. 1920 for research into diseases of farm animals; Dir. W. B. MARTIN, PH.D., M.R.C.V.S., D.V.S.M.; Sec. F. B. COUTTS; publ. *Annual Report.*

**Animal Virus Research Institute:** Pirbright, Woking, Surrey; investigates animal viruses with particular reference to foot-and-mouth disease; library 1,500 vols.; Dir. R. F. SELLERS; Sec. C. D. QUINTON.

**Central Veterinary Laboratory (Ministry of Agriculture, Fisheries and Food):** New Haw, Weybridge, Surrey, KT15 3NB; f. 1917 for research into diseases of farm animals and poultry; joint library with Commonwealth Bureau of Animal Health (50,000 vols., 975 periodicals); Dir. A. J. STEVENS, M.A., B.V.SC.; Laboratory Sec. B. A. BATH; Librarian D. E. GRAY, F.L.A.

**Centre for Overseas Pest Research:** College House, Wright's Lane, London, W8 5SJ; f. 1971; a scientific unit of the Overseas Development Administration; research in the fields of agriculture and public health; aims to help developing countries solve problems caused by crop pests (especially those of major food staples) and disease vectors; 105 scientific staff; library of 80,000 books and reprints; Dir. P. T. HASKELL, C.M.G., PH.D., F.I.BIOL.; publs. *Annual Reports†, Anti-Locust Bulletins and Memoirs†, Tropical Pest Bulletins†, Pest Control Manuals†* (all irregular), *Tropical Pest Management, Tsetse and Trypanosomiasis Information Quarterly, Termite Abstracts* (all quarterly).

**Commonwealth Agricultural Bureaux:** *see* International Chapter, sub-section 'Agriculture'.

**Commonwealth Forestry Institute:** (*see under* University of Oxford).

**East Malling Research Station:** East Malling, Maidstone, Kent; f. 1913 for the promotion of experiments in horticulture; Dir. I. J. GRAHAM-BRYCE; publs. *Annual Report, Journal of Horticultural Science* (joint publication with Long Ashton Research Station).

**Forestry Commission Research and Development Division:** f. 1919 to advance forest technology; graduate staff of 75; library of 7,800 vols.; Dir. of Research and Development D. R. JOHNSTON; comprises two research stations with biological sections for arboriculture, silviculture, tree seeds, genetics, wildlife, entomology, pathology, site studies, physiology, and service sections for statistics, work study, field surveys, photography, library, research information; publ. *Report on Forest Research* (annually). The two research stations are:

**Forest Research Station:** Alice Holt Lodge, Wrecclesham, Farnham, Surrey; Chief Research Officer D. A. BURDEKIN.

**Northern Research Station:** Forestry Commission, Roslin, Midlothian, Scotland; Chief Research Officer D. T. SEAL.

**Glasshouse Crops Research Institute:** Worthing Road, Rustington, Littlehampton, West Sussex, BN16 3PU; f. 1953 for research on glasshouse crops and mushrooms, and on bulbs, flowers and shrubs grown in the open; library of 8,000 vols.; 360 journals received; 190 scientific and technical staff; Dir. D. RUDD-JONES, C.B.E., M.A., PH.D., F.I.BIOL.; publs. *Annual Report†, Growers' Bulletins* (irregular).

**Grassland Research Institute:** Hurley, nr. Maidenhead, Berks.; f. 1949 to promote research and other scientific studies in grassland husbandry, including establishment, productivity, quality and management of forage crops and in systems of animal production; 80 research staff; library of 9,830 vols., and 1,210 current periodicals; Dir. Prof. A. LAZENBY, M.S., M.A., PH.D.; Sec. D. B. CURRIE, M.B.I.M.; publs. *Annual Report, Technical Reports*.

**Hannah Research Institute:** Ayr, KA6 5HL, Scotland; f. 1928 for studies relating to the production and utilization of milk; scientific and support staff of 150; library of 1,200 vols., 200 periodicals; Dir. Prof. M. PEAKER, PH.D.; Sec. N. A. D. MCCANCE, M.B.I.M.; publs. *Annual Report†, Technical Bulletins* (jointly with Nat. Inst. for Research in Dairying).

**Hill Farming Research Organisation:** Bush Estate, Penicuik, Midlothian, EH26 0PY; f. 1954; research in hill soils, plant production and utilization, and sheep, cattle and red deer nutrition and production; Dir. J. EADIE, B.SC.(AGR.); Sec. H. C. M. MCLEOD; publ. *Triennial Report†*.

**Hop Research Department:** (*see under* Wye College).

**Houghton Poultry Research Station:** Houghton, Huntingdon, Cambs., PE17 2DA; f. 1948; research into avian diseases; library; Dir. P. M. BIGGS, PH.D., D.SC., D.V.M., F.R.C.V.S., F.R.C.PATH., F.I.BIOL., F.R.S.; Sec. J. R. ANDREWS, B.SC., A.H.A.; publs. *Biennial Report†, Current Research in Poultry Science* (weekly).

**John Innes Institute:** Colney Lane, Norwich, NR4 7UH; f. 1910 by private bequest, now grant-aided; for research in genetics, plant breeding, virology and ultra-structural studies; Dir. Prof. H. W. WOOLHOUSE, PH.D.; Sec. Miss C. M. YEOMANS, M.A.; publ. *Annual Report†*.

**Long Ashton Research Station (University of Bristol):** Long Ashton, Bristol, BS18 9AF; f. 1903 as National Fruit and Cider Institute, which was in 1912 incorporated in the Research Station; basic studies of plant metabolism, research into fruit culture and related subjects, microclimatology and the effects of weather on crop productivity, control of diseases and pests of agricultural and horticultural crops, microbiological and quality assessment studies on cider, fruit juices and wines, home food storage and preservation; financed mainly by A.R.C. and Ministry of Agriculture, Fisheries and Food; Dir. Prof. J. M. HIRST, D.SC., PH.D., F.R.S.; Sec. W. P. WEATHERHOGG, B.SC.(ECON.), F.C.A.; publ. *Annual Report†*.

**Macaulay Institute for Soil Research, The:** Craigiebuckler, Aberdeen, AB9 2QJ; f. 1930; there are nine main departments: mineral soils, peat and forest soils, spectrochemistry, soil organic chemistry, plant physiology, microbiology, soil fertility, statistics, and soil survey; scientific staff of c. 110; library of 6,000 vols., 500 journals; Dir. T. S. WEST, PH.D., D.SC., C.CHEM., F.R.I.C., F.R.S.E.; Sec. Miss E. A. PIGGOTT; publs. *Annual Report†, Soil Survey of Scotland Publications†*.

**National Institute for Research in Dairying:** (*see* under University of Reading).

**National Institute of Agricultural Botany:** Huntingdon Rd., Cambridge, CB3 0LE; f. 1919 to promote the improvement of existing varieties of seeds, plants and crops in the United Kingdom; includes the Official Seed Testing Station for England and Wales, and other branches which are particularly concerned with crop variety testing and description, seed certification and seed production techniques; 6,500 mems.; Dir. G. MILBOURN, PH.D.; publs. *Annual Report, Journal,* and leaflets.

**National Institute of Agricultural Engineering:** Wrest Park, Silsoe, Bedford, MK45 4HS; Dir. Prof. R. L. BELL, PH.D., F.I.M., F.INST.P.; Sec. I. J. A. GUNN, A.C.C.A.

**National Vegetable Research Station:** Wellesbourne, Warwick; f. 1949; conducts research to improve the culture and quality of vegetables grown in the open; 8 Research Sections; library receives 400 scientific journals; a Vegetable Gene Bank, funded by OXFAM, opened 1980; Dir. Prof. J. K. A. BLEASDALE, PH.D., F.I.BIOL.; Sec. A. A. DALBY, M.B.E.; Librarian D. A. WOODROFFE, B.SC.; publs. *Annual Report†, Practical Guide Leaflets for Gardeners*.

**Plant Breeding Institute:** Maris Lane, Trumpington, Cambridge, CB2 2LQ; f. 1912 as Cambridge University Plant Breeding Institute, established 1952 as a separate institute to promote and undertake research and investigations of a pure and applied scientific nature on plant breeding for the improvement of agricultural crops, the production of new varieties of arable and herbage plants and the development of breeding techniques; Dir. P. R. DAY, PH.D.; Sec. D. R. HADDEN, F.C.I.S., M.B.I.M.; publ. *Annual Report*.

**Rothamsted Experimental Station:** Harpenden, Herts., AL5 2JQ; f. 1843 for research in soil and plant growth; Rothamsted is also the headquarters of the Soil Survey of England and Wales and the Commonwealth Bureau of Soils; about 80,000 volumes in library; Scientific Staff 475; Dir. LESLIE FOWDEN, PH.D., F.R.S.; Sec. W. BARNES, F.C.A.; publs. *Annual Report, Rothamsted Guide, Yields of the Field Experiments,* etc.

**Rowett Research Institute:** Bucksburn, Aberdeen, AB2 9SB; f. 1913 for research in animal nutrition and allied sciences; 172 scientists; Reid Library of 8,000 vols. and 750 current journals; Dir. Sir KENNETH BLAXTER, F.R.S.; Heads of Depts.: Protein Biochemistry, R. H. SMITH, PH.D.; Lipid Biochemistry, G. A. GARTON, PH.D., D.SC., F.R.S.E., F.R.S. (Deputy Dir.); Microbial Biochemistry, P. N. HOBSON, PH.D., D.SC., F.R.S.E.; Experimental Pathology, B. F. FELL, PH.D., M.R.C.V.S.; Physiology, R. N. B. KAY, PH.D., F.R.S.E.; Energy Metabolism, J. C. MACRAE, PH.D.; Applied Nutrition, A. S. JONES, PH.D.; Nutritional Biochemistry, C. F. MILLS, M.SC., PH.D., F.R.S.E.; Biometry, A. W. BOYNE, B.SC., F.R.S.E.; Veterinary Pathology, G.A. SHARMAN, B.SC., M.R.C.V.S.; Chemical and Physical Analysis, J. DAVIDSON, PH.D.; Sec. J. BISHOP, F.C.I.S.; Duthie Experimental Farm, H. DENERLEY, B.SC.(AGRIC.); Librarian H. P. MARTIN; Engineering Services, S. A. ABEL, B.SC.(ENG.), M.I.E.E.; publ. *Annual Report of Studies in Animal Nutrition and Allied Sciences†*.

**Scottish Crop Research Institute:** Invergowrie, Dundee, DD2 5DA; f. 1980 by amalgamation of Scottish Horticultural Research Institute and Scottish Plant Breeding Station; aims to improve the productivity and quality of crops, particularly those grown in northern Britain, by studying their breeding, culture and protection from diseases and pests; fundamental research contributes to the establishment of scientific principles; research on potato, spring barley (especially for malting), forage brassicas (especially swede, rape and kale), raspberry and blackcurrant; Dir. C. E. TAYLOR, PH.D., F.R.S.E., F.I.BIOL; publ. *Annual Report*.

**Scottish Institute of Agricultural Engineering:** Bush Estate, Penicuik, Midlothian; Dir. Dr. D. P. BLIGHT, M.SC., PH.D., C.ENG., F.I.MECH.E.; Sec. C. G. WILLIAMSON, F.C.I.S., M.B.I.M.

**Slough Laboratory** (Ministry of Agriculture, Fisheries and Food Agricultural Development and Advisory Service): London Rd., Slough, SL3 7HJ; f. 1940, present name

U.K. (GREAT BRITAIN)

1979 (fmrly. Pest Infestation Control Laboratory); research and advice on preservation of stored agricultural products; biology and control of vertebrate and invertebrate pests of stored products; micro-organisms in stored products; vertebrate pests of crops; and related subjects, e.g. biochemistry and toxicology, environmental effects of pesticides; Dir. G. H. O. BURGESS, PH.D., F.R.S.E., F.I.F.S.T.

**Welsh Plant Breeding Station (University College of Wales):** Plas Gogerddan, nr. Aberystwyth, Dyfed, SY23 3EB; f. 1919 for the study of the breeding, genetics, physiology, cytology and nutritive value of grasses, clovers and cereals; the production of improved varieties; the study of disease resistance, plant ecology, grassland agronomy and the general management and improvement of lowland and hill pastures; Dir. Prof. J. P. COOPER, PH.D., D.SC., F.R.S., F.I.BIOL.; Sec. T. G. HELLER, F.C.I.S., A.P.M.I.; publs. *Annual Report†, Reprints, Technical Bulletins†.*

**Woburn Experimental Station (Lawes Agricultural Trust):** Husborne Crawley, Bedford; f. 1876 for the investigation of manurial and other problems of British crops; run as outstation of Rothamsted Experimental Station; Dir. L. FOWDEN, PH.D., F.R.S.; publ. *Annual Report.*

ECONOMICS, LAW AND POLITICS

**Economic Research Council:** 55 Park Lane, London, W1Y 3DH; f. 1943 as a non-profit-making research and educational organization in the field of economics and monetary practice; Pres. Rt. Hon. Lord BEECHING; Chair. DAMON DE LASZLO; Hon. Sec. EDWARD HOLLOWAY; publ. *Britain and Overseas* (quarterly).

**Henley Centre for Forecasting:** 2-4 Tudor St., Blackfriars, London, EC4Y 0AA; f. 1974 to promote and develop business and environmental forecasting; a non-profit organization, affiliated to the Administrative Staff College (q.v.); aims to make its research available to a wide audience in business, education and government; forecasts based on specific sets of assumptions about changes in political, social and environmental factors; holds seminars and training programmes; 32 full-time staff, 40 forecasting contributors; Chair. Prof. T. KEMPNER; Dir. HYWEL JONES; publs. *Framework Forecasts for the U.K., Forecasts of Exchange Rate Movements, Measuring Portfolio Performance, The Director's Guide* (monthly), *Planning Consumer Markets, The UK Leisure Markets, Costs and Prices, Framework Forecasts for the EEC Economies, Investment Markets* (quarterly).

**International Institute for Strategic Studies, The:** 23 Tavistock St., London, WC2E 7NQ; f. 1958; aims to promote discussion and research on the problems of defence, disarmament and international security in the nuclear age; international membership and Council; 1,436 mems. and 578 assoc. mems.; Chair. of the Council Dr. ERNST VAN DER BEUGEL; Dir. Dr. CHRISTOPH BERTRAM; publs. *Survival* (6 a year), *The Military Balance, Strategic Survey* (annual), *Adelphi Papers* (8-10 a year), Studies in International Security.

**Institute for the Study of Conflict:** 12/12A Golden Square, London, W1R 3AF; f. 1970 for the advancement of research into the causes and manifestations of insurgency and political violence; library of c. 7,000 vols., 200 periodicals; Chair. Prof. LEONARD SCHAPIRO; Dir. MICHAEL GOODWIN; Defence Services Consultant Major-Gen. F. A. H. LING, C.B., C.B.E., D.S.O., D.L.; publs. *Conflict Studies, Annual of Power and Conflict,* special reports.

**National Institute of Economic and Social Research:** 2 Dean Trench St., Smith Square, London, SW1P 3HE; f. 1938; Pres. The Rt. Hon. Lord ROLL, K.C.M.G., C.B.; Dir. G. D. N. WORSWICK, F.B.A.; Sec. Mrs. K. JONES;

WORLD OF LEARNING

publs. *Economic and Social Studies, Occasional Papers, Joint Studies in Public Policy, Annual Report, Economic Review* (quarterly), *Discussion Papers.* Has attached:

**Social Science Research Council Designated Research Centre in Comparative Industrial Structure and Efficiency:** f. 1981; study of sources of productivity differences between Britain and other advanced industrial countries; 5 staff; Dir. S. J. PRAIS, SC.D.

**Overseas Development Institute:** 10-11 Percy St., London, W1P 0JB; f. 1960 to act as a research and information centre on overseas development issues and problems; library of 11,000 vols.; Chair. Sir GEORGE BISHOP; Dir. ROBERT WOOD; publs. *ODI Review* (2 a year), *Periodicals Reference Bulletin†* (6 a year), research work in the form of books, pamphlets and briefing papers.

**Policy Studies Institute (PSI):** 1/2 Castle Lane, London, SW1E 6PR; f. 1978 (fmrly. PEP); independent; studies questions of economic and social policies and the working of political institutions; Pres. Lord ROLL, K.C.M.G., C.B., Lord SEEBOHM; Chair. of Council Sir MONTY FINNISTON, F.R.S.; Dirs. JOHN PINDER, O.B.E., RICHARD DAVIES (Admin. and External Relations); publs. *PSI Reports, Studies in European Politics, Discussion Papers, Research Papers.*

EDUCATION

**Institute for Cultural Research:** P.O.B. 13, Tunbridge Wells, Kent; f. 1966; to promote and conduct research and advance public education in man's heritage of knowledge; Dir. of Studies The Sayed IDRIES SHAH; Chair. of Council ROBERT CECIL, C.M.G., M.A.; Chair. of Trustees Prof. D. B. FRY, PH.D.; Hon. Sec. DAVID PENDLEBURY, M.A.; publs. intercultural monographs†.

**National Foundation for Educational Research in England and Wales:** The Mere, Upton Park, Slough, Berks., SL1 2DQ; f. 1947; to study problems arising within the national educational system, to disseminate information on its findings and to collaborate on a national and international basis with other educational and research bodies; Pres. SECRETARY OF STATE FOR EDUCATION AND SCIENCE; Chair. A. W. S. HUTCHINGS, M.A., C.B.E.; Dir. ALFRED YATES, M.A., M.ED., F.B.PS.S.; publs. *Educational Research* (3 a year), *Educational Research News, Research Reports* (various), etc.

**Society for Research into Higher Education Ltd.:** at the University, Guildford, GU2 5XH; f. 1964 to collect and disseminate information about research into and developments in higher education and to encourage research into higher education; 370 individual mems., 240 corporate mems.; Chair. Dr. D. A. BLIGH; Admin. R. EUSTACE; publs. *Abstracts* (quarterly), *Studies in Higher Education, Evaluation Newsletter* (2 a year), *International Newsletter* (termly), *Bulletin* (every 6 weeks), *Leverhulme Commission Reports,* monographs, occasional publications, pamphlets.

HISTORY, GEOGRAPHY AND ARCHAEOLOGY

**Leo Baeck Institute:** 4 Devonshire St., London, W.1; f. 1955; an international research institute for the history of German-speaking Jewry; Dir. Dr. ARNOLD PAUCKER; publs. *Year Book,* symposium volumes, monographs, etc.

**Scott Polar Research Institute:** Lensfield Rd., Cambridge, CB2 1ER; f. 1921; research and information centre on the Polar regions; exhibits; 15,000 vols., 850 periodicals; Dir. Dr. G. DE Q. ROBIN; publs. *Polar Record, Recent Polar Literature, Recent Polar and Glaciological Literature.*

LANGUAGE AND LITERATURE

**Modern Humanities Research Association:** f. at Cambridge in 1918 with the object of encouraging advanced studies in modern and medieval languages and literatures; approx. 1,100 mems.; Hon. Sec. Prof. D. A. WELLS, M.A., PH.D., The Queen's University of Belfast, Belfast, BT7 1NN; publs. *Modern Language Review* (quarterly), *Annual Bibliography of English Language and Literature*, *Yearbook of English Studies*, *The Year's Work in Modern Language Studies*, *The Slavonic and East European Review* (quarterly), *Publications Series*, *MHRA Texts and Dissertations*, *Annual Bulletin*, *MHRA Style Book*.

**Orthological Institute:** 1 Lincoln's Inn Fields, London, W.C.2; f. 1927 by C. K. Ogden; co-operates with the Basic English Foundation; Dir. MARK HAYMON; Trustees of the Basic English Foundation: Prof. JOSEPH LAUWERYS, Dr. G. BURNISTON BROWN, MARK HAYMON.

## MEDICINE

**Medical Research Council:** 20 Park Crescent, London, W1N 4AL; inc. 1920; its principal objectives are to promote the balanced development of medical and related biological research and to advance knowledge that will lead to improved health care; it employs its own research staff in over 60 establishments; also provides grants to enable individual scientists to undertake research programmes and projects, thus complementing the research resources of the universities, polytechnics and hospitals; research training is supported by means of fellowships and studentships; Chair. The Rt. Hon. The Lord SHEPHERD; Deputy Chair. and Sec. J. L. GOWANS, C.B.E., M.D., D.SC., D.PHIL., F.R.C.P., F.R.S.; Second Sec. S. G. OWEN, C.B.E., M.D., F.R.C.P.; publs. *Handbook*, *Annual Report*.

The Council's own research activities are mainly undertaken in the following establishments:

**National Institute for Medical Research:** Mill Hill, London, NW7 1AA; divisions: animal, bacterial infectivity, biochemistry, biophysics, biological ultrastructure, developmental biology, gene structure and expression, genetics, immunology, microbiology, molecular pharmacology, parasitology, neurophysiology and neuropharmacology, virology; laboratories of developmental biochemistry, lipid and general chemistry, leprosy and mycobacterial research, peptide chemistry, neurobiology, endocrine physiology and pharmacology, computing; department of engineering; Dir. Sir ARNOLD BURGEN, M.D., F.R.C.P., F.R.S.

**Institute of Hearing Research:** University of Nottingham, University Park, Nottingham, NG7 2RD; Dir. M. HAGGARD, PH.D.

**Clinical Research Centre:** Watford Rd., Harrow, Middx., HA1 3UJ; divisions of clinical cell biology, clinical sciences, communicable diseases, anaesthesia, computing and statistics, clinical chemistry, bioengineering, immunological genetics, immunological medicine, inherited metabolic diseases, electron microscopy, immunochemical genetics, perinatal medicine, rheumatology, comparative medicine, histopathology research group, perinatal medicine, psychiatry; radioisotopes division, haematology section, transplantation section, radiology division; Dir. C. C. BOOTH, M.D., F.R.C.P.

**M.R.C. Unit on Neural Mechanisms of Behaviour:** 3 Malet Place, London, WC1E 7JG; Dir. I. STEELE RUSSELL, PH.D.

**M.R.C. Biostatistics Unit:** Hills Rd., Cambridge, CB2 2QH; Dir. I. SUTHERLAND, D.PHIL.

**M.R.C. Blood Group Unit:** University College London, Wolfson House, Stephenson Way, London, NW1 2HE; Dir. RUTH SANGER, PH.D., F.R.S.

**M.R.C. Blood Pressure Unit:** Western Infirmary, Glasgow, G11 6NT; Dir. A. F. LEVER, M.B., B.SC., F.R.C.P., F.R.S.E.

**M.R.C. Brain Metabolism Unit:** University Dept. of Pharmacology, 1 George Square, Edinburgh, EH8 9JZ; Dir. Dr. G. FINK, M.D., D.PHIL.

**M.R.C. Clinical Oncology and Radiotherapeutics Unit:** Medical School, Hills Rd., Cambridge, CB2 2HQ; Hon. Dir. Prof. N. M. BLEEHEN, B.M., B.SC., F.R.C.P., F.R.C.R.

**M.R.C. Cyclotron Unit:** Hammersmith Hospital, Ducane Rd., London, W12 0HS, and Western General Hospital, Crewe Rd., Edinburgh, EH4 2XU; Dir. D. D. VONBERG, B.SC.

**M.R.C. Dental Unit:** Dental School, Lower Maudlin St., Bristol, BS1 2LY; Hon. Dir. Prof. A. I. DARLING, C.B.E., M.D.S., D.D.SC., M.R.C.S., F.D.S.R.C.S., F.R.C.PATH.

**M.R.C. Environmental Epidemiology Unit:** South Academic Block, Southampton General Hospital, Tremona Rd., Southampton; Dir. Prof. DONALD ACHESON.

**M.R.C. Epidemiology Unit, South Wales:** 4 Richmond Rd., Cardiff, CF2 3AS; Dir. P. C. ELWOOD, M.D., M.R.C.P., F.F.C.M.

**M.R.C. Clinical Genetics Unit:** Institute of Child Health, 30 Guilford St., London, WC1N 1EH; Dir. C. O. CARTER, D.M., F.R.C.P.

**M.R.C. Human Biochemical Genetics Unit:** The Galton Laboratory, University College London, Wolfson House, 4 Stephenson Way, London, NW1 2HE; Dir. D. A. HOPKINSON, M.D.

**M.R.C. Molecular Haematology Unit:** Nuffield Dept. of Clinical Medicine, Radcliffe Infirmary, Oxford, OX2 6HF; Dir. Prof. D. J. WETHERALL, M.D., F.R C.P., F.R.C.PATH., F.R.S.

**M.R.C. Cellular Immunology Unit:** Sir William Dunn School of Pathology, Oxford, OX1 3RE; Dir. Dr. A. WILLIAMS.

**M.R.C. Immunochemistry Unit:** University Dept. of Biochemistry, South Parks Rd., Oxford, OX1 3QU; Hon. Dir. Prof. R. R. PORTER, PH.D., F.R.S.

**M.R.C. Industrial Injuries and Burns Unit:** Birmingham Accident Hospital, Bath Row, Birmingham, B15 1NA; Dir. J. P. BULL, C.B.E., M.D., F.R.C.P.

**M.R.C. Laboratories, The Gambia:** Fajara, Gambia, W. Africa; Dir. B. M. GREENWOOD, M.D., M.R.C.P.

**M.R.C. Laboratories, Jamaica:** University of the West Indies, Mona, Kingston 7, Jamaica, West Indies; Dir. G. R. SERJEANT, M.D., M.A., M.R.C.P.

**M.R.C. Laboratory Animals Centre:** M.R.C. Laboratories, Woodmansterne Rd., Carshalton, Surrey, SM5 4EF; Dir. D. G. WHITTINGHAM, PH.D., F.R.C.V.S.

**M.R.C. Mineral Metabolism Unit:** The General Infirmary, Great George St., Leeds, LS1 3EX; Dir. Prof. B. E. C. NORDIN, M.D., D.SC., F.R.C.P.

**M.R.C. Laboratory of Molecular Biology:** University Post-graduate Medical School, Hills Rd., Cambridge, CB2 2QH; Dir. S. BRENNER, M.B., D.PHIL., F.R.S.

**M.R.C. Neuroendocrinology Unit:** Newcastle General Hospital, Westgate Rd., Newcastle upon Tyne, NE4 6BE; Dir. J. A. EDWARDSON, PH.D.

**Dunn Nutrition Unit:** Milton Rd., Cambridge, CB4 1XJ; Dir. R. G. WHITEHEAD, M.A., PH.D., F.I.BIOL.

**M.R.C. Perceptual and Cognitive Performance Unit:** Experimental Psychology Laboratory, University of Sussex, Falmer, Brighton, BN1 9QY; Dir. Prof. W. P. Colquhoun, Ph.D.

**M.R.C. Pneumoconiosis Unit:** Llandough Hospital, Penarth, Glam., CF6 1XW; Dir. P. C. Elmes, M.D., F.R.C.P.

**M.R.C. Unit for Epidemiological Studies in Psychiatry:** University Dept. of Psychiatry, Royal Edinburgh Hospital, Morningside Park, Edinburgh, EH10 5HF; Dir. N. B. Kreitman, M.D., M.R.C.P.E., F.R.C.Psych., D.P.M.

**M.R.C. Neurological Prostheses Unit:** Institute of Psychiatry, De Crespigny Park, Denmark Hill, London, SE5 8AF; Hon. Dir. Prof. G. S. Brindley, M.D., F.R.C.P., F.R.S.

**M.R.C. Clinical Psychiatry Unit:** Graylingwell Hospital, Chichester, Sussex; Dir. P. Sainsbury, M.D., F.R.C.P., F.R.C.Psych., D.P.M.

**M.R.C. Social Psychiatry Unit:** Institute of Psychiatry, De Crespigny Park, London, SE5 8AF; Dir. Prof. J. K. Wing, M.D., Ph.D., F.R.C.Psych., D.P.M.

**M.R.C. Applied Psychology Unit:** 15 Chaucer Rd., Cambridge, CB2 2EF; Dir. A. D. Baddeley, Ph.D.

**M.R.C. Development Psychology Unit:** Drayton House, Gordon St., London, WC1N 0AN; Dir. N. O'Connor, Ph.D.

**M.R.C. Clinical Population Cytogenetics Unit:** Western General Hospital, Crewe Rd., Edinburgh, EH4 2XU; Dir. Prof. H. J. Evans, Ph.D., F.R.S.E.

**M.R.C. Radiobiology Unit:** Harwell, Didcot, Oxon., OX11 0RD; Dir. J. Vennart, D.Sc., F.Inst.P.

**M.R.C. Unit on the Experimental Pathology of Skin:** The Medical School, Birmingham, B15 2TJ; Dir. G. M. A. Gray, D.Sc. (acting).

**M.R.C. Medical Sociology Unit:** Institute of Medical Sociology, Westburn Rd., Aberdeen, AB9 2ZE; Dir. Prof. R. Illsley, Ph.D.

**M.R.C. Toxicology Unit:** M.R.C. Laboratories, Woodmansterne Rd., Carshalton, Surrey, SM5 4EF; Dir. T. A. Connors, Ph.D., D.Sc., F.I.Biol.

**M.R.C. Trauma Unit:** University of Manchester Medical School, Stopford Bldg., Oxford Rd., Manchester, M13 9PL; Dir. H. B. Stoner, M.D., F.R.C.Path.

**M.R.C. Tuberculosis and Chest Diseases Unit:** Brompton Hospital, Fulham Rd., London, SW3 6HP; Dir. W. Fox, C.M.G., M.D., F.R.C.P., F.F.C.M.

**M.R.C. Unit for Laboratory Studies of Tuberculosis:** Royal Postgraduate Medical School, Ducane Rd., London, W12 0HS; Hon. Dir. Prof. D. A. Mitchison, M.B., F.R.C.P., M.R.C.Path.

**M.R.C. Virology Unit:** Institute of Virology, Church St., Glasgow, G11 5JR; Hon. Dir. Prof. J. H. Subak-Sharpe, Ph.D., F.R.S.E.

**M.R.C. Biochemical Parasitology Unit:** Molteno Institute, Downing St., Cambridge, CB2 3EE; Dir. B. A. Newton, Ph.D., M.R.C.Path., F.I.Biol., F.R.I.C.

**M.R.C. Social and Applied Psychology Unit:** University Department of Psychology, Sheffield, S10 2TN; Dir. P. B. Warr, Ph.D.

**M.R.C. Cell Mutation Unit:** University of Sussex, Falmer, Brighton, Sussex, BN1 9QG; Dir. Prof. B. A. Bridges, Ph.D.

**M.R.C. Unit on Development and Integration of Behaviour:** Sub-department of Animal Behaviour, Madingley, Cambridge, CB3 8AA; Hon. Dir. Prof. R. A. Hinde, M.A., Sc.D., D.Phil., F.R.S.

**M.R.C. Lipid Metabolism Unit:** Hammersmith Hospital, Ducane Rd., London, W12 0HS; Dir. N. B. Myant, D.M., B.Sc., F.R.C.P.

**M.R.C. Leukaemia Unit:** Royal Postgraduate Medical School, Ducane Rd., London, W12 0HS; Hon. Dir. Prof. D. A. G. Galton, M.D., F.R.C.P.

**M.R.C. Hearing and Balance Unit:** Institute of Neurology, The National Hospital, Queen Square, London, WC1N 3BG; Dir. J. D. Hood, Ph.D., D.Sc., F.Inst.P.

**M.R.C. Epidemiology and Medical Care Unit:** Northwick Park Hospital, Watford Rd., Harrow, Middx., HA1 3UJ; Dir. T. W. Meade, M.A., B.M., M.R.C.P., F.F.C.M.

**M.R.C. Neurochemical Pharmacology Unit:** University Dept. of Pharmacology, Hills Rd., Cambridge, CB2 2QD; Dir. L. L. Iversen, Ph.D.

**M.R.C. Clinical Pharmacology Unit:** University Dept. of Clinical Pharmacology, Radcliffe Infirmary, Oxford, OX2 6HE; Hon. Dir. Prof. D. G. Grahame-Smith, M.B., Ph.D., F.R.C.P.

**M.R.C. Reproductive Biology Unit:** Centre for Reproductive Biology, 37 Chalmers St., Edinburgh; Dir. Prof. R. V. Short, Sc.D., F.R.C.V.S., F.R.S., F.R.S.E.

**M.R.C. Mammalian Genome Unit:** University Dept. of Zoology, West Mains Rd., Edinburgh, EH9 3JT; Dir. E. M. Southern, Ph.D.

**M.R.C. Cell Biophysics Unit:** Dept. of Biophysics, University of London, King's College, 26–29 Drury Lane, London, WC2B 5RL; Dir. Prof. B. B. Boycott, F.R.S.

**M.R.C. Mammalian Development Unit:** University College London, Wolfson House, 4 Stephenson Way, London, NW1 2HE; Dir. Miss A. McLaren, D.Phil., F.R.S.

**M.R.C. Developmental Neurobiology Unit:** 33 St. John's Mews, London, W.C.1; Dir. R. Balázs, Dr.Med., Dr.Phil.

**M.R.C. Mechanisms in Tumour Immunity Unit:** M.R.C. Centre, University Medical School, Hills Rd., Cambridge, CB2 2QH; Hon. Dir. Prof. P. J. Lachmann, Sc.D., F.R.C.P.

**M.R.C. Laboratories, Carshalton:** Woodmansterne Rd., Carshalton, Surrey, SM5 4EF; Admin. Officer B. H. Goodfellow.

---

**Arthritis and Rheumatism Council for Research, The:** 41 Eagle St., London, WC1R 4AR; f. 1936 to organize research into the causes and means of treatment of rheumatism, arthritis, and allied diseases; to encourage teaching, and to stimulate public authorities to provide treatment; Pres. Lord Porritt, G.C.M.G., G.C.V.O., C.B.E., F.R.C.P., F.R.C.S.; Gen. Sec. M. C. G. Andrews, C.B.E.

**Asthma Research Council:** 12 Pembridge Square, London, W2 4EH; f. 1927 to promote research into asthma and its allied disorders; Patron H.R.H. The Duchess of Gloucester; Chair. D. Walters, M.B.E., M.P.; Hon. Treas. D. E. Franklin.

**Beatson Institute for Cancer Research:** Garscube Estate, Switchback Rd., Glasgow, G61 1BD, Scotland; f. 1910, renamed 1967; research in molecular pathology, particularly studies on the molecular biology of cellular differentiation in relation to cancer; staff of 60; library of 500 vols. and 40 journals; Dir. Dr. J. Paul.

**British Society for Research on Ageing:** f. 1954 to encourage gerontological research in Great Britain by acting as a forum for the report and discussion of new advances in ageing research; open to all who are actively engaged in experimental gerontology; 140 mems.; Pres. Prof. D. Bellamy; Hon. Sec. Dr. C. Rowlatt, Dept. of Cell Pathology, Imperial Cancer Research Fund, Box 123, Lincoln's Inn Fields, London, WC2A 3PX.

RESEARCH INSTITUTES — U.K. (GREAT BRITAIN)

**Burden Neurological Institute:** Stoke Lane, Stapleton, Bristol; f. 1939 to conduct research in neurology and psychiatry; library of 4,000 vols.; Dir. Dr. R. COOPER; Sec. R. D. A. JONES.

**Bureau of Hygiene and Tropical Diseases:** Keppel St., London, WC1E 7HT; f. 1908 as Sleeping Sickness Bureau; Dir. R. SCHRAM, M.A., M.D.; Sec. A. H. PHIPPS, B.COM.; publs. *Abstracts on Hygiene and Communicable Diseases†, Tropical Diseases Bulletin†* (both monthly).

**Central Public Health Laboratory:** Colindale Avenue, London, NW9 5HT; f. 1946; central laboratory of the Public Health Laboratory Service, 61 Colindale Ave., London, NW9 5EQ, providing a microbiological service for the control of the spread of infectious diseases; 350 staff; library of 20,000 vols.; Dir. Prof. A. A. GLYNN, M.D., F.R.C.P.; Division of Hospital Infection Dir. Dr. P. D. MEERS, M.D., F.R.C.PATH.; Division of Enteric Pathogens Dir. Dr. B. ROWE, M.A., M.B., D.T.M.&H.; Epidemiological Research Laboratory Dir. Dr. T. M. POLLOCK, M.B., CH.B., F.R.C.P.(GLASG.), F.F.C.M.; Food Hygiene Laboratory Dir. Dr. R. J. GILBERT, M.PHARM, PH.D., M.C.R.PATH.; National Collection of Type Cultures Curator Dr. L. R. HILL, D.SC., F.I.BIOL.; Division of Microbiological Reagents and Quality Control Dir. Dr. P. S. GARDNER, M.D.; Virus Reference Laboratory Dir. Dr. M. S. PEREIRA, M.D.

**Imperial Cancer Research Fund:** Lincoln's Inn Fields, London, WC2A 3PX; f. 1902; library of 18,000 vols.; Chair. Prof. Sir ERIC SCOWEN, M.D., D.SC., F.R.C.P., F.R.C.S., F.R.C.P.E.; Dir. of Research W. F. BODMER, PH.D., F.R.S.; Sec. A. B. L. CLARKE, O.B.E.; publs. *Annual Report, Scientific Report* (annually).

**Institute of Cancer Research:** 34 Sumner Pl., London, SW7 3NU; f. 1910; Dir. Dr. ROBIN WEISS; Prof. of Immunobiology Prof. A. J. S. DAVIES; Prof. of Chemistry Prof. A. B. FOSTER; Prof. of Organic Chemistry Prof. W. C. J. ROSS; Prof. of Physics applied to Medicine Prof. G. E. ADAMS; Prof. of Epidemiology Prof. M. R. ALDERSON; Prof. of Radiobiology Prof. P. ALEXANDER; Prof. of Tumour Pathology Prof. N. F. C. GOWING; Prof. of Experimental Pathology Prof. A. M. NEVILLE; Prof. of Radiotherapy Prof. M. J. PECKHAM; Prof. of Medicine (vacant).

**Lister Institute of Preventive Medicine:** *see* under University of London.

**Liverpool School of Tropical Medicine:** Pembroke Place, Liverpool, L3 5QA; f. 1898 and received its Charter of Incorporation 1905; governed by a Council representative of the University of Liverpool and the merchants and shipowners of Liverpool; its objects are to train medical and paramedical personnel proceeding to or coming from the tropics in all aspects of individual or community medicine in the tropics, to conduct original research into tropical diseases and their control, and to organize and conduct clinical and prophylactic measures against tropical diseases; Dean Prof. Chevalier H. M. GILLES, K.O.S.J., M.D., F.R.C.P., F.F.C.M., D.T.M.&H.; publs. *Annals of Tropical Medicine and Parasitology, Annals of Tropical Paediatrics.*

**Mathilda and Terence Kennedy Institute of Rheumatology:** Bute Gardens, London, W6 7DW; f. 1966; conducts research into the causes and cure of the rheumatic diseases; Dir. I. H. M. MUIR, C.B.E.; Gen. Sec. F. B. CHARLESWORTH.

**Paterson Laboratories:** Christie Hospital and Holt Radium Institute, Manchester Area Health Authority (Teaching) South District, Manchester, M20 9BX; f. 1932; conducts basic cancer research; 180 mems.; Dir. L. G. LAJTHA, M.D., D.PHIL., F.R.C.P.(E.), F.R.C.PATH.

**Public Health Laboratory Service Centre for Applied Microbiology and Research:** Porton Down, Salisbury, Wilts., SP4 0JG; diagnostic methods, prophylaxis and treatment for bacterial and viral diseases; diagnostic reagents for clinical biochemical tests; mechanisms of microbial pathogenicity; vaccines and immunoprophylactics and production up to clinical trial level; microbiological safety; continuous culture of micro-organisms; development of processes for the production and purification of bacterial enzymes and other microbial products; freeze drying of biological materials; environmental hygiene; Dir. Dr. P. M. SUTTON.

**Ross Institute of Tropical Hygiene:** Keppel St., London, WC1 7HT; f. 1926 as a memorial to the late Sir Ronald Ross; it has since 1934 been a Dept. of the London School of Hygiene and Tropical Medicine; its objects are the teaching of tropical hygiene, the promotion of public health schemes in the tropics, particularly in relation to industry, and research both at home and in the field overseas; Chair. W. WILSON MAYNE, O.B.E., B.SC., M.I.BIOL.; Dir. Prof. D. J. BRADLEY, M.A., D.M., M.R.C.PATH., F.I.BIOL., F.F.C.M.; Organizing Sec. L. G. PONSFORD, LL.M.

**Strangeways Research Laboratory:** Wort's Causeway, Cambridge, CB1 4RN; f. 1912; research into cell biology, developmental biology, cancer, rheumatoid arthritis; Dir. J. T. DINGLE, D.SC.

**Wellcome Laboratories of Tropical Medicine:** Langley Court, Beckenham, Kent, BR3 3BS; Head O. D. STANDEN, D.SC., M.SC.

**Wellcome Research Laboratories:** Langley Court, Beckenham, Kent, BR3 3BS; Group Research and Development Dir. J. R. VANE, D.SC., F.R.S.; Dir. of Administration W. DENCH, B.PHARM., M.P.S., F.B.I.R.A.

**West Midland Institute of Geriatric Medicine and Gerontology:** c/o Moseley Hall Hospital, Alcester Rd., Moseley, Birmingham, B13 8JL; f. 1971; the first institute of its kind in the U.K.; to promote and advance science and medicine relating to the development of gerontology and of medicine in old age; 174 mems.; small specialist library; Dir. Dr. O. H. D. PORTSMOUTH; Sec. Dr. A. V. BARFORD.

NATURAL SCIENCES

**Natural Environment Research Council:** Polaris House, North Star Ave., Swindon, SN2 1EU; established by Royal Charter 1965; the natural environmental sciences supported by the Council include geology, geophysics and geochemistry; physical oceanography and marine ecology; hydrology, freshwater ecology; terrestrial ecology and some aspects of meteorology; Council also makes awards for postgraduate training, research grants and fellowships; Chair. Sir HERMAN BONDI, K.C.B., F.R.S.

The component institutes of the Council are:

**Institute of Geological Sciences:** Exhibition Rd., London, SW7 2DE; incorporates the Geological Survey of Great Britain, the Geological Museum and the Overseas Geological Surveys; library is one of largest geological libraries in the world (150,000 maps); offices also at Edinburgh, Leeds, Nottingham, Belfast, Exeter; Dir. Dr. G. M. BROWN, F.R.S., F.R.S.E.

**Institute of Oceanographic Sciences:** Wormley Laboratory, Wormley, Godalming, Surrey, GU8 5UB; Bidston Observatory, Bidston, Birkenhead, L43 7RA; Taunton Laboratory, Crossway, Taunton, TA1 2DW; Dir. A. S. LAUGHTON, PH.D.

**Institute for Marine Environmental Research:** Project Place, Plymouth, PL1 3DH; Dir. R. S. GLOVER, B.SC., F.R.S.E.

**Institute of Marine Biochemistry:** St. Fitticks Rd., Aberdeen, AB1 3RA; Dir. P. T. GRANT, PH.D.

**Sea Mammal Research Unit:** c/o British Antarctic Survey, Madingley Rd., Cambridge, CB3 0ET; Dir. R. M. LAWS, PH.D.; Officer in charge J. HARWOOD.

**Institute of Hydrology:** Maclean Bldg., Crowmarsh Gifford, Wallingford, Oxon., OX10 8BB; Dir. J. S. G. MCCULLOCH, PH.D., F.INST.P.

**Institute of Terrestrial Ecology:** 68 Hills Rd., Cambridge, CB2 1LA; research and advisory service in conservation and wildlife management; research stations at Merlewood, Monks Wood, Furzebrook, Edinburgh, Banchory, Bangor, Cambridge; Dir. J. N. R. JEFFERS.

**Unit of Virology:** 5 South Parks Rd., Oxford, OX1 3RB; Dir. T. W. TINSLEY, O.B.E., M.A., D.SC., F.I.BIOL.

**British Antarctic Survey:** Madingley Rd., Cambridge, CB3 0ET; Dir. R. M. LAWS, PH.D.

**Unit of Comparative Plant Ecology:** Dept. of Botany, University of Sheffield, S10 2TN; Head of Unit I. H. RORISON, PH.D.

Grant-aided establishments:

**Marine Biological Association of the United Kingdom:** See under Learned Societies.

**Scottish Marine Biological Association:** See under Learned Societies.

**Unit of Marine Invertebrate Biology:** Marine Science Laboratories, Menai Bridge, Gwynedd, LL59 5EH; Hon. Dir. Prof. D. J. CRISP, C.B.E., F.R.S.

**Freshwater Biological Association:** See under Learned Societies.

Special services:

**NERC Scientific Services:** Polaris House, North Star Ave., Swindon, SN2 1EU; Dir. B. F. RULE, M.SC., M.B.C.S.

**Planning and Special Services:** Polaris House, North Star Ave., Swindon, SN2 1EU; Head J. A. MCGINNETY, PH.D.

**NERC Computing Service:** c/o Institute of Oceanographic Sciences, Bidston Observatory, Birkenhead, Merseyside, L43 2RA; Head B. J. HINDE, B.SC.

**NERC Research Vessel Services:** No. 1 Dock, Barry, South Glamorgan, CF6 6UZ; Head L. M. SKINNER, PH.D.

---

**Science and Engineering Research Council:** Polaris House, North Star Ave., Swindon, SN2 1ET; f. 1965; covers a large field of fundamental science; supports research in engineering and technology in universities. Its primary purpose is to sustain standards of research and postgraduate education in universities and polytechnics. Its charter makes provision for it to carry out research and development through its own establishments; to encourage and support similar research by any other person or body; to provide and operate equipment for common use by universities, technical colleges and like institutions; to make grants for postgraduate studies and to disseminate knowledge of science and technology. *Chairman of Council:* Prof. J. F. C. KINGMAN, F.R.S. *Secretary:* BRIAN W. OAKLEY.

The estimated annual budget is around £216.75 million and total staff about 2,900.

The Council is responsible for the following research establishments:

**Royal Greenwich Observatory:** Herstmonceux Castle, Hailsham, East Sussex, BN27 1RP; f. 1675; supports university research in ground-based optical astronomy through provision of telescopes and modern instruments; responsible for the procurement and operation of the optical telescope for the La Palma Observatory being provided by the SERC for U.K. astronomers; has a Starlink data processing centre and a pulsed laser for satellite laser ranging, used in collaboration with universities; collaborates with South African Astronomical Observatory and maintains the Time Service; Dir. Prof. A. BOKSENBERG, F.R.S.; publs. *Annual Report, Nautical, Air and Star Almanac, Astronomical Almanac* (jointly with U.S.A.), various reports of observations.

**Royal Observatory, Edinburgh:** Blackford Hill, Edinburgh, EH9 3HJ; f. 1818; manages the 1.2 metre Schmidt telescope in Australia and the 3.8 metre infra-red telescope in Hawaii; houses the Dept. of Astronomy of Edinburgh University; Dir. and Astronomer Royal for Scotland Prof. MALCOLM S. LONGAIR; publs. *Annual Report*, scientific publs. and communications.

**Rutherford Appleton Laboratory:** Chilton, Didcot, Oxon., OX11 0QX; fosters university research in particle physics and co-ordinates the U.K.'s efforts in this field; also uses particle accelerators elsewhere, e.g. at CERN in Geneva; a new high-intensity pulsed neutron source is under construction; research in plasma physics and the development of interactive and distributed computing systems; the laboratory is the focal point of SERC's work in microelectronics, robotics and energy; supports university space research and is responsible for rockets, satellites and high altitude balloons used for geophysical and astrophysical experiments; research on the propagation of radio waves and on the ultra-violet and X-ray emission spectra of high temperature astrophysical sources using spacecraft; Dir. Dr. G. MANNING; publs. *Annual Report*, scientific and technical publs.

**Daresbury Laboratory:** Daresbury, Warrington, Cheshire, WA4 4AD; f. 1958; centre for international research in nuclear structure physics and in the applications of synchrotron radiation; has a 2 GeV electron storage ring for synchrotron radiation research and a tandem Van de Graaff accelerator for research on nuclear structure; collaborates with universities to cover research in physics, chemistry, biology, etc.; Dir. Prof. L. L. GREEN; publs. *Annual Report*, scientific and technical publs.

---

**Cambridge University Institute of Astronomy:** The Observatories, Madingley Rd., Cambridge, CB3 0HA; incorporating former Observatory f. 1824; Solar Physics Observatory f. 1913; Institute of Theoretical Astronomy f. 1967; 70 staff; library of 13,000 vols.; work on observational and theoretical astrophysics; Dir. Prof. M. J. REES; publ. *Annual Report*†.

**Fulmer Research Institute, Ltd.:** Stoke Poges, Slough, Berks., SL2 4QD; f. 1946; owned by the Institute of Physics; the institute carries out contract research, principally in the fields of metallurgy, plastics and polymers, ceramics, physical, inorganic and organic chemistry, solid state physics and engineering for Government and industrial sponsors, both British and Overseas; 250 staff; library of 10,000 vols.; Managing Dir. W. E. DUCKWORTH; publ. *FRI Newsletter* (quarterly).

**Institute of Zoology:** Zoological Society of London, Regent's Park, London, NW1 4RY; f. 1964; depts. of reproduction, nutrition, genetics, infectious diseases, veterinary research, and Curator's research depts.; incorporates the **Wellcome Laboratories of Comparative Physiology** and the **Nuffield Laboratories of Comparative Medicine;** studies aimed at the scientific improvement of conservation, breeding and management of animals in captivity and in the wild, as well as comparative aspects of human physiology and medicine; 80 staff; library and publs.: see Zoological Society of London; Dir. J. P. Hearn, M.SC., PH.D., F.I.BIOL.

**Meteorological Office:** London Rd., Bracknell, Berks., RG12 2SZ; f. 1855; the state weather service; Dir.-Gen. Sir John Mason, C.B., D.SC., F.R.S.; publs. weather reports, *Geophysical Memoirs*, *Scientific papers*, *Meteorological Magazine*, *Marine Observer*, etc.

**Mullard Radio Astronomy Observatory:** Cavendish Laboratory, Cambridge; f. 1945; 75 staff; Dir. Prof. Sir Martin Ryle; publs. numerous scientific papers.

**National Computing Centre Ltd., The:** Oxford Rd., Manchester, M1 7ED; f. 1966; a non-profit-distributing organization financed by industry, commerce and government; promotes the wider and more effective use of computers; gives information, advice and training, supplies software packages, promotes standards and codes of practice, co-operates with, and co-ordinates the work of, members and other organization concerned with computers and their use; 300 staff; Chair. Prof. J. H. H. Merriman, C.B., O.B.E., M.SC., M.INST.P., C.ENG., F.I.E.E., F.K.C.; Dir. D. R. Fairbairn; publ. *N.C.C. Interface* (monthly).

**Nuffield Radio Astronomy Laboratories: Jodrell Bank** (University of Manchester): Macclesfield, Cheshire; the station has seven large steerable radio telescopes, including the Mark 1A 250-ft. diameter radio telescope; these can be directed to follow radio objects in any part of the sky; work includes research on the galactic and extra-galactic radio emissions; observations of radio emission from quasars, pulsars and flare stars; multi-telescope interferometry and very long base-line interferometry; tracking of lunar and planetary space probes; Dir. Prof. Graham Smith, F.R.S.

**Royal Botanic Garden:** Edinburgh, EH3 5LR; The National Botanic Garden of Scotland; f. 1670; taxonomic research; courses leading to diploma in horticulture; outstations—Younger Botanic Garden, near Dunoon, Argyll; Logan Botanic Garden, Stranraer, Wigtownshire; Dawyck Arboretum, Stobo, Peebles; Herbarium of *c.* 1,700,000 specimens; library: see Special Libraries; Regius Keeper D. Henderson; publ. *Notes from the Royal Botanic Garden, Edinburgh†*.

**Royal Botanic Gardens:** Kew, Richmond, Surrey; f. 1759 by Princess Augusta of Saxe-Gotha, Dowager Princess of Wales; became a National Botanic Garden 1841; taxonomic and economic botany and horticulture; Dir. Prof. Arthur Bell; publs. *Kew Bulletin†* (quarterly), *Index Kewensis* (every 5 years), *Hooker's Icones Plantarum†* (annually), *Kew Record* (annually), floras and monographs.

**United Kingdom Atomic Energy Authority:** 11 Charles II St., London, SW1Y 4QP; f. 1954 to take over responsibility for research and development in atomic energy; may now also undertake certain research and development in other fields; Chair. Dr. W. Marshall, C.B.E., F.R.S.; Sec. P. J. Searby, C.B.E.; publ. *Atom* (monthly).

   Atomic Energy Establishment: Winfrith, Dorchester, Dorset; Dir. H. Cartwright, C.B.E.

   Culham Laboratory: Culham, Abingdon, Oxon.; Dir. Dr. W. M. Lomer.

   Atomic Energy Research Establishment: Harwell, Oxon.; Dir. Dr. L. E. J. Roberts, C.B.E.

   Northern Division: Risley, Warrington, Lancs.; Man. Dir. Dr. T. N. Marsham, C.B.E.

**University Marine Biological Station:** Millport, Isle of Cumbrae, Scotland; f. 1896, re-organized 1970 as University Station for provision of teaching and research facilities in Marine Biology primarily for universities of London and Glasgow but also for other universities; for supply of marine specimens to U.K. universities; 40 staff; library of 2,000 vols.; Dir. Prof. J. A. Allen; Sec. Miss E. M. Palfalvy; publ. *Annual Report*.

**University Observatory:** Dept. of Astrophysics, Oxford; f. *c.* 1870; teaching and research in astronomy and atomic spectroscopy, with particular reference to solar, stellar and extragalactic physics, cosmology and theoretical astrophysics; library of approx. 6,000 books; 7 academic staff; Dir. D. E. Blackwell.

**University of London Observatory:** Mill Hill Park, London, N.W.7; f. 1929; teaching and research in astronomy; Dir. Prof. R. Wilson.

**Wildfowl Trust:** Slimbridge, Glos.; f. 1946; 20,000 mems.; concerned with all aspects of the biology of the Anatidae, particularly those related to conservation, research and education; the world's largest comparative collection of living wildfowl is maintained at Slimbridge; other centres open to the public all year round at Arundel, Sussex; Martin Mere, Lancs.; Peakirk, Cambs.; Washington, Tyne and Wear; Welney, Norfolk; Caerlaverock, Dumfriesshire (1st Sept. to 15th May); Hon. Dir. Sir Peter Scott, C.B.E., D.SC., LL.D.; Dir. Research Prof. G. V. T. Matthews, M.A., PH.D.; publs. *Wildfowl†* (annually), *Wildfowl News* (2 a year).

PHILOSOPHY AND PSYCHOLOGY

**Institute of Psychophysical Research:** 118 Banbury Rd., Oxford, OX2 6JU; f. 1961; carries out academic research in the fields of philosophy, psychology and theoretical physics, and their inter-relationships; Dir. C. E. Green, B.LITT., M.A.; publ. *Proceedings†* (irregular).

RELIGION, SOCIOLOGY AND ANTHROPOLOGY

**Institute for the Study and Treatment of Delinquency:** 34 Surrey St., Croydon, Surrey; f. 1931 to initiate and promote scientific research into the causes and prevention of crime; founder of the Portman Clinic, an out-patient clinic for diagnosis and treatment of delinquents, with an advisory service to courts; Pres. Lord Kilbrandon, P.C.; Chair. of Council Prof. Gordon Trasler, J.P.; Gen. Sec. Miss E. Saville, M.B.E.; publs. *British Journal of Criminology* (quarterly), *Annual Report*, monographs and pamphlets.

**Social Science Research Council:** 1 Temple Ave., London, EC4Y 0BD; f. 1965; makes grants to assist research in universities, polytechnics and independent institutions; financial support to postgraduate students and provides information on the social sciences; Chair. M. V. Posner; Sec. C. S. Smith; publs. *SSRC Newsletter†* (3 a year), *SSRC Annual Report†*, *Research Supported by the SSRC†* (annually).

**Tavistock Institute of Human Relations:** Tavistock Centre, Belsize Lane, London, NW3 5BA; incorporated 1947; study of human relations in conditions of well-being, conflict or breakdown in the family, the work group, the community and the larger organization; disciplines range from clinical psychology to operational research; library of 18,000 vols.; Sec. P. M. Foster, D.F.C., M.ED.; publ. *Human Relations* (monthly).

TECHNOLOGY

Government Department Research Establishments concentrate on research and development that is in the national interest, and serve three main purposes: they contribute to the efficiency of industry as a whole, work on specific problems within particular industries, and help central and local authorities to provide necessary services; the establishments are grouped under the relevant Departments as follows:

*Department of Industry Research Establishments:*

**Computer Aided Design Centre:** Madingley Rd., Cambridge, CB3 0HB; Dir. A. I. LLEWELYN, O.B.E., B.SC.; publs. various.

**Laboratory of the Government Chemist:** Cornwall House, Stamford St., London, SE1 9NQ; f. 1842; provision of scientific advice and a comprehensive analytical service to government depts., other official organizations and where appropriate the private sector; research in analytical chemistry; staff of c. 380; library of c. 8,000 vols., 500 periodicals; Government Chemist Dr. R. F. COLEMAN, D.SC., C.CHEM., F.R.S.C.; publs. *Report of the Government Chemist* (annually), etc.

**National Engineering Laboratory:** East Kilbride, Glasgow, G75 0QU; f. 1947 for mechanical engineering research, development and testing; Dir. P. I. FREEMAN, PH.D.; publ. *Research Reports*, Conference Publications.

**National Physical Laboratory:** Teddington, Middx., TW11 0LW; f. 1900; national standards of measurement; definitive data with regard to engineering materials; computing technique; Dir. P. DEAN, C.B., PH.D., F.INST.P., F.I.M.A.; publs. various.

**Torry Research Station:** (see under University of Aberdeen).

**Warren Spring Laboratory:** Stevenage, Herts.; f. 1959; research on industrial technology and environmental technology; Dir. A. J. ROBINSON, PH.D., C.ENG., A.R.S.M., F.I.M.M.; publs. various.

*Ministry of Defence Research Establishments:*

**Admiralty Marine Technology Establishment:** Teddington, Middlesex; Dir. A. B. MITCHELL.

**Admiralty Surface Weapons Establishment:** Portsdown, Portsmouth, Hants.; Dir. K. F. SLATER.

**Admiralty Underwater Weapons Establishment:** Portland, Dorset; library of 15,000 vols., 50,000 reports; Head of Library and Information Services: M. G. SIMS; Dir. I. L. DAVIES.

**Aeroplane and Armament Experimental Establishment:** Boscombe Down, Salisbury, Wiltshire; Commandant Air Cdre. R. J. SPIERS, O.B.E., F.R.AE.S.

**Chemical Defence Establishment:** Porton Down, Salisbury, Wilts.; Dir. Dr. R. G. H. WATSON.

**Military Vehicles and Engineering Establishment:** Chobham Lane, Chertsey, Surrey; Dir. J. ELLIS.

**National Gas Turbine Establishment:** Pyestock, Farnborough, Hants.; Dir. W. H. TURNER.

**National Remote Sensing Centre:** Space Dept., Royal Aircraft Establishment, Farnborough, Hants., GU14 6TD; f. 1980 to promote the use of remote sensing data in the U.K.; theoretical and development work in remote sensing technology incl. microwave/target interaction, image manipulation and analysis techniques; processes and analyses data from remote sensing satellites; acquires data from meteorological satellites; 30 staff; Man. G. J. DAVISON; publs. *Remote Sensing Bulletin*† (quarterly), reports (available as RAE Technical Publications).

**Propellants, Explosives and Rocket Motor Establishment:** Powdermill Lane, Waltham Abbey, Essex, EN9 1BP; research and development of explosives, propellants, materials, chemistry; also at Westcott, nr. Aylesbury, Bucks., HP18 0NZ: research and development of rocket motor technology; Dir. Dr. B. H. NEWMAN.

**Royal Aircraft Establishment:** Farnborough, Hants.; Dir. T. H. KERR.

**Royal Armament Research and Development Establishment:** Fort Halstead, Sevenoaks, Kent; Dir. Dr. F. H. PANTON, M.B.E.

**Royal Signals and Radar Establishment:** Malvern, Worcs., WR14 3PS; Dir. A. SMART.

*Departments of the Environment and Transport Research Establishments:*

**Building Research Establishment:** Garston, Watford, Herts., WD2 7JR; f. 1972 by merger of the Building Research Station, the Fire Research Station and the Forest Products Research Laboratory; Dir. Dr. I. DUNSTAN; publs. *BRE News*, *Building Research Establishment Digests*, etc.

**Transport and Road Research Laboratory:** Crowthorne, Berkshire; estab. 1933; currently controlled by Department of Transport; research on road materials and construction, road traffic, transportation and safety; 53,500 books and pamphlets and 900 journals in library; Dir. R. J. BRIDLE, B.SC., F.ENG., F.I.C.E., F.I.H.E.; publs. *Annual Reports*, *Text Books*, *Technical Papers*, *T.R.R.L. Reports* and *Road Notes*.

**Water Research Centre:** Elder Way, Stevenage, Herts., and Henley Rd., Medmenham, P.O.B. 16, Marlow, Bucks.; f. 1974 (by amalgamation of two laboratories); U.K. centre for research on water pollution and treatment of water and waste-water; an Industrial Research Association financed by members; Dir. J. L. VAN DER POST, B.SC., C.ENG., F.I.MECH.E., F.I.GAS.E.; publs. *Annual Reports*, *Technical Reports*, *WRC Information*† (weekly), *WRC Newsheet*.

---

**British Ceramic Research Association:** Queens Rd., Penkhull, Stoke-on-Trent, Staffs., ST4 7LQ; f. 1948; research into properties of raw materials and products of the pottery, refractories and clay building materials industries; manufacturing processes; design and performance of machinery and kilns; performance and high-temperature physics and chemistry of refractories and industrial ceramics; strength of brick masonry and stresses in buried clay pipe-lines; improved methods of chemical and physical testing; c. 300 mems.; library of 13,000 vols. and 40,000 pamphlets; Chair. A. J. OWEN; Dir. D. W. F. JAMES, PH.D.; Sec. N. J. BRAMHALL, B.A.; publs. papers, reports, *British Ceramic Abstracts*†.

**BHRA Fluid Engineering** (British Hydromechanics Research Association): Cranfield, Bedford, MK43 0AJ; f. 1947; covers fluid engineering on a broad front; specializes in physical and mathematical modelling of flow problems, high-pressure technology, pumps and the transport of solids by pipeline; sealing technology; mems.: over 200 companies; Dir. of Research G. F. W. ADLER; Sec. R. CHADWICK; Head of Information Dept. and Library H. S. STEPHENS.

**British Glass Industry Research Association:** Northumberland Rd., Sheffield, S10 2UA; f. 1955; Chair. N. JACKSON, C.ENG., M.I.MECH.E., F.INST.E., M.I.NUC.E.

**British Ship Research Association:** Wallsend Research Station, Wallsend, Tyne and Wear, NE28 6UY; f. 1944; Dir. and Sec. D. GOODRICH; publ. *Journal of Abstracts* (monthly).

**Centre for the Study of Industrial Innovation:** River Cottage, Riversdale, Bourne End, Bucks., SL8 5EB; f. 1970; economic study and analysis of specific and general topics in the field of industrial innovation; Dir. E. P. HAWTHORNE.

**Construction Industry Research and Information Association:** 6 Storey's Gate, London, SW1P 3AU; research into construction and offshore engineering; Dir. Dr.

L. S. BLAKE; Sec. J. B. BEHR; publs. *Annual Report, News Letter* (every 2 months), Reports, Technical Notes.

**Foundation for Business Responsibilities:** 40 Doughty St., London, WC1N 2LF; f. 1966 as Industrial Educational and Research Foundation; to enable directors, members of the civil service, members of Parliament and trade union leaders to examine the principles and responsibilities underlying business decisions; Chair. of the Trustees Sir JOHN REISS, B.E.M.; Dir. MICHAEL IVENS.

**Malaysian Rubber Producers' Research Association:** Tun Abdul Razak Laboratory, Brickendonbury, Hertford, SG13 8NL; f. 1938; research and development on natural rubber; library of 3,500 books and 200 periodicals, information retrieval system containing 35,000 items; Dir. of Research Dr. L. MULLINS; publs. *Annual Report, Rubber Developments* (quarterly), *NR Technology* (quarterly), *Technical Bulletins List of Publications* (quarterly), various information sheets.

**National Research Development Corporation:** Kingsgate House, 66-74 Victoria St., London, SW1E 6SL; f. 1949; an independent public corporation which promotes adoption, by the granting of manufacturing licences, of new products and processes invented in government laboratories, universities, and elsewhere, advancing money where necessary to bring them to a commercially viable stage; assists industrial development; library of 2,000 vols., and 200 periodicals; Chair. Sir FREDERICK WOOD; Man. Dir. J. C. CAIN, PH.D., M.R.S.C., F.I.BIOL.; Head of Public Relations B. S. W. MANN, C.ENG., M.I.MECH.E., M.I.INF.SC.; publs. *Bulletin* (2 a year), reports and pamphlets.

**Production Engineering Research Association (PERA):** Melton Mowbray, Leics., LE13 0PB; f. 1946; an independent research, consultancy, training and advisory organization; specializes in all aspects of manufacture, including manpower, machinery, materials, methods, management and marketing; undertakes specialized manufacture; Dir.-Gen. Prof. WILFRED B. HEGINBOTHAM, O.B.E., D.SC., PH.D.

**Scottish Universities' Research and Reactor Centre:** East Kilbride, Glasgow, G75 0QU; f. 1963; provides research and teaching facilities in reactor physics, radiochemistry, nuclear physics, activation analysis, radiation chemistry, nuclear medicine, radiation protection, geochronology, isotope geology, stable isotope geochemistry and carbon dating (NERC Radiocarbon Lab. on site); Dir. Prof. H. W. WILSON, PH.D., F.INST.P., F.R.S.E.

**Tropical Products Institute:** 56-62 Gray's Inn Rd., London, WC1X 8LU; research and development work on the handling, preservation, processing, quality control, storage, marketing and utilization of the plant and animal products of the tropics and sub-tropics; scientific, technical and economic advisory service for developing countries; library and information service; staff of 360; Dir. Dr. E. M. THAIN, PH.D., C.CHEM., F.R.S.C.; publs. *Tropical Science*† (quarterly), *T.P.I. Reports, Biennial Report, Oil Palm News* (annually), *Tropical Stored Products Information* (3 a year), *Library Accessions Bulletin* (monthly), *Crop and Product Digest* (series), *Tropical Products Institute Newsletter* (3 a year), *Rural Technology Guides* (series), *Postharvest leaflets* (series).

## LIBRARIES AND ARCHIVES

*Achives:* The collections in many libraries listed below are not confined to printed books but include quantities of archives and manuscripts. In nearly every English county and in several in Wales there is a County Record Office, usually in the County town. A full list of these and of other archive repositories is given in *Record Repositories in Great Britain* (H.M.S.O.).

### NATIONAL ARCHIVES

**Public Record Office:** Ruskin Ave., Kew, Richmond, Surrey, TW9 4DU and Chancery Lane, WC2A 1LR; national archives of the United Kingdom; over 50 million documents; museum exhibits include the Domesday Book, the 1225 Magna Carta, royal autographs and historical and biographical documents spanning eight centuries; Keeper of Public Records A. W. MABBS; the Office's numerous publications are listed in H.M.S.O.'s *British National Archives*.

*Libraries:* The selection of libraries given below is classified as follows:
  National Libraries.
  Government Libraries.
  Public Libraries.
  Special Libraries.
  University and College Libraries.

### NATIONAL LIBRARIES
#### THE BRITISH LIBRARY

Founded 1973 under the British Library Act. Formed from the former British Museum library departments, National Central Library, British National Bibliography Ltd., and the National Lending Library for Science and Technology. It has three main divisions: Reference, Lending and Bibliographic Services.

BOARD OF MANAGEMENT:
2 Sheraton St., London, W1V 4BH.

*Chairman:* Sir FREDERICK DAINTON, F.R.S.
*Deputy Chairman and Chief Executive:* Sir HARRY HOOKWAY.

Publications: *The British Library Journal* (2 a year), *Annual Report, British Library News* (monthly).

**Reference Division:** Great Russell St., London, WC1B 3DG; contains over 10,000,000 printed books, about 81,000 Western and 37,000 Oriental MSS., 100,000 charters and rolls, 18,000 detached seals and casts of seals, 3,000 Greek and Latin papyri, and a fine collection of Egyptian papyri; public reading rooms for research, admission by reader's pass; exhibition galleries of books, maps, MSS. and postage stamps are open to the general public in Great Russell St., London, WC1B 3DG; Dir.-Gen. A. WILSON, F.L.A.; publs. bibliographic catalogues.

The Reference Division has four major departments:

*Department of Printed Books:* the most comprehensive copyright library of the United Kingdom, with large collections of early and foreign books and periodicals; there are sub-departments housing official papers, maps, music and postage stamps, the Newspaper Library (Colindale Ave., London, NW9 5HE) and the Library Association Library (7 Ridgmount St., London, WC1E 7AE); Keepers R. J. FULFORD, I. P. GIBB.

*Department of Manuscripts:* covers Western history, art and literature, including manuscripts, maps and music, from the earliest times to the present day; Dir. and Keeper D. P. WALEY.

*Department of Oriental MSS. and Printed Books:* 14 Store St., London, WC1E 7DG; covers the languages and literature of Asia and North Africa; especially rich in Hebrew, Arabic, Persian, Indian and Chinese MSS., and ancient versions of the Bible; over 400,000 printed books, incl. 8th- and 9th-century Japanese and Chinese; Keeper G. E. MARRISON.

*Science Reference Library:* principal public reference library in the United Kingdom for contemporary literature of physical sciences, technology, engineering, the life sciences and business information; Dir. M. W. HILL; publs. *Guide to S.R.L., Aids to Readers, Periodical Publications in the S.R.L., S.R.L. News, Guide to Government department and other libraries,* etc.

*Holborn Reading Room:* 25 Southampton Buildings, London, WC2A 1AW; f. as Patent Office Library 1855; 25,000 periodicals, 85,000 vols.; comprehensive collection of world patents literature.

*Aldwych Reading Room:* 9 Kean St., Drury Lane, London, WC2B 4AT; f. 1966; complements Holborn Branch collection on sciences, specializing in life and earth sciences; 25,000 periodicals, 70,000 vols. and pamphlets.

**Lending Division:** Boston Spa, Wetherby, West Yorks., LS23 7BQ; combines the resources of the former National Central Library and the former National Lending Library for Science and Technology; c. 4,450,000 vols., 56,000 current periodicals and c. 3,000,000 documents in microform; national centre for interlibrary lending; IFLA Office for International Lending; the Gift and Exchange Section is a major centre for the redistribution of surplus library materials; also contains the U.K. Medlars Service; Dir.-Gen. M. B. LINE, F.L.A.; publs. *Interlending Review* (quarterly), *Index of Conference Proceedings Received* (monthly with cumulations), *Current Serials Received* (annually), *British Reports, Translations and Theses* (monthly), *Keyword Index to Serial Titles: KIST* (quarterly).

**Bibliographic Services Division:** 2 Sheraton St., London, W1V 4BH; creates and publishes, in print and machine-readable forms, bibliographic records of items deposited in its Copyright Receipt Office (legal depository for U.K. and Irish publs.), audiovisual materials, music, serials, etc.; acts as National Serials Data Centre for the assignment of International Standard Serial Numbers; provides computer-driven local catalogue services (LOCAS) for other divisions of British Library and other U.K. libraries; operates on-line British Library Automated Information Service (BLAISE); Dir.-Gen. P. R. LEWIS; publs. *British National Bibliography* (weekly), *British Catalogue of Audiovisual Materials, British Catalogue of Music, British Education Index, Books in English* (microfiche), *Serials in the British Library, Research in British Universities, Polytechnics and Colleges.*

**Research and Development Department:** 2 Sheraton St., London, W1V 4BH; incorporates the functions of the fmr. Office of Scientific and Technical Information (OSTI); promotes and supports research and development related to libraries and information in all fields, and to this end awards research grants and contracts to outside bodies; Dir. B. J. PERRY (acting).

**National Library of Scotland:** George IV Bridge, Edinburgh, EH1 1EW; formerly known as the Advocates' Library; f. 1680s; contains about 4,000,000 vols. and pamphlets and a large collection of MSS.; under Copyright legislation may claim any book, etc., published in the United Kingdom and Ireland; Chair. of the Trustees M. F. STRACHAN, M.B.E., F.R.S.E.; Librarian E. F. D. ROBERTS, PH.D., F.R.S.E.; Keeper of MSS. T. I. RAE, PH.D.; Keepers of Printed Books J. R. SEATON, W. H. BROWN, M.SC., F.L.A., R. DONALDSON, PH.D., I. D. MCGOWAN; Sec. B. G. HUTTON.

*National Library of Scotland Lending Services:* Lawnmarket, Edinburgh, EH1 2PJ; f. 1921 as Scottish Central Library, merged with Nat. Library of Scotland 1974; maintains a stock of scarce and expensive books to supplement the reserves of Scottish public libraries, and to act as the headquarters for Scottish inter-library co-operation; c. 80,000 vols.; houses Scottish Union Catalogue recording locations for c. 800,000 works.

**National Library of Wales:** Aberystwyth, Dyfed; f. 1907; one of the six copyright libraries of the British Isles; c. 2,000,000 printed books, 30,000 MSS., over 3,500,000 deeds and documents and 120,000 maps, prints and drawings, including the finest existing Welsh collection; diaries and correspondence of David Lloyd George; Librarian R. GERAINT GRUFFYDD, D.PHIL.; publs. *The National Library of Wales Journal* (twice yearly), *Bibliotheca Celtica* (annually).

## GOVERNMENT LIBRARIES
### LONDON

**Departments of Industry and Trade. Common Services: Libraries:** 1 Victoria St., SW1 0ET; Head of Library Services F. COCHRANE, F.L.A., D.G.A.; publ. *Publications* (annual list of Departmental documents).

**Department of Industry Ashdown House Library:** 123 Victoria St., SW1E 6RB; British industry and industrial policy; the emphasis is on material published in the last ten years; Librarian Mrs. M. Y. KEARY, F.L.A.; publs. *Periodicals and Abstracts List, Statistics List.*

**Department of Trade Library:** 1 Victoria St., London, SW1H 0ET; f. 1950; mainly current material covering social sciences, descriptive economics; Librarian P. KIRWAN, M.A., F.L.A.; branch library:

*Solicitor's Library:* Monsanto House, 10–18 Victoria St., SW1H 0NQ; English and EEC law with emphasis on commercial and industrial subjects; Librarian N. A. HASKER, LL.B., A.L.A.

**Department of Trade Marine Library:** Sunley House, 90 High Holborn, London, WC1V 6LP; f. 1968; material on marine safety; employment, safety and health of seamen; safety of navigation search and rescue; oil pollution; Librarian Mrs. J. WRIGHT, B.A.

**Department of Trade Statistics and Market Intelligence Library:** Export House, 50 Ludgate Hill, London, EC4M 7HU; f. 1962; material on foreign and international official statistics; foreign trade directories; U.K. official statistics; public reference library; Librarian Miss M. E. COLLINS, B.SC., A.L.A.

**Business Statistics Office Library:** Cardiff Rd., Newport, Gwent, NPT 1XG; f. 1969; statistical methodology and U.K. official statistics; provides enquiry and information service; Librarian P. C. MCSHANE, M.A., A.L.A.

**Department of Energy Library:** Thames House South, Millbank, London, SW1P 4QJ; material on energy resources, policy and technology; economics of energy; Librarian Mrs. R. GOONESENA, B.A., A.L.A.; publs. *Dept. of Energy Publications in Print* (irregular).

**Offshore Supplies Office Library:** Alhambra House, 45 Waterloo St., Glasgow, G2 6AS; f. 1974; current material on all aspects of the offshore oil and gas industry; Librarian Mrs. A. DEMPSTER, B.A., A.L.A.

**Monopolies and Mergers Commission Library:** 48 Carey St., London, WC2A 2JT; f. 1970; material on monopoly, competition and anti-trust; industrial economics; Librarian Miss M. J. AITCHISON, A.L.A.

**Office of Fair Trading Library:** Field House, Breams Bldgs., London, EC4 1PR; f. 1973; material on consumer affairs; competition; consumer credit; monopolies; mergers and restrictive practices; Librarian Mrs. J. M. TITCOMBE, A.L.A.

**Foreign and Commonwealth Office Library:** Sanctuary Buildings, Great Smith St., SW1P 3BZ; additional service point in Downing St., SW1A 2AL. The library serving the Overseas Development Administration is situated in Eland House, Stag Place, SW1E 5DH. The library specializes in publications on international relations and diplomacy and the history, economy, politics and law of foreign and Commonwealth countries; includes books on early travel, diplomatic memoirs, treaty collections and material on all aspects of overseas development and technical assistance; about 750,000 volumes, mainly in European languages, long runs of periodicals and a map collection; reference library only; Librarian H. HANNAM, A.L.A.

**Department of Education and Science Library:** Elizabeth House, York Rd., S.E.1; f. 1896; contains over 183,000 vols.; the largest section consists of books and official publications dealing with the organization and administration of education; there is also a representative collection of books on theory of education, methods of teaching, psychology, educational buildings and equipment; Librarian DAVID N. ALLUM, B.A., A.L.A.; publs. *Library Bulletin* (monthly), subject bibliographies.

**Departments of the Environment and Transport Library:** 2 Marsham St., SW1P 3EB; provides information for the staff of the Department on housing, environmental and regional planning, pollution, highways, local government, natural resources, new towns, town and country planning, roads, ports, docks and harbours, traffic, transport, recreation, urban renewal, water supply and sewerage; Librarian W. PEARSON, M.B.E., B.SC.(ECON.), A.L.A.; publs. *Library Bulletin* (fortnightly, with a monthly supplement (legislation, circulars, technical memoranda), *Annual List of Publications, Register of Research and Surveys* (annually), Bibliographies.

**Department of Health and Social Security Library:** Alexander Fleming House, Elephant and Castle, London, SE1 6BY; f. 1834; contains over 200,000 vols. and pamphlets and 1,600 current periodicals on public health, health services, medicine, hospitals, social security and social welfare; Librarian Miss A. M. C. KAHN, M.B.E., B.A., F.L.A.; publs. *Hospital Abstracts, Current Literature on Health Services, Health Buildings Library Bulletin, Social Security Library Bulletin, Social Service Abstracts, Current Literature on Occupational Pensions* (all monthly), *Nursing Research Abstracts* (quarterly, in co-operation with the Nursing Division).

**Home Office Library:** 50 Queen Anne's Gate, SW1H 9AT; c. 53,000 vols., 7,500 microforms; social sciences, especially parliamentary material, criminal law, criminology, penology and community relations; available to researchers for reference by arrangement; Librarian D. B. GIBSON, F.L.A.; publ. *Home Office List of Publications* (annually).

**House of Commons Library:** London, SW1A 0AA; f. 1818; contains over 150,000 volumes, including Parliamentary Papers; the reference library files contain more than 1,500 periodicals and newspapers; the research division issues internal reference sheets, background papers and memoranda on subjects of current interest to Members; the branch library in the Norman Shaw North building handles enquiries on Parliament from the general public; Librarian DAVID MENHENNET, M.A., D.PHIL.

**House of Lords Library:** Old Palace Yard, Westminster, SW1A 0PW; f. 1826; contains about 90,000 volumes, legal and Parliamentary, history and general literature; Librarian ROGER H. V. C. MORGAN.

**India Office Library:** (Foreign and Commonwealth Office): 197 Blackfriars Rd., SE1 8NG; f. 1801; contains about 300,000 European and Oriental printed books, 20,000 Oriental MSS., 14,000 British paintings and drawings relating principally to India and the East, 10,000 Oriental drawings and miniatures and 170,000 photographs; Dir. B. C. BLOOMFIELD, M.A., F.L.A.; publs. *Annual Report, Guide* and catalogues of the collection.

**India Office Records:** (Foreign and Commonwealth Office): 197 Blackfriars Rd., SE1 8NG; London archives of British administration in India (East India Company 1600–1858, Board of Control 1784–1858, India Office 1858–1947, Burma Office 1937–48); some 175,000 vols., files and boxes of official records, 70,000 vols. of Government publs.; 30,000 maps; private papers of soldiers and civilians who served, travelled or resided in South Asia, 10,500 vols. and boxes; Dir. B. C. BLOOMFIELD, M.A., F.L.A.; publs. *Annual Report*, Lists and guides.

**Ministry of Agriculture, Fisheries and Food Library:** 3 Whitehall Place, SW1A 2HH; f. 1889; 160,000 vols., some 2,000 current periodicals and serials; includes Cowan and Cotton Libraries (books and periodicals on apiculture) and Punnett collection (poultry genetics); Librarian F. C. HIRST, O.B.E., F.L.A.; publs. *Plant Varieties and Seeds Gazette†* (monthly), *MAFF Publications: agriculture and food catalogue* (2 a year), *Plant Pathology†* (quarterly), Bulletins and Leaflets†.

*Branch Library:* Great Westminster House, Horseferry Rd., SW1P 2AE; approx. 30,000 vols., 620 current periodicals; Librarian Miss S. J. KEW, A.L.A.

*Branch Library:* Government Bldgs., Hook Rise South, Tolworth, Surbiton, Surrey, KT6 7NF; c. 1,300 vols., 12,500 pamphlets and reprints, 200 current periodicals; Librarian R. M. PARK, M.A., A.L.A.

**Ministry of Defence (Whitehall) Library:** Old War Office, Whitehall, SW1A 2EU; main library contains c. 900,000 vols. and pamphlets; sections: Defence Studies (Defence policy, history of regiments, British army campaigns); Scientific and Technical (aircraft, ships, weapons, computers and electronics, management systems and related subjects); General (international and domestic politics, economics, biographies, languages, geography, travel); a branch library serves the MOD Procurement Executive and contains 40,000 vols., 1,300 periodicals; Librarian J. C. ANDREWS, F.L.A.; publs. *Preview* (new books, monthly), *Reconnaissance* (periodical articles, monthly).

**Naval Historical Library:** Ministry of Defence, Empress State Bldg., Lillie Rd., SW6 1TR; f. 1810; 230,000 items; mainly maritime collections and associated subjects; reference only; Head of Library J. D. BROWN.

**Property Services Agency (Dept. of the Environment) Library:** C Block, Whitgift Centre, Wellesley Rd., Croydon, CR9 3LY; building and civil engineering design and construction; 50 branch technical libraries in the U.K. and overseas; special library: *Management and Training* (Cardington R.A.F. Station, Beds.); 150,000 vols., 700 current periodicals in main library; Chief Librarian C. E. ROGERS; publs. *Current Information in the Construction Industry†* (fortnightly), *Construction References†* (2 a year), bibliographies†, lists of reprints and translations, *PSA in Print* (annually).

**Treasury and Cabinet Office Library:** Parliament St., SW1P 3AG; 90,000 vols.; 700 periodicals; covers economics, finance and public administration; includes the library of the Central Statistical Office; Librarian J. H. WORMALD, B.SC.(ECON.), A.L.A.

**Tropical Products Institute Library:** 56-62 Gray's Inn Rd., WC1X 8LU; f. 1895; a scientific unit of the Overseas Development Administration, Foreign and Commonwealth Office, specializing in tropical plant and animal products with particular emphasis on post-harvest aspects; c. 100,000 items and 1,250 current periodical titles; Head of Library and Information Services J. A. WRIGHT, A.L.A.; publs. *Accession Bulletin* (c. 6 a year), *List of Current Periodicals* (annually).

PROVINCES

**National Meteorological Library:** London Rd., Bracknell, Berks., RG12 2SZ; f. 1870; approx. 135,000 vols. and 37,000 pamphlets; the national library for meteorology, climatology; and includes comprehensive records of data published by British and foreign institutions; Librarian E. W. C. HARRIS.

## PUBLIC LIBRARIES
### LONDON

**Barking and Dagenham Public Libraries:** Central Library, Barking, Essex, IG11 7NB; f. 1888; 470,000 vols.; Librarian LESLIE CANNON, F.L.A.

**Barnet Public Libraries:** Ravensfield House, The Burroughs, Hendon, NW4 4BE; f. 1965; 904,564 vols.; Librarian D. A. RUDDOM, A.L.A.

**Bexley Public Libraries:** Administrative Offices, Hall Place, Bourne Rd., Bexley, Kent; c. 500,000 vols.; 14 brs.; 2 mobile libraries, ref. library; Local History and Kent collections; Librarian G. BARNET.

**Brent Library Service:** 2–12 Grange Rd., Willesden Green, NW10 2QY; f. 1965; 725,000 vols.; 13 brs., mobile library, hospital library, housebound service, Grange Museum of Local History; Librarian and Curator J. N. CLARKE, M.A., A.L.A.

**Bromley Public Libraries:** Central Library, High St., Bromley, BR1 1EX; f. 1894; 867,093 vols.; 53,117 audio items; Librarian D. M. LAVERICK, F.L.A.

**Camden Public Libraries:** St. Pancras Library, 100 Euston Rd., London, NW1 2AJ; over 950,000 vols.; Dir. of Libraries and Arts F. D. COLE, F.L.A.

**Croydon Public Libraries:** Katharine St., Croydon, CR9 1ET; f. 1888; 550,000 vols.; Librarian A. O. MEAKIN, F.L.A.

**Ealing Public Libraries:** Walpole Park, Ealing, W5 5EQ; f. 1965; 623,329 vols.; Librarian M. W. MOSS, M.A., F.L.A.

**Enfield Public Libraries:** Central Library, Cecil Rd., Enfield, Middx., EN2 6TW; f. 1965; 700,000 vols.; 15 brs., 3 reference libraries, mobile library; Borough Librarian P. N. TURNER, F.L.A.

**Greenwich Public Libraries:** Greenwich Library, Woolwich Rd., SE10 0RL; f. 1905; 627,534 vols., 56,166 gramophone records, 7,200 tape cassettes; Borough Librarian J. LOWRY, B.A., A.L.A.

**Hackney Public Libraries:** Central Library, Mare St., Hackney, E8 1HG; f. 1908; 765,471 vols.; 16 brs. 3 ref. libraries; special collections: automobile engineering aviation, mechanic trades, woodwork and furniture, local history, John Dawson Collection, Defoe Collection; Librarian F. E. AYLEY, A.L.A. (acting); publ. *Preface* (quarterly).

**Hammersmith and Fulham Public Libraries:** Central Library, Shepherds Bush Rd., London, W6 7AT; 500,000 vols.; special collections include sociology, law, politics, civil administration, Christianity and early children's books; Librarian T. J. RIX, F.R.S.A., F.L.A.

**Haringey Libraries:** Central Library, High Rd., Wood Green, London, N22 6XD; Controller of Libraries W. S. H. ASHMORE, F.L.A.

**Harrow Public Library Service:** P.O. Box 4, Civic Centre, Harrow, HA1 2UU; f. 1965; 445,088 vols.; Librarian A. W. BALL, B.A., F.L.A.

**Havering Public Libraries:** Central Library, St. Edward's Way, Romford, Essex, RM1 3AR; c. 500,000 vols.; 9 brs., Arts Centre; Borough Librarian and Arts Officer D. A. PARTRIDGE, F.L.A.; publs. *Local Government Annotations* (*LOGA*) (monthly) on behalf of Advisory Body of Librarians—London Boroughs Association.

**Hillingdon Borough Libraries:** 22 High St., Uxbridge, Middx. UB8 1JN; f. 1965; 500,000 vols.; Librarian P. COLEHAN, F.L.A.

**Hounslow Library Services:** Dept. of Arts and Recreation, The Civic Centre, Lampton Rd., Hounslow, Middx. TW3 4DN; f. 1965; Librarian B. R. WALKINSHAW, B.A., A.L.A.

**Islington Libraries:** Central Library, 2 Fieldway Crescent, London, N5 1PF; f. 1905; 544,357 vols.; Borough Librarian R. G. SURRIDGE, M.A., F.R.S.A., F.L.A.

**Kensington and Chelsea Libraries and Art Service:** Central Library, Phillimore Walk, London, W.8; f. 1888; 520,000 vols.; the system includes the Chelsea Library, Chelsea Old Town Hall, Kings Rd., London, S.W.3; 4 brs., mobile library, art gallery at Leighton House, 12 Holland Park Rd., London, W.14; special collections: biography, languages, folklore, costume and local history; Borough Librarian and Arts Officer C. J. KOSTER, B.A., A.L.A.

**Kingston-upon-Thames Public Libraries:** Guildhall, Kingston-upon-Thames, Surrey, KT1 1EU; f. 1882; 330,000 vols.; Librarian G. P. ANDREW, A.L.A., F.B.I.M.

**Lambeth Public Libraries:** 164 Clapham Park Rd., London, SW4 7DD; f. 1888; over 950,000 vols.; Asst. Dir. Libraries JANET A. HILL.

**Lewisham Library Service:** Administrative Offices, 170 Bromley Rd., London, SE6 2UZ; f. 1890; 729,000 vols.; 17 brs., 2 reference libraries, Archives and Local History section, 1 medical library; Chief Librarian K. R. COX, A.L.A.; publ. *Comtech:* Commercial and Technical information review.

**Merton Public Libraries:** Administrative Offices, Merton Cottage, Church Path, S.W.19; f. 1965; 500,000 vols.; special collections: cricket, macroeconomics, tennis, world history; Librarian (vacant).

**Newham Public Libraries:** East Ham Library, High St. South, London, E6 4EL; f. 1965; 448,000 vols., 39,000 reference stock, 8,000 gramophone records; Librarian EDWARD MAY, B.A., A.L.A.

**Redbridge Public Libraries:** Central Library, Oakfield Rd., Ilford, Essex, IG1 1EA; Adult and reference 455,000 vols., Junior 119,000 vols., gramophone records and tapes 19,000; 10 brs., 2 mobile libraries, central ref. library; special collections: Photography and Social Pathology; Librarian F. C. KENNERLEY, F.L.A.; publ. *Introduction to Service* (irregularly).

**Richmond upon Thames Public Libraries:** Richmond Central Library, Little Green, Richmond, Surrey; f. 1880; 359,886 vols.; Librarian D. JONES, M.A., F.L.A.

**Southwark Public Libraries:** Admin. Dept., 20–22 Lordship Lane, SE22 8HN; 762,000 vols.; 45,152 records and tapes; 18 brs.; music library; Art Gallery; 2 museums; Librarian K. A. DOUGHTY, F.L.A.

**Sutton Libraries and Arts Services:** Central Library, St. Nicholas Way, Sutton, Surrey, SM1 1EA; f. 1936; 509,000 vols.; Borough Librarian R. SMITH, F.L.A., A.I.M.ENT.

**Tower Hamlets Public Libraries:** Central Library, Bancroft Rd., London, E1 4DQ; f. 1965; 466,763 vols.; special collections: General, American, French, German, Portuguese literature and texts; Yiddish, Hebrew and Judaica collections; Local History library; collection of books in Urdu, Bengali, Punjabi, Hindi and Gujerati; gramophone records and tape cassettes; Librarian D. T. ELLIOTT, B.A., M.L.S., F.L.A., M.B.I.M., M.INST.R.M.

**Upper Norwood Public Library:** Westow Hill, SE19 1TJ; collection on the Crystal Palace and its historical background; Librarian Mrs. P. SCOTT, A.L.A.

**Waltham Forest Public Libraries:** Central Library, High St., Walthamstow, London, E17 7JN; f. 1893; c. 650,000 vols.; special collections: Land Economics, Housing, Town Planning, Interior Decorating and Furnishing, Russia, Polar Regions, Domestic Economy; Librarian J. W. HOWES, F.L.A.

**Wandsworth Public Libraries:** Administrative Dept., Battersea District Library, 265 Lavender Hill, London, SW11 1JB; f. 1885; 943,874 vols.; 12 brs.; 2 reference libraries, 6 music libraries; special collections: architecture, town planning, European history, geography and travel, occult sciences, local history, early children's books, William Blake, G. A. Henty; Librarian D. F. PARKER, F.L.A., M.B.I.M.; publs. *Wandpetls Newsletter*, *Local History Slide Catalogue*, *Local History Portfolios of Prints* (Wandsworth, Battersea and Putney).

**Westminster City Libraries:** Central Administration, Marylebone Rd., NW1 5PS; total stock of books and other materials 1,871,710; City Librarian MELVYN BARNES, D.M.A., A.L.A., F.B.I.M.; the system includes the following libraries:

*Central Reference Library:* St. Martin's St., WC2H 7HP; 493,273 vols. covering the humanities, pure sciences, commerce and technology; British and foreign directories; over 1,000 current periodicals; Fine Arts Library; Pavlova Memorial Library; 28,000 maps; microfilm and microcard readers.

*Central Music Library:* Buckingham Palace Rd., SW1W 9UD; 91,600 items.

*Westminster History* and *Archives Dept.:* Buckingham Palace Rd., SW1W 9UD; 181,100 archives.

*Medical Library:* Marylebone Rd., NW1 5PS; 27,300 items.

*District Libraries:* Buckingham Palace Rd., SW1W 9UD, South Audley St., W1Y 5DJ, Gt. Smith St., SW1P 3DG, Rampayne St., SW1V 2PU, Charing Cross Rd., WC2H 0HG, Sutherland Ave., W9 2QT, Porchester Rd., W2 5DU, Circus Rd., NW8 6PD, Marylebone Rd., NW1 5PS, Church St., NW8 8EU, Little Portland St., W1N 5AG; Harrow Rd., W10 4NE.

### PROVINCES

**Avon County Library:** Central Library, College Green, Bristol, BS1 5TL; 57 brs., 11 mobile libraries (including 2 for schools); reference library; commerce and industry, fine art, music; 1,722,112 vols.; Dir. E. GRIMSHAW, F.L.A.

**Bedfordshire County Library:** County Hall, Bedford; f. 1925, reorganized 1974; District Libraries at Bedford, Biggleswade, Dunstable, Leighton Buzzard, Luton; special collections: Mott-Harrison collection of Bunyan life and works, Fowler collection of historical source material (County Hall); aeronautics, automobile engineering, picture lending collection, slides, audio-visual (district libraries); 1,250,000 vols.; gramophone records; 24 brs., 9 mobile libraries; special services for hospitals, housebound readers, local government, schools and young people; County Librarian C. MURIS, M.A., F.L.A.

**Berkshire County Library:** Shire Hall, Shinfield Park, Reading RG2 9XD; f. 1924; 1,018,946 vols.; 40 brs.; 8 mobile libraries (including 2 for schools and 2 for elderly and housebound); music and drama, British standards, selective H.M.S.O. since 1962, microfilm computer catalogue; County Librarian M. E. ASSER, F.L.A.

**Birmingham Public Libraries:** Central Library, Chamberlain Sq., Birmingham, B3 3HQ; f. 1861; 45 brs.; Reference Library f. 1866; Departments: Fine Arts (including John Ash Oberammergau Passion Play Collection), History and Geography (including Sir Benjamin Stone Collection of photographs and Marston Rudland Collection of Engraved Portraits), Language and Literature (including King's Norton Parish Library, Sheldon Rector's Library, Parker Collection of children's books, Samuel Johnson, Milton, Cervantes, Baskerville and War Poetry Collections, Early Printed Books, Fine Bindings and Private Press Books, and Shakespeare Library (f. 1864, 42,000 vols. in 87 languages), Local Studies (including Boulton and Watt, and Priestley Collections, Diocesan Record Office for Birmingham), Music Library, Philosophy and Religion, Quick Reference and Commercial Information, Science and Technology (including Patents), Social Sciences; United Nations depository; 1,140,000 vols. including 128 incunabula; City Librarian B. H. BAUMFIELD, F.L.A., F.R.S.A., F.B.I.M.

**Bradford Public Libraries:** Prince's Way, Bradford, BD1 1NN; 1,426,025 vols.; 36 libraries provide general collections; Central Library specializes in: Commerce, Science and Technology, Social Sciences, Music, Art, Local Studies, Archives, Asian Languages; Chief Librarian W. DAVIES, F.L.A.

**Buckinghamshire County Library:** County Offices, Walton St., Aylesbury, Bucks., HP20 1UU; f. 1918; 1,000,000 vols.; 44 full and part-time brs.; Country Librarian C. RIPPON, F.L.A.

**Cambridgeshire Libraries:** County Library H.Q., Princes St., Huntingdon, Cambs. PE18 6NS; 1,322,486 vols.; 55 brs., 9 mobile libraries; County Librarian B. A. DWYER, B.A., A.L.A. (acting).

**Cheshire Libraries and Museums:** 91 Hoole Rd., Chester, CH2 3NG; f. 1922; 1,700,000 vols.; 39 full-time, 12 part-time, 4 dual use brs., 6 public mobile libraries, 2 school mobile libraries, 2 trailer libraries and 3 research libraries; H.Q. special collections; Educational Resources Library; Dir. of Libraries and Museums PATRICK D. GEE, F.L.A.

**Cleveland County Libraries:** Central Library, Victoria Square, Middlesbrough, TS1 2AY; f. 1974; 1,176,000 vols.; 42 brs.; County Librarian F. REGAN, M.A., F.L.A., F.R.S.A.

**Cornwall County Library:** Old County Hall, Station Rd., Truro, Cornwall, TR1 3UV; f. 1925; 317,637 vols.; 29 brs., 10 mobile libraries; County Librarian J. E. FARMER, A.L.A.

**Coventry Public Library:** Administration and Reference Libraries, Bayley Lane, Coventry; 486,200 vols.; special collections on the motor industry, cycle industry, local history, George Eliot, trade unions and industrial relations; Dir. A. DAVIS.

**Derbyshire County Library:** County Offices, Matlock, Derbyshire, DE4 3AG; f. 1923; 1,746,718 vols.; 67 brs.; County Librarian P. D. GRATTON, B.A., D.P.A., F.L.A., F.R.S.A.

**Devon Library Services:** Barley House, Isleworth Rd., Exeter, EX4 1RQ; f. 1974; 2,000,000 vols.; 74 brs., 17 mobile libraries; County Librarian ALISON SHUTE.

*Area Libraries:*

North Devon: Vicarage St., Barnstaple, EX32 7EJ; Area Librarian K. HUNT, F.L.A.

South Devon: Lymington Rd., Torquay, TQ1 3DT; Area Librarian P. BOTTRILL, B.A., A.L.A.

Central Devon: Castle St., Exeter, EX4 3PQ; Area Librarian P. W. ELLIS, A.L.A.

East Devon: 40 Exeter Rd., Exmouth, EX8 1PS; Area Librarian M. MAGUIRE, A.L.A.

West Devon: Drake Circus, Plymouth, PL4 8AL; Area Librarian J. R. ELLIOTT, F.L.A.

**Dorset County Library:** Colliton Park, Dorchester, Dorset; f. 1920, reorganized 1974; 1,464,531 vols.; 53 brs.; 5 mobile libraries; special collections: Dorset Collection, Thomas Hardy Collection, Powys Collection; County Librarian H. E. RADFORD, F.L.A.; publs. *Annual Report, Subject Index.*

*West Area Headquarters:* Dorset County Library, Colliton Park, Dorchester; Assistant County Librarian (West Area) Miss J. M. RHODES, A.L.A.

*Central Area Headquarters:* Arndale Library, The Arndale Centre, Poole; Assistant County Librarian (Central Area) Miss S. J. SENIOR, B.A., D.M.A., F.L.A.

*East Area Headquarters:* Lansdowne Library, The Lansdowne, Bournemouth; Assistant County Librarian (East Area) H. N. HEISSIG, B.A., F.L.A.

**Durham County Library:** P.O. Box, County Hall, Durham; f. 1923; 1,600,000 vols.; 39 full-time brs., 29 part-time brs. 1 trailer, 6 mobile and 6 travelling libraries; County Librarian S. C. DEAN, F.L.A.

**Essex County Library:** County Library Headquarters, Goldlay Gardens, Chelmsford, Essex, CM2 0EW; 2,582,000 vols.; County Librarian BARRY LANGTON, A.L.A.

**Gloucestershire County Library:** Shire Hall, Quayside Wing, Gloucester, GL1 2HY; County Librarian B. STRADLING, F.L.A.

**Hampshire County Library:** 81 North Walls, Winchester, Hampshire, SO23 8BY; f. 1974; 3,434,619 vols.; 71 brs.; 22 mobile libraries; County Librarian J. C. BEARD, F.L.A.

**Hereford and Worcester County Libraries:** Love's Grove, Castle St., Worcester; f. 1974 as result of local government reorganization; 1,159,000 vols.; 20 full-time and 11 part-time service points, 3 school and 13 public mobile libraries, 2 college libraries and 1 architectural library; County Librarian Miss A. P. BARNES, M.A., F.L.A., F.R.S.A.

**Hertfordshire Library Service:** County Hall, Hertford; f. 1925; 3,600,000 vols.; 48 brs.; 13 mobile libraries; special collections: drama, music, local history; County Librarian E. M. BROOME, F.L.A.

**Humberside County Libraries:** Central Library, Albion St., Hull; 2,500,000 vols.; many special collections incl. whaling, shipping and trawling, iron and steel, John Wesley, Winifred Holtby, Andrew Marvell, Wilberforce, slavery, Napoleon; Dir. of Leisure Services R. G. ROBERTS, D.M.S., F.L.A., F.I.M.ENT.; various publs.

**Kent County Library:** Springfield, Maidstone, Kent; f. 1921; 3,500,000 vols.; Librarian DEAN HARRISON, M.A., F.L.A.

**Lancashire Library:** 143 Corporation St., Preston, PR1 8RH; f. 1924; 3,582,474 vols.; 110 brs., 13 mobile libraries; County Librarian MICHAEL J. DOLAN, A.L.A.

**Leeds City Libraries:** Municipal Bldgs., Calverley St., Leeds, LS1 3AB; 1,859,000 vols.; numerous special collections including fine botanical books, Jewish and Hebrew books, military history, patents, H.M.S.O. publications, Unesco documents, archives and maps; Librarian DEREK WILLIAMSON, M.A., F.L.A.

**Leicestershire Libraries and Information Service:** Thames Tower, 2 Navigation St., Leicester, LE1 3TZ; f. 1974; 2,000,000 vols.; sound recordings, pictures, films, filmstrips, slides, microforms; 76 libraries, 8 mobile libraries; County Librarian G. E. SMITH, O.B.E., F.L.A.; publs. local studies, abstracts, reports and booklists.

**Lincolnshire County Library:** Brayford House, Lucy Tower St., Lincoln, LN1 1XN; f. 1974 from 7 former Lincolnshire library authorities; 1,383,166 vols.; 48 brs., 13 mobile libraries, 2 trailer libraries; special collections: Agriculture, Lincolnshire material, Alfred Tennyson; County Librarian R. A. CARROLL, B.A., F.L.A.

**Liverpool City Libraries:** Brown, Picton and Hornby Libraries, William Brown St., Liverpool, Lancs., L3 8EW; f. 1852; 2,504,268 vols., pamphlets, MSS. etc.; Reference Library (Bibliographical Unit and Philosophy and Religion Library); Hornby Library (rare books, fine bindings, manuscripts and prints); Commercial and Social Sciences Library; Arts and Recreations Library; Music and Records Library; Commonwealth, American and International Libraries; Record Office and Local History Library (permanent exhibition *Liverpool from 1207*); Technical Library; Ladsirlac Industrial Library Services and Municipal Research Library; City Librarian RALPH MALBON.

**Manchester Public Libraries:** Central Library, St. Peter's Square, Manchester, M2 5PD; f. 1852; 2,129,358 vols.; includes social sciences, commercial, technical, arts, music, language and literature, local history, archives, Jewish and general libraries; two library theatres with resident company; 26 district libraries, with 4 mobile libraries, also libraries in old people's homes, hospitals and prisons; Dir. D. OWEN, B.A., A.L.A.

**Newcastle upon Tyne City Libraries:** Princess Square, off New Bridge St., NE99 1MC; f. 1880; 1,100,000 vols.; Thomas Bewick Collection (wood engravings), Thomlinson Library (theological), local collections, music, commercial and technical collections; all H.M.S.O. publications since 1958; Librarian A. WALLACE, F.L.A.

**Norfolk County Library:** County Hall, Norwich, NR1 2DH; f. 1925, reorganized 1974; 1,556,041 vols.; 3 divisional libraries; 43 brs.; 13 mobile libraries; County Librarian D. P. MORTLOCK, F.L.A.

**Northamptonshire Libraries:** 27 Guildhall Rd., Northampton, NN1 1EF; f. 1927; 1,224,620 vols.; 37,607 sound recordings; 5 full-time and 30 part-time brs.; County Leisure and Libraries Officer R. WRIGHT, F.L.A.; publs. *LOG* (weekly list of local government articles), *What the Papers Say* (daily), *DISCAT* (monthly).

**Northumberland County Library:** The Willows, Morpeth, Northumberland; f. 1924; 573,000 vols.; 31 brs., 7 mobile libraries; special collections: local history, drama, poetry, technical and commercial; County Librarian G. E. LAUGHTON, F.L.A.

**Nottinghamshire County Library:** Central Library, Angel Row, Nottingham; f. 1974; 569,125 vols.; special collections include local history, D. H. Lawrence, Byron and Robin Hood collections; Dir. of Leisure Services W. HEYCOCK.

**Oxfordshire County Libraries:** Holton, Oxford, OX9 1QQ; 900,000 vols.; 4,000 maps, 3,000 prints, 2,500 slides, 35,000 photographs of local history; 6,000 scores and 6,000 sound recordings; 17 full-time and 26 part-time libraries; 8 mobile libraries; 350 school libraries; County Librarian LEONARD WHITE, F.L.A.

**Sheffield City Libraries:** Central Library, Surrey St., Sheffield, S1 1XZ; f. 1856; 1,837,894 vols. (excluding sound recordings and MSS.); 37 br. libraries, 3 mobile libraries and 1 travelling library; Arts and Humanities Library (incl. private press books, Whitworth collection of organ books, books printed in England 1765–79); Science and Technology Library (incl. World Metal Index, British Patents (1617 to date); Business Library; Local Studies and Archives (incl. Arundel Castle MSS., Fairbank map collection, Edmund Burke's correspondence, parish records for Sheffield Archdeaconry; Wentworth Woodhouse Muniments, Carpenter Collection); photocopying and microfilm equipment; Dir. R. F. ATKINS, F.L.A.

**Shropshire County Library:** Column House, 7 London Rd., Shrewsbury. Shropshire; f. 1925; 725,000 vols., gramophone records; microfilm and computer catalogues; 32brs., 5 mobile and 3 trailer libraries; County Librarian A. J. CROWE, F.L.A.; reprints books on local history.

**Somerset County Library:** Mount St., Bridgwater, Somerset; f. 1919; 830,000 vols.; 33 brs., 9 mobile libraries; County Librarian R. J. STOAKLEY, F.L.A.

**Staffordshire County Library:** Friars Terrace, Stafford ST17 4AY; f. 1916; 3,222,607 vols., 52,985 gramophone records; 44 full-time and 34 part-time brs., 7 mobile libraries; schools service includes books, project collections, gramophone records, films and filmstrips; technical and commercial information services; County Librarian L. J. LIVESEY, F.L.A.; publs. *UPDATE: Current Awareness Bulletin* (monthly), *CONTACT: Abstracts on Local Government* (monthly).

**Suffolk County Library:** County Hall, St. Helen's St., Ipswich IP4 2JS; f. 1974 by amalgamation of former Suffolk library authorities; County Librarian P. R. LABDON, F.L.A.

**Surrey County Library:** West St., Dorking; 1,579,758 vols.; County Librarian J. A. SAUNDERS, A.L.A.

**East Sussex County Library:** Southdown House, 44 St. Anne's Crescent, Lewes, East Sussex, BN7 1SQ; 1,750,000 vols.; 30 full-time and 14 part-time brs.; County Librarian J. N. ALLEN, B.A., F.L.A.

**(West) Sussex County Council Library Service:** Tower St., Chichester, Sussex; f. 1925; 1,140,000 vols.; 31 full-time and 6 part-time brs., 7 mobile libraries; County Librarian R. J. HUSE, F.L.A.

**Warwickshire County Library:** The Butts, Warwick, CV34 4SS; f. 1920; 1,128,000 vols.; 36 brs.; County Librarian T. W. HOWARD, F.L.A.; publ. *Annual Report*.

**Wiltshire Library and Museum Service:** Library and Museum Service Headquarters, Bythesea Rd., Trowbridge, Wilts.; f. 1919; 2,001,200 vols., gramophone records, cassettes, slides, films, etc.; 44 brs., 6 mobile libraries; special collections: Wiltshire, agriculture, cricket, food technology, life of Christ, railways and railway engineering; Dir. FREDERICK HALLWORTH, O.B.E., F.L.A., F.R.G.S.; publs. *Biennial Report, Lackham Library Bulletin* (10 a year).

**Yorkshire (North) County Library:** County Library Headquarters, Grammar School Lane, Northallerton, Yorks., DL6 1DF; f. 1974; 1,357,630 vols.; 19 full-time, 42 part-time libraries, 21 mobile libraries, 2 voluntary centres; special collections: local history and topography, drama, music, early children's literature; Sitwell Collection; Petyt Library relating to 17th ecntury; Sir John Marriott Collection of modern European history; Spa/Mineral waters, from 1572; Bertram Unne Photograph Collection (Yorkshire 1945–75); County Librarian DOROTHY M. HUDSON, F.L.A.; publs. occasional.

## SCOTLAND

**Dundee District Libraries:** Central Library, The Wellgate, Dundee, DD1 1DB; 13 brs. and 1 part-time br., mobile library; 520,000 vols.; Chief Librarian DUNCAN M. TORBET, F.L.A.

**Edinburgh City Libraries:** Central Library, George IV Bridge, Edinburgh, EH1 1EG; f. 1890; 1,197,403 items; 21 brs., 4 mobile libraries; special collections: Edinburgh Room (contains information on life in Edinburgh and on Scott, Stevenson, Ballantyne; press cuttings; 68,649 items), Scottish (especially genealogy; 76,265 items), Music (includes indexes to songs and instrumental music; 52,688 items), Fine Art (includes costume; large collection of prints; 90,526 items); Audio library: 11,325 items; City Librarian A. P. SHEARMAN, B.A., F.L.A.

**Glasgow District Libraries:** Glasgow; includes The Mitchell Library; f. 1874 (*see below*); Commercial Library with Library of Patents and 44 district libraries; 2,735,234 vols.; special collections of books for the blind and foreign literature and local history; Dir. W. A. G. ALISON, F.L.A.; publ. *Annual Report*.

**Mitchell Library:** North St., Glasgow, G3 7DN; f. 1874; 1,042,438 vols.; special collections: on Glasgow (20,000 vols.), music (35,000 vols.), Robert Burns (3,500 vols.), and Scottish poetry (9,000 vols.); Librarian R. A. GILLESPIE, F.L.A. The Library receives a copy of every publication issued by H.M.S.O., and is also a Depository Library for the unrestricted publications of the United Nations, Unesco and FAO.

**Kirkcaldy District Library:** East Fergus Place, Kirkcaldy, Fife KY1 1XT; f. 1975 after reorganization; 340,000 vols.; Librarian RONALD McLAREN, A.L.A.

**Renfrew District Libraries:** Marchfield Ave., Paisley, Renfrewshire, PA3 2RJ; f. 1920, reorganized 1975; 502,000 vols.; 26 brs., toy library, local government library, 2 mobile libraries; Chief Librarian JOSEPH D. HENDRY, M.A., F.L.A., F.S.A.(SCOT.), A.M.B.I.M.

## WALES

**Clwyd Library Service:** County Civic Centre, Mold, CH7 6NW; f. 1974 (previously Flintshire, Denbighshire, part of Merioneth, Colwyn Bay, Flint, Rhyl and Wrexham Library Services); 1.5 million vols.; 6 area libraries, 21 full-time brs., 28 part-time libraries, 17 mobile libraries; special collections of Arthurian literature and local history; County Librarian GLYN DAVIES, F.L.A., F.R.S.A.

**Dyfed County Library:** Public Library, St. Peter's St., Carmarthen, SA31 1LN; f. 1974; 818,077 vols.; 47 brs.; special collections: Francis Green MSS., Henry Owen Library (5,000 vols., historical and local), part of the library of the Carmarthenshire Antiquarian Society; County Librarian (vacant).

**Gwent County Library:** County Library H.Q. ,County Hall, Cwmbran, Gwent, NP44 2XL; f. 1974; 902,000 vols.; 32 brs.; County Librarian M. F. A. ELLIOTT, F.L.A., L.R.A.M.

**Gwynedd Library Service:** Maesincla, Caernarfon, Gwynedd; f. 1974; 848,126 vols.; 44 brs.; County Librarian GEOFFREY THOMAS, B.A., F.L.A.

**Mid Glamorgan County Library:** Coed Parc, Park St., Bridgend, Mid.-Glam., CF31 4BA; f. 1974; 785,186 vols.; 11 full-time and 18 part-time brs.; County Librarian R. W. DAVIES, F.L.A.

**Powys County Library:** Cefnllys Rd., Llandrindod Wells, Powys, LD1 5LD; f. 1974; 633,000 vols.; 24 brs.; special local history collection; County Librarian GEORGE LLEWELLYN, F.L.A.

**South Glamorgan County Libraries:** Central Library, Cardiff, S. Glam., CF1 2QU; f. 1974 after reorganization; 1,222,000 vols.; 33 br. libraries; County Librarian G. A. DART, F.L.A.

**Cardiff Central Library:** f. 1862; Reference Dept., including patents (except specifications), maps, prints, periodicals, Societies' libraries; Research dept., including MSS., deeds, documents, incunabula, large Welsh and other special reference collections; Commercial dept., Lending dept., and music and gramophone record collections.

## SPECIAL LIBRARIES

### LONDON

**Aslib Library:** 3 Belgrave Square, SW1X 8PL; c. 16,000 vols. on documentation, information science, special libraries and related subjects, 370 current periodicals of the world and about 25,000 references to articles, reports, etc., on library and information science; Librarian Miss V. K. GILBERT, B.A., M.I. INF. SCI.; publ. monthly current awareness lists in *Aslib Information*.

**Bray Libraries (SPCK):** Holy Trinity Church, Marylebone Rd., London, N.W.1; f. 1730 by Dr. Thomas Bray (1658–1730) to set up and administer libraries at home and abroad for the use of the clergy and the laity; libraries in Australia, Africa, Japan, New Guinea and elsewhere, as well as in the U.K.

**British and Foreign Bible Society's Library:** 146 Queen Victoria St., EC4V 4BX; f. 1804; largest collection of printed Bibles (over 28,000 vols. of Scripture in more than 2,000 languages); Librarian ALAN F. JESSON, M.L.S., A.L.A.; publs. *Word in Action*† (3 a year), library guide, sectional catalogues.

**British Architectural Library:** R.I.B.A., 66 Portland Place, W1N 4AD; f. 1834; with c. 130,000 vols., 680 current periodicals, 400 dead runs, c. 40,000 photographs, c. 100,000 MSS., and an important collection of c. 250,000 drawings (housed at 21 Portman Square, W1H 9HF), is one of the most complete architectural libraries; Librarian D. E. DEAN, M.A., A.L.A., F.R.S.A.; publs. *Architectural Periodicals Index* (quarterly), *R.I.B.A. Booklist* (annually).

**British Broadcasting Corporation Reference Library:** Broadcasting House, London, W1A 1AA; f. 1927; 170,000 vols., 1,500 British and foreign periodicals; Librarian G. L. HIGGENS, F.L.A.

**B.B.C. Music Library:** Yalding House, 156 Great Portland St., London, W1N 6AJ; over 250,000 sets of music, 5,000 vols. of reference material; Librarian M. MILLER, M.A., L.R.A.M., F.L.A.

**British Institute of Recorded Sound:** 29 Exhibition Rd., S.W.7; f. 1955; national archive of sound recordings; contains over 300,000 discs and tape recordings of music, drama and literature, language and dialect, speeches and events, wildlife sounds, etc.; library of books, periodicals, and record manufacturers' catalogues from all countries; Dir. Dr. ANTHONY KING; publ. *Recorded Sound*† (2 a year).

**British Medical Association Library:** Tavistock Square, WC1H 9JP; f. 1887; 90,000 vols., 5,000 periodicals; Librarian D. J. WRIGHT, B.A., A.L.A.

**British Museum (Natural History) Library:** Cromwell Rd., SW7 5BD; f. 1881; 750,000 vols. on biological and earth sciences (zoology, entomology, botany, palaeontology inc. physical anthropology and mineralogy); Librarian A. P. HARVEY, M.I.INF.SCI.; publs. *Bulletin British Museum Natural History*† (5 series: *Botany, Entomology, Geology, Historical, Zoology*) (irregular), scientific books, leaflets and special publications.

**British Theatre Association Library:** 9 Fitzroy Square, W1P 6AE; f. 1919; 250,000 vols. inc. several hundred MSS.; special collections include William Archer Collection (books, programmes), Nugent Monck Collection (prompt copies, privately printed plays, etc.); available to members only; Librarian ENID FOSTER.

**Canning House Library:** The Hispanic and Luso-Brazilian Council, Canning House, 2 Belgrave Square, S.W.1; f. 1943; 50,000 vols., and cultural and economic periodicals; Librarian Miss M. C. YOUNGER, B.LIB., A.L.A.; publs. *British Bulletin of Publications on Latin America, the Caribbean, Portugal and Spain* (2 a year).

**Church Missionary Society Library:** 157 Waterloo Rd., SE1 8UU; f. 1799; approx. 20,000 vols.; religion, social sciences, history, language, description and travel; special collections include James Long Bequest (books on Islam and Buddhism); Librarian Miss J. M. WOODS; Archivist Miss R. A. KEEN.

**College of Arms:** Queen Victoria St., EC4V 4BT; c. 30,000 vols.; genealogical and heraldic collections; Registrar and Librarian J. P. BROOKE-LITTLE, M.V.O., M.A., F.S.A., F.S.G., F.H.S. (Norroy and Ulster King of Arms).

**Congregational Library:** Memorial Hall, 2 Fleet Lane, E.C.4; f. 1830; contains about 40,000 vols., mainly relating to Church history, the history and activities of the Nonconformists, theology, religious liberty and hymnology.

**H.M. Customs and Excise Library:** King's Beam House, Mark Lane, EC3 7HE; f. 1671; contains about 40,000 vols.; also departmental museum; Head of Library Services S. R. PRESTIDGE.

**Dr. Williams's Library:** 14 Gordon Square, WC1H 0AG; opened 1729; contains c. 132,000 vols., a lending library of theological, philosophical and historical works; Librarian JOHN CREASEY, M.A., A.L.A.; publs. *Catalogue of Accessions 1900-1950, 1951-1960, 1961-1970*, *Bulletin of Accessions* (annual), *Lectures of Friends of Dr. Williams's Library* (annual), occasional papers.

**Friends' Library:** Friends' House, Euston Rd., NW1 2BJ; f. 1673; the official library of the Society of Friends (Quakers) in Great Britain and the repository of its archives; contains about 14,000 vols., 20,000 pamphlets, and 4,000 vols. of MSS., as well as prints and photographs; Librarian EDWARD H. MILLIGAN.

**Geological Society Library:** Burlington House, Piccadilly, London, W1V 0JU; f. 1807; c. 300,000 vols., 38,000 maps; lending restricted to the U.K.; back-up library to British Lending Library; personal access to facilities restricted to Fellowship; Librarian Mrs. E. R. NUTT.

**Gray's Inn Library:** South Square, Gray's Inn, WC1R 5EU; f. c. 1522; 40,000 vols.; Legal Reference Library, for members of Gray's Inn, others admitted on application; special collections: 12th–14th century MSS., Baconiana; Librarian P. C. BEDDINGHAM.

**Guildhall Library** (Library of the Corporation of London): Aldermanbury, EC2P 2EJ; f. about 1425; contains 150,000 printed books, etc., more than 80,000 series of MSS., 30,000 prints and 30,000 maps; general reference library, particularly rich in books on all aspects of London history; the MSS. collection consists mainly of City parochial records, records of the City Livery Companies, London diocesan records, and records of major London commercial institutions; City Librarian GODFREY THOMPSON, M.A., F.S.A., F.L.A.; publ. *Guildhall Studies in London History* (2 a year).

**City Business Library:** Gillett House, Basinghall St., London, EC2V 5BX; contains British and foreign directories, newspapers, trade papers, statistics and all aspects of commerce and management; Business Librarian M. J. CAMPBELL, A.L.A.

**Hirsch Music Library:** British Library, Great Russell St., W.C.1; purchased for the nation in 1946; a unique collection of music, musical treatises and theoretical works prior to 1800, full operatic scores and complete and first editions of the classics with an extensive collection of musical literature from the nineteenth and twentieth centuries; Music Librarian O. W. NEIGHBOUR.

**Inner London Education Authority Education Library:** County Hall, Westminster Bridge, SE1 7PB; f. 1909; c. 200,000 vols., general collection, emphasis on history, theory and methods of education and child study; Librarian PAMELA MUNNS, A.L.A.

*Reference Library and Information Service:* 275 Kennington Lane, SE11 5Q2; f. 1972; current learning/teaching materials to F. E. level; books and A/V items.

**Inner Temple Library:** Temple, London, E.C.4; f. c. 1500; c. 90,000 vols.; mostly legal and historical; contains in addition to U.K. law and legal history, an extensive collection of law relating to the British Commonwealth. Collection of 10,000 MSS., including Petyt MSS., available to the public (on special application) for historical research; Librarian W. W. S. BREEM.

**Inns of Court Bar Library and Probate Library:** Royal Courts of Justice, Strand, WC2A 2LL; f. 1883; contains 25,000 vols.; Librarian C. L. FISHER, M.B.E.

**Institute of Contemporary History—Wiener Library:** 4 Devonshire St., W.1; f. in Amsterdam in 1934 by Dr. Alfred Wiener, moved to London 1939; about 100,000 vols. and newspapers, magazines, press cuttings, photos and other documents on Nazism, Fascism, anti-Semitism, racialism, refugee and minority problems, Jewish history and contemporary European, Jewish and Middle Eastern history; Librarian Mrs. CHRISTA WICHMANN; publs. *The Wiener Library Bulletin, The Wiener Library Catalogue Series, Journal of Contemporary History.*

**Institute of Geological Sciences Reference Library of Geology:** Geological Museum, Exhibition Rd., SW7 2DE; f. 1837; incorporating the libraries of the Geological Survey and Museum and the Overseas Geological Surveys; 300,000 vols., 3,000 (titles) current serials, over 150,000 maps, 60,000 pamphlets, 20,000 archives; national collection of 25,000 photographs illustrating British scenery and geology; regional collections in branch libraries at Edinburgh, Keyworth (Nottingham) and Leeds; Chief Librarian and Archivist K. J. SPENCER, F.L.A.

**Institution of Electrical Engineers' Library:** Savoy Place, WC2R 0BL; f. 1871; the main collection contains over 30,000 books, 20,000 bound volumes of periodicals, 20,000 reports, pamphlets, etc.; over 700 periodicals are received; special collections of historical electrical works: Sir Francis Ronalds Collection (6,000 vols. and pamphlets), Silvanus P. Thompson Library (4,500 vols. and 8,000 pamphlets), Faraday MSS., and library, notebooks and MSS. of Oliver Heaviside; also holds Library of British Computer Society (5,000 vols., 3,000 pamphlets and 100 periodicals); Librarian JANET P. TOMLINSON, A.L.A.A.; publs. numerous journals, abstracts and papers on physics, electronics, electrical engineering, etc.

**Lambeth Palace Library:** Lambeth SE1 7JU; f. 1610; contains about 150,000 printed items and 3,000 vols. of MSS. dating back to the 9th century, also a considerable number of archives; Librarian and Archivist E. G. W. BILL, M.A.

**Law Society Library:** Chancery Lane, London, WC2A 1PL; f. 1828; 65,000 vols., primarily English legal material; Librarian F. P. RICHARDSON, F.L.A.

**Library Association Library:** see British Library.

**Lincoln's Inn Library:** Holborn, W.C.2; in existence 1475; with 100,000 vols. and 2,000 vols. of MSS., including the Hale Collection, is the oldest law library in London; Librarian R. WALKER.

**Linnean Society Library:** Burlington House, Piccadilly, W1V 0LQ; f. 1788; contains about 90,000 vols. on natural history, including Linnaeus's own library and a collection of manuscripts, engravings and portraits; Librarian GAVIN BRIDSON; publs. *Biological Journal, Botanical Journal, Zoological Journal* (all 8 a year), *Synopses of the British Fauna* (occasional), *Symposia* volumes (annually).

**London Library:** 14 St. James's Square, SW1Y 4LG; f. 1841; c. 1,000,000 vols. covering a wide range of subjects and languages; subscription circulating and reference library; an educational charity under Royal Charter; Librarian DOUGLAS MATTHEWS, B.A., F.L.A.

**London Oratory Library:** Brompton Rd., South Kensington, S.W.7; f. 1854; contains 40,000 vols. and 3,000 pamphlets on Theology and Church History; separate library (4,000 vols.) of David Lewis, Tractarian convert.

**Marx Memorial Library:** Marx House, 37 Clerkenwell Green, London, E.C.1; f. 1933; approx. 20,000 vols.; 25,000 pamphlets, files of Labour, Socialist and Communist periodicals; research, reading and lending; lectures, study courses and discussion conferences; Librarian CHARLES HALL; publ. *Biennial Bulletin.*

**Metals Society Library:** 1 Carlton House Terrace, S.W.1; f. 1869; 30,000 vols.; Librarian G. TURPIE, B.SC.; publs. *Isips* (weekly subject profiles), *World Calendar of Forthcoming Meetings* (quarterly), *International Metals Publications* (monthly), *Transactions.*

**Middle Temple Library (The Hon. Society of the):** Middle Temple Lane, EC4Y 9BT; f. 1641; contains c. 125,000 vols. of works on British, Commonwealth, American, Public International and European Communities law; Librarian and Keeper of the Records Miss E. McNEILL, B.A., D.L.S., A.T.C.L., A.L.A.

**National Film Archive:** 81 Dean St., London, W1V 6AA; f. 1935 as a division of the British Film Institute; preserves for posterity, and makes available for study, cinematograph films and TV programmes, stills, posters and set designs of artistic and historical value; Curator DAVID FRANCIS.

**Royal Academy of Arts Library:** Burlington House, W.1; f. 1768; over 15,000 vols. on the fine arts and standard reference books; also original drawings, MSS. and engravings; Librarian Miss CONSTANCE-ANNE PARKER.

**Royal Asiatic Society Library:** 56 Queen Anne St., W.1; f. 1823; c. 100,000 vols. dealing with Asia, and 2,000 Oriental MSS.; Librarian Dr. R. K. P. PANKHURST; publs. *Journal of the Royal Asiatic Society* (2 a year), monographs.

**Royal Astronomical Society Library:** Burlington House, Piccadilly, London, W1V 0NL; f. 1820; c. 25,000 vols. and archives; Librarian Mrs. E. LAKE, B.SC.

**Royal Botanic Gardens, Library and Archives Division:** Kew, Richmond, Surrey; f. 1852; over 120,000 vols., 3,000 periodicals, 140,000 pamphlets, 170,000 plant illustrations; statutory place of deposit;· registered files and 250,000 letters and MSS.; Chief Librarian and Archivist Miss S. M. D. FITZGERALD, B.A., A.L.A.; publs. *Kew Record of Taxonomic Literature* (annually), *Author and Classified Catalogues, List of Periodicals.*

**Royal College of Physicians' Library:** 11 St. Andrew's Place, Regent's Park, London, NW1 4LE; f. 1518; confined to the history of medicine, with a bias towards medical biography, but rich in 16th- and 17th-century books covering the whole field of learning, also a small collection of books on medical education; contains 48,000 books and pamphlets (incl. over 100 incunabula), 3,000 MSS. (Western and Oriental), 5,000 autograph letters, 12,000 engraved portraits and photographs and 2,800 slides (mainly portraits); Harveian Librarian Sir GORDON WOLSTENHOLME, O.B.E., F.R.C.S.; Librarian DENNIS COLE, M.A., A.L.A.; publs. *Munk's Roll* (Lives of Fellows of the College) 5 vols. 1876–1968, *Evan Bedford Library of Cardiology: catalogue,* exhibition catalogues, etc.

**Royal College of Surgeons of England Library:** 35–43 Lincoln's Inn Fields, WC2A 3PN; f. 1800; medical and surgical books and 650 current periodicals; 130,000 volumes; Librarian E. H. CORNELIUS, M.A., A.L.A.; publs. *History of College the* (1959), *English Books before 1701* (1963), *Ann,als† Catalogues of Hunterian Museum.*

**Royal College of Veterinary Surgeons' Wellcome Library:** 32 Belgrave Square, SW1X 8PQ; open to all qualified veterinary surgeons; 25,000 vols.; Librarian Miss B. HORDER, B.A., A.L.A.

**Royal Commonwealth Society Library:** Northumberland Ave., WC2N 5BJ; f. 1868; contains 400,000 vols. and pamphlets relating to the countries of the Commonwealth; Librarian D. H. SIMPSON, M.A., F.L.A.; publ. *Library Notes* (6 a year).

**Royal Geographical Society Library:** Kensington Gore, SW7 2AR; f. 1830; contains 100,000 vols. on geography; 600,000 maps and charts, 4,000 atlases, large selection of gazetteers and expedition reports in the Map Room; Librarian G. S. DUGDALE; publ. *The Geographical Journal†* (3 a year).

**Royal Institute of International Affairs Library:** 10 St. James's Square, London, SW1Y 4LE; f. 1920; over 158,000 vols., c. 630 current periodicals; Librarian Mrs. N. M. GALLIMORE, L. ÈS.L., DIP.LIB.

    **Press Library:** over 20,000 box files of classified cuttings from the international press dating from 1924 (only 1940 onwards available at present); Press Librarian Miss S. J. BOYDE, M.A., DIP. LIB.

**Royal Institution of Great Britain Library:** 21 Albemarle St., W.1; f. 1799; 50,000 vols. on all branches of science; 150 periodicals currently received; special collections: scientific biography, social relations of science, popular science, history of science, early scientific books and journals especially of 18th and 19th centuries, photochemistry, X-ray crystallography; archives and MSS. of many scientists who have worked at the Institution, including Davy, Faraday, Tyndall, Dewar and the Braggs; Librarian Mrs. I. M. MCCABE, M.SC., DIP. LIB.

**Royal National Institute for the Deaf Library and Information Services:** 105 Gower St., London, WC1E 6AH; f. 1911; 10,000 books and 300 current journals on all aspects of sound, hearing, speech and language; Librarian M. E. PLACKETT, A.L.A.; publ. *Hearing* (every 2 months).

**Royal Society Library:** 6 Carlton House Terrace, SW1Y 5AG; f. 1660; c. 150,000 vols.; Librarian N. H. ROBINSON.

**Royal Society of Chemistry Library:** Burlington House, Piccadilly, W1V 0BN; f. 1841; over 70,000 vols.; is a fine collection of works on chemistry and cognate subjects; special collection of books on alchemy and early chemistry; Librarian R. G. GRIFFIN, F.L.A.

**Royal Society of Medicine Library:** 1 Wimpole St., W1M 8AE; f. 1805; important medical library, comprising c. 500,000 vols., c. 2,000 current periodicals; extended 1953, by benefaction from the Wellcome Trust; lending restricted to members; back-up library to British Library; Librarian D. W. C. STEWART.

**Royal United Services Institute for Defence Studies Library:** Whitehall, London, SW1A 2ET; f. 1831 as the Royal United Service Institution Library; about 100,000 vols., 200 periodicals on British defence and related subjects, international affairs.

**St. Bride Printing Library:** Bride Lane, Fleet St., E.C.4; f. 1895; devoted to works on printing and the allied crafts; contains about 30,000 vols.; Librarian J. M. MOSLEY.

**St. Paul's Cathedral Library:** E.C.4; f. 1707; containing old works on theology and Greek and Latin classics, also some interesting MSS.; upwards of 13,500 vols. and 11,500 pamphlets; Librarian FRANK ATKINSON.

**Science Museum Library:** South Kensington, SW7 5NH; a national library of pure and applied science and the history of science and technology, with c. 465,000 vols. including 21,000 periodicals, of which some 6,300 titles are current; photocopying and information services; Keeper L. R. DAY, M.SC.

**Sion College Library:** Victoria Embankment, EC4Y 0DN; f. 1630; contains about 100,000 vols., including MSS., mostly theological; Librarian Miss J. M. OWEN, B.A., A.L.A.

**Sir John Soane's House and Museum Library:** 13 Lincoln's Inn Fields, W.C.2; f. 1837; contains Sir John Soane's collection of some 8,000 vols. on art, antiquities, architecture, classical and general literature; Curator and Librarian Sir JOHN SUMMERSON, C.B.E., F.B.A., A.R.I.B.A.

**Societies for the Promotion of Hellenic and Roman Studies Library:** 31–34 Gordon Square, London, WC1H 0PP; f. 1879; in association with London University Institute of Classical Studies; contains over 55,000 vols. on classical archaeology, history, and literature; classified collection of over 5,000 coloured slides; Librarian Miss A. E. HEALEY, B.A., A.L.A.

**Society of Antiquaries Library:** Burlington House, Piccadilly, W1V 0HS; f. 1707; contains more than 130,000 books and 650 current periodicals on British and Foreign archaeology and history, heraldry, genealogy, etc., MSS., prints, drawings, early printed books, brass rubbings, seal casts; Librarian J. H. HOPKINS, M.A.; publs. *Antiquaries Journal†* (2 a year), *Archaeologia†*, research reports† (occasionally).

**Supreme Court Library:** Royal Courts of Justice, Strand, London, WC2A 2LL; f. 1970; common law library; 150,000 vols.; Librarian K. W. BEST, M.B.E., F.L.A.

**United Nations Information Centre Library:** 14-15 Stratford Place, W.1; contains all United Nations documents and publications, and selection of publications from the specialized agencies; Librarian Miss M. P. FARQUHAR, B.A., A.L.A.

**Victoria and Albert Museum, Library of the:** South Kensington, SW7 2RL; f. 1837; contains over 600,000 vols.; is the national collection of works on the fine and applied arts; the Dyce and Forster libraries number about 32,000 vols., mostly English literature, history and drama; other special collections include fine bookbindings, the Clements Collection of British Armorial Bookbindings, 20th-century French illustrated books and the Guy Little collection of children's books; Keeper of the Library R. W. LIGHTBOWN, M.A., F.S.A., F.R.A.S.

**Wellcome Institute for the History of Medicine Library:** 183 Euston Rd., NW1 2BP; f. c. 1890, opened to public 1949; over 600 incunabula; c. 400,000 books; broadsides; 50,000 pamphlets, 2,670 periodical titles; 5,000 Western MSS.; 9,000 Oriental MSS. in over 30 languages; 100,000 autograph letters; 100,000 prints, drawings, paintings; 9,000 photographic slides, 38,000 negatives; 650 microforms, 20 films; medical imprints of the colonial Americans 1557–1833; Librarian E. J. FREEMAN, B.A., A.L.A.; publs. *Medical History* (quarterly), *Current Work in the History of Medicine* (bibliographical quarterly).

**Westminster Chapter Library:** Westminster Abbey, S.W.1; f. 1623–25; contains about 14,000 vols., mainly 17th- and 18th-century, predominantly theological but with general literature and 16th- and 17th-century music; remarkable collection of Abbey Records and other documents, etc.; Librarian H. M. NIXON, M.A., F.S.A.; Keeper of Muniments N. H. MACMICHAEL, F.S.A., F.R.HIST.S.

**Zoological Society Library:** Regent's Park, N.W.1; f. 1826; contains about 150,000 vols. of works and periodicals connected with zoology; Librarian R. FISH, F.L.A.

PROVINCES

**Canterbury Cathedral Archives and Library and City Record Office:** Canterbury; f. probably about 597; in continuous existence since 11th century; contains c. 50,000 printed books, administrative MSS. of the Dean and Chapter, Canterbury Diocesan Archives (excluding probate and testamentary records), Canterbury City archives; Canon-Librarian Rev. Canon A. M. ALLCHIN, M.A.; Archivist and Dir. Miss A. M. OAKLEY, M.A., A.L.A., F.S.A.

**Chetham's Library:** Long Millgate, Manchester, M3 1SB; f. 1653 as a free public reference library; c. 70,000 vols.

including many 17th and 18th century works; Librarian Miss A. C. SNAPE, M.A.

**Dean Savage Reference Library:** 14 The Close, Lichfield, Staffs.; f. 1924; *c.* 5,000 vols., mostly theology and ecclesiastical history; for use, apply to Head of Special Collections, Main Library, University of Birmingham, B15 2TT.

**East Asian History of Science Library:** 16 Brooklands Ave., Cambridge, CB2 2BB; f. from collections assembled since 1942 by Dr. Joseph Needham of Caius College, from sources in China and the West, primarily intended for the researches on which is based the series "Science and Civilisation in China" (20 vols. planned, about half already published); governed by the East Asian History of Science Trust (f. 1968), an educational charity; a unique specialist collection of books, periodicals, off-prints, MSS. in Asian and European languages, also archival and iconographic material (notes, photographs, maps, microfilms, etc.); open to research scholars by appointment; Librarian Dr. MICHAEL SALT.

**Exeter Cathedral Library:** Bishop's Palace, Exeter, EX1 1HX; f. 11th century when Bishop Leofric gave 66 manuscript volumes to the Cathedral Church; over 30,000 vols. including *Exeter Book of Old English Poetry* and *Exon Domesday*; administered by the University of Exeter; Librarian J. F. STIRLING, J.P., M.A.

**Indian Institute Library:** Broad St., Oxford; f. 1883, classical and modern South Asian studies; 85,000 vols.; including government reports and periodicals; Librarian J. B. KATZ; see also Bodleian Library.

**National Library for the Blind:** Cromwell Rd., Bredbury, Stockport, SK6 2SG; f. 1882; contains 350,000 vols., including music, in Braille and Moon types; Librarian and Dir.-Gen. Dr. W. A. MUNFORD.

**Norwich Cathedral Dean and Chapter Library:** Norwich, Norfolk; a medieval monastic (Benedictine) foundation; over 8,000 vols., some incunabula and MSS.; Librarian Cathedral Office, The Close, Norwich, NR1 4EH.

**Peterborough Cathedral Library:** Peterborough; contains *c.* 8,000 vols., some important medieval MSS. and many early printed books; books printed before 1800 are now deposited in the Cambridge University Library, save those of local concern; Librarian Canon T. R. CHRISTIE, M.A.

**Prince Consort's Army Library:** Knollys Rd., Aldershot, Hants., GU11 1PS; f. 1860; military studies library, 20,000 vols., and Army historical library, 25,000 vols.; Librarian Mrs. J. L. SEARS, A.L.A.

**Ripon Cathedral Library:** Ripon, Yorks.; f. 1608; mainly old books including a rare Caxton and many incunabula; some important 15th–16th century printed books, early MSS. Service Books, 13th–15th-century MSS., Books of Hours, 13th-century Bible, a collector's library of Anthony Higgins, f. 1570, preserved almost intact, etc.; Librarian Canon D. G. FORD.

**St. Deiniol's Residential Library:** Hawarden, Deeside, Clwyd, CH5 3DF; f. 1895 by W. E. Gladstone; 120,000 vols., 40,000 pamphlets, and MSS. material; mainly theology, philosophy, history (esp. 19th century), classics, English and European literature; accommodation for 39 students; Warden and Chief Librarian Rev. PETER J. JAGGER, M.A., M.PHIL., F.R.HIST.S.

**Salisbury Cathedral Library:** The Cathedral, Salisbury, Wilts.; f. 11th century; contains books, medieval MSS., and an original Magna Carta, dated June 15th, 1215; open only to *bona fide* research students by appointment; Librarian SUZANNE EWARD.

**Shakespeare Centre:** Stratford-upon-Avon, Warwicks.; f. 1964; *c.* 40,000 vols., comprising the collections of the Shakespeare Birthplace Trust and the Royal Shakespeare Theatre Library; Dir. and Librarian Dr. LEVI FOX, O.B.E., D.L., M.A., F.S.A., F.R.HIST.S., F.R.S.L.

**Tyndale Library:** 36 Selwyn Gardens, Cambridge, CB3 9BA; f. 1944; the research centre of the Tyndale Fellowship for Biblical and Theological Research; intended for postgraduate study in biblically-related fields, with a view to promoting evangelical scholarship; *c.* 20,000 vols.; Librarian C. J. HEMER, PH.D.; publ. *Tyndale Bulletin*† (annually).

**York Minster Library:** Dean's Park, York, YO1 2JD; f. 7th/8th century, refounded *c.* 1410; 75,000 vols., 80 incunabula, 80 mediaeval MSS., 200 music MSS.; special collections include Civil War Tracts and Yorkshire local history (10,000 vols.); Librarian Canon R. CANT.

## SCOTLAND

**Royal Botanic Garden Library:** Edinburgh, EH3 5LR; f. 1670; incorporates the botanical libraries of the Plinian (1841), Wernerian (1858) and Botanical (1872) societies of Edinburgh, Dr. John Hope (1899), Cleghorn Memorial Library (1941) and Mr. Robert Scarlett (1975); compiles indexes to Monographs, Floras, Gardens, botanists, botanical expeditions, etc.; bibliography of literature on Ericales 1753–; research on early Natural History Societies; 80,000 vols., including pre-Linnean literature on botany, horticulture, agriculture and medicine; 70,000 pamphlets and separates; 3,400 (1,500 current) periodicals; extensive collection of botanical drawings and prints, photographs, cuttings, etc., correspondence, diaries, maps, plans, MSS., etc., relating to the early Regius Keepers and Curators and botanists and horticulturists in Britain and abroad; Librarian M. V. MATHEW, B.A., D.L.SC., A.L.A.; publs. *Notes from the Royal Botanic Garden*† (irregular), *British Fungus Flora* (irregular), *RBG Edinburgh Department Publication Series*, *Periodicals Holding List* (irregular), *Catalogue of Plants*, various guides.

**Royal College of Physicians and Surgeons of Glasgow Library:** 234 St. Vincent St., Glasgow, G2 5RJ; f. 1599; 150,000 vols.; Librarian A. M. RODGER, B.A., A.L.A.; publ. *Scottish Medical Journal*.

**Royal College of Physicians of Edinburgh Library:** 9 Queen St., Edinburgh, EH2 1JQ; f. 1681; *c.* 200,000 vols.; open to all medically qualified persons; emphasis on new clinical medicine; particularly rich in the early sources of medical knowledge and its periodical collection; over 1,000 vols. of MSS.; Librarian Miss J. P. S. FERGUSON, M.A., A.L.A.

**Royal Society of Edinburgh Library:** 22–24 George St., Edinburgh, EH2 2PQ; f. 1783; 300,000 vols.; David Hume MSS.; Librarian W. H. RUTHERFORD, F.C.I.S.

**Scottish Record Office:** P.O.B. 36, H.M. General Register House, Edinburgh, EH1 3YY; national archives of Scotland; local and church records and records of Scottish government and law from 12th to 20th centuries; contains also many groups of deposited private and business muniments; Keeper of the Records of Scotland JOHN IMRIE, M.A., LL.D.

**Signet Library:** Parliament Square, Edinburgh; date of foundation 1722, but there were Writers to H.M. Signet as early as 1460; *c.* 65,000 vols.; in the Library of the Society of Writers to Her Majesty's Signet are special collections of Scottish literature, genealogies, legal literature, including that of the British Commonwealth; Librarian GEORGE H. BALLANTYNE, M.A., F.L.A.

## WALES

**Library of the National Museum of Wales:** Cathays Park, Cardiff, CF1 3NP, Glam.; f. 1907; books and periodicals relevant to the Museum collections; also houses libraries of Cardiff Naturalists Society and Cambrian Archaeological Association; 106,000 vols.; Librarian W. J. JONES, F.L.A.

## UNIVERSITY AND COLLEGE LIBRARIES

### London

**British Library of Political and Economic Science:** London School of Economics, 10 Portugal St., WC2A 2HD; f. 1896; over 750,000 bound vols. and numerous other items covering economics, political science, law (especially international), sociology, history, geography, etc., legislative and administrative reports, important deposits of official documents, and special collections, including MSS.; Librarian D. A. CLARKE, M.A.; publs. *Guide to the Library*, *A London Bibliography of the Social Sciences* (annually), *Classified Catalogue of a Collection of Works on Publishing and Bookselling in the British Library of Political and Economic Science*, *Outline of the Resources of the Library*, *Interim Check-List of the Publications of Sidney and Beatrice Webb*.

**Guy's Hospital Medical School: The Wills Library:** St. Thomas's St., SE1 9RT; f. 1903; 30,000 vols.; Wills Librarian JEAN FARMER; publ. *Guy's Hospital Gazette*† (monthly).

**Imperial College Libraries:** South Kensington, SW7 2AZ; include College (Lyon Playfair) Library, f. 1962; Haldane Library of non-scientific literature, and 17 departmental libraries; 400,000 vols.; College Librarian ADRIAN WHITWORTH, M.A.

**Institute of Advanced Legal Studies Library:** 17 Russell Square, WC1B 5DR; f. 1947; *c.* 144,000 vols., *c.* 2,400 current periodicals; comprehensive collection of legal literature (except for Oriental laws and literature of East European law in East European languages), with special emphasis on English law, the legal systems of the Commonwealth, United States law, Western European law, Latin American law, international law; Librarian W. A. F. P. STEINER, LL.M., M.A., A.L.A.; publs. *List of current legal research topics* (annual), *List of official committees, commissions and other bodies concerned with the reform of the law* (every 2 years), *Index to foreign legal periodicals* (quarterly).

**Institute of Historical Research Library:** University of London, Senate House, London, WC1E 7HU; f. 1921; 125,000 vols.; Librarian WILLIAM KELLAWAY, M.A.; publs. *Bulletin*, *Historical Research for University Degrees in the United Kingdom* (annual), *Teachers of History in the Universities of the United Kingdom* (annual), *Writings on British History*.

**King's College Library:** Strand, WC2R 2LS; f. 1829; contains *c.* 435,000 vols.; Librarian IAN ANGUS, M.A., DIP. LIB.

**The London Hospital Medical College Library:** Turner St., London, E1 2AD; f. 1785; 27,000 vols.; Librarian P. S. HOCKNEY, B.SC., A.L.A., M.I.INF.SCI.

**London School of Hygiene and Tropical Medicine Library:** Keppel St., Gower St., WC1E 7HT; f. 1924; *c.* 65,000 vols., 1,400 current periodicals; tropical and preventive medicine in all aspects, many series of medical reports; Librarian V. J. GLANVILLE, A.L.A.; publ. *Dictionary Catalogue*.

**Middlesex Hospital Medical School: Boldero Library:** Riding House St., London, W1P 7PN; f. 1835; medical and ancillary sciences; 20,000 vols.; Librarian Mrs. J. CROPPER, B.SC.

**Queen Mary College Library:** Mile End Rd., London, E1 4NS; f. 1887; 240,000 vols.; Librarian T. H. BOWYER, B.SC., F.L.A.

**Royal Academy of Music Library:** Marylebone Rd., NW1 5HT; f. 1823; 90,000 vols., 25,000 sets of orchestral parts, gramophone records; special collections include Sir Henry Wood Library, Angelina Goetz Library; Librarian Miss M. J. HARINGTON, B.A., L.R.A.M.

**Royal College of Music Library:** Prince Consort Rd., South Kensington, SW7 2BS; f. 1883; *The Parry Room Library*: antiquarian printed and manuscript music, collected editions, periodicals, admission by Reader's Ticket only; *Wolfson Lending Library*: *c.* 150,000 vols., scores, gramophone records, primarily for use of college members; Chief Librarian PAMELA THOMPSON, B.A.; Reference Librarian CHRISTOPHER BORNET, M.A.

**School of Oriental and African Studies Library:** (University of London), Malet St., WC1E 7HP; f. 1916; over 520,000 vols. and pamphlets, 5,000 periodicals, 2,300 MSS. and archive collections dealing with Oriental and African languages, literature, philosophy, religions, history, law, cultural anthropology, art and archaeology, social sciences; back-up library to the British Library for loans; Librarian V. T. H. PARRY, M.A., DIP.LIB., F.L.A.

**School of Slavonic and East European Studies Library:** University of London, Senate House, WC1E 7HU; f. 1915; 220,000 vols. on the history, language and literature of Russia, Finland, and the countries of eastern and south-eastern Europe; Librarian J. E. O. SCREEN, M.A., PH.D., A.L.A.

**St. Mary's Hospital Medical School Library:** Norfolk Place, Paddington, W2 1PG; f. 1854; 29,000 vols.; Librarian N. D. PALMER, B.A., A.L.A.

**University College Library:** Gower St., WC1E 6BT; f. 1828; contains over 900,000 books and periodicals, and includes several special collections of great value, e.g. manuscripts of Jeremy Bentham, papers of Sir Edwin Chadwick, C. H. Barlow Dante collection augmented by libraries of Sir John Rotton and Mr. H. St. John Brooks, J. T. Graves mathematical library, Whitley Stokes Celtic library, C. K. Ogden library including correspondence of Lord Brougham, and scripts and letters of George Orwell; houses Mocatta library of Anglo-Judaica, and libraries of Biographical Society, British Society of Franciscan Studies, Folklore Society, Geologists' Association, Hertfordshire Natural History Society, Huguenot Society, London Mathematical Society, Malacological Society, Philological Society, Royal Historical Society, Viking Society for Northern Research; Librarian J. W. SCOTT, B.A., A.L.A.

**University College Clinical Sciences Library:** University St., W.C.1; f. 1907; 35,000 vols.; Librarian G. R. PEACOCK, B.A., A.L.A.

**University of London Library:** Senate House, WC1E 7HU; f. 1838; primarily for members of the University, contains over 1,000,000 vols. for reference and loan, including several special collections, e.g., the Goldsmiths' Library of Economic Literature, the Quick Memorial Library of old educational books and the history of education, the Durning-Lawrence Library of Elizabethan-Jacobean Literature, particularly strong in Shakespeare and Sir Francis Bacon, the Harry Price Library of Magical Literature, the Sterling Library of early editions, mainly of English Literature, Carlton Shorthand Library, Bromhead Library of Books on London, the United States Library, Family Welfare Association Library, Malcolm Morley Theatre collection; Dir. DOUGLAS J. FOSKETT, O.B.E., M.A., F.L.A., F.R.S.A.

### Provinces

**University of Aston in Birmingham Library:** Gosta Green, Birmingham, B4 7ET; f. 1895; 170,000 vols., 106,000 bound periodicals; Comrie collection of Mathematical tables; Librarian CHARLES R. BURMAN, B.A., F.L.A.; publs. *Library Newsletter* (2 a term), *Higher Education Current Awareness Bulletin*† (fortnightly), *Current Contents Bulletins*† (fortnightly), *Library Guide*†, *Special Subject Guides*†.

**University of Bath Library:** Claverton Down, Bath, BA2 7AY; 170,000 vols.; contains Sir Isaac Pitman's Library; University Librarian J. H. LAMBLE, M.A., A.L.A.

**University of Birmingham Library:** P.O.B. 363, Edgbaston, Birmingham, B15 2TT; f. 1880 (as Mason Science College Library); 1,300,000 vols., 8,000 current periodicals, 200,000 MSS.; special collections include: archives of Joseph, Austen and Neville Chamberlain, W. H. Dawson, Francis Brett Young, Harriet Martineau, Bishop E. W. Barnes, Sir Oliver Lodge, John Galsworthy (partial); St. Mary's, Warwick and Bengeworth parish libraries, Wigan Library from Bewdley, Worcs., Baskerville collection, Selbourne Library; Birmingham and Midland Institute pamphlet collection; Librarian A. NICHOLLS, B.A., A.L.A. (acting); publs. *Guide to the Library* (annually), *Regulations* (irregular), *Librarian's Report* (annually), *Special Guides* (irregular), *Quick lists* (irregular), *Library Information Sheets* (irregular).

**Bodleian Library:** Oxford, OX1 3BG; the library of Oxford University; f. 1602; contains about 4,250,000 printed vols., 50,000 MSS.; includes the Old Library, the Radcliffe Camera, New Library and four dependent libraries: the Radcliffe Science Library, the Law Library, the Indian Institute Library and Rhodes House Library (for the history of the British Commonwealth and of the United States); a Copyright library, entitled to a free copy of every book published in the U.K.; Librarian (vacant); publ. *The Bodleian Library Record* (1 or 2 a year).

**University of Bradford Library:** Bradford, Yorks., BD7 1DP; f. 1966; c. 360,000 vols.; Librarian F. EARNSHAW, B.A., A.L.A.; publs. *Annual Report†, Library Bulletin†, Know your Library†*, occasional bibliographies and guides†.

**University of Bristol Library:** Tyndall Ave., Bristol, BS8 1TJ; f. 1923; 900,000 vols.; special collections include the English novel to 1850, the Sir Allen Lane Penguin collection, business histories, early medicine, mathematics, chemistry and physics, Pinney Papers (17th–19th centuries), I. K. Brunel workbooks and papers, British philosophers, landscape gardening, courtesy books, General Election addresses (part of the National Liberal Club Library), Wigglesworth Ornithological Library, EDC, Addington Symonds Papers, Papers of the Somerset Miners' Association; Librarian N. HIGHAM, M.A., A.L.A.

**University of Cambridge Archives:** The University Library, West Rd., Cambridge, CB3 9DR; collection includes: charters of privilege, statutes, Grace books, royal letters and mandates, foundation deeds, letters-patent, transcripts, university ecclesiastical and civil jurisdiction, university departmental records, records of the University Press, etc.; Keeper of the Archives Mrs. D. M. OWEN, M.A., F.S.A.

**University of Cambridge Library:** West Rd., Cambridge; a Copyright library; contains over 3,000,000 printed books, over 15,000 MSS., large collections of papers and correspondence, and 780,000 maps; the collections have been accumulating since the beginning of the 15th century; Librarian F. W. RATCLIFFE, M.A., PH.D.

*College Libraries:*

**Christ's College Library:** f. 1448, refounded 1506; 50,000 vols., incunabula, periodicals; special collections: works of John Milton, including over 100 items published before 1700, Charles Lesingham Smith collection of early mathematical and scientific works, William Robertson Smith Oriental Library, Sir Stephen Gazelee collection of Coptic studies, A. H. Wratislaw collection of Slavonic language and literature, W. H. D. Rouse collection of Indian studies and pre-16th century English books; Librarian C. P. COURTNEY, PH.D.

**Churchill College Library:** f. 1960; 33,500 vols.; special collections, extensive political, military and scientific archives mainly of the late 19th and 20th centuries; Librarian A. L. R. FINDLAY, M.A., PH.D.; Keeper of Archives CORRELLI BARNETT, M.A.

**Clare College Library:** f. 1326; comprises Fellows' Library (8,000 vols.) and Forbes Library (12,000 vols.); special collections: Cecil Sharp MSS.; Forbes Librarian R. D. GOODER, PH.D.; Fellows' Librarian N. O. WEISS, PH.D.

**Corpus Christi College Library:** f. 14th century; 5,000 vols.; special collections: Parker bequest of MSS. and early printed books, Lewis collection of coins, gems and other antiquities; Librarian R. I. PAGE, LITT.D.

**Downing College Library:** f. 1800; special collections of Bowtell MSS. relating to the city and university of Cambridge, 500 vols. of naval history and navigation and large collection of law, Civil War and Commonwealth newspapers; Librarian P. GAY, SC.D.

**Emmanuel College Library:** f. 1584; 320 MSS. from 12th century to the present, 70,000 vols. with large number of pre-18th century works; Librarian R. G. G. COLEMAN, M.A.

**Fitzwilliam College Library:** f. 1869; 25,000 vols.; Librarian J. STREET, M.A., PH.D.

**Girton College Library:** f. 1869; 65,000 vols., 120 periodicals; special collections: Newall collection of Scandinavian material, Frere collection of Hebrew MSS., Crews collection of Judeo-Spanish material, Somerville collection of mathematics, Bibas collection of 18th-century French works, Blackburn collection of women's rights materials; Librarian MARGARET GASKELL, M.A.

**Gonville and Caius College Library:** f. 1348; 32,000 vols., 1,000 MSS. related to medieval law and science; special collections: 17th century heraldic and genealogical records, Charles Doughty's "Word Notes"; Librarian J. H. PRYNNE, M.A.

**Jesus College Old Library:** f. 1500; c. 8,600 vols., 39 incunabula, 80 medieval MSS. from north-country monasteries, 17 oriental MSS.; special collections: Civil War tracts, military science, large theological collection; Keeper of the Old Library, D. J. V. FISHER.

**King's College Library:** f. 1441; 125,000 vols.; special collections: music, MSS. of Sir Isaac Newton (available on microfilm in the University Library), 20th-century literary MSS., notably major collections of Rupert Brooke, E. M. Forster and T. S. Eliot; Librarian P. J. CROFT, M.A.

**Magdalene College Old Library:** MSS. of works by Thomas Hardy, Rudyard Kipling and T. S. Eliot and 33 MSS., including a 14th-century Apocalypse; incunabula, including Caxton's 2nd edition of Chaucer's Canterbury Tales, foreign-printed books of 16th, 17th and 18th centuries, early theological works; Diaries of A. C. Benson and W. R. Inge; 6,000 vols.; Librarian Dr. R. LUCKETT.

**Newnham College Library:** f. 1897; 8 medieval MSS., incunabula, early editions of poets, dramatists and chroniclers of 16th and 17th centuries; Librarian A. PHILLIPS, M.A.

**Pembroke College Library:** f. 1347; 40,200 vols., medieval MSS.; special collections: papers of Gray, C. Smart, William Mason, R. Storrs; Librarian R. C. TREBILCOCK, M.A.

**Pepys Library (Magdalene College):** f. 1724 in its present location; 3,000 vols. in original bookcases; Pepys's own collection (MSS., books, music, maps, prints and drawings), not added to since 1704; Pepys's own catalogue; special collections: Pepys MSS. (including Diary), medieval MSS., naval and historical MSS. (mostly English, 16th- and 17th-century), calligraphic collection, prints of London and Westminster, incunabula, broadside ballads, plays, etc.; Librarian R. C. LATHAM, C.B.E., M.A.

**Peterhouse (Perne) Library:** f. 1594; 280 medieval MSS., 16th- and 17th-century musical MSS. (on permanent deposit in University Library); 25,000 vols., 60 incunabula; special collections: first editions of classics in science, series of early liturgical books; Librarian Prof. E. J. KENNEY, M.A., F.B.A.

**Queens' College Library:** f. 1448; 22 medieval MSS., 31 incunabula, over 33,000 vols.; catalogue by Thomas Hartwell Horne (1827); Milner collection of works on history of Reformation and 18th-century science and mathematics; Librarian I. R. WRIGHT, M.A.

**St. Catharine's College Library:** f. 18th century; MSS., 30 incunabula, 24,000 vols.; special collections: 17th century political and religious tracts, 184 vols. of 18th century medical works (Addenbrooke collection), medieval Romance literature, Spanish books and MSS. of 16th and 17th centuries; Librarian J. R. SHAKESHAFT, M.A., PH.D.

**St. John's College Library:** f. 1624; MSS.; special collections: 15th century books, early French and Italian works, Benlowes collection of 17th-century poems, Matthew Prior folios, Sir Soulden Lawrence law collection, Thomas Gisborne collection of 18th-century books, Samuel Butler collection, Smith collection of Rabelais literature, Wordsworthiana, mathematical works of historical interest from libraries of Adams, Todhunter and Pendlebury, Thomas à Kempis bequest, Hugh Gatty Library; Librarian A. G. LEE, M.A.

**Selwyn College Library:** f. 1930; 30,000 vols., MSS., incunabula; special collections: diaries and papers of George Augustus Selwyn (1809–78) Primate of New Zealand and later Bishop of Lichfield, MSS. and correspondence of Brooke Foss Westcott (1825–1901) Bishop of Durham, large collection of theological works including 3,000 19th-century English ecclesiastical pamphlets; Librarian A. P. VLASTO, M.A., PH.D.

**Sidney Sussex College Library:** f. 16th century; 7,300 vols., 106 MSS., incunabula; special collections: 18th and 19th century mathematical books; Taylor Mathematical Library (separately administered); Librarian M. STEWART.

**Trinity College Library:** f. 1546; MSS.; 150,000 vols.; Western MSS. collection includes: 138 Greek MSS., medieval MSS. including 10th-century Gospels, Canterbury Psalter and the Apocalypse, large number of literary MSS. including Milton's shorter poems, Tennyson's poetical drafts, works by Thackeray, FitzGerald, Macaulay, A. E. Housman, Capell collection of Shakespeareana, numerous MSS. of Newton, Bentley, Whewell and Houghton; letters and MSS. of 17th, 18th, 19th and 20th centuries; Oriental MSS.; 740 incunabula; special collections of printed books include: collection of canon Law and Bibles, Julius Hare collection of German theology and philosophy, Rothschild library of 18th-century English literature, French and Italian books, classical pamphlets, 19th-century mathematical books, 800 volumes from the library of Isaac Newton, Civil War tracts, large collection of 18th- and 19th-century English books; microfilms, photostats, xerographic and bromide prints; Librarian P. GASKELL, M.A., PH.D., D.LITT.

**Trinity Hall Library:** f. 1600; 15,000 vols., 31 MSS.; special collections: early canon law, Larman Bequest of books and MSS. relating to Reformation and Tudor periods, particularly heraldry, ecclesiastical history and theology; Librarian J. CREMONA, M.A., PH.D.

*Special Libraries:*

**Balfour and Newton Library:** Department of Zoology, Downing St., Cambridge; Balfour Library f. 1883, Newton Library f. 1907; 18,000 vols., 17,500 periodicals, over 100,000 reprints; special collections: Newton and Strickland collections of ornithology, McAndrew collection of conchology, Watson collection of malacology; Librarian R. HUGHES.

**Marshall Library of Economics:** Sidgwick Ave., Cambridge, CB3 9DB; f. 1925; 72,500 vols.; special collections: Pryme collection of economic literature, mostly dating from before 1840; Librarian Miss M. HANNIGAN.

**Squire Law Library:** The Old Schools, Cambridge; f. 1904; 88,000 vols.; special collections: Roman law, legal history, conflict of laws, international law, political biographies; research library; Librarian G. G. E. HUGHES.

**University of Durham Library:** Palace Green, Durham; f. 1833; c. 600,000 vols.; special collections include those formed by Bishop Cosin, Dr. Routh, Bishop Maltby and Dr. Winterbottom, and the Sharp Library from Bamburgh Castle, 200 incunabula, First Folio Shakespeare, old bindings and medieval MSS., Oriental Section containing over 130,000 items and Sudan Archive, Science Section containing over 90,000 items, Education section containing c. 30,000 items; Librarian Miss A. M. MCAULAY, B.A., F.L.A.; publs. Durham University Library publications (occasional).

**University of East Anglia Library:** University Plain, Norwich, NR4 7TJ; 500,000 vols.; Librarian W. L. GUTTSMAN, M.SC.(ECON.).

**University of Essex Library:** P.O.B. 24, Colchester, CO4 3UA; f. 1964; c. 300,000 vols., 2,800 current periodicals; Librarian F. J. FRIEND, B.A.

**University of Exeter Library:** Prince of Wales Rd., Exeter, EX4 4PT; f. 1937; 630,000 vols.; administers Exeter Cathedral Library (*q.v.*), and Library of Devon and Exeter Institution (36,000 vols.); Librarian J. F. STIRLING, J.P., M.A.

**University of Hull: The Brynmor Jones Library:** Cottingham Rd., Hull, Yorkshire; f. 1928; 600,000 vols.; special collections, South East Asia, British Labour history; Librarian P. A. LARKIN, C.B.E., M.A., C.LITT., F.R.S.L., F.L.A.

**John Rylands University Library of Manchester:** University of Manchester, Oxford Rd., Manchester, M13 9PP; f. 1972 by merger of John Rylands Library (f. 1900) with Manchester University Library (f. 1851); c. 3,350,000 vols. and c. 8,000 current periodical titles; special collections include: Althorp collection of Earl Spencer (3,000 incunabula), Christie collection (classical Renaissance), Freeman collection (history), Bullock collection (Italian 16th century), Partington collection (history of chemistry), collections on Jewish Haskalah literature, Methodism (including Methodist Archives and Research Centre) and literature of dissent, French Revolution, labour history, history of science and medicine; large reference and research library in the humanities, science and medicine; 17,000 European and Oriental MSS. notably the collection of the Earls of Crawford and Balcarres; several million deeds and charters; *Manchester Guardian* archives; numerous tracts, journals, and broadsides of 17th and 18th centuries, English and French, Mazarinades; rare bindings and association copies; Jevons, Tout, Auchinleck and numerous collections of papers, literary, industrial, military, etc.; c. 600,000 titles in microform; Dir. M. A. PEGG, PH.D.; publ. *Bulletin* (2 a year).

**University of Keele Library:** Keele, Staffs., ST5 5BG; f. 1949; 496,000 vols.; Librarian J. M. WOOD, M.A., F.L.A.

**University of Kent Library:** Canterbury; 400,000 vols.; humanities, social sciences, mathematics, natural and physical sciences; Librarian W. J. SIMPSON, B.A., DIP.LIB.STUD., A.L.A., F.R.S.A.

**University of Lancaster Library:** Bailrigg, Lancaster, LA1 4YH; f. 1963; 550,000 vols., pamphlets and other items, 3,250 current serials; special collections include Comenius Library (Central and South-eastern Europe), Quaker Collection, Redlich collection (music); Librarian ARTHUR DAVIES, B.A., A.L.A.; publs. *Annual Report*, Serials list (irregular), Bibliographic guides (irregular).

**University of Leeds Library:** Leeds, LS2 9JT; f. 1874; 1,611,997 vols. and pamphlets including the Brotherton Collection which contains 50,471 vols. and pamphlets and a large number of MSS., deeds and letters; Librarian D. Cox, B.A., A.L.A.; publs. *Leeds Studies in English†, Leeds texts and monographs†, Proceedings of the Leeds Philosophical and Literary Society: literary and historical section†, Proceedings of the Leeds Philosophical and Literary Society: scientific section†, Proceedings of the Yorkshire Geological Society†, University of Leeds review†.*

**University of Leicester Library:** University Rd., Leicester; f. 1921; special collections of local history of England and Wales, Transport History and French memoirs, Fairclough Collection on 17th century studies; 620,000 vols.; Librarian D. G. F. WALKER, M.A., LL.B.

**University of Liverpool Library:** P.O.B. 123, Liverpool, L69 3DA; f. 1881; over 1,000,000 vols., over 6,000 current periodicals; special collections include 254 incunabula, the T. G. Rylands collection (early cartography, Lancashire and Cheshire history), the William Blake collection, the Scott Macfie collection (gypsy studies), the William Noble collection (modern private presses), the Knowsley collection (17th–19th-century English pamphlets), the Peers collection (Spanish Civil War), and the Fraser collection (c. 900 books and pamphlets on tobacco; also much material on positivism and secularism); Latin-American collection specializing in Peru and Brazil; modern MS. holdings include the Rathbone, Blanco White, Brunner and Glasier papers; the School of Education Library contains an important collection of children's books; Librarian V. E. KNIGHT, M.A., PH.D.; publs. *Periodicals Finding List* (irregular), *Annual Report*.

**University of Newcastle upon Tyne Library:** Newcastle upon Tyne; f. 1871 as Library of Durham College of Physical Science; 520,000 vols.; special collections include the Heslop Collection of English dictionaries, Gertrude Bell Oriental Collection, Pybus Medical (historical) Collection, etc.; Librarian Dr. B. J. ENRIGHT; Library publications issued occasionally.

**University of Nottingham Library:** University Park, Nottingham, NG7 2RD; f. (University College) 1881; c. 700,000 vols. and pamphlets; 4,600 current periodicals; MSS. and archives (Portland, Newcastle, Middleton, Manvers, etc.) c. 2,000,000 items; special collections include D. H. Lawrence, early children's books, French Revolution, meteorology, ornithology; includes Agriculture Library (Sutton Bonington) and Medical Library; Librarian P. A. HOARE, M.A., A.L.A.

**Open University Library:** Walton Hall, Milton Keynes, MK7 6AA; f. 1969; 100,000 vols.; special collection in Educational Technology; Librarian D. J. SIMPSON.

**University of Oxford Library** (*see* Bodleian Library).

*College Libraries:*

**Balliol College Library:** f. 1263; 70,000 vols.; Librarian Mrs. P. A. BULLOCH, D.PHIL.

**Brasenose College Library:** 38,000 vols.; Librarian P. J. JONES, M.A., D.PHIL.

**Christ Church Library:** 130,000 vols.; Librarian J. F. A. MASON, M.A., D.PHIL., F.S.A., F.R.HIST.S.

**Codrington Library (All Souls College):** Oxford, OX1 4AL; f. 1710; 110,000 vols.; special collections: medieval and modern history, military history and law; Librarian J. S. G. SIMMONS, O.B.E., M.A., F.L.A.

**Corpus Christi College Library:** f. 1517; 60,000 vols., MSS.; special collections: incunabula, early English printed books, 17th- and 18th-century Italian books, English, French and German books on 19th-century philosophy; Librarian T. H. ASTON, M.A.

**Exeter College Library:** Librarian Dr. J. R. MADDICOTT, M.A., D.PHIL., F.R.HIST.S.

**Hertford College Library:** Librarian N. G. MCCRUM M.A., D.PHIL., D.SC.

**Jesus College Library:** f. 1571; 20,000 vols.; special collections: Celtic collection, library of Lord Herbert of Cherbury, works by and on T. E. Lawrence (of Arabia); Librarian J. D. WALSH, M.A., PH.D.; Archivist D. A. REES, M.A., D.PHIL.

**Keble College Library:** f. 1876; c. 40,000 vols. in working library; special collections: medieval MSS., incunabula and early printed books, Millard collection, Hatchett-Jackson collection, Port-Royal, John Keble's own library, part of Henry Liddon's library; Fellow Librarian Dr. D. C. POTTS.

**Lincoln College Library:** f. 1427; 30,000 vols.; Librarian Mrs. A. DELAHAYE.

**Magdalen College Library:** f. 1458; 49,000 vols.; special collections: 16th- to 18th-century books, late medieval English history; Librarian G. L. HARRISS, M.A., D.PHIL.

**Merton College Library:** Librarian J. R. L. HIGHFIELD, M.A., D.PHIL.

**New College Library:** f. 1379; 90,000 vols.; special collections: medieval MSS., incunabula, early archives; Librarian the Rev. G. V. BENNETT, M.A., D.PHIL.; publ. *The Archives of New College Oxford*.

**Oriel College Library:** f. 1326; 40,000 vols.; special collection of personages who attended Oriel College; Librarian W. E. PARRY, M.A., D.PHIL.

**Pembroke College Library:** f. 1883; 33,500 vols.; Chandler collection of Aristotelia; Librarian Dr. J. D. FLEEMAN.

**Queen's College Library:** 130,000 vols.; Librarian R. A. C. PARKER, M.A., D.PHIL.

**St. Edmund Hall Library:** f. 17th century; 40,000 vols.; Librarian S. E. WERNBERG-MØLLER, M.A.

**St. John's College Library:** 80,000 vols.; Librarian H. M. COLVIN, C.B.E., M.A., F.B.A., F.R.HIST.S.

**Trinity College Library:** Librarian M. MACLAGAN, M.A., F.S.A. (acting).

**University College Library:** f. 1249; 20,000 vols.; special collections are deposited in the Bodleian Library (*see* above) with the exception of small collection of Lord Attlee's post-war papers; Librarian R. PARK.

**Wadham College Library:** f. 1613; 50,000 vols.; special collections: 16th-century theology, 17th-century science; Persian history and literature; Librarian Dr. J. D. GURNEY.

**Worcester College Library:** f. 1714; 75,000 vols.; special collections: Clarke Papers (Civil War and Commonwealth documents), architectural books and drawings (Inigo Jones, Hawksmoor), English poetry and drama from 1550–1750, Pottinger collection of 19th-century pamphlets; Librarian LESLEY MONTGOMERY.

*Special Libraries:*

**Ashmolean Library:** Beaumont St., Oxford, OX1 2PH; f. 1969, but fmrly. dept. of Ashmolean Museum, f. 1683; 152,000 vols.; archaeology, ancient history and ancient Near Eastern studies, and Byzantine studies, numismatics, classical languages and literature, Western art and architecture. Special collections include Grenfell and Hunt Papyrological Library, Griffith Egyptological Library, Haverfield and Richmond Archives and original documentation of principal archaeological expeditions and explorations and classification of artefacts; Librarian B. MCGREGOR.

**Taylor Institution Library:** St. Giles, Oxford, OX1 3NA; f. 1845; 300,000 vols.; Continental European languages and literature, medieval and modern, including general and historical background material and in particular older and modern editions of French, German, Italian, Russian, Spanish and Portuguese literature; literature of modern Latin America, Celtic studies, modern Greek; philology and general linguistics; special collections: Voltaire and the French Enlightenment, Anglo-German literary relations, B. Constant, G. B. Guarini, East German literature; Librarian G. G. BARBER.

**University of Reading Library:** Whiteknights, Reading, RG6 2AE; f. 1892; approx. 650,000 vols., 5,500 current periodicals; special collections include Overstone Library, Stenton Library on English history, Cole Library on early zoology, Finzi collections of music and English poetry, Turner collection of French Revolution pamphlets, agricultural history, children's books, archives of British publishers; Librarian J. THOMPSON, B.A., F.L.A.

**University of Salford Library:** Salford, M5 4WT; f. 1957; 300,000 vols.; Librarian A. C. BUBB, B.A., F.L.A.; publs. *Guides.*

**Selly Oak Colleges Library:** Birmingham, B29 6LE; f. 1921; social studies, anthropology, religion and mission, world area studies, development aid, Islamics; 60,000 vols., 3,000 Arabic and Syriac MSS.; Greek papyri; Librarian Miss F. H. B. WILLIAMS, M.A., DIP. LIB.

**University of Sheffield Library:** Western Bank, Sheffield, S. Yorks., S10 2TN; over 800,000 books and pamphlets; special collections include Sir Charles Firth's collection of 17th-century tracts; Librarian C. K. BALMFORTH, M.A., F.L.A.

**University of Southampton Library:** Southampton, SO9 5NH; Main and Departmental libraries about 600,000 vols., about 6,300 current periodicals, Wessex Medical Library, Ford Collection of Parliamentary Papers (1801 to date), Cope collection of Hampshire material, Perkins Agricultural Library, Parkes Library (relationship between Jewish and non-Jewish worlds), Hampshire Field Club Library; Librarian B. NAYLOR, M.A., A.L.A.

**University of Surrey Library:** Stag Hill, Guildford, Surrey; f. 1894; 250,000 vols., 2,800 current periodicals; Librarian R. F. EATWELL, M.A., F.L.A.; publ. *Current Awareness Bulletin.*

**University of Sussex Library:** Falmer, Brighton, BN1 9QL; 450,000 vols.; Librarian Miss E. M. RODGER, B.SC., A.L.A.

**University of Warwick Library:** Gibbet Hill Rd., Coventry; f. 1963; 550,000 vols.; special collections: British and foreign statistical serials (trade, finance, production), current and retrospective, Economics Working Papers, pre-1948 collections of Howard League for Penal Reform, Modern Records Centre (labour history, industrial relations, politics); Librarian P. E. TUCKER, M.A., B.LITT., A.L.A.

**University of York Library:** Heslington, York, YO1 5DD; f. 1963; 300,000 vols.; Librarian HARRY FAIRHURST, M.A.

SCOTLAND

**University of Aberdeen Library:** New Library, Meston Walk, Old Aberdeen, AB9 2UE; f. 1494; c. 1,000,000 vols.; McBean Jacobite Collection, O'Dell railway collection, Taylor psalmody collection, Gregory, Melvin and other special collections; Librarian J. M. SMETHURST, B.A., A.L.A.

**University of Dundee Library:** Dundee, DD1 4HN; f. 1881; 400,000 vols.; Librarian J. R. BARKER, M.A., F.L.A.

**University of Edinburgh Library:** George Square, Edinburgh, EH8 9LJ; f. 1580; nearly 2,000,000 vols.; Drummond (of Hawthornden) Collection; Laing Charters and MSS.; Halliwell-Phillipps Collection; MSS. on Scottish history and the Scottish literary renaissance; includes the Central Medical Library, Centre of European Governmental Studies Library, Law Library, New College Library (Faculty of Divinity) and Royal (Dick) School of Veterinary Studies Libraries; Librarian Miss BRENDA E. MOON, M.A., F.L.A.; publ. *Abstract of the Library Report†.*

**University of Glasgow Library:** Hillhead St., Glasgow, G12 8QE; f. 15th century; 1,300,000 vols.; incorporates Trinity College Glasgow Library (Church of Scotland); Hunterian Books and MSS., Euing Collections of the Bible and music, Hamilton Collection of philosophy, Ferguson Collection of the history of chemistry, Stirling Maxwell Collection of Emblem books, J. M. Whistler archive, David Murray regional history collection; Librarian H. J. HEANEY, M.A., F.L.A.

**Heriot-Watt University: Cameron Smail Library:** Riccarton, Edinburgh, EH14 4AS and Chambers St., Edinburgh, EH1 1HX; f. 1821; 100,000 vols., 1,500 periodicals; Librarian A. ANDERSON, M.A., F.L.A.; publs. *Annual Report, Readers' Guide.*

**University of St. Andrews Library:** St. Andrews, Fife; f. 1412; 700,000 vols., MSS., maps and numerous special collections, including Donaldson (Classics and Education), J. D. Forbes (Science), and Von Hügel (Theology and Philosophy); Librarian A. G. MACKENZIE.

**University of Stirling Library:** Stirling; f. 1966; 300,000 vols., 2,600 periodicals; collection of works of Sir Walter Scott and contemporaries, bibliography room with Albion and Columbian presses, I.U.P. set of 19th-century government publications; facilities for on-line information retrieval; Librarian P. G. PEACOCK.

**Strathclyde University: The Andersonian Library:** 101 St. James' Rd., Glasgow, G4 0NS; f. 1796; 387,000 vols.; Anderson collection (founder's library), Young collection (alchemy and early chemistry), Laing collection (18th- and 19th-century mathematics); Librarian C. G. WOOD, M.A., F.L.A.

WALES

**University of Wales Libraries.**

**University College of Wales Library:** Penglais, Aberystwyth, Dyfed, SY23 3DZ; f. 1872; 450,000 vols., 3,000 periodicals; special collections: Gregynog

LIBRARIES AND ARCHIVES, MUSEUMS AND ART GALLERIES — U.K. (GREAT BRITAIN)

Press books and 20th-century private press books; George Powell Collection (19th-century English and French literature, fine art and music); Rudler Collection of geological pamphlets; Duff Collection of pamphlets (Classics); League of Nations Documents Collection; Librarian W. W. DIENEMAN, M.A., A.L.A.; publs. *Bulletin of the Board of Celtic Studies†, Cambrian Law Review†, Interstate†.*

**University College of North Wales Library:** Bangor; f. 1884; 400,000 vols.; Librarian L. G. HEYWOOD, M.A.

**University College, Cardiff, Library:** P.O.B. 78, Cathays Park, Cardiff, CF1 1XL; f. 1883; 440,000 vols.; Salisbury Library (Welsh and Celtic Studies), EEC Documentation Centre, UN Depository, Youth Movement Archive, Brett collection of Tennysoniana, Ifor Powell collection of pamphlets on 20th-century affairs, Mazzini collection; Librarian R. J. E. HORRILL, B.A.

**University College of Swansea Library:** Singleton Park, Swansea; 500,000 vols. and pamphlets; Librarian Miss M. I. COOPER, B.A., F.L.A.

**Welsh National School of Medicine Library:** Heath Park, Cardiff, CF4 4XN; f. 1931; 50,000 vols., including Branch and outlier libraries plus Historical Collection; Librarian R. J. DANNATT, B.A., A.L.A.

**University of Wales Institute of Science and Technology Library:** King Edward VII Ave., Cardiff, CF1 3NU; 150,000 vols.; Librarian J. K. ROBERTS, M.SC., A.L.A.

**St. David's University College Library:** Lampetert, Dyfed, SA48 7ED; 130,000 vols., including Tract collection of 9,000 items; Librarian G. P. LILLEY, M.A., DIP.LIB., F.L.A.; publ. *Cambria†, Trivium†.*

## MUSEUMS AND ART GALLERIES

### ENGLAND

#### LONDON

**British Museum:** Great Russell St., W.C.1; f. 1753 in pursuance of the will of Sir Hans Sloane, and with the addition of the Cottonian and Harleian Libraries; opened 1759; present buildings begun 1823. Collections and exhibitions of prehistoric, Egyptian, Assyrian, medieval, oriental and other arts; prints, drawings, ceramics and coins. Ethnographical collections are displayed at Museum of Mankind, 6 Burlington Gardens, W.1. Many catalogues and reproductions are published. Chair. of Board of Trustees The Lord TREND; Dir. Dr. DAVID WILSON, F.S.A.; Sec. G. B. MORRIS; Keepers of Departments: Prints and Drawings J. K. ROWLANDS; Egyptian Antiquities T. G. H. JAMES; Western Asiatic Antiquities E. SOLLBERGER; Greek and Roman Antiquities B. F. COOK; Medieval and Later Antiquities N. M. STRATFORD; Oriental Antiquities L. R. H. SMITH; Ethnography M. D. MCLEOD; Prehistoric and Romano-British Antiquities I. H. LONGWORTH; Coins and Medals R. A. G. CARSON; Research Laboratory M. S. TITE; Conservation and Technical Services (vacant).

**British Museum (Natural History):** Cromwell Rd., South Kensington, SW7 5BD; originates from the Natural History Departments of the British Museum, Bloomsbury, transferred to the present address 1881–85, and a branch comprising the Zoological Museum at Tring, Herts; in 1963 the Natural History Museum became a separate institution with its own body of trustees; Chair. of the Board of Trustees T. R. E. SOUTHWOOD, D.SC., F.R.S.; Dir. R. H. HEDLEY, D.SC., F.I.BIOL.; Keeper of Zoology J. G. SHEALS, PH.D., F.I.BIOL.; Keeper of Entomology L. A. MOUND, D.SC.; Keeper of Palaeontology H. W. BALL, PH.D.; Keeper of Mineralogy A. C. BISHOP, PH.D.; Keeper of Botany J. F. M. CANNON, B.SC.; Head of Dept. of Public Services R. S. MILES, D.SC.; Head of Dept. of Central Services G. B. CORBET, PH.D.; Head of Dept. of Library Services A. F. HARVEY, A.I.INF.SC.; library: see Special Libraries.

**Carlyle's House:** 24 Cheyne Row, Chelsea, S.W.3; built 1708; occupied by the Carlyles 1834–81; National Trust property; contains Carlyle's books, paintings and furniture; Curator Col. JAMES EDGAR.

**Courtauld Institute Galleries, University of London:** Woburn Square, London, WC1H 0AA; f. 1958; comprises the Samuel Courtauld collection of French Impressionist and Post-Impressionist paintings, the Princes Gate Collection of Old Master paintings and drawings (especially Michelangelo and Rubens), the Lee and Gambier-Perry collections of Old Masters, the Roger Fry collection of early 20th-century French and English paintings, the Witt collection of Old Master drawings and the William Spooner collection of English landscape drawings and watercolours; Dir. Dr. DENNIS FARR.

**Cuming Museum (Borough of Southwark):** 157 Walworth Rd., London, SE17 1RS; f. 1902; archaeological evidence for local history, Roman, medieval and post-medieval finds; the Lovett collection of London superstitions; Curator K. A. DOUGHTY, F.L.A.

**Dulwich Picture Gallery:** College Rd., Dulwich, S.E.21; built 1814 by Sir John Soane to house collection of Old Masters including Rembrandt, Rubens, Cuyp, Van Dyck, Teniers, Poussin, Claude, Watteau, Raphael, Tiepolo, Gainsborough, Murillo, etc.; Dir. G. A. WATERFIELD, M.A.

**Geffrye Museum:** Kingsland Rd., E2 8EA; f. 1914; contains a small but excellent collection of furniture and domestic objects arranged in a series of period rooms from 1600 to 1939; reconstruction of John Evelyn's "Closet of Curiosities"; costume display; reference library of books and periodicals on the arts and social history, temporary exhibitions, children's centre (Saturdays and holidays); Dir. JEFFERY DANIELS, M.A.

**Geological Museum** (Museum of Practical Geology): Exhibition Rd., South Kensington, SW7 2DE; f. 1837; part of the Institute of Geological Sciences administered by the Natural Environment Research Council (q.v.); exhibitions include *The Story of the Earth*; *Britain before Man*; *British Fossils*; an extensive display of gemstones showing them in their parent rock associations, in their natural crystal form and final cut state; the regional geology and scenery of Great Britain; fine collections of British fossils, rocks and minerals, and minerals and metallic ores illustrating the geology of economically important mineral deposits throughout the world. There are also extensive reserve collections of fossils, rocks, minerals and building and decorative stones for reference and research. There is a regular programme of talks, demonstrations and films; programme free on request; Dir. G. M. BROWN, D.SC., F.R.S.; Curator F. W. DUNNING, O.B.E., B.SC.

**Hampton Court Palace:** East Molesey, Surrey, KT8 9AU; contains a collection of paintings and tapestries, including Andrea Mantegna's nine great tempera paintings of "The Triumph of Julius Caesar"; Surveyor of the Queen's Pictures Sir OLIVER MILLAR, K.C.V.O., F.B.A., F.S.A.; Superintendent of the Royal Collection J. COWELL.

**Horniman Museum and Library:** London Rd., Forest Hill, SE23 3PQ; f. 1901; ethnographical collection from all parts of the world (including tools, musical instruments, the arts, magic and religion), and exhibits related to the natural history of animals; education centre; Aquarium; library of 35,000 vols., mainly on anthropology, prehistory, art, ethnomusicology and natural history; free lectures and concerts on subjects connected with the exhibits are given in autumn and winter; Dir. D. M. BOSTON, O.B.E., M.A.; Deputy Dir. J. MOSS-ECCARDT, A.M.A.; Keepers: (Ethnography) Mrs. V. E. VOWLES, F.M.A., (Musicology) Mrs. F. PALMER, (Education) Mrs. E. D. GOODHEW, PH.D., A.R.C.S., D.I.C., (Natural History) P. E. J. WHEATCROFT, PH.D., A.M.A.; Librarian D. W. ALLEN, B.SC., A.L.A.

**Imperial War Museum:** Lambeth Rd., SE1 6HZ; a national museum and picture gallery; f. in 1917, illustrating and recording every aspect of the various operations in which the Armed Forces of the British Commonwealth have been engaged since 1914; contains many exhibits, over 10,000 works of art, 5,000,000 photographs, archive on British and foreign documents, more than 40 million feet of film and a growing collection of sound records; library of 100,000 vols., 25,000 pamphlets, 5,000 sets of periodicals, 15,000 maps and drawings; Vice-Pres. and Chair. of the Board of Trustees Marshal of the R.A.F. Sir JOHN GRANDY, G.C.B., K.B.E., D.S.O.; Dir. Dr. A. N. FRANKLAND, C.B.E., D.F.C.

**Iveagh Bequest:** Kenwood, Hampstead Lane, NW3 7JR; left to the nation by Edward Cecil Guinness, first Earl of Iveagh, in 1927; includes paintings of British, Dutch, Flemish and French Schools, housed in an 18th-century mansion containing a fine Adam library; summer exhibitions on aspects of 18th-century art; Admin. Trustee Greater London Council; Curator JOHN JACOB, M.A., F.M.A.; publs. catalogues†.

**Livesey Museum (Borough of Southwark):** 682 Old Kent Rd., London, SE15 1JF; f. 1974; variety of changing exhibitions of Borough and beyond; Curator K. A. DOUGHTY.

**Museum of London:** London Wall, E.C.2; formed from amalgamation of London Museum and Guildhall Museum; London from earliest days to the present; displays the Lord Mayor's golden coach, etc.; Museum of the Year 1978; Chair. of Board of Govs. MICHAEL ROBBINS; Dir. MAX HEBDITCH.

**National Army Museum:** Royal Hospital Rd., SW3 4HT; f. 1960; displays depicting the history of the British Army since 1485, the Indian Army until Independence in 1947, and colonial forces; reference collections of books, MSS., prints and early photographs; uniforms including decorations and badges; weapons; painting, silver, china, models; personal relics; Dir. W. REID, F.S.A., F.M.A.

**National Gallery:** Trafalgar Square, W.C.2; f. 1824; contains examples of all the principal European schools up to early 20th century; a selection of British painters from Hogarth to Turner; public lectures on most weekdays; Chair. Lord ANNAN; Dir. Sir MICHAEL LEVEY; Keeper ALLAN BRAHAM; Scientific Adviser R. H. G. THOMSON; Chief Restorer MARTIN WYLD.

**National Maritime Museum:** Greenwich, S.E.10; established 1934, opened 1937; illustrates British maritime history as exemplified by the work of the Royal Navy, Merchant Shipping, Fishing industry, marine archaeology, explorers and yachtsmen; the collection includes portraits and sea pieces, models, prints and drawings, instruments, maps and charts, seals, uniforms, weapons, medals and relics, ships' draughts, a library of books and MSS.; New Neptune Hall contains the paddle tug *Reliant*, small boats, boat-building shed, figureheads, new displays of ship models; Barge House includes State barges from the 17th century; the Museum includes the Queen's House, a royal palace built by Inigo Jones which houses 16th- and 17th-century treasures, and the Old Royal Observatory where the displays illustrate the work, largely concerned with time and navigation, which was done here, and a planetarium; Dir. Dr. BASIL GREENHILL, C.B., C.M.G.

**National Portrait Gallery:** St. Martin's Place, WC2H 0HE; f. 1856; collection contains over 9,000 portraits of eminent British men and women of the last 500 years; activities include lectures, exhibitions; Dir. Dr. J. T. HAYES, M.A., PH.D., F.S.A.; Chair. of Trustees Lord KENYON, C.B.E., B.A., D.L., F.S.A.

**National Postal Museum:** King Edward Bldg., King Edward St., EC1A 1LP; f. 1966, reopened in new premises 1969; collection of stamps, essays, drawings and official documents dating back to Rowland Hills' proposals for Uniform Penny Postage in 1837–39; also the Post Office collection of stamps of the world and of British 20th-century stamps, and the philatelic archives (1855–1965) of Thomas De La Rue and Co., security printers; Curator W. RAIFE WELLSTED.

**Public Record Office:** *see* under National Archives.

**Royal Air Force Museum:** Hendon, NW9 5LL; f. 1963, opened 1972; attached to the Ministry of Defence; exhibits material recording the history of the Royal Flying Corps, the Royal Naval Air Service, the Royal Air Force, and aviation generally; activities cover many aspects of aviation, including military, civil, artistic, scientific, industrial and political; archives and library of 100,000 vols.; Dir. Dr. J. I. TANNER, M.A., PH.D., F.L.A., F.M.A., F.R.Ae.S., F.R.HIST.S., F.S.A.

  **Battle of Britain Museum:** opened 1978; contains a unique collection of British, German and Italian aircraft, which were engaged in the great air battle of 1940; Dir. as above.

**Royal College of Music Museum of Instruments:** Prince Consort Rd., South Kensington, S.W.7; f. 1883; includes Donaldson, Tagore, Hipkins and Ridley collections; Curator Mrs. ELIZABETH WELLS.

**Royal College of Surgeons Museum:** Lincoln's Inn Fields, WC2A 3PN; formed upon the Hunterian Collection purchased by Parliament in 1799; opened in 1813 when there were about 13,682 specimens; many additions both to buildings and collections have been made since the first opening; part of the buildings and many valuable items were destroyed in 1941; since the war 4 new museums have been built and many specimens replaced; Conservator of the Anatomical Museum R. M. H. MCMINN, PH.D., M.D.; Curator of the Hunterian Museum ELIZABETH ALLEN, M.I.BIOL.; Conservator of the Pathological Museum J. L. TURK, D.SC., M.D., M.R.C.PATH.; Curator of the Pathological Museum M. S. ISRAEL, M.R.C.P., M.R.C.PATH.; Hon. Curator of the Odontological Museum A. E. W. MILES, L.R.C.P., M.R.C.S., F.D.S.R.C.S., F.F.D.R.C.S.I.; Hon. Curator of Historical Surgical Instruments Sir ERIC RICHES, M.C., F.R.C.S.

**Science Museum:** South Kensington, SW7 2DD; f. 1857; the National Museum of Science and Industry; Dir. Dame MARGARET WESTON, D.B.E., B.SC., C.ENG., M.I.E.E.; Keeper Physics Dept. Dr. D. B. THOMAS, M.SC., PH.D.; Keeper Chemistry Dept. R. G. W. ANDERSON, M.A., D.PHIL.; Keeper Electrical Engineering and Communications Dept. E. J. S. BECKLAKE, PH.D., F.B.I.S.; Keeper Transport Dept. G. W. B. LACEY, B.SC., A.R.AE.S.; Keeper Mechanical and Civil Engineering Dept. J. T. VAN RIEMSDIJK, B.A.; Keeper Earth and Space Sciences Dept. J. WARTNABY, M.SC., PH.D.; Dept. of Museum Services Keeper D. A. ROBINSON, M.A., D.PHIL.; Museum Supt. (vacant); Science Library: *see* Libraries (London).

**Sir John Soane's House and Museum:** 13 Lincoln's Inn Fields, W.C.2; built in 1812 by Sir John Soane, Architect of Bank of England; est. by Act of Parliament 1833, for the promotion of the study of architecture and allied arts; Curator Sir JOHN SUMMERSON, C.B.E., F.B.A., A.R.I.B.A.; library: *see* Special Libraries.

**South London Art Gallery** (*Borough of Southwark*): Peckham Rd., SE5 8UH; f. 1891; frequent exhibitions of paintings in oils and water colours, prints, etchings and sculptures; the permanent collection is exhibited from time to time; Curator K. A. DOUGHTY, F.L.A.

**Tate Gallery:** Millbank, SW1P 4RG; f. 1897 by Sir Henry Tate; comprises the British Collection: mainly painting from *c.* 1550 to *c.* 1875, including works by Hogarth, Blake, Constable, Turner and the Pre-Raphaelites; Modern Collection: paintings, sculptures, drawings and prints from *c.* 1875 to the present; total works: over 10,000 including *c.* 5,000 prints; Dir. ALAN BOWNESS, C.B.E.

**Tower of London Armouries:** E.C.3; the national collection of arms and armour, illustrating their development from the Middle Ages to 1914 and including the armour of the Tudor and Stuart sovereigns and other historic relics, and with an Oriental Section; reference library; Master of the Armouries A. V. B. NORMAN, B.A., F.S.A., F.S.A.(SCOT.).

**Victoria and Albert Museum:** S. Kensington, SW7 2RL; f. 1852, under the Office of Arts and Libraries; a museum of Fine and Applied Arts of all countries, periods and styles: Dir. Dr. ROY STRONG, PH.D., F.S.A.; Keepers of Museum Depts.: Sculpture, A. F. RADCLIFFE; Ceramics, J. V. G. MALLET; Prints, Drawings and Paintings, C. KAUFFMAN; Metalwork, C. BLAIR; Textiles, T. LEVEY; Furniture, P. K. THORNTON; Indian, R. W. SKELTON; Far Eastern, J. G. AYERS; Museum Services, JOHN PHYSICK; Library, R. W. LIGHTBOWN.

**Apsley House** (*The Wellington Museum*): 149 Piccadilly, W.1; opened to the public 1952; contains paintings, silver, porcelain, orders and decorations, and personal relics of the first Duke of Wellington; Officer-in-Charge (vacant).

**Bethnal Green Museum of Childhood:** Cambridge Heath Rd., E.2; f. 1872; British painting and art objects, ceramics, costumes, textiles, furniture and toys; Officer-in-Charge ANTHONY BURTON.

**Ham House:** near Richmond, Surrey; country house built in 1610 and enlarged by Elizabeth, Duchess of Lauderdale; contains much of the original furniture and interior ornament.

**Osterley Park House:** Osterley, Middx.; 16th-century house remodelled by Robert Adam.

**Wallace Collection:** Hertford House, Manchester Square, W1M 6BN; f. 1900; outstanding collections of pictures miniatures, sculpture, French furniture, clocks, ceramics, Sèvres porcelain, bronzes, arms and armour and *objets d'art*, bequeathed to the nation in 1897 by Lady Wallace; Dir. J. INGAMELLS.

**Wellcome Museum of Medical Science:** The Wellcome Bldg., 183 Euston Rd., NW1 2BP; illustrated accounts of diseases prevalent in tropical and sub-tropical areas; pathological, entomological and other specimens, photomicrographs and abstracts of recent medical literature; primarily for medical graduates and undergraduates tutorial facilities; Dir. Dr. A. J. DUGGAN, M.D., F.R.C.P., F.M.A.

**Whitechapel Art Gallery:** Whitechapel High St., E1 7QX; f. 1901; temporary exhibitions, principally of modern or contemporary art; no permanent collection; charitable trust supported by the Arts Council, Greater London Council, local authorities and charitable bodies; Chair. of Trustees STEPHEN KEYNES; Dir. NICHOLAS SEROTA.

PROVINCES

The following is a selection from the many provincial museums of England. Arrangement is alphabetically by towns:

**Bowes Museum, The:** Barnard Castle, Co. Durham; collections formed 1840–75 by John and Josephine Bowes mainly of all forms of Continental Fine and Decorative Arts; f. at Barnard Castle 1869, since when there have been additions of British Decorative Arts, including series of English rooms from 16th to 19th centuries, music, costumes, local history and archaeology galleries; originally a private trust, now administered by Durham County Council; Curator Mrs. E. CONRAN, M.A., F.M.A.; Keeper of Art B. CROSSLING, PH.L.

**Holburne of Menstrie Museum:** University of Bath, Great Pulteney St., Bath, Avon; f. 1882; pictures, miniatures, silver, ceramics, glass, furniture, etc., in an 18th-century building; Crafts Study Centre; Curator Mrs. PHILIPPA BISHOP.

**The American Museum in Britain:** Claverton Manor, nr. Bath; f. 1959, opened 1961; first American museum in Europe; aims at illustrating the development of American decorative arts from 17th to 19th centuries; library; Dir. IAN MCCALLUM, A.R.I.B.A.

**Birmingham Museums and Art Gallery:** Chamberlain Sq., Birmingham, B3 3DH; f. 1867; Departments of Fine and Applied Art (foreign schools from Renaissance, English from 17th century, early English watercolours and Pre-Raphaelite paintings and drawings, sculpture, silver, ceramics and textile collections); Archaeology, Ethnography and Local History (collections from Ancient Egypt, Ur, Nineveh, Jericho, Nimrud, Vinca, Jerusalem, Petra and Vounos (Cyprus) in the Old World, Mexico and Peru in the New, Prehistoric, Roman and British Medieval antiquities); Pacific ethnography collection; British coin collection; Natural History; comprehensive collections of minerals, gemstones and molluscs, British birds, lepidoptera and coleoptera; Midland flora; Dir. MICHAEL DIAMOND, M.A., F.M.A.

*Branch Museums:* Department of Science and Industry; f. 1950; early industrial machinery and illustrations of scientific principles, locomotive hall; Aston Hall (Jacobean house furnished with textile and furniture collections); Blakesley Hall (Tudor house with collections of local history); Weoley Castle (archaeological site), Sarehole Mill (18th-century watermill once used for corn milling and blade grinding, restored 1969–74); Birmingham Nature Centre, Cannon Hill.

**Rhodes Memorial Museum and Commonwealth Centre:** South Rd., Bishop's Stortford, Herts.; f. 1938; Cecil Rhodes' birthplace preserved, with 15 rooms of exhibits relating to his life and times and South Africa; Man./Sec. ROBERT B. CROOKS.

**Blackburn Museum and Art Gallery:** Library St., Blackburn, Lancs., BB1 7AJ; f. 1860; coins and medieval MSS., Japanese prints, fine and decorative arts, ethnography, natural history and the museum of East Lancashire Regiment; also the Lewis Museum of Textile Machinery and the Turton Tower folk museum; Dir. PAUL SYKES.

**Royal Pavilion, Art Gallery and Museums, Brighton:** f. 1851; Dir. JOHN MORLEY, M.A., F.M.A.

*Brighton Art Gallery and Museum:* Church St., Brighton, Sussex; collection of early and modern paintings, water-colours, prints and drawings; English pottery and porcelain, including the Willett Collection;

decorative art and furniture of Art Nouveau and Art Deco periods; ethnography and archaeology; musical instruments; Brighton history.

*Royal Pavilion:* Brighton; once the marine palace of King George IV and other monarchs (1787–1846); interior decorations restored and original furniture.

*Booth Museum of Natural History:* Dyke Road, Brighton; display of birds; reference collections of eggs, insects, minerals, palaeontology, osteology, skins and herbaria; gallery of vertebrate evolution.

*Preston Manor:* Preston Park; furnished Georgian house, rebuilt 1738, and re-modelled 1905; home of the Stanford family for nearly 200 years; illustrates the way of life of a rich family before the First World War.

*Grange Art Gallery and Museum:* Rottingdean; toys, Sussex folk-life, Rudyard Kiplingiana.

**City of Bristol Museum and Art Gallery:** Queen's Rd., Bristol, BS8 1RL; also Red Lodge, Park Row (16th century), Georgian House (18th century), Chatterton House Museum, Blaise Castle House Museum, St. Nicholas Church Museum, Bristol Industrial Museum (Princes Wharf); Kingsweston Roman Villa and Sea Mills Roman Site, Fairbairn Steam Crane (City Docks); Controller D. G. HARMER, M.A., J.P.; Dir. of City Museum NICHOLAS THOMAS, M.A., F.S.A., F.M.A.; Dir. of City Art Gallery A. WILSON, M.A., F.S.A., F.M.A.; publs. guides, catalogues, *Half-yearly Bulletin*, etc.

**Towneley Hall Art Gallery and Museums:** Towneley Hall, Burnley, Lancs.; f. 1902; 17th- to 20th-century oils; early English water colours; collections of period furniture, ivories, 18th-century glassware and oriental ceramics; archaeological specimens and militaria; Hall built from c. 1350; Curator HUBERT R. RIGG, F.M.A., F.R.S.A., F.S.A.(SCOT.).

**Museum of Local Crafts and Industries:** Adjacent to Towneley Hall; f. 1971.

*Natural History Centre:* Adjacent to Towneley Hall; f. 1981.

**Fitzwilliam Museum:** Trumpington St., Cambridge, CB2 1RB; f. 1816; art collections of the University; paintings, drawings, prints, sculpture; coins and medals; ceramics, glass, textiles, arms and armour and other applied arts; Greek, Roman, western Asiatic and Egyptian antiquities; library of 80,000 vols. and medieval, literary and music MSS., autograph letters; early printed books, printed music, books on history of art; Dir. Prof. A. M. JAFFÉ, D.LITT., F.R.S.A.; publ. *Annual Report*†.

**Museum of Archaeology and Anthropology:** Downing St., Cambridge, CB2 3DZ; f. 1883; Curator D. W. PHILLIPSON, M.A., PH.D.

**University Museum of Zoology:** Downing St., Cambridge; f. 1819; Dir. K. A. JOYSEY, M.A., PH.D.

**Jane Austen's House:** Main St., Chawton, Alton, Hampshire; f. 1949; portraits, documents, furniture and objects relating to Jane Austen and her family; Dir. F. E. CARPENTER.

**The Weald and Downland Open Air Museum:** Singleton, Chichester, Sussex; f. 1971 to save interesting examples of vernacular architecture in the area which have been threatened with demolition; so far 15 buildings ranging from early medieval times to 19th century have been re-erected on the site, which should eventually house 50 buildings; Pres. Lord EGREMONT; Museum Dir. CHRISTOPHER S. H. ZEUNER; Research Dir. R. HARRIS; Hon. Sec. M. HOLDSWORTH; publs. Guide Books and educational material for schools†.

**Corinium Museum:** Park St., Cirencester, Glos.; one of the country's leading collections of Roman material; mosaic pavements, sculpture, military and civil tombstones, household domestic utensils, personal ornaments, and Samian and coarse pottery, all giving ample evidence of the importance and wealth of Corinium, which was the second largest town in Roman Britain; regional museum for the Cotswolds; Curator D. J. VINER, B.A., A.M.A., F.S.A.

**Cotswold Countryside Collection:** Northleach, Glos.; includes the Lloyd-Baker Collection of agricultural history: wagons, horse-drawn implements and tools; originally a House of Correction, its history is displayed in a reconstructed cell block.

**Colchester and Essex Museum:** The Castle, Colchester, Essex, CO1 1TJ; f. 1860 from the collections of Essex Archaeological Society; local antiquities and natural history; maintained by the Borough Council. The large collections are from Colchester and Essex, and the Roman section is particularly extensive. Three branch museums (Natural History, Later Antiquities, Social History). Curator D. T.-D. CLARKE, M.A., F.S.A., F.M.A.; publs. *Annual Report, Local Archaeological Monographs*.

**Wiltshire Archaeological and Natural History Society Museum:** Long St., Devizes, Wilts.; f. 1853; Bronze Age, Iron Age, Roman and Natural History collections; library of over 8,000 vols.; Curator F. K. ANNABLE, B.A., F.S.A., F.M.A.; publ. *Wiltshire Archaeological and Natural History Magazine*† (annually).

**Doncaster Museum and Art Gallery:** Chequer Rd., Doncaster, Yorks.; f. 1909; regional natural history, geology, archaeology and local history collections; permanent art collection, paintings, ceramics and glass; frequent temporary exhibitions; Curator T. G. MANBY, M.A., F.S.A., F.M.A.; publs. *Museum and Art Gallery Publications* 8vo and 4to series (irregular), *Catalogues*.

**Dorset County Museum and Natural History and Archaeological Society:** Dorchester; Museum f. 1846, Society f. 1875, merged in 1928; aims to encourage an active interest in natural history, archaeology, the fine arts, geology, literature, and the local history of Dorset; lectures, conferences and seminars are held in the Museum in winter and spring; Pres. Mrs. J. C. WALTON; publ. *The Proceedings of the Dorset Natural History and Archaeological Society* (annually).

**Gulbenkian Museum of Oriental Art and Archaeology:** University of Durham, Elvet Hill, Durham; f. 1960; collections of international status of oriental art and archaeology covering Ancient Egypt and the Near East, the Indian sub-continent, Japan and S.E. Asia; Duke of Northumberland's collection of Egyptian antiquities; MacDonald collection of Chinese ceramics; Charles Hardinge collection of Chinese jades; Keeper JOHN RUFFLE, M.A., F.S.A.

**Gloucester Museums:** Gloucester; Curator J. F. RHODES. The museums are as follows:

**City Museum and Art Gallery:** Brunswick Rd.; f. 1859; natural science, archaeology (before A.D. 1500), and applied art; temporary art exhibitions.

**Bishop Hooper's Lodging:** 99–103 Westgate St.; history of the city from A.D. 1500; bygone crafts and industries of Gloucestershire.

**Grantham Museum:** St. Peter's Hill, Grantham; f. 1922; exhibits material relating to the archaeology and history of Grantham and district; special collection relating to Sir Isaac Newton; Dir. A. J. H. GUNSTONE, F.S.A.

**Dove Cottage and Wordsworth Museum (The Dove Cottage Trust):** Dove Cottage, Town End, Grasmere, Ambleside, Cumbria; f. 1890; Wordsworth's Cottage containing original furniture and collection of personal effects, and a museum containing MSS., portraits and first editions, objects relating to the poet and to rural life of the period; library of 4,000 vols. and MSS.; Librarian Dr. P. LAVER; Enquiries: Mrs. O. A. WEST; publ. *Friends of Dove Cottage Newsletter* (annually).

**Thurrock Borough Museum:** Orsett Rd., Grays, Essex, RM17 5DX; f. 1956; archaeology and history of Thurrock with accent on the growth of technology in a Thamesside landscape; Curator RANDAL BINGLEY.

**Thurrock Riverside Museum:** Civic Sq., Tilbury, Essex; f. 1977; archaeology and history of the River Thames between Purfleet and Fobbing; Curator RANDAL BINGLEY.

**Guernsey Museum and Art Gallery:** Candie Gardens, St. Peter Port, Guernsey; f. 1978 (as Lukis Museum 1909); tells story of the island and its people; includes art gallery displaying pictures of Guernsey and by Guernsey painters, and audio visual theatre; offers education service; maritime and military brs. at Fort Grey and Castle Cornet; Curator Mrs. H. R. COLE; publs. museum guides, *Annual Report*.

**Disraeli Museum:** Hughenden Manor, High Wycombe, Bucks.; contains Disraeli's books, furniture, paintings and personal effects; property of the National Trust (*q.v.*).

**Tolson Memorial Museum:** Ravensknowle Park, Wakefield Rd., Huddersfield, HD5 8DJ, Yorks.; opened 1922; illustrates natural and human history of the district; geology, botany, zoology, pre-history, folk-life, toys, development of woollen industry, collection of horse-drawn vehicles; Dir. V. C. SMITH, F.M.A.

**Ironbridge Gorge Museum:** Ironbridge, Telford, Shropshire, TF8 7AW; f. 1968; preserves and displays the industrial and social remains of the East Shropshire Coalfield; 3-mile site on the river Severn comprising: Coalbrookdale Museum and Abraham Darby Furnace Site, Ironbridge with the Severn Wharf and Warehouse, the Iron Bridge (built 1779), Blists Hill Open Air Museum, Coalport China Works Museum; reference library of *c.* 20,000 vols.; Dir. NEIL COSSONS, M.A., F.S.A., F.M.A.

**Abbot Hall Art Gallery and Museum of Lakeland Life and Industry:** Kendal, Cumbria, LA9 5AL; f. 1962 (gallery), 1971 (museum); gallery provides schedule of changing exhibitions of local and international interest; houses permanent collections of primarily 18th-century furniture, paintings and objets d'art, modern paintings, sculpture and drawings; museum features the working and social life of the area; talks and tours provided; library of 300 vols.; Dir. Miss M. E. BURKETT, O.B.E., B.A., F.M.A.,; Curator of Museum J. W. ANSTEE.

**Leeds City Museums:** Municipal Bldgs., Leeds, Yorks., LS1 3AA; f. 1820 for the preservation and display of objects of ethnographical, biological, geological, and archaeological importance, and for the furtherance of adult and child education by visual means. The City Museum houses natural history, ethnology and archaeology; the Abbey House Museum illustrates the folk life of the people of Yorkshire over the last two hundred years whilst the ruins of the adjacent Kirkstall Abbey are among the finest examples of early Cistercian architecture in the country. The Science and Industry Museum is housed in the recently acquired Armley Mill; Dir. P. C. D. BREARS, A.M.A.; publs. Guides and Catalogues.

**Temple Newsam House:** Leeds, LS15 0AE; opened to the public 1923; Tudor-Stuart house, birthplace of Lord Darnley; contains extensive collections of paintings and the decorative arts; Dir. ROBERT ROWE, C.B.E., M.A., F.M.A.; publs. *Leeds Arts Calendar* (twice yearly), *Guides* and *Catalogues*.

**Leeds City Art Gallery:** Municipal Bldgs., Leeds, LS1 3AA; f. 1888; English, French and Italian paintings of the 17th, 18th and 19th centuries; early English water-colours, including Kitson and Lupton collections; modern paintings and sculpture; Print Room and Art Library; Dir. and publs. as above.

**Lotherton Hall:** Aberford, near Leeds; opened to the public 1969; 19th- and 20th-century country house; Gascoigne Collection of 17th–19th-century furniture, silver, ceramics, costume and paintings; modern crafts; oriental gallery; Dir. and publs. as above.

**Leicestershire Museums, Art Galleries and Records Service:** 96 New Walk, Leicester, LE1 6TD; f. 1849; sections of antiquities, biology, earth sciences, fine and decorative arts, technology, education and interpretation; Leicestershire Record Office repository for official and private archives; branch museums: Jewry Wall Museum of Archaeology, Melton Carnegie Museum, Newarke Houses, Belgrave Hall, Guildhall, Wygston's House, Museum of Technology, Museum of the Royal Leicestershire Regt., Rutland County Museum, Oakham Castle, The Old Manor House at Donington-le-Heath; library of 15,000 vols.; Dir. P. J. BOYLAN, B.SC., F.G.S., F.M.A., M.B.I.M.

**Lincoln City and County Museum:** Broadgate, Lincoln; f. 1906; exhibits natural history, archaeological and historical collections relating to Lincolnshire; large collection of Roman antiquities from Lincoln; fine collection of armour and arms; Dir. A. J. H. GUNSTONE, B.A., F.S.A., F.M.A.; Keeper A. J. WHITE, M.A., A.M.A.

**Museum of Lincolnshire Life:** Burton Rd., Lincoln; f. 1969; displays illustrating the social, agricultural and industrial history of Lincolnshire over the last three centuries; Keeper Mrs. C. M. WILSON, A.M.A.

**Skegness Church Farm Museum:** Church Rd. South, Skegness, Lincs.; f. 1976; a complex of 18th- and 19th-century farmhouse and agricultural buildings with displays of agricultural equipment typical of the area; farmhouse furnished to period *c.* 1900; Keeper Mrs. C. M. WILSON, A.M.A.

**Usher Art Gallery:** Lindum Rd., Lincoln; f. 1927; exhibits the Usher collection of watches, miniatures, porcelain, *objets d'art*, etc.; special collection of works by Peter De Wint and a general collection of paintings, sculpture and decorative art objects; extensive collection of coins and tokens from Lincolnshire; Keeper R. H. WOOD, DIP.A.D.

**Merseyside County Museum:** William Brown St., Liverpool, L3 8EN; f. 1851, rebuilt 1964–69; outstanding collections include the Mayer-Fejérvàry Gothic ivories, the Bryan Faussett group of Anglo-Saxon antiquities, the Lord Derby and Tristram ornithological collections; gallery displays include material relating to Local History and Natural History, Shipping, Egyptology, Ethnology, Decorative Art, Transport and the King's Regiment; there is an Aquarium and Planetarium; education programme, information services and environmental conservation work; branch museums: Speke Hall, Croxteth Country Park, and Maritime Museum; Dir. RICHARD FOSTER, M.A., F.S.A., F.M.A.; publs. various, including *Annual Report*†, *Bulletin*† (occasional), guides, catalogues, etc.

**Walker Art Gallery:** William Brown St., Liverpool, L3 8EL; f. 1873; English paintings, Impressionist and Old Master paintings, particularly Italian and Netherlandish Primitives, English and European drawings, water-colours and sculpture; Dir. TIMOTHY STEVENS, M.A.

**Manchester City Art Galleries:** City Art Gallery, Mosley St., Manchester, M2 3JL; f. 1823; British painting, old masters and decorative arts; other galleries: Gallery of Modern Art, Queens' Park Art Gallery, Platt

Hall (clothes since the 17th century), Wythenshawe Hall, Heaton Hall and Fletcher Moss Museum and Art Gallery; Dir. TIMOTHY CLIFFORD; publs. *Concise Catalogue of British Paintings* (Vol. I artists born before 1850, Vol. II artists born after 1850)†, *Concise Catalogue of Foreign Paintings*†.

**Manchester Museum:** The University, Manchester, M13 9PL; f. 1821; archaeology (including Egyptology), ethnology, geology, botany, zoology, entomology; education and exhibition services; Dir. ALAN WARHURST, B.A., F.S.A., F.M.A.

**North Western Museum of Science and Industry:** 97 Grosvenor St., Manchester, M1 7HF; f. 1969; collections on the history of science and technology, scientific equipment, machinery including early textile mill machines, photographs and drawings; Dir. R. L. HILLS, M.A., PH.D., D.I.C.

**Hancock Museum:** Barras Bridge, Newcastle upon Tyne, NE2 4PT; f. 1829, present building 1884; general zoology, ornithology, geology, botany and ethnology; headquarters of Northumberland Wildlife Trust Ltd. and the Natural History Society of Northumbria; museum administered jointly by the Natural History Society of Northumbria and the University of Newcastle upon Tyne; Curator A. M. TYNAN, B.SC., F.M.A.

**Tyne and Wear County Council Museums:** Dir. J. M. A. THOMPSON, M.A., A.M.A.

  **Laing Art Gallery and Museum:** Higham Place, Newcastle upon Tyne, NE1 8AG; f. 1904; Art Gallery contains water-colours of British School from 17th century onwards, British oil paintings (18th-20th centuries), sculpture, engravings, etchings, Japanese colour prints; Museum contains Egyptian, Greek and Roman antiquities, decorative and industrial art, Oriental arms and armour; annexe at Higham Place Gallery.

  **John George Joicey Museum:** City Rd., Newcastle upon Tyne, NE1 2AS; furniture, local exhibits, European arms and armour; sited in 17th-century almshouse which is the only brick building of Renaissance architecture in Newcastle.

  **Museum of Science and Engineering:** West Blandford St., Newcastle upon Tyne; f. 1981; three large galleries with displays of stationary engines showing development of motive power, and regular temporary exhibitions.

**Museum of Antiquities of the University and the Society of Antiquaries of Newcastle upon Tyne:** Department of Archaeology, The University, Newcastle upon Tyne; f. 1813; prehistoric, Roman and Medieval collections, scale models of Hadrian's Wall, reproductions of Roman arms and armour, and reconstruction of a Temple of Mithras; library of 5,000 items relating to Hadrian's Wall, British, Continental and Mediterranean archaeology; Keeper D. J. SMITH, PH.D., F.S.A.

**Norfolk Museums Service:** Norwich, Norfolk, NR1 3JU; incorporates the following museums: in Norwich, *Castle Museum* (local social and cultural history, natural history, porcelain, art, crafts, archaeology), *Bridewell Museum* (local industries and crafts in medieval house), *Strangers' Hall Museum* (15th-century domestic articles and furnishings), *St. Peter Hungate* (ecclesiastical art, medieval illuminated books, church plate, etc.); in Great Yarmouth, *Maritime Museum for East Anglia, Tolhouse Museum, Exhibition Galleries, Elizabethan House Museum* (domestic life, toys, porcelain, glassware); in King's Lynn, *Lynn Museum* (history, natural history and geology of West Norfolk), *Museum of Social History*; in Thetford, *Ancient House Museum*; in Walsingham, *Shirehall Museum* (18th-century court room and display on pilgrim history); in Gressenhall, *Norfolk Rural Life Museum* (farm tools and implements, engines, Craftsmen's Row and Cherry Tree cottage); in Cromer, *Cromer Museum* (history, geology and natural history); Dir. F. W. CHEETHAM, O.B.E., B.A., F.M.A.

**Nottingham City Museum and Art Gallery:** The Castle, Nottingham, NG1 6EL; f. 1878; archaeology and ethnography; fine and applied arts; reference library of 2,500 vols.; Dir. B. LOUGHBROUGH, M.A., F.M.A.

**Nottingham Natural History Museum:** Wollaton Hall, Nottingham; f. 1867; collections of botanical, zoological, and geological material; extensive British and foreign herbaria, Crowfoot collection of exotic butterflies, Pearson collection of European butterflies, Fowler collection of British Coleoptera, Hollier collection of Wenlock Limestone fossils, Carrington series of Mountain Limestone fossils; reference library of approx. 5,000 vols.; controlled by Nottingham City Council; Curator B. R. P. PLAYLE, M.SC., A.M.A.

**Ashmolean Museum:** Oxford; f. 1683; contains the art and archaeological collections of the University of Oxford; British, European, Mediterranean, Egyptian and Near Eastern archaeology; Italian, Dutch, Flemish, French and English oil paintings; Old Master and modern drawings, water-colours and prints; miniatures; European ceramics; sculpture and bronzes; English silver; objects of applied art; Hope collection of engraved portraits; coins and medals of all countries and periods; Chinese and Japanese porcelain, paintings and lacquer; Chinese bronzes, Tibetan art; Indian sculpture and painting; Islamic pottery and metalwork; Dir. D. T. PIPER, C.B.E., M.A.

**Museum of Modern Art Oxford:** 30 Pembroke St., Oxford, OX1 1BP; f. 1966; 20th-century painting, sculpture, photography, prints, drawings, film, and occasionally aspects of design and architecture; lectures, seminars, etc.; reference library; Dir. DAVID ELLIOTT.

**Plymouth Museum and Art Gallery:** Drake Circus, Plymouth, Devon; f. 1897 to illustrate the arts and sciences of the West Country; comprises the Cottonian Collection of early printed and illuminated books, Old Master engravings and drawings, and portraits by Sir Joshua Reynolds; the Clarendon Collection of portraits of English worthies; silver; William Cookworthy's Plymouth and Bristol porcelain; natural history, archaeology and local history; the Museum administers Buckland Abbey, former home of Sir Francis Drake (vested in National Trust since 1948), now a Drake, Maritime and West Country Folk Museum (f. 1951), the Elizabethan House (f. 1930), 32 New St., and the Merchant's House (f. 1977), 33 St. Andrew's St. (16–17th-century); Dir. J. BARBER, M.A., F.S.A., A.M.A.

**Lady Lever Art Gallery, The:** Port Sunlight, Wirral, Merseyside; gift made to the public in 1922 by William Hesketh, First Viscount Leverhulme in memory of his wife, Elizabeth Ellen, Lady Lever; collection includes paintings and drawings of the British School (from the late 17th century), sculpture, 18th-century English furniture, Chinese ceramics, Wedgwood and textiles; Dir. TIMOTHY STEVENS, M.A.

**Harris Museum and Art Gallery:** Market Square, Preston, Lancs., PR1 2PP; f. 1882; specialist collections in the fields of fine art, decorative art, archaeology, natural history, including works by the Devis family, the Newsham Bequest of 19th-century paintings and sculpture, and the Cedric Houghton Bequest of ceramics; Dir. MICHAEL CROSS.

**Reading Museum and Art Gallery:** Reading, Berks.; f. 1883 to collect, preserve and exhibit objects of art, archaeology and science, especially of the district; special collections: Silchester collection of Romano-British remains; Dir. C. A. SIZER, B.SC., F.G.S., F.M.A.

**Institute of Agricultural History and Museum of English Rural Life:** University of Reading, Whiteknights, Reading, Berks., RG6 2AG; f. 1951; national collection of objects, photographs and records of English agricultural history; special collection of archives and publications of agricultural engineering industry; bibliographical unit of classified references to the printed literature of British agricultural history; library of 10,000 vols.; Dir. E. J. T. COLLINS, PH.D.

**Pilkington Glass Museum:** Prescot Rd., St. Helens, Merseyside, WA10 3TT; f. 1964; illustrates the evolution of glassmaking techniques, and how the product has been used since Phoenician times; private museum, forming an integral part of the head office complex of Pilkington Bros. Ltd. (f. 1826 as St. Helens Crown Glass Co.); reference library of 1,000 vols.; Curator I. M. BURGOYNE.

**Salisbury and South Wiltshire Museum:** The King's House, 65 The Close, Salisbury, Wilts; f. 1860; Curator P. R. SAUNDERS, B.A., A.M.A.; publ. *Annual Report*.

**Oates Memorial Library and Museum and Gilbert White Museum:** The Wakes, Selborne, Alton, Hants.; f. 1954; private museum funded by the Oates Memorial Trust; consists of two museums in an historic house, and a 5-acre garden; Dir. Dr. JUNE CHATFIELD; publs. guides.

*Gilbert White Museum:* exhibits on Gilbert White and Selborne with some natural history; in the garden plants of Gilbert White's time are grown.

*Oates Memorial Museum:* display on exploration in Africa by Frank Oates (late 19th century) and in Antarctica by Lawrence Oates; Oates Memorial Library consists of books on natural history and Antarctica and Africa (available by arrangement).

*Gilbert White Field Studies Centre:* for use by local schools and colleges.

**Sheffield City Museum:** Weston Park, Sheffield, Yorks., S10 2TP; f. 1875; collections of Sheffield silver, Old Sheffield Plate, British and European cutlery, coins and medals, ceramics, local archaeology, natural sciences, local geology, etc.; library of 7,000 vols.; Dir. JOHN E. BARTLETT, M.A., F.S.A., F.M.A.; publs. occasional publications on collections and on Sheffield region.

**Abbeydale Industrial Hamlet:** Abbeydale Rd. South; opened 1970; an 18th-century scytheworks with Huntsman type crucible steel furnace, tilt-hammers, grinding-shop and hand forges; Dir. as City Museum.

**Bishops' House:** Meersbrook Park; opened 1976; a late 15th-century timber-framed domestic building with 16th- and 17th-century additions; Dir. as City Museum.

**Shepherd Wheel:** Whiteley Wood; opened 1975; a Sheffield 'Little Mesters' water-powered grinding shop; Dir. as City Museum.

**Graves Art Gallery:** Surrey St., Sheffield; f. 1936; English, Italian Renaissance and Netherlands paintings; Dir. H. FRANK CONSTANTINE, F.M.A.

**Mappin Art Gallery.**

**Southampton Art Gallery:** Dept. of Leisure Services, Civic Centre, Southampton, Hants.; f. 1916 by a Bequest Fund for purchase and display of works of art; new building opened 1939; collections include Continental Old Masters, French 19th- and 20th-century School, British painting from the 18th century to present day, with emphasis on the Camden Town School; library of 1,000 vols.; activities include a temporary exhibition programme, an information centre and Artshop and the establishment of a community education service; Curator A. B. RAINCE, B.A., A.M.A.

**Atkinson Art Gallery:** Lord St., Southport, Merseyside; f. 1878 for the exhibition of the town's permanent collection; 18th-, 19th- and 20th-century British oils and watercolours, modern and contemporary prints; Keeper of Fine Art DIANA DE BUSSY, M.A.

**Stoke-on-Trent City Museum and Art Gallery:** Broad St., Hanley, Stoke-on-Trent, Staffs.; one of the finest collections of ceramics in the world with emphasis on Staffordshire pottery and porcelain; depts. of Fine Art, Decorative Art, Natural History, Archaeology and Social History; also administers Ford Green Hall, Smallthorne, a timber-framed building of c. 1580, and the Spitfire Museum in Hanley; Dir. A. R. MOUNTFORD, M.A., F.S.A., F.M.A.; publs. *Journal of Ceramic History, Annual Report of the Museum Archaeological Society*.

**Wakefield Art Gallery:** Wentworth Terrace, Wakefield, W. Yorks.; Museums and Art Galleries Officer Mrs. GILLIAN SPENCER, M.A.

**Elizabethan Exhibition Gallery:** Brook St., Wakefield.

**Wakefield Museum:** Wood St., Wakefield.

**Pontefract Museum:** Salter Rd., Pontefract.

**Wolverhampton Art Gallery and Museum:** Lichfield St., Wolverhampton, W. Midlands; f. 1885; works by 18th-, 19th- and 20th-century English painters, English Water-colours and Oriental works of art; Bantock House, Bantock Park, contains fine examples of English enamels, Japanning and English porcelain; Branch Museum at Bilston contains local history exhibits and English enamels; Curator DAVID RODGERS, M.A.

**Castle Museum, York:** f. 1938; England's first major folk museum; Kirk collection illustrates English life in the 17th–20th centuries; the adjacent Debtor's Prison (opened 1952) contains early crafts and costumes, militaria and armour collections; nearby is the "York Story" at the Heritage Centre, Castlegate, f. 1975 to interpret the social and architectural history of the City of York; Curator Dr. G. D. NICOLSON.

**National Railway Museum:** Leeman Road, York, YO2 4XJ; f. 1975; part of the Science Museum (q.v.); houses a large part of the National Collection of Railway Relics; full-size locomotives, carriages, and rolling stock, models, signalling equipment, railway relics, posters, prints, photographs and paintings; reference library of 10,000 vols.; Keeper Dr. J. A. COILEY, M.A.

**York City Art Gallery:** Exhibition Square, York; f. 1879; permanent collection consists of paintings of the Italian, Dutch, Flemish, German, French, Spanish and British Schools and includes the Lycett Green Collection (presented through the N.A.C.F. 1955); there is a collection of works by William Etty, R.A. and other York artists; a collection of modern stoneware pottery and an extensive collection of prints and drawings, largely devoted to the topography of York; library of 5,000 vols.; Curator RICHARD GREEN, M.A.; publ. *Preview*† (3 a year).

**Yorkshire Museum:** Museum Gardens, York, YO1 2DR; f. 1822; important and extensive collections of British archaeology, especially from Roman York, geology, biology and Yorkshire ceramics; Curator T. M. CLEGG, F.M.A., M.B.O.U.

## WALES

**Borough of Newport Museum and Art Gallery:** John Frost Square, Newport, Gwent; f. 1888; special collections of Roman material from Caerleon and Caerwent; oils, early English water-colours and prints; natural and local history collections; Curator C. J. NEWBERY, B.A., A.M.A.

**Museum of Welsh Antiquities, University College of North Wales:** Ffordd Gwynedd, Bangor, Gwynedd; f. 1894; collects and exhibits antiquities relating to North Wales; Roman, Dark Age relics, furniture, crafts, costumes, prints and maps; art gallery; Curator JOHN ELLIS JONES.

**National Museum of Wales** (*Amgueddfa Genedlaethol Cymru*): Cathays Park, Cardiff, CF1 3NP; f. 1907; a museum of the natural sciences, archaeology, industry and art with special reference to Wales; brs.: Welsh Folk Musuem at St. Fagans; Welsh Industrial and Maritime Museum, Cardiff; the Turner House art gallery at Penarth; the Legionary Museum at Caerleon; Museum of the Woollen Industry, Drefach Felindre, Dyfed; Welsh State Museum, Llanberis, Gwynedd; Welsh Industrial and Maritime Museum, Cardiff; Yr Hen Gapel (The Old Chapel Museum), Tre'r-ddôl, Dyfed; Segontium Roman Fort Museum, Caernarfon, Gwynedd; Oviel Evyri (environmental gallery), Llanberis, Gwynedd; Pres. Col. Sir WILLIAM CRAWSHAY, D.S.O., F.R.D., T.D., D.L., LL.D.; Dir. D. A. BASSETT, PH.D.; Sec. D. W. DYKES, M.A.; publ. *Annual Report*†.

## SCOTLAND

**Aberdeen Art Gallery and Museums:** Art Gallery and Museums Department, Schoolhill, Aberdeen, AB9 1FQ; library of 3,000 vols. and 6,000 catalogues; Dir. IAN McKENZIE SMITH; contains:

*Aberdeen Art Gallery:* Schoolhill, Aberdeen; f. 1885; fine and decorative arts; major collection of 20th-century British art; James McBey print room and reference library; educational services.

*James Dun's House:* 61 Schoolhill, Aberdeen; f. 1975; temporary exhibitions museum.

*Provost Skene's House:* Guestrow, Aberdeen; f. 1953; 17th-century historic house; period rooms; local history.

*Provost Ross's House.*

*Maritime Museum:* Shiprow, Aberdeen; f. 1980.

**Burns Museum:** Alloway, Ayrshire; MSS. and correspondence of the poet Robert Burns; Curator J. LETHAM CONNELL.

**Dumfries Museum:** Corberry Hill, Dumfries; building erected as a windmill *c.* 1790; f. 1835 as an observatory; exhibits Roman relics, Stone and Bronze Age artefacts, natural and local history from Dumfries and Galloway; incorporates Dumfries Museum, Thornhill Museum, Langholm Museum and Myrseth Museum collections; MSS. concerning Burns, Carlyle, Scott, Barrie; camera obscura; period rooms at Old Bridge House (1660) nearby; Sanquhar Museum in Adam-designed Town House (1753) covers local history and geology; Curator A. E. TRUCKELL, M.B.E., F.S.A., F.S.A.(SCOT.), F.M.A., M.A.

**Dundee City Art Gallery and Museum:** Albert Square, Dundee, DD1 1DA; f. 1873; Flemish, Dutch, French and British painting, especially Scottish Schools, prints and drawings; regional collections of archaeology, history, natural history, botany and geology; Dir. J. D. BOYD, D.A., F.M.A., F.S.A.(SCOT.), F.R.S.A.; publs. works on archaeology, history, natural history, whaling, art, etc., *Annual Report*.

*Barrack Street Museum:* Dundee, DD1 1PG; shipping and local industries, etc.; Dir. as above.

*Broughty Castle Museum:* Dundee, DD5 2BE; history of Broughty Ferry, Tay whaling, natural history of the Tay, arms and armour; Dir. as above.

*Camperdown House:* Camperdown Park, Dundee, DD2 4FT; history of golf, personalia of Adm. Adam Duncan and the Duncans of Camperdown; Dir. as above.

*Mill's Observatory:* Balgay Hill; Cooke astronomical telescope, planetarium and other instruments; Dir. as above.

*St. Mary's Tower:* Dundee, DD1 4DG; 15th-century bell-tower, only portion remaining of pre-Reformation church of St. Mary; site museum and viewpoint; Dir. J. D. BOYD.

**Edinburgh City Museums and Art Galleries:** comprise Huntly House (museum headquarters), 142 Canongate (local history), Canongate Tolbooth (temporary exhibitions and Tartan display), Museum of Childhood, 38 High St., Lady Stair's House, Lawnmarket (collection of Scott, Burns and Stevenson), City Art Centre, Market St. (temporary exhibitions and 19th- and 20th-century artists), Lauriston Castle, Cramond Rd. South (furniture collection), Queensferry Museum, South Queensferry (local history); City Curator HERBERT COUTTS, S.B.ST.J., F.M.A., F.S.A.(SCOT.).

**Glasgow Museums and Art Galleries:** Kelvingrove, Glasgow; art collection f. 1856, now extensive, with pictures representative of Italian, Dutch, Flemish and French Schools, including Rembrandt, Rubens, Giorgione and a particularly strong group of French Impressionists; collection of British, especially Scottish art; British domestic, Colonial and Scandinavian silver and Scottish communion plate, items from Burrell Collection of paintings, stained glass, furniture, tapestries, etc.; sculpture, ceramics, *objets d'art*; good collections of European arms and armour; archaeological and ethnographic collections; the Natural History department contains birds, mammals, and is especially rich in geological material; library of 50,000 vols. and periodicals; branch museums include Museum of Transport, Pollok House (an 18th-century period house in Adam style containing an important collection of Spanish paintings), People's Palace (Glasgow's museum of local history), Haggs Castle museum for children, St. Enoch Exhibition Centre; Dir. ALISDAIR A. AULD, D.A., F.M.A., F.R.S.A.; publs. *Calendar of Events* (quarterly), *Scottish Art Review*†, guides†, catalogues†, etc.

**Hunterian Museum:** Glasgow University, Glasgow, G12 8QQ; f. 1807; geological, prehistoric, Roman and ethnographical collections and the Hunterian Coin Cabinet; art collection (incl. works by Chardin, Reynolds, Stubbs, Whistler and C. R. Mackintosh) in Hunterian Art Gallery; zoological and anatomical collections in university depts. of Zoology and Anatomy; Dir. Prof. FRANK WILLETT, M.A., F.R.S.E.

**Hunterian Art Gallery:** Hillhead St.; unrivalled collections of C. R. Mackintosh and J. M. Whistler; works by Chardin, Stubbs and Reynolds; Scottish painting from the 18th century to the present; Old Master and modern prints.

**Kirkcaldy Museums and Art Gallery:** War Memorial Gardens, Kirkcaldy, Fife; f. 1925; local history, archaeology, earth and natural sciences, transport, industrial history, decorative arts, costume, ceramics; 19th- and 20th-century Scottish paintings; Dir. A. SNEDDON, LL.B.; publs. catalogue, worksheets.

**National Gallery of Scotland:** The Mound, Edinburgh, EH2 2EL; f. 1859; permanent collection of European and Scottish paintings, etc., up to 1900; Dir. COLIN THOMPSON, M.A.; Keeper HUGH MACANDREW, M.A.; Keeper of Prints and Drawings KEITH ANDREWS, M.A., D.LITT., F.S.A.; Restorer JOHN DICK; Education and Information CHRISTOPHER JOHNSTONE, B.A.; publs. *News* describing new accessions and exhibitions of the 3 National Galleries (quarterly), *Annual Report*.

**Scottish National Portrait Gallery:** Queen St., Edinburgh, EH2 1JD; f. 1882; portraits of Scottish historical interest; an extensive reference section of engravings and photographs of portraits; Dir. as above; Keeper ROBIN HUTCHISON, M.A.

**Scottish National Gallery of Modern Art:** Inverleith House, Royal Botanic Garden, Edinburgh, EH3 5LR; f. 1960; paintings, drawings, prints and sculptures Scottish and Continental 20th-century; Dir. as above; Keeper DOUGLAS HALL, B.A., F.M.A.

**National Museum of Antiquities of Scotland:** Queen St., Edinburgh, EH2 1JD; f. 1780; prehistoric, Roman, medieval and recent collections from Scotland; also Agricultural Museum, Ingliston; accessions, etc., published in the *Proceedings of the Society of Antiquaries of Scotland;* Dir. A. FENTON.

**Royal Scottish Museum:** Chambers St., Edinburgh, EH1 1JF; f. 1854; a national museum with collections covering the decorative arts of the world, archaeology and ethnography, natural history, geology, and science and technology; Dir. NORMAN TEBBLE, D.SC., F.R.S.E.; Keepers: Art and Archaeology, R. ODDY, M.A ; Natural History, A. S. CLARKE, PH.D.; Technology, J. D. STORER, B.SC., A.F.R.AE.S.; Geology, C. D. WATERSTON, D.SC., PH.D., F.R.S.E., F.M.A.; Librarian Miss D. C. F. SMITH, M.A., A.L.A.

**Scottish Fisheries Museum, The:** St. Ayles, Harbourhead, Anstruther, Fife; f. 1969; visual historical record of every aspect of the Scottish Fishing Industry and modern methods and trends; small marine aquarium; reference library of 350 vols.; Curator (vacant); publ. *Newsletter*† (annually).

# UNIVERSITIES AND UNIVERSITY COLLEGES

## UNIVERSITY OF ABERDEEN
ABERDEEN, AB9 1FX
Telephone: 0224-40241.
Telex: 73458.
Founded 1495.

*Chancellor:* Rt. Hon. Lord POLWARTH, T.D., D.L.

*Vice-Chancellor and Principal:* Prof. G. P. MCNICOL, PH.D., M.D.

*Secretary and Clerk and Registrar to the General Council:* T. B. SKINNER, M.A.

*Librarian:* J. M. SMETHURST, B.A., A.L.A.

Library: see Libraries.

Number of teachers: 1,236, including 82 professors.

Number of students: 5,975.

Publications: *Aberdeen University Calendar†, Aberdeen University Review†, Aberdeen University Study Series†, Northern Scotland†, Undergraduate Prospectus†.*

### DEANS:
*Faculty of Arts and Social Sciences:* A. RUTHERFORD, M.A., B.LITT.
*Faculty of Science:* E. M. PATTERSON, PH.D.
*Faculty of Divinity:* I. H. MARSHALL, PH.D.
*Faculty of Law:* P. N. LOVE, M.A., LL.B.
*Faculty of Medicine:* A. L. STALKER, T.D., D.L., M.D., F.R.C.PATH.

### PROFESSORS AND HEADS OF DEPARTMENTS:

*Faculty of Arts and Social Sciences:*
BARNES, J. C., M.A., Italian (Head of Dept.)
BEALEY, F. W., B.SC.ECON., Politics
BRIDGES, R. C., PH.D., History (Head of Dept.)
CAMERON, J. R., M.A., B.PHIL., Logic
CARTER, I. R., PH.D., Institute for the Study of Sparsely Populated Areas (Dir.)
CHADWICK, C., M.A., D.U., French
CRAM, D. F., PH.D., Linguistics (Head of Dept.)
CUMMINS, J. G., PH.D., Spanish (Head of Dept.)
DODD, R. H., Music (Head of Dept.)
DRAPER, R. P., PH.D., English
FARRINGTON, B. F., M.A., Language Laboratory (Head of Dept.)
FOWLIE, I. M., M.A., Moral Philosophy (Head of Dept.)
FRASER, ELIZABETH D., M.A., ED.B., PH.D., Psychology
GASKIN, M., D.F.C., M.A., Political Economy
GREENWOOD, D. E., M.A., Dir. of Centre for Defence Studies
HARGREAVES, J. D., M.A., History
ILLSLEY, R., C.B.E., PH.D., Institute of Medical Sociology
LAIDLAW, J. C., M.A., PH.D., French
MACAULAY, D., M.A., Celtic (Head of Dept.)
MELLOR, R. E. H., B.A., F.R.G.S., Geography
MOORE, R. S., PH.D., Sociology
MORLEY, M. F., B.A., F.C.A., Accountancy
NISBET, J. D., O.B.E., M.A., PH.D., Education
PAYNE, P. L., PH.D., F.R.HIST.S., Economic History
PEARCE, D. W., M.A., Political Economy
RAMSEY, P. H., M.A., D.PHIL., History
RIST, J. M., M.A., F.R.S.CAN., Classics
RITCHIE, W., PH.D., Geography
ROCHFORD, G., B.A., B.SC., Social Work Studies
RUTHERFORD, A., M.A., B.LITT., English
SALZEN, E. A. PH.D., Psychology
SCOBBIE, I., M.A., Scandinavian Studies (Head of Dept.)
SYMONS, J. R., PH.D., Psychology
WALLS, A. F., M.A., B.LITT., Religious Studies
WILKIE, J. R., M.A., German
WILKINSON, P., M.A., International Relations

*Faculty of Science:*
BROWN, P. E., PH.D., F.G.S., F.R.S.E., Geology
DUNNET, G. M., PH.D., F.R.S.E., F.I.BIOL., Zoology
GIMINGHAM, C. H., SC.D., PH.D., F.R.S.E., F.I.BIOL., Botany
GREENHALGH, J. F. D., M.A., M.S., PH.D., Agriculture
HAMILTON, W. A., PH.D., F.R.S.E., Microbiology
HUBBUCK, J. R., M.A., D.PHIL., Mathematics
KEIR, H. M., PH.D., D.SC., C.CHEM., F.R.S.E., F.I.BIOL., F.R.S.C., Biochemistry
KERRIDGE, D. F., B.SC., F.I.S., Statistics
LODGE, G. A., PH.D., F.I.BIOL., Agriculture
MARR, G. V., D.SC., PH.D., Natural Philosophy
MARSH, J. S., M.A., Agriculture
MARTIN, A., M.S., F.R.AG.S., Agriculture
MATTHEWS, J. D., B.SC.FOR., F.R.S.E., F.I.FOR., F.I.BIOL., F.R.S.A., Forestry
MEARES, P., M.A., PH.D., SC.D., D.SC., C.CHEM., F.R.S.C., F.R.S.E., Physical Chemistry
MOLLAND, A. G., M.A., PH.D., History and Philosophy of Science (Head of Dept.)
MORDUE, W., PH.D., D.SC., F.I.BIOL., Zoology
MURRAY, A. M., PH.D., F.B.C.S., Computing Science (Head of Dept.)
OGSTON, D., M.D., PH.D., D.SC., F.R.C.P., F.R.C.P.E., Physiology
PARSONS, J. W., PH.D., Soil Science
PATTERSON, E. M., PH.D., F.R.S.E., F.I.M.A., Mathematics
REID, S. R., PH.D., A.F.I.M.A., Engineering Science
ROBERTSON, F. W., PH.D., D.SC., F.I.BIOL., F.R.S.E., Genetics
SMITH, J. R., PH.D., C.ENG., M.I.E.E., M.I.E.E.E., F.R.S.A., Engineering
TAIT, E. A., B.SC., F.G.S., Geology
TAYLOR, H. F. W., PH.D., D.SC., C.CHEM., F.R.S.C., F.I.CERAM., F.R.S.A., F.R.S.E., Inorganic Chemistry
THOMSON, R. H., D.SC., PH.D., C.CHEM., F.R.S.C., F.R.S.A., F.R.S.E., Organic Chemistry
WHITEMAN, A. J., PH.D., F.G.S., F.I.PET., Geology

*Faculty of Divinity:*
BARBOUR, R. A. S., M.C., M.A., D.D., S.T.M., New Testament Exegesis
JOHNSTONE, W., M.A., B.D., Hebrew
MAIN, A., PH.D., Practical Theology
MARSHALL, I. H., M.A., PH.D., New Testament Exegesis
TORRANCE, J. B., M.A., B.D., Systematic Theology
YULE, G. S. S., M.A., Church History

*Faculty of Law:*
LOVE, P. N., M.A., LL.B., Conveyancing and Professional Practice of Law
LYALL, F., M.A., PH.D., LL.M., Public Law
MACCORMACK, G. D., LL.B., M.A., D.PHIL., Jurisprudence
MACLEARY, A. R., M.SC., F.R.I.C.S., F.R.T.P.I., M.B.I.M., F.R.S.A., Land Economy
MESTON, M. C., M.A., LL.B., J.D., Private Law

*Faculty of Medicine:*
ASHCROFT, G. W., M.B., CH.B., D.SC., F.R.C.P.E., F.R.S.E., F.R.C.PSYCH., Psychiatry
CAMPBELL, A. G. M., M.B., CH.B., F.R.C.P., Child Health
CLEGG, E. J., M.D., PH.D., F.I.BIOL., Anatomy
DOUGLAS, A. S., D.SC., M.D., F.R.C.P., F.R.C.P.E., F.R.C.P.G., F.R.C.PATH., Medicine
FRAZER, S. C., M.B., CH.B., PH.D., F.R.S.E., F.R.C.PATH., Chemical Pathology
HORNE, C. H. W., M.D., D.SC., M.R.C.PATH., Immunopathology
KLOPPER, A. I., M.D., PH.D., F.R.C.O.G., Reproductive Endocrinology
MACGILLIVRAY, I., M.D., F.R.C.P.G., F.R.C.O.G., Obstetrics and Gynaecology
MACLEOD, M., M.D., Renal Medicine
MALLARD, J. R., PH.D., D.SC., C.ENG., F.I.E.E., F.INST.P., F.R.C.PATH., F.R.S.E., Medical Physics
MILTON, A. S., M.A., D.PHIL., Pharmacology
NORMAN, J. N., D.SC., M.D., PH.D., F.R.C.S.E., F.R.C.S.G., F.I.BIOL., Institute of Environmental and Offshore Medicine
PENNINGTON, T. H., M.B., B.S., PH.D., M.R.C.PATH., Bacteriology
POSTLETHWAITE, R., B.SC., M.D., F.R.C.PATH., Virology
RICHARDSON, I. M., J.P., M.D., PH.D., D.PH., F.R.C.P.E., F.R.C.G.P., General Practice
SMITH, G., M.B.E., D.SC., M.D., CH.M., F.R.C.S.G., F.R.S.E., F.R.C.S.E., F.A.C.S., F.C.C.P., F.I.BIOL., Surgery
STALKER, A. L., T.D., D.L., M.D., F.R.C.PATH., Pathology
WALKER, W., M.A., M.B., CH.B., F.R.C.P., F.R.C.P.E., Therapeutics and Clinical Pharmacology
WEIR, R. D., M.D., D.PH., F.R.C.P., F.F.C.M., Community Medicine

### READERS:

*Faculty of Arts and Social Sciences:*
CRAWFORD, T., M.A., English
DEREGOWSKI, J. B., PH.D., Psychology
DUKES, P., M.A., PH.D., History
FORSYTH, J., M.A., Russian
GRAY, M., M.A., Economic History
HARGREAVES, H., M.A., English
HASTINGS, A., S.T.D., Religious Studies
IRWIN, D. G., M.A., PH.D., F.S.A., F.R.S.A., History of Art
KEMP, A. G., M.A., Political Economy
MCDIARMID, M. P., M.A., B.LITT., English
MACFARLANE, L. J., PH.D., History

# UNIVERSITIES

SHORT, A., B.SC.ECON., M.A., B.LITT., Politics
TURNER, B. S., PH.D., Sociology

*Faculty of Science:*

BATES, W. J., PH.D., Natural Philosophy
BOWLING, D. J. F., PH.D., Botany
CAMERON, G. G., PH.D., D.SC., F.R.S.E., Chemistry
CHALMERS, R. A., PH.D., D.SC., F.R.S.E., Chemistry
FOTHERGILL, J. E., PH.D., F.R.S.E., Biochemistry
GLASSER, F. P., PH.D., D.SC., Chemistry
GLASSER, L. S. D., PH.D., D.SC., F.INST.P., Chemistry
MCGEOUGH, J. A., PH.D., C.ENG., M.I.MECH.E., M.I.M., Engineering
MCKEAN, D. C., M.A., D.PHIL., D.SC., Chemistry
MCKENZIE, J., M.D., F.S.A.(SCOT)., Developmental Biology
MATTHEW, G. D., PH.D., C.ENG., M.I.C.E., Engineering
MURRAY, J. S., B.SC.FOR., Forestry
NELSON, J. B., D.PHIL., Zoology
PONTING, F. W., M.A., PH.D., Mathematics
PORTEOUS, J. W., PH.D., F.R.S.E., F.R.S.A., F.I.BIOL., Biochemistry
RICHARDS, J. C. S., PH.D., F.INST.P., C.ENG., M.I.E.E., F.R.S.E., Natural Philosophy
WHITE, A. J., M.SC., PH.D., Mathematics

*Faculty of Medicine:*

BEWSHER, P. D., M.D., F.R.C.P.E., Therapeutics and Clinical Pharmacology
DENDY, P. P., PH.D., Bio-Medical Physics and Bio-Engineering
ETTINGER, K. V., M.SC., PH.D., M.S.E.E., C.ENG., M.I.E.E., Bio-medical Physics and Bio-Engineering
INNES, G., M.D., D.P.H., M.R.C.PSYCH., F.F.C.M., Community Medicine
LEES, G. M., PH.D., Pharmacology
MCLAUCHLAN, J., CH.M., Surgery
PETRIE, J. C., M.B., CH.B., Therapeutics and Clinical Pharmacology
SUTHERLAND, H. W., M.B., CH.B., D.OBST.R.C.O.G., F.R.C.O.G., Obstetrics and Gynaecology
WHEATLEY, D. N., PH.D., Pathology

ASSOCIATED INSTITUTES:

**Macaulay Institute for Soil Research:** see under Research Institutes.

**Marine Laboratory of the Department of Agriculture and Fisheries for Scotland.**
Director: B. B. PARRISH, C.B.E., B.SC., F.R.S.E., F.I.BIOL.

**Rowett Research Institute:** see under Research Institutes.

**Torry Research Station (M.A.F.F.).**
Director: J. J. CONNELL, PH.D., F.I.F.S.T.

**Institute of Marine Biochemistry (N.E.R.C.):** see under Natural Environment Research Council.

**Institute of Terrestrial Ecology (N.E.R.C.):** see under Natural Environment Research Council.

# UNIVERSITY OF ASTON IN BIRMINGHAM

GOSTA GREEN, BIRMINGHAM
B4 7ET

Telephone: 021-359 3611.

Telex: 336997.

Founded as Municipal Technical School 1895, College of Advanced Technology 1956, University Charter 1966.

*Chancellor:* Sir ADRIAN CADBURY, M.A.
*Vice-Chancellor:* Prof. F. W. CRAWFORD, PH.D., D.ENG., D.SC., C.ENG., F.I.E.E., F.I.E.E.E., F.INST.P., F.A.P.S., F.I.M.A.
*Senior Pro-Vice-Chancellor:* Prof. J. E. FLOOD, PH.D., C.G.I.A., C.ENG., F.I.E.E., F.I.E.R.E.
*Registrar and University Secretary:* K. N. HOUGHTON, M.A.
*Librarian:* C. R. BURMAN, B.A., F.L.A.

Number of teachers: 523.
Number of students: 5,512.

Publications: *Undergraduate Prospectus, Guide to Postgraduate Studies, Calendar, Guide for Overseas Students, A Guide to Aston, Annual Report and Accounts, Regulations.*

DEANS:

*Faculty of Engineering:* Prof. I. L. DILLAMORE, PH.D., D.SC., C.ENG., F.I.M.
*Faculty of Management:* R. L. AMEY, B.A., C.ENG., F.I.MECH.E.
*Faculty of Science:* A. BARNSLEY, B.SC., M.I.M.M., C.ENG., M.I.GEOL., F.G.S.
*Faculty of Social Sciences and Humanities:* Prof. F. E. KNOWLES, M.A., M.SC.

PROFESSORS:

AGER, D. E., B.A., PH.D., Modern Languages (Head of Department)
BARKER, P. E., PH.D., C.ENG., D.SC., F.I.CHEM.E., Chemical Engineering
BARNBY, J. T., PH.D., C.ENG., F.I.M., Mechanical Behaviour of Materials
BELL, C. R., B.A., M.SC.(ECON.), Sociology and Social History (Head of Department)
BLAIR, J. A., PH.D., D.SC., C.CHEM., F.R.S.C., Chemistry
BOOTH, R. T., J.P., PH.D., D.I.C., M.I.MECH.E., C.ENG., M.I.I.S.O., Safety and Hygiene
BRAUN, E., M.SC., PH.D., DR.RER.NAT., Solid State Physics (Head of Technology Policy Unit)
BROWN, M. R. W., M.SC., PH.D., D.SC., F.P.S., M.I.BIOL., Pharmaceutical Microbiology
CHILD, J., M.A., PH.D., Organizational Behaviour
DAVIES, E. J., PH.D., D.SC., C.ENG., F.I.E.E., SEN.MEM.I.E.E., Electrical Engineering
DAVIS, E. W., M.A., Business and Finance
DILLAMORE, I. L., D.SC., PH.D., Metallurgy and Materials Engineering (Head of Department)
EDWARDS, E., PH.D., M.R.AE.S., F.B.PS.S., Applied Psychology
FERRY, C. B., B.PHARM., PH.D., F.P.S., Pharmacology (Head of Department of Pharmacy)
FLOOD, J. E., D.SC.(ENG.), PH.D., C.G.I.A., C.ENG., F.I.E.E., F.I.E.R.E., Electrical and Electronic Engineering

# U.K. (GREAT BRITAIN)

FOSTER, K., M.A., PH.D., C.ENG., M.I.MECH.E., Mechanical Engineering (Head of Department)
GUTTERIDGE, W. F., M.B.E., M.A., International Studies (Head of Political and Economic Studies Group)
HARDING, G. F. A., PH.D., A.B.PS.S., Clinical Neurophysiology
HAWKES, D. D., M.SC., PH.D., F.G.S., M.I.GEOL., Geology
HOLMES, M., PH.D., D.SC., C.ENG., F.I.C.E., F.I.STRUCT.E., Civil Engineering (Head of Department)
HSU, T. C., PH.D., Applied Mechanics
HUNT, S. E., PH.D., F.INST.P., F.I.NUC.E., Physics (Head of Department)
JACKSON, D. A. S., B.A., B.PHIL., Business Economics
JEFFREYS, G. V., M.SC., PH.D., F.R.I.C., C.ENG., F.I.CHEM.E., Chemical Engineering (Head of Department)
JEPSON, W. B., M.SC., C.ENG., M.I.C.E., Construction and Environmental Health
KNOWLES, F. E., M.A., M.SC., Language
LAWDEN, D. F., M.A., SC.D., F.R.S.(N.Z.), F.I.M.A., Mathematical Physics (Head of Department)
LEWIS, C. D., M.SC., PH.D., C.ENG., M.I.PROD.E., M.I.E.E., Operations Management
LOVERIDGE, R., M.A., M.SC., Manpower Management
MCWHINNIE, W. R., PH.D., D.SC., C.CHEM., F.R.S.C., Chemistry (Head of Department)
MATTY, A. J., PH.D., D.SC., F.I.BIOL., Biological Sciences (Head of Department)
MULLINEUX, N., PH.D., F.I.M.A., Mathematics
MULVEY, T., D.SC., F.INST.P., C.ENG., F.I.E.E., Electron Physics
NEAL, W. E. J., PH.D., F.INST.P., C.ENG., F.I.E.E., M.O.S.A., Applied Thermodynamics and Energy Studies
PAGE, F. M., PH.D., SC.D., Chemistry
PICK, H. J., PH.D., C.ENG., F.I.M., F.I.MECH.E., Materials Technology
PORTER, K. E., PH.D., C.ENG., F.I.CHEM.E., Chemical Engineering
PRATT, A. W., D.SC., F.INST.P., Construction and Environmental Health (Head of Department)
PUGH, G. J. F., PH.D., D.SC., F.I.BIOL., Biological Sciences
REX, J. A., PH.D., Ethnic Relations
ROSE, E. A., M.SC., F.R.T.P.I., A.R.I.B.A., F.R.S.A., Architectural Planning and Urban Studies
SANSOME, D. H., PH.D., C.ENG., F.I.MECH.E., Applied Plasticity
SCOTT, G., B.A., B.SC., F.R.S.C., Polymer Chemistry
SINGLETON, W. T., M.A., D.SC., Applied Psychology (Head of Department)
STEVENS, M. F. G., PH.D., M.P.S., Experimental Chemotherapy
THORNLEY, R. H., M.SC.(TECH), PH.D., D.SC., A.M.C.T., C.ENG., F.I.MECH.E., F.I.PROD.E., M.J.S.M.E., Production Engineering (Head of Department of Production Technology and Production Management)
WHITFIELD, R. C., PH.D., M.A., M.ED., Education
WIBBERLEY, D. G., PH.D., D.SC., C.CHEM., F.R.I.C., Medicinal Chemistry

AFFILIATED INSTITUTE:

**Social Science Research Council Unit on Ethnic Relations:** Dir. Prof. J. A. REX, PH.D.

## UNIVERSITY OF BATH
CLAVERTON DOWN,
BATH, BA2 7AY
Telephone: (0225) 61244.

Founded 1856, designated College of Advanced Technology 1960, independent institution with direct-grant status 1962, University Charter 1966.

*Chancellor:* Lord KEARTON OF WHITCHURCH, K.T., O.B.E., F.R.S.
*Vice-Chancellor:* P. T. MATTHEWS, C.B.E., M.A., PH.D., F.R.S.
*Pro-Vice-Chancellors:* R. E. THOMAS, O.B.E., M.COM., LL.D., C.B.I.M., J. F. EASTHAM, D.SC., PH.D., C.ENG., F.I.E.E., F.R.S.E.
*Secretary and Registrar:* G. S. HORNER, M.A., D.M.A.
*Librarian:* J. H. LAMBLE, M.A., A.L.A.
Library: *see* Libraries.
Number of teachers: 367.
Number of students: 3,589.

### HEADS OF SCHOOLS:

*Architecture and Building Engineering:* Prof. M. BRAWNE, M.A., M.ARCH., F.R.I.B.A.
*Biological Sciences:* Prof. A. H. ROSE, D.SC., PH.D., F.I.BIOL.
*Chemistry:* F. S. STONE, D.SC., PH.D., C.CHEM, F.R.I.C.
*Chemical Engineering:* Prof. W. J. THOMAS, D.SC., PH.D., D.I.C., F.I.CHEM.E., C.ENG.
*Education:* Prof. J. J. THOMPSON, M.A., PH.D., F.R.S.C.
*Electrical Engineering:* Prof. J. F. EASTHAM, D.SC., PH.D., C.ENG., F.I.E.E., F.R.S.E.
*Engineering:* Prof. D. E. BOWNS, PH.D., C.ENG., M.I.MECH.E., F.INST.M.C.
*Humanities and Social Sciences:* Prof. R E. KLEIN, B.A.
*Management:* Prof. R. E. THOMAS, O.B.E., M.COM., C.B.I.M.
*Materials Science:* Prof. B. HARRIS, D.SC., PH.D., C.ENG., F.INST.P., M.I.M., C.ENG.
*Modern Languages:* Prof. J. COVENEY, B.A., D. DE L'U.
*Mathematics:* Prof. R. SIBSON, M.A., PH.D.
*Pharmacy:* Prof. R. T. PARFITT, PH.D., M.P.S., C.CHEM., F.R.S.C.
*Physics:* Prof. H. O. BERKTAY, PH.D., F.I.A.

### DIRECTORS:

*Centre for Adult Studies:* H. E. FRANK, B.SC.(ECON.)
*Centre for European Industrial Studies:* Prof. B. T. BAYLISS, PH.D.
*Bath Institute of Medical Engineering:* S. C. LILLICRAP, A.R.C.S., PH.D., D.I.C. (acting)
*Southwestern Industrial Research Ltd.:* M. R. FORSEY, B.SC., A.M.INST.F.
*Computer Unit:* Prof. J. P. FITCH, M.A., PH.D.

### PROFESSORS:

ANCILL, R. J., M.D., PH.D., M.R.C.S., L.R.C.P., F.R.C.PATH., F.I.BIOL., F.R.S.A., Pharmacology
AUSTWICK, K., M.SC., PH.D., F.S.S., J.P., Education
BAYLISS, B. T., PH.D.
BERKTAY, H. O., PH.D., F.I.A., Physics
BLACK, J., PH.D., C.ENG., F.I.MECH.E., F.R.AE.S., Engineering
BOWNS, D. E., PH.D., C.ENG., M.I.MECH.E., F.INST.M.C., Engineering
BRAWNE, M., M.A., M.ARCH., F.R.I.B.A., Architecture
BUTLER, G. P. G., PH.D., German
CAMPBELL, N. M., PH.D., C.CHEM., F.R.S.C., Chemistry
COLLARD, D., M.A., Economics
COTGROVE, S. F., PH.D., Sociology
COVENEY, J., DR.DE.L'UNIV., French
DIPROSE, K. V., B.A., F.I.M.A., Control Engineering
EASTHAM, J. F., D.SC., PH.D., C.ENG., F.I.E.E., F.R.S.E., Power Engineering
FITCH, J. P., PH.D., Software Engineering
HAPPOLD, E., C.ENG., F.I.C.E., F.I.STRUCT.E., F.I.O.B., Building Engineering
HARRIS, B., D.SC., PH.D., F.INST.P., M.I.M., C.ENG., Materials Science
HENSHAW, G. G., PH.D., Plant Biology
KLEIN, R. E., B.A., Social Policy and Administration
MANGHAM, I. L., PH.D., Management Development
PARFITT, R. T., PH.D., M.P.S., C.CHEM., F.R.S.C., Pharmaceutical and Medicinal Chemistry
REES, J. E., PH.D., M.P.S., Pharmaceutics
ROSE, A. H., D.SC., PH.D., Microbiology
ROZZI, T. E., PH.D., M.I.E.E., M.I.E.E.E., Electronic Engineering
SANDFORD, C. T., M.A.(ECON.), Political Economy
SAUNDERS, G. A., PH.D., D.I.C., F.INST.P., Physics
SIBSON, R., M.A., PH.D., Statistics
STONE, F. S., D.SC., PH.D., C.CHEM., F.R.S.C., Chemistry
THOMAS, R. E., M.COM., F.B.I.M., Business Administration
THOMAS, W. J., O.B.E., D.SC., PH.D., D.I.C., F.I.CHEM.E., C.ENG., Chemical Engineering
THOMPSON, J. J., M.A., PH.D., F.R.S.C., Education
TOMKINS, C. R., M.SC., I.P.F.A., Business Finance
WALLACE, F. J., D.SC., PH.D., C.ENG., F.I.MECH.E., Engineering
WEITZMAN, P. D. J., M.A., D.PHIL., Biochemistry
WILLIS, J. R., PH.D., D.I.C., F.I.M.A., Applied Mathematics

## UNIVERSITY OF BIRMINGHAM
P.O.B. 363, BIRMINGHAM B15 2TT
Telephone: 021-472-1301.

Founded 1900.

*Chancellor:* Sir PETER SCOTT, C.B.E., D.S.C., M.A.
*Pro-Chancellor:* C. BEALE, T.D., M.A.
*Vice-Chancellor and Principal:* Prof. E. A. MARSLAND, PH.D., F.D.S.R.C.S., F.R.C.PATH.
*Pro-Vice-Chancellor and Vice-Principal:* Prof. J. D. FAGE, M.A., PH.D.
*Registrar:* W. R. G. LEWIS, B.A.
*Secretary:* H. HARRIS, B.SC., LL.B., D.P.A., F.C.I.S.
*Librarian:* A. NICHOLLS, B.A., A.L.A. (acting).
Library: *see* Libraries.
Number of teachers: 1,106, including 142 professors.
Number of full-time students: 8,687.

Publications: Annually: *Reports, Calendar, Prospectus, Faculty Handbooks and Information Pamphlets, Medical Graduates' News Letter, Shakespeare Survey, Midland History, Gazette* (4 issues per year), *Educational Review* (each term), *Birmingham University Chemical Engineer*† (3 a year), *Department of Transportation Research Journal*† (every 2 years).

### DEANS:

*Faculty of Science and Engineering:* D. G. WALKER, PH.D., D.SC.
*Faculty of Arts:* J. T. BOULTON, PH.D.
*Faculty of Medicine and Dentistry:* O. L. WADE, M.A., M.D., B.CHIR., F.R.C.P., F.R.C.P.I.
*Faculty of Commerce and Social Science:* G. E. CHERRY, B.A.
*Faculty of Law:* R. R. PENNINGTON, LL.D.
*Faculty of Education:* R. GULLIFORD, B.A.

### DIRECTORS:

*Birmingham Radiation Centre:* Prof. J. WALKER, D.SC., PH.D., F.INST.P.
*Cancer Epidemiology Research Unit:* J. A. H. WATERHOUSE, PH.D., M.A.
*Centre for Russian and East European Studies:* Prof. D. M. NUTI, M.A., PH.D.
*Centre of West African Studies:* Prof. J. D. FAGE, M.A., PH.D.
*Centre for Child Study:* (vacant).
*Centre for Contemporary Cultural Studies:* J. R. B. JOHNSON, PH.D.
*Drama and Theatre Arts:* J. B. POWELL, M.A.
*Extramural Studies:* A. A. M. PARKER, M.A., F.R.S.A.
*Film Analysis Unit:* Prof. D. C. COLLEY, M.A., PH.D.
*Health Services Management Centre:* Prof. D. T. E. WILLIAMS, PH.D.
*Health Services Research Centre:* Prof. E. G. KNOX, M.D., F.R.C.P.
*Institute of Local Government Studies:* Prof. J. D. STEWART, M.A., D.PHIL.
*Centre for Urban and Regional Studies:* Prof. A. S. TRAVIS, B.A., F.R.T.P.I., F.R.S.A.
*Institute for Engineering Production (Lucas):* Prof. K. B. HALEY, PH.D.
*Shakespeare Institute (Stratford):* Prof. J. P. BROCKBANK, PH.D.
*Institute of Child Health:* Prof. A. S. MCNEISH, M.SC., M.B., CH.B., F.R.C.P.
*Institute for the Study of Worship and Religious Architecture:* Rev. Prof. J. G. DAVIES, M.A., D.D.
*Centre for Materials Science:* D. W. JONES, PH.D.
*Institute of Judicial Administration:* Prof. I. R. SCOTT, PH.D.
*Research Centre for the Education of the Visually Handicapped:* M. J. TOBIN, PH.D.

*Centre for Byzantine Studies:* Prof. A. A. M. BRYER, M.A., D.PHIL.

PROFESSORS:

*Faculty of Science and Engineering:*
ALLANSON, J. T., M.SC., C.ENG., M.I.E.E., Electronic and Electrical Engineering
BARKER, S. A., PH.D., D.SC., C.CHEM., F.R.S.C., Carbohydrate Chemistry
BELL, T., PH.D., Metallurgy
BLEASDALE, J. K. A., PH.D., Plant Biology
BORG, N., D.SC., C.ENG., F.I.C.E., F.I.MUN.E., F.R.S.H., Transportation
BRIDGEWATER, J., Chemical Engineering
BROADHURST, P. L., M.A., PH.D., D.SC., F.I.BIOL., F.B.PS.S., Psychology
COLLEY, D. C., PH.D., High Energy Physics
COPAS, J. B., PH.D., Statistics
CUNINGHAME-GREEN, R. A., M.A., PH.D., F.B.C.S., F.I.M.A., Industrial Mathematics
DAVIES, J. T., M.A., SC.D., M.SC., PH.D., D.SC., C.ENG., F.I.CHEM.E., Chemical Engineering
DOWELL, J. D., PH.D., Elementary Particle Physics
DOWNTON, F., D.SC., D.I.C., Statistics
FINLAYSON, L. H., PH.D., D.SC., Zoology and Comparative Physiology
GARRETT, B.SC., Geological Sciences
GRIFFITHS, D. H., PH.D., M.SC., F.G.S., Geophysics
HALEY, K. B., B.SC., PH.D., F.I.M.A., Operational Research in Engineering Production
HALLAM, A., M.A., PH.D., F.G.S., Geological Sciences
HAMLIN, M. J., B.SC., D.I.C., M.S.A.I.C.E., F.I.W.E.S., F.I.P.H.E., M.INST.W.P.C., M.A.S.C.E., Water Engineering
HAWKES, J. G., M.A., PH.D., SC.D., Plant Biology
HUGHES, B. P., PH.D., D.SC., M.I.C.E., C.ENG., F.I.STRUCT.E., Civil Engineering
INNES, N. L., D.SC., PH.D., Genetics
JARRATT, P., PH.D., F.I.M.A., F.B.C.S., F.S.S., Computing
JINKS, J. L., PH.D., D.SC., F.I.BIOL., F.R.S., Genetics
JONES, A. S., PH.D., D.SC., Chemistry
LIVINGSTONE, D., M.SC., PH.D., Pure Mathematics
LLEWELLYN, J., M.SC., PH.D., D.SC., F.I BIOL., Parasitology
MATHER, Sir KENNETH, C.B.E., D.SC., F.R.S., Genetics
McCLEVERTY, J. A., PH.D., D.I.C., Inorganic Chemistry
McQUILLAN, A. D., C.ENG., PH.D., F.I.M., Physical Metallurgy
MORRISON, G. C., PH.D., F.INST.P., Nuclear Structure
NIENOW, A. W., PH.D., Chemical Engineering
PRIME, H. A., M.SC., C.ENG., F.I.E.E., Electronic and Electrical Engineering
RAILLY, J. W., PH.D., M.SC., C.ENG., F.I.MECH.E., Turbo-Machinery
ROBB, J. C., D.SC., PH.D., F.R.S.C., C.CHEM., Physical Chemistry
ROWE, G. W., M.A., PH.D., D.SC., C.ENG., F.I.MECH.E., F.INST.P., Mechanical Engineering
SHEARMAN, E. D. R., B.SC., C.ENG., F.I.E.E., S M.I.E.E.E., Electronic and Electrical Engineering
SKYRME, T. H. R., M.A., Mathematical Physics
SMALLMAN, R. E., PH.D., D.SC., F.I.M., C.ENG., Metallurgy
SMITH, H., PH.D., D.SC., F.R.C.PATH., F.R.S., Microbiology
TATLOW, J. C., PH.D., D.SC., F.R.S.C., C.CHEM., Organic Chemistry
TEMPLE, P. H., M.A., PH.D., F.G.S., Geography
THOMAS, D., M.A., PH.D., Geography
TOBIAS, S. A., M.A., PH.D., D.SC., C.ENG., F.I.MECH.E., F.I.PROD.E., F.R.S.A., Mechanical Engineering
TUCKER, D. G., PH.D., D.SC., C.ENG., F.I.E.E., F I.E.R.E., History of Technology
VINEN, W. F., M.A., PH.D., F.R.S., Physics
WAGNER, A. O., PH.D., Pure Mathematics
WALKER, J., D.SC., PH.D., F.INST.P., Applied Nuclear Science
WARNER, N. A., PH.D., F.I.M.M., F.I.M., F.I.CHEM.E., C.ENG., Minerals Engineering
WILLMORE, A. P., PH.D., Space Research
WILSON, A. J. C., M.SC., PH.D., F.INST.P., F.I.M., F.R.S., Crystallography
WITTRICK, W. H., M.A., SC.D., PH.D., F.ENG., M.I.C.E., F.R.AE.S., F.A.A., F.R.S., Civil Engineering
WRIGHT, G. T., PH.D., D.SC., M.INST.P., Electronic Engineering

*Faculty of Arts:*
BOULTON, J. T., PH.D., English Studies
BROCKBANK, J. P., M.A., PH.D., English Language and Literature
BRYER, A. A. M., M.A., D.PHIL., F.S.A., Byzantine Studies
BURNS, C. A., PH.D., French
CAMPBELL, A. E., M.A., PH.D., American History
DAVIES, Rev. J. G., M.A., D.D., Theology
DAVIS, R. H. C., M.A., F.B.A., Medieval History
DOUGLAS, A. E., M.A., Latin
FAGE, J. D., M.A., PH.D., African History
GRENVILLE, J. A. S., B.A., PH.D., Modern History
HICK, J. H., M.A., D.LITT., D.PHIL., Theology
HILTON, R. H., B.A., D.PHIL., F.B.A., Medieval Social History
HOLLENWEGER, W. J., TH.D., Mission
KEYS, I. C. B., C.B.E., M.A., D.MUS., F.R.C.O., Music
LAMBERT, W. G., M.A., F.B.A., Assyriology
LODGE, D. J., M.A., PH.D., Modern English Literature
LOMAX, D. W., M.A., D.PHIL., Spanish
McNAIR, P. M. J., M.A., D.PHIL., PH.D., Italian Language and Literature
MILES, H. A. D., M.A., Fine Arts
POMPA, L., M.A., PH.D., Philosophy
REES, JOAN, PH.D., English Literature
RICKETTS, P. T., PH.D., French
SHEPHERD, G. T., M.A., Medieval English Language and Literature
SINCLAIR, J. M., M.A., Modern English Language
SMITH, R. E. F. M.A., Russian
SUBIOTTO, A. V., M.A., PH.D., German
TOMLINSON, R. A., M.A., F.S.A., Ancient History and Archaeology

*Faculty of Medicine and Dentistry:*
ASHTON, E. H., PH.D., D.SC., Anatomy
ASHTON, F., M.B., CH.M., F.R.C.S., Surgery
AYLIFFE, G. A. J., B.SC., M.D., CH.B., Medical Microbiology
BACON, P. A., B.A., M.B., B.CHIR., Rheumatology
BEVAN, P. G., CH.M., F.R.C.S., Surgery
BISHOP, J. M., M.D., D.SC., F.R.C.P., Medicine
BLUGLASS, R. S., M.D., F.R.C.PSYCH., D.P.M., Forensic Psychiatry
BRADLEY, P. B., PH.D., D.SC., F.I.BIOL., Pharmacology
BREWER, D. B., M.D., F.R.C.PATH., Morbid Anatomy
BROWNE, R. M., D.D.S., PH.D., F.D.S.R.C.S., F.R.C.PATH., Oral Pathology
BUTT, W. R., PH.D., D.SC., F.R.C.S., Endocrinology
CURRAN, R. C., M.D., F.R.C.P., F.R.S.E., F.R.C.PATH., Pathology
DRURY, M., O.B.E., M.B., CH.B., F.R.C.P., General Practice
FOSTER, T. D., M.D.S., F.D.S.R.C.S., D.ORTH.R.C.S., Children's Dentistry and Orthodontics
HARDWICKE, J., M.B., B.S., M.D., F.R.C.PATH., M.R.C.P., Experimental Pathology
HARNDEN, D. G., PH.D., F.I.BIOL., M.R.C.PATH., Cancer Studies
HARRINGTON, J. M., M.SC., M.B., M.R.C.P., M.F.O.M., Occupational Health
HILTON, S. M., M.A., M.B., B.CHIR., PH.D., Physiology
HITCHCOCK, E. R., M.B., CH.M., F.R.C.S., F.R.C.S.ED., Neurosurgery
HOFFENBERG, R., M.D., PH.D., F.R.C.P., Medicine
ISAACS, B., M.D., F.R.C.P.ED., Geriatric Medicine
JAMES, P. M. C., V.R.D., M.D.S., D.P.D., L.D.S.R.C.S., Dental Health
KNOX, E. G., M.D., F.R.C.P., F.F.C.M., Social Medicine
LITTLER, W. A., M.D., F.R.C.P., Cardiology
MACLENNAN, I. C. M., M.B.B.S., PH.D., M.R.C.PATH., Immunology
McNEISH, A. S., M.B., CH.B., M.SC., F.R.C.P., Paediatrics and Child Health
MARSLAND, E. A., PH.D., B.D.S., F.R.C.PATH., F.D.S.R.C.S., Oral Pathology
NEWTON, J. R., M.D., F.R.C.O.G., Obstetrics and Gynaecology
O'CONNOR, B. T., M.S., M.CH.ORTH., F.R.A.C.S., F.R.C.S., Orthopaedic Surgery
OWEN, J. J. T., M.A., M.D., Anatomy
ROBINSON, J. S., M.D., D.A., F.F.A.R.C.S., Anaesthetics
SHOVELTON, D. S., B.SC., B.D.S., F.D.S.R.C.S., Conservative Dentistry
SLANEY, G., M.S., M.B., CH.M., F.R.C.S., Surgery
SMITH, W. T., M.D., F.R.C.P., F.R.C.PATH., Neuropathology
STUART, J., M.D., F.R.C.P.ED., F.R.C.PATH., Haematology
TOMLIN, H. R., M.D.S., L.D.S.R.C.S.ED., Dental Prosthetics
TRETHOWAN, Sir WILLIAM, C.B.E., M.A., M.B., B.CHIR., F.R.C.P., F.R.A.C.P., F.R.C. PSYCH., F.A.N.Z.C.P., D.P.M., Psychiatry
WADE, O. L., M.D., M.B., B.CHIR., F.R.C.P., F.R.C.P.I., Therapeutics and Clinical Pharmacology
WALTON, K. W., PH.D., D.SC., M.D., M.R.C.S., L.R.C.P., F.R.C.PATH., Investigative Pathology
WHITFIELD, I. C., D.SC., PH.D., F.R.I.C., Neuro-communications
WHITEHEAD, T. P., PH.D., M.C.B., M.R.C.PATH., F.R.S.C., Clinical Chemistry
WOLSTENCROFT, J. H., M.A., PH.D., Physiology

*Faculty of Commerce and Social Science:*
BROWN, N. G., B.SC., B.A., F.R.MET.S., International Security Affairs
CHERRY, G. E., B.A., F.T.P.I., F.R.I.C.S., Urban and Regional Planning
COLLIS, A. T., B.SC.(ECON.), Social Administration
DAVEY, K. J., M.A., M.SOC.SC., Development Administration

DAVIES, R. W., PH.D., Soviet Economic Studies
DEAKIN, N. D., M.A., D.PHIL., Social Administration
FORD, J. L., M.A., Economics
GAMBLING, T. E., B.COM., PH.D., F.C.A., Accounting
HARRIS, J. R., M.A., PH.D., Economic and Social History
HININGS, C. R., B.A., Organizational Studies
HOPKINS, A. G., PH.D., Economic History
KING, M. A., M.A., Investment
KRONSJÖ, T. O. M., FIL.K., FIL.LIC., Economic Planning
LANE, D. S., D.PHIL., Sociology
LITTLECHILD, S. C., PH.D., Commerce
MINKES, A. L., M.A., Business Organization
NUTI, D. M., M.A., PH.D., Political Economy
OLSEN, M. R., M.SC., PH.D., Social Administration
PATTANAIK, P. K., PH.D., Mathematical Economics
SAMUELS, J. M., B.COM., F.C.C.A., Business Finance
**STEWART, J. D., M.A., D.PHIL., Local Government and Administration**
TRAVIS, A. S., B.A., F.R.T.P.I., F.R.S.A., Urban and Regional Studies
WIGHTMAN, D. R., PH.D., International Economic Organization

*Faculty of Law:*
**BROWN, L. N., M.A., LL.B., DR. en DROIT, Comparative Law**
HAND, G. J., M.A., D.PHIL., F.R.HIST.S., M.R.I.A., Jurisprudence
HARVEY, B. W., M.A., LL.M., Property Law
**PENNINGTON, R. R., LL.D., Commercial Law**
SCOTT, I. R., PH.D., Law

*Faculty of Education:*
CLARK, M. M., PH.D., D.LITT., Educational Psychology
DEARDEN, R. F., PH.D., History and Philosophy of Education
GULLIFORD, R., B.A., Special Education
HUGHES, M. G., PH.D., BAR.-AT-LAW, Social and Administrative Studies in Education
TAYLOR, P. H., M.ED., Curriculum Studies

*Department of Biochemistry:*
GILBERT, G. A., M.A., PH.D., SC.D., F.R.S., Biochemistry
HOUGH, J.S., PH.D., D.SC., F.I.BIOL., Brewing Science and Industrial Biochemistry
PERRY, S. V., PH.D., SC.D., F.R.S., Biochemistry (Head of Dept.)
WALKER, D. G., PH.D., D.SC., Biochemistry

READERS:

*Faculty of Science and Engineering:*
ADIE, R. J., O.B.E., PH.D., F.G.S., Antarctic Geology
BEEVERS, C. J., D.SC., PH.D., F.I.M., C.ENG., Engineering Materials
BOOTH, D. A., M.A., D.SC., PH.D., Physiological Psychology
BURDON, J., PH.D., D.SC., Organic Chemistry
CARTER, J. W., PH.D., D.SC., C.ENG., F.I.CHEM.E., F.R.S.C., Chemical Engineering
COOPE, G. R., PH.D., D.SC., F.G.S., Quaternary Studies
COOPER, D. C., M.SC., PH.D., C.ENG., A.M.I.E.E., Electronic Engineering

DAVIES, R., PH.D., C.ENG., M.I.MECH.E., M.I.M., Engineering Plasticity
ENGLAND, J. B. A., PH.D., Nuclear Physics
FELDMAN, M. P., PH.D., F.B.PS.S., Clinical Psychology
GLEN, J. W., M.A., PH.D., M.INST.P., Ice Physics
HOARE, A. H. M., D.PHIL., Algebra
KERR, J. A., D.SC., PH.D., Chemical Kinetics
KING, R. F., PH.D., Geophysics
KOSTERLITZ, J. M., D.PHIL., Mathematical Physics
LACY, E. D., B.SC., A.R.C.S., F.G.S., Geochemistry
LAWSON, G. J., PH.D., C.CHEM., F.R.S.C., C.ENG., F.I.M.M., Minerals Engineering
LEES, G., PH.D., D.SC., F.G.S., F.I.H.E., Highway Engineering
LONG, R., PH.D., M.R.S.C., C.ENG., F.INST.F., Chemical Engineering
LORETTO, M. H., D.SC., Materials Science
MACKAY, G. M., PH.D., S.M., M.I.C.E., C.ENG., F.I.MECH.E., Traffic Safety
MACLEAN, T. S. M., PH.D., C.ENG., M.I.E.E., Electromagnetism
MAJER, J. R., D.SC., PH.D., D.I.C., C.CHEM., M.R.S.C., Chemistry
MOSELEY, F., E.R.D., D.SC., PH.D., F.G.S., Geology
O'CONNOR, D. A., D.SC., M.INST.P., Crystal Physics
OLIVER, D. R., PH.D., D.SC., Chemical Engineering
PATRICK, C. R., PH.D., D.SC., C.CHEM., F.R.S.C., Physical Chemistry
PEAKER, F. W., PH.D., Physical Chemistry
PRATT, J. N., PH.D., D.SC., C.ENG., F.INST.P., F.I.M., Metallurgical Thermochemistry
RIDDIFORD, L., PH.D., D.SC., M.SC., F.INST.P., High Energy Physics
ROBERTS, W. T., M.SC., PH.D., M.INST.P., Applied Metallurgy
RUSHTON, K. R., PH.D., D.SC., C.ENG., M.I.C.E., M.I.W.E.S., Civil Engineering
SMITH, D., PH.D., D.SC., Space Research
STEPHEN, W. I., PH.D., D.SC., C.CHEM., F.R.S.C., Analytical Chemistry
STEPHENS, R., PH.D., D.SC., Organic Chemistry
WARWICK, G. T., M.B.E., PH.D., F.G.S., Geomorphology
WELLS, C. F., D.SC., PH.D., C.CHEM., F.R.S.C., Inorganic Chemistry
WELSBY, V. G., PH.D., D.SC., C.ENG., F.I.E.E., F.I.E.R.E., Electrical Engineering

*Faculty of Arts:*
BIRDSALL, J. N., M.A., PH.D., F.R.A.S., New Testament Studies and Textual Criticism
EATON, J. H., M.A., Old Testament Studies
FAULKES, A. R., M.A., B.LITT., Old Icelandic
FORTUNE, N. C., PH.D., Music
GELLING, MARGARET, PH.D., English Place Name Studies
GELLING, P. S., M.A., F.S.A., Ancient History and Archaeology
HONAN, P., M.A., PH.D., English Literature
JOUBERT, J., B.MUS., F.R.A.M., Music
KNECHT, R. J., M.A., French History
SIMMONS, R. C., M.A., PH.D., American History

*Faculty of Medicine and Dentistry:*
ANSELL, G. B., D.SC., M.A., PH.D., Neurochemistry

BERRY, M., M.B., CH.B., PH.D., D.SC., Neuroanatomy
BULL, J. P., M.A., M.D., B.CHIR., M.R.C.S., F.R.C.P., Traumatology
CHANCE, M. R. A., PH.D., D.SC., F.I.BIOL., Ethology
COOTE, J. H., PH.D., Physiology
FLEWETT, T. H., M.D., B.CH., B.A.O., F.R.C.P., F.R.C.PATH., Clinical Virology
HEATH, D. A., M.B., CH.B., F.R.C.P., Medicine
HUDLICKA, OLGA, M.D., PH.D., D.SC., Physiology
JONES, E. L., M.D., M.R.C.S., L.R.C.P., M.R.C.PATH., Pathology
KEIGHLEY, M. R. B., M.S., F.R.C.S., Surgery
LING, N. R., PH.D., M.R.C.PATH., Immunology
OSBORNE, M. P., PH.D., D.SC., Neurobiology
RACK, P. M. H., M.A., M.B., B.CHIR., F.R.C.S., Experimental Neurology
SEVITT, S., M.SC., M.D., B.CH., B.A.O., F.R.C.P.I., F.R.C.PATH., Pathology
STANWORTH, D. R., PH.D., D.SC., F.R.C.PATH., Immunology
THOMAS, G. H., PH.D., D.I.C., Steroid Endocrinology
THOMPSON, H., M.D., CH.B., F.R.C.PATH., Pathology
WATERHOUSE, J. A. H., PH.D., M.A., Medical Statistics
WILSON, H. J., D.SC., PH.D., C.CHEM., F.R.I.C., Dental Materials

*Faculty of Education:*
BROCKLEHURST, J. B., M.A., D.MUS., Music Education
TOBIN, M. J., PH.D., Special Education

*Department of Biochemistry:*
BRAY, H. G., PH.D., D.SC., Biochemistry
FINEAN, J. B., PH.D., D.SC., Molecular Biology
JAMES, SYBIL P., PH.D., D.SC., F.R.C.PATH., Biochemistry
TEALE, F. W. J., PH.D., Physical Biochemistry

*Centre for Russian and East European Studies:*
HANSON, P., PH.D., Soviet Economics

*Centre of West African Studies:*
PEIL, MARGARET, M.A., PH.D., Sociology

*Department of Extramural Studies:*
GOULDER, M. D., M.A., D.D., Biblical Studies

LLOYD EVANS, G., PH.D., Dramatic Literature

# UNIVERSITY OF BRADFORD

BRADFORD, WEST YORKSHIRE, BD7 1DP

Telephone: 0274-33466.

Founded 1957 as Bradford Institute of Technology; University Charter 1966.
Academic year: October to June (three terms).

*Chancellor:* The Rt. Hon. Sir HAROLD WILSON, K.G., O.B.E., M.P., M.A., F.R.S.

*Pro-Chancellor:* A. J. THAYRE, C.B.E., B.COM., F.S.S.

*Vice-Chancellor and Principal:* J. C. WEST, C.B.E., PH.D., D.SC., F.I.E.E.

*Registrar and Secretary:* I. M. SANDERSON, M.B.E., B.SC.

*Librarian:* F. EARNSHAW, B.A., A.L.A.

**Number of teachers:** 700.
**Number of students:** 5,300.

UNIVERSITIES                                                                                                                U.K. (GREAT BRITAIN)

Publications: *University Calendar, University Undergraduate Prospectus, University Postgraduate Prospectus, Course and Research Booklets.*

### DEANS:

*Board of Studies in Engineering:* P. B. MELLOR, PH.D., C.ENG., M.I.MECH.E.
*Board of Studies in Life Sciences:* D. W. MATHIESON, PH.D., C.CHEM., F.R.S.C.
*Board of Studies in Physical Sciences:* C. D. KEMP, B.SC., F.I.S.
*Board of Studies in Social Sciences:* J. M. O'CONNELL, M.A., PH.D.

### PROFESSORS:

ALLEN, SHEILA, B.A., Sociology
BAKER, T. G., PH.D., D.SC., F.I.BIOL., F.R.S.E., M.R.C.PATH., Medical Sciences
BARNETT, S., PH.D., F.I.M.A., Applied Mathematics
BARRY, B. W., PH.D., M.P.S., C.CHEM., F.R.S.C., Pharmaceutical Technology
BEARD, RUTH, M.SC., M.A., PH.D., Educational Studies
BIJL, D., M.A., DR.SC., F.R.S.E., Materials Science
BOTTOMLEY, J. A., M.A., PH.D., Economics
BROWN, G., PH.D., Nuclear Physics
CAIRNS, J. H., PH.D., C.ENG., F.I.M., Industrial Technology
CHRISTIE, MARGARET J., PH.D., A.I.M.L.T., F.B.P.S., Psychology
COLES, P. H., M.A., History
DELANY, M. J., M.SC., D.SC., F.L.S., Environmental Sciences
DOYLE, P., M.A.(ECON.), M.S., PH.D., Marketing
EDWARDS, D. T., M.SC., PH.D., Project Planning Centre for Developing Countries
EDWARDS, M. F., PH.D., C.ENG., M.I.CHEM.E., Chemical Engineering
FRASER, D., PH.D., F.R.HIST.S., History
GOODMAN, I., M.SC., PH.D., A.R.T.C.S., C.CHEM., F.R.S.C., Polymeric Materials
HANSON, C., PH.D., C.ENG., C.CHEM., F.R.S.C., F.I.CHEM.E., F.I.M.M., Chemical Engineering
HELLIWELL, J. B., PH.D., F.R.S.E., F.I.M.A., Mathematics (Engineering)
HICKSON, D. J., M.SC.(TECH.), A.C.I.S., Behavioural Studies
HIGGINS, J. C., M.A., M.SC., PH.D., C.ENG., M.I.E.E., Management Sciences
HOWSON, D. P., D.SC., C.ENG., F.I.E.E., F.I.E.R.E., Electrical and Electronic Engineering
KEMP, C. D., B.SC., F.I.S., Statistics
LEACH, G. D. H., M.SC., PH.D., F.P.S., M.I.BIOL., Pharmacology
LEES, E., M.SC., PH.D., F.I.BIOL., Biological Sciences
LOCKYER, K. G., B.SC., C.ENG., M.I.E.E., M.B.I.M., Operations Management
LONG, D. A., M.A., D.PHIL., Structural Chemistry
MATHIESON, D. W., B.SC., PH.D., F.R.S.C., Pharmaceutical Chemistry
MELLOR, P. B., PH.D., C.ENG., M.I.MECH.E., Mechanical Engineering
MERRETT, M. J., PH.D., Botany
MYLROI, M. G., PH.D., F.INST.M.C., Control Engineering
O'CONNELL, J. M., M.A., PH.D., Peace Studies
ORD-SMITH, R. A. J., PH.D., F.B.C.S., F.I.M.A., Computer Science
PAGE, C. W., C.ENG., F.R.S.C., M.I.CHEM.E., Chemical Engineering
PETTIT, P. N., M.A., L.PH., PH.D., Philosophy

ROBINSON, P. D., M.A., D.PHIL., Mathematics
ROSE, HILARY A., B.A., Applied Social Studies
SHAW, G., D.I.C., PH.D., D.SC., F.R.S.C., A.C.R.S., Organic Chemistry
SHEPHERD, W., PH.D., D.SC.(ENG.), C.ENG., F.I.E.E., S.M.I.E.E., Electrical Power Applications
SIMMONS, J. G., PH.D., D.SC., C.ENG., F.I.E.R.E., F.I.E.E., F.INST.P., Micro-Electronics
STONIER, T. T., M.S., PH.D., Science and Society
TILFORD, R. B., B.A., M.SC.(ECON.), Modern Languages
WALKER, V., D.I.C., C.ENG., M.I.MECH.E., Mechanical Engineering
WATSON, P. A., PH.D., C.ENG., M.I.E.E., Communication Engineering
WEARNE, S. H., B.SC., D.I.C., PH.D., C.ENG., Technological Management
WILBY, C. B., PH.D., C.ENG., F.I.C.E., F.I.STRUCT.E., Civil and Structural Engineering
WILLIS, F. M., B.A., Modern Languages

### READERS:

CHILDS, T. H. C., M.A., PH.D., Tribology
COURT, W. E., M.PHARM., PH.D., F.P.S., Pharmacognosy
COYLE, R. G., PH.D., A.R.S.M., Systems Dynamics
DYSON, E., PH.D., F.T.I., Textile Engineering
EARLAND, C., M.SC., PH.D., A.R.C.S., F.R.S.C., Man-Made Fibres and Textile Chemistry
GELDART, D., PH.D., C.ENG., Chemical Engineering
JONES, D. W., PH.D., F.R.S.C., F.INST.P., Structural and Inorganic Chemistry
JONES, H. W., M.A., PH.D., F.R.HIST.S., History
LANCASTER, P. R., PH.D., C.ENG., M.I.MECH.E., Mechanical Engineering
McGIVERING, I. C., M.A., Organizational Behaviour
MULLEY, B. A., PH.D., M.R.S.C., M.P.S., Pharmaceutics
NAYLOR, R. J., PH.D., M.P.S., Pharmacology
SALTER, R. J., PH.D., C.ENG., M.I.C.E., Civil Engineering
SHEPHERD, W., PH.D., M.A.SC., C.ENG., F.I.E.E., Electrical Engineering
STEADMAN, R., M.SC., PH.D., F.INST.P., Materials Science
THOMAS, C. B., M.SC., PH.D., Physical Electronics
WHEELOCK, J. V., PH.D., Physiological Chemistry
WRONSKI, A., D.I.C., PH.D., Materials Science
WYATT, H. V., PH.D., F.I.BIOL., Microbiology

### ATTACHED INSTITUTES:

**University of Bradford Management Centre:** Emm Lane, Bradford, West Yorks., BD9 4JL; f. 1963; library of 20,000 vols.; 50 teachers; 300 undergraduate, 120 postgraduate, 50 Doctoral students; Dir. Prof. J. C. HIGGINS; Librarian N. HUNTER.

**Project Planning Centre for Developing Countries:** University of Bradford, Bradford, BD7 1DP, West Yorks.; f. 1969; 17 teachers, 3 research staff; short courses, in U.K. and overseas, in selected topics: industrial, rural, development banking, agro-industrial, infrastructure, health, education, tourism, regional projects; 12-month taught Master's programme in National Development and Project Planning; Dir. Prof. D. T. EDWARDS, M.SC., PH.D.

## UNIVERSITY OF BRISTOL
BRISTOL BS8 1TH
Telephone: 24161.

Founded 1909, previously established as University College, Bristol, 1876.

*Visitor:* H.M. THE QUEEN.
*Chancellor:* Prof. DOROTHY HODGKIN, O.M., M.A., PH.D., D.SC., LL.D., F.R.C.P., F.R.S.
*Pro-Chancellors:* Sir REGINALD VERDON-SMITH, D.L., M.A., B.C.L., D.SC., LL.D., HUGH ROGERS, M.A., D.SC., LL.D., R. S. W. CLARKE, J.P., LL.D.
*Vice-Chancellor:* Sir ALEC MERRISON, D.L., PH.D., D.SC., LL.D., F.R.S
*Pro-Vice-Chancellors:* Prof. P. HAGGETT, PH.D., Prof. P. H. PETTIT, M.A., Prof. R. T. SEVERN, PH.D., D.SC.
*Registrar and Secretary:* E. C. WRIGHT, M.A.
*Librarian:* N. HIGHAM, M.A., A.L.A.

Library: *see* Libraries.

Number of teachers: 2,000, including 100 professors.

Number of students (full-time and part-time): 6,992.

Publications: *Calendar, Univ. of Bristol Register* and Faculty Prospectuses.

### DEANS:

*Faculty of Arts:* Prof. K. INGHAM, O.B.E., M.C., M.A., D.PHIL.
*Faculty of Science:* Prof. R. N. DIXON, PH.D., D.SC.
*Faculty of Medicine:* Prof. D. C. BERRY, M.D.S., PH.D.
*Faculty of Engineering:* Prof. R. D. MILNE, M.SC., PH.D.
*Faculty of Law:* Prof. M. P. FURMSTON, M.A., LL.M.
*Faculty of Social Sciences:* Prof. H. TAJFEL, M.A., PH.D.
*Faculty of Education:* Prof. P. ROBINSON, M.A., D.PHIL.

### PROFESSORS:

(some professors serve in more than one faculty)

*Faculty of Arts:*
ALEXANDER, P., B.A., B.SC., Philosophy
ASHWORTH, W., PH.D., Economic and Social History
BURROW, J. A., M.A., English
COSTELOE, M. P., PH.D., Hispanic and Latin American Studies
GOULD, J. P., M.A., Greek
HOWARTH, W. D., M.A., Classical French Literature
INGHAM, K., O.B.E., M.C., M.A., D.PHIL., History
KENT, The Rev. J. H. S., M.A., PH.D., Theology
MASON, H. T., D.PHIL., French Language and Literature

U.K. (GREAT BRITAIN)

MORTON, A., PH.D., Philosophy
NINEHAM, The Rev. D. E., D.D., Theology
NORTHAM, J. R., M.A., PH.D., Modern and Comparative Drama
REISS, H. S., M.A., PH.D., German
ROGERS, J. W. P., M.A., PH.D., English
ROSS, C. D., M.A., D.PHIL., Medieval History
RUDD, W. J. N., M.A., PH.D., Latin
VINCENT, J. R., M.A., PH.D., Modern History
WARREN, P. M., M.A., PH.D., F.S.A., Ancient History and Classical Archaeology
WARREN, R. H. C., M.A., MUS.D., Music
WICKHAM, G. W. G., M.A., D.PHIL., Drama

*Faculty of Science:*
BAILEY, A. J., Biochemistry
BERRY, M. V., PH.D., Physics
BROWN, JOHN, M.A., PH.D., Experimental Psychology
CHAMBERS, R. G., M.A., PH.D., Physics
CHAPPELL, J. B., PH.D., Biochemistry
DINELEY, D. L., B.SC., PH.D., Geology
DIXON, R. N., PH.D., Theoretical Chemistry
DRAZIN, P. G., PH.D., Mathematics
EGLINTON, G., PH.D., D.SC., Organic Geochemistry
ENDERBY, J. E., PH.D., Physics
EVERETT, D. H., M.B.E., M.A., D.PHIL., D.SC., F.R.S.E., Physical Chemistry
FOLLETT, B. K., PH.D., Zoology
FOWLER, P. H., D.SC., F.R.S., Physics
GUTFREUND, H., PH.D., Physical Biochemistry
HIRST, J. M., D.SC., PH.D., F.R.S., Agricultural and Horticultural Science
HUGHES, G. M., PH.D., SC.D., Zoology
KELLER, A., DIPL. CHEM., PH.D. F.R.S., Polymer Science
LANG, A. R., PH.D., F.R.S., Physics
MACMILLAN, J., PH.D., D.SC., Organic Chemistry
MARSTRAND, J. M., M.A., D.PHIL., Pure Mathematics
NYE, J. F., M.A., PH.D., Physics
OTTEWILL, R. H., M.A., PH.D., Colloid Science
ROGERS, M. H., PH.D., Computer Science
ROUND, F. E., PH.D., D.SC., Botany
SHEPHERDSON, J. C., M.A., Pure Mathematics
STONE, F. G. A., M.A., PH.D., SC.D., Inorganic Chemistry
WALSBY, A. E., PH.D., Botany
WHITING, M. C., M.A., PH.D., Organic Chemistry
ZIMAN, J. M., M.A., M.SC., D.PHIL., F.R.S., Theoretical Physics

*Faculty of Medicine:*
ANDERSON, D. J., B.D.S., M.SC., PH.D., L.D.S.R.C.S., Oral Biology
BERRY, D. C., M.D.S., PH.D., Dental Surgery
BOURNE, F. J., PH.D., M.R.C.V.S., Veterinary Medicine
BRADFORD, E. W., M.D.S., D.D.SC., Dental Surgery
BULLER, A. J., M.B., M.R.C.P., Physiology
BUTLER, N. R., M.D., F.R.C.P., D.C.H., Child Health
CHAPPELL, J. B., PH.D., Biochemistry
CLAMP, J. R., PH.D., M.D., F.R.I.C., Experimental Surgery
COLLEY, J. R. T., B.SC., M.D., B.S., M.R.C.S., L.R.C.P., M.F.C.M., Community Health
DARLING, A. I., C.B.E., M.D.S., D.D.SC., F.D.S.R.C.S., F.F.D., R.C.S.I., F.C.PATH., M.R.C.S., L.R.C.P., Dental Surgery

DAVIES, E. RHYS, Diagnostic Radiology
EPSTEIN, M. A., M.A., M.D., PH.D., D.SC., F.R.C.PATH., F.R.S., Pathology
GREGORY, R. L., M.A., F.R.M.S., F.R.S.E., Neuropsychology
GUTFREUND, PH.D., Physical Biochemistry
LINCOLN, D. W., PH.D., Anatomy
MATTHEWS, B., PH.D., L.D.S.R.C.S., Physiology
MITCHELL, J. F., M.A., PH.D., F.I.BIOL., Pharmacology
MITCHELL, J. P., M.B., M.S., F.R.C.S., F.R.C.S.E., Urology
MORGAN, H. G., M.D., F.R.C.P., F.R.C. PSYCH., Mental Health
PEACOCK, J. H., M.B., CH.M., F.R.C.S., Surgical Sciences
PEARSON, H., PH.D., F.R.C.V.S., Veterinary Surgery
PICKERING, B. T., PH.D., D.SC., Anatomy
PORTER, D. G., M.SC., B.VET.MED., PH.D., M.R.C.V.S., Pre-Clinical Veterinary Studies
PRYS-ROBERTS, C., M.A., D.M., PH.D., F.F.A.R.C.S., Anaesthetics
READ, A. E. A., M.D., F.R.C.P., Medicine
SILVER, I. A., M.A., M.R.C.V.S., Comparative Pathology
SPELLER, D. C. E., M.A., B.M., B.CH., M.R.C.P., M.R.C.PATH., Clinical Bacteriology
STIRRAT, G. M., Obstetrics and Gynaecology
WEBSTER, A. J. F., M.A., PH.D., M.R.C.V.S., Animal Husbandry
WILLIAMSON, R. C. N., M.B., M.CHIR., F.R.C.S., Surgery

*Faculty of Engineering:*
ANDREW, C., M.A., PH.D., M.I.MECH.E., Applied Mechanics
BIRD, B. M., M.SC., PH.D., Electrical Engineering
CRABTREE, L. F., PH.D., Aeronautical Engineering
DAGLESS, E. L., Microelectronics
MCLEOD, R. K., B.ARCH., A.R.I.B.A., Architecture
MILNE, R. D. M.SC., PH.D., F.I.M.A., F.R.AE.S., Engineering Mathematics
ROGERS, G. F. C., B.SC., F.I.MECH.E., Engineering Thermodynamics
SANDER, K. F., PH.D., M.I.E.E., Electronic Engineering
SEVERN, R. T., PH.D., D.SC., Civil Engineering
SMITH, I., M.A., LL.D., A.R.I.B.A., R.W.A., Architecture

*Faculty of Law:*
FURMSTON, M. P., M.A., LL.M., Law
HORNBY, J. A., M.A., LL.B., Law
PETTIT, P. H., M.A., Equity

*Faculty of Social Sciences:*
ASHWORTH, W., PH.D., Economic and Social History
BANTON, M. P., PH.D., D.SC., Sociology
BENNATHAN, E., M.A., M.COMM., Political Economy
BROWN, JOHN, M.A., PH.D., Experimental Psychology
BUITER, W. H., PH.D., Economics
DEATON, A. S., M.A., PH.D., Econometrics
HAGGETT, P., M.A., PH.D., Urban and Regional Geography
PARSLOE, PHYLLIDA, B.A., Social Work
SIMMONS, I. G., PH.D., F.S.A., Geography
SMITH, I., M.A., LL.D., A.R.I.B.A., R.W.A., Architecture
TAJFEL, H., M.A., PH.D., Social Psychology
TOWNSEND, P. B., Social Policy

WORLD OF LEARNING

WHITTINGTON, G., M.A., PH.D., F.C.A., Accounting and Finance

*Faculty of Education:*
FORD, B., M.A.
HOYLE, E., B.SC.(SOC.), M.A.(ED.)
ROBINSON, W. P., M.A., D.PHIL.

READERS:
(some staff serve in more than one faculty)

*Faculty of Arts:*
ALFORD, B. W. E., PH.D., Economic History
BRAUN, E., PH.D., Drama
LAMBERT, M. D., M.A., B.LITT., Medieval History
MACQUEEN, J. G., M.A., Classics and Ancient Middle Eastern Studies
ROWELL, G. R., M.A., Theatre History
TOMLINSON, A. C., M.A., F.R.S.L., English Poetry
WARMINGTON, B. H., M.A., Ancient History
WILLIAMS, C. J. F., M.A., D.PHIL., Philosophy
WILSON, NELLY, D. DE L'UNIV., French

*Faculty of Science:*
ALDER, R. W., D.PHIL., D.SC., Organic Chemistry
ARRIDGE, R. G. C., M.A., Physics
ASHBEE, K. H. G., PH.D., D.SC., Metallurgy and Ceramics
ATKINS, E. D. T., D.SC., Physics
BARRON, T. H. K., M.A., D.PHIL., Theoretical Chemistry
BEECH, F. W., PH.D., D.SC., Microbiology
BYRDE, R. J. W., PH.D., Plant Pathology
CARR, J. G., PH.D., D.SC., Microbiology
CLEAVE, J. P., PH.D., Mathematics
COTTINGHAM, W. N., PH.D., Physics
COX, A. P., PH.D., D.SC., Physical Chemistry
CROOK, J. H., PH.D., Psychology
CURTIS, L. F., PH.D., Geography
DENTON, R. M., M.A., PH.D., D.SC., Biochemistry
DUNCAN, F. G., M.A., F.B.C.S., Computer Science
DUNNING, W. J., M.B.E., PH.D., Physical Chemistry
EVANS, D. V., PH.D., F.R.AE.S., F.I.M.A., Mathematics
GIBSON, W. M., M.A., PH.D., Physics
GREEN, M., PH.D., D.SC., Inorganic Chemistry
GYORFFY, B. L., PH.D., Physics
HEWITT, E. J., PH.D., D.SC., Plant Physiology
HINDLEY, J., PH.D., Biochemistry
HOLBROOK, J. J., PH.D., D.SC., Biochemistry
JONES, O. T. G., PH.D., Biochemistry
MCOMIE, J. F. W., M.A., D.PHIL., D.SC., Organic Chemistry
MADELIN, M. F., PH.D., Mycology
MALOS, J., PH.D., Physics
MAXWELL, J. R., PH.D., Organic Geochemistry
MILLER, P. J., PH.D., Zoology
MUIRHEAD, HILARY, M.A., PH.D., Biochemistry
NEVILLE, A. C., M.A., PH.D., Zoology
NEWMAN, E. I., PH.D., D.SC., Ecology
NICKLESS, G., PH.D., Analytical Chemistry
PENNYCUICK, C. J., M.A., PH.D., Zoology
PEREGRINE, D. H., PH.D., Mathematics
ROBERTS, T. A., PH.D., Food Bacteriology
SAVAGE, R. J. G., PH.D., Vertebrate Palaeontology
SLATER, M., PH.D., Mathematics

1480

## UNIVERSITIES

STEEDS, J. W., PH.D., Electron Microscopy
THOMPSON, T. E., PH.D., D.SC., Zoology
TIMMS, P. L., D.PHIL., Inorganic Chemistry
WATSON, H. C., PH.D., D.SC., Molecular Biophysics
WILLIAMS, J., M.B, CH.B., PH.D., Biochemistry
WOODWARD, P., PH.D., Chemical Crystallography

*Faculty of Medicine:*
ARMSTRONG, D. M., PH.D., Physiology
BHOOLA, K. D., M.D., PH.D., B.A.O., Pharmacology
BILLINGTON, W. D., PH.D., Reproductive Immunology
BROWN, P. S., B.A., B.M., B.CH., M.R.C.P., Pharmacology
DUNN, P. M., M.A., M.D., B.CHIR., M.R.C.P., D.CH., D.OBST.R.C.O.G., Child Health
HARTOG, M., M.A., D.M., F.R.C.P., Medicine
HEATON, K. W., M.D., F.R.C.P., Medicine
HOLBROOK, J. J., PH.D., D.SC., Biochemistry
HOLMES, J. R., M.V.SC., PH.D., M.R.C.V.S., Veterinary Medicine
KEEN, P. M., PH.D., M.R.C.V.S., Pharmacology
LANYON, L. E., PH.D., M.R.C.V.S., Veterinary Anatomy
LEWIS, D. M., B.A., M.B., B.CH., PH.D., M.R.C.S., L.R.C.P., Physiology
LINTON, A. H., M.SC., PH.D., F.R.C.PATH., Veterinary Bacteriology
LUCKE, J. N., PH.D., M.R.C.V.S., D.V.A., Veterinary Surgery (Anaesthesia)
PURVES, M. J., M.D., PH.D., F.R.C.P., Physiology
SMITH, R. N., PH.D., D.SC., F.R.C.V.S., Veterinary Anatomy
TAYLOR, R. B., PH.D., M.R.C.V.S., Immunology
THOMAS, R. C., PH.D., Physiology
WEAVER, BARBARA M. Q., PH.D., F.R.C.V.S., D.V.A., Veterinary Anaesthesia

*Faculty of Engineering:*
ADAMS, R. D., PH.D., Mechanical Engineering
BROADWAY, A. R. W., PH.D., Electrical Engineering
CULLIMORE, M. S. G., PH.D., F.I.STRUCT.E., M.WELD.I., Civil Engineering
ELLISON, E. G., PH.D., M.I.MECH.E., Mechanical Engineering
FONG, W., PH.D., D.SC., F.I.E.E., Electrical Engineering
LAWSON, T. V., B.SC., D.I.C., F.R.AE.S., M.I.MECH.E., F.R.MET.S., Industrial Aerodynamics
LYNN, P. A., D.I.C., PH.D., M.I.E.E., Electronic Engineering
SIMPSON, A., DIP.TECH., PH.D., D.SC., A.F.R.AE.S., A.F.I.M.A., Aeronautical Engineering

*Faculty of Social Sciences:*
ALFORD, B. W. E., PH.D., Economic History
BARRETT, E. C., PH.D., Geography
BROOME, J. R., PH.D., Economics
CLAY, C. G. A., PH.D., Economic History
CROOK, J. H., PH.D., Psychology
CURTIS, L. F., PH.D., Geography
EGGINTON, D. A., B.SC.(ECON)., F.C.A., Accountancy
GILES, H., PH.D., Psychology
HAMNETT, T. G. I., PH.D., Sociology
HILARY LAND, C. M., B.SC., Social Administration
LECOMBER, J. R. C., M.A., Economics

*Faculty of Education:*
INGLIS, F. C., M.PHIL., PH.D., Education

### ASSOCIATED INSTITUTIONS:

**The Baptist College:** Woodland Road, Bristol, BS8 IUN; f. 1679.
*Principal:* Rev. W. M. WEST, DR.TH.

**Wesley College:** Henbury Hill, Bristol, BS10 7QD; f. 1842; Theological College.
*Principal:* Rev. W. D. STACEY, PH.D.

**Bath College of Higher Education.**
*Principal:* N. P. PAYNE, M.SC.

**College of St. Paul and St. Mary:** Cheltenham, Glos.
*Principal:* G. D. BARNES, M.PHIL.

**Bristol Polytechnic Faculty of Education:** Bristol.
*Chairman:* HARRY ELLIS.


## BRUNEL UNIVERSITY
UXBRIDGE,
MIDDLESEX, UB8 3PH
Telephone: (0895) 37188.

Founded 1957 as Brunel College of Technology; College of Advanced Technology 1962; University Charter 1966.

Academic year: September to July.

*Chancellor:* The Rt. Hon. The Earl of HALSBURY, B.SC., F.R.S., F.R.S.C., F.INST.P., C.ENG., F.I.PROD.E., C.CHEM.
*Pro-Chancellor:* P. E. TRIER, M.A., C.ENG., F.I.E.E., F.INST.P.
*Vice-Chancellor and Principal:* Prof. R. E. D. BISHOP, C.B.E., F.ENG., F.R.S.
*Pro-Vice-Chancellor:* Prof. J. BURNETT, M.A., LL.B., PH.D.
*Vice-Principal:* Prof. R. J. TERRY, PH.D., D.SC., F.I.BIOL.
*Secretary General:* D. NEAVE, B.A., LL.M.
*Academic Registrar:* E. R. CHANDLER, M.A.
*Librarian:* C. E. N. CHILDS, B.A.
Library: see Libraries.
Number of teachers: 296.
Number of students: 4,370.

Publications: *Prospectus of First Degree Courses, Graduate Studies* (both annually), *Brunel Bulletin* (2 a year), *Annual Report.*

### HEADS OF SCHOOLS:
*Biological Sciences:* Prof. T. F. SLATER, PH.D., D.SC., F.R.S.C., F.I.BIOL., C.CHEM.
*Chemistry:* C. F. BELL, M.A., D.PHIL., C.CHEM., F.R.S.C.
*Engineering:* Prof. T. O. JEFFRIES, M.A., D.PHIL., C.ENG., F.I.E.E.
*Materials:* Prof. M. J. BEVIS, PH.D., C.ENG., F.INST.P., F.I.M.
*Mathematical Studies:* (vacant).
*Social Sciences:* Prof. The Lord VAIZEY OF GREENWICH, M.A., D.TECH., D.LITT.

### HEADS OF DEPARTMENTS:
*Applied Biology:* Prof. T. G. ONIONS, PH.D., F.I.BIOL.
*Biochemistry:* Prof. T. F. SLATER, PH.D., D.SC., F.I.BIOL., C.CHEM., F.R.S.C.
*Applied Chemistry:* Prof. K. S. W. SING, PH.D., D.SC., C.CHEM., F.R.S.C.
*Industrial Chemistry:* Prof. G. C. BOND, PH.D., D.SC., C.CHEM., F.R.S.C.
*Cybernetics:* Prof. F. H. GEORGE, M.A., PH.D., F.S.S., F.B.C.S., F.INST.C.SC.
*Design Technology:* Prof. B. L. MYERS, ASSOC.R.C.A.
*Education:* R. SCHOFIELD, B.SC., M.INST.P.
*Building Technology:* W. G. OWEN, B.SC., C.ENG., M.I.E.E. (acting).
*Electrical Engineering & Electronics:* Prof. D. W. LEWIN, D.SC., C.ENG., F.B.C.S., F.I.E.R.E., F.I.E.E., M.I.E.E.E., M.INST.P., M.INST.M.C.
*Engineering & Management Systems:* Prof. R. WILD, M.SC., PH.D., WH.F., C.ENG., M.I.MECH.E., M.I.PROD.E.
*Mechanical Engineering:* Prof. A. W. CROOK, D.SC., C.ENG., F.INST.P., F.I.MECH.E.
*Production Technology:* Prof. R. W. NEW, D.TECH., A.M.C.T., C.ENG., F.I.MECH.E., F.I.PROD.E., M.B.I.M.
*Metallurgy:* Prof. C. BODSWORTH, M.MET., PH.D., C.ENG., F.I.M.
*Non-Metallic Materials:* Prof. M. J. BEVIS, PH.D., C.ENG., F.INST.P., F.I.M.
*Computer Science:* Prof. M. L. V. PITTEWAY, M.A., PH.D., SC.D., F.I.M.A., F.B.C.S., F.INST.P.
*Mathematics:* G. D. SMITH, M.SC., F.I.M.A.
*Statistics & Operational Research:* (vacant).
*Physics:* Prof. C. A. HOGARTH, PH.D., D.SC., F.INST.P.
*Economics:* Prof. W. ELKAN, PH.D.
*Government:* Prof. M. KOGAN, M.A.
*Law:* Prof. T. M. PARTINGTON, LL.B.
*Psychology:* Prof. L. HUDSON, M.A., PH.D.
*Sociology & Social Anthropology:* Prof. M. K. HOPKINS, M.A.

### PROFESSORS:
ALEKSANDER, I., PH.D., C.ENG., M.I.E.E., M.I.E.E.E., M.B.C.S., F.CYB.SOC., Electronics
BURNETT, J., M.A., LL.B., PH.D., Social History
FELTHAM, P., PH.D., D.SC., Applied Physics
GORE, P. H., PH.D., D.SC., C.CHEM., F.R.S.C., Applied Chemistry
JENNINGS, B. R., PH.D., D.SC., F.INST.P., Experimental Physics
KEMPNER, T., B.SC.(ECON), F.B.I.M., Principal, Administrative Staff College, Henley
KOGAN, M., M.A., Government and Social Administration
MUSGRAVE, G., M.SC., C.ENG., M.I.E.E., M.INST.M.C., Digital Systems
OGDEN, R. W., M.A., PH.D., Mathematics
REYNOLDS, A. J., PH.D., D.I.C., C.ENG., M.I.MECH.E., Mechanical Engineering

WHITEMAN, J. R., PH.D., Numerical Analysis

ATTACHED INSTITUTES:

**Institute of Computational Mathematics:** Dir. Prof. J. R. WHITEMAN, PH.D.

**Institute of Industrial Training:** Dir. A. DANIELS, B.SC.

**Institute of Organisation and Social Studies:** Dir. Prof. E. JAQUES, M.A., M.D., PH.D., F R.C.PSYCH.

## THE UNIVERSITY COLLEGE AT BUCKINGHAM

BUCKINGHAM, MK18 1EG
Telephone: 02802-4161.

Founded 1973 (first student intake 1976).

Private control; Academic year: January to December (4 10-week terms).

*Visitor:* Lord HAILSHAM OF ST. MARYLEBONE, P.C., C.H., F.R.S., D.C.L.
*Chairman of Council:* E. W. I. PALAMOUNTAIN, M.A.
*Principal:* Prof. ALAN PEACOCK, D.SC., M.A., F.B.A.
*Vice-Principal:* Prof. PETER WATSON, M.SC., F.C.A.
*Bursar:* PETER QUICK, M.A., F.C.C.A.
*Academic Registrar:* SIMON ELLIS, M.A.
*Librarian:* JOHN E. PEMBERTON, M.A., F.L.A., F.R.S.A.

Number of teachers: 45.
Number of students: 420.

Publication: *Prospectus*† (annually).

CHAIRMEN OF BOARDS OF STUDIES:

*Accounting and Financial Management:* Prof. P. L. WATSON, M.SC., F.C.A.
*Economics:* G. K. SHAW, PH.D.
*European Studies:* V. A. R. B. DURAND, M.A.
*History, Politics & English Literature:* Dr. J. C. CLARKE, D.PHIL.
*Law:* Prof. D. C. M. YARDLEY, LL.B., D.PHIL.
*Life Sciences:* Prof. A. J. BROOK, PH.D., D.SC., F.R.S.E.
*Politics, Economics and Law:* M. B. SKINNER, PH.D.

PROFESSORS:

BROOK, A. J., PH.D., D.SC., F.R.S.E., Life Sciences
BURN, E. H., B.C.L., M.A., Law
COVENEY, J., B.A., DR.UNIV., F.R.S.A., Modern Languages
PEACOCK, A. T., D.SC., M.A., F.B.A., Economics
SETON, F., D.PHIL., Economics
SHAW, G. K., PH.D., Economics
VEREKER, C. H., M.A., D.PHIL., Social and Political Theory
WATSON, P. L., M.SC., F.C.A., Accounting and Financial Management
WILSON, T., PH.D., F.B.A., Economics
WOLFSOHN, H. A., B.A., Politics
YARDLEY, D. C. M., D.PHIL., Law

## UNIVERSITY OF CAMBRIDGE

CAMBRIDGE
Telephone: 358933 (Central Offices)

Founded in the 13th Century.

*Chancellor:* H.R.H. The Prince PHILIP, Duke of EDINBURGH, K.G., K.T.
*Vice-Chancellor:* Prof. F. H. HINSLEY, O.B.E., M.A.
*High Steward:* The Rt. Hon. the Lord DEVLIN, M.A., HON. LL.D.
*Orator:* F. H. STUBBINGS, M.A., PH.D.
*Registrary:* R. E. MACPHERSON, M.A.
*Secretary-General of the Faculties:* A. D. I. NICOL, M.A., PH.D.
*Librarian:* F. W. RATCLIFFE, M.A.

Fitzwilliam Museum: see Museums.
Number of teaching staff: approx. 1,500.
Number of students: 8,209 men, 3,270 women, total 11,479.

Publications: *Admissions Prospectus, Graduate Studies Prospectus* (annually), *Statutes and Ordinances of the University, Cambridge University Reporter* (weekly during full-term and occasionally at other times), *The Cambridge University Handbook* (annually), *List of Members,* Supplements to the *Historical Register.*

UNIVERSITY TEACHING OFFICERS:

The initials in brackets appearing after each professor's name and subject represent the College or Institute to which he is attached. The key is given below:

Cai.—Gonville and Caius College.
Cth.—St. Catharine's College.
Chr.—Christ's College.
Chu.—Churchill College.
Cl.—Clare College.
Cl. H.—Clare Hall.
C.C.—Corpus Christi College.
Dar.—Darwin College.
Dow.—Downing College.
Ed.—St. Edmund's House.
Em.—Emmanuel College.
F.—Fitzwilliam College.
G.—Girton College.
H.H.—Hughes Hall.
Ho.—Homerton College.
Je —Jesus College.
Jn.—St. John's College.
K.—King's College.
L.C.—Lucy Cavendish Collegiate Society.
M.—Magdalene College.
N.H.—New Hall.
N.—Newnham College.
Pem.—Pembroke College.
Pet.—Peterhouse.
Q.—Queens' College.
R.—Robinson College.
Se.—Selwyn College.
Sid.—Sidney Sussex College.
T.—Trinity College.
T.H.—Trinity Hall.
W.—Wolfson College.

*Faculty of Architecture and History of Art:*

PROFESSORS:

JAFFÉ, A. M., LITT.D., History of Western Art (K.)
WILSON, C. A. ST. J., M.A., Architecture (Pem.)

READERS:

ECHENIQUE, M., M.A., Architecture and Urban Studies (Chu.)
HENDERSON, G. D. S., M.A., PH.D., Medieval Art (Dow.)

*Faculty of Classics:*

PROFESSORS:

ALLEN, W. S., M.A., PH.D., Comparative Philology (T.)
CROOK, J. A., M.A., Ancient History (Jn.)
KENNEY, E. J., M.A., Latin (Pet.)
KIRK, G. S., LITT.D., F.B.A., Greek—Regius (T.)
OWEN, G. E. L., M.A., Ancient Philosophy (K.)
SNODGRASS, A. M., M.A., PH.D., Classical Archaeology (Cl.)

READERS:

CHADWICK, J., LITT.D., F.B.A., Greek Language and Classics (Dow.)
LLOYD, G. E. R., M.A., PH.D., Ancient Philosophy and Science (K.)

*Faculty of Divinity:*

PROFESSORS:

CHADWICK, Rev. H., D.D., Divinity—Regius (M.)
HOOKER, Miss M. D., M.A., PH.D., Divinity (R.)
LASH, N. L. A., M.A., B.D., Divinity—Norris-Hulse (Ed.)

READER:

BAMMEL, E., M.A., Early Christian and Jewish Studies (Ed.)

*Faculty of English:*

PROFESSORS:

CLEMOES, P. A. M., PH.D., F.R.HIST.S., Anglo-Saxon (Em.)
HOLLOWAY, J., LITT.D., Modern English (Q.)
JACK, I. R. J., LITT.D., English (Pem.)
KERMODE, J. F., M.A., English Literature (K.)
RICKS, C. B., M.A., English (Chr.)
STEVENS, J. E., C.B.E., M.A., PH.D., Medieval and Renaissance English (M.)
WILLIAMS, R. H., LITT.D., Drama (Je.)

READERS:

BEER, J. B., M.A., PH.D., English Literature (Pet.)
BREWER, D. S., LITT.D., Medieval English (Em.)
PAGE, R. I., LITT.D., Old English and Old Norse Philology (C.C.)
STOREY, G., M.A., English Literature (T.H.)
TANNER, P. A., M.A., PH.D., American Literature (K.)

*Faculty of Modern and Medieval Languages:*

PROFESSORS:

BARRÈRE, J. B. M., M.A., French Literature (Jn.)
BOYDE, P., PH.D., Italian (Jn.)
FORSTER, L. W., LITT.D., German (Se.)
GREEN, D. H., M.A., German (T.)
LEIGH, R. A., C.B.E., LITT.D., French (T.)
LEWITTER, L. R., M.A., PH.D., Slavonic Studies (Chr.)

# UNIVERSITIES

## U.K. (GREAT BRITAIN)

MATTHEWS, P. H., M.A., Linguistics (Jn.)
NISBET, H. B., Modern Languages
RICKARD, P., PH.D., French (Em.)
SMITH, C. C., M.A., PH.D., Spanish (Cth.)

### READERS:
COLEMAN, D., M.A., French Literature (N.H.)
DRONKE, E. P. M., M.A., Medieval Latin Literature (Cl. H.)

### Faculty of Music:
#### PROFESSOR:
GOEHR, A., M.A., Music (T.H.)

### Faculty of Oriental Studies:
#### PROFESSORS:
BROUGH, J., M.A., F.B.A., Sanskrit (Jn.)
EMERTON, Rev. J. A., D.D., Hebrew—Regius (Jn.)
SERJEANT, R. B., PH.D., Arabic (T.)

#### READERS:
ALLCHIN, F. R., M.A., Indian Studies (Chu.)
GERSHEVITCH, I., M.A., F.B.A., Iranian Studies (Je.)
NORMAN, K. R., M.A., Indian Studies (Dow.)
RAY, J. D., M.A., Egyptology (Se.)

### Faculty of Economics and Politics:
#### PROFESSORS:
BARNES, J. A., D.SC., M.A., Sociology (Chu.)
DEANE, Miss P. M., M.A., Economic History (N.)
GODLEY, Hon. W. A. H., Applied Economics (K.)
HAHN, F. H., M.A., Economics (Chu.)
MATTHEWS, R. C. O., M.A., Political Economy (Cl.)
NEILD, R. R., M.A., Economics (T.)
TURNER, H. A. F., M.A., Industrial Relations (Chu.)

### Faculty of Education:
#### PROFESSOR:
HIRST, P. H., M.A., Education (W.)

### Faculty of History:
#### PROFESSORS:
BEALES, D. E. D., M.A., PH.D., Modern History (Sid.)
BROOKE, C. N. L., LITT.D., Ecclesiastical History (Cai.)
CHADWICK, Rev. W. O., D.D., F.B.A., Modern History—Regius (Se.)
ELTON, G. R., LITT.D., F.B.A., English Constitutional History (Cl.)
FIELDHOUSE, D. K., Imperial and Naval History
HINSLEY, F. H., O.B.E., M.A., History of International Relations (Jn.)
HOLT, J. C., M.A., F.S.A., Medieval History (F.)
SKINNER, Q. R. D., M.A., Political Science (Chr.)
SUPPLE, B. E., PH.D., Economic History (Chr.)

#### READERS:
BAYLY, C. A., PH.D., Smuts (Cth.)
COWLING, M. J., M.A., Modern English History (Pet.)
DUNN, J. M., M.A., Politics (K.)
FORBES, D., M.A., History of Modern Political Thought (Cl.)
ILIFFE, J., M.A., PH.D., African History (Jn.)
LASLETT, T. P. R., LITT.D., Politics and the History of Social Structure (T.)

### Faculty of Law:
#### PROFESSORS:
BOWETT, D. W., LL.D., International Law (Q.)
JOLOWICZ, J. A., M.A., Comparative Law (T.)
JONES, G. H., LL.D., Laws of England (T.)
MILSOM, S. F. C., M.A., F.B.A., Law (Jn.)
PARRY, C., LL.D., International Law (Dow.)
STEIN, P. G., M.A., LL.B., Civil Law—Regius (Q.)
WADE, H. R. W., LL.D., Q.C., F.B.A., English Law (Cai.)
WALKER, N. D., C.B.E., LITT.D., Criminology (K.)
WEST, D. J., LITT.D., Clinical Criminology (Dar.)

#### READERS:
LAUTERPACHT, E., M.A., International Law (T.)
O'HIGGINS, P., M.A., PH.D., Labour Law (Chr.)
WEIR, J. A., M.A., Law (T.)
WILLIAMS, D. G. T., M.A., LL.B., Public Law (W.)
YALE, D. E. C., M.A., LL.B., English Legal History (Chr.)

### Faculty of Philosophy:
#### PROFESSORS:
ANSCOMBE, Miss G. E. M., M.A., Philosophy (N.H.)
SMILEY, T. J., M.A., PH.D., Philosophy (Cl.)

#### READER:
LEWY, C., M.A., PH.D., Philosophy (T.)

### Faculty of Engineering:
#### PROFESSORS:
ASHBY, M. F., M.A., PH.D., Engineering (Cl.H.)
BECK, A. H. W., M.A., Engineering (C.C.)
BRANDON, P. S., M.A., Electrical Engineering (Je.)
FFOWCS WILLIAMS, J. E., M.A., Engineering (Em.)
HEYMAN, J., M.A., PH.D., Engineering (Pet.)
JOHNSON, K. L., M.A., Engineering (Je.)
JOHNSON, W., M.A., Mechanics (F.)
MACFARLANE, A. G. J., SC.D., Engineering (Se.)
MAIR, W. A., C.B.E., M.A., Aeronautical Engineering (Dow.)
NEWLAND, D. E., M.A., SC.D., Engineering (Se.)
SCHOFIELD, A. N., M.A., Engineering (Chu.)
SHERCLIFF, J. A., M.A., PH.D., Applied Thermodynamics (T.)

#### READERS:
CALLADINE, C. R., SC.D., Structural Mechanics (Pet.)
CARROLL, J. E., M.A., PH.D., Solid State Electronics (Q.)
DWIGHT, J. B., M.A., M.SC., Structural Engineering (M.)
FALLSIDE, F., M.A., Electrical Engineering (T.H.)
FULLER, A. T., SC.D., Control Engineering (Chu.)
SMITH, K. C. A., PH.D., Electrical Engineering (F.)
SQUIRE, L. C., M.A., Engineering (Chu.)
WHITEHEAD, D. S., M.A., PH.D., Engineering (Je.)

### Faculty of Geography and Geology:
#### PROFESSORS:
CHISHOLM, M. D. I., M.A., Geography (Cth.)
CHORLEY, R. J., SC.D., Geography (Sid.)
JACOBS, J. A., M.A., Geophysics (Dar.)
OXBURGH, E. R., M.A., Mineralogy and Petrology (T. H.)
WHITTINGTON, H. B., M.A., F.R.S., Geology (Sid.)

#### READERS:
ARMSTRONG, T. E., M A., PH.D., Arctic Studies (Cl. H.)
FARMER, B. H., M.A., South Asian Geography (Jn.)
HARLAND, W. B., M.A., Tectonic Geology (Cai.)
LONG, J. V. P., PH.D., Physics of Geochemical Measurement (Chr.)
MCKENZIE, D. P., M.A., PH.D., Tectonics (K.)
MATTHEWS, D. H., M.A., PH.D., F.R.S., Marine Geology (K.)
MCCONNELL, J. D. C., M.A., PH.D., Mineralogy (Chu.)

### Faculty of Mathematics:
#### PROFESSORS:
ADAMS, J. F., M.A., PH.D., F.R.S., Astronomy and Geometry (T.)
BAKER, A., M.A., PH.D., Pure Mathematics (T.)
BATCHELOR, G. K., PH.D., F.R.S., Applied Mathematics (T.)
CASSELS, J. W. S., PH.D., F.R.S., Pure Mathematics (T.)
HAWKING, S. W., PH.D., Mathematics (Cai.)
KENDALL, D. G., M.A., F.R.S., Mathematical Statistics (Chu.)
MOFFATT, H. K., PH.D., Mathematical Physics (T.)
POWELL, M. J. D., SC.D., Applied Numerical Analysis (Pem.)
SWINNERTON-DYER, Sir PETER, M.A., F.R.S., Mathematics (Cth.)
TAYLOR, J. C., M.A., PH.D., Mathematical Physics (R.)
THOMPSON, J. G., M.A., Mathematics (Chu.)
WHITTLE, P., M.A., Mathematics for Operational Research (Chu.)

#### READERS:
ALLAN, G. R., M.A., PH.D., Functional Analysis (Chu.)
CONWAY, J. H., M.A., PH.D., Pure Mathematics (Cai.)
FRIEDLANDER, F. G., PH.D., Partial Differential Equations (T.)
GARLING, D. J. H., SC.D., Mathematical Analysis (Jn.)
HUNT, J. C. R., M.A., PH.D., Fluid Mechanics (T.)
LANDSHOFF, P. V., M.A., PH.D., Mathematical Physics (T.)
ROSEBLADE, J. E., PH.D., Algebra (Je.)
WEISS, N. O., M.A., PH.D., Astrophysics (Cl.)

### Faculty of Physics and Chemistry:
#### PROFESSORS:
BATTERSBY, A. R., SC.D., F.R.S., Organic Chemistry (Cth.)
BUCKINGHAM, A. D., PH.D., F.R.S., Chemistry (Pem.)
COOK, A. H., SC.D., F.R.S., Natural Philosophy (K.)
EDWARDS, Sir SAMUEL, M.A., PH.D., F.R.S., Physics (Cai.)
HEINE, V., PH.D., F.R.S., Physics (Cl.)
HEWISH, A., M.A., PH.D., F.R.S., Radio Astronomy (Chu.)
HONEYCOMBE, R. W. K., PH.D., Metallurgy (Cl.H.)

JOSEPHSON, B. D., M.A., PH.D., F.R.S., Physics (T.)
LEWIS, J., SC.D., F.R.S., Chemistry (R.)
LYNDEN-BELL, D., M.A., PH.D., F.R.S., Astrophysics (Cl.)
PIPPARD, Sir BRIAN, SC.D., F.R.S., Physics—Cavendish (Cl. H.)
RAPHAEL, R. A., M.A., F.R.S., Organic Chemistry (Chr.)
REES, M. J., M.A., PH.D., Astronomy and Experimental Philosophy (K.)
RYLE, Sir MARTIN, M.A., F.R.S., Radio Astronomy (T.)
THOMAS, J. M., M.A., Physical Chemistry (K.)
THRUSH, B. A., SC.D., Physical Chemistry (Em.)

READERS:

BALDWIN, J. E., PH.D., Radio Astronomy (Q.)
BROWN, D. McG., SC.D., Organic Chemistry (K.)
BUDDEN, K. G., M.A., PH.D., F.R.S., Physics (Jn.)
CHARLES, J. A., SC.D., Process Metallurgy (Jn.)
EDEN, R. J., M.A., PH.D., Theoretical Physics (Cl. H.)
HARLEY-MASON, J., SC.D., Organic Chemistry (C.C.)
HOWIE, A., PH.D., Physics (Chu.)
JOHNSON, B. F. G., M.A., Inorganic Chemistry (F.)
KNOTT, J. F., PH.D., Mechanical Metallurgy (Chu.)
MADDOCK, A. G., SC.D., Radiochemistry (Cth.)
TOWNSEND, A. A., PH.D., F.R.S., Experimental Fluid Mechanics (Em.)
WILLIAMS, D. H., SC.D., Organic Chemistry (Chu.)
YOFFE, A. D., SC.D., Physics (Dar.)

*Faculty of Archaeology and Anthropology:*

PROFESSORS:

COLES, J. M., M.A., European Prehistory (F.)
GOODY, J. R., SC.D., Social Anthropology (Jn.)
RENFREW, A. C., SC.D., Archaeology (Jn.)

READER:

MACFARLANE, A. D. J., PH.D., Historical Anthropology (K.)

*Faculty of Biology (A):*

PROFESSORS:

BEAMENT, Sir JAMES, SC.D., F.R.S., Agriculture (Q.)
HORN, G., SC.D., Zoology (K.)
THODAY, J. M., SC.D., F.R.S., Genetics (Em.)
WEST, R. G., SC.D., F.R.S., Botany (Cl.)

READERS:

ASHBURNER, M., SC.D., Developmental Genetics (Chu.)
BATESON, P. P. G. B., SC.D., Animal Behaviour (K.)
EVANS, G. C., SC.D., Experimental Ecology (Jn.)
MACROBBIE, Miss E. A. C., M.A., Plant Biophysics (G.)
RISHBETH, J., SC.D., F.R.S., Plant Pathology (C.C.)
TREHERNE, J. E., SC.D., Invertebrate Physiology (Dow.)
WELLS, M. J., SC.D., Zoology (Chu.)
WHITEHOUSE, H. L. K., SC.D., Genetic Recombination (Dar.)

*Faculty of Biology (B):*

PROFESSORS:

ADRIAN, Lord, M.A., M.D., Cell Physiology (Chu.)

COOMBS, R. R. A., SC.D., F.R.S., Biology (C.C.)
CUTHBERT, A. W., M.A., Pharmacology (Je.)
GLYNN, I. M., M.D., Membrane Physiology (T.)
GRESHAM, G. A., M.D., SC.D., Morbid Anatomy and Histology (Je.)
HARRISON, R. J., M.D., F.R.S., Anatomy (Dow.)
HAYDON, D. A., M.A., F.R.S., Membrane Biophysics (T.H.)
JEWELL, P. A., M.A., PH.D., Physiology of Reproduction (Jn.)
KEYNES, R. D., SC.D., Physiology (Chu.)
KORNBERG, Sir HANS, SC.D., F.R.S., Biochemistry (Chr.)
LACHMANN, P. J., SC.D., Tumour Immunology (Chr.)
MACKINTOSH, N. J., Experimental Psychology (K.)
NORTHCOTE, D. H., SC.D., F.R.S., Plant Biochemistry (Sid.)
SHUTE, C. C. D., M.D., Histology (Chr.)
WILDY, P., M.A., M.B., B.CHIR., Pathology (Cai.)

READERS:

CAMPBELL, F. W., M.A., Neurosensory Physiology (Jn.)
COMLINE, R. S., SC.D., Veterinary Physiology (Cth.)
EDWARDS, R. G., M.A., Physiology (Chu.)
FITZSIMONS, J. T., M.D., SC.D., Physiology (Cai.)
HERBERTSON, B. M., M.A., Morbid Anatomy and Histology (F.)
IVERSON, Mrs. S. D., PH.D., Physiological Psychology (Je.)
MATTHEWS, E. K., M.A., Pharmacology (Jn.)
MERTON, P. A., M.A., M.B., B.CHIR., Human Physiology (T.)
METCALFE, J. C., M.A., PH.D., Biochemistry (Dar.)
MUNRO, A. J., M.A., PH.D., Immunology (Chr.)
PERHAM, R. N., SC.D., Biochemistry of Macromolecular Structures (Jn.)

*Faculty of Clinical Medicine:*

PROFESSORS:

ACHESON, R. M., M.A., SC.D., F.R.C.P., Community Medicine (Chu.)
BLEEHEN, N. M., M.A., F.R.C.P., Clinical Oncology (Jn.)
BUTTERFIELD, Sir JOHN, O.B.E., M.A., M.D., F.R.C.P., Physic—Regius (Dow.)
CALNE, R. Y., M.A., F.R.C.S., F.R.S., Surgery (T. H.)
DAVIS, J. A., M.A., Paediatrics (Pet.)
DOUGLAS, C. P., M.A., F.R.C.O.G., Obstetrics and Gynaecology (Em.)
HALES, C. N., M.D., Clinical Biochemistry (Dow.)
HAYHOE, F. G. J., M.D., F.R.C.P., Haematological Medicine (Dar.)
MILLS, I. H., M.D., F.R.C.P., Medicine (Chu.)
ROTH, Sir MARTIN, M.D., F.R.C.P., Psychiatry (T.)
SHERWOOD, T., M.A., Radiology

READERS:

EDWARDS, A. W. F., SC.D., Mathematical Biology (Cai.)
WALSHE, J. M., SC.D., Metabolic Disease (T. H.)

*Department of Chemical Engineering:*

PROFESSOR:

DAVIDSON, J. F., SC.D., F.R.S., Chemical Engineering (T.)

READER:

KENNEY, C. N., M.A., PH.D., Chemical Engineering (F.)

*Department of Clinical Veterinary Medicine:*

PROFESSORS:

SOULSBY, E. J. L., M.A., Animal Pathology (W.)
STEELE-BODGER, A., Veterinary Clinical Studies (Cai.)

READER:

HALL, L. W., M.A., Comparative Anaesthesia (G.)

*Computer Laboratory:*

PROFESSORS:

NEEDHAM, R. M., M.A., PH.D., Computer Systems (W.)
WHEELER, D. J., PH.D., Computer Science (Dar.)

*Department of History and Philosophy of Science:*

PROFESSOR:

HESSE, Miss M. B., M.A., Philosophy of Science (W.)

READER:

WHITESIDE, D. T., PH.D., History of Mathematics (Chu.)

*Department of Land Economy:*

PROFESSOR:

CAMERON, G. C., M.A. (W.)

*University Library:*

LIBRARIAN:

RATCLIFFE, F. W., M.A. (C.C.)

MEN'S COLLEGES:

(in order of their foundation)

**Peterhouse:** f. 1284.
Master: Lord DACRE OF GLANTON, M.A., F.B.A.

**Pembroke College:** f. 1347.
Master: Prof. Lord ADRIAN, M.D.

**Corpus Christi College:** f. 1352.
Master: M. W. MCCRUM, M.A.

**Magdalene College:** f. 1542.
Master: Sir DERMAN CHRISTOPHERSON, PH.D., F.R.S.

WOMEN'S COLLEGES:

**Newnham College:** f. 1871.
Principal: Mrs. JEAN FLOUD, C.B.E., B.SC.(ECON.), M.A.

**New Hall:** f. 1954.
President: Mrs. VALERIE L. PEARL.

**Lucy Cavendish Collegiate Society:** f. 1964 (Approved Society 1965).
President: Lady BOWDEN, M.A.

MIXED COLLEGES:

**Christ's College:** f. 1505 for men; women admitted 1978.
Master: Prof. J. H. PLUMB, LITT.D., F.B.A.

**Churchill College:** f. 1960 for men; women admitted 1972.
Master: Prof. Sir WILLIAM HAWTHORNE, C.B.E., M.A., F.R.S., F.R.AE.S., F.I.MECH.E.

**Clare College:** f. 1326 for men; women admitted 1972.
Master: R. C. O. MATTHEWS, M.A., F.B.A.

**Downing College:** f. 1800 for men; women admitted 1978.
*Master:* Prof. Sir JOHN BUTTERFIELD, O.B.E.

**Emmanuel College:** f. 1584 for men; women admitted 1978.
*Master:* D. S. BREWER, LITT.D.

**Fitzwilliam College:** f. 1966 for men; women admitted 1978.
*Master:* J. C. HOLT, M.A.

**Girton College:** f. 1869 for women; men admitted 1977.
*Mistress:* Mrs. B. E. RYMAN, M.A., PH.D.

**Gonville and Caius College:** f. 1348 for men; women admitted 1978.
*Master:* H. W. R. WADE, M.A., LL.D., D.C.L., F.B.A.

**Homerton College:** f. 1824 as a Training College (Approved Society 1977); men re-admitted 1978.
*Principal:* Miss A. C. SHRUBSOLE, M.A.

**Hughes Hall:** f. 1885 as the Cambridge Training College for Women (Approved Society 1968).
*President:* Prof. R. D'AETH, PH.D.

**Jesus College:** f. 1496 for men; women admitted 1978.
*Master:* Sir ALAN COTTRELL, SC.D., F.R.S.

**King's College:** f. 1441 for men; women admitted 1972.
*Provost:* B. A. O. WILLIAMS, M.A.

**Queens' College:** f. 1448 for men; women admitted 1979.
*President:* Prof. D. W. BOWETT, LL.D.

**Robinson College:** f. 1977.
*Warden:* Prof. J. LEWIS, SC.D., F.R.S.

**St. Catharine's College:** f. 1473 for men; women admitted 1978.
*Master:* Prof. Sir PETER SWINNERTON-DYER, Bt., M.A., F.R.S.

**St. Edmund's House:** f. 1896 for men; (Approved Foundation 1975); women admitted 1978.
*Master:* Rev. J. S. COVENTRY, M.A., S.T.L.

**St. John's College:** f. 1511 for men; women admitted 1981.
*Master:* Prof. J. H. HINSLEY, O.B.E., M.A.

**Selwyn College:** f. 1882 for men; women admitted 1976.
*Master:* Rev. Prof. W. O. CHADWICK, D.D., F.B.A.

**Sidney Sussex College:** f. 1596 for men; women admitted 1976.
*Master:* Prof. D. H. NORTHCOTE, PH.D., SC.D., F.R.S.

**Trinity College:** f. 1546 for men; women admitted 1977.
*Master:* Prof. Sir ALAN HODGKIN, O.M., K.B.E., SC.D., F.R.S.

**Trinity Hall:** f. 1350 for men; women admitted 1977.
*Master:* T. M. SUGDEN, C.B.E., SC.D., F.R.S.

MIXED COLLEGES FOR GRADUATE STUDENTS:

**Clare Hall:** f. 1966 (Approved Foundation).
*President:* Sir MICHAEL STOKER, M.A., M.D.

**Darwin College:** f. 1964.
*Master:* Prof. Sir MOSES FINLEY, M.A., PH.D., F.B.A.

**Wolfson College:** f. 1965.
*President:* D. G. T. WILLIAMS, M.A., LL.B.

ATTACHED INSTITUTES:

**Audio-Visual Aids Unit.**
*Head:* M. A. GIENKE, M.A. (H.H.).

**Centre of African Studies.**
*Director:* A. T. GROVE, M.A. (Dow.)

**Centre of International Studies.**
*Director:* Prof. F. H. HINSLEY, M.A. (Jn.)

**Centre of Latin American Studies.**
*Director:* D. A. BRADING, M.A. (Ed.)

**Centre of South Asian Studies.**
*Director:* B. H. FARMER, M.A. (Jn.)

**School of the Biological Sciences.**
*Secretary:* G. R. ANDERSON, M.A. (Se.)

**School of the Physical Sciences.**
*Secretary:* J. R. PAYNE, M.A. (Chr.)

## THE CITY UNIVERSITY
NORTHAMPTON SQUARE,
LONDON EC1V 0HB
Telephone: 01-253 4399.

Founded 1896; formerly Northampton College of Advanced Technology; University Charter 1966.

Academic year: September to July.

*Chancellor:* The Lord Mayor of London.
*Vice-Chancellor and Principal:* R. N. FRANKLIN, M.E., M.A., D.PHIL., D.SC.
*Pro-Vice-Chancellors:* C. F. CULLIS, M.A., D.SC., D.PHIL., C.CHEM., F.R.S.C., K. R. KIRTON, M.A.
*Academic Registrar:* L. A. FAIRBAIRN, PH.D.
*Librarian:* S. J. TEAGUE, B.SC.(ECON.), F.L.A., F.R.S.A.

Number of teachers: 308.
Number of students: 3,000.

Publications: *Undergraduate Prospectus†, Postgraduate Prospectus†, Quest†* (1 a year), *City News†* (every 2 months).

HEADS OF DEPARTMENTS:

*Civil Engineering:* Prof. P. O. WOLF, B.SC.(ENG.), A.K.C., C.ENG., F.I.C.E., F.I.W.E.S., F.A.S.C.E., F.R.MET.S., M.I.A.H.R., M.A.G.U.
*Mechanical Engineering:* Prof. J. C. LEVY, PH.D., M.S., C.ENG., F.I.MECH.E., M.R.AE.S., A.C.G.I.
*Electrical and Electronic Engineering:* Prof. A. J. ELLISON, D.SC.(ENG.), C.ENG., F.I.MECH.E., F.I.E.E., S.M.I.E.E.
*Systems Science:* Prof. P. K. M'PHERSON, S.M., M.A., C.ENG., F.I.MECH.E., F.INST.M.C., F.I.MAR.E., C.N.I.
*Aeronautics:* S. BUCHANAN, B.SC.(ENG.), C.ENG., F.R.AE.S. (acting).
*Mathematics:* Prof. M. A. JASWON, M.A., PH.D., F.I.M.A.
*Computer Science:* Prof. V. E. PRICE, M.A., PH.D., F.I.M.A., F.B.C.S.
*Physics:* Prof. L. FINKELSTEIN, M.SC., C.ENG., M.INST.P., M.I.E.E., F.INST.M.C.
*Chemistry:* C. F. CULLIS, M.A., D.SC., D. PHIL., C.CHEM., F.R.I.C.
*Optometry and Visual Science:* Prof. G. M. DUNN, F.B.O.A.H.D., D.C.L.P., D.ORTH., F.S.M.C.
*Social Science and Humanities:* Prof. C. D. HARBURY, PH.D.
*City University Business School:* Prof. J. A. P. TREASURE, PH.D. (Dean).
*Centre for Information Science:* Prof. R. T. BOTTLE, PH.D., C.CHEM., F.R.I.C., F.L.A., F.INF.SC. (Dir.)
*Centre for Arts and Related Studies:* D. E. P. JENKINS, B.SC., C.ENG., M.I.E.E.
*Centre for Banking and International Finance:* Prof. B. GRIFFITHS, M.SC.(ECON.) (Dir.).
*Centre for Educational Technology:* L. F. EVANS, M.I.M., A.I.CERAM.

PROFESSORS:

BEENSTOCK, M., PH.D., Finance and Investment
BROWN, A. F., M.A., PH.D., F.INST.P., F.I.M. F.R.S.E., Physics
DAVIDSON, R. S., A.R.I.C., PH.D., Organic Chemistry
DONALDSON, J. D., D.SC., PH.D., C.CHEM., F.R.I.C., Industrial Chemistry
DONE, G. T. S., PH.D., C.ENG., M.I.MECH.E., M.R.AE.S., Applied Mechanics
FLETCHER, R. J., M.SC., D.ORTH., Optometry
FOX, A. J., PH.D., Social Statistics
GIBSON, J. E., D.SC., PH.D., C.ENG., F.I.C.E., F.I.STRUCT.E., M.I.A.S.S., Civil Engineering Structures
GOODHARDT, G. J., M.A., F.S.S., Consumer Studies
HOUSE, H., PH.D., C.ENG., M.I.E.E., High Voltage Engineering
KESSLER, S., B.SC.(ECON.), Industrial Relations
MURRAY, H., PH.D., Export Management
ROBERTS, P. D., PH.D., C.ENG., M.I.E.E., M.INST.M.C., Control Engineering
RUSKELL, G. L., PH.D., Ocular Anatomy
STEWARD, E. G., D.SC., PH.D., F.INST.P., Physics and Molecular Medicine
TUNSTALL, C. J., B.A., Sociology

READERS:

ATKINSON, J. H., PH.D., M.A., A.C.G.I., Soil Mechanics
COLEMAN, J. D., M.SC., C.ENG., F.I.C.E., F.INST.P., F.I.M.A., F.I.H.E., F.G.S., F.R.MET.S., Civil Engineering
DAVIES, A. C., M.PHIL., PH.D., C.ENG., M.I.E.E., S.M.I.E.E.E., Electrical and Electronic Engineering
EAGLES, P. M., M.SC., PH.D., Mathematics
ISLAM, M. A., PH.D., Mathematics
MATHON, J., PH.D., Mathematics
PADGHAM, C. A., M.SC., PH.D., D.I.C., A.R.C.S., F.INST.P., Optometry and Visual Science
RICKMAN, H. P., M.A., D.PHIL., Philosophy
STOPS, D. W., D.I.C., PH.D., C.ENG., A.R.C.S., M.INST.P., M.I.E.E., Physics

TAYLOR, B., B.SC.(Econ.), Portfolio Investment
TSEUNG, A. C. C., PH.D., F.R.S.C., F.I.CERAM., A.I.M., F.INST.F., C.ENG., Chemistry

## UNIVERSITY OF DUNDEE
DUNDEE, DD1 4HN
Telephone: 0382-23181.

Founded 1881 as University College, Dundee; Royal Charter granted in 1967.

*Chancellor:* The Rt. Hon. the Earl of DALHOUSIE, K.T., G.C.V.O., G.B.E., M.C., LL.D.
*Rector:* The Rt. Hon. Lord MACKIE OF BENSHIE, C.B.E., D.S.O., D.F.C.
*Principal and Vice-Chancellor:* A. M. NEVILLE, M.C., D.SC., F.I.STRUCT.E., F.R.S.E.
*Secretary:* R. SEATON, M.A., LL.B.
*Librarian:* J. R. BARKER, M.A., F.L.A.

Library: *see* Libraries.

Number of full-time teachers: 423, including 61 professors.

Number of students: 3,362 full-time.

Publications: *University Calendar, Prospectus, Contact.*

### DEANS:

*Faculty of Medicine and Dentistry:* Prof. I. A. D. BOUCHIER, M.D.
*Faculty of Science:* Prof. K. J. STANDLEY, M.A., D.PHIL., F.R.S.E., F.INST.P.
*Faculty of Law:* Prof. I. D. WILLOCK, M.A., PH.D.
*Faculty of Engineering and Applied Science:* A. J. O. CRUICKSHANK, PH.D., C.ENG., F.I.E.E., F.R.S.E.
*Faculty of Arts and Social Sciences:* Prof. C. BLAKE, R.L.D., F.R.S.E.
*Faculty of Environmental Studies:* M. R. JONES, B.ARCH., M.C.D., M.L.A., A.R.I.B.A., A.R.I.A.S.

### PROFESSORS:

*Faculty of Medicine and Dentistry:*
ANDERSON, J. N., M.D.S., Dental Prosthetics
BATCHELOR, Sir IVOR R. C., C.B.E., M.B., CH.B., D.P.M., F.R.C.P.(E.), F.R.S.(E.), F.R.C.PSYCH., Psychiatry
BECK, J. S., B.SC., M.D., F.R.C.P.(E.), F.R.C.P.(G.), M.R.C.PATH., Pathology
BOUCHIER, I. A. D., M.D., F.R.C.P., F.R.C.P.E., Medicine
CHISHOLM, D. M., PH.D., F.D.S.R.C.P.S., Dental Surgery
COWLEY, G. C., D.D.S., Periodontology, Community Dentistry
CROOKS, J., M.D., F.R.C.P., F.R.C.P.(E.), F.R.C.P.(G.), Pharmacology and Therapeutics
CUSCHIERI, A., M.D., CH.M., F.R.C.S., F.R.C.S.E., Surgery
DICK, D. A. T., M.B., CH.B., M.A., D.PHIL., D.SC., Anatomy
DUGUID, J. P., C.B.E., B.SC., M.D., F.R.C.PATH., Bacteriology
GRIEVE, A. R., D.D.S., F.D.S.R.C.S.E., Conservative Dentistry
GRIFFITHS, P. D., B.SC., M.D., L.R.C.P., M.R.C.S., F.R.C.PATH., Biochemical Medicine
HARDEN, R. M., M.D., F.R.C.P.G., Medical Education
HOWIE, P. W., M.D., M.R.C.O.G., Obstetrics and Gynaecology
KNOX, J. D. E., M.D., F.R.C.P.(E.), F.R.C.G.P., General Practice
LOWE, K. G., M.D., F.R.C.P., F.R.C.P.(E.), F.R.C.P.(G.), Medicine
McEWEN, J. D., L.D.S., D.D.O.R.F.P.S.G., Orthodontics, Child Dental Health
MAIR, A., M.D., D.P.H., D.I.H., F.R.C.P.(E.), F.F.C.M., F.R.S.E., Community and Occupational Medicine
MARTIN, J. H., PH.D., F.INST.P., F.R.S.A., Medical Biophysics
MITCHELL, R. G., M.D., F.R.C.P.E., D.C.H., Child Health
MURDOCH, G., M.B., CH.B., F.R.C.S.E., Orthopaedic and Traumatic Surgery
STEVENSON, I. H., PH.D., Pharmacology
TUNSTALL PEDOE, H. D., M.A., M.D., Cardiovascular Epidemiology

*Faculty of Science:*
BRIMACOMBE, J. S., PH.D., D.SC., C.CHEM., F.R.S.C., F.R.S.E., Chemistry
COHEN, P., PH.D., Enzymology
CORBET, P. S., PH.D., D.SC., SC.D., Zoology
CRACKNELL, A. P., M.A., D.PHIL., M.SC., F.INST.P., F.R.S.E., Theoretical Physic,
DUTTON, G. J. F., PH.D., D.SC., F.R.S.E., Biochemistry
EVERITT, W. N., B.SC., M.A., D.PHIL., F.I.M.A., F.R.S.E., Mathematics
FOSTER, R., M.A., D.PHIL., D.SC., C.CHEM., F.R.S.C., F.R.S.E., Physical Organic Chemistry
GARLAND, P. B., M.A., M.B., B.CH., PH.D., F.R.S.E., Biochemistry
JONES, D. S., M.B.E., M.A., D.SC., F.I.M.A., F.R.S.E., F.R.S., Applied Mathematics
LAMBERT, J. D., PH.D., F.I.M.A., F.R.S.E., Mathematics
MACDONALD, S. G. G., M.A., PH.D., F.INST.P., F.I.M.A., Physics
MITCHELL, A. R., PH.D., D.SC., F.R.S.E., F.I.M.A., Numerical Analysis
RAMSAY, D. M., PH.D., F.G.S., Geology
RAVEN, J. A., M.A., PH.D., Biological Sciences
ROCHESTER, C. H., PH.D., D.SC., C.CHEM., F.R.S.C., Chemistry
SLEEMAN, B. D., PH.D., D.SC., F.I.M.A., F.R.S.E., Applied Analysis
SPEAR, W. E., PH.D., D.SC., F.INST.P., F.R.S., F.R.S.E., Physics
SPRENT, P., B.SC., PH.D., F.I.M.A., F.R.S.E., Mathematical Statistics
STANDLEY, K. J., M.A., D.PHIL., F.R.S.E., F.INST.P., Physics
STEWART, W. D. P., PH.D., D.SC., F.I.BIOL., F.R.S., F.R.S.E., Biological Sciences

*Faculty of Law:*
DAINTITH, T. C., M.A., Public Law
GRINYER, S. R., M.SC., F.C.A., Accountancy
McDONALD, A. J., B.A., LL.B., W.S., Conveyancing
WILKINSON, A. B., M.A., LL.B., Private Law
WILLOCK, I. D., M.A., LL.B., PH.D., Jurisprudence

*Faculty of Engineering and Applied Science:*
BARR, A. D. S., PH.D., C.ENG., F.I.MECH.E., Mechanical Engineering
MAKIN, B., PH.D., M.I.E.E., C.ENG., Electrical Engineering
NEWELL, A. R., PH.D., C.ENG., M.I.E.E., Electronics and Micro-computer systems
VARDY, A. E., PH.D., M.I.C.E., Civil Engineering

*Faculty of Arts and Social Sciences:*
BARTLETT, C. J., PH.D., F.R.HIST.S., International History
BLAKE, C., M.A., PH.D., F.R.S.E., Applied Economics
CAIRD, J. B., M.A., D. DE L'U., Geography
COOPER, N. L., M.A., B.PHIL., Moral Philosophy
KENNEDY, R. A., B.A., PH.D., F.B.PS.S., Psychology
LAST, R. W., PH.D., Modern Languages
MAPSTONE, ELISABETH, M.A., Social Administration
NEWTON, K., PH.D., Politics
NORTON-SMITH, J., M.A., B.LITT., F.R.S.A., English
PARISH, P. J., B.A., F.R.HIST.S., Modern Social and Economic History

ATTACHED INSTITUTE:

**Centre for Petroleum and Mineral Law Studies:** Park Place, Dundee, DD1 4HN; f. 1977; a unit of the Faculty of Law; teaching, research and publications on the law relating to petroleum, minerals and other natural resources; offers one-year Diploma in Petroleum Law; collection of 2,000 documents; Dir. Prof. TERENCE DAINTITH; publs. occasional publications†.

## UNIVERSITY OF DURHAM
OLD SHIRE HALL, DURHAM, DH1 3HP.
Telephone: 64466.

Founded 1832.

*Chancellor:* Dame MARGOT FONTEYN DE ARIAS.
*Vice-Chancellor:* F. G. T. HOLLIDAY, C.B.E., B.SC., F.R.S.E.
*Pro-Vice-Chancellors:* J. L. BROOKS, M.A., E. SUNDERLAND, M.A., PH.D.
*Registrar and Secretary:* I. E. GRAHAM, M.A.
*Librarian:* AGNES M. MCAULAY, B.A., F.L.A.

Library: *see* Libraries.

Number of teaching staff: 504, including 52 professors.

Number of students: 4,701.

Publications: *Durham University Journal, Durham University Gazette, Durham Research Review.*

### DEANS:

*Divinity:* Very Rev. J. F. McHUGH, S.T.D., L.S.S., PH.L.
*Arts:* P. J. FITZPATRICK, PH.D., S.T.L.
*Science:* Prof. H. MARSH, S.M., M.A., PH.D., C.ENG., F.I.MECH.E.
*Music:* D. J. WILKS, B.A., B.MUS., F.R.C.O.
*Education:* R. J. T. BROWN, M.A.
*Social Sciences:* J. A. BECKFORD, PH.D.
*Law:* Prof. B. SMYTHE, LL.B.

### PROFESSORS:
(some professors serve in more than one faculty)

*Faculty of Divinity:*
BARRETT, Rev. C. K., M.A., D.D., F.B.A.
JONES, Rev. Canon D. R., M.A.
SYKES, Rev. Canon S. W., M.A.

*Faculty of Arts:*
BRIDGWATER, W. P., M.A., B.LITT., German
BROOKS, J. L., M.A., Spanish

CRAIK, T. W., M.A., PH.D., English
FLETCHER, D. J., M.A., French
HARRIS, J. R., M.A., D.PHIL., Egyptology
HARRISON, W., M.A., Russian
HARVEY, P. D. A., M.A., D.PHIL., Medieval History
JONES, C., M.A., B.LITT., English Language
MACPHERSON, I. R., PH.D., Spanish
STOKES, M. C., M.A., Greek
TOWNEND, G. B., M.A., Latin
WARD, W. R., M.A., D.PHIL., Modern History
WATSON, J. R., M.A., PH.D., English
WILSON, D. B., D.D'UNIV., French

*Faculty of Social Sciences:*
ABRAMS, P., M.A., PH.D., Sociology
CRAMP, ROSEMARY J., M.A., B.LITT., F.S.A., F.R.HIST.S., Archaeology
CREEDY, J., B.SC., B.PHIL., Economics
KAIM-CAUDLE, B.SC.(ECON.), BAR.-AT-LAW, Social Policy
MILNE, A. J. M., PH.D., Political Theory and Institutions
O'BRIEN, D. P., B.SC.(ECON.), PH.D., Economics
SKERRATT, L. C. L., B.SC.(ECON.), Accounting
SPOONER, F. C., M.A., PH.D., Economic History
SUNDERLAND, E., M.A., PH.D., Anthropology

*Faculty of Science:*
ATTEWELL, P. B., PH.D., D.ENG., C.ENG., M.I.C.E., M.I.M.M., F.G.S., Engineering Geology
BARKER, D., M.A., D.PHIL., D.SC., Zoology
BOTT, M. H. P., M.A., PH.D., F.R.S., F.G.S., F.R.A.S., Geophysics
BOULTER, D., M.A., D.PHIL., Botany
BOWEN-JONES, H., M.A., Geography
BRANSDEN, B. H., PH.D., F.INST.P., Theoretical Physics
CHAMBERS, R. D., PH.D., D.SC., F.R.S.C., Organic Chemistry
CLARK, D. T., PH.D., F.R.S.C., F.P.R.I., Organic Chemistry
CLARKE, J. I., M.A., PH.D., Geography
DEWEY, J. F., PH.D., Geology
HIGGINS, P. J., M.A., PH.D., Pure Mathematics
HIGGINSON, G. R., PH.D., M.I.MECH.E., M.I.C.E., C.ENG., Engineering Science
MARSH, H., S.M., M.A., PH.D., C.ENG., F.I.MECH.E., Engineering Science
MARTIN, A. D., PH.D., Theoretical Physics
ROBERTS, G. G., PH.D., D.SC., F.INST.P., Applied Physics
SIMMONS, I. G., PH.D., F.S.A., Geography
SQUIRES, E. J., PH.D., F.INST.P., Applied Mathematics
STERLING, M. J. H., PH.D., C.ENG., M.I.E.E., M.INST.M.C., Engineering Science
WILLMORE, T. J., M.SC., PH.D., D.SC., F.I.M.A., Pure Mathematics
WOLFENDALE, A. W., PH.D., D.SC., F.INST.P., F.R.A.S., F.R.S., Physics

*Faculty of Music:*
TAYLOR, E. R., M.A., D.MUS., A.R.C.O.

*Faculty of Education:*
BATHO, G. R., M.A., F.R.HIST.S.
COFFIELD, F. J., M.A., M.ED.

*Faculty of Law:*
DOWRICK, F. E., M.A., BAR.-AT-LAW
SMYTHE, B., LL.B., BAR.-AT-LAW

*University Business School:*
BAKER, H. C., B.SC., M.A., C.B.I.M., Business Studies

READERS:
*Faculty of Divinity:*
BONNER, G., M.A., Theology

*Faculty of Arts:*
DOYLE, A. I., M.A., PH.D., Bibliography
FAGG, J. E., M.A., Palaeography and Diplomatic
FITZPATRICK, P. J., PH.D., S.T.L., Philosophy
JAMES, M. E., M.A., History
KUHN, K. H., PH.D., Coptic
MORRALL, E. J., M.A., PH.D., Medieval German Literature
PRESTWICH, M. C., M.A., D.PHIL., History
SMEED, J. W., M.A., PH.D., Modern German Literature
THOMAS, J. D., M.A., PH.D., Papyrology

*Faculty of Social Sciences:*
BROWN, R. K., B.A., Sociology
CHAPMAN, R. A., M.A., PH.D., M.B.I.M., Politics

*Faculty of Science:*
BESAG, J. E., B.SC., Mathematical Statistics
BOWLER, K., PH.D., Animal Physiology
CORNER, W. D., PH.D., D.SC., Physics
COULSON, J. C., PH.D., D.SC., Animal Ecology
DAVIES, L., PH.D., Entomology
DEWDNEY, J. C., M.A., Geography
EMELEUS, C. H., M.SC., D.PHIL., F.G.S., Geology
FAIRLIE, D. B., PH.D., Applied Mathematics
GRANGER, G. W., PH.D., Psychology
JOHNSON, G. A. L., PH.D., D.SC., F.G.S.
KOHNSTAM, G., PH.D., Physical Chemistry
MAJOR, J. V., PH.D., F.INST.P., Physics
PAYNE, J. W., PH.D., Biochemistry
SMITH, R. A., PH.D., Mathematics
WADE, K., PH.D., D.SC., Chemistry
WHITTON, M. A., PH.D., Botany
WOODS, J., PH.D., F.INST.P., Applied Physics

*Faculty of Education:*
MAY, P. R., J.P., B.A.

*Faculty of Law:*
SMITH, A. T. H., M.A., LL.M.

COLLEGES:
**University Office:** Old Shire Hall, Durham, DH1 3HP.
*Warden:* F. G. T. HOLLIDAY, C.B.E., B.SC., F.R.S.E.

**University College:** f. 1833.
*Master:* E. C. SALTHOUSE, PH.D., C.ENG., M.I.E.E.

**Hatfield College:** f. 1846.
*Master:* J. P. BARBER, M.A., PH.D.

**Grey College:** f. 1959.
*Master:* E. HALLADAY, M.A.

**Van Mildert College:** f. 1963.
*Master:* P. W. KENT, J.P., M.A., PH.D., D.PHIL., D.SC., D.LITT., F.R.S.C.

**Collingwood College:** f. 1972.
*Master:* J. A. TUCK, M.A., PH.D.

**College of St. Hild and St. Bede:** f. 1975.
*Principal:* J. V. ARMITAGE, PH.D.

**St. Chad's College:** f. 1904.
*Principal:* Rev. R. C. TROUNSON, M.A.

**St. John's College:** f. 1909.
*Principal:* Miss D. R. ETCHELLS, M.A., B.D.

**Ushaw College:** f. 1808.
*President:* Rt. Rev. P. M. COOKSON, S.T.D., L.S.S.

**St. Cuthbert's Society:** f. 1871; known as non-Collegiate until 1947.
*Principal:* Prof. J. L. BROOKS, M.A.

**St. Mary's College:** f. 1899.
*Principal:* Miss JOAN M. KENWORTHY, M.A., B.LITT.

**St. Aidan's College:** f. 1895; known as Home Students until 1947, and St. Aidan's Society until 1961.
*Principal:* Miss IRENE HINDMARSH, J.P., M.A.

**Trevelyan College:** f. 1965.
*Principal:* Miss DEBORAH LAVIN, M.A.

**The Graduate Society:** f. 1965.
*Principal:* G. KOHNSTAM, PH.D.

AFFILIATED COLLEGE:
**Codrington College:** Barbados, British West Indies.

# UNIVERSITY OF EAST ANGLIA
NORWICH, NR4 7TJ
Telephone: 0603 56161.

Founded 1961.

*Chancellor:* The Rt. Hon. the Lord FRANKS OF HEADINGTON, O.M., G.C.M.G., K.C.B., C.B.E., P.C., M.A., F.B.A.

*Vice-Chancellor:* Prof. M. W. THOMPSON, D.SC., F.INST.P.

*Pro-Vice-Chancellors:* Prof. J. R. JONES, M.A., PH.D., Prof. N. E. CUSACK, PH.D.

*Registrar and Secretary:* M. G. E. PAULSON-ELLIS, M.A., F.C.A.

*Librarian:* W. L. GUTTSMAN, M.SC. (ECON.).

Number of teachers: 385.
Number of students: 4,343.

Publications: *The University of East Anglia Prospectus, Calendar, Vice-Chancellor's Annual Report.*

DEANS:
*School of Biological Sciences:* M. J. SELWYN, M.A., PH.D.
*School of Chemical Sciences:* Prof. M. J. FRAZER, PH.D.
*School of Computing Studies and Accountancy:* P. A. DEARNLEY, PH.D.
*School of Development Studies:* O. G. R. BELSHAW, M.A.
*School of Economic and Social Studies:* A. E. B. HEADING, M.A.
*School of Education:* W. ETHERINGTON, M.A., M.ED.
*School of English and American Studies:* H. R. TEMPERLEY, M.A., PH.D., F.R.HIST.S.
*School of Environmental Sciences:* Prof. A. YOUNG, M.A., PH.D.

*School of Fine Arts and Music:* Prof. P. G. ASTON, D.PHIL.
*School of Law:* J. G. MILLER, LL.M., PH.D.
*School of Mathematics and Physics:* Prof. P. CHADWICK, PH.D., SC.D., F.R.S.
*School of Modern Languages and European History:* J. D. ELSWORTH, M.A., PH.D.

PROFESSORS:

*School of Biological Sciences:*
DAVIES, D. D., PH.D., Biology
DAVIES, D. R., PH.D., Applied Genetics
DIXON, A. F. G., D.PHIL., Biology
FOLKES, B. F., PH.D., Biology
HOPWOOD, D. A., M.A., PH.D., D.SC., F.I.BIOL, F.R.S., Genetics
ROJAS, E. E., M.SC., PH.D., Biology
WOOLHOUSE, H. W., PH.D., Biology

*School of Chemical Sciences:*
FRAZER, M. J., PH.D., C.CHEM., Chemical Education
HARRIS, M. A., PH.D., Chemistry
KETTLE, S. F. A., PH.D., C.CHEM., F.R.S.C., Chemistry
MCKILLOP, A., PH.D., Chemistry
SHEPPARD, N., M.A., PH.D., F.R.S., C.CHEM., Chemistry

*School of Computing Studies and Accountancy:*
BHASKAR, K. N., M.SC.(ECON.), Accountancy and Finance
HOUSDEN, R. J. W., M.A., PH.D., DIP.N.A., F.I.M.A., F.B.C.S., Computing Studies
STOCKER, P. M., M.SC., F.I.M.A., F.B.C.S., Computing Studies

*School of Development Studies:*
FRANK, A. G., M.A., PH.D., Social Change
LIVINGSTONE, I., M.A., Development Economics

*School of Economic and Social Studies:*
CHURCH, R. A., PH.D., F.R.HIST.S., Economic History
DAVIES, M., PH.D., Social Work
DUNCAN, G. C., D.PHIL., Politics
EMERSON, A. R., PH.D. Sociology
GRICE, G. R., M.A., PH.D., Philosophy
HILL, T. P., M.A., Economics
HOLLIS, J. M., J.P., M.A., Philosophy
PARIKH, A., L.M.COM., M.SC., Economics
SCHWEINBERGER, A. G., PH.D., Economics
TEICHOVA, ALICE, PH.D., C.SC., Economic History

*School of Education:*
BROWN, G., M.ED., PH.D.
SOCKETT, H. T., M.A., PH.D.
WILKINSON, A. M., M.A., PH.D.

*School of English and American Studies:*
ALMANSI, G., M.A., English and Comparative Literature
ASHTON, R., PH.D., F.R.HIST.S., English History
BRADBURY, M. S., M.A., PH.D., F.R.S.L., American Studies
BROADBENT, J. B., M.A., PH.D., English Literature
BROOKE, N. S., M.A., English Literature
FOWLER, R. G., M.A., English and Linguistics
JONES, J. R., M.A., PH.D., English History
TEMPERLEY, H. R., M.A., PH.D., American Studies

*School of Environmental Sciences:*
CLAYTON, K. M., M.SC., PH.D., Environmental Sciences
FUNNELL, B. M., M.A., PH.D., Environmental Sciences
O'RIORDAN, T., M.A., M.S., PH.D., Environmental Sciences
VINE, F. J., PH.D., F.R.S., Environmental Sciences
YOUNG, A., M.A., PH.D., Environmental Sciences

*School of Fine Arts and Music:*
ASTON, P. G., D.PHIL., G.B.S.M., F.T.C.L., A.R.C.M., Music
MARTINDALE, A. H. R., M.A., F.S.A., Professor of Visual Arts

*School of Law:*
MILLER, J. G., LL.M., PH.D., Law

*School of Mathematics and Physics:*
CHADWICK, P., PH.D., SC.D., F.R.S., Mathematics
CUSACK, N. E., PH.D., F.INST.P., Physics
GLAUERT, M. B., M.A., D.SC., D.I.C., F.I.M.A., Mathematics
OSBORNE, D. V., M.A., PH.D., F.R.S.E., Physics
RILEY, N., PH.D., F.I.M.A., Applied Mathematics
YOUNG, W. H., PH.D., F.INST.P., Theoretical Physics

*School of Modern Languages and European History:*
FLETCHER, J. W. J., M.A., DIP.D'ET.SUP., Comparative Literature
MCFARLANE, J. W., M.A., B.LITT., European Literature
MOSSE, W. E., M.A., PH.D., European Literature
ROWLEY, B. A., M.A., PH.D., European Literature

READERS:

*School of Biological Sciences:*
CLARKE, C. H., PH.D.
CROGHAN, P. C., M.A., PH.D.
GREENWOOD, C., PH.D.
HEWITT, G. M., PH.D.
KEARN, G. C., PH.D., D.SC.
SHELTON, G., M.A., PH.D.
SIMS, A. P., PH.D.

*School of Chemical Sciences:*
PACKER, K. J., PH.D.
POWELL, O. B., PH.D.

*School of Computing Studies and Accountancy:*
BRISTON, R. J., B.SC., F.C.A.

*School of Development Studies:*
BELSHAW, D. G. R., M.A.

*School of Economic and Social Studies:*
SCOTT-TAGGART, M. J., M.A.

*School of English and American Studies:*
BIGSBY, C. W. E., M.A., PH.D.
CLARKE, C. C., M.A.
DYSON, A. E., M.A., M.LITT.
HASSELL SMITH, A.
KENNEDY, P. M., D.PHIL., F.R.HIST.S.
THOMPSON, R. F.

*School of Environmental Sciences:*
BOULTON, G. S., PH.D.
LISS, P. S.
MCCAVE, I. N., M.A., PH.D.
MOSELEY, M. J., PH.D.
MOSS, B., PH.D.

*School of Mathematics and Physics:*
MORLAND, L. W., PH.D., F.I.M.A.
REEVE, J. E., M.SC.
WEST, R. N., PH.D., F.INST.P.

*School of Modern Languages and European Studies:*
DUFEU, V. M., PH.D.
SHAFFER, ELINOR S., M.A., PH.D.

ASSOCIATED RESEARCH INSTITUTES:

**Explosives Research and Development Establishment (Ministry of Technology):** Powdermill Lane, Waltham Abbey, Essex.

**Fisheries Laboratory (Ministry of Agriculture, Fisheries and Food):** Pakefield Rd., Lowestoft; Dir. A. PRESTON, B.SC.

**Food Research Institute (Agricultural Research Council):** Colney Lane, Norwich, NR4 7UA; Dir. R. F. CURTIS, PH.D., D.SC., F.R.I.C., F.I.F.S.T.

**John Innes Institute:** Colney Lane, Norwich, NR4 7UH; Dir. Prof. H. W. WOOLHOUSE, PH.D.

**Norfolk and Norwich Institute for Medical Education:** Norfolk and Norwich Hospital, Norwich, NR1 3SR.

# UNIVERSITY OF EDINBURGH
EDINBURGH, EH8 9YL
Telephone: 031-667-1011.
Telex: 727442 (UNIVED G).
Founded 1583.

Private control; Academic year: October 1st to September 30th.

*Chancellor:* H.R.H. The Prince PHILIP, Duke of EDINBURGH, K.G., K.T., P.C., O.M., G.B.E., LL.D., F.R.S.
*Vice-Chancellor and Principal:* J. H. BURNETT, M.A., D.PHIL., F.R.S.E., F.I.BIOL.
*Rector:* Very Rev. ANTHONY ROSS, O.P., S.T.L., F.S.A.SCOT.
*Secretary:* A. M. CURRIE, O.B.E., B.A., B.LITT.
*Librarian:* Miss B. E. MOON, M.A., F.L.A.
Library: see Libraries.
Number of teaching staff: 1,350, including 152 professors.
Number of students: 10,398.
Publication: *Edinburgh University Calendar.*

DEANS:

*Faculty of Divinity:* Rev. A. C. ROSS, M.A., B.D., S.T.M., PH.D.
*Faculty of Law:* Prof. A. W. BRADLEY, M.A., LL.B.
*Faculty of Medicine:* Prof. G. J. ROMANES, C.B.E., PH.D., M.B., CH.B., F.R.C.S.E., F.R.S.E.
*Faculty of Arts:* Prof. K. A. FOWLER, PH.D., F.R.HIST.S.
*Faculty of Science:* Prof. M. M. YEOMAN, PH.D., F.R.S.E.
*Faculty of Music:* Prof. M. TILMOUTH, PH.D.
*Faculty of Social Sciences:* Prof. C. B. WILSON, PH.D.
*Faculty of Veterinary Medicine:* Prof. K. M. DYCE, D.V.M.&S., M.R.C.V.S.

PROFESSORS:

*Faculty of Divinity:*
ANDERSON, G. W., M.A., D.D., TEOL.D., F.B.A., F.R.S.E., Hebrew and Old Testament Studies

ANDERSON, H., M.A., PH.D., D.D., New Testament Language, Literature and Theology
CHEYNE, A. C., M.A., B.LITT., B.D., Ecclesiastical History
FORRESTER, D. B., M.A., B.D., D.PHIL., Christian Ethics and Practical Theology
MACKEY, J. P., L.PH., S.T.L., D.D., PH.D., Systematic Theology
MCINTYRE, The Very Rev. J., M.A., B.D., D.LITT., D.D., F.R.S.E., Divinity

*Faculty of Law:*
BIRKS, P. B. H., LL.M., Civil Law
BLACK, R., LL.M., Scots Law
BRADLEY, A. W., M.A., LL.B., Constitutional Law
MCCLINTOCK, F. H., B.SC., M.A., Criminology
MACCORMICK, D. N., M.A., Public Law
MACGIBBON, I. C., M.A., LL.B., PH.D., Public International Law
NOBLE, I. W., M.A., LL.B., W.S., Conveyancing
WILSON, W. A., M.A., LL.B., Scots Law

*Faculty of Medicine:*
AITKEN, R. C. B., M.D., F.R.C.P.E., F.R.C.PSYCH., Rehabilitation Studies
BAIRD, D. T., B.A., M.B., CH.B., D.SC., F.R.C.P.E., F.R.C.O.G., Obstetrics and Gynaecology
BEST, J. J. K., M.B., CH.B., M.SC., M.R.C.P., D.M.R.D., F.R.C.R., Medical Radiology
BOYD, G. S., PH.D., F.R.S.C., F.R.S.E., Biochemistry
CHARLTON, G., M.D.S., F.D.S.R.C.S., Conservative Dentistry
CHISHOLM, G. D., CH.M., F.R.C.S., F.R.C.S.E., Surgery
COLLEE, J. G., M.D., F.R.C.P.E., F.R.C.PATH., Bacteriology
CURRIE, Sir ALASTAIR, B.SC., M.B., CH.B., F.R.C.P., F.R.C.S.E., F.R.C.PATH., F.R.S.E., Pathology
DUNCAN, W., M.B., CH.B., D.M.R.T., F.R.C.P.E., F.R.C.S.E., F.R.C.R., Radiotherapy
EDWARDS, C. R. W., M.D., F.R.C.P., F.R.C.P.E., Medicine
EMERY, A. E. H., M.D., PH.D., D.SC., F.R.C.P.E., M.F.C.M., F.R.S.E., Human Genetics
FARQUHAR, J. W., M.D., F.R.C.P.E., Child Life and Health
FLENLEY, D. C., B.SC., M.B., CH.B., PH.D., F.R.C.P.E., F.R.C.P., Respiratory Medicine
FORFAR, J. O., M.C., B.SC., M.D., F.R.C.P.E., F.R.C.P., F.R.C.P.G., F.A.C.N., F.R.S.E., D.C.H., Child Life and Health
FORREST, A. P. M. B.SC., M.D., CH.M., F.R.C.S.E., F.R.C.S., F.R.C.S.G., F.R.S.E., Clinical Surgery
GINSBORG, B. L., PH.D., F.R.S.E., Pharmacology
GIRDWOOD, R. H., M.D., F.R.C.P., F.R.C.P.E., F.R.C.PATH., F.R.S.E., Therapeutics
GREENING, J. R., D.SC., PH.D., F.INST.P., F.R.S.E., Medical Physics
HOWIE, J. G. R., M.D., PH.D., F.R.C.G.P., General Practice
HUGHES, S. P. F., M.S., L.R.C.P., F.R.C.S., F.R.C.S.E., F.R.C.S.I., Orthopaedic Surgery
HUNTER, J. A. A., M.D., F.R.C.P.E., Dermatology
KENDELL, R. E., M.A., M.D., F.R.C.P., F.R.C.PSYCH., Psychiatry
MACLENNAN, W. D., F.R.C.S., F.D.S., H.D.D., L.D.S., Oral Surgery
MASON, J. K., C.B.E., M.D., D.C.P., D.M.J., F.R.C.PATH., D.T.M. & H., Forensic Medicine

MILLER, J. D., M.D., PH.D., F.R.C.S.E., F.R.C.S.G., F.A.C.S., Surgical Neurology
NUKI, G., M.B., B.S., M.R.C.S., F.R.C.P., F.R.C.P.E., Rheumatology
OLIVER, M. F., M.D., F.R.C.P., F.R.C.P.E., F.F.C.M., Cardiology
OSWALD, I., M.A., M.D., D.SC., D.P.M., F.R.C.PSYCH., Psychiatry
PHILLIPS, C. I., M.D., PH.D., M.SC., D.P.H., F.R.C.S.E., F.R.C.S., D.O., Ophthalmology
ROBERTSON, J. D., M.D., F.R.C.P.E., F.R.C.S.E., F.F.A.R.C.S., D.A., Anaesthetics
ROBSON, J. S., M.D., F.R.C.P.E., F.R.C.P., Medicine
ROMANES, G. J., C.B.E., B.A., PH.D., M.B., CH.B., F.R.C.S.E., F.R.S.E., Anatomy
SMYTH, J. F., M.A., M.D., M.SC., M.R.C.P., Medical Oncology
SOUTHAM, J. C., M.A., M.B., B.CHIR., B.CH.D., M.R.C.PATH., Oral Medicine and Oral Pathology
STOCKWELL, R. A., M.B., B.S., PH.D., Anatomy
SUTCLIFFE, P., M.CH.D., PH.D., Preventive Dentistry
WALTON, H. J., M.D., PH.D., F.R.C.P.E., F.R.C.PSYCH., D.P.M., Psychiatry
WATSON, W. E., M.D., B.S., D.PHIL., M.R.C.P., F.R.C.S., Physiology
WATT, D. M., PH.D., F.D.S., H.D.D., L.D.S., Restorative Dentistry
WHITBY, L. G., M.A., PH.D., M.D., F.R.C.P., F.R.C.P.E., F.R.C.PATH., F.R.S.E., Clinical Chemistry
WILLIAMSON, J., M.B., CH.B., F.R.C.P.E., Geriatric Medicine

*Faculty of Arts:*
ASHER, R. E., PH.D., Linguistics
BARROW, G. W. S., M.A., D.LITT., F.B.A., F.R.S.E., Scottish History and Paleography
BORTHWICK, E. K., PH.D., Greek
BRAND, C. P., M.A., PH.D., Italian
CAMPBELL, I. M., M.A., Humanity
CORDER, S. P., B.A., Applied Linguistics
DICKINSON, H. T., M.A., PH.D., F.R.HIST.S., History
ELWELL-SUTTON, L. P., B.A., Persian
FIELDING, K. J., M.A., D.PHIL., F.R.S.E., English Literature
FORBES, E. G., PH.D., M.SC., M.LITT., F.R.A.S., History of Science
FOWLER, A. D. S., M.A., D.PHIL., D.LITT., F.B.A., English Literature
FOWLER, K. A., PH.D., F.R.HIST.S., Medieval History
FRANCE, P., M.A., D.PHIL., French
FURNESS, N. A., DR.PHIL., German
GILLIES, W., M.A., F.S.A.SCOT., Celtic
HARDING, D. W., M.A., D.PHIL., Archaeology
HEPBURN, R. W., M.A., PH.D., Moral Philosophy
HURFORD, J. R., PH.D., General Linguistics
LARKIN, M. J. M., M.A., PH.D., History
MACQUEEN, J., M.A., Scottish Literature and Oral Tradition
RENWICK, J. P., M.A., PH.D., French
RILEY, E. C., M.A., Spanish
ROBSON, W. W., M.A., English Literature
SHAW, D. L., M.A., PH.D., Latin American Studies
SHEPPERSON, G. A., M.A., Commonwealth and American History
SPRIGGE, T. L. S., PH.D., Logic and Metaphysics
THORNE, J. P., M.A., B.LITT., English Language
WARD, D., M.A., Russian

*Faculty of Science:*
BONSALL, F. F., M.A., D.SC., F.R.S.E., F.R.S., Mathematics

BURSTALL, R. M., M.SC., PH.D., Computer Science
COCHRAN, W., PH.D., M.A., F.R.S., F.R.S.E., Natural Philosophy
COLLINS, J. H., M.SC., F.ENG., F.I.E.E., F.INST.P., F.I.E.E.E., F.I.E.R.E., Electrical Engineering
COWLEY, R. A., M.A., PH.D., F.R.S.E., F.R.S., Physics
CRAIG, G. Y., D., F.R.S.E., Geology
CREER, K. M., M.A., PH.D., SC.D., F.R.A.S., Geophysics
DAVIS, P. H., D.SC., PH.D., F.R.S.E., Plant Taxonomy
DONOVAN, R. J., PH.D., C.CHEM., F.R.S.C., F.R.S.E., Physical Chemistry
EBSWORTH, E. A. V., SC.D., M.A., PH.D., C.CHEM., F.R.S.C., F.R.S.E., Chemistry
FARAGO, P. S., M.A., DR.PHIL., F.INST.P., F.R.S.E., Physics
FINCHAM, J. R. S., PH.D., SC.D., F.R.S., F.R.S.E., Genetics
FINNEY, D. J., C.B.E., M.A., SC.D., F.R.S., F.R.S.E., Statistics
HENDRY, A. W., PH.D., D.SC., F.I.C.E., F.I.STRUCT.E., F.R.S.E., Civil Engineering
HIGGS, P. W., PH.D., F.R.S.E., Theoretical Physics
JARVIS, P. G., M.A., PH.D., D.FIL., F.R.S.E., Forestry and Natural Resources
KEMBALL, C., M.A., SC.D., C.CHEM., F.R.S.C., M.R.I.A., F.R.S.E., F.R.S., Chemistry
KING, J. L., M.A., PH.D., F.I.M.A., Mechanical Engineering
KNOX, J. H., PH.D., D.SC., F.R.S.C., C.CHEM., F.R.S.E., Physical Chemistry
LONGAIR, M. S., M.A., PH.D., F.R.S.E., Astronomy
MACKIE, A. G., M.A., PH.D., F.R.S.E., Applied Mathematics
MANNING, A. W. G., D.PHIL., F.R.S.E., Natural History
MAVOR, J., PH.D., C.ENG., M.I.E.E., M.I.E.E.E., M.I.E.R.E., M.INST.P., Microelectronics
MICHAELSON, S., B.SC., A.R.C.S., F.I.M.A., F.R.S.E., F.R.S.A., F.B.C.S., Computer Science
MICHIE, D., M.A., D.PHIL., D.SC., F.Z.S., F.R.S.E., F.B.C.S., Machine Intelligence
MITCHISON, J. M., SC.D., F.R.S.E., F.R.S., F.I.BIOL., Zoology
MURRAY, K., PH.D., F.R.S., Molecular Biology
OWEN, A. E., PH.D., M.R.S.C., F.INST.P., F.R.S.E., Physical Electronics
PRESCOTT, J. H. D., PH.D., M.I.BIOL., Animal Production
RASBASH, D. J., PH.D., A.R.C.S., D.I.C., F.I.CHEM.E., F.I.FIRE.E., C.ENG., Fire Engineering
REES, E. G., M.A., PH.D., Mathematics
ROBERTSON, N. F., C.B.E., M.A., PH.D., F.R.S.E., Agriculture and Rural Economy
SCOTT, A. I., M.A., D.SC., PH.D., F.R.S., F.R.S.E., Organic Chemistry
STEWART, Sir FREDERICK, PH.D., D.SC., F.R.S.E., F.R.S., Geology
WALLACE, D. J., PH.D., Mathematical Physics
WILKINSON, J. F., M.A., PH.D., Microbiology
YEOMAN, M. M., M.SC., PH.D., F.R.S.E., Botany

*Faculty of Music:*
LEIGHTON, K., M.A., D.MUS., L.R.A.M., Music
TILMOUTH, M., M.A., PH.D., Music

*Faculty of Social Sciences:*
 ALTSCHUL, Miss A. T., B.A., M.SC., S.R.N., R.M.N., R.N.T., F.R.C.N., Nursing Studies
 ANDERSON, M., M.A., D.PHIL., Politics
 ANDERSON, M., M.A., PH.D., Economic History
 BEHREND, Miss HILDE, B.SC.(ECON.), PH.D., Industrial Relations
 COKE, S., M.A., International Business
 COPPOCK, J. T., M.A., PH.D., F.B.A., F.R.S.E., Geography
 DONALDSON-SALTER, Mrs. M. C., PH.D., Developmental Psychology
 ENTWISTLE, N. J., PH.D., F.B.PS.S., Education
 ERICKSON, J., M.A., Politics
 HUNT, N. C., C.B.E., PH.D., Business Studies
 JOHNSON-MARSHALL, P. E. A., C.M.G., M.A., R.I.B.A., F.R.T.P.I., DIST.T.P., Urban Design and Regional Planning
 LEE, T. A., M.SC., C.A., A.T.I.I., Accountancy and Finance
 LITTLEJOHN, J., A.P.D.A., PH.D., Social Anthropology
 MITCHISON, Mrs. R., M.A., Social History
 ODDIE, G. B., B.ARCH., R.I.B.A., F.R.I.A.S., DIP.T.P., Architecture
 POGGI, G., M.A., PH.D., Sociology
 SINFIELD, R. A., B.A., Social Policy
 STEWART, I. G., M.A., Economics
 VANDOME, P., M.A., Econometrics
 VOWLES, D. M., M.A., B.SC., D.PHIL., Psychology
 WATSON, J. W., M.A., PH.D., LL.D., F.R.S.E., F.R.S.CAN., Geography
 WILLIAMS, H. P., M.A., PH.D., Management Science
 WILSON, C. B., PH.D., Architectural Science
 WOLFE, J. N., M.A., B.LITT., Economics

*Faculty of Veterinary Medicine:*
 ALEXANDER, F., D.SC., PH.D., M.R.C.V.S., F.R.S.E., Veterinary Pharmacology
 BAXTER, J. T., M.A., PH.D., M.R.C.V.S., F.I.BIOL., Veterinary Medicine
 BROCKLESBY, D. W., DR.VET.MED., M.R.C.PATH., M.R.C.V.S., Tropical Animal Health
 CAMPBELL, J. R., B.V.M.S., PH.D., F.R.C.V.S., Veterinary Surgery
 DYCE, K. M., D.V.M. & S., M.R.C.V.S., Veterinary Anatomy
 FERGUSON, G. S., T.D., B.SC., M.R.C.V.S., D.V.S.M., Animal Health
 IGGO, A., M.AGRIC.SC., D.SC., PH.D., F.R.S.E., F.R.S., Veterinary Physiology

CONSTITUENT COLLEGE:

**New College:** f. 1846.
 *Principal:* Rev. A. C. ROSS, M.A., B.D., S.T.M., PH.D.

ATTACHED INSTITUTE:

**Institute for Advanced Studies in the Humanities:** 17 Buccleuch Place, Edinburgh, EH8 9LN; Dir. Prof. (Emer.) D. DAICHES, D.PHIL., PH.D., LITT.D., D.LITT., D.UNIV., F.R.S.E.

ASSOCIATED INSTITUTIONS:

**Centre of Rural Economy.**

**East of Scotland College:** *see* under Colleges.

# UNIVERSITY OF ESSEX
WIVENHOE PARK,
COLCHESTER, CO4 3SQ
Telephone: 0206-862286.
Telex: 98440 (UNILAB G).

Founded 1961.

*Chancellor:* Lord BUTLER OF SAFFRON WALDEN, K.G., C.H., M.A., D.C.L., LL.D., D.U., LITT.D., D.L.
*Pro-Chancellor and Chairman of Council:* J. E. TABOR, O.B.E., M.A., D.L.
*Vice-Chancellor:* A. E. SLOMAN, C.B.E., M.A., D.PHIL., D.U.
*Pro-Vice-Chancellor (Academic):* Prof. J. F. P. BLONDEL, L. EN DR., B.LIT.
*Pro-Vice-Chancellor (Services):* Prof. K. F. BOWDEN, M.SC., PH.D.
*Pro-Vice-Chancellor (Social):* Prof. A. SPICER, B.A., L. ÈS L.
*Registrar:* E. NEWCOMB, B.A.
*Librarian:* F. J. FRIEND, B.A.

Number of teaching staff: *c.* 270.
Number of students: *c.* 2,900.

Publications: *Calendar†* (annual), *Prospectus†* (annual), *Vice-Chancellor's Report†* (annual), *Graduate Studies†* (annual).

DEANS:

*School of Comparative Studies:* Prof. H. NEWBY, PH.D.
*School of Law:* Prof. A. D. YATES, M.A.
*School of Mathematical Studies:* Prof. C. B. WINSTEN, M.A.
*School of Science and Engineering:* Prof. D. J. BARBER PH.D.
*School of Social Studies:* P. J. FRANK, B.A.
*Dean of Students:* J. R. MILLER, PH.D.

PROFESSORS:

BARBER, D. J., Physics
BERGSTROM, A. R., Economics
BLONDEL, J. F. P. Government
BOWDEN, K. F., Computer Science
BROOKER, R. A., Computing Science
BROTHERSTON, J. G., Literature
BROYDEN, C. G., Computer Science
BUDGE, I., Government
CATTERMOLE, K. W., Telecommunication Systems
CHAPLIN, G. B. B., Electrical Engineering Science
CHICHILNISKY, G., Economics
CIOFFI, F., Philosophy
COHEN, S., Sociology
GORDON, M., Chemistry
GRAY, T. R. G., Biology
HART, C., Literature
HEAL, G. M., Economics
KING, A., Government
LOCKWOOD, D., Sociology
LOUDON, R., Physics
PEARSON, G., Literature
PODRO, M. I., Art
PROUDMAN, I., Mathematics
SÄRLVIK, B. H., Government
SHIRE, J. G. M., Biology
SPICER, A., Language and Linguistics
TATHAM, M. A. A., Language and Linguistics
TERRY, A. H., Literature
TURNER, J. A., Electrical Engineering Science
WILKS, Y., Language and Linguistics
WINSTEN, C. B., Mathematics
WOOLF, S. J., History
YATES, A. D., Law

READERS:

ATKIN, R. H., Mathematics
BARKER, A., Government
BOWDEN, K., Chemistry
BULLEN, G. J., Chemistry
BUTTERFIELD, R. W., Literature
COLLIER, S. D. W., History
CREWE, I. M., Government
EDWARDS, M., Literature
EVANS, B. G., Electrical Engineering
FARLIE, D. J. G., Mathematics
FIDLER, J. K., Electrical Engineering
GRAY, R. J., Literature
HOSKING, G. A., History
HUGHES, T. P., Physics
LUBASZ, H., History
MACKINNON, L., Physics
MARSDEN, D., Sociology
NEWBY, H., Sociology
O'NEIL, O. S., Philosophy
PUTTFARKEN, T., Art
RIDLEY, B. K., Physics
RUDD, E., Sociology
SCAZZOCCHIO, C., Biology
SCHOFIELD, N. J., Economics
TAYLOR, M. J., Government
THOMPSON, P. R., Sociology
TILLETT, J. G., Chemistry
TILLEY, D. R., Physics
WEXLER, P. J., Language and Linguistics

# UNIVERSITY OF EXETER
EXETER, EX4 4QJ
Telephone: 77911.

University College 1922,
University 1955.

*Chancellor:* (vacant).
*Vice-Chancellor:* H. KAY, C.B.E., M.A., PH.D.
*Academic Registrar and Secretary:* K. T. NASH, M.A.
*Librarian:* J. F. STIRLING, J.P., M.A.
Library: *see* Libraries.

Number of teachers: 500 full-time, including 50 professors.
Number of students: approx. 5,000 men and women.

Publications: *Annual Report, Calendar, Prospectus, Graduate Prospectuses, Gazette* (termly), *Newsletter* (2 a term).

DEANS:

*Faculty of Arts:* Prof. J. H. FOX, B.A., D.DE L'U.
*Faculty of Law:* J. W. BRIDGE, LL.M., PH.D.
*Faculty of Science:* Prof. J. WEBSTER, PH.D., D.SC., F.I.BIOL.
*Faculty of Applied Science:* Prof. J. C. R. TURNER, M.A., PH.D., SC.D., F.I.CHEM.E., C.ENG.
*Faculty of Education:* Prof. J. C. DANCY, M.A.
*Faculty of Social Studies:* Prof. M. M. GOLDSMITH, PH.D.

PROFESSORS AND
HEADS OF DEPARTMENTS:

*Faculty of Arts:*
 ATKINSON, R. F., B.A., B.PHIL., Philosophy
 COCKRELL, C. R. S., B.A., Russian
 CORBIN, P. F., PH.D., English

Doe, P. M., M.A., Music
Flower, J. E., M.A., PH.D., French
Fox, J. H., D. DE L'U., French
Holdsworth, C. J., M.A., PH.D., F.R.HIST.S., Medieval History
Porter, Rev. Canon J. R., M.A., Theology
Ravenhill, W. L. D., M.A., PH.D., Human and Regional Geography
Roots, I. A., M.A., F.R.HIST.S., History
Salgado, G., PH.D., English Literature
Shaban, M. A., A.M., PH.D., Arabic and Islamic Studies
Straw, A., PH.D., Geography
Thomson, P. W., M.A., Drama
Todd, M., B.A., F.S.A., Archaeology
Whinnom, K., M.A., Spanish
Wiseman, T. P., M.A., D.PHIL., Classics
Wood, M., PH.D., English
Yates, W. E., M.A., PH.D., German
Youings, Miss J. A., PH.D., F.R.HIST.S., English Social History

*Faculty of Science:*
Abel, E. W., PH.D., D.SC., F.R.I.C., Inorganic Chemistry
Ashford, J. R., M.A., PH.D., Mathematical Statistics and Operational Research
Bishop, E., D.SC., F.R.I.C., Analytical Chemistry
Campbell, J. A., M.SC., M.A., M.S., D.PHIL., Computer Science
Davies, D. R., PH.D., D.SC., Applied Mathematics
Eiser, J. R., PH.D., Psychology
Fowler, G. N., PH.D., F.INST.P., A.R.C.S., F.I.M.A., F.R.MET.S., Theoretical Physics
Howe, M. J. A., PH.D., Psychology
Leadbetter, A. J., PH.D., D.SC., Physical Chemistry
Murray, J. W., PH.D., A.R.C.S., D.I.C., F.G.S., Geology
Nichols, D., M.A., D.PHIL., Biological Sciences
Rees, D., M.A., SC.D., F.R.S., Pure Mathematics
Reid, R. L., M.A., F.B.PS.S., Psychology
Schofield, K., PH.D., D.SC., Organic Chemistry
Webster, J., PH.D., D.SC., Biological Sciences
Wyatt, A. F. G., D.PHIL., Physics

*Faculty of Applied Science:*
Edmunds, H. G., PH.D., F.I.MECH.E., Engineering Science
Flower, J. O., PH.D., M.I.E.E., F.I.MAR.E., Engineering Science
Turner, J. C. R., M.A., PH.D., F.I.CHEM.E., C.ENG., F.C.S., Chemical Engineering

*Faculty of Social Studies:*
Black, J., M.A., Economic Theory
Goldsmith, M. M., A.B., PH.D., Political Theory
Leaper, R. A. B., C.B.E., M.A., Social Administration
Minchinton, W. E., B.SC.(ECON.), F.R.HIST.S., Economic History
Mitchell, G. D., M.B.E., B.SC.(ECON.), F.R.A.I., Sociology
Parker, R. H., B.SC.(ECON.), F.C.A., Accountancy
Shaw, M. T., M.SC., Politics
Walker, D., M.A., Economics

*Faculty of Law:*
Bridge, J. W., LL.M., PH.D., Public Law
Lasok, D., L.EN.DR., LL.D., PH.D., DR. JURIS., European Law
Parker, C. F., M.A., LL.B., Law

*Faculty of Education:*
Burghes, D. N., PH.D.
Dancy, J. C., M.A., Education
Daveney, T. F., B.A., Adult Education
Pring, R. A., PH.D., Education
Wragg, E. C., M.ED., PH.D., Education (Director)

*Postgraduate Medical School:*
Mattingly, D., M.B., B.S., M.R.C.P. (Director)

*Institute of Biometry and Community Medicine:*
Canvin, R. W., M.SC. (Director)

*Institute of Cornish Studies:*
Thomas, A. C., M.A., DIP.ARCH., F.S.A. (Director)

*Language Centre:*
Hartmann, R. R. K., D.COMM., M.A.

*Teaching Services Centre:*
Bligh, D. A., PH.D.

READERS:

*Faculty of Arts:*
Alberich, J. M., PH.D., Modern Spanish Literature
Faulkner, P., M.A., English
Garland, Mary, PH.D., German
Harley, J. B., PH.D., Geography
Hudson, Rev. W. D., M.A., B.D., PH.D., Moral Philosophy
Keene, G. B., PH.D., Logic
Langford, S. G., PH.D., Social Philosophy
Noakes, J. D., D.PHIL., F.R.HIST.S., Modern European History
Orme, N. I., M.A., D.PHIL., F.R.HIST.S., History
Perry, N., PH.D., Post-Classical French Studies
Richards, D. J., M.A., B.LITT., Russian
Swanton, M. J., PH.D., English Medieval Studies
Walling, D. E., PH.D., Physical Geography
Watts, D. A., M.A., D.U., Classical French Literature
Wolffe, B. P., M.A., D.PHIL., F.R.HIST.S., Medieval History

*Faculty of Science:*
Coe, K., M.A., PH.D., F.G.S., Petrology
Crout, D. H. G., PH.D., Organic Chemistry
Drabble, J. R., PH.D., F.INST.P., Solid State Physics
Flack, F. C., PH.D., Medical Physics
Fryer, J. G., PH.D., Statistics
Klein, G., M.SC., PH.D., Applied Mathematics
Kline, P., M.ED., PH.D., Psychometrics
Meads, R. E., M.A., D.PHIL., Nuclear Spectroscopy
Moodie, R. B., PH.D., Physical-Organic Chemistry
Odoni, R. W. K., PH.D., Number Theory
Phillips, I. D. J., PH.D., Plant Physiology
Pitt, D., PH.D., Plant Pathology
Proctor, M. C. F., M.A., PH.D., Plant Ecology
Rosseinsky, D. R., PH.D., D.SC., Physical Chemistry
Rosser, W. G. V., M.SC., PH.D., Electromagnetism

*Faculty of Applied Science:*
Brookes, C. A., PH.D., C.ENG., F.I.M., Engineering Materials
Zienkiewicz, H. K., M.SC., PH.D., C.ENG., F.R.AE.S., Mechanics of Fluids

*Faculty of Social Studies:*
Corner, D. C., M.A., PH.D., Business Finance
Dowse, R. E., PH.D., Politics
Hewitt, Miss M., PH.D., Social Institutions

Meyer, F. V., PH.D., International Economics
Oliver, F. R., M.A., S.D., D.PHIL., Economic and Social Statistics
Turner, B. A., PH.D., Sociology of Organizations

*Faculty of Education:*
King, R. A., M.SC., PH.D., Education

ATTACHED INSTITUTES:

**Centre for Arab Gulf Studies:** f. 1979; documentation, research, publication on the Arab Gulf, and postgraduate training; Dir. Prof. M. A. Shaban, A.M., PH.D.

**Institute of Population Studies:** Hoopern House, 101 Pennsylvania Rd., Exeter EX4 6DT; f. 1978; training in population research, particularly in issues for developing countries; communicating population issues; research in acceptability of family planning and related issues, e.g. evaluation of services; 10 staff; Dirs. Prof. G. D. Mitchell, Dr. R. Snowden.

# UNIVERSITY OF GLASGOW

GLASGOW, G12 8QQ.

Telephone: 041-339-8855.

Founded 1451, reconstituted 1577.

Academic year: October to June.

*Chancellor:* Sir Alexander Cairncross, K.C.M.G., M.A., PH.D., LL.D., D.LITT., D.SC.(ECON.), D.UNIV.
*Vice-Chancellor and Principal:* Prof. Alwyn Williams, PH.D., D.SC., F.R.S.E., M.R.I.A., F.G.S., F.R.S.
*Vice-Principals:* Prof. A. M. Potter, M.A., PH.D., Prof. W. Mulligan, M.SC., PH.D., Prof. D. Flint, T.D., M.A., B.L., C.A.
*Rector:* Reginald Bosanquet.
*Registrar:* J. McCargow, M.A.
*Librarian:* H. J. Heaney, M.A.

Library: see Libraries.

Number of teaching staff: 1,157, including 167 professors.

Number of students: 11,041.

Publications†: *Glasgow University Publications, Geology Department Papers, Soviet Studies* (quarterly). *Glasgow University Calendar* (annually), occasional publications of the University of Glasgow Press.

† Exchanges on a selective basis.

DEANS:

*Faculty of Arts:* E. K. C. Varty, M.A., PH.D.
*Faculty of Science:* D. W. A. Sharp, M.A., PH.D.
*Faculty of Medicine:* B. Jennett, M.D.
*Faculty of Law:* W. A. Harland, M.D., PH.D.
*Faculty of Divinity:* A. D. Galloway, PH.D.
*Faculty of Engineering:* A. Coull, PH.D.
*Faculty of Veterinary Medicine:* D. D. Lawson, B.SC., M.R.C.V.S., D.V.R.
*Faculty of Social Sciences:* Andrew S. Skinner, M.A., B.LITT.

PROFESSORS:

*Faculties of Arts and Social Sciences:*
ALCOCK, L., M.A., F.S.A., F.R.S.E., Archaeology
BOWN, L. J., O.B.E., D.UNIV., Adult and Continuing Education
BROWN, A. L., M.A., D.PHIL., Medieval History
BROWN, P. M., M.A., D.PHIL., Italian—Stevenson Chair
BUTTER, P. H., M.A., English Literature
CHECKLAND, S. G., M.A., M.COMM., PH.D., F.B.A., Economic History
DONNISON, D. V., D.LITT., LL.D., Town and Regional Planning
DOWNIE, R. S., M.A., Moral Philosophy
DREW, K. P. A., M.A., English Literature
DRYDEN, M. M., M.B.A., PH.D., Management Studies
DUNCAN, A. A. M., M.A., Scottish History and Literature
ELDRIDGE, J. E. T., M.A., Sociology
FARR, R. MacL., M.A., PH.D., Psychology
FINCH, R. G., M.A., PH.D., German
GRANT, N. D. C., M.A., M.ED., PH.D., Education
HENRY, P., M.A., Slavonic Languages
HOOK, A. D., M.A., PH.D., English Literature—Bradley Chair
HOUSTON, G. F. B., M.A., B.LITT., Political Economy
HUNTER, L. C., M.A., D.PHIL., Applied Economics
LARNER, J. P., M.A., Medieval History
MACDONALD, HUGH J., M.A., PH.D., Music
McDONALD, J. B. I., M.A., Drama
MACDOWELL, D. M., M.A., Greek
MACMILLAN, A., M.A., F.R.I.A.S., R.I.B.A., Architecture
MARTIN, F. M., B.A., PH.D., Social Administration
NOVE, A., D.AGR., F.B.A., Economics
PICKVANCE, R., B.A., History of Fine Art
POTTER, A. M., M.A., PH.D., Politics—James Bryce Chair
ROBBINS, K. G., M.A., D.PHIL., History
ROUND, N. G., M.A., D.PHIL., Hispanic Studies
SAMUELS, M. L., M.A., English Language
SCHAPER, E., DR.PHIL., Aesthetic Philosophy
SKINNER, A. S., M.A., B.LITT., Political Economy
SLAVEN, A., M.A., B.LITT., Business History
SMETHURST, C., M.A., B.LITT., French
THOMSON, A. W. J., M.S., PH.D., Business Policy
THOMSON, D. S., M.A., Celtic
VARTY, E. K. C., B.A., PH.D., French
WALSH, P. G., M.A., PH.D., Humanity
WEIR, D. T. H., B.A., Organizational Behaviour
WILSON, T., O.B.E., M.A., PH.D., F.B.A., Political Economy
WILSON, T. B., M.A., B.MUS., Adult and Continuing Education—Music

*Faculty of Science:*
BONEY, A. D., PH.D., D.SC., Botany
BOWES, D. R., PH.D., D.SC., F.R.S.E., Geology
BROOKS, C. J. W., PH.D., D.SC., Chemistry
BURDON, R. H., PH.D., Biochemistry
CAPON, B., PH.D., Chemistry
CUNNINGHAM, J. M. M., C.B.E., PH.D., Agriculture
CURTIS, A. S. G., M.A., PH.D., Cell Biology
DREVER, R. W. P., PH.D., Natural Philosophy
FERRIER, R. P., M.A., PH.D., Natural Philosophy
GILLES, D. C., PH.D., Computing Science
GRASSIE, N. G., PH.D., D.SC., Chemistry
GUNN, J. C., C.B.E., M.A., D.SC., Natural Philosophy
HOPKINS, C. A., PH.D., Zoology
HUGHES, I. S., PH.D., Natural Philosophy
HUNTER, J., M.A., PH.D., Mathematics
KIRBY, G. W., M.A., PH.D., SC.D., Chemistry
LAING, E. W., M.A., PH.D., Natural Philosophy
LEAKE, B. E., PH.D., D.SC., Geology
MOORHOUSE, R. G., M.A., PH.D., Natural Philosophy
MUNN, W. D., M.A., PH.D., D.SC., Mathematics
OVERTON, K. H., PH.D., D.SC., Chemistry
PEAKER, M., PH.D., Dairy Science
PETRIE, G., M.A., B.SC.(PH.E.), Geography
RANKIN, R. A., M.A., PH.D., SC.D., Mathematics
REID, J. M., M.A., Natural Philosophy
ROBERTSON, J. D., PH.D., SC.D., Zoology
ROY, A. E., PH.D., F.R.S.E., Astronomy
SHARP, D. W. A., M.A., PH.D., Inorganic Chemistry
SHERRATT, D. J., PH.D., Genetics
SIM, G. A., PH.D., Chemistry
SNEDDON, I. N., O.B.E., M.A., D.SC., Mathematics
SWEET, P. A., M.A., PH.D., F.R.S.E., Astronomy
THOMPSON, I. B., M.A., PH.D., Geography
THOMSON, S. J., PH.D., D.SC., Chemistry
TIVY, J., PH.D., Geography
VICKERMAN, K., M.A., PH.D., D.SC., Zoology
WARDLAW, A. C., PH.D., D.SC., Microbiology
WILKINS, M. B., PH.D., D.SC., Botany

*Faculty of Medicine:*
ADAMS, J. H., M.B., CH.B., PH.D., Neuropathology
ANDERSON, J. R., C.B.E., M.D., LL.D., Pathology
ARNEIL, G. C., M.D., PH.D., Child Health
BAIN, W., M.D., Cardiac Surgery
BARBER, J. H., J.P., M.D., General Practice—Norie-Miller Chair
BOND, M. R., M.D., PH.D., Psychological Medicine
BOYD, I. A., M.D., PH.D., D.SC., Physiology
CAIRD, F. I., M.A., D.M., Geriatric Medicine
CALMAN, K. C., B.SC., M.D., PH.D., Oncology—Cancer Research Campaign Chair
CAMPBELL, D., M.B., CH.B., Anaesthesia
CARTER, D. C., M.D., Surgery
COCKBURN, J., M.D., Child Health
DURNIN, J. V. G. A., M.A., M.B.CH.B., D.SC., Physiology
FERGUSON-SMITH, M.A., M.B., B.CH., Medical Genetics
FOULDS, W. S., M.D., CH.M., Ophthalmology
GENTLES, J. C., PH.D., Dermatology
GEORGE, W. D., M.B., B.S., Surgery
GILLESPIE, J. S., M.B., CH.B., PH.D., Pharmacology
GOLDBERG, A., M.D., Practice of Medicine
GOUDIE, R. B., M.D., Pathology
GRIST, N. R., B.SC., M.B., CH.B., Infectious Diseases
HAMBLEN, D., M.B., B.S., PH.D., Orthopaedics
HARLAND, W. A., M.D., PH.D., Forensic Medicine
HARPER, A. M., M.D., Surgery
HUTTER, O. F., PH.D., Physiology
JENNETT, W. B., M.D., Neurosurgery
KENNEDY, A. C., M.D., Medicine
LAWRIE, T. D. V., B.SC., M.D., Medical Cardiology
LEDINGHAM, I. M., M.B., CH.B., Surgery
LEE, W. R., M.D., Ophthalmic Pathology
LENIHAN, J. M. A., O.B.E., M.SC., PH.D., Clinical Physics
LUFFINGHAM, J. K., B.D.S., PH.D., F.D.S., D.ORTH., R.C.S., Orthodontics
McGOWAN, D. A., M.D.S., Oral Surgery
MacGREGOR, A. R., PH.D., F.D.S., Prosthodontics
MACKIE, R. M. L., M.D., Dermatology
MACNAUGHTON, M. C., M.D., Obstetrics and Gynaecology
MacSWEEN, R. N. M., B.SC., M.D., Pathology
MASON, D. K., B.D.S., M.D., F.D.S., Oral Medicine
MORGAN, H. G., B.SC., M.B., CH.B., Pathological Biochemistry
PARROTT, D. M. V., D.SC., PH.D., Bacteriology and Immunology
PATERSON, R. C., M.D.S., PH.D., Conservative Dentistry
REID, J. L., B.A., B.CH.P., D.M., M.R.C.P., Materia Medica
SCOTHORNE, R. J., B.SC., M.D., Anatomy
SIMPSON, J. A., M.D., F.R.S.E., Neurology
SMELLIE, R. M. S., D.SC., PH.D., Biochemistry
SPENCE, A. A., M.D., Anaesthesia
STEWART, G. T., B.SC., M.D., Community Medicine
STONE, F. H., M.B.CH.B., Child and Adolescent Psychiatry
SUBAK-SHARPE, J. H., PH.D., Virology
TEASDALE, G. M., M.B., B.S., Neurosurgery
TIMBURY, G. C., M.B.CH.B., Postgraduate Medical Education
TIMBURY, M. C., M.D., PH.D., Bacteriology and Immunology
WHEATLEY, D., M.B., CH.B., CH.M., Cardiac Surgery
WHITFIELD, C. R., M.D., F.R.C.O.E., Midwifery

*Faculty of Veterinary Medicine:*
ARMOUR, J., PH.D., M.R.C.V.S., Veterinary Pathology
DOUGLAS, T. A., PH.D., M.R.C.V.S., Veterinary Biochemistry
FISHER, E. W., PH.D., D.V.M., M.R.C.V.S., Veterinary Medicine
HEMINGWAY, R. G., M.SC., PH.D., Animal Husbandry
JARRETT, W. F. H., PH.D., M.R.C.V.S., F.R.S., Veterinary Parasitology
LAWSON, D. D., B.SC., M.R.C.V.S., D.V.R., Veterinary Surgery
McINTYRE, W. I. M., PH.D., M.R.C.V.S., Veterinary Medicine
MULLIGAN, W., M.SC., PH.D., Veterinary Physiology
SELMAN, I. E., PH.D., M.R.S.V.S., Veterinary Medicine
URQUHART, G. M., PH.D., M.R.C.V.S., Veterinary Parasitology
WRIGHT, N. G., PH.D., D.V.M., M.R.C.V.S., Veterinary Anatomy

*Faculty of Law:*
CAMPBELL, T. D., M.A., PH.D., Jurisprudence
COWIE, G. S., M.A., LL.B., Public Law
FLINT, D., T.D., M.A., B.L., C.A., Accountancy
GORDON, W. M., M.A., LL.B., PH.D., Civil Law
GRAY, S. J., PH.D., A.C.C.A., Accountancy
INGLIS, J. A. M., M.A., LL.B., Conveyancing
JACK, R. B., M.A., LL.B., Mercantile Law
LEWIS, M., B.A., Taxation
SHAW, J. C., B.L., C.A., Accountancy
WALKER, D. M., Q.C., M.A., PH.D., LL.D., F.B.A., Private Law

*Faculty of Divinity:*
BEST, E., M.A., B.D., PH.D., Biblical Criticism

DAVIDSON, R., M.A., B.D., Old Testament and Semitic Studies
FREND, W. H. C., T.D., M.A., D.PHIL., D.D., Ecclesiastical History
GALLOWAY, A. D., M.A., B.D., PH.D., S.T.M., Divinity
MACDONALD, J., M.A., B.D., PH.D., S.T.M., Old Testament and Semitic Studies

*Faculty of Engineering:*
BARLOW, A. J., PH.D., Electrical Engineering
COULL, A., PH.D., Civil Engineering
FAULKNER, D., PH.D., R.C.N.C., F.R.I.N.A., M.A.S.N.A.M.E., Naval Architecture
LAMB, J., D.SC., PH.D., Electrical Engineering
RICHARDS, B. E., PH.D., Aeronautics and Fluid Mechanics
SCOTT, B. F., PH.D., Mechanical Engineering
SUTHERLANDS, H. B., S.M., Civil Engineering

READERS:
ALEXANDER, W. D., M.D., F.R.C.P.GLAS., F.R.C.P.ED., Practice of Medicine
BARRON, L. D., D.PHIL., Chemistry
BEHAN, P. O., M.B.CH.B., Neurology
BERRIE, A. M. M., PH.D., Botany
BLUCK, B. J., PH.D., Geology
BROWN, J. C., PH.D., Astronomy
BUCHANAN, G. L., PH.D., D.SC., Chemistry
CALOW, P., PH.D., Zoology
CATTO, MARY E., M.D., Pathology
CLANCHY, M. T., M.A., PH.D., Medieval History
CONNOLLY, J. D., PH.D., Chemistry
COWAN, I. B., M.A., PH.D., Scottish History
DARGIE, J. D., PH.D., Veterinary Physiology
DOWSON, H. R., PH.D., Mathematics
DUNSMUIR, R., M.SC., PH.D., Electronics and Electrical Engineering
EDE, D. A., M.S., PH.D., Zoology
ELLIOTT, C. G., M.SC., PH.D., Botany
FELL, G. S., PH.D., Pathological Biochemistry
FEWSON, C. A., PH.D., Biochemistry
FULTON, W. F. M., B.SC., M.D., Materia Medica
GRAHAM, D. I., M.B., B.CH., PH.D., Neuropathology
GRANT, J. K., PH.D., Steroid Biochemistry
GRIFFITHS, I. R., PH.D., Veterinary Surgery
HILLMAN, J. R., PH.D., Botany
HOBSBAUM, P. D., M.A., PH.D., English Literature
HOLLINGSWORTH, T. H., M.A., PH.D., Social and Economic Research
HOLMES, P. H., PH.D., M.R.C.V.S., Veterinary Physiology
HUTCHINSON, S. A., T.D., PH.D., Botany
JARDINE, W. G., M.SC., PH.D., Geology
JENNETT, S. M., M.D., PH.D., Physiology
JENNINGS, F. W., M.AGRIC., PH.D., Veterinary Pathology
KEANE, S. M., M.A., LL.B., PH.D., C.A., Accountancy
KEATES, J. S., O.B.E., M.A., Geography
KELLAS, J. G., M.A., PH.D., Politics
KELLETT, J. R., M.A., PH.D., Economic History
LEVER, W. F., M.A., D.PHIL., Social and Economic Research
LUNT, D. A., Dental Anatomy
MCNEILL, I. C, PH.D., D.SC., Chemistry
MACFARLANE, P. W., PH.D., Medical Cardiology
MADELEY, C. R., M.D., Infectious Diseases
MADEN, B. E. H., M.A., PH.D., Biochemistry
MILBURN, J. A., PH.D., Botany
MULVEY, C., M.A., Social and Economic Research

MURISON, D. D., M.A., English Language and Literature
PARR, J. B., PH.D., Social and Economic Research
PARSONS, F. V., PH.D., History
PIRIE, H. M., M.R.C.V.S., PH.D., Veterinary Pathology
PITTS, J., PH.D., Biochemistry
PRENTICE, C. R. M., M.D., Practice of Medicine
PRICE, R. J., PH.D., Geography
REID, G. L., M.A., Applied Economics
SANDISON, A. T., B.SC., M.D., Pathology
SANFORD, A. J., PH.D., Psychology
SCOTT, A. M., M.C., M.A., Scottish Literature
SIMPSON, H. W., M.D., PH.D., Pathology
SINHA, R. P., PH.D., Political Economy
SKILLICORN, I. O., PH.D., Natural Philosophy
SMITH, L. D., B.SC., Political Economy
STEPHEN, K. W., B.D.S., F.D.S., Oral Medicine
THOMSON, J. A., M.D., PH.D., Practice of Medicine
TONER, P. G., D.SC., M.B., CH.B., Pathology
TYLER, J. K., PH.D., Chemistry
WAKELIN, D., PH.D., Zoology
WHALEY, K., M.D., PH.D., Pathology
WHITEHEAD, R. R., M.SC., PH.D., Natural Philosophy
WILKINSON, C. D., B.A., PH.D., Electronics and Electrical Engineering
WILKINSON, P. C., M.D., Bacteriology and Immunology
WONG, H. H. Y., PH.D., Aeronautics and Fluid Mechanics

ASSOCIATED COLLEGE:

**West of Scotland Agricultural College:** (*see* under Colleges).

ATTACHED INSTITUTIONS:

**Building Services Research Unit:** University of Glasgow, G12 8RZ.

**Scottish Universities Research Reactor Centre:** East Kilbride, Lanarkshire; see under Research Institutes.

**Medical Research Council Virology Unit:** Institute of Virology, Church St., Glasgow, G11 5JR; experimental virus research unit; Hon. Dir. Prof. H. SUBAK-SHARPE, PH.D.

**Medical Research Council Blood Pressure Unit:** Western Infirmary, Glasgow, G11 6NT; blood pressure research unit; Dir. A. F. LEVER, M.B., B.SC., F.R.C.P.

**Science and Engineering Research Council Data Analysis Unit (Natural Philosophy).**

**Beatson Institute for Cancer Research:** (Royal Beatson Memorial Hospital) Garscube Estate, Bearsden, Glasgow.

**Social Paediatric and Obstetric Research Group:** 64 Oakfield Ave., Glasgow, G12.

**Glasgow Institute of Radiotherapeutics:** Western Infirmary, Glasgow, G11 6NT; f. 1966; research in radiotherapeutics and clinical oncology, teaching; Dir. K. E. HALNAN.

**Wellcome Surgical Research Institute:** Garscube Estate, Bearsden Rd., Bearsden, Glasgow.

**Institute of Soviet and East European Studies:** 9 Southpark Terrace, Glasgow, G12 8LG; f. 1963; research, teaching and editorial activities on the U.S.S.R. and Eastern Europe in all fields of social sciences; library of 16,000 vols. and pamphlets, mostly in Russian and other East European languages; Dir. W. V. WALLACE; publ. *Soviet Studies* (quarterly).

## HERIOT-WATT UNIVERSITY
EDINBURGH, EH1 1HX

Telephone: (031)-225-8432.

Founded 1821 as School of Arts, Heriot-Watt College 1885, University Charter 1966.

*Chancellor:* The Rt. Hon. The Lord THOMSON OF MONIFIETH, P.C., LL.D., D.LITT., D.SC.
*Principal and Vice-Chancellor:* T. L. JOHNSTON, PH.D., F.R.S.E.
*Vice-Principal:* Prof. A. R. ROGERS, F.P.S., F.R.S.C.
*Secretary:* D. I. CAMERON, J.P., B.L., C.A.
*Librarian:* A. ANDERSON, M.A., F.L.A.

Number of teachers: c. 325.
Number of students: c. 3,200.

Publications: *Guide for Applicants, Guide to Postgraduate Study and Research, Faculty Handbooks* (all annually), *Annual Report*.

DEANS:
*Faculty of Science:* Prof. S. D. SMITH, PH.D., D.SC., F.R.S.E., F.R.S.
*Faculty of Engineering:* Prof. C. W. NUTT, PH.D., D.SC., M.I.CHEM.E., F.R.S.C.
*Faculty of Economic and Social Studies:* P. J. WELHAM, PH.D.
*Faculty of Environmental Studies:* D. N. SKINNER, B.ARCH., M.L.ARCH., I.L.A., R.I.B.A.

PROFESSORS:
*Faculty of Economic and Social Studies:*
BUXTON, N. K., M.A., PH.D., Economics
HOME, G., International Banking
MACKAY, D. I., Economics
RODGER, L. W., Business Organization
SMALL, J. R., Accountancy and Finance
STANFORTH, A. M., Languages
THOMPSON, A. E., Economics of Government

*Faculty of Engineering:*
BOLTON, A., Civil Engineering
DAVIDSON, C. W., Electrical and Electronic Engineering
EDWARDS, A. D., Civil Engineering
HALLIWELL, A. R., Offshore Engineering
HEATH, F. G., Computer Engineering
NICOLL, G. R., Electrical and Electronic Engineering
NUTT, C. W., Chemical and Process Engineering
PATTEN, T. D., Mechanical Engineering
RORKE, J., Mechanical Engineering
STEWART, G., Petroleum Engineering
TORRANCE, V. B., Building

*Faculty of Environmental Studies:*
DUNBAR-NASMITH, J. D., Architecture
MELVILLE, I. S., Town and Country Planning

U.K. (GREAT BRITAIN)

Faculty of Science:
  Brown, C. M., Microbiology
  Buchanan, J. G., Organic Chemistry
  Gilbert, J. C., Pharmacology
  Gowenlock, B. G., Chemistry
  Gray, J. R., Actuarial Mathematics and Statistics
  Harper, P. G., Theoretical Physics
  Knops, R. J., Mathematics
  Manners, D. J., Brewing and Biochemistry
  McCutcheon, J. J., Actuarial Studies
  Rogers, A. R., Pharmacy
  Smith, S. D., Physics
  Williams, M. H., Computer Science
  Williamson, J. H., Mathematics

READERS:

Faculty of Engineering:
  Cowan, J., Civil Engineering
  Dickson, A., Mechanical Engineering
  Helszajn, J., Electrical and Electronic Engineering

Faculty of Science:
  Ball, J. M., Mathematics
  Milligan, R., Physics
  Mollison, D., Actuarial Mathematics and Statistics
  Peckham, G. E., Physics
  Pidgeon, C. R., Physics
  Thomas, H. G., Mathematics

ATTACHED INSTITUTES:

**Esmée Fairbairn Research Centre:** Heriot-Watt University, Chambers St., Edinburgh EH1 1HX; Dir. Prof. K. G. Lumsden, M.A., PH.D.

**Institute of Offshore Engineering:** Heriot-Watt University Research Park, Riccarton, Currie, Edinburgh EH14 4AS; Dir. C. S. Johnston, PH.D.

ASSOCIATED INSTITUTION:

**Edinburgh College of Art:** see under Colleges.

## THE UNIVERSITY OF HULL
COTTINGHAM ROAD,
HULL, HU6 7RX
Telephone: (0482) 46311.
Founded 1927.

Chancellor: The Rt. Hon. Lord Wilberforce, P.C., C.M.G., O.B.E., M.A.

Vice-Chancellor: Sir Roy Marshall, C.B.E., M.A., PH.D., LL.D.

Pro-Vice-Chancellors: Prof. H. K. Bevan, J.P., LL.M., BAR.-AT-LAW, Prof. M. R. House, M.A., PH.D., F.G.S.

Registrar: F. T. Mattison, M.A., LL.B.

Librarian: P. A. Larkin, C.B.E., C.LIT., M.A., D.LIT., D.LITT., F.L.A., F.R.S.L.

Library: see Libraries.

Number of teachers: 540, including 66 professors.

Number of students (full-time): 5,500.

Publications: Calendar, Annual Report, Prospectus, Departmental Pamphlets.

DEANS:

Faculty of Arts: J. A. V. Chapple, M.A.

Faculty of Science: J. Friend, PH.D., F.I.BIOL.
Faculty of Social Sciences: V. G. K. Pons, M.SOC.SC., PH.D.
Faculty of Law: P. B. Fairest, M.A., LL.B.

PROFESSORS:

Faculty of Arts:
  Andrews, K. R., PH.D., History
  Brett, R. L., B.A., B.LITT., English Language and Literature
  Chapple, J. A. V., M.A., English Language and Literature
  Connell-Smith, G. E., PH.D., F.R.HIST.S., Contemporary History
  Earl, D. C., M.A., PH.D., Classics
  Flint, J. M., M.A., PH.D., Hispanic Studies
  Fudge, E. C., M.A., PH.D., Linguistics
  Ginestier, P., L. ÈS L., D.E.S., D. DE L'U, Modern French Literature
  **Hanson, Rev. A. T., M.A., D.D., Theology**
  Ireson, J. C., M.A., D. ÈS L., Modern French Literature
  Jennings, B., M.A., Adult Education
  King, P. K., M.A., Modern Dutch Studies
  Lehmann, A. G., M.A., D.PHIL., European Studies
  McClelland, V. A., M.A., PH.D., F.R.S.A., Education Studies
  McInnes, E. O., M.A., PH.D., German
  Moloney, B., M.A., PH.D., Italian
  Moore, G. H., M.A., American Literature
  Newbould, B., B.MUS., M.A., Music
  Peace, R. A., M.A., B.LITT., Russian Studies
  Pickford, C. E., M.A., D. ÈS L., Medieval French Literature
  Pollard, A., B.A., B.LITT., English
  Speck, W. A., D.PHIL., History
  White, A. R., PH.D., Philosophy
  Whybray, Rev. R. N., M.A., D.PHIL., Hebrew and Old Testament Studies
  Wilton-Ely, J., M.A., F.S.A., History of Art

Faculty of Science:
  Appleton, J. H., M.A., M.SC., PH.D., Geography
  Baldwin, R. R., M.A., PH.D., C.CHEM., F.R.S.C., Physical Chemistry
  Brener, J. M., PH.D., Psychology
  Bryant, F. J., PH.D., D.SC., Physics
  Chapman, N. B., M.A., PH.D., C.CHEM., F.R.S.C., Chemistry
  Clarke, A. D. B., C.B.E., PH.D., F.B.PS.S., Psychology
  Cole, G. H. A., PH.D., D.SC., F.R.A.S., F.INST.P., Theoretical Physics.
  Cook, G. B., M.A., PH.D., Computer Studies
  **Dawes, E. A., PH.D., D.SC., F.I.BIOL.,** C.CHEM., F.R.S.C., Biochemistry
  Donaldson, I. M. L., M.B., CH.B., M.A., M.R.C.P., M.R.C.P.ED., F.Z.S., Zoology
  Dunham, A. C., M.A., D.PHIL., M.I.M.M., F.G.S., Industrial Mineralogy
  Elliott, R. J., M.A., PH.D., Pure Mathematics
  Friend, J., PH.D., F.I.BIOL., Plant Biology
  Goldspink, G., PH.D., SC.D., F.R.S.M., Zoology
  Gray, G. W., PH.D., C.CHEM., F.R.S.C., Organic Chemistry
  **Higginson, W. C. E., M.A., D.PHIL.,** C.CHEM., F.R.S.C., Inorganic Chemistry
  **House, M. R., M.A., PH.D., F.G.S., Geology**
  Jones, D. A., M.A., D.PHIL., F.I.BIOL., Genetics
  Morris, W. D., PH.D., F.I.MECH.E., C.ENG., Mechanical Engineering

  Neale, J. W., PH.D., D.SC., F.G.S., F.L.S., Micropalaeontology
  Patmore, J. A., J.P., B.LITT., M.A., Geography
  Phillips, J. G., PH.D., D.SC., F.I.BIOL., F.A.Z., F.R.S.M., F.R.S., Wolfson Institute
  Poots, G., PH.D., D.SC., Applied Mathematics
  Pugh, A., PH.D., C.ENG., F.I.E.E., F.I.E.R.E., Electronic Engineering
  **Ramsden, S. A., D.PHIL., Applied Physics**
  Ward, R. C., PH.D., Geography
  Wilkinson, H. R., M.A., Geography

Faculty of Social Sciences:
  Cigno, A., PH.D., Economic Theory
  Cunnison, I. G., M.A., D.PHIL., Social Anthropology
  Dodd, C. H., M.A., Politics
  Hayward, J. E. S., PH.D., Politics
  Hooper, D. F., PH.D., Social Work Studies
  Kitchen, J., B.SC.(ECON.), F.C.A., Accounting
  Lancaster, A., PH.D., Econometrics
  McDonnell, H., M.B., CH.B., M.SC., M.F.C.M., F.R.S.M., F.S.S., Health Studies
  Pons, V. G. K., M.SOC.SC., PH.D., Sociology
  Saville, J., B.SC.(ECON.), Economic and Social History
  Smith, G. A., PH.D., Social Administration
  Wilson, J. S. G., M.A., DIP.COM., Economics and Commerce

Faculty of Law:
  Bevan, H. K., J.P., LL.B., BAR.-AT-LAW
  Fairest, P. B., M.A., LL.B.

READERS:

Faculty of Arts:
  Borland, Mrs. W. M. D., M.A., Golden Age Literature
  Chilton, C. W., M.A., PH.D., Classics
  Clarke, Mrs. A. M., PH.D., F.B.PS.S., Educational Psychology
  Hedges, A. J., M.A., B.MUS., Music (Composition)
  Ryder, T. T. B., M.A., PH.D., Classics
  Taylor, P. A. M., M.A., PH.D., American Studies

Faculty of Science:
  Boatman, D. J., PH.D., M.A., Plant Ecology
  Cavenett, B. C., PH.D., M.INST.P., Solid State Physics
  Coley-Smith, J R., PH.D., D.SC., Plant Pathology
  Collinson, C. D., PH.D., Applied Mathematics
  De Boer, G., M.A., Geography
  Goldsworthy, G. J., PH.D., Comparative Endocrinology
  Hagston, W. E., PH.D., Theoretical Physics
  Harris, A., M.A., PH.D., Geography
  Killingbeck, J. P., PH.D., D.SC., Theoretical Physics
  Nowell, N. W., PH.D., Endocrinology
  Pearson, D. B., PH.D., Mathematical Physics
  Peel, A. J., PH.D., Plant Physiology
  Pert, G. J., PH.D., A.R.C.S., Applied Physics
  Phillips, J. P., N. M.A., PH.D., Mathematical Methods in Clinical Psychology
  Ratledge, C., PH.D., C.CHEM., F.R.S.C., Biochemistry
  Shorter, D., D.PHIL., C.CHEM., F.R.S.C., Chemistry
  Sudd, J. H., M.A., PH.D., Entomology

THRELFALL, D. R., PH.D., D.SC., Plant Biochemistry
TOWNSHEND, A., PH.D., D.SC., C.CHEM., F.R.S.C.
WALKER, R. W., PH.D., Physical Chemistry
WELLS, P. B., PH.D., C.CHEM., F.R.S.C., Physical Chemistry
WILKINSON, S. G., PH.D., Organic Chemistry

*Faculty of Social Sciences:*
ASAD, T., M.A., D.PHIL., Social Anthropology
KEMP, T., B.SC.(ECON.), Economic and Social History
LAWSON, Mrs. R. M., M.COM., D.SOC.SC., South-East Asian Economics
PAREKH, B. C., M.A., PH.D., Politics

ATTACHED INSTITUTES AND CENTRES:
*Institute of Education:* Dir. Prof. V. A. MCCLELLAND, M.A., PH.D., F.R.S.A.
*Centre for South-East Asian Studies:* Dir. D. K. BASSETT, PH.D.
*Institute of European Studies:* Dir. Prof. A. G. LEHMANN, M.A., D.PHIL.
*Institute for Health Studies:* Dir. Prof. H. MCDONNELL, M.B., CH.B., M.SC., M.F.C.M., F.R.S.M., F.S.S.
*Institute of Modern Dutch Studies:* Dir. Prof. P. K. KING, M.A.
*Institute of Nursing Studies:* Dir. Miss M. CLARKE, S.R.N., R.N.T., B.SC., M.PHIL.
*Wolfson Institute* (Gerontology): S.E.R.C. Senior Research Fellow, Wolfson Professor and Dir. Prof. J. G. PHILLIPS, PH.D., D.SC., F.I.BIOL., F.A.Z., F.R.S.M., F.R.S.
*Centre for the Joint Study of Economics, Politics and Sociology:* Dir. Prof. J. S. G. WILSON, M.A.
*Audio-Visual Centre:* Dir. (vacant.)
*Computer Centre:* Dir. D. W. BEARD, M.SC., PH.D.
*Language Teaching Centre:* Controller: Prof. P. K. KING, M.A.

## UNIVERSITY OF KEELE
KEELE,
STAFFORDSHIRE, ST5 5BG
Telephone: 0782-621111.

**Founded as University College of North Staffordshire 1949, University of Keele 1962.**

*Chancellor:* H.R.H. THE PRINCESS MARGARET, COUNTESS OF SNOWDON, C.I., G.C.V.O.
*Vice-Chancellor:* DAVID HARRISON, M.A., PH.D., SC.D., F.R.I.C., F.I.CHEM.E.
*Registrar:* J. F. N. HODGKINSON, O.B.E., M.A.
*Librarian:* J. M. WOOD, M.A., F.L.A.
Library: see Libraries.
**Number of teaching staff: 308, including 34 professors.**
Number of students: 2,837 undergraduates, 311 full-time postgraduates.
Publication: *University Calendar.*

PROFESSORS:
*Board of Humanities:*
ADAMS, D. K., M.A., A.M., D.PHIL., American Studies
BANCE, A. F., PH.D., German
BROOME, J. H., PH.D., D.U., French
CHARLTON, J. M. T., M.A., F.S.A., Classics
DICKINSON, P., M.A., F.R.C.O., L.R.A.M., A.R.C.M., Music
GOLDMAN, A. M., A.M., PH.D., American Studies
LAMPERT, E., L. ÈS L., D.PHIL., F.R.S.L., Russian Studies
RIVET, A. L. F., M.A., F.S.A., Classics
ROBERTS, M. A. M., M.A., English
ROLO, P. J. V., M.A., F.R.HIST.S., History
SWINBURNE, R. G., B.PHIL., M.A., Philosophy

*Board of Social Sciences:*
DWYER, D. J., PH.D., Geography
EGGLESTON, S. J., B.SC.(ECON.), M.A., D.LITT., Education
FISHMAN, L., PH.D., Economics
FRANKENBERG, R. J., M.A.(ECON.), PH.D., Sociology and Social Anthropology
HARRISON, M., B.A.(ECON.), D.E.S., D.PHIL., Politics
HUNTER, I. M. L., D.PHIL., Psychology
HUTT, S. J., M.A., Psychology
JAMES, A. M., B.SC.(ECON.), International Relations
KAY, M. R., LL.B., PH.D., BAR.-AT-LAW, Law
KEMPA, R. F., ING.CHEM., PH.D., Science Education
STEVENSON, OLIVE, M.A., Social Policy and Social Work
THOMPSON, D., LL.B., PH.D., BAR.-AT-LAW, Law

*Board of Natural Sciences:*
ABER, G. M., M.D., PH.D., F.R.C.P., Postgraduate Medicine
ARME, C., PH.D., F.I.BIOL., Biological Sciences
EVANS, E. F., PH.D., Communication and Neuroscience
FULLER, W., PH.D., A.K.C., F.INST.P., Physics
HUTCHINSON, E. C., M.D., F.R.C.P., Postgraduate Medicine
KELLING, G., PH.D., F.G.S., Geology
KENDALL, P. C., PH.D., F.I.M.A., F.R.A.S., Mathematics
LLOYD, J. B., D.SC., PH.D., F.P.S., F.R.S.C., Biological Sciences
MACKAY, D. M., PH.D., F.INST.P., Communication
MILLAR, I. T., PH.D., C.CHEM., F.R.S.C., Chemistry
MORTIMER, C. T., PH.D., D.SC., C.CHEM., F.R.S.C., Inorganic Chemistry
PLESCH, P. H., M.A., SC.D., C.CHEM., F.R.S.C., Chemistry
REEVES, C. M., M.A., PH.D., F.B.C.S., F.I.M.A., Computer Science

*Adult Education:*
DYSON, R. F., PH.D., Director

READERS:
*Board of Humanities:*
DAY, J. P. DE C., M.A., Philosophy
GOMME, A. H., J.P., M.A., PH.D., English
KILLHAM, E. J., M.A., English
LEES, J. D., M.A., PH.D., American Studies
RAW, BARBARA, M.A., F.S.A., English

*Board of Social Sciences:*
AKEHURST, M. B., M.A., LL.B., D.U., BAR.-AT-LAW, Law
DERBYSHIRE, E., M.SC., PH.D., F.G.S., Physical Geography
RICHARDSON, J. J., PH.D., Communication and Neuroscience

*Board of Natural Sciences:*
BORRELL, P., PH.D., C.CHEM., F.R.S.C., Chemistry
HAMMOND, P., PH.D., Communication and Neuroscience

HOLLOWAY, D. G., PH.D., F.INST.P., Physics
JONES, G., PH.D., D.SC., C.CHEM., F.R.S.C., Chemistry
LAINÉ, D. C., PH.D., D.SC., C.ENG., F.I.E.E., F.INST.P., Physics
LIEBECK, H., M.A., M.SC., PH.D., Mathematics
MORGAN, E. D., D.PHIL., C.CHEM., F.R.S.C., Chemistry
PARK, R. G., PH.D., F.G.S., M.I.GEOL., Geology
STEEL, W. M., M.B., CH.B., F.R.C.S., Postgraduate Medicine
SMITH, P., PH.D., F.I.M.A., Mathematics
YARDLEY, H. J., PH.D., Biological Sciences

## UNIVERSITY OF KENT AT CANTERBURY
CANTERBURY,
KENT, CT2 7NZ
Telephone: (0227) 66822.

Founded 1965.
Academic year: October to June.

*Chancellor:* The Rt. Hon. J. GRIMOND, M.P., T.D., LL.D., D.C.L.
*Vice-Chancellor:* D. J. E. INGRAM, M.A., D.PHIL., D.SC., F.INST.P.
*Deputy Vice-Chancellor:* M. J. C. VILE, M.A., PH.D.
*Pro-Vice-Chancellors:* M. IRWIN, B.A., B.LITT., G. RICKAYZEN, PH.D., F.INST.P.
*Registrar and Finance Officer:* A. D. LINFOOT, M.A.
*Librarian:* W. J. SIMPSON, B.A., A.L.A., F.R.S.A.

Number of teachers: 468.
Number of students: 4,317.

Publications: *Prospectus, Graduate Studies Handbooks, Gazette, Vice-Chancellor's Annual Report.*

DEANS:
*Faculty of Humanities:* C. H. WAKE, M.A., D.U.
*Faculty of Social Sciences:* J. J. HUGHES, B.SC.(ECON.)
*Faculty of Natural Sciences:* Prof. G. RICKAYZEN, PH.D.
*School of Mathematical Studies:* Prof. G. B. WETHERILL, PH.D., A.R.C.S., D.I.C. (Chairman).

*Faculty of Humanities:*

PROFESSORS:
BIRMINGHAM, D., PH.D., Modern History
BUTLER, R. J., M.A., Philosophy
COLLINSON, P., M.A., PH.D., F.R.HIST.S., F.A.A.H., History
DAVISON, P., M.A., PH.D., English and American Literature
FOAKES, R. A., M.A., PH.D., English and American Literature
GIBSON, R. D. D., PH.D., French
GREGOR, I. C. S., PH.D., Modern English Literature
HOLT, S. C., M.A., PH.D., European Studies
IRWIN, M., B.A., B.LITT., English Literature
KINKEAD-WEEKES, M., M.A., English and American Literature

Mylne, Vivienne G., ph.d., chev. des palmes academiques, French
Read, D., m.a., b.litt., ph.d., f.r.hist.s., Modern English History
Swanston, H. F. G., m.a., m.litt., ph.d., Theology

READERS:

Bann, S., m.a., ph.d., Modern Cultural Studies
Bolt, Christine A., ph.d., American History
Cardinal, R. T., m.a., ph.d., Comparative Literature
Hampshire, P., m.a., d.litt., French
James, W. L. G., m.a., d.phil., Victorian and Modern Literature
Radford, C. J., d.phil., Philosophy
Wake, C. H., m.a., d.u., Modern French and African Literature

*Faculty of Natural Sciences:*

PROFESSORS:

Brown, J. B., d.phil., Experimental Physics
Connor, J. A., m.a., ph.d., Inorganic Chemistry
Jennison, R. C., ph.d., f.r.a.s., f.inst.p., c.eng., f.i.e.e., f.r.s.a., Physical Electronics
Lanigan, M. J., m.sc., ph.d., Digital Electronics
Powles, J. G., m.sc., ph.d., d. ès s., f.inst.p., Physics
Rickayzen, G., ph.d., Theoretical Physics
Stacey, K. A., ph.d., d.i.c., f.i.biol., Molecular Biology

READERS:

Cain, R. B., ph.d., d.sc., f.l.s., Biology
Gutteridge, W. E., m.a., ph.d., Biochemical Parasitology
Jackson, D. A., ph.d., Experimental Physics
Knowles, C. J., ph.d., Biochemistry
Lyle, S. J., ph.d., d.sc., a.r.i.c., Chemistry
McDonnell, J. A. M., ph.d., Space Sciences
Parker, E. A., m.a., ph.d., f.r.a.s., Radio Communications
Sobhy, M. I., ph.d., Electronics
Strange, J. H., ph.d., f.inst.p., Physics
Williams, A., m.a., d.phil., Organic Chemistry

*Faculty of Social Sciences:*

PROFESSORS:

Allingham, M., m.a.(econ.), ph.d., Economic Theory
Bird, P. A., b.sc.(econ.), f.c.a., Accounting
Davies, B. P., m.a., d.phil., d.p.s.a., Social Policy
Flowerdew, A. D. J., m.a., Management Science
George, V., m.a., ph.d., Social Administration and Social Work
McLellan, D. T., m.a., d.phil., Political Theory
Metcalf, D., m.a.(econ.), ph.d., Economics
Mingay, G. E., ph.d., Agrarian History
Pahl, R. E., m.a., ph.d., Sociology
Palley, Claire D. T., ll.b., ph.d., Law
Pressnell, L. S., ph.d., Economic and Social History
Seymour-Ure, C. K., m.a., d.phil., Government
Simpson, A. W. B., m.a., d.c.l., j.p., Law
Stephenson, G. M., ph.d., f.b.ps.s., Social Psychology
Stirling, P., m.a., d.phil., Sociology

Thirwall, A. P., m.a., ph.d., Applied Economics
Vile, M. J. C., m.a., ph.d., Political Science
Warren, M. D., m.d., b.s., d.p.h., d.i.h., f.r.c.p., f.f.c.m., Social Medicine

READERS:

Armstrong, W. A., ph.d., Social and Demographic History
Burton, J. W., ph.d., d.sc., International Relations
Craven, J. A. G., b.a., Economics
Davis, J. H. R., ph.d., Social Anthropology
Duncanson, D. J., o.b.e., m.a., ph.d., South-East Asian Studies
Groom, A. J. R., m.a., d. ès sc., International Relations
Hooker, M. B., ll.m., Comparative Law
Kumar, J. K., m.a., m.sc., ph.d., Sociology
Macdonald, M. G., m.a., ll.m., f.c.a., Accounting and Taxation

*School of Mathematical Studies:*

PROFESSORS:

Chisholm, J. S. R., m.a., ph.d., m.r.i.a., Applied Mathematics
Noble, M. E., m.a., ph.d., Pure Mathematics
Wetherill, G. B., ph.d., a.r.c.s., d.i.c., Statistics

READERS:

Common, A. K., ph.d., Applied Mathematics
Moran, S., m.sc., ph.d., Pure Mathematics

ATTACHED INSTITUTES:

**Computing Laboratory.**
Director: E. B. Spratt, ph.d., f.i.m.a., m.b.c.s.
Professor: P. J. Brown, m.a., ph.d., f.b.c.s., Computer Science.

**Unit for the History, Philosophy and Social Relations of Science.**
Professor: M. P. Crosland, m.sc., ph.d.

**Institute of Languages and Linguistics.**
Director: J. Martin, m.a.

**School of Continuing Education.**
Director: A. T. Barbrook, ph.d.

# UNIVERSITY OF LANCASTER

BAILRIGG, LANCASTER, LA1 4YW
Telephone: Lancaster (0524) 65201.
Telex: 65111 Lancul G.
Founded 1964.

*Chancellor:* H.R.H. Princess Alexandra.
*Pro-Chancellor:* Sir Alastair Pilkington, m.a., d.tech., d.eng., f.r.s.
*Vice-Chancellor:* Prof. P. A. Reynolds, m.a.
*Secretary:* G. M. Cockburn, m.a.
*Registrar:* M. D. Forster, m.a., b.sc. (Econ.)
*Librarian:* Arthur Davies, b.a., a.l.a.
Library: see Libraries.
Number of teachers: 470.

Number of full-time students: c. 4,000 undergraduate, 600 postgraduate.

Publications: *Undergraduate Prospectus*†, *Graduate Studies Prospectus*†, *Graduate Studies Prospectus*† (School of Management and Organisational Sciences) (each annually), *Annual Report.*

The university has no faculties; boards of studies are responsible for the co-ordination of courses.

PROFESSORS:

Arafat, W. N., Arabic and Islamic Studies
Bellany, I., Politics
Bennett, S. N., Educational Research
Benson, J. H., Philosophy
Bevington, J. C., Chemistry
Bowker, Rev. J. W., Religious Studies
Bray, R. W., Music
Brunner, Elizabeth, Economics
Candlin, C. N., Linguistics
Carroll, D. R., English Literature
Checkland, P. B., Systems
Clegg, A. B., Nuclear Physics
Clenshaw, C. W., Mathematics
Fairbairn, W. M., Theoretical Physics
French, M. J., Engineering
Hadley, R. D., Social Administration
Harris, S. L., Engineering
Higman, B., Computer Studies
Holmes, G. S., History
Hussey, S. S., English Language and Medieval Literature
Johnson, J. H., Geography
Krejčí, J., European Studies
Lawrence, R. J., Marketing
Lawrenson, T. E., Theatre Studies
Leech, G. N., Linguistics
Levy, P. M., Psychology
Lloyd, E. H., Mathematics
MacBean, A. I., Economics
Mansfield, T. A., Biological Sciences
Mercer, A., Operational Research
Morgan, K. J., Chemistry
Murray, W. A., English
O'Donnell, T., Hydrology
Peasnell, K. V., Accounting and Finance
Perkin, H. J., Social History
Pigott, C. D., Biological Sciences
Potts, W. T. W., Biological Sciences
Richmond, J., Religious Studies
Ross, A. M., Educational Research
Shennan, J. H., History
Sherry, N., English Literature
Shimmin, Sylvia B. N., Behaviour in Organizations
Sibley, F. N., Philosophy
Simpson, M. G., Operational Research
Smart, N., Religious Studies
Stamp, E., Accounting Theory
Townsend, H., Economics
Tredgold, R. H., Physics
Tutt, N., Applied Social Studies
Vaughan, Michalina E. F., Sociology
Wallington, P. T., Law
Wardman, H. W., French Studies
Williams, G. L., Educational Planning
Woolrych, A. H., History
Young, P. C., Environmental Sciences
Zeman, Z. A. B., Central and South-Eastern European Studies

READERS:

Bowker, Margaret, History of Education
Devlin, K. J., Mathematics
Fielder, G., Environmental Sciences
Foster, F., Physics
Fox, R., History of Science
Heaton, F. W., Biological Sciences
Hodge, P., Chemistry

# UNIVERSITIES

HUNT, S., Biological Sciences
KERSHAW, D., Mathematics
LEE, P. M., Physics
MORGAN, MARGERY M., English Literature
SAMPSON, G. R., Linguistics
SMALL, R. W. H., Crystallography
SMOKER, P. L., Peace and Conflict Research
TAYLOR, J., Economics
TUCKER, R. W., Physics
WILLIAMS, L. A. J., Environmental Sciences

## UNIVERSITY OF LEEDS
LEEDS, LS2 9JT
Telephone: (0532) 31751.
Telex: 557939.
Founded 1904.

*Chancellor:* H.R.H. The Duchess of KENT, G.C.V.O.
*Pro-Chancellor:* Sir RICHARD GRAHAM, Bt., O.B.E., D.L.
*Vice-Chancellor:* (vacant).
*Pro-Vice-Chancellor:* Prof. B. HOGAN, LL.B.
*Registrar:* J. J. WALSH, M.A.
*Librarian:* D. COX, B.A., A.L.A.
Library: see Libraries.
Number of teachers: 1,115.
Number of students: 9,164 undergraduates, 1,663 postgraduates.

Publications: *University Calendar†, Guide to Applicants†, Leeds University Review, Guide to Current Research, Register of Graduates.*

### DEANS:

*Faculty of Arts:* Prof. D. E. JENKINS, M.A.
*Faculty of Economic and Social Studies:* D. WARWICK, PH.D.
*Faculty of Education:* W. B. STEPHENS, M.A.(ED.).
*Faculty of Law:* Prof. G. N. GLOVER, LL.B.
*Faculty of Science:* A. WREN, M.A.
*Faculty of Engineering:* R. D. MACKEY, PH.D.
*Faculty of Medicine:* Prof. D. R. WOOD, B.M., B.CH., M.A., F.I.BIOL.

### PROFESSORS:

*Faculty of Arts:*
ARNOTT, W. G., M.A., PH.D., Greek Language and Literature
BARNARD, J., M.A., B.LITT., English Literature
BARNARD, L. W., M.A., PH.D., Theology and Religious Studies
BUTLER, L. A. S., M.A., PH.D., F.S.A., Archaeology
CROSS, A., M.A., PH.D., Russian
DAVIES, G. A., M.A., D.PHIL., Spanish and Portuguese
DILKS, D. N., B.A., International History
DOWNER, G. B., B.A., Chinese Studies
GIBBONS, B. C., M.A., PH.D., English Literature
HOLLAND, R. F., M.A., B.PHIL., Philosophy
HOOK, B. G., B.A., Chinese Studies
HOPE, T. E., D.SC., M.A., PH.D., French Language and Literature
JENKINS, D. E., M.A., Theology and Religious Studies
KNIGHT, K. G., M.A., PH.D., German Language and Literatture
MILLIGAN, M. O., M.A., Philosophy
MATTINGLY, H. B., M.A., Ancient History
MORPURGO, J. E., D.H.L., D.LITT., LIT.D., American Literature
O'DONNELL, W. R., M.A., Linguistics and Phonetics
RUSHTON, J. G., M.A., D.PHIL., Music
SAWYER, P. H., M.A., Medieval History
SHIPPEY, T. A., M.A., English Language and Medieval English Literature
TAYLOR, A. J., M.A., F.R.H.S., Modern History
TAYLOR, J., M.A., History
THODY, P., M.A., French Literature
WHITE, D. M., M.A., PH.D., Italian Language and Literature
WOODMAN, A. J., PH.D., Latin Language and Literature
YOUNG, M. J. L., M.A., PH.D., F.R.A.S., Semitic Studies

*Faculty of Economic and Social Studies:*
ALLEN, V. L., PH.D., Sociology of the Industrial Society
BAUMAN, Z., M.A., PH.D., Sociology
BEETHAM, D., M.A.(ECON.), Politics
BERESFORD, M. W., M.A., Economic History
BUTTERWORTH, J., M.SC., PH.D., Management Studies
CROSSLEY, J. R., B.SC.(ECON.), Industrial Relations
GREVE, J., B.SC.(ECON.), Social Policy and Administration
GWILLIAM, K. M., B.A., Transport Economics
JONES, G. R. J., M.A., F.S.A., Historical Geography
KIRKBY, M. J., PH.D., Geography
MAUNDERS, K. T., B.SC., F.C.C.A., Business Finance and Accounting
PHILLIPS, G. D. A., M.SC., Econometrics
RAINNIE, G. F., M.A., Economic Studies
SURREY, M., M.A., Economics
WARWICK, D., PH.D., Sociology
WILSON, A. G., M.A., Urban and Social Geography

*Faculty of Education:*
GODSEN, P. H. J. H., M.A., PH.D., Education
JEPSON, N. A., PH.D., Adult Education
LAYTON, D., M.A., M.SC., Education (Science)
SUTHERLAND, MARGARET B., M.ED., PH.D., Education

*Faculty of Law:*
DRAKE, C. D., M.A., LL.B., BAR.-AT-LAW, English Law
HOGAN, T. B., LL.B., BAR.-AT-LAW, Common Law
ROGERS, W. V. H., M.A., BAR.-AT-LAW, Common Law

*Faculty of Science:*
ALEXANDER, R. McN., M.A., PH.D., D.SC., F.I.BIOL., Zoology
AYSCOUGH, P. B., M.A., PH.D., SC.D., F.R.S.C., Physical Chemistry
BRIDEN, J. C., M.A., PH.D., F.G.S., F.R.A.S., Geophysics
CARE, A. D., PH.D., D.SC., B.V.M.S., M.R.C.V.S., Animal Physiology and Nutrition
COVE, D. J., M.A., PH.D., Genetics
CRIGHTON, D. G., M.A., PH.D., Applied Mathematical Studies
DRAKE, F. R., PH.D., Genetics

## U.K. (GREAT BRITAIN)

DUGDALE, J. S., M.A., D.PHIL., F.R.S.C., Physics
ELSTON, J., PH.D., F.I.BIOL., Crop Science
FRANCIS, E. H., D.SC., F.R.S.E., F.G.S., Earth Sciences
GOLDIE, A. W., M.A., Pure Mathematics
GOLDSWORTHY, F. A., M.SC., PH.D., F.I.M.A., Applied Mathematics
GRAY, P., M.A., PH.D., SC.D., F.R.S.C., Physical Chemistry
GREENWOOD, N. N., D.SC., Inorganic and Structural Chemistry
HOLLIMAN, F. G., M.A., PH.D., F.R.S.C., Organic Chemistry
JONES, H. GWYNNE, B.SC., F.B.PS.S., Psychology
LANCE, E. C., M.A., PH.D., Pure Mathematics
LEE, D. L., PH.D., F.I.BIOL., Agricultural Zoology
LEEDALE, G. F., PH.D., D.SC., Botany
MARDIA, K. V., M.SC., PH.D., D.SC., F.A.S.A., F.I.M.S., Applied Statistics
MARSDEN, P. L., PH.D., F.INST.P., Physics
MORGAN, G. J., M.SC., PH.D., F.INST.P., Theoretical Physics
NORTH, A. C. T., PH.D., M.INST.P., Biophysics
PRICE, H. L., M.A., M.SC., PH.D., C.ENG., F.R.AE.S., F.I.M.A., Mathematics for Applied Science
SAMMES, P. G., PH.D., D.SC., D.I.C., M.R.S.C., C.CHEM., Organic Chemistry
SHAW, B. L., PH.D., F.R.S., Inorganic and Structural Chemistry
SMITH, K., PH.D., Computational Science
WARD, I. M., M.A., P.DHIL., F.INST.P., F.P.R.I., Physics

*Faculty of Engineering:*
BRADLEY, D., PH.D., C.ENG., M.I.MECH.E., F.INST.P., Mechanical Engineering
BROOK, R. J., SC.D., Ceramics
COLE, B. N., PH.D., C.ENG., F.I.MECH.E., Mechanical Engineering
CUSENS, A. R., PH.D., C.ENG., F.I.C.E., F.R.S.E., F.I.STRUCT.E., Civil Engineering
DIXON-LEWIS, G., M.A., D.PHIL., Fuel and Energy
DOWSON, D., PH.D., D.SC., C.ENG., F.I.MECH.E., F.A.S.M.E., A.S.L.E., Engineering Fluid Mechanics
GROSBERG, P., M.SC.(ENG.), PH.D., C.ENG., M.I.MECH.E., F.T.I., Textile Engineering
GUILE, A. E., PH.D., D.SC.(ENG.), C.ENG., F.I.E.E., Electrical and Electronic Engineering
HASELDEN, G. G., D.SC., PH.D., D.I.C., A.C.G.I., C.ENG., F.I.CHEM.E., F.I.I.P., S.F.INST.E., F.R.P.S., Chemical Engineering
LAWRENSON, P. J., D.SC., C.ENG., F.I.E.E., F.I.E.E.E., F.ENG., Electrical Engineering
McGREAVY, C., D.ENG., C.ENG., F.I.CHEM.E., F.B.C.S., Chemical Engineering
McINTYRE, J. E., B.SC., C.CHEM., F.R.S.C., F.T.I., Textile Industries
MARA, D., PH.D., M.I.C.E., M.I.P.H.E., M.I.BIOL., Civil Engineering
MATTHEWS, P. A., PH.D., C.ENG., M.I.E.E., F.I.E.E.E., Electrical and Electronic Engineering
MAY, A. D., M.A., C.ENG., M.I.C.E., M.I.H.E., F.C.I.T., Transport Engineering
NUTTING, J., M.A., SC.D., PH.D., C.ENG., F.I.M., Metallurgy

RATTEE, I. D., O.B.E., B.SC., F.R.S.C., A.R.C.S., Colour Chemistry and Dyeing
RHODES, J. D., PH.D., D.SC., F.I.E.E.E., C.ENG., M.I.E.E., Electrical and Electronic Engineering
ROBINSON, DAVID S., PH.D., Food Science
SMITH, G. H., PH.D., Animal Physiology and Nutrition
WILLIAMS, A., PH.D., C.ENG., F.R.S.C., F.INST.E., F.INST.PET., F.I.GAS.E., Fuel and Combustion Science
YOUNG, P. A., M.A., PH.D., C.ENG., F.I.M.M., F.I.MIN.E., Mining and Mineral Sciences

*Faculty of Medicine:*
BARRETT, A. M., PH.D., Pharmacology
BASKER, R. M., M.D.S., L.D.S.R.C.S., M.G.D.S.R.C.S., Dental Prosthetics
BEVIS, D. C. A., M.B., CH.B., F.R.C.O.G., Obstetrics and Gynaecology (St. James's University Hospital)
BIRD, C. C., PH.D., F.R.C.PATH., Pathology
BURCH, P. R. J., M.A., PH.D., Medical Physics
CLARK, E. R., PH.D., M.P.S., C.CHEM., F.R.S.C., Pharmacology
COOKE, Mrs. E. MARY, B.SC., M.D., L.R.C.P., M.R.C.S., F.R.C., Clinical Microbiology
COOPER, E. H., M.D., B.S., D PHIL., D.SC., F.R.C.P., Experimental Pathology and Cancer Research
CRABB, H. S. M., M.D.S., PH.D., F.D.S.R.C.S., Conservative Dentistry
DICKSON, R., Orthopaedic Surgery
ELLIS, R. E., PH.D., Medical Physics
GEE, D. J., M.B., B.S., F.R.C.PATH., D.M.J., Forensic Medicine
GILES, G. R., M.D., F.R.C.S., Surgery (St James's University Hospital)
GOWLAND, G., PH.D., F.R.C.PATH., Immunology
HERVEY, G. R., M.A., M.B., B.CHIR., PH.D., Physiology
HOLMES, R. L., M.B., CH.B., PH.D., D.SC., Anatomy
HOPPER, F. E., M.D.S., F.D.S.R.C.S., F.F.D.R.C.S.I., Dental Surgery
JACKSON, D., D.D.S., M.D.S., L.D.S., Children's Dentistry
JOHNSTON, D., M.D., F.R.C.S.E., F.R.C.S.G., Surgery (Leeds General Infirmary)
JOSLIN, C. A. F., M.B., B.S., F.R.C.R., D.M.R.T., M.I.E.R.E., C.ENG., Radiotherapy
LINDEN, R. J., M.B., CH.B., PH.D., D.SC., F.R.C.P., Cadiovascular Studies
LOSOWSKY, M. S., M.D., F.R.C.P., Medicine (St James's University Hospital)
MCDOWALL, G. M. D., M.D., F.F.A.R.C.S., Anaesthesia
MAINWARING, W. I. P., PH.D., D.SC., Biochemistry
MEADOW, S. R., M.A., F.R.C.P., D.OBST.R.C.O.G., D.C.H., Paediatrics and Child Health (St. James's University Hospital)
MINDHAM, R. H. S., M.D., F.R.C.P., F.R.C.PSYCH., D.C.H., Psychiatry
MOORE, W. J., D.SC., PH.D., Anatomy with relation to Dentistry
MORGAN, D. B., M.D., M.R.C.PATH., Chemical Pathology
RICHARDS, I. D. G., M.D., PH.D., F.R.C.P., D.P.H., F.F.C.M., Community Medicine and General Practice
ROBINSON, DONALD S., M.A., PH.D., Biochemistry
SCOTT, J. S., M.D., F.R.C.S.(ED.), F.R.C.O.G., Obstetrics and Gynaecology (Leeds Maternity Hospital)
SMITHELLS, R. W., M.B., B.S., F.R.C.P., D.C.H., Paediatrics and Child Health
STITCH, S. R., PH.D., F.R.S.C., Steroid Endocrinology
WATSON, D. H., PH.D., F.I.BIOL., General Microbiology
WOOD, D. R., B.M., B.CH., B.SC., M.A., Applied Pharmacology
WRIGHT, V., M.D., F.R.C.P., Rheumatology

READERS:

*Faculty of Arts:*
BRIDGE, F. R., PH.D., International History
HARTLEY, B. R., M.A., F.S.A., Archaeology
MUIR, LYNETTE R., PH.D., French
OLBY, R. C., M.A., D.PHIL., History and Philosophy of Science
RAVETZ, J. R., PH.D., History and Philosophy of Science
THOMPSON, R. L., M.A., Celtic Studies
WANGERMANN, E., M.A., D.PHIL., Modern History
WOODS, J. A., M.A., Modern History

*Faculty of Economics and Social Studies:*
REES, P. H., M.A., PH.D., Geography

*Faculty of Science:*
BROADHEAD, E., M.A., D.PHIL., Animal Ecology
CARSON, A. S., M.SC., PH.D., D.SC., Physical Chemistry
COLLINSON, E., M.A., PH.D., Physical Chemistry
DALES, H. G., M.A., PH.D., Pure Mathematics
EVANS, L. V., PH.D., D.SC., Plant Sciences
HARBERD, D. J., M.SC., D.SC., Agricultural Botany
HILLAS, A. M., PH.D., Cosmic Physics
JENNINGS, J. B., PH.D., D.SC., Invertebrate Zoology
KNORRING, O. VON, M.SC., PH.D., Mineral Chemistry
MCCONNELL, J. C., PH.D., Pure Mathematics
ROBSON, J. C., PH.D., Pure Mathematics
RUBIO, J. E., E.D., M.S., PH.D., Applied Mathematics
TURNER, J. R. G., PH.D., Genetics
WATSON, A. A., PH.D., Cosmic Physics

*Faculty of Engineering:*
BENNETT, E. W., PH.D., C.ENG., F.I.C.E., M.I.STRUCT.E., Civil Engineering
BLAZYNSKI, T. Z., PH.D., C.ENG., M.I.MECH.E., Mechanical Engineering
DENTON, M. J., D.SC., Textile Industries
FOX, J. A., B.SC., C.ENG., Civil Engineering
JOHNSON, D. J., M.SC., PH.D., Textile Physics
MOBBS, F. R., M.SC., D.I.C., Mechanical Engineering
MORGAN, D. V., M.SC., PH.D., C.ENG., F.INST.P., M.I.E.E., Electrical Engineering
PARSONS, B., PH.D., C.ENG., Mechanical Engineering
SCULLY, J. C., M.A., PH.D., Corrosion Science
STAINSBY, G., M.A., PH.D., C.CHEM., F.R.I.C., Food Science
TRUTER, E. V., PH.D., D.SC., Textile Chemistry

*Faculty of Medicine:*
BROWN, S. B., PH.D., Biochemistry
DAWSON, J. B., PH.D., Medical Physics
DOMBAL, F. T. DE, M.A., M.D., F.R.C.S., Surgery
ELLIS, F. R., PH.D., D.A., F.F.A.R.C.S., Anaesthesia
HULLIN, R. P., M.SC., PH.D., Biochemistry
OAKEY, R. E., PH.D., D.SC., F.R.S.C., Steroid Endocrinology
SMITH, W. D. A., O.B.E., M.D., D.A., F.F.A.R.C.S., Anaesthesia
SUTHERLAND, T. W., M.D., F.R.C.PATH., Pathology

AFFILIATED COLLEGES:

**College of the Resurrection:** Mirfield, Yorks.; f. 1902 by the Community of the Resurrection for the training of priests.
*Principal:* Rev. B. GREEN, C.R., M.A.
*Vice-Principal:* Rev. D. LLOYD, C.R., M.A.
*Secretary:* Bro. D. WILSON, C.R.
*Registrar:* Rev. C. HARRISON, C.R., M.A.
Number of tutors: 5.
Number of students: 44 men.

**College of Ripon and York St. John:** York; f. 1841; Ripon; f. 1862; College of Higher Education.
*Principal:* G. P. MCGREGOR, M.ED., D.PHIL., F.R.S.A.
*Vice-Principal:* Rev. H. T. BATEY, M.A.
*Registrar:* S. D. ILLINGWORTH, B.SC.
*Senior Administrative Officer:* R. WILKINSON, B.COM., A.I.C.A.
Number of teachers: 175.
Number of students: 1,700.

## UNIVERSITY OF LEICESTER

UNIVERSITY ROAD,
LEICESTER, LEI 7RH
Telephone: (0533) 554455.
Telex: 34 11 98.
Telegrams: University, Leicester.

University College founded 1918; Charter 1950; University Charter 1957.

*Chancellor:* Prof. Sir ALAN HODGKIN, O.M., K.B.E., M.A., SC.D., M.D., D.SC., F.R.S.
*Vice-Chancellor:* M. SHOCK, M.A.
*Registrar:* M. A. BAATZ, M.A.
*Librarian:* D. G. F. WALKER, M.A., LL.B., A.L.A.

Library: see Libraries.
Number of teachers: 535, including 58 professors.
Number of students (full-time): 4,823.

Publications: *Calendar, Prospectus* (annually), *Annual Report.*

DEANS:

*Faculty of Arts:* Prof. H. B. WILSON, M.A.
*Faculty of Science:* Prof. R. WHITTAM, PH.D., M.A., F.R.S.
*Faculty of Social Sciences:* J. BONNER, B.SC.(ECON.), B.PHIL.
*Faculty of Law:* Prof. D. G. BARNSLEY, LL.M.
*Faculty of Medicine:* Prof. R. KILPATRICK, C.B.E., M.D., F.R.C.P.

**PROFESSORS:**

*Faculty of Arts:*
BERNBAUM, G., B.SC.(ECON.), F.R.S.A., Education
COLLINS, P. A. W., M.A., English Literature
CUNNINGHAM, J. S., B.A., B.LITT., English
EVERITT, A. M., M.A., PH.D., F.S.A., F.R.HIST.S., English Local History
FITTON BROWN, A. D., M.A., Classics
HEMMINGS, F. W. J., M.A., D.PHIL., French Literature
HERRMANN, L. J., M.A., F.S.A., History of Art
McWILLIAM, G. H., M.A., Italian
MARTIN, G. H., M.A., D.PHIL., F.S.A., F.R.HIST.S., History
MEGAW, J. V. S., M.A., F.S.A., Archaeology
PATERSON, J. H., M.A., Geography
WARNER, G., M.A., F.R.HIST.S., Modern History
WILLSON, H. B., M.A., German
WRIGHT, D. S., M.A., Education

*Faculty of Science:*
BEEBY, J. L., M.A., PH.D., Theoretical Physics
DAVIES, R. O., M.A., PH.D., Pure Mathematics
DAVIS, E. A., PH.D., Experimental Physics
FREEMAN, P. R., M.A., PH.D., Mathematical Statistics
JONES, T. B., PH.D., D.SC., F.INST.P., Ionospheric Physics
MACGREGOR, H. C., PH.D., Zoology
MACLELLAN, G. D. S., M.A., PH.D., C.ENG., F.I.MECH.E., F.I.E.E., Engineering
MEADOWS, A. J., M.A., D.PHIL., M.SC., Astronomy; History of Science; Primary Communications
PEACOCK, R. D., PH.D., D.SC., Inorganic Chemistry
PONTER, A. R. S., PH.D., M.A., A.R.C.S., Engineering
POUNDS, K. A., PH.D., F.R.S., Space Physics
SLUCKIN, W., PH.D., F.B.PS.S., Psychology
SMITH, H., D.SC., PH.D., F.I.BIOL., Botany
SYMONS, M. C. R., PH.D., D.SC., F.R.S.C., Physical Chemistry
TARNEY, J., PH.D., F.G.S., Geology
TRIPPETT, S., M.A., PH.D., SC.D., Organic Chemistry

*Faculty of the Social Sciences:*
ALDCROFT, D. H., PH.D., Economic and Social History
BANKS, J. A., M.A., Sociology
BANKS, OLIVE, PH.D., Sociology
JACKSON, P. M., PH.D., Economics; Public Sector Economics
PATERSON, J. H., M.A., Geography
SPENCE, J. E., B.A., B.SC.(ECON.), Politics

*Faculty of Law:*
BARNSLEY, D. G., LL.M., Law
DASHWOOD, A., M.A., Law
GRIEW, E. J., M.A., LL.B., BAR.-AT-LAW, Law
GRODECKI, J. K., M.A., B.EN DR., BAR.-AT-LAW, Law

*Faculty of Medicine:*
BECK, F., M.D., D.SC., L.R.C.P., M.R.C.S., Anatomy
BELL, P. R. F., M.D., F.R.C.S., Surgery
BLAKELEY, A. G. H., D.PHIL., B.M.B.CH., Applied Physiology
BRAMMAR, W. J., PH.D., Biochemistry
BRANDON, S., M.D., D.P.M., D.C.H., F.R.C.PSYCH., M.R.C.P., Psychiatry
CLARKE, M., M.B.B.S., M.R.C.S., L.R.C.P., D.P.H., M.F.C.M., Epidemiology
KILPATRICK, R., C.B.E., M.D., F.R.C.P., Pharmacology and Therapeutics
MACVICAR, J., M.D., F.R.C.S., F.R.C.O.G., Obstetrics and Gynaecology
MARINKER, M., M.B.B.S., F.R.C.G.P., General Practice
PRITCHARD, R. H., PH.D., Genetics
ROSENTHAL, A. R., M.D., Ophthalmology
SHAW, W. V., B.A., M.D., Biochemistry
SIMPSON, H., M.D., M.D., F.R.C.P.E., D.C.H., D.OBST.R.C.O.G., Child Health
SMITH, G., M.D., M.R.C.S., L.R.C.P., F.F.A.R.C.S., Anaesthesia
SNEATH, P. H. A., M.A., M.D., D.DE L'U., M.R.C.S., L.R.C.P., Microbiology
SWALES, J. D., M.A., M.D., F.R.C.P., Medicine
WALKER, F., PH.D., M.D., F.R.C.PATH., Pathology
WHITTAM, R., PH.D., M.A., F.R.S., Physiology

*Centre for Mass Communication Research:*
HALLORAN, J. D., D.SC. (Director)

*Primary Communications Research Centre:*
MEADOWS, A. J., M.A., D.PHIL., M.SC. (Head)

*Public Sector Economics Research Centre:*
JACKSON, P. M., PH.D. (Director)

*Victorian Studies Centre:*
COLLINS, P. A. W., M.A. (Chairman)

# UNIVERSITY OF LIVERPOOL
P.O.B. 147,
LIVERPOOL, L69 3BX
Telephone: 051-709-6022.
Telex: 627095.
Founded by Royal Charter, 1903.

*Chancellor:* The Rt. Hon. the Viscount LEVERHULME, T.D., J.P., B.A., LL.D.
*Pro-Chancellor:* A. W. BEESTON, J.P., M.SC., PH.D., F.R.S.C., C.CHEM., M.I.T.M.A., C.P.A.
*Vice-Chancellor:* Emeritus Prof. R. F. WHELAN, M.D., PH.D., D.SC., F.R.C.P., F.R.A.C.P., F.A.C.E., F.A.A.
*Pro-Vice-Chancellors:* Prof. P. W. EDWARDS, M.A., PH.D., Prof. D. H. JENNINGS, M.A., D.PHIL., F.I.BIOL., Prof. A. S. KING, PH.D., M.R.C.V.S.
*Registrar:* H. H. BURCHNALL, M.A.
*Librarian:* V. E. KNIGHT, M.A., PH.D.

Number of teachers: 992 including 121 professors.

Number of students: 8,091.

Publications: *Town Planning Review* (quarterly), *Bulletin of Hispanic Studies* (quarterly), *Third World Planning Review* (2 a year), *Calendar* (annually), *Recorder* (termly).

**DEANS:**
*Faculty of Arts:* Mrs. IRENE COLLINS, M.A., B.LITT., F.R.HIST.S.
*Faculty of Science:* Prof. A. LEDWITH, D.SC., PH.D., C.CHEM., M.R.S.C.
*Faculty of Medicine:* Prof. E. D. FARMER, M.A., M.D.S., F.R.C.PATH., F.D.S.R.C.S.
*Faculty of Law:* Prof. J. K. MACLEOD, PH.D., BAR. AT LAW.
*Faculty of Engineering Science:* Prof. G. D. GALLETLY, SC.D., D.ENG., C.ENG., F.I.C.E., F.I.MECH.E.
*Faculty of Veterinary Science:* Prof. R. J. FITZPATRICK, PH.D., M.R.C.V.S.
*Faculty of Social and Environmental Studies:* Dr. N. T. BOADEN, M.A., PH.D.

**PROFESSORS:**

*Faculty of Arts:*
ALLOTT, MIRIAM, M.A., PH.D., Modern English Literature
CAIRNS, F., M.A., Latin
CROSS, J. E., M.A., FIL.DR., English Language
DAVIES, J. K., M.A., D.PHIL., Ancient History and Classical Archaeology
EDWARDS, P. W., M.A., PH.D., English Literature
HAIR, P. E. H., M.A., D.PHIL., Modern History
HARDING, A., M.A., F.R.HIST.S., F.S.A.S., Medieval History
HENNOCK, E. P., M.A., PH.D., F.R.HIST.S., Modern History
LLOYD, A. C., M.A., Philosophy
LONG, A. A., PH.D., Greek
McMILLIN, A. B., PH.D., Russian
McWATTERS, K. G., B.A., D. DE L'U., French
REDDICK, J., M.A., D.PHIL., German
RICKETTS, P. T., PH.D., French
SHORE, A. F., M.A., Egyptology
SMALLMAN, F. B. R., M.A., B.MUS., A.R.C.O., Music

*School of Education:*
BLYTH, W. A. L., M.A., M.ED., PH.D., Education
STONES, E., M.A., PH.D., Education

*Faculty of Science:*
BATHURST, R. G. C., D.SC., PH.D., A.R.C.S., F.G.S., Geology
BOWDEN, K. F., D.SC., F.INST.P., Oceanography
BRADSHAW, A. D., M.A., PH.D., F.I.BIOL., Botany
CAIN, A. J., M.A., D.PHIL., Zoology
CASSELS, J. M., M.A., PH.D., F.R.S., Physics
COLLINGE, B., PH.D., Physics
CRAPPER, G. D., PH.D., Applied Mathematics
DELVES, L. M., M.SC., D.PHIL., F.INST.P., F.I.M.A., Computational Science
DUNCAN, C. J., PH.D., Zoology
EYRE, B. L., D.SC., C.ENG., F.I.M., F.INST.P., Materials Science
FLINN, D., D.SC., PH.D., A.R.C.S., D.I.C., F.G.S., Geology
GLOVER, J., PH.D., D.SC., C.CHEM., M.R.S.C., Biochemistry
GOODWIN, T. W., C.B.E., D.SC., C.CHEM., F.R.S.C., F.I.BIOL., F.R.S., Biochemistry
GREEN, L. L., M.A., PH.D., F.INST.P., Experimental Physics
GRIMLEY, T. B., PH.D., Inorganic, Physical and Industrial Chemistry
HOLLIDAY, A. K., PH.D., D.SC., C.CHEM., F.R.S.C., Inorganic Chemistry
HOLT, J. R., PH.D., F.INST.P., F.R.S., Experimental Physics
JENNINGS, D. H., M.A., D.PHIL., F.I.BIOL., Botany
JOHNSON, C. E., M.A., D.PHIL., F.INST.P., Experimental Physics
KING, D. A., PH.D., SC.D., M.INST.P., F.R.S.C., Physical Chemistry

LEDWITH, A., D.SC., PH.D., C.CHEM., M.R.S.C., Inorganic, Physical and Industrial Chemistry
MICHAEL, C., M.A., D.PHIL., Theoretical Physics
NAYLOR, E., PH.D., D.SC., F.I.BIOL., Marine Biology
OLDROYD, J. G., M.A., PH.D., SC.D., Applied Mathematics
PERKINS, H. R., PH.D., D.SC., F.I.BIOL., Microbiology
RILEY, J. P., PH.D., D.SC., C.CHEM., F.R.S.C., Oceanography
RITCHIE, D. A., PH.D., F.R.S.E., F.I.BIOL., Genetics
SAMPFORD, M. R., M.A., D.PHIL., A.R.C.S., Mathematical Statistics
SUTHERLAND, I. O., M.A., PH.D., Organic Chemistry
TAYLOR, S. J., PH.D., Pure Mathematics
WALL, C. T. C., PH.D., F.R.S., Pure Mathematics
WILSON, R. L., M.SC., PH.D., D.I.C., Geophysics

*Faculty of Medicine:*
BEAZLEY, J. M., M.D., F.R.C.O.G., Obstetrics and Gynaecology
BELLINGHAM, A. J., M.B., B.S., F.R.C.P., Haematology
BENTLEY, G., M.B., CH.M., F.R.C.S., Orthopaedic and Accident Surgery
BRECKENRIDGE, A. M., M.D., M.SC., F.R.C.P., Clinical Pharmacology
COPELAND, J. R. M., M.A., M.D., B.CHIR., F.R.C.P., D.P.M., F.R.C.PSYCH., Psychiatry
EVANS, D. A. PRICE, M.D., PH.D., D.SC., F.R.C.P., Medicine
FARMER, E. D., M.A., M.D.S., F.R.C.PATH., F.D.S.R.C.S., Dental Surgery
FENDALL, N. R. E., M.D., D.P.H., F.F.C.M., International Community Health
FLETCHER, J. P., B.D.S., F.D.S.R.C.S., Dental Surgery
GILLES, Chevalier H. M., K.ST.J., M.D., F.R.C.P., F.F.C.M., F.M.C.P.H.(NIG.), D.T.M. & H., Tropical Medicine
HARRIS, F., M.D., M.MED.(PAED.), F.R.C.P., Child Health
HARRISON, R. G., M.A., D.M., Anatomy
HEATH, D. A., M.D., PH.D., D.SC., F.R.C.P., F.R.C.PATH., Pathology
HENDRICKSE, R. G., M.D., F.R.C.P., F.R.C.P.ED., F.M.C.(NIG.), Tropical Paediatrics
HOPKINS, C. R., PH.D., Medical Cell Biology
LISTER, J., M.D., F.R.C.S., Paediatric Surgery
MCCARTHY, K., M.D., F.R.C.PATH., Medical Microbiology
MACDONALD, W. W., D.SC., PH.D., F.I.BIOL., Medical Entomology
MILLS, G. L., M.B., CH.B., M.R.C.S., L.R.C.P., D.OBST.R.C.O.G., F.R.C.P., F.R.C.P.E., Geriatric Medicine
MUMFORD, J. M., M.SC., PH.D., M.S., F.D.S.R.C.S., Operative Dental Surgery
NELSON, G. S., M.D., D.SC., F.R.C.PATH., D.A.P.E., D.T.M.&H., Parasitology
OLIVER, W. M., V.R.D., M.D.S., F.D.S.R.C.S.E., D.R.D.R.C.S.E., Dental Health
PETERSON, O. H., M.D., Physiology
PHAROAH, P. O. D., M.D., M.SC., M.F.C.M., Community Health
SHIELDS, R., M.D., F.R.C.S.ED., F.R.C.S., Surgery
STELL, P. M., CH.M., F.R.C.S., A.I.L., Oto-Rhino-Laryngology
UTTING, J. E., J.P., M.A., M.B., B.CHIR., F.F.A.R.C.S., Anaesthesia

WHITEHOUSE, G. H., M.B., B.S., M.R.C.P., D.M.R.D., F.R.C.R., A.K.C., Diagnostic Radiology
WOODROW, J. C., M.D., F.R.C.P., Medicine

*Faculty of Law:*
HUDSON, A. H., M.A., LL.B., PH.D., BAR. AT LAW, Common Law
MACLEOD, J. K., PH.D., BAR.-AT-LAW, Law
PARKER, D. B., LL.B., BAR.-AT-LAW, Law

*Faculty of Engineering Science:*
CRAGGS, J. D., M.SC., PH.D., F.INST.P., Electronic Engineering
GALLETLY, G. D., SC.D., D.ENG., C.ENG., F.I.C.E., F.I.MECH.E., Applied Mechanics
HOLMES, P., PH.D., C.ENG., M.I.C.E., Maritime Civil Engineering
HULL, D., PH.D., D.SC., C.ENG., F.I.M., F.P.R.I., Materials Engineering
JONES, N., M.SC., PH.D., D.SC., C.ENG., F.I.MECH.E., Mechanical Engineering
LECK, J. H., M.ENG., PH.D., C.ENG., F.I.E.E., F.INST.P., Electrical Engineering
NORBURY, J. F., M.ENG., PH.D., C.ENG., F.I.MECH.E., F.R.AE.S., Mechanical Engineering
PARBROOK, H. D., PH.D., C.ENG., F.I.MECH.E., M.INST.P., Building Engineering
SAWKO, F., D.SC., C.ENG., M.I.C.E., M.I.STRUCT.E., M.AM.SOC.C.E., Civil Engineering

*Faculty of Veterinary Science:*
CLARKSON, M. J., D.V.SC., PH.D., M.R.C.V.S., Veterinary Preventive Medicine
FINN, C. A., PH.D., M.R.C.V.S., Veterinary Physiology
FITZPATRICK, R. J., PH.D., M.R.C.V.S., Veterinary Clinical Studies
FORD, E. J. H., D.V.SC., F.R.C.V.S., F.R.C.PATH., Veterinary Clinical Studies
KELLY, D. F., M.A., PH.D., B.V.SC., M.R.C.V.S., F.R.C.PATH., Veterinary Pathology
KING, A. S., PH.D., M.R.C.V.S., Veterinary Anatomy
KING, J. O. L., M.V.SC., PH.D., F.R.C.V.S., F.I.BIOL., Animal Husbandry

*Faculty of Social and Environmental Studies:*
BROADBRIDGE, S. A., PH.D., Economic History
BROMLEY, D. B., PH.D., F.B.PS.S., Psychology
DIX, G. B., B.A., M.L.A., DIP.T.P., R.I.B.A., F.R.T.P.I., Civic Design
HALLIDAY, J. S., PH.D., F.INST.P., Industrial Studies
LAWTON, R., M.A., Geography
MARCEAU, JANE, PH.D., Sociology
MINFORD, A. P. L., M.SC., PH.D., Applied Economics
MORRIS, R. C., M.SC., F.C.A., Accounting
NOBAY, A. R., PH.D., Economic Science
OLDFIELD, F., M.A., PH.D., Geography
PEEL, J. D. Y., M.A., PH.D., Sociology
PROTHERO, R. M., M.A., PH.D., Geography
PROUDLOVE, J. A., M.ENG., F.I.MUN.E., F.C.I.T., Transport Studies
RIDLEY, F. F., O.B.E., PH.D., Political Theory and Institutions
SMITH, C. T., M.A., Latin-American Geography
TARN, J. N., PH.D., R.I.B.A., F.R.HIST.S., Architecture

*Institute of Extension Studies:*
RHODES, E., M.A. (Director).

*Computer Laboratory:*
ALTY, J. L., PH.D., M.B.C.S. (Director).

AFFILIATED INSTITUTION:
**Liverpool School of Tropical Medicine:** see Research Institutes.

# UNIVERSITY OF LONDON
SENATE HOUSE,
LONDON, WC1E 7HU
Telephone: 01-636 8000.
Telegrams: University, London.

Founded 1836 as an examining body; became also a teaching body in 1898.

*Chancellor:* H.R.H. The PRINCESS ANNE, Mrs. MARK PHILLIPS.
*Vice-Chancellor:* Prof. R. QUIRK, C.B.E., M.A., PH.D., D.LIT., FIL.DR., D.H.C., F.B.A.
*Principal:* J. R. STEWART, C.B.E., M.A.
*Academic Registrar:* P. F. VOWLES, M.A.
*Director of Extra-Mural Studies:* Prof. B. H. GROOMBRIDGE, B.SC.
*Director of Library and Goldsmiths' Librarian:* D. J. FOSKETT, M.A., F.L.A.
*Library: see Libraries.*
Number of appointed teachers: 1,661.
Number of internal students: 54,037.
Number of external students: 20,353.

DEANS:

*Faculty of Theology:* Prof. The Rev. Canon G. R. DUNSTAN, M.A., D.D., F.S.A.
*Faculty of Arts:* Prof. C. V. BOCK, M.A., DR.PHIL.
*Faculty of Laws:* Prof. A. R. MELLOWS, PH.D., LL.D.
*Faculty of Music:* S. GLASSER, M.A.
*Faculty of Medicine:* Prof. L. P. LE QUESNE, M.CH., D.M., F.R.C.S., F.R.A.C.S.
*Faculty of Science:* Prof. R. A. HOWIE, M.A., PH.D., SC.D.
*Faculty of Engineering:* Prof. J. W. MULLIN, PH.D., D.SC., F.I.CHEM.E., F.R.S.C.
*Faculty of Economics:* Prof. ADELA A. NEVITT, B.SC.(ECON.).
*Faculty of Education:* Prof. P. J. BLACK, PH.D.

PROFESSORS:

The initials in brackets appearing after each professor's name and subject represent the College or Institute to which he is attached. The key is given below:

Bfd. C.—Bedford College.
Bk. C.—Birkbeck College.
Ch. X H.M.S.—Charing Cross Hospital Medical School.
Chel. C.—Chelsea College.
Guy's H.M.S.—Guy's Hospital Medical School.
I.C.—Imperial College.
Inst. Arch.—Institute of Archaeology.
Inst. Bas. Med. Sci.—Institute of Basic Medical Sciences.

Inst. Can. Res.—Institute of Cancer Research.
Inst. Dermat.—Institute of Dermatology.
Inst. Educ.—Institute of Education.
Inst. Hist. Res.—Institute of Historical Research.
Inst. L. & O.—Institute of Laryngology and Otology.
Inst. Latin Amer. St.—Institute of Latin American Studies.
Inst. Neurol.—Institute of Neurology.
Inst. Oph.—Institute of Ophthalmology.
Inst. Orth.—Institute of Orthopaedics.
Inst. Psych.—Institute of Psychiatry.
Inst. U.S. Studs.—Institute of United States Studies.
K.C.L.—King's College London.
K.C.H.M.S.—King's College Hospital Medical School.
L.S. Dent. Surg.—Royal Dental Hospital of London School of Dental Surgery.
L.S.E.—London School of Economics.
L.S. Hyg. & Trop. Med.—London School of Hygiene and Tropical Medicine.
Lond. H.M.C.—London Hospital Medical College.
Middx. H.M.S.—Middlesex Hospital Medical School.
Q.E.C.—Queen Elizabeth College.
Q.M.C.—Queen Mary College.
R.H.C.—Royal Holloway College.
R.F.H.S.M. — Royal Free Hospital School of Medicine.
R.P.M.S.—Royal Postgraduate Medical School.
R. Vet. C.—Royal Veterinary College.
Sch. Pharm.—School of Pharmacy.
S.O.A.S.—School of Oriental and African Studies.
S.S.E.E.S.—School of Slavonic and Eastern European Studies.
St. Bart.'s H.M.C.—St. Bartholomew's Hospital Medical College.
St. G.'s H.M.S.—St. George's Hospital Medical School.
St. My.'s H.M.S.—St. Mary's Hospital Medical School.
St. Thos.'s H.M.S.—St. Thomas's Hospital Medical School.
U.C.L.—University College London.
Warb. I.—Warburg Institute.
Wfd. C.—Westfield College.
West. M.S.—Westminster Medical School.
Wye C.—Wye College.

Details of all Colleges and Institutes follow the professor list.

*Faculty of Theology:*
ACKROYD, Rev. P. R., M.TH., M.A., PH.D., D.D., Old Testament Studies (K.C.L.)
DUNSTAN, Rev. Canon G. R., M.A., F.S.A., Moral and Social Theology (K.C.L.)
HALL, S. G., M.A., B.D., Ecclesiastical History (K.C.L.)
OWEN, Rev. H. P., M.A., Christian Doctrine (K.C.L.)
STANTON, G. N., M.A., PH.D., New Testament Studies (K.C.L.)
SUTHERLAND, S. R., M.A., History and Philosophy of Religion (K.C.L.)

*Faculty of Arts:*
ABRAMSKY, C. A., B.A., Hebrew and Jewish Studies (U.C.L.)
ALEXANDER, R. N., M.A., B.LITT., English Language and Literature (Q.M.C.)
ALLOTT, MIRIAM, M.A., PH.D., English (Bk.C.)
ANDERSON, M. S., M.A., PH.D., International History (L.S.E.)
ANDRZEJEWSKI, B. W., M.A., PH.D., Cushitic Languages and Literatures (S.O.A.S.)
AQUILECCHIA, G., M.A., DOTT.LETT., Italian (Bfd.C.)
BALLHATCHET, K. A., M.A., PH.D., History of South Asia (S.O.A.S.)
BARBER, W. H., M.A., D.PHIL., French (Bk.C.)
BARRON, J. P., M.A., D.PHIL., Greek Language and Literature (U.C.L.)
BATELY, JANET M., M.A., English Language and Medieval Literature (K.C.L.)
BAWDEN, C. R., PH.D., F.B.A., Mongolian (S.O.A.S.)
BAXANDALL, M. D. K., M.A., History of the Classical Tradition (Warb. I.)
BEASLEY, W. G., PH.D., History of the Far East (S.O.A.S.)
BISHOP, D., A.R.I.C.S., A.M.I.C.C., Building (U.C.L.)
BOCK, C. V., M.A., DR.PHIL., German (Wfd.C.)
BOURNE, K., PH.D., International History (L.S.E.)
BOWIE, M. M., M.A., D.PHIL., French Language and Literature (Q.M.C.)
BOYCE, NORAH E. M., PH.D., Iranian Studies (S.O.A.S.)
BROWN, R. A., M.A., D.PHIL., F.S.A., History (K.C.L.)
BROWN, T. J., M.A., F.S.A., Palaeography (K.C.L.)
BURCHER, R. K., PH.D., Naval Architecture (U.C.L.)
BURNS, J. H., M.A., PH.D., History of Political Thought (U.C.L.)
CAMERON, A. M., M.A., PH.D., Ancient History (K.C.L.)
CAMPOS, C. L., L. ès L., PH.D., French (Brit. Inst. in Paris)
CARNOCHAN, J., B.A., Phonetics (S.O.A.S.)
CHALKER, J., M.A., English (Wfd. C.)
CHAPMAN, R., M.A., PH.D., English Studies (L.S.E.)
CHAUDHURI, K. N., PH.D., Economic History of Asia (S.O.A.S.)
CHRISTIE, I. R., M A., British History (U.C.L.)
COHEN, A., M.A., PH.D., Anthropology of Africa and Near East (S.O.A.S.)
COLDSTREAM, J. N., M.A., F.B.A., F.S.A., Archaeology (Aegean) (Bfd.C.)
CORBETT, P. E., M.A., Classical Art and Archaeology (U.C.L.)
COURTNEY, E., M.A., Latin Language and Literature (K.C.L.)
COWAN, C. D., M.A., PH.D., Oriental History (S.O.A.S.)
COWAN, P. D., PH.D., A.R.I.B.A., Planning Studies (U.C.L.)
CRISP, O., PH.D., Russian Economic History (S.S.E.E.S.)
CUMMINS, J. S., PH.D., Hispanic Studies (U.C.L.)
CUSHING, G. F., M.A., PH.D., Hungarian Language and Literature (S.S.E.E.S.)
DEYERMOND, A. D., M.A., Spanish (Wfd. C.)
DIXON, P., M.A., English (Wfd. C.)
DRAGE, C.-L., M.A., PH.D., Russian (S.S.E.E.S.)

DU BOULAY, F. R. H., M.A., Medieval History (Bfd. C.)
DUNN, C. J., PH.D., Japanese (S.O.A.S.)
EVANS, D. H., M.A., D. DE L'UNIV., Romance Philology (Q.M.C.)
EVANS, J. D., M.A., PH.D., LITT.D., F.S.A., F.B.A., Archaeology (Inst. Arch.)
EVISON, V. I., D.LITT., Archaeology of the Anglo-Saxon period (Bk. C.)
EWBANK, INGA-STINA, M.A., FIL.KAND., English Literature (Bfd. C.)
FAHY, C. F., M.A., PH.D., Italian (Bk. C.)
FLOUD, R. C., D.PHIL., Modern History (Bk. C.)
FOOTE, P. G., M.A., Old Scandinavian (U.C.L.)
FOURCIN, A. J., PH.D., Experimental Phonetics (U.C.L.)
FOWLER, F. M., M.A., D.PHIL., German Language and Literature (Q.M.C.)
FREEBORN, R. H., M.A., D.PHIL., Russian Literature (S.S.E.E.S.)
GELLNER, E. A., PH.D., Philosophy with special reference to Sociology (L.S.E.)
GIANGRANDE, G., DOTT.FIL., PH.D., Classics (Bk. C.)
GIMSON, A. C., B.A., Phonetics (U.C.L.)
GLENDINNING, O. N. V., PH.D., Spanish (Q.M.C.)
GOODYEAR, F. R. D., PH.D., Latin (Bfd. C.)
GOWING, L. B., C.B.E., M.A., Fine Art (U.C.L.)
GRAHAM, A. C., PH.D., Classical Chinese (S.O.A.S.)
GRAY, J. R., M.A., PH.D., History of Africa (S.O.A.S.)
HALE, J. R., M.A., Italian (U.C.L.)
HAMLYN, D. W., M.A., Philosophy (Bk. C.)
HANDLEY, E. W., M.A., F.B.A., Greek (U.C.L.)
HARDY, BARBARA, M.A., English Literature (Bk. C.)
HARRIS, D. R., B.LITT., M.A., PH.D., Human Environment (Inst. Arch.)
HARVEY, L. P., D.PHIL., Spanish (K.C.L.)
HEALY, J.F., M.A., PH.D., Classics (R.H.C.)
HENDERSON, EUGENIE J. A., B.A., Phonetics (S.O.A.S.)
HILL, A. G., M.A., B.LITT., English Language and Literature (R.H.C.)
HOBSBAWM, E. J. E., PH.D., Economic and Social History (Bk. C.)
HODDER, B. W., M.A., PH.D., Geography (S.O.A.S.)
HODSON, F. R., PH.D., Prehistoric Archaeology (Inst. Arch.)
HOLT, P. M. M.A., D.PHIL., D.LITT., History of the Near and Middle East (S.O.A.S.)
HUNT, J. D., M.A., PH.D., English Literature (Bfd.C.)
ILERSIC, A. R., M.SC.(ECON.), Social Studies (Bfd. C.)
INNES, G., M.A., PH.D., West African Languages (S.O.A.S.)
JOHNSON, D. W. J., B.A., B.LITT., French History (U.C.L.)
JOHNSTONE, T. M., PH.D., Arabic (S.O.A.S.)
JONES, M. A.. M.A., D.PHIL., American History (U.C.L.)
JUDEN, B. V., M.A., French Language and Literature (R.H.C.)
KITSON, M. W. L., M.A., History of Art (Courtauld Inst. Art)
KOENIGSBERGER, H. G., M.A., PH.D., History (K.C.L.)
LA FONTAINE, J., PH.D., Anthropology (L.S.E.)
LANG, D. M., D.LIT., LITT.D., DR.PHILOL. SC., Caucasian Studies (S.O.A.S.)

LASKO, P. E., B.A., History of Art (Courtauld Inst. Art)
LAWRENCE, C. H., D.PHIL., Medieval History (Bfd. C.)
LEAKEY, F. W., PH.D., French Language and Literature (Bfd. C.)
LESLIE, R. F., PH.D., Modern History (Q.M.C.)
LEWIS, I. M., B.SC., B.LITT., D.PHIL., Anthropology (L.S.E.)
LOYN, H. R., D.LITT., History (Wfd. C.)
LOWENTHAL, D., M.A., PH.D., Geography (U.C.L.)
LYNCH, J., M.A., PH.D., Hispanic and Latin American History (Inst. Latin Amer. St.)
MARSHALL, J. H., M.A., D.PHIL., Romance Philology (Wfd.C.)
MARSHALL, P. J., D.PHIL., Imperial History (K.C.L.)
MAXWELL, R. M., B.ARCH., A.R.I.B.A., Architecture (U.C.L.)
MAYER, A. C., PH.D., Asian Anthropology (S.O.A.S.)
MEIJER, R. P., PH.D., Dutch Language and Literature (Bfd. C.)
MENAGE, V. L., M.A., PH.D., Turkish (S.O.A.S.)
MILLAR, F. G. B., D.PHIL., Ancient History (U.C.L.)
MILLER, K., M.A., Modern English Literature (U.C.L.)
MILNER, G. B., M.A., PH.D., Austronesian Studies (S.O.A.S.)
MORGAN, W. B., M.A., PH.D., Geography (K.C.L.)
MUSGROVE, J., B.ARCH., Environmental Design and Engineering (U.C.L.)
NICOL, D. M., M.A., PH.D., Modern Greek and Byzantine History, Language and Literature (K.C.L.)
OATES, E. E. D. M., M.A., F.S.A., Western Asiatic Archaeology (Inst. Archaeology)
OLIVER, R. A., M.A., PH.D., History of Africa (S.O.A.S.)
O'NEILL, P. G., PH.D., Japanese (S.O.A.S.)
OUSTON, P. A., M.A., PH.D., French Language and Literature (K.C.L.)
PEAKE, C. H., M.A., English (Q.M.C.)
POLLARD, D. E., PH.D., Chinese (S.O.A.S.)
QUIRK, R., C.B.E., M.A., PH.D., D.LIT., English Language and Literature (U.C.L.)
RAPHAEL, D. D., M.A., D.PHIL., Philosophy (I.C.)
RECKERT, S., M.LITT., PH.D., Portuguese (K.C.L.)
RILEY-SMITH, J. S. C., M.A., PH.D., History (R.H.C.)
ROBINS, R. H., M.A., General Linguistics (S.O.A.S.)
ROSSER, K. C., M.A., PH.D., Development Planning (U.C.L.)
SAMILOV, M., M.A., PH.D., Comparative Philology of the Slavonic Languages (S.S.E.E.S.)
SANDERSON, G. N., M.A., PH.D., Modern History (R.H.C.)
SCHRAM, S. R., PH.D., Politics, with special reference to China (S.O.A.S.)
SCREECH, M. A., D.LITT., French Language and Literature (U.C.L.)
SETON-WATSON, G. H. N., C.B.E., M.A., Russian History (S.S.E.E.S.)
SHARROCK, R., M.A., English Language and Literature (K.C.L.)
SHORTO, H. L., M.A., Mon-Khmer Studies (S.O.A.S.)
SIMMONDS, E. H. S., M.A., Languages and Literatures of South East Asia (S.O.A.S.)
SMITH, D. M., PH.D., Geography (Q.M.C.)

SMITH, H. S., M.A., Egyptology (U.C.L.)
SNELLGROVE, D. L., M.A., PH.D., D.LITT., Tibetan (S.O.A.S.)
SORABJI, R. R. K., B.PHIL., M.A., Ancient Philosophy (K.C.L.).
SPENCE, N. C. W., PH.D., French Linguistics (Bfd.C.)
STEER, J., M.A., History of Art (Bk.C.)
STERN, J. P., M.A., PH.D., German (U.C.L.)
STRATHERN, A. J., M.A., PH.D., Anthropology (U.C.L.)
SWALES, M. W., M.A., PH.D., German (U.C.L.)
SWART, K. W., JUR.CAND., LITT.D., Dutch History and Institutions (U.C.L.)
THOMPSON, F. M. L., D.PHIL., History (Inst. Hist. Res.)
ULLENDORFF, E., M.A., D.PHIL., D.LITT., F.B.A., Semitic Languages (S.O.A.S.)
UNDERWOOD, V. P., PH.D., D.-ÈS-L., French (U.C.L.)
VAREY, J. E., PH.D., Spanish (Wfd. C.)
VATIKIOTIS, P. J., PH.D., Politics with special reference to the Near and Middle East (S.O.A.S.)
VICKERY, B. C., M.A., F.L.A., Library Studies (U.C.L.)
WALKER, R. M., PH.D., Spanish (Bk. C.)
WATKINS, J. W. N., D.SC., M.A., Philosophy (L.S.E.)
WATSON, A. I., PH.D., Spanish (Bk. C.)
WATSON, N. F., B.ARCH., A.R.I.B.A., Architecture (U.C.L.)
WATSON, W., M.A., F.S.A., F.B.A., Chinese Art and Archaeology (S.O.A.S.)
WATT, D. C., M.A., International History (L.S.E.)
WELLS, G. A., M.A., PH.D., German (Bk. C.)
WEST, M. L., PH.D., Greek (Bfd. C.)
WHITE, J. E. C. T., M.A., PH.D., History of Art (U.C.L.)
WILKES, J. J., PH.D., Archaeology of the Roman Provinces (Inst. Arch.)
WILKS, M. J., M.A., PH.D., Medieval History (Bk. C.)
WILLCOCK, M. M., B.A., Latin (U.C.L.)
WILLIAMS, G., PH.D., History (Q.M.C.)
WINCH, P. G., B.PHIL., Philosophy (K.C.L.)
WISBEY, R. A., M.A., DR.PHIL., German (K.C.L.)
WISEMAN, D. J., O.B.E., M.A., Assyriology (S.O.A.S.)
WOLLHEIM, R. A., M.A., F.B.A., Philosophy of Mind and Logic (U.C.L.)
WORTH, K. J., M.A., PH.D., Drama and Theatre Studies (R.H.C.)
WRIGHT, E., M.A., American History (Inst. U.S. Studs.)
WRIGHT, J. C., M.A., Sanskrit (S.O.A.S.)
YUILL, W. E., M.A., German (Bfd. C.)
ZARNECKI, G., C.B.E., M.A., PH.D., F.B.A., F.S.A., History of Art (Courtauld Inst. Art)

*Faculty of Laws:*

ADAMS, J. E., LL.B., Law (Q.M.C.)
ALLOTT, A. N., M.A., PH.D., African Law (S.O.A.S.)
BOYLE, A. J., LL.M., Law (Q.M.C.)
BUTLER, W. E., M.A., PH.D., D.SC., J.D., Comparative Law (U.C.L.)
CHENG, B., LIC. EN DROIT., PH.D., LL.D., Air and Space Law (U.C.L.)
CORNISH, W. R., LL.B., B.C.L., English Law (L.S.E.)
COULSON, N. J., M.A., Oriental Laws (S.O.A.S.)
DERRETT, J. D. M., M.A., PH.D., D.C.L., Oriental Laws (S.O.A.S.)
DIAMOND, A. L., LL.M., Law (Inst. Adv. Legal Studies)

GOODE, R. M., LL.B., Credit and Commercial Law (Q.M.C.)
GRIFFITH, J. A. G., LL.M., Public Law (L.S.E.)
GRUNFELD, C., M.A., Law (L.S.E.)
GUEST, A. G., M.A., English Law (K.C.L.)
HIGGINS, ROSALYN, M.A., J.S.D., International Law (L.S.E.)
IVAMY, E. R. H., PH.D., LL.D., Law (U.C.L.)
JACOBS, F. G., M.A., D.PHIL., European Law (K.C.L.)
JOWELL, J. L., M.A., LL.M., S.J.D., Public Law (U.C.L.)
LAHORE, J., M.A., LL.M., Intellectual Property Law (Q.M.C.)
LLOYD OF HAMPSTEAD, Lord, M.A., LL.D., Jurisprudence (U.C.L.)
MELLOWS, A. R., LL.M., PH.D., LL.D., Law of Property (K.C.L.)
READ, J. S., LL.B., Comparative Public Law with special reference to Africa (S.O.A.S.)
RIDEOUT, R. W., PH.D., Labour Law (U.C.L.)
RYDER, E. C., LL.B., M.A., English Law (U.C.L.)
SCAMELL, E. H., LL.M., English Law (U.C.L.)
SIMMONDS, K. R., M.A., D.PHIL., International Law (Q.M.C.)
WEDDERBURN, Lord, LL.B., M.A., Commercial Law (L.S.E.)
ZANDER, M., LL.M., Law (L.S.E.)

*Faculty of Music:*

SPINK, I. W. A., M.A., F.T.C.L., A.R.C.M., Music (R.H.C.)
TROWELL, B. L., M.A., PH.D., Music (K.C.L.)
WHITTALL, A. M., A.T.C.L., A.R.C.O., M.A., PH.D., Musical Theory and Analysis (K.C.L.)

*Faculty of Medicine:*

ADAMS, A. P., M.B., B.S., M.R.C.S., L.R.C.P., F.F.A.R.C.S., PH.D., Anaesthetics (Guy's H.M.S.)
ADAMS, C. W. M., M.A., M.D., D.SC., M.R.C.PATH., Pathology (Guy's H.M.S.)
ADAMS, G. E., PH.D., D.SC., Physics as Applied to Medicine (inst. Cancer Research)
ADLER, M. W., M.B., B.S., M.D., M.R.C.P., M.F.C.M., Genito-Urinary Medicine (Middx.H.M.S.)
ALBERMAN, E. D., M.A., M.B., B.CHIR., M.D., D.PHIL., M.F.C.M., M.R.C.P., F.F.C.M., Clinical Epidemiology (Lond. H.M.C. and St. Bart.'s H.M.C.)
ALEXANDER, A. G., B.D.S., M.D.S., F.D.S.R.C.S., Conservative Dentistry (U.C.L.)
ALLDRED, H., D.D.S., Conservative Dentistry (Lond. H.M.C.)
ANDERSON, J., M.A., B.SC., M.D., F.R.C.P., Medicine (K.C.H.M.S.)
ANDERSON, J. A. D., M.A., M.D., D.R.C.O.G., D.P.H., M.R.C.G.P., F.F.C.M., Community Medicine (Guy's H.M.S.)
ANDERSON, R. H., B.SC., M.D., M.R.C.PATH., Paediatric Cardiac Morphology (Cardiothoracic Inst.)
ARDEN, G. B., PH.D., Neurophysiology (Inst. Oph.)
ARMSTRONG, W. G., M.SC., PH.D., Biochemistry in Relation to Dentistry (L.S. Dent. Surg.)
ARNSTEIN, H. R. V., PH.D., D.SC., Biochemistry (K.C.L.)
AZZOPARDI, J. G., M.D., D.C.P., D.PATH., M.R.C.PATH., Oncology (R.P.M.S.)
BACHELARD, H. S., M.SC., PH.D., Biochemistry (St. Thos's H.M.S.)
BAGSHAWE, K. D., M.D., M.R.C.P., Medical Oncology (Ch. XH.M.S.)

BAKER, J. B. E., B.M., B.CH., B.SC., M.A., Pharmacology (Ch. XH.M.S.)
BAKER, P. F., M.A., PH.D., F.R.S., Physiology (K.C.L.)
BANATVALA, J. E., M.A., M.D., D.CH., D.PH., Clinical Virology (St. Thos's H.M.S.)
BARON, D. N., D.SC., M.D., F.R.C.P., F.R.C.PATH., Chemical Pathology (R.F.H.S.M.)
BARRATT, T. M., M.B., B.CHIR., F.R.C.P., Paediatric Nephrology (Inst. Child Health)
BATCHELOR, J. R., M.A., B.CHIR., M.B., M.D., M.R.C.S., L.R.C.P., Tissue Immunology (R.P.M.S.)
BAUM, M., M.B.CH.B., F.R.C.S., CH.M., Surgery (K.C.H.M.S.)
BEARD, R. W., B.CHIR., M.D., M.R.C.O.G., Obstetrics and Gynaecology (St. My.'s H.M.S.)
BELLAIRS, A. D'A., M.A., D.SC., M.R.C.S., L.R.C.P., Vertebrate Morphology (St. My.'s H.M.S.)
BELLAIRS, M. RUTH, PH.D., Embryology (U.C.L.)
BENNETT, A., PH.D., D.SC., Pharmacology (K.C.H.M.S.)
BENTALL, H. H., M.B., B.S., F.R.C.S., Cardiac Surgery (R.P.M.S.)
BERMAN, D. S., D.ORTH.R.C.S., D.D.P.H.R.C.S., PH.D., Child Dental Health (London H.M.C.)
BERRY, C. L., M.D., M.R.C.PATH., Morbid Anatomy (Lond. H.M.C.)
BERRY, R. J., M.A., PH.D., Oncology (Middx. H.M.S.)
BESSER, G. M., B.SC., M.D., F.R.C.P., Endocrinology (St. Bart.'s H.M.C.)
BICKNELL, D. JOAN, M.B.CH.B., M.D. F.R.C.P., Psychiatry of Mental Handicap (St. G.'s H.M.S.)
BILLING, BARBARA H., PH.D., Biochemistry as applied to Medicine (R.F.H.S.M.)
BIRD, A. C., M.D., D.O., F.R.C.P., Clinical Ophthalmology (Inst. Oph.)
BISCOE, T. J., B.SC., M.B., B.S., Physiology (U.C.L.)
BISSET, G. W., D.PHIL., L.R.C.P., M.R.C.S., Pharmacology (St. Thos.'s H.M.S.)
BLACKWOOD, H. J. J., B.D.S., M.D., F.F.D., F.C.PATH., F.F.A.R.C.S.I., Oral Anatomy (L.S. Dent. Surg.)
BLANDY, J. P., M.A., D.M., M.CH., F.R.C.S., Urology (London H.M.C.)
BLUMGART, L. H., M.D., F.R.C.S., Surgery (R.P.M.S.)
BOLTON, T. B., M.A., PH.D., Pharmacology (St. G.'s H.M.S.)
BORN, G. V. R., D.PHIL., M.A., Pharmacology (K.C.L.)
BOWEN, D. A. L., M.A., D.PATH., D.M.J., M.R.C.PATH., F.R.C.P., F.R.C.PATH., Forensic Medicine (Ch. X.H.M.S.)
BOYDE, A., PH.D., L.D.S.R.C.S., Dental Anatomy (U.C.L.)
BRADBURY, M. W. B., D.M., Physiology (K.C.L.)
BRADEN, M., B.SC., PH.D., Materials Science in Dentistry (Lond. H.M.C.)
BRADLEY, D. J., Tropical Hygiene (L.S. Hyg. & Trop. Med.)
BRANT, H. A., M.D., F.R.C.O.G., F.R.C.S., F.R.C.P., Clinical Obstetrics and Gynaecology (U.C.L.)
BRASS, W., M.A., Medical Demography (L.S. Hyg. & Trop. Med.)
BREATHNACH, A. S., M.SC., M.D., Anatomy (St. My.'s H.M.S.)
BRENT, L., B.SC., PH.D., Immunology (St. My.'s H.M.S.)
BRINDLEY, G. S., M.D., M.R.C.S., L.R.C.P., F.R.S., Physiology (Inst. Psychiatry)

BRITTON, H. G., B.SC., M.B., B.CHIR., PH.D., F.R.I.C., Chemical Physiology (St. My's H.M.S.)
BROOKS, R. V., PH.D., D.SC., F.R.C.PATH., Chemical Endocrinology (St. Thos.'s H.M.S.)
BROWN, D. A., PH.D., Pharmacology (Sch. Pharm.)
BROWSE, N. L., M.D., F.R.C.S., Surgery (St. Thos.'s H.M.S.)
BRUMFITT, W., M.B., B.S., PH.D., M.R.C.P., F.R.C.PATH., Medical Microbiology (R.F.H.S.M.)
BURNSTOCK, G., PH.D., M.SC., D.SC., Anatomy (U.C.L.)
CAMERON, I. R., D.M., M.R.C.P., Medicine (St. Thos.'s H.M.S.)
CAMERON, J. M., PH.D., M.D., D.M.J., M.R.C.PATH., Forensic Medicine (Lond. H.M.C.)
CAMERON, J. S., M.D., M.R.C.P., Renal Medicine (Guy's H.M.S.)
CAMPBELL, P. N., PH.D., D.SC., Biochemistry (Middx. H.M.S.)
CAMPBELL, S., M.B., CH.B., M.R.C.O.G., Obstetrics and Gynaecology (K.C.H.M.S.)
CARLESS, J. E., B.PHARM., M.SC., PH.D., Pharmaceutics (Sch. Pharm.)
CARTER, C. O., M.A., D.M., F.R.C.P., Clinical Genetics (Inst. Child Health)
CAVANAGH, J. B., M.D., M.R.C.P., Applied Neurobiology (Inst. Neurology)
CAWLEY, R. H., PH.D., D.P.M., M.R.C.P., F.R.C.PSYCH., Psychological Medicine (Inst. Psych. & K.C.H.M.S.)
CAWSON, R. A., B.D.S., M.D., M.C.PATH., L.M.S.S.A., F.D.S.R.C.S., Oral Medicine and Pathology (Guy's H.M.S.)
CHANTLER, C., M.A., M.B., B.CHIR., M.R.C.P., Paediatric Nephrology (Guy's H.M.S.)
CHARD, T., M.D., M.R.C.O.G., Reproductive Physiology (Lond. H.M.C. and St. Bart's H.M.C.)
CLAIREAUX, A. E., M.D., F.R.C.P., F.R.C.O.G., F.R.C.PATH., Histopathology (Inst. Child Health)
CLARK, C. G., CH.M., M.D., F.R.C.S., Surgery (U.C.L.)
CLARK, T. J. H., M.D., F.R.C.P., Thoracic Medicine (Guy's H.M.S.)
CLARKE, PATRICIA H., M.A., D.SC., Biochemistry (Microbial) (U.C.L.)
COHEN, R. D., M.A., M.B., B.CHIR., M.D., M.R.C.P., Metabolic Medicine (Lond. H.M.C.)
COHEN, S., C.B.E., PH.D., M.D., F.C.PATH., F.R.S., Chemical Pathology (Guy's H.M.S.)
COLE, D. F., PH.D., Physiology (Inst. Oph.)
COLLIER, L. H., M.B., B.S., M.R.C.S., L.R.C.P., M.D., Virology (Lond. H.M.C.)
COLLINS, W. P., PH.D., D.SC., F.R.I.C., Reproductive Biochemistry (K.C.H.M.S.)
CONWAY, C. M., D.A., F.F.A.R.C.S., Anaesthetics (West.M.S.)
CORRIN, B., M.B., M.D., M.R.C.PATH., Thoracic Pathology (Cardiothoracic Inst.)
COTCHIN, E., D.SC., M.R.C.V.S., Veterinary Pathology (R. Vet. C.)
CRAFT, I., Obstetrics and Gynaecology (R.F.H.S.M.)
CRANSTON, W. I., M.A., M.D., F.R.C.P., Medicine (St. Thos.'s H.M.S.)
CRAWFORD, N., PH.D., Biochemistry (Inst. Bas. Med. Sci.)
CREESE, R., M.B., B.S., PH.D., Physiology (St.My.'s H.M.S.)
CRISP, A. H., M.D., D.SC., F.R.C.P., F.R.C.P., F.R.C.PSYCH., Psychiatry (St. G.'s H.M.S.)

CURREY, H. L. F., M.MED., F.R.C.P., Rheumatology (Lond. H.M.C.)
CURSON, I., B.D.S., F.D.S.R.C.S., Conservative Dentistry (K.C.H.M.S.)
CURZEN, P., B.SC., M.D., L.R.C.P., M.R.C.S., F.R.C.O.G., Obstetrics and Gynaecology (West. M.S.)
CURZON, G., D.SC., Neurochemistry (Inst. of Neurology)
DALY, M. DE B., M.A., M.D., SC.D., Physiology (St. Bart.'s H.M.C.)
DAROUGAR, S., M.D., Public Health Ophthalmology (Inst. Oph.)
DATTA, N., M.D., F.R.C.PATH., Microbial Genetics (R.P.M.S.)
DATTA, S. P., B.SC., M.B., B.S., Medical Biochemistry (U.C.L.)
DAVIDSON, G., D.SC., Entomology as applied to Malaria (L.S. Hyg. & Trop. Med.)
DAVIES, A. J. S., PH.D., Immunobiology (Inst. Cancer Research)
DAVIES, D. S., PH.D., Biochemical Pharmacology (R.P.M.S. )
DAVIES, M. J., M.D., L.R.C.P., M.R.C.S., M.R.C.PATH., Cardio-Vascular Pathology (St. G.'s H.M.S.)
DAVISON, A. N., B.PHARM., PH.D., D.SC., F.P.S., Neurochemistry (Inst. of Neurology)
DAY, M. H., M.B., B.S., PH.D., L.R.C.P., M.R.C.S., Anatomy (St. Thos's H.M.S.)
DEWHURST, Sir JOHN, M.B., CH.B., M.R.C.O.P., F.R.C.S.E., Obstetrics and Gynaecology (Inst. Obstetrics)
DICKINSON, C. J., B.SC., M.A., D.M., M.R.C.P., Medicine (St. Bart.'s H.M.C.)
DILLY, P. N., M.SC., M.B., B.S., PH.D., G.M., Structural Biology (St. G.'s H.M.S.)
DODD, B. E., M.SC., PH.D., D.SC., Blood Group Serology (Lond. H.M.C.)
DOLLERY, C. T., M.B., B.S., B.SC., CH.B., F.R.C.P., Clinical Pharmacology (R.P.M.S.)
DONOVAN, B. T., PH.D., Neuroendocrinology (Inst. Psych.)
DOWLING, R. H., M.D., F.R.C.P., Gastroenterology (Guy's H.M.S.)
DU BOULAY, E. P. G. H., D.M.R.D., F.R.C.P., F.F.R., Neuroradiology (Inst. Neurology)
DUBOWITZ, V., D.C.H., M.D., M.R.C.P., Paediatrics (Inst. Child Health)
DUCHEN, L. W., PH.D., D.C.P., M.R.C.PATH., Neuropathology (Inst. Neurology)
DUCKWORTH, R., B.D.S., M.D., M.C.PATH., F.D.S.R.C.S., Oral Medicine (Lond. H.M.C.)
DUDGEON, J. A., C.B.E., M.C., T.D., D.L., M.A., M.D., F.R.C.P., F.R.C.PATH., Microbiology (Inst. Child Health)
DUDLEY, H. A. F., M.B., CH.M., F.R.C.S.E., F.R.A.C.S., Surgery (St. My.'s H.M.S.)
DUMONDE, D. C., M.A., M.B., B.CHIR., PH.D., M.D., F.R.C.PATH., Immunology (St. Thos.'s H.M.S.)
EDWARDS, J. G., M.A., B.M., B.CH., D.P.M., D.M., M.R.C.P., M.R.C.PSYCH., Addiction Behaviour (Inst. Psych.)
EDWARDS, R. H. T., PH.D., M.R.C.P., Human Metabolism (U.C.L.)
ELDER, M. G., M.D., M.R.C.O.G., F.R.S.C.E., Obstetrics and Gynaecology (Inst. Obstetrics)
ELLIS, H., M.CH., D.M., F.R.C.S., Surgery (West. M.S.)
EVANS, D. J., M.B., B.CHIR., Tissue Pathology (R.P.M.S.)
EXTON-SMITH, A. N., M.A., M.B., B.CHIR., M.D., F.R.C.P., Geriatric Medicine (U.C.L.)
FAIRWEATHER, D. V. I., M.D., F.R.C.O.G., Obstetrics and Gynaecology (U.C.L.)

FATT, P., PH.D., F.R.S., Biophysics (U.C.L.)
FEINSTEIN, A., PH.D., M.D., Immunology (R.P.M.S.)
FESTENSTEIN, H., M.B., CH.B., M.R.C.PATH., Immunology (Lond. H.M.C. and St. Bart's H.M.C.)
FISHER, R. F., M.B., B.S., L.R.C.P., F.R.C.S., M.D., PH.D., D.SC., Biophysical Ophthalmology (Inst. Oph.)
FLECK, A., M.B., CH.B., PH.D., F.R.I.C., M.R.C.PATH., F.R.S., Chemical Pathology (Ch. X.H.M.S.)
FLOYER, M. A., M.A., M.D., F.R.C.P., Medicine (Lond. H.M.C.)
FLUTE, P. T., M.D., M.C.PATH., Haematology (St. G.'s H.M.S.)
FLYNN, F. V., M.D., M.R.C.P., M.C.PATH., Chemical Pathology (U.C.L.)
FOX, W., M.D., F.R.C.P., Community Therapeutics (Cardiothoracic Inst.)
GALTON, D. A. G., M.D., F.R.C.P., Haematological Oncology (R.P.M.S.)
GAMBLE, H. J., M.SC., PH.D., Neuroanatomy (St. Thos.'s H.M.S.)
GARNER, A., M.D., Pathology (Inst. Oph.)
GARRETT, J. R., B.SC., M.B., B.S., PH.D., L.D.S., L.R.C.S., M.R.C.PATH., Oral Pathology (K.C.H.M.S.)
GILLIATT, R. W., M.A., D.M., F.R.C.P., Clinical Neurology (Inst. Neurology)
GLENISTER, T. W., T.D., M.B., B.S., PH.D., D.SC., Anatomy (Ch. X H.M.S.)
GLOSTER, J., PH.D., M.D., Experimental Ophthalmology (Inst. Oph.)
GOLDSMITH, R., B.A., M.B., B.CH., Physiology (Chel. C.)
GOODWIN, J. F., M.D., F.R.C.P., Clinical Cardiology (R.P.M.S.)
GOWING, N. F. C., M.D., F.R.C.PATH., Tumour Pathology (Inst. Cancer Research)
GRAHAM, P. J., M.B., B.CHIR., D.P.M., F.R.C.P., F.R.C.PSYCH., Child Psychiatry (Inst. Child Health)
GREAVES, M. W., M.A., M.B., PH.D., F.R.C.P., Dermatology (Inst. Dermat.)
GREEN, J. H., M.A., M.B., B.CHIR., PH.D., Physiology (Middx. H.M.S.)
GRIMES, A. J., PH.D., Experimental Haematology (St. Thos's H.M.S.)
GUNN, J., M.D., M.R.C.PSYCH., Forensic Psychiatry (Inst. Psych.)
GUZ, A., M.D., M.R.C.P., Medicine (Ch. XH.M.S.)
HARDISTY, R. M., M.D., M.R.C.P., F.C.PATH., Haematology (Inst. Child Health)
HARKNESS, R. D. M. I.-K., B.SC., M.B., B.S., Physiology (U.C.L.)
HARRIS, J. W. S., M.A., M.B., B.S., PH.D., M.R.C.O.G., Anatomy (R.F.H.S.M.)
HARRIS, M., M.D., F.D.S.R.C.S., Oral Surgery (Inst. Dent. Surg.)
HARRIS, P. C., PH.D., M.D., F.R.C.P., Cardiology (Cardiothoracic Inst.)
HARRISON, D. F. N., M.D., F.R.C.S., Laryngology and Otology (Inst. Laryngology)
HAWKINS, D. F., M.B.B.S., PH.D., M.R.C.O.G., Obstetric Therapeutics (Inst. Obstetrics)
HAYWARD, J. C., PH.D., Nursing Studies (Chel. C.)
HEALY, M. J. R., B.A., Medical Statistics (L.S. Hyg. & Trop. Med.)
HEARD, B. E., B.E., B.SC., M.B., CH.B., M.D., F.R.C.PATH., F.R.C.P., Histopathology (Cardiothoracic Inst.)
HEATH, R. B., M.D., Virology (Lond. H.M.C. and St. Bart's H.M.C.)
HERMON-TAYLOR, J., M.CHIR., Surgery (St. G.'s H.M.S.)
HICKS, R. M., PH.D., D.SC., Experimental Pathology (Middx. H.M.S.)

HIGGINS, P. M., M.B.B.S., M.R.C.P., General Practice (Guy's H.M.S.)
HILL, D. K., M.A., SC.D., F.R.S., Biophysics (R.P.M.S.)
HILSON, G. R. F., M.D., F.C.PATH., Bacteriology (St. G.'s H.M.S.)
HINCHCLIFFE, R., PH.D., M.D., D.L.O., F.R.C.P.E., Medicine—Audiological (Inst. L. & O.)
HINTON, J. M., M.D., M.R.C.P., D.P.M., Psychiatry (Middx. H.M.S.)
HIRSCH, S. R., M.PHIL., M.D., M.R.C.P., M.R.C.PSYCH., Psychiatry (Ch. XH.M.S.)
HJELM, N. M., M.D., Chemical Pathology (Inst. Child Health)
HOBBIGER, F., PH.D., M.D., D.SC., Pharmacology (Middx. H.M.S.)
HOBBS, J. R., M.D., D.OBST.R.C.O.G., M.R.C.P., M.C.PATH., Chemical Pathology (West. M.S.)
HOBBS, K. E. F., M.B., B.S., CH.M., F.R.C.S., Surgery (R.F.H.S.M.)
HOBKIRK, J. A., B.D.S., PH.D., F.D.S.R.C.S., Dental Prosthetics (Inst. Dent.Surg.)
HOBSLEY, M., M.A., M.CHIR., PH.D., F.R.C.S., Surgical Science (Middx. H.M.S.)
HODGES, J. R., B.PHARM., PH.D., D.SC., Pharmacology (R.F.H.S.M.)
HODKINSON, H. M., B.M., B.CH., M.A., F.R.C.P., D.M., Geriatric Medicine (R.P.M.S.)
HOFFBRAND, A. V., M.A., D.M., M.R.C.P., D.C.P., M.R.C.PATH., Haematology (R.F.H.S.M.)
HOLBOROW, E. J., M.B., B.CHIR., M.R.C.S., M.D., F.R.C.PATH., F.R.C.P., Immunopathology (Lond. H.M.C.)
HOLLAND, W. W., B.SC., B.S., M.D., Clinical Epidemiology and Social Medicine (St. Thos.'s H.M.S.)
HOLT, K. S., M.D., F.R.C.P., Developmental Paediatrics (Inst. Child Health)
HOUSTON, W. J. B., B.D.S., Orthodontics (L.S. Dent. Surg.)
HOWE, A., PH.D., Physiology (Chel. C.)
HUEHNS, E. R., PH.D., M.D., M.R.C.PATH., Haematology (U.C.L.)
HUNTER, W. H., B.SC., PH.D., Pharmaceutical Chemistry (Chel. C.)
HURLEY, ROSALINDE, M.D., L.R.C.P., M.R.C.S., M.R.C.PATH., Microbiology (Inst. Obstetrics)
HUTT, M.S.R., M.D., M.R.C.S., F.R.C.P., F.R.C.PATH., Geographical Pathology (St. Thos.'s H.M.S.)
HUXLEY, Sir ANDREW F., M.A., D.SC, M.D., F.R.S., Physiology (U.C.L.)
JAMES, D. W., M.B., B.S., Anatomy (U.C.L.)
JAMES, V. H. T., PH.D, D.SC., F.R.I.C., Chemical Pathology (St. My.'s H.M.S.)
JEFFCOATE, S. L., B.A., M.B., B.CHIR., PH.D., Biochemical Endocrinology (Inst. Obstetrics and Gynaecology)
JEFFERYS, Mrs. M., B.SC.(ECON.), Medical Sociology (Bfd.C.)
JENKINS, G. C., M.B.B.S., PH.D., M.R.C.PATH., Haematology (Lond. H.M.C.)
JENKINS, J. S., M.D., F.R.C.P., Endocrinology—Clinical (St. G.'s H.M.S.)
JENKINSON, D. H., M.SC., PH.D., Pharmacology (U.C.L.)
JOELS, N., M.B., B.S., PH.D., Physiology (St. Bart.'s H.M.C.)
JOHNSON, F. R. B.A.O., M.D., Anatomy (Lond. H.M.C.)
JOHNSON, N. W., L.D.S., M.D.SC., F.D.S.R.C.S., F.A.C.D.S., Oral Pathology (Lond. H.M.C.)
JONES, A. E., M.D., M.R.C.P., D.M.R.T., Radiotherapy (St. Bart.'s H.M.C.)

JONES, B. R., M.B. CH.B., D.F.R.C.S., Preventive Ophthalmology (Inst. Oph.)
JONES, E. WILSON, M.B., B.CHIR., M.R.C.P., Dermatological Pathology (Inst. Dermat.)
JUDAH, J. D., B.A., B.M., B.CH., M.R.C.P., Experimental Pathology (U.C.L.)
JUKES, M. G. M., M.A., D.M., Veterinary Physiology (R.Vet.C.)
KAKKAR, V. V., M.B., B.S., F.R.C.S., Surgical Science (K.C.H.M.S.)
KAY, A. B., M.B., CH.B., M.A., PH.D., D.SC., F.R.C.P., M.R.C.PATH., Clinical Immunology (Cardiothoracic Inst.)
KEATINGE, W. R., M.A., M.B., B.CHIR., PH.D., Physiology (Lond. H.M.C.)
KEEN, H., M.D., M.R.C.P., Human Metabolism (Guy's H.M.S.)
KELLY, J. S., M.B., CH.B., PH.D., M.A., Pharmacology (St. G.'s H.M.S.)
KETTERER, B., M.SC., PH.D., Biochemistry (Middx. H.M.S.)
KRAMER, I. R. H., M.D.S., F.D.S.R.C.S. (ENG.), F.R.C.PATH., Oral Pathology (Inst. Dent. Surg.)
LADER, M. H., M.B., CH.B., PH.D., M.D., D.SC., D.P.M., M.R.C.PSYCH., Clinical Psychopharmacology (Inst. Psych.)
LAING, J. A., PH.D., M.R.C.V.S., Animal Husbandry and Veterinary Hygiene (R. Vet. C.)
LAMBERT, H. P., M.A., M.D., F.R.C.P., Microbial Diseases (St. G.'s H.M.S.)
LANDON, J., M.D., M.R.C.S., L.R.C.P., Chemical Pathology (St. Bart.'s H.M.C.)
LANT, A. F., PH.D., F.R.C.P., F.R.C.P.E., Clinical Pharmacology and Therapeutics (West M.S.)
LANTOS, P. L., M.D., PH.D., M.R.C.PATH., Neuropathology (Inst. Psych.)
LAURENCE, D. R., M.D., F.R.C.P., Pharmacology and Therapeutics (U.C.L.)
LAWLER, S. D., M.B.B.S., M.D., F.R.C. PATH., M.R.C.P., Human Genetics (Inst. Can. Res.)
LEHNER, T., M.D., B.D.S., F.D.S.R.C.S., M.R.C.PATH., Oral Immunology (Guy's H.M.S.)
LEIGHTON, B. C., M.D.S., D.ORTH.R.C.S., Orthodontics (K.C.H.M.S.)
LE QUESNE, L. P., M.A., M.CH., D.M., F.R.C.S., Surgery (Middx. H.M.S.)
LENNARD-JONES, J. E., M.A., M.D., F.R.C.P., Gastroenterology (Lond. H.M.C.)
LESSOF, M. H., M.A., M.D., F.R.C.P., Medicine (Guy's H.M.S.)
LEWIS, B., PH.D., M.D., M.R.C.P., M.R.C.PATH., Chemical Pathology (St. Thos.'s H.M.S.)
LEWIS, G. P., PH.D., Pharmacology (Inst. Bas. Med. Sci.)
LEWIS, O. J., M.D., Anatomy (St. Bart.'s H.M.C.)
LISHMAN, W. A., M.D., M.R.C.P., Neuropsychiatry (Inst. Psych.)
LLOYD, JUNE K., M.D., F.R.C.P., Child Health (St. G.'s H.M.S.)
LOGAN, R. F. L., M.D., F.R.C.P., D.I.H., Organization of Medical Care (L.S.Hyg. & Trop. Med.)
LUCY, J. A., B.SC., M.A., PH.D., Biochemistry (R.F.H.S.M.)
LUZZATTO, L., M.D., Haematology (R.P.M.S.)
MACARTNEY, F. J., B.A., B.CH., M.B., M.R.C.P., Paediatric Cardiology (Inst. Child Health)
McCOLL, I., M.S., F.R.C.S., Surgery (Guy's H.M.S.)
MACDONALD, I., PH.D., D.SC., M.D., D.OBST.R.C.O.G., Applied Physiology (Guy's H.M.S.)

MACDONALD, W. I., PH.D., F.R.C.P., Clinical Neurology (Inst. Neurology)
MACINTYRE, I., M.B., CH.B., PH.D., D.SC., M.R.C.PATH., Endocrine Chemistry (R.P.M.S.)
MACINTYRE, N., M.D., F.R.C.P., Medicine (R.F.H.S.M.)
MACKENZIE, D. W. R., PH.D., Medical Mycology (L.S. Hyg. & Trop. Med.)
MCLEAN, P., PH.D., D.SC., Biochemistry (Middx. H.M.S.)
MCMINN, R. M. H., PH.D., M.D., Anatomy (Inst. Basic Med. Sci.)
MAGNUS, I. A., M.A., M.D., F.R.C.P., Photobiology (Inst. Derm.)
MAINI, R. N., B.A., M.B., B.CHIR., F.R.C.P., Immunology of Rheumatic Disease (Ch. XH.M.S.)
MALPAS, J. S., M.B., B.S., D.PHIL., F.R.C.P., Medical Oncology (St. Bart.'s H.M.C.)
MANT, A. K., M.D., M.R.C.PATH., Forensic Medicine (Guy's H.M.S.)
MARKS, I. M., M.B., D.PH., M.R.C.PSYCH., Experimental Psychopathology (Inst. Psych.)
MARLEY, E., M.A., M.B., B.CHIR., M.D., D.SC., D.P.M., F.R.C.P., Pharmacology (Inst. Psych.)
MARSDEN, C. D., M.SC., M.D., B.S., M.R.C.P., Neurology (Inst. Psych. K.C.H.M.S.)
MARSHALL, J., M.D., M.R.C.P., Clinical Neurology (Inst. Neurology)
MASERI, A., M.D., Cardiovascular Medicine (R.P.M.S.)
MATHEWS, A. M., PH.D., Psychology (St. G.'s H.M.S.)
MATTHEWS, D. M., PH.D., M.D., M.C.PATH., Experimental Chemical Pathology (West M.S.)
MELROSE, D. G., B.M., B.CH., M.A., M.R.C.P., F.R.C.S., Surgical Science (R.P.M.S.)
MICHAELS, L., M.D., M.R.C.PATH., F.R.C.P.(C.), Pathology (Inst. Laryngology)
MILEDI, R., B.SC., M.D., F.R.S., Biophysics (U.C.L.)
MILLARD, P. H., M.B., B.S., M.R.C.S., F.R.C.P., Geriatric Medicine (St. G.'s H.M.S.)
MILLER, D. L., M.A., D.PH., M.D., F.R.C.P., F.F.C.M., Community Medicine (Middx. H.M.S.)
MILLS, J. R. E., M.SC., D.D.S., F.D.S., F.D.S.R.C.S., Orthodontics (Inst. Dent. Surg.)
MIMS, C. A. C., B.S., M.D., Microbiology (Guy's H.M.S.)
MITCHISON, D. A., M.B., M.CHIR., Bacteriology (Infectious Diseases) (R.P.M.S.)
MOLLIN, D. L., B.SC., M.B., CH.B., M.C.PATH., M.R.C.P., Haematology (St. Bart.'s H.M.C.)
MONGAR, J. L., PH.D., Pharmacology (U.C.L.)
MORLEY, D. C., M.B., B.CHIR., M.A., M.D., D.CH., Tropical Child Health (Inst. Child Health)
MORRELL, D. C., M.B.B.S., M.R.C.P., D.OBST.R.C.O.G., F.R.C.G.P., General Practice (St. Thos.'s H.M.S.)
MORRIS, N. F., M.D., F.R.C.O.G., Obstetrics and Gynaecology (Ch. X H.M.S.)
MORTIMER, K. V., PH.D., L.D.S.R.C.S., Conservative Dentistry (L.S. Dent. Surg.)
MOSS, D. W., PH.D., D.SC., Clinical Enzymology (R.P.M.S.)
MOSS, J. P., PH.D., Orthodontics (U.C.L.)
MOWBRAY, J. F., B.A., M.B., B.CHIR., M.R.C.P., Immunopathology (St. My.'s H.M.S.)

NAYLOR, M. N., PH.D., F.D.S.R.C.S., Preventive Dentistry (Guy's H.M.S.)
NAYLOR, P. F. D., Dermatology (St. Thos.'s H.M.C.)
NEIL, E., M.D., D.SC., Physiology (Middx. H.M.S.)
NEILL, D. J., D.F.C., M.D.S., F.D.S.R.C.S., Prosthetic Dentistry (Guy's H.M.S.)
NEVILLE, A. M., CH.B., PH.D., M.D., M.R.C.PATH., Experimental Pathology (Inst. Cancer Research)
NEWSOM-DAVIS, J. M., M.A., M.D., M.R.C.P., Neurology (R.F.H.S.M. and Inst. Neurol.)
NEWTON, J. M., PH.D., Pharmaceutics (Chel. C.)
NIAS, A. H. W., D.M., D.M.R.T., F.Q.C.R., Cancer Research (St. Thos's H.M.S.)
NOAKES, D. E., PH.D., M.R.C.V.S., Veterinary Obstetrics and Diseases of Reproduction (R. Vet. C.)
NOBLE, W. C., PH.D., D.SC., Microbiology (Inst. Dermat.)
O'NEIL, R., B.D.S., M.R.C.S., L.R.C.P., F.D.S.R.C.S., Oral Surgery (U.C.L.)
OPPÉ, T. E., M.B., B.S., D.CH., F.R.C.P., Paediatrics (St. My.'s H.M.S.)
OWEN, J. A., B.SC., PH.D., M.D., M.C.PATH., Chemical Pathology (St. G.'s H.M.S.)
PANAYI, G. S., B.A., M.B., M.D., M.R.C.P., Rheumatology (Guy's H.M.S.)
PASTERNAK, C. A., D.PHIL., Biochemistry (St. G.'s H.M.S.)
PATTISON, J. R., D.M., Medical Microbiology (K.C.H.M.S.)
PAYKEL, E. S., M.D., M.R.C.P., M.R.C.PSYCH., Psychiatry (St. G.'s H.M.S.)
PAYNE, J. P., M.B., CH.B., D.A., F.F.A.R.C.S., Anaesthesia (Lond. H.M.C.)
PEART, W. S., M.D., F.R.S., F.R.C.P., Medicine (St. My.'s H.M.S.)
PECKHAM, M. J., M.A., M.D., D.M.R.T., F.F.R., Radiotherapy (Inst. Cancer Research)
PENNY, R. H. C., PH.D., F.R.C.V.S., M.A.C.V.SC., Clinical Veterinary Medicine (R. Vet. C.)
PETERS, D. K., M.B., B.CH., M.R.C.P., Medicine (R.P.M.S.)
PETERS, W., M.A., B.S., M.R.C.S., D.T.M. & H., M.D., D.SC., F.R.C.P., Medical Protozoology (L.S. Hyg. & Trop. Med.)
PHILLIPS, I., M.A., M.D., M.R.C.PATH., Microbiology—Medical (St. Thos.'s H.M.S.)
PICTON, D. C. A., B.D.S., B.SC., PH.D., F.D.S.R.C.S., Experimental and Preventive Dentistry (U.C.L.)
PILKINGTON, T. R. E., M.D., F.R.C.P., Medicine (St. G.'s H.M.S.)
PLAYFAIR, J. H. L., PH.D., Immunology (Middx. H.M.S.)
POND, D. A., M.A., M.D., F.R.C.P., D.P.M., Psychiatry (Lond. H.M.C.)
PORTER, K. A., D.SC., M.D., Pathology (St. Mary's H.M.S.)
POSWILLO, D. E., B.D.S., F.D.S.R.C.S., D.D.S., F.R.A.C.D.S., F.I.BIOL., M.R.C.PATH., D.SC., Oral Surgery (L.S. Dent. Surg.)
PRICHARD, B. N. C., M.SC., M.B.B.S., M.R.C.P., Clinical Pharmacology (U.C.L.)
PRIEST, R. G., B.S., D.P.M., M.D., M.R.C.P.E., M.R.C.PSYCH., Psychiatry (St. My.'s H.M.S.)
PROPHET, A. S., C.B.E., DD..S., F.D.S., Dental Surgery (U.C.L.)
QUILLIAM, J. P., M.D., M.B., B.S., D.SC., M.R.C.P., Pharmacology (St. Bart.'s M.!l C.)

RANG, H. P., M.SC., M.B., B.S., D.PHIL., M.A., Pharmacology (U.C.L.)
REES, L. H., M.B., B.S., M.R.C.P., M.SC., M.R.C.PATH., Chemical Endocrinology (St. Bart.'s H.M.C.)
RENWICK, J. H., M.B., CH.B., PH.D., D.SC., M.F.C.M., F.R.C.P., Human Genetics and Teratology (L.S. Hyg. & Trop. Med.)
REYNOLDS, E. O. R., M.D., D.CH., F.R.C.P., Paediatrics—Neonatal (U.C.L.)
RICHARDS, P., M.B.B.CHIR., M.A., PH.D., M.D., F.R.C.P., Medicine (St. My.'s H.M.S.)
RITCHIE, H. D., M.A., CH.M., F.R.C.S., Surgery (Lond. H.M.C.)
ROBERTSON, W. B., B.SC., M.D., Histopathology (St. G.'s H.M.S.)
ROBINSON, B. F., M.D., F.R.C.P., Cardiovascular Medicine (St. G.'s H.M.S.)
ROBINSON, R. J., M.A., D.PHIL., D.CH., F.R.C.P., Paediatrics (Guy's H.M.S.)
ROBSON, E. B., PH.D., Human Genetics (U.C.L.)
ROBSON, J. G., C.B.E., M.B., CH.B., D.A., F.F.A.R.C.S., Anaesthetics (R.P.M.S.)
RODNIGHT, R. B., D.SC., Neurochemistry (Inst. Psych.)
ROITT, I. M., D.PHIL., Immunology (Middx. H.M.S.)
ROSE, G. A., M.A., M.D., M.R.C.P., Epidemiology and Preventive Medicine (L.S. Hyg. & Trop. Med.)
ROWE, A. H. R., M.D.S., F.D.S.R.C.S., Conservative Dental Surgery (Guy's H.M.S.)
RUSSELL, G. F. M., M.D., F.R.C.P., Psychiatry (Inst. Psych.)
RUTTER, M. L., M.D., M.R.C.P., Child Psychiatry (Inst. Psych.)
RYMAN, BRENDA E., M.A., PH.D., Biochemistry (Ch. X H.M.S.)
SANDLER, M., M.B., CH.B., M.D., M.R.C.P., F.R.C.PATH, Chemical Pathology (Inst. Obstetrics)
SAUNDERS, K. B., M.B.B.CHIR., M.A., M.D., F.R.C.P., Medicine (St.G.'s H.M.S.)
SCHEUER, P. J., F.D., F.R.C.PATH., Clinical Histopathology (R.F.H.S.M.)
SCOPES, J. W., PH.D., M.R.C.P., Paediatrics (St. Thos.'s H.M.S.)
SCOTT, G. B. D., M.D., Histopathology (R.F.H.S.M.)
SCRUTTON, M. C., M.A., D.PHIL., Biochemistry (K.C.)
SEARS, T. A., PH.D., Neurophysiology (Inst. Neurology)
SELWYN, S., B.SC., M.D., M.R.C.PATH., Medical Microbiology (West M.S.)
SEMPLE, S. J. G., M.D., F.R.C.P., Medicine (Middx. H.M.S.)
SEVER, P. S., M.A., M.B.B.CHIR., PH.D., M.R.C.P., Clinical Pharmacology and Therapeutics (St. My.'s H.M.S.)
SEWARD, G. R., M.B., B.S., M.D.S., F.D.S, R.C.S., Oral Surgery (Lond. H.M.C.)
SHAPER, A. G., M.B., CH.B., D.T.M., & H., M.R.C.PATH., F.R.C.P., F.F.C.M., Clinical Epidemiology (R.F.H.S.M.)
SHEPHERD, M., M.A., M.D., M.R.C.P., D.P.M., Epidemiological Psychiatry (Inst. Psych.)
SHERLOCK, Dame SHEILA, D.B.E., M.D., F.R.C.P., Medicine (R.F.H.S.M.)
SILVER, P. H. S., M.B. B.S., PH.D., Anatomy (Middx. H.M.S.)
SIMS, P., PH.D., Carcinogen Biochemistry (Inst. Can. Res.)
SIMS, W., PH.D., M.S., F.D.S.R.C.S., Microbiology in Relation to Dentistry (L.S. Dent. Surg.)
SIRS, J. A., PH.D., Biophysics (St. My.'s H.M.S.)

SLOPER, J. C., M.A., M.D., M.R.C.P., F.R.C.PATH., Experimental Pathology (Ch. X H.M.S.)
SMAJE, L. H., B.SC., M.B., B.S., PH.D., Physiology (Ch. XH.M.S.)
SMITH, I. K. M., M.SC., M.R.C.V.S., Veterinary Microbiology and Parasitology (R. Vet. C.)
SMITH, J. F., B.A., M.B., B.CHIR., M.R.C.P., Morbid Anatomy (U.C.L.)
SMITH, M. J. H., M.PHARM., PH.D., F.R.I.C., Chemical Pathology (K.C.H.M.S.)
SMITH, N. J. D., B.D.S., M.SC., M.PHIL., Dental Radiology (K.C.H.M.S.)
SMITH, S. E., M.A., B.M.B.CH., Applied Pharmacology and Therapeutics (St. Thos.'s H.M.S.)
SÖNKSEN, P. H., M.D., M.R.C.P., Endocrinology (St. Thos.'s H.M.S.)
SOOTHILL, J. F., M.A., M.B., B.CHIR., M.R.C.P., M.R.C.PATH., Immunology (Inst. Child Health)
SOWRAY, J. H., B.D.S., M.R.C.S., L.R.C.P., F.D.S., Oral Surgery (K.C.H.M.S.)
SPECTOR, R. G., Applied Pharmacology (Guy's H.M.S.)
SPECTOR, W. G., M.A., M.B., B.CH., M.R.C.P., Pathology (St. Bart.'s H.M.C.)
SPEIRS, R. L., PH.D., Physiology in relation to Dentistry (Lond. H.M.C.)
SPITZ, L., M.B., CH.B., F.R.C.S., Paediatric Surgery (Inst. Child Health)
STEINBERG, HANNAH, PH.D., Psychopharmacology (U.C.L.)
STEINER, R. E., B.A.O., M.D., F.R.C.P., F.F.R., D.M.R.D., Diagnostic Radiology (R.P.M.S.)
STERN, H., M.B., CH.B., PH.D., M.R.C.PATH, Virology (St. G.'s H.M.S.)
STEWART, J. W., M.B., B.S., Haematology (Middx. H.M.S.)
STRANG, L. B., M.D., M.R.C.P., Paediatrics (U.C.L.)
STROUD, C. E., M.B., B.CH., M.R.C.P., D.C.H., Child Health (K.C.H.M.S.)
SYMMERS, W. ST. C., PH.D., M.D., M.R.C.P.ED., F.R.C.P., Histopathology (Ch. X H.M.S.)
SYMON, L., M.B., CH.B., F.R.C.S., F.R.C.S.E., Neurological Surgery (Inst. Neurology)
TANNER, J. M., D.SC., PH.D., M.D., M.R.C.P., Child Health and Growth (Inst. Child Health)
TAYLOR, A., B.SC., M.B., B.S., Physiology (St. Thos.'s H.M.S.)
TAYLOR, D. E. M., M.B., CH.B., B.SC., F.R.C.S., Applied Physiology (Inst. Bas. Med. Sci.)
TAYLOR, G. W., M.S., F.R.C.S., Surgery (St. Bart.'s H.M.C.)
TAYLOR, K. W., M.A., M.B., M.CHIR., PH.D., Biochemistry (Lond. H.M.C.)
TAYLOR, R. W., M.D., M.R.C.O.G., Obstetrics and Gynaecology (St. Thos.'s H.M.S.)
THOMAS, P. K., B.SC., M.D., M.R.C.P., Neurology (R.F.H.S.M.)
TIGHE, J. R., B.SC., M.B., B.CH., M.D., F.R.C.P., M.R.C.PATH., Histopathology (St. Thos.'s H.M.S.)
TROUNCE, J. R., M.D., F.R.C.P., Clinical Pharmacology (Guy's H.M.S.)
TULLEY, W. J., B.D.S., F.D.S., PH.D., Orthodontics (Guy's H.M.S.)
TURK, J. L., M.D., D.SC., Pathology (Inst. Bas. Med. Sci.)
TURNER, D. R., M.B., PH.D., M.R.C.PATH., Histopathology (Guy's H.M.S.)
TURNER, P., B.SC., M.D., M.B.B.S., M.R.C.P., Clinical Pharmacology (St. Bart.'s H.M.C.)
TURNER-WARWICK (Mrs.), MARGARET E. H., D.M., PH.D., F.R.C.P., Thoracic Medicine (Cardiothoracic Inst.)

VAUGHAN, L. C., D.SC., F.R.C.V.S., Veterinary Surgery (R. Vet. C.)
VERE, D. W., M.D., M.R.C.P., Therapeutics (Lond. H.M.C.)
WAKELING, A., M.B., CH.B., PH.D., Psychiatry (R.F.H.S.M.)
WALKER, P. G., PH.D., Chemical Pathology (Inst. Orth.)
WALL, P. D., M.A., D.M., Anatomy (U.C.L.)
WATERLOW, J. C., M.D., SC.D., F.R.C.P., Human Nutrition (L.S. Hyg. & Trop. Med.)
WATERS, N. E., M.SC., PH.D., Physical Sciences in relation to Dentistry (L.S. Dent. Surg.)
WATERSON, A. P., M.D., M.R.C.P., Virology (R.P.M.S.)
WATKINS, E. S., M.B., CH.B., B.SC., M.D., F.R.C.S., Neurosurgery (Lond. H.M.C.)
WATSON, J. P., M.A., M.D., D.CH., D.P.M., M.R.C.P., M.R.C.PSYCH., Psychiatry (Guy's H.M.S.)
WATSON, R. M., M.D.S., F.D.S.R C.S., Dental Prosthetics (K.C.H.M.S.)
WEBSTER, K. E., M.B.B.S., B.SC., PH.D., Anatomy (K.C.L.)
WEINBREN, H. K., B.SC., M.B.B.CH., M.D., F.R.C.PATH., Experimental Pathology (R.P.M.S.)
WELBOURN, R. B., M.A., M.D., F.R.C.S., Surgical Endocrinology (R.P.M.S.)
WETHERLEY-MEIN, G., B.A., M.D., Haematology (St. Thos.'s H.M.S.)
WHITE, J. M., M.B., CH.B., Haematology (K.C.H.M.S.)
WICKRAMASINGHE, S. N., M.B., B.S., PH.D., Haematology (St. My.'s H.M.S.)
WIDDICOMBE, J. G., M.A., D.PHIL., D.M., Physiology (St. G.'s H.M.S.)
WILKIE, D. R., M.D., M.R.C.P., F.R.S., Physiology (U.C.L.)
WILLIAM, E. S., M.D., PH.D., Nuclear Medicine (Middx. H.M.S.)
WILLIAMS, J. D., B.SC., M.B., CH.B., D.C.P., M.D., M.R.C.P., Medical Microbiology (Lond. H.M.C.)
WILLIAMSON, R., M.SC., PH.D., Biochemistry (St. My.'s H.M.S.)
WILLOUGHBY, D. A., PH.D., M C.PATH., F.I.BIOL., Experimental Pathology (St. Bart.'s H.M.C.)
WILLS, E. D., M.A., M.SC., PH.D., Biochemistry (St. Bart.'s H.M.C.)
WING, J. K., PH.D., M.D., D.P.M., Social Psychiatry (Inst. Psych. & L.S. Hyg. & Trop. Med.)
WINNER, H. I., M.A., M.D., F.C.PATH., Medical Microbiology (Ch. X H.M.S.)
WINTER, G. B., B.D.S., M.B., B.S., D.C.H., F.D.S., Children's Dentistry (L.S. Dent. Surg.)
WOLFF, O. H., M.A., M.D., F.R.C.P., Child Health (Inst. Child Health)
WOLPERT, L., PH.D., Biology as Applied to Medicine (Mddx. H.M.S.)
WOOD, C. B. S., B.A., M.B., B.CHIR., D.CH., M.R.C.P., Child Health (St. Bart.'s H.M.C. & Lond. H.M.C.)
WOOLF, N., M.B., CH.B., M.MED., PH.D., M.R.C.PATH, Histopathology (Middx. H.M.S.)
WOOTTON, I. D. P., M.A., M.B., B.CHIR., PH.D., F.R.I.C., Chemical Pathology (R.P.M.S.)
WRIGHT, E. A., M.D., M.R.C.P., Morbid Anatomy (K.C.H.M.S.)
WRIGHT, N. A., M.D., PH.D., M.R.C.PATH., Histopathology (R.P.M.S.)
WRONG, O. M., B.M., B.CH., M.A., D.M., F.R.C.P., Medicine (U.C.L.)
WYARD, S. J., PH.D., D.SC., Physics applied to Medicine (Guy's H.M.S.)
WYLLIE, J. H., M.D., F.R.C.S., F.R.C.S.E., Surgical Studies (U.C.L.)

WYNN, V., M.D., M.R.C.P., F.C.PATH., Human Metabolism (St. My.'s H.M.S.)
YOUNG, I. M., M.SC., PH.D., Perinatal Physiology (St. Thos.'s H.M.S.)
YUDILEVICH, D., M.SC., Physiology (Q.E.C.)
ZUCKERMAN, A. J., M.SC., M.D., M.R.C.S., L.R.C.P., D.OBST.R.C.O.G., M.R.C.PATH., Microbiology (L.S. Hyg. & Trop. Med.)

*Faculty of Science:*
ALBERY, W. J., M.A., D.PHIL., Physical Chemistry (I.C.)
ALEXANDER, P., PH.D., D.SC., Radiobiology (Inst. Cancer Research)
ALLEN, G., PH.D., F.INST.P., F.R.S., Chemical Technology (I.C.)
ALLEN, J. A., Marine Biology (Marine Biological Station, Millport)
ALLSOP, R. E., PH.D., Transport Studies (U.C.L.)
AUDLEY, R. J., PH.D., Psychology (U.C.L.)
AUDLEY-CHARLES, M. G., PH.D., Geology (Q.M.C.)
AYLETT, B. J., M.A., PH.D., Chemistry (Wfd. C.)
BAILEY, ANITA I., M.SC., Interface Science (I.C.)
BAKER, D. A., PH.D., Agricultural Botany (Wye C.)
BARBER, J., M.SC., PH.D., Plant Physiology (I.C.)
BARNARD, E. A., PH.D., Physiological Biochemistry (I.C.)
BARNARD, T., PH.D., Micropalaeontology (U.C.L.)
BARTON, D. E., PH.D., Statistics (Q.M.C.)
BASTIN, J. A., M.A., PH.D., Physics (Q.M.C.)
BAUM, H., B.SC., PH.D., Biochemistry (Chel. C.)
BECKETT, A. H., D.SC., PH.D., F.P.S., F.R.S.C., Pharmacy (Chel. C.)
BELL, E. A., M.A., PH.D., Biology (K.C.L.)
BELL, G. M., M.A., D.PHIL., Applied Mathematics (Chel. C.)
BELL, P. R., M.A., PH.D., Botany (U.C.L.)
BELLAMY, E. H., M.A., PH.D., Physics (Wfd. C.)
BENDER, A. E., PH.D., Nutrition and Dietetics (Q.E.C.)
BERRY, R. J., M.A., PH.D., D.SC., Genetics (U.C.L.)
BEVAN, E. A., M.A., PH.D., Genetics (Q.M.C.)
BILLIMORIA, J. D., PH.D., D.SC., Lipid Biology (West M.S.)
BINMORE, K. G., PH.D., Mathematics (L.S.E.)
BLOW, D. M., PH.D., F.R.S., Biophysics (I.C.)
BLUNDELL, D. J., PH.D., Environmental Geology (Chel. C.)
BLUNDELL, T. L., D.PHIL., Crystallography (Bk. C.)
BOHM, D. J., B.S., PH.D., Theoretical Physics (Bk. C.)
BONDI, Sir HERMANN, M.A., F.R.S., Mathematics (K.C.L.)
BONNETT, R., PH.D., Organic Chemistry (Q.M.C.)
BONNOR, W. B., D.SC., PH.D., Mathematics (Q.E.C.)
BOYCOTT, B. B., B.SC., F.R.S., Biology (K.C.L.)
BOYD, R. L. F., C.B.E., B.SC.(ENG.), PH.D., F.R.S., Physics (U.C.L.)
BRADBEER, J. W., PH.D., Botany (K.C.L.)
BRADFORD, H. F., PH.D., D.SC., Neurochemistry (I.C.)
BRADLEY, D. C., PH.D., D.SC., Inorganic Chemistry (Q.M.C.)

BRITTON, J. L., M.SC., PH.D., Pure Mathematics (Q.E.C.)
BROWN, E. H., PH.D., Geography (U.C.L.)
BUGG, D. V., PH.D., Nuclear Physics (Q.M.C.)
BURGE, E. J., M.A., PH.D., Physics (Chel. C.)
BURGE, R. E., PH.D., D.SC., Physics (Q.E.C.)
BURGESS, D. D., M.A., PH.D., Spectroscopy (I.C.)
BUTTERWORTH, I., PH.D., Physics (I.C.)
CARO, C. G., B.SC., M.D., F.R.C.P.E., Physiological Mechanics (I.C.)
CASTILLEJO, L., B.SC.(ENG.), B.A., Physics (U.C.L.)
CHALONER, W. G., PH.D., Botany (Bfd. C.)
CHAPMAN, D., PH.D., D.SC., Biophysical Chemistry (R.F.H.S.M.)
CHAPMAN, G., M.A., PH.D., Zoology (Q.E.C.)
CHARAP, J. M., M.A., PH.D., Theoretical Physics (Q.M.C.)
CHEESMAN, D. F., PH.D., Biochemistry (Bfd. C.)
CLOUDSLEY-THOMPSON, J. L., M.A., PH.D., D.SC., Zoology (Bk. C.)
COHN, P. M., M.A., PH.D., Mathematics (Bfd. C.)
COLE, MONICA M., PH.D., Geography (Bfd. C.)
COLES, B. R., D.PHIL., Solid State Physics (I.C.)
COLTHEART, M., M.A., PH.D., Psychology (Bk. C.)
CONOLLY, B., M.A., Mathematics and Operational Research (Chel. C.)
CONWAY, G. R., PH.D., Environmental Technology (I.C.)
COOKE, R. U., M.SC., PH.D., Geography (U.C.L.)
COOPER, D. C., PH.D., Computer Science (U.C.L.)
COULOURIS, G. F., B.SC., Computer Systems (Q.M.C.)
COX, C. B., PH.D., D.SC., Zoology (K.C.L.)
COX, D. R., M.A., PH.D., F.R.S., Statistics (I.C.)
COX, F. E. G., PH.D., D.SC., Zoology (K.C.L.)
CROOK, E. M., M.SC., PH.D., Biochemistry (St. Bart.'s H.M.C.)
DALES, R. P., PH.D., Zoology (Bfd. C.)
DAVIES, A. G., PH.D., D.SC., Chemistry (U.C.L.)
DAVIES, E. B., D.PHIL., Mathematics (K.C.L.)
DIPLOCK, A. T., D.SC., Biochemistry (Guy's H.M.S.)
DOBBS, E. R., PH.D., Physics (Bfd. C.)
DODGE, J. D., PH.D., Botany (R.H.C.)
DONOVAN, B., PH.D., D.SC., F.I.P., Physics (Wfd. C.)
DONOVAN, D. T., PH.D., D.SC., Geology (U.C.L.)
DOYLE, F. H., D.M.R.D., F.F.R., Radiological Science (R.P.M.S.)
DUCKETT, J. G., PH.D., Botany (Q.M.C.)
DUNGEY, J. W., PH.D., Physics (I.C.)
EASTHAM, M. S. P., M.A., D.PHIL., Pure Mathematics (Chel. C.)
EGGLESTON, H. G., M.A., PH.D., SC.D., Pure Mathematics (R.H.C.)
EKINS, R. P., M.A., PH.D., Biophysics (Middx. H.M.S.)
ELLIOTT, W. S., M.A., F.I.E.E., F.INST.P., Computing (I.C.)
ESSAM, J. W., PH.D., Mathematics (Wfd. C.)
EYSENCK, H. J., PH.D., D.SC., Psychology (Inst. Psych.)
FERSHT, A. R., PH.D., Chemistry (I.C.)
FLORENTIN, J. J., PH.D., Computer Science (Bk. C.)

FOSS, B. M., M.A., Psychology (Bfd. C.)
FOSTER, A. B., PH.D., D.SC., Chemistry (Inst. Cancer Research)
GAHAN, P. B., PH.D., Botany (Q.E.C.)
GINSBURG, M., PH.D., D.SC., Pharmacology (Chel. C.)
GODWIN, H. J., M.A., Statistics and Computer Science (R.H.C.)
GOLD, V., PH.D., D.SC., F.R.S., Chemistry (K.C.L.)
GOLDSACK, S. J., PH.D., Computing Science (I.C.)
GOLDSTEIN, H., B.SC., Statistical Methods (Inst. Educ.)
GRANT, E. H., PH.D., Experimental Physics (Q.E.C.)
GREEN, J., D.SC., PH.D., Zoology (Wfd. C.)
GREENBAUM, A. L., D.SC., PH.D., Biochemistry (U.C.L.)
GRIFFITH, T. C., PH.D., D.SC., Physics (U.C.L.)
GROVES, G. V., M.A., PH.D., Physics (U.C.L.)
GRUENBERG, K. W., PH.D., Pure Mathematics (Q.M.C.)
HAINES, M. G., PH.D., Physics (I.C.)
HAJNAL, J., M.A., F.B.A., Statistics (L.S.E.)
HALL, D. O., PH.D., Biology (K.C.L.)
HART, M., PH.D., Physics (K.C.L.)
HARTLEY, B. S., M.A., PH.D., Biochemistry (I.C.)
HASSELL, M. P., M.A., D.PHIL., Insect Ecology (I.C.)
HASTED, J. B., M.A., D.PHIL., Experimental Physics (Bk. C.)
HAYMAN, W. K., M.A., SC.D., F.R.S., Pure Mathematics (I.C.)
HAYWARD, J. C., PH.D., Nursing Studies (Chel. C.)
HEDDLE, D. W. O., PH.D., Physics (R.H.C.)
HERRIOT, P., M.ED., PH.D., Occupational Psychology (Bk. C.)
HEYMANN, F. F., B.SC.(ENG.), PH.D., Physics (U.C.L.)
HOCKING, L. M., PH.D., Mathematics (U.C.L.)
HOLGATE, P., B.SC., Statistics (Bk. C.)
HOLMES, W., PH.D., D.SC., Agriculture (Wye C.)
HOLT, S. J., PH.D., D.SC., F.R.I.C., Experimental Biochemistry (Mddx. H.M.S.)
HOUGH, L., PH.D., D.SC., F.R.I.C., Chemistry (Q.E.C.)
HOWARTH, D. J., PH.D., Computing Science (I.C.)
HOWIE, R. A., M.A., PH.D., SC.D., Mineralogy (K.C.L.)
HUGHES, D. R., M.A., PH.D., Mathematics (Wfd. C.)
HUGHES, J., PH.D., Pharmacological Biochemistry (I.C.)
ILIFFE, J. K., M.A., Information Systems Science and Technology (Q.M.C.)
JAMES, A. M., M.A., D.PHIL., D.SC., F.R.S.C., Physical Chemistry (Bfd. C.)
JENNINGS, R. E., PH.D., Physics (U.C.L.)
JONSCHER, A. K., PH.D., Solid State Electronics (Chel. C.)
KALMUS, P. I. P., PH.D., Nuclear Physics (Q.M.C.)
KEMBER, N. F., PH.D., D.SC., Biophysics (St. Bart.'s H.M.C.)
KHABAZA, I. M., M.A., Computing Science (Q.M.C.)
KIBBLE, T. W. B., M.A., PH.D., Theoretical Physics (I.C.)
KILMISTER, C. W., PH.D., Applied Mathematics (K.C.L.)
KING, P. J. H., M.SC., Computer Science (Bk. C.)
KIRK, D. N., D.SC., F.R.S.C., Chemistry (Wfd. C.)

KIRSTEIN, P. T., M.SC., PH.D., D.SC.(ENG.), Computer Systems (U.C.L.)
KNILL, J. L., PH.D., Engineering Geology (I.C.)
LANDIN, P. J., M.A., Computing Science (Q.M.C.)
LARMAN, D. G., PH.D., Mathematics (U.C.L.)
LEADER, E., M.S., PH.D., Theoretical Physics (Wfd. C.)
LEES, A. D., M.A., PH.D., SC.D., F.R.S., Insect Physiology (I.C.)
LEHMAN, M. M., PH.D., Computing Science (I.C.)
LEVY, J. F., B.SC., Wood Science (I.C.)
LEWIS, C. T., M.A., PH.D., Zoology (R.H.C.)
LINDSAY, P. A., PH.D., Physical Electronics (K.C.L.)
LINDOP, P. J., M.B., B.S., PH.D., D.SC., M.R.C.P.
Radiation Biology (St. Bart.'s H.M.C.)
MACDONALD, I. G., M.A., Pure Mathematics (Q.M.C.)
McDOWELL, M. R. C., M.A., PH.D., Applied Mathematics (R.H.C.)
McGLASHAN, M. L., D.SC., PH.D., F.R.S.C., Chemistry (U.C.L.)
MANNERS, G., M.A., Geography (U.C.L.)
MARCH, P. V., PH.D., Physics (Wfd. C.)
MARTIN, D. H., PH.D., Physics (Q.M.C.)
MASON, R. G., M.SC., PH.D., Pure Geophysics (I.C.)
MASON, S. F., M.A., D.PHIL., D.SC., Chemistry (K.C.L.)
MATHEWS, A. M., PH.D., Psychology (St. G.'s H.M.S.)
MATHIAS, A. P., PH.D., Bio-chemistry (U.C.L.)
MILLEN, D. J., PH.D., D.SC., Chemistry (U.C.L.)
MITCHISON, N. A., D.PHIL., F.R.S., Zoology and Comparative Anatomy (U.C.L.)
MOORE, D. W., M.A., PH.D., Applied Mathematics (I.C.)
MOORE, J. H., PH.D., D.SC., F.R.S.C., Biochemistry in relation to Agriculture in the University of London (Wye C.)
MORGAN, M. J., PH.D., Psychology (U.C.L.)
MORRIS, H. R., PH.D., Biological Chemistry (I.C.)
MORTON, I. D., M.SC., PH.D., F.R.S.C., F.N.Z.I.C., F.I.F.S.T., Food Science (Q.E.C.)
MOSES, V., M.A., PH.D., D.SC., Microbiology (Q.M.C.)
NEW, G. H. C., M.A., D.PHIL., Non-Linear Optics (I.C.)
ORR, J. S., Physics—Medical (R.P.M.S.)
OVEREND, W. G., D.SC., Chemistry (Bk. C.)
PATRICK, A. D., PH.D., Enzymology (Inst. Child Health)
PENDRY, J. B., M.A., PH.D., Theoretical Solid State Physics (I.C.)
PERCIVAL, I. C., PH.D., Applied Mathematics (Q.M.C.)
PERKINS, M. J., PH.D., Chemistry (Chel. C.)
PETERSON, P. J., M.SC., PH.D., Botany (Wfd. C.)
PICKARD, D. H., B.A., Marketing (Wye C.)
PIPER, F. C., PH.D., Mathematics (Wfd. C.)
PIRANI, F. A. E., M.A., PH.D., D.SC., Rational Mechanics (Q.M.C.)
PIRT, S. J., PH.D., F.I.BIOL., Microbiology (Q.E.C.)
POST, H. R., PH.D., Philosophy of Natural Sciences (Chel. C.)

POWER, E. A., M.SC., PH.D., Mathematics (U.C.L.)
PRATT, P. L., PH.D., Crystal Physics (I.C.)
PRENTICE, J. E., PH.D., Geology (K.C.L.)
PRIDHAM, J. B., PH.D., D.SC., Biochemistry (R.H.C.)
PRITCHARD, J., PH.D., Physical Chemistry (Q.M.C.)
PUGH, J. C., M.A., PH.D., Geography (K.C.L.)
PYE, J. D., PH.D., Zoology (Q.M.C.)
RABIN, B. R., M.SC., PH.D., Biochemistry (U.C.L.)
RACHMAN, S., PH.D., Abnormal Psychology (Inst. Psych.)
RAFF, M. C., M.D.C.M., F.R.C.P.S., Biology (U.C.L.)
RANDALL, E. W., D.PHIL., Inorganic Chemistry (Q.M.C.)
RATTANSI, P. M., M.A., PH.D., History and Philosophy of Science (U.C.L.)
REES, C. W., PH.D., Organic Chemistry (I.C.)
REES, K. R., PH.D., D.SC., Biochemical Pathology (U.C.L.)
REESE, C. B., PH.D., M.A., SC.D., Chemistry (K.C.L.)
REUTER, G. E. H., M.A., Mathematics (I.C.)
RIDD, J. H., PH.D., D.SC., Chemistry (U.C.L.)
RING, J., PH.D., F.INST.P., F.R.A.S., Physics (I.C.)
ROBINSON, D., PH.D., Biochemistry (Q.E.C.)
ROGERS, C. A., D.SC., F.R.S., Mathematics (U.C.L.)
ROSS, W. C. J., D.SC., Organic Chemistry (Inst. Cancer Research)
ROTH, K. F., M.SC., PH.D., F.R.S., Pure Mathematics (Theory of Numbers) (I.C.)
ROXBURGH, I. W., PH.D., Applied Mathematics (Q.M.C.)
SALAM, A., M.A., PH.D., F.R.S., Theoretical Physics (I.C.)
SAMET, P. A., PH.D., Computer Science (U.C.L.)
SATCHELL, D. P. N., PH.D., Chemistry (K.C.L.)
SAUNDERS, L., PH.D., D.SC., F.R.S.C., Pharmaceutical Chemistry (Sch. Pharm.)
SCHWABE, W. W., D.SC., Horticulture (Wye C.)
SCORER, R. S., PH.D., Theoretical Mechanics (I.C.)
SEATON, M. J., PH.D., Physics (U.C.L.)
SHARMA, C. S., M.SC., D.PHIL., Applied Mathematics (Bk. C.)
SHAW, R. A., PH.D., D.SC., F.R.S.C., Chemistry (Bk. C.)
SHEARMAN, D. J., D.SC., Sedimentology (I.C.)
SIMONS, H. A. B., M.A., PH.D., Physics as applied to Medicine (R.F.H.S.M.)
SINGER, K., PH.D., Physical Chemistry (R.H.C.)
SMITH, A. J., PH.D., Geology (Bfd. C.)
SMITH, C. A. B., PH.D., Biometry (U.C.L.)
SMITH, J. A. S., M.A., D.PHIL., Chemistry (Q.E.C.)
SMITH, J. T., PH.D., M.P.S., Pharmaceutical Microbiology (Sch. Pharm.)
SMITH, R. L., PH.D., Biochemical Pharmacology (St. My.'s H.M.S.)
SMYTH, J. D., PH.D., D.SC., Parasitology (I.C.)
SONDHEIMER, E. H., M.A., D.SC., PH.D., Mathematics (Wfd. C.)
SPENCE, D. A., PH.D., D.SC., Mathematics (I.C.)
SPYER, K. M., PH.D., D.SC., Physiology (R.F.H.S.M.)

STEWART, G. R., PH.D., Botany (Bk. C.)
STEWARTSON, K., M.A., PH.D., F.R.S., Mathematics (U.C.L.)
STONE, M., PH.D., Probability and Statistics (U.C.L.)
STONELEY, R., M.A., PH.D., Petroleum Geology (I.C.)
STREATER, R. F., PH.D., Applied Mathematics (Bfd. C.)
STUART, J. T., PH.D., F.R.S., Theoretical Fluid Mechanics (I.C.)
SUMMERFIELD, A., B.SC.TECH., B.SC., Psychology (Bk. C.)
SUTTON, J., PH.D., D.SC., F.R.S., Geology (I.C.)
SYKES, K. W., M.A., D.PHIL., Physical Chemistry (Q.M.C.)
TAIT, J. F., PH.D., F.R.S., Physics as applied to Medicine (Middx. H.M.S.)
TAYLOR, J. G., M.A., PH.D., Mathematics (K.C.L.)
THOMPSON, J. M. T., M.A., SC.D., Structural Mechanics (U.C.L.)
THORNES, J. B., M.SC., PH.D., Physical Geography (Bfd. C.)
TIFFEN, R. W., PH.D., D.SC., Applied Mathematics (Bk. C.)
TOBE, M. L., PH.D., Chemistry (U.C.L.)
TYRRELL, H. J. V., M.A., D.SC., Physical and Inorganic Chemistry (Chel. C.)
VARMA, M. R. G., D.SC., Medical Entomology (L.S. Hyg. & Trop. Med.)
VAUGHAN, R. C., PH.D., Pure Mathematics (I.C.)
VERNON, C. A., D.SC., Chemistry (U.C.L.)
WATSON, B. W., PH.D., F.I.P., Applied Medical Electronics (St. Bart's H.M.C.)
WATSON, JANET V., PH.D., Geology (I.C.)
WAY, M. J., M.A., D.SC., Applied Entomology (I.C.)
WEALE, R. A., D.SC., Visual Science (Inst. Oph.)
WEBBE, G., D.SC., Applied Parasitology (L.S. Hyg. & Trop. Med.)
WEHRFRITZ, B. A., F. PH.D., Pure Mathematics (Q.M.C.)
WEINBERG, F. J., PH.D., D.SC., Combustion Physics (I.C.)
WELFORD, W. T., D.SC., Physics (I.C.)
WEST, T. S., PH.D., D.SC., F.R.S.C., Analytical Chemistry (I.C.)
WHALLEY, W. B., D.SC., F.R.S.C., Chemistry (Sch. Pharm.)
WILKINSON, Sir GEOFFREY, PH.D., F.R.S., Inorganic Chemistry (I.C.)
WILKINSON, G. R., PH.D., Physics (K.C.L.)
WILLIAMS, G. H., PH.D., D.SC., F.R.S.C., Chemistry (Bfd. C.)
WILSON, R., C.B.E., PH.D., F.R.S., Astronomy (U.C.L.)
WILLS, E. D., PH.D., Biochemistry (St. Barts.'s H.M.C.)
WOHLFARTH, E. P., PH.D., D.SC., Theoretical Magnetism (I.C.)
WOLFENDEN, K., B.SC., M.A., Information Processing (U.C.L.)
WOOD, R. K. S., PH.D., F.I.BIOL., Plant Pathology (I.C.)

*Faculty of Engineering:*
AITCHISON, C. S., B.SC., F.I.E.E., Electronics (Chel. C.)
AMBRASEYS, N. N., PH.D., Engineering Seismology (I.C.)
ANDERSON, J. C., M.SC., PH.D., D.SC. (ENG.), Electrical Materials (I.C.)
ANDREWS, E. H., D.SC., F.INST.P., Materials (Q.M.C.)
ASH, E. A., PH.D., Electrical Engineering (U.C.L.)
BONFIELD, W., PH.D., Materials (Q.M.C.)
BRADSHAW, P., B.A., Experimental Aerodynamics (I.C.)
BROWN, E. H., PH.D., Structural Analysis (I.C.)

BROWN, E. T., M.ENG.SC., PH.D., Rock Mechanics (I.C.)
BURKIN, A. R., M.SC., PH.D., F.R.I.C., Hydrometallurgy (I.C.)
BURLAND, J. B., M.SC.(ENG.), PH.D., M.I.C.E., Soil Mechanics (I.C.)
CAMERON, A., M.SC., PH.D., D.SC.(ENG.), Lubrication Engineering (I.C.)
CLARRICOATS, P. J. B., PH.D., Electrical Engineering (Q.M.C.)
COHEN, E., M.SC., PH.D., Mineral Technology (I.C.)
DAVIES, D. E. N., PH.D., D.SC., Electrical Engineering (U.C.L.)
DAVIES, R. M., M.S., PH.D., Bioengineering (U.C.L.)
DOUGILL, J., W. PH.D., F.I.C.E., F.A.S.E.C., Concrete Structures and Technology (I.C.)
DOWLING, P. J., B.E., D.I.C., PH.D., Steel Structures (I.C.)
EARLES, S. W. E., PH.D., Mechanical Engineering (K.C.L.)
EILON, S., PH.D., Management Science (I.C.)
FREEMAN, E. M., PH.D., F.I.E.E., Applied Electromagnetics (I.C.)
GIBSON, R. E., PH.D., D.SC.(ENG.), F.I.C.E., Engineering Science (K.C.L.)
GOPINATH, A., M.TECH., PH.D., D.ENG., Electronics (Chel. C.)
GOSNEY, W. B., B.SC.(ENG.), Refrigeration Engineering (K.C.L.)
GRANT, P. J., M.A., PH.D., Nuclear Power (I.C.)
GRIEVESON, P., PH.D., D.I.C., Applied Metallurgy (I.C.)
GROOTENHUIS, P., PH.D., D.SC.(ENG.), Engineering Science—Mechanical (I.C.)
HANCOCK, G. J., PH.D., Aeroelasticity (Q.M.C.)
HUSBAND, T. M., M.A., PH.D., Engineering Manufacture (I.C.)
HUTCHINSON, J. N., PH.D., M.I.C.E., F.G.S., Engineering Geomorphology (I.C.)
IVES, K. J., PH.D., Public Health Engineering (U.C.L.)
JANOTA, M. S., M.SC., PH.D., D.SC., M.I.MECH.E., Mechanical Engineering (Q.M.C.)
JEFFES, J. H. E., M.A., PH.D., D.SC. (ENG.), Extraction Metallurgy (I.C.)
KEMP, K. O., PH.D., Civil Engineering (U.C.L.)
LAITHWAITE, E. R., M.SC., PH.D., Heavy Electrical Engineering (I.C.)
LAMBERT, T. H., B.SC.(ENG.), PH.D., Mechanical Engineering (U.C.L.)
LAUGHTON, M. A., PH.D., D.SC.(ENG.), Electrical and Electronic Engineering (Q.M.C.)
LESLIE, D. C., M.A., D.PHIL., Nuclear Engineering (Q.M.C.)
LILLY, M. D., PH.D., D.SC., Biochemical Engineering (U.C.L.)
MAYNE, D. Q., M.SC., Control Theory (I.C.)
MULLIN, J. W., PH.D., D.SC., F.I.CHEM.E., F.R.S.C., Chemical Engineering (U.C.L.)
MUNRO, J., PH.D., Civil Engineering Systems (I.C.)
MURGATROYD, W., M.A., PH.D., Thermal Power (I.C.)
NEAL, B. G., M.A., PH.D., SC.D., F.I.C.E., Civil Engineering (I.C.)
OWEN, P. R., C.B.E., M.SC., F.R.S., Aviation (I.C.)
PASHLEY, D. W., PH.D., F.INST.P., F.R.S., Materials (I.C.)
PEARSON, J. R. A., A.M., PH.D., Chemical Engineering (I.C.)

Poskitt, T. J., ph.d., m.i.c.e., Civil Engineering (Q.M.C.)
Redwood, M., d.sc.(eng.), Electrical and Electronic Engineering (Q.M.C.)
Rowe, P. N., ph.d., d.sc.(eng.), Chemical Engineering (U.C.L.)
Rydill, L. J., o.b.e., m.r.i.n.a., r.c.n.c., c.eng., Naval Architecture (U.C.L.)
Sargent, R. W. H., ph.d., Chemical Engineering (I.C.)
Sawistowski, H., ph.d., Chemical Engineering (I.C.)
Sayers, B. McA., m.sc., ph.d., Electrical Engineering applied to Medicine (I.C.)
Scales, J. T., f.r.c.s., l.r.c.p., c.i.mech.e., Biomedical Engineering (Inst. Orth.)
Shaw, C. T., m.sc., Mining (I.C.)
Smart, A. D. G., Urban Planning (U.C.L.)
Spalding, D. B., ph.d., Heat Transfer (I.C.)
Swanson, S. A. V., ph.d., Biomechanics (I.C.)
Turner, C. E., ph.d., d.sc.(eng.), Materials in Mechanical Engineering (I.C.)
Turner, C. W., ph.d., Electrical Engineering (K.C.L.)
Turner, L. F., ph.d., Digital Communication (I.C.)
Wall, C. G., ph.d., Petroleum Engineering (I.C.)
Westcott, J. H., ph.d., d.sc., Control Systems (I.C.)
Whitelaw, J. H., ph.d., Convective Heat Transfer (I.C.)
Williams, J. G., ph.d., d.sc.(eng.), Polymer Engineering (I.C.)
Williams, M. M. R., ph.d., d.sc., Nuclear Engineering (Q.M.C.)
Williams, T. J., ph.d., d.sc., f.i.mech.e., Mechanical Engineering (K.C.L.)
Woods, W. A., ph.d., d.eng., Mechanical Engineering (Q.M.C.)

*Faculty of Economics and Political Science (including Commerce and Industry):*
Abel-Smith, B., ph.d., Social Administration (L.S.E.)
Atkinson, A. B., b.a., Economics (L.S.E.)
Barker, T. C., m.a., ph.d., f.r.hist.s., Economic History (L.S.E.)
Bartholomew, D. J., ph.d., Statistics (L.S.E.)
Bauer, P. T., m.a., Economics with special reference to Under-Developed Countries and Economic Development (L.S.E.)
Britton, D. K., m.a., Agricultural Economics (Wye C.)
Brown, G. W., ph.d., Sociology (Bfd. C.)
Carsberg, B. V., m.sc.(econ.), m.a. (econ.), f.i.c.a., Accounting (L.S.E.)
Coddington, A., b.sc., d.phil., Economics (Q.M.C.)
Cohen, P. S., ph.d., Sociology (L.S.E.)
Corry, B. A., ph.d., Economics (Q.M.C.)
Cranston, M. W., b.litt., f.r.s.l., Political Science (L.S.E.)
Crick, B., ph.d., Politics (Bk. C.)
Dasgupta, P. S., ph.d., Economics (L.S.E.)
Day, A. C. L., b.a., Economics (L.S.E.)
Dev, F. S. D., m.sc., Accounting (L.S.E.)
Douglas, A. S., m.a., ph.d., Computational Methods (L.S.E.)
Durbin, J., m.a., Statistics (L.S.E.)
Erickson, C. J., m.a., ph.d., Economic History (L.S.E.)
Foldes, L. P., m.sc.(econ.), Economics (L.S.E.)

Hart, O. S. D.'A., m.a., ph.d., Economics (L.S.E.)
Henderson, P. D., m.a., Political Economy (U.C.L.)
Himmelweit, Hildegard T., m.a., ph.d., Social Psychology (L.S.E.)
Hines, A. G., b.sc.(econ.), Economics (Bk. C.)
Howe, C. B., m.a., ph.d., Economics with reference to Asia (S.O.A.S.)
Jones, E., m.sc., ph.d., Geography (L.S.E.)
Jones, G. W., m.a., d.phil., Government (L.S.E.)
Kedourie, E., b.sc.(econ.), Politics (L.S.E.)
Land, Ailsa H., ph.d., Operational Research (L.S.E.)
Layard, P. R. G., m.sc.(econ.), Economics (L.S.E.)
Letwin, W., ph.d., Political Science (L.S.E.)
Little, A., ph.d., Social Administration (Bfd. C.)
MacDonald, J. S., m.a., ph.d., Social Policy (Chel. C.)
McGregor, Rt. Hon. Lord, b.sc.(econ.), Social Institutions (Bfd. C.)
McRae, D. G., m.a., Sociology (L.S.E.)
Marris, R. L., m.a., sc.d., Economics (Bk. C.)
Martin, D. A., ph.d., Sociology (L.S.E.)
Morishima, M., m.a., Economics (L.S.E.)
Morris, T. P., ph.d., Social Institutions (L.S.E.)
Morris-Jones, W. H., b.sc.(econ.), Commonwealth Affairs (Inst. Commonwealth Studies)
Myint, M. H., m.a., ph.d., d.litt., Economics (L.S.E.)
Nevitt, Adela A., b.sc.(econ.), Social Administration (L.S.E.)
Nickell, S. J., b.a., m.sc., Economics (L.S.E.)
Nish, I. H., ph.d., International History (L.S.E.)
Northedge, F. S., b.sc.(econ.), ph.d., International Relations (L.S.E.)
Peston, M. H., b.sc.(econ.), Economics (Q.M.C.)
Pinker, R. A., m.sc.econ., Social Work Studies (L.S.E.)
Plowman, D. E. G., m.a., Social Administration (L.S.E.)
Portes, R. D., m.a., d.phil., Economics (Bk.C.)
Prest, A. R., m.a., ph.d., Economics with special reference to Economics of the Public Sector (L.S.E.)
Reader, D. H., m.a., ph.d., Social Studies (Chel. C.)
Roberts, B. C., m.a., Industrial Relations (L.S.E.)
Sargan, J. D., b.a., Econometrics (L.S.E.)
Self, P. J. O., m.a., Public Administration (L.S.E.)
Silberston, Z. A., m.a., Economics (I.C.)
Spraos, J., m.a., Political Economy (U.C.L.)
Strange, S., b.sc.(econ.), International Relations (L.S.E.)
Stuart, A., d.sc.(econ.), Statistics (L.S.E.)
Thurley, K. E., b.sc.(econ.), Industrial Relations with special reference to Personnel Management (L.S.E.)
Walker, K. R., d.phil., Economics with reference to Asia (S.O.A.S.)
Wibberley, G. P., m.sc., ph.d., Country side Planning (Wye C.)
Wiles, P. J. de la F., m.a., Russian Social and Economic Studies (L.S.E. and S.S.E.E.S.)

Wise, M. J., m.c., ph.d., Geography (L.S.E.)
Wrigley, E. A., ph.d., Population Studies (L.S.E.)
Yamey, B. S., c.b.e., b.com., Economics (L.S.E.)

*Faculty of Education:*
Aspin, D. N., ph.d., Education (K.C.L.)
Bernstein, B. B., ph.d., d.litt., Sociology of Education (Inst. Educ.)
Black, P. J., Science Education (Chel. C.)
Blackstone, T., ph.d., Educational Administration (Inst. Educ.)
Blaug, M., m.a., ph.d., Economics of Education (Inst. Educ.)
Charlton, K., m.a., ed.b., History of Education (K.C.L.)
Davies, W. B., m.a., Education (Chel. C.)
Francis, Hazel, ph.d., Educational Psychology (Inst. Educ.)
Graves, N. J., m.a., ph.d., Geography Education (Inst. Educ.)
Groombridge, B. H., b.a., Adult Education (Dept. of Extra-Mural Studies)
Hindley, C. B., m.b., ch.b., b.sc., Child Development (Inst. Educ.)
Holmes, B., ph.d., Education (Inst. Educ.)
Johnson, D. C., ph.d., Mathematics Education (Chel. C.)
Lawton, D., ph.d., Education (Inst. Educ.)
Lucas, A. M., ph.d., Science Curriculum Studies (Chel. C.)
MacLeod, R. M., ph.d., Science of Education (Inst. Educ.)
Peters, R. S., ph.d., Philosophy of Education (Inst. Educ.)
Rosen, H., ph.d., Education, English (Inst. Educ.)
Skilbeck, M., m.a., ph.d., Education with special reference to Curriculum Studies (Inst. Ed.)
Swanwick, K., l.r.a.m., g.r.s.m., a.r.c.o., m.ed., ph.d., Music Education (Inst. Educ.)
Wedell, K., ph.d., Educational Psychology with reference to children with special needs (Inst. Educ.)
Widdowson, H. G., m.a., ph.d., Education (Inst. Educ.)
Williams, P. R. C., b.a., Education in Developing Countries (Inst. Educ.)

Schools of the University:

(Numbers given are appointed and recognized teachers, and students registered with the University)

I. *Schools in receipt of U.G.C. Grants*
(a) Non-Medical

**Bedford College:** Inner Circle, Regent's Park, NW1 4NS; f. 1849, incorporated 1869, chartered 1909, 1911, 1957, 1965 and 1973.

*Principal:* J. N. Black, m.a., d.phil., d.sc., f.r.s.e., f.i.biol.

*Secretary:* Maj. Gen. S. M. O'H. Abraham (rtd.), c.b., m.c., b.a.

*Registrar:* L. P. Turnbull, m.sc.

Library of over 200,000 vols.
Number of teachers: 169 including 28 professors.

Number of students: 1,641.

Deans:
*Faculty of Arts:* Prof. W. E. Yuill, m.a.

*Faculty of Science:* Prof. E. R. DOBBS, PH.D., D.SC., F.INST.P., F.I.O.A.

**Birkbeck College:** Malet St., WC1E 7HX; f. 1823; Charter of Incorporation 1926.
*Master:* Prof. W. G. OVEREND, PH.D., D.SC., C.CHEM., F.R.S.C.
*Secretary:* R. E. SWAINSON, M.A.
*Registrar:* H. L. SNAITH, M.A.

Number of teachers: 194, including 34 professors.
Number of students: 261 full-time, 2,186 part-time.

Publications: *College Calendar†, College Prospectus†.*

DEANS:

*Faculty of Arts:* Prof. M. J. WILKS, M.A., PH.D., F.R.HIST.S.
*Faculty of Science:* J. T. TEMPLE, M.A., PH.D.
*Faculty of Economics:* Prof. RICHARD PORTES, M.A., D.PHIL.

**Chelsea College University of London:** Manresa Rd., Chelsea, SW3 6LX; f. as S.W. London Polytechnic in 1891; in 1957 it was nominated as a College of Advanced Technology and from August 1966 was admitted as a grant-receiving School of the University.
*Principal:* C. F. PHELPS, M.A., D.PHIL.
*Secretary:* W. C. SLADE, B.SC., A.C.M.A.
*Academic Registrar:* F. R. FINCH, M.A., M.B.I.M.

Library: 110,000 volumes, 800 periodical publications.
Number of students: 1,957 full-time, 548 part-time.

Publications: *Prospectus†, Postgraduate Studies†, Annual Report†, Science Chelsea* (periodically).

**Imperial College of Science and Technology:** South Kensington, SW7 2AZ; formed 1907 by federation of Royal College of Science, Royal School of Mines, and City and Guilds College.
*Rector:* Lord FLOWERS, M.A., M.SC., D.SC., F.INST.P., F.R.S.
*Secretary:* J. H. SMITH, C.B.E., B.A.
*Registrar:* P. E. MEE, M.B.E., T.D., B.SC.(ECON.).

Number of teachers: 660, including 90 professors.
Number of students: 4,546.

DEANS:

*Royal College of Science:* Prof. M. D. BLOW, PH.D., F.R.S.
*Royal School of Mines:* Prof. J. L. KNILL, PH.D., A.R.C.S., C.ENG., M.I.C.E., F.G.S., M.I.GEOL.
*City and Guilds College:* Prof. E. H. BROWN, PH.D., D.I.C., C.ENG., M.I.C.E.

**King's College:** Strand, WC2R 2LS; f. 1829.
*Principal:* Sir NEIL CAMERON, G.C.B., C.B.E., D.S.O., D.F.C., A.E.
*Secretary:* H. F. PATTERSON, M.A.
*Registrar:* J. D. MCCORMACK, B.A.
Library: see Libraries.
Number of teachers: 355, including 68 professors.
Number of students: 3,200.

DEANS:

*Faculty of Arts:* L. P. HARVEY, M.A., D.PHIL.
*Faculty of Laws:* F. G. JACOBS, M.A., D.PHIL.
*Faculty of Natural Science:* E. A. BELL, M.A., PH.D., C.CHEM., F.R.S.C.
*Faculty of Medical Sciences:* K. E. WEBSTER, M.B., B.S.
*Faculty of Engineering:* S. W. E. EARLES, D.SC.(ENG.), PH.D., A.K.C., C.ENG., F.I.MECH.E.
*Faculty of Theology:* S. R. SUTHERLAND, M.A.
*Faculty of Education:* K. C. CHARLTON, M.A., M.ED.
*Faculty of Music:* A. M. WHITTALL, M.A., PH.D., A.T.C.L., A.R.C.O.

**London School of Economics and Political Science:** Houghton Street, Aldwych, WC2A 2AE; f. 1895.
*Director:* Prof. R. G. DAHRENDORF.
*Academic Secretary:* J. ALCOCK, B.A.
*Secretary for Finance and Administrative Services:* J. PIKE, C.B.E., M.A.
Library: see Libraries.
Number of teachers: 303.
Number of research staff: 23.

Number of students: 3,700 full-time, 595 part-time.

Publications: *Economica* (quarterly journal of economics, economic history, and statistics), *The British Journal of Sociology* (quarterly), *British Journal of Industrial Relations, Journal of Transport Economics and Policy* (both three times a year), *New Series, Reprints of Scarce Works on Political Economy, Monographs on Social Anthropology, International Studies Monographs, Millenium: Journal of International Studies, Law and Economics, Occasional Papers on Social Administration, Greater London Papers, Geographical Papers, A London Bibliography of the Social Sciences, L.S.E. Research Monographs, L.S.E. Studies on Education,* Inaugural and other lectures†.

ATTACHED INSTITUTES:

**Business History Unit:** f. 1978 jointly with Imperial College of Science and Technology to promote research into business history, including technological aspects; Dir. Dr. L. HANNAH.

**Centre for Labour Economics:** f. 1974 (successor to the Higher Education Research Unit) to undertake research in labour economics, especially unemployment, income distribution and incentives; a S.S.R.C. Designated Research Centre; Head Prof. P. R. G. LAYARD.

**Centre for International Studies:** f. 1967 to promote research in international studies, particularly Soviet and Chinese studies and European studies; Chair. of Steering Committee Prof. I. H. NISH.

**Greater London Group:** f. 1958 to undertake research and publication in problems of Greater London and the South-East Region; consists of academic teachers of the School with a small professional research staff; Chair. Prof. P. J. O. SELF.

**International Centre for Economics and Related Disciplines:** f. 1978 to promote research into applied economics and related fields; Chair. Prof. A. B. ATKINSON.

**Population Investigation Committee:** f. 1936 to promote and undertake research into population questions; collaborates in the L.S.E. postgraduate programme in demography; Chair. Prof. R. G. DAHRENDORF.

---

**Queen Elizabeth College:** Campden Hill Rd., W8 7AH; f. 1908; offers courses leading to the B.Sc., and postgraduate degrees and diplomas both by research and taught courses.
*Principal:* ROBERT S. BARNES, D.SC., F.INST.P., F.I.M.
*Secretary:* W. M. G. BOMPAS, M.A., C.ENG., M.I.MECH.E.
*Academic Registrar:* D. LEA, M.A.
Library of 25,000 vols.
Number of teachers: 113.
Number of students: 1,100.

Publications: *Prospectus, Annual Report.*

**Queen Mary College:** Mile End Road, London, E1 4NS; f. 1887.
*Principal:* Sir JAMES MENTER, M.A., PH.D., SC.D., F.R.S.
*Secretary:* G. G. WILLIAMS, B.A.
Library: see Libraries.
Number of teaching staff: 325, including 52 professors.
Number of students: 3,315.

Publications: *Prospectus, Annual Report.*

DEANS:

*Faculty of Arts:* Prof. M. M. BOWIE, M.A., D.PHIL.
*Faculty of Science:* Prof. V. MOSES, M.A., PH.D., D.SC.
*Faculty of Engineering:* Prof. D. C. LESLIE, M.A., D.PHIL.

*Faculty of Law:* Prof. K. R. Simmonds, M.A., D.PHIL.
*Faculty of Social Studies:* T. A. Smith, B.SC.

**Royal Holloway College:** Egham Hill, Egham, Surrey, TW20 0EX; f. 1883 opened by Queen Victoria in 1886; residential college for men and women; Faculties of Arts, Science and Music.
*Principal:* L. H. Butler, M.A., D.PHIL.
*Secretary:* R. Hardy, M.A., LL.B.
*Registrar:* Miss J. L. Hurn, B.A.
*Librarian:* B. J. C. Wintour, B.A., A.L.A.

Library of over 140,000 vols.
Number of teachers: 135, including 17 professors.
Number of students: 1,500.
Publications: *Prospectus*† (May), *Calendar* (October), *Report* (January).

DEANS:
*Faculties of Arts and Music:* W. A. Davenport, M.A.
*Faculty of Science:* Prof. D. W. O. Heddle, PH.D., F.INST.P., F.R.A.S.

**Royal Veterinary College:** Royal College St., London, NW1 0TU; f. 1791.
*Principal and Dean:* Dr. A. O. Betts, M.A., PH.D., M.R.C.V.S.
*Secretary and Bursar:* D. W. Gordon-Brown, B.A., D.M.S.
*Registrar:* Miss Ann Tribble, M.A.

Library of 30,000 vols.
Number of teachers: 78.
Number of students: 400.

**School of Oriental and African Studies:** Malet St., WC1E 7HP; t. 1916.
*Director:* Prof. C. D. Cowan, M.A., PH.D.
*Secretary:* C. C. Moore, M.A.
Library: *see* Libraries.
Number of teachers: 197.
Number of students: 940.
Publications: *The Bulletin*, *Journal of African Law*, *Calendar*, *Annual Report*.

**Contemporary China Institute:** f. 1968; supports advanced research and training in modern Chinese studies, promotes publications, attempts to disseminate knowledge of contemporary China to a wide audience; runs a fellowship programme; Head Dr. H. D. R. Baker; publs. *The China Quarterly*, *Modern China Studies International Bulletin* (annually).

**The School of Pharmacy:** 29-39 Brunswick Square, WC1N 1AX; f. 1842.
*Dean:* F. Fish, PH.D., F.P.S.
*Clerk to the Council and Secretary:* B. Symondson, A.C.I.S., F.A.A.I., M.I.D.P.M.

Number of teachers: 50, including 6 professors.
Number of students: 356.

**University College:** Gower Street, WC1E 6BT; f. 1826.
*Provost:* Sir James Lighthill, D.SC., F.R.AE.S., F.I.M.A., F.R.S.
*Registrar:* J. W. Arterton, B.A.
*Secretary:* J. R. Tovell, F.C.A.
Library: *see* Libraries.
Number of teachers: 666, including 120 professors.
Number of students: 6,700.
Publication: *Calendar*.

DEANS:
*Faculty of Arts:* D. W. J. Johnson, B.A., B.LITT.
*Faculty of Science:* P. R. Bell, M.A.
*Faculty of Laws:* J. L. Jowell, M.A., LL.M., S.J.D.
*Faculty of Engineering:* D. E. N. Davies, D.SC., F.ENG., F.I.E.E., F.I.E.R.E.
*Faculty of Clinical Sciences:* A. S. Prophet, C.B.E., D.D.S., F.D.S.R.C.S., F.F.D.R.C.S.I.
*Faculty of Medical Sciences:* A. P. Mathias, PH.D.
*Faculty of Environmental Studies:* D. Bishop, C.ENG., M.I.C.E.

**Westfield College:** Kidderpore Ave., Hampstead, NW3 7ST; f. 1882.
*Principal:* B. Thwaites, M.A., PH.D., F.I.M.A.
*Secretary:* R. C. Parkin.
*Registrar:* Miss J. M. Sims, M.A.

Library of 131,969 vols.
Number of teachers: 117, including 19 professors.
Number of full-time students: 1,186.
Publications: *Prospectus*, *Annual Report*.

DEANS:
*Faculty of Arts:* Prof. A. D. Deyermond, M.A., B.LITT.
*Faculty of Science:* J. Griffith, PH.D.

**Wye College:** Wye, Ashford, Kent; f. 1447, incorporates the South-Eastern Agricultural College and the Swanley Horticultural College; courses in Agriculture, Horticulture and related sciences, Agricultural Economics including management and marketing, Rural Environment Studies, Agrarian Development.
*Principal:* I. A. M. Lucas, C.B.E., M.SC., F.R.AG.S.
*Secretary:* R. E. Wyatt, M.B.E., B.SC., M.A.
*Librarian:* E. Mary Lucas, B.SC., A.L.A.

Library of 30,000 vols.
Number of students: 530.

**Centre for European Agricultural Studies:** f. 1973; research and post-experience seminars in the fields of agricultural finance and taxation, comparative agricultural technology, rural and regional planning, commodity studies, European agriculture and relationships with Third World economies.

---

*(b)* Undergraduate Medical and Dental

**Charing Cross Hospital Medical School:** The Reynolds Building, St. Dunstan's Rd., London, W6 8RP; f. 1834.
*Dean:* Prof. T. W. Glenister, C.B.E., T.D., M.B., B.S., PH.D., D.SC.
*Secretary:* G. K. Buckley, M.A., F.H.A.
Library of 30,000 vols.
Number of teachers: 104.
Number of students: 600.
Publications: *Prospectus* (annually), *Annual Report*.

**Guy's Hospital Dental School:** London Bridge, SE1 9RT; f. 1888.
*Dean:* J. C. Houston, M.D., F.R.C.P.
*Secretary:* D. G. Bompas, C.M.G., M.A.
Number of students: 423.

**Guy's Hospital Medical School:** London Bridge, SE1 9RT; f. 1769.
*Dean:* J. C. Houston, M.D., F.R.C.P.
*Secretary:* D. G. Bompas, C.M.G., M.A.
Library: *see* Libraries.
Number of students: 801.
Publication: *Guy's Hospital Gazette*† (monthly).

**King's College Hospital Medical School:** Denmark Hill, SE5 8RX; f. 1831.
*Dean:* L. T. Cotton, M.CH., F.R.C.S.
*Secretary:* D. J. Britten, B.SC. (ECON.).
Library of 20,000 vols.
Number of teachers: 144 medical, 39 dental.
Number of clinical undergraduate students: 285 medical, 181 dental.

**London Hospital Medical College, The:** Turner Street, E.1; f. 1785.
*Dean:* Sir John Ellis, M.B.E., M.A., M.D., F.R.C.P.
*Secretary:* J. W. Walmsley.
Library: *see* Libraries.
Number of teachers: 280.
Number of students: 530 medical, 268 dental, 18 science.

**Middlesex Hospital Medical School, The:** Mortimer Street, W1P 7PN; f. 1835.
*Dean:* Sir Douglas Ranger, M.B., B.S., F.R.C.S.
*Secretary:* D. E. Eardley, B.SC., M.INST.P., M.I.E.E.
Number of students: 520.

**Royal Dental Hospital of London, School of Dental Surgery:** 32 Leicester Square, WC2H 7LJ; f. 1858.
*Dean:* Prof. W. J. B. Houston, B.D.S., PH.D., F.D.S., D.ORTH.
*School Secretary:* E. G. Smith.
Library of 4,500 vols.
Number of teachers: 80.
Number of students: 234.

**Royal Free Hospital School of Medicine:** Rowland Hill Street, NW3 2PF; f. 1874.

*Dean:* B. B. MacGillivray, b.sc., m.b., b.s., f.r.c.p.
*Secretary:* G. W. Fenn, m.a.
　Number of full-time teachers: 92, including 21 professors.
　Number of students: 565.

**St. Bartholomew's Hospital Medical College:** West Smithfield, E.C.1; f. 1662.
*Dean:* I. Kelsey Fry, d.m., f.r.c.p., f.r.c.r.
*Secretary:* D. J. Brown, m.b.e., m.a.
　Number of teachers: 120.
　Number of students: 830.

**St George's Hospital Medical School:** Cranmer Terrace, Tooting, SW17 0RE; f. 1751.
*Dean:* R. D. Lowe, m.d., ph.d., f.r.c.p.
*Secretary:* E. Fairhurst, m.a.
*Academic Registrar:* J. A. Bursey, b.a.
　Library of 24,000 vols.
　Number of students: 490.
　Publications: *School Prospectus*†, *Report*.

**St. Mary's Hospital Medical School:** Norfolk Place, Paddington, W2 1PG; f. 1854.
*Dean:* Prof. P. Richards, m.a., m.d., ph.d., f.r.c.p.
*Secretary:* K. Lockyer, b.a.
　Number of students: 546.

**St. Thomas's Hospital Medical School:** Lambeth Palace Rd., SE1 7EH; hospital f. 1106.
*Dean:* Brian Creamer, m.d., b.s., f.r.c.p.
*Secretary:* V. H. Warren, m.a.
　Number of students: 498.

**Westminster Medical School:** Horseferry Rd., Westminster, SW1P 2AR; f. 1834.
*Dean:* Dr. P. A. Emerson, m.a., m.d., f.r.c.p.
*Secretary:* R. A. M. Forrest, b.a.
　Number of teachers: 100.
　Number of students: *c.* 300.

(c) Postgraduate Medical

**British Postgraduate Medical Federation:** 33 Millman St., WC1N 3EJ; established by the University of London in 1945; admitted as a School of the University in 1947.
*Director:* David Innes Williams, m.d., m.chir., f.r.c.s.
*Secretary:* Michael E. Coops, m.a., ll.b.

INSTITUTES OF THE FEDERATION:

**Institute of Basic Medical Sciences:** Royal College of Surgeons of England, 35–43 Lincoln's Inn Fields, WC2A 3PN; f. 1951.
*Dean:* Prof. A. J. Harding Rains, m.s., f.r.c.s.
*Secretary:* Michael E. Coops, m.a., ll.b.

**Institute of Cancer Research, Royal Cancer Hospital:** 34 Sumner Place, SW7 3NU.
*Director:* R. A. Weiss, ph.d.
*Dean:* C. B. Cameron, m.d.
　Library of 35,000 vols.

**Cardiothoracic Institute:** Fulham Road, S.W.3; in association with the Brompton Hospital, the London Chest Hospital and National Heart Hospital; f. 1946; library of 15,000 vols.
*Dean:* Dr. E. E. Keal, m.d., f.r.c.p.
*Secretary:* Irene F. Oddy, b.a.

**Institute of Child Health:** 30 Guilford St., WC1N 1EH; associated with the Hospitals for Sick Children, Great Ormond St.
*Dean:* Prof. O. H. Wolff, m.a., m.d., f.r.c.p.

**Institute of Dental Surgery:** Eastman Dental Hospital, Gray's Inn Road, WC1X 8LD.
*Dean:* Prof. I. R. H. Kramer, m.d.s., f.d.s.r.c.s., f.f.d., f.r.a.c.d.s., f.r.c.path.

**Institute of Dermatology:** St. John's Hospital for Diseases of the Skin, Lisle Street, Leicester Square, WC2H 7BJ.
*Dean:* E. Wilson Jones, m.b., b.chir., f.r.c.p., f.r.c.path.

**Institute of Laryngology and Otology:** The Royal National Throat, Nose and Ear Hospital, 330 Gray's Inn Rd., W.C.1; f. January 1946; teaching and research, oto-rhino-laryngology.
*Dean:* R. Pracy, f.r.c.s.
*Secretary:* B. A. Blatch, b.sc.
　Publications: *Annual Reports*, *Syllabus* (irregular).

**Institute of Neurology:** The National Hospital, Queen Square, WC1N 3BG; f. 1938; 16,000 vols.
*Dean:* P. C. Gautier-Smith, m.a., m.d., f.r.c.p.
　Publication: *Annual Report*†.

**Institute of Obstetrics and Gynaecology:** Queen Charlotte's Maternity Hospital, Goldhawk Road, W6 0XG (associated also with the Hammersmith Hospital and Chelsea Hospital for Women); M.R.C.O.G. and other higher degree courses; advanced education for surgeons and trainees).
*Dean:* Prof. Sir John Dewhurst, f.r.c.s.(e.), f.r.c.o.g.
*Secretary:* Mrs. P. Adrigan.

**Institute of Ophthalmology:** Judd Street, W.C.1 (associated with Moorfields Eye Hospital); f. 1947; postgraduate teaching and research in eye disease and prevention of blindness; library of 13,000 vols.
*Dean:* B. S. Jay, m.d., f.r.c.s.
*Secretary and Registrar:* F. C. Keegan, f.c.i.s.
　Publication: *Annual Report*.

**Institute of Orthopaedics:** Royal National Orthopaedic Hospital, Brockley Hill, Stanmore, Middx., HA7 4LP.
*Dean:* E. L. Trickey, f.r.c.s.
*Secretary:* C. H. Audaer, b.a., f.a.a.i., a.m.b.i.m.

**Institute of Psychiatry:** De Crespigny Park, Denmark Hill, SE5 8AF.
*Dean:* J. L. T. Birley, b.a., b.m., f.r.c.p., f.r.c.psych., d.p.m.

**Institute of Urology (University of London):** 172–176 Shaftesbury Ave., W.C.2 (associated with the St. Peter's Hospitals).
*Dean:* J. P. Pryor, m.s., f.r.c.s.

---

**London School of Hygiene and Tropical Medicine** (incorporating the Ross Institute and the T.U.C. Centenary Institute): Keppel St., WC1E 7HT; f. 1924, opened 1929.
*Dean:* Dr. C. E. G. Smith.
　Library: *see* Libraries.
　Number of teachers: 125.
　Number of students: *c.* 1,100.
　Publications: *Memoir Series*, *The Journal of Helminthology*, *The Journal of Tropical Medicine and Hygiene*.

**Royal Postgraduate Medical School:** Hammersmith Hospital, Ducane Rd., W12 0HS; f. 1935.
*Dean:* Malcolm Godfrey, m.b., b.s., f.r.c.p.
　Library of 24,000 vols., 610 current periodicals.
　Number of teachers: 161.
　Number of students: *c.* 1,900.

*II. Schools not in receipt of U.G.C. Grants*

**Heythrop College:** 11–13 Cavendish Square, W1M 0AN; courses lead to the B.D., the M.Th., the Ph.D. in the Faculty of Theology and B.A. in philosophy and theology, M.A. in philosophy; library of 150,000 vols.
*Principal:* Rev. F. X. Walker, s.j., ph.d. (acting).
*Secretary and Registrar:* Rev. J. F. Colliston, s.j., b.a., s.t.l.
　Number of teachers: 24.
　Number of students: 150.

**Lister Institute of Preventive Medicine:** Elstree, Herts., WD6 3AX; inc. 1891 to support research into biomedicine.
*Chairman of Governing Body:* Prof. A. Neuberger, c.b.e., m.d., f.r.c.p., f.r.c.path., f.r.s.
*Secretary:* G. J. Roderick, b.com.

## UNIVERSITY OF LONDON

UNIVERSITY INSTITUTES:

**Courtauld Institute of Art:** *see* under Colleges.

**Institute of Advanced Legal Studies:** 17 Russell Square, WC1B 5DR; f. 1947; provides a centre for postgraduate legal studies and legal research.
*Director:* Prof. A. L. DIAMOND, LL.M.
*Secretary:* J. A. BOXHALL, M.A.
*Librarian:* W. A. F. P. STEINER, LL.M., M.A., F.L.A.
Library: see Libraries.

**Institute of Archaeology:** 31–34 Gordon Square, WC1H 0PY; f. 1936.
*Director:* Prof. J. D. EVANS, M.A., PH.D., LITT.D., F.B.A., F.S.A.
*Secretary:* I. K. ORCHARDSON, M.A., PH.D.
Number of teachers: 22.
Number of students: 200.
Publications: *Annual Bulletin*† and occasional publications.

**Institute of Classical Studies:** 31–34 Gordon Square, WC1H 0PY; f. 1953; library of basic research books complemented by the library of the Hellenic and Roman Societies (joint library of 55,000 volumes); research courses and seminars held for postgraduate students.
*Director:* Prof. E. W. HANDLEY, M.A., F.B.A.
*Secretary:* ALICIA TOTOLOS, B.A.
Publications: *Bulletin* (annually), *Bulletin Supplements* (occasional).

**Institute of Commonwealth Studies:** 27 Russell Square, WC1B 5DS; f. 1949; for postgraduate research in social sciences and recent history relating to the Commonwealth; library of 90,000 vols.
*Director:* Prof. W. H. MORRIS-JONES, B.SC.(ECON.).
*Secretary:* P. H. LYON, PH.D.
*Librarian:* Mrs. P. LARBY, M.A., F.L.A.

**Institute of Education:** 20 Bedford Way, London, WC1H 0AL; f. by London County Council as London Day Training College in 1902, transferred to control of University of London in 1932; advanced studies and research in education; higher degrees; Associateship; advanced diploma courses; postgraduate teacher training.
*Director:* W. TAYLOR, PH.D., D.SC., LITT.D.
*Secretary:* E. W. EARLE, B.A.
Number of students: 2,695.
Library of c. 210,000 vols., 1,900 periodicals.
Publications: *Calendar*†, *Annual Report*†, *Studies in Education*† (monographs), *Bedford Way Papers*† (occasional papers), *Education Libraries Bulletin* (termly) and supplements (occasional).

ATTACHED INSTITUTE:

**Thomas Coram Research Unit:** 41 Brunswick Square, WC1N 1AZ; f. 1974 with support from the Dept. of Health and Social Security, Thomas Coram Fndn., and other bodies; now a S.S.R.C. Designated Research Centre; research in health, education and development of normal and handicapped children; Dir. BARBARA TIZARD, PH.D.

---

**Institute of Germanic Studies:** 29 Russell Square, WC1B 5DP; f. 1950 for postgraduate research; 922 mems.
*Hon. Director:* Prof. J. P. STERN, M.A., PH.D., LITT.D.
*Deputy Director:* J. L. FLOOD, M.A., PH.D.
*Secretary:* KARIN HELLMER.
*Librarian:* W. ABBEY, B.A., A.L.A.
Library of 48,000 vols.
Publications: *Annual Report*, *Theses in Germanic Studies at British Universities* (annually), *Publications*, *Bithell Series of Dissertations*, *Bithell Memorial Lectures* (annually).

**Institute of Historical Research:** Senate House, WC1E 7HU; f. 1921.
*Director:* Prof. F. M. L. THOMPSON, M.A., D.PHIL., F.B.A.
*Secretary and Librarian:* WILLIAM KELLAWAY, M.A., F.L.A.
Library: see Libraries.

**Institute of Latin American Studies:** 31 Tavistock Square, WC1H 9HA; f. 1965 to promote Latin American studies at graduate level and to provide for discussion and collaboration between members of the University and other interested persons.
*Director:* Prof. JOHN LYNCH, M.A., PH.D.
*Secretary:* HAROLD BLAKEMORE, PH.D.
*Librarian:* CAROLE TRAVIS, B.A., A.L.A.
Publications: *Latin American Monographs* (irregular), *Theses in Latin American Studies*† (annually), *Latin American Studies in the Universities of the United Kingdom*† (annually), *Staff Research in Progress or Recently Completed in the Humanities and the Social Sciences*† (annually), *Miscellaneous Publications* (irregular).

**School of Slavonic and East European Studies:** University of London, WC1E 7HU; f. 1915.
*Director:* M. A. BRANCH, PH.D.
*Clerk to the Council:* P. ROBINSON, M.I.P.M., J.P.
*Registrar:* SUSAN PENNEY, B.A.
Number of teachers: 46, including 7 professors.
Number of students: 276 full-time, 23 part-time.
Publication: *The Slavonic and East European Review*† (quarterly).

**Institute of United States Studies:** 31 Tavistock Square, W.C.1; f. 1965 to promote and co-ordinate graduate work in American studies in the University and to assist liaison between teachers of American subjects in other universities.
*Director:* Prof. E. WRIGHT, M.A.
*Secretary:* J. H. DANIELS, M.A., D.PHIL.
*Librarian:* ANGELA PHILLIPS, B.A., A.L.A.
Publication: *American Studies Bibliography* on microfiche (quarterly and annually).

**Warburg Institute:** Woburn Square, WC1H 0AB; f. 1905 for the study of cultural and intellectual history and the history of the classical tradition.
*Director:* Prof. J. B. TRAPP, M.A., F.B.A.
Publications: *Studies* (monographs), *Journal of the Warburg and Courtauld Institutes*, *Corpus Platonicum Medii Aevi*, *Mediaeval and Renaissance Studies*, *Warburg Institute Surveys*.

**British Institute in Paris (Department of French):** 11 rue de Constantine, 75007 Paris; f. in 1894 as "Guilde Internationale", attached to University of Paris 1927, incorporated in University of London 1969.
*Director:* Prof. C. L. CAMPOS, L. ÈS L., PH.D.
*Head of French Department:* Mrs. E. WILLIAMSON, PH.D., M. ÈS L.
*London Secretary:* Miss J. FENTON, British Institute in Paris, University of London, Senate House, London, W.C.1.

**Mullard Space Science Laboratory:** Dept. of Physics and Astronomy, University College London, Holmbury St. Mary, Dorking, RH5 6NT, Surrey.

INSTITUTIONS WITH RECOGNIZED TEACHERS

The following institutions, although not constituent bodies of the University, have some recognized teachers of the University of London on their staffs.

**Goldsmiths' College:** Lewisham Way, New Cross, SE14 6NW; f. 1905; first and postgraduate internal degrees; professional studies and advanced courses in education, music, art and design and social sciences; adult studies.
*Warden:* RICHARD HOGGART, M.A., LITT.D., D.UNIV., D. ÈS L.
Library of 200,000 vols.
Number of staff: 368.
Number of students (of the university) 2,968, others 495 (full-time), 50 (part-time).

Publications: *Undergraduate Prospectus†, Postgraduate Prospectus†, Annual Report.*

Jews' College.

London Business School.

**Royal Academy of Music.**

**Royal College of Music.**

**Trinity College of Music.**

Research Institutes

National Institute for Medical Research (*Medicine*).

Rothamsted Experimental Station (*Agriculture*).

## LOUGHBOROUGH UNIVERSITY OF TECHNOLOGY
LOUGHBOROUGH, LEICS.

Telephone: Loughborough 63171.

*Formerly* Loughborough College of Technology; University Charter 1966.

Academic year: October to July (three terms).

*Chancellor:* Sir ARNOLD HALL, M.A., F.ENG., F.R.S.

*Senior Pro-Chancellor:* H. W. FRENCH, C.B.E., B.SC., C.ENG., F.I.E.E., F.INST.P., F.C.P.

*Vice-Chancellor:* C. C. BUTLER, PH.D., D.SC., M.INST.P., F.R.S.

*Senior Pro-Vice-Chancellor:* Prof. J. SIZER, B.A., F.C.M.A., F.B.I.M., F.R.S.A.

*Pro-Vice-Chancellor:* R. L. CANNELL, M.ENG., C.ENG., F.I.E.E.

*Registrar:* H. BROOKS, B.SC.(ECON.), F.I.C.S.

*Librarian:* Prof. A. J. EVANS, B.PHARM., PH.D., F.L.A., M.I.INF.SC.

Library contains 600,000 vols.

Number of teachers: 500.

Number of students: 6,241.

Publications: *Gazette†* (quarterly), *Calendar†, Undergraduate Prospectus†, Postgraduate Prospectus†, Student Manual†.*

### DEANS:

*School of Engineering:* Prof. J. N. BUTTERS, PH.D., C.ENG., F.INST.P., F.I.E.E., M.I.MECH.E.

*School of Pure Applied Science:* Prof. K. W. BENTLEY, D.PHIL., D.SC., F.R.S.E.

*School of Human and Environmental Studies:* Prof. D. SWANN, PH.D.

*School of Educational Studies:* Prof. J. LUCAS, PH.D.

### PROFESSORS:

ADAMTHWAITE, A. P., PH.D., F.R.HIST.S., History

ASHFORD, N. J., PH.D., M.S.C.E., C.ENG., F.I.C.E., F.C.I.T., M.A.S.C.E., Transport Planning

BAJPAI, A. C., M.SC., F.I.M.A., F.B.C.S., COMP.I.E.E., Mathematical Education

BELL, R., PH.D., D.SC., C.ENG., M.I.MECH.E., M.I.E.E., Manufacturing Technology

BENTLEY, K. W., M.A., D.PHIL., D.SC., F.R.S.E., Organic Chemistry

BIRLEY, A. W., M.A., D.PHIL., F.P.R.I., Polymer Technology

BRITTAN, K. W., PH.D., D.I.C., Creative Design

BROCK, G. C., PH.D., C.ENG., F.I.C.E., Civil Engineering

BUTLIN, R. A., M.A., F.R.G.S., Geography

BUTTERS, J. N., PH.D., C.ENG., F.INST.P., F.I.E.E., M.I.MECH.E., Mechanical Engineering

CAMPBELL, D. S., D.SC., D.I.C., C.ENG., F.I.E.R.E., F.INST.P., S.M.I.E.E.E., Component Technology

CANTOR, L. M., M.A., Education

CARTER, F. T. C., M.A., Modern Languages

CHERNS, A. B., M.A., F.B.PS.S., Social Sciences

COHEN, L., M.A., M.ED., PH.D., Education

DENT, J. C., M.S., PH.D., C.ENG., M.I.MECH.E., Mechanical Engineering

DOWNS, B., M.ENG., C.ENG., M.I.MECH.E., Mechanical Engineering

ELLIOTT, C. K., PH.D., F.B.PS.S., Human Resource Management

EVANS, A. J., B.PHARM., PH.D., F.L.A., M.I.INF.SC., University Librarian

EVANS, D. J., D.SC., PH.D., F.I.M.A., F.B.C.S., Computing

FRESHWATER, D. C., PH.D., D.L.C.(SCI.), C.ENG., F.I.CHEM.E., Chemical Engineering

GREGORY, G., M.A., M.S., M.SC., PH.D., Management Sciences

GRIFFITHS, J. W. R., PH.D., C.ENG., F.I.E.E., F.I.E.R.E., Electronics

HALES, F. D., PH.D., C.ENG., M.I.MECH.E., F.I.M.A., M.B.C.S., Surface Transport

HAMPSON, N. A., D.SC., PH.D., C.CHEM., F.R.S.C., A.R.T.C.S., Applied Electrochemistry

HAVARD-WILLIAMS, P., M.A., A.L.A., A.N.Z.L.A., F.L.A.I., F.B.I.M., Library Studies

HIGGIN, G. W., M.A., PH.D., Continuing Management Education

JOHNS, D. J., M.SC.(ENG.), PH.D., C.ENG., F.R.AE.S., A.F.A.I.A.A., F.I.O.A., F.C.I.T., M.A.E.S.I., Transport Technology

JONES, L. L., M.A., C.ENG., M.I.C.E., M.I.STRUCT.E., Structural Engineering

KIRK, N. S., PH.D., Consumer Ergonomics

LEES, F. P., M.A., PH.D., A.C.G.I., C.ENG., F.I.CHEM.E., F.I.PLANT.E., M.B.C.S., F.INST.M.C., Plant Engineering

LLEWELLYN, D. T., B.SC.(ECON.), Money and Banking

LUCAS, J., PH.D., English

MANN, J., PH.D., M.I.E., Chemical Engineering

MARSHALL, W. A., M.B., CH.B., PH.D., F.I.BIOL., Human Biology

MENZIES, I. A., PH.D., D.SC., D.I.C., C.CHEM., F.R.I.C., F.I.M., F.I.CORR.T., F.I.M.F., C.ENG., M.I.M.M., Materials Engineering

MILLLER, J. N., M.A., PH.D., C.CHEM., F.R.S.C., Analytical Chemistry

RAFFLE, J. R., PH.D., C.ENG., M.I.C.E., F.INST.P., F.R.S.A., Physics

SHACKEL, B., M.A., F.B.PS.S., Human Sciences

SIZER, J., B.A., F.C.M.A., M.B.I.M., F.R.S.A., Financial Management

SMITH, I. R., PH.D., D.SC., C.ENG., F.I.E.E., Electrical Power Engineering

STOREY, C., B.SC., F.I.M.A., Industrial Mathematics

SURY, R. J., PH.D., C.ENG., M.I.MECH.E., F.I.PROD.E., Engineering Production

SWANN, D., B.A., PH.D., Economics

THOMASON, H., M.SC., PH.D., Physical Education and Recreational Science

TRIMBLE, E. G., B.SC., C.ENG., F.I.C.E., M.I.MECH.E., M.I.STRUCT.E., Construction Management

WEBB, A., M.SC.(ECON.), Social Administration

WILKINSON, F., M.A., PH.D., F.R.S.C., Physical Chemistry

WRAY, G. R., PH.D., D.SC., F.ENG., A.M.C.T.S., F.T.I., F.I.MECH.E., F.R.S.A., Mechanical Engineering

### READERS:

ALEXANDER, A. J., M.SC., PH.D., C.ENG., M.I.MECH.E., M.R.AE.S., Mechanical Engineering

ALLWOOD, R. J., PH.D., Civil Engineering

BLOIS, K. J., B.A., Marketing

CLARK, A. P., M.A., PH.D., C.ENG., D.I.C., M.I.E.R.E., Electronic and Electrical Engineering

DAVIES, T. H., M.A., C.ENG., M.I.MECH.E., Courtaulds Reader in Mechanisms

DUNCAN, A. M., M.A., M.SC., PH.D., History and Philosophy of Science and Technology

FOGG, A. G., PH.D., A.R.T.C.S., C.CHEM., F.R.S.C., Analytical Chemistry

HAMLEY, E. J., PH.D., M.I.BIOL., Human Biology

HEANEY, H., D.SC., PH.D., C.CHEM., F.R.I.C., A.R.T.C.S., Organic Chemistry

JONES, P. R. M., M.SC., PH.D., Human Functional Anatomy

MARPLES, PH.D., C.CHEM., F.R.S.C., Organic Chemistry

MASSEY, A. G., M.SC., D.SC., C.CHEM., F.R.I.C., Inorganic Chemistry

NEWCOMB, T. P., M.SC., D.SC., F.INST.P., C.ENG., F.I.MECH.E., Transport Technology

PUGH, S., B.SC.(ENG.), C.ENG., M.I.MECH.E., Smallpeice Reader in Engineering Design

RICHARDS, J. M., PH.D., A.K.C., A.INST.P., A.F.I.M.A., F.R.MET.S., Electronic and Electrical Engineering

STEVENS, S. J., M.SC., PH.D., D.C.AE., C.ENG., M.I.MECH.E., M.R.AE.S., Transport Technology

STONE, P. T., B.SC., A.B.PS.S., F.C.I.B.S., Vision and Lighting

STURGESS, J. W., M.SC., PH.D., F.INST.P., C.ENG., M.I.E.E., F.R.S.A., Physics

### ATTACHED INSTITUTES:

**Institute of Polymer Technology:** Dir. Prof. A. W. BIRLEY, M.A., D.PHIL., F.P.R.I.

**Centre for Transport Engineering Practice:** Dir. G. G. LUCAS, M.SC., PH.D., C.ENG., M.I.MECH.E.

**Engineering Design Centre:** Dir. (vacant).

**Centre for Industrial Studies:** Dir. D. J. BILLAU, M.SC., C.ENG., PH.D., M.I.MECH.E., F.I.PROD.E.

**Centre for Extension Studies:** Dir. R. L. CANNELL, M.ENG., C.ENG., F.I.E.E.

**Institute for Consumer Ergonomics:** Dir. Prof. N. S. KIRK, PH.D.

**Computer Centre:** Dir. D. C. HOGG, M.A., A.F.I.M.A., F.B.C.S.

**Centre for the Advancement of Mathematical Education in Technology:** Dir. Prof. A. C. BAJPAI, M.SC., F.I.M.A., COMP.I.E.E.

# VICTORIA UNIVERSITY OF MANCHESTER

OXFORD RD.,
MANCHESTER, M13 9PL
Telephone: 061-273 3333.

Founded 1903.

*Chancellor:* His Grace the Duke of DEVONSHIRE, P.C., M.C., J.P., V.L., LL.D.

*Vice-Chancellor:* Prof. M. RICHMOND, PH.D.

*Registrar:* K. E. KITCHEN, B.A.

*Librarian:* M. A. PEGG, PH.D.

Library: see John Rylands University Library of Manchester.

Number of teachers: 1,832 full-time.
Number of students: 16,576 (including 4,181 in the Faculty of Technology and 150 postgraduates in the Faculty of Business Administration).

Publications: University: *Calendar, Grants and Awards, General Information, Student Accommodation;* Faculty: *Prospectuses* and *Notes for Applicants, Postgraduate Courses,* booklets, etc.; U.M.I.S.T.: *Guide for Applicants Seeking Admission to Undergraduate Courses,* departmental prospectuses, *Postgraduate Studies and Research,* etc.

## DEANS:

*Faculty of Arts:* MARGARET L. M. YOUNG, M.A., L. ÈS L., PH.D.
*Faculty of Business Administration:* Prof. A. M. McCOSH, D.B.A., C.A.
*Faculty of Economic and Social Studies:* S. A. MOORE, M.A.(ECON.), M.B.C.S.
*Faculty of Education:* D. McNAIR, M.ED.
*Faculty of Law:* Prof. GILLIAN M. WHITE, M.A., PH.D.
*Faculty of Medicine:* Prof. J. M. EVANSON, M.SC., M.B., CH.B., F.R.C.P.
*Faculty of Music:* M. AITCHISON, M.A., MUS.B., L.R.A.M.
*Faculty of Science:* Prof. J. ZUSSMAN, PH.D., D.PHIL., F.INST.P.
*Faculty of Technology:* Prof. J. W. S. HEARLE, PH.D., D.SC., F.INST.P., F.T.I.; see also University of Manchester Institute of Science and Technology.
*Faculty of Theology:* Rev. D. A. PAILIN, PH.D.

## PROFESSORS:

*Faculty of Arts:*
BELL, J. A. M., B.ARCH., M.C.D., PH.D., R.I.B.A., M.R.T.P.I., Architecture
BIRD, G. H., M.A., Philosophy
BIRLEY, A. R., M.A., D.PHIL., F.S.A., Ancient History
BOSWORTH, C. E., M.A., PH.D., Arabic Studies
COLLINGE, N. E., M.C., M.A., PH.D., Comparative Philology
COX, C. B., M.A., M.LITT., English Literature
DANNATT, J. T., M.A., A.R.A., R.I.B.A., Architecture
DODWELL, C. R., M.A., PH.D., LITT.D., F.R.HIST.S., F.S.A., F.B.A., History of Art
DOUGLAS, I., PH.D., Physical Geography
DOVELL, P., B.ARCH., M.C.D., M.A., R.I.B.A., M.R.T.P.I., Urban Design
DUMBRECK, J. C., M.A., Russian
GRIFFITH, T. G., M.A., B.LITT., Italian Language and Literature
HOGG, R. M., M.A., PH.D., English Language and Medieval English Literature
HYDE, J. K., D.PHIL., Medieval History
JOCELYN, H. D., M.A., PH.D., Latin
JONES, G. D. B., M.A., D.PHIL., F.S.A., Archaeology
KANTOROWICH, R. H., B.ARCH., M.A., R.I.B.A., F.R.T.P.I., Town and Country Planning
KELLER, R. E., DR.PHIL., M.A., German Language and Medieval German Literature
KERFERD, G. B., M.A., Greek
LEWIS, J. PARRY, B.SC., M.A., Economics of Regions and Towns
LINDARS, Rev. B., S.S.F., M.A., D.D., Biblical Criticism and Exegesis
MARSHALL, P. D., M.A., PH.D., American History and Institutions
MUSSON, A. E., M.A., Economic History
PALMER, D. J., M.A., B.LITT., English Literature
PULLAN, B. S., M.A., PH.D., Modern History
RAMSDEN, H., M.A., DR.FIL. & LET., Spanish Language and Literature
RANGER, T. O., M.A., D.PHIL., Modern History
RICHARDS, K. R., M.A., Drama
ROBINSON, D. G., M.A., F.R.T.P.I., Regional Planning
ROBSON, B. T., M.A., PH.D., Geography
RODGERS, H. B., M.A., Geography
ROTHWELL, W., M.A., D.U., French Language and Medieval French Literature
SUTCLIFFE, F. E., M.A., PH.D., Classical French Literature
WELLAND, D. S. R., M.A., PH.D., American Literature

*Faculty of Business Administration:*
ARMSTRONG, E. G. A., M.COM., PH.D., Industrial Relations
CHANNON, D. F., B.SC., D.B.A., Marketing
COLLCUTT, R. H., B.SC.(ENG.), M.B.A., Operational Research
HAGUE, D. C., B.SC., M.COM., M.B.A., Managerial Economics
LAWSON, G. H., M.A.(ECON.), M.A.B., A.A.C.C.A., Business Finance
LUPTON, T., M.A., PH.D., Organizational Behaviour
McCOSH, A. M., B.SC., D.B.A., C.A., Management Accounting
MORRIS, J. F., M.B.A., PH.D., Management Development
MUMFORD, ENID, M.A., PH.D., F.I.P.M., Organizational Behaviour
STAPLETON, R. C., PH.D., Business Finance
WOOD, D., M.COM., PH.D., Business Economics

*Faculty of Economic and Social Studies:*
ARNOLD, J. A., M.SC., A.C.A., Accounting
ARTIS, M. J., M.A.ECON., Economics
AUSTIN, D. G., B.A., M.A.(ECON.), Government
COLMAN, D. R., M.S., PH.D., Agricultural Economics
COPPOCK, D. J., B.A.(ECON.,) Economics
FORSYTH, G., B.A.(ECON.), Social Administration
HAGUE, D. C., M.COM., M.B.A., Managerial Economics
METCALFE, J. S., M.SC., Economics
MUSSON, A. E., M.A., Economic History
PARRY, G. B., PH.D., Government
PETERS, E. L., M.A., M.A.(ECON.), D.PHIL., Social Anthropology
ROBERTS, B. R., A.M., PH.D., Sociology
SHANIN, T., M.A.(ECON.), PH.D., Sociology
STEEDMAN, I. W., PH.D., Economics
TORDOFF, W., M.A., M.A.(ECON.), PH.D., Government
WHITE, D. J., M.A., M.A.(ECON.), M.SC., PH.D., Decision Theory
WILLIAMS, R., M.A., Government and Science Policy
WORSLEY, P. M., M.A.(ECON.), PH.D., Sociology

*Faculty of Education:*
MITTLER, P. J., M.A., M.ED., PH.D., Special Education
MUSGROVE, F., M.ED., PH.D., Education
SMITHERS, A. G., M.SC., PH.D., A.B.PS.S., Education
TAYLOR, I. G., M.D., D.P.H., F.R.C.P., Audiology and Education of the Deaf
TURNER, J. D., M.A., Adult and Higher Education

*Faculty of Law:*
BROMLEY, P. M., M.A., LL.M., Law
FARRAND, J. T., LL.D., Law
STREET, H., C.B.E., PH.D., LL.D., F.B.A., English Law
WHITE, GILLIAN M., M.A., LL.B., PH.D., International Law

*Faculty of Medicine (including Dental School):*
ADAMS, P. H., M.B., CH.B., M.SC., PH.D., M.R.C.P., Medicine
BEECH, H. R., PH.D., F.B.PS.S., Clinical Psychology
BLACKLOCK, N. J., O.B.E., M.B., CH.B., F.R.C.S., Urological Surgery
BOYD, R. D. H., M.A., M.B., B.CHIR., F.R.C.P., Child Health and Paediatrics
BROCKLEHURST, J. C., M.D., F.R.C.P.ED., Geriatrics
CASE, R. M., PH.D., Physiology
CROWTHER, D., M.A., M.B., B.CHIR., M.SC., PH.D., M.R.C.P., Clinical Oncology
DOBBING, J., M.SC., M.B., B.S., M.R.C.P., F.R.C.PATH., Child Growth and Development
ELSTEIN, M., M.D., M.R.C.O.G., Obstetrics and Gynaecology
EVANSON, J. M., M.SC., M.B., CH.B., F.R.C.P., Medicine
FORD, W. L., M.B., CH.B., M.A., M.SC., D.PHIL., M.R.C.P.ED., M.R.C.PATH., Experimental Pathology
FOX, B. W., PH.D., F L.S., Experimental Chemotherapy
FOX, H., M.D., M.R.C.PATH., Reproductive Pathology
FOX, R. A., B.SC., M.D., F.A.C.P., F.R.C.P.CAN., Geriatric Medicine
GALASKO, C. S. B., CH.M., M.SC., F.R.C.S., Orthopaedic Surgery
GARDNER, D. L., M.A., M.D., PH.D., F.R.C.P., F.R.C.PATH., Histopathology
GILLESPIE, I. E., M.D., M.SC., F.R.C.S., Surgery
GOLDBERG, D. P., M.A., D.M., M.SC., D.P.M., F.R.C.P., F.R.C.PSYCH., Psychiatry
GOSLING, J. A., M.D., Anatomy
GRANT, A. A., D.D.SC., M.SC., F.R.A.C.D.S., Prosthetic Dentistry
GRANT, M. E., D.PHIL., Medical Biochemistry
GREEN, R., M.B., CH.B., Physiology
HARRIS, P. F., M.SC., M.D., Anatomy
HEALEY, T. E. J., B.SC.,M.D., F.F.A.R.C.S., Anaesthesia
HOLLOWAY, P. J., PH.D., Child Dental Health
HOUNSFIELD, G. N., C.B.E., M.D., D.SC., D.TECH., F.R.S., Imaging Sciences (Professorial Fellow)

HOUSTON, I. B., M.D., D.C.H., M.R.C.P., Child Health
IRVING, M. H., M.D., CH.M., M.SC., F.R.C.S., Surgery
ISHERWOOD, I., M.B., CH.B., M.R.C.P., D.M.R.D., F.R.C.R., F.F.R., Diagnostic Radiology
**JACKSON, D. S.**, PH.D., **Medical Biochemistry**
JAYSON, M. I. V., M.D., F.R.C.P., Rheumatology
JONES, J. H., M.D., M.SC., F.F.D.R.C.S.I., F.R.C.PATH., Oral Medicine
**KESSEL, W. I. N.**, M.A., M.SC., M.D., D.P.M., F.R.C.P., F.R.C.PSYCH., **Psychiatry**
LAJTHA, L. G., M.D., D.PHIL., M.SC., F.R.C.PATH., Experimental Oncology
LECK, I. M., M.B., CH.B., PH.D., F.F.C.M., Community Medicine
LEE, W. R., M.D., M.SC., D.I.H., F.R.C.P., Occupational Health
McFARLANE, Lady, M.SC., M.A., S.R.N., S.C.M., F.R.C.N., Nursing
MAWER, G. E., M.B., CH.B., M.SC., PH.D., M.R.C.P.ED., Clinical Pharmacology
METCALFE, D. H. H., M.A., M.B., B.CHIR., F.R.C.G.P., General Practice
MOORE, J. R., M.D.S., M.SC., F.D.S.R.C.S., Oral Surgery
NIXON, G. S., D.D.SC., PH.D., M.SC., H.D.D., F.D.S., R.C.P.S.GLAS., F.D.S., D.R.D., R.C.S.ED., Conservative Dentistry
PULLAN, B. R., M.SC., PH.D., Medical Biophysics
RATCLIFFE, J. G., Chemical Pathology
**SCHNIEDEN, H.**, M.D., M.SC., **Pharmacology, Materia Medica and Therapeutics**
SELLWOOD, R. A., CH.M., M.SC., F.R.C.S., Surgery
SMITH, ALWYN, M.B., CH.B., M.SC., PH.D., D.P.H., F.R.C.P.GLAS., F.F.C.M., F.R.C.G.P., Epidemiology and Social Oncology
STANBURY, S. W., M.D., F.R.C.P., Medicine
TAYLOR, D. C., M.D., D.P.M., M.R.C.P., F.R.C.PSYCH., Child and Adolescent Psychiatry
THOMAS, S., B.SC., M.SC., M.D., Physiology
TINDALL, V. R., M.D., M.SC., F.R.C.S., F.R.C.O.G., Obstetrics and Gynaecology
TURNBERG, L. A., M.D., F.R.C.P., Medicine
YATES, P. O., M.D., F.R.C.PATH., Neuropathology

*Faculty of Music:*
KEMP, I. M., M.A., Music

*Faculty of Science:*
BAGNALL, K. W., PH.D., D.SC., C.CHEM., F.R.S.C., Inorganic Chemistry
BARKER, G. R., D.SC., PH.D., C.CHEM., F.R.S.C., Biochemistry
BAXENDALE, J. H., D.SC., Physical Chemistry
BLACKBURN, N., M.SC., PH.D., Pure Mathematics
BRYN JONES, C., Computing Science
**BYERS BROWN, W.**, D.SC., **Theoretical Chemistry**
COOPER, R., PH.D., D.SC., C.ENG., F.I.E.E., Electrical Engineering
CUTTER, E. G., PH.D., D.SC., F.R.S.E., Botany
DAVIES, J. G., M.A., PH.D., Radio Astronomy
DAVIES, R. D., PH.D., D.SC., Radio Astronomy
DONNACHIE, A., M.SC., PH.D., Theoretical Physics
EDWARDS, D. B. G., M.SC., PH.D., M.I.E.E., Computer Engineering
ELDER, J. W., M.SC., PH.D., Geophysics

ELWORTHY, P. H., B.PHARM., PH.D., D.SC., C.CHEM., M.R.S.C., M.P.S., Pharmacy
FRANKLIN, T. J., PH.D., Biochemistry (Professional Fellow)
GIBBONS, M., M.SC., PH.D., Liberal Studies in Science
GRICE, R., M.A., PH.D., Physical Chemistry
**GUTHRIE, D. M.**, PH.D., F.R.S.E., **Zoology**
HALL, H. E., B.A., PH.D., M.SC., Physics
HALL, W. B., M.S.C., C.ENG., F.I.MECH.E., F.I.NUCL.E., Nuclear Engineering
HALLIDAY, M. S., M.A., PH.D., Psychology
HARTLEY, B., M.A., PH.D., Pure Mathematics
**HOFFMAN, G. R.**, PH.D., **Electrical Engineering**
HORNE, M. R., O.B.E., M.A., M.SC., PH.D., SC.D., F.ENG., F.I.C.E., F.I.STRUCT.E., Civil Engineering
ILLINGWORTH, C. R., B.A., M.SC., Applied Mathematics
JOHANNESEN, N. H., M.SC., DR.TECHN., C.ENG., F.I.MECH.E., F.R.AE.S., M.A.I.A.A., Mechanics of Fluids
KAHN, F. D., M.A., M.SC., D.PHIL., Astronomy
McDOWELL, D. M., M.SC., PH.D., C.ENG., F.I.C.E., M.AM.SOC.C.E., Civil Engineering
MACKENZIE, W. S., M.A., M.SC., PH.D., F.R.S.E., Petrology
MOORE, M. A., B.A., D.PHIL., Theoretical Physics
MORRIS, D., PH.D., Computer Programming
MORTON, A. J., M.SC., C.ENG., F.I.MECH.E., M.I.MAR.E., M.INST.F., Mechanical Engineering
MURPHY, P. G., B.A., M.S., M.SC., PH.D., Physics
PAPANGELOU, F., M.SC., PH.D., Mathematical Statistics
PHILLIPS, W. R., M.SC., PH.D., Physics
POGSON, C. I., PH.D., Biochemistry
READ, F. H., M.SC., D.SC., F.INST.P., Physics
REASON, J. T., PH.D., Psychology
ROWE, P. W., PH.D., D.SC., C.ENG., F.I.C.E., M.I.W.E., Soil Mechanics
ROWLAND, M., PH.D., M.P.S., Pharmacy
SKINNER, H. A., D.PHIL., F.R.S.C., Physical Chemistry
SMITH, EDWIN, M.SC., PH.D., C.ENG., F.I.M., Metallurgy
STANLEY, P., PH.D., C.ENG., M.I.MECH.E., F.INST.P., Mechanical Engineering
SUMNER, F. H., PH.D., F.B.C.S., Microprocessor Applications
SUTHERLAND, J. K., D.SC., PH.D., Organic Chemistry
SWINBURNE, T. R., D.I.C., PH.D., D.SC., A.R.C.S., M.I.BIOL., Cryptogamic Botany
TALLENTIRE, A., PH.D., F.P.S., Pharmacy
TRINCI, A. P. J., Cryptogamic Botany
TRUEMAN, E. R., D.SC., Zoology
URSELL, F. J., M.A., M.SC., SC.D., F.R.S., Applied Mathematics
WALSH, JOAN E., M.A., D.PHIL., Numerical Analysis
WILLIAMS, R., M.A., Government and Science Policy
WILLMOTT, J. C., M.SC., PH.D., F.INST.P., Physics
YATES, C. E. M., PH.D., Mathematical Logic
ZUSSMAN, J., M.A., M.SC., PH.D., D.PHIL., F.INST.P., Geology

*Faculty of Technology (in the University Institute of Science and Technology):*
ASHMORE, P. G., M.A., M.SC., PH.D., C.CHEM., F.R.S.C., Chemistry

ASPINALL, D., PH.D., F.B.C.S., C.ENG., F.I.E.E., Computation
ATKINSON, B., PH.D., C.ENG., F.I.CHEM.E., Chemical Engineering
BECK, M. S., PH.D., D.SC., F.I.E.E., M.INST.M.C., Instrumentation
BLACK, G., M.SC., PH.D., D.I.C., F.INST.P., F.B.C.S., Computation
BRODA, P. M. A., PH.D., Applied Molecular Biology
BROTTON, D. M., PH.D., D.SC., C.ENG., F.I.C.E., F.I.STRUCT.E., Civil and Structural Engineering
BULLOUGH, R. K., M.A., M.SC., PH.D., F.INST.P., Mathematical Physics
BURBERRY, P. J., M.SC.(ARCH.), M.SC., R.I.B.A., F.I.O.B., Building
BURDEKIN, F. M., .A., PH.D., C.ENG., M.I.C.E., M.I.MECH.E., F.WELD.I., Civil and Structural Engineering
BUSH, S. F., M.A., PH.D., C.ENG., M.I.MECH.E., M.I.CHEM.E., Polymer Engineering
CARDWELL, D. S. L., PH.D., D.SC., History of Science and Technology
COOPER, C. B., PH.D., C.ENG., F.I.E.E., Electrical Engineering
COOPER, C. L., M.B.A., PH.D., Management Educational Methods
CRONLY-DILLON, J. R., M.A., M.SC., PH.D., Ophthalmic Optics
CRUICKSHANK, D. W. J., M.A., PH.D., SC.D., C.CHEM., F.R.S.C., Chemistry
DAVIES, B. J., M.SC., C.ENG., F.I.MECH.E., F.I.E.E., F.I.PROD.E., Manufacturing Technology
EDDY, A. A., M.A., D.PHIL., M.SC.TECH., Biochemistry
ENTWISTLE, K. M., M.SC., PH.D., C.ENG., F.I.M., Metallurgy
FARRELL, P. G., Electrical Engineering
GOODMAN, J. F. B., M.SC., PH.D., F.I.P.M., Industrial Relations
HANKINS, H. C. A., PH.D., C.ENG., F.I.E.E., Communications Engineering
HASZELDINE, R. N., PH.D., D.SC., SC.D., C.CHEM., F.R.S.C., F.R.S., Chemistry
**HEARLE, J. W. S.**, M.A., SC.D., PH.D., F.INST.P., F.T.I., **Textile Technology**
HOLLIER, R. H., M.SC., PH.D., C.ENG., M.I.PROD.E., M.I.MECH.E., F.I.M.H., Operations Management
HOPKINS, H. G., D.SC., F.I.M.A., F.A.S.M.E., Mathematics
KIRKBRIGHT, G. F., PH.D., D.SC., C.CHEM., F.R.S.C., Analytical Sciences
KROPHOLLER, H. W., M.SC., C.ENG., M.I.CHEM.E., Paper Science
LATHAM, J., PH.D., D.SC., D.I.C., F.INST.P., Physics
LAUNDER, B. E., D.SC.(ENG.), SC.D., Mechanical Engineering
MILWARD, A. S., M.A., PH.D., European Studies
MUNRO, N., PH.D., C.ENG., M.I.E.E., M.A.I.E.E.E., Applied Control Engineering
PALMER, A. C., PH.D., Civil Engineering
PAYNE, PH.D., C.ENG., M.I.E.R.E., Instrumentation
PETERS, R. H., PH.D., D.SC., C.COL., F.S.D.C., F.T.I., Polymer and Fibre Science
PICKERING, J. F., PH.D., Industrial Economics
PILCHER, R., M.SC., C.ENG., F.I.C.E., F.I.O.B., M.I.STRUCT.E., M.A.S.C.E., Building
POWNER, E. T., M.SC.TECH., C.ENG., M.I.E.E., Applied Microelectronics
**PRIESTLEY, M. B.**, M.A., PH.D., **Statistics**
RAMAGE, R., PH.D., C.CHEM., F.R.S.C., Chemistry

RHODERICK, E. H., M.A., M.SC., PH.D., C.ENG., F.INST.P., F.I.E.E., Solid-State Electronics
RICHARDS, B., M.SC., PH.D., F.B.C.S., F.I.M.A., Computation
RIPPIN, D. W. T., PH.D., C.ENG., M.I.CHEM.E., Chemical Engineering
ROSE-INNES, A. C., M.A., D.PHIL., D.SC., F.INST.P., Physics and Electrical Engineering
ROSENBROCK, H. H., PH.D., D.SC., C.ENG., F.I.E.E., F.I.CHEM.E., F.INST.M.C., F.R.S., Control Engineering
RUSBRIDGE, M. G., M.A., PH.D., M.SC., F.INST.P., F.R.MET.S., Physics
SAGER, J. C., M.A., M.SC., F.I.L., Modern Languages
SINGH, M. G., PH.D., D. ÈS SC., C.ENG., M.I.E.E., Control Engineering
SMITH, R., M.SC., PH.D., Marketing
WELSH, J., M.SC., PH.D., Software Engineering
WINTERBONE, D. E., PH.D., C.ENG., M.I.MECH.E., Mechanical Engineering
WOOD, G. C., M.A., PH.D., SC.D., C.ENG., F.I.M., C.CHEM., F.R.S.C., F.I.CORR.T., F.I.M.F., Corrosion Science
WOODBURN, E. T., PH.D., C.ENG., M.I.CHEM.E., M.S.A.CHEM.I., M.S.A.I.CHEM.E., Chemical Engineering

*Faculty of Theology:*
DYSON, A. O., M.A., D.PHIL., Social and Pastoral Theology
HANSON, Rt. Rev. R. P. C., M.A., M.A.(THEOL.), D.D., M.R.I.A., Historical and Contemporary Theology
LINDARS, Rev. B., S.S.F., D.D., Biblical Criticism and Exegesis
LING, T. O., M.A., M.A.(THEOL.), B.D., PH.D., Comparative Religion

*Departments not assigned to Faculties:*
ASHMORE, O., M.A., F.S.A., Extra-Mural Studies
LIVINGSTONE, A. S., M.S., M.A.(ECON.), Administrative Studies for Overseas Visiting Fellows
MITTLER, P. J., M.A., M.ED., PH.D., Dir., Hester Adrian Research Centre

READERS:
*Faculty of Arts:*
ALEXANDER, J. J. G., M.A., D.PHIL., History of Art
BLAMIRES, D. M., M.A., PH.D., German
BOGDANOW, FANNI, M.A., PH.D., French
BRICE, W. C., M.A., Geography
COX, R. G., M.A., PH.D., English Literature
GARDINER, S. C., M.A., PH.D., Slavonic Languages
HENRY, D. P., PH.D., Philosophy
JOHN, E., M.A., History
LATHAM, J. D., M.A., D.PHIL., Arabic
THORNLEY, D. G., B.A., R.I.B.A., Architecture
WETHERILL, P. M., M.A., D.U., French
WOOD-JONES, R. B., M.A., PH.D., R.I.B.A., F.S.A., Architecture

*Faculty of Business Administration:*
WILLMER, M. A. P., B.SC., M.A., D.C.AE., Operational Research

*Faculty of Economic and Social Studies:*
FARNIE, D. A., M.A., PH.D., Economic History
MEDHURST, K. N., M.A., PH.D., Government
STUBBS, D. C., M.A., PH.D., Economics
WRIGHT, M. W., D.PHIL., Government

*Faculty of Education:*
JOHN, J. E. J., B.SC., Audiology

*Faculty of Medicine:*
BAMFORD, F. N., M.D., D.P.H., D.C.H., Development Paediatrics
BARIC, L., PH.D., Health Education
CHAPMAN, J. A., PH.D., F.INST.P., Medical Biophysics
CHARLESWORTH, D., M.D., F.R.C.S., Surgery
COOMBE, E. C., D.SC., PH.D., C.CHEM., F.R.I.C., Dental Materials Science
ELDER, J. B., M.D., F.R.C.S., Surgery
FOSTER, R. W., PH.D., M.B., B.S., Pharmacology
GOWENLOCK, A. H., M.SC., M.B., CH.B., PH.D., F.R.C.PATH., F.R.I.C., Chemical Pathology
HARRIS, R., B.SC., M.D., D.T.M.&H., M.R.C.P., Medical Genetics
HOBSON, R. F., B.A., M.D., F.R.C.P., D.P.M., F.R.C.PSYCH., Psychotherapy
MOORE, W. M. O., M.B., B.CH., C.P.H., F.R.C.O.G., Obstetrics and Gynaecology
PAUL, D. H., PH.D., Physiology
PRESTON, N. W., M.D., DIP.BACT., F.R.C.PATH., Bacteriology
RUSSELL, C., PH.D., Oral Microbiology
SCHWARZ, V., PH.D., Chemical Pathology
STEVEN, F. S., PH.D., D.SC., Medical Biochemistry
TURNER, E. P., M.SC., D.D.S., L.D.S.R.C.S., Oral Pathology
WEISS, J. B., M.SC., D.C.C., Medical Biochemistry
WILLIAMS, G., M.D., PH.D., F.R.C.PATH., Pathology

*Faculty of Music:*
AITCHISON, M., M.A., MUS.B., L.R.A.M., Music

*Faculty of Science:*
ANNAND, W. J. D., D.SC., C.ENG., F.I.MECH.E., A.F.R.AE.S., Engineering
ASKEW, R. R., D.PHIL., Entomology
AXON, H. J., D.PHIL., Metallurgy
BAKER, C. T. H., M.A., D.PHIL., Mathematics
BAKER, R. R., Zoology
BLOWER, J. G., M.SC., Ecology
BU'LOCK, J. D., PH.D., Microbial Chemistry
BUTLER, R. D., PH.D., Cytology
CAMM, G. L., M.A., D.PHIL., Mathematics
CONNOR, J. N. L., M.A., D.PHIL., Chemistry
COOK, L. M., D.PHIL., Zoology
DORMER, K. J., PH.D., Botany
DOWKER, J. S., PH.D., Theoretical Physics
GOLDFARB, L. J. B., M.SC., PH.D., Theoretical Physics
HILLIER, I. H., PH.D., D.I.C., Chemistry
IRVINE, J. M., M.SC., PH.D., Theoretical Physics
LEAK, G. M., PH.D., F.INST.P., C.ENG., F.I.M., Metallurgy
LITTING, C. N. W., PH.D., C.ENG., M.I.E.E., F.INST.P., Electrical Engineering
MANDL, F., M.A., D.PHIL., Theoretical Physics
MEABURN, J., PH.D., D.SC., Astronomy
MILLS, O. S., B.SC., Chemistry
NICHOLLS, G. D., M.A., PH.D., Geochemistry
PALMER, H. P., D.PHIL., D.SC., Radio-Astronomy
PARIS, J. B., PH.D., Mathematics
ROBINSON, B., M.SC., PH.D., Pharmacy
SHELTON, R. A. J., PH.D., C.ENG., F.I.M., M.I.M.M., Metallurgy
SMITH, G. F., M.SC., PH.D., Chemistry
SMITH, I. M., M.S., PH.D., C.ENG., M.I.C.E., Engineering
WALSH, D., PH.D., Radio Astronomy

WATSON, E. J., M.A., Mathematics
WOOD, R. J., PH.D., Genetics

*Faculty of Technology:*
ASHWORTH, V., PH.D., C.CHEM., M.R.S.C., M.I.CORR.T., Corrosion Science Engineering
BANKS, R. E., PH.D., D.SC., C.CHEM., F.R.S.C., Chemistry
BARBER, M., M.A., D.PHIL., Chemistry
BRAMELLER, A., PH.D., D.SC., C.ENG., F.I.E.E., M.I.GASE., A.F.I.M.A., Electrical Power Systems
CHALMERS, B. J., PH.D., D.SC., C.ENG., F.I.E.E., Electrical Engineering
DAVIES, G. A., B.SC., PH.D., C.ENG., M.I.CHEM.E., Chemical Engineering
EVANS, P. E., M.A., PH.D., D.SC., Materials Science
GEAKE, J. E., PH.D., D.SC., F.INST.P., Physics
GOTT, G. F., PH.D., C.ENG., M.I.E.E., Electrical Engineering and Electronics
HATTON, A. P., M.SC.TECH., PH.D., D.SC., C.ENG., F.I.MECH.E., Heat Transfer
HAWKYARD, J. B., PH.D., C.ENG., M.I.MECH.E., Mechanical Engineering
HOWARD, G. J., PH.D., Polymer and Fibre Science
HOWELL, F. T., M.SC., PH.D., A.I.MIN.E., F.G.S., Engineering Geology
KITCHING, R., PH.D., D.SC., C.ENG., F.I.MECH.E., Mechanical Engineering
KITCHINGMAN, W. J., M.SC.TECH., PH.D., D.SC., C.ENG., M.I.M., F.INST.P., Metallurgy
KULIKOWSKI, J. J., M.SC.ENG., PH.D., Ophthalmic Optics
MCAULIFFE, C. A., D.PHIL., D.SC., Chemistry
MILLER, J. D. A., PH.D., F.I.BIOL., Corrosion Science
MUNN, R. W., PH.D., Chemistry
ROBERTS, G. K., PH.D., European Studies
SKORECKI, J., B.SC.(ENG.), M.SC.TECH., PH.D., D.SC., C.ENG., F.I.MECH.E., Mechanical Engineering
STAINTHORP, F. P., B.SC.TECH., PH.D., C.ENG., F.I.CHEM.E., M.INST.M.C., Chemical Engineering
STEPTO, R. F. T., PH.D., Polymer and Fibre Science
TIPPING, A. E., PH.D., D.SC., C.CHEM., F.R.S.C., Chemistry
WHITEHOUSE, N. D., M.SC., C.ENG., M.I.MECH.E., Internal Combustion Engines

ASSOCIATED INSTITUTE:
**University of Manchester Institute of Science and Technology:** P.O.B. 88, Sackville St., Manchester, M60 1QD; f. 1824 as Manchester Mechanics' Institute; Faculty of Technology in the University of Manchester since 1905; governed by a Court of Governors and a Council created under Royal Charter which established the Institute in 1956.

*Visitor:* H.R.H. The Prince PHILIP, Duke of EDINBURGH, K.G., K.T., P.C., O.M., G.B.E., F.R.S.

*Principal:* Prof. R. N. HASZELDINE, M.A., PH.D., D.SC., SC.D., C.CHEM., F.R.I.C., F.R.S.

*Secretary and Registrar:* D. H. MCWILLIAM, B.A.

*Librarian:* E. D. G. ROBINSON, J.P., M.A., A.L.A.

The library contains c. 132,000 vols., 1,100 periodicals, etc.

### ATTACHED INSTITUTES:

**Manchester Business School:** Booth St. West, Manchester, M15 6PB; includes the Faculty of Business Administration in the University, but is governed by its own Council, which includes business representatives; postgraduate and post-experience courses and research projects; University courses for Dip.B.A. and M.B.A., also research facilities for M.B.Sc. and Ph.D.
*Director:* Prof. T. LUPTON, M.A., PH.D.

**Manchester Museum:** *see* under Museums.

**Whitworth Art Gallery:** Oxford Rd., Manchester; Dir. Prof. C. R. DODWELL, M.A., PH.D., LITT.D., F.R.HIST.S., F.B.A., F.S.A.

**Hester Adrian Research Centre for the Study of Learning Processes in the Mentally Handicapped:** c/o The University, Manchester, M13 9PL; Dir. Prof. P. J. MITTLER, M.A., M.ED., PH.D.

**Centre for Urban and Regional Research:** c/o The University, Manchester, M13 9PL; Dir. Prof. J. PARRY LEWIS, B.SC., M.A.

**Pollution Research Unit:** c/o The University, Manchester, M13 9PL; Dir. Prof. M. GIBBONS, PH.D.

**Centre for Youth Studies:** c/o Faculty of Education, The University, Manchester, M13 9PL; Dir. C. MURRAY, M.PHIL., PH.D.

**Centre for Overseas Educational Development:** c/o Faculty of Education, The University, Manchester, M13 9PL; Chair. of Cttee. Prof. J. D. TURNER, M.A.

**Manchester-Sheffield-U.M.I.S.T. School of Probability and Statistics:** c/o Dept. of Mathematics, U.M.I.S.T., P.O.B. 88, Sackville St., Manchester, M60 1QD; Dir. Prof. R. M. LOYNES, PH.D.

**Manchester University Centre for the Study of Chronic Rheumatism:** c/o Medical School, The University, Manchester M13 9PT; f. 1947; Dir. Prof. M. I. V. JAYSON, M.D., F.R.C.P.

---

## UNIVERSITY OF NEWCASTLE UPON TYNE
NEWCASTLE UPON TYNE,
NE1 7RU

Telephone: Newcastle 328511.

Founded 1851, incorporated as separate University in 1963.

*Chancellor:* His Grace the Duke of NORTHUMBERLAND, K.G., P.C., T.D., D.C.L., K.ST.J., F.R.S.

*Vice-Chancellor:* Prof. L. W. MARTIN, M.A., PH.D.

*Pro-Vice-Chancellors:* Prof. J. R. O'CALLAGHAN, M.SC., C.ENG., F.I.MECH.E., Prof. D. H. WHIFFEN, M.A., D.PHIL, D.SC., C.CHEM., F.R.S.C., F.R.S.

*Registrar:* W. R. ANDREW, M.A.

*Librarian:* B. J. ENRIGHT, M.A., D.PHIL.

Number of teachers: 852, including 119 professors.

Number of students: 7,718.

Publications: *Calendar, Undergraduate Prospectus, Postgraduate Prospectus, Vice-Chancellor's Report, William Henry Charlton Memorial Lectures.*

### DEANS:

*Faculty of Medicine:* Prof. D. A. SHAW, M.B., CH.B., F.R.C.P., F.R.C.P.(E.) (Medicine); Prof. R. STORER, L.D.S., M.SC., F.D.S.R.C.S. (Dentistry).

*Faculty of Arts:* Prof. J. A. CANNON, M.A., PH.D.

*Faculty of Science:* Prof. D. G. MURCHISON, PH.D., F.G.S., F.R.S.E.

*Faculty of Engineering:* Prof. J. D. THORNTON, PH.D., D.SC., C.CHEM., F.R.S.C., C.ENG., F.I.CHEM.E.

*Faculty of Social Sciences:* Prof. H. B. BERRINGTON, B.SC. (ECON.).

*Faculty of Law:* Prof. J. B. CLARK, M.A., LL.B.

*Faculty of Agriculture:* P. W. ARNOLD, M A., PH.D.

*Faculty of Education:* J. J. C. MCCABE, M.ED., M.INST.P.

### PROFESSORS:

*Faculty of Arts:*
ADAMS, N. E. A., A.R.C.A., R.A., Fine Art
BAILEY, R. N., M.A., PH.D., F.S.A., Anglo-Saxon Civilization
BRENIKOV, P., M.A., F.R.T.P.I., Town and Country Planning
CANNON, J. A., M.A., PH.D., History
DANBY, M. W., M.A., A.R.I.B.A., Architecture
FARMER, B., M.A., R.I.B.A., Architecture
**HARDY, A. C.,** M.A., B.ARCH., DIP.T.P., A.R.I.B.A., M.R.T.P.I., Building Science
HARRISON, R. M., M.A., F.S.A., Archaeology
**HONIGMANN, E. A. J.,** M.A., D.LITT., English Literature
JOBEY, G., D.S.O., M.A., F.S.A., Prehistoric Archaeology
JONES, W. G., M.A., PH.D., Scandinavian Studies
MATTHEWS, D., C.B.E., M.A., D.MUS., F.R.A.M., Music
MCCORD, N., PH.D., Social History
MENHENNET, A., M.A., D.PHIL., German
SAUNDERS, T. J., PH.D., Greek
SHEFTON, B. B., M.A., Greek Art and Archaeology
STRANG, BARBARA M. H., M.A., English Language, General Linguistics
STRANG, C., M.A., Philosophy
WATT, J. A., PH.D., Medieval History
WEST, D. A., M.A., Latin
YARROW, P. J., M.A., D.U., French

*Faculty of Social Sciences:*
BELL, KATHLEEN, M., C.B.E., B.A. (ADMIN.), Social Studies
BERRINGTON, H. B., B.SC.(ECON) Politics
COLLISON, P., M.A., PH.D., Social Studies
JONES-LEE, M. W., D.PHIL., Economics
ROWLEY, C. K., PH.D., Economics
TIMMS, N. W., M.A., Social Work Studies

*Faculty of Law:*
CLARK, J. B., M.A., LL.B., Law
**ELLIOTT, D. W.,** LL.B., Law
OGUS, A. I., M.A., Law

*Faculty of Medicine:*
ALBERTI, K. G. M. M., M.A., D.PHIL., F.R.C.P., M.R.C.PATH., Clinical Biochemistry
**ALLAN, D. N.,** D.D.S., M.D.S., Operative Dental Surgery
ALLEN, A., M.A., D.PHIL., Physiological Biochemistry
BLAIR, E. L., M.D., F.R.C.P., Physiology
BODDY, K., PH.D., D.SC., F.INST.P., F.R.S.(E.), Medical Physics
CROMBIE, A. L., M.B., CH.B., F.R.C.S.ED., Ophthalmology
EASTOE, J. E., PH.D., D.SC., A.R.C.S., D.I.C., Oral Physiology
ECCLESTON, D., PH.D., D.SC., F.R.C. PSYCH., Psychiatry
EVANS, J. G., M.A., F.R.C.P., M.F.C.M., F.S.S., Geriatrics
HANKINSON, J., M.B., B.S., F.R.C.S., Neurosurgery
HARRIS, J. B., PH.D., M.P.S., F.I.BIOL., Experimental Neurology
HULL, C. J., M.B., B.S., M.R.C.S., L.R.C.P., F.F.A.R.C.S., Anaesthesia
JOHNSTON, I. D. A., M.B., M.CH., B.A.O., F.R.C.S., Surgery
JULIAN, D. G., M.A., M.D., F.R.C.P., F.R.C.P.ED., F.R.A.C.P., Cardiology
KERR, D. N. S., M.B., CH.B., M.SC., F.R.C.P., F.R.C.P.ED., Medicine
KOLVIN, I., M.D., F.R.C.PSYCH., Child Psychiatry
MCCALLUM, R. I., M.D., D.SC., M.R.C.S., F.R.C.P., F.F.O.M., Occupational Health and Hygiene
MADELEY, C. R., M.D., Clinical Virology
MILLER, J. S. G., M.A., D.PHIL., Anatomy
MURRAY, J. J., M.CH.D., PH.D., F.D.S.R.C.S., Child Dental Health
**NEWELL, D. J.,** M.A., PH.D., F.S.S., Medical Statistics
PARKHOUSE, J., M.D., CH.B., M.A., M.SC., F.F.A.R.C.S., D.A., Postgraduate Medical Education
RAWLINS, M. D., M.D., F.R.C.P., Clinical Pharmacology
ROBERTS, D. F., M.A., SC.D., D.PHIL., F.I.BIOL., Human Genetics
RUSSELL, J. K., M.D., CH.B., F.R.C.O.G., Obstetrics and Gynaecology
SHAW, D. A., M.B., CH.B., F.R.C.P., F.R.C.P.ED., Clinical Neurology
**SHUSTER, S.,** M.B., PH.D., F.R.C.P., Dermatology
SOAMES, J. V., PH.D., M.R.C.PATH., M.D.S.R.C.P.S.GLAS., Oral Pathology
**STEVENS, J.,** M.A., M.D., F.R.C.S., F.R.C.S.ED., F.R.C.S.(G.), Orthopaedic and Traumatic Surgery
**STORER, R.,** L.D.S., M.SC., F.D.S.R.C.S., Prosthodontics
STUART, A. E., M.B., PH.D., F.R.C.P.(E.), F.R.S.E., M.R.C.PATH., Pathology
SUSSMAN, M., PH.D., F.I.BIOL., Bacteriology
THOMPSON, J. W., M.B., PH.D., M.R.C.P., Pharmacology
TOMLINSON, B. E., C.B.E., M.D., F.R.C.P., F.R.C.PATH., Pathology
**WALDER, D. N.,** M.D.,CH.M., F.R.C.S., F.R.C.S.ED., Surgical Science
WALKER, J. H., M.D., F.R.C.G.P., F.F.C.M., Family and Community Medicine
WALKER, W., M.D., D.SC., F.R.C.P., F.R.C.PATH., Haematology
WALTON, Sir JOHN, T.D., M.D., D.SC., F.R.C.P., Neurology
**WEBB, J. K. G.,** O.B.E., M.A., B.M., B.CH., F.R.C.P., Child Health

# UNIVERSITIES

U.K. (GREAT BRITAIN)

*Faculty of Science:*
ARCHIBALD, A. R., PH.D., Microbiological Chemistry
BADDILEY, Sir JAMES, PH.D., D.SC., F.R.S.E., F.R.S., Chemical Microbiology
BURTON, K., M.A., PH.D., F.R.S., Biochemistry
CANN, J. R., PH.D., Geology
CLARK, R. B., D.SC., PH.D., F.Z.S., F.L.S., F.I.BIOL., F.R.S.E., Zoology
DAVIES, P. C. W., PH.D., Theoretical Physics
DEARMAN, W. R., PH.D., A.R.C.S., F.G.S., Engineering Geology
DOLDER, K., PH.D., A.R.C.S., F.INST.P., Atomic Physics
FREEMAN, N. C., PH.D., F.I.M.A., Applied Mathematics
GLOVER, S. W., M.A., PH.D., SC.D., F.I.BIOL., Genetics
GODDARD, J. B., PH.D., Regional Development Studies
HAMMERTON, M., PH.D., F.B.PS.S., Psychology
HORROCKS, G., M.A., PH.D., Pure Mathematics
JOHNSON, B. E., PH.D., F.R.S., Pure Mathematics
MURCHISON, D. G., PH.D., F.G.S., F.R.S.E., Organic Petrology
PAIN, R. H., M.A., PH.D., Physical Biochemistry
PLACKETT, R. L., M.A., SC.D., F.S.S., Statistics
RANDELL, B., B.SC., A.R.C.S., F.B.C.S., Computing Science
RINGROSE, J. R., M.A., PH.D., F.R.S.E., F.R.S., Pure Mathematics
ROBERTS, P. H., M.A., PH.D., SC.D., F.R.A.S., F.R.S., Applied Mathematics
RUNCORN, S. K., M.A., SC.D., PH.D., F.INST.P., F.R.A.S., F.R.S., Physics
SHAW, J., M.A., Comparative Physiology
SIMPSON, E. S., M.A., PH.D, Geography
SWAN, G. A., PH.D., D.SC., C.CHEM., F.R.S.C., Organic Chemistry
SYKES, A. G., PH.D., D.SC., F.R.S.C., Inorganic Chemistry
WHIFFEN, D. H., M.A., D.PHIL., D.SC., C.CHEM., F.R.S.C., F.R.S., Physical Chemistry
WHITFIELD, H., A.R.C.S., D.I.C., F.B.C.S., Computing and Data Processing

*Faculty of Engineering:*
CALDWELL, J. B., O.B.E., PH.D., F.ENG., F.R.I.N.A., M.I.STRUCT.E., Naval Architecture and Shipbuilding
DENNESS, B., M.SC., PH.D., D.I.C., C.ENG., M.I.C.E., M.I.M.M., F.G.S., Ocean Engineering
FELLS, I., M.A. PH.D., F.ENG., F.INST.E., C.CHEM., F.R.S.C., Energy Conversion
GALLAGHER, C. C., M.SC.TECH., PH.D., M.I.MECH.E., M.I.PROD.E., Industrial Management
GOODRIDGE, F., PH.D., C.CHEM., F.R.S.C., C.ENG., F.I.CHEM.E., Electrochemical Engineering
HARRIS, M. R., B.SC.(ENG.), C.ENG., F.I.E.E., Electrical Engineering
HILLS, P. J., M.SC., C.ENG., M.I.C.E., F.I.H.E., M.C.I.T., Transport Engineering
HOLT, A. G. J., PH.D., D.SC., F.I.E.E., F.I.E.R.E., Electrical Engineering
JACK, K. H., PH.D., SC.D., C.CHEM., F.R.S.C., F.R.S., Applied Crystal Chemistry
JEFFREY, A., PH.D., D.SC., F.I.M.A., F.R.S.E., Engineering Mathematics
KINNIMENT, D. J., M.SC., PH.D., C.ENG., M.I.E.E., M.I.E.E.E., Electronic Engineering
KONG, F. K., PH.D., Structural Engineering
LEWIS, R. I., M.A., PH.D., C.ENG., M.I.MECH.E., Fluid Mechanics and Thermodynamics
MAUNDER, L., O.B.E., SC.D., PH.D., F.ENG., F.I.MECH.E., Mechanical Engineering
NOVAK, P., ING.DR., DR.SC., C.ENG., F.I.C.E., F.I.W.E.S., F.F.B., Civil and Hydrauilc Engineering
PARKINS, R. N., PH.D., D.SC., C.ENG., F.I.M., Metallurgy and Engineering Materials
PESCOD, M. B., O.B.E., S.M., C.ENG., F.I.C.E., F.I.P.H.E., M.I.W.P.C., Environmental Control Engineering
THOMPSON, R. V., PH.D., M.ENG., C.ENG., F.I.MAR.E., F.I.MECH.E., F.S.E., Marine Engineering
THORNTON, J. D., PH.D., D.SC., C.CHEM., F.R.S.C., C.ENG., F.I.CHEM.E., Chemical Engineering

*Faculty of Agriculture:*
ARMSTRONG, D. G., PH.D., D.SC., C.CHEM., F.R.S.C., F.I.BIOL., F.R.S.E., Agricultural Biochemistry and Nutrition
ARNOLD, P. W., M.A., PH.D., Soil Science
ASHTON, J., M.A., M.LITT., M.S., Agricultural Economics
DICKSON, G. R., PH.D., F.I.BIOL., Agriculture
O'CALLAGHAN, J. R., B.E., M.SC., C.ENG., F.I.MECH.E., Agricultural Engineering
RITSON, C., M.AGR.SC., Agricultural Marketing
RUSSELL, G. E., M.A., PH.D., SC.D., F.I.BIOL., F.R.E.S., Agricultural Biology

*Faculty of Education:*
EDWARDS, A. D., M.A., M.PHIL., PH.D., Education

## READERS:
*Faculty of Arts:*
DERRY, J. W., M.A., PH.D., Modern History
DOWNING, M. F., M.SC., F.L.I., Landscape Design
GILLAM, J. P., M.A., F.S.A., Archaeology
HOLLAND, R. B., M.A., A.R.I.B.A., History of Art
LAZENBY, J. F., M.A., Ancient History
SAWYER, Rev. J. F. A., M.A., B.D., PH.D., Religious Studies
WILLIS, P., PH.D., F.R.I.B.A., History of Architecture
WOOF, R. S., M.A., PH.D., English Literature

*Faculty of Social Sciences:*
DAVEY, A. G., B.A., A.B.PS.S., Applied Social Studies
DENNIS, N., B.SC.(ECON.), Social Studies
SUGDEN, R., M.SC.ECON., Economics

*Faculty of Medicine:*
AHERNE, W. A., M.D., PH.D., F.R.C.PATH., Histopathology
COTES, J. E., M.A., D.M., F.R.C.P., M.F.O.M., Pulmonary Physiology
DAWES, J. D. K., M.D., F.R.C.S., Ear, Nose and Throat Studies
DICK, W. C., M.D., F.R.C.P., Rheumatology
ELLIS, H. A., M.D., PH.D., F.R.C.PATH., Pathology
FERREIRA, H. G., M.D., PH.D., Physiology
FOSTER, J. B., M.D., F.R.C.P., Clinical Neurology
GARSIDE, R. F., PH.D., F.B.PS.S., Clinical Psychology
HALLY, A. D., M.D., Anatomy
JAMES, O. F. W., M.A., M.R.C.P., Geriatrics
PARKIN, J. M., M.D., F.R.C.P., Paediatrics
PENNINGTON, R. J. T., PH.D., D.SC., F.R.S.E., Neurochemistry
RUGG-GUNN, A. J., R.D., B.D.S., PH.D., F.D.S.R.C.S.ED., Preventive Dentistry
TAYLOR, W., PH.D., Steroid Biochemistry
THODY, A. J., PH.D., Experimental Dermatology
WATSON, A. J., M.D., F.R.C.PATH., Pathology

*Faculty of Science:*
ANDERSON, J. A., M.A., D.PHIL., F.S.S., F.I.M.A., Statistics
ARMSTRONG, R. D., PH.D., D.SC., A.R.C.S., C.CHEM., F.R.S.C., Electrochemical Mechanisms
ARST, H. N., PH.D., SC.D., Genetics
CARMODY, P. J., M.A., F.R.I.C.S., Surveying
COLLINSON, D. W., PH.D., F.R.A.S., Experimental Palaeomagnetism
COVINGTON, A. K., PH.D., D.SC., C.CHEM., F.R.S.C., Physical Chemistry
EMMERSON, P. T., PH.D., Biochemistry
GIRDLER, R. W., PH.D., F.R.A.S., F.G.S., Geophysics
HARRISON, J. A., PH.D., D.SC., Electrochemistry
JAROS, M., PH.D., Theoretical Physics
LISTER, H., PH.D., F.R.S.E., Physical Geography
LITTLEWOOD, A. B., M.A., D.PHIL., Inorganic Chemistry
MARSH, H., PH.D., D.SC., Carbon Science
MOLYNEUX, L., PH.D., M.B.C.S., Physical Instrumentation
MOSS, BETTY L., M.SC., PH.D., F.L.S., Phycology
PANCHEN, A. L., M.A., PH.D., SC.D., Vertebrate Zoology
ROSE, J. S., M.A., D.SC., PH.D., Algebra
SCHOLES, G., PH.D., D.SC., C.CHEM., F.R.S.C., Radiation Chemistry
SOWARD, A. M., M.A., PH.D., Fluid Mechanics
STOODLEY, R. J., PH.D., Organic Chemistry
TARLING, D. H., PH.D., F.R.A.S., F.G.S., Palaeomagnetism
TOZER, D. C., PH.D., Theoretical Geophysics
WASSERMAN, G. D., PH.D., F.I.M.A., Theory and Philosophy of Biology

*Faculty of Engineering:*
BROWN, J. E., PH.D., C.ENG., F.I.E.E., Electrical Engineering
BUXTON, I. L., PH.D., C.ENG., F.R.I.N.A., Marine Transport
FARMER, I. W., PH.D., C.ENG., M.I.C.E., F.I.MIN.E., F.I.M.M., Mining Engineering
JOHNSON, G. R., PH.D., Biomedical Engineering
PETRIE, C. J. S., M.A., PH.D., Theoretical and Applied Rheology

*Faculty of Agriculture:*
REECE, A. R., M.SC.(AGR.ENG.), PH.D., C.ENG., M.I.MECH.E., Agricultural Engineering

*Faculty of Education:*
MOSELEY, D. V., M.A., Applied Psychology
WALLIS, P. J., M.A., F.I.M.A., F.R.HIST.S., Bibliography of Education

# UNIVERSITY OF NOTTINGHAM
UNIVERSITY PARK, NOTTINGHAM, NG7 2RD
Telephone: 0602-56101.
Founded 1948.

*Chancellor:* Sir GORDON HOBDAY PH.D., LL.D., F.R.S.C.

*Pro-Chancellor:* J. CAMERON-GIFFORD, D.SC.

*Vice-Chancellor:* B. C. L. WEEDON, C.B.E., PH.D., D.SC., D.TECH., A.R.C.S., D.I.C., C.CHEM., F.R.S.C., F.R.S.

*Registrar:* G. E. CHANDLER, B.A.

*Librarian:* P. A. HOARE, M.A., A.L.A.

Library: see Libraries.

Number of teachers: 1,000.
Number of students: 6,900.

Publications: Calendar, Prospectuses, Gazette, Annual Report.

### DEANS:

*Agricultural Science:* R. A. LAWRIE, PH.D., SC.D., D.SC.
*Arts:* R. L. STOREY, M.A., PH.D.
*Education:* M. CRAFT, PH.D.
*Engineering:* W. SMITH, PH.D.
*Law and Social Sciences:* R. H. OSBORNE, PH.D.
*Medicine:* R. E. COUPLAND, M.D., PH.D., D.SC.
*Science:* L. CROMBIE, PH.D., D.SC.

### PROFESSORS:

ANDREW, E. R., M.A., PH.D., SC.D., D.SC., F.INST.P., F.R.S.E., Experimental Physics
ARIE, T. H. D., M.A., M.R.C.P., D.P.M., F.R.C.PSYCH., F.F.C.M., Health Care of the Elderly
ASHKENAZI, V., C.E., D.PHIL., D.SC., C.ENG., F.I.C.E., F.I.M.A., F.R.I.C.S., F.S.C.E., Engineering Surveying
ATKINSON, T., D.I.C., PH.D., C.ENG., F.I.MIN.E., F.I.M.M., F.I.E.E., M.I.MECH.E., Mining Engineering
BAKER, P. E., D.PHIL., F.G.S., Geology
BALDWIN, R. W., PH.D., M.R.C.PATH., F.I.BIOL., Tumour Biology
BENT, I. D., M.A., PH.D., A.R.C.O., Music
BEURLE, R. L., PH.D., C.ENG., A.C.G.I., F.I.E.E., F.I.E.R.E., F.INST.P., Electronic Engineering
BIRMINGHAM, A. T., M.B., B.SC., Pharmacology
BLAMEY, R. W., M.A., M.D., F.R.C.S., Surgery
BURGESS, D. A., PH.D., Pure Mathematics
BURKHARDT, H., M.A., PH.D., Mathematical Education
BURWELL, R. G., B.SC., M.D., F.R.C.S., Human Morphology and Experimental Orthopaedics
BYCROFT, B. W., PH.D., Pharmaceutical Chemistry
CAMERON, K., PH.D., FIL.DR., F.R.HIST.S., F.B.A., English Language
CARTER, L. R., D.PHIL., F.C.I.I., Insurance Studies
CHALLIS, L. J., M.A., D.PHIL., Low Temperature Physics
CLARKE, B. C., D.PHIL., Genetics
CLOUGH, S., PH.D., Physics
COATES, R. C., PH.D., F.ENG., F.I.C.E., F.I.STRUCT.E., Civil Engineering
COATS, A W., M.SC.(ECON.), PH.D., Economic and Social History
COCKING, E. C. D., D.SC., PH.D., F.I.BIOL., Botany
COLE, J. P., M.A., PH.D., Regional Geography
COOPER, J. E., B.CH., D.P.M., F.R.C.P., F.R.C.PSYCH., Psychiatry
CORLETT, E. N., M.ENG., PH.D., C.ENG., F.I.PROD.E., F.I.MECH.E., A.B.PS.S., F.H.F.S., Production Engineering and Production Management
COUPLAND, R. E., PH.D., M.D., D.SC., F.R.S.E., Human Morphology
CRAFT, M., PH.D., Education
CROMBIE, L., PH.D., D.SC., C.CHEM., F.R.S.C., F.R.S., Organic Chemistry
CROSSLAND, J., M.A., PH.D., F.I.BIOL., Pharmacology
DAVIS, S. S., PH.D., C.CHEM., F.R.S.C., M.P.S., Pharmacy
DAWSON, I. M. P., M.A., M.D., F.R.C.P., F.R.C.PATH., Pathology
DOYLE, W., M.A., D.PHIL., F.R.HIST.S., Modern History
EGGLESTON, J. F., B.SC., F.I.BIOL., Education
ELEY, D. D., O.B.E., PH.D., SC.D., F.R.I.C., F.R.S., Physical Chemistry
ELWOOD, J. M., M.D., F.R.C.P.(C.), Community Health
FELL, CHRISTINE, M.A., F.R.HIST.S., Early English Studies
FENTEM, P. H., M.SC., M.B., CH.B., Physiology
FESSLER, H., PH.D., C.ENG., F.I.MECH.E., Experimental Stress Analysis
GOULD, S. J., M.A., Sociology
GREENFIELD, A. D. M., C.B.E., M.B., B.S., D.SC., F.R.C.P., Physiology
HALL, G. G., M.A., PH.D., F.I.M.A., Applied Mathematics
HAMPTON, J. R., M.A., D.M., D.PHIL., F.R.C.P., Cardiology
HARDCASTLE, J. D., M.A., M.CHIR., M.R.C.P., F.R.C.S., Surgery
HARRIS, D. J., LL.B., PH.D., Public International Law
HARRISON, J., M.A., Philosophy
HAWTHORNE, J. N., PH.D., D.SC., F.I.BIOL., Biochemistry
HEMMING, F. W., PH.D., A.R.I.C., Biochemistry
HIGMAN, F. M., M.A., B.LITT., French
HODGES, D. J., PH.D., C.ENG., F.I.MIN.E., F.INST.F., F.G.S., Mine Surveying
HOWARTH, C. I., M.A., D.PHIL., Psychology
HULL, D., B.SC., M.B., CH.B., F.R.C.P., D.CH., D.OBST.R.C.O.G., Child Health
IVINS, J. D., M.SC.(AGRIC.), PH.D., F.R.AG.S., Agriculture
JONES, M. V., PH.D., Slavonic Studies
KAVANAGH, D. A., M.A., Politics
KING, C. A. M., PH.D., SC.D., F.R.G.S., F.G.S., Physical Geography
KING, T. J., M.A., D.PHIL., Chemistry
KINSLEY, Rev. J., M.A., PH.D., D.LITT., F.R.S.L., F.R.HIST.S., F.B.A., English
LAMMING, G. E., M.S., PH.D., D.SC., F.I.BIOL., Animal Physiology
LANGMAN, M. J. S., M.D., F.R.C.P., Therapeutics
LAWRIE, R. A., PH.D., D.SC., SC.D., F.R.S.E., F.R.S.C., F.I.F.S.T., Food Science
LEACH, J. S. L., PH.D., C.ENG., F.INST.P., F.I.M., F.I.CORR.T., Metallurgy and Materials Science
LEES, D. S., PH.D., F.C.A., Industrial Economics
LEWIS, D., M.A., M.SC., PH.D., D.SC., F.R.S.C., Applied Biochemistry
LIEBESCHUETZ, J. H. W. G., PH.D., Classics and Ancient History
LUNZER, E. A., M.A., PH.D., Educational Psychology
MANSFIELD, P., PH.D., Physics
MARKUS, R., A. PH.D., F.R.HIST.S., Medieval History
MARSH, D. C., M.COM., Social Administration and Social Work
MILNER, A. D., M.D., F.R.C.P., Child Health
MITCHELL, J. E., M.A., PH.D., Political Economy
MITCHELL, J. R. A., M.A., M.D., D.PHIL., F.R.C.P., Medicine
MONTEITH, J. L., PH.D., D.I.C., F.INST.P., F.I.BIOL., F.R.S., F.R.S.E., Environmental Physics
MOUGHTIN, J. C., M.C.D., M.A., PH.D., F.R.ANTH.I., R.I.B.A., M.R.T.P.I., Planning Studies
NASH, W. F., M.SC., PH.D., F.INST.P., Physics
NEWSON, L. J., PH.D., Child Development
O'GRADY, F. W., M.SC., M.D., F.R.C.PATH., Microbiology
OSBORNE, R. H., PH.D., Economic Geography
OWEN, M. J., M.S., PH.D., C.ENG., F.I.MECH.E., F.P.R.I., Reinforced Plastics
PARKINSON, J. R., B.COM., Economics
PATTENDEN, G., PH.D., Organic Chemistry
PELL, P. S., PH.D., C.ENG., F.I.C.E., F.I.STRUCT.E., Civil Engineering
PRICHARD, A. M., LL.B., Property Law
RAYNER, A. J., M.A., PH.D., Agricultural Economics
REGAN, D. E., PH.D., Local Government
RILEY, C., B.ARCH., M.C.D., A.R.I.B.A., F.R.S.A., Architecture
SIEFKEN, H. G., DR.PHIL., German
SIMONS, J. P., PH.D., D.SC., C.CHEM., F.R.S.C., Physical Chemistry
SMART, A., M.A., D.A., F.S.A., F.R.S.A., Fine Art
SMITH, A. F. M., M.A., M.SC., PH.D., Mathematical Statistics
SMITH, A. G., D.I.C., C.ENG., F.I.MECH.E., M.R.AE.S., Thermodynamics
SMITH, J. C., Q.C., M.A., LL.M., F.B.A., Common Law
SMITH, W., PH.D., D.I.C., A.C.G.I., C.ENG., F.I.CHEM.E., Chemical Engineering
SPENCER, A. J. M., M.A., PH.D., D.SC., Theoretical Mechanics
STEPHENS, M. D., M.A., M.ED., PH.D., Adult Education
STEVENS, K. W. H., M.A., D.PHIL., Theoretical Physics
STOREY, R. L., M.A., PH.D., F.R.HIST.S., English History
SYMONDS, E. M., M.D., F.R.C.O.G., Obstetrics and Gynaecology
TATE, R. B., M.A., PH.D., Hispanic Studies
TEW, J. H. B., PH.D., Money and Banking
THOMAS, Rev. J. HEYWOOD, S.T.M., D.D., Christian Theology
TURNER, J. J., M.A., PH.D., C.CHEM., F.R.S.C., Inorganic Chemistry
USHERWOOD, P. N. R., PH.D., F.I.BIOL., F.R.S.E., Zoology
WAKELIN, D., PH.D., D.SC., Zoology
WARBURTON, G. B., M.A., PH.D., C.ENG., F.I.MECH.E., F.R.S.E., Applied Mechanics
WAUGH, W., M.A., M.B., M.CHIR., F.R.C.S., Orthopaedic and Accident Surgery
WHITTINGTON, W. J., PH.D., Agricultural Botany
WILLCOCKS, A. J., PH.D., F.I.S.W., Social Administration
WOODBINE, M., M.SC., PH.D., F.R.S.C., F.I.BIOL., Agricultural Microbiology
WORTHINGTON, B. S., B.SC., M.B., B.S., D.M.R.D., F.R.C.R., Radiology
WRIGHT, A., M.SC., PH.D., D.SC., Electrical Engineering

### READERS:

AMOS, A. T., PH.D., D.I.C., Mathematics
BATES, C. A., PH.D., Theoretical Physics
BENNETT, T., PH.D., Physiology
BERRY, H. M., English Language
BONNEY, M. C., F.B.C.S., F.B.P.I.C.S., Production Engineering and Production Management
BRINDLEY, D. N., PH.D., D.SC., Biochemistry
BROWN, S. F., PH.D., C.ENG., M.I.C.E., F.I.H.E., Civil Engineering
BUTTERY, P. J., PH.D., Applied Biochemistry
CARDWELL, R. A., PH.D., Hispanic Studies

# UNIVERSITIES

## U.K. (GREAT BRITAIN)

CHAPMAN, S. D., M.A., PH.D., Textile History
CHILDS, D. H., PH.D., Politics
CLARKE, K. U., PH.D., D.SC., F.I.BIOL., Zoology
COATES, K. S., Sociology and Industrial Relations
COLE, D. J. A., PH.D., Animal Production
COLEMAN, G., PH.D., Biochemistry
CRAIK, D. J., PH.D., Physical Chemistry
DANIELS, J. C., M.ED., PH.D., Education
DUNN, J. D. G., M.A., B.D., PH.D., Theology
ELLIOTT, R. B., PH.D., F.G.S., Geology
EVANS, W. C., PH.D., D.SC., F.P.S., Phytochemistry
GRANSDEN, ANTONIA, M.A., PH.D., F.R.HIST.S., F.S.A., Medieval History
GREEN, W. A., PH.D., Theoretical Mechanics
HUDSON, R. L., D.PHIL., Mathematics
HUGO, W. B., PH.D., F.P.S., Pharmaceutical Microbiology
JOHNS, P. B., M.SC., PH.D., C.ENG., M.I.E.E., Electrical and Electronic Engineering
LICHTAROWICZ, A., PH.D., C.ENG., M.I.MECH.E., M.A.S.M.E., Fluid Power
LOGAN, N., PH.D., C.CHEM., F.R.S.C., Inorganic Chemistry
MCPHERSON, M. J., PH.D., C.ENG., M.I.MIN.E., M.I.M.M., Mining Engineering
MASSER, D. W., PH.D., Pure Mathematics
MAYER, R. J., PH.D., D.SC., Biochemistry
MOORE, W. S., M.A., PH.D., F.INST.P., Experimental Physics
MORRIS, B., PH.D., Zoology
MORRIS, R., PH.D., Zoology
NEWBOLD, P., PH.D., Mathematics
PEBERDY, J. F., PH.D., F.I.BIOL., Plant Microbiology
POWER, G., M.B.E., M.A., PH.D., F.INST.P., Mathematics
PULHAM, R. J., PH.D., Inorganic Chemistry
ROCHESTER, C. H., PH.D., D.SC., F.R.S.C., Physical Chemistry
RODWAY, A. E., M.A., PH.D., English Studies
ROGERS, T. G., J.P., PH.D., Theoretical Mechanics
ROSE, A., D.SC., F.I.M.A., Mathematics
RUDHAM, R., PH.D., C.CHEM., F.R.S.C., Physical Chemistry
SHEARD, F. W., PH.D., Theoretical Physics
SNELL, C., M.SC., Stress Analysis
THOMAS, J. E., M.A., D.PHIL., Adult Education
TITOW, J. Z., M.A., PH.D., Medieval Economic and Social History
TUCK, B., PH.D., D.SC., C.ENG., M.I.E.E., F.INST.P., Electrical and Electronic Engineering
UNSWORTH, M. H., PH.D., Environmental Physics
WALLWORK, S. C., M.A., D.PHIL., F.INST.P., Physical Chemistry
WATERHOUSE, R. B., J.P., M.A., PH.D., F.I.M., Metallurgy and Materials Science
WATTS, M. R., D.PHIL., F.R.HIST.S., Modern History
WHITING, D. A., PH.D., D.SC., F.R.S.C., Organic Chemistry
WHITTAKER, B. N., PH.D., C.ENG., F.I.MIN.E., F.I.M.M., Mining Engineering
WILLIS, M. R., PH.D., Physical Chemistry
WOODALL, D. R., M.A., PH.D., Pure Mathematics

## OPEN UNIVERSITY
### WALTON HALL, MILTON KEYNES, MK7 6AA BUCKINGHAMSHIRE

Telephone: 0908-74066.

Founded 1969.

Academic year: February to December; teaching takes place in the first ten months, with examinations in October/November. Correspondence courses fully integrated with broadcasts on B.B.C. 2 television and V.H.F. radio, and residential summer schools. Students are over the age of 21, working in full-time employment and studying for an O.U. degree in their spare time. Associate students study single courses of a vocational or personal interest. Apart from the Walton headquarters, there are 13 regions administering c. 260 study centres throughout the country.

Chancellor: LORD BRIGGS, M.A., B.SC. (ECON.).
Pro-Chancellor: Sir PETER THORNTON, K.C.B.
Vice-Chancellor: Dr. J. H. HORLOCK, M.A., PH.D., SC.D., F.ENG., F.R.S.
Secretary: D. J. CLINCH, M.B.A.
Librarian and Director of Media Resources: D. J. SIMPSON, B.SC.(ECON.), F.L.A.

Number of full-time teachers: c. 500.
Number of part-time students: c. 80,000.

### DEANS:
Faculty of Arts: Prof. A. J. B. MARWICK, M.A., B.LITT., F.R.HIST.S.
Faculty of Educational Sciences: J. M. BYNNER, PH.D.
Faculty of Mathematics: M. CRAMPIN, PH.D.
Faculty of Science: Prof. M. PENTZ, M.SC., M.SC.(ENG.).
Faculty of Social Sciences: F. G. CASTLES, B.A.
Faculty of Technology: Prof. J. J. SPARKES, PH.D., M.I.E.E., S.M.I.E.E., C.ENG.

### DIRECTORS OF UNITS:
Institute of Educational Technology: Prof D. G. HAWKRIDGE, M.A., B.ED., PH.D.
Regional Tutorial Services: D. A. GRUGSON (acting).

### PROFESSORS:
BRANNAN, D. A., PH.D., Mathematics
CHAPMAN, P. F., M.A., PH.D., Energy Studies
DRAKE, M., M.A., PH.D., Social Sciences
ELLIOTT, G. F., M.A., PH.D., Physics
GASS, I. G., D.SC., PH.D., F.G.S., Earth Science
GLATTER, R., M.A., Educational Studies
GREENE, J. M., M.A., PH.D., Psychology
HALL, S., M.A., Sociology
HARRIS, L., M.SC., Economics
HAWKRIDGE, D. G., M.A., PH.D., Applied Educational Sciences
HAYNES, L. J., PH.D., F.R.S.C., D.I.C., A.R.C.S., C.CHEM., Chemistry
HENDRIE, G., M.A., PH.D., F.R.C.O., A.R.C.M., Music
HOLISTER, G. S., M.SC., PH.D., C.ENG., M.I.MECH.E., M.I.C.E., A.INST.P., F.R.AE.S., Engineering Science
JAMES, W., B.A., Educational Studies
LEARMONTH, A. T. A., M.A., PH.D., Geography
LEWIS, B. N., B.SC., Applied Educational Sciences

LEWIS, T., M.A., D.SC., Mathematics
MARTIN, C. G., M.A., Literature
MARWICK, A. J. B., M.A., B.LITT., F.R.HIST.S., History
MERRITT, J. E., B.A., A.B.PS.S., Educational Studies
MURRAY, D. J., M.A., D.PHIL., Government
NEIL, M. W., PH.D., F.R.S.C., Applied Educational Sciences
NEWEY, C. W. A., PH.D., Materials Science
NUTTALL, D. L., M.A., PH.D., A.B.PS.S., Educational Studies
PARKINSON, A. G., M.SC., PH.D., D.I.C., C.ENG., M.R.I.N.A., Engineering Mechanics
PENGELLY, R. M., PH.D., F.B.C.S., Mathematics
PENROSE, O., PH.D., Mathematics
ROSE, S. P. R., PH.D., F.I.BIOL., F.R.S.A., Biology
SCHARF, A., PH.D., Art History
SMITH, R. C., M.SC., PH.D., F.R.MET.S., D.I.C., F.I.M.A., Mathematics
SPARKES, J. J., PH.D., C.ENG., M.I.E.E., S.M.I.E.E., Electronics Design and Communications
STANNARD, F. R., PH.D., Physics
SWIFT, D. F., M.A., PH.D., Educational Studies
VESEY, G. N. A., M.A., M.LITT., Philosophy

### READERS:
BLACKBURN, D. A., PH.D., Engineering Science
BLUNDEN, J. R., PH.D., Geography
CASTLES, F. G., B.A., Political Science
CLARK, H. F., PH.L., S.T.L., D.D., Religious Studies
CRECRAFT, D. I., PH.D., M.S., C.ENG., M.I.E.E., M.I.E.R.E., Electronics Design and Communications
FLEGG, H. G., M.A., F.I.M.A., F.R.MET.S., C.ENG., M.I.E.E., M.R.AE.S., Mathematics
FURBANK, P. N., M.A., Literature
HILL, R. R., PH.D., M.R.S.C., Chemistry
HUSSEY, M. J. L., PH.D., M.I.ENV.SCI., Technological Education
MACDONALD-ROSS, M., B.SC., Textual Communication
NELSON, R., M.SC., F.I.M.A., F.B.C.S., Mathematics
PORTEOUS, A., M.ENG., F.I.MECH.E., C.ENG., M.I.CHEM.E., M.I.S.W.M., Engineering Mechanics
REID, C. N., PH.D., C.ENG., F.I.M., Materials Science
ROWNTREE, D. G. F., B.SC., Educational Development
RUSSELL, C. A., PH.D., D.SC., C.CHEM., F.R.S.C., History of Science and Technology
SMITH, P. J., PH.D., D.I.C., A.R.C.S., F.R.A.S., Earth Science
STONE, B. E., M.A., Literature
VARLEY, MARGARET E., M.A., PH.D., F.I.BIOL., F.L.S., Biology
WALTON, A. J., M.SC., PH.D., Physics
WRIGHT, J. B., M.A., F.G.S., Earth Science

## UNIVERSITY OF OXFORD
### OXFORD

Telephone: 56747.

Postal Address:
University Offices, Wellington Square, Oxford, OX1 2JD.

Originated 13th Century.

Chancellor: Rt. Hon. H. MACMILLAN, O.M., P.C., D.C.L.
Vice-Chancellor: GEOFFREY J. WARNOCK, M.A.

Registrar: A. J. DOREY, D.PHIL.
Secretary of Faculties: R. BUTLER, M.A.
Deputy Registrar: A. L. FLEET, M.A.
 Library: see Bodleian Library.
 Ashmolean Museum: see Museums.
 Number of teachers: c. 1,500, including c. 150 professors.
 Number of students: 12,354.
 Publication: Oxford University Gazette.

## UNIVERSITY TEACHING OFFICERS:

The initials in brackets appearing after each professor's name and subject represent the College to which he is attached. The key is given below:

All S.—All Souls College.
Ball.—Balliol College.
Bras.—Brasenose College.
Camp.—Campion Hall.
Ch. Ch.—Christ Church.
Corp.—Corpus Christi College.
Exeter—Exeter College.
Greyf.—Greyfriars.
Green—Green College.
Hertf.—Hertford College.
Jesus—Jesus College.
Keble—Keble College.
L.M.H.—Lady Margaret Hall.
Linacre—Linacre College.
Linc.—Lincoln College.
Magd.—Magdalen College.
Mansf.—Mansfield College.
Mert.—Merton College.
New—New College.
Nuff.—Nuffield College.
Oriel—Oriel College.
Pemb.—Pembroke College.
Qu.—The Queen's College.
Reg. P.—Regent's Park College.
S. Ann.—St. Anne's College.
S. Ant.—St. Antony's College.
S. Ben.—St. Benet's Hall.
S. Cat.—St. Catherine's College.
S. Cross—St. Cross College.
S. Edm.—St. Edmund Hall.
S. Hil.—St. Hilda's College.
S. Hug.—St. Hugh's College.
S. Joh.—St. John's College.
S. Pet.—St. Peter's College.
Som.—Somerville College.
Trin.—Trinity College.
Univ.—University College.
Wadh.—Wadham College.
Wolfs.—Wolfson College.
Worc.—Worcester College.

*Faculty of Anthropology and Geography:*

PROFESSORS:

CUNLIFFE, B. W., D.PHIL., F.S.A., European Archaeology (Keble)
GOTTMANN, I. J., D. ÈS L., F.B.A., Geography (Hertf.)
HARRISON, G. A., D.PHIL., Biological Anthropology (Linacre)
HOUSE, J. W., D.LITT., Geography (S. Pet.)
NEEDHAM, R., D.LITT., Social Anthropology (All S.)

READERS:

LIENHARDT, R. G., D.PHIL., Social Anthropology (Wolfs.)
SWEETING, Miss M. M., PH.D., Geography (S. Hug.)

*Faculty of Biological and Agricultural Sciences:*

PROFESSORS:

ARMITAGE, P., PH.D., Biomathematics (S. Pet.)
EDWARDS, J. H., M.B., B.CHIR., F.R.C.P., F.R.S., Genetics
MANDELSTAM, J., PH.D., F.R.S., Microbiology (Linacre)
PHILLIPS, Sir DAVID, PH.D., F.R.S., Molecular Biophysics (Corp.)
POORE, M. E. D., PH.D., Forest Science (S. Joh.)
PORTER, R. R., PH.D., F.R.S., Biochemistry (Trin.)
SMITH, D. C., D.PHIL., F.R.S., Rural Economy (S. Joh.)
SOUTHWOOD, T. R. E., PH.D., D.SC., F.R.S., Zoology (Mert.)
SPENCER-SMITH, D., PH.D., Entomology
WHATLEY, F. R., PH.D., F.R.S., Botany (Magd.)

DIRECTOR:

Institute of Agricultural Economics: G. H. PETERS, M.SC. (Wolfs.).

READERS:

CLOWES, F. A. L., D.PHIL., D.SC., Botany (Magd.)
DALZIEL, K., PH.D., F.R.S., Biochemistry
McFARLAND, D. J., D.PHIL., Animal Behaviour (Ball.)
NYE, P. H., M.A., Soil Science (S. Cross)
PARSONS, D. S., D.M., Physiological Biochemistry (Mert.)
PHILLIPSON, J., PH.D., Animal Ecology (Linacre)

*Faculty of Clinical Medicine:*

PROFESSORS:

DAWES, G. S., C.B.E., D.M., F.R.S., F.R.C.P., F.R.C.O.G., F.A.C.O.G., Medical Research (Worc.)
DUTHIE, R. B., CH.M., F.R.C.S.E., F.R.C.S., F.A.C.S., Orthopaedic Surgery (Worc.)
GELDER, M. G., D.M., F.R.C.P., F.R.C. PSYCH., W. A. Handley Professor of Psychiatry (Mert.)
GRAHAME-SMITH, D. G., PH.D., F.R.C.P., Clinical Pharmacology (Corp.)
HARRIS, H., D.PHIL., F.R.C.P., F.R.S., (CH.CH.)
MATTHEWS, W. B., D.M., F.R.C.P., Clinical Neurology (S. Edm.)
McGEE, J. O'D., PH.D.,M.D., M.R.C.PATH., Morbid Anatomy (Linacre)
MORRIS, P. J., PH.D., F.R.C.S., F.R.A.C.S., F.A.C.S., Surgery (Ball.)
RANDLE, P. J., PH.D., M.D., Clinical Biochemistry (Hertf.)
SLEIGHT, P., D.M., F.R.C.P., Cardiovascular Medicine (Exeter)
SYKES, M. K., B.CHIR., F.F.R.A.C.S., Anaesthetics (Pemb.)
TIZARD, J. P. M., C.B.E., B.M., F.R.C.P., Paediatrics (Jesus)
TURNBULL, A. C., M.D., CH.B., F.R.C.O.G., Obstetrics and Gynaecology (Oriel)
VESSEY, M. P., M.D., Social and Community Medicine (S. Cross)
WEATHERALL, D. J., M.D., F.R.C.P., F.R.C.PATH., F.R.S., Clinical Medicine (Magd.)

DIRECTOR:

POTTER, J. M., D.M., F.R.C.S., Postgraduate Medical Education and Training (Wadh.)

READERS:

BRON, A. J., D.O., F.R.C.S., Ophthalmology
LEDINGHAM, J. G. G., D.M., F.R.C.P., Medicine (New)
PETO, R., M.SC., Cancer Studies
TARIN, D., D.M., Pathology (Green)

*Department of Educational Studies:*

DIRECTOR:

JUDGE, H. G., PH.D., (Bras.)

READER:

HARGREAVES, D. H., D.PHIL. (Jesus)

*Department for External Studies:*

DIRECTOR:

SMETHURST, R. G., M.A. (Worc.)

*Faculty of English Language and Literature:*

PROFESSORS:

BAYLEY, J. O., M.A., English Literature (S. Cat.)
CAREY, J., D.PHIL., English Literature (Mert.)
ELLMANN, R., PH.D., F.B.A., English Literature (New)
GRAY, D., English Language and Literature (L.M.H.)
JONES, H. J. F., M.A., Poetry (Merton)
STANLEY, E. G., PH.D., Anglo-Saxon (Pemb.)

READERS:

DRONKE, U. M., B.LITT., Ancient Icelandic Literature and Antiquities (Linacre)
FOXON, D. F., M.A., F.B.A., Textual Criticism (Wadh.)
JONES, E. L., PH.D., English Literature (Magd.)
WEAVER, M. L. H. L., PH.D., American Literature (Linacre)

*Faculty of Fine Art:*

PROFESSOR:

BROWN, J., PH.D., Fine Art

RUSKIN MASTER OF DRAWING:
MORSBERGER, P., M.A. (New)

*Faculty of Modern History:*

PROFESSORS:

COBB, R. C., C.B.E., M.A., F.B.A., Modern History (Worc.)
GOWING, Mrs. M. M., C.B.E., M.A., F.B.A., History of Science (Linacre)
HASKELL, F. J. H., F.B.A., History of Art (Trin.)
HOWARD, M. E., C.B.E., M.C., D.LITT., F.B.A., Modern History—Regius (Oriel)
MATHIAS, P., M.A., F.B.A., Economic History (All S.)
OBOLENSKY, Prince DIMITRI, PH.D., D.LITT., F.B.A., F.S.A., F.R.HIST.S., Russian and Balkan History (Ch. Ch.)
PATTERSON, J. J., PH.D., American History
PLATT, D. C. M., D.PHIL., History of Latin America (S. Ant.)
POLE, J. R., PH.D., F.R.H.S., American History and Institutions (S. Cat.)
ROBINSON, R. E., C.B.E., PH.D., History of the British Commonwealth (Ball.)
STOCKWIN, J. A. A., PH.D., Modern Japanese Studies
WALLACE-HADRILL, J. M., D.LITT., F.B.A., Modern History (All S.)

READERS:

CHAPLAIS, P. T. V. M., PH.D., F.B.A., F.R.HIST.S., Diplomatic History (Wadh.)
COLVIN, H. M., C.B.E., M.A., F.B.A., F.R.HIST.S., Architectural History (S. Joh.)

UNIVERSITIES U.K. (GREAT BRITAIN)

RAYCHAUDHURI, T., D.PHIL., Modern South Asian History (S. Ant.)
THIRSK, Mrs. I. J., PH.D., F.B.A., F.R.HIST.S., Economic History (S. Hil.)
THOMAS, K. V., M.A., F.B.A., Modern History (S. Joh.)
WEBSTER, C., D.SC., History of Medicine (Corp.)

*Faculty of Law:*

PROFESSORS:

ATIYAH, P. S., F.B.A., D.C.L., English Law (S. Joh.)
BROWNLIE, I., Q.C., D.PHIL., D.C.L., F.B.A., Public International Law (All S.)
DWORKIN, R. M., M.A., F.B.A., Jurisprudence (Univ.)
HONORÉ, A. M., D.C.L., Civil Law—Regius (All S.)
RUDDEN, B. A., PH.D., Comparative Law (Bras.)
TREITEL, G. H., English Law (All S.)

READERS:

BARTON, J. L., B.C.L., M.A., Roman Law (Mert.)
FINNIS, J. M., D.PHIL., Laws of the British Commonwealth and United States (Univ.)
HOOD, R., PH.D., Criminology (All S.)
REYNOLDS, F. M. B., B.C.L., M.A., Law (Worc.)
TAPPER, C. F. H., B.C.L., M.A. (Magd.)

*Faculty of Literae Humaniores:*

PROFESSORS:

ACKRILL, J. L., M.A., F.B.A., History of Philosophy (Bras.)
BOARDMAN, J., M.A., F.B.A., F.S.A., Classical Archaeology and Art (Linc.)
BRUNT, P. A., M.A., F.B.A., Ancient History (Bras.)
DUMMETT, M. A. E., M.A., F.B.A., Logic (New)
FORREST, W. G. G., M.A., Ancient History (New)
FRERE, S. S., C.B.E., D.LITT., F.B.A., F.S.A., Archaeology of the Roman Empire (All S.)
HARE, R. M., M.A., F.B.A., Moral Philosophy (Corp.)
LLOYD-JONES, P. H. J., M.A., F.B.A., Greek—Regius (Ch. Ch.)
MORPURGO-DAVIES, Mrs. A., M.A., Comparative Philology (Som.)
NISBET, R. G. M., M.A., F.B.A., Latin Language and Literature (Corp.)
SCOTT, D. S., PH.D., F.B.A., Mathematical Logic (Mert.)
STRAWSON, Sir PETER, M.A., F.B.A., Metaphysical Philosophy (Magd.)

READERS:

COULTON, J. J., PH.D., Classical Archaeology (Mert.)
FRASER, P. M., M.C., M.A., F.B.A., Hellenistic History (All S.)
GANDY, R. O., PH.D., Mathematical Logic (Wolfs.)
MACKIE, J. L., M.A., F.B.A., Philosophy (Univ.)
PEARS, D. F., M.A., F.B.A., Philosophy (Ch. Ch.)
RUSSELL, D. A F. M., M.A., F.B.A., Classical Literature (S. Joh.)

*Faculty of Mathematics:*

PROFESSORS:

ATIYAH, M. F., PH.D., F.R.S., Mathematics (Royal Society Research) (S. Cat.)
BROOKE-BENJAMIN, T., M.ENG., PH.D., F.R.S., Natural Philosophy (Qu.)
FOX, L., D.PHIL., D.SC., Numerical Analysis (Ball.)

HIGMAN, G., D.PHIL., F.R.S., Pure Mathematics (Magd.)
HOARE, C. A. R., M.A., D.F.B.C.S., Computation (Wolfs.).
JAMES, I. M., D.PHIL., F.R.S., Geometry (New)
KINGMAN, J. F. C., D.SC., F.R.S., Mathematics (S. Ann.)
PENROSE, R., PH.D., F.R.S., Mathematics (Wadh.)
WOODS, L. C., D.PHIL., D.SC., Mathematics (Theory of Plasma) (Ball.)

READERS:

BIRCH, B. J., PH.D., F.R.S., Mathematics (Bras.)
EDWARDS, D. A., D.PHIL., Mathematics (Linc.)
GANDY, R. O., PH.D., Mathematics (Wolfs.)
MURRAY, J. D., PH.D., D.SC., F.R.S.E., Mathematics (Corp.)
SEGAL, G. B., D.PHIL., Mathematics (S. Cat.)

*Faculty of Medieval and Modern Languages:*

PROFESSORS:

EVANS, D. E., D.PHIL., Celtic Literature (Jesus)
FENNELL, J. L. I., PH.D., Russian (New)
GANZ, P. F., PH.D., German (St. Edm.)
GRAYSON, C., M.A., F.B.A., Italian Studies (Magd.)
HARRIS, R., D.PHIL., General Linguistics (Worc.)
McFARLANE, I. D., M.B.E., D.U., F.B.A., French Literature (Wadh.)
MANGO, C., D.U., F.B.A., Byzantine and Modern Greek Language and Literature (Exeter)
MICHAEL, I. D. L., PH.D., Spanish Studies (Exeter)
POSNER, R., D.PHIL., Romance Languages (S. Hug.)
PRAWER, S. S., D.PHIL., D.LITT., LITT.D., F.B.A., German Language and Literature (Qu.)
SHACKLETON, R., D.LITT., F.B.A., French Literature (Bras.)

READERS:

RAITT, A. W., D.PHIL., F.R.S.L., French Literature (Magd.)
SEIFFERT, L., PH.D., German (Hertf.)

*Faculty of Music:*

PROFESSOR:

ARNOLD, D. M., B.MUS., A.R.C.M., F.B.A. (Wadh.)

*Faculty of Oriental Studies:*

PROFESSORS:

BAINES, J. R., D.PHIL., Egyptology (Qu.)
BARR, J., B.D., F.B.A., Hebrew—Regius (Ch. Ch.)
DOWSETT, C. J. F., D.PHIL., F.B.A., Armenian Studies (Pemb.)
GOMBRICH, R. F., D.PHIL., Sanskrit (Ball.)
MADELUNG, W. F., PH.D., Arabic (S. Joh.)
MATILAL, B. K., PH.D., Eastern Religions and Ethics (All S.)
VAN DER LOON, P., M.A., D.R.S., Chinese (Univ.)

READERS:

VERMES, G., D.THEOL., Jewish Studies (Wolfs.)
WERNBERG-MÖLLER, P., D.PHIL., Semitic Philology (S. Pet.)

*Faculty of Physical Sciences:*

PROFESSORS:

ALLEN, K. W., PH.D., Nuclear Structure (Ball.)
BALDWIN, J. E., PH.D., F.R.S., Organic Chemistry
BLACKWELL, D. E., PH.D., Astronomy (New)
CHRISTIAN, J. W., D.PHIL., F.R.S., Physical Metallurgy (S. Edm.)
DALITZ, R. H., PH.D., F.R.S., Research Professor of the Royal Society, Theoretical Physics (All S.)
ELLIOTT, R. J., D.PHIL., F.R.S., Theoretical Physics (New)
GOODENOUGH, J. B., PH.D., Inorganic Chemistry (S. Cat.)
HEMP, W. S., M.A., F.R.AE.S., Structural Engineering (Keble)
HIRSCH, Sir PETER, D.PHIL., F.R.S., Metallurgy (S. Edm.)
HOUGHTON, J. T., D.PHIL., F.R.S., Atmospheric Physics (Jesus)
MARCH, N. H., PH.D., Theoretical Chemistry (Univ.)
MITCHELL, E. W. J., C.B.E., PH.D., Experimental Philosophy
PAIGE, E. G. S., PH.D., Engineering (S. Joh.)
PERKINS, D. H., PH.D., F.R.S., Elementary Particle Physics (S. Cat.)
ROWLINSON, J. S., D.PHIL., F.R.S., F.R.S.C., F.I.CHEM.E., Physical Chemistry (Exeter)
SANDARS, P. G. H., D.PHIL., Experimental Physics (Ch. Ch.)
VINCENT, E. A., PH.D., Geology (Univ.)
WILLIAMS, R. J. P., D.PHIL., F.R.S., Royal Society Napier Research Professor, Inorganic Chemistry (Wadh.)
WROTH, C. P., PH.D., Engineering Science (Bras.)

READERS:

BARROW, R. F., D.PHIL., Physical Chemistry (Exeter)
GRACE, M. A., D.PHIL., F.R.S., Nuclear Physics (Ch. Ch.)
LLEWELLYN SMITH, C. H., D.PHIL., Theoretical Physics (S. Joh.)
MOORBATH, S., D.PHIL., D.SC., F.R.S., Geology (Linacre)
ROSENBERG, H. M., D.PHIL., Physics (S. Cat.)
SCHULTZ, D. L., D.PHIL., Engineering Science (S. Cat.)
TER HAAR, D., D.SC., PH.D., F.R.S.E., Theoretical Physics (Magd.)
TURNER, D. W., PH.D., F.R.S., Physical Chemistry (Ball.)
WHELAN, M. J., D.PHIL., F.R.S., Physical Examination of Materials (Linacre)
WHITTAKER, E. J. W., PH.D., F.I.P., Mineralogy (S. Cross)
YOUNG, G. T., D.SC., PH.D., F.R.S.C., Chemistry (Jesus)

*Faculty of Physiological Sciences:*

PROFESSORS:

BLAKEMORE, C. B., PH.D., Physiology (Magd.)
BROWNLEE, G. G., PH.D., Chemical Pathology (Linc.)
GARDNER, R. L., PH.D., Pathology, Royal Society Research (Ch. Ch.)
PATON, Sir WILLIAM, C.B.E., D.M., F.R.S., F.R.C.P., Pharmacology (Ball.)
PHILLIPS, C. G., D.M., F.R.S., F.R.C.P., Anatomy (Hertf.)

READERS:

GORDON, G., D.M., Sensory Physiology (Bras.)
GORDON, S., PH.D., Experimental Pathology (Exeter)

Matthews, P. B. C., D.M., D.SC., F.R.S., Physiology of Motor Control (Ch. Ch.)
Porterfield, J. S., M.D., Bacteriology (Wadh.)
Powell, T. P. S., M.D., F.R.C.S., F.R.S., Neuroanatomy (S. Joh.)

*Faculty of Psychological Studies:*

PROFESSORS:
Bryant, P. E., PH.D., Psychology (Wolfs.)
Cowey, A., D.PHIL., Physiological Psychology (Linc.)
Weiskrantz, L., PH.D., F.R.S., Psychology (Magd.)

READER:
Argyle, J. M., M.A., Social Psychology (Wolfs.)

*Faculty of Social Studies:*

PROFESSORS:
Brown, J. A. C., M.A., Applied Economics (Mert.)
Bull, H., B.PHIL., International Relations (Ball.)
Finer, S. E., M.A., F.R.HIST.S., Government and Public Administration (All S.)
Halsey, A. H., PH.D., Social and Administrative Studies (Nuff.)
Hendry, D. F., PH.D., Economics
Kirkwood, K., M.A., Race Relations (S. Ant.)
Mirrlees, J. A., PH.D., Economics (Nuff.)
Sen, A. K., PH.D., F.B.A., Political Economy (All S.)

DIRECTORS:
Goodwin, P. B., PH.D., Transport Studies (acting)
Jackson, E. F., M.A., Institute of Economics and Statistics (S. Ant.)

READERS:
Beckerman, W., D.PHIL., Economics (Ball.)
Bliss, C. J., PH.D., International Economics (Nuff.)
Hammersley, J. M., D.SC., F.R.S., Mathematical Statistics (Trin.)
Hood, R. G., D.PHIL., Criminology (All S.)
Johnson, N., M.A., Comparative Study of Institutions (Nuff.)
Kaser, M. C., M.A., Economics (S. Ant.)
Madden, A. F., B.LITT., D.PHIL., F.R. HIST.S., Commonwealth Government (Nuff.)
Roberts, E. A., International Relations
Ryan, A. J., M.A., Politics (New)
Wilson, B. R., PH.D., Sociology (All S.)

*Faculty of Theology:*

PROFESSORS:
Caird, Rev. G. B., D.PHIL., D.D., F.B.A., Exegesis of Holy Scripture (Qu.)
Macquarrie, Rev. J., PH.D., D.LITT., Divinity (Ch. Ch.)
McManners, Rev. J., D.LITT., F.B.A., F.A.H.A., F.R.HIST.S., Ecclesiastical History—Regius (Ch. Ch.)
Mitchell, B. G., M.A., Philosophy of the Christian Religion (Oriel)
Nicholson, Rev. E. W., D.D., Interpretation of Holy Scripture (Oriel)
O'Donovan, Rev. O. M. T., D.PHIL., Moral and Pastoral Theology (from May 1982)
Wiles, Rev. M. F., D.D., F.B.A., Divinity (Ch. Ch.)

COLLEGES:
**All Souls College:** f. 1438; for Fellows only.
*Warden:* F. P. Neill, Q.C., B.C.L.

**Balliol College:** f. 1263.
*Master:* A. J. P. Kenny, D.PHIL., F.B.A., F.R.S.E.

**Brasenose College:** f. 1509.
*Principal:* J. K. B. M. Nicholas, M.A.

**Christ Church:** f. 1546.
*Dean:* The Very Rev. E. W. Heaton, M.A.

**Corpus Christi College:** f. 1517.
*President:* Sir Kenneth Dover, D.LITT., F.R.S.E., F.B.A.

**Exeter College:** f. 1314.
*Rector:* W. G. Barr, M.A.

**Green College:** f. 1979, for graduates.
*Warden:* Sir Richard Doll, O.B.E., D.M., F.R.S.

**Hertford College:** f. 1874.
*Principal:* J. R. Torrance, M.A. (acting).

**Jesus College:** f. 1571.
*Principal:* Sir John Habakkuk, M.A., F.B.A.

**Keble College:** f. 1870.
*Warden:* C. J. E. Ball, M.A.

**Lady Margaret Hall:** f. 1878.
*Principal:* D. M. Stewart, M.A.

**Linacre College:** f. 1962, as Linacre House, for graduates.
*Principal:* J. B. Bamborough, M.A.

**Lincoln College:** f. 1427.
*Rector:* The Rt. Hon. Lord Trend, P.C., G.C.B., C.V.O., M.A.

**Magdalen College:** f. 1458.
*President:* K. B. Griffin, D.PHIL.

**Merton College:** f. 1264.
*Warden:* Sir Rex Richards, D.PHIL., D.SC., F.R.S.

**New College:** f. 1379.
*Warden:* A. H. Cooke, M.B.E., D.PHIL.

**Nuffield College:** f. 1937, for graduates.
*Warden:* M. G. Brock, C.B.E., M.A.

**Oriel College:** f. 1326.
*Vice-Provost:* W. E. Parry, D.PHIL.

**Pembroke College:** f. 1624.
*Master:* Sir Geoffrey Arthur, K.C.M.G., M.A.

**The Queen's College:** f. 1340.
*Provost:* The Rt. Hon. Lord Blake, M.A., F.B.A.

**St. Anne's College:** f. 1893 (as Society of Oxford Home Students).
*Principal:* Mrs. Nancy K. Trenaman, M.A.

**St. Antony's College:** f. 1950, for graduates.
*Warden:* A. R. M. Carr, M.A.

**St. Catherine's College:** f. 1868, reconstituted as a full College 1962.
*Master:* Sir Patrick Nairne, G.C.B., M.C.

**St. Cross College:** f. 1965, for graduates.
*Master:* G. H. Stafford, C.B.E., PH.D., F.R.S., F.INST.P.

**St. Edmund Hall:** f. ca. 1278.
*Principal:* Sir Ieuan Maddock, C.B., O.B.E., M.A., F.R.S.

**St. Hilda's College:** f. 1893.
*Principal:* Mrs. G. M. Moore, J.P., M.A.

**St. Hugh's College:** f. 1886.
*Principal:* Miss M. R. Trickett, M.A.

**St. John's College:** f. 1555.
*President:* Sir John Kendrew, C.B.E., SC.D., F.R.S.

**St. Peter's College:** f. 1929 as St. Peter's Hall.
*Master:* G. E. Aylmer, D.PHIL., F.B.A.

**Somerville College:** f. 1879.
*Principal:* Miss D. M. S. D. Park, C.M.G., O.B.E., M.A.

**Trinity College:** f. 1554.
*President:* A. M. Quinton, M.A., F.B.A.

**University College:** f. 1249.
*Master:* Lord Goodman, C.H., LL.M.

**Wadham College:** f. 1612.
*Warden:* Sir Stuart Hampshire, M.A., F.B.A.

**Wolfson College:** f. 1965, for graduates.
*President:* The Hon. Sir Henry Fisher, Q.C., M.A.

**Worcester College:** f. 1714.
*Provost:* Lord Briggs, M.A., F.B.A.

PERMANENT PRIVATE HALLS
**Campion Hall:** f. 1896.
*Master:* Rev. P. Edwards, M.A.

**Greyfriars:** f. 1910.
*Warden:* Rev. M. J. Mann, O.F.M.

**Mansfield College:** f. 1885.
*Principal:* D. A. Sykes, D.PHIL.

**Regent's Park College:** f. 1810.
*Principal:* Rev. B. R. White, D.PHIL.

**St. Benet's Hall:** f. 1897.
*Master:* Rev. P. D. Holdsworth, M.A., O.S.B., S.T.L.

ATTACHED INSTITUTES:
**Institute of Commonwealth Studies:** Queen Elizabeth House, 21 St. Giles, Oxford; f. 1945.
*Director:* A. D. Hazlewood, M.PHIL.

**Ruskin School of Drawing and Fine Art:** *see* under Colleges.

**Commonwealth Forestry Institute:** South Parks Rd., Oxford; f. 1924 for research and higher studies in forestry; *Dir.* Prof. M. E. D. Poore, D.PHIL.

**Maison Française:** *see* under Learned Societies.

**Oxford Centre for Management Studies:** see under Colleges.

**Centre for Postgraduate Hebrew Studies:** Principal D. PATTERSON, PH.D.

**Centre for Socio-Legal Studies:** Dirs. D. R. HARRIS, B.C.L., R. M. HARTWELL, D.PHIL.

# UNIVERSITY OF READING
READING, BERKSHIRE, RG6 2AH

Telephone: (0734) 85123.

University Extension College established 1892; University Charter granted 1926.

*Chancellor:* The Rt. Hon. Lord SHERFIELD, G.C.B., G.C.M.G., D.C.L., LL.D., F.I.C.E.
*Vice-Chancellor:* Dr. E. S. PAGE, M.A., PH.D.
*Deputy Vice-Chancellor:* Prof. G. W. A. FOWLES, PH.D., D.SC., C.CHEM., F.R.I.C.
*Registrar:* J. F. JOHNSON, B.A.
*Librarian:* J. THOMPSON, B.A., F.L.A.

Library: see Libraries.

Number of teachers: 650, including 86 professors.

Number of students: 6,489.

Publication: *Proceedings of the University* (annually).

### DEANS:
*Faculty of Letters and Social Sciences:* F. ROBERTSON, M.A.
*Faculty of Science:* Prof. A. WILD, PH.D.
*Faculty of Agriculture and Food:* Prof. G. M. H. WAITES, M.A., PH.D., F.I.BIOL.
*Faculty of Urban and Regional Studies:* Prof. H. W. E. DAVIES, M.SC.(ECON.), M.R.T.P.I.
*School of Education:* Prof. R. WILSON, B.A. (Chair.).

### PROFESSORS:
(some professors serve in more than one faculty)

*Faculty of Letters and Social Sciences:*
ANDRESKI, S. L., M.SC.(ECON.), PH.D., Sociology
BIDDISS, M. D., PH.D., F.R.HIST.S., History
BROMWICH, M., B.SC.(ECON.), Finance and Accounting
CAMPBELL, P. W., M.A., Politics
CASSON, M. C., Economics
COUPE, W. A., M.A., PH.D., German
CRYSTAL, D., PH.D., Linguistic Science
DAVIES, MARGARET C., M.A., D.UNIV., French
DAVIS, R., M.A., D.PHIL., Psychology
DOWNES, J. K., PH.D., F.S.A., History of Art
DUNNING, J. H., PH.D., D.PHIL., International Investment and Business Studies
VAN EMDEN, W. G., PH.D., French
FLETCHER, I., PH.D., English
FLETCHER, R., PH.D., Sociology
FLEW, A. G. N., M.A., D.LITT., Philosophy
FROY, M., DIP.FINE ART, Fine Art
GREGORY, R. G., M.A., D.PHIL., Politics
GURR, A. J., M.A., PH.D., English
HALL, P. G., M.A., PH.D., Geography
HART, P. E., B.SC.(ECON.), Economics
HUFTON, OLWEN, PH.D., F.R.HIST.S., History
JACKSON, P., LL.B., B.C.L., M.A., BAR., Law
LEPSCHY, G. C., D.LETT., Italian
LOCKWOOD, W. B., M.A., D.LITT., Germanic and Indo-European Philology
MATTHEW, D. J. A., M.A., D.PHIL., History
MATTHEWS, P. H., M.A., Linguistic Science
MORGAN, E. V., M.A., Economics
PALMER, F. R., M.A., F.B.A., Linguistic Science
PALMER, N. E., Law
PARKINSON, G. H. R., M.A., D.PHIL., Philosophy
REDFERN, W. D., M.A., PH.D., French
SALVESEN, C. G., B.A., B.LITT., English
TWYMAN, M. L., PH.D., Typography and Graphic Communication
WARBURTON, D. M., A.M., PH.D., Psychology
WILLIAMS, R. D., M.A., Classics
WISHART, P. C. A., B.MUS., F.G.S.M., Music

*Faculty of Science:*
ALLEN, J. R. L., D.SC., Geology
ALLEN, P., F.R.S., M.A., PH.D., Geology
ATKINS, A. G., Mechanical Engineering
BAILEY, D. K., M.A., PH.D., Geology
BRYCE-SMITH, D., D.SC., C.CHEM., F.R.S.C., Organic Chemistry
CURNOW, R. N., PH.D., Applied Statistics
DAVIS, R., M.A., D.PHIL., Psychology
DILS, R. R., PH.D., D.SC., C.CHEM., F.R.S.C., F.I.BIOL., Physiology & Biochemistry
DUNN, P. D., PH.D., F.I.E.E., C.ENG., F.I.MECH.E., Engineering Science
VAN EMDEN, H. F., PH.D., Applied Entomology
EVANS, J. T., PH.D., D.SC., Physics
FAULKNER, E. A., M.A., PH.D., C.ENG., F.I.E.E., F.I.E.R.E., Solid State Electronics
FELLGETT, P. B., M.A., PH.D., F.R.S.E., F.B.C.S., C.ENG., F.I.E.E., F.I.E.R.E., F.INST.M.C., Cybernetics
FOWLES, G. W. A., B.SC., PH.D., D.SC., C.CHEM., F.R.S.C., Inorganic Chemistry
FREY, H. M., M.A., D.PHIL., C.CHEM., F.R.S.C., Physical Chemistry
HALL, P. G., M.A., PH.D., Geography
HARBORNE, J. B., PH.D., D.SC., Botany
HEYWOOD, V. H., PH.D., D.SC., Botany
HIRST, W., PH.D., D.SC., F.INST.P., C.ENG., F.I.MECH.E., Tribology
HOCKNEY, R. W., M.A., PH.D., Computer Science
HOPKINS, H. H., D.SC., D. ÈS SC., F.INST.P., F.R.S., Applied Optics
HUNT, J. N., PH.D., D.I.C., A.R.C.S., F.R.MET.S., F.R.A.S., F.I.M.A., Applied Mathematics
KAPLAN, C., M.SC., M.B., CH.B., F.R.C.PATH., Microbiology
McCOMBIE, C. W., M.A., PH.D., F.R.S.E., Physics
MILLS, I. M., B.SC., D.PHIL., Chemical Spectroscopy
MOORE, D. M., PH.D., Botany
MORTON, K. W., M.A., PH.D., Applied Mathematics
NASH-WILLIAMS, C.ST.J.A., M.A., PH.D., F.R.S.E., Pure Mathematics
NEWMAN, R. C., PH.D., F.INST.P., Physics
NURSTEN, H. E., PH.D., D.SC., C.CHEM., F.R.S.C., F.I.F.S.T., Food Science
PEARCE, R. P., PH.D., F.R.S.E., F.R.MET.S., Meteorology
SERIES, G. W., M.A., D.PHIL., D.SC., F.R.S., Physics
SEWELL, M. J., PH.D., D.SC., F.I.M.A., Applied Mathematics
SIMKISS, K., PH.D., D.SC., Zoology
WAITES, G. M. H., M.A., PH.D., F.I.BIOL., Physiology & Biochemistry
WILD, A., PH.D., Soil Science
WILLIAMS, G., B.SC., Zoology
WRIGHT, J. D. M., M.A., D.PHIL., F.R.S.E., Pure Mathematics

*Faculty of Agriculture and Food:*
BLAKEBROUGH, N., M.SC.TECH., PH.D., C.ENG., F.I.CHEM.E., Food Technology
BUNTING, A. H., C.M.G., M.SC., D.PHIL., LL.D., F.I.BIOL., Agricultural Development Overseas
McINERNEY, J. P., PH.D., Agricultural Economics and Management
PEGG, G. F., M.SC., PH.D., Horticulture
ROBERTS, E. H., PH.D., D.SC., F.I.BIOL., Crop Production
ROLFE, E. J., B.SC., M.CHEM.A., C.CHEM., F.R.S.C., F.I.F.S.T., Food Technology
SPEDDING, C. R. W., M.SC., PH.D., D.SC., F.I.BIOL., Agricultural Systems
TUCK, R. H., M.A., Agricultural Economics and Management
WILD, A., PH.D., Soil Science
WILLIAMS, W., D.SC., F.I.BIOL., Agricultural Botany

*Faculty of Urban and Regional Studies:*
BENNETT, J., A.R.I.C.S., Quantity Surveying
BIGGS, W. D., PH.D., F.I.M., Building Technology
DAVIES, H. W. E., M.SC.(ECON.), M.R.T.P.I., Planning
HOWES, C. K., Land Management

*School of Education:*
WILSON, R., B.A.
WRIGLEY, J., C.B.E., M.ED., PH.D., F.B.PS.S.

### ATTACHED INSTITUTION:
**National Institute for Research in Dairying:** Shinfield, Reading, RG2 9AT; f. 1912 for the investigation of problems in dairying and allied subjects; more than 20,000 vols. and 35,000 pamphlets in library and over 450 current journals, Dir. J. W. G. PORTER, M.A., PH.D., F.I.BIOL.; Sec. L. C. FITZGERALD; publ. *Annual Report*.

### AFFILIATED INSTITUTE:
**College of Estate Management:** see under Colleges.

# UNIVERSITY OF ST. ANDREWS
ST. ANDREWS, FIFE, SCOTLAND

Telephone: 76161.

Founded 1410.

*Chancellor:* Sir KENNETH J. DOVER, M.A., D.LITT., LL.D., F.B.A.
*Rector:* TIM BROOKE-TAYLOR, M.A.
*Principal and Vice-Chancellor:* J. STEVEN WATSON, M.A., D.LITT., D.H.L., D.H., F.R.HIST.S., F.R.S.E.
*Vice-Principal:* Prof. M. A. JEEVES, M.A., PH.D., F.B.PS.S., F.A.P.S., F.R.S.E.
*Secretary and Registrar:* M. J. B. LOWE, PH.D.
*Quaestor and Factor:* C. P. GORDON, C.A.
*Librarian:* A. G. MACKENZIE, M.A, A.L.A.

Library: see Libraries.

Number of teachers: 335, including 55 professors.
Number of students: 3,578.

### DEANS:

*Faculty of Arts:* K. M. MacIver, M.A., PH.D.
*Faculty of Science:* D. M. Finlayson, PH.D.
*Faculty of Divinity:* Prof. J. K. Cameron, M.A., B.D., PH.D., F.R.HIST.S.

### PROFESSORS:

*Faculty of Arts:*

Adam, R. J., M.A., F.R.HIST.S., Social History
Bayley, P. C., M.A., English Literature
Branscombe, P. J., M.A., PH.D., German (Austrian Studies)
Brumfitt, J. H., M.A., D.PHIL., French
Bullough, D. A., M.A., F.S.A., F.R.HIST.S., Medieval History
Christian, R. F., M.A., Russian
Gifford, D. J., T.D., M.A., B.LITT., Spanish
Grinyer, P. M., M.A., PH.D., Economics (Finance and Investment)
Kemp, M. J., M.A., Fine Arts
Kenyon, J. P., PH.D., D.LITT., Modern History
Kidd, I. G., M.A., Greek
Kimbell, D. R. B., M.A., D.PHIL., L.R.A.M., Music
Levi, A. H. T., M.A., D.PHIL., French Language and Literature
Mayo, B., M.A., Moral Philosophy
Mulder, J. W. F., M.A., D.PHIL., Linguistics
Ogilvie, R. M., M.A., D.LITT., F.B.A., F.S.A., F.S.A.SCOT., F.R.S.E., Latin
Owen, D. D. R., M.A., PH.D., French
Rickman, G. E., M.A., D.PHIL., F.S.A., Ancient History (Roman)
Robson, P., M.SC., M.A., Economics
Smout, T. C., M.A., PH.D., Scottish History
Taylor, S. S. B., PH.D., French
Watt, D. E. R., D.PHIL., Scottish Church History
Woodward, L. J., M.A., Spanish
Wright, C. J. G., M.A., PH.D., B.PHIL., Logic and Metaphysics

*Faculty of Science:*

Allen, J. W., M.A., Physics
Blyth, T. S., D. ÈS SC., D.SC., F.R.S.E., F.I.M.A., Pure Mathematics
Callan, H. G., M.A., D.SC., F.R.S., F.R.S.E., Natural History
Cole, A. J., M.SC., PH.D., F.B.C.S., Computing Science
Cormack, R. M., M.A., PH.D., F.R.S.E., Statistics
Cornwell, J. F., PH.D., F.R.S.E., Theoretical Physics
Crawford, R. M. M., D.SC., F.R.S.E., Plant Ecology
Curle, S. N., M.SC., PH.D., F.R.S.E., Applied Mathematics
Dingle, R. B., PH.D., F.R.S.E., Theoretical Physics
Gunstone, F. D., PH.D., D.SC., F.R.S.E., F.R.I.C., Chemistry
Howie, J. M., D.PHIL., D.SC., F.R.S.E., Pure Mathematics
Jeeves, M. A., M.A., PH.D., Psychology
Lamb, J. F., M.B., CH.B., PH.D., Physiology
Laverack, M. S., PH.D., F.I.BIOL., F.R.S.E., Marine Biology
Proudfoot, V. B., PH.D., F.S.A., F.R.S.E., Geography
Reid, D. H., PH.D., D.SC., F.R.S.E., Chemistry
Serafini-Fracassini, A., M.D., PH.D., Biochemistry
Smith, J. W., M.D., CH.B., Regional Anatomy
Spence, D. H. N., PH.D., F.R.S.E., Botany
Stibbs, D. W. N., M.SC., D.PHIL., F.R.A.S., F.R.S.E., Astronomy
Stradling, R. A., M.A., D.PHIL., Natural Philosophy
Tedder, Lord, M.A., SC.D., PH.D., D.SC., F.R.S.E., F.R.I.C., Chemistry
Thomas, D. B., D.SC., M.B., B.S., F.I.BIOL., F.R.C.PATH., F.R.S.E., Anatomy
Tristram, G. R., PH.D., F.I.BIOL., F.R.S.E., Biochemistry
Walton, E. K., PH.D., F.R.S.E., Geology
Wyatt P. A. H., PH.D., F.R.S.E., F.R.I.C., Chemistry

*Faculty of Divinity:*

Cameron, J. K., M.A., B.D., PH.D., F.R.HIST.S., Ecclesiastical History
McKane, Rev. W., M.A., PH.D., Hebrew and Oriental Languages
Shaw, D. W. D., M.A., LL.B., B.D., Divinity
Whyte, J. A., M.A., Practical Theology and Christian Ethics
Wilson, R. M., M.A., B.D., PH.D., F.B.A., Biblical Criticism

## UNIVERSITY OF SALFORD
SALFORD, M5 4WT, LANCS.
Telephone: 061-736-5843.

Founded 1896 as the Royal Technical Institute, later Royal College of Advanced Technology, University Charter granted April 1967.

Academic year: September to July.

*Chancellor:* H.R.H. The Prince Philip, Duke of Edinburgh, K.G., P.C., K.T., O.M., G.M.B.E., F.R.S.
*Pro-Chancellors:* D. W. Hill, C.B.E., PH.D., D.SC., C.CHEM., F.R.S.C., F.T.I., T. J. Lunt, B.SC., Rt. Rev. E. R. Wickham, B.D., Bishop of Middleton.
*Vice-Chancellor:* Prof. J. M. Ashworth, PH.D., D.SC., F.I.BIOL.
*Pro-Vice-Chancellors:* Prof. E. R. Bryan, M.SC.(ENG.), PH.D., D.SC., C.ENG., F.I.C.E., F.I.STRUCT.E., Prof. M. B. Harris, M.A., PH.D., E. Parker, M.SC., C.ENG., M.I.-MECH.E., M.R.AE.S.
*Registrar:* S. R. Bosworth, B.A.
*Librarian:* A. C. Bubb, B.A., F.L.A

Number of teachers: 502.
Number of students: 4,541.

### PROFESSORS:

Ashworth, G. W., C.B.E., B.ARCH., M.C.D., R.I.B.A., P.P.R.T.P.I., Urban Environmental Studies
Baric, Lorraine F., PH.D., F.R.A.I., M.A.S.A., Sociology and Anthropology
Bark, L. S., D.SC., C.CHEM., F.R.S.C., Analytical Chemistry
Birss, R. R., PH.D., D.SC., D.I.C., C.ENG., M.I.E.E., F.INST.P., Physics
Bryan, E. R., M.SC.(ENG.), PH.D., D.SC., C.ENG., F.I.C.E., F.I.STRUCT.E., Structural Engineering
Burgess, R. A., B.ARCH., R.I.B.A., F.I.O.B., F.I.M.S., M.B.I.M., Construction
Calderwood, J. H., M.ENG., PH.D., C.ENG., F.I.EE., F.INST.P., Electrical Engineering.
Carter, G., PH.D., C.ENG., F.INST.P., Physical Electronics
Chisholm, A. W. J., C.ENG., F.I.MECH.E., F.I.PROD.E., Mechanical Engineering
Crossley, T. R., PH.D., C.ENG., M.R.AE.S., Manufacturing Systems Engineering
Cundall, R. B., PH.D., C.CHEM., F.R.S.C., Biochemistry
Davies, J. M., PH.D., D.SC., C.ENG., F.I.C.E., F.I.STRUCT.E., Structural Engineering
Easson, A., D.PHIL., English
Edwards, J., M.SC., PH.D., Orthopaedic Mechanics
Gamlen, G. A., M.SC., PH.D., C.CHEM., M.R.S.C., Chemistry
Gee, K. P., PH.D., Accountancy
Goddard, L. S., PH.D., Mathematics
Gray, J. O., M.SC., PH.D., C.ENG., F.I.E.E., Control Engineering
Halling, J., M.ENG., PH.D., D.I.C., F.C.G.I., C.ENG., F.I.PROD.E., F.I.MECH.E., Engineering Tribology
Hampshire, M. J., PH.D., F.INST.P., Solid State Electronics
Harris, M. B., M.A., PH.D., Romance Linguistics
Holland, F. A., M.SC., PH.D., D.I.C., C.ENG., F.I.CHEM.E., Chemical Engineering
Livesey, J. L., PH.D., D.I.C., C.ENG., M.I.MECH.E., M.A.I.A.A., Fluid Mechanics
Lord, P., M.SC.(TECH.), PH.D., C.ENG., F.INST.P., F.I.O.A., M.I.E.E., Acoustics
McKinlay, H., M.A., B.LITT., Management Studies
Marquand, D. I., B.A., Contemporary History and Politics
Millward, R., PH.D., Economics
Molyneux, D. H., M.A., PH.D., Biology
Moss, R. P., PH.D., Geography
Orville-Thomas, W. J., PH.D., D.SC., C.CHEM., F.R.S.C., Physical Chemistry
Porter, B., M.A., PH.D., D.SC., C.ENG., M.I.MECH.E., M.INST.M.C., S.M.I.E.E.E., Engineering Dynamics and Control
Robertson-Mellor, G. R., M.A., Modern Languages
Sack, R. A., PH.D., F.I.M.A., F.INST.P., Mathematics
Smith, A., D.A., A.T.D., F.M.A., Art and Industry
Sumner, M. T., B.A.(ECON.), Economics
Sutcliffe, H., M.A., PH.D., C.ENG., F.I.E.E., F.I.E.R.E., Electronic Engineering
Tebble, R. S., PH.D., D.SC., F.INST.P., Physics
Villiers, T. A., PH.D., F.L.S., Biology
Walkden, F., PH.D., F.I.M.A., Applied Mathematics and Computing
White, H. P., M.A., M.C.I.T., Geography
Wilson, E. M., M.SC., PH.D., C.ENG., F.I.C.E., F.A.S.C.E., Hydraulic Engineering
Wyn-Jones, E., PH.D., D.SC., D.PHIL., Physical Chemistry
Yates, B., PH.D., F.INST.P., Physics

### READERS:

Bannister, A., M.C., M.SC., C.ENG., F.I.C.E., Civil Engineering
Bryan, M. E., PH.D., Electrical Engineering
Catterall, R., PH.D., D.SC., C.CHEM., M.R.S.C., Chemistry
Clark, J., PH.D., D.SC., C.CHEM., F.R.S.C., Chemistry
Dollimore, D., J.P., PH.D., D.SC., C.CHEM., F.R.S.C., Chemistry
Ford, R. D., PH.D., F.I.O.A., Applied Acoustics
Grant, W. A., PH.D., M.INST.P., Electrical Engineering

HICKEY, L. D., M.A., LL.B., LIC. EN FIL., DR. EN FIL. Y LETRAS, Barrister-at-Law, Modern Languages
HICKMOTT, P. W., PH.D., D.SC., C.CHEM., F.R.S.C., Chemistry
HUGHES, R., PH.D., D.SC., C.ENG., F.I.CHEM.E., Chemical Engineering
MALTBY, D., PH.D., A.C.G.I., C.ENG., M.I.C.E., M.C.I.T., M.I.H.E., Civil Engineering
METH-COHN, O., PH.D., D.SC., A.R.T.C.S., C.CHEM., M.R.S.C., Chemistry
MODINOS, A., PH.D., M.INST.P., Electrical Engineering
PARR, M. J., PH.D., Biology
RAYMOND, S., M.SC.(TECH.), PH.D., DIP.T.P., C.ENG., F.I.C.E., M.R.T.P.I., M.I.H.E., Civil Engineering
SCHEINMANN, F., PH.D., D.SC., M.A., A.R.T.C.S., F.PHYTOCHEM. SOC., Chemistry
TAYLOR, P. L., M.A., C.ENG., F.I.E.E., F.I.M.A., Electrical Engineering
TEER, D. G., D.I.C., F.INST.P., F.I.M., Mechanical Engineering
TEMPEST, W., PH.D., Electrical Engineering
THOMASON, P. F., PH.D., C.ENG., M.I.M., A.R.T.C.S., Mechanical Engineering
TOPHAM, N., B.SC.(ECON.), Economics
WRAGG, A., M.A., PH.D., F.I.M.A., Mathematics
ZDRAVKOVIC, M. M., M.SC., PH.D., Mechanical Engineering

ATTACHED INSTITUTES:

**Centre for Development Studies:** Dir. M. B. GLEAVE, M.A.

**Centre for Leisure Studies:** Dir. M. A. SMITH, B.SC.

**Centre for Transport Studies:** Dir. T. CONSTANTINE, PH.D., C.ENG., F.I.C.E., F.I.MUN.E.

**Centre for Tribological Studies:** Dir. J. HALLING, M.ENG., PH.D., D.I.C., F.C.G.I., C.ENG., F.I.MECH.E., F.I.PROD.E.

**Centre for Underwater Science and Technology:** Dir. R. S. TEBBLE, PH.D., D.SC., F.INST.P.

**Environmental Institute:** Dir. G. W. ASHWORTH, C.B.E., B.ARCH., M.C.D., R.I.B.A., P.P.R.T.P.I.

**Industrial Centre for Design and Manufacturing Engineering:** Gen. Man. B. D. RICHARDSON, M.SC., C.ENG., M.I.MECH.E., M.I.PROD.E.

**Salford Orthopaedic Appliance Unit:** Medical Dir. J. C. GRIFFITHS, M.B., CH.B., F.R.C.S., CH.M.

## UNIVERSITY OF SHEFFIELD
SHEFFIELD, S10 2TN
Telephone: 78555.
Telex: 54348 ULSHEF G.
Founded 1905.

*Chancellor:* Sir FREDERICK DAINTON, M.A., PH.D., SC.D., C.CHEM., F.R.S.C., F.R.S.
*Pro-Chancellors:* C. S. BARKER, B.A., D. B. HARRISON, J.P., LL.M.
*Vice-Chancellor:* Prof. G. D. SIMS, O.B.E., D.I.C., M.SC., PH.D., F.ENG., F.I.E.E., F.I.E.R.E., F.C.G.I.

*Pro-Vice-Chancellors:* Prof. G. CLAYTON, M.A., Prof. G. W. GREENWOOD, D.MET., PH.D., C.ENG., F.INST.P., F.I.M., Prof. S. GREGORY, M.A., PH.D.
*Registrar and Secretary:* F. J. ORTON, B.SC., B.LITT.
*Librarian:* C. K. BALMFORTH, M.A., F.L.A.
Library: see Libraries.
Number of full-time teaching staff: 952.
Number of students: 7,852.
Publications: *Calendar*†, *Annual Report, Faculty Undergraduate and Postgraduate and General prospectuses, Faculty Handbooks, Staff Handbook* (annually), *Newsletter* (fortnightly).

DEANS:

*Faculty of Arts:* Prof. W. F. BLAKE, M.A., B.LITT.
*Faculty of Pure Science:* Prof. W. GALBRAITH, PH.D., F.INST.P.
*Faculty of Medicine:* Prof. D. S. MUNRO, M.D., F.R.C.P.
*Faculty of Law:* Prof. A. E. BOTTOMS, M.A., PH.D.
*Faculty of Engineering:* Prof. T. H. HANNA, PH.D., C.ENG., F.I.C.E.
*Faculty of Materials:* Prof. B. A. BILBY, PH.D., F.R.S.
*Faculty of Social Sciences:* Prof. R. J. NICHOLSON, M.A.
*Faculty of Architectural Studies:* Prof. F. I. MASSER, PH.D., M.C.D., M.R.T.P.I.
*Faculty of Educational Studies:* Prof. M. F. LYNCH, PH.D., A.R.S.C., M.INST.INF.SCI.

PROFESSORS:
(Some staff serve in more than one faculty)

*Faculty of Arts:*
BLAKE, N. F., M.A., B.LITT., English Language
BRANIGAN, K., PH.D., F.S.A., Prehistory and Archaeology
CARR, W., J.P., PH.D., History
CROSSLAND, R. A., M.A., Greek
GARDEN, E. J. C., D.MUS., F.R.C.O., A.R.A.M., A.R.C.M., Music
GRAHAM, G. K., M.A., D.PHIL., English Literature
HALEY, K. H. D., M.A., B.LITT., Modern History
HEATHCOTE, A. A., M.A., Hispanic Studies
LUSCOMBE, D. E., M.A., PH.D., Medieval History
MOSLEY, D. J., M.A., PH.D., Ancient History and Classical Archaeology
NIDDITCH, P. H., M.A., PH.D., Philosophy
RITCHIE, J. M., M.A., DR.PHIL., Germanic Studies
ROGERSON, J. W., M.A., D.D., Biblical Studies
WILLIAMS, D., PH.D., French

*Faculty of Pure Science:*
ATHERTON, N. M., PH.D., M.INST.P., Physical Chemistry
BACON, G. E., M.A., SC.D., PH.D., F.INST.P., Physics
BALL, J. N., PH.D., Zoology
BANKS, P., M.A., D.PHIL., Biochemistry
BARER, R., M.C., M.A., B.SC., M.B., B.S., Human Biology and Anatomy
BARNETT, V., M.SC., PH.D., F.I.S., Probability and Statistics

COLLINS, W. D., PH.D., D.SC., Applied and Computational Mathematics
CONNOLLY, K. J., PH.D., F.B.PS.S., Psychology
CRANGLE, J., PH.D., F.INST.P., Physics
DAWSON, J. B., PH.D., D.SC., F.R.S.E., Geology
DOWNIE, C., D.SC., PH.D., F.G.S., Geology
EBLING, F. J. G., D.SC., PH.D., F.I.BIOL., Zoology
FRISBY, J. P., PH.D., Psychology
GALBRAITH, W., PH.D., F.INST.P., Nuclear Physics
GREGORY, S., M.A., PH.D., Geography
HARRISON, P. M., M.A., D.PHIL., Biochemistry
HASLAM, E., PH.D., Chemistry
HUNTER, S. C., PH.D., Applied and Computational Mathematics
JOHNSTON, R. J., M.A., PH.D., Geography
KAISER, T. R., M.SC., D.SC., D.PHIL., F.R.A.S., Space Physics
LOYNES, R. M., DIP.STAT., PH.D., Probability and Statistics
MAITLIS, P. M., D.SC., PH.D., Inorganic Chemistry
McWEENY, R., D.PHIL., C.CHEM., F.R.S.C., F.INST.P., Theoretical Chemistry
MIRSKY, L., M.SC., PH.D., Pure Mathematics
NORTHCOTT, D. G., M.A., PH.D., F.R.S., Pure Mathematics
OLLIS, W. D., PH.D., F.R.S.C., F.R.S., F.R.S.A., Organic Chemistry
PYM, J. S., PH.D., Pure Mathematics
QUAYLE, J. R., M.A., PH.D., F.R.S., Microbiology
ROPER, J. A., PH.D., F.R.S.E., Genetics
SCRATCHERD, T., M.B., B.S., M.D., F.R.C.P., Physiology
TURNER, G., F.R.S., M.A., D.PHIL., F.R.A.S., Physics
ULLMANN, J. R., M.A., PH.D., Computer Science
WALKER, A. M., M.A., Probability and Statistics
WALKER, D. A., D.SC., PH.D., F.I.BIOL., F.R.S., Biology
WATERS, R. S., M.A., Physical Geography
WILLIS, A. J., D.SC., PH.D., F.I.BIOL., Botany

*Faculty of Medicine:*
BANKS, P., M.A., D.PHIL., Biochemistry
BARER, R., M.C., M.A., M.B., B.S., HON. F.R.M.S., Human Biology and Anatomy
BLACK, M. M., M.SC., PH.D., F.INST.P., C.ENG., M.R.AE.S., Medical Physics and Clinical Engineering
BRAMLEY, P. A., M.B., CH.B., B.D.S., M.R.C.S., L.R.C.P., F.D.S.R.C.S., Dental Surgery
BURKE, P. H., M.D.S., F.D.S.R.C.S., D.D.OR.F.P.S., Child Dental Health
CLARK, R. G., M.B., CH.B., F.R.C.S., Surgery
COOKE, I. D., M.B., B.S., D.G.O., F.R.C.O.G., Obstetrics and Gynaecology
CRANE, W. A. J., M.D., F.R.C.P., F.R.C.PATH., Pathology
DUCKWORTH, T., M.B., CH.B., F.R.C.S., Orthopaedics
HARRISON, P. M., M.A., D.PHIL., Biochemistry
HENRY, L., M.D., M.R.C.P., F.R.C.PATH., Pathology
HUDSON, G., M.SC., M.B., CH.B., D.SC., M.D., F.R.C.PATH., Experimental Haematology
JENNER, F. A., M.B., CH.B., PH.D., M.R.C.P., D.P.M., F.R.C.PSYCH., Psychiatry
JOHNS, R. B., PH.D., L.D.S.R.C.S., Restorative Dentistry

JOHNSON, A. G., M.CHIR., F.R.C.S., Surgery
KNOWELDEN, J., M.D., F.R.C.P., F.F.C.M., D.PH., J.P., Community Medicine
MCENTEGART, M. G., M.D., F.R.C.PATH., Medical Microbiology
MILNER, R. D. G., M.D., M.A., PH.D., F.R.C.P., Paediatrics
MUNRO, D. S., M.D., F.R.C.P., Medicine
POTTER, C. W., PH.D., M.R.C.PATH., Virology
RICHMOND, J., M.D., F.R.C.P., Medicine
RUSSELL, R. G. G., M.A., M.B., B.CHIR., PH.D., D.M., M.R.C.P., M.R.C.PATH., Human Metabolism and Clinical Biochemistry
SCRATCHERD, T., M.B., M.D., F.R.C.P., Physiology
SHARP, F., M.D., F.R.C.O.G., M.B.CH.B., D.OBST., Obstetrics and Gynaecology
SMITH, C. J., B.D.S., PH.D., L.D.S.R.C.S., M.R.C.PATH., Oral Pathology
THORNTON, J. A., M.D., D.A., M.B.B.S., F.F.A.R.C.S., Anaesthetics
WILKES, E., O.B.E., M.A., M.B., B.CHIR., F.R.C.P., F.R.C.G.P., M.R.C.PSYCH., Community Care and General Practice
WOODS, H. F., B.M., B.CH., D.PHIL., M.R.C.P., Clinical Pharmacology and Therapeutics

*Faculty of Law:*
BATTERSBY, G., B.A., J.P., Law
BOTTOMS, A. E., M.A., DIP.CRIM., PH.D., Criminological and Socio-Legal Studies
LEWIS, N., LL.B., Law
MCCLEAN, J. D., B.C.L., M.A., Law
WOOD, Sir JOHN, C.B.E., LL.M., Law

*Faculty of Engineering:*
ANDERSON, A. P., PH.D., Electronic and Electrical Engineering
BARNARD, J. A., D SC., PH.D., A.R.C.S., D.I.C., C.ENG., F.I.CHEM.E., Chemical Engineering and Fuel Technology
BENSON, F. A., D.L., M.ENG., D.ENG., PH.D., C.ENG., F.I.E.E., F.I.E.E.E., F.C.I.B.S., Electronic and Electrical Engineering
BOND, D., PH.D., C.ENG., F.I.C.E., F.I.STRUCT.E., Civil and Structural Engineering
DUGDALE, D. E., D.SC., PH.D., Mechanical Engineering (Cutting Tool Technology)
HANNA, T. H., PH.D., C.ENG., F.I.C.E., Civil and Structural Engineering
HOBSON, G. S., PH.D., Electronic and Electrical Engineering
MILLER, K. J., PH.D., M.A., C.ENG., M.I.MECH.E., M.I.PROD.E., M.I.M., A.C.G.I., Mechanical Engineering
NICHOLSON, H., D.ENG., M.A., C.ENG, F.I.E.E., M.I.MECH.E., Control Engineering
ROBSON, P. N., PH.D., F.I.E.E., F.I.E.E.E., Electronic and Electrical Engineering
ROYLE, J. K., M.SC.TECH., PH.D., C.ENG., F.I.MECH.E., F.R.AE.S., Mechanical Engineering
SWITHENBANK, J., PH.D., M.AMER. I.CHEM.E., F.ENG, F.INST.E., A.INST.P., Chemical Engineering and Fuel Technology

*Faculty of Materials:*
ARGENT, B. B., PH.D., D.MET., C.ENG., F.I.M., Metallurgy
BILBY, B. A., PH.D., F.R.S., Theory of Materials
DAVIES, G. J., M.A., PH.D., SC.D., C.ENG., F.I.M., M.I.MECH.E., Metallurgy
ESHELBY, J. D., PH.D., F.R.S., Theory of Materials

GREENWOOD, G. W., D.MET., PH.D., C.ENG., F.INST.P., F.I.M., Metallurgy
RAWSON, H., M.SC.TECH., D.SC.TECH., C.ENG., F.I.M.A., F.I.M., F.S.G.T., Ceramics, Glasses and Polymers

*Faculty of Social Sciences:*
CLAYTON, G., M.A., Applied Economics
CONNOLLY, PH.D., F.B., PS.S. Psychology
FRISBY, J. P., PH.D., Psychology
GREGORY, S., M.A., PH.D., Geography
JOHNSTON, R. J., M.A., PH.D., Geography
LOWE, E. A., B.SC.(ECON.). F.C.A., A.C.I.S., Accounting and Financial Management
NICHOLSON, R. J., M.A., Econometrics
NORMAN, J. M., M.SC., PH.D., Management Studies
SAINSBURY, E. E., M.A., Social Administration
WARRENDER, J. H., M.A., Political Theory and Institutions
WATERS, R. S., M.A., Geography
WESTERGAARD, J. H, B.SC.(ECON)., Sociological Studies

*Faculty of Architectural Studies:*
GOSLING, D., DIP.T.P., M.ARCH., M.C.P., R.I.B.A., A.R.I.A.S., M.R.T.P.I., F.R.S.A., Architecture
MASSER, F. I., PH.D., M.C.D., M.R.T.P.I., Town and Regional Planning
MURTA, K. H., B.ARCH., DIP.ARCH. F.R.I.B.A., Architecture
PAGE, J. K., B.A., F.C.I.B.S., Building Science
WEDDLE, A. E., B.ARCH., DIP.T.P., Landscape Architecture

*Faculty of Educational Studies:*
BOLTON, N., PH.D., Education
LYNCH, M. F., PH.D., C.CHEM., M.INST.INF.SCI., Postgraduate School of Librarianship and Information Science
ROACH, J. P. C., M.A., PH.D., Education
RODERICK, G. W., PH.D., M.A., M.INST.P., Continuing Education
SAUNDERS, W. L., M.A., F.L.A., F.I.INF. SCI., Information Studies

## UNIVERSITY OF SOUTHAMPTON
HIGHFIELD.
SOUTHAMPTON, SO9 5NH
Telephone: 0703-559122.

Founded 1952; opened as the Hartley Institution 1862; incorporated as the Hartley University College 1902.

*Chancellor:* Lord ROLL OF IPSDEN K.C.M.G., C.B., B.COM., PH.D., D.SC., D.SOC.SC., LL.D.

*Vice-Chancellor:* Prof. J. M. ROBERTS, M.A., D.PHIL.

*Deputy Vice-Chancellors:* Prof. J. H. BIRD, PH.D., F.C.I.T., F.R.G.S., Prof. B. L. CLARKSON, PH.D., C.ENG., F.R.AE.S., F.S.E.E., F.I.O.A.

*Secretary and Registrar:* D. A. SCHOFIELD, M.A.

*Academic Registrar:* Miss A. E. CLARKE, J.P., B.A.

*Librarian:* B. NAYLOR, M.A., DIP.LIB., A.L.A.

Library: see Libraries.

Number of full-time teaching staff: 714 including 112 professors.
Number of students: 6,083.

Publications: *Calendar†, Undergraduate Prospectus, Postgraduate Prospectus, Departmental Reports and Research Reports, Annual Report, Research Report and Publications, Inaugural, Foundation and Memorial Lectures.*

DEANS:

*Faculty of Arts:* W. N. INCE, M.A., DR. DE L'UNIV.
*Faculty of Science:* Prof. N. B. H. JONATHAN, PH.D.
*Faculty of Engineering and Applied Science:* Prof. R. C. SMITH, PH.D., F.INST.P.
*Faculty of Social Sciences:* Prof. D. HOLT, PH.D.
*Faculty of Educational Studies:* Prof. P. J. KELLY, M.A., PH.D., F.I.BIOL.
*Faculty of Law:* Prof. G. DWORKIN, LL.B.
*Faculty of Medicine:* Prof. J. B. L. HOWELL, M.B., B.S., PH.D., F.R.C.P.
*Faculty of Mathematical Studies:* Prof. P. T. LANDSBERG, PH.D., D.SC., F.R.S.E., F.INST.P., F.I.M.A.

PROFESSORS:

*Faculty of Arts:*
ARMSTRONG, I. M., PH.D., English
BELLOS, D. M., M.A., D.PHIL., French
EVANS, P. A., M.A., D.MUS., F.R.C.O., Music
INCE, W. N., M.A., D. DE L'UNIV., French
MANSER, A. R., M.A., B.PHIL., Philosophy
MICHAEL, I. D. L., B.A., PH.D., Spanish
MORRIS, Rev. C., M.A., F.R.HIST.S., Medieval History
PAPST, E. E., M.A., German
RANKIN, H. D., M.A., Classics
SAMBROOK, A. J., M.A., PH.D., English
SMITH, A. J., M.A., English
SMITH, P., M.A., D.PHIL., F.R.HIST.S., Modern History
UCKO, P. J., PH.D., F.S.A., Archaeology

*Faculty of Science:*
BAKER, R., PH.D., Chemistry
BARNES, K. J., PH.D., F.INST.P., Theoretical Physics
BEATTIE, I. R., M.A., PH.D., D.SC., Chemistry
BIRD, J. H., PH.D., F.C.I.T., F.R.G.S., Geography
CARRINGTON, A., M.A., PH.D., F.R.S., Chemistry
CHARNOCK, H., M.SC., D.I.C., F.R.S., Physical Oceanography
COOKSON, R. C., PH.D., C.CHEM., F.R.S.C., F.R.S., Chemistry
FLEISCHMANN, M., PH.D., A.R.C.S., C.CHEM., F.R.S.C., Chemistry, Electro-Chemistry
GREGORY, K. J., PH.D., F.R.G.S., Geography
HODSON, F., PH.D., F.G.S., Geology
HALL, J. L., D.PHIL., A.R.C.S.
HUTCHINSON, G. W., M.A., PH.D., F.R.S.A., F.R.A.S., Physics
JONATHAN, N. B. H., PH.D., Chemistry
KERKUT, G. A., M.A., PH.D., SC.D., F.I.BIOL., Physiology and Biochemistry
LEE, E. W., PH.D., F.I.E.E., F.INST.P., Physics
LOCKWOOD, A. P. M., M.A., PH.D., F.I.BIOL., Marine Biology
LUCKHURST, G. R., PH.D., Chemistry
NESBITT, R. W., PH.D., F.G.S.A., Geology
SLEIGH, M. A., PH.D., D.SC., F.I.BIOL., Biology
SMALL, R. J., M.A., PH.D., Geography

# UNIVERSITIES — U.K. (GREAT BRITAIN)

### Faculty of Engineering and Applied Science:
BAILEY, A. J., PH.D., C.ENG., M.I.E.E., Applied Electrostatics
BETTS, J. A., PH.D., C.ENG., M.I.E.E., Communications
BRAY, K. N. C., M.SE., PH.D., C.ENG., M.A.I.A.A., M.R.AE.S., Gas Dynamics
BRIGNELL, J. E., PH.D., M.INST.P., Electronics
BUTTERFIELD, R., D.SC., D.I.C., C.ENG., M.I.C.E., M.I.STRUCT.E., Soil Mechanics
CHADWICK, G. A., M.A., PH.D., C.ENG., F.I.M., Engineering Materials
CHEESEMAN, I. C., PH.D., A.R.C.S., C.ENG., F.R.AE.S., F.C.I.T., Helicopter Engineering
CLARKSON, B. L., PH.D., C.ENG., F.R.AE.S., F.S.E.E., F.I.O.A., Vibration Studies
DAVIES, P. O. A. L., PH.D., C.ENG.AUST., C.ENG., F.I.MECH.E., Experimental Fluid Dynamics
DOAK, P. E., M.S., F.I.O.A., Acoustics
GAMBLING, W. A., PH.D., D.SC., F.I.E.R.E., F.I.E.E., F.ENG., Electronics
GOODRICH, G. J., B.SC., C.ENG., F.R.I.N.A., Ship Science
HAMMOND, P., M.A., C.ENG., F.I.E.E., M.I.MECH.E., Electrical Power Engineering
HUTTON, S. P., D.ENG., PH.D., C.ENG., F.I.MECH.E., M.I.C.E., M.R.AE.S., Mechanical Engineering
KEMHADJIAN, H. A., M.SC.(ENG.), C.ENG., F.I.E.E., Integrated Circuit Technology
LARGE, J. B., M.S., F.I.O.A., M.B.A.C., Applied Acoustics
LILLEY, G. M., O.B.E., M.SC.(ENG.), D.I.C., C.ENG, F.R.AE.S., M.I.MECH.E., F.I.M.A., M.I.A.A., Aeronautics and Astronautics
MORICE, P. B., PH.D., D.SC., C.ENG., F.I.C.E., F.I.STRUCT.E., Civil Engineering
NICHOLS, K. G., M.SC., M.INST.P., C.ENG., F.I.E.R.E., Electronics
NIGHTINGALE, J. M., PH.D., WH.F., WH.SC., M.I.E.E., Control Engineering
PARKIN, P. H., B.SC., F.I.O.A., Research Prof.
PRIEDE, T., D.SC.(ENG.), PH.D., INZ.MECH., F.ENG., F.I.MECH.E., M.S.A.E., Automobile Engineering
RICHARDS, E. J., O.B.E., M.A., D.SC., F.ENG., F.R.AE.S., F.I.MECH.E., Research Professor
ROBINSON, D. W., D.SC., C.ENG., A.C.G.I., M.I.E.E., Research Professor
SMITH, R. C., PH.D., F.INST.P., Physical Electronics
WILLIAMS, T. E. H., C.B.E., M.SC., PH.D., C.ENG., F.I.C.E., F.INST.H.E., M.I.STRUCT.E., F.C.I.T., F.R.S.A., Civil Engineering

### Faculty of Social Sciences:
BOURN, A. M., B.SC.(ECON.), F.C.A., Accounting
GALE, A., F.B.PS.S., Psychology
HILTON, K., PH.D., A.C.I.S., Financial Control
HOLT, D., PH.D., Social Statistics
MARTIN, J. P., M.A., PH.D., Sociology and Social Administration
MIZON, G. E., M.SC.(ECON.), M.A., PH.D., Econometrics
PLANT, R., PH.D., Politics
PRITCHARD, C., M.A., A.A.P.S.W., Social Work Studies
RICHARDS, P. G., PH.D., British Government
SMITH, J. H., B.A., Sociology
TRASLER, G. B., M.A., PH.D., F.B.PS.S., Psychology
WICKENS, M. R., M.SC.(ECON.), Applied Economics

### Faculty of Educational Studies:
FORDHAM, P. E., B.A., Adult Education
KELLY, P. J., M.A., PH.D., F.I.BIOL., Education

### Faculty of Law:
DWORKIN, G., LL.B., Law
JACKSON, D. C., B.C.L., M.A., Law
WILSON, J. F., M.A., Law

### Faculty of Medicine:
ACHESON, E. D., M.A., D.M., F.R.C.P., F.F.C.M., Clinical Epidemiology
AKHTAR, M., M.SC., PH.D., D.I.C., F.R.S., Biochemistry
BAIN, M. B., CH.B., M.D., F.R.C.G.P., D.CH., D.OBST.R.C.O.G., Primary Medical Care
BARKER, D. J. P., PH.D., M.D., F.R.C.P., F.F.C.M., Clinical Epidemiology
BULMER, D., M.A., M.D., D.SC., Human Morphology
CLAYTON, B. E., PH.D., M.D., F.R.C.P., F.R.C.PATH., Chemical Pathology and Human Metabolism
DENNIS, K. J., M.B., CH.B., F.R.C.S.EDIN., F.R.C.O.G., Human Reproduction and Obstetrics
GEORGE, C. F., B.SC., M.D., F.R.C.P., Clinical Pharmacology
GIBBONS, J. L., M.D., F.R.C.P., F.R.C. PSYCH., D.P.M., Psychiatry
HALL, M. R. P., M.A., B.M., B.CH., F.R.C.P., F.R.C.P.(E.), Geriatric Medicine
HOWELL, J. B. L., M.B., B.S., PH.D., F.R.C.P., Medicine
KERKUT, G. A., M.A., PH.D., SC.D., F.I.BIOL., Neurophysiology
LEE, H. A., B.SC., M.B., B.S., F.R.C.P., Metabolic Medicine
MAYOR, D., B.SC., M.B., CH.B., F.R.C.S.(E.), Human Morphology
MUNDAY, K. A., PH.D., F.I.BIOL., Physiology and Pharmacology
NORMAN, J., M.B., CH.B., PH.D., F.F.A.-R.C.S., Anaesthetics
NORMAND, I. C. S., M.A., D.M., F.R.C.P., Child Health
POLAK, A., M.D., F.R.C.P., Renal Medicine
RHODES, P., B.CHIR., M.A., F.R.C.S., F.R.C.O.G., F.R.A.C.M.A., Postgraduate Medical Education
SHEARER, J. R., M.B., CH.B., PH.D., F.R.C.S., Orthopaedic Surgery
SHELLEY, T., M.SC., PH.D., Medical Physics
STEVENSON, G. T., M.D., D.PHIL., Immuno-chemistry
TAYLOR, I., M.D., CH.M., F.R.C.S., Surgery
TAYLOR, T. G., M.A., PH.D., F.I.BIOL., Nutrition
WATERS, W. E., M.B., B.S., F.F.C.M., D.I.H., Community Medicine
WATT, P. J., M.D., M.R.C.P., Microbiology
WELLER, R. O., M.D., PH.D., M.R.C.PATH., Neuropathology
WHITEHOUSE, J. M. A., M.A., M.D., M.R.C.P., Medical Oncology
WRIGHT, D. H., B.SC., M.D., F.R.C.PATH., Pathology
WRIGHT, R., M.A., M.D., D.PHIL., F.R.C.P., Medicine

### Faculty of Mathematical Studies:
BARRON, D. W., M.A., PH.D., F.B.C.S., Computer Studies
GRIFFITHS, H. B., M.SC., PH.D., F.I.M.A., Pure Mathematics
LANDSBERG, P. T., PH.D., D.SC., F.R.S.E., F.INST.P., F.I.M.A., Applied Mathematics
ROBERTSON, S. A., PH.D., F.R.S.E., Pure Mathematics
SMITH, T. M. F., B.SC.(ECON.), Statistics
TOCHER, K. D., PH.D., D.SC., Operational Research

## READERS:
### Faculty of Arts:
BROWN, D. C., M.A., B.MUS., PH.D., L.T.C.L., Music
HAFFENDEN, P. S., PH.D., F.R.HIST.S., History
HANNA, A. J., PH.D., History
MATHER, F. C., M.A., F.R.HIST.S., History
PLATT, C. P. S., M.A., PH.D., F.S.A., F.R.HIST.S., History
PUGH, T. B., M.A., B.LITT., History
SPARKES, PH.D., Classics

### Faculty of Science:
BELL, L. G. E., PH.D., C.CHEM., M.R.S.C., F.I.BIOL., Biology
BEWICK, A., PH.D., Chemistry
BURTON, J. D., PH.D., C.CHEM., F.R.S.C., Chemical Oceanography
EMSLEY, J. W., PH.D., Chemistry
HENDRA, P. J., PH.D., D.SC., Chemistry
HOPKINS, B. J., PH.D., F.INST.P., Physics
JERRARD, H. G., PH.D., F.INST.P., Physics
MACLEAN, N., PH.D., M.I.BIOL., S.D.A., Biology
MANNERS, J. G., M.A., PH.D., M.I.BIOL., Biology

### Faculty of Engineering and Applied Science:
ALLEN, H. G., PH.D., C.ENG., F.I.STRUCT.-ENG., M.I.C.E., Civil Engineering
BINNS, K. J., D.SC., C.ENG., M.I.E.E., A.F.I.M.A., Electrical Engineering
BREBBIA, C. A., PH.D., Civil Engineering
CARRE, B. A., M.A., PH.D., C.ENG., M.I.E.E., F.B.C.S., Electronics
FARRAR, R. A., PH.D., C.ENG., D.I.C., M.I.M., A.R.S.M., Mechanical Engineering
FISHER, M. J., PH.D., Sound and Vibration Research
MEAD, D. J., D.C.AE., PH.D., C.ENG., F.R.AE.S., Aeronautics and Astronautics
RICE, C. G., M.SC., F.INST.P., F.I.O.A., Subjective Acoustics
SCURLOCK, R. G., M.A., D.PHIL., F.INST.P., Cryogenics
WEEDY, B. M., PH.D., C.ENG., M.I.E.E., Electrical Power Systems
WILMSHURST, T. H., PH.D., Electronics
WILLOUGHBY, A. F. W., PH.D., C.ENG., A.R.S.M., D.I.C., M.I.M., Mechanical Engineering

### Faculty of Social Sciences:
CALVERT, P. A. R., A.M., M.A., PH.D., F.R.HIST.S., Politics
CHAPMAN, C. B., M.SC., P.ENG., PH.D., Management Sciences
GLASTONBURY, B. S., B.A., Applied Social Studies
HART, H., PH.D., F.C.A., Accounting
HILL, D. M., PH.D., Politics
McKENNELL, A. C., M.A., PH.D., F.B.PS.S., Methodology of Attitude Surveys
McKENZIE, G. W., M.A., PH.D., International Economics
MATTHEWS, W. A., PH.D., Psychology
SIDDLE, D. A., PH.D., A.B.PS.S., Psychophysiology

### Faculty of Educational Studies:
FEUCHTWANGER, E. J., M.A., PH.D., F.R.HIST.S., Defence Studies

### Faculty of Law:
CRONIN, J. B., LL.B., Law
GANZ, G., LL.M., Law
SAMUELS, H. A., B.A., Law

### Faculty of Medicine:
WALKER, R. J., PH.D., D.SC., M.I.BIOL., Neurophysiology

Woodruff, G. N., ph.d., Physiology and Pharmacology

*Faculty of Mathematical Studies:*
Davies, H. J., ph.d., Mathematics
Howson, A. G., m.sc., ph.d., f.i.m.a., Mathematical Curriculum Studies
John, J. A., ph.d., Mathematics
Kirby, D., ph.d., Mathematics
Westcott, B. S., ph.d., f.i.m.a., Mathematics

## UNIVERSITY OF STIRLING
STIRLING, FK9 4LA
Telephone: (0876) 3171.
Telex: 778874.
Founded 1967.

Academic year: September to May (two semesters).

*Chancellor:* Sir Montague Finniston, f.r.s.
*Principal:* Sir Kenneth Alexander, ll.d., d.univ., f.r.s.e.
*Secretary:* R. G. Bomont, j.p., b.sc. (econ.), i.p.f.a.
*Deputy Secretary (Registrar):* F. Smyth, ll.b.
*Librarian:* P. G. Peacock, b.a., a.l.a.

Number of teachers: 260.
Number of students: 2,900.

Publications: *Annual Prospectuses, Annual Report, Calendar.*

Professors:

Allen, D. H., ph.d., c.eng., f.i.chem.e., f.r.s.a., Management Science and Technology Studies
Brown, C. V., ph.d., Economics
Campbell, R. H., m.a., ph.d., Economic History
Cannon, T., b.sc., Business Studies
Cowie, J. M. G., ph.d., c.chem., f.r.s.c., f.r.s.e., Chemistry
Dickinson, J. P., ph.d., a.a.s.a., a.c.i.s., Accountancy
Duncan, J., m.sc., ph.d., f.r.s.e., Mathematics
Dunn, T. A., m.a., ph.d., English Studies
Duthie, J. H., m.a., ph.d., Education
Holden, J. M., ll.b., ph.d., ll.d., a.i.b., Business Law
Jeffares, A. N., m.a., ph.d., d.phil., d. de l'univ., f.a.h.a., f.r.s.l., f.r.s.e., English Studies
Jimack, P. D., ph.d., French
Kleinpoppen, H., dr.rer.nat. et habil., f.inst.p., f.a.p.s., f.r.a.s., Experimental Physics
Loasby, B. J., m.litt., Management Economics
Lockerbie, S. I. J., m.a., ph.d., French
McEwen, P., ph.d., f.b.ps.s., Psychology
Medhurst, K. N., ph.d., Political Studies
Morrison, A. T., m.ed., f.b.ps.s., Education
Muntz, W. R. A., d.phil., Biology
Patz, D. H., m.s., ph.d., Accountancy
Roberts, R. J., ph.d., m.r.c.path., m.r.c.v.s., f.r.s.e., Aquaculture
Tennant, N. W., ph.d.
Thomas, M. F., m.a., ph.d., Earth and Environmental Science
Timms, D. W. G., ph.d., Sociology
Trainer, J., m.a., ph.d., German
Turner, C., ph.d., Sociology
Waddell, D. A. G., m.a., d.phil., f.r.hist.s., Modern History
Wallace, D. A. R., ph.d., f.r.s.e., Mathematics

Wilson, L. B., d.sc., f.b.c.s., Computing Science

Readers:
Hay, R. W., ph.d., c.chem., f.r.s.c., f.n.z.i.c., f.r.s.e., Chemistry
Marshall, E. A., m.a., ll.b., ph.d., Business Law
Mayhead, R., m.a., English Studies
McIntyre, D. I., m.a., m.ed., Education
Roberts, J. S., ph.d., f.r.s.c., Chemistry
Woodward, J. F., b.sc., f.i.struct.e., m.i.c.e., m.b.i.m.

Attached Institutes:
**Institute of Aquaculture:** Dir. Prof. R. J. Roberts.

## UNIVERSITY OF STRATHCLYDE
GEORGE STREET, GLASGOW, G1 1XW.
Telephone: 041-552-4400.

Founded 1796 under the title of Anderson's Institution; affiliated to the University of Glasgow between 1913 and 1964; presented with University Charter 1964.

Academic year: October to June.

*Chancellor:* The Rt. Hon. Lord Todd of Trumpington, o.m., m.a., d.sc., d.phil., c.chem., f.r.s.c., p.p.r.s.
*Principal and Vice-Chancellor:* G. J. Hills, ph.d., d.sc., c.chem., f.r.s.c.
*Vice-Principal:* Prof. W. E. Tyler, m.a., f.l.a.
*Registrar:* D. W. J. Morrell, m.a., ll.b.
*Librarian:* C. G. Wood, m.a., f.l.a.

Number of full-time teachers: 753.
Number of full-time students: 6,668.

Publications: *Annual Report†, University Calendar, Prospectus†, Postgraduate Booklets†, Continuing Education Programme.*

Deans:

*School of Mathematics, Physics and Computer Science:* Prof. G. Eason, m.sc., ph.d., f.i.m.a., f.r.s.e.
*School of Chemical and Materials Sciences:* Prof. P. L. Pauson, ph.d., c.chem., f.r.s.c., f.r.s.e.
*School of Mechanical and Chemical Engineering and Naval Architecture:* J. T. Webster, b.sc., a.r.c.s.t., c.eng., f.i.mech.e.
*School of Civil and Mining Engineering and Applied Geology:* Prof. P. McL. D. Duff, ph.d., f.i.m.m., f.g.s., f.r.s.e.
*School of Electrical and Electronic Engineering:* J. E. Matthews, ph.d., c.eng., f.i.e.e.
*School of Architecture, Building Science and Planning:* P. A. Reed, b.a., r.i.b.a.
*School of Biological Sciences:* John A. Blain, ph.d.
*School of Pharmaceutical Sciences:* Prof. A. T. Florence, ph.d., a.r.c.s.t., c.chem., f.r.s.c.

*School of Arts and Social Studies:* Prof. J. Butt, ph.d.
*School of Business and Administration:* Prof. M. J. Baker, t.d., b.a., b.sc.(econ.). d.b.a., f.inst.m.

Professors:

Anderson, W., ph.d., f.p.s., Pharmacy
Bain, A. D., m.a., ph.d., f.r.s.e., Monetary and Financial Economics
Baker, M. J., b.a., b.sc.(econ.), d.b.a., f.inst.m., Marketing
Barr, D. I. H., ph.d., d.r.t.c., f.i.c.e., Civil Engineering
Beavis, J. R. S., b.a.(econ.), f.c.a., f.h.c.i.m.a., Hotel Management
Bell, H. B., ph.d., a.r.c.s.t., f.i.m., Extraction Metallurgy
Beveridge, G. S. G., ph.d., f.i.chem.e., f.r.s.e., Chemical and Process Engineering
Bowey, Angela M., ph.d., Strathclyde Business School
Bowman, W. C., b.pharm., ph.d., d.sc., f.p.s., f.i.biol., f.r.s.e., Pharmacology
Burns, C. B., m.a., ll.b., ph.d., Business Law
Butler, D. S., b.a., f.i.m.a., Numerical Analysis
Butt, J., ph.d., Economic History
Carbery, T. F., m.sc.(econ.), ph.d., d.p.a., Office Organization
Clark, J. G., b.a., d.u.p., French Studies
Clunies-Ross, A. I., m.a., Economics
Colin, A. J. T., m.a., f.b.c.s., f.i.e.e., Computer Science
Donaldson, W. A., m.a., Operational Research
Duff, P. McL. D., ph.d., f.i.m.m., f.g.s., f.r.s.e., Applied Geology
Eason, G., m.sc., ph.d., f.i.m.a., f.r.s.e., Mathematics for Applied Scientists
Eisner, E., ph.d., f.inst.p., f.acoust. soc. amer., f.r.s.e., Applied Physics
Fletcher, W. W., ph.d., f.l.s., f.i.biol., f.r.s.e., Biology
Florence, A. T., ph.d., a.r.c.s.t., c.chem., f.r.s.c., m.p.s., Pharmacy
Gennard, J., m.a., Industrial Relations
Graham, N. B., ph.d., c.chem., f.r.s.c., f.c.i.c., f.p.r.i., Chemical Technology
Grimble, M. J., m.sc., ph.d., Electrical Engineering
Gunn, L. A., m.a., Administration
Harper, A. J., m.a., ph.d., German Studies
Harvey, J. M., m.s., ph.d., a.r.c.s.t., f.i.mech.e., Mechanics of Materials
Hawthorn, J., ph.d., a.r.c.s.t., c.chem., f.r.s.c., f.i.biol., f.i.f.s.t., f.r.s.e., Food Science and Nutrition
Hood, N., m.a., m.litt., Strathclyde Business School
Howe, G. M., m.sc., ph.d., d.sc., f.r.g.s., f.r.met.s., f.r.s.e., Geography
Hughes, J., b.sc., f.i.mech.e., f.i.s.p.o., Prosthetics and Orthotics
Hutchison, W. M., ph.d., d.sc., f.l.s., f.i.biol., f.r.s.e., Parasitology
Irving, G., m.a., ph.d., Natural Philosophy
Jahoda, G., m.sc., ph.d., Psychology
Kennerley, J. A. M., m.sc., c.eng., m.i.mech.e., f.i.m.a., f.r.a.e.s., Director of Strathclyde Business School
Kuo, C., ph.d., f.r.i.n.a., Shipbuilding and Naval Architecture
Leslie, F. M., ph.d., f.i.m.a., f.inst.p., Mathematics
Livingstone, J. M., m.a., m.sc.(econ.), ph.d., m.b.i.m., Marketing
MacCabe, C. M. J., ph.d., English Studies
MacLaren, J. F. T., ph.d., a.r.c.s.t., c.eng., f.i.mech.e., f.inst.e., Thermodynamics and Mechanics of Fluids

# UNIVERSITIES

MACLEOD, I. A., PH.D., Structural Engineering
MCGILVRAY, J. W., M.A., M.LITT., Dir. Fraser of Allander Institute for Research on the Scottish Economy
MCKINLAY, D. G., PH.D., F.I.C.E., F.A.S.C.E., F.G.S., Mechanics of Soils
MARKUS, T. A., M.A., M.ARCH.(M.I.T.), R.I.B.A., Building Science
MARSHALL, R. D., M.SC., PH.D., C.CHEM., F.R.S.C., Biochemistry
MAVER, T. W., PH.D., M.C.I.B.S., Architecture and Building Science
MAXWELL, G. M., PH.D., F.I.MIN.E., F.I.Q., Mining and Petroleum Engineering
MILLER, I. P., PH.D., S.S.C., N.P., Law
MORCOS-ASAAD, F. N., M.ARCH., S.M. (M.I.T.), PH.D., M.A.S.C.E., R.I.B.A., F.R.I.A.S., Architecture
NORTH, A. M., PH.D., D.SC., SC.D., F.R.S.C., F.R.S.E., Physical Chemistry
PACK, D. C., C.B.E., M.A., D.SC., F.I.M.A., F.E.I.S., F.R.S.E., Mathematics
PARRATT, J. R., PH.D., D.SC., F.P.S., F.I.BIOL., Physiology and Pharmacology
PAUL, J. P., PH.D., A.R.C.S.T., C.ENG., F.I.MECH.E., F.B.O.A., F.I.S.P.O., F.R.S.A., Bioengineering
PAUSON, P. L., PH.D., C.CHEM., F.R.C.S., F.R.S.E., Organic Chemistry
PERKINS, P. G., PH.D., D.SC., C.CHEM., F.R.S.C., F.INST.P., F.R.S.E., Inorganic Chemistry
PETCH, N. J., PH.D., D.MET., F.I.M., F.R.S., Metallurgy
ROACH, G. F., PH.D., F.R.A.S., F.I.M.A., F.R.S.E., Mathematics
ROSE, R., D.PHIL., Politics
ROSIE, A. M., M.SC., PH.D., F.I.E.E., Electronic Science and Telecommunications
ROSS, D. S., PH.D., A.R.C.S.T., F.I.PROD.E., F.I.MECH.E., F.B.I.M., Production Management and Manufacturing Technology
SANDISON, A. G., M.A., PH.D., English Studies
SCHAFFER, H. R., PH.D., Psychology
SHAW, R. K., PH.D., F.B.I.M., Technology and Business Studies
SHERWOOD, J. N., PH.D., D.SC., C.CHEM., F.R.S.C., F.R.S.E., Physical Chemistry
SIMPSON, D. R. F., M.A., PH.D., Research Prof., Fraser of Allander Institute for Research on the Scottish Economy
SIMPSON, H. C., S.M., SC.D., F.INST.P., F.I.MECH.E., F.R.S.E., Thermodynamics and Heat Transfer
SMITH, A. L. S., PH.D., F.INST.P., Experimental Physics
SMITH, J. E., M.SC., PH.D., D.SC., F.I.BIOL., F.R.S.E., Applied Microbiology
SPENCE, J., PH.D., D.SC., C.ENG., F.I.MECH.E., Mechanics of Materials
STENLAKE, J. B., PH.D., D.SC., C.CHEM., F.P.S., F.R.S.C., F.R.S.E., Pharmacy
SYKES, A. J. M., M.A., PH.D., Sociology
TEDFORD, D. J., PH.D., F.I.E.E., F.INST.P., F.R.S.E., Electrical Engineering
TILSTONE, W. J., PH.D., M.R.C.PATH., Forensic Science
TYLER, W. E., M.A., F.L.A., Librarianship
WANNOP, U. A., M.A., M.C.D., Urban Planning
WARD, J. T., M.A., PH.D., F.R.HIST.S., Modern History
WILKIE, W. R., M.A., F.I.SC.B., Administration
WOOD, G. C., PH.D., Pharmacy
WOOD, H. C. S., PH.D., C.CHEM., F.R.S.C., F.R.S.E., Organic Chemistry

## READERS:

AITKEN, W. G., PH.D., F.I.M.M., F.G.S., Applied Geology
BENGOUGH, W. I., PH.D., D.SC., Polymer Science
BLADON, P., PH.D., D.I.C., C.CHEM., M.R.S.C., Organic Chemistry
BLAIN, J. A., PH.D., Biochemistry
BROWN, D. H., J.P., PH.D., D.SC., Inorganic Chemistry
BROWN, J., PH.D., A.R.C.S.T., C.ENG., F.I.MECH.E., F.INST.R., Dynamics and Control
CAMERON, D., PH.D., F.I.P.M., Strathclyde Business School
COACKLEY, P., PH.D., C.CHEM., F.R.S.C., A.M.C.T., F.I.P.H.E., M.I.W.P.C., Civil Engineering
DAWSON, MARY, PH.D., F.P.S., Pharmacy
DUCKWORTH, R. B., PH.D., F.I.F.S.T., Food Science and Nutrition
FABIAN, D. J., PH.D., D.SC., F.I.M., F.INST.P., Metallurgy
FARISH, O., PH.D., C.ENG., F.I.E.E., M.INST.P., S.M.I.E.E.E., Electrical Engineering
FORSYTH, D. J. C., M.A., Economics
FRAILE, M., DR.FIL. Y LET., Spanish
GRAY, R. B., M.A., PH.D., Industrial Relations
GREEN, A. L., PH.D., Biochemistry
HENDRY, R., PH.D., C.ENG., F.I.CHEM.E., Chemical and Process Engineering
HOWIE, A. J., M.A., PH.D., F.I.M.A., Statistics
JACKSON, G., PH.D., History
JAMES, B. G. S., B.A., Marketing
KIRKPATRICK, W. M., PH.D., A.R.C.S.T., M.I.C.E., M.I.STRUCT.E., M.A.S.C.E., Civil Engineering
KIRKWOOD, R. C., PH.D., Biology
KNOX, G. R., PH.D., Organic Chemistry
LOWNDES, J. S., PH.D., F.I.M.A., Mathematics
MCGREGOR, D. R., PH.D., Computer Science
MACGREGOR, J., M.SC., PH.D., F.I.BIOL., Bioengineering
MACLEOD, C. J., PH.D., C.ENG., M.I.E.E., Electronic Science and Telecommunications
MARSHALL, I. G., PH.D., Physiology and Pharmacology
MATTHEWS, J. E., PH.D., F.I.E.E., Electrical Engineering
MILLINGTON, P. F., M.SC., PH.D., F.R.M.S., Bioengineering
MORRIS, E. N., M.SC., F.I.W.SC., Architecture and Building Science
MORRISON, W. R., PH.D., D.SC., A.R.C.S.T., F.R.S.C., F.R.S.E., Food Science and Nutrition
NONHEBEL, D. C., D.PHIL., C.CHEM., F.R.S.C., F.R.S.E., Organic Chemistry
OTTAWAY, J. M., PH.D., D.SC., C.CHEM., F.R.S.C., Inorganic Chemistry
PANTELOURIS, E. M., PH.D., D.SC., Biology
PENDER, J. T., B.SC., A.R.C.S.T., C.ENG., M.I.E.E., Electrical Engineering
PROCTOR, G. R., PH.D., C.CHEM., F.R.S.C., Organic Chemistry
ROONEY, D. H., PH.D., A.R.C.S.T., C.ENG., F.I.MECH.E., Thermodynamics and Mechanics of Fluids
SHARPE, J. W., M.A., F.INST.P., F.R.S.E., Natural Philosophy
SMITH, A. L. M., M.A., Politics
SMITH, K., PH.D., Geography
STUART, A. U., B.SC., C.ENG., M.I.MECH.E., M.I.PROD.E., M.I.E.M., Production Management and Manufacturing Technology
SWINBANKS, D. B., B.SC., A.C.G.I., D.I.C., M.R.AE.S., C.ENG., M.I.MECH.E., Thermodynamics and Mechanics of Fluids
TOOTH, A. S., M.SC., PH.D., A.M.C.T., C.ENG., F.I.MECH.E., Mechanics of Materials
WADE, T. L. B., PH.D., Russian
WARD, A., PH.D., F.R.A.S., Applied Physics
WATON, N. G., PH.D., Physiology and Pharmacology
WEBSTER, J. T., B.SC., A.R.C.S.T., C.ENG., F.I.MECH.E., Engineering Design and Drawing
WOOD, W. S., M.B.E., PH.D., C.ENG., F.I.E.E., Electrical Engineering
ZEITLIN, I. J., PH.D., M.I.BIOL., Physiology and Pharmacology

## ATTACHED INSTITUTES:

**Centre for Industrial Innovation:** 100 Montrose St., Glasgow, G4 0LZ; Dir. E. R. NORTH, B.SC.

**Centre for the Study of Public Policy:** McCance Bldg., 16 Richmond St., Glasgow, G1 1XQ; Dir. Prof. R. ROSE, D.PHIL.

**David Livingstone Institute of Overseas Development Studies:** McCance Bldg., 16 Richmond St., Glasgow, G1 1XQ; Dir J. PICKETT, B.SC.(ECON.), M.LITT.

**Fraser of Allander Institute for Research on the Scottish Economy (Dept. of Economics):** 100 Montrose St., Glasgow, G4 0LZ; Dir. Prof. J. W. MCGILVRAY, M.A., M.LITT.

**National Centre for Training and Education in Prosthetics and Orthotics:** Balmanno Building, 73 Rottenrow, Glasgow, G4 0NG; Dir. Prof. J. HUGHES, B.SC., F.I.MECH.E., F.I.S.P.O.

# UNIVERSITY OF SURREY
## GUILDFORD, SURREY, GU2 5XH

Telephone 0483-71281.

Telex: 859331.

Founded as Battersea Polytechnic Institute 1891; designated a College of Advanced Technology 1956; University Charter 1966.

*Chancellor:* H.R.H. The Duke of KENT, G.C.M.G., G.C.V.O.
*Vice-Chancellor:* A. KELLY, PH.D., SC.D., F.INST.P., C.ENG., F.I.M., F.ENG., F.R.S.
*Pro-Vice-Chancellors:* V. S. GRIFFITHS, PH.D., C.CHEM., F.R.S.C., F.INST.P., O. PICK, D.IUR.
*Academic Registrar:* G. HAIGH, PH.D., D.I.C., M.INST.P.
*Librarian:* R. F. EATWELL, M.A., F.L.A.

Number of teachers: 381 full-time.
Number of students: 3,525.

Publications: *Prospectus†, Prospectus of Postgraduate Courses and Research Studies†, Report of the Vice-Chancellor†* (annually).

## DEANS:

*Faculty of Biological and Chemical Sciences:* Prof. N. MARKS, M.A., D.M., F.R.C.P., F.R.C.P.(E.), F.R.C.PATH.
*Faculty of Engineering:* Prof. I. M. ALLISON, PH.D., C.ENG., M.R.AE.S.
*Faculty of Human Studies:* B. POCKNEY, B.A., B.SC.(ECON.).
*Faculty of Mathematical and Physical Sciences:* Prof. M. B. WALDRON, PH.D., C.ENG., F.I.M.

PROFESSORS AND
HEADS OF DEPARTMENTS:

*University Professor:*
SMITH BRINDLE, R., D.MUS., Music

*Faculty Professor:*
GRIFFITHS, V. S., PH.D., C.CHEM., F.R.S.C., F.INST.P., Combustion Chemistry

*Faculty of Biological and Chemical Sciences:*
ARMSTRONG-ESTHER, C. A., PH.D., S.R.N., R.N.T., M.I.BIOL., Nursing Studies
BRIDGES, J. W., PH.D., Toxicology
DAVIS, P. R., M.B. PH.D., L.R.C.P., F.R.C.S., F.I.BIOL., Human Biology
DICKERSON, J. W. T., PH.D., F.I.BIOL., F.R.S.H., F.I.F.S.T., Human Nutrition
ELVIDGE, J. A., PH.D., D.SC., D.I.C., A.R.C.S., C.CHEM., F.R.S.C., Organic Chemistry
MARKS, V., M.A., D.M., F.R.C.P., F.R.C.P.(E.), F.R.C.PATH., Clinical Biochemistry
PARKE, D. V. W., PH.D., D.SC., C.CHEM., F.R.S.C., F.I.BIOL., F.R.C.PATH., Biochemistry
SMITH, J. E., PH.D., M.R.C.V.S., F.I.BIOL., Microbiology

*Faculty of Engineering:*
ALLISON, I. M., PH.D., C.ENG., M.R.AE.S., Experimental Mechanics
BENYON, J. D. E., PH.D., C.ENG., F.I.E.E., F.I.E.R.E., Electronic and Electrical Engineering
CARNEGIE, W., PH.D., C.ENG., M.I.MAR.E., Vibrations
CLIFT, R., M.A., PH.D., C.ENG., M.I.CHEM.E., Chemical Engineering
MAKOWSKI, Z. S., PH.D., D.I.C., C.ENG., F.I.C.E., M.A.S.C.E., Civil Engineering
SIMONS, N. E., M.A., PH.D., D.SC.ENG., C.ENG., F.I.C.E., F.G.S., Geotechnical Engineering
STEPHENS, K. G., PH.D., F.INST.P., C.ENG., F.I.E.E., Electronic and Electrical Engineering
WALKER, A. C., A.R.C.S.T., PH.D., D.SC., C.ENG., M.I.MECH.E., M.I.C.E., Buckling of Structures

*Faculty of Human Studies:*
ABELL, P., PH.D., Sociology
ARCHER, B. H., M.A., PH.D., Hotel, Catering and Tourism Management
FORBES, S., M.A., MUS.D., A.R.C.O., L.R.A.M., A.R.C.M., Music
FREYNE, J. P., B.SC.(ECON.), Director of General Studies
HAWARD, L. R. C., M.A., DR.PSY., F.B.PS.S., Psychology
HEALEY, F. G., M.A. PH.D., Linguistic and International Studies (French)
IRVING, R. J., M.SC., PH.D., C.CHEM., F.R.S.C., Home Economics
JAMES, D. E., M.ED., A.B.P.S.S., M.I.BIOL., F.R.S.H., F.R.S.A., Adult Education
LEE, T. R., M.A., PH.D., F.B.PS.S., Psychology
NAILON, P. W., M.PHIL., F.H.C.I.M.A., Hotel and Catering Management
PICK, O., B.A., D.IUR., Linguistic and International Studies (International Relations)
POCKNEY, B. P., B.SC.(ECON.), B.A., Russian Studies
REEVES, N. B. R., M.A., D.PHIL., Linguistic and International Studies (German)
ROBINSON, C., B.A.(ECON.), F.S.S., Economics
SMITH BRINDLE, R., D.MUS., Music
THAKUR, S. C., M.A., PH.D., Philosophy
TROPP, A., PH.D., Sociology

*Faculty of Mathematical and Physical Sciences:*
BAILEY, J. E., PH.D., C.ENG., F.I.M., M.INST.P., F.I.CERAM., Materials Technology
CASTLE, J. E., PH.D., C.CHEM., F.R.S.C., F.I.CORR.T., Applied Interface Science
CROCKER, A. G., PH.D., D.SC., A.R.C.S., F.INST.P., F.I.M., Solid State Physics
GOODWIN, T. F., C.ENG., F.B.C.S., M.R.AE.S., Director of Computing Unit
JACKSON, DAPHNE F., PH.D., D.SC., A.R.C.S., F.INST.P., Nuclear Physics
PUTTICK, K. E., PH.D., M.INST.P., Solid State Physics
ROBINSON, P. M., PH.D., Statistics/Operational Research
WALDRON, M. B., PH.D., C.ENG., F.I.M., Metallurgy
WILLIAMS, W. E., PH.D., D.SC., F.I.M.A., Mathematics

READERS:

*Faculty of Biological and Chemical Sciences:*
ABRAHAM, M. H., PH.D., D.SC., C.CHEM., F.R.S.C., Organic Chemistry
BUTLER, M., PH.D., M.I.BIOL., Virology
HILLMAN, H., M.B., B.S., PH.D., M.R.C.S., L.R.C.P., Physiology
JACKSON, R. M., PH.D., M.I.BIOL., Plant Microbiology
KING, L. J., PH.D., Biochemistry
LADD, M. F. C., M.SC., PH.D., D.SC., C.CHEM., F.R.S.C., F.INST.P., Crystallography
LARKWORTHY, L. F., PH.D., D.SC., C.CHEM., F.R.S.C., Inorganic Chemistry
LEE, W. H., PH.D., C.CHEM., F.R.S.C., Physical Chemistry
LEWIS, D., M.SC., PH.D., M.INST.P., Crystallography
REED, E., PH.D., D.SC., C.CHEM., F.R.S.C., Analytical Biochemistry
SNELL, K., PH.D., Biochemistry
WALKER, R., PH.D., C.CHEM., M.R.S.C., F.I.F.S.T., Food Science
WRIGHT, J. W., M.B.B.S., M.SC., M.R.C.P., M.R.C.PATH., Metabolic Medicine

*Faculty of Engineering:*
BRADBURY, L. J. S., PH.D., Fluid Mechanics
BYWATER, R. E. H., PH.D., C.ENG., M.I.E.E., M.B.C.S., Computer and Control Engineering
DAVIS, Q. V., B.SC.(ENG.), C.ENG., F.I.E.E., F.INST.P., Telecommunications
HANNANT, D. J., PH.D., C.ENG., M.I.C.E., Concrete Technology
MOLES, F. D., B.SC.TECH., C.ENG., M.INST.F., Fuel Technology
NOOSHIN, H., PH.D., D.I.C., Structural Engineering
PARKER, G. A., PH.D., C.ENG., F.I. MECH.E., M.A.S.M.E., M.INST.M.C., Fluid Control Systems
SUPPLE, W. J., PH..D, C.ENG., M.I.C.E., Structural Engineering
THOMAS, W. J., PH.D., C.CHEM., F.R.S.C., C.ENG., M.I.CHEM.E., M.INST.E., DIP.CHEM.E., Chemical Engineering

*Faculty of Human Studies:*
BAGLEY, C., M.A.(SOC.), D.PHIL., Sociology
BURKART, A. J., M.A., F.T.S., Tourism
CANTER, D. V., PH.D., F.B.PS.S., Psychology
COOPER, D. E., M.A., Philosophy
HABER, L. F., PH.D., Economics
MATTHEWS, W., D.PHIL., Russian Studies
THOMPSON, J., PH.D., Food Studies

*Faculty of Mathematical and Physical Sciences:*
CORNBLEET, S., PH.D., F.I.M.A., Microwave Physics
DAVIES, M., M.SC., PH.D., D.I.C., A.R.C.S., F.I.M.A., Numerical Analysis
FOULDS, K. W. H., PH.D., C.ENG., F.I.E.E., M.I.E.E.E., Microwave Physics
JOHNSON, R. C., PH.D., F.INST.P., Nuclear Physics
MIODOWNIK, A. P., PH.D., C.ENG., F.I.M., Physical Metallurgy
MORSE, C. T., PH.D., Computing
QUILLIAM, J. E. H., M.SC., M.B.C.S., Computing (Head of Special Projects)
ROBERTSON, M. M., M.A., PH.D., Pure Mathematics
SHAIL, R., PH.D., F.I.M.A., Applied Mathematics

ATTACHED INSTITUTES:

**Institute for Educational Technology:**
f. 1967; research and innovation in teaching and learning in higher and secondary education; Dir. Prof. L. R. B. ELTON, M.A., D.SC., F.INST.P., F.I.M.A., F.R.S.A.

**Robens Institute of Industrial and Environmental Health and Safety:**
f. 1979; incorporates the fmr. Wolfson Bioanalytical Centre and five additional units: materials handling research, isolator (gnotobiotics), industrial biomedical epidemiology and health care research, and toxicology; carries out research and provides information; advisory and investigative service; training centre; Dir. Prof. J. W. BRIDGES, PH.D.

# UNIVERSITY OF SUSSEX
FALMER, BRIGHTON, SUSSEX, BN1 9RH

Telephone: Brighton (0273) 606755.

Founded 1961.

*Chancellor:* Lord SHAWCROSS, P.C., G.B.E., Q.C.
*Vice-Chancellor:* Prof. Sir DENYS WILKINSON, M.A., PH.D., SC.D., F.R.S.
*Pro-Vice-Chancellor:* Prof. J. L. LYONS, M.A., PH.D., F.B.A.
*Pro-Vice-Chancellor (Arts and Social Studies):* Prof. M. M. McGOWAN, PH.D.
*Pro-Vice-Chancellor (Science):* Prof. R. J. BLIN-STOYLE, M.A., D.PHIL., F.INST.P., F.R.S.
*Chairman of Education:* Prof. R. A. BECHER, M.A.
*Registrar:* G. LOCKWOOD, D.PHIL.
*Librarian:* Miss E. M. RODGER, B.SC., A.L.A.

Library: see Libraries.

Number of teachers: 476.
Number of students: 4,600.

Publications: *Guide for Applicants, B.A. and B.Sc. degrees, Graduate Studies in Science, Graduate Prospectus—Arts and Social Studies, Annual Report, University Guide.*

DEANS:

*School of African and Asian Studies:* P. K. CHAUDHURI, B.A., M.SC.

UNIVERSITIES U.K. (GREAT BRITAIN)

*School of Biological Sciences:* Prof. R. J. ANDREW, M.A., PH.D.
*School of Cultural and Community Studies:* Prof. W. M. LAMONT, PH.D.
*School of Engineering and Applied Sciences:* Prof. R. L. GRIMSDALE, PH.D.
*School of English and American Studies:* J. S. WHITLEY, M.A.
*School of European Studies:* Prof. G. F. A. BEST, PH.D.
*School of Mathematical and Physical Sciences:* Prof. J. P. ELLIOTT, PH.D.
*School of Chemistry and Molecular Sciences:* Prof. J. N. MURRELL, PH.D.
*School of Social Sciences:* Prof. D. N. WINCH, PH.D.
*Graduate School in Arts and Social Studies:* Prof. B. D. GRAHAM, M.A., PH.D.

PROFESSORS:

ANDREW, R. J., M.A., PH.D., Animal Behaviour
ATHERTON, D. P., PH.D., D.SC., Electrical Engineering
BARNA, T., C.B.E., PH.D., Economics
BATHER, J. A., PH.D., DIP.STATS., Mathematics and Statistics
BAYLEY, F. J., PH.D., D.SC., C.ENG, F.I.MECH E., Mechanical and Structural Engineering
BECHER, R. A., M.A., Education
BEST, G. F. A., M.A., PH.D., History
BLIN-STOYLE, R. J., M.A., D.PHIL., F.INST.P., F.R.S., Theoretical Physics
BODEN, M. A., M.A., A.M., PH.D., Philosophy
BOTTOMORE, T. B., M.SC.(ECON.), Sociology
BREWER, D. F., M.A., D.PHIL., Physics
BRIDGES, B. A., PH.D., Prof. Fellow, Dir. M.R.C. Cell Mutation Unit
BROWN, J. R., M.A., B.LITT., PH.D., English
CHALMERS, A. D., M.A., Social Psychology
COHN, N. R., M.A., D.LITT., Columbus Centre
COLE, R. J., PH.D., Development Genetics
COLQUHOUN, W. P., M.A., PH.D., Prof. Fellow, Dir. M.R.C. Perceptual and Cognitive Performance Unit
CORNFORTH, Sir JOHN W., C.B.E., M.SC., D.PHIL., C.CHEM., F.R.I.C., F.R.S., Chemistry
CRUICKSHANK, J., M.A., PH.D., LITT.D., French
DARTNALL, H. J. A., PH.D., D.SC., F.R.I.C., Biological Sciences
DORE, R. P., B.A., F.B.A., Prof. Fellow, Institute of Development Studies
DUCHÊNE, L. F., B.SC.(ECON.), Dir. Sussex European Research Centre
EABORN, C., PH.D., D.SC., C.CHEM., F.R.I.C., F.R.S., Chemistry
EDGLEY, R., B.A., B.PHIL., Philosophy
EDMUNDS, D. E., PH.D., Mathematics
ELKINS, T. H., B.A., Geography
ELLIOTT, J. P., PH.D., Theoretical Physics
EPPEL, E. M., M.A., M.ED., Dir. Centre for Continuing Education
EPSTEIN, A. L., LL.B., PH.D., Social Anthropology
EPSTEIN, Mrs. T. S., PH.D., Prof. Fellow, School of African and Asian Studies
FRAENKEL, L. E., M.A.SC., Partial Differential Equations
FREEMAN, C., D.PHIL., Science Policy
GRAHAM, B. D., M.A., PH.D., Politics
GREEN, R. H., M.A., LL.D., Prof. Fellow, Institute of Development Studies
GRIMSDALE, R. L., M.SC., PH.D., C.ENG., M.I.E.E., F.B.C.S., Electronics

GROSS, R. A., M.A., PH.D., American Studies
HARRISON, J. F. C., M.A., PH.D., History
HARVEY, J. D., M.A., MUS.D., PH.D., Music
HOLLAND, L. A., D.SC., F.INST.P., F.I.E.E., C.ENG., F.S.G.T., Physics
JAYAWANT, B. V., PH.D., D.SC., C.ENG., F.I.E.E., Electrical and Systems Engineering
JENKINS, A. D., PH.D., D.SC., C.CHEM., F.R.I.C., Polymer Science
JOHNSON, A. W., M.A., PH.D., SC.D., C.CHEM., F.R.I.C., F.R.S., Chemistry, Dir. A.R.C. Unit of Invertebrate Chemistry and Physiology
JOHNSON-LAIRD, P. N., PH.D., Experimental Psychology
DE KADT, E. J., M.A., PH.D., Prof. Fellow, Institute of Development Studies
KARMILOFF-SMITH, A. D., PH.D., Prof. Fellow, Developmental Psychology
LACEY, C., PH.D., Education
LAMONT, W. M., History and Education
LAPPERT, M. F., PH.D., D.SC., C.CHEM., F.R.S.C., F.R.S., Chemistry
LEGGETT, A. J., M.A., D.PHIL., Theoretical Physics
LERNER, L. D., M.A., English
LIPTON, M., B.A., Prof. Fellow, Institute of Development Studies
LLOYD, P. C., M.A., D.PHIL., Social Anthropology
LONGUET-HIGGINS, H. C., M.A., D.PHIL., D.UNIV., F.R.S., F.R.S.E., Perception and Cognition
LYNTON, N. C., B.A., History of Art
LYONS, J., M.A., PH.D., F.B.A., Linguistics
McCAPRA, F., PH.D., D.I.C., Chemistry
McGOWAN, Miss M. M., PH.D., French
MacKENZIE, N. I., B.SC.(ECON.), Education
MASON, R., PH.D., C.CHEM., F.R.I.C., F.INST.P., F.R.S., Chemistry
MAYNARD SMITH, J., B.A., B.SC., F.R.S., Biology
MESTEL, L., B.A., M.SC., PH.D., F.R.S., Astronomy
MESZAROS, I., PH.D., Philosophy
MINHAS, B. S., M.A., M.S., PH.D., Prof. Fellow, Institute of Development Studies
MORRISON, S. L., M.B., F.R.C.P., F.F.C.M., Prof. Fellow, Centre for Medical Research
MURRELL, J. N., PH.D., C.CHEM., F.R.I.C., Chemistry
MUTTER, R. P. C., M.A., English
NUTTALL, A. D., M.A., B.LITT., English
POCOCK, D. F., B.LITT., M.A., D.PHIL., F.R.A.I., Social Anthropology
POSTGATE, J. R., M.A., D.PHIL., D.SC., F.INST.BIOL., F.R.S., Microbiology
PREVEZER, S., M.A., LL.M., Law
RIVETT, B. H. P., M.SC., Operational Research
RÖHL, J. C. G., M.A., PH.D., History
SCHAFFER, B. B., B.SC., PH.D., Prof. Fellow, Institute of Development Studies
SCOTT, D. B., M.A., D.SC., F.I.M.A., Mathematics
SEERS, D., M.A., C.M.G., Prof. Fellow, Institute of Development Studies
SHALL, S., M.SC., M.B., B.CH., PH.D., Biochemistry
SMITH, K. F., M.A., PH.D., F.INST.P., Experimental Physics
SMITH, M. A. M., D.PHIL., Economics
SUNKEL, O., B.A., Prof. Fellow, Institute of Development Studies
SUTCLIFFE, J. F., PH.D., D.SC., F.INST.BIOL., Plant Physiology
SUTHERLAND, N. S., M.A., D.PHIL., Experimental Psychology
SYMONDS, N. D., B.A., B.SC., PH.D., Microbial Genetics
TAYLER, R. J., M.A., PH.D., Astronomy

TAYLOR, R. J., M.A., PH.D., L.R.A.M., German
THORLBY, A. K., M.A., PH.D., Comparative Literature
THORNE, C. G., M.A., International Relations
VAITSOS, C. V., M.A., PH.D., Prof. Fellow, Institute of Development Studies
WARD, G. N., M.A., F.I.M.A., Mathematics
WILKINSON, Sir DENYS, M.A., PH.D., SC.D., F.R.S., Physics
WINCH, D. N., PH.D., Economics

READERS:

ALLEN, L., PH.D., D.SC., D.I.C., A.R.C.S., F.INST.P., Experimental Physics
BARTON, G., M.A., D.PHIL., Theoretical Physics
BAILEY, A. J., B.A., Education
BEEFORTH, T. H., M.A., M.INST.P., C.ENG., M.I.E.E., Electronics Engineering
BENEWICK, R. J., M.A., PH.D., Politics
BOTT, R. W., B.SC., C.CHEM., F.R.I.C., Molecular Sciences
BRAY, R. C., PH.D., SC.D., Biochemistry
BROWN, M. G., B.SC., M.A., C.CHEM., F.R.I.C., Education and Chemistry
BROWN, R., M.A., History
BURROW, J. W., M.A., PH.D., Intellectual History
BURRELL, D. J., B.A., Education
BURROWS, C. R., PH.D., Mechanical and Structural Engineering
BUSHELL, P. J., M.A., D.PHIL., Mathematics
BYRNE, J., M.SC., PH.D., Experimental Physics
CARLEBACH, J. I., M.LITT., DIP.SOC., DIP.CRIM., D.PHIL., Sociology
CARSANIGA, G., DOTT.LETT., Italian
CHAUDHURI, P. K., B.A., M.SC., Economics
CLARK, N. G., PH.D., History and Social Studies of Science
CLARKE, G. M., M.A., F.I.S., Mathematics
COHEN, C. D., B.SC., Economics
COOK, Miss P. L., M.A., PH.D., Economics
COOPER, G. J., PH.D., Mathematics
CRAIG, G. W., M.A., French
CRAVEN, A. H., M.SC., PH.D., C.ENG., Mathematics
CROMWELL, Miss V., M.A., History
DARWIN, C. J., M.A., PH.D., Experimental Psychology
DEARLOVE, J. N., M.A., D.PHIL., Politics
DIFFEY, T. J., PH.D., Philosophy
DOMBEY, N. D., PH.D., Theoretical Physics
DUNWOODY, M. J., PH.D., Mathematics
ERAUT, M. R., M.A., PH.D., Education
ERTL, M. E., M.SC., PH.D., Materials Science
FINN, C. B. P., M.A., D.PHIL., M.INST.P., Experimental Physics
GAZDAR, G. J. M., M.A., PH.D., Linguistics
GIEDYMIN, J., M.A., M.ECON., PH.D., Logic and Scientific Method
GOODWIN, B. C., M.SC., Developmental Biology
GRIFFITHS, I. L., PH.D., Geography
GRILLO, R. D., PH.D., Social Anthropology
GUHA, R., M.A., History
HACKEL, S., M.A., D.PHIL., Russian Studies
HAMILTON, W. D., M.SC., PH.D., F.INST.P., Experimental Physics
HANSON, J. R., M.A., D.SC., PH.D., D.I.C., C.CHEM., F.R.I.C., Molecular Sciences
HANKEY, Miss A. T., PH.D., Classical and Medieval Studies
HARRISON, B. J., M.A., PH.D., Philosophy
HAWKINS, M. J., M.A., History
HOGAN, D. F., M.A., Education
HOLMES, R., PH.D., C.ENG., F.I.MECH.E., Mechanical and Structural Engineering
JACKSON, R. A., M.A., D.PHIL., Molecular Sciences

1533

JENKINS, C., M.A., PH.D., French
JOSIPOVICI, G. D., B.A., English
JOHN, S. B., M.A., French
JONES, N. B., M.ENG., D.PHIL., Control Electrical and Systems Engineering
KEDWARD, H. R., M.A., B.PHIL., History
KITCH, M. J., M.A., History
KROTO, H. W., PH.D., Molecular Sciences
LAND, M. F., PH.D., Neurobiology
LANGMUIR, Mrs. E. H., M.A., PH.D., History of Art
LLOYD, Mrs. B. B., M.A., PH.D., Social Psychology
LÖB, L., DR.PHIL., German
MARTELLI, G. E. G., DOTT.FIS., LIT.DOT.FIS.SUP., Experimental Physics
MCCAFFERY, R. J., PH.D., Molecular Sciences
MACGILLIVRAY, A. J., PH.D., Biochemistry
MAYO, P. R., PH.D., Developmental Psychology
MEDCALF, S. E., M.A., B.LITT., English
MIDDLEMAS, R. K., D.PHIL., History
MILNER-GULLAND, R. R., M.A., Russian Studies
NIXON, J.-F., PH.D., D.SC., Molecular Science
OGLEY, R. C., B.A., International Relations
OLDFIELD, D. E., M.A., English
OSBORNE, J., PH.D., German
OWEN, J. M., D.PHIL., Mechanical and Structural Engineering
PLATT, Miss J. A., M.A., Sociology
PRICKETT, A. T. S., M.A., PH.D., English
ROBERTS, J. B., M.A., PH.D., Mechanical and Structural Engineering
ROGERS, Miss R. H., M.SC., PH.D., F.I.M.A., Mathematics
ROSS, A. M., M.A., PH.D., English
ROSSELLI, J., PH.D., History
RUSSELL, I. J., PH.D., Neurobiology
SANTS, H. J., M.A., Developmental Psychology
SCHULKIND, E. W., B.A., D.U., French History and Literature
SIMMONDS, J. E., M.A., Social Administration
SIMPSON, A. W., PH.D., Materials Science
SINFIELD, A. J., M.A., English
SLOMAN, A., D.PHIL., Philosophy
SMITH, J. D., M.A., PH.D., Molecular Sciences
SMITH, B. L., J.P., M.A., PH.D., Experimental Physics
SMITH, P. B., PH.D., Social Psychology
SPRIGGE, T. L. S., M.A., PH.D., Philosophy
SPRINGFORD, M. J., PH.D., M.INST.P., Experimental Physics
STREETER, D. T., B.SC., Ecology
THOMAS, J. D., PH.D., Ecology
THOMSON, Miss P., M.A., English
TOWNSEND, P. D., PH.D., Experimental Physics
TURNER, R. E., M.A., PH.D., Theoretical Physics
VENABLES, J. A., M.A., PH.D., F.INST.P., Experimental Physics
WALL, D. G., B.SC.(ECON.), Economics
WALLIS, M., M.A., PH.D., Biochemistry
WALTON, D. R. M., M.A., D.SC., C.CHEM., F.R.I.C., Molecular Sciences
WARREN, N., M.A., Social Psychology
WATTS, C. T., M.A., PH.D., English
WEIR, A. J., M.A., PH.D., Mathematics
WEST, R. W., D.PHIL., Education
WHITEMAN, K. J., M.A., Mathematics
WHITLEY, J. S., M.A., English
WILKINSON, R. H., PH.D., American Studies
WOOD, D. P. J., M.A., PH.D., History
WOOLLONS, D. J., PH.D., C.ENG., M.I.E.E., Electronics and Computer Science
WRAITH, G. C., M.A., PH.D., Mathematics
WRIGLEY, C. C., M.A., History
YEO, C. S., D.PHIL., History

ATTACHED INSTITUTES:

**Science Policy Research Unit:** Dir. Prof. C. FREEMAN.

**A.R.C. Unit of Invertebrate Chemistry and Physiology:** Dir. Prof. A. W. JOHNSON.

**A.R.C. Unit of Nitrogen Fixation:** Dir. Prof. J. R. POSTGATE.

**M.R.C. Perceptual and Cognitive Performance Unit:** Dir. Prof. W. P. COLQUHOUN.

**M.R.C. Cell Mutation Unit:** Dir. Prof. B. A. BRIDGES.

**Sussex European Research Centre:** Dir. Prof. L. F. DUCHÊNE.

**Institute of Development Studies:** Dir. (vacant).

**Institute of Manpower Studies:** Pres. P. WALTERS.


## UNIVERSITY OF WALES
UNIVERSITY REGISTRY,
KING EDWARD VII AVE.,
CATHAYS PARK,
CARDIFF, CF1 3NS
Telephone: 22656.
Founded 1893.

*Chancellor:* H.R.H. The Prince CHARLES, Prince of WALES.
*Pro-Chancellor:* The Rt. Hon. Lord EDMUND-DAVIES, P.C., LL.D., B.C.L.
*Vice-Chancellor:* C. W. L. BEVAN, C.B.E., D.SC., F.R.S.C.
*Registrar:* E. W. JONES, B.SC.
Libraries: *see* Libraries.

The University of Wales Press publishes learned works and periodicals in Welsh and English.

Includes the following 7 Colleges:

**University College of Wales:** Aberystwyth; Telephone 3177; f. 1872; Language of instruction: English, with some courses in Welsh; Academic year: October to December, January to March, April to June.
*President:* The Rt. Hon. The Lord CLEDWYN, C.H., P.C.
*Vice-Presidents:* BEN G. JONES, C.B.E., LL.B., Sir MELVYN ROSSER, F.C.A.
*Principal:* GARETH OWEN, D.SC., M.R.I.A., F.I.BIOL.
*Vice-Principal:* Prof. HAROLD CARTER, M.A.
*Registrar:* T. A. OWEN, M.A.
Library: *see* Libraries.

Number of teachers: 340, including 46 professors.

Number of students: 2,676 undergraduate and 499 postgraduate.

Publications: *University of Wales Calendar, Prospectus, Postgraduate Prospectus, Llawlyfr, Newsletter—Llythyr Newyddion.*

DEANS:
*Faculty of Arts:* Prof. D. HAY, M.A., PH.D.
*Faculty of Science:* Prof. H. REES, D.SC., PH.D., F.R.S.
*Faculty of Education:* Prof. J. R. WEBSTER, M.A., PH.D.
*Faculty of Economic and Social Studies:* D. STEEDS, B.A.
*Faculty of Law:* Prof. J. A. ANDREWS, M.A., B.C.L., J.P., BAR.-AT-LAW.

PROFESSORS:
ANDREWS, J. A., M.A., B.C.L., BAR.-AT-LAW, Law
BATEMAN, D. I., M.A., Agricultural Economics
CARTER, HAROLD, M.A., Human Geography
COOPER, J. P., F.R.S., PH.D., D.SC., F.I.BIOL., Agricultural Botany
DAVIES, R. R., D.PHIL., F.R.HIST.S., History
DAVIES, W., M.SC., PH.D., D.SC., M.I.M.M., F.G.S., Applied Geology
DIETRICH, B. C., PH.D., Classics
DODSON, C. J., M.A., Education
EMERY, G., M.A., F.B.C.S., Computer Science
EVANS, E., M.A., PH.D., Irish
FRYDE, E. B., M.A., D.PHIL., F.R.HIST.S., History
GARNETT, J. C., M.SC.(ECON.), International Politics
GOWAN, IVOR, M.A., Political Science
HAINES, M., PH.D., Agricultural Marketing
HALL, M. A., PH.D., A.R.C.S., Botany
HAYES, J. D., PH.D., Agriculture
HEADING, JOHN, M.A., PH.D., Applied Mathematics
HELLER, H. G., Organic Chemistry
JONES, B. M., D.SC., Zoology
JONES, G. L., PH.D., German, Swedish and Russian
JONES, I. G., M.A., F.R.HIST.S., Welsh History
JONES, R. M., PH.D., Welsh Language and Literature
JONES, W. J., M.SC., PH.D., Chemistry
KIDSON, C., PH.D., Physical Geography
KING, H. K., M.A., PH.D., F.R.I.C., F.INST.BIOL., Biochemistry and Agricultural Biochemistry
MACVE, R. H., M.A., M.SC., A.C.A., Accounting
MATHUR, P. N., M.A., Economics
MILLS, M., M.A., D.PHIL., English
MORRIS, A. O., PH.D., Pure Mathematics
MORRIS, D. W., PH.D., Agriculture
MORRIS, J. G., D.PHIL., F.I.BIOL., Microbiology
MOSELEY, T. H., M.A., LL.B., BAR.-AT-LAW, Law
O'HARA, M. J., M.A., PH.D., Geology
PARROTT, H. I., M.A., D.MUS., F.T.C.L., A.R.C.O., Music
PRICE, G., M.A., D. DE L'U., Romance Studies
REES, G. L., M.A., Economics
REES, H., F.R.S., D.SC., PH.D., Agricultural Botany
ROBERTS, T. A., M.A., D.PHIL., Philosophy
SLAY, D., M.A., English
THOMAS, L., PH.D., D.SC., F.INST.P., Physics
THOMAS, P. D. G., M.A., PH.D., F.R.HIST.S., History
TWIDDY, N. D., PH.D., F.INST.P., Physics
VAN VELSEN, J., LL.B., PH.D., Sociology and Social Anthropology
WALTERS, K., M.SC., PH.D., Applied Mathematics
WEBSTER, J. R., M.A., PH.D., Education
WILLIAMS, G., PH.D., D.SC., Physical Chemistry

## UNIVERSITIES — U.K. (GREAT BRITAIN)

ATTACHED INSTITUTE:
**Welsh Plant Breeding Station:** see under Research Institutes.

### University College of North Wales:
Bangor; Telephone: Bangor 51151, f. 1884.

*President:* Rt. Hon. Lord KENYON, C.B.E., D.L., LL.D.
*Principal:* Sir CHARLES EVANS, B.M.; M.A., D.SC., F.R.C.S.
*Secretary and Registrar:* E. HUGHES, B.A.
*Librarian:* L. J. G. HEYWOOD, M.A.
Library: see Libraries.
Number of teaching staff: 352 including 35 professors.
Number of students: 3,109.

Publications: *Gazette* (termly), *Annual Report, Prospectus, Guide to Courses* (annually), *Prospectus for Non-Graduating Students* (irregular), *Summer School Brochure* (annually), *Conference Accommodation Brochure* (irregular).

DEANS:
*Faculty of Arts:* Prof. M. WILCOX, M.A., B.D., PH.D.
*Faculty of Science:* Prof. T. J. M. BOYD, PH.D., F.INST.P.

PROFESSORS:
*Faculty of Arts:*
ANDERSON, M. J., B.A., Drama
BUSST, A. J. L., PH.D., French and Romance Studies
HUNTER, G. B. B., M.A., Philosophy
JONES, A. R., B.A., B.LITT., English
JONES, B. L., M.A., Welsh
KING, R. D., PH.D., Social Theory and Institutions
LOADES, D. M., PH.D., F.R.HIST.S., History
MATHIAS, W., D.MUS., Music
RADFORD, A., PH.D., Linguistics
REVELL, J. R. S., B.SC.(ECON.), M.A., Economics
SMITH, M. F., M.A., M.LITT., F.S.A., Classics
THOMAS, G., M.A., D.PHIL., Welsh
WILCOX, Rev. M., B.D., M.A., PH.D., Biblical Studies
WILLIAMS, I. W., PH.D., Education
WILLIAMS, J. G., M.A., Welsh History
WILLIAMS, P., M.A., PH.D., F.B.PS.S., Education

*Faculty of Science:*
BOYD, T. J. M., PH.D., Applied Mathematics
BROWN, R., M.A., D.PHIL., Pure Mathematics
CRISP, D. J., C.B.E., M.A., PH.D., SC.D., F.R.S., Marine Biology
DARBYSHIRE, J., D.SC., F.INST.P., Physical Oceanography
FOGG, G. E., PH.D., SC.D., F.R.S., Marine Biology
GREIG-SMITH, P., M.A., SC.D., F.L.S., Plant Biology
HARPER, J. L., M.A., D.PHIL., F.R.S., Botany
LACEY, W. S., PH.D., D.SC., F.L.S., F.G.S., Plant Biology
LEWIS, T. J., M.SC., D.SC., PH.D., C.ENG., F.I.E.E., F.INST.P., Electrical Materials Science
MILES, T. R., M.A., PH.D., F.B.PS.S., Psychology
OWEN, J. B., PH.D., M.A., F.I.BIOL., Agriculture
PAUL, R. J. A., D.SC., C.ENG., F.R.AE.S., F.I.E.E., F.I.MECH.E., F.B.C.S., Electronic Engineering
RIBBONS, D. W., PH.D., D.SC., Biochemistry and Soil Science
ROCHE, L., M.F., PH.D., Forestry
SAGAR, G. R., M.A., D.PHIL., Agricultural Botany
SHERIDAN, J., M.A., D.PHIL., D.SC., F.R.I.C., Physical and Inorganic Chemistry
STEPHENSON, I. M., M.SC., PH.D., C.ENG., M.I.E.E., Electronics
STIRLING, C. J. M., PH.D., D.SC., C.CHEM., F.R.I.C., Organic Chemistry
WILCOCK, W. L., PH.D., F.R.A.S., Physics

HEADS OF DEPARTMENT:
*Faculty of Arts:*
ROBERTS, A., LL.B., M.A., Extra-Mural Studies
*Faculty of Science:*
HOBART, J., B.SC., F.R.E.S., Animal Biology

READERS:
*Faculty of Arts:*
KERRIDGE, ERIC, PH.D., F.R.HIST.S., Economics
REES, B., M.A., Welsh
THOMAS, G., M.A., D.PHIL., Welsh
THRALL, Miss M. E., M.A., PH.D., Biblical Studies
WHITLEY, Rev. C. F., M.A., B.D., PH.D., Biblical Studies

*Faculty of Science:*
CHAMBERS, LL. G., D.SC., Mathematics
DORSETT, D. A., PH.D., D.SC., Marine Biology
JONES, W. C., M.A., PH.D., SC.D., Zoology
SIMPSON, J. H., PH.D., Physical Oceanography
SMITH, A. J. E., M.A., D.PHIL., D.SC., Plant Biology
TAYLOR SMITH, D., B.SC., D.I.C., Physical Oceanography
TURVEY, J. R., PH.D., D.SC., F.R.I.C., Physical and Molecular Sciences
WYNN JONES, R. G., Biochemistry and Soil Science
WYNN PARRY, D., M.SC., D.SC., Plant Biology

ATTACHED INSTITUTES:
**Inter-University Institute of Engineering Control:** f. 1967 to promote co-operation in teaching and research by linking postgraduate work at Universities of Sussex and Warwick and University College of North Wales; Dir. Prof. R. J. A. PAUL.

**Institute of Economic Research:** f. 1969; research in regional economics, economics of developing countries, tourism and economics of ports, policy-making and planning; data analysis; Dirs. R. R. MACKAY, M.A., J. FLETCHER, M.A.

**Institute of European Finance:** f. 1973; Jt. Dirs. Prof. J. R. S. REVELL, J. E. MAYCOCK, B.COM., F.I.B.

**Industrial Development Unit:** f. 1968 to establish liaison with the electronics industry and to undertake provision to the industry of specialized high-voltage equipment; Dir. Dr. J. CHUBB.

**Unit of Marine Invertebrate Biology (N.E.R.C.):** See under Natural Environment Research Council.

---

### University College, Cardiff:
P.O.B. 78, Cardiff, CF1 1XL; Telephone: Cardiff 44211; f. 1883, incorporated by Royal Charter 1884.

*President:* The Rt. Hon. The Lord ELWYN-JONES, P.C., C.H., M.A.
*Principal:* C. W. L. BEVAN, C.B.E., D.SC., C.CHEM., F.R.S.C.
*Vice-Principal (Administration) and Registrar:* L. A. MORITZ, M.A., D.PHIL.
Library: see Libraries.
Number of teaching staff: 543, including 75 professors.
Number of students: 5,593.

Publications: *Prospectus* (annually), *Annual Report, Newsletter* (9 a year), *Safety Handbook* (annually).

DEANS:
*Faculty of Arts:* D. E. HILL, J.P., M.A.
*Faculty of Economic and Social Studies:* D. R. THOMAS, M.A., B.PHIL.(ECON.)
*Faculty of Law:* Prof. J. C. W. WYLIE, LL.M.
*Faculty of Science:* W. A. L. EVANS, M.SC., PH.D.
*Faculty of Applied Science:* T. T. LEWIS, B.SC., C.ENG., M.I.MECH.E.
*Faculty of Theology:* M. DURRANT, B.A., B.PHIL.
*Faculty of Education:* Prof. A. TAYLOR, M.A.

PROFESSORS:
(Some professors serve in more than one faculty.)
*Faculties of Arts, Education, Music and Theology:*
AGUIRRE, J. M., LIC. EN D., PH.D., Hispanic Studies
ATKINSON, R. J. C., C.B.E., M.A., F.S.A., Archaeology
BEETLESTONE, J. G., PH.D., D.SC., Science Education
BROOKS, M., PH.D., F.G.S., F.R.A.S., Geology
DEAN, W. T., PH.D., D.SC., F.G.S., Geology
EVANS, J. L., M.A., D.PHIL., Philosophy and History of Wales
FOULKES, P., M.A., PH.D., German
GILLESPIE, G. T., M.A., PH.D., German
GRIFFITHS, R. M., M.A., PH.D., French
HAWKES, T. F., M.A., PH.D., English
HEARDER, H., PH.D., Modern History
HENRIQUES, URSULA R. Q., M.A., B.LITT., PH.D., History
HODDINOTT, A., D.MUS., Music
JARRETT, M. G., PH.D., F.S.A., Archaeology
JONES, F. J., M.A., D.U.P., Italian
KELSALL, M. M., M.A., B.LITT., English
LEWIS, C. W., B.A., F.S.A., F.R.HIST.S., Welsh
McPHERSON, T. H., M.A., Philosophy
PIERCE, G. O., M.A., History of Wales
ROBBINS LANDON, H. C., D.MUS., Music
SAGGS, H. W. F., M.TH., M.A., PH.D., F.S.A., Semitic Languages and Religious Studies

SHERGOLD, N. D., M.A., PH.D., Hispanic Studies
TAYLOR, A., M.A., Education
WALCOT, P., M.A., PH.D., Classics
WILLIAMS, G. A., M.A., PH.D., History

*Faculty of Economic and Social Studies:*
ALBROW, M. C., PH.D., Sociology
BLACKMAN, D. E., PH.D., F.B.PS.S., Psychology
COXON, A. P. M., PH.D., Sociology
CROSS, J. A., M.A., PH.D., Politics
FRENCH, E. A., PH.D., BAR.-AT-LAW, Accountancy and Financial Control
GEORGE, K. D., M.A., Economics
HOPKIN, Sir BRYAN, C.B.E., M.A., Economics
JONES, H., PH.D., Social Administration
JONES, R. E., M.A., Politics
REES, R., M.SC.ECON., Economics
THOMASON, G. F., M.A., PH.D., Industrial Relations

*Faculty of Law:*
CALVERT, H. G., LL.M.
FARRAR, J. H., LL.M., Solicitor
SHERIDAN, L. A., LL.D., PH.D., BAR.-AT-LAW
WYLIE, J. C. W., LL.D.

*Faculty of Science:*
BELLAMY, D., D.PHIL., F.I.BIOL., Zoology
BROOKS, M., PH.D., F.G.S., F.R.A.S., Geology
CHURCHHOUSE, R. F., M.A., PH.D., F.B.C.S., F.I.M.A., F.R.A.S., Computing Mathematics
DAVIES, R. O., M.SC., D.PHIL., Physics
DEAN, W. T., PH.D., D.SC., F.G.S., Geology
DISNEY, M. J., PH.D., F.R.A.S., Applied Mathematics and Astronomy
DODGSON, K. S., PH.D., D.SC., F.I.BIOL., Biochemistry
ERASMUS, D. A., PH.D., D.SC., Zoology
EVANS, W. D., D.PHIL., Pure Mathematics
GILLARD, R. D., PH.D., Inorganic Chemistry
HOOLEY, C., M.A., SC.D., Pure Mathematics
HUGHES, D. E., M.A., D.SC., PH.D., F.I.BIOL., Microbiology
JACKSON, A. H., M.A., PH.D., SC.D., F.R.S.C., Organic Chemistry
KEMP, K. W., PH.D., F.I.S., F.I.M.A., Mathematical Statistics, Operational Research
LEVER, J. D., M.A., M.D., SC.D., Anatomy
LLOYD, D., PH.D., D.SC., Microbiology
MOFFATT, D. B., M.D., F.R.C.S., Anatomy
PICKLES, V. R., M.A., M.D., D.C.H., Physiology
ROBERTS, M. W., PH.D., D.SC., Chemistry
SMITH, A. G., PH.D., Plant Science
TAYLOR, C. A., PH.D., D.SC., F.INST.P., Physics
WEIGOLD, J., M.SC., PH.D., D.SC., Pure Mathematics
WHITTLE, E., M.SC., PH.D., D.SC., Chemistry
WICKRAMASINGHE, N. C., M.A., PH.D., SC.D., F.R.A.S., Applied Mathematics and Astronomy

*Faculty of Applied Science:*
BRINKWORTH, B., M.SC.ENG., PH.D., Mechanical Engineering and Energy Studies
BROWN, K. M., PH.D., F.I.MIN.E., F.I.Q.
GOVETT, G. J. S., PH.D., D.SC., Mineral Exploitation
HEALEY, M., M.SC., PH.D., Electrical and Electronic Engineering
LLOYD, H. K. M., PH.D., F.I.M., Metallurgy and Materials Science
MAJID, K. I., PH.D., D.SC., Civil and Structural Engineering
MARKLAND, E., PH.D., D.SC., F.I.MECH.E., F.I.C.E., Mechanical Engineering and Energy Studies
THOMPSON, J. E., PH.D., D.ENG., F.INST. P., F.I.M., Electrical and Electronic Engineering

ATTACHED INSTITUTES:

**School of Home Economics:** Dir. A. R. MATHIESON, O.B.E., PH.D., F.R.I.C., F.R.S.A.

**David Owen Centre for Population Growth Studies:** Dir. CASPAR BROOK.

**Computing Centre:** Dir. J. C. BALDWIN, D.PHIL.

**Extra-Mural Studies:** Dir. J. SELWYN DAVIES, B.A.

**University Industry Centre (C.U.I.C.):** Man. J. C. JONES.

**Sherman Theatre:** Dir. G. J. AXWORTHY, M.A.

**Centre for Journalism Studies:** Dir. R. J. BOSTON, M.A.

**Centre for Educational Technology:** Dir. G. D. MOSS, PH.D.

**University College, Cardiff, English Centre for Overseas Students (C.U.E.C.O.S.):** Dir. Sqn. Ldr. J. F. HARRIS.

---

**University College of Swansea:** Singleton Park, Swansea, SA2 8PP; Telephone: 0792-205678; f. 1920; Academic year: October to December, January to March, April to June.
*President:* Sir JOHN HABAKKUK, M.A., D.LITT., F.B.A.
*Principal:* Prof. R. W. STEEL, M.A., D.SC.
*Vice-Principals:* Prof. J. DUTTON, PH.D., F.INST.P., Prof. R. B. GRAVENOR, M.SC., PH.D., Prof. I. M. WILLIAMS, M.A.
*Registrar:* ANEURIN DAVIES, M.A.
Library: see Libraries.
Number of teaching staff: 445.
Number of students: 3,860.

DEANS:

*Faculty of Arts:* Prof. C. COLLARD, M.A., M.LITT.
*Faculty of Economic and Social Studies:* Prof. D. T. HERBERT, PH.D.
*Faculty of Science:* Prof. D. V. AGER, D.SC., PH.D., D.I.C., F.G.S.
*Faculty of Applied Science:* D. M. E. CHRISTIE, M.SC.
*Faculty of Education:* Prof. M. CHAZAN, M.A., F.B.PS.S.

PROFESSORS:

*Faculty of Arts:*
ANGLO, S., PH.D., History of Ideas
COLLARD, C., M.A., M.LITT., Classics
GREENLEAF, W. H., PH.D., Political Theory and Government
MINOGUE, V., M.A., M.LITT., French
PHILLIPS, D. Z., M.A., Philosophy
ROBERTS, B. F., M.A., PH.D., Welsh
SHANNON, R. T., M.A., PH.D., Modern History
WAIDSON, H. M., M.A., D.PHIL., German
WILLIAMS, G., C.B.E., M.A., D.LITT., F.R.HIST.S., History
WOODWARD, J. B., M.A., D.PHIL., Russian Language and Literature

*Faculty of Economic and Social Studies:*
BROADY, M., B.A., Social Policy and Social Work
COLE, W. A., M.A., PH.D., Economic History
ELLIOTT, C. M., D.PHIL., Development Policy and Planning
HANSEL, C. E. M., M.A., Psychology
MAPES, R. E. A., B.A., B.LITT., Medical Sociology
NEVIN, E. T., M.A., PH.D., Economics
PETHYBRIDGE, R. W., M.A., D.ÈS SC. POL., Russian and East European Studies
WILLIAMS, W. M., M.A., Sociology and Anthropology

*Faculty of Education:*
CHAZAN, M., M.A.

*Faculty of Science:*
AGER, D. V., D.SC., PH.D., D.I.C., F.G.S., Geology
BANNER, F. T., D.SC., PH.D., F.G.S., Oceanography
BEARDMORE, J. A., PH.D., Genetics
BETTERIDGE, D., PH.D., D.SC., Chemistry
BEYNON, J. H., D.SC., F.R.S. (Royal Society Research Prof.)
BROWN, E. G., PH.D., D.SC., F.R.S.C., Biochemistry
DUTTON, J., PH.D., Physics
HAWKES, A. G., PH.D., Statistics
HERBERT, D. T., PH.D., Geography
MORGAN, C. G., M.SC., PH.D., Physics
NIBLETT, G. B. F., M.SC., PH.D., BAR.-AT-LAW, Computer Science
OWEN, T. R., M.SC., Geology
PELTER, A., M.SC., PH.D. Organic Chemistry
PURNELL, J. H., M.A., PH.D., Physical Chemistry
RYLAND, J. S., M.A., PH.D., D.SC., Zoology
STEPHENS, N., M.SC., PH.D., Geography
SYMONS, L., PH.D., Geography
SYRETT, P. J., M.A., D.SC., Botany
TEMPERLEY, H. N. V., M.A., SC.D., Applied Mathematics
THONEMANN, P. C., M.SC., D.PHIL., Physics
WESTON, J. D., PH.D., D.SC., Pure Mathematics
WILLIAMS, D., M.A., D.PHIL., Pure Mathematics

*Faculty of Applied Science:*
ALEXANDER, J. M., D.SC., PH.D., Mechanical Engineering
BARKER, H. A., PH.D., Electrical Engineering
GRAVENOR, R. B., M.SC., PH.D., A.R.S.C., Management Science
RICHARDSON, J. F., O.B.E., D.SC., PH.D., Chemical Engineering
SINGER, A. R. E., PH.D., Metallurgy
ZIENKIEWICZ, O. C., PH.D., D.SC., F.R.S., Civil Engineering

**Welsh National School of Medicine:** Heath Park, Cardiff, CF4 4XN; Telephone: 755944; incorporated as an Independent School of the University of Wales by Royal Charter in 1931.
*President:* Sir CENNYDD TRAHERNE, K.G., T.D., LL.D., M.A., J.P., K.ST.J.

*Provost:* Prof. H. L. DUTHIE, M.D., C.R.M., F.R.C.S.(ED.).
*Director and Dean of Postgraduate Studies:* D. H. MAKINSON, M.A., M.B., F.R.C.P.
*Dean of Dental School:* B. E. D. COOKE, M.D.S., F.D.S., L.R.C.P., M.R.C.S., F.R.C.PATH.
*Dean of Clinical Studies:* G. S. KILPATRICK, M.D., F.R.C.P.(ED.), F.R.C.P.
*Registrar and Secretary:* T. R. SAUNDERS, B.A.
Library: see Libraries.
Number of teaching staff: 162, including 25 clinical professors.
Number of clinical students: 660.

PROFESSORS:

ASSCHER, A. W., B.SC., M.D., F.R.C.P., Renal Medicine
BLOOM, A. L., M.D., F.R.C.PATH., M.R.C.P., Haematology
CAMPBELL, H., M.A., M.B., F.R.C.P., B.S., F.S.S., F.F.C.M., Medical Statistics
DAVIS, R. H., M.A., D.M., F.R.C.G.P., General Practice
ELDER, G. H., M.D., F.R.C.PATH., Medical Biochemistry
EVANS, K. T., M.B., CH.B., F.R.C.P., D.M.R.D., F.R.C.R., Diagnostic Radiology
GRAY, O. P., M.B., CH.B., D.C.H., F.R.C.P., Child Health
GRIFFITHS, K., PH.D., Cancer Research (Steroid Biochemistry)
HALL, R., B.SC., B.S., M.D., F.R.C.P., Medicine
HENDERSON, A. H., B.A., M.B., B.CHIR., F.R.C.P., Cardiology
HIBBARD, B. M., M.D., PH.D., F.R.C.O.G., Obstetrics and Gynaecology
HUGHES, L. E., M.B., B.S., D.S., F.R.A.C.S., F.R.C.S., Surgery
JACOBS, A., M.D., F.R.C.PATH., F.R.C.P., Haematology
KILPATRICK, G. S., M.D., F.R.C.P.ED., F.R.C.P., Tuberculosis and Chest Diseases
KNIGHT, B. H., B.CH., M.D., F.R.C.PATH., D.M.J., Forensic Pathology
LAURENCE, K. M., M.A., M.B., CH.B., D.SC., F.R.C.PATH., M.R.C.P., Child Health
MAPLESON, W. W., PH.D., D.SC., F.INST.P., Anaesthetics
MARKS, R., B.SC., M.B., B.S., D.T.M.&H., F.R.C.P., Dermatology
MCKIBBIN, B., M.D., M.SC., F.R.C.S., Traumatic and Orthopaedic Surgery
RAWNSLEY, K., M.B., CH.B., F.R.C.P., D.P.M., F.R.C.PSYCH., Psychological Medicine
RICHENS, A., B.SC., M.B., B.S., PH.D., F.R.C.P., Pharmacology
ROBERTS, C. J., M.D., PH.D., D.P.H., D.OBST.R.C.O.G., Community Medicine
VICKERS, M. D. A., M.B., B.S., D.A., F.F.A.R.C.S., Anaesthetics
WATKINS, J. F., M.D., B.CHIR., M.A., DIP.BACT., Medical Microbiology
WILLIAMS, E. D., M.A., M.B., B.CH., F.R.C.PATH., F.R.C.P., Pathology

*Dentistry:*

BATES, J. F., B.D.S., M.SC., D.D.S., Restorative Dentistry
COOKE, B. E. D., M.D.S., F.D.S., L.R.C.P., M.R.C.S., F.R.C.PATH., Oral Medicine
DOLBY, A. E., M.D., F.D.S., Periodontology
ECCLES, J. D., B.D.S., PH.D., F.D.S., Conservative Dentistry
MILLER, J., M.D.S., D.D.S., F.D.S., Children's Dentistry, Preventive Dentistry
ROBERTSON, N. R. E., B.D.S., D.D.S., D.D.O., F.D.S.R.C.P.S., Orthodontics

READERS:

ADAMS, D., M.D.S., PH.D., Oral Biology
DODGE, J. A., M.D., F.R.C.P., D.C.M., Child Health
HARPER, P. S., D.M., F.R.C.P., Medicine
KEYSER, J. W., M.SC., PH.D., F.R.I.C., F.R.C.PATH., Medical Biochemistry
PEARSON, J. F., M.D., F.R.C.O.G., Obstetrics and Gynaecology
SALAMAN, J. R., M.A., M.B., M.CHIR., F.R.C.S., Surgery
STAFFORD, G. D., T.D., L.D.S., M.SC., PH.D., Restorative Dentistry
STARK, J. M., M.D., F.R.C.PATH., Medical Microbiology

**Saint David's University College:** Lampeter, Dyfed, SA48 7ED; Telephone: Lampeter 422351; founded 1822; College opened St. David's Day 1827; first Royal Charter granted 1827, with later Charters 1852, 1865, 1896 and 1963; affiliated to Oxford Univ. 1880 and Cambridge Univ. 1883; inc. as constituent institution of the University of Wales 1971; Academic year: October to December, January to March, April to June.

*Visitor:* Rt. Rev. E. M. ROBERTS, M.A., Bishop of St. David's.
*Principal:* Prof. B. R. MORRIS, M.A., D.PHIL.
*Academic Registrar:* A. M. S. KENWRIGHT, M.A.
Library: see Libraries.
Number of teaching staff: 75, including 9 professors.
Number of students: 700.
Publications: *Prospectus, Trivium*† (academic journal), *Cambria*† (geographical journal).

PROFESSORS:

*Faculty of Arts:*
BEAUMONT, P., PH.D., Geography
CAVENDISH, A. P., B.A., Philosophy
DUCKHAM, B. F., M.A., F.R.HIST.S., History
EVANS, D. S., M.A., B.D., D.LITT., Welsh
GEORGE, F. W. A., PH.D., French
LOFMARK, C. J., M.A., PH.D., German
SKILTON, M. A., M.A., M.LITT., English
WOOD, T., M.A., B.D., Theology

**University of Wales Institute of Science and Technology (UWIST):** King Edward VII Ave., Cardiff, CF1 3NU; Tel.: Cardiff 42522; f. 1866 and formerly the Welsh College of Advanced Technology; incorporated by Royal Charter in 1967 as constituent institution of the University of Wales. Academic year: September to June. First Degree courses are given in five Schools of Studies: Applied Sciences, Arts, Business and Law, Engineering, Environmental Design, and Health and Life Sciences.

*President:* Sir JULIAN HODGE, K.ST.J., LL.D.
*Vice-President:* G. FORBES HAYES, C.ST.J., M.A., M.I.MECH.E.
*Principal:* A. F. TROTMAN-DICKENSON, M.A., PH.D., D.SC.
*Vice-Principal:* Prof. D. WALLIS, B.SC., F.B.PS.S.
*Registrar:* F. HARRIS-JONES, M.A.
Library: see Libraries.
Number of teachers: 267 (48 part-time).
Number of students: 2,970, including 354 postgraduates.
Publications: *Prospectus, Annual Report.*

DEANS:

*School of Applied Sciences:* Prof. J. KING, M.SC., M.R.I.N.A., M.N.I., M.R.IN., M.C.I.T.
*School of Arts, Business and Law:* Prof. R. MANSFIELD, PH.D.
*School of Engineering:* Prof. D. J. HARRIS, O.B.E., PH.D., C.ENG., F.I.E.E., F.I.E.R.E.
*School of Environmental Design:* Prof. A. R. LIPMAN, M.A., PH.D.
*School of Health and Life Sciences:* Prof. P. A. PARISH, M.B., CH.B., M.D., M.R.C.S., M.F.C.M., F.R.C.G.P.

PROFESSORS:

BATCHELOR, B. G., PH.D., C.ENG., M.I.E.E., Electronics
BATTY, J. M., B.A., M.R.T.P.I., Town Planning
BRATCHELL, D. F., PH.D., English
BROWN, E. D., LL.M., PH.D., Law
BRUTON, M. J., M.SC.ENG., D.I.C., M.R.T.P.I., M.I.H.E., M.C.I.T., Town Planning
BULL, A. T., PH.D., F.I.BIOL., Applied Biology
CADWALLADER, F. J. J., LL.M., PH.D., Law
COUPER, A. D., M.A., PH.D., F.C.I.T., M.R.IN., F.N.I., Maritime Studies
DAVIES, GETHYN, PH.D., Applied Economics
DAVIES, GLYN, B.A., M.SC.(ECON.), Applied Economics, Banking and Finance
DUNCAN, K. D., PH.D., F.B.PS.S., Applied Psychology
EDWARDS, R. W., D.SC., F.I.BIOL., M.I.W.P.C., Applied Biology
EYNON, J. M., F.R.I.B.A., F.S.A., Architecture
GEDDES, J. D., PH.D., C.ENG., F.I.C.E., F.ASCE., M.I.H.E., F.G.S., Civil Engineering and Building Technology
GOSS, R. O., M.A., PH.D., F.C.I.T., F.N.I., Maritime Studies
GROVES, R. E. V., M.SC., PH.D., F.C.A., Business Administration and Accountancy
HARRIS, D. J., O.B.E., PH.D., C.ENG., F.I.E.E., F.I.E.R.E., Physics, Electronics and Electrical Engineering
LIPMAN, A. R., M.A., PH.D., A.R.I.B.A., Architecture
JONES, E. E., PH.D., F.I.M.A., F.INST.P., Mathematics
KELLAWAY, I. W., PH.D., M.P.S., Pharmacy
KING, J., M.SC., M.R.IN., F.N.I., M.R.I.N.A., Maritime Studies
MANSFIELD, R., M.A., PH.D., Business Administration and Accountancy
MILLODOT, M., O.D., M.SC., PH.D., F.A.A.O., F.A.A.A.S., Optometry
O'SULLIVAN, P. E., PH.D., Architecture
PARISH, P. A., M.D., CH.B., M.R.C.S., F.R.C.G.P., Pharmacy
PARROTT, J. E., PH.D., D.SC., F.INST.P., Physics, Electronics and Electrical Engineering

U.K. (GREAT BRITAIN)

PATCHETT, K. W., LL.M., Law
SPENCER, P. S. J., PH.D., F.I.BIOL., M.P.S., Pharmacy
TOWILL, D. R., D.SC., C.ENG., M.I.PROD.E., F.I.E.R.E., Mechanical Engineering and Engineering Production
WALLIS, D., B.SC., F.B.PS.S., Applied Psychology
WILLIAMS, D. R., PH.D., D.SC., C.CHEM., F.R.S.C., Chemistry
WILLIAMS, F. W., M.A., PH.D., C.ENG., M.I.C.E., M.I.STRUCT.E., Civil Engineering and Building Technology

READERS:

ASKAM, V., PH.D., F.P.S., Pharmacy
BROWN, A., M.SC., PH.D., C.ENG., F.I.MECH.E., M.A.S.M.E., Mechanical Engineering and Engineering Production
FOULKES, D. L., LL.M., BAR.-AT-LAW, Law
HUGHES, R. E., M.A., PH.D., F.I.BIOL., Applied Biology
NICHOLLS, P. J., PH.D., C.CHEM., F.R.S.C., F.I.BIOL., Pharmacy
PARK, G. S., D.SC., PH.D., C.CHEM., F.R.S.C., Chemistry
RUSSELL, A. D., PH.D., D.SC., M.P.S., M.R.C.PATH., Pharmacy
THOMAS, D. S., M.A., PH.D., English
THOMAS, J. D. R., D.SC., C.CHEM., F.R.S.C., Chemistry
WATERS, R. T., PH.D., C.ENG., M.I.E.E., M.INST.P., Physics, Electronics and Electrical Engineering

## UNIVERSITY OF WARWICK

COVENTRY, CV4 7AL
Telephone: (0203)-24011.

Charter granted March 1965.

Academic year: October to December, January to March, April to June (three terms).

*Chancellor:* Lord Justice SCARMAN, P.C., O.B.E., M.A.

*Pro-Chancellor:* Sir ARTHUR VICK, O.B.E., PH.D.

*Vice-Chancellor:* J. B. BUTTERWORTH, J.P., D.L., M.A.

*Pro-Vice-Chancellors:* A. G. FORD, M.A., D.PHIL., B. BERGONZI, M.A., B.LITT., A. J. FORTY, PH.D., D.SC.

*Secretary and Registrar:* A. ROWE-EVANS, B.A.

*Academic Registrar:* M. L. SHATTOCK, M.A.

*Librarian:* P. E. TUCKER, M.A., B.LITT., A.L.A.

Number of teachers: 500.
Number of students: 5,250.

Annual Publications: *Guide to First Degree Courses*†, *Graduate Studies Prospectuses*†, *Vice-Chancellor's Report to Court*†.

PROFESSORS:

*Faculty of Arts:*
BERGHAHN, V. R., M.A., PH.D., History
BERGONZI, B., M.A., B.LITT., English
BOOTH, M. R., M.A., PH.D., Theatre Studies
CHARLTON, D. G., M.A., PH.D., French Studies
GARDNER, J. R., M.A., PH.D., F.S.A., History of Art
HARRISON, R. J., M.A., D.PHIL., Social History

HENNESSY, C. A. M., M.A., D.PHIL., History
MALLETT, M. E., M.A., D.PHIL., History
MULRYNE, J. R., M.A., PH.D., English
OSBORNE, J., PH.D., German Studies
PRESTON, J., M.A., B.LITT., English
RAWSON, C. J., M.A., B.LITT., English
SCARISBRICK, J. J., M.A., PH.D., History

*Faculty of Science:*
BHATTACHARYYA, K., M.SC., PH.D., Engineering (Manufacturing Systems)
BURKE, D. C., PH.D., Biological Sciences
BUTCHER, P. N., PH.D., Physics (Theoretical Physics)
BUXTON, J. N., M.A., Computer Science
CARTER, R. W., M.A., PH.D., Mathematics
CLARK, V. M., M.A., PH.D., Chemistry and Molecular Sciences
DOUCE, J. L., PH.D., D.SC., Engineering (Electrical Science)
EELLS, J., PH.D., Mathematics
ELLIS, R. J., PH.D., Biological Sciences
EPSTEIN, D. B. A., PH.D., Mathematics
FORTY, A. J., PH.D., D.SC., Physics
GREEN, J. A., PH.D., Mathematics
HARRISON, P. J., B.SC., Statistics
JENNINGS, K. R., M.A., D.PHIL., Chemistry and Molecular Sciences (Physical Chemistry)
JOHNSON, R. P., M.A., Engineering (Civil Engineering)
KELLY, D. P., PH.D., D.SC., Environmental Sciences
KEMP, T. J., M.A., D.PHIL., D.SC., Chemistry and Molecular Sciences
MCMILLAN, P. W., PH.D., D.SC.TECH., Physics
PARRY, W., M.SC., PH.D., Mathematics
PATERSON, M. S., M.A., PH.D., Computer Science
RAMSAY, T. A., B.SC., M.B., CH.B., F.R.F.P.S., M.R.C.P., F.R.C.S., F.F.C.M., Postgraduate Medical Education
RHODES, R. G., M.SC., PH.D., Engineering
SEYMOUR, E. F. W., M.A., D.PHIL., Physics
WALLBRIDGE, M. G. H., PH.D., Chemistry and Molecular Sciences (Inorganic Chemistry)
WHITEHOUSE, D. J., PH.D., Mechanical Engineering
WHITTENBURY, R., M.SC., PH.D., Biological Sciences
ZEEMAN, E. C., M.A., PH.D., F.R.S., Mathematics

*Faculty of Educational Studies:*
LAWRENCE, J. G., M.A., Education
SCHWARZENBERGER, R. L. E., M.A., PH.D., Science Education
SHIPMAN, M. D., PH.D., Education
SKEMP, R. R., M.A., PH.D., Education

*Faculty of Social Studies:*
ANNETT, J., M.A., D.PHIL., Psychology
ARCHER, MARGARET S., PH.D., Sociology
BAIN, G. S., M.A., D.PHIL., Industrial and Business Studies
COHEN, R., M.SC., PH.D., Sociology
COWLING, K. G., PH.D., Economics (Industrial Economics)
FAWTHROP, R. A., PH.D., Industrial and Business Studies (Financial Management)
FORD, A. G., M.A., D.PHIL., Economics
GHAI, Y. P., LL.M., Law
GRIFFITHS, A. PHILLIPS, B.PHIL., Philosophy
HARRISON, K. W. S., D.PHIL., Economics
HOULDEN, B. T., PH.D., Industrial and Business Studies
LEONARD, P. T., M.SC.(ECON.) Applied Social Studies
LIVELY, J. F., M.A., Politics
LOCKE, D. B., M.A., B.PHIL., Philosophy
MCAUSLAN, J. P. W. B., B.A., B.C.L., Law

WORLD OF LEARNING

MILLER, C. J., LL.M., Law
MILLER, M. H., M.A., PH.D., Economics
PETTIGREW, A. M., PH.D., Industrial and Business Studies (Organizational Behaviour)
ROBERTS, K., Economic Theory
SKIDELSKY, R., M.A., D.PHIL., International Studies
STACEY, MARGARET, B.SC.(ECON.), Sociology
STERN, N. H., M.A., D.PHIL., Economics
TOMLINSON, R. C., M.A., Industrial and Business Studies
TWINING, W. L., M.A., J.D., Law
URWIN, D. W., M.A., PH.D., Politics
WALLIS, K. F., M.SC.TECH., PH.D., Econometrics
WATERWORTH, J. D., B.SC.(ECON.), Industrial and Business Studies (Marketing)
WILSON, G. P., M.A., LL.B., Law

READERS:

*Faculty of Arts:*
BEAVER, H. L., M.A., English
BULLIVANT, R., PH.D., German Studies
GOODE, J. A., PH.D., English
GRANSDEN, K. W., M.A., English
HALL, H. G., M.A., PH.D., French
KAMEN, H. A. F., M.A., D.PHIL., History
KOCHAN, L., M.A., PH.D., History
LEWIS, G., M.A., D.PHIL., History
RIGHTER, W. H., M.A., B.LITT., English

*Faculty of Science:*
DALTON, H., PH.D., Biological Sciences
ELWORTHY, K. D., M.A., D.PHIL., Mathematics
GOLDING, B. T., M.SC., PH.D., Chemistry and Molecular Sciences
GRIFFITHS, D. E., M.A., PH.D., Chemistry and Molecular Sciences
HAWKES, T. O., M.A., PH.D., Mathematics
HUTCHINSON, D. W., PH.D., Chemistry and Molecular Sciences
MYKURA, H., PH.D., D.SC., Physics
PARK, D. M. R., M.A., PH.D., Computer Science
PRITCHARD, A. J., PH.D., Engineering (Control Theory)
ROURKE, C. P., M.A., PH.D., Mathematics
ROWLANDS, G., PH.D., Physics
SANDERSON, B. J., PH.D., Mathematics
SCHMIDT, K., DR.PHIL., Mathematics
SHURMER, H. V., PH.D., D.SC., Engineering
STONEHEWER, S. E., M.A., PH.D., Mathematics
WALTERS, P., D.PHIL., Mathematics
WOODLAND, H. R., M.A., D.PHIL., Biological Sciences (Genetics)

*Faculty of Social Studies:*
ANDERMAN, S. D., LL.M., M.SC., Law
BARRETT, D. C., S.J., PH.D., Philosophy
BOOTHROYD, H., B.SC., Industrial and Business Studies (Operational Research)
GALLIE, D., M.SC., PH.D., Sociology
HAACK, SUSAN W., B.PHIL., PH.D., Philosophy
HOLDCROFT, D., B.A., Philosophy
HYMAN, R., D.PHIL., Industrial and Business Studies
SEADE, J. K., D.PHIL., Philosophy
TRIGG, R. H., M.A., D.PHIL., Philosophy

ATTACHED RESEARCH INSTITUTES:

**Mathematics Research Centre:** f. 1965; Dir. Prof. E. C. ZEEMAN, M.A., PH.D.

**Centre for the Study of Social History:** f. 1968; Dir. Prof. R. J. HARRISON, M.A., D.PHIL.

UNIVERSITIES, POLYTECHNIC LEVEL INSTITUTIONS
U.K. (GREAT BRITAIN)

**Inter-University Institute of Engineering Control:** f. 1969; Dir. Prof. J. L. DOUCE, PH.D., D.SC., C.ENG., F.I.E.E.

**Centre for Research in Industry, Business and Administration:** f. 1969; Dirs. Prof. J. R. PERRIN, M.B.A., PH.D., Prof. R. C. TOMLINSON, M.A., C.ENG.

**Social Science Research Council Industrial Relations Research Unit:** f. 1969; Dir. Prof. G. S. BAIN, M.A., D.PHIL.

**Control Theory Centre:** f. 1970; Dir. A. J. PRITCHARD, PH.D.

**Centre for Micro-engineering and Metrology:** f. 1980; Dir. Prof. D. J. WHITEHOUSE, PH.D., C.ENG., M.I.E.E., F.I.PROD.E.

**Legal Research Institute:** f. 1978; Dir. Prof. Y. P. GHAI, LL.M.

**Mathematics Education Research Centre:** f. 1979; Dir. Prof. R. R. SKEMP, M.A., PH.D.

**Research Centre on the Mathematical Modelling of Clinical Tests:** f. 1979; Dir. Prof. A. G. MCDONALD, B.SC.

**Development Economics Research Centre:** f. 1980; Dir. Prof. N. H. STERN, M.A., D.PHIL.

**Institute for Employment Research:** f. 1981; Dir. R. M. LINDLEY, M.SC., PH.D.

## UNIVERSITY OF YORK

HESLINGTON, YORK, YO1 5DD

Telephone: 0904-59861.

Founded 1963.

Academic year: October to June (three terms).

*Chancellor:* Lord SWANN, M.A., PH.D., D.UNIV., F.R.S., F.R.S.E.
*Pro-Chancellors:* The Most Revd. and Rt. Hon. S. Y. BLANCH, M.A., A. S. RYMER, O.B.E., J.P., D.UNIV., L. E. WADDILOVE, C.B.E., J.P., D.UNIV.
*Vice-Chancellor:* Prof. S. B. SAUL, PH.D.

*Registrar:* ANNE RIDDELL.
*Librarian:* H. FAIRHURST, M.A.

Library: see Libraries.

Number of teachers: 320.
Number of students: 3,400.

Publications: *Undergraduate Prospectus†, Graduate Prospectus†* (annual).

PROFESSORS:
ARTHURS, A. M., M.A., D.SC., Mathematics
BERTHOUD, J. A., B.A., English
BLAKE, D. L., M.A., Music
BLOODWORTH, G. G., M.A., PH.D., Electronics
BOSSY, J. A., PH.D., History
BRONK, J. R., A.B., D.PHIL., Biochemistry
COOPER, R. A., M.A., Social and Economic Statistics
CORNISH, F. H. J., M.A., D.PHIL., Mathematics
CULYER, A. J., B.A., Economics
CURREY, J. D., M.A., D.PHIL., Biology
DOBSON, R. B., M.A., D.PHIL., History
DOSSER, D. G. M., B.SC.(ECON.), Economics
DUNSIRE, A., M.A., Politics
FEINSTEIN, C. H., PH.D., Economic and Social History
HAMPSON, N., M.A., D.UNIV., F.B.A., History
HARRIS, B. A., M.A., English
HEAVENS, O. S., PH.D., D.SC., D.UNIV., Physics
JONES, KATHLEEN, PH.D., Social Administration
LEECH, RACHEL M., M.A., D.PHIL., Biology
LEFF, G., PH.D., LITT.D., History
LE PAGE, R. B., PH.D., Language
LISTER, I., M.A., Education
MOODIE, G. C., M.A., Politics
MULKAY, M., M.A., PH.D., Sociology
NORMAN, R. O. C., M.A., D.SC., F.R.S., Chemistry
PEARSALL, D. A., M.A., English
PRUTTON, M., PH.D., Physics
PYLE, I. C., M.A., PH.D., Computer Science
RAHTZ, P. A., M.A., Archaeology
TAYLOR, L. J., M.A., Sociology
VENABLES, P. H., PH.D., D.SC., Psychology
WADDINGTON, D. J., PH.D., D.I.C., Chemical Education
WHITAKER, DOROTHY S., M.A., PH.D., Social Work
WILLIAMS, A. H., B.COM., Economics
WILLIAMSON, M. H., M.A., D.PHIL., Biology
WISE, D., O.B.E., B.ARCH., Architecture
WISEMAN, J., B.SC.(ECON.), Applied Economics
WOOLFSON, M. M., M.A., PH.D., D.SC., Theoretical Physics

READERS:
BURNETT-HALL, D. G., M.A., F.B.C.S., Computer Science
BUTTERWORTH, E. D., O.B.E., M.A., Community Work
CHADWICK, M. J., M.A., PH.D., Biology
COONEY, E. W., B.SC.(ECON.), Economic and Social History
CROSS, M. CLAIRE, M.A., PH.D., History
DODSON, G. G., M.SC., PH.D., Chemistry
GILBERT, B. C., M.A., D.PHIL., Chemistry
GODFREY, L. G., M.SC., Social and Economic Statistics
HALL, R., M.A., Philosophy
HARTLEY, K., PH.D., Economics
HESTER, R. E., D.SC., PH.D., Chemistry
HUTTON, J. P., M.A., Social and Economic Statistics
IONS, E. S. A., M.A., B.LITT., Politics
MAYNARD, A. K., B.PHIL., Social and Economic Statistics
MATTHEW, J. A. D., PH.D., Physics
MOODY, A. D., M.A., English
ROBARDS, A. W., PH.D., D.SC., Biology
SAWYER, M. C., M.SC.(ECON.), Economics
SHEIL-SMALL, T. B., PH.D., Mathematics
SIMMONS, P. J., M.SC.(ECON.), PH.D., Economics
WILSON, R. A., PH.D., Biology

ATTACHED INSTITUTES:
**Borthwick Institute of Historical Research:** St. Anthony's Hall, Peaseholme Green, York, YO1 2PW; Dir. Dr. D. M. SMITH, M.A., PH.D.

**Institute of Advanced Architectural Studies:** King's Manor, York, YO1 2EP; Dir. Prof. D. WISE, O.B.E., B.ARCH., DIP.T.P., R.I.B.A.

**Institute of Social and Economic Research:** University of York, Heslington, York, YO1 5DD; Dir. Prof. J. WISEMAN, B.SC.(ECON.).

**Centre for Medieval Studies:** Dirs. Prof. R. B. DOBSON, M.A., D.PHIL., Prof. D. A. PEARSALL, M.A.

**Centre for Southern African Studies:** Dir. C. R. HILL, M.A.

# POLYTECHNIC LEVEL INSTITUTIONS

## CITY OF BIRMINGHAM POLYTECHNIC

PERRY BARR, BIRMINGHAM, B42 2SU

Telephone: 021-356-6911.

Founded 1971.

Constituent Colleges: Birmingham College of Art, Birmingham College of Commerce, Birmingham School of Music, North Birmingham Technical College, South Birmingham Technical College, City of Birmingham College of Education, Bordesley College of Education, Anstey College of Physical Education.

*Director:* R. J. W. HAMMOND, B.A.

*Secretary:* W. S. GALE, D.M.A.
*Librarian:* M. M. HADCROFT, M.A., A.L.A., A.I.INF.SC.

Library of 300,000 vols.

Number of teachers: 740.
Number of students: 8,922 (including part-time).

DEANS:
*Faculty of Art and Design:* P. L. FIELD.
*Faculty of the Built Environment:* D. W. EDDEN.
*Faculty of Business Studies and Law:* H. W. H. CAWTHORNE.
*Faculty of Education and Teacher Training:* D. E. HELLAWELL.
*Faculty of Engineering and Science:* R. R. WHITWORTH.
*Faculty of Social Sciences and Arts:* C. SPECTOR.

HEADS OF DEPARTMENTS:
BALL, R. W., Mathematics and Statistics
BARLOW, B. J., History of Art and Complementary Studies
CHOYCE, A. G., Business and Management Studies
COOK, B., Fine Art
CORBETT, I., Mechanical and Production Engineering
DALTON, P. J., Law
DAVIS, W. A., Government and Economics
FITZJOHN, B. S., English and Foreign Languages
FOX, E. S., Librarianship

HANCOCK, N., Education Studies and Undergraduate Teacher Training
HARDIE, P., Visual Communication
HEMMING, G., Electrical Engineering
HITCHEN, J. M., Science
LEYLAND, D. G., Planning and Landscape
McARDLE, I. W. M., Sociology and Applied Social Studies
POTTER, R. W., Three Dimensional Design
PRICE, E., Art Education and Foundation Studies
SKINNER, D. W. H., Construction and Surveying
TOMLINSON, D., Fashion and Textiles
WATKINS, B. R., Curricular Studies and Postgraduate Teacher Training

*Birmingham School of Music:*
CARUS, L.

## BRIGHTON POLYTECHNIC
MOULSECOOMB,
BRIGHTON, BN2 4AT

Telephone: (0273)-693655.

Founded 1970.

Constituent Colleges: Brighton College of Art, Brighton College of Technology, Brighton College of Education, East Sussex College of Higher Education.

*Director:* G. R. HALL, B.SC., F.ENG., F.R.I.C., S.F.INST.E.
*Deputy Director:* J. C. PARKINSON, M.B.E., T.D., PH.D., F.R.S.C., F.P.S.
*Secretary and Clerk to the Council:* G. R. GARDENER, M.TH.
*Head of Learning Resources:* C. L. HEWITT, B.SC.(ECON.), M.A.

Library of 330,000 vols.

Number of teachers: 515 (full-time).
Number of students: 4,091 (full-time).

### DEANS AND FACULTY CHAIRMEN:

*Faculty of Art and Design:* R. PLUMMER, A.R.C.A.
*Faculty of Education Studies:* K. L. GARDNER, M.A., F.I.M.A.
*Faculty of Engineering and Environmental Studies:* F. LEE, B.SC.TECH., C.ENG., F.I.C.E.
*Faculty of Management and Informatics:* A. BLACKLEDGE, M.PHIL., F.I.M.A.
*Faculty of Natural and Life Sciences:* J. D. DONALD, B.SC., C.CHEM., F.R.S.C., F.L.S.
*Faculty of Social and Cultural Sciences:* IDA M. WEBB, M.ED., PH.D.

### HEADS OF DEPARTMENTS:

BARKER, I. R. L., M.A., PH.D., C.CHEM., F.R.S.C., Chemistry
BELL, R. G., M.SC., A.F.I.M.A., Mathematics (acting)
BURKE, G. M., M.ED., Chelsea School of Human Movement
CLARKSON, M. W., B.A., Education (Primary)
COBB, A., N.D.D., Visual Communication
CRAMP, B. G. W., M.A., Community Studies
CROOK, J. M., Three Dimensional Design
DAVIS, D., A.T.D., PH.D., Art Teacher Education Centre
FITZGERALD, P. G., B.SC., M.INST.M., Business Studies
HAYNES, R., M.PHIL., Art History
HEATER, D. B., B.A., Humanities
HOGG, W. K., PH.D., F.I.E.E., Electrical and Electronic Engineering
IRWIN, G., Fine Art (Painting and Sculpture)
LOMAX, J. P., M.A.(ARCH.), PH.D., A.R.I.B.A., Architecture and Interior Design
LONGLEY, D., M.SC.(TECH.), PH.D., C.ENG., F.I.E.E., Computing and Cybernetics
MAILLARDET, F. J., PH.D., C.ENG., M.I.MECH.E., Mechanical and Production Engineering
MARES, C., M.A., Language Studies
McBETH, G. W., PH.D., Physics
MELLOR, V., B.A., Education (Secondary) (acting)
MILES, J., M.A., Fashion and Textiles
NUNNS, R. E., M.A., F.C.A., Finance and Accountancy
PARKER, M. S., M.SC., PH.D., M.P.S., M.I.BIOL., Pharmacy
QUINN, J., M.PHIL., C.ENG., F.I.PROD.E., F.B.I.M., F.I.I.M., Management Centre
ROSE, P. D., N.D.D., A.T.D., Combined Arts
RUTLAND, P. J., PH.D., F.I.O.B., F.I.A.S., A.M.A.T.M., Building
STAYNES, B. W., PH.D., C.ENG., Civil Engineering (acting)
TURNER, C., B.SC., A.L.A., M.I.I.S., Librarianship
WHITE, H. J., M.A., Education (Eastbourne)

## BRISTOL POLYTECHNIC
COLDHARBOUR LANE,
FRENCHAY,
BRISTOL, BS16 1QY

Telephone: (0272) 656261.

Founded 1969.

*Director:* Dr. WILLIAM BIRCH.
*Chief Administrative Officer:* E. KINDER, F.C.I.S., F.B.I.M.
*Academic Registrar:* Miss H. K. GREENAWAY, B.A.
*Librarian:* J. C. HARTAS, B.COM., A.L.A.

Library of 300,000 vols.

Number of teachers: 700.

Number of students: 4,500 full-time and sandwich, 4,100 part-time.

### HEADS OF DEPARTMENTS:

*Faculty of Accounting, Business and Management:*
BOLT, G. J., B.SC.(ECON.), M.A., F.INST.M., F.B.I.M., Business Studies
GILLIES, J. P., F.C.A., F.C.M.A., Accounting and Finance
HAXELL, J. D., B.A., D.M.S., Public Services Management
HAZLEHURST, R. J., M.SC., C.ENG., M.I.PROD.E., Management Studies
HOLMES, P. W. DE LANCE, B.SC.(ECON.), M.SC., F.B.I.M., F.I.I.M., South West Regional Management Centre

*Faculty of Art and Design:*
CHALKER, J. B., A.R.C.A., R.W.A., A.S.I.A., Design
CLEMENTS, J., N.D.D., Graphic Design
LANCASTER, J., M.PHIL., N.D.D., A.T.D., D.A.E., F.S.A.E., Art Education (School)
PASCOE, E., D.F.A.(LOND.), F.R.B.S., R.W.A., Fine Art

*Faculty of Computing, Mathematics and Science:*
CHUDLEY, C. T., PH.D., M.INST.P., F.I.M.A., Computer Studies and Mathematics
GREEN, T., PH.D., C.CHEM., F.R.S.C., M.I.BIOL., Science

*Faculty of Education:*
ELLIS, H. B., M.ED., Professional Studies in Education
WOODMAN, P. F., B.A., M.ED., Education Studies (acting)

*Faculty of Humanities, Social Science, Languages and Law:*
MARSHALL, D. M., M.A., F.I.L., Modern Languages
OLIVER, W. P., M.A., LL.B., Law
TAUBMAN, R., M.A., Humanities
TOZER, W., V.R.D., M.A., B.SC.(ECON.), A.M.B.I.M., Economics and Social Science

*Faculty of Technology:*
COCKS, F. D., PH.D., C.ENG., M.I.E.E., Engineering
CUSACK, M. M., M.PHIL., M.C.I.O.B., F.B.I.M., M.I.ENV.SC., Construction and Environmental Health
HUTTON, B. J., B.A., M.SC., M.I.H.E., M.R.T.P.I., Town and Country Planning
SPEDDING, A. H., PH.D., C.ENG., M.I.STRUCT.E., A.R.I.C.S., A.I.Q.S., Surveying

## COVENTRY (LANCHESTER) POLYTECHNIC
PRIORY ST.,
COVENTRY, CV1 5FB

Telephone: (0203) 24166.

Founded 1970.

*Director:* G. V. HOLROYDE, B.SC., A.R.C.O.
*Deputy Director:* M. E. FOSS, PH.D., C.CHEM., F.R.S.C.
*Assistant Director (Administration):* P. D. HEATH, M.A.
*Librarian:* J. FLETCHER, M.A., A.L.A.

Library of 200,000 vols.

Number of teachers: 544.

Number of students: 4,567 full-time, 1,358 part-time, total 5,925.

### DEANS:

*Faculty of Art and Design:* D. C. BROADHEAD, A.R.C.A., F.S.I.A.D.
*Faculty of Engineering:* W. B. PALMER, M.A., PH.D., C.ENG., F.I.MECH.E.
*Faculty of Applied Sciences:* B. RAY, M.SC., PH.D., C.ENG., M.I.E.E., F.INST.P.
*Faculty of Social Science and Public Policy:* O. W. FURLEY, M.A., B.LITT.
*Faculty of Business:* B. NICOL, M.A., PH.D., M.I.P.M.

### HEADS OF DEPARTMENTS:

*Faculty of Art and Design:*
BRICKWOOD, A., M.DES., R.C.A., A.S.I.A., Industrial Design
HARRISON, A. E., M.I.S.A.D., M.S.T.D., Graphic Design
PHILLIPS, D., LL.B., L.G.S.M., F.R.S.A., Art History and Communication
SAXTON C., D.F.A., Art
STAIR, N., B.A., Centre for Media Studies

*Faculty of Engineering:*
BELLAMY, N. W., PH.D., C.ENG., F.I.E.E., Electrical and Electronic Engineering
HARVEY, S. J., PH.D., C.ENG., M.I.MECH.E., Combined Engineering

STOUT, K., PH.D., Production Engineering
STRINGER, P. E., PH.D., C.ENG., F.I.E.E., Systems and Control
WALKER, H. E., M.ENG., C.ENG., F.I.C.E., F.I.MUN.E., F.I.O.B., Civil Engineering and Building
WALLIS, J. D., M.A., S.M., C.ENG., F.I.MECH.E., MEM.A.S.M.E., Mechanical Engineering

*Faculty of Applied Science:*
BRAITHWAITE, G. R., M.SC., F.S.S., F.I.M.A., Statistics and Operational Research
COOPER, R., M.A., D.PHIL., F.I.BIOL., Biological Sciences
JAMES, D. J. G., PH.D., F.I.M.A., Mathematics
LOADER, J. J., M.SC., PH.D., Computer Science
OUBRIDGE, J. O. V., PH.D., C.CHEM., F.R.S.C., Applied Chemistry
RANDALL, R. F. Y., PH.D., F.INST.P., A.R.P.S., Materials and Energy Science
SMITH, D. E., PH.D., F.R.G.S., Geography

*Faculty of Social Science and Public Policy:*
CRISPIN, G., M.PHIL., Urban and Regional Planning
FURLEY, O. W., M.A., B.LITT., Politics and History
HURREN, H. A., M.A., D.PHIL., F.I.L., Language Studies
JUNOD, Miss V., M.A., M.A.T.S.W.E., Applied Social Studies

*Faculty of Business:*
NABIEL, E., M.A.(POL.SC.), PH.D., D.SC.(ECON.), Economics
NICOL, B. N., M.A., PH.D., M.I.P.M., Management Studies
ROYALL, D. V. E., M.A., LL.B., Legal Studies
SPURRELL, D. J., B.SC., Business Studies

## DUNDEE COLLEGE OF TECHNOLOGY

BELL ST., DUNDEE, DD1 1HG

Telephone: 0382-27225.

Founded 1911.

*Principal:* H. G. CUMING, M.A., PH.D., D.I.C., C.ENG., F.I.M.A., M.R.AE.S.

Library of 74,000 vols.
Number of teachers: 153 full-time, 70 part-time.
Number of students: 1,500 full-time, 850 part-time.

Faculties of Engineering and Construction (depts. of civil engineering, electrical and electronic engineering, mechanical and industrial engineering, surveying and building), Management and Social Studies (depts. of accountancy and economics, business studies), Science (depts. of mathematics and computer studies, molecular and life sciences, physics, textile science, audio-visual and reprographic unit).

## GLASGOW COLLEGE OF TECHNOLOGY

COWCADDENS RD., GLASGOW, G4 0BA

Telephone: 041-332-7090.

Founded 1971.

Academic year: September to June.

*Director:* REGINALD J. BEALE, PH.D., C.ENG., F.I.MECH.E.
*Depute Directors:* B. R. McMANUS, PH.D., C.ENG., M.I.PROD.E., N. G. MEADOWS, PH.D., C.ENG., M.I.E.E., F.B.I.M.

Number of teachers: 350.
Number of students: 3,400 full-time, 4,000 part-time.
Publications: *Prospectus of Full-time Courses, Prospectus of Part-time Courses* (annually).

HEADS OF DEPARTMENTS:

BENSON, L., A.C.M.A., F.B.I.M., Management Studies
BEZZANT, R. J., B.SC., C.CHEM., F.R.S.C., Chemistry and Metallurgy
BUSH, P. W., PH.D., Humanities
CAREY, R., M.A., Politics
COLLINGTON, E., C.A., A.C.M.A., A.T.I.I., Finance and Accounting
CURTIS, G. H., PH.D., M.INST.P., C.ENG., M.I.E.E., F.I.E.R.E., Electrical and Electronic Engineering
DALGLEISH, R., M.SC., Economics
DICKSON, A., PH.D., Sociology
DOBBIE, H. G., B.SC.(ECON.), A.S.C.C., Business Administration
EDGAR, D., M.ED., F.B.C.S., Computer Studies
GILLOTT, H. F., M.SC.(TECH.), A.M.C.T., F.B.O.A., Ophthalmic Optics
JAMIESON, A. M., B.SC., A.F.I.M.A., Mathematics
KELLINGTON, S. H., PH.D., Physics
LOGAN, W. W., M.A., Health and Nursing Studies
MacCONNELL, J. T., PH.D., M.I.BIOL., Biological Studies
PHILLIPS, R., PH.D., Psychology
STEELE, J. T., B.A., F.C.I.I., Banking and Insurance
THOMSON, F., B.SC., C.ENG., A.R.C.S.T., F.I.MECH.E., Mechanical and Civil Engineering
WRIGHT, M., LL.M., M.B.I.M., Law and Public Administration

## HATFIELD POLYTECHNIC

HATFIELD, HERTFORDSHIRE

Telephone: 07072-68100.
Telex: 262413.

Founded 1952 as Hatfield College of Technology, attained present status 1969.

*Director:* Sir NORMAN LINDOP, M.SC., F.R.S.C. (to April 1982).
*Deputy Director:* J. M. ILLSTON, PH.D., D.SC., C.ENG., F.I.C.E.
*Librarian:* D. E. BAGLEY, M.A., F.L.A.

Library of 150,000 vols.
Number of teachers: 400.
Number of students: 4,500.

DEANS:

*School of Engineering:* R. BARRETT, PH.D., C.ENG., F.I.E.E.
*School of Humanities:* D. HUTCHINSON, M.A.
*School of Information Sciences:* R. W. SHARP, PH.D., A.R.C.S., F.B.C.S.
*School of Natural Sciences:* W. BOARDMAN, PH.D., M.SC., C.CHEM., F.R.S.C., A.R.T.C.S.

*School of Business and Social Sciences:* R. S. L. MARTIN, J.P., LL.B., M.A., BAR.

ATTACHED INSTITUTES:

**Hatfield Polytechnic Observatory:** Bayfordbury, Hertford, Herts.; f. 1970; teaching of astronomy at all levels and research particularly into aspects of photo-electric and infra-red astronomy; library of 200 vols. and a number of periodicals; Dir. J. C. D. MARSH, M.SC., C.ENG., M.I.E.R.E., F.R.A.S.

**National Institute for Careers Education and Counselling:** f. 1975 by Careers Research and Advisory Centre and the Polytechnic to advance the development of guidance services in the U.K. through education and training, research and development work.

**National Reprographic Centre for Documentation:** f. 1967 with a grant from the Office for Scientific and Technical Information (Dept. of Education and Science); govt. support now under British Library; advisory and consultancy service on microform and reprographic systems and techniques; abstracting and information service.

## HUDDERSFIELD POLYTECHNIC

QUEENSGATE, HUDDERSFIELD, W. YORKSHIRE, HD1 3DH

Telephone: 0484-22288.

Founded 1841, formerly Huddersfield College of Technology, attained present status 1970.

*Rector:* K. J. DURRANDS, M.SC., C.ENG., F.I.MECH.E., F.I.E.E., F.I.PROD.E.
*Registrar:* M. E. BOND, M.A.

Library of c. 240,000 vols.
Number of teachers: 520.
Number of students: 4,000 full-time, 2,500 part-time.

DEANS:

*Faculty of Arts:* (vacant).
*Faculty of Business:* P. S. HAILS, B.SC.(ECON.), F.INST.M., M.B.I.M.
*Faculty of Education:* D. LEGGE, PH.D., F.B.PS.S.
*Faculty of Engineering:* R. G. BARWICK, B.SC., C.ENG., M.I.E.E.
*Faculty of Sciences:* R. LIVINGSTONE, PH.D., C.CHEM., F.R.I.C.
*Research:* M. S. BURNIP, M.SC., PH.D., F.T.I., A.M.S.C.T.

HEADS OF DEPARTMENTS:

BARWICK, R. G., B.SC., C.ENG., M.I.E.E., Systems
BELCHER, M. G., N.D.D., F.B.D.S., F.S.I.A.D., F.R.S.A., Art and Design
BULLINGHAM, J. M., M.SC., PH.D., Electrical and Electronic Engineering
BURNIP, M. S., M.SC., PH.D., F.T.I., A.M.S.C.T., Textile Industries
FLINN, J. W., B.SC., Postgraduate and In-Service F.E. Studies
FORWARD, A., PH.D., R.I.B.A., F.R.I.A.S., Architecture and Construction Studies

U.K. (GREAT BRITAIN)

GLEW, G., M.SC., F.H.C.I.M.A., M.I.BIOL., A.I.F.S.T., Catering Studies
GRANT, B., B.COM., M.ED., Pre-Service F.E. Studies
HAILS, P. S., B.SC.(ECON.), F.INST.M., M.B.I.M., Management Studies
HEWITT, C. R., M.LITT., M.B.I.M., Extra-Mural Centres
JACOBS, A., M.A., Music
LEA, E. C., B.SC.(ECON.), Marketing Studies
LEGGE, D., PH.D., F.B.PS.C., Behavioural Sciences
MURPHY, B., M.SC., A.I.M.T.A., D.M.A., A.M.B.I.M., Accountancy and Professional Studies
NEWBOLD, D. E., M.A., B.LITT., D.PHIL., Education
O'CONNELL, J., B.A., History and Political Studies
SHAW, R., B.SC., M.A., C.ENG., F.B.C.S., F.I.M.A., A.F.R.AE.S., Computer Studies and Mathematics
TWIGG, E., B.A., M.ED., Staff Development
WHITE, W., M.SC., PH.D., Physical Education

## KINGSTON POLYTECHNIC
PENRHYN RD.,
KINGSTON UPON THAMES,
SURREY, KT1 2EE
Telephone: 01-549 1366.

Founded 1970.

Constituent Colleges: Gipsy Hill College of Education, Kingston College of Art, Kingston College of Technology.

*Director:* L. E. LAWLEY, PH.D., F.INST.P.
*Deputy Director:* A. H. S. MATTERSON, M.A., D.PHIL.
*Registrar:* R. B. HILL, M.A., M.SC.
*Librarian:* N. POLLARD, B.A., A.L.A.

Library of 300,000 vols.

Number of teachers: 450.
Number of students: 5,100.

Publications: Prospectuses, *Academic Awards: Research Report* (biennially).

HEADS OF SCHOOLS AND DEPARTMENTS:

BERRY, D., B.A., DIP.ARCH., F.R.I.B.A., Architecture
BROOKER, Mrs. D., A.R.C.A., Fashion
COBB, C. H., PH.D., Arts and Languages
COEKIN, J. A., PH.D., C.ENG., F.I.E.E., Electrical and Electronic Engineering
DANIEL, S. S., M.SC.(ECON.), Economics and Politics
ESTEVE-COLL, Mrs. E. A. L., B.A., A.L.A., Learning Resources
FYFE, D. J., PH.D., Mathematics
GODFREY, R. J., PH.D., Education Studies
KENNEA, T. D., PH.D., Geography
LLOYD, J. M., B.SC.(ECON.), Business
LLOYD JONES, P., PH.D., A.R.C.S., Three-Dimensional Design
LONG, R., PH.D., C.CHEM., F.R.S C., Chemical and Physical Sciences
MILLAR, J., A.R.C.A., R.B.A., Fine Art
POTTS, C. E., N.D.D., A.S.T.D., F.R.S.A., F.S.I.A. Graphic Design
REED, D. M., B.SC. (ECON.), M.A., DIP.ECON.POL.SC., Sociology
RENTON, B. D., LL.M., PH.D., A.C.I.S., Law
SIMM, D. H., B.SC.(ENG.), C.ENG., F.I.C.E., M.I.W.E.S., Civil Engineering
SMITH, M. P., PH.D., Liberal Studies

TOWNSEND, J. P., PH.D., C.ENG., M.I.MECH.E., F.I.PROD.E., Management Education
WHITE, Mrs. D. P., M.SC., F.R.I.C.S., Surveying
WHITTEN, D. G.; B.SC., A.R.C.S., F.G.S., Geology
WOOLVET, G. A., M.TECH., D.I.C., C.ENG., M.I.MECH.E., M.R.AE.S., M.I.E.E., M.INST.M.C., Mechanical Aeronautical and Production Engineering

## LEEDS POLYTECHNIC
CALVERLEY ST.,
LEEDS, LS1 3HE
Telephone: (0532) 462971.

Founded 1970.

*Director:* P. J. NUTTGENS, M.A., PH.D., A.R.I.B.A.
*Head of Administration:* A. J. H. HAMBLIN, PH.D., C.CHEM., M.R.S.C., F.B.I.M.
*Librarian:* J. H. FLINT, F.L.A.

Library of 300,000 vols.

Number of teachers: 725 full-time, 400 part-time.
Number of students: 5,000 full-time, 5,000 part-time.

HEADS OF SCHOOLS:

*Accounting and Applied Economics:* R. J. BULL, B.SC.(ECON.), A.C.C.A.
*Architecture and Landscape:* W. T. BRADSHAW, DIP.ARCH., F.R.I.B.A.
*Carnegie School of Physical Education and Human Movement Studies:* C. E. BOND, M.ED., D.L.C.
*Constructional Studies:* G. A. GRANT, B.SC.TECH., C.ENG., F.I.C.E., F.I.MUN.E., F.I.O.B.
*Creative Arts and Design:* F. RUBNER, F.S.I.A.D., F.R.S.A.
*Education:* A. L. NICHOLAS, M.A., F.I.L., BAR.-AT-LAW.
*Electrical Engineering:* J. N. HUTCHINSON, M.SC.(ENG.), C.ENG., M.I.E.E.
*Health and Applied Science:* K. R. FELL, PH.D., F.P.S., M.I.BIOL.
*Home and Institutional Studies:* R. H. BENSON, DIP.TEX.IND., M.B.I.M., M.H.C.I.M.A.
*Humanities and Contemporary Studies:* A. MCGREGOR, B.A.
*International Studies:* B. B. WOODMAN, PH.D., F.I.L.
*Law:* J. F. MYERS, M.A., LL.B., BAR.-AT-LAW.
*Librarianship:* D. E. DAVINSON, B.SC. (ECON.), D.P.A., F.L.A.
*Management and Business Studies:* A. C. HALL, B.A.(ECON.), F.C.I.S., F.I.M.C., F.B.I.M., I.C.M.A.
*Mathematics and Computing:* J. J. KIELY, M.SC., F.I.M.A.
*Mechanical and Production Engineering:* R. E. SCHOFIELD, M.SC., PH.D., C.ENG., M.I.MECH.E., F.I.PROD.E., A.M.C.S.T.
*Social Studies:* J. G. HAGGETT, LL.B., A.A.P.S.W.
*Town Planning:* R. A. MORDEY, B.A., M.C.D., M.R.T.P.I.

## LEICESTER POLYTECHNIC
P.O.B. 143, LEICESTER, LE1 9BH
Telephone: (0533) 551551.

Founded 1969.

*Director:* D. P. BETHEL, A.R.W.A., A.T.D., F.S.A.E., F.S.I.A.D.
*Deputy Director:* S. COTSON, PH.D., C.CHEM., F.R.S.C.
*Secretary:* (vacant).
*Librarian:* S. R. GADSDEN, M.L.S., A.L.A.

Number of teachers: 600.
Number of students: 5,000 full-time, 3,000 part-time.

DEANS:

*Faculty of Art and Design:* Mrs. M. B. W. STEWART, M.A.
*Faculty of Business:* A. CLARK, LL.B., Barrister, A.C.I.S.
*Faculty of Education, Humanities and Social Science:* F. W. BARTLETT, B.A.
*Faculty of Science:* F. NEWCOMBE, PH.D., A.R.C.S.T., M.I.BIOL., M.P.S.
*Faculty of Technology and Construction:* D. L. MUNDEN, B.SC., C.TEXT., F.T.I.

HEADS OF SCHOOLS AND DEPARTMENTS:

*Faculty of Art and Design:*
HODGE, A. W., DES.R.C.A., M.S.I.A.D., Industrial Design
HOSKIN, J., Fine Art
MORGAN, P., DES.R.C.A., Fashion and Design
REA, P., A.R.C.A., F.S.T.D., F.R.S.A., Graphics
STEWART, M., M.A., Art History
WITTS, N., B.A., Expressive Arts

*Faculty of Business:*
BARON, P. J., M.S., Economics and Accounting (acting)
CLARK, A., LL.B., BAR.-AT-LAW, A.C.I.S., Law
CONWAY, D. E., M.A., F.B.C.S., F.I.M.A., Mathematics, Computing and Statistics

*Faculty of Education, Humanities and Social Science:*
BARTLETT, F. W., B.A., Social and Community Studies
HIORNS, J. N., B.A., Humanities
HONEY, J. R. DE S., D.PHIL., Education

*Faculty of Science:*
ELLIOT, M. C., PH.D., M.I.BIOL., Life Sciences
GRUNWELL, P., M.A., PH.D., Speech Pathology
NEWCOMBE, F., PH.D., A.R.C.S.T., M.I.BIOL., M.P.S., Pharmacy
OXLEY, D. P., PH.D., M.INST.P., Physics
POLLOCK, J. M., PH.D., D.I.C., F.R.S.C., Chemistry

*Faculty of Technology and Construction:*
CHIDDICK, D. M., M.SC., A.R.I.C.S., Building, Surveying and Land Economy
MATOFF, T. R., D.ARCH., R.I.B.A., Architecture
MCKAY, J., B.SC., C.ENG., M.I.E.E., Electronic and Electrical Engineering
MUNDEN, D. L., B.SC., C.TEXT., F.T.I., Textile and Knitwear Technology
PICKEN, D. J., M.A., PH.D., C.ENG., F.I.MECH.E., M.I.PROD.E., Mechanical and Production Engineering

## LIVERPOOL POLYTECHNIC
RODNEY HOUSE,
70 MOUNT PLEASANT,
LIVERPOOL, L3 5UX

Telephone: (051)-708-6620.

Founded 1970.

*Rector:* GERALD BULMER, M.A., PH.D., C.CHEM., F.R.S.C.
*Deputy Rector:* C. M. ATKINSON, PH.D., C.CHEM., F.R.S.C.
*Senior Administrative Officer:* HUGH BEGLEY, D.M.A., F.C.I.S.
*Academic Registrar:* J. M. CHARLES, M.A.
*Librarian:* D. H. REVILL.

Number of teachers: 630 full-time.

Number of students: 4,623 full-time and sandwich; 492 short full-time and block release, 2,814 part-time.

Faculties of: Construction; Engineering; Science; Art and Design; Business and Management Studies; Humanities and Social Studies; Education and Community Studies.

## POLYTECHNIC OF CENTRAL LONDON
309 REGENT ST.,
LONDON, W1R 8AL

Telephone: (01)-580-2020.

Founded 1970.

*Rector:* Prof. COLIN ADAMSON, M.SC. (ENG.), D.SC., C.ENG., F.I.E.E., F.I.E.E.E.
*Secretary and Chief Administrative Officer:* H. G. JELF, C.B.E., M.A.
*Librarian:* NEIL F. MCLEAN, B.A., A.L.A.

Library of 250,000 vols.

Number of students: 3,715 full-time, 7,144 part-time, 12,500 short course.

### DEANS:
*School of Communication:* T. B. JONES, M.A.
*School of Engineering and Science:* Prof. G. HOLT, PH.D.
*School of the Environment:* F. C. GARRISON, M.ED.
*School of Languages:* Prof. P. P. NEWMARK, B.A.
*School of Law:* M. A. COMMONS, M.A., LL.M.
*School of Management Studies:* C. E. CHAMBERS, B.A.
*School of the Social Sciences and Business Studies:* A. S. TAYLOR, M.SC. (ECON.)
*London Regional Management Centre:* P. J. O'BRIEN, T.D., M.A.

## CITY OF LONDON POLYTECHNIC
117/119 HOUNDSDITCH,
LONDON, EC3A 7BU

Telephone: (01)-283 1030.

Founded 1970.

*Provost:* J. MICHAEL EDWARDS, Q.C., M.A., B.C.L., F.B.I.M.

*Chief Administrative Officer:* PETER BURRELL, I.P.F.A., M.B.I.M.
*Chief Librarian:* Mrs. R. PANKHURST, M.A., A.L.A.

Number of teachers: 400 full-time, 500 part-time.

Number of students: 15,000.

Publications: *Guide for Applicants* (annually), *Report* (annually), *Research Review*† (biennially).

### HEADS OF DEPARTMENTS:
*School of Business Studies:*
BELCHER, M., B.A., A.I.L., Secretarial Studies
GERSON, R., B.A., Politics
HARVEY, M., M.SC., F.R.S.A., A.C.C.A., F.C.I.S., Accountancy and Taxation
OLIVER, Lady, M.A., BARR., Law
PALMER, O. W., M.SC., M.INST.M.S.M., M.I.P.A., M.A.A., Management and Marketing
POWELL, W. R., B.A., F.R.G.S., Modern Languages
REBMANN-HUBER, Z., M.A.SC., M.SC., Management Science
STEBBINGS, W. H., F.C.I.S., F.C.I.T., Transport and Insurance
TOFT, K. S., M.SC.(ECON.), A.I.B., Economics and Banking
WHITE, C. L., PH.D., Sociology

*School of Science and Technology:*
CLARKE, M., PH.D., D.SC.(ENG.), C.ENG., C.CHEM., F.R.S.C., F.I.M., F.I.CORR.T., F.I.M.F., Metallurgy and Materials
CROWNE, C. W. P., PH.D., C.CHEM., M.R.S.C., Chemistry
CURRIE, L. C., B.A., C.ENG., A.M.I.A.A.P., A.B.PS.S., A.M.I.PROD.E., Psychology
DROMGOOLE, N. A., M.A., General Studies
GODDARD, J., PH.D., A.R.C.S., D.I.C., F.INST.P., Physics
MEIRION-JONES, G. I., M.PHIL., PH.D., Geography
MORRIS, K. M. L., N.D.A., M.SC., PH.D., Biological Sciences
SKELHORN, R. R., PH.D., F.G.S., Geology

*School of Art:*
HUNTLEY, D. W., F.R.B.S., N.D.D., A.T.C., Fine and Applied Art
LAWS, T., Silversmithing, Jewellery and Allied Crafts

*School of Navigation:*
KEMP, J. F., PH.D., F.R.I.N.

## POLYTECHNIC OF NORTH LONDON
HOLLOWAY, LONDON, N7 8DB.

Telephone: (01)-607-2789.

Founded 1971.

Departments at: Holloway Rd., London, N.7; Essex Rd., London, N.1; Highbury Grove, London, N.5; Kentish Town, N.W.5.

*Director:* Dr. D. MACDOWALL.
*Secretary:* P. KNIGHT, F.C.I.S.
*Academic Registrar:* R. F. HALL, B.SC.
*Librarian:* S. FRANCIS, F.L.A.

Library of over 150,000 vols.

Number of teachers: 490.

Number of students: 5,500, full- and part-time.

### HEADS OF DEPARTMENTS:
BARTON, Dr. J. C., Physics
BRANDON, Dr. P., Geography and Geology
BRISCOE, W., Environmental Design (acting)
CHAMPNESS, C. J., Law
CLARK, C. R., Business Studies
DORWARD, Dr. N. M., Accounting and Administrative Studies
GLAZER, Dr. J., National College of Rubber Technology
GOODMAN, Dr. E., Mathematics
JAMES, R., Extension Studies
JONES, S., Teaching Studies
KLIGER, Dr. B. N., Food and Biological Sciences
McGARRY, K., Librarianship
MEADOWS, R. G., Electronic and Communications Engineering
OWSTON, Dr. P. G., Chemistry
PARRY, N. C., Sociology
TONKS, P., Management Studies

## NORTH EAST LONDON POLYTECHNIC
ROMFORD RD., STRATFORD,
LONDON, E15 4LZ

Telephone: (01)-555-0811.

Founded 1970.

Organized in three precincts: West Ham Precinct, Romford Rd., Stratford, London, E15 4LZ; Waltham Forest Precinct, Forest Rd., Walthamstow, London, E17 4JB; Barking Precinct, Longbridge Rd., Dagenham, Essex, RM8 2AS; and in the Anglian Regional Management Centre, Danbury Park, Danbury, nr. Chelmsford, Essex, CM3 4AT.

*Director:* Dr. G. S. BROSAN, T.D., PH.D., C.ENG., F.I.E.E., F.I.PROD.E., F.I.M.A.
*Chief Administrative Officer:* C. MILNER, M.PHIL., A.M.B.I.M., A.M.I.P.M., M.I.T.O.
*Librarian:* P. W. PLUMB, J.P., F.L.A.

Library of over 300,000 vols. and 3,300 current periodicals. Also houses the library of the former National Institute of Industrial Psychology.

Number of teachers: *c.* 775 full-time.

Number of students: 4,050 full-time and 3,600 part-time.

### DEANS:
*Faculty of Art and Design:* P. J. BOURNE.
*Faculty of Business:* A. HALE.
*Faculty of Engineering:* J. THOMPSON.
*Faculty of Environmental Studies:* Dr. J. L. TAYLOR.
*Faculty of Arts:* J. F. ROSSITER.
*Faculty of Human Sciences:* Dr. J. RADFORD.
*Faculty of Science:* G. WRIGHT.
*Anglian Regional Management Centre:* B. A. LITTLEWOOD.

### HEADS OF DEPARTMENTS:
ACKROYD, Dr. G. F., Mechanical Engineering (B).
AL NAIB, S. K., Civil Engineering (W.F.)
BEEDHAM, G. E., Biology (W.H.)
BOADLE, A. J., Management Development (A.R.M.C.)

CASSELL, J. B., Chemical Engineering (B.)
CAUSON, A. C., Computing Services (W.F.)
CHADWICK, G. F., Education (B.)
CRICKMORE, L. S., Humanities (B.)
DAVIES, J. L., Management (Public Services) (A.R.M.C.)
DYE, P., Science Degree Course (W.H.)
FRITH, N. L., Architecture (W.F.)
HALE, A., Systems and Computing (B).
HARGREAVES, M. K., Chemistry (W.H.)
HILL, S. F., Services to Industry (A.M.R.C.)
HOLLWEY, J. R., Land Surveying (W.F.)
JACKSON, S. A., Production Engineering (B.)
JONES, R., Health and Social Studies (W.H.)
LICHTENSTEIN, E. A., Law (B.)
LOWNDES, R., Manpower Studies (A.R.M.C.)
MOSERT, H., Accounting and Finance (B.)
NEVILLE, J. E., Paramedical Sciences (W.H.)
OVERALL, J. R., General Surveying and Construction (W.F.)
PEPPER, J. V., Mathematics (W.H.)
PLANT, J., Business Studies (B.) (acting)
POWNEY, J., Education (B.)
PRESTON, A. E., Dean of Students (B.)
REICH, B., Psychology (W.H.)
RUSTIN, M., Sociology (W.H.)
SALMON, M. J., Applied Economic Studies (B.)
SIM, A. C., Electrical Engineering (B.)
WHITEREAD, T., Humanities (B.)
WRIGHT, G., Applied Physics (W.H.)

## MANCHESTER POLYTECHNIC
ALL SAINTS BUILDING,
ALL SAINTS,
MANCHESTER, M15 6BH

Telephone: 061-2286171.

Founded 1970.

Academic year: September to July.

*Director:* K. GREEN, M.A.
*Deputy Director:* D. HAMER, PH.D., F.R.S.A.
*Assistant Directors:* F. R. HOLTERMAN, A.R.C.A., F.R.S.A. (Academic); C. H. BROOKES, PH.D., M.I.BIOL., A.R.S.C. (Personnel).
*Secretary:* R. O. YEO, B.A.
*Librarian:* I. ROGERSON, M.L.S., A.L.A.

Number of teachers: 1,021.

Number of students: 5,901 full-time, 1,769 sandwich, 5,634 part-time.

### DEANS:
*Faculty of Art and Design:* D. WAIN-HOBSON, A.R.C.A.
*Faculty of Community Studies:* D. JOHNSON, B.A., F.C.I.S. (acting).
*Faculty of Humanities:* D. J. MELLING, M.A. (acting).
*Faculty of Management and Business:* J. H. HEPBURN, B.SC., F.B.C.S., M.B.I.M.
*John Dalton Faculty of Technology:* P. R. FALKNER, M.A., C.CHEM., F.R.S.C.
*Hollings Faculty:* G. WILSON, PH.D., C.ENG., M.I.CHEM.E.

HEADS OF DEPARTMENTS:
*Faculty of Art and Design:*
BILLANY, K. D., Visual Studies
CONNOLLY, A. L. J., Comunication Arts and Design
DARKE, M. H., Architecture and Landscape
HENSLER, D., Fine Art
JEWITT, T. S., Printing Technology
MORRELL, W. A., Textiles/Fashion
THOMAS, H. A. C., Three Dimensional Design

*Faculty of Community Studies:*
DAY, A. E., Library and Information Studies
FLETCHER, D. E., Environmental and Geographical Studies
JOHNSON, D., Applied Community Studies
ROBERTS, D. A., Social Science

*Faculty of Humanities:*
GARRETT, B. W., Languages
HOPKIN, J. H., English and History
JEREMIAH, D., History of Art and Design
MELLING, D. J., General Studies

*Faculty of Management and Business:*
BAMFORD, G. G., Economics and Economic History
JOWETT, A., Accounting and Finance
SWANN, K., Management
WEBB, M. H. J., Business Studies

*John Dalton Faculty of Technology:*
BASHFORD, V. G., Polymer Technology
CALDWELL, R., Biological Sciences
FIDO, A. T., Metallurgy
MATHER, J., Mechanical, Production and Chemical Engineering
MEECH, B. R., Physics, Mathematics and Computing
ROBINSON, P. J., Chemistry
SIMCOX, G. E., Electrical and Electronic Engineering

*Hollings Faculty:*
GIBSON, W. G., Clothing Design and Technology
SMITH, B. R., Food Manufacture and Distribution
WILSON, G., Hotel, Catering and Institutional Management

EXTRA FACULTY UNITS:
*Law:* S. B. MARSH, J.P., B.COM., LL.B., PH.D., BARR.-AT-LAW.
*Staff Development and Educational Methods Units:* B. HOLLINSHEAD, B.SC., M.I.BIOL.
*Institute of Advanced Studies:* J. LANGRISH, M.SC., PH.D.

## MIDDLESEX POLYTECHNIC
ADMISSIONS OFFICE,
114 CHASE SIDE, SOUTHGATE,
LONDON, N14 5PN

Telephone: 01-886 6599.

Designated 1973; comprises the former Enfield and Hendon Colleges of Technology, Hornsey College of Art, New College of Speech and Drama, Trent Park College of Education and the College of All Saints.

*Director:* R. M. W. RICKETT, PH.D., F.R.S.C.
*Deputy Director:* M. M. EDWARDS, PH.D., M.B.I.M.

*Academic Registrar:* D. THATCHER, B.SC.
*Head of Library Services:* J. COWLEY, B.A., F.L.A.

DEANS:
*Art and Design:* P. GREEN, A.R.E., A.S.I.A., A.T.C.
*Business Studies and Management:* D. HARPER, B.A.
*Education and Performing Arts:* A. D. GRADY, M.A., PH.D.
*Engineering, Science and Mathematics:* J. OSBORNE-MOSS, B.SC.(ENG.), C.ENG., F.I.MECH.E.
*Humanities:* R. GUNTER, M.A. (acting).
*Social Science:* A. J. HOLT, B.A.(PHIL.), B.A.(SOC.).

## NAPIER COLLEGE
COLINTON RD., EDINBURGH
EH10 5DT

Telephone: 031-447 7070.

SIGHTHILL COURT,
EDINBURGH EH11 4BN

Telephone: 031-443 6061.

Founded 1964.

Academic year: August to July.

*Principal:* J. DUNNING, C.B.E., B.SC., M.ED., M.A., A.M.C.T., C.ENG., M.I.M., F.E.I.S.
*Associate Principal:* A. RAE, M.A., F.I.L., F.B.I.M.
*Senior Depute Principal:* R. TEALE, M.A., C.ENG., F.I.E.E., F.INST.P.
*Academic Registrar:* R. W. STEVENSON, M.A.
*Librarian:* J. L. BATE, M.A., F.L.A.

Number of teachers: 390.

Number of students: *c.* 3,300 full-time, 3,400 part-time.

DEANS:
*Faculty of Humanities:* A. BARRON, B.A., M.B.I.M.
*Faculty of Professional Studies:* J. MURRAY, B.SC., A.R.C.S.T., C.ENG., F.I.PROD.E., F.I.MECH.E., F.B.I.M.
*Faculty of Science:* D. F. LEACH, B.SC., F.I.M.A., M.INST.P.
*Faculty of Technology:* W. A. TURMEAU, PH.D., C.ENG., F.I.MECH.E.

HEADS OF DEPARTMENTS:
*Faculty of Humanities:*
BUTTERWORTH, D. N., M.A., Music
CAMPBELL, I., B.A., M.I.O.P., L.C.G., Printing and Publishing (acting)
DAVIDSON, H. L., M.B.I.M., Catering and Hotel Studies
DRESNER, H., M.A., Languages
MCARTHUR, P. M., A.C.I.I., Physical Education
PASHLEY, D., F.I.I.P., F.R.P.S., Photography
RENTON, R. S., A.S.I.A.D., F.B.I.D., F.R.S.A., F.S.A.SCOT., Design

*Faculty of Professional Studies:*
BOWIE, A., B.A., C.A., F.C.C.A., F.B.I.M., Accounting
FIELD, D. J., B.A., Law
JOLLY, J. D., M.B.E., M.A., Management

LINDSAY, D. W., M.LITT., Industrial Studies and Social Studies
MCCULLOCH, J. C., B.COM., M.A., Business Studies
MILLAR, G. P., D.S.C., C.A., Banking and Insurance
STEWART, D. W. N., Office Administration

*Faculty of Science:*
ANDERSON, K. J., PH.D., F.I.BIOL., C.CHEM., F.R.S.C., Biological Science
CAMPBELL, A. G., M.SC., F.INST.P., Physics
CHUTER, I. H., M.SC., M.B.C.S., Computer Studies
FIELDING, G. T., M.SC., F.I.MA., F.S.S., Mathematics
MILBURN, G. H. W., PH.D., C.CHEM., F.R.S.C., M.B.I.M., Chemistry

*Faculty of Technology:*
BEARDS, P. H., B.SC., C.ENG., F.I.E.E., Electrical and Electronic Engineering
CORP, R., M.ENG., C.ENG., M.I.STRUCT.E., Civil Engineering
DALE, A., B.SC., F.C.I.O.B., Building and Surveying
WATSON, A., T.D., M.SC., PH.D., C.ENG., F.I.MECH.E., M.I.E.E., Mechanical Engineering
YOUNG, A. R., M.SC., C.ENG., M.I.PROD.E., M.I.MAR.E., Industrial Engineering

## NEWCASTLE UPON TYNE POLYTECHNIC
ELLISON BUILDING,
ELLISON PLACE,
NEWCASTLE UPON TYNE,
NE1 8ST

Telephone: (0632)-326002.

Founded 1969.

*Director:* Prof. LAING BARDEN, PH.D., D.SC., F.I.C.E., F.G.S.
*Chief Administrative Officer:* R. HOPKINSON, B.SC.
*Librarian:* Prof. K. G. E. HARRIS, M.A., F.L.A.

Library of 420,000 vols.
Number of teachers: 750 (full-time).
Number of students: 5,470 full-time, 3,750 part-time.

DEANS:
*Faculty of Art and Design:* Prof. T. BROMLY, A.T.D.
*Faculty of Business and Management:* G. MITCHELL, B.A., F.B.I.M., F.R.S.A.
*Faculty of Community and Social Studies:* A. R. KING, PH.D.
*Faculty of Construction and Applied Science:* G. C. RENDALL, B.SC., C.ENG., M.I.C.E.
*Faculty of Education:* R. L. SNOWDON, M.ED., F.R.S.A.
*Faculty of Engineering:* G. NEEDHAM, M.SC., PH.D., C.ENG., M.I.MECH.E., A.M.C.T.
*Faculty of Humanities:* J. COLLERTON, B.A.
*Faculty of Professional Studies:* Prof. J. REAR, M.A.

HEADS OF SCHOOLS:
*Faculty of Art and Design:*
BROMLY, Mrs. M., A.T.D., Fashion
BROMLY, Prof. T., A.T.D., Fine Art
BURKE, T. A., N.D.D., F.R.S.A., Industrial Design
DOWNING, Mrs. J., A.T.D., D.A.E.S., Creative and Performing Arts
OLIVER, J. N., B.SC., Art History
SLADE, J., M.SC., A.R.C.A., M.S.I.A.D., Graphic Design

*Faculty of Business and Management:*
CASSELLS, D., M.SC., Business Analysis
GIBSON, Prof. R. D., M.SC., PH.D., Mathematics, Statistics and Computing
HARRIS, N. D., M.SC.TECH., M.B.I.M., F.I.I.M., F.M.S., F.I.M.H., Operations Management
LYNN, R., M.A., Marketing and Distribution
POTTS, A., M.A., M.ED., Business Administration

*Faculty of Community and Social Studies:*
EVERITT, Mrs. K. A. M., M.A., Social Work and Community Studies
HANNON, J., B.SC., Occupational Studies
VEIT-WILSON, J. H., M.A., Applied Social Science
WATSON, D. W., M.PHIL., PH.D., Behavioural Science

*Faculty of Construction and Applied Science:*
BOOTH, D., PH.D., C.CHEM., F.R.S.C., Chemical and Life Sciences
NEWALL, A. J., PH.D., C.ENG., M.I.GAS.E., Construction and Building Services
RENSHAW, W. E., A.R.I.C.S., F.R.G.S., Surveying

*Faculty of Education:*
CORNISH, M., M.A., Teaching Studies
GOLIGHTLY, Mrs. L. C., M.SC., M.I.BIOL., Home Economics Studies
MURPHY, F., M.A., Education Studies

*Faculty of Engineering:*
ARMSTRONG, C., PH.D., F.I.MECH.E., C.ENG., Power Engineering
RITCHEY, A., B.SC., C.ENG., M.I.E.E., Electronic Engineering
STRAFFORD, Prof. K. N., M.SC., PH.D., F.I.CORR.T., F.I.M., C.ENG.
WILSON, J., PH.D., M.INST.P., Physics

*Faculty of Humanities:*
BUSWELL, R. J., B.A., Geography and Environmental Studies
CALDWELL, W., F.L.A., Librarianship
HUBSCH, P., M.A., Modern Languages
PAGE, H. M., M.A., PH.D., English and History

*Faculty of Professional Studies:*
ELCOCK, H. J., M.A., M.PHIL., PH.D., Government
KENNY, P. H., LL.M., Solicitor, Law
LOMBARD, W., B.SC.(ECON.), F.C.A., Accountancy
ROPER, B. A., M.A.(ECON.), F.R.S.S., Economics

## NORTH STAFFORDSHIRE POLYTECHNIC
COLLEGE RD.,
STOKE ON TRENT
Telephone: 0785-45531.

BEACONSIDE, STAFFORD
Telephone: 0782-52331.

MADELEY, NR. CREWE
Telephone: 0785-53511.

Founded 1970.

*Director:* J. F. DICKENSON, PH.D., C.ENG., F.I.MECH.E.
*Deputy Directors:* W. E. LEWIS, PH.D., C.ENG., M.I.E.E., R. S. PARADISE, B.SC.(ENG.), C.ENG., F.I.MECH.E., K. B. THOMPSON, M.A., M.ED.
*Secretary and Chief Administrative Officer:* H. C. JOHNSTONE, M.A.
*Academic Registrar:* R. A. BOTT, B.SC.(ECON.), D.M.A.
*Librarian:* E. S. WATERSON, M.A., F.L.A.

Number of teachers: 480.
Number of students: 2,800 full-time, 2,200 part-time.

HEADS OF DEPARTMENTS:
*Ceramic Technology:* G. J. GITTENS, PH.D., C.CHEM., F.R.S.C., F.I.CERAM.
*Chemistry:* W. K. WILFE, M.SC., C.CHEM., F.R.S.C.
*Physics:* J. B. WILLIAMS, M.SC., F.INST.P., M.I.NUC.E.
*Art History and Complementary Studies:* Mrs. F. I. SWANN, B.A.
*Fine Art:* C. MELBOURNE, A.R.C.A., F.R.S.A.
*Graphic Design and Printing:* C. SWANN, F.S.I.A.
*Three-Dimensional Design (Ceramics):* K. E. W. WRIGHT, A.T.D., M.S.I.A.
*Business and Legal Studies:* A. D. RAMSAY, B.COM., DIP.COM., M.B.I.M.
*Economics:* J. L. BRIDGE, PH.D.
*Management Studies:* A. J. H. KITLEY, M.SC., D.M.S., M.I.P.M., F.B.I.M.
*Education and Teaching Studies:* J. KENNEDY, M.A., F.R.HIST.S.
*Humanities:* J. K. SHELTON, M.A., PH.D., DIP.ED., A.T.C.M.
*International Relations and Politics:* A. E. THORNDIKE, J.P., M.SC., PH.D.
*Geography and Sociology:* G. KAY, M.A., PH.D., F.R.G.S.
*Electrical and Electronic Engineering:* (vacant).
*Mechanical and Civil Engineering:* E. JACKSON, M.SC.(TECH.), C.ENG., M.I.MECH.E.
*Mining Engineering:* T. BRERETON, PH.D., C.ENG., F.I.MIN.E., M.I.M.M., F.INST.F.
*Bio-Medical Engineering Unit:* O. F. PHOENIX, B.SC.(ENG.), C.ENG., F.I.MECH, A.R.AE.S.
*Computing:* H. L. W. JACKSON, M.SC., PH.D., M.INST.P., F.I.M.A., F.B.C.S.
*Mathematics:* H. G. MARTIN, PH.D., F.I.M.A., F.B.C.S., M.INST.P.
*Computer Centre:* D. M. MELLUISH, M.A., M.SC., F.B.C.S., A.F.I.M.A.
*Physical Education:* A. HARGREAVES, M.A.

## OXFORD POLYTECHNIC
GYPSY LANE, HEADINGTON,
OXFORD, OX3 0BP
Telephone: (0865)-64777.

Founded 1970, formerly Oxford College of Technology; amalgamated with Lady Spencer Churchill College of Education 1976.

*Director:* B. L. TONGE, PH.D., C.CHEM., F.R.S.C., M.B.I.M.

U.K. (GREAT BRITAIN)

*Deputy Director:* V. T. OWEN, M.A., B.LITT.
*Academic Secretary:* R. M. TULLOCH, M.A.
*Registrar:* M. S. LEWIS, PH.D.
*Librarian:* P. F. JACKSON, A.L.A.
   Library of 160,000 vols.
   Number of teachers: 440.
   Number of students: 3,592 full-time, 1,000 part-time.

DEANS:

*Faculty of Architecture, Planning and Estate Management:* H. D. THOMAS, M.A., M.C.D., M.R.T.P.I.
*Faculty of Educational Studies:* C. I. CULLINGFORD, M.A., M.PHIL.
*Faculty of Educational Studies:* J. M. TAYLOR, M.A.
*Faculty of Technology:* P. D. GODDARD, M.SC., C.ENG., M.I.C.E., M.I.STRUCT.E., F.I.O.B.
*Faculty of Modern Studies:* C. A. HORN, PH.D., M.SC., LL.B., M.B.I.M., F.C.I.S., F.O.W.S.O.M.

HEADS OF DEPARTMENTS:

BARBER, C. R., Social Studies
CARTER, F. L., Educational Development
CLARK, B. E., Mathematics, Statistics and Computing
CLARK, R. J., Management and Business Studies
DORWARD, L. F., Engineering
FRANCIS, E. C., Design
GLASSON, J., Town Planning
GODDARD, P. D., Construction
HARDING, A. J., Modern Languages
HODGES, M., Education
MADGWICK, P., Law, Politics and Economics
MAGUIRE, R., Architecture
MOBBS, D. R. A., Biology
MURRAY, R. G., Humanities
O'CONNOR, J., Catering Management
REA, W. J., Geology and Physical Science
TAYLOR, V. W., Estate Management

## PAISLEY COLLEGE OF TECHNOLOGY
HIGH STREET, PAISLEY,
RENFREWSHIRE, PA1 2BE
   Telephone: 041-887 1241.
   Telex: 778951 PCT LIB.

Founded 1897.

Academic year: September to June.

*Principal:* THOMAS M. HOWIE, B.SC., C.ENG., F.I.C.E.
*Vice-Principal:* THOMAS C. DOWNIE, PH.D., C.CHEM., F.R.S.C.
*Registrar:* JOHN M. OSWALD, M.B.E., B.SC., A.R.C.S.T.
*Librarian:* HAMISH MACLACHLAN, M.A., F.L.A.
   Number of teachers: 231 full-time.
   Number of students: 2,300 full-time, 300 part-time.
   Publications: *College Prospectus, Annual Report, Research Report.*

DEANS:

*Faculty of Engineering:* Prof. IAIN A. MACLEOD, PH.D., C.ENG., M.I.C.E., M.I.STRUCT.E.

*Faculty of Science:* Prof. JOHN C. SMYTH, PH.D., F.I.BIOL., F.L.S.
*Faculty of Social Planning and Management Sciences:* PETER J. SLOANE, PH.D.

HEADS OF DEPARTMENTS:

ANDERSON, Prof. J., M.SC., C.ENG., F.I.MECH.E., F.I.PROD.E., Mechanical and Production Engineering
BARR, Prof. L. W., PH.D., F.INST.P., F.R.S.E., Physics
BURNSIDE, Prof. R. R., PH.D., F.I.M.A., Mathematics and Computing
DAVIS, Prof. L. E., PH.D., C.ENG., F.I.E.E., S.M.I.E.E., Electrical and Electronic Engineering
FOSTER, Prof. J. O., M.A., PH.D., Politics and Sociology
MACLEOD, I., PH.D., C.ENG., M.I.C.E., M.I.STRUCT.E., Civil Engineering
MILLINGTON, Prof. A. F., B.SC., F.R.I.C.S., Land Economics
SHELDON, Prof. H. N., M.A., Social Studies
SLOANE, P. J., PH.D., Economics and Management
SMYTH, Prof. J. C., PH.D., F.I.BIOL., F.L.S., Biology
TRUSCOTT, Prof. T. G., PH.D., C.CHEM., F.R.S.C., Chemistry

ATTACHED INSTITUTES:

*Alcohol Studies Centre:* Dir. W. M. SAUNDERS, M.PHIL.
*Local Government Unit:* Dir. R. YOUNG, M.A.
*Centre for Liaison with Industry and Commerce:* Dir. J. A. WYLIE, B.SC., C.CHEM., M.R.S.C.
*Materials and Components Developing and Testing Association:* Dir. E. DOWNEY, B.SC., C.ENG., M.I.C.E., M.I.STRUCT.E., M.INST.H.E.
*Microelectronics Educational Development Centre:* Dir. Dr. P. WILLIAMS, PH.D., M.INST.P., C.ENG., M.I.E.E.
*Scottish School of Non-Destructive Testing:* Dir. W. MCEWAN, B.SC., C.ENG., M.I.MECH.E., M.INST.W.

## PLYMOUTH POLYTECHNIC
DRAKE CIRCUS,
PLYMOUTH, PL4 8AA
   Telephone: (0752)-21312.

Founded 1970.

*Director:* R. F. ROBBINS, PH.D., C.CHEM., F.R.I.C.
*Deputy Directors:* I. C. CANNON, PH.D.; Capt. G. R. HUGHES, M.B.E., M.C.INST.T., F.N.I.
*Chief Administrative Officer:* R. G. BARKER, M.A.
*Head of Learning Resources Centre:* I. D. SIDGREAVES, B.A., A.L.A.
   Number of staff: 380.
   Number of students: 3,100 full-time and sandwich, 1,800 part-time.
   Publications: *Annual Report†, Prospectuses.*

DEANS:

*Faculty of Maritime Studies:* D. H. MOREBY, PH.D., M.N.I.
*Faculty of Science:* K. C. C. BANCROFT, PH.D., C.CHEM., F.R.S.C., M.I.ENV.SCI.

WORLD OF LEARNING

*Faculty of Technology:* C. M. GILLETT, J.P., PH.D., M.INST.P., C.ENG., M.I.E.E.
*Business School:* S. H. STARKS, M.SC.
*Faculty of Social Science:* G. PAYNE, M.A.

HEADS OF DEPARTMENTS:

*Faculty of Maritime Science:*
FIFIELD, L. W., F.R.I.N., F.N.I., M.C.I.T., Maritime Science
GREGORY, I., M.N.I., Marine Technology
RICH, C. A., M.SC., D.M.S., F.N.I., M.C.I.T., A.M.B.I.M., Shipping and Transport
*Faculty of Science:*
ANGUS, R. K., D.PHIL., M.INST.P., Environmental Sciences
GOODRIDGE J. C., PH.D., Geographical Sciences
HEATH, L. A. F., PH.D., F.I.BIOL., M.I.ENV.SCI., Biological Sciences
*Faculty of Technology:*
HENSON, C. S., B.SC.(ENG.), A.G.C.I., C.ENG., M.I.E.E., Communications Engineering
HOWARTH, M. J., PH.D., F.I.M.A., Mathematics, Statistics and Computing
KENNEDY, C. K., M.SC., PH.D., C.ENG., M.I.C.E., Civil Engineering
RABLEY, D. R. S., B.SC.(ENG.), C.ENG., F.I.MECH.E., M.I.MAR.E., M.I.PROD.E., M.B.I.M., Mechanical Engineering
WEBSTER, B. R., B.SC.(ENG.), C.ENG., F.I.E.E., F.I.E.R.E., Electrical Engineering
*Plymouth Business School:*
FROST, R. D., B.A., M.B.A., Management Studies
HARVEY, D. A., M.SC., I.P.F.A., Business Studies
*Social Science:*
GIARCHI, G. G., M.A., C.Q.S.W., Social Work
LEE, A. N., PH.D., Social and Political Studies
WOOKEY, P. E., PH.D., Psychology

## PORTSMOUTH POLYTECHNIC
MUSEUM RD.,
PORTSMOUTH, PO1 2QQ
   Telephone: (0705)-827681.

Founded 1870 as Portsmouth School of Science and Art.

*President:* W. DAVEY, C.B.E., PH.D., F.R.I.C.
*Deputy President:* R. PARKER, PH.D., F.INST.P.
*Vice-Presidents:* D. J. WILLIAMS, B.SC., M.A., A.K.C., P. S. HASKELL, M.B.E., J.P., M.SC., PH.D., P. F. MILLS, B.A., M.SC., F.I.M.A.
*Secretary and Registrar:* Brig. B. R. BIGGS, F.B.I.M.
*Librarian:* W. G. GALE, B.A., A.L.A.
   Library of 350,000 vols.
   Number of teachers: 700.
   Number of students: 5,376 full-time and sandwich, 955 part-time.

HEADS OF DEPARTMENTS, FACULTIES AND SCHOOLS:

BRANDON, P. S., M.SC., A.R.I.C.S., Surveying
BROADBENT, G. H., B.A.(ARCH.), A.R.I.B.A., Architecture

CAHM, E. S. H., B.A., Languages and Area Studies
CHANDLER, D. C., PH.D., W.SCH., C.ENG., F.I.MECH.E., Mechanical Engineering and Naval Architecture
DELLOW, F., M.PHIL., C.ENG., F.I.E.E., Electronic and Electrical Engineering
GRIFFIN, J. W., PH.D., C.CHEM., F.R.S.C., Chemistry and Geology
HIBBERT, F. A., M.A., PH.D., Biological Sciences
HYMAN, S., PH.D., F.C.I.S., M.B.I.M., Management Studies
LEWIS, O. J., M.A., M.SC., A.F.I.M.A., Mathematics (acting)
MILLARD, G. C., M.A., PH.D., Historical and Literary Studies
PERKS, F., PH.D., F.P.S., C.CHEM., F.R.I.C., D.B.A., Pharmacy
PODOLSKI, T. M., M.COM., PH.D., Economics
POWELL, M. T. G., B.SC., M.INST.P., Computing Centre
RAWKINS, T. H., B.A., M.I.B.G., Geography
ROLLS, I. F., M.A.(ED.), A.R.C.S., M.INST.P., Educational Studies
SCANE, J. G., M.SC., F.INST.P., Physics
STEAD, P. A., B.SC., C.ENG., M.I.C.E., M.I.W.E.S., Civil Engineering
TAYLOR, N., A.T.C., Fine Art
VAIL, J. R., M.SC., PH.D., D.SC., C.ENG., F.I.M.M., F.G.S., Geology
WRIGHT, R. W. G., M.SC.(ECON.), M.B.S.A., Social Studies

## PRESTON POLYTECHNIC
CORPORATION ST.,
PRESTON, PR1 2TQ

Telephone: (0772)-22141.
Founded 1956 as Harris College, 1973 as Preston Polytechnic.

Academic year: September to July.

*Director:* H. D. LAW, PH.D., C.CHEM., F.R.S.C.
*Deputy Directors:* S. SKIDMORE, PH.D., C.CHEM., F.R.S.C., G. T. FOWLER, M.A.
*Chief Administrative Officer:* T. G. GOODWIN, M.A.
*Librarian:* J. R. EDGAR, M.A., F.L.A.

Number of teachers: 380.
Number of students: 2,520 full-time, 3,000 part-time.

Publications: prospectus of full-time courses†, prospectus of part-time courses†.

### DEANS:
*Faculty of Art and Design:* T. METCALFE, A.R.C.A., A.S.I.A.
*Faculty of Business and Management:* B. G. BOOTH, M.SC., F.S.S.
*Faculty of Science and Technology:* J. J. BETTS, PH.D., C.CHEM., F.R.S.C.
*Faculty of Social Studies and Humanities:* G. T. FOWLER, M.A. (acting).

### HEADS OF DEPARTMENTS:
*Faculty of Business and Management:*
LIVESEY, Prof. F., B.A.(ECON.), Economics and Business Studies
SQUIRES, T. J., M.SC., F.B.I.M., Management Studies
THOMAS, P. A., LL.M., Law
WALLIS, R. W., B.COM., I.P.F.A., Accounting and Finance
*Faculty of Science and Technology:*
CLAPP, D. M., PH.D., C.ENG., M.R.AE.S., F.I.MECH.E., Mechanical and Production Engineering
PALMER, A., B.SC.(TECH.)., C.ENG., M.I.E.E., Electrical and Electronic Engineering
RYAN, T. M., B.SC., F.R.I.C.S., F.I.Q.S., Construction and Urban Studies
SHORT, A. M., PH.D., F.INST.M.C., F.INST.P., Sciences
WALSH, D. W., M.SC., Mathematics, Statistics and Computing

*Faculty of Social Studies and Humanities:*
HENIG, S., M.A., Social Studies
PROBYN, H. E., M.PHIL., Language and Humanities
YOUNG, P. M., B.A., M.SC., Psychology

ATTACHED INSTITUTE:
*Lancastrian School of Management:* Eastcliff, Preston; Dean E. K. LANGHAM, B.SC.(ECON.), C.ENG., M.I.MECH.E., F.I.PROD.E.

## ROBERT GORDON'S INSTITUTE OF TECHNOLOGY
SCHOOLHILL,
ABERDEEN AB9 1FR

Telephone: 0224-574511.

*Principal:* PETER CLARKE, PH.D.

Library of 135,000 vols.
Number of teachers: 270.
Number of students: 3,000 full-time, 3,000 part-time.

Faculties of Arts, Engineering, and Science Technology. Schools of art, architecture, business management, chemistry, electronic and electrical engineering, hotel and institutional administration, home economics, librarianship, mathematics, mechanical and off-shore engineering, nutrition, pharmacy, physics, social studies.

## SHEFFIELD CITY POLYTECHNIC
POND ST., SHEFFIELD S1 1WB

Telephone: (0742)-20911.

Founded 1969.
Constituent Colleges: Sheffield Polytechnic, Sheffield City College of Education, Totley-Thornbridge College of Education, Lady Mabel College of Education.

Academic year: September to July.
*Principal:* Rev. Canon G. TOLLEY, M.SC., PH.D., F.R.S.C., C.B.I.M.
*Deputy Principal:* D. THACKER, B.SC., C.ENG., F.I.M.
*Assistant Principal (Personnel and Resource Management):* A. R. CORBETT, J.P., M.I.P.M., M.B.I.M.
*Assistant Principal (Academic and Student Affairs):* J. C. EARLS, PH.D., C.ENG., F.I.E.E., M.B.I.M.
*Secretary:* A. M. DAVIS, B.A.
*Librarian:* D. T. LEWIS, M.ED., A.L.A.

Library of 440,000 vols.
Number of teachers: 780.
Number of students: 6,000 full-time.

### DEANS:
*Faculty of Art and Design:* J. T. BRIGHTON, M.A.
*Faculty of Business and Management Studies:* C. J. SUTTON, M.A., PH.D.
*Faculty of Social Studies:* R. V. BAILEY, B.A.
*Faculty of Education:* G. Q. CRAIG, M.A.
*Faculty of Humanities:* R. N. L. ABSALOM, B.A., F.I.L.
*Faculty of Engineering:* A. F. FULWOOD, B.SC.(ENG.), C.ENG., F.I.C.E., F.I.STRUCT.E., F.I.O.B.
*Faculty of Science:* M. GOLDSTEIN, B.SC., PH.D., C.CHEM., F.R.S.C.

### HEADS OF DEPARTMENTS:
*Faculty of Art and Design:*
BRIGHTON, J. T., M.A., History of Art
MACDONALD, B., B.A., Sculpture
TOWNLEY, J., D.F.A., A.T.D., A.R.E., Painting and Printmaking
TYSSEN, J. K., DES.R.C.A., Design
*Faculty of Business and Management Studies:*
GLADWELL, D. C., M.A., F.R.S.A., F.H.C.I.M.A., Hotel and Catering Studies and Home Economics
LEWIS, A. L., B.SC.(ECON.), Management Studies
SUTTON, C. J., M.A., PH.D., Economics and Business Studies
WILMOTT, R. A., B.SC.(ECON.), A.C.I.S., Accountancy and Company Administration
WOOD, E. G., B.COM., M.I.M.C., M.B.I.M., Director, Sheffield Centre for Innovation and Productivity
*Faculty of Social Studies:*
BAILEY, R. V., B.A., Applied Social Studies
CHALLINOR, J., B.ED., S.R.N., S.C.M., Health Studies
HAIGH, R. H., B.SC.(ECON.), M.A., Political Studies
HEBDEN, R. E., M.A., PH.D., Geography and Environmental Studies
LEAKER, A. M. D., B.SC., M.A., DIP.T.P., F.R.I.C.S., M.R.T.P.I., A.I.M.H., A.M.B.I.M., Urban and Regional Studies
*Faculty of Education:*
ALDERSON, G. J. K., M.A., PH.D., Physical Education and Human Movement Studies
CARLSON, B., M.A., Education Studies
CRAIG, G. Q., M.A., Professional Studies
HUDSON, H., M.B.E., B.COM., Education Services
WATSON, L. E., M.A., Education Management
*Faculty of Humanities:*
ABSALOM, R. N. L., B.A., F.I.L., Modern Languages
AINSWORTH, M., M.A., English
BUNTING, J., B.A., M.ED., L.R.A.M., A.R.C.M., L.T.C.L., Section of Music
CASHDAN, A., M.A., M.ED., F.B.PS.S., Communication Studies
SALT, J., M.A., History
*Faculty of Engineering:*
ABRAHAM, D., M.SC., C.ENG., F.I.E.E., M.R.AE.S., Electrical and Electronic Engineering
BARDSLEY, O., M.A., M.SC., C.ENG., M.R.AE.S., Mechanical and Production Engineering
FULWOOD, A. F., B.SC., C.ENG., F.I.C.E., F.I.STRUCT.E., F.I.O.B., Civil Engineering
WATERWORTH, H. W., M.A., A.R.I.C.S., F.I.O.B., A.I.Q.S., Building

*Faculty of Science:*
DAVIES, D. A., PH.D., F.INST.P., Applied Physics
DRAFFAN, I., M.SC., M.B.C.S., M.D.P.M.A., Computer Studies
FLETCHER, B. H., PH.D., M.I.BIOL., Biological Sciences
GILCHRIST, W. G., M.SC., PH.D., A.R.C.S., F.S.S., F.I.M.A., F.I.S., Mathematics and Statistics
GOLDSTEIN, M., PH.D., C.CHEM., F.R.S.C., Chemistry
HILLS, A. W. D., M.A., PH.D., D.I.C., M.I.M.M., C.ENG., F.I.M., Metallurgy

## POLYTECHNIC OF THE SOUTH BANK

BOROUGH RD., LONDON, SE1 0AA.

Telephone: (01)-928-8989.

Founded 1971.

Academic year: September to July.

*Director:* R. J. BEISHON, D.PHIL., C.ENG., M.I.M.
*Academic Registrar:* D. FOSTER, D.L.C., M.ED., F.B.I.M.
*Librarian:* D. F. W. HAWES, M.A., F.L.A., F.R.S.A.

Library of 298,500 vols.
Number of teachers: 600.
Number of students: 4,000 full-time, 3,000 part-time.

Publication: *Prospectus†* (annually).

### DEANS:

*Faculty of Administrative Studies:* P. M. WEAVER.
*Faculty of Science and Engineering:* Dr. J. M. DUBBEY.
*Faculty of Built Environment:* J. RATCLIFFE.
*Faculty of Education, Human and Social Studies:* M. H. CROWTHER.

### HEADS OF DEPARTMENTS:

*Faculty of Administrative Studies:*
HAWORTH, C. H., Modern Languages
WATSON, C. H., Accountancy, Finance and Information Studies
WEAVER, P. M., Law and Government

*Faculty of Science and Engineering:*
DUBBEY, Dr. J. M., Mathematical Sciences and Computing
JENNINGS, Dr. C. B., Mechanical and Production Engineering
JOHNS, Dr. W. R., Chemical Engineering
KAPOSI, Dr. A., Electrical and Electronic Engineering
KIDMAN, F. G., National Bakery School
WELLER, Dr. B. E., Physical Science and Technology
WIX, Dr. P., Applied Biology and Food Science

*Faculty of Built Environment:*
CHONG, Dr. C. V. Y., Construction Science and Materials
HAENLEIN, H., Architecture
LANE, S. J., Building Economics
McCONNELL, R. S., Town Planning
RATCLIFFE, J., Estate Management
SCOTT, Dr. D. R., Environmental Science and Technology
SLANEY, J. R., Civil and Structural Engineering
WEBB, R. T., Construction Mathematics
WILDER, L., Building Administration

*Faculty of Education, Human and Social Studies:*
CROWTHER, M. H., Home Economics
McGINTY, D. A., Professional Education Studies
NEWMAN, Dr. O., Social Sciences
OWEN, G., Nursing and Community Health Studies
TYAS, J. G. M., Humanities
WISKER, A., Arts

## SUNDERLAND POLYTECHNIC

CHESTER RD., SUNDERLAND, SR1 3SD

Telephone: (0783)-76191.

Telex: 537037.

Founded 1969.

Academic year: September to June.

*Rector:* E. P. HART, PH.D., C.CHEM., F.R.S.C.
*Deputy Rector:* R. COWELL, PH.D.
*Chief Administrative Officer:* M. SKILLETER, C.B.E., LL.B., F.C.I.S.
*Librarian:* N. HUNTER, M.A., B.SC., LL.B., A.L.A.

Library of 150,000 vols.
Number of teachers: 389.
Number of students: 4,788.

### DEANS:

*Faculty of Art and Design:* M. YEOMANS, D.F.A., A.T.C., A.R.G.O., F.R.S.A.
*Faculty of Engineering:* D. LYNCH, B.SC., C.ENG., F.R.I.N.A.
*Faculty of Humanities:* E. W. L. HUGHES, B.A.
*Faculty of Science:* A. PEAT, B.SC.
*Faculty of Pharmaceutical Sciences:* B. HEMSWORTH, M.A., PH.D., M.P.S.
*Faculty of Education:* H. WEBSTER, M.A.

## TEESSIDE POLYTECHNIC

BOROUGH RD., MIDDLESBROUGH, CLEVELAND, TS1 3BA

Telephone: (0642)-244176.

Founded 1929 as Constantine College of Technology, attained present status 1970.

*Director:* Dr. MICHAEL LONGFIELD.
*Chief Administrative Officer:* D. S. CLARKE, M.A.
*Librarian:* W. R. MOSS, B.A., F.L.A.

Library of 80,000 vols.
Number of teachers: 300.
Number of students: 4,000.

Degree courses in Art and Design, Computer Science, Mathematics, Business Studies, Chemical, Civil, Mechanical, Instrumentation and Control Engineering, Humanities and Social Studies.

### HEADS OF DEPARTMENTS:

*Business and Professional Studies:* H. C. BRIDGER, B.COM., B.C.L., F.C.I.S.

*Management:* J. M. WRIGHT, M.SC., C.ENG., M.I.MECH.E., M.I.GAS.E.
*Humanities:* H. McL. CURRIE, M.A.
*Administration and Social Studies:* L. J. TASKER.
*Art and Design:* S. SPEDDING, DIP.F.A.
*Mathematics and Statistics:* (vacant).
*Computer Science:* C. A. G. WEBSTER, PH.D.
*Chemical Engineering:* C. J. LIDDLE, M.SC., PH.D., D.I.C.
*Chemistry:* V. MOSS, PH.D., F.R.S.C.
*Metallurgy and Materials:* R. J. HEY, B.SC., F.I.M.
*Civil and Structural Engineering:* W. M. JENKINS, PH.D., C.ENG., F.I.C.E.
*Mechanical Engineering:* L. J. HODSON, B.SC., C.ENG., M.I.MECH.E.
*Electrical, Instrumentation and Control Engineering:* L. J. HERBST, PH.D., F.INST.P., C.ENG.
*Health and Community Studies:* E. E. GLOVER.

## THAMES POLYTECHNIC

WELLINGTON ST., WOOLWICH, LONDON, SE18 6PF

Telephone: (01)-854-2030.

Founded 1970.

Previously Woolwich Polytechnic.

*Director:* Dr. N. SINGER.
*Academic Registrar:* A. MAYFIELD.
*Librarian:* R. S. EAGLE.

Library of 160,000 vols.
Number of teachers: 330.
Number of students: 4,907.

Publications: *Thames Papers in Political Economy*; *Literature and History, A New Journal for the Humanities*.

### DEANS:

*Faculty of Engineering:* Dr. J. S. MASON.
*Faculty of Architecture and Surveying:* J. D. A. McWILLIAM.
*Faculty of Science and Mathematics:* M. D. MORISETTI.
*Faculty of Business, Social Sciences and Humanities:* Dr. G. KOOLMAN.
*Dartford Faculty of Education and Movement Studies:* M. G. BRUCE.

### HEADS OF SCHOOLS:

BATTERSBY, G. A., Electrical Engineering
BRUCE, M. G., Education and Teaching Studies
CURRELL, B. R., Chemistry
HAWKINS, A. T., Civil Engineering
HOBBS, J. M., Mathematics, Statistics and Computing
JOHNSTONE, J. C., Movement and Recreation Studies
KOOLMAN, G., Social Sciences
McWILLIAM, J. D. A., Surveying
MASON, J. S., Mechanical Engineering
MORISETTI, M. D., Biological Sciences
PAUL, J., Architecture
PITT, Miss V. J., Humanities
RANDALL, G. K., Business Administration
WILLIAMS, J. L., Materials Science and Physics

## TRENT POLYTECHNIC
BURTON ST.,
NOTTINGHAM, NG1 4BU
Telephone: 0602-48248.

Telex: 377534.

Founded 1970.

Academic year: September to July.

*Director:* E. A. FREEMAN, M.A., PH.D., D.SC., F.I.E.E., F.I.M.A.

*Assistant Director and Chief Administrative Officer:* D. B. DAVIES, D.P.A.

*Academic Registrar:* A. E. FOSTER, D.M.A.

*Librarian:* D. DAINTREE, M.A., F.L.A.

Library of 300,000 vols.

Number of teachers: 800.

**Number of students:** 6,000 **full-time,** 7,000 **part-time.**

### DEANS:

*Faculty of Art and Design:* R. D. ARCHER, A.R.C.A.

*Faculty of Business:* Prof. G. S. HARDERN, B.A.(ECON.), LL.B., A.C.M.A.

*Faculty of Education Studies:* Prof. W. C. MIDDLEBROOK, M.A.

*Faculty of Engineering and Science:* Prof. R. STOCK, PH.D., C.CHEM., F.R.S.C.

*Faculty of Environmental Studies:* Prof. I. H. SEELEY, M.A., PH.D., F.R.I.C.S., C.ENG.

*Faculty of Human Sciences:* J. D. STANCER, M.SC.(ECON.), PH.D.

*Faculty of Modern Studies:* R. J. FIELDING, B.SC.(ECON.), M.PHIL.

### HEADS OF DEPARTMENTS:

ASHWORTH, E., B.SC., In-Service Education
BARRATT, B., M.ENG., C.ENG., F.I.MIN.E., Mining
BROWN, J., M.SC., C.ENG., F.I.C.E., F.I.STRUCT.E., Civil and Structural Engineering
BURNS, R. W., M.SC., PH.D., C.ENG., M.I.E.E., M.I.E.R.E., M.INST.P., Electrical and Electronic Engineering
CARD, Prof. R., LL.M., Legal Studies
CARRUTHERS, D. W., B.A., Fine Art
CLARK, Prof. P. L., PH.D., R.I.B.A., CH.ARCH., Building and Environmental Health
FIELDING, R. J., M.PHIL., History and Geography
GEAR, Prof. A. R. E., PH.D., Business Studies
GLEN, D. M., Visual Communication
HARRISON, Prof. G. B., M.A., School Technology, Craft and Design
HOLLAWAY, A. L., A.R.C.A., Three-Dimensional Design
JOHNSON, P., M.SC., Mathematical Sciences
MAGILL, W. B. B., B.A., B.D., Literature, Languages and Philosophy
MERCER, C. K., PH.D., M.I.BIOL., Life Sciences (acting)
MIDDLEBROOK, Prof. W. C., M.A., Education Studies
NEWTON, Prof. E. W., Fashion and Textiles
RAINS, C. E., M.ED., M.PHIL., Creative Arts
RICHARDS, N. D., M.A., M.SC.(HYG.), PH.D., Social Studies
ROBINS, Prof. D. L. J., PH.D., F.R.T.P.I., Town and Country Planning
RODGERS, A. R., M.A., F.B.I.M., F.R.ECON.S., F.S.S., Management Studies
SEELEY, Prof. I. H., M.A., PH.D., F.R.I.C.S., C.ENG., Surveying
SENEQUE, Prof. P. J. C., M.COMM., Accounting and Finance
STANCER, J. D., M.SC.(ECON.), PH.D., Economics and Public Administration
STOCK, Prof. R., PH.D., C.CHEM., F.R.S.C., Physical Sciences
THOMPSON, Prof. P. J., M.SC., C.ENG., F.I.MECH.E., F.I.PROD.E., Mechanical and Production Engineering
WILLOCK, J., F.T.I., F.R.S.A., Fashion and Textiles

## POLYTECHNIC OF WALES
LLANTWIT RD., TREFOREST, PONTYPRIDD, MID GLAMORGAN, CF37 1DL
Telephone: 0443-405133.

Founded 1913 as South Wales and Monmouth School of Mines; in 1956 became Glamorgan College of Technology; in 1970 became Glamorgan Polytechnic; merged with Glamorgan College of Education to become Polytechnic of Wales 1975.

*Director:* J. D. DAVIES, M.SC., PH.D., D.SC., C.ENG., F.I.C.E., F.I.STRUCT.E.

*Deputy Directors:* F. J. HYBART, PH.D. FR.S.C., C. ROBERTS, M.A., M.B.I.M.

*Chief Administrative Officer:* P. GILLIBRAND, B.A.(ECON.), D.M.A.

*Academic Registrar:* C. M. LAWTHOM, M.ED.

*Librarian:* G. W. EWINS, B.SC. (ECON.), A.L.A.

Library of 160,000 vols., 2,000 current periodicals.

Number of teachers: 350.

Number of students: 2,600 full-time, 1,200 part-time, total 3,800.

Includes Degree, H.N.D., T.E.C. and B.E.C. courses, Sandwich courses.

### DEANS:

*Faculty of Environmental Studies:* R. D. MCMURRAY, B.SC., C.ENG., F.I.C.E., F.I.O.B.

*Faculty of Engineering Studies:* G. H. THOMPSON, M.SC., C.ENG., F.I.E.E.

*Faculty of Professional Studies:* R. ROBERTS, M.SC., M.I.P.M., M.B.I.M.

### HEADS OF DEPARTMENTS:

*Faculty of Environmental Studies:*
BIKER, A. J., M.SC., A.R.I.C.S., A.R.V.A., Estate Management and Quantity Surveying
MCMURRAY, R. D., B.SC., C.ENG., F.I.C.E., F.I.O.B., Civil Engineering and Building
MORGAN, L., C.ENG., F.R.I.C.S., F.I.MIN.E., Mining and Mine Surveying

*Faculty of Engineering Studies:*
BASSETT, M. B., M.SC.TECH., PH.D., C.ENG., F.I.MECH.E., F.I.PROD.E., F.I.PLANT.E., F.B.P.I.C.S., Mechanical and Production Engineering
GEORGE, W. O., PH.D., D.SC., C.CHEM., F.R.S.C., Science
GREEN, D. J., M.SC., F.B.C.A., F.I.M.A., Mathematics and Computer Science
THOMPSON, G. H., M.SC., C.ENG., F.I.E.E., Electrical Engineering

*Faculty of Professional Studies:*
HAWKINS, P. J. L., M.SC.(ECON.), PH.D., Social Studies
HILL, J. D., M.A., F.B.I.M., Business and Administrative Studies
ROBERTS, R., M.SC., M.I.P.M., M.B.I.M., Management and Legal Studies
SLATER, M., M.A., PH.D., Arts and Languages

## THE POLYTECHNIC WOLVERHAMPTON
THE MOLINEUX, MOLINEUX ST., WOLVERHAMPTON, WV1 1SB
Telephone: (0902) 710654.

Founded 1969.

Constituent Colleges: Wolverhampton College of Art, Wolverhampton College of Technology, Dudley College of Education, Wolverhampton Teachers' College for Day Students and Wolverhampton Technical Teachers' College.

*Director:* G. A. SEABROOKE, LL.B., F.B.I.M.

*Deputy Director:* C. J. M. LEE, M.SC., C.ENG., M.I.MECH.E.

*Secretary:* G. R. BROOKS, B.A.

*Librarian:* Mrs. S. G. AYERST, B.SC., M.I.INF.SC.

Library of 200,000 vols.

Number of teachers: 625.

**Number of students:** 4,000 **full-time,** 3,000 **part-time.**

*Publications: West Midland Studies, Journal of Industrial Affairs, The Dudley Journal.*

### DEANS:

*Faculty of Art and Design:* E. CLEMENTS, DES.R.C.A., F.S.I.A., F.R.S.A.

*Faculty of Education:* D. J. MORTIMER, B.SC., M.ED.

*Faculty of Engineering:* C. J. M. LEE, M.SC., C.ENG., M.I.MECH.E.

*Faculty of Humanities:* H. SMITH, M.A., LL.B., PH.D.

*Faculty of Science:* J. A. SANDBACH, M.SC., F.R.S.C., C.CHEM., F.B.I.M.

*Faculty of Social Science:* (vacant).

### HEADS OF DEPARTMENTS:

*Faculty of Art and Design:*
POTTER, H., DES.R.C.A., M.S.I.A., A.I.B.D., Design
ROWE, N., N.D.D., DIP.F.A., Fine Art

*Faculty of Education:*
ANDREWS, M. A., B.A., M.ED., Teaching and Curriculum Studies II
CLARK, A. S., B.SC.(ECON.), M.A., Education Studies
TEMPLE, M. V., M.A., Teaching and Curriculum Studies I

*Faculty of Engineering:*
COURTEN, D. S., J.P., B.SC.(ENG.), C.ENG., F.I.MUN.E., F.C.I.O.B., M.I.H.E., Building and Civil Engineering

EASTOP, T. D., PH.D., C.ENG., M.I.MECH.E., M.I.MAR.E., Mechanical and Production Engineering
JONES, R., PH.D., C.ENG., M.I.PROD.E., Industrial and Electrical Engineering

*Faculty of Humanities:*
SHEPPARD, P. E., B.A., Arts
WHITE, J. E. G., M.A., L.-ES-L., Languages and European Studies

*Faculty of Science:*
MCLAREN, J., PH.D., F.R.S.C., Physical Sciences
POWELL, A. J., M.A., F.I.M.A., M.B.C.S., Computing and Mathematical Sciences
WEBBER, F. C., PH.D., M.I.BIOL., Biological Sciences

*Faculty of Social Science:*
CROCKETT, J., M.A., LL.M., Legal Studies

WILDSMITH, J. R., M.A., M.SOC.SC., Economics and Social Sciences

*School of Business and Management Studies:*
LUCEY, T., M.SOC.SC., F.C.M.A., M.B.C.S.

*Management Centre:*
ASHBY, D. C., M.SC., PH.D., F.I.W.M., C.ENG., F.I.MIN.E., F.M.B.I.M.

# COLLEGES

Due to space limitations, we are restricted to giving a selection of colleges in the U.K. The degree courses run by these Colleges (unless otherwise stated) lead to degrees awarded by the Council for National Academic Awards (q.v.) and are comparable to courses at British universities.

## AGRICULTURE

**East of Scotland College of Agriculture:** West Mains Rd., Edinburgh, EH9 3JG; f. 1901; associated with the University of Edinburgh; degree courses in Agriculture, Animal Production Science, Crop Production Science, Agricultural Science and Agricultural Economics; Higher Diploma and Diploma courses in Agriculture; College Certificate in Farming Practice; 50 teachers, 330 students; library of 13,000 vols., 450 serials, 20,000 pamphlets; Principal Prof. N. F. ROBERTSON, C.B.E., M.A., PH.D., F.R.S.E.

**Harper Adams Agricultural College** (incorporating National Institute of Poultry Husbandry): Newport, Shropshire; est. 1901; four-year sandwich course for B.Sc. in Agricultural Technology; three-year sandwich courses for H.N.D. in Agriculture, H.N.D. in Agricultural Marketing and Business Administration, H.N.D. in Agricultural Engineering; two-year sandwich course for O.N.D. in Poultry; one-year post degree/diploma course in Crop Protection; one-year H.N.D. Preparatory course; Principal A. G. HARRIS, N.D.A., M.I.AG.E., M.I.BIOL., A.R.AG.S.

**Lancashire College of Agriculture and Horticulture:** Myerscough Hall, Billsborrow, Preston, PR3 0RY; f. 1890; 51 teachers, 240 students; library of 16,000 vols.; Principal F. A. W. PEREGRINE, N.D.A., F.R.AG.S.

**North of Scotland College of Agriculture:** 581 King St., Aberdeen; f. 1904; associated with the University of Aberdeen; 75 teachers; 300 students; library of 20,000 vols.; Principal G. A. LODGE, PH.D.; Dir. of Studies M. H. D. F. FYFE; publs. *Annual Report*†, *Research, Investigations and Field Trials*† (annual).

**Royal Agricultural College:** Cirencester, Glos.; f. 1845; College Diplomas in Agriculture and Estate Management, and National and Professional qualifications; Advanced Diploma in Farm Management; Principal H. V. HUGHES, B.SC.

**Seale-Hayne Agricultural College:** Newton Abbot, Devon; f. 1912; 500 students; Diploma in Technology of Food; H.N.D. courses in Agriculture, Rural Resources and their Management, Applied Biology, Food Technology; degree course in Agriculture; post-graduate and post-H.N.D. supplementary courses in Farm Management (3 options—general Farm Management, Milk Production, Amenity Agriculture and Recreation Management); Management Studies; Principal G. J. DOWRICK, B.SC., PH.D., F.I.BIOL.

**Shuttleworth Agricultural College:** Old Warden Park, Bedfordshire, SG18 9DX; f. 1944; farms 370 hectares, estate of 1,900 hectares; residential college for 250 students; H.N.D. courses in General Agriculture and Arable Option, O.N.D. in Agriculture; one-year farming course for college certificate; Principal J. E. SCOTT, M.S., F.R.AG.S.

**Welsh Agricultural College:** Llanbadarn Fawr, Aberystwyth, SY23 3AL; f. 1971; library of c. 24,000 vols.; 17 lecturers, 180 students; Principal Prof. D. W. MORRIS, PH.D.; Chief Administrative Officer W. PUGH EVANS, D.M.A.

**West of Scotland Agricultural College:** Auchincruive, Ayr, KA6 5HW; f. 1899; associated with the Universities of Strathclyde and Glasgow; education, advisory and research and development work; 70 teachers, 460 students; library of 10,000 vols.; Principal J. M. M. CUNNINGHAM.

**Writtle Agricultural College:** Writtle, Chelmsford, CM1 3RR; courses in Agriculture, Agricultural Engineering and Horticulture.

**Wye College:** *see* under University of London.

## ART

The colleges listed below (unless otherwise stated) are those which run courses leading to the Diploma in Art and Design, comparable to first degree courses at British universities, awarded by the C.N.A.A. (q.v.).

**Bath Academy of Art:** Corsham, Wiltshire, SN13 0DB; f. 1946; B.A. (Hons.) degree courses in Fine Art, Visual Communication—Graphic Design, Three-Dimensional Design, Ceramics; one-year Foundation course in Art and Design; 53 teachers, 250–300 students; library of 23,000 vols.; Principal M. G. FINN, A.R.C.A., F.R.S.A.

**Camberwell School of Art and Crafts:** Peckham Rd., London, SE5 8UF; Hons. degree courses in Fine Art, Graphic Design, Ceramics and Metalwork, Textiles; Principal I. E. TREGARTHEN JENKIN, M.A.

**City of Canterbury College of Art:** New Dover Rd., Canterbury, Kent, CT1 3AN; f. 1882; B.A. (Hons.) degree courses in Fine Art and Graphic Design; B.A. and diploma courses in Architecture; diploma courses in Graphic Design and Fashion/Textiles; 53 full-time and 91 part-time teachers, 500 students; library of 26,039 vols.; Principal G. G. BELLAMY, DES.R.C.A.; Vice-Principal BARRY KIRK, A.R.C.A.; Chief Admin. Officer DAVID HAMPSON, B.SC.(SOC.).

**Central School of Art and Design:** Southampton Row, London, WC1B 4AP; f. 1896; degree courses in Fine Art, Graphic and Three-dimensional Design, Textiles, Theatre; course in Foundation Studies; M.A. courses in Graphic Design and Industrial Design; 490 students; library of 26,000 vols.; Principal T. PANNELL, DES.R.C.A., F.S.I.A.D., A.T.I.; Vice-Principal P. BIRD, B.A., A.T.D.

**Chelsea School of Art:** Manresa Rd., London, SW3 6LS; f. 1895; degree courses in Fine Art; library of 18,000 vols.; Principal F. BRILL.

**City and Guilds of London Art School:** 124 Kennington Park Rd., London, S.E.11; f. 1879; 3-year diploma courses in Painting, Graphic Arts, Sculpture, Sculpture Carving of Stone and Wood, Restoration of Wood and Stone; 2-year certificate courses in Lettering, Printmaking, Woodcarving and Gilding, Decora-

## COLLEGES

tive Arts; number of teaching staff: 30; Chair. Commodore CHARLES NOBLE, C.B.E., D.SC., V.R.D., R.N.R.; Principal ROGER DE GREY, R.A.

**Courtauld Institute of Art:** 20 Portman Square, London, W1H 0BE; f. 1932; affiliated to the University of London; undergraduate and postgraduate courses in the History of European Art; diploma course in Conservation of Paintings; 20 teachers, 196 full-time and 145 part-time students; Dir. Prof. P. E. LASKO, B.A., F.S.A.; Registrar D. J. WALLACE, B.SC.; publ. *Journal of the Warburg and Courtauld Institutes* (annually).

**Duncan of Jordanstone College of Art:** Perth Rd., Dundee; Schools of Architecture, Town Planning, Design (Textile, Graphic, Illustration/Printmaking, Ceramics, Silversmithing and Jewellery, Interior Design, Product Design), Drawing and Painting, Sculpture, Home Economics, Catering and Institutional Management, Department of Printing; 100 full-time and 60 part-time teachers, 850 full-time and 500 part-time students; Principal M. LACOME, F.R.S.A., M.S.I.A., M.S.T.D., M.INST.P.

**Edinburgh College of Art:** Lauriston Place, Edinburgh, EH3 9DF; f. 1907; Departments of Architecture, Town and Country Planning; Schools of Drawing and Painting, Design and Crafts, Sculpture; Principal G. T. N. Ross; Sec. and Treas. JOHN J. NICE, D.M.A.

**Exeter College of Art and Design:** Earl Richards Rd. North, Exeter, Devon, EX2 6AS; f. 1835; degree courses in Graphic Design (Illustration, Typography and Photography) and Fine Art (Painting, Sculpture, Ceramics, Printmaking and Art History); diploma in Printing (two-year); Publishing and Book Production for Graduates (one-year); 350 students; library of 16,000 vols., 45,000 slides; Principal CLIFFORD FISHWICK, A.T.D.; Chief Admin. Officer W. A. COBB.

**Falmouth School of Art:** 27 Woodlane, Falmouth, Cornwall; f. 1947; foundation art course and B.A. (Hons.) course in Fine Art; 25 teachers, c. 150 students; Principal T. A. CROSS, D.F.A.; Registrar H. N. METCALFE.

**Glasgow School of Art:** 167 Renfrew St., Glasgow, G3 6RQ; f. 1840; B.A. courses in Fine Art and Design, Town and Country Planning, and (in conjunction with Glasgow University) Architecture; Dir. ANTHONY E. JONES, M.F.A., DIP.A.D.; Sec. and Treas. F. W. KEAN, C.A., A.C.M.A.

**Gloucestershire College of Art and Design:** Pittville, Cheltenham, Glos. and Brunswick Rd., Gloucester; f. 1968 from the amalgamation of the Cheltenham and City of Gloucester Colleges of Art and Stroud School of Art; B.A. (Hons.) degrees awarded in Fine Art (Painting, Printmaking, Sculpture), Textiles and Fashion; foundation course in Art and Design; designated diploma courses in Architecture; B.A. degree courses in Landscape Architecture and Town Planning; vocational courses in Graphics and Technical Graphics, Photography, Printing, Display and Fashion, Painting and Decorating; 96 teachers, 630 students; library of 30,000 vols.; Principal JAMES MARTIN, D.A. (EDIN.); Registrar L. WOODWARD, D.E.M.

**Hamilton Kerr Institute:** Whittlesford, Cambridge, CB2 4NE; f. 1976; dept. of Fitzwilliam Museum, Univ. of Cambridge; postgraduate course in conservation and restoration of easel paintings; 5 teachers, 6 full-time students; Dir. N. BROMMELLE.

**Loughborough College of Art and Design:** Radmoor, Loughborough, Leicestershire; degree courses in Fine Art, Three-dimensional Design, Textiles/Fashion; vocational diploma courses in Fashion, Graphic Design; one-year foundation course.

**Maidstone College of Art:** Oakwood Park, Oakwood Rd., Maidstone, Kent; f. 1867; CNAA courses in Fine Art, Graphic Design; full- and part-time printing courses; 38 full-time and 75 part-time teachers, 300 full-time and 120 part-time students; Principal K. GRIBBLE, D.F.A., F.R.S.A., A.S.I.A., A.R.W.A.; Chief Admin. Officer M. F. CHAPMAN, D.M.A.; publ. *Vision* (occasional).

**Norwich School of Art:** St. George St., Norwich, Norfolk, NR3 1BB; f. 1846; degree courses in Fine Art and Graphic Design, Foundation course and Vocational Design course; 30 full-time lecturers; Principal W. G. ENGLISH.

**Ravensbourne College of Art and Design:** Walden Rd., Chislehurst, Kent, BR7 5SN; f. 1962; B.A. degree courses in Fine Art, Graphic and Three-dimensional Design, Fashion/Textiles; 56 full-time and 60 part-time teachers, 500 students; library of 15,000 vols., 20,000 slides; Principal N. FREWING, DES.R.C.A., F.S.I.A.D.; Registrar A. H. LOCKE, J.P., B.A., F.I.L.

**Royal Academy Schools:** Burlington House, Piccadilly, London, W1V 0DS; f. 1768; Schools of Painting and Sculpture; Keeper P. GREENHAM, C.B.E., B.A., R.A.; Curator W. WOODINGTON, R.P., R.B.A.

**Royal College of Art:** Kensington Gore, London, SW7 2EU; f. 1837, awarded Charter 1967 empowering it to grant its own degrees; postgraduate institution receiving direct grant from D.E.S.; Schools of Ceramics and Glass, Environmental Design, Fashion Design, Film and Television, Furniture Design, Graphic Arts, Industrial Design, Painting, Sculpture, Silversmithing and Jewellery, Textile Design; Depts. of Cultural History, Design Management, Design Research, Environmental Media, Photography, Design Education Unit; 580 students; Visitor H.R.H. The Duke of EDINBURGH, K.G., K.T.; Provost Sir HUGH CASSON; Rector and Vice-Provost Prof. LIONEL MARCH, M.A., SC.D.; Registrar B. COOPER, B.A., A.M.B.I.M.; publ. *Yearbook*.

PROFESSORS:

ARCHER, B., C.B.E., DR.R.C.A., C.ENG., M.I.MECH.E., M.I.E.D., Design Education and Design Research
BENNEY, G., R.D.I., DES.R.C.A., Silversmithing and Jewellery
BROGDEN, J., DES.R.C.A., Fashion Design
DE FRANCIA, P., Painting
FRAYLING, C., M.A., PH.D., Cultural History
HEDGECOE, J., DR.R.C.A., F.S.I.A.D., Photography
HEIGHT, F., DES.R.C.A., C.ENG., M.I.MECH.E., F.S.I.A.D., Industrial Design
HERITAGE, R., C.B.E., R.D.I., DES.R.C.A., F.S.I.A.D., Furniture Design
KING, P., C.B.E., A.R.A., Sculpture
MILLER, J., A.A.DIP., R.I.B.A., Environmental Design
NICHOLSON, R., A.R.C.A., F.S.I.A.D., Textile Design
QUEENSBERRY, Lord, F.S.I.A.D., Ceramics and Glass
SMITH, B., B.SC.(ENG.), C.ENG., M.I.MECH.E., F.I.PROD.E., F.B.I.M., F.INST.M., F.I.M.C., Design Management
SPENCER, H., R.D.I., DR.R.C.A., Graphic Arts

**Ruskin School of Drawing and Fine Art:** 74 High St., Oxford; f. 1871; dept. of the University of Oxford; 3-year degree course in Fine Art; 60 students; Principal P. MORSBERGER, M.A.

**St. Martin's School of Art:** 107/111 Charing Cross Rd., London, WC2H 0DU; f. 1854; M.A. course in Fashion and B.A. courses in Fine Art, Graphic Design, Textiles and Fashion; 1,000 students; Principal I. SIMPSON, A.R.C.A.; Secretary and Registrar P. J. R. HERMAN.

**School of Architecture, Architectural Association:** 34–36 Bedford Square, London, WC1B 3ES; instituted 1847; 5-year course leading to AA Dipl. and exemption from the R.I.B.A. Part 2 exam.; postgraduate courses and research in Architecture, Planning & Urban Design; 500 students; 4,000 mems.; library of 29,000 vols.; Chair. A. S. BOYARSKY, B.ARCH., M.R.P., M.R.A.I.C., T.P.L.C.; publ. *AA Quarterly*.

**Slade School of Fine Art:** University College, Gower St., London, W.C.1;

f. 1871; degree courses in Drawing and Painting with instruction in History of Art, Print-making and Film; postgraduate courses in Drawing, Painting, Print-making (Etching, Engraving, Silkscreen, Lithography), Theatre Design, Sculpture, Electronic (Computer) art and mixed media forms; supervision is given to those studying for higher degrees in the historical and theoretical Study of Film; Univ. of London B.A. degree in Fine Art, Higher Diploma in Fine Art, M.Phil./Ph.D. in Film Studies; 200 students; Slade Prof. LAWRENCE GOWING, C.B.E.; Sec. MURRAY WATSON, M.A.

**Stourbridge College of Technology and Art:** Church St., Stourbridge, DY8 1LY; f. 1853 as School of Design; degree courses in Fine Art, Three-dimensional Design (Glass/Ceramics); 35 full-time and 4 part-time teachers, 250 students; library of 18,000 vols. and 55,000 slides; Principal T. H. JENKINS, B.SC., A.M.B.I.M., A.F.I.M.A.; Chief Administrative Officer A. J. EVANS, M.INST.A.M., A.S.C.T.; publ. Prospectus of courses.

**University of London, Goldsmiths' College (School of Art and Design):** Lewisham Way, New Cross, SE14 6NW; f. 1893; first degree courses in Fine Art, Embroidery & Textiles; combined degrees in Art/Dance, Art/Education, Art/Religious Studies; Communication Studies with Sociology or Education; M.A. in Fine Art; postgraduate diplomas in Art History, Art Therapy, Ceramics, Communication Studies, Fine Art and Graphics, Embroidery/Textiles; A.T.C. and L.D.A.D. (Communication and Graphics) Foundation courses; 56 full-time staff, 95 part-time specialists, 550 full-time or joint degree students; Dean P. K. STEEL (acting).

**West Surrey College of Art and Design:** Falkner Rd., Farnham, Surrey; degree courses in Fine Art, Textiles, Ceramics/Glass/Metals, Photography, Film and Video, Animation; foundation course; library of 50,000 vols.; 650 students; Principal L. W. STOPPANI, A.R.C.A., F.S.A.E.

**Wimbledon School of Art:** Merton Hall Rd., Wimbledon, London, SW19 3QA; f. 1890; Hons. degree in Art and Design, courses in Fine Art Painting, Fine Art Sculpture, Theatre Design; own diploma in Graphic Design; Certificate in Theatre Wardrobe; Foundation Course; library of 22,000 vols.; 340 students; Principal MYLES MURPHY.

**Winchester School of Art:** Park Ave., Winchester; f. c. 1870; Hons. degree courses in Fine Art, Painting, Sculpture and Printmaking, Printed and Woven Textiles; Research Diploma in Textiles; Foundation course; 22 full-time and 76 part-time teachers; library of 12,000 vols. and slide collection; Principal D. C. SHERLOCK, B.A., M.PHIL., M.S.D.I., F.R.S.A.; Registrar R. J. STAINER, D.M.A., M.I.L.G.A.

### BUSINESS AND COMMERCE

**Aberdeen College of Commerce:** Holburn St., Aberdeen, AB9 2YT, Scotland; f. 1959; courses in Accounting and Legal Studies, General Studies, Business Studies, Secretarial Studies, English and Communication, Languages, Mathematics, Computing and Science; Office Administration Studies; library of 18,000 vols.; 173 full-time teachers; 1,600 full-time, 3,500 part-time students; Principal B. EDWARDS, B.SC.(ECON.), B.COM., M.LITT., M.I.S., F.S.S.; Registrar H. A. FORREST; Librarian M. SMITH, A.L.A.

**Administrative Staff College:** see Henley—the Management College.

**Central College of Commerce:** 300 Cathedral St., Glasgow, G1 2TA; f. 1962; courses in Business Studies, Distribution, English and General Studies, Hairdressing; 84 full-time, 127 part-time teachers, 850 full-time, 4,500 part-time students; library of 30,000 vols.; Principal D. C. HORN; Registrar F. H. MCCROSSAN.

**College of Estate Management:** Whiteknights, Reading, Berks., RG6 2AW. f. 1919; courses for external B.Sc. degree in Estate Management of the University of Reading and for the examinations of the professional societies dealing with the use, development, valuation and management of land and buildings; Principal P. W. HUNTSMAN, B.SC., F.R.I.C.S.; Sec. D. E. TUCKER, M.A.

**College of Production Technology and School of Business Administration:** 5 Elwick Rd., Ashford, Kent; f. 1949; Pres. Dr. DOUGLAS R. WOODLEY; Registrar Mrs. J. M. CROSBY.

**Dundee College of Commerce:** 30 Constitution Rd., Dundee, DD3 6TB; f. 1956; 122 full-time and 25 part-time teachers, 3,550 students; library of 17,000 vols.; Principal C. M. BROWN, B.SC.(ENG.), C.ENG., M.I.PROD.E., M.B.I.M.; Depute Principal D. HOOD, M.A., LL.B., BAR.-AT-LAW.

**Henley—the Management College:** Greenlands, Henley-on-Thames, Oxfordshire, RG9 3AU; f. 1946 as the Administrative Staff College; various residential courses for managers and administrators already holding important positions to prepare them for still greater responsibilities; special courses; research projects; higher degrees and postgraduate courses; 35 teachers, 90 students; library of 18,000 vols.; Principal Prof. T. KEMPNER, B.SC.(ECON.), C.B.I.M.; Registrar J. R. LIVEING, F.B.I.M.; Librarian Miss GAIL THOMAS; publs. *Journal of General Management*, Occasional and College Papers.

**London Business School:** Sussex Place, Regent's Park, London NW1 4SA; f. 1965; two-year courses leading to the M.Sc. degree and three-year courses leading to the Ph.D. degree of London University; 37 teachers, 230 students; Principal Prof. R. J. BALL, M.A., PH.D.

PROFESSORS:

BALL, R. J., Economics
BEESLEY, M. E., Economics
BERRY, D. F., Business Administration
BREALEY, R. A., Portfolio Investment
CHAMBERS, D. J., Operational Research
ECCLES, A. J., Business Administration
EHRENBERG, A. S. C., Marketing
HEATH, J. B., Economics
HOPWOOD, A., Accounting and Financial Reporting
HUNT, J. W., Human Relations
MOORE, P. G., Statistics and Operational Research
NICHOLSON, T. A. J., Production Management
PUGH, D. S., Organizational Behaviour
PYM, D. L., Organizational Behaviour
REID, W., Accounting and Financial Control
SIMMONDS, K., Marketing and International Business
STOPFORD, J. M., International Business

**Oxford Centre for Management Studies:** Kennington Rd., Kennington, Oxford, OX1 5NY; f. 1965; independent of but linked with the University of Oxford; nine-week Senior Managers Development programme leading to the Oxford University Certificate in Management Studies; 3-week Fundamental Issues in Management programme; company courses specially designed to meet the needs of sponsoring organizations; corporate strategy seminars; top management briefings; individual management development programmes; teaching for the M.Phil. degree of Oxford University; Dir. UWE KITZINGER, C.B.E., M.A., B.LITT.

### MUSIC AND DRAMATIC ART

**Bristol Old Vic Theatre School:** 1 and 2 Downside Rd., Clifton, Bristol; in association with the Bristol Old Vic Company and Drama Dept. of the Univ. of Bristol; courses in acting, design, directing and technical aspects of the theatre; Principal C. DENYS.

**Central School of Speech and Drama:** Embassy Theatre, Swiss Cottage, London, NW3 3HY; f. 1906; c. 40 staff, c. 300 students; departments of Stage, Teaching of Speech and Drama, Speech Therapy; Principal GEORGE KITSON; Registrar RENEE HOSKING.

**Guildhall School of Music and Drama:** Barbican, London, EC2Y 8DT; f. by the Corporation of London in 1880 and administered by the Music Cttee.; Professorial staff 270; c. 1,600 students; Principal JOHN HOSIER, M.A., F.G.S.M.; Dir. of Music L. EAST, M.MUS., F.G.S.M.; Dir. of Drama TONY CHURCH, M.A.; Dir. of Administration GEORGE DERBYSHIRE. LL.B.

**London Academy of Music and Dramatic Art:** Tower House, 226 Cromwell Rd., London, S.W.5; professional theatrical training, acting and stage management; Dir. of Administration and Technical Courses ROBERT STANTON; Dir. of Acting School ROGER CROUCHER.

**National Film School:** Beaconsfield Film Studios, Station Rd., Beaconsfield, Bucks.; f. 1970; professional 3-year training for film and television with broadly based background of humane studies; small information library; Chair. Lord LLOYD of HAMPSTEAD; Dir. COLIN YOUNG.

**Royal Academy of Dramatic Art (R.A.D.A.):** 62 Gower St., London, WC1E 6ED; f. 1904; courses: Acting (7 terms), Stage Management, Scene Painting and Design, Stage Carpentry (all 4 terms); Principal HUGH CRUTTWELL; Administrator-Registrar RICHARD O'DONOGHUE.

**Royal Academy of Music:** Marylebone Road, London, N.W.1; f. 1822; inc. by Royal Charter 1830; professorial staff 140, students 650 full-time study only; Pres. H.R.H. Princess ALICE, The Duchess of GLOUCESTER; Principal Sir ANTHONY LEWIS, C.B.E., M.A., MUS.B.(CANTAB.), HON. R.A.M.; Warden NOEL COX, B.MUS., F.R.A.M.; Administrator G. HAMBLING; Registrar R. GOLDING, M.A., HON. R.A.M.; publs. *Prospectus*, *R.A.M. Magazine* (termly), *L.R.A.M. Syllabus* (annually).

**Royal College of Music:** Prince Consort Rd., South Kensington, London, S.W.7; f. 1883; 700 pupils; Dir. Sir DAVID WILLCOCKS, C.B.E., M.C., MUS.B., F.R.C.M., F.R.C.O.; Registrar MICHAEL GOUGH MATTHEWS, F.R.C.M., A.R.C.O.

**Royal College of Organists:** Kensington Gore, London, SW7 2QS; f. 1864, inc. by Royal Charter 1893; Hon. Sec. STEPHEN CLEOBURY, M.A., MUS.B.

**Royal Military School of Music:** Kneller Hall, Twickenham, Middlesex; a military school established 1857 for the purpose of training the non-commissioned officer for the position of bandmaster and young soldiers as solo performers; 50 students, 250 pupils; Commandant Col. D. T. L. BEATH; Dir. of Music Lt.-Col. G. E. EVANS, The Blues and Royals; Adjutant Lt.-Col. S. C. SEELHOFF, M.B.E., Royal Scots Dragoon Guards.

**Royal Northern College of Music:** 124 Oxford Rd., Manchester, M13 9RD; amalgamation of Royal Manchester College of Music and Northern School of Music; Royal Charter 1923 and 1973; library of 45,000 vols.; Pres. H.R.H. The Duchess of KENT; Principal JOHN MANDUELL, F.R.A.M., F.R.N.C.M.

**Royal School of Church Music:** Addington Palace, Croydon, CR9 5AD; f. 1927, inc. 1930; centre for training church musicians; world-wide membership of affiliated choirs; Chair. of Council The BISHOP OF BATH AND WELLS; Dir. LIONEL DAKERS, D.MUS., F.R.A.M., F.R.C.O.(CHM), A.D.C.M., F.R.C.M.; publs. *Church Music* (quarterly), *World of Church Music* (annually).

**Royal Scottish Academy of Music and Drama:** St. George's Place, Glasgow, G2 1BS; f. 1890 as The Glasgow Athenaeum, became The Scottish National Academy of Music 1928, The Royal Scottish Academy of Music 1944 and the Royal Scottish Academy of Music and Drama 1968; teaching staff 100; c. 400 students; Principal D. LUMSDEN, M.A., D.PHIL.; Sec. J. O. MAVOR, M.A.

**Trinity College of Music:** Mandeville Place, London, W1M 6AQ; f. 1872; full-time diploma courses (3-4 years) to equip students as teachers or performers; 400 full-time and 50 part-time students; Pres. YEHUDI MENUHIN, K.B.E.; Principal MEREDITH DAVIES, M.A., B.MUS., F.R.C.M., F.R.C.O.; publ. *T.C.M. Bulletin* (bi-annually).

SCIENCE AND TECHNOLOGY

**Camborne School of Mines:** Trevenson, Pool, Redruth, Cornwall, TR15 3SE; f. 1859; 24 teachers, 200 students; library of 8,000 vols.; Principal P. HACKETT, PH.D., C.ENG., F.I.M.M.; Registrar H. D. HOY, M.PHIL.; publs. *Annual Journal†*, annual prospectus.

**Cranfield Institute of Technology:** Cranfield, Bedfordshire; f. 1946 as College of Aeronautics, awarded Charter 1969 to grant own degrees, although not listed by the University Grants Committee; Nat. College of Agricultural Engineering (q.v.) became a School of the Institute 1975; provides postgraduate and post-experience master-degree and doctoral-degree courses of study and research and short courses in several branches of science, engineering, technology and management orientated towards design, development, manufacture and organization in industry; Schools of Aeronautics, Agricultural Engineering (NCAE), Automotive Studies, Mechanical Engineering, Production Studies, Management; Departments of Design of Machine Systems, Fluid Engineering, Electronic System Design, Social Policy, Materials, Mathematics; Centre for Transport Studies of Engineering Design, Cranfield Unit for Precision Engineering, Cranfield Product Engineering Centre, Ecological Physics Research Unit, National Materials Handling Centre; 1,100 postgraduate students, 5,500 short-course students; library of 30,000 vols.; Vice-Chancellor Sir HENRY CHILVER, PH.D., D.SC., M.A., F.ENG.; Registrar A. J. I. DAVIES, B.A.; publ. *Reports†* (irregular).

**Glasgow College of Building and Printing:** 60 North Hanover St., Glasgow, G1 2BP; f. 1972 by amalgamation of Colleges of Building (f. 1927) and Printing (f. 1925); library of 30,000 vols.; 207 teachers; 650 full-time and 3,000 part-time students; Principal D. McEWAN, B.SC., C.ENG., M.I.MUN.E., F.C.I.O.B.; Academic Registrar J. K. GRAHAM, M.A.; Registrar Mrs. J. C. BLACKBURN; publ. *Prospectus†*.

**National College of Agricultural Engineering:** Silsoe, Bedford, MK45 4DT; f. 1961 (became a School of the Cranfield Institute of Technology 1975, and now comprises the Faculty of Agricultural Engineering, Food Production and Rural Land Use); full-time residential courses leading to B.Sc., postgraduate Diploma, M.Sc. or Ph.D. in Agricultural Engineering; wide range of postgraduate options; 40 academic staff; 136 undergraduate students, 136 graduate students; library of over 25,000 vols.; Head Prof. B. A. MAY, B.SC., N.D.AGR.E., C.ENG., M.I MECH.E., F.I.AGR.E.; publs. *NCAE Occasional Papers* (irregular), *Consultancy and Research brochures*, *Newsletter* (3 a year), *Prospectus*.

**Royal Military College of Science:** Shrivenham, Swindon, Wilts.; f. 1864; officer students and civilians holding Shrivenham Scholarships, County Awards and Army Cadetships are prepared for degrees in Engineering and Applied Science under auspices of Council for National Academic Awards (CNAA); Army Officers from the Home and Commonwealth armies take postgraduate courses and officers of the three services take specialist scientific courses; residential; 100 teachers, including 7 full and 13 assoc. profs.; library of 80,000 vols.; Commandant Maj.-Gen. R. F. VINCENT, D.S.O.; Dean F. J. M. FARLEY, M.A., PH.D., SC.D., F.INST.P., F.R.S.; Academic Registrar Lt.-Col. (retd.) P. J. KNOTT, M.A.

**Royal Naval College, Greenwich:** London, SE10 9NN; f. 1873; courses in Nuclear Science and Technology to C.N.A.A. M.Sc. level, junior, intermediate and senior courses in Naval Staff Training; library of 40,000 vols.; Pres. Rear-Adm. J. H. CARLILL, O.B.E.; Dir. of Studies and Dean of the College Capt. G. N. DAVIS, B.SC., R.N.

# NORTHERN IRELAND

Population 1,538,800

## LEARNED SOCIETIES AND RESEARCH INSTITUTES

**Agricultural Research Institute of Northern Ireland:** Hillsborough, Co. Down; Dir. Prof. J. C. MURDOCH, PH.D.; Sec. W. J. HANNA, F.C.I.S.

**Arts Council of Northern Ireland:** 181A Stranmillis Rd., Belfast, BT9 5DU; f. 1943; the Council is charged with developing the practice and appreciation of the arts throughout Northern Ireland. It maintains a gallery and subvents the Ulster Orchestra, Theatre, Ballet and Opera Companies, literary publications and festivals; Chair. Dr. A. S. WORRALL, O.B.E.; Dir. K. JAMISON, O.B.E.; publs. *Annual Report*, catalogues.

**Belfast Natural History and Philosophical Society:** c/o Linen Hall Library, 17 Donegall Sq. N., Belfast; f. 1821; 100 mems.; Hon. Sec. N. MCNEILLY, M.B.E., B.A.; publ. *Proceedings and Reports*.

**Observatory, The:** Armagh; f. 1790 by Primate Robinson; variable star research; it possesses an 18/12-in. Schmidt telescope and a 10-in. refractor; library of 5,000 vols.; Dir. Dr. MART DE GROOT; Sec. Miss SHEELAGH GREW; publs. *Armagh Observatory Contributions*† and *Leaflets*†.

**Ulster Archaeological Society:** Archaeology Dept., The Queen's University of Belfast, Belfast, BT7 1NN; 370 mems.; Pres. A. E. P. COLLINS; Hon. Sec. R. S. J. CLARKE; publ. *Ulster Journal of Archaeology*† (annually).

**Veterinary Research Laboratories:** Stormont, Belfast; part of Department of Agriculture; library of 8,000 vols.; Dir. Prof. C. DOW, PH.D., B.V.M.S., M.R.C.V.S., F.R.C.PATH.

## LIBRARIES

**Belfast Library and Society for Promoting Knowledge (Linen Hall Library):** Donegall Sq. N., Belfast; f. 1788; c. 200,000 vols.; 1,700 mems. and subscribers; special features are the Gibson Collection of Burns and Burnsiana, the Ewart Collection of books on textile manufactures, Belfast-printed books, etc., and the Belshaw Collection; Librarian J. R. R. ADAMS, F.L.A.

**Belfast Public Libraries:** Central Library, Royal Ave., Belfast, BT1 1EA; f. 1888: 16 branch libraries, 4 part-time centres and 2 mobile libraries; Central Lending Library 36,000 vols.; Central Reserve Collection 100,000 vols.; Humanities and General Reference Library 102,000 vols.; Irish Library 40,000 books, pamphlets and MSS. on all aspects of Ireland, Ulster and Belfast; Fine Arts and Literature 74,000 vols.; Music Library 12,000 vols., 24,000 scores, 24,000 records/cassettes; Business, Science and Technology Library 68,000 vols.; other special collections: Bibliographies, Government and Agency Publications, Patents, Rare Books; microfilm holdings, reader/printers; Chief Librarian I. A. CRAWLEY, F.L.A.

**Magee University College Library:** Northland Rd., Londonderry, BT48 7JL; f. 1865; 98,000 books and pamphlets; special collections: Spalding Collection on Eastern civilizations, Irish Collection, Irish Presbyterianism, Londonderry Local Collection, and Incunabula; MSS include Steward, Deuchanel and Witherow Collections; Librarian GRAHAM WHITE, M.A., F.L.A.

**New University of Ulster Library:** Coleraine, Co. Londonderry, BT52 1SA; f. 1968; c. 185,000 vols. and pamphlets; considerable holdings of microtexts; European Documentation Centre; Special collections: Henry Morris Irish Collection; Headlam-Morley Collection relating to World War I; Paul Ricard Collection relating to World War II; Stelfox Natural History Collection; MSS. of Denis Johnston; Henry Davis Gift of incunabula and rare books; Librarian F. J. E. HURST, M.A., A.L.A., F.L.A.I.

**North-Eastern Education and Library Board, Library Service:** Demesne Ave., Ballymena, Co. Antrim; f. 1922, reorganized 1973; 1,807,298 vols.; 36 brs., 13 mobile libraries; Chief Librarian J. P. E. FRANCIS, B.A., F.L.A.; publs. *Library Bulletin* (quarterly), *Local Collection* (quarterly), *Professional, Commercial and Technical Bulletin* (monthly), *Public Services Information Bulletin* (monthly), *Select List of Additions* (monthly), *Northern Ireland Local Studies List* (2 a year).

**Public Library:** Armagh; f. 1771 by Primate Richard Robinson; Ref. Dept. about 30,000 vols., Lending Dept. about 10,000; Dean Swanzy's special collection of genealogical works and Army Lists; history, theology, philosophy; largely antiquarian; MSS. include copies of Primatial Registers from 1362; (genealogical research not undertaken); Keeper Very Rev. JOHN R. M. CROOKS, M.A.

**Queen's University Library:** Belfast; f. 1849; 860,000 books, pamphlets, manuscripts, theses and microforms; special collections: Hibernica Collection (incl. R. M. Henry Collection, O'Rahilly Collection), Antrim Presbytery Library, MacDouall Collection (Philology), Hamilton Harty Music Collection, Thomas Percy Library; Librarian A. BLAMIRE, M.A., A.L.A.; publs. *Irish Naturalists Journal*† (quarterly), *Northern Ireland Legal Quarterly*†, *Wiles Lectures*† (annual), *Inaugural Lectures*†, *Statistical and Social Inquiry Society of Ireland Journal*† (annual).

**South Eastern Education & Library Board:** Windmill Hill, Ballynahinch, Co. Down; f. 1973; 23 brs., 7 mobile libraries; 825,000 vols.; Chief Librarian D. H. WELCH, F.L.A.; publs. *Drumlin: books and pamphlets added to the Irish Collection* (every 2 months), *Public Services Information Bulletin* (monthly) in co-operation with other N. Ireland library services.

**Southern Education and Library Board, Library Service:** Brownlow Rd., Legahory, Craigavon, Co. Armagh; f. 1973; 19 brs., 11 mobile libraries; 1,094,605 vols.; Chief Librarian W. R. H. CARSON.

## MUSEUMS

**County Museum:** The Mall East, Armagh; f. 1935; collection of material illustrative of local history, antiquities and natural history; Curator D. R. M. WEATHERUP, F.M.A.

**Ulster Folk and Transport Museum:** Cultra Manor, Holywood, Co. Down; a national Museum comprising the Ulster Folk Museum and the former Belfast Transport Museum; library of 15,000 vols.; Chair. of Board of Trustees J. LL. MACQUITTY, Q.C.; Dir. G. B. THOMPSON, O.B.E., M.SC., F.M.A.; publs. *Ulster Folklife*† (annual), *Ulster Folk and Transport Museum Year Book*†.

MUSEUMS, UNIVERSITIES AND COLLEGES U.K. (NORTHERN IRELAND)

**Folk Museum:** f. 1958; opened to public 1964; 136-acre estate in which authentic buildings illustrating Ulster folk-life are being re-erected; twelve reconstructions complete, three in progress.

**Transport Museum:** f. 1962, merged with Folk Museum 1967; being transferred to new premises in a 40-acre site adjoining the Folk Museum's estate; first group of new transport galleries opened May 1976.

**Ulster Museum:** Botanic Gardens, Belfast, BT9 5AB; est. under municipal management 1890 in the Central Public Library; transferred to new building 1929; since April 1962 national museum administered by Board of Trustees; contains collections of fine and applied arts, coins, medals, Irish antiquities, ethnography, industrial technology, local history, and natural sciences; library of 12,000 vols.; Dir. Dr. W. A. McCutcheon, M.A., F.S.A., F.R.G.S.

# UNIVERSITIES AND COLLEGES

## NEW UNIVERSITY OF ULSTER
COLERAINE, CO. LONDONDERRY
Telephone: Coleraine 4141.

Founded 1965; opened October 1968.

Chancellor: Lord Grey of Naunton, G.C.M.G., G.C.V.O., O.B.E.
Vice-Chancellor: W. H. Cockcroft, M.A., D.PHIL.
Registrar: W. T. Ewing, J.P., M.A., LL.B.
Librarian: F. J. E. Hurst, M.A., F.L.A.I.
Number of teachers: 250.
Number of students: 2,000, including c. 500 postgraduates.
Publications: *Undergraduate Prospectus, Postgraduate Prospectus, Bulletin* (weekly during term-time), *Calendar. Report to the Court.*

### Deans:
School of Social Sciences: J. E. Spencer, B.SC.(ECON.).
School of Physical Sciences: G. T. Best, PH.D.
School of Humanities: Kenneth Jones, M.A.
Education Centre: J. E. Nesbitt, M.A., PH.D.
School of Biological and Environmental Studies: K. L. Wallwork, M.A., PH.D.
Institute of Continuing Education: Alan Rogers, M.A., PH.D., F.R.HIST.S., F.S.A.

### Professors:
School of Biological and Environmental Studies:
BARBOUR, K. M., B.LITT., M.A., D.PHIL., Geography
LYNN, R., M.A., PH.D., Psychology
MACFADYEN, A., M.A., D.SC., F.INST.BIOL., Biology
NEWBOULD, P. J., PH.D., F.INST.BIOL., Environmental Science
WOOD, R. B., PH.D., Biology

Education Centre:
JENKINS, D. R., M.A.
NESBITT, J. E., M.A., PH.D.

School of Social Sciences:
CARTER, D. T., M.A., M.S., D.PHIL., Social Work
GIBSON, N. J., PH.D., M.R.I.A., Economics
MORTON-WILLIAMS, P. M., PH.D., Sociology and Social Anthropology
SPENCER, J. E., B.SC.(ECON.), Economics

School of Humanities:
JOLLES, F. E. F. M.A. DR.PHIL., German
MACMATHÚNA, S., PH.D., Irish Studies
MANNING, B. S., M.A., D.PHIL., History
NICHOLL, H. F., M.A., M.LITT., Philosophy
THOMSON, A. W., M.A., English

School of Physical Sciences:
BEST, G. T., PH.D., F.I.P., Physics
GRUNDON, M. F., M.A., D.PHIL., M.R.I.A., F.R.S.C., Chemistry
HENSTOCK, R. M.A., PH.D., F.I.M.A., F.R.A.S., Mathematics
SWINTON, F. L., PH.D., F.R.S.E., Chemistry
WILLIAMS, R. H., M.A., PH.D., D.SC., F.I.P., Physics
YOUNG, A., PH.D., F.B.C.S., F.I.M.A., F.R.A.S., Mathematics

Institute of Continuing Education:
ROGERS, A., M.A., PH.D., F.R.HIST.S., F.S.A.

### Incorporated College:

**Magee University College:** Northland Rd., Londonderry, BT48 7JL; Tel.: Londonderry 65621. Opened in 1865. During the existence of the Royal University of Ireland (1879-1908) the college was one of the five recognized institutions composing that university; since 1970 it has been associated with the New University of Ulster and in 1972 became the centre for an Institute of Continuing Education; Dir. Prof. Alan Rogers, M.A., PH.D., F.R.HIST.S., F.S.A.; College Admin. Officer J. W. Taggart; Library: see Libraries.

## QUEEN'S UNIVERSITY OF BELFAST
UNIVERSITY RD.,
BELFAST, BT7 1NN
Telephone: Belfast 0232-45133.
Telex: QUBADM 74487.

Founded as Queen's College in 1845, received University Charter in 1908.

State control; Language of instruction: English; Academic year: October to September.

Chancellor: The Rt. Hon. Lord Ashby of Brandon, D.SC., M.A., F.R.S.
Pro-Chancellors: The Rt. Rev. Mgr. A. H. Ryan, PH.D., D.D., D.LIT., J. M. Benn, C.B., M.A.
President and Vice-Chancellor: P. Froggatt, M.A., M.D., PH.D., D.P.H., F.F.C.M., F.R.C.P.I., F.R.C.P., F.F.O.M., F.F.C.M.IRE., M.R.I.A.
Pro-Vice-Chancellors: Prof. B. Crossland, C.B.E., PH.D., D.SC., F.I.MECH. E., F.I.PROD.E., M.R.I.A., F.R.S., Prof. J. Braidwood, M.A.
Secretary: R. G. Topping, V.R.D., M.A.
Secretary to Academic Council: A. H. Graham, M.A.
Librarian: A. Blamire, M.A., A.L.A.
Library: see Libraries.
Number of full-time academic staff: 830, including 105 professors.
Number of students: 6,248 full-time, 960 part-time.

Publications: *Calendar, General Prospectus, Faculty Prospectuses†, Postgraduate Prospectus†, Adult Education Prospectus†, Student Accommodation Handbook†, Faculty Handbooks†, Entrance Regulations and Information Handbook†, General University Regulations and Rules of Discipline, Higher Degrees and Postgraduate Courses Handbook†, Scholarships Handbook†, Institute of Professional Legal Studies Handbook†* (all annual).

### Deans:
Faculty of Arts: Prof. C. B. Radford.
Faculty of Science: Prof. E. W. Simon.
Faculty of Law and Jurisprudence: Prof. G. Hornsey.
Faculty of Medcine: Prof. A. H. G. Love.
Faculty of Economics and Social Sciences: Prof. R. Wallis.
Faculty of Engineering: Prof. P. P. Benham.
Faculty of Theology: Prof. M. J. McGann.
Faculty of Agriculture and Food Science: Prof. C. Dow.
Faculty of Education: Prof. J. F. Fulton.

### Professors:
Faculty of Arts:
ASTIN, A. E., M.A., M.R.I.A., Ancient History
BLACKING, J. A. R., M.A., PH.D., D.LITT. F.R.A.I., Social Anthropology
BRAIDWOOD, J., M.A., English Language and Literature
CRONIN, J., M.A., English
EVANS, J. D. G., M.A., PH.D., Logic and Metaphysics
GOODING, D. W., M.A., PH.D., M.R.I.A., Old Testament Greek

1555

GREER, DAVID C., M.A., Music
HARKNESS, D. W., M.A., PH.D., F.R.HIST.S., Irish History
HUXLEY, G. L., M.A., F.S.A., M.R.I.A., Greek
McEVOY, J. J., D.PHIL., M.A., M.S.I.E.P.M., Scholastic Philosophy
McGANN, M. J., B.LITT., M.A., Latin
RADFORD, C. B., M.A., PH.D., French
RUSSELL-GEBBETT, P. S. N., M.A., PH.D., Spanish
SINGH, G., M.A., PH.D., DOTT.LETT., Italian
SMALLWOOD, E. MARY, M.A., PH.D., F.S.A., Romano-Jewish History
STOCKMAN, G., M.A., PH.D., Celtic
WARREN, W. L., M.A., D.PHIL., M.R.I.A., F.R.HIST.S., F.R.S.L., Modern History
WELLS, D. A., M.A., PH.D., German
WHEELER, M. C. C., M.A., M.LITT., Slavonic Studies

*Faculty of Science:*
BATES, Sir DAVID, D.SC., M.R.I.A., F.R.S., Theoretical Physics (Special Research Chair)
BROWN, K., M.A., A.PS.S.I., F.B.PS.S., Psychology
BURKE, P. G., PH.D., M.R.I.A., F.INST.P., F.R.S., Mathematical Physics
BURNS, D. T., PH.D., D.SC., F.I.C.I., C.CHEM., F.R.S.C., Analytical Chemistry
D'ARCY, P. F., O.B.E., PH.D., D.SC., F.P.S., C.CHEM., F.R.S.C., M.P.S.N.I., Pharmacy
ELMORE, D. T., PH.D., A.R.C.S., Biochemistry
GILBODY, H. B., PH.D., F.INST.P., M.R.I.A., Physics
GLOCKLING, F., PH.D., D.SC., Inorganic Chemistry
GRIGG, R. GRAD.R.S.C., PH.D., Organic Chemistry
IVIN, K. J., PH.D., SC.D., C.CHEM., F.R.S.C., M.R.I.A., Physical Chemistry
KIRK, W., B.A., F.S.A.SCOT., Geography
LISSBERGER, P. H., PH.D., F.INST.P., Physics
MADDOX, I. J., PH.D., D.SC., F.I.M.A., Pure Mathematics
MARTIN, S. J., M.SC., PH.D., Gene Biochemistry
MOISEIWITSCH, B. L., PH.D., M.R.I.A., Applied Mathematics
ROONEY, J. T., PH.D., Catalytic Chemistry
SCHWARZACHER, W., D.PHIL., F.G.S., Mathematical Geology
SIMON, E. W., M.A., D.PHIL., D.SC., M.R.I.A., F.I.BIOL., Botany
SMITH, F. J., PH.D., F.I.M.A., F.B.C.S., M.R.I.A., Computer Science
THREADGOLD, L. T., PH.D., SC.D., F.I.BIOL., Zoology
WRIGHT, A. D., PH.D., F.G.S., Geology

*Faculty of Law:*
CAMPBELL, C. M., LL.B., Jurisprudence
GREER, DESMOND S., B.C.L., LL.B., Law
HORNSEY, G., LL.M., Public Law

*Faculty of Medicine:*
ADAMS, C. P., M.D.S., F.D.S.R.C.S., F.F.D.R.C.S.I., D.ORTH.R.C.S., Orthodontics
ALLDRITT, W. A. S., M.D.S., F.D.S.R.C.S., F.F.D.R.C.S.I., Periodontics
ALLEN, INGRID V., M.D., F.R.C.PATH., Neuropathology
ARCHER, D. B., M.B., D.O., F.R.C.S., Ophthalmology
BRIDGES, J. B., T.D., B.SC., M.D., Physiology
BRIDGES, J. M., M.D., F.R.C.P.ED., F.R.C.PATH., Haematology
BUCHANAN, K. D., PH.D., M.D., F.R.C.P.G., F.R.C.P.ED., F.R.C.P., Metabolic Medicine
CARRÉ, I. J., M.A., M.D., F.R.C.P., F.R.C.P.I., D.C.H., Child Health
CINNAMOND, M. J., M.B., F.R.C.S.E., Otorhinolaryngology
CLARKE, R. S. J., M.D., PH.D., F.F.A.R.C.S., Clinical Anaesthetics
DUNDEE, J. W., M.D., PH.D., F.F.A.R.C.S., M.R.C.P., Anaesthetics
ELWOOD, J., M.D., PH.D., D.P.H., M.R.C.S., F.F.C.M., D.I.H., Social and Preventive Medicine
FENTON, G. W., M.B., F.R.C.P.ED., F.R.C.PSYCH., M.R.C.P., D.P.M., Mental Health
FRASER, K. B., M.C., M.D., D.SC., F.R.S.E., Microbiology
GILLIES, R. R., M.D., F.R.C.P.ED., F.R.C.PATH., D.P.H., Clinical Bacteriology
GREENFIELD, A. A., PH.D., F.I.S., Medical Statistics
HARRISON, T. J., M.D., PH.D., Anatomy
IRWIN, W. G., M.D., D.OBST.R.C.O.G., F.R.C.G.P., General Practice
LEWIS, S. A., PH.D., A.B.PS.S., Psychology Applied to Medicine
LOVE, A. H. G., B.SC., M.D., F.R.C.P., F.R.C.P.I., Gastro-Enterology
LOWRY, W. S. B., M.SC., M.B., D.M.R.T., F.R.C.R., F.R.C.P.I., Cancer Studies
McDEVITT, D. G., D.SC., M.D., F.R.C.P., F.R.C.P.I., Clinical Pharmacology
McKEOWN, E. FLORENCE, M.D., D.SC., F.R.C.PATH., F.R.C.P., Morbid Anatomy
MEBAN, C., M.D., PH.D., Anatomy
NEVIN, N. C., B.SC., M.D., F.R.C.P., Medical Genetics
O'BRIEN, F. V., B.D.S., M.B., F.D.S.R.C.P.S., Dental Surgery
PINKERTON, J. H. McK., M.D., F.R.C.O.G., F.R.C.P.I., Midwifery and Gynaecology
RODDIE, I. C., T.D., M.D., D.SC., F.R.C.P.I., M.R.I.A., Physiology
ROY, A. D., M.B., CH.B., F.R.C.S., F.R.C.S.ED., F.R.C.S.I., F.A.C.S., Surgery
SHANKS, R. G., D.SC., M.D., F.R.C.P., F.R.C.P.ED., Therapeutics and Pharmacology
STEWART, D. J., M.D.S., F.D.S.R.C.S., F.F.D.R.C.S.I., Paediatric and Preventive Dentistry
STOUT, R. W., M.D., F.R.C.P., Geriatric Medicine
SWALLOW, J. N., M.D.S., Restorative Dentistry
THOMPSON, W., B.SC., M.D., F.R.C.O.G., Midwifery and Gynaecology
VALLANCE-OWEN, J., M.A., M.D., F.R.C.P., F.R.C.P.I., F.R.C.PATH., Medicine
WALLACE, W. F. M., B.SC., M.D., M.R.C.P., Applied Physiology
WILSON, R. I., M.B.E., M.B., F.R.C.S.E., F.R.C.S.I., Orthopaedic Surgery

*Faculty of Economics and Social Sciences:*
BATES, J. A., PH.D., C.B.I.M., Business Economics
BLACK, R. D. C., B.COMM., M.A., PH.D., M.R.I.A., F.B.A., Economics
BLACK, W., PH.D., Applied Economics
BROWN, M. J., M.S.W., PH.D., Social Administration and Social Work
EHRLICH, C., PH.D., Economic and Social History
O'LEARY, C., M.A., D.PHIL., Political Science
PERKS, R. W., B.A., M.SC., F.C.M.A., M.B.I.M., Accounting
WALLIS, R., D.PHIL., Sociology

*Faculty of Engineering:*
BENHAM, P. P., PH.D., D.SC., C.ENG., F.I.MECH.E., F.P.R.I., F.R.AE.S., M.R.I.A., Aeronautical Engineering
BLAIR, G. P., PH.D., D.SC., C.ENG., F.I.MECH.E., F.S.A.E., Mechanical Engineering
CROSSLAND, B., C.B.E., PH.D., D.SC., F.I.MECH.E., F.I.PROD.E., F.WELD.I., M.R.I.A., F.ENG., F.R.S., Mechanical Engineering
HOGG, B. W., PH.D., C.ENG., M.I.E.E., S.M.I.E.E., Electrical Engineering
JENNINGS, A., D.SC., C.ENG., F.I.M.A., M.R.AE.S., M.I.STRUCT.E., Civil Engineering
KIDD, W. J., B.ARCH., R.I.B.A., Architecture
LONG, A. E., PH.D., C.ENG., M.I.C.E., M.I.STRUCT.E., Civil Engineering
ROBERTS, A. P., D.I.C., F.I.M.A., Engineering Mathematics
RYAN, W. D., M.SC., PH.D., C.ENG., F.I.E.E., Electronics

*Faculty of Agriculture and Food Science:*
DOW, C., B.V.M.S., PH.D., M.R.C.V.S., F.R.C.PATH., Comparative Pathology
FURNESS, G. W., M.SC., Agricultural Economics
HOLDING, A. J., PH.D., M.S., Agricultural Bacteriology
MARKS, R. J., M.SC., PH.D., M.I.BIOL., Agricultural Zoology
MURDOCH, J. C., PH.D., Crop and Animal Production
TODD, J. R., M.AGR., PH.D., C.CHEM., F.R.S.C., F.I.F.S.T., Agricultural Chemistry
WRIGHT, C. E., PH.D., F.I.BIOL., Agricultural Botany

*Faculty of Education:*
BANFIELD, J., M.A., PH.D., Dir. of Extra-Mural Studies
CATHCART, H. R., M.A., PH.D., Education
FULTON, J. F., M.A., PH.D., Education
KNOX, H. M., M.A., M.ED., PH.D., Education
NICHOLS, A. K., M.ED., Dir. of Physical Education

READERS:

*Faculty of Arts:*
BROOME, P., PH.D., French
DEVLIN, D. D., M.A., English
GRAY, J., M.A., F.R.HIST.S., Modern History
HAMILTON, J. N., M.A., PH.D., Celtic
SCOTT, A. B., D.PHIL., Latin
STEWART, A. T. Q., M.A., PH.D., F.R.HIST.S., Irish History

*Faculty of Science:*
ARMITAGE, D. H., PH.D., Pure Mathematics
BATES, B., M.SC., D.I.C., PH.D., M.INST.P., Physics
BELL, K. L., M.A., PH.D., Applied Mathematics and Theoretical Physics
BOAL, F. W., M.S., PH.D., Geography
BOYD, D. K., PH.D., D.SC., C.CHEM., M.R.S.C., Organic Chemistry
BROWN, W. P., M.A., PH.D., F.B.PS.S., F.PS.S.I., Psychology
BUCHANAN, R. H., PH.D., Geography
COMMON, R., PH.D., Geography
CROTHERS, D. S. F., M.A., PH.D., F.INST.P., F.I.M.A., Applied Mathematics and Theoretical Physics
DAVIES, R. J. H., M.A., PH.D., Biochemistry
GALWEY, A. K., D.I.C., PH.D., D.SC., C.CHEM., F.R.S.C., Physical Chemistry
GOTTO, R. V., D.SC., Zoology
GRIMSHAW, J., PH.D., D.SC., C.CHEM., F.R.S.C., Organic Chemistry
HALTON, D. W., PH.D., M.I.BIOL., Zoology
HAMILTON, J. N., M.A., PH.D., Celtic
HIBBERT, A., M.A., D.PHIL., Applied Mathematics and Theoretical Physics
JOHN, P. C. L., PH.D., Botany

# UNIVERSITIES AND COLLEGES

JOHNSTON, A. R., PH.D., Physics
KINGSTON, A. E., PH.D., Applied Mathematics and Theoretical Physics
LEWIS, F. A., PH.D., Inorganic Chemistry
MURPHY, R. F., PH.D., Biochemistry
NELSON, S. M., D.PHIL., M.SC., PH.D., C.CHEM., M.R.S.C., Inorganic Chemistry
PARK, D., PH.D., D.SC., Botany
PERROTT, R. H., PH.D., M.B.C.S., Computer Science
PINK, R. C., D.SC., C.CHEM., M.R.S.C., Physical Chemistry
PRESTON, J., PH.D., Geology
ROBINSON, P. M., PH.D., Botany
RUDGE, M. R. H., PH.D., Applied Mathematics and Theoretical Physics
SMITH, D. L., PH.D., Botany
STEER, M. W., PH.D., Botany
STEWART, A. L., PH.D., Applied Mathematics and Theoretical Physics
SVEHLA, G., PH.D., D.SC., C.CHEM., F.R.S.C., Analytical Chemistry
SWAIN, S., PH.D., Applied Mathematics and Theoretical Physics
WRIGHT, A. L., B.COMM., M.A., Economics

*Faculty of Law:*
KNIGHT, M. T., M.A., LL.D., Common Law

*Faculty of Medicine:*
ALLEN, J. D., M.D., Physiology
MCNEILL, T. A., B.SC., M.D., Immunobiology
MERRETT, J. D., PH.D., Medical Statistics
PARKS, T. G., M.B., M.CH., F.R.C.S.ED., Surgical Science
RICHARDSON, A., B.DS., D.P.D., M.SC., F.F.D.R.C.S.I., D.ORTH.R.C.S., Orthodontics

*Faculty of Economics and Social Sciences:*
BROWN, K. D., M.A., PH.D., F.R.HIST.S., Economic and Social History
CLARKSON, L. A., PH.D., Economic and Social History
WHYTE, J. H., M.A., PH.D., M.R.I.A., Political Science
WRIGHT, A. L., M.A., Economics

*Faculty of Engineering:*
BAHRANI, A., M.SC., PH.D., C.ENG., F.I.MECH.E., F.WELD.I., M.I.M., Mechanical and Industrial Engineering
DUNWOODY, J., PH.D., C.ENG., M.I.MECH.E., F.I.M.A., Engineering Mathematics
MONDS, F. C., PH.D., Electrical and Electronic Engineering
NEWMANN, M. M., PH.D., Engineering Mathematics
STEWART, J. A. C., PH.D., Electrical and Electronic Engineering

*Faculty of Agriculture and Food Science:*
GORDON, F. J., PH.D., Crop and Animal Production
JACKSON, N., M.A., PH.D., D.SC., C.CHEM., F.R.S.C., F.I.BIOL., Agricultural and Food Chemistry
LOGAN, C., PH.D., Mycology and Plant Pathology
PATTERSON, J. T., D.I.C., PH.D., F.I.F.S.T., Agricultural and Food Bacteriology

*Faculty of Education:*
MUINZER, L. A., M.A., PH.D., Extra-Mural Studies

ATTACHED INSTITUTES:

**Institute of Irish Studies:** Dir. (vacant).

**Institute of Professional Legal Studies:** Dir. J. H. S. ELLIOTT, B.C.L., B.A., LL.B., Solicitor.

# THE UNION THEOLOGICAL COLLEGE
BOTANIC AVE.,
BELFAST 7
Telephone: 25374.

Founded 1978 as result of merger of Assembly's College (founded 1847) and Magee Theological College, Londonderry. The members of faculty constitute the Presbyterian Theological Faculty, Ireland, which grants the theological degrees of B.D. and D.D. It is situated in close proximity to Queen's University and is a recognized College of the University.

*Principal:* Rev. Prof. E. A. RUSSELL, M.TH., D.D.
*Vice-Principal:* Rev. Prof. J. R. BOYD, B.A., B.D.
*Secretary:* Rev. Prof. J. S. MCIVOR, B.A., B.D., PH.D.
*Warden:* Rev. Prof. J. R. BOYD, B.A., B.D.
*Librarian:* Miss ANNE MCCONNELL, M.A., B.D.

Library: 22,000 vols.
Number of teachers: 8, including 5 professors.
Number of students: 70.

PROFESSORS:

BOYD, Rev. J. R., B.A., B.D., Christian Ethics
HOLMES, Rev. R. F. G., M.A., M.LITT., Church History
MCIVOR, Rev. J. S., PH.D., Old Testament
RUSSELL, Rev. E. A., B.A., M.TH., D.D., New Testament
THOMPSON, Rev. J., PH.D., Systematic Theology

# U.K. (NORTHERN IRELAND)

# BELFAST COLLEGE OF TECHNOLOGY
BELFAST, BT1 6DJ

Erected by the Council of the County Borough of Belfast, under the control of the Belfast Education and Library Board. Founded 1901. Opened in 1907.

*Principal:* W. F. K. KERR, M.SC., PH.D., C.ENG., F.I.MECH.E.
*Vice-Principal:* G. MCBRATNEY, B.SC., C.ENG., F.I.MECH.E.
*Registrar:* (vacant).

# ULSTER POLYTECHNIC
SHORE RD.,
NEWTOWNABBEY,
CO. ANTRIM, BT37 0QB
Telephone: Whiteabbey 65131.
Founded 1971.

State control; Language of Instruction: English; Academic year: September to July.

*Rector:* DEREK BIRLEY, M.A.
*Pro-Rectors:* ANNE E. H. DUFTON, M.A., R. I. HOUSTON, M.S., M.I.E.E., R. H. MCGUIGAN, PH.D., C.ENG., F.I.MECH.E., M.I.PROD.E., O. M. WHITE, M.SC., PH.D., F.INST.P.
*Academic Registrar:* P. J. CONWAY, B.A.
*Librarian:* B. G. BAGGETT, B.SC., M.I.INF.SC.

Number of teachers: 577.
Number of students: 4,500 full-time and sandwich, 3,200 part-time.

DEANS:

*Arts:* Prof. R. J. GAVIN, M.A., PH.D.
*Business and Management:* Prof. J. A. O'REILLY, B.COMM., M.B.A., M.H.C.I.M.A.
*Science:* Prof. J. A. MAGOWAN, M.SC., PH.D.
*Social and Health Sciences:* Prof. R. A. F. ELLIS, B.A., A.B.PS.S.
*Technology:* Prof. D. MCCLOY, PH.D., D.SC., D.I.C., C.ENG., F.I.MECH.E., F.R.AE.F.
*Education:* (vacant).

# UNITED KINGDOM
## OVERSEAS TERRITORIES AND PROTECTED STATES

## ASCENSION ISLAND

**Ascension Historical Society:** Fort Hayes Museum, Georgetown; information on the South Atlantic islands of Ascension, St. Helena and Tristan da Cunha, especially their unique natural history; Chair. Wing Commdr. KENNETH H. PICKUP, R.A.F.

**Fort Hayes Museum:** Georgetown; museum in 19th-century fort; local volcanic geology and natural history displays; collection of hand-blown bottles; naval artefacts; amateur astronomical observatory; library of Ascension and St. Helena material, early maps, photographs and paintings.

## BERMUDA
### LEARNED SOCIETIES

**Astronomical Society of Bermuda:** P.O.B. 1054, Hamilton 5; Pres. MORLEY E. B. NASH, M.D.; Sec. C. MCGONAGLE; publs. *Bermuda Sky Watch, Cosmos*.

**Bermuda Audubon Society:** P.O.B. 1328, Hamilton 5; Pres. DAVID WINGATE, M.B.E., D.SC.; publ. *Newsletter*.

**Bermuda Society of Arts:** Art Gallery, City Hall, P.O.B. 1202, Hamilton 5; f. 1956; 300 mems.; Pres. Dr. MARJORIE BEAN; Curator Mrs. VALERIE WEDDUP.

**Bermuda National Trust:** P.O.B. 61, Hamilton 5; f. 1970 to promote the preservation of lands and buildings of natural or historic interest; 2,000 mems.; Pres. GERALD SIMONS; Dir. W. S. ZUILL; publ. *Newsletter* (quarterly).

**Bermuda Historical Society:** Par-la-Ville, Hamilton; 120 mems.; Pres. Sir DUDLEY SPURLING, Kt., C.B.E., J.P.

**Bermuda Technical Society:** P.O.B. 151, Hamilton 5; c. 85 mems.; Pres. W. R. HOLLAND; Sec. ALLAN BLUNDELL.

**Royal Commonwealth Society, Bermuda Branch:** P.O.B. 1245, Hamilton 5; Chair. JOHN GILBERT; Hon. Sec. IAN K. M. ESSLEMONT.

**St. George's Historical Society:** Cnr. Duke of Kent St. and Featherbed Alley, St. George's; 109 mems.; Pres. Mrs. W. OLIVEY; Curator Mrs. ELIZABETH E. FRITH.

### RESEARCH INSTITUTES

**Bermuda Department of Agriculture and Fisheries:** P.O.B. 834, Hamilton 5, Bermuda; f. 1898; Dir. IDWAL W. HUGHES, M.S.A., PH.D.; Asst. Dirs. EDWARD A. MANUEL, B.S.A. (Agriculture), JAMES BURNETT-HERKES, M.SC., PH.D. (Fisheries); publs. *Annual Report, Monthly Bulletin*, occasional special reports.

**Bermuda Biological Station for Research:** Ferry Reach 1-15; f. 1903; research in nearly all aspects of marine sciences and oceanography; summer courses organized in marine invertebrates, embryology, geology, etc. and high school and college facilities for instruction in marine sciences; a 65 ft. research ship is attached to the station, also a number of smaller boats for inshore work; library of over 13,000 vols.; Pres. Dr. W. REDWOOD WRIGHT; Dir. Dr. WOLFGANG STERRER; publs *Contributions†, Special Publications*.

### LIBRARIES AND MUSEUMS

**Bermuda Aquarium, Museum and Zoo:** P.O.B. 145, The Flatts, Smiths 3; f. 1928; live zoological collection, local natural history and other exhibits; 1,500 mems. (Bermuda Zoological Soc.); library of 2,000 vols.; Curator RICHARD J. WINCHELL; publ. *Critter Talk* (quarterly).

**Bermuda Archives:** Government Administration Building, Hamilton 5-24; f. 1949; only repository for official and non-governmental records; Archivist HELEN ROWE.

**Bermuda Library:** Par-la-Ville, Hamilton 5-31; f. 1839; national and public library services; 140,000 vols.; special collection of Bermudiana; br. libraries in St. George's and Somerset; Librarian Mrs. MARY SKIFFINGTON, B.A., A.L.A.

**Bermuda Maritime Museum:** P.O.B. 273, Somerset 9; f. 1975; area includes fortress of Bermuda Dockyard and exhibits representing Bermuda maritime history; Chair. Dr. J. C. ARNELL; Sec. J. D. ROBINSON; Dir. Dr. E. C. HARRIS; publ. *Ratlines†* (2 a year).

**Confederate Museum:** (mailing address: P.O.B. 61, Hamilton 5); situated in St. George's; administered by the Bermuda National Trust; displays depicting Bermuda's role in the American Civil War; collection of antique furniture; Dir. W. S. ZUILL.

**President Henry Tucker House:** (mailing address: P.O.B. 61, Hamilton 5); situated in St. George's; administered by the Bermuda National Trust; historic house with period furniture; Dir. W. S. ZUILL.

**Verdmont:** Collector's Hill, Smith's Parish (P.O.B. 61, Hamilton); administered by Bermuda National Trust; historic house with period furniture; Dir. W. S. ZUILL.

### COLLEGE
#### BERMUDA COLLEGE

PROSPECT, DEVONSHIRE

*Chief Executive Officer:* A. C. H. HALLETT.

Number of teachers: c. 90.
Number of students: c. 2,000 (day and evening).

HEADS OF DEPARTMENTS:
*Commerce and Technology:* B. I. GUISHARD, B.A., B.ED., F.B.I.M.
*Academic Studies:* G. COOK, D.PHIL.
*Hotel Technology:* (vacant).

## GIBRALTAR
### LEARNED SOCIETIES

**Gibraltar Ornithological Society:** c/o Gibraltar Museum, Bomb House Lane; f. 1978; 168 mems.; Chair. CLIVE FINLAYSON; Sec. J. E. CORTES; publs. *Alectorist†, Newsletter* (annually).

**The Gibraltar Society:** John Mackintosh Hall, Gibraltar; f. 1929; for the advancement of general knowledge of Gibraltar and its environs; 301 mems.; Chair. E. A. J. CANESSA; Hon. Sec. E. F. J. GARCIA.

## LIBRARIES AND MUSEUM

**Gibraltar Garrison Library:** f. 1793; extensive reference section, 38,000 vols.; Sec. J. M. SEARLE.

**Gibraltar Library Service:** 310 Main St.; f. 1977; 5,000 vols.; Librarian MELVYN ROSE, B.SC., M.I.BIOL.

**Gibraltar Museum:** Bomb House Lane; f. 1930; controlled by a Committee of Management appointed by the Governor; collection of local Natural History, Archaeology (especially Palaeolithic and Phoenician) and History (especially Local and Military); Curator/Archivist J. BENSUSAN.

# HONG KONG

## LEARNED SOCIETIES AND RESEARCH INSTITUTES

**Asia Foundation, The:** P.O.B. 1738, Hong Kong; f. 1954; one of 14 branches of the main organization in the U.S.A. (q.v.); to support Asian social, educational, economic and cultural development, and regional co-operation among Asian countries; Rep. FRANK E. DINES.

**British Council:** Easey Commercial Bldg., 253-61 Hennessy Rd., Wanchai; Rep. O. R. SIDDLE; library: see Libraries.

**Goethe Institut:** 141 Des Voeux Rd. Central, P.O.B. 5531, Hong Kong; f. 1962; Concerts, Filmshows, Exhibitions, Lectures; information service; Language classes; Library of 4,650 vols.; Dir. Dr. R. THOMA.

**Hong Kong Chinese PEN Centre:** Victoria Park Mansion, 15th floor, Flat A, Paterson St.; f. 1955; 85 mems.; library of 1,600 vols.; Pres. HO CHIA-HUA; Sec. WILLIAM HSU; publ. *PEN News* (weekly in Chinese).

**Hong Kong Library Association:** c/o The Library, University of Hong Kong, Pokfulam Rd.; f. 1958; 300 mems.; Chair. TIMOTHY CHOW; Hon. Sec. ALEX NG; publs. *Journal, Newsletter*.

**Hong Kong Medical Association:** P.O.B. 1957, General Post Office, Hong Kong; f. 1920 to promote the welfare and protect the lawful interests of the medical profession, to promote co-operation with national and international medical societies, and to work for the advancement of medical science; 1,850 mems.; Pres. Dr. DAVID C. T. WONG; Hon. Sec. Dr. LEE KIN HUNG; publ. *Bulletin†* (annually).

**Hong Kong Surgical Society:** c/o Federation of Medical Societies, Duke of Windsor Bldg., 4th Floor, 15 Hennessy Rd.; f. 1964 to promote, disseminate and advance knowledge of surgery among fellows and mems. of the society; organizes lectures, discussions, social and academic programmes, etc.; 200 mems.; Pres. Dr. C. H. LEONG; Sec. Dr. K. S. LEE; publ. *Journal†*.

**Royal Asiatic Society, Hong Kong Branch:** P.O.B. 3864, Hong Kong; f. 1847, re-established 1959; for the encouragement of the arts, science and literature in relation to Asia, particularly Hong Kong; lectures and social activities; 452 mems., 108 overseas mems.; library of 1,014 vols.; Pres. Dr. M. TOPLEY; Hon. Sec. Mrs. M. O'HARA; publ. *Journal†*.

**Royal Observatory, Hong Kong:** f. 1884; library of 20,000 vols.; Dir. J. P. PEACOCK; publs. *Meteorological Results* (annually), *Astronomical Tables and Star Charts* (annually), *Departmental Reports* (annually), *Extracts of Meteorological Observations* (monthly), *Weather Summaries* (monthly), *Weather Maps* (daily), *Rainfall Chart* (monthly and annually), *Technical Note†* (irregularly), *Climatological Note†* (irregularly), *Technical Memoir†* (irregularly), *Forecasters' Note* (irregularly), *Magnetic Results, Marine Climatological Summaries* (annually).

**Union Research Institute:** 9 College Rd., Kowloon; f. 1951; private institution affiliated to Union Cultural Organization Ltd.; studies of contemporary Chinese affairs, including material, research and publication programmes; 31 mems.; library of 30,000 vols.; Dir. WILLIAM HSU; Sec.-Gen. WANG TSIEN-WU; publs. *Chung-hua Yueh-pao* (China Monthly), *Union Research Service* (twice a week in English).

## LIBRARIES

**British Council Library:** Easey Commercial Bldg., 253-61 Hennessy Rd., Wanchai; 9,314 vols., 110 periodicals; Librarian Mrs. C. H. JEN.

**Chinese University of Hong Kong University Library System:** Shatin, New Territories, f. 1963; 3 branch libraries, Chung Chi College Library; f. 1951; New Asia College Library; f. 1949; United College Library, f. 1956; over 714,000 vols. in Oriental and Western languages, 5,733 current periodicals and 10,042 reels of microfilms; special collections: rare Chinese books, Korean 13th-century *Tripitake* printed from wood blocks, 6,980 Tun Huang MSS.; modern Chinese drama comprising c. 1,850 titles; collection of 56 oracle bones; University Librarian LAI-BING KAN, M.A., M.L.S., PH.D., A.L.A.A., M.I.INF.SC.

**Hong Kong Junior Chamber of Commerce Libraries:** 24 Ice House St., 4th Floor, Hong Kong; 27 branch libraries for children.

**Hong Kong Polytechnic Library:** Kowloon, Hong Kong; f. 1972; 200,000 vols., mostly in English; over 5,000 current periodicals, a comprehensive collection of standards and a collection of non-print materials; Librarian BARRY L. BURTON, B.A., A.L.A.A., M.B.I.M.; publ. *Hongkongiana*.

**New Territories Public Libraries, Cultural Services Department:** Park-In Commercial Centre, 24th Floor, Dundas St., Kowloon, Hong Kong; Tsuen Wan Branch: f. 1974; Cheung Chau Branch: f. 1977; Tai Po Branch: f. 1977; Sha Tin Branch: f. 1977; Sheung Shui Branch: f. 1978; Tuen Mun Branch: f. 1978; Yuen Long Branch: f. 1979; Kwai Chung Branch: f. 1979; Tai O Branch: f. 1980; Mobile: f. 1981; joint bookstock of 44,379 vols. in English, 125,234 vols. in Chinese, 285 titles of current newspapers and periodicals, 1,110 items of audio-visual material; reference, adult and junior libraries, newspapers and periodicals reading rooms, study rooms, audio-visual services, extension activities; Chief Librarian ALEX NG; publ. *Catalogue of books printed in Hong Kong* (quarterly).

**Sun Yat-Sen Library:** 172-174 Boundary St., Kowloon; f. 1953; public library; 110,000 vols.; Dir. L. S. WONG; Librarian D. Y. LIN, M.F., LL.D.

**University of Hong Kong Main Library:** f. 1911; contains about 315,000 vols. in Western languages, including the Hong Kong and Morrison collections; c. 3,400 current periodicals; Librarian H. A. RYDINGS, M.B.E., M.A., A.L.A.

  **Fung Ping Shan Library:** f. 1932; in the same building; about 220,000 vols. in Chinese and other oriental languages.

  **Medical Library:** Sassoon Rd.; 49,000 vols., 700 current periodicals.

  **Law Library:** Knowles Bldg., Bonham Rd.; f. 1969; 18,000 vols., 300 current periodicals.

**Urban Council Libraries:** City Hall, Edinburgh Pl., Hong Kong; f. 1962; Waterloo Rd. Branch: f. 1965; Pok Fu Lam Branch: f. 1970; Yau Ma Tei Branch: f. 1971; Ping Shek Branch: f. 1972; Kwun Tong Branch: f. 1975; Kowloon Mobile Library: f. 1976; Sham Shui Po Branch, Western Branch: f. 1977; Mei Foo Branch, Hong Kong Mobile: f. 1978; Wan Chai Branch, Chai Wan Branch: f. 1979; North Point Branch: f. 1981;

joint bookstock of 334,394 vols. in English, 698,445 vols. in Chinese, 618 titles of current newspapers and periodicals, 17,419 items of audio-visual material; reference, adult and junior libraries; Chief Librarian TIMOTHY A. CHOW, L. ÈS L., DIP.LIB., A.L.A.A.

## MUSEUMS

**Hong Kong Museum of Art:** Edinburgh Place, Hong Kong; f. 1962; Chinese antiquities, incl. the Henry Yeung collection; historical paintings, prints and drawings of Hong Kong, Macao and China, incl. Chater, Sayer, Law and Ho Tung collections; contemporary works by local artists; Curator LAURENCE C. S. TAM.

**Hong Kong Museum of History:** 4th Floor, Star House, Salisbury Rd., Kowloon, Hong Kong; f. 1975; archaeology, ethnology and local history of Hong Kong, incl. the Fr. Raphael Maglioni and Fr. Daniel J. Finn archaeological collections from Hong Kong and South China; Chinese fishing junk models; historical photographs; active excavations and field work; Lei Cheng Uk Han Tomb and branch museum; Curator B. A. V. PEACOCK.

## UNIVERSITIES AND COLLEGES

### UNIVERSITY OF HONG KONG
POKFULAM RD., HONG KONG
Telephone: 5-468161.
Founded 1911.

*Chancellor:* H.E. THE GOVERNOR OF HONG KONG.
*Pro-Chancellor:* Sir ALBERT RODRIGUES, C.B.E., E.D., LL.D., J.P.
*Vice-Chancellor:* RAYSON LISUNG HUANG, C.B.E., D.PHIL., D.SC., J.P.
*Pro-Vice-Chancellors:* Prof. L. K. YOUNG, M.A., D.PHIL., J.P., Prof. J. B. GIBSON, O.B.E., M.D., F.R.C.P., F.R.C. PATH.
*Treasurer:* M. G. R. SANDBERG, O.B.E., J.P.
*Dean of Students:* P. M. WHYTE, B.A.
*Registrar:* E. L. ALLEYNE, M.B.E., B.A., M.LITT., J.P.
*Secretary:* N. J. GILLANDERS, LL.B., F.C.I.S., F.C.M.A., F.S.C.A., J.P.
*Librarian:* H. A. RYDINGS, M.B.E., M.A., A.L.A.

Number of teaching staff: 580 full-time.
Number of students: 6,308.

Publications: *Calendar†, Vice-Chancellor's Report†, Univ. Gazette†, Undergrad* (students), *Interflow*.

DEANS:
*Faculty of Arts:* Dr. N. LEE, M.A., PH.D.
*Faculty of Science:* Prof. S. C. CHAN, PH.D., D.SC., F.R.S.C., F.R.S.A.
*Faculty of Medicine:* Prof. A. C. L. HSIEH, M.D., D.SC.
*Faculty of Engineering:* Prof. Y. K. CHEUNG, PH.D., D.SC., C.ENG., F.I.C.E., F.I.STRUCT.E., F.I.E., F.A.S.C.E., F.H.K.I.E.
*Faculty of Social Sciences:* Dr. S. C. FAN, PH.D., F.I.S., F.S.S.

PROFESSORS:
AITCHISON, J., M.A., D.SC., F.R.S., Statistics
BINNIE DAWSON, J. L. M., R.D., D.PHIL., F.B.PS.S., Psychology
BOYDE, T. R. C., B.SC., M.D., Biochemistry
BRIMER, M. A., M.A., Education
BROOK, A. H., L.D.S.R.C.S., B.D.S., F.D.S., M.D.S., Children's Dentistry and Orthodontics
BRUGES, E. A., PH.D., F.I.MECH.E., F.I.MAR.E., M.A.S.M.E., Mechanical Engineering
CHAN, D. K. O., M.SC., PH.D., Zoology
CHAN, S. C., PH.D., D.SC., F.R.S.C., F.R.S.A., Chemistry
CHAN, T. K., M.B., B.S., F.R.C.P., Medicine
CHEN, Y. M., D.SC., Mathematics
CHENG, F. C. Y., M.B., B.S., F.R.C.S., F.A.C.S., F.R.A.C.S., Surgery
CHEUNG, Y. K., PH.D., D.SC., F.I.C.E., F.I.STRUCT.E., F.I.E., F.A.S.C.E., F.H.K.I.E., Civil Engineering
CLARK, R. K. F., B.D.S., PH.D., L.D.S.R.C.S., F.D.S., R.C.P.S., Prosthetic Dentistry
COOKE, B. L., PH.D., Education
DAVIES, W. I. R., M.SC., B.D.S., L.D.S.R.C.S., Periodontics and Public Health
ELLIS, A. J., D.PHIL., D.SC., Mathematics
EVANS, D. M. E., LL.B., B.C.L., J.P., Law
FEARNHEAD, R. W., M.D.S., L.D.S.R.C.S., D.SC., Oral Anatomy
GIBSON, J. B., O.B.E., M.D., F.R.C.P., F.R.C.PATH., Pathology
GRANT, C. J., PH.D., Geography
GRIFFITHS, D. A., PH.D., D.SC., Botany
GROVES, M. C., D.PHIL., Sociology
HARRIS, P. B., PH.D., D.LITT., Political Science
HO, P. Y.; PH.D., D.SC., F.INST.P., F.A.H.A., Chinese
HODGE, P., M.A., Social Work
HOWE, G. L., F.D.S.R.C.S., L.R.C.P., M.R.C.S., M.D.S., F.F.D.R.C.S., Oral Surgery and Medicine
HSIEH, A. C. L., M.D., D.SC., Physiology
HWANG, J. C. C., M.SC., PH.D., Physiology
KING, F. H. H., M.A., D.PHIL., Economics
KWOK, R. Y. W., M.S.(ARCH.), M.S., PH.D., Urban Studies and Planning
LEONG, C. Y., M.B., B.S., F.R.C.S., Orthopaedic Surgery
LEUNG, W. S., PH.D., M.SC., C.ENG., F.I.E.E., F.I.E.R.E., SEN.M.I.E.E.E., Electrical Engineering
LISOWSKI, F. P., L.M., PH.D., L.R.C.P.I., L.R.C.S.I., Anatomy
LOFTS, B., PH.D., D.SC., F.I.BIOL., Zoology
LORD, R., M.A., Dir. Language Centre
LUMB, P., D.SC.(ENG.), D.I.C., F.I.C.E., F.A.S.C.E., F.G.S., Civil Engineering
LYE, K. C., B.ARCH , M.F.A., M.R.A.I.C., R.I.B.A., Architecture
MA, H. K., M.B., B.S., F.R.C.O.G., J.P., Obstetrics and Gynaecology
MOK, C. K., M.B., B.S., F.R.C.S., F.A.C.S., Surgery
MOORE, F.C.T., D.PHIL., Philosophy
NEWMAN, D. J., A.R.C.S., PH.D., D.SC., F.F.I.P., Physics
NG, M. H., PH.D., Microbiology
ONG, Tan Sri G. B., O.B.E., M.D., M.B B.S., F.R.C.S., F.A.C.S., F.R.A.C.S., F.G.S., J.P., Surgery
PAYNE, D. S., PH.D., F.R.S.C., A.R.C.S., Chemistry
RENSON, C. E., L.D.S.R.C.S., PH.D., D.D.P.H.R.C.S., Conservative Dentistry
RIPPLE, R. E., M.S., PH.D., Psychology
SHORTRIDGE, K. F., PH.D., Microbiology
TODD, D., M.D., F.R.C.P., F.R.A.C.P., J.P., Medicine
TSO, S. C., M.B., B.S., F.R.C.P., Medicine
WILLOUGHBY, P. G., LL.M., Law
WONG, J., B.SC., M.B., B.S., PH.D., F.R.A.C.S., Surgery
YEUNG, C. Y., M.B., B.S., D.C.H., F.R.C.P., Paediatrics
YOUNG, L. K., M.A., D.PHIL., J.P., History
YOUNG, R. T. T., M.D., F.R.C.P., F.R.A.C.P., J.P., Medicine

### THE CHINESE UNIVERSITY OF HONG KONG
SHATIN, NEW TERRITORIES, HONG KONG
Telephone: 0-633111.
Founded 1963

Chung Chi College, New Asia College and United College are Foundation Colleges of the University (*see below*). Principal languages of instruction: Chinese and English; Academic year: August to July. The University is controlled by a self-governing corporation.

*Chancellor:* H. E. THE GOVERNOR OF HONG KONG.
*Vice-Chancellor:* Prof. MA LIN, PH.D., J.P.
*Pro-Vice-Chancellors:* G. H. CHOA, C.B.E., M.D., F.R.C.P., F.F.C.M., D.T.M. & H., J.P.; B. HSU, PH.D., F.I.P., F.I.O.P.
*Treasurer:* The Hon. Q. W. LEE, C.B.E., LL.D., J.P.
*Secretary:* F. C. CHEN, M.A., PH.D.
*Registrar:* J. T. S. CHEN, LL.B., LIC.SC. ECON. ET POL., D.LITT., ORDRE DES PALMES ACADEMIQUES.
*Librarian:* LAI-BING KAN, M.A., M.L.S., PH.D., A.L.A.A.

Library: *see* Libraries.

Number of teachers: 503 full-time, 80 part-time.
Number of students: 4,796 full-time, 609 part-time.

Publications: *University Calendar* (annual), *University Bulletin* (quarterly), *Journal of The Chinese University of Hong Kong* (annual), *Journal of the Institute of Chinese Studies* (annual), *Renditions* (Chinese-English Translation Magazine, 2 a year), etc.

DEANS:

*Graduate School:* S. W. TAM, PH.D.
*Faculty of Arts:* D. C. LAU, M.A., LL.D.
*Faculty of Business Administration:* K. C. MUN, M.A., PH.D.
*Faculty of Medicine:* G. H. CHOA, C.B.E., M.D., D.T.M. & H., F.R.C.P., F.F.C.M.
*Faculty of Science:* L. B. THROWER, O.B.E., M.SC., F.L.S., PH.D.
*Faculty of Social Science:* R. P. L. LEE, PH.D.

PROFESSORS:

CHAN, Y. W., PH.D., Physics
CHANG, S. D., M.A., PH.D., Geography
CHANG, S. T., M.S., PH.D., Biology
CHEN, C. F., M.S., PH.D., Electronics
CHEN, C. N., M.B., M.SC., Psychiatry
CHEN, T. C., M.A., PH.D., I.E.E.E., Computer Science and Electronics
CHOA, G. H., C.B.E., M.D., D.T.M. & H., F.R.C.P., J.P., Administrative Medicine
DONNAN, S. P. B., M.SC., M.PHIL., Community Medicine
ESPY, J. L., S.M., D.B.A., Lingnan Institute of Business Administration
GARDINER, J. E., M.A., PH.D., Pharmacology
GWILT, D., MUS.B., Music
HAMANN, W. C., M.D., PH.D., Physiology
HSING, M. H., B.A., Economics
HSU, B., PH.D., F.I.P., F.I.O.P., Physics
HSUEH, S. S., M.A., Government and Public Administration
JOHNSON, F. C., M.A., ED.D., English
JONES, J. F., M.SW., M.A.P.A., PH.D., Social Work
LAU, D. C., M.A., LL.D., Chinese Language and Literature
LEE, J. C. K., PH.D., Morbid Anatomy
LIU, S. H., M.A., PH.D., Philosophy
LOH, S. C., PH.D., Computer Science
RICHES, D. J., B.SC., M.B., B.S., PH.D., M.R.C.S., L.R.C.P., Anatomy
THROWER, L. B., O.B.E., M.SC., F.L.S., PH.D., J.P., Biology
TO, C. Y., M.A., PH.D., School of Education
YU, T., M.A., Journalism and Communication Studies

CONSTITUENT COLLEGES AND INSTITUTES:

**Chung Chi College:** f. 1951.
*College Head:* P. Y. K. FU, PH.D.
Number of teachers: 153 (full-time).
Number of students: 1,445 (full-time).

**New Asia College:** f. 1949.
*College Head:* AMBROSE Y. C. KING, PH.D.
Number of teachers: 141 (full-time).
Number of students: 1,375 (full-time).

**United College:** f. 1956.
*College Head:* T. C. CHEN, M.A., PH.D., I.E.E.E.
Number of teachers 152 (full-time).
Number of students: 1,597 (full-time).

**School of Education:** f. 1965; 574 students (95 full-time); Dir. C. Y. TO, PH.D.

**Graduate School:** f. 1966; 284 students; Dean S. W. TAM, PH.D.

**Department of Extramural Studies:** f. 1965; Dir. T. C. LAI, M.A., DIP.AD.ED., J.P.

**Institute of Chinese Studies:** f. 1967; Dir. T. K. CHENG, PH.D.

**Institute of Social Studies and Humanities:** f. 1965; Dir. M. H. HSING, B.A.

**Institute of Science and Technology:** f. 1965; Dir. H. M. CHANG, M.SC., PH.D.

## HONG KONG POLYTECHNIC
### KOWLOON

Founded 1972 (formerly Hong Kong Technical College). Autonomous control, financed mainly from the University and Polytechnic Grants Committee; Language of instruction: English.

*President:* H.E. the Governor of Hong Kong, Sir MURRAY MACLEHOSE, G.B.E., K.C.M.G., K.C.V.O., M.A.
*Chairman of Council:* The Hon. Sir SZE-YUEN CHUNG, C.B.E., D.SC., PH.D., C.ENG., F.I.MECH.E., F.I.PROD.E., C.B.I.M., J.P.
*Director:* K. L. C. LEGG, O.B.E., M.SC., PH.D., C.ENG., F.H.K.I.E., F.I.MECH.E., F.R.AE.S., F.C.I.T., J.P.
*Deputy Director:* CHING YUEN-KAI, M.B.E., PH.D., D.I.C., C.ENG., M.I.E.R.E., F.I.E.E., J.P.
*Secretary to Council and Aide to Director:* S. F. BAILEY, C.B.E., BAR.-AT-LAW.

Library: *see* Libraries.

Number of teachers: 820 full-time.

Number of students: 7,660 full-time, 3,500 day release (part-time), 13,400 evening.

Publications: *Prospectus*†, *Annual Report*†, *Handbook for Full-time Students*, *Handbook for Part-time Students*, *Part-Time Day Release Handbook*, *Library Handbook*, *Consultancy Handbook*.

HEADS OF DEPARTMENTS:

BARNES, P. F. R., M.A., Languages
BROMFIELD, A. C., Master Mariner, M.R.I.N., M.N.I., F.B.I.M., Nautical Studies
CHAN, KA-KU, M.SC., F.S.D.C., F.T.I., C.COL., Textiles and Clothing
CHANG, SZE-SHEN, PH.D., C.ENG., F.I.MECH.E., M.I.PROD.E., F.H.K.I.E., Mechanical and Marine Engineering
DERMONT, A. R., F.C.I.S., M.INST.AM., M.B.I.M., Accountancy (acting)
FARR, M. B., M.A., Design
GINSBURG, K. M., PH.D., C.ENG., A.C.T., F.I.M., Applied Science
HAIGH, P., B.A., F.B.I.M., M.I.I.M., Business and Management Studies
LEES, L. H., M.SC., PH.D., M.I.E.E., P.ENG., C.ENG., M.I E.E.E., SEN.M.A.I.I.E., M.H.K.I.E., Electrical Engineering
LEWIS, W. H. P., PH.D., F.I.M.L.S., M.R.C.PATH., Medical and Health Care
LINDSAY, D. V., C.ENG., F.I.MECH.E., M.I.PROD.E., M.I.MAR.E., M.I.PLANT.E., M.H.K.I.E., M.I.M. & C., M.I.T.O., Industrial Centre
MACQUARRIE, L. B., M.S.W., Social Work
MEAD, G P., M.TECH., C.A.S., CERT.ED., L.I.M.A., F.B.C.S., F.I.D.P., Computing Studies
RICHARDSON, S., M.SC., PH.D., C.ENG., F.I.MECH.E., F.I.PROD.E., F.B.I.M., F.H.K.I.E., Production and Industrial Engineering
SLATER, B. E., F.H.C.I.M.A., D.M.S., M.B.I.M., Institutional Management and Catering Studies
STRINGER, R. D., F.R.I.C.S., F.C.I.O.B., Building and Surveying
TANG, CHE-HONG, IRVING, D.SC., F.I.M.A., F.B.C.S., Mathematical Studies
WARD, H. S., PH.D., C.ENG., M.I.C.E., Civil and Structural Engineering
WONG, SOOK-LEUNG, JOSHUA, PH.D., C.ENG., F.I.E.R.E., M.I.E.E.E., Electronic Engineering

**Morrison Hill Technical Institute:** 6 Oi Kwan Rd., Wanchai, Hong Kong; f. 1969; courses in commercial studies, construction, electrical engineering, mechanical engineering and general studies; 88 full-time and 550 part-time teachers; 12,000 full-time and part-time students; library of c. 15,100 vols.; Principal ALICK FONG-YAN; Vice-Principal TSANG HING-SEN.

# MONTSERRAT

**Montserrat Public Library:** Plymouth; operates mobile library service; c. 17,000 vols.

# ST. HELENA

**St. Helena Heritage Society:** Broadway House, Jamestown; f. 1979; c. 60 mems.; aims to awaken public interest in and appreciation of the geography, history, natural history, architecture and culture of St. Helena; to promote high standards of planning and architecture; to secure the preservation of natural features, flora and fauna, wrecks of historic interest, etc.; museum; Chair. Ven. Archdeacon LINDSAY; Sec. ERIC M. GEORGE.

# UNITED STATES OF AMERICA
Population 216,817,000

## ACADEMIES

### NATIONAL ACADEMY OF SCIENCES—NATIONAL ACADEMY OF ENGINEERING—INSTITUTE OF MEDICINE—NATIONAL RESEARCH COUNCIL

2101 Constitution Ave., Washington, D.C. 20418.

The National Academy of Sciences is a private non-profitmaking organization dedicated to the advancement of science and its use for general welfare. Its Congressional charter of 1863 calls upon it to serve as an independent adviser to the Federal Government in science and technology and provides it with broad authority to determine its organization. Membership (currently about 1,325) is by election only and is in recognition of research accomplishments.

In December 1964, a National Academy of Engineering was created under the charter of the Academy of Sciences as a parallel organization, autonomous in the selection of its membership but co-ordinated with the Academy of Sciences in the provision of advice to the Federal Government.

The Institute of Medicine was chartered by the National Academy of Sciences in 1970 in recognition of the problems posed in the provision of adequate health services. The Institute identifies important issues that relate to health and medicine, initiates and conducts studies of national policy and planning for health care, responds to requests from the federal government for studies and advice, and establishes liaison with societies in the field.

The National Research Council was established by the Academy of Sciences in 1916 to permit a broader association of scientists and engineers in the work of the Academy. The Research Council is now the principal operating agency of both Academies, carrying out studies by means of appointed committees of scientists and engineers. Policies for the work of the Research Council are established by a Governing Board, consisting of representatives of the elected councils of the two Academies and of the Institute of Medicine.

### NATIONAL ACADEMY OF SCIENCES
Founded 1863.

*President:* FRANK PRESS.
*Vice-President:* JAMES D. EBERT.
*Home Secretary:* BRYCE CRAWFORD.
*Foreign Secretary:* THOMAS F. MALONE.
*Treasurer:* ELKAN R. BLOUT.
*Executive Officer:* PAUL L. SITTON.
*Comptroller:* DAVID WILLIAMS.
*Council of the Academy:* PAUL BERG, BRYCE CRAWFORD, JAMES D. EBERT, HERBERT FRIEDMAN, RALPH E. GOMORY, DANIEL E. KOSHLAND, ELWOOD JENSEN, ROBERT MCADAMS, ELIZABETH MILLER, WILLIAM NIERENBERG, GEORGE E. PALADE, FRANK PRESS, JOHN D. ROBERTS, I. M. SINGER, LEWIS THOMAS.

The Academy is divided into the following Sections, to which members are assigned at their own choice:

11 Mathematics
12 Astronomy
13 Physics
14 Chemistry
15 Geology
16 Geophysics
21 Biochemistry
22 Cellular and Developmental Biology
23 Physiological and Pharmacological Sciences
24 Neurobiology
25 Botany
26 Genetics
27 Population Biology, Evolution, Ecology
31 Engineering
32 Applied Biology
33 Applied Physical and Mathematical Sciences
41 Medical Genetics, Hematology, Oncology
42 Medical Physiology, Edocrinology, Metabolism
43 Medical Microbiology and Immunology
51 Anthropology
52 Psychology
53 Social and Political Sciences
54 Economic Sciences

MEMBERS:

21 ABELES, ROBERT H., Graduate Department of Biochemistry, Brandeis University, Waltham, Mass. 02154.
15 ABELSON, PHILIP H., Science Magazine, 1515 Massachusetts Ave., N.W., Washington, D.C. 20005.
13 ADAIR, ROBERT K., Department of Physics, Yale University, 217 Prospect St., New Haven, Conn. 06520.
51 ADAMS, ROBERT MCCORMICK, The Oriental Institute, 1155 East 58th St., Chicago, Ill. 60637.
26 ADELBERG, EDWARD A., Department of Human Genetics, Yale University, 333 Cedar St., New Haven, Conn. 06510.
32 ADKISSON, PERRY L., Texas A & M University, College Station, Texas 77843.
21 ADLER, JULIUS, Depts. of Biochemistry and Genetics, Univ. of Wisconsin, Madison, Wis. 53706.
13 ADLER, STEPHEN LOUIS, School of Natural Sciences, Institute of Advanced Study, Princeton, N.J. 08540.
33 AGNEW, HAROLD M., General Atomic Co., P.O.B. 81608, San Diego, Calif. 92138.
11 AHLFORS, LARS V., PH.D., Department of Mathematics, Harvard University, Cambridge, Mass. 02138.
42 AHRENS, EDWARD H., Jr., Rockefeller University, 1230 York Ave., New York, N.Y. 10021.
16 AKI, KEIITI, Massachusetts Institute of Technology, Cambridge, Mass. 02139.
ALBERTS, BRUCE M., University of California, San Francisco, Calif. 94143.
14 ALBERTY, ROBERT A., School of Science, Massachusetts Institute of Technology, Cambridge, Mass. 02139.
14 ALDER, BERNI J., Lawrence Livermore Laboratory, P.O.B. 808, Livermore, Calif. 94550.
27 ALEXANDER, RICHARD D., Museum of Zoology, University of Michigan, Ann Arbor, Mich. 48109.
27 ALLARD, ROBERT W., Department of Genetics, University of California, Davis, Calif. 95616.
15 ALLEN, CLARENCE R., Seismological Laboratory, California Institute of Technology, Pasadena, Calif. 91125.
12 ALLER, LAWRENCE HUGH, Department of Astronomy, University of California, Los Angeles, Calif. 90024.
53 ALMOND, GABRIEL ABRAHAM, Dept. of Political Science, Stanford University, Stanford, Calif. 94305.
13 ALVAREZ, LUIS W., Lawrence Berkeley Laboratory, University of California, Berkeley, Calif. 94720.
21 AMES, BRUCE NATHAN, Department of Biochemistry, University of California, Berkeley, Calif. 94720.
16 ANDERS, EDWARD, Enrico Fermi Institute, University of Chicago, Chicago, Ill. 60637.
13 ANDERSON, CARL D., California Institute of Technology, Pasadena, Calif. 91125.

13 ANDERSON, HERBERT L., Los Alamos Scientific Laboratory, Mail Stop 434, Los Alamos, N.M. 87545.
16 ANDERSON, KINSEY A., University of California, Berkeley, Calif. 94720.
13 ANDERSON, PHILIP W., Room 1D-26B, Bell Telephone Laboratories, Inc., 600 Mountain Ave., Murray Hill, N.J. 07974.
33 ANDERSON, THEODORE W., Department of Statistics, Stanford University, Stanford, Calif. 94305.
26 ANDERSON, THOMAS FOXEN, Institute for Cancer Research, 7701 Burholme Avenue, Philadelphia, Pa. 19111.
25 ANDREWS, HENRY NATHANIEL, Jr., R.F.D.I., Box 146, Laconia, N.H. 03246.
21 ANFINSEN, CHRISTIAN BOEHMER, National Institutes of Health, Bethesda, Md. 20014.
16 ARNOLD, JAMES RICHARD, Dept. of Chemistry, B-017 University of California, San Diego, La Jolla, Calif. 92093.
25 **ARNOLD, WILLIAM ARCHIBALD**, Biology Division, Oak Ridge National Laboratory, P.O.B. Y, Oak Ridge, Tenn. 37830.
21 ARNON, DANIEL I., 251 Hilgard Hall, University of California, Berkeley, Calif. 94720.
54 ARROW, KENNETH J., Stanford University, Stanford, Calif. 94305.
11 ARTIN, MICHAEL, Dept. of Mathematics, 2-239 Massachusetts Institute of Technology, Cambridge, Mass. 02138.
21 ASHWELL, G. GILBERT, National Institutes of Health, Bethesda, Md. 20205.
33 ASTIN, ALLEN V., 5008 Battery Lane, Bethesda, Md. 20014.
52 ATKINSON, RICHARD C., National Science Foundation, Room 520, 1800 G St., N.W., Washington, D.C. 20550.
43 AUSTEN, K. FRANK, Harvard Medical School, Robert B. Brigham Hospital, Parker Hill Ave., Boston, Mass. 02120.
43 AUSTRIAN, ROBERT, University of Pennsylvania School of Medicine, Philadelphia, Pa. 19104.
24 AXELROD, JULIUS, National Institute of Mental Health, 9000 Rockville Pike, Bethesda, Md. 20205.
27 AYALA, FRANCISCO J., University of California, Davis, Calif. 95616.
53 AYDELOTTE, WILLIAM O., Department of History, University of Iowa, Iowa City, Ia. 52242.
12 BABCOCK, HORACE W., Hale Observatories, 813 Santa Barbara St., Pasadena, Calif. 91101.
13 BACHER, ROBERT F., B.S., PH.D., California Institute of Technology, Pasadena, Calif. 91125.
33 BACKUS, GEORGE E., University of California, San Diego, La Jolla, Calif. 92093.
33 BACKUS, JOHN, IBM Research Labroatory, 5600 Cottle Rd., San José, Calif. 95193.
12 BAHCALL, JOHN N., School of Natural Sciences, Institute for Advanced Study, Princeton, N.J. 08540.
13 BAINBRIDGE, KENNETH T., M.S., A.M., PH.D., 5 Nobscot Rd., Weston, Mass. 02193.
12 **BAKER, JAMES G.**, Harvard College Observatory, Cambridge, Mass. 02138.
51 BAKER, PAUL T., Pennsylvania State University, University Park, Pa. 16802.
14 BAKER, W. O., Bell Laboratories, Inc., Murray Hill, N.J. 07974.
14 BALDESCHWIELER, JOHN D., California Institute of Technology, Pasadena, Calif. 91125.
21 BALDWIN, ROBERT L., Stanford University, Stanford, Calif. 94305.
21 BALLOU, CLINTON EDWARD, Department of Biochemistry, University of California, Berkeley, Calif. 94720.
43 BALTIMORE, DAVID, Department of Biology, Massachusetts Institute of Technology, Cambridge, Mass. 02139.
25 BANKS, HARLAN P., Cornell University, Ithaca, N.Y. 14853.
13 **BARDEEN, JOHN**, University of Illinois, Urbana, Ill. 61801.
25 **BARGHOORN, ELSO S.**, The Biological Laboratories, Harvard University, Cambridge, Mass. 02138.
13 BARGMANN, VALENTINE, Princeton University, Princeton, N.J. 08540.
21 **BARKER, HORACE A., PH.D.**, Department of Biochemistry, University of California, Berkeley, Calif. 94720.
31 BARRETT, C. S., Denver Research Institute, University of Denver, Denver, Colo. 80208.
13 BARSCHALL, HENRY H., University of Wisconsin, Madison, Wis. 53706.
14 BARTLETT, PAUL D., Department of Chemistry, Texas Christian University, Fort Worth, Tex. 76129.
15 BARTON, PAUL B., Jr., U.S. Geological Survey National Center, M.S.959, Reston, Va. 22092.
42 BARTTER, FREDERIC C., University of Texas Health Science Center, 7400 Merton Minton Blvd., San Antonio, Tex. 78284.

14 BASOLO, FRED, Northwestern University, Evanston, Ill. 60201.
52 BEACH, FRANK AMBROSE, Department of Psychology, University of California, Berkeley, Calif. 94720.
26 BEADLE, G. W., 5630 Ingleside Ave., Chicago, Ill. 60637.
33 BEAN, CHARLES P., General Electric Co., P.O.B. 8, Schenectady, N.Y. 12301.
41 BEARN, ALEXANDER G., Merck, Sharp and Dohme International, P.O.B. 2000, Rahway, N.J. 07065.
BEAUCHAMP, JESSE L., California Institute of Technology, Pasadena, Calif. 91125.
54 BECKER, GARY STANLEY, Department of Economics, University of Chicago, 1126 East 59th St., Chicago, Ill. 60637.
43 BEESON, PAUL B., Seattle Veterans Administration Hospital, Seattle, Wash. 98108.
25 BEEVERS, HARRY, University of California, Santa Cruz, Calif. 95064.
24 BEIDLER, LLOYD M., Department of Biological Science, Florida State University, Tallahassee, Fla. 32306.
21 BEINERT, ABRAM, Harvard University, Cambridge, Mass. 02138.
43 BENACERRAF, BARUJ, Department of Pathology, Harvard Medical School, 25 Shattuck Street, Boston, Mass. 02115.
14 **BENDER, MYRON L.**, Northwestern University, Evanston, Ill. 60201.
42 BENDITT, EARL PHILIP, Department of Pathology, University of Washington School of Medicine, Seattle, Wash. 98195.
BENEDEK, GEORGE B., Department of Physics, Massachusetts Institute of Technology, Cambridge, Mass. 02139.
31 **BENEDICT, MANSON**, Massachusetts Institute of Technology, Cambridge, Mass. 02139.
BENNETT, MICHAEL V. L., Office of the Director, Division of Cellular Neurobiology, Albert Einstein College of Medicine.
25 BENSON, ANDREW A., Scripps Institution of Oceanography, University of California, San Diego, La Jolla, Calif. 92093.
BENSON, SIDNEY W., Department of Chemistry, University of Southern California, Los Angeles, Calif. 90007.
26 **BENZER, SEYMOUR**, California Institute of Technology, Pasadena, Calif. 91125.
21 BERG, PAUL, Department of Biochemistry, Stanford University School of Medicine, Stanford, Calif. 94305.
54 BERGSON, ABRAM, Harvard University, Cambridge, Mass. 02138.
33 BERKSON, JOSEPH, Mayo Clinic, Rochester, Minn. 55901.
51 BERLIN, OVERTON BRENT, University of California, Berkeley, Calif. 94720.
42 BERLINER, ROBERT W., Yale University School of Medicine, New Haven, Conn. 06510.
23 BERN, HOWARD A., Department of Zoology, University of California, Berkeley, Calif. 94720.
14 BERNSTEIN, RICHARD B., Dept. of Chemistry, Columbia University, New York, N.Y. 10027.
14 BERRY, R. STEPHEN, University of Chicago, Chicago, Ill. 60637.
53 BERRY, BRIAN J. L., Old Tavern Farm, 471 Massachusetts Ave., West Acton, Mass. 01720.
11 **BERS, LIPMAN**, Department of Mathematics, Columbia University, New York, N.Y. 10027.
14 BERSON, JEROME A., Department of Chemistry, Yale University, New Haven, Conn. 06520.
13 **BETHE, H. A., PH.D.**, Cornell University, Ithaca, N.Y. 14853
41 BEUTLER, ERNEST, Scripps Clinic and Research Foundation, 10666 North Torrey Pines Rd., La Jolla, Calif. 92037.
23 BEYER, KARL, Pennsylvania State University, Hershey, Pa. 17033.
14 BIGELEISEN, JACOB, State University of New York, Stony Brook, N.Y. 11794.
11 BING, R. H., Department of Mathematics, University of Texas, Austin, Tex. 78712.
11 **BIRKHOFF, GARRETT**, Harvard University, Cambridge, Mass. 02138.
43 BISHOP, J. MICHAEL, University of California, San Francisco, Calif. 94143.
31 BISPLINGHOFF, RAYMOND L., Office of the Director for Research and Development, Tyco Laboratories, Inc., Exeter, N.H. 03833.
13 BJORKEN, JAMES D., Stanford Linear Accelerator Center, Stanford University, P.O.B. 4349, Stanford, Calif. 94305.
25 BJÖRKMAN, OLLE, Carnegie Institute of Washington, 290 Panama St., Stanford, Calif. 94305.
11 BLACKWELL, DAVID H., University of California, Berkeley, Calif. 94720.
53 BLALOCK, H. M., Jr., 18425 17th Ave., N.W., Seattle, Wash. 98177.

53 BLAU, PETER M., Columbia University, New York, N.Y. 10027.
25 BLINKS, LAWRENCE R., Hopkins Marine Station of Stanford University, Pacific Grove, Calif. 93950.
13 BLOCH, FELIX, Stanford University, Stanford, Calif. 94305.
14 BLOCH, HERMAN S., 9700 Kevdale Ave., Skokie, Ill. 60076.
21 BLOCH, KONRAD E., Harvard University, 12 Oxford St., Cambridge, Mass. 02138.
13 BLOEMBERGEN, NICOLAAS, Pierce Hall, Harvard University, Cambridge, Mass. 02138.
24 BLOOM, FLOYD ELLIOT, Office of the Director, Arthur V. Davis Center for Behavioral Neurology, The Salk Institute, P.O.B. 1809, San Diego, Calif. 92112.
21 BLOUT, ELKAN R., Harvard Medical School, Boston, Mass. 02115.
41 BLUMBERG, BARUCH S., Institute for Cancer Research, 7701 Barholme Ave., Fox Chase, Philadelphia, Pa. 19111.
11 BOCHNER, SALOMON, PH.D., Department of Mathematics, Rice University, Houston, Texas 77001.
33 BODE, H. W., Harvard University, Cambridge, Mass. 02138.
22 BODENSTEIN, DIETRICH H. F. A., Department of Biology, University of Virginia, Charlottesville, Va. 22903.
24 BODIAN, DAVID, School of Medicine, Johns Hopkins University, 1721 Madison St., Baltimore, Md. 21205.
14 BOEKELHEIDE, VIRGIL CARL, University of Oregon, Eugene, Ore. 97403.
25 BOGORAD, LAWRENCE, The Biological Laboratories, Harvard University, Cambridge, Mass. 02138.
25 BOLD, HAROLD C., Department of Botany, University of Texas, Austin, Tex. 78712.
22 BONNER, JAMES FREDERICK, A.B., PH.D., California Institute of Technology, Pasadena, Calif. 91125.
22 BONNER, JOHN T., Department of Biology, Princeton University, Princeton, N.J. 08540.
16 BOOKER, HENRY G., University of California, San Diego, La Jolla, Calif. 92093.
53 BORCHERT, JOHN R., Department of Geography, University of Minnesota, Minneapolis, Minn. 55455.
32 BORLAUG, NORMAN E., International Maize and Wheat Improvement Center, Londres 40, Mexico 6, D.F., Mexico.
32 BORMANN, FREDERICK H., Greeley Memorial Laboratory, School of Forestry and Environmental Studies, Yale University, 370 Prospect St., New Haven, Conn. 06511.
11 BOSE, RAJ C., Department of Mathematics, Colorado State University, Fort Collins, Colo. 80523.
BOTSTEIN, DAVID, Department of Biology, Massachusetts Institute of Technology, Cambridge, Mass. 02139.
11 BOTT, RAOUL, Department of Mathematics, Harvard University, 1 Oxford St., Cambridge, Mass. 02138.
14 BOUDART, MICHEL, Department of Chemical Engineering, Stanford University, Stanford, Calif. 94305.
53 BOULDING, KENNETH E., Institute of Behavioral Science, University of Colorado, Boulder, Colo. 80309.
14 BOVEY, FRANK A., Bell Laboratories, 600 Mountain Ave., Murray Hill, N.J. 07974.
52 BOWER, GORDON H., Department of Psychology, Stanford University, Stanford, Calif. 94305.
15 BOYD, F. R., Jr., Geophysical Laboratory, Carnegie Institution of Washington, Washington, D.C. 20008.
21 BOYER, P. D., Molecular Biology Institute, University of California, Los Angeles, Calif. 90024.
BOYNTON, ROBERT M., Department of Psychology, University of California, San Diego, La Jolla, Calif. 92093.
43 BOYSE, EDWARD, Sloan-Kettering Institute for Cancer Research, 410 East 68th St., New York, N.Y. 10021.
15 BRACE, WILLIAM F., Department of Earth and Planetary Sciences, Massachusetts Institute of Technology, Cambridge, Mass. 02139.
13 BRADBURY, NORRIS E., 1451 47th St., Los Alamos, N.M. 87544.
21 BRADY, ROSCOE O., National Institutes of Health, Bethesda, Md. 20205.
51 BRAIDWOOD, ROBERT JOHN, RR5, Box 316, La Porte, Ind. 46350.
32 BRAKKE, MYRON K., University of Nebraska, Lincoln, Neb 68583.
33 BRANSCOMB, LEWIS M., IBM Corporation, Old Orchard Rd., Armonk, N.Y. 10504.
BRANTON, DANIEL, The Biological Laboratories, Harvard University, Cambridge, Mass. 02138.
13 BRATTAIN, WALTER H., Whitman College, Walla Walla, Wash. 99362.
14 BRAUMAN, JOHN I., Department of Chemistry, Stanford University, Calif. 94305.

25 BRAUN, ARMIN C., Rockefeller University, New York, N.Y. 10021.
42 BRAUNWALD, EUGENE, Harvard Medical School, Boston, Mass. 02215.
14 BRESLOW, RONALD, Columbia University, New York, N.Y. 10027.
14 BREWER, LEO, University of California, Berkeley, Calif. 94720.
13 BREWER, RICHARD G., IBM Research Laboratory, San Jose, Calif.
BRIDGES, WILLIAM B., Department of Electrical and Applied Physics, California Institute of Technology, Pasadena, Calif. 91125.
22 BRIGGS, ROBERT WILLIAM, Indiana University, Bloomington, Ind. 47401.
25 BRIGGS, WINSLOW R., Department of Plant Biology, Carnegie Institution of Washington, 290 Panama St., Stanford, Calif. 94305.
24 BRINK, FRANK, Jr., Rockefeller University, New York, N.Y. 10021.
26 BRINK, R. ALEXANDER, Dept. of Genetics, University of Wisconsin, Madison, Wis. 53706.
41 BRINKHOUS, KENNETH M., Department of Pathology, University of North Carolina School of Medicine, Chapel Hill, N.C. 27514.
26 BRITTEN, ROY J., Kerckhoff Marine Laboratory, California Institute of Technology, 101 Dahlia St., Corona del Mar, Calif. 92625.
23 BROBECK, JOHN R., 224 Vassar Ave., Swarthmore, Pa. 19081.
13 BRODE, ROBERT BIGHAM, PH.D., University of California, Berkeley, Calif. 94720.
23 BRODIE, BERNARD B., Pennsylvania State University College of Medicine, Hershey, Pa. 16802.
16 BROEKER, WALLACE S., Lamont-Doherty Geological Observatory of Columbia University, Palisades, N.Y. 10964.
23 BROOKS, CHANDLER McC., Department of Physiology, Box 31, State University of New York Downstate Medical Center, 450 Clarkson Ave., Brooklyn, N.Y. 11203.
33 BROOKS, HARVEY, Harvard University, Cambridge, Mass. 02138.
BROOKS, NORMAN H., Department of Environmental and Civil Engineering, California Institute of Technology, Pasadena, Calif. 91125.
11 BROWDER, FELIX E., Department of Mathematics, University of Chicago, 5734 University Ave., Chicago, Ill. 60637.
11 BROWDER, WILLIAM, Princeton University, Princeton, N.J. 08540.
22 BROWN, DONALD D., Department of Embryology, Carnegie Institution of Washington, 115 West University Parkway, Baltimore, Md. 21210.
13 BROWN, GERALD E., Physics Dept., State University of New York, Stony Brook, N.Y. 11794.
31 BROWN, HAROLD, Secretary of Defense, Washington, D.C. 20301.
16 BROWN, HARRISON S., East-West Center, 1777 East-West Rd., Honolulu, Hawaii 96848.
14 BROWN, HERBERT C., Purdue University, Lafayette, Ind. 47907.
41 BROWN, MICHAEL S., University of Texas Health Science Center, Dallas, Tex. 75235.
52 BROWN, ROGER W., Department of Psychology and Social Relations, Harvard University, 33 Kirkland St., Cambridge, Mass. 02138.
32 BROWN, WILLIAM L., Pioneer Hi-Bred International, Inc., Des Moines, Ia.
13 BRUECKNER, K. A., University of California, San Diego, La Jolla, Calif. 92093.
14 BRUICE, THOMAS C., Department of Chemistry, University of California, Santa Barbara, Calif. 93106.
31 BRYSON, ARTHUR E., Jr., Department of Aeronautics and Astronautics, Stanford University, Stanford, Calif. 94305.
21 BUCHANAN, JOHN MACHLIN, Massachusetts Institute of Technology, Cambridge, Mass. 02139.
14 BÜCHI, GEORGE H., Massachusetts Institute of Technology, Cambridge, Mass. 02139.
31 BUCHSBAUM, S. J., Bell Laboratories, Crawford Corner Rd., Holmdel, N.J. 07733.
33 BUDIANSKY, BERNARD, Division of Applied Sciences, Harvard University, Cambridge, Mass. 02138.
31 BUECHE, ARTHUR M., General Electric Co., 3135 Easton Turnpike, Fairfield, Conn. 06431.
15 BUERGER, M. J., S.M., PH.D Institute of Materials Science, University of Connecticut, U-136, Storrs, Conn. 06268.

24 BULLOCK, THEODORE H., School of Medicine, University of California, San Diego, La Jolla, Calif. 92093.
12 BURBIDGE, E. MARGARET, Dept. of Physics, University of California, San Diego, La Jolla, Calif. 92093.
12 BURKE, BERNARD F., Department of Physics, Massachusetts Institute of Technology, Cambridge, Mass. 02139.
42 BURNS, JOHN J., Hoffmann-La Roche Inc., Nutley, N.J. 07110.
25 BURRIS, R. H., University of Wisconsin, Madison, Wis. 53706.
33 BURSTEIN, ELIAS, University of Pennsylvania, Philadelphia, Pa. 19104.
32 BURTON, GLENN W., U.S. Dept. of Agriculture, Georgia Coastal Plain Experiment Station, Tifton, Ga. 31794.
25 BUTLER, WARREN L., Dept. of Biology, University of California, San Diego, La Jolla, Calif. 92093.
16 BYERS, HORACE R., 1036 Fairway, Santa Barbara, Calif. 93108.

33 CAHN, JOHN W., National Bureau of Standards, Bldg. 223, Room A153, Washington, D.C. 20234.
32 CAINE, STANLEY A., Environmental Studies, University of California, Santa Cruz, Calif 95060.
14 CAIRNS, T. L., P.O.B. 3941, Greenville, Del. 19807.
11 CALDERÓN, ALBERTO P., Dept. of Mathematics, University of Chicago, 5734 University, Chicago, Ill. 60637.
14 CALVIN, MELVIN, University of California, Berkeley, Calif. 94720.
16 CAMERON, A. G. W., Harvard College Observatory, 60 Garden St., Cambridge, Mass. 02138.
26 CAMPBELL, ALLAN M., Department of Biological Sciences, Stanford University, Stanford, Calif. 94305.
53 CAMPBELL, ANGUS, University of Michigan, Ann Arbor, Mich. 48109.
53 CAMPBELL, DONALD T., Department of Psychology, Northwestern University, Evanston, Ill. 60201.
43 CANNON, PAUL R., Box 79, Route 2, Yorkville, Ill. 60560.
33 CARRIER, GEORGE F., Division of Engineering and Applied Physics, Pierce Hall, Harvard University, Cambridge, Mass. 02138.
27 CARSON, HAMPTON L., School of Medicine, University of Hawaii, 1960 East-West Rd., Honolulu, Hawaii 96822.
21 CARTER, H. E., A.M., PH.D., University of Arizona, Tucson, Ariz. 85721.
33 CASE, KENNETH M., Rockefeller University, 1230 York Ave., New York, N.Y. 10021.
16 CHAMBERLAIN, JOSEPH W., Department of Space Physics and Astronomy, Rice University, Houston, Tex. 77001.
13 CHAMBERLAIN, OWEN, Lawrence Berkeley Laboratory, University of California, Berkeley, Calif. 94720.
21 CHANCE, BRITTON, University of Pennsylvania, Philadelphia, Pa. 19104.
12 CHANDRASEKHAR, S., Laboratory for Astrophysics and Space Research, 933 East 56th Street, Chicago, Ill. 60637.
51 CHANG, KWANG-CHIH, Peabody Museum, Harvard University, Cambridge, Mass. 02138.
43 CHANOCK, ROBERT M., Laboratory of Infectious Diseases, National Institutes of Health, Bethesda, Md. 20205.
14 CHAPMAN, ORVILLE L., Department of Chemistry, University of California, Los Angeles, Calif. 90024.
21 CHARGAFF, ERWIN, Cell Chemistry Laboratory, The Roosevelt Hospital, 428 West 59th St., New York, N.Y. 10019.
16 CHARNEY, JULE GREGORY, Department of Meteorology, Massachusetts Institute of Technology, Cambridge, Mass. 02139.
22 CHASE, MERRILL W., Rockefeller University, 1230 York Ave., New York, N.Y. 10021.
11 CHERN, SHIING-SHEN, University of California, Berkeley, Calif. 94720.
33 CHERNOFF, HERMAN, Massachusetts Institute of Technology, Cambridge, Mass. 02139.
13 CHEW, GEOFFREY FOUCAR, University of California, Berkeley, Calif. 94720.
31 CHODOROW, MARVIN, Edward L. Ginzton Laboratory, Stanford University, Stanford, Calif. 94305.
51 CHOMSKY, A. NOAM, Department of Foreign Literatures and Linguistics Massachusetts Institute of Technology, Cambridge, Mass. 02139.
43 CHOPPIN, PURNELL W., Rockefeller University, 1230 York Ave., New York, N.Y. 10021.
13 CHRISTY, ROBERT F., California Institute of Technology, Pasadena, Calif. 91125.
11 CHURCH, ALONZO, University of California, 405 Hilgard Ave., Los Angeles, Calif. 90024.
12 CLARK, GEORGE W., Massachusetts Institute of Technology, Cambridge, Mass. 02139.

25 CLAYTON, RODERICK K., 111 Brandon Place, Ithaca, N.Y. 14850.
42 CLEMENTS, JOHN A., Cardiovascular Research Institute, University of California, San Francisco, Calif. 94143.
33 CLOGSTON, ALBERT M., Bell Laboratories, 600 Mountain Ave., Murray Hill, N.J. 07974.
14 CLOSS, GERHARD L., Department of Chemistry, University of Chicago, 5735 South Ellis Ave., Chicago, Ill. 60637.
15 CLOUD, PRESTON, U.S. Geological Survey, Biogeology Clean Laboratory, University of California, Santa Barbara, Calif. 93106.
31 CLOUGH, RAY, University of California, Berkeley, Calif. 94720.
53 COALE, ANSLEY J., Office of Population Research, Princeton University, 21 Prospect Ave., Princeton, N.J. 08540.
32 COCKERHAM, C. CLARK, Department of Statistics, North Carolina State University, Box 5457, Raleigh, N.C. 27607.
12 CODE, ARTHUR D., Washburn Observatory, University of Wisconsin, 475 North Charter St., Madison, Wis. 53706.
24 COHEN, MELVIN J., Department of Biology, Kline Biology Tower, Yale University, New Haven, Conn. 06520.
33 COHEN, MORREL H., University of Chicago, Chicago, Il. 60637.
31 COHEN, MORRIS, Massachusetts Institute of Technology, Cambridge, Mass. 02139.
11 COHEN, PAUL J., Department of Mathematics, Stanford University, Stanford, Calif. 94305.
21 COHEN, PHILIP P., Department of Physiological Chemistry, 694 Medical Sciences Building, University of Wisconsin, Madison, Wis. 53706.
21 COHEN, SEYMOUR STANLEY, Dept. of Pharmacological Sciences, School of Basic Health Sciences, State University of New York, Stony Brook, N.Y. 11794.
22 COHEN, STANLEY, Vanderbilt University School of Medicine, Nashville, Tenn. 37240.
26 COHEN, STANLEY N., Stanford University School of Medicine, Stanford, Calif. 94305.
21 COHN, MILDRED, Dept. of Biochemistry and Biophysics, University of Pennsylvania School of Medicine, Philadelphia, Pa. 19104.
41 COHN, ZANVIL A., Rockefeller University, New York, N.Y. 10021.
27 COLBERT, EDWIN H., Museum of Northern Arizona, Fort Valley Rd., P.O.B., 720, Flagstaff, Ariz. 86001.
33 COLE, JULIAN D., Mechanics and Structures Department, University of California, Los Angeles, Calif. 90024.
23 COLE, KENNETH S., 2404 Loring St., San Diego, Calif. 92109.
53 COLEMAN, JAMES S., Department of Sociology, University of Chicago, Chicago, Ill. 60637.
15 COLEMAN, ROBERT G., U.S. Geological Survey, Menlo Park, Calif.
13 COLEMAN, SIDNEY, Harvard University, Cambridge, Mass. 02138.
31 COLLINS, SAMUEL C., 12322 River View Rd., Oxon Hill, Md. 20022.
14 COLLMAN, JAMES P., Department of Chemistry, Stanford University, Stanford, Calif. 94305.
21 COLOWICK, SIDNEY P., Department of Microbiology, Vanderbilt University School of Medicine, Nashville, Tenn. 37232.
15 COLSON, ELIZABETH F., Dept. of Anthropology, University of California, Berkeley, Calif. 94720.
23 COMROE, JULIUS H., JR., Cardiovascular Research Institute, University of California, San Francisco, Calif. 94143.
51 CONKLIN, HAROLD C., Department of Anthropology, Yale University, New Haven, Conn. 06520.
42 CONN, J. W., Admiralty Point, Apt. W-703, 2369 Gulf Shore Blvd., Naples, Fla. 33940.
14 CONNICK, ROBERT E., College of Chemistry, University of California, Berkeley, Calif. 94720.
53 CONVERSE, PHILIP E., Institute for Social Research, University of Michigan, Ann Arbor, Mich. 48106.
13 COOL, RODNEY L., Rockefeller University, New York, N.Y. 10021.
51 COON, CARLETON S., 207 Concord Street, Gloucester, Mass. 01930.
13 COOPER, LEON N., Department of Physics, Brown University, Providence, R.I. 02912.
14 COREY, E. J., Harvard University, 12 Oxford Street, Cambridge, Mass. 02138.
21 CORI, CARL F., M.D., Massachusetts General Hospital, Fruit Street, Boston, Mass. 02114.
14 COTTON, F. ALBERT, Department of Chemistry, Texas A & M University, College Station, Texas 77843.

25 COUCH, JOHN N., A.M., PH.D., University of North Carolina, Chapel Hill, N.C. 27514.
13 COURANT, ERNEST D., Building 902, Brookhaven National Laboratory, Upton, N.Y. 11973.
23 COURNAND, ANDRÉ FREDERIC, Columbia University, College of Physicians and Surgeons, 630 West 168th St., New York, N.Y. 10032.
32 COWLING, ELLIS BREVIER, North Carolina State University, Box 5485, Raleigh, N.C. 27607.
16 COX, ALLAN V., Stanford University, Stanford, Calif. 94305.
16 CRAIG, HARMON, Scripps Institution of Oceanography, A-020, University of California, San Diego, La Jolla, Calif. 92093.
14 CRAM, DONALD J., University of California, Los Angeles, Calif. 90024.
13 CRANE, H. RICHARD, Physics Department, University of Michigan, Ann Arbor, Mich. 48109.
14 CRAWFORD, BRYCE, Jr., University of Minnesota, Minneapolis, Minn. 55455.
13 CREUTZ, EDWARD C., Bishop Museum, P.O.B. 6037, Honolulu, Hawaii 96818.
13 CREWE, ALBERT V., Physical Sciences Division, Eckhart Hall, University of Chicago, Ill. 60637.
14 CRISTOL, STANLEY J., Department of Chemistry, University of Colorado, Boulder, Colo. 80309.
53 CRONBACH, LEE J., School of Education, Stanford University, Stanford, Calif. 94305.
13 CRONIN, JAMES WATSON, Enrico Fermi Institute, University of Chicago, Chicago, Ill. 60637.
CRONKITE, EUGENE P., Office of the Chairman, Medical Department, Medical Research Center, Brookhaven National Laboratory, Upton, N.Y. 11973.
26 CROW, JAMES F., University of Wisconsin, Madison, Wis. 53706.
CROWELL, JOHN C., Department of Geology, University of California, Santa Barbara, Calif. 93106.
14 CURTIN, DAVID Y., Department of Chemistry, University of Illinois, Urbana, Ill. 61801.
31 CUTLER, C. CHAPIN, Ginzton Laboratory, Stanford University, Stanford, Calif. 94305.
53 DAHL, ROBERT A., Department of Political Science, Yale University, New Haven, Conn. 06520.
33 DANTZIG, GEORGE B., Operations Research Department, Stanford University, Stanford, Calif. 94305.
32 DARBY, WILLIAM J., The Nutrition Foundation, Inc., 489 Fifth Ave., New York, N.Y. 10017.
27 DARLINGTON, PHILIP J., Jr., 71 Juniper Rd., Belmont, Mass. 02178.
31 DARLINGTON, SIDNEY, University of New Hampshire, 8 Fogg Drive, Durham, N.H. 03824.
22 DARNELL, JAMES E., Jr., Rockefeller University, New York, N.Y. 10021.
14 DAUBEN, WILLIAM G., Department of Chemistry, University of California, Berkeley, Calif. 94720.
23 DAVENPORT, HORACE W., Department of Physiology, University of Michigan School of Medicine, Ann Arbor, Mich. 48109.
31 DAVID, E. E., Jr., Office of the President, Exxon Research and Engineering Co., P.O.B. 101, Florham, N.J. 07932.
21 DAVIDSON, NORMAN R., California Institute of Technology, Pasadena, Calif. 91125.
21 DAVIE, EARL W., University of Washington, Seattle, Wash. 98195.
21 DAVIES, DAVID R., National Institutes of Health, Bethesda, Md. 20205.
21 DAVIS, BERNARD D., Bacterial Physiology Unit, Harvard Medical School, 25 Shattuck St., Boston, Mass. 02115.
32 DAVIS, GEORGE K., Institute of Food and Agricultural Sciences, University of Florida, Gainesville, Fla. 32611.
24 DAVIS, HALLOWELL, 7526 Cornell Ave., University City, Mo. 63160.
53 DAVIS, KINGSLEY, Population Research Laboratory, University of Southern California, University Park, Los Angeles, Calif. 90007.
DAWID, IGOR B., Section of Developmental Biochemistry, National Cancer Institute, National Institutes of Health, Bethesda, Md. 20205.
33 DAWSON, JOHN M., Dept. of Physics, University of California, 405 Hilgard Ave., Los Angeles, Calif. 90024.
54 DEBREU, GERARD, Dept. of Economics, University of California, Berkeley, Calif. 94720.
31 DEERE, DON U., 6834 S.W. 35th Way, Gainsville, Fla. 32601.
DEEVEY, EDWARD S., Jr., Florida State Museum, University of Florida, Gainesville, Fla. 32611.
13 DEHMELT, HANS, University of Washington, Seattle, Wash. 98195.

51 DE LAGUNA, FREDERICA, 221 Roberts Rd., Bryn Mawr, Pa. 19010.
21 DELUCA, H. F., University of Wisconsin, Madison, Wis. 53706.
31 DEN HARTOG, J. P., E.E., PH.D., Massachusetts Institute of Technology, Cambridge, Mass. 02139.
24 DETHIER, VINCENT G., Department of Zoology, University of Massachusetts, Amherst, Mass. 01002.
53 DEUTSCH, KARL W., Faculty of Arts and Sciences, Littauer 213, Harvard University, Cambridge, Mass. 02138.
13 DEUTSCH, MARTIN, Laboratory for Nuclear Science, Massachusetts Institute of Technology, Cambridge, Mass. 02139.
52 DE VALOIS, RUSSELL L., Department of Psychology, University of California, Berkeley, Calif. 94720.
27 DIAMOND, JARED M., University of California, Los Angeles, Calif. 90024.
13 DICKE, ROBERT H., Joseph Henry Laboratories, Physics Department, Princeton University, Princeton, N.J. 08540.
32 DIENER, THEODOR O., Plant Virology Laboratory, U.S. Dept. of Agriculture, Agricultural Research Center, Beltsville, Md. 20705.
21 DISCHE, ZACHARIAS, Department of Ophthalmology, College of Physicians and Surgeons, 630 W. 168th St., New York, N.Y. 10032.
43 DIXON, FRANK J., Scripps Clinic and Research Foundation, 10666 North Torrey Pines Rd., La Jolla, Calif. 92037.
14 DJERASSI, CARL, Stanford University, Stanford. Calif. 94305.
14 DOERING, WILLIAM VON EGGERS, 53 Francis Ave., Cambridge, Mass. 02138.
26 DOERMANN, AUGUST H., Department of Genetics, SK-50, University of Washington, Seattle, Wash. 98195.
21 DOISY, E. A., A.B., M.S., PH.D., St. Louis University School of Medicine, 1402 South Grand Boulevard, St. Louis. Mo. 63104.
42 DOLE, VINCENT P., Rockefeller University, New York, N.Y 10021.
11 DOOB, J. L., 208 W. High St., Urbana, Ill. 61801.
42 DORFMAN, ALBERT, Department of Pediatrics, University of Chicago, 5825 Maryland Ave., Chicago, Ill. 60637.
42 DORFMAN, RALPH I., 10465 Berkshire Drive, Los Altos Hills, Calif. 94022.
21 DOTY, PAUL M., Harvard University, 12 Oxford St., Cambridge, Mass. 02138.
24 DOWLING, JOHN E., The Biological Laboratories, Harvard University, 16 Divinity Ave., Cambridge, Mass. 02138.
12 DRAKE, F. D., National Astronomy and Ionosphere Center Space Sciences Building, Cornell University, Ithaca, N.Y 14853.
31 DRAPER, CHARLES STARK, Charles Stark Draper Laboratory, Inc., 555 Technology Square, Cambridge, Mass. 02139.
13 DRELL, SIDNEY D., Stanford University, P.O.B. 4349, Stanford, Calif. 94305.
14 DRICKAMER, HARRY G., University of Illinois, Urbana, Ill. 61801.
13 DUBRIDGE, L. A., A.M., PH.D., 5309 Cantante, Laguna Hills, Calif. 92653.
33 DUFFIN, R. J., Department of Mathematics, Carnegie-Mellon University, Schenley Park, Pittsburgh, Pa. 15213
22 DULBECCO, RENATO, The Salk Institute, P.O.B. 1809, San Diego, Calif. 92112.
53 DUNCAN, OTIS DUDLEY, Department of Sociology, University of Arizona, Tucson, Ariz. 85721.
21 DUWEZ, POL E., W. M. Keck Laboratory of Engineering Materials, California Institute of Technology, Pasadena, Calif. 91125.
13 DYSON, FREEMAN JOHN, Institute for Advanced Study, Princeton, N.J. 08540.
22 EALE, HARRY, Albert Einstein College of Medicine, Bronx N.Y. 10461.
22 EBERT, JAMES D., Carnegie Institution of Washington, Washington, D.C. 20005.
21 EDELMAN, GERALD M., Rockefeller University, New York, N.Y. 10021.
42 EDELMAN, ISIDORE S., Columbia University College of Physicians and Surgeons, 630 West 168th St., New York, N.Y. 10032.
31 EDGERTON, HAROLD E., Department of Electrical Engineering, Massachusetts Institute of Technology, Cambridge, Mass. 02139.
27 EDMONDSON, W. THOMAS, Department of Zoology, University of Washington, Seattle, Wash. 98195.
21 EDSALL, JOHN T., A.B., M.D., The Biological Laboratories, Harvard University, 16 Divinity Avenue, Cambridge, Mass. 02138.

51 EGGAN, F. R., University of Chicago, 1126 East 59th St., Chicago, Ill. 60637.
11 EILENBERG, SAMUEL, Columbia University, New York, N.Y. 10027.
22 EISEN, HERMAN N., Center for Cancer Research, Massachusetts Institute of Technology, Cambridge, Mass. 02139.
27 EISNER, THOMAS, Cornell University, Ithaca, N.Y. 14853.
31 ELIAS, PETER, Department of Electrical Engineering and Computer Science, Room NE43-839, M.I.T., Cambridge, Mass. 02139.
14 ELIEL, ERNEST L., Department of Chemistry, University of North Carolina, Chapel Hill. N.C. 27514.
14 EL-SAYED, MOSTAFA A., University of California, Los Angeles, Calif. 90024.
15 EMERY, KENNETH O., 74 Ransom Rd., Falmouth, Mass. 02540.
14 EMMETT, PAUL H., 23 Da Vinci, Lake Oswego, Ore. 97034.
31 EMMONS, HOWARD W., Pierce Hall, Harvard University, Cambridge, Mass. 02138.
22 ENDERS, JOHN F., M.A., PH.D., 64 Colbourne Crescent, Brookline, Mass. 02146.
15 ENGEL, ALBERT E. J., Scripps Institution of Oceanography, University of California, San Diego, A-020, La Jolla, Calif. 92093.
25 EPSTEIN, EMANUEL, Dept. of Land, Air and Water Resources, University of California, Davis, Calif. 95616.
16 EPSTEIN, SAMUEL, Division of Geological and Planetary Sciences, California Institute of Technology, Pasadena, Calif. 91125.
15 ERNST, W. G., Dept. of Earth and Space Sciences, University of California, Los Angeles, Calif. 90024.
21 ESTABROOK, RONALD W., University of Texas Health Science Center, 5323 Harry Hines Blvd., Dallas, Tex. 75235.
52 ESTES, WILLIAM K., Rockefeller University, New York, N.Y. 10021.
15 EUGSTER, HANS P., Department of Earth and Planetary Sciences, Johns Hopkins University, Baltimore, Md. 21218.
25 EVANS, HAROLD J., Department of Botany and Plant Pathology, Oregon State University, Corvallis, Ore. 97331.
27 EVANS, HOWARD E., Dept. of Zoology and Entomology, Colorado State University Fort Collins, Co. 80523.
24 EVARTS, EDWARD V., Building 36, Room 2D10, National Institute of Mental Health, Bethesda, Md. 20014.
14 EYRING, HENRY, B.A., M.S., PH.D., Department of Chemistry, University of Utah, Salt Lake City. Utah 84112.
13 FAIRBANK, WILLIAM M., Stanford University, Stanford, Calif. 94305.
31 FANO, ROBERT M., Dept. of Electrical Engineering and Computer Science, NE43-533, M.I.T., Cambridge, Mass. 02139.
13 FANO, UGO, University of Chicago, 1118 East 58th St., Chicago, Ill. 60637.
22 FAWCETT, DON W., Department of Anatomy, Harvard Medical School, 25 Shattuck St., Boston, Mass. 02115.
11 FEDERER, HERBERT, 287 Elmgrove Ave., Providence, R.I. 02906.
11 FEFFERMAN, CHARLES, Princeton University, Princeton, N.J. 08540.
13 FEHER, GEORGE, Dept. of Physics, B-019, University of California, San Diego, La Jolla, Calif. 92093.
11 FEIT, WALTER, Dept. of Mathematics, Yale University, P.O.B. 2155, Yale Station, New Haven, Conn. 06520.
21 FELSENFELD, GARY, Laboratory of Molecular Biology, NIAMDD, National Institutes of Health, Bethesda, Md. 20205.
14 FERRY, JOHN D., University of Wisconsin, Madison, Wis. 53706.
13 FESHBACH, HERMAN, Massachusetts Institute of Technology, Cambridge, Mass. 02139.
52 FESTINGER, LEON, Department of Psychology, New School for Social Research, 65 Fifth Ave., New York, N.Y. 10003.
41 FINCH, CLEMENT A., University of Washington School of Medicine, Seattle, Wash. 98195.
FINK, GERALD R., Department of Genetics, Cornell University, Ithaca, N.Y. 14853.
43 FINLAND, MAXWELL, Boston City Hospital, Boston, Mass. 02118.
21 FISCHER, EDMOND H., Department of Biochemistry, University of Washington, Seattle, Wash. 98195.
31 FISK, JAMES BROWN, Lee's Hill Rd., Box 85, Basking Ridge, N.J. 07920.
13 FITCH, VAL L., Joseph Henry Laboratories, Princeton University, Box 708, Princeton, N.J., 08440.

14 FIXMAN, MARSHALL, Colorado State University, Fort Collins, Colorado 80523.
51 FLANNERY, KENT V., University of Michigan, Ann Arbor, Mich. 48109.
31 FLETCHER, HARVEY, PH.D., D.S., 276 Eyring Science Center, Brigham Young University, Provo, Utah 84602.
24 FLEXNER, LOUIS B., School of Medicine, University of Pennsylvania. Philadelphia, Pa. 19104.
14 FLORY, PAUL JOHN, M.S., PH.D., Department of Chemistry, Stanford University, Stanford, Calif. 94305.
14 FLYGARE, W. H., Noyes Chemical Laboratory, University of Illinois, Urbana, Ill. 61801.
54 FOGEL, ROBERT W., Dept. of Economics, Harvard University, Cambridge, Mass. 02138.
14 FOLKERS, KARL AUGUST, University of Texas, Austin, Texas 78712.
16 FORBUSH, SCOTT ELLSWORTH, Carnegie Institute of Washington, 5241 Broad Branch Rd., N.W., Washington, D.C. 20015.
23 FORSTER, ROBERT E., Department of Physiology, School of Medicine, University of Pennsylvania, Philadelphia, Pa. 19104.
51 FOSTER, GEORGE McC., Jr., Department of Anthropology University of California, Berkeley, Calif. 94720.
13 FOWLER, WILLIAM A., California Institute of Technology, Pasadena, Calif. 91125.
22 FRAENKEL, GOTTFRIED S., University of Illinois, Urbana, Ill. 61801.
21 FRAENKEL-CONRAT, HEINZ L., Virus Laboratory, University of California, Berkeley, Calif. 94720.
43 FRANKLIN, EDWARD, New York University Medical Center, New York, N.Y. 10003.
13 FRAUENFELDER, HANS, Department of Physics, University of Illinois, Urbana, Ill. 61801.
42 FREDRICKSON, DONALD S., Office of the Director, National Institutes of Health, Bethesda, Md. 20205.
53 FREEDMAN, RONALD, Population Studies Center, University of Michigan, 1225 South University Ave., Ann Arbor, Mich. 48109.
25 FRENCH, C. STACEY, Carnegie Institution of Washington, Stanford, Calif. 94305.
FRIDOVICH, IRWIN, Department of Biochemistry, Duke University Medical Center, Durham, N.C. 27706.
14 FRIED, JOSEF, Department of Chemistry, University of Chicago, Chicago, Ill. 60637.
21 FRIEDKIN, MORRIS E., Basic Science Bldg. 4080, M-001. University of California, San Diego, La Jolla, Calif. 92093.
14 FRIEDLANDER, GERHART, Department of Chemistry, Brookhaven National Laboratory, Upton, N.Y. 11973.
12 FRIEDMAN, HERBERT, United States Naval Research Laboratory (Code 7100), Washington, D.C. 20375.
54 FRIEDMAN, MILTON, Hoover Institution, Stanford University, Stanford, Calif. 94305.
11 FRIEDRICHS, KURT OTTO, Courant Institute of Mathematical Sciences, New York University, New York, N.Y. 10012.
FRIEMAN, EDWARD A., Office of the Associate Director, Plasma Physics Laboratory, Princeton University, Princeton, N.J. 08540.
41 FRIEND, CHARLOTTE, Mount Sinai School of Medicine, City University of New York, Fifth and 100th St., New York, N.Y. 10029.
21 FRUTON, JOSEPH S., Yale University, 350 Kline Biology Tower, New Haven, Conn. 06520.
16 FULTZ, DAVE, Department of Geophysical Sciences, University of Chicago, 5734 South Ellis Ave., Chicago, Ill. 60637.
31 FURTH, HAROLD P., Princeton University, P.O.B. 451, Princeton, N.J. 08540.
14 FUSON, R. C., A.M., PH.D, University of Illinois, Urbana, Ill. 61801.
24 GAJDUSEK, D. CARLETON, National Institute of Neurological Diseases and Stroke, National Institutes of Health, Bethesda, Md. 20205.
52 GALAMBOS, ROBERT, University of California, San Diego, La Jolla, Calif. 02003.
22 GALL, JOSEPH G., Department of Biology, 418 Kline Biology Tower. Yale University, New Haven, Conn. 06520.
33 GARABEDIAN, PAUL R., New York University, 251 Mercer St., New York, N.Y. 10012.
22 GAREN, ALAN, Yale University, Box 1937, Yale Station, New Haven, Conn. 06520.
51 GARN, STANLEY M., Center for Human Growth and Development, University of Michigan, 1111 East Catherine St., Ann Arbor, Mich. 48109.

52 GARNER, WENDELL R., Department of Psychology, Yale University, New Haven, Conn. 06520.
15 GARRELS, ROBERT M., Department of Geological Sciences, Northwestern University, Evanston, Ill. 60201.
13 GARWIN, RICHARD L., Thomas J. Watson Research Center, IBM Corporation, P.O.B. 218, Yorktown Heights, N.Y. 10598.
14 GATES, MARSHALL DEMOTTE, Jr., Dept. of Chemistry, University of Rochester, Rochester, N.Y. 14627.
33 GEBALLE, THEODORE H., Department of Applied Physics, Stanford University, Stanford, Calif. 94305.
51 GEERTZ, CLIFFORD J., Institute for Advanced Study, Princeton, N.J. 08540.
21 GEIDUSCHEK, E. PETER, Department of Biology, University of California, San Diego, P.O.B. 109, La Jolla, Calif. 92093.
13 GELL-MANN, MURRAY, California Institute of Technology, Pasadena, Calif. 91125.
43 GERSHON, RICHARD K., Yale University School of Medicine, New Haven, Conn. 06520.
12 GIACCONI, RICCARDO, Center for Astrophysics, 60 Garden St., Cambridge, Mass. 02138.
33 GIAEVER IVAR, General Electric Co., Research and Development Center, P.O.B. 8, Schenectady, N.Y. 12301.
14 GIAUQUE, WILLIAM F., B.S., PH.D., SC.D., University of California, Berkeley, Calif. 02154.
25 GIBBS, MARTIN, Department of Biology, Brandeis University, Waltham, Mass. 02154.
41 GIBLETT, ELOISE R., Puget Sound Blood Center, Seattle, Wash.
52 GIBSON, ELEANOR J., Department of Psychology, Cornell University, Ithaca, N.Y. 14853.
16 GILBERT, J. FREEMAN, Institute of Geophysics and Planetary Physics, A-025, University of California, San Diego, La Jolla, Calif. 92093.
21 GILBERT, WALTER, Biological Laboratories, Harvard University, 16 Divinity Ave., Cambridge, Mass. 02138.
26 GILES, NORMAN H., Dept. of Zoology, University of Georgia, Athens, Ga. 30602.
23 GILMAN, ALFRED, Department of Pharmacology, Yale University School of Medicine, 333 Cedar St., New Haven, Conn. 06510.
14 GILMAN, HENRY, 3221 Oakland St., Ames, Iowa 50010.
31 GILRUTH, ROBERT R., 5128 Park Ave., Dickinson, Tex. 77539.
31 GINZTON, E. L., Varian Associates, 611 Hansen Way, Palo Alto, Calif. 94303.
13 GLASER, DONALD ARTHUR, University of California, Berkeley, Calif. 94720.
13 GLASHOW, SHELDON L., 30 Prescott St., Brookline, Mass. 02146.
26 GLASS, HIRAM BENTLEY, State University of New York, Stony Brook, N.Y. 11790.
11 GLEASON, ANDREW M., Harvard University, 1 Oxford St., Cambridge, Mass. 02138.
25 GODDARD, DAVID ROCKWELL, PH.D., National Academy of Sciences, 2101 Constitution Ave., Washington, D.C. 20418.
24 GOEBEL, WALTHER FREDERICK, Rockefeller University, New York, N.Y. 10021.
16 GOLD, THOMAS, Cornell University, Ithaca, N.Y. 14853.
16 GOLDBERG, EDWARD D., University of California, San Diego, La Jolla, Calif. 92093.
12 GOLDBERG, LEO, Kitt Peak National Observatory, 950 N. Cherry Ave., P.O.B. 26732, Tucson, Ariz. 85726.
13 GOLDBERGER, M. L., California Institute of Technology, 340-32 Pasadena, Calif. 91125.
13 GOLDHABER, GERTRUDE S., Brookhaven National Laboratory, Upton, N.Y. 11973.
13 GOLDHABER, MAURICE, Brookhaven National Laboratory, Upton, N.Y. 11973.
16 GOLDREICH, PETER M., Division of Geological and Planetary Sciences, California Institute of Technology, Pasadena, Calif. 91125.
23 GOLDSTEIN, AVRAM, Addiction Research Foundation, Palo Alto, Calif.
41 GOLDSTEIN, JOSEPH L., University of Texas Health Center, Dallas, Tex. 75235.
33 GOLDSTINE, HERMAN H., 175 Fairway Drive, Princeton, N.J. 08540.
  GOMER, ROBERT, Office of the Director, The James Franck Institute, University of Chicago, Ill. 60637.
33 GOMORY, R. E., Thomas J. Watson Research Center, IBM Corporation, P.O.B. 218, Yorktown Heights, N.Y. 10598.
43 GOOD, ROBERT A., Office of the President and Director, Sloan-Kettering Institute for Cancer Research, 410 East 68th St., New York, N.Y. 10021.
51 GOODENOUGH, WARD H., Department of Anthropology, University of Pennsylvania Museum, 33rd and Spruce Sts., Philadelphia, Pa. 19104.
53 GOODMAN, LEO A., Department of Statistics, University of Chicago, 1118 East 58th St., Chicago, Ill. 60637.
23 GOODMAN, LOUIS S., University of Utah, Salt Lake City, Utah 84132.
16 GOODY, RICHARD M., Pierce Hall, Harvard University, Cambridge, Mass. 02138.
14 GORDON, ROY G., Department of Chemistry, Harvard University, 12 Oxford St., Cambridge, Mass. 02138.
33 GORDON, WILLIAM E., Rice University, Houston, Tex. 77001.
13 GORDY, WALTER, Duke University, Durham, N.C. 27706.
42 GOTTSCHALK, CARL W., Department of Medicine, University of North Carolina School of Medicine, Chapel Hill, N.C. 27514.
31 GOULD, ROY W., California Institute of Technology, Pasadena, Calif. 91125.
33 GRAD, HAROLD, Courant Institute of Mathematical Sciences, 251 Mercer St., New York, N.Y. 10012.
27 GRANT, VERNE E., Department of Botany, University of Texas, Austin, Tex. 78712.
14 GRAY, HARRY B., Division of Chemistry and Chemical Engineering, California Institute of Technology, Pasadena, Calif. 91125.
21 GREEN, DAVID EZRA, University of Wisconsin, 1710 University Avenue, Madison, Wis. 53706.
52 GREEN, DAVID M., Harvard University, 33 Kirkland St., Cambridge, Mass. 02138.
22 GREEN, HOWARD, Room 56-535, M.I.T., 77 Massachusetts Ave., Cambridge, Mass. 02139.
26 GREEN, M. M., University of California, Davis, Calif. 95616.
51 GREENBERG, JOSEPH H., Stanford University, Stanford, Calif. 94305.
24 GREENGARD, PAUL, Yale University School of Medicine, 333 Cedar St., New Haven, Conn. 06510.
12 GREENSTEIN, JESSE L., California Institute of Technology, Pasadena, Calif. 91125.
13 GREISEN, KENNETH I., Dept. of Astronomy, Cornell University, Ithaca, N.Y. 14853.
24 GRIFFIN, DONALD R., Rockefeller University, New York, N.Y. 10021.
51 GRIFFIN, JAMES B., University of Michigan, Ann Arbor, Mich. 48104.
11 GRIFFITHS, PHILIP A., Harvard University, Cambridge, Mass. 02138.
54 GRILICHES, ZVI, Littauer Center, Harvard University, Cambridge, Mass. 02138.
22 GROBSTEIN, CLIFFORD, Science, Technology and Public Affairs, University of California, San Diego, La Jolla, Calif. 92093.
42 GROSS, JEROME, Developmental Biology Laboratory, Massachusetts General Hospital, Boston, Mass. 02114.
41 GROSS, LUDWIK, Cancer Research Unit, Veterans Administration Hospital, 130 West Kingsbridge Rd., Bronx, N.Y. 10468.
42 GROSS, ROBERT E., Box 493, Brattleboro, Vermont 05301.
24 GRUNDFEST, HARRY, Columbia University, 630 West 168th St., New York, N.Y. 10032.
14 GRUNWALD, ERNEST, Department of Chemistry, Brandeis University, Waltham, Mass. 02154.
52 GUILFORD, JOY P., P.O.B. 1288, Beverly Hills, Calif. 90213.
42 GUILLEMIN, ROGER C. L., Department of Neuroendocrinology, Salk Institute for Biological Studies, P.O.B. 1809, San Diego, Calif. 92112.
12 GUNN, JAMES E., Hale Observatories, California Institute of Technology, 813 Santa Barbara St., Pasadena, Calif. 91101.
21 GUNSALUS, IRWIN C., Biochemistry Department, 420 Roger Adams Laboratory, University of Illinois, Urbana, Ill. 61801.
14 GUTOWSKY, H. S., Department of Chemistry, University of Illinois, Urbana, Ill. 61801.

51 HAAS, MARY R., University of California, Berkeley, Calif. 94720.
22 HABEL, KARL, Room 108E, Reading Institute of Rehabilitation, RD 1, Box 252, Reading, Pa. 19607.
14 HACKERMAN, NORMAN, Office of the President, Rice University, P.O.B. 1892, Houston, Tex. 77001.
31 HAENSEL, VLADIMIR, Universal Oil Products Co., 10 UOP Plaza, Des Plaines, Ill. 60016.
22 HAGINS, WILLIAM A., National Institutes of Health, Bethesda, Md. 20205.

23 HAGIWARA, SUSUMU, University of California, Los Angeles, Calif. 90024.
33 HAGSTRUM, HOMER D., Bell Telephone Laboratories, Inc., 600 Mountain Ave., Murray Hill, N.J. 07974.
13 HAHN, E. L., Department of Physics, University of California, Berkeley, Calif. 94720.
13 HALL, ROBERT N., General Electric Corporate Research and Development, P.O.B. 8, Schenectady, N.Y. 12301.
32 HALVER, JOHN E., College of Fisheries, University of Washington, Seattle, Wash. 98195.
24 HAMBURGER, VIKTOR, PH.D., Washington University, St. Louis, Mo. 63130.
14 HAMMES, GORDON G., Department of Chemistry, Cornell University, Ithaca, N.Y. 14853.
14 HAMMOND, GEORGE S., Allied Chemical Corpn., P.O.B. 1021R, Morristown, N.J. 07960.
21 HANDLER, PHILIP, National Academy of Sciences, Washington, D.C. 20418.
31 HANNAY, N. BRUCE, Bell Telephone Laboratories Inc., 600 Mountain Ave., Murray Hill, N.J. 07974.
33 HANSEN, MORRIS H., 5212 Goddard Rd., Bethesda, Md. 20014.
32 HANSON, ROBERT P., University of Wisconsin, 1655 Linden Drive, Madison, Wis. 53706.
23 HARDY, JAMES D., John B. Pierce Foundation Laboratory, 290 Congress Ave., New Haven, Conn. 06519.
HARISH-CHANDRA, Department of Mathematics, Institute for Advanced Study, Olden Lane, Princeton, N.J. 08540.
14 HARKER, DAVID, 23 High St., Buffalo, N.Y. 14203.
32 HARLAN, JACK R., Department of Agronomy, S-516 Turner Hall, University of Illinois, Urbana, Ill. 61801.
52 HARLOW, HARRY F., B.A., PH.D., 672 Roller Coaster Rd., Tucson, Ariz. 85704.
32 HARRAR, J. G., 125 Puritan Drive, Scarsdale, N.Y. 10583.
21 HARRINGTON, WILLIAM F., McCollum-Pratt Institute, Johns Hopkins University, Baltimore, Md. 21218.
31 HARRIS, CYRIL M., Columbia University, New York, N.Y. 10027.
HARRIS, STEPHEN E., Department of Electrical Engineering and Applied Physics, Edward L. Ginzton Laboratory, Stanford University, Calif. 94305.
33 HARRIS, ZELLIG S., Department of Linguistics, University of Pennsylvania, 401 Williams Hall, Philadelphia, Pa. 19174.
24 HARTLINE, HALDAN KEFFER, Rockefeller University, New York, N.Y. 10021.
26 HASKINS, CARYL P., Suite 600, 2100 M St., N.W., Washington, D.C. 20037.
27 HASLER, ARTHUR D., University of Wisconsin, Madison, Wis. 53706.
21 HAUROWITZ, FELIX, Department of Chemistry, Indiana University, Bloomington, Ind. 47401.
16 HAURWITZ, BERNHARD, Department of Atmospheric Science, Colorado State University, Fort Collins, Colo. 80523.
51 HAURY, EMIL W., Department of Anthropology, University of Arizona, Tucson, Ariz. 85721.
53 HAUSER, PHILIP M., Population Research Center, University of Chicago, 1126 East 59th St., Chicago, Ill. 60637.
14 HAWTHORNE, M. FREDERICK, Department of Chemistry, University of California, Los Angeles, Calif. 90024.
15 HEDBERG, HOLLIS D., 118 Library Place, Princeton, N.J. 08540.
12 HEESCHEN, DAVID S., National Radio Astronomy Observatory, Edgemont Rd., Charlottesville, Va. 22901.
32 HEGSTED, DAVID M., Department of Nutrition, Harvard University School of Public Health, 665 Huntington Ave., Boston, Mass. 02115.
41 HEIDELBERGER, CHARLES, University of Southern California Cancer Center, 1721 North Griffin Ave., Los Angeles, Calif. 90031.
43 HEIDELBERGER, MICHAEL, B.S., A.M., PH.D., New York University School of Medicine, 550 First Avenue, New York, N.Y. 10016.
52 HELD, RICHARD M., E10-137, Department of Psychology, Massachusetts Institute of Technology, Cambridge, Mass. 02139.
16 HELLIWELL, R. A., Radioscience Laboratory, Stanford University, Stanford, Calif. 94305.
26 HELSINKI, DONALD R., University of California, San Diego, La Jolla, Calif. 92093.
41 HENLE, GERTRUDE, Children's Hospital of Philadelphia, 34th St. and Civic Center Blvd., Philadelphia, Pa. 19104.
43 HENLE, WERNER, Joseph Stokes Jr. Research Institute, Children's Hospital of Philadelphia, Philadelphia, Pa. 19104.

13 HENLEY, ERNEST M., University of Washington, Seattle, Wash. 98195.
21 HEPPEL, LEON A., Section of Biochemistry and Molecular Biology, Cornell University, Ithaca, N.Y. 14853.
32 HEPTING, GEORGE H., 11 Maplewood Rd., Asheville, N.C. 28804.
13 HERB, R. G., National Electrostatics Corporation, P.O.B. 117, Graber Rd., Middleton, Wis. 53562.
12 HERBIG, GEORGE HOWARD, Lick Observatory, University of California, Santa Cruz, Calif. 95064.
12 HERGET, PAUL, Cincinnati Observatory, Cincinnati, Ohio 45208.
13 HERRING, WILLIAM C., Stanford University, Stanford, Calif. 94305.
14 HERSCHBACH, DUDLEY R., Department of Chemistry, Harvard University, 12 Oxford St., Cambridge, Mass. 02138.
26 HERSHEY, ALFRED DAY, RD Box 1640, Moores Hill Rd., Syosset, N.Y. 11791.
42 HERTZ, ROY, Department of Pharmacology, George Washington University, 2300 Eye St., N.W., Washington, D.C. 20037.
31 HEWLETT, WILLIAM R., Hewlett-Packard Company, 1501 Page Mill Rd., Palo Alto, Calif. 94304.
14 HILDEBRAND, JOEL H., B.S., PH.D., 500 Coventry Rd., Berkeley (Kensington), Calif. 94707.
52 HILGARD, ERNEST R., Stanford University, Stanford, Calif. 94305.
21 HILL, ROBERT L., Department of Biochemistry, Duke University Medical Centre, Durham N.C. 27710.
21 HILL, TERRELL L., National Institute of Arthritis and Metabolic Diseases, National Institutes of Health, Bethesda, Md. 20205.
43 HIRSCH, JAMES G., Rockefeller University, New York, N.Y. 10021.
14 HIRSCHFELDER, JOSEPH O., B.S., PH.D., Theoretical Chemistry Institute, University of Wisconsin, Madison, Wis. 53706.
52 HIRSH, IRA J., Central Institute for the Deaf, 818 South Euclid, St. Louis, Mo. 63110.
43 HIRST, GEORGE K., Public Health Research Institute Inc., 455 First Ave., New York, N.Y. 10016.
21 HITCHINGS, GEORGE H., 4022 Bristol Rd., Durham, N.C. 27707.
14 HOARD, J. L., Department of Chemistry, Cornell University, Ithaca, N. Y. 14853.
52 HOCHBERG, JULIAN, Columbia University, New York, N.Y. 10027.
11 HOCHSCHILD, GERHARD P., University of California, Berkeley, Calif. 94720.
51 HOCKETT, CHARLES F., Department of Anthropology, Cornell University, Ithaca, N.Y. 14853.
11 HOEFFDING, WASSILY, Department of Statistics, University of North Carolina, Chapel Hill, N.C. 27514.
HOFFMAN, JOSEPH F., Department of Physiology, Yale University School of Medicine, New Haven, Conn. 06520.
14 HOFFMANN, ROALD, Department of Chemistry, Cornell University, Ithaca, N.Y. 14853.
21 HOFMANN, KLAUS, University of Pittsburgh School of Medicine, Pittsburgh, Pa. 15261.
13 HOFSTADTER, ROBERT, Department of Physics, Stanford University, Stanford, Calif. 94305.
22 HOGNESS, DAVID S., Department of Biochemistry, Stanford University Medical Center, Stanford, Calif. 94305.
HOLE, FRANK, Department of Anthropology, Yale University, New Haven, Conn. 06520.
26 HOLLAENDER, ALEXANDER, Associated Universities Inc., 1717 Massachusetts Ave., N.W., Washington, D.C. 20036.
15 HOLLAND, H. D., Harvard University, Cambridge, Mass. 02138.
22 HOLLEY, ROBERT W., Salk Institute for Biological Studies, P.O.B. 1809, San Diego, Calif. 92112.
14 HOLM, RICHARD H., Department of Chemistry, Stanford University, Stanford, Calif. 94305.
HOLMAN, RALPH T., Office of the Executive Director, Hormel Institute, University of Minnesota, Austin.
HOLSTEIN, THEODORE D., Department of Physics, University of California, Los Angeles, Calif. 90024.
22 HOLTFRETER, JOHANNES, Biological Laboratories, University of Rochester, Rochester, N.Y. 14627.
53 HOMANS, GEORGE C., Department of Sociology, William James Hall 480, Harvard University, Cambridge, Mass. 02138.
13 HOPFIELD, JOHN J., Department of Physics, Joseph Henry Laboratories, Princeton University, Princeton, N.J. 08544.

21 HORECKER, B. L., Roche Institute of Molecular Biology, Nutley, N.J. 07110.
14 HORNIG, DONALD F., Harvard School of Public Health, 665 Huntington Ave., Boston, Mass. 02115.
26 HOROWITZ, NORMAN H., California Institute of Technology, Pasadena, Calif. 91125.
32 HORSFALL, JAMES G., Connecticut Agricultural Experiment Station, Box 1106, New Haven, Conn. 06504.
43 HORSTMANN, DOROTHY M., Yale University School of Medicine, 333 Cedar St., New Haven, Conn. 06510.
22 HOTCHKISS, ROLLIN D., Rockefeller University, New York, N.Y. 10021.
31 HOTTEL, HOYT C., Room 12-110, Department of Chemical Engineering, Massachusetts Institute of Technology, Cambridge, Mass. 02139.
31 HOUSNER, GEORGE W., Division of Engineering and Applied Science, California Institute of Technology, Pasadena, Calif. 91125.
54 HOUTHAKKER, HENDRIK S., 218 Littauer Center, Harvard University, Cambridge, Mass. 02138.
33 HOWARD, LOUIS N., Dept. of Mathematics, 2-377 Massachusetts Institute of Technology, Cambridge, Mass. 02139.
51 HOWELL, F. CLARK, Department of Anthropology, University of California, Berkeley, Calif. 94720.
51 HOWELLS, W. W., Peabody Museum, Harvard University, Cambridge, Mass. 02138.
15 HUBBERT, M. KING, 5208 Westwood Drive, N.W., Washington, D.C. 20016.
24 HUBEL, DAVID H., Department of Neurobiology, Harvard Medical School, 25 Shattuck St., Boston, Mass. 02115.
43 HUEBNER, ROBERT J., National Institutes of Health, Bethesda, Md. 20205.
41 HUGGINS, CHARLES BRENTON, M.D., M.SC., D.SC., University of Chicago, 950 East 59th Street, Chicago, Ill. 60637.
13 HUGHES, VERNON W., Department of Physics, Yale University, New Haven, Conn. 06520.
14 HUIZENGA, JOHN R., Department of Chemistry, University of Rochester, River Station, Rochester, N.Y. 14627.
51 HULSE, FREDERICK S., Department of Anthropology, University of Arizona, Tucson, Ariz. 85721.
31 HUNSAKER, J. C., M.S., SC.D., Massachusetts Institute of Technology, Cambridge, Mass. 02139.
HUNTEN, DONALD M., Department of Planetary Sciences, University of Arizona, Tucson, Ariz. 85721.
52 HURVICH, LEO M., Department of Psychology, University of Pennsylvania, 3815 Walnut St., Philadelphia, Pa. 19104.
54 HURWICZ, LEONID, Department of Economics, University of Minnesota, Minneapolis, Minn. 55455.
21 HURWITZ, JERARD, Department of Developmental Biology and Cancer, Albert Einstein College of Medicine, 1300 Morris Park Ave., Bronx, N.Y. 10461.
27 HUTCHINSON, GEORGE EVELYN, M.A., Yale University, New Haven, Conn. 06520.
14 HUTCHISON, CLYDE A., Jr., University of Chicago, Chicago, Ill. 60637.
15 IMBRIE, JOHN, Dept. of Geological Sciences, Brown University, Providence, R.I. 02912.
13 INGHRAM, MARK G., University of Chicago, Chicago, Ill. 60637.
INKELES, ALEX, Department of Sociology, Hoover Institution, Stanford University, Calif. 94305.
26 IRWIN, MALCOLM ROBERT, M.S., PH.D., University of Wisconsin, Madison, Wis. 53706.
42 ISSELBACHER, KURT J., Gastrointestinal Unit, Massachusetts General Hospital, Boston, Mass. 02114.
41 ITANO, HARVEY A., University of California, San Diego, La Jolla, Calif. 92093.
41 JACOBSON, LEON O., University of Chicago, 950 East 59th Street, Chicago, Ill. 60637.
11 JACOBSON, NATHAN, Yale University, New Haven, Conn. 06520.
25 JAGENDORF, ANDRÉ T., Cornell University, Ithaca, N.Y. 14853.
15 JAMES, HAROLD LLOYD, United States Geological Survey, 1617 Washington St., Port Townsend, Wash. 98368.
52 JAMESON, DOROTHEA, Department of Psychology, University of Pennsylvania, 3815 Walnut St., Philadelphia, Pa. 19104.
13 JAVAN, ALI, Department of Physics, Massachusetts Institute of Technology, Cambridge, Mass. 02139.
21 JENCKS, WILLIAM P., Graduate Department of Biochemistry, Brandeis University, Waltham, Mass. 02154.
51 JENNINGS, JESSE D., Dept. of Anthropology, University of Utah, Salt Lake City, Utah 84112.
42 JENSEN, ELWOOD V., University of Chicago, 950 East 59th St., Chicago, Ill. 60637.

33 JOHN, FRITZ, Courant Institute of Mathematical Sciences, 251 Mercer St., New York, N.Y. 10012.
31 JOHNSON, CLARENCE L., Lockheed Aircraft Corporation, Burbank. Calif. 91503.
14 JOHNSON, WILLIAM S., Department of Chemistry, Stanford University, Stanford, Calif. 94305.
14 JOHNSTON, HAROLD S., University of California, Berkeley, Calif. 94720.
JOKLIK, WOLFGANG K., Office of the Chairman, Department of Microbiology and Immunology, Duke University Medical Center, Durham, N.C. 27706.
JONES, ROBERT T., NASA Ames Research Center, Moffat Field, Calif.
54 JORGENSON, DALE W., Littauer Center, Harvard University, Cambridge, Mass. 02138.
21 KABAT.ELVIN, A., Columbia University College of Physicians and Surgeons, 701 West 168th St., New York, N.Y. 10032.
11 KAC, MARK, Rockefeller University, New York, N.Y. 10021.
13 KADANOFF, LEO P., James Franck Institute, University of Chicago, Chicago, Ill. 60637.
26 KAISER, A. DALE, Stanford University School of Medicine, Stanford, Calif. 94305.
21 KALCKAR, HERMAN M., Massachusetts General Hospital, Boston, Mass. 02115.
21 KAMEN, MARTIN DAVID, University of California, San Diego, La Jolla, Calif. 92093.
24 KANDEL, ERIC R., Columbia University College of Physicians and Surgeons, 630 West 168th St., New York, N.Y. 10032.
33 KANTROWITZ, ARTHUR, 1010 Memorial Drive, Cambridge, Mass. 02138.
41 KAPLAN, HENRY S., Department of Radiology, Stanford University Medical Center, Stanford, Calif. 94305.
33 KAPLAN, JOSEPH, 1565 Kelton Ave., Los Angeles, Calif. 90024.
21 KAPLAN, NATHAN O., Department of Chemistry, University of California, San Diego, La Jolla, Calif. 92093
11 KAPLANSKY, IRVING, University of Chicago, Chicago, Ill. 60637.
14 KARLE, ISABELLA L., Laboratory for the Structure of Matter, U.S. Naval Research Laboratory, Code 6030, Washington, D.C. 20735.
14 KARLE, JEROME, Code 6030, Laboratory for the Structure of Matter, Naval Research Laboratory, Washington, D.C. 20375.
33 KARLIN, SAMUEL, Department of Mathematics, Stanford University, Stanford, Calif. 94305.
33 KARP, RICHARD M., University of California, Berkeley, Calif. 94720.
14 KARPLUS, MARTIN, Department of Chemistry, Harvard University, 12 Oxford St., Cambridge, Mass. 02138.
14 KASHA, MICHAEL, Institute of Molecular Biophysics, Florida State University, Tallahassee, Fla. 32306.
53 KATES, ROBERT W., 10 Einhorn Rd., Worcester, Mass. 01609.
14 KATZ, JOSEPH J., Chemistry Division, Argonne National Laboratory, 9700 South Cass Ave., Argonne, Ill. 60639.
14 KAUFMAN, FREDERICK, University of Pittsburgh, Pittsburgh, Pa. 15260.
14 KAUZMANN, WALTER J., Princeton University, Princeton, N.J. 08540.
33 KELLER, JOSEPH B., Courant Institute of Mathematical Sciences, New York University, 251 Mercer St., N.Y. 10012.
12 KELLERMANN, KENNETH I., National Radio Astronomy Observatory, P.O.B. 2, Greenbank, W. Va. 24944.
53 KELLEY, HAROLD H., University of California, Los Angeles, Calif. 90024.
32 KELMAN, ARTHUR, Department of Plant Pathology, University of Wisconsin, 1630 Linden Drive, Madison, Wis. 53706.
24 KENNEDY, DONALD, Stanford University, Stanford, Calif. 94305.
21 KENNEDY, EUGENE P., Harvard Medical School, 25 Shattuck St., Boston, Mass. 02115.
13 KERST, DONALD WILLIAM, B.A., PH.D., University of Wisconsin, Madison, Wis. 53706.
24 KETY, SEYMOUR SOLOMON, Mailman Research Center, McLean Hospital, 115 Mill St., Belmont, Mass. 02178.
53 KEYFITZ, NATHAN, William James Hall, Room 480, Harvard University, Cambridge, Mass. 02138.
21 KHORANA, H. GOBIND. Department of Biology and Chemistry, Massachusetts Institute of Technology, Cambridge, Mass. 02139.

# NATIONAL ACADEMY OF SCIENCES    UNITED STATES OF AMERICA

11 KIEFER, JACK C., Statistics Dept., University of California, Berkeley, Calif. 94720.
43 KILBOURNE, EDWIN D., Dept. of Microbiology, Mt. Sinai School of Medicine, 1 Gustave Levy Place, at 100 St. and 5th Ave., New York, N.Y. 10029.
31 KINZEL, AUGUSTUS B., 1738 Castellana Rd., La Jolla, Calif. 92037.
KIPNIS, DAVID M., Office of the Chairman, Department of Medicine, Washington University School of Medicine, St. Louis, Mo. 63130.
14 KISTIAKOWSKY, G. B., PH.D., Harvard University, 12 Oxford Street, Cambridge, Mass. 02138.
13 KITTEL, CHARLES, University of California, Berkeley, Calif. 94720.
11 KLEENE, STEPHEN C., University of Wisconsin, Madison, Wis. 53706.
54 KLEIN, LAWRENCE R., Economics Department, University of Pennsylvania, Philadelphia, Pa. 19104.
13 KLEIN, MARTIN J., Dept. of Physics, Yale University, Box 2036, Yale Station, New Haven, Conn. 06520.
14 KLEMPERER, WILLIAM A., Harvard University, Cambridge, Mass. 02138.
21 KLOTZ, IRVING M., Department of Chemistry, Northwestern University, Evanston, Ill. 60201.
32 KNIPLING, E. F., 2623 Military Rd., Arlington, Va. 22207.
16 KNOPOFF, LEON, Institute of Geophysics and Planetary Physics, University of California, Los Angeles, Calif. 90024.
33 KNUTH, DONALD E., Computer Science Department, Stanford University, Stanford, Calif. 94305.
24 KOELLE, GEORGE B., Department of Pharmacology, University of Pennsylvania School of Medicine, Philadelphia, Pa. 19104.
13 KOHN, WALTER, University of California, San Diego, La Jolla, Calif. 92093.
14 KOLTHOFF, IZAAK MAURITS, School of Chemistry, University of Minnesota, Minneapolis, Minn. 55455.
54 KOOPMANS, TJALLING C., Yale University, New Haven, Conn. 06520.
22 KOPROWSKI, HILARY, The Wistar Institute, 36th St. at Spruce, Philadelphia, Pa. 19104.
21 KORNBERG, ARTHUR, Stanford University Medical School, Stanford, Calif. 94305.
21 KOSHLAND, DANIEL E., Jr., Department of Biochemistry, University of California, Berkeley, Calif. 94720.
KOSHLAND, MARIAN E., Department of Molecular Biology, University of California, Berkeley, Calif. 94720.
11 KOSTANT, BERTRAM, Room 2-282, M.I.T., Cambridge, Mass. 02139.
12 KRAFT, ROBERT P., Lick Observatory, University of California, Santa Cruz, Calif. 95064.
25 KRAMER, PAUL J., Duke University, Durham, N.C. 27706.
21 KRAMPITZ, LESTER O., Dept. of Microbiology, Case Western Reserve University, Cleveland, Ohio 44106.
43 KRAUSE, RICHARD M., National Institute of Allergy and Infectious Diseases, National Institutes of Health, Bethesda, Md. 20205.
12 KRAUSHAAR, WILLIAM L., Department of Physics, University of Wisconsin, 475 North Charter St., Madison, Wis. 53706.
15 KRAUSKOPF, KONRAD B., School of Earth Sciences, Stanford University, Stanford, Calif. 94305.
23 KRAYER, OTTO, 3940 East Timrod St., Apt. 202, Tucson, Ariz. 85711.
21 KREBS, EDWIN G., Dept. of Pharmacology, SJ-30, University of Washington, Seattle, Wash. 98195.
51 KROGMAN, W. M., Lancaster Cleft Palate Clinic, 24 North Lime St., Lancaster, Pa. 17602.
13 KROLL, NORMAN M., Department of Physics, P.O.B. 109. University of California, San Diego, La Jolla, Calif. 92093.
43 KRUGMAN, SAUL, New York University Medical Centre, 550 First Ave., New York, N.Y. 10016.
33 KRUSKAL, MARTIN, Princeton University, Princeton, N.J. 08540.
53 KUHN, THOMAS, Massachusetts Institute of Technology, Cambridge, Mass. 02139.
43 KUNKEL, HENRY G., Rockefeller University, New York, N.Y. 10021.
13 KUSCH, P., University of Texas, Dallas, Box 688, Richardson, Tex. 75080.
54 KUZNETS, SIMON, 67 Francis Ave., Cambridge, Mass. 02138.
52 LACEY, JOHN I., Wright State University School of Medicine, Yellow Springs, O.
15 LACHENBRUCH, ARTHUR H., U.S. Geological Survey, 345 Middlefield Rd., Menlo Park, Calif. 94025.
13 LAMB, WILLIS EUGENE, Jr., Department of Physics, University of Arizona, Tucson, Ariz. 85721.

13 LAND, EDWIN H., Polaroid Corpn., Cambridge, Mass. 02139.
25 LANG, ANTON, MSU/ERDA Plant Research Laboratory, Michigan State University, East Lansing, Mich. 48824.
15 LANGBEIN, WALTER B., 4452 North 38th St., Arlington, Va. 22207.
21 LARDY, HENRY ARNOLD, Institute for Enzyme Research, University of Wisconsin, Madison, Wis. 53706.
24 LARRABEE, MARTIN G., Johns Hopkins University, Baltimore, Md. 21218.
43 LAWRENCE, H. SHERWOOD, New York University Medical Center, 550 First Ave., New York, N.Y. 10016.
33 LAX, BENJAMIN, Massachusetts Institute of Technology, Cambridge, Mass. 02139.
11 LAX, PETER D., Courant Institute of Mathematical Sciences, 251 Mercer St., New York, N.Y. 10012.
42 LEAF, ALEXANDER, Massachusetts General Hospital, Boston, Mass. 02114.
33 LEBOWITZ, JOEL L., Rutgers University, New Brunswick, N.J. 08903.
22 LEDER, PHILIP, National Institutes of Health, Bethesda, Md. 20205.
26 LEDERBERG, JOSHUA, Rockefeller University, 1230 York Ave., New York, N.Y. 10021.
13 LEDERMAN, LEON M., Columbia University, 538 West 120th Street, New York, N.Y. 10027.
13 LEE, TSUNG-DAO, Columbia University, New York, N.Y. 10027.
14 LEE, YUAN, University of California, Berkeley, Calif. 94720.
21 LEHMAN, ISRAEL R., Dept. of Biochemistry, Stanford, University School of Medicine, Stanford, Calif. 94305.
33 LEHMANN, ERICH L., Statistics Dept., University of California, Berkeley, Calif. 94720.
21 LEHNINGER, A. L., Johns Hopkins University, 725 North Wolfe St., Baltimore, Md. 21205.
12 LEIGHTON, R. B., California Institute of Technology, Pasadena, Calif. 91125.
14 LEONARD, NELSON J., Department of Chemistry, University of Illinois, Urbana, Ill. 61801.
54 LEONTIEF, WASSILY, Institute for Economic Analysis, 215 Mercer St., New York, N.Y. 10012.
32 LEOPOLD, A. STARKER, School of Forestry, University of California, Berkeley, Calif. 94720.
25 LEOPOLD, ESTELLA BERGERE, Quaternary Research Center, University of Washington, Seattle, Wash. 98195.
15 LEOPOLD, LUNA B., Dept. of Geology and Geophysics, Earth Sciences Building, University of California, Berkeley, Calif. 94720.
42 LERNER, AARON B., Department of Dermatology, School of Medicine, Yale University, New Haven, Conn. 06510.
54 LERNER, ABBA P., Florida State University, Tallahassee, Fla. 32306.
24 LEVI-MONTALCINI, RITA, Via G. Romagnosi 18/A, 00196, Rome, Italy.
41 LEVINE, PHILIP, Ortho Research Foundation, Raritan, N.J 08869.
26 LEVINTHAL, CYRUS, Department of Biological Sciences, Columbia University, New York, N.Y. 10027.
26 LEWIS, EDWARD B., California Institute of Technology, Pasadena, Calif. 91125.
11 LEWY, HANS, University of California, Berkeley, Calif. 94720.
21 LI, CHOH HAO, Hormone Research Laboratory, University of California, San Francisco, Calif. 94143.
52 LIBERMAN, ALVIN M., Department of Psychology, University of Connecticut, Storrs, Conn. 06268.
31 LICKLIDER, J. C. R., 40 Pleasant View Rd., Arlington, Mass. 02174.
LIDDLE, GRANT W., Office of the Chairman, Vanderbilt University School of Medicine, Nashville, Tenn. 37240.
42 LIEBERMAN, SEYMOUR, College of Physicians and Surgeons, 630 West 168th St., New York, N.Y. 10032.
33 LIEPMANN, HANS W., Graduate Aeronautical Laboratories, California Institute of Technology, Pasadena, Calif. 91125.
LIKENS, GENE E., Section of Ecology and Systematics, Cornell University, Ithaca, N.Y. 14853.
33 LIN, CHIA-CHIAO, Massachusetts Institute of Technology, Cambridge, Mass. 02139.
26 LINDSLEY, DAN L., Jr., Department of Biology, University of California, San Diego, La Jolla, Calif. 92093.
52 LINDSLEY, DONALD B., University of California, Los Angeles, Calif. 90024.
16 LINDZEN, RICHARD S., 301 Lake Ave., Newton, Mass. 02161.
21 LIPMANN, FRITZ ALBERT, Rockefeller University, New York, N.Y. 10021.
14 LIPSCOMB, WILLIAM N., Harvard University, 12 Oxford Street, Cambridge, Mass. 02138.

53 LIPSET, S. M., Dept. of Political Sciences and Sociology, Stanford University, Stanford, Calif. 94305.
41 LITTLEFIELD, JOHN W., Johns Hopkins Hospital, Baltimore, Md. 21205.
13 LIVINGSTON, M. STANLEY, 1005 Calle Largo, Santa Fe, N.M. 87501.
41 LONDON, IRVING M., Harvard-MIT Program in Health Sciences and Technology, 77 Massachusetts Ave., Cambridge, Mass. 02139.
14 LONG, FRANKLIN A., Cornell University, Ithaca, N.Y. 14853
24 LORENTE DE Nó, RAFAEL, University of California School of Medicine, Los Angeles, Calif. 90024.
16 LORENZ, EDWARD N., Department of Meteorology, M.I.T., Cambridge, Mass. 02139.
51 LOUNSBURY, FLOYD G., Yale University, New Haven, Conn. 06520.
15 LOVERING, THOMAS SEWARD, Apt. 186 Northview, 2663 Tallant Rd., Santa Barbara, Calif. 93105.
13 LOW, FRANCIS E., Room 6-313, Department of Physics, Massachusetts Institute of Technology, Cambridge, Mass. 02139.
12 LOW, FRANK J., Lunar and Planetary Laboratory, University of Arizona, Tucson, Ariz. 85721.
15 LOWENSTAM, HEINZ A., California Institute of Technology, Pasadena, Calif. 91125.
21 LOWRY, OLIVER H., Washington University, 660 South Euclid, St. Louis, Mo. 63110.
   LUCAS, ROBERT E., Jr., Department of Economics, University of Chicago, Chicago, Ill. 60637.
52 LUCE, R. DUNCAN, William James Hall, Harvard University, Cambridge, Mass. 02138.
21 LURIA, S. E., Department of Biology, Massachusetts Institute of Technology, Cambridge, Mass. 02139.
13 LUTTINGER, J. M., Department of Physics, Columbia University, New York, N.Y. 10027.
12 LUYTEN, WILLEM J., 211 Space Science Center, University of Minnesota, Minneapolis, Minn. 55455.
12 LYNDS, ROGER, Aura Inc., Kitt Peak National Observatory, 950 North Cherry Ave., P.O.B. 26732, Tucson, Ariz. 85726.

16 MACDONALD, GORDON J. F., 308 Murdough Center, Dartmouth College, Hanover, N.H. 03755.
33 MACDONALD, J. Ross, Department of Physics and Astronomy, University of North Carolina, Chapel Hill, N.C. 27514.
11 MACKEY, GEORGE W., Harvard University, Cambridge, Mass. 02138.
11 MACLANE, SAUNDERS, A.M., D.PHIL., University of Chicago, Chicago, Ill. 60637.
51 MACNEISH, RICHARD S., R.S. Peabody Foundation for Archaeology, Box 71, Andover, Mass. 01810.
21 MAGASANIK, BORIS, Massachusetts Institute of Technology, Cambridge, Mass. 02139.
14 MAHAN, BRUCE H., Department of Chemistry, University of California, Berkeley, Calif. 94720.
31 MAIMAN, THEODORE H., TRW Inc., Los Angeles, Calif.
16 MALKUS, WILLEM V. R., Department of Mathematics, Massachusetts Institute of Technology, Cambridge, Mass. 02139.
16 MALONE, THOMAS F., Holcomb Research Institute, Butler University, Indianapolis, Ind. 46208.
32 MANGELSDORF, P. C., 510 Caswell Rd., Chapel Hill, N.C. 27514.
53 MARCH, JAMES G., School of Education, Stanford University, Stanford, Calif. 94305.
14 MARCUS, R. A., California Institute of Technology, Pasadena, California 91125.
21 MARGOLIASH, E., Dept. of Biochemistry and Molecular Biology, Northwestern University, Evanston, Ill. 60201.
14 MARGRAVE, JOHN L., Office of Advanced Studies and Research, Rice University, P.O.B. 1892, Houston, Tex. 77001.
14 MARK, H. F., Polytechnic Institute of Brooklyn, Brooklyn, N.Y. 11201.
22 MARKERT, CLEMENT L., Department of Biology, Yale University, New Haven, Conn. 06520.
41 MARKS, PAUL A., College of Physicians and Surgeons, Columbia University, 630 West 168th St., New York, N.Y. 10032.
24 MARLER, PETER R., Rockefeller University, Center for Field Research, Tyrrel Rd., Millbrook, N.Y. 12545.
13 MARSHAK, ROBERT EUGENE, City College of New York, Convent Ave. and 138th St., New York, N.Y. 10031.
13 MARTIN, PAUL, Lyman Laboratory, Harvard University, Cambridge, Mass. 02138.

14 MARVEL, C. S., A.B., PH.D., University of Arizona, Tucson, Ariz. 85721.
31 MATHEWS, MAX V., Bell Laboratories, 600 Mountain Ave., Murray Hill, N.J. 07974.
12 MAYALL, NICHOLAS ULRICH, 5945 Mina Vista, Tucson, Ariz. 85718.
14 MAYER, JOSEPH E., Department of Chemistry, University of California, San Diego, La Jolla, Calif. 92037.
43 MAYER, MANFRED M., Johns Hopkins University School of Medicine, 725 North Wolfe St., Baltimore, Md. 21205.
27 MAYR, ERNST, Museum of Comparative Zoology, Oxford St., Cambridge, Mass. 02138.
22 MAZIA, DANIEL, Department of Zoology, University of California, Berkeley, Calif. 94720.
43 MCCARTY, MACLYN, Rockefeller University, New York, N.Y. 10021.
26 MCCLINTOCK, BARBARA, Cold Spring Harbor Laboratory, Cold Spring Harbor, N.Y. 11724.
14 MCCONNELL, HARDEN M., Stanford University, Stanford, Calif. 94305.
   MCDANIEL, BOYCE D., Office of the Director, Laboratory of Nuclear Studies, Cornell University, Ithaca, N.Y. 14853.
43 MCDERMOTT, WALSH, Robert Wood Johnson Foundation, P.O.B. 2316, Princeton. N.J. 08540.
43 MCDEVITT, HUGH O'NEILL, Stanford University School of Medicine, Stanford, Calif. 94305.
21 MCELROY, W. D., Office of the Chancellor, University of California, San Diego, La Jolla, Calif. 92093.
   MCFADDEN, DANIEL L., Department of Economics, Massachusetts Institute of Technology, Cambridge, Mass. 02139.
31 MCKAY, KENNETH G., Bell Telephone Laboratories Inc., 600 Mountain Ave., Murray Hill, N.J. 07974.
11 MCKEAN, HENRY P., Courant Institute of Mathematical Sciences, New York, N.Y.
54 MCKENZIE, LIONEL W., University of Rochester, Rochester, N.Y. 14627.
41 MCKUSICK, VICTOR A., Department of Medicine, Johns Hopkins Hospital, Baltimore, Md. 21205.
13 MCMILLAN, EDWIN M., University of California, Berkeley, Calif. 94720.
   MCSHANE, E. J., 209 Maury Ave., Charlottesville, Va. 22903.
14 MEINWALD, JERROLD, Dept. of Chemistry, Cornell University, Ithaca, N.Y. 14853.
21 MEISTER, ALTON, Cornell University Medical College, 1300 York Avenue, New York, N.Y. 10021.
15 MENARD, H. WILLIAM, U.S. Geological Survey, National Center-MS 101, 12201 Sunrise Valley Drive, Reston, Va. 22092.
21 MERRIFIELD, R. BRUCE, Rockefeller University, New York, N.Y. 10021.
53 MERTON, ROBERT K., Columbia University, New York, N.Y. 10027.
32 MERTZ, EDWIN T., Department of Biochemistry, Purdue University, West Lafayette, Ind. 49707.
26 MESELSON, MATTHEW S., Harvard University, Cambridge, Mass. 02138.
32 METCALF, ROBERT L., Department of Entomology, University of Illinois, Urbana, Ill. 61801.
21 MEYER, KARL, Columbia University College of Physicians and Surgeons, 630 West 168th St., New York, N.Y. 10032.
27 MICHENER, CHARLES D., University of Kansas, Lawrence, Kan. 66045
   MIHALAS, DIMITRI, High Altitude Observatory, Boulder, Colo.
13 MILES, JOHN W., University of California, San Diego, La Jolla, Calif. 92093.
43 MILLER, C. PHILLIP, 5757 Kimbark Avenue, Chicago, Ill. 60637.
41 MILLER, ELIZABETH C., McArdle Laboratory for Cancer Research, University of Wisconsin, 450 North Randall Ave., Madison, Wis. 53706.
52 MILLER, GEORGE A., Rockefeller University, New York, N.Y. 10021.
41 MILLER, JAMES A., McArdle Laboratory for Cancer Research, University of Wisconsin, 450 North Randall Ave., Madison, Wis. 53706.
52 MILLER, NEAL ELGAR, Rockefeller University, New York, N.Y. 10021.
22 MILLER, OSCAR L., Jr., Dept. of Biology, University of Virginia, Charlottesville, Va. 22901.
21 MILLER, STANLEY L., Department of Chemistry, University of California, San Diego, La Jolla, Calif. 92093.
11 MILNOR, JOHN W., The Institute for Advanced Study, Princeton, N.J. 08540.
33 MINDLIN, R. D., 89 Deer Hill Drive, Ridgefield, Conn., 06877.

33 MINSKY, MARVIN L., The Artificial Intelligence Laboratory, Massachusetts Institute of Technology, 545 Technology Square, Cambridge, Mass. 02139.
26 MINTZ, BEATRICE, Institute for Cancer Research, 7701 Burholme Ave., Fox Chase, Philadelphia, Pa. 19111.
14 MISLOW, KURT M., Department of Chemistry, Princeton University, Princeton, N.J. 08540.
54 MODIGLIANI, FRANCO, Sloan School of Management, Massachusetts Institute of Technology, Cambridge, Mass. 02139.
11 MONTGOMERY, DEANE, School of Mathematics, The Institute for Advanced Study, Princeton, N.J. 08540.
33 MONTROLL, ELLIOTT W., University of Rochester, Rochester, N.Y. 14627.
MOORE, FRANCIS D., Harvard Medical School, Cambridge, Mass. 02138.
27 MOORE, JOHN A., Department of Biology, University of California, Riverside, Calif. 92521.
21 MOORE, STANFORD, Rockefeller University, New York, N.Y. 10021.
21 MORALES, MANUEL F., Cardiovascular Research Institute, University of California, San Francisco, Calif. 94143.
54 MORGAN, JAMES N., Survey Research Center, Institute for Social Research, University of Michigan, Ann Arbor, Mich. 48106.
12 MORGAN, W. W., Yerkes Observatory, University of Chicago, Williams Bay, Wis. 53191.
11 MORREY, CHARLES B., Jr., 210 Yale Ave., Berkeley, Calif. 94708.
13 MORRISON, PHILIP, Massachusetts Institute of Technology, Cambridge, Mass. 02139.
13 MORSE, PHILIP M., 126 Wildwood St., Winchester, Mass. 01890.
22 MOSCONA, ARON A., University of Chicago, 920 East 58th St., Chicago, Ill. 60637.
11 MOSER, JÜRGEN K., Courant Institute of Mathematical Sciences, New York University, 251 Mercer St., New York, N.Y. 10012.
33 MOSTELLER, C. FREDERICK, Dept. of Mathematical Sciences, Science Center, Room 604, Harvard University, 1 Oxford St., Cambridge, Mass. 02138.
11 MOSTOW, G. D., Department of Mathematics, Box 2155, Yale Station, Yale University, New Haven, Conn. 06520.
41 MOTULSKY, ARNO G., Division of Medical Genetics, University of Washington, Seattle, Wash. 98195.
24 MOUNTCASTLE, VERNON B., School of Medicine, Johns Hopkins University, 725 North Wolfe St., Baltimore, Md. 21205.
51 MOVIUS, HALLAM L., Peabody Museum, Harvard University, Cambridge, Mass. 02138.
14 MUETTERTIES, EARL L., Department of Chemistry, University of California, Berkeley, Calif. 94720.
43 MÜLLER-EBERHARD, HANS J., Department of Molecular Immunology, Scripps Clinic and Research Foundation, 10666 North Torrey Pines Rd., La Jolla, Calif. 92037.
14 MULLIKEN, ROBERT S., B.S., PH.D., University of Chicago, Chicago, Ill. 60637.
11 MUMFORD, DAVID B., Department of Mathematics, Harvard University, Cambridge, Mass. 02138.
12 MÜNCH, GUIDO, Max-Planck-Institut für Astronomie, 69 Heidelberg 1, Königstuhl, Fed. Rep. of Germany.
16 MUNK, WALTER H., University of California, San Diego, La Jolla, Calif. 92093.
32 MUNRO, H. N., Department of Nutrition and Food Science, 56-225, Massachusetts Institute of Technology, Cambridge, Mass. 02139.
51 MURDOCK, GEORGE PETER, Wynnewood Plaza, Apt. 107, Wynnewood, Pa. 19096.
25 MYERS, JACK, Department of Zoology, University of Texas, Austin, Tex. 78712.
21 NACHMANSOHN, DAVID, Columbia University College of Physicians and Surgeons, 630 West 168th Street, New York, N.Y. 10032.
53 NAGEL, ERNEST, Philosophy Hall, Columbia University New York, N.Y. 10027.
13 NAMBU, YOICHIRO, The Enrico Fermi Institute, University of Chicago, 5630 Ellis Ave., Chicago, Ill. 60637.
21 NATHANS, D., Johns Hopkins University School of Medicine, 725 North Wolfe St., Baltimore, Md. 21205.
24 NAUTA, WALLE J. H., Department of Psychology, Massachusetts Institute of Technology, Cambridge, Mass. 02139.
26 NEEL, JAMES V., University of Michigan Medical School, Ann Arbor, Mich. 48109.
52 NEFF, WILLIAM DUWAYNE, Center for Neural Sciences, Indiana University, Bloomington, Ind. 47401.
32 NELSON, OLIVER E., University of Wisconsin, Madison, Wis. 53706.
54 NERLOVE, MARC, Northwestern University, Evanston, Ill. 60201.
21 NEUFELD, ELIZABETH F., National Institutes of Health, Bldg. 10, 9-N238, Bethesda, Md. 20205.
12 NEUGEBAUER, GERRY, George W. Downs Laboratory of Physics. California Institute of Technology, Pasadena, Calif. 91125.
12 NEUGEBAUER, OTTO E., Brown University, Box 1900, Providence, R.I. 02912.
21 NEURATH, HANS, University of Washington, Seattle, Washington 98195.
53 NEWCOMB, THEODORE M., 1045 Cedar Bend Drive, Ann Arbor, Mich. 48105.
52 NEWELL, ALLEN, Carnegie-Mellon University, Schenley Park, Pittsburgh, Pa. 15213.
15 NEWELL, NORMAN D., American Museum of Natural History, Central Park West at 79th St., New York, N.Y. 10024.
14 NEWMAN, MELVIN S., Ohio State University, Columbus, Ohio 43210.
16 NEY, EDWARD P., School of Physics and Astronomy, University of Minnesota, Minneapolis, Minn. 55455.
11 NEYMAN, JERZY, University of California, Berkeley, Calif. 94720.
13 NIER, ALFRED OTTO C., M.S., PH.D., University of Minnesota, Minneapolis, Minn. 55455.
16 NIERENBERG, WILLIAM A., Scripps Institution of Oceanography, University of California, San Diego, La Jolla, Calif. 92093.
11 NIRENBERG, LOUIS, New York University, 251 Mercer Street, New York, N.Y. 10012.
21 NIRENBERG, MARSHALL WARREN, Laboratory of Biochemical Genetics, National Heart Institute, Bethesda, Md. 20205.
21 NOMURA, MASAYASU, Institute for Enzyme Research, University of Wisconsin, 1710 University Ave., Madison, Wis. 53706.
22 NOVIKOFF, ALEX B., Department of Pathology, Albert Einstein College of Medicine, 1300 Morris Park Ave., Bronx, N.Y. 10461.
41 NOWELL, PETER C., School of Medicine, University of Pennsylvania, Philadelphia, Pa. 19104.
31 NOYCE, ROBERT N., Intel Corporation, Santa Clara, Calif.
14 NOYES, RICHARD M., Dept. of Chemistry, University of Oregon, Eugene, Ore. 97403.
14 NOYES, W. ALBERT, Jr., S.B., PH.D., LL.D., D.SC., University of Texas, Austin, Tex. 78712.
13 O'BRIEN, BRIAN, Box 166, Woodstock, Conn. 06281.
21 OCHOA, SEVERO, Roche Institute of Molecular Biology, Nutley, N.J. 07110.
32 ODUM, EUGENE P., Institute of Ecology, University of Georgia, Athens, Ga. 30602.
OHNO, SUSUMU, Office of the Chairman, Department of Biology, City of Hope National Medical Center, Duarte, Calif.
14 OLAH, GEORGE A., Dept. of Chemistry, University of Southern California, Los Angeles, Calif. 90007.
43 OLD, LLOYD J., Sloan-Kettering Institute for Cancer Research, 410 East 68th St., New York, N.Y. 10021.
31 OLIVER, B. M., Hewlett-Packard Company, 1501 Page Mill Rd., Palo Alto, Calif. 94304.
51 OLIVER, DOUGLAS, University of Hawaii, 4051 Black Point Rd., Honolulu, Hawaii 96816.
27 OLSON, EVERETT C., University of California, Los Angeles, Calif. 90024.
31 OLSON, HARRY F., 71 Palmer Square, Princeton, N.J. 08540.
21 ONCLEY, J. L., A.B., PH.D., University of Michigan, Ann Arbor, Mich. 48105.
ORNSTEIN, DONALD S., Department of Mathematics, Stanford University, Calif. 94305.
31 OROWAN, EGON, 44 Paysan Terrace, Belmont, Mass. 02178.
21 OSBORN, MARY J., University of Connecticut Health Center, Farmington, Conn. 06032.
53 OSGOOD, CHARLES E., Institute of Communications Research, University of Illinois, Urbana, Ill. 61801.
12 OSTERBROCK, DONALD E., Lick Observatory, University of California, Santa Cruz, Calif. 95064.
12 OSTRIKER, JEREMIAH P., Princeton University Observatory, Princeton, N.J. 08540.
13 OVERHAUSER, ALBERT W., Department of Physics, Purdue University, West Lafayette, Ind. 47907.
26 OWEN, RAY D., California Institute of Technology, Pasadena, Calif. 91125.
42 PAGE, IRVINE H., Cleveland Clinic, 9500 Euclid Ave., Cleveland, Ohio 44106.
13 PAIS, ABRAHAM, Rockefeller University, New York, N.Y. 10021.

13 Pake, George E., Xerox Research Center, 3333 Coyote Hill Rd., Palo Alto, Calif. 94304.
22 Palade, George E., Yale University School of Medicine, 333 Cedar St., New Haven, Conn. 06510.
24 Palay, Sanford L., Harvard Medical School, 25 Shattuck St., Boston, Mass. 02115.
13 Panofsky, Wolfgang K. H., Stanford University, P.O.B. 4349, Stanford, Calif. 94305.
23 Pappenheimer, A. M., Jr., The Biological Laboratories, Harvard University, 16 Divinity Ave., Cambridge, Mass. 02138.
23 Pappenheimer, John R., Harvard Medical School, 25 Shattuck Street, Boston, Mass. 02115.
22 Pardee, Arthur B., Sidney Farber Cancer Center, 44 Binney St., Boston, Mass. 02115.
12 Parker, Eugene N., Laboratory for Astrophysics, 933 East 56th St., Chicago, Ill. 60637.
14 Parr, Robert G., Department of Chemistry, University of North Carolina, Chapel Hill, N.C. 27514.
31 Patel, C. Kumar N., Physical Research Laboratory, Bell Laboratories, Holmdel, N.J. 07974.
25 Patrick, Ruth, Academy of Natural Sciences, 19th and The Parkway, Philadelphia, Pa. 19103.
14 Pauling, Linus, sc.d., Big Sur, Calif. 93920.
31 Pearson, Gerald L., Stanford Electronics Laboratories, Stanford University, Stanford, Calif. 94305.
14 Pearson, Ralph G., Dept. of Chemistry, University of California, Santa Barbara, Calif. 93106.
16 Pekeris, Chaim L., The Weizmann Institute of Science, Rehovot, Israel.
12 Penzias, Arno A., Crawford Hill Laboratory, Bell Laboratories, Box 400, Holmdel, N.J. 07733.
Perkins, David, Department of Biological Sciences, Stanford University, Calif. 94305.
Perl, Martin L., Stanford Linear Accelerator Center, Stanford University, Calif. 94305.
14 Perlman, I., 14th-29th November St., Jerusalem, Israel.
22 Perry, Robert P., Institute for Cancer Research and the University of Pennsylvania, 7701 Burholme Ave., Philadelphia, Pa. 19111.
16 Pettengill, Gordon, Massachusetts Institute of Technology, Cambridge, Mass. 02139.
15 Pettijohn, F. J., Johns Hopkins University, Baltimore, Md. 21218.
14 Pettit, R., Department of Chemistry, University of Texas, Austin, Tex. 78712.
52 Pfaffmann, Carl, Rockefeller University, New York, N.Y. 10021.
31 Pfann, W. G., Bell Laboratories, 600 Mountain Ave., Murray Hill, N.J. 07974.
33 Phillips, James C., Bell Telephone Laboratories, 600 Mountain Ave., Murray Hill, N.J. 07974.
16 Phillips, Norman A., 4609 Keppler Place, Camp Springs, Md. 20031.
21 Phillips, William D., Dept. of Chemistry, Washington University, St. Louis, Mo. 63130.
31 Pickering, William H., California Institute of Technology, Pasadena, Calif. 91125.
31 Pierce, J. R., California Institute of Technology, Pasadena, Calif. 91125.
31 Pigford, Robert L., Dept. of Chemical Engineering, University of Delaware, Newark, Del. 19711.
14 Pimentel, George C., National Science Foundation, Washington, D.C. 20550.
13 Pines, David, Department of Physics, University of Illinois, Urbana, Ill. 61801.
31 Piore, E. R. 115 Central Park West, New York, N.Y. 10023.
24 Pittendrigh, Colin S., Hopkins Marine Station, Pacific Grove, Stanford University, Calif. 93950.
14 Pitzer, Kenneth Sanborn, b.s., ph.d., Department of Chemistry, University of California, Berkeley, Calif. 94720.
11 Polya, George, 2260 Dartmouth St., Palo Alto, Calif. 94306.
42 Popper, Hans, City University of New York, Fifth Ave. and 100th St., New York, N.Y. 10029.
22 Porter, Keith Roberts, Department of Molecular, Cellular and Developmental Biology, University of Colorado, Boulder, Colo. 80302.
Posner, Michael I., Department of Psychology, University of Oregon, Eugene, Ore. 97403.
52 Postman, Leo J., Department of Psychology, University of California, Berkeley, Calif. 94720.
Potter, Michael, National Cancer Institute, National Institutes of Health, Bethesda, Md. 20205.
41 Potter, Van R., University of Wisconsin Medical Center, 450 North Randall Ave., Madison, Wis. 53706.

13 Pound, R. V., Harvard University, Cambridge, Mass. 02138.
33 Prausnitz, John M., Department of Chemical Engineering, University of California, Berkeley, Calif. 94720.
26 Preer, John R., Jr., Dept. of Biology, Indiana University, Bloomington, Ind. 47402.
22 Prescott, David Marshall, Genetisches Institut, d. Justus-Liebig-Universität, 6300 Giessen, Federal Republic of Germany.
16 Press, Frank, Executive Office of the President, Room 360, Washington, D.C. 20500.
12 Preston, George W., California Institute of Technology, 813 Santa Barbara St., Pasadena, Calif. 91101.
16 Price, P. Buford, Jr., Department of Physics, University of California, Berkeley, Calif. 94720.
13 Primakoff, Henry, University of Pennsylvania, Philadelphia, Pa. 19104.
22 Prosser, C. Ladd, Department of Physiology, University of Illinois, Urbana, Ill. 61801.
26 Ptashne, Mark, Harvard University, 16 Divinity Ave., Cambridge, Mass. 02138.
22 Puck, Theodore T., Dept. of Biophysics, University of Colorado Medical Center, Denver, Colo. 80262.
31 Puckett, Allen E., Hughes Aircraft Co., Mail Station A/159, Centinela and Teale Sts., Culver City, Calif. 90230.
13 Purcell, E. M., b.s., a.m., ph.d., Harvard University, Cambridge, Mass. 02138.
43 Putnam, Frank W., Department of Zoology, Jordan Hall 206, Indiana University, Bloomington, Ind. 47405.
31 Quate, C. F., Ginzton Laboratories, Stanford University, Stanford, Calif. 94305.
11 Quillen, Daniel G., Room 2-237, M.I.T., Cambridge, Mass. 02139.
11 Quine, Willard V. O., Harvard University, Cambridge, Mass. 02138.
13 Rabi, I. I., 450 Riverside Drive, New York, N.Y. 10027.
Rabinowitz, Jesse C., Department of Biochemistry, University of California, Berkeley, Calif. 94720.
21 Racker, Efraim, Cornell University, Ithaca, N.Y. 14853.
54 Radner, Roy, Department of Economics, 250 Barrows Hall, University of California, Berkeley, Calif. 94720.
23 Rahn, Hermann, State University of New York Buffalo, N.Y. 14214.
13 Rainwater, L. James, Columbia University, New York, N.Y. 10027.
42 Rall, J. Edward, National Institutes of Health, Bethesda, Md. 20205.
43 Rammelkamp, Charles H., Department of Medicine, Cleveland Metropolitan General Hospital, 3395 Scranton Rd., Cleveland, Ohio 44109.
31 Ramo, Simon, TRW Inc., One Space Park, Redondo Beach, Calif. 90278.
13 Ramsey, Norman F., Harvard University, Cambridge, Mass. 02138.
41 Ranney, Helen M., Department of Medicine, University Hospital, 225 West Dickinson St., San Diego, Calif. 92103.
25 Raper, Kenneth Bryan, University of Wisconsin, Madison, Wis. 53706.
31 Rasmussen, Norman C., Massachusetts Institute of Technology, Cambridge, Mass. 02139.
52 Ratliff, Floyd, Rockefeller University, New York, N.Y. 10021.
21 Ratner, Sarah, Department of Biochemistry, Public Health Research Institute City of New York, Inc., 455 First Ave., New York, N.Y. 10016.
41 Ratnoff, Oscar D., University Hospitals of Cleveland, Cleveland, Ohio 44106.
15 Raup, David M., Field Museum of Natural History, Roosevelt Rd. and Lake Shore Drive, Chicago, Ill. 60605.
25 Raven, Peter H., Missouri Botanical Garden, 2345 Tower Grove Ave., St. Louis. Mo. 63110.
13 Redfield, Alfred G., Brandeis University, Waltham, Mass. 02154.
21 Reed, Lester J., Department of Chemistry, Clayton Foundation Biochemical Institute, University of Texas, Austin, Tex. 78712.
16 Reed, Richard J., University of Washington, Seattle, Wash. 98195.
16 Reichelderfer, Francis W., a.b., d.sc., 3031 Sedgwick St., N.W., Washington, D.C. 20008.
14 Reilley, Charles N., Venable and Kenan Laboratories, 045A, Chapel Hill, N.C. 27514.
13 Reines, Frederick, University of California, Irvine, Calif. 92717.

33 REISS, HOWARD, University of California, Los Angeles, Calif. 90024.
14 RENTZEPIS, PETER M., Physical and Inorganic Chemistry Research Dept., Bell Telephone Laboratories Inc., 600 Mountain Ave., Murray Hill, N.J. 07974.
16 REVELLE, ROGER, Dept. of Political Science, University of Calif., San Diego, La Jolla, Calif. 92093.
16 REYNOLDS, JOHN H., University of California, Berkeley, Calif. 94720.
RHINES, PETER E., Woods Hole Oceanographic Institution, Woods Hole, Mass. 02543.
26 RHOADES, M. M., M.S., PH.D., Indiana University, Bloomington, Ind. 47401.
RICE, JAMES R., Department of Theoretical and Applied Mechanics, Brown University, Providence, R.I. 02912.
14 RICE, STUART A., University of Chicago, 5640 Ellis Ave., Chicago, Ill. 60637.
21 RICH, ALEXANDER, Department of Biology, Massachusetts Institute of Technology, Cambridge, Mass. 02139.
21 RICHARDS, FREDERIC M., 69 Andrews Rd., Guilford, Conn. 06437.
13 RICHTER, BURTON, Stanford University, Stanford, Calif. 94305.
52 RICHTER, CURT PAUL, Johns Hopkins Hospital, Baltimore, Md. 21205.
32 RICK, CHARLES M., Jr., Department of Vegetable Crops, University of California, Davis, Calif. 95616.
52 RIGGS, LORRIN A., Brown University, Providence, R.I. 02912.
53 RIKER, WILLIAM H., Department of Political Science, University of Rochester, Rochester, N.Y. 14627.
27 RIPLEY, SIDNEY DILLON II, Smithsonian Institution, Washington, D.C. 20560.
22 RIS, HANS, Department of Zoology, University of Wisconsin, Madison, Wis. 53706.
43 ROBBINS, FREDERICK C., Case Western Reserve School of Medicine, 2119 Abington Rd., Cleveland, O. 44106.
11 ROBBINS, HERBERT E., 17 Woodhull Rd., East Setauket, N.Y. 11733.
14 ROBERTS, JOHN D., California Institute of Technology, Pasadena, Calif. 91125.
11 ROBINSON, JULIA, University of California, Berkeley, Calif. 94720.
15 RODGERS, JOHN, Department of Geology and Geophysics, Yale University, New Haven, Conn. 06520.
43 ROIZMAN, BERNARD, University of Chicago, 910 East 58th St., Chicago, Ill. 60637.
25 ROLLINS, REED C., Gray Herbarium, Harvard University, 22 Divinity Ave., Cambridge, Mass. 02138.
26 ROMAN, HERSCHEL L., Department of Genetics, University of Washington, Seattle, Wash. 98195.
21 ROSE, IRWIN, Institute for Cancer Research, 7701 Burholme Ave., Philadelphia, Pa. 19111.
24 ROSE, JERZY E., Laboratory of Neurophysiology, 283 Medical Sciences Building, University of Wisconsin, Madison, Wis. 53706.
21 ROSEMAN, SAUL, Department of Biology and McCollum-Pratt Institute, Johns Hopkins University, Charles and 34th Sts., Baltimore, Md. 21218.
31 ROSENBLITH, WALTER A., Room 3-240, Massachusetts Institute of Technology, Cambridge, Mass. 02139.
33 ROSENBLUTH, MARSHALL N., Institute for Advanced Study, Princeton, N.J. 08540.
52 ROSENZWEIG, MARK R., University of California, Berkeley, Calif. 94720.
14 ROSS, JOHN, Room 6-123, Massachusetts Institute of Technology, Cambridge, Mass. 02139.
13 ROSSI, BRUNO BENEDETTO, PH.D., Massachusetts Institute of Technology, Cambridge, Mass. 02139.
14 ROSSINI, FREDERICK D., 2131 N.E. 58 Court, Fort Lauderdale, Fla. 33308.
51 ROUSE, IRVING, Yale University, Box 2114, Yale Station, New Haven, Conn. 06520.
43 ROWE, WALLACE P., National Institutes of Health, Building 7, Room 304, Bethesda, Md. 20205.
14 ROWLAND, FRANK S., University of California, Irvine, Calif. 92717.
43 RUBIN, A. HARRY, W.M. Stanley Hall, University of California, Berkeley, Calif. 94720.
RUBIN, VERA C., Department of Terrestrial Magnetism, Carnegie Institution of Washington, D.C. 20005.
41 RUDDLE, FRANCIS H., Department of Biology, Yale University, New Haven, Conn. 06520.
13 RUDERMAN, MALVIN A., Pupin Physics Laboratories, Columbia University, New York, N.Y. 10027.

26 RUSSELL, ELIZABETH S., The Jackson Laboratory, Bar Harbor, Maine 04609.
26 RUSSELL, WILLIAM L., Biology Division, Oak Ridge National Laboratory, P.O.B. Y, Oak Ridge, Tenn. 37830.
43 SABIN, ALBERT B., Medical University of South Carolina, 171 Ashley Ave., Charleston, S.C. 29401.
13 SACHS, ROBERT G., Enrico Fermi Institute, University of Chicago, 5630 Ellis Ave., Chicago, Ill. 60637.
26 SAGER, RUTH, Sidney Farber Cancer Institute, 44 Binney St., Boston, Mass. 02115.
32 SALISBURY, G. W., University of Illinois, Urbana, Ill. 61801.
12 SALPETER, E. E., Laboratory of Nuclear Studies, Cornell University, Ithaca, N.Y. 14853.
54 SAMUELSON, PAUL A., Department of Economics, Massachusetts Institute of Technology, Cambridge, Mass. 02139.
12 SANDAGE, ALLAN R., Hale Observatories, 813 Santa Barbara St., Pasadena, Calif. 91101.
14 SARETT, LEWIS H., Merck and Co. Inc., P.O.B. 2000, Rahway, N.J. 07065.
23 SAWYER, CHARLES H., University of California School of Medicine, Los Angeles, Calif. 90024.
54 SCARF, HERBERT E., Department of Economics, Yale University, Box 2125, Yale Station, New Haven, Conn. 06520.
21 SCHACHMAN, HOWARD K., University of California, Berkeley, Calif. 94720.
31 SCHAIRER, GEORGE S., The Boeing Company, P.O.B. 3707, M.S. 10-47, Seattle, Wash. 98124.
42 SCHALLY, ANDREW V., 1601 Perdido St., New Orleans, La. 70146.
24 SCHARRER, BERTA V., Department of Anatomy, Albert Einstein College of Medicine, Bronx, N.Y. 10461.
13 SCHAWLOW, ARTHUR L., Department of Physics, Stanford University, Stanford, Calif. 94305.
14 SCHERAGA, H. A., Cornell University, Ithaca, N.Y. 14853.
11 SCHIFFER, M. M., Department of Mathematics, Stanford University, Stanford, Calif. 94305.
21 SCHIMKE, ROBERT T., Department of Biological Sciences, Stanford University, Stanford, Calif. 94305.
42 SCHMID, RUDI, Department of Medicine, University of California, San Francisco, Calif. 94143.
21 SCHMIDT, GERHARD, Tufts University School of Medicine, 136 Harrison Ave., Boston, Mass. 02111.
23 SCHMIDT-NIELSEN, KNUT, Duke University, Durham, N.C. 27706.
24 SCHMITT, FRANCIS OTTO, Neurosciences Research Program, Massachusetts Institute of Technology, 165 Allandale St., Jamaica Plain, Mass. 02130.
22 SCHNEIDERMAN, HOWARD A., Center for Pathobiology, University of California, Irvine, Calif. 92717.
13 SCHRIEFFER, J. ROBERT, Department of Physics, University of Pennsylvania, Philadelphia, Pa. 19104.
32 SCHULTES, RICHARD E., Botanical Museum of Harvard University, Oxford St., Cambridge, Mass 02138.
54 SCHULTZ, THEODORE W., Department of Economics, University of Chicago, 1126 East 59th St., Chicago, Ill. 60637.
33 SCHWARTZ, JACOB T., Department of Computer Science, Courant Institute of Mathematical Sciences, New York University, 251 Mercer St., New York, N.Y. 10012.
13 SCHWARTZ, MELVIN, Department of Physics, Stanford University, Stanford, Calif. 94305.
12 SCHWARZSCHILD, MARTIN, Princeton University Observatory, Peyton Hall, Princeton, N.J. 08540.
13 SCHWINGER, JULIAN, Department of Physics, University of California, 405 Hilgard Ave., Los Angeles, Calif. 90024.
32 SCRIMSHAW, NEVIN S., Department of Nutrition and Food Science, Massachusetts Institute of Technology, Cambridge, Mass. 02139.
14 SEABORG, GLENN THEODORE, Lawrence Berkeley Laboratory, University of California, Berkeley, Calif. 94720.
32 SEARS, ERNEST ROBERT, U.S. Department of Agriculture, 108 Curtis Hall, University of Missouri, Columbia, Mo. 65201.
31 SEARS, WILLIAM R., Department of Aerospace and Mechanical Engineering, University of Arizona, Tucson, Ariz. 85721.
42 SEEGMILLER, J. EDWIN, Department of Medicine, University of California, San Diego, School of Medicine, La Jolla, Calif. 92093.
11 SEGAL, IRVING E., 2-244, Department of Mathematics, Massachusetts Institute of Technology, Cambridge, Mass. 02139.
13 SEGRÈ, EMILIO, University of California, Berkeley, Calif. 94720.

13 SEITZ, FREDERICK, Rockefeller University, New York, N.Y. 10021.
32 SEQUEIRA, LUIS, University of Wisconsin, Madison, Wis. 53706.
13 SERBER, ROBERT, Columbia University, New York, N.Y. 10027.
11 SERRIN, JAMES B., University of Minnesota, Minneapolis, Minn. 55455.
26 SETLOW, RICHARD B., Brookhaven National Laboratory, Upton, N.Y. 11973.
53 SEWELL, WILLIAM H., Department of Sociology, University of Wisconsin, Madison, Wis. 53706.
12 SHANE, C. D., P.O. Box 582, Santa Cruz, Calif. 95061.
11 SHANNON, CLAUDE E., 5 Cambridge St., Winchester, Mass. 01890.
42 SHANNON, JAMES A., 7935 S.W. Westgate Way, Portland, Ore. 97227.
31 SHAPIRO, ASCHER H., Massachusetts Institute of Technology, Cambridge, Mass. 02139.
51 SHAPIRO, H. L., A.M., PH.D., American Museum of Natural History, Central Park West at 79th St., New York, N.Y. 10024.
12 SHAPIRO, IRWIN I., Department of Earth and Planetary Sciences and Department of Physics, 54–620, Massachusetts Institute of Technology, Cambridge, Mass. 02139.
54 SHAPLEY, LLOYD S., Rand Corpn., 1700 Main St., Santa Monica, Calif. 90406.
15 SHARP, ROBERT P., Division of Geological and Planetary Sciences, California Institute of Technology, Pasadena, Calif. 91125.
SHATKIN, AARON J., Laboratory of Molecular Virology, Roche Institute of Molecular Biology, Nutley, N.J.
14 SHEEHAN, JOHN C., Massachusetts Institute of Technology, Cambridge, Mass. 02139.
21 SHEMIN, DAVID, Department of Biochemistry and Molecular Biology, Northwestern University, Evanston, Ill. 60201.
52 SHEPARD, ROGER N., Stanford University, Stanford, Calif. 94305.
14 SHIRLEY, DAVID A., University of California, Berkeley, Calif. 94720.
31 SHOCKLEY, WILLIAM, B.SC., PH.D., Stanford Electronics Laboratories, Stanford University, Stanford, Calif. 94305.
15 SHOEMAKER, EUGENE M., U.S. Geological Survey, Flagstaff, Ariz.
33 SHULL, CLIFFORD G., Department of Physics, Massachusetts Institute of Technology, Cambridge, Mass. 02139.
14 SHULL, HARRISON, Rensselaer Polytechnic Institute, Troy, N.Y. 12181.
21 SHULMAN, ROBERT G., Biophysics Department, Bell Laboratories, Murray Hill, N.J. 07974.
24 SIDMAN, RICHARD L., Children's Hospital Medical Center, 300 Longwood Ave., Boston, Mass. 02115.
22 SIEKEVITZ, PHILIP, Rockefeller University, 1230 York Ave., New York, N.Y., 10021.
15 SILVER, LEON THEODORE, California Institute of Technology, Pasadena, Calif. 91125.
14 SIMMONS, H. E., Jr., Experimental Station, E.I. du Pont de Nemours and Co. Inc., Wilmington, Delaware 19898.
53 SIMON, HERBERT A., Department of Psychology, Carnegie-Mellon University, Pittsburgh, Pa. 15213.
SIMONS, EVWYN L., Department of Anthropology and Anatomy, Duke Primate Center, Duke University, Durham, N.C. 27706.
15 SIMPSON, G. G., PH.D., 5151 East Holmes St., Tucson, Ariz. 85711.
13 SIMPSON, JOHN A., The Enrico Fermi Institute for Nuclear Studies, University of Chicago, Chicago, Ill. 60637.
14 SINFELT, JOHN H., Corporate Research Laboratories, Exxon Research and Engineering Co., P.O. Box 45, Linden, N.J. 07036.
11 SINGER, ISADORE M., University of California, Berkeley, Calif. 94720.
21 SINGER, MAXINE F., National Institutes of Health, Bethesda, Md. 20205.
21 SINGER, S. J., Department of Biology, University of California, San Diego, La Jolla, Calif. 92037.
21 SINSHEIMER, ROBERT LOUIS, Division of Biology, California Institute of Technology, Pasadena, Calif. 91125.
14 SKELL, PHILIP S., Davey Laboratory, University Park, Pa. 16802.
52 SKINNER, BURRHUS FREDERIC, M.A., PH.D., Harvard University, Cambridge, Mass. 02138.
51 SKINNER, G. WILLIAM, Stanford University, Stanford, Calif. 04305.
25 SKOOG, FOLKE K., University of Wisconsin, Madison, Wis. 53706.

33 SLEPIAN, DAVID, Bell Laboratories, 600 Mountain Ave., Murray Hill, N.J. 07974.
13 SLICHTER, CHARLES P., Department of Physics, University of Illinois, Urbana. Ill. 61801.
11 SMALE, STEPHEN, Department of Mathematics, University of California, Berkeley, Calif. 94720.
25 SMITH, ALBERT C., Dept. of Botany, 3190 Maile Way, University of Hawaii, Honolulu, Hawaii 96822.
33 SMITH, CYRIL STANLEY, 31 Madison St., Cambridge, Mass. 02138.
21 SMITH, EMIL L., University of California Medical Center, Los Angeles, Calif. 90024.
11 SMITH, PAUL A., B.S., PH.D., Columbia University, New York, N.Y. 10027.
SMITH, RAY F., Department of Entomological Sciences University of California, Berkeley, Calif. 94720.
26 SMITHIES, OLIVER, Laboratory of Genetics, University of Wisconsin, Madison, Wis. 53706.
14 SMYTH, CHARLES P., Frick Chemical Laboratory, Princeton University, Princeton, N.J. 08540.
21 SNELL, ESMOND E., University of Texas, Austin, Texas 78712.
43 SNELL, GEORGE D., 21 Atlantic Ave., Bar Harbor, Me. 04609.
24 SNYDER, SOLOMON H., Johns Hopkins University School of Medicine, Baltimore, Md. 21218.
24 SOKOLOFF, LOUIS, National Institutes of Health, Bethesda, Md. 20205.
52 SOLOMON, RICHARD L., 3815 Walnut St., Philadelphia, Pa. 19104.
54 SOLOW, ROBERT M., E52-383, Department of Economics, Massachusetts Institute of Technology, Cambridge, Mass. 02139.
14 SOMORJAI, G. A., University of California, Berkeley, Calif. 94720.
26 SONNEBORN, TRACY M., A.B., PH.D., Indiana University, Bloomington, Ind. 47401.
13 SOROKIN, PETER P., IBM Corpn., P.O.B., 218, Yorktown Heights, N.Y. 10598.
14 SPEDDING, F. H., Iowa State University, Ames, Iowa 50010.
11 SPENCER, D. C., Department of Mathematics, Princeton University, Princeton, N.J. 08540.
52 SPERRY, ROGER W., Division of Biology, California Institute of Technology, Pasadena, Calif. 91125.
51 SPICER, EDWARD H., Department of Anthropology, College of Liberal Arts, University of Arizona, Tucson, Ariz. 85721.
41 SPIEGELMAN, SOL, Columbia University, 701 West 168th St., New York, N.Y. 10032.
SPITZER, FRANK, Department of Mathematics, Cornell University, Ithaca, N.Y. 14853.
12 SPITZER, LYMAN, Jr., Princeton University Observatory, Peyton Hall, Princeton, N.J. 08540.
51 SPOEHR, ALEXANDER, Department of Anthropology, University of Pittsburgh, Pittsburgh, Pa. 15213.
32 SPRAGUE, G. F., Department of Agronomy, University of Illinois, Urbana, Ill. 61801.
25 SRB, ADRIAN M., Cornell University, Ithaca, N.Y. 14853.
21 STADTMAN, E. R., National Heart, Lung and Blood Institute, National Institutes of Health, Bethesda, Md. 20205.
STADTMAN, THRESSA C., Intermediary Metabolism and Bioenergetics Section, National Heart, Lung and Blood Institute, National Institutes of Health, Bethesda, Md. 20205.
26 STAHL, FRANKLIN W., Institute of Molecular Biology, University of Oregon, Eugene, Ore. 97403.
25 STARR, RICHARD C., Department of Botany, University of Texas, Austin, Tex. 78712.
27 STEBBINS, G. LEDYARD, University of California, Davis, Calif. 95616.
11 STEIN, CHARLES M., 821 Santa Fe Ave., Stanford, Calif. 94305.
11 STEIN, ELIAS M., Department of Mathematics, Princeton University, Princeton, N.J. 08540.
13 STEINBERGER, J., CERN, Geneva 23, Switzerland.
21 STEINER, DONALD F., Department of Biochemistry, University of Chicago, 920 East 58th St., Chicago, Ill. 60637.
52 STELLAR, ELIOT, 102 College Hall, University of Pennsylvania, Philadelphia, Pa. 19174.
32 STEPHENS, STANLEY G., 3219 Darien Drive, Raleigh, N.C. 27607.
33 STERNBERG, ELI, California Institute of Technology, Pasadena, Calif. 91125.

42 STETTEN, DEWITT, Jr., National Institutes of Health, Bldg. 1, Bethesda, Md. 20205.
31 STEVER, H. GUYFORD, 1528 33rd St., N.W., Washington, D.C. 20007.
51 STEWART, THOMAS D., Smithsonian Institution, Washington, D.C. 20560.
54 STIGLER, GEORGE J., Walgreen Foundation, University of Chicago, 5836 Greenwood Ave., Chicago, Ill. 60637.
14 STOCKMAYER, W. H., Dartmouth College, Hanover, N.H. 03755.
22 STOECKENIUS, WALTHER, Cardiovascular Research Institute, Room 1315-M, University of California, San Francisco, Calif. 94143.
33 STOKER, J. J., Courant Institute of Mathematical Sciences, New York University, 251 Mercer Street, New York, N.Y. 10012.
16 STOMMEL, HENRY M., Woods Hole Oceanographic Institution, Woods Hole, Mass. 02543.
11 STONE, MARSHALL H., Department of Mathematics, University of Massachusetts, Amherst, Mass. 01002.
14 STORK, GILBERT, Department of Chemistry, Columbia University, New York, N.Y. 10027.
31 STRATTON, JULIUS ADAMS, S.M., SC.D., Massachusetts Institute of Technology, 77 Massachusetts Ave., Cambridge, Mass. 02139.
22 STRAUS, WILLIAM L., Jr., 7111 Park Heights Ave., Apt. 506, Baltimore, Md. 21215.
13 STREET, JABEZ C., P.O. Box 336, East Falmouth, Mass. 02536.
26 STREISINGER, GEORGE, Institute of Molecular Biology, University of Oregon, Eugene, Or. 97403.
14 STREITWIESER, ANDREW, University of California, Berkeley, Calif. 94720.
21 STROMINGER, JACK LEONARD, Biological Laboratories, Harvard University, Cambridge, Mass. 02138.
25 STUMPF, P. K., Dept. of Biochemistry and Biophysics, University of California, Davis, Calif. 95616.
21 STURTEVANT, JULIAN M., Department of Chemistry, Kline Chemistry Laboratory, Yale University, New Haven, Conn. 06520.
16 SUESS, HANS E., Department of Chemistry, University of California, San Diego, La Jolla, Calif. 92093.
13 SUHL, HARRY, Department of Physics, B-019 Revelle College, University of California, San Diego, La Jolla, Calif. 92093.
31 SUITS, C. G., A.B., D.SC., Crosswinds, Pilot Knob, N.Y. 12844.
52 SUPPES, PATRICK, Institute for Mathematical Studies in Social Sciences, Stanford University, Ventura Hall, Stanford, Calif. 94305.
31 SUTHERLAND, IVAN E., 256-80, California Institute of Technology, Pasadena, Calif. 91125.
11 SWAN, RICHARD G., Department of Mathematics, University of Chicago, 5734 University Ave., Chicago, Ill. 60637.
22 SWIFT, HEWSON H., Department of Biology, University of Chicago, Chicago, Ill. 60637.
16 SYKES, LYNN R., Lamont-Doherty Geological Observatory, Columbia University, Palisades, N.Y. 10964.
21 SZENT-GYÖRGYI, ALBERT, P.O.B. 187, Woods Hole, Mass. 02543.
21 TABOR, HERBERT, National Institute of Arthritis, Metabolism, and Digestive Diseases, National Institutes of Health, Bethesda, Md. 20205.
43 TALMAGE, DAVID W., University of Colorado Medical Center, Denver, Colo. 80220.
43 TAMM, IGOR, Rockefeller University, 1230 York Ave., New York, N.Y. 10021.
21 TANFORD, CHARLES, Department of Biochemistry, Duke University Medical Center, Durham, N.C. 27710.
TANNER, CHAMP B., Department of Soil Science, University of Wisconsin, Madison, Wis. 53706.
14 TARBELL, D. S., Department of Chemistry, Vanderbilt University, Nashville, Tenn. 37235.
11 TARSKI, ALFRED, 462 Michigan Ave., Berkeley, Calif. 94707.
11 TATE, JOHN T., Harvard University, Cambridge, Mass. 02138.
14 TAUBE, HENRY, Dept. of Chemistry, Stanford University, Stanford, Calif. 94305.
42 TAUSSIG, HELEN B., Apt. 158, Crosslands, Kennett Square, Pa. 19348.
TAYLOR, HUGH P., Jr., Division of Geological and Planetary Science, California Institute of Technology, Pasadena, Calif. 91125.
26 TAYLOR, JAMES H., Institute of Molecular Biophysics, Florida State University, Tallahassee, Fla. 32306.
TAYLOR, JOSEPH H., Jr., Department of Physics and Astronomy, University of Massachusetts at Amherst, Mass. 01003.
52 TEITELBAUM, PHILIP, Department of Psychology, University of Illinois, Champaign, Ill. 61820.
13 TELEGDI, VALENTINE L., University of Chicago, 5630 Ellis Ave., Chicago, Ill. 60637.
13 TELLER, EDWARD, Lawrence Livermore Laboratory, P.O.B. 808, Livermore, Calif. 94550.
26 TEMIN, HOWARD M., University of Wisconsin Medical Center, Madison, Wis. 53706.
24 TEMKIN, OWSEI, 419 Alabama Rd., Towson, Md. 21204.
31 TERMAN, F. E., 445 El Escarpado, Stanford, Calif. 94305.
25 THIMANN, KENNETH VIVIAN, University of California, Santa Cruz, Calif. 95064.
31 THOMAS, CHARLES ALLEN, 7701 Forsyth Boulevard, St. Louis, Mo. 63105.
43 THOMAS, LEWIS, Office of the President, Memorial Sloan-Kettering Cancer Center, 1275 York Ave., New York, N.Y. 10021.
33 THOMAS, LLEWELLYN HILLETH, 3012 Wycliff Rd., Raleigh, N.C. 27607.
11 THOMAS, T. Y., 249 North Glenroy Ave., Los Angeles, Calif. 90049.
15 THOMPSON, JAMES B., Jr., Dept. of Geological Sciences, Harvard University, Cambridge, Mass. 02138.
11 THOMPSON, JOHN G., Department of Pure Mathematics, University of Cambridge, 16 Mill Lane, Cambridge CB2 1SB, England.
52 THOMPSON, RICHARD F., University of California, Irvine, Calif. 92717.
12 THORNE, KIP S., 130-33, California Institute of Technology, Pasadena, Calif. 91125.
31 TIEN, PING KING, Dept. of Electron Physics, Bell Telephone Laboratories Inc., Crawfords Corner Rd., Holmdel, N.J. 07733.
TILLY, CHARLES, Departments of Sociology and History, University of Michigan, Ann Arbor, Mich. 48109.
15 TILTON, GEORGE R., Dept. of Geological Sciences, University of California, Santa Barbara, Calif. 93106.
13 TING, SAMUEL C. C., Massachusetts Institute of Technology, Bldg. 44, Cambridge, Mass. 02139.
13 TINKHAM, MICHAEL, Department of Physics, Harvard University, Cambridge, Mass. 02138.
14 TISHLER, MAX, Department of Chemistry, Wesleyan University, Middletown, Conn. 06457.
54 TOBIN, JAMES, Department of Economics, Yale University, Box 2125, Yale Station, New Haven, Conn. 06520.
TORREY, JOHN G., Department of Biology, Harvard Forest, Petersham, Mass.
12 TOUSEY, RICHARD, United States Naval Research Laboratory (Code 7140), Washington, D.C. 20375.
13 TOWNES, CHARLES H., Department of Physics, University of California, Berkeley, Calif. 94720.
22 TRAGER, WILLIAM, Rockefeller University, New York, N.Y. 10021.
13 TREIMAN, SAM B., Joseph Henry Laboratories, Jadwin Hall, P.O.B. 708, Princeton University, Princeton, N.J. 08540.
14 TROST, BARRY M., University of Wisconsin, Madison, Wis. 53706.
33 TUKEY, JOHN W., Bell Laboratories 2C-580, 600 Mountain Ave., Murray Hill, N.J. 07974.
14 TURKEVICH, ANTHONY L., The Enrico Fermi Institute for Nuclear Studies, University of Chicago, Chicago, Ill. 60637.
33 TURNBULL, DAVID, Harvard University, Cambridge, Mass. 02138.
15 TURNER, FRANCIS J., University of California, Berkeley, Calif. 94720.
TURRO, NICHOLAS J., Department of Chemistry, Columbia University, New York, N.Y. 10027.
21 UDENFRIEND, SIDNEY, Roche Institute of Molecular Biology, Nutley, N.J. 07110.
13 UHLENBECK, GEORGE E., Rockefeller University, New York. N.Y. 10021.
11 ULAM, S. M., University of Florida, Gainesville, Fla. 32609.
21 UMBARGER, H. EDWIN, Department of Biological Sciences, Purdue University, West Lafayette, Ind. 47907.
52 UNDERWOOD, BENTON J., Department of Psychology, Northwestern University, Evanston, Ill. 60201.
21 VAGELOS, P. ROY, Merck, Sharp & Dohme Research Laboratories, Rahway, N.J. 07065.
41 VALENTINE, WILLIAM N., University of California, Los Angeles, Calif. 90024.
21 VALLEE, BERT L., Department of Biochemistry, Harvard Medical School, 721 Huntington Ave., Boston, Mass. 02115.
16 VAN ALLEN, JAMES A., Dept. of Physics and Astronomy, State University of Iowa, Iowa City, Ia. 52242.

14 VAN TAMELEN, EUGENE E., Stanford University, Stanford, Calif. 94305.
VELICK, SIDNEY F., Department of Biological Chemistry, University of Utah, Salt Lake City, Utah 84112.
16 VERHOOGEN, JOHN, University of California, Berkeley, Calif. 94720.
16 VILLARD, OSWALD GARRISON, Jr., Radioscience Laboratory, Stanford University, Stanford, Calif. 94305.
23 VISSCHER, MAURICE B., 120 Melbourne Ave., S.E., Minneapolis, Minn. 55414.
51 VOGT, E. Z., Jr., Harvard University, Cambridge, Mass. 02138.
43 VOGT, PETER K., University of Southern California School of Medicine, Los Angeles, Calif. 90007.
21 VON HIPPEL, PETER H., Institute of Molecular Biology, University of Oregon, Eugene, Ore. 97403.
32 WADLEIGH, CECIL H., 5621 Whitefield Chapel Rd., Lanham, Md. 20801.
26 WAELSCH, SALOME G., Albert Einstein College of Medicine, 1300 Morris P Park Ave., Bronx, New York, 10461.
32 WAGGONER, PAUL E., Connecticut Agricultural Experiment Station, P.O.B. 1106, 123 Huntington St., New Haven, Conn. 06504.
21 WALD, GEORGE, M.A., PH.D., Harvard University, 16 Divinity Ave., Cambridge, Mass. 02138.
32 WALKER, J. C., M.S., PH.D., 14016 Newcastle Drive, Sun City, Ariz. 85351.
16 WALKER, ROBERT M., Department of Physics, Box 1105, Washington University, St. Louis, Mo. 63130.
14 WALL, FREDERICK T., San Diego State University, San Diego, Calif. 92182.
51 WALLACE, ANTHONY F. C., Department of Anthropology, University of Pennsylvania, University Museum, Philadelphia, Pa. 19174.
14 WALLING, CHEVES T., Department of Chemistry, University of Utah, Salt Lake City, Utah 84112.
14 WARNER, J. C., 4742 Center Ave., Apt. 301, Pittsburgh, Pa. 15213.
51 WASHBURN, SHERWOOD L., University of California, Berkeley, Calif. 94720.
16 WASSERBURG, GERALD J., Division of Geological and Planetary Sciences, California Institute of Technology, Pasadena, Calif. 91125.
15 WATERS, AARON C., 308 Moore St., Santa Cruz, Calif. 95060.
42 WATSON, CECIL JAMES, University of Minnesota Medical Unit, Northwestern Hospital, Minneapolis, Minn. 55407.
21 WATSON, JAMES D., Cold Spring Harbor Laboratory, Cold Spring Harbor, Long Island, N.Y. 11724.
13 WATSON, KENNETH M., Department of Physics, University of California, Berkeley, Calif. 94720.
14 WAUGH, J. S., Department of Chemistry, Massachusetts Institute of Technology, Cambridge, Mass. 02139.
31 WEBER, ERNST, P.O.B. 1619, Tryon, N.C. 28782.
21 WEBER, GREGORIO, Department of Biochemistry, Roger Adams Laboratory, University of Illinois, Urbana, Ill. 61801.
51 WEDEL, WALDO R., Department of Anthropology, Smithsonian Institution, Washington, D.C. 20560.
33 WEINBERG, ALVIN M., Office of the Director, Institute for Energy Analysis, P.O.B. 117, Oak Ridge, Tenn. 37830.
13 WEINBERG, STEVEN, Department of Physics, Harvard University, Cambridge, Mass. 02138.
21 WEINHOUSE, SIDNEY, Temple University School of Medicine, 3420 North Board St., Philadelphia, Pa. 19140.
22 WEISS, PAUL ALFRED, Rockefeller University, New York, N.Y. 10021.
13 WEISSKOPF, VICTOR F., Massachusetts Institute of Technology, Cambridge, Mass. 02139.
14 WEISSMAN, S. I., Louderman Hall, Washington University, St. Louis, Mo. 63130.
43 WELLER, THOMAS H., Harvard School of Public Health, 665 Huntington Ave., Boston, Mass. 02115.
15 WELLS, JOHN W., Cornell University, Ithaca, N.Y. 14853.
25 WENT, FRITS W., Desert Research Institute, University of Nevada, Reno, Nev. 89507.
14 WESTHEIMER, FRANK H., Harvard University, 12 Oxford St., Cambridge, Mass. 02138.
16 WETHERILL, GEORGE W., Carnegie Institution of Washington, 5241 Broad Branch Rd., N.W., Washington, D.C. 20015.
52 WEVER, ERNEST G., Princeton University, Princeton, N.J. 08540.
13 WHEATLEY, JOHN C., Department of Physics, Revelle College, University of California, San Diego, La Jolla, Calif. 92093.

13 WHEELER, JOHN A., Department of Physics, University of Texas, Austin, Tex. 78712.
31 WHINNERY, JOHN R., Department of Electrical Engineering and Computer Sciences, University of California, Berkeley, Calif. 94720.
12 WHIPPLE, FRED L., Astrophysical Observatory, Smithsonian Institution, Cambridge, Mass. 02138.
15 WHITE, DONALD E., U.S. Geological Survey, 345 Middlefield Rd., Menlo Park, Calif. 94025.
53 WHITE, GILBERT F., Institute of Behavioral Science, University of Colorado, Boulder, Colo. 80309.
53 WHITE, HARRISON C., Department of Sociology, William James Hall, Harvard University, Cambridge, Mass. 02138.
11 WHITEHEAD, GEORGE W., Room 2-284, Department of Mathematics, Massachusetts Institute of Technology, Cambridge, Mass. 02139.
14 WHITESIDES, GEORGE M., Room 18-298, M.I.T., Cambridge, Mass. 02139.
12 WHITFORD, ALBERT E., Lick Observatory, University of California, Santa Cruz, Calif. 95064.
11 WHITNEY, HASSLER, MUS.B., PH.D., The Institute for Advanced Study, Princeton, N.J. 08540.
14 WIBERG, KENNETH, Dept. of Chemistry, Yale University, New Haven, Conn. 06520.
13 WICK, GIAN-CARLO, Scuola Normale Superiore, Piazza Del Cavalleri, 56100 Pisa, Italy.
14 WIDOM, BENJAMIN, Department of Chemistry, Cornell University, Ithaca, N.Y. 14853.
31 WIESNER, JEROME B., Massachusetts Institute of Technology, Cambridge, Mass. 02139.
13 WIGHTMAN, ARTHUR S., Joseph Henry Laboratories, Princeton University, Princeton, N.J. 08544.
13 WIGNER, EUGENE P., DR.ENG., Princeton University, Princeton, N.J. 08540.
11 WILDER, R. L., University of California, Santa Barbara, Calif. 93106.
51 WILLEY, GORDON R., Peabody Museum, Harvard University, Cambridge, Mass. 02138.
22 WILLIAMS, CARROLL M., The Biological Laboratories, Harvard University, 16 Divinity Ave., Cambridge, Mass. 02138.
14 WILLIAMS, JOHN W., University of Wisconsin, Madison, Wis. 53706.
21 WILLIAMS, ROBLEY C., Department of Molecular Biology, University of California, Berkeley, Calif. 94720.
21 WILLIAMS, ROGER J., Clayton Foundation Biochemical Institute, University of Texas, Austin, Tex. 78712.
14 WILSON, E. BRIGHT, Jr., B.S., A.M., PH.D., Harvard University, 12 Oxford St., Cambridge, Mass. 02138.
27 WILSON, EDWARD O., Museum of Comparative Zoology Laboratories, Harvard University, Cambridge, Mass. 02138.
13 WILSON, KENNETH G., Laboratory of Nuclear Studies, Cornell University, Ithaca, N.Y. 14853.
12 WILSON, OLIN C., Hale Observatories, 813 Santa Barbara St., Pasadena, Calif. 91101.
25 WILSON, PERRY W., Department of Bacteriology, University of Wisconsin, Madison, Wis. 53706.
13 WILSON, ROBERT R., Fermi National Accelerator Laboratory, P.O.B. 500, Batavia, Ill. 60510.
12 WILSON, ROBERT W., Bell Telephone Laboratories, P.O. Box 400, Holmdel, N.J. 07733.
33 WINOGRAD, SHMUEL, T. J. Watson Research Center, P.O.B. 218, Yorktown Heights, N.Y. 10598.
41 WINTROBE, M. M., College of Medicine, University of Utah, 50 North Medical Drive, Salt Lake City, Utah 84132.
26 WITKIN, EVELYN M., Douglass College, Rutgers University, New Brunswick, N.J. 08540.
14 WITKOP, BERNHARD, National Institute of Arthritis, Metabolism and Digestive Diseases, National Institutes of Health, Bethesda, Md. 20205.
32 WOGAN, GERALD N., Massachusetts Institute of Technology, Cambridge, Mass. 02139.
WOLFE, RALPH S., Department of Microbiology, University of Illinois, Urbana, Ill. 61801.
13 WOLFENSTEIN, LINCOLN, Carnegie-Mellon University, Pittsburgh, Pa. 15213.
11 WOLFOWITZ, J., Department of Mathematics, University of South Florida, Tampa, Fla. 33620.
31 WOLMAN, ABEL, Johns Hopkins University, Baltimore, Md. 21218.
53 WOLPERT, JULIAN, School of Architecture and Urban Planning and Woodrow Wilson School, Princeton University, Princeton, N.J. 08540.
21 WOOD, HARLAND G., Department of Biochemistry, Case Western Reserve University, Cleveland, Ohio 44106.

## NATIONAL ACADEMY OF SCIENCES — UNITED STATES OF AMERICA

26 Wood, William B. III, Dept. of Molecular, Cellular and Developmental Biology, University of Colorado, Boulder, Colo. 80309.
31 Wooldridge, Dean E., 4545 Via Esperanza, Santa Barbara, Calif. 93110.
24 Woolsey, Clinton N., 106 Virginia Terrace, Madison, Wis. 53705.
15 Wright, H. E., Jr., University of Minnesota, 310 Pillsbury Drive, Minneapolis, Minn. 55455.
13 Wu, Chien-Shiung, Department of Physics, Columbia University, New York, N.Y. 10027.
16 Wulf, Oliver Reynolds, California Institute of Technology, Pasadena, Calif. 91125.
16 Wunsch, Carl, Dept. of Earth and Planetary Sciences, Room 54-914, M.I.T., Cambridge, Mass. 02139.
21 Wyman, Jeffries, Istituto Regina Elena, Viale Regina Elena 291, Rome 00161, Italy.
42 Wyngaarden, James B., Department of Medicine, Duke University Medical Center, Durham, N.C. 27710.
42 Yalow, Rosalyn S., Veterans Administration Hospital, 130 W. Kingsbridge Rd., Bronx, N.Y. 10468.
13 Yang, Chen Ning, Dept. of Physics, State University of New York, Stony Brook, N.Y. 11794.
26 Yanofsky, Charles, Stanford Univ., Stanford, Calif. 94305.
15 Yoder, Hatten S., Jr., Carnegie Institution of Washington, 2801 Upton St., N.W., Washington, D.C. 20008.
13 Zacharias, Jerrold R., 32 Clifton St., Belmont, Mass. 02178.
21 Zamecnik, Paul C., Massachusetts General Hospital, Boston, Mass. 02114.
14 Zare, Richard N., Dept. of Chemistry, Stanford University, Stanford, Calif. 94305.
15 Zen, E-An, U.S. Geological Survey, National Center, Mail Stop 959, Reston, Va. 22092.
33 Zener, Clarence, Carnegie-Mellon University, Schenley Park, Pittsburgh, Pa. 15213.
32 Zentmyer, George A., University of California, Riverside, Calif. 92521.
14 Zimm, Bruno Hasbrouck, Dept. of Chemistry, University of California, San Diego, La Jolla, Calif. 92093.
14 Zimmerman, Howard E., University of Wisconsin, Madison, Wis. 53706.
26 Zinder, Norton D., Rockefeller Univ., New York, N.Y. 10021.
31 Zinn, Walter H., 1155 Ford Lane, Dunedin, Fla. 33528.
22 Zirkle, Raymond E., 4675 West Red Rock Drive, Perry Park SWDC, Larkspur, Colo. 80118.
33 Zwanzig, Robert W., Institute for Physical Science and Technology, University of Maryland, College Park, Md. 20742.
31 Zworykin, Vladimir K., R.C.A. Laboratories, Princeton, N.J. 08540.
11 Zygmund, Antoni, Dept. of Mathematics, University of Chicago, Chicago, Ill. 60637.

### Members Emeriti:

Anderson, Charles A., Mount San Antonio Gardens, B21 900 East Harrison Ave., Pomona, Calif. 91767.
Billings, Marland P., Harvard University, Cambridge, Mass. 02138.
Birch, A. Francis, Harvard Univ., Cambridge, Mass. 02138.
Bleakney, Walker, 4681 La Espada Drive, Santa Barbara, Calif. 93111.
Bok, Bart J., University of Arizona, Tucson, Ariz. 85721.
Breit, Gregory, State University of New York, Buffalo, N.Y. 14260.
Burns, Robert K., The Bridgewater Home, Bridgewater, Va. 22812.
Castle, W. B., Harvard Medical School, Brookline, Mass.
Chalmers, Bruce, Harvard Univ., Cambridge, Mass. 02138.
Chipman, John, 19 Lorena Rd., Winchester, Mass. 01890.
Coggeshall, Lowell T., Route 2, Foley, Ala. 36535.
Corner, George W., American Philosophical Society, 104 South Fifth St., Philadelphia, Pa. 19106.
Doell, Richard R., P.O. Box 1463, El Granada, Calif. 94018.
Dubos, René, Rockefeller University, New York, N.Y. 10021.
Elsasser, Walter M., Dept. of Earth and Planetary Sciences, Johns Hopkins University, Baltimore, Md. 21218.
Emerson, Sterling, 1207 Morada Place, Altadena, Calif. 91001.
Esau, Katherine, University of California, Santa Barbara, Calif. 93106.
Friedmann, Herbert, 350 South Fuller Ave., Apt. 12H, Los Angeles, Calif. 90036.
Fuoss, Raymond M., Hamden, Conn.
Greenewalt, Crawford H., E.I. du Pont de Nemours & Co. Inc., Wilmington, Dela. 19898.
Hammett, Louis P., 288 Medford Leas, Medford, N.J. 08055.
Hastings, A. Baird, 2130 Vallecitos, Apt. 147, La Jolla, Calif. 92037.
Johnson, John R., Deer Valley Farm, Townshend, Vt. 05353.
Kemble, Edwin C., 8 Ash St. Place, Cambridge, Mass. 02138.
King, Charles G., 192 Kendel at Longwood, Kennett Square, Pa. 19348.
Landis, Eugene M., 1547 Silver Creek Drive, Hellertown, Pa. 18055.
Lloyd, David P., New Cottage, Greatham, Pulborough, RH20 2ES, Sussex, England.
Longsworth, Lewis G., 144-60 29th Ave., Flushing, N.Y. 11354.
Lush, Jay L., Dept. of Animal Science, 239 Kildee Hall, Iowa State University, Ames, Iowa 50011.
Magoun, Horace W., 427 25th St., Santa Monica, Calif. 90402.
Nolan, Thomas B., 2219 California St., N.W., Washington, D.C. 20008.
Northrop, John H., P.O.B. 1387, Wickenburg, Ariz. 85358.
Raymond, Arthur E., 73 Oakmont Drive, Los Angeles, Calif. 90049.
Redfield, Alfred C., 14 Maury Lane, Woods Hole, Mass. 02543.
Riker, A. J., 2760 East Eighth St., Tucson, Ariz. 85716.
Rose, William C., University of Illinois, Urbana, Ill. 61801.
Schmidt, C. F., 15462 Gulf Blvd., Madeira Beach, Fla. 33708.
Stern, Curt, 225 Chumalia St., 7, San Leandro, Calif. 94577.
Tuttle, O. Frank, Tucson, Ariz.
Tuve, Merle A., 135 Hesketh St., Chevy Chase, Md. 20015.
Van Niel, C. B., Carmel, Calif.
Wetmore, Ralph H., 12 Francis Ave., Cambridge, Mass. 02138.
Woodring, Wendell P., National Museum of Natural History, Washington, D.C. 20560.
Wright, Sewall, University of Wisconsin, Madison, Wis. 53706.
Wyckoff, Ralph W., 4715 E. Fort Lowell Rd., Tucson, Ariz. 85712.
Zariski, Oscar, 122 Sewall Ave., Brookline, Mass. 02146.

### Foreign Associates:

13 Abragam, Anatole, Centre d'Etudes Nucléaires de Saclay, B.P. 2, 91190 Gif-sur-Yvette, France.
33 Aigrain, Pierre R., 8 Square Henry Paté, Paris 75016, France.
11 Alexandroff, Paul S., Mathematical Institute of the Academy of Sciences of the U.S.S.R., Bolshaya Kalushskaya 19, Moscow, U.S.S.R.
16 Alfvén, Hannes, University of California, San Diego, La Jolla, Calif. 92093.
13 Amaldi, Edoardo, University of Rome, Piazzale delle Scienze 5, Rome, Italy.
12 Ambartsumian, V., Burakan Astronomical Observatory, Erevan, Armenia, U.S.S.R.
43 Andrewes, Sir Christopher Howard, Overchalke, Coombe Bissett, Salisbury, Wilts., England.
11 Atiyah, Michael F., Mathematical Institute, University of Oxford, 24-29 St. Giles, Oxford, OX1 3LB, England.
26 Auerbach, Charlotte, Institute of Animal Genetics, West Mains Rd., Edinburgh, EH9 3JN, Scotland.
14 Bartlett, Neil, University of California, Berkeley, Calif. 94720.
14 Barton, Sir Derek, Institut de Chimie des Substances Naturelles, 91190 Gif-sur-Yvette, France.
22 Beerman, Wolfgang, Max-Planck-Institut für Biologie, Spemannstr. 7400 Tübingen 1, Fed. Rep. of Germany.
14 Bell, Ronald Percy, 5 Park Villa Court, Leeds LS5 1EB, England.
21 Bergström, Sune, Karolinska Institutet, S10401, Stockholm, Sweden.
51 Bernal, Ignacio, Mexico City, Mexico.
13 Biermann, Ludwig, Max-Planck-Institute for Physics and Astrophysics, Foehringer Ring 6, 8000 Munich 40, Federal Republic of Germany.
16 Blamont, Jacques Emile, University of Paris, France.
Bodmer, Walter F., Imperial Cancer Research Fund Laboratories, London, England.
13 Bogolubov, Nikolai N., Joint Institute for Nuclear Research, Dubna Main Post Office, P.O.B. 79, Moscow, U.S.S.R.
13 Bohr, Aage Niels, Department of Physics, Niels Bohr Institute, Blegdamsvej 17, Copenhagen, Denmark.

12 BOLTON, JOHN G., A.N.R.A.O., N.S.W., Australia.
22 BRACHET, JEAN, Laboratoire de Morphologie Animale, 67 rue des Chevaux, Rhode-St.-Genèse, Belgium.
21 BRAUNSTEIN, ALEKSANDR E., Novoslobodskaya ul., 57/65, KV. 24, Moscow, U.S.S.R
26 BRENNER, SYDNEY, University Postgraduate School, Hills Rd., Cambridge, CB2 2QH, England.
32 BRESSANI, RICARDO, Institute of Nutrition of Central America and Panama, Carretera Roosevelt, Zona 11, Guatemala City, Guatemala.
52 BROADBENT, DONALD E., University of Oxford, Dept. of Applied Psychology, South Parks Rd., Oxford, OX1 3UD, England.
13 DE BROGLIE, Prince LOUIS, 94 rue Perronet, Neuilly-sur-Seine, France.
25 BÜNNING, ERWIN, Institut für Biologie, 74 Tübingen, Auf der Morgenstelle, Federal Republic of Germany.
43 BURNET, Sir MACFARLANE, 48 Monomeath Ave., Canterbury, 3126 Victoria, Australia.
11 CARTAN, HENRI PAUL, 95 blvd. Jourdan, 75014-Paris, France.
33 CASIMIR, H. B. G., De Zegge 7, Heeze, Netherlands.
26 CATCHESIDE, D. G., Waite Agricultural Research Institute, Glen Osmond, South Australia 5064.
26 CAVALLI-SFORZA, L. L., Stanford University School of Medicine, Stanford, Calif. 94305.
51 CLARK, J. G. D., The Master's Lodge, Peterhouse, Cambridge, CB2 1QY, England.
15 COOMBS, DOUGLAS S., Dept. of Geology, University of Otago, Box 56, Dunedin, New Zealand.
14 CORNFORTH, Sir JOHN W., School of Molecular Sciences, University of Sussex, Falmer, Brighton, BN1 9QJ, England.
31 COTTRELL, Sir ALAN HOWARD, The Master's Lodge, Jesus College, Cambridge, England.
31 COUSTEAU, JACQUES Y., c/o Cousteau Society, 777 Third Ave., New York, N.Y. 10017.
 COWAN, W. MAXWELL, Developmental Neurobiology Laboratory, Salk Institute, San Diego, Calif. 92138.
21 CRICK, FRANCIS, Salk Institute for Biological Studies, San Diego, Calif. 92112.
53 DAHRENDORF, RALF, London School of Economics and Political Science, University of London, London, WC2A 2AE, England.
 DAUSSET, JEAN B. G. J., Laboratoire Immunogénétique de la Transplantation Humaine, Hôpital St. Louis, Paris, France.
11 DIRAC, PAUL ADRIEN MAURICE, Florida State University, Tallahassee, Fla. 32306.
26 DUBININ, N. P., Institute of General Genetics, Academy of Sciences of the U.S.S.R. Moscow B-133, Moscow, U.S.S.R.
41 DE DUVE, CHRISTIAN, International Institute of Cellular and Molecular Pathology, Av. Hippocrate 75, B1200 Brussels, Belgium.
25 DUYSENS, LOUIS N. M., Dept. of Biophysics, State University of Leiden, Wassenaarseweg 78, Leiden, Netherlands.
23 ECCLES, Sir JOHN, Cá a la Grá, Contra, CH-6611, Switzerland.
14 EIGEN, MANFRED, Max-Planck-Institut für Physikalische Chemie, Bunsenstrasse 10, 3400 Göttingen, Germany.
21 ENGELHARDT, W. A., Institute of Molecular Biology, Academy of Sciences of the U.S.S.R., Vavilov Str. 32, Moscow B-312, U.S.S.R.
11 ERDÖS, PAUL, Hungarian Academy of Sciences, Budapest, Hungary.
31 ESAKI, LEO, IBM Corpn., Yorktown Heights, N.Y. 10598.
14 ESCHENMOSER, ALBERT J., Eidgenössische Technische Hochschule Zürich, Laboratorium für Organische Chemie, Universitätsstrasse 16, CH-8092, Zurich, Switzerland.
23 VON EULER, U. S., Karolinska Institutet, S-10401 Stockholm 60, Sweden.
43 FENNER, FRANK, Centre for Resource and Environmental Studies, Australian National University, Canberra, A.C.T. 2600, Australia.
25 FREY-WYSSLING, A. F., Institut für Allgemeine Botanik, E.T.H., Universitätstrasse 2, Zurich, Switzerland.
24 VON FRISCH, U. S., Uber der Klause 10, 8000 Munich, Federal Republic of Germany.
 FUKUI, KENICHI, Department of Hydrocarbon Chemistry, Kyoto University, Kyoto, Japan.
15 GANSSER, AUGUSTO, Geologisches Institut, Eidgenössische Technische Hochschule, Sonneggstrasse 5, Zurich, Switzerland.
25 GAUTHERET, ROBERT, Paris, France.

43 GEAR, JAMES H. S., Institute for Virology, S.A. Institute for Medical Research, P.O.B. 1038, Johannesburg 2000, South Africa.
16 GEISS, JOHANNES, Institute of Physics, University of Berne, Sidlerstr. 5, 3012 Berne, Switzerland.
11 GELFAND, ISRAEL M., Laboratory of Mathematical Methods in Biology, Moscow State University, Moscow, 117234, U.S.S.R.
 GINZBURG, VITALI L., Department of Theoretical Physics, Lebedev Institute, Moscow, U.S.S.R.
32 GLEN, ROBERT, 4523 Juniper Place, Victoria, B.C., V8N 3K1, Canada.
15 GOGUEL, JEAN, Ecole Nationale Supérieure des Mines, 100 rue du Bac, Paris VIIe, France.
23 GRANIT, RAGNAR, The Nobel Institute for Neurophysiology, Karolinska Institutet, Stockholm 60, Sweden.
32 GURDON, J. B., M.R.C. Laboratory for Molecular Biology, Hills Rd., Cambridge CB2 2QH, England.
25 GUSTAFSSON, C. ÅKE T., Institute of Genetics, Lund University, Sölvegaten 29, S-223, 62 Lund, Sweden.
26 HARRIS, HARRY, Department of Human Genetics, University of Pennsylvania, Philadelphia, Pa. 19104.
15 HARRISON, J. M., 4 Kippewa Drive, Ottawa K1S 3G4, Canada.
31 HAWTHORNE, W. R., University Engineering Laboratory, Cambridge University, Trumpington St., Cambridge, England.
21 HAYAISHI, OSAMU, Department of Medical Chemistry, Kyoto University Faculty of Medicine, Sakyo-ku, Kyoto 606, Japan.
25 HEBB, DONALD O., Dalhousie University, Halifax, N. S. B3H 4J1, Canada.
13 HERZBERG, GERHARD, National Research Council, Ottawa 7, Ont., K1A OR6, Canada.
54 HICKS, Sir JOHN R., All Souls College, Oxford, England.
25 HILL, R., Department of Biochemistry, Cambridge University, Cambridge CB2 1QW, U.K.
27 HINDE, ROBERT A., M.R.C. Unit on Development and Integration of Behaviour, University of Cambridge, Madingley, Cambridge, CB3 8AA, England.
23 HODGKIN, Sir ALAN L., Trinity College, Cambridge CB2 1TQ, England.
14 HODGKIN, DOROTHY C., Chemical Crystallography Laboratory, 9 Parks Rd., Oxford OX1 3PD, England.
11 HÖRMANDER, LARS, Department of Mathematics, University of Lund, Sweden.
12 HOYLE, Sir FRED, Cockley Moor, Dockray, Penrith, Cumberland, CA11 0LG, England.
23 HUXLEY, Sir ANDREW F., University College, London, Gower St., London WC1E 6BT, England.
21 HUXLEY, HUGH E., M.R.C. Laboratory of Molecular Biology, Cambridge, CB2 2QH, England.
12 VAN DE HULST, HENDRIK, Sterrewacht, Leiden, Huygens Laboratorium, Wassenaarseweg 78, Leiden 2405, Netherlands.
31 INOSE, HIROSHI, Dept. of Electronic Engineering, University of Tokyo, Bunkyo-Ku, Tokyo, Japan.
22 JACOB, FRANÇOIS, Institut Pasteur, 25 rue du Docteur Roux, Paris XVe, France.
16 JEFFREYS, Sir HAROLD, St. John's College, Cambridge, England.
43 JERNE, NIELS K., Basel Institute for Immunology, 487 Grenzacherstr., CH-4058 Basel, Switzerland.
25 JOLIOT, PIERRE A., Institut de Biologie Physico-Chimique, 13 rue Pierre et Marie Curie, 75005 Paris, France.
33 JOST, RES, Institute for Theoretical Physics, E.T.H., CH8093, Zurich, Switzerland.
13 KAPITZA, PETER L., S.I. Vavilov Institute of Physical Problems, Academy of Sciences of the U.S.S.R., Moscow, U.S.S.R.
21 KATCHALSKI-KATZIR, EPHRAIM, The Weizmann Institute of Science, Rehovot, Israel.
13 KATZ, Sir BERNARD, Department of Biophysics, University College, London, England.
16 KEILIS-BOROK, VLADIMIR I, Institute of Physics of the Earth, Academy of Sciences, Moscow, U.S.S.R.
21 KENDREW, JOHN COWDREY, Medical Research Council, Laboratory of Molecular Biology, Hills Rd., Cambridge CB2 2QH, England.
26 KIHARA, HITOSHI, Kihara Institute for Biological Research, Mutsakawa 3-122-21, Yokohama, Japan.
26 KIMURA, MOTOO, National Institute of Genetics, Mishima, 411 Japan.
41 KLEIN, GEORGE, Institutet fär Tumörbiologi, Karolinska Institutet, 104 01 Stockholm 60, Sweden.

## NATIONAL ACADEMY OF SCIENCES — UNITED STATES OF AMERICA

11 KODAIRA, KUNIHIKO, Department of Mathematics, Gakushuin University, 1-5-1 Mejiro, Toshima, Tokyo, Japan.
51 VON KOENIGSWALD, G. H. RALPH, Forschungsinstitut Senckenberg, Senckenberganlage 25, 6 Frankfurt a.M., Federal Republic of Germany.
11 KOLMOGOROV, ANDREJ N., Moscow State University, Moscow, U.S.S.R.
21 KREBS, Sir HANS A., Nuffield Department of Clinical Medicine, Radcliffe Infirmary, Oxford, England.
KREIN, MARK GRIGOR'EVICH, Odessa Institute of Civil Engineering, Odessa, U.S.S.R.
13 KUBO, RYOGO, Department of Physics, University of Tokyo, Hongo Bunkyo-Ku, Tokyo, Japan.
16 LAL, DEVENDRA, Physical Research Laboratory, Navrangpura, Ahmedabad 380009, India.
51 LARSEN, HELGE E., Ethnographical Dept., Danish National Museum, 10 Ny Vestergade, DK1471 Copenhagen K, Denmark.
14 LEHN, JEAN-MARIE P., Université Louis Pasteur, Strasbourg, France.
21 LELOIR, LUIS F., Instituto de Investigaciones Bioquimicas, Obligado 2490, Buenos Aires, Argentina.
11 LERAY, JEAN. Collège de France, 11 Place Marcelin-Berthelot, Paris Ve, France.
51 LÉVI-STRAUSS, CLAUDE, Laboratoire d'Anthropologie Sociale, Collège de France, 11 place Marcelin-Berthelot, 75231 Paris Cedex 05, France.
33 LIGHTHILL, Sir M. JAMES, University College, London, England.
24 LINDAUER, MARTIN, Department of Zoology and Comparative Physiology, Bayerische-Julius-Maximilians Universität, Würzburg, Federal Republic of Germany.
14 LONGUET-HIGGINS, HUGH C., Centre for Research on Perception and Cognition, Laboratory of Experimental Psychology, University of Sussex, Falmer, Brighton BN1 9QY, England.
15 LONGUET-HIGGINS, MICHAEL S., University of Cambridge, Silver St., Cambridge CB3 9EW, England.
24 LORENZ, KONRAD, Max-Planck-Institut für Vergl. Verhaltensforschung, Abt. 4, Tiersoziologie A-3422, Altenberg, Austria.
42 LUFT, ROLF, Dept. of Endocrinology and Metabolism, Karolinska Institutet, 104 01, Stockholm 60, Sweden.
22 LWOFF, ANDRÉ, Institut Pasteur, 25 rue du Docteur Roux, 75274 Paris Cedex 15, France.
26 LYON, MARY F., MRC Radiobiology Unit, Harwell, Didcot, Oxon OX11 0RD, England.
54 MALINVAUD, EDMOND, Institut National de la Statistique et des Etudes Economiques, 18 blvd. Pinard, 75675 Paris 14, France
15 McLAREN, DIGBY J., Geological Survey of Canada, 601 Booth St., Ottawa, Ont. K1A 0E8, Canada.
42 McMICHAEL, Sir JOHN, 2 North Sq., London, NW11 7AA, England.
MEADE, JAMES, Department of Applied Economics, Cambridge University, Cambridge, England.
22 MEDAWAR, Sir PETER B., Clinical Research Centre, Watford Rd., Harrow, Middlesex, HA1 3UJ, England.
52 MILNER, BRENDA, Department of Neurology, Montreal Neurological Institute, Quebec, Canada.
MILSTEIN, CÉSAR, Protein Chemistry Subdivision, Medical Research Council Laboratory of Molecular Biology, Cambridge, England.
21 MITCHELL, PETER, Glynn Research Ltd., Glynn House, Bodmin, Cornwall, PL30 4AU, England.
14 MIZUSHIMA, S., 2-10-6, Tamagawa-Denenchofu, Setagayaku, Tokyo, Japan.
16 MONIN, ANDREI S., Institute of Oceanology, Academy of Sciences of the U.S.S.R., Moscow, U.S.S.R.
13 MÖSSBAUER, RUDOLF L., Dept. of Physics, Technical University, D-8046 Garching, Munich, Fed. Rep. of Germany.
13 MOTT, Sir NEVILLE, University of Cambridge, Cavendish Laboratory, Madingley Rd., Cambridge CB3 0HE, England.
13 MOTTELSON, BEN R., Nordisk Institut for Teoretisk Atomfysik, Copenhagen ø, Denmark.
16 NAGATA, TAKESI, National Institute of Polar Research, Itabashi, Tokyo 173, Japan.
21 NEEDHAM, JOSEPH, East Asian History of Science Library, 16 Brooklands Ave., Cambridge, England.
13 NE'EMAN, YUVAL, Tel-Aviv University, Tel-Aviv, Israel.
16 NICOLET, MARCEL, Brussels University, 30 Ave. Den Doorn, 1180 Brussels, Belgium.

43 NOSSAL, Sir GUSTAV J. V., Royal Melbourne Hospital, Victoria 3050, Australia.
30 OCCHIALINI, GIUSEPPE, Institute of Physical Science, University of Milan, Via Celoria 16, 20133 Milan, Italy.
12 OORT, JAN, Observatory of Leiden, Leiden, The Netherlands.
12 ÖPIK, ERNST J., Armagh Observatory, Armagh, BT61 9DG, N. Ireland.
43 OUDIN, JACQUES, Institut Pasteur, 28 rue du Docteur Roux, Paris 15e, France.
13 PEIERLS, Sir RUDOLF, Nuclear Physics Laboratory, Keble Rd., Oxford OX1 3RH, England.
33 PENNEY, Lord, Wantage, Oxon., England.
21 PERUTZ, MAX F., University Postgraduate Medical School, Cambridge, CB2 2QH, England.
41 PICKERING, Sir GEORGE, Cairns Library, Radcliffe Infirmary, Oxford, OX2 6HE, U.K.
14 POLANYI, JOHN C., University of Toronto, 80 St. George's St., 262 Lash Miller, Toronto, M5S 1A1, Canada.
14 POPLE, JOHN A., Dept. of Chemistry, Carnegie-Mellon University, Pittsburgh, Pa. 15213.
14 PORTER, Sir GEORGE, The Royal Institution, 21 Albemarle, St., London, W1X 4BS, England.
43 PORTER, RODNEY ROBERT, Department of Biochemistry, University of Oxford, South Parks Rd., Oxford OX1 3QU, England.
14 PRELOG, V., Laboratorium für organische Chemie, Eidgenössische Technische Hochschule, Zürich, Switzerland.
14 PRIGOGINE, I., University of Brussels, Serv. de Chimie Physique II, Blvd. du Triomphe, 1050 Brussels, Belgium.
32 RAMALINGASWAMI, VULIMIRI, All India Institute of Medical Sciences, Ansari Nagar, New Delhi 110016, India.
21 REICHARD, PETER A., Karolinska Institute, Stockholm, Sweden.
14 REICHEL-DOLMATOFF, GERARDO, Latin American Center, University of California, Los Angeles.
14 REICHSTEIN, TADEUS, Organisch-chemische Anstalt, St. Johanns-Ring 19, Basle, Switzerland.
27 RENSCH, BERNHARD, Zoologisches Institut der Westfälischen Wilhelms-Universität, 44 Münster (Westf.), Federal Republic of Germany.
15 RINGWOOD, A. E., Australian National University, Research School of Earth Sciences, Institute of Advanced Studies, P.O.B. 4, Canberra 2600, Australia.
32 ROBERTSON, ALAN, Institute of Animal Genetics, West Mains Rd., Edinburgh EH9 3JN, Scotland.
25 ROBERTSON, Sir RUTHERFORD N., Australian National University, Box 4, P.O. Canberra, A.C.T., Australia 2600.
31 ROCHA, MANUEL C. M., Av. Estados Unidos da America 95-3° Dt°., Lisbon 5, Portugal.
31 ROSENBLUETH, EMILIO, Instituto de Ingenieria, Ciudad Universitaria, Mexico, D.F., Mexico.
31 ROY, MAURICE, 86 Avenue Niel, Paris XVII, France.
12 RYLE, Sir MARTIN, Cavendish Laboratory, Madingley Rd., Cambridge CB3 0HE, U.K.
13 SAKHAROV, ANDREI, P. N. Lebedev Institute of Physics, Academy of Sciences of the U.S.S.R., 14 Leninsky Prospekt, Moscow, U.S.S.R.
13 SALAM, ABDUS, Blackett Laboratory, Imperial College, London, S.W.7, England.
21 SANGER, FREDERICK, University Postgraduate Medical School, Cambridge, CB2 2QH, England.
12 SCHMIDT, MAARTEN, Hale Observatories, 813 Santa Barbara St., Pasadena, Calif. 91101.
21 SELA, MICHAEL, Office of the President, Weizmann Institute of Science, Rehovot, Israel.
14 SEMENOV, NIKOLAI N., Institute of Chemical Physics, Vorobyevskoye chaussee 2, Moscow, V-133, U.S.S.R.
11 SERRE, JEAN-PIERRE, Collège de France, 75231 Paris Cedex 05, France.
11 SHAFAREVICH, IGOR R., Mathematical Institute of the U.S.S.R. Academy of Sciences, Ul. Vavilova 42, Moscow 117333, U.S.S.R.
12 SHKLOVSKY, I. S., Astrophysical Department, Institute of Space Research, Academy of Sciences of the U.S.S.R., 14 Leninsky Prospekt, Moscow, U.S.S.R.
25 SLATYER, RALPH O., Department of Environmental Biology, Australian National University, Canberra, Australia.
52 SOKOLOV, EUGENE N., Faculty of Psychology, Moscow State University, Moscow, U.S.S.R.
22 STANIER, ROGER Y., Institut Pasteur, 28 rue du Docteur Roux, 75274 Paris Cedex 15, France.
12 STRÖMGREN, BENGT, Cph Observatory, Østervoldgade 3, DK-1350 Copenhagen K, Denmark.

32 Swaminathan, M. S., Indian Council of Agricultural Research, Krishi Bhavan, Dr. Rajendra Prasad Rd., New Delhi, 110001, India.
12 Swings, P., Institut d'Astrophysique, Université de Liège, Cointe-Ougree, Belgium.
22 Szentágothai, János, 1st Department of Anatomy, Semmelweis University Medical School, Tüzoltó utca 58, Budapest IX, Hungary.
25 Takhtajan, Armen L., Komarov Botanical Institute, 2 Prof. Popov St., Leningrad 197022, U.S.S.R.
25 Tamiya, H., Shinjuku-ku, Shimo-ochiai, Tokyo, 3-9-10, Japan (161).
21 Theorell, Hugo, Nobel Institute of Medicine, Stockholm 60, Sweden.
53 Tinbergen, J., Erasmus University, Rotterdam 3016, The Netherlands.
24 Tinbergen, N., Department of Zoology, Animal Behaviour Research Group, South Parks Rd., Oxford, OX1 3PS, England.
14 Todd, Lord, University Chemical Laboratory, University of Cambridge, Lensfield Rd., Cambridge, England.
15 Trümpy, Daniel R., Geologisches Institut, Eidgenössische Technische Hochschule, CH-8092 Zurich, Switzerland.
23 Ussing, Hans H., Copenhagen, Denmark.
16 Uyeda, Seida, Earthquake Research Institute, University of Tokyo, Tokyo, Japan.
13 Van Hove, Léon, European Organization for Nuclear Research, Geneva, Switzerland.
31 Wagner, Carl, Max-Planck-Institut für Physikalische Chemie, Bunsenstrasse 10, 34 Göttingen, Federal Republic of Germany.
41 Waldenström, Jan G., Dept. of Medicine, General Hospital, Malmö, Sweden.
Weibel, Ewald Rudolf, Department of Anatomy, University of Berne, Berne, Switzerland.
11 Weil, André, Institute for Advanced Study, Princeton, N.J. 08540.
von Wettstein, Diter H., Department of Physiology, Carlsberg Laboratory, Copenhagen, Denmark.
White, Michael J. D., Department of Genetics, University of Melbourne, Victoria, Australia.
22 Wigglesworth, Sir Vincent B., Department of Zoology, University of Cambridge, Downing St., Cambridge CB2 3EJ, England.
11 Wilkes, M. V., The Computer Laboratory, Corn Exchange St., Cambridge CB2 3QG, England.
14 Wilkinson, Geoffrey, Department of Chemistry, Imperial College of Science and Technology, London SW7 2AY, England.
15 Wilson, J. Tuzo, Office of the Director-General, Ontario Science Centre, 770 Don Mills Rd., Don Mills, Ont. M3C 1T3, Canada.
Wyllie, Peter John, Department of Geophysical Sciences, University of Chicago, Chicago, Ill. 60637.
12 Zeldovich, Yakov, Institute of Applied Mathematics, Academy of Sciences of the U.S.S.R., Moscow 12547, U.S.S.R.

### NATIONAL ACADEMY OF ENGINEERING
Founded 1964.

*President:* Courtland D. Perkins.
*Vice-President:* Ralph Landau.
*Home Secretary:* Harold Liebowitz.
*Foreign Secretary:* N. Bruce Hannay.
*Treasurer:* Frederic A. L. Holloway.

#### MEMBERS:

Aaron, Robert, Bell Telephone Laboratories, Holmdel, N.J 07733 (1979).
Abramson, H. Norman, Engineering Sciences Division, Southwest Research Institute, P.O. Drawer 28510, San Antonio, Tex. 78284 (1976).
Ackermann, William C., P.O.B. 232, Urbana, Ill. 61801 (1967).
Acrivos, Andreas, Dept. of Chemical Engineering, Stanford University, Stanford, Calif. 94305 (1977).
Adamson, Arthur P., General Electric Co., Cincinnati, Ohio 45215 (1980).
Adcock, Willis A., Texas Instruments Inc., P.O.B. 5012, Dallas, Tex. 75222 (1974).
Adler, Dr. Robert, Zenith Center, 1000 Milwaukee Ave., Glenview, Ill. 60025 (1967).

Agnew, Harold M., Los Alamos Scientific Laboratory of the University of California, P.O.B. 1663, Los Alamos, N.M. 87545 (1976).
Agnew, William G., General Motors Research Laboratories, 12 Mile and Mound Rds., Warren, Mich. 48090 (1974).
Albaugh, Frederic W., 2534 Harris Ave., Richland, Wash. 99352 (1978).
Alexander, William D., P.O.B. 707, Litchfield Beach, Pauley Is., S.C. 29585 (1978).
Alfrey, Turner, Jr., Dow Chemical Co., 1702 Bldg., Midland, Mich. 48640 (1977).
Allen, Clarence R., Seismological Laboratory 252-21, California Institute of Technology, Pasadena, Calif. 91125 (1976).
Allen, Herbert, Cameron Iron Works, Inc., P.O.B. 1212, Houston, Tex. 77001 (1979).
Allen, Lew, Jr., The Pentagon, Room 4E-929, Washington, D.C. 20330 (1978).
Alvarez, Dr. Luis W., University of California, Berkeley, Calif. 94720 (1969).
Amdahl, Dr. Gene Myron, Amdahl Corpn., 1160 Kern Ave., Sunnyvale, Calif. 94086 (1967).
Amirikian, Arsham, Amirikian Engineering Co., 35 Wisconsin Circle, Suite 500, Chevy Chase, Md. 20015 (1980).
Amundson, Neal R., Dept. of Chemical Engineering, University of Houston, Houston, Tex. 77004 (1970).
Ancker-Johnson, Dr. Betsy, Argonne National Laboratory, 9700 Cass Ave., Argonne, Ill. 60439 (1975).
Anderson, Arthur G., IBM Corpn., Monterey and Cottle Rds., San Jose, Calif. 95193.
Anderson, Arthur R., ABAM Engineers Inc., 1127 Port of Tacoma Rd., Tacoma, Wash. 98421 (1977).
Anderson, John G., General Electric Co., 100 Woodlawn Ave., Pittsfield, Mass. 01201 (1979).
Ang, Alfredo H.-S., University of Illinois at Urbana-Champaign, 3129E Civil Engineering Building, Urbana, Ill. 61801 (1976).
Apstein, Maurice, School of Engineering and Applied Science, George Washington University, Washington, D.C. 20052 (1977).
Arbiter, Nathaniel, X9 Ranch, Vail, Ariz. 85641 (1977).
Aris, Dr. Rutherford, Department of Chemical Engineering and Materials Science, University of Minnesota, Minneapolis, Minn. 55455.
Armstrong, Neil A., Cardwell International Ltd., 31 North Broadway, Lebanon, Ohio (1978).
Arnold, Philip M., P.O.B. 1457, Bartlesville, Okla. 74003 (1970).
Arnold, W. Howard, Westinghouse Electric Corpn., Box 355, Pittsburgh, Pa. 15230 (1974).
Ashley, Dr. Holt, Stanford University, Stanford, Calif. 94305 (1970).
Atkin, Rupert L., TRW Automotive World-wide, 34201 Van Dyke, Warren, Mich. 48092.
Atwood, Donald J., Detroit Diesel Allison Division, Gen. Motors Corpn., 13400 West Outer Drive, Detroit, Mich. 48228 (1980).
Atwood, J. Leland, P.O.B. 90343, Airport Station, Los Angeles, Calif. 90009 (1974).
Auerbach, Isaac L., 121 North Broad St., Philadelphia, Pa. 19107 (1974).
Austin, Dr. James B., 114 Buckingham Rd., Pittsburgh, Pa. 15215 (1967).
Austin, T. Louis, Texas Utilities Co., 2001 Bryan Tower, Dallas, Tex. 75201 (1979).
Avery, Robert, Argonne National Laboratory, 9700 South Cass Ave., Argonne, Ill. 60439 (1978).
Avila, Charles F., 272 Atlantic Ave., Swampscott, Mass. 01907 (1968).
Babb, Albert L., Dept. of Nuclear Engineering, University of Washington, Seattle, Washington 98195 (1972).
Bachman, Walter C., Wayside, Short Hills, New Jersey 07078 (1967).
Backus, John W., IBM Research Laboratory, 91 St. Germain Ave., San Francisco, Calif. 94114 (1977).
Bacon, Vinton W., University of Wisconsin, Milwaukee, Wis. 53201 (1969).
Bailey, Stuart L., Atlantic Research Corpn., 5390 Cherokee Ave., Alexandria, Va. 22314 (1973).
**Bainer, Roy**, University of California, Davis, **Calif. 95616** (1965).
Baird, Jack A., American Telephone and Telegraph Co., 195 Broadway, New York, N.Y. 10007 (1971).
Baker, James G., C-12 Harvard College Observatory, 60 Garden St., Cambridge, Mass. 02138 (1979).
Baker, Robert A., Sr., 285 Clinton Place, Hackensack, N.J. 07601 (1967).

## NATIONAL ACADEMY OF ENGINEERING

BAKER, Dr. W. O., Bell Laboratories, 600 Mountain Ave., Murray Hill, N.J., 07974.
BALLHAUS, Dr. WILLIAM F., Beckman Instruments Inc., 2500 Harbor Blvd., Fullerton, Calif. 92634 (1973).
BANDEL, HANNSKARL, Severud-Perrone-Sturm-Bandel, 415 Lexington Ave., New York, N.Y. 10017 (1978).
BANKS, HARVEY O., Camp Dresser & McKee Inc., 710 South Broadway, Walnut Creek, Belmont, Calif. 94596 (1973).
BARDEEN, JOHN, Dept. of Physics, University of Illinois, Urbana, Ill. 61801 (1972).
BARKAN, PHILIP, Design Division, Stanford Univ., Stanford, Calif. 94305 (1980).
BARLOW, EDWARD J., Jr., 611 Hansen Way, Palo Alto, Calif. 94303 (1968).
BARNES, HOWARD C., Chas. T. Main Inc., Southeast Tower, Prudential Center, Boston, Mass. 02199 (1974).
BARON, MELVIN L., Weidlinger Associates, 110 East 59th St., New York, N.Y. 10022 (1978).
BARON, SEYMOUR, Burns and Roe, Inc., 700 Kinderkamack Road, Oradell, N.J. 07649 (1980).
BARON, THOMAS, Shell Development Co., One Shell Plaza, P.O.B. 2463, Houston, Tex. 77001 (1977).
BARR, HARRY F., 25620 Meadowdale Lane, Franklin, Mich. 48025 (1965).
BARROW, THOMAS D., Exxon Corpn., 1251 Ave. of the Americas, New York, N.Y. 10020 (1974).
BARTHOLD, LIONEL O., Power Technologies, Inc., P.O.B. 1058, Schenectady, N.Y. 12301 (1981).
BARUCH, JORDAN J., U.S. Dept. of Commerce, Washington, D.C. 20230 (1974).
BATCHELOR, JOHN W., 11709 Joan Drive, Pittsburgh, Pa. 15235 (1980).
BATTIN, RICHARD H., Charles Stark Draper Laboratory Inc., Cambridge, Mass. 02142 (1974).
BAUER, ROBERT F., 811 West 7th St., Los Angeles, Calif. 90017 (1969).
BAXTER, SAMUEL S., 7048 Castor Ave., Philadelphia, Pa. 19149 (1970).
BEARD, LEO R., Center for Research in Water Resources, University of Texas at Austin, 10100 Burnet Rd , Austin, Tex. 78758 (1975).
BEATON, ROY H., General Electric Co., 175 Curtner Ave., San Jose, Calif. 95125 (1977).
BEATTIE, HORACE S., IBM Corpn., Deepwood Drive, Lexington, Ky. 40505 (1976).
BECHTEL, STEPHEN D., Jr., Bechtel Group of Companies, 50 Beale St., San Francisco, Calif. 94105 (1975).
BECK, PAUL A., 204 Metallurgy and Mining Building, University of Illinois, Urbana, Ill. 61801 (1981).
BECKMAN, Dr. ARNOLD O., P.O.B. C-19600, Irvine, Calif. 92713 (1967).
BEEDLE, LYNN S., Fritz Engineering Laboratory, Lehigh University, Bethlehem, Pa. 18015 (1972).
BEHNKE, WALLACE B., Commonwealth Edison Co., 1 First National Plaza, P.O.B. 767, Chicago, Ill. 60690 (1980).
BELL, C. GORDON, Digital Equipment Corpn., 146 Main St., Maynard, Mass. 01754 (1977).
BELL, MILO C., University of Washington, Seattle, Wash. 98195 (1968).
BELLMAN, RICHARD E., University of Southern California, University Park, Los Angeles, Calif. 90007 (1977).
BELLPORT, BERNARD P., 855 Terra California Drive 4, Walnut Creek, Calif. 94595 (1970).
BENEDICT, Dr. MANSON, Massachusetts Institute of Technology, Cambridge, Mass. 02139 (1967).
BERANEK, Dr. LEO L., Boston Broadcasters Inc., Needham, Mass. 02192 (1966).
BERG, DANIEL, Westinghouse Electric Corpn., Gateway Center, Room 144, Pittsburgh, Pa. 15222 (1976).
BERGEN, WILLIAM B., P.O.B. 747, St. Michaels, Md. 21663 (1974).
BERGER, BERNARD B., University of Massachusetts, Marston Hall-Rm. 21, Amherst, Mass. 01003 (1979).
BERKEY, DONALD C., General Electric Co., P.O.B. 7600, Stamford, Conn. 06904 (1979).
BERLEKAMP, ELWYN R., University of California, Berkeley, Calif. 94720 (1977).
BERRY, Dr. DONALD S., Northwestern University, Evanston, Ill. 60201 (1966).
BINGER, WILSON V., Tippetts-Abbett-McCarthy-Stratton, 345 Park Ave., New York, N.Y. 10022.
BIOT, Dr. MAURICE A., Avenue Paul Hymans 117, 1200 Brussels, Belgium (1967).
BIRD, R. BYRON, The University of Wisconsin, Madison, Wis. 53706 (1969).

## UNITED STATES OF AMERICA

BISPLINGHOFF, Dr. RAYMOND L., Tyco Laboratories Inc., Tyco Park, Exeter, N.H. 03833.
BITZER, DONALD L., University of Illinois, Urbana, Ill. 61801 (1974).
BLASINGAME, BENJAMIN P., Delco Electronics Division, General Motors Corporation, 6767 Hollister Ave., Goleta, Calif. 93017 (1971).
BLECHER, FRANKLIN H., Bell Telephone Laboratories, Whippany Rd., Whippany, N.J. 07981 (1979).
BLEICH, HANS H., 12 West 72nd St., New York, N.Y. 10023 (1978).
BLICKWEDE, DONALD J., Bethlehem Steel Corpn., Bethlehem, Pa. 18016 (1976).
BLOCH, ERICH, IBM Corpn., East Fishkill Facility, Route 52, Hopewell Junction, N.Y. 12533 (1980).
BLOOR, W. SPENCER, Leeds & Northrup, A Unit (General Signal Corpn.), North Wales, Pa. 19454 (1979).
BLUME, Dr. JOHN A., 130 Jessie St., San Francisco, Calif. 94105 (1969).
BOBECK, ANDREW H., Bell Laboratories, Room 2D 352, 600 Mountain Ave., Murray Hill, N.J. 07974.
‡BODE, Dr. HENDRIK W., Harvard University, Cambridge, Mass. 02138 (1964).
BOGDANOFF, Dr. JOHN L., Purdue University, 120 A & ES Building, West Lafayette, Ind. 47907.
BOGDONOFF, SEYMOUR M., Dept. of Aerospace and Mechanical Sciences, Princeton University, Princeton, N.J. 08540 (1977).
BOILEAU, OLIVER C., General Dynamics Corpn., Pierre Laclede Center, 7733 Forsyth Blvd., St. Louis, Miss. 63105 (1979).
BOLEY, Dr. BRUNO A., Technological Institute, Northwestern University, Evanston, Ill. 60201.
BOLT, BRUCE A., University of California, Berkeley, Calif. 94720 (1978).
BOLT, RICHARD H., 50 Moulton St., Cambridge, Mass. 02138 (1978).
BOUDART, MICHEL, Dept. of Chemical Engineering, Stanford University, Stanford, Calif. 94305 (1979).
BOULGER, FRANCIS W., Battelle Columbus Laboratories, 505 King Ave., Columbus, Ohio 43201 (1978).
BOUNDY, Dr. RAY H., 600 South Ocean Blvd., Apt. 1503, Boca Raton, Fla. 33432 (1967).
BOVAY, HARRY E., Jr., Bovay Engineers Inc., 5009 Caroline St., Houston, Tex. 77004 (1978).
BOWHILL, SIDNEY A., University of Illinois, Urbana, Ill. 61801 (1971).
BOYD, Dr. JAMES, 282 Del Mesa Carmel, Carmel, Calif. 92921 (1967).
BOYER, RAYMOND F., Midland Macromolecular Institute, 1910 West St. Andrews Drive, Midlands, Mich. 48640 (1978).
BOYER, VINCENT S., Philadelphia Electric Co., 2301 Market St., Philadelphia, Pa. 19101 (1980).
BOYLE, WILLARD S., P.O.B. 179, Wallace, Nova Scotia, Canada (1974).
BRANNON, H. RAYMOND, Exxon Production Research Co., P.O.B. 2189, Houston, Tex. 77001 (1980).
BRANSCOMB, LEWIS M., IBM Corpn., Old Orchard Rd., Armonk, 10504 (1974).
BRAY, A. PHILIP, General Electric Co., 175 Curtner Ave., San Jose, Calif. 95125 (1979).
BREAKWELL, JOHN V., Department of Aeronautics and Astronautics, Stanford University, Stanford, Calif. 94305 (1981).
BREEN, JOHN E., The University of Texas at Austin, ECJ Hall 4.200, Austin, Tex. 78712 (1976).
BRENNER, HOWARD, Dept. of Chemical Engineering, Univ. of Rochester, Rochester, N.Y. 14627 (1980).
BRESLER, BORIS, Wiss, Janney, Elstner & Associates, Inc., 5801 Christie Ave., Suite 485, Emeryville, Calif. 94608 (1979).
BRIAN, Dr. P. L. THIBAUT, Corporate Engineering Air Products and Chemicals Inc., P.O.B. 538, Allentown, Pa. 18105.
BRIDGES, WILLIAM B., California Institute of Technology, Room 116-81, Pasadena, Calif. 91125 (1977).
BRINCKERHOFF, CHARLES M., 784 Park Avenue, New York, N.Y. 10021 (1976).
BROMBERG, Dr. ROBERT, TRW Systems Group One Space, Park, Redondo Beach, Calif. 90278 (1969).
BROOKS, FREDERICK P., Jr., Department of Computer Science, University of North Carolina, Chapel Hill, N.C. 27514 (1976).
BROOKS, Dr. HARVEY, Harvard University, Cambridge, Mass. 02138 (1968).
BROOKS, Dr. NORMAN H., California Institute of Technology, Pasadena, Calif. 91125 (1973).
BROUGHTON, DONALD B., Engineering Research and Development Division, UOP Process Division, 20 UOP Plaza, Des Plaines, Ill. 60016 (1976).

BROWN, Dr. ALFRED E., Celanese Research Co., P.O.B. 1000, Summit, N.J. 07901.
BROWN, BURTON P., 50 Brown St., Baldwinsville, N.Y. 13027 (1973).
BROWN, DAVID, Two Park Ave., New York, N.Y. 10016 (1978).
BROWN, Dr. GEORGE H., 117 Hunt Drive, Princeton, N.J. 08540 (1965).
BROWN, Dr. GORDON S., 8126 North Madrid Drive, Tucson, Ariz. 85704 (1965).
BROWN, Dr. HAROLD, The Pentagon, Room 3E-880, Washington, D.C. 20301 (1967).
BROWN, Dr. H. J. U., University of Houston, 4400 Calhoun St., Houston, Tex. 77004 (1975).
BRUMER, MILTON, 6750 Entrada Place, Boca Raton, Fla. 33433 (1969).
BRYSON, ARTHUR E., Jr., Stanford University, Stanford, Calif. (1970).
BUCHSBAUM, Dr. SOLOMON J., Communications Sciences Division, Bell Laboratories, Crawford Corner Rd., Holmdel, N.J. 07733 (1973).
BUCKLEY, PAGE SCOTT, Control Systems, Design Division, Engineering Department, E.I. du Pont de Nemours and Co., Wilmington, Del. 19898 (1981).
BUCY, J. FRED, Jr., Texas Instruments Inc., P.O.B. 5484, Dallas, Tex. 75222 (1974).
BUDIANSKY, BERNARD, Division of Engineering and Applied Physics, Harvard University, Cambridge, Mass. 02138 (1976).
BUECHE, ARTHUR M., General Electric Co., P.O.B. 8, Schenectady, N.Y. 12301 (1974).
BURKE, JOSEPH E., 33 Forest Rd., Burnt Hills, N.Y. 12027 (1976).
BURKS, G. EDWIN, 3320 North Bigelow, Peoria, Ill. 61604 (1978).
BURNETT, Dr. JAMES ROBERT, TRW Systems Group, One Space Park, Redondo Beach, Calif. 90728.
BURNHAM, D. C., Westinghouse Electric Corpn., Gateway Center, Pittsburgh, Pa. 15222 (1968).
BUSEMANN, ADOLF, 970 Lincoln Place, Boulder, Colo. 80302 (1970).
BUSH, SPENCER H., Battelle Northwest Laboratories, P.O.B. 999, Richland, Wash. 99352 (1970).
CAIRNS, Dr. ROBERT W., 900 Burnt Mills Rd., Box 4095, Wilmington, Dela. 19807 (1969).
CAMRAS, MARVIN, IIT Research Institute, 10 West 35th St., Chicago, Ill. 60616 (1976).
CANNON, Dr. ROBERT H., Jr., California Institute of Technology, Pasadena, Calif. 91125 (1973).
CAPLAN, JOHN D., Research Laboratories, General Motors Corpn., 12 Mile and Mounds Rds., Warren, Mich. 48090 (1973).
CARLSON, ROY W., 55 Maryland Ave., Berkeley, Calif. 94707 (1974).
CARRIER, GEORGE F., Harvard University, Cambridge, Mass. 02138 (1974).
CASAGRANDE, Dr. ARTHUR, Harvard University, Cambridge, Mass. 02138 (1966).
CASAGRANDE, LEO, Casagrande Consultants, 40 Massachusetts Ave., Arlington, Mass. 02174 (1974).
CASSIDY, Lt.-Gen. WILLIAM F., 1848 River Shore Drive, Indialantic, Florida 32903 (1967).
CERMAK, Dr. JACK E., Fluid Mechanics Program, Dept. of Civil Engineering, Colorado State University, Fort Collins, Colo. 80521 (1973).
**CHADWICK, Dr. WALLACE L., 904 Pacific Mutual Building, 523 West Sixth Street, Los Angeles, Calif. 90014 (1965).**
CHAMBERS, CARL C., Estero Woods Village, Apt. 322, Estero, Fla. 33928 (1970).
CHAO, BEI TSE, Department of Mechanical and Industrial Engineering, University of Illinois at Urbana-Champaign, Urbana, Ill. 61801 (1981).
CHAPMAN, Dr. DEAN R., Dept. of Aeronautics/Astronautics and Mechanical Engineering, Stanford Univ., Stanford, Calif. 94305 (1975).
CHARPIE, Dr. ROBERT A., Cabot Corpn., 125 High St., Boston, Mass. 02110 (1975).
CHARYK, Dr. JOSEPH V., Communications Satellite Corpn., 950 L'Enfant Plaza, S.W., Washington, D.C. 20024 (1973).
**CHENEA, Dr. PAUL F., General Motors Corporation, Research Laboratories, Warren, Mich. 48090 (1969).**
CHESEBROUGH, HARRY E., 471 Dunston Rd., Bloomfield Hills, Mich. 48013 (1967).
CHESTNUT, HAROLD, Corporate Research & Development, General Electric Co., One River Rd., Schenectady, N.Y. 12345 (1974).
CHODOROW, Dr. MARVIN, Stanford University, Stanford, Calif. 94305 (1967).
CHOW, Dr. VEN T., Hydrosystems Laboratory, University of Illinois, Urbana, Ill. 61801 (1973).

CHURCHILL, STUART W., University of Pennsylvania, Philadelphia, Pa. 19174 (1974).
‡CISLER, WALKER L., 1300 Washington Boulevard Bldg., Detroit, Mich. 48226 (1964).
CLARKE, Lt.-Gen. FREDERICK J. (Retd.), Tippetts-Abbett-McCarthy-Stratton, 1101 15th St., N.W., Suite 700, Washington, D.C. 20005 (1973).
CLAUSER, FRANCIS H., California Institute of Technology, Pasadena, Calif. 91109 (1970).
CLEARY, Dr. EDWARD J., 32088 Waterside Lane, Westlake Village, Calif. 91361 (1967).
CLEVELAND, F. ALLEN, Lockheed Corpn., P.O.B. 551, Burbank, Calif. 91520 (1980).
CLEWELL, DAYTON H., 34 Driftway Lane, Darien, Conn. 06820 (1976).
**CLOUGH, Dr. RAY W., University of California, Berkeley, Calif. 94720 (1968).**
CLUFF, LLOYD S., Woodward-Clyde Consultants, 3 Embarcadero Center, Suite 700, San Francisco, Calif. 94111 (1978).
COBLE, ROBERT L., Dept. of Materials Science and Engineering, M.I.T., Cambridge, Mass. 02139 (1978).
COCKE, JOHN, T. J. Watson Research Center, P.O.B. 218, Yorktown Heights, N.Y. 10566 (1979).
CODD, EDGAR F., IBM Research Laboratory, San Jose, Calif. 95193 (1981).
COFFIN, Dr. LOUIS F., Jr., General Electric Research and Development Center, P.O.B. 8, Schenectady, N.Y. 12301.
COHEN, EDWARD, Ammann & Whitney, Two Worlds Trade Center, New York, N.Y. 10047.
COHEN, Dr. KARL P., 928 California Ave., Palo Alto, Calif. 94303 (1967).
COHEN, MORRIS, Dept. of Metallurgy and Materials Science, M.I.T., Cambridge, Mass. 02139 (1972).
COHN, NATHAN, 1457 Noble Rd., Jenkintown, Pa. 19046 (1969).
COLE, JULIAN D., University of California, 5732 Boelter Hall, Los Angeles, Calif. 90024 (1976).
COLLINS, Dr. ARTHUR A., Arthur A. Collins Inc., 13601 Preston Rd., Dallas, Tex. 75240.
COLTMAN, JOHN W., Westinghouse Research Laboratories, Beulah Road, Pittsburgh, Pa. 15232 (1976).
COMPTON, W. DALE, Ford Motor Co., Dearborn, Mich. 48121 (1981).
CONCORDIA, CHARLES, London Square, 12 Hampton, Clifton Park, N.Y. 12065 (1978).
CONWELL, ESTHER M., Xerox Corpn., Xerox Sq. W114, Rochester, N.Y. 14644 (1980).
COOK, THOMAS B., Jr., Sandia National Laboratories, Livermore, Calif. 94550 (1981).
COOKE, J. BARRY, Holiday Plaza, Suite 400, San Rafael, Calif. 94903 (1979).
COOPER, FRANKLIN S., Haskins Laboratories, 270 Crown St., New Haven, Conn. 06510. (1976).
COPELAND, NORMAN A., 9000 Du Pont Bldg., Wilmington, Del. 19898 (1977).
CORBATÓ, FERNANDO J., M.I.T., Cambridge, Mass. 02139 (1976).
CORCORAN, WILLIAM H., Dept. of Chemical Engineering, Calif. Inst. of Technology, Mail Code 206-41, Pasadena, Calif. 91125 (1980).
CORE, JESSE F., Pennsylvania State University, State College, Penn. 16801 (1981).
CORNELL, C. ALLIN, Massachusetts Institute of Technology, Cambridge, Mass. 02139 (1981).
CORRSIN, STANLEY, Dept. of Chemical Engineering, Johns Hopkins Univ., Baltimore, Md. 21218 (1980).
CORRY, ANDREW F., Boston Edison Co., 800 Boylston St., Boston, Mass. 02199 (1978).
CORSON, DALE R., 617 Clark Hall, Ithaca, N.Y. 14583 (1981).
CORTRIGHT, EDGAR M., Owens-Illinois Inc., P.O.B. 1035, Toledo, Ohio 43666 (1973).
COVERT, EUGENE E., M.I.T., Bldg. 31, Room 265, Cambridge, Mass. 02139 (1976).
CRAGON, HARVEY G., Texas Instruments Inc., P.O.B. 225012, MS72, Dallas, Tex. 75265 (1978).
CRAIN, CULLEN M., Rand Corpn., 1700 Main St., Santa Monica, Calif. 90406 (1980).
CRANDALL, STEPHEN H., M.I.T., Room 3-360, Cambridge, Mass. 02139 (1977).
CRANE, L. STANLEY, Southern Railways Co., P.O.B. 1808, Washington, D.C. 20013 (1978).
CRAVEN, JOHN P., University of Hawaii, 2540 Dole St., Honolulu, Hawaii 96822 (1970).
CREAGAN, ROBERT J., Energy Systems Analysis, Westinghouse Research and Development Center, Pittsburgh, Pa. 15235 (1981).

# NATIONAL ACADEMY OF ENGINEERING — UNITED STATES OF AMERICA

CROCCO, LUIGI, 24 rue Vignon, 75009 Paris, France (1979).
CROMBIE, DOUGLASS D., Nat. Telecommunications and Information Admin., U.S. Dept. of Commerce, Boulder, Colo. 80303 (1980).
CROOKE, ROBERT C., Global Marine Development Inc., 2302 Martin St., Irvine, Calif. 92715 (1981).
CROSS, RALPH E., The Cross Company, Fraser, Mich. 48026 (1968).
CRUZ, JOSE B., Jr., Co-ordinated Science Lab., Room 4-111, Univ. of Illinois, Urbana, Ill. 61801 (1980).
CULLER, FLOYD L., Jr., Electric Power Research Institute, 3412 Hillview Ave., Palo Alto, Calif. 94303.
CULLUM, A. EARL, Jr., Inwood Post Office, P.O.B. 7004, Dallas, Tex. 75209 (1970).
CURRIE, MALCOLM R., Missile Systems Group, Hughes Aircraft Co., 26/N-10, Canoga Park, Calif. 91304 (1971).
CUTLER, C. CHAPIN, Bell Laboratories, Crawford Corner Rd., Holmdel, N.J. 07733 (1970).
DACEY, Dr. GEORGE C., Bell Laboratories, Crawford Corner Rd., Holmdel, N.J. 07733 (1973).
DAHLSTROM, Dr. DONALD A., Envirotech Corpn., 414 West Third South, Salt Lake City, Utah 84110 (1975).
DAILY, Dr. JAMES W., University of Michigan, Ann Arbor, Mich. 48104 (1975).
DAKIN, THOMAS W., Westinghouse Research and Development Center, 1310 Beulah Rd., Pittsburgh, Pa. 15235 (1981).
D'APPOLONIA, Dr. ELIO, D'Appolonia Consulting Engineers, Inc., 10 Duff Rd., Pittsburgh, Pa. 15235 (1977).
DARLINGTON, Dr. SIDNEY, University of New Hampshire, 8 Fogg Drive, Durham, N.H. 03824.
DAVENPORT, Dr. LEE L., GTE Laboratories Inc., 1 Stamford Forum, Stamford, Conn. 06904 (1973).
DAVENPORT, Dr. WILBUR B., Jr., M.I.T., Room 38-401, Cambridge, Mass. 02139 (1975).
DAVID, Dr. EDWARD E., Jr., Exxon Research and Engineering Co., P.O.B. 101, Florham Park, N.J. 07932 (1966).
DAVIS, Dr. FRANK W., 6328 Curzon, Fort Worth, Tex. 76116 (1967).
DAVIS, HARMER E., University of California, Berkeley, Calif. 94720 (1967).
DAVIS, RUTH M., The Pentagon, Room 3E114, Washington, D.C. 20301 (1976).
DAVIS, WILLARD KENNETH, Bechtel Corporation, San Francisco, Calif. (1970).
DEAN, ROBERT C., Creare Innovations Inc., P.O.B. 68, Hanover, N.H. 03755 (1977).
DEAN, ROBERT G., Dept. of Civil Engineering, Univ. of Delaware, 130 DuPont Hall, Newark, Dela. 19711 (1980).
DEBRA, DANIEL B., Department of Aeronautics and Astronautics, Stanford University, Stanford, Calif. 94305 (1981).
DEBUS, Dr. KURT H., 280 Bahama Blvd., Cocoa Beach, Fla. 32931.
DECKER, RAYMOND F., INCO Ltd., 1 New York Plaza, New York, N.Y. 10004 (1980).
DEERE, Dr. DON U., 6834 S.W. 35th Way, Gainesville, Fla. 32601 (1967).
DEGENKOLB, HENRY J., Degenkolb and Associates, 350 Sansome St., Room 500, San Francisco, Calif. 94104 (1977).
DELAUER, Dr. RICHARD D., TRW Inc., One Space Park, Redondo Beach, Calif. 90278 (1969).
DEMARIA, ANTHONY J., United Technologies Research Center, Silver Lane, East Hartford, Conn. 06108 (1976).
DEN HARTOG, Dr. JACOB P., M.I.T., Room 3-262, Cambridge, Mass. 02139.
DESCHAMPS, GEORGES A., Dept. of Electrical Engineering, University of Illinois, Urbana, Ill. 61801 (1978).
DESOER, CHARLES A., Dept. of Electrical Engineering and Computer Sciences, University of California, Berkeley, Calif. 94720 (1977).
DESSAUER, Dr. JOHN H., P.O.B. 373, 57 Monroe Ave., Pittsford, N.Y. 14534 (1967).
DICKEMAN, RAYMOND L., Seattle Trust Co., 10655 N.E. 4th St., Bellevue, Wash. 98004 (1978).
DICKIESON, ALTON C., 18018 Conquistador Drive, Sun City West, Ariz. 85375 (1970).
DIETRICH, Dr. JOSEPH R., 165 Wood Pond Rd., West Hertford, Conn. 06107 (1975).
DILLARD, JOSEPH K., Westinghouse Electric Corporation, 700 Braddock Ave., East Pittsburgh, Pa. 15112.
DINNEEN, Dr. GERALD P., Asst. Secretary of Defense, The Pentagon, Room 3E282, Washington, D.C. 20301 (1975).
DIRKS, LESLIE C., Central Intelligence Agency, Washington, D.C. 20505 (1970).
DOLAN, JOHN E., American Electric Power Corpn., 180 East Broad St., Columbus, Ohio 43215 (1980).

DONALDSON, COLMAN DUPONT, Aeronautical Research Associates of Princeton, Inc., 50 Washington Rd., P.O.B. 2229, Princeton, N.J. 08540 (1979).
DONOVAN, ALLEN F., P.O.B. 92957, Los Angeles, Calif. 90009 (1969).
DOUGLAS, WALTER S., Parsons, Brinckerhoff, Quade & Douglas, One Penn Plaza, 250 34th St., New York, N.Y. 10001 (1967).
DOUMA, JACOB H., Hydraulic Design Branch, Office of the Chief of Engineers, Department of the Army, Washington D.C. (1971).
DRAKE, ROBERT M., Jr., Special Asst. to the President, University of Kentucky, Lexington, Ky. 40506 (1974).
DRAPER, CHARLES S., Charles Stark Draper Laboratory Inc., 68 Albany St., Cambridge, Mass. 02139 (1965).
DRESSELHAUS, MILDRED S., Massachusetts Institute of Technology, Cambridge, Mass. 02139 (1974).
DRICKHAMER, HARRY G., Dept. of Chemical Engineering, University of Illinois, Urbana, Ill. 61801 (1979).
DRUCKER, Dr. DANIEL C., University of Illinois, Urbana, Ill 61801 (1967).
DUFFY, ROBERT A., Charles Stark Draper Lab., Inc., 555 Technology Sq., Cambridge, Mass. 02139 (1980).
DUKLER, A. E., Dean of Engineering, Univ. of Houston, 4800 Calhoun St., Houston, Tex. 77004 (1977).
DUWEZ, POL, Calif. Inst. of Technology, Pasadena, Calif. 91125 (1979).
DYER, IRA, Department of Ocean Engineering, M.I.T., Cambridge, Mass. 02139 (1976).
EBERHART, HOWARD D., College of Engineering, King Abdulaziz Univ., P.O.B. 1540, Jeddah, Saudi Arabia (1977).
ECKERT, ERNST R. G., University of Minnesota, Minneapolis, Minn. (1970).
ECKERT, Dr. J. PRESPER, UNIVAC, Division of Sperry-Rand Corpn., P.O.B. 500, Blue Bell, Pa. 19422 (1967).
EDGERTON, Dr. HAROLD E., Massachusetts Institute of Technology, Cambridge, Mass. 02139 (1966).
EDLUND, MILTON C., Virginia Polytechnic Institute and State University, Blacksburg, Va. 24061 (1976).
EGGERS, ALFRED J., Jr., Lockheed Palo Alto Research Laboratories, 3251 Hanover St., Bldg. 201, Palo Alto, Calif. 94304 (1972).
EISENBERG, PHILLIP, Hydronautics Inc., 7210 Pindell School Rd., Laurel, Md. 20810 (1974).
EISENBUD, MERRIL, New York University Medical Center, 550 First Ave., New York, N.Y. 10016 (1977).
ELDER, REX A., Bechtel Incorporated, 50 Beale St., San Francisco, Calif. 94119 (1978).
ELDRED, KENNETH McK., Bolt Beranek and Newman Inc., 50 Moulton St., Cambridge, Mass. 02138 (1975).
ELIAS, PETER, M.I.T., Cambridge, Mass. 02139 (1979).
ELIASSEN, ROLF, Metcalf & Eddy Inc., 1029 Corporation Way, Palo Alto, Calif. 94305 (1971).
ELKINS, LINCOLN F., Sohio Petroleum Co., 50 Penn Place, Suite 1100, Oklahoma City, Okla. 73118 (1980).
ELKINS, LLOYD E., Amoco Production Company, Research Center, P.O.B. 591, Tulsa, Okla. 74102 (1976).
ELLIOTT, Dr. JOHN F., M.I.T. Room 8-109, Cambridge, Mass. 02139.
ELLIOTT, MARTIN A., 13623 Alchester Lane, Houston, Tex. 77079 (1976).
ELMENDORF, CHARLES H. III, 34 Cross Gates Rd., Madison, N.J. 07940 (1971).
ELMS, JAMES C., 112 Kings Place, Newport Beach, Calif. 92663 (1974).
ELSTON, CHARLES W., 1 River Road, Schenectady, N.Y. 12345 (1967).
EMMONS, Dr. HOWARD W., Harvard University, Cambridge, Mass. 02138 (1965).
ENGELBRECHT, RICHARD S., University of Illinois at Urbana-Champaign, 3230 Civil Engineering Building, Urbana, Ill. 61801 (1976).
‡ENGSTROM, Dr. ELMER W., Apt. 31-01, Meadow Lakes, Hightstown, N.J. 08520 (1964).
ESHLEMAN, R. VON, Stanford University, Stanford, Calif. 94305 (1978).
ESTCOURT, VIVIAN F., Bechtel Power Corpn., P.O.B. 3965, San Francisco, Calif. 94119 (1981).
ESTES, ELLIOTT M., General Motors Corporation, 3044 West Grand Boulevard, Detroit, Mich. 48202 (1976).
ETHERINGTON, HAROLD, 84 Lighthouse Drive, Jupiter, Fla. 33458 (1978).
EVANS, BOB O., IBM Corporation, White Plains, N.Y. 10604 (1970).
EVANS, DAVID C., Evans and Sutherland Computer Corpn., 580 Arapeen Drive, Salt Lake City, Utah 84108 (1978).

EVANS, Dr. ERSEL A., P.O.B. 1970, Richland, Wash. 99352.
EVERETT, JAMES L., III, Philadelphia Electric Co., 2301 Market St., Philadelphia, Pa. 19101 (1974).
EVERETT, ROBERT R., MITRE Corpn., P.O.B. 208, Bedford, Mass. 01730 (1979).
EVERHART, THOMAS E., Dept. of Engineering and Computer Sciences, University of California, Berkeley, Calif. 94720 (1978).
‡EVERITT, Dr. WILLIAM L., University of Illinois, Urbana, Ill. 61801 (1964).
FADUM, RALPH E., School of Engineering, N.C. State University, 229 Riddick Bldg., Raleigh, N.C. 27607 (1975).
FAGET, MAXIME A., National Aeronautics and Space Administration, Houston, Tex. 77058 (1970).
FAIR, JAMES R., Dept. of Chemical Engineering, Univ. of Texas at Austin, Austin, Tex. 78712 (1974).
FANO, Dr. ROBERT M., Dept. of Electrical Engineering, M.I.T., Cambridge, Mass. 02139 (1973).
FEELY, FRANK F., Exxon Research and Engineering Co., P.O.B. 101, Florham Park, N.J. 07932 (1979).
FEINSTEIN, JOSEPH, Varian Associates, 611 Hansen Way, Palo Alto, Calif. 94303 (1976).
FELKER, JEAN HOWARD, Bell Laboratories, P.O.B. 2020, New Brunswick, N.J. 08903 (1974).
FELSEN, LEOPOLD B., Polytechnic Inst. of New York, 333 Jay St., Brooklyn, N.Y. 11201 (1977).
FENVES, STEVEN J., Carnegie-Mellon University, Schenley Park, Pittsburgh, Pa 15213 (1976).
FERENCE, MICHAEL, Jr., Anglers Cove 12-203, 1456 N.E. Ocean Blvd., Stuart, Fla. 33494 (1971).
FERGUSON, PHIL M., University of Texas at Austin, 3102 Beverly Rd., Austin, Tex. 78703 (1973).
FETTERS, Dr. KARL L., 7099 Oak Drive, Poland, O. 44514 (1965).
FIELD, A. J., 650 South Grand Ave., Suite 900, Los Angeles, Calif. 90017 (1974).
FIELD, Dr. LESTER M., 4139 Via Marina 8-805, Marina del Rey, Calif. 90291 (1967).
FIELD, MICHAEL, Metcut Research Associates, Inc., 3980 Rosslyn Drive, Cincinnati, Ohio 45209 (1976).
FINE, Dr. MORRIS E., Technological Institute, Northwestern University, Evanston, Ill. 60201 (1973).
FINK, DANIEL J., General Electric Co., Valley Forge Space Center, P.O.B. 8555, Philadelphia, Pa. 19101 (1974).
FINK, DONALD G., 103-B Heritage Hills, Somers, N.Y. 10589 (1969).
FINNIE, IAIN, Dept. of Mechanical Engineering, University of California, Berkeley, Calif. 94720 (1979).
FISCHER, IRENE K., 301 Philadelphia Ave., Takoma Park, Maryland 20012 (1979).
FISHER, HAROLD W., P.O.B. 1792, Duxbury, Mass. 02332 (1969).
FISHER, JOHN C., 189 Forts Ferry Rd., Latham, N.Y. 12110 (1981).
FISK, Dr. JAMES B., Lees Hill Rd., Box 85, Basking Ridge, N.J. 07920 (1966).
FLANAGAN, JAMES L., Bell Telephone Laboratories, 600Mountain Ave., Room 2D540, Murray Hill, N.J. 07974 (1978).
FLAWN, PETER T., University of Texas, San Antonio, Tex. 78284 (1974).
FLAX, Dr. ALEXANDER H., 400 Army-Navy Drive, Arlington, Va. 22202 (1967).
FLEMINGS, MERTON C., Department of Materials Science and Engineering, Room 8-407, Cambridge, Mass. 02139 (1976).
FLETCHER, JAMES C., School of Engineering, University of Pittsburgh, 232 Benedum Hall, Pittsburgh, Pa. 15261 (1970).
FOLSOM, Dr. RICHARD G., 585 Oakville Crossroad, Napa, Calif. 94558 (1965).
FONTANA, Dr. MARS G., The Ohio State University, Columbus, O. 43210 (1967).
FORRESTER, Dr. JAY W., Massachusetts Institute of Technology, Cambridge, Mass. 02139 (1967).
FOSTER, Dr. JOHN S., Jr., TRW Inc., 23555 Euclid Ave., Cleveland, Ohio 44117 (1969).
FOX, GERARD F., Howard Needles Tammen and Bergendoff, 1345 Avenue of the Americas, New York, N.Y. 10019 (1976).
FRANK, RICHARD S., 6028 North Wedgewood Lane, Peoria, Ill. 61614 (1980).
FRAZIER, J. EARL, Frazier-Simplex, Inc., 436 E. Beau St., P.O.B. 493, Washington, Pa. 15301 (1978).
FREY, Dr. DONALD N., Bell & Howell Co., 7100 McCormick Blvd., Chicago, Ill. 60645 (1967).
FREUDENSTEIN, FERDINAND, Columbia University, Seeley W. Mudd Building, New York, N.Y. 10027 (1979).
FRIEDLANDER, Dr. SHELDON K., California Institute of Technology, Pasadena, Calif. 91125.

FROSCH, ROBERT A., NASA, Washington, D.C. 20546 (1971).
FRYE, JOHN C., Geological Society of America, 3300 Penrose Place, Boulder, Colo. 80301 (1971).
FU, KUNG-SUN, Department of Electrical Engineering, Purdue University, West Lafayette, Ind. 47907 (1976).
FUBINI, Dr. EUGENE G., E. G. Fubini Consultants Ltd., 1901 North Fort Myer Drive, Arlington, Va. 22209 (1966).
FUCIK, E. MONTFORD, Harza Engineering Co., 150 South Wacker Drive, Chicago, Ill. 60606 (1974).
FUERSTENAU, DOUGLAS W., Department of Materials Science and Engineering, University of California, Berkeley, Calif. 94720 (1976).
FUHRMAN, ROBERT A., Lockheed Missiles and Space Company, Inc., P.O.B. 504, Sunnyvale, Calif. 94088 (1976).
FUNG, YUAN-CHENG B., University of California, San Diego, La Jolla, Calif. 92093 (1979).
GADEN, ELMER L., Jr., University of Vermont, Votey Bldg., Burlington, Vt. 05401 (1974).
GAGGE, A. PHARO, Yale University, 290 Congress Ave., New Haven, Conn. 06519 (1979).
GAGNEBIN, ALBERT P., INCO Ltd., One New York Plaza, New York, N.Y. 10004 (1974).
GALAMBOS, THEODORE V., Washington University, Box 1130, St. Louis, Mo. 63130 (1979).
GALLAGER, ROBERT G., M.I.T., Room 35-206, Cambridge, Mass. 02139 (1979).
GALLOWAY, WILLIAM J., Bolt Beranek & Newman Inc., 21120 Vanowen St., Canoga Park, Calif. 91303 (1979).
GARBARINI, EDGAR J., Bechtel group of cos., 50 Beale St., San Francisco, Calif. 94105 (1980).
GARWIN, RICHARD L., IBM T.J. Watson Research Center, P.O.B. Watson 218, Yorktown Heights, N.Y. 10598 (1978).
GASICH, WELKO E., Northrop Corpn., 3901 West Broadway, Hawthorne, Calif. 90250 (1979).
GAUTREAUX, MARCELIAN F., Ethyl Corpn., P.O.B. 341, Baton Rouge, La. 70821 (1977).
GAVIN, JOHN G., Jr., Grumman Aerospace Corpn., Bethpage, Long Island, N.Y. 11714 (1974).
GEE, EDWIN A., International Paper Co., 220 East 42nd St., New York, N.Y. 10017 (1979).
GEER, RONALD L., Shell Oil Co., One Shell Plaza, P.O.B. 2463, Houston, Tex. 77001 (1977).
GEIST, JACOB M., Air Products & Chemicals Inc., P.O.B. 538, Allentown, Pa. 18105 (1980).
GERWICK, BEN C., Jr., University of California, Berkeley, 500 Sansome St., San Francisco, Calif. 94111 (1973).
GETTING, Dr. IVAN A., P.O.B. 92957, Los Angeles, Calif. 90005 (1968).
GEYER, JOHN C., 710 Bosley Rd., Cockeysville, Md. 21030 (1970).
GIAEVER, Dr. IVAR, General Electric Corporate Research and Development Center, Room 3C32, P.O.B. 8, Schenectady, N.Y 12301.
GIBBONS, JAMES F., Stanford University, Stanford, Calif. 94305 (1974).
GILKESON, ROBERT F., Philadelphia Electric Co., 2301 Market St., Philadelphia, Pa. 19101 (1978).
GILMAN, Dr. JOHN J., Allied Chemical Corpn., P.O.B. 1021R, Morristown, N.J. 07960.
GILRUTH, Dr. ROBERT R., 5128 Park Ave., Dickinson, Tex. 77539 (1968).
GINSBURG, CHARLES P., Ampex Corpn., 401 Broadway, Redwood City, Calif. 94063 (1973).
GINZTON, Dr. EDWARD L., 611 Hansen Way, Palo Alto, Calif. 94303 (1965).
GLASER, EDWARD L., Ampex Corpn., 200 North Nash St., El Segundo, Calif. 90245 (1977).
GLENNAN, Dr. T. KEITH, 11483 Waterview Cluster, Reston, Va. 22090 (1967).
GLOYNA, EARNEST F., University of Texas, Austin, Tex. 78712 (1970).
GOLAND, MARTIN, Southwest Research Institute, P.O. Drawer 28510, San Antonio, Tex. 78284 (1967).
GOLOMB, SOLOMON W., University of Southern California, Los Angeles, Calif. 90007 (1976).
GOMORY, Dr. RALPH E., IBM Watson Research Center, P.O.B. 218, Yorktown Heights, N.Y. 10598.
GOODENOUGH, JOHN B., Inorganic Chemistry Laboratory, Oxford University, South Parks Rd., Oxford, England (1976).
GOODING, ROBERT C., 1305 Trinity Drive, Alexandria, Va. 22314 (1976).
GORDON, EUGENE I., Bell Telephone Laboratories, Murray Hill, N.J. 07974 (1979).
GORDON, Dr. WILLIAM E., Rice University, P.O.B. 1892, Houston, Tex. 77001.

GORNOWSKI, EDWARD J., Exxon Research and Engineering Company, P.O.B. 101, Florham Park, N.J. 07932 (1971).
GOULD, ROY W., California Institute of Technology, Pasadena, Calif. 91125 (1971).
GOULD, WILLIAM R., Southern California Edison Co., 2244 Walnut Grove Ave., Rosemead, Calif. 91770 (1973).
GRAFF, GEORGE S., McDonnell Aircraft Co., P.O.B. 516, St. Louis, Mo. 63166 (1981).
GRANGER, Dr. JOHN V. N., Science and Technology Counselor, U.S. Embassy, Grosvenor Sq., London, W.1, England.
GRANT, NICHOLAS J., Dept. of Materials Science and Engineering, M.I.T., Room 8-305, Cambridge, Mass. 02139 (1980).
GRAY, Dr. PAUL E., M.I.T., Room 3-208, Cambridge, Mass. 02139.
GREEN, PAUL E., Jr., IBM Corpn., Old Orchard Rd., Armonk, N.Y. 10504 (1981).
GROSH, Dr. RICHARD J., Ranco Inc., 701 West 5th Ave., P.O.B. 8369, Columbus, Ohio 43201 (1969).
GROSS, ERIC T. B., Rensselaer Polytechnic Institute, Troy, N.Y. 12181 (1978).
GROVE, ANDREW S., Intel Corpn., 3065 Bowers Ave., Santa Clara, Calif. 95051 (1979).
GUNNESS, ROBERT C., One First National Plaza, Suite 2656, Chicago, Ill. 60603 (1969).
GYFTOPOULOS, ELIAS P., Massachusetts Institute of Technology, Cambridge, Mass. 02139 (1981).
HADDAD, JERRIER A., Old Orchard Road, Armonk, N.Y. 10504 (1968).
HAENSEL, VLADIMIR, Universal Oil Products Co., 10 UOP Plaza, Des Plaines, Ill. 60016 (1974).
HAFSTAD, Dr. LAWRENCE R., RFD 1, Chester, Md. 21619 (1968).
‡HAIDER, MICHAEL L., 1 Rockefeller Plaza, New York N.Y. 10020 (1964).
HAIT, Dr. JAMES, 435 Toyama Drive, Sunnyvale, Calif. 94086 (1967).
HALBOUTY, MICHEL T., 5100 Westheimer Rd., Houston, Tex. 77056 (1979).
HALL, ALBERT C., Box 315c, Queenstown, Md. 21658 (1970).
HALL, ROBERT N., General Electric Co. Research and Development Center, P.O.B. 8, Schenectady, N.Y. 12301 (1978).
HALL, Dr. WILLIAM J., University of Illinois, Urbana, Ill. 61801 (1968).
HAMILTON, WILLIAM T., Boeing Commercial Airplane Co., P.O.B. 3707, MS 78-50, Seattle, Wash. 98124 (1978).
HAMMING, KENNETH W., 527 Meadow Drive West, Wilmette, Ill. 60091 (1974).
HAMMING, RICHARD, Naval Postgraduate School, Code 52HG, Monterey, Calif. 93940 (1980).
HAMMOND, DAVID G., Daniel, Mann, Johnson and Mendenhall, 201 N. Charles St., Suite 1900, Baltimore, Md. 21201 (1981).
HANCOCK, JOHN C., Purdue University, West Lafayette, Ind. 47907 (1974).
HANEY, PAUL D., Black & Veatch Consulting Engineers, P.O.B. 8405, Kansas City, Mo. 64114 (1974).
HANNAY, N. BRUCE, Bell Laboratories, 600 Mountain Ave., Murray Hill, N.J. 07974 (1974).
HANRATTY, THOMAS J., University of Illinois, Urbana, Ill. 61801 (1974).
HANSEN, ARTHUR G., Purdue University, West Lafayette, Ind. 47907 (1976).
HANSEN, GRANT L., System Development Corpn., 2500 Colorado Ave., Santa Monica, Calif. 90406 (1977).
HAPPEL, JOHN, Catalyst Research Corpn., 450 East Edsall Blvd., Palisades Park, N.J. 07650 (1981).
HARDER, EDWIN L., 1204 Milton Avenue, Pittsburgh, Pa. 15218 (1976).
HARLEMAN DONALD R. F., Massachusetts Institute of Technology, Cambridge, Mass. 02139 (1974).
HARPER, JOHN D., Aluminium Company of America, Pittsburgh, Pa. 15219 (1971).
HARRINGTON, DEAN B., General Electric Co., Building 59 W. Room 117, 1 River Rd., Schenectady, N.Y. 12345 (1981).
HARRIS, Dr. CYRIL M., Columbia University, 1330 Mudd, New York, N.Y. 10027.
HARRIS, MILTON, 3300 Whitehaven St., N.W., Suite 500, Washington, D.C. 20007. (1976)
HARRIS, STEPHEN E., Ginzton Laboratory, Stanford University, Stanford, Calif. 94305 (1977).
HARRIS, WILLIAM J., Asscn. of American Railroads, 1920 L St. N.W., Washington, D.C. 20036 (1977).
HARTER, GEORGE A., TRW Equipment Group, 23555 Euclid Ave., T/M 3630, Cleveland, O. 44117 (1981).
HARTLEY, FRED L., Union Oil Co. of California, P.O.B. 7600, Los Angeles, Calif. 90051 (1980).

HARVEY, DOUGLASS C., Eastman Kodak Co., 343 State St., Rochester, N.Y. 14650 (1981).
HARWOOD, JULIUS J., Ford Motor Co., P.O.B. 2053, Dearborn, Mich. 48121 (1977).
HATSOPOULOS, GEORGE N., Thermo Electric Corpn., 101 First Ave., Waltham, Mass. 02139 (1978).
HAUS, HERMANN A., M.I.T., Room 36-351, Cambridge, Mass. 02139 (1976).
HAUSPURG, ARTHUR, Consolidated Edison Company of New York, Inc., 4 Irving Place, New York, N.Y. 10003 (1976).
HAWKINS, Dr. W. LINCOLN, Bell Laboratories, 600 Mountain Ave., Murray Hill, N.J. 07974.
HAWKINS, WILLIS M., Lockheed California Co., P.O.B. 551 Burbank, Calif. 91520 (1966).
HAYES, Maj.-Gen. THOMAS J., III (Retd.), International Engineering Co. Inc., 220 Montgomery St., San Francisco, Calif. 94104.
HAYES, Dr. WALLACE D., Princeton University, Princeton, N.J. 08540.
HAZEN, RICHARD, Hazen and Sawyer, 360 Lexington Ave., New York, N.Y. 10017 (1974).
HEDRICK, IRA G., Grumman Aerospace Corpn., Bethpage, Long Island, N.Y. 11714 (1974).
HEILMEIER, GEORGE H., Texas Instruments Inc., P.O.B. 225474, M.S. 400, Dallas, Tex. 75265 (1979).
HEINEMANN, EDWARD H., Heinemann Asscs., Box 1795, Rancho Santa Fe, Calif. 92067 (1965).
HEINEMANN, HEINZ, Lawrence Berkeley Laboratories, Bldg. 62, University of California, Berkeley, Calif. 94720 (1976).
HELLWARTH, ROBERT W., University of Southern California, Los Angeles, Calif. 90007 (1977).
HEMSWORTH, MARTIN C., General Electric Co., J44, Cincinnati, Ohio 45215 (1980).
HENDRIE, JOSEPH M., Nuclear Regulatory Commission, Washington, D.C. 20555 (1976).
HERMAN, ROBERT, Traffic Science Dept., General Motors Research Laboratories, Warren, Mich. 48090 (1978).
HERRMANN, GEORGE, Department of Mechanical Engineering, Stanford University, Stanford, Calif. 94305 (1981).
HERTZBERG, ABRAHAM, 120 Aerospace Research Laboratory FL-10, University of Washington, Seattle, Wash. 98195 (1976).
HERWALD, Dr. S. W., Westinghouse Electric Corpn., Gateway Center, Pittsburgh, Pa. 15222 (1967).
HESS, WILMOT N., Environmental Research Laboratories, National Oceanic and Atmospheric Administration, Boulder, Colo. 80302 (1976).
HEWLETT, Dr. WILLIAM R., 1501 Page Mill Rd., Palo Alto, Calif. 94304 (1965).
HIBBARD, Dr. WALTER R., Jr., College of Engineering, Virginia Polytechnic Institute and State University, Blacksburg, Va. 24061 (1966).
HILLIER, Dr. JAMES, 22 Arreton Rd., Princeton, N.J. 08540 (1967).
HIRTH, JOHN P., Ohio State University, 116 West 19th Ave., Columbus, O. 43210 (1974).
HITTINGER, WILLIAM C., RCA Corporation, David Sarnoff Research Center, Princeton, N.J. 08540 (1976).
HOAG, DAVID G., The Charles Stark Draper Laboratory, Inc., 555 Technology Square, M.S. 70, Cambridge, Mass. 02139 (1979).
HOCOTT, CLAUDE R., University of Texas at Austin, Austin, 78712 (1974).
HODGE, PHILIP G., Jr., University of Minnesota, Aero 107, Minneapolis, Minn. 55455 (1977).
HOFF, Dr. NICHOLAS J., Rensselaer Polytechnic Institute, Troy, N.Y. 12181 (1965).
HOFFMAN, JOHN D., Nat. Measurement Lab., Nat. Bureau of Standards, U.S. Dept. of Commerce, Washington, D.C. 20234 (1980).
HOGAN, C. LESTER, Fairchild Camera and Instrument Corpn., 464 Ellis St., Mountain View, Calif. 94042 (1977).
HOGG, DAVID C., National Oceanic and Atmospheric Administration, Boulder, Colo. 80302 (1978).
HOGNESTAD, Dr. EIVIND, Portland Cement Asscn., Old Orchard Rd., Skokie, Ill. 60076 (1973).
‡HOLBROOK, Dr. GEORGE E., 409 Milton Drive, Wilmington, Del. 19802 (1964).
HOLLEY, CHARLES H., General Electric Company, One River Rd., Schenectady, N.Y. 12345 (1976).
HOLLIS, Dr. MARK D., 411 Lone Palm Drive, Lakeland, Fla. 33801 (1967).
HOLLISTER, Dr. SOLOMON C., 5 Parkway Place, Ithaca, N.Y. 14850 (1973).

‡Hollomon, Dr. J. Herbert, Massachusetts Institute of Technology, Cambridge, Mass. 02139 (1964).
Holloway, Dr. Frederick A. L., Exxon Corpn., 220 Park Ave., Florham Park, N.J. 07932 (1965).
Holloway, Dr. Marshall G., 217 Pirates Place, Jupiter, Fla. 33458 (1967).
Holmes, D. Brainerd, Raytheon Co., 141 Spring St., Lexington, Mass. 02173 (1977).
Holonyak, Dr. Nick, Jr., University of Illinois—Urbana, Urbana, Ill. 61801 (1973).
Holtby, Kenneth F., Boeing Commercial Airplane Co., P.O.B. 3707, M.S. 79-35, Seattle, Wash. 98124 (1979).
Hood, Edward E., Jr., General Electric Co., Fairfield, Conn. 06431 (1980).
Hooven, Frederick J., Thayer School of Engineering, Dartmouth College, Hanover, N.H. 03755 (1979).
Hopper, Capt. Grace M., U.S. Dept. of the Navy, OP-916D, The Pentagon, BD 770, Washington, D.C. 20350 (1973).
Hornbeck, Dr. John A., Bell Laboratories, 600 Mountain Ave., Murray Hill, N.J. 07974.
Horton, Billy M., Case Western Reserve University, Cleveland, Ohio 44106 (1979).
Hosler, Charles L., Jr., College of Earth and Mineral Sciences, Pennsylvania State University, Deike Building, University Park, Pa. 16802 (1978).
Hottel, Hoyt C., Massachusetts Institute of Technology, Cambridge, Mass. 02139 (1974).
Hougen, Olaf A., University of Wisconsin, Madison, Wis. 53706 (1974).
**Housner, Dr. George W., California Institute of** Technology, **Pasadena. Calif. 91109 (1965).**
Howard, William J., Sandia Laboratories, Albuquerque, N.M. 87185 (1979).
Hrones, Dr. John A., Case Western Reserve University, 10900 Euclid Ave., Cleveland, Ohio 44106.
Hudson, Dr. Donald E., California Institute of Technology, 1201 East California Blvd., Pasadena, Calif. 91125 (1973).
Hudson, Herbert E., Jr., Water & Air Research, Inc., P.O.B. 1121, Gainsville, Fla. 32602 (1978).
Huebner, George J., 720 Oakdale Rd., Ann Arbor, Mich. 48105.
**Huggins, William Herbert,** Johns Hopkins University, Baltimore, Md. 21218 (1970).
Hulm, John K., Westinghaus Electric Corpn., Research & Development Center, 1310 Beulah Rd., Pittsburgh, Pa. 15235 (1980).
Humphrey, Dr. Arthur E., University of Pennsylvania, 107 Towne Bldg., Philadelphia, Pa. 19174 (1973).
Hunsaker, Dr. Jerome C., 10 Louisburg Square, Boston, Mass. 02108 (1967).
Ingard, K. Uno, M.I.T., Room 31-268, Cambridge, Mass. 02139 (1980).
Irwin, George R., University of Maryland, College Park, Md. 20740 (1977).
Isakoff, Sheldon E., Engineering Dept., Louviers 1278, E.I. du Pont de Nemours & Co. Inc., Wilmington, Dela. 19898 (1980).
Iselin, Donald G., Naval Facilities Engineering Command, 200 Stovall St., Alexandria, Va. 22332 (1980).
Iverson, Kenneth E., T. J. Watson Research Centre, P.O.B. 218, Yorktown Heights, N.Y. 10598 (1979).
Jacobs, J. Donovan, 500 Sansome St., San Francisco, Calif. 94111 (1969).
**Jacobs, Dr. John E., Northwestern University, Evanston, Ill. 60201 (1969).**
Jaffee, Dr. Robert I., Electric Power Research Institute, 3412 Hillview Ave., P.O.B. 10412, Palo Alto, Calif. 94304 (1969).
Jaicks, Frederick G., Inland Steel Co., 30 West Monroe St., Chicago, Ill. 60603 (1979).
Jarrett, Noel, Alcoa Laboratories, Alcoa Center, Pa. 15069 (1979).
Jeffs, George W., 2230 East Imperial Highway, El Segundo, Calif. 90245 (1978).
Jennings, Burgess H., Northwestern University, 1500 Sheridan Rd., Wilmette, Ill. 60091 (1977).
Jennings, Paul C., California Inst. of Technology, Pasadena, Calif. 91125 (1977).
Joel, Amos E., Jr., Bell Laboratories, Room 2C-632, Holmdel, N.J. 07733 (1981).
Johnson, Dr. Clarence L., 2555 North Hollywood Way, P.O.B. 551, Burbank, Calif. 91503 (1965).
Johnson, Dr. H. Richard, Watkins-Johnson Co., 3333 Hillview Ave., Palo Alto, Calif. 94304 (1973).
Johnson, I. Birger, 1508 Barclay Place, Schenectady, N.Y. 12309 (1980).

Johnson, James R., Physical Sciences Laboratory Research, 3M Company, St. Paul, Minn. 55133 (1972).
Johnson, Joe W., Department of Civil Engineering, University of California, 412 O'Brien Hall, Berkeley, Calif. 94720 (1976).
Johnson, Reynold B., Education Engineering Associates, 550 Hamilton Ave., Palo Alto, Calif. 94301 (1981).
Johnson, Robert L., McDonnell Douglas Astronautics Company, 5301 Bolsa Avenue, Huntington Beach, Calif. 92647 (1976).
Johnson, Wendell E., 1524 Woodacre Drive, McLean, Va. 22101 (1970).
Johnson, Dr. Wilfrid E., P.O.B. 963, Richland, Wash. 99352 (1968).
Johnson, Dr. Woodrow E., Westinghouse Electric Corpn., 2001 Lebanon Rd., West Mifflin, Pa. 15122 (1968).
Johnston, Bruce G., 5025 E. Calle Barril, Tucson, Ariz. 85718 (1979).
Johnston, Roy G., Brandow and Johnston Associates, 1660 West Third St., Los Angeles, Calif. 90017 (1981).
Jones, Robert T., Ames Research Center, NASA, Moffett Field, Calif. 94035 (1973).
Jonsson, J. Erik, Texas Instruments Inc., Dallas, Tex. 75201 (1971).
Jordan, Donald J., 113 Evergreen Lane, Glastonbury, Conn. 06033 (1976).
Jordan, Dr. Edward C., University of Illinois, Urbana, Ill. 61801 (1967).
Jordan, Dr. Richard C., University of Minnesota, 125 Mechanical Engineering Bldg., Minneapolis, Minn. 55455.
Kalb, John W., Ohio Brass Co., Frank Black Research Center, Wadsworth, Ohio 44281 (1980).
Kaman, Charles H., Kaman Corpn., Bloomfield, Conn. 06002 (1967).
Kane, Edward R., E.I. du Pont de Nemours & Co., Ltd., Wilmington, Del. 19898 (1979).
Kane, Eneas D., Standard Oil Co. of California, 225 Bush St., San Francisco, Calif. 94104 (1977).
Kantrowitz, Arthur R., AVCO Everett Research Laboratory Inc., 2385 Revere Beach Parkway, Everett, Mass. 02149 (1977).
Katz, Dr. Donald L., The University of Michigan, Ann Arbor, Mich. 48104 (1968).
Kays, William M., School of Engineering, Stanford University, Stanford, Calif. 94305 (1977).
Kear, Bernard H., United Technologies Research Center, Silver Lane, East Hartford, Conn. 06108 (1979).
Keil, Dr. Alfred A. H., Massachusetts Institute of Technology, Cambridge, Mass. 02139 (1966).
Kellogg, Herbert H., Columbia University, Seeley W. Mudd Building, New York, N.Y. 10027 (1978).
Kennedy, Dr. John F., University of Iowa, Iowa City, Iowa 52242 (1973).
Kerrebrock, Jack L., M.I.T., Room 33-207, Cambridge, Mass. 02139 (1978).
Kesler, Clyde E., University of Illinois at Urbana-Champaign, Civil Engineering Building, Urbana, Ill. 61801 (1977).
Kessler, George W., 720 Williams Drive, Winter Park, Fla. 32789 (1969).
Ketchledge, Raymond W., Bell Laboratories, Naperville, Ill. 60540 (1970).
Keulegan, Garbis H., U.S.A.E. Waterways Experiment Station, P.O.B. 631, Vicksburg, Miss. 39180 (1979).
Keyes, Robert W., IBM T.J. Watson Research Center, P.O.B. 218, Yorktown Heights, N.Y. 10598 (1976).
Khan, Dr. Fazlur R., Skidmore, Owings & Merrill, 30 West Monroe St., Chicago, Ill. 60603 (1973).
**Kiely, John R., 50 Beale Street, San Francisco, Calif. 94119 (1967).**
Kilby, Jack S., 5924 Royal Lane, Dallas, Tex. 75230 (1967).
Kilgore, Lee A., Cline Hollow Rd., R.D. 3, Export, Pa. 15632 (1976).
Killian, Dr. James R., Jr., Massachusetts Institute of Technology, Cambridge, Mass. 02139 (1967).
Kimbark, Edward W., Bonneville Power Administration, U.S. Department of Energy, P.O.B. 3621-EOB, Portland, Or. 97208 (1979).
Kimmons, George H., Tennessee Valley Authority, Room W12A9, Knoxville, Tenn. 37401 (1980).
King, C. Judson, Department of Chemical Engineering, University of California, Berkeley, Calif. 94720 (1981).
Kingery, Dr. W. David, M.I.T., Cambridge, Mass. 02139.
Kino, Gordon S., W.W. Hansen Laboratories of Physics, Stanford University, Stanford, Calif. 94305 (1976).
‡Kinzel, Dr. Augustus B., 1738 Castellana Rd., La Jolla, Calif. 92037 (1964).

KIRCHMAYER, LEON K., General Electric Co., 1 River Rd., Schenectady, N.Y. 12345 (1979).
KIRKBRIDE, Dr. CHALMER G., 1629 K St., N.W., Washington, D.C. 20006 (1967).
KLEBANOFF, PHILIP S., National Engineering Laboratory, National Bureau of Standards, Department of Commerce, Washington, D.C. 20234 (1981).
KLEINROCK, LEONARD, School of Engineering and Applied Science, Univ. of California at Los Angeles, Boelter Hall 3732, Los Angeles, Calif. 90024 (1980).
KLINE, STEPHEN J., Department of Mechanical Engineering, Stanford University, Stanford, Calif. 94305 (1981).
KNOWLES, HUGH S., 3100 North Mannheim Rd., Franklin Park, Ill. 60131 (1969).
KNUTH, DONALD E., Department of Computer Science, Stanford University, Stanford, Calif. 94305 (1981).
KOBAYASHI, SHIRO, Prof. of Mechanical Engineering, Univ. of California, Berkeley, Calif. 94720 (1980).
KOCH, LEONARD J., Illinois Power Co., 500 South 27th St., Decatur, Ill. 62525 (1981).
KOHLER, MAX ADAM, 402 Dennis Ave., Silver Spring, Md. 20901 (1981).
KOUTS, HERBERT J. C., Dept. of Nuclear Energy, Brookhaven National Laboratory, Upton, N.Y. 11973 (1978).
KRAFT, CHRISTOPHER COLUMBUS, Jr., Lyndon B. Johnson Space Center, NASA, Houston, Tex. 77058 (1970).
KRAUS, JOHN D., Ohio State University, Columbus, Ohio 43210 (1972).
KRESSEL, HENRY, RCA Laboratories, David Sarnoff Research Center, Princeton, N.J. 08540 (1980).
KUESEL, THOMAS R., Parsons Brinckerhogg Quade & Douglas Inc., One Penn Plaza, 250 West 34th St., New York, N.Y. 10001 (1977).
KUH, Dr. ERNEST S., University of California, Berkeley, Calif. 94720.
KUHRT, WESLEY A., United Technologies Corpn., 1 Financial Plaza, Hartford, Conn. 06101 (1980).

LAFFERTY, JAMES M., General Electric Co., P.O. Box 43, Schenectady, N.Y. 12301 (1981).
LAMBE, T. WILLIAM, M.I.T., Cambridge, Mass. 02139 (1972).
LAMBERTSEN, CHRISTIAN J., Institute for Environmental Medicine, University of Pennsylvania Medical Center, G-2, Philadelphia, Pa. 19104 (1977).
LAMM, A. UNO, 365 Moseley Rd., Hillsborough, Calif. 94010 (1979).
**LAND, Dr. EDWIN H., 730 Main Street, Cambridge, Mass. 02139 (1965).**
LANDAU, RALPH, Halcon International Inc., 2 Park Ave., New York, N.Y. 10016 (1972).
LANDAUER, ROLF W., IBM T.J. Watson Research Center, P.O.B. 218, Yorktown Heights, N.Y. 10598 (1978).
‡LANDIS, JAMES N., 2701 Golden Rain Rd., Walnut Creek, Calif. 94595 (1964).
LANDIS, JOHN W., Stone and Webster Engineering Corpn., P.O. Box 2325, Boston, Mass. 02107 (1981).
**LANDSBERG, Dr. HELMUT E., The University of Maryland, College Park, Md. 20742 (1966).**
LANDWEBER, LOUIS, Inst. of Hydraulic Research, Univ. of Iowa, Iowa City, Ia. 52242 (1980).
LANG, MARTIN, Camp Dresser & McKee Inc., 1 World Trade Center, Suite 2637, New York, N.Y. 10048 (1980).
LANG, WILLIAM W., IBM Corpn., Building 704, Poughkeepsie, N.Y. 12602 (1978).
LARSON, Dr. CLARENCE E., 6514 Bradley Blvd., Bethesda, Md. 20034 (1973).
LARSON, THURSTON E., Illinois State Water Survey, P.O.B. 232, Urbana, Ill. 61801 (1978).
LATHAM, ALLEN, Jr., Haemonetics Corpn., 8 Erie Drive, Natick, Mass. 01760 (1969).
LAUDISE, ROBERT A., Bell Laboratories, Room 1A-264, Murray Hill, N.J. 07974 (1980).
LAUFER, JOHN, Dept. of Aerospace Engineering, University of Southern California, Los Angeles, Calif. 90007 (1977).
LAW, HAROLD B., 145 Van Dyke Rd., Hopewell, N.J. 08525 (1979).
LAWLER, JOSEPH C., Camp Dresser & McKee Inc., 1 Center Plaza, Boston, Mass. 02108 (1973).
LAWROSKI, Dr. STEPHEN, 9700 South Cass Ave., Argonne, Ill. 60439 (1969).
LEATHERS, J. F. M., The Dow Chemical Co., 2030 Dow Center, Abbott Rd., Midland, Mich. 48640 (1978).
LEDERER, JEROME F., 468-D Calle Cadiz, Laguna Hills, Calif. 92653 (1967).
LEE, Dr. E. H., Stanford University, Stanford, Calif. 94305.

LEE, GRIFF C., J. Ray McDermott & Co. Inc., P.O.B. 60035, New Orleans, La. 70160 (1980).
LEE, Dr. THOMAS H., General Electric Co., Fairfield, Conn. 06431.
LEE, WILLIAM S., Duke Power Co., P.O.B. 2178, Charlotte, N.C. 28242 (1978).
LEES, LESTER, Graduate Aeronautical Laboratories, California Institute of Technology, Pasadena, Calif. 91109 (1971).
LEHAN, FRANK W., 1696 East Valley Rd., Santa Barbara, Calif. 93108 (1970).
LeMESSURIER, WILLIAM J., Sippican Consultants International, Inc., 1033 Massachusetts Ave., Cambridge, Mass. 02138 (1978).
LEPS, THOMAS M., Thomas M. Leps Inc., 177 Watkins Ave., Atherton, Calif. 94025 (1973).
LEVENSON, MILTON, Electric Power Research Institute, 3413 Hillview Ave., Palo Alto, Calif. 94304 (1976).
LEVERENZ, HUMBOLDT W., 35 Westcott Rd., Princeton, N.J. 08540 (1970).
LEVY, SALOMON, S. Levy Inc., Suite 1050, 1901 S. Bascom Ave., Campbell, Calif. 45008 (1974).
LEWIS, DAVID S., General Dynamics Corpn., Pierre Laclede Center, St. Louis, Mo. 63105 (1971).
LEWIS, W. DEMING, Lehigh University, Bethlehem, Pa. 18015 (1967).
LI, TINGYE, Bell Laboratories, Crawford Hill Lab., Box 400, Holmdel, N.J. 07733 (1980).
LIEBOWITZ, Dr. HAROLD, George Washington University, Washington, D.C. 20052.
LIEPMANN, HANS W., California Institute of Technology, Pasadena, Calif. 91109 (1965).
LIGHTFOOT, EDWIN N., Jr., University of Wisconsin-Madison, 1415 Johnson Drive, Madison, Wis. 53706 (1979).
LIN, T. Y., 315 Bay St., San Francisco, Calif. 94133 (1967).
LINDEN, HENRY R., Institute of Gas Technology, 3424 South State St., Chicago, Ill. 60616 (1974).
‡LINDER, CLARENCE H., 1334 Ruffner Rd., Schenectady, N.Y. 12309 (1964).
LINDVALL, FREDERICK C., Lindvall, Richter and Assocs., 825 W. Colorado Blvd., Los Angeles, Calif. 90041 (1967).
LING, DONALD P., 1816 Nakomis Court N.E., Albuquerque, New Mexico 87112 (1967).
LING, FREDERICK F., Dept. of Mechanical Engineering, Rensselaer Polytechnic Institute, Troy, N.Y 12181 (1977).
LING, JOSEPH T., Division of Environmental Engineering and Pollution Control, 3M Company, 900 Bush Ave., Box 33331, St. Paul, Minn. 55133 (1976).
LINSLEY, RAY K., Hydrocomp. Inc., 1502 Page Mill Rd., Palo Alto, Calif. 94304 (1976).
LINVILL, JOHN G., Stanford University, Stanford, Calif. 94305 (1971).
LISCHER, LUDWIG F., Commonwealth Edison Co., P.O.B. 767, Chicago, Ill. 60690 (1978).
LITTLE, C. GORDON, National Oceanic and Atmospheric Administration, Boulder, Colo. 80302 (1974).
LOEWY, ROBERT G., Rensselaer Polytechnic Institute, 110 8th St., Troy, N.Y. 12181 (1971).
LOGAN, JOHN A., Rose-Hulman Institute of Technology, 5500 Wabash Ave., Terre Haute, Ind. 47803 (1968).
LONDON, A. L., Stanford University, Stanford, Calif. 94305 (1979).
LONGWELL, JOHN P., M.I.T., Room 66-554, Cambridge, Mass. 02139 (1976).
LOOFBOURROW, ALAN G., 183 East Long Lake Rd., Bloomfield Hills, Mich. 48013 (1977).
LOUGHLIN, BERNARD D., Hazeltine Corpn., Greenlawn, N.Y. 11740 (1967).
LOVELACE, ALAN M., NASA, Washington, D.C. 20546 (1974).
Low, GEORGE M., Rensselaer Polytechnic Institute, 110 8th St., Troy, N.Y. 12181 (1970).
Low, JOHN R., Jr., 635 McAlawy Rd., Charlotte, N.C. 28211 (1978).
LOWE, JOHN, III, Tippetts-Abbett-McCarthy-Stratton, 345 Park Ave., New York, N.Y. 10022 (1974).
LUCAS, WILLIAM R., National Aeronautics and Space Administration, Marshall Space Flight Center, Ala. 35812 (1978).
LUCKY, ROBERT W., Bell Telephone Laboratories, 600 Mountain Ave., Room 7B202, Murray Hill, N.J. 07974 (1978).
LUDWIG, HARVEY F., Southeast Asia Technology Co. Ltd., 87 Sukhumvit Rd., Bangkok, Thailand (1969).
LUDWIG, JOHN H., 43 Alston Place, Santa Barbara, Calif. 93108 (1971).
LUERSSEN, FRANK W., Inland Steel Co., 3210 Watling St., East Chicago, Ind. 46312 (1977).

LUNDIN, BRUCE T., 5629 Columbia Rd., North Olmstead, Ohio 44070 (1976).
LUNDSTROM, LOUIS C., General Motors Corpn., Technical Center, Warren, Mich. 48090 (1977).
LUSTMAN, BENJAMIN, Westinghouse Bettis Atomic Power Laboratory, P.O.B. 79, Mifflin, Pa. 15122 (1968).
MACCREADY, PAUL B., Jr., AeroVironment, Inc., 145 Vista Ave., Pasadena, Calif. 91107 (1979).
MACDONALD, J. ROSS, Univ of North Carolina, Chapel Hill, N.C. 27514 (1970).
MACDONNELL, W. D., Kelsey-Hayes Co., 38481 Huron River Drive, Romulus, Mich. 48174 (1968).
MACKENZIE, JOHN D., Engineering and Applied Science Materials Department, University of California, 6532 Boelter Hall, Los Angeles, Calif. 90024 (1976).
MACMILLAN, DOUGLAS C., General Dynamics Corpn., Quincy, Mass. 02169 (1967).
MACPHERSON, HERBERT G., 102 Orchard Circle, Oak Ridge, Tenn. 37830 (1978).
MAGER, ARTUR, Aerospace Corpn., P.O.B. 92957, Los Angeles, Calif. 90009 (1977).
MAIMAN, THEODORE H., TRW Electronics, 10880 Wilshire Blvd., Los Angeles, Calif. 90024 (1967).
MALOZEMOFF, PLATO, 300 Park Avenue, New York, N.Y. 10022 (1969).
MANLY, WILLIAM D., Cabot Corpn., Kokomo, Ind. 46901 (1974).
MANN, Dr. ROBERT W., M.I.T., 77 Massachusetts Ave., Room 3-439. Cambridge, Mass. 02139 (1973).
MAR, JAMES WAH, Massachusetts Institute of Technology, Cambridge, Mass. 02139 (1981).
MARBLE, FRANK E., California Institute of Technology, Pasadena, Calif. 91109 (1974).
MARCATILI, ENRIQUE A. J., Transmission and Circuit Research Department, Bell Laboratories, Box 400, Holmdel, N.J. 07733 (1976).
MARCUVITZ, NATHAN, Polytechnic Institute of New York, Route 110, Farmingdale, N.Y. 11735 (1978).
MARK, HANS, Ames Research Center, NASA, Moffett Field, Calif. 94035 (1976).
MARSHALL, W. ROBERT, University of Wisconsin, Madison, Wis. 53706 (1967).
MARTIN, THOMAS L., Jr., Illinois Institute of Technology, 3300 South Federal St., Chicago, Ill. 60616 (1971).
MASON, Dr. EDWARD A., Standard Oil Co. (Indiana), Amoco Research Center, P.O.B. 400, Naperville, Ill. 60540 (1975).
MATHEWS, MAX V., Bell Telephone Laboratories, 600 Mountain Ave., Room 2D-554, Murray Hill, N.J. 07974 (1979).
MATSUDA, FUJIO, University of Hawaii, 2444 Dole St., Honolulu, Hawaii 96822 (1974).
MAUCH, HANS A., Mauch Laboratories Inc., 3035 Dryden Rd., Dayton, Ohio 45439 (1973).
MAURER, ROBERT D., Corning Glass Works, Corning, N.Y. 14830 (1979).
MAY, WALTER G., Exxon Research and Engineering Co., Linden, N.J. 07036 (1978).
MAYO, JOHN S., Bell Telephone Laboratories, 600 Mountain Ave., Murray Hill, N.J. 17974 (1979).
MCAFEE, Dr. JERRY, Gulf Oil Corpn., P.O.B. 1166, Pittsburgh, Pa. 15230 (1967).
MCCABE, WARREN L., Highland Farms, Black Mountain, N.C. 28711 (1978).
MCCARTHY, GERALD T., 94 Colt Rd., Summit, N.J. 07901 (197.3)
MCCARTHY, JOHN F., Jr., NASA-Lewis Research Center, 21000 Brookpark Rd., Cleveland, O. 44135 (1981).
MCCARTY, PERRY L., Dept. of Civil Engineering, Stanford University, Stanford, Calif. 94305 (1977).
MCCLELLAND, BRAMLETTE, McClelland Engineers, Inc., 6100 Hillcroft, Houston, Tex. 77081 (1979).
**MCCUNE, FRANCIS K., 1564 Danny Drive, Sarasota, Fla. 33580 (1966).**
MCCUNE, WILLIAM J., Jr., Polaroid Corpn., 549 Technology Square, Cambridge, Mass. 02139 (1979).
MCKAY, Dr. KENNETH G., Bell Laboratories, 600 Mountain Ave., Murray Hill, N.J. 07974 (1968).
MCKETTA, JOHN J., University of Texas, Austin, Tex. 78712 (1970).
MCKINNEY, ROSS E., Dept. of Civil Engineering, University of Kansas, 4002 Learned Hall, Lawrence, Kansas 66045 (1977).
MCLUCAS, Dr. JOHN L., COMSAT General Corpn., 950 L'Enfant Plaza, S.W., Washington, D.C. 20024 (1969).
MCMAHON, CHARLES J., Jr., Dept. of Materials Science and Engineering, K1, Univ. of Pennsylvania, Philadelphia, Pa. 19104 (1980).
MCMASTER, ROBERT C., 6435 Dublin Rd., Delaware, O. 43015 (1970).

MCMILLAN, Dr. BROCKWAY, Bell Laboratories Inc., Whippany, N.J. 07981 (1969).
MECHLIN, GEORGE F., Jr., Ocean Research and Engineering Center, Westinghouse Electric Corpn., Pittsburgh, Pa. 15235 (1971).
MEINDL, JAMES D., Stanford University, Stanford, Calif. 94305 (1978).
MEISEL, SEYMOUR L., Mobil Research and Development Corpn., 150 East 42nd St., New York, N.Y. 10017 (1981).
MERCHANT, Dr. M. EUGENE, Cincinnati Milacron Inc., 4701 Marburg Ave., Cincinnati, Ohio 45209.
MERGLER, HARRY W., Glennan Lab. 518, Case Western Reserve Univ., University Circle, Cleveland, Ohio 44106 (1980).
METTLER, Dr. RUBEN F., TRW Inc., 23555 Euclid Ave., Cleveland, O. 44117 (1965).
METZGER, SIDNEY, Communications Satellite Corporation, 950 L'Enfant Plaza, Washington, D.C. 20024 (1976).
METZLER, DWIGHT F., Kansas Dept. of Health and Environment, Forbes Field, Bldg. 740, Topeka, Kan. 66620 (1973).
METZNER, ARTHUR B., University of Delaware, Newark, Del. 19711 (1979).
MEYERAND, RUSSELL G., Jr., United Technologies Research Center, Silver Lane, East Hartford, Conn. 06108 (1978).
MICHAEL, HAROLD L., Purdue University, West Lafayette, Ind. 47907.
MICHAELS, ALAN S., Stanford University, Stanford, Calif. 94305 (1979).
MICKLEY, HAROLD S., Stauffer Chemical Co., Westport, Conn. 06880 (1978).
MILLAR, Dr. GORDON H., Deere & Co., Moline, Ill. 61265.
MILLER, Dr. OTTO N., 555 Market St., San Francisco, Calif. 94105 (1968).
MILLER, RENE H., Massachusetts Institute of Technology, Cambridge, Mass. 02139 (1968).
MILLER, STEWART E., Bell Laboratories, Crawford Hill Laboratory, Box 400, Holmdel, N.J. 07733 (1973).
MILLIKEN, FRANK R., Kennecott Copper Corpn., 161 East 42nd St., New York, N.Y. 10017.
MILLS, G. ALEXANDER, Energy Research & Development Admin., 20 Massachusetts Ave., N.W., Room 4103, Washington, D.C. 20545 (1977).
MINDLIN, Dr. RAYMOND D., Columbia University, New York, N.Y. 10027 (1966).
MISCH, HERBERT L., Ford Motor Company, The American Road, Dearborn, Mich. 48121 (1976).
MITCHELL, JAMES K., Department of Civil Engineering, University of California, 440 Davis Hall, Berkeley, Calif. 94720 (1976).
MOELLER, DADE W., School of Public Health, Harvard University, Boston, Mass. 02115 (1978).
MOLL, JOHN L., Hewlett-Packard Co., 1501 Page Mill Rd., Palo Alto, Calif. 94304 (1974).
MONISMITH, CARL C., Prof. of Civil Engineering, Univ. of California, 215 McLaughlin Hall, Berkeley, Calif. 94720 (1980).
MOORE, GORDON E., Intel Corporation, 3065 Bowers Ave., Santa Clara, Calif. 95051 (1976).
MOORE, JOHN R., Actron Division of McDonnell Douglas Corpn., 700 Royal Oaks Drive, Monrovia, Calif. 91016 (1978).
MOORE, WILLIAM W., Dames & Moore, 500 Sansome St., San Francisco, Calif. 94111 (1978).
MORGAN, JAMES J., California Institute of Technology, Pasadena, Calif. 91125 (1978).
MORGAN, PAUL W., 822 Roslyn Ave., West Chester, Pa. 19380 (1977).
MORRIS, JOHN W., U.S. Army Corps of Engineers, 1000 Independence Ave., S.W., Washington, D.C. 20314 (1979).
MORROW, WALTER E., Lincoln Laboratory, M.I.T., P.O.B. 73, Lexington, Mass. 02173 (1978).
MORSE, RICHARD S., 193 Winding River Rd., Wellesley, Mass. 02181 (1976).
MUELLER, Dr. GEORGE E., System Development Corpn., 2500 Colorado Ave., Santa Monica, Calif. 90406 (1967).
MUESER, WILLIAM H., Quarry Lane, Route 2, P.O.B. 52, Bedford Village, N.Y. 10506 (1978).
MULLIGAN, JAMES H., Jr., School of Engineering, University of California, Irvine, Calif. 92664 (1974).
MUMMA, Rear Adm. A. G., U.S.N. (Ret.), 66 Minnisink Rd., Short Hills, N.J. 07078 (1976).
MURDEN, WILLIAM R., Jr., Water Resources Support Center, Kingman Bldg., Fort Belvoir, Va. 22060 (1979).
MURPHY, Dr. EUGENE F., 252 Seventh Ave., New York, N.Y. 10001 (1968).
MURRAY, PETER, Westinghouse Advanced Reactors Division, Westinghouse Electric Corporation, Madison, Pa. 15663 (1976).

MYERS, DALE D., U.S. Dept. of Energy, 201 Old Executive Bldg., Washington, D.C. 20585 (1974).
MYERS, Dr. PHILIP S., University of Wisconsin—Madison, 1500 Johnson Drive, Madison, Wis. 53706 (1973).
NAGEL, THEODORE J., American Electric Power Service Corpn., 2 Broadway, New York, N.Y. 10004 (1973).
NEAL, RICHARD B., Stanford Linear Accelerator Center, Stanford University, Stanford, Calif. 94305 (1979).
NEUMANN, GERHARD, General Electric Company, 1000 Western Ave., Lynn, Mass. 01910 (1970).
NEWELL, ALLEN, Prof. of Computer Science, Carnegie-Mellon Univ., Schenley Park, Pittsburgh, Pa. 15213 (1980).
NEWMAN, JOSEPH H., Tishman Research Corpn., 666 Fifth Ave., New York, N.Y. 10019 (1973).
NICHOLS, Maj.-Gen. KENNETH D., 16715 Thurston Rd., Dickerson, Md. 20753 (1968).
NOBLE, CHARLES C., Chas. T. Main, Inc., Prudential Center, Boston, Mass. 02199 (1981).
NOYCE, Dr. ROBERT N., Intel Corpn., 3065 Bowers Ave., Santa Clara, Calif. 95051 (1969).
OBLAD, Dr. ALEX G., University of Utah, Salt Lake City, Utah 84112.
O'BRIEN, BRIAN, Box 166, Woodstock, Conn. 06281 (1981).
O'BRIEN, MORROUGH P., University of California, Richmond, Calif. 94802 (1969).
O'CONNOR, DONALD J., Manhattan College, Manhattan College Parkway, Bronx, N.Y. 10471 (1978).
ODER, FREDERIC C. E., Lockheed Missile and Space Co. Inc., P.O.B. 504, Sunnyvale, Calif. 94086 (1980).
OKRENT, DAVID, University of California, Los Angeles, Calif. 90024 (1974).
OKUN, Dr. DANIEL A., School of Public Health, University of North Carolina, Chapel Hill, N.C. 27514 (1973).
OLD, Dr. BRUCE S., 25 Acorn Park, Cambridge, Mass. 02140 (1968).
OLDSHUE, JAMES Y., Mixing Equipment Co., Unit of General Signal, 135 Mt. Read Blvd., Rochester, N.Y. 14611 (1980).
OLIVER, Dr. BERNARD M., 1501 Page Mill Road, Palo Alto, Calif. 94304 (1966).
OLSEN, KENNETH H., Digital Equipment Corpn., 146 Main St., Maynard, Mass. 01754 (1977).
O'NEILL, EUGENE F., Transmission Terminals and Maintenance Division, Bell Laboratories, Holmdel, N.J. 07733 (1976).
O'NEILL, Dr. RUSSELL R., University of California, Los Angeles, Calif. 90024.
ONGERTH, HENRY J., Water Sanitation Section, California Department of Health, 2151 Berkeley Way, Berkeley, Calif. 94704 (1976).
OPPENHEIM, ANTONI K., University of California, Berkeley, Calif. 94720 (1978).
OSBORN, Dr. ELBURT F., Carnegie Institution of Washington, 2801 Upton St., N.W., Washington, D.C. 20008 (1968).
OSTERBERG, Dr. JORJ O., Northwestern University, Evanston, Ill. 60201.
OSTRACH, SIMON, Case Western Reserve University, Cleveland, Ohio 44106 (1978).
OWEN, WALTER S., Dept. of Materials Science and Engineering, M.I.T., Room 8-309, Cambridge, Mass. 02139 (1977).
PACKARD, DAVID, Hewlett-Packard Co., 1501 Page Mill Rd., Palo Alto, Calif. 94304 (1971).
PAIGE, Dr. HILLIARD W., International Energy Assocs., Ltd., 2600 Virginia Ave., Suite 505, Washington, D.C. 20037 (1968).
PAINE, Dr. THOMAS O., Northrop Corpn., 1800 Century Park East, Century City, Los Angeles, Calif. 90067 (1973).
PALLADINO, Dr. NUNZIO J., The Pennsylvania State University, University Park, Pa. 16802 (1967).
PARKER, EARL R., University of California, Berkeley, Calif. 94720 (1960).
PARKER, HERBERT M., HMP Associates, Inc., 2030 Harris Ave., Richland, Wash. 99352 (1978).
PARKER, JACK S., General Electric Company, 3135 Easton Turnpike, Fairfield, Conn. 06431 (1976).
PARKER, NORMAN F., Varian Associates, 611 Hansen Way, Palo Alto, Calif. 94303 (1976).
PARKS, ROBERT J., California Institute of Technology, 4800 Oak Grove Drive, Pasadena, Calif. 91103 (1973).
PARME, ALFRED L., 6787 Avda. Andorra, La Jolla, Calif. 92307 (1974).
PASK, Dr. JOSEPH A., University of California, Hearst Mining Building, Berkeley, Calif. 94720.
PATEL, C. KUMAR N., Bell Telephone Laboratories, Murray Hill, N.J. 07974 (1978).
PAXTON, HAROLD W., United States Steel Corpn., 600 Grant St., Pittsburgh, Pa. 15230 (1978).

PEARSON, Dr. GERALD L., Stanford University, Stanford, Calif. 94305 (1968).
PECK, Dr. RALPH B., 1101 Warm Sands Drive, S.E., Albuquerque, New Mexico 87123 (1965).
PEDERSON, DONALD O., University of California, Berkeley, Calif. 94720 (1974).
PELLINI, WILLIAM S., Mayflower Rd., P.O.B. 68, Carver, Mass. 02330 (1974).
PELTIER, EUGENE J., Sverdrup & Parcel & Associates, Inc., 800 North 12th Blvd., St. Louis, Mo. 63101 (1979).
PENNELL, MAYNARD L., 1545 N.E. 143rd St., Seattle, Wash. 98125 (1968).
PENNER, STANFORD S., University of California, San Diego, Room B-1010, La Jolla, Calif. 92093 (1977).
PENZIEN, JOSEPH, Dept. of Civil Engineering, University of California, Berkeley, Calif. 94720 (1977).
PERKINS, COURTLAND D., National Academy of Engineering, 2101 Constitution Ave., N.W., Washington, D.C. 20418 (1969).
PERKINS, KENDALL, P.O.B. 516, St. Louis, Mo. 63108 (1970).
PERLIS, ALAN J., Dept. of Computer Science, Yale University, 10 Hillhouse Ave., New Haven, Conn. 06520 (1977).
PERRY, WILLIAM J., Office of the Secretary of Defense, The Pentagon, Room 3E-1006, Washington, D.C. 20301 (1970).
PETERS, Dr. MAX S., University of Colorado, Boulder, Colo. 80302 (1969).
PETERSON, Dr. ALLEN M., Stanford University, Stanford, Calif. 94305 (1973).
PETERSON, DEAN F., Agency for International Development, Washington, D.C. 20523 (1974).
PETERSON, HAROLD A., 121 West Calle Montana Jack, Green Valley, Ariz. 85614 (1978).
PETRONE, Dr. ROCCO A., National Center for Resource Recovery, Inc., 1211 Connecticut Ave., N.W., Suite 800, Washington, D.C. 20036.
PETTIT, Dr. JOSEPH M., Georgia Institute of Technology, 225 North Ave., N.W., Atlanta, Ga. 30332 (1967).
PHILLIPS, Gen. SAMUEL C., TRW Energy Products Group, 9841 Airport Blvd., Suite 1500, Los Angeles, Calif. 90045 (1971).
PHILLIPS, THOMAS L., Raytheon Company, Lexington, Mass. 02173 (1971).
‡PICKERING, Dr. WILLIAM H., California Institute of Technology, Pasadena, Calif. 91103 (1964).
PIERCE, Dr. JOHN R., California Institute of Technology, Pasadena, Calif. 91109 (1965).
PIGFORD, ROBERT L., Dept. of Chemical Engineering, University of Delaware, Newark, Del. 19711 (1971).
PIGFORD, THOMAS H., Department of Nuclear Engineering, University of California, 4101 Etcheverry Hall, Berkeley, Calif. 94720 (1976).
PIKARSKY, MILTON, Regional Transportation Authority, P.O.B. 3858, Chicago, Ill. 60654 (1973).
PINGS, CORNELIUS J., California Institute of Technology, Pasadena, Calif. 91125 (1981).
PIORE, Dr. EMANUEL R., 115 Central Park West, New York, N.Y. 10023 (1966).
PISTER, KARL S., Dept. of Civil Engineering, Univ. of California, Berkeley, Calif. 94720 (1980).
PLESSET, MILTON S., California Institute of Technology, Room 104-44, Pasadena, Calif. 91125 (1979).
PLUMMER, JAMES W., P.O.B. 504, Sunnyvale, Calif. 94086 (1978).
PLUNKETT, ROBERT, University of Minnesota, Minneapolis, Minn. 55455 (1974).
POETTMANN, FRED H., Marathon Oil Co., P.O.B. 269, Littleton, Colo. 80160 (1978).
POPOV, EGOR P., Department of Civil Engineering, University of California, 725 Davis Hall, Berkeley, Calif. 94720 (1976).
POTTER, Dr. DAVID S., General Motors Corpn., Technical Center, Warren, Mich. 48090 (1973).
POUNDSTONE, WILLIAM N., Consolidation Coal Co., Consol Plaza, 1800 Washington Rd., Pittsburgh, Pa. 15241 (1977).
PRATER, C. DWIGHT, Mobil Research and Development Corpn., Paulsboro, N.J. 08066 (1977).
PRATT, PERRY W., 296 Hollister Way West, Glastonbury, Conn. 06033 (1967).
PRAUSNITZ, JOHN M., University of California, Berkeley, Calif. 94720 (1979).
PROBSTEIN, RONALD F., M.I.T., Room 3-246, Cambridge, Mass. 02139 (1977).
PROMISEL, NATHAN E., 12519 Davan Drive, Silver Spring, Md. 20904 (1978).
PUCKETT, Dr. ALLEN E., Hughes Aircraft Company, Centinela and Teale Sts., Culver City, Calif. 90230 (1965).
QUATE, CALVIN F., Stanford University, Stanford, Calif. 94305 (1970).
QUENEAU, PAUL E., Thayer School of Engineering, Dartmouth College, Hanover, N.H. 03755 (1981).

QUINN, JOHN A., Dept. of Chemical and Biochemical Engineering, University of Pennsylvania, Philadelphia, Pa. 19104 (1978).
RABINOW, JACOB, National Bureau of Standards, U.S. Department of Commerce, Washington, D.C. 20234 (1976).
RADER, LOUIS T., University of Virginia, Charlottesville, Va. 22901 (1970).
RAJCHMAN, Dr. JAN A., 268 Edgerstoune Rd., Princeton, N.J. 08540 (1966).
RAMEY, HENRY J., Jr., Stanford University, Stanford, Calif. 94305 (1981).
‡RAMO, Dr. SIMON, TRW Inc., One Space Park, Redondo Beach, Calif. 90278 (1964).
RAND, Dr. WILLIAM B. W., 34 Avon Rd., Kensington, Calif. 94707 (1973).
RANNIE, W. DUNCAN, California Institute of Technology, 1201 E. California St., Pasadena, Calif. 91125 (1979).
RASMUSSEN, NORMAN C., M.I.T., Room 24-102, Cambridge, Mass. 02139 (1977).
‡RAYMOND, ARTHUR E., 73 Oakmont Drive, Los Angeles, Calif. 90049 (1964).
RECHTIN, EBERHARDT, Hewlett-Packard Co., 1501 Page Mill Rd., Palo Alto, Calif. 94304 (1968).
REED, CHARLES E., General Electric Co., Fairfield, Conn. 06431 (1969).
REED, EUGENE D., Sandia Laboratories, Room 245, Bldg. 802, Albuquerque, N.M. 87115 (1971).
REED, IRVING S., University of Southern California, 510 Powell Hall, Los Angeles, Calif. 90007 (1979).
REES, Dr. EBERHARD F. M., 3917 Panorama Drive, S.E., Huntsville, Ala. 35801 (1973).
REESE, Dr. LYMON C., University of Texas at Austin, 10. 338 Cockrell Hall, Austin, Tex. 78712.
REICHL, ERIC H., Conoco Coal Development Co., Pa. 15129.
REID, ROBERT C., Massachusetts Institute of Technology, Cambridge, Mass. 02139 (1980).
REISSNER, ERIC, Department of Applied Mechanics and Engineering Sciences, University of California, San Diego, La Jolla, Calif. 92093 (1976).
RESWICK, JAMES B., Surgical Services, Room 121-HB Building, Rancho Los Amigos Hospital, Downey, Calif. 90242 (1976).
REYNOLDS, WILLIAM C., Stanford University, Stanford, Calif. 94305 (1979).
RICE, JAMES R., Division of Engineering, Box D, Brown Univ., Providence, R.I. 02912 (1980).
RICE, STEPHEN O., Dept. of Applied Physics and Information Science, University of California, San Diego, La Jolla, Calif. 92093 (1977).
RICH, BEN R., Advanced Development Projects, Lockheed California Co., Burbank, Calif. 91520 (1981).
RICHARDS, ROBERT B., General Electric Company, 310 De Guigne Drive, Mail Code S05, Sunnyvale, Calif. 94086 (1970).
RICHARDSON, HERBERT H., Dept. of Mechanical Engineering, M.I.T., 77 Massachusetts Ave., Room 3-173, Cambridge, Mass. 02139 (1980).
RICHART, Dr. FRANK E., Jr., The University of Michigan, Ann Arbor, Mich. 48104 (1969).
RICKOVER, Adm. H. G., U.S.N., U.S. Atomic Energy Commission, Washington, D.C. 20545 (1967).
ROBECK, GORDON G., U.S. Environmental Protection Agency, 26 West Saint Clair St., Cincinatti, O. 45268 (1980).
ROBERTS, GEORGE A., Teledyne, Inc., 1901 Ave. of the Stars, Los Angeles, Calif. 90067 (1978).
ROBERTS, LAWRENCE G., Telenet Communications Corpn., 1950 17th St., N.W., Suite 850, Washington, D.C. 20036 (1978).
ROBERTSON, LESLIE E., Skilling, Helle, Christiansen, Robertson, 230 Park Ave., 1216, New York, N.Y. 10017.
ROBINSON, DENIS M., High Voltage Engineering Corporation, Burlington, Mass. 01803 (1970).
ROBINSON, THOMAS B., Black & Veatch, P.O.B. 8405, Kansas City, Mo. 64114 (1979).
ROCHELEAU, ROBERT F., E.I. du Pont de Nemours and Co., Wilmington, Del. 19898 (1981).
RODDIS, LOUIS H., Jr., 110 Broad St., Charleston, S.C. 29401 (1967).
ROE, KENNETH A., Burns and Roe, Inc., 550 Kinderkamack Rd., Oradell, N.J. 07649 (1978).
ROHLICH, GERARD ADDISON, University of Texas, Austin, Tex. 78712 (1970).
ROHSENHOW, Dr. WARREN M., M.I.T., Room 3156, Cambridge, Mass. 02139.
ROOT, Dr. L. EUGENE, 1340 Hillview Drive, Menlo Park, Calif. 94025 (1965).
ROSE, ALBERT, Boston University, Boston, Mass. 02215 (1975).

ROSEN, Dr. HAROLD A., Hughes Aircraft Co., P.O.B. 92919, Airport Station, Los Angeles, Calif. 90009 (1973).
ROSENBAUM, JOE B., 1149 Mercedes Way, Salt Lake City, Utah 84108 (1973).
ROSENBERG, PAUL, Paul Rosenberg Associates, 330 Fifth Ave., Pelham, N.Y. 10803 (1970).
ROSENBLITH, Dr. WALTER A., M.I.T., 77 Massachusetts Ave., Room 3-240, Cambridge, Mass. 02139 (1973).
ROSHKO, ANATOL, California Institute of Technology, Mail Code 105-50, Pasadena, Calif. 91125 (1978).
ROSS, Dr. IAN M., Bell Laboratories, Murray Hill, N.J. 07974 (1973).
ROSS, PHILIP N., P.O.B. 336, Irvington, Va. 22480 (1968).
ROUSE, Dr. HUNTER, 10814 Mimosa Drive, Sun City, Ariz. 80523 (1966).
ROWAND, WILL H., P.O.B. 6485, Litchfield Park, Ariz. 85340 (1968).
ROWE, JOSEPH E., Case Institute of Technology, Case Western Reserve University, 10900 Euclid Ave., Crawford Hall, Cleveland, Ohio 44106 (1977).
ROY, Dr. RUSTUM, Pennsylvania State University, 202 Materials Research Laboratory, University Park, Pa. 16802 (1973).
RUDD, DALE F., University of Wisconsin-Madison, Madison, Wis. 537056 (1978).
RUMMEL, ROBERT W., Rummel Associates Inc., 908 South Power Rd., Mesa, Ariz. 85206 (1973).
RUMSEY, VICTOR H., Dept. of Electrical Engineering and Computer Sciences, Univ. of California at San Diego, Mail Code CO14, La Jolla, Calif. 92093 (1980).
RUSSELL, ALLEN S., Aluminium Co. of America, 1501 Alcoa Building, Pittsburgh, Pa. 15219 (1976).
RUTLEDGE, Dr. PHILIP C., 81 Heritage Hill Rd., New Canaan, Conn. 06840 (1968).

SAFFER, ALFRED, Oxirane International, 120 Alexander St., Princeton, N.J. 08540 (1978).
SAMMET, JEAN E., IBM Corpn., 545 Technology Square, Cambridge, Mass. 02139 (1977).
SANDBERG, IRWIN W., Mathematics and Statistics Research Center, Bell Laboratories, Murray Hill, N.J. 07974.
SARKARIA, GURMUKH S., International Engineering Co., Inc., 180 Howard St., San Francisco, Calif. 94105 (1981).
SAVAGE, WARREN F., Materials Division, Rensselaer Polytechnic Institute, Troy, N.Y. 12181 (1981).
SAVILLE, THORNDIKE, Jr., Coastal Engineering Research Center, Kingman Bldg., Fort Belvoir, Va. 22060 (1977).
SCHADE, HENRY A., 88 Norwood Ave., Kensington, Calif. 94707 (1973).
SCHAEFER, JACOB W., Bell Laboratories, Murray Hill, N.J. 07974 (1980).
SCHAIRER, GEORGE S., Boeing Co., P.O.B. 3999, Seattle, Wash. 98124 (1967).
SCHECHTER, ROBERT S., Department of Petroleum Engineering, University of Texas at Austin, Austin, Tex. 78712 (1976).
SCHEY, JOHN A., Department of Mechanical Engineering, University of Waterloo, Waterloo, Ontario, Canada N2L 3G1 (1981).
SCHMITT, OTTO H., University of Minnesota, Minneapolis, Minn. 55455 (1979).
SCHMITT, ROLAND W., General Electric Research and Development Center, P.O.B. 8, Schenectady, N.Y. 12301 (1978).
SCHRIEVER, Gen. BERNARD A., U.S.A.F., Schriever & McKee Inc., 1025 Connecticut Ave., N.W., Washington, D.C. 20036 (1967).
SCHROEDER, MANFRED R., Universitaet Goettingen, Rieswartenweg 8, D-3400 Goettingen, Federal Republic of Germany (1979).
SCHROEPFER, GEORGE J., 5343 Clinton Ave., S. Minneapolis, Minn. 55419 (1981).
SCHUBAUER, GALEN B., 5609 Gloster Rd., Washington, D.C. 20016 (1980).
SCHUHMANN, REINHARDT, Jr., School of Materials Engineering, Purdue University, West Lafayette, Ind. 97907 (1976.)
SCHURMAN, GLENN A., Chevron Petroleum (U.K.) Ltd., Chevron House, 93 Wigmore St., London W1H 9AA, U.K. (1980).
SCHWAN, Dr. HERMAN P., University of Pennsylvania, Philadelphia, Pa. 19174.
SCISSON, SIDNEY E., Fenix & Scisson Inc., P.O.B. 15609, Tulsa, Okla. 74112 (1977).
SCORDELIS, ALEXANDER C., University of California, 729 Davis Hall, Berkeley, Calif. 94720 (1978).
SCOTT, RONALD F., California Institute of Technology, Pasadena, Calif. 91109 (1974).
SCRIVEN, L. E., University of Minnesota, Minneapolis, Minn. 55455 (1978).

NATIONAL ACADEMY OF ENGINEERING — UNITED STATES OF AMERICA

SEAMANS, ROBERT C., Jr., M.I.T., 77 Massachusetts Ave., Room 1-206, Cambridge, Mass. 02139 (1968).
SEARS, WILLIAM R., University of Arizona, Tucson, Ariz. 85721 (1968).
SEBAN, RALPH A., University of California, Berkeley, Calif. 94720 (1978).
SEED, H. BOLTON, University of California, Berkeley, Calif. 94720 (1970).
SEVERUD, FRED N., 415 Lexington Avenue, New York, N.Y. 10017 (1968).
SHAPIRO, ASCHER H., Massachusetts Institute of Technology, Cambridge, Mass. 02139 (1974).
SHAW, Dr. MILTON C., Arizona State University, Room ECG-247, Tempe, Ariz. 85281 (1968).
SHEA, JOSEPH F., Raytheon Company, 141 Spring St., Lexington, Mass. 02173 (1971).
SHEA, Dr. TIMOTHY E., 92 Pine Grove Avenue, Summit, N.J. 07901 (1967).
SHEETS, Dr. HERMAN E., University of Rhode Island, Kingston, R.I. 02881 (1967).
SHEPHERD, MARK, Jr., Texas Instruments Inc., 13500 North Central Expressway, Dallas, Tex. 75222 (1970).
SHEPHERD, Dr. WILLIAM G., University of Minnesota, Minneapolis, Minn. 55455 (1969).
SHERBY, OLEG D., Stanford University, Stanford, Calif. 94305 (1979).
SHEWMON, PAUL G., Ohio State University, 116 West 19th Ave., Columbus, Ohio 43210 (1979).
SHINOZUKA, MASANOBU, Columbia University, New York, N.Y. 10027 (1978).
SHOUPP, Dr. WILLIAM E., 343 Maple Ave., Pittsburgh, Pa. 15218 (1967).
SIEGMAN, Dr. ANTHONY E., Stanford University, Stanford, Calif. 94305 (1973).
SIESS, Dr. CHESTER P., University of Illinois, Urbana, Ill. 61801 (1967).
SILVERSTEIN, Dr. ABE, 21160 Seabury Ave., Fairview Park, O. 44126 (1967).
SIMPSON, JOHN W., 2055 Outlook Drive, Pittsburgh, Pa. 15241 (1966).
SINCLAIR, Dr. DONALD B., 250 Beacon St., Boston, Mass. 02116 (1965).
SINFELT, Dr. JOHN H., Exxon Research and Engineering Co., P.O.B. 45, Linden, N.J. 07036.
SINGLETON, HENRY E., Teledyne, Inc., 1901 Ave. of the Stars, Los Angeles, Calif. 90067 (1979).
SJOBERG, SIGURD A., Lyndon B. Johnson Space Center, NASA, Houston, Tex. 77058 (1974).
SKILLING, JOHN B., 2200 The Financial Center, 1215 Fourth Ave., Seattle, Wash. 98161 (1965).
SKROMME, LAWRENCE H., Sperry New Holland, New Holland, Pa. 17557 (1978).
SLEPIAN, DAVID, Mathematical Studies Dept., Bell Laboratories, Murray Hill, N.J. 07974 (1976).
SLICHTER, WILLIAM P., Materials Science and Engineering Division, Bell Laboratories, Murray Hill, N.J. 07974 (1976).
SLIEPCEVICH, CEDOMIR M., University of Oklahoma, Norman, Okla. 73069 (1972).
SMELT, RONALD, Lockheed Aircraft Corporation, Burbank, Calif. 91520 (1971).
SMITH, Dr. JOE M., University of California, Davis, Calif. 95616.
SMITH, Rear Adm. LEVERING, U.S.N. (Ret.), 1462 Waggaman Circle, McLean, Va. 22101 (1965).
SMITH, Dr. MARK K., P.O.B. 189, Norwich, Conn. 05055 (1967).
SMITH, ROBERT L., University of Kansas, Lawrence, Kansas 66045.
SMITH, Dr. WILBUR S., 4500 Jackson Blvd., Columbia, S.C. 29209 (1968).
SMULLIN, LOUIS D., Massachusetts Institute of Technology, Cambridge, Mass. 02139 (1970).
SNITZER, ELIAS, United Technologies Research Center, (M.S. 92), East Hartford, Conn. 06108 (1979).
SNYDER, Rear Admiral J. EDWARD, Hoffman II, 200 Stovall St., Alexandria, Va. 22332 (1979).
SOLOMON, Dr. GEORGE E., TRW Inc., One Space Park, Redondo Beach, Calif. 90278 (1967).
SOZEN, METE AVNI, University of Illinois at Urbana-Champaign, 3112 Civil Engineering Bldg., Urbana, Ill. 61801 (1977).
SPAGHT, Dr. MONROE E., Royal Dutch Petroleum Co., Shell Centre, London, SE1 7NA, England (1969).
SPARKS, Dr. MORGAN, Sandia Laboratories, Albuquerque, N.M. 87115 (1973).
SPOELHOF, CHARLES P., Kodak Apparatus Division, Eastman Kodak Co., 901 Elmgrove Rd., Rochester, N.Y. 14650 (1981).

SQUIRE, ALEXANDER, Westinghouse Electric Corpn., P.O.B. 355, Pittsburgh, Pa. 15230 (1979).
SQUIRES, ARTHUR M., Virginia Polytechnic Institute and State University, Blacksburg, Va. 24061 (1977).
SQUIRES, LOMBARD, 939 Nelsons Walk, Naples, Fla. 33940 (1967).
STAEHLE, ROGER W., Ohio State University, 116 West 19th Ave., Columbus, Ohio 43210 (1978).
STARBIRD, Lt.-Gen. ALFRED D. (retd.), 7208 Regent Drive, Alexandria, Va. 22307 (1973).
STARR, Dr. CHAUNCEY, Electric Power Research Institute, 3412 Hillview Ave., Palo Alto, Calif. 94304 (1965).
STARR, EUGENE C., Bonneville Power Administration, P.O.B. 3621-E1C, Portland, Ore. 97208 (1977).
STASZESKY, FRANCIS M., Boston Edison Co., 800 Boylston St., Boston, Mass. 02199 (1979).
STEINBERG, MORRIS A., Lockheed Aircraft Corpn., P.O.B. 551, Burbank, Calif. 91520 (1977).
STEINER, JOHN E., The Boeing Co., P.O.B. 3707, MS 10-17, Seattle, Wash. 98124 (1978).
STEKLY, Z. J. JOHN, Magnetic Corpn. of America Inc., 179 Bear Hill, Waltham, Mass. 02154 (1981).
STERN, ARTHUR C., School of Public Health, University of North Carolina, Chapel Hill, N.C. 27514 (1976).
STERN, THEODORE, Westinghouse Electric Corpn., Gateway Center, Pittsburgh, Pa. 15222 (1979).
STERNBERG, Dr. ELI, California Institute of Technology, Pasadena, Calif. 91125.
STERNLICHT, BENO, Mechanical Technology Inc., 968 Albany Shaker Rd., Latham, N.Y. 12110 (1980).
STEVER, Dr. H. GUYFORD, 1528 33rd St., N.W., Washington, D.C. 20007 (1965).
STEWART, ROBERT E., Texas A. & M. University, College Station, Texas 77843 (1978).
STIBITZ, GEORGE R., Department of Physiology, Dartmouth Medical School, Hanover, N.H. 03755 (1981).
STONE, HENRY E., Nuclear Engineering Division, General Electric Co., 175 Curtner Ave., San Jose, Calif. 95125 (1981).
STOOKEY, STANLEY D., Corning Glass Works, Corning, N.Y. 14830 (1977).
STRAITON, ARCHIE W., University of Texas at Austin, Austin, Tex. 78712 (1976).
STRATTON, JAMES H., 3913 Watson Place, N.W., Washington, D.C. 20016 (1981).
‡STRATTON, Dr. JULIUS A., Massachusetts Institute of Technology, Cambridge, Mass. 02139 (1964).
‡SUITS, C. G., "Crosswinds", Pilot Knob, N.Y. 12844 (1964).
SUMMERFIELD, MARTIN, New York University, Barney Building, 5th Floor, 26-36 Stuyvesant St., New York, N.Y. 10003 (1979).
SUOMI, Dr. VERNER E., The University of Wisconsin, Madison, Wis. 53706 (1966).
SUTHERLAND, Dr. IVAN E., California Institute of Technology, 256-80, Pasadena, Calif. 91125 (1973).
SWABB, LAWRENCE E., Jr., Exxon Research & Engineering Co., P.O.B. 101, Florham Park, N.J. 07932 (1977).
SWEARINGEN, JOHN E., Jr., Standard Oil Co. (Indiana), 200 East Randolph Drive, Chicago, Ill. 60601 (1969).
SWEARINGEN, JUDSON S., Rotoflow Corpn., 2235 Carmelina Ave., Los Angeles, Calif. 90064 (1977).
SWENSON, GEORGE W., Jr., University of Illinois at Urbana-Champaign, Urbana, Ill. 61801 (1978).
SWERLING, PETER, 2811 Wilshire Blvd., Santa Monica, Calif. 90403 (1978).
SWIGER, WILLIAM F., Stone & Webster Engineering Corpn., Boston, Mass. 02107 (1980).
SYVERTSON, CLARENCE A., Ames Research Center, NASA, Moffett Field, Calif. 94035 (1981).
SZE, MORGAN C., Engineering Development Center, Lummus Company, 1515 Broad St., Bloomfield, N.J. 07003 (1976).
TANENBAUM, MORRIS, American Telephone and Telegraph Co., 295 North Maple Ave., Basking Ridge, N.J. 07920 (1972).
TATLOW, RICHARD H., III, 630 Third Avenue, New York, N.Y. 10017 (1967).
TAYLOR, CHARLES E., University of Illinois, Urbana, Ill. 61801 (1979).
TAYLOR, JOHN J., Westinghouse Electric Corpn., Pittsburgh, Pa. 15230 (1974).
TEAL, Dr. GORDON K., 5222 Park Lane, Dallas, Tex. 75220 (1969).
TEDESKO, Dr. ANTON, 26 Brookside Circle, Bronxville, N.Y. 10708 (1967).
TELLEP, DANIEL M., Lockheed Missiles and Space Co., Inc., Sunnyvale, Calif. 94086 (1979).
TENENBAUM, MICHAEL, Inland Steel Co., 30 West Monroe St., Chicago, Ill. 60603 (1974).
‡TERMAN, Dr. FREDERICK E., Stanford University, Stanford, Calif. 14305 (1964).

THIELE, ERNEST W., 1625 Hinman Ave., Evanston, Ill. 60201 (1980).
‡THOMAS, CHARLES A., 7701 Forsyth Blvd., St. Louis, Mo. 63105 (1964).
THOMAS, HAROLD A., Jr., Harvard University, 120 Pierce Hall, Cambridge, Mass. 02138 (1976).
THOMPSON, KEN L., Bell Laboratories, 600 Mountain Ave., MH 2C-423, Murray Hill, N.J. 07974 (1980).
THON, J. GEORGE, 465 Barbara Way, Hillsborough, Calif. 94010.
THRODAHL, MONTE C., Monsanto Co., 800 North Lindbergh Blvd., Mail Zone DID, St. Louis, Mo. 63166 (1980).
THÜRLIMANN, BRUNO, Pfannenstiel Strasse 56, 8132 Egg (ZH), Switzerland (1978).
TIEN, CHANG-LIN, Department of Mechanical Engineering, University of California, Berkeley, Calif. 94720 (1976).
TIEN, Dr. PING KING, Bell Laboratories, Holmdel, N.J. 07733.
TILLINGHAST, JOHN A., American Electric Power Service Corpn., 2 Broadway, New York, N.Y. 10004 (1974).
TIMMERHAUS, Dr. KLAUS D., University of Colorado, Boulder, Colo. 80302.
TODD, Dr. FREDERICK H., Sea Lodge, 10B Harbour Rd., Beadnell, Chathill, NE67 5BS, Northumberland, England (1965).
TOWNSEND, Dr. JOHN W., Jr., Fairchild Space & Electronics Co., 20301 Century Blvd., Germantown, Md. 20767 (1975).
TRIBUS, Dr. MYRON, M.I.T., Room 9-215, Cambridge, Mass. 02139 (1973).
TRUMP, JOHN G., M.I.T., High Voltage Research Laboratory, Bldg. N-10, Cambridge, Mass. 02139 (1977).
TRUXAL, Dr. JOHN G., State University of New York, Stony Brook, N.Y. 10017 (1965).
TULIN, MARSHALL P., Hydronautics, Inc., 7210 Pindell School Rd., Laurel, Md. 20810 (1979).
TURNER, Dr. HOWARD S., Turner Construction Co., 150 East 42nd St., New York, N.Y. 10017 (1973).
VANDERSLICE, THOMAS A., General Telephone and Electronics, 1 Stamford Forum, Stamford, Conn. 06904 (1980).
VAN DER ZIEL, ALDERT, 139 Electrical Engineering Building, University of Minnesota, 123 Church St., Minneapolis, Minn. 55455 (1978).
VAN DYKE, MILTON D., Stanford University, Durand Building, Stanford, Calif. 94305 (1976).
VANONI, VITO, California Institute of Technology, Pasadena, Calif. 91125 (1977).
VAN UITERT, LE GRAND, Bell Laboratories, 600 Mountain Avenue, Murray Hill, N.J. 07974 (1981).
VAN VALKENBURG, Dr. MAC E., University of Illinois, Urbana, Ill. 61801 (1973).
VASSELL, GREGORY S., American Electric Power Service Corpn., 2 Broadway, New York, N.Y. 10004 (1980).
VELETSOS, ANESTIS S., Rice University, Houston, Tex. 77001 (1979).
VERSNYDER, FRANCIS L., Materials Technology Department, United Technologies Research Center, East Hartford, Conn. 06101 (1981).
VIEST, IVAN, Bethlehem Steel Corpn., GSO, Bethlehem, Pa. 18016 (1978).
VILLARD, Dr. OSWALD G., Jr., Stanford University, Menlo Park, Calif. 94305 (1966).
VITERBI, ANDREW J., Linkabit Corpn., 10453 Roselle St., San Diego, Calif. 92121 (1978).
VOGEL, HERBERT D., 601-2 Washington Bldg., Washington, D.C. 20005 (1977).
VOLLUM, C. HOWARD, Tektronix, Inc., P.O.B. 500, Beaverton, Ore. 97077 (1977).
VON GIERKE, HENNING E., Aerospace Medical Research Laboratory/BB, Wright Patterson Air Force Base, Ohio 45433 (1976).
VON HIPPEL, ARTHUR R., M.I.T., Room 38-377, Cambridge, Mass. 02139 (1977).
VON OHAIN, HANS J. P., 5598 Folkestone Drive, Dayton, Ohio 45459 (1980).

WACHTMAN, JOHN B., Jr., Inorganic Materials Division, National Bureau of Standards, U.S. Department of Commerce, Washington, D.C. 20234 (1976).
WADSWORTH, MILTON E., University of Utah, Room 209, W.C. Browning Building, Salt Lake City, Utah 84112 (1979).
WAGNER, AUBREY J., 201 Whittington Drive, Knoxville, Tenn. 37919 (1973).
WAGNER, HARVEY A., 1300 Washington Blvd. Bldg., Detroit, Mich. 48226 (1970).
WAIT, JAMES R., National Oceanic and Atmospheric Administration, Boulder, Colo. 80023 (1977).
‡WALKER, Dr. ERIC A., Pennsylvania State University, 222 Hammond Bldg., University Park, Pa. 16802 (1964).
WATKINS, Dr. DEAN A., 3333 Hillview Ave., Palo Alto, Calif. 94304 (1968).

WAYNICK, Dr. ARTHUR H., Pennsylvania State University, University Park, Pa. 16802.
‡WEBER, Dr. ERNST, P.O.B. 1619, Tryon, N.C. 28782 (1964).
WEBER, EUGENE W., 2700 Virginia Ave., N.W., Apartment 601, Washington, D.C. 20037 (1979).
WEBSTER, WILLIAM M., RCA Laboratories, David Sarnoff Research Centre, Princeton, N.J. 08540 (1976).
WEEKS, WILFORD F., U.S. Army Cold Regions Research and Engineering Laboratory, Hanover, N.H. 03755 (1979).
WEERTMAN, JOHANNES, The Technological Institute, Northwestern University, Evanston, Ill. 60201 (1976).
WEHAUSEN, JOHN V., Dept. of Naval Architecture, Univ. of California, Berkeley, Calif. 94720 (1980).
WEI, JAMES, Chemical Engineering Dept., M.I.T., Cambridge, Mass. 02139 (1978).
WEINBERG, Dr. ALVIN M., P.O.B. 117, Oak Ridge, Tenn. 37830.
WEISZ, PAUL B., Mobil Research and Development Corpn., P.O.B. 1025, Princeton, N.J. 08540 (1977).
WELCH, JASPER A., National Security Council, Washington, D.C. 20506 (1980).
WELCH, LLOYD .R., University of Southern California, 502 Powell Hall, Los Angeles, Calif. 90007 (1979).
WELLS, Dr. EDWARD C., P.O.B. 3707, Seattle, Wash. 98124 (1967).
WENK, Dr. EDWARD, Jr., University of Washington, Seattle, Wash. 98195 (1969).
WENTORF, ROBERT H., Jr., General Electric Research and Development Center (K-1), P.O.B. 8, Schenectady, N.Y. 12345 (1979).
WENZEL, JAMES G., Lockheed Missiles and Space Co. Inc., P.O.B. 504, Organization 57-01-Building 150, Sunnyvale, Calif. 94088.
WERNICK, JACK H., Bell Telephone Laboratories, 600 Mountain Ave., Murray Hill, N.J. 07974 (1979).
WERTHEIM, Rear-Adm. ROBERT H., U.S. Dept. of the Navy, Washington, D.C. 20376 (1977).
WESSENAUER, G. O., 2931 Nurick Drive, Chattanooga, Tenn. 37415 (1968).
WEST, JOHN M., Combustion Engineering, Inc., 1000 Prospect Hill Rd., Windsor, Conn. 06095 (1979).
WESTON, ROY F., Roy F. Weston Inc., Weston Way, West Chester, Pa. 19280 (1976).
WESTWATER, JAMES W., University of Illinois, Urbana, Ill. 61801 (1974).
WESTWOOD, ALBERT R. C., Martin Marietta Laboratories, 1450 South Rolling Rd., Baltimore, Md. 21227 (1980).
WHEATON, ELMER P., 127 Solana Rd., Portola Valley, Calif. 94205 (1967).
WHEELON, ALBERT D., Hughes Aircraft Co., El Segundo, Calif. 90245 (1970).
WHINNERY, Dr. JOHN R., University of California, Berkeley, Calif. 94720 (1965).
WHITBY, KENNETH T., University of Minnesota, Minneapolis, Minn. 55455 (1978).
WHITCOMB, RICHARD T., Transonic Aerodynamics Branch, Langley Research Center, NASA, Hampton, Va. 23665 (1976).
WHITE, Dr. DAVID C., M.I.T., Room E40-131, Cambridge, Mass 02139.
WHITE, Dr. ROBERT M., National Research Council, 2101 Constitution Ave., N.W., Washington, D.C. 20418 (1968).
WHITMAN, Dr. ROBERT V., M.I.T., Room 1-382, Cambridge, Mass. 02139.
WIDMER, ROBERT H., General Dynamic Corpn., Pierre Laclede Center, St. Louis, Mo. 63105 (1977).
WIEGEL, ROBERT L., University of California, 412 O'Brien Hall, Berkeley, Calif. 94720.
WIESNER, Dr. JEROME B., Massachusetts Institute of Technology, Cambridge, Mass. 02139 (1966).
WILBUR, LYMAN D., 4502 Hillcrest Drive, Boise, Ida. 83705 (1967).
WILKE, Dr. CHARLES R., University of California, Berkeley, Calif. 94720.
WILKINS, J. ERNEST, Jr., EG & G Idaho Inc., P.O.B. 1625, Idaho Falls, Idaho 83401 (1976).
WILLENBROCK, Dr. F. KARL, Southern Methodist University, Dallas, Tex. 75725.
WILSON, GERALD L., M.I.T., 77 Massachusetts Ave., Room 10-171, Cambridge, Mass. 02139 (1980).
WILSON, STANLEY D., 1105 North 38th St., Seattle, Wash. 98103 (1967).
WILSON, THORNTON A., Boeing Co., P.O.B. 3707, Seattle, Wash. 98124 (1974).
WINTER, GEORGE, Cornell University, Ithaca, N.Y. 14850 (1097).
WITHINGTON, HOLDEN W., Boeing Commercial Airplane Co., P.O.B. 3707, M.S. 77-97, Seattle, Wash. 98124 (1980).

WOLFE, BERTRAM, General Electric Co., 175 Curtner Ave., M/C 845, San Jose, Calif. 95125 (1980).
WOLL, EDWARD, Aircraft Engine Business Group, General Electric Co., 1000 Western Ave., Lynn, Mass. 01910 (1977).
WOLMAN, Dr. ABEL, The Johns Hopkins University, Baltimore, Md. 21218 (1965).
WOOD, CARLOS C., 686 Lockford St., Lodi, Calif. 95240 (1967).
WOODSON, Dr. HERBERT H., University of Texas at Austin, Engineering Science Building 236, Austin, Tex. 78712.
WOOLDRIDGE, DEAN E., 4545 Via Esperanza, Santa Barbara, Calif. 93110 (1977).
YARDLEY, JOHN F., NASA, Washington, D.C. 20546 (1977).
YARIV, AMMON, California Institute of Technology, Mail Stop 116-81, Pasadena, Calif. 91125 (1976).
YEE, ALFRED A., Alfred A. Yee and Associates, Inc., Suite 810, 1441 Jaouikabu Boulevard, Honolulu, Hawaii 96814 (1976).
YIH, CHIA-SHUN, Prof. of Fluid Mechanics, Univ. of Michigan, Ann Arbor, Mich. 48109 (1980).
YOUNG, LAURENCE R., M.I.T., Room 37-207, Cambridge, Mass. 02139 (1980).
ZADEH, Dr. LOTFI A., University of California, Berkeley, Calif. 94720 (1973).
ZEBROSKI, EDWIN L., Nuclear Safety Analysis Center, Electric Power Research Institute, 3412 Hillview Ave., Palo Alto, Calif. 94303 (1981).
ZINN, WALTER H., 2940 Bay Meadow Court, Clearwater, Fla. 33519 (1974).
ZWORYKIN, Dr. VLADIMIR K., David Sarnoff Research Center, Princeton, N.J. 08540 (1965).

‡ Founding member.

## INSTITUTE OF MEDICINE

Founded 1970

*President:* FREDERICK C. ROBBINS.

### MEMBERS:

ABDELLAH, FAYE G.
ABRAMS, HERBERT L.
AFFELDT, JOHN E.
AIKEN, LINDA H.
ALBERTY, R. A.
ALPERT, JOEL J.
ALTMAN, STUART H.
ANDREOLI, KATHLEEN G.
ANLYAN, W. G.
ARMISTEAD, W. W.
ARROW, KENNETH J.
ASPER, SAMUEL P.
ATKINSON, RICHARD C.
AUSTEN, W. GERALD
AYDELOTTE, MYRTLE K.
AZARNOFF, DANIEL L.
BAKER, WILLIAM O.
BARCHAS, JACK D.
BARGER, A. CLIFFORD
BARONDESS, JEREMIAH A.
BATEMAN, MILDRED M.
BECK, JOHN C.
BENNETT, IVAN L., Jr.
BERG, PAUL
BERGSTRÖM, SUNE
BERLINER, ROBERT W.
BERNE, ROBERT M.
BEVAN, WILLIAM
BLANPAIN, JAN E. G.
BLENDON, ROBERT J.
BLOUT, ELKAN R.
BOK, DEREK C.
BRAUNWALD, EUGENE
BRESLOW, LESTER
BRICKER, NEAL S.
BRIM, ORVILLE G.
BRISTOW, LONNIE R.
BRODIE, H. KEITH H.
BRYANT, JOHN H.
BRYANT, THOMAS E.
BULGER, ROGER J.
BURNS, JOHN J.
BURT, ROBERT A.
BURWELL, E. L.
BUSSE, EWALD W.
BUSSMAN, JOHN W.
BUTLER, LEWIS H.
BUTLER, ROBERT N.
CALABRESI, GUIDO
CALHOUN, NOAH R.
CALLAHAN, DANIEL
CAPRON, ALEXANDER M.
CAREY, WILLIAM D.
CHALMERS, THOMAS C.
CHASE, ROBERT A.
CHILDS, BARTON
CHOW, RITA K.
CHRISTMAN, LUTHER
CLARKSON, THOMAS W.
CLEMENTE, CARMINE D.
CLEVER, LINDA H.
CLIFTON, JAMES A.
CLUFF, LEIGHTON E.
COBB, JEWEL P.
COBBS, PRICE M.
COHEN, D. WALTER
COHEN, SEYMOUR S.
COLES, ANNA L. B.
COLES, ROBERT
COOKE, ROBERT E.
COOPER, JOHN A. D.
COOPER, THEODORE
COWAN, W. MAXWELL
COX, JEROME R., Jr.
CRAVALHO, ERNEST G.
CRAWSHAW, RALPH
CROMWELL, FLORENCE S.
CRONKHITE, LEONARD W., Jr.
CROSS, HAROLD D.
CUMMINGS, MARTIN M.
DADDARIO, EMILIO
DAINES, WILLIAM P.
DANFORTH, WILLIAM H.
DAVIS, EDGAR G.
DAVIS, KAREN
DENENBERG, HERBERT S.
DENNY, FLOYD W.
DERZON, ROBERT A.
DETWEILER, DAVID K.
DICKSON, JAMES F., III
DIXON, ANDREW D.
DJERASSI, CARL
DORFMAN, ALBERT
DOWDA, F. WILLIAM
DUMMETT, CLIFTON O.
DUSTAN, HARRIET P.
DUVAL, MERLIN K., Jr.
EBERT, JAMES D.
EDWARDS, ADRIAN L.
EGDAHL, RICHARD H.
EISDORFER, CARL
EISEN, HERMAN N.
EISENBERG, LEON
ELGEE, NEIL G.
ELINSON, JACK
ELLWOOD, PAUL M., Jr.
ENGLISH, JOSEPH
ENTHOVEN, ALAIN
ESTABROOK, RONALD W.
ESTES, E. HARVEY, Jr.
EVANS, EDWIN C.
EVANS, JOHN R.
FAGIN, CLAIRE M.
FARBER, SAUL J.
FARQUHAR, JOHN W.
FEDERMAN, DANIEL D.
FEIN, RASHI
FEINSTEIN, ALVAN R.
FELCH, WILLIAM C.
FELDMAN, JACOB J.
FELDSTEIN, MARTIN S.
FELTS, WILLIAM R.
FISCHER, A. ALAN
FLAGLE, CHARLES D.
FLEMING, SCOTT
FOEGE, WILLIAM H.
FORD, LORETTA C.
FORDHAM, CHRISTOPHER C., III
FOSTER, HENRY W., Jr.
FOX, MAURICE S.
FOX, RENEE C.
FRAZIER, HOWARD S.
FREDRICKSON, DONALD S.
FREEDMAN, DANIEL X.
FREI, EMIL, III
FREIDSON, ELIOT
FRIED, CHARLES
FUCHS, VICTOR R.
GAMBLE, JOHN R.
GILBERT, FRED I.
GINSBERG, HAROLD S.
GLASER, ROBERT J.
GLASSER, MELVIN A.
GOOD, ROBERT A.
GOTTSCHALK, CARL W.
GOYAN, JERE E.
GRAYSTON, J. THOMAS
GREENBERG, BERNARD
GREENE, JOHN C.
GREENLICK, MERWYN
GROBE, JAMES I.
GROBSTEIN, CLIFFORD
GRONVALL, JOHN A.
GROSS, RUTH T.
GUNTER, LAURIE M.
GUZE, SAMUEL B.
HAGGERTY, ROBERT J.
HALPERN, CHARLES R.
HAMBURG, BEATRIX A. M.
HAMBURG, DAVID A.
HANFT, RUTH S.
HARRIS, JEAN L.
HAUGHTON, JAMES G.
HAWTHORNE, EDWARD
HAYES, GEORGE J.
HAYNES, M. ALFRED
HAYWOOD, H. CARL
HENDERSON, DONALD A.
HENDERSON, MAUREEN
HERSHEY, NATHAN
HESS, ARTHUR E.
HEYSSEL, ROBERT
HIATT, HOWARD H.
HILDRETH, EUGENE A.
HILL, GENEVIEVE T.
HILL, ROBERT L.
HIRSCH, JAMES G.
HOBBS, NICHOLAS
HOGNESS, JOHN R.
HOLLOMAN, JOHN L. S.
HUGHES, JAMES P.
HUTT, PETER BARTON
IGLEHART, JOHN K.
ISSELBACHER, KURT J.
JACKSON, CARMAULT B., Jr.
JACOX, ADA K.
JOHNSON, JEAN E.
JOHNSON, MARIE-LOUISE
JONES, STANLEY B.
JONSEN, ALBERT R.
KARL, MICHAEL M.
KATZ, JAY
KATZ, MICHAEL
KATZ, SIDNEY
KELLY, JAMES F.
KEMPE, C. HENRY
KENNEDY, DONALD
KERR, I. LAWRENCE
KETY, SEYMOUR S.
KIBRICK, ANNE
KINNARD, WILLIAM J., Jr.
KIPNIS, DAVID M.
KIRKLAND, LANE
KITTREDGE, JOHN K.
KLARMAN, HERBERT E.
KLERMAN, GERALD L.
KORSCH, BARBARA M.
KOUNTZ, SAMUEL L.
KRAUSE, RICHARD M.
KREVANS, JULIUS R.
LAMBERTSEN, ELEANOR C.
LAWRENCE, ROBERT S.
LAWTON, BEN R.
LEAF, ALEXANDER
LEDERBERG, JOSHUA
LEE, PHILIP R.
LEFFALL, LASALLE D., Jr.
LEHNINGER, ALBERT L.
LEVINE, SOL
LEVINTHAL, CYRUS
LEVIT, EDITH J.
LEVY, GERHARD
LEVY, ROBERT I.
LEWIS, CHARLES E.
LEWIS, IRVING J.
LINDHEIM, ROSLYN
LINDZEY, GARDNER
LOEB, VIRGIL, Jr.
LONDON, IRVING M.
LONG, ROBERT C.
LOWENSTEIN, LEAH M.
LUBIC, RUTH WATSON
LYTHCOTT, GEORGE
MACCOBY, ELEANOR E.
MACMAHON, BRIAN
MAGASANIK, BORIS
MAHONEY, MARGARET E.
MANLEY, AUDREY FORBES
MANN, MARION
MANN, ROBERT W.
MARKERT, CLEMENT L.
MARKS, PAUL A.
MARSTON, ROBERT Q.
MARTINSON, IDA M. SATHER
MAUKSCH, INGEBORG G.
MCATEE, PATRICIA A.
MCCALLUM, CHARLES A.
MCLACHLAN, GORDON
MCMAHON, JOHN A.
MCNERNEY, WALTER J.
MECHANIC, DAVID
MEDALIE, JACK H.
MELLINKOFF, SHERMAN M.
MELMON, KENNETH L.
MENNINGER, W. WALTER
MERIGAN, THOMAS C.
MERRILL, RICHARD A.
MICHAEL, MAX, Jr.
MILLER, MORTON D.
MORRIS, ALVIN L.
MORRISON, MILNOR B.
MOSER, ROBERT H.

## UNITED STATES OF AMERICA

**Members**—*Continued*

Moses, Lincoln E.
Mosteller, C. Frederick
Motulsky, Arno G.
Murray, Robert F.
Neel, James V.
Nelson, Alan
Newhouse, Joseph P.
Newman, Howard N.
Old, Lloyd J.
Omenn, Gilbert S.
Orloff, Jack
Pardee, Arthur B.
Pellegrino, Edmund D.
Perkoff, Gerald T.
Perrin, Edward B.
Perry, J. Warren
Petersdorf, Robert G.
Piel, Gerard
Pierce, Chester M.
Platt, Kenneth A.
Price, James G.
Prout, Curtis
Puck, Theodore T.
Rabkin, Mitchell T.
Rall, David P.
Ranney, Helen M.
Reinhardt, Uwe E.
Reitemeier, Richard J.
Relman, Arnold S.
Reswick, James B.
Rice, Dorothy P.
Rich, Clayton
Richmond, Julius
Riecken, Henry W.
Robbins, Frederick C.
Roberts, Doris E.
Robins, Lee N.
Roemer, Milton I.
Rogers, David E.
Rogers, Paul G.
Rosenkrantz, Barbara G.
Rosenthal, Gerald D.
Ross, Richard S.
Roy, William R.
Rubenstein, Edward
Ryan, Kenneth J.
Sabiston, David C., Jr.
Sanders, Charles A.
Sanford, Jay P.
Sarett, Lewis H.
Schelling, Thomas C.
Schoen, Max H.
Schorr, Lisbeth Bamberger
Schwartz, William B.
Scitovsky, Anne A.
Scott, W. Richard
Scribner, Belding H.
Seegmiller, J. Edwin
Seldin, Donald W.
Selikoff, Irving J.
Shannon, Iris R.
Sheldon, Eleanor B.
Sherman, John F.
Shinefield, Henry R.
Shires, G. Tom
Shirley, Aaron

Shreffler, Donald C.
Silver, Henry K.
Singer, Maxine F.
Sinkford, Jeanne
Sinsheimer, Robert L.
Smith, Richard A.
Solnit, Albert J.
Solomon, David H.
Spellman, Mitchell
Spencer, William A.
Spivak, Jonathan M.
Sprague, Charles C.
Starfield, Barbara
Stark, Nathan J.
Stevens, Rosemary
Straus, Robert
Strominger, Jack L.
Sullivan, Louis W.
Swanson, August G.
Swazey, Judith P.
Talley, Robert Boyd
Talmage, David W.
Tarlov, Alvin R.
Taylor, Carl E.
Terenzio, Joseph V.
Thier, Samuel O.
Thomas, Andrew L.
Thompson, Alvin J.
Tornyay, Rheba de
Tosteson, Daniel
Turner, John B.
Tyroler, H. A.
Upton, Arthur C.
Vagelos, P. Roy
Van Citters, Robert L.
Vohs, James A.
Wald, Patricia M.
Ward, L. Emmerson
Warren, James V.
Warren, Kenneth S.
Watson, C. Gordon
Watts, Charles D.
Watts, Malcolm S. M.
Weinstein, I. Bernard
Weinstein, Irwin M.
Weisbrod, Burton A.
Weller, Thomas H.
White, Jack E.
White, Kerr L.
Wilbur, Richard S.
Wildgen, J. Jerome
Williams, Bryan
Williams, Carroll M.
Williams, T. Franklin
Wilson, Marjorie P.
Wilson, Ruby L.
Wise, Harold
Woods, Geraldine P.
Wyngaarden, James B.
Yancey, Asa G.
Yarmolinsky, Adam
Yerby, Alonzo S.
Young, Frank E.
Zaffaroni, Alejandro
Zuidema, George D.

Senior Members:

Abelson, Philip R.
Ahrens, E. H., Jr.
Axelrod, Julius
Ball, Robert M.
Barnes, Allan C.
Baumgartner, Leona
Bazelon, David
Bearn, Alexander G.
Beeson, Paul B.
Bloch, Konrad E.
Branscomb, Lewis M.
Branson, Herman R.
Brinkhous, Kenneth M.

Brodie, Bernard B.
Brooks, Harvey
Burket, George E., Jr.
Chapman, Carleton B.
Cherkasky, Martin
Child, Charles G.
Clausen, John A.
Cohen, Wilbur J.
Collen, Morris F.
Comroe, Julius H., Jr.
Conn, Jerome W.
Cope, Oliver
Crow, James F.

Daniels, Arlene K.
Davis, Bernard D.
Densen, Paul M.
Deuschle, Kurt W.
Dole, Vincent P.
Donabedian, Avedis
Dunlop, John T.
Dunning, James M.
Ebert, Robert H.
Elam, Lloyd C.
Ellis, Effie O.
Freund, Paul A.
Galagan, Donald J.
Garwin, Richard L.
Gell-Mann, Murray
Ginzberg, Eli
Giorgi, Elsie A.
Harrington, Donald C.
Haviland, James W.
Hillenbrand, Harold
Ingram, Alvin J.
Jacobson, Leon O.
Kaplan, Henry S.
Keene, Clifford H.
Kirklin, John W.
Kunkel, Henry G.
Lasagna, Louis
Leone, Lucile P.
Lilienfeld, Abraham
Luria, S. E.
McCarty, Maclyn
McDermott, Walsh
Meister, Alton
Merton, Robert K.
Meselson, Matthew S.
Millis, John S.
Mills, George H.
Murphy, Franklin D.
Myers, Jack D.

Nabrit, Samuel N.
Nelson, Norton
Nelson, Russell A.
Newton, Quigg
Nirenberg, Marshall
Odegaard, Charles E.
Page, Irvine H.
Pake, George E.
Palade, George E.
Pettengill, Daniel W.
Piore, Nora
Price, Don K.
Rahn, Hermann
Rammelkamp, Charles H.
Ramsey, Paul
Redlich, F. C.
Riley, Matilda W.
Rosenblith, Walter A.
Rushmer, Robert F.
Saward, Ernest
Schlotfeldt, Rozella M.
Schultze, Charles L.
Scrimshaw, Nevin S.
Shanas, Ethel
Shannon, James A.
Shapiro, Sam
Sheps, Cecil G.
Smith, Lloyd H., Jr.
Sognnaes, Reidar F.
Somers, Anne R.
Somers, Herman M.
Stead, Eugene A., Jr.
Tenney, S. Marsh
Thomas, Lewis
Volker, Joseph F.
Ward, Paul D.
Wilbur, Dwight Locke
Zamecnik, Paul C.

## NATIONAL RESEARCH COUNCIL
Founded 1916.

The Council works through commissions and assemblies, each with its special boards and committees of scientific and technical experts.

*Assembly of Behavioral and Social Sciences:* J. Wolpert.

*Assembly of Engineering:* H. G. Stever.

*Assembly of Life Sciences:* F. W. Putnam.

  *Division of Biological Sciences:* A. Kelman.

  *Division of Medical Sciences:* J. G. Hirsch.

*Assembly of Mathematical and Physical Sciences:* H. Friedman.

  *Office of Chemistry and Chemical Technology:* T. L. Cairns.

  *Office of Earth Sciences:* J. C. Crowell.

  *Office of Mathematical Sciences:* W. Browder.

  *Office of Physical Sciences:* W. A. Fowler.

*Commission on Human Resources:* H. Shull.

*Commission on International Relations:* T. F. Malone.

*Commission on Natural Resources:* R. M. White.

*Commission on Sociotechnical Systems:* E. W. Montroll.

## NATIONAL ACADEMY OF EDUCATION
11 DUPONT CIRCLE, SUITE 130,
WASHINGTON, D.C. 20036

Founded 1965.

The National Academy of Education is organized by distinguished scholars "to create a forum which will set the highest standards for educational inquiry and discussion." It parallels in general purposes, programmes and prestige the National Academy of Sciences. It operates with private and foundation funds. A majority of the members and foreign associates are outstanding university scholars from the behavioural sciences, the humanities and education, who have made notable contributions to educational scholarship. The members-at-large are distinguished practitioners. The principal function is to stimulate fruitful lines of research. Activities have included task force studies leading to advisory reports and publications, programmes of support to identify and encourage promising scholars of education at the early post-doctoral stage, and efforts to raise the level of public discourse concerning key educational issues. The Academy meets twice a year.

*President:* STEPHEN K. BAILEY.
*Vice-President:* JOHN B. CARROLL.
*Executive Director:* JUDITH B. MCGLAUGHLIN.
*Secretary-Treasurer:* MARTIN TROW.

### Section I: The History & Philosophy of Education

LAWRENCE A. CREMIN (Chairman)
BERNARD BAILYN
PATRICIA A. GRAHAM
THOMAS F. GREEN
OSCAR HANDLIN
DIANE RAVITCH
FREDERICK RUDOLPH
ISRAEL SCHEFFLER
DAVID TYACK

### Section II: The Politics, Economics, Sociology & Anthropology of Education

NATHAN GLAZER (Chairman)
STEPHEN K. BAILEY
GARY S. BECKER
CHARLES E. BIDWELL
BURTON R. CLARK
JAMES S. COLEMAN
LAMBROS COMITAS
ROBERT LEVINE
SEYMOUR MARTIN LIPSET
ROBERT K. MERTON
JACOB MINCER
DAVID RIESMAN
ALICE M. RIVLIN
THOMAS SOWELL
MARTIN TROW

### Section III: The Psychology of Education

ROBERT M. GAGNÉ (Chairman)
RICHARD C. ANDERSON
RICHARD C. ATKINSON
BENJAMIN S. BLOOM
URIE BRONFENBRENNER
JEROME S. BRUNER
JOHN B. CARROLL
JEANNE S. CHALL
LEE J. CRONBACH
ELEANOR J. GIBSON
ROBERT GLASER
WALLACE E. LAMBERT
WILBERT J. MCKEACHIE
JULIAN C. STANLEY, Jr.
ROBERT L. THORNDIKE

### Section IV: The Study of Educational Practice

H. THOMAS JAMES (Chairman)
KENNETH B. CLARK
K. PATRICIA CROSS
NATHANIEL L. GAGE
J. W. GETZELS
JOHN I. GOODLAD
EDMUND W. GORDON
ELIZABETH P. HAGEN
CYRIL O. HOULE
PHILIP W. JACKSON
MICHAEL KIRST
HOPE J. LEICHTER
JAMES G. MARCH
LEE S. SHULMAN
PATRICK SUPPES

### Members-at-Large

JOHN H. FISCHER
JOHN W. GARDNER
ALEXANDER HEARD
THEODORE M. HESBURGH
ROGER W. HEYNS
FRANCIS KEPPEL
CLARK KERR
MARTIN MEYERSON
EWALD B. NYQUIST
JAMES A. PERKINS
WILBUR SCHRAMM
CLIFTON R. WHARTON, Jr.
WILLARD WIRTZ

### Members Emeriti

BRUNO BETTELHEIM
HOWARD R. BOWEN
GUY T. BUSWELL
ROALD F. CAMPBELL
FRANCIS S. CHASE
JOHN L. CHILDS
ERIK H. ERIKSON
JOHN C. FLANAGAN
WILLIAM K. FRANKENA
NELSON GOODMAN
ROBERT J. HAVIGHURST
ERNEST R. HILGARD
SIDNEY HOOK
EVERETT C. HUGHES
FRITZ MACHLUP
T. R. MCCONNELL
WILBUR SCHRAMM
T. W. SCHULTZ
JOSEPH J. SCHWAB
RALPH W. TYLER
HELEN M. WALKER

### Foreign Associates

JOSEPH BEN-DAVID
A. H. HALSEY
TORSTEN HUSÉN
BÄRBEL INHELDER
MICHIO NAGAI
RICHARD S. PETERS
NATHAN ROTENSTREICH
JAN SZCZEPAŃSKI

### Foreign Associates Emeriti

ERIC ASHBY
ANNA FREUD
Lord ROBBINS
PHILIPS E. VERNON

**Academy of Natural Sciences of Philadelphia, The:** 19th and the Parkway, Philadelphia, Pa. 19103; f. 1812; natural history museum; research in systematics and evolutionary biology, ecology, limnology and geology; large study collections of plants, animals and fossils of world-wide scope; teaching at all levels; 3,300 mems.; 185,000-volume research library; Chair. of Board HOWARD P. BROKAW; Librarian SYLVA S. BAKER; publs. *Proceedings†, Notulae Naturae†, Monographs†, Frontiers†*, special publications.

**American Academy and Institute of Arts and Letters:** 633 West 155th St., New York, N.Y. 10032; f. 1898; 250 mems.; Pres. ARTHUR M. SCHLESINGER, Jr.; Sec. WILLIAM MEREDITH.

**American Academy of Arts and Sciences:** Norton's Woods, 136 Irving St., Cambridge, Mass. 02138; f. 1780; 2,600 mems.; Pres. MILTON KATZ; Sec. NATHAN GLAZER; Exec. Officer JOHN VOSS; publs. *Daedalus* (quarterly), *Bulletin* (monthly), *Records* (annually).

**California Academy of Sciences:** Golden Gate Park, San Francisco, Calif. 94118; f. 1853 for the advancement of natural sciences through public education and research, incorporated under the laws of the State of California 1871; 14,000 mems. incl. 300 Fellows; maintains a public museum of natural history, the Steinhart Aquarium, the Simpson African Hall, the Morrison Planetarium (Dir. LEE SIMON), a scientific library of 85,000 vols. (Librarian RAY BRIAN), and research departments with large scientific collections; Departments: Aquatic Biology (Dir. JOHN E. MCCOSKER), Botany (Curator DENNIS BREEDLOVE), Entomology (Curator DAVID KAVANAGH), Exhibits (Chair. JOHN E. MCCOSKER (acting), Herpetology (Curator ALAN LEVITON), Invertebrate Zoology (Curator WELTON LEE), Ornithology and Mammalogy (Curator LUIS BAPTISTA), Geology (Curator PETER RODDA); Dir. of Research WILLIAM N. ESCHMEYER; Pres. RICHARD JAHNS; Admin. Dir. GEORGE LINDSAY; publs. *Proceedings†, Newsletter* (monthly), *Pacific Discovery* (every 2 months), *Annual Report†, Occasional Papers†*.

**Chicago Academy of Sciences:** 2001 North Clark St., Chicago, Ill. 60614; f. 1857; 950 mems.; exhibits on the natural history of the Chicago region; study collections of many areas in North America; teaching at college level; a technical scientific library; Pres. JEFFREY R. SHORT, Jr.; Sec. JACK COWEN, M.D.; Dir. W. J. BEECHER, PH.D.; publs. *Natural History Miscellanea†, Museum Activities†, Bulletin.*

**Connecticut Academy of Arts and Sciences:** Drawer 93A, Yale Station, New Haven, Conn. 06520; f. 1799; 300 mems.; library merged with Yale University Library; Pres. FRED C. ROBINSON; Sec. DOROTHEA RUDNICK; publs. *Transactions†, Memoirs†* (both irregular).

**Maryland Academy of Sciences:** 601 Light St., Baltimore, Md.; f. 1797, as an educational and scientific institution, and for the diffusion and explanation of scientific information to the public; controls Maryland Science Center; 3,200 mems.; Chair. HOWARD I. SCAGGS; Pres. Dr. OWEN M. PHILLIPS; Exec. Dir. JAMES R. BACKSTROM; publ. *Monthly Newsletter.*

**New York Academy of Sciences:** 2 East 63rd St., New York, N.Y. 10021; f. 1817; 27,000 mems.; Pres. JOEL L. LEBOWITZ; Vice-Pres. CRAIG D. BURRELL, DOROTHY CUNNINGHAM, MERRIL EISENBUD, HEINZ R. PAGELS, LUCIE WOOD SAUNDERS; Exec. Dir. SIDNEY BOROWITZ; Section Chairs. VERA D. RUBIN, RALPH SOLECKI (Anthropology), NATHAN M. REISS (Atmospheric Sciences), BARBARA PETRACK (Biochemistry),

JAMES P. QUIGLEY (Biological Sciences), BABETTE B. WEKSLER (Biomedical Sciences), FRANK LANDSBERGER (Biophysics), R. J. H. VOORHOEVE (Catalysis), VASSIL ST. GEORGIEV (Chemical Sciences), GEORGE GUGEL (Computer and Information Sciences), EDWARD COHEN (Engineering), NORBERT ROBERTS (Environmental Sciences), ALLISON PALMER (Geological Sciences), VIRGINIA SEXTON (History, Philosophy and Ethical Issues of Science and Technology), MYRON YOUDIN (Instrumentation), VIRGINIA TELLER (Linguistics), LOUIS V. QUINTAS (Mathematics), MARVIN WEINSTEIN (Microbiology), MARC S. LAZARUS (Organometallic Chemistry), VITTORIO CANUTO (Physical Sciences), S. W. SHALABY (Polymer Science), HELMUT E. ADLER, CYNTHIA P. DEUTSCH (Psychology), BIANCA L. ROSENBERG (Science and Public Policy), WILLARD J. JACOBSON (Science Education); publs. *Annals, The Sciences*.

**Ohio Academy of Science:** 445 King Ave., Columbus, Ohio 43201; f. 1891; 2,000 mems.; Pres. JOHN L. CRITES; Exec. Officer LYNN EDWARD ELFNER; publs. *The Ohio Journal of Science: Ohio Academy of Science News, Ohio's Natural Heritage*.

**Southern California Academy of Sciences:** c/o Natural History Museum of Los Angeles County, 900 Exposition Blvd., Los Angeles, Calif. 90007; f. 1891; 450 mems.; library of 6,000 vols.; Pres. Dr. F. G. HOCHBERG; Sec. Dr. CAMM C. SWIFT; publs. *Bulletin* (3 issues annually), *Memoirs* (irregularly).

For medical academies, *see under* Medicine.

# LEARNED SOCIETIES

## GENERAL

**American Council of Learned Societies:** 800 Third Ave., New York, N.Y. 110022; f. 1919; 43 societies concerned with the humanities and the humanistic aspects of the social sciences; Pres. Dr. R. M. LUMIANSKY; publs. *Annual Report, Newsletter* (quarterly).

## AMERICAN PHILOSOPHICAL SOCIETY
(Held at Philadelphia for Promoting Useful Knowledge)
104 AND 105 SOUTH FIFTH ST.,
PHILADELPHIA, PA. 19106
Founded 1743.

The American Philosophical Society, the oldest learned society in the United States, was founded by Benjamin Franklin. Members (500 U.S. citizens and 100 foreign) are elected by the Society on the basis of distinction in any field of learning. There are five classes of membership: exact sciences, natural sciences, social sciences, humanities and members at large. The Society meets twice a year (April, November) for symposia, lectures and the reading of papers. It makes grants for research, conducts a distinguished library rich in historical MSS., chiefly relating to the history of science in America (*see* Special Libraries), and awards prizes including the Magellanic Premium, the oldest American scientific award. The Society owns two buildings: Philosophical Hall (1789, a National Historical Landmark) and Library Hall. Both buildings contain numerous valuable portraits (paintings and statuary) of distinguished former members.

*President:* JONATHAN E. RHOADS, M.D., D.MED.SCI., LITT.D., LL.D.

*Executive Officer:* WHITFIELD J. BELL, Jr., PH.D., LITT.D., LL.D.

Publications: *Transactions†, Proceedings†*, individual monographs (*Memoirs*), *Year Book†*.

**National Foundation on the Arts and the Humanities:** Washington, D.C. 20506; f. 1965 as an independent agency in the Executive Branch of Government to develop and promote a broadly conceived national policy of support for the humanities and the arts in the United States. It is composed of:

**National Endowment for the Arts:** f. 1965 to establish and carry out a programme of grants-in-aid to non-profit groups, individuals of exceptional talent and state art agencies, which will promote progress in the arts; Chair. LIVINGSTONE BIDDLE.

**National Endowment for the Humanities:** f. 1965 to establish and carry out a programme supporting projects of research, education and public activity in the humanities; Chair. Dr. JOSEPH DUFFEY.

**National Council on the Arts:** appointed 1964, advises the Chairman of the National Endowment for the Arts on policies, programmes and procedures and reviews applications for financial assistance; 26 private citizen members appointed by the President for six-year terms (approx. one-third of the appointments expire every two years); Chair. of Council is Chair. of the Arts Endowment.

**National Council on the Humanities:** appointed 1966; advises the Chairman of the National Endowment for the Humanities on policies, programmes and procedures and reviews applications for financial assistance; 26 private citizen mems. appointed by the President for six-year terms (approx. one-third of the appointments expire every two years); Chair. of Council is Chair. of the Humanities Endowment.

**Federal Council on the Arts and the Humanities:** f. 1965 to co-ordinate the activities of the two Endowments with related Federal agencies; mems. include the Chairmen of the two Endowments; the Commissioner, Office of Education, Dept. of Health, Education and Welfare; the Secretary of the Smithsonian Institution; the Director of the National Science Foundation; the Librarian of Congress; the Director of the National Gallery of Art; the Chairman of the Commission of Fine Arts; The Archivist of the United States; Asst. Secretary for Educational and Cultural Affairs, Dept. of State; Director, National Park Service, Dept. of the Interior; Commissioner, Public Buildings Service, General Services Administration; Exec. Secretary, Senate Commission on Arts and Antiquities; Secretary of Commerce; Secretary of Housing and Urban Development; Secretary, Department of Transportation; Administrator, General Services Administration; Chair. National Museum Services Board; Director, Institute of Museum Services; a member of the House of Representatives.

## SMITHSONIAN INSTITUTION
WASHINGTON, D.C. 20560
Founded 1846.

For the "increase and diffusion of knowledge among men" by bequest of James Smithson.

*Chancellor:* WARREN E. BURGER, Chief Justice of the United States.

*Secretary (Presiding Officer):* S. DILLON RIPLEY, B.A., PH.D.

*Director, Smithsonian Institution Libraries:* Dr. ROBERT MALOY.

Library: see Libraries.

Publications: *Smithsonian Year, Smithsonian Contributions to Astrophysics, Smithsonian Studies in Air and Space, Smithsonian Contributions to Anthropology, Smithsonian Contributions to Botany, Smithsonian Contributions to the*

*Earth Sciences, Smithsonian Contributions to the Marine Sciences, Smithsonian Contributions to Paleobiology, Smithsonian Contributions to Zoology, Smithsonian Studies in History and Technology, Freer Gallery of Art Oriental Studies, Freer Gallery of Art Occasional Papers, Ars Orientalis*, also exhibit catalogues, pamphlets, books and special publications.

### THE ESTABLISHMENT:

President of the United States, Vice-President of the United States, Chief Justice of the United States, Secretary of State, Secretary of the Treasury, Secretary of Defense, Attorney General, Secretary of the Interior, Secretary of Agriculture, Secretary of Commerce, Secretary of Labor, Secretary of Health and Human Services, Secretary of Housing and Urban Development, Secretary of Transportation, Secretary of Energy.

### BOARD OF REGENTS:

WARREN E. BURGER (Chief Justice of the United States) (Chancellor), GEORGE H. W. BUSH (The Vice-President of the United States), HENRY M. JACKSON (Member of the Senate), E. J. GARN (Member of the Senate), BARRY GOLDWATER (Member of the Senate), JOSEPH DiGENOVA (Member of the Senate), SILVIO O. CONTE (Member of the House of Representatives), NORMAN Y. MINETA (Member of the House of Representatives), EDWARD BOLAND (Member of the House of Representatives), DAVID C. ACHESON, ANNE ARMSTRONG, JOHN PAUL AUSTIN, WILLIAM G. BOWEN, WILLIAM A. M. BURDEN, MURRAY GELL-MANN, CARYL P. HASKINS, A. LEON HIGGINBOTHAM, Jr., CARLISLE H. HUMELSINE, JAMES E. WEBB (Citizen Members).

### EXECUTIVE COMMITTEE OF THE BOARD OF REGENTS:

WARREN E. BURGER (Chancellor), JAMES E. WEBB (Chair.), CARYL P. HASKINS, WILLIAM A. M. BURDEN, S. DILLON RIPLEY (Sec.).

## BUREAUX UNDER THE ADMINISTRATION OF THE SMITHSONIAN INSTITUTION
(see also under relevant sections)

Anacostia Neighborhood Museum: Dir. JOHN R. KINARD, B.D.
Archives of American Art: Dir. W. E. WOOLFENDEN, M.A.
Chesapeake Bay Center for Environmental Studies: Dir. J. K. SULLIVAN, M.S., PH.D.
Cooper-Hewitt Museum: Dir. L. M. TAYLOR.
Fort Pierce (Florida) Bureau: Dir. (vacant).
Freer Gallery of Art: Dir. T. LAWTON, M.A., PH.D.
International Exchange Service: Dir. J. ESTES.
Hirshhorn Museum and Sculpture Garden: Dir. A. LERNER, B.A.
Museum of African Art: Dir. WARREN M. ROBBINS, M.A., L.H.D., LL.D.
National Air and Space Museum: Dir. N. W. HINNERS, M.S., PH.D.
National Armed Forces Museum Advisory Board: Exec. Sec. J. S. HUTCHINS, B.S.
National Museum of American Art: Dir. HARRY LOWE (acting).
National Museum of American History: Dir. ROGER G. KENNEDY, LL.B.
National Museum of Natural History: Dir. RICHARD S. FISKE, M.S.E., PH.D.
National Portrait Gallery: Dir. (vacant).
National Zoological Park: Dir. T. H. REED, D.V.M.
Radiation Biology Laboratory: Dir. W. H. KLEIN, PH.D.
Renwick Gallery: Dir. LLOYD E. HERMAN, M.A.
Smithsonian Science Information Exchange, Inc.: Pres. DAVID F. HERSEY, M.S., PH.D.
Smithsonian Astrophysical Observatory: Dir. G. B. FIELD, PH.D.
Smithsonian Tropical Research Institute: Balboa, Panama; Dir. I. RUBINOFF, M.A., PH.D.

*The following bureaux are separately administered:*
John F. Kennedy Center for the Performing Arts: Chair. R. L. STEVENS, D.H.L., LL.D.
National Gallery of Art: Dir. J. CARTER BROWN, M.B.A., M.A., LL.D.
Woodrow Wilson International Center for Scholars: Dir. J. H. BILLINGTON, D.PHIL.

### AGRICULTURE AND VETERINARY SCIENCE

**Agricultural History Society:** Business Office: Economic Research Service, Room 140, 500 12th St., S.W., Washington, D.C. 20250; f. 1919 to stimulate interest in, promote the study of, and facilitate research and publication on the history of agriculture; incorporated 1924 as a non-profit organization; Pres. JEROME BLUM; Sec. WAYNE D. RASMUSSEN; publ. *Agricultural History* (quarterly).

**American Dairy Science Association:** 309 W. Clark St., Champaign, Ill. 61820; 2,145 mems., 693 affiliated mems.; Pres. J. H. MARTIN; Exec. Sec. C. J. CRUSE; publ. *Journal of Dairy Science* (monthly).

**American Forestry Association:** 1319 18th St., N.W., Washington, D.C. 20036; f. 1875; 65,000 mems.; Exec. Vice-Pres. REXFORD A. RESLER.

**American Society for Horticultural Science:** 701 North Saint Asaph St., Alexandria, Va. 22314; f. 1903; 4,500 mems.; field of activities, to promote and encourage scientific research and education in all branches of horticulture; Dir. CECIL BLACKWELL; publs. *Hortscience, Journal* (every 2 months).

**American Society of Agricultural Engineers:** P.O.B. 410, 2950 Niles Rd., St. Joseph, Mich. 49085; f. 1907; 11,000 mems.; Pres. Dr. G. W. ISAACS; Exec. Vice-Pres. J. L. BUTT; publs. *Agricultural Engineering* (monthly), *Transactions* (every 2 months), *Agricultural Engineers Yearbook*.

**American Society of Agronomy:** 677 South Segoe Rd., Madison, Wis. 53711; f. 1907; 11,000 mems.; Exec. Vice-Pres. MATTHIAS STELLY; publs. *Agronomy Journal* (bi-monthly), *Crops and Soils* (9 a year), *Agronomy Monographs, Agronomy News* (bi-monthly), *Agronomy Abstracts* (annually), *ASA Special Publication Series, Journal of Environmental Quality* (quarterly), *Journal of Agronomic Education* (annually).

**American Society of Animal Science:** c/o Claude J. Cruse, Exec. Secretary, 309 W. Clark St., Champaign, Ill. 61820; promotes development of sciences beneficial to animal production; 4,500 mems.; Pres. R. OLTJEN; Sec.-Treas. I. OMTVEDT; publ. *Journal of Animal Science* (monthly).

**American Veterinary Medical Association:** 930 North Meacham Rd., Schaumburg, Ill. 60196; f. 1863; 34,000 mems.; Exec. Vice-Pres. Dr. D. A. PRICE; publs. *Journal of the A.V.M.A.* (fortnightly) and *American Journal of Veterinary Research* (monthly).

**Council for Agricultural Science and Technology:** 250 Memorial Union, Ames, Iowa 50011; inc. 1972; aims to advance the understanding and use of agricultural science and technology by co-ordinating efforts of scientific agricultural societies, by improving communication between branches of agricultural science and technology and by co-operating with other scientific organizations on matters of common interest; 4,500 mems.; Pres. Dr. R. P. UPCHURCH; Exec. Vice-Pres. Dr. CHARLES A. BLACK; publs. *Reports, Comments from CAST, News from CAST, Papers*, special publications.

**Poultry Science Association Inc.:** Business Man. CLAUDE CRUSE, 309 W. Clark St., Champaign, Ill. 61820; publ. *Poultry Science* (monthly).

**Society for Range Management:** 2760 West Fifth Ave., Denver, Colo. 80204; f. 1948 to develop understanding of range ecosystems and of the principles applicable to the management of range resources; 6,000 mems. worldwide; publs. *Journal of Range Management* (bi-monthly) and *Rangelands* (bi-monthly).

**Society of American Foresters:** 5400 Grosvenor Lane, Bethesda, Md. 20814; f. 1900; 19,000 mems.; Pres. THOMAS B. BORDEN; Exec. Vice-Pres. JOHN C. BARBER; publs. *Journal of Forestry* (monthly), *Forest Science, Southern Journal of Applied Forestry* (quarterly).

**Soil Science Society of America:** f. 1936; 5,700 mems.; associated with the American Society of Agronomy; Exec. Vice-Pres. Dr. MATTHIAS STELLY, 677 South Segoe Rd., Madison, Wis. 53711; publ. *Journal* (every 2 months).

### ARCHITECTURE AND TOWN PLANNING

**American Institute of Architects:** 1735 New York Ave., N.W., Washington, D.C. 20006; f. 1857; 35,000 mems.; library of 19,000 vols.; Exec. Vice-Pres. DAVID OLAN MEEKER, Jr.; publs. *AIA Journal, Memo.*

**American Planning Association:** 1776 Massachusetts Ave., N.W., Washington, D.C. 20036; f. 1978 (an amalgamation of the American Institute of Planners and the American Society of Planning Officials); 22,000 mems.; Exec. Dir. ISRAEL STOLLMAN; publs. *APA Journal* (quarterly), *Planning, APA News, PAS reports and memos* (monthly), *Land Use Law and Zoning Digest* (11 a year).

**American Society of Landscape Architects, Inc.:** 1900 M St., N.W., Suite 750, Washington, D.C. 20036; f. 1899, inc. 1916 as a professional association; 5,300 mems. and affiliates; Exec. Dir. EDWARD H. ABLE, Jr.; publs. *Landscape Architecture News Digest* (monthly), *Landscape Architecture* (quarterly), *Landscape Architectural Technical Information Series* (quarterly), *Members' Handbook* (annually).

**National Trust for Historic Preservation in the United States:** 1785 Massachusetts Ave., N.W., Washington, D.C. 20036; f. 1949 to encourage preservation of buildings, sites and objects significant in American history and culture; 160,000 mems.; library of 8,000 vols.; Pres. MICHAEL L. AINSLIE; Corp. Sec. WILL AREY; publs. *Historic Preservation* (every 2 months), *Preservation News* (monthly), etc.

**Society of Architectural Historians:** 1700 Walnut St., Suite 716, Philadelphia, Pa. 19103; f. 1940; 4,500 mems.; Pres. DAVID GEBHARD; Sec. DAVID T. VAN ZANTEN; Exec. Sec. PAULETTE OLSON; publs. *Journal* (quarterly), *Newsletter* (6 a year).

### THE ARTS

**American Council for the Arts:** 570 Seventh Ave., New York, N.Y. 10018; f. 1960 to promote the interests of the arts through advocacy, publication and information exchange; c. 1,100 mems.; library of c. 10,000 items; Pres. EDWARD M. BLOCK; Exec. Dir. W. GRANT BROWNRIGG; publs. *American Arts* (every 2 months), *UpDate* (monthly).

**American Federation of Arts:** 41 East 65th St., New York, N.Y. 10021; f. 1909; non-profit educational organization; aims to broaden the knowledge and appreciation of the arts of the past and present; organizes exhibitions throughout the U.S.A. and abroad; Pres. ARTHUR D. EMIL; Dir. WILDER GREEN; publ. *AFA Newsletter* (3 a year).

**American Musicological Society:** 201 South 34th St., Philadelphia, Pa. 19104; f. 1934; 3,500 mems.; Pres. HOWARD MAYER BROWN; Exec. Dir. ALVIN H. JOHNSON; publs. *Journal* (3 a year) and *Newsletter* (2 a year).

**American Society for Aesthetics:** C.W. Post Center of Long Island University, Greenvale, N.Y. 11548; f. 1942; study, research, discussion and publication in aesthetics and the arts; 1,000 mems.; Pres. FRANCIS SPARSHOTT; Sec.-Treas. ARNOLD BERLEANT; publs. *Journal of Aesthetics and Art Criticism* (quarterly), *ASA Newsletter*.

**American Society for Theatre Research:** c/o Dept. of English, Queens College of the City University of New York, Flushing, N.Y. 11367; f. 1956; serves needs of theatre historians and fosters knowledge of the theatre in the U.S.A. and overseas; 605 mems.; Pres. Prof. JOSEPH W. DONOHUE; Sec. Prof. MARGARET LOFTUS RANALD; publs. *ASTR Newsletter†, Theatre Survey†* (2 a year).

**American Society of Composers, Authors and Publishers (ASCAP):** 1 Lincoln Plaza, New York, N.Y. 10023; f. 1914; issues licences for public performance of members' copyright works; mems.: 17,850 authors and composers, 7,458 publishers; a non-profit-making society; Pres. HAL DAVID.

**Archives of American Art:** Smithsonian Institution, 41 East 65th St., New York, N.Y. 10021; Processing and Reference Centre: N.M.AA-PG Bldg., Smithsonian Institution, Washington, D.C. 20560; f. 1954; documents relating to American art in the original and on microfilm; approx. 7,000,000 items; regional centres in Boston, Detroit, New York, San Francisco and Washington; Dir. WILLIAM E. WOOLFENDEN; Curator GARNETT MCCOY; publ. *Journal* (quarterly).

**Center for Creative Photography:** University of Arizona, 843 East University Blvd., Tucson, Ariz. 85719; f. 1975; a unique resource for the study and history of photography; extensive collection of prints and other materials related to the life and works of 20th-century photographers comprises a computer-catalogued archive; houses the life-time archives of Ansel Adams, Wynn Bullock, Harry Callahan, Aaron Siskind, Frederick Sommer, W. Eugene Smith, etc.; open to the public; library of 3,000 vols.; Dir. JAMES L. ENYEART; publ. *Center for Creative Photography†* (research publ., c. 5 a year).

**College Art Association of America:** 16 East 52nd St., New York, N.Y. 10022; f. 1912 to further scholarship and excellence in the teaching and practice of art and art history; 7,000 individual, 1,800 institutional mems.; Sec. JOHN R. MARTIN; publs. *Art Bulletin, Art Journal* (quarterly), monographs.

**Graphic Arts Technical Foundation, Inc.:** 4615 Forbes Ave., Pittsburgh, Pa. 15213; f. 1924; 3,100 mems.; library of over 2,500 vols.; non-profit scientific, technical and educational organization serving the international graphic communications community; conducts technical seminars and workshops on various aspects of graphic communications; Pres. WILLIAM J. MARINER; Exec. Dir. GILBERT W. BASSETT; publs. *Graphic Arts Abstracts* (monthly), *Capsule Report* (10 a year), *International News* (10 a year), *Health and Safety News, Environmental Control Report* (quarterly), *Education Report* (2 a year), technical services and research project reports, techno-economic forecasts, quality control devices and audio-visuals.

**Hispanic Society of America:** 613 West 155th St., New York, N.Y. 10032; f. 1904; 400 mems.; professional research staff; reference library and museum; Dir. THEODORE S. BEARDSLEY, Jr.; numerous publs.

**National Academy of Design:** 1083 Fifth Ave., New York, N.Y. 10028; f. 1825; membership composed exclusively of artists, divided into two groups, Associates and Academicians; sections: painting, sculpture, water colour, graphic arts, architecture; Pres. ROBERT S. HUTCHINS, N.A.; Corresp. Sec. XAVIER GONZALEZ; Dir. JOHN DOBKIN.

LEARNED SOCIETIES　　　　　　　　　　　　　　　　　　　　　　　　　UNITED STATES OF AMERICA

**Art 8chool of the National Academy:** 5 East 89th St., New York; Dir. JOHN DOBKIN.

**National Music Council:** 250 West 54th St., Room 300, New York, N.Y. 10019; f. 1940, chartered by Congress 1957; non-profit organization; aims to provide a forum for the discussion of the country's national music affairs, and to act as a force to strengthen the importance of music in the nation's life and culture; 65 member orgs.; publ. *Bulletin* (2 a year).

**National Sculpture Society:** 15 East 26th St., New York, N.Y. 10010; f. 1893, inc. 1896; 350 mems.; Exec. Dir. CLAIRE A. STEIN; publ. *National Sculpture Review* (quarterly).

**National Society of Mural Painters, Inc.:** c/o American Federation of Arts, 41 East 65th St., New York, N.Y. 10021; f. 1893, inc. 1895; 200 mems.; Sec. HELEN TREADWELL; publ. *Newsletter* (irregular).

**Society for Ethnomusicology, Inc.:** P.O.B. 2984, Ann Arbor, Mich. 48106; 2,100 mems.; Pres. GERARD BEHAGUE; Sec. CHARLOTTE FRISBIE; publs. *Ethnomusicology, Newsletter* (3 a year), special series.

### BIBLIOGRAPHY AND LIBRARY SCIENCE

**American Association of Law Libraries:** 53 West Jackson Blvd., Chicago; f. 1906; 3,200 mems.; Pres. ROGER JACOBS; Sec. SHIRLEY R. BYSIEWICZ; publs. *Law Library Journal* (quarterly), *Index to Foreign Legal Periodicals* (quarterly), *Directory of Law Libraries* (biennial), *Current Publications* (monthly).

**American Library Association:** 50 East Huron St., Chicago, Ill. 60611; f. 1876; 35,000 mems.; library of *c.* 19,000 vols.; Dir. ROBERT WEDGEWORTH; publs. *American Libraries* (monthly), *Booklist* (fortnightly), *Choice* (monthly), *Journal of Library Automation* (quarterly), *College and Research Libraries* (bi-monthly), *Library Resources and Technical Services* (quarterly), *School Media Quarterly, Top of the News* (quarterly), *Library Technology Reports* (every 2 months), *RQ* (quarterly), *Newsletter on Intellectual Freedom* (every 2 months), and over 20 other serial publications.

**American Society for Information Science (ASIS):** 1815 N. Lynn St., Suite 800, Arlington, Va. 22209; f. 1937; concerned with the development of advanced methodologies and techniques that contribute to the more efficient use of information; acts as a bridge between research and development and the requirements of diverse types of information systems; comprises managers, designers and users of information systems and technology; over 4,000 mems.; Pres. MARGARET T. FISCHER; Man. Dir. SAMUEL B. BEATTY; publs. *Journal, Bulletin* (every 2 months), *Annual Review of Information Science and Technology, Annual Proceedings*.

**American Theological Library Association:** f. 1947; inc. 1973; 600 mems.; Pres. JERRY CAMPBELL; Exec. Sec. AL HURD, 1421 Ramblewood Drive, East Lansing, Mich. 48823; publs. *Proceedings* (annual), *Newsletter* (quarterly), *Religion Index I: Periodical Literature* (2 a year), *Religion Index II: Multi-Author Works* (annually).

**Art Libraries Society of North America (ARLIS/NA):** 3775 Bear Creek Circle, Tucson, Ariz. 85715; f. 1972; sponsors conference and workshops, distributes publications, grants awards for art book publishing and student essays on visual librarianship (George Wittenborn Award); 1,050 mems. world-wide; affiliated with ARLIS (U.K.); Chair. CAROLINE BACKLUND; Exec. Sec. PAMELA J. PARRY; publ. *Newsletter*† (5 a year).

**Association of American Library Schools:** f. 1915; 103 institutional mems., 750 personal mems.; Exec. Sec. JANET C. PHILLIPS, 471 Park Lane, State College, Pa. 16801; publ. *Journal of Education for Librarianship* (5 a year).

**Association of Research Libraries:** 1527 New Hampshire Ave., N.W., Washington, D.C. 20036; f. 1932; 111 institutional members; Exec. Dir. RALPH E. MCCOY; publs. *ARL Newsletter, ARL Salary Survey, ARL Statistics, ARL Minutes*.

**Association of Visual Science Librarians:** f. 1968 to foster collective and individual acquisition and dissemination of visual science information, to improve services to those seeking such information and to develop libraries' standards; 48 mems. of which 13 outside the U.S.A.; Chair. F. ELEANOR WARNER, Librarian, New England College of Optometry, 420 Beacon St., Boston, Mass. 02115; publs. *Vision Union List of Serials, Ph.D. Theses in Physiological Optics, Guidelines and Standards for Visual Science Libraries serving Optometric Institutions, A Library Guide to Indexes and Abstract Journals for Vision Literature*†.

**Bibliographical Society of America:** P.O.B. 397, Grand Central Station, New York, N.Y. 10163; f. 1904, inc. 1927; 1,500 mems.; Exec. Sec. DEIRDRE C. STAM; publ. *Papers* (quarterly).

**Bibliographical Society of the University of Virginia:** c/o University of Virginia Library, Charlottesville, Va. 22901; f. 1947; an international society of bibliographers; 1,500 mems.; Sec.-Treas. RAY W. FRANTZ, Jr.; publ. *Studies in Bibliography* (annual).

**California Library Association:** 717 K St., Suite 300, Sacramento, Calif. 95814; f. 1896; 3,500 mems.; Exec. Dir. S. B. MOSES; Pres. CAROL ARONOFF; publ. *CLA Newsletter* (monthly).

**California Media and Library Educators Association:** 1575 Old Bayshore Hwy., Suite 204, Burlingame, Calif. 94010; Pres. MARIAN D. COPELAND; publ. *CMLEA Journal* (2 a year).

**Catholic Library Association:** f. 1921; 3,365 mems.; Exec. Dir. M. RICHARD WILT, 461 W. Lancaster Ave., Haverford, Pa. 19041; publs. *Catholic Library World* (monthly), *Catholic Periodical and Literature Index* (every 2 months), etc.

**Council of National Library and Information Associations:** 461 West Lancaster Ave., Haverford, Pa. 19041; f. 1942; 19 mem. asscns.; Chair. JOHN T. CORRIGAN; Sec.-Treas. ERICH MEYERHOFF.

**Council on Library Resources:** 1 Dupont Circle, N.W., Washington, D.C. 20036; f. 1956; to develop resources and services of libraries and library co-operation; Pres. WARREN J. HAAS; publ. *Annual Report*.

**Inter-American Bibliographical and Library Association:** P.O.B. 600583, North Miami Beach, Fla. 33160; f. 1930; 250 mems.; Pres. A. CURTIS WILGUS; Sec.-Treas. MAGDALEN M. PANDO; publ. *Doors to Latin America*† (quarterly).

**Medical Library Association:** c/o R. BRAUDE, McGoogan Library of Medicine, 42nd and Dewey Ave., Omaha, NE 68105; f. 1898; 5,000 mems.; the association supports and encourages medical and allied scientific libraries, promotes the exchange of medical literature among its institutional members, and improves the professional qualifications and status of medical librarians; publs. *Bulletin, MLA News*, etc.

**Music Library Association:** 343 South Main, Room 205, Ann Arbor, Mich. 48108; f. 1931; 1,850 mems.; publs. *Notes* (quarterly), *Music Cataloging Bulletin* (monthly), *MLA Index Series* (irregular), *Brief Rules for the Cataloging of Music, Technical Reports—Information for Music Media Specialists* (irregular).

**Society of American Archivists:** f. 1936; a professional association of persons and institutions active or interested in the acquisition, preservation, management, and servicing of documentary materials; 3,000 mems. (international); Pres. MAYNARD BRICHFORD; Exec. Dir.

ANN MORGAN CAMPBELL, 330 S. Wells, Apt. 810, Chicago 60606; publs. *The American Archivist* (quarterly), *SAA Newsletter* (6 a year).

**Special Libraries Association:** 235 Park Ave. South, New York, N.Y. 10003; f. 1909; 11,500 mems.; specialized library and specialized information services; Exec. Dir. D. R. BENDER; publs. include *Special Libraries* (quarterly), *SpeciaList* (monthly).

**Theatre Library Association:** f. 1937; 500 mems.; Pres. LOUIS A. RACHOW; Sec.-Treas. RICHARD M. BUCK, Performing Arts Research Centre, 111 Amsterdam Ave., New York, N.Y. 10023; publs. *Broadside* (quarterly), *Performing Arts Resources* (annually).

### ECONOMICS, LAW AND POLITICS

**Academy of Political Science:** 619 W. 114th St., New York, N.Y. 10025; f. 1880; 10,200 mems.; Pres. R. H. CONNERY; publs. *Political Science Quarterly†, Proceedings†* (2 a year).

**American Academy of Political and Social Science:** 3937 Chestnut St., Philadelphia, Pa. 19104; f. 1889; c. 11,000 mems.; Pres. MARVIN E. WOLFGANG; Business Man. Mrs. INGEBORG HESSLER; publ. *The Annals* (bimonthly).

**American Accounting Association:** 5717 Bessie Drive, Sarasota, Fla. 33577; f. 1916; professional society for educators, practitioners and students of accounting; 15,000 mems.; Pres. JOSEPH A. SILVOSO; Admin. Sec. PAUL L. GERHARDT; publs. *The Accounting Review*, monographs, surveys.

**American Arbitration Association:** 140 West 51st St., New York, N.Y. 10020; f. 1926; administration of arbitration, mediation and elections in resolving disputes in areas of automobile accident, commercial, community, labour, no-fault and international claims; conducts educational and training programmes, seminars, conferences and skill-building sessions; 4,400 mems., 50,000 arbitrators on national panel; library of 16,000 vols., 330 periodical titles; Pres. ROBERT COULSON; publs. *Arbitration Journal†* (quarterly), *News and Views* (quarterly), *Summary of Labor Arbitration Awards* (monthly), *Arbitration in the Schools* (monthly), *Labor Arbitration in Government* (monthly), *New York No-Fault Arbitration Reports* (monthly), *Lawyers' Arbitration Letter* (quarterly), *Digest of Court Decisions* (quarterly).

**American Bar Association:** 1155 East 60th St., Chicago, Ill. 60637; f. 1878; 275,000 mems.; library of 50,000 vols.; Sec. F. WM. MCCALPIN; publs. *Journal* (monthly), *Reports* (annual), *Bar Leader* (every 2 months).

**American Economic Association:** 1313 21st Ave. South, Nashville, Tenn. 37212; f. 1885 to encourage economic discussion, research and the issue of publications on economic subjects; 19,000 mems. and 6,000 subscribers; Sec. ELTON HINSHAW; publs. *American Economic Review*, *Papers and Proceedings*, *Journal of Economic Literature*, *Index of Economic Articles*.

**American Finance Association:** c/o Graduate School of Business Administration, New York University, 100 Trinity Place, New York, N.Y. 10006; f. 1940 to make available knowledge on current developments in the field of finance; 4,000 mems.; Sec.-Treas. Dr. ROBERT G. HAWKINS; publ. *Journal of Finance* (5 times a year).

**American Judicature Society:** 200 West Monroe St., Suite 1606, Chicago, Ill. 60606; f. 1913 to promote the effective administration of justice; 35,000 mems.; Exec. Dir. GEORGE H. WILLIAMS; publs. *Judicature* (monthly), *Update* (every 2 months).

**American Law Institute:** 4025 Chestnut St., Philadelphia, Pa. 19104; f. 1923 to promote the clarification and simplification of the law; research work; 2,502 mems.; library of 4,600 vols.; Pres. ROSWELL B. PERKINS; Dir. HERBERT WECHSLER; Exec. Vice-Pres. PAUL A. WOLKIN.

**American Law Institute-American Bar Association Committee on Continuing Professional Education:** 4025 Chestnut St., Philadelphia, Pa. 19104; f. 1947 to organize, develop and carry out a national programme of continuing education of the bar; 9,000 vols. in library; Exec. Dir. PAUL A. WOLKIN; publs. *The Practical Lawyer†* (every 6 weeks), *ALI-ABA CLE Review†* (weekly), *ALI-ABA Course Materials Journal†* (every 2 months), *CLE Register†* (monthly), *Practice Texts*, *Practice Handbooks*, etc.

**American Peace Society:** 4000 Albemarle St., N.W., Washington, D.C. 20016; f. 1828; Pres. Dr. EVRON M. KIRKPATRICK; Sec. L. EUGENE HEDBURG; publ. *World Affairs* (quarterly).

**American Political Science Association:** 1527 New Hampshire Ave., N.W., Washington, D.C. 20036; f. 1903; 16,000 mems.; Exec. Dir. EVRON M. KIRKPATRICK; publs. *The American Political Science Review* (quarterly), *P.S.* (quarterly).

**American Society for Political and Legal Philosophy:** c/o The Sec., Prof. M. P. GOLDING, Dept. of Philosophy, Duke Univ., Durham, N.C. 27708; f. 1955; 500 mems.; Pres. Prof. J. SHKLAR; publ. *NOMOS* (Yearbook).

**American Society for Public Administration:** 1225 Connecticut Ave., N.W., Washington, D.C. 20036; f. 1939; 17,500 mems.; national and regional conferences, management institutes, personnel exchange; chapters in local centres; Exec. Dir. KEITH F. MULROONEY; publs. *Public Administration Times* (fortnightly), *Public Administration Review* (every 2 months).

**American Society of International Law:** 2223 Massachusetts Ave., N.W., Washington, D.C. 20008; f. 1906, inc. 1950; 5,200 mems.; 22,000 vols.; Exec. Dir. SEYMOUR J. RUBIN; Pres. MONROE LEIGH; publs. *International Legal Materials* (every 2 months), *The American Journal of International Law* (quarterly), *Proceedings* (annual), *Newsletter*, books and occasional publications.

**American Statistical Association:** 806 15th St., N.W., Washington, D.C. 20005; f. 1839; 15,000 mems.; Sec.-Treas. FRED C. LEONE; publs. *Journal*, *The American Statistician*, *Technometrics*, *Amstat News*, *Journal of Educational Statistics*, *Current Index to Statistics*.

**Association of American Law Schools:** Suite 370, One Dupont Circle, N.W., Washington, D.C. 20036; f. 1900 for the improvement of the legal profession through legal education; 138 institutional mems.; Exec. Dir. JOHN A. BAUMAN; publs. *Proceedings* (annual), *Directory of Law Teachers* (annual), *Journal of Legal Education* (5 a year), *Newsletter* (quarterly), *Research Bulletin* (2 a year), *Legal Affairs Manual*.

**Atlantic Council of the United States:** 1616 H St., N.W., Washington, D.C. 20006; f. 1962; aims to advance the security and economic strength of the U.S.A. and other nations of the North Atlantic, to reinforce existing Atlantic institutions, to unite the efforts of the Atlantic nations for their peace, stability and material well-being and to encourage and assist the development of free, representative and democratic political institutions; non-profit making organization, funded by corporations, foundations, labour unions and private individuals with an annual budget of c. $735,000; Chair. KENNETH RUSH; Sec. TOM KILLEFER; Dir. Gen. FRANCIS O. WILCOX; publs.† *Atlantic Community Quarterly*, *Atlantic Community News*.

**Carnegie Endowment for International Peace:** 11 Dupont Circle, N.W., Washington, D.C. 20036; f. 1910; conducts its own programmes of research, discussion, publication and education in international affairs and American foreign policy, and international law and organization; engages in joint ventures with other organizations to extend dialogue on world affairs issues; library of c. 8,000 vols.; Pres. THOMAS LOWE HUGHES; 27 trustees; publ. *Foreign Policy* (quarterly).

**Council for European Studies:** 1404 International Affairs Building, Columbia University, New York, N.Y. 10027; f. 1970; a consortium of Western European studies programs at over 40 universities in the U.S.A.; affiliated with Columbia Univ.; aims to encourage greater scholarly interest in Western Europe, to emphasize the commonality of problems that face the nations of Western Europe and North America; sponsors research, information services, graduate student training; holds conferences, etc.; mems.: 800 individuals, 50 universities; Exec. Sec. Dr. IOANNIS SINANOGLOU; publ. *European Studies Newsletter†* (every 2 months).

**Council of State Governments:** Iron Works Pike, Lexington, Ky. 40578; f. 1933; offices in Washington, D.C., New York, Atlanta, Chicago and San Francisco; a joint governmental agency established by the States for service to the States; publs. *State Government* (quarterly), *State Government News* (monthly), *The Book of the States* (biennially, even-numbered years, with supplements issued in odd-numbered years), *Suggested State Legislation* (annual), *Legislative Session Sheet* (weekly), *National Association of Attorneys General* (annual), *Legislative Research Checklist* (quarterly), and many volumes of reports, research, etc.

**Council on Foreign Relations, Inc.:** 58 East 68th St., New York, N.Y. 10021; f. 1921; 2,100 mems.; Foreign Relations Library of 40,000 vols., 300 periodicals, clippings files; Chair. DAVID ROCKEFELLER; Pres. WINSTON LORD; Vice-Pres. and Sec. JOHN TEMPLE SWING; publs. *Foreign Affairs* (5 a year), and books on major issues of U.S. foreign policy.

**Economic History Association:** Eleutherian Mills Historical Library, P.O.B. 3630, Wilmington, Del. 19807; f. 1941 to encourage and promote teaching, research and publication in all fields of economic history; 1,230 mems., 2,340 library mems., 280 foreign mems.; Pres. ALLAN BOGUE; Sec. R. D. WILLIAMS; publ. *Journal of Economic History* (quarterly).

**Federal Bar Association:** 1815 H St., N.W., Washington, D.C. 20006; f. 1920; 15,000 mems.; 99 Chapters; over 70 committees in fields of federal law; Exec. Dir. J. THOMAS ROULAND; Asst. Dir. PAMELA WUNDERLICH; publs. *Federal Bar Journal, Federal Bar News*.

**Foreign Policy Association, Inc.:** 205 Lexington Ave., New York, N.Y. 10016; f. 1918; object: to promote citizen education in world affairs, to assist organizations, communities and educational institutions to develop programmes for citizen understanding and constructive participation in world affairs, and to advance public understanding of foreign policy problems through national programmes and publications of a non-partisan character based upon the principles of freedom, justice and democracy; Chair. CARTER L. BURGESS; publs. *Headline Series* (5 a year), *Great Decisions* (yearly), *Foreign Policy Briefs* (in presidential election years).

**Institute of Management Sciences, The (TIMS):** 146 Westminster St., Providence, R.I. 02903; f. 1953; 6,800 mems.; Pres. ARTHUR M. GEOFFRION; publs. *Management Science* (monthly), *Interfaces* (every 2 months), *Mathematics of Operations Research* (quarterly).

**Institute for Mediterranean Affairs:** 428 East 83rd St., New York, N.Y. 10028; established under charter of the University of the State of New York to evolve a better understanding of the historical background and contemporary political and socio-economic problems of the nations and regions that border on the Mediterranean Sea; to analyse the various tensions in the Eastern Mediterranean and to investigate the basic problems of the area; special attention is given to the Israeli-Arab conflict; 250 Academic Advisory mems.; Pres. Prof. SEYMOUR M. FINGER; Chair. Prof. NASROLLAH S. FATEMI; Vice-Chair. Prof. ABBA P. LERNER; Dir. SAMUEL A. MERLIN; publ. *The Mediterranean Survey* (bulletin, irregular).

**Inter-American Statistical Institute (IASI):** c/o Gen. Secretariat of the O.A.S., Washington, D.C. 20006, U.S.A.; f. 1940; 596 mems.; fosters statistical development in the Western Hemisphere; Pres. WALTER E. DUFFETT (Canada), Vice-Pres. J. RUBÉN ORELLANA (Ecuador), VÍCTOR OCHSENIUS (Chile), JUAN MANUEL CABALLERO (Panama), CARMEN P. MCFARLANE (Jamaica); Sec.-Gen. TULO H. MONTENEGRO; publ. *Estadística* (2 a year).

**Library of International Relations:** 666 North Lake Shore Drive, Chicago, Ill. 60611; f. 1932; non-profit institution supported by voluntary contributions; founded to stimulate interest and research in international problems; holds Round Table discussions for members; conducts seminars on special areas for business executives; offers special services to businesses and to academic institutions; 500 mems.; has a specialized collection of 352,000 books, documents and pamphlets, and more than 1,000 magazines coming from all over the world; Pres. JAMES H. DEVRIES; Sec. ELOISE RE QUA.

**Society of Actuaries:** 208 S. La Salle Street, Chicago, Ill. 60604; Communications Man. LINDA M. DELGADILLO.

**Twentieth Century Fund:** 41 East 70th St., New York, N.Y. 10021; f. 1919 by the late Edward A. Filene as an endowed foundation for public policy research on major economic, political and social institutions and issues; Chair. of the Board of Trustees DON K. PRICE; Vice-Chair. of the Board and Chair. of Exec. Cttee. PETER A. A. BERLE; Dir. M. J. ROSSANT; publs. *Annual Report, Newsletter*, studies and task force reports.

**Universities Field Staff International-Institute of World Affairs:** Twin Lakes, Salisbury, Conn. 06668; f. 1924; summer seminar for graduate and advanced students interested in economics, law, international affairs, government service, education; partial scholarships; 2,000 graduate mems. for 100 countries.

**World Peace Foundation:** 22 Batterymarch St., Boston, Mass. 02109; f. 1910: an operating foundation which does not give outside grants; policy-oriented studies in world affairs; research into international organization, American public opinion on foreign policy, U.S.-Canada relations, etc.; Dir. and Sec. ALFRED O. HERO; sponsors publ. *International Organization* (quarterly).

### EDUCATION

**Adult Education Association of the U.S.A.:** 810 Eighteenth St., N.W., Washington, D.C. 20006; f. 1951; a non-profit membership organization established "to increase lifelong learning opportunities for all people"; 3,000 mems., 3,000 subscribers; Exec. Dir. LLOYD DAVIS; publs. *Adult Education* (quarterly), *Lifelong Learning: The Adult Years* (monthly).

**Alfred P. Sloan Foundation:** 630 Fifth Ave., New York, N.Y. 10111; f. 1934; makes grants for projects in science and technology, economics and management, and related higher education; Pres. ALBERT REES; publ. *Report* (annually).

**American Association for Higher Education:** One Dupont Circle, Suite 780, Washington, D.C. 20036; f. 1870; sponsors projects and programs that will improve the quality of American higher education; 6,160 mems.; Pres. RUSSELL EDGERTON; publs. *Current Issues in Higher Education, Research Reports, AAHE Bulletin, Journal of Higher Education.*

**American Association of State Colleges and Universities:** One Dupont Circle, N.W., Washington, D.C. 20036; f. 1961 to improve higher education within its member institutions through co-operative planning, through studies and research on common educational problems, and through the development of a more unified programme of action; 342 mems.; 31 assoc. mems.; Pres. ALLAN W. OSTAR; publs. *Memo* (fortnightly), *OFP Reports (Office of Federal Programs), Proceedings* (annually).

**American Association of University Professors:** One Dupont Circle, N.W., Washington, D.C. 20036; f. 1915; 77,000 mems.; Pres. HENRY YOST; Gen. Sec. IRVING SPITZBERG; publ. *Academe: Bulletin of the AAUP* (8 a year).

**American Council on Education:** One Dupont Circle, Washington, D.C. 20036; f. 1918; 1,600 member institutions and associations; Pres. J. W. PELTASON; publs. *Educational Record* (quarterly), *Higher Education and National Affairs* (weekly).

**American Vocational Association, Inc.:** 2020 North Fourteenth St., Arlington, Va. 22201; f. 1925; 55,000 mems.; Exec. Dir. GENE BOTTOMS; publ. *Voc Ed* (8 a year), *Yearbook.*

**Association of American Colleges, Inc.:** 1818 R St., N.W., Washington, D.C. 20009; f. 1915 to promote liberal learning in all its forms in all types of post-secondary institutions; 600 mems.; Pres. MARK H. CURTIS; publs. *Liberal Education* (quarterly), *Forum for Liberal Education* (8 a year).

**Association of American Universities:** One Dupont Circle, N.W., Washington, D.C. 20036; f. 1900; 50 mems.; Pres. THOMAS A. BARTLETT.

**Association of Theological Schools in the United States and Canada:** P.O.B. 130, Vandalia, Ohio 45377; f. 1918 as Conference of Theological Schools, est. 1938 as American Association of Theological Schools; promotes improvement of theological education, provides information on theological schools and encourages communication between parties interested in the subject; 196 member schools; Pres. HARVEY H. GUTHRIE; Exec. Dir. LEON PACALA; publs. *Bulletin, Directory, Theological Education* (2 a year).

**Carnegie Corporation of New York:** 437 Madison Ave., New York, N.Y. 10022; f. 1911 by Andrew Carnegie for the advancement of knowledge and understanding among peoples of the U.S. and of the British Overseas Commonwealth; primary interests: education and public affairs; grants principally to colleges and universities and professional and educational organizations; 17 trustees; Pres. ALAN PIFER; Sec. SARA L. ENGELHARDT; publs. *Annual* and *Quarterly Reports.*

**Carnegie Foundation for the Advancement of Teaching:** 1785 Massachusetts Ave., N.W., Washington, D.C. 20036; f. 1905 to provide pensions for college teachers (the list of beneficiaries has been closed) and to conduct educational studies; 25 Trustees; Pres. ERNEST L. BOYER; Sec. Treas. JEAN VAN GORDEN; publ. *Annual Report.*

**Council for Basic Education:** 725 15th St., N.W., Washington, D.C. 20005; f. 1956; a private organization to encourage high academic standards in American public schools; 6,200 mems.; Exec. Dir. A. GRAHAM DOWN.

**Ford Foundation:** 320 East 43rd St., New York, N.Y. 10017; f. 1936; a non-profit corporation, dedicated to the advancement of human welfare, principally through the support of education, research and demonstration; Chair. of Board ALEXANDER HEARD; Pres. FRANKLIN A. THOMAS.

**Foundation Center, The:** formerly The Foundation Library Center, 888 Seventh Ave., New York, N.Y. 10106; offices in Washington, San Francisco, Cleveland; f. 1956; makes available information about philanthropic foundations; maintains a full collection of foundation reports; library of 2,500 vols., 3,000 pamphlets and articles, 6,500 foundation reports, computer files of foundation grants, aperture card system containing foundation IRS returns; Pres. THOMAS R. BUCKMAN; Dir. Public Services CAROL M. KURZIG; publs. *Foundation Grants Index* (every 2 months and annual cumulation), *Foundation Directory* (every 2 years), *Foundation Center Source Book Profiles* (every 2 months), Comsearch Printouts (annually), *Foundation Center National Data Book* (annually), *Foundation Grants to Individuals* (every 2 years), *About Foundations.*

**John Simon Guggenheim Memorial Foundation:** 90 Park Ave., New York, N.Y. 10016; f. 1925; offers Fellowships for research in any field of knowledge and for artistic creation in any of the fine arts, including music; Pres. GORDON N. RAY; Vice-Pres. G. THOMAS TANSELLE; Sec. STEPHEN L. SCHLESINGER; publs. *Annual Announcement of Fellowships, Reports of the President and Treasurer.*

**Institute of International Education:** 809 United Nations Plaza, New York, N.Y. 10017; f. 1919; private non-profit agency which develops, administers and programs educational and cultural exchange between U.S.A. and more than 100 other countries; conducts conferences, special studies and seminars to analyse and evaluate development in the field of educational exchange; six regional offices, overseas offices in Bangkok, Hong Kong and Mexico City; library of 6,000 vols.; Pres. WALLACE B. EDGERTON; publs. *Annual Report, Open Doors, World Higher Education Communique* (quarterly), *Vacation Study Abroad, U.S. College-Sponsored Programs Abroad* (both annually).

**National Education Association of the United States:** 1201 16th St. N.W., Washington, D.C. 20036; f. 1857; 1,600,000 mems., c. 100,000 life mems.; Exec. Dir. TERRY E. HERNDON; Dir. in each State; publs. *Today's Education* (quarterly), *NEA Reporter* (9 times each year).

**National Society for the Study of Education:** 5835 Kimbark Avenue, Chicago, Ill. 60637; f. 1901; 5,500 mems.; Sec. KENNETH J. REHAGE; publ. *Yearbook.*

**Philosophy of Education Society:** c/o Sec.-Treas. Dr. C. J. B. MACMILLAN, Dept. of Educational Research, Development and Foundations, College of Education, Florida State Univ., Tallahassee, Fla. 32306; f. 1941; 950 mems.; exists to promote discussion and analysis of philosophy and education and to improve the teaching and research in philosophy and education; publs. *Educational Theory* (quarterly), *Proceedings of the PES* (annually).

**Rockefeller Foundation:** 1133 Ave. of the Americas, New York, N.Y. 10036; f. 1913 to promote the well-being of mankind. Current concentration is on problems of hunger, international relations, population, health, equal opportunity and the arts and humanities; Chair. of Board THEODORE M. HESBURGH; Pres. RICHARD W. LYMAN; publs. *President's Review and Annual Report†, R.F. Illustrated†, Working Papers†,* occasional Special Reports.

**W. K. Kellogg Foundation:** 400 North Ave., Battle Creek, Mich. 49016; f. 1930; administers funds for non-partisan, non-profit agricultural, educational, and health activities in the public interest; Pres. RUSSELL G. MAWBY; Sec. JOANNE M. DREWNO; publ. *Annual Report*.

**Woodrow Wilson International Center for Scholars:** Smithsonian Institution Bldg., Washington, D.C. 20560; f. 1968 "to symbolize and strengthen the fruitful relation between the world of learning and the world of public affairs"; residential fellowship program organized in five divisions: historical and cultural studies, social and political studies and the division of resources, environment and interdependence, Kennan Institute for advanced Russian studies and Latin American programme; up to 40 scholars, approx. half from the U.S.A., of both academic and non-academic occupations; periods of study of up to one year; library of 15,000 vols., 400 periodicals; Chair. of Board of Trustees WILLIAM J. BAROODY; Dir. JAMES H. BILLINGTON; Admin. Officer WILLIAM M. DUNN; see also Smithsonian Institution.

### HISTORY, GEOGRAPHY AND ARCHAEOLOGY

#### History

**American Antiquarian Society:** 185 Salisbury St., Worcester, Mass. 01609; f. 1812; a learned society and research library concerned with American history before 1877; 610,000 vols., 500,000 manuscripts, 3 million newspaper issues, 70,000 graphics; 378 mems.; Dir. MARCUS A. MCCORISON; publ. *Proceedings* (2 a year).

**American Association for State and Local History:** 1400 Eighth Ave. South, Nashville, Tenn. 37203; f. 1940; 7,000 mems.; successor to Conference of Historical Societies; objects: exchange of information on local and regional history and historical societies, and dissemination in scholarly and popular publications of professional material and interpretative articles; Dir. GERALD W. GEORGE; publs. *History News* (monthly; professional news), *Bulletins* (irregular; professional data), *Directory of Historical Societies and Agencies in the United States and Canada* (biennially), technical leaflets, etc.

**American Catholic Historical Association:** The Catholic University of America, Washington, D.C. 20064; f. 1919 to promote interest in the history of the Catholic Church broadly considered; research work; 1,100 mems.; Sec. ROBERT TRISCO; publ. *Catholic Historical Review†* (quarterly).

**American Historical Association:** 400 A St., S.E., Washington, D.C. 20003; f. 1884; c. 14,000 mems.; Pres. BERNARD BAILYN; Exec. Dir. SAMUEL R. GAMMON; publs. *American Historical Review* (5 a year), *AHA Newsletter* (9 a year), *Employment Information Bulletin* (quarterly with 4 supplements), *Annual Report*, *Program*, various historical pamphlets.

**American Irish Historical Society:** 991 Fifth Ave., New York, N.Y. 10028; f. 1897; research in the history of the Irish in America; 500 mems.; library of 25,000 vols.; Dir. T. M. BAYNE; Librarian and Archivist Dr. WILLIAM GRIFFIN; publ. *The Recorder* (annual).

**American-Jewish Historical Society:** 2 Thornton Rd., Waltham, Mass. 02154; f. 1892; formed to collect and publish material bearing upon the history of America, and to promote the study of Jewish history in general as related to American-Jewish history; library of 66,000 vols., 6,000,000 MSS., contains many rare and valuable manuscripts, some of the 16th, 17th and 18th centuries; 3,800 mems.; Librarian Dr. NATHAN M. KAGANOFF; publs. *American Jewish History*, monographs.

**American Numismatic Society:** Broadway at 156th St., New York, N.Y. 10032; f. 1858; 2,065 mems.; Pres. HARRY W. BASS, Jr.; Chief Curator WILLIAM E. METCALF; Dir. and Sec. LESLIE A. ELAM; publs. *Numismatic Literature* (bi-annual), *Numismatic Notes and Monographs, Numismatic Studies, Museum Notes, Sylloge Nummorum Graecorum, The Collection of the American Numismatic Society*.

**American Society for Eighteenth-Century Studies:** 421 Denney Hall, Ohio State University, Columbus, Ohio 43210; f. 1969, inc. 1970; independent society; works through publications and meetings to foster interest and encourage investigation in the achievements of the 18th century in America and Europe; c. 1,800 mems.; Pres. ROGER HAHN; Exec. Sec. RONALD C. ROSBOTTOM; publs. *Eighteenth-Century Studies* (quarterly), *Studies in Eighteenth-Century Culture* (annually), *ASECS News Circular* (quarterly).

**American Society of Church History:** 305 E. Country Club Lane, Wallingford, Pa. 19086; f. 1888, reorganized 1906; 1,500 mems. and 1,475 subscribers; Sec. WILLIAM B. MILLER; publ. *Church History* (quarterly).

**American Swedish Historical Foundation and Museum:** 1900 Pattison Avenue, Philadelphia, Pa. 19145; f. 1926; the Foundation was established to collect, preserve, and to tell the story of the contributions made to the development of America by those of Swedish background. It maintains a large museum built in the style of a Swedish manor and housing both temporary exhibitions and permanent collections, among which is the finest collection of old Scandinavian silver in America; the two libraries hold 12,500 vols.; c. 1,000 mems.; Chair. EDWIN R. BRODÉN; Dir. LYNN C. MALMGREN; publ. *Newsletter* (every 2 months).

**California Historical Society:** 2090 Jackson St., San Francisco, Calif. 94109; f. 1871; non-profit making institution inc. under the laws of the State of California; includes an art museum; organizes historic tours, lectures, films, exhibitions and inter-museum loans; 8,500 mems.; library of 50,000 vols., rare MSS., pamphlets and maps, 200,000 historic photographs; brs. in Los Angeles and San Marino; Dir. PAMELA L. SEAGER (acting); Pres. Board of Trustees ROBERT J. BANNING; publs. *Quarterly Journal†, California History†*, books, pamphlets, bulletins, catalogues.

**Concord Antiquarian Society:** Lexington Road and Cambridge Turnpike, Concord, Mass. 01742; f. 1886; 1,200 mems.; Pres. Mrs. WILLIAM F. A. STRIDE; Admin. Mrs. THOMAS G. DOIG; publs. *Handbook, Exhibition Catalogs, Newsletter* (quarterly).

**Dallas Historical Society:** The Hall of State, Dallas, Tex. 75226: f. 1922; collection of historical materials; the Society has the custody of the Hall of State (*q.v.* Museums), which it operates as a museum and archives of Texas history; 1,500 mems.; library of 8,000 vols., also archive items, periodical and newspaper collections and 15,000 museum items; Pres. JOE M. DEALEY; Dir. JOHN W. CRAIN.

**Historical Society of Pennsylvania:** 1300 Locust St., Philadelphia, Pa. 19107; f. 1824; 3,200 mems.; library (*see* Libraries), archives, museum; Pres. JOHN W. ECKMAN; Sec. HOWARD H. LEWIS; Dir. JAMES E. MOONEY; publ. *The Pennsylvania Magazine of History and Biography* (quarterly).

**Institute of Early American History and Culture:** P.O.B. 220, Williamsburg, Va. 23187; f. 1943; two 2-year post-doctoral fellowships; Dir. THAD W. TATE; publs. *William and Mary Quarterly*, monographs, documents and bibliographies on American history to 1815, *News Letter* (2 or 3 per year), *Handbook*.

**Long Island Historical Society:** 128 Pierrepont St., Brooklyn, N.Y. 11201; f. 1863; library of 125,000 vols.; 1,250 mems.; Pres. IRVING CHOBAN; Dir. RUSSELL BASTEDO; publ. *The Journal of Long Island History*.

**Maryland Historical Society:** 201 West Monument St., Baltimore, Md. 21201; f. 1844; 6,500 mems.; museum and library: *see* under Museums; Pres. FRANK WELLER; Dir. ROMAINE S. SOMERVILLE; publs. *The Archives of Maryland, Maryland Historical Magazine*† (quarterly), *News and Notes, Maryland Magazine of Genealogy*† (2 a year).

**Massachusetts Historical Society:** 1154 Boylston St., Boston, Mass. 02215; f. 1791; oldest Historical Society in U.S.; library: *see* Libraries; Dir. LOUIS L. TUCKER; Librarian JOHN D. CUSHING; publs. *Proceedings*, etc.

**Medieval Academy of America:** 1430 Massachusetts Ave., Cambridge, Mass. 02138; inc. 1925 for the conduct, encouragement, promotion, and support of research, publication, and instruction in medieval records, literature, languages, art, archaeology, history, philosophy, science, life, and all other aspects of medieval civilization; approx. 4,000 mems.; Pres. ROBERT M. LUMIANSKY; Exec. Dir. LUKE H. WENGER; publs. *Speculum: A Journal of Medieval Studies* (quarterly), *Publications 1–90, Speculum Anniversary Monographs 1–7*.

**Minnesota Historical Society:** Saint Paul, Minnesota 55101; f. 1849; 8,000 mems.; library of over 400,000 vols. with extensive MSS., newspaper and picture depts., 30 historic sites; Pres. CURTIS L. ROY; Sec. and Dir. RUSSELL W. FRIDLEY; publs. *Minnesota History* (quarterly), *Roots* (3 a year), *Minnesota History News* (every 2 months).

**New York Historical Society:** 170 Central Park West, New York, N.Y. 10024; f. 1804; 2,000 mems. (all grades); museum of American history including portraits, landscapes and genre paintings; library of 600,000 vols., 1,000,000 MSS.; Dir. JAMES J. HESLIN.

**Oregon Historical Society:** Portland, Oregon 97205; f. 1873; 6,000 mems.; 40,000 books, 1,600,000 photographs, 12,000 maps, many pamphlets, serials and newspapers; original MSS., 10,000,000 pieces; museum artifacts from neolithic period to discovery, settlement of Oregon Country, Pacific Northwest; Dir. THOMAS VAUGHAN; publs. *Oregon Historical Quarterly*†, *Newsletter*†.

**Organization of American Historians:** 112 North Bryan St., Bloomington, Ind. 47401; f. 1907 to promote historical study in American history; attached to Indiana University; 8,500 indiv. mems., 3,500 institutional mems.; Pres. GERDA LERNER; Exec. Sec. JOAN HOFF WILSON; publs.† *Journal of American History, Program for Annual Meeting, Newsletter*.

**Pilgrim Society:** 75 Court St., Plymouth, Mass. 02360; f. 1820; 850 mems.; library of 12,000 vols. and Rare Manuscript Collections dealing with the Plymouth Colony; the Society maintains Pilgrim Hall, the oldest public museum in North America. Collections of Pilgrim decorative arts, furnishings, pre-historic Indian collections. Maintains the National Monument to the Forefathers and Coles Hill; Dir. LAURENCE R. PIZER; publs. books and pamphlets.

**Presbyterian Historical Society:** 425 Lombard St., Philadelphia, Pa. 19147; f. 1852; library of 117,000 vols. and 2,000,000 MSS.; Pres. Mrs. W. J. ATKINS; Sec. WILLIAM B. MILLER; publs. *Journal* (quarterly), *Annual Report, Publication Series*.

**Renaissance Society of America:** 1161 Amsterdam Ave., New York, N.Y. 10027; f. 1954; 1,695 individual mems., 1,205 library mems.; Exec. Dir. EUGENE RICE; publ. *Renaissance Quarterly*.

**Rhode Island Historical Society:** 52 Power St., Providence, R.I. 02906; f. 1822; administers: John Brown House: 18th-century museum house, R.I.; decorative arts, furniture, paintings, silver and pewter; library, 121 Hope St., 200,000 vols.; historical and genealogical; large graphics and MSS. collection; Museum of Rhode Island History: Aldrich House, 110 Benevolent St.; 2,700 mems.; Dir. ALBERT T. KLYBERG; Librarian PAUL R. CAMPBELL; Curator ANN LeVEQUE; publ. *Rhode Island History* (quarterly).

**Society of American Historians:** 610 Fayerweather Hall, Columbia University, New York 10027; f. 1939; 250 fellows; Pres. WALTER LORD; Sec. KENNETH T. JACKSON.

**State Historical Society of Wisconsin:** 816 State St., Madison, Wis. 53706; f. 1846; 6,000 mems.; 902,579 vols. including pamphlets and government documents; 131,811 microfilms, 380,758 sheet microformats, 48,000,000 MSS., 30,400 cu. ft. archives, 4,000 atlases, 50,000 sheet maps, 1,000,000 pictures and negatives; Dir. RICHARD ALTON ERNEY; publs. *Wisconsin Magazine of History* (quarterly), *Columns* (every 2 months).

**Vermont Historical Society:** 109 State St., Pavilion Building, Montpelier, Vt. 05602; f. 1838; objects: educational work in Vermont and American history; collection of books, documents, and MSS. relating to Vermont; publication of historical magazines and books; maintenance of State Museum and Kent Tavern Museum; 2,700 mems.; library of 40,000 vols.; Pres. DEBORAH CLIFFORD; Dir. WESTON A. CATE, Jr.; publs. *Vermont History* (quarterly), *Vermont History News* (6 a year), *Booklist* (annually).

**Western Reserve Historical Society:** 10825 East Blvd., Cleveland, Ohio 44106; f. 1867; maintains a historical museum, auto-aviation museum, five historical sites; 3,300 mems.; library of over 200,000 vols., 100,000 prints and photos, 5,000,000 MSS; Pres. PAUL W. WALTER; Exec. Dir. THEODORE A. SANDE; publ. *News* (every 2 months).

## Geography

**American Geographical Society:** Suite 1501, 25 West 39th St., New York, N.Y. 10018; f. 1852; 1,500 Fellows; Pres. JOHN E. GOULD; Dir. Dr. SARAH KERR MYERS; publs. journals: *Geographical Review* (quarterly), *Focus* (5 a year).

**American Society of Limnology and Oceanography:** f. 1936; 4,000 mems.; Sec. C. L. SCHELSKE, Great Lakes Research Division, Univ. of Michigan, Ann Arbor, Mich. 48109; publ. *Limnology and Oceanography* (bi-monthly).

**Association of American Geographers:** 1710 16th St., N.W., Washington, D.C. 20009; f. 1904; 6,000 mems.; Exec. Dir. PATRICIA J. McWETHY; publs. *Annals, The Professional Geographer*.

**National Geographic Society:** 17th and M Streets, N.W., Washington, D.C. 20036; f. 1888; organized for the increase and diffusion of geographic knowledge; library of 60,000 vols.; Chair. of Board of Trustees MELVIN M. PAYNE; Editor WILBUR E. GARRETT; Pres. GILBERT M. GROSVENOR; publs. *National Geographic*† (monthly) and *National Geographic World* (monthly), maps, books, atlases and filmstrips.

**Society of Woman Geographers:** 1619 New Hampshire Ave., N.W., Washington, D.C. 20009; f. 1925; 450 mems.; Pres. ELIZABETH FAGG OLDS; Sec. Mrs. BETTY GUYOT; publs. *Annual Bulletin, Newsletter*.

## Archaeology

**Archaeological Institute of America:** 53 Park Place, New York, N.Y. 10007; f. 1879; 7,500 mems.; Pres. ROBERT H. DYSON, Jr.; Exec. Dir. EUGENE L. STERUD; publs.

*American Journal of Archaeology*† (quarterly), 4,500 subscribers, *Archaeology*† (illustrated, every 2 months), 24,000 subscribers.

**Arizona Archaeological and Historical Society:** Arizona State Museum, Univ. of Arizona, Tucson, Arizona 85721; f. 1916; 550 mems.; Pres. Dr. GERD SCHLOSS; Sec. SHARON F. URBAN; publ. *The Kiva*.

### INTERNATIONAL CULTURAL INSTITUTES

**Asia Foundation:** P.O.B. 3223, San Francisco, Calif. 94119 (Main Office); offices in Washington and 12 Asian countries; f. 1954; 3,370 vols. on current Asian and world affairs; aims to assist Asian economic and social development through private American assistance to Asian public and private organizations, voluntary associations, institutions and individuals working to further social and economic progress within their societies; provides "seed money" grants in the fields of rural and community development; food and nutrition; population and community health; law and justice; communications, books and libraries; management, employment and economic development; cultural exchange for Asian-American understanding; Chair. Board of Trustees RUSSELL G. SMITH; Pres. HAYDN WILLIAMS; Sec. TURNER H. McBAINE; publs. *The Asian Student Orientation Handbook*, *President's Review*, *The Asia Foundation News*.

**Austrian Institute:** 11 East 52nd St., New York, N.Y. 10022; f. 1963; Government office responsible for cultural and scientific affairs, etc., under Austrian Federal Ministry of Foreign Affairs; library of 5,000 vols.; films, slides, etc., reference library; Dir. Dr. FRITZ COCRON.

**Belgian-American Educational Foundation, Inc.:** 420 Lexington Ave., New York, N.Y. 10017; f. 1920 to promote academic and scientific exchange by providing grants to scholars and graduate students for study and work in the other country; Pres. EMILE L. BOULPAEP.

**British Council:** British Embassy, 3100 Massachusetts Ave., N.W., Washington, D.C. 20008; Cultural Attaché H. R. CROOKE.

**English-Speaking Union of the United States:** 16 East 69th St., New York, N.Y. 10021; f. 1920; Chair. KINGMAN BREWSTER; Pres. JOHN I. B. McCULLOCH; Exec. Dir. JOHN D. WALKER; publ. *News*; 86 brs. in U.S.A.

**French Institute/Alliance Française/Federation of French Alliances in the United States:** 22 East 60th St., New York, N.Y. 10022; f. 1911 (A.F. de N.Y. f. 1898, Federation 1902); 7,750 mems.; library of 35,000 vols.; classes, lectures, films, scholarships; Senior Dir. V. MILLIGAN; Exec. Dir. J. VALLIER; publ. *French Bibliography* (annual).

**Goethe House, New York—German Cultural Center:** 1014 Fifth Ave., New York, N.Y. 10028; br. of Goethe Institut, Munich; promotes cultural exchange between the United States and Germany through lectures, films, concerts and exhibitions; language information division for teachers of German; runs German-American Partnership Program (GAPP); library of 16,000 vols. and *c.* 100 periodicals in German and English and selection of records; Dir. Dr. CHRISTOPH WECKER.

**Goethe Institut:** 530 Bush St., San Francisco, Calif. 94108; f. 1968; library of 8,000 vols.; Dir. ERNST SCHÜRMANN.

### LANGUAGE AND LITERATURE

**American Association for the Advancement of the Humanities:** 918 16th St., N.W., Suite 601, Washington, D.C. 20006; f. 1977; supports the work of humanists, fosters communication and co-operation among them, promotes public understanding of the humanities, and seeks to increase the contribution of the humanities to American life; activities include speaking out for the values of the humanities and for the cultivation of basic literary, historical and related skills; representing and providing information about the humanities before public and private agencies; undertaking research; investigating and reporting on issues that affect the humanities; cultivating improved press coverage of the humanities and of the accomplishments of teachers, scholars and writers in the humanities; 2,789 individual, 63 institutional mems., 177 subscriptions; Chair. JAMES M. BANNER, Jr.; Sec.-Treas. THEODORE K. RABB; publ. *Humanities Report*† (monthly).

**American Classical League:** Miami University, Oxford, Ohio; f. 1918; 3,000 mems.; Sec. JOAN MYERS; publ. *The Classical Outlook* (quarterly).

**American Center of P.E.N.:** 47 Fifth Ave., New York, N.Y. 10003; f. 1922 to promote friendship and intellectual co-operation among writers, the exchange of ideas and freedom of expression; conferences, workshops, emergency fund for writers, translation prize; administers Ernest Hemingway Foundation Award for first novels; sponsors 5 prizes for distinguished literary translation; programme for inmate-writers in American prisons; 1,800 mems.; library of 1,000 vols.; Pres. BERNARD MALAMUD; Exec. Sec. KAREN KENNERLY; publs. *Grants and Awards Available to American Writers* (annual), *Newsletter* (quarterly), various books and reports.

**American Comparative Literature Association:** Dept. of Comparative Literature, State University of New York, Binghamton, N.Y. 13901; f. 1960 to further the growth of comparative literature in the U.S.A.; 700 mems.; Pres. A. OWEN ALDRIDGE; Sec.-Treas. FREDERICK GARBER; publ. *ACLA Newsletter*.

**American Dialect Society:** c/o Exec. Sec., Dept. of English, Univ. of Western Ontario, London, Ont., N6A 3K7, Canada; f. 1889; approx. 800 mems.; study of the English language in North America, together with other languages or dialects of other languages influencing it or being influenced by it; extensive dictionary being compiled on dialect of the United States and Canada; Pres. Prof. JOHN ALGEO; Exec. Sec. H. R. WILSON; publs. *Publication*, *Newsletter* (thrice yearly), *American Speech* (quarterly), occasional monographs.

**American Philological Association:** f. 1869; study of classical languages, literatures and history; 2,950 mems.; Sec. ROGER BAGNALL, Dept. of Classics, 617 Hamilton Hall, Columbia University, New York, N.Y. 10027; publs. *Transactions* (annual), *Newsletters* (quarterly), *Philological Monographs*, *American Classical Studies*, *Text Series*, Special Publications.

**Hispanic Society of America:** (*see* under The Arts).

**Linguistic Society of America:** 3520 Prospect St., Washington, D.C. 20007; f. 1924; annual and summer meetings, linguistic institute; 4,500 mems.; 1,900 libraries, foreign and domestic; Pres. WILLIAM LABOV; Sec.-Treas. VICTORIA A. FROMKIN; publs. *Language* (quarterly), *LSA Bulletin* (quarterly).

**Modern Language Association of America:** 62 Fifth Ave., New York, N.Y. 10011; f. 1883; 30,000 mems.; Exec. Dir. Prof. JOEL CONARROE; publs. *PMLA* (6 a year), *MLA International Bibliography of Books and Articles on the Modern Languages and Literatures* (annually), *MLA Directory of Periodicals* (every 2 years).

**North American Spanish Language Academy/Academia Norteamericana de la Lengua Española:** 613 West 155th St., New York, N.Y. 10032; f. 1976; mem. of Asociación de Academias de la Lengua Española; 28 Academicians; Dir. CARLOS F. McHALE; Sec. GUMERSINDO YÉPEZ; publ. *Boletín*.

**Poetry Society of America:** 15 Gramercy Park, New York, N.Y. 10003; f. 1910; 1,100 mems.; service organization for poets and readers of poetry; library of 5,000 vols.;

Admin. Dir. DEBORAH GIMELSON; publ. *Bulletin*† (quarterly).

**Society of Biblical Literature:** f. 1880; study of biblical and related literature, language, history, religions; 4,800 mems.; Pres. BERNHARD ANDERSON; Exec. Sec. PAUL J. ACHTEMEIER, Union Theological Seminary, 3401 Brook Rd., Richmond, Va. 23227; publs. *Journal of Biblical Literature*† (quarterly), *Semeia*† (occasional).

**Speech Communication Association:** 5105 Backlick Rd., Annandale, Va. 22003; f. 1914; 6,000 mems.; Exec. Sec. WILLIAM WORK; publs. *Quarterly Journal of Speech*, *Communication Monographs* (quarterly), *Communication Education* (quarterly), *Directory* (annual), *Directory of Graduate Programs* (every 2 years), *Free Speech Yearbook*, *International and Intercultural Communication Annual*.

## MEDICINE

**Aerospace Medical Association:** Washington National Airport, Washington, D.C. 20001; f. 1929; advancement of Aerospace Medicine, Life Sciences, Bio-astronautics and Environmental Medicine; annual awards; 3,600 mems.; Exec. Vice-Pres. RUFUS R. HESSBERG., M.D.; publ. *Aviation, Space and Environmental Medicine* (monthly).

**American Academy of Allergy:** 611 East Wells St., Milwaukee, Wis. 53202; f. 1943; 2,981 mems.; Pres. K. FRANK AUSTEN, M.D.; publ. *The Journal of Allergy and Clinical Immunology*.

**American Academy of Family Physicians, The:** 1740 West 92nd St., Kansas City, Mo. 64114; f. 1947; promotes and maintains high standards in the general/family practice of medicine; 48,000 mems.; Pres. SAM A. NIXON, M.D.; Exec. Dir. ROGER TUSKEN; publs. *American Family Physician*, *AAFP Reporter* (both monthly).

**American Academy of Ophthalmology:** 1833 Fillmore St., P.O.B. 7424, San Francisco, Calif. 94120; f. 1896; Exec. Vice-Pres. BRUCE E. SPIVEY; publs. *Ophthalmology*, *Argus* (monthly), *The Ophthalmologist* (quarterly).

**American Academy of Otolaryngology-Head and Neck Surgery:** 15 Second St., S.W., Rochester, Minn. 55901; f. 1896; 5,599 mems.; Exec. Vice-Pres. WESLEY H. BRADLEY, M.D.; publ. *Otolaryngology-Head and Neck Surgery* (every 2 months).

**American Academy of Pediatrics:** f. 1930; 21,166 mems.; Exec. Dir. Dr. R. G. FRAZIER, 1801 Hinman Ave., P.O.B. 1034, Evanston, Ill. 60204; publ. *Pediatrics*.

**American Academy of Periodontology:** 211 East Chicago Ave., Chicago, Ill. 60611; f. 1914; 3,700 mems.; Pres. ROBERT L. REEVES; Sec. ROBERT W. KOCH; publ. *Journal of Periodontology* (monthly).

**American Association of Anatomists:** Department of Anatomy, Medical College of Virginia, Richmond, Va. 23298; f. 1888; 2,753 mems.; Pres. Dr. SANFORD L. PALAY; Sec.-Treas. Dr. WILLIAM P. JOLLIE; publs. *American Journal of Anatomy*, *Anatomical Record*, *Journal of Comparative Neurology*.

**American Association of Immunologists:** 9650 Rockville Pike, Bethesda, Md. 20014; f. 1913; independent body for the exchange of information and advancement of knowledge in immunology and related fields; c. 3,000 mems.; Pres. D. B. AMOS; Sec.-Treas. HENRY METZGER; publ. *Journal of Immunology*.

**American Association of Pathologists, Inc.:** 9650 Rockville Pike, Bethesda, Md. 20014; f. 1976; Pres. VINCENT T. MARCHESI; Sec.-Treas. PAUL E. LACY; publ. *American Journal of Pathology* (monthly).

**American Cancer Society Inc.:** 777 Third Ave., New York, N.Y., 10017; f. 1913; voluntary health agency; library of over 16,000 vols.; Exec. Vice-Pres. LANE W. ADAMS; publs. *Cancer News*† (2 a year), *Cancer* (2 a month), *Ca—A Cancer Journal for Clinicians*† (every 2 months), *World Smoking & Health* (quarterly).

**American College of Obstetricians and Gynecologists:** 600 Maryland, S.W., Suite 300, Washington, D.C. 20024; f. 1951; 22,600 mems.; Pres. GEORGE M. RYAN, Jr. M.D.; Sec. WILLIAM T. MOXSON, M.D.; publ. *Obstetrics and Gynecology* (monthly).

**American College of Physicians:** 4200 Pine St., Philadelphia, Pa. 19104; f. 1915; 15,260 Fellows, 154 Masters, 15,524 mems., 16,481 Associates; Exec. Dir. ROBERT MOSER, M.D.; publ. *Annals of Internal Medicine* (monthly).

**American College of Surgeons:** 55 East Erie St., Chicago, Ill. 60611; f. 1913; 43,000 Fellows; Dir. Dr. C. ROLLINS HANLON; Sec. W. EUGENE STERN, M.D.; publs. *Surgery, Gynecology and Obstetrics* (monthly), *Yearbook* (triennially), *Bulletin*† (monthly).

**American Dental Association:** 211 East Chicago Ave., Chicago, Ill. 60611; f. 1859; 133,000 mems.; library of 30,000 vols.; Exec. Dir. JOHN M. COADY, D.D.S.; publs. *Journal* (monthly), *ADA News* (weekly), *Journal of Oral Surgery* (monthly), *Washington News Bulletin* (irregular), *Index to Dental Literature* (quarterly), *Dental Abstracts* (monthly), *Journal of Endodontics* (monthly), *American Dental Directory* (annual), *Accepted Dental Therapeutics* (every 2 years), *Guide to Dental Materials and Devices* (every 2 years).

**American Dietetic Association, The:** 430 North Michigan Ave., Chicago, Ill. 60611; f. 1917 to advance the science of dietetics; to promote education in these and allied fields; 44,000 mems.; library of 1,500 vols.; Pres. EDNA P. LANGHOLZ, R.D.; Sec.-Treas. DONNA WATSON, R.D.; publ. *Journal* (monthly).

**American Geriatrics Society:** 10 Columbus Circle, New York 10019; f. 1942; 9,000 mems.; Pres. IRWIN HILLIARD, M.D.; Exec. Dir. KATHRYN S. HENDERSON; publ. *Journal of the American Geriatrics Society*.

**American Gynecological and Obstetrical Society:** f. 1981; 171 Fellows, 83 Life Fellows, 43 Hon. Fellows; Sec. Dr. T. T. HAYASHI, Magee Womens' Hospital, Pittsburgh, Pa. 15213.

**American Heart Association:** 7320 Greenville Ave., Dallas, Tex. 75231; 130,000 mems.; supports cardiovascular research and bring its benefits to the public through professional education and community service programmes, to co-ordinate efforts of all medical and lay groups in combating cardiovascular diseases, and to inform the public of progress in the cardiovascular field; Pres. HARRIET DUSTAN, M.D.; Exec. Vice-Pres. WILLIAM W. MOORE; publs. *Stroke*†, *Circulation*†, *Circulation Research*†, *Modern Concepts of Cardiovascular Disease*†, *Cardiovascular Nursing*†, *Current Concepts of Cerebrovascular Disease—Stroke*.

**American Hospital Association:** 840 North Lake Shore Drive, Chicago, Ill. 60611; f. 1898 to promote public welfare through leadership and assistance to members in provision of better health care and services for all; 31,314 personal mems.; 6,162 institutional mems.; library of 32,000 vols.; Pres. JOHN ALEXANDER MCMAHON; publ. *Hospital Week* (weekly).

**American Institute of Nutrition:** 9650 Rockville Pike, Bethesda, Md. 20014; f. 1928 to develop and extend knowledge of nutrition and to facilitate personal contact between investigators in nutrition and related fields of interest; 2,000 mems.; Pres. R. E. OLSON; Sec. P. B. SWAN; publ. *The Journal of Nutrition*.

**American Laryngological, Rhinological and Otological Society, Inc. (Triological Society):** f. 1895; approx. 700 mems.; Exec. Sec. WILLIAM M. TRIBLE, M.D.; Admin. Asst. ANN R. HOLM, 2954 Dorman Rd., Broomall, Pa. 19008.

**American Lung Association:** 1740 Broadway, New York, N.Y. 10019; f. 1904 as the National Association for the

Study and Prevention of Tuberculosis; Pres. EDMUND CASEY, M.D.; Man. Dir. JAMES A. SWOMLEY; publ. *ALA Bulletin* (10 a year); 150 affiliated associations throughout the country.

The Medical Section of the ALA, the American Thoracic Society, has a membership of over 8,400, including some 700 pulmonary physicians in foreign countries; Exec. Sec. SANDY IANNOTTA; publ. *American Review of Respiratory Disease* (monthly).

**American Medical Association:** 535 North Dearborn St., Chicago, Ill. 60610; f. 1847; 213,940 mems.; Pres. HOYT D. GARDNER, M.D.; Exec. Vice-Pres. JAMES H. SAMMONS, M.D.; publs. *Journal* (weekly), *American Medical News* (weekly), nine special journals (monthly), *American Medical Directory* (irregular).

**American Medical Technologists:** 710 Higgins Rd., Park Ridge, Ill. 60068; f. 1939; 14,700 mems.; Pres. JOHN SHERER; Vice-Pres. DOROTHY LEWIS; Sec. JOHN HEGGERS; publ. *Journal* (every 2 months).

**American Medical Women's Association, Inc.:** 465 Grand St., New York, N.Y. 10002; f. 1915; professional asscn. for women physicians; Pres. CHRISTINE E. HAYCOCK, M.D.; Exec. Dir. LORRAINE LOESEL; publ. *Journal* (monthly).

**American Neurological Association:** c/o Bowman Gray School of Medicine, Winston-Salem, N.C. 27103; f. 1875; 706 mems.; Pres. LEWIS P. ROWLAND; Sec.-Treas. JAMES F. TOOLE; publ. *Transactions* (annually).

**American Occupational Therapy Association, Inc.:** 1383 Picard Drive, Rockville, Md. 20850; f. 1917; 31,000 mems.; Pres. MAE D. HIGHTOWER-VANDAMM, O.T.R.; Exec. Dir. JAMES J. GARIBALDI; publs. *The American Journal of Occupational Therapy* (monthly), *Newspaper* (monthly).

**American Optometric Association, Inc.:** 243 N. Lindbergh Blvd., St. Louis, Mo. 63141; f. 1898 to promote the art and science of optometry, to improve vision care and health of the public; 20,300 mems.; Exec. Dir. RICHARD W. AVERILL; publs. *Journal* (monthly), *News* (fortnightly).

**American Pediatric Society:** f. 1888; 855 active mems.; Sec.-Treas. DAVID GOLDRING, M.D., P.O.B. 14871, St. Louis, Mo. 63178.

**American Physical Therapy Association:** 1156 15th St., N.W., Washington, D.C. 20005; f. 1921, inc. 1930; to develop and improve physical therapy education, practice and research; 31,035 mems.; Exec. Dir. ROYCE P. NOLAND; publs. *Physical Therapy* (journal), *Progress Report*.

**American Physiological Society:** 9650 Rockville Pike, Bethesda, Maryland 20014; f. 1887; 5,300 mems.; Exec. Sec. ORR E. REYNOLDS; publs. *American Journal of Physiology* (consolidated) and various specialist journals.

**American Psychiatric Association:** 1700 15th St., N.W., Washington, D.C. 20009; f. 1844; 24,000 mems.; Sec. H. KEITH H. BRODIE, M.D.; Med. Dir. MELVIN SABSHIN; publ. *American Journal of Psychiatry* (monthly).

**American Public Health Association:** 1015 15th St., N.W., Washington, D.C. 20005; f. 1872; interests include environment, personal health services, social factors, manpower and training in public health; 30,000 mems.; Exec. Dir. WILLIAM H. MCBEATH, M.D., M.P.H.; publs. *American Journal of Public Health* (monthly), *The Nation's Health* (monthly).

**American Rheumatism Association:** Arthritis Fndn., 3400 Peach Tree Rd., N.E., Atlanta, Ga. 30326; 3,200 mems.; Exec. Sec. LYNN BONFIGLIO.

**American Roentgen Ray Society:** f. 1900; 1,500 active mems.; Sec. RAYMOND A. GAGLIARDI, M.D., 800 Woodward Ave., Pontiac, Mich. 48053; publ. *American Journal of Roentgenology* (monthly).

**American Society for Clinical Investigation:** f. 1907; c. 1,800 mems.; Pres. PHILIP W. MAJERUS, M.D., Dept. of Hematology-Oncology, Washington Univ. School of Medicine, St. Louis, Mo. 63110; Vice-Pres. ROBERT W. SCHRIER, M.D.; publ. *Journal of Clinical Investigation* (monthly).

**American Society for Medical Technology:** 5555 West Loop S., Suite 200, Bellaire, Tex. 77401; f. 1933; c. 29,000 mems.; there are constituent societies according to states, and district societies within the states; Exec. Vice-Pres. GARY L. MORGAN; publs. *American Journal of Medical Technology*, *ASMT News* (monthly).

**American Society for Microbiology:** 1913 I St., N.W., Washington, D.C. 20006; f. 1899, under present name 1961; 31,000 mems.; Pres. Dr. FREDERICK C. NEIDHARDT; Exec. Dir. RILEY D. HOUSEWRIGHT; Exec. Sec. R. W. SARBER; publs. *Journal of Bacteriology*, *Applied and Environmental Microbiology*, *Journal of Virology*, *Infection and Immunity* (monthly), *ASM News*, *Antimicrobial Agents and Chemotherapy*, *Journal of Clinical Microbiology*, *Molecular and Cellular Biology* (monthly), *International Journal of Systematic Bacteriology*, *Microbiological Reviews* (quarterly), *Abstracts of the Annual Meeting* (annually).

**American Society for Pharmacology and Experimental Therapeutics, Inc.:** 9650 Rockville Pike, Bethesda, Md. 20014; f. 1908; 3,049 mems.; Pres. Dr. WILLIAM FLEMING; Exec. Officer Dr. HOUSTON BAKER; publs. *Journal of Pharmacology and Experimental Therapeutics*, *Rational Drug Therapy*, *Clinical Pharmacology and Therapeutics* (monthly), *Drug Metabolism and Disposition*, *Molecular Pharmacology* (every 2 months), *Pharmacological Reviews*, *The Pharmacologist*, *Drug Metabolism Newsletter* (quarterly).

**American Society of Clinical Hypnosis:** 2250 East Devon Ave., Suite 336, Des Plaines, Ill. 60018; f. 1957; an independent organization of professional people in medicine, dentistry, and psychology who share scientific and clinical interests in hypnosis; aims to provide educational programmes to further understanding and acceptance of hypnosis as an important tool of ethical clinical medicine and scientific research; 4,200 mems.; Pres. HAROLD P. GOLAN, D.M.D.; Sec. SHELDON P. COHEN, M.D.; publ. *The American Journal of Clinical Hypnosis†* (quarterly).

**American Society of Clinical Pathologists:** 2100 West Harrison St., Chicago, Ill. 60612; f. 1922; over 20,000 mems.; library of 25,000 vols.; Pres. JOHN BERNARD HENRY, M.D.; Sec. L. P. JAMES, JR., M.D.; publs. *American Journal of Clinical Pathology*, *Laboratory Medicine*.

**American Society of Human Genetics:** Medical College of Virginia, Box 33, MCV Station, Richmond, Va. 23298; 2,000 mems.; Pres. BARBARA BOWMAN, PH.D.; Sec. JUDITH A. BROWN, PH.D.; publ. *American Journal of Human Genetics* (every 2 months).

**American Society of Tropical Medicine and Hygiene:** P.O.B. 46502, Parkdale Branch, Cincinnati, Oh. 45246; f. 1903; 2,100 mems.; Sec.-Treas. Dr. M. HOEKENGA; publs. *American Journal of Tropical Medicine and Hygiene*, *Tropical Medicine and Hygiene News*.

**American Speech-Language-Hearing Association:** 10801 Rockville Pike, Rockville, Md. 20852; f. 1925; 36,000 mems.; Exec. Sec. FREDERICK T. SPAHR, PH.D.; publs. *Journal of Speech and Hearing Disorders* (quarterly), *Journal of Speech and Hearing Research* (quarterly), *Asha* (monthly), *Language Speech and Hearing Services in Schools* (quarterly).

UNITED STATES OF AMERICA

**American Surgical Association:** f. 1880; 650 mems.; Sec. W. GERALD AUSTEN, Dept. of Surgery, Massachusetts General Hospital, 32 Fruit St., Boston, Mass. 02114; publs. *Transactions* (annual), *Annals of Surgery*.

**American Urological Association, Inc.:** 1120 North Charles St., Baltimore, Md. 21201; f. 1902; 5,100 mems.; Pres. Dr. DAVID A. CULP; Sec. Dr. HERBERT BRENDLER; publ. *Journal of Urology*.

**Armed Forces Institute of Pathology:** 6825 16th St., N.W., Washington, D.C. 20306; est. 1862 as Army Medical Museum, changed to Armed Forces Institute of Pathology in 1949; it is the central laboratory of pathology for the Department of Defence serving the needs of the U.S. Army, Navy, Air Force, the Veterans' Administration and of other Federal agencies. It is organized into: Center for Advanced Pathology, Center for Advanced Medical Education, AFIP Repository and Research Services, Medical Illustration Services and Armed Forces Medical Museum; Dir. Capt. ELGIN C. COWART, Jr., M.C., U.S. Navy.

**Association of American Medical Colleges:** Suite 200, One Dupont Circle, N.W., Washington, D.C. 20036; f. 1876; 123 operational U.S. medical schools, over 400 teaching hospitals; Pres. JOHN A. D. COOPER, M.D., PH.D.; publs. *Journal of Medical Education* (monthly), *AAMC Directory of Medical Education*, *AAMC Curriculum Directory* (annually).

**Association of American Physicians:** f. 1886; 800 mems.; Sec. J. WILSON, Univ. of Texas Southwestern Medical School, 5323 Harry Hines Blvd., Dallas, Texas 75235; publ. *Transactions* (annually).

**Center for the Study of Aging and Human Development:** Duke University, Durham, N.C. 27710; f. 1955; trains researchers and clinicians with particular emphasis on post-doctoral training in physiological and behavioural aspects of aging; lectures, seminars and publications; Geriatric Evaluation and Treatment Clinic for direct service and in-service professional training; co-sponsors Duke Institute for Learning in Retirement; Dir. GEORGE L. MADDOX, PH.D.

**College of Physicians of Philadelphia:** 19 South 22nd St., Philadelphia, Pa. 19103; f. 1788 (College, f. 1787); Mid-Eastern Regional Medical Library of 300,236 vols.; 1,730 Fellows; Pres. LEWIS W. BLUEME, M.D.; publ. *Transactions and Studies*†.

**Commonwealth Fund, The:** 1 East 75th St., New York, N.Y.; f. 1918; grants for experimental and developmental programmes to strengthen medical education; Chair. of Board C. SIMS FARR; Pres. MARGARET E. MAHONEY; publ. *Annual Report*.

**Gerontological Society of America, The:** 1835 K St., N.W., Suite 305, Washington, D.C. 20006; 6,000 mems.; Exec. Dir. JANICE M. CALDWELL, D.P.H.; publs. *Journal of Gerontology*, *The Gerontologist*.

**Gorgas Memorial Institute of Tropical and Preventive Medicine, Inc.:** 2001 Wisconsin Ave., N.W., Washington, D.C. 20007; f. 1921; non-profit, biomedical research and training organization; Pres. JACK W. MILLAR, M.D.; Vice-Pres. PHILLIP E. WINTER, M.D.; Sec. MARY E. CORNING; Research Agency: Gorgas Memorial Laboratory, Apartado 6991, Panama 5, R. de P.; Dir. (vacant); publs. *Annual Report*†, *Scientific Papers*†.

**Industrial Health Foundation, Inc.:** 5231 Centre Ave., Pittsburgh, Pa. 15232; f. 1935; a non-profit organization for the advancement of healthy working conditions in industry; 150 member companies and associations; library of 2,000 vols.; Chair. CALHOUN L. H. HOWARD; Pres. D. C. BRAUN, M.D.; publs. *Industrial Hygiene Digest* (monthly), special technical bulletins.

**Institute of Medicine:** see National Academy of Sciences.

**John A. Hartford Foundation, Inc.:** 405 Lexington Avenue, New York, N.Y. 10174; f. 1929 by John A. Hartford and George L. Hartford; runs fellowship programme to sponsor careers in research and academic medicine, a health care financing programme and an energy programme; Pres. LEONARD DALSEMER; Exec. Dir. ROBERT F. HIGGINS; publs. *Bulletin* (2 a year), *Annual Report*.

**John and Mary R. Markle Foundation:** 50 Rockefeller Plaza, New York, N.Y. 10020; f. 1927 by an endowment given by John Markle, chartered by the State of New York; seeks to improve mass media and realize the potential of communications technology; Pres. LLOYD N. MORRISETT; Sec. VIRGINIA DUNLAP; publ. *Annual Report*.

**Medical Society of the State of New York:** 420 Lakeville Rd., Lake Success, New York, N.Y. 11042; f. 1807; 26,000 mems.; Exec. Vice-Pres. EDWARD SIEGEL, M.D.; publs. *New York State Journal of Medicine* (monthly), *Medical Directory of New York State* (every 2 years), *News of New York* (every 2 months).

**National Foundation:** 800 Second Ave., New York, N.Y. 10017; f. 1938 as The National Foundation for Infantile Paralysis Inc., name and programme changed in 1958; present activities include broad basic and clinical research in birth defects, patient care through a network of 100 birth defects centres, professional education and support of the Salk Institute for Biological Studies; membership: 3,100 chapters; Pres. BASIL O'CONNOR; publ. *Annual Report*.

**National Mental Health Association:** 1800 North Kent St., Suite 200, Arlington, Va. 22209; f. 1950; 45 State Divisions, 850 Local Chapters; Pres. HILDA ROBBINS; Exec. Dir. RICHARD C. HUNTER (acting); publ. *In Touch*.

**National Society for Medical Research:** 1029 Vermont Ave., N.W., Suite 700, Washington, D.C. 20005; f. 1946; Pres. Dr. JOHN F. SHERMAN; Exec. Dir. WILLIAM M. SAMUELS; publ. *NSMR Bulletin*† (monthly).

**New York Academy of Medicine:** 2 East 103rd St., New York, N.Y. 10029; f. 1847; 3,500 mems.; library: see Libraries; Pres. Dr. NORBERT ROBERTS; Sec. Dr. FIDELIO A. JIMENEZ; publ. *Bulletin* (monthly).

**Radiological Society of North America, Inc.:** 1415 W. 22nd St., Oak Brook, Ill. 50621; f. 1915; 11,282 mems.; Pres. HILLIER L. BAKER, M.D.; Sec. JAMES J. MCCORT, M.D.; publ. *Radiology*.

**Society of Medical Jurisprudence:** 237 East 86th St., New York, N.Y. 10028; org. and inc. 1883; investigation, study and advancement of the science of medical jurisprudence, and the attainment of a higher standard of medical testimony; members must be physicians, lawyers, chemists or forensic odontologists of good standing in their respective professions, or teachers in approved Law or Medical Schools; total membership 550–600; Sec. RITA FARRELL; publ. *Proceedings* (intermittent).

MUSEOLOGY

**American Association of Museums:** 1055 Thomas Jefferson St., N.W., Washington, D.C. 20007; f. 1906; promotes museums as cultural resources and represents interests of museum profession; membership consists of 4,450 individuals, 1,230 institutions and 330 libraries, 575 trustees, 240 foreign mems.; the Association is governed by a board of councillors, who are museum directors; Pres. KENNETH STARR; Dir. LAWRENCE L. REGER; publs. *Museum News* (6 a year), *Aviso* (monthly), series of technical papers, *The Official Museum Directory*.

**Association of Art Museum Directors:** P.O.B. 10082, Savannah, Ga. 31412; f. 1916 to promote the development of a scholarly and creative role for art museums and their directors in the cultural life of the nation; to apply its members' knowledge and experience in the field of art to the promotion of the public good; to encourage communication among art museums and their directors; 150 mems.; Pres. RALPH T. COE; Sec. THOMAS N. MAYTHAM.

## NATURAL SCIENCES
### General

**American Association for the Advancement of Science:** 1515 Massachusetts Ave., N.W., Washington, D.C. 20005; f. 1848; 138,000 mems.; Pres. D. ALLAN BROMLEY; Exec. Officer WILLIAM D. CAREY; publs. *Science* (weekly), *Science 81* (monthly), *AAAS Science Books & Films* (5 a year), *Science* Compendia, cassettes and cassette albums, etc.

**Buffalo Society of Natural Sciences:** Humboldt Parkway, Buffalo, N.Y. 14211; org. 1861; 2,100 mems.; administers the Buffalo Museum of Science; astronomy, anthropology, biology, botany, conchology, entomology, geology, ornithology, palaeontology, primitive and oriental art, mycology, zoology; solar and lunar observatory; library of 40,000 vols.; education dept.; lectures, loan exhibits; Pres. CLIFFORD J. AWALD; Dir. ERNST E. BOTH (acting); publs. *Calendar* (monthly), *Collections*† (quarterly), *Report*† (annually), *Bulletin*†.

**Cranbrook Institute of Science:** 500 Lone Pine Rd., P.O.B. 801, Bloomfield Hills, Mich. 48013; f. 1930; a non-profit making organization with exhibits and educational programmes in astronomy, mineralogy, geology, botany, zoology, ecology, anthropology, mathematics and physics; 5,000 mems.; library of 16,000 vols.; Dir. KATHLEEN K. ROTH; publs. *Bulletins, Newsletter, Annual Reports*, etc.

**Franklin Institute:** Benjamin Franklin Parkway, at 20th St., Philadelphia, Pa. 19103; f. 1824; is a non-profit organization engaged in scientific and technological research; its committee on Science and Arts awards the "Franklin" Medal and a number of other medals and certificates of merit; Franklin Research Center, see under Research Institutes; the Bartol Research Foundation (Newark, Del.), est. 1921, performs basic research in cosmic radiation and nuclear physics; library of 300,000 vols., 4,000 periodicals, especially strong in physical sciences; the collection of patents numbers over 6 million; 6,000 mems.; the Institute incorporates the Science Museum and the Fels Planetarium (a Zeiss planetarium) and houses the Benjamin Franklin National Memorial; there is an observatory open to the public; Pres. BOWEN C. DEES; Chair. RICHARD T. NALLE, Jr.; publs. *Journal, Institute News*† (every 2 months).

**History of Science Society:** f. 1924; 1,500 mems.; Sec. SALLY GREGORY KOHLSTEDT, Maxwell School, Syracuse University, Syracuse, N.Y. 13210; publs. *Isis* (quarterly), *HSS Newsletter* (quarterly).

**Mellon Institute:** (see Carnegie-Mellon University under Universities).

**National Science Foundation (NSF):** 1800 G St., N.W., Washington, D.C. 20550; f. 1950; independent agency of the U.S. Government concerned with the advancement of science in the U.S.; it sponsors scientific research, encourages and supports improvements in science education and fosters scientific information exchange, though does not itself conduct research or carry out education projects; administers the U.S. Antarctic Research Program, International Decade of Ocean Exploration, Global Atmospheric Research Program, Ocean Sediment Coring Program; finances five national research centres; a 25-member National Science Board (Chair. LEWIS M. BRANSCOMB) including the NSF Director (Dr. JOHN SLAUGHTER) develops the Foundation's plans and policies and guides its operation; publs. *Mosaic* (6 a year), *Antarctic Journal of the United States* (quarterly), *Bulletin* (10 a year).

**National Science Teachers Association:** 1742 Connecticut Ave., N.W., Washington, D.C. 20009; est. 1895, re-organized 1944, to advance science teaching and science education at elementary, secondary and college levels; 20,000 mems.; Pres. SARAH E. KLEIN; Exec. Dir. BILL G. ALDRIDGE; publs. *The Science Teacher, Science and Children, Journal of College Science Teaching*.

**Sigma Xi, the Scientific Research Society:** 345 Whitney Ave., New Haven, Conn. 06511; f. 1886 for the encouragement of scientific research; over 200,000 mems.; Pres. HERBERT E. LONGENECKER; Exec. Dir. THOMAS T. HOLME; publ. *American Scientist* (every 2 months).

**World Future Society:** 4916 St. Elmo Ave., Washington, D.C. 20014; f. 1966; private, non-profit organization promoting free discussion and study of alternative futures especially on scientific or technological themes; 40,000 mems.; Pres. EDWARD S. CORNISH; Sec. GRAHAM T. T. MOLITOR; publs. *The Futurist, Bulletin* (every 2 months), *Future Survey* (monthly).

### Biological Sciences

**American Genetic Association:** 818 18th St., N.W., Washington, D.C. 20006; f. 1903; 1,650 mems.; Sec. Dr. K. P. BOVARD; publ. *Journal of Heredity* (bi-monthly).

**American Institute of Biological Sciences:** 1401 Wilson Blvd., Arlington, Va. 22209; f. 1947; mems.: 40 professional societies and 8 industrial firms; 7,500 individual mems.; Pres. Dr. FOREST W. STEARNS; Exec. Dir. Dr. ARTHUR C. GENTILE; publ. *BioScience* (monthly).

**American Malacological Union Inc., The:** 3706 Rice Blvd., Houston, Tex. 77005; f. 1931; study of phylum Mollusca—taxonomy, anatomy, commercial fisheries, medical and palaeontological aspects; 750 mems.; Pres. Dr. RICHARD S. HOUBRICK; Recording Sec. CONSTANCE E. BOONE; publ. *Bulletin* (annually).

**American Ornithologists' Union:** Museum of Natural History, 2559 Puesta del Sol Rd., Santa Barbara, Ca. 93105 f. 1883; scientific study of birds; 4,000 mems.; Pres. JAMES R. KING; Sec. DENNIS M. POWER; publs. *The Auk*† (quarterly), *Ornithological Monographs* (irregular), *Check-List of North American Birds*.

**American Phytopathological Society:** f. 1908; 3,700 mems.; Exec. Vice-Pres. R. J. TARLETON, 3340 Pilot Knob Rd., St. Paul, Minn. 55121; publs. *Phytopathology, Phytopathological Classics, Phytopathological Monographs, Plant Disease Compendia Series, Directory of Members*.

**American Society of Ichthyologists and Herpetologists:** Dept. of Ichthyology, American Museum of Natural History, New York, N.Y. 10024; f. 1913; 3,673 mems. and subscribers; Sec. DONN E. ROSEN; publ. *Copeia* (quarterly).

**American Society of Mammalogists:** f. 1919, inc. 1920; 3,600 mems.; object of the Society is the promotion of interest in Mammalogy by holding meetings, issuing serial or other publications, and aiding research; five classes of mems., all elective: Annual, Life, Patron, Honorary and Emeritus; the Society is affiliated with the American Institute of Biological Sciences and the International Union for the Conservation of Nature; Sec.-Treas. Dr. GORDON L. KIRKLAND, Jr., c/o The

Vertebrate Museum, Shippensburg State College, Shippensburg, Pa. 17257; publs. *Journal of Mammalogy* (quarterly), *Mammalian Species* (irregular) and occasional monographs.

**American Society of Naturalists:** f. 1883; 655 mems.; Pres. Prof. RICHARD C. LEWONTIN; Sec. Prof. ROGER MILKMAN, Dept. of Zoology, Univ. of Iowa, Iowa City, Ia. 52242; publ. *The American Naturalist* (monthly).

**American Society of Parasitologists:** f. 1924; 1,800 mems.; Sec.-Treas. C. R. PAGE, III, Dept. of Biology, Tulane University, New Orleans, La. 70118; publ. *The Journal of Parasitology* (bi-monthly).

**American Society for Photobiology:** 4720 Montgomery Lane, Bethesda, Md. 20014; f. 1972; 700 mems.; Pres. A. LAMOLA; Exec. Sec. R. J. BURK, Jr.; publs. *Photochemistry* and *Photobiology* (monthly), *Newsletter* (bi-monthly).

**American Society of Zoologists:** f. 1913; to arrange meetings and publish journal; 4,500 mems.; Business Man. MARY WILEY, Box 2739, California Lutheran College, Thousand Oaks, Calif. 91360; publ. *American Zoologist* (quarterly).

**Biophysical Society:** 9650 Rockville Pike, Room 404, Bethesda, Md. 20014; f. 1957; 3,500 mems.; Pres. Dr. LEE D. PEACHEY; Sec. Dr. WINONA BARKER; publs. *Biophysical Journal*, abstracts of annual meetings.

**Botanical Society of America, Inc.:** School of Biological Sciences, Univ. of Kentucky, Lexington, Ky. 40506; f. 1906; 3,000 mems.; Sec. CAROL C. BASKIN; publs. *American Journal of Botany* (monthly), *Plant Science Bulletin* (6 a year), *Guide to Graduate Study in the U.S. and Canada* (irregular), *Directory* (every 2 or 3 years).

**Ecological Society of America:** f. 1915; 6,200 mems.; Sec. Dr. EDWARD J. KORMONDY, Dept. of Botany and Microbiology, Univ. of Oklahoma, Norman, Okla. 73019; publs. *Bulletin* (quarterly), *Ecology* (every 2 months), *Ecological Monographs* (quarterly).

**Entomological Society of America:** f. 1953 by the union of the American Association of Economic Entomologists (f. 1889) and the former Entomological Society of America (f. 1906); 8,300 mems.; Exec. Dir. DARRYL HANSEN, 4603 Calvert Rd., College Park, Maryland 20740; publs. *Annals of the Entomological Society of America* (bi-monthly), *Journal of Economic Entomology* (bi-monthly), *Environmental Entomology* (bi-monthly), *Bulletin* (quarterly), *Insecticide and Acaricide Tests* (annually), *Miscellaneous Publications of the E.S.A.* (irregular), *Pesticide Handbook—Entoma* (biennial), *Pesticide Index* (biennial).

**Environmental Mutagen Society:** 4720 Montgomery Lane, Bethesda, Md. 20014; f. 1969; 500 mems.; promotion of basic and applied studies of mutagenesis; makes an annual award; Pres. J. DRAKE; Administrative Officer R. J. BURK, Jr.; publ. *Mutation Research*.

**Federation of American Societies for Experimental Biology:** 9650 Rockville Pike, Bethesda, Maryland 20014; f. 1913; member societies—American Physiological Society, American Society of Biological Chemists, American Society for Pharmacology and Experimental Therapeutics, American Association of Pathologists, American Institute of Nutrition, American Association of Immunologists; Exec. Dir. ROBERT W. KRAUSS; publ. *Federation Proceedings* (monthly).

**Genetics Society of America:** c/o Business Office, P.O. Drawer U, University Sta. Austin, Tex. 78712; f. 1916; 3,200 mems.; Editor G. LEFEVRE; publ. *Genetics* (monthly).

**Mycological Society of America:** f. 1931; 1,500 mems.; Sec.-Treas. ROGER D. GOOS, Dept. of Botany, University of Rhode Island, Kingston, R.I. 02881; publs. *Mycologia* (every 2 months), *MSA Newsletter* (2 a year), *Mycologia Memoirs* (irregular).

**National Audubon Society:** 950 Third Ave., New York, N.Y. 10022; f. 1905; membership: approx. 370,000; c. 400 local chapters; library of 18,000 books and periodical titles; Pres. RUSSELL W. PETERSON, Sr.; Vice-Pres. PAUL HOWARD; publs. *Audubon* (every 2 months), *American Birds* (every 2 months).

**National Wildlife Federation:** 1412 16th St., N.W., Washington, D.C. 20036; f. 1936; 4,600,000 mems. and supporters; Pres. C. CLIFTON YOUNG; Exec. Vice-Pres. JAY D. HAIR; publs. *Conservation Report*, *National Wildlife Magazine†*, *International Wildlife Magazine†*, *Ranger Rick's Nature Magazine†*, *Conservation Directory*.

**Natural Resources Council of America:** Chair. LOUIS S. CLAPPER; Exec. Sec. (vacant), Box 20, Tracy's Landing, Md. 20869.

**The Nature Conservancy:** 1800 North Kent St. (No. 800), Arlington, Va. 22209; f. 1950, inc. in 1951; preservation of ecological diversity through protection of natural areas; 105,000 mems.; Pres. WILLIAM D. BLAIR, Jr.; publ. *Nature Conservancy News†* (every 2 months).

**Society for Developmental Biology:** f. 1939; c. 1,400 mems.; Sec. CLAUDIA FORET, 89 Depot Rd., Eliot, Me. 03903; publs. *Developmental Biology* (monthly), *Annual Symposia*.

**Society for Economic Botany:** Systematic and Evolutionary Biology, The Biological Sciences Group, Univ. of Connecticut, Storrs, Conn. 06268; f. 1959; 600 mems.; Pres. Dr. HARRY S. FONG; Sec. Dr. GREGORY J. ANDERSON; publ. *Economic Botany* (quarterly).

**Society of Vertebrate Paleontology:** Pres. FARISH A. JENKINS, Jr.; Sec.-Treas. BRUCE J. MACFADDEN, Florida State Museum, Univ. of Florida, Gainesville, Fla. 32611.

**Wildlife Management Institute:** 709 Wire Building, Washington, D.C. 20005; inc. 1946; 400 mems.; Pres. DANIEL A. POOLE; Vice-Pres. L. R. JAHN; publs. *North American Wildlife and Natural Resources Conference Transactions* (annual), *Outdoor News Bulletin* (bi-weekly).

**Wildlife Society, Inc., The:** 5410 Grosvenor Lane, Washington, D.C. 20014; f. 1937 to develop and promote sound stewardship of wildlife resources and of the environments upon which wildlife and man depend, to undertake an active role in preventing man-induced environmental degradation, to increase awareness and appreciation of wildlife values and to seek the highest standards in all activities of the wildlife profession; 8,000 mems.; Dir. RICHARD N. DENNEY; publs. *Journal of Wildlife Management*, *Wildlife Society Bulletin* (quarterly), *Wildlife Monographs*.

## Mathematics

**American Mathematical Society:** P.O.B. 6248, Providence, R.I. 02940; f. at Columbia Univ. in 1888 as the New York Mathematical Society; inc. 1923 as American Mathematical Society; membership 19,200; Sec. Prof. EVERETT PITCHER; Exec. Dir. Dr. WILLIAM J. LE VEQUE; publs. *Bulletin* (every 2 months), *Proceedings*, *Transactions*, *Mathematical Reviews* (monthly), *Mathematics of Computation* (quarterly), and others.

**Dozenal Society of America:** Math. Dept., Nassau Community College, Garden City, N.Y. 11530; inc. 1944; 115 mems; Chair. CHARLES BAGLEY; Pres. GENE ZIRKEL; publ. *Dozenal Journal* (1 or 2 a year).

**Industrial Mathematics Society:** P.O.B. 159, Roseville, Mich. 48066; f. 1949 to promote a better understanding of how mathematics may be used in the solution of complex problems in industry and various professions; 110 mems.; Pres. ROBERT SCHMIDT; Sec. NACLANE F. WAUGH; publ. *Industrial Mathematics* (2 a year).

**Mathematical Association of America, Inc.:** 1529 18th St., N.W. Washington, D.C. 20036; f. 1915; 19,000 mems.; Sec. D. P. ROSELLE; Exec. Dir. A. B. WILLCOX; publs. *American Mathematical Monthly* (10 a year), *Mathematics Magazine*† (5 a year), *Two-Year College Mathematics Journal* (5 a year), monographs, studies, notes.

### Physical Sciences

**Acoustical Society of America:** 335 East 45th St., New York, N.Y. 10017; f. 1929; 5,700 mems.; Pres. DAVID M. GREEN; Admin. Sec. BETTY H. GOODFRIEND; publ. *Journal* (monthly).

**American Association of Petroleum Geologists:** Box 979, Tulsa, Oklahoma 74101; f. 1917; 30,000 mems.; Exec. Dir. FRED A. DIX, Jr.; publs. *Bulletin*†, *AAPG Explorer* (monthly).

**American Astronomical Society:** Louisiana State Univ. Observatory, Box BK, Baton Rouge, La. 70803; f. 1899, inc. 1928; 3,700 mems.; Sec. Prof. ARLO U. LANDOLT; publs. *The Astronomical Journal* (monthly), *Bulletin* (quarterly), *The Astrophysical Journal* (2 a month), *AAS Photo Bulletin* (3 a year).

**American Chemical Society:** 1155 16th St., N.W., Washington, D.C. 20036; f. 1876; 120,000 mems.; Pres. Dr. ROBERT W. PARRY; Exec. Dir. Dr. RAYMOND P. MARIELLA; publs. include: *CHEMTECH, Chemical and Engineering News, Analytical Chemistry, Chemical Abstracts* and its various services, *Journal of Physical Chemistry, Journal* and others.

**American Crystallographic Association:** 335 E. 45th St., New York, N.Y. 10017; f. 1950; 1,800 mems.; crystallography and the application of diffraction methods to the study of the arrangement of atoms in matter; Pres. JEROME B. COHEN; Sec. Dr. K. ANN KERR; publs. *Newsletter* (every 2 months), *Program and Abstracts* (booklets, 2 a year), *Transactions* (annually).

**American Geological Institute:** 5205 Leesburg Pike, Falls Church, Va. 22041; f. 1948; 36,000 mems.; Exec. Dir. A. G. UNKLESBAY; publs. *Geotimes, International Geology Review, Bibliography and Index of Geology* (monthly), *Earth Science* (quarterly).

**American Geophysical Union:** 2000 Florida Ave., N.W., Washington, D.C. 20009; f. 1919; 13,000 mems.; has ten sections: Geodesy; Seismology; Meteorology; Geomagnetism and Palaeomagnetism; Oceanography; Volcanology, Geochemistry and Petrology; Hydrology; Tectonophysics; Planetology; Solar-Planetary Relations; Pres. J. TUZO WILSON; Exec. Dir. A. F. SPILHAUS, Jr.; publs. *Journal of Geophysical Research* (3 monthly sections), *Eos* (weekly), *Review of Geophysics and Space Physics* (quarterly), *Geophysical Research Letters* (monthly), and others.

**American Institute of Chemists:** 7315 Wisconsin Ave., Washington, D.C. 20014; f. 1923; 5,000 mems.; Pres. Dr. ROY L. WHISTLER; Exec. Dir. DAVID A. H. ROETHEL; publs. *The Chemist*† (monthly), *Professional Directory* (every 2 years).

**American Institute of Physics:** 335 East 45th St., New York, N.Y. 10017; f. 1931; composed of nine societies with total membership of approx. 60,000; Dir. H. WILLIAM KOCH; Sec. JOHN C. JOHNSON; 45 publs. including journals, bulletins, translated Russian and Chinese journals and secondary information services.

**American Meteorological Society:** f. 1919, inc. 1920; 9,600 mems.; Pres. Dr. ROBERT M. WHITE; Exec. Dir. Dr. KENNETH C. SPENGLER, 45 Beacon St., Boston, Mass. 02108; publs. *Bulletin, Meteorological Monographs. Meteorological and Geoastrophysical Abstracts, Journal of Physical Oceanography, Journal of the Atmospheric Sciences, Journal of Applied Meteorology, Monthly Weather Review, Historical Monographs*.

**American Microscopical Society:** Dept. of Biology, Bridgeport University, Bridgeport, Conn. 06602; f. 1878; 855 mems. and 699 subscribers; Treas. H. A. JAMES; publ. *Transactions* (quarterly).

**American Nuclear Society:** 555 North Kensington Ave., La Grange Park, Ill. 60525; f. 1954; 16 professional divisions and two technical groups: Alternative Energy Technologies and Systems, Fusion Energy, Education, Environmental Sciences, Isotopes and Radiation, Materials Science and Technology, Mathematics and Computation, Nuclear Criticality Safety, Fuel Cycle and Waste Management, Nuclear Reactor Safety, Power, Radiation Protection and Shielding, Reactor Operations, Reactor Physics, Remote Systems Technology, Thermal Hydraulics, Technical Group for Human Factor Systems; 47 local sections, 8 overseas local sections (one in Japan, one in Latin America, 4 in Europe, one in Taiwan, one in Ghana); 55 student branches; 13,000 mems. including 1,100 overseas mems. in 40 countries; 185 organization mems.; Pres. CORWIN RICKARD; Exec. Dir. OCTAVE J. DU TEMPLE; publs. *Nuclear Science and Engineering, Nuclear Report* (monthly), *Nuclear News* (15 a year), *Nuclear Technology* (15 a year), *Transactions* (2 a year), *Proceedings of the Remote Systems Technology, Buyers' Guide* (annually), *Washington Newsletter*, nuclear standards, technical monographs and topical meeting proceedings.

**American Pharmaceutical Association:** 2215 Constitution Avenue N.W., Washington, D.C. 20037; f. 1852; 56,000 mems.; Pres. and Chief Exec. Officer Dr. WILLIAM S. APPLE; publs. *American Pharmacy, Journal of Pharmaceutical Sciences* (monthly), *Contemporary Pharmacy Practice* (quarterly), *Pharmacy Weekly*.

**American Physical Society:** 335 East 45th St., New York, N.Y. 10017; f. 1899; 30,000 mems.; Sec. Dr. W. W. HAVENS, Jr.; publs. *Bulletin, Physical Review, Reviews of Modern Physics, Physical Review Letters*.

**American Society of Biological Chemists, Inc.:** 9650 Rockville Pike, Bethesda, Md. 20014; f. 1906; 5,000 mems.; Exec. Officer C. C. HANCOCK; publ. *Journal of Biological Chemistry* (twice-monthly).

**Electrochemical Society, Inc.:** 10 South Main St., Pennington, N.J. 08534; f. 1902; approx. 5,300 mems.; Exec. Sec. V. H. BRANNEKY; publs. *Journal* (12 issues annually), softbound symposium volumes, hardbound monograph series.

**Electron Microscopy Society of America:** Oak Ridge National Laboratory, P.O.B. X, Oak Ridge, Tenn. 37830; f. 1942; annual meeting, presenting technical papers and exhibits; aims to increase and diffuse knowledge of electron microscopy and related instruments and results obtained through their use; 3,400 mems.; Sec. FRANCES BALL; publs. *Proceedings* (annually), *Bulletin* (2 a year).

**Geochemical Society:** Dept. of Geological Studies, Virginia Polytechnic Institute, Blacksburg, Va. 24061; f. 1955; 1,400 mems.; Pres. G. R. TILTON; Sec. T. TAKAHASHI; publ. *Geochimica et Cosmochimica Acta*.

**Geological Society of America, Inc.:** P.O.B. 9140, 3300 Penrose Place, Boulder, Colo. 80301; f. 1888; total membership 12,720; Exec. Dir. JOHN C. FRYE; publs. *Geology* (monthly), *Bulletin* (monthly), *Special Papers, Maps and Charts, Memoirs, Treatise on Invertebrate Paleontology* (irregularly), *Abstracts with Programs* (7 issues annually).

**Mineralogical Society of America:** 2000 Florida St., N.W., Washington, D.C. 20009; f. 1919; 2,600 mems.; Pres. G. V. GIBBS; Sec. M. CHARLES GILBERT; publ. *The American Mineralogist* (every 2 months).

**Oak Ridge Associated Universities, Inc.:** P.O.B. 117, Oak Ridge, Tenn. 37830; f. 1946; educational and research corporation of c. 50 colleges and universities; seeks to help the U.S. Dept. of Energy, other private and governmental organizations, and its member institutions to solve societal problems relating to energy, health and the environment; among these activities are co-operative university-DOE laboratory programmes, including graduate-level training opportunities and research-participation opportunities for faculty and students; public and professional education in subjects related to energy and the environment; clinical and preclinical research in radiopharmaceuticals and the effects on health of energy technologies; a marmoset research centre; manpower training for high-technology industry; Exec. Dir. Dr. PHILIP L. JOHNSON.

**Optical Society of America:** 1816 Jefferson Place, N.W., Washington, D.C. 20036; f. 1916; a national organization devoted to the advancement of optics and the service of all who are interested in any phase of that science; member Society of American Institute of Physics; 8,000 mems.; Pres. ANTHONY J. DEMARIA; Exec. Dir. JARUS W. QUINN; publs. *Journal, Applied Optics* (2 a month), *Optics Letters* (monthly).

**Paleontological Society:** f. 1909 to publish and disseminate palaeontological research; 1,650 mems.; associated with the Geological Society of America; Sec. WALTER C. SWEET, Dept. of Geology, Ohio State University, Columbus, Ohio 43210; publs. *Journal of Paleontology* (every 2 months), *The Paleontological Society Memoirs* (irregular), *Paleobiology* (quarterly), *News and Notes* (quarterly).

**Seismological Society of America:** 2620 Telegraph Ave., Berkeley, Calif. 94704; f. 1906; 1,700 mems.; seismology, earthquake engineering, earthquake geology, etc.; Sec. LANE R. JOHNSON; publ. *Bulletin* (bi-monthly).

**Society of Economic Geologists:** 185 Estes St., Lakewood, Colo. 80226; f. 1920; 1,500 mems.; Sec. A. L. BROKAW; publ. *Economic Geology* (8 a year).

**Society of Economic Paleontologists and Mineralogists:** P.O.B. 4756, Tulsa, Okla. 74104; f. 1926; 5,500 mems.; Sec.-Treas. RONALD D. PERKINS; publs. *Journal of Paleontology* (bi-monthly), *Journal of Sedimentary Petrology* (quarterly).

PHILOSOPHY AND PSYCHOLOGY

**American Philosophical Association:** f. 1900; 6,200 mems.; to promote the exchange of ideas among philosophers, to encourage creative and scholarly activity in philosophy and to facilitate the professional work of teachers of philosophy; Chair. RUTH BARCAN MARCUS; Sec. JOHN O'CONNOR, Univ. of Delaware, Newark, Del. 19711; publs. *Proceedings and Addresses of APA members, Jobs for Philosophers, Grants and Fellowships of Interest to Philosophers, Guidebook for Publishing Philosophy, Role of Philosophy in Higher Education.*

**American Psychological Association:** f. 1892; 50,000 mems.; Exec. Officer MICHAEL PALLAK, 1200 17th St., N.W., Washington, D.C. 20036; publs. *American Psychologist* (monthly), *APA Monitor* (monthly), *Psychological Abstracts* (monthly), and sixteen others.

**Metaphysical Society of America:** c/o Sec./Treas., EUGENE T. LONG, Dept. of Philosophy, University of South Carolina, Columbia, S.C. 29208; 700 mems.; f. 1950 to study metaphysical problems without regard to professional, racial, religious and regional boundaries; Pres. THOMAS LANGAN.

**Philosophy of Science Association:** Philosophy Dept., Michigan State University, East Lansing, Mich. 48824; f. 1934 to further studies and free discussion in the field of philosophy of science; 1,000 mems.; Pres. ERNAN MCMULLIN; Exec. Sec. PETER D. ASQUITH; publs. *Philosophy of Science* (quarterly), *Newsletter* (quarterly), *Proceedings of Biennial Meetings.*

**Psychometric Society:** Davie Hall, University of North Carolina, Chapel Hill, N.C. 27514; f. 1935; 1,400 mems.; Sec. MARK APPELBAUM; publ. *Psychometrika* (quarterly).

RELIGION, SOCIOLOGY AND ANTHROPOLOGY

**African Studies Association:** 255 Kinsey Hall, Univ. of California, Los Angeles, Calif. 90024; f. 1957; 2,300 mems.; encourages research and collects and disseminates information on Africa; Pres. Prof. NORMAN BENNETT; Sec. DONALD COSENTINO; publs. *Review, Newsletter, Issue.*

**American Academy of Religion:** Dept. of Religious Studies, California State University, Chico, Chico, Calif. 95929; f. 1909; society for teachers of and researchers into religion and religious studies; informs members of current developments within the field and of new materials and opportunities for study grants and research funds; 4,600 mems.; Pres. GORDON KAUFMAN; Sec. JUDITH PLASKOW; Exec. Dir. CHARLES E. WINQUIST; publs. *Journal, Journal Thematic Supplement, Studies in Religion Series, Academy Series, Texts and Translations Series.*

**American Anthropological Association:** 1703 New Hampshire Ave., N.W., Washington, D.C. 20009; f. 1902; 10,400 mems.; Pres. WILLIAM C. STURTEVANT; Exec. Dir. E. J. LEHMAN; publs. *American Anthropologist* (quarterly), *Anthropology Newsletter* (9 a year), *Guide to Departments of Anthropology* (annually).

**American Folklore Society, Inc.:** 1703 New Hampshire Ave., N.W., Washington, D.C. 20009; f. 1888; 1,500 mems.; Sec.-Treas. CHARLES CAMP; publs. *Journal of American Folklore* (quarterly), *Publications.*

**American Oriental Society:** 329 Sterling Memorial Library, Yale Station, New Haven, Conn.; f. 1842; 1,900 mems.; library of 19,560 vols.; Pres. RICHARD MATHER; Sec. STANLEY INSLER; publs. *Journal†* (quarterly), *Monograph Series.*

**American Personnel and Guidance Association:** 5203 Leesburg Pike, Falls Church, Va. 22041; f. 1952; counselling, guidance and student personnel services; 42,000 mems.; 13 divisions: American College Personnel Asscn., Asscn. for Counsellor Education and Supervision, National Vocational Guidance Asscn., Asscn. for Humanistic Education and Development, American School Counselor Asscn., American Rehabilitation Counseling Asscn., Asscn. for Measurement and Evaluation in Guidance, National Employment Counselors Asscn., Asscn. of Non-White Concerns in Personnel and Guidance, Asscn. for Religion and Values in Counseling, Asscn. of Specialists in Group Work, Public Offender Counselors Asscn., American Mental Health Counselors Asscn.; Exec. Dir. Dr. CHARLES L. LEWIS; publs. 16 periodicals on aspects of counselling, guidance and personnel.

**American Society for Ethnohistory:** Dept. of Anthropology, Midwestern State University, Wichita Falls, Tex. 76308; f. 1954; 1,200 mems.; to promote and encourage research into the documentary history of the culture of primitive peoples, and related problems; Sec.-Treas. J. E. AYRES; publ. *Ethnohistory* (quarterly).

**American Sociological Association:** 1722 N St., N.W., Washington, D.C. 20036; f. 1905; 14,500 mems.; Pres. ERVING GOFFMAN; Exec. Officer RUSSELL DYNES; publs. *The American Sociological Review* (every 2 months), *Sociology of Education, The American Sociologist, Journal of Health and Social Behavior, Social Psychology* (quarterly), *Contemporary Sociology* (every 2 months).

**American Studies Association:** 307 College Hall/CO, University of Pennsylvania, Philadelphia, Pa. 19104; f. 1951; research and teaching in the field of U.S. culture; 3,000 individual mems., 200 institutions; Pres. ROBERT F. BERKHOFER; Exec. Dir. ROBERTA K. GLADOWSKI; publ. *American Quarterly*.

**Association for Asian Studies, Inc.:** 1 Lane Hall, University of Michigan, Ann Arbor, Mich. 48109; f. 1941; 5000 mems.; Sec.-Treas. RHOADS MURPHEY; publs. *Bibliography of Asian Studies* (annually), *Journal of Asian Studies* (quarterly), *Asian Studies Newsletter* (5 a year), *Doctoral Dissertations on Asia, Membership Directory* (irregularly).

**Association for the Study of Afro-American Life and History, Inc.:** 1401 14th St., N.W., Washington, D.C. 20005; f. 1915; 30,000 mems.; publs. *Afro-American History Bulletin* (8 a year), *Journal of Afro-American History* (quarterly).

**National Institute of Social Sciences:** 150 Amsterdam Ave., New York, N.Y. 10023; f. 1899; 850 mems.; Pres. J. SINCLAIR ARMSTRONG; Sec. BRUCE E. BALDING.

**Pacific Sociological Association:** Dept. of Sociology, Arizona State University, Tempe, Ariz. 85287; 823 mems.; Pres. LOIS B. DEFLEUR; Sec.-Treas. FRED B. LINDSTROM; publ. *Pacific Sociological Review*.

**Population Association of America, Inc.:** P.O.B. 14182, Benjamin Franklin Station, Washington, D.C. 20044; f. 1932; 2,500 mems.; Pres. J. S. SIEGEL; publs. *Demography, Population Index, PAA Affairs*.

**The Population Council, Inc.:** 1 Dag Hammarskjold Plaza, New York, N.Y. 10017; Center for Biomedical Research, Tower Building, 1230 York Ave. at 64th St., New York, N.Y. 10021; f. 1952; non-governmental and non-profitmaking organization; aims to enhance human welfare in the following areas: human reproductive biomedicine, social science relevant to the understanding of public policy issues; health, family planning and other population related programmes to strengthen local, national and regional institutions; publications for scientists, policy-makers and the concerned public training of population specialists; Chair. Board of Trustees ROBERT H. EBERT; Pres. GEORGE ZEIDENSTEIN; Vice-Pres. and Dir. Centre for Biomedical Research C. WAYNE BARDIN; Vice-Pres. and Dir. Centre for Policy Research PAUL DEMENY; Vice-Pres. and Treas. JAMES BAUSCH; Vice-Pres. and Dir. International Programs GEORGE F. BROWN; publs. *Annual Reports, Studies in Family Planning, Population and Development Review, Fact Books*, public issues papers and monographs.

**Religious Research Association:** P.O.B. 303, Manhattanville Station, New York, N.Y. 10027; f. 1959; aims to increase understanding of the function of religion in persons and society through application of social scientific and other scholarly methods; to promote religious research; to co-operate with other societies and individuals interested in the study of religion; c. 400 mems.; Pres. DAVID O. MOBERG; Sec. CONSTANT H. JACQUET; publ. *Review of Religious Research†*.

**Russell Sage Foundation:** 230 Park Ave., New York, N.Y. 10017; inc. 1907 to promote improvement of social and living conditions in the United States; supports social science research in policy analysis, culture, citizenship and institutions; Chair. OSCAR M. RUEBHAUSEN; Pres. MARSHALL A. ROBINSON; Sec. WARREN H. BACON; publs. research findings in book form, books-in-print catalogue, *Annual Report*.

**Society for Applied Anthropology:** 1703 New Hampshire Ave., N.W., Washington, D.C. 20009; f. 1941; 2,400 mems.; Pres. WILLIS SIBLEY; publs. *Human Organization* (quarterly), *Practicing Anthropology, Monograph Series*.

**Society for the Study of Evolution:** EPO Biology, Univ. of Colorado, Boulder, Colo. 80302; f. 1946 to promote the study of organic evolution and the integration of the various fields of science concerned with evolution; Pres. O. SOLBRIG; Sec. JEFFERY MITTON; publ. *Evolution*.

TECHNOLOGY

**American Ceramic Society, Inc.:** 65 Ceramic Dr., Columbus, Ohio 43214; f. 1899; 7,625 individual mems., 242 corporation mems.; Exec. Dir. ARTHUR L. FRIEDBERG; publs. *Journal, Communications, Ceramic Bulletin* (monthly), *Ceramic Abstracts, Ceramic Engineering and Science Proceedings* (every 2 months).

**American Consulting Engineers Council:** 1015 15th St., N.W., Washington, D.C. 20005; f. 1910; 3,650 mems.; Exec. Vice-Pres. L. SPILLER; publ. *Directory*.

**American Institute of Aeronautics and Astronautics:** 1290 Ave. of the Americas, N.Y. 10104; f. 1932; 24,336 professional, 4,039 student mems.; Pres. G. GAVIN; Exec. Sec. JAMES HARFORD; publs. *Astronautics & Aeronautics* (includes *AIAA Bulletin*), *Journal, Journal of Spacecraft and Rockets, Journal of Aircraft, Journal of Energy, Journal of Hydronautics, International Aerospace Abstracts, AIAA Journal, Journal of Guidance and Control*.

**American Institute of Chemical Engineers:** 345 East 47th St., New York, N.Y. 10017; f. 1908; 52,000 mems.; Pres. W. K. DAVIS; Exec. Dir. J. CHARLES FORMAN; publs. *A.I.Ch.E. Journal* (bi-monthly), *Chemical Engineering Progress* (monthly), *International Chemical Engineering, Energy Progress, Environmental Progress, Plant/Operations Progress* (all quarterly), *Monograph and Symposium Series*.

**American Institute of Industrial Engineers, Inc.:** 25 Technology Park Atlanta, Norcross, Ga. 30092; f. 1948; 37,000 mems.; Exec. Dir. DAVID BELDEN; publs. *Industrial Engineering* (monthly), *AIIE Transactions, The Engineering Economist* (quarterly).

**American Institute of Mining, Metallurgical and Petroleum Engineers, Inc.:** 345 East 47th St., New York, N.Y. 10017; f. 1871; 73,000 mems.; Pres. WILLIAM H. WISE; Exec. Dir. JOE B. ALFORD; publs. *Mining Engineering, Journal of Metals, Iron and Steelmaker, Journal of Petroleum Technology* (monthly), *Metallurgical Transactions A* (monthly), *Metallurgical Transactions B* (quarterly), *Society of Petroleum Engineers Journal* (every 2 months), *Society of Mining Engineers Transactions and Society of Petroleum Engineers Transactions* (annually).

**American Iron and Steel Institute:** 1000 16th St., N.W., Washington, D.C. 20036; f. 1908; 2,614 mems.; Pres. ROBERT B. PEABODY; Exec. Vice-Pres. and Treas. JAMES F. COLLINS.

**American National Standards Institute:** 1430 Broadway, New York, N.Y. 10018; f. 1918; mems. 900 companies, 200 organizations; library of 13,000 vols.; Pres. WILLIAM H. GATENBY; Exec. Vice-Pres. and Sec. DONALD L. PEYTON; publ. *Reporter/Standards Action* (bi-weekly).

**American Society for Engineering Education:** f. 1893; 13,000 mems., 550 institutional mems.; for the improvement of higher and continuing education for engineers and engineering technologists including teaching, counselling, research, ethics, etc.; Exec. Dir. D. E. MARLOWE, Suite 400, One Dupont Circle, Washington, D.C. 20036; publs. *Engineering Education* (8 a year), *Engineering Education News* (monthly), *Chemical Engineering Education, Civil Engineering Education, Computers in Education Transactions, Engineering Economist, Mechanical Engineering News, Technos*

**American Society for Metals:** Metals Park, Ohio 44073; f. 1913; 50,000 mems.; Man. Dir. A. R. PUTNAM; publs. *Metal Progress* (monthly), *Metallurgical Transactions A* (monthly) & *B* (quarterly) (with TMS-AIME), *ASM News* (monthly), *Metals Abstracts* (monthly), *Metals Abstracts Index* (monthly), *Metal Progress Databook* (annually), *Metal Progress Heat Treating Buyer's Guide & Directory* (annually), *International Metals Reviews* (every 2 months, with The Metals Society), *Ironmaking and Steelmaking* (every 2 months), *Digest Series* (9 publications monthly), *Journal of Materials for Energy Systems, Journal of Applied Metalworking, Journal of Heat Treating* (all quarterly), *Alloys Index*.

**American Society for Testing and Materials (ASTM):** 1916 Race St., Philadelphia, Pa. 19103; inc. 1902; voluntary concensus standards; 30,000 mems.; Pres. W. T. CAVANAUGH; publs. *Proceedings* (annually), *ASTM Book of Standards* (annually), *Journal of Testing and Evaluation* (bi-monthly), *Standardization News* (monthly), *Journal of Forensic Sciences* (quarterly), *Composites Technology Review* (quarterly), *Geotechnical Testing Journal* (quarterly), *Cement, Concrete and Aggregates* (2 a year).

**American Society of Agricultural Engineers:** Box 410, Saint Joseph, Michigan 49085; f. 1907; 11,000 mems.; Exec. Vice-Pres. J. L. BUTT; publs. *Agricultural Engineering* (monthly), *Agricultural Engineers' Yearbook* (annual), *Transactions of the A.S.A.E.* (bi-monthly), proceedings and books.

**American Society of Civil Engineers:** 345 East 47th St., New York, N.Y. 10017; f. 1852; 68,000 mems.; Exec. Dir. EUGENE ZWOYER; publs. *Proceedings* (monthly), *Transactions* (annually), *Civil Engineering, ASCE* (monthly), *ASCE Publications Abstracts* (bi-monthly).

**American Society of Heating, Refrigerating and Air-Conditioning Engineers, Inc.:** 1791 Tullie Circle, N.E., Atlanta, Ga. 30329; f. 1959 by merger of the American Society of Heating and Ventilating Engineers and the American Society of Refrigerating Engineers; approx. 44,000 mems.; Sec. and Exec. Vice-Pres. A. T. BOGGS III; publs. *ASHRAE Journal* (monthly), *ASHRAE Handbook & Product Directory, Standards, Transactions* (annually), *Research Bulletins*.

**American Society of Mechanical Engineers:** United Engineering Center, 345 East 47th St., New York, N.Y. 10017; f. 1880; 95,000 mems.; Pres. ORVAL L. LEWIS; Exec. Dir. and Sec. R. B. FINCH; publs. *Mechanical Engineering* (monthly), *Applied Mechanics Reviews* (monthly), *Transactions* (divided into 11 periodicals, each published quarterly): *Journal of Engineering for Power, Journal of Engineering for Industry, Journal of Applied Mechanics, Journal of Heat Transfer, Journal of Lubrication Technology, Journal of Dynamic Systems, Measurement and Control, Journal of Fluids Engineering, Journal of Engineering Materials and Technology, Journal of Pressure Vessel Technology, Journal of Biochemical Engineering, Journal of Mechanical Design*.

**American Society of Naval Engineers, Inc.:** 1012 '14th St., N.W., Suite 807, Washington, D.C. 20005; f. 1888; over 5,000 mems.; Pres. Vice-Adm. C. R. BRYAN, U.S.N., retd.; Sec.-Treas. Capt. JAMES L. McVOY, retd.; publ. *Naval Engineers Journal* (6 a year).

**American Society of Photogrammetry:** 105 North Virginia Ave., Falls Church, Va. 22046; f. 1934; 7,500 mems.; Exec. Dir. WILLIAM D. FRENCH; publs. *Manuals of Photogrammetry, Color Aerial Photography, Manual of Remote Sensing, Handbook of Non-Topographic Photogrammetry, Photogrammetric Engineering and Remote Sensing†* (monthly).

**American Welding Society:** 2501 N.W. 7th St., Miami, Fla. 33125; f. 1919; 30,000 mems.; Exec. Dir. J. E. DATO; publs. *Welding Journal* (monthly), *Welding Handbook* (biennial).

**Association of Consulting Chemists and Chemical Engineers, Inc.:** Suite 92, 50 E. 41st St., New York, N.Y. 10017; f. 1928; 125 mems.; Exec. Sec. A. K. PETERSON; publ. *Consulting Services*.

**Edison Electric Institute:** 1111 19th St., N.W., Washington, D.C. 20036; f. 1933; mems. U.S. investor-owned electric companies; Pres. WILLIAM McCOLLAM, Jr.

**Illuminating Engineering Society of North America:** 345 East 47th St., New York, N.Y. 10017; f. 1906; 9,500 mems.; Exec. Vice-Pres. M. G. MELDEN; publs. *Lighting Design and Application* (monthly), *Journal* (quarterly), *IES Lighting Handbooks* (2 vols.—Reference and Application, alternately every 5 years).

**Industrial Designers Society of America, Inc.:** 6802 Poplar Place, McLean, Va. 22101; f. 1965 through merger of American Society of Industrial Designers (f. 1944), Industrial Designers Institute (f. 1938) and Industrial Design Education Association; 1,500 mems.; Exec. Dir. BRIAN J. WYNNE.

**Institute of Electrical and Electronics Engineers, Inc.:** 345 East 47th St., New York, N.Y. 10017; f. 1884; 200,000 mems.; Exec. Dir. R. M. EMBERSON; publs. *IEEE Spectrum* (monthly), *Proceedings* (monthly), *IEEE Journal of Solid State Circuits*, specialized conference records.

**Institute of Food Technologists:** 221 North La Salle St., Chicago, Ill. 60601; f. 1939; 18,000 mems.; Pres. Dr. F. J. FRANCIS; Exec. Dir. CALVERT L. WILLEY; publs. *Food Technology* (monthly), *Journal of Food Science* (bi-monthly).

**Instrument Society of America:** P.O.B. 12277, 67 Alexander Drive, Research Triangle Park, N.C. 27709; f. 1945; 26,000 mems.; Exec. Dir. D. R. HARTING; Pres. J. R. MIDDLETON; conferences and symposia, exhibits, short courses, special interest divisions, films, audio and video cassettes; publs. *Instrumentation Technology* (monthly), *ISA Transactions* (quarterly), *ISA Instrumentation Index* (quarterly), *InTech*, proceedings, standards, monographs, references, compendia, study guides.

**International Communication Association:** formerly National Society for the Study of Communication; f. 1950 to bring together academics and professionals concerned with research and application of human communication; 2,100 mems.; Pres. STEVEN H. CHAFFEE; Exec. Sec. ROBERT L. COX, Balcones Research Center, 10100 Burnet Rd., Austin, Tex. 78758; publs. *The Journal of Communication, Human Communication Research, Membership Directory, Program* (annual), *The ICA Newsletter, The Communication Yearbook*.

**Mining and Metallurgical Society of America:** 230 Park Ave., New York, N.Y. 10169; Pres. MILTON H. WARD.

**National Association of Power Engineers, Inc.:** 176 West Adams St., Suite 1914, Chicago, Ill. 60603; f. 1882; 12,000 mems.; Man. H. L. PATTON; publ. *National Engineer* (monthly).

**National Society of Professional Engineers:** 2029 K St., N.W., Washington, D.C. 20006; f. 1934; professional aspects of engineering; 80,000 mems.; Exec. Dir. DONALD G. WEINERT; publs. *Professional Engineer, Engineering Times* (monthly).

**Society for the History of Technology:** Dept. of History, UCSB, Santa Barbara, Calif. 93106; concerned with history of technological devices and processes, relations of technology with science, politics, social change, the arts and humanities, and economics; affiliated to the American Association for the Advancement of Science, the American Council of Learned Societies and the Engineers Joint Council; 2,000 mems.; Pres. THOMAS P. HUGHES; Sec. Dr. CARROLL W. PURSELL, Jr.; publs. *Technology and Culture* (quarterly), *Monograph Series*.

**Society of Automotive Engineers, Inc.:** 400 Commonwealth Drive, Warrendale, Pa. 15096; f. 1905; 39,000 mems.; Sec. and Gen. Man. JOSEPH GILBERT; publs. *SAE Transactions, SAE Handbook* (annually), *Automotive Engineering* (monthly).

**Society of Naval Architects and Marine Engineers:** One World Trade Center, Suite 1369, New York, N.Y. 10048; f. 1893; c. 13,000 mems.; Sec. and Exec. Dir. ROBERT G. MENDE.

**Society of Rheology:** 335 East 45th St., New York, N.Y. 10017; f. 1929; Pres. E. B. BAGLEY; Sec. M. T. SHAW; publs. *Rheology Bulletin* (irregular), *Journal of Rheology* (every 2 months).

**United Engineering Trustees, Inc.:** 345 East 47th St., New York, N.Y. 10017; f. 1904 as a joint corporate agency of the major national engineering societies, to administer substantial trust funds for the advancement of the engineering arts and sciences, including ownership and administration of Engineering Societies Library (q.v.), Engineering Foundation, United Engineering Center, and several awards; library of over 200,000 vols.; Pres. OSCAR BRAY; Sec. and Gen. Man. ALEXANDER KORWEK.

**Engineering Foundation:** 345 East 47th St., New York, N.Y. 10017; f. 1914 by 5 major engineering societies to administer trust funds for the furtherance of research in science and engineering and the advancement in any other manner of the profession of engineering and the good of mankind; 19 mems.; Sec. JOHN A. ZECCA; publ. *Annual Report*.

## RESEARCH INSTITUTES

*More than 90 per cent of research in America is conducted by the universities and private industry. Most of the organizations listed below are independent, non-profit-making institutions.*

### AGRICULTURE AND VETERINARY SCIENCE

**Agricultural Research Institute:** 2100 Pennsylvania Ave., N.W., Washington, D.C. 20037; f. 1951; 150 mems.; Pres. DONALD W. BARTON; publs. *Newsletter* (quarterly), *Proceedings* (annual).

**Forest Products Research Society:** 2801 Marshall Court, Madison, Wis. 53705; f. 1947; 5,000 mems. from 62 countries; Exec. Vice-Pres. ARTHUR B. BRAUNER; publs. *Journal* (monthly), *Wood Science* (quarterly).

### BIBLIOGRAPHY AND LIBRARY SCIENCE

**Institute for Scientific Information:** 3501 Market St., University City Science Center, Philadelphia, Pa. 19104; f. 1960; periodicals library of 6,500 titles; Pres. Dr. EUGENE GARFIELD; Vice-Pres. and Treas. MARVIN SCHROEDER; publs. *Journal Citation Reports, Science Citation Index, Social Sciences Citation Index, Arts and Humanities Citation Index, Index to Scientific and Technical Proceedings, Index to Scientific Reviews, Index to Social Sciences and Humanities Proceedings, Automatic Subject Citation Alert (ASCA), Ascatopics, Current Abstracts of Chemistry and Index Chemicus, Encyclopaedia Chimica Internationalis, Chemical Substructure Index, Index Chemicus Registry System, Current Bibliographic Directory to the Arts and Sciences, ISI Magnetic Tapes, Scisearch, Social Scisearch, Index to Scientific and Technical Proceedings and Books, Automatic New Structure Alert (ANSA)* and *Current Contents* in the following editions: *Agriculture, Biology and Environmental Sciences; Social and Behavioral Sciences; Physical, Chemical and Earth Sciences; Engineering, Technology and Applied Sciences; Life Sciences; Clinical Practice.*

**National Federation of Abstracting and Indexing Services:** 112 South 16th St., Philadelphia, Pa. 19102; f. 1958; 44 mems.; Pres. E. K. GANNETT; Exec. Dir. M. LYNNE NEUFELD; publs. *NFAIS Newsletter, Report Series, State-of-the-Art Publications*.

### ECONOMICS, LAW AND POLITICS

**Brookings Institution:** 1775 Massachusetts Ave., N.W., Washington, D.C. 20036; f. 1927; 120 professional mems.; library of 50,000 vols.; research, education, and publishing in the fields of economics, government, and foreign policy; Pres. BRUCE K. MACLAURY; publs. *Brookings Bulletin* (quarterly), *Brookings Papers on Economic Activity* (3 a year), *Reprint Series* (irregular).

**East-West Center:** 1777 East-West Rd., Honolulu, Hawaii 96848; f. 1960; financed largely by U.S. Congress with contributions from Asian Pacific countries to promote better relations and understanding among peoples of Asia, the Pacific and the U.S.A.; provides awards to 1,500 scholars, authorities, researchers, graduate students, managers, to work on problems which are actual or potential sources of difference between East and West; consists of five institutes: Communication, Culture Learning, Environment and Policy, Population, and Resource Systems; undertakes open grants and special projects; Pres. VICTOR HAO LI; publs. *East-West Perspectives, Asian and Pacific Census Forum, Culture Learning Institute Report, East-West Resource Systems Institute Newsletter, Language Planning Newsletter, Environment and Policy Newsletter.*

**(Robert Maynard) Hutchins Center for the Study of Democratic Institutions:** Box 4068, Santa Barbara, Calif. 93103; f. 1959, name changed 1979; Chair. MORRIS L. LEVINSON; Pres. ROBERT M. HUTCHINS; Sec. and Treas. PETER TAGGER; publs. *The Center Magazine, World Issues* (every 2 months).

**Marketing Science Institute:** 14 Story St., Cambridge, Mass. 02138; f. 1962 to contribute to improved marketing performance by developing objective, factual information about marketing practices and their effects by devising and testing new methods for analysing these facts, and by appraising social and economic issues related to marketing; Chair. HENRY SCHACHTE; Exec. Dir. STEPHEN A. GREYSER.

**National Bureau of Economic Research:** 1050 Massachusetts Ave., Cambridge, Mass. 02138; f. 1920; fundamental qualitative analysis of the U.S. economy; 50 Dirs.; Pres. MARTIN FELDSTEIN; Exec. Dir. DAVID HARTMAN.

**Scripps Foundation for Research in Population Problems and Gerontology Center:** Miami University, 327 Hoyt, Oxford, Ohio 45056; f. 1922; 8 mems.; library of 4,000 vols.; Dir. ROBERT C. ATCHLEY.

### EDUCATION

**American Educational Research Association:** 1230 17th St., N.W., Washington, D.C. 20036; f. 1915; 13,000 mems.; Exec. Officer WILLIAM J. RUSSELL; publs. *American Educational Research Journal, Review of Educational Research, Educational Researcher, Review* of Research in Education, Journal of Educational Statistics, Educational Evaluation and Policy Analysis, Contemporary Educational Reviews.

**National Institute of Education:** 1200 19th St. N.W., Washington, D.C. 20208; f. 1972 by Congress; part of the U.S. Dept. of Education; main government agency supporting educational research; aims to promote educational equity and improve the quality of educational practice; three programme areas: Teaching and Learning, Educational Policy and Organization, Dissemination and Improvement of Practice; Dir. MILTON GOLDBERG; publs. Publications and Papers, NIE Information, reports.

HISTORY, GEOGRAPHY AND ARCHAEOLOGY

**Center for Reformation Research:** 6477 San Bonita Ave., St. Louis, Mo. 63105; f. 1957; microfilm library of original MSS. and printed materials of the 15th and 16th centuries; reference library; Exec. Dir. WILLIAM MALTBY; publs. Newsletter, Sixteenth-Century Bibliography (occasionally).

**Leo Baeck Institute, Inc.:** 129 East 73rd St., New York, N.Y. 10021; f. 1954; research and publication about the history of German-speaking Jews; library of 60,000 vols., archives and art collection; Pres. Dr. M. GRUENEWALD; Sec. F. GRUBEL; publs. LBI Yearbook, Bulletin (in German), LBI News, Library and Archives News.

**Mississippi Bureau of Geology:** P.O.B. 5348, Jackson, Missisippi 39216; f. 1850; research into the resources of the State; library of 60,000 vols.; Dir. A. R. BICKER, Jr.; publs. Bulletins, Information Series, Environmenta Geology Series, Mississipi Geology.

**Paleontological Research Institution:** 1259 Trumansburg Rd., Ithaca, N.Y. 14850; f. 1932; over 600 mems.; library of 50,000 vols.; Dir. Dr. PETER R. HOOVER; publs. Bulletins of American Paleontology†, Palaeontographica Americana†, etc.

**School of American Research:** Box 2188, Santa Fé, New Mexico 87501; f. 1907; conducts research in archaeology; grants to four resident scholars annually; advanced seminars in anthropology; anthropological publications; extensive collections in Southwest Indian art; 1,400 mems.; library of 6,000 vols.; Pres. DOUGLAS W. SCHWARTZ; Chair. JASON W. KELLAHIN.

MEDICINE

**American Association for Cancer Research, Inc.:** 1275 York Ave., New York, N.Y. 10021; f. 1907; 3,455 mems.; Pres. Dr. SIDNEY WEINHOUSE; Sec.-Treas. Dr. FREDERICK S. PHILIPS; publ. Cancer Research (monthly).

**American Federation for Clinical Research:** 6900 Grove Rd., Thorofare, N.J. 08086; f. 1940; 10,600 Mems.; Pres. SUZANNE OPARIL, M.D.; publ. Clinical Research (5 a year).

**Association for Research in Nervous and Mental Disease, Inc.:** c/o Secretary, B. COHEN, Mt. Sinai School of Medicine, 100th St. at 5th Ave., New York, N.Y. 10029; f. 1920; 1,500 mems.

**Association for Research in Vision and Ophthalmology, Inc.:** P.O.B. 1001, Wy Kagyl Station, New Rochelle, N.Y. 10804; f. 1928; 2,100 mems.; Chair. GUNTHER VON NOORDEN, M.D.; Sec.-Treas. PAUL HENKIND, M.D., PH.D.; publ. Investigative Ophthalmology and Visual Science.

**Eye Research Institute of the Retina Foundation:** 20 Staniford St., Boston, Mass. 02114; f. 1950; basic and clinical research on causes, prevention and treatment of eye diseases, development of diagnostic and therapeutic devices, instruments and techniques for ophthalmology, study of normal and abnormal characteristics of processes of vision; 200 mems.; Pres. CHARLES L. SCHEPENS, M.D.; Vice-Pres. H. MACKENZIE FREEMAN, M.D.; publs. Biennial Report, Monographs and Conferences.

**Fels Research Institute:** Livermore St., Yellow Springs, Ohio 45387; f. 1929; studies in human development and additional research projects in biochemistry, genetics, psychology, psycho-physiology, neurophysiology; Scientific Dir. BEATRICE C. LASEY (acting).

**Institute for Cancer Research:** 7701 Burholme Ave., Fox Chase Cancer Center, Philadelphia, Pa. 19111; f. 1926; library of 20,000 vols. including 4,300 monographs and 419 scientific journals; Pres. and Dir. Dr. ALFRED J. KNUDSON; Sec.-Treas. F. J. McKAY; publ. Scientific Report† (annually).

**Institutes of Medical Sciences, The:** 2200 Webster St., San Francisco, Calif. 94115; f. 1959; private research organization conducting patient-oriented research in heart disease, visual sciences, health research and neurology; Pres. GRAHAM WIDDOWSON, PH.D.

**Jackson Laboratory:** Bar Harbor, Maine 04609; f. 1929; research in mammalian genetics; 50 staff mems.; library of 20,000 books; Dir. Dr. BARBARA H.SANFORD; publs. Annual Report†, Training for Research (annually), JAX (quarterly).

**Lovelace Foundation for Medical Education and Research:** 5200 Gibson Blvd., S.E., Albuquerque, New Mexico 87108; f. 1947 to aid, engage in, conduct and foster medical, surgical and scientific research and investigation; 207 mems.; library of 26,477 books and bound journals, with 481 current periodicals; Chief Exec. Officer DONALD E. KILGORE, Jr.; Dir. of Research Administration ROGER O. MCCLELLAN; publs. Annual Report, research and educational reports.

**Mayo Foundation:** Rochester, Minn. 55901; f. 1919; clinical medicine, medical research and education; library of 200,000 vols. and 3,000 periodicals; Chair. Board of Trustees S. F. KEATING; Chair. Board of Govs. W. E. MAYBERRY; Admin. R. C. ROESLER; publ. Mayo Clinic Proceedings (monthly).

**Menninger Foundation:** Box 829, Topeka, Kansas 66601; f. 1925 as a non-profit centre for treatment and prevention research and professional education in psychiatry; medical library of 35,000 vols.; Pres. ROY MENNINGER, M.D.; Vice-Pres. IRVING SHEFFEL; Chief of Professional Services COTTER HIRSCHBERG, M.D.; publs. TPR, Menninger Perspective, Bulletin of the Menninger Clinic.

**National Institutes of Health:** U.S. Department of Health and Human Services, Public Health Service, Bethesda, Md. 20205; principal agency of D.H.H.S. for biomedical research, research training, and biomedical communications; appropriations $3,500 million; Dir. (vacant).

*National Institute of Child Health and Human Development:* f. 1963; supports, fosters and co-ordinates research and training in areas of maternal health, child health and human development, focusing on the continuing process of growth and development, biological and behavioural; Dir. NORMAN KRETCHMER, M.D., PH.D.

*National Institute of Arthritis, Diabetes and Digestive and Kidney Diseases:* f. 1950; conducts and supports research into diseases comprising the most crippling afflictions, including arthritis, diabetes and other hereditary errors of metabolism, digestive diseases, endocrine gland disorders, diseases of the blood and bone; also orthopaedics, dermatology and nutrition; Dir. G. DONALD WHEDON, M.D.

*National Heart, Lung, and Blood Institute:* f. 1948 as National Heart Institute, redesignated 1969 and 1976; performs and supports research in diseases of the heart, blood vessels, lungs (exclusive of pulmonary malignancies) and blood; Dir. ROBERT I. LEVY, M.D.

*National Cancer Institute:* f. 1937; supports broad research programmes into the causes, detection and diagnosis, and treatment of cancer; co-operates with State and local health agencies and voluntary bodies; Dir. VINCENT T. DEVITA, Jr., M.D.

*National Institute of Allergy and Infectious Diseases:* f. 1955; conducts and supports research in microbiology aimed at solving new problems in allergic diseases and unresolved problems in bacterial diseases, and at developing a useful body of knowledge in the viral diseases; Dir. RICHARD B. KRAUSE, M.D.

*National Institute of Dental Research:* f. 1948; research concerned with problems of dental caries and periodontal disease, with special emphasis on treatment, control and prevention; Dir. DAVID B. SCOTT, D.D.S.

*National Institute of Neurological and Communicative Disorders and Stroke:* f. 1950; conducts, fosters, and co-ordinates research on the causes, prevention, diagnosis and treatment of the neurological, sensory, and communicative disorders; Dir. MURRAY GOLDSTEIN, D.O. (acting).

*National Institute of General Medical Sciences:* f. 1963; supports a programme of research and training in the health sciences; Dir. RUTH L. KIRSCHSTEIN, M.D.

*National Institute of Environmental Health Sciences:* f. 1969; conducts, fosters and co-ordinates research on the biological effects of chemical, physical, and biological substances present in or introduced into the environment; Dir. DAVID P. RALL, M.D., PH.D.

*National Eye Institute:* f. 1968; conducts and supports research and training relating to blinding eye diseases and visual disorders, including research and training in the special health problems and requirements of the blind; conducts and supports investigations into the basic sciences relating to the mechanisms of sight and visual functions; Dir. CARL KUPFER, M.D.

*National Institute on Aging:* f. 1974; conducts and supports biomedical, social and behavioural research and training related to the ageing process and diseases and other special problems and needs of the aged; Dir. ROBERT N. BUTLER, M.D.

*National Library of Medicine:* (see National Libraries).

**Naval Aerospace Medical Institute:** Pensacola, Florida 32508; f. 1939; training in aviation and aerospace medicine; library of 20,000 vols.; Commanding Officer Capt. R. PAUL CAUDILL, Jr.

**Pasadena Foundation for Medical Research:** 99 North El Molino, Pasadena, Calif. 91101; f. 1952; oncology, cell biology, differentiated cell culture, prostatic cancer, educational and documentary films in biology; Founding Dir. Dr. GEORGE S. SHARP; Exec. Dir. WILLIAM OPEL; publ. *Annual Report†*.

**Radiation Research Society:** 4720 Montgomery Lane, Bethesda, Md. 20014; f. 1952; 1,500 mems.; Pres. R. H. SCHULER; Exec. Dir. R. J. BURK, Jr.; publs. *Radiation Research* (monthly), *Newsletter* (bi-monthly).

**Sloan-Kettering Institute for Cancer Research:** 410 East 68th St., New York, N.Y. 10021; f. 1945; research in physical and biological sciences relating to cancer; postdoctoral research training in laboratory investigations with scientific staff; graduate instruction through Cornell University; research unit of Memorial Sloan-Kettering Cancer Center; Dir. Dr. R. A. GOOD; publ. *Annual Report.*

**Society for Pediatric Research:** f. 1929; Sec.-Treas. Dr. JOHN JOHNSON, University of New Mexico School of Medicine, Albuquerque, N.M. 87131; publ. *The Society for Pediatric Research Program and Abstracts* (annually).

**Southwest Foundation for Research and Education:** P.O.B. 28147, San Antonio, Tex. 78284; f. 1941; basic research in biomedical sciences; Pres. MARTIN GOLAND; Sec.-Treas. E. F. FEITH; publs. *Progress in Biomedical Research* (quarterly), *Annual Report.*

**Wistar Institute of Anatomy and Biology:** 36th and Spruce Sts., Philadelphia, Pa. 19104; f. 1892; cellular and sub-cellular research in human diseases; library of 5,000 vols.; Dir. HILARY KOPROWSKI, M.D.

### NATURAL SCIENCES
#### General

**Battelle Memorial Institute:** 505 King Ave., Columbus, Ohio 43201; f. 1925 as a non-profit, public-purpose organization to engage in research, assist education, and to develop, license and dispose of technology; conducts research and development on a contract basis for industry, Government and individuals in the physical, life and social/behavioural sciences; 7,200 staff mems.; library of more than 150,000 vols.; major laboratories in Columbus (Ohio), Richland and Seattle (Washington), Frankfurt-am-Main and Geneva; offices in Algiers, London, Paris, Milan, Atlanta, Huntsville, Houston, Palo Alto, Spokane and Washington (D.C.); Pres. S. L. FAWCETT.

**Carnegie Institution of Washington:** 1530 P Street, N.W., Washington, D.C. 20005; f. 1902 "to encourage, in the broadest and most liberal manner, investigation research and discovery, and the application of knowledge to the improvement of mankind"; research and education in the biological and physical sciences; 80 faculty mems.; Chair. Board of Trustees WILLIAM R. HEWLETT; Pres. JAMES D. EBERT; publs. *Year Book, Report of the President, Academic Catalog*, monograph series; the Institution has the following Departments:

**Mount Wilson and Las Campanas Observatories:** 813 Santa Barbara St., Pasadena, Calif. 91101; f. 1904 as Mount Wilson Observatory; Dir. Dr. GEORGE PRESTON.

**Geophysical Laboratory:** 2801 Upton St., N.W., Washington, D.C. 20008; f. 1906; Dir. H. S. YODER, Jr.

**Department of Terrestrial Magnetism:** 5241 Broad Branch Road, N.W., Washington, D.C. 20015; f. 1904; Dir. GEORGE W. WETHERILL.

**Department of Plant Biology:** Stanford, Calif. 94305; f. 1903 as Desert Laboratory; Dir. WINSLOW F. BRIGGS.

**Department of Embryology:** 115 West University Parkway, Baltimore, Maryland 21210; f. 1914; Dir. DONALD D. BROWN.

**Center for Short-Lived Phenomena:** 138 Mt. Auburn St., Cambridge, Mass. 02138; f. 1968; receives, co-ordinates and disseminates information on short-lived natural events (volcanic eruptions, meteorite falls, etc.), sudden changes in biological and ecological systems such as animal migrations and colonizations, major occurrences of temporary pollution; c. 3,000 registered correspondents in 145 countries; Dir. RICHARD GOLOB; publ. *Weekly Newsletter.*

**Midwest Research Institute:** 425 Volker Blvd., Kansas City, Mo. 64110; f. 1944; 550 mems.; specialization in chemistry, biological sciences, toxicology, health sciences, economics, management sciences, human services, applied mathematics, environmental science, energy, safety; Pres. JOHN MCKELVEY; Sec. MARTIN N. SCHULER; publs. *Annual Report†, MRI Quarterly†*.

**New England Institute:** 90 Grove St., P.O.B. 308, Ridgefield, Conn. 06877; f. 1954; interdisciplinary research and education in natural sciences, medicine, physics, environmental studies, social sciences, etc.; library of 5,000 vols.; Chair. of Board JOHN H. HELLER; Pres. EMILE G. BLIZNAKOV; Sec. ROBERT T. TATE, Jr.

**Rand Corporation, The:** 1700 Main St., Santa Monica, Calif. 90406; f. 1948; br. in Washington; research on matters affecting the public interest: urban development, education, civil and criminal justice, regulatory policies and institutions, health, housing, energy, military strategy, etc.; funds from the Air Force, government agencies and the private sector; 568 research staff; Pres. Dr. DONALD B. RICE; Chair. DONALD H. RUMSFELD; publs. research reports, quarterly and annual indexes with abstracts of all unclassified publs., *Rand Research Review* (3 a year), research reports and bibliographies of publs. in selected subject areas.

**Southern Research Institute:** 2000 Ninth Ave., South, Birmingham, Ala. 35205; f. 1941; applied research on chemotherapeutic agents and techniques, carcinogenesis, pollution control, instrumentation, analytical procedures, biomaterials and bioengineering, polymeric materials, fibres and fabrics, economic studies, other fields; technical library of 36,000 vols.; Pres. HOWARD E. SKIPPER; Exec. Vice-Pres. R. D. OSGOOD, Jr.; Sec. ANDREW WYPER, Jr.; 575 employees; publ. *Southern Research Institute Bulletin*.

**Virginia Institute for Scientific Research:** Science Center W-106, University of Richmond, Va. 23173; f. 1949; Dir. Dr. J. SAMUEL GILLESPIE, Jr.; Sec. Dr. CHARLES H. WHEELER, III.

Biological Sciences

**Boyce Thompson Institute for Plant Research, Inc.:** Cornell University, Ithaca, N.Y. 14853; f. 1924; research on plants, including biochemistry, plant physiology, plant pathology, entomology, air and water pollution, pesticides; library of 41,000 vols.; Chair. WILLIAM T. SMITH; Man. Dir. ROY A. YOUNG; Sec. DEWAYNE C. TORGESON; publ. *Annual Reports†*.

**Cold Spring Harbor Laboratory:** P.O.B. 100, Cold Spring Harbor, New York 11724; f. 1890, chartered under present title 1962; library of 25,000 vols.; Dir. Dr. J. D. WATSON; Admin. Dir. W. R. UDRY; publs. *Symposia on Quantitative Biology* (annually), *C.S.H. Monographs* (irregular), *Abstracts of Papers, Annual Report†, C.S.H. Conferences on Cell Proliferation* (annually), *Reports in the Neurosciences, Banbury Reports* (irregular).

**Marine Biological Laboratory:** Woods Hole, Falmouth, Mass. 02543; inc. 1888; formerly a summer institution, currently an active research and teaching station throughout the year; offers courses and seminars on ecology, behaviour, developmental biology, neurobiology, comparative pathology of marine invertebrates and biological techniques; library of over 150,000 vols., 3,000 periodicals; Pres. and Dir. PAUL R. GROSS; Chair. of Board PROSSER GIFFORD; publs. *Annual Bulletin, Annual Report* (annually).

**Moss Landing Marine Laboratories:** P.O.B. 223, Moss Landing, Calif. 95039; f. 1966; research, education and public service in the marine sciences; Dir. Dr. JOHN H. MARTIN.

**Mote Marine Laboratory, Inc.:** 1600 City Island Park, Sarasota, Fla. 33577; f. 1955; independent, non-profit organization with educational affiliation to Cornell University; marine research, bioacoustics, biomedical and elasmobranch biology, estuarine ecology, neurobiology and behaviour of sharks; 63 mems.; library of 2,500 vols., 15,000 reprints on marine biology; Pres. WILLIAM R. MOTE; Dir. WILLIAM H. TAFT, PH.D.; publs. *Contributions from the Mote Marine Laboratory†, Collected Papers†, Quarterly Newsletter†*.

**New England Aquarium:** Central Wharf, Boston, Mass. 02110; f. 1957; 12,000 mems.; public aquarium; research programmes; library of 1,500 vols.; Pres. Mrs. JOSIAH A. SPAULDING; Exec. Dir. JOHN H. PRESCOTT; publs. *Aquasphere* (3 a year), *Aqualog* (6 a year).

**New York Botanical Garden:** Bronx, N.Y. 10458; f. 1891; 8,000 mems.; 250 acres of gardens, plant collections and wild areas, including a National Landmark conservatory; museum building includes exhibit hall, 3.8 million specimen herbarium; library of 95,000 vols., 215,000 other items; Pres. JAMES M. HESTER; publs. *Garden Magazine, Economic Botany, Mycologia, Botanical Review, North American Flora, Memoirs, Brittonia, The Native Orchids of Florida*, and *Newsletter*.

**Salk Institute for Biological Studies:** P.O.B. 85800, San Diego, Calif. 92138; f. 1960; 450 mems.; advanced biological research in cancer, neuro-endocrinology, developmental neurobiology, behavioural neurobiology, peptide biology, developmental biology, molecular biology, pre-biotic chemistry, immunology and language studies; library; Pres. Dr. FREDERIC DE HOFFMANN; Founding Dir. JONAS E. SALK.

**Society for Experimental Biology and Medicine:** 630 West 168th St., New York, N.Y. 10032; f. 1903; 3,500 mems., 3,500 subscribers; Sec. and Man. Editor M. R. NOCENTI; publ. *Proceedings* (11 issues a year).

**World Life Research Institute:** 23000 Grand Terrace Rd., Colton, Calif. 92324; f. 1959; research into marine biotoxicology, terrrestrial phytochemistry and water pollution; Dir. BRUCE W. HALSTEAD.

**Worcester Foundation for Experimental Biology:** 222 Maple Ave., Shrewsbury, Mass. 01545; f. 1944; independent biomedical research centre; emphasis on regulatory biology, especially the study of normal and cancer cell growth, neurobiology, endocrine and reproductive biology; conducts joint Ph.D. program with Clark University and Worcester Polytechnic Inst.; staff of 250, including 47 faculty level scientists; library of 25,000 vols.; Pres. and Scientific Dir. MAHLON B. HOAGLAND, M.D.; Exec. Dir. and Vice-Pres. FEDERICO WELSCH, M.D., PH.D.; publs. *Research Reporter* (quarterly), *Report of Research* (annually), *Annual Report*.

Physical Sciences

**Argonne National Laboratory:** 9700 South Cass Ave., Argonne, Ill. 60439; f. 1946; research and development in all phases of science and engineering relating to nuclear and non-nuclear energy, with broad programmes of fundamental research in physical, biomedical and environmental sciences, staff of c. 5,300; library of 150,000 vols. and 750,000 technical reports; Laboratory Dir. W. E. MASSEY, PH.D.; publ. *Report* (annually).

**Arthur J. Dyer Observatory:** Vanderbilt University, Nashville, Tenn. 37240; f. 1952; specializes in research on local structure of the Milky Way, photo-electric photometry of eclipsing binaries and variable stars, external galaxies and galactic nebulae; equipped with combination 60-cm. reflecting and Baker-Schmidt telescope and 30-cm. Cassegrain reflecting telescope; Observatory Library contains 6,000 vols.; Dir. A. M. HEISER.

**Association of Universities for Research in Astronomy, Inc. (AURA):** 1002 N. Warren Ave., Tucson, Ariz. 85719; f. 1957; operates the Kitt Peak National Observatory, Arizona, the Sacramento Peak Observatory, New

Mexico, the Space Telescope Science Institute, Baltimore, Md. and the Cerro Tololo Inter-American Observatory, Chile; library of 30,000 vols.; Pres. Dr. JOHN M. TEEM; Sec. Dr. ALBERT B. WEAVER; publ. *Contributions from the Kitt Peak National Observatory, the Space Telescope Science Institute and the Cerro Tololo Inter-American Observatory.*

**Franklin Research Center:** The Franklin Institute, Benjamin Franklin Parkway at 20th St., Philadelphia, Pa. 19103; contract research in the fields of science information services, systems science, physical and life sciences and engineering; Pres. (vacant); Vice-Pres. (Admin.) JOHN R. STOVER.

**Goddard Institute for Space Studies:** 2880 Broadway, New York, N.Y. 10025; astronomy, astrophysics, meteorology, planetary atmospheres; library of 15,000 vols.; Dir. Dr. ROBERT JASTROW.

**Institute of Polar Studies:** Ohio State University, Columbus, Ohio 43210; f. 1960; geology, glaciology, atmospheric sciences, pedology, history, palynology, marine biology, astronomy in polar regions; 60 mems.; library of 10,000 vols.; Dir. D. H. ELLIOT; publ. *Report*† (irregular).

**Lick Observatory:** Mount Hamilton, Calif. 95140; attached to the University of California, Santa Cruz Campus; f. 1888; optical astronomy and astrophysics; Dir. D. E. OSTERBROCK, PH.D.

**Lowell Observatory:** Box 1269, Flagstaff, Ariz. 86002; f. 1894; library of 12,000 vols.; 25 staff; Dir. A. A. HOAG; publ. *Bulletin*†.

**Lunar and Planetary Institute:** 3303 NASA Rd. 1, Houston, Texas 77058; f. 1968 to promote and support research in lunar and planetary studies; library of 8,000 vols., 130 periodicals; computerized bibliography of lunar and planetary literature; photo-map library containing all extra-terrestrial lunar photography, Mariner, Viking and Voyager satellite photography; photo-map library is a NASA Regional Planetary Image Center; Dir. ROGER J. PHILLIPS; publ. *Lunar and Planetary Information Bulletin*† (quarterly).

**Maria Mitchell Observatory:** The Nantucket Maria Mitchell Asscn., Vestal St., Nantucket, Mass. 02554; f. 1902; research, research training, public lectures and viewings; library of 3,000 vols.; Dir. Dr. EMILIA PISANI BELSERENE; publ. *Annual Report*†.

**National Astronomy and Ionosphere Center:** Space Sciences Building, Cornell University, Ithaca, N.Y. 14853; f. 1971; independent research centre funded by the U.S. National Science Foundation and operated by Cornell Univ. (but not a Cornell facility); c. 24 staff; Dir. Prof. FRANK D. DRAKE; Admin. Dir. EUGENE F. BARTELL; publs. reports of experiments and observations.

**Arecibo Observatory:** P.O.B. 995, Arecibo, Puerto Rico 00612; f. 1964; became part of NAIC in 1971; world's largest radio/radar telescope available for use by all scientists from all over the world; small library; c. 150 staff; Dir. of Operations Dr. HAROLD D. CRAFT, Jr.

**National Center for Atmospheric Research (NCAR):** P.O.B. 3000, Boulder, Colo. 80307; f. 1960; sponsored by National Science Foundation; operated by the University Corpn. for Atmospheric Research (UCAR); research in weather prediction, causes of climatic trends, solar processes and influences of the sun on weather and climate, convective storms, and global air quality; 650 staff mems.; library of 52,000 items (incl. 5,000 vols. of meteorological data), 500 journals received regularly; Dir. Dr. WILMOT N. HESS; publs. *Atmospheric Technology*† (2 a year), *UCAR Newsletter*† (monthly), *Annual Report*, *NCAR Technical Notes*† (irregularly), *Publications Announcement*† (2 a year).

**National Radio Astronomy Observatory:** P.O.B. 2, Green Bank, West Virginia, and Edgemont Rd., Charlottesville, Virginia, and Suite 100, 2010 North Forbes Blvd., Tucson, Ariz., and P.O.B. O, Socorro, New Mexico; f. 1956; research in radio astronomy, radio astronomy electronics, design of radio telescopes; observing radio telescopes include a 300-ft. transit radio telescope, a 140-ft. equatorial radio telescope, three 85-ft. telescopes, a 27 element array of 82-ft. radio telescopes in New Mexico and a 36-ft. milimetre-wave radio telescope; operated by Associated Universities, Inc., under contract with the National Science Foundation of Washington, D.C.; 383 staff, of which 107 are scientists and engineers; library of 21,000 vols.; Dir. MORTON ROBERTS.

**Rare-Earth Information Center (RIC):** Energy and Mineral Resources Research Institute, Iowa State University, Ames, Iowa 50011; f. 1966; emphasis on metallurgy and solid state physics; 22,000 vols., including reports, conference proceedings and journals; Dir. KARL A. GSCHNEIDNER, Jr.; publs. *Rare-Earth Information Center News*† (quarterly), occasional bibliographies†, compilations†, and critical reviews.

**Sacramento Peak Observatory:** Sunspot, New Mexico 88349; f. 1952; operated by AURA, Inc. (*q.v.*); national centre for solar research; offers telescope use to astronomical community; 52 employees, including 10 astrophysicists; library of 7,500 vols.; Dir. J. B. ZIRKER; publs. research papers.

**Smithsonian Astrophysical Observatory:** 60 Garden St., Cambridge, Mass. 02138; a bureau of the Smithsonian Institution (*see under Learned Societies*); mem. of the Harvard-Smithsonian Center for Astrophysics; research in radio astronomy, theoretical astrophysics, planetary and lunar science, atomic and molecular physics, geoastronomy, high-energy astrophysics, optical and infra-red astronomy, solar and stellar physics; Dir. G. B. FIELD, PH.D.

**Sproul Observatory:** Swarthmore, Pa. 19081; f. 1911; attached to Swarthmore College; 61-cm. Long Focus Refractor; astrometric research; library of 6,000 vols.; Dir. SARAH LEE LIPPINCOTT; publs. *Sproul Observatory Reprints*† (irregular).

**United States Naval Observatory:** 34th and Massachusetts Ave., N.W., Washington, D.C. 20390; f. 1830; positional astronomy, astrometry, double stars, earth rotation, precise time measurement, celestial mechanics; library of 75,000 vols.; substation at Flagstaff, Arizona; stellar parallaxes, photometry; Superintendent Capt. R. A. VOHDEN; Scientific Dir. Dr. GART WESTERHOUT; publs. *Astronomical Almanac, Nautical Almanac, Air Almanac, Almanac for Computers, Astronomical Phenomena, NavObs Circulars, Astronomical Papers, Time Service Bulletins.*

**Warner and Swasey Observatory:** 1975 Taylor Rd., East Cleveland, Ohio 44112; f. 1920; astronomical research and education (observational facility of the department of astronomy at Case Western Reserve University); library of 15,000 vols.; Dir. PETER PESCH.

**Woods Hole Oceanographic Institution:** Woods Hole, Mass. 02543; f. 1930; research in physical, chemical and biological oceanography, marine geology and marine geophysics, ocean acoustics, ocean engineering and marine policy; conducts joint PH.D. programme with Massachusetts Inst. of Technology, postdoctoral fellowship programme and summer student fellowship programme; joint library with Marine Biological Laboratory of 150,000 vols. and 5,000 periodical titles; Pres. PAUL M. FYE; Dir. JOHN H. STEELE; publs. *Collected Reprints* (annually), *Oceanus* (quarterly), *Woods Hole Notes* (bi-monthly).

**Yale Observatory:** Yale University, Box 6666, 260 Whitney Ave., New Haven, Conn. 06511; publ. *Transactions.*

**Yerkes Observatory:** Williams Bay, Wis. 53191; Department of Astronomy and Astrophysics of the Univ. of Chicago; f. 1897; Dir. Dr. L. M. Hobbs.

## Philosophy and Psychology

**American Society for Psychical Research, Inc.:** 5 West 73rd St., New York, N.Y. 10023; f. 1885; 2,600 mems.; library of 6,500 vols.; Chester Carlson Research Fellow Dr. Karlis Osis; Exec. Sec. Laura F. Knipe; publs. *Journal, Newsletter* (quarterly).

**Eastern Pennsylvania Psychiatric Institute:** Henry Ave. and Abbotsford Rd., Philadelphia, Pa. 19129; f. 1956; library of 27,800 vols. relating to the behavioural sciences; Dir. Charles Shagass, M.D. (acting).

**Institute for Philosophical Research:** 101 East Ontario St., Chicago, Ill. 60611; f. 1952; for the study of philosophy from ancient Greek times to the present day; library of 10,000 vols.; Pres. and Dir. Mortimer J. Adler; Sec.-Treas. Theresa Panek; publ. *Concepts in Western Thought.*

## Religion, Sociology and Anthropology

**American Institute for Research in the Behavioral Sciences:** 135 North Bellefield Ave., Pittsburgh, Pa. 15213; f. 1946; Dir. Dr. Melvin H. Rudov; Pres. and Chief Exec. Officer Dr. S. Rains Wallace; Sec. Dr. Frederick B. Davis; publs. *Behavioral Sciences Newsletter* (fortnightly), *Creative Talent Awards* (annual monograph).

Office in Palo Alto. 1791 Arastradero Rd.; Dir. and Chair. Dr. John C. Flanagan.

Office in Bangkok, Thailand: P.O.B. 11-45; Dir. Dr. Paul A. Schwarz.

Offices in Maryland: 10605 Concord St., Kensington, Md.; Dir. Dr. Preston S. Abbott; and 8555 16th St., Silver Spring, Md.; Dir. Dr. Edwin A. Fleishman.

**American Schools of Oriental Research:** 126 Inman St., Cambridge, Mass. 02139; f. 1900; approx. 2,000 mems.; Pres. Philip J. King; support activities of independent archaeological institutions abroad: The Albright Institute of Archeological Research, Jerusalem, Israel, the American Centre of Oriental Research in Amman, Jordan and the Cyprus American Archaeological Research Institute, Nicosia, Cyprus; publs. *Biblical Archaeologist†* (quarterly), *Bulletin†* (quarterly), *Journal of Cuneiform Studies†* (quarterly), *The Annual.*

**Center for Advanced Study in the Behavioral Sciences:** 202 Junipero Serra Blvd., Stanford, Calif. 94305; f. 1954; Dir. Dr. Gardner Lindzey.

**Middle American Research Institute:** Tulane University, New Orleans, Louisiana 70118; f. 1924; for research, education, and publications related to Mexico and Central America; supports publication, archaeological excavation and research in humanities and social sciences; small museum gallery; anthropological collections; Dir. E. Wyllys Andrews V.

**Middle East Institute:** 1761 N St., N.W., Washington, D.C. 20036; f. 1946; to develop and maintain facilities for research, publication and dissemination of information, with a view to developing in the United States a more thorough understanding of the countries of the Middle East; holds an annual conference on Middle East affairs; 1,900 mems.; Pres. Hon. L. Dean Brown; publ. *Middle East Journal* (quarterly).

**Social Science Research Council:** 605 Third Ave., New York, N.Y. 10158; f. 1923; to advance research in the social sciences in a variety of ways: appointment of committees of scholars to set priorities and make plans for critical areas of social research; improvement of research training through training institutes and fellowship programmes; support of individual research through post-doctoral grants; sponsorship of research conferences, often interdisciplinary and international; sponsorship of books and other research publications that may result from these activities; Pres. Kenneth Prewitt; publ. *Items* (quarterly).

**Wenner-Gren Foundation for Anthropological Research, Inc.** (formerly The Viking Fund, Inc.): 1865 Broadway, New York, N.Y. 10023; inc. 1941; promotes and supports research internationally in anthropology and related sciences; offers Third World Fellowships; Dir. of Research Lita Osmundsen.

## Technology

**Brookhaven National Laboratory:** Upton, Long Island, N.Y. 11973; f. 1947; operated by Associated Universities, Inc., under contract with the U.S. Dept. of Energy; basic and applied research by staff and visiting scientists in the fields of energy, particle accelerators, physics, medicine, biology, chemistry, applied sciences, mathematics, and the environment, including the design, development, acquisition and operation of large-scale facilities too costly or complex for an individual university; training of scientists and engineers; dissemination of scientific and technical knowledge; library of 110,000 vols.; staff: 750 research, 400 professional, 690 technicians, 1,200 general; Dir. Dr. George H. Vineyard; publ. *Biennial Report.*

**Building Research Advisory Board:** 2101 Constitution Ave., N.W., Washington, D.C. 20418; f. 1949 as a unit of the Nat. Academy of Sciences—Nat. Research Council; undertakes activities concerned with the development and application of technology to serve society's needs for housing, building and related community and environmental design and development.

**Combustion Institute:** 986 Union Trust Building, Pittsburgh, Pa. 15219; f. 1954; 2,500 mems.; Pres. R. Friedman; Exec. Sec. Marge C. Salamony; publs. *Combustion and Flame* (monthly), *Proceedings of Symposium (International) on Combustion* (biennially).

**Herty Foundation:** P.O.B. 1963, Savannah, Ga. 31402; f. 1938; research and development of all fibrous materials, particularly forest and agricultural products and synthetic fibres; Dir. Dr. J. Robert Hart.

**Industrial Research Institute, Inc.:** 100 Park Ave., New York, N.Y. 10017; f. 1938; 275 mem. companies; Exec. Dir. Charles F. Larson; publ. *Research Management* (bi-monthly).

**Institute of Textile Technology:** P.O.B. 391, Charlottesville, Va. 22902; f. 1944; research, graduate education and information programmes for the textile industry; library of 50,000 vols.; Pres. C. G. Tewksbury; Dean R. A. Barnhardt; publ. *Textile Technology Digest†* (monthly).

**National Aeronautics and Space Administration (NASA):** 27 official addresses, of which the main research centres are:

**Lyndon B. Johnson Space Center:** NASA, Houston, Texas 77058; f. 1961; the Johnson Space Center is responsible for the design, development and testing of manned spacecraft and associated systems, for the selection and training of astronauts and for the operation of manned space flights; Johnson Space Center Technical Library of 49,000 vols., 550,000 technical reports, 600 periodicals; Dir. C. C. Kraft, Jr.; Dir. of Engineering and Development M. A. Faget; Dir. of Data Systems and Analysis H. W. Tindall; Dir. of Space and Life Sciences Richard S. Johnston; Dir. of Flight Operations George W. S. Abbey; Dir. of Administration and Program Support P. H. Whitbeck; Dir. of Center Operations J. V. Piland; Dir. of Safety, Reliability and Quality Assurance M. L. Raines; Man. Program Operations Office Donald D. Arabian; attached laboratory:

**White Sands Test Facility:** Las Cruces, New Mexico; f. 1965; conducts developmental and operational tests of spacecraft engines and associated propulsion systems, conducts tests in such areas as materials technology, contamination control, precision cleaning, conducts environmental evaluations of special components and systems, coordinates NASA test projects on White Sands Missile Range.

**Goddard Space Flight Center:** NASA, Greenbelt, Md. 20771; f. 1959; space research; 3,500 mems.; library of 57,000 vols., 35,000 periodicals; Dir. (vacant).

**Ames Research Center:** National Aeronautics and Space Administration, Moffett Field, Calif. 94035; Dir. CLARENCE A. SYVERTSON.

**John F. Kennedy Space Center:** National Aeronautics and Space Administration, Fla. 32899; f. 1962; previously Launch Operations Center; space vehicle launch facility; library of 32,000 vols., 106,000 documents and reports, 589 periodicals; 160,000 specifications and standards; Dir. LEE R. SCHERER.

**Langley Research Center:** National Aeronautics and Space Administration, Hampton, Va. 23665; Dir. Dr. D. P. HEARTH.

**Lewis Research Center:** National Aeronautics and Space Administration, 21000 Brookpark Road, Cleveland, Ohio 44135; Dir. B. LUBARSKY (acting).

**George C. Marshall Space Flight Center:** National Aeronautics and Space Administration, Alabama 35812; f. 1960; Dir. Dr. W. R. LUCAS.

**National Bureau of Standards:** Washington, D.C. 20234; f. 1901 by act of Congress (re-organized 1978) to strengthen and advance national science and technology; provides services to Government and industry; a technical basis for equity in trade; and technical services to promote public safety; Dir. Dr. ERNEST AMBLER; publs. *Dimensions* (monthly), *Journal of Research*.

Organized in three sections:

**National Measurement Laboratory:** provides national system of physical, chemical and materials measurement and co-ordinates system with measurement systems of other nations; offers advisory, research and calibration services and standard reference material; consists of centres of: absolute physical quantities; radiation research; chemical physics; analytical chemistry; materials science.

**National Engineering Laboratory:** provides technology and technical services in public and private sectors to address national needs and solve national problems in the public interest; consists of centres of: applied mathematics; electronics and electrical engineering; manufacturing engineering; building technology; fire research; consumer product technology; chemical engineering.

**Institute for Computer Sciences and Technology:** conducts research and provides scientific and technical services to aid federal agencies in selection, acquisition, application and use of computer technology to improve effectiveness and economy in Government operations; manages Federal Information Processing Standards Program; provides technical foundation for computer-related policies of the Federal Government; includes centres for programming science and technology and computer systems engineering.

**SRI International:** 333 Ravenswood Ave., Menlo Park, California 94025; f. 1946 (fmrly. Stanford Research Institute); centre for diversified research for industry and government in pure and applied science; over 3,200 staff mems. and over 16,000 completed projects; brs. in Washington, D.C., New York, Chicago, Juneau, Honolulu; overseas offices in London, Stockholm, Zurich, Tokyo, Paris, Milan, Bonn, Amsterdam, Taipei, Melbourne, Djakarta, Mexico City, Toronto, Calgary, Edmonton, Ottawa; Pres. WILLIAM F. MILLER; Dir. TERENCE CULLINAN; publ. *SRI Journal* (monthly).

**System Development Corporation:** 2500 Colorado Ave., Santa Monica, Calif. 90406; f. 1957; design and development of information systems; social science studies and evaluation; online interactive multi-disciplinary bibliographical retrieval system includes over 70 data bases; library of 100,000 vols.; Pres. Dr. GEORGE E. MUELLER.

**Textile Research Institute:** Princeton, N.J. 08540; f. 1930; basic research and graduate education in the physical and engineering sciences relating to fibrous materials; 80 corporate mems., 169 individual mems.; library of 5,000 vols.; Pres. L. REBENFELD; publs. *Notes on Research, Textile Research Journal*.

## LIBRARIES

*There are many thousands of libraries in the United States, ranging from the small town library of a few hundred volumes to the library in the large city where the number may be reckoned in millions. As limitation of space makes it impossible to list all these, we give a selection classified as follows:*

National Libraries.
Government Libraries.
Public Libraries (over 600,000 vols.).
Special Libraries.
State Libraries (over 500,000 vols.).
University Libraries.

### NATIONAL LIBRARIES

**Library of Congress, The:** Washington, D.C. 20540; f. 1800; contains over 80 million items, including *c.* 20 million books and pamphlets; the operations, activities and personnel of the library are divided into eight departments—Office of the Librarian, Management, National Programs, Research Services, Congressional Research Service, Processing Services, Law Library and Copyright Office. Collections include one million vols. on Hispanic and Portuguese culture, and the largest collection of Russian literature outside the Soviet Union. Special collections:

*Books for the blind and physically handicapped:* 30,000 music scores, textbooks and instructional materials in braille, large type and recorded media, 4,000 titles in braille and 15,000 recorded on discs, and on tapes, reproduced in thousands of copies and available in more than 160 co-operating regional and sub-regional libraries in the United States and its territories.

*Cartography:* 3,670,121 maps, atlases, globes, etc.

*Folk Music:* over 30,000 recordings on cylinders, discs, wires and tapes dating back to 1980; 300,000 selections of folksong, folk music, folk tale, oral history and lore; 225,000 sheets of manuscript material; 3,500 folk-related books and periodicals; dissertations, fieldnotes tape transcriptions.

## UNITED STATES OF AMERICA

*Law:* over 1.7 million items, including material on American, British, Hispanic, European, Far Eastern, Near Eastern and African Law.

*Manuscripts: c.* 35 million manuscripts relating to American history and civilization, including the papers of American Presidents from George Washington to Calvin Coolidge, other statesmen and diplomats, and men and women of letters.

*Microform:* 3,477,675 microforms.

*Motion Pictures, Broadcasts and Sound Recordings:* 281,270 reels, early film dating from 1894 with emphasis on American films from 1912–42; over 1,000,000 recordings, some in special collections; Berliner, Joe Berger, John Secrist, Raymond Swing, OWI, U.S. Marine Corps Combat Records, Artists and House of Representatives Debates.

*Music:* 6,000,000 items of music and music literature.

*Orientalia:* more than 1,265,000 vols. in Chinese, Japanese, Korean and languages of Southern Asia; *c.* 114,000 in Hebraic; 110,000 in Near Eastern.

*Prints and Photographs:* over 10,000,000 items, among them early daguerreotypes, Mathew Brady photographs, and the work of contemporary photographers; fine prints, posters and architectural collections.

*Rare Books:* over 500,000 items, including the largest collection of incunabula in the Western Hemisphere.

*Periodicals:* includes newspapers, Government Publications and other serial publications.

The Library's priority remains service to the Congress of the United States, but it now performs, in its role as the national library, services to other libraries which include: development of scientific schemes of classification (Library of Congress and Dewey Decimal), subject headings, and cataloguing embracing the whole field of printed matter; a centralized acquisition and cataloguing programme in which publications are acquired worldwide and cataloguing data distributed to other libraries by means of printed cards, machine-readable tapes, and printed book catalogues; editing for publication a *National Union Catalogue, Pre-1956 Imprints,* which will have 11 million entries for significant holdings of major American libraries; publication of the *National Union Catalogue,* a record of acquisitions by American libraries since 1955; an inter-library loan system; the exchange of duplicates with other libraries; and the provision of advice on technical matters relating to the preservation and restoration of library collections.

Services to the public include: registration of creative work for copyright; use of 2 general and 18 special reading rooms; reference and bibliographic services; research and referral services in science and technology; photoduplication for a fee of items in the collections not subject to copyright or other restrictions; chamber music concerts and literary programmes; lectures and symposia, such as the series in observance of the Bicentennial of American Independence; publication of guides, catalogues, proceedings, facsimiles of rare items in the collections, etc.; sale of recordings of poetry and folk music; exhibits in Library buildings; slide/sound presentation: "America's Library"; guided tours; Librarian Dr. DANIEL J. BOORSTIN; publs. *Library of Congress Publications in Print* (annually), *Calendar of Events* (monthly), *Information for Readers, Special Facilities for Research* (available upon request).

**National Agricultural Library:** U.S. Dept. of Agriculture, Beltsville, Md. 20705; 1,500,000 vols.; agriculture and the related sciences; especially collection of botany, zoology, chemistry, veterinary medicine, forestry, plant pathology, general agriculture; Dir. RICHARD A. FARLEY.

**National Archives and Records Service:** National Archives Bldg., 8th St. at Pennsylvania Ave., N.W., Washington, D.C. 20408; the National Archives, created as an independent agency in 1934, was transferred in 1949 to the newly established General Services Administration, in which it became the National Archives and Records Service; it now consists of the Offices of the National Archives, Programme Support, Program Development, Federal Records Centers, Public Programs and Exhibits, the Federal Register, Presidential Libraries and Records and Information Management. NARS administers a Federal archive system of 23 institutions, including 15 national records centers and 8 Presidential libraries. It selects, preserves and administers Federal Records of enduring value and prescribes standards and methods for the efficient management of current records of the Federal Government. On permanent display in the Exhibition Hall are the Declaration of Independence, the Constitution of the United States, and the Bill of Rights (facsimiles of these and other documents are for sale); NARS publishes aids to the use of records in custody there and reproduces bodies of records of high research value on microfilm, positive prints of which are for sale; Archivist of the United States Dr. ROBERT M. WARNER; Deputy Archivist of the United States Dr. EDWARD WELDON; publ. *Prologue: The Journal of the National Archives.*

**National Library of Medicine:** Bethesda, Maryland 20209; formerly Armed Forces Medical Library; f. 1836; 1,500,000 vols., journals, theses on medicine and health-related sciences; 490,000 vols. on the history of medicine, plus MSS.; 65,000 prints and photographs; the library possesses a computerized information retrieval system; Dir. MARTIN M. CUMMINGS, M.D.; publs. *Index Medicus, Cumulated Index Medicus. Abridged Index Medicus, Bibliography of the History of Medicine, NLM Current Catalog, NLM Audiovisuals Catalog.*

## GOVERNMENT LIBRARIES

### WASHINGTON, D.C.

**Army Library:** Department of the Army, Military District of Washington, Room 1A 518, The Pentagon, Washington, D.C. 20310; f. 1944; combines the resources of 28 former War Dept. libraries into one central collection in the Pentagon; 200,000 vols., and 1,000,000 documents; special collections on military arts and sciences, unit histories, military law; and Army administrative, training and technical publications; provides publications to 270 field law libraries; Dir. MARY L. SHAFFER.

**Department of Commerce Library:** 14th and Constitution Ave., N.W., Washington, D.C. 20230; f. 1913; 250,000 vols., 50,000 vols. microform; Dir. Dr. STANLEY J. BOUGAS.

**Bureau of the Census Library:** Federal Office Bldg. No. 3, Room 2455, Washington, D.C. 20233; f. 1952; 250,000 vols.; Librarian BETTY BAXTRESSER.

**National Oceanic and Atmospheric Administration, Environmental Data and Information Service, Environmental Science Information Center, Library**

LIBRARIES UNITED STATES OF AMERICA

and Information Services Division: WSC 4, 6009 Executive Blvd., Rockville, Md. 20852; 500,000 vols.; Chief Librarian ELIZABETH J. YEATES.

*Miami/Coral Gables Center:* 15 Rickenbacker Causeway, Miami, Fla. 22149; f. 1970; 26,524 vols., 18,000 microforms, 2,965 maps and charts; Librarian ROBERT M. TING.

(NOAA also has 30 libraries and information centres holding specialized collections.)

Boulder Laboratories Library: Boulder, Colo. 80302; f. 1851; 112,000 vols. and 212,000 microfiche; Librarian Dr. JOAN M. MAIER.

National Bureau of Standards Library: Administration Bldg., Room E01, Route 70 S and Quince Rd., Gaithersburg, Md. 20760; f. 1912; 175,000 vols.; Librarian PATRICIA W. BERGER.

Patent Office Scientific Library: 2021 Jefferson Davis Hwy., Arlington, Va. 20231; f. 1836; 200,000 vols., 28,000,000 foreign patent documents; Librarian ELIZABETH PAN, PH.D.

Department of Health, and Human Services Libraries: 330 Independence Ave., S.W., 20201:

Department Library: 700,000 vols.; located Headquarters Building; Dir. KANARDY L. TAYLOR.

National Institutes of Health Library: 100,000 vols., located National Institutes of Health, Bethesda, Md.; Librarian SEYMOUR I. TAINE.

St. Elizabeths Hospital Library: 24,000 vols.; located Hospital Grounds, Washington, D.C.; Librarian LAWRENCE MOORE.

Social Security Administration Library: 40,000 vols.; located Baltimore, Md.; Librarian Miss ANITA GOLDSTEIN.

Department of Justice Library: 10th St. and Constitution Ave., N.W. 20530; f. 1831; 275.000 vols., principally Anglo-American legal and related materials; Library Director MAUREEN M. MOORE.

Department of Labor Library: 200 Constitution Ave., N.W., 20210; f. 1885; 535,000 vols., 3,200 current periodical titles; Librarian ANDRE C. WHISENTON.

Department of State Library: 2201 C St., N.W. 20520; f. 1789; 600,000 vols.; materials relate primarily to the economic, political and social conditions in foreign areas, international economic relations and diplomatic history; Librarian CONRAD P. EATON.

Department of the Interior Libraries: Washington, D.C. 20240.

Natural Resources Library of the U.S. Department of the Interior: Room 1140, Interior Building, 18th and C Streets, N.W.; f. 1949 by amalgamation of 8 existing Interior Libraries at Washington; 850,000 vols.; over 14,000 serials and 4,000 periodicals received; is the main library in the Department's National Natural Resources Library and Information System (NNRLIS): a network of over 400 field libraries serving the Bureaux and offices of the Department; subjects include the conservation and development of natural resources; automated information services; interlibrary loans service; copy facilities; open to the public; Dir. PHILLIP M. HAYMOND; publs. Bibliographies, available from U.S. National Technical Information Service.

Geological Survey Library: National Center, mail stop 950, 12201 Sunrise Valley Drive, Reston, Va. 22092; f. 1879; 600,000 vols., 250,000 maps, 250,000 pamphlets; 8,500 serial and periodical titles received; comprehensive working and research library; interlibrary loan service; open to the public; Chief Librarian GEORGE H. GOODWIN, Jr.

Department of the Treasury Library: 15th and Pennsylvania Ave., 20220; 125,000 vols. (primarily economic and legal); special collections: taxation, public finance, international economic affairs; Library Dir. ANNE E. STEWART.

House of Representatives Library: Cannon House Office Bldg. B-18, Washington, D.C. 20515; f. 1792; 100,000 vols., and special bound collections of all House of Representatives publications since *c.* 1800; Librarian E. RAYMOND LEWIS.

Navy Department Library: Bldg. 220, Washington Navy Yard, D.C. 20374; f. 1798; 150,000 vols.; and various bureau and office libraries and special collections; Librarian STANLEY KALKUS.

Senate Library: Capitol Building, Washington, D.C. 20510; f. 1871; 250,000 vols., including special collection of Legislative Proceedings and Documents from 1774; the work of the Senate Library is essentially that of research and reference for the use of the Senate and its committees; principal services rendered include legislative and general reference, automated legislative information retrieval, Micrographics Center and photoduplication facilities; Librarian ROGER K. HALEY; publs. *Nomination and Election of the President and Vice-President* (quadrennially), *Senate Election, Expulsion and Censure Cases from 1789 to 1972, Proposed Amendments to the Constitution of the United States, Presidential Vetoes, Index of Congressional Committee Hearings.*

U.S. Energy Research and Development Administration Library: Washington, D.C. 20545; f. 1947; 30,000 titles, 500,000 reports; collection includes books, journals, reports and legislation relating to all aspects of energy; Librarian C. NEIL SHERMAN; publs. *Library Accessions List, ERDA Headquarters Reports* (monthly).

Veterans Administration, Library Division: Veterans Administration Central Office, 810 Vermont Ave. N.W., Washington, D.C. 20420; planning, policy, development, training, centralized support services for the V.A. Library Network (VALNET); this comprises 340 hospital and general libraries in 175 health care facilities (combined holdings *c.* 2,000,000 vols., *c.* 500,000 audio visuals, 5,000 journals) and network access to bibliographic data bases through 105 VA Online Centers; Chief KARLN RENNINGER.

## PUBLIC LIBRARIES
(with a total number of volumes over 600,000)

ALABAMA

Birmingham Public and Jefferson County Free Library: 2020 Park Place, Birmingham, Ala. 35203; f. 1909; 1,018,380 vols.; special collections: Agee Cartographical Collection (including Joseph H. Woodward Collection), Collins Collection of the Dance, Scruggs Philately Collection, Department of Southern History and Literature, government documents; archives, manuscripts, micro forms, phono records, telephone reference-DIALOG Online Computer reference service, programme for senior citizens, County Audio-Visual Department, special service for Blind and Physically Handicapped; 11 brs., 2 bookmobiles; Dir. GEORGE R. STEWART.

1625

## ARIZONA

**City of Phoenix Public Library:** 12 East McDowell Rd., Phoenix, Az. 85004; f. 1901; 1,149,391 vols., 33,215 periodicals; also A/V material; Dir. W. R. HENDERSON.

## CALIFORNIA

**Los Angeles County Public Library System:** 320 West Temple St., Los Angeles, 90012; 4,555,486 vols.; 114 community, mobile and institutional libraries; 6 regional headquarters; Librarian LINDA F. CRISMOND.

**Los Angeles Public Library:** 630 West 5th St., Los Angeles, 90071; f. 1872; 4,161,905 vols.; Librarian WYMAN H. JONES.

**San Diego Public Library:** 820 E St., San Diego, Calif. 92101; f. 1882; 1,645,912 vols.; City Librarian WILLIAM W. SANNWALD.

**San Francisco Public Library:** Civic Center, San Francisco, 94102; 1,701,815 vols.; City Librarian JOHN C. FRANTZ.

## COLORADO

**Denver Public Library:** 1357 Broadway, Denver; f. 1889; 1,732,225 vols.; specializes in Western U.S. history, conservation of natural resources, energy and the environment, genealogy, Napoleon, fine printing, folk music; City Librarian HENRY G. SHEAROUSE, Jr.; publs. *The News*† (6 a year), *Newsletter* (fish and wildlife reference service, quarterly).

## DISTRICT OF COLUMBIA

**Public Library of the District of Columbia:** 901 G St., N.W., Washington, D.C. 20001; f. 1896; Martin Luther King Memorial Library, 20 branches, Special Services Division; 1,371,084 vols.; Dir. HARDY R. FRANKLIN, PH.D.

## FLORIDA

**Miami-Dade Public Library:** 1 Biscayne Blvd., Miami, Fla. 33132; f. 1942; 1,770,000 vols.; 3 regional libraries; 24 brs., 1 Artmobile, 5 bookmobiles; specializes in Florida history, 16mm. films, Spanish books, urban affairs, genealogy; Dir. E. F. SINTZ.

## GEORGIA

**Atlanta Public Library:** 1 Margaret Mitchell Sq., N.W., Atlanta, Georgia 30303; f. 1867; 1,600,000 vols., 60,000 recordings and cassettes; Dir. JOSEPH V. ZAVODNY (acting).

## ILLINOIS

**Chicago Public Library:** 425 North Michigan Ave., Chicago 60611; f. 1872; 4,263,442 vols.; Commissioner DONALD J. SAGER.

## INDIANA

**Allen County Public Library:** 900 Webster St., Fort Wayne; f. 1894; over 1,600,000 vols.; 11 brs., 5 bookmobiles; Dir. RICK J. ASHTON.

**Indianapolis-Marion County Public Library:** 40 East St. Clair St., Indianapolis, Ind. 46204; f. 1873; 1,400,000 vols.; 23 branches, 2 bookmobiles; Dir. RAYMOND E. GNAT; publ. *Reading in Indianapolis*.

## KENTUCKY

**Louisville Free Public Library:** Fourth and York Sts., Louisville, Kentucky 40203; f. 1902; 1,139,534 vols.; Film Services with 3,000 films, 1,500 filmstrips, 122 sets of 35mm. slides, 36,000 phono-discs, 70,000 programmes on electronic tape; operates two FM radio stations for music and educational programmes; 20 brs., 3 bookmobiles; special Kentucky History Collection; houses a "Louisville Art Gallery"; Talking Book Library for the blind and physically handicapped; service for the deaf; Dir. R. S. KOZLOWSKI.

## LOUISIANA

**New Orleans Public Library:** 219 Loyola Ave., New Orleans, La. 70140; f. 1843; 713,264 vols.; 11 brs. and 2 bookmobiles; Librarian M. E. WRIGHT, Jr.

## MARYLAND

**Enoch Pratt Free Library:** 400 Cathedral St., Baltimore, Md. 21201; f. 1886; special H. L. Mencken collection; 2,157,077 vols., 6,009 films, 31,074 recordings; Dir. ANNA CURRY; publ. *Menckeniana* (quarterly).

## MASSACHUSETTS

**Boston Public Library and Eastern Massachusetts Regional Public Library System:** Copley Square, Boston, Mass. 02117; f. 1852; believed to be the oldest free municipal library supported by taxation in any city of the world; 4,153,674 vols.; Dir. and Librarian PHILIP J. MCNIFF.

**Springfield City Library:** 220 State St., Springfield, Mass. 01103; f. 1857; 685,239 vols.; 8 brs. and one bookmobile; Headquarters of Western Regional Public Library System; Dir. ROBERT E. WAGENKNECHT; publ. *Bulletin*†.

**Worcester Public Library and Central Massachusetts Regional Library System:** Salem Square, Worcester, 01608; f. 1859; 601,392 vols.; Librarian JOSEPH S. HOPKINS.

## MICHIGAN

**Detroit Public Library:** 5201 Woodward Ave., Detroit, Mich. 48202; f. 1865; 2,507,495 vols., 172,500 maps, 24,000 microfilms, 48,000 microfiche, 2,000 films, 950,000 pictures; special collections on Automotive history, Burton Historical Collection (Michigan, Great Lakes and Old North-west Territory), Labor History Collection; Dir. Mrs. JANE HALE MORGAN.

## MINNESOTA

**Minneapolis Public Library and Information Center:** 300 Nicollet Mall, Minneapolis, Minn. 55401; f. 1885; 1,578,166 vols.; Dir. JOSEPH KIMBROUGH.

**Saint Paul Public Library:** 90 West 4th St., Saint Paul, Minn. 55102; f. 1882; 759,289 vols.; Dir. GERALD W. STEENBERG.

## MISSOURI

**Kansas City Public Library:** 311 East 12th St., Kansas City, Missouri 64106; f. 1873; 1,221,646 vols.; Dir. HAROLD R. JENKINS.

**St. Louis County Library:** 1640 S. Lindbergh Blvd., St. Louis, Missouri 63131; f. 1946; 1,599,013 vols.; 15 brs. and 20 bookmobiles; Dir. DONNELL J. GAERTNER.

**St. Louis Public Library:** 1301 Olive St., St. Louis, Missouri 63103; f. 1865; 1,365,000 vols.; 2 bookmobiles; Librarian and Exec. Dir. JOAN COLLETT; publs. *Index to St. Louis Magazines and Obituaries* (quarterly), *Missouri Union List of Serial Publications*.

## NEW JERSEY

**Newark Public Library:** Newark, P.O.B. 630; f. 1888; 1,180,493 catalogued vols., 924,814 catalogued non-book items, 1,696,441 uncatalogued items, 411,531 periodicals, 1,015,095 prints, pictures and art slides; collections: art, music, science, technology, business, New Jersey history, fine printing, black studies, Newark Evening News Morgue; Dir. THOMAS J. ALRUTZ; publs. *Business Literature* (10 a year), *Annual Report*, etc.

## NEW YORK

**Brooklyn Public Library:** Grand Army Plaza, Brooklyn, N.Y. 11238; f. 1896; consolidated with the Brooklyn Library 1902; Brooklyn history; special programs include: media centre, El Centro Hispano de Informacion, Education and Job Information centres, prison

# LIBRARIES

service, reading improvement and literacy programme; 3,816,450 items; borough-wide library system of 57 brs., Business Library and Central Library; Dir. KENNETH F. DUCHAC.

**Buffalo and Erie County Public Library:** Lafayette Square, Buffalo; f. 1954 as an amalgamation of three libraries; 3,267,472 vols.; Dir. PAUL M. ROONEY.

**New York Public Library:** Fifth Ave. and 42nd St., New York 10018; f. 1895 by the consolidation of Astor and Lennox Libraries; 9,000,000 vols. (not including manuscripts, maps, microfilms, phono-records, prints and sheet music), over 30,000 periodicals and newspapers; over 80 branch libraries; special collections include Berg collection of English and American literature, Arents collection of books on tobacco and books in parts, and the Spencer collection of illustrated books; Dir. EDWIN S. HOLMGREN. Research Libraries: 6 million vols., 11 million manuscripts; Research Dir. DAVID H. STAM.

**Queens Borough Public Library:** 89-11 Merrick Blvd., Jamaica, N.Y. 11432; organized 1896, inc. 1907; central reference and research centre with 57 branch libraries and 4,003,923 vols.; special collection Long Island history and genealogy; picture collection of over a million and a half pictures; Dir. CONSTANCE B. COOKE.

**Rochester Public Library:** 115 South Ave., Rochester, N.Y. 14604; f. 1912; 932,182 vols.; 10 brs., 2 bookmobiles; Dir. LINDA M. BRETZ; publ. *Rochester History* (quarterly).

### NORTH CAROLINA

**Public Library of Charlotte and Mecklenburg County:** 310 N. Tryon St., Charlotte, N.C. 28202; f. 1903; 715,580 vols.; Dir. ARIAL A. STEPHENS; publ. *Program Suggestions for Clubs and Study Groups* (annual).

### OHIO

**Akron-Summit County Public Library:** 55 South Main St., Akron 44326; f. 1874; 971,003 vols.; Librarian/Dir. STEVEN HAWK; publs. *Annual Report*†, *The Owlet*†.

**Cleveland Public Library:** 325 Superior Ave., Cleveland 44114; f. 1869; 2,418,323 vols.; 33 neighbourhood branches; bookmobile and Books-By-Mail service; the John G. White endowed collection of Folklore, Orientalia and Chess; large circulating collection of films and sound recordings; services to hospitals, the homebound, the physically handicapped and the blind; telephone reference service; paid research service; Dir. Dr. ERVIN J. GAINES; publ. *Index to Cleveland Newspapers* (monthly).

**Dayton and Montgomery County Public Library:** 215 East Third St., Dayton 45402; f. 1805; 1,381,400 vols., 19 brs.; bookmobile service; service to homebound, elderly and blind; circulating collection of 16 mm. films, records and cassettes; Dir. JOHN S. WALLACH; publs. *Annual Report, Business Industry Technology Service*†.

**Public Library of Cincinnati and Hamilton County:** 800 Vine St., Cincinnati 45202; f. 1853; 3,242,497 vols.; 125,612 maps; 39 brs.; Regional Library for the Blind and Physically Handicapped, institutions/Books-by-Mail/Bookmobile dept.; specializes in local history, genealogy, theology, art, music, theatre, oral history; Librarian JAMES R. HUNT.

**Public Library of Columbus and Franklin County:** 28 South Hamilton Rd., Columbus 43213; 1,191,490 vols., 21 brs.; Dir. RICHARD T. SWEENEY.

**Toledo-Lucas County Public Library:** 325 Michigan St., Toledo; consolidated 1970; 1,261,986 vols.; Dir. ARDATH DANFORD.

# UNITED STATES OF AMERICA

### OREGON

**Library Association of Portland—Multnomah County Library:** 801 S.W. Tenth Ave., Portland, Ore. 97205; f. 1864; over 1 million vols.; 14 branches; Librarian JAMES BURGHARDT.

### PENNSYLVANIA

**Carnegie Library of Pittsburgh:** 4400 Forbes Ave., Pittsburgh, Pa. 15213; f. 1895; 2,357,963 vols., c. 66,000 of which are in foreign languages; 19 brs., all with their own collections, and 5 mobile libraries; Dir. ANTHONY A. MARTIN.

**Free Library of Philadelphia:** Logan Sq., Philadelphia, Pa. 19103; 48 brs. throughout the city and 3 regional libraries; f. 1891; 2,933,732 vols.; special collections include: Fleisher orchestral music; Carson history of the common law; Widener incunabula; Drinker Choral Library; Lewis Illuminated MSS., European and Oriental; History of the Automobile; Elkins Americana, Dickens, Goldsmith, Poe; Lewis cuneiform tablets; Rosenbach children's books of the 18th and 19th centuries; children's illustrators, Beatrix Potter, Arthur Rackham; theatre collection; Dir. KEITH DOMS.

### RHODE ISLAND

**Providence Public Library:** 150 Empire St., Providence 02903; 631,908 vols.; Dir. ANNALEE M. BUNDY.

### TENNESSEE

**Memphis and Shelby County Public Library and Information Center:** 1850 Peabody Ave., Memphis; f. 1893; 1,600,000 vols.; CATV and colour videotaping studio; information and referral service (LINC-Library Information Center); Dir. ROBERT B. CRONEBERGER; publs. *LINC's Latest* (monthly), *Kaleidoscope* (monthly), *Chronicle* (quarterly), *Undercurrent* (monthly).

### TEXAS

**Dallas Public Library:** 1954 Commerce St., Dallas; 2,747,184 system holdings; Dir. Mrs. L. M. BRADSHAW.

**Fort Worth Public Library:** 300 Taylor St., Fort Worth, Tex. 76102; f. 1901; 646,313 vols.; reference, bibliographical, circulation and extension services; special collections include Bibliography, Bookplates, Early Children's Books, Earth Science, Genealogy and Oral History; Dir. LINDA ALLMAND.

**Houston Public Library:** Civic Center, 500 McKinney Ave., Houston, 77002; 2,345,634 vols.; Dir. D. M. HENINGTON.

### VIRGINIA

**Fairfax County Public Library:** 5502 Port Royal Rd., Springfield, Va. 22151; f. 1939; 1,374,266 vols.; 17 branches, 2 bookmobiles; also films, phonodiscs, microfilm, periodicals; Dir. WILLIAM L. WHITESIDES.

### WASHINGTON

**Seattle Public Library:** 1000 4th Ave., Seattle 98104; f. 1891; 1,515,680 vols.; special collections: Aeronautics, Pacific Northwest Americana; 23 br. libraries; Librarian RONALD A. DUBBERLY.

### WISCONSIN

**Milwaukee Public Library:** 814 West Wisconsin Ave., Milwaukee 53233; f. 1878; 2,355,842 vols.; special collections include Great Lakes marine collection, cookbooks, H. G. Wells, definitive editions of collected works of British and American authors, Charles King collection, Harry Franck collection, genealogy; depository for U.S. Federal Documents, U.S. Geologic Survey, U.S. Defence Mapping Agency maps and U.S. Patent Office; 12 br. libraries, Wisconsin Regional Library for the Blind and Physically Handicapped headquarters, 4 mobile libraries, 3 library vans; Librarian HENRY E. BATES, Jr.

## SPECIAL LIBRARIES

### ALASKA

**Alaska Historical Library:** Pouch G, State Office Bldg., Juneau, Alaska 99811; f. 1900, name changed 1967; an Alaska/Arctic research library housing the Wickersham collection, Alaska newspapers, MSS. and photographs; 29,000 vols.; Librarian PHYLLIS DE MUTH; publ. *Northern Libraries Bulletin* (3 a year).

### CALIFORNIA

**Hoover Institution on War, Revolution and Peace:** Stanford, Calif. 94305; f. 1919; centre of documentation and research on international and domestic political, social and economic change in the 20th century; over 1.5 million vols. and approx. 4,000 archival units on the causes and consequences of war and revolutionary movements, and man's endeavour to achieve peace; with particular emphasis on the rise and spread of communism and other totalitarian movements; international studies programme on U.S.S.R. and Eastern Europe, Africa and Middle East, Asia and Pacific, Western Europe; research programme on political, economic and social problems in the United States; independent, within the framework of Stanford University; Dir. W. GLENN CAMPBELL.

**Huntington Library, Art Gallery and Botanical Gardens:** San Marino, Calif. 91108; estab. 1919 by the late Henry E. Huntington as a free research library, art gallery, museum, and botanical garden; library collections include 330,254 rare books, more than five million MSS., a large print collection and a working reference library of 242,943 vols.; available to scholars and others engaged in research work, on application to the Registrar; the collections are limited to British and American history and literature; particular strengths include English medieval and Renaissance, British drama, American colonial, American Civil War, American frontier, 19th- and 20th-century literary MSS.; separate reference libraries are located in the Botanical Department and Art Gallery, the latter including 75,000 photographs of paintings and 6,000 British drawings; public programmes, lectures, exhibitions; research programme includes fellowships, grants, and publication of the *Huntington Library Quarterly*† and other scholarly works; Dir. JAMES THORPE; Librarian DANIEL H. WOODWARD; see also Museums and Art Galleries.

**Los Angeles County Law Library:** 391 West First St., Los Angeles, Calif. 90012; f. 1891; 663,507 vols.; Librarian RICHARD T. IAMELE.

**San Francisco Law Library:** 436 City Hall, San Francisco 94102; 238,831 vols., main library; 30,367 vols., branch library; Librarians H. E. ROWE, J. H. HAUFF.

### DISTRICT OF COLUMBIA

**Association of American Railroads, Economics and Finance Department Library:** Room 523, American Railroads Bldg., 1920 L St., N.W., Washington, D.C. 20036; f. 1910; 50,000 vols.; collection on transportation economics, history, and future developments all over the world; Librarian JOHN MCLEOD.

**Dumbarton Oaks Research Library and Collection:** 1703 32nd St., Washington, D.C. 20007; donated in 1940 to Harvard University by Mr. and Mrs. Robert Woods Bliss as a research centre in the Byzantine and Médieval Humanities; research library of over 100,000 vols.; collections of early Christian and Byzantine art, and of Pre-Columbian art of Central and South America; research programmes in Byzantine and Pre-Columbian studies, history of landscape architecture; Dir. GILES CONSTABLE; Librarian IRENE VASLEF; publs. *Dumbarton Oaks Papers* (Byzantine, annually), *Dumbarton Oaks Studies* (Byzantine, irregularly), *Studies in Pre-Columbian Art and Archaeology* (irregularly), *Conference Proceedings* (Pre-Columbian, irregularly), *Colloquium Papers* (Landscape Architecture, irregularly).

**Folger Shakespeare Library:** Washington, D.C.; dedicated 1932; collections comprise: the world's largest collection of original editions and reprints of Shakespeare; more than 50 per cent of the extant titles of English Renaissance books, 1475–1640; one of the most significant collections in the Western Hemisphere for the study of British civilization between 1500 and 1700; Continental books of 16th and 17th centuries; 185 vols. 18th-century Strozzi MSS.; a Dryden collection; English plays, 1641–1700; about 100,000 books of 18th, 19th and 20th centuries, dealing with the Elizabethan age; approximately 250,000 play bills; some 50,000 MSS. of 16th and 17th centuries relating to the life and times of Shakespeare; approximately 50,000 literary and theatrical prints and engravings; Programmes: Fellowships; Institute of Renaissance and 18th-century studies; theatre programme; lectures; poetry readings; concerts; exhibitions; administered by Trustees of Amherst College; Dir. Dr. O. B. HARDISON, Jr.

**Smithsonian Institution Libraries:** General Library, National Museum of Natural History Building, 10th and Constitution Ave., N.W., 20560; 950,000 vols.; brs. include: General Library, Anthropology Branch Library, Botany Branch Library, Cooper-Hewitt Museum of Decorative Arts and Design Branch Library, Entomology Branch Library, National Air and Space Museum Branch Library, National Museum of American History and Technology Branch Library, National Museum of Natural History Branch Library, Museum of African Art Branch Library, National Zoological Park Branch Library, Smithsonian Astrophysical Observatory Branch Library, Smithsonian Radiation Biology Laboratory Branch Library, Smithsonian Tropical Research Institute Branch Library and, affiliated, The Woodrow Wilson International Center for Scholars Library; Dir. Dr. ROBERT MALOY.

### ILLINOIS

**American Medical Association Division of Library and Archival Services:** 535 North Dearborn St., Chicago, Ill. 60610; f. 1911; 140,000 vols.; specializes in clinical medicine, sociology and economics of medicine, international health, history of American Medical Association and health education; Dir. SUSAN CRAWFORD, PH.D.

**Cook County Law Library:** 2900 Chicago Civic Center, Chicago, Ill. 60602; f. 1966; 200,000 vols.; Exec. Librarian WILLIAM J. POWERS; publs. *C.C.L.L. Newsletter, C.C.L.L. Selected New Acquisitions*.

**Illinois State Historical Library:** Springfield, Ill.: f. 1889; 155,000 vols., 6,200,000 MSS.; special collections, including Illinois history, Lincolniana, Civil War, Illinois newspapers, genealogy, Mormon history, Mid-West Americana MSS.; State Historian OLIVE S. FOSTER (acting); publs. *Collections, Journal of the Illinois State Historical Society, Illinois History, Occasional Papers*.

**John Crerar Library:** 35 West 33rd St., Chicago, Ill. 60616; f. 1894; about 1,250,000 vols. and pamphlets on the basic sciences, mathematics, astronomy, physics, chemistry, geology, and the biological sciences, and their applications in agriculture, medicine, and all branches of engineering; Exec. Dir. and Librarian

WILLIAM S. BUDINGTON; publs. *Translations Register-Index*† (monthly), *Leukemia Abstracts*† (monthly).

**Library of International Relations:** see under Learned Societies.

**Newberry Library:** 60 West Walton St., Chicago, Ill. 60610; f. 1887; a free public reference library of over 1,300,000 vols. in the humanities, with special collections on the American Indians, the history of printing, music, American and English history and literature, exploration and early cartography, Portugal, the Renaissance in England and Europe, European history from the Renaissance to 1815, the Philippine Islands; Latin American history and literature of the colonial period; maintains research and educational programmes in its Center for the History of Cartography, Center for the History of the American Indian, and Family and Community History Center; Pres. and Librarian L. W. TOWNER.

### IOWA

**Herbert Hoover Presidential Library and Museum:** West Branch, Iowa 52358; f. 1962; official and personal papers of 31st President of U.S.A.; also 94 MS. collections; 22,843 vols., 5,529,750 MSS., 24,511 photos, 251 sound recordings and 135,174 ft. of film, 2,621 rolls of microfilm, 9,478 pages of oral history, 4,166 museum objects; Dir. THOMAS T. THALKEN.

### KANSAS

**Dwight D. Eisenhower Library:** Abilene, Kansas 67410; f. 1962; manuscripts, presidential and personal papers related to former President Eisenhower, and manuscripts of important persons in the Eisenhower administration and in the General's military career; 18,000,000 manuscript materials, 20,000 vols., photographic collection of 100,000 items, audio tapes and films; Dir. Dr. J. E. WICKMAN.

**Kansas State Historical Society Library:** 120 West Tenth, Topeka 66612; f. 1875; 300,000 vols.; state archives, newspapers and census, state historical museum, archaeology; Exec. Dir. JOSEPH W. SNELL; publ. *Kansas History: A Journal of the Central Plains*.

### MASSACHUSETTS

**American Antiquarian Society Library:** 185 Salisbury St., Worcester 01609; f. 1812; 628,000 vols.; Americana to 1876; Dir. M. A. MCCORISON; publs. *Proceedings* and monographs.

**Francis A. Countway Library of Medicine:** 10 Shattuck St., Boston, Mass. 02115; f. 1965; a combination of the Harvard Medical Library and Boston Medical Library; 480,000 vols.; Librarian C. R. LE SUEUR.

**Library of the Boston Athenaeum:** 10½ Beacon St., Boston Mass. 02108; f. 1807; independent research library; 600,000 vols.; history, biography, English and American literature and fine decorative arts; special collections include Confederate States imprints, books from libraries of George Washington, Gen. Henry Knox and Bishop Cheverus, the King's Chapel Collection (1698), Gypsy literature, private press publications, 19th-century tracts, early U.S. Government documents and the Charles E. Mason print collection; conservation dept. for preservation of library materials; Dir. and Librarian RODNEY ARMSTRONG.

**Massachusetts Historical Society Library:** 1154 Boylston St., Boston, Mass. 02215; f. 1791; 450,000 vols.; large collection of American historical MSS; Librarian JOHN D. CUSHING.

### MINNESOTA

**James Jerome Hill Reference Library:** 76-80 West 4th St., Saint Paul, Minn. 55102; f. 1921; 200,000 vols.; business, economics and transport; Exec. Dir. Dr. VIRGIL F. MASSMAN.

**Minnesota Historical Society Library:** 690 Cedar St., Saint Paul, Minn. 55101; f. 1849; 300,000 vols.; North American history particularly relating to Minnesota and the Upper Midwest (especially travel accounts, fur trade, Scandinavian and other immigration, labour, political and church history, railroad records, local history and geneaology); several million pamphlets, documents, newspapers, films, maps, photographs, tapes, artifacts, and MSS.; Dir. RUSSELL W. FRIDLEY.

### MISSOURI

**Harry S. Truman Library:** Independence, Mo. 64050; dedicated 1957; manuscripts, printed materials, photographs, sound recordings, oral history interviews and museum materials relating to the career and administration of former President Truman; 12,363,360 MSS., 74,446 photographs, 44,380 vols., 75,028 other printed items; administered by the Archivist of the United States, ROBERT M. WARNER; Dir. BENEDICT K. ZOBRIST.

**Pope John XXIII Foundation Library:** Ecumenical and Research Center, 5225 Rockhill Rd., Kansas City, Mo. 64110; f. 1933; 10,000 vols. on religion; Librarian Mrs MARJORIE COPELAND.

### NEW YORK

**American Museum of Natural History Library:** Central Park West at 79th St., New York, N.Y. 10024; 325,000 vols., 6,000 periodicals; natural history; Chief Librarian Miss NINA J. ROOT.

**Association of the Bar of the City of New York Library:** 42 West 44th St., New York, N.Y. 10036; 369,000 vols.; law; Librarian ANTHONY P. GRECH.

**Engineering Societies Library:** 345 East 47th St., New York, N.Y. 10017; f. 1913; 250,000 vols.; Dir. S. KIRK CABEEN.

**Franklin D. Roosevelt Library:** Hyde Park, New York 12538; dedicated 1941; manuscripts, photographs, printed and museum materials concerning the life and times of Franklin and Eleanor Roosevelt, incl. 9,000 lin. ft. of his papers, many papers of his contemporaries and associates; 16 million MSS. pages, 127,000 photographs, 40,000 books, 84,000 other printed items, 22,000 museum items; administered by the National Archives and Records Service of the General Services Administration; Dir. WILLIAM R. EMERSON.

**Hispanic Society of America Library:** Broadway, between 155th and 156th Streets, New York, N.Y. 10032; f. 1904; over 100,000 manuscripts; 15,000 books printed before 1701, including 250 incunabula; over 100,000 later books; art, history and literature of Spain, Portugal and colonial Hispanic America; clipping and photographic files; Curator JEAN R. LONGLAND.

**Jewish Theological Seminary of America Library:** 3080 Broadway, New York, N.Y. 10027; c. 240,000 vols.; c. 10,000 MSS., c. 23,000 leaves of Cairo Genizah, Archives, Louis Ginzberg Microfilm Library (foreign collections of Hebrew MSS.); incunabula; Bible Rabbinics, Jewish History, Liturgy, Theology, Early Yiddish, Hebrew Literature, History of Science and Medicine; Haggadahs; Megillot (Esther scrolls); Ketuboth (marriage contracts); Prints and Photographs; Librarian Dr. MENAHEM SCHMELZER.

**Medical Research Library of Brooklyn:** 450 Clarkson Ave., Brooklyn, New York 11203; the joint library of the Academy of Medicine of Brooklyn, Inc., f. 1845, and the State University of New York, Downstate Medical Center, f. 1860; 241,548 vols.; Dir. KENNETH E. MOODY.

**Mercantile Library Association:** 17 East 47th St., New York, N.Y. 10017; f. 1820; 1,900 mems.; 186,000 vols.; Librarian CLAIRE J. ROTH; Pres. MICHAEL THERRY.

UNITED STATES OF AMERICA

**New York Academy of Medicine Library:** 2 East 103rd St., New York, N.Y. 10029; f. 1847; 459,462 vols., 180,615 catalogued pamphlets, 274,241 catalogued illustrations and portraits; Librarian BRETT A. KIRKPATRICK.

**New York Law Institute Library:** 120 Broadway, New York, N.Y. 10271; f. 1828; 230,000 vols.; 1,450 reels of microfilm; 16,300 microfiches; law library for practising attorneys; Librarian SIEGLINDE H. ROTHSCHILD.

**Pierpont Morgan Library:** 29 East 36th St., New York, N.Y. 10016; f. 1924; collections formed by J. Pierpont Morgan, with additions made by his son and others; among its treasures are: Mediaeval and Renaissance MSS. from 6th to 16th centuries; Constance Missal, Gutenberg Bibles and other printed books from the inception of printing, c. 1450 to the 20th century; Assyrian and Babylonian seals, cylinders, and cuneiform tablets; Egyptian, Greek and other papyri; music MSS. and letters from 15th to 20th centuries; historical letters and documents from 11th to 20th centuries; bookbindings; early children's books; prints and master drawings; paintings, sculpture, and art objects; Dir CHARLES A. RYSKAMP.

**Union Theological Seminary Library:** 3041 Broadway at Reinhold Niebuhr Place (120th St.), New York, N.Y. 10027; f. 1836; 555,000 vols., 30,000 pieces in microform, 1,500 periodical subscriptions, 1,000 audio tapes, etc.; incorporates Missionary Research library; Dir. RICHARD D. SPOOR.

**United Nations Library—Dag Hammarskjöld Library:** United Nations Plaza, New York 10017; f. 1946; dedicated 1961; special collections of documents on the UN, Specialized Agencies and the League of Nations; collections of books, periodicals and government documents on international law and relations, economics, statistics and on other topics of concern to the UN; activities and history of the UN; international affairs 1918-45; official gazettes of all countries; 380,000 vols., 15,000 serials, 80,000 maps; Dir. Dr. V. ORLOV.

**U.S. Military Academy Library:** West Point, N.Y. 10996; f. 1802; 400,000 bound vols.; military-historical, academic, government documents, MSS., rare books and special collections; Librarian, Historian and Archivist E. A. WEISS; publ. *USMA Library Bulletins* (irregular).

PENNSYLVANIA

**American Philosophical Society Library:** 105 South 5th St., Philadelphia, Pa. 19106; f. 1743; 157,850 vols., c. 5,000,000 MSS. microfilm; special collections on Benjamin Franklin, history of science, genetics, quantum physics, Darwinism, American Indian linguistics, Thomas Paine; Librarian EDWARD C. CARTER II; publs. *Annual Report, Library Publications* (irregular), *Mendel Newsletter* (irregular).

**Historical Society of Pennsylvania Library:** 1300 Locust St., Philadelphia 19107; f. 1824; 500,000 vols. and pamphlets, over 14,000,000 MSS.; historical and genealogical material on the original colonies and surrounding states; Librarian JOHN H. PLATT.

WISCONSIN

**American Geographical Society Collection of the University of Wisconsin-Milwaukee Library:** P.O.B. 399, Milwaukee, Wis. 53201; 186,000 vols., 373,000 maps, 6,090 atlases, 71 globes, 33,700 pamphlets, 45,900 photographs; Curator Dr. ROMAN DRAZNIOWSKY; publs. *Current Geographical Publications*† (10 a year).

## STATE LIBRARIES
(with a total number of volumes over 500,000)

**Arizona Department of Library, Archives and Public Records:** Capitol Building, Phoenix, Ariz. 85007; f. 1864; law, government, Arizona and Southwest history, genealogy, federal and state documents, library extension service, archives, public records; 1,154,713 vols.; Dir. Mrs. SHARON WOMACK (acting).

**California State Library:** P.O.B. 2037, Sacramento, Calif. 95809; f. 1850; 378,000 vols., 2,500,000 government publications; library service to State Government; preservation of California materials; government document depository; law library; books for the blind, and physically handicapped service; administrator of state and federal aid to public libraries; State Librarian GARY E. STRONG; publs. *California State Publications* (monthly), *California Library Statistics and Directory* (annually).

**Connecticut State Library:** 231 Capitol Ave., Hartford, Conn. 06115; f. 1850; 650,000 vols., 1,000,000 government documents, 19,000 cu. ft. of MSS. and state archives; Connecticut newspapers, genealogy, history, law, legislative reference; State Librarian CLARENCE WALTERS; publs. *Connecticut State Library Newsletter* (irregular), *Checklist of Publications of Connecticut State Agencies* (monthly).

**Hawaii State Library:** Box 2360, Honolulu, Hawaii 96804; 1,090,044 vols.; State Librarian RUTH S. ITAMURA.

**Illinois State Library:** Springfield, Ill. 62756; f. 1842; over 2.5 million items and documents; Librarian KATHRYN J. GESTERFIELD; publ. *Illinois Libraries* (monthly except July and August).

**Indiana State Library:** 140 North Senate Ave., Indianapolis 46204; f. 1825; to provide library service to state government, advice and counsel to the libraries and librarians of the state, reference service and materials for local school, public, special, and academic libraries; genealogy and special research collections; library for Indiana Academy of Science; 800,000 items; Dir, C. RAY EWICK; publs. *Indiana Libraries* (quarterly). *Focus on Indiana Libraries* (monthly).

**Kansas State Library:** State House, Topeka, Kansas 66612; f. 1854; law, legislative reference, library services to the blind and handicapped; 800,000 vols.; State Librarian ERNESTINE GILLILAND.

**Kentucky Department of Library and Archives:** Box 537, Berry Hill, Frankfort, Ky. 40602; 4,140,000 vols.; Librarian JAMES A. NELSON.

**State Library of Massachusetts:** 341 State House, Boston, Mass. 02133; f. 1826; 822,083 vols.; a government and public affairs library serving the information and research needs of the executive and legislative branches of Massachusetts State government; depository for printed documents of the same and for selected federal documents; collections especially strong in public law, public affairs, state and local history; State Librarian JAMES H. FISH; publ. *Commonwealth of Massachusetts Publications Received by the State Library* (quarterly).

**Michigan State Library:** 735 E. Michigan Ave., P.O.B. 30007, Lansing, Mich. 48909; f. 1837; approx. 1,500,000 vols.; operates the State Library for the Blind and the State Law Library; Librarian FRANCIS X. SCANNELL; publs. *Michigan's Public Libraries Annual Statistics, Of Timely Interest, Michigan Documents, Michigan in Books, Family Trails, Michigan Periodical Index, Michigan Newspapers on Microfilm, Michigan Education Resources.*

## LIBRARIES

**New Hampshire State Library:** 20 Park St., Concord, N.H.; 787,203 vols.; Librarian Mrs. SHIRLEY ADAMOVICH (acting).

**New Jersey State Library:** 185 W. State St., Trenton, N.J. 08625; 700,000 vols.; Dir. R. H. MCDONOUGH.

**New York State Library:** Albany, New York 12230; includes pamphlets, MSS.; collections of American and especially New York State history; newspapers and periodicals, Government publications, genealogy, Library for the Blind and Visually Handicapped; 4.5 million items; Dir. PETER J. PAULSON.

*Reference Services:* Principal Librarian (vacant).

*Legislative and Governmental Services:* Principal Librarian JACQUELINE ENEQUIST.

*Collection Management/Network Services:* Principal Librarian JOHN VAN DER VEER JUDD.

*Collection Acquisition and Processing:* Principal Librarian W. DE ALLEAUME.

Publs. *Bookmark, Checklist of Official Publications of the State of New York,* etc.

**State Library of Ohio:** Columbus, Ohio; f. 1817; 1,040,728 vols.; a special library for State government, incl. periodicals, documents, pamphlets, services and microforms; special collection of management, political science, genealogy and local history; State Librarian RICHARD M. CHESKI.

**Oregon State Library:** State Library Building, Salem, Oregon 97310; f. 1905; 1,094,546 vols.; provides service for the Legislature, state agencies and state officials; Librarian MARCIA LOWELL; publ. *Checklist of Official Publications.*

**State Library of Pennsylvania:** Box 1601, Harrisburg, Pa. 17105; 943,224 vols.; government, political science, education, social work, sociology, American and especially Pennsylvania history, urban affairs, library science, law, genealogy; Collection of Pennsylvania newspapers; maps; State Librarian ELLIOT L. SHELKROT; publs. *Year's Work in Pennsylvania Studies, Checklist of Official Pennsylvania Publications* (monthly).

**Virginia State Library:** 11th and Capitol St., Richmond, Va. 23219; f. 1823; 551,000 vols.; Virginia, Confederate and Southern history, genealogy; archive collection of 20,000,000 pieces; 75,000 maps; Librarian DONALD R. HAYNES; publs. *Virginia Cavalcade* (quarterly), *Checklist of Virginia State Publications, Statistics, Virginia State Publications in Print* (annual).

**Washington State Library:** Olympia, Wash. 98504; f. 1853; 528,743 books and periodicals, 886,836 federal and state documents; 39,512 microfiche, 25,000 microfilm, 4,961 films; Dir. RODERICK G. SWARTZ.

### SELECTED UNIVERSITY LIBRARIES
(arranged alphabetically by States)

**University of Alabama Library:** University, Ala. 35486; f. 1828; regional depository for federal documents; departmental libraries for business, education, engineering, sciences; special collections on Alabama and Southern history and literature; 1,250,000 vols.; Librarian JAMES F. WYATT, PH.D.

**University of Arizona Library:** Tucson, Ariz. 85721; f. 1891; 2,766,187 vols.; Librarian W. DAVID LAIRD, M.S.; publs. occasional papers†.

**Stanford University Libraries:** Stanford, Calif. 94305; f. 1885; 4,487,553 vols., including the Green Library (1,609,881), Hoover Institution on War, Revolution and Peace (1,214,620 vols.), the J. Henry Meyer Memorial Library for under-graduates (140,344 vols.) and 45 departmental and school libraries, of which the major ones are: Lane Medical Library (276,562 vols.), Law Library (250,553 vols.), Cubberley Education Library (99,537 vols.), Branner Earth Sciences Library (62,311 vols.), J. Hugh Jackson Business Library (264,270 vols.), Food Research Institute Library (69,860 vols.), Linear Accelerator Center Library (92,272 vols.), Falconer Biology Library (61,762 vols.), Hopkins Marine Station Library (21,686 vols.), Mathematical and Computer Sciences Library (40,469 vols.), Swain Chemistry Library (27,444 vols.), Art (101,079 vols.), Music (43,794 vols.), Physics (30,505 vols.), Engineering (73,097 vols.); special collections: Transportation, Sir Isaac Newton, Typography, Music, English and American Literature; Technical Information Service serving business and industry; Dir. of Libraries DAVID C. WEBER.

**University of California Libraries:** Berkeley, Calif. 94720; f. 1868; total of 17,544,833 vols. in 10 libraries, which, with the number of volumes and names of librarians, are:

Berkeley: 5,753,731; J. A. ROSENTHAL, M.A., M.S.L.S.
Davis: 1,606,266; B. KREISSMAN, PH.D.
Hastings College of the Law: 167,549; D. F. HENKE, J.D., M.LL.
Irvine: 939,012; C. J. BOYER, M.L.S., PH.D.
Los Angeles: 4,234,835; R. SHANK, D.L.S.
Riverside: 983,200; JOAN CHAMBERS, M.L.S.
San Diego: 1,332,525; MILLICENT D. ABELL, M.A., M.L.S.
San Francisco: 486,389; D. BISHOP, B.A., M.S.
Santa Barbara: 1,375,227; A. VEANER, M.L.S.
Santa Cruz: 619,669; A. J. DYSON, M.S.L.S.

**University of Southern California Library:** Los Angeles, Calif. Z90007; f. 1880; 1,866,161 vols.; Librarian R. L. KIDMAN, M.S.

**University of Colorado Libraries:** Boulder, Colo. 80309; f. 1876; 1,852,904 vols.; Dir. CLYDE WALTON.

**University of Connecticut Library:** Storrs, Conn. 06268; f. 1881; 1,775,000 vols.; Dir. JOHN P. MCDONALD; Librarian NORMAN D. STEVENS; publ. *University of Connecticut Bibliography Series*† (irregular).

**Yale University Library:** New Haven, Conn.; f. 1701; 7,072,345 vols.; each of the 12 Undergraduate Colleges has its own library; the following list gives the principal departmental libraries, with the total of volumes:

| | |
|---|---:|
| Main Library (Sterling Memorial, Beinecke & Cross Campus) | 4,392,939 |
| American Oriental Society | 21,534 |
| Anthropology | 13,646 |
| Art | 65,413 |
| Babylonian Collection | 5,326 |
| Chemistry | 12,314 |
| Classics | 18,228 |
| College Libraries | 79,314 |
| Cowles Foundation | 8,509 |
| Divinity | 317,130 |
| Drama | 21,279 |
| Economic Growth Center | 35,975 |
| Engineering and Applied Science | 25,692 |
| Epidemiology and Public Health | 13,749 |
| Forestry and Environmental Studies | 124,023 |
| Geology | 82,804 |
| German Reading Room | 1,051 |
| German Seminar | 6,613 |

| History Seminar | 4,795 |
| Indological and Linguistic Seminar | 5,176 |
| Kline Science | 320,620 |
| Law | 582,893 |
| Mathematics | 21,742 |
| Medical | 442,211 |
| Music | 101,883 |
| Observatory | 14,968 |
| Ornithology | 7,260 |
| Palmer-Schreiber | 6,887 |
| Philosophy | 2,999 |
| Semitic Reference | 1,172 |
| Sinological Seminar | 11,000 |
| Social Science | 42,166 |
| Statistics | 3,216 |
| Storage Collection | 224,269 |
| Yale Center for British Art and British Studies (Rare Book) | 20,148 |
| Yale Center for British Art and British Studies (Reference) | 13,401 |

Librarian RUTHERFORD D. ROGERS; publ. *Gazette*†.

**Florida State University Library:** Tallahassee, Fla. 32306; f. 1853; 1,400,000 vols.; Dir. C. E. MILLER, M.S.L.S.; publs. *Notes in Anthropology, Contributions of the Sedimentological Research Laboratory, Journal of Hispanic Philology*, etc.

**University of Florida Libraries:** Gainesville, Fla. 32611; f. 1901; 2,079,344 vols.; Dir. G. A. HARRER.

**Northwestern University Libraries:** Evanston, Ill. 60201; f. 1856; 2,748,182 vols.; Northwestern University Library (humanities and social sciences, with special collections relating to Africa, French Revolution, Siege and Commune of Paris 1870-1871, Horace, Spanish Civil War, Spanish Drama, Modern Movements in Art, Literature and Politics, Maps); five branch libraries (transportation, science-engineering, geology, mathematics, music); three professional libraries (dentistry, law, medicine) and the Schaffner Library in Chicago; University Librarian JOHN P. MCGOWAN.

**University of Chicago Library:** Chicago, Ill. 60637; f. 1892; over 4,200,000 vols., including the Joseph Regenstein Library, Harper (College) Memorial Library and 6 departmental libraries and professional school libraries; research collections (including special collections), for research in most areas in the humanities, law, business, and the social, biological and physical sciences; Dir. MARTIN RUNKLE.

**University of Illinois (Urbana-Champaign) Library:** Urbana, Ill. 61801; f. 1867; 5,936,823 vols., 3,150,338 manuscripts, maps, microtexts and other items; special collections in classical literature and history, English literature including Milton and Shakespeare, Western U.S. history, Lincolniana, Italian history, music, architecture, science and technology; University Librarian HUGH ATKINSON, M.S.

**Indiana University Library System:** Bloomington, Ind. 47405; f. 1829; 5,029,534 vols., 1,569,211 microforms, 3,812,020 MSS., 290,249 music scores, 242,512 slides, 429,372 maps and charts; government publications; Dean of Libraries ELAINE F. SLOAN.

**Purdue University Libraries:** West Lafayette, Ind. 47907; f. 1869; 1,300,000 vols.; Dir. JOSEPH M. DAGNESE.

**University of Notre Dame Libraries:** Notre Dame, Ind. 46556; f. 1873; 1,380,000 vols.; Dir. ROBERT C. MILLER.

**Iowa State University Libraries:** Ames, Iowa 50011; f. 1870; 1,400,000 vols., 1,200,000 microforms, 17,607 serials, special collections in agricultural history, entomology, botany, conservation and veterinary medicine; Dean WARREN B. KUHN, M.S.

**University of Iowa Libraries:** Iowa City, Iowa 52242; f. 1847; 2,136,899 vols., 12 departmental libraries; special collections; Dean of Library Administration LESLIE W. DUNLAP, M.A., B.S.L.S., PH.D.; University Librarian DALE M. BENTZ, B.A., B.S.L.S., M.S.

**Kansas State University of Agriculture and Applied Science, Farrell Library:** Manhattan, Kansas 66506; f. 1863; 900,000 vols., 11,200 serials, 1,500,000 microforms, 570,000 government documents, 100,000 maps, 10,000 sound recordings, 8,000 scores, 5,500 slides, 2,300 tapes; 4 brs. (Veterinary Medical, Chemistry, Physics, Architecture and Design); special collections in cookbooks, Linnaeana, Robert Graves; Dean of Libraries MARY R. MAGRUDER; publs. *Library Bibliography Series* (irregular), *KSU Library Cassette Series on Library Technology* (irregular).

**University of Kansas Libraries:** Lawrence, Kans. 66045; f. 1866; 1,900,000 vols., 800,000 microforms; includes Watson (central) Library, Kenneth Spencer Research Library, and 6 branch and departmental libraries; Dean of Libraries JIM RANZ; publs. *Books and Libraries at the University of Kansas*†, *Bibliographical Contributions*†, *University of Kansas Publications, Library Series*†.

**University of Kentucky Libraries:** Lexington, Kentucky 40506; f. 1909; 1,792,048 vols., 2,010,756 microforms, 130,375 maps, 33,866 current serials; 14 departmental and collegiate libraries; UN, federal and state depositories; King Library Press; University and audio-visual archives; large collection of Kentuckiana, special collections in French and Spanish drama 1600-1900, on Ohio Valley, modern political manuscript collections, broadside ballads and chapbooks, Cortot collection of music theory, typography, history of books; Dir. PAUL A. WILLIS.

**Louisiana State University Library:** Baton Rouge, La.; f. 1860; 1,818,059 vols.; UN, federal and state depositories; special collections include E. A. McIlhenny Natural History Collection, Louisiana Collection, sugar technology, Lincolniana, petroleum, bibliograph collection, crawfish, archives on Lower Mississippi Valley; Dir. GEORGE J. GUIDRY, Jr.; publs. *Statistics of Southern College and University Libraries, Library Lectures*.

**Tulane University of Louisiana Libraries:** New Orleans, La. 70118; f. 1834; 1,400,000 vols. (incl. Law, Medicine and six other collections); special collections on New Orleans, Louisiana and Southern U.S. history; Latin American archaeology, art, economics and political science; Librarian WILLIAM NEWMAN.

**Johns Hopkins University Libraries:** Baltimore, Md. 21218; f. 1876; total of 2,214,300 vols.; consists of:

Arts and Sciences Division: Baltimore, Md. 21218; including the Milton S. Eisenhower Library, Albert D. Hutzler Undergraduate Library, and John Work Garrett Rare Book Library; Librarian SUSAN K. MARTIN.

William H. Welch Medical Library: Baltimore, Md. 21205; Librarian Dr. RICHARD A. POLACSEK.

School of Hygiene and Public Health Library; Librarian BARBARA ZELNIK (acting).

School of Advanced International Studies Library: Washington, D.C. 20036 (Librarian PETER PROMEN) and Bologna, Italy (Librarian ALDO ROSSI).

Applied Physics Laboratory Library: Laurel, Md. 20810; Librarian ROBERT KEPPLE.

**University of Maryland Libraries:** College Park, Md. 20742; f. 1813; consists of:

College Park Campus Libraries: 1,231,540 vols.; Dir. H. JOANNE HARRAR.

Baltimore County Campus Library: Catonsville, Md.; 310,396 vols.; Librarian A. RAIMO.

Eastern Shore Campus Library: Princess Anne, Md.; 106,000 vols.; Librarian JESSIE SMITH.

Health Sciences Library: Baltimore, Md.; 218,486 vols.; Librarian CYRIL FENG.

School of Law Library: Baltimore, Md.; 150,000 vols.; Librarian L. KIEFER.

**Boston University Libraries:** Boston, Mass. 02215; f. 1870; 1,371,000 vols., 20,750 periodicals; Dir. JOHN LAUCUS, A.B., M.S.

**Harvard University Library:** Cambridge, Mass. 02138; f. 1638; the oldest library in the U.S.A.; the total of 10,082,663 vols. is divided among some 90 libraries and central collection which is housed in the Widener, Houghton, Pusey, Lamont, Hilles, Cabot Science Centre, Harvard-Yenching, Littauer, Loeb Music, Tozzet and Fine Arts Libraries; important collections in nearly every field of learning, and over 3,700 vols. printed before 1501; Dir. OSCAR HANDLIN; Harvard College Librarian YEN-TSAI FÊNG; publ. *Harvard Library Bulletin*† (quarterly). The largest special libraries, with number of vols. and names of librarians, are:

Andover-Harvard Theological Library: 355,583 vols.; MARIA GROSSMANN.

Baker Library for Business Administration: 526,528 vols.; MARY CHATFIELD.

Countway Library for Medicine: 493,916 vols.; C. ROBIN LESUEUR.

Harvard-Yenching Library: 588,151 vols.; EUGENE W. WU.

Houghton Library for Rare Books and MSS.: 294,904 vols.; WILLIAM H. BOND.

Law School Library: 1,345,411 vols.; HARRY MARTIN.

Littauer Library: 424,423 vols.; J. C. DAMASKOS.

Museum of Comparative Zoology Library: 225,302 vols.; EVA JONAS.

**Massachusetts Institute of Technology Libraries:** Cambridge, Mass. 02139; f. 1861; 1,759,971 books and pamphlets, 18,849 periodicals; Dir. of Libraries JAY K. LUCKER.

**Michigan State University Libraries:** East Lansing, Mich. 48824; f. 1855; 2,615,000 vols. and 10 departmental libraries and special collections; Dir. R. E. CHAPIN, PH.D.

**University of Michigan Library:** Ann Arbor, Mich. 48109; over 5,400,000 vols., including the special collections in the Business Administration Library, William L. Clements Library of American History, the Law Library, Michigan Historical Collections, Flint Campus Library, Dearborn Campus Library and 21 divisional libraries; Dir. RICHARD M. DOUGHERTY, PH.D.

**Wayne State University Libraries:** Detroit, Mich. 48202; 1,950,000 vols. in 5 library units: education, general, law, medicine, science; Dir. V. M. PINGS, PH.D.

**University of Minnesota Library:** Minneapolis, Minn.; f. 1851; 3,250,000 vols.; general and 20 departmental libraries; Dir. ELDRED SMITH.

**St. Louis University Libraries:** 3655 W. Pine Blvd., St. Louis, Mo. 63108; f. 1818; 863,445 vols.; Dir. W. P. COLE; publ. *Manuscripta*† (3 a year).

**University of Missouri Library:** Columbia, Mo. 65201; f. 1839; 2,000,000 vols. in general and 9 departmental libraries on Columbia Campus; 616,043 vols. in general and six departmental libraries on Kansas City Campus; 300,000 vols. on the Rolla Campus; 320,000 vols. in one library on the St. Louis Campus; special collections of Western Historical MSS. and Missouriana; Dirs. of Libraries: JOHN H. GRIBBIN, PH.D., Columbia; KENNETH LABUDDE, PH.D., Kansas City; RONALD G. BOHLEY, M.L.S., Rolla; RONALD D. KRASH, M.L.S., St. Louis.

**University of Nebraska Libraries:** Lincoln, Neb. 68588; f. 1869; 2,000,000 vols. in combined libraries plus UN and federal and map depositories; 20,000 serials; microfacsimile and archive depts.; collections supporting 9 colleges, 5 schools and 42 PH.D. programmes in Lincoln, 7 colleges and 1 school in Omaha; Dean G. A. RUDOLPH.

**Princeton University Library:** Princeton, N.J. 08540; f. 1746; about 3,000,000 vols.; special collections include Robert Garrett collection of Arabic and Mediaeval MSS., the Gest Oriental Library (250,000 vols.), the William Seymour theatre collection, the Rollins collection of Western Americana, the archives of Eugène de Beauharnais, Morris L. Parrish collection of Victorian novelists, Cyrus H. McCormick and Grenville Kane collections of Early Americana, John Foster Dulles Library of Diplomatic History, etc.; Librarian DONALD W. KOEPP; publ. *Chronicle*.

**Rutgers University Libraries:** New Brunswick, N.J. 08901; f. 1766; c. 2,000,000 vols.; 17 additional libraries on Rutgers campuses in New Brunswick, Camden and Newark with specialized collections in medicine, physics, mathematics, microbiology, art, alcohol studies, labour/management relations, urban research and law; Librarian HENDRIK EDELMAN.

**Columbia University Libraries:** New York, N.Y. 10027; f. 1754; c. 5,000,000 vols.; there are 26 departmental and professional school libraries with important collections in architecture, business, law, medicine, engineering, the sciences, humanities and social sciences; University Librarian PATRICIA BATTIN.

**Cornell University Libraries:** Ithaca, N.Y. 14853; f. 1865; 4,300,000 vols.; Librarian LOUIS E. MARTIN.

**Five Associated University Libraries:** co-ordinates the libraries of the University of Rochester, Cornell University, Syracuse University, the State Universities of New York at Binghamton and Buffalo; Liaison Officer Mrs. MARIE B. KUNDER, 757 Ostrom Ave., Syracuse, N.Y. 13210.

**New York University Libraries:** New York, N.Y. 10012; f. 1835; 2,302,000 vols.; Dean CARLTON C. ROCHELL, PH.D.

**Syracuse University Library:** 222 Waverly Ave., Syracuse, N.Y. 13210; f. 1870; 1,752,453 vols.; Dir. DONALD C. ANTHONY.

**University of Rochester Libraries:** Rochester, N.Y. 14627; f. 1850; 1,900,000 vols.; includes Sibley Music Library and Edward G. Miner Library; Dir. JAMES F. WYATT.

**Duke University Library:** Durham, N.C. 27706; f. 1838; 3,100,000 vols.; British history and literature of 17th to 19th centuries; general European history since 1870; French Revolution; Church history of Reformation; American and Latin American history; Southern Americana; French, English, Italian and American literature; international law; ten special libraries; Librarian ELVIN E. STROWD (acting).

**University of North Carolina Library:** Chapel Hill, N.C. 27514; f. 1795; 2,487,122 vols., 1,329,557 microforms; special collections on North Carolina, Southern Americana, on the Origin and Development of the Book, on American drama, Dickens, Shaw, Spanish drama, Federal and State documents, Latin America, Napoleon and the French Revolution, Johnson and Boswell, Mazarinades, Music, and Southern historical MSS.; 10 departmental libraries in scientific and other fields; Librarian JAMES F. GOVAN.

**Case Western Reserve University Libraries:** Cleveland, Ohio 44106; f. 1826; 1,591,912 vols., 13,283 current periodicals and 273,015 microforms in five administrative units:

University Libraries: Freiberger Library (humanities and social sciences), Sears Library (science, technology, business, management, geology), Kulas Music Library, Astronomy Library; Dir. JAMES V. JONES.

Cleveland Health Sciences Library (medicine, dentistry, nursing); Dir. ROBERT G. CHESHIER.

School of Applied Social Sciences; Librarian VLATKA IVANISEVIC.

School of Law; Librarian SIMON GOREN.

School of Library Science; Librarian BETTINA MACAYEAL.

Special collections include Early American Children's Books, German Literature and Philology, History of Medicine, History of Printing, History of Science and Technology, Environmental Sciences, Natural History, Public Housing and Urban Development.

**Ohio State University Libraries:** 1858 Neil Ave. Mall, Columbus, Ohio 43210; f. 1870; 3,497,902 vols.; 1,300,866 other items; Dir. of Libraries WILLIAM J. STUDER.

**University of Cincinnati Library:** Cincinnati, Ohio 45221; f. 1819; 1.3 million vols.; comprises a general library, and 15 departmental libraries; includes special collections on classics, modern Greek, and history of medicine; Librarian CHARLES B. OSBURN, PH.D.

**University of Oklahoma Library:** Norman, Oklahoma 73019; f. 1892; 1,850,000 vols.; special collections in western history, business and economic history and history of science; Librarian SUL H. LEE.

**University of Oregon Library:** Eugene, Oregon 97403; f. 1876; 1,503,000 vols.; 283,000 government documents; 329,000 maps; 41,000 microfilm reels; 738,000 other microforms; Librarian G. W. SHIPMAN, A.M.L.S., M.A.

**Pennsylvania State University Libraries:** University Park, Pa. 16802; 2,300,000 vols.; 2,100,000 microforms, 250,000 maps, 1,042,000 government documents, 24,000 serials; comprises Central Library, 5 departmental brs., 19 branch campuses, Hershey Medical Centre Library; special collections: American Literature (Fred Lewis Pattee); Australian Art and Literature; Gift Books, Emblem Books; German Literature in translation (Allison-Shelley); Joseph Priestly; Renaissance; Williamscote Library (18th-century English, History, Theology and Classics); Utopian Literature; Labour History; Australiana; Vance Packard; John O'Hara; Conrad Richter, Theodore Roethke, Kenneth Burke; U.S. Steel Workers of America Archives; Dean of Libraries STUART FORTH.

**University of Pennsylvania Library:** Philadelphia, Pa. 19104; f. 1750; 2,900,000 vols.; central library and 20 departmental and affiliated libraries; Archaeology, Leibniz, Descartes, History of Philosophy and Science, Baltic Languages and Literature (especially Saulys Collection of Lithuanian materials), History of Chemistry (Edgar Fahs Smith collection), French Revolution, Aristotelianism, Occam, Medieval History, Inquisition (Henry C. Lea Library), English and European Bibles, Italian Renaissance Literature (Macauley Collection), Spanish Literature of the Golden Age (Rennert and Crawford Collections), Spanish Linguistics (Gillet Collection), Shakespeareana (Furness Library), Restoration Drama, 18th- and early 19th-century English fiction, Jonathan Swift, Thomas Paine, American drama, fiction, and poetry: Walt Whitman, Washington Irving, Robert Montgomery Bird, Theodore Dreiser, James Farrell; Middle-High German (Bechstein and part of Ehrismann Collection), Old French, Friesian, Indic MSS., South Asia, History of Economics (especially 18th and early 19th centuries), History of Education, Cryptography, Spiritualism, Programmschriften, Elzevir Imprints, Franklin Imprints,. early Americana, the American West, Canadiana; Dir. RICHARD DEGENNARO.

**University of Pittsburgh Libraries:** Pittsburgh, Pa. 15260; f. 1873; 19 separate libraries on or near Main Campus and 4 regional campus libraries in Bradford, Greensburg, Johnstown and Titusville; 3,504,467 vols. including microforms; Dir. Mrs. GLENORA ROSSELL.

**Brown University Library:** Providence. R.I. 02912; f. 1767; 1,530,000 vols.; Librarian C. J. SCHMIDT.

**University of Tennessee Libraries:** Knoxville, Tenn. 37916; f. 1794; 1,436,000 vols.; Dir. DONALD R. HUNT.

**Vanderbilt University Library:** Nashville, Tenn. 37203; estab. 1873; 1939–79 associated with Joint University Libraries; over 1,450,000 vols., incl. Central/Science Library and 5 professional school libraries (Divinity, Education, Law, Management and Medical); Dir. FRANK P. GRISHAM.

**University of Texas System Libraries:** Austin, Tex. 78712; f. 1883; 3,878,535 vols.; also Arlington 528,860 vols., El Paso 482,831 vols.; Permian Basin 282,178 vols.; San Antonio 199,938 vols.; Health Science Center, Houston 38,600 vols.; Health Science Center, Dallas 129,008 vols.; Health Science Center, San Antonio 88,154 vols.; Medical Branch, Galveston 162,097; Dir. at Austin H. W. BILLINGS, M.L.S.

**University of Utah Library:** Salt Lake City, Utah 84112; f. 1850; 1,990,000 vols., 17,249 serial titles; special collections: archives, Middle East, MSS., rare books, Western Americana, oral history; U.S. State and U.N. documents depository; Dir. R. K. HANSON.

**University of Virginia Library:** Charlottesville, Va. 22901; f. 1819; 2,431,322 vols.; special collection on American History, including McGregor Library of American History and the Barrett Library of American Literature, Massey Faulkner collection, Streeter collection on Southeastern Railways, Optics, Evolution, Thomas Jefferson, Edgar Allan Poe, Walt Whitman, Greek and Latin literature, Nuclear Energy, Music, International Law, History of Printing, Gothic novels, inter alia; Librarian RAY W. FRANTZ.

**University of Washington Libraries:** Seattle, Wash.; f. 1862; 4,025,369 vols.; 47,000 current serials, 3,019,186 microforms; includes Law Library (separately administered; Librarian ROBERT C. BERRING), Health Sciences Library, Odegaard Undergraduate Library, East Asia Library, Pacific North-west Collection of Americana and 17 br. libraries; Dir. MERLE N. BOYLAN.

**West Virginia University Library:** Morgantown, W. Va.; f. 1867; 1,622,000 vols.; Dir. R. F. MUNN.

**University of Wisconsin Library:** Madison, Wis. 53706; f. 1848; 3,631,669 vols.; special collections on pharmacy, Scandinavian literature, Gaelic literature and history, and modern Polish literature, history of science, history of Calvinism, socialist and labour movements; English, American, French, German, Icelandic, Irish, Spanish literature and history, etc.; Dir. JOSEPH H. TREYZ, M.S.

# MUSEUMS AND ART GALLERIES

MUSEUMS. *The following list includes most of the best known and special museums in the United States, but it is of necessity a selection only.*

*"The Official Museums Directory" published by the American Association of Museums and the Smithsonian Institution should be consulted for more detailed information.*

**Adams National Historic Site:** P.O.B. 531, 135 Adams St., Quincy, Mass. 02169; donated to the U.S. in December 1946, by the Adams Memorial Society; designated a national historic site under the administration of the National Park Service of the Department of the Interior; built in 1731 by Major Leonard Vassall of Boston; bought by John Adams in 1787. At the end of his term he lived in the house until his death in 1826. The house then passed to his son, John Quincy Adams, in the middle of his term as sixth President. After his death in 1848 the house passed to his son, Charles Francis Adams, Minister to England during the Civil War. The Adams family continued to live there until the death in 1927 of Brooks Adams, the fourth son of Charles Francis Adams. The house, contents, and garden are as the Adams family left them. The separate stone library, standing in the garden, was built in 1870 by Charles Francis Adams. It contains an estimated 14,000 volumes, comprising most of the libraries of John Quincy Adams and Charles Francis Adams and some of the libraries of John Adams, Charles Francis Adams II, Henry Adams and Brooks.

**Adler Planetarium, The:** 1300 South Lake Shore Drive, Chicago, Ill. 60605; f. 1930 by Max Adler; the circular planetarium chamber seats 400 persons, with a hemispherical dome 68 feet wide and Zeiss VI projector; the exhibition areas contain a comprehensive collection of astronomical instruments, mostly ranging from the 15th century; exhibits in astronomy and related sciences; uni-directional Universe Theatre; library of about 5,000 vols.; lecture hall seating 120 persons; classrooms; photographic laboratories; optical shop; art, wood, and metal shops; 8-inch coelostat and projection spectrograph; several telescopes including a 16-inch diam. Cassegrain-Newtonian reflector. Programme includes classes in astronomy, navigation, and telescope making; graded school programme; public observation sessions, demonstrations, lectures and films and sponsorship of amateur astronomical societies; Dir. Dr. JOSEPH M. CHAMBERLAIN; publs. *Sky Show*† and *Course Brochures*†.

**Alaska State Museum:** Pouch FM, Juneau, Alaska 99811; f. 1900, opened to the public 1920; outstanding collection of Eskimo, Tlingit and Haida, Athapaskan, and Aleut artifacts; also contemporary and historic art, natural history specimens, and a limited historic collection; Dir. ALAN MUNRO.

**American Museum of Natural History:** Central Park West at 79th St., New York, N.Y. 10024; inc. 1869; departments: animal behaviour, anthropology, astronomy and the American Museum—Hayden Planetarium (*see* below), education, entomology, herpetology, ichthyology, fossil and living invertebrates, mammalogy, mineralogy, ornithology, vertebrate paleontology; library: see Libraries; Pres. Board of Trustees ROBERT G. GOELET; Dir. THOMAS D. NICHOLSON, PH.D.; Controller PAULINE MEISLER; publs. *Natural History Magazine, American Museum Novitates, A.M.N.H. Bulletin, Curator, Anthropological Papers, Micropaleontology Press.*

**Hayden Planetarium:** 81st St. and Central Park West, New York, N.Y. 10024; f. 1935; by rays of light from Zeiss projector on a 75-foot dome, about 9,000 stars are shown in the Planetarium heavens; several times in the year a new sky-show is presented dealing dramatically and scientifically with the various aspects of the heavens; courses and special lectures; Chair. and Associate Astronomer Dr. MARK R. CHARTRAND III; Astronomer Dr. KENNETH L. FRANKLIN.

**American Museum of Science and Energy:** P.O.B. 117, Oak Ridge, Tenn. 37830; f. 1949; operated for the U.S. Department of Energy by the Museum Division of the Oak Ridge Associated Universities; Chair. ROBERT F. CONTENT.

**Arizona State Museum:** Univ. of Arizona, Tucson, Arizona 85721; f. 1893; devoted to the study of south-western archaeology and the living Indians of the region, and engaged in archaeological, ethnohistoric and ethnological research, excavation and field work in Arizona; library of 32,000 vols.; archaeological publication series; Dir. RAYMOND H. THOMPSON, PH.D.

**Art Institute of Chicago:** Michigan Avenue at Adams Street, Chicago, Ill. 60603; f. 1879; 65,000 mems.; American painting and sculpture; 13th to 20th-century European painting; mediaeval and Renaissance art; prints and drawings; sculpture; Oriental arts (of 5,000 years); primitive art; textiles; decorative arts; photography; School of Art; Ryerson Library, f. 1901; Burnham Library, f. 1912; total of 129,000 vols. and 180,000 slides on art and architecture; also Junior Museum; Pres. E. LAURENCE CHALMERS; Vice-Pres. LARRY TER MOLEN, ROBERT MARS, DONALD J. IRVING; Sec. LINDA STARKS; publs. *Calendar, Annual Report, Museum Studies, Bulletin*, exhibition catalogues. *See also under* "Colleges".

**Asian Art Museum of San Francisco, The Avery Brundage Collection:** Golden Gate Park, San Francisco, Calif. 94118; f. 1969; museum and centre of research on outstanding collections of Chinese, Japanese, Korean, Indian, South-East Asian, Lamaist and Islamic art; library of 14,000 vols.; Dir. and Chief Curator YVON D'ARGENCÉ.

**Baltimore Museum of Art:** Art Museum Drive, Baltimore, Md. 21218; f. 1914; collections include 2nd-6th century Antioch Mosaics, Epstein and Jacobs collection of Old Masters, 17th-20th century American paintings, Cone collection of 19th and 20th century French paintings, drawings and sculptures, May collection of 20th century European paintings and sculptures, 60,000 prints and drawings from 15th century to modern times, Gallagher Memorial Collection of contemporary American paintings, Wurtzburger collection of primitive art, Wurtzburger Collection of 20th-century sculpture; collections of American and European decorative arts; library of 35,000 vols.; Pres. CALMAN J. ZAMOISKI, Jr.; Dir. ARNOLD L. LEHMAN; publ. *Calendar of Events.*

**Barnes Foundation Collection:** Merion Station, Montgomery County, Pa. 19066; f. 1922 by Dr. Albert C. Barnes; offers courses in the philosophy and appreciation of art; collection of 1,000 paintings, including works by El Greco, Titian, Goya, Rubens, Renoir, Cézanne, Picasso, Matisse and Van Gogh; also sculpture, antique furniture and wrought iron; Arboretum, with courses in botany and horticulture; Pres. SIDNEY W. FRICK; Vice-Pres. VIOLETTE DE MAZIA; Treas. GIRARD BANK; publ. *Journal of the Art Department*†.

**Bernice P. Bishop Museum:** P.O.B. 19000A, 1355 Kalihi St., Honolulu, Hawaii 96819; f. 1889; devoted to the study of natural and cultural history in the Pacific; depts. of anthropology, botany, education, entomology, history, ichthyology, zoology, malacology; Hawaii Immigrant Heritage Preservation Center; Herbarium Pacificum; museum ship "Falls of Clyde"; library of 85,000 vols., 360,000 historic photographs; maps and art works; Dir. Dr. EDWARD C. CREUTZ; publs. *Journal of Medical Entomology* (and *Supplements*), *Pacific Insects*, *Pacific Insects Monographs*, *Insects of Micronesia*, *Department of Anthropology Reports*, *Pacific Anthropological Records*, bulletins†, occasional papers†, special publications and annual reports†.

**Boston Museum of Fine Arts:** Boston, Mass. 02115; a private corporation; incorp. 1870; departments of Asiatic art with outstanding collection of Chinese and Japanese sculpture, painting, and ceramics, Indian and Mohammedan art; Egyptian art with important Old Kingdom Collection; Classical art with Greek and Roman sculpture, coins, and seals; American and European decorative arts with American furniture, silver, Medieval and Renaissance European sculpture, English and American silver; paintings of Europe and America, stressing French Impressionist, American Colonial and 19th-century works; large department of Prints and Drawings; department of Textiles with Coptic, 17th-19th century European and American textiles, costumes, and tapestries, Contemporary Art (since 1945), department of education, Art School; library of 105,000 books, 86,000 pamphlets; Dir. JAN FONTEIN; publs. *MFA Preview* (calendar of events, every 2 months), *Bulletin* (annually), catalogues, handbooks.

**Brooklyn Botanic Garden and Arboretum:** 1000 Washington Ave., Brooklyn, N.Y. 11215; f. 1910; library of 55,000 vols., c. 10,000 species and varieties; education programs, guided tours, plant information service; Pres. DONALD E. MOORE; publs. *Plants and Gardens* (quarterly), *Annual Report*, *Contributions*.

**Brooklyn Children's Museum:** 145 Brooklyn Ave., Brooklyn, N.Y. 11213; f. 1899; world's first children's museum; teaching collection of more than 50,000 authentic objects chiefly in cultural history, natural history, technology; full-scale technological exhibits (i.e. windmill, greenhouse, steam engine, stream, gristmill); Children's Resource Library; Portable Loan Collection for schools; performing arts spaces; continuing participatory activities for general public, school classes, groups; workshops; staff research library; retail Marketplace; Friends of 'BCM membership group; Dir. LLOYD HEZEKIAH; publ. *Balloooon* (every 2 months).

**Brooklyn Museum:** Eastern Parkway, Brooklyn, N.Y. 11238; estab. 1890; aboriginal American art; Peruvian textiles; pre-Columbian gold; Costa Rican sculpture; collections from Africa, Melanesia and Polynesia; collections from China, Korea, Southeast Asia, Japan, India and Persia; Colonial South American art; American period rooms; American and European paintings; Prints and Drawings; Ancient art of the Near East, Egypt, Greece and Rome; American and European costumes; American glass, pewter and silver; costumes gallery; art reference library and Egyptological library (70,000 books and periodicals); Dir. MICHAEL BOTWINICK.

**Buffalo Fine Arts Academy** (*incorporating Albright-Knox Art Gallery* (*dedicated* 1905)): 1285 Elmwood Ave., Buffalo, N.Y. 14222; f. 1862; collection of 19th and 20th-century paintings, with emphasis on American and European contemporary artists; sculpture 3,000 B.C. to present day; prints and drawings; Chair. SEYMOUR H. KNOX; Pres. SAMUEL D. MAGAVERN; Sec. ROY W. DOOLITTLE; Dir. (Art Gallery) ROBERT T. BUCK, Jr.; Chief Curator DOUGLAS G. SCHULTZ; Curator of Education CHRISTO PHER B. CROSMAN.

**Buffalo Museum of Science:** Humboldt Parkway, Buffalo, N.Y. 14211; building opened 1929; administered by Buffalo Society of Natural Sciences; Exhibit halls tell the story of science in natural sequence and full colour; anthropology, astronomy, biology, botany, conchology, entomology, geology, ornithology, palaeontology, primitive and oriental art, zoology; library of 40,000 vols.; solar and lunar observatory, loan collections, lectures, motion pictures, day and evening classes, etc.; Pres. CLIFFORD J. AWALD; Dir. ERNST E. BOTH (acting); publs. *Collections/BSNS*†, *Calendar* (monthly) and *Buffalo Society of Natural Sciences Bulletin*†.

**Buhl Planetarium and Institute of Popular Science:** Allegheny Square, Pittsburgh, Pa. 15212; opened 1939; five galleries are devoted to exhibits in earth-space and physical sciences; the auditorium, seating 490 spectators, is equipped with a Zeiss planetarium projector for presentations of astronomical science; a lecture hall, seating 240 persons, is equipped for laboratory demonstrations, science films, and the use of micro-projector, epidiascope, and similar visual teaching devices; educational programme in science extends from elementary to collegiate and adult level; in the observatory a 10-inch siderostat telescope is available to the public: classes in astronomy, short-wave radio, model rocketry, physics, chemistry, geology, etc.; 8 lesson vacation courses on space-age science for children; Exec. Dir. C. F. WAPIENNIK.

**California Palace of the Legion of Honor:** Lincoln Park, San Francisco, Calif. 94121; f. 1924; museum of fine arts; French paintings from the 16th-20th centuries; French original room interiors; French and Flemish tapestries; sculpture by Auguste Rodin; Achenbach Foundation for Graphic Arts has largest collection of prints and drawings in the Western U.S.; Dir. IAN MCKIBBIN WHITE; publ. *Monthly Calendar of Events*†; see also M. H. de Young Memorial Museum.

**Cincinnati Art Museum:** Eden Park, Cincinnati, Ohio 45202; inc. 1881; permanent collections include: Paintings—Europe (12th-20th century), including Mary Emery, Mary Hanna and Mary E. Johnston collections; China (13th-17th century); America (18th-20th century); Sculpture—Nabataean antiquities from Khirbet Tannur; Egyptian, including Millard F. and Edna F. Shelt collections; Greek, Roman, Medieval, Renaissance, Near and Far Eastern and Modern sculpture; Prints and Drawings—Europe (15th-20th century); America (17th-20th century); Miniatures— India (16th-18th century); Persia (11th-17th century); Primitive Cultures—Artifacts (6th-19th century) from N. and S. America and Africa; Decorative Arts— European arms and armour, Chinese bronzes and pottery (ancient to 13th century); Near-Eastern pottery, silver, textiles, bronzes and gold; European and American period rooms, ceramics, silver, glass, lace, tapestries and costumes; the Arthur Joseph collection of Meissen porcelain is on permanent loan; the W. T. H. Howe collection of early American glass; the William H. Doane collection of musical instruments; temporary exhibitions; library of 43,000 vols. with 225,000 pamphlets and clippings and 16,500 mounted pictures; Dir. MILLARD F. ROGERS, Jr.; publ. *Bulletin* (annually).

**Cleveland Health Education Museum:** 8911 Euclid Ave., Cleveland, Ohio 44106; incorporated 1936, opened 1940; founded by doctors, dentists, etc.; lectures, exhibits, models, films, covering all aspects of health; permanent exhibits; outstanding collection of 100 models on human reproduction; the "Transparent Woman"; the mechanical "brain"; the "chromosome puff"; the Upjohn "Defense of Life"; Department of Education working with schools in Greater Cleveland; Dir. LOWELL F. BERNARD: publ. *Health News* (monthly).

**Cleveland Museum of Art:** 11150 East Blvd., Cleveland, Ohio 44106; inc. 1913, opened 1916; collections include paintings, sculpture, prints and drawings, textiles and decorative arts from the ancient world, the Orient, Europe, the Americas, Africa and Oceania; library of 107,000 books and periodicals; Pres. JAMES H. DEMPSEY; Dir. SHERMAN E. LEE; publs. *Bulletin*† (10 a year), *News & Calendar* (every 2 months).

**Cleveland Museum of Natural History:** Wade Oval, University Circle, Cleveland, Ohio; f. 1920; comprises Natural History Museum, Mueller Planetarium and Observatory, Cleveland Aquarium, Kelley's Island and Fern Lake Reservations; collections in all fields, with particular emphasis on the northern half of Ohio, including Upper Devonian Fossil Fishes; also vertebrates, insects, shells, minerals, precious and semi-precious stones, and botanical and ethnological materials; dept. of physical anthropology responsible for the discovery and naming of new species of early man, A. afarensis; the Museum has sponsored or participated in several expeditions to Africa, islands of the South Atlantic, vicinity of the North Pole, the Azuero Peninsula of Panama, and various parts of North America; many study collections, including Elizabeth Lucas collection of floral reproductions, the Hamann-Todd skeletal collection; mounted Jurassic cetiosaurid, Haplocanthosaurus; library of 50,000 vols.; Dir. Dr. H. D. MAHAN; publs. *The Explorer* (quarterly), *Kirtlandia*† (scientific papers), *The Cleveland Bird Calendar* (quarterly), *Tracks* (bi-monthly members' newsletter).

**Colonial Williamsburg Foundation:** Goodwin Building Williamsburg, Va. 23185; f. 1926; preservation project and 173-acre outdoor museum with nearly 500 preserved, restored, and reconstructed buildings with over 225 period rooms open to public; more than 90 acres of period gardens and greens; collection of 18th-century English and American furniture and domestic objects; library of 50,000 vols.; audiovisual and publication programmes; demonstration of 36 crafts by 100 craftsmen; operates Carter's Grove Plantation (1754 manor house on James River) and Bassett Hall (original 18th-century house, local residence of John D. Rockefeller when instrumental in restoring 18th-century capital of Virginia colony; Chair. CARLISLE H. HUMELSINE; Pres. CHARLES R. LONGSWORTH; publs. *Annual Report, Colonial Williamsburg Today* (quarterly newsletter).

**Cooper-Hewitt Museum, Smithsonian Institution's National Museum of Design:** 2 East 91 St., New York, N.Y. 10028; administered by the Smithsonian Institution (*see* under Learned Societies); formerly Cooper Union Museum; f. 1895; 300,000 items, including collections of original drawings and designs for architecture and the decorative arts; 15th- to 20th-century prints; textiles, lace, woodwork and furniture, ceramics, glass, etc.; drawings and paintings by F. E. Church, W. Homer and other 19th-century American artists; library of 33,000 vols.; Picture Reference Library of 1,500,000 illustrations; 15,000 auction catalogues, archives of colour, pattern, textiles, symbols, interior design, advertising; Dir. Mrs. LISA TAYLOR.

**Currier Gallery of Art:** 192 Orange Street, Manchester, New Hampshire; f. 1929; galleries devoted to oils, water colours, prints, decorative arts and sculpture; permanent collection contains works by Copley, Degas, G. B Tiepolo, Stuart, Homer, Raeburn, Monet, Tintoretto, Constable, Corot, Ruysdael, Mabuse, van Cleve, Rouault, Matisse, Perugino, Picasso and contemporary American painters; 18th- and 19th-century furniture, glass, silver, pewter; frequent loan exhibitions, lectures, concerts, children's programmes; Dir. ROBERT M. DOTY; publ. *Bulletin*.

**Denver Art Museum:** 100 West 14th Ave. Parkway, Denver, Colo. 80204; f. 1893 as Artists' Club of Denver; new building opened 1971; art education programmes for children and adults; collections of world art represent almost every period and culture in history; regular changing exhibitions and special events; Dir. THOMAS N. MAYTHAM; publs. monthly newsletter†, regular catalogues and publications†.

**Denver Museum of Natural History:** City Park, Denver, Colo. 80205; f. and incorporated 1900; departments: anthropology, graphic design, birds, geology, mammals, palaeontology; American Indian Hall; Pres. ALLAN PHIPPS; Dir. CHARLES T. CROCKETT; Sec. CHRISTOPHER DOBBINS; publs. *Annual Reports, Popular Series, Museum Pictorial*.

**Detroit Institute of Arts:** 5200 Woodward Ave., Detroit, Mich. 48202; f. 1885; comprehensive collection from prehistoric to contemporary times; rich collection of American, Dutch, Flemish, French, Italian and German Expressionist painting; French-Canadian silver, African, Oriental and Modern art; graphic arts; American and European decorative arts; Theatre arts collection; library of 50,000 vols.; Dir. FREDERICK J. CUMMINGS; Sec. ROBERT T. WESTON; publs. *Bulletin*† (quarterly), *Calendar* (10 a year).

**Edison Institute, The:** Greenfield Village and Henry Ford Museum, Dearborn, Mich.; f. 1929; general museum of American history covering 260 acres; American decorative arts, transportation, steam and electrical power, communication agriculture, lighting, home arts, 100 historic houses and craft shops; Robert Hudson Tannahill Research Library contains 100,000 research books, pamphlets, leaflets, clippings and other ephemera, 50,000 letters, MSS. and documents; Ford Archives contain 14 million books, MSS., records, and 400,000 photographic negatives; Chair. of the Board WILLIAM CLAY FORD; Pres. Dr. HAROLD SKRAMSTAD; publ. *The Herald* (quarterly).

**Fels Planetarium of the Franklin Institute:** Philadelphia, Pa. 19103; The Zeiss Planetarium can show the skies in the past, present, or future for extended periods; seats 350; graded school programme; classes in astronomy; Dir. H. G. HAMILTON.

**Field Museum of Natural History:** Roosevelt Rd. At Lake Shore Drive, Chicago, Ill. 60605; f. by Marshall Field in 1893; departments: anthropology, botany, geology, zoology (birds, fishes, insects, invertebrates, mammals, reptiles and amphibians); library: 200,000 vols.; large collection of books on China, including several thousand in Chinese; Ornithological Section includes many rare and beautifully illustrated vols.; Dir. LORIN I. NEVLING, Jr.; publs. *Field Museum of Natural History Bulletin, General Guide, Fieldiana*† (technical publications in anthropology, botany, geology, and zoology), exhibition catalogues, various other publs.

**Fogg Art Museum:** *see* William Hayes Fogg Art Museum.

**Franklin Institute Science Museum and Planetarium:** Benjamin Franklin Parkway, at 20th St., Philadelphia, Pa. 19103; f. 1824; exhibits and demonstrations in physical sciences and technology; research laboratories; meetings and lectures; 8,000 mems.; library of 3,000 vols., 4,000 periodicals, patent file; Dir. JOEL N. BLOOM.

**Freer Gallery of Art:** Jefferson Drive at 12th St., S.W., Washington, D.C. 20560; administered by the Smithsonian Institution (*see* under Learned Societies); established 1906; opened 1923; devoted to research on the outstanding collections of Chinese, Japanese, Indian and Islamic art; gift of the late Charles L. Freer, of Detroit; large collection of the works of James McNeill Whistler and his contemporaries; library of 25,000 vols.; Dir. THOMAS LAWTON, M.F.A., PH.D.; publs. *Annual Report, Occasional Papers, Oriental Studies, Ars Orientalis*, etc.

**Frick Collection:** 1 East 70th St., New York, N.Y. 10021; opened 1935; important collection of 13th- to 19th-century European paintings; Italian Renaissance bronzes and furniture; Limoges enamels of the Renaissance; French 18th-century sculpture, furniture and porcelains; Oriental porcelains; rotating exhibitions of drawings and prints; the works of art, most of them assembled by the late industrialist Henry Clay Frick, are arranged with a freedom and flexibility that retain the atmosphere of his former residence; Dir. EVERETT FAHY.

**Griffith Observatory and Planetarium:** 2800 East Observatory Rd., Los Angeles, Calif. 90027; opened 1935; three main divisions: the Observatory, with Zeiss twin 12-inch and 9½-inch refracting telescopes and three solar telescopes; the Hall of Science, with over 100 exhibits; the Theatre of the Heavens, with its Zeiss planetarium and space travel projectors; Dir. Dr. E. C. KRUPP; publ. *The Griffith Observer*† (illustrated, monthly).

**Guggenheim Museum:** (*see* Solomon R. Guggenheim Museum).

**Hall of State:** Dallas, Tex. 75226; f. 1936; museum and archives of Southwestern United States history, operated by Dallas Historical Society (*see* Learned Soceities); library of 10,000 vols. and 1,500,000 archival items; Pres. JOE M. DEALEY.

**Henry Francis du Pont Winterthur Museum:** Winterthur, Del. 19735; f. 1930; collection of American furniture and domestic objects arranged in over 200 period settings from 17th century to 1840; library of 47,500 vols.; Dir. JAMES MORTON SMITH; publ. *Winterthur Portfolio* (quarterly).

**Hirshhorn Museum and Sculpture Garden:** Independence Ave. at 8th St., S.W., Washington, D.C. 20560; est. 1966, opened 1974; administered by the Smithsonian Institution; contemporary American and European art; 19th- and 20th-century sculpture; research library of 10,000 vols.; Dir. ABRAM LERNER, B.A.

**Hispanic Society of America Museum, The:** Broadway, between 155th and 156th Streets, New York, N.Y. 10032; f. 1904; free museum concentrated on the culture of the Iberian Peninsula: paintings (14th to 20th centuries), sculpture (13th to 20th centuries), archaeology, decorative arts (ceramics, textiles, metalwork, furniture); reference library and files; Dir. Dr. THEODORE S. BEARDSLEY, Jr.; Curator Dr. P. E. MULLER.

**Honolulu Academy of Arts:** 900 South Beretania St., Honolulu, Hawaii 96814; f. 1927; museum and school; Western and Asian art collections; educational programmes for adults and young people; theatre with frequent programmes; special exhibitions; 5,000 mems.; 24,000 vols.; Pres. HENRY B. CLARK; Dir. JAMES W. FOSTER; Sec. Mrs. L. B. HALL; publ. *Calendar News*, monthly bulletin for members.

**Huntington Library, Art Gallery and Botanical Gardens:** San Marino, California 91108; f. 1919 by the late Henry E. Huntington as a free research library, art gallery, museum, and botanical garden.

**Art Gallery** (formerly residence of the founder) contains chiefly 18th-century British and European portraits and landscapes; 18th-century French sculpture and decorative arts (English and French furniture, French tapestries, English miniatures, English silver, etc.).

**Botanical Gardens,** open to public: Desert Garden, Camellia Gardens, Japanese Garden; Dir. JAMES THORPE; Curators: Art ROBERT WARK, Botanical Gardens MYRON KIMNACH; Dir. of Admin. and Public Services SUZANNE W. HULL. *See also* Libraries.

**Illinois State Museum:** Dickson Mounds Museum, Lewistown, Ill. 61542; f. 1965; anthropology museum; exhibits: New World prehistory, prehistoric Indian village and burial mound; archaeological field research and Laboratories; Dir. (vacant); publ. *Dickson Mounds Museum Anthropological Studies*.

**Jewish Museum, The:** 1109 Fifth Ave., New York, N.Y. 10028; f. 1904; Jewish Ceremonial Art; changing contemporary exhibits of Jewish interest; special events, films, lectures, etc.; Dir. JOAN ROSENBAUM; publs. catalogues of exhibits, etc.

**J. Paul Getty Museum:** 17985 Pacific Coast Highway, Malibu, Calif. 90265; f. 1953; a fine collection of Greek and Roman antiquities, Renaissance and Baroque paintings and French decorative arts is housed in a re-creation of a Roman seaside villa, the Villa dei Papyri, which was destroyed by the eruption of Vesuvius in A.D. 79; library of c. 30,000 vols.; Dir. STEPHEN GARRETT; publ. *Publications*†.

**John G. Shedd Aquarium:** 1200 South Lake Shore Drive, Chicago, Ill. 60605; opened 1930; John Graves Shedd, shortly before his death in 1926, presented $3,000,000 to the people of Chicago with which to build an aquarium; exhibits only living specimens of aquatic life; at the end of the collecting season there is in the Aquarium an average of 4,500 specimens, representing about 554 distinct species; new exhibit, the Coral Reef, depicts corals and 75 species of marine fish native to Caribbean reefs; library of 1,200 vols.; Dir. WILLIAM P. BRAKER; publ. *Aquaticus* (quarterly newsletter).

**Kansas City Museum of Regional History:** 3218 Gladstone, Kansas City, Mo. 64123; f. 1939; administered by Kansas City Museum Association for the City of Kansas City; American Indian artifacts, costume and textile collection, planetarium; archives and reference library; Dir. GREGG F. STOCK.

**Lincoln Park Zoological Gardens:** 2200 North Cannon Drive, Chicago, Ill. 60614; f. 1874; 2,100 specimens of mammals, birds, reptiles, and amphibians; farm; owned and operated by the Chicago Park District; specialities: great apes, lemurs, small mammals, perching birds, snakes; special programmes: Farm in the Zoo, Travelling Zoo and Endangered Species educational programmes; scientific studies include chromosome analysis, nutrition, behaviour, reproductive biology, physiology, South American field work; Dir. Dr. LESTER E. FISHER; publs. *Guide Book* (annually), *The Ark* (quarterly), *Animal Inventory* (annually).

**Los Angeles County Museum of Natural History:** 900 Exposition Blvd., Los Angeles, Calif. 90007; f. 1910; Western U.S.A. and American History, New World ethnology and archaeology, palaeontology, geology, mineralogy, botany, ichthyology, mammalogy, entomology, herpetology, invertebrate zoology, ornithology; 10,000 mems.; library of 90,000 vols.; Pres. Board of Governors ED. N. HARRISON; Chair. Museum Foundation RICHARD VOLPERT; Dir. WILLIAM B. LEE; publs. *Science Series*† (irregular), *Terra* (*Museum Alliance Quarterly*), *Contributions in Science*† (irregular), *Bulletins*† (Science), *Bulletins of History Division* (irregular).

**Marineland of Florida (Marineland, Inc.):** Rt. 1, Box 122, St. Augustine, Fla. 32084; f. 1938; includes two

Oceanariums, 11 marine exhibits and a research laboratory for work on marine life; houses C. V. Whitney Marine Research Laboratory; large library of texts and periodicals on aquatic sciences; Curator R. L. JENKINS; Chair. C. V. WHITNEY.

**Mariners Museum, The:** Museum Drive, Newport News, Va. 23606; f. 1930 by Archer M. Huntington; international maritime history collection includes all periods and lake, river and canal navigation, as well as oceans and seas; major categories: complete small craft; engines; vessel fittings, gear, ornaments and furnishings; tools; instruments; weaponry; whaling and fishing gear; lifesaving equipment; sailors' clothing and personal possessions; models; scrimshaw and marine decorative arts; print and painting collection; special exhibitions; library of c. 60,000 books and pamphlets, 6,000 maps and charts, and 160,000 photographs; Dir. WILLIAM D. WILKINSON; publ. *Journal* (quarterly).

**Metropolitan Museum of Art, The:** Fifth Ave. and 82nd St., New York, N.Y. 10028; f. 1870; Departments: American Paintings and Sculpture, American Decorative Arts, Arms and Armour, Ancient Near Eastern Art, Costume Institute, Education (including Junior Museum), Egyptian Art, Drawings, European Paintings, European Sculpture and Decorative Arts, Far-Eastern Art, Greek and Roman Art, Islamic Art, Medieval Art, Primitive Art, Musical Instruments, Prints and Photographs, Twentieth Century Art; the Museum Library contains 250,000 books, 1,200 periodical titles; photograph and slide library; 35,000 mems.; Pres. WILLIAM B. MACOMBER; Dir. PHILIPPE DE MONTEBELLO; publs. *The Bulletin, Calendar of Events, Annual Report, Special Exhibition Catalogues*, etc.

**The Cloisters:** a branch of the Metropolitan Museum of Art, is located in Fort Tryon Park, New York; f. 1926; devoted to European medieval art.

**M. H. de Young Memorial Museum:** Golden Gate Park, San Francisco, Calif. 94118; f. 1895; large collection of European and American art, paintings, sculpture; original period rooms; tapestries, furniture and other decorative arts illustrating Western cultures from ancient Egypt, Greece and Rome to the 20th century; traditional arts of Africa, Oceania, and the Americas; the Samuel H. Kress collection of European paintings, Roscoe and Margaret Oakes collection of European painting and decorative arts; the Dr. T. Edward and Tullah Hanley collection of European and American painting; John D. Rockefeller III collection of American painting; Dir. IAN MCKIBBIN WHITE.
(*See* also California Palace of the Legion of Honor.)

**Minneapolis Society of Fine Arts, The:** 2400 Third Ave. South, Minneapolis, Minn. 55404; f. 1883; 13,000 mems.; library of 20,000 vols.; sponsors The Minneapolis Institute of Arts and the Minneapolis College of Art and Design; the Institute: collection of 65,000 objects representing nearly every school and period of art, including European and American paintings, sculpture, decorative arts, period rooms, prints and drawings, photography, Oriental, African, Oceanic, Ancient and Native North and South American Arts; Minnich collection of botanical, zoological and fashion prints, paintings by Rembrandt, El Greco, Goya, Manet, Renoir, Matisse; Alfred F. Pillsbury collection of ancient Chinese jades and bronzes, etc.; Dir. SAMUEL SACHS II; publ. *Bulletin* (annual).

**Montclair Art Museum:** 3 South Mountain Ave., Montclair, N.J.; opened 1914; paintings, sculpture (largely American); Rand American Indian Art collection; Chinese Snuffbottle collection: American, European and Oriental prints; the Whitney Silver Collection; changing exhibitions; reference library of c. 8,000 vols.; 13,000 colour slides; Dir. ROBERT J. KOENIG; publ. *Bulletin* (every 2 months Sept.-June).

**Morehead Planetarium:** University of North Carolina, at Chapel Hill; f. 1947, opened 1949; Carl Zeiss Planetarium Model VI Instrument, Observatory with 24-inch reflector telescope, Memorial Rotunda, Copernican Orrery, Scientific and Art Exhibitions, etc.; daily public programmes; training laboratory for U.S. Astronauts; Dir. A. F. JENZANO.

**Museum and Library of Maryland History, Maryland Historical Society:** 201 West Monument St., Baltimore, Md. 21201; f. 1844; exhibits Francis Scott Key's original MS of The Star-Spangled Banner; portrait gallery and 7 period rooms; over 2,000 paintings and miniatures; 700 pieces of furniture; sculpture, drawings, silver; ceramics; jewellery, textiles; library of over 90,000 vols., etc.; manuscript room includes Calvert Papers, papers of Benjamin Henry Latrobe, over 1,300 letters and documents of the Lords Baltimore and their families, genealogical collection and many hundreds of prints and drawings; maritime collection emphasizing crafts of Chesapeake Bay; Pres. FRANK H. WELLER, Jr.; Dir. ROMAINE S. SOMERVILLE; publ. *News and Notes* (every 2 months).

**Museum of Fine Arts, The:** 1001 Bissonnet St., Houston, Tex. 77005; incorporated in 1924; 10,000 vols., 7,000 pamphlets; art of ancient Egypt, Greece and Rome; European paintings and bronzes 15th-20th centuries; Oriental, South-west Indian and pre-Columbian art, native arts from Africa, Australia and the South Pacific Islands; contemporary European and American painting and sculpture; incorporates The Bayou Bend Collection of American furniture and paintings and English and American decorative arts, and Museum School of Art; Pres. ALEXANDER MCLANAHAN; Dir. WILLIAM C. AGEE; publ. *Bulletin*† (quarterly).

**Museum of Modern Art, The:** 11 West 53rd St., New York, N.Y. 10019; f. 1929; collection and changing exhibitions, international in scope, of paintings, drawings, prints, sculptures, industrial and graphic design, photographs and architecture dating from 1880s; large collection of American, British, French, German and Russian films, about 800 of which are available to educational organizations; daily film showings; modern art library of 40,000 vols.; organizes exhibitions in all the visual arts for circulation all over the world; Dir. RICHARD E. OLDENBURG; publs. monographs, catalogues, etc.

**Museum of New Mexico:** P.O.B. 2087, Santa Fé, N.M. 87503; f. 1909; a State agency, under Board of Regents appointed by Governor, divisions in anthropology, history, fine arts, international folk art, state monuments located in separate buildings; custody of combined libraries approx. 20,000 vols.; Dir. JEAN M. WEBER; publs. *El Palacio* (quarterly), popular and scientific books, monographs, reports.

**Museum of Science and Charles Hayden Planetarium:** Science Park, Boston, Mass. 02114; f. 1830; exhibits on Astronomy, Natural History, Physical Science, technology, man and medicine; library of 40,000 vols. and pamphlets; Dir. RICHARD O. HOWE (acting); publs. *Reports*† (annual), *Newsletter*† (10 a year).

**Museum of Science and Industry:** 57th St. and Lake Shore Drive, Chicago, Ill. 60637; f. by Julius Rosenwald, chartered 1926, opened 1933; agriculture, metals, power, physics, chemistry, electronics, plastics, transportation, mathematics, petroleum, food, space engineering, communications and medical sciences; exhibits include full-size coal mine, German submarine, walk-through model of human heart, Colleen Moore's Fairy Castle, "Yesterday's Main Street", "The Circus", full-size farm, actual Apollo 8 spacecraft, 747 jetliner cabin, and exhibits on space exploration and energy research; Pres. and Dir. Dr. VICTOR J. DANILOV; publ. *Progress*† (bi-monthly).

**Museum of the American Indian** (Heye Foundation): Broadway at 155th St., New York, N.Y. 10032; f. 1916; dedicated to the preservation, study, exhibition and collection of the material culture of the aborigines of the Western Hemisphere; Indian Information Center of current resources on American Indians; library of 40,000 vols., 70,000 photographs and negatives; Dir. ROLAND W. FORCE, PH.D.; publs. *Contributions* (25 vols.), *Notes and Monographs* (12 vols.), *Miscellaneous* series, *Indian Notes* (quarterly).

**Museum of the City of New York:** Fifth Avenue at 103rd St., New York, 10029; f. 1923; history museum; exhibits include Cityrama, Dutch Gallery, Marine Gallery, New York Doll's Houses; library of 10,000 vols.; Dir. J. V. NOBLE; publs. *Report* (annual), *Bulletin* (quarterly).

**National Air and Space Museum:** Washington, D.C. 20560; administered by the Smithsonian Institution (*see* under Learned Societies); f. 1946 to record the national development of aeronautics and astronautics; to collect, preserve, and display aeronautical and astronautical equipment of historical interest and significance; and to provide educational material for the historical study of aeronautics and astronautics. The collection contains original full-size aircraft, spacecraft, recovered space exploration vehicles, engines, instruments, flight clothing, accessories of technical, historical, and biographical interest, scale models, and extensive reference data; ibrary of 24,000 vols. and journals; photographic collection; Dir. NOEL W. HINNERS.

**National Gallery of Art:** 4th St. and Constitution Ave. N.W., Washington, D.C. 20565; a separately administered Bureau of the Smithsonian Institution (*see* under Learned Societies); estab. 1937, West Building opened 1941, East Building 1978; paintings, sculpture, prints, and drawings, and examples of decorative arts; library of 90,000 vols., 1,380 periodicals; photographic archives; slide collection; Pres. JOHN R. STEVENSON; Dir. J. CARTER BROWN; Administrator JOSEPH G. ENGLISH; publs. *Studies in the History of Art, Kress Foundation Studies in the History of European Art, The A. W. Mellon Lectures in the Fine Arts, The Ailsa Mellon Bruce Studies in American Art*.

**National Museum of American Art:** 8th and G Sts., N.W., Washington, D.C. 20560; administered by the Smithsonian Institution (*see* under Learned Societies); f. 1846; American painting, sculpture, prints and drawings, particularly of the 19th and 20th centuries; specialized library of 40,000 vols., collection of 50,000 slides and 33,000 photographs; research and educational programmes; Dir. (vacant).

**National Museum of American History:** 14th St., Constitution Ave., Washington, D.C. 20560; administered by the Smithsonian Institution (*see* under Learned Societies); collections depicting American cultural, civil and military history, and the history of science and technology; Dir. ROGER G. KENNEDY.

**National Museum of Natural History:** Washington, D.C. 20560; a branch of the Smithsonian Institution (*see* Learned Societies); depository of the national collections, containing over 57 million catalogued items. It is especially rich in the natural science and anthropology of the Americas, including zoology, entomology, botany, geology, palaeontology, archaeology, ethnology, and physical anthropology; also houses exhibits relating to the natural sciences and anthropology; research staff of approx. 110 scientists; Dir. RICHARD S. FISKE; publs. *Smithsonian Contributions* (separate series for Anthropology, Botany, Earth Sciences, Paleobiology, Zoology and Marine Sciences).

**National Portrait Gallery:** 8th at F St., N.W., Washington, D.C. 20560; administered by the Smithsonian Institution (*see* under Learned Societies); f. 1962; portraits of persons who have made significant contributions to the history, development or culture of the people of the United States; library of 41,000 vols.; Dir. (vacant).

**Nelson-Atkins Gallery of Art:** Rockhill at 45th, 4525 Oak St., Kansas City, Mo. 64111; estab. 1926 under the will of Mr. Nelson for the purchase of works of fine arts such as paintings, engravings, sculptures, tapestries and decorative arts; the collection, begun in 1930, was opened to the public in 1933; library of 32,000 vols.; Dir. RALPH T. COE; publs. *Bulletin†, Gallery Events†*.

**New Orleans Museum of Art:** P.O.B. 19123, New Orleans, La. 70179; f. 1911; paintings, sculpture, photography, glass, prints and drawings; Oriental jades, ceramics, screens and bronzes; ancient glass and Graeco-Roman ceramics; Samuel H. Kress collection (Italian Renaissance paintings); Hyams collection (late 19th-century French Barbizon and salon paintings); 18th-, 19th- and 20th-century American, and 19th- and 20th-century Louisiana art; Latin American Spanish Colonial painting, sculpture and decorative arts; Pre-Columbian sculpture collection from Central and South America; African sculpture; Billups collection (European and American glass); Latter-Schlesinger collection (18th-century portrait miniatures); Victor K. Kiam collection of 20th-century European and American painting and sculpture; Victor K. Kiam collection of African, Oceanic, Northwest Coast American Indian sculpture; Japanese screen and scroll paintings from the Edo Period; library of 7,200 vols.; Dir. E. JOHN BULLARD; publs. *Arts Quarterly*, occasional papers and catalogues.

**New York Cultural Center in association with Fairleigh Dickinson University:** 2 Columbus Circle, New York, N.Y. 10019; f. 1964 by Huntington Hartford; Dir. MARIO AMAYA; Curator SUSAN GINSBURG; publs. *Realism Now, 75 Years of the Comics, Women Chose Women, 3D into 2D, Drawing for Sculpture, French Master Drawings of the 17th and 18th Centuries in North American Collections*.

**Oriental Institute of the University of Chicago:** 1155 East 58th St., Chicago, Illinois 60637; f. 1919; 60 mems.; research in the early and advanced civilizations of the Near East; Collection started 1896; over 70,000 objects, derived mainly from the Oriental Institute's field work, representing the art, religion and daily life of ancient Egypt, Nubia, Assyria, Babylonia, Persia, Palestine, Syria, Anatolia, Libya and Cyprus, and early Christian and Islamic material; Dir. ROBERT MCC. ADAMS; Curator JOHN CARSWELL.

**Peabody Museum of Archaeology and Ethnology:** Harvard University, Cambridge, Mass. 02138; f. 1866 by George Peabody. The Museum works in the closest co-operation with the Department of Anthropology of Harvard, and much of the research is jointly determined. Since its founding, more than 800 expeditions have been sent to every continent, resulting, with the addition of important gifts and purchases, in the building up of one of the most comprehensive collections of ethnology, archaeology, and physical anthropology in the United States. The first scientific studies of Maya archaeology were made under its direction, and its collections from this area, and from Middle America generally, are extremely important. There are also collections of Old World archaeology. The American School of Prehistoric Research is a department of the Museum and conducts excavations in the Old World. In ethnology, the material from the Pacific Islands is important, and the Museum is also rich in material representing the native tribes of Africa, of South America, and of the Plains and North-west Coast Indians of North America, where some of the objects date from the Lewis and

Clark expedition of 1806. The archaeology of the south-western United States, including the Pueblo Indian area, is also strongly represented. The Tozzer Library with its 110,000 books and pamphlets, covers the entire field of anthropology. Dir. C. C. LAMBERG-KARLOVSKY; publs. *Papers, Memoirs, Bulletins, Monographs,* American School of Prehistoric Research *Bulletins* and special publications of the Peabody Museum Press.

**Peabody Museum of Natural History:** 170 Whitney Ave., New Haven, Connecticut 06511; affiliated with Yale University; f. by a gift of George Peabody, 1866; extensive collections in the fields of anthropology, meteorites, botany, palaeobotany, invertebrate palaeontology, mineralogy, oceanography, vertebrate palaeontology, invertebrate zoology and vertebrate zoology, scientific instruments, each with its own Curator; also Yale Peabody Museum Field Station; Dir. K. M. WAAGE, PH.D.; publs. *Bulletin, Postilla, Discovery.*

**Peabody Museum of Salem:** East India Sq., Salem, Mass. 01970; f. 1799; maritime history, ethnology and local natural history; library of 100,000 vols.; Dir. PETER FETCHKO; publ. *American Neptune* (quarterly).

**Pennsylvania Academy of the Fine Arts, The:** Broad and Cherry Sts., Philadelphia, Pa. 19102; f. 1805; collection of 18th–20th-century American painting, sculpture, graphics; special exhibitions yearly; important archive; Pres. CHARLES E. MATHER; Sec. and Dir. RICHARD J. BOYLE; publs. *Annual Report†, Newsletter†*.

**Philadelphia Museum of Art:** Parkway at 26th St., Philadelphia, Pa. 19130; incorp. 1876; 100,000 vols.; paintings, graphics, sculpture and decorative arts from medieval to contemporary times representing European, American, and Far Eastern Art; Pres. ROBERT MONTGOMERY SCOTT; Dir. JEAN SUTHERLAND BOGGS; publs. *Bulletin* (quarterly), *Newsletter* (monthly), exhibition catalogues.

**Rochester Museum and Science Center:** 657 East Ave. at Goodman St., Rochester, N.Y. 14603; f.1912; natural science, anthropology, history, and technology; library of 20,000 vols.; Strasenburgh Planetarium: computerized, Zeiss projector, exhibits, daily astronomy and space-science shows in Star Theater; 800-acre Cumming Nature Center in the nearby Bristol Hills; Museum Dir. C. F. HAYES III; Planetarium Dir. D. S. HALL; Exec. Dir. RICHARD C. SCHULTZ; publ. *RMSC News†.*

**Roosevelt's Little White House:** Warm Springs, Ga.; remains as it was when the President died here in 1945; mementoes and film of Roosevelt in Georgia; under direction of Georgia Dept. of Natural Resources.

**San Diego Museum of Art:** Balboa Park, P.O.B. 2107, San Diego, Calif. 92112; Renaissance and Baroque paintings of Spanish, Italian, Dutch, Flemish and French schools; major works by Greco, Zurbaran, Goya, Crivelli, Titian, Tiepolo, Guardi, Rubens, Rembrandt, Ruysdael, Hals, David, Matisse, Braque; early and contemporary American artists; Asiatic arts and sculpture, graphics and decorative arts from many countries; art library of several thousand vols.; lectures, concerts, and classes are provided; Dir. STEVEN BREZZO.

**San Diego Society of Natural History Museum:** P.O.B. 1390, San Diego, Calif. 92112; founded 1874 to further the knowledge of natural history and the conservation of natural resources; 2,900 mems.; library of 60,000 vols.; Dir. Dr. CHARLES McLAUGHLIN; publs. *Transactions†, Memoirs†,* Occasional Papers† (irregular).

**San Francisco Museum of Modern Art:** Van Ness at McAllister St., San Francisco, Calif. 94102; f. 1921 by the San Francisco Art Association; modern art; contains 10 galleries; permanent collection includes: Clyfford Still Collection; Josef Albers Foundation gift; Albert Bender Collection of 20th-century American and European paintings, Harriet Levy and Sarah and Michael Stein Memorial Collections of modern French paintings emphasizing early Matisse; William Gerstle Collection; other important paintings and sculpture by North and South American and European contemporaries; large photography and graphics collection; reference library with emphasis on periodicals and contemporary art; *c.* 30 special exhibitions annually; Pres. EUGENE E. TREFETHEN, Jr.; Dir. HENRY T. HOPKINS; publs. calendar of events (every 2 months), catalogue of special exhibitions.

**San Jacinto Museum of History Association:** P.O.B. 758, San Jacinto Monument, Deer Park, Texas 77536; f. 1939; exhibits outline the history of Texas from the time of Cortes to the Civil War; library of 15,000 vols.; Pres. PAUL G. BELL, Jr.; Dir. J. C. MARTIN.

**Science Museum of Minnesota:** 30 East 10th St., St. Paul, Minn. 55102; f. 1907; research and exhibits in anthropology, biology and palaeontology, omnitheater (planetarium), two nature centres, technology, and branch planetarium and exhibits in Minneapolis; library of 15,000 vols.; Pres. Dr. WENDELL A. MORDY; Dir. PHILIP S. TAYLOR; publs. *Scientific Publications—New Series†* (irregular), *Monographs†* (irregular), *Encounters* (monthly).

**Smith College Museum of Art:** Northampton, Mass.; f. 1879; collections include examples from most periods and cultures with special emphasis on European and American paintings, sculpture, drawings, prints and photographs of the 17th–20th centuries; Dir. CHARLES CHETHAM; Curator of Painting and Assoc. Dir. BETSY B. JONES.

**Snow Entomological Museum:** University of Kansas, Lawrence, Kan.; f. 1870; primarily North American insects, with worldwide representation of bees, aquatic Hemiptera, Mecoptera; Dir. C. D. MICHENER; Curator G. W. BYERS.

**Solomon R. Guggenheim Museum, The:** 1071 Fifth Ave., New York, N.Y. 10028; f. 1937; the building designed by Frank Lloyd Wright; the permanent collection of approx. 4,000 works since the Post-Impressionist era, augmented by the Justin K. Thannhauser Collection of Impressionist and Post-Impressionist masterpieces, includes large collections of Brancusi sculptures, Kandinsky paintings and graphics, and works by Klee, also important paintings by Chagall, Delaunay, Dubuffet, Léger, Marc, Mondrian and Picasso; a continuous programme of loan exhibitions is presented, drawn from its own collection and from leading public and private collections throughout the world; research library of *c.* 20,000 vols.; Dir. THOMAS M. MESSER; Dir. of Exhibitions DIANE WALDMAN; Senior Curator Dr. LOUISE A. SVENDSEN; publs. exhibition catalogues†.

**Spencer Museum of Art, University of Kansas:** Lawrence, Kan. 66045; f. 1928; specializes in 17th- and 18th-century German and Austrian art, American painting, graphics and photographs, American, European and Oriental decorative art, Japanese Edo Painting and contemporary Chinese painting; 45,000 vols. in Murphy Library of Art History; Dir. CHARLES ELDREDGE; publs. *Register* (2 a year) and exhibition catalogues.

**St. Louis Art Museum, The:** Forest Park, St. Louis, Mo. 63110; f. 1907; municipally owned and supported collection of about 20,000 art objects; important collections of American, European and Asian painting, sculpture and decorative arts, pre-Columbian and Oceanic art; library of 26,000 vols.; Dir. JAMES D. BURKE; publs. *Bulletin†, Annual Report†.*

**Texas Memorial Museum:** Campus of the University of Texas, Austin, Tex. 78705; f. 1936; civic and natural history of Texas, minerals, fossils, palaeontology, vertebrate and invertebrate zoology, geology, anthropology, archaeology; radiocarbon, materials conservation, and vertebrate palaeontology laboratories; Dir. Dr. WILLIAM G. REEDER; publs. *Bulletin†, Pearce-Sellards Series†, Miscellaneous Papers, TMM Newsletter†, Museum Notes†* (all irregular).

**University Art Museum:** University of California, 2626 Bancroft Way, Berkeley, Calif. 94720; f. 1970; 10 exhibition galleries, sculpture garden, the Pacific Film Archive; permanent collection of Asian and western art; Hans Hoffman collection; serves the university community with exhibitions, study collections, etc.; receives travelling exhibitions from the major American museums; Dir. JAMES ELLIOTT.

**University of Alabama Museum of Natural History:** P.O.B. 5897, Alabama 35486; Dir. Dr. JOSEPH O. VOGEL.

**University Museum, The:** University of Pennsylvania, 33rd and Spruce Sts., Philadelphia, Pa. 19104; f. 1887; archaeological collection from Old and New Worlds; ethnology from the New World, Oceania and Africa; Near Eastern tablet collection of 25,000 documents; Museum Applied Science centre for Archaeology carries out research in physical sciences, especially dating techniques, ancient metallurgical processes and the detection of forgeries; radiocarbon and thermoluminescence dating available; the museum also acts as a teaching organization and leads expeditions overseas; library of 75,000 vols.; Dir. ROBERT H. DYSON, Jr. (acting); publs. *Expedition†* (quarterly), *Museum Applied Science Center for Archaeology (MASCA) Journal, Publications of the Babylonian Fund*, monographs.

**Virginia Museum of Fine Arts:** Boulevard and Grove, Richmond, Va. 23221; f. 1934; three "Artmobiles"; statewide network of local and regional arts organizations and loan programme offering exhibition material to State Service Member Groups; repertory theatre company; film, music and dance programmes; permanent collections include Russian Imperial jewelled objects by Fabergé, ancient Greek, Roman and Byzantine objects and sculptures; Indian, Chinese, Japanese, medieval, renaissance, and baroque paintings and sculptures; English and American decorative arts and paintings; contemporary art; library of 35,000 vols.; Dir. R. PETER MOOZ; publs. *Bulletin†* (9 a year), *Arts in Virginia†* (3 a year), catalogues of exhibitions and of European and ancient art†, *Fabergé†*.

**Wadsworth Atheneum:** Hartford, Conn. 06103; f. 1842; art through the ages; Gallery of the Senses, for sighted and blind; Auerbach library of 18,000 vols.; Pres. BURTON TREMAINE, Jr.; publs. *Atheneum Calendar* (every 2 months), exhibition catalogues†.

**Walker Art Center:** Vineland Place, Minneapolis, Minn, 55403; f. 1927; 20th-century paintings, drawings, prints, sculpture, photography; Dir. MARTIN FRIEDMAN; publs. *Design Quarterly, Monthly Calendar of Events*, exhibition catalogues.

**Walters Art Gallery:** 600 North Charles St., Baltimore, Maryland 21201; f. 1931; over 25,000 objects; the exhibits are arranged in historical and chronological sequence and comprise: Egyptian art, Ancient East, Minoan and Mycenaean art, Greek, Etruscan and Roman art, Near-Eastern art, Coptic art, Byzantine art, pre-Romanesque and Romanesque, early Gothic art, later Gothic art, Renaissance sculpture and decorative arts, manuscript illumination, incunabula, Italian painting, Renaissance and Northern Renaissance art, 17th-, 18th- and 19th-century art, Far-Eastern art, Ancient American art, 19th-century American art; 3,000 mems.; library of 75,000 vols.; Dir. RICHARD H. RANDALL, Jr.; publs. *Journal* (anually), *Annual Report, Bulletin* (monthly, Oct.–May).

**Wheelwright Museum, The** (*formerly Museum of Navaho Ceremonial Art*): P.O.B. 5153, Santa Fé, New Mexico 87501; f. by Mary C. Wheelwright; incorp. 1937; houses collections of pottery, basketry, textiles, jewellery and other items of Southern Athabascan cultures; Dir. SUSAN MCGREEVY.

**Whitney Museum of American Art:** 945 Madison Ave., New York, N.Y. 10021; f. 1930; established for the encouragement and advancement of contemporary American art; special exhibitions include Whitney biennial and historical surveys; Dir. TOM ARMSTRONG; Administrator PALMER B. WALD.

**William Hayes Fogg Art Museum:** Harvard University, Cambridge, Mass. 02138; f. 1895; Fine Arts collection covering prehistoric to modern Eastern and Western art; houses Harvard's Fine Arts Department and serves as a laboratory for training museum officials, art historians and conservators; houses Harvard's Fine Arts Library of 190,000 vols., 730,000 photographs, 340,000 slides; Dir. SEYMOUR SLIVE; publs. *Annual Report*, exhibition catalogues, quarterly newsletter.

**Worcester Art Museum:** 55 Salisbury St., Worcester, Mass. 01608; f. 1896; illustrates the evolution of art from early Egyptian civilization to modern times; especially notable are ancient Egyptian, classical, Oriental and medieval sculpture; mosaics from Antioch; a French Romanesque Chapter House; a Gothic tapestry of the Last Judgment; Italian and other European schools of painting of the 13th to 20th centuries; English, French, and American collections from the 18th century to the present day; pre-Columbian art; Japanese prints; library of 35,000 vols.; Pres. HENRY B. DEWEY; Dir. RICHARD STUART TEITZ; Chief Curator JAMES A. WELU; Administrator W. ARTHUR GAGNÉ; publs. *Calendar* (quarterly), *Journal* (annually), Catalogues.

# UNIVERSITIES AND COLLEGES

*Due to space limitations we give a selection only, which is based on the list of accredited institutions as published by the American Council on Education.*

*Arranged alphabetically by State.*

## ALABAMA

### ALABAMA STATE UNIVERSITY
915 SOUTH JACKSON ST., P.O.B. 271, MONTGOMERY, ALABAMA 36195

Founded 1874 as college, attained university status 1969.

*President:* (vacant).
*Vice-President for Academic Affairs:* Dr. WILLIAM S. EDMONDS.
*Vice-President for Business and Finance:* FREDDIE GALLOT.
*Vice-President for University Advancement:* CHARLES VARNER.
*Director, Public Relations and Information Services:* JOHN KNIGHT, Jr.
*Vice-President for Student Affairs:* Dr. JOHNNY SHEPPARD.
*Vice-President for Planning and Analysis:* Dr. JOHN BAKER, Jr.

Library of 195,142 vols.
Number of students: 4,066.

Publications: *Alabama State University Bulletin* (annually), *Alumni Newsletter, Impact.*

DEANS:
*College of Education:* Dr. GORDON BLISS.
*College of Business Administration:* Dr. PERCY VAUGHN.
*College of Arts and Sciences:* Dr. EUNICE MOORE.
*University College:* Dr. ROBERT THOMSON.
*Graduate Studies:* Dr. LEROY BELL, Jr.
*Evening and Weekend College:* Dr. ARCHIE MOORE.
*School of Music:* Dr. OTIS D. SIMMONS.

### ATHENS STATE COLLEGE
ATHENS, ALABAMA 35611
Telephone: 232-1802.
Founded 1822.

*President:* Dr. SIDNEY E. SANDRIDGE.
*Director of Admissions:* LARRY McCOY.
*Librarian:* J. D. BALLEW.

The library contains 70,000 vols.
Number of teachers: 59.
Number of students: 1,250.

### AUBURN UNIVERSITY
AUBURN, ALABAMA 36849
Telephone: (205) 826-4000.
Land-grant State University.

Founded in 1856 as The East Alabama Male College, became Alabama Agricultural and Mechanical College 1872, Alabama Polytechnic Institute 1899, Auburn University 1960.

*President:* H. HANLY FUNDERBURK, Jr.
*Vice-Presidents:* J. GRADY COX (*Executive*), TAYLOR D. LITTLETON (*Academic Affairs*), CHESTER C. CARROLL (*Research*), STANLEY P. WILSON (*Agriculture, Home Economics, Veterinary Medicine*).
*Director of University Relations:* DANIEL C. HOLSENBECK.

Library of 1,100,000 bound vols., 1,300,000 microforms, numerous special collections and government document collections.

Number of teachers: 1,076.
Number of students: 18,603.

Publications: *The Auburn Plainsman* (weekly), *Glomerata* (annually), *Southern Humanities Review* (quarterly), *Public Sector* (quarterly), *AES Highlights* (monthly), *Circle* (quarterly), *The Auburn Pharmacist* (quarterly), *Engineering Research Activities* (annually), *The Auburn Veterinarian* (quarterly).

DEANS:
*Agricultural Instruction:* R. DENNIS ROUSE.
*Agricultural Research:* GALE BUCHANAN.
*Agricultural Extension:* J. MICHAEL SPROTT.
*Architecture and Fine Arts:* E. KEITH McPHEETERS.
*Arts and Sciences:* EDWARD H. HOBBS.
*Business:* GEORGE R. HORTON, Jr.
*Education:* JACK E. BLACKBURN.
*Engineering:* CHESTER C. CARROLL (acting).
*Home Economics:* RUTH L. GALBRAITH.
*Nursing:* MARY F. WOODY.
*Pharmacy:* BEN F. COOPER.
*Veterinary Medicine:* JOHN T. VAUGHAN.
*Graduate School:* PAUL F. PARKS.
*Students:* W. HAROLD GRANT.
*General Extension and Public Service:* GENE A. BRAMLETT.

### BIRMINGHAM-SOUTHERN COLLEGE
800 8TH AVE., BIRMINGHAM, ALABAMA 35254.

Southern University founded in Greensboro 1856, Birmingham College opened 1898; consolidated as Birmingham-Southern College 1918.

*President:* NEAL R. BERTE.
*Vice-President for Academic Affairs:* EDMUND MOOMAW.
*Vice-President for Admissions Services:* ROBERT DORTCH.
*Vice-President for Development and Public Relations:* ROBERTA WEBB.
*Librarian:* BARBARA G. SCOTT.

The library contains 126,000 vols.
Number of teachers: 96.
Number of students: 1,452.

### HUNTINGDON COLLEGE
1500 E. FAIRVIEW AVENUE, MONTGOMERY, ALABAMA 36106
Telephone: (205) 265-0511.
Founded 1854.

*President:* Dr. ALLEN K. JACKSON.
*Registrar:* JEAN RODGERS.
*Dean:* Dr. WILLARD D. TOP.
*Librarian:* ROBERT E. CHAPEL.

The library contains 86,600 vols.
Number of teachers: 45.
Number of students: 600.

### JACKSONVILLE STATE UNIVERSITY
JACKSONVILLE, ALABAMA 36265
Telephone: (205) 435-9820.
Founded 1883.

*President:* Dr. ERNEST STONE.
*Vice-President for Academic Affairs:* Dr. THERON E. MONTGOMERY.
*Vice-President for Business Affairs:* CHARLES C. ROWE.
*Dean of Admissions:* Dr. H. B. WOODWARD, III.
*Dean of Students:* Dr. DON SCHMITZ.
*Librarian:* Dr. A. MILLICAN.

The library contains 227,000 vols.
Number of teachers: 305.
Number of students: 7,222.

### LIVINGSTON UNIVERSITY
LIVINGSTON, ALABAMA 35470
Telephone: 652-9661.
Founded 1835.

*President:* ASA N. GREEN.
*Registrar:* CLARENCE EGBERT.

The library contains 103,000 vols.
Number of teachers: c. 75.
Number of students: 1,250.

### OAKWOOD COLLEGE
HUNTSVILLE, ALABAMA 35806
Telephone: 837-1630.
Founded 1896.

*President:* C. B. ROCK.
*Dean of the College:* M. A. WARREN.
*Registrar:* LILLIAN GREEN.
*Librarian:* Miss JANNITH LEWIS.

The library contains 58,000 vols.
Number of teachers: 58.
Number of students: 1,120.

## SAMFORD UNIVERSITY
800 LAKESHORE DRIVE,
BIRMINGHAM, ALABAMA 35229

Founded 1841.

*President:* LESLIE S. WRIGHT, M.A., LL.D., PED.D., L.H.D.
*Vice-President for Academic Affairs:* RURIC E. WHEELER, M.S., PH.D.
*Registrar:* TRAVIS JORDAN TINDAL, M.S., ED.D.
*Librarian:* F. W. HEMBOLD, B.A., M.A.

Number of teachers: 267, including 59 professors.
Number of students: 3,921.
Publication: *Bulletin*.

DEANS:

*Cumberland School of Law:* D. E. CORLEY, J.D.
*School of Business:* WM. D. GEER, M.A., D.B.A.
*School of Education:* JOHN T. CARTER, M.S., ED.D.
*School of Music:* C. H. RHEA, M.MUS.ED., ED.D.
*College of Arts and Sciences:* LEE N. ALLEN, M.S., PH.D.
*School of Pharmacy:* J. WINTTER, PH.D.
*School of Graduate Studies:* LEE N. ALLEN.
*Ida V. Moffett School of Nursing:* MARTHA HEARN, M.S., ED.D.

## SPRING HILL COLLEGE
MOBILE, ALABAMA 36608
Telephone: (205) 460-2011.

Founded 1830.

*President:* Rev. PAUL S. TIPTON, S.J.
*Academic Dean:* Dr. J. P. MACNAMARA.
*Dean of Students:* JOHN M. BURTON.
*Administrative Assistant to President:* ADELE S. GWATKIN.
*Director of Development:* ROBERT P. JOHNSON.
*Vice-President for Finance:* JOHN R. OESTER.
*Librarian:* MARCIA M. FINDLEY.

The library contains 118,000 vols.
Number of teachers: 80.
Number of students: 900.

## TROY STATE UNIVERSITY SYSTEM
TROY, ALABAMA 36081
Telephone: (205) 566-3000.

Founded 1887.

*President:* RALPH W. ADAMS.
*Vice-Presidents:* JAMES D. C. ROBINSON, EDWARD F. BARNETT, JAMES E. BAILEY, Jr., ROBERT M. PAUL, DONALD J. GIBSON, GENE ELROD.
*Assistant to the President:* FREDDIE W. WOOD.

*Registrar:* WALTER SULLIVAN.
*Librarian:* KENNETH CROSLIN.

The library contains 295,006 vols.
Number of teachers: 656.
Number of students: 12,805.

## TUSKEGEE INSTITUTE
ALABAMA 36088
Telephone: 727-8011.

Founded 1881.

*President:* Dr. L. H. FOSTER.
*Student Affairs:* Dr. W. J. SAPP.
*Business Affairs:* L. A. WILLIAMS.
*Development Affairs:* Dr. VELMA L. BLACKWELL.
*Registrar:* Mrs. DOROTHY CONLEY.
*Librarian:* Mrs. ANNIE G. KING.

The library contains 250,000 vols.
Number of teachers: 399.
Number of students: 3,465.

DEANS:

*Arts and Sciences:* Dr. O. C. WILLIAMSON.
*Applied Sciences:* Dr. G. E. COOPER.
*Education:* Dr. G. W. TAYLOR.
*Engineering:* Dr. Z. W. DYBCZAK.
*Nursing:* Dr. LAURANNE SAMS.
*Veterinary Medicine:* Dr. W. C. BOWIE.

## UNIVERSITY OF ALABAMA
UNIVERSITY, ALABAMA 35486
Telephone: (205) 348-6010.

Founded 1831.

*President:* JOAB L. THOMAS, M.A., PH.D.
*Academic Vice-President:* E. ROGER SAYERS, M.S., PH.D. (acting).
*Vice-President for Planning and Operations:* JOSEPH T. SUTTON, M.A., PH.D.
*Vice-President for Financial Affairs and Treasurer:* ROBERT A. WRIGHT, B.S. (acting).
*Vice-President for Student Affairs:* ALBERT S. MILES, PH.D.
*Library:* see Libraries.

Number of teachers: 1,022.
Number of students: 17,918.

Publications: *Alabama Business†, Alabama Law Review†, Revista de Estudios Hispanicos†, South Eastern Latin Americanist†, Alabama Review†, Alumni News†, The Journal of the Legal Profession, Law and Psychology Review*.

DEANS:

*College of Arts and Sciences:* D. E. JONES, M.S., PH.D.
*College of Commerce and Business Administration:* HERBERT H. MITCHELL, M.S., PH.D.
*College of Community Health Sciences:* WILMER J. COGGINS, M.D.
*College of Education:* M. L. ROBERTS, Jr., M.A., L.H.D. (acting).
*College of Engineering:* WILLIAM J. HATCHER, Jr., M.S., PH.D. (acting).

*Graduate School of Library Service:* J. D. RAMER, D.L.S.
*Graduate School:* WILLIAM H. MACMILLAN, PH.D.
*School of Home Economics:* Miss M. A. CRENSHAW, M.S., PH.D.
*School of Law:* ALLEN E. SMITH, L.L.B.
*School of Social Work:* JAMES H. WARD, M.S.W., PH.D.
*New College:* BERNARD J. SLOAN, M.A., PH.D.
*School of Communication:* WILLIAM H. MELSON, M.A.C., PH.D.
*Capstone College of Nursing:* KATHRYN CROSSLAND, M.S.N., ED.D.

## UNIVERSITY OF ALABAMA IN BIRMINGHAM
BIRMINGHAM, ALABAMA 35294

Founded 1966.

*President:* S. RICHARDSON HILL, Jr., M.D.
*Vice-President for Health Affairs:* CHARLES A. MCCALLUM, D.M.D., M.D.
*Vice-President University College:* THOMAS K. HEARN, Jr., PH.D.
*Vice-President for Administration:* J. DUDLEY PEWITT, D.B.A.
*Vice-President for Institutional Advancement and Legal Affairs:* (vacant).
*Vice-President for Finance:* JERRY D. YOUNG, D.B.A.
*Vice-President for Research and Graduate Studies:* ROBERT P. GLAZE, PH.D.
*Vice-President for Student Affairs:* JOHN D. JONES, ED.D.

Number of teachers: 1,530 (1,384 full-time).
Number of students: 14,448.

Publications: *Alabama Journal of Medical Sciences†* (quarterly), *Beacon†* (monthly), *Medical Center†* (every 2 months), *UAB Report†* (weekly), catalogues†, bulletins†.

DEANS:

*Graduate School:* BLAINE A. BROWNELL, PH.D., KENNETH J. ROOZEN, PH.D.
*School of Medicine:* JAMES A. PITTMAN, Jr., M.D.
*School of Dentistry:* LEONARD H. ROBINSON, D.M.D., M.D.
*School of Optometry:* HENRY B. PETERS, O.D.
*School of Nursing:* MARIE L. O'KOREN, ED.D.
*School of Community and Allied Health:* KEITH D. BLAYNEY, PH.D.
*School of Business:* M. GENE NEWPORT, PH.D.
*School of Education:* MILLY COWLES, PH.D.
*School of Engineering:* JAMES H. WOODWARD, PH.D.
*School of Humanities:* JAMES RACHELS, PH.D.
*School of Natural Sciences and Mathematics:* LEE R. SUMMERLIN, Jr. PH.D. (acting).
*School of Social and Behavioral Sciences:* GEORGE E. PASSEY, PH.D.

## UNIVERSITY OF ALABAMA IN HUNTSVILLE
HUNTSVILLE, ALABAMA 35899
Founded 1950.
President: John C. Wright, Ph.D.
Vice-President (Academic Affairs) and Dean of the Faculty: Elmer E. Anderson, Ph.D.
Number of teachers: 200.
Number of students: 4,035.
Publications: Bulletins.

DEANS:
School of Science and Engineering: G. Dimopoullos.
School of Humanities and Behavioral Sciences: J. Rogers.
School of Primary Medical Care: Colin Campbell.
School of Nursing: Dr. Etta Anne Hincker.
School of Graduate Studies and Research: N. F. Audeh.

## UNIVERSITY OF MONTEVALLO
MONTEVALLO, ALABAMA 35115
Telephone: 665-2521.
Founded 1896.
President: Dr. James F. Vickrey, Jr.
Academic Vice-President: Dr. Russell G. Warren.
Dean of Students: Dr. Joseph W. Hamer.
Director, Admissions and Records: Larry A. Peevy.
Librarian: R. B. Somers.

The library contains 155,550 vols., 1,346 magazines, 15 newspapers.
Number of teachers: 156.
Number of students: 2,593.

## UNIVERSITY OF NORTH ALABAMA
FLORENCE, ALABAMA 35630
Telephone: 766-4100.
Founded 1872 as a State institution.
President: R. M. Guillot.
Director of Admissions: J. H. Allen.
Librarian: Miss Ruth Dacus.

The library contains 140,562 vols.
Number of teachers: 203 full-time, 23 part-time.
Number of students: 5,000.

## UNIVERSITY OF SOUTH ALABAMA
307 UNIVERSITY BLVD., MOBILE, ALABAMA 36688
Telephone: (205) 460-6101.
Founded 1963.
President: Dr. F. P. Whiddon.
Vice-President for Academic Affairs: Dr. James R. Bobo.
Assistant to the President: Dr. Ralph W. Jones.
Director of Admissions: David Stearns.
Executive Director of Development: William Pipas.
Registrar: Carolyn Parham.
Librarian: Dr. C. Lowry.

The library contains 206,850 vols.
Number of teachers: 349.
Number of students: 8,005.

DEANS:
College of Education: Dr. G. Uhlig.
College of Business and Management Studies: Dr. D. Mosley.
College of Arts and Sciences: Dr. W. W. Kaempfer.
College of Medicine: Dr. S. Crawford.
College of Engineering: Dr. H. Rodriguez.
College of Allied Health: Dr. Patsy Covey.
School of Nursing: Dr. Dora Blackmon.
Division of Student Personnel: Dr. M. Howell.
School of Continuing Education and Special Programs: Dr. E. Bunnell.

# ALASKA

## ALASKA PACIFIC UNIVERSITY
ANCHORAGE, ALASKA 99504
Telephone: (907) 276-8181.
Founded 1957 as Alaska Methodist University, name changed 1979.
President: Glenn A. Olds.
Provost: Raghbir S. Basi.
Registrar: Jeanette Brooks.
Librarian: Jack O'Bar.

The library contains 255,487 vols.
Number of teachers: 36.
Number of students: 300.

## UNIVERSITY OF ALASKA STATEWIDE SYSTEM
FAIRBANKS, ALASKA 99701
Telephone: (907) 479-7311.
Founded 1915 as Alaska Agricultural College and School of Mines; university status 1935; consists of 3 major urban campuses and 10 community colleges.
President: Dr. Jay Barton.
Vice-President for Academic Affairs and Institutional Planning: Dr. Woodworth G. Thrombley.
Executive Vice-President: Dr. Sherman Carter.
Director of Information Services: Gerald E. Bowkett.
President of Board of Regents: Edward B. Rasmuson.
Number of teachers: c. 900.
Number of students: c. 27,000.
Publications: Now in the North (quarterly), program catalogues from various units of the university.

CHANCELLORS:
Fairbanks Campus: Dr. Howard Cutler.
Anchorage Campus: Dr. Frank Harrison.
Juneau Campus: Dr. Michael E. Paradise.
Community Colleges, Extension and Rural Education: Dr. Patrick O'Rourke.

# ARIZONA

## ARIZONA STATE UNIVERSITY
TEMPE, ARIZONA 85281
Telephone: (602) 965-9011.
Founded 1885.
President: Dr. J. Russell Nelson.
Provost/Academic Vice-President: Dr. Paige E. Mulhollan.
Vice-President for Business Affairs: Jack G. Penick.
Vice-President for Student Affairs: Dr. G. F. Hamm.
Registrar: Enos Underwood.
Librarian: Dr. Donald E. Riggs.

The library contains 1,534,000 vols.
Number of teachers: 1,230.
Number of students: 36,159.
Publications: various.

DEANS:
College of Architecture: H. Burgess.
College of Business Administration: Dr. William E. Reif (acting).
College of Education: Dr. Robert T. Stout.
College of Engineering and Applied Sciences: Dr. Clovis R. Haden.
College of Fine Arts: Dr. Jules Heller.
College of Law: Dr. Alan A. Matheson.
College of Liberal Arts: Dr. Guido G. Weigend.
College of Nursing: Dr. Juanita F. Murphy.
College of Public Programs: Nicholas L. Henry.
School of Social Work: Dr. Ismael Dieppa.

## NORTHERN ARIZONA UNIVERSITY
FLAGSTAFF, ARIZONA 86011
Telephone: 523-9011
Founded 1899.
President: Eugene M. Hughes.
Dean of Admissions and New Student Programs: Dr. Marge Cibik.
Librarian: Dr. Robert Kemper.

The library contains 1,400,000 vols.
Number of teachers: 575.
Number of students: 12,407.

## UNIVERSITY OF ARIZONA
TUCSON, ARIZONA 85721
Telephone: (602) 626-0111.
Founded 1885.
Academic year: August to May (two terms).

*President:* JOHN P. SCHAEFER, PH.D.
*Executive Vice-President:* A. B. WEAVER, PH.D.
*Vice-President for Administrative Services:* ROBERT A. PETERSON, M.B.A.
*Vice-President for Planning and Budgeting:* GARY M. MUNSINGER, PH.D.
*Vice-President for Research:* A. R. KASSANDER, PH.D.
*Vice-President for Student Relations:* RICHARD M. EDWARDS, PH.D.
*Registrar:* DAVID BUTLER, M.B.A.
*Librarian:* W. DAVID LAIRD, M.S.
Library: *see* Libraries.
Number of teachers: 2,200.
Number of students: 30,900.

Publications: *Arizona Quarterly* (Literature), *Arizona Law Review, Arizona and the West* (Quarterly Journal of History), *Hispanic American Historical Review* (quarterly), *Record†, Bulletin†, Business and Economic Review†* (monthly), *Books of the Southwest†*, agricultural publications.

### DEANS:

*Administration:* F. P. GAINES, PH.D.
*Admissions and Records:* D. L. WINDSOR, M.A.
*College of Agriculture:* BARTLEY CARDON, PH.D.
*College of Architecture:* R. GOURLEY, M.ARCH.
*College of Business and Public Administration:* K. R. SMITH, PH.D.
*College of Earth Sciences:* HUGH ODISHAW, M.A.
*College of Education:* F. R. PAULSEN, ED.D.
*College of Engineering:* R. H. GALLAGHER, PH.D.
*College of Fine Arts:* ROBERT WERNER, PH.D. (acting).
*College of Law:* R. C. HENDERSON, LL.M.
*College of Liberal Arts:* PAUL ROSENBLATT, PH.D.
*College of Medicine:* L. J. KETTEL, M.D.
*College of Mines:* WILLIAM COSART, PH.D. (acting).
*College of Nursing:* GLADYS E. SORENSEN, D.ED.
*College of Pharmacy:* J. R. COLE, PH.D.
*Graduate College:* L. B. JONES, PH.D.
*Students:* R. S. SVOB, M.A.

### PROFESSORS:

*College of Agriculture:*
ALCORN, S. M., Plant Pathology
ALLEN, R., Plant Pathology
ANGUS, R. C., Agricultural Economics
BARTELS, P. G., Plant Sciences
BEMIS, W. P., Plant Sciences
BERRY, J. W., Nutrition and Food Science
BOHN, H. L., Soils, Water and Engineering
BRIGGS, R. E., Plant Sciences
BROWN, W. H., Animal Science
CHIASSON, R. B., Veterinary Science
CHRISTOPHERSON, V. A., Home Economics
DANIEL, T. C., Renewable Natural Resources
DAY, A. D., Plant Sciences
DENNIS, R. E., Plant Sciences
DEUTSCHMAN, A. J., Nutrition and Food Science
DEWHIRST, L. W., Veterinary Science
DOBRENZ, A. K., Plant Sciences
DUTT, G. R., Soils, Water and Engineering
ENDRIZZI, J. E., Plant Sciences
FANGMEIER, D. D., Soils, Water and Engineering
FAZIO, S., Plant Sciences
FEASTER, C. V., Plant Sciences
FFOLLIOTT, P. F., Watershed Management
FIRCH, R. S., Agricultural Economics
FISHER, W. D., Plant Sciences
FOGEL, M. M., Watershed Management
FOSTER, R. E., Plant Sciences
FOX, R. W., Agricultural Economics
FREVERT, R. K., Agricultural Engineering
FULLER, W. H., Soils, Water and Engineering
GAY, L. W., Watershed Management
GERHARDT, P. D., Entomology
GILBERTSON, R. L., Plant Pathology
GOLL, D. E., Nutrition and Food Science
GRAHAM, G. J., Agricultural Communications
HALE, W. H., Animal Science
HAMILTON, K. C., Plant Sciences
HARTSHORNE, D. J., Nutrition and Food Science
HATHORN, S., Agricultural Economics
HAVENS, W. H., Landscape Architecture
HILLMAN, J. S., Agricultural Economics
HINE, R. B., Plant Pathology
HOGAN, L. M., Plant Sciences
HULL, H. M., Watershed Management
HUNGERFORD, C. R., Wildlife Ecology
JACKSON, E. B., Plant Sciences
JACOBS, C. O., Agricultural Education
JENSEN, M. H., Plant Sciences
JONES, W. D., Landscape Architecture
JORDAN, G. L., Range Management
KATTERMAN, F. R. H., Plant Sciences
KEARNS, J. R., Home Economics
KIGHT, M. A., Home Economics
KING, D. A., Renewable Natural Resources, Agricultural Economics
KIRCHER, H., W. Nutrition and Food Sciences
KLEMMEDSON, J. O., Range Management
KNEEBONE, W. R., Plant Sciences
KNORR, A. J., Home Economics
KNORR, P. N., Renewable Natural Resources
KUEHL, R. O., Quantitative Studies
MANNING, D. E., Home Economics
MARCHELLO, J. A., Nutrition and Food Science
MARÉ, C. J., Veterinary Science
MARTIN, S. C., Range Management
MARTIN, W. E., Agricultural Economics
MATLOCK, W. G. Soils, Water and Engineering
McCAUGHEY, W. F., Nutrition and Food Science
McCLURE, M. A., Plant Pathology
McCORMICK, F. G., Agricultural Education
McDANIEL, R. G., Plant Sciences
METCALFE, D. S., Plant Sciences
MOORE, L., Entomology
NELSON, M. R., Plant Pathology
NIELSON, M. W., Entomology
NIGH, E. L., Plant Pathology
NUTTING, W. L., Entomology
OEBKER, N. F., Plant Sciences
OGDEN, P. R., Range Management
OLSON, K. S., Agricultural Education
PEW, W. D., Plant Sciences
POST, D. F., Soils, Water and Engineering
RAMAGE, R. T., Plant Sciences
RAY, D. E., Animal Sciences
REED, R. E., Veterinary Science
REID, B. L., Animal Science, Nutrition and Food Science
RICE, R. R., Home Economics
RICE, R. W., Animal Sciences
RODNEY, D. R., Plant Sciences
ROLLINS, F. D., Animal Science, Nutrition and Food Science
RUBIS, D. D., Plant Sciences
SACAMANO, C. M., Plant Sciences
SCHMUTZ, E. M., Range Management
SCHONHORST, M. H., Plant Sciences
SCHUH, J. D., Animal Science
SELKE, M. R., Animal Science
SHARPLES, G. C., Plant Sciences
SHIVELY, J. N., Veterinary Science
SMITH, N. S., Wildlife Ecology
SOWLS, L. K., Wildlife Ecology
STANGHELLINI, M. E., Plant Pathology
STITH, L. S., Plant Sciences
STOTT, G. H., Animal Science
STROENLEIN, J. L., Soils, Water and Engineering
STUBBLEFIELD, T., Agricultural Economics
STULL, J. W., Nutrition and Food Science
TAYLOR, B. B., Plant Sciences
THAMES, J. L., Watershed Management
THEURER, C. B., Animal Science
TUCKER, T. C., Soils, Water and Engineering
TUTTLE, D. M., Entomology
UPCHURCH, R. P., Plant Sciences
VAVICH, M. G., Nutrition and Food Science
VOIGT, R. L., Plant Sciences
WAGLE, R. F., Watershed Management
WARE, G. W., Entomology
WARRICK, A. W., Soils, Water and Engineering
WATSON, T. F., Entomology
WEBER, C. W., Nutrition and Food Science, Animal Science
WERNER, F. G., Entomology
WIERSMA, F., Soils, Water and Engineering
WRIGHT, L. N., Plant Sciences
ZUBE, E. H., Renewable Natural Resources
ZWOLINSKI, M. J., Watershed Management

*College of Architecture:*
ALBANESE, C. A.
GIEBNER, R. C.
GOURLEY, R.
GREEN, E. C.
HECK, G.
LOCKARD, W. K.
McCONNELL, R. E.
MATTER, F.
MILLER, A. E.
SOBIN, H.

*College of Business and Public Administration:*
BAREFIELD, R. M., Accounting
BARRETT, W. B., Accounting
BLOOM, C. C., Public Policy, Planning and Administration
BOWEN, D. L., Public Policy, Planning and Administration
BRYSON, P. J., Economics
BUEHLER, J. E., Economics
CARPENTER, R. D., Public Policy, Planning and Administration
CHASE, R. B., Management
DIXON, H. A., Accounting
FLIPPO, E. B., Management
FRANK, H. J., Economics
GIBSON, L. J., Geography and Regional Development

## UNIVERSITIES AND COLLEGES—ARIZONA (UNIVERSITY OF)

Hawkins, C. A., Finance and Real Estate
Hecht, M. E., Geography and Regional Development
Herber, B. P., Economics
Kleespie, D. L., Accounting
La Salle, J. F., Management Information Systems
Logan, J. P., Management
Lynn, E. S., Accounting
Mann, L. D., Public Policy, Planning and Administration
Marshall, R. H., Economics
McIff, L. H., Accounting
McMillan, S. C., Management
Morrison, J. M., Public Policy, Planning and Administration
Mulligan, R. A., Public Policy, Planning and Administration
Munsinger, G. M., Marketing
Myers, L. A., Accounting
Navin, T. R., Management
Newman, J. W., Marketing
Nunamaker, J. F., Management Information Systems
Ostlund, L. E., Marketing
Pederson, L. R., Geography and Regional Development
Reeves, R. W., Geography and Regional Development
Roos, N. R., Finance and Real Estate
Saarinen, T. F., Geography and Regional Development
Shanno, D. F., Management Information Systems
Silvers, A. L., Public Policy, Planning and Administration
Smith, V. L., Economics
Summers, G. W., Management
Taylor, L. D., Economics
Weber, J. E., Management
Wells, D. A., Economics
Wenders, J. T., Economics
Wert, J. E., Finance and Real Estate
Williams, N., Geography and Regional Development

*College of Earth Sciences:*
Anthony, J. W., Geosciences
Bannister, B., Tree-Ring Laboratory
Bull, W. B., Geosciences
Coney, P. J., Geosciences
Damon, P. E., Geosciences
Davis, S. N., Hydrology and Water Resources
Dean, J. S., Tree-Ring Laboratory
Duckstein, L., Hydrology and Water Resources
Evans, D. D., Hydrology and Water Resources
Ferguson, C. W., Tree-Ring Laboratory
Fritts, H. C., Tree-Ring Laboratory
Guilbert, J. M., Geosciences
Harshbarger, J. W., Hydrology and Water Resources
Haynes, C. V., Geosciences
Ince, S., Hydrology and Water Resources
La Marche, V. C., Tree-Ring Laboratory
Maddock, T., Hydrology and Water Resources
Martin, P. S., Geosciences
McCullough, E. J., Geosciences
Nagy, B., Geosciences
Neuman, S. P., Hydrology and Water Resources
Odishaw, H., Geosciences
Resnick, S. D., Hydrology and Water Resources
Robinson, W. J., Tree-Ring Laboratory
Schreiber, J. F., Geosciences
Simpson, E. S., Hydrology and Water Resources
Simpson, G. G., Geosciences
Smiley, T. L., Geosciences
Stokes, M. A., Tree-Ring Laboratory
Sumner, J. S., Geosciences
Titley, S. R., Geosciences

*College of Education:*
Aleamoni, L. M., Educational Psychology
Allen, P. M., Secondary Education
Allen, R. V., Elementary Education
Altman, E., Library Science
Anderson, W. K., Higher Education
Antley, E. M., Reading
Barnes, W. D., Secondary Education
Bergan, J. R., Educational Psychology
Berliner, D. C., Educational Psychology
Blake, R. F., Educational Foundations and Administration
Blecha, M. K., Elementary Education
Brown, E. D., Elementary Education
Butler, H. E., Educational Foundations and Administration
Calmes, R. E., Educational Psychology
Chalfant, J. C., Special Education
Chilcott, J. H., Educational Foundations and Administration
Christensen, O. C., Counseling and Guidance
Clark, D. C., Secondary Education
Daldrup, R. J., Counseling and Guidance
Danielson, P. J., Counseling and Guidance
Dickinson, D. C., Library Science
Fillerup, J., Elementary Education
Gaines, F. P., Educational Foundations and Administration
Gavlak, E. S., Secondary Education
Goodman, K. S., Elementary Education
Goodman, Y. M., Elementary Education
Grant, A. T., Higher Education
Grant, R. T., Educational Foundations and Administration
Harcleroad, F., Higher Education
Hillman, B. W., Counseling and Guidance
Johnson, B. G., Rehabilitation
Johnson, R. K., Library Science
Kidwell, R. A., Business and Career Education
Kirk, S. A., Special Education
Klein, R. L., Secondary Education
Knief, L. M., Educational Psychology
Krebs, R. C., Secondary Education
Langen, H. J., Business and Career Education
Leigh, H. W., Secondary Education
Leshin, G., Special Education
Leslie, L., Higher Education
Letson, R. J., Secondary Education
Maxwell, M. F., Science Library
McCarthy, J. M., Special Education
Melnik, A., Reading
Merritt, C. B., Educational Psychology
Nash, P. N., Elementary Education
Nicholson, G. I., Educational Psychology
Olson, W. L., Special Education
Paulsen, F. R., Educational Foundations and Administration
Ranniger, B. J., Elementary Education
Sabers, D. L., Educational Psychology
Saunders, T. F., Educational Foundations and Administration
Smith, K. J., Reading
Smith, M. C., Secondary Education
Steinbrenner, A. H., Secondary Education
Stokes, M. B., Educational Foundations and Administration
Strand, W. H., Educational Foundations and Administration
Thornburg, H. D., Educational Psychology
Trejo, A. D., Library Science
Turechek, A. G., Rehabilitation
Wilson, H. B., Educational Foundations and Administration

*College of Engineering:*
Anderson, R., Aerospace and Mechanical Engineering
Bottaccini, M., Aerospace and Mechanical Engineering
Carlile, R. N., Electrical Engineering
Christensen, H. D., Aerospace and Mechanical Engineering
Da Deppo, D. A., Civil Engineering and Engineering Mechanics
Duckstein, L., Systems and Industrial Engineering
Dudley, D. G., Electrical Engineering
Evans, W. H., Electrical Engineering
Fahey, W. J., Electrical Engineering
Ferrell, W. R., Systems and Industrial Engineering
Gallagher, R. H., Civil Engineering
Hamilton, D. J., Electrical Engineering
Hausenbauer, C., Electrical Engineering
Hessemer, R. A., Electrical Engineering
Hetrick, D. L., Nuclear and Energy Engineering
Hilberry, N., Nuclear and Energy Engineering
Hill, F. J., Electrical Engineering
Hoenig, S. A., Electrical Engineering
Huelsman, L. P., Electrical Engineering
Hunt, B. R., Systems and Industrial Engineering
Ince, S., Civil Engineering and Engineering Mechanics
Jimenez, R. A., Civil Engineering and Engineering Mechanics
Jones, R. C., Electrical Engineering
Kamel, H. A., Aerospace and Mechanical Engineering
Kececioglu, D., Aerospace and Mechanical Engineering
Kerwin, W. J., Electrical Engineering
Kinney, R. B., Aerospace and Mechanical Engineering
Korn, G. A., Electrical Engineering
Kriegh, J. D., Civil Engineering and Engineering Mechanics
Laursen, E. M., Civil Engineering and Engineering Mechanics
Malvick, A. J., Civil Engineering and Engineering Mechanics
Mattson, R. H., Electrical Engineering
McEligot, D. M., Aerospace and Mechanical Engineering
Miklofsky, H. A., Civil Engineering and Engineering Mechanics
Morse, R. L., Nuclear and Energy Engineering
Newlin, P. B., Civil Engineering and Engineering Mechanics
Parks, E. K., Aerospace and Mechanical Engineering
Perkins, H. C., Aerospace and Mechanical Engineering
Petersen, R. E., Aerospace and Mechanical Engineering
Peterson, G. R., Electrical Engineering
Phillips, R. A., Civil Engineering and Engineering Mechanics
Post, R. G., Nuclear and Energy Engineering
Ramberg, J. S., Systems and Industrial Engineering
Reagan, J. A., Electrical Engineering
Richard, R. M., Civil Engineering and Engineering Mechanics
Rogers, W. L., Aerospace and Mechanical Engineering
Schultz, D. G., Systems and Industrial Engineering
Scott, L. B., Jr., Aerospace and Mechanical Engineering
Seale, R. L., Nuclear and Energy Engineering

SEARS, W. R., Aerospace and Mechanical Engineering
SEEBASS, A. R., Aerospace and Mechanical Engineering
SIERKA, R. A., Civil Engineering and Engineering Mechanics
SULTAN, H. A., Civil Engineering and Engineering Mechanics
THOMSON, Q. R., Aerospace and Mechanical Engineering
TRIFFET, T., Civil Engineering and Engineering Mechanics
VINCENT, T. L., Aerospace and Mechanical Engineering
WACKS, M. E., Nuclear and Energy Engineering
WAIT, J. V., Electrical Engineering
WYMORE, A. W., Systems and Industrial Engineering
YAKOWITZ, S., Systems and Industrial Engineering
YAPPEL, A. R., Aerospace and Mechanical Engineering

*College of Fine Arts:*
ANDERSON, W. H., Art
ANTHONY, J. R., Music
BARRECA, F. R., Radio—TV
BOONE, D. R., Speech and Hearing Sciences
BURROUGHS, R. C., Drama
CONANT, H., Art
CONLEY, E. T., Music
DAY, L., Music
DENNISTON, D. G., Art
EPPERSON, G., Music
ERLINGS, B. R., Music
EWBANK, H. L., Speech Communication
FERRELL, J. R., Music
GORIN, I., Music
GROSSMAN, M. K., Art
HARTSELL, O. M., Music
HASKIN, D. M., Art
HELDT, C. R., Art
HIXON, T. J., Speech and Hearing Sciences
HODGSON, W. R., Speech and Hearing Sciences
HULL, R. L., Music
KEYWORTH, R. A., Drama
KING, A. A., Speech Communication
LABAN, F. K., Speech Communication
LEE, J. K., Music
LITTLER, C. A., Art
MARRONEY, P. R., Drama
MARSH, O., Music
MCDONALD, S., Music
MCMILLAN, R. W., Art
MCMILLAN, T. M., Music
MOSHER, E., Music
MUCZYNSKI, R., Music
MURPHY, E. W., Music
PEARLMAN, L., Music
PETERS, R. E., Music
PRITCHARD, W. D., Music
QUINN, R. M., Art
REICH, S., Art
SCHROEDER, L. R., Art
SCOTT, J. P., Art
SHELTON, R. L., Speech and Hearing Sciences
SKINNER, P. H., Speech and Hearing Sciences
WERNER, R. J., Music
ZUMBRO, N., Music

*College of Law:*
ANDREWS, A. W.
ARES, C. E.
BOYD, W. E.
CLARK, R. E.
DAVIS, R. J.
DOBBS, D. B.
ECKHARDT, A. G.
HEGLAND, K. F.
HENDERSON, R. C.

HOFFMAN, J.
IRWIN, J. J.
KOZOLCHYK, B.
LIVERMORE, J. M.
RAPPEPORT, J. J.
SCHUESSLER, T. L.
SMITH, C. M.
SPECE, R. G.
TORMEY, T. J.
VAN SLYCK, W. N.
WEXLER, D. B.
WOODS, W. D.

*College of Liberal Arts:*
ADAMEC, L. W., Oriental Studies
ALLEN, R. C., Romance Languages
ANGEL, J. R., Astronomy
APOSHIAN, H. V., Cellular and Developmental Biology
BAGNARA, J. T., General Biology
BAILEY, D. C., Oriental Studies
BARFIELD, M., Chemistry
BARRETT, B. R., Physics
BARROW, L., Romance Languages
BARTELS, P. H., Microbiology
BARTLETT, N. R., Psychology
BASHKIN, S., Physics
BASSO, K. H., Anthropology
BATEMAN, H. E., History
BATES, R. B., Chemistry
BATTAN, L. J., Atmospheric Sciences
BENSON, C. T., Mathematics
BHATTACHARYA, R. N., Mathematics
BICKEL, W. S., Physics, Microbiology
BLITZER, L., Physics
BOWEN, T., Physics
BRILLHART, J. D., Mathematics
BROWDER, R. P., History
BROWN, A. D., Romance Languages
BROWN, J. H., Ecology and Evolutionary Biology
CALDER, W. A., Ecology and Evolutionary Biology
CALDWELL, R. L., Philosophy
CANFIELD, J. D., English
CAPPONI, G., Romance Languages
CARSON, D. W., Journalism
CARTER, H. E., Chemistry and Biochemistry
CARTER, P. A., History
CHAMBERS, R. H., Physics
CHANDOLA, A. C., Oriental Studies
CHEEMA, M. S., Mathematics
CHILCOTT, J. H., Anthropology
CLARK, L. D., English
CLARKE, J. W., Political Science
CLAY, J. R., Mathematics
COAN, R. W., Psychology
COCKRUM, E. L., Ecology and Evolutionary Biology
CORTNER, R. C., Political Science
COWAN, J. L., Philosophy
CULBERT, T. P., Anthropology
CURTIS, R. F., Sociology
DANIEL, T. C., Psychology
DAVIS, J. E., Romance Languages
DAWSON, G. A., Atmospheric Sciences
DELORIA, V., Political Science
DEMOREST, J.-J., Romance Languages
DENNY, J. L., Mathematics
DEVER, W. G., Oriental Studies
DIEBOLD, A. R., Anthropology
DINNERSTEIN, L., History
DOMINO, G., Psychology
DONAHUE, D. J., Physics
DONOHOE, J., History
DRYDEN, E. A., English
DUFNER, M., German
DULLES, J. W. F., History
DUNCAN, B., Sociology
DUNCAN, O. D., Sociology
EISNER, S., English
EMRICK, R. M., Physics
ENEMARK, J. H., Chemistry
ERICKSON, M. L., Sociology

EVANS, W. H., Atmospheric Sciences and Electrical Engineering
FAN, C.-Y., Physics
FEINBERG, J., Philosophy
FELTHAM, R. D., Chemistry
FERNANDO, Q., Chemistry, Pharmacology and Toxicology
FERRIS, W. R., Cellular and Developmental Biology
FIFE, P. C., Mathematics
FITCH, W. S., Astronomy
FORSTER, L. S., Chemistry
FRANKEN, P. A., Physics
FREISER, H., Chemistry
GARCIA, J. D., Physics
GEHRELS, A. M., Lunar and Planetary Laboratory
GREELEY, A. M., Sociology
GREENLEE, W. M., Mathematics
GRISWOLD, R. E., Computer Science
GROEMER, H., Mathematics
GROVE, L., Mathematics
GRYTING, L. A. T., Romance Languages
GYURKO, L. A., Romance Languages
HADLEY, M. E., General Biology
HALL, H. K., Chemistry
HAMBLIN, R. L., Sociology
HARRIS, R. M., General Biology
HAURY, E. W., Anthropology
HAYNES, C. V., Anthropology
HEED, W. B., Ecology and Evolutionary Biology
HENDERSON, R. N., Anthropology
HENDRICKSON, J. R., Ecology and Evolutionary Biology
HERMAN, B. M., Atmospheric Sciences
HILL, H. A., Physics
HINTON, H. P., History
HOFFMANN, W. F., Astronomy
HOSHAW, R. W., Ecology and Evolutionary Biology
HOSLEY, R., English
HRUBY, V. J., Chemistry
HSIAO, S., Psychology
HUBBARD, W. B., Planetary Sciences
HUFFMANN, D. R., Physics
HUNTEN, D M., Planetary Sciences
INGRAM, H., Political Science
INMAN, B. J., English
ITTELSON, W. H., Psychology
IVENTOSCH, H., Romance Languages
JELINEK, A. J., Anthropology
JENKINS, E. W., Physics
JENSEN, H., Philosophy
JETER, W. S., Microbiology
JOKIPII, J. R., Astronomy and Planetary Sciences
JONES, L. B., Chemistry
JOYNER, C., Political Science
JUST, K. W., Physics
KAHN, M. W., Psychology
KASSANDER, A. R., Atmospheric Sciences
KECK, K., Cellular and Developmental Biology
KELLER, P. C., Chemistry
KELLEY, A. E., Chemistry
KESSLER, J. O., Physics
KETCHAM, C. H., English
KILKSON, R., Microbiology, Physics
KING, J. E., Psychology
KOHLER, S., Physics
KUKOLICH, S. G., Chemistry
LAMB, G. L., Mathematics
LAMB, U., History
LAMB, W. E., Physics
LANSING, R. W., Psychology
LEAVITT, J. A., Physics
LEHRER, A. J., Linguistics
LEHRER, K. E., Philosophy
LEONARD, R. C., Sociology
LEVY, J. E., Anthropology
LIEBERSON, S., Sociology
LIPPINCOTT, W. T., Chemistry
LOMEN, D. O., Mathematics
LOMONT, J. S., Mathematics

LONGACRE, W. A., Anthropology
LOVELOCK, D., Mathematics
LOW, F. J., Astronomy
LOWE, C. H., Ecology and Evolutionary Biology
LUDOVICI, P. P., Microbiology
LYTLE, C. M., Political Science
MACKINNON, W. J., Psychology
MADISON, P., Psychology
MAHAR, J. M., Oriental Studies
MAHMOUD, H. M., Physics
MALIK, J., Russian and Slavic Languages
MANGELSDORF, P., Journalism
MARQUART, D. I., Psychology
MARTIN, J. W., Romance Languages
MARVEL, C. S., Chemistry
MASON, C. T., Ecology and Evolutionary Biology
McCAULEY, W. J., General Biology
McCULLEN, J. D., Physics
McELROY, J. H., English
McINTYRE, L. C., Physics
McLAUGHLIN, D. W., Mathematics
McNIECE, G. M., English
MEAD, A. R., General Biology
MEINEL, A. B., Astronomy
MENDELSON, N. H., Cellular and Developmental Biology
MERING, J. V., History
MEYER, M. C., History
MILLER, W. B., General Biology
MILO, R. D., Philosophy
MORSE, R. L., Physics
MULLER, E. N., Political Science
MULVANEY, J. E., Chemistry
MURPHY, J. G., Philosophy
MYERS, D. E., Mathematics
NELSON, D. A., Romance Languages
NETTING, R. M., Anthropology
NICHOLS, R. L., History
NUNAMAKER, J. F., Computer Science
OFFICER, J. E., Anthropology
O'LEARY, J. W., Cellular and Developmental Biology
OLSEN, S. J., Anthropology
OLSON, G. B., Microbiology
O'MALLEY, R. E., Mathematics
OSWALD, J. G., History
PARKER, T. W., History
PARMENTER, R. H., Physics
PICKENS, P., Cellular and Developmental Biology
PIERCE, R. S., Mathematics
POLLOCK, J. L., Philosophy
PROMIS, J. M. O., Romance Languages
QAFISHEH, H. A., Oriental Studies
RAAB, F. V., Philosophy
REITAN, R. M., Psychology
RIDGE, G. W., Journalism
RIVERO, E. S., Romance Languages
ROBINS, H. F., English
ROBINSON, C., English
ROBSON, J. W., Physics
ROEMER, E., Astronomy
ROSALDO, R. I., Romance Languages
ROSENBERG, C. I., Romance Languages
ROSENBLATT, P., English
ROSENZWEIG, M. L., Ecology and Evolutionary Biology
RUND, H., Mathematics
RUSK, J. G., Political Science
SALMON, W. C., Philosophy
SALZMAN, W. R., Chemistry
SCADRON, M. D., Physics
SCHAEFER, J. P., Chemistry
SCHOTLAND, R. M., Atmospheric Sciences
SCHULTZ, W. R., Oriental Studies
SEEBASS, A. R., Mathematics
SEELEY, M. G., Chemistry
SELLARS, W., Philosophy
SELLERS, W. D., Atmospheric Sciences
SERKOWSKI, K. M., Lunar and Planetary Laboratory
SHELTON, R. W., English
SIGWORTH, O. F., English

SONETT, C. P., Planetary Sciences
STALEY, D. O., Atmospheric Sciences
STARK, R. W., Physics
STEELINK, C., Chemistry
STEINBRENNER, A. H., Mathematics
STINI, W. A., Anthropology
STONER, J. O., Physics
STRITTMATTER, P. A., Astronomy
SWIHART, T. L., Astronomy
TAO, Y.-S., Oriental Studies
TER HORST, R., Romance Languages
THOMPSON, R. H., Anthropology
THOMSON, D. A., Ecology and Evolutionary Biology
TIFFT, W. G., Astronomy
TINSLY, R. L., German
TOMA, P. A., Political Science
TOMIZUKA, C. T., Physics
TRIFAN, D., Mathematics
TURNER, P. R., Anthropology
TWOMEY, S. A., Atmospheric Sciences
UNDERWOOD, J. H., Anthropology
VIGNERY, J. R., History
WAHLKE, J. C., Political Science
WANGSNESS, R. K., Physics
WEAVER, A. B., Physics
WEAVER, T., Anthropology
WEBER, J. E., Statistics
WEINSTEIN, D., History
WEYMANN, R. J., Astronomy
WHEELER, L., Psychology
WILD, P. T., English
WILLIAMS, E. J., Political Science
WILLIAMS, R. E., Astronomy
WILSKA, A. P., Physics
WILSON, C. E., Political Science
WILSON, G. S., Chemistry
WING, W. H., Physics
WISE, E. N., Chemistry
WOLOSHIN, D. J., German
WOOLF, N. J., Astronomy
WRENN, R. L., Psychology
WYCKOFF, R. W. G., Physics, Microbiology
YALL, I., Microbiology
YOSHINO, I. R., Sociology
YOUNGGREN, N. A., General Biology
ZAGONA, S. V., Psychology

*College of Medicine:*
ABRAMS, H. K., Family and Community Medicine
ALEPA, F. P., Internal Medicine
ANGEVINE, J. B., Anatomy
BARBEE, R. A., Internal Medicine
BARRETT, H., Radiology
BEIGEL, A., Psychiatry
BENSON, B., Anatomy
BERNSTEIN, H., Microbiology
BOONE, D. R., Surgery
BOYER, J. T., Internal Medicine
BRENDAL, K., Pharmacology
BRESSLER, R., Pharmacology, Internal Medicine
BROSIN, H. W., Psychiatry
BROWN, B. R., Anaesthesiology, Pharmacology
BURKS, T. F., Pharmacology
BURROWS, B., Internal Medicine
CAPP, M. P., Radiology
CHRISTIAN, C. D., Obstetrics and Gynaecology, Anatomy
CHVAPIL, M., Surgery
COMERCI, G. D., Paediatrics, Family and Community Medicine
CORRIGAN, J. J., Paediatrics
DANTZLER, W. H., Physiology
DAVIS, J. R., Pathology
DENNY, W. F., Internal Medicine
DRACH, G. W., Surgery
DROEGEMULLER, W., Obstetrics and Gynaecology
EWY, G. A., Internal Medicine
FINLEY, P. R., Pathology
FREUNDLICH, I. M., Radiology
FULGINITI, V. A., Paediatrics

GOLDBERG, S. J., Paediatrics
GORE, R. W., Physiology
HODGSON, W. R., Surgery
HUESTIS, D. W., Pathology
HUXTABLE, R. J., Pharmacology
JOHNSON, P. C., Physiology
JONES, S. E., Internal Medicine
KETTEL, L. J., Internal Medicine
KNUDSON, R., Internal Medicine
KRUTZSCH, P. H., Anatomy
LAYTON, J. M., Pathology
LEVENSON, A. I., Psychiatry
LYNCH, P. J., Internal Medicine
MARCUS, F. I., Internal Medicine
MORKIN, E., Internal Medicine
MOUNT, D. W., Microbiology
NORTON, L. W., Surgery
NUDELMAN, S., Radiology
NUGENT, C. A., Internal Medicine
OGDEN, D. A., Internal Medicine
PAPLANUS, S. H., Pathology
PATTON, D., Radiology
PELTIER, L. F., Surgery
PRESENT, A. J., Radiology
RACY, J. C., Psychiatry
RAY, C. G., Pathology, Paediatrics
RUSSELL, D. H., Pharmacology
SALMON, S. A., Internal Medicine
SHAW, J. R., Family and Community Medicine
SIBLEY, W. A., Neurology
SMITH, J. W., Internal Medicine
SPIZIZEN, J., Microbiology
STUART, D. G., Physiology
SWINDELL, W., Radiology
THOMPSON, H. C., Paediatrics, Family and Community Medicine
WANGENSTEEN, S. L., Surgery
WITTE, C. L., Surgery
WITTE, M. H., Surgical Biology
WOLFE, W. L., Radiology
ZUKOSKI, C. F., Surgery

*College of Mines:*
DEMER, L. J., Metallurgical Engineering
DOTSON, J. C., Mining and Geological Engineering
DRESHER, W. H., Metallurgical Engineering
EDWARDS, R. M., Chemical Engineering
GROSS, J. F., Chemical Engineering
HARRIS, D. P., Mining and Geological Engineering
KEATING, K. L., Metallurgical Engineering
KIM, Y. C., Mining and Geological Engineering
MORRIS, T. M., Metallurgical Engineering
PETERS, W. C., Mining and Geological Engineering
RANDOLPH, A. D., Chemical Engineering
REHM, T. R., Chemical Engineering
RIEBER, M., Mining and Geological Engineering
WENDT, J. O., Chemical Engineering
WHITE, D. H., Chemical Engineering

*College of Nursing:*
KAY, M. A.
McCORD, B. A.
PUTT, A. M.
SORENSEN, G. E.

*College of Pharmacy:*
BREWER, W. R., Pharmaceutical Sciences
BURTON, L. E., Pharmaceutical Sciences
CHIN, L., Pharmacology and Toxicology
CLAYTON, J. W., Pharmacology and Toxicology
COLE, J. R., Pharmaceutical Sciences
MARTIN, A. R., Pharmaceutical Sciences
PICCHIONI, A. L., Pharmacology and Toxicology
REMERS, W. A., Pharmaceutical Sciences
ZAPOTOCKY, J. A., Pharmaceutical Sciences

UNITED STATES OF AMERICA

General Departments:
ATWATER, A. E., Physical Education
BALTES, P. A., Military Science
CUSANOVICH, M., Biochemistry
DUNN, D. R., Physical Education
JENSEN, R. G., Biochemistry
KING, W. H., Health Education
MILLER, D., Physical Education
NELSON, L. O., Continuing Education
REES, F. D., Health Education
ROBY, F. B., Physical Education
ROBY, M. P., Physical Education
RUPLEY, J. A., Biochemistry
SMITH, D. W., Health-Related Professions
STRACK, D. H., Physical Education
SVOB, R. S., Physical Education
TOLLIN, G., Biochemistry
WELLS, M. A., Biochemistry
WILMORE, J. H., Physical Education
WILSON, J. M., Physical Education

## ARKANSAS

### ARKANSAS COLLEGE
P.O. BOX 2317, BATESVILLE, ARKANSAS 72501

Telephone: (501) 793-9813.
Founded 1872.
*President:* WILLIAM H. DUNKLIN (acting).
*Vice-President for Finance:* RICHARD S. THOMAS.
*Vice-President for Planning:* Dr. ROBERTA BROWN.
*Dean:* JOHN T. DAHLQUIST.
*Dean of Students:* DENNIS W. WRIGHT.
*Director of Admissions:* JOHN THOMPSON.
The library contains 72,000 vols.
Number of teachers: 35.
Number of students: 535.

### ARKANSAS STATE UNIVERSITY
STATE UNIVERSITY, ARKANSAS 72467

Telephone: (501) 972-2100.
Founded 1909.
*President:* RAY THORNTON.
*Registrar:* GRETA S. MACK.
*Librarian:* JAMES W. HANSARD.
The library contains 519,600 vols.
Number of teachers: 330.
Number of students: 7,423.

### ARKANSAS TECH UNIVERSITY
RUSSELLVILLE, ARKANSAS 72801

Telephone: 968-0389.
Founded 1909.
*President:* KENNETH KERSH.
*Registrar:* CHARLES M. SHELTON.
*Librarian:* W. A. VAUGHN.
The library contains 155,000 vols.
Number of teachers: 140.
Number of students: 3,200.

### COLLEGE OF THE OZARKS
CLARKSVILLE, ARKANSAS 72830

Telephone: 754-2788.
Founded 1834.
*President:* JOHN F. BURHORN, Jr.
*Registrar:* P. R. PITTMAN.
*Librarian:* TERRENCE MECH.
The library contains 108,000 vols.
Number of teachers: 39.
Number of students: 720.

### HARDING UNIVERSITY
SEARCY, ARKANSAS 72143

Telephone: (501) 268-6161.
Founded 1924.
*President:* Dr. CLIFTON L. GANUS, Jr.
*Registrar:* V. BECKETT.
*Librarian:* Miss WINNIE BELL.
The library contains 190,000 vols.
Number of teachers: 165.
Number of students: 3,081.

### HENDERSON STATE UNIVERSITY
ARKADELPHIA, ARKANSAS 71923

Telephone: (501) 246-5511.
Founded 1890 as church-related college; became a state institution in 1929.
*President:* Dr. M. B. GARRISON.
*Registrar:* H. LUCHT.
*Librarian:* Dr. G. GARRY WARREN.
The library contains 175,000 volumes.
Number of teachers: 170.
Number of students: 3,000.

### HENDRIX COLLEGE
CONWAY, ARKANSAS 72032

Telephone: (501) 329-6811.
Founded 1884.
*President:* JOE B. HATCHER.
*Registrar:* ALBERT M. RAYMOND.
*Librarian:* Dr. HENRY ALSMEYER.
The library contains 140,000 vols.
Number of teachers: 60.
Number of students: 1,037.

### JOHN BROWN UNIVERSITY*
P.O.B. 600, SILOAM SPRINGS, ARKANSAS 72761

Telephone: (501) 524-3131.
Founded 1919.
*President:* Dr. J. E. BROWN.
*Dean:* Dr. R. E. COX.
*Librarian:* G. ROGERS.
Number of teachers: c. 50.
Number of students: 585.

* No reply received to our questionnaire this year.

WORLD OF LEARNING

### PHILANDER SMITH COLLEGE
812 WEST 13TH ST., LITTLE ROCK, ARKANSAS 72203

Telephone: FR. 5-9845.
Founded 1877.
*President:* GRANT S. SHOCKLEY.
*Registrar:* Mrs. DOROTHY FRAIZER.
*Librarian:* MAXINE LEWIS.
Number of teachers: c. 60.
Number of students: 600.

### UNIVERSITY OF ARKANSAS
FAYETTEVILLE, ARKANSAS 72701

Telephone: 575-2000.
Established 1871. Opened 1872.
*President:* JAMES E. MARTIN, M.S., PH.D.
*Vice-President for Academic Affairs:* CHARLES W. OXFORD, PH.D.
*Vice-President for Agriculture:* JOHN WILLIAM GOODWIN, M.S. PH.D.
*Vice-President for Fiscal Affairs:* FRED S. VORSANGER, M.B.A.
*Director of Libraries:* R. V. POPE, B.S., M.S.L.S.
*Director of Museum:* C. R. McGIMSEY, M.A., PH.D.
Number of teachers: main campus 809, total 1,730.
Number of students: main campus 15,600, total 32,500.

DEANS:
*College of Agriculture and Home Economics:* G. HARDY, PH.D.
*College of Arts and Sciences:* J. GUILDS, PH.D.
**College of Business Administration:** J. P. OWEN, M.B.A., PH.D.
*College of Education:* F. J. VESCOLANI, M.A., ED.D.
*College of Engineering:* J. E. HALLIGAN, PH.D.
*Graduate School:* J. J. HUDSON, M.A., PH.D.
*School of Law:* D. EPSTEIN, J.D., LL.M.
*School of Architecture:* C. MURRAY SMART, B.ARCH., M.S.
*Division of Continuing Education:* HUGH L. MILLS, M.S., ED.D.

### UNIVERSITY OF ARKANSAS AT LITTLE ROCK
33RD & UNIVERSITY, LITTLE ROCK, ARKANSAS 72204

Telephone: 569-3000.
Founded 1927.
*Chancellor:* Dr. G. ROBERT ROSS.
*Executive Vice-Chancellor for Academic Affairs:* Dr. J. H. FRIBOURGH.
*Vice-Chancellor for Finance:* FRANCIS L. ROBINSON.
*Vice-Chancellor for Student Affairs:* Dr. DOROTHY TRUEX.
*Registrar:* HAROLD DUERKSEN.

*Librarian:* J. A. Allen.

The library contains 234,000 vols.
**Number of teachers:** 471.
**Number of students:** 10,038.

### UNIVERSITY OF ARKANSAS AT MONTICELLO
MONTICELLO, ARKANSAS 71655
Telephone: (501) 367-6811.
Founded 1909.

*Chancellor:* Dr. Fred J. Taylor.
*Registrar:* R. L. Kirchman.
*Librarian:* William F. Droessler.

The library contains 80,000 vols.
**Number of teachers:** 104.
**Number of students:** 1,608.

### UNIVERSITY OF ARKANSAS AT PINE BLUFF
PINE BLUFF, ARKANSAS 71601

*Chancellor:* Herman B. Smith, Jr., M.S., Ph.D.
**Number of students:** 3,000.
Liberal arts and teacher education; first degrees.

## CALIFORNIA

### ARMSTRONG COLLEGE
2222 HAROLD WAY,
BERKELEY, CALIFORNIA 94704
Telephone: (415) 848-2500.
Founded 1918.

*President:* John E. Armstrong.
*Registrar:* J. Robert Bercaw.
*Librarian:* Gary Tombleson.

The library contains 20,000 vols.
**Number of teachers:** 50.
**Number of students:** 625.

### ART CENTRE COLLEGE OF DESIGN
1700 LIDA ST.,
PASADENA, CALIFORNIA 91103
Telephone: (213) 577-1700.
Founded 1930.

*President:* Donald R. Kubly.
*Admissions Director/Registrar:* Rosa Maria Zaldivar.
*Librarian:* Elizabeth Stockley.

Departments of Communications Design, Film, Illustration, Industrial Design, Painting, Photography.
**Number of teachers:** 192.
**Number of students:** 1,150.

### AZUSA PACIFIC UNIVERSITY
HIGHWAY 66 at CITRUS AVENUE,
AZUSA, CALIFORNIA 91702
Telephone: (213) 969-3434.
Founded 1899.

*President:* Dr. Paul E. Sago.

*Dean of the College:* Dr. Don Grant.
*Director of Admissions:* Larry Brooks.
*Librarian:* Ed Peterman.

The library contains 286,085 vols.
**Number of teachers:** 90 full-time, 27 part-time.
**Number of students:** 1,505.

### BETHANY BIBLE COLLEGE
800 BETHANY DRIVE,
SANTA CRUZ,
CALIFORNIA 95066
Telephone: 438-3800.
Founded 1919.

*President:* Richard Foth.
*Registrar:* Miss C. Wilson.
*Academic Dean:* Charles Pace.
*Librarians:* Arnold McLellan, Ed Koetitz.

The library contains 48,198 vols.
**Number of teachers:** 32 (including 10 part-time).
**Number of students:** 645.

### BIOLA UNIVERSITY
13800 BIOLA AVENUE,
LA MIRADA, CALIFORNIA 90639
Telephone: (213) 944-0351.
Founded 1908.

*President:* J. Richard Chase.
*Registrar:* Greg Vaughan.
*Dean of Admissions:* Wayne Chute.
*Librarian:* Gerald Gooden.

The library contains 165,000 vols.
**Number of teachers:** 233.
**Number of students:** 3,181.

### CALIFORNIA BAPTIST COLLEGE
8432 MAGNOLIA AVENUE,
RIVERSIDE, CALIFORNIA 92504
Telephone: 689-5771.
Founded 1950.

*President:* Dr. James R. Staples, B.D., Ed.D.
*Dean:* Stephen Carleton, M.A., Ph.D.
*Registrar:* D. W. Hokett, B.D., M.Ed.

The library contains 103,000 vols.
**Number of teachers:** 50.
**Number of students:** 985.

### CALIFORNIA COLLEGE OF ARTS AND CRAFTS
5212 BROADWAY, OAKLAND,
CALIFORNIA 94618
Telephone: 653-8118.
Founded 1907.

*President:* Harry X. Ford.
*Dean of Admissions:* Jean Thomma.
*Librarian:* R. Harper.

The library contains 25,000 vols.
**Number of teachers:** 167.
**Number of students:** 977.

### CALIFORNIA COLLEGE OF PODIATRIC MEDICINE
BOX 7855, RINCON ANNEX,
SAN FRANCISCO,
CALIFORNIA 94120
Telephone: (415) 563-3444.
Founded 1914.

*President and Chief Executive Officer:* Stanley Burnham, Ed.D.
*Vice-President and Academic Dean:* Paul R. Scherer, D.P.M.
*Librarian:* L. Shapiro, M.L.S.

The library contains 7,500 vols., 8,000 periodicals.
**Number of teachers:** 81.
**Number of students:** 391.

### CALIFORNIA INSTITUTE OF INTEGRAL STUDIES
3494 21ST ST., SAN FRANCISCO,
CALIFORNIA 94110
Telephone: (415) 648-1489, 648-3949,
Founded 1968.

*President:* Dr. Theodore M. Vestal.
*Vice-President:* Mrs. Bina P. Chaudhuri.
*Dean:* Dr. Ralph Metzner.
*Registrar:* Dr. Ira Rechtshaffer.
*Librarian:* Vern Haddick.

The library contains 19,000 vols.
**Number of teachers:** 35.
**Number of students:** 170.
*Publication: Integral Review* (annually).

### CALIFORNIA INSTITUTE OF TECHNOLOGY
PASADENA, CALIFORNIA 91125
Telephone: (213) 795-6811.
Founded 1891. Private.

*President:* Marvin L. Goldberger, Ph.D.
*Vice-President and Provost:* John D. Roberts, Ph.D.
*Vice-President for Business and Finance and Treasurer:* D. W. Morrison, M.B.A.
*Vice-President for Institute Relations:* E. R. Wilson.
*Vice-President for Student Affairs:* James J. Morgan, Ph.D.
*Director of Admissions:* S. L. Huntley, Ph.D.
*Dean of Students:* David W. Wales, Ph.D.
*Controller:* R. T. Baker, B.S.
*Secretary:* H. C. Martel, Ph.D.
*Registrar:* L. G. Bonner, Ph.D.
*Librarian:* J. E. Tallman, B.A.

The library contains 340,000 vols.
**Number of teachers:** 300.
**Number of students:** 1,709.
Publications: *Engineering and Science, Caltech News.*

## UNITED STATES OF AMERICA

**Chairmen of Divisions:**
*Biology:* L. E. Hood, Ph.D.
*Chemistry and Chemical Engineering:* H. B. Gray, Ph.D.
*Engineering and Applied Science:* R. W. Gould, Ph.D.
*Geological and Planetary Sciences:* W. Barclay Kamb, Ph.D.
*Humanities:* R. G. Noll, Ph.D.
*Physics, Mathematics and Astronomy:* R. E. Vogt, Ph.D.

**Professors:**

Acosta, A. J., Ph.D., Mechanical Engineering
Ahrens, T. J., Ph.D., Geophysics
Albee, A. L., Ph.D., Geology
Allen, C. R., Ph.D., Geology and Geophysics
Anderson, D. L., Ph.D., Geophysics
Anson, F. C., Ph.D., Analytical Chemistry
Apostol, T. M., Ph.D., Mathematics
Aschbacher, M., Ph.D., Mathematics
Attardi, G., M.D., Biology
Babcock, Jr., C. D., Ph.D., Aeronautics
Baldeschwieler, J. D., Ph.D., Chemistry
Barish, B. C., Ph.D., Physics
Barnes, C. A., Ph.D., Physics
Beauchamp, J. L., Ph.D., Chemistry
Benton, J. F., Ph.D., History
Benzer, S., Ph.D., D.Sc., Neuroscience
Berg, H. C., Ph.D., Biology
Boehm, F. H., Ph.D., Physics
Bonner, J. F., Ph.D., Biology
Bridges, W. B., Ph.D., Electrical Engineering and Applied Physics
Brokaw, C. J., Ph.D., Biology
Brooks, N. H., Ph.D., Environmental Science and Civil Engineering
Brown, G. L., Ph.D., Aeronautics
Burnett, D. S., Ph.D., Nuclear Geochemistry
Caughey, T. K., Ph.D., Applied Mechanics
Chan, S. I., Ph.D., Chemical Physics
Christy, R. F., Ph.D., Theoretical Physics
Clark, J. K., Ph.D., English
Clauser, F. H., Ph.D., Engineering
Cohen, D. S., Ph.D., Applied Mathematics
Cohen, M. H., Ph.D., Radio Astronomy
Coles, D. E., Ph.D., Aeronautics
Corcoran, W. H., Ph.D., Chemical Engineering
Corngold, N., Ph.D., Applied Science
Cowan, E. W., Ph.D., Physics
Culick, F. E. C., Ph.D., Jet Propulsion and Applied Physics
Davidson, E. H., Ph.D., Biology
Davidson, N. R., Ph.D., Chemistry
Davis, L., Ph.D., Economics
Davis, L., Jr., Ph.D., Theoretical Physics
Dean, R. A., Ph.D., Mathematics
DePrima, C. R., Ph.D., Mathematics
Dickerson, R. E., Ph.D., Physical Chemistry
Dilworth, R. P., Ph.D., Mathematics
Dreyer, W. J., Ph.D., Biology
Elliot, D. C., Ph.D., History
Epstein, S., Ph.D., Geochemistry
Evans, D. A., Ph.D., Chemistry
Fay, P., Ph.D., History
Fender, D. H., Ph.D., Biology and Applied Science
Ferejohn, J. A., Ph.D., Political Science
Feynman, R. P., Ph.D., Theoretical Physics
Fiorina, M. P., Ph.D., Political Science
Fowler, W. A., Ph.D., Physics
Franklin, J. N., Ph.D., Applied Mathematics
Frautschi, S. C., Ph.D., Theoretical Physics
Fuller, F. B., Ph.D., Mathematics
Garmire, G. P., Ph.D., Physics
Gavalas, G. R., Ph.D., Chemical Engineering

Gell-Mann, M., Ph.D., Sc.D., D.Sc., Theoretical Physics
Goddard, III, W. A., Ph.D., Chemistry and Applied Physics
Goldreich, P. M., Ph.D., Planetary Science and Astronomy
Gomez, R., Ph.D., Physics
Goodstein, D. L., Ph.D., Physics and Applied Science
Gould, R. W., Ph.D., Applied Physics
Gray, H. B., Ph.D., Chemistry
Greenstein, J. L., Ph.D., Astrophysics
Grether, D. M., Ph.D., Economics
Grubbs, R. H., Ph.D., Chemistry
Gunn, J. E., Ph.D., Astronomy
Hall, M., Jr., Ph.D., Mathematics
Hood, L. E., M.D., Ph.D., Biology
Horowitz, N. H., Ph.D., Biology
Housner, G. W., Ph.D., Engineering
Hudson, D. E., Ph.D., Mechanical Engineering and Applied Mechanics
Humphrey, F. B., Ph.D., Electrical Engineering
Ingersoll, A. P., Ph.D., Planetary Science
Ireland, R. E., Ph.D., Organic Chemistry
Iwan, W. D., Ph.D., Applied Mechanics
Jennings, P. C., Ph.D., Applied Mechanics
Jones, W. T., Ph.D., Philosophy
Kamb, W. B., Ph.D., Geology and Geophysics
Kanamori, H., Ph.D., Geophysics
Kavanagh, R. W., Ph.D., Physics
Keller, H. B., Ph.D., Applied Mathematics
Klein, B. H., Ph.D., Economics
Knauss, W. G., Ph.D., Aeronautics
Knowles, J. K., Ph.D., Applied Mechanics
Konishi, M., Ph.D., Biology
Kreiss, H. O., Dr.tech., Applied Mathematics
Kubota, T., Ph.D., Aeronautics
Kuppermann, A., Ph.D., Chemical Physics
Lagerstrom, P., Ph.D., Applied Mathematics
Langmuir, R. V., Ph.D., Electrical Engineering
Leal, L. G., Ph.D., Chemical Engineering
Lees, L., M.S., Environmental Engineering and Aeronautics
Leighton, R. B., Ph.D., Physics
Levine, M. E., LL.B., Law and Social Change in the Technological Society
Lewis, E. B., Ph.D., Biology
Liepmann, H. W., Ph.D., Aeronautics
List, E. J., Ph.D., Environmental Engineering Science
Lorden, G., Ph.D., Mathematics
Lowenstam, H., Ph.D., Palaeoecology
Luxemburg, W. A. J., Ph.D., Mathematics
McCaldin, J. O., Ph.D., Applied Science and Electrical Engineering
McCann, G. D., Ph.D., Applied Science
McGill, T. C., Ph.D., Applied Physics
McKee, J. E., Sc.D., Environmental Engineering
McKoy, V., Ph.D., Theoretical Chemistry
Mandel, O., Ph.D., English
Marble, F. E., Ph.D., Jet Propulsion and Mechanical Engineering
Marcus, R. A., Ph.D., Chemistry
Mayer, J. W., Ph.D., Electrical Engineering
Mayhew, G. P., Ph.D., English
Mead, C. A., Ph.D., Electrical Engineering and Computer Science
Mercereau, J. E., Ph.D., D.Sc., Physics and Applied Science
Middlebrook, R. D., Ph.D., Electrical Engineering
Miklowitz, J., Ph.D., Applied Mechanics
Mitchell, H. K., Ph.D., Biology
Moffet, A. T., Ph.D., Radio Astronomy
Morgan, J. J., Ph.D., Environmental Engineering Science

Muhleman, D. O., Ph.D., Planetary Science
Munger, E. S., Ph.D., Geography
Murray, B. C., Ph.D., Planetary Science
Neugebauer, G., Ph.D., Physics
Nicolet, M., Ph.D., Electrical Engineering
Noll, R. G., Ph.D., Economics
North, W. J., Ph.D., Environmental Science
Oke, J. B., Ph.D., Astronomy
Oliver, R. W., Ph.D., Economics
Owen, R. D., Ph.D., Sc.D., Biology
Papas, C. H., Ph.D., Electrical Engineering
Paul, R. W., Ph.D., History
Peck, C. W., Ph.D., Physics
Pickering, W. H., Ph.D., Electrical Engineering
Pierce, J. R., Ph.D., D.Sc., D.Eng., Ed., LL.D., Engineering
Pine, J., Ph.D., Physics
Pings, C. J., Ph.D., Chemical Engineering and Chemical Physics
Plesset, M. S., Ph.D., Engineering Science
Plott, C. R., Ph.D., Economics
Quirk, J. P., Ph.D., Economics
Raftery, M. A., Ph.D., Sc.D., Chemical Biology
Raichlen, F., Sc.D., Civil Engineering
Rannie, W. D., Ph.D., Jet Propulsion and Mechanical Engineering
Revel, J., Ph.D., Biology
Richards, J. H., Ph.D., Organic Chemistry
Roberts, J. D., Ph.D., Dr.rer.nat., Sc.D., Chemistry
Rosenstone, R. A., Ph.D., History
Roshko, A., Ph.D., Aeronautics
Ryser, H. J., Ph.D., Mathematics
Sabersky, R. H., Ph.D., Mechanical Engineering
Saffman, P. G., Ph.D., Applied Mathematics
Sargent, W. L. W., Ph.D., Astronomy
Schmidt, M., Ph.D., Sc.D., Astronomy
Sciulli, F. J., Ph.D., Physics
Scott, R. F., Sc.D., Civil Engineering
Scudder, T., Ph.D., Anthropology
Seinfeld, J. H., Ph.D., Chemical Engineering
Shair, F. H., Ph.D., Chemical Engineering
Sharp, R. P., Ph.D., Geology
Shoemaker, E. M., Ph.D., Sc.D., Geology
Silver, L. T., Ph.D., Geology
Smith, H. D., Ph.D., LH.D., English
Sperry, R. W., Ph.D., D.Sc., Psychobiology
Sternberg, E., Ph.D., Mechanics
Stewart, H. J., Ph.D., Aeronautics
Stone, Jr., E. C., Ph.D., Physics
Strumwasser, F., Ph.D., Biology
Sturtevant, B., Ph.D., Aeronautics
Taylor, H. P., Jr., Ph.D., Geology
Thompson, F. B., Ph.D., Applied Science and Computer Science
Thorne, K. S., Ph.D., Theoretical Physics
Todd, J., B.Sc., Mathematics
Tombrello, T. A., Jr., Ph.D., Physics
Tschoegl, N. W., Ph.D., Chemical Engineering
Vogt, R. E., Ph.D., Physics
Vreeland, T., Jr., Ph.D., Materials Science
Wales, D. B., Ph.D., Mathematics
Walker, R. L., Ph.D., Physics
Wasserburg, G. J., Ph.D., Geology and Geophysics
Wayland, J. H., Ph.D., Engineering Science
Weinberg, W. H., Ph.D., Chemical Engineering and Chemical Physics
Westphal, J. A., B.S., Planetary Science
Whaling, W., Ph.D., Physics
Whitham, G. B., Ph.D., Applied Mathematics
Wilts, C. H., Ph.D., Electrical Engineering
Wood, D. S., Ph.D., Materials Science
Wu, T. Y.-T., Ph.D., Engineering Science

UNIVERSITIES AND COLLEGES—CALIFORNIA

YARIV, A., PH.D., Electrical Engineering and Applied Physics
ZACHARIASEN, F., PH.D., Theoretical Physics
ZIRIN, H., PH.D., Astrophysics
ZUKOSKI, E. E., PH.D., Jet Propulsion and Mechanical Engineering
ZWEIG, G., PH.D., Theoretical Physics

## CALIFORNIA INSTITUTE OF THE ARTS
24700 McBEAN PARKWAY, VALENCIA, CALIFORNIA 91355

Established 1961; Schools of Art and Design, Music, Theatre, Dance, Film and Video.

*President:* ROBERT J. FITZPATRICK.

Number of teachers: 145.
Number of students: 750.

## CALIFORNIA LUTHERAN COLLEGE
THOUSAND OAKS, CALIFORNIA 91360

Telephone: (805) 492-2411.

Founded 1959.

*President:* JERRY H. MILLER.
*Vice-President for Academic Affairs:* DAVID E. SCHRAMM.
*Vice-President for Financial Affairs:* A. D. BUCHANAN.
*Vice-President for Development:* GARY E. ERICKSON.
*Vice-President for Admissions:* WILLIAM HAMM.
*Dean for Student Affairs:* RONALD KRAGTHORPE.
*Director of Admissions:* RONALD TIMMONS.
*Registrar:* ALAN SCOTT.
*Librarian:* AINA ABRAHAMSON.

The library contains 100,000 vols.
Number of teachers: 143.
Number of students: 1,880.

## CALIFORNIA STATE UNIVERSITY AND COLLEGES
400 GOLDEN SHORE, CALIFORNIA 90802

Co-ordinating agency for 19 state universities and colleges.

*Chancellor:* GLENN S. DUMKE.

## CALIFORNIA POLYTECHNIC STATE UNIVERSITY
SAN LUIS OBISPO, CALIFORNIA 93407

Founded 1901.

*President:* WARREN J. BAKER, M.A., PH.D.
*Executive Vice-President:* D. W. ANDREWS, M.A., PH.D.
*Vice-President for Academic Affairs:* HAZEL J. JONES, M.A., ED.D.
*Dean of Students:* RUSSELL H. BROWN, M.A., PH.D.

The library contains 584,199 vols.
Number of teachers: 931.
Number of students: 16,048.
Publications: *Mustang Daily, Cal Poly Today* (quarterly).

DEANS:
*School of Agriculture and Natural Resources:* HOWARD C. BROWN, M.S., PH.D.
*School of Architecture and Environmental Design:* G. J. HASSLEIN, F.A.I.A.
*School of Business:* ROBERT K. COE, M.A., PH.D.
*School of Communicative Arts and Humanities:* JON M. ERICSON, M.A., PH.D.
*School of Engineering and Technology:* ROBERT G. VALPEY, M.S., PH.D.
*School of Human Development and Education:* C. C. CUMMINS, M.S., ED.D.
*School of Science and Mathematics:* WILLIAM C. LANGWORTHY, PH.D.

## CALIFORNIA STATE COLLEGE, BAKERSFIELD
9001 STOCKDALE HIGHWAY, BAKERSFIELD, CALIFORNIA 93309

Founded 1965.

Courses in Liberal Arts, Science, Mathematics and Nursing.

*President:* Dr. JACOB P. FRANKEL.
*Vice-President:* Dr. PHILIP M. RICE.
*Dean for Administration:* Dr. KENNETH SECOR.
*Dean of Students:* Dr. GEORGE B. HIBBARD.

Library of 190,000 vols.
Number of teachers: 150.
Number of students: 3,050.

## CALIFORNIA STATE COLLEGE, SAN BERNARDINO
5500 STATE COLLEGE PARKWAY, SAN BERNARDINO, CALIFORNIA 92407

Telephone: (714) 887-7401.

Founded 1960.

Liberal Arts college with several applied programmes offering a broad range of first degrees, several teaching credentials and master degrees in selected fields.

*President:* J. M. PFAU, PH.D.
*Vice-President for Academic Affairs:* GERALD SCHERBA, PH.D.
*Vice-President for Administration:* JOSEPH K. THOMAS, ED.D.
*Dean of Students:* KENTON L. MONROE, PH.D.
*Librarian:* A. NELSON, M.A.L.S.

The library contains 262,238 vols.
Number of teachers: c. 181.
Number of students: 4,383.

## CALIFORNIA STATE COLLEGE, STANISLAUS
TURLOCK, CALIFORNIA 95380

Telephone: (209) 633-2201.

Founded 1957.

*President:* Dr. WALTER OLSON.
*Vice-President for Academic Affairs:* Dr. REUBEN TORCH.
*Director of Admissions:* E. J. AUBERT.
*Librarian:* R. D. GALLOWAY.

The library contains 245,000 vols.
Number of teachers: 213.
Number of students: 4,200.

## CALIFORNIA STATE POLYTECHNIC UNIVERSITY, POMONA
3801 WEST TEMPLE AVE., POMONA, CALIFORNIA 91768

Telephone: (714) 598-4726.

Founded 1938.

*President:* Dr. HUGH O. LA BOUNTY, Jr.
*Registrar:* ROBERT L. LOSSER.
*Librarian:* HAROLD F. WELLS.

The library contains 340,000 vols.
Number of teachers: 800.
Number of students: 14,800.

DEANS:
*School of Agriculture:* TONY J. CUNHA.
*School of Arts:* ERNEST D. ROSE.
*School of Business:* DAVID G. FOLEY.
*School of Engineering:* BEAUMONT DAVISON.
*School of Environmental Design:* JERE S. FRENCH.
*School of Science:* RALPH W. AMES.
*Teacher Preparation Center:* ALVIN H. THOMPSON.

## CALIFORNIA STATE UNIVERSITY, CHICO
CHICO, CALIFORNIA 95929

Telephone: (916) 895-6116.

Founded 1887.

*President:* Dr. ROBIN WILSON.
*Director of Admissions:* Dr. KENNETH EDSON.
*Vice-President for Academic Affairs:* Dr. ROBERT FREDENBURG.
*Vice-President for Administration:* Dr. ALLAN FORBES.
*Director, Area and Interdisciplinary Programs:* Dr. CLARK DAVIS.

DEANS:
*Undergraduate Programs:* Dr. PATRICIA BROSE.
*Student Affairs:* Dr. BETTY LOU RAKER.
*School of Agriculture and Home Economics:* Dr. LUCAS CALPOUZOS.
*School of Applied Sciences:* Dr. GARY WATTERS.
*School of Behavioral and Social Sciences:* Dr. JAMES HAEHN.

*School of Business:* Dr. Andrew Sikula.
*School of Education:* Dr. Arley Howsden.
*School of Humanities and Fine Arts:* Dr. Lois Christensen.
*School of Natural Sciences:* Dr. William Stephens.
*Graduate School:* Dr. John Morgan.

The library contains 530,000 vols.

Number of teachers: 939.
Number of students: 13,410.

### CALIFORNIA STATE UNIVERSITY, DOMINGUEZ HILLS
CARSON, CALIFORNIA 90747

Telephone: (213) 516-3300.

Founded 1960.

*President:* D. R. Gerth.
*Vice-Presidents:* D. A. MacPhee, D. J. Karber.
*Registrar:* K. Finlay.
*Librarian:* P. Wesley.

The library contains 247,000 vols.

Number of teachers: 300.
Number of students: 8,000.

#### DEANS:
*Humanities and Fine Arts:* H. Caldwell.
*Natural Sciences and Mathematics:* S. Wiley.
*Social and Behavioral Sciences:* J. Fenton.
*Education:* G. R. Walker.
*Management:* J. Harris (acting).

### CALIFORNIA STATE UNIVERSITY, FRESNO
FRESNO, CALIFORNIA 93740

Telephone: (209) 294-2000.

Founded 1911.

*President:* Harold H. Haak.
*Director of Admission and Records:* K. Davies.
*Librarian:* Lillie Parker.

The library contains 600,000 vols.

Number of teachers: 720.
Number of students: 15,553.

### CALIFORNIA STATE UNIVERSITY, FULLERTON
FULLERTON, CALIFORNIA 92634

Telephone: (714) 773-2011.

Founded 1957.

*President:* Dr. Jewel Plummer Cobb.
*Registrar:* J. B. Sweeney.
*Library Director:* E. W. Toy, Jr.

The library contains 508,564 vols.

Number of teachers: 800.
Number of students: 22,000.

### CALIFORNIA STATE UNIVERSITY, HAYWARD
HAYWARD, CALIFORNIA 94542

Telephone: 881-3000.

Founded 1957.

*President:* Ellis E. McCune.
*Director of Admissions:* Judith Hirsch.
*Librarian:* Melissa Rose.

The library contains 600,000 vols.

Number of teachers: 500.
Number of students: 10,000.

### CALIFORNIA STATE UNIVERSITY, LONG BEACH
1250 BELLFLOWER BLVD., LONG BEACH, CALIFORNIA 90840

Telephone: (213) 498-4111.

Founded 1949.

*President:* Dr. Stephen Horn.
*Director of Admissions and Records:* Leonard Kreutner.
*Library Director:* Dr. Peter Spyers-Duran.

The library contains 738,077 vols.

Number of teachers: 874 full-time, 898 part-time.
Number of students: 30,096.

### CALIFORNIA STATE UNIVERSITY, LOS ANGELES
5151 STATE UNIVERSITY DRIVE, LOS ANGELES, CALIFORNIA 90032

Telephone: (213) 224-0111.

Founded 1947.

*President:* James M. Rosser.
*Vice-President for Academic Affairs:* Philip Vaird (acting).
*Vice-President for Administration:* Patricia McCoy.
*Librarian:* M. Polan.

The library contains 895,000 vols.

Number of teachers: 800 full-time, 600 part-time.
Number of students: 22,500.

### CALIFORNIA STATE UNIVERSITY, NORTHRIDGE
18111 NORDHOFF STREET, NORTHRIDGE, CALIFORNIA 91330

Telephone: 885-3777.

Founded 1958.

*President:* James W. Cleary.
*Director of Admissions and Records:* Ned Reynolds.
*Librarian:* Norman Tanis.

The library contains 700,000 vols., 175,000 maps.

Number of teachers: 1,400.
Number of students: 27,500.

#### DEANS:
*School of the Arts:* R. Heidsiek.
*School of Business Administration and Economics:* J. Robertson.
*School of Communication and Professional Studies:* L. Glass.
*School of Education:* A. LaBue.
*School of Engineering and Computer Science:* C. Sanders.
*School of Humanities:* J. Richfield.
*School of Science and Mathematics:* D. Bianchi.
*School of Social and Behavioral Sciences:* W. Knowles.

### CALIFORNIA STATE UNIVERSITY, SACRAMENTO
6000 J ST., SACRAMENTO, CALIFORNIA 95819

Telephone: (916) 454-6011.

Founded 1947.

*President:* W. Lloyd Johns.
*Director of Admissions and Records:* D. Anderson.
*Librarian:* J. Ball.

The library contains 570,137 vols.

Number of teachers: 900.
Number of students: 20,700.

#### DEANS:
*School of Arts and Sciences:* Roger Leezer.
*School of Business and Public Administration:* Austin J. Gerber.
*School of Education:* James R. Neal.
*School of Engineering:* Donald H. Gillott.
*School of Social Work:* Paul Walsma.

### CHAPMAN COLLEGE
333 NORTH GLASSELL STREET, ORANGE, CALIFORNIA 92666

Telephone: (714) 997-6611.

Founded 1861.

*President:* G. T. Smith.
*Executive Assistant to the President:* G. Maxine Preston.
*Dean of the Faculty:* Cameron Sinclair.
*Registrar:* E. E. Owens.
*Dean of Admissions:* Anthony Garcia.
*Librarian:* Janice Shawl.

The library contains 169,186 vols.

Number of teachers: 96 full-time, 56 part-time.
Number of students: 1,582.

### CLAREMONT GRADUATE SCHOOL
10TH & COLLEGE, CLAREMONT, CALIFORNIA 91711

Telephone: (714) 621-8000.

Founded 1925.

*President:* John D. Maguire.
*Dean of the Graduate School:* Paul A. Albrecht.
*Librarian:* P. Barkey.

Number of teachers: 300 (including faculty members from The Claremont Colleges).

Number of students: 1,500.

## COLLEGE OF NOTRE DAME
RALSTON AVENUE,
BELMONT, CALIFORNIA 94002
Telephone: 593-1601.
Founded 1851; Chartered 1868.
President: Sister VERONICA SKILLIN.
Registrar: DIANE MERTZ.
Director of Admissions: KRISTINE ZAVOLI.
Librarian: Sister CATHERINE PELLITIER.

The library contains 89,098 vols.
Number of teachers: 140.
Number of students: 1,342.

## FRESNO PACIFIC COLLEGE
1717 SOUTH CHESTNUT AVE.,
FRESNO, CALIFORNIA 93702
Telephone: (209) 251-7194.
Founded 1944.
President: EDMUND JANZEN.
Dean of Academic Affairs: DALTON REIMER.
Registrar: Mrs. ADINA SCHMIDT.
Librarian: A. PAULS.

The library contains 54,298 vols.
Number of teachers: 40.
Number of students: 775.

## GOLDEN GATE UNIVERSITY
536 MISSION STREET,
SAN FRANCISCO,
CALIFORNIA 94105
Telephone: (415) 391-7800.
Founded 1901.
President: OTTO W. BUTZ.
Registrar: MICHAEL STUBLAREC.
Librarian: HAROLD KORF.

The library contains 250,000 vols.
Number of teachers: 800.
Number of students: 9,560.

## HARVEY MUDD COLLEGE
KINGSTON HALL, CLAREMONT
CALIFORNIA 91711
Telephone: (714) 621-8120.
Founded 1955.
Courses in science and engineering.
President: D. K. BAKER.
Registrar: N. KRUGER.
Dean of Faculty: B. S. TANENBAUM.
Dean of Students: W. GANN.
Dean of Admission: E. R. WALKER.
Library Director: PATRICK BARKEY.

The library contains over 1,000,000 vols. (shared with the Claremont Colleges).
Number of teachers: 60.
Number of students: 498.

## HOLY NAMES COLLEGE
3500 MOUNTAIN BOULEVARD,
OAKLAND, CALIFORNIA 94619
Telephone: (415) 436-0111.
Founded 1868.
Four-year, co-educational liberal arts college.

President: Sister IRENE WOODWARD.
Vice-President for Administration: KEVIN M. DIRAN.
Dean of Academic Affairs: VELMA B. RICHMOND.
Director of Admissions and Financial Aid: Sister JACQUELYN SLATER.
Librarian: Sister HELEN CLARE HOWATT.

The library contains 92,000 vols.
Number of teachers: 86.
Number of students: 666.

## HUMBOLDT STATE UNIVERSITY
ARCATA, CALIFORNIA 95521
Telephone: (707) 826-3011.
Founded 1913.
President: Dr. ALISTAIR W. McCRONE.
Dean of Admissions and Records: ROBERT HANNIGAN.
Librarian: DAVID K. OYLER.

The library contains 244,000 vols.
Number of teachers: 402.
Number of students: 7,500.

## LOMA LINDA UNIVERSITY
LOMA LINDA, CALIFORNIA 92354
Telephone: 796-7311 and 785-2000.
Founded 1905.
President: V. NORSKOV OLSEN, PH.D., DR.THEOL.
Vice-Presidents: NORMAN J. WOODS, PH.D., TRACY R. TEELE, M.ED., W. J. BLACKER, MARLOWE H. SCHAFFNER, M.D., EDWARD C. WINES, M.A.
Director, Admissions and Records: ARNO KUTZNER, PH.D.
Director of Libraries: H. MAYNARD LOWRY, PH.D.

The libraries contain 356,845 vols. and periodicals.
Number of teachers: 1,580.
Number of students: 5,127.

Publications: Bulletins, Handbooks, University Scope, Criterion, University Observer, Adventist Heritage.

### DEANS:
College of Arts and Sciences: VERN R. ANDRESS, PH.D.
School of Health: ANDREW HAYNAL, M.D., M.P.H.
School of Education: W. H. MEIER, ED.D.
School of Medicine: G. GORDON HADLEY, M.D.
School of Dentistry: JUDSON KLOOSTER, D.D.S.
Graduate School: MAURICE D. HODGEN, ED.D.
School of Nursing: HELEN KING, PH.D.
School of Allied Health Professions: I. C. WOODWARD, PH.D.

## LOYOLA MARYMOUNT UNIVERSITY
7101 WEST 80 STREET,
LOS ANGELES, CALIFORNIA 90045
Telephone: (213) 642-2700.
Founded 1911.
Founded by Vincentian Fathers as St. Vincent's College 1865, taken over by Jesuit Fathers 1911, name changed to Loyola College 1918, Loyola Univ. and Marymount College merged 1973.
President: Rev. DONALD MERRIFIELD, S.J.
Executive Vice-President: Dr. JAMES E. FOXWORTHY.
Academic Vice-President: Rev. JOHN D. CUDDIGAN, S.J.
Vice-President for Student Affairs: Dr. HENRY F. DURAND.
Provost: Sr. JOAN TREACY, R.S.H.M.
Vice-President for University Relations: KENNETH J. DAPONTE.
Registrar: ROSE ST. ONGE.
Director of Admissions: M. L. L'HEUREUX.

The library contains 176,000 vols.
Number of teachers: 293.
Number of students: 4,867.

### DEANS:
Business: R. L. WILLIAMSON, PH.D.
Science and Engineering: Dr. J. P. CALLINAN.
Law: T. A. BRUINSMA.
Liberal Arts: Rev. A. B. BRZOSKA, S.J.
College of Fine and Communication Arts: Dr. P. CLOTHIER.
Graduate Division: Dr. A. F. TURHOLLOW.

## MILLS COLLEGE
OAKLAND, CALIFORNIA 94613
Founded as a Seminary 1852, as a College 1885.
President: MARY S. METZ.
Dean of the Faculty: CHARLES E. LARSEN.
Dean of Students: DOROTHY KELLER.
Director of Graduate Study: ALLAN E. WENDT.
Librarian: (vacant).

The library contains 195,000 vols.
Number of teachers: 132.
Number of students: 932.

Publications: The Mills Stream, The Crest (annually), Bulletin of Mills College, Mills Quarterly (alumnae).

## MONTEREY INSTITUTE OF INTERNATIONAL STUDIES
425 VAN BUREN ST.,
MONTEREY, CALIFORNIA 93940
Founded 1955.
President: Dr. WILLIAM G. CRAIG.
Academic Dean: Dr. GLYNN WOOD.
Admissions Officer: Dr. ELIZABETH BROOKS.

UNITED STATES OF AMERICA

*Vice-President for Administration:* Dr. NATHAN DICKMEYER.

The library contains 43,000 vols.
Number of students: 475.

### MOUNT ST. MARY'S COLLEGE
12001 CHALON ROAD,
LOS ANGELES, CALIFORNIA 90049
Telephone: (213) 476-2237.
Founded 1925.

*President:* Sister MAGDALEN COUGHLIN.
*Dean of Academic Development:* Rev. MATTHEW DELANEY.
*Registrar and Director of Admissions:* Sister HELEN OSWALD.
*Librarian:* Mrs. ERIKA CONDON.

The library contains 131,440 vols.
Number of teachers: 130.
Number of students: 1,100.

**Doheny Campus:** 10 Chester Place, Los Angeles, California 90007; Tel. (213) 476-0450; f. 1962.
*Graduate and Extended Day Programs:* Sister PAULETTE GLADIS.
*Associate in Arts Degree Program:* Sister MARIE LOYOLA SANDERS.

### NORTHROP UNIVERSITY
INGLEWOOD, CALIFORNIA 90306
Telephone: (213) 641-3470.
Founded 1942.

*President:* Dr. B. J. SHELL.
*Director of Admissions:* JUDSON W. STAPLES.
*Director of Records:* Mrs. CATHLEEN KATZ.
*Librarian:* CHERE NEGAARD.

The library contains 63,802 bound vols.
Number of teachers: 106 full-time, 33 part time.
Number of students: 1,300.

Includes: College of Engineering, College of Engineering Technology, School of Business and Management, School of Law, Aviation Technician School and Language Institute. Programs leading to Associate, Bachelor and Master degrees; the Law School offers a Juris Doctor degree and a Tax Program.

### OCCIDENTAL COLLEGE
LOS ANGELES, CALIFORNIA 90041
Founded 1887.

*President:* RICHARD C. GILMAN, PH.D., LL.D., L.H.D.
*Executive Vice-President:* ROBERT L. BOVINETTE.
*Vice-President for Planning and Development:* LEE O. CASE.
*Dean of the Faculty:* JAMES W. ENGLAND, M.A., PH.D.
*Registrar:* EVELYNE B. GLASER, B.A.
*Dean of Students:* BRIGIDA A. KNAUER, M.A.
*Dean of Admissions:* JAMES MONTOYA, M.A.

The library contains 350,000 vols.

Number of teachers: 114 full-time, 35 part-time.
Number of students: 1,650.

### OTIS ART INSTITUTE OF PARSONS SCHOOL OF DESIGN
2401 WILSHIRE BOULEVARD,
LOS ANGELES, CALIFORNIA 90057
Telephone: (213) 387-5288.
Founded 1918.

*Dean of the College:* NEIL HOFFMAN.
*Gallery Director:* HAL GLICKSMAN.
*Registrar:* LYNN JORDAN.

The library contains 15,000 vols.
Number of teachers: 25 (day).
Number of students: 400 (day).

### PACIFIC OAKS COLLEGE
5 AND 6 WESTMORELAND PLACE,
PASADENA, CALIFORNIA 91103
Telephone: (213) 795-9161.
Founded 1945.

*Provost:* ELIZABETH HERRICK.
*Registrar:* JOANNE JONES.
*Dean of Academic Programs:* KAREN FITE.
*Dean of Students:* VIVIAN HOLLAND.
*Librarian:* CHERYL HADLEY.

The library contains 20,000 vols.
Number of teachers: 35.
Number of students: 290.

### PACIFIC UNION COLLEGE
ANGWIN, CALIFORNIA 94508
Founded 1882.

*President:* J. W. CASSELL, Jr., PH.D.
*Dean:* GORDON MADGWICK, PH.D.
*Registrar:* CHARLES T. SMITH, Jr., PH.D.
*Business Manager:* R. A. STRICKLAND, B.S.
*Chief Librarian:* CLARENCE SLETWICK, M.L.S.

The library contains 140,000 vols.
Number of teachers: 126.
Number of students: 1,000 men, 1,000 women, total 2,000.

Publications: *College Bulletin, Student Handbook, P.U.C. Viewpoint* (quarterly).

### PEPPERDINE UNIVERSITY
24255 PACIFI CCOAST HIGHWAY,
MALIBU, CALIFORNIA 90265

Founded 1937 as college, attained university status 1970.

*President:* HOWARD A. WHITE.
*Chancellor:* M. NORVEL YOUNG.
*Librarian:* Mrs. D. MOORE.

The library contains 366,571 vols.
Number of teachers: 236 full-time, including 66 professors.

Number of students: 6,800.
Publication: *Pepperdine People* (quarterly).

### PITZER COLLEGE
MILLS AVE., CLAREMONT,
CALIFORNIA 91711
Telephone: (714) 621-8000
Founded 1963.

*President:* FRANK L. ELLSWORTH.
*Registrar:* Mrs. A. MABERRY.
*Librarian:* PATRICK BARKEY.

The library contains 440,000 volumes.
Number of teachers: 70.
Number of students: 760.

### POMONA COLLEGE
SUMNER HALL,
CLAREMONT, CALIFORNIA 91711
Founded 1887.

*President:* DAVID ALEXANDER, D.PHIL.
*Vice-President and Dean:* R. T. VOELKEL, TH.D.
*Associate Dean:* R. STANTON HALES, M.A., PH.D.
*Vice-President and Dean of Students:* RICHARD A. FASS, PH.D.
*Dean of Admissions:* R. FRED ZUKER, M.ED., PH.D.
*Registrar:* M. ARMSTRONG, M.A.

The library contains 1,020,000 vols.
Number of teachers: 130.
Number of students: 1,350.

Publication: *Bulletin* (6 a year).

### ST. JOHN'S COLLEGE*
5118 E. SEMINARY RD.,
CAMARILLO, CALIFORNIA 93010.
Telephone: 482-2755.
Founded 1927.

*President:* Rev. JAMES M. GALVIN, C.M
*Registrar:* Rev. GEORGE WEBER, C.M.
*Librarian:* Sister M. RUTH, I.H.M.

The library contains 33,000 vols.
Number of teachers: 14.
Number of students: 248.

* No reply received to our questionnaire this year.

### ST. MARY'S COLLEGE OF CALIFORNIA
MORAGA, CALIFORNIA 94575
Telephone: (415) 376-4411.
Founded 1863.

Colleges of Liberal Arts, Science and Economics; Graduate programs in Theology, Education, Business, Psychology and Health, Physical Education and Recreation.

*President:* Brother MEL ANDERSON, F.S.C.
*Registrar:* BARBARA BURTON, B.A.

UNIVERSITIES AND COLLEGES—CALIFORNIA U.S.A.

*Librarian:* Bro. Casimir Reichlin, F.S.C., M.S., L.S.

The library contains 137,989 vols.
Number of teachers: 244.
Number of students: 2,781.

### SAN DIEGO STATE UNIVERSITY
SAN DIEGO, CALIFORNIA 92182
Telephone: (714) 265-5200.
Founded 1897.

*President:* Thomas B. Day.
*Vice-President, Academic Affairs:* A. W. Johnson.
*Director of University Affairs:* Paul Steen.
*Chairman of Senate:* William H. Phillips.
*Director of Admissions and Records:* Nancy Sprotte.
*Dean of Students:* Daniel B. Nowak.
*Librarian:* Ned V. Joy (acting).

Number of teachers: 1,133 full-time, 719 part-time, total 1,852.
Number of students: 33,000 undergraduate and graduate.

Publications: *Aztec Report* (Alumni Magazine), *The Aztec Engineer*, *Business Inquiry*.

#### DEANS:
*Business Administration:* Allan R. Bailey.
*Engineering:* Jay H. Harris.
*Arts and Letters:* Robert C. Detweiler.
*Education:* Robert Nardelli (acting).
*Graduate Studies:* James W. Cobble.
*Human Services:* Harriet G. Kopp (acting).
*Professional Studies:* Jerry Mandel.
*Sciences:* Donald R. Short.

### SAN FRANCISCO CONSERVATORY OF MUSIC
1201 ORTEGA STREET,
SAN FRANCISCO,
CALIFORNIA 94122
Telephone: 564-8086.
Founded 1917.

*President:* Milton Salkind.
*Dean:* Richard Howe.
*Admissions Officer:* Mrs. Colleen Katzowitz.

The library contains 17,500 vols. and 6,000 audio-visual titles.
Number of teachers: 68.
Number of students: 225.

### SAN FRANCISCO STATE UNIVERSITY
1600 HOLLOWAY AVE.,
SAN FRANCISCO,
CALIFORNIA 94132
Founded 1899.

*President:* Dr. Paul F. Romberg.

*Provost:* Dr. Donald Garrity.
*Vice-President for Administrative Affairs:* Dr. Konnilyn Feig.
*Comptroller:* A. L. Leidy.
*Director of Admissions and Records:* Dr. Charles A. Stone.
*Dean of Faculty Affairs:* Dr. L. Ianni.
*Dean of Students:* Dr. L. L. Kroeker.
*Librarian:* Dr. Frank A. Schneider.

The library contains 508,500 vols.
Number of teachers: 1,450.
Number of students: 24,335.

### SAN JOSÉ STATE UNIVERSITY
SAN JOSE, CALIFORNIA 95192
Telephone: (408) 277-3456.
Founded 1857.

*President:* Dr. Gail Fullerton.
*Director, Admissions and Records:* Clyde B. Brewer.
*Library Director:* Maureen Pastine.

The library contains 700,000 vols.
Number of teachers: 1,570.
Number of students: 25,338.

### SCRIPPS COLLEGE
10th AND COLUMBIA,
CLAREMONT, CALIFORNIA 91711
Telephone: (714) 621-8149.
Founded 1926.

*President:* John H. Chandler.
*Vice-President for Development and Public Relations:* Floyd C. Ethridge.
*Dean of Faculty:* Paula Goldsmid.
*Dean of Students:* Daryl G. Smith.
*Registrar:* Helen L. Ketchum.
*Director of Admissions:* Janet E. A. Burback.
*Librarian:* Judy B. Harvey-Sahak.

Library: 87,000 vols. in Denison Library, Scripps College; 1,020,000 vols. in the Honnold Library of The Claremont Colleges.
Number of teachers: 80.
Number of students: 575.

### SONOMA STATE UNIVERSITY
ROHNERT PARK,
CALIFORNIA 94928
Telephone: (707) 664-2880.
Founded 1960.

*President:* Peter Diamandopoulos.
*Registrar:* F. H. Jorgensen.
*Director of Admissions and Records:* Frank Tansey.
*Librarian:* Ruth Hafter.

The library contains 287,000 vols., 35,000 periodicals.
Number of teachers: 286 (full-time), 135 (part-time).
Number of students: 5,508.

### SOUTHERN CALIFORNIA COLLEGE
COSTA MESA, CALIFORNIA 92626
Telephone: (714) 556-3610.
Founded 1920.

*President:* Wayne E. Kraiss.
*Academic Dean:* Klaude Kendrick.
*Librarian:* Kenneth Tracy.

The library contains 66,000 vols.
Number of teachers: 30 full-time.
Number of students: 695.

### SOUTHERN CALIFORNIA COLLEGE OF OPTOMETRY
2001 ASSOCIATED ROAD,
FULLERTON, CALIFORNIA 92631
Founded 1904.

*President:* R. L. Hopping, o.d.
*Dean:* Douglas Poorman, ph.d.
*Comptroller:* Robert Baird, c.p.a.
*Librarian:* Mrs. P. Carlson, m.s.l.s.

The library contains 8,000 vols.
Number of teachers: 84.
Number of students: 410.

Publications: *The Alumniscope*, *The Reflex* (annual).

### STANFORD UNIVERSITY
STANFORD, CALIFORNIA 94305
Telephone: (415) 497-2300.
Founded 1885.

*President:* Donald Kennedy.
*Vice-President and Provost:* (vacant).
*Academic Secretary:* Eric Hutchinson.
*Dean of Admissions:* Fred A. Hargadon.
*Dean of Student Affairs:* James W. Lyons.
*Registrar:* Sally Mahoney.
*Libraries Director:* D. C. Weber.

Library: see Libraries.
Number of teachers: 1,737, including 601 full professors.
Number of students: 12,618.

Publications: *Stanford Law Review*, *Stanford Observer* (8 a year), *Alumni Almanac* (quarterly).

#### DEANS:
*Graduate School of Business:* Rene C. McPherson.
*School of Earth Sciences:* Allan V. Cox.
*School of Education:* J. Myron Atkin.
*School of Engineering:* W. Kays.
*School of Humanities and Sciences:* Halsey L. Royden.
*School of Law:* Charles J. Meyers.
*School of Medicine:* Lawrence G. Crowley (acting).
*Hoover Institution:* W. G. Campbell (Director).
*Physical Education and Athletics:* F. A. Geiger (Director).

#### PROFESSORS:
Abbott, D. P., Biology
Abbott, Isabella A., Biology
Acrivos, A., Chemical Engineering
Adams, J. L., Mechanical Engineering

AGRAS, W. S., Psychiatry
ALEGRÍA, F., Spanish
AMEMIYA, T., Economics
AMSTERDAM, A. G., Law
ANDERSON, T. W. Jr., Statistics and Economics
ANDERSSON, T. M., German
ANGELL, J. B., Electrical Engineering
ASHLEY, H., Aeronautics and Astronautics
ATKINSON, R. C., Psychology and Education
BABCOCK, BARBARA, Law
BACH, G. L., Economics and Public Policy
BAGANOFF, D., Aeronautics and Astronautics
BAGSHAW, M. A., Radiology
BALDWIN, R. L., Biochemistry
BALLAM, J., Stanford Linear Accelerator Center
BANDURA, A., Social Sciences
BARCHOS, J., Psychiatry
BARKAN, P., Mechanical Engineering
BARNETT, W. G., Law
BARTON, J. H., Law
BATES, C. W., Materials Science and Engineering
BAUM, D., Paediatrics
BAXTER, W. F., Law
BAYLOR, D. A., Neurobiology
BEAVER, W. H., Accounting
BEFU, H., Anthropology
BEM, D. J., Psychology
BENSCH, K. G., Pathology
BERG, P., Biochemistry
BERG, P. W., Mathematics
BERGER, J., Sociology
BERNFIELD, M. R., Paediatrics
BERSHADER, D., Aerophysics
BIENENSTOCK, A. I., Applied Physics, Materials Science and Engineering
BJORKEN, J. D., Stanford Linear Accelerator Center
BLANK, N., Radiology
BLANKENBECLER, R., Stanford Linear Accelerator Center
BONNER, W. A., Chemistry
BOUDART, M. J., Chemical Engineering and Chemistry
BOWER, G. H., Psychology
BOYLE, C. K., Art
BRACEWELL, R. N., Electrical Engineering
BRAUMAN, J. J., Chemistry
BREAKWELL, J. V., Aeronautics and Astronautics
BREITROSE, H. S., Communication
BREST, P. A., Law
BRIDGES, E. M., Education
BRIGGS, W. R., Biology
BRIGHAM, W., Petrol Engineering
BRODSKY, S., Stanford Linear Accelerator Center
BRODY, R. A., Political Science
BROWN, B. W., JR., Biostatistics
BRYSON, A. E., Jr., Engineering
BUBE, R. H., Materials Science
BUNEMAN, O., Electrical Engineering
BUNKER, J. P., Anaesthesia
BUSH, R. N., Education
CALFEE, R. C., Education and Psychology
CAMPBELL, A. M., Biology
CANN, H., Paediatrics and Genetics
CAPELLETTI, M., Law
CARNOCHAN, W. B., English
CARNOY, M., Education
CASTANEDA, A., Education
CAVALLI-SFORZA, L. L., Genetics
CHANG, I. D., Aeronautics and Astronautics
CHAO, C. C., Aeronautical Engineering
CHASE, R. A., Surgery
CHILTON, E. G., Mechanical Engineering
CHODOROW, M., Applied Physics and Electrical Engineering
CHOW, K. L., Medicine
CHOWNING, J. M., Music
CHUNG, K L., Mathematics
CLAERBOUT, J. F., Geophysics

CLARK, H. H., Psychology
CLAYTON, R. B., Biochemistry in Psychiatry
CLEBSCH, W. A., Religion and Humanities
CLOUGH, G. W., Civil Engineering
COHEN, A., Music
COHEN, B. P., Sociology
COHEN, E. G., Education
COHEN, E. N., Anaesthesia
COHEN, P. J., Mathematics
COHEN, S. N., Medicine
COHEN, W., Law
COHN, R. G., French
COLADARDCI, A. P., Education and Psychology
COLE, W., Speech and Drama
COLLINS, J. A., Surgery
COLLMAN, J. P., Chemistry
COMPTON, R. R., Geology
CONNOLLY, T. J., Mechanical Engineering
COOTNER, P. H., Finance (G.S.B.)
COTTLE, R. W., Operations Research
COVER, T. M., Electrical Engineering and Statistics
COX, A. V., Geophysics
CRAIG, G. A., Humanities
CREGER, W. P., Medicine
CRONBACH, L. J., Education and Psychology
CROWLEY, L. G., Surgery
CUTLER, C. C., Applied Physics
CUTLER, R. W. P., Neurology
DALLIN, A., History and Political Science
DANTZIG, G. B., Transportation Sciences
DAVID, P. A. Economics
DAVIS, R. T., Marketing—Graduate School of Business
DE BRA, D. B., Aeronautics and Astronautics
DEGLER, C. N., American History
DEKKER, G. G., English
DEMENT, W. C., Psychiatry
DEMSKI, J. S., Information and Accounting
DICKINSON, W. R., Geology
DICKSON, F. W., Geology
DIEN, A. E., Chinese
DJERASSI, C., Chemistry
DONIACH, S., Applied Physics
DORFMAN, R. F., Pathology
DORNBUSCH, S. M., Sociology
DOUGLAS, JAMES, Civil Engineering
DREKMEIER, C., Political Science
DRELL, S. D., Stanford Linear Accelerator Center
DUNN, D. A., Engineering
DUUS, P., History
EASTMAN, R. H., Chemistry
EAVES, B. C., Operations Research
EDWARDS, M., Classics
EFRON, B., Statistics
EHRLICH, P. R., Biology
EHRLICH, T., Law
EISNER, E. W., Education and Art
EITNER, L. E. A., Fine Arts
ELSEN, A., Art History
ENTHOVEN, ALAIN, Public and Private Management
EPEL, D., Blioogy
ESHLEMAN, V. R., Electrical Engineering
ESSLIN, M., Drama
EULAU, H., Political Science (G.S.B.)
EUSTIS, R., H. Mechanical Engineering
EVANS, J. M., English
EVITT, W. R., Geology
FAGEN, R. R., Political Science
FAINSTAT, T., Gynaecology and Obstetrics
FAIRBANK, W. M., Physics
FALCON, W. P., Economics
FARBER, EUGENE M., Dermatology
FARQUHAR, J. W., Medicine
FEFERMAN, S., Mathematics and Philosophy
FEHRENBACHER, D. E., American History
FEIGEN, G. A., Physiology
FEIGENBAUM, E. A., Computer Science
FELDMAN, M. W., Biology
FERGUSON, C. A., Linguistics

FERZIGER, J. H., Mechanical Engineering
FETTER, A. L., Physics
FIDO, F., Italian
FIFER, C. N., English
FINN, R., Mathematics
FLAVELL, J., Psychology
FLOYD, R. W., Computer Science
FLYNN, MICHAEL, Electrical Engineering
FOLLESDAL, D., Philosophy
FONDAHL, J. W., Civil Engineering
FORSTER, K. W., Art
FRAKE, C. O., Anthropology
FRANCO, J., Spanish and Portuguese
FRANKLIN, G. F., Electrical Engineering
FRANKLIN, M. A., Law
FRANZINI, J. B., Civil Engineering
FRIEDENTHAL, J. H., Law
FRIEDMAN, L. M., Law
FUCHS, V. R., Economics
FUHRMAN, F. A., Experimental Medicine
GAGE, N. L., Education
GANESAN, A. T., Genetics
GANZ, L., Psychology
GEBALLE, T. H., Applied Physics and Materials Science
GELPI, A. J., English
GEORGE, A. L., Political Science
GERE, J. M., Civil Engineering
GERMANE, G. E., Transportation and Logistics, Graduate School of Business
GEROW, B. A., Anthropology
GIBBONS, J. F., Electrical Engineering
GIBBS, J. L., Jr., Anthropology
GIBSON, C. D., Community and Preventive Medicine
GICOVATE, B., Spanish
GILBARG, D., Mathematics
GILLESPIE, G., German
GILMAN, F. J., SLAC
GIRARD, R. A., Law
GIRAUD, R., French
GOLDSTEIN, A., Pharmacology
GOLDSTEIN, P. L., Law
GOLUB, G. H., Computer Science
GONDA, T. A., Psychiatry
GOOD, E. M., Religion and Classics
GOODE, W. J., Sociology
GOODMAN, J. W., Electrical Engineering
GOULD, W. B., Law
GOVAN, D. E., Surgery
GRAY, R. W., Food Research Institute
GREEN, P. B., Biology
GREENBERG, J. H., Social Sciences
GREY, T. C., Law
GROSS, R. E., Education
GROSS, RUTH T., Paediatrics
GUERARD, A. J., Literature
GULEVICH, G., Psychiatry
GUNTHER, G., Law
GURLEY, J. G., Economics
HACKING, I., Philosophy
HANAWALT, P. C., Biology
HANBERY, J. W., Surgery
HANCOCK, E. W., Medicine
HANNA, S. S., Physics
HANSCH, T. W., Physics
HARBAUGH, J. W., Geology
HARMAN, W. W., Electrical Engineering
HARRIS, D. J., Economics
HARRIS, S. E., Electrical Engineering
HARRISON, D. C., Medicine
HARRISON, J. M., Business
HARRISON, W. A., Applied Physics
HARVEY, V. A., Religious Studies
HASTORF, A. H., III, Psychology
HAUSMAN, W., Industrial Engineering
HAWLEY, N. S., Mathematics
HEINRICHS, W. L., Gynaecology and Obstetrics
HELLIWELL, R. A., Electrical Engineering
HERRING, W. C., Applied Physics
HERRIOT, J. G., Computer Science
HERRMANN, G., Applied Mechanics and Civil Engineering
HERZENBERG, L. A., Genetics
HESS, R. D., Child Education

HESTER, R. M., French
HICKMAN, B. G., Economics
HILLIER, F. S., Operations Research
HINTIKKA, K. J. J., Philosophy
HOFSTADTER, R., Physics
HOGAN, W. W., Engineering-Economics
HOGNESS, D. S., Biochemistry
HOLLISTER, L. E., Medicine
HOLM, R. H., Chemistry
HOLM, R. W., Biology
HOLMAN, H. R., Medicine
HORN, R. A., Political Science
HORNGREN, C. T., Accounting (G.S.B.)
HOROWITZ, L., Psychology
HORSLEY, I., Music
HOULE, G. L., Music
HOWARD, D. R., English
HOWARD, R. A., Engineering—Economic Systems
HOWELL, J. E., Economics, Graduate School of Business
HSU, E. Y., Civil Engineering
HUGGINS, R. A., Materials Science
HULTENG, J. L., Communication
HULTGREN, H. N., Medicine
HUTCHINSON, E., Chemistry
IGLEHART, D. L., Operations Research
IKE, N., Political Science
INKELES, A., Education
IRESON, W. G., Industrial Engineering
JACOBSTEIN, J. M., Law Librarian and Professor of Law
JAEDICKE, R. K., Accounting (G.S.B.)
JAHNS, R. H., Geology
JAMESON, M. H., Classics
JARDETZKY, O., Pharmacology
JOHNS, M. V., Jr., Statistics
JOHNSON, W. S., Chemistry
JOHNSTON, B. F. Food Research Institute
JOHNSTON, J. P., Mechanical Engineering
JONES, H. H., Radiology
JOSLING, T. E., Food Research Institute
JUILLAND, A. G., French
KAHN, M. S., Art
KAILATH, T., Electrical Engineering
KAISER, A. D., Biochemistry
KALLMAN, R. F., Radiology
KALMAN, S. M., Pharmacology
KANE, T. R., Applied Mechanics and Mechanical Engineering
KAPLAN, H. S., Medicine
KAPLAN, J., Law
KARAMCHETI, K., Aeronautics and Astronautics
KARLIN, S., Mathematics
KATCHADOURIAN, H. A., Psychiatry
KAYS, W. M., Mechanical Engineering
KEMPSON, R. L., Pathology
KENNEDY, D., Human Biology
KEOHANE, N., Political Science
KEOHANE, R. O., Political Science
KINO, G. S., Electrical Engineering
KIRK, D., Population Studies
KLINE, S. J., Mechanical Engineering
KNUTH, D. E., Computer Science
KOPELL, B., Psychiatry
KORN, D., Pathology
KORNBERG, A., Biochemistry
KORNBERG, R. D., Structural Biology
KOVACH, R. L., Geophysics
KREISEL, G., Logic and Mathematics
KRETCHMER, N., Paediatrics
KRIER, J. E., Law
KRISS, J. P., Radiology and Medicine
KRUGER, C. H., Mechanical Engineering
KRUGER, P., Civil Engineering
KRUMBOLTZ, J. D., Education and Psychology
KUHN, W. E., Music and Education
KURZ, M., Economics
LANGMUIR, G. I., History
LARSON, C. P., Anaesthesia
LAU, L. J. Y., Economics
LEAVITT, H. J., Organizational Behavior and Psychology (G.S.B.)

LEE, E. H., Applied Mechanics and Aeronautics and Astronautics
LEHMAN, I. R., Biochemistry
LEIDERMAN, P. H., Psychiatry
LEITH, D. W. G. S., Stanford Linear Accelerator Center
LEVIN, H. M., Education
LEVINE, H., Mathematics
LEVINE, S., Psychology in Psychiatry
LEWIS, J. W., Chinese Politics
LI, V., International Studies
LIEBERMAN, G. J., Statistics and Operations Research
LINDENBERGER, H. S., Humanities
LINVILL, J. G., Electrical Engineering
LINVILL, W. K., Engineering Economic Systems
LIPSET, S. M., Political Science and Sociology
LITTLE, W. A., Physics
LITZENBERGER, R. H., Business
LIU, J. J., Chinese
LOBDELL, F., Art
LOFTIS, J., English
LOHNES, W. F. W., German
LONDON, A. L., Mechanical Engineering
LUENBERGER, D. G., Engineering-Economic Systems
LUETSCHER, J. A., Jr., Medicine
LUTH, W. C., Geology
LUZZATTI, L., Paediatrics
LYMAN, R. W., History
LYON, R. J. P., Earth Sciences
LYONS, C. R., Dramatic Literature
MACOVSKI, A., Electrical Engineering
McCARTHY, J., Computer Science
McCARTY, P. L., Civil Engineering
McCLUSKEY, E. J., Electrical Engineering and Computer Science
McCONNELL, H. M., Chemistry
McDEVITT, H. O., Medicine
McDONALD, J. G., Finance, (G.S.B.)
McGREGOR, J. L., Mathematics
McKIM, R. H., Mechanical Engineering
McKINNON, R. I., Economics
McMAHAN, U. J., Neurobiology
McWHORTER, M. M., Electrical Engineering
MACCOBY, E., Psychology
MADIX, R. J., Chemical Engineering
MAFFLY, R. H., Medicine
MANLEY, J. F., Political Science
MANN, J. K., Law
MANNE, A. S., Economics and Operations Research
MANNING, L. A., Electrical Engineering
MANSOUR, T. E., Pharmacology
MARCH, J. G., Political Science and Sociology
MARK, J. B. D., Surgery
MARSDEN, S. S., Jr., Petroleum Engineering
MARSHALL, H. R., Political Science
MASON, D. M., Chemical Engineering
MASSY, W. F., Business Administration
MAYERS, J., Aeronautical Engineering
MAYHEW, L. B., Education
MAZZE, R. I., Anaesthesia
MEIER, G. M., International Economics Graduate School of Business
MEINDL, J. D., Electrical Engineering
MERIGAN, T. C., Jr., Medicine
MERRYMAN, J. H., Law
MEYER, J. W., Sociology
MEYERHOF, W. E., Physics
MEYERS, C. J., Law
MILGRAM, R. J., Mathematics
MILLER, A. R., Management (G.S.B.)
MILLER, D. C., Art
MILLER, J. R., III, Business Administration
MILLER, R. G., Jr., Statistics
MILLER, W. F., Computer Science
MISCHEL, W., Psychology
MITCHNER, M., Mechanical Engineering
MOFFAT, R. J., Mechanical Engineering
MOMADAY, M. S., English

MOMMSEN, K., German
MONTGOMERY, D. B., Management
MOONEY, H. A., Biology
MOOS, R. H., Psychology in Psychiatry
MORAVCSIK, J. M., Philosophy
MORSE, R. M., History
MOSER, T. C., English
MOSES, L. E., Statistics and Preventive Medicine
MOSHER, H. S., Chemistry
MOZLEY, R. F., Stanford Linear Accelerator Center
MUELLER-VOLMER, K., German
MUTH, R. F., Economics
NAGEL, D. A., Surgery
NANNEY, H. B., Music
NELSEN, T. S., Surgery
NELSON, L. M., Communication
NEWMAN-GORDON, P., French
NICHOLLS, J. G., Physiology
NIVISON, D. S., Chinese and Philosophy
NIX, W. D., Materials Science
NIXON, J. E., Education and Physical Education
NORTH, R. C., Political Science
NORTHWAY, W. H., Radiology and Paediatrics
NOYES, H. P., Stanford Linear Accelerator Center
OBERHELMAN, H. A., Jr., Surgery
OLIVEIRA, N., Art
OLKIN, I., Statistics and Education
ORNSTEIN, D., Mathematics
OSSERMAN, R., Mathematics
OXLEY, G. M., International Business, Graduate School of Business
PAFFENBARGER, R. S., Medicine
PANOFSKY, W. K. H., Stanford Linear Accelerator Center
PANTELL, R. H., Electrical Engineering
PARET, P., History
PARKER, E. B., Communication
PARKER, H. W. Civil Engineering
PARKS, G. A., Mineral Engineering
PARLEE, N. A. D., Extractive Metallurgy
PECORA, R., Chemistry
PERKINS, D. D., Biology
PERL, M. L., Stanford Linear Accelerator Center
PERRY, J., Philosophy
PETERSON, A. M., Electrical Engineering
PHILLIPS, J. H. Jr., Biology
PHILLIPS, R., Mathematics
PITTENDRIGH, C. S. Biology
POLITZER, R. L., Education and Romance Linguistics
PORTERFIELD, J. T. S., Finance, Graduate School of Business
POUND, G. M., Materials Science
PRIBRAM, K. H., Psychiatry and Psychology
PRINCE, D. A., Neurology
PROSSER, E., Dramatic Literature and Criticism
QUATE, C. F., Applied Physics and Electrical Engineering
RABIN, R. L., Law
RAMEY, H. J., Petroleum Engineering
RATNER, L. G., Music
RAUBITSCHEK, A. E., Humanities
RAY, H., Marketing
RAY, P. M., Biology
REAVEN, G. M., Medicine
REBHOLZ, R., English
REGNERY, D. C., Biology
REMINGTON, J. S., Medicine
REMSON, I., Geology
REYNOLDS, C. W., Food Research Institute
REYNOLDS, W. C., Mechanical Engineering
RICHARDS, C. W., Civil Engineering
RICHTER, B., Stanford Linear Accelerator Center
RITSON, D. M., Physics
RIVERS, W. L., Communication
ROBERTSON, C. R., Chemical Engineering

ROBERTSON, W. VAN B., Biochemistry in Paediatrics
ROBIN, E., Medicine and Physiology
ROBINSON, W. S., Medicine
ROGERS, E. M., Communication
ROGGEVEEN, V. J., Civil Engineering
ROSENBERG, N., Economics
ROSENBERG, S. A., Medicine and Radiology
ROSENHAN, D., Law and Psychology
ROSSE, J. N., Economics
ROTH, B., Mechanical Engineering
ROWEN, H. S., Public Management
ROYDEN, H. L., Mathematics
RUBINSTEIN, L. J., Pathology
RUOTOLO, L. P., English
RUSSELL, D. A., Drama
RYAN, L. V., English
SAMELSON, H., Mathematics
SARTORI, G., Political Science
SCHAWLOW, A. L., Physics
SCHIMKE, R. T., Pharmacology and Biology
SCHRADER, H. W., Drama
SCHRIER, S. L., Medicine
SCHUBERT, E. D., Speech and Hearing Sciences
SCHULMAN, I., Paediatrics
SCHWARTZ, H. C., Paediatrics
SCHWARTZ, M., Physics
SCHWERDT, C. E., Medical Microbiology
SCHWETTMAN, H. A., Physics
SCOTT, K. E., Law
SCOTT, W. R., Sociology
SCOWCROFT, R. P., English
SERBEIN, O. N., Jr., Insurance, Graduate School of Business
SHAH, H. C., Civil Engineering
SHARPE, W. F., Finance (G.S.B.)
SHARPLESS, K. B., Chemistry
SHEPARD, R. N., Psychology
SHER, B. D., Law
SHER, R., Mechanical Engineering
SHERBY, O. D., Materials Science
SHOOTER, E. M., Genetics
SHULTZ, G. P., Management
SHUMWAY, N. E., Surgery
SHYNE, J. C., Materials Science
SIEGEL, A. E., Psychology in Psychiatry
SIEGEL, B. J., Anthropology
SIEGMAN, A. E., Electrical Engineering
SIEGMUND, D. O., Statistics
SIMMONS, F. B., Surgery
SIMONE, J. V., Paediatrics
SITGREAVES, B. R., Education
SIU, Y.-T., Mathematics
SKINNER, G. W., Anthropology
SMITH, K. C., Radiology
SMITH, L. C., Music
SMITH, R. J., Electrical Engineering
SNOW, R. E., Education
SOLOMON, E., Finance, Graduate School of Business
SOLOMON, H., Statistics and Education
SPICER, W. E., Electrical Engineering and Materials Science
SPITZ, L. W., History
SPREITER, J. R., Applied Mechanics, Aeronautics, Astronautics
SPUDICH, J. A., Structural Biology
SRINIVASAN, V., G.S.B.
STAMEY, T. A., Surgery
STANSKY, P. D. L., History
STARK, G. R., Biochemistry
STARRETT, D. A., Economics
STEELE, C. R., Aeronautics and Astronautics
STEIN, C. M., Statistics
STEVENSON, D. A., Materials Science
STOCKER, B. A. D., Medical Microbiology
STONE, W. H., English
STREET, R. L., Civil Engineering
STRYER, L., Cell Biology
STURROCK, P. A., Engineering Science and Applied Physics
SULLIVAN, D. M., Oriental Art
SUNSHINE, P., Paediatrics

SUPPES, P., Philosophy, Statistics and Education
SUSSKIND, L., Physics
TAUBE, H., Chemistry
TAYLOR, R. E., Stanford Linear Accelerator Center
TEXTOR, R. B., Education and Anthropology
THOMAS, E. A. C., Psychology
THOMAS, J. H., Biology
THOMPSON, D. A., Industrial Engineering
THOMPSON, G. A., Geophysics
THORESEN, C. E., Education
TILLER, W. A., Materials Science
TRAUGOTT, E. C., Linguistics and English
TRIMPI, W. W., English
TRISKA, J. F., Political Science
TUTTLE, D. F. Jr., Electrical Engineering
TYACK, D. B., Education
UEDA, M., Japanese and Comparative Literature
URMSON, J. O., Philosophy
UELAND, K., Gynaecology and Obstetrics
VAN ANDEL, T. H., Geology
VAN CAMPEN, J. A., Slavic Languages
VAN DYKE, M. D., Aeronautics and Astronautics
VAN HORNE, J. C., Finance (G.S.B.)
VAN SLYKE, L. P., History
VAN TAMELEN, E. E., Chemistry
VEINOTT, A. F., Jr., Operations Research
VILLARD, O. G., Jr., Electrical Engineering
VINCENTI, W. G., Aeronautics and Astronautics
VOSTI, K. L., Medicine
VUCINICH, W. S., History
WAGONER, R. V., Physics
WALD, M. S., Law
WALECKA, J. D., Physics
WARD, R. E., Political Science
WATERMAN, A. T., Jr., Electrical Engineering
WATT, I. P., English
WEAVER, W., Jr., Civil Engineering
WEBB, E. J., Organizational Behaviour (G.S.B.)
WEINSTEIN, L., French
WEISSBLUTH, M., Applied Physics
WESSELLS, N. K., Biology
WHITE, R. L., Electrical Engineering and Materials Science
WIDROW, B., Electrical Engineering
WILDE, D. J., Chemical Engineering
WILKINSON, J. W., Computer Science
WILLIAMS, H. R., Law
WILSON, J. L., Surgery
WILSON, R. B., Decision Sciences (G.S.B.)
WIRTH, J. D., History
WOJCICKI, S. G., Physics
WOODWARD, D. W., Biology
WRIGHT, G., History
WYNTER, S., Spanish and Portuguese
YALOM, I. D., Psychiatry
YANOFSKY, C., Biology
YAU, S. T., Mathematics
YEARIAN, M. R., Physics
YOTOPOULOS, P. A., Food Research Institute
ZARE, R. N., Chemistry
ZATZ, L. M., Radiology
ZBORALSKE, F. F., Radiology
ZELDITCH, M., Jr., Sociology
ZIMBARDO, P. G., Psychology

## U.S. INTERNATIONAL UNIVERSITY

10455 POMERADO ROAD, SAN DIEGO, CALIFORNIA 92131
Telephone: (714) 271-4300.

Founded 1952.

Private university.

*President:* WILLIAM C. RUST, PH.D.

*Vice-Presidents:* WAYNE L. ALLISON, PH.D., RANDALL C. PHILLIPS, D.D.

INTERNATIONAL CAMPUSES:

**Universidad Internacional de Mexico:** Georgia 123, Col. Napoles, Mexico 18, D.F.

**International University—Europe:** The Avenue, Bushey, Watford, WD2 2LN, England.

**International University—Africa:** Nairobi, Kenya; Dir. VIRGIL BERGMAN.

## U.S. NAVAL POSTGRADUATE SCHOOL

MONTEREY, CALIFORNIA 93940

Founded 1909.

Courses in Engineering (Mechanical, Electrical and Aeronautical), Science (Oceanography, Meteorology, Physics, Computer Science), Policy Science (Management Specializations), Operationally Oriented Programs (Antisubmarine Warfare, Command, Control and Communications, Intelligence, Electronic Warfare Systems).

*Superintendent:* Rear-Admiral JOHN J. EKELUND.
*Chief Faculty Administrative Officer:* Dr. JACK R. BORSTING.
*Librarian:* PAUL SPINKS.

Library of 558,000 vols. (including microform).

Number of teachers: 250.
Number of students: 1,200.

Publications: *Catalogue* (biennial), *This Week in the Library* (weekly), *Library Periodical Holdings List* (annually), *Technical Reports, Research Papers* (irregular).

## UNIVERSITY OF CALIFORNIA

Founded 1868.

System-wide Administrative Offices: University Hall, Berkeley, California 94720. Campuses at Berkeley, Davis, Irvine, Los Angeles, Riverside, San Diego, San Francisco, Santa Barbara, and Santa Cruz.

UNIVERSITY-WIDE OFFICERS:
*President:* DAVID S. SAXON, PH.D.
*Vice-President:* WILLIAM B. FRETTER, PH.D.
*Academic Vice-President:* JAMES S. ALBERTSON (acting).
*Vice-President (Agricultural Sciences):* J. B. KENDRICK, Jr., PH.D.
*Vice-President (Academic and Staff Personnel Relations):* ARCHIE KLEINGARTNER, PH.D.
*Vice-President (Financial and Business Management):* BALDWIN G. LAMSON, M.D.

OFFICERS OF THE REGENTS:
*General Counsel of the Regents:* DONALD L. REIDHAAR, LL.D.

## UNIVERSITIES AND COLLEGES—CALIFORNIA (UNIVERSITY OF) — U.S.A.

*Secretary of the Regents:* Marjorie J Woolman.
*Treasurer of the Regents:* Herbert M. Gordon, b.a.
Library: see Libraries.
Number of teachers: c. 6,253.
Number of students: c. 135,000.

### University of California, Berkeley
Berkeley, California 94720.
Telephone: (415) 642-2331.
Established 1872.
*Chancellor:* I. M. Heyman, b.a., ll.b.
*Vice-Chancellor (Administration):* R. F. Kerley, b.s.
*Provosts:* G. J. Maslach, R. B. Park.
*University Librarian:* J. A. Rosenthal.
Number of teachers: 3,100.
Number of students: 28,500.

#### Deans:
*Graduate Division:* Robert R. Brown (acting).
*College of Environmental Design:* Richard Bender.
*College of Chemistry:* Norman E. Phillips.
*College of Engineering:* E. S. Kuh, ph.d.
*College of Letters and Science:* R. B. Park, ph.d.
*College of Natural Resources:* David Schlegel (acting).
*School of Business Administration:* Earl Cheit.
*School of Education:* Robert B. Ruddell (acting).
*School of Journalism:* Edwin R. Bayley.
*School of Law:* Sanford S. Kadish, ph.d.
*School of Library and Information Studies:* Michael K. Buckland.
*School of Optometry:* Irving Fatt (acting).
*School of Public Health:* Warren Winkelstein, Jr., m.d.
*Graduate School of Public Policy:* Allan P. Sindler.
*School of Social Welfare:* Harry Specht.

#### Chairmen of Departments:
*College of Letters and Science:*
 Aerospace Studies: Reagan H. Beane.
 Afro-American Studies: W. Banks.
 Anthropology: (vacant).
 Astronomy: John Gaustad.
 Bacteriology and Immunology: Leon Wofsy.
 Biochemistry: J. Rabinowitz.
 Biology: William A. Jensen, ph.d.
 Botany: O. R. Collins.
 Classics: (vacant).
 Comparative Literature: L. Janette Richardson, ph.d.
 Dramatic Art: W. I. Oliver.
 Economics: Bent Hansen, ph.d.
 English: Ralph W. Rader.
 French: Leo Bersani, ph.d.
 Geography: James J. Parsons, ph.d.
 Geology and Geophysics: Thomas V. McEvilly.
 German: Hinrich C. Seeba, dr.phil.
 History: Robert J. Brentano.
 History of Art: R. Middlekaufe.
 Italian: Arnolfo B. Ferruolo.
 Linguistics: Karl E. Zimmer, ph.d.
 Mathematics: S. Kobayashi.
 Medical Physics: A. Bearden.
 Military Science: Monte Ray Bullard.
 Molecular Biology: H. Echols.
 Music: L. Moe.
 Naval Science: Frank T. Watkins.
 Near Eastern Studies: Wolfgang J. Heimpel, ph.d.
 Oriental Languages: Lewis Lancaster.
 Palaeontology: William B. N. Berry.
 Philosophy: B. Stroud.
 Physical Education: Mary Lou Norrie, ph.d.
 Physics: J. D. Jackson.
 Physiology-Anatomy: P. Timiras.
 Political Science: Chalmers Johnson.
 Practice of Art: Jerrold Ballaine, m.r.a.
 Psychology: Stephen E. Glickman, ph.d.
 Rhetoric: William J. Brandt.
 Scandinavian: J. Lindow.
 Slavic Languages and Literatures: R. Hughes.
 Sociology: R. Bellah.
 South and Southeast Asian Languages and Literature: Barend A. Van Nooten, ph.d.
 Spanish and Portuguese: A. Askins.
 Special Programs Division: W. B. Slottman.
 Statistics: Peter Bickel.
 Zoology: P. Licht.

*College of Chemistry:*
 Chemical Engineering: C. Judson King, sc.d.
 Chemistry: Joseph Cerny.
 Education: G. Clifford.

*College of Engineering:*
 Civil Engineering: Carl L. Monismith.
 Hydraulic and Sanitary Engineering: Jerome F. Thomas, ph.d.
 Structural Engineering and Structural Mechanics: Milos Polivka.
 Transportation Engineering: K. Crandall.
 Electrical Engineering and Computer Sciences: D. J. Sakrison.
 Industrial Engineering and Operations Research: William S. Jewell.
 Materials Science and Engineering: R. H. Blagg.
 Mechanical Engineering: Chang-Lin Tien, ph.d.
 Naval Architecture: John V. Wehausen, ph.d.
 Nuclear Engineering: Thomas H. Pigford, ph.d.

*College of Environmental Design:*
 Architecture: Joseph Esherick, b.arch.
 City and Regional Planning: A. Jacobs.
 Landscape Architecture: R. Tetlow.
 Ethnic Studies: Ronald Takaki.

*College of Natural Resources:*
 Conservation and Resource Studies: Paul Gersper.
 Forestry and Resource Management: D. E. Teegarden.
 Agricultural and Resource Economics: James N. Boles, ph.d.
 Cell Physiology: B. Buchanan.
 Entomological Sciences: Evert I. Schlinger, ph.d.
 Forestry and Conservation: D. E. Teegarden.
 Genetics: Seymour Fogel, ph.d.
 Nutritional Sciences: Doris Calloway.
 Plant Pathology: A. R. Weinhold.
 Soils and Plant Nutrition: K. Babcock.

*School of Public Health:*
 Biomedical and Environmental Health Sciences: Leonard Syme.
 Social Administrative Health Services: R. Bailey.

*University Extension:* Milton R. Stern.

### University of California, Davis
Davis, California 95616
Established 1905.
*Chancellor:* J. H. Meyer, ph.d.
*Executive Vice-Chancellor:* E. W. Learn, ph.d.
*Vice-Chancellor (Academic Affairs):* L. H. Mayhew, ph.d.
*Vice-Chancellor (Student Affairs):* T. B. Dutton, ph.d.
*Vice-Chancellor (Business and Finance):* J. F. Sullivan, ph.d.
*Registrar:* M. C. Skinner, ed.d.
*Librarian:* B. Kreissman, ph.d.
Number of students: 18,887.

#### Deans:
*College of Agriculture and Environmental Sciences:* C. E. Hess, ph.d.
*College of Letters and Science:* L. J. Andrews, ph.d.
*College of Engineering:* J. D. Kemper, ph.d.
*School of Law:* F. Bartosic, l.l.m.
*School of Medicine:* H. E. Williams, m.d.
*School of Veterinary Medicine:* W. R. Pritchard, d.v.m., ph.d., j.d.
*Graduate Division:* A. G. Marr, ph.d.

### University of California, Irvine
Irvine, California 92717
Telephone: (714) 833-5011.
Opened 1965.
State control; three quarter terms.
*Chancellor:* Daniel G. Aldrich, Jr., ph.d.
*Executive Vice-Chancellor:* James L. McGaugh.
*Vice-Chancellor for Academic Affairs:* William J. Lillyman.
*Vice-Chancellor (Student Affairs):* John M. Whiteley.

Vice-Chancellor (Business and Finance): LEON SCHWARTZ.
University Librarian: CALVIN BOYER.

Number of teachers: 580.
Number of students: 10,200 full-time.

Publications: *UCI General Catalogue*†, *UCI Journal*† (newspaper), *Humanities Review*†, and numerous student publications.

### DEANS:

School of:
  Biological Sciences: NORMAN M. WEINBERGER (acting).
  Fine Arts: WILLIAM HOLMES (acting).
  Humanities: HAROLD TOLIVER (acting).
  Physical Sciences: MYRON BANDER.
  Social Sciences: LINTON C. FREEMAN.
  Engineering: A. V. STUBBERUD.
Graduate School of Management: LYMAN W. PORTER.
College of Medicine: STANLEY VAN DEN NOORT.
Teacher Education: RITA W. PETERSON.
Information and Computer Science: JULIAN FELDMAN.
Program in Social Ecology: JOSEPH DIMENTO.
Graduate Studies and Research: JAIME RODRIGUEZ.
Undergraduate Studies: GUY J. SIRCELLO.

### PROFESSORS:

ALDRICH, DANIEL G., Jr., Biological Sciences
ANGRESS, RUTH, PH.D., German
ARDITTI, J., PH.D., Biological Sciences
ARMENTROUT, S. A., M.D., Medicine
ARONOWITZ, S., PH.D., Comparative Culture and Social Science
ARQUILLA, E. R., M.D., PH.D., Pathology
ARTHUR, P. D., PH.D., Mechanical Engineering
ATSATT, P. R., PH.D., Ecology and Evolutionary Biology
BALL, E. A., PH.D., Developmental and Cell Biology
BANDER, M., PH.D., Physics
BARNES, C. W., Jr., PH.D., Electrical Engineering
BARNEY, S. A., English and Comparative Literature
BARRUTIA, R., Spanish and Portuguese
BARTLETT, R. H., M.D., Surgery
BATCHELDER, W., PH.D., Psychology
BENFORD, G. A., Physics
BERK, J. E., M.D., Medicine
BERKOWITZ, L. B., Classics
BERNS, M. W., PH.D., Biological Sciences
BERSHAD, N. J., PH.D., Electrical Engineering
BINDER, A., PH.D., Social Ecology
BIRNBAUM, I., PH.D., Psychology
BORK, A. M., PH.D., Physics
BOSTICK, W. L., M.D., Pathology
BOUGHEY, A. S., PH.D., Social Ecology
BRANT, D. A., PH.D., Chemistry
BRAUNSTEIN, M. L., PH.D., Psychology
BREBBIA, C., PH.D., Engineering
BROWN, G. W., PH.D., Administration
BROWN, H. O., English and Comparative Literature
BRUCE, D. L., M.D., Anaesthesiology
BRUNNER, T. F., PH.D., Classics
BRYANT, P. J., PH.D., Biological Sciences

BUTLER, E. W., Social Sciences
CALDERWOOD, J. L., English and Comparative Literature
CALL, J. D., M.D., Psychiatry and Human Behaviour
CAMPBELL, B., PH.D., Physiology
CAMPBELL, R. D., PH.D., Biology
CANCIAN, F., PH.D., Anthropology
CANNONITO, F. B., PH.D., Mathematics
CASERIO, MAJORIE C., Chemistry
CASSUTO, A., Music
CHEN, H. H., Physics
CLECAK, P., PH.D., Comparative Culture and Social Science
COHEN, R. S., D.F.A., Drama
COLACLIDES, P., PH.D., Classics
COLBY, B. N., Social Sciences
CONNOLLY, J. E., M.D., Surgery
CORNSWEET, T. N., PH.D., Sociology
COTMAN, C., PH.D., Psychobiology
CROCKER, T. T., Community and Environmental Medicine
CULLEN, B. F., M.D., Anaesthesiology
CUNNINGHAM, D. D., PH.D., Medical Microbiology, Molecular Biology and Biochemistry
DARLING, D. A., PH.D., Mathematics
DAVIS, R. H., PH.D., Biology
DEARDEN, L. C., PH.D., Anatomy and Radiology
DELAP, T., Studio Art
DEMALLAC-SAUZIER, G., PH.D., Russian
DIGGINS, J. P., PH.D., History
DISAIA, P., M.D., Obstetrics and Gynaecology
DIXON, P. S., PH.D., Population and Environmental Biology
DOEDENS, R. J., Chemistry
DONATO, E., French/Italian
DONOGHUE, W. F., PH.D., Mathematics
DUBIN, R., PH.D., Social Sciences, Administration
DURE-SMITH, P., M.D., Radiology
ECKSTEIN, H. H., Social Sciences
EKLOF, P. C., Mathematics
FAGIN, H., Administration
FELDMAN, J., Psychology and Information Science
FIELDING, G. F., PH.D., Social Science and Administration
FLINK, J., PH.D., Comparative Culture
FOLTZ, E. L., M.D., Surgery
FREEMAN, F., PH.D., Chemistry
FREEMAN, L. C., Social Sciences
FREEMAN, R. K., M.D., Obstetrics and Gynaecology
FRIED, M. D., PH.D., Mathematics
FRIOU, G. U., M.D., Medicine
FROMAN, L. A., Jr., PH.D., Social Sciences
FURNAS, D. W., M.D., Surgery
GAMO, H., PH.D., Electrical Engineering
GARRISON, E. C., PH.D., Drama
GAZZANIGA, A. B., M.D., Surgery
GEIS, G. L., Social Ecology
GIOLLI, R. A., PH.D., Psychobiology and Anatomy
GLOBUS, G. G., M.D., Psychiatry
GOTTSCHALK, L. A., M.D., Psychiatry and Human Behaviour
GRAHAM, J. H., M.D., Medicine
GRANGER, G. A., PH.D., Immunology
GREENBERGER, ELLEN, PH.D., Social Ecology
GUINN, V. P., PH.D., Chemistry
GWINUP, G., M.D., Medicine
HALL, O., M.F.A., English and Comparative Literature
HALL, P. F., Functional Correlates, Gynaecology and Obstetrics
HATFIELD, G. W., PH.D., Biology
HEHRE, W. J., Chemistry
HEINEY, D. W., PH.D., Comparative Literature
HENRY, W. L., M.D., Medicine
HODGE, H. C., PH.D., Community and Environmental Medicine

HOLLADAY, J. C., PH.D., Mathematics
HOLLANDER, D., M.D., Medicine
HOLMES, W. C., Music
HUBERT, J. D., PH.D., French
HUBERT, R. R., PH.D., French and Comparative Literature
HUSTZI, J. B., Music
HUXTABLE, R. F., M.D., Paediatrics
HYDE, L., M.D., Pulmonary Medicine
INDOW, T., Social Sciences
IRVINE, S. R., Ophthalmology
ISER, W., PH.D., English
ISERI, L. T., M.D., Medicine
JOHNSTON, J., PH.D., Economics
JONES, J., PH.D., Radiological Sciences
JONES, J. P., M.F.A., Studio Art
JORGENSEN, J. G., Comparative Culture
JOSEPHSON, R. K., PH.D., Biological Sciences and Psychobiology
JUBERG, R. K., PH.D., Mathematics
KALISCH, G. K., PH.D., Mathematics
KAPLAN, H. S., Pathology
KARAMARDIAN, K., PH.D., Mathematics and Administration
KASSOUF, S. T., PH.D., Economics
KATZ, J., M.D., Paediatrics
KEY, M. R., PH.D., Linguistics and Humanities
KRAEMER, K. L., PH.D., Administration and Public Policy Research Organization
KRASSNER, S. M., SC.D., Medical Microbiology
KRIEGER, M., PH.D., English and Comparative Literature
KUNZE, R. A., PH.D., Mathematics
LAMBERT, J. F., PH.D., Philosophy
LAVE, C. A., Social Sciences
LEE, E. K. C., Chemistry
LEHNERT, H., PH.D., German
LENHOFF, H. M., Development and Cell Biology
LENTRICCIA, F., PH.D., English
LEOPOLD, I. H., M.D., D.SC., Surgery
LILLYMAN, W. J., PH.D., German
LORING, E., Fine Arts
LUDWIG, F. C., M.D., Pathology
LYNCH, G. S., PH.D., Psychobiology
McCLURE, J. H., M.D., Obstetrics and Gynaecology
McCULLOCH, S. C., PH.D., History
McGAUGH, J. L., PH.D., Psychobiology
McGUIRE, J. W., PH.D., Administration
McIVER, R. T., Chemistry
McLAUGHLIN, C. S., PH.D., Biochemistry
McMICHAEL, J., PH.D., English
MACMILLEN, R. E., Ecology and Evolutionary Biology
MARADUDIN, A. A., PH.D., Physics
MARGOLIS, J., PH.D., Economics
MARGULIES, N., Administration
MARTIN, D. C., M.D., Surgery
MARTIN, J. H., PH.D., English and Comparative Literature
MAYER, M. E., PH.D., Physics
MEHRA, J., Physics
MELDEN, A. I., PH.D., Philosophy
MENTON, S., PH.D., Spanish and Portuguese
METZGER, D. G., Social Sciences
MEYER, H. C., PH.D., History
MICHELSON, W. M., Social Ecology
MILLER, D. R., M.D., Surgery
MILLS, D. L., PH.D., Physics
MILNE, E., M.B., CH.B., F.F.R., Radiological Sciences
MOLDAVE, K., PH.D., Biochemistry
MONTGOMERY, R. L., PH.D., English and Comparative Literature
MOOD, A. M., PH.D., Administration
MOORE, H. W., Chemistry
MORAN, E. M., M.D., Paediatrics
MOSIER, H. D., M.D., Paediatrics
MOYED, H. S., M.D., Microbiology
MULLIGAN, J. H., PH.D., Electrical Engineering
NAGEL, B., PH.D., German

NARENS, L. E., Social Sciences
NELSON, T. L., M.D., Paediatrics
NICOLSON, G., PH.D., Biology
NOBLE, E., Psychiatry and Human Behaviour
ODEGARD, P. S., Music
OLIN, S., PH.D., History
ORJUELA, H., PH.D., Spanish
OVERMAN, L. E., Chemistry
PALLEY, J., PH.D., Spanish
PARKER, W. H., PH.D., Physics
PARSONS, T. D., Philosophy
PATTISON, E. M., M.D., Psychiatry
PETERS, R. L., PH.D., English and Comparative Literature
PIKE, N. C., PH.D., Philosophy
PORTER, L. W., PH.D., Administration
PORTER, R. W., Surgery
POSTER, M. S., PH.D., History
PRIBRAM, H. W., M.B., CH.B., Radiology
QUINLIVAN, L. G., M.D., Obstetrics and Gynaecology
REARDON, B. P., PH.D., Classics
RECKER, W. W., PH.D., Engineering
REGOSIN, R. L., PH.D., French
REINES, F., PH.D., Physics
RESNIKOFF, H. L., PH.D., Mathematics
ROBERTS, G. O., PH.D., Sociology and Comparative Culture
ROMNEY, A. K., PH.D., Social Sciences
ROSTOKER, N., Physics
ROWLAND, F. S., PH.D., Chemistry
RUSSO, B., Mathematics
RYAN, M. P., History
RYNN, N., PH.D., Engineering and Physics
SAINE, T. P., PH.D., German
SANDMAN, C. A., Psychiatry and Psychobiology
SANTAS, G. X., PH.D., Philosophy
SASSIN, J. F., M.D., Neurology, Psychobiology
SAUNDERS, R. M., PH.D., Electrical Engineering
SCHEINBERG, S., PH.D., Mathematics
SCHERFIG, J., PH.D., Civil and Environmental Engineering
SCHNEIDERMAN, H. A., Development and Cell Biology
SCHULTZ, J., PH.D., Physics
SHAW, G. L., PH.D., Physics
SHEPHERD, R., Engineering
SIMON, M., ED.D., English and Education
SIRCELLO, G., PH.D., Philosophy
SKLANSKY, J., ENG.SC.D., Electrical Engineering
SLIM, H. C., Music
SPEAR, G. S., M.D., Pathology
SPERLING, D. R., M.D., Paediatrics, Radiology
STARR, A., M.D., Psychobiology and Neurology
STEIN, J. J., Radiological Sciences
STEIN, L., Medical Pharmacology and Therapeutics
STEMMER, E. A., M.D., Surgery
STEPHENS, G. C., PH.D., Biology
STERNER, J. H., Community and Environmental Medicine
STUBBERUD, A. R., Engineering
SWETT, J. E., PH.D., Anatomy
SYPHERD, P. S., Medical Microbiology, Molecular Biology and Biochemistry
TAFT, R. W. PH.D., Chemistry
TASHJIAN, D. L., PH.D., Comparative Culture
TEWARI, K. K., PH.D., Biochemistry
THOMAS, O. P., PH.D., Linguistics and Education
THOMPSON, R. F., PH.D., Psychobiology
THORP, E. O., PH.D., Mathematics
THRUPP, L. D., M.D., Infectious Diseases
TILLES, J. G., M.D., Infectious Diseases
TOBIS, J. S., M.D., Physical Medicine and Rehabilitation
TOLIVER, H., PH.D., English and Comparative Literature
TONGE, F. Jr., PH.D., Information and Computer Science
TRIPLETT, R., Drama
TUCKER, H. G., PH.D., Mathematics
TURNER, J. H., Social Sciences
UHR, C. G., Administration
USHIODA, S., Physics
VALENTA, L. J. V., PH.D., Endocrinology
VAN DEN NOORT, S., Medicine
VAN HOVEN, G., Physics
VERMUND, H., M.D., Radiological Sciences
VERZEANO, M. L., PH.D., Psychobiology
VILLEGAS, J., PH.D., Spanish and Portuguese
VINAS, D. B., Spanish
VOLK, B. W., M.D., Pathology
WALLIS, R. F., PH.D., Physics
WALTER, H., Physiology
WARNER, R. C., PH.D., Biochemistry
WATT, W. C., PH.D., Social Science
WATSON, J. D., Microbiology and Biological Sciences
WEINBERGER, N. M., PH.D., Psychobiology
WEINSTEIN, G., Medicine
WERNER, C., Social Sciences
WEXLER, K. N., PH.D., Psychology
WHALEN, R. E., PH.D., Psychobiology
WHIPPLE, G. H., M.D., Cardiology
WHITE, D. R., Social Sciences
WHITE, G. T. PH.D., History
WHITE, J. L., Programme in Comparative Culture
WHITE, S. H., PH.D., Physiology, Biology
WHITELEY, J. M., Programme in Social Ecology
WHITLEY, R. J., Mathematics
WOLFSBERG., M, PH.D., Chemistry
WOODBURNE, M. O., Physical Sciences
WRIGHT, C. P., M.F.A., English
WULFF, D. L., PH.D., Biochemistry
YEH, J. J., PH.D., Mathematics
YELLOTT, J. I., Jr., Social Sciences

# University of California, Los Angeles (UCLA)

LOS ANGELES, CALIFORNIA 90024
Telephone: (213) 825-4321.
Established 1919.

*Chancellor:* CHARLES E. YOUNG, PH.D.
*Executive Vice-Chancellor:* WILLIAM D. SCHAEFER, PH.D.
*Vice-Chancellor (Administration):* J. W. HOBSON, M.A.
*Vice-Chancellor (Academic):* C. Z. WILSON, PH.D
*Vice-Chancellor (Student Affairs):* W. C. DOBY, M.A., ED.D.
*Vice-Chancellor (Faculty Relations):* H. W. HOROWITZ, LL.B., S.J.D.
*Vice-Chancellor (Institutional Relations):* ELWIN V. SVENSON.
*Librarian:* R. SHANK, D.L.S.
*Registrar:* S. CHIN, M.B.A.

Number of teachers: 3,100.
Number of students: 30,180.

### DEANS:

*School of Architecture and Urban Planning:* H. S. PERLOFF, PH.D.
*College of Letters and Science:* E. J. WEBER, M.LITT.
*School of Engineering and Applied Science:* R. O'NEILL, PH.D.
*College of Fine Arts:* R. GRAY, M.F.A.
*Graduate School of Management:* J. C. LAFORCE, PH.D.
*School of Dentistry:* J. R. HOOLEY, D.D.S.
*School of Education:* J. I. GOODLAD, PH.D.
*School of Law:* W. D. WARREN, J.S.D.
*Graduate School of Library and Information Science:* R. H. HAYES, PH.D.
*School of Medicine:* S. M. MELLINKOFF, M.D.
*School of Nursing:* M. E. RERES, ED.D.
*School of Public Health:* ROGER DETELS, M.D., M.S.
*School of Social Welfare:* M. F. CONNERY, D.S.W.
*Graduate Division:* VICTORIA A. FROMKIN, PH.D.
*Students:* (vacant).

### PROFESSORS:

*Aerospace Studies:*
BRENNAN, W. F., M.S.

*Anatomy:*
BOK, P. D., PH.D.
BUCHWALD, N. A., PH.D.
CLEMENTE, CARMINE D., PH.D
COOPER, E. L., PH.D.
ELDRED, E., M.D.
GORSKI, R. A., PH.D.
KRUGER, L., PH.D.
MAXWELL, D. S., PH.D.
MURPHY, F. D., M.D.
PEASE, D. C., PH.D.
SAWYER, C. H., PH.D.
SCHEIBEL, A. B., M.D.
SCHLAG, J., M.D.
SEGUNDO, J. P., M.D.
SILVA, G. D., F.D.S., M.R.C.S., L.R.C.P.
TOWERS, B., M.R.C.S., L.R.C.P.
YOUNG, R. W., PH.D.

*Anaesthesiology:*
BAUER, R. O., M.D.
BELLVILLE, J. W., M.D.
KATZ, R. L., M.D.
LEE, C. M., M.D.
PATTERSON, R. W., M.D.
RUBINSTEIN, E. H., M.D., PH.D.
SULLIVAN, S. F., M.D.
WALTS, L. F., M.D.

*Anthropology:*
DONNAN, C. B., PH.D.
HILL, J. N., PH.D.
MAQUET, J., PH.D.
MEIGHAN, C. W., PH.D.
MOERMAN, M., PH.D.
NICHOLSON, H. B., PH.D.
OSWALT, W. H., PH.D.
WILBERT, J., PH.D.
WILLIAMS, B. J., PH.D.

*Architecture and Urban Planning:*
ADELSON, M., PH.D.
ARONI, S., PH.D.
BURNS, L. S., PH.D.
FRIEDMANN, J., PH.D.
GIVONI, B., PH.D.
KAMNITZER, P., M.ARCH., M.S.
MARRIS, P. H., B.A.
MILNE, M. A., M.ARCH.
MITCHELL, W. J., M.E.D.
MOORE, C. W., PH.D.
PERLOFF, H. S., PH.D.
SCHULITZ, H. C., M.A.D.
SOJA, E. W., PH.D.
STEA, D., PH.D.
VREELAND, T. R., Jr., M.ARCH.
WACHS, M., PH.D.

*Art:*
AMATO, S., B.F.A.
BLOCH, F. M., PH.D.
BOIME, A., PH.D.
BRICE, W. J., M.A.
BROWN, R. B., M.A.

Carter, J. B., M.A.
Downey, S. B., PH.D.
Elgart, E. J., M.F.A.
Heinecken, R., M.A.
**Jennings, T.**, M.A.
Kester, J. B., M.A.
Mihich, V.
Mullican, A. L.
Neuhart, J. A., A.A.
**Nunes, G. M.**, M.A.
Pedretti, C. N., M.A.
**Stussy, J.**, M.F.A.
Werckmeister, O. K., PH.D.

*Astronomy:*
**Abell, G. O.**, PH.D.
Aller, L. H., PH.D.
Coroniti, F., PH.D.
Epps, H., PH.D.
Ford, H. C., PH.D.
Plavec, M. M., D.SC.
Ulrich, R. K., PH.D.

*Atmospheric Sciences:*
Arakawa, A., D.SC.
Edinger, J. G., PH.D.
Pruppacher, H. R., PH.D.
Siscoe, G. L., PH.D.
Thorne, R. M., PH.D.
Venkateswaran, S. V., PH.D
Wurtele, M. G., PH.D.
Yanai, M., D.SC.

*Biological Chemistry:*
Delange, R. J., PH.D.
Fulco, A. J., PH.D.
Glitz, D. G., PH.D.
**Harary, I.**, PH.D.
Mead, J. F., PH.D.
Pierce, J. G., PH.D.
Popjak, G. J., D.SC., M.D.
Roberts, S., PH.D.
Sigman, D. S., PH.D.
Slater, R. B., PH.D.
Zabin, I., PH.D.

*Biology:*
Barber, A. A., PH.D.
Bartholomew, G. A., PH.D.
Cascarano, J., PH.D.
Chapman, D. J., PH.D.
Clark, W. R., PH.D.
Cody, M. L., PH.D.
Collias, N. E., PH.D.
Ebersold, W. T., PH.D.
Eckert, R. O., PH.D.
Edney, E. B., PH.D.
Engelmann, F., PH.D.
Fessler, J. H., PH.D.
Gordon, M. S., PH.D.
Gorman, G. C., PH.D.
Howell, T. R., PH.D.
James, T. W., PH.D.
Kavanau, J. L., PH.D.
Lake, J. A., PH.D.
Laties, G. G., PH.D.
Lewis, F. H., PH.D.
Lunt, O. R., PH.D.
MacInnis, A. J., PH.D.
Muscatine, L., PH.D.
Nobel, P. S., PH.D.
Roberts, Clara M., PH.D.
Phinney, B. O., Jr., PH.D.
Ray, D. S., PH.D.
Salser, W. A., PH.D.
Siegel, R. W., PH.D.
Simpson, L., PH.D.
Thompson, H. J., PH.D.
Thornber, J. P., PH.D.
Vaughn, P. P., PH.D.

*Biomathematics:*
Afifi, A. A., PH.D.
Clark, V. A., PH.D.
**Dixon, W. J.**, PH.D.
Dunn, O. J., PH.D.
Elashoff, R. M., PH.D.
**Jenden, D. J.**, M.B.

**Massey, F. J.**, PH.D.
Newton, C. M., M.D., PH.D.

*Chemistry:*
**Anet, F. A.**, PH.D.
Atkinson, D. E., PH.D.
Baur, M. E., PH.D.
Bayes, K. D., PH.D.
**Boyer, P. D.**, PH.D.
Chapman, O. L., PH.D.
Cram, D. J., PH.D.
Dickerson, R. E., PH.D.
Eisenberg, D. S., PH.D.
**El Sayed, M.**, PH.D.
Farrington, P. S., PH.D.
Foote, C. S., PH.D.
Hawthorne, M. F., PH.D.
Kaesz, H. D., PH.D.
Kivelson, D., PH.D.
Knobler, C. M., PH.D.
McMillan, W. G., Jr., PH.D
McTague, J. P., PH.D.
Nicol, M. F., PH.D.
Reiss, H., PH.D.
Schumaker, V. N., PH.D.
Scott, R. L., PH.D.
Smith, R. A., PH.D.
Stevens, R. V., PH.D.
Trueblood, K. N., PH.D.
Wasson, J. T., PH.D.
**West, C. A.**, PH.D.

*Classics:*
Levine, P., PH.D.
Löfstedt, B. T. M., PH.D.
Puhvel, J., PH.D.

*Dance:*
Gilbert, P. S.,
Scothorn, C. J., M.A.
Snyder, A. F., M.A.
Thomas, E. L., PH.D.

*Dentistry:*
Barber, T. K., D.D.S., M.S.
Bernard, G. W., D.D.S., D.HP.
Beumer, J., D.D.S., M.S.
Caputo, A. A., M.S., PH.D.
Carranza, F. A., Jr., D.D.S., DR.ODONT.
Chaconas, S. J., D.D.S., M.S.
Dixon, A. D., D.D.S., M.D.S., PH.D., D.SC.
**Flocken, J. E.**, D.M.D.
Goldberg, L. J., PH.D., D.D.S.
Grenfell, J. W., D.M.D.
Hargis, H. W., D.D.S.
Junge, D., PH.D.
Kapur, K. K., D.M.D.
Kenney, E. B., D.D.S., M.S.
**Kratochvil, F. J.**, D.D.S.
Lucatorto, F. M., D.D.S.
Richter, W. A., D.M.D., M.S.
Ruhlman, C. D., D.M.D.
Schoen, M. H., D.D.S., DR.P.H.
Silva, G. D., F.D.S., M.R.C.S., L.R.C.P.
Thye, R., D.M.D.
Weinstock, A., D.D.S., PH.D.
White, S. C., D.D.S.
Wolcott, R. B., D.D.S

*Earth and Space Sciences:*
Anderson, O. L., PH.D.
Boettcher, A. L., PH.D.
Busse, F. H., DR.SC.NAT.
**Carlisle, D.**, PH.D.
**Christie, J. M.**, PH.D.
Coleman, P. J., Jr., PH.D.
Dollase, W. A., PH.D.
Ernst, W. G., PH.D.
**Hall, C. A.**, Jr., PH.D.
Kaplan, I. R., PH.D.
Kaula, W., M.S., D.SC.
Kivelson, M., PH.D.
**Loeblich, Helen T.**, PH.D.
McPherron, R. L., PH.D.
Nelson, C. A., PH.D.
**Oertel, G.**, DR.RER.NAT.
Rosenfeld, J. L., PH.D.
Schopf, J. W., PH.D.

Schubert, G., PH.D.
Shreve, R. L., PH.D.
Wasson, J. T., PH.D.
Watson, K. De P., PH.D.

*Economics:*
**Allen, W. R.**, PH.D.
Clower, R. W., B.LITT.
Darby, M. R., PH.D.
Demsetz, H., PH.D.
**Hilton, G. W.**, PH.D.
Hirsch, W. Z., PH.D.
Hirsileifer, J., PH.D.
Intriligator, M. D., PH.D.
Klein, B., PH.D.
Leamer, E. E., PH.D.
Leijonhufvud, A. S., PH.D.
McCall, J. J., PH.D.
Riley, J. G., PH.D.
**Somers, H. M.**, PH.D.
Sowell, T., PH.D.
Thompson, E. A., PH.D.
Welch, F. R., PH.D.

*Education:*
Alkin, M. C., M.A., ED.D.
Astin, A. W., PH.D.
Astin, H. S., PH.D.
Baker, E. L., ED.D.
Berry, G. L., ED.D.
Bruno, J. E., PH.D.
Clark, B. R., PH.D.
Cohen, A. M., PH.D.
Cohen, S., PH.D.
**Coleman, J. C.**, PH.D.
Crabtree, C., PH.D.
Dorr, A., PH.D.
Erickson, L. W., ED.D.
Feshbach, N. D., PH.D.
Goodlad, J. I., PH.D., L.H.D., LL.D.
Gordon, C. W., PH.D.
Hewett, F. M., PH.D.
Keislar, E. R., PH.D.
Keogh, B. K., PH.D.
Kintzer, F. C., ED.D.
LaBelle, T. J., PH.D.
McNeil, J. D., ED.D.
Popham, W. J., ED.D.
Shavelson, R. J., PH.D.
Silberman, H. F., ED.D.
Skager, R. W., PH.D.
Solman, L. C., PH.D.
**Sorenson, A. G.**, PH.D.
Tyler, L., ED.D.
Weinberg, C., ED.D.
Wilson, C. Z., PH.D.
Wittrock, M. C., PH.D.

*Engineering:*
Allen, F. G., PH.D.
Ardell, A. J., PH.D.
Avizienis, A. A., PH.D.
**Balakrishnan, A. V.**, PH.D.
Bennion, D., PH.D.
**Buchberg, H.**, M.S.
Bunshah, R. F., D.SC.
Bussell, B., PH.D.
Cantor, D. G., PH.D.
Carlyle, J. W., PH.D.
Casperson, L. W., PH.D.
Catton, I., PH.D.
**Charwat, A. F.**, PH.D.
Chen, F. F., PH.D.
Chu, W. W., PH.D.
Cole, J. D., PH.D.
Conn, R. W., PH.D.
Di Stefano, J. J., PH.D.
Dong, S. B., PH.D.
Douglass, D. L., PH.D.
Dracup, J. A., PH.D.
Dubowsky, S., SC.D.
Edwards, D. K., PH.D.
**Elliott, R. S.**, PH.D.
**Estrin, G.**, PH.D.
Forrester, A. T., PH.D.
**Forster, H. K.**, PH.D.

UNIVERSITIES AND COLLEGES—CALIFORNIA (UNIVERSITY OF)     U.S.A.

FOURNEY, M. E., PH.D.
FREDERKING, T. H., PH.D.
FRIEDLANDER, S. K., PH.D.
FRIEDMANN, P. P., D.SC.
GREIBACH, S. A., PH.D.
HART, G. C., PH.D.
INGERSOLL, A. C., PH.D.
JACOBSEN, S. E., PH.D.
KARPLUS, W. J., PH.D.
KASTENBERG, W. E., PH.D.
KELLY, R. E., SC.D.
KLEINROCK, L., PH.D.
KLINGER, A., PH.D.
KNAPP, W. J., SC.D.
KNUTH, E. L., PH.D.
LEIPOLD, M. H., PH.D.
LEONDES, C. T., PH.D.
LEVAN, N., PH.D.
LIU, C. Y., PH.D.
LYMAN, J. H., PH.D.
MACKENZIE, J. D., PH.D
MCCUTCHAN, J. W., M.S.
MCNAMEE, L. P., PH.D.
MAL, A. K., PH.D.
MARTIN, D. F., PH.D.
MASSEY, J. L., PH.D.
MEECHAM, W. C., PH.D.
MELKANOFF, M., PH.D.
MILLER, B. L., PH.D.
MILLS, A. F., PH.D.
MINGORI, D. L., PH.D.
MORGAN, A. J. A., PH.D
MUKI, R., PH.D.
MUNTZ, E. R., PH.D.
NELSON, R. B., SC.D.
NOBE, K., PH.D.
NOTTAGE H. B., PH.D
O'BRIEN, P. F., M.S.
OKRENT, D., PH.D.
OMURA, J. K., PH.D.
O'NEILL, R. R., PH.D.
ONO, K., PH.D.
ORCHARD, H. J., M.S.
PEARL, J., PH.D.
PERRINE, R. L., PH.D.
PINNOW, D. A., PH.D.
PLESSET, M. S., PH.D.
POMRANING, G. C., PH.D.
ROBINSON, L. B., PH.D.
ROSENSTEIN, A. B., PH.D
RUBINSTEIN, M. F., PH.D
SCHMIT, L. A., M.S.
SCHOTT, F. W., PH.D.
SHABAIK, A. H., PH.D.
SINES, G. H., Jr., PH.D.
STAFSUDD, O. M., PH.D.
STARR, C., PH.D.
STERN, R., PH.D.
TEMES, G. C., PH.D.
VAN VORST, W. D., PH.D.
VIDAL, J. J., PH.D.
VISWANATHAN, C. R., PH.D.
WAGNER, C. N., DR.RER.NAT.
WANG, P. K., PH.D.
WAZZAN, A. R., PH.D.
WESTMANN, R. A., PH.D.
WIBERG, D. M., PH.D.
WILLSON, A. N., Jr., PH.D.
YAO, K., PH.D.
YEH, C. W., PH.D.
YEH, W. W., PH.D.
YUE, A. S., PH.D.

*English:*
ALLEN, M. J., PH.D.
BEDIENT, C. B., PH.D.
BOWEN, J. D., PH.D.
CALDER, D. G., PH.D.
CAMPBELL, R. N., PH.D.
CROSS, R. K., PH.D.
DEARING, V. A., PH.D.
DENT, R. W., PH.D.
FORD, P. K., PH.D.
GEORGES, R. A., PH.D.
GOLDBERG, G. J., PH.D.
GUFFEY, G. R., PH.D.

GULLANS, C. B., PH.D.
KELLY, H. A., PH.D.
KESSLER, J., PH.D.
KINSMAN, R. S., PH.D.
KREIGER, M.
LANHAM, R. A., PH.D.
LEHAN, R. D., PH.D.
NEVIUS, B. R., PH.D.
NOVAK, M. E., PH.D.
POVEY, J. F., PH.D.
RIDDEL, J., PH.D.
RIDLEY, F. H., PH.D.
ROPER, A. H., PH.D.
ROUSSEAU, G. S., PH.D.
SCHAEFER, W. D., PH.D.
SELLIN, P. R., PH.D.
SHEATS, P. D., PH.D.
TENNYSON, G. B., PH.D.
THORSLEV, P. L., Jr., PH.D.
WELSH, A., PH.D.
WILGUS, D. K., PH.D.
YEAZELL, R. B., PH.D.

*French:*
BENSIMON, M., PH.D.
GANS, E. L., PH.D.
NOUTY, H. M., D. ès L.

*Geography:*
BENNETT, C. F., Jr., PH.D.
BERGER, C. R., PH.D.
CLARK, W. A., PH.D.
DUNBAR, G. S., PH.D.
KOSTANICK, H. L., PH.D.
MCKNIGHT, T. L., PH.D
NELSON, H. J., PH.D.
ORME, A. R., PH.D.
SAUER, J. D., PH.D.
SCOTT, A. J., PH.D.
TERJUNG, W. H., PH.D.
THROWER, N. J. W., PH.D.
WALTER, H., PH.D.

*Germanic Languages:*
BAHR, E., PH.D.
BÄUML, F. H., PH.D.
CHAPMAN, K. G., PH.D.
NEHRING, W., PH.D.
SHIDELER, R. P., PH.D.
SOBEL, E., PH.D.
WAGENER, H., PH.D.
WARD, D. J., PH.D.
WILBUR, T. H., PH.D.

*History:*
APPLEBY, J. O., PH.D.
BOLLE, K., PH.D.
BENSON, R. L., PH.D.
BURNS, E. B., PH.D.
BURNS, R. I., PH.D.
BURR, R. N., PH.D.
CHAMBERS, M. H., PH.D.
CLASEN, C., PH.D.
COBEN, S., PH.D.
DALLEK, R., PH.D.
EHRET, C., PH.D.
FUNKENSTEIN, A., PH.D.
GALBRAITH, J. S., PH.D.
GATELL, F. O., PH.D.
GOMEZ-QUINONES, J., PH.D.
HOVANNISIAN, R. G., PH.D.
HOWE, D. W., PH.D.
HUNDLEY, N. C., PH.D.
KEDDIE, N., PH.D.
KREKIC, B., PH.D.
LASLETT, J. H., PH.D.
LOCKHART, J., PH.D.
LOSSKY, A., PH.D.
LOWENBERG, P. J., PH.D.
MARSOT, A., PH.D.
MARTINES, L., PH.D.
NASH, G. D., PH.D.
OBICHERE, B. I., PH.D.
POSNANSKY, M., PH.D.
ROGGER, H., PH.D.
ROUSE, R. H., PH.D.
SAR DESAI, D. R., PH.D.

SAXTON, A. P., PH.D.
SHAW, S., PH.D.
VRYONIS, S., PH.D.
WEBER, E. J., M.A.
WESTMAN, R. S., C.PH.
WILKE, J. W., PH.D.
WOHL, R. A., PH.D.
WOLPERT, S., PH.D.

*Italian:*
CECCHETTI, G., PH.D.
CHIAPPELLI, F., D.I.L.
COTTINO-JONES, M., PH.D.

*Journalism:*
WILCOX, W., PH.D.

*Kinesiology:*
BARNARD, R. J., PH.D.
BROWN, CAMILLE, ED.D.
CRATTY, B. J., ED.D.
EDGERTON, V. R.
EGSTROM, G. H., PH.D.
GARDNER, G. W., PH.D.
KEOGH, J. F., ED.D.
MILLER, N. P., ED.D.
MOREHOUSE, L. E., PH.D.
SMITH, J. L., PH.D.

*Law:*
AARON, B., LL.B.
ABEL, R. L., LL.B.
ABRAMS, N., J.D.
ALLEYNE, R. H., Jr., LL.B.
ANDERSON, A. G., J.D.
ASIMOW, M. R., PH.D.
BAUMAN, J. A., J.S.D.
BINDER, D. A., LL.B.
BLUMBERG, G. G., J.D.
BRUDNO, BARBARA, J.D.
DELGADO, R., J.D.
DUKEMINIER, J. J., Jr., LL.B.
EISENBERG, T., J.D.
FLETCHER, G. P., M.CL.
GOLDBERG, C. E., J.D.
GRAHAM, K. W., Jr., J.D.
HAGMAN, D. G., LL.M.
HOROWITZ, H. W., LL.B., LL.M.
JONES, E. A., Jr., LL.B.
JORDAN, R. L., LL.B.
KARST, K. L., LL.B.
KLEIN, W. A., LL.B.
KRIER, J. E., J.D.
LETWIN, L., LL.B.
LIEBELER, W. J., J.D.
MCGEE, H. W., Jr., J.D.
MCGOVERN, W., Jr., LL.B.
MELLINKOFF, D., LL.B.
MORRIS, H., LL.B., D.PHIL.
NIMMER, M. B., LL.B.
PRAGER, S. W., J.D.
PRICE, M. E., LL.B.
ROSETT, A. I., LL.B.
SCHWARTZ, G. T., LL.B., J.D.
SCHWARTZ, M. L., LL.B.
SIEGEL, S., J.D.
SUMNER, J. D., Jr., LL.M., J.S.D.
YEAZELL, S. C., J.D.

*Library Service:*
BORKO, H., PH.D.
EVANS, G. E., PH.D.
GARDNER, R. K., PH.D.
HAYES, R. M., PH.D.
SHANK, R., D.L.S.
VOSPER, R. G., M.A.

*Linguistics:*
ANDERSON, S. R., PH.D.
ANTILLA, R. A., PH.D.
BRIGHT, W. O., PH.D.
FROMKIN, V. A., PH.D.
GIVÓN, T., PH.D.
KEENAN, E. L., PH.D.
LADEFOGED, P., PH.D.
SCHACHTER, P. M., PH.D.
STOCKWELL, R. P., PH.D.
THOMPSON, S. A., PH.D.
WELMERS, W. E., PH.D.

*Management:*
ANDREWS, R. B., PH.D.
BETTMAN, J., PH.D.
BUCKLEY, J. W., D.B.A.
BUFFA, E. S., PH.D.
BURNS, L. S., PH.D.
CARRABINO, J. D., PH.D.
CASE, F. E., D.SC.
CULBERT, S. A., PH.D.
DAVIS, L. E., M.S.
EITEMAN, D. K., PH.D.
ERLENKOTTER, D., PH.D.
FLAMHOLTZ, E. G., PH.D.
FOGEL, W. A., PH.D.
GEOFFRION, A. M., PH.D.
GRAVES, G. W., PH.D.
HOFFLANDER, A. E., PH.D.
HUTCHINSON, J. E., PH.D.
JACKSON, J. R., PH.D.
KASSARJIAN, H. H., PH.D.
KIRCHER, P., PH.D., C.P.A.
LIENTZ, B. P., PH.D.
LIPPMAN, S. A., PH.D.
MACQUEEN, J. B., PH.D.
MASON, R. H., PH.D.
MASSARIK, F., PH.D.
MITCHELL, D. J., PH.D.
MITTELBACH, F. G., M.A.
NELSON, R. T., PH.D.
NICOLS, A., PH.D.
NISKANEN, W. A., PH.D.
OUCHI, W. G., PH.D.
RAIA, A. P., PH.D.
ROLL, R. W., PH.D.
SHELTON, J. P., PH.D.
SPROWLS, R. C., PH.D.
TANNENBAUM, R., PH.D.
WESTON, J. F., PH.D.
WILLIAMS, H. M., J.D.
WILLIAMS, R. M., PH.D.

*Mathematics:*
ARENS, R. F., PH.D.
BABBITT, D. G., PH.D.
BAKER, K. A., PH.D.
BALAKRISHNAN, A. V., PH.D.
BLATTNER, R. J., PH.D.
BROWN, R. F., PH.D.
CANTOR, D. G., PH.D.
CHANG, C. C., PH.D.
CODDINGTON, E. A., PH.D.
COLE, J. D., PH.D.
CURTIS, P. C., Jr., PH.D.
DYE, H. A., PH.D.
EDWARDS, R., PH.D.
EFFROS, E. G., PH.D.
ENGUIST, B., PH.D.
FATTONINI, H. O., PH.D.
FERGUSON, T. S., PH.D.
GAMELIN, T. W., PH.D.
GARNETT, J., PH.D.
GIESEKER, D., PH.D.
GORDON, B., PH.D.
GREENE, R. E., PH.D.
GROSSMAN, N., PH.D.
HALES, A. W., PH.D.
HORN, A., PH.D.
HU, S.-T., PH.D.
JENNRICH, R. I., PH.D.
JOHNSON, P. B., PH.D.
KOOSIS, P. J., PH.D.
LIGGETT, T. M., PH.D.
MARTIN, D. A., S.B.
MIECH, R. J., PH.D.
MOSCHOVAKIS, Y. N., PH.D.
O'NEILL, B., PH.D.
OSHER, S. J., PH.D.
PAIGE, L. J., PH.D.
PORT, S. C., PH.D.
RALSTON, J. V., PH.D.
REDHEFFER, R. M., PH.D.
ROTHSCHILD, B., PH.D.
SARIO, L. R., PH.D.
SCHACHER, M. M., PH.D.
SHAPLEY, L. S.
STEINBERG, R., PH.D.
STRAUS, E. G., PH.D.
TAKESAKI, M., PH.D.
VARADARAIAN, V. S., PH.D.
WHITE, J. H., PH.D.
YLVISAKER, N. D., PH.D.

*Microbiology:*
COLLIER, R. J., PH.D.
EISERLING, F. A., PH.D.
FOX, C. F., PH.D.
LASCELLES, JUNE, PH.D.
MARTINEZ, R. J., PH.D.
NIERLICH, D. P., PH.D.
PICKETT, M. J., PH.D.
RITTENBERG, S. C., PH.D.
ROMIG, W. R., PH.D.
SERCARZ, E. E., PH.D.
WILCOX, G. L., PH.D.

*Microbiology and Immunology*
FAHEY, J. L., M.D.
HILDEMANN, W. H., PH.D.
HOWARD, D. H., PH.D.
IMAGAWA, D. T., PH.D.
MILLER, J. N., M.D.
NAYAK, D. P., PH.D.
RASMUSSEN, A. F., Jr., M.D., PH.D.
STEVENS, J. G., PH.D.
VOGE, M., PH.D.
WALL, T. R., PH.D.
WETTSTEIN, F. O., PH.D.
WORK, T. H., M.D., PH.D.

*Medicine:*
ADAMS, W. S., M.D.
BARNETT, E. V., M.D.
BEALL, G. N., M.D.
BLAHD, W. H., M.D.
BROWN, J., M.D.
CHOPRA, I. J., M.D.
CLINE, M. J., M.D.
DAYTON, S., M.D.
FAHEY, J. L., M.D.
FIGUEROA, W. G., M.D.
FINEGOLD, S. M. M.D.
FINK, KATHRYN F., PH.D.
FISHER, D. A., M.D.
GOLDBERG, L. S., M.D.
GUZE, L. B., M.D.
HERSHMAN, J. M., M.D.
HEWITT, W. L., M.D.
JOHNSON, B. L., M.D.
KABAK, M. M., M.D.
KALEYANIDES, G. J., M.D.
KATTUS, A. A., Jr., M.D.
KLEEMAN, C. R., M.D.
KORENMAN, S. G., M.D.
LANGER, G. A., M.D.
LEVY, L., PH.D.
LEWIS, C. E., M.D., D.SC.
LIEBERMAN, J., PH.D.
MACALPIN, R. N., M.D.
MELLINKOFF, S. M., M.D.
MOMMAERTS, W. F. H. M., PH.D.
PAULUS, H. E., M.D.
PEARCE, M. L., M.D.
PEARSON, C. M., M.D.
PERLOFF, J., M.D.
POPS, M. A., M.D.
REISNER, R. M., M.D.
ROSS, G., M.R.C.P.
SAMBHI, M. P., PH.D.
SAMLOFF, M. I., PH.D.
SCHULTZE, R. G., M.D.
SCHWABE, A. D., M.D.
SHAH, P. M., M.D.
SHINABERGER, J., M.D.
SHINE, K. I., M.D.
SIMMONS, D. H., M.D., PH.D.
SOLOMON, D. H., M.D.
SPARKES, R. S., M.D.
SWERDLOFF, R. S., M.D.
TANAKA, K. R., M.D.
TIERNEY, D, F., M.D.
TYAN, M. L., M.D.
VALENTINE, W. N., M.D.
WALSH, J. H., M.D.
WASSERMAN, K., PH.D., M.D.
WITTENSTEIN, G. J., M.D.
WORDEN, R. E., M.D.

*Military Science and Tactics:*
JULIAN, R. H., M.S.E.

*Music:*
BARKIN, E., PH.D.
BRADSHAW, M. C., PH.D.
CROSSLEY-HOLLAND, P. C., M.A.
D'ACCONE, F. A., PH.D.
DES MARAIS, P. E., M.A.
GEROW, M., PH.D.
GOLLNER, M., PH.D.
HAMMOND, F. F., PH.D.
HARMON, T. F., PH.D.
HUDSON, R. A., PH.D.
HUTCHINSON, W. R., PH.D.
JAIRAZBHOY, N., PH.D.
LAZAROF, H., M.F.A.
MORTON, D., PH.D.
NKETIA, J. H.
REANEY, G., M.A.
SCHWADRON, A. A., MUS.A.D.
STEVENSON, R. M., PH.D.
TRAVIS, R. E., M.A.
TUSLER, R., PH.D.
WILGUS, D. K., PH.D.

*Naval Science:*
THOMPSON, G. I., M.A., M.S.

*Near Eastern Languages and Cultures:*
BANANI, A., PH.D.
BAND, A. J., PH.D.
BODROGLIGETI, A., PH.D.
BONEBAKKER, S., PH.D.
BUCCELLATI, G., PH.D.
DAVIDSON, H. A., PH.D.
POONAWALA, I. K., PH.D.
SANJIAN, A. K., PH.D.
SCHMIDT, H., PH.D.
SEGERT, S., L.SC.

*Neurology:*
HERRMANN, C., M.D.
MARKHAM, C. H., M.D.
OLDENDORF, W. H., M.D.
TOURTELLOTTE, W. W., PH.D., M.D.
WALTER, R. D., M.D.
WEIL, M. L., M.D.
WOLFGRAM, F., PH.D.

*Nursing:*
LEWIS, C. E., M.D.
MOIDEL, H. C., M.A.
RERES, M., ED.D.
SERAYDARIAN, M., PH.D.
VREDEVOE, D. L., PH.D.

*Obstetrics and Gynaecology:*
ASSALI, N. S., M.D.
BASHORE, R. A., M.D.
BRINKMAN, C., M.D.
CUSHNER, I. M., M.P.H., M.D.
DIGNAM, W. J., PH.D.
JUDD, H. L., M.D.
LAGASSE, L. D., M.D.
LEBHERZ, T. B., M.D.
MARSHALL, J. R., M.D.
MOORE, J. G., M.D.

*Ophthalmology:*
CHRISTENSEN, R. E., M.D.
HEPLER, R. S., M.D.
KREIGER, A. E., M.D.
PETTIT, T. H., M.D.
STRAATSMA, B. R., M.D.

*Oriental Languages:*
SCHARFE, H., PH.D.

*Pathology:*
BALUDA, M. A., PH.D.
BROWN, W. J., M.D.
COULSON, W. F., M.D.

Foos, R. Y., M.D.
Lamson, B. G., M.D.
Latta, H., M.D.
Lubran, M. M., PH.D., M.D.
Martin, W. J., PH.D.
Myhre, B. A., PH.D., M.D.
Porter, D. D., M.D.
Rodgerson, D. O., PH.D.
Smith, G. S., M.D.
Vanlancker, J. L., M.D.
Verity, M. A., M.D.
Waisman, J., M.D.
Walford, R. L., M.D.
Zamboni, L., M.D.

*Paediatrics:*
Ament, M. E., M.D.
Cherry, J. D., M.D.
Fielding, J. E., M.D., M.P.H., M.B.A.
Fine, R. N., M.D.
Fisher, D. A., M.D.
Friedman, W. F., M.D.
Heiner, D. C., M.D.
Imagawa, D. T., PH.D.
Jarmakani, J. M., M.D.
Kaplan, S., M.D.
Moss, A. J., M.D.
Parmelee, A. H., M.D.
Philippart, M., M.D.
Schain, R. J., M.D.
St. Geme, J. W., Jr., M.D.
Stiehm, E. R., PH.D.
Towers, B., M.R.C.S., L.R.C.P.

*Pharmacology:*
Bevan, J. A., M.B., B.S.
Cho, A. K., PH.D.
George, R., PH.D.
Hewitt, W. L., M.D.
Jarvik, M. E., M.D., PH.D.
Jenden, D. J., M.D.
Lomax, P., M.D.
Taylor, D., M.A., M.D.
Thompson, J. H., M.D.

*Philosophy:*
Adams, M. M., PH.D.
Adams, R. M., PH.D.
Albritton, R., PH.D.
Burge, C. T., PH.D.
Donnellan, K. S., PH.D.
Foot, P. R., M.A.
Furth, M., PH.D.
Kaplan, D. B., PH.D.
Yost, R. M., Jr., PH.D.

*Physics:*
Abers, E. S., PH.D.
Braunstein, R., PH.D.
Byers, Nina, PH.D.
Chaikin, P. M., PH.D.
Chester, M., PH.D.
Clark, W. G., PH.D.
Cornwall, J. M., PH.D.
Coroniti, F., PH.D.
Dawson, J. M., PH.D.
Finkelstein, R. J., PH.D.
Forrester, A. T., PH.D.
Fried, B., PH.D.
Fronsdal, C., PH.D.
Gruner, G., PH.D.
Haddock, R. P., PH.D.
Holstein, T. D., PH.D.
Igo, G. J., PH.D.
Kennel, C. F., PH.D.
Knopoff, L., PH.D.
Moszkowski, S. A., PH.D.
Nefkens, B. M., PH.D.
Norton, R. E., PH.D.
Orbach, R. L., PH.D.
Pincus, P. A., PH.D.
Rudnick, Isadore, PH.D.
Sakurai, J. J., PH.D.
Satten, R. A., PH.D.
Saxon, D. S., PH.D.
Schlein, P., PH.D.
Schwinger, J. S., PH.D.
Slater, W. E., PH.D.

Stork, D. H., PH.D.
Ticho, H. K. PH.D.
Whitten, C. A., PH.D.
Wong, C. W., PH.D.
Wong, A. Y., PH.D.
Wong, E. Y., PH.D.

*Physiology:*
Bezanilla, F. J., PH.D.
Brady, A. J., PH.D.
Buchwald, J. S., PH.D.
Ciani, S., PH.D.
Diamond, J. M., PH.D.
Eisenman, G., M.D.
Grinnell, A. D., PH.D.
Hagiwara, S., M.D., PH.D.
Jeffrey, B. M., PH.D.
Langer, G. A., M.D.
Mommaerts, W. F. H. M., PH.D.
Ross, G., M.R.C.P.
Simmons, D. H., M.D., PH.D.
Sonnenschein, R. R., M.D., PH.D.
Wright, E. M., PH.D.

*Political Science:*
Ashcraft, R. E., PH.D.
Baerwald, H. H., PH.D.
Baum, R. D., PH.D.
Bernstein, I., PH.D.
Bollens, J. C., PH.D.
Cattell, D. T., PH.D.
Coleman, J. S., PH.D.
Dogan, M., PH.D.
Englebert, E. A., PH.D.
Fried, R. C., PH.D.
Gerstein, R. S., PH.D.
Gonzalez, E., PH.D.
Hoffenberg, M., PH.D.
Kerr, M. H., PH.D.
Kolkowicz, R., PH.D.
Korbonski, A., PH.D.
Lofchie, M. F., PH.D.
Marvick, D., PH.D.
Nixon, C. R., PH.D.
Rapoport, D. C., PH.D.
Ries, J. C., PH.D.
Rogowski, R. L., PH.D.
Sisson, J. R., PH.D.
Sklar, R. L., PH.D.
Wilkinson, D. O., PH.D.
Wolfenstein, E. V., M.A.
Young, C. E., PH.D.

*Psychiatry and Biobehavioural Sciences:*
Buchwald, N. A., PH.D.
Colby, K. M., M.D.
Fish, Barbara, M.D.
Fluharty, A. L., PH.D.
Fuster, J. M., M.D.
Garcia, J., PH.D.
Greenblatt, M., M.D.
Grossman, H. J., M.D.
Hewett, F. M., PH.D.
Jarvik, L. F., M.D., PH.D.
Jarvik, M. E., M.D., PH.D.
Jeffrey, B. W., PH.D.
Jerison, H. J., PH.D.
Langness, L., PH.D.
Marsh, J. T., PH.D.
May, P. R. A., M.D.
McGlothlin, W. H., PH.D.
McGuire, M. T., M.D.
Mensh, I. N., PH.D.
Popjak, G. J., M.D.
Price-Williams, D. R., PH.D.
Rubin, R. T., M.D.
Scheibel, A. B., M.D.
Schwartz, D. A., M.D.
Shapiro, D., PH.D.
Shneidman, E. S., PH.D.
Silverstein, A. B., PH.D.
Simmons, J. Q., M.D.
Stoller, R. J., M.D.
Straker, M., M.D.
Tarjan, G., M.D.
Walter, R. D., M.D.
West, L. J., M.D.

Worden, R., M.D.
Yamamoto, J., M.D.

*Psychology:*
Baker, B. L., PH.D.
Bentler, P. M., PH.D.
Bjork, R. A., PH.D.
Broen, W. E., PH.D.
Butcher, L. L., PH.D.
Carterette, E. C., PH.D.
Centers, R., PH.D.
Coleman, J. C., PH.D.
Collins, B. E., PH.D.
Comrey, A. L., PH.D.
Ellison, G. D., PH.D.
Feshbach, S., PH.D.
Friedman, M. P., PH.D.
Gerard, H. B., PH.D.
Goldstein, M. J., PH.D.
Greenfield, P. M., PH.D.
Henker, B. A., PH.D.
Henley, N. M., PH.D.
Holman, E. W., PH.D.
Houston, J. P., PH.D.
Jeffrey, W. E., PH.D.
Kelley, H. H., PH.D.
Krasne, F., PH.D.
Liebeskind, J. C., PH.D.
Lovaas, O. I., PH.D., LITT.D.
Madsen, M. C., PH.D.
Maltzman, I. M., PH.D.
Mehrabian, A., PH.D.
Nakamura, C. Y., PH.D.
Novin, D., PH.D.
Padilla, A. M., PH.D.
Parducci, A., PH.D.
Raven, B. H., PH.D.
Sears, D. O., PH.D.
Sheehan, J. G., PH.D.
Shure, G. H., PH.D.
Sue, S., PH.D.
Thomas, J. P., PH.D.
Weiner, B., PH.D.

*Public Health:*
Afifi, A. A., PH.D.
Alfin-Slater, R. B., PH.D.
Ash, L. R., PH.D.
Barr, A. R., D.SC.
Blake, J., PH.D.
Breslow, L., M.D., M.P.H
Clark, V. A., PH.D.
Detels, R., M.S., M.D.
Dixon, W. J., PH.D.
Dunn, O. J., PH.D.
Hopkins, C. E., PH.D.
Jelliffe, D. B., M.D.
Kar, S. B., PH.D.
Katz, A. H., M.A., D.S.W.
Lewis, C. E., D.SC.
Mah, R. A., PH.D.
Massey F. J. Jr., PH.D
Neumann, A. K., M.P.H., M.D
Rada, E. L., PH.D.
Schacher, J. F., PH.D.
Swendseid, M. E., PH.D
Torrens, P. R., M.D., M.P.H
Wilner, D M., PH.D
Work, T. H., M.D.

*Radiology:*
Bennett, L. R., M.D.
Gold, R. H., M.D.
Greenfield, M. A., PH.D
Hanafee, W. N., M.D.
Jorgens, J., M.D.
Juillard, G. J., M.D.
Langdon, E. A., M.D.
MacDonald, N. S., PH.D
Norman, A., PH D
Parker, R. G., M.D.
Phelps, M. E., PH.D.
Smathers, J. B., PH.D.
Stekel, R. J., M.D.
Tabrisky, J., M.D.
Webber, M. M., M.D.
Wilson, G. H., M.D.
Withers, H. R., PH.D.

*Slavic Languages:*
ALBIJANIC, A., PH.D.
BIRNBAUM, H., PH.D.
GIMBUTAS, M., PH.D.
EEKMAN, T., PH.D.
FLIER, M. S., PH.D.
HARPER, K. E., PH.D.
MARKOV, V., PH.D.
SHAPIRO, M., PH.D.
WORTH, D. S., PH.D.

*Social Welfare:*
COHEN, J., D.S.S.
CONNERY, M. F., D.S.W.
GIOVANNONI, J. M., PH.D.
KATZ, A. H., M.A., D.S.W.
KITANO, H. H., PH.D.

*Sociology:*
ALVAREZ, R., PH.D.
BONACICH, P., PH.D.
FREEMAN, H. E., PH.D.
GARFINKEL, H., PH.D.
GORDON, C. W., PH.D.
GRUSKY, O., PH.D.
KITANO, H. H., PH.D.
LEVINE, G. N., PH.D.
LIGHT, I. H., PH.D.
OPPENHEIMER, V. K., M.D.
SABAGH, G., PH.D.
SEEMAN, M., PH.D.
SHURE, G. H., PH.D.
TENHOUTEN, W. D., PH.D.
TURNER, R. H., PH.D.
TREIMAN, D. J., PH.D.
ZEITLIN, M., PH.D.

*Spanish and Portuguese:*
ARORA, S. L., PH.D.
BARCIA, J. R., LIC. FYL.
BENITEZ, R. A., PH.D.
GIMENO, J., PH.D.
HULET, C. L., PH.D.
JOHNSON, C. B., PH.D.
MORRIS, B., M.A.
OTERO, C. P., PH.D.
OVIEDO, J. M., PH.D.
ROBE, S. L., PH.D.

*Speech:*
PHELPS, W. W., PH.D.
WILCOX, W., PH.D.

*Surgery:*
AMSTUTZ, H. C., M.D.
BARKER, W. F., M.D.
CRANDALL, P. H., M.D.
FONKALSRUD, E. W., M.D.
GOODWIN, W. E., M.D.
HONRUBIA, V., M.D.
KAUFMAN, J. J., M.D.
MALONEY, J. V., Jr., M.D.
MORTON, D. L., M.D.
MULDER, D. G., M.D.
RAND, R. W., M.D.
STERN, W. E., M.D.
TERASAKI, P. I., PH.D.
WARD, P. H., M.D.
ZAREM, H. A., M.D.

*Theatre Arts:*
ADAMS, W. B., M.A.
CLARKE, S. M., B.A.
CAUBLE, J. R., M.A.
CRABS, D. B., M.A.
CORRIGAN, R. F., M.A.
FRIEDMAN, A. B., PH.D.
GOODMAN, P., PH.D.
HAWKINS, C., R. M.A.
HELSTEIN, M., M.F.A., PH.D.
LATOURETTE, F. D., M.L.
MUELLER, C. R., PH.D.
STOUMEN, L. C., PH.D.
WOLLOCK, A. V., PH.D.
YOUNG, J. W., M.A.

ATTACHED INSTITUTE:
**Latin American Center:** f. 1959; 60 undergraduate, 55 graduate students; Dir. Dr. J. WILBERT.

## University of California, Riverside

RIVERSIDE, CALIFORNIA 92521
Telephone: 714-787-1012.
Established 1907.
State control.

*Chancellor:* TOMÁS RIVERA, PH.D.
*Vice-Chancellor:* CARLTON R. BOVELL, PH.D.
*Vice-Chancellor (Student Affairs):* LOUIS J. LEO, J.D.
*Vice-Chancellor (Administration):* ELEANOR MONTAGUE, M.A., M.B.A.
*Registrar:* RONALD M. SLOMINSKI, M.B.A.
*Librarian:* JOAN CHAMBERS, M.L.A.

Number of teachers: 389.
Number of students: 4,600.

DEANS:

*College of Natural and Agricultural Sciences:* I. W. SHERMAN, PH.D.
*College of Humanities and Social Science:* D. H. WARREN, PH.D.
*Graduate School of Administration:* J. EARLEY, PH.D. (acting).
*School of Education:* I. BALOW, PH.D.
*Graduate School:* LELAND M. SHANNON, PH.D.

PROFESSORS:

ADRIAN, C. R., PH.D., Political Science
ALCALA, H. R., PH.D., Spanish
ANDERSON, E. N., PH.D., Anthropology
APROBERTS, R., PH.D., English
ARNOLD, B. C., PH.D., Statistics
ASCHMANN, H. H., PH.D., Geography
AYLLON, C., PH.D., Spanish
BALOW, I. H., PH.D., Education
BARKIN, K. D., PH.D., History
BARNES, M. M., PH.D., Entomology
BARRICELLI, J.-P., PH.D., Romance Languages and Comparative Literature
BARTNICKI-GARCIA, S., PH.D., Plant Pathology
BEALS, A. R., PH.D., Anthropology
BELSER, W. L., PH.D., Microbiology
BINGHAM, F. T., PH.D., Soils and Plant Nutrition
BITTERS, W. P., PH.D., Horticultural Science
BLOCK, R. E., PH.D., Mathematics
BONACICH, E. M., PH.D., Sociology
BRADSHAW, W. T., M.A., Studio Art
BRINKERHOFF, D. M., PH.D., Art
BROADBENT, S. M., PH.D., Anthropology
BROWN, L. R., PH.D., Entomology
BRUNER, L. J., PH.D., Physics
BUTLER, E. W., PH.D., Sociology
CAMPBELL, L. G., PH.D., History
CANNELL, G. H., PH.D., Soil Physics
CARLSON, J. S., PH.D., Education
CARNEY, F. M., PH.D., Political Science
CARROTT, R. G., PH.D., Art History
CASTRO, C. E., PH.D., Nematology
CHALMERS, B. T., PH.D., Mathematics
CHILCOTE, R. H., PH.D., Political Science
COGGINS, C. W., Jr., PH.D., Plant Physiology
COHEN, L. H., PH.D., Geology
COOPER, K. W., PH.D., Biology
CORTES, C. E., PH.D., History/Chicano Studies
CRAWFORD, J. C., PH.D., Music
CUMMINGS, F. W., PH.D., Physics
DAVIAU, D. G., PH.D., German
DE BACH, P. H., PH.D., Biological Control
DE PILLIS, J. E., PH.D., Mathematics
DESAI, B. R., PH.D., Physics
DESJARDINS, P. R., PH.D., Plant Pathology
DUGGER, W. M., PH.D., Botany
DUNN, M. F., PH.D., Biochemistry
ECKERT, J. W., PH.D., Plant Pathology
EDMUNDS, S. W., M.A., Administration
EIGNER, E. M., PH.D., English
EKMAN, E., PH.D., History
ELDERS, W. A., PH.D., Geological Sciences
EMBLETON, T. W., PH.D., Horticultural Science
ENDO, R. M., PH.D., Plant Pathology
ERWIN, D. C., PH.D., Plant Pathology
ESSICK, R. N., PH.D., English
EVERETT, G. E., PH.D., Physics
EYMAN, R. K., PH.D., Education
FOCHT, D. D., PH.D., Soil and Environmental Sciences
FUKUTO, T. R., PH.D., Entomology
FUNG, S. Y., PH.D., Physics
GABLE, F. K., PH.D., Music
GAFFNEY, M., PH.D., Economics
GARDINER, K. W., Administration/Environmental Science
GAUSTAD, E. S., PH.D., History
GEORGHIOU, G. P., PH.D., Entomology
GERICKE, P. O., PH.D., Spanish
GOEDEN, R. D., PH.D., Biological Control
GOKHALE, D. V., PH.D., Statistics
GRIFFIN, B. R., PH.D., French
GUNTHER, F. A., PH.D., Entomology
GURTOV, M., PH.D., Political Science
HALBERG, C. J. A., Jr., PH.D., Mathematics
HALL, A. E., PH.D., Botany and Plant Sciences
HALL, I. M., PH.D., Insect Pathology
HANSON, E. M., PH.D., GSA/Education
HARPER, L. H., PH.D., Mathematics
HARRAH, D., PH.D., Philosophy
HEATH, R. L., PH.D., Botany and Plant Sciences
HELMKAMP, G. K., PH.D., Chemistry
HENDRICK, I. G., ED.D., Education
HINE, R. V., PH.D., History
HOLTEN, D. D., PH.D., Biochemistry
JACKSON, M., PH.D., Sociology
JOHNS, D. C., PH.D., Music
JOHNSON, H. W., PH.D., Chemistry
JOHNSON, O. A., PH.D., Philosophy
JORDAN, L. S., PH.D., Horticultural Sciences
KAUS, P. E., PH.D., Physics
KEARNEY, M., PH.D., Anthropology
KEEN, N. T., PH.D., Plant Pathology
KERNAN, ANNE, PH.D., Physics
KNOX, G. A., PH.D., English
KOGIKU, K. C., PH.D., Economics
LABANAUSKAS, C. K., PH.D., Horticulture
LEGNER, E. F., PH.D., Biological Control
LETEY, J., Jr., PH.D., Soil Physics
LIPPERT, L. F., Plant Sciences
LIU, N. L., PH.D., Physics
MACLAUGHLIN, D. E., PH.D., Physics
MACMILLAN, D., PH.D., Education
MCCOLLUM, D. C., PH.D., Physics
MCMURTRY, J. A., PH.D., Entomology
MAGNUS, B., PH.D., Philosophy
MANKAU, R., PH.D., Nematology
MARCH, R. B., PH.D., Entomology
MAYHEW, W. W., PH.D., Life Sciences
MEGENNEY, W. W., PH.D., Literatures and Languages
MERCER, J. R., PH.D., Sociology
METCALF, F. T., PH.D., Mathematics
MEYER, M. M., PH.D., Sociology
MILLER, T. A., Entomology
MOORE, J. A., PH.D., Biology
MULLA, M. S., PH.D., Entomology
MUNNECKE, D. E., PH.D., Plant Pathology
MURASHIGE, T., PH.D., Horticulture
MURPHY, M. A., PH.D., Geological Sciences
MYERS, A. K., PH.D., Psychology
NACHMAN, M., PH.D., Psychology
NEUMAN, R. C., PH.D., Chemistry
NOLTMAN, E. A. G., PH.D., M.D., Biochemistry
NORMAN, A. W., PH.D., Biochemistry
OATMAN, E. R., PH.D., Entomology

OKAMURA, W. H., PH.D., Chemistry
OLSEN, R. W., PH.D., Biomedical Sciences
ORANS, M., PH.D., Anthropology
ORTTUNG, W. H., PH.D., Chemistry
PAGE, A. L., PH.D., Soil Science
PARSONS, J. B., Jr., PH.D., Far Eastern History and Culture
PAULING, E. C., PH.D., Biology
PEASE, R. W., PH.D., Earth Sciences
PENGELLEY, E. T., PH.D., Biology
PERKINS, V L., PH.D., History
PETRINOVIICH, L., PH.D., Psychology
PITTS, J. N., Jr., PH.D., Chemistry
POE, R. T., PH.D., Physics
POLLAK, M., PH.D., Physics
PRATT, P. F., PH.D., Soil Science
PRESS, S. J., PH.D., Statistics
RADOYCE, L., M.A., German and Russian
RANSOM, R. L., PH.D., Economics
RAO, M. M., PH.D., Mathematics
RATLIFF, L. J., PH.D., Mathematics
RAVITCH, N., PH.D., History
REAGAN, M. D., PH.D., Political Science
RETTIG, M. F., PH.D., Chemistry
REYNOLDS, H. T., PH.D., Entomology
REYNOLDS, W. H., M.F.A., Music
RHINE, R. J., PH.D., Psychology
RISSO, R. D., PH.D., Theatre
RIVERA, T., PH.D., Literatures and Languages
ROBINSON, P. T., PH.D., Geology
RUIBAL, R., PH.D., Zoology
SAWYER, D. T., PH.D., Chemistry
SCHLUNDT, C. L., PH.D., Dance
SCHMIDT, H. H., PH.D., Chemistry
SCHWARTZ, M., PH.D., Political Science
SCORA, R. W., PH.D., Botany
SEMANCIK, J., PH.D., Plant Physiology
SHANNON, L. M., PH.D., Biochemistry
SHAPIRO, V. L., PH.D., Mathematics
SHEN, B. C., PH.D., Physics
SHERMAN, H. J., PH.D., JUR.D., Economics
SHERMAN, I. W., PH.D., Zoology
SHOEMAKER, V. H., PH.D., Biology
SIMANEK, E., PH.D., Physics
SIMS, J. J., Plant Pathology
SINCLAIR, B., PH.D., Political Science
SINGER, H., PH.D., Education
SINGER, R. D., PH.D., Psychology
SOOST, R. K., PH.D., Genetics
SPERLING, S. E., PH.D., Psychology
SPOSITO, G., PH.D., Soil Science
STAFNEY, J. D., PH.D., Mathematics
STANLEY, J. L., PH.D., Political Science
STEADMAN, J. M., PH.D., English
STEPHENS, E. R., PH.D., Environmental Science
STERN, V. M., PH.D., Entomology
STEWART, S. N., PH.D., English
STOLTZFUS, B. F., PH.D., French
STOLZY, L. H., PH.D., Soil Physics
STRALKA, A. R., PH.D., Mathematics
STRICKLER, F. L., PH.D., Dance
STROMBOTNE, J. S., M.F.A., Art
TAYLOR, O. C., PH.D., Plant Sciences
THOMASON, I. J., PH.D., Nematology
THOMSON, W. W., PH.D., Biology
TING, I. P., PH.D., Biology
TOBEY, R. C., PH.D., History
TOMLINSON-KEASEY, C., PH.D., Psychology
TSAO, P. H., PH.D., Plant Pathology
TURNER, A. C., PH.D., Political Science
TURNER, J. H., PH.D., Sociology
TZENG, O., PH.D., Psychology
VAN DEUSEN, L. M., PH.D., English
VAN GUNDY, S. D., PH.D., Nematology
VASEK, F. C., PH.D., Botany and Plant Sciences
VICKERY, J. B., PH.D., English
WARREN, D. H., PH.D., Psychology
WAY, H. F., Jr., PH.D., Political Science
WEATHERS, L. G., PH.D., Plant Pathology
WEDDING, R. T., PH.D., Biochemistry
WHITE, R. S., PH.D., Physics
WILD, R. L., PH.D., Physics
WILKINS, C. L., PH.D., Chemistry
WING, R. M., PH.D., Chemistry
WOODBURNE, M. O., PH.D., Geology
WRIGHT, L., PH.D., Philosophy
YERMANOS, D. M., PH.D., Agronomy
YOUNGER, V. B., PH.D., Agronomy

## University of California, San Diego

LA JOLLA,
CALIFORNIA 92093
Telephone: 452-3135.

Became part of the University 1912.

*Chancellor:* RICHARD ATKINSON, PH.D.
*Vice-Chancellor (Academic Affairs):* JOHN W. MILES, PH.D.
*Vice-Chancellor (Financial Management):* HERMAN D. JOHNSON.
*Vice-Chancellor (Health Sciences) and Dean of the School of Medicine:* ROBERT PETERSDORF, M.D.
*Vice Chancellor (Undergraduate Affairs):* JOSEPH W. WATSON, PH.D.
*Vice-Chancellor (Marine Sciences) and Director of Scripps Institution of Oceanography:* W. A. NIERENBERG, PH.D.
*Dean of Graduate Studies and Research:* MANUEL ROTENBERG, PH.D.
*Provost of Revelle College:* WOO CHIA-WEI, PH.D.
*Provost of John Muir College:* J. L. STEWART, PH.D.
*Provost of the Third College:* FAUSTINA SOLIS, M.S.W. (acting)
*Provost of the Fourth College:* MERVYN L. RUDEE, PH.D.
*Registrar and Admissions Officer:* RONALD J. BOWKER.
*Librarian:* MILLICENT ABELL.

Number of teachers: 820.
Number of students: 11,360.

Publications: *UCSD General Catalog, UCSD Graduate Studies, UCSD School of Medicine Catalog, UCSD Summer Session* (all annuals), *Explore* (University Extension Catalog).

PROFESSORS:

*Anthropology:*
BAILEY, F. G.
D'ANDRADE, R.
LEVY, R.
SCHWARTZ, T.
SPIRO, M.
SWARTZ, M.
TUZIN, D.

*Applied Mechanics and Engineering Sciences:*
MILLER, D. (Chairman)
BRADNER, H.
ELLIS, A.
FUNG, Y.-C.
HEGEMIER, G.
INTAGLIETTA, M.
LIBBY, P.
LIN, S.-C.
MIDDLEMAN, S.
MILES, J.
NACHBAR, W.
OLFE, D.
PENNER, S.
REISSNER, E.
ROBERSON, R.
SCHNEIDER, A.
SORENSON, H.
SWORDER, D.
VAN ATTA, D.
WOO, S.
ZWEIFACH, B.

*Biology:*
GEIDUSCHEK, E. (Chairman)
BUTLER, W.
CHRISPEELS, M.
DUTTON, R.
FRIEDKIN, M.
GREEN, M.
GROBSTEIN, C.
HAYASHI, M.
HELINSKI, D.
HOLLAND, J.
LINDSLEY, D.
LOOMIS, W.
MCELROY, W.
MILLS, S.
MONTAL, S. M.
SALTMAN, P.
SATO, G.
SIMON, M.
SINGER, J.
STERN, H.
TOKUYASU, K.
VARON, S.
WILLS, C.
XUONG, N.-H.

*Chemistry:*
DOOLITTLE, R. (Chairman)
ABELSON, J.
ALLISON, W.
ARNOLD, J.
DELUCA, M.
DENNIS, E.
GOODMAN, M.
KAMEN, M.
KAPLAN, N.
KEARNS, D.
KRAUT, J.
MARTI, K.
MAYER, J.
MCMORRIS, T.
MILLER, S.
PERIN, C.
SCHRAUZER, G.
SHULER, K.
SUESS, H.
TRAYLOR, T.
VOLD, R.
WENKERT, E.
WILSON, K.
XUONG, N.-H.
ZIMM, B.

*Drama:*
ADDISON, M. (Chairman)
CHRISTMAS, E.
GAFFNEY, F.
SCHNEIDER, A. L.
WAGNER, A.

*Economics:*
CONLISK, J. (Chairman)
ATTIYEH, R.
BEAR, D.
ENGLE, R.
GRANGER, C.
GROVES, T.
HELLER, W.
HOOPER, J.
RAMANATHAN, R.
STARR, R.

*Electrical Engineering and Computer Science:*
ANDERSON, V. (Chairman)
ALFVEN, H.
BOOKER, H.
BOWLES, K.
CHANG, W.
COLES, W.
FEJER, J.

FREDMAN, M.
HELSTROM, C.
HU, T.
LAU, S.
LEE, S. H.
LUGANNANI, R.
LUO, H.-L.
MASRY, E.
RICKETT, B.
ROTENBERG, M.
RUDEE, M. L.
RUMSEY, V.
SAVITCH, W.

*History:*
RINGROSE, D. (Chairman)
CESPEDES, C.
CHODOROW, S.
HUGHES, H. S.
JACKSON, G.
METZGER, T.
MITCHELL, A.
POMEROY, E.
RAPPAPORT, A.
RUIZ, R.
SCHEIBER, H.
SCOBIE, J.

*Linguistics:*
NEWMARK, L. (Chairman)
KLIMA, E.
KURODA, S.-Y.
LANGACKER, R.
LANGDON, M.
PERLMUTTER, D.
SCHANE, S.

*Literature:*
LYON, J. (Chairman)
BERMAN, R.
BLANCO, C.
CASALDUERO, J.
CATALAN, D.
CONCHA, J.
COOPER, C.
DE CERTEAU, M.
ELLIOTT, R.
FRENK, M.
FUSSELL, E.
LETTAU, R.
PEARCE, R.
PRIETO, A.
STEWART, J.
WESLING, D.
WIERSCHIN, M.
WRIGHT, A.
YIP, W.-L.

*Mathematics:*
HALKIN, H. (Chairman)
ANDERSON, D.
BENDER, E.
BISHOP, E.
BUNCH, J.
ENRIGHT, T.
EVANS, J.
FILLMORE, J.
FITZGERALD, C.
FRANKEL, T.
GARSIA, A.
GETOOR, R.
GRAGG, W.
HELTON, J.
LIN, J.
MANASTER, A.
OLSHEN, R.
REISSNER, E.
RODIN, B.
ROHRL, H.
ROSENBLATT, M.
SHARPE, M.
SMALL, L.
SMITH, D. R.
STARK, H.
WARSCHAWSKI, S.
WILLIAMSON, S.
WULBERT, D.

*Music:*
REYNOLDS, R. (Chairman)
ERICKSON, R.
FARRELL, P.
MOORE, F. R.
NEE, T.
NEGYESY, J.
OGDON, W.
OLIVEROS, P.
RANDS, B.
REYNOLDS, R.
SILBER, J.
TURETZKY, B.

*Philosophy:*
ALLISON, H. (Chairman)
LEE, E.
MOORE, S.
OLAFSON, F.
STROLL, A.
VENDLER, Z.

*Physics:*
LOVBERG, R. (Chairman)
BRUECKNER, K.
BURBIDGE, M.
BURBIDGE, G.
CHEN, J.
FEHER, G.
FRAZER, W.
GOODKIND, J.
GOULD, R.
HALPERN, F.
KOHN, W.
KROLL, N.
LIEBERMANN, L.
MA, S.-K.
MALMBERG, J.
MAPLE, M. B.
MASEK, G.
MCILWAIN, C.
MONTAL, S. M.
NIERENBERG, W.
O'NEIL, T.
PETERSON, L.
PICCIONI, O.
SCHULTZ, S.
SHAM, L. J.
SUHL, H.
SWANSON, R.
THOMPSON, W.
VERNON, W.
WHEATLEY, J.
WONG, D.
WOO, C.-W.
XUONG, N.-H.
YORK, H.

*Political Science:*
LAKOFF, S. (Chairman)
CORNELIUS, W.
LIJPHART, A.
REVELLE, R.

*Psychology:*
REYNOLDS, G. (Chairman)
ANDERSON, N.
ATKINSON, R. C.
BOYNTON, R.
COLE, M.
DEUTSCH, J. A.
EBBESEN, E.
FANTINO, E.
MANDLER, G.
MANDLER, J.
NORMAN, D.
RUMELHART, D.

*Scripps Institution of Oceanography:*
ROSENBLATT, R. (Chairman)
ANDERSON, V.
ARRHENIUS, G.
ARTHUR, R.
BACKUS, G.
BADA, J.
BENSON, A.
BERGER, W.

BRADNER, H.
BRUNE, J.
BULLOCK, T.
COX, C.
CRAIG, H.
CURRAY, J.
DAVIS, R.
DUNTLEY, S.
ENGEL, A.
ENRIGHT, J.
FAULKNER, D. J.
FOX, D.
GILBERT, J. F.
GOLDBERG, E.
HAMMEL, H.
HAUBRICH, R.
HAWKINS, J.
HAXO, F.
HEILIGENBERG, W.
HENDERSHOTT, M.
HESSLER, R.
HOLLAND, N.
INMAN, D.
JOHNSON, M.
KEELING, C.
LAL, D.
LEWIN, R.
MCGOWAN, J.
MENARD, H. W.
MULLIN, M.
MUNK, W.
NEWMAN, W.
NIERENBERG, W.
PARKER, R.
PHLEGER, F.
RAITT, R.
RAKESTRAW, N.
REID, J.
REVELLE, R.
SHEPARD, F.
SHOR, G.
SOMERO, G.
SOMERVILLE, R.
SPIESS, F.
SUESS, H. E.
VACQUIER, V.
VACQUIER, V. D.
VANATTA, C.
VOLCANI, B.
WATSON, K.
WHITE, F.
WINTERER, E.
ZOBELL, C.

*Sociology:*
BERGER, B. (Chairman)
CICOUREL, A.
DAVIS, F.
DOUGLAS, J.
GRANA, C.
GUSFIELD, J.
WISEMAN, J.

*Visual Arts:*
ANTIN, D. (Chairman)
ANTIN, E.
COHEN, H.
FARBER, M.
HARRISON, N.
KAHR, M.
KAPROW, A.
SCANGA, I.

*Third College:*
SCHILLER, H.
THOMAS, C.

*School of Medicine:*

*Anaesthesiology:*
SAIDMAN, L. (Chairman)
KATZ, J.
SHAPIRO, H.
SMITH, N. T.

*Community and Family Medicine:*
BARRETT-CONNOR, E. (Acting Chairman)
HOWELL, D.

UNIVERSITIES AND COLLEGES—CALIFORNIA (UNIVERSITY OF) U.S.A.

SHIMKIN, M.
SIMON, H.
STOKES, J.

*Medicine:*
RANNEY, H. (Chairman)
BARRETT-CONNOR, E.
BLANTZ, R.
BRAUDE, A.
BYFIELD, J.
CODE, C.
COPPAGE, W.
COVELL, J.
DAYTON, S.
DEFTOS, L.
DULBECCO, R.
FANESTIL, D.
GILL, G.
GOULIAN, M.
GRUNDY, S.
HARDISON, W.
HENDERSON, L.
HOFMANN, A.
HOLLINGSWORTH, J.
ISENBERG, J.
JONES, O. W.
KARLINER, J.
KNIAZEFF, A.
MAYER, S.
MENDELSOHN, J.
MOSER, K.
OXMAN, M.
RAPAPORT, S.
ROSS, J.
SEEGMILLER, J.
SHABETAI, R.
STEINBERG, D.
STOUGHTON, R.
TAYLOR, P.
WEST, J.
WHEELER, H.
WHITE, F.
ZVAIFLER, N.

*Neurosciences:*
WIEDERHOLT, W. (Chairman)
BICKFORD, R.
BULLOCK, T.
GALAMBOS, R.
HILLYARD, S.
LIVINGSTON, R.
O'BRIEN, J.
SPOONER, C.
TSCHIRGI, R.

*Pathology:*
LAMPERT, P. (Chairman)
ALEXANDER, N.
BENIRSCHKE, K.
BLOOR, C.
BRAUDE, A.
DAVIS, C.
DULBECCO, R.
HOUGIE, C.
ITANO, H.
MASOUREDIS, S.
OXMAN, M.
SELL, S.
STOUGHTON, R.
ZETTNER, A.

*Paediatrics:*
NYHAN, W. (Chairman)
CONNOR, J.
GLUCK, L.
HAMBURGER, R.
HOWELL, D.
MENDOZA, S.
SCHNEIDER, J.

*Psychiatry:*
JUDD, L. (Chairman)
BARONDES, S.
GROVES, P. M.
JANOWSKY, D.
MANDELL, A.

PENN, N.
SCHUCKIT, M.
SEGAL, D.
SQUIRE, L.
STORMS, L.

*Radiology:*
BERK, R. (Chairman)
AMBERG, J.
ASHBURN, W.
BAILY, N.
BOOKSTEIN, J.
BYFIELD, J.
FRIEDMAN, P.
HALPERN, S.
HIGGINS, C.
KERBER, C.
LASSER, E.
LEOPOLD, G.
RESNICK, D.
TALNER, L.
VERBA, J.
WARD, J.
WICKBOM, I.

*Reproductive Medicine:*
YEN, S. (Chairman)
BENIRSCHKE, K.
GLUCK, L.
HOLLINGSWORTH, D.
LEIN, A.
LUCAS, W.

*Surgery:*
AKESON, W. (acting Chairman)
ALKSNE, J.
BERNSTEIN, E.
CODE, C.
CONVERY, F.
FARRIS, J.
FRONEK, A.
HALASZ, N.
LEE, S.
NAHUM, A.
NICKEL, V.
ORLOFF, M.
PESKIN, G.
PETERS, R.
PILCH, Y.
SCHMIDT, J.
SEVEL, D.
SHAPIRO, H.
UTLEY, J. R.
WILSON, D.
WOO, S.

## University of California, San Francisco

3RD AND PARNASSUS AVENUES,
SAN FRANCISCO, CALIFORNIA 94143
Established 1873.

*Chancellor:* FRANCIS A. SOOY, M.D.
*Vice-Chancellor (Administration):* E. K. ERICKSON, M.B.A.
*Vice-Chancellor (Academic Affairs):* L. L. BENNETT, M.A., PH.D., M.D
*Dean of Students:* P. LINDBERG.
*Registrar:* PETER MASSEY.
*Librarian:* D. BISHOP, B.A., M.S.

Number of teachers: 824.
Number of students: 3,182.

DEANS:

*School of Dentistry:* B. W. PAVONE, D.D.S.
*School of Pharmacy:* J. E. GOYAN, PH.D
*School of Medicine:* J. R. KREVANS, A.B., M.D.
*School of Nursing:* MARJORIE S. DUNLAP, M.P.S., ED.D.
*Graduate Division:* H. A. HARPER, PH.D.

DIRECTORS:
*Hospitals and Clinics:* ROBERT A. DERZON.
*Langley Porter Neuropsychiatric Institute:* R. S. WALLERSTEIN, M.D.

## University of California, Santa Barbara

SANTA BARBARA, CALIFORNIA 93106
Telephone: (805) 961-2311.

Established 1891; became part of the University 1944.

*Chancellor:* ROBERT A. HUTTENBACK, PH.D.
*Vice-Chancellor:* ROBERT S. MICHAELSEN, PH.D.
*Vice-Chancellor (Student and Community Affairs):* EDWARD E. BIRCH, PH.D.
*Assistant Chancellors:* ROBERT E. BASON (University Relations), ROGER HORTON (Budget and Administrative Operations), RICHARD W. JENSEN (Planning and Analysis).
*Assistant Vice-Chancellors:* ROBERT J. KROES (Administrative Services), ROBERT J. CAMERON (Staff Personnel), GERALD J. LARSON, PH.D. (Academic Affairs), MARVIN MARCUS, PH.D. (Research and Academic Development).
*Registrar and Dean of Admissions:* C. MCKINNEY, PH.D.
*Librarian:* ALLEN B. VEANER.

Number of teachers: 1,100.
Number of students: 14,430.

DEANS:

*College of Letters and Science:* DAVID A. SPRECHER, PH.D.
*College of Engineering:* JOHN E. MYERS, PH.D.
*College of Creative Studies:* M. MUDRICK, PH.D. (Provost).
*Graduate Division:* DAVID S. SIMONETT, PH.D.
*Graduate School of Education:* NAFTALY GLASMAN, PH.D.
*Instructional Development:* RICHARD E. OGLESBY, PH.D.

PROFESSORS:

AHLERS, G., Physics
AKEMANN, C. A., Mathematics
ALEXANDER, ALEC P., Economics
ANDERSON, S. V., Political Science
ARNTZ, M. A., Art
ATHANASSAKIS, A. N., Classics
ATKINS, S. P., German and Slavic Languages and Literature
ATWATER, T. H., Geological Sciences
AYRES, L. M., Art and Art History
BACHMUTH, S. O., Mathematics
BADASH, L., History
BAKER, G. E., Political Science
BALDWIN, J. A., Electrical Engineering
BALDWIN, J. D., Sociology
BANERJEE, S., Chemical and Nuclear Engineering
BARRETT, P. H., Physics
BARRON, C. A., Spanish and Portuguese
BARY, D., Spanish and Portuguese
BELCHIOR, M. L., Spanish and Portuguese
BERK, R. A., Sociology
BILLIGMEIER, R. H., Sociology

BLUM, G. S., Psychology
BOEHME, T. K., Mathematics
BOHANNAN, P., Anthropology
BONADEO, A. A., Italian
BOOK, R., Mathematics
BORDEN, M., History
BOTKIN, D. B., Environmental Studies
BOWERS, E., English
BOWERS, M. T., Chemistry
BOYAN, N. J., Education
BRADAC, J. J., Speech
BREWER, M. B., Psychology
BROKENSHA, D. W., Anthropology
BROWN, D. E., Anthropology
BROWN, G., Art
BROWN, G. I., Education
BROWNLEE, W. E., History
BRUCH, J. C., Jr., Mechanical and Environmental Engineering
BRUCKNER, A. M., Mathematics
BRUICE, T. C., Chemistry
BRUNO, J., Computer Science
BUGENTAL, D. E., Psychology
BUNTON, C. A., Chemistry
CALDWELL, D. O., Physics
CAMBERN, M. J., Mathematics
CANNELL, D. S., Physics
CAPPS, W. H., Religious Studies,
CARBON, J. A., Biology
CARLISLE, H. J., Psychology
CARLOS, M. L., Anthropology
CARROLL, J., English
CASE, J. F., Biological Sciences
CAVAT, I. C., Art
CEDER, J. G., Mathematics
CHAFFEE, R., Ergonomics and Physical Education
CHEN, C. I. Y., History
CLARKE, H. W., Classics
COFFMANN, E. G., Jr., Computer Science
COLE, H. M., Art
COLLINS, R. O., History
COMANOR, W. S., Economics
COMSTOCK, W. R., Religious Studies
CONNELL, J. H., Biological Sciences
COOLEY, T. F., Economics
CORTRIGHT, S. M., Art and Art History
COTTON, J. W., Educational Psychology
CRESSEY, D. R., Sociology
CRONSHAW, J., Biological Sciences
CROUCH, R. L., Economics
CROWELL, J. C., Geology
CUSHING, J. E., Jr., Biological Sciences
DAVIDSON, R. H., Political Sciences
DE CANIO, S., Economics
DECONDE, A., History
DELATTRE, GENEVIEVE, French and Italian
DELCHIARO, M. A., Arts and Art History
DIEMER, E. L., Music
DJORDJEVIC, D., History
DOLE, W. E., Jr., Art
DORRA, H., Art
EBELING, A. W., Biological Sciences
EISBERG, R. M., Physics
ENGLESBERG, E., Biological Sciences
ERASMUS, C. J., Anthropology
ERNEST, J. A., Mathematics
ESTES, J. E., Geography
EXNER, R. C., German and Slavic
FAGAN B., Anthropology
FAN, K., Mathematics
FARWELL, B., Art and Art History
FENECH, H. J., Chemical and Nuclear Engineering
FINGARETTE, H., Philosophy
FISHER, R. V., Geological Sciences
FISHER, S., Sociology
FLACKS, R., Sociology
FLEMING, B. N., Philosophy
FOLEY, J., Psychology
FONTANA, J., Electrical Engineering
FORD, P. C., Chemistry
FRECH, H. E., Economics
FRICKER, P. R., Music and Creative Studies

FRIESEN, A., History
FROST, F. J., History
FROST, W., English
FUENTES, V. F., Spanish and Portuguese
FUKUI, H., Political Science
FULCO, J. R., Physics
FULLER, M. D., Geological Sciences
GALLO, M., Spanish and Portuguese
GEBHARD, D. S., Art
GERBER, S. E., Speech
GERIG, J. T. C., Chemistry
GERSHO, A., Electrical and Computer Engineering
GERSTEIN, L. J., Mathematics
GIBOR, A., PH.D., Biological Sciences
GILLESPIE, J. E., Music
GLASMAN, N. S., Education
GLENN, S. L., Dramatic Art
GOGEL, W. C., Psychology
GOLD, D., Sociology
GOLLEDGE, R. G., Geography
GOLLIN, A. M., History
GOODRICH, C. S., German and Slavic Languages
GOTTSCHALK, G., German and Slavic Languages
GOTTSDANKER, R. M., Psychology
GUSS, D. L., English
HAMILTON, D. L., Psychology
HAMMOND, P. E., Religious Studies
HANLEY, T., Speech
HANNA, O. T., Chemical and Nuclear Engineering
HANRIEDER, W., Political Science
HANSMA, P. K., Physics
HARDING, T. G., Anthropology
HARRIS, D. O., Chemistry
HARROP, J., Dramatic Art
HARTLE, J. B., Physics
HATCH, E., Anthropology
HETZRON, R., Germanic and Slavic Languages
HICKMAN, R. S., Mechanical and Environmental Engineering
HIGGINS, J. W., Psychology
HOFFMEISTER, G., Comparative Literature
HOLLISTER, C. W., History
HOLMES, R. W., Biological Sciences
HOLMES, W. N., Biological Sciences
HONE, D., Physics
HOPSON, C. A., Geology
HOSFORD, R. E., Education
HOWARD, J. A., Electrical and Computer Engineering
HSU, D. M., Music
HSU, I. C. Y., History
HUBBARD, A. T., Chemistry
HUBERT, L. J., Education
HUTTENBACK, R. A., History
IANNACCONE, L., Education
IYER, R., Political Sciences
JACCARINO, V., Physics and Creative Studies
JACOBS, G., Psychology
JACOBS, W. R., History
JENCKS, C., Sociology
JOHNSEN, E. C., Mathematics
JOHNSON, D. B., German and Slavic Languages
JOHNSON, M., Economics
JORDAN, B., Classics
KASKA, W. C., Chemistry
KELLEY, R. L., History
KELLY, P. J., Mathematics
KENDLER, H. H., Psychology
KENDLER, T. S., Psychology
KENNEDY, J. H., Chemistry
KING, J. L., Biological Sciences
KIRKER, H. C., History
KIRTMAN, B., Chemistry
KOEGEL, R. L., Speech
KOTZEBUE, K. L., Electrical Engineering
KROEMER, H., Electrical and Computer Engineering
LARIS, P. C., Biological Sciences

LARSON, G. J., Religious Studies
LEE, N. L., Biological Sciences
LEIPNIK, R. B., Mathematics
LEWIS, H. W., Physics
LICK, W., Mechanical and Environmental Engineering
LIU, A. P., Political Science
LOOMIS, E. W., English
LUYENDYK, B. P., Geological Sciences
LYTLE, L. D., Psychology
MADSEN, W., Anthropology
MAHLENDORF, U. R., German
MALECOT, A., French and Italian
MANN, D. E., Political Science
MARCUS, M., Mathematics
MARK, P. A., Dramatic Art
MARSAK, L. M., History
MARSCHALL, E., Mechanical and Environmental Engineering
MARTIN, R. M., Chemistry
MARTÍNEZ-LÓPEZ, E., Spanish and Portuguese
MATTHAEI, G. L., Electrical Engineering
MCCARTHY, P. J., English
MCCLINTOCK, C. G., Psychology
MCCURDY, B. S., Art and Art History
MEAD, W. J., Economics
MELLER, P. T., Art and Art History
MELLICHAMP, D. A., Chemical and Nuclear Engineering
MERCER, L. J., Economics
MERCIER, V. H., English
MERKL, P. H., Political Science
MERZ, J. L., Electrical and Computer Engineering
MESSICK, D. M., Psychology
METIU, H. I., Chemistry
MICHAEL, E., Ergonomics and Physical Education
MICHAELSEN, R. S., Religious Studies
MILLER, G. H., Chemistry
MILLER, W. C., Mathematics
MILLETT, K. C., Mathematics
MILLIKAN, R., Chemistry
MILSTEIN, F., Mechanical and Environmental Engineering
MINC, H., Mathematics
MITCHELL, T. P., Mechanical Engineering
MITRA, S. K., Electrical and Computer Engineering
MOCHIZUKI, H. Y., Mathematics
MOIR, A., Art
MOLOTCH, H. L., Sociology
MOORE, J. D., Mathematics
MORGAN, W. D., Economics
MORRISON, R. J., Physics
MORSE, D., Biological Sciences
MOSELEY, M. F., Jr., Biological Sciences
MUDRICK, M., English
MULLER, W. H., Biological Sciences
MURDOCH, W., Biological Science
MURRAY, J., French and Italian
MYERS, J. E., Chemical and Nuclear Engineering
NASH, A. E. K., Political Science
NASH, R. W., History
NELSON, W., Music
NEUSHUL, M., Biological Sciences
NEWMANN, M., Mathematics
NORRIS, R. M., Geological Sciences
ODETTE, G. R., Chemical and Nuclear Engineering
OFFEN, H. W., Chemistry
OGLESBY, R. E., History
OMER, G. T. ST., English
ORDUNG, P. F., Electrical Engineering
ORIAS. E., Biological Sciences
OUTCALT, D. L., Mathematics
PAI, K., German and Slavic Languages
PALKE, W. E., Chemistry
PANIKKAR, R., Religious Studies
PEALE, S. J., Physics
PEARCE, D. R., English
PEARSON, B. A., Religious Studies
PEARSON, R. G. Chemistry

PHILLIPS, A. W., Spanish and Portuguese
PHILLIPS, L., Economics
PIERSON, C. J., Art and Art History
PIPPENGER, J. E., Economics
PRITCHARD, G. O., Chemistry
PRITCHETT, C. H., Political Science
PROFIO, A. E., Chemical and Nuclear Engineering
PURSELL, C. W., Jr., History
QUIMBY, R., Speech
REARDON, W. R., Dramatic Art
REMAK, J., History
RENEHAN, R. F., Classics
REYNOLDS, R. W., Psychology
REYNOLDS, W. A., Spanish
RHODES, I. B., Electrical and Computer Engineering
RICKBORN, B. B. F., Chemistry
RIDLAND, J., English
RINKER, R. G., Chemical and Nuclear Engineering
ROBERTSON, J. B., Mathematics
ROCHELLE, R., Ergonomics and Physical Education
ROSE, M., English
ROSS, I. K., Biology
RUSSELL, J. B., History
SANDALL, O. C., Chemical and Nuclear Engineering
SAWYER, R. F., Physics
SCALAPINO, D. J., Physics
SCHEFF, T., Sociology
SCHNEIDAU, H. N., English
SCHOELL, E. R., Speech
SCHRIEFFER, J. R., Physics
SCHROCK, T. S., Political Science
SCHWARTZ, A. M., Linguistics
SCHWYZER, H., Philosophy
SEBORG, D. E., Chemical and Nuclear Engineering
SEMMEL, M. I., Education
SENGUPTA, J. K., Economics
SERVICE, E. R., Anthropology
SESONSKE, A., Philosophy
SHAPIRO, P., Economics
SHAPIRO, S. B., Education
SHARRER, H. L., Spanish and Portuguese
SHIBUTANI, T., Sociology
SIMONETT, D., Geography
SIMONS, S. O., Mathematics
SKALNIK, J. G., Electrical Engineering
SLOSS, J. M., Mathematics
SMART, N. R., Religious Studies
SMITH, D. M., Biological Sciences
SMITH, J. D., Art and Art History
SOBEL, M., Mathematics
SONQUIST, J. A., Sociology
SPAULDING, A. C., Anthropology
SPRECHER, D. A., Mathematics
STATES, B., Dramatic Art
STEAR, E. B., Electrical Engineering
STEPHENS, A., English
STEPHENS, T. E., Military Science
STEWART, G., English
ST. OMER, G., English
STOUGH, C., Philosophy
SUGAR, R., Physics
SULLIVAN, J. P., Classics
SWANDER, H., English
SWEENEY, BEATRICE M., Biological Sciences
SYLVESTER, A. G., Geological Sciences
TABORSKY, G., Biological Sciences
TALBOTT, J., History
TEMMER, M. J., French
THOMAS, R. C., Art
THOMAS, R. M., Education
THOMPSON, R. C., Mathematics
TILTON, G. R., Geological Sciences
TOBIN, R. W., French
TOBLER, W. R., Geography
TRENCH, R., Biological Sciences
TRIPLETT, E. L., Biological Sciences
TURNER, H., Political Science
VALENTINE, J. W., Biological Sciences

VOTEY, H. L., Jr., Economics
WADE, G., Electrical Engineering
WALKER, P. D., French and Italian
WALKER, W. C., Physics
WALTERS, J. L., Biological Sciences
WATERMAN, J., Germanic and Slavic Languages and Literature
WEAVER, D. W., Geological Sciences
WEISS, M. L., Mathematics
WENNER, A. M., Biological Sciences
WESSON, R. G., Political Science
WILCZEK, F., Physics
WILKINS, B. T., Philosophy
WILSON, C. H., Jr., Music
WILSON, L., Biological Sciences
WISE, W. S., Geological Sciences
WONG, R. Y., Mathematics
WOOD, R. C., Electrical Engineering
YAQUB, A., Mathematics
YOUNG, D. C., Classics
ZELMANOWITZ, J., Mathematics
ZIMMER, J., Education
ZIMMERMAN, D., Sociology
ZIMMERMAN, E. L., English
ZYTOWSKI, C. B., Music

ATTACHED INSTITUTES:

**Center for Chicano Studies.**
**Community and Organization Research Institute.**
**Computer Systems Laboratory.**
**Institute for the Interdisciplinary Applications of Algebra and Combinatorics**
**Institute of Environmental Stress.**
**Institute of Religious Studies.**
**Intercampus Institute for Research of Particle Accelerators.**
**Marine Science Institute.**
**Quantum Institute.**
**Robert M. Hutchins Center for the Study of Democratic Institutions:** see under Research Institutes.
**Social Process Research Institute.**

## University of California, Santa Cruz

SANTA CRUZ, CALIFORNIA 95064
Telephone: (408) 429-0111.
Chartered 1961; Opened 1965.

*Chancellor:* ROBERT L. SINSHEIMER.
*Academic Vice-Chancellor:* JOHN A. MARCUM.
*Librarian:* ALLAN J. DYSON.

Number of teachers: c. 350.
Number of students: 6,364.

DEANS:

*Humanities and Arts:* HELENE MOGLEN.
*Natural Sciences:* WILLIAM T. DOYLE.
*Social Sciences:* (vacant).

PROVOSTS:

*Cowell College:* JOHN DIZIKES.
*Adlai E. Stevenson College:* DAVID E. KAUN.
*Crown College:* SIEGFRIED PUKNAT.
*Merrill College:* GEORGE VON DER MUHLL.
*College V:* PHILIP F. NELSON.
*Kresge College:* HELENE MOGLEN.
*Oakes College:* J. HERMAN BLAKE.
*College Eight:* (vacant).

RESEARCH UNITS:

**Coastal Marine Study Center:** Dir. WILLAM T. DOYLE.
**Lick Observatory:** Dir. (vacant).

## UNIVERSITY OF LA VERNE

LA VERNE, CALIFORNIA 91750
Telephone: (714) 593-3511.
Founded 1891.

*President:* ARMEN SARAFIAN.
*Vice-Presidents:* W. DONALD CLAGUE (Academic), THOMAS HALL (Development), ALTON MORSE (Business Services).
*Directors:* MICHAEL WELCH (Admissions and Financial Aid), VIRGIL WILKINSON (Personnel).
*Registrar:* MARILYN DAVIES.
*Librarian:* MARLIN HECKMAN.

Library of 113,000 vols., Law library of 70,000 vols.
Number of teachers: 78 full-time, 235 part-time.
Number of students: 1,900.

DEANS:

*Student Services:* SHARON AGLER.
*Undergraduate:* JACQUELINE P. DOUD.
*School of Continuing Education:* JAMES MANOLIS.
*College of Law:* CHARLES DOSKOW.
*American Armenian International College:* GARBIS YEGHIAYAN.

## UNIVERSITY OF REDLANDS

REDLANDS, CALIFORNIA 92373
Telephone: 793-2121.
Founded 1907; Private.

*President:* DOUGLAS R. MOORE, B.A., S.T.B., PH.D.
*Vice-President for Academic Affairs:* GERALD O. GATES, PH.D.
*Registrar:* NORA McLAUGHLIN, B.A.
*Library Director:* ROGER BATY, PH.D.

The library contains 265,029 vols.
Number of teachers: 109.
Number of students: 1,100.
Publication: *Redlands Report.*

DEANS:

*Curriculum:* JOHN P. BROWNFIELD, M.F.A.
*Interdisciplinary Studies:* H. BEN DILLOW, M.A.
*Graduate Studies:* ROBERT L. STUART, PH.D.

AFFILIATED CENTRES:

**Alfred North Whitehead Center for Lifelong Learning:** f. 1976; 1,200 students; Dean DONALD C. KLECKNER, PH.D.
**Johnston Center for Individualized Learning:** f. 1969; 40 students; Dir. KATHY SHUMAKER, PH.D.

## UNIVERSITY OF SAN DIEGO
ALCALA PARK, SAN DIEGO,
CALIFORNIA 92110

Telephone: (714) 291-6480

Founded 1949.

*President:* Dr. AUTHOR E. HUGHES.
*Vice-President and Provost:* Sister SALLY FURAY.
*Vice-President for University Relations:* Dr. WILLIAM L. PICKETT.
*Vice-President for Business Affairs:* JOHN D. BOYCE.
*Vice-President for Student Affairs:* THOMAS F. BURKE.
*Librarian:* MARIAN HOLLEMAN.

### DEANS:

*School of Law:* SHELDON KRONTZ.
*College of Arts and Sciences:* Dr. C. JOSEPH PUSATERI.
*School of Education:* Dr. EDWARD F. DE ROCHE.
*School of Business Administration:* Dr. JAMES BURNS.
*School of Nursing:* Dr. IRENE PALMER.
*School of Graduate and Continuing Education:* Dr. RAYMOND BRANDES.

The library contains 343,929 vols.
Number of teachers: 264.
Number of students: 4,428.


## UNIVERSITY OF SAN FRANCISCO
GOLDEN GATE AND PARKER STREETS,
SAN FRANCISCO,
CALIFORNIA 94117.

Telephone: (415) 666-6886.

Founded 1855; Private; Jesuit.

*Resident:* Rev. JOHN J. LO SCHIAVO, S.J.
*Vice-Presidents:* Rev. JOSEPH ANGILELLA, S.J. (*Academic*), Dr. ANNE DOLAN (*Student Development*), ALFRED P. ALESSANDRI (*University Relations*), Dr. DOUGLAS D. DAVIS (*Administration and University Legal Adviser*).
*Secretary:* Rev. P. P. CALLAGHAN, S.J.
*Librarian:* PAUL E. BIRKEL.

The library contains 366,000 vols.
Number of teachers: 250.
Number of students: 6,500.

Publications: *Wasmann Journal*, *Law Review* (both bi-annually), *U.S.F. Quarterly*, *U.S.F. Report*, *U.S.F. Alumnus* (all quarterly).

### DEANS AND DIRECTORS:

*Admissions and Records:* GABRIEL P. CAPETO.
*Colleges of Liberal Arts and Science:* DAVID A. HARNETT.
*Business Administration:* BERNARD L. MARTIN.
*School of Law:* JOSEPH T. HENKE.
*Nursing:* JOAN L. GREEN (acting).
*School of Education:* WAYNE DOYLE (acting).

*Continuing Education:* COLIN SILVERTHORNE.


## UNIVERSITY OF SANTA CLARA
SANTA CLARA,
CALIFORNIA 95053

Telephone: (408) 984-4256.

Founded 1851. Private.

*President:* WILLIAM J. REWAK, S.J.
*Academic Vice-President:* PAUL LOCATELLI, S.J.
*Chancellor:* PATRICK A. DONOHOE, S.J.
*Vice-President for Finance:* JOSE A. DEBASA.
*Vice-President for University Relations:* EUGENE F. GERWE.
*Vice-President for Student Services:* PAUL L. MOORE.
*Librarian:* V. NOVAK.

The library contains 450,000 vols.
Number of teachers: 243.
Number of students: 7,101.

Publications: *Santa Clara*, *Redwood*, *The Owl*, *Santa Clara Today*.

### DEANS:

*College of Arts and Sciences:* JOSEPH L. SUBBIONDO.
*School of Engineering:* R. J. PARDEN.
*School of Law:* G. J. ALEXANDER.
*School of Business:* ANDRÉ L. DELBECQ.


## UNIVERSITY OF SOUTHERN CALIFORNIA
UNIVERSITY PARK,
LOS ANGELES, CALIFORNIA 90007

Telephone: (213) 743-2311.

Established 1879; Incorporated and opened 1880.

*President:* JAMES H. ZUMBERGE, PH.D.
*Senior Vice-Presidents:* CORNELIUS J. PINGS, PH.D. (Academic Affairs), JON C. STRAUSS, PH.D. (Administration), MICHAEL RADOCK, M.A. (Development and University Relations).
*Vice-President, Governmental Affairs:* HOUSTON I. FLOURNOY, PH.D.
*Vice-President, Health Affairs:* J. VAN DER MEULEN, M.D.
*Vice-President, Student Affairs:* JAMES R. APPLETON, PH.D.
*Vice-President, Business Affairs:* A. D. LAZZARO, B.S.
*Registrar:* CAROLE JONES, A.B. (acting).
*Director of Admissions:* JAY BERGER, PH.D.
*Librarian:* ROY L. KIDMAN, M.S.
*Library: see* Libraries.

Number of teachers: 2,700.
Number of students: 28,129.

Publication: *Bulletin* (monthly).

### DEANS:

*College of Letters, Arts and Sciences:* DAVID H. MALONE, PH.D. (acting).
*Graduate School:* CHARLES E. OXNARD, PH.D., D.SC.

*School of Architecture:* ROBERT S. HARRIS, M.F.A.
*School of Business Administration:* JACK STEELE, D.B.A.
*School of Dentistry:* WILLIAM H. CRAWFORD, Jr., D.D.S.
*School of Education:* JOHN B. ORR, PH.D. (acting).
*School of Engineering:* Z. A. KAPRIELIAN, PH.D.
*School of Fine Arts:* JOHN S. GORDON, M.F.A.
*School of Law:* SCOTT BICE, J.D.
*School of Library Science:* ROGER C. GREER, PH.D.
*School of Medicine:* A. W. MATHIES, Jr., PH.D., M.D.
*School of Performing Arts:* GRANT BEGLARIAN, D.M.A.
*School of Pharmacy:* J. A. BILES, PH.D.
*School of Public Administration:* ROBERT P. BILLER, PH.D.
*School of Social Work:* ROBERT W. ROBERTS, PH.D.
*College of Continuing Education, Evening College, Summer Session:* ROSALIND LORING, M.A.
*Annenberg School of Communications:* PETER CLARKE, PH.D.
*Leonard Davis School of Gerontology:* JAMES E. BIRREN, PH.D.
*Institute of Safety and Systems Management:* JOHN V. GRIMALDI, PH.D. (acting).


## UNIVERSITY OF THE PACIFIC
STOCKTON, CALIFORNIA 95211

Telephone: 946-2011.

Founded as California Wesleyan College 1851; name changed to University of the Pacific 1852; consolidated with Napa College 1896; name changed to College of the Pacific 1911; name changed to University of the Pacific 1961; Private control.

*President:* STANLEY E. MCCAFFREY.
*Academic Vice-President:* C. J. HAND.
*Financial Vice-President:* R. R. WINTERBERG.
*Vice-President-Executive Assistant:* C. L. DOCHTERMAN.
*Dean of Admissions:* E. L. MEDFORD.
*Vice-President for Student Life:* JUDITH M. CHAMBERS.
*Dean of Academic Records and Institutional Research and University Registrar:* LEE C. FENNELL.
*Librarian:* HIRAM DAVIS.

The library contains 300,000 vols.
Number of teachers: 371.
Number of students: 6,004.

Publications: *Pacific Review*, *Pacific Historian*, *Pacifican*, *Contact Point* (Dental School), *De Minimus* (School of Law).

### DEANS:

*Business and Public Administration:* ELLIOT H. KLINE.
*Education:* O. T. JARVIS.
*Engineering:* R. L. HEYBORNE.
*Graduate School:* R. W. SMITH III.

UNIVERSITIES AND COLLEGES—CALIFORNIA, COLORADO U.S.A.

*Liberal Arts:* R. A. WHITEKER.
*Music:* C. E. NOSSE.
*Pharmacy:* L. C. MARTINELLI.
*Covell College:* G. L. CALDWELL.
*School of Dentistry:* ARTHUR DUGONI.
*School of Law:* G. D. SCHABER.

## WEST COAST UNIVERSITY
440 SHATTO PLACE,
LOS ANGELES, CALIFORNIA 90020
Telephone: (213) 487-4433.

Founded 1909.

*President:* Dr. ROBERT M. L. BAKER, Jr.
*Executive Vice-President and Provost:* Dr. C. B. GAMBRELL.
*Secretary and Treasurer:* Dr. PHILIP HAMMEL.
*Registrar:* Mrs. ESTHER HUGHES.
*Librarian:* Ms. BETH HOWELL.

The library contains 20,000 vols.
Number of teachers: 200.
Number of students: 1,350.

## WESTMONT COLLEGE
955 LA PAZ ROAD,
SANTA BARBARA,
CALIFORNIA 93108
Telephone: 969-5051.

Founded 1940.

*President:* Dr. DAVID K. WINTER.
*Vice-President and Academic Dean:* Dr. TOM ANDREWS.
*Registrar:* Mrs. ARLEEN SHENNUM.
*Director of Learning Resources:* JOHN D. MURRAY.

The library contains 120,000 vols.
Number of teachers: 58.
Number of students: 1,075.

## WHITTIER COLLEGE
WHITTIER, CALIFORNIA 90608
Telephone: (213) 693-0771.

Founded 1901.

*President:* EUGENE S. MILLS.
*Dean:* RICHARD J. WOOD.
*Librarian:* PHILIP M. O'BRIEN.

Number of teachers: 100.
Number of students: 1,400.
Publication: *The Rock* (quarterly).

# COLORADO

## ADAMS STATE COLLEGE OF COLORADO
ALAMOSA, COLORADO 81102
Telephone: 589-7341.

Founded 1921.

*President:* WILLIAM M. FULKERSON, Jr.
*Vice-President for Academic Affairs:* GLENN BURNHAM, ED.D. (acting).
*Vice-President for Business and Financial Affairs:* LEONARD MCLEAN, M.A.

*Dean of Graduate Studies:* LLOYD SWENSON, ED.D.
*Registrar and Director of Admissions:* WAYNE FARLEY, M.A.
*Librarian:* NELLIE HASFJORD, M.A.

The library contains 158,993 vols.
Number of teachers: 104.
Number of students: 2,000.

## COLORADO COLLEGE
COLORADO SPRINGS,
COLORADO 80903

Chartered 1874.

*President:* LLOYD E. WORNER.
*General Secretary:* W. ROBERT BROSSMAN.
*Business Manager:* R. W. BROUGHTON.
*Librarian:* G. V. FAGAN.

Number of teachers: 160.
Number of students: 1,820.

DEANS:

*College:* R. C. BRADLEY.
*Students:* M. F. TAYLOR, Jr.
*Admissions:* R. E. WOOD.
*Summer School:* GILBERT R. JOHNS.
*Women:* LAUREL MCLEOD.
*Director of Alumni Affairs:* B. YALICH.

## COLORADO SCHOOL OF MINES
GOLDEN, COLORADO 80401
Telephone: (303) 279-0300.

Founded 1874.

A university of mineral resources.

*President:* GUY T. MCBRIDE, Jr.
*Vice-President for Business Affairs:* W. GORDON SCOTT.
*Vice-President for Academic Affairs and Dean of the Faculty:* WILLIAM M. MUELLER.
*Vice-President for Institutional Planning and Development:* J. G. WELLES.
*Dean of Graduate Studies and Research:* JOHN O. GOLDEN.
*Dean of Students:* MICHAEL NYIKOS.
*Director of Admissions:* A. W. YOUNG.
*Librarian:* HARTLEY K. PHINNEY, Jr.

Library of 225,000 vols.
Number of teachers: 200.
Number of students: 3,070.
Publications: *Quarterly of the Colorado School of Mines, Mineral Industries Bulletin.*

## COLORADO STATE UNIVERSITY
FORT COLLINS, COLORADO 80521

Founded 1870 as The Agricultural College of Colorado; became a State institution in 1876, a land-grant college in 1879.

*President:* R. E. CHRISTOFFERSEN, PH.D.
*Executive Director:* EUGENE T. PETRONE, M.A.
*Treasurer:* J. R. HEHN, PH.D.
*Executive Vice-President:* C. O. NEIDT, PH.D. (acting).

*Vice-President for Research:* GEORGE G. OLSON, PH.D.
*Vice-President for Finance:* M. A. BINKLEY, PH.D.
*Registrar and Director of Admissions:* L. L. OVERTURF, M.S.
*Director of Libraries:* L. W. ANDERSON, PH.D.

The library contains 900,000 vols.
Number of teachers: 1,200.
Number of students: 11,000 men, 7,000 women, total 18,000.

DEANS:

*College of Business:* D. W. DOBLER, PH.D.
*College of Engineering:* L. V. BALDWIN, PH.D.
*College of Forestry and Natural Resources:* J. M. HUGHES, PH.D.
*College of Natural Sciences:* W. B. COOK, PH.D.
*College of Agriculture:* D. D. JOHNSON, PH.D.
*College of Veterinary Medicine:* R. D. PHEMISTER, D.V.M.
*College of Humanities and Social Sciences:* F. J. VATTANO, PH.D.
*College of Home Economics:* HELEN F. MCHUGH, M.S., PH.D.
*College of Professional Studies:* W. JOHNSON, PH.D.
*Graduate School:* P. T. BRYANT, PH.D. (acting).

ASSOCIATED INSTITUTIONS:

*Colorado Agricultural Experimental Station.*
  Director: J. P. JORDON, PH.D.
*Extension Service.*
  Director: L. W. WATTS, M.S.
*Colorado State Forest Service.*
  State Forester: T. B. BORDEN, M.S.
*Rocky Mountain Forest and Range Experiment Station.*
  Director: C. M. LOVELESS, PH.D.
*Colorado Co-operative Wildlife Research Unit.*
  Leader: R. M. HOPPER.
*Colorado Co-operative Fishery Research Unit.*
  Leader: D. L. HORAK.

## COLORADO WOMEN'S COLLEGE
1800 PONTIAC ST.,
DENVER, COLORADO 80220
Telephone: (303) 394-6012.

Founded 1888.

*President:* Dr. SHERRY MANNING.
*Dean of Faculty:* Dr. ELAYNE DONOHUE.
*Director of Admissions:* MICHAEL BIERY.
*Librarian:* P. N. FRAME.

The library contains 133,000 volumes.
Number of teachers: 39.
Number of students: 450.

### FORT LEWIS COLLEGE
COLLEGE HEIGHTS,
DURANGO, COLORADO 81301
Telephone: 247-7184.

Founded 1911.

*President:* REXER BERNDT.
*Director of Admissions:* HARLAN STEINE.
*Librarian:* R. GOBBLE.

The library contains 226,000 vols.
Number of teachers: 165.
Number of students: 3,400.

### LORETTO HEIGHTS COLLEGE
3001 SOUTH FEDERAL BLVD.,
DENVER, COLORADO 80236
Telephone: (303) 936-8441.

Founded 1918.

*President:* ADELE PHELAN.
*Vice-President and Academic Dean:* ANTHONY PARIMANATH.
*Dean of Campus Life:* ADELIA TYLER.
*Director of Admissions and Financial Aid:* M. CONSTANCE CAMPBELL.
*Librarian:* AGNES MYERS.

The library contains 93,000 vols.
Number of teachers: 101.
Number of students: 800.

### UNIVERSITY OF COLORADO
BOULDER,
COLORADO 80309

Incorporated 1861, opened 1877.

*President:* ARNOLD R. WEBER.
*Vice-President for Administration:* THEODORE VOLSKY Jr., PH.D.
*Vice-President for Budget and Planning:* JOHN W. BARTRAM, B.A.
*Assistant Vice-President for Finance and Treasurer:* HERBERT R. DUNHAM, B.S.
*Secretary of the University and Board of Regents:* H. H. ARNOLD, LL.B.
*Director of Student Administrative Services:* WILLIAM A. DOUGLAS, M.A.
Library: see Libraries.

Publications: *College Catalog* (annually), *Colorado Alumnus* (monthly for 10 months), *Colorado Business Review* (monthly), *Colorado Quarterly*, *English Language Notes*, *East European Quarterly*, *University of Colorado Law Review*, *Colorado Engineer*, *Arctic and Alpine Research* (quarterly), *Computer Newsletter* (9 times per year), and University of Colorado Studies series covering various subjects.

#### University of Colorado at Boulder
BOULDER, COLORADO 80309
*Chancellor:* J. RUSSELL NELSON, PH.D.
*Vice-Chancellor for Administration:* TED TEDESCO, M.P.A.
*Vice-Chancellor for Academic Affairs and Dean of Faculties:* MILTON E. LIPETZ, PH.D.

Number of students: 21,727.

DEANS:
*College of Environmental Design:* DWAYNE NUZUM, PH.D.
*College of Business and Administration:* WILLIAM H. BAUGHN, M.A.
*School of Education:* RICHARD TURNER, PH.D.
*School of Journalism:* RUSSELL E. SHAIN, PH.D.
*School of Law:* THOMAS G. BROWN, LL.B.
*School of Medicine:* ROY SCHWARTZ, M.O.
*School of Nursing:* BETTY S. WILLIAMS, D.P.H.
*Graduate School:* MILTON E. LIPETZ, PH.D.
*College of Arts and Sciences:* WILLIAM E. BRIGGS, M.A., PH.D.
*College of Engineering:* WILLIAM J. PIETENPOL, PH.D.
*College of Music:* ROBERT FINK, M.MUS.ED., PH.D.
*School of Pharmacy:* V. GENE ERWIN, PH.D.
*School of Dentistry:* THOMAS J. BOMBERG, D.D.S.
*Continuing Education and Summer Session:* P. JOHN LYMBEROPOULOS, PH.D.

#### University of Colorado at Colorado Springs
COLORADO SPRINGS, COLORADO 80907
*Chancellor:* DONALD SCHWARTZ, PH.D.
Number of students: 3,288.

#### University of Colorado at Denver
DENVER, COLORADO 80202
*hancellor:* (vacant).
Number of students: 8,097.

### UNIVERSITY OF DENVER
DENVER, COLORADO 80208
Telephone: 753-1964.
Telex: 910-931-2532.

Founded 1864.

Private control; Academic year: September to June.

*Chancellor:* ROSS PRITCHARD.
*Vice-Chancellor for Academic Affairs:* IRVING B. WEINER.
*Vice-Chancellor for Institutional Advancement:* LEONARD MEYER.
*Vice-Chancellor for Student Affairs:* THOMAS G. GOODALE.
*Vice-Chancellor for Financial Affairs and Treasurer:* RICHARD H. HARRINGTON.
*Registrar:* J. POMMREHN.
*Librarian:* M. SCHERTZ.

The library contains 1,603,764 vols.
Number of teachers: 486 full-time, 105 part-time, total 591.
Number of students: 8,391.

Publications: *Denver Law Journal of International Law and Policy*, *Denver Law Journal* (quarterly), *Denver Quarterly*, *Clarion* (2 a week), *Today* (fortnightly), *K-Book* (annually), *University of Denver News* (quarterly).

DEANS:
*Arts and Sciences:* KENNETH PURCELL.
*Business Administration:* R. BRANDENBURG.
*Law:* DANIEL HOFFMAN.
*Graduate School of Arts and Sciences:* M. KIME.
*Graduate School of Librarianship and Information Management:* B. FRANCKOWIAK.
*Graduate School of International Studies:* B. ABRAHAMSSON (acting).
*Graduate School of Social Work:* L. MCCUMMINGS.

PROFESSORS:
*College of Arts and Sciences:*
ADAMS, P., Education
AMME, R. C., Physics
ANDERSON, D., Foreign Languages and Literature
BARANY, G., History
BARBOUR, A., Speech Communication
BARCUS, J. R., Physics
BARDWELL, G. E., Mathematics
BEALL, C. P., Political Science
BERNAL, M., Psychology
BLEISTEIN, N., Mathematics
BOKLUND, G. K., English
BRANDOM, W., Biological Sciences
BRECK, A. DU P., History
CAMPOS, J., Psychology
CARPENTER, S., Physics
CARROLL, A., Education
CHAPMAN, G. W., English
CHASSON R. L., Physics
CLEIN, M., Physical Education
COHEN, J., Mathematics
CRANE, T., History
DANCE, F. E. X., Speech Communication
DAVINE, R., Music
DAVIS, J., Education
DORN, W. S., Mathematics
DORSETT, L., History
DRABEK, T. E., Sociology
DRISCOLL, W. T., Biological Sciences
EATON, G., Chemistry
EPSTEIN, S., English
EVERHART, E., Physics
FEE, R. D., Music
FELDMAN, B., English
GEDDES, C., History
GLORFELD, L., Speech Communication
GOLDBERG, A., Speech Communication
GOLLOB, H., Psychology
GREENBERG, H., Mathematics
GUDDER, S. P., Mathematics
HAITH, M., Psychology
HARTER, S., Psychology
HOFFMAN, RUTH I., Mathematics
HORN, J., Psychology
HUGHES, D., History
IONA, M., Physics
JAMES, S., English
JONES, N., Psychology
KEATS, D., Music
KEY, W. H., Sociology
KING, E. W., Education
KIRK, J., Religious Studies
LARSON, C., Speech
LEYDEN, D., Chemistry

MANSELL, G., Art
MARCHAND, J.-P., Mathematics
MENDELSOHN, H., Mass Communications
MOORE, W. E., Sociology and Law
MURCRAY, D., Physics
NEWKIRK, J. B., Chemistry
OLSON, G., Physical Education
PATEL, V. L., Physics
PFNISTER, A., Education
PHILLIPS, JEANNE S., Psychology
PRATHER, R., Mathematics
PURCELL, K., Psychology
RAFFEL, B., English
RECHARD, D., Mathematics
RITCHIE, H. M., Theatre
RUDD, R., Geography
SCHMIDT-COLLERUS, J., Chemistry
SLAICHERT, W. M., Education
SMITH, D., Chemistry
SPILKA, B., Psychology
STICKLER, W. C., Chemistry
STONE, G., Biological Sciences
STRAWN, M., Art
TRIPP, R., English
TUTTLE, E., Physics
VAN DER MERWE, A., Physics
WALSH, V., Economics
WATT, N., Psychology
WILLIAMS, J. E., English
WYAND M., Economics

*College of Law:*
ALTONIN, W.
BEANEY, W. M.
BLUMENTHAL, M.
BRODY, B.
CARVER, J.
COCO, A.
DUFFORD, P.
JAMISON, F. W.
KESSELMAN, J. J., Accounting and Law
KRENDL, C.
LAWSON, H.
LINN, J. P.
LITTLEFIELD, N.
MARSH, T. G.
MOORE, W. E., Law and Sociology
MUNCH, C.
NANDA, V. P.
REESE, J. H.
ROSENBERG, H. L.
TIFFANY, L. P.
WALKER, T. B.
WALLACE, J. E.
WINOKUR, J.
YEGGE, R. B.

*College of Business Administration:*
BARDWELL, G., Statistics and Mathematics
BOZEMAN, B., Business Law
BRITTAN, M. R., Statistics
CAMPBELL, S., Statistics
DRURY, D., Economics
FIRMIN, P., Accountancy
FLETCHER, D., Administrative Sciences
FOSTER, G., Administrative Sciences
GIST, R. R., Marketing Management
GRIMSTAD, C. R., Accounting
HALTERMAN, C., Administrative Sciences
JOHNSTON, J., Business Law
JONES, D. E., Administrative Sciences
KESSELMAN, J. J., Accounting
KUARK, J. Y., Statistics and Economics
MASON, A., Finance and Management
McCROSKEY, J., Finance
SORENSEN, J., Accounting
SOTIRIOUS, C., Administrative Sciences
VARDAMAN, G., Administrative Sciences
VON STROH, G., Administrative Sciences
WALTHER, J. V., Finance

*Graduate Schools (Professional):*
ANCELL, H., Social Work
BARNETT, ELEANOR M., Social Work
BAYLEY, D., International Studies
BOLTE, K., Social Work
BRIDGES, J., Social Work
CAPORASO, J., International Studies
GOGGIN, M. K., Librarianship
JORGENSON, J. Social Work
KAPLAN, I., Social Work
KLEPINGER, B., Social Work
McCANN, C. W., Social Work
SHEPHERD, G., International Studies
SHERMAN, E., Social Work
SZYLIOWICZ, J. S., International Studies

ATTACHED INSTITUTE:
**Denver Research Institute:** Dir. SHIRLEY H. JOHNSON, Jr.

## UNIVERSITY OF NORTHERN COLORADO
GREELEY, COLORADO 80639

Telephone (303) 351-1890.

Founded 1889 as the State Normal School; name changed to Colorado State Teachers' College 1911, to Colorado State College of Education in 1935, to Colorado State College in 1957; present name adopted in 1970.

*President:* ROBERT C. DICKESON, PH.D.
*Vice-President for Academic Affairs:* CHALRES W. MANNING, PH.D.
*Registrar:* CHARLES SELDEN, M.S.
*Vice-President for Administrative Services:* A. E. BARNHART, ED.D.
*Vice-President for Student Affairs:* GERALD E. TANNER, PH.D.
*Vice-President for University Development:* JOHN L. BURKE, B.A.
*Librarian:* CLAUDE J. JOHNS, Jr., PH.D.
Number of teachers: 620.
Number of students: 10,870.
Publications: *Bulletin, Alumni Notes, Alumni News Letter, Journal of Research Services.*

DEANS:
*Graduate School:* B. R. BROWN.
*School of Business:* R. DOLPHIN, Jr.
*College of Education:* O. L. TRAINER.
*School of Health, Physical Education and Recreation:* M. PUTHOFF.
*School of Industrial Technology and Home Economics:* W. R. ERWIN, ED.D.
*College of Arts and Science:* A. E. BENT.
*College of Performing and Visual Arts:* J. E. MILLER, PH.D.
*School of Nursing:* D. ARLTON (acting).

## UNIVERSITY OF SOUTHERN COLORADO
2200 BONFORTE BOULEVARD, PUEBLO, COLORADO 81001

Telephone: (303) 549-0123.

Founded as Junior College 1933, Southern Colorado State College 1961, present name 1975.

*President:* LYLE C. WILCOX.
*Librarian:* Mrs. B. MOORE (acting).
The library contains 18,000 vols.
Number of teachers: 293.
Number of students: 5,637.

## WESTERN STATE COLLEGE OF COLORADO
GUNNISON, COLORADO 81230

Telephone: 943-0120.

Founded 1901.

*President:* Dr. JOHN P. MELLON.
*Registrar:* L. H. HALL.
*Librarian:* J. C. GARRALDA.
The library contains 130,000 vols.
Number of teachers: 135.
Number of students: 3,200.

# CONNECTICUT

## ALBERTUS MAGNUS COLLEGE
NEW HAVEN, CONNECTICUT 06511

Telephone: 777-6631.

Liberal Arts College for women.

Founded 1925.

*President:* Sister FRANCIS DE SALES HEFFERNAN.
*Dean:* Sister M. FAITH DARGAN.
*Director of Admissions:* Sister MICHELE RYAN.
*Librarian:* Sister M. WILMA LYNCH.
The library contains 87,413 vols.
Number of teachers: 55.
Number of students: 565.

## CENTRAL CONNECTICUT STATE COLLEGE
NEW BRITAIN, CONNECTICUT 06050

Telephone: (203) 827-7203.

Founded 1849.

*President:* F. DON JAMES.
*Registrar:* CARL BECK.
*Librarian:* R. MASSMANN, Director of Library Services.
The library contains 313,245 vols.
Number of teachers: 416.
Number of students: 12,061.

## CONNECTICUT COLLEGE
NEW LONDON, CONNECTICUT 06320

Founded 1911.

*President:* OAKES AMES, PH.D.
*Secretary of the College and Assistant to the President for College Relations:* JANE R. BREDESON, B.A.
*Registrar:* ROBERT LEE RHYNE, PH.D.
*Dean of Admissions:* JEANETTE B. HERSEY, B.S.
*Office of Graduate Studies:* R. FRANCIS JOHNSON, TH.D.
*Dean of the College:* ALICE JOHNSON, PH.D.
*Dean of the Faculty:* R. FRANCIS JOHNSON, TH.D.
*Dean of Student Affairs:* MARGARET WATSON, A.B.

Librarian: BRIAN D. ROGERS, M.S.L.S.
The library contains 363,000 vols.
Number of teachers: 197 (full-time and part-time).
Number of students: 1,670.

## EASTERN CONNECTICUT STATE COLLEGE
83 WINDHAM ST., WILLIMANTIC, CONNECTICUT 06226

Telephone: (203) 456-2231.

Founded 1889, refounded as Willimantic State College 1959, name changed 1967.

President: CHARLES R. WEBB.
Director of Admissions and Research: ARTHUR C. FORST.
Librarian: OLIVER HAYES.
The library contains 95,000 vols.
Number of teachers: 115.
Number of students: 2,553.

## FAIRFIELD UNIVERSITY
FAIRFIELD, CONNECTICUT 06430

Telephone: (203) 255-5411.

Founded 1942.

School of Arts and Sciences, Business, Nursing, Education and Communication, Continuing Education.

President: Rev. ALOYSIUS P. KELLEY, S.J.
Provost: Dr. JOHN A. BARONE.
Academic Vice-President: Rev. CHRISTOPHER F. MOONEY, S.J.
Vice-President, Business and Finance: JOHN M. HICKSON.
Vice-President, Student Services: WILLIAM P. SCHIMPF.
Vice-President for Development and Public Relations: GEORGE E. DIFFLEY.
University Registrar: ROBERT C. RUSSO.
Registrar, Graduate Schools: ROBERT GRIFFIN.
Librarian: BARBARA D. BRYAN.
The library contains 312,887 vols.
Number of teachers: 299.
Number of students: Undergraduate 4,091, Graduate 971.

DEANS:
College of Arts and Sciences: Dr. STEPHEN L. WEBER.
School of Business: Dr. JOHN GRIFFIN.
Graduate School of Communication: THEODORE A. CHENEY (acting).
Graduate School of Education: Dr. ROBERT PITT.
School of Nursing: Dr. PHYLLIS PORTER.
School of Continuing Education: Dr. WILLIAM MURPHY.

## HARTFORD GRADUATE CENTER
275 WINDSOR ST., HARTFORD, CONNECTICUT 06120

Telephone: (203) 549-3600.

Founded 1955.

President: Dr. HOMER D. BABBIDGE, Jr.
Director of Student Affairs: REBECCA M. FRIEDMAN.
Librarian: D. L. EVANS.
The library contains 25,000 vols.
Number of teachers: 22 full-time, 100 part-time.
Number of students: 1,300.

## QUINNIPIAC COLLEGE
HAMDEN, CONNECTICUT 06518

Telephone: (203) 288-5251.

Founded 1929.
Independent.

President: RICHARD A. TERRY.
Provost and Vice-President for Academic Affairs: HARRY L. BENNETT.
Registrar: DOROTHY LAURIA WHITE.
Librarian: MILDRED B. TANOFSKY.
The library contains 125,000 vols.
Number of teachers: 376.
Number of students: 2,322 full-time, 1,579 part-time.

DEANS:
School of Allied Health and Natural Science: MARLIN DEARDEN.
School of Business: LEON V. HIRSCH.
School of Liberal Arts: D. R. ELKINS, M. H. WOSKOW.
Continuing Education: NOEL G. BISHOP.

## SAINT JOSEPH COLLEGE
1678 ASYLUM AVENUE, WEST HARTFORD, CONNECTICUT 06117

Telephone: 232-4571.

Founded 1932.

President: Sister MARY CONSOLATA.
Academic Dean: Dr. FRED GILLIARD.
Registrar: KATHLEEN M. DEVINE.
Librarian: ALICE M. ANGELO.
The library contains 99,725 vols.
Number of teachers: 115.
Number of students: 1,525.

## SOUTHERN CONNECTICUT STATE COLLEGE
501 CRESCENT STREET, NEW HAVEN, CONNECTICUT 06515

Telephone: (203) 397-4000.

Founded 1893.

Liberal Arts, Teacher and Career Education.

President: Dr. FRANK HARRISON.
Vice-President: ROBERT A. NOWLAN, Jr.
Vice-President for Administrative Affairs: J. CLAUDE SCHEUERMAN.
Dean of Arts and Sciences: MARTIN J. ANISMAN.
Dean of Graduate Studies: ELLA A. ERWAY.
Dean of Professional Studies: ROCCO ORLANDO.
Dean of Student Affairs: MARTIN J. CURRY.
Director of Public Affairs: JOHN MATTIA.
Registrar: JOHN D. BRERETON.
Librarian: RICHARD HEGEL.
The library contains 385,611 vols.
Number of teachers: 417 full-time, 199 part-time.
Number of students: 11,368.

## TRINITY COLLEGE
HARTFORD, CONNECTICUT 06106

Founded 1823.

President: JAMES F. ENGLISH, Jr.
Vice-President: THOMAS A. SMITH.
Vice-President for Finance and Planning: JAMES F. ENGLISH, Jr.
Treasurer: ROBERT A. PEDEMONTI.
Secretary of the Faculty: J. BARD McNULTY.
Librarian: RALPH EMERICK.
The library contains 635,000 vols.
Number of full-time teachers: 138, including 58 professors.
Number of students: 1,806.

Publications: Tripod, Review, Trinity Reporter, Cesare Barbieri Courier.

DEAN:
Faculty: ANDREW G. DE ROCCO.

## UNITED STATES COAST GUARD ACADEMY
NEW LONDON, CONNECTICUT 06320

Telephone: (203) 443-8463.

Founded 1876.

President: Rear-Admiral MALCOLM E. CLARK (Superintendent).
Director of Admissions: Capt. ROBERT T. GETMAN.
Librarian: P. H. JOHNSON.
The library contains 108,000 vols.
Number of teachers: 120.
Number of students: 996.

## UNIVERSITY OF BRIDGEPORT
BRIDGEPORT, CONNECTICUT 06602

Telephone: (203) 576-4000.

Founded 1927.

President: LELAND MILES.
Vice-President of Academic Affairs: EDWIN G. EIGEL, Jr.

## UNIVERSITIES AND COLLEGES—CONNECTICUT (UNIVERSITY OF) — U.S.A.

*Vice-President for Administration and Finance:* HENRY J. HENEGHAN, Jr.
*Vice-President of University Relations:* JOHN J. COX.
*Vice-President for Enrollment Planning:* WARREN K. COOPER.
*Dean of Student Life:* JACQUELINE D. BENAMATI.
*Librarian:* JUDITH HUNT.

The library contains 317,290 vols.
Number of teachers: 285 full-time, 110 part-time, total 395.
Number of students: 3,617 full-time, 3,189 part-time, total 6,806.

### DEANS:

*College of Arts and Humanities:* J. RUSSELL NAZZARO.
*College of Business and Public Management:* JOHN MULCAHY.
*College of Science and Engineering:* RICHARD HILL.
*College of Health Sciences:* JOSEPH NESCHASEK.
*College of Law:* HOWARD A. GLIKSTEIN.

## UNIVERSITY OF CONNECTICUT
STORRS, CONNECTICUT 06268
Telephone: (203) 486-2000.

Established 1881 as The Storrs Agricultural School; opened to women in 1893 and name changed to Storrs Agricultural College, to Connecticut Agricultural College in 1899, to Connecticut State College 1933, and in 1939 to The University of Connecticut.

*President:* JOHN A. DIBIAGGIO, D.D.S., M.A.
*Vice-President (Academic Affairs):* K. G. WILSON, PH.D.
*Vice-President (Health Affairs):* JAMES E. MULVIHILL, D.M.D.
*Vice-President (Student Affairs):* FRANK A. NAPOLITANO, PH.D.
*Vice-President for Financial Affairs:* ARTHUR L. GILLIS, PH.D.
*Vice-President for Graduate Education and Research:* ANTHONY T. DIBENEDETTO, PH.D.
*Registrar:* THOMAS J. BURKE, M.A.
*Librarian:* J. P. McDONALD, M.S.L.S.
Library: see Libraries.
Number of teachers: 1,562 (full-time).
Number of students: 21,874.

Publications: *Connecticut Alumnus* (quarterly), *University of Connecticut Bulletin* (4 times a year), *Advanced and Graduate Courses* (twice yearly), *Graduate Engineering, Science and Statistics Courses* (twice yearly), *Summer Sessions Bulletin* (annual), *University Chronicle* (weekly).

### DEANS:

*College of Agriculture and Natural Resources:* E. J. KERSTING, D.V.M., M.S.
*College of Liberal Arts and Sciences:* J. A. ELIAS, PH.D.

*School of Business Administration:* R. J. PATTEN, PH.D.
*School of Dental Medicine:* HARALD LÖE, D.D.S.
*School of Education:* MARK R. SHIBLES, PH.D.
*School of Engineering:* P. W. McFADDEN, PH.D.
*School of Extended and Continuing Education:* GALVIN G. GALL, M.A.
*School of Fine Arts:* JEROME M. BIRDMAN, PH.D.
*School of Home Economics and Family Studies:* ROBERT G. RYDER, PH.D.
*School of Law:* P. I. BLUMBERG, J.D.
*School of Medicine:* ROBERT U. MASSEY, M.D.
*School of Nursing:* MARLENE KRAMER, PH.D.
*School of Pharmacy:* KARL A. NIEFORTH, PH.D.
*School of Allied Health Professions:* PAULINE FITZ, M.A., R.D.
*Ratcliffe Hicks School of Agriculture:* J. P. H. BRAND, PH.D. (Director).
*School of Social Work:* ROBERT GREEN, D.P.A.

### DIRECTORS:

*Institute of Cellular Biology:* PAUL F. GOETINCK, PH.D.
*Institute of Marine Sciences:* SUNG Y. FENG, PH.D.
*Institute of Materials Science:* L. V. AZAROFF, PH.D.
*Institute of Water Resources:* VICTOR E. SCOTTRON, D.ENG.
*Urban Research Institute:* M. J. TENZER, PH.D.
*Center for Black Studies:* F. L. BASS, ED.D.
*Center for Animal Care:* PHILIP D. FICHANDLER, D.V.M.
*Institute for Social Inquiry:* E. C. LADD, Jr., PH.D.
*Computer Center:* H. S. PETER JONES, M.SC.
*Office of Institutional Research:* LOIS E. TORRENCE, PH.D.
*Director of Development:* RAYMOND J. BUCK, Jr., A.B. (acting).

### PROFESSORS:

*College of Agriculture and Natural Resources:*
ALDRICH, R. A., PH.D., Agricultural Engineering
ARONSON, R. F., M.S., Agricultural Extension
BENSON, R. H., PH.D., Animal Industries
BRAND, J. P. H., PH.D., Agricultural Economics
BROWN, L. R., PH.D., Animal Industries
BETHUNE, J. E., PH.D., Forest Research
BRYANT, E. S., D.V.M., Pathobiology
BURKE, C. N., PH.D., Pathobiology
CARPENTER, E., Jr., PH.D., Ornamental Horticulture
COWAN, W. A., PH.D., Animal Industries
CZAJKOWSKI, J. M., ED.D., Foods and Nutrition
DANIELS, E. E., D.V.M., Nutritional Sciences
ECKER, G. A., PH.D., Farm Management

EMMERT, F. H., PH.D., Plant Nutrition
FARRISH, R. O. P., PH.D., Agricultural Economics
FAVRETTI, R. J., M.S., M.L.A., Landscape Architecture
FELLOWS, I. F., PH.D., Agricultural Economics
FETTERMAN, ELSIE B., PH.D., Family Economics and Management
FREDRICKSON, T. N., D.V.M., PH.D., Pathobiology
GAUNYA, W. S., PH.D., Animal Industries
GOETINCK, P. F., PH.D., Animal Genetics
GUTTAY, A. J. R., PH.D., Agronomy
HALE, N. S., PH.D., Animal Husbandry
JENSEN, R. G., PH.D., Nutritional Sciences
KHAIRALLAH, E. A., PH.D., Biology
KENNARD, W., PH.D., Plant Physiology
KERSTING, E. J., D.V.M., M.S., Pathobiology
KINSMAN, D. M., PH.D., Animal Industries
KLEIN, N. W., PH.D., Animal Genetics
KNOX, K. L., PH.D., Nutritional Sciences
KOTHS, J. S., PH.D., Floriculture
KOTTKE, M. W., PH.D., Agricultural Economics
LANE, DORIS A., M.A., Home Economics
LEE, T., PH.D., Agricultural Economics
LUCAS, J. J., PH.D., Biometrics
MALKUS, L. A., PH.D., Animal Industries
McDOWELL, R. D., PH.D., Wildlife Ecology
MEADE, A. R., M.S., M.A., Cooperative Extension and Research
NIELSEN, S. W., PH.D., A.C.V.P., Pathobiology
PETERS, R. A., PH.D., Agronomy
PIERRO, L. J., PH.D., Animal Genetics
PRINCE, R. P., M.S., Agricultural Engineering
RIDEOUT, A. H., PH.D., Cooperative Extension
SAVOS, M. G., PH.D., Entomology
SEAVER, S. K., PH.D., Agricultural Economics
SOMES, R. G., PH.D., Animal Genetics
STERN, D. N., D.V.M., Pathobiology
STITTS, D. G., PH.D., Agricultural Economics
TOURTELLOTTE, M. E., PH.D., Pathobiology
VANDER HEIDE, L., PH.D., Pathobiology
VAN KRUININGEN, H. J., D.V.M., PH.D., Pathobiology
WASHKO, W. W., PH.D., Agronomy
WAXMAN, S., PH.D., Ornamental Horticulture
WENGEL, R. W., PH.D., Agronomy
WHITWORTH, W. R., PH.D., National Resources Conservation
WILLIAMS, L. F., M.S., Pathobiology
WYAND, D. S., D.V.M., Pathobiology
YANG, T., D.V.M., PH.D., Pathobiology

*College of Liberal Arts and Sciences:*
ABBOTT, J. L., PH.D., English
ABRAHAMSON, M., PH.D., Sociology
ABRAMSON, A. S., PH.D., Linguistics
AIGNER, J. S., PH.D., Anthropology
ALLEN, G. J., PH.D., Psychology
ALLEN, J. L., PH.D., Geography
ANDREWS, O., PH.D., Romance and Classical Languages
AZAROFF, L., PH.D., Physics
BARBERET, G. J., PH.D., Romance and Classical Languages
BARON, R., PH.D., Psychology
BARRALL, E. M. I., PH.D., Chemistry
BARTH, P. S., PH.D., Economics
BARTRAM, R. H., PH.D., Physics
BECK, C., PH.D., Political Science
BEST, P. E., PH.D., Physics

BIZZICCARI, A., D.PHIL., Romance and Classical Languages
BLACK, R. F., PH.D., Geology
BOBBITT, J. M., PH.D., Chemistry
BOER, C. W., PH.D., English
BOHN, R. K., PH.D., Chemistry
BOOTH, E. J. R., PH.D., Economics
BROWN, R. D., PH.D., History
BRUSH, A. H., PH.D., Biology
BUDNICK, J. I., PH.D., Physics
BUTLER, FRANCELIA M., PH.D., English
CAMBON, G., D.PHIL., Romance and Classical Languages
CAMERON, J. A., PH.D., Biology
CARLSON, E. W., PH.D., English
CARY, J. B., PH.D., English
CAZEL, F. A., Jr., PH.D., History
CHAMBERLAND, B., PH.D., Chemistry
CHANCE, N. A., PH.D., Anthropology
CHAPPLE, W. D., PH.D., Biology
CHIANG, A. C., PH.D., Economics
CHINSKY, J. M., PH.D., Psychology
CHIN, R., PH.D., Economics
CHOVNICK, A., PH.D., Genetics
CLARK, H., PH.D., Biology
CLARK, N. B., PH.D., Biology
COHEN, A. K., PH.D., Sociology
COLE, G. F., PH.D., Political Science
COLLINS, R. P., PH.D., Biology
COONS, R. E., PH.D., History
COOPER, F. S., PH.D. History
CROSBY, D. H., PH.D., Germanic and Slavic Languages
CUMMINGS, I. P., PH.D., English
CURRY, P. O., PH.D., History
DAMMAN, A. W. H., PH.D., Biology
DAMON, D. H., PH.D., Physics
D'ANTONIO, W. V., PH.D., Sociology
DAVID, C. W., PH.D., Chemistry
DAVIS, I. R., PH.D., Political Science
DAVIS, J. M., PH.D., English
DAVIS, N. T., PH.D., Biology
DEHLINGER, P., PH.D., Geology
DENENBERG, V. H., PH.D., Bio-behavioural Sciences, Psychology
DICKERMAN, E. H., PH.D., History
DICKERSON, D. J., PH.D., Psychology
DOEG, K. A., PH.D., Biology
DOMBROWSKI, R. S., PH.D., Romance and Classical Languages
DOTSON, F., PH.D., Sociology
DUBOIS, R. M., M.B.A., Colonel, Field Artillery, Military Science
DUFFY, R. J., PH.D., Communication Sciences
ELIAS, J. A., PH.D., Philosophy
ELLING, R. H., PH.D., Behavioural Sciences and Community Medicine
ELLINGTON, J. W., Philosophy
EMMEL, HILDEGARD, PH.D., Germanic and Slavic Languages
FARINA, A., PH.D., Psychology
FARIS, J. C., PH.D., Anthropology
FENG, S. Y., PH.D., Biology
FITCH, R. M., PH.D., Chemistry
FRANKEL, P. H., PH.D., Geology
FRITZ, C. A., Jr., PH.D., Philosophy
FRUEH, A. J., PH.D., Geology
GERSON, L. L., PH.D., Political Sciences
GETTER, H., PH.D., Psychology
GIACOBINI, E., DR.MED.SCI., Biobehavioural Sciences
GILLIAM, O. R., PH.D., Physics
GINSBURG, B. E., PH.D., Bio-behavioural Sciences
GIOLAS, T. G., PH.D., Communication Sciences
GOETINCK, P. F., PH.D., Animal Genetics
GOLDMAN, B., PH.D., Biobehavioural Sciences
GOLDSTONE, H. I., PH.D., English
GORDON, M., PH.D., Biobehavioural Sciences
GORDON, M. W., PH.D., Sociology
GOSSELIN, R., PH.D., Mathematics

GREENE, J. C., PH.D., History
GUGLER, J. N. M., PH.D., Sociology
HAHN, Y., PH.D., Physics
HAKMILLER, K. L., PH.D., Psychology
HALL, J. J., PH.D., English
HALLER, K., PH.D., Physics
HAMILL, H. M., PH.D., History
HANCOCK, R. N., PH.D., Philosophy
HEISS, J. S., PH.D., Sociology
HEMPHILL, G. T., PH.D., English
HEYWOOD, S. M., PH.D., Biology
HILL, E., M.S., Journalism
HOGLUND, A. W., PH.D., History
HUANG, S. J., PH.D., Chemistry
ISLAM, M. M., PH.D., Physics
JACOBUS, L. A., PH.D., English
JOHNSON, J. F., PH.D., Chemistry
JOHNSON, J. R., PH.D., Art
KAPLOWITT, S. J., PH.D., Germanic and Slavic Languages
KATZ, L., PH.D., Chemistry
KATZ, L., PH.D., Psychology
KAUFMAN, H. M., PH.D., Psychology
KEGELES, G., PH.D., Biology
KESSEL, Q. C., PH.D., Physics
KHAIRALLAH, E. A., PH.D., Biology
KIM, I. J., PH.D., Political Science
KIND, C. A., PH.D., Biology
KINKADE, R. P., PH.D., Romance and Classical Languages
KIRK, I., PH.D., Germanic and Slavic Languages
KLEIN, N., PH.D., Animal Genetics
KLEMENS, P. G., PH.D., Physics
KNAUERHASE, R., PH.D., Economics
KOGAN, N., PH.D., Political Sciences
KORT, F., PH.D., Political Sciences
KOSTINER, E. S., PH.D., Chemistry
KRAUSE, R. A., PH.D., Chemistry
KUPPERMAN, J. J., PH.D., Philosophy
LADD, E. C., PH.D., Political Science
LANDIN, J., PH.D., Mathematics
LANG, B., PH.D., Philosophy
LAUFER, H., PH.D., Biology
LAUGHLIN, W. S., PH.D., Bio-behavioural Sciences, Anthropology
LEACOCK, S., PH.D., Anthropology
LEADBETTER, E. R., PH.D., Biology
LEDERER, H., PH.D., Germanic and Slavic Languages
LERMAN, J. W., PH.D., Communication Sciences
LERMAN, M., PH.D., Mathematics
LIBERMAN, A. M., PH.D., Psychology
LINDLEY, T. F., PH.D., Philosophy
LITT, E., PH.D., Political Science
LOUGEE, R. W., PH.D., History
LOWE, C. A., PH.D., Psychology
LUCAS-LENARD, J., PH.D., Biology
MACIUIKA, B. V., PH.D., History
McGRADE, A. S., PH.D., Philosophy
McHUGH, M. P., PH.D., Romance and Classical Languages
McLAUGHLIN, C. A., PH.D., English
MARCUS, P. I., PH.D., Biology
MASTERTON, W. L., PH.D., Chemistry
MATTINGLY, I. G., PH.D., Linguistics
MEAD, R. G., Jr., PH.D., Romance and Classical Languages
MEDLICOTT, A. G., Jr., PH.D., English
MEYER, P. H., PH.D., Romance and Classical Languages
MOELLER, C. W., PH.D., Chemistry
MOSHER, D. L., PH.D., Psychology
MOYNIHAN, W. T., PH.D., English
MUGNAINI, E., M.D., Bio-behavioural Sciences
NAMENWIRTH, J. Z., PH.D., Sociology
NASH, D. J., PH.D., Sociology and Anthropology
NEUWIRTH, J. H., PH.D., Mathematics
NEWMYER, R. K., PH.D., History
NOETHER, EMILIANA P., PH.D., History
NOETHER, G. E., PH.D., Statistics

OBUCHOWSKI, C. W., PH.D., Romance and Classical Languages
O'HARA, J. D., PH.D., English
OWEN, C. A., Jr., B.LIT., English
PATERSON, T. G., PH.D., History
PELTO, P. J., PH.D., Anthropology
PENNER, L., PH.D., Biology
PHILPOTTS, A. R., PH.D., Geology and Geophysics
PIERRO, L. J., PH.D., Animal Genetics
PILAR, G., M.D., Biology
PLANK, J., PH.D., Political Science
POLLACK, E., PH.D., Physics
PROSER, M. N., PH.D., English
RANEY, G. N., PH.D., Mathematics
RAWITSCHER, G. H., PH.D., Physics
REED, H. A., PH.D., History
REPASE, D. E., PH.D., Political Science
RETTENMEYER, C., PH.D., Biology
RING, K., PH.D., Psychology
ROACH, J. L., PH.D., Sociology
ROBERTS, T. J., PH.D., English
ROHNER, R. P., PH.D., Anthropology
ROLLIN, A. R., PH.D., Psychology
ROLLINS, C. D., D.PHIL., Philosophy
ROMANO, A., PH.D., Biology
ROSEN, W., PH.D., English
ROSS, M., PH.D., Communication Sciences
ROTH, S. J., PH.D., Biology
ROTTER, J. B., PH.D., Psychology
RUMNEY, G. R., PH.D., Geography
RUSSEK, A., PH.D., Physics
RYFF, J. V., Mathematics
SACHS, B. D., PH.D., Psychology
SACHS, J. S., PH.D., Communication Sciences
SALTER, E., M.A., English
SAN JUAN, E., Jr., PH.D., English
SCHAEFER, C. W., PH.D., Biology
SCHOR, R., PH.D., Physics
SCHULTZ, R. J., PH.D., Biology
SCHUSTER, T., PH.D., Biology
SCHWARZ, J. C., PH.D., Psychology
SCULLY, J. J., PH.D., English
SEIDMAN, H., PH.D., Political Science
SHAFFER, J. A., PH.D., Philosophy
SHANKWEILER, D. P., PH.D., Psychology
SHAW, R. E., PH.D., Psychology
SINCLAIR, K. V., PH.D., LIT.D., Romance and Classical Languages
SINGER, M., PH.D., Economics
SINICROPI, G., PH.D., Romance and Classical Languages
SLATER, J. A., PH.D., Biology
SMITH, J., PH.D., Psychology
SMITH, S. R., PH.D., Chemistry
SMITH, W. W., PH.D., Physics
SPENCER, D. E., PH.D., Mathematics
SPENCER, H. E., PH.D., Art
SPEYER, J. F., PH.D., Biology
SPIEGEL, E., PH.D., Mathematics
STAVE, B. M., PH.D., History
STERN, M. R., PH.D., English
STREAMS, F. A., PH.D., Biology
SUITS, T. A., PH.D., Romance and Classical Languages
TANAKA, J., PH.D., Chemistry
THATCHER, M. B., PH.D., Political Science
THOMAN, E., PH.D., Biobehavioural Sciences
THORKELSON, H. J., PH.D., Economics
TOLLEFSON, J. L., PH.D., Mathematics
TOKES, R. L., PH.D., Political Science
TORRENCE, L. E., PH.D., Political Science
TRAINOR, F. R., PH.D., Biology
TURNER, F. C., PH.D., Political Science
TURVEY, M., PH.D., Psychology
UHLIG, L., PH.D., Germanic and Slavic Languages
VAN DUSEN, A., PH.D., History
VASINGTON, F. D., PH.D., Biology
VAUGHAN, W. R., PH.D., Chemistry

WACHMAN, M., PH.D., Mathematics
WACHTEL, A., PH.D., Biology
WARD, A. M., PH.D., History
WARDWELL. W. I., PH.D., Sociology
WARKOV, S., PH.D., Sociology
WEHRLE, E. S., PH.D., History
WEINER, P., PH.D., Economics
WELLS, A. F., D.SC., Chemistry
WERBOFF, J., PH.D., Psychology
WETHERELL, D. F., PH.D., Biology
WETZEL, R. M., PH.D., Biology
WEXLER, I., PH.D., Economics
WILCOX, T. W., M.A., English
WILKENFELD, R. B., PH.D., English
WILSON, K. G., PH.D., English
WILSON, MARTHA, PH.D., Psychology
WILSON, W. A., PH.D., Psychology
WINROB, R. M., PH.D., Psychiatry
WITRYOL, S., PH.D., Psychology
WOLK, E. S., PH.D., Mathematics
WOOD, D. E., PH.D., Chemistry
WRIGHT, A. W., PH.D., Economics
YPHANTIS, D. A., PH.D., Biology
ZEAMAN, B. H., PH.D., Psychology
ZEAMAN, D., PH.D., Psychology

*School of Allied Health Professions:*
ADAMS, F. G., D.D.S.
BAUER, J., M.S.
FITZ, P. A., M.A., R.D.
KASKA, V., M.S., R.P.T.

*School of Business Administration:*
BOYCE, B. N., S.P.R.A., PH.D., Finance and Real Estate
CLOSE, D. B., PH.D., C.P.C.U., Insurance
CURCURU, E. H., PH.D., Industrial Administration
DUKER, J. M., PH.D., Marketing
EMERZIAN, A. D., PH.D., Industrial Administration
FISCHER, D. E., D.B.A., C.F.A., Finance
HEMPEL, D. J., PH.D., Marketing
HIGGINS, J. W., M.S., C.P.A., Accounting
HOLZMAN, R. S., PH.D., Accounting
JOHNSON, H. M., PH.D., Finance
JOHNSON, K. B., D.B.A., Finance
KINNARD, W., PH.D., Finance
KNIFFIN, F. W., D.B.A., M.A., Marketing
MALINOWSKI, Z. S., PH.D., Business
MALSBURY, D. R., ED.D., Business Environment and Policy
MESSNER, S. D., D.B.A., Finance and Real Estate
MORRISON, T. A., PH.D., C.P.A., Accounting
NORGAARD, CORINE T., PH.D., Accounting
NORGAARD, R. L., PH.D., Finance
PATTEN, R. J., PH.D., Accounting
ROTHSTEIN, M., PH.D., Management and Administrative Sciences
SAUNDERS, C. B., D.B.A., Business Environment and Policy
SOUERWINE, A. H., PH.D., Industrial Administration
SPIRER, H. F., PH.D., Management and Administrative Sciences
TUCKER, E. W., S.J.D., Business Law
WEBER, K. L., M.A., Aerospace Studies
WENDEL, R. F., PH.D., Marketing
WILDE, D. U., PH.D., Information Systems Administration
WRIGHT, A. W., PH.D., Business Environment and Policy
WYMAN, H. E., PH.D., Accounting
YANOUZAS, J. N., PH.D., Industrial Administration

*School of Dental Medicine:*
BAUM, L., D.M.D., Restorative Dentistry
BRONNER, F., D.D.S., Oral Biology
BURSTONE, C. J., D.D.S., Orthodontics
CASTALDI, C. R., D.D.S., M.S.D., Paediatric Dentistry
CUTLER, L., D.D.S., Oral Diagnosis
GAY, T., PH.D., Oral Biology
KATZ, E. P., PH.D., Oral Biology
KOLLAR, E. J., PH.D., Oral Biology
LANGELAND, K., D.D.S., PH.D., Endodontics
LEVINE, P. T., D.D.S., Oral Biology
LÖE, HARALD, D.D.S., Periodontics
MUMFORD, G., D.D.S., PH.D., General Dentistry
NALBANDIAN, J., D.M.D., General Dentistry
NANDA, R., D.D.S., Orthodontics
NORTON, L. A., D.M.D., Orthodontics
NUKI, K., D.D.S., Periodontics
REISKIN, A., D.D.S., Oral Radiology
ROBERTSON, P. B., D.D.S., Periodontics
RODAN, G. A., PH.D., Oral Biology
SPANGBERG, L. S. W., D.D.S., PH.D., Endodontics
TANZER, J., D.M.D., PH.D., General Dentistry
WEINSTEIN, S., D.D.S., PH.D., Oral Biology
YAEGER, J. J., D.D.S., PH.D., Oral Biology

*School of Education:*
ATKYNS, G. C., PH.D., Education
BASS, F. L., ED.D., Education
BLICK, D. J., PH.D., Science Education
BLOOMER, R. H., ED.D., Educational Psychology
BRAZZIEL. W. F., PH.D., Education
BRUBACHER, J. W., PH.D., Educational Administration
CALDER, C. R., Jr., PH.D., Education
DAIGON, A., ED.D., Education
DEMPSEY, R., PH.D., Education
DYRLI, O. E., ED.D., Elementary Education
FAIT, H. F., PH.D., Physical Education
FLYNN, J. T., ED.D., Educational Psychology
GABLE, R., ED.D., Education
GLENNON, V. J., PH.D., Education
GOODKIND, T. B., PH.D., Elementary Education
HARTLEY, H. J., ED.D., Educational Administration
HOOD, B. L., PH.D., Education
KAHN, H., PH.D., Educational Psychology
LACONTE, R. T., ED.D., Secondary Education
LIBERMAN, I., PH.D., Educational Psychology
MALSBARY, D. R., ED.D., Business Education
NORRIS, R. B., ED.D., Education
OSBORN, BARBARA L., PH.D., Home Economics Education
OWEN, S., PH.D., Education
PAPPANIKOU, A. J., ED.D., Educational Psychology
PROTHEROE, D. W., ED.D., Elementary Education
RENZULLI, J., ED.D., Educational Psychology
ROBERTS, A. D., ED.D., Education
ROE, W. H., PH.D., Education
ROGERS, V. R., PH.D., Education
ROSS, C., PH.D., Education
RUCKER, C. N., PH.D., Educational Psychology
SHAW, R. A., ED.D., Secondary Education
SHEATHELM, H. H., PH.D., Educational Administration
SHEEHAN, T. J., PH.D., Education
SHIBLES, M. R., PH.D., Education
SHIVERS, J. S., PH.D., Physical Education
SLEEMAN, P. J., ED.D., Education
STONE, F., ED.D., Education
STRAUCH, J. D., ED.D., Education
WEINLAND, T. P., PH.D., Education

WHINFIELD, R. W., PH.D., Higher, Technical and Adult Education
WICAS, E., ED.D., Educational Psychology

*School of Engineering:*
BELL, J. P., SC.D., Chemical Engineering
BENNETT, C. O., D.ENG., Chemical Engineering
BOCK, P., D.ENG., Hydrology and Water Resources
BOOTH, T. L., PH.D., Electrical Engineering
BOWLEY, W. W., PH.D., Mechanical Engineering
CAMPBELL, G. S., PH.D., Aerospace Engineering
CARNEY, J. F., III, PH.D., Civil Engineering
CHIEN, YI-TZUU, PH.D., Electrical Engineering
CLAPP, P. C., PH.D., Metallurgy
COUGHLIN, R. W., PH.D., Chemical Engineering
DABORA, E. K., PH.D., Mechanical Engineering
DEVEREUX, O. F., PH.D., Metallurgy
DIBENEDETTO, A. T., PH.D., Chemical Engineering
GALLIGAN, J., PH.D., Metallurgy
GANT, E. V., M.S., Civil Engineering
GARRETT, R. E., PH.D., Mechanical Engineering
GARTNER, J. R., PH.D., Mechanical Engineering
GREENE, N. D., PH.D., Metallurgy
HEALY, K. A., SC.D., P.E., Civil Engineering
HILDING, W. E., PH.D., Mechanical Engineering
HOWARD, G. M., PH.D., Chemical Engineering
JOHNSTON, E. R., D.S., Civil Engineering
KARTESTUNCER, H., D.ING., Civil Engineering
KATTAMIS, T., SC.D., Metallurgy
KLEI, H. E., PH.D., Chemical Engineering
KLEINMAN, D. L., SC.D., Electrical Engineering
KNAPP, C. H., PH.D., Electrical Engineering
KOCHENBURGER, R., SC.D., Electrical Engineering
KOENIG, H. A., PH.D., Mechanical Engineering
LONG, R. P., PH.D., Civil Engineering
LYDERSEN, A., PH.D., Chemical Engineering
McEVILY, A. J., D.ENG.SC., Metallurgy
McFADDEN, P. W., PH.D., Mechanical Engineering
MELEHY, M. A., PH.D., Electrical Engineering
NORTHROP, R. B., PH.D., Electrical Engineering
NOWOTNY, H., DR.TECHN., Metallurgy
PITKIN, E. T., PH.D., Mechanical Engineering
SCHULTZ, C. W., PH.D., Electrical Engineering
SCOTTRON, V., D.ENG., Civil Engineering
SOLECKI, R., D.SC., Mechanical Engineering
STEPHENS, J. E., PH.D., Civil Engineering
STEPHENSON, R. M., PH.D., Chemical Engineering
STRUTT, P. R., PH.D., Metallurgy
STUTZMAN, L. F., PH.D., Chemical Engineering
SUNDSTROM, D. W., PH.D., Chemical Engineering
SUPRYNOWICZ, V. A., PH.D., Electrical Engineering
WIDMER, W. J., S.M., Civil Engineering

*School of Fine Arts:*

BALLARD, F. W., M.A., Dramatic Arts
BIRDMAN, J. M., PH.D., Dramatic Arts
COLEMAN, R., M.A., Music
CROSSGROVE, R., M.F.A., Art
DOUDERA, G., B.F.A., Art
EVERSOLE, J. A., ED.D., Music
FAWCETT, J., B.F.A., Art
FORMAN, K., M.A., Art
GILLESPIE, A. E., M.S., Music
GREGORIC, M. T., PH.D., Dramatic Art
GREGOROPOULOS, J., B.A., Art
HEILWEIL, D., M.A., Dramatic Arts
HELLER, J. J., PH.D., Music
HERR, J. H., PH.D., Dramatic Arts
HITCHCOCK, R. F., M.A., Art
JOHNSON, J. R., PH.D., Art
JUEL-LARSEN, P., D.M.A., Music
KATTER, N. E., PH.D., Dramatic Arts
KLITZ, B., PH.D., Music
LAZLOFFY, J., M.MUS., Music
MURRAY, D. L., PH.D., Dramatic Arts
NEGORO, MINNIE, M.F.A., Art
O'CONNOR, E. J. P., ED.D., Music
PARKER, W. E., M.F.A., Art
PATRYLAK, D. J., M.MUS., Music
POELLEIN, J. A., D.M.A., Music
ROJO, J. N., M.F.A., Dramatic Arts
SEEBER, L. A., M.MUS., Music
SMITH, H., M.MUS., Music
SOMER, A., PH.D., Music
SPENCER, R. E., PH.D., Art
SWIBOLD, R. E., B.ARCH., Architecture
THORNTON, R. S., M.F.A., Art
ZELANSKI, P. J., M.F.A., Art

*School of Home Economics:*

DREYER, A. S., PH.D., Child Development and Family Relations
KELLER, E. D., PH.D., Child Development and Family Relations
NICHOLSON, C. K., PH.D., Human Development and Family Relations
OSBORN, B. L., PH.D., Home Economics Education
ROSENCRANZ, H. A., PH.D., Human Development and Family Relations
ROSENCRANZ, MARYLOU, PH.D., Clothing. Textiles and Interior Design
RYDER, R., PH.D., Human Development and Family Relations

*School of Law:*

BARD, R. L., M.A., LL.B.
BECKER, L. E., Jr., A.B., LL.B.
BIRMINGHAM, R., J.D., PH.D.
BLUMBERG, P. I., A.B., J.D.
BYSIEWICZ, SHIRLEY R., LL.B.
CADY, F. C., LL.B.
CULLISON, A. D., B.S., J.D., LL.M.
DAVIS, C., LL.B.
KAY, R. S., J.D.
KURLANTZICK, L. S., LL.B.
LAPLANTE, J. A., LL.M.
LEVY, N., J.S.D.
MORAWETZ, T. H., PH.D.
MCGILL, H. C., B.A., LL.B.
ORLAND, L., LL.B.
POMP, R. D., J.D.
SACKS, H. R., LL.B.
SCANLON, C., LL.M.
SHEA, C., LL.M.
SHUCHMAN, P., LL.B.
SNYDER, L. B., LL.M.
SOIFER, A., J.D., M.U.S.
SUSCO, W. W., J.D.
TAIT, C. C., LL.B.
TONDRO, R. J., LL.B.
WEISBROD, C. A., LL.B.
WHITMAN, R., LL.B.
WOLFSON, N., A.B., J.D.

*School of Medicine:*

ANTAR, M. A., M.B., B.CH., PH.D., Nuclear Medicine
BAILIT, H. L., D.M.D., PH.D., Biobehavioural Sciences and Community Health
BECKER, E. L., M.D., PH.D., Pathology
BERGER, A., M.D., Family Medicine
BERLIN, R. D., M.D., Physiology
BIGAZZI, P., M.D., Pathology
BLECHNER, J. N., M.D., Obstetrics and Gynaecology
BOYLAN, J., M.D., Medicine
COHEN, S., M.D., Pathology
COOPERSTEIN, S. J., PH.D., Anatomy
CROOG, S., PH.D., Psychiatry, Behavioural Sciences and Community Health
DAVIDOFF, F. F., M.D., Medicine
DEUTSCHER, M., PH.D., Biochemistry
ELLING, R. H., PH.D., Community Medicine and Health Care
FEINSTEIN, M. B., PH.D., Pharmacology
FISS, H., PH.D., Psychiatry
FLEESON, W., M.D., Psychiatry
FOSTER, J., M.D., Surgery
GLASEL, J. A., PH.D., Biochemistry
GLUECK, B., M.D., Physiology
GOLDSCHREIDER, I., M.D., Pathology
GONDOS, B., M.D., Pathology
GOSSLING, H., M.D., Surgery
GRASSO, J. A., PH.D., Anatomy
HAMILTON, T. S., M.D., Community Medicine and Health Care
HINZ, C. F., M.D., Medical and Paediatrics
HOSAIN, F., PH.D., Nuclear Medicine
HOYER, L. W., M.D., Medicine
JAFFEE, J., M.D., Psychiatry
JUNGAS, R. L., PH.D., Physiology
KATZ, A., M.D., Medicine
KEGELES, S. S., PH.D., Behavioural Sciences and Community Health
MAHER, J. C., M.D., Medicine
MARKOWITZ, M., M.D., General Paediatrics
MASSEY, R. U., M.D., Medicine
MEYER, R., M.D., Psychiatry
MOREST, D. K., M.D., Anatomy
MORSE, E. E., M.D., Laboratory Medicine
O'ROURKE, J., M.D., Surgery
OSBORN, MARY J., PH.D., Microbiology
PATTERSON, J. W., M.D., PH.D., D.SC., Physiology
PEROVITCH, M. N., M.D., Radiology
POMERLEAU, O., PH.D., Psychiatry
RAISZ, L., M.D., Medicine
RESSLER, C., PH.D., Pharmacology
RIPPEY, R., PH.D., Health Education
ROBERTS, M. P., M.D., Surgery and Neurology-Neurosurgery
ROTHENBERG, A., M.D., Psychiatry
ROTHFIELD, L. I., M.D., Microbiology
ROTHFIELD, NAOMI, M.D., Medicine
SCHEIG, R., M.D., Medicine
SCHENKMAN, J. B., PH.D., Pharmacology
SHA'AFI, R. I., PH.D., Physiology
SHEEHAN, T. J., PH.D., Health Education
SIGMAN, E. M., M.D., Surgery
SPACKMAN, T., M.D., Radiology
SPENCER, R. P., M.D., Nuclear Medicine
SPICKER, S., PH.D., Community Medicine and Health Care
STABENAU, J. R., M.D., Psychiatry
STRITTMATTER, P., PH.D., Biochemistry
SULAVIK, S., M.D., Medicine
SUNDERMAN, F. W., M.D., Laboratory Medicine
TANZER, M. L., M.D., Biochemistry
TENNANT, R., M.D., Pathobiology
THOMPSON, H. G., M.D., Neurology and Neurosurgery
TILTON, R. C., PH.D., Laboratory Medicine
TOPAZIAN, R., D.D.S., Oral Surgery
VIOLA, M., M.D., Medicine
VOLLE, R. L., PH.D., Pharmacology
WALKER, J. E. C., M.D., M.SC., Community Medicine and Health Care
WARD, P. A., M.D., Pathology
WERBOFF, J., PH.D., Behavioural Sciences and Community Health
WIESEL, B., M.D., Psychiatry
WINTROB, R. M., M.D., Psychiatry

*School of Nursing:*

HAYES, JANICE E., PH.D.
INFANTE, M. S., ED.D.
KRAMER, M., PH.D.
WHITE, MARGUERITE B., ED.D.

*School of Pharmacy:*

DICAPUA, R. A., PH.D., Immunology
EDWARDS, J. M., PH.D., Pharmacognosy
HITE, G. J., PH.D., Medicinal Chemistry
KELLEHER, W. J., PH.D., Pharmacognosy
NIEFORTH, K. A., PH.D., Medical Chemistry
ROSENBERG, P., PH.D., Pharmacology
SCHWARTING, A. E., PH.D., Pharmacognosy
SIMONELLI, A. P., PH.D., Pharmaceutics
SKAUEN, D. M., PH.D., Pharmacy

*School of Social Work:*

ALISSI, A. S., PH.D.
BOATMAN, LOUISE, M.S.
BOK, M., PH.D.
COLEMAN, M., M.S.W.
DUBINS, I. G., M.S.
ECHOLS, IVOR, PH.D.
GERMAIN, C. B., PH.D.
GOROFF, N. N., M.S.S.A.
GREEN, R., PH.D.
LITTLE, V., PH.D.
LUTZ, W. A., M.A., M.S.
MALUCCIO, A. N., M.A., D.S.W.
NEWMAN, J., M.S.S.S.
PICHEY, J. R., M.S.W.
PINNER, E. L., PH.D.
SELIG, R., M.S.W.
STUART, A., PH.D.
TURNER, N., S.M.A.
WEINER, M., M.G.A.
WILLIAMS, R. C., M.S.S.S.
WU, YUEN-CHI, PH.D.

## UNIVERSITY OF HARTFORD

200 BLOOMFIELD AVENUE,
WEST HARTFORD,
CONNECTICUT 06117

Telephone: (203) 243-4100.

Founded 1877.

*President:* Dr. STEPHEN J. TRACHTENBERG.

*Provost and Vice-President:* Dr. CAROL GUARDO.

*Vice-President for Administration:* (vacant).

*Treasurer and Vice-President:* Dr. MICHAEL BRITTON.

*Dean of Students:* DORIS COSTER.

*Registrar:* RICHARD WHITESIDE.

*Director of Admissions:* (vacant).

*Business Manager:* V. TEDESCHI.

*Librarian:* J. MCGAVERN.

Library of 275,000 vols.

**Number of teachers:** 300 full-time.

**Number of students:** 4,000 full-time undergraduates, 2,600 part-time undergraduates, 420 full-time graduates, 2,300 part-time graduates.

DEANS:

Hartford Art School: EDWIN E. STEIN.
College of Arts and Sciences: Dr. JAMES S. VINSON.
School of Business and Public Administration: WALTER McCANN.
College of Basic Studies: Dr. ARTHUR H. AUTEN.
College of Education: Dr. I. S. STARR.
College of Engineering: Dr. T. S. LEWIS.
Hartt College of Music: DONALD HARRIS.
Ward Technical College: JOHN D. DRISCOLL.

## UNIVERSITY OF NEW HAVEN
WEST HAVEN,
CONNECTICUT 06516
Telephone: (203) 934-6321.
Founded 1920.

President: PHILIP S. KAPLAN.
Registrar: JOSEPH P. MACIONUS.
Dean of Admissions and Financial Aid: JOHN BENEVENTO.
Librarian: S. M. BAKER, Jr.

The library contains 140,230 vols., 93,699 documents and 23,084 bound periodicals.
Number of teachers: 146 full-time, 280 part-time.
Number of students: 7,531.

## WESLEYAN UNIVERSITY
HIGH ST., MIDDLETOWN
CONNECTICUT 06457
Telephone: 347-9411.
Chartered 1831.

President: COLIN G. CAMPBELL.
Provost: W. KERR, PH.D.
Dean of Admissions: KARL FURSTENBERG, M.B.A.
Secretary: W. KERR, PH.D.
Librarian: J. ROBERT ADAMS, M.A.

The library contains 750,000 vols.
Number of teachers: 300.
Number of students: 2,500.

Publication: Bulletin (quarterly).

## WESTERN CONNECTICUT STATE COLLEGE
DANBURY, CONNECTICUT 06810
Telephone: (203) 792-1400.
Founded 1903.

President: ROBERT M. BURSI.
Registrar: WILLIAM McKEE.
Administrative Officer: Dr. GILBERT TEAL.
Librarian: ROBERT BLAISDELL.
Number of teachers: 225.
Number of students: 5,248.

DEANS:
Academic Dean: Dr. GERTRUDE BRAUN.
Graduate Studies: Dr. M. JACK RUDNER.
Director of Teacher Education: Dr. STEPHEN LOVATT.

## YALE UNIVERSITY
NEW HAVEN,
CONNECTICUT 06520
Telephone: (203) 436-4771.

Founded in 1701, named Yale College in 1718. Transition to University status took place from 1810 to 1861.
Private control.

President: A. BARTLETT GIAMATTI, PH.D.
Provost: GEORGES MAY, PH.D.
Secretary: H. CHAUNCEY, Jr., B.A.
Vice-President for Finance and Administration: JERALD L. STEVENS, M.B.A.
University Officer for Development and Alumni Affairs: JOHN A. WILKINSON, M.A.T.
Librarian: R. D. ROGERS, M.A.
Library: see Libraries.
Number of teachers: c. 1,500.
Number of students: c. 9,000.

Publications: Yale Review, Yale Journal of Biology and Medicine, Yale Law Journal, Yale Alumni Magazine, American Journal of Science, Library Gazette, Bulletin of Art Gallery Associates, American Scientist, Journal of American Oriental Society, Journal of Biological Chemistry, Yale Divinity News, Journal of the History of Medicine and Allied Sciences, Journal of Music Theory, Yale Forest School News, Yale Scientific Magazine.

DEANS:

Yale College: HOWARD R. LAMAR, PH.D.
School of Architecture: CESAR PELLI, M.S.ARCH.
Graduate School: KEITH S. THOMPSON, PH.D.
Divinity School: Rev. LEANDER E. KECK, PH.D.
School of Forestry and Environmental Studies: CHARLES H. W. FOSTER, PH.D.
Law School: HARRY H. WELLINGTON, LL.B.
School of Medicine: ROBERT W. BERLINER, M.D., SC.D.
School of Music: FRANK P. TIRRO, PH.D.
School of Nursing: DONNA K. DIERS, M.S.N.
School of Drama: LLOYD RICHARDS, M.A.
School of Organization and Management: GEOFFREY C. HAZARD, Jr., LL.B. (acting).

PROFESSORS:
Faculty of Arts and Sciences (Yale College and Graduate School):
AABOE, A. H., PH.D., History of Science
ABELSON, R. P., PH.D., Psychology
ADAIR, R. K., PH.D., Physics
AHLSTROM, S. E., PH.D., American and Modern Religious History
ANDERSON, J. R., Psychology
ANSCOMBE, F. J., M.A., Statistics
APPELQUIST, T. W., PH.D., Physics
APTER, D. E., PH.D., Political Science and Sociology
BARGHOORN, F. C., PH.D., Political Science
BARKER, R. C., M.ENG., PH.D., Applied Science
BAUMER, F. L., PH.D., History
BEALS, R. W., Mathematics
BEHLER, E., PH.D., German
BELL, W., PH.D., Sociology
BENNETT, W. R., PH.D., Engineering and Applied Science
BERINGER, E. R., PH.D., Physics
BERNER, R. A., PH.D., Geology and Geophysics
BERNSTEIN, IRA B., PH.D., Applied Science
BERSON, J. A., PH.D., Chemistry
BLASSINGAME, J. W., PH.D., History
BLOOM, H. I., P.H.D., Humanities
BLUM, J. M., PH.D., History
BOCKELMAN, C. K., PH.D., Physics
BOORMAN, S. A., PH.D., Sociology
BORROFF, MARIE, PH.D., English
BOWMAN, W. S., Jr., M.A., Law and Economics
BRAINARD, W. C., PH.D., Economics
BROMLEY, D. A., PH.D., Physics
BROOKS, P. P., PH.D., French and Comparative Literature
BROWN, D., PH.D., Economics
BRUMBAUGH, R. S., PH.D., Philosophy
BUXTON, C. E., PH.D., Psychology
CAHN, W. B., History of Art
CANNON, B. C., PH.D., History of Music
CHANG, K-C., PH.D., Anthropology
CHANG, R. K., PH.D., Engineering and Applied Science
CHILD, I. L., PH.D., Psychology
CHU, B.-T., PH.D., Engineering and Applied Science
CHUPKA, W. A., PH.D., Chemistry
CLARK, B. R., PH.D., Sociology
CLARK, S. P., Jr., PH.D., Geophysics
COE, M. D., PH.D., Anthropology
COHEN, M. J., PH.D., Biology
COLE, A. T., Jr., PH.D., Classics
CONKLIN, H. C., PH.D., Anthropology
COOKE, M. G., PH.D., English
COOPER, R. N., PH.D., Economics
CORREA, G., PH.D., Spanish
COWGILL, W. C., PH.D., Linguistics
CROSBY, S. McK., PH.D., History of Art
CROTHERS, D. M., PH.D., Chemistry and Molecular Biophysics
CROWDER, R. G., PH.D., Psychology
CROWLEY, J. B., PH.D., History
CULLER, A. D., PH.D., English
CUNNINGHAM, W. J., PH.D., Engineering and Applied Science
DAHL, R. A., PH.D., Political Science
DAVIS, C. T., PH.D., Afro-American Studies and English
DAVIS, D. B., PH.D., History
DE MAN, P., PH.D., French and Comparative Literature
DEMARQUE, P., PH.D., Astrophysics
DEMETZ, P., DR.PHIL., German and Comparative Literature
DIAZ-ALEJANDRO, C. F., PH.D., Economics
DOOB, L. W., PH.D., Psychology
DUPRE, L. K., PH.D., Religious Studies
DURAN, M., PH.D., Spanish
DYEN, I., PH.D., Malayo-Polynesian Comparative Linguistics
ERIKSON, K., PH.D., Sociology
ERLICH, V., PH.D., Russian Literature
EVENSON, R. E., Economics

FALLER, J. W., PH.D., Chemistry
FEI, J. C.-H., PH.D., Economics
FEIDELSON, C., PH.D., English
FEIT, W., PH.D., Mathematics
FENN, J. B., PH.D., Applied Science and Chemistry
FESLER, J. W., PH.D., Government
FETTER, R. B., D.B.A., Administrative Sciences
FITCH, F. B., PH.D., Philosophy
FIXMAN, M., PH.D., Chemistry
FOGELIN, R. J., PH.D., Philosophy
FORTE, A., M.A., Theory of Music
FRANKEL, H. H., PH.D., Chinese Literature
FRANKFURT, H. C., PH.D., Philosophy
FRUTON, J. S., PH.D., Biochemistry
GALL, J. G., PH.D., Biology and Molecular Biophysics
GALSTON, A. W., PH.D., Botany
GAREN, A., PH.D., Molecular Biophysics
GARLAND, H., PH.D., Mathematics
GARNER, W. R., PH.D., Psychology
GATZKE, H. W., PH.D., History
GAUDON, J. A. M., D.L., French Literature
GAY, P., PH.D., History
GEANAKOPLOS, D. J., PH.D., History and Religious Studies
GLIER, PH.D., German
GOLDSMITH, T. H., PH.D., Biology
GORDON, R. B., D.ENG., Applied Science and Geophysics
GOULD, T. F., PH.D., Classics
GREENBERG, J. S., PH.D., Physics
GREENE, T. McL., PH.D., English and Comparative Literature
GURSEY, F., PH.D., Physics
HALL, J. W., PH.D., History
HALLO, W. W., PH.D., Assyriology
HAMBURGER, J., PH.D., Political Science
HANSON, A. C., PH.D., History of Art
HARRIES, K., PH.D., Philosophy
HARTIGAN, J. A., PH.D., Statistics
HARTMAN, G., PH.D., English and Comparative Literature
HARTMAN, W. D., PH.D., Biology
HAVERKAMP-BEGEMANN, E., PH.D., History of Art
HENNING, B. D., PH.D., History
HERBERT, R. L., PH.D., History of Art
HERINGTON, C. J., M.A., Greek
HERSEY, G. L., History of Art
HERZENBERG, A., PH.D., D.SC., Engineering and Applied Science
HIRSHFIELD, J. L., PH.D., Applied Science
HOLLANDER, J., English
HOWE, R. E., PH.D., Mathematics
HUGHES, V. W., PH.D., Physics
HUNTER, G. K., English
HUTCHINSON, F., M.A., SC.D., Biophysics
IRONS, E. T., PH.D., Computer Science
JACKSON, R. L., PH.D., Russian Literature
JACOBSON, N., PH.D., Mathematics
JAMESON, F. R., PH.D., French
JANIS, I. L., PH.D., Psychology
KAGAN, D., PH.D., History and Classics
KAKUTANI, S., PH.D., Mathematics
KANTER, R. M., PH.D., Sociology
KAZEMZADEH, F., PH.D., History
KESSEN, W., PH.D., Psychology
KLEIN, M. J., PH.D., History of Physics
KLEVORICK, A. K., PH.D., Law and Economics
KOOPMANS, T. C., PH.D., Economics
KÖRNER, S., PH.D., Philosophy
KRAMER, G. H., PH.D., Political Science
KUBLER, G. A., PH.D., History of Art
LAMAR, H. R., PH.D., American History
LANE, R. E., PH.D., Political Science
LANG, S., Mathematics
LA PALOMBARA, J., PH.D., Political Science

LARSON, R. B., PH.D., Astronomy
LEE, R., Mathematics
LENGYEL, P., PH.D., Molecular Biophysics
LEONHARD, W., PH.D., History
LEWIS, H. B., PH.D., Psychology
LEWIS, R. W. B., PH.D., English and American Studies
LIBERMAN, A. M., PH.D., Linguistics
LICHTEN, W. L., PH.D., Physics
LINDBLOM, C. E., PH.D., Economics and Political Science
LINZ, J. J., PH.D., Sociology and Political Science
LOPEZ, R. S., PH.D., History
LORD, G. DeF., Jr., PH.D., English
LOUNSBURY, F. G., PH.D., Anthropology
LYONS, P. A., PH.D., Chemistry
MACAVOY, P. W., PH.D., Organization and Management and Economics
MACDOWELL, S. W., PH.D., Physics
MACINTYRE, A. J., PH.D., Mathematics
MACK, M., PH.D., English
MACMULLEN, R., PH.D., History and Classics
McCLELLAN, E., Japanese Literature
McCLURE, R. D., Astronomy
McGUIRE, W. J., PH.D., Psychology
MARCUS, R. B., PH.D., Philosophy
MARKERT, C. L., PH.D., Biology
MARTIN, S. E., PH.D., Far Eastern Linguistics
MARTZ, L. L., PH.D., English
MASSEY, W. S., PH.D., Mathematics
MAY, G. M., PH.D., French
MAYHEW, D. R., PH.D., Political Science
MEEKS, W. A., B.D., PH.D., Religious Studies
MERRIMAN, D., PH.D., Biology
METLITZKI, D., PH.D., English
MILLER, J. H., PH.D., English
MILLER, J. P., PH.D., Social Science
MILLER, R. S., Wildlife Ecology and Biology
MISKIMIN, H. A., PH.D., History
MONTGOMERY, C. F., M.A., History of Art
MONTIAS, J. M., PH.D., Economics
MORGAN, E. S., PH.D., History
MOROWITZ, H. J., PH.D., Molecular Biophysics
MORSE, A. S., PH.D., Engineering and Applied Science
MORSE, R. McG., PH.D., History
MOSTOW, G. D., PH.D., Mathematics
MYERS, J. K., PH.D., Sociology
NARENDRA, K. S., PH.D., Engineering and Applied Science
NATANSON, M., PH.D., Philosophy
NELSON, L., Jr., PH.D., Comparative Literature
NELSON, R. R., PH.D., Economics
NORDHAUS, W. D., PH.D., Economics
ONAT, E. T., D.SC., Engineering and Applied Science
ORCUTT, G. H., PH.D., Economics, Urban Studies
ORVILLE, P. M., PH.D., Petrology
OSTROM, J. H., PH.D., Geology and Geophysics
OZMENT, S. E., PH.D., Religious Studies
PALISCA, C. V., PH.D., History of Music
PARKER, P. D. M., PH.D., Physics
PARKER, W. N., PH.D., Economics
PATRICK, H. T., PH.D., Economics
PATTERSON, A. P., Jr., PH.D., Chemistry
PAULSON, R. H., PH.D., English
PECK, M. J., PH.D., Economics
PELIKAN, J. J., Jr., PH.D., Ecclesiastical History
PERLIS, A. J., PH.D., SC.D., Computer Science
PHILLIPS, A., DR.ENG., Engineering and Applied Science
PICCHIO, R. P., DR.LETT., Slavic Literatures

PILBEAM, D. R., PH.D., Anthropology
PLANTINGA, L. B., PH.D., History of Music
POLLITT, J. J., PH.D., Classical Archaeology and History of Art
POPE, M. H., PH.D., Semitic Languages
PORTER, C. A., PH.D., French
POSPISIL, L. J., PH.D., Anthropology
POULSON, D. F., PH.D., Biology
POWELL, R. P., PH.D., Economics
PRICE, D. J. DE S., PH.D., History of Science
PRICE, M. M., PH.D., English
PROWN, J. D., PH.D., History of Art
RAE, D. W., PH.D., Political Science
RANIS, G., PH.D., Economics
REISS, A. J., Jr., PH.D., Sociology
RESCORLA, R. A., PH.D., Psychology
REYNOLDS, L. G., PH.D., LL.D., Economics
RHOADS, D. C., PH.D., Geology
RICHARDS, F. M., PH.D., Molecular Biophysics
RICKART, C. E., PH.D., Mathematics
ROBERTSON, W. D., D.SC., Applied Science
ROBINSON, F. C., PH.D., English
RODGERS, J., PH.D., Geology
RODRIGUEZ-MONEGAL, E., PH.D., Latin-American Literature
ROSENBAUM, J. L., Biology
ROSENTHAL, F., DR.PHIL., Near Eastern Languages
ROSNER, D. E., PH.D., Engineering and Applied Science
ROUSE, I., PH.D., Anthropology
RUDDLE, F. H., PH.D., Biology and Human Genetics
RUGGLES, R., PH.D., Economics
RUSSETT, B. M., PH.D., Political Science
SALTZMAN, B., PH.D., Geology and Geophysics
SAMMONS, J. L., PH.D., German Literature
SANDWEISS, J., PH.D., Physics
SARASON, S. B., PH.D., Psychology
SAUNDERS, M., PH.D., Chemistry
SCARF, H. E., PH.D., Economics
SCHANK, R. C., Computer Science and Psychology
SCHEFFLER, H. W., PH.D., Anthropology
SCHENKER, A. M., PH.D., Slavic Linguistics
SCHOOLFIELD, G. C., PH.D., German and Scandinavian Literatures
SCHRADER, G. A., Jr., PH.D., Philosophy
SCHULTHEISS, P. M., PH.D., Engineering and Applied Science
SCHULTZ, H. L., PH.D., Physics
SCHULTZ, M. H., PH.D., Computer Science
SCHULZ, T. P., PH.D., Economics of Population
SCOTT, A. I., D.SC., PH.D., Chemistry
SCOTT, J. C., Political Science
SCULLY, V. J., Jr., PH.D., History of Art
SELIGMAN, G. B., PH.D., Mathematics
SHAUMYAN, S. K., DR.SCI., Linguistics
SHEFFIELD, F. D., PH.D., Psychology
SHESTACK, A., M.A., History of Art
SHUBIK, M., PH.D., Mathematics, Institutional Economics
SIBLEY, C. G., Biology, Ornithology
SIMONS, E. L., PH.D., D.PHIL., Geology
SIMPSON, W. K., PH.D., Egyptology
SINANOGLU, O., PH.D., Molecular Biophysics and Chemistry
SINGER, J. L., PH.D., Psychology
SIU, Y-T., PH.D., Mathematics
SKINNER, B. J., PH.D., Geology and Geophysics
SMITH, G. G., PH.D., History
SMITH, J. E., PH.D., Philosophy
SÖLL, D. G., PH.D., Molecular Biophysics and Biochemistry

# UNIVERSITIES AND COLLEGES—CONNECTICUT (YALE UNIVERSITY) U.S.A.

SOMMERFIELD, C. M., PH.D., Physics
SPENCE, J. D., PH.D., History
STANKIEWICZ, E., PH.D., Slavic Linguistics
STANLEY, E. G., PH.D., English
STEPAN, A. C., PH.D., Political Science
STIMSON, H. M., PH.D., Chinese Linguistics
STOWE, B. B., PH.D., Biology
STRYER, L., M.D., Molecular Biophysics and Biochemistry
SUSSEX, I. M., PH.D., Biology
SYLVESTER, R. S., PH.D., English
SZCZARBA, R. H., PH.D., Mathematics
TAFT, H. D., PH.D., Physics
TAMAGAWA, T., D.SC., Mathematics
THOMPSON, L. M., D.LITT., History
THOMPSON, R. F., PH.D., History of Art
THOMSON, K. S., PH.D., Biology
TOBIN, J., PH.D., Economics
TRACHTENBERG, A., PH.D., American Studies and English
TRIFFIN, R., PH.D., JUR.D., Economics
TRINKAUS, J. P., PH.D., Biology
TUFTE, E. R., Political Science and Statistics
TUREKIAN, K. K., PH.D., Geology and Geophysics
TURNER, H. A., Jr., PH.D., History
TUTEUR, F. B., M.ENG., PH.D., Engineering and Applied Science
VALESIO, P., PH.D., Italian Linguistics
VAN ALTENA, W. F., PH.D., Astronomy
VERONIS, G., PH.D., Geology and Applied Science
WAAGE, K. M., PH.D., Geology
WAGNER, A. R., PH.D., Psychology
WAITE, W. G., PH.D., History of Music
WAITH, E. M., PH.D., English
WALKER, C. A., D.ENG., Engineering
WANDYCZ, P. S., History
WASSERMAN, H. H., PH.D., Chemistry
WATERMAN, T. H., PH.D., Biology
WEGENER, P. P., SC.D., Applied Science
WEINSTEIN, S., PH.D., Buddhist Studies
WELLS, R. S., 3rd., PH.D., Linguistics and Philosophy
WESTERFIELD, H. B., PH.D., Political Science
WHEELER, R. G., PH.D., Engineering and Applied Science
WHEELER, S., PH.D., Law and Sociology
WHITAKER, T. R., PH.D., English
WIBERG, K. B., PH.D., Chemistry
WILLIAMS, G. W., M.A., Classics
WINKS, R. W., PH.D., History
WOLF, W. P., PH.D., Engineering and Applied Science
YU, Y., History
ZIGLER, E. F., PH.D., Psychology
ZWEIG, F., PH.D., Engineering and Applied Science

*School of Medicine:*

ABLOW, R. C., M.D., Clinical Diagnostic Radiology and Paediatrics
ADELBERG, E. A., PH.D., Human Genetics
AGHAJANIAN, G. K., M.D., Psychiatry and Pharmacology
ANDRIOLE, V. T., M.D., Medicine
ASTRACHAN, B. M., M.D., Clinical Psychiatry
ATKINS, E., M.D., Medicine
BARNETT, R. N., Pathology
BARRNETT, R. J., M.D., Cytology
BAUE, A. E., M.D., Surgery
BERLINER, R. W., M.D., Medicine and Physiology
BERTINO, J. R., M.D., Medicine, Pharmacology
BITENSKY, M. W., M.D., Pathology
BLACK, F. L., PH.D., Epidemiology
BLATT, S. J., PH.D., Psychiatry and Psychology
BOUHUYS, A., M.D., PH.D., Medicine and Epidemiology
BOVE, J. R., M.A., M.D., Laboratory Medicine
BOWERS, M. B., M.D., Psychiatry
BRAVERMAN, I. M., M.D., Dermatology
BREG, W. R., Clinical Human Genetics and Paediatrics
BYCK, R., Clinical Pharmacology and Psychiatry
CAHOW, C. E., Clinical Surgery
CANELLAKIS E. S., PH.D., Pharmacology
CARTER, D., Pathology
CARTER, D. M., Dermatology
CASALS-ARIET, J., M.D., Epidemiology
CHANDLER, W. K., M.D., Physiology
CHRISMAN, O. D., Orthopaedic Surgery
CLEMENT, D. H., Paediatrics
COHART, E. M., M.D., M.P.H. Public Health
COHEN, L. S., M.A., M.D., Medicine
COLE, J. W., M.D., Surgery
COLEMAN, J. E., M.D., PH.D., Molecular Biophysics and Biochemistry
COLEMAN, J., Public Health and Psychiatry
COLLINS, W. F. Jr., M.D., Neurosurgery
COMER, J. P., M.D., Psychiatry
CONN, H. O., M.D., Medicine
COOPER, J. R., PH.D., Pharmacology
COTLIER, E., Ophthalmology and Visual Science
CRELIN, E. S., Jr., PH.D., Anatomy
DAVEY, L. M., Surgery
DAVIS, C. D., M.D., Obstetrics and Gynaecology
DOLAN, T. F., M.D., Clinical Paediatrics
DONALDSON, R. M., M.D., Medicine
DOUGLAS, W. W., M.D., Pharmacology
DOWNING, S. E., M.D., Pathology
DOWNS, W. G., Epidemiology
DUBOIS, A. B., M.D., Epidemiology and Physiology
EBBERT, A., Jr., M.D., Clinical Medicine
EDELSON, M., M.D., Psychiatry
EISENSTADT, J. M., Human Genetics
ERRERA, P. L., M.A., M.D., Clinical Psychiatry
EVANS, A. S., M.D., M.P.H., Epidemiology
FARQUHAR, M. G., PH.D., Cell Biology
FEINSTEIN, A. R., M.D., Medicine, Epidemiology
FISCHER, J. J., M.D., PH.D., Therapeutic Radiology
FLECK, S., M.D., Psychiatry
FLYNN, J. P., PH.D., Psychology
FORBES, T. R., PH.D., Anatomy
GERSHON, R. K., M.D., Pathology
GIEBISCH, G. M.D., Physiology
GIFFORD, R. H., M.D., Clinical Medicine
GILLIS, C. N., PH.D., Anaesthesiology
GLASER, G. H., M.D., MED.SC.D., Neurology
GLENN, W. W. L., M.D., Surgery
GLICKMAN, M. G., Clinical Diagnostic Radiology
GOFFINET, J. A., M.D., Clinical Medicine
GOLDENBERG, I. S., M.D., Clinical Surgery
GOLDSTEIN, P. S., Paediatrics
GOODYER, A. V. N., M.D., Medicine
GOTTSCHALK, A., M.D., Diagnostic Radiology
GREEN, R. H., Medicine
GREENE, N. M., M.D., Anaesthesiology
GREENGARD, P., PH.D., Pharmacology
GREENSPAN, R. H., M.D., Diagnostic Radiology
GRYBOSKI, J. D., Paediatrics
HANDSCHUMACHER, R. E., PH.D., Pharmacology
HAYES, M. A., M.D., PH.D., Surgery
HENINGER, G., M.D., Clinical Psychiatry
HESS, O. W., Obstetrics and Gynaecology
HODSON, C. T., M.D., Diagnostic Radiology
HOFFMAN, J. F., PH.D., Physiology
HOFFER, P. B., Diagnostic Radiology
HORSTMANN, DOROTHY M., M.D., D.SC., Epidemiology and Paediatrics
HOWARD, R. O., Ophthalmology
HOWARD-FLANDERS, P., PH.D., Radiobiology and Molecular Biophysics
HSIUNG, G. D., PH.D., Laboratory Medicine
IGERSHEIMER, W. W., Psychiatry
IRWIN, G. A. L., Diagnostic Radiology
JACKSON, S. W., M.D., Clinical Psychiatry
JAMIESON, J. D., PH.D., Cell Biology
JATLOW, P. I., M.D., Laboratory Medicine
JOHNSTON, W. D., Dental Surgery
JONAS, A. M., D.V.M., Health Science Resources
KANTOR, F. S., M.D., Medicine
KAPLOW, L. S., M.D., Pathology and Laboratory Medicine
KASE, N. G., M.D., Obstetrics and Gynaecology
KASHGARIAN, M., M.D., Pathology
KASL S. V., PH.D., Epidemiology
KIER, E. L., M.D., Diagnostic Radiology
KIRCHNER, J. A., M.D., Otolaryngology
KITAHATA, L. M., M.D., Anaesthesiology
KLATSKIN, E. H., PH.D., Clinical Psychology
KLATSKIN, G., M.D. Medicine
KLAUS, S. N., M.D., Dermatology
KLEBER, H. D., M.D., Clinical Psychiatry
KONIGSBERG, W., PH.D., Molecular Biophysics and Biochemistry
KRIZEK, T. J., M.D., Plastic Surgery
KUSHLAN, S. D., Medicine
LATTANZI, W. E., Paediatrics
LAVIETES, P. H., Medicine and Public Health
LEAVY, S. A., Psychiatry
LERNER, A. B., PH.D., M.D., Dermatology
LERNER, M. R., M.D., Clinical Dermatology
LEVINE, R. J., M.D., Medicine
LEVINSON, D. J., PH.D., Psychology
LEVITIN, H., M.D., Clinical Medicine
LEVY, L. L., Neurology
LEWIS, M., M.D., Clinical Paediatrics and Psychology
LIDZ, R. W., Psychiatry
LIDZ, T., M.D., Psychiatry
LIFTON, R. J., M.D., Psychiatry
LINDENMUTH, W. W., Surgery
LIPSKY, S. R., M.D., Physical Medicine
LOEWALD, H., Psychiatry
LOWMAN, R. M., M.D., Diagnostic Radiology
LYTTON, B., M.D., Urology
MCALLISTER, W. B., M.D., Clinical Pathology
MCCOLLUM, R. W., M.D., Epidemiology
MCGUIRE, J. S., Jr., M.D., Dermatology
MAAS, J. W., M.D., Psychiatry
MAHL, G. F., PH.D., Psychology
MALAWISTA, S. E., M.D., Medicine
MANUELIDIS, E. E., M.D., Pathology
MARCHESI, V. T., M.D., Pathology
MARSH, J. C., Clinical Medicine
MATTSON, R. H., Neurology
MEIGS, J. W., Epidemiology
MILLER, I. G., Paediatrics
MILLER, W. H., M.D., Ophthalmology
MILSTONE, J. H., M.D., Pathology
MORRIS, J. M., M.D., Gynaecology
NIEDERMAN, J. C., Epidemiology and Medicine
NORTON, N., Social Work in Psychiatry
ONGLEY, P. A., Paediatrics
OSTFELD, A. M., M.D., Epidemiology and Public Health
PALADE, G. E., M.D., Cell Biology
PASTERNAK, M., Psychiatry
PEARSON, H. A., M.D., Pediatrics
PELLEGRINO, E. D., Medicine

PICKETT, L. K., M.D., Clinical Surgery and Paediatrics
PINCUS, J. H., M.D., Neurology
PRELINGER, E., Psychology in Psychiatry
PROVENCE, SALLY. A., M.D., Paediatrics
PRUSOFF, W. H., M.S., PH.D., Pharmacology
RADDING, C. M., M.D., Medicine and Molecular Biophysics and Biochemistry
RASMUSSEN, H., M.D., Medicine and Cell Biology
REISER, M. F. M.D., Psychiatry
RICHARDS, F. F., M.D., Medicine
RIEDEL, D. C., M.S., PH.D., Public Health
RITCHIE, J. M., PH.D., SC.D., Pharmacology
RITVO, S., Psychiatry
ROOT, R. K., M.D., Medicine
ROSEN, G., M.D., PH.D., History of Medicine
ROSENBERG, L. E., M.D., Human Genetics, Medicine, and Paediatrics
ROTH, O., Medicine
ROTHENBERG, A., Psychiatry
ROWE, D. S., M.D., Clinical Paediatrics and Public Health
SARTORELLI, A. C., PH.D., Pharmacology
SCHOWALTER, J. E., M.D., Clinical Paediatrics and Psychiatry
SCHULZ, R. J., PH.D., Clinical Therapeutic Radiology
SEARS, M. L., M.D., Ophthalmology
SELIGSON, D., M.D., Laboratory Medicine
SHOPE, R. E., M.D., Epidemiology
SILVER, G. A., M.D., M.P.H., Public Health
SIMMONDS, S., PH.D., Molecular Biophysics and Biochemistry
SINGER, J. L., Psychology
SOLITAIRE, G. B., Pathology
SOLNIT, A. J., M.D., Paediatrics and Psychiatry
SON, Y. H., Clinical Therapeutic Radiolog
SOUTHWICK, W. O., M.D., Orthopaedic Surgery
SPIRO, H. M., M.D., Medicine
STANSEL, H. C., M.D., Clinical Surgery
STEVENS, C. F., M.D., PH.D., Physiology
STOLWIJK, J. A. J., Environmental Health
STORER, E. H., M.A., M.D., Surgery
STUBBLEFIELD, R. L., Psychiatry
TALNER, N. S., M.D., Paediatrics and Diagnostic Radiology
TAUB, A., Anaesthesiology
THIER, S. O., M.D., Medicine
THOMPSON, J. D., B.S., Public Health
TISCHLER, G. L., M.D., Clinical Psychiatry
TREFFERS, H. P., PH.D., Pathology
VON GRAEVENITZ, A. W. C., M.D., Laboratory Medicine
WAKSMAN, B. H., M.D., Pathology
WARSHAW, J. B., M.D., Paediatrics and Obstetrics and Gynaecology
WEISS, R., M.D., Urology
WEISSMAN, S. M., M.D., Human Genetics, Medicine, and Molecular Biophysics and Biochemistry
WESSEL, M. A., Paediatrics
WEXLER, H., Psychiatry
WHITE, A. A., Biomechanics
WHITE, C., M.D., Public Health
WHITTEMORE, R., Paediatrics
WRIGHT, H. K., M.D., Surgery
YESNER, R., M.D., Pathology

*School of Law:*
ACKERMAN, B. A., LL.B.
BISHOP, J. W., Jr., LL.B., M.A.
BITTKER, B. I., LL.B., M.A.
BLACK, C. L., LL.B., M.A.
BORK, R.
BOWMAN, W. S., Jr., M.A.
BROWN, R. S., Jr., LL.B., M.A.
BURT, R. A.
CALABRESI, G., LL.B., M.A.
CHIRELSTEIN, M. A., J.D.
CLARK, E., LL.B., M.A.
CLARK, R. C.
COVER, R. M., LL.B.
DAMASKA, M.
DEUTSCH, J. G., LL.B., PH.D.
DUKE, S. B., LL.M.
FISS, O. M., LL.B.
GILMORE, G., PH.D.
GOLDSTEIN, A. S., LL.B., M.A.
GOLDSTEIN, J., LL.B., PH.D.
HAZARD, G. C., Jr., LL.B.
JOHNSTONE, Q., J.S.D.
KATZ, J., M.D.
KLEVORICK, A. K., PH.D.
LEFF, A. A., LL.B.
LIPSON, L. S., LL.B., M.A.
MARSHALL, B., LL.B., M.A.
MASHAW, J.
PETERS, ELLEN A., LL.B., M.A.
REISMAN, W. M., B.A., J.S.D.
ROSTOW, E. V., M.A., LL.D.
SIMON, J. G., LL.B., M.A.
WELLINGTON, H. H., M.A., LL.B.
WHEELER, S., PH.D.
WINTER, R. K., Jr., LL.B.

*Divinity School:*
ADAMS, Rev. H. B., Pastoral Theology
BURGESS, Rev. J. M., Ministry
AHLSTROM, S. E., PH.D., Modern Religious History
CHILDS, B. S., TH.D., Old Testament
DAHL, N. A., TH.D., New Testament
DITTES, J. E., PH.D., Psychology of Religion
DOBIHAL, E. F., Jr., PH.D., Pastoral Care
FORMAN, C. W., PH.D., Missions
FREI, H. W., PH.D., Religious Studies
GEANAKOPLOS, D. J., PH.D., History and Religious Studies
HEIN, N. J., PH.D., Comparative Religion
HOLMER, P. L., PH.D., LITT.D., LL.D., Theology
JOHNSON, Rev. R. C., S.T.M., PH.D., D.D., Theology
KAVANAGH, A. J., O.S.B., S.T.D., Liturgics
KECK, L. E., PH.D., New Testament
KELSEY, D. H., PH.D., Theology
LINDBECK, G. A., PH.D., Theology
MILLER, Rev. R. C., PH.D., S.T.D., D.D., Christian Education
MUEHL, E. W., LL.B., LL.D., D.D., Practical Theology
POPE, M. H., PH.D., Semitic Languages
NOUWEN, H., Pastoral Theology
WILLIAMS, C. W., PH.D., Religion

*School of Forestry and Environmental Studies:*
BORMANN, F. H., PH.D., Forest Ecology
BURCH, W. R., Jr., PH.D., Forest Sociology
FOSTER, C. H., PH.D., Forestry
FURNIVAL, G. M., D.F., Forest Management
GALSTON, A. W., PH.D., Botany and Forestry
MERGEN, F., M.F., PH.D., Forestry
MILLER, R. S., D.PHIL., Wildlife Ecology
REIFSNYDER, W. E., M.F., PH.D., Forest Meteorology
SMITH, D. M., M.F., PH.D., Silviculture
STOWE, B. B., PH.D., Biology and Forestry
VOIGT, G. K., PH.D., Forest Soils
WORRELL, A. C., M.F., PH.D., Forest Policy

*School of Art:*
BAILEY, W. H., M.F.A., Art
CHAET, B. R., B.S.ED., Painting
EISENMAN, A., M.A., Graphic Design
PETERDI, G. F., M.A., Printmaking

*School of Architecture:*
GEHNER, M. D., M.ARCH., Architectural Engineering
PELLI, C., M.S.ARCH., Dean
SPIEGEL, H., B.S.ARCH., M.ENG., Architectural Engineering

*School of Music:*
BAKER, R. S., S.M.D., L.H.D.
CURRIER, D. R., M.M.
DAVENNY, W. M., MUS.M.
FRENCH, R. F., M.A.
HEATH, F. F., Jr., M.M., Choral Music
KRIGBAUM, C. R., M.F.A.
NELSON, P., PH.D.
PARISOT, A. S., M.A.
STERN, B. G., M.S.
TIRRO, F. P., PH.D.
WILSON, K., MUS.M.

*School of Organization and Management:*
ACKERMAN, B. A., LL.B., Law
BERNEY, P. R., Accounting
CALABRESI, G., LL.B., Law
COOPER, R. N., PH.D., Economics
FETTER, R. B., D.B.A., Administrative Sciences
ISAACSON, L., Practice of Management
LINDBLOM, C. E., PH.D., Political and Social Science
MACAVOY, P. W., PH.D., Economics and Management
NELSON, R. R., PH.D., Economics
PECK, M. J., PH.D., Economics
POLSBY, N. W., PH.D., Economics and Management
ROSS, S. A., Economics
SARASON, S. B., PH.D., Psychology
SHUBIK, M., PH.D., Economics
VROOM, V. H., PH.D., Psychology
WINTER, S. G., PH.D., Economics and Management

*School of Drama:*
RICHARDS, L., M.A., English

AFFILIATED INSTITUTES:

**Institute for Sacred Music:** Dir. JON D. BAILEY.

**Institution for Social and Policy Studies:** Dir. CHARLES E. LINDBLOM, PH.D.

# DELAWARE

## DELAWARE STATE COLLEGE
DUPONT HIGHWAY,
DOVER, DELAWARE 19901
Telephone: 302-736-4901.

Founded 1891.

*President:* Dr. LUNA I. MISHOE.
*Registrar:* JEAN A. WILSON.
*Librarian:* Dr. DANIEL COONS.

The library contains 107,438 vols., 22,000 microtexts.

Number of teachers: 146.
Number of students: 2,124.

## UNIVERSITY OF DELAWARE
NEWARK, DELAWARE 19711
Telephone: 738-2000.

Founded 1833 from the Newark Academy founded in 1765; Chartered 1769.

Academic year: September to June (two terms).

*President:* E. ARTHUR TRABANT, PH.D.
*Provost and Vice-President for Academic Affairs:* L. LEON CAMPBELL, PH.D.
*Vice-President for Student Affairs:* STUART J. SHARKEY.
*Librarian:* SUSAN BRYNTESON.

Number of teachers: 798.
Number of students: 8,821 men, 10,174 women, total 18,997.

University publications: *Bibliography of Faculty Publications, The University News, Catalogue, Bulletins.*

### DEANS:

*College of Agricultural Sciences:* D. F. CROSSAN, PH.D.
*College of Arts and Science:* HELEN GOULDNER, PH.D.
*College of Business and Economics:* ERIC BRUCKER, PH.D.
*College of Education:* FRANK BRUSH MURRAY.
*College of Engineering:* IRWIN G. GREENFIELD, PH.D.
*College of Human Resources:* ALEXANDER DOBERENZ, PH.D.
*College of Nursing:* EDITH ANDERSON, PH.D.
*College of Marine Studies:* W. S. GAITHER, PH.D.
*College of Physical Education, Athletics and Recreation:* DAVID M. NELSON.
*College of Urban Affairs and Public Policy:* DAVID AMES.

### PROFESSORS:

ALLEN, LeR., Education
AMES, D. L., Urban Affairs and Public Policy
ANDERSON, E., Nursing
ARNSDORF, V., Education
BARNETT, A. Electrical Engineering
BAXTER, W., Mathematics
BELLAMY, D. P., Mathematical Sciences
BEN-ISRAEL, A., Mathematics
BENNETT, A. LeR., Political Science
BENTON, W. J., Animal Science and Agricultural Biochemistry
BIEBUYCK, D. P., Anthropology
BILINSKY, Y., Political Science
BILLON, S. A., Business Administration
BIRCHENALL, C. E., Metallurgy
BISCHOFF, K., Biomedical Engineering
BOER, K., Engineering
BOHNER, C. H., English
BOHNING, E., Languages and Literature
BOLGIANO, L. P., Electrical Engineering
BOORD, R. L., Life and Health Sciences
BORDEN, G. A., Communication
BOWEN, Z., English
BOWIE, N. E., Philosophy
BOYER, W. W., Jr., Political Science
BRABNER, G., Education
BRAUN, T. E. D., Languages and Literature
BRAY, D. P., Entomology
BRILL, T. B., Chemistry
BROCKENBROUGH, T. W., Civil Engineering
BROWN, C. H., Urban Affairs and Public Policy
BROWN, H., Art Conservation
BROWN, R. P., Theatre
BURBUTIS, P. P., Entomology
BURMEISTER, J. L., Chemistry
BUSHMAN, R. L., History
CADY, H. L., Music
CALLAHAN, R., History
CAMPBELL, L. L., Life and Health Sciences
CARON, D. M., Entomology and Applied Ecology
CARRIKER, M., Marine Studies
CAVINESS, B. F., Computer and Information Sciences
CHAMBLISS, W., Sociology
CHESSON, E., Jr., Civil Engineering
CHOU, T. W., Mechanical and Aerospace Engineering
CHRISTENSEN, M. A., English
CICALA, G., Psychology
CLARK, A. M., Life and Health Sciences
COLE, G. L., Agriculture and Food Economics
COLMAN, R. F., Chemistry
COLTON, D., Mathematics
COOPER, C. B., Physics
COPE, M., Art History
COULET DU GARD, R., Languages and Literature
COX, R. L., English
CRAVEN, E. W., Art History
CRONIN, T. E., Political Science
CROSSAN, D., Plant Science
CROUSE, J. H., Educational Studies
CURTIS, C. R., Plant Science
CURTIS, J., History
DA CUNHA, J., Art
DAIBER, F. C., Marine Studies and Life and Health Sciences
DANBERG, J., Mechanical and Aerospace Engineering
DANIELS, W. B., Physics
DAVISON, R., English
DEAN, R. G., Civil Engineering and Marine Studies
DeHAVEN, A. L., Nursing
DENN, M., Chemical Engineering
DENSON, C. D., Chemical Engineering
DILLEY, F., Philosophy
DIPIETRO, R., Languages and Literature
DIRENZO, G., Sociology
DOBERENZ, A., Food Science and Human Nutrition
DUNHAM, C. W., Plant Science
DUNN, A. H., III, Business Administration
EDINGTON, J. W., Mechanical and Aerospace Engineering
ELLIS, J. D., History
ELTERICH, G. J., Agriculture and Food Economics
EXLINE, R. V., Psychology
FARBER, D., Electrical Engineering
FARKAS, D. F., Food Science and Human Nutrition
FARNHAM-DIGGORY, S., Educational Studies
FIELDHOUSE, D. J., Plant Science
FLETCHER, W. A., History
FRANCIS, D. W., Life and Health Sciences
GAITHER, W. S., Marine Studies
GATES, B. C., Chemical Engineering
GAUDY, Jr., A., Civil Engineering
GIBBS, R., Marine Studies
GILBERT, R. P., Mathematics
GOODRICH, R., Mathematics
GOULDNER, H., Sociology
GRANDA, A. M., Life and Health Sciences
GREENBERG, M. D., Mechanical and Aerospace Engineering
GREENFIELD, I. G., Mechanical and Aerospace Engineering, Metallurgy
HAENLEIN, G. F. W., Animal Science
HALIO, J., English
HALPRIN, A., Physics
HASKELL, M., Urban Affairs
HAUTY, G. T., Psychology
HECK, R. F., Chemistry
HILL, R. N., Physics
HOERL, A., Mathematical Sciences
HOGAN, R. C., English
HOMER, W. I., Art History
HSIAO, G. C., Mathematics
HUNSPERGER, R., Electrical Engineering
HUTCHINSON, H. D., Economics
HUTHMACHER, J. J., History
INCIARDI, J. A., Sociology
IZARD, C., Psychology
KATZER, J., Chemical Engineering
KERNER, E. H., Physics
KERR, A., Civil Engineering
KING, J. R., Music
KING, N. R., Theatre
KIRCH, M. S., Languages and Literature
KLEINMAN, R., Mathematics
KLEMAS, V., Marine Studies
KRAFT, J. C., Geology
KRAMER, J. J., Electrical Engineering
KULACKI, F. A., Mechanical and Aerospace Engineering
KWART, H., Chemistry
LAMB, D. E., Computer and Information Sciences, Chemical Engineering
LEMAY, J. A. L., English
LESLIE, C., Life and Health Sciences
LEWIS, K. R., Economics
LIBERA, R., Mathematics
LIVINGSTON, A., Mathematics
LUKASHEVICH, S., History
LURIE, E., Life and Health Sciences and History
LUTZ, B. C., Electrical Engineering
McCULLOUGH, R., Chemical Engineering
McLAREN, J. C., Languages and Literature
MANGONE, G., Marine Studies and Political Science
MARKELL, W., Accounting
MARTIN, R. E., English
MATHER, J. R., Geography
MAW, W. H., Educational Studies
MEAKIN, J. D., Energy Conversion, Mechanical Engineering and Materials Science
MERRILL, J. M., History and Marine Studies
MERRILL, T., English
METZNER, A. B., Chemical Engineering
MEYER, D., History
MITCHELL, W., Plant Science
MOODY, W. B., Education Development
MOORE, J. A., Chemistry
MOREHART, A. L., Plant Science
MOSBERG, L., Educational Studies
MOSS, J. F., Art
MOSZYNSKI, J. R., Mechanical and Aerospace Engineering
MUNROE, J. A., History
MUNSON, M. S. B., Chemistry
MURPHY, L. C., Individual and Family Studies
MURRAY, F., Education
MURRAY, R. B., Physics
NASHED, M. Z., Mathematics
NEALE, D. C., Education
NELSON, D. M., Physical Education
NEUTS, M., Computer and Information Sciences; Mathematics
NICHOLLS, R. L., Civil Engineering
NOGGLE, J., Chemistry
NORMAN, R. A., Business Administration
NORTON, D. L., Philosophy
OLSON, J. H., Chemical Engineering
PALLEY, M. L., Political Science
PARKER, H., English
PELLICCIARO, E. J., Mathematics
PETTIGREW, E., Urban Affairs and Public Policy
PIGFORD, R. L., Chemical Engineering
PIKULSKI, J. J., Educational Development
PIPES, R. B., Mechanical and Aerospace
POHLEN, M. F., Business Administration
RAYMOND, H. R., Physical Education
RECHNITZ, G., Chemistry
REITNOUR, C. M., Animal Science and Agricultural Biochemistry
REMAGE, R., Jr., Mathematics
REYNOLDS, H. T., Political Science
ROBINSON, C. E., English
ROSENBERGER, J. K., Animal Science and Agricultural Biochemistry

Ross, B. E., Education
Rowe, C. A., Art
Runnels, T., Animal Science and Agricultural Biochemistry
Russell, T. W. F., Chemical Engineering
Rylander, C. R., Physical Education
Salsbury, R. L., Animal Science and Agricultural Biochemistry
Sandler, S. I., Chemical Engineering
Sasser, M., Plant Science
Saydam, T., Computer and Information Sciences
Scarborough, E. N., Agricultural Engineering
Scarpitti, F. R., Sociology
Schmidt, B. G., Business Administration
Schuit, G. A., Chemical Engineering
Schultz, D. A., Urban Affairs and Public Policy
Schultz, J., Chemical Engineering
Schwartz, N. E., Anthropology
Schweizer, E., Chemistry
Scott, J., Business Administration
Seidel, B. S., Mechanical and Aerospace Engineering
Settles, B., Individual and Family Studies
Sharnoff, M., Physics
Shurtleff, B., Art
Siegel, J., Psychology
Sloane, A. A., Business Administration
Slover, C., Mathematics
Smith, J. M., History
Smith, R. C., Agricultural and Food Economics
Snodgrass, W. D., English
Somers, G. F., Life and Health Sciences; Marine Studies
South, F. E., Life and Health Sciences
Spielman, L. A., Civil and Chemical Engineering
Spinski, V., Art
Staiger, R. C., Education Development
Stakgold, I., Mathematics; Civil, Mechanical and Aerospace Engineering
Stark, R., Mathematical Sciences, Civil Engineering
Steiner, R., Languages and Literature
Stetson, M. H., Life and Health Sciences
Stiles, A. B., Chemical Engineering
Stillman, D., Art History
Stokes, G. A., Nursing
Straka, G., History
Stretcher, M. A., Chemical Engineering
Sussman, M. B., Individual and Family Studies
Swain, F. M., Geology and Marine Studies
Tannian, F. X., Urban Affairs and Public Policy
Teel, M. R., Plant Science
Teis, D., Art
Toensmeyer, U. C., Agriculture and Food Economics
Trabant, E. A., Engineering
Travis, L. E., Computer and Information Sciences
Tripp, M. R., Life and Health Sciences
Vagenas, P. T., Theatre
Valbuena, A. J., Languages and Literature
Venezky, R., Education
Vincent, W. S., Life and Health Sciences
Vinson, J. R., Mechanical and Aerospace Engineering; Marine Studies
Walpole, E. W., Agricultural Engineering
Wang, Hsiang, Civil Engineering and Marine Studies
Warren, R., Urban Affairs and Public Policy; Marine Studies
Warter, P., Electrical Engineering
Weaver, J. W., Textiles, Design and Consumer Economics
Weinacht, R. J., Mathematics
Wetlaufer, D. B., Chemistry
Williams, F. E., Physics
Wilson, C., Educational Development
Wolters, R. B., History
Wood, R. H., Chemistry
Wriston, J. C., Jr., Chemistry
Wu, J., Marine Studies and Civil Engineering
Yang, C. Y., Civil Engineering
Yolles, S., Chemistry
Young, M., Mechanical and Aerospace Engineering
Zikakis, J. P., Animal Science and Agricultural Biochemistry
Zimmerman, J., Mechanical and Aerospace Engineering
Zsoldos, L., Economics
Zuckerman, M., Psychology

# DISTRICT OF COLUMBIA

## AMERICAN UNIVERSITY
MASSACHUSETTS AND NEBRASKA AVES., N.W., WASHINGTON, D.C. 20016

Telephone: (202) 686-2000.

Chartered 1893.

*President:* Richard E. Berendzen.
*Provost:* Milton Greenberg.
*Vice-President for Development:* L. Victor Atchison.
*Dean of Admissions and Financial Aid:* Rebecca R. Dixon.
*Registrar:* Donald W. Bunis.
*Librarian:* Donald Dennis.

Number of teachers: 430.
Number of students: 12,500.

### Deans:

*College of Arts and Sciences:* Frank Turaj.
*Kogod College of Business and Administration:* Herbert E. Striner.
*School of Nursing:* Laura Kummer.
*Washington College of Law:* Thomas Buergenthal.
*Division of Continuing Education:* Thomas A. Coffey.
*College of Public and International Affairs:* Robert E. Cleary.

## CATHOLIC UNIVERSITY OF AMERICA
FOURTH ST. AND MICHIGAN AVE., N.E., WASHINGTON, D.C. 20064

Telephone: (202) 635-5000.

Incorporated 1887; Chartered by the Congress of the United States 1889.

*Chancellor:* H.E. Cardinal William W. Baum.
*President:* Edmund D. Pellegrino.
*Executive Vice-President and Provost:* C. J. Nuesse, ph.d., ll.d.
*Vice-President for Administration and Finance:* Richard C. Applegate, m.a.
*Vice-President for Development:* Eugene J. Kennedy.
*Vice-President for Student Affairs:* Bro. Nivard Scheel, c.f.x., ph.d.
*Registrar:* Joseph C. Michalowicz, m.e.e.
*Director of Admissions:* Robert Talbot.
*Director of Financial Aid:* Kevin Gallagher.
*Director of Information Systems and Planning:* E. D. Jordan, ph.d.
*Director of Libraries:* L. R. Wagner, m.s.l.s.

Number of teachers: 533.
Number of students: 7,400.

Publications: *The Anthropological Quarterly, The Catholic Historical Review* (quarterly).

### Deans:

*School of Arts and Sciences:* Eugene R. Kennedy, ph.d.
*School of Education:* Raymond J. Steimel, ph.d.
*School of Engineering and Architecture:* G. E. McDuffie, ph.d.
*School of Law:* John L. Garvey, s.j.d.
*School of Music:* Dr. T. Mastroianni, d.mus.
*School of Nursing:* Virginia C. Conley, ed.d.
*School of Philosophy:* J. P. Dougherty, ph.d.
*School of Religious Studies:* Rev. Carl J. Peter, ph.d., s.t.d.
*School of Social Service:* Joan W. Mullaney, d.s.w.

## GALLAUDET COLLEGE
7TH ST. AND FLORIDA AVE., N.E. WASHINGTON, D.C. 20052

Telephone: (202) 447-0314.

Founded 1864.

*President:* E. C. Merrill, Jr.
*Director of Admissions and Records:* Gerald M. Jordan.
*Dean of Graduate School:* Gilbert Delgado.
*Librarian:* Fern Edwards.

The library contains 150,000 vols.
Number of teachers: 190.

## THE GEORGE WASHINGTON UNIVERSITY
WASHINGTON, D.C. 20052

Telephone: 676-6000.

Founded 1821.

Private control; Academic year: September to May.

*President:* Lloyd H. Elliott, ed.d., ll.d.
*Provost and Vice-President for Academic Affairs:* Harold F. Bright, ph.d.
*Vice-President for Development:* S. Alpert, m.d.
*Vice-President for Administration and Research:* C. J. Lange, ph.d.
*Vice-President for Policy Studies and Special Projects:* L. H. Mayo, j.s.d., ll.b., b.s.
*Vice-President and Treasurer:* C. E. Diehl, m.b.a.

# UNIVERSITIES AND COLLEGES—DISTRICT OF COLUMBIA U.S.A.

*Vice-President for Medical Affairs:* R. P. KAUFMAN, M.D.
*Vice-President for Student Affairs:* WILLIAM P. SMITH, Jr., M.B.A.
*Director of Admissions:* J. Y. RUTH, A.B.
*Registrar:* R. GEBHARDTSBAUER, M.A.
*University Librarian:* J. B. ALSIP, M.LN.

The library contains 1,137,225 vols.
**Number of teachers:** 2,981.
**Number of students:** 20,844.

### DEANS:

*Columbian College of Arts and Sciences:* C. D. LINTON, PH.D.
*The National Law Center:* J. A. BARRON, LL.M.
*Academic Affairs (Medical Center):* L. T. BOWLES, M.D.
*Administrative Affairs (Medical Center):* P. S. BIRNBAUM, M.S. IN M.E.
*Clinical Affairs (Medical Center):* D. S. O'LEARY, M.D.
*Education:* E. W. KELLY, Jr., PH.D.
*Engineering:* H. LIEBOWITZ, D.AE.E.
*Government and Business Administration:* N. LOESER, D.B.A.
*Graduate School of Arts and Sciences:* H. SOLOMON, PH.D.
*Continuing Education and Summer Sessions:* W. F. E. LONG, PH.D.
*Public and International Affairs:* B. M. SAPIN, PH.D.

### PROFESSORS:

(many professors serve in more than one school)

*Columbian College of Arts and Sciences:*
*Graduate School of Arts and Sciences:*
*School of Public and International Affairs:*

ABRAVANEL, E., Psychology
AFFRONTI, L. F., Microbiology
ALBERT, E. N., Anatomy
ALLAN, F. D., Anatomy
ALLEE, J. G., English
ASCHHEIM, J., Economics
ATKINS, D. L., Biological Sciences
BAILEY, J. M., Biochemistry
BARI, R. A., Mathematics
BARTH, J. R., Economics
BEILSKI, L. S., Speech and Drama
BERGMANN, O., Physics
BLOOM, S., Pathology
BOWLING, L. S., Speech and Drama
BRIGHT, H. F., Statistics
BRITT, A. D., Chemistry
BROWN, R. G., Sociology
BURKS, J. F., Romance Languages and Literature
CALDWELL, W. E., Psychology
CARESS, E. A., Chemistry
CARROLL, G. V., Geology
CASSIDY, M. M., Physiology
CISIN, IRA H., Sociology
COATES, A. G., Geology
COHN, V. H., Pharmacology
COURTLESS, T. F., Sociology
CUNLIFFE, M. F., American Studies and History
DAVISON, R. H., History
DEPAUW, L. G., History
DUNN, R. M., Economics
EISENSTEIN, J. C., Physics
ETZIONI, A., Sociology
FILIPESCU, N., Chemistry
FRENCH, R. S., Philosophy
FREY, J. A., Romance Languages and Literature
GANZ, R. N., English
GASTWIRTH, J. L., Statistics
GOLDFARB, R. S., Economics
GOLDSTEIN, A. L., Biochemistry
GORDON, M. F., Geography
GREENHOUSE, S. W., Statistics
GRUBAR, F. S. Art
GYORGY A., International Affairs
HABER, S. E., Economics
HASKETT, R. C., History
HIGHFILL, P. H., English
HILL, P. P., History
HILLIS, J. W., Speech
HILTEBEITEL, A. J., Religion
HINTON, H. C., International Affairs
HOBBS, H. H., Physics
HOLMAN, M. A., Economics
HSIEH, C. Y., Economics
HUANG, KUN-YEN, Microbiology
HUGH, R., Microbiology
HUMPHREY, R. L., Anthropology
JACKSON, M. J., Physiology
JOHNSON, T. N., Anatomy
JONES, R. G., Religion
JUNGHENN, H. D., Mathematics
KATZ, I. J., Mathematics
KENDRICK, J. W., Economics
KENNEY, R. A., Physiology
KENNY, R. W., History
KENYON, H., Mathematics
KIM, Y. C., Political Science
KIND, P. D., Microbiology
KING, J. C., German Language and Literature
KIRSCH, A. D., Statistics
KLAREN, P. F., History
KOERING, M. J., Anatomy
KRULFELD, R. M., Anthropology
LANGE, C. J., Psychology
LAVINE, THELMA Z., Philosophy
LEBLANC, H. L., Political Science
LENGERMANN, P. M., Sociology
LEVITAN, S. A., Economics
LEVY, B. I., Psychology
LEVY, J. B., Chemistry
LEWIS, J. F., Geology
LEWIS, R. K., Anthropology
LILLIEFORS, H. W., Statistics
LINDHOLM, R. C., Geology
LINTON, C. D., English
LIVERMAN, T. P., Mathematics
LOGSDON, J. M., International Affairs
LONG, W. F. E., Economics
LOWE, J. C., Geography
MANDEL, H. G., Pharmacology
MAZEL, P., Pharmacology
MAZZEO, G., Romance Languages and Literature
MERGEN, B. M., American Studies
MILLAR, J. W., Epidemiology
MILLER, F. N., Pathology
MILLER, J. C., Psychology
MONDALE, C. C., American Studies
MORGAN, J. A., Political Science
MOSEL, J. N., Psychology
MOSER, C. A., Slavic Languages and Literature
NATOV, N. N., Slavic Languages and Literature
NELSON, N. D., Mathematics
NIMER, B., Political Science
O'REAR, C. E., Forensic Science
PACKER, R. K., Biological Sciences
PARRIS, R., Music
PERROS, T. P., Chemistry
PETROV, V., International Affairs
PHILLIPS, E. L., Psychology
PRATS, F., Physics
PURCELL, R. E., Political Science
REESING, J. P., English
REICH, B., Political Science
REICH, M., Microbiology
REYNOLDS, W. M., Speech and Drama
RICE, C. E., Psychology
ROBB, J. W., Romance Languages and Literature
ROBINSON, L. F., Art
ROTHBLAT, L. A., Psychology
ROWLEY, D. A., Chemistry
SACHAR, H. M., History
SAPIN, B. M., International Affairs
SCHIFF, S. O., Zoology
SCHLAGEL, R. H., Philosophy
SCHMIDT, W. E., Chemistry
SCHWOERER, L. G., History
SHARKEY, R. P., History
SHIH, C., Chinese
SIDRANSKY, H., Pathology
SIEGEL, F. R., Geochemistry
SIGUR, G. J., International Affairs
SILBER, D. E., Psychology
SMITH, B. W., Biochemistry
SMYTHE, R. T., Statistics
SNELL, R. S., Anatomy
SOLOMON, HENRY, Economics
STAMBUK, G., International Affairs
STEINER, C., German
STEINER, G., Music
STEPHENS, R. W., Sociology
STEWART, C. T., Economics
STEWART, P. L., Sociology
STRAW, J. A., Pharmacology
TAAM, CHOY TAK, Mathematics
TELLER, D. H., Art
THOENELT, K., German
THORNTON, R. C., History
TIDBALL, C. S., Physiology
TIDBALL, M. E., Physiology
TURNBULL, C. M., Anthropology
VAHOUNY, G. V., Biochemistry
WALK, R. D., Psychology
WALKER, R. H., American Civilization
WALLACE, D. D., Religion
WALLACE, R. A., Sociology
WAYNE, S. J., Political Science
WEI, LEE-JEN, Statistics
WHITE, D. G., Chemistry
YAKOBSON, HELEN B., Slav Language and Literature
YEIDE, H. E., Religion
ZUCHELLI, A. J., Physics

*National Law Center:*
ALBERT, J. M.
BANZHAF, J. F.
BARRON, J. A.
BROWN, J. M.
CAPLAN, G. M.
CHANDLER, J. P.
CIBINIC, J.
DIENES, C. T.
HAMBRICK, J. R.
HEAD, A. K.
KAYTON, I.
LOWTHER, D. C.
MALLISON, W. T.
MAYO, L. H.
MERRIFIELD, L. S.
NASH, R. C.
PARK, R. E.
POCK, M. A.
POTTS, E. A.
REITZE, A. W.
ROBINSON, D.
ROTHSCHILD, D. P.
SCHILLER, L. A.
SCHWARTZ, T. M.
SEIDELSON, D. E.
SHARPE, D. J.
SIRULNIK, E. S.
SOLOMON, L. D.
STARRS, J. E.
STEVENSON, R. B.
WEAVER, D. B.
WESTON, G. E.
ZENOFF, E.

*School of Government and Business Administration:*
ADAMS, E. B., Management Science

AMLING, F., Business Administration
BIRNBAUM, P. S., Health Services Administration
BLACK, GUY, Business Administration
BROWN, D. S., Public Administration
BURDETSKY, B., Business Administration
CHITWOOD, S. R., Public Administration
DARR, K. J., Health Services Administration
DEVOLITES, M. C., Health Services Administration
DIVITA, S. F., Business Administration
DYER, R. F., Business Administration
EASTIN, R. B., Business Administration
EL-ANSARY, A. I., Business Administration
ELDRIDGE, R. W., Business Administration
ERICSON, R. F., Management Science
FULLER, S. S., Urban and Regional Planning
GALLAGHER, M. G., Accounting
GINTZIG, L. I., Health Services Administration
GRUB, P. D., Business Administration
HALAL, N. E., Management Science
HANDORF, W. C., Business Administration
HARMON, M. M., Public Administration
HARVEY, J. B., Management Science
HILMY, J., Accounting
KEEGAN, W. J., Business Administration
KURTZ, F. C., Accounting
LAUTER, G. P., Business Administration
LEWIS, E. J. B., Accounting
LIPPITT, G., Management Science
LOESER, N. M., Business Administration
MASTRO, A. J., Accounting
McGRATH, D. C., Urban Planning
PAIK, C. M., Accounting
REEVES, P. N., Health Services Administration
ROMAN, D. D., Management Science
VAILL, P. B., Management Science
ZWICK, J., Business Administration

*Medical Center:*
ABRAMSON, F. P., Pharmacology
ADAMS, J. P., Orthopaedic Surgery
ALPERT, S., Anaesthesiology
ARMALY, M. F., Ophthalmology
AVERY, G. B., Child Health and Development
BACOS, J. M., Medicine
BAKER, W. P., Medicine
BARTER, R. H., Obstetrics and Gynaecology
BARTH, W. F., Medicine
BATTLE, C. U., Child Health and Development
BECKER, K. L., Medicine
BELMAN, A. B., Urology
BOWLES, L. T., Surgery
CASTELL, D. O., Medicine
CHANOCK, R. M., Child Health and Development
CHENG, T. O., Medicine
COAKLEY, C. S., Anaesthesiology
CONNERS, C. K., Psychiatry and Behavioural Sciences
CRAFT, J. B., Anaesthesiology
CURTIN, J. A., Medicine
DAVIS, D. O., Radiology
DELANEY, D. W., Child Health and Development
DEVITA, V. T., Medicine
DUNBAR, B. S., Anaesthesiology
ECKELMAN, W. C., Radiology
EGAN, J. H., Psychiatry and Behavioural Sciences
EINHORN, A. H., Child Health and Development
ELGART, M. L., Dermatology
ENG, G. D., Child Health and Development

EPSTEIN, B. S., Anaesthesiology
FEFFER, H. L., Orthopaedic Surgery
FELTS, W. R., Medicine
FINKELSTEIN, J. D., Medicine
FORTUNE, W. P., Orthopaedic Surgery
FRIENDLY, D. S., Ophthalmology
GREEN, F. C., Child Health and Development
HEAD, M., Medical and Public Affairs
HERER, G. R., Child Health and Development
HICKS, J. M. B., Child Health and Development
HIGGINS, G. A., Surgery
HSU, I. I., Medicine
HUNG, W., Child Health and Development
KAUFMAN, R. P., Medicine
KEIMOWITZ, R. I., Medicine
KENMORE, P. I., Orthopaedic Surgery
KLUBES, P., Pharmacology
KOBRINE, A. I., Neurological Surgery
KRAMER, N. C., Medicine
KURZ, R. B., Psychiatry and Behavioural Sciences
LAROSA, J. C., Medicine
LEIKIN, S. L., Child Health and Development
LESSIN, L. S., Medicine
LETTERMAN, G. S., Surgery
LEWICKI, A. M., Radiology
LICHTMANN, M. W., Anaesthesiology
LINDSAY, J., Medicine
MAJD, M., Radiology
MARSH, W. L., Pathology
MATTHEWS, M. J., Pathology
McGOWAN, L., Obstetrics and Gynaecology
McKAY, D. W., Orthopaedic Surgery
McSWEENEY, W. J., Radiology
MILHORAT, T. H., Neurological Surgery
MILLER, H. C., Urology
MOLINARI, G. F., Neurology
MORALES, G. A., Anaesthesiology
MOVASSAGHI, N., Child Health and Development
NEVIASER, R. J., Orthopaedic Surgery
NOSHPITZ, J. D., Psychiatry and Behavioural Sciences
O'LEARY, D. S., Medicine
OLMSTED, W. W., Radiology
O'REILLY, S., Neurology
OTT, J. E., Health Care Sciences
PARRISH, A. E., Medicine
PARROTT, R. H., Child Health and Development
PERLIN, S., Psychiatry and Behavioural Sciences
PERRY, L. W., Child Health and Development
PIEMME, T. E., Health Care Sciences
PIERCE, L. E., Medicine
PIPBERGER, H. V., Clinical Engineering
RANDOLPH, J. G., Surgery
REBA, R. C., Radiology
REISS, D., Psychiatry and Behavioural Sciences
RIOS, J. C., Medicine
RIZZOLI, H. V., Neurological Surgery
ROCKOFF, S. D., Radiology
ROGERS, C., Radiology
ROSENQUIST, G. C., Child Health and Development
ROSS, A. M., Medicine
SAUERBRUNN, B. J. L., Radiology
SCHECHTER, G. P., Medicine
SCHULMAN, J. D., Obstetrics and Gynaecology
SCOTT, L. P., Child Health and Development
SHELBURNE, S. A., Neurology
SHORB, P. E., Surgery
SIDBURY, J. B., Child Health and Development
SIMON, E. R., Medicine

SLY, R. M., Child Health and Development
SMITH, B. H., Pathology
SPAGNOLO, S. V., Medicine
STEINGLASS, P. J., Psychiatry and Behavioural Sciences
TAMAGNA, I. G., Medicine
TSANGARIS, N. T., Surgery
TUAZON, C. U., Medicine
VALASKE, M. J., Pathology
VAN HOUTEN, R. J., Anaesthesiology
VARGHESE, P. J., Medicine
VARMA, V. M., Radiology
WAXMAN, B., Obstetrics and Gynaecology
WEBSTER, T. G., Psychiatry and Behavioural Sciences
WEINGOLD, A. B., Obstetrics and Gynaecology
WEINTRAUB, H. D., Anaesthesiology
WERNER, M., Pathology
WIENER, J. M., Psychiatry and Behavioural Sciences
WITORSCH, P., Medicine
WOLFF, F. W., Medicine
YAMAMOTO, W. S., Clinical Engineering
ZIMMERMAN, H. J., Medicine
ZIMMERMAN, J. E., Anaesthesiology

*School of Education:*
BAKER, R. E., Education
BOSWELL, J. G., Education
BREEN, J. L., Human Kinetics and Leisure Studies
BRENNER, M. B., Education
BROWN, F. J., Education
COTTRELL, R. S., Special Education
DUBOIS, E. E., Education
ELLIOTT, L. H., Education
FERRANTE, R., Education
HAWKINS, D. E., Human Kinetics and Leisure Studies
HORRWORTH, G. L., Education
HUNT, J. D., Human Kinetics and Leisure Studies
IVES, R. J. K., Special Education
KAVRUCK, S., Education
KELLY, E. W., Education
KULAWIEC, E. P., Education
LINKOWSKI, D. C., Education
MARINACCIO, A., Education
McINTYRE, M., Education
MOORE, D. A., Education
NADLER, L., Education
PARATORE, S. R., Education
PAUP, D. C., Human Kinetics and Leisure Studies
RASHID, MARTHA, N. Education
SHOTEL, J. R., Special Education
SNODGRASS, J. E., Human Kinetics and Leisure Studies
STALLINGS, LORETTA M., Human Kinetics and Leisure Studies
TILLMAN, R., Education
VONTRESS, C. E., Education
WINKLER, L., Education

*School of Engineering and Applied Science:*
ABD-ALLA, A. M., Engineering
ARKILIC, G. M., Applied Science
CAMBEL, A. B., Engineering
CRAFTON, P. A., Engineering Administration
EFTIS, J., Engineering
EISENBERG, M. F., Engineering
ESTERLING, D. M., Engineering
FALK, J. E., Operations Research
FEIR, J. E., Civil Engineering
FIACCO, A. V., Operations Research
FOX, R. R., Engineering Mechanics
FRIEDMAN, A. D., Electrical Engineering
GILMORE, C. M., Engineering
GOULARD, R., Engineering
GROSS, D., Operations Research
HELGERT, H. J., Engineering

1690

UNIVERSITIES AND COLLEGES—DISTRICT OF COLUMBIA U.S.A.

Heller, R. B., Electrical Engineering
Kahn, W. K., Electrical Engineering
Kaufman, R. E., Engineering
Kaye, J., Engineering Administration
Kiper, A. M., Engineering
Lang, R. H., Engineering
Lee, T. N., Engineering
Liebowitz, H., Engineering
Mahmood, K., Engineering
Marlow, W. H., Operations Research
Maurer, W. D., Computer Science
McCormick, G. P., Operations Research
Meltzer, A. C., Electrical Engineering
Myers, M. K., Engineering
Noor, A. K., Engineering
Pickholtz, R. L., Electrical Engineering
Rothman, S., Engineering Administration
Sewell, H. B., Engineering Administration
Shane, P. S., Engineering Administration
Singpurwalla, N. D., Operations Research
Soland, R. M., Operations Research
Steiner, H. M., Engineering Administration
Toridis, T. G., Engineering
Waters, R. C., Engineering Administration
Whitesides, J. L., Engineering
Yang, J. N., Engineering
Yuan, S. W., Engineering

## GEORGETOWN UNIVERSITY
37TH AND O STREETS, N.W.,
WASHINGTON, D.C. 20057

Telephone: (202) 625-0100.

Founded in 1789 as the first Catholic University in the U.S.A.

*President:* Timothy S. Healy, S.J., Ph.D.
*Chancellor of the Medical Center:* Matthew F. McNulty, Jr.
*Executive Vice-President for Academic Affairs and Provost:* J. Donald Freeze, S.J.
*Executive Vice-President for Law Center Affairs:* David J. McCarthy, Jr.
*Secretary:* Virginia M. Keeler.
*Librarian:* J. E. Jeffs, M.S.L.S.

The library contains 1,200,000 vols.
Number of teachers: 925 full-time, 450 part-time.
Number of students: 11,960.

Publications: *Georgetown Medical Bulletin* (quarterly), *The Georgetown Law Journal* (6 a year), *Law and Policy in International Business* (3 a year), *Georgetown Today* (2 a month), *The Hoya, Res Ipsa Loquitur, Domesday Book.*

### Deans:
*College of Arts and Sciences:* Royden B. Davis, S.J., J.D.
*Graduate School:* Richard B. Schwartz, Ph.D.
*School of Medicine:* John B. Henry, M.D.
*Law Center:* David J. McCarthy, Jr.
*School of Dentistry:* Robert J. Taylor, D.D.S. (acting).
*School of Nursing:* Elizabeth M. Hughes, Ph.D.

*Edmund A. Walsh School of Foreign Service:* Peter F. Krogh, Ph.D.
*School of Languages and Linguistics:* James E. Alatis, Ph.D.
*School of Business Administration:* Ronald L. Smith, Ph.D.
*School for Summer and Continuing Education:* Michael J. Collins, Ph.D.

Attached Institutes:

**Georgetown Center for Strategic and International Studies:** 1800 K St., N.W., Washington, D.C. 20006; f. 1962 to advance the understanding of international policy issues through the study of world problems and conferences; Chair. David M. Abshire, Ph.D.

**Joseph and Rose Kennedy Institute of Ethics:** 3520 Prospect St., N.W., Washington, D.C. 20057; f. 1971 to study ethical and related policy issues in medicine, biology, population, food distribution and economic development; Dir. Thomas J. King, Ph.D.

## HOWARD UNIVERSITY
2400 SIXTH STREET, N.W.,
WASHINGTON, D.C. 20059

Telephone: (202) 636-6100.

Founded 1867.

Private control; Academic year: September to May (two terms).

*President:* James E. Cheek, Ph.D.
*Vice-President for Academic Affairs:* Lorraine A. Williams, Ph.D.
*Vice-President for Administration and Secretary of the University:* Owen D. Nichols, Ed.D.
*Vice-President for Business and Fiscal Affairs-Treasurer:* Caspa L. Harris, C.P.A., J.D.
*Vice-President for Development and University Relations:* Roger D. Estep, D.V.M.
*Vice-President for Health Affairs:* Carlton P. Alexis, M.D.
*Vice-President for Student Affairs:* Carl E. Anderson, Ed.D.
*Director of Libraries:* Binford H. Conley, M.A.

The library contains 1,012,493 vols.
Number of teachers: 1,922.
Number of students: 11,748.

Publications: *Journal of Negro Education* (quarterly), *Journal of Religious Thought* (2 a year), *Howard Law Review* (quarterly), *New Directions Magazine* (quarterly), *Right on the Campus.*

### Deans:
*College of Dentistry:* Jean C. Sinkford, Ph.D.
*College of Liberal Arts:* R. L. Owens, Ph.D.

*College of Medicine:* Russell L. Miller, M.D.
*College of Pharmacy:* Wendell P. Hill, Pharm.D.
*College of Fine Arts:* Thomas J. Flagg, M.A.
*College of Nursing:* Anna B. Coles, Ph.D.
*School of Religion:* Lawrence N. Jones, Ph.D.
*School of Social Work:* Jay Chunn, Ph.D.
*Graduate School:* Edward W. Hawthorne, Ph.D., M.D.
*School of Allied Health Sciences:* Harley E. Flack, Ph.D.
*School of Engineering:* Lucius M. Walker, Ph.D. (acting).
*School of Law:* Wiley Branton, J.D.
*School of Architecture and Planning:* Prof. Harry Robinson, III, M.C.U.D.
*School of Communication:* Lionel C. Barrow, Ph.D.
*School of Education:* Willie T. Howard, Ed.D.
*School of Business and Public Administration:* M. Wilson, Ph.D.
*School of Human Ecology:* Cecile Edwards, Ph.D.
*Summer School:* Graham Johnson, M.A.

## SOUTHEASTERN UNIVERSITY
501 EYE ST., S.W.,
WASHINGTON, D.C. 20024

Telephone: (202) 488-8162.

Founded 1879. First and Master's degrees in Business and Public Administration.

*President:* Dr. Harry K. Miller, Jr.
*Dean of Graduate Studies:* Dr. J. Lee Westrate.
*Dean of Undergraduate Studies:* Dr. Beverly L. Elson.
*Director of Student Affairs:* Dr. Jean Rees.
*Librarian:* Lawrence A. Himmelfarb.
Library of 20,000 vols.
Number of teachers: 154.
Number of students: 1,850.

## TRINITY COLLEGE
WASHINGTON, D.C. 20017

Telephone: (202) 269-2000.

Founded 1897.

Roman Catholic liberal arts college for women, sponsored by Sisters of Notre Dame of Namur.

*President:* Sister Rose Ann Fleming.
*Vice-President:* Sister Margaret Finnegan.
*Academic Dean:* Dr. Jean Willke.
*Treasurer:* Sister Dorothy McCormick, S.N.D.
*Dean of Students:* Winifred E. Coleman.
*Director of Admissions:* Marga McNally.

*Director of Institutional Research:* Dr. KAREN KERSHENSTEIN.
*Business Officer:* ELLSWORTH KRAMER.
*Librarian:* Sister DOROTHY BEACH, S.N.D.

The library contains over 150,000 vols.

Number of teachers: 50 full-time, 30 part-time.

Number of students: 535 full-time, 279 part-time.

Publications: *Trinity College Record, Trinity Times, Trinilogue, Alumnae Journal, Trinity College Newsletter*†.

## UNIVERSITY OF THE DISTRICT OF COLUMBIA

Founded 1977; a public urban land-grant university organized on three campuses from existing colleges; first degree programmes.

### Harvard Street Campus
11TH AND HARVARD STS., N.W., WASHINGTON, D.C. 20009

Telephone: 673-7000.

*President:* LISLE C. CARTER, Jr.
Number of students: 15,096.

### Mount Vernon Square Campus
1331 H ST., N.W., WASHINGTON, D.C. 20005

Telephone: 727-2448.

*President:* (vacant).
Number of students: 7,660.

### Van Ness Campus
4200 CONNECTICUT AVE., N.W., WASHINGTON, D.C. 20008

Telephone: 282-7550.

*President:* (vacant).
Number of students: 4,900.

## FLORIDA

### BARRY COLLEGE
11300 N.E. 2ND AVENUE, MIAMI, FLORIDA 33161

Telephone: 758-3392.

Founded 1940.

*President:* Sister JEANNE O'LAUGHLIN, O.P.
*Vice-President for Academic Affairs:* Dr. PATRICK LEE.
*Librarian:* Sister M. FRANZ LANG, O.P.

The library contains 116,243 vols.
Number of teachers: 100.
Number of students: 1,800.

DEANS:

*Business:* R. WILLIAM MORELL, PH.D.
*Arts and Sciences:* ANDRE COTE, PH.D.
*Continuing Education:* TONI POWELL, PH.D.

*Nursing:* Sister JUDITH BALCERSKI, O.P.
*School of Social Work:* JOHN M. RILEY, PH.D.
*Education:* JOHN W. MAGUIRE, PH.D.

### BETHUNE-COOKMAN COLLEGE
640 SECOND AVENUE, DAYTONA BEACH, FLORIDA 32015

Telephone: (904) 255-1401.

Founded 1904.

*President:* OSWALD P. BRONSON, PH.D.
*Executive Vice-President:* Dr. R. J. GAINOUS, Jr.
*Vice-President for Academic Affairs and Dean of the Faculty:* CLEO S. HIGGINS, PH.D.
*Vice-President for Fiscal Affairs:* ERNEST C. COOK.
*Vice-President for Development and Planning:* LEO P. ELLIS.
*Vice-President for Student Affairs:* CLARENCE N. CHILDS.
*Registrar and Director of Admissions:* JAMES C. WYMES, Sr.
*Librarian:* GLADYS M. GREENE.

The library contains 99,762 vols.

Number of teachers: 99 full-time, 18 part-time.
Number of students: 1,472 full-time, 155 part-time.

### BISCAYNE COLLEGE
16400 N.W. 32ND AVE., MIAMI, FLORIDA 33054

Telephone: (305) 625-6000.

Founded 1962.

*President:* Fr. PATRICK H. O'NEILL, O.S.A.
*Dean of the College:* Fr. JAMES J. MCCARTNEY, O.S.A.
*Dean of Admissions:* JAMES T. PARKER, PH.D.
*Academic Deans:* JOHN J. WELDON, PH.D., Fr. FRANCISCO RODRIGUEZ, O.S.A.
*Librarian:* MARGARET ELLISTON.

Library of 100,000 vols.
Number of teachers: 100.
Number of students: 3,000.

### FLORIDA AGRICULTURAL AND MECHANICAL UNIVERSITY
TALLAHASSEE, FLORIDA 32307

Telephone: 222-8030-904.

Founded 1887.

*President:* WALTER L. SMITH, M.ED., PH.D.
*Executive Vice-President:* HARRY S. BLANTON, PH.D.
*Vice-President of Administration and Fiscal Affairs:* ROBERT CARROLL, M.S., PH.D.

*Vice-President for Academic Affairs:* GERTRUDE SIMMONS, M.S., PH.D.
*Vice-President for Student Affairs:* TIMOTHY L. LANGSTON, M.S., E.ED.
*Librarian:* N. E. GAYMON, M.S.L.S., PH.D.

The library contains 294,240 vols.

Number of teachers: 398.
Number of students: 6,011.

DEANS:

*College of Architecture:* RICHARD K. CHALMERS, M.ARCH.
*College of Education:* EVELYN B. MARTIN, M.A., ED.D. (acting).
*College of Humanities and Social Sciences:* L. W. NEYLAND, M.A., PH.D.
*College of Science and Technology:* CHARLES C. KIDD, M.S.E., M.S., PH.D.
*School of Business and Industry:* SYBIL C. MOBLEY, M.B.A., PH.D.
*School of Nursing:* GEORGIE C. LABADIE, M.S., ED.D.
*School of Pharmacy:* CHARLES WALKER, M.S., PH.D.
*Military Science:* Lt.-Col. CHARLES HOBBS, P.M.S.
*Navy ROTC:* Capt. O. M. BROOKS.

### FLORIDA ATLANTIC UNIVERSITY
BOCA RATON, FLORIDA 33431

Telephone: (305) 395-5100.

Founded 1961.

*President:* Dr. GLENWOOD L. CREECH.
*Vice-President for Academic Affairs:* Dr. KENNETH MICHELS.
*Registrar:* R. M. KOSER, Jr.
*Librarian:* HARRY SKALLERUP.

The library contains 300,000 volumes.

Number of teachers: 300.
Number of students: 7,000.

DEANS:

*College of Business and Public Administration:* G. LUING.
*College of Education:* (vacant).
*College of Engineering:* Dr. D. O. AKHURST.
*College of Humanities:* Dr. J. SUBERMAN.
*College of Science:* Dr. EARL BAKER.
*College of Social Science:* Dr. ROBERT J. HUCKSHORN.

### FLORIDA INSTITUTE OF TECHNOLOGY
P.O.B. 1150, MELBOURNE, FLORIDA 32901

Telephone: (305) 723-3701.

*President:* JEROME P. KEUPER.
*Vice-President for Academic Affairs:* J. E. MILLER.
*Vice-President for Financial Affairs:* JOHN W. SIMMONS.
*Vice-President for Public Affairs:* TOM ADAMS.

UNIVERSITIES AND COLLEGES—FLORIDA U.S.A.

*Vice-President for Student Affairs:* BARRY A. FULLERTON.
*Vice-President for Administrative Affairs:* R. A. WORK, Jr.
*Director of Admissions:* ROBERT S. HEIDINGER.
*Executive Director, Jensen Beach Campus:* ERNEST E. TEALEY.
*Registrar:* GEORGE S. JONES, III.
*Director of Libraries:* L. L. HENSON.

Number of students: 6,000.

DEANS:

*School of Science and Engineering:* ANDREW W. REVAY, Jr.
*School of Management and Humanities:* JAMES T. STOMS.
*School of Professional Psychology:* CHARLES D. CORMAN.
*School of Aeronautics:* J. A. LAUDERBAUGH.
*Graduate Studies and Research:* H. P. WEBER.


## FLORIDA MEMORIAL COLLEGE
15800 N.W. 42ND AVE., MIAMI, FLORIDA 33054
Telephone: (305) 625-4141.
Founded 1879.

*President:* Dr. WILLIE C. ROBINSON.
*Librarian:* Mrs. EDNA J. WILLIAMS.

The library contains 80,000 vols.
Number of teachers: 44.
Number of students: 1,210.


## FLORIDA SOUTHERN COLLEGE
LAKELAND, FLORIDA 33802
Telephone: (813) 683-5521.
Founded 1885.

*President:* Dr. ROBERT A. DAVIS.
*Admissions:* WILLIAM B. STEPHENS.
*Librarian:* G. LAWRENCE STALLINGS.

The library contains 150,000 vols.
Number of teachers: 83.
Number of students: 1,735 full-time, 93 part-time.


## FLORIDA STATE UNIVERSITY
TALLAHASSEE, FLORIDA 32306
Telephone: 644-1234.

Founded 1857 as the Seminary West of the Suwannee River, and later became the Florida State College, became the Florida State College for Women 1905, became co-educational and attained university status 1947.

Academic year: September to April (two semesters).

*Chancellor of the State University System:* BARBARA W. NEWELL, PH.D.
*President:* B. F. SLIGER, PH.D.
*Vice-President for Academic Affairs:* AUGUSTUS B. TURNBULL, III, PH.D.
*Vice-President for Administration:* B. J. HODGE, PH.D.

*Vice-President for University Relations:* PATRICK HOGAN, B.S.
*Dean of the Faculties:* DAISY P. FLORY, PH.D.
*Registrar:* T. C. BURNETTE, M.B.A.
*Librarian:* CHARLES E. MILLER, M.S.L.S.
Library: see Libraries.
Number of teachers: 1,379.
Number of students: 22,424.
Publication: *Bulletin.*

DEANS:

*College of Arts and Sciences:* W. BAUM, PH.D.
*College of Business:* E. R. SOLOMON, PH.D.
*College of Communication:* T. CLEVENGER, PH.D.
*School of Criminology:* E. CZAJKOSKI, D.P.A.
*College of Education:* J. L. GANT, PH.D.
*School of Graduate Studies and Research:* R. M. JOHNSON, PH.D.
*School of Home Economics:* MARGARET A. SITTON, ED.D.
*College of Law:* L. O. SLAGLE, L.L.B.
*School of Library Science:* H. GOLDSTEIN. ED.D.
*School of Music:* R. GLIDDEN, PH.D.
*School of Nursing:* EMILIE D. HENNING, ED.D.
*College of Social Sciences:* W. D. MAZEK, PH.D.
*School of Social Work:* D. BARDILL, PH.D.
*School of Theatre:* R. G. FALLON, M.A.
*School of Visual Arts:* JERRY DRAPER, PH.D.

PROFESSORS:

ABCARIAN, G., PH.D., Government
ACOSTA, P. B., Nutrition and Food Science
ADAIR, C. H., ED.D., Social Studies Education
AKER, G. F., PH.D., Adult Education
ALBRIGHT, J., Physics
ALDERSON, J., M.S., Social Work
ALLEN, R., Education
ALLEY, J., PH.D., Music
AMMERMAN, D., History
ANDREWS, J. J., PH.D., Mathematics
ANG, J. S., Finance
ANTHONY, W., PH.D., Management
ARMER, J. M., PH.D., Sociology
ATKINS, B., PH.D., Government
BAILEY, J. S., Psychology
BAKER, H. D., PH.D., Psychology
BALKUS, K., Urban Regional Planning
BANGHART, F. W., ED.D., Education
BARCILON, A., PH.D., Meteorology
BARDILL, D., Social Work
BARTLETT, R. A., PH.D., History
BASSIN, A., PH.D., Criminology
BASU, D., Statistics
BAUM, W., PH.D., Meteorology
BAYER, A. E., PH.D., Sociology
BEARD, J., PH.D., Education
BEARD, R., PH.D., Philosophy
BECK, E. R., PH.D., History
BECK, P., PH.D., Government
BEIDLER, L. M., PH.D., Biological Science
BELL, F. W., PH.D., Economics
BELL, T., Art
BENDER, L., ED.D., Higher Education
BERKLEY, M., Psychology
BETTEN, N., History
BICKLEY, B., PH.D., English
BJERREGARD, C., M.M., Music
BLACK H. A., C.P.A., PH.D., Accounting

BLAKE, G. K., ED.D., Education
BLAZEK, R. D., Library Science
BODA, J., D.M.A., Music
BRADLEY, R. A., PH.D., Statistics
BRANSON, R., PH.D., Education
BREWER, J. K., PH.D., Education Systems
BRIGGS, L. J., PH.D., Educational Research
BRIGHAM, J., Psychology
BROCK, V., PH.D., English
BRUECKHEIMER, W. K., PH.D., Geography
BRYANT, J., PH.D., Mathematics
BUCHER, F., PH.D., Visual Arts
BURCK, H., PH.D., Education
BURGE, J., PH.D., Nursing
BURKMAN, E., Jr., ED.D., Education
BURROWAY, JANET, M.A., English
BURTON, D. L., PH.D., English Education
BURTON, E., Movement Science and Physical Education
CAMPBELL, T. M., PH.D., History
CANCALON, E., PH.D., Modern Languages
CANNON, FRANCES, ED.D., Education
CANNISTRARO, P., PH.D., History
CANTERBERY, E. R., PH.D., Economics
CAPPS, W., D.M., Music
CAREY, J., PH.D., Religion
CHAMPION, J. E., C.P.A., PH.D., Accounting
CHAN, C. Y., Mathematics
CHICK, JOYCE, PH.D., Education
CHOPPIN, G. R., PH.D., Chemistry
CIANNELLA, Y., B.A., Music
CLARK, R., PH.D., Chemistry
CLEVENGER, T., PH.D., Speech
COLBERG, M. R., PH.D., Economics
COOK, E., PH.D., Anthropology
CRAMER, W., ED.D., Music
CREASON, D., Theatre
CROFT, J., Music
CROSBY, H., Law
CUNNINGHAM, L. S., PH.D., Religion
CZAJKOSKI, E. H., D.P.A., Criminology
DANCY, R., Philosophy
DANN, E., Music
DARST, D., Modern Languages
DAVIS, B. H., PH.D., English
DAVIS, R. H., PH.D., Physics
DAWIRS, H. N., PH.D., Communication
DEASY, LEILA, PH.D., Social Welfare
DEBUSK, A. G., PH.D., Biological Science
DEKLOET, S., PH.D., Biological Science
DELANEY, C. O., M.M., Music
DENMARK, E. T., PH.D., Mathematics Education
DESHAIES, A., M.F.A., Art
DESLOGE, E. A., PH.D., Physics
DETAR, D. F., PH.D., Chemistry
DEVORE, G., PH.D., Geology
DICK, W., PH.D., Education
DICKSON, D., LL.B., PH.D., Law
DIRAC, P., PH.D., Physics
DOUGHERTY, R., PH.D., Chemistry
DOWNING, P., Economics and Policy Sciences
DYBDAHL, F., Music
DYE, T. R., PH.D., Government
DYSON, J., PH.D., Government
EASTON, D., PH.D., Biological Science
EDNEY, C. W., PH.D., Communication
EDWARDS, S., PH.D., Physics
EHRHARDT, C. W., J.D., Law
EISENBERG, D., PH.D., Modern Languages
ELAM, J., Biological Science
ELFNER, L., PH.D., Psychology
ELLIOTT, F., PH.D., Biological Sciences
EVERETT, P. W., PH.D., Physical Education and Recreation
FALLON, R., M.A., Theatre
FAUST, F., Criminology
FENDRICH, J., PH.D., Sociology
FERNALD, E., PH.D., Geography
FLANAGAN, S. C., Government
FLETCHER, H., PH.D., Education
FLETCHER, N., PH.D., Physics
FLORY, D., PH.D., Government
FORDYCE, P. R., M.S., Education

1693

Foster, G., ph.d., Education
Fowler, D., English
Fowler, Nancy, ph.d., Music
Fox, J. D., ph.d., Physics
Fox, V. B., ph.d., Criminology
Frechette, E., ed.d., Education
Frick, H. L., ph.d., Education
Frieden, E., ph.d., Chemistry
Friedmann, I., ph.d., Biology
Fulton, R., ph.d., Chemistry
Gagne, R., ph.d., Educational Research
Gallups, W., Business and Accounting
Gapinski, J., ph.d., Economics
Garrett, B., ph.d., Chemistry
George, L. C., Law
Gilmer, R., ph.d., Mathematics
Givens, Azzurra, ph.d., Modern Languages
Gleeson, T. A., ph.d., Meteorology
Glick, H. R., Government
Glick, R. E., ph.d., Chemistry
Glidden, R., ph.d., Music
Glotzbach, H., ed.d., Music
Golden, L., ph.d., Classics
Goldstein, Harold, ed.d., Library Science
Goldstein, Harris, Social Work
Gombosi, M., m.a., Music
Good, R., ph.d., Education
Goudeau, J. M., ph.d., Library Science
Gould, L. C., Criminology
Grant, S. R., ed.d., Education
Gray, R. B., ph.d., Government
Graziadei, P., Biology
Greaves, R., ph.d., History
Grigg, C. M., ph.d., Sociology
Grimm, Betty J., Music
Grosslight, J. H., ph.d., Psychology
Gruender, D., ph.d., Philosophy
Guice, B., ed.d., Education
Gunn, B., ph.d., Marketing
Gwartney, J., ph.d., Economics
Hafner, L., ed.d., Education
Hagopian, V., ph.d., Physics
Halpern, P., ph.d., History
Hansen, J., ph.d., Education
Hanson, M. A., ph.d., Statistics
Hardee, Melvene D., ph.d., Higher Education
Harper, G. M., ph.d., English
Harsanyi, J., b.m., Music
Hart, T. L., Library Science
Haworth, C., ph.d., Economics
Hazelrigg, L. E., Sociology
Heard, W. H., ph.d., Biological Science
Heck, W. R., ph.d., Accounting
Heerema, N., ph.d., Mathematics
Hendrickson, Norejane, ph.d., Home and Family Life
Henning, E., ed.d., Nursing
Herndon, R., ph.d., Environment Studies
Herrnkind, W., ph.d., Biological Science
Herz, W., ph.d., Chemistry
Hess, S. L., ph.d., Meteorology
Hicks, Mary W., ph.d., Home and Family Life
Hills, J. R., ph.d., Education
Hinely, W. H., ed.d., Education
Hintikka, J., ph.d., Philosophy
Hodge, B. J., ph.d., Management
Hodges, D. C., ph.d., Philosophy
Hoetker, W. J., ed.d., Education
Hofer, K., ph.d., Biological Science
Hoffman, K. B., Chemistry
Hokanson, J. E., ph.d., Psychology
Holbrook, A., ph.d., Audiology and Speech Pathology
Hollander, M., ph.d., Statistics
Homann, P., ph.d., Biological Science
Hornby, B., Theatre
Horward, D., ph.d., History
Howard, L. N., Mathematics and Computer Science
Hsueh, Y., Oceanography
Hudson, W. W., Social Work

Hughes, W., ed.d., Music
Hunt, R. H., ph.d., Physics
Hunter, C., ph.d., Mathematics
Ice, R., ph.d., Religion
Jahoda, G., d.l.s., Library Science
Jeffery, C., ph.d., Criminology
Jenks, F. L., Curriculum and Instruction
Jensen, R., ph.d., Accounting
Jogdeo, K., Mathematics
Johnsen, R. H., ph.d., Chemistry
Johnson, D. J., Movement Science and Physical Education
Johnson, F. C., ph.d., Education
Johnson, R. H., d.m., Music
Johnson, R. M., ph.d., Biological Science
Jones, B. J., ph.d., Movement Science and Physical Education
Jones, G. R., ed.d., Education
Jones, J. P., ph.d., History
Jones, W. R., ph.d., Religion
Jordan, C. L., ph.d., Meteorology
Kaelin, E., ph.d., Philosophy
Kalin, R., ph.d., Education
Kandel, A., Mathematics and Computer Science
Kasha, M., ph.d., Chemistry
Kassouny, Margaret E., ph.d., Food and Nutrition
Kaufman, R., Instructional Systems Development
Kemper, K., ph.d., Physics
Kennedy, R. H., ll.b., Law
Kennedy, W., ph.d., Psychology
Kenshalo, D. R., ph.d., Psychology
Kerr, J. R., d.b.a., Marketing
Keuchel, E. F., History
Kilenyi, E., Jr., Music
King, D. C., Marketing
King, T. R., ph.d., Communication
Kinloch, G., ph.d., Sociology
Kinoshita, S., ph.d., Mathematics
Kirby, D., English
Kirk, C., ed.d., Music
Kittles, E., ph.d., Clothing and Textiles
Koster, R., College Programmes
Kraft, R., ph.d., Education
Krehbiel, C., m.m.e., Music
Kreimer, H. F., ph.d., Mathematics
Krishef, C., ph.d., Social Work
Krishnamurti, R., ph.d., Oceanography
Krishnamurti, T., ph.d., Meteorology
Kromhout, R. A., ph.d., Physics
Kropp, R. P., ed.d., Higher Education
Kuhn, Marylou, ph.d., Art Education
Lacher, R., ph.d., Mathematics
Laird, W., ph.d., Economics
Lannutti, J. E., ph.d., Physics
Laseur, N., ph.d., Meteorology
Lathrop, R., ph.d., Education
Lazier, G., ph.d., Theatre
Leamon, M. P., ph.d., Education
Leffler, J. E., ph.d., Chemistry
Lerner, A., ph.d., Economics
Lewis, J. R., ph.d., Risk Management
Light, R., ph.d., Chemistry
Lilly, C. C., Risk and Insurance
Lin, P. E., Statistics
Linder, B., ph.d., Chemistry
Lipner, H., ph.d., Biological Science
Litton, M., ed.d., Education
Livingston, R., Biological Science
Loper, D., ph.d., Mathematics
Louwenaar, K., Music
Lu, J., ph.d., Modern Languages
Luebkemann, H., ed.d., Education
Lunstrum, J. P., ed.d., Education
McArthur, C. W., ph.d., Mathematics
Macesich, G., ph.d., Economics
McConnell, H. L., ph.d., Geography
McElrath, J., English
McHugh, W., j.d., Law
McIntyre, E., ph.d., Accounting
McWilliams, R., ph.d., Mathematics
Madsen, Charles, Jr., ph.d., Psychology

Madsen, Clifford, ph.d., Music
Mandelkern, L., ph.d., Molecular Biophysics
Mann, C. K., ph.d., Chemistry
Mariscal, R., ph.d., Biological Science
Marshall, R., ph.d., Business Management
Martin, M., College Programmes
Martin, P. Y., Social Work
Massialas, B., ph.d., Education
Masterton, B., ph.d., Psychology
Matthews, C., Education
May, J. G., ph.d., Psychology
Mazek, W., ph.d., Economics
Meeter, D., ph.d., Statistics
Megargee, E., ph.d., Psychology
Mellon, E. K., Chemistry
Menzel, M., ph.d., Biological Science
Menzel, R. W., ph.d., Oceanography
Miles, E. P., Jr., ph.d., Mathematics
Miller, K. S., Psychology and Sociology
Minnick, W. C., ph.d., Communication
Mohr, Lillian H., ph.d., Home and Family Life
Moore, John, ph.d., History
Moore, W. L., Religion
Morgan, R. M., ph.d., Education
Morris, H., ph.d., English
Morse, J. M., Law
Mott, J., ph.d., Mathematics
Moulton, G. C., Physics
Moulton, W. G., ph.d., Physics
Mundy, J., ed.d., Human Services and Studies
Nam, C. B., ph.d., Sociology
Nation, W. B., ph.d., Marketing
Nelson, J. W., ph.d., Physics
Nichols, E. D., ph.d., Mathematics
O'Brien, J. J., ph.d., Meteorology and Oceanography
O'Sullivan, P., ph.d., Geography
Oeltjen, J., j.d., Law
Oldson, W., ph.d., History
Olsen, C., Theatre
Orcutt, J., ph.d., Sociology
Osmond, J. K., ph.d., Geology
Osteryoung, J., Finance
Ozanne, U., Marketing
Page, W. J., Social Work and Public Administration
Palmer, M., ph.d., Government
Paredes, J. A., ph.d., Anthropology
Pargman, D., ph.d., Education
Parsons, M. B., ph.d., Government
Patton, D. J., ph.d., Geography
Pearman, J. R., ph.d., Economics
Pestle, R., ph.d., Home Economics Education
Petrovich, F., Physics
Pfeffer, R., ph.d., Meteorology
Phifer, G., ph.d., Communication
Philpott, R. J., ph.d., Physics
Piccard, P. J., ph.d., Government
Piersol, J., Music
Pitts, J. E., ph.d., Finance
Plendl, H., ph.d., Physics
Plescia, J., ph.d., Classics
Pribic, E., Modern Languages
Price, L., ph.d., Communication
Priest, J. F., ph.d., Religion
Proschan, F., ph.d., Statistics
Ragland, P., ph.d., Geology
Rapp, D., ph.d., Home and Family Life
Rashotte, M., ph.d., Psychology
Rasmussen, D., ph.d., Economics
Rasmussen, L. V., ph.d., Education
Reardon, R., Human Services and Studies
Reaver, J. R., ph.d., English
Redfield, D., ed.d., Education
Reese, H. J., ed.d., Education
Reich, J., Classics
Rhodes, A. L., ph.d., Sociology
Rhodes, W., ph.d., Chemistry
Richardson, J., ph.d., History
Ritchie, M., ed.d., Education

UNIVERSITIES AND COLLEGES—FLORIDA U.S.A.

Roady, E. E., ph.d., Government
Robson, D., ph.d., Physics
Roche, J., Art
Rockwood, C., ph.d., Economics
Rockwood, P., ph.d., Marketing
Rogers, W., ph.d., History
Rubenstein, R., ph.d., Religion
Sandon, L., Religion
Saltiel, J., ph.d., Chemistry
Scarborough, B. B., ph.d., Psychology
Schendel, L. L., ph.d., Audiology and Speech Pathology
Schiffman, H., d.m., Music
Schroeder, E. M., j.d., Law
Schroeder, W., ph.d., Education
Schwartz, L., ed.d., Education
Schwartz, M., ph.d., Chemistry
Sethuraman, J., ph.d., Statistics
Sheline, R. K., ph.d., Chemistry and Physics
Shelton, W. N., ph.d., Physics
Short, R. B., ph.d., Biological Science
Shrode, W. A., d.b.a., Management
Simberloff, D., ph.d., Biological Science
Simmons, J. S., ph.d., English
Singer, R., ph.d., Education
Sitton, Margaret, ed.d., Home Economics
Skibinsky, M., Statistics
Skofronick, J., ph.d., Physics
Slagle, L. O., Law
Sliger, B. F., ph.d., Economics
Sly, D., ph.d., Economics
Smith, D. D., ph.d., Sociology
Smith, E. H., ed.d., Education
Smith, J. C., ph.d., Psychology
Smith, Nancy, ph.d., Dance
Snyder, W. R., ph.d., Education
Sobel, I., ph.d., Economics
Solomon, E. R., ph.d., Risk and Insurance
Sorensen, P., ph.d., Economics
Sparkman, Marjorie, ph.d., Nursing
Stakenas, R., ph.d., Educational Research
Standley, F., ph.d., English
St. Angelo, D., Government
Stauber, A., Risk and Insurance
Stephens, J. J., ph.d., Meteorology
Stimson, J. A., Government
Stoker, H. W., Jr., ph.d., Education
Stowell, D. C., Theatre
Strane, R., Theatre
Streem, J., m.s., Music
Sturges, W., ph.d., Oceanography
Stuy, J., ph.d., Biology
Sumners, De W., ph.d., Mathematics
Swain, C. W., ph.d., Religion
Tam, C., ph.d., Mathematics
Tanenbaum, J., ph.d., History
Tanner, W. F., ph.d., Geology
Taylor, J., ph.d., Music
Taylor, J. H., ph.d., Biological Science
Thomas, A., d.m.a., Music
Thomas, H. B., Educational Leadership
Thomas, M., History
Thompson, M. Lynette, ph.d., Classics
Thompson, W. R., Government
Tschinkel, W. R., Biological Science
Tucker, A., ph.d., Education
Turnbull, A. B., Public Administration
Turner, R., ph.d., History
Turner, Robert, ph.d., Finance
Vance, M. M., ph.d., History
Van Der Creek, W., ll.m., Law
Vanderhill, B. G., ph.d., Geography
VanDoren, J., ll.b., Law
VanOrden, P., ed.d., Library Science
Vaughan, S., Theatre
Vickers, T., ph.d., Chemistry
Vinson, J. K., Law
Voich, D., ph.d., Management
Wagner, R. B., Economics
Walborsky, H. M., ph.d., Chemistry
Waldby, H. O., ph.d., Government
Waldo, G., ph.d., Criminology

Walmsley, W., m.a., Art
Wang, Y. L., ph.d., Physics
Warden, Jessie A., ph.d., Clothing and Textiles
Weale, M. J., ph.d., Interior Design
Weidner, D., j.d., Law
Wellborn, C., ph.d., Religion
Weller, R., ph.d., Sociology
Wells, Lucy Janet, ed.d., Education
White, D. C., m.d., ph.d., Biological Science
White, J. A., Jr., ph.d., Music
Whitney, G., ph.d., Psychology
Wiese, L., ph.d., Biological Science
Wilkens, P., ph.d., Management
Williams, H., ph.d., Modern Languages
Williams, T., ph.d., Biological Science
Wills, H., ph.d., Education
Winchester, J. W., ph.d., Oceanography
Winsberg, M., ph.d., Geography
Winstead, W. O., Music
Winters, S. S., ph.d., Geology
Wise, S. W., Geology
Wright, J. L., ph.d., History
Wright, T., m.m., Music
Wyatt, J., ph.d., Modern Languages
Wynot, E., ph.d., History
Yerger, R. W., ph.d., Biological Science
Yetter, J., ll.m., Law
Young, E., ph.d., Mathematics
Young, W., ph.d., Business and Finance
Yost, G., Jr., ph.d., English
Zenz, G. J., ph.d., Marketing

## JACKSONVILLE UNIVERSITY

JACKSONVILLE, FLORIDA 32211

Telephone: (904) 744-3950.

Founded 1934.

*President:* Dr. Frances B. Kinne.

*Dean of Faculties:* Dr. John E. Trainer, Jr.

*Director of Admissions:* J. Bradford Sargent.

*Registrar:* Lewis D. Bullard.

*Librarian:* Thomas H. Gunn.

The library contains 237,595 vols.

Number of teachers: 105 full-time, 77 part-time.

Number of students: 2,428.

## NEW COLLEGE OF THE UNIVERSITY OF SOUTH FLORIDA

5700 N. TAMIAMI TRAIL, SARASOTA, FLORIDA 33580

Telephone: 355-7671.

Founded 1960.

*Provost:* Dr. Eugene Lewis.

*Admissions:* Roberto Noya.

The library contains approx. 145,000 vols.

Number of teachers: 44.
Number of students: 450.

Divisional Chairmen:
*Humanities:* Dr. James G. Moseley.
*Social Sciences:* Dr. Robert Benedetti.
*Natural Sciences:* Dr. Peter A. Kazaks.

## ROLLINS COLLEGE

WINTER PARK, FLORIDA 32789

Telephone:
(305) 646-2120 (President's Office)
(305) 646-2000 (Information Office)

Founded 1885.

*President:* Thaddeus Seymour.
*Provost:* Robert D. Marcus.
*Registrar:* Bettina Beer.
*Director of Admissions:* Julia H. Ingraham.
*Librarian:* Patricia Delks.

The library contains 174,667 vols.
Number of teachers: 112.
Number of students: 4,227.

## SAINT LEO COLLEGE

P.O.B. 2187,
SAINT LEO, FLORIDA 33574

Telephone: (904) 588-8200.

Founded 1889.

Private control, Catholic.

*President:* Dr. Thomas B. Southard.
*Vice-President for Academic Affairs:* Dr. Robert C. Gould.
*Vice-President for Student Affairs:* Dr. Robert L. Ackerman.
*Registrar:* A. James Christiansen.
*Librarian:* Sister Dorothy Neuhofer.

The library contains 55,000 vols.
Number of teachers: 49.
Number of students: 1,000.

## STETSON UNIVERSITY

DeLAND, FLORIDA 32720

Telephone: (904) 734-4121.

Established as De Land Academy 1883; chartered as De Land University 1887; name changed 1889; related to the Baptist Churches of Florida.

Academic year: September to June.

*President:* Pope A. Duncan.
*Vice-President and Dean of the University:* Thomas J. Turner.
*Vice-President for Development:* H. Douglas Lee.
*Vice-President for Finance and Planning:* H. Graves Edmondson.
*Dean of Students:* Garth Jenkins.

The libraries contain over 284,000 catalogued items.

Number of teachers: 121 in DeLand; 21 at College of Law, St. Petersburg.

Number of students: 2,246 in DeLand; 450 at College of Law.

*Publications: The Stetson University Bulletin, The Cupola.*

## UNIVERSITY OF FLORIDA

GAINESVILLE, FLORIDA 32611

Telephone: (904) 392-3261.

Founded 1853.

*President:* Robert Q. Marston, m.d.

UNITED STATES OF AMERICA

*Vice-President for Academic Affairs:* R. A. BRYAN, PH.D.
*Vice-President for Agricultural Affairs:* K. Q. TEFERTILLER, PH.D.
*Vice-President for Health Affairs:* KENNETH F. FINGER (acting).
*Vice-President for Administrative Affairs:* W. E. ELMORE, B.S., C.P.A.
*Vice-President for Alumni Development:* A. WIGGINS, B.S.
*University Registrar:* L. V. VOYLES, B.A.
*Director of Libraries:* G. HARRER, PH.D.
*Director, Florida State Museum:* F. W. KING, PH.D.

Library: see Libraries.
Number of teachers: 2,614.
Number of students: 33,242.

Publications include: *Journal of Politics, Southern Folklore Quarterly, University of Florida Law Review, Florida Historical Quarterly, Latin American Studies Association Newsletter.*

### DEANS:

*Architecture:* M. T. JAROSZEWICZ, M.A.
*Business Administration:* R. F. LANZILLOTTI. PH.D.
*Continuing Education:* J. W. KNIGHT, ED.D.
*Education:* D. C. SMITH, PH.D.
*Engineering:* W. H. CHEN, PH.D.
*Fine Arts:* J. J. SABATELLA, M.F.A.
*Graduate School:* FRANCIS STEHLI, PH.D.
*Journalism and Communications:* R. L. LOWENSTEIN, PH.D.
*Law:* FRANK T. READ, J.D.
*Liberal Arts and Sciences:* C. F. SIDMAN, PH.D.
*Physical Education:* C. A. BOYD, ED.D.
*Medicine:* W. DEAL, M.D.
*Nursing:* LOIS MALOSANOS, PH.D.
*Pharmacy:* M. A. SCHWARTZ, PH.D.
*Health Related Professions:* RICHARD GUTEKUNST, PH.D.
*Dentistry:* D. L. ALLEN, D.D.S.
*Agriculture:* GERALD ZACHARIAH, PH.D.
*Forestry:* A. C. MACE, PH.D.
*Agriculture (Extension):* J. T. WOESTE, PH.D.
*Agriculture (Research):* F. A. WOOD, PH.D.
*Veterinary Medicine:* E. BESCH (acting).

### PROFESSORS:

*University College:*
  BARINGER, W. E., PH.D., American Institutions
  BENTLEY, G. R., PH.D., Comprehensive Logic
  BOWERS, R. H., Jr., PH.D., Comprehensive English
  CHILDERS, W. C., PH.D., Comprehensive English
  DERRICK, C., PH.D., Humanities
  DOHERTY, H. J., Jr., PH.D., American Institutions
  DUNKLE, J. R., PH.D., Physical Sciences
  FRAZER, W., PH.D., Comprehensive English
  GRAEFFE, A. D., PH.D., Humanities
  GRATER, H., PH.D., Comprehensive Logic
  HAINES, L. F., PH.D., Comprehensive Logic

  HAMMOND, E. A., PH.D., American Institutions
  HELLSTROM, W., PH.D., Comprehensive English
  HODGES, J. R., PH.D., Comprehensive English
  JOHNSON, IRMGARD, PH.D., Humanities
  KRAMER, S., PH.D., Comprehensive Logic
  MARCUS, R. B., ED.D., Physical Sciences
  PENROD, J., PH.D., Comprehensive English
  PIRKLE, E. C., PH.D., Physical Sciences
  ROBERTS, L., PH.D., Physical Sciences
  STANDLEY, G. B., PH.D., Comprehensive Logic
  SUNWALL, J., PH.D., Humanities
  THURSTON, P. T., PH.D., Comprehensive Logic
  WALKER, B., M.A., Comprehensive English

*Architecture:*
  BUTT, A. F., M.ARCH., Architecture
  EPPES, B. G., M.S., Building Construction
  HALPERIN, D. A., PH.D., Building Construction
  KINZEY, B. Y., Jr., M.S., Architecture
  REEVES, F. B., M.ARCH., Architecture
  SMITH, H. H., M.L.A., Landscape Architecture
  WAGNER, W. G., M.ARCH., Architecture

*Arts and Sciences:*
  ADAMS, E. D., PH.D., Physics and Astronomy
  ALLEN, J. J., PH.D., Romance Languages and Literature
  ANTHONY, D. S., PH.D., Botany
  BAILEY, T. L., III, PH.D., Physics and Astronomy
  BALLARD, S. S., PH.D., Physics
  BATTISTE, M. A., PH.D., Chemistry
  BAXTER, J. F., PH.D., Chemistry
  BEDNAREK, A. R., PH.D., Mathematics
  BERARDO, F. M., PH.D., Sociology
  BERNER, L., PH.D., Zoology
  BIGELOW, G. E., PH.D., English
  BREY, W. S., Jr., PH.D., Chemistry
  BRODKORB, P., PH.D., Zoology
  BROOKS, J. K., PH.D., Mathematics
  BROYLES, A. A., PH.D., Physics and Astronomy
  BUSHNELL, D., PH.D., History
  BUTLER, G. B., PH.D.. Chemistry
  CARR, A. F., PH.D.. Zoology
  CARR, T. D., PH.D., Physics and Astronomy
  CHALMERS, D. M., PH.D., History
  CONNER, J. W., PH.D., Romance Languages and Literature
  DEWSBURY, D. A., PH.D., Psychology
  DOUGHTY, P. L., PH.D., Anthropology
  DRESDNER, R. D., PH.D., Chemistry
  FAIRBANKS. C. H., PH.D., Anthropology
  FLOWERS, J. W., PH.D., Physics and Astronomy
  FUNK, A. L., PH.D., History
  GARRETT, R. E., PH.D., Physics and Astronomy
  GAY-CROSIER, R., PH.D., Romance Languages and Literature
  GREEN, A. E., PH.D., Physics and Astronomy
  GRIFFIN, G. M., PH.D., Geology
  HANRAHAN, R. J., PH.D., Chemistry
  HARING, E. S., PH.D., Philosophy
  HIERS, H., PH.D., Religion
  HILL, S. S., Jr., PH.D., Religion
  HOLLIEN, H., PH.D., Linguistics
  HOWER, A., PH.D., Romance Languages and Literature
  JOHNSON, F. C., II, PH.D., Zoology
  JONES, W. M., PH.D., Chemistry
  LEMARCHAND, R., PH.D., Political Science

  LESLIE, G. R., PH.D., Sociology
  LISCA, P., PH.D., English
  LOWDIN, P. O., PH.D., Chemistry
  MAHON, J. K., PH.D., History
  MATURO, F. J., Jr., PH.D., Zoology
  M'CALISTER, L. N., PH.D., History
  MCNAB, B. K., PH.D., Zoology
  MEYER, M. E., PH.D., Psychology
  MUSCHLITZ, E. E., Jr., PH.D., Chemistry
  NICOL, D., PH.D., Zoology
  NIDDRIE, D. L., PH.D., Geography
  OHRN, N. Y., PH.D., Chemistry
  OMER, G. C., Jr., PH.D., Physics and Astronomy
  PALENIK, G. J., PH.D., Chemistry
  PAUL, H. W., PH.D., History
  PENNYPACKER, H. S., Jr., PH.D., Psychology
  PEPINSKY, R., PH.D., Physics and Astronomy
  PERSON, WL. B., PH.D., Chemistry
  PICKARD, J. B., PH.D., English
  POP-STOJANOVIC, Z. R., PH.D., Mathematics
  POPOV, V. M., PH.D., Mathematics
  RAO, P. V., PH.D., Statistics
  ROBINSON, W. R., PH.D., English
  RYSCHKEWITSCH, G. E., PH.D., Chemistry
  SAW, J. G., PH.D., Statistics
  SHANOR, L., PH.D., Botany
  SHAW, M. E., PH.D., Psychology
  SMITH, A. G., PH.D., Physics and Astronomy
  SPANIER, J. W., PH.D., Political Science
  STAHMER, H. M.. PH.D., Religion
  SWANSON, B. E., PH.D., Political Science
  TEW, R. E., PH.D., Speech
  VANDIVER, J. S., PH.D., Sociology
  WAGLEY, C. W., PH.D., Anthropology
  WEBB, W. B., PH.D., Psychology
  WELTNER, W., Jr. PH.D., Chemistry
  WILLIAMS, A. L., PH.D., English
  WINEFORDNER, J. D., PH.D., Chemistry
  WOOD, F. B., PH.D., Physics and Astronomy
  WOODRUFF, W., PH.D., History
  ZEMAN, J. J., PH.D., Philosophy
  ZILLER, R. C., PH.D., Psychology
  ZOLTEWICZ, J. A., PH.D., Chemistry

*Business Administration:*
  BRIGHAM, E. F., PH.D., Finance and Insurance
  CHAMPION, J. M., PH.D., Management
  FOX, W. M., PH.D., Management
  FRAZER, W. J., Jr., PH.D., Economics
  HOROWITZ, I., PH.D., Management
  HOWARD, W. M., PH.D., Finance and Insurance
  MATTHEWS, C. A., PH.D., Finance, Insurance
  THOMPSON, R. B., PH.D., Marketing
  YU, S. C., PH.D., Accounting

*Education:*
  ALEXANDER, S. K., Jr., ED.D., Education Administration
  AVILA, D. L., ED.D., Foundations
  CREWS, R., ED.D., Instructional Leadership
  CURRAN, R. L., PH.D., Foundations
  FILLMER, H. T., PH.D., Instructional Leadership
  GUERTIN, W. H. PH.D., Foundations
  HASS, C. G., ED.D., Instructional Leadership
  HEDGES, W. D., ED.D., Instructional Leadership
  HENSEL, J. W., PH.D., Instructional Leadership
  HIPPLE, T. W., PH.D., Instructional Leadership
  LEWIS, A. J., PH.D., Instructional Leadership

## UNIVERSITIES AND COLLEGES—FLORIDA (UNIVERSITY OF) — U.S.A.

McGuire, V., ed.d., Subject Specialization
Myers, R. B., ed.d., General Teacher Education
Myrick, R. D., ph.d., Counselor Education
Newell, J. M., ph.d., Foundations
Nunnery, M. Y., ed.d., Education Administration
Reid, W. R., ph.d., Special Education
Renner, R. R., ph.d., Foundations
Riker, H. C., ed.d., Counselor Education
Soar, R. S., ph.d., Foundations
Todd, E. A., ed.d., Subject Specialization
Wattenbarger, J. L., ed.d., Educational Administration
Wenzel, E. L., ed.d., Instructional Leadership
Williams, E. L., ph.d., Student Services
Wittmer, P. J., ph.d., Counselor Education
Wolking, W. D., ph.d., Special Education

*Engineering:*
Block, S. S., ph.d., Chemical Engineering
Christensen, B. A., ph.d., Civil Engineering
Dalton, G. R., ph.d., Nuclear Engineering
Dehoff, R. T., sc.d., Materials Sciences
Ebcioglu, I. K., ph.d., Engineering Sciences
Elgerd, O.I., d.sc., Electrical Engineering
Fahien, R. W., ph.d., Chemical Engineering
Farber, E. A., ph.d., Mechanical Engineering
Gaither, R. B., ph.d., Mechanical Engineering
Hoover, J. W., m.s.ae., Engineering Science
Hren, J. J., ph.d., Materials Sciences and Engineering
Irey, R. K., ph.d., Mechanical Engineering
Lindgren, E. R., d.r.sc., Engineering Science and Mechanics
Mahig, J., ph.d., Mechanical Engineering
Odum, H. T., ph.d., Environmental Engineering
Oliver, C. C., ph.d., Mechanical Engineering
Omalley, J. R., ph.d., Electrical Engineering
Pyatt, E. E., dr. eng., Environmental Engineering Science
Roan, V. P., Jr., ph.d., Mechanical Engineering
Schaub, J. H., ph.d., Civil Engineering
Schneider, R. T., ph.d., Nuclear Engineering
Self, M. W., ph.d., Civil Engineering
Smith, J. R., ph.d., Electrical Engineering
Smutz, M., ph.d., General Engineering
Spangler, B. D., m.s., Civil Engineering
Tesar, D., ph.d., Mechanical Engineering
Tou, J. T., d.n.g., Computer and Information Science
Tyner, M., ph.d., Chemical Engineering
Uman, M. A., ph.d., Electrical Engineering
Verink, E. D., Jr., ph.d., Materials Sciences and Engineering
Walker, R. D., Jr., m.s., Chemical Engineering

*Fine Arts:*
Bowles, R. W., m.s., Music
Craven, R. C., Jr., m.f.a., Art
Grissom, E. E., m.f.a., Art
Hale, J. P., m.s., Music
Kushner, D. Z., ph.d., Music
Poole, R., m.a., Music
Troupin, E. C., m.m., Music
Uelsmann, J. N., m.f.a., Art
Williams, H. D., m.ed., Art
Wilmot, D. L., m.a., Music

*Graduate School:*
Wahl, F. M., ph.d., Geology

*Latin American Studies:*
Carter, W. E., ph.d., Anthropology
Suarez, A., ll.b., Law

*Journalism and Communications:*
Christiansen, K. A., ed.d., Broadcasting
Davis, H. G., m.a., Journalism
Edwardson, M. N., ph.d., Broadcasting
Pierce, F. N., ph.d., Advertising

*Law:*
Baldwin, F. N., ll.m.
Delony, D., ll.m.
Freeland, J. J., ll.b.
Glicksberg, M., ll.m.
Gordon, M. W., j.d.
Hughes, K. B., s.j.d.
Hunt, E. L., ll.m.
Jones, E. M., j.s.d.
Little, J. W., m.s.
McCoy, F. T., m.a.
Macdonald, W. D., s.j.d.
Probert, W., j.s.d.
Quarles, J. C., ll.b.
Smith, D. T., ll.b.
Van Alstyne, W., Jr., s.j.d.
Weyrauch, W. O., j.s.d.

*Physical Education and Health:*
Hicks, Dora A., ed.d., Health Education and Safety
Leavitt, Norma M., ed.d., P.E. Professional Curriculum
Leilich, R. E., r.ed., General Physical Education
Moore, C. A., ph.d., General Physical Education

*Medicine:*
Agee, O. F., m.d., Radiology
Andersen, T. W., m.d., Anaesthesiology
Ayoub, E. M. m.d., Paediatrics
Boyce, R. P., ph.d., Biochemistry
Cassin, S., ph.d., Physiology
Debusk, F. L., m.d., Paediatrics
Eitzman, D. V., m.d., Paediatrics
Finlayson, B., ph.d., Surgery
Fregly, M. J., ph.d., Physiology
Fried, M., ph.d., Biochemistry
Garcia-Bengoche, F., m.d., Neurosurgery
Gifford, G. E., ph.d., Microbiology
Hill, H. M., m.d., Neuroscience
Kaude, J. V., m.d., Radiology
Leibman, K. C., ph.d., Pharmacology
Maren, T. H., m.d., Pharmacology
Mauderli, W., d.sc., Radiology
Michael, M., Jr., m.d., General Medicine
Million, R. R., Radiology
Modell, J. H., m.d., Anaesthesiology
Noyes, W. D., m.d., Medicine
Otis, A. B., ph.d., Physiology
Perkins, H. M., m.d., Anaesthesiology
Pfaff, W. W., m.d., Surgery
Rhoton, A. L., Jr., m.d., Neurosurgery
Ross, M. H., ph.d., Anatomy
Rubin, M. L., m.d., Ophthalmology
Shands, J. W., Jr., m.d., Microbiology
Smith, R. T., m.d., Pathology
Stainsby, W. N., sc.d., Physiology

Vanmeirop, L. H., m.d., Paediatrics
Williams, C. M., ph.d., Radiology
Woodward, E. R., m.d., Surgery

*Nursing:*
Barton, P. H., d.ed., Education
Knowles, Lois N., m.a., Nursing

*Pharmacy:*
Garrett, E. R., ph.d.
Rao, K. V., ph.d.
Villalonga, F. A., ph.d.

*Health Related Professions:*
Bzoch, K. R., ph.d., Communicative Disorders
Davis, H. C., ph.d., Clinical Psychology
Perry, N. W., Jr., ph.d., Clinical Psychology

*Dentistry:*
Balanoff, N., ph.d., Dentistry
Bennett, C. G., d.d.s., Dentistry
Collett, W. K., sc.d., Oral Medicine
Fast, T. B., d.d.s., Oral Medicine
Fischlschweiger, W., ph.d., Basic Dentistry
Garrington, G. E., m.s., Oral Medicine
Lundeen, H. C., b.a., Dentistry
Mckenzie, R. S., ph.d., Basic Dentistry
Mahan, P. E., ph.d., Dental Education
Stanley, H. R., d.d.s., Oral Medicine

*Agriculture and Forestry:*
Ahmed, E. M., ph.d., Food Technology and Nutrition
Ammerman, C. B., ph.d., Animal Science
Biggs, R. H., ph.d., Fruit Crops
Blue, W. G., ph.d., Soils
Brasher, J. J., ph.d., Extension Administration
Caldwell, R. E., ph.d., Soils
Carpenter, J. W., ph.d., Animal Science
Clark, H. B., ph.d., Food and Resource Economics
Combs, G. E., Jr., ph.d., Animal Science
Conrad, J. H., ph.d., Animal Science
Cook, A. A., ph.d., Plant Pathology
Covey, C. D., ph.d., Food and Resource Economics
Dean, C. E., ph.d., Agronomy
Dennison, R. A., ph.d., Food Technology and Nutrition
Eastwood, R. A., ph.d., Food and Resource Economics
Edds. G. T.. ph.d., Veterinary Science
Edwardson, J. R., ph.d., Agronomy
Elkins, V. L., m.s., Food and Resource Economics
Eno, C. F., ph.d., Soils
Feaster, J. P., ph.d., Animal Science
Fiskell, J. G., ph.d., Soils
Freeman, T. E., ph.d., Plant Pathology
Fry, J. L., ph.d., Poultry Science
Gerber, J. F., ph.d., Soils
Green, V. E., ph.d., Agronomy
Habeck, D. H., ph.d., Entomology
Hall, C. B., ph.d., Vegetable Crops
Hammond, L. C., ph.d., Soils
Harms, R. H., ph.d., Poultry Science
Harrison, D. S., ms.ag., Agricultural Engineering
Hentges, J. F., Jr., ph.d., Animal Science
Horner, E. S., ph.d., Agronomy
Humphreys, T. E., ph.d.
Joiner, J. N., ph.d., Ornamental Horticulture
Jones, D. W., m.s.a., Agronomy
Kerr, S. H., ph.d., Entomology
Koger, M., ph.d., Animal Science
Langham, M. R., ph.d., Food and Resource Economics
Locascio, S. J., ph.d., Vegetable Crops
Marshall, S. P., ph.d., Dairy Science
Matthews, R. F., ph.d., Food Science

McCLOUD, D. E., PH.D., Agronomy
McPHERSON, W. W., PH.D., Food and Resource Economics
MOORE, J. E., PH.D., Animal Science
MORRILL, O. L., ED.D., Extension Administration
MOTT, G. D., PH.D., Agronomy
MOXLEY, C. C., PH.D., Food and Resource Economics
MULLINS, J. T., PH.D., Botany
MYERS, J., M.S., Agricultural Engineering
NATION, J. L., PH.D., Entomology
NORDEN, ALLAN J., PH.D., Agronomy
PALMER, A. Z., PH.D., Animal Science
PERRY, V. G., PH.D., Research Administration
PFAHLER, P. L., PH.D., Agronomy
POLOPOLUS, L., PH.D., Food and Resource Economics
PRITCHETT, W. L., PH.D., Soils
PURDY, L. H., PH.D., Agricultural Engineering
REDDISH, R. L., PH.D., Animal Science
ROBERTS, D. A., PH.D., Plant Pathology
ROBERTSON, W. K., PH.D., Soils
ROBINSON, F. A., M.S., Entomology
RODGERS, E. G., PH.D., Agronomy
ROTHWELL, D. F., PH.D., Soils
RUELKE, O. C., PH.D., Agronomy
SCHENK, N. C., PH.D., Agronomy
SHEEHAN, T. J., PH.D., Ornamental Horticulture
SHIRLEY, R. L., PH.D., Animal Science
SIMPSON, C. F., PH.D., Veterinary Science
SMART, G. C., Jr., PH.D., Entomology
SMITH, C. N., PH.D., Food and Resource Economics
SOULE, J., PH.D., Fruit Crops
SPINKS, D. O., PH.D., Soils
STALL, R. E., PH.D., Plant Pathology
VAN HORN, H. H., PH.D., Dairy Science
WALKER, T. J., PH.D., Entomology
WALLACE, H. D., PH.D., Animal Science
WARNICK, A. C., PH.D., Animal Science
WEST, S. H., PH.D., Agronomy
WHITCOMB, W. H., PH.D., Entomology
WHITE, F. H., PH.D., Veterinary Science
WILCOX, C. J., PH.D., Dairy Science
WILKINSON, R. C., PH.D., Entomology
WILKOWSKE, H. H., PH.D., Food Science

## UNIVERSITY OF MIAMI
CORAL GABLES, FLORIDA 33124
Chartered 1925.
Telephone: (305) 284-2211.
Private control; Academic year: August to May (two terms).

*President:* Dr. EDWARD T. FOOTE, II.
*Provost and Executive Vice-President:* Dr. CLARENCE G. STUCKWISCH (acting).
*Vice-President for Financial Affairs:* DAVID LIEBERMAN.
*Vice-President for Business Affairs:* OLIVER G. F. BONNERT.
*Vice-President for Medical Affairs and Dean:* Dr. BERNARD J. FOGEL (acting).
*Vice-President for Development Affairs:* EDWARD G. COLL, A.B.
*Vice-President for Student Affairs:* W. R. BUTLER, ED.D.

*Dean of Students:* WILLIAM B. SHEEDER, M.A.
*Registrar:* SIDNEY WEISBURD, M.B.A.
*Librarian:* FRANK RODGERS.

The library contains 1,343,422 vols.
Number of teachers: 1,348 full-time, 450 part-time, total 1,789.
Number of students: 17,105

Publications: *The Miami Hurricane* (student bi-weekly newspaper), *Ibis* (yearbook), *Journal of Inter-American Studies* (quarterly), *World Affairs* (quarterly), *University Bulletins.*

### DEANS:
*Graduate Studies and Research:* CLARENCE G. STUCKWISCH, PH.D.
*College of Arts and Sciences:* ARTHUR W. BROWN, PH.D.
*School of Business Administration:* Dr. CARL E. B. MCKENRY (acting).
*School of Education:* LOU KLEINMAN, PH.D.
*School of Engineering and Architecture:* NORMAN G. EINSPRUCH, PH.D.
*School of Law:* SOIA MENTSCHIKOFF, LL.D.
*School of Medicine:* Dr. BERNARD J. FOGEL.
*School of Music:* W. F. LEE, PH.D.
*School of Nursing:* Dr. EVELYN R. BARRITT.
*School of Continuing Studies:* M. R. ALLEN, PH.D.
*Rosenstiel School of Marine and Atmospheric Sciences:* Dr. WARREN J. WISBY (acting).

### ATTACHED INSTITUTES:
**Centre for Theoretical Studies:** f. 1964 Dir. B. KURSUNOGLU, PH.D.

**Centre for Advanced International Studies:** f. 1964; Dir. Dr. HAIM SHAKED (acting).

**Institute for Molecular and Cellular Evolution:** f. 1964; Dir. SIDNEY W. FOX, PH.D.

## UNIVERSITY OF SOUTH FLORIDA
4202 EAST FOWLER AVE., TAMPA, FLORIDA 33620
Telephone: 974-2011.
Founded 1956, classes commenced 1960.
State control; Academic year: September to August (semester system).

*President:* JOHN LOTT BROWN.
*Registrar:* DOUGLAS MCCULLOUGH.
*Vice-President of Academic Affairs:* GREGORY M. O'BRIEN.
*Vice-President of Student Affairs:* DANIEL R. WALBOLT.
*Vice-President for Finance and Administration:* ALBERT C. HARTLEY.
*Vice-President for University Relations:* JOSEPH BUSTA.
*Vice-President of Employment Relations and Legal Affairs:* STEVEN G. WENZEL.
*Librarian:* Mrs. MARY LOU HARKNESS.

The library contains 787,321 vols.
Number of teachers: 1,265.
Number of students: 25,000.

### DEANS:
*College of Business Administration:* Dr. ROBERT G. COX.
*College of Education:* WILLIAM G. KATZENMEYER.
*College of Engineering:* GLENN A. BURDICK.
*College of Fine Arts:* HARRISON W. COVINGTON.
*College of Medicine:* ANDOR SZENTIVANYI.
*College of Nursing:* Dr. GWENDOLINE MACDONALD.
*College of Arts and Letters:* JAMES F. STRANGE.
*College of Natural Sciences:* Dr. JAMES RAY.
*College of Social and Behavioural Sciences:* Dr. TRAVIS NORTHCUTT.
*Regional Campus Affairs:* JAMES B. HECK.
*USF at Sarasota:* ROBERT BARYLSKI.
*USF at Fort Myers:* ROY I. MUMME.
*USF at St. Petersburg:* JOHN HINZ.
*New College of USF:* EUGENE LEWIS (Provost).

## UNIVERSITY OF TAMPA
TAMPA, FLORIDA 33606
Telephone: 253-8861.
Founded 1931.

*President:* RICHARD D. CHESHIRE.
*Provost:* EDWIN F. WILDE.
*Vice-President for Business and Finance:* RUDOLPH E. KOLETIC.
*Vice-President for Public Affairs:* J. MARK LONO.
*Vice-President for Facilities Planning:* JOHN D. TELFER.
*Secretary:* JOHN D. TELFER.
*Librarian:* Mrs. LYDIA ACOSTA.

The library contains 175,000 vols.
Number of teachers: 85 full-time.
Number of students: 2,350.

# GEORGIA

## AGNES SCOTT COLLEGE
DECATUR, GEORGIA 30030
Undergraduate liberal arts college for women.
Founded 1889.

*President:* MARVIN B. PERRY, Jr., PH.D.
*Dean of College:* JULIA T. GARY, PH.D.
*Dean of Students:* MARTHA C. KIRKLAND, M.A.
*Registrar:* LEA ANN G. HUDSON, B.A.
*Director of Admissions:* JUDITH M. TINDEL, B.A.
*Librarian:* JUDITH JENSEN, L.M.S.

The library contains 160,000 vols.
Number of teachers: 67, including 21 professors.
Number of students: 560.
Publications: *Bulletin, Alumnae Quarterly*.

## ALBANY STATE COLLEGE
ALBANY, GEORGIA 31705
Telephone: 439-4095.
Founded 1903.

President: BILLY C. BLACK.
Director of Admissions: DOROTHY B. HUBBARD.
Librarian: Dr. GUY C. CRAFT.

The library contains 125,620 vols.
Number of teachers: 125.
Number of students: 1,500.

## ATLANTA UNIVERSITY
ATLANTA, GEORGIA 30314
Founded 1865; Chartered 1867.

President: CLEVELAND L. DENNARD.
Treasurer: DWIGHT C. MINTON.
Registrar: G. H. TAYLOR.

The library contains 380,000 vols.
Number of teachers: 135 full-time.
Number of students: 1,691.

Publications: *Atlanta University Bulletin*† (quarterly), *Phylon*†, *The Atlanta University Review of Race and Culture* (quarterly).

DEANS:
Education: BARBARA HATTON (acting).
Business Administration: AUGUSTUS H. STERNE.
Arts and Sciences: B. F. HUDSON, Jr.
Social Work: CLARENCE COLEMAN.
School of Library and Information Studies: VIRGINIA L. JONES.

## BERRY COLLEGE
MOUNT BERRY, GEORGIA 30149
Founded 1902.

President: GLORIA M. SHATTO.
Dean of Students: THOMAS W. CARVER.
Dean of the College: L. DOYLE MATHIS.
Dean of Admissions: THOMAS C. GLOVER.
Registrar: GARY WOOLLEY.

The library contains 330,326 vols.
Number of teachers: 82 full-time and 22 part-time.
Number of students: 1,607.
Publication: *Admissions Catalog*†.

## CLARK COLLEGE
240 CHESTNUT ST., S.W.,
ATLANTA, GEORGIA 30314
Telephone: (404) 681-3080.
Founded 1869.

President: ELIAS BLAKE, Jr.
Director of Admissions: CLIFTON RAWLES.
Director of Business Affairs: NATHANIEL WILLIAMS.
Dean of Faculty and Instruction: Dr. WINFRED HARRIS.
Dean of Students: CURTIS D. GILLESPIE.
Librarian: Mrs. FANNIE B. HOGAN.

The library contains 72,000 vols.
Number of teachers: 129.
Number of students: 2,086.

Publications: *The Panther* (term-time student journal), *The Communicator* (quarterly).

## EMORY UNIVERSITY
ATLANTA, GEORGIA 30322
Telephone: 329-6036.
Related to the United Methodist Church.
Chartered as Emory College 1836, University 1915.

President: JAMES T. LANEY, PH.D.
Executive Vice-President and Dean of Faculties: CHARLES T. LESTER, PH.D.
Vice-President for Business: O. E. MYERS, Jr., M.A.
Vice-President for Arts and Sciences: JOHN M. PALMS, PH.D.
Vice-President for Finance and Treasurer: HUGH E. HILLIARD, C.P.A.
Vice-President for Health Affairs and Director of the Woodruff Medical Centre: E. GARLAND HERNDON, M.D.
Executive Director of Development: JOHN W. STEPHENSON, M.B.A.
Director of Admissions: C. N. WATSON, A.M.
Registrar: CHARLES R. NICOLAYSEN.
Director of Libraries: HERBERT JOHNSON, M.A.

The library contains 1,636,344 vols.
Number of teachers: 1,173 (full-time).
Number of students: 7,977.

Publications: *Emory Magazine, Emory Law Journal, Medicine at Emory*.

DEANS:
Emory College: DAVID L. MINTER, PH.D.
Oxford College (Oxford): WILLIAM MONCRIEF, PH.D.
Campus Life: WILLIAM H. FOX, PH.D.
Business Administration: GEORGE M. PARKS, PH.D.
Dentistry: CHARLES A. WALDRON, D.D.S.
Graduate School: ELLEN P. MICKIEWICZ, PH.D.
School of Law: THOMAS D. MORGAN, J.D.
School of Medicine: JAMES F. GLENN, M.D.
School of Nursing: EDNA M. GREXTON, D.P.H.
School of Theology: JIM L. WAITS, D.D.

## FORT VALLEY STATE COLLEGE
FORT VALLEY, GEORGIA 31030
Telephone: 825-8281.
Founded 1895.

President: C. W. PETTIGREW.
Dean of the Faculty: W. S. M. BANKS, II.
Associate Dean: THOMAS BARRETT.
Registrar: EDWARD GRAENING.
Librarian: Miss HOMIE REGULUS.

The library contains 140,797 vols.
Number of teachers: 152.
Number of students: 2,000.

## GEORGIA COLLEGE MILLEDGEVILLE
MILLEDGEVILLE, GEORGIA 31061
Chartered in 1889 as Georgia Normal and Industrial College; name changed 1922 to Georgia State College for Women and 1961 to The Woman's College of Georgia. Its present name dates from 1967 when it became a co-educational institution.

President: Dr. EDWIN G. SPEIR, Jr.
Vice-President: RALPH W. HEMPHILL.
Vice-President for Business and Finance: W. L. EDDINS.
Registrar and Director of Admissions: R. L. COX, Jr.
Dean of Students: Dr. PAUL A. BENSON.

Number of books in library: 144,525.
Number of teachers: 147.
Number of students: 3,369.
Publication: *Bulletin* (12 a year).

## GEORGIA INSTITUTE OF TECHNOLOGY
ATLANTA, GEORGIA 30332
Telephone: (404) 894-2000.
Chartered 1885.

President: JOSEPH M. PETTIT, PH.D.
Registrar: FRANK E. ROPER Jr., M.S.I.E.
Vice-President, Academic Affairs: J. R. STEVENSON, PH.D. (acting).
Vice-President, Business and Finance: GENE M. NORDBY, PH.D.
Vice-President, Institute Relations and Development: P. WARREN HEERNANN, M.S.
Vice-President, Planning: CLYDE D. ROBBINS, PH.D.
Vice-President, Research: A. P. SHEPPARD, PH.D. (acting).
Librarian: E. GRAHAM ROBERTS, PH.D.
Executive Secretary: JANICE GOSDIN, B.S.

The library contains 890,000 vols.
Number of teachers: 950.
Number of students: 11,500.

Publications: *The Technique, Engineer, Blue Print*.

DEANS:
College of Architecture: WILLIAM L. FASH, M.ARCH.

*College of Engineering:* WILLIAM M. SANGSTER, PH.D.
*College of Management:* CHARLES GEARING, PH.D.
*College of Science and Liberal Studies:* HENRY S. VALK, PH.D.
*Graduate Studies:* JAMES J. BYNUM, PH.D. (acting).
*Students:* JAMES E. DULL, M.ED.

SCHOOL DIRECTORS:

*Aerospace Engineering:* ARNOLD L. DUCOFFE, PH.D.
*Biology:* JOHN W. CRENSHAW, PH.D.
*Ceramic Engineering:* JOSEPH L. PENTECOST, PH.D.
*Chemical Engineering:* D. W. POEHLEIN, PH.D.
*Chemistry:* J. AARON BERTRAND, PH.D.
*Civil Engineering:* JOHN F. FITZGERALD, D.SC.
*Electrical Engineering:* DEMETRIUS T. PARIS, PH.D.
*Engineering Science and Mechanics:* MILTON E. RAVILLE, PH.D.
*Health Systems:* HAROLD E. SMALLEY, PH.D.
*Geophysical Sciences:* CHARLES E. WEAVER, PH.D.
*Information and Computer Science:* RAYMOND MIELER, PH.D.
*Industrial and Systems Engineering:* M. E. THOMAS, PH.D.
*Mathematics:* L. A. KARLOVITZ, PH.D.
*Mechanical Engineering:* STOTHE P. KEZIOS, PH.D.
*Nuclear Engineering:* LYNN E. WEAVER, PH.D.
*Physics:* CHARLES BRADEN, PH.D. (acting).
*Psychology:* EDWARD H. LOVELAND, PH.D.
*Textile Engineering:* W. C. LINCHER, PH.D. (acting).

ACADEMIC DEPARTMENT DIRECTORS:

*Air Force Aerospace Studies:* JAMES PRIEST.
*English:* KARL M. MURPHY, PH.D.
*Military Science:* DAVID GARVIN, M.S.
*Modern Languages:* LOUIS J. ZAHN, PH.D.
*Music:* GREGORY COLSON, M.A.
*Naval Science:* GERALD HENSON.
*Physical Education and Recreation:* JAMES K. REEDY, PH.D.
*Social Science:* JON JOHNSTON, M.S. (acting).

ATTACHED CENTERS AND INSTITUTES:

**Engineering Experiment Station:** Dir. DONALD J. GRACE, PH.D.

**Georgia Tech Research Institute:** Gen. Man. WILLIAM H. BORCHERT, M.S.

**Interdisciplinary Programmes:** JACK SPURLOCK, PH.D.

**Health Systems Research Center:** Dir. HAROLD E. SMALLEY, PH.D.

**Environmental Resources Center:** Dir. BERND KAHN, PH.D.

### GEORGIA SOUTHERN COLLEGE
STATESBORO, GEORGIA 30458
Telephone: (912) 681-5211.
Founded 1906.

*President:* Dr. DALE W. LICK.
*Vice-President:* Dr. CHARLES J. AUSTIN.
*Vice-President of Business and Finance:* WILLIAM COOK.
*Dean of Students:* Dr. JOHN F. NOLEN.
*Registrar:* DON COLEMAN.
*Librarian:* KENNETH WALTER.
  The library contains 300,000 vols.
  Number of teachers: 360.
  Number of students: 6,800.

### GEORGIA STATE UNIVERSITY
UNIVERSITY PLAZA,
ATLANTA, GEORGIA 30303
Telephone: 658-2000.
Founded 1913.

*President:* Dr. NOAH LANGDALE, Jr.
*Executive Vice-President and Provost:* Dr. WILLIAM M. SUTTLES.
*Vice-President for Academic Affairs:* Dr. ELI A. ZUBAY.
*Vice-President for Academic Services:* Dr. KATHLEEN D. CROUCH.
*Vice-President for Student Services:* Dr. WILLIAM S. PATRICK.
*Vice-President for Urban Affairs:* Dr. EDMUND W. HUGHES.
*Vice-President for Financial Affairs:* Dr. ROGER O. MILLER.
*University Librarian:* Dr. RALPH E. RUSSELL.
  The library contains 630,000 vols. plus microforms.
  Number of teachers: c. 1,000.
  Number of students: c. 20,000.
  Publications: *Business Review, Foreign Languages Beacon, Studies in Literary Imagination.*

DEANS:

*College of Allied Health Sciences:* Dr. J. RHODES HAVERTY.
*College of Arts and Sciences:* Dr. CLYDE FAULKNER (acting).
*College of Business Administration:* Dr. KENNETH BLACK, Jr.
*College of Education:* Dr. SHERMAN R. DAY.
*College of General Studies:* Dr. CHARLES E. HOPKINS.
*College of Urban Life:* Dr. WILLIAM W. NASH.

### LA GRANGE COLLEGE
LA GRANGE, GEORGIA 30240
Telephone: (404) 882-2911.
Founded 1831.

*President:* Dr. WALTER Y. MURPHY.
*Registrar:* JIMMY G. HERRING.
*Dean of Admissions:* JOHN T. HELTON.

*Librarian:* FRANK W. LEWIS.
  The library contains 70,000 vols.
  Number of teachers: 58.
  Number of students: 947.

### MERCER UNIVERSITY
MACON, GEORGIA 31207
Telephone: (912) 745-6811.
Chartered 1833.
Private control, Baptist.

*Chancellor:* RUFUS C. HARRIS.
*President:* R. KIRBY GODSEY.
*Registrar:* T. M. TRIMBLE.
*Business Officer:* ROBERT A. SKELTON.
*Librarian:* D. L. METTS, Jr.
  Number of teachers: 150.
  Number of students: 5,000.
  Publication: *Mercer University Bulletin.*

DEANS:

*Liberal Arts College:* ROLLIN S. ARMOUR.
*Director of Graduate Studies:* P. CABLE.
*Law:* GLENN CLARK (acting).
*Medicine:* WILLIAM BRISTOL.
*Mercer University in Atlanta:* JEAN HENDRICKS.
*Pharmacy:* O. LITTLEJOHN.
*Summer Session:* JOANNA WATSON.
*Director of Admissions:* JOSEPH MCDANIEL.

### MOREHOUSE COLLEGE
223 CHESTNUT STREET S.W.,
ATLANTA, GEORGIA 30314
Telephone: Murray 8-4223.
Founded 1867.

*President:* HUGH M. GLOSTER.
*Registrar:* PHILLIP REDRICK.
*Academic Dean:* W. J. HUBERT.
*Librarian:* Mrs. JESSIE E. EBANKS.
  The library contains 298,496 vols.
  Number of teachers: 112 full-time.
  Number of students: 1,950.

### MORRIS BROWN COLLEGE
643 HUNTER STREET, S.W.,
ATLANTA, GEORGIA 30314
Telephone: 525-7831.
Founded 1881.

*President:* Dr. ROBERT THREATT.
*Director of Admissions and Records:* Mrs. LUCILLE S. WILLIAMS.
*Vice-President for Academic Affairs:* Dr. WILLIE F. PAYNE.
*Librarian:* Mrs. V. W. JENKINS.
  The library contains 45,706 vols.
  Number of teachers: 94.
  Number of students: 1,560.

## NORTH GEORGIA COLLEGE
DAHLONEGA, GEORGIA 30597
Telephone: 404-864-3391.
Founded 1873.
*President:* John H. Owen.
*Registrar:* Gary R. Steffey.
*Librarian:* Mrs. Marjorie J. Clark.
The library contains 107,410 vols.
Number of teachers: 94.
Number of students: 1,930.
Publication: *North Georgia College Bulletin Series.*

## OGLETHORPE UNIVERSITY
ATLANTA, GEORGIA 30319
Telephone: (404) 261-1441.
Founded 1835.
*President:* Manning M. Pattillo, Jr.
*Registrar:* G. Malcolm Amerson.
*Director of Admissions:* James A. Nesbitt.
*Librarian:* T. W. Chandler, Jr.
The library contains 63,000 bound vols.
Number of teachers: 45.
Number of students: 847.
Publications: *The Tower* (2 a year), *The Stormy Petrel* (fortnightly).

## PAINE COLLEGE
AUGUSTA, GEORGIA 30910
Telephone: (404) 722-4471.
Founded 1882.
*President:* Julius S. Scott, Jr.
*Registrar:* Mrs. Patricia B. Steele.
*Librarian:* Mrs. Millie Parker.
The library contains 81,000 vols.
Number of teachers: 56.
Number of students: 757.

## PIEDMONT COLLEGE
DEMOREST, GEORGIA 30535
Telephone: (404) 723-8301.
Founded 1897.
*President:* Dr. James E. Walter.
*Registrar:* Nolan Mix.
*Dean:* Dr. Mary C. Lane.
*Librarian:* David Pratt.
The library contains 65,000 volumes.
Number of teachers: 30.
Number of students: 400.

## SAVANNAH STATE COLLEGE
SAVANNAH, GEORGIA 31404
Telephone: 356-2240.
Founded 1890.
*President:* Dr. Clyde W. Hall (acting).
*Registrar:* John B. Clemmons.
*Librarian:* Andrew J. McLemore.
The library contains 116,951 vols.
Number of teachers: 127.
Number of students: 2,008.

## SHORTER COLLEGE
ROME, GEORGIA 30161
Telephone: (404) 291-2121.
Founded 1873.
*President:* Dr. Randall H. Minor.
*Academic Dean:* Dr. Charles W. Whitworth.
*Business Manager:* Weston Plymale.
*Director of Admissions:* Miss Pat Hart.
*Registrar:* Mrs. Katharine Lovvorn.
*Dean of the Division of Student Services:* Dr. Craig Allee.
*Director of Placement:* Marvin Russell.
*Director of College Relations:* Robert D. Chisholm.
*Librarian:* Mrs. Mary Mac Mosley.
The library contains 83,269 vols.
Number of teachers: 64.
Number of students: 813.

## SPELMAN COLLEGE
350 SPELMAN LANE S.W.,
ATLANTA, GEORGIA 30314
Telephone: 681-3643.
Founded 1881.
*President:* Donald M. Stewart.
*Registrar:* Mrs. Jeanne Allen.
*Librarian:* Hulda Wilson.
The library contains 49,324 vols. and 350 periodicals.
Number of teachers: 117.
Number of students: 1,366.

## UNIVERSITY OF GEORGIA
ATHENS, GEORGIA 30602
Telephone: 542-3030.
Incorporated by Act of General Assembly January 27, 1785, established 1801.
*President:* Fred C. Davison, D.V.M., Ph.D.
*Vice-President for Academic Affairs:* Dr. Virginia Y. Trotter, M.S., Ph.D.
*Vice-President for Research:* R. C. Anderson, M.A., Ph.D.
*Vice-President for Services:* S. E. Younts, M.S., Ph.D.
*Vice-President for Business and Finance:* A. W. Barber, M.B.A.
*Vice-President for Development and University Relations:* H. Perk Robins, B.S.
*Vice-President for Student Affairs:* Dwight Douglas, Ed.D.
*Registrar:* Bruce T. Shutt, M.S., Ph.D.
*Librarian:* David F. Bishop, B.M., M.S.L.S.
The library contains 2,065,000 vols.
Number of teachers: 1,578.
Number of students: 23,470.

DEANS:
*Graduate School:* John C. Dowling, Ph.D.
*College of Agriculture:* William P. Flatt.
*College of Arts and Sciences:* Dr. W. J. Payne, Ph.D.
*College of Business Administration:* W. C. Flewellen, M.S., Ph.D.
*College of Education:* Kathryn A. Blake.
*School of Environmental Design:* Robert P. Nicholls, M.L.A.
*School of Forestry:* Leon A. Hargreaves, Jr., Ph.D.
*School of Home Economics:* Emily H. Pou, Ph.D.
*School of Journalism:* Scott M. Cutlip, Ph.M.
*School of Law:* James Ralph Beaird, LL.M.
*School of Pharmacy:* Howard C. Ansel, Ph.D.
*School of Veterinary Medicine:* David P. Anderson, Ph.D.
*School of Social Work:* C. A. Stewart, M.A., M.S.S.W., Ph.D.

## VALDOSTA STATE COLLEGE
NORTH PATTERSON STREET,
VALDOSTA, GEORGIA 31601
Telephone: (912) 247-3233.
Founded 1906.
*President:* Hugh C. Bailey.
*Vice-President and Dean of Faculties:* W. Ray Cleere.
*Registrar:* Arthur L. Bostock, Jr.
*Librarian:* David L. Ince.
The library contains 240,000 vols
Number of teachers: 209.
Number of students: 4,900.

## WESLEYAN COLLEGE
MACON, GEORGIA 31297
Telephone: (912) 477-1110.
Founded 1836.
*President:* Fred W. Hicks.
*Dean:* Kayron McMinn.
*Director of Admissions:* Burton Fite.
*Librarian:* Hasseltine Roberts.
The library contains 115,000 vols.
Number of teachers: 36.
Number of students: 422.

## WEST GEORGIA COLLEGE
CARROLLTON, GEORGIA 30118
Telephone: (404) 834-1388.
Founded 1933 (senior college status, 1957).

President: Dr. MAURICE K. TOWNSEND.
Vice-President and Dean of Faculties: Dr. JOHN T. LEWIS.
Dean of Graduate School: Dr. B. W. GRIFFITH, Jr.
Registrar: Dr. GORDON E. FINNIE.
Director of Admissions: C. DOYLE BICKERS.
Librarian: CHARLES E. BEARD.

The library contains 1,016,461 vols. and other articles.

Number of teachers: 242.
Number of students: 5,271.

Publications: *West Georgia College Annual Report, Library Annual Report, Registrar's Report.*

## HAWAII

### BRIGHAM YOUNG UNIVERSITY, HAWAII CAMPUS
LAIE, OAHU, HAWAII 96762
Telephone: 293-3211.
Founded 1955.

President: J. ELLIOT CAMERON.
Vice-President for Academics: ERIC B. SHUMWAY.
Registrar: CHARLES GOO.
Dean: ERIC B. SHUMWAY.
Librarian: RICHARD PEARSON.

The library contains 150,000 vols.

Number of teachers: 97.
Number of students: 1,840.

### CHAMINADE UNIVERSITY OF HONOLULU
3140 WAIALAE AVENUE,
HONOLULU, HAWAII 96816
Telephone: 7354711.
Founded 1955.

President: Rev. DAVID H. SCHUYLER, S.M.
Vice-President and Academic Dean: DAWES N. HIU, PH.D.
Director of Admissions: WILLIAM F. MURRAY, PH.D.
Registrar: Bro. HERMAN GERBER, S.M.
Dean of Students: Mrs. SHARYN GOO.
Librarian: MARIAN HUBBARD.

The library contains 50,000 vols.

Number of teachers: 109.
Number of students: 1,459 full-time.

Publications: *Newsletter* (quarterly), *Silversword, Aulama, 'Ahinahina.*

### UNIVERSITY OF HAWAII
2444 DOLE ST.,
HONOLULU, HAWAII 96822

Founded 1907, University of Hawaii 1920. A state-wide system, including university and community colleges.

President: FUJIO MATSUDA, SC.D.
Vice-President for Academic Affairs: DAVID A. HEENAN.
Vice-President for Administration: HAROLD MASUMOTO, J.D.
Chancellor for Community Colleges: DEWEY KIM, M.P.A.
Chancellor for Manoa: DURWARD LONG, PH.D.
Chancellor for Hilo: STEPHEN MITCHELL, PH.D.
Chancellor for West Oahu: RALPH MIWA, PH.D.

Publications: *Bulletins.*

### University of Hawaii at Hilo
1400 KAPIOLANI ST., HILO 96720
Liberal Arts College.

Chancellor: STEPHEN R. MITCHELL, PH.D.

DEANS:
College of Arts and Sciences: DAVID C. PURCELL, Jr.
College of Agriculture: FREDERICK TOM.
Provost, Hawaii Community College: MITSUGU SUMADA.

Number of students: 3,000.

### University of Hawaii at Manoa
2500 CAMPUS RD.,
HONOLULU, HAWAII 96822

Chancellor: DURWARD LONG, PH.D.
Assistant Vice-Chancellor for Faculty Affairs: ROBERT PRAHLER (acting).
Provost and Dean, College of Arts and Sciences: DAVID CONTOIS (acting).
Librarian: DON L. BOSSEAU.
Number of students: 20,319.

DEANS:
College of Arts and Sciences:
  Faculty of Arts and Humanities: REX A. WADE.
  Faculty of Languages, Linguistics and Literature: RICHARD K. SEYMOUR.
  Faculty of Natural Sciences: ROBERT L. PECSOK.
  Faculty of Social Sciences: DEANE E. NEUBAUER.
College of Business Administration: H. DAVID BESS (acting).
College of Continuing Education and Community Service: WESLEY T. PARK.
College of Education: ANDREW W. S.IN.
College of Engineering: REGINALD H. F. YOUNG (acting).
College of Tropical Agriculture and Human Resources: NOEL P. KEFFORD (acting).
Graduate Division: BARBARA Z. SIEGEL (acting).
School of Architecture: ELMER E. BOTSAI.
School of Law: MARVIN J. ANDERSON (acting).
Graduate School of Library Studies: IRA W. HARRIS.
School of Medicine: TERENCE A. ROGERS.
School of Nursing: HESSEL FLITTER (acting).
School of Public Health: JERROLD M. MICHAEL.
School of Social Work: DANIEL S. SANDERS.
School of Travel Industry Management: CHUCK Y. GEE.
Student Affairs: ELY MEYERSON.
Summer Session: ROBERT K. SAKAI.

## IDAHO

### COLLEGE OF IDAHO
2112 CLEVELAND BLVD.,
CALDWELL, IDAHO 83605
Telephone: (208) 459-5011.
Founded 1891.

President: ARTHUR H. DEROSIER, Jr.
Registrar: WILLIAM E. WALLACE.
Librarian: R. G. ELLIOTT.

The library contains 115,000 vols.
Number of teachers: 45.
Number of students: 854.

### IDAHO STATE UNIVERSITY
POCATELLO, IDAHO 83201
Telephone: (208) 236-0211.
Founded 1901.

President: Dr. MYRON L. COULTER.
Vice-President for Academic Affairs: Dr. WILLIAM W. CHMURNY.
Vice-President for Administration: Dr. CLIFFORD TRUMP.
Financial Vice-President: PHILIP H. EASTMAN.
Dean of Student Affairs: JAY G. JENSEN.
Registrar: DAROLD H. CHAMBERS.
Librarian: RONALD J. SWANSON.

The library contains 260,226 vols.
Number of teachers: 369.
Number of students: 11,689.

### NORTHWEST NAZARENE COLLEGE
NAMPA, IDAHO 83651
Telephone: 467-8011.
Founded 1913.

President: KENNETH H. PEARSALL.
Vice-President for Academic Affairs: Dr. G. FORD.
Registrar: Mrs. WANDA MCMICHAEL.
Director of Admissions: B. WEBB.
Librarian: Miss EDITH LANCASTER.

The library contains 81,550 vols.

Number of teachers: 75.
Number of students: 1,313.

### UNIVERSITY OF IDAHO
MOSCOW, IDAHO 83843
Telephone: 885-6111.
Chartered 1889.

UNIVERSITIES AND COLLEGES—IDAHO, ILLINOIS U.S.A.

*President:* RICHARD D. GIBB, PH.D.
*Vice-President for Academic Affairs and Research:* ROBERT R. FURGASON, PH.D.
*Financial Vice-President/Bursar:* DAVID L. MCKINNEY, M.B.A.
*Co-ordinator of Student Services:* TERRY R. ARMSTRONG, ED.D.
*Director of Admissions/Registrar:* M. E. TELIN, M.ED.
*Librarian:* W. S. OWENS, M.A., L.S.
The library contains 1,000,000 vols.
Number of teachers: 700.
Number of students: 8,500.

DEANS:

*Graduate School:* ARTHUR R. GITTINS, PH.D.
*Agriculture:* RAYMOND MILLER, PH.D.
*Business and Economics:* CHARLES D. MCQUILLEN, PH.D.
*Education:* E. V. SAMUELSON, ED.D.
*Engineering:* RICHARD WILLIAMS, PH.D.
*Forestry:* J. H. EHRENREICH, PH.D.
*Instructional Services:* WARREN S. OWENS, M.A.L.S.
*Law:* CLIFF F. THOMPSON, J.D.
*Letters and Science:* E. K. RAUNIO, PH.D.
*Mines and Earth Resources:* M. M. MILLER, PH.D.

## ILLINOIS

### AUGUSTANA COLLEGE
ROCK ISLAND, ILLINOIS 61201

Founded 1860.

*President:* THOMAS TREDWAY.
*Vice-President:* H. W. SUNDELIUS.
*Director of Institutional Research and Records:* TIMOTHY SCHERMER.
*Director of Admissions:* RALPH E. STARENKO.
*Director of Career Planning and Placement:* (vacant).
*Librarian:* JOHN CALDWELL.
The library contains 239,363 vols.
Number of teachers: 117 full-time, 39 part-time (including 31 full professors).
Number of students: 2,275 full-time, 159 part-time, total 2,434.

DEANS:

*College:* H. W. SUNDELIUS.
*Students:* JOHN W. HULLETT.

### BLACKBURN COLLEGE
700 COLLEGE AVENUE,
CARLINVILLE, ILLINOIS 62626

Telephone: (217) 854-3231.

Founded 1857.

*President:* JOHN ALBERTI, PH.D.
*Provost and Dean:* ARTHUR H. DARKEN.
*Director of Admissions and Records:* DONALD GIX.
*Librarian:* R. L. UNDERBRINK.

The library contains 65,000 vols.
Number of teachers: 38.
Number of students: 539.

### BRADLEY UNIVERSITY
PEORIA, ILLINOIS 61625

Telephone: Peoria 676-7611.

Founded 1897.

*President:* Dr. MARTIN G. ABEGG.
*Vice-President for Academic Affairs:* Dr. JOHN C. HITT.
*Vice-President for Development:* Dr. IAN T. STURROCK.
*Assistant to the President and Dean of Student Services:* Dr. JAMES H. ERICKSON.
*Assistant Vice-President for Life Planning:* Dr. THOMAS HUDDLESTON, Jr.
*Director of Admissions:* ROBERT VOSS.
*Director of Financial Aid:* DAVID PARDIECK.
*Director of Institutional Research and Registrar:* Miss RUTH JASS.
*Librarian:* Dr. ROBERT A. JONES.
Number of teachers: 284.
Number of students: 5,750.

DEANS:

*College of Liberal Arts and Sciences:* Dr. MAX H. KELE.
*Graduate School:* Dr. JAMES BALLOWE.
*College of Business Administration:* Dr. J. TAYLOR SIMS.
*College of Communications and Fine Arts:* Dr. PHILIP WEINBERG.
*College of Education:* Dr. LARRY K. BRIGHT.
*College of Engineering and Technology:* Dr. JAMES B. MATTHEWS.
*College of Continuing Education:* Dr. DONALD M. ALBANITO.
*College of Health Sciences:* Dr. JAMES M. MULLENDORE.

### CHICAGO STATE UNIVERSITY
95TH ST. AT KING DRIVE,
CHICAGO, ILLINOIS 60628

Telephone: (312) 995-2000.

Founded 1867.

State control; Academic year: September to August (three terms).

*President:* BENJAMIN H. ALEXANDER.
*Provost and Academic Vice-President:* WILLIAM W. SUTTON.
*Vice-President for Planning, Finance and Student Support:* PAUL BRINKMAN.
*Librarian:* PATRICK LEONARD.
Number of teachers: 421.
Number of students: 6,998.

Publications: *Illinois Schools Journal* (quarterly), *Second Century* (quarterly alumni magazine), *Campus Line* (quarterly newsletter), annual catalogues.

### COLLEGE OF ST. FRANCIS
500 WILCOX ST.,
JOLIET, ILLINOIS 60435

Telephone: (815) 740-3360.

Founded 1930.

*President:* Dr. JOHN C. ORR.
*Academic Vice-President:* Dr. PHILIP STEINKRAUSS.
*Director of Libraries:* Sr. CAROL ANN NOVAK, O.S.F.
The library contains 119,000 vols.
Number of teachers: 170.
Number of students: 3,251.

Publications: *Bulletin* (annually), *Magazine* (quarterly).

### DEPAUL UNIVERSITY
CHICAGO, ILLINOIS 60604

Telephone: (312) 321-8000.

Chartered as Saint Vincent's College 1898, as DePaul University 1907.

*Chancellor:* Rev. J. R. CORTELYOU, C.M.
*President:* Rev. J. T. RICHARDSON, C.M.
*Treasurer:* Rev. J. PATRICK MURPHY, C.M., A.M.
*Vice-President for Business Affairs:* RALPH BEAUDOIN.
*Vice-President and Dean of Faculties:* Dr. PATRICIA EWERS.
*Vice-President for Student Affairs:* Very Rev. EDWARD F. RILEY, C.M.
*Vice-President for Development and Public Relations:* HERBERT NEWMAN.
*Vice-President for Planning:* HOWARD SULKIN, PH.D.
*Registrar:* R. L. HOEFLER.
*Librarian:* GLENN SCHARFENORTH.
The library contains 390,000 vols.
Number of teachers: 398 (full-time).
Number of students: 13,356.

Publications: *De Paul Magazine* (quarterly), *De Paulia* (weekly), *Law Review* (half-yearly), *Newsline* (bi-weekly).

DEANS:

*Arts and Science:* Dr. RICHARD J. MEISTER.
*Commerce:* Bro. LEO RYAN, C.S.V.
*Graduate:* Dr. JOHN MASTERSON.
*Law:* ELWIN GRIFFITH.
*Music:* FREDERICK MILLER, D.M.A.
*Education:* Dr. WILMA LONGSTREET.
*School for New Learning:* DAVID O. JUSTICE.

### EASTERN ILLINOIS UNIVERSITY
CHARLESTON, ILLINOIS 61920

Telephone: 581-2021.

Founded 1895.

*President:* Dr. DANIEL E. MARVIN, Jr.
*Vice-President for Student Affairs:* Dr. G. D. WILLIAMS.
*Vice-President for Academic Affairs:* Dr. STANLEY RIVES.
*Vice-President for Business Affairs:* Dr. GEORGE MILLER.
*Librarian:* Dr. WILSON LUQUIRE.

Number of teachers: 600.
Number of students: 10,774.
Publication: *Eastern Illinois University General Catalog.*

DEANS:
*School of Education:* Dr. FRANK LUTZ.
*Graduate School:* Dr. LARRY WILLIAMS.
*Arts and Sciences:* Dr. JOHN LAIBLE.

## ELMHURST COLLEGE
190 PROSPECT STREET,
ELMHURST, ILLINOIS 60126
Telephone: (312) 279-4100.

Founded 1871.

*President:* IVAN E. FRICK.
*Dean of College:* PETER SCHMIECHEN.
*Dean of Students:* JAMES CUNNINGHAM.
*Director of Admissions and Financial Aid:* MICHAEL E. DESSIMOZ.
*Director of Development and Public Relations:* KENNETH E. BARTELS.
*Librarian:* MELVIN J. KLATT.

The library contains 141,000 vols.
Number of teachers: 102 (Day Session).
Number of students: 1,708 Day Session, 1,052 Evening Session.

## EUREKA COLLEGE
EUREKA, ILLINOIS 61530
Telephone: (309) 467-3721.

Founded 1855.

*President:* Dr. DANIEL D. GILBERT.
*Dean of the College:* Dr. JERRY D. MCCOY.
*Dean of Admissions:* GEORGE HEARNE.
*Librarian:* DIANE CAUGHRON.

The library contains 78,000 vols.
Number of teachers: 36.
Number of students: 470.

## GEORGE WILLIAMS COLLEGE
555 31ST STREET, DOWNERS GROVE, ILLINOIS 60515
Telephone: 964-3100.

Founded 1890.

*President:* Dr. RICHARD E. HAMLIN.
*Vice-President and Dean of the College:* Dr. J. CLIFFORD HOLMES.
*Registrar:* LAWRENCE J. BORGIONE.
*Librarian:* MARILYN T. THOMPSON.

The library contains 90,000 vols.
Number of teachers: 79 full-time.
Number of students: 1,320.

## GREENVILLE COLLEGE
GREENVILLE, ILLINOIS 62246
Telephone: (618) 664-1840.

Founded 1892.

*President:* Dr. W. RICHARD STEPHENS.
*Vice-President for Academic Affairs and Dean of Faculty:* Dr. RICHARD L. HOLEMON.
*Director of Admissions:* THOMAS D. MORGAN.

The library contains 95,373 vols.
Number of teachers: 50 full-time.
Number of students: 858.
Publication: *Record* (quarterly).

## ILLINOIS BENEDICTINE COLLEGE
LISLE, ILLINOIS 60532
Telephone: (312) 968-7270.

Founded 1887 as St. Procopius College.

*President:* Dr. RICHARD C. BECKER.
*Executive Vice-President:* THOMAS J. DYBA.
*Director of Admissions:* THOMAS RICH.
*Director of Library Services:* B. THOMPSON.

The library contains 100,000 vols.
Number of teachers: 109.
Number of students: 1,500.
Publications: *Illinois Benedictine Magazine*† (quarterly), *Alumni Bulletin*† (quarterly), *President's Annual Report*†.

## ILLINOIS COLLEGE
JACKSONVILLE, ILLINOIS 62650
Telephone: (217) 245-7126.

Founded 1829.

*President:* DONALD C. MUNDINGER.
*Director of Admissions:* MARTHA CLARK.
*Librarian:* R. L. PRATT.

The library contains 90,000 vols.
Number of teachers: 49.
Number of students: 850.

## ILLINOIS INSTITUTE OF TECHNOLOGY
3300 S. FEDERAL ST.,
CHICAGO, ILLINOIS 60616

Formed 1940 by consolidation of Armour Institute of Technology (founded 1892), Lewis Institute (founded 1896).

*President:* T. L. MARTIN, Jr., PH.D.
*Executive Vice-President and Provost:* S. A. GURALNICK, PH.D.
*Vice-President for Finance and Treasurer:* G. B. FENNER, M.B.A.
*Vice-President for Business Affairs:* M. T. TRACHT, A.D.
*Vice-President for Marketing:* A. MCCLURE, B.S.
*Vice-President and Executive Secretary to the Board of Trustees:* M. W. BATES, B.S.
*Admissions and Financial Aid:* W. E. SHACKELFORD, M.MUS.
*Registrar:* M. I. EDISON, M.B.A.
*Librarian:* H. BIBLO, M.E.

The libraries contain 1,444,765 vols.
Number of teachers: 285 full-time, 456 part-time, total 741.
Number of students: 7,056.
Publications: bulletins, research publications.

DEANS:
*College of Architecture, Planning and Design:* G. R. MCSHEFFREY, DIPL. ARCH.
*Armour College of Engineering:* A. VACROUX, PH.D. (acting).
*Lewis College of Sciences and Letters:* R. FILLER, PH.D.
*Chicago-Kent College of Law of I.I.T.:* L. M. COLLENS, J.D.
*Harold Leonard Stuart School of Management and Finance:* A. A. BLUM, PH.D.

DIRECTORS:
*Division of Academic Services:* J. T. DYGDON, M.B.A.
*School of Advanced Studies:* G. T. HIGGINS, PH.D.
*Division of Student Life:* J. W. VICE, A.M.
*Division of Student Counselling:* J. G. FRIEDLAND, PH.D.
*Division of Student Development:* G. E. COOK, M.S.
*Information Services:* J. E. CLOHISY.

AFFILIATED INSTITUTES:
**IIT Research Institute:** f. 1936.
**Institute of Gas Technology:** f. 1941.

## ILLINOIS STATE UNIVERSITY
NORMAL, ILLINOIS 61761
Founded 1857.

*President:* LLOYD I. WATKINS.
*Vice-President and Provost:* LEON E. BOOTHE.
*Director of Admissions:* WILBUR VENERABLE.
*Director of Libraries:* J. W. KRAUS.

Number of teachers: 975.
Number of students: 19,717.

DEANS:
*Undergraduate School:* EUGENE JABKER.
*Graduate School:* C. A. WHITE.
*College of Applied Science and Technology:* JACK E. RAZOR.
*College of Arts and Sciences:* C. EDWARD STREETER.
*College of Business:* ANDREW T. NAPPI.
*College of Education:* BENJAMIN C. HUBBARD.
*College of Fine Arts:* C. BOLEN.
*College of Continuing Education and Public Service:* EDWARD T. ANDERSON.

## ILLINOIS WESLEYAN UNIVERSITY
BLOOMINGTON, ILLINOIS 61701
Chartered 1853.

*President:* ROBERT S. ECKLEY, PH.D.
*Dean:* WENDELL W. HESS, PH.D.
*Business Manager:* KENNETH C. BROWNING.
*Director of Admissions:* J. R. RUOTI.
*Registrar:* J. R. BARBOUR.
*Librarian:* C. D. HIGHUM.

Number of teachers: 124.
Number of students: 1,616.
Publication: *Bulletin* (monthly).

DEANS:

*Dean of Students:* GLENN J. SWICHTENBERG, PH.D.

## KNOX COLLEGE
GALESBURG, ILLINOIS 61401
Founded 1837.

*President:* E. INMAN FOX, PH.D.
*Vice-President for Finance and Treasurer:* LAWRENCE W. LARSON, D.B.A.
*Dean of College and Vice-President for Academic Affairs:* MARY L. EYSENBACH, PH.D.
*Dean of Students:* JACK D. FITZGERALD, PH.D.
*Librarian:* DOUGLAS L. WILSON, PH.D.

The library contains 170,000 vols.
Number of teachers: 85, including 30 professors.
Number of students: 1,050.

Publications: *Knox Bulletin*, *Catalog and Report* (financial statement), *Knox Alumnus* (quarterly), *Directory*, *Knox Idea* (viewbook).

## LAKE FOREST COLLEGE
LAKE FOREST, ILLINOIS 60045
Founded 1857.
Four-year Liberal Arts College.

*President:* EUGENE HOTCHKISS III, PH.D.
*Dean of the Faculty:* BAILEY DONNALLY (acting).
*Registrar:* RUTHANE BOPP, M.A.
*Vice-President for Business Affairs:* THEODORE CARLUS, M.B.A., C.P.A.
*Dean of Student Affairs:* DAVID M. BYERS, M.DIV.
*Librarian:* ARTHUR MILLER, Jr., PH.D

Number of teachers: 83.
Number of students: 1,050.

Publications: *The Stentor*† (weekly), *Spectrum* (6 times a year), *Tusitala* (annually).

## LEWIS UNIVERSITY
ROUTE 53,
ROMEOVILLE, ILLINOIS 60441
Telephone: (815) 838-0500.
Founded 1932.

*President:* Bro. EDWARD FALLON, F.S.C. (acting).
*Vice-President for Academic Affairs:* Dr. DAVID V. CURTIS.
*Vice-President for Business and Finance:* WAYNE DRAUDT (acting).
*Dean of Student Services:* Dr. PAUL KAISER.
*Registrar:* ROBERT KEMPIAK.
*Director of Libraries:* (vacant).

The library contains 110,000 vols.
Number of teachers: 175.
Number of students: 3,000.

DEANS:

*College of Arts and Sciences:* Bro. RAPHAEL MASCARI, F.S.C.
*College of Business:* Dr. KEVIN SPIESS.
*College of Nursing:* Dr. KATHLEEN FENNER.

## LOYOLA UNIVERSITY
CHICAGO, ILLINOIS 60611

Chartered as St. Ignatius College 1870; incorporated as Loyola University 1909.

*President:* Rev. RAYMOND C. BAUMHART, S.J.
*Chancellor:* Rev. JOHN H. REINKE, S.J.
*Provost for the Medical Center:* Dr. RICHARD A. MATRE.
*Vice-President and Dean of Faculties:* Dr. RONALD E. WALKER.
*Vice-President for Student Services:* MARIETTE LeBLANC.
*Vice-President for University and Campus Ministry:* Rev. DONALD J. HAYES, S.J.
*Vice-President and Assistant to the President:* Dr. JAMES D. BARRY.
*Vice-President for Finance:* KARL ZEISLER.
*Vice-President for Administration:* JOHN F. LANGDON.
*Vice-President for Development and Public Relations:* W. D. CONROYD.
*Vice-President for Personnel:* JOHN P. MURRAY.
*Director of Registration and Records:* GEORGE A. HOSTERT, Jr.
*Director of University Libraries:* Dr. ROBERT ENNEN.

The library contains 747,613 vols.
Number of teachers: 1,800.
Number of students: 14,909.

Publications: *Mid-America*, *Dialogue*, *Cadence*, *Restoration and 18th Century Theatre Research*, *Loyola University Psychometric Laboratory Bulletin*, *Journal of the Loyola Historical Society*, *The Business Journal*.

DEANS:

*College of Arts and Sciences (Lake Shore, co-educational):* Rev. LAWRENCE BIONDI, S.J. (acting).
*College of Arts and Sciences (Lewis Towers, co-educational):* Rev. JOHN E. FESTLE, S.J. (Associate Dean).
*University College:* Dr. HENRY R. MALECKI.
*School of Business Administration:* Dr. DONALD G. MEYER.
*Graduate School:* Dr. FRANCIS J. CATANIA.
*School of Law:* CHARLES W. MURDOCK.
*School of Medicine:* Dr. CLARENCE N. PEISS.
*Jesuit School of Theology in Chicago:* Rev. JOHN J. BEGLEY, S.J.
*School of Dentistry:* Dr. RAFFAELE SURIANO.
*School of Social Work:* Dr. CHARLES T. O'REILLY.
*School of Education:* Dr. GERALD L. GUTEK.
*School of Nursing:* Dr. JULIA A. LANE.
*Niles College of Loyola University:* Rev. MARTIN N. WINTERS.
*Graduate School of Business:* Dr. TASSOS G. MALLIARIS (Director).
*Institute of Industrial Relations:* Dr. ALAN J. FREDIAN (Director).
*Institute of Pastoral Studies:* Rev. JEROME O'LEARY, O.P.
*Parmly Hearing Institute:* Dr. WILLIAM A. YOST (Director).
*Erickson Institute of Early Education:* Dr. JOAN COSTELLO.
*Loyola Guidance Centre:* Dr. J. CLIFFORD KASPAR (Director).
*Rome Centre of Liberal Arts, Italy:* Rev. JOHN J. KILGALLEN, S.J.

## MACMURRAY COLLEGE
JACKSONVILLE, ILLINOIS 62650
Founded 1846.

*President:* Dr. B. G. STEPHENS, PH.D.
*Business Manager:* WOLFGANG HERTWECK, M.P.S.
*Dean:* EDWARD J. MITCHELL, PH.D.
*Librarian:* RONALD B. DANIELS, M.L.S.

The library contains 145,000 vols.
Number of teachers: 52, including 15 professors.
Number of students: 743.

Publications: *The Daily Other* (Student Newspaper), *Student Yearbook*, *Annual Catalog*, *MacMurray College News*†, *Montage*.

## MILLIKIN UNIVERSITY
DECATUR, ILLINOIS 62522
Founded 1901.

*President:* Dr. J. ROGER MILLER.
*Provost and Vice-President for Academic Affairs:* Dr. C. RICHARD DECKER.
*Registrar:* Dr. JAMES R. G. OLSON.
*Vice-President for Student Development:* JOSEPH H. HOUSTON.
*Director of the Library:* Dr. CHARLES HALE.

Number of students: 1,530.

Publications: *Millikin University Alumni Bulletin* (quarterly), *Meet Millikin* (quarterly), *The Decaturian* (fortnightly).

DEANS:

*College of Arts and Sciences:* GERALD A. REDFORD.
*School of Music:* Dr. A. WESLEY TOWER.
*School of Business and Industrial Management:* RICHARD A. MANNWEILER.
*School of Nursing:* Dr. MARY SHANKS.

## MONMOUTH COLLEGE
700 EAST BROADWAY,
MONMOUTH, ILLINOIS 61462

Telephone: (309) 457-2311.

Founded 1853.

*President:* Dr. BRUCE HAYWOOD.
*Registrar:* Dr. MILTON L. BOWMNA.
*Librarian:* H. HAUGE.

The library contains 182,000 vols.

Number of teachers: 70.
Number of students: 650.

## MUNDELEIN COLLEGE
6363 SHERIDAN ROAD,
CHICAGO, ILLINOIS 60660

Telephone: (312) 262-8100.

Founded 1930.

*President:* Sister SUSAN RINK, B.V.M.
*Registrar:* Dr. STUART A. GOLDMAN.
*Academic Dean:* Dr. JEAN SWEAT.
*Director of Learning Resources:* E. PRZYBYLSKI.

The library contains 134,267 vols.

Number of teachers: 132.
Number of students: 1,491.

## NATIONAL COLLEGE OF EDUCATION
2840 SHERIDAN ROAD,
EVANSTON, ILLINOIS 60201

Telephone: (312) 256-5150.

Founded 1886.

*President:* ORLEY R. HERRON.
*Registrar:* BETTY L. BURNS.
*Dean of Undergraduate Admissions:* GALE STRAUS.
*Librarian:* E. ARTHUR STUNARD.

The library contains 115,000 vols.

Number of teachers: 94 full-time, 150 part-time.
Number of students: 4,635.

DEANS:

*Graduate School:* DARRELL BLOOM.
*School of Continuing Studies:* WILLIAM ROBINSON.
*Undergraduate College:* EDWARD RISINGER (acting).

## NORTH CENTRAL COLLEGE
30 N. BRAINARD,
NAPERVILLE, ILLINOIS 60540

Telephone: (312) 420-3400.

Founded 1861.

*President:* GAEL D. SWING.
*Director of Admissions:* LLOYD KRUMLAUF.
*Librarian:* HARRIET ARKLIE.

The library contains 95,000 vols.

Number of teachers: 74.
Number of students: 1,198.

## NORTH PARK COLLEGE AND THEOLOGICAL SEMINARY
5125 NORTH SPAULDING AVE.,
CHICAGO, ILLINOIS 60625

Telephone: (312) 583-2700.

Founded 1891.

*President:* Rev. WILLIAM R. HAUSMAN.
*Dean:* Dr. QUENTIN D NELSON.
*Vice-President for Academic Affairs:* Dr. ROBERT SANDIN.
*Director of Records:* Dr. ELMER H. OST.
*Dean of Admissions:* J. E. LUNDEEN.
*Librarian:* Miss BETTY J. HIGHFIELD.

The library contains 390,600 vols.

Number of teachers: 77 full-time, 41 part-time.
Number of students: 1,346.

## NORTHEASTERN ILLINOIS UNIVERSITY
BRYN MAWR AT ST. LOUIS AVE.,
CHICAGO, ILLINOIS 60625

Telephone: (312) 583-4050.

Founded 1961.

*President:* Dr. RONALD WILLIAMS.
*Provost:* Dr. JOHN COWNIE.
*Vice-President for Administrative Affairs:* Dr. W. H. LIENEMANN.
*Vice-President for Student Affairs:* Dr. DANIEL C. KIELSON.
*Vice-President for Development and Public Affairs:* DONN BICHSEL.
*Dean of Student Development:* Dr. R. KIPP HASSELL.
*Director for Admissions and Records:* Dr. ERIC MOCH.
*University Librarian and Director of Learning Services:* Dr. MELVIN GEORGE.

The library contains 390,600 vols.
Number of teachers: 500.
Number of students: 10,346.

DEANS:

*Graduate College:* Dr. V. F. MALEK.
*College of Education:* Dr. AHMED FAREED.
*College of Arts and Sciences:* Dr. F. W. DOBBS.
*Center for Program Development:* Dr. REYNOLD FELDMAN.

## NORTHERN ILLINOIS UNIVERSITY
DEKALB, ILLINOIS 60115

Founded 1895.

*President:* WILLIAM R. MONAT.
*Assistants to President:* W. J. PEMBROKE, K. L. BEASLEY.
*Vice-President and Provost:* JOHN E. LA TOURETTE.
*Vice-President of Student Affairs:* HARRY J. CANON.
*Vice-President, Business Affairs:* R. J. SMITH.
*Director of Development and Alumni Relations:* RICHARD W. UBL.
*Director, University Libraries:* JEAN A. MAJOR.

The library contains 1,100,461 vols. and 530,032 document items.

Number of students: 22,506 (3,558 Extension).

DEANS:

*Graduate School:* DEAN JAROS.
*College of Continuing Education:* CLIVE C. VERI.
*College of Business:* JAMES D. BENSON.
*College of Education:* JOHN H. JOHANSEN.
*College of Professional Studies:* PEGGY SULLIVAN.
*College of Visual and Performing Arts:* R. W. BUGGERT.
*College of Liberal Arts and Sciences:* JAMES D. NORRIS.
*College of Law:* LEONARD STRICKMAN.
*International Programs:* DANIEL WIT.

## NORTHWESTERN UNIVERSITY
EVANSTON, ILLINOIS 60201

Telephone: (312) 492-3741.

Founded 1851.

Private control; Academic year: September to June.

*President:* ROBERT H. STROTZ, PH.D.
*Provost:* RAYMOND W. MACK, PH.D.
*Senior Vice-President for Business and Finance:* LEE ELLIS.
*Vice-President for Research and Dean of Science:* DAVID MINTZER, PH.D.
*Vice-President for Student Affairs:* JIM G. CARLETON, PH.D.
*Vice-President for Institutional Advancement:* JOHN FIELDS, M.B.A.
*Vice-President for Development:* ALLIN W. PROUDFOOT.
*Vice-President for Institutional Relations:* W. I. IHLANFELD, PH.D.
*Registrar:* DONALD G. GWINN, PH.D.
*Librarian:* J. P. MCGOWAN, M.A.

Library: see Libraries.

Number of teachers (full-time): 1,305.
Number of students (full-time): 11,948.

Publications: *Tri-Quarterly* (3 a year), *Alumni News* (6 a year), *Northwestern Engineer* (quarterly), *The Bridge* (quarterly), *The Black Law Journal* (3 a year), *Journal of Criminal Law and Criminology* (quarterly), *Northwestern University Journal of International Law and Business* (2 a year), *The Reporter* (quarterly), *Northwestern University Law Review*.

DEANS:

*Graduate School:* CLARENCE VER STEEG, PH.D.
*Dental School:* N. OLSEN, D.D.S., M.S.D.
*Medical School:* J. E. ECKENHOFF, M.D.
*Kellogg Graduate School of Management:* D. P. JACOBS, PH.D.
*School of Education:* DAVID E. WILEY, PH.D.
*Medill School of Journalism:* IRA W. COLE, M.S.
*School of Law:* DAVID S. RUDER, J.D.

UNIVERSITIES AND COLLEGES—ILLINOIS U.S.A.

*School of Music:* T. MILLER, MUS.A.D., D.MUS.
*School of Speech:* R. V. WOOD, PH.D.
*Technological Institute:* B. A. BOLEY, SC.D.
*Division of Continuing Education:* ELLEN CORLEY, PH.D.
*College of Arts and Sciences:* RUDOLPH H. WEINGARTNER, PH.D.
*Summer Session:* ROBERT L. CHURCH, PH.D.

HEADS OF DEPARTMENTS:

*College of Arts and Sciences:*
  *African-American Studies:* WILLIAM EXUM.
  *Anthropology:* OSWALD WERNER.
  *Art:* EDWARD F. PASCHKE.
  *Art History:* DAVID VAN ZANTEN.
  *Biochemistry and Molecular Biology:* EMANUEL MARGOLIASH.
  *Biological Sciences:* SIDNEY B. SIMPSON (acting).
  *Chemistry:* LOUIS A. ALLRED.
  *Classics:* JOHN WRIGHT.
  *Economics:* DALE MORTENSEN.
  *English:* HAROLD KAPLAN (acting).
  *French and Italian:* GERALD MEAD.
  *Geography:* MICHAEL DACEY.
  *Geological Sciences:* E. H. T. WHITTEN.
  *German:* VOLKER O. DURR.
  *History:* DAVID JORAVSKY.
  *History and Literature of Religions:* EDMUND F. PERRY.
  *Linguistics:* GILBERT KRULEE.
  *Mathematics:* MEYER DWASS.
  *Philosophy:* EDWIN M. CURLEY.
  *Physics and Astronomy:* KUNDAN S. SINGWI.
  *Political Science:* JENNETH JANDA.
  *Psychology:* RICHARD R. BOOTZIN.
  *Slavic Languages:* IRWIN WEIL.
  *Sociology:* ARNOLD S. FELDMAN.
  *Spanish and Portuguese:* CYRUS DECOSTER.

*Kellogg Graduate School of Management:*
  *Accounting and Information Systems:* BALA V. BALACHANDRAN.
  *Finance:* JOHN BOYD.
  *Marketing:* SIDNEY J. LEVY.
  *Organization Behavior:* ROBERT DEWAR.
  *Policy and Environment:* LAWRENCE LAVENGOOD.
  *Managerial Economics and Decision Sciences:* MARK SATTERTHWAITE.

*Medill School of Journalism:*
  *Graduate Advertising:* VERNON R. FRYBURGER.
  *Editorial, Undergraduate:* CRAIG KLUGMAN.

*School of of Music:*
  *Church Music and Organ:* R. G. ENRIGHT.
  *Conducting and Performing Organization:* JOHN PAYNTER.
  *Music Education:* BENNETT REIMER.
  *Music History and Literature:* THEODORE KARP.
  *Performance:*
    *Piano:* ARTHUR TOLLEFSON.
    *Strings:* MYRON KARTMAN.
    *Voice:* RICHARD E. ALDERSON.
    *Winds and Percussion:* FRED HEMKE.
  *Theory and Composition:* JOHN BUCCHERI.

*School of Speech:*
  *Communication Studies:* DAVID H. ZAREFSKY.
  *Communicative Disorders:* ROY A. KOENIGSKNECHT.
  *Interpretation:* LILLA A. HESTON.
  *Radio, TV, Film:* JACK C. ELLIS.
  *Speech Education:* KATHLEEN M. GALVIN.
  *Theatre:* LESLIE A. HINDERYCKX.

*Technological Institute:*
  *Chemical Engineering:* JOSHUA S. DRANOFF.
  *Civil Engineering:* RAYMOND J. KRIZEK.
  *Electrical Engineering and Computer Sciences:* S. S. YAU.
  *Engineering Sciences and Applied Mathematics:* RAYMOND A. KLIPHARDT.
  *Industrial Engineering and Management Sciences:* ARTHUR P. HURTER.
  *Materials Science and Engineering:* MICHAEL M. MESHII.
  *Mechanical and Nuclear Engineering:* M. C. YUEN.

*Dental School:*
  *Biological Materials:* EVAN H. GREENER.
  *Cleft Palate:* MORTON S. ROSEN.
  *Dental Hygiene:* PATRICIA PHAGAN.
  *Endodontics:* MICHAEL A. HEUER.
  *Fixed Prosthodontics:* GILBERT I. BRINSDEN.
  *Operative Dentistry:* RUSSELL ANDERSON (acting).
  *Oral Biology:* ARTHUR VEIS.
  *Oral Diagnosis:* STEPHEN SMITH, THOMAS M. LUND (Radiology).
  *Oral and Maxillofacial Surgery:* DONALD E. CASEY.
  *Orthodontics:* HAROLD T. PERRY, Jr.
  *Pedodontics:* R. WILLIAM CORNELL.
  *Periodontics:* PETER J. ROBINSON.
  *Removable Prosthodontics:* ROSS L. TAYLOR.

*Medical and Dental Schools Basic Sciences (Combined):*
  *Anatomy:* JOSEPH PYSH.
  *Microbiology-Immunology:* PHILIP PATERSON.
  *Pathology:* DANTA SCARPELLI.
  *Pharmacology:* TOSHIO NARAHASHI.
  *Physiology:* JAMES C. HOUK.
  *Molecular Biology:* ROBERT H. ROWND.

*Medical School:*
  *Anesthesia:* EDWARD A. BRUNNER.
  *Cancer Center:* NATHANIEL BERLIN.
  *Community Medicine:* JEREMIAH STAMLER.
  *Dermatology:* HENRY H. ROENIGK, Jr.
  *Endocrinology, Metabolism and Nutrition:* NORBERT FREINKEL.
  *Medicine:* ROY PATTERSON.
  *Neurology:* DONALD H. HARTER.
  *Obstetrics and Gynecology:* JOHN J. SCIARRA.
  *Ophthalmology:* DAVID SHOCH.
  *Orthopedic Surgery:* MICHAEL SCHAFER.
  *Otolaryngology and Maxillofacial Surgery:* GEORGE SISSON.
  *Pediatrics:* HENRY L. NADLER.
  *Psychiatry:* HAROLD VISOTSKY.
  *Radiology:* LEE F. ROGERS.
  *Rehabilitation Medicine:* HENRY B. BETTS.
  *Surgery:* JOHN M. BEAL.
  *Urology:* JOHN T. GRAYHACK.

### OLIVET NAZARENE COLLEGE
P.O.B. 592, KANKAKEE, ILLINOIS 60901
Telephone: (815) 939-5011.
Founded 1907.

*President:* LESLIE PARROTT, PH.D.
*Registrar:* JIM KNIGHT, M.S.
*Dean of Admissions:* R. QUANSTROM.
*Librarian:* A. WIENS, M.S.
The library contains 100,000 volumes.
Number of teachers: 110.
Number of students: 2,150.

### PRINCIPIA COLLEGE
ELSAH, ILLINOIS 62028
Telephone: (618) 374-2131.
Founded 1910.

*President:* ARTHUR F. SCHULZ, Jr., M.A.
*Dean:* JOHN E. G. BOYMAN, M.A.
*Dean of the Faculty:* MARY LU FENNELL., M.A., PH.D.
*Registrar:* CAROLYN BOOTH, B.A.
*Director of Admissions:* MARTHA QUIRK, B.A.
*Librarian:* PATRICIA STEVENS, M.S.L.S.
The library contains 125,000 vols.
Number of teachers: 90.
Number of students: 875.

### QUINCY COLLEGE
1831 COLLEGE AVENUE, QUINCY, ILLINOIS 62301
Telephone: (217) 222-8020.
Founded 1859; Chartered in 1873.

*President:* Rev. GABRIEL BRINKMAN, O.F.M.
*Registrar:* EDWARD MAYER.
*Dean of Admissions:* R. SMITH.
*Academic Dean:* K. CONROY.
*Dean of Students:* J. CERNECH.
*Business Manager:* T. MILLER.
*Librarian:* Rev. V. KINGERY, O.F.M.
The library contains 200,000 vols.
Number of teachers: 95.
Number of students: 1,750.

### ROCKFORD COLLEGE
5050 EAST STATE ST., ROCKFORD, ILLINOIS 61101
Co-educational college founded 1847.

*President:* NORMAN L. STEWART, PH.D.

*Vice-President and Dean of the College:* G. E. WESNER, PH.D.
*Dean of Enrolment Planning:* CHARLES WHARTON, M.A.
*Librarian:* J. T. MICHNA, M.S.
  The library contains 125,000 vols.
  Number of teachers: 57, including 16 professors.
  Number of students: 850 women, 650 men, total 1,100.
  Publications: *Bulletin†, Information Pamphlet.*

## ROOSEVELT UNIVERSITY
430 SOUTH MICHIGAN AVENUE, CHICAGO, ILLINOIS 60605
Telephone: 341-3500.
Founded 1945.

*President:* ROLF A. WEIL, PH.D.
*Controller:* H. BLAND, C.P.A.
*Registrar:* D. E. STEERE, M.S.
*Librarian:* A. JONES, M.A.
  The library contains 310,000 vols.
  Number of teachers: 456 (184 full-time and 272 part-time).
  Number of students: 7,000.
  Publications: *Business and Society, Annual Catalogs, Roosevelt University Magazine.*

DEANS:
*Faculties and Graduate Division:* ALFRED L. MOYE, PH.D.
*College of Arts and Science:* JEROME FLEMING, PH.D.
*College of Business Administration:* DOUGLAS F. LAMONT, PH.D.
*Chicago Musical College:* GEORGE H. WILSON, PH.D. (acting)
*College of Continuing Education:* LEE PORTER, ED.D.
*College of Education:* CURTIS C. MELNICK, ED.D. (acting).
*Students:* DOMINIC MARTIA, PH.D.

## ROSARY COLLEGE
RIVER FOREST, ILLINOIS 60305
Founded 1901.

*President:* Sister CANDIDA LUND.
*Academic Dean:* NORMAN CARROLL.
*Dean of Admissions:* JOHN BALLHEIM.
*Registrar:* SHIRLEY HAINES.
*Vice-President for Business Affairs:* JOHN P. BRADY.
*Director of Development:* Sister VIRGINIA TURNER.
*Dean of Graduate School of Library Science:* Sister LAURETTA MCCUSKER.
*Librarian:* Sister MARY FIELD.
  The library contains 227,000 vols.
  Number of teachers: 127.
  Number of students: 1,575.

## SAINT XAVIER COLLEGE
3700 WEST 103RD ST., CHICAGO, ILLINOIS 60655
Telephone: 779-3300.
Founded 1847.

*President:* Sister M. IRENAEUS CHEKOURAS.
*Director of Admissions:* ROBERT J. FITZPATRICK.
*Librarian:* CHRISTOPHER MILLSON-MARTULA.
  The library contains 67,000 vols.
  Number of teachers: 107.
  Number of students: 2,133.

## SCHOOL OF THE ART INSTITUTE OF CHICAGO
COLUMBUS DRIVE AND JACKSON BOULEVARD, CHICAGO, ILLINOIS 60603
Telephone: (312) 443-3700.
Founded 1866.

*Director:* DONALD J. IRVING.
*Dean:* ROGER GILMORE.
  Libraries of 141,470 vols.
  Number of teachers: 160.
  Number of students: 1,157.

## SHIMER COLLEGE
438 N. SHERIDAN RD., WAUKEGAN, ILLINOIS 60085
Telephone: (312) 623-8400.
Founded 1853.

*Executive Officer:* DON P. MOON.
*Dean of the College:* RICHARD W. BEESON.
*Librarian:* MARGUERITE P. MCBRIDE.
  The library contains 31,000 vols.
  Number of teachers: 26.
  Number of students: 167.

## SOUTHERN ILLINOIS UNIVERSITY —CARBONDALE
CARBONDALE, ILLINOIS 62901
Telephone: (618) 453-2121.
Founded 1869; State control.

*President:* ALBERT SOMIT, PH.D.
*Director of Admissions:* B. K. BROWNING, PH.D.
  The library contains 1,700,000 vols.
  Number of students: 22,693.
  Publication: *The Daily Egyptian.*

DEANS:
*Graduate School:* JOHN JACKSON, PH.D. (acting).
*College of Education:* E. J. CLARK, PH.D.
*College of Liberal Arts:* JAMES LIGHT, PH.D.
*College of Science:* NORMAN J. DOORENBOS, PH.D.
*School of Agriculture:* G. H. KROENING, PH.D.
*School of Business and Administration:* JOHN DARLING, PH.D.
*College of Communications and Fine Arts:* C. B. HUNT, PH.D.
*School of Technical Careers:* A. L. PRATT, ED.D.
*College of Human Resources:* SAMUEL GOLDMAN, PH.D.

*College of Engineering and Technology:* KENNETH TEMPELMEYER, PH.D.
*School of Law:* DAN HOPSON, LL.M.
*Student Affairs:* BRUCE R. SWINBURNE, PH.D.
*School of Medicine:* R. H. MOY, M.D.
*Library Affairs:* KENNETH PETERSON, PH.D.
*General Academic Programmes:* JEWELL FRIEND, PH.D.
*Continuing Education:* ROBERT RATCLIFFE, PH.D.

## SOUTHERN ILLINOIS UNIVERSITY —EDWARDSVILLE
EDWARDSVILLE, ILLINOIS 62026
Telephone: (618) 692-2475.
Founded 1957; State control.

*President:* EARL LAZERSON.
*Vice-President and Provost:* BARBARA J. TETERS.
*Directors:* JAMES R. BUCK (Development and Public Affairs), LUTHER D. STATLER (Supporting Services), EARL S. BEARD (Personnel Services), JOHN R. REINER (Planning and Resource Management).
  The library contains 705,000 vols.
  Number of students: 11,342.
  Publications: *Papers on Language and Literature†, Sou'Western.*

DEANS:
*School of Business:* D. J. WERNER, PH.D.
*School of Education:* F. DONALD CARVER, PH.D.
*School of Fine Arts and Communications:* H. L. WHITE, PH.D.
*School of Humanities:* CAROL A. KEENE, PH.D.
*School of Science and Technology:* THOMAS P. ANDERSON.
*School of Social Science:* SUZANNE JACOBITTI, PH.D.
*Dean of Students:* DANIEL K. DOELGER, PH.D.
*School of Dental Medicine:* HERBERT BUTTS.
*University College:* H. L. WHITE, PH.D.
*Graduate School:* VAUGHNIE LINDSAY, PH.D.
*School of Nursing:* P. R. FORNI, PH.D.
*Lovejoy Library:* JOHN C. ABBOTT, PH.D. (Director).

## UNIVERSITY OF CHICAGO
5801 S. ELLIS AVE., CHICAGO, ILLINOIS 60637
Telephone: 753-3001.

Incorporated in 1857 as the first University of Chicago, and in 1890 as the University of Chicago (at the present site).

*President:* HANNA H. GRAY.
*Provost:* D. GALE JOHNSON.
*Vice-President for Business and Finance:* WILILAM B. CANNON.

UNIVERSITIES AND COLLEGES—ILLINOIS U.S.A.

*Vice-President for Academic Resources and Planning:* JONATHAN F. FANTON.
*Vice-President for Community Affairs:* JONATHAN KLEINBARD.
*Vice-President for Public Affairs:* D. J. R. BRUCKNER.
*Vice-President and Dean of Students:* C. D. O'CONNELL.
*Vice-President and Comptroller:* H. E. BELL.
*Treasurer:* MARY PETRIE.
*Registrar:* MAXINE H. SULLIVAN.
Library: see Libraries.
Number of teachers: 1,021.
Number of students: 7,937.

DEANS:

*The College:* JONATHAN Z. SMITH.
*School of Business:* R. N. ROSETT.
*Divinity School:* J. M. KITAGAWA.
*Graduate Library School:* DON R. SWANSON.
*Law School:* GERHARD CASPER.
*School of Medicine:* ROBERT B. URETZ.
*School of Social Service Administration:* MARGARET K. ROSENHEIM.
*Graduate School of Education:* P. W. JACKSON.
*Students:* C. D. O'CONNELL.
*Biological Sciences:* ROBERT B. URETZ.
*Humanities:* K. J. WEINTRAUB.
*Physical Sciences:* A. V. CREWE.
*Social Sciences:* W. H. KRUSKAL.


## UNIVERSITY OF ILLINOIS

URBANA, ILLINOIS 61801

Telephone: (217) 333-1000.
Chartered 1867.
State control.

*President:* STANLEY O. IKENBERRY, PH.D.
*Executive Vice-President:* R. W. BRADY, PH.D.
*Vice-President for Academic Affairs:* PETER E. YANKWICH, PH.D.
Library: see Libraries.
Number of teachers: 4,852 (fulltime).
Number of students: 60,705.

### University of Illinois at Urbana-Champaign

URBANA, ILLINOIS 61801
Telephone: (217) 333-1000.

*Chancellor:* J. E. CRIBBETT, J.D. (acting).
*Vice-Chancellor for Academic Affairs:* E. L. GOLDWASSER, PH.D.
*Vice-Chancellor for Administrative Affairs:* D. F. WENDEL.
*Vice-Chancellor for Campus Affairs:* S. R. LEVY.
*Vice-Chancellor for Research:* T. L. BROWN.

*Director of Admission and Records:* G. R. ENGELGAU (acting).
*Librarian:* H. C. ATKINSON.

DEANS:

*College of Liberal Arts and Sciences:* W. F. PROKASY, PH.D.
*College of Commerce and Business Administration:* V. K. ZIMMERMANN, PH.D., C.P.A.
*College of Engineering:* D. C. DRUCKER, PH.D.
*College of Agriculture:* O. G. BENTLEY, PH.D.
*College of Education:* J. R. BURNETT, PH.D.
*College of Fine and Applied Arts:* J. H. MCKENZIE, M.A.
*College of Law:* P. H. HAY, J.D.
*College of Communications:* J. W. CAREY, PH.D.
*College of Applied Life Studies:* A. V. SAPORA, PH.D. (acting).
*School of Social Work:* F. H. ITZEN, M.A. (acting).
*Graduate College:* T. L. BROWN, PH.D.
*College of Veterinary Medicine:* R. E. DIERKS, PH.D., D.V.H.
*School of Basic Medical Sciences:* D. K. BLOOMFIELD, M.D.
*Graduate School of Library Science:* C. H. DAVIS, PH.D.
*Office of Continuing Education and Public Service:* D. A. DAHL, ED.D. (Director).
*Institute for Environmental Studies:* B. B. EWING, PH.D. (Director).
*Institute of Aviation:* H. L. TAYLOR, PH.D.
*Institute of Labor and Industrial Relations:* W. H. FRANKE, PH.D. (Director).

PROFESSORS:

*College of Agriculture:*
*Agricultural Administration:*
EVANS, J. F., Agricultural Communications

*Agricultural Economics:*
BAKER, C. B.
BARRY, P. J.
BOCK, C. A.
BRINEGAR, G. K.
BURDGE, R. J.
CLAAR, J. B.
DOVRING, F., Land Economics
DUE, JEAN M.
ENGLAND, G. M., Food Marketing
ERICKSON, D. E., Farm Management Extension
FETTIG, L. P.
FLIEGEL, F. C., Rural Sociology
FREY, T. L., Agricultural Finance
GUITHER, H. D., Agricultural Policy
HALCROW, H. G.
HERBST, J. H., Farm Management
HILL, L. D., Agricultural Marketing
HINTON, R. A., Farm Management
JUDGE, G. G.
KESLER, R. P., Farm Management
LEUTHOLD, R. M.
MUELLER, A. G., Farm Management
PADBERG, D. I.
ROBINSON, J. W., Jr., Rural Economy
ROUSH, J. R.
SCHMIDT, S. C., Agricultural Marketing and Policy
SCHWEITZER, H. J.

SCOTT, J. T., Farm Management and Production Economics
SEITZ, W. D.
SIMS, F. M., Farm Management Extension
SMITH, D. G.
SOFRANKO, A. J., Rural Sociology
SPITZE, R. G.
STICE, L. F., Grain Marketing Extension
SWANSON, E. R., Farm Management and Production Economics
THOMPSON, W. N., Farm Management and Policy
VAN ES, J. C.
WEST, V. I., Rural Sociology
WILKEN, D. F., Farm Management Extension
WILLIAMS, M. S.

*Agricultural Engineering:*
BUTLER, B. J.
CURTIS, J. O.
DAY, D. L.
DRABLOS, C. J. W.
ESPENSCHIED, R. F.
GOERING, C. E.
HUNT, D. L.
JEDELE, D. G.
JONES, B. A.
LEMBKE, W. D.
MUEHLING, A.
OLVER, E. F.
RODDA, E. D.
SHOVE, G. C.
SIEMENS, J. C.
STEINBERG, M. P.
WAKELAND, H. L.
YOERGER, R. R.

*Agricultural Entomology:*
JAYCOP, E. R.
KOGAN, M.
LUCKMANN, W. H.
METCALF, R. L.
MOORE, S.
WALDBAUER, G. P.

*Agronomy:*
ALEXANDER, D. E., Plant Genetics
BEAVERS, A. H., Soil Mineralogy
BROWN, C. M., Plant Breeding
BURGER, A. W.
CARMER, S. G., Biometry
DEWET, J. M. J., Plant Cytogenics
DUDLEY, J. W., Plant Genetics
FEHRENBACHER, J. B., Pedology
GRAFFIS, D. W., Forage Crop Extension
HADLEY, H. H., Plant Genetics
HAGEMAN, R. H., Plant Genetics
HANSON, J. B., Plant Physiology
HARLAN, J. R., Plant Genetics
HASSETT, J. J., Soils
HINESLY, T. D., Soil Ecology
HITTLE, CARL B., Plant Breeding
HOEFST, R. C., Soil Fertility
HOWELL, R. W.
HYMOWITZ, T., Plant Genetics
JACKOBS, J. A., Crop Production
JONES, R. L., Soil Mineralogy and Ecology
KNAKE, E. L., Weed Extension
KOEPPE, D. E., Plant Physiology
KURTZ, L. T., Soil Fertility
LAMBERT, R. J., Plant Genetics
LAUGHNAN, J. R., Plant Genetics
MCGLAMERY, M.D.
MCKIBBEN, G. E.
MILLER, D. A., Plant Breeding
OSCHWALD, W. R.
PECK, T. R., Soil Chemistry
SCOTT, W. O., Crop Extension
SEIF, R. D., Biometry
SLIFE, F. W., Crop Production
STEVENSON, F. J., Soil Chemistry
THORNE, M. D.

WALKER, W. M., Biometry and Data Processing
WELCH, L. F.
WIDHOLM, J. M., Plant Physiology

*Animal Science:*
BAKER, D. H.
BANKS, E. M.
BECKER, D. E.
BENTLEY, O. G.
CORBIN, J. E.
CURTIS, S. E.
DZIUK, P. J.
FORBES, R. M., Nutritional Biochemistry
GARRIGUS, U. S.
HARRISON, P. C.
HOLLIS, G. R.
JENSEN, A. H., Animal Nutrition
JOHNSON, H. S., Poultry Extension
MISTRY, S. P., Biochemistry
NORTON, H. W., Statistical Design and Analysis
RASMUSEN, B. A., Animal Genetics
RICKETTS, G. E.
RIDLEN, S. F., Poultry Extension

*County Agricultural Extension:*
BANNON, J. J.

*Dairy Science:*
BRYANT, M. P., Microbiology
CAMPBELL, J. R., Dairy Husbandry
CLARK, J. H., Nutrition
CRAGLE, R. G.
DAVIS, C. L., Nutrition
GOMES, W. R.
HAYS, R. L., Physiology
HUTJENS, M. F.
LARSON, B. L., Biological Chemistry
LODGE, J. R., Physiology

*Family and Consumer Economics:*
DUNSING, M. M.
MAGRABI, F. M.

*Food Science:*
JOHNSTON, P. V.
KUMMEROW, F. A., Food Chemistry
NELSON, R. A.
NISHIDA, T.
PERKINS, E. G.
RODDA, E. D.
SIEDLER, A. J.
STEINBERG, M. P., Food Engineering
TOBIAS, J., Dairy Technology
VISEK, W. J.
WEI, L. S.
WHITNEY, R. McL., Food Chemistry
WITTER, L. D., Food Microbiology

*Foods and Nutrition:*
HACKLER, L. R.
OREILLY, L. E.

*Forestry:*
BAZZAZ, F.
CLOW, P., Wood Science
GILMORE, A. R.
KARR, J. R.
KOEPPE, D. E.
PERCIVAL, D. H., Research, Wood Technology and Utilization
ROLFE, G. L.

*Human Development and Family Ecology:*
SMITH, R. B.

*Horticulture:*
CARBONNEAU, M. C., Floriculture Extension
COURTER, J. W.
DAYTON, D. F., Plant Breeding
DICKINSON, D. B., Jr., Plant Physiology
GEORGE, W. L., Jr.
HOPEN, H. J.

NELSON, W. R., Jr.
REBEIZ, C. A., Plant Physiology
RHODES, A. M.
SIMONS, R. K., Pomology
SPLITTSTOESSER, W. E., Plant Physiology
TITUS, J. S., Pomology

*Plant Pathology:*
FORD, R. E.
GOODMAN, R. M.
GOTTLIEB, D.
SHAW, P. D., Biochemistry
SHURTLEFF, M. C.
SINCLAIR, J. B.

*Textiles and Interior Design:*
MEAD, M. E., Clothing

*Veterinary Programs in Agriculture:*
BEVILL, R. F.
BUCK, W. B.
DIERKS, R. E.
FITZGERALD, P. R., Veterinary Research
HANSEN, L. E., Veterinary Research
JACKSON, G. L.
LEVINE, N. D., Veterinary Research
MANSFIELD, M. E.
McQUEEN, R. O.
PICKARD, J. R.
RISTIC, M.
SEGRE, D.
SIMON, J., Pathology and Hygiene
WAGNER, W. C.
WOODS, G. T., Veterinary Research

*Vocational Agriculture:*
COURSON, R. L.
ESPENSHIED, R. F.
HERBST, J. H.

**College of Commerce and Business Administration:**

*Accountancy:*
BEDFORD, N. M.
BRIGHTON, G. D.
FESS, P. E.
HOLZER, H. P.
JOHNSON, O. E.
McKEOWN, J. C.
MANES, R. P.
NEUMANN, F. L.
PERRY, K. W.
SCHOENFELD, H. M.
SMITH, C. H.
ZIMMERMAN, V. K.

*Business Administration:*
ANDREASEN, A. R.
BEDFORD, N. M.
EVANS, R. V.
FERBER, R.
GARDNER, D. M., Marketing
HILL, R. M.
HINOMOTO, H.
LINOWES, D. F.
NEGANDHI, A. R.
OLDHAM, G. R.
PONDY, L. R.
PRIMEAUX, W. J., Jr.
ROBERTS, D. M.
ROTH, A. E.
ROWLAND, K. M.
SALANCIK, G. R.
SCHOENFELD, H. M.
SHETH, J. N.
SIMON, J. L.
SUDMAN, S.
THOMAS, H.
THOMAS, W. E., Jr.
WINTER, F. M.

*Economics:*
BAER, W.
BRANDIS, R.

BREMS, H. J.
DUE, J. F.
FERBER, M. A.
FERBER, R.
FRANKEL, M.
GIERTZ, J. F.
GOTTHEIL, F. M.
HARTMAN, P. T.
HEINS, A. J.
HODGMAN, D. R.
JUDGE, G. G.
McMAHON, W. H.
MILLAR, J. R.
MIRMAN, L.
NEAL, L. O.
NEWBOLD, P.
PHILLIPS, J. D., Jr.
RESEK, R. W.
SCHRAN, P.
SHUPP, F. R.
SIMON, J. L.
SPRENKLE, C. M.
TAIRA, K.
USELDING, P. J.
WELLS, P. J.
YANCEY, T. A.

*Finance:*
BRYAN, W. R.
CAMMACK, T. E.
DOHERTY, N. A.
GENTRY, J. A.
LEE, C. F.
LINKE, C. M.

*Bureau of Economics and Business Research:*
FERBER, R. (Research)
PHILLIPS, J. D., Jr. (Research)
RESEK, R. W.
USELDING, P. J.

**College of Education:**
Administration, Higher and Continuing Education:
BURLINGAME, M.
CORBALLY, J. E.
HENDERSON, R. A.
HOUSE, E. R.
SERGIOVANNI, T. Y.

*Educational Psychology:*
ANDERSON, R. C.
BRASKAMP, L. A.
CAMPIONE, A. B.
GOULET, L. R.
GRONLUND, N. E.
HAM, W. S.
HARMON, L. W.
HILL, J. H.
HILL, K. T.
HUMPHREYS, L. G.
JONES, R. S.
LINN, R. L.
McCONKIE, G. W.
MAEHR, M. L.
McINTYRE, C. J.
ORTONY, A. J.
ROSENSHINE, B.
STAKE, R. E.
TATSUOKA, M.
WEST, C. K.
ZACCARIA, J.

*Elementary and Early Childhood Education:*
DAVIS, R. B.
DENNY, T.
DURKIN, M. D.
EASLEY, J. A., Jr.
EVERTTS, E.
KATZ, L. G., Early Childhood Education
LERCH, H. H.
MANOLAKES, T.
PEARSON, P. D.
PURVES, A. C., English
RATHS, J. D.

# UNIVERSITIES AND COLLEGES—ILLINOIS (UNIVERSITY OF) U.S.A.

RODGERS, F. A.
RUBIN, L. J.
SHORESMAN, P. B., Science Education

*Educational Policy Studies:*
BURNETT, J. R., Philosophy of Education
ENNIS, R. H., Philosophy of Education
FEINBERG, W.
KARIER, C. J., History of Education
MCMURRAY, F., Philosophy of Education
PESHKIN, A. J., Comparative Education
SMITH, R. A., Cultural and Educational Policy
TROIKE, R. O.
VIOLAS, P. C., History of Education

*Secondary and Continuing Education:*
BRAUNFELD, P. G.
COLWELL, R. J.
COX, C. B.
JOHNSON, W. D..
METCALF, L. E
ROSEN, S.
TRAVERS, K. J.
WALKER, J. L.
WESTBURY, I. D.

*Special Education:*
HENDERSON, R. A.
JORDAN, LAURA J.
KARNES, MERLE
LILLY, M. S.
SPRAGUE, R. L.

*Vocational and Technical Education:*
EVANS, R. N.
GRIGGS, M. B.
HEMP, P. E.
KAZANAS, H. C.
SPITZE, H. T.
TOMLINSON, R. W.
WENTLING, T. L.

**College of Engineering:**
*Aeronautical Engineering:*
BOND, C. E.
HILTON, H. H.
HOPKINS, C. O.
KRIER, H.
LIN, YUKEWNG M.
ORMSBEE, A. I.
PRUSSING, J. E.
ROSCOE, S. N.
SENTMAN, L. H., III
STREHLOW, R. A.
YEN, SHEE MANG.
ZAK, A. R.

*Ceramic Engineering:*
BERGER, R. L.
BERGERON, C. G.
BROWN, S. D.
NELSON, J. A.
PAYNE, D. A.
WILLIAMS, W. S.
YOUNG, J. F.

*Chemical Engineering:*
ALKIRE, R. C.
DRICKAMER, H. G.
ECKERT, C. A.
HANRATTY, T. J.
SCHMITZ, R. A.
WESTWATER, J. W.

*Civil Engineering:*
ANG, A.
BAERWALD, J. E., Transportation and Traffic Engineering
BARENBERG, E. J.
BERGER, R. L.
BOYCE, D. E., Transportation and Regional Science
CHILTON, A. B.
CHOW, VEN TE

CORDING, E. J.
DAVISSON, M. T.
DEMPSEY, B. J.
DRUCKER, D. C.
ENGELBRECHT, R., Environmental Engineering
EUBANKS, R. A.
EWING, B. B.
GAMBLE, W. L.
GURFINKEL, G.
HALL, W. J.
HALTIWANGER, J. D.
HENDRON, A. J., Jr.
HERRIN, M.
KARARA, H. M.
KESLER, C. E.
KHACHATURIAN, N.
LAWRENCE, F. V.
LIEBMAN, J. C., Environmental Engineering
LOPEZ, L. A.
LOWRY, W. P.
MELIN, J. W.
MESRI, G.
MOSBORG, R. J.
MURTHA, J. P., Structural and Hydraulic Engineering
PECKNOLD, D.
PFEFFER, J. T., Sanitary Engineering
ROBINSON, A. R.
SCHNOBRICH, W. C.
SINNAMON, G. K.
SNOEYINK, V. L.
SOZEN, M. A.
STALLMEYER, J. E.
STUKEL, J. J.
TANG, W.
THOMPSON, M. R.
UBN, Y.-K.
WONG, K. W.
YEN, B. C.
YOUNG, U. F.

*Computer Science:*
GEAR, C. W.
KUCK, D. L.
LEVY, A.
LIU, C. L.
MULLER, D. E.
MUROGA, S.
POPPELBAUM, W.
PREPARATA, F. P.
RAY, S. R.
ROBERTSON, J. E.
SAMEH, A. H.
SLOTNICK, D. L.
SNYDER, J. N.

*Electrical Engineering:*
ALBRIGHT, W. G.
ANNER, G. E.
BITZER, D. L.
BOWHILL, S. A.
BROWN, R. M.
CHIEN, R. T.
COLEMAN, P. D.
CROWLEY, J. M.
CRUZ, J. B., Jr.
DAVIDSON, E. S.
DESCHAMPS, G. A.
DE TEMPLE, T. A.
DUNN, F.
DYSON, J. D.
EMERY, W. L.
ERNST, E. W.
GADDY, O. L.
GARDNER, C. S.
HADDAD, A. H.
HANDLER, P.
HANG, D. F.
HELM, M. S.
HESS, K.
HOLONYAK, N., Jr.
HOLSHOUSER, D. F.
HUANG, T. S.

HUNSINGER, B. J.
KOKOTOVIC, P. V.
KUO, B.
LEE, S. W.
LIU, C. H.
LO, Y. T.
MAST, P. E.
MAYEDA, W.
MAYES, P. E.
METZE, G. A.
MILEY, G. H.
MITTRA, R.
MUROGA, S.
MURRELL, T. A.
PERKINS, W. R.
PINES, D.
POPPELBAUM, W.
PREPARATA, F. B.
PURSLEY, M. B.
RAO, N. N.
RAY, S. R.
ROBERTSON, J. E.
SAH, CHIH TANG
SECHRIST, C. F., Jr.
SMITH, L. G.
STILLMAN, G. E.
STREETMAN, B. G.
SWENSON, G. W., Jr.
TRICK, T. N.
TURNBULL, R. J.
VAN VALKENBURG, M. E.
VERDEYEN, J. T.
WAX, N.
YEH, KUNG CHIE

*General Engineering:*
CONRY, T. F.
DOBROVOLNY, J. S.
KUZNETSOV, E. N.

*Highway Traffic Safety Center:*
BAERWALD, J. E.

*Mechanical and Industrial Engineering:*
ADDY, A. L.
BAREITHER, H. D.
BAYNE, J. W.
CHAO, BEI TSE
CHATO, J. C.
CHEN, M. M.
CHOW, WEN LUNG
FRIEDERICH, A. G.
GREENE, J. E.
HERTIG, B. A.
JONES, B. G.
KORST, H. H.
LEACH, J. L.
LECKIE, F. A.
MARTIN, R. J.
PIGAGE, L. C., Industrial Engineering
SOO, SHAO LEE
STOECKER, W. F.
STUKEL, J. J.
WHITE, R. A.
YEN, S. M.

*Metallurgy and Mining Engineering:*
ALTSTETTER, C. J., Physical Metallurgy
BIRNBAUM, H. K., Physical Metallurgy
BOHL, R. W., Metallurgy
DE WITTE, A. J., Petroleum Engineering
EHRLICH, G., Physical Metallurgy
LAWRENCE, F. V., Metallurgical Engineering
METZGER, M., Physical Metallurgy
ROWLAND, T. J., Physical Metallurgy
WAYMAN, C. M., Metallurgy Engineering
WERT, C. A., Physical Metallurgy

*Nuclear Engineering:*
AXFORD, R. A.
CHAO, BEI TSE
CHILTON, A. B.
DORNING, J. J., Jr.
HANG, D. F.
JONES, B. G.

Miley, G. H.
Turnbull, R. J.
Wehring, B.

### Physics:
Alpert, D.
Anderson, A. C.
Ascoli, G.
Axel, P.
Baym, G. A.
Brown, F. C.
Brown, R. M.
Brussel, M. K.
Cahn, J. H.
Chang, S. J.
Debrunner, P. G.
Dow, J. D.
Eisenstein, B. I.
Flynn, C. P.
Frauenfelder, H.
Ginsberg, D. M.
Goldwasser, E. L.
Granato, A. V.
Handler, P.
Hanson, A. O.
Holloway, L. E.
Hummel, J. P.
Iben, I., Jr.
Jackson, E. A.
Jones, L. M.
Klein, M. V.
Koehler, J.
Koester, L. J., Jr.
Kogut, J. B.
Kruse, U. E.
Kunz, A. B.
Lamb, F. K.
Lazarus, D.
Mapother, D. E.
McMillan, W. L.
Mochel, J. M.
O'Halloran, T. A., Jr.
Pandharipande, V. R.
Pethick, C. J.
Pines, D.
Propst, F. M.
Raether, M.
Ravenhall, D. G.
Sah, Chih Tang
Salamon, M. B.
Sard, R. D.
Satterthwaite, C. B
Simmons, R. O.
Slichter, C. P.
Smith, J. H.
Snyder, J. N.
Stapleton, H. J.
Sullivan, J. D.
Watson, W. D.
Wattenberg, A.
Williams, W. S.
Wolfe, J. P.
Wortis, M.
Wright, J. A.
Wyld, H. W., Jr.

### Theoretical and Applied Mechanics:
Buckmaster, J. D.
Carlson, D. E.
Clark, M. E.
Corten, H. T.
Costello, G.
Drucker, D. C.
Eubanks, R. A.
Kesler, C. E.
Leckie, F. A.
Miller, R. E.
Morrow, J.
Robertson, J. M.
Shield, R. T.
Sidebottom, O. M.
Walker, J. S.
Worley, W. J.

### College of Fine and Applied Arts:
#### Architecture:
Baker, J. S.
Bianchini, A. C.
Clayton, G. T.
Creese, W. L.
Ding, G. D.
Eng, W.
Forester, R. A.
Katz, R. D.
Lanford, S. T.
Lewis, W. H.
Link, R. P.
Miller, H. J.
Notaras, A.
O'Connell, W. J.
Replinger, J. G.
Schousboe, I.
Shick, W. L.
Swing, J. H.
Tavis, R. L.
Winkelhake, C. A.
Young, H. C.

#### Art and Design:
Betts, E. H.
Bodnar, P.
Bradshaw, G. R.
Breen, H. F., Jr.
Briggs, C. W.
Fagan, P.
Fehl, P.
Foster, G. N.
Frith, D. E.
Gallo, F.
Gunter, F. E.
Hardiman, G. W.
Jackson, B. M.
Lansing, K. M.
McFarland, N. T.
Moore, A. D.
Perlman, R.
Pilcher, D. W.
Price, L. H.
Rowan, D. M.
Regehr, C. C.
Sato, S.
Savage, J. A.
Sinsabaugh, A. R.
Sterkel, R. W.
Von Neumann, R. A.
Wicks, E. C.
Youngman, W. R.
Zagorski, E. J.
Zernich, T., Jr.
Ziff, J.

#### Urban and Regional Planning:
Blair, L. F.
Boyce, D. E.
Forrest, C. W., Jr.
Freund, E. C.
Goodman, W. I.
Guttenberg, A. Z.

#### Landscape Architecture:
Keith, W. M.
Nelson, W. R., Jr.
Riley, R. B.
Slotnick, D. L.

#### School of Music:
Bailey, J. L.
Bays, R. E.
Begian, H.
Berry, E. S., Jr.
Brun, H.
Carter, A. M.
Coggins, W. R.
Colwell, R. J.
Dalheim, E. L.
Divirgilio, N.
Drake, K. O.
Edlefsen, B. E.
Elyn, M.
Fredrickson, L. T.
Garvey, J. C.
Gray, R. E.
Gunsalas, D. C.
Gushee, L. A.
Hamilton, J.
Heiles, W. H.
Hoffman, M. E.
Holden, T. L.
Johnston, B. B., Jr.
Krolick, E. J.
Krummel, D. W
Leonhard, C.
Lloyd, D.
Luca, S.
Lyke, J. B.
Martirano, S.
McDowell, A. J.
McKenzie, J. H.
Murray, A. D.
Nettl, B.
Perantoni, D. T.
Perich, G.
Powell, M. E.
Richards, Claire L.
Ringer, A. L.
Sanders, D. W.
Shapiro, J.
Siwe, T. V.
Smith, R. B.
Temperley, N.
Thomas, R. E.
Vermel, P.
Warfield, W. C.
Wilson, Grace E.
Wisniewski, T. J.
Wustman, J. C.
Zonn, P. N.

#### Dance:
Blossom, B.

#### Theatre:
Ahart, J. C.
Behringer, Clara, M.
Hobgood, B. M.
Knight, D.
Works, B. R.

### College of Communications:
#### Advertising:
Barban, A. M.
Rotzoll, K. B.
White, G. E.

#### Journalism:
Carey, J. W.
Evans, J. F.
Guback, T. H.
Littlewood, T. B.
Peterson, T. B.

### College of Law:
Benfield, M. W., Jr.
Cribbet, J. E.
Fellows, M. L.
Findley, R. W.
Frampton, G. T.
Graham, M. H.
Hay, P. H.
Krause, H. D.
Lafave, W. R.
Landers, J. M.
Maggs, P. B.
Marcus, P.
McCord, J. H.
Morgan, T. D.
Nowak, J. E.
Painter, W. H.
Reisner, R.
Rotunda, R. D.
Shoben, E. W.
Simon, R. J.
Stone, V. J.

### College of Liberal Arts and Sciences:
#### Anthropology:
Bruner, E. M.
Casagrande, J. B.
Cunningham, C. E.
Giles, E.

GOULD, H. A.
GROVE, D. C.
LATHRAP, D. W.
LEHMAN, F. K.
NETTL, B.
PLATH, D. W.
SHIMKIN, D. B.
UCHENDU, V. C.
WHITTEN, N. E., Jr.
ZUIDEMA, R. T.

*Asian Studies:*
CHENG, C. C.
COHEN, S. P.
GOULD, H. A.
JACOBS, N.
PLATH, D. W.
SHRAN, P.
YU, G. T.

*Astronomy:*
IBEN, I., Jr.
KALER, J. B.
LAMB, F. K.
OLSON, E. C.
ROSEN, S.
SNYDER, L. E.
SWENSON, G. W., Jr.
TRURAN, J. W.
WATSON, W. D.
YOSS, K. M.

*Botany:*
BAZZAZ, F.
CAROTHERS, Z. B.
CRANG, R. F. E.
DEWET, J. M.
DICKINSON, D. B., Jr.
GOVINDJEE
HANSON, J. B.
HOFFMAN, L. R.
MEINS, F., Jr.
PHILLIPS, T. L.
SEIGLER, D.
TUVESON, R. W.

*Chemistry and Chemical Engineering:*
ALKIRE, R. G., Chemical Engineering
APPLEQUIST, D., Chemistry
BEAK, P., Chemistry
BELFORD, R. L., Chemistry
BROWN, T. L., Chemistry
CHANDLER, D., Chemistry
CLARK, J. M., Jr., Biochemistry
COATES, R. M., Chemistry
CONRAD, H. E., Biochemistry
CURTIN, D. Y., Chemistry
DRAGO, R. S., Chemistry
DRICKAMER, H. G., Chemical Engineering and Chemistry
ECKERT, C. A., Chemical Engineering
FAULKNER, L. Z., Chemistry
GUNSALUS, I. C., Biochemistry
GUTOWSKY, H. S., Chemistry
HAGER, L. P., Biochemistry
HAIGHT, G. P., Jr., Chemistry
HANRATTY, T. J., Chemical Engineering
HENDRICKSON, D. N., Chemistry
HUMMEL, J. P., Chemistry
JONAS, J., Chemistry
KATZENELLENBOGEN, J. A., Chemistry
LEONARD, N. J., Chemistry and Biochemistry
MARTIN, J. C., Chemistry
PAUL, I. C., Chemistry
RINEHART, K. L., Chemistry
SCHMITZ, R. A., Chemical Engineering
SCHUSTER, G. B., Chemistry
SHAPLEY, J. R., Chemistry
SMITH, S. G., Chemistry and Chemical Education
SWITZER, R. L., Biochemistry
UHLENBECK, O. C., Biochemistry
WEBER, G., Biochemistry
WESTWATER, J. W., Chemical Engineering
YANKWICH, P. E., Chemistry

*Classics:*
BATEMAN, J. J.
BROWNE, G. M.
JACOBSON, H.
MARCOVICH, M.
SCHOEDEL, W. R.
ZGUSTA, LADISLAV

*Comparative Literature:*
ALDRIDGE, A. O.
BENSTOCK, B.
HOLLERER, W.
JOST, F.
KNUST, H.
MARCHAND, J. W.
NELSON, R. J.
TIKKU, G. L.

*Ecology, Ethology and Evolution:*
BANKS, E. M.
FRAZZETTA, T. H.
GETZ, L. L.
GHENT, A. W.
HIRSCH, J.
HOFFMEISTER, D. F.
KARR, J. R.
LOWRY, W. P.
SALMON, M.
WILLSON, M. F.

*English:*
ALTENBERND, A. L.
ASTON, K. O.
BARKSDALE, R. K.
BENSTOCK, B.
BRANDABUR, E. J.
CAMPBELL, J. J.
CURLEY, D.
DICKEE, M.
FRAYNE, J. P.
FRIEDMAN, J.
GARRETT, P. K.
HALSBAND, R.
HENDRICK, G.
HURT, J. B.
KACHRU, Y.
KINNAMON, K.
KRAMER, D. V.
LIEBERMAN, L. J.
ROGERS, R. W.
SANDERS, C.
SHUMAN, R. D.
STEIN, A.
STILLINGER, J. C.
STILLINGER, N. B.
TIBBETTS, A. M.
WATTS, E. S.
WEEKS, F. W.
WILKIE, B. F.
WILSON, H. W.

*Entomology:*
FRIEDMAN, S.
GHENT, A. W.
JAYCOX, E. R.
KOGAN, M.
LARSEN, J. R., Jr.
METCALF, R. J..
SELANDER, R. B.
STERNBURG, J. G.
WALDBAUER, G. P.
WILLIS, J. H.

*French:*
ALDRIDGE, A. O.
BOWEN, B. C.
DELEY, H. C., Jr.
GAENG, P. A.
HAIDU, P.
JAHIEL, E.
JOST, F.
MAINIOUS, B. H.
MARTY, F., Italian
NACHTMANN, F. W.
NELSON, R. J.

*Genetics and Development:*
KRUIDENIER, F. J.
LAUGHNAN, J. R.
MEINS, F., Jr.
NANNEY, D. L.
SELANDER, R. B.
STEFFENSEN, D. M.
STOCUM, D. L.
TUVESON, R. W.
WATTERSON, R. L.
WHITT, G. S.
WILLIS, J. H.
WOESE, C. R.

*Geography:*
ALEXANDER, C. S.
FELLMANN, J. D.
GETIS, A.
KARARA, H. M.
LOWRY, W. P.
ROEPKE, H. G.
SHIMKIN, D. B.
THOMPSON, J.

*Geology:*
BLAKE, D. B.
CAROZZI, A.
DOMENICO, P. A.
GRAF, D. E.
HENDERSON, D. M.
HOWER, J.
KLEIN, G. D.
LANGENHEIM, R. I.
MANN, C. J.
SANDBERG, P. A.

*Germanic Languages and Literatures:*
ANTONSEN, E.
HAILE, H. G.
HOLLERER, W.
KNUST, H.
LORBE, R. E.
MARCHAND, J. W.
MITCHELL, P. M.
RAUCH, I.

*History:*
ARNSTEIN, W. L.
BATES, J. L.
BERNARD, P. P.
CRAWFORD, R. B.
DAWN, C. E.
EASTMAN, L. E.
FARNHAM, W. D.
HILL, B. D.
HITCHINS, K.
JAHER, S. C.
JOHANNSEN, R. W.
KLING, B. B.
LOVE, J. L.
McCOLLEY, R. M.
McKAY, J. P.
NICHOLS, J. A.
QUELLER, D. E.
SCHROEDER, P. W.
SOLBERG, W. U.
SPENCE, C. C.
SUTTON, R. M.

*Linguistics:*
ANTONSEN, E.
ASTON, KATHARINE
BLAYLOCK, W. C.
BROWNE, G. M.
CHENG, C.-C.
DAWSON, C. L.
GAENG, P. A.
KACHRU, B. B.
KACHRU, Y.
KENSTOWICZ, M. J.
KISSEBERTH, C. W.
LEHMAN, F. K.
MACLAY, H. S.
MARCHAND, J. E.
RAUCH, I.
SALTARELLI, M.

1713

Tikku, G. L.
Zgusta, J. W.

### Mathematics:
Albrecht, F. R.
Appel, K. I.
Ash, R. B.
Bank, S. B.
Bartle, R. G.
Bateman, P. T.
Berg, I. D.
Berkson, E. R.
Berndt, B. C.
Bishop, R. L.
Blumenthal, S.
Bohrer, R. E.
Boone, W. W.
Braunfeld, P. G.
Buckmaster, J. D.
Burkholder, D. L.
Carroll, R. W.
Chen, K. T.
Dade, E. C.
Day, M. M.
Diamond, H. G.
Evans, E. G., Jr.
Fossum, R. M.
Gear, C. W.
Goldberg, S. I.
Gray, J. W.
Griffith, P. A.
Haken, W.
Halberstam, H.
Hamstrom, Mary E.
Helms, L. L.
Janusz, G. J.
Jerrard, R. P.
Jockusch, C. G., Jr.
Jogdeo, S. S.
Kamber, F. W.
Kaufman, R. P.
Knight, F. B.
Langebartel, R. G.
Loeb, P. A.
McEliece, R. J.
Miles, J. B.
Muller, D. E.
Osborn, H.
Parker, E. T.
Peressini, A. L.
Philipp, W.
Porta, H. A.
Portnay, S. L.
Ranga, Rao R.
Reiner, I.
Robinson, D. S.
Rothman, N. J.
Rotman, J. J.
Rubel, L. A.
Schupp, P. E.
Scott, E. J.
Stolarsky, K. B.
Stout, W. F.
Suzuki, M.
Takeuti, G.
Ting, T. W.
Tondeur, P. M.
Uhl, J. J., Jr.
Ullom, S. V.
Walter, J. H.
Weichsel, P. M.
Wijsman, R. A.

### Microbiology:
Bryant, M. D.
Cronan, J. E., Jr.
DeMoss, R. D.
Kallio, R. E.
Kaplan, S.
Konisky, J.
Meyer, R. C.
Reichmann, M. E.
Savage, D. C.
Voss, E. W., Jr.
Woese, C. R.
Wolfe, R. S.

### Philosophy:
Caton, C. E.
Diggs, B. J.
Schacht, R. L.
Shwayder, D. S.
Tiebout, H. M., Jr.
Wallace, J. D.

### Physiology and Biophysics:
Barr, L.
Buetow, D. E., Physiology
Connor, J. A.
Crofts, A. R., Biophysics
Donchin, E.
Ducoff, H. S.
Dunn, F., Biophysics
Ebrey, T. G.
Govindjec, Biophysics
Heath, J. E., Physiology
Helman, S. I.
Hertig, B. A.
Larsen, J. R., Jr., Physiology
Ramirez, V. D., Physiology
Satinoff, E.
Sleator, W. W.
Swartz, H. M., Biophysics
Twardock, A. R.
Weber, G.
Willis, J. S., Physiology

### Political Science:
Casper, D.
Cohen, S. P.
Davis, M.
Glad, B.
Gove, S. K.
Kanet, R. E.
Kolodziej, E. A.
Merritt, R.
Monypenny, P.
Nagel, S. S.
Orfield, G. A.
Scott, R. E.
Seligman, L. G.
Wirt, F. M.
Yu, G. T.
Zinnes, D. A.

### Psychology:
Adams, J. A.
Anderson, R. C.
Banks, E. M.
Bernstein, D. A.
Birch, J. D.
Campione, A. B.
Campione, J. C.
Clore, G. L., Jr.
Cohen, J. B.
Costin, F.
Davis, J. H.
Donchin, E.
Dulany, D. E., Jr.
Dweck, C. S.
Eriksen, C. W.
Fishbein, M.
Greenough, W. T.
Hake, H. W.
Hall, W. S.
Hill, K. T.
Hirsch, J.
Hopkins, C. O.
Hulin, C. L.
Humphreys, L. G.
Kanfer, F. H.
Komorita, S. S.
Laughlin, P. R.
Linn, R. L.
McGrath, J. E.
Medin, D. L.
Osgood, C. E.
Parke, R. D.
Prokasy, W. F.
Paul, G. L.
Rappaport, J.
Satinoff, E.
Seldman, E.
Sprague, R. L.
Swarr, R. R.
Tatsuoka, M.
Teitelbaum, P.
Triandis, H. C.
Wagman, M.
Weir, M. W.
Wyer, R. S., Jr.

### Religious Studies:
Schoedel, W. R.

### Slavic Languages and Literature:
Dawson, C. L.
Friedberg, M.
Kenstowicz, M. J.
Pachmuss, T.

### Sociology:
Bordua, D. J.
Choldin, H. M.
Denzin, N. K.
Fliegel, F. C.
Form, W. H.
Gorecki, J.
Huber, J.
Jacobs, N.
Johnson, H. M.
Karsh, B.
Lueschen, G.
Robinson, J. W., Jr.
Simon, R. J.
Sofranko, A. J.
Spaeth, J. L.
Sudman, S.
Van Es, J. C.

### Spanish, Italian and Portuguese:
Baldwin, S. W., Jr., Spanish and Italian
Blaylock, W. C., Spanish
Dutton, B., Spanish
Lott, R. E., Spanish
Pasquariello, A. M., Spanish
Porgueras, A., Spanish
Preto-Rodas, R.
Saltarelli, M., Spanish

### Speech Communication:
Andersen, K. E.
Bateman, J. J.
Delia, J. G.
Mueller, H. L.
Nebergall, R. E.

### Speech and Hearing Science:
Bigler, R. C.
Kim, C. W.
O'Neill, J. J.
Quigley, S. P.
Zemlin, W. R.

### Library:
#### Library Administration:
Atkinson, H. C.
Brichford, M. J.
Deal, C. W.
Gorman, M.
Huff, W. H.
Miller, L. H.
McClellan, W. M.
Rinkel, G. K.
Satterlee, Marilyn
Shtohryn, D. M.
Wert, L. M.
Williams, M. E.
Wong, S.

#### Graduate School of Library Science:
Davis, C.
Goldhor, H.
Krummel, D. W.
Lancaster, F. W.
Williams, M. E.

### Radio Isotope Laboratory:
NYSTROM, F. R.

### College of Applied Life Studies:
#### Health and Safety:
CRESWELL, W. H., Jr., Health Education
MORTIMER, R. G.
STONE, D. B.

#### Physical Education:
CHESKA, ALYCE T.
LOY, J. W., Jr.
LUESCHEN, G.
MARTENS, R.
MASSEY, B. H.
MATTHEWS, D. O.
THOMPSON, M. M.
WRIGHT, R. G.

#### Leisure Studies:
BANNON, J. J.

#### Rehabilitation-Education Services:
NUGENT, T. J.

### College of Veterinary Medicine:
#### Clinical Medicine:
BRODIE, B.
DAVIS, L. E.
DORNER, J. L.
GUSTAFSSON, B. K.
HELPER, L. C.
SCHILLER, A. G.
SMALL, E.
SMITH, C. W.
THURMON, J. C.
WHITMORE, H. L.

#### Pathobiology:
BRYAN, H. S.
DIERKS, R. E.
DORNER, J. L.
FITZGERALD, P. R., Veterinary Parasitology
HANSON, L. E.
LEVINE, N. D., Veterinary Parasitology
MANSFIELD, M. E.
MEYER, R. C.
PICKARD, J. R.
RISTIC, M.
SHADDUCK, J. A.
SIMON, J.
TODD, K. S., Veterinary Parasitology
TOMPKINS, W. A.
WATRACH, A. M.
WOODS, G. T., Veterinary Microbiology and Public Health

#### Biosciences:
BEVILL, R. F., Jr.
BUCK, W. B.
DAVIS, L. M.
HANSEN, L. G.
JACKSON, G. L.
MCQUEEN, R. D.
METCALF, R. L.
SAFANIE, A. H.
THURMON, J. C.
TWARDOCK, A. R.
WAGNER, W. C.

### School of Social Work:
BALGOPAL, P. R.
BRIELAND, D.
COSTIN, LELA
HENDERSON, C. H.
ITZIN, F. H.
MECH, E. V.
TABER, M. A.

### School of Basic Medical Sciences:
BLOOMFIELD, D. K.
CLARK, J. M., Jr.

DEMOSS, R. D.
GHENT, A. W.
HAGER, L. P.
HEATH, J. E.
LEESON, C. R.
LEVY, A. H.
RAMIREZ, V. D.
REICHMANN, M. E.
SAVAGE, D. C.
SCHOENBERG, M. D.
SIEDLER, A. J.
SNYDER, J. N.
SPRAGUE, R. L.
SWITZER, R. L.
VISEK, W. J.
WATTERSON, R. L.
WEBER, G.
ZEMLIN, W. R.

### School of Clinical Medicine:
ABSOLON, K. B.
BLOOMFIELD, D. K.
GANS, H.
LEONARD, A.
LEVY, A. H.
NELSON, R. A.
SHARP, J. T.
SIEGEL, I. A.
THURSH, D. R.
VISEK, W. J.

## University of Illinois at Chicago Circle

P.O.B. 4348, CHICAGO, ILLINOIS 60680

Telephone: 996-3000.

Chancellor: DONALD H. RIDDLE, PH.D.
Vice-Chancellors: RICHARD WARD, RICHARD JOHNSON.
University Librarian: BEVERLY A. LYNCH.

Number of students: 20,663.

### DEANS:
Architecture, Art and Urban Sciences: ALAN M. VOORHEES.
Business Administration: RALPH WESTFALL.
Engineering: PAUL PASLAY.
Liberal Arts and Sciences: ELMER B. HADLEY.
Education: MAURICE J. EASH.
Health, Physical Education and Recreation: S. L. FORDHAM, ED.D. (Director).
Graduate College: J. ROCEK, PH.D.
Jane Addams College of Social Work: SHIRLEY M. BUTTRICK.
Urban Sciences: C. J. ORLEBEKE, PH.D.

## University of Illinois at the Medical Center, Chicago

P.O.B. 6998, CHICAGO, ILLINOIS 60680

Telephone: 996-7000.

Chancellor: J. S. BEGANDO, PH.D.
Vice-Chancellor for Academic Affairs: ALEXANDER M. SCHMIDT, PH.D.
Vice-Chancellor for Administrative Services: RICHARD H. WARD, D.CRIM. (acting).
Vice-Chancellor for Health Services: ALEXANDER M. SCHMIDT, M.D.

### DEANS:
Graduate College: KAREN M. HIIEMAE, PH.D. (acting).
College of Dentistry: S. H. YALE, D.D.S.
College of Medicine: M. C. CREDITOR (acting).
Abraham Lincoln School of Medicine: P. M. FORMAN.
School of Basic Medical Sciences at Chicago: EDWARD P. COHEN, M.D.
School of Basic Medical Sciences at Urbana-Champaign: D. K. BLOOMFIELD, M.D.
School of Clinical Medicine at Urbana-Champaign: D. K. BLOOMFIELD.
Peoria School of Medicine: JERRY I. NEWMAN, M.D. (acting).
Rockford School of Medicine: CLIFFORD R. GRULEE, M.D.
College of Nursing: HELEN K. GRACE, PH.D.
College of Pharmacy: HENRI R. MANASSE, PH.D. (acting).
College of Associated Health Professions: T. W. BECKHAM.
School of Public Health: V. DIEFENBACH.

### DIRECTORS:
Division of Services for Crippled Children: EDWARD F. LIS, M.D.
University of Illinois Hospital: MARVIN C. MILES.
Institution for Tuberculosis Research: RAY G. CRISPEN, PH.D.

## WESTERN ILLINOIS UNIVERSITY
MACOMB, ILLINOIS 61455

Telephone: 295-1414.

Founded 1899.

President: LESLIE F. MALPASS.
Provost and Academic Vice-President: BRUCE H. CARPENTER.
Vice-President for Student Affairs: R. D. GIERHAN.
Dean of Admissions and Records: F. E. FESS.
Librarian: PEARCE S. GROVE.

Number of teachers: 702.
Number of students: 13,352.

Publications: Undergraduate Catalog, Graduate Catalog, Summer Sessions Bulletin, Mississippi Valley Review, Essays in Literature.

### DEANS:
College of Arts and Sciences: ROBERT L. KINDRICK.
College of Education: DAVID R. TAYLOR.
College of Applied Sciences: RODNEY J. FINK.
College of Business: H. C. NUDD.
College of Fine Arts: F. D. SUYCOTT, Jr.
College of Health, Physical Education and Recreation: W. L. LAKIE.
School of Graduate Studies: SUZANNE REID.
Summer Sessions: ROGER D. FORD.

### WHEATON COLLEGE
WHEATON, ILLINOIS 60187

Founded 1860.

*President:* Dr. HUDSON T. ARMERDING, PH.D.
*Registrar:* PATRICK L. MILLER, M.A.
*Director of Admissions:* STUART O. MICHAEL, M.DIV.
*Vice-President for Academic Affairs:* W. KRIEGBAUM, PH.D.
*Vice-President for Finance:* DAVID JOHNSTON, PH.D.
*Vice-President for Student Development:* Dr. HENRY W. NELSON, D.ED.
*Vice-President for Development:* Dr. NORMAN EDWARDS, D.P.S.
*Dean of Graduate School:* J. E. PLUEDDEMANN, PH.D. (acting).
*Dean:* Dr. P. VELTMAN, PH.D.
*Dean of Conservatory:* H. M. BEST, S.M.D.
*Librarian:* PAUL SNEZEK, M.A.

The library contains over 210,000 items.

Number of teachers: 140, including 52 professors.

Number of students: 1,291 men, 1,231 women, total 2,522.

Publications: *InForm* (5 times a year), *Literary Magazine* (3 times a year), *Record* (weekly), *Tower* (year book).

## INDIANA

### ANDERSON COLLEGE
ANDERSON, INDIANA 46011

Telephone: (317) 649-9071.

Founded 1917.

*President:* Dr. ROBERT H. REARDON.
*Vice-President for Academic Affairs and Dean of the College:* Dr. ROBERT A. NICHOLSON.
*Dean of the Faculty:* Dr. DUANE HOAK.
*Registrar:* LUCILLE STRAWN.
*Librarian:* RICHARD SNYDER.

The library contains 119,000 vols.

Number of teachers: 101.
Number of students: 2,005.

### BALL STATE UNIVERSITY
MUNCIE, INDIANA 47306

Telephone: 317-289-1241.

Founded 1918.

*President:* ROBERT P. BELL.
*Vice-Presidents:* Dr. M. C. BEYERL, Dr. ROBERT E. LINSON, Dr. JAMES V. KOCH, THOMAS J. KINGHORN.
*Registrar:* J. W. ESPEY.
*Librarian:* Dr. MICHAEL B. WOOD.

The library contains 1,205,110 vols.

Number of teachers: 926.
Number of students: 17,557.

Publications: *Forum*† (quarterly), *The Steinbeck Quarterly*, *Indiana Social Studies Quarterly*, *Business Review*† (2 a year), *Teacher Educator*† (4 a year), *Proceedings of the Indiana Academy of Social Sciences* (annually), *22 Young Indiana Writers* (annually), *Ball State University Faculty Lectures*† (annually), *Ball State Monographs*† (irregularly), *Geographical Survey* (quarterly).

### BUTLER UNIVERSITY
4600 SUNSET AVE., INDIANAPOLIS, INDIANA 46208

Telephone: 283-8000

Founded 1855; private control.

*President:* JOHN G. JOHNSON.
*Vice-President for Academic Affairs:* PAUL R. STEWART.
*Vice-President for Financial Development:* WM. O. POWELL, Jr.
*Vice-President for Business Affairs and Treasurer:* WM. H. TEMPLETON.
*Registrar:* R. E. CAWTHORNE.
*Librarian:* R. A. DAVIS.

Number of teachers: 250.
Number of students: 3,800.

### CALUMET COLLEGE
HAMMOND, INDIANA 46394

Telephone: (219)473-7770.

Founded 1951.

*President:* Rev. LOUIS OSTERHAGE.
*Registrar:* JAY GOULD.
*Librarian:* JON L. IGLAR.

The library contains 90,000 vols.

Number of teachers: 55.
Number of students: 1,400.

### DEPAUW UNIVERSITY
GREENCASTLE, INDIANA 46135

Chartered 1837 as Indiana Asbury University, name changed 1884.

*President:* RICHARD F. ROSSER, PH.D.
*Provost:* D. DODGE JOHNSON, PH.D.
*Dean of Faculty:* JAMES L. COOPER, PH.D.
*Vice-President for Finance and Comptroller:* FRED S. SILANDER, PH.D.
*Executive Vice-President for External Relations:* ROBERT G. BOTTOMS, D.MIN.
*Registrar:* E. S. YPMA, PH.D.
*Librarian:* J. A. MARTINDALE, M.A.L.S.

The library contains 350,000 volumes.

Number of teachers: 145 full-time, 55 part-time.
Number of students: 1,106 men, 1,324 women, total 2,430.

Publications: *Bulletin* (annual), *The Alumnus* (quarterly).

DIRECTORS:
*Music:* CASSEL GRUBB, M.MUS.
*Nursing:* CHARMAINE SMITH, M.S.N.
*Graduate Studies:* J. R. ANDERSON, PH.D.

### EARLHAM COLLEGE
RICHMOND, INDIANA 47374

Founded 1847.

*President:* FRANKLIN W. WALLIN.
*Vice-President for Business Affairs:* G. RICHARD WYNN.
*Vice-President for Development:* RICHARD LANCASTER.
*Provost and Dean of Academic Affairs:* LEONARD CLARK.
*Librarian:* EVAN FARBER.

Number of teachers: 109.
Number of students: 1,115.

Publications: *Earlhamite*, *Earlham Post* (weekly), *Crucible* (bi-annual by students), *Sargasso* (annual by students), *Earlham College Bulletin* (annual).

DEANS:
*College:* LEONARD CLARK.
*Students:* SUSAN CRIM.

### FRANKLIN COLLEGE
FRANKLIN, INDIANA 46131

Telephone: (317) 736-8441.

Founded 1834.

*President:* EDWIN A. PENN.
*Dean:* LAWRENCE BRYAN.
*Vice-President for Admissions and Financial Aid:* NOLAN COOPER.
*Librarian:* R. COWARD.

The library contains 86,000 vols.

Number of teachers: 48 full-time, 8 part-time.
Number of students: 650.

### GOSHEN COLLEGE
GOSHEN, INDIANA 46526

Telephone: 533-3161.

Founded 1894.

*President:* J. LAWRENCE BURKHOLDER.
*Registrar:* J. D. NYCE.
*Librarian:* D. YODER.

The library contains 134,650 vols.

Number of teachers: 85.
Number of students: 1,314.

### HANOVER COLLEGE
HANOVER, INDIANA 47243

First instruction 1827; Chartered 1829.

Private control, Presbyterian.

*President:* JOHN E. HORNER, M.A., PH.D., LL.D., LITT.D., L.H.D.
*Vice-President for Academic Affairs:* STANLEY P. CAINE, M.S., PH.D.

UNIVERSITIES AND COLLEGES—INDIANA U.S.A.

*Vice-President for Student Affairs:*
DAVID A. PALMER, M.A., PH.D.
The library contains 250,000 vols.
Number of teachers: 71.
Number of students: 1,012.

## HUNTINGTON COLLEGE
HUNTINGTON, INDIANA 46750
Telephone: 356-6000.
Founded 1897.

*President:* Dr. EUGENE B. HABECKER.
*Academic Dean:* Dr. GERALD G. WINKLEMAN.
*Director of Admissions:* JOHN C. SCHAFER.
*Registrar:* Mrs. IMOGENE M. PALMER.
*Librarian:* ROBERT E. KAEHR.
The library contains 52,000 vols.
Number of staff: 40.
Number of students: 552.

## INDIANA CENTRAL UNIVERSITY
1400 EAST HANNA AVE.,
INDIANAPOLIS, INDIANA 46227
Telephone: (317) 788-3368.
Founded 1902.

*President:* Dr. GENE E. SEASE.
*Vice-President:* Dr. LYNN R. YOUNGBLOOD.
*Registrar:* W. D. LAWRENCE.
*Academic Dean:* Dr. NOEL BAKER.
*Director of Admissions:* D. J. HUFFMAN.
*Librarian:* Mrs. F. WILSON.
The library contains 116,859 vols.
Number of teachers: 120 full-time.
Number of students: 1,300 full-time, 2,150 part-time.

## INDIANA INSTITUTE OF TECHNOLOGY
1600 E. WASHINGTON,
FORT WAYNE, INDIANA 46803
Telephone: (219) 422-5561.
Founded 1930.

*President:* THOMAS F. SCULLY.
*Director of Student Services:* JOHN ACKERMAN.
*Librarian:* JEANNE ROTHGEB.
The library contains 45,000 volumes.
Number of teachers: 50.
Number of students: 700.
Schools of Engineering, Sciences and Business.

## INDIANA STATE UNIVERSITY
TERRE HAUTE, INDIANA 47809
Telephone: 232-6311.
Founded 1865.

*President:* RICHARD G. LANDINI.
*Vice-President for Academic Affairs:* RICHARD M. CLOKEY.

*Senior Vice-President and Treasurer:* J. K. MOULTON.
*Vice-President for Development and Public Affairs:* ORIN DAHL.
*Vice-President for Student Affairs:* Dr. J. W. TRUITT.
*Registrar:* WILLIAM R. OSMON.
*Director of Admissions and University High School Relations:* JOHN BUSH.
*Librarian:* RONALD G. LEACH.
The library contains 844,994 vols.
Number of teachers: 668.
Number of students: 12,362.

## INDIANA UNIVERSITY
BLOOMINGTON, INDIANA 47405
(Other Campuses at Fort Wayne, Kokomo, Gary, South Bend, Indianapolis, New Albany, Richmond, Indiana).
Telephone: (812) 332-0211.

Established 1820 as a State Seminary, opened 1824, became Indiana College 1828, attained university status 1838, became State University 1852.

*President:* JOHN W. RYAN, PH.D.
*Chancellor:* H. B WELLS, M.A., LL.D.
*Vice-Presidents:* W. G. PINNELL, D.B.A., E. G. WILLIAMS, D.B.A., G. W. IRWIN, Jr., M.D., K. R. R. GROS LOUIS, PH.D.
*Registrar and Director of Admissions:* M. D. SCHERER.
*Dean of Libraries:* ELAINE SLOAN.
*Library:* see Libraries.
Number of teachers: 1,441 (Bloomington), 1,865 (all other campuses), full-time.
Number of students: 31,877 (Bloomington), 47,596 (all other campuses), full- and part-time.
Publications: *University Bulletin* (30 times a year), *Indiana Magazine of History* (quarterly), *Indiana Law Journal* (quarterly), *Journal of Mathematics and Mechanics*, *International Journal of American Linguistics*, *Indiana Folklore* (quarterly), *Journal of Victorian Studies*, *Indiana Business Review* (monthly), *Business Horizons* (quarterly).

## MANCHESTER COLLEGE
604 COLLEGE AVENUE,
NORTH MANCHESTER,
INDIANA 46962
Telephone: (219) 982-2141.
Founded 1889.

*President:* A. BLAIR HELMAN.
*Academic Dean:* ROBERT S. KELLER.
*Dean of Students:* STANLEY B. ESCOTT.
*Treasurer:* ELDON E. FAHS.
*Registrar:* R. H. PAINE.
*Director of Admissions:* DORALEEN SCHEETZ-HOLLAR.
*Librarian:* J. A. WILLMERT.

The library contains 152,000 vols.
Number of teachers: 79 full-time.
Number of students: 1,189 full-time.
Publications: *Bulletin* (monthly), *The Oak Leaves* (student weekly), *The Aurora* (annual).

## MARIAN COLLEGE
3200 COLD SPRING RD.,
INDIANAPOLIS, INDIANA 46222
Telephone: 924-3291.
Founded 1851.

*President:* LOUIS GATTO, PH.D.
*Director of Development and College Relations:* ALAN LISLE, M.S., M.A.
*Dean of Academic Affairs:* Sister MARGARETTA BLACK, O.S.F., PH.D.
*Dean of Student Services:* WILLIAM H. WOODMAN, PH.D.
*Business Manager and Controller:* Col. L. W. WAGNER, B.S.
*Librarian:* Sister THERESE WENTE, O.S.F., M.A.
The library contains 105,000 vols.
Number of teachers: 85.
Number of students: 850.

## MARION COLLEGE
MARION, INDIANA 46952
Telephone: (317) 674-6901.
Founded 1920.

*President:* ROBERT R. LUCKEY.
*Director of Records:* JAMES BLACKBURN.
*Dean of College:* JAMES B. BARNES.
*Librarian:* H. BOYCE.
The library contains 97,981 vols.
Number of teachers: 100.
Number of students: 1,100.

## PURDUE UNIVERSITY
WEST LAFAYETTE,
INDIANA 47907
Telephone: (317) 494-6000.

Founded 1869; Instruction commenced 1874.
State control; Academic year: August to May.

*President:* ARTHUR G. HANSEN, PH.D., D.ENG., D.SC.
*Executive Vice-President and Provost:* FELIX HAAS, M.S., PH.D.
*Executive Vice-President and Treasurer:* F. R. FORD, B.S.M.E., M.S.I.M., PH.D.
*Vice-President for Research and Dean of the Graduate School:* STRUTHER ARNOTT, B.SC., PH.D.
*Vice-President for Student Services:* W. J. FISCHANG, B.S., PH.D.
*Vice-President for Development:* JOHN S. DAY, M.B.A., D.C.S.
*Vice-President for Housing and Food Services:* JOHN C. SMALLEY, B.S.
*Vice-President and Dean of Academic Services:* D. R. BROWN, B.S., M.S., PH.D.

Vice-President for Physical Facilities: WALTER W. WADE, B.S.P.S.E.
Vice-President and Associate Provost: R. A. GREENKORN, B.S., M.S., PH.D.
Vice-President for Business Services and Assistant Treasurer: C. B. WISE, B.S.I.M.
Registrar: BETTY M. SUDARTH, PH.D.
Director of Admissions: JAMES R. KRAYNAK, M.S.ED.
Director of Libraries: J. M. DAGNESE, M.A., M.S.L.S.

The libraries contain 1,424,896 vols.
Number of teachers: 2,078 West Lafayette campus; 882 regional campuses.
Number of students: 32,366 (13,487 additional students at regional campuses).

Publications: *University Bulletins, Purdue University Press Books, Modern Fiction Studies.*

### DEANS:

School of Agriculture: B. J. LISKA, M.S., PH.D.
School of Veterinary Medicine: J. J. STOCKTON, D.V.M., M.S., PH.D.
School of Consumer and Family Sciences: N. H. COMPTON, M.S., PH.D.
Schools of Engineering: J. C. HANCOCK, M.S.E.E., PH.D.
School of Management: K. V. SMITH, M.B.A., PH.D.
Schools of Pharmacy and Pharmacal Sciences, Nursing and Health Services: V. E. TYLER, M.S., PH.D.
School of Humanities, Social Science and Education: R. L. RINGEL, M.S., PH.D.
School of Technology: G. W. MCNELLY, M.S., PH.D.
School of Science: A. H. CLARK, M.A., PH.D.
Graduate School: STRUTHER ARNOTT, PH.D.
Dean of Students: B. I. COOK, M.A., PH.D.

### PROFESSORS:

School of Agriculture:

*Agricultural Economics:*
ATKINSON, J. H.
BABB, E. M.
BACHE, D. H.
BLAKE, B. F.
DOERING, O. C.
DOWNEY, W. D.
FARRIS, P. L.
FARRIS, W. S.
JONES, B. F.
KADLEC, J. E.
KEHRBERG, E. W.
KOHLS, R. L.
MILLER, W. L.
MORRIS, W. H. M.
OESTERLE, E. C.
POND, M. T.
ROBBINS, P. R.
SCHRADER, L. F.
SHARPLES, J. A.
TAYLOR, R. W.
THOMAS, D. W.

*Agricultural Engineering:*
DALE, A. C.
FOSTER, G. H.
HINKLE, C. N.
HUGGINS, L. F.
ISAACS, G. W.
LIEN, R. M.
LILJEDAHL, J. B.
MCKENZIE, B. A.
MONKE, E. J.
PEART, R. M.

*Agronomy:*
AHLRICHS, J. L.
AXTELL, J. D.
BARBER, S. A.
BAUMAN, L. F.
BAUMGARDNER, M. F.
BRONSON, R. D.
CHRISTMAS, E. P.
CRANE, P. L.
DALE, R. F.
DANIEL, W. H.
FRANZMEIER, D. P.
GLOVER, D. V.
HILST, A. R.
HOLT, D. A.
LECHTENBERG, V. L.
LOW, P. F.
MANNERING, J. V.
MCFEE, W. W.
MOLDENHAUER, W. C.
NELSON, D. W.
NELSON, W. L.
NEWMAN, J. E.
NYQUIST, W. E.
OHLROGGE, A. J.
PATTERSON F. L.
PHILLIPS, M. W.
RHYKERD, C. L.
SOMMERS, L. E.
SWEARINGEN, M. L.
WHITE, J. L.
WIERSMA, D.
WILCOX, J. R.

*Animal Sciences:*
ABERLE, E. D.
ALBRIGHT, J. L.
ALLISTON, C. W.
ANDERSON, V. L.
BELL, A. E.
CLINE, T. R.
CUNNINGHAM, M. D.
FORREST, J. C.
FOSTER, J. R.
HARRINGTON, R. B
HARRIS, D. L.
HUNSLEY, R. E.
JONES, H. W.
JUDGE, M. D.
KEENAN, T. W.
LISKA, B. J.
LONG, J.
MALVEN, P. V.
MARTIN T. G.
MAYROSE, V. B.
NOLLER, C. H.
OUTHOUSE, J. B.
PERRY, T. W.
PLUMLEE, M. P.
ROGLER, J. C.
STADELMAN, W. J.
STOB, M.
WOODS, W. R.

*Biochemistry:*
AXELROD, B.
BRANDT, K. G.
BUTLER, L. G.
CARLSON, D. M.
HERMODSON, M. A.
KIM, K.
KOHLAW, G. B.
KROGMANN, D. W.
PARKER, H. E.
REGNIER, F. E.
RODWELL, V. W.
SCHALL, E. D.
SOMERVILLE, R. L.
WEINER, H.
ZALKIN, H.

*Botany and Plant Pathology:*
ATHOW, K. L.
BRACKER, C. E.
CURTIS, R. W.
GREEN, R. J.
HENNEN, J. F.
HODGES, T. K.
HUBER, D. M.
KENAGA, C. B.
LISTER, R. M.
ROSS, M. A.
SCHREIBER, M. M.
SCOTT, D. H.
SHANER, G. E.
TOMES, M. L.
TSAI, C. Y.
TUITE, J. F.
WILLIAMS, E. B.
WILLIAMS, J. L.

*Entomology:*
BENNETT, G. W.
EDWARDS, C. R.
FERRIS, J. M.
FERRIS, V. R.
GALLUN, R. L.
HOLLINGWORTH, R. M.
MATTHEW, D. L.
ORTMAN, E. E.
OSMUN, J. V.
PASCHKE, J. D.
SCHUDER, D. L.
WILSON, M. C.

*Forestry and Natural Resources:*
BEERS, T. W.
BYRNES, W. R.
CALLAHAN, J. C.
CARTER, M. C.
CHANEY, W. R.
ECKELMAN, C. A.
HOFFER, R. M.
HUNT, M. O.
MERRITT, C.
MILLER, C. I.
MOSER, J. W.
MUMFORD, R. E.
SUDDARTH, S. K.

*Horticulture:*
CARPENTER, P. L.
CHERRY, J. H.
EMERSON, F. H.
ERICKSON, H. T.
FLINT, H. L.
HAFEN, L.
HAYDEN, R. A.
HOFF, J. E.
JANICK, J.
MOSER, B. C.
NELSON, P. E.
ROMANOWSKI, R. R.
SULLIVAN, G. H.
TIGCHELAAR, E. C.
WILCOX, G. E.

School of Veterinary Medicine:
ALLEN, A. R., Medical Communications
MEYER, K. B., Continuing Education and Extension

*Large Animal Clinics:*
AMSTUTZ, H. E.
CALLAHAN, C. J.
FESSLER, J. F.
MORTER, R. L.
PAGE, E. H.
RUNNELS, L. J.

*Small Animal Clinics:*
BLAKEMORE, J. C.
BLEVINS, W. E.
WEIRICH, W. E.

## UNIVERSITIES AND COLLEGES—INDIANA, U.S.A.

*Veterinary Anatomy:*
Hinsman, E. J.
Stromberg, M. W.
Stump, J. E.
VanSickle, D. C.

*Veterinary Microbiology, Pathology, and Public Health:*
Armstrong, C. H.
Burnstein, T.
Carlton, W. W.
Claflin, R. M.
Freeman, M. J.
Gaafar, S. M.
Gustafson, D. P.
Haelterman, E. O.
Hooper, B. E.
Jones, R. K.
Kirkham, W. W.
Morse, E. V.
Olander, H. J.
Robinson, F. R.
Stockton, J. J.
VanVleet, J. E.
Winterfield, R. W.

*Veterinary Physiology and Pharmacology:*
Bottoms, G. D.
Coppoc, G. L.
Goetsch, G. D.
Jackson, H. D.
Neher, G. M.
Tacker, W. A.

*School of Consumer and Family Sciences:*
*Child Development and Family Studies:*
Compton, N. H.
Denton, G. W.
Kerckhoff, R. K.
Lewis, R. A.

*Consumer Sciences and Retailing:*
Conte, M.
Rennebohm, F. H.

*Foods and Nutrition:*
Abernathy, R. P.
Fuqua, M. E.
Kirksey, A.
Pratt, D. E.
Story, Jon A.

*Restaurant, Hotel and Institutional Management:*
Cioch, J. J.

*Schools of Engineering:*
*Aeronautics and Astronautics:*
Drake, J. W.
Gustafson, W. A.
Marshall, F. J.
Osborn, J. R.
Sun, C. T.
Yang, H. T. Y.

*Chemical Engineering:*
Albright, L. F.
Andres, R. P.
Chao, K. C.
Delgass, W. N.
Eckert, R. E.
Emery, A. H.
Greenkorn, R. A.
Kessler, D. P.
Koppel, L. B.
Lim, H. C.
Ramkrishna, D.
Reklaitis, G.
Squires, R. G.
Tsao, G. T.
Wankat, P. C.
Williams, T. J.

*Civil Engineering:*
Altschaeffl, A. G.
Anderson, V. L.
Botkin, K. E.
Chen, W.
Curtis, K. S.
Delleur, J. W.
Diamond, S.
Dolch, W. L.
Etzel, J. E.
Grady, C. P. L.
Gutzwiller, M. J.
Harr, M. E.
Havers, J. A.
Hittle, J. E.
Judd, W. R.
Kirsch, E. J.
Lee, R. H.
Leonards, G. A.
Lovell, C. W.
McEntyre, J. G.
McLaughlin, J. F.
Michael, H. L.
Mikhail, E. M.
Miles, R. D.
Rao, R. A.
Satterly, G. T.
Sinha, K. C.
Ting, E. C.
Toebes, G. H.
Waling, J. L.
Wood, L. E.
Yao, J. T. Q.
Yoder, E. J.

*Electrical Engineering:*
Carroll, D. P.
Chen, C. L.
Coates, C. L.
Cooper, G. R.
El-Abiad, A. H.
Friedlaender, F. J
Fu, King-Sun
Fukunaga, K.
Geddes, L. A.
Gunshor, R. L.
Haas, V. B.
Hancock, J. C.
Hayt, W. H.
Heydt, G. T.
Huang, T. S.
Kak, A. J.
Kashyap, R. L.
Koivo, A. J.
Krause, P. C.
Landgrebe, D. A.
Lin, P. N.
Lindenlaub, J. C.
Lipo, T. A.
Luh, J. Y.-S.
McGillem, C. D.
Mowle, F. J.
Neudeck, G. W.
Newhouse, V. L.
Pierret, R. F.
Saridis, G. N.
Schwartz, R. J.
Silva, L. F.
Thompson, H. W.
Vest, R. W.
Weeks, W. L.

*Freshman Engineering:*
Boyle, T. A.
Butler, B.
LeBold, W. K.
McDowell, R. W.
Smith, C. P.

*Industrial Engineering:*
Barany, J. W.
Barash, M. M.
Leimkuhler, F. F.
Moodie, C. L.
Morin, T. L.
Petersen, C. C.
Ravindran, A.
Salvendy, G.
Solberg, J. J.
Sparrow, F. T.
Sweet, A. L.
Talavage, J. J.

*Mechanical Engineering:*
Bergdolt, V. E.
Brown, C. L.
Citron, S. J.
Cohen, R.
Crocker, M. J.
DeWitt, D. P.
Fox, R. W.
Goldschmidt, V. E.
Hall, A. S.
Hamilton, J. F.
Hillberry, B. M.
Hoffman, J. D.
Holowenko, A. R.
Incropera, F.
L'Ecuyer, M. R.
Lefebvre, A. H.
Leidenfrost, W.
Liley, P. E.
McDonald, A. T.
Mellor, A. M.
Morse, F. B.
Phillips, W. M.
Sgandren, F.
Schiff, A. J.
Schoenhals, R. J.
Skifstad, J. G.
Soedel, W.
Stevenson, W. H.
Thompson, H. D.
Tiederman, W. G.
Tree, D. R.
Viskanta, R.

*Materials Engineering:*
Dayananda, M. A.
Grace, R. E.
Hruska, S. J.
Liedl, G. L.
Sato, H.
Schuhmann, R.

*Nuclear Engineering:*
Hungerford, H. E.
Lykoudis, P. S.
Ott, K.
Sesonske, A.
Theofanous, T. G.

*School of Management:*
*Administrative Sciences:*
King, D. C.
Sherwood, J. J.

*Economics:*
Carlson, J. A.
Carr, C. R.
Hendershott, P. H.
Horwich, G.
Hu, S. C.
Kadiyala, K. R.
Moore, J. C.
Papke, J. A.
Sparrow, F. T.
Weidenaar, D. J.
Whinston, A. B.
Wiley, J. W.

*Management:*
Bass, F. M.
Carr, C. R.
Cooper, A. C.
Day, J. S.
Johnson, R. W.
King, D. C.
Lawrence, C.
Lewellen, W. G.
Moskowitz, H.
Pessemier, E. A.
Scaletta, P. J.

Schendel, D. E.
Schlarbaum, G. G.
Schultz, R. L.
Smith, K. V.
Tse, J. Y. D.
Ullmann, J. C.
Whinston, A. B.
Wright, G. P.

Schools of Pharmacy and Pharmacal Sciences, Nursing and Health Science:
Banker, G. S.
Belcastro, P. F.
Born, G.
Borowitz, J.
Byrn, S. R.
Carlson, G. P.
Cassady, J.
Chalmers, R. K.
Christian, J. E.
Evanson, R. V.
Floss, H. G.
Geddes, L. E.
Heinstein, P. F.
Hem, S. L.
Johnson, H. R.
Kessler, W. V.
Kildsig, D. O.
Knevel, A. M.
Landolt, R. R.
Mack, D. O.
McLaughlin, J. L.
Maickel, R. P.
Morre, D. J.
Peck, G.
Robbers, J. E.
Shaw, S. M.
Sperandio, G. J.
Spratto, G. R.
Stokes, E. R.
Tyler, V. E.
Yim, G. K.
Yost, K. J.
Ziemer, P. L.

School of Humanities, Social Science and Education:

Creative Arts:
Beelke, R. G.
Dorn, C. M.
Miller, D. E.
O'Connor, J. A.
Phillips, I. V.
Pounders, A. J.
Reed, R. B.
Stocking, C. M.
Vevers, A. M.
Watson, L. H.

Audiology and Speech Sciences:
Binnie, C.
Goldstein, D. P.
Leonard, L. B.
Lloyd, L. L.
Noll, J. D.
Ringel, R. L.
Weinberg, B.

Communication:
Berg, D. M.
Kildahl, E. E.
Redding, W. C.
Stevens, G. E.
Stewart, C. J.
Tompkins, P. K.
Trachtman, L. E.
Webb, R.

Education:
Asher J. W.
DeVito, A.
Evans, W.
Feldhusen, J.
Georgeoff, P. J.
Herron, J. D.
Hicks, C. R.

Isaacson, L. E.
Johnson, R.
Kane, R.
Krockover, G.
Lamb, P. M.
Linden, K.
Lloyd, L. L.
Lowe, P. K.
McDaniel, E.
Nelson, N. J.
Nelson, R. C.
Nicholson, E.
Richardson, W. B.
Salen, G. P.
Shertzer, B. E.
Stone, S. C.
Wheatley, G.

English:
Adler, J. H.
Bache, W. B.
Church, M.
DeVitis, A. A.
Evans, W. H.
Goldstein, S. M.
Gottfried, L. A.
Lauterbach, E. S.
Lawry, J. S.
Light, M.
Lokke, V. L.
Magliola, R. R.
Myers, N. N.
Neufeldt, L. N.
Raskin, V.
Reichard, H. M.
Stafford, W. T.
Stefanile, F. N.
Stuckey, W. J.
Thompson, G. R.
Voorhees, R. J.

History:
Berthrong, D. J.
Jones, O. L.
Rothenberg, G. E.
Woodman, H. D.

Foreign Languages and Literature:
Beer, J. M. A.
Carraciolo-Trejo, E.
Chandler, A. A.
Marti de Cid, D.
Pasco, A. H.
Pfanner, H.
Ruiz-Ramon, F.
Walther, D. H.
Whitby, W. M.

Philosophy:
McBride, W. L.
Rowe, W. L.
Schrag, C. O.

Physical Education, Health and Recreation Studies:
Annarino, A. A.
Hanson, D. L.
Ismail, A. H.
Lamb, D. R.
Theobald, W. F.
Veenker, C. H.
Widule, C. J.

Political Science:
Beres, L. R.
Caputo, D. A.
Hale, M. Q.
Kofmehl, K. T.
Stegenga, J. A.
Theen, R. H. W.
Weinstein, M. A.

Psychological Sciences:
Baron, R. A.
Brown, D. R.
Capaldi, E. D.
Capaldi, E. J.

Cicirelli, V. G.
Deaux, K.
Eagly, A. H.
Gruen, G. E.
Ilgen, D. R.
Jacoby, J.
Kantowitz, B. H.
Linden, J. D.
Martin, W. E.
Naylor, J. C.
Ottinger, D. R.
Powley, T. L.
Rychlak, J. F.
Schonemann, P.
Sorkin, R. D.
Swensen, C. H.
Townsend, J. T.
Wachs, T. D.
Wasserman, G. W.
Wilms, J. H.
Winer, B. J.

Sociology and Anthropology:
Anderson, J.
Eichhorn, R. L.
Hirsch, W.
Kanin, E. J.
McGee, R. J.
Patchen, M.
Perrucci, R.
Waddell, J. O.
Williams, M.

School of Science:

Biological Sciences:
Altman, J.
Arnott, S.
Aronson, A. I.
Brenchley, J. E.
Chiscon, J. A.
Cramer, W. A.
Crane, F. L.
Das, G. D.
Dilley, R. A.
Gilham, P. T.
Golub, E. S.
Jaffe, L.
Lovett, J. S.
Morre, D. J.
Moskowitz, M.
Nakajima, S.
Nakajima, Y.
Ostroy, S. E.
Pak, W. L.
Pinto, L. H.
Postlethwait, S. N.
Ray, W. J.
Rossmann, M. G.
Simon, E. H.
Smith, L. D.
Tessman, I.
Umbarger, H. E.
Williams, L. S.
Winfree, A. T.

Chemistry:
Angell, C. A.
Benkeser, R. A.
Brewster, J. H.
Cooks, R. G.
Daly, P. J.
Davenport, D. A.
Diestler, D. J.
Edgell, W. F.
Fong, F. K.
Grimley, R. T.
Herron, J. D.
Honig, J. M.
Laskowski, M.
Light, A.
Lipschutz, M. E.
Livingston, R. L.
Lytle, F. E.
Margerum, D. W.
Markley, J. L.

Morrison, H. A.
Mueller, C. R.
Muller, N.
Negishi, E.
Pardue, H. L.
Porile, N. T.
Richardson, J. W.
Robinson, W. R.
Sneen, R. A.
Truce, W. E.
Van Etten, R. L.
Walton, R. A.
Wolinsky, J.

*Geosciences:*

Agee, E. M.
Hinze, W. J.
Kullerud, G.
Levandowski, D. W.
Melhorn, W. N.
Meyer, H. O. A.
Smith, P. J.

*Mathematical Sciences:*

Abhyankar, S.
Baouendi, M. S.
Baxter, G.
Becker, J. C.
Berkovitz, L. D.
Branges, Louis de
Brown, L. G.
Clark, A. H.
Cumberbatch, E.
Davis, B. J.
Drasin, D.
Fuller, W. R.
Gambill, R. A.
Gottlieb, D. H.
Haas, F.
Heinzer, W.
Hunt, R. A.
Jerison, M.
Kaplan, S.
Keedy, M. L.
Krabbe, G. L.
Lillo, J. C.
Lipman, J.
Mullikin, T. W.
Neugebauer, C.
Pollard, H.
Price, J. J.
Putnam, C. R.
Rubin, J.
Sawyer, S.
Schultz, R. E.
Silverman, E.
Thoe, D.
Thurber, J. K.
Wang, J. S. P.
Weitsman, A.
Weston, V. H.
Zachmanoglou, E. C.
Zink, R. E.

*Physics:*

Andrew, K. L.
Ascarelli, G.
Balazs, L. A. P.
Barnes, V. E.
Becker, W. M.
Bray, R.
Capps, R. H.
Carmony, D. D.
Colella, R.
Fischbach, E.
Fowler, E. C.
Fuchs, N. H.
Furdyna, J. K.
Gaidos, J. A.
Garfinkel, A. F.
Gartenhaus, S.
Grabowski, Z. W.
Gutay, L. J.
Johnson, O. E.
Keesom, P. H.
Kim, Y. E.

Kuo, T. K.
Loeffler, F. J.
McIlwain, R. L.
MacKay, J. W.
Mieher, R. L.
Miller, D. H.
Mullen, J. G.
Overhauser, A. W.
Palfrey, T. R.
Pearlman, N.
Prohofsky, E. W.
Ramdas, A. K.
Rodriguez, S.
Rosen, S. P.
Scharenberg, R. P.
Simms, P. C.
Sladek, R. J.
Steffen, R. M.
Sugawara, M.
Tendam, D. J.
Tubis, A.
Willmann, R. B.

*Statistics:*

Anderson, V. L.
Berger, J. O.
Gleser, L. J.
Gupta, S. S.
Hicks, C. R.
Moore, D. S.
Pillai, K. C. S.
Puri, P. S.
Rubin, H.
Studden, W. J.
Yackel, J. W.

*Computer Sciences:*

Buchi, J. R.
Conte, S. D.
Denning, P. J.
Gautschi, W.
Rice, J. R.
Rosen, S.
Young, P. R.

*School of Technology:*

*Applied Technology:*
McNelly, G. W.

*Aviation Technology:*
Blatchley, E. R.
Duncan, W. P.
Maris, J. R.
Treager, I. E.

*Building Construction:*
Moss, D. D.
Snyder, J. H.

*Electrical Engineering Technology:*
Hoeche, V. W.
Hubele, R. C.
Lentz, C. E.
Rainey, G. L.

*General Studies:*
Schwarz, R. F.
Smith, D. R.

*Industrial Education:*
Carrel, J. J.
Eddy, M.
Mason, W H.
McVicker, H. E.
Neher, L. D.
Sams, D.
Suess, A. R.

*Mechanical Engineering Technology:*
Banton, H. L.
Pritchett, S. L.
Travis, H. T.

*Supervision:*
Bobillo, R. M.
Hull, T. F.
Windle, J. L.

*Technology:*
Lisack, J. P.

## ROSE-HULMAN INSTITUTE OF TECHNOLOGY

5500 WABASH AVENUE,
TERRE HAUTE, INDIANA 47803

Founded 1874.

*President:* Dr. Samuel F. Hulbert.
*Vice-President for Financial Affairs and Business Manager:* R. J. Miller.
*Dean:* J. R. Eierfert.
*Registrar:* L. W. Harmening.
*Librarian:* H. Cole, Jr. (Director of the Library).

The library contains 40,000 volumes.

Number of teachers: 90.
Number of students: 1,250.

Publication: *Bulletin* (bi-annually).

## SAINT FRANCIS COLLEGE*

2701 SPRING ST.,
FORT WAYNE, INDIANA 46808

Telephone: 432-3551.

Founded 1890.

*President:* Sister M. J. Scheetz.
*Registrar:* Sister M. Agnes.
*Librarian:* Sister M. Ida.

Number of teachers: 100.
Number of students: 1,211.

* No reply received to our questionnaire this year.

## SAINT JOSEPH'S COLLEGE

RENSSELAER, INDIANA 47978

Telephone: (219) 866-7111.

Founded 1889.

*President:* Charles Banet.
*Registrar:* C. Robbins.
*Librarian:* R. Vigeant.

The library contains 120,000 vols.

Number of teachers: 65.
Number of students: 1,002.

## SAINT MARY-OF-THE-WOODS COLLEGE

SAINT MARY-OF-THE-WOODS, INDIANA 47876

Telephone: (812) 535-4141.

Founded 1840.

*President:* Sister Jeanne Knoerle, s.p.

*Vice-President for Academic Affairs:* Sister Suzanne Dailey, s.p. (acting).
*Vice-President for Development:* Jean Fuqua, s.p.
*Vice-President for Business Affairs:* Alice Ann Rhinesmith, s.p.
*Vice-President for Student Affairs:* Sister Kathleen Desautels, s.p. (acting).

*Registrar:* CHARLES W. WATSON.
*Dean of Admissions:* TERRI GRASSO, S.P.
*Librarian:* Sister EMILY WALSH.

The library contains 131,000 vols.
Number of teachers: 58 full-time, 20 part-time, total 78.
Number of students: 978.

### SAINT MARY'S COLLEGE
NOTRE DAME, INDIANA 46556
Founded 1844.

*President:* Dr. JOHN M. DUGGAN.
*Vice-President and Dean of Faculty:* Dr. WILLIAM A. HICKEY.
*Vice-President for College Relations:* LAWRENCE DURANCE.
*Dean of Student Affairs:* Dr. KATHLEEN M. RICE.
*Controller:* JASON D. LINDOWER, Jr.

The library contains 145,600 vols.
Number of students: 1,819.

Publications: *Courier, Saint Mary's Reports* (quarterly), *Blue Mantle, Chimes* (annually).

### TAYLOR UNIVERSITY
UPLAND, INDIANA 46989
Telephone: (317) 998-2751.
Founded 1846.

Duration of academic year: September to May (three terms).

*President:* Dr. GREGG O. LEHMAN.
*Director of Records:* CARMEN TAYLOR.
*Dean of Admissions:* RONALD L. KELLER.
*Librarian:* Miss ALICE HOLCOMBE.

The library contains 129,000 vols.
Number of teachers: 84.
Number of students: 1,582.

Publications: *Profile, Taylor University Magazine, Taylor Club News.*

### UNIVERSITY OF EVANSVILLE
P.O.B. 329,
EVANSVILLE, INDIANA 47702
Founded 1854.

*President:* Dr. WALLACE B. GRAVES.
*Registrar:* KENNETH H. JONES.
*Vice-President for Academic Affairs:* MALCOLM H. FORBES.
*Vice-President for Student Affairs:* THORNTON B. PATBERG.
*Vice-President for Administration:* Dr. FRANK S. MCKENNA.
*Vice-President for Development:* JAMES W. LADD.
*Director of Admissions:* STEPHEN D. GRISSOM.

Number of teachers: 200, including 41 professors.

Number of students: 2,154 men, 3,026 women, total 5,180 (day and evening).

Publication: *The Crescent.*

DEANS:
*College of Alternative Programs:* Dr. ROGER H. SUBLETT.
*College of Arts and Sciences:* Dr. SAMUEL E. LONGMIRE.
*School of Business Administration:* Dr. GARY A. LYNCH.
*School of Engineering:* Dr. JOHN R. TOOLEY.
*School of Nursing:* Dr. LOIS J. MERRILL.
*School of Education:* Dr. RONALD E. GOLDENBERG.
*College of Fine Arts:* VINCENT L. ANGOTTI.
*School of Graduate Studies:* Dr. RONALD E. GOLDENBERG.
*Learning Resources:* Dr. P. GRADY MOREIN.
*Students:* B. JAMES DAWSON.

### UNIVERSITY OF NOTRE DAME
NOTRE DAME, INDIANA 46556
Telephone: (219) 283-6011.
Founded 1842.

*President:* Rev. THEODORE M. HESBURGH, C.S.C., S.T.D.
*Executive Vice-President:* Rev. E. P. JOYCE, C.S.C., C.P.A.
*General Counsel:* PHILIP J. FACCENDA, J.D.
*Provost:* O. TIMOTHY O'MEARA, PH.D.
*Vice-President for Advanced Studies:* ROBERT E. GORDON, PH.D.
*Vice-President for Business Affairs:* THOMAS J. MASON, M.B.A., C.P.A.
*Vice-President for Student Affairs:* Rev. JOHN L. VANWOLVLEAR, C.S.C., M.A.
*Vice-President for Public Relations and Development:* J. W. FRICK, PH.D.
*Director of Admissions:* JOHN T. GOLDRICK, M.A.
*Registrar:* RICHARD J. SULLIVAN, M.B.A.
*Librarian:* ROBERT C. MILLER, M.S., M.A.
*Archivist:* WENDY C. SCHLERETH, PH.D.
*Library:* see Libraries.

Number of teachers: 749.
Number of students: 8,750.

Publications: *The Scholastic, American Midland Naturalist, Review of Politics, Publications in Medieval Studies, Notre Dame Lawyer, Technical Review, The Juggler, Journal of Symbolic Logic, Notre Dame Student Business Review, The Observer, The Dome. Notre Dame Magazine, The American Journal of Jurisprudence, Notre Dame Report, The History Teacher, Science Quarterly, Texts and Studies in the History of Medieval Education.*

DEANS:
*Freshman Year of Studies:* EMIL T. HOFMAN, PH.D.
*Faculty of Arts and Letters:* ISABEL CHARLES, PH.D.
*Faculty of Business Administration:* YUSAKU FURUHASHI, PH.D. (acting).
*Faculty of Engineering:* J. C. HOGAN, PH.D.
*Faculty of Law:* DAVID T. LINK, J.D.
*Faculty of Science:* B. WALDMAN, PH.D.
*Continuing Education:* T. P. BERGIN, D.S.S.
*Administration:* L. M. CORBACI, M.A.

ATTACHED INSTITUTES:
Lobund Laboratory (Microbiology).
Institute for International Studies.
Center for the Study of Man in Contemporary Society.
Urban Studies Institute.
Radiation Laboratory.
Center for the Study of Human Rights.
Center for Constitutional Studies.
Thomas and Alberta White Center.
Center for the Study of American Catholicism.

### VALPARAISO UNIVERSITY
VALPARAISO, INDIANA 46383
Telephone: (219) 462-5115.
Founded 1859.

*President:* Dr. R. V. SCHNABEL.
*Registrar:* P. THUNE.
*Director of Admissions:* WARREN MULLER.
*Librarian:* EDWIN A. JOHNSON.

The library contains 324,000 vols.
Number of teachers: 301.
Number of students: 3,912.

### WABASH COLLEGE
CRAWFORDSVILLE, INDIANA 47933
Telephone: (317) 362-1400.
Founded 1832.

*President:* LEWIS SALTER.
*Registrar:* THEODORE BEDRICK.
*Librarian:* LAWRENCE FRYE.

The library contains 291,990 vols.
Number of teachers: 75.
Number of students: 800.

## IOWA

### BUENA VISTA COLLEGE
STORM LAKE, IOWA 50588
Telephone: (712) 749-2351.
Founded 1891.

*President:* KEITH G. BRISCOE.
*Dean of Faculty:* FREDERIC D. BROWN, PH.D.

The library contains 73,000 vols.
Number of teachers: 50.
Number of students: 1,300.

## CENTRAL COLLEGE
PELLA, IOWA 50219
Telephone: (515) 628-4151.
Founded 1853.

*President:* K. J. WELLER.
*Vice-President for Finance:* R. FROELICH.
*Academic Dean:* H. KOLENBRANDER.
*Librarian:* C. PERRY.

The library contains 120,000 vols.
**Number of students:** 1,500.
Publications: *The Central Bulletin, The Central Ray, The Pelican.*

## CLARKE COLLEGE
1550 CLARKE DRIVE,
DUBUQUE, IOWA 52001
Telephone: (319) 588-6300.
Founded 1843.

*President:* MENEVE DUNHAM, PH.D.
*Vice-President for Academic Affairs:* THOMAS MCCARVER.
*Dean for Student Development:* PATRICK CONLON.
*Admissions Director:* EDWIN REGER.
*Registrar:* Sister MARY EUGENA SULLIVAN, B.V.M.
*Librarian:* Sister KATHLEEN MULLIN, B.V.M.

The library contains 121,000 vols.
**Number of teachers:** 70.
**Number of students:** 840.
Publication: *On Campus* (quarterly).

## COE COLLEGE
CEDAR RAPIDS, IOWA 52402
Telephone: (319) 399-8000.
Founded 1851.

*President:* LEO L. NUSSBAUM.
*Registrar:* JOHN JACKOBS.
*Vice-President and Dean:* J. PRESTON COLE.
*Vice-President for Business Affairs:* WERNER SNOW.
*Vice-President for Development:* PETER J. LAUGEN.
*Director of Admissions:* CHRISTINE GALLOWAY.
*Dean of Student Services:* LYNNEA HALBERG.
*Librarian:* RICHARD DOYLE.

The library contains 180,235 vols.
**Number of teachers:** 80.
**Number of students:** 1,243.
Publications: *Courier* (quarterly), *Bulletin* (annually).

## CORNELL COLLEGE
MOUNT VERNON, IOWA 52314
Telephone: (319) 895-8811.
Founded 1853.

*President:* Dr. PHILIP B. SECOR.

*Dean of the College:* Dr. ROBERT P. LEWIS.
*Vice-President for Business Affairs and Treasurer:* CHARLES M. COCHRAN.
*Dean of Students:* DONNA M. HUNTER.
*Director of Library Services:* STUART A. STIFFLER.

The library contains 172,000 vols.
**Number of teachers:** 66.
**Number of students:** 922.

## DORDT COLLEGE
SIOUX CENTER, IOWA 51250
Telephone: (712) 722-3771.
Founded 1955.

*President:* Rev. B. J. HAAN.
*Academic Dean:* Dr. DOUGLAS RIBBENS.
*Dean of Students:* Rev. JOHN HULST.
*Director of Admissions:* HOWARD HALL.
*Librarian:* Miss HESTER HOLLAAR.

The library contains 90,000 vols.
**Number of teachers:** 69 full-time, 8 part-time.
**Number of students:** 1,200.

## DRAKE UNIVERSITY
26TH ST. AND UNIVERSITY AVE.,
DES MOINES, IOWA 50311
Chartered 1881.
Telephone: (515) 271-2011.

Private control; Academic year: September to May (two terms).

*President:* W. C. MILLER, PH.D., LL.D.
*Vice-President, Academic Administration:* J. W. KOLKA, J.D., PH.D.
*Vice-President, Business and Finance:* C. A. KASTEN, B.A., M.B.A.
*Vice-President, Institutional Development:* K. E. DOVE, B.S.
*Vice-President, Student Life:* D. V. ADAMS, M.A., ED.D.
*Registrar:* R. C. SCHEETZ, B.A.
*Director of Institutional Research:* L. M. LANDIS, M.S., ED., PH.D.
*Director of Libraries:* W. A. STOPPEL, M.A., PH.D.

The library contains 415,000 vols. and 2,250 periodicals.
**Number of teachers:** 276 full-time, 26 part-time.
**Number of students:** 4,510 full-time, 2,082 part-time.
Publications: *Drake Law Review, Drake Perspectives* (quarterly).

DEANS:
*Law School:* R. M. CALKINS, B.A., J.D.
*Continuing Education:* P. D. LANGERMAN, M.S., PH.D.
*Graduate School:* E. L. CANFIELD, M.A., PH.D.
*College of Business Administration:* R. G. PEEBLER, M.A., C.P.A.
*College of Education:* A. SCHWARTZ, M.A., PH.D.

*College of Fine Arts:* J. E. ERLENBACH, M.M., PH.D.
*School of Journalism:* H. STRENTZ, M.A., PH.D.
*College of Liberal Arts:* PATSY H. SAMPSON.
*College of Pharmacy:* C. BOYD GRANBERG, M.S., PH.D.

## GRACELAND COLLEGE
LAMONI, IOWA 50140
Telephone: (515) 784-5000.
Founded 1895.

*President:* JOE E. HANNA.
*Vice-President for Academic Affairs and Dean of Faculty:* PAUL M. EDWARDS.
*Vice-President for Financial Affairs:* RALPH E. WOUTERS.
*Vice-President for Student Affairs:* NEWELL R. YATES.
*Registrar:* J. T. CLOSSON.
*Librarian:* VOLANTE H. RUSSELL.

The library contains 91,000 vols.
**Number of teachers:** 87.
**Number of students:** 1,309.

## GRINNELL COLLEGE
GRINNELL, IOWA 50112
Founded 1846.

*President:* GEORGE A. DRAKE, M.A., PH.D.
*Executive Vice-President:* W. S. WALKER, M.A., PH.D.
*Dean of Student Affairs:* JAMES TEDERMAN, M.A.,
*Librarian:* C. MCKEE, A.M.L.S.

Library of 250,000 vols.
**Number of teachers:** 123, including 44 professors.
**Number of students:** 685 men, 549 women, total 1,234.

## IOWA STATE UNIVERSITY OF SCIENCE AND TECHNOLOGY
AMES, IOWA 50011
Telephone: (515) 294-1840.
Founded 1858.

*President:* W. R. PARKS, PH.D.
*Vice-President for Business and Finance:* W. R. MOORE, B.S.
*Vice-President for Academic Affairs:* G. C. CHRISTENSEN, D.V.M., M.S., PH.D.
*Vice-President for Information and Development:* C. HAMILTON, B.S.
*Vice-President for Research:* D. J. ZAFFARANO, PH.D.
*Vice-President for Student Affairs:* THOMAS B. THIELEN, PH.D.

Library: see Libraries.
**Number of students:** 24,268.

Publications: *The Agriculturist, The Iowa Engineer, Outlook, Ethos, The Veterinary Student, Engineering Research, Iowa State Daily, Iowa State Journal of Research, Iowa Stater.*

### Deans:

Agriculture: Lee Roy Kolmer, ph.d.
Design: Michael P. Brooks, ph.d.
Education: V. S. Lagomarcino, ph.d.
Engineering: D. R. Boylan, Jr., ph.d.
Graduate College: D. J. Zaffarano, ph.d.
Home Economics: Ruth E. Deacon, ph.d.
Sciences and Humanities: Wallace A. Russell, ph.d.
Veterinary Medicine: Phillip T. Pearson, ph.d.
Admissions and Records: Fred C. Schlunz, m.a.
University Extension: Robert L. Crom, ph.d.
Students: Jon C. Dalton, ed.d.
Library Services: Warren B. Kuhn, m.l.s.

### Professors:

*College of Agriculture:*
Amemiya, M., ph.d., Agronomy
Anderson, I. C., m.s., ph.d., Agronomy
Anderson, L. L., ph.d., Animal Science
Atherly, A. G., ph.d., Genetics
Atkins, R. E., ph.d., Agronomy
Bachmann, R. W., ph.d., Animal Ecology
Baumel, P., ph.d., Agricultural Economics
Bauske, R. J., ph.d., Horticulture
Beer, C. E., ph.d., Agricultural Engineering
Beitz, D. C., ph.d., Animal Science, Biochemistry and Biophysics
Beneke, R. R., ph.d., Agricultural Economics
Benson, G. O., ph.d., Agronomy
Blinn, E. G., m.s., Journalism and Mass Communication
Boehlje, M. D., ph.d., Agricultural Economics
Bohlen, J. M., ph.d., Sociology
Boyd, D. E., ph.d., Journalism and Mass Communication
Brackelsberg, P. O., ph.d., Animal Science
Bratton, C. G., m.s., Journalism and Mass Communication
Bremner, J. M., ph.d., Agronomy
Buchele, W. F., m.s., ph.d., Agricultural Engineering
Buck, G. J., ph.d., Horticulture
Bultena, G. L., ph.d., Sociology
Burris, J. S., ph.d., Plant Pathology
Burroughs, W., ph.d., Animal Science
Carlander, K. D., ph.d., Animal Ecology
Carlson, I. T., ph.d., Agronomy
Carlson, R. E., ph.d., Agronomy
Christian, L. L., ph.d., Animal Science
Crawford, H. R., ph.d., Agricultural Education and Secondary Education
Crom, R. I., ph.d., Journalism and Mass Communication
Countryman, D. W., ph.d., Forestry
Dahm, P. A., m.a., ph.d., Entomology
Denisen, E. L., m.s., ph.d., Horticulture
Dewitt, J. R., ph.d., Entomology
Dinsmore, J. J., ph.d., Animal Ecology
Disney, R. L., b.a., Journalism and Mass Communication
Emmerson, J. T., ph.d., Journalism and Mass Communication
Epstein, A. H., ph.d., Botany
Ewan, R. C., ph.d., Animal Science
Ewing, S. A., ph.d., Animal Science
Fehr, W. R., ph.d., Agronomy
Fenton, T. E., ph.d., Agronomy
Foreman, C. F., m.s., ph.d., Animal Science
Freeman, A. E., m.s., ph.d., Animal Science (Dairy Science)
Frey, K. J., ph.d., Agronomy
Futrell, G. A., ph.d., Agricultural Economics
George, J. R., ph.d., Agronomy
Giese, H., m.s.(a.e.), arch.e., Agricultural Engineering
Goudy, W. J., ph.d., Sociology
Gratto, C. P., ph.d., Agricultural Economics
Graves, D. J., ph.d., Biochemistry and Biophysics
Green, D. E., ph.d., Agronomy
Hall, C. V., ph.d., Horticulture
Hamilton, C., b.s., Journalism and Mass Communication
Hammond, E. G., m.a., ph.d., Food Technology
Hanway, J. J., m.s., ph.d., Agronomy
Harl, N. E., ph.d., Economics
Harris, D. G., ph.d., Economics
Haynes, E. H., ph.d., Animal Science
Hazen, T. E., m.s., ph.d., Agricultural Engineering
Heady, E. O., m.s., ph.d., Agricultural Economics
Hodges, C. F., ph.d., Horticulture
Hoerner, T. A., ph.d., Agricultural Engineering
Hoffman, M. P., ph.d., Animal Science
Hopkins, F. S., Jr., ph.d., Forestry
Hvistendahl, J. K., ph.d., Journalism and Mass Communication
Imsande, J. D., ph.d., Genetics-Biochemistry and Biophysics
Jacobson, N. L., m.s., ph.d., Animal Science, Dairy Science
James, S. C., ph.d., Agricultural Economics
Jennings, V. M., ph.d., Plant Pathology Seed and Weed Sciences
Johnson, H. P., m.s., ph.d., Agricultural Engineering
Jurgens, M. H., ph.d., Animal Science
Kahan, R. S., ph.d., Journalism and Mass Communication
Kahler, A. A., ph.d., Agricultural Education
Kiser, J. J., m.s., Animal Science
Kline, E. A., m.s., ph.d., Animal Science
Klonglan, G., ph.d., Sociology
Kolmer, L. R., ph.d., Economics
Kraft, A. A., ph.d., Food Technology
Kunerth, W. F., m.s., Journalism and Mass Communication
Ladd, G. W., m.a., ph.d., Agricultural Economics
LaGrange, W. F., m.s., Animal Science
Lagrange, W. S., ph.d., Food Technology
Lawrence, R. L., ph.d., Education
Lewis, R. E., ph.d., Entomology
Lovely, G., b.s., Agricultural Engineering
Lush, J. L., m.s., ph.d., Animal Science
McClelland, J. B., m.s., ph.d., Agricultural Education
McGilliard, A. D., ph.d., Animal Science
McNabb, H. S., m.s., ph.d., Plant Pathology
Mahlstede, J. P., ph.d., Horticulture
Manwiller, F. G., ph.d., Forestry
Marion, W. W., ph.d., Food Technology
Marley, S. J., ph.d., Agricultural Engineering
Marvin, K. R., m.s., Journalism and Mass Communication
Melvin, S. W., ph.d., Agricultural Engineering
Menzel, B. W., ph.d., Animal Ecology
Meyer, V. M., m.s., Agricultural Engineering
Miller, W. J., ph.d., Genetics
Moorman, R. B., ph.d., Animal Ecology
Nichols, H. E., m.s., Horticulture
Nordskog, A. W., m.s., ph.d., Animal Science
Norton, D. C., m.sc., ph.d., Plant Pathology
Nyvall, R. F., ph.d., Plant Pathology
Owings, W. J., ph.d., Animal Science
Parrish, F. C., Jr., ph.d., Animal Science
Parsons, G. E., ph.d., Agricultural Education
Paulsen, A. A., ph.d., Agricultural Economics
Pearce, R. B., ph.d., Agronomy
Pedersen, J. H., m.s., ph.d., Agricultural Engineering
Pedigo, L. P., ph.d., Entomology
Pesek, J. T., Jr., ph.d., Agronomy
Peterson, P. A., ph.d., Agronomy
Pollard, M. L., ph.d., Journalism and Mass Communication
Powers, R. C., ph.d., Rural Sociology
Prestemon, D. R., ph.d., Forestry
Robertson, D. S., ph.d., Genetics
Robinson, J. L., m.s., ph.d., Agronomy
Robson, R. M., ph.d., Animal Science, Biochemistry and Biophysics
Rowley, W. A., ph.d., Entomology
Russell, W. A., m.s., ph.d., Agronomy
Rust, R. E., m.s., Animal Science
Schafer, J. W., Jr., ph.d., Agronomy
Scholtes, W. H., m.s., ph.d., Agronomy
Scott, A. D., ph.d., Agronomy
Scott, J. T., m.b.a., ph.d., Agricultural Economics and Rural Sociology
Self, H. L., m.s., ph.d., Animal Science
Sell, J. L., ph.d., Animal Science
Shaw, R. H., ph.d., Climatology
Shelley, J. D., b.j., Journalism and Mass Communication
Shibles, R. M., ph.d., Agronomy
Skadberg, J. M., ph.d., Economics
Skrdla, W. H., ph.d., Agronomy
Smith, R. J., ph.d., Agricultural Engineering
Speer, V. C., m.s., ph.d., Animal Science
Stadler, Joan K., ph.d., Genetics
Staniforth, D. W., m.sc., ph.d., Botany Agronomy
Stevermer, E. J., ph.d., Animal Science
Stockdale, H. J., ph.d., Entomology
Stritzel, J. A., m.s., ph.d., Agronomy
Stromer, M. H., ph.d., Food Technology
Summerfelt, R. C., ph.d., Animal Ecology
Tabatabai, M. A., ph.d., Agronomy
Tait, J. L., ph.d., Sociology and Anthropology
Thomas, B. H., ph.d., Biochemistry
Thompson, H. E., ph.d., Agronomy
Thompson, L. M., m.s., ph.d., Agronomy
Thomson, G. W., m.s., ph.d., Forestry
Timmons, J. F., m.a., ph.d., Agricultural Economics
Tipton, C. L., ph.d., Biochemistry and Biophysics
Trenkle, A. H., ph.d., Animal Science
Troeh, F. R., m.s., Agronomy
Van Fossen, L. D., m.voc.ed., Agricultural Engineering
Voelker, D. E., m.s., Animal Science

Voss, R. D., ph.d., Agronomy
Walker, H. W., m.s., ph.d., Food Technology
Warner, D. R., ph.d., Animal Science
Webb, J. R., ph.d., Agronomy
**Wedin, W. F.**, m.s., ph.d., Agronomy
Weigle, J. L., ph.d., Horticulture
Welshons, W. J., ph.d., Genetics
Wickersham, T. W., m.s., Animal Science
Willham, R. L., ph.d., Animal Science
Williams, D. L., d.ed., Agricultural Education, Secondary Education
Wisner, R. N., ph.d., Agricultural Economics
**Woolley, D. G.**, m.s., ph.d., Agronomy
Wunder, W. W., ph.d., Animal Science
Yarbrough, J. P., ph.d., Journalism and Mass Communication
Young, J. W., ph.d., Animal Science
Zimmerman, D. R., ph.d., Animal Science
**Zmolek, W. G.**, m.s., Animal Science

*College of Design:*
Allen, P. M., m.f.a., Art and Design
Brooks, M. P., ph.d., Community and Regional Planning
Carpenter, K. E., m.arch., Architecture
Danielson, D. R., m.s., Art and Design
Dyas, R. W., m.l.a., Landscape Architecture
Fenimore, R. D., m.s., Art and Design
Fitzsimmons, J. R., m.l.a., Landscape Architecture
Gottfried, H. W., ph.d., Art and Design
Harvey, R. R., m.l.a., Landscape Architecture
Heemstra, H. C., m.arch., Architecture
Heggen, R. D., m.f.a., Art and Design
Held, S. E., m.s., Art and Design
Kainlauri, E. O., ph.d., Architecture
Kitzman, M. J., m.m.a., Architecture
Lane, K. F., m.l.a., Landscape Architecture
McKeown, D. I., m.s., Architecture
Mahayni, R. G., ph.d., Community and Regional Planning
Meixner, Mary L., m.a., Home Economics Studies
Miller, E. S., m.f.a., Art and Design
Roberts, J. M., m.l.a., Landscape Architecture
Rutledge, A. J., m.l.a., Landscape Architecture
Shank, W. I., m.a., Architecture
Shao, P. P. W., m.f.a., Architecture
Slater, B. J., m.s., Architecture
Sontag, J., ph.d., Art and Design
Stone, V. F., b.arch., Architecture
Woods, J. E., ph.d., Architecture and Mechanical Engineering

*College of Education:*
Ahmann, J. S., ph.d., Professional Studies
Beard, J. R., ed.d., Elementary Education
Boyles, N., ph.d., Secondary Education
Breiter, J. C., ed.d., Elementary Education
Canute, R. J., ed.d., Professional Studies
**Dilts, H. E.**, ph.d., Secondary Education
Downs, G. E., ed.d., Elementary Education
Ebbers, L. H., ph.d., Professional Studies
Engel, R. A., ph.d., Professional Studies
Forker, B. E., ph.d., Physical Education

Frye, M. Virginia, ph.d., Physical Education
Glass, L. W., ph.d., Secondary Education
Hopper, G. C., ed.d., Guidance and Counselling
Howe, T. G., ph.d., Professional Studies
Hunter, W. A., ph.d., Professional Studies
Jones, C. W., ph.d., Professional Studies
Kizer, G. A., ph.d., Professional Studies
Kniker, C. R., ed.d., Secondary Education
Lagomarcino, V., ph.d., Professional Studies
Manatt, R. P., ph.d., Professional Studies
Menze, L. E., b.s., Physical Education
Miller, W. G., ph.d., Industrial Education
Netusil, A., ph.d., Professional Studies
Nichols, H. J., ph.d. Physical Education
Parks, G. A., ed.d., Industrial Education
Pellegreno, D. D., ed.d., Professional Studies
Schloerke, W. C., ed.d., Secondary Education
Schneider, L. R., m.s., Physical Education, Secondary Education
Sherick, A. M., m.s., Industrial Education
Smith, L. G., ph.d., Secondary Education
Thomas, R. A., ph.d., Professional Studies
Toman, B., m.s., Physical Education
Volker, R. P., ph.d., Secondary Education
Warren, R. D., ph.d., Professional Studies
**Wolansky, W.**, ed.d., Industrial Education

*College of Engineering*
**Abraham, W. H.**, ph.d., Chemical Engineering
Anderson, D. A., ph.d., Aerospace Engineering
Arnold, L. K., m.s., ph.d., Chemical Engineering
Austin, T. A., ph.d., Civil Engineering
Bahadur, S., ph.d., Mechanical Engineering
Basart, J. P., ph.d., Electrical Engineering
**Baumann, E. R.**, m.s., ph.d., Civil Engineering
Baumgarten, J. R., ph.d., Mechanical Engineering
Bautista, R. G., ph.d., Chemical Engineering
Berard, M. F., ph.d., Materials Science and Engineering
Berger, R. W., ph.d., Industrial Engineering
Bergles, A. E., ph.d., Mechanical Engineering
Boylan, D. R., ph.d., Chemical Engineering
Brearley, H. C., ph.d., Electrical Engineering, Computer Science
Brewer, K. A., ph.d., Civil Engineering
Brockman, W. H., ph.d., Electrical Engineering
Brown, R. G., m.s., ph.d., Electrical Engineering
Burger, C. P., ph.d., Engineering Science and Mechanics
Burkhart, L. E., m.s., ph.d., Chemical Engineering
Burnett, G., Jr., m.s., ph.d., Nuclear Engineering

Camp, R. C., ph.d., Electrical Engineering
Carstens, R. L., ph.d., Civil Engineering
Cleasby, J. L., m.s., ph.d., Civil Engineering
Cook, W. J., ph.d., Mechanical Engineering
Cowles, H., m.s., ph.d., Industrial Engineering
Danofsky, R. A., ph.d., Nuclear Engineering
De Jong, P. S., m.s., Freshman Engineering
**Demirel, T.**, ph.d., Civil Engineering
Dodd, C. M., cer.e., Materials Science and Engineering
Dougal, M. D., ph.d., Civil Engineering
Eide, A. R., ph.d., Freshman Engineering
Ekberg, C. E., m.s., ph.d., Civil Engineering
Fellinger, R. C., m.s., Mechanical Engineering
**Fouad, Abdel**, ph.d., Electrical Engineering
Graham, F. M., ph.d., Engineering Science and Mechanics
Greer, R. T., ph.d., Engineering Science and Mechanics
Greimann, L. F., ph.d., Civil Engineering
**Griffen, D. L.**, m.s., j.d., Industrial Engineering
Hale, H. W., m.s., ph.d., Electrical Engineering
Hall, J. L., ph.d., Mechanical Engineering
Handy, R. L., m.s., ph.d., Civil Engineering
**Hardy, R. L.**, b.s.c.e., dr.-ing., Civil Engineering
Henkin, A., ph.d., Mechanical Engineering
Hill, J. C., ph.d., Chemical Engineering
Hoover, J. M., m.s., Civil Engineering
Hsieh, H. C., ph.d., Electrical Engineering
Hsu, C. T., ph.d., Aerospace Engineering
Hunter, O., ph.d., Materials Science and Engineering
Iversen, J. D., ph.d., Aerospace Engineering
Jeyapalan, K., ph.d., Civil Engineering
Jones, E. C., ph.d., Electrical Engineering
Junkhan, G. H., ph.d., Mechanical Engineering
Kavanagh, P., ph.d., Mechanical Engineering
Kayser, F. X., sc.d., Materials Science and Engineering
Klaiber, F. W., ph.d., Civil Engineering
Koerber, G. G., m.s., ph.d., Electrical Engineering
Kopplin, J. O., ph.d., Electrical Engineering
Larsen, W. L., ph.d., Materials Science and Engineering
Larson, J. L., Jr., m.s., Mechanical Engineering
Larson, M. A., m.s., ph.d., Chemical Engineering
Lee, Dah-Yinn, ph.d., Civil Engineering
Lohnes, R., ph.d., Civil Engineering
McConnell, K. G., ph.d., Engineering Science and Mechanics
McDaniel, T. J., ph.d., Aerospace Engineering
McGee, T. D., m.s., ph.d., Materials Science and Engineering
McRoberts, K. L., ph.d., Industrial Engineering

Mahmoud, A. A., ph.d., Electrical Engineering
Mashaw, L. H., b.s., Freshman Engineering
Michel, A. N., ph.d., Electrical Engineering
Mickle, J. L., ph.d., Civil Engineering
Mischke, C. R., m.s., ph.d., Mechanical Engineering
Montag, G. M., ph.d., Industrial Engineering
Moore, W. R., b.s., Industrial Engineering
Morgan, P. E., m.s., Civil Engineering
Munson, B. R., ph.d., Engineering Science and Mechanics
Nariboli, G. A., ph.d., Engineering Science and Mechanics
Nilsson, J. W., ph.d., Electrical Engineering
Northup, L. L., ph.d., Freshman Engineering
Okiiski, T. H., ph.d., Mechanical Engineering
Oulman, C. S., ph.d., Civil Engineering
Patterson, J. W., ph.d., Materials Science and Engineering
Patterson, R. E., b.s., Engineering Extension
Peters, L. C., ph.d., Mechanical Engineering
Peterson, P. W., ph.d., Engineering Research Institute, Aerospace Engineering
Pierson, B. L., ph.d., Aerospace Engineering
Pletcher, R. H., ph.d., Mechanical Engineering
Pohm, A. V., ph.d., Electrical Engineering
Porter, M. L., ph.d., Civil Engineering
Post, R. E., ph.d., Electrical Engineering
Potter, A. G., ph.d., Electrical Engineering
Pulsifer, A. H., ph.d., Chemical Engineering and Nuclear Engineering
Read, A. A., ph.d., Electrical Engineering
Reilly, P. J., ph.d., Chemical Engineering
Riley, W. F., m.s., Engineering Science and Mechanics
Ring, S. L., ph.d., Civil Engineering
Roberts, D. M., m.sc., ph.d., Nuclear Engineering
Rogge, T. R., ph.d., Engineering Science and Mechanics
Rohach, A. F., ph.d., Nuclear Engineering
Sanders, C. G., m.a., Freshman Engineering
Sanders, W. W., ph.d., Civil Engineering
Schmerr, L. W., ph.d., Engineering Science and Mechanics
Seagrave, R. C., ph.d., Chemical Engineering
Serovy, G. K., ph.d., Mechanical Engineering
Smay, T. A., ph.d., Electrical Engineering
Smith, C. E., ph.d., Industrial Engineering
Smith, G. W., m.s., ph.d., Industrial Engineering
Spangler, M. G., m.s., Civil Engineering
Swift, C. S., ph.d., Electrical Engineering
Tamashunas, V., m.s., Industrial Engineering
Tannehill, J. C., ph.d., Aerospace Engineering
Townsend, C. L., ph.d., Electrical Engineering
Triska, C. J., ph.d., Electrical Engineering
Tsai, Yu-Min, ph.d., Engineering Science and Mechanics
Ulrichson, D. L., ph.d., Chemical Engineering
Vaughn, R. C., m.i.e., Industrial Engineering
Verhoeven, J., ph.d., Materials Science and Engineering
Weiss, H. J., d.sc., Engineering Science and Mechanics
Wheelock, T. D., ph.d., Chemical Engineering
Wilder, D. R., ph.d., Materials Science and Engineering
Willett, R. M., ph.d., Electrical Engineering
Wilson, L. N., ph.d., Aerospace Engineering
Young, D. F., ph.d., Engineering Science and Mechanics
Young, J. C., ph.d., Civil Engineering
Zingg, R., ph.d., Electrical Engineering, Computer Science

*College of Home Economics:*
Anderson, J. M., m.s., Home Economics
Beavers, I., ph.d., Home Economics Education
Bivens, G. E., ph.d., Family Environment
Brewer, Wilma D., m.s., ph.d., Food and Nutrition
Clark, S. G., ph.d., Child Development
Coulson, R. W., ph.d., Child Development
Deacon, Ruth, ph.d., Family Environment
Dupont, Jacqueline, ph.d., Food and Nutrition
Elliott, E. A., ph.d., Home Economics Education
Fanslow, A. M., ph.d., Home Economics Education
Galejs, Irma, ph.d., Child Development
Garcia, P. A., ph.d., Food and Nutrition
Hathcock, J. N., ph.d., Food and Nutrition
Heltsley, M. E., ph.d., Family Environment
Huepenbecker, A. L., ph.d., Textiles and Clothing
Hughes, R. P., ph.d., Home Economics Education, Secondary Education
McKinley, Marjorie M., m.a., ph.d., Institution Management
Olson, P. J., m.s., Food and Nutrition
Osman, E. M., ph.d., Food and Nutrition
Pease, Damaris, m.s., ph.d., Child Development
Peet, Louise J., m.a., ph.d., Family Environment
Pickett, Mary S., ph.d., Family Environment
Powers, E. A., ph.d., Family Environment
Roderuck, Charlotte E., m.s., ph.d., Food and Nutrition
Schwieder, E. W., ph.d., Family Environment
Stockdale, D. F., ph.d., Child Development
Winakor, Thora G., m.s., ph.d., Textiles and Clothing

*College of Sciences and Humanities:*
Abian, A., m.s., ph.d., Mathematics
Allen, E. S., ph.d., Mathematics
Angelici, R. J., ph.d., Chemistry
Applequist, J. B., ph.d., Biochemistry-Biophysics
Apt, L. J., ph.d., History
Athreya, K. B., ph.d., Mathematics and Statistics
Avant, L. L., ph.d., Psychology
Balinsky, J., ph.d., Zoology
Barnes, R. G., m.a., ph.d., Physics
Barnes, W. E., s.m., ph.d., Mathematics
Barton, T. J., ph.d., Chemistry
Bataille, R. R., ph.d., English
Beavers, W. I., ph.d., Physics
Benson, D. R., m.a., ph.d., English
Bernard, R. W., ph.d., Foreign Languages and Literatures
Biggs, D. L., m.a., ph.d., Earth Science
Bleyle, C. O., ph.d., Music
Bishop, S. H., ph.d., Zoology
Boles, D. E., ph.d., Political Science
Borgen, F. H., ph.d., Psychology
Bowen, G. H., ph.d., Physics
Brown, D. W., m.b.a., Business Administration
Brown, F. G., ph.d., Psychology, Secondary Education
Brown, G. G., ph.d., Zoology
Bruner, C. H., m.a., Foreign Languages and Literatures
Bruner, D. K., a.m., ph.d., English
Burkhalter, N. L., m.m., ph.d., Music, Secondary Education
Buttrey, B. W., m.s., ph.d., Zoology
Cain, B. E., ph.d., Mathematics
Carlson, B. C., m.a., ph.d., Physics and Mathematics
Carlson, O. N., ph.d., Materials Science and Engineering
Charles, D. C., ph.d., Psychology and Secondary Education
Chen, C. W., ph.d., Materials Science and Engineering
Clem, J. R., ph.d., Physics
Cohen, H., ph.d., Sociology
Colwell, P., ph.d., Mathematics
Coolbaugh, R. C., ph.d., Botany
Corbett, J. D., ph.d., Chemistry
Cornette, J. L., ph.d., Mathematics
Courteau, J., ph.d., Foreign Languages and Literatures
Cox, C. P., m.a., Statistics
Cox, D. F., ph.d., Statistics
Cravens, H., ph.d., History
Crow, G. P., m.a., Air Force Aerospace Studies
Dahiya, R. S., ph.d., Mathematics
David, H. A., ph.d., Statistics
David, H. T., m.a., ph.d., Statistics and Industrial Engineering
Davies, P. G., ph.d., English
Dean, D. G., ph.d., Sociology
Dearin, R., ph.d., Speech
Dickson, S. E., ph.d., Mathematics
Dobson, J. M., ph.d., History
Dolphin, W. D., ph.d., Zoology
Dorfman, G. A., ph.d., Political Science
Dow, J. R., ph.d., Foreign Languages and Literatures
Drewes, C. D., ph.d., Zoology
Drexler, M. B., ph.d., Speech
Dunham, J., ph.d., Zoology
Durand, D. P., ph.d., Microbiology
Edwards, D. C., ph.d., Psychology
Elrod, J. W., ph.d., Philosophy
Espenson, J. H., ph.d., Chemistry
Faden, A. M., ph.d., Economics
Fassell, V. A., ph.d., Chemistry
Feinberg, L., ph.d., English
Fink, A., ph.d., Mathematics
Finnemore, D., ph.d., Physics
Firestone, A., ph.d., Physics
Fletcher, L. B., ph.d., Economics
Fox, K. A., m.a., ph.d., Economics
Franzen, H. F., ph.d., Chemistry
French, D., d.sc., ph.d., Biochemistry, Biophysics
Frink, O., ph.d., Foreign Languages and Literatures

Fritz, J. S., ph.d., Chemistry
Fromm, H. J., ph.d., Biochemistry
Fuchs, R., ph.d., Physics
Fuller, W. A., m.s., ph.d., Statistics
Galejs, J. E., m.a., Library
Galyon, A. E., Jr., ph.d., English
Gerstein, B. C., ph.d., Chemistry
Ghosh, Malay, ph.d., Statistics
Gilman, H., ph.d., Chemistry
Gradwohl, D. M., ph.d., Sociology and Anthropology
Graupera, A., m.a., Foreign Languages and Literatures
Groeneveld, R. A., ph.d., Statistics
Grossman, A. S., ph.d., Physics
Gschneidner, K. A., ph.d., Materials Science and Engineering
Hadwiger, D. F., ph.d., Political Science
Haggard, F. E., ph.d., English
Hammer, C. L., ph.d., Physics
Han, C.-P., ph.d., Statistics
Handy, C. B., ph.d., Business Administration
Hannum, T. E., ph.d., Psychology
Hansen, R. S., ph.d., Chemistry
Hartman, P. A., m.s., ph.d., Microbiology
Harville, D. A., ph.d., Statistics
Hentzel, I. R., ph.d., Mathematics
Herrnstadt, R. L., m.s., ph.d., English
Hickman, R. D., ph.d., Statistics
Hill, J. C., ph.d., Physics
Hinz, P. N., ph.d., Statistics and Forestry
Hodges, L. R., ph.d., Physics
Hoffman, D. K., ph.d., Chemistry
Holt, J. G., ph.d., Microbiology
Homer, R. H., ph.d., Mathematics
Hoover, L. L., ph.d., Business Administration
Horner, H. T., Jr., ph.d., Botany
Horowitz, J., ph.d., Biochemistry and Biophysics
Hotchkiss, D., ph.d., Statistics
Hutton, W., Jr., ph.d., Chemistry
Isaacson, D. I., ph.d., Statistics and Mathematics
Isely, D., m.s., ph.d., Botany
Jacobson, R. A., ph.d., Chemistry
Johnson, D. C., ph.d., Chemistry
Johnson, Q. C., ph.d., English
Jumper, W. C., m.a., ph.d., English and Speech
Kahn, A. S., ph.d., Psychology
Karas, G. G., m.s., ph.d., Psychology
Keith, P. M., ph.d., Sociology and Anthropology, Professional Studies
Keller, C., ph.d., History
Keller, R. F., ph.d., Mathematics, Computer Science
Kempthorne, O., m.a., sc.d., Statistics
Kennedy, W. J., ph.d., Statistics
Kernan, W. J., ph.d., Physics
Kirkendall, R., ph.d., History
Kihl, Y. W., ph.d., Political Science
Klemke, E. D., ph.d., Philosophy
Kliewer, K. L., ph.d., Physics
Knaphus, G., ph.d., Botany and Secondary Education
Kottman, R. N., ph.d., History
Kratochvil, M. R., a.m., English and Secondary Education
Kuhn, W. B., m.l.s., Library
Lacasa, Judith A., ph.d., Foreign Languages and Literatures
Lamb, R. C., ph.d., Physics
Lambert, R. J., m.s., ph.d., Mathematics
Lamotte, C. E., ph.d., Botany
Lando, H. A., ph.d., Psychology
Lapan, H. E., ph.d., Economics
Larson, R. L., m.s., Naval Science and Tactics
Lassila, K. E., ph.d., Physics
Layton, W. L., ph.d., Psychology
Lemish, J., ph.d., Earth Science

Lersten, N. R., ph.d., Botany
Levine, H. A., ph.d., Mathematics
Lewis, E. C., m.a., ph.d., Psychology
Lockhart, W. R., ph.d., Microbiology
Loudenback, Lynn J., ph.d., Business Administration
Lowitt, R., ph.d., History
Lowrie, J. A., ph.d., English
Luckett, D. G., m.a., ph.d., Economics
Luecke, G. R., ph.d., Mathematics
Lynch, D. W., m.s., ph.d., Physics
McCarley, R. F., ph.d., Chemistry
McJimsey, G. T., ph.d., History
McNee, J. C., a.m.l.s., Library
McVicker, C. D., m.a., ph.d., Foreign Languages and Literatures
Maple, C. G., m.a., d.sc., Mathematics and Computer Science
Martin, D. S., ph.d., Chemistry
Mathews, J. C., ph.d., Mathematics
Meeden, G. D., ph.d., Statistics
Meeker, W. Q., Jr., ph.d., Statistics
Merrill, W. C., ph.d., Economics
Metzler, D. E., ph.d., Biochemistry
Meyer, C. W., m.a., ph.d., Economics
Miller, R. K., ph.d., Mathematics
Morris, W. D., ph.d., Foreign Languages and Literatures
Muchinsky, P. M., ph.d., Psychology
Mulford, C. L., ph.d., Sociology
Mutchmor, J., ph.d., Zoology
Nevins, D., ph.d., Botany
Nordlie, B. E., ph.d., Earth Science
Olorunsola, V. A., ph.d., Political Science
Olson, J. A., ph.d., Biochemistry and Biophysics
Palmer, R. C., a.m., ph.d., English
Parks, W. R., m.a., ph.d., Political Science
Pattee, P. A., ph.d., Microbiology
Peglar, G. W., s.m., ph.d., Mathematics
Peters, R. H., ph.d., Psychology
Peterson, D., ph.d., Materials Science and Engineering
Pigozzi, D. L., ph.d., Mathematics
Pohl, R. W., ph.d., Botany
Pollak, E., ph.d., Statistics and Genetics
Powell, J. E., ph.d., Chemistry
Prescott, J. R., ph.d., Economics
Pursey, D. L., b.s., ph.d., Physics
Quinn, L. Y., ph.d., Microbiology
Rahman, M.-U., ph.d., Earth Sciences
Rasmussen, J., ph.d., Political Science, Secondary Education
Redmond, J. R., ph.d., Zoology
Reschly, D. J., ph.d., Psychology and Professional Studies
Ross, D. K., ph.d., Physics
Rudolph, W. B., ph.d., Mathematics and Secondary Education
Rue, N. L., m.a., Military Science and Tactics
Ruedenberg, K., ph.d., Chemistry
Russell, G. A., m.s., ph.d., Chemistry
Russell, W. A., ph.d., Psychology
Sanderson, D. E., m.s., ph.d., Mathematics
Schafer, R., ph.d., Sociology
Schofield, R. E., ph.d., History
Schuster, D. H., ph.d., Psychology
Seifert, G., ph.d., Mathematics
Seifert, K. E., ph.d., Earth Science
Shadle, H. L., ph.d., Business Administration
Small, G. J., ph.d., Chemistry
Smith, F. G., Botany
Smith, J. F., ph.d., Materials Science and Engineering
Sposito, V. A., ph.d., Statistics
Stanford, J. L., ph.d., Physics
Starleaf, D. R., ph.d., Economics
Stassis, C., ph.d., Physics

Steiner, A., ph.d., Mathematics
Steiner, E. F., ph.d., Mathematics
Stephenson, J. A., ph.d., Economics
Stewart, C. R., ph.d., Botany
Stewart, R. M., ph.d., Computer Science
Strahan, R. F., ph.d., Statistics and Psychology
Svec, H. J., ph.d., Chemistry
Swenson, C. A., ph.d., Physics
Swenson, R. W., ph.d., Botany
Swift, A. G., ph.d., Music
Talbot, R. B., ph.d., Political Science
Thomas, R. W., ph.d., Economics
Tiffany, L. H., m.s., ph.d., Botany
Tondra, R. J., ph.d., Mathematics
Trahanovsky, W. S., ph.d., Chemistry
Trivedi, R. K., ph.d., Materials Science and Engineering
Turnage, T. W., ph.d., Psychology
Ulmer, M. J., ph.d., Zoology
Underhill, W. R., ph.d., Speech
Van Iten, R. J., ph.d., Philosophy
Vandewetering, H., ph.d., Economics
Vary, J. P., ph.d., Physics
Verkade, J. G., ph.d., Chemistry
Voigt, A. F., m.a., ph.d., Chemistry
Vondra, C. F., ph.d., Earth Science
von Grabow, R. H., d.m.a., Music
von Wittich, Barbara, ph.d., Foreign Languages and Literatures
Warman, R. E., ph.d., Psychology
Warner, C. M., ph.d., Biochemistry and Biophysics
Warren, D. M., ph.d., Sociology and Anthropology
Weber, T. A., ph.d., Physics
Wechsler, M., ph.d., Materials Science and Engineering
White, G. C., ph.d., Music
Whiteford, M. B., ph.d., Sociology and Anthropology
Williams, F. D., ph.d., Microbiology
Williams, S. A., ph.d., Physics
Wilson, G. P., m.a., ph.d., Speech
Wilt, A. F., ph.d., History
Wohn, F. K., ph.d., Physics
Wolf, E. L., ph.d., Physics
Wolins, L., m.a., ph.d., Psychology and Statistics
Woods, D. G., ph.d., Music and Secondary Education
Wright, F. M., m.s., ph.d., Mathematics
Yarger, D. N., ph.d., Earth Science
Yates, N. W., m.a., ph.d., English
Yates, S. M., ph.d., Library
Yeung, E. S., ph.d., Chemistry
Young, Bing-Lin, ph.d., Physics
Zaffarano, D. J., ph.d., Physics
Zbaracki, R. J., ph.d., English, Secondary Education
Zober, M., litt.m., ph.d., Business Administration
Zytowski, D., ed.d., Psychology

*College of Veterinary Medicine:*
Ahrens, F. A., ph.d., Veterinary Pharmacology, Physiology
Andrews, J. J., d.v.m., Veterinary Pathology
Baker, D. L., d.v.m., Veterinary Clinical Sciences
Bal, H. S., ph.d., Veterinary Anatomy
Beran, G., ph.d., Veterinary Microbiology and Preventive Medicine
Carithers, J. R., ph.d., Veterinary Anatomy
Carithers, R. W., ph.d., Veterinary Clinical Sciences
Carson, T. L., ph.d., Veterinary Pathology
Chastain, C. B., d.v.m., m.s., Veterinary Clinical Medicine
Cholvin, N. R., m.s., ph.d., Veterinary Physiology and Pharmacology
Christensen, G. C., ph.d., Veterinary Anatomy

CLARK, T. L., D.V.M., Veterinary Clinical Sciences
DELLMANN, N. D., PH.D., Veterinary Anatomy
DRAPER, D. D., PH.D., Veterinary Anatomy
DYER, D. C., PH.D., Veterinary Pharmacology, Physiology
ENESS, P. G., D.V.M., Veterinary Clinical Sciences
ENGEN, R. L., PH.D., Veterinary Physiology and Pharmacology
EVANS, L. E., PH.D., Veterinary Clinical Sciences
FLATT, R., PH.D., Veterinary Pathology
GHOSHAL, N. G., PH.D., Veterinary Anatomy
GLOCK, R. D., PH.D., Veterinary Pathology
GOUGH, P. M., PH.D., Veterinary Microbiology and Preventive Medicine
GRAHAM, D. L., PH.D., Veterinary Pathology
GREVE, J., PH.D., Veterinary Pathology
GRIER, R. L., PH.D., Veterinary Clinical Sciences
HARRIS, D. L., PH.D., Veterinary Microbiology, Preventive Medicine
HEMBROUGH, F. B., PH.D., Veterinary Physiology and Pharmacology
HERRICK, J. B., M.S., Veterinary Clinical Sciences
HILL, H. T., PH.D., Veterinary Microbiology and Preventive Medicine
HOEFLE, W. D., D.V.M., Veterinary Clinical Sciences
HOFSTAD, M S., D.V.M., PH.D., Veterinary Microbiology
HOGLE, R. M., D.V.M., Veterinary Microbiology and Preventive Medicine
JENSEN, L. A., D.V.M., Veterinary Microbiology and Preventive Medicine
JESKA, E. L., PH.D., Veterinary Pathology
KAEBERLE, M. L., D.V.M., M.S., Veterinary Microbiology
KEMP, R. L., D.V.M., PH.D., Veterinary Pathology
KLUGE, J. P., D.V.M., PH.D., Veterinary Pathology
KRAMER, T. T., PH.D., Veterinary Microbiology and Preventive Medicine
KUNESH, J. P., PH.D., Veterinary Clinical Sciences
LEDET, A. E., PH.D., Veterinary Pathology
LLOYD, W. E., P.H.D, Veterinary Pathology
LUNDVALL, R. L., M.S., Veterinary Clinical Sciences
NELSON, C. L., D.V.M., Veterinary Microbiology and Preventive Medicine
PACKER, R. A., PH.D., Veterinary Microbiology
PEARSON, P. T., D.V.M., PH.D., Veterinary Clinical Sciences
RANDIC, M., PH.D., Veterinary Pharmacology, Physiology
REECE, W. O., PH.D., Veterinary Physiology and Pharmacology
REED, D. E., PH.D., Microbiology
ROSS, R. F., PH.D., Research Institute
SCHWARTE, L. H., M.S., PH.D., Veterinary Pathology
SEATON, V. A., D.V.M., Veterinary Pathology
SWENSON, M. J., D.V.M., PH.D., Veterinary Physiology and Pharmacology
SWITZER, W. P., D.V.M., PH.D., Veterinary Microbiology
THOEN, C. O., PH.D., Microbiology
VAN METER, W. G., PH.D., Veterinary Pharmacology, Physiology
WASS, W. M., D.V.M., PH.D., Veterinary Clinical Sciences
WOODE, G., D.V.MED., Veterinary Microbiology
ZIMMERMANN, W. J., PH.D., Veterinary Pathology

ATTACHED RESEARCH INSTITUTES:

**Agriculture and Home Economics Experiment Station:** Dir. LEE R. KOLMER.

**Center for Agricultural and Rural Development:** Dir. EARL O. HEADY.

**Center for Industrial Research and Service:** Dir. DAVID H. SWANSON.

**Computation Center:** Dir. CLAIR G. MAPLE.

**Energy and Mineral Resources Research Institute:** Dir. ROBERT S. HANSEN.

**Engineering Research Institute:** Dir. DAVID R. BOYLAN.

**Home Economics Research Institute:** Dir. RUTH E. DEACON.

**Industrial Relations Centre:** Professor in Charge PAUL M. MUCHINSKY.

**Mining and Mineral Resources Research Institute:** Dir. RAY W. FISHER.

**Research Institute for Studies in Education:** Dir. RICHARD D. WARREN.

**Science and Humanities Research Institute:** Dir. WALLACE A. RUSSELL.

**Statistical Laboratory:** Dir. HERBERT A. DAVID.

**Veterinary Medical Diagnostic Laboratory:** Professor and Head VAUGHN A. SEATON.

**Veterinary Medical Research Institute:** Dir. PHILLIP T. PEARSON.

**Water Resources Research Institute:** Dir. MERWIN A. DOUGAL.

**World Food Institute:** Dir. CHARLOTTE E. RODERUCK.

## IOWA WESLEYAN COLLEGE
MOUNT PLEASANT, IOWA 52641

Telephone: 385-8021.

Founded 1842.

*President:* LOUIS A. HASELMAYER.
*Registrar, Financial Aid and Director of Admissions:* EDWARD KROPA.
*Director of Library Services:* ALAN DOOLITTLE.

The library contains 91,000 vols.
Number of teachers: 52.
Number of students: 600.

## LORAS COLLEGE
1450 ALTA VISTA,
DUBUQUE, IOWA 52001

Telephone: (319) 588-7100.

Founded 1839.

*President:* PASQUALE DI PASQUALE, Jr., PH.D.
*Registrar:* G. B. NOONAN.
*Librarian:* R. KLEIN.

The library contains 231,000 vols.
Number of teachers: 116.
Number of students: 1,868.

## LUTHER COLLEGE
DECORAH, IOWA 52101

Telephone: (319) 387-2000.

Founded 1861.

*President:* H. GEORGE ANDERSON.
*Registrar:* LOYAL D. RUE.
*Librarian:* LEIGH JORDAHL.

The library contains 250,000 vols.
Number of teachers: 170.
Number of students: 2,100.

## MARYCREST COLLEGE
1607 WEST 12TH STREET
DAVENPORT, IOWA 52804

Telephone: 326-9512.

Founded 1939.

*President:* Dr. A. LYNN BRYANT.
*Registrar:* Mrs. ELIZABETH SHORE.
*Librarian:* Sister JOAN SHEIL, C.H.M.

The library contains 89,000 vols.
Number of teachers: 73.
Number of students: 1,035.

## MORNINGSIDE COLLEGE
1501 MORNINGSIDE AVENUE,
SIOUX CITY, IOWA 51106

Telephone: 274-5000.

Founded 1893

*President:* Dr. MILES TOMMERAASEN.
*Registrar:* Dr. KENNETH W. SCHEMPF.
*Director of Admissions:* FRED ERBES.
*Director of Library:* CHARLES LE MASTER.

The library contains 121,000 vols.
Number of teachers: 83.
Number of students: 1,450.

## MOUNT MERCY COLLEGE
1330 ELMHURST DRIVE N.E.,
CEDAR RAPIDS, IOWA 52402

Telephone: (319) 363-8213.

Founded 1928.

*President:* Dr. THOMAS R. FELD.
*Registrar:* Sister MARY MICHAELINE MEEHAN.
*Librarian:* DAVID L. FERCH.

The library contains 61,000 vols.
Number of teachers: 86.
Number of students: 1,066.

## NORTHWESTERN COLLEGE
ORANGE CITY, IOWA 51041

Telephone: (712) 737-4821.

Founded 1882.

*President:* FRIEDHELM RADANDT.

UNIVERSITIES AND COLLEGES—IOWA                                                                                                                                          U.S.A.

*Academic Dean:* HAROLD HEIE.
*Director of Admissions:* RON DE JONG.
*Vice-President for Development:* ROBERT WALLINGA.
*Vice-President for Financial Affairs:* PAUL MUYSKENS.
*Director of Church Relations:* JOHN DEWILD.
*Director of Financial Aid:* R. SIMMELINK.
*Dean of Student Development:* JAMES VANDER MEULEN.
*Registrar:* HAROLD VANDER LAAN.
*Librarian:* A. HIELKEMA.

The library contains 125,000 vols.
Number of teachers: 52.
Number of students: 910.

## ST. AMBROSE COLLEGE
518 WEST LOCUST ST., DAVENPORT, IOWA 52803
Telephone: (319) 383-8800.
Founded 1882.

*President:* Dr. WILLIAM J. BAKROW.
*Senior Vice-President for Academic Affairs:* DONALD J. MOELLER.
*Provost, Long Range Planning:* Rev. F. J. MCMAHAN.
*Admissions Dean:* J. TIMOTHY BARRY.
*Librarian:* CORINNE POTTER.

The library contains 100,000 vols.
Number of teachers: 150.
Number of students: 1,956.

Publications: *Ambrose Scene* (quarterly), *Paper S.A.C.* (weekly), *Oaks* (Year Book).

## SIMPSON COLLEGE
INDIANOLA, IOWA 50125
Founded 1860.

*President:* ROBERT E. MCBRIDE.
*Vice-President and Dean of Academic Affairs:* R. MELVIN HENDERSON.
*Librarian:* J. CHRISTOPHER.

The library contains 109,000 vols.
Number of teachers: 60.
Number of students: 850.

Publications: *Simpson Alumnus* (quarterly), *Bulletin* (annually).

## UNIVERSITY OF DUBUQUE
2050 UNIVERSITY AVE., DUBUQUE, IOWA 52001
Telephone: (319) 589-3000.
Founded 1852.

*President:* W. F. PETERSON.
*Dean of the College of Liberal Arts:* JOSEPH V. STEWART.
*Director of Student Services, College:* C. BUNTING.
*Dean of the Theological Seminary:* Dr. HERBERT E. MANNING.
*University Librarian:* DUNCAN BROCKWAY.

The College library contains 75,000 vols. and periodicals.
The Seminary library contains 219,546 vols. and periodicals.
Number of students: College 1,064, Seminary 183.

## UNIVERSITY OF IOWA*
IOWA CITY, IOWA 52242
Telephone: (319) 353-3120
Founded 1847.

State control; Academic year: August to May (two terms and summer session).

*President:* WILLARD L. BOYD, Jr., LL.M., S.J.D.
*Vice-President for Student Affairs and Dean for Academic Affairs:* P. G. HUBBARD, M.S., PH.D.
*Vice-President for Academic Affairs and Dean of the Faculties:* MAY BRODBECK, M.A., PH.D.
*Vice-President for Finance and University Services:* EDWARD H. JENNINGS, PH.D.
*Vice-President for Administrative Services:* W. SHANHOUSE, B.S.
*Vice-President for Educational Development and Research:* D. C. SPRIESTERSBACH, M.A., PH.D.
*Treasurer:* R. B. MOSSMAN, B.S.C.
*Registrar:* W. A. COX, M.S.
*Admissions:* JOHN E. MOORE, M.A.
*Continuing Education:* R. F. RAY, M.A., PH.D.
*Students:* M. L. HUIT, M.A.
*Dean of Library Administration:* L. W. DUNLAP, M.A., B.S.L.S., PH.D.

Number of teachers: c. 2,500.
Number of students: 24,153.

### DEANS:
*Liberal Arts:* HOWARD LASTER.
*Law:* N. WILLIAM HINES, LL.B.
*Medicine:* JOHN W. ECKSTEIN.
*Dentistry:* JAMES H. MCLERAN.
*Pharmacy:* DALE E. WURSTER, PH.D.
*Graduate:* D. C. SPRIESTERSBACH, M.A., PH.D.
*Engineering:* ROBERT G. HERING, PH.D.
*Education:* H. R. JONES, M.A., PH.D.
*Business Administration:* B. L. BARNES, M.B.A., PH.D., C.P.A.
*Nursing:* EVELYN C. BARRITT, PH.D.
*Advanced Studies:* RUDOLPH W. SCHULZ, PH.D.

* No reply received to our questionnaire this year.

## UNIVERSITY OF NORTHERN IOWA
CEDAR FALLS, IOWA 50614
Telephone: (319) 273-2311.
Founded 1876.

*President:* JOHN J. KAMERICK.
*Registrar:* ROBERT LEAHY.
*Librarian:* D. O. ROD.

The library contains 520,000 vols.
Number of teachers: 550 full-time, 150 part-time.
Number of students: 11,098.

## UPPER IOWA UNIVERSITY
FAYETTE, IOWA 52142
Telephone: (319) 425-3311.
Founded 1857.

*President:* Dr. DARCY C. COYLE.
*Academic Dean:* WILLIAM DRAKE.
*Dean of Students:* BRAULIC CABALLERO.
*Registrar:* LOIS Y. WILCOX.
*Librarian:* BECKY WADIAN.

The library contains 105,000 vols.
Number of teachers: 36.
Number of students: 2,100.

## WARTBURG COLLEGE
WAVERLY, IOWA 50677
Telephone: 352-1200.
Founded 1852.

*President:* Rev. ROBERT L. VOGEL.
*Vice-President for Financial Affairs:* W. FREDRICK, Jr.
*Dean of Faculty:* Dr. EDWIN H. WELCH.
*Registrar:* HAROLD SUNDET.
*Director of Admissions:* DREW BOSTER.
*Librarian:* DONAVON SCHMOLL.

The library contains 130,000 vols.
Number of teachers: 78.
Number of students: 1,094.

## WESTMAR COLLEGE
LE MARS, IOWA 51031
Telephone: (712) 546-7081.
Founded 1890.

Four-year Liberal Arts College.

*President:* Dr. JOHN F. COURTER.
*Dean:* Dr. STEPHEN GOOD.
*Registrar:* JENEIL MENEFEE.
*Librarian:* UNHI KANG.

The library contains 89,500 vols.
Number of teachers: 41.
Number of students: 650.

# KANSAS

## BAKER UNIVERSITY
(United Methodist)
BALDWIN CITY, KANSAS 66006
Telephone: 594-6451.
Chartered 1858.

*President:* Dr. RALPH M. TANNER.
*Provost and Dean:* Dr. C. E. PETERSON, Jr.
*Dean of Students:* FRED WEBB, M.S.
*Director of University Relations:* MURRAY BLACKWELDER.
*Treasurer:* DOROTHY SUTTON.
*Registrar:* MAUREEN WATERS.
*Librarian:* Dr. JOHN FORBES.

Number of teachers: 61.
Number of students: 850.

Publications: *Orange, Wildcat, Baker World.*

## BENEDICTINE COLLEGE
ATCHISON, KANSAS 66002

Founded 1924, name changed 1971 as result of merger of College of St. Benedict's and Mount St. Scholastica College.

*President:* Fr. GERARD SENECAL, O.S.B.
*Academic Dean:* Sister KATHERINE DELANEY, O.S.B.
*Registrar:* Sister DELORES WAGNER.

The library contains 274,000 vols.
Number of teachers: 74.
Number of students: 1,095.

## BETHANY COLLEGE
LINDSBORG, KANSAS 67456
Telephone: (913) 227-3312.
Founded 1881.

*President:* Dr. ARVIN HAHN.
*Dean:* Dr. ALAN STEINBACH.
*Registrar:* HAZEL SCHELPER.
*Librarian:* DIXIE LANNING.

The library contains 82,293 vols.
Number of teachers: 50.
Number of students: 855.

## BETHEL COLLEGE
NORTH NEWTON, KANSAS 67117
Telephone: (316) 283-2500.
Founded 1887.

*President:* Dr. HAROLD J. SCHULTZ.
*Academic Dean:* Dr. MARION DECKERT.
*Librarian:* MARTHA STUCKY.

The library contains 98,000 vols.
Number of teachers: 43 full-time, 29 part-time, total 72.
Number of students: 682.
Publications: *Bulletin, Mennonite Life.*

## EMPORIA STATE UNIVERSITY
1200 COMMERCIAL,
EMPORIA, KANSAS 66801
Telephone: (316) 343-1200.

Founded 1857, university status 1976.

*President:* JOHN E. VISSER.

Library of 597,621 vols.
Number of students: 4,461 undergraduates, 1,950 graduates.

## FORT HAYS STATE UNIVERSITY
HAYS, KANSAS 67601
Founded 1902.

*President:* Dr. G. W. TOMANEK.
*Vice-President for Academic Affairs:* Dr. JAMES J. MURPHY.
*Vice-President for Administration and Finance:* Dr. DALE JOHANSEN.
*Vice-President for Student Affairs:* Dr. B. D. JELLISON.

*Registrar:* JAMES V. KELLERMAN.
*Institutional Research Director:* KAY A. DEY.
*Librarian:* Dr. DEAN WILLARD.

The library contains 663,000 vols.
Number of teachers: 292.
Number of students: 5,863.
Publications: *Leader, Reveille, Fort Hays Studies.*

DEANS:
*Arts and Sciences:* Dr. LELAND BARTHOLOMEW.
*Nursing:* Dr. ELAINE HARVEY.
*Education:* Dr. LAVIER L. STAVEN.
*Graduate Faculty:* Dr. JAMES L. FORSYTHE.
*Students:* Dr. B. D. JELLISON.

## FRIENDS UNIVERSITY
2100 UNIVERSITY AVE.,
WICHITA, KANSAS 67213
Telephone: (316) 261-5800.
Founded 1898.

Liberal Arts; four-year course.

*President:* Dr. RICHARD FELIX.
*Dean:* Dr. HARPER COLE.
*Registrar:* Dr. LEROY BRIGHTUP.
*Business Manager:* BILLY D. WARNER.
*Director of Learning Resources Center:* Dr. HANS BYNAGLE.
*Director of Public Relations:* Dr. RONALD R. SCHMIDT.
*Dean of Students:* MERLE R. JOHNSON.

The library contains 87,000 vols.
Number of teachers: 75.
Number of students: 935.
Publication: *Focus* (quarterly).

## KANSAS STATE UNIVERSITY OF AGRICULTURE AND APPLIED SCIENCE
MANHATTAN, KANSAS 66506
Telephone: (913) 532-6011.

Founded as Kansas State Agricultural College 1863; name changed by Act of State Legislature 1931 and 1959.

*President:* DUANE C. ACKER.
*Provost:* OWEN KOEPPE.
*Vice-President, University Facilities:* G. CROSS.
*Vice-President for Student Affairs:* C. E. PETERS.
*Vice-President, Business Affairs:* D. D. BEATTY.
*Librarian:* MARY MAGRUDER.
Library: see Libraries.
Number of students: 18,619.
Publications: *General Catalog, Student Catalog, Summer School Catalog, K-Stater, Extension Bulletins, Collegian, Engineering Bulletins, Dimensions.*

DEANS:
*Graduate School:* R. F. KRUH.
*Agriculture:* JOHN O. DUNBAR.
*College of Engineering:* D. E. RATHBONE.

*College of Architecture and Design:* B. FOERSTER.
*College of Arts and Sciences:* W. STAMEY.
*College of Home Economics:* RUTH M. HOEFLIN.
*College of Veterinary Medicine:* D. TROTTER.
*Division of Extension:* FRED SOBERING.
*College of Education:* JORDAN B. UTSEY.
*College of Business Administration:* R. A. LYNN.

## KANSAS WESLEYAN UNIVERSITY
SALINA, KANSAS 67401
Telephone: (913) 827-5541.
Founded 1886.

*President:* DANIEL L. BRATTON.
*Registrar:* Mrs. ROBERTA NELSON.
*Librarian:* DARRYL B. PODOLL.

The library contains 62,000 vols.
Number of teachers: 33.
Number of students: 428.

## MARYMOUNT COLLEGE OF KANSAS
EAST IRON AVE.
AND MARYMOUNT RD.,
SALINA, KANSAS 67401
Founded 1922.

*President:* Dr. JOHN P. MURRY.
*Academic Dean:* Dr. WILLIAM MEDLAND.
*Dean of Students:* TODD REYNOLDS.

The library contains 92,103 vols.
Number of teachers: 72.
Number of students: 832.

## OTTAWA UNIVERSITY
10TH & CEDAR STREETS,
OTTAWA, KANSAS 66067
Telephone: (913) 242-5200.
Founded 1865.

*President:* ROBERT E. SHAW.
*Registrar:* Mrs. ANNABELLE PENCE.
*Dean:* HAROLD D. GERMER.
*Director of Admissions:* TERRY D. MATHIAS.
*Librarian:* MARION RIOTH.

The library contains 90,000 vols.
Number of teachers: 75.
Number of students: 895.

## PITTSBURG STATE UNIVERSITY
1700 SOUTH BROADWAY,
PITTSBURG, KANSAS 66762
Telephone: 231-7000.
Founded 1903.

*President:* JAMES B. APPLEBERRY.
*Registrar:* Dr. LEE R. CHRISTENSEN.
*Librarian:* STEVENS W. HILYARD.

The library contains 359,000 vols.
Number of teachers: 321.
Number of students: 5,267.

# UNIVERSITIES AND COLLEGES—KANSAS (UNIVERSITY OF) U.S.A.

DEANS:
*School of Arts and Sciences:* Dr. R. C. WELTY.
*School of Education:* Dr. WESLEY J. SANDNESS.
*School of Technology:* Dr. W. P. SPENCE.
*Graduate Studies:* Dr. J. D. HAGGARD.
*Kelce School of Business and Economics:* Dr. RICHARD K. HAY.

## SAINT MARY COLLEGE
LEAVENWORTH, KANSAS 66048
Telephone: (913) 682-5151.
Founded 1923.
Liberal arts college for women.
*President:* Sister MARY JANET MCGILLEY, PH.D.
*Dean:* Sister SUE MILLER, PH.D.
*Registrar:* SANDRA VAN HOOSE, M.A.
*Librarian:* Sister ANNA ROSE HANNE, M.L.
*Dean of Students:* Sister MARY ELIZABETH KELLY, M.S.ED.

The library contains over 110,000 vols.
Number of teachers: 77.
Number of students: 798.

## SAINT MARY OF THE PLAINS COLLEGE
240 SAN JOSE DRIVE,
DODGE CITY, KANSAS 67801
Telephone: 225-4171.
Founded 1952.
*President:* MICHAEL J. MCCARTHY.
*Registrar:* VINCENT T. LAUDICK.
*Librarian:* Sister HILDEGARDE STRUBLE, C.S.J.

The library contains 57,000 volumes.
Number of teachers: 48.
Number of students: 660.

## SOUTHWESTERN COLLEGE
100 COLLEGE,
WINFIELD, KANSAS 67156
Telephone: (316) 221-4150.
Founded 1885.
*President:* Dr. ROBERT PAUL SESSIONS.
*Registrar:* RALPH DECKER.
*Academic Dean:* Dr. ROBERT EVANS.
*Director of Admissions:* CARL PAGLES.
*Librarian:* D. NUTTER.

The library contains over 100,000 vols.
Number of teachers: 46.
Number of students: 652.

## STERLING COLLEGE
STERLING, KANSAS 67579
Telephone: (316) 278-2173.
Founded 1887.
*President:* Dr. CHARLES W. SCHOENHERR.
*Registrar:* ROBERT M. REED, Jr.

*Librarian:* Mrs. LOUISE SNYDER.
The library contains 60,000 volumes.
Number of teachers: 42.
Number of students: 550.

## TABOR COLLEGE
400 SOUTH JEFFERSON,
HILLSBORO, KANSAS 67063
Founded 1908.
*President:* Rev. VERNON E. JANZEN.
*Vice-President:* Dr. TED W. NICKEL.
*Dean of Academic Affairs:* Dr. STANLEY A. CLARK.
*Dean of Student Development:* JACK BRAUN.
*Director of Institutional Advancement:* Dr. ALLEN GRUNAU.

The library contains 60,000 vols.
Number of students: 478.

## UNIVERSITY OF KANSAS
LAWRENCE, KANSAS 66045
Telephone: (913) 864-2700.
State University, under the Kansas Board of Regents.
Organized by the Legislature 1864. Opened 1866.
*Chancellor:* GENE A. BUDIG, ED.D.
*Executive Secretary:* R. VON ENDE, M.A.
*Librarian:* J. RANZ, PH.D.

Number of teachers: 1,362.

### Lawrence Campus:
*Executive Vice-Chancellor:* R. P. COBB, PH.D.
*Vice-Chancellor for Academic Affairs:* DEANELL R. TACHA, J.D.
*Vice-Chancellor for Research, Graduate Studies and Public Service:* F. HOROWITZ, PH.D.
*Vice-Chancellor for Student Affairs:* D. AMBLER, PH.D.

DEANS:
*Admissions and Records:* G. DYCK, ED.D.
*Graduate School:* F. HOROWITZ, PH.D.
*College of Liberal Arts and Sciences:* ROBERT LINEBERRY, PH.D.
*School of Business:* JOHN TOLLEFSON, PH.D.
*School of Education:* D. P. SCANNELL, PH.D.
*School of Engineering:* D. C. KRAFT, PH.D.
*School of Architecture and Urban Design:* W. MAX LUCAS, PH.D.
*School of Fine Arts:* J. MOESER, D.M.A.
*School of Journalism:* D. BRINKMAN, PH.D.
*School of Law:* MICHAEL J. DAVIS, J.D.
*School of Pharmacy:* H. L. MOSSBERG, PH.D.
*School of Social Welfare:* D. HARDCASTLE, PH.D.
*Student Life:* C. SMITH, PH.D.
*Student Services:* D. ALDERSON, M.S.

PROFESSORS:
*College of Liberal Arts and Sciences:*
AANGEENBRUG, R., Geography and Meteorology
ADAMS, R., Chemistry
AKAGI, J., Microbiology
ALEXANDER, J., History
ALLEN, K. E., Human Development and Family Life
AMMAR, R. G., Physics and Astronomy
ANGINO, E. E., Geology
ARGERSINGER, W. J., Chemistry
ARMITAGE, K., Physiology and Cell Biology, Systematics and Ecology
ARMSTRONG, T., Physics and Astronomy
ASHLOCK, P., Biological Sciences
ATKINS, G. D., English
AUGELLI, J. P., Geography and Meteorology
BAER, D., Human Development and Family Life
BALFOUR, W., Physiology and Cell Biology
BARON, F. E., German
BATSON, C. D., Psychology
BAUMGARTEL, H., Psychology
BAUR, E., Sociology
BAVEL, Z., Computer Science
BAXTER, R., Botany
BEARD, D., Physics and Astronomy
BEARSE, R., Physics and Astronomy
BEER, R. E., Entomology, Systematics and Ecology
BELL, W., Entomology, Physiology and Cell Biology
BENSON, R., Geology
BERGERON, D. M., English
BICKFORD, M., Geology
BLUBAUGH, J., Speech and Drama
BOON, J. P., French and Italian
BORCHARDT, R. T., Biochemistry
BORCHERT, R., Botany, Physiology and Cell Biology
BORN, D. G., Human Development and Family Life
BOVEE, E., Physiology and Cell Biology
BOYD, B. English
BRANDT, J. F., Speech and Drama
BREHM, J. W., Psychology
BREWER, J. W., Mathematics
BRICKE, J. J., Philosophy
BRICKER, C. E., Chemistry
BRUSHWOOD, J. S., Spanish and Portuguese
BULGREN, W., Computer Science
BULLER, C., Microbiology
BUNCE, J. W., Mathematics
BURCHILL, B., Physiology and Cell Biology
BURGSTAHLER, A., Chemistry
BURTON, P., Physiology and Cell Biology
BUSHELL, D. G., Human Development and Family Life
BYERS, G. W., Entomology, Systematics and Ecology
BYRNE, M. C., Speech and Drama
CAMPBELL, K. K., Speech and Drama
CAMPBELL, P. N., Speech and Drama
CARLSON, R., Chemistry
CASAGRANDE, P., English
CHAMBERLIN, V., Spanish and Portuguese
CHERNISS, M., English
CHRISTOFFERSEN, R., Chemistry
CIENCIALA, A. M., History
CLARK, J. G., History
COBB, R., English
COIL, W. H., Systematics and Ecology
COLE, R., Philosophy
CONBOY, W. A., Speech
CONRAD, J. L., Slavic Languages and Literature
CONRAD, P., Mathematics

1731

Contoski, V., English
Craig, B. M., French and Italian
Crawford, M. H., Anthropology
Crockett, W. H., Speech and Drama, Psychology
Cross, F., Systematics and Ecology
Culvahouse, J., Physics and Astronomy
Daicoff, D., Economics
Dardess, J. W., History
Davidson, J., Physics and Astronomy
Davis, J., Speech and Drama
Davis, R. E., Physics and Astronomy
Debicki, A. P., Spanish and Portuguese
De George, R., Philosophy
Dellwig, L. F., Geology
Denney, D., Psychology
Denney, N. W., Psychology
Dick, E. S., German
Dienes, L., Geography and Meteorology
Dinneen, D., Linguistics, French and Italian
Dort, W., Geology
Downs, C. W., Speech and Drama
Draper, L. R., Microbiology
Drayton, A. D., African Studies
Drury, J. W., Political Science
Duellman, W. E., Systematics and Ecology
Duncan, T. E., Mathematics
Eagleman, J. R., Geography and Meteorology
Eldredge, C. C., History of Art
El Hodiri, M., Economics
Etzel, B. S., Human Development and Family Life
Everett, G. E., Chemistry
Fields, J. E., Political Science
Findlay, R., Speech and Drama
Fletcher, W., Soviet and East European Studies
Freeman, B. C., French and Italian
Friauf, R. J., Physics
Friesen, B. S., Biochemistry, Radiation Biophysics
Gagen, Jean, English
Galton, H., Slavic Language and Literature
Galvin, F., Mathematics
Genova, A. C., Philosophy
Giffin, K., Speech
Gilbert, W., History
Gilles, P., Chemistry
Givens, R., Chemistry
Gold, J., English
Goldhammer, P., Physics and Astronomy
Goodman, G., History
Greaves, R. F., History
Gridley, R. E., English
Grier, E., English
Griffin, C., History
Gump, P. V., Psychology
Gunn, J., English
Hallenbeck, R. C., Psychology
Hambleton, W., Geology
Hamrick, J. L., Botany, Systematics and Ecology
Hanson, F. A., Anthropology
Harder, M. A., Political Science
Hardin, R. E., English
Harmony, M., Chemistry
Hedrick, P. W., Systematics and Ecology
Heller, F. H., Political Science
Hersh, R., Biochemistry
Hierl, P., Chemistry
Himes, R. H., Biochemistry
Himmelberg, C., Mathematics
Hiner, N. R., History, Education
Hoffmann, R. S., Systematics and Ecology
Holmes, D. S., Psychology
Hopkins, B. L., Human Development and Family Life

Horowitz, F., Human Development and Family Life
Horowitz, Floyd, English
Houston, B. K., Psychology
Houston, L. L., Biochemistry
Huelsbergan, H., German
Humphrey, P., Systematics and Ecology
Hurst, G. C., East Asian Languages and Cultures, History
Huston, Aletha, Human Development and Family Life
Huyser, E., Chemistry
Ingemann, Frances, Linguistics
Iwamoto, R., Chemistry
Jander, R., Entomology, Systematics and Ecology
Janzen, J. M., Anthropology
Jenks, G. F., Geography and Meteorology
Jerkovich, G., Soviet and East European Studies
Johnson, A., Anthropology
Johnson, J. T., French and Italian
Johnson, M. L., English
Johnson, W. S., East Asian Languages and Cultures
Johnston, R., Systematics and Ecology
Kaesler, R. L., Geology
Katzman, D. M., History
Kay, R., History
Kellas, G. A., Psychology
Ketzel, C., Political Science
Kitos, P., Biochemistry
Kleinberg, J., Chemistry
Krone, R., Physics and Astronomy
Kuhlke, W., Speech and Drama
Kwak, N., Physics and Astronomy
Lacy, N. J., French and Italian
Laird, R., Political Science
Lande, C. M., Political Science
Landgrebe, J., Chemistry
Landsberg, M., English
LeBlanc, J., Human Development and Family Life
Lee, C.-J., Political Science, East Asian Studies
Levine, C. H., Political Science
Levine, S., English
Li, C. T., History of Art
Lichtwardt, R. W., Botany
Lineberry, R. L., Political Science
Linkugel, W., Speech and Drama
Linton, B. A., Speech and Drama
Longhurst, J., History
Lundsgaarde, H. P., Anthropology
Maggiora, G., Biochemistry
Maranell, G., Sociology
Martin, E. J., Psychology
Martin, R., Philosophy
Masinton, C., English
Maurer, J., Slavic Languages and Literatures
Maurer, W. R., German
McCarthy, P., Mathematics
McColl, R. W., Geography and Meteorology; East Asian Languages and Cultures
McCoy, D. R., History
McGregor, R., Botany
McKinney, H. L., History
McNall, S. G., Sociology
Mendelson, J., Psychology
Mengel, R., Systematics and Ecology
Merrill, W. M., Geology
Michel, J. F., Speech and Drama
Michener, C., Entomology, Systematics and Ecology
Miller, L. K., Human Development and Family Life
Moos, F., Anthropology
Morotz, G., Geography and Meteorology
Mostert, P., Mathematics
Mulder, J. B., Physiology and Cell Biology
Munczek, H. J., Physics and Astronomy

Nehring, E., Political Science
Nelick, F. C., English
Nelson, L., History
Neuringer, C., Psychology
Nunley, R. E., Geography and Meteorology
Olsen, R. R., Economics
Orel, H., English
Otani, Y., Economics
Paludan, P., History
Palumbo, D., Political Science
Paretsky, D., Microbiology
Parson, D., Speech and Drama
Patton, B., Speech and Drama
Percival, W. K., Linguistics
Phillips, O. C., Classics
Piekalkiewicz, J. A., Political Science
Porter, J., Mathematics
Prete, S., Classics
Prosser, F. W., Physics and Astronomy
Quadagno, D. M., Physiology and Cell Biology
Quinn, D., English
Reiber, F. M., Design
Reynolds, C., Chemistry
Risley, T., Human Development and Family Life
Robertson, D. C., Microbiology
Robison, R. A., Geology
Robinson, W. S., History
Rosenfeld, H., Psychology
Rowell, A. J., Geology
Ruhe, E. L., English
Salinas, N., Mathematics
Sapp, R., Physics and Astronomy
Saricks, A., History
Sariola, S., Sociology
Saul, N. E., History
Schlager, G., Biological Sciences
Schowen, R. L., Chemistry
Schultz, E. A., English
Schweppe, E. J., Computer Science
Scott, W. O., English
Seaver, J. E., History
Sedelow, S., Computer Science
Sedelow, W., Computer Science
Semb., G. B., Human Development and Family Life
Senior, J., Classics and Comparative Literature
Shaffer, H., Soviet and East European Studies, Economics
Shankel, D., Microbiology, Biological Sciences
Shapiro, G., Philosophy
Shaw, E. I., Physiology and Cell Biology, Radiation Biophysics
Shelly, M., Psychology
Sheridan, R., Economics
Sherman, J., Human Development and Family Life
Shirer, H. W., Physiology and Cell Biology
Shontz, F. C., Psychology
Slade, N., Biological Sciences
Smith, A. J., Psychology
Smith, R. J., Anthropology
Snyder, C., Psychology
Souza, R., Spanish and Portuguese
Spires, R. C., Spanish and Portuguese
Springer, H. S., English
Squier, R. J., Anthropology
Srinivasan, T. P., Mathematics
Stammler, H., Slavic Languages and Literatures
Stannard, J., History of Science
Stansifer, C., History, Latin American Area Studies
Stokstad, M., History of Art
Stump, R., Physics and Astronomy
Sutton, M. K., English
Szeptycki, P., Mathematics
Taylor, L., Religious Studies

TAYLOR, O., Entomology, Systematics and Ecology
TITUS, J. E., Political Science
TOMASEK, R., Political Science
TORRES, A. M., Botany
TSUBAKI, A., Speech and Drama, East Asian Languages and Cultures
TUTTLE, W., History
UNRUH, W., Physics and Astronomy
VAN SCHMUS, W., Geology
VAN VLECK, F. S., Mathematics
VERDU, A., Philosophy
VINCENT, J. S., Spanish and Portuguese
WAGGONER, G. R., English
WALLACE, V., Computer Science
WARRINER, C., Sociology
WEAVER, R., Biological Sciences
WEIR, J. A., Physiology and Cell Biology
WEISS, T., Economics
WELCH, R., Psychology
WELLS, P. V., Botany, Systematics and Ecology
WHITE, A., Anthropology
WHITE, K. S., French and Italian
WIKE, E. L., Psychology
WILLER, D., Sociology
WILLINGHAM, J., English
WILLIS, R., Speech and Drama
WILLNER, A. R., Political Science
WILLNER, D., Anthropology
WILSON, T. A., History
WISEMAN, G., Physics and Astronomy
WOELFEL, J., Philosophy, Religious Studies
WOLF, M., Human Development and Family Life
WOLFE, H. G., Physiology and Cell Biology
WONG, K.-W., Physics and Astronomy
WOODYARD, G. W., Spanish and Portuguese
WORTH, G., English
WRIGHT, BEATRICE, Psychology
WRIGHT, J. B., Speech and Drama
WRIGHT, J. C., Human Development and Family Life
WRIGHTSMAN, L. S., Psychology
WU, DE-MIN, Economics
WYTTENBACH, C., Physiology and Cell Biology
YETMAN, N., Sociology and American Studies
YOCHIM, J. M., Physiology and Cell Biology
ZELLER, E., Geology
ZIMBRICK, J., Biochemistry, Radiation Biophysics
ZUTHER, G. H. W., English

*School of Architecture and Urban Design:*
BENJAMIN, B.
BESINGER, C
BLACK, A.
DEAN, T. S.
HELMS, R. N.
KAHN, C. H.
LUCAS, W. M.
MICHEL, L. F.
MORLEY, J.
PAPANEK, V.

*School of Business:*
BARRON, F. H., Business
BAUMGARTEL, H. J., Organizational Behaviour
COGGER, K., Business
FITCH, H. G., Business
FORD, N. E., Jr., Business
GAUMNITZ, J. E., Business
JOY, O. M., Business
KNAPPER, A. R., Business
KROGH, H. C., Insurance, Finance
LESSIG, V. P., Business
MACKENZIE, K. D., Organization and Administration
MCNISH, J. H., Business Law
MITCHELL, W. S., Accounting
PINCHES, G., Business
PINET, F., Business
SHERR, L. A., Statistics, Operations Research
STETTLER, H. F., Accounting
THOMAS, A. L., Accounting
TOLLEFSON, J. O., Marketing, Quantitative Methods
YU, P., Business

*School of Education:*
ALLEY, G. R., Special Education
BARRIENTOS, I. L., Administration, Foundations, Higher Education
BUDIG, G. A., Educational Policies and Administration
BUSHELL, D. G., Curriculum and Instruction
CAPPS, L., Curriculum and Instruction
CHAFFIN, J. D., Special Education
CLARK, G. M., Special Education
DUERKSEN, G. L., Art, Music Education and Music Therapy
FINE, M., Educational Psychology and Research
GALLAGHER, P., Special Education
GLASNAPP, D., Educational Psychology and Research
GUENTHER, J., Curriculum and Instruction
GUESS, P. D., Special Education
HAACK, P. A., Art, Music Education and Music Therapy
HARGISS, G. F., Art, Music Education and Music Therapy
HAVLICEK, L. L., Educational Psychology and Research
HECK, E., Counseling
HILLESHEIM, J. W., Administration, Foundations, Higher Education
HINER, N. R., Administration, Foundations, Higher Education
HOUCHINS, R., Special Education
HOHN, R., Educational Psychology and Research
LASHIER, W., Curriculum and Instruction
LINDSLEY, O. R., Administration, Foundations, Higher Education
MEYER, E. L., Special Education
MISKEL, C., Administration, Foundations and Higher Education
OSNESS, W. H., Health, Physical Education and Recreation
RADOCY, R. E., Art, Music Education and Music Therapy
RIDGWAY, R. W., Curriculum and Instruction
RUESCHHOFF, P. H., Art, Music Education and Music Therapy
RUNDQUIST, R. M., Counselling
SCANNELL, D. P., Educational Psychology and Research
SCHIEFELBUSCH, R. L., Special Education
SCHILD, A. H., Curriculum and Instruction
STUCKY, M., Administration, Foundations, Higher Education
SUNDBYE, N.W., Curriculum and Instruction
SWARTZ, M. E., Curriculum and Instruction
TURNBULL, H. R., Special Education
WHELAN, R. J., Special Education

*School of Engineering:*
ANGINO, E. E., Civil Engineering
BAER, C. J., Mechanical Engineering
BARR, B. G., Mechanical Engineering
BAULEKE, M. P., Mechanical Engineering
BIGGS, A. W., Electrical Engineering
BISHOP, K. A., Chemical and Petroleum Engineering
BREIPOHL, A. M., Electrical Engineering
BURKHEAD, C. E., Civil Engineering
BURMEISTER, L. C., Mechanical Engineering
CRISP, J. N., Mechanical Engineering
DAUGHERTY, D., Electrical Engineering
EASLEY, J., Civil Engineering
FOREMAN, G. W., Mechanical Engineering
FUNG, A., Electrical Engineering
GREEN, D. W., Chemical and Petroleum Engineering
HOLTZMAN, J. C., Electrical Engineering
KELLY, G. L., Electrical Engineering
KRAFT, D. C., Civil Engineering
KUZMANOVIC, B. O., Civil Engineering
LAN, C. E., Aerospace Engineering
LEE, J., Civil Engineering
LENZEN, K. H., Civil Engineering
LEONARD, R. J., Civil Engineering
MCBRIDE, E. J., Mechanical Engineering
MCKINNEY, R. E., Civil Engineering
MCNOWN, J. S., Civil Engineering
MALONEY, J. O., Chemical and Petroleum Engineering
MESLER, R. B., Chemical and Petroleum Engineering
METZLER, D. E., Civil Engineering
MOORE, R. K., Electrical Engineering
MUIRHEAD, V., Aerospace Engineering
POGGE, E., Civil Engineering
PRESTON, F. W., Chemical and Petroleum Engineering
ROLFE, S. T., Civil Engineering
ROSE, K. E., Mechanical Engineering
ROSKAM, J., Aerospace Engineering
ROSSON, H. F., Chemical and Petroleum Engineering
RUMMER, D., Electrical Engineering
SHIRER, H. W., Physiology and Cell Biology, Electrical Engineering
SMITH, H. W., Aerospace Engineering
SMITH, R. L., Civil Engineering
SWIFT, G. W., Chemical and Petroleum Engineering
TALLEY, H. E., Electrical Engineering
ULABY, F., Electrical Engineering
UNZ, H., Electrical Engineering
WALAS, S. M., Chemical and Petroleum Engineering
WILLEMS, N., Civil Engineering
WILLHITE, G. P., Chemical and Petroleum Engineering
YU, Y. S., Civil Engineering

*School of Fine Arts:*
ANGELETTI, R., Music Performance
BOBERG, G. R., Music Performance
BOYAJIAN, H. N., Music Performance
BOYLE, A. L., Design
BRANHAM, R. L., Design
CLARK, J. B., Music History
COSTA, J. C., Music Performance
DYKES, D., Design
FLEISHER, L., Music Performance
FOSTER, R. E., Music Ensembles
GERKEN, A., Music Theory
GREEN, M. S., Voice
HIXON, G., Design
HOAG, C. K., Music, Theory and Composition
LAWNER, G., Music Ensembles
LING, M., Music Performance
MCKAY, J. S., Design
MATTILA, E. C., Music Theory
MAXEY, L. S., Music Performance
MILLER, L. D., Occupational Therapy
MOESER, J., Music Performance
PAIGE, N., Music Performance
POLILOSKE, D. T., Music History
POZDRO, J. W., Music Theory and Composition
RALSTON, J., Music Ensembles
REIBER, F. M., Design
SCHEID, L. D., Music Performance

Schira, R., Art
Shimomura, R., Art
Shumway, S. N., Music Theory
Smith, K., Music Performance
Sudlow, R. N., Art
Talleur, J. J., Art
Tefft, E., Art
Thompson, P., Art
Vaccaro, N. D., Art

*School of Journalism:*
Bremner, J. B., Editing, Critical Writing
Brinkman, D., Journalism
Dart, P., Broadcasting and Film History
Dary, D., Journalism
Day, J. L., Journalism
Jess, P., Reporting, Editing, Law of Communication
Jugenheimer, D. W., Advertising, Management
Linton, B. A., TV and Film Production
Pickett, C. M., History, Reporting, Editing
Young, L., Journalism

*School of Law:*
Ainsworth, M.
Casad, R. C.
Clark, B.
Coggins, G. C.
Davis, M. J.
Dickinson, M. J.
Goetz, R. A.
Hecker, E. W.
Heller, F. H.
Kelly, W. A.
Kissam, P
Lovitch, F. B.
Meyer, K.
Murphy, J. F.
Rose, L. M.
Shapiro, S.
Tacha, D.
Westerheke, W. E.
Wheeler, M.
Wilson, P. E.

*School of Pharmacy:*
Faiman, M. D., Pharmacology and Toxicology
Grunewald, G. L., Medicinal Chemistry
Hanzlik, R. O., Medicinal Chemistry
Higuchi, T., Pharmaceutical Chemistry
Lindenbaum, S., Pharmaceutical Chemistry
Martin, F. G., Pharmacy Practice
Mertes, M. P., Medicinal Chemistry
Mitscher, L. A., Medicinal Chemistry
Mossberg, H. E., Pharmacy Practice
Repta, A., Pharmaceutical Chemistry
Rutledge, C. O., Pharmacology and Toxicology
Rytting, J. H., Pharmaceutical Chemistry
Stella, V., Pharmaceutical Chemistry
Sternson, L. A., Pharmaceutical Chemistry
Wenzel, D. G., Pharmacology and Toxicology
Wiley, R. A., Medicinal Chemistry

*School of Social Welfare:*
Chambers, D. E., Social Policy, Child Welfare Research
Dailey, D. M., Research, Human Sexuality, Clinical Practice
Gordon, M. S., Field Practicum, Practice, Supervision
Hardcastle, D. A., Social Policy
Katz, A. J., Social Policy, Community Mental Health, Administration
Leon, H., Clinical Practice, Human Behaviour
Taylor, J. B., Research, Community Mental Health, Behaviour

**College of Health Sciences and Hospital (Kansas City and Wichita):**

*Executive Vice-Chancellor:* D. Waxman, M.D.

*Vice-Chancellor for Clinical Affairs:* C. Hartman, M.D.

*Vice-Chancellor for Hospital Administration:* M. Chiga, M.D.

*Vice-Chancellor for Academic Affairs:* J. Meek, M.D.

Deans:

*School of Medicine (Kansas City):* Marvin Dunn, M.D.
*School of Medicine (Wichita):* William Reals.
*School of Nursing:* D. Geitgey, R.N., Ed.D.
*School of Allied Health:* S. Norton, Ph.D.

Professors:

Abdou, N. I., M.D., Ph.D., Medicine
Amelunxen, R., Ph.D., Microbiology
Anderson, H. C., M.D., Pathology
Arakawa, K., M.D., Anaesthesiology
Arnold, W. N., Ph.D., Biochemistry
Asher, M. A., M.D., Surgery
Azarnoff, D. L., M.D., Medicine and Pharmacology
Bahr, R. T., Sr., Ph.D., Nursing
Bailie, M. D., M.D., Paediatrics
Barnhorst, D. A., M.D., Cardiothoracic Surgery
Batnitzky, S., M.D., Diagnostic Radiology
Behbehani, A. M., Ph.D., Pathology
Bergin, J. J., M.D., Medicine
Bolinger, R. E., M.D., Medicine
Brackett, C. E., M.D., Surgery (Neurosurgery)
Bunag, R. D., M.D., M.A., Pharmacology
Butterfield, E., Ph.D., Paediatrics
Cameron, W. J., M.D., Gynaecology and Obstetrics
Chang, C. H. J., M.D., Diagnostic Radiology
Chapman, A., Ph.D., Anatomy
Chard, Marilyn A., R.N., Ed.D., Paediatric Nursing
Cheng, C. C., Ph.D., Pharmacology
Chiga, M., M.D., Pathology
Chin, T. D. Y., M.D., Community Health and Medicine
Cho, C. T., M.D., Ph.D., Paediatrics and Microbiology
Clancy, B., R.N., Nursing
Clancy, R. L., Ph.D., Physiology
Cohn, D., M.D., Biochemistry
Cook, J. D., M.D., Medicine
Cooke, A. R., M.D., Medicine
Cuppage, F. E., M.D., Pathology
Dickmann, Zeev, Ph.D., Obstetrics and Gynaecology
Diederich, D. A., M.D., Medicine
Diedrich, W. M., Ph.D., Hearing and Speech
Donatelle, E. P., M.D., Family and Community Medicine
Doull, J., M.D., Ph.D., Pharmacology and Toxicology
Dujovne, C., M.D., Medicine and Pharmacology
Dunn, M. I., M.D., Medicine
Dwyer, S. J., Ph.D., Diagnostic Radiology
Ebner, K. E., Ph.D., Biochemistry
Festoff, Barry W., M.D., Neurology
Fisher, H. F., M.D., Ph.D., Biochemistry
Foltz, F. M., Ph.D., Anatomy
Foret, J. D., M.D., Surgery

Fox, H. A., M.D., Paediatrics
Frakes, Elizabeth, M.S., Nutrition
Frenkel, J. K., M.D., Ph.D., Pathology
Friesen, S. R., M.D., Ph.D., Surgery
Fulton, R. T., Ph.D., Hearing and Speech
Geitgey, D. A., Ed.D., Nursing
Goldberg, I. D., Ph.D., Microbiology
Gonzalez, N., M.D., Physiology
Goodwin, D. W., M.D., Psychiatry
Grantham, J., M.D., Medicine
Greenberger, N. J., M.D., Medicine
Greenwald, G. S., Ph.D., Obstetrics and Gynaecology and Physiology
Guthrie, R., M.D., Paediatrics
Hardin, C. A., M.D., Surgery
Hassanein, K., Ph.D., Biometry
Hermreck, A., M.D., Ph.D., Surgery
Hiebert, J. M., M.D., Surgery
Holden, D. M., M.D., Family and Community Medicine and Paediatrics
Holmes, F. F., M.D., Medicine
Hoogstraten, B., M.D., Medicine
Houchins, R., Ph.D., Hearing and Speech
Hudson, B. G., Biochemistry
Hudson, R. P., M.D., History of Medicine, Medicine
Hurwitz, A., M.D., Medicine and Pharmacology
Jacobs, R. R., M.D., Surgery
Jensen, T., Ph.D., Microbiology
Jerome, N., Ph.D., Community Health
Jewell, W. R., M.D., Clinical Surgery
Johnson, D. C., Ph.D., Obstetrics and Gynaecology and Physiology
Justesen, D. R., Ph.D., Psychiatry
Kalivas, J., M.D., Medicine
Kennedy, J. A., M.D., Medicine
Kepes, J., M.D., Pathology
Kerby, G. R., M.D., Medicine
Kimmel, J. R., M.D., Ph.D., Biochemistry
Klaassen, C., Ph.D., Pharmacology
Knauff, H. S., M.D., Oto-Rhino-Laryngology
Knox, A. W., Ph.D., Hearing and Speech
Krampitz, S., Ph.D., Nursing
Krantz, K., M.D., Obstetrics, Gynaecology and Anatomy
Kyner, J. L., M.D., Medicine
Lansky, S. B., M.D., Paediatrics and Psychiatry
Lawwill, T. M. W., Ophthalmology
Laybourne, P. C., Jr., M.D., Psychiatry, Family Practice
Lee, K. R., M.D., Diagnostic Radiology
Lemoine, A. N., M.D., Ophthalmology
Levine, Errol, Ph.D., Diagnostic Radiology
Lewis, H. D., Jr., M.D., Medicine
Liu, C., M.D., Paediatrics and Medicine
Lowman, J. T., M.D., Paediatrics
Lukert, B., M.D., Medicine
Lynch, S., M.D., Medicine
McReynolds, L., Ph.D., Hearing and Speech
Maguire, M. H., Ph.D., Pharmacology
Manning, R. T., M.D., Internal Medicine
Mansfield, C. M., M.D., Radiation Therapy
Masters, F. W., M.D., Surgery
Mathewson, H. S., M.D., Clinical Anaesthesiology
Mattioli, L., M.D., Paediatrics
Matzke, H. A., Ph.D., Anatomy
Mayfield, D. G., M.D., Psychiatry
Mebust, W. K., M.D., Surgery
Meek, J. C., M.D., Medicine
Melnykovych, G., Ph.D., Microbiology
Miles, M., Ph.D., Nursing
Miller, June, Ed.D., Hearing and Speech
Mills, R. C., Ph.D., Biochemistry
Mohn, M. P., Ph.D., Anatomy
Nelson, S., M.D., Pharmacology
Nelson, W. P., M.D., Medicine
Noelken, M., Ph.D., Biochemistry
Norton, S., Ph.D., Pharmacology

UNIVERSITIES AND COLLEGES—KANSAS, KENTUCKY U.S.A.

OTHMER, E., M.D., PH.D., Psychiatry
PIERCE, G. E., M.D., Surgery
POISNER, A. M., M.D., Pharmacology
PRESTON, D. F., M.D., Diagnostic Radiology
PROUD, G. O., M.D., Oto-Rhino-Laryngology
PUGH, D. M., M.D., Medicine
REALS, W. J., M.D., Pathology
RECKLING, F. W., M.D., Surgery
REDFORD, J. B., M.D., Rehabilitation Medicine
RHODES, J. B., M.D., Medicine
RISING, J., M.D., Family Practice
ROBINSON, D. W., M.D., Surgery
ROBINSON, R. G., M.D., Diagnostic Radiology
RUTH, W. E., M.D., Medicine
SAMSON, F. E., Jr., PH.D., Physiology
SCHIEFELBUSCH, R., PH.D., Hearing and Speech
SCHIMKE, R. NEIL, M.D., Medicine and Paediatrics
STECHSCHULTE, D. J., M.D., Medicine
SULLIVAN, L. P., PH.D., Physiology
SVOBODA, D. J., M.D., Pathology
TARR, M., PH.D., Physiology
TEMPLETON, A. W., M.D., Diagnostic Radiology
THOMPSON, A. M., PH.D., Physiology
THURSTON, H. I., R.N., Nursing
TORBETT, M. P., PH.D., Nursing
UYEKI, E. M., PH.D., Pharmacology
VAN LEEUWEN, G. J., M.D., Paediatrics
VATS, T. S., M.D., Paediatrics
VOTH, D., M.D., Internal Medicine
WALASZEK, E. J., PH.D., Pharmacology
WALKER, J. D., M.D., Family Practice
WATANABE, I., M.D., Pathology
WAXMAN, D., M.D., Medicine
WERDER, A. A., PH.D., Microbiology
WOLKOFF, A. S., M.D., Obstetrics and Gynaecology
WONG, K. P., Biochemistry
YOUNGSTROM, KARL A., M.O., PH.D., Anatomy and Diagnostic Radiology
ZIEGLER, D. K., M.D., Neurology

## WASHBURN UNIVERSITY OF TOPEKA
17TH AND COLLEGE STREETS, TOPEKA, KANSAS 66621

Telephone: 295-6300.

President: JOHN L. GREEN, Jr., PH.D.
Vice-President for Academic Affairs: C. R. HAYWOOD, PH.D.
Vice-President for Student Affairs: L. L. DODSON, ED.D.
Vice-President for Institutional Advancement: W. MERLE HILL, PH.D.
Vice-President for Financial Affairs and Treasurer: LOUIS E. MOSIMAN.
Registrar: ELINOR SAVILLE, M.A.
Director of Admissions: JOHN E. TRIGGS, ED.S.
Librarian: CHARLENE HURT, M.L.

The library contains 250,048 vols.
Number of teachers: 310.
Number of students: 6,031.

Publications: Washburn Alumni, Washburn Law School Journal.

DEANS:

Law: CARL MONK, J.D.
School of Business: RICHARD E. OLSON, PH.D.
Special Instructional Programs: JAMES M. YOUNG, PH.D.
College of Arts and Sciences: PAUL S. SALTER, PH.D.

## WICHITA STATE UNIVERSITY
WICHITA, KANSAS 67208

Founded 1895 as Fairmount College (Congregational), control transferred to City of Wichita 1926, added to the Kansas state higher education system 1964.

President: C. D. AHLBERG, M.A., PH.D.
Vice-President for Academic Affairs and Dean of Faculties: J. B. BREAZEALE, M.S., PH.D.
Vice-President for Student Affairs and Dean of Students: J. J. RHATIGAN, M.A., PH.D.
Vice-President for Business Affairs: R. D. LOWE, B.S.B.A., C.P.A.
Vice-President for Academic Resources Development: M. H. BUSH, M.A., PH.D.
Dean of Libraries and Media Resources: J. G. SCHAD, M.L.S.

The library contains 654,827 vols.
Number of teachers: 509 full-time, 168 part-time, total 667.
Number of students: 8,234 men, 8,389 women, total 16,621.

Publications: University Studies†, Sunflower†, Wichita State University Magazine, Wichita State Alumni News.

DEANS:

Admissions and Records: C. R. WENTWORTH, M.A., PH.D.
Liberal Arts and Sciences: P. J. MAGELLI, M.S., PH.D.
Education: L. M. CHAFFEE, M.ED., PH.D.
Fine Arts: G. B. TERWILLIGER, M.A., ED.D.
Engineering: W. J. WILHELM, M.S., PH.D.
Business Administration: D. SHARP. M.B.A., PH.D.
Health Related Professions: S. D. RODENBERG, A.M., PH.D.
Graduate: L. M. BENNINGFIELD, M.S.E.E., PH.D.
University College: D. E. McFARLAND, M.S., PH.D.
Continuing Education: C. R. WENTWORTH, M.A., PH.D. (acting).

# KENTUCKY

## BELLARMINE COLLEGE
NEWBURG RD., LOUISVILLE, KENTUCKY 40205

Telephone: 452-8211.

Founded 1950.

President: Dr. EUGENE V. PETRIK.
Dean of Admissions and Educational Services: ROBERT G. PFAADT.
Librarian: JOAN WETTIG.

The library contains 88,500 vols.
Number of teachers: 73.
Number of students: 2,300.

## BEREA COLLEGE
BEREA, KENTUCKY 40404
Founded 1855.

President: WILLIS D. WEATHERFORD.
Vice-President for Finance and Secretary: L. JONES.
Academic Vice-President and Dean: WILLIAM STOLTE.
Business Vice-President: K. WARMING.
Registrar: JAMES MASTERS.
Librarian: THOMAS KIRK.

The library contains 231,000 vols.
Number of teachers: 150.
Number of students: 1,434.

## CAMPBELLSVILLE COLLEGE
CAMPBELLSVILLE, KENTUCKY 42718

Telephone: (502) 465-8158.

Founded 1906.

President: Dr. W. R. DAVENPORT.
Librarian: B. H. PARSLEY.

The library contains 90,000 vols.
Number of teachers: 44.
Number of students: 700.

## CENTRE COLLEGE OF KENTUCKY
DANVILLE, KENTUCKY 40422

Telephone: (606) 236-5211.

Founded 1819.

President: THOMAS A. SPRAGENS.
Provost and Dean: EDGAR C. RECKARD.

The library contains 135,000 vols. and 700 periodicals.

Number of teachers: 70.
Number of students: 750-800.

## CUMBERLAND COLLEGE
WILLIAMSBURG, KENTUCKY 40769

Telephone: (606) 549-2200

Founded 1889.

President: JIM TAYLOR.
Registrar: ROGER BAKER.
Academic Dean: Dr. E. C. MASDEN.
Dean of College Personnel: Dr. J. P. DUKE.
Librarian: ROBERT WILLIAMS.

The library contains 93,000 vols.
Number of teachers: 105.
Number of students: 2,000.

## EASTERN KENTUCKY UNIVERSITY
RICHMOND, KENTUCKY 40475

Telephone: 622-0111.

Founded 1906.

President: J. C. POWELL.
Vice-President for Academic Affairs and Research: JOHN D. ROWLETT.
Vice-President for Administration: J. C. POWELL.
Registrar: DONALD SMITH.
Librarian: E. WEYHRAUCH.

The library contains 500,000 vols.
Number of teachers: 725.
Number of students: 13,668.

### GEORGETOWN COLLEGE
GEORGETOWN, KENTUCKY 40324

Telephone: (502) 863-8011.

Founded 1829.

*President:* Dr. BEN M. ELROD.
*Chancellor:* Dr. ROBERT L. MILLS.
*Academic Dean:* Dr. JOE LEWIS (acting).
*Director of Business Affairs:* Dr. TOM E. BENBERG.
*Director of Development:* RICHARD CARLTON.
*Director of Admissions:* DON DE BORDE.
*Librarian:* JANE LANSON.

The library contains 120,601 vols.
Number of teachers: 93.
Number of students: 1,270.

### KENTUCKY STATE UNIVERSITY
FRANKFORT, KENTUCKY 40601

Telephone: (502) 564-2550.

Founded 1886.

*President:* W. A. BUTTS, PH.D.
*Vice-President:* (vacant).
*Director of Admissions:* FRED WILLIAMS.
*Director of Libraries:* DONALD W. LYONS.

The library contains 234,223 vols.
Number of teachers: 101.
Number of students: 2,342.

### KENTUCKY WESLEYAN COLLEGE
3000 FREDERICA STREET, OWENSBORO, KENTUCKY 42301

Telephone: 926-3111.

Founded 1858.

*President:* LUTHER W. WHITE III.
*Dean:* Dr. DONALD D. DOUGLASS.
*Registrar:* Dr. GUS PARIS.
*Librarian:* D. KING.

The library contains 81,000 vols.
Number of teachers: 52.
Number of students: 666 full-time, 250 part-time.

### MOREHEAD STATE UNIVERSITY
MOREHEAD, KENTUCKY 40351

Telephone: (606) 783-2221.

Founded 1922.

*President:* Dr. MORRIS L. NORFLEET.
*Director of Admissions:* Dr. RANDAL HART.
*Librarian:* Dr. J. ELLIS.

The library contains 344,809 vols.
Number of teachers: 300.
Number of students: 4,511 full-time, 2,575 part-time.

### MURRAY STATE UNIVERSITY
UNIVERSITY STATION, MURRAY, KENTUCKY 42071

Telephone: 762-3011.

Founded 1922.

*President:* CONSTANTINE CURRIS.

*Registrar:* WILSON GANTT.
*Librarian:* EDWIN STROHECKER.

The library contains 350,000 vols.
Number of teachers: 360.
Number of students: 5,422 full-time, 2,419 part-time.

### PIKEVILLE COLLEGE
PIKEVILLE, KENTUCKY 41501

Telephone: (606) 432-9200.

Founded 1889.

*President:* Dr. JACKSON O. HALL.
*Vice-President for Academic Affairs:* Dr. MARIE V. TARPEY.
*Librarian:* WILLIAM AGUILAR.

The library contains 82,000 vols.
Number of teachers: 52.
Number of students: 612.

### SPALDING COLLEGE
851 SOUTH FOURTH STREET, LOUISVILLE, KENTUCKY 40203

Telephone: (502) 585-9911.

Founded 1814.

Four-year Liberal Arts College.

*President:* Dr. EILEEN M. EGAN, S.C.N., PH.D.
*Assistant to the President:* VINCENT I. BROSKY, M.A.
*Director of Business and Financial Affairs:* GERALD H. OESWEIN, B.A.
*Director of Admissions:* MARY P. NOLAN, M.A.
*Academic Dean:* Dr. EDWARD G. SMITH.
*Director of Student Services:* Sister BRIDGID CLIFFORD, M.A.
*Library Director:* LUCILLE SCHAUER, M.S.L.S.

The library contains 98,694 vols.
Number of teachers: 91.
Number of students: 980.

### THOMAS MORE COLLEGE
P.O.B 85, FORT MITCHELL, KENTUCKY 41017

Telephone: 341-5800.

Founded 1921.

*President:* ROBERT J. GIROUX.
*Registrar:* JOAN YELTON.
*Librarian:* Sister M. ADRIENNE RIEHLE, S.N.D.

The library contains 90,000 vols.
Number of teachers: 58.
Number of students: 1,002.

### TRANSYLVANIA UNIVERSITY
300 N. BROADWAY, LEXINGTON, KENTUCKY 40508

Telephone: 233-8111.

Founded 1780 as Transylvania College, attained university status 1970.

*President:* IRVIN E. LUNGER (acting).
*Vice-President and Dean of the College:* ASA ALAN HUMPHRIES, Jr.
*Vice-President for Finance:* CHARLES L. SHEARER.
*Director of Student Affairs:* LAWRENCE TRUAX (acting).
*Registrar:* JOANNE WITTE.
*Librarian:* JOHN SHERIDAN.

The library contains 100,581 vols.
Number of teachers: 52.
Number of students: 788.

### UNION COLLEGE
BARBOURVILLE, KENTUCKY 40906

Telephone: (606) 546-4151.

Founded 1879.

*President:* MAHLON A. MILLER.
*Registrar:* EDWIN LE MASTER.
*Dean of Faculty:* DWIGHT C. STEWART.
*Dean of Graduate Academic Affairs:* WARREN ROBBINS.
*Executive Vice-President:* ROBERT D. CAREY.
*Director of Admissions:* JAMES GARNER.
*Librarian:* J. B. MCFERRIN.

The library contains 74,431 vols.
Number of teachers: 50.
Number of students: 950.

### UNIVERSITY OF KENTUCKY
LEXINGTON, KENTUCKY 40506

Telephone: 258-9000.

Founded 1865.

Academic year: August to May.

*President:* Dr. OTIS A. SINGLETARY.
*Vice-President for Administration:* Dr. DONALD B. CLAPP.
*Vice-President for Academic Affairs:* Dr. ART GALLAHER.
*Vice-President for University Relations:* Dr. RAY R. HORNBACK.
*Vice-President for Student Affairs:* Dr. ROBERT G. ZUMWINKLE.
*Vice-President for Business Affairs and Treasurer:* JACK C. BLANTON.
*Vice-President for the Albert B. Chandler Medical Center:* Dr. PETER P. BOSOMWORTH.
*Vice-President for the Community College System:* Dr. CHARLES WETHINGTON.
*Vice-President for Minority Affairs:* Dr. JOHN T. SMITH.
*Dean of Admissions and Registrar:* E. W. OCKERMAN, ED.D.
*Director of Libraries:* PAUL A. WILLIS. J.D.

Library: *see* Libraries.
Number of teachers: 1,980.
Number of students: 42,258.

Publications: *Agricultural Experimental Station Bulletin, Bureau of Business Research Bulletin, Bureau of Community Service Bulletin, Bureau of Government Research Bulletin, Bureau* of School Service Bulletin, Engineering Experiment Station Bulletin, Kentucky Alumnus, Kentucky Engineer, Kentucky Law Journal, Report to Kentucky Schools, University of Kentucky Buletin.

DEANS:

College of Agriculture: Dr. CHARLES E. BARNHART.
College of Arts and Sciences: Dr. MICHAEL BAER.
College of Communications: HERBERT N. DRENNON (acting).
College of Engineering: Dr. ROGER EICHHORN.
College of Fine Arts: Dr. J. ROBERT WILLS.
College of Home Economics: Dr. MARJORIE STEWART.
College of Law: Dr. THOMAS P. LEWIS.
College of Education: Dr. GEORGE W. DENEMARK.
College of Business and Economics: Dr. WILLIAM W. ECTON.
College of Pharmacy: Dr. JOSEPH V. SWINTOSKY.
College of Medicine: Dr. D. KAY CLAWSON.
College of Nursing: Dr. MARION E. MCKENNA.
College of Dentistry: Dr. MERRILL W. PACKER.
College of Allied Health Professions: Dr. JOSEPH HAMBURG.
College of Architecture: Prof. ANTHONY EARDLEY.
College of Library Science: Dr. T. W. SINEATH.
College of Social Professions: S. ZAFAR HASAN.
Graduate School: Dr. W. C. ROYSTER.
Undergraduate Studies: Dr. CHARLES ROWELL (acting).
University Extension: Dr. STEPHEN LANGSTON.
Community College System: Dr. CHARLES WETHINGTON (Vice-President).
Community College Directors:
Ashland Community College: Dr. R. L. GOODPASTER.
Elizabethtown Community College: Dr. J. S. OWEN.
Hazard Community College: Dr. J. M. JOLLY.
Henderson Community College: Dr. MARSHALL ARNOLD.
Hopkinsville Community College: Dr. T. L. RILEY.
Jefferson Community College (Louisville): Dr. R. HORVATH.
Lexington Technical Institute: W. N. PRICE.
Madisonville Community College: Dr. ARTHUR D. STUMPF.
Maysville Community College: Dr. J. SHIRES.
Paducah Community College: Dr. D. J. CLEMENS.
Prestonsburg Community College: Dr. H. A. CAMPBELL.
Somerset Community College: Dr. R. D. KELLEY.
Southeast Community College (Cumberland): Dr. LARRY STANLEY.

## UNIVERSITY OF LOUISVILLE
LOUISVILLE, KENTUCKY 40292
Founded 1798.

President: DONALD C. SWAIN.
Executive Vice-President: WILLIAM F. EKSTROM.
Vice-President for Academic Affairs: HERBERT GARFINKEL.
Vice-President for Administration: N. F. ELBERT.
Vice-President for Student Affairs: EDWARD H. HAMMOND.
Vice-President for University Relations: STEPHEN B. BING.
Director of Academic Services: BRUCE BURSACK.
Dean of Libraries: JOHN T. DEMOS.

Publications: The Cardinal, University of Louisville Quarterly, Thoroughbred (annually).

DEANS:
Arts and Sciences: LOIS S. CRONHOLM.
Medicine: DONALD KMETZ (acting).
Law: HAROLD G. WREN.
Graduate School: X. JOSEPH MUSACCHIA.
Dentistry: FREDERICK PARKINS.
Engineering (Speed Scientific School): EARL GERHARD.
Music: JERRY W. BALL.
Social Work (Graduate): ROGER M. LIND.
School of Education: RAPHAEL NYSTRAND.
University College: LEICESTER MOISE (acting).
Business School: WILLIAM H. PETERS.
School of Police Administration: JOHN C. KLOTTER.

## WESTERN KENTUCKY UNIVERSITY
COLLEGE HEIGHTS,
BOWLING GREEN,
KENTUCKY 42101
Telephone: (502) 745-0111.
Founded 1906.

President: Dr. DONALD W. ZACHARIAS.
Vice-President (Academic Affairs): Dr. JAMES L. DAVIS.
Vice-President (Student Affairs): Dr. JOHN D. MINTON.
Vice-President (Business Affairs): HARRY K. LARGEN.
Registrar: Dr. STEPHEN HOUSE.

The library contains 700,000 vols.
Number of teachers: 670.
Number of students: 13,500.

# LOUISIANA

## CENTENARY COLLEGE OF LOUISIANA
P.O.B. 4188,
CENTENARY STATION,
SHREVEPORT, LOUISIANA 71104
Telephone: 869-5011.
Founded 1825.

President: Dr. DONALD A. WEBB.
Dean of College: Dr. DOROTHY B. GWIN.
Dean of Students: RICHARD ANDERS.
Registrar: JOHNSON WATTS.
Librarian: JAMES VOLNY.

Number of teachers: 67.
Number of students: 1,016.
Publications: Yoncopin† (annually), Conglomerate†, Scuttlebutt†, Dimensions†, This Is Centenary†.

## DILLARD UNIVERSITY
2601 GENTILLY BLVD.,
NEW ORLEANS, LOUISIANA 70122
Telephone: 283-8822.
Founded 1869.

President: Dr. SAMUEL DUBOIS COOK.
Registrar: Dr. C. L. REYNOLDS.
Director of Admissions: Mrs. VERNESE B. O'NEAL.
Librarian: Dr. CAROLE R. TAYLOR.

The library contains 122,220 vols.
Number of teachers: 90.
Number of students: 1,248.

## GRAMBLING STATE UNIVERSITY
GRAMBLING, LOUISIANA 71245
Telephone: 247-6941.
Founded 1901.

President: JOSEPH B. JOHNSON.
Registrar: Mrs. RUBY W. BILLUPS.
Librarian: Mrs. PAULINE LEE.

The library contains 186,893 volumes.

## LOUISIANA COLLEGE*
PINEVILLE, LOUISIANA 71360
Telephone: (318) 487-7011.

Founded 1906. College of Liberal Arts and Sciences owned by the Louisiana Baptist Convention.

President: ROBERT L. LYNN.
Academic Dean: Dr. E. EUGENE HALL.
Registrar: Miss DOROTHY CALHOON.
Librarian: LANDRUM SALLEY.

The library contains 75,000 volumes.
Number of teachers: 60.
Number of students: 1,260.

* No reply received to our questionnaire this year.

## LOUISIANA STATE UNIVERSITY SYSTEM
BATON ROUGE,
LOUISIANA 70803
Founded 1860.

President: MARTIN D. WOODIN.

Library of 3,600,000 vols.
Number of students: 54,000.

## LOUISIANA STATE UNIVERSITY
BATON ROUGE, LOUISIANA 70803
Telephone: (504) 388-3202.
Founded 1860.

*Chancellor:* JAMES H. WHARTON, PH.D.
*Director of Academic Services:* A. L. CLARY, M.A.
*Vice-Chancellor for Academic Affairs:* CAROLYN HARGRAVE, PH.D.
*Vice-Chancellor for Administrative Services:* JAMES W. REDDOCH, PH.D.
*Vice-Chancellor for Research:* SEAN P. McGLYNN, PH.D.
*Vice-Chancellor for Business Affairs:* QUINN M. COCO, B.S.
*Vice-Chancellor for Student Affairs:* JAMES W. REDDOCH, PH.D.
*Chancellor of Law Center:* WILLIAM D. HAWKLAND, J.D., LL.M.
*Director of Libraries:* GEORGE J. GUIDRY, JR., M.A.
Number of students: 26,500.

### DEANS:

*Junior Division:* V. CANGELOSI.
*General College:* R. D. HAY.
*Division of Continuing Education:* F. A. McCAMERON, PH.D.
*College of Agriculture:* R. H. HANCHEY, PH.D.
*College of Arts and Sciences:* HENRY L. SNYDER, PH.D.
*College of Chemistry and Physics:* H. B. WILLIAMS, PH.D.
**College of Business Administration:** DONALD WOODLAND, PH.D.
*College of Education:* C. W. SMITH, PH.D.
*College of Engineering:* RICHARD MATULA, PH.D.
*School of Social Welfare:* B. MOHAN, PH.D.
*School of Library and Information Science:* MARIE L. CAIRNS, PH.D. (acting).
*School of Music:* LYLE MERRIMAN, PH.D.
*School of Design:* J. L. NEILSON, B.A.
*School of Veterinary Medicine:* E. D. BESCH, D.V.M., PH.D.
*University College:* R. L. W. SCHMIDT, PH.D.

### LOUISIANA STATE UNIVERSITY AT ALEXANDRIA
ALEXANDRIA, LOUISIANA 71301

*Chancellor:* Dr. SAM HAGER FRANK.
Number of students: 1,506.

### LOUISIANA STATE UNIVERSITY AT EUNICE
EUNICE, LOUISIANA 70535

*Chancellor:* ANTHONY MUMPHREY, PH.D.
*Director of Academic Affairs and Services:* DONALD O. ROGERS, PH.D.
*Registrar:* RICHARD COLLIER.
*Head of Division of Liberal Arts:* JAMES L. MOORE, PH.D.
*Head of Sciences:* WILLIAM J. LEMBECK, PH.D.
*Head of Nursing and Allied Health:* IRMA A. ANDRUS.
*Director of Development:* JOHN L. COUVILLION, PH.D.

*Director of Business Affairs:* LEROY J. STARK.
Number of students: 1,410.

### LOUISIANA STATE UNIVERSITY MEDICAL CENTER
NEW ORLEANS, LOUISIANA 70112

*Chancellor:* ALLEN A. COPPING, D.D.S.
Number of students: 2,600.

### DEANS:
*School of Medicine (New Orleans):* PAUL F. LARSON, M.D.
*School of Medicine (Shreveport):* PERRY G. RIGBY, M.D. (acting).
*School of Graduate Studies:* JOHN C. FINERTY, PH.D.
*School of Dentistry:* JACK H. RAYSON, D.D.S.
*School of Allied Health Professions:* STANLEY H. ABADIE, PH.D.
*School of Nursing:* HELEN DUNN, D.P.H.

### LOUISIANA STATE UNIVERSITY IN SHREVEPORT
8515 YOUREE DRIVE, SHREVEPORT, LOUISIANA 71115
Founded 1967.

*Chancellor:* E. GRADY BOGUE, ED.D.
*Vice-Chancellor for Academic Affairs:* Dr. GARY BRASHIER.
*Vice-Chancellor for Business Affairs:* Dr. A. J. HOWELL.
*Vice-Chancellor for Student Affairs:* Dr. JIMMIE SMITH.
Number of students: 3,755.

### LOUISIANA TECH UNIVERSITY
RUSTON, LOUISIANA 71272

Chartered 1894 as Louisiana Industrial Institute and College; name changed to Louisiana Industrial Institute 1898; became Louisiana Polytechnic Institute 1921, became Louisiana Tech University 1970.

*President:* F. JAY TAYLOR, PH.D.
*Vice-President for Academic Affairs:* D. D. RENEAU, PH.D.
*Vice-President for Administrative Affairs:* GEORGE BYRNSIDE, B.S.
*Vice-President for Student Affairs:* E. S. FOSTER, M.S.
*Registrar:* ELEANOR S. ROCKETT, M.S.
*Director of Libraries:* DUDLEY YATES, PH.D.

The library contains 1,300,000 vols.
Number of teachers: 400.
Number of students: 10,000.

### DEANS:
*College of Life Sciences:* H. B. BARKER, PH.D.
*College of Arts and Sciences:* P. J. PENNINGTON, PH.D.
*College of Administration and Business:* B. R. OWENS, PH.D.

*College of Education:* B. J. COLLINSWORTH, ED.D.
*College of Engineering:* J. J. THIGPEN, PH.D.
*College of Home Economics:* (vacant).
*Graduate School:* Dr. JOHN MAXFIELD, PH.D.
*Division of Admissions, Basic and Career Studies:* Mrs. PATSY LEWIS, M.A.

### LOYOLA UNIVERSITY
6363 ST. CHARLES AVE., NEW ORLEANS, LOUISIANA 70118
Telephone: (504) 865-2011.

Founded 1905 as Loyola College. Chartered as University 1912.

*President:* Rev. JAMES C. CARTER, S.J.
*Vice-President for Academic Affairs:* Dr. ROBERT A. PRESTON.
*Vice-President for Business and Finance:* J. L. ECKHOLDT.
*Vice-President for Communications:* Rev. THOMAS H. CLANCY, S.J.
*Vice-President for Institutional Advancement:* CHARLES E. YOUNG.
*Vice-President for Student Affairs:* VINCENT P. KNIPFING.
*Director of Admissions:* Dr. REBECCA BRECHTEL.
*Librarian:* MARY LEE SWEET.

The library contains 300,000 vols.
Number of teachers: 240.
Number of students: 3,639.
Publications: *New Orleans Review, Loyola Law Review.*

### DEANS:
*College of Arts and Sciences:* Dr. MARIA FALCO.
*College of Business Administration:* Dr. JOSEPH BONIN.
*School of Law:* MARCEL GARSAUD.
*College of Music:* Dr. DAVID SWANZY.
*City College:* Dr. FREDRICK J. DOBNEY.
*Dean of Campus Ministry:* Rev. THOMAS MADDEN, S.J.

### McNEESE STATE UNIVERSITY
LAKE CHARLES, LOUISIANA 70609
Telephone: (318) 477-2520.

Founded 1939.
*President:* Dr. JACK V. DOLAND.
*Registrar:* MISS LINDA FINLEY.
*Librarian:* RICHARD REID.

Number of teachers: 337.
Number of students: 6,025.
Publications: *The Log, The Corral, The McNeese Review, The Contraband* (weekly), *Alumni Newsletter* (monthly).

### DEANS:
*School of Education:* Dr. LOUIS RZEPKA.
*Graduate School:* Dr. JUDITH MORGAN.
*School of Liberal Arts:* Dr. RICHEY NOVAK.
*School of the Sciences:* Dr. BOBBY E. HANKINS.

*School of Business:* Dr. ELDON BAILEY.
*School of Engineering and Technology:* Dr. CARROLL KARKALITS.

## NICHOLLS STATE UNIVERSITY
THIBODAUX, LOUISIANA 70301
Telephone: (504) 446-8111.

Opened in 1948 as a junior college of Louisiana State University; became Francis T. Nicholls State College 1956, attained university status 1970.

*President:* Dr. VERNON F. GALLIANO.
*Vice-President and Provost:* Dr. DONALD J. AYO.
*Vice-President, Academic Affairs:* Dr. O. E. LOVELL, Jr.
*Vice-President, Business Affairs:* MAURICE R. CHARITAT.
*Vice-President, Student Affairs:* Dr. G. G. VARVARO.
*Library Director:* Dr. RANDALL A. DETRO.

The library contains 186,904 vols. and periodicals and 306,886 microforms.
Number of teachers: 220 (full-time).
Number of students: 6,481.

DEANS:

*Dean of Development and Personnel Services:* Dr. GARY J. WHIPPLE.
*Dean of Admissions and Registrar:* S. DAN MONTZ, Jr.
*Dean of Men:* WILLIAM L. DUNCAN.
*Dean of Women:* BONNIE JEAN BOURG.
*College of Business Administration:* Dr. RIDLEY J. GROS, Jr.
*College of Education:* Dr. D. G. JOSEPH.
*College of Liberal Arts:* Dr. NOLAN P. LECOMPTE, Jr.
*College of Life Science and Technology:* C. J. FALCON.
*College of Sciences:* Dr. MERLIN M. OHMER.
*Graduate School:* Dr. VERN A. PITRE.

## NORTHEAST LOUISIANA UNIVERSITY
NORTHEAST STATION, MONROE, LOUISIANA 71209
Telephone: (318) 342-2011.

Founded 1931 as college, attained university status 1970.

*President:* DWIGHT D. VINES, D.B.A.
*Registrar:* BARRY M. DELCAMBRE, M.A.
*Librarian:* LARRY D. LARASON, PH.D.

The library contains 649,146 vols.
Number of teachers: 356.
Number of students: 9,175.

## NORTHWESTERN STATE UNIVERSITY OF LOUISIANA
NATCHITOCHES, LOUISIANA 71457
Telephone: (318) 357-5701.

Founded 1884 as college, attained university status 1970.

*President:* RENÉ J. BIENVENU.

*Registrar:* AUSTIN TEMPLE.
*Librarian:* WILLIAM BUCHANAN.

The library contains 470,000 vols.
Number of teachers: 300.
Number of students: 6,500.

## OUR LADY OF HOLY CROSS COLLEGE
4123 WOODLAND DRIVE, NEW ORLEANS, LOUISIANA 70114
Telephone: (504) 394-7744.

Founded 1916.

*President:* Dr. WALTER S. MAESTRI.
*Registrar:* Sister ANN LOUISE ARNO, M.S.C.
*Librarian:* Sister EVELYN EASON, M.S.C.

The library contains 58,211 vols.
Number of teachers: 81.
Number of students: 1,754.

## ST. MARY'S DOMINICAN COLLEGE
7214 ST. CHARLES AVENUE, NEW ORLEANS, LOUISIANA 70118
Telephone: 865-7761.

Founded 1910.

*President:* Dr. MARY G. SHEA, I.H.M.
*Registrar:* KATHERINE ALITO.
*Librarian:* ELAINE WILTSE MOUNT.

The library contains 78,000 vols.
Number of teachers: 76.
Number of students: 850.

## SOUTHEASTERN LOUISIANA UNIVERSITY
UNIVERSITY STATION, HAMMOND, LOUISIANA 70402
Telephone: 549-2000.

Founded 1925 as college, attained university status 1970.

*President:* Dr. J. LARRY CRAIN.
*Registrar:* Dr. JAMES B. DAVIS.
*Librarian:* Dr. F. L. GREAVES, Jr.

The library contains 219,845 vols.
Number of teachers: 260 full-time.
Number of students: 7,700.

## SOUTHERN UNIVERSITY
BATON ROUGE, LOUISIANA 70813

Founded 1880.

*President:* JESSE N. STONE, Jr.
*Chancellor Baton Rouge Campus:* ROOSEVELT STEPTOE.
*System Vice-President for Academic Affairs:* JAMES J. PRESTAGE.
*Vice-President for Student Affairs and Community Services:* CLARENCE M. COLLIER.
*Vice-President for Research and Planning:* LEWIS L. WHITE.

*Vice-President for Finance and Business Affairs:* TOLOR E. WHITE.
*Registrar:* C. H. CHAPMAN.
*Librarian:* Mrs. GEORGIA BROWN.

The library contains 268,842 vols.
Number of teachers: 430.
Number of students: 9,512.

## TULANE UNIVERSITY OF LOUISIANA
NEW ORLEANS, LOUISIANA 70118
Telephone: 865-5000.

Founded 1834 as Medical College of Louisiana, became Tulane University of Louisiana 1884.

*President:* EAMON M. KELLY, PH.D.
*Vice-Presidents:* PAUL McFARLAND, M.B.A. (Business and Finance), FREDERICK STARR, PH.D. (Academic Affairs), DONALD R. MOORE, J.D. (Student Services), WARREN A. JOHNSON, M.A. (Development).
*Provost:* FRANCIS L. LAWRENCE, PH.D. (acting).
*Director of Admissions:* JILL JONKER, B.A. (acting) (Tulane), LOIS CONRAD, M.A. (Newcomb).
*Director of Registration and Records:* EARL D. RETIF, J.D.
*Director of Libraries:* WILLIAM NEWMAN, M.L.S.
Library: see Libraries.

Number of teachers: 799 (670 full-time).
Number of students: 10,040.

DEANS AND DIRECTORS:

*College of Arts and Sciences:* J. E. GORDON, PH.D.
*Newcomb College for Women:* RAYMOND A. ESTHUS, PH.D. (acting).
*Graduate School of Business Administration:* MEYER FELDBERG, PH.D.
*School of Engineering:* H. A. THOMPSON, PH.D.
*School of Architecture:* RONALD C. FILSON, B.ARCH.
*School of Law:* PAUL R. VERKUIL, J.S.D.
*Graduate School:* FRANCIS L. LAWRENCE, PH.D. (acting).
*School of Medicine:* J. T. HAMLIN III, M.D.
*School of Public Health and Tropical Medicine:* J. E. BANTA, M.P.H., M.D.
*School of Social Work:* HELEN CASSIDY, M.S.W. (acting).
*University College and Summer School:* LOUIS BARRILLEAUX, PH.D.

PROFESSORS:

ADROUNY, G. A., PH.D., Biochemistry
AKDAMAR, K., Medicine
ALWORTH, W., PH.D., Chemistry
ANDRE, T. J., LL.M., Law
ANDREWS, E. W., PH.D., Anthropology
APPLE, D. J., Medicine
ARCOS, J. C., L.SC., Medicine
ARGUS, M. F., PH.D., Medicine
ARIMURA, A., DR.MED.SC., Medicine
ASSAD, T. J., PH.D., English
BAMFORTH, S. S., PH.D., Biology
BARRON, P. L., Law
BATIZA, R., LL.B., Law
BATSON, H., Medicine

BECK, C. H., PH.D., Electrical Engineering
BECKWITH, R. E., PH.D., Management Science
BELTRAN-MORA, G. S., M.D., Medicine
BENNETT, J. W., PH.D., Biology
BILODEAU, INA, PH.D., Psychology
BLESSEY, W. E., C.E., Civil Engineering
BOLLIER, E. P., PH.D., English
BOOTHBY, N. B., M.F.A., Art
BOUDREAUX, K., PH.D., Business
BOUGERE, M. B., PH.D., Education
BOWERS, C. Y., M.D., Medicine
BRICKER, V. E., Anthropology
BRITO, D. L., Economics
BRIZZEE, K. R., PH.D., Biomedical Science
BROSMAN, C. H., PH.D., French
BROWN, W. B., PH.D., History
BRUCE, R. N., Jr., PH.D., Civil Engineering
BRUNSTETTER, R. W., M.D., Psychiatry and Neurology
BUCCINO, S., PH.D., Physics
BURNS, K. F., PH.D., D.V.M., D.V.SC., Comparative Medicine
CALDWELL, D. R., Medicine
CALOGNE, W. F., Jr., B.ARCH., Architecture
CARTER, C. H., PH.D., History
CARTER, J. M., M.D., Nutrition
CARTER, M. K., M.D., Pharmacology
CASSIDY, HELEN E., M.S.W., Social Work
CHIRINO, F. P., Medicine
CLEMMER, D. I., PH.D., Epidemiology
CLEMMER, J., Art
CLINE, B. L., Tropical Medicine
COCHRANE, J. D., PH.D., Political Science
COHEN, J., PH.D., English
COHEN, W., PH.D., Biochemistry
COMARDA, R. M., M.S.W., Social Work
CONWAY, E. D., PH.D., Mathematics
COOK, R. G., PH.D., English
COUCH, H. C., LL.B., Law
COWIN, S. C., PH.D., Mechanical Engineering
CRONVICH, J. A., M.S., S.M., Medicine and Electrical Engineering
DALIA, F. J., PH.D., Civil Engineering
DARENSBOURG, D., PH.D., Chemistry
DARENSBOURG, M. Y., PH.D., Chemistry
DAUNS, J., Mathematics
DAVIDSON, J. F., PH.D., Political Science
DAVIS, C. T., PH.D., History
DELGADO, R., M.D., Environmental Health Sciences
DIEM, J. E., PH.D., Mathematics
DOMER, F. R., PH.D., Pharmacology
DOMINGUE, G. J., PH.D., Microbiology
DRAKE, R. L., PH.D., Electrical Engineering
DUNDEE, H., PH.D., Biology
DURHAM, F. E., PH.D., Physics
EDMONSON, M. S., PH.D., Anthropology
EPPS, A. C., Medicine
EPSTEIN, A. W., M.D., Psychiatry and Neurology
ESTHUS, R. A., PH.D., History
EVANS, B. B., M.D., Urology
FINGERMAN, M., PH.D., Biology
FINNERAN, R. J., PH.D., English
FISCHER, J. L., PH.D., Anthropology
FISHER, J. W., PH.D., Pharmacology
FONT, R. G., M.D., Medicine
FORCE, R., LL.M., Law
FRAZER, R. M., PH.D., Classics
FREUDENBERGER, H., PH.D., Economics
FRIEDMAN, LORRAINE, PH.D., Microbiology
FRITCHIE, C. J., PH.D., Chemistry
FUCHS, L., PH.D., Mathematics
FULLER, H., J.D., Law
GALLANT, D. M., M.D., Psychiatry and Neurology
GEORGE, W., Pharmacology
GERALL, A. A., PH.D., Psychology
GILES, T. D., M.D., Medicine
GOLDSTEIN, J. A., PH.D., Mathematics
GOODMAN, A. J., PH.D., Physics
GOODMAN, S. S., PH.D., Economics
GOTTLIEB, A. A., M.D., Microbiology

GOTZKOWSKY, B. K., PH.D., Slavonic Languages
GRILLET, P. A., PH.D., Mathematics
GUM, O. B., PH.D., M.D., Medicine
GUNNING, G. E., PH.D., Biology
GUTH P. S., PH.D., Pharmacology
GWYN, W. B., PH.D., Political Science
HACK, M. H., PH.D., Medicine
HADDAD, R. J., Medicine
HAMILTON, DE W. C., Jr., PH.D., Mechanical Engineering
HAMRICK, J. T., M.D., M.P.H., Health Services Administration
HARKIN, D. L., M.D., Pathology, Anatomy
HARRIS, W. H., Pathology
HAYDEN, R. G., PH.D., Social Work
HEATH, R. G., D.M.SC., M.D., Psychiatry and Neurology
HENDRICKSON, G. W., M.F.A., Speech and Theatre
HOFMANN, K. H., PH.D., Mathematics
HRUBECKY, H. F., Engineering
HYMAN, A. L., M.D., Surgery
ICHINOSE, H., M.D., Pathology
IZAWA, C., Psychology
JACOBUS, O. J., PH.D., Chemistry
JOHNSON, E. J., PH.D., Microbiology and Immunology
JOHNSON, H. A., M.D., Pathology
JOHNSON, H. McK., Geology and Geophysics
JOHNSON, M. K., Microbiology
JONES, J. W., Surgery
KADOWITZ, P., Pharmacology
KASTIN, A. J., M.D., Medicine
KERSTEIN, M. D., Medicine
KING, A. R., PH.D., Anthropology
KIRBY, R., M.D., Anaesthesiology
KNILL, R. J., PH.D., Mathematics
KOENIG, F. W., PH.D., Sociology
KREMENTZ, E. T., M.D., Surgery
KTSANES, T., PH.D., Sociology
LAGUAITE, JEANETTE K., PH.D., Oto-Laryngology
LAMANTIA, J. R., Jr., B.ARCH., Architecture
LAVALLE, I. H., D.B.A., Management Science
LAW, V. J., PH.D., Chemical Engineering
LEVINE, A., PH.D., Statistics
LEWIS, P. H., Political Science
LEWY, J. E., Medicine
LI, Y., PH.D., Biochemistry
LITTLE, M. D., PH.D., Tropical Medicine
LLEWELLYN, R. C., M.D., Neuro-Surgery
LLOYD, G. A., Social Work
LOVETT, W. A., PH.D., Law
LUMSDEN, R., PH.D., Biology
LUZA, R., PH.D., History
MAGUE, J. T., PH.D., Chemistry
McDOUGAL, L. L., III, LL.M., Law
McGHEE, T., PH.D., Engineering
MCPHEETERS, D. W., PH.D., Spanish
MCPHERSON, G. L., PH.D., Chemistry
MALEK, E. A., PH.D., Parasitology
MALONE, B. C., History
MARTINEZ, J. L., M.S., Mechanical Engineering
MASON, H. L., PH.D., Political Science
MECKSTROTH, G. R., PH.D., Radiology
MILES, H. H. W., M.D., Psychiatry and Neurology
MILLER, M. J., PH.D., Tropical Medicine and Parasitology
MINDAK, W., PH.D., Business
MISLOVE, M., PH.D., Mathematics
MIZELL, M., PH.D., Biology and Anatomy
MOGABGAB, W. J., M.D., Medicine
MONACHINO, F. L., M.M., Music
MONTGOMERY, T. A., PH.D., Spanish and Portuguese
MONTY, J. R., PH.D., French
MORRISS, R. H., PH.D., Physics
MOULDER, P. V., Surgery
MOUTON, W. J., Jr., M.S.C.E., Architecture
NICE, C. M., Jr., M.D., PH.D., Radiology

NICHOLS, R. L., Surgery
NICO, W. R., Mathematics
NIKLAUS, J. L., PH.D., Civil Engineering
OAKLAND, W., PH.D., Economics
OLIVERA, O. H., PH.D., Spanish and Portuguese
O'NEAL, E. C., PH.D., Psychology
ORIHEL, T. C., PH.D., Tropical Medicine and Parasitology
OSAKWE, C. O., J.S.D., Law
PALMER, V. V., LL.M., Law
PAOLINI, G., PH.D., Spanish and Portuguese
PARK, J. B., PH.D., Biomedical Engineering
PARSLEY, R., PH.D., Earth Sciences
PARTRIDGE, E. B., PH.D., English
PATTERSON, A. J., D.T.M. & H., Tropical Medicine and International Health
PEACOCK, E. E., M.D., Surgery
PEEBLES, E. M., Anatomy
PERCY, B. P., LL.B., Law
PERNOLL, M. L., Medicine
PETERS, B. G., PH.D., Political Science
PEYRONNIN, C. A., M.S., Mechanical Engineering
PHILLIPS, J. H., M.D., Medicine
PIERCE, R., J.D., Law
PIERCE, W. A., Jr., PH.D., Microbiology and Immunology
PIZER, D., PH.D., English
POESCH, J. J., PH.D., Art History
POWELL, R., PH.D., Architecture
PRESTON, R. E., PH.D., Music
PURRINGTON, R. D., PH.D., Physics
PUYAU, F. A., M.D., Paediatrics and Radiology
QUIGLEY, F. D., PH.D., Mathematics
RAY, C. T., M.D., Medicine
RECK, A. J., PH.D., Philosophy
REDMAN, H., Jr., PH.D., French
REED, R. J., M.D., Pathology
RICHARDSON, D. E., Neurosurgery
RIEISS, F. K., LL.M., Business Studies
ROBERTS, J. A., M.D., Urology
ROBERTS, LOUISE, PH.D., Philosophy
ROBERTSON, D., PH.D., Art History
ROBINS, R. S., PH.D., Political Science
ROBINSON, L. H., M.D., Psychology
RODRIGUEZ, R. P., Medicine
ROGERS, J. T., Jr., PH.D., Mathematics
ROMAN, P. M., PH.D., Sociology
ROSENCRANS, S. I., PH.D., Mathematics
RYAN, J. R., Medicine
RYAN, R. F., M.D., Plastic Surgery
SALVAGGIO, J. E., M.D., Medicine
SCHALLY, A. V., PH.D., Medicine
SCHENKER, R. L., B.ARCH., Architecture
SCHLEGEL, J. U., M.D., PH.D., Urology and Surgery
SCHOENBAUM, T. J., Law
SCHOR, N. A., Pathology
SETO, Y. J., PH.D., Electrical Engineering
SHAPIRA, E., Pathology
SIMMONS, J. L., PH.D., English
SKINNER, H. C., PH.D., Geology
SMALLEY, A. E., PH.D., Biology
SMITH, M. P., PH.D., Political Science
SMITHER, W. J., PH.D., Spanish and Portuguese
SOGIN, H. N., PH.D., Mechanical Engineering
SOUTHERLAND, F., M.P.H., Social Work
SPERRY, C. J., M.S., Electrical Engineering
STEELE, R. H., PH.D., Biochemistry
STEG, J. L., M.A., Art
STERNBERG, W. H., B.A., M.D., Pathology
STJERNHOLM, R. L., PH.D., Biochemistry
STUCKEY, W. J., Jr., M.D., Medicine
SULZER, J. L., PH.D., Psychology
SUTTKUS, R. D., PH.D., Biology
SWEENEY, J. M., LL.B., Law
TABB, H. G., B.S., Oto-Laryngology
TANNER, J. E., PH.D., Economics
THIEN, L. B., PH.D., Biology
THREEFOOT, S. A., M.D., Medicine
TRIVIGNO, PAT., M.A., Art

Trufant, S. A., Medicine
Turner, W. K., M.ARCH., Architecture
Van Biskerk, W. C., PH.D., Biomedical Engineering
Vliet, D. H., PH.D., Electrical Engineering
Vokes, E. H., PH.D., Earth Sciences
Volpe, E. P., PH.D., Biology
Walker, L. B., PH.D., Anatomy
Wallin, J. D., Medicine
Waring, W. W., M.D., Paediatrics
Watts, R. G., PH.D., Mechanical Engineering
Webb, W., M.D., Surgery
Weill, H., M.D., Medicine
Weinstein, A., PH.D., Biomedical Engineering
Welden, A. L., PH.D., Biology
Whittemore, R., PH.D., Philosophy
Wilkins, B., PH.D., Chemical Engineering
Woodward, R. E., PH.D., History
Yaeger, R. G., PH.D., Tropical Medicine and Parasitology
Yard, R. N., PH.D., Physical Education
Yates, R. D., PH.D., Anatomy
Yiannopoulos, A., J.S.D., Law

Attached Institutes:

**Center for Latin American Studies:** f. 1966; Dir. R. E. Greenleaf, PH.D.

**Center for Public Policy Studies:** f. 1978; Dir. B. Guy Peters, PH.D.

**Delta Regional Primate Research Center:** f. 1964; Dir. P. J. Gerone, SC.D.

**Middle American Research Institute:** see under Research Institutes.

**Center for Business History Studies:** f. 1975; Dir. B. H. Wall, PH.D.

## UNIVERSITY OF NEW ORLEANS
NEW ORLEANS, LOUISIANA 70122

Telephone: (504) 283-0366.

Established in 1956 by Act 60 of Louisiana State Legislature. Metropolitan campus of the Louisiana State University System.

*Chancellor:* Leon J. V. Richelle, M.D., PH.D.
*Vice-Chancellor for Academic Affairs:* Cooper R. Mackin, PH.D.
*Vice-Chancellor for Business Affairs:* George D. D'Aquin, Jr., B.C.S.
*Vice-Chancellor for Student Affairs:* Edgar E. Burks, M.A.
*Vice-Chancellor for Development and Research Services:* Jerome P. Dickhaus, M.A.
*Director of Admissions and Records:* S. Mark Strickland, M.B.A.
*Director of Library:* Donald D. Hendricks, PH.D.

The library contains 750,000 vols.
Number of teachers: 650.
Number of students: 15,000.

Publications: *Statistical Abstract of Louisiana, Mississippi Valley Journal of Business and Economics, Division of Business and Economic Research Studies and Reports, Community Outreach, The UNO Graduate School Program.*

Deans:

*Graduate School:* Robert S. Jordan, PH.D.
*College of Business Administration:* John E. Altazan, PH.D.
*College of Education:* Milton L. Ferguson, ED.D.
*College of Sciences:* David Dunn, PH.D.
*School of Engineering:* Fritz E. Dohse, PH.D.
*Junior Division:* James W. Ellis, PH.D.
*Metropolitan College:* Gordon Mueller, PH.D.
*Dean of Student Development:* E. Frank Masingill, PH.D.

## UNIVERSITY OF SOUTHWESTERN LOUISIANA
U.S.L. STATION, LAFAYETTE, LOUISIANA 70504

Telephone: (318) 264-6000.

Founded 1898.

*President:* R. Authement.
*Registrar:* W. Champagne.
*Librarian:* Donald Saporito.

The library contains 460,847 vols.
Number of teachers: 601.
Number of students: 13,865.

Publications: *The USL History Series†, Publications of the Institute of French Studies* (irregular), *USL International Research Series†* (irregular), *Southwestern Review†* (annually), *Louisiana History* (quarterly), *Attakapas Gazette†* (quarterly), *Revue de Louisiana†* (2 a year).

## XAVIER UNIVERSITY OF LOUISIANA
7325 PALMETTO ST., NEW ORLEANS, LOUISIANA 70125

Telephone: (504) 486-7411.

Founded 1915.

*President:* Norman C. Francis.
*Director of Admissions:* Dr. Alfred Guillaume.
*Director of Student Financial Aid:* Linda Chapital.
*Librarian:* Leslie Morris.

The library contains 100,000 volumes.
Number of teachers: 133.
Number of students: 2,003.

Deans:

*University Dean:* Sister Rosemarie Kleinhaus, S.B.S.
*College of Arts & Sciences:* Dr. Alfred J. Guillaume.
*College of Pharmacy:* Warren P. McKenna (acting).
*Graduate School:* Dr. Louis Castenell.

# MAINE

## BATES COLLEGE
LEWISTON, MAINE 04240

Telephone: (207) 782-5531.

Founded 1855.

*President:* Dr. Thomas H. Reynolds.
*Dean of Faculty:* Dr. Carl B. Straub.
*Dean of Admissions:* William C. Hiss.
*Librarian:* Joseph J. Derbyshire.

The library contains 256,000 vols.
Number of teachers: 130.
Number of students: 1,449.

## BOWDOIN COLLEGE
BRUNSWICK, MAINE 04011

Incorporated 1794.

*President:* A. LeRoy Greason, PH.D.
*Vice-President for Development:* John L. Heyl, A.B.
*Registrar:* Rhoda Z. Bernstein, A.B.
*Treasurer:* Dudley H. Woodall, M.B.A.
*Dean of Faculty:* Alfred H. Fuchs, PH.D.
*Dean of College:* Robert C. Wilhelm, PH.D.
*Dean of Students:* Allen L. Springer, M.A.L.D.
*Librarian:* A. Monke, M.S.

The library contains 605,000 vols.
Number of teachers: 100.
Number of students: 786 men, 587 women.

Publications: *Bowdoin Alumnus* (quarterly).

## COLBY COLLEGE
WATERVILLE, MAINE 04901

Founded 1813.

*President:* William R. Cotter.
*Vice-President:* S. A. Nicholson.
*Treasurer:* Karl Broekhuizen.
*Dean of Faculty:* P. B. Dorain.
*Dean of Students:* Earl H. Smith.
*Dean of Admissions:* H. Carroll.
*Librarian:* Suanne Muehlner.

The library contains 315,000 volumes.
Number of teachers: 160, including 42 professors.
Number of students: 1,663.

Publications: *Library Quarterly†, Colby Alumnus†, Colby†, Annual Catalog†.*

## NASSON COLLEGE
MAIN STREET, SPRINGVALE, MAINE 04083

Telephone: (207) 324-5340.

Founded 1912.

*President:* Edgar B. Schick.
*Registrar:* William W. Hoag.
*Director-Librarian:* R. J. Berkley.

The library contains 126,500 vols.
Number of teachers: 41.
Number of students: 625.

### SAINT JOSEPH'S COLLEGE
NORTH WINDHAM, MAINE 04062
Telephone: 892-6766.

Founded 1912.

*President:* Dr. ANTHONY R. SANTORO.
*Registrar:* Sister MARY ALINE.
*Academic Dean:* SR. M. DOLORES SABLONE.
*Librarian:* Sister FLEURETTE KENNON.
  The library contains over 50,000 vols.
  Number of teachers: 50.
  Number of students: 500 (External 4,000).

### UNIVERSITY OF MAINE AT FARMINGTON
FARMINGTON, MAINE 04938
Telephone: (207) 778-3501.

Founded 1864 as college, attained university status 1970.

*President:* Dr. HARLAN A. PHILIPPI (acting).
*Vice-President for Academic Affairs:* Dr. THEODORE P. EMERY, Jr.
*Vice-President for Finance and Administration:* ROGER G. SPEAR.
*Director of Admissions:* J. A. McLAUGHLIN.
*Librarian:* JOHN BURNHAM.
  The library contains 86,000 vols.
  Number of teachers: 105.
  Number of students: 1,700.

### UNIVERSITY OF MAINE AT ORONO
ORONO, MAINE 04469
Telephone: Orono 581-1110.

Founded 1865.

*President:* KENNETH W. ALLEN, PH.D. (acting).
*Vice-President for Academic Affairs:* HENRY O. HOOPEE, PH.D. (acting).
*Registrar:* JOHN COLLINS.
*Vice-President for Student Affairs:* THOMAS ACETO, ED.D.
*Vice-President for Finance and Administration:* JOHN D. COUPE, PH.D. (acting).
*Vice-President for Research and Public Service:* F. R. HUTCHINSON, PH.D.
*Librarian:* J. MACCAMPBELL, PH.D.
  Number of teachers: 596.
  Number of students: 6,207 men, 5,367 women, total 11,574.
  Publications: *Bulletin, Maine Studies, Agricultural Experimental Station Publications, Co-operative Extension Bulletins, Technology Experiment Station Publications.*

DEANS:

*College of Life Sciences and Agriculture:* KENNETH E. WING, PH.D.
*College of Arts and Sciences:* KARL WEBB, PH.D.
*College of Business Administration:* W. S. DEVINO, PH.D.
*College of Engineering and Science:* JAMES CLAPP, PH.D.
*College of Education:* ROBERT COBB, ED.D.
*Graduate School:* DONNA B. EVANS, PH.D. (acting).

### UNIVERSITY OF SOUTHERN MAINE
PORTLAND, MAINE 04103
Telephone: (207) 839-6771.

Founded 1878.

*President:* ROBERT L. WOODBURY.
*Registrar:* JOHN F. KEYSOR.
*Director of Admissions:* GORDON S. BIGELOW (acting).
*Librarian:* STEPHEN J. RENO (acting).
  The library contains 287,801 volumes.
  Number of teachers: 350.
  Number of students: 8,200.

## MARYLAND

### COLUMBIA UNION COLLEGE
TAKOMA PARK, MARYLAND 20012
Telephone: (301) 270-9200.

Founded 1904.

Private (Seventh-day Adventist) Liberal Arts college.

*President:* Dr. WILLIAM LOVELESS.
*Dean:* Dr. FRED HAUCK.
*Director of Development:* FENTON FROOM.
*Director of Religious Activities:* N. JOHNSON.
*Registrar:* J. GURUBATHAM.
*Librarian:* MARGARET VON HAKE.
  The library contains 95,000 vols.
  Number of teachers: 100.
  Number of students: 884.
  Publications: *The Sligonian* (weekly), *The Columbian* (quarterly), *The Bulletin, Columbia Perspectives* (bi-annually), *Golden Memories, Montage* (annually).

### COPPIN STATE COLLEGE
2500 WEST NORTH AVENUE, BALTIMORE, MARYLAND 21216
Telephone: 383-4500.

Founded 1900.

*President:* CALVIN W. BURNETT.
*Vice-President for Academic Affairs:* CASSELL LAWSON.
*Vice-President for Business & Finance:* JOSEPH HASKINS, Jr.
*Vice-President for Institutional Planning & Development:* ROBERT B. CHAPMAN, III.
*Vice-President for Student Affairs:* RONALD K. DESOUZA.
*Registrar:* MARVIN G. LOGAN.
*Librarian:* JOSEPH A. BOYCE.
  The library contains 113,303 vols.
  Number of teachers: 137 full-time, 45 part-time.
  Number of students: 2,538 undergraduates, 255 postgraduates, total 2,793.

### FROSTBURG STATE COLLEGE
COLLEGE AVENUE, FROSTBURG, MARYLAND 21532
Telephone: 689-4000.

Founded 1898.

*President:* NELSON P. GUILD.
*Registrar:* THOMAS A. BILGER.
*Director of Admissions:* D. SANFORD.
*Librarian:* J. J. ZIMMERMAN.
  The library contains 265,000 vols.
  Number of teachers: 185.
  Number of students: 3,200.

### GOUCHER COLLEGE
TOWSON, MARYLAND 21204

Founded 1885.

*President:* RHODA M. DORSEY.
*Dean:* JAMES BILLET.
*Dean of Students:* JULIE COLLIER-ADAMS.
*Registrar:* MARTIN BERLINROOD.
*Director of Admission:* JANIS L. BOSTER.
*Librarian:* BETTY KONDAYAN.
  Number of teachers: 128, including 31 professors.
  Number of students: 1,070 women, 16 men.
  Publications: *Weekly, Donnybrook Fair, Preface, The Goucher Quarterly, Goucher College Catalog, President's Bulletin.*

### HOOD COLLEGE
FREDERICK, MARYLAND 21701

Founded 1893.

*President:* MARTHA E. CHURCH, PH.D., SC.D.
*Provost:* CHRISTINE A. YOUNG, PH.D.
*Vice-President for Administration and Finance:* JOSEPH PASTORE.
*Vice-President for Development and External Relations:* ROBERT O. WHITE.
*Registrar:* LORETTA M. BASSLER, A.M.
*Librarian:* LLOYD F. WAGNER.
  The library contains 125,615 vols.
  Number of teachers: 87 full-time, 77 part-time.
  Number of students: 1,783.
  Publications: *Catalogue, Prospectus, Alumnae Magazine, Graduate Bulletin.*

DEANS:

*Student Affairs:* E. SUSAN KELLOGG, A.M.
*Graduate Program:* MARVIN E. FARBSTEIN, ED.D.
*Academic Affairs:* MARY S. METZ, PH.D.

## JOHNS HOPKINS UNIVERSITY
BALTIMORE, MARYLAND 21218
Telephone: (301) 338-8000.
Founded 1876.
Private control; Academic year: September to June.

*President:* STEVEN MULLER, PH.D.
*Provost:* RICHARD P. LONGAKER, PH.D.
*Vice-Provost:* RICHARD A. ZDANIS, PH.D.
*Vice-President for Finance and Management Systems:* ROBERT C. BOWIE.
*Vice-President for Health Divisions:* RICHARD S. ROSS, M.D.
*Vice-President for Public Affairs:* ROSS JONES, M.S.
*Registrar:* ROBERT E. CYPHERS, M.ED.
*Librarian:* SUSAN K. MARTIN.

Library: see Libraries.
Number of full-time teachers: 1,389.
Number of students: 10,272.

### DEANS:

*Homewood Faculties:* GEORGE E. OWEN, PH.D.
*School of Arts and Sciences:* SIGMUND R. SUSKIND, PH.D.
*School of Engineering:* V. DAVID VANDELINDE, PH.D.
*School of Medicine:* RICHARD S. ROSS, M.D.
*School of Hygiene and Public Health:* DONALD A. HENDERSON, M.D., M.P.H.
*Evening College:* ROMAN J. VERHAALEN, PH.D.
*School of Advanced International Studies:* GEORGE R. PACKARD, PH.D.
*Peabody Conservatory of Music* (Affiliated Institution): ELLIOTT W. GALKIN, PH.D. (Director)
*Applied Physics Laboratory:* CARL O. BOSTROM, PH.D. (Director).

### PROFESSORS:

*Homewood Faculties (Arts and Sciences and Engineering):*
ACHINSTEIN, P., PH.D., Philosophy
ACKERS, G. K., PH.D., Biology
ARMSTRONG, L., Jr., PH.D., Physics
ARROWSMITH, W., PH.D., Classics and Writing Seminars
BALASSA, BELA, PH.D., Political Economy
BALDWIN, J., PH.D., History
BARKER, S. F., PH.D., Philosophy
BARTH, J., M.A., Writing Seminars and English
BEER, M., PH.D., Biophysics
BENTON, G. S., PH.D., Earth and Planetary Science
BESSMAN, M., PH.D., Biology
BLASS, E. M., PH.D., Psychology
BOARDMAN, J. M., PH.D., Mathematics
BRAND, L., PH.D., Biology
BRAUDY, L., PH.D., English
BRUSH, L. M., PH.D., Geography and Environmental Engineering; Earth and Planetary Sciences
CAMERON, S., PH.D., English
CARAMAZZA, A., PH.D., Psychology
CARLSON, F. D., PH.D., Biophysics
CHAPANIS, A., PH.D., Psychology
CHIEN, C.-Y., PH.D., Physics
CHRIST, C. F., PH.D., Political Economy
CLAY, D., PH.D., Classics
COHEN, D., PH.D., History and Anthropology
COHON, J., PH.D., Geography and Environmental Engineering
CONE, R. A., PH.D., Biophysics
COOPER, J. S., PH.D., Near Eastern Studies
COROTIS, R., PH.D., Civil Engineering, Materials Science and Engineering
CORRSIN, S., PH.D., Chemical Engineering
COWAN, D., PH.D., Chemistry
CRENSON, M., PH.D., Political Science
CUMMINGS, M., PH.D., Political Science
CURTIN, P., PH.D., History
DAGDIGIAN, P., PH.D., Chemistry
DAVIDSEN, A., PH.D., Physics
DAVIDSON, F. M., PH.D., Electrical Engineering
DEFAUX, G., PH.D., Romance Languages
DEMPSEY, C., PH.D., History of Art
DE SOTO, C. B., PH.D., Psychology
DIETZE, G., DR. JUR., PH.D., S.J.D., Political Science
DOERING, J., PH.D., Chemistry
DOMOKOS, G., PH.D., Physics
DYCKMAN, J. W., PH.D., Geography and Environmental Engineering
EDIDIN, M., PH.D., Biology
EGETH, H., PH.D., Psychology
ELLIOTT, D., PH.D., Earth and Planetary Sciences
ENTWISLE, DORIS, PH.D., Social Relations; Engineering
ERICKSEN, J. R., PH.D., Mechanics
EUGSTER, H. P., DR.SCI.NAT., Earth and Planetary Science
FELDMAN, G., PH.D., Physics
FELDMAN, P., PH.D., Physics
FISH, S., PH.D., English
FISHER, G. W., PH.D., Earth and Planetary Science
FISHER, J., PH.D., Geography and Environmental Engineering
FITZGERALD, E. R., PH.D., Mechanics
FLATHMAN, R. C., PH.D., Political Science
FLEISHMAN, A., PH.D., English
FORSTER, R., PH.D., History
FREEHLING, W. W., PH.D., History
FRIED, M., PH.D., Humanities and History of Art
FULTON, T., PH.D., Physics
GALAMBOS, L. P., PH.D., History
GARVEY, W., PH.D., Psychology
GOEDICKE, H., PH.D., Near Eastern Studies
GOLDMAN, A., PH.D., Mathematical Sciences
GOLDSTEIN, M., D.SC., Electrical and Biomedical Engineering
GOLDTHWAITE, R., PH.D., History
GORE, W. C., D.ENG., Electrical Engineering
GREEN, B. F., PH.D., Psychology
GREEN, R. E., Jr., PH.D., Civil Engineering; Materials Science and Engineering
GREENBERGER, M., PH.D., Mathematical Science
GREENE, J., PH.D., History
GRYDER, J., PH.D., Chemistry
HANKE, S., PH.D., Geography and Environmental Engineering, Political Economy
HANNAWAY, O., PH.D., History of Science
HARDIE, L. A., PH.D., Earth and Planetary Science
HARRINGTON, W. F., PH.D., Biology
HARTMAN, P. E., PH.D., Biology
HARVEY, D., PH.D., Geography and Environmental Engineering
HENRY, R., PH.D., Physics
HIGHAM, J., PH.D., History
HILLERS, D., PH.D., Near Eastern Studies
HOGAN, R., PH.D., Psychology, Social Relations
HORN, R., PH.D., Mathematical Sciences
HOWARD, J. W., PH.D., Political Science
HUANG, R. C., PH.D., Biology
HUGGINS, W. H., SC.D., Electrical Engineering
HULSE, S. H., PH.D., Psychology
IGUSA, J.-I., PH.D., Mathematics
IRWIN, J., PH.D., Writing Seminars, English
JACKSON, J. B. C., PH.D., Economics and Political Science
JOSEPH, R., PH.D., Electrical Engineering
JUDD, B., PH.D., Physics
JUDSON, H. F., B.A., Writing Seminars and History of Science
KAGAN, R., PH.D., History
KARGON, R. H., PH.D., History of Science
KARNI, E., PH.D., Political Economy
KATZ, J. L., PH.D., Chemical Engineering
KEMPF, G., PH.D., Mathematics
KENNER, H., PH.D., English
KESSLER, H., PH.D., History of Art
KHAN, M., PH.D., Political Economy
KIM, C. W., PH.D., Physics
KITAIGORODSKII, S., PH.D., Earth and Planetary Sciences
KNIGHT, F., PH.D., History
KOSARAJU, S. R., PH.D., Electrical Engineering
KOSKI, W. S., PH.D., Chemistry
KURTH, LIESELOTTE E., PH.D., German
LARRABEE, M. G., PH.D., Biophysics
LEE, Y. C., PH.D., Biology
LEE, Y. K., PH.D., Physics
LIDKE, V., PH.D., History
LISKA, G., PH.D., Political Science
LONG, R. R., PH.D., Earth and Planetary Science, Mechanics
LONGAKER, R., PH.D., Political Science
LOVE, W., PH.D., Biophysics
LUCK, G., PH.D., Classics
LYNN, K. S., PH.D., History
MACKSEY, R., PH.D., Humanistic Studies
MADANSKY, L., PH.D., Physics
MARSH, B., PH.D., Economics and Political Science
MARTIN, E., PH.D., Anthropology
McCLAIN, W. H., PH.D., German
McDILL, E., PH.D., Social Relations
MEYER, G., PH.D., Electical Engineering
MEYER, J. P., PH.D., Mathematics
MINTZ, S., PH.D., Anthropology
MOOS, H. W., PH.D., Physics
MOUDRIANAKIS, E., PH.D., Biology
MULLER, S., PH.D., Political Science
MURR, B. L., PH.D., Chemistry
NADDOR, E., PH.D., Mathematical Science
NAGELE, R., PH.D., German
NEWMAN, P., D.SC., Political Economy
NICKON, A., PH.D., Chemistry
OLSON, P., PH.D., Romance Languages
OLTON, D. S., PH.D., Psychology
O'MELIA, C. R., PH.D., Geography and Environmental Engineering
ONO, T., PH.D., Mathematics
ORGEL, S., PH.D., English
OWEN, G. E., PH.D., Physics
PALMER, C. H., Jr., PH.D., Electrical Engineering
PEABODY, R. L., PH.D., Political Science
PEVSNER, A., PH.D., Physics
PHILLIPS, O. M., PH.D., Earth and Planetary Science
POCOCK, J. G., PH.D., History
POLAND, D., PH.D., Chemistry
POND, R. B., B.S., Civil Engineering; Materials Science and Engineering
PORTES, A., PH.D., Social Relations
POSNER, G. H., PH.D., Chemistry
PRICE, K., PH.D., Philosophy and Education
PRICE, R., PH.D., Anthropology
RANUM, O., PH.D., History

REVELLE, C., PH.D., Geography and Environmental Engineering
**ROBINSON, D. W., PH.D., Chemistry**
ROSE, H., PH.D., Political Economy
ROSE, W. L., PH.D., Medicine
ROSEMAN, S., PH.D., History
**ROURKE, F. E., PH.D., Political Science**
RUGH, W. J., III, PH.D., Electrical Engineering
RUSSELL-WOOD, A. J. R., PH.D., History
SACCONE, E., DOT. IN LETT., Romance Languages
**SACHS, D., PH.D., Philosophy**
**SAMPSON, J. H., PH.D., Mathematics**
SCHNEEWIND, J. B., PH.D., Philosophy
SCHWARZ, W., DR.ENG., Chemical Engineering
**SELIGER, H., PH.D., Biology**
SERFLING, R. J., PH.D., Mathematical Sciences
SHALIKA, J., PH.D., Mathematics
SHEARN, A., PH.D., Biology
SHIFFMAN, B., PH.D., Mathematics
SIEBER, H., PH.D., Romance Languages
**SILVERSTONE, H. J., PH.D., Chemistry**
**SMITH, T., PH.D., Education and History**
SPRING, D., PH.D., History
STANLEY, J., ED.D., Psychology
STANLEY, S., PH.D., Earth and Planetary Sciences
STRAUSS, M., PH.D., Psychology
STRUEVER, NANCY, PH.D., Humanities and History
**SUSKIND, S. R., PH.D., Biology**
**TORGERSON, W., PH.D., Psychology**
TRUESDELL, C., PH.D., Mechanics
**TUCKER, R. W., PH.D., Political Science**
VANDELINDE, V. D., PH.D., Electrical Engineering
VERHEYEN, E., PH.D., History of Art
**WALKER, J. C., PH.D., Physics**
WALKER, M., PH.D., History
WALTERS, A., PH.D., Political Economy
WALTERS, R., PH.D., History
WESTGATE, C., PH.D., Electrical Engineering
**WHITE, E. H., PH.D., Chemistry**
WILSON, W. S., PH.D., Mathematics
WOLMAN, M. G., PH.D., Geography and Environmental Engineering
ZDANIS, R. A., PH.D., Physics
ZIFF, L., PH.D., English

*Faculty of Medicine:*
AUGUST, J. T., M.D., Pharmacology and Experimental Therapeutics
**BAKER, R. R., M.D., Surgery and Oncology**
BARTLETT, JOHN C., M.D., Medicine
BAYLESS, T. M., M.D., Medicine
BELL, W. R., M.D., Medicine
BOYER, S. H., IV, M.D., Medicine
BRADY, J. V., PH.D., Psychiatry
BRUSILOW, S. W., M.D., Paediatrics
CAMERON, J. L., M.D., Surgery
CHARACHES, S., M.D., Medicine and Laboratory Medicine
**CHILDS, B., M.D., Paediatrics**
COFFEY, D. S., PH.D., Urology, Pharmacology and Experimental Therapeutics and Oncology
COYLE, J. T., Jr., M.D., Pharmacology and Experimental Therapeutics, Neuroscience and Psychiatry
**DINTZIS, H. M., PH.D., Biophysics**
**DONNER, M. W., M.D., Radiology**
DORST, J. P., M.D., Radiology and Paediatrics
DRACHMAN, D. B., M.D., Neurology
ENGLUND, P. T., PH.D., Physiological Chemistry
ERNST, C. B., M.B., Surgery
**FROST, J. K., M.D., Pathology**
GOTT, V. L., M.D., Cardiac Surgery
GREEN, W. R., M.D., Ophthalmology
HALLER, J. A., Jr., M.D., Paediatric Surgery and Emergency Medicine
HENDRIX, T. R., M.D., Medicine
**HEPTINSTALL, R. H., M.D., Pathology**
HEYSSEL, R. M., M.D., Medicine
HOOPES, J. E., M.D., Plastic Surgery
HUGHES, W. T., Jr., M.D., Paediatrics—Infectious Diseases
**ISHIZAKA, K., M.D., Medicine and Immunology**
ISHIZAKA, T., Medicine and Immunology
JEFFS, R. D., M.D., Paediatric Urology
**JOHNS, R. J., M.D., Biomedical Engineering and Medicine**
JOHNSON, R. T., M.D., Neurology and Microbiology
KAZAZIAN, H. H., M.D., Paediatrics
KELLY, T. J., Jr., M.D., PH.D., Molecular Biology and Genetics
KIDD, B. S. L., M.D., Paediatric Cardiology
KING, T. M., M.D., PH.D., Gynaecology and Obstetrics
KISHIMOTO, Y., PH.D., Neurology
KUHAR, M. J., PH.D., Neuroscience, Psychiatry, Pharmacology and Experimental Therapeutics
**LANE, M. D., PH.D., Physiological Chemistry**
**LEHNINGER, A. L., PH.D., Physiological Chemistry**
**LENNARZ, W. J., PH.D., Physiological Chemistry**
LEVIN, J., M.D., Medicine
LICHTENSTEIN, L. M., M.D., Medicine
LIETMAN, P. S., M.D., PH.D., Medicine, Pediatrics, Pharmacology and Experimental Therapeutics
LITTLEFIELD, J. W., M.D., Paediatrics
LONG, D. M., M.D., PH.D., Neurological Surgery
McHUGH, P. R., M.D., Psychiatry
**McKHANN, G. M., M.D., Neurology**
**McKUSICK, V. A., M.D., Medicine**
MADDREY, W. C., M.D., Medicine
MARGOLIS, S., M.D., Medicine
MAYER, M. M., PH.D., Immunology
MIGEON, B. R., M.D., Paediatrics
**MIGEON, C. J., M.D., Paediatrics**
MILDVAN, A. S., M.D., Physiological Chemistry
**MILNOR, W. R., M.D., Physiology**
MONEY, J. W., PH.D., Medical Psychology
MOSER, H. W., M.D., Neurology and Paediatrics
MOUNTCASTLE, V. B., M.D., Physiology and Neuroscience
MURPHY, E. A., M.D., SC.D., Medicine
**NAGER, G. T., M.D., Laryngology and Otology**
NATHANS, D., M.D., Molecular Biology and Genetics
NEY, R. L., M.D., Medicine
NORMAN, P. S., M.D., Medicine
**ORDER, S. E., M.D., Oncology and Radiology**
OWENS, A. H., Jr., M.D., Medicine and Oncology
PATZ, A., M.D., Ophthalmology
PEDERSEN, P. L., PH.D., Physiological Chemistry
PERMUTT, S., M.D., Medicine and Anaesthesiology
PIERCE, N. F., M.D., Medicine
POGGIO, G. F., M.D., Physiology and Neuroscience
**POLACSEK, R. A., M.D., Medical Bibliography**
POLLARD, T. D., M.D., Anatomy
PRICE, D. L., M.D., Neuropathology
RILEY, L. H., Jr., M.D., Orthopaedic Surgery
ROBINSON, C. H., PH.D., Pharmacology and Experimental Therapeutics
ROBINSON, D. A., DR.ENG., Ophthalmology and Biomedical Engineering
ROGERS, M. C., M.D., Anaesthesiology and Paediatrics
ROSENBAUM, A. E., M.D., Radiology
ROSS, R. S., M.D., Medicine
SACHS, M. B., PH.D., Biomedical Engineering
SACK, R. B., M.D., SC.D., Medicine
**SAGAWA, K., M.D., PH.D., Biomedical Engineering**
**SANTOS, G. W., M.D., Oncology and Medicine**
SCHMEISSER, G., Jr., M.D., Orthopaedic Surgery
SCHUSTER, M. M., M.D., Medicine
SHEPARD, R. H., M.D., Biomedical Engineering and Physiology
SIEBENS, A. A., M.D., Surgery (Rehabilitation) and Medicine
SIEGELMAN, S. S., M.D., Radiology
**SILVERSTEIN, A. M., PH.D., Ophthalmology**
SMITH, G. W., M.D., Surgery
SMITH, H. O., M.D., Molecular Biology and Genetics
SNYDER, S. H., M.D., Neuroscience, Pharmacology and Experimental Therapeutics and Psychiatry
**STEVENSON, L. G., M.D., PH.D., History of Medicine**
TALALAY, P., M.D., Pharmacology and Experimental Therapeutics
**UDVARHELYI, G. B., M.D., Neurological Surgery**
WAALKES, T. P., M.D., PH.D., Oncology
**WAGNER, H. N., Jr., M.D., Radiology and Medicine**
WALKER, A., PH.D., Cell Biology and Anatomy
WALKER, W. G., M.D., Medicine
WALSER, McK., M.D., Pharmacology and Experimental Therapeutics and Medicine
WALSH, P. C., M.D., Urology
WEISFELDT, M., M.D., Medicine
WEISS, B., M.D., Molecular Biology and Genetics
WHITE, R. I., M.D., Radiology and Medicine
**WILLIAMS, G. M., M.D., Surgery**
YARDLEY, J. H., M.D., Pathology
ZIERLER, K. L., M.D., Physiology and Medicine
ZIEVE, P. D., M.D., Medicine
ZINKHAM, W. H., M.D., Paediatrics and Oncology
ZUIDEMA, G. D., M.D., Surgery

*School of Hygiene and Public Health:*
ABBEY, H., SC.D., Biostatistics
ANNAU, Z., PH.D., Environmental Health Sciences
**BAKER, T. D., M.D., M.P.H., International Health**
BANG, F. B., M.D., Pathobiology
BRENNER, M. H., PH.D., Health Services Administration
BRIGHT, M., PH.D., Behavioural Sciences
BROMBERGER-BARNEA, B., PH.D., Environmental Health Sciences
BUSHEL, A., D.D.S., M.P.H., Health Services Administration
CHOW, L. P., M.D., DR.P.H., Population Dynamics
COHEN, B., PH.D., M.P.H., Epidemiology
**COMSTOCK, G. W., M.D., DR.P.H., Epidemiology**
CORN, M., PH.D., Environmental Health Sciences
CORNELY, D. A., M.D., M.P.H., Maternal and Child Health
DANNENBERG, A. M., Jr., M.D., PH.D., Environmental Health Sciences
DAVIS, K., PH.D., Health Services Administration

DIAMOND, E. L., PH.D., Epidemiology
DUNCAN, D. B., PH.D., Biostatistics
EMMETT, E. A., M.B., M.S., Environmental Health Sciences
EWING, L. E., PH.D., Population Dynamics
FITZGERALD, R. S., PH.D., Environmental Health Sciences
FLAGLE, C. D., D.ENG., Health Services Administration
GITTELSOHN, A. M., PH.D., M.P.H., Biostatistics
GOLDBERG, A. M., PH.D., Environmental Health Sciences
GOODMAN, H. C., M.D., Pathobiology
GORDIS, L., M.D., DR.PH., Epidemiology
GRAHAM, G. G., M.D., International Health
GRAY, R., M.B., M.SC., Population Dynamics
GREEN, G. M., M.D., Environmental Health Sciences
GROSSMAN, L., PH.D., Biochemistry
GRUENBERG, E. M., M.D., DR.P.H., Mental Hygiene
HENDERSON, D. A., M.D., M.P.H., Health Services Administration
HSU, Y. C., M.D., Pathobiology
HUANG, P. C., PH.D., Biochemistry
KANTNER, J. F., PH.D., Population Dynamics
KAWATA, K., M.P.H., DR.P.H., Environmental Health Sciences
KIMBALL, A. W., PH.D., Biostatistics
KRAMER, M. S., SC.D., Mental Hygiene
KRUSE, C. W., DR.P.H., Environmental Health Sciences
LERNER, M., PH.D., Health Services Administration
LEVINE, M. L., M.D., DR.P.H., Epidemiology
LEVY, D. A., M.D., Biochemistry
LILIENFELD, A. M., M.D., M.P.H., SC.D., Epidemiology
MANDELL, W., PH.D., M.P.H., Mental Hygiene
MATANOSKI, G. M., M.D., M.P.H., DR.P.H., Epidemiology
MEINERT, C. L., PH.D., Epidemiology
MENKES, H. A., M.D., Environmental Health Sciences
MONK, M., PH.D., Epidemiology
NAVARRO, V., M.D., D.M.S.A., DR.P.H., Health Services Administration
PAIGE, D. M., M.D., M.P.H., Maternal and Child Health
PARKER, R. D., PH.D., Health Services Administration
PROCTOR, D. F., M.D., Environmental Health Sciences
REINKE, W. A., PH.D., International Health
RIDER, R. V., SC.D., Population Dynamics
ROHDE, C. A., PH.D., Biostatistics
ROSS, A., PH.D., Biostatistics
ROYALL, R. M., PH.D., Biostatistics
RUBIN, R. J., PH.D., Environmental Health Sciences
SCHILLER, E. L., SC.D., Pathobiology
SCHOENRICH, E. H., M.D., M.P.H., Health Services Administration
SCHUETZ, A. W., PH.D., Population Dynamics
SELTSER, R., M.D., M.P.H., Epidemiology
SHAH, K. V., M.B.B.S., DR.P.H., Pathobiology
SHAPIRO, S., B.S., Health Services Administration
SHELOKOV, A., M.D., Epidemiology
SIRAGELDIN, I. A., PH.D., Population Dynamics
SLADEN, W. J. L., M.D., PH.D., Pathobiology

STARFIELD, B. H., M.D., M.P.H., Health Services Administration
SWIFT, D. L., PH.D., Environmental Health Sciences
SYKES, Z. M., Jr., PH.D., Population Dynamics
SZKLO, M., M.D., M.P.H., DR.P.H., Epidemiology
TAYLOR, C. E., M.D., DR.P.H., International Health
TONASCIA, J., PH.D., Biostatistics
TRPIS, M., PH.D., Pathobiology
TS'O, P. O. P., PH.D., Biochemistry
WANG, S. Y., PH.D., Environmental Health Sciences
WHITE, P. E., PH.D., Behavioural Sciences
WILLIAMSON, J. W., M.D., Health Services Administration
YOUNG, J. P., D.ENG., Health Services Administration
ZELNIK, M., PH.D., Population Dynamics
ZIRKIN, B., PH.D., Population Dynamics

*School of Advanced International Studies:*
CALLEO, D., PH.D., European Studies
DINERSTEIN, H. S., PH.D., Soviet Studies
DORAN, CHARLES F., PH.D., Canadian Studies and International Relations
FRANK, I., PH.D., International Economics
HANSEN, R. D., PH.D., International Organizations
KHADDURI, M., PH.D., Middle East Studies
LISKA, G., PH.D., Political Science
LYSTAD, R. A., PH.D., African Studies
OSGOOD, R. C., PH.D., American Foreign Policy
ROETT, R., PH.D., Latin American Studies
SCHWEBEL, S. M., LL.B., International Law
TUCKER, ROBERT W., PH.D., Political Science
ZARTMAN, I. W., PH.D., African Studies

# MARYLAND INSTITUTE, COLLEGE OF ART

1300 WEST MT. ROYAL AVE.,
BALTIMORE, MARYLAND 21217

Telephone: (301) 669-9200.

Founded 1826.

*President:* FRED LAZARUS IV.
*Registrar:* Miss ANN HEETHER.
*Academic Dean:* Dr. T. KLITZKE.
*Librarian:* J. STONEHAM.

The library contains 30,000 vols.
Number of teachers: 85.
Number of students: 1,305.

# MORGAN STATE UNIVERSITY

HILLEN RD. AND
COLD SPRING LANE
BALTIMORE, MARYLAND 21239

Founded 1867.

*President:* Dr. ANDREW BILLINGSLEY.
*Vice-President for Academic Affairs:* Dr. HARRIET PEAT TRADER.
*Vice-President for Finance and Management:* ABRAHAM MOORE.
*Dean of the College of Arts and Sciences:* Dr. TALBERT O. SHAW.
*Registrar:* HOUSTON STANBURY.

*Director of Library:* KAREN ROBERTSON.

The library contains 403,711 vols.
Number of teachers: 299.
Number of students: 5,297.

# MOUNT SAINT MARY'S COLLEGE

EMMITSBURG, MARYLAND 21727

Telephone: (301) 447-6122.

Founded 1808.

*President:* Dr. ROBERT J. WICKENHEISER.
*Dean:* Dr. JOHN W. CAMPBELL.
*Registrar:* G. BAKER.
*Librarian:* Dr. STEPHEN ROCKWOOD.

The library contains 105,000 vols.
Number of teachers: 73.
Number of students: 1,305.

# SAINT JOHN'S COLLEGE

ANNAPOLIS, MARYLAND 21404

Founded as King William School 1696.

*President:* EDWIN J. DELATTRE.
*Provost:* J. BURCHENAL AULT.
*Dean:* EDWARD G. SPARROW, Jr.
*Treasurer:* C. T. ELZEY.
*Registrar:* NANCY WINTER.
*Director of College Relations:* THOMAS PARRAN, Jr.
*Director of Admissions:* JOHN CHRISTENSEN.
*Librarian:* CHARLOTTE FLETCHER.

The library contains c. 71,000 vols.
Number of teachers: 56.
Number of students: 386.

For Santa Fe branch *see* under New Mexico.

# ST. MARY'S SEMINARY AND UNIVERSITY

5400 ROLAND AVE.,
BALTIMORE, MARYLAND 21210

Telephone: (301) 323-3200.

Founded 1791.

*President and Rector:* Rev. ROBERT F. LEAVITT, S.S.
*Vice-President for Resource/Development:* Rev. JAMES W. LOTHAMER, S.S.
*Academic Dean:* Sr. PATRICIA SMITH, R.S.M.
*Treasurer:* RICHARD G. CHILDS, B.S.
*Director of Financial Aid:* PRISCILLA GORDON.
*Publications:* St. Mary's Bulletin (quarterly), *Catalogues*.

The libraries contain 153,975 vols.
Number of teachers: 29 full-time, 52 part-time, total 81.
Number of students: 177 full-time, 178 part-time, total 355.

UNITED STATES OF AMERICA

## SALISBURY STATE COLLEGE*
SALISBURY, MARYLAND 21801

Telephone: (301) 546-3261.

Founded 1925.

*President:* T. E. BELLAVANCE.
*Academic Dean:* Dr. T. L. ERSKINE.
*Registrar:* DOROTHY L. POWELL.
*Dean of Students:* O. ROBINSON.
*Director of Business:* G. HOWATT.
*Director of Information:* W. FOX.
*Director of Admissions:* MARGARET HOPKINS.
*Librarian:* J. T. THRASH.

The library contains 120,000 vols.
Number of teachers: 200.
Number of students: 4,427.

\* No reply received to our questionnaire this year.


## TOWSON STATE UNIVERSITY
YORK ROAD,
BALTIMORE, MARYLAND 21204

Telephone: (301) 321-2000.

Founded 1866.

*President:* HOKE SMITH.
*Registrar:* G. A. SARTORI.
*Director of Admissions:* LINDA COLLINS.
*Vice-President for Academic Affairs:* PATRICIA R. PLANTE.
*Vice-President, Business and Finance:* DONALD MCCULLOH.
*Vice-President, Student Affairs:* DOROTHY SIEGEL.
*Vice-President, Institutional Development:* SALLY V. SOURIS.
*Librarian:* THOMAS E. STRADER.

The library contains 372,000 vols.
Number of teachers: 965.
Number of students: 15,528.

Publication: *Towson State Journal of International Affairs* (2 a year).


## UNITED STATES NAVAL ACADEMY
ANNAPOLIS, MARYLAND 21402

Founded 1845.

*Superintendent:* Vice-Admiral EDWARD C. WALLER, U.S.N.
*Commandant of Midshipmen:* Capt. LEON A. EDNEY, U.S.N.
*Academic Dean:* B. M. DAVIDSON, PH.D.
*Associate Dean:* R. D. MATHIEU, PH.D.
*Dean of Admissions:* Rear-Admiral R. W. MCNITT, U.S.N. (retd.), M.S.
*Assistant Deans:* Capt. N. C. COLLIER, U.S.N., M.S., Cdr. J. M. PETROVICH U.S.N., M.B.A., Prof. J. F. KELLEY, PH.D.
*Registrar:* Assoc. Prof. R. L. DAVIS, PH.D.
*Director of Museum:* Prof. W. W. JEFFRIES, PH.D.
*Librarian:* Prof. R. A. EVANS, A.B., M.L.S.

The library contains 500,000 volumes.
Number of teachers: 549.
Number of students (midshipmen): 4,627.

Publications: *USNA Catalogue, Lucky Bag, The Log, Shipmate.*

DIVISION DIRECTORS:
*Engineering and Weapons:* Capt. J. R. ESHMAN, U.S.N., M.S.
*English and History:* Col. J. A. McGINN, U.S.M.C., ED.M.
*Mathematics and Science:* Capt. R. L. REASONOVER, U.S.N., M.S.
*Professional Development:* Capt. T. D. PAULSEN, U.S.N.
*U.S. and International Studies:* Capt. J. A. JOCKELL, U.S.N., M.A.
*Athletics:* Capt. J. O. COPPEDGE, U.S.N. (retd.), M.A.


## UNIVERSITY OF BALTIMORE
CHARLES AT MOUNT ROYAL,
BALTIMORE, MARYLAND 21201

Telephone: (301) 727-6350.

Founded 1925.

*President:* Dr. H. MEBANE TURNER.
*Dean of Admissions:* Mrs. CATHRYN FEATHER.
*Librarian:* JOAN BOURNE (acting).

The library contains 303,000 vols.
Number of teachers: 119 full-time, 134 part-time.
Number of students: 1,972 full-time, 3,425 part-time.

DEANS:
*Law:* LAURENCE M. KATZ.
*Liberal Arts:* Dr. NEIL J. KLEINMAN.
*Business:* Dr. FRED KELLY.
*Graduate:* Dr. FRED HOPKINS.


## UNIVERSITY OF MARYLAND SYSTEM
ADELPHI,
MARYLAND 20783

Founded 1807.

*President:* JOHN S. TOLL.
*Executive Vice-President:* ALBIN O. KUHN.
*Vice-Presidents:* WARREN W. BRANDT (General Administration), DAVID ADAMANY (Academic Affairs), DAVID S. SPARKS (Graduate Studies and Research), FRANK L. BENTZ, Jr. (Agricultural Affairs and Legislative Relations), ROBERT G. SMITH (University Development).
*Registrar:* WILLIAM C. SPANN.
*Librarian:* H. JOANNE HARRAR.


### University of Maryland at College Park
COLLEGE PARK, MARYLAND 20742

Telephone: (301) 474-0100.
Founded 1859.

*Chancellor:* ROBERT L. GLUCKSTERN.

Number of students: 37,864.

Divisions of: Agricultural and Life Sciences; Mathematics and Physical Sciences; Engineering; Arts and Humanities; Human and Community

WORLD OF LEARNING

Resources. Each division contains academic departments and professional colleges.

The library contains 1,403,568 vols.

### University of Maryland at Baltimore
BALTIMORE, MARYLAND 21201

Founded 1807.

*Chancellor:* ALBIN O. KUHN.

Number of students: 4,495.

Schools of Dentistry, Law, Medicine, Nursing, Pharmacy, Social Work and Community Planning, University of Maryland Hospital, Maryland Institute for Emergency Medical Services.

The libraries contain 346,000 vols.

### University of Maryland, Baltimore County
5401 WILKENS AVENUE,
CATONSVILLE, MARYLAND 21228

Founded 1963.

*Chancellor:* JOHN W. DORSEY.
*Vice-Chancellors:* WALTER S. JONES (Academic Affairs), SALLIE A. GIFFEN (Administration), SCOTT T. RICKARD (Student Affairs).
*Dean of Arts and Sciences:* RICHARD F. NEVILLE.

Publications: *Undergraduate Catalog, Graduate Catalog* (annually).

The library contains 325,000 vols. and 3,100 journals.

Number of teachers: 448, including 251 professors.

Number of students: 5,828 undergraduates, 479 graduates.

### University of Maryland, Eastern Shore
PRINCESS ANNE, MARYLAND 21853

Telephone: (301) 651-2200.

Founded 1886.

Liberal Studies, Professional Studies and Experimental Studies.

*Chancellor:* WILLIAM P. HYTCHE.
*Vice-Chancellor, Academic Affairs:* JODELLANO J. STATOM.
*Vice-Chancellor, Administrative Affairs:* JOEL C. MACK.
*Vice-Chancellor, Student Affairs:* HERMAN FRANKLIN.
*Dean of Research:* C. DENNIS IGNASIAS.
*Librarian:* JESSIE C. SMITH.
*Director of Admissions and Registration:* JAMES B. EWERS.

The library contains 85,000 vols.
Number of teachers: 80.
Number of students: 1,009.


## WASHINGTON COLLEGE
CHESTERTOWN,
MARYLAND 21620

Telephone: (301) 778-2800.

Founded 1782.

*President:* Dr. JOSEPH H. MCLAIN.
*Registrar:* ERMON N. FOSTER.
*Dean:* GARRY E. CLARKE.
*Director of Admissions:* A. M. DI MAGGIO.
*Librarian:* BETTY WASSON.
  The library contains 130,000 vols.
  Number of teachers: 69.
  Number of students: 750.

## WESTERN MARYLAND COLLEGE
WESTMINSTER, MARYLAND 21157.
Telephone: 848-7000.
Founded 1867.

*President:* RALPH C. JOHN.
*Vice-President and Dean of Academic Affairs:* WILLIAM MCCORMICK, Jr.
*Vice-President for Business Affairs:* PHILIP B. SCHAEFFER.
*Vice-President for Development:* JAMES F. RIDENOUR.
*Vice-President for Student Affairs:* C. WRAY MOWBRAY, Jr.
*Registrar, Director of Records and Institutional Information:* HILBERT HUGHLETT DAWKINS, Jr.
*Librarian:* G. T. BACHMANN, Jr.
  The library contains 123,363 vols.
  Number of teachers: 127.
  Number of students: 1,386.

## MASSACHUSETTS

### AMERICAN INTERNATIONAL COLLEGE
SPRINGFIELD, MASSACHUSETTS 01109
Telephone: (413) 737-7000.
Founded 1885.

*President:* HARRY J. COURNIOTES.
*Dean of Admissions:* JOHN R. FALLON.
*Registrar:* Mrs. ESTHER F. HANSEN.
*Librarian:* Dr. SUSAN LEE.
  The library contains 100,000 vols.
  Number of teachers: 126 full-time, 34 part-time.
  Number of students: 2,200.

### AMHERST COLLEGE
AMHERST, MASSACHUSETTS 01002
Telephone: (413) 542-2000.
Founded 1821; Chartered 1825.

*President:* JULIAN H. GIBBS.
*General Secretary:* J. L. CALLAHAN, Jr., B.A.
*Secretary for Public Affairs:* D. C. WILSON, M.A.
*Registrar:* G. M. MAGER, A.M., PH.D.
*Treasurer:* GEORGE B. MAY, B.A.
*Comptroller:* MARVIN R. KUIPERS, B.A.
*Dean of the Faculty:* MARY CATHERINE BATESON, PH.D.
*Dean of Students:* J. BISHOP, PH.D.
*Dean of Admission:* EDWARD B. WALL, B.A.

  The library contains 530,000 vols.
  Number of teachers: 160.
  Number of students: 1,500.

### ANNA MARIA COLLEGE
PAXTON, MASSACHUSETTS 01612
Telephone: (617) 757-4586.
Founded 1946.

*President:* Sister BERNADETTE MADORE, S.S.A., PH.D.
*Dean:* LOUISE N. SOLDANI, PH.D.
*Registrar:* Sister ROLLANDE QUINTAL, S.S.A.
  The library contains 50,000 vols.
  Number of teachers: 104.
  Number of students: 1,507.

### ASSUMPTION COLLEGE
500 SALISBURY STREET, WORCESTER, MASSACHUSETTS 01609
Telephone: 752-5615.
Founded 1904.

*President:* JOSEPH H. HAGAN.
*Dean of Admissions and Financial Aid:* T. E. DUNN.
*Dean of Academic Affairs:* RICHARD A. OEHLING.
*Librarian:* PHILIPPE L. POISSON.
  The library contains 153,000 vols.
  Number of teachers: 137.
  Number of students: 2,592.

### ATLANTIC UNION COLLEGE
SOUTH LANCASTER, MASSACHUSETTS 01561
Telephone: 365-4561.
Founded 1882.

*President:* LARRY M. LEWIS.
*Registrar:* J. D. MUSTARD.
*Librarian:* O. R. SCHMIDT.
  The library contains 99,000 vols.
  Number of teachers: 86.
  Number of students: 680.

### BABSON COLLEGE
BABSON PARK, (WELLESLEY), MASSACHUSETTS 02157
Telephone: 235-1200.
Founded 1919; College of Management.

*President:* Dr. WILLIAM R. DILL.
*Vice-President (Academic Affairs):* Dr. MELVYN R. COPEN.
*Vice-President (Financial Affairs):* J. PUTNEY.
*Vice-President (Student Affairs):* P. STAAKE, Jr.
*Vice-President (College Resources):* CHARLES D. THOMPSON.
*Director of Admission:* JOSEPH B. CARVER.
*Librarian:* J. A. BOUDREAU.
  The library contains 82,000 vols.
  Number of teachers: 115.
  Number of students: 3,115.
  Publications: *College Catalogs*† (annual), *Alumni Bulletin*† (quarterly).

### BENTLEY COLLEGE
WALTHAM, MASSACHUSETTS 02154
Founded 1917.

*President:* Dr. GREGORY H. ADAMIAN.
*Vice-President for Academic Affairs:* Dr. JOHN T. NICHOL.
*Vice-President for Business and Finance:* R. L. LENINGTON.
*Vice-President for Institutional Advancement:* DAVID W. ELLIS.
*Vice-President for Student Affairs:* Dr. THOMAS H. ZARLE.
  The library contains 102,130 vols.
  Number of teachers: 291.
  Number of students: 7,600.

### BOSTON COLLEGE
CHESTNUT HILL, MASSACHUSETTS 02167
Founded 1863 by the Society of Jesus.

*President:* Rev. J. DONALD MONAN, S.J., PH.D.
*Financial Vice-President:* J. R. SMITH, M.B.A.
*Academic Vice-President:* Rev. JOSEPH A. PANUSKA, S.J., PH.D.
*Director of Libraries:* THOMAS O'CONNELL, D.C.L.
  The library contains 1,000,000 vols.
  Number of teachers: 865, including 132 full professors.
  Number of students: 14,445.
  Publications: *Stylus, Annual Survey of Massachusetts Law, Boston College Law Review, Boston College Magazine.*

DEANS:

*College of Arts and Sciences:* Rev. WILLIAM B. NEENAN, S.J., PH.D.
*Graduate School of Arts and Sciences:* DONALD J. WHITE, PH.D.
*School of Management:* JOHN J. NEUHAUSER, PH.D.
*Evening College of Arts, Sciences, and Business Administration:* Rev. J. A. WOODS, S.J., ED.D.
*School of Education:* MARY D. GRIFFIN, PH.D.
*School of Nursing:* MARY A. DINEEN, ED.D.
*Law School:* R. G. HUBER, LL.M.
*Graduate School of Social Work:* JUNE G. HOPPS, PH.D.
*Summer Session:* Rev. G. R. FUIR, S.J., A.M., S.T.L.

### BOSTON STATE COLLEGE
625 HUNTINGTON AVENUE, BOSTON, MASSACHUSETTS 02115
Telephone: 731-3300.
Founded 1852.

President: ROBERT V. MCCARTHY.
Registrar: JANE CURRIER.
Librarian: MARY R. GORMAN.

The library contains 155,298 vols.
Number of teachers: 280.
Number of students: 5,231.

## BOSTON UNIVERSITY
### 147 BAY STATE RD., BOSTON, MASSACHUSETTS 02215

Telephone: (617) 353-2000.

Founded 1839, Chartered 1869.

Private control; Academic year: September to May (two semesters), June to August (summer session).

President: JOHN R. SILBER.
Provost: ROBERT MAYFIELD (acting).
Vice-Presidents: RICHARD EGDAHL (Academic Affairs, Health), DANIEL FINN (University Relations), MARY-JANE HEMPERLEY (Administrative Services), ROBERT MAYFIELD (External Programs), CHARLES SMITH (Business and Financial Affairs), ROBERT FELDMAN (Development), GERALD GROSS (Arts, Publications, Media), DEAN DONER (Overseas Program), ROBERT BERGENHEIM (Labor and Public Relations).
Registrar: JON V. HAYWOOD.
Librarian: JOHN LAUCUS.

Library: see Libraries.
Number of teachers: 2,513.
Number of students: 28,509.

Publications: Journal of Education, Boston University Law Review, Bostonia Today, Journal of Field Archaeology.

### DEANS:
College of Basic Studies: BRENDAN GILBANE.
College of Engineering: LOUIS PADULO.
College of Liberal Arts: GEOFFREY BANNISTER.
Graduate School: GEOFFREY BANNISTER.
Metropolitan College: IRWIN PRICE.
Program in Artisanry: JERE OSGOOD.
Sargent College of Allied Health Professions: DAVID HERSHENSON.
School of Education: PAUL WARREN.
School for the Arts: GERALD GROSS (acting).
School of Graduate Dentistry: SPENCER FRANKL.
School of Law: WILLIAM SCHWARTZ.
School of Management: HENRY MORGAN.
School of Medicine: JOHN SANDSON.
School of Nursing: ANN BURGESS.
School of Public Communications: DONIS DONDIS.
School of Social Work: HUBERT E. JONES.
School of Theology: RICHARD NESMITH.

## BRANDEIS UNIVERSITY
### 415 SOUTH ST., WALTHAM, MASSACHUSETTS 02254

Telephone: (617) 647-2000.

Founded 1948.

President: Dr. MARVER H. BERNSTEIN, PH.D.
Chancellor: Dr. ABRAM L. SACHAR, PH.D., LITT.D.
Financial Affairs and University Treasurer: L. G. LOOMIS, M.B.A.
Development: (vacant).
Administrative Affairs: P. T. VAN AKEN, M.B.A., B.A.
Admissions: D. GOULD, M.S.ED.
Library Director: BESSIE K. HAHN.

Number of teachers: 354.
Number of students: 2,800 undergraduate, 650 graduate students.

### DEANS:
Faculty, Arts and Sciences: A. P. CARTER, PH.D.
Graduate School, Arts and Sciences: R. ART, PH.D.
College, Arts and Sciences: A. O. KLEIN, PH.D.
Florence Heller School for Advanced Studies in Social Welfare: S. ALTMAN, PH.D.

### DEPARTMENT CHAIRMEN:
Creative Arts:
  Fine Arts: ROBERT MAEDA, PH.D., JOACHIM GAEHDE, PH.D.
  Music: ALLAN KEILER, PH.D.
  Theater Arts: THEODORE KAZANOFF, M.A.

Humanities:
  Classical and Oriental Studies: IAN TODD, PH.D.
  English and American Literature: ALAN LEVITAN, PH.D.
  Linguistics: RAY JACKENDOFF, PH.D.
  German and Slavic: R. SZULKIN, PH.D.
  Jewish Communal Service: BERNARD REISMAN, PH.D.
  Near Eastern and Judaic Studies: MARVIN FOX, PH.D.
  Philosophy and History of Ideas: (vacant).
  Romance and Comparative Literature: MURRAY SACHS, PH.D.

Science:
  Biochemistry: R. ABELES, PH.D.
  Biology: CHANDLER FULTON, PH.D.
  Chemistry: COLIN STEEL, PH.D.
  Mathematics: DAVID BUCHSBAUM, PH.D.
  Photobiology Institute: JEROME A. SCHIFF, PH.D.
  Physics: HOWARD SCHNITZER, PH.D.
  Rosenstiel Medical Science Research Center: H. O. HALVORSON, PH.D. (Director).

Social Science:
  African and Afro-American Studies: WELLINGTON W. NYANGONI, PH.D.
  American Studies: L. H. FUCHS, PH.D.
  Anthropology: ROBERT HUNT, PH.D.
  Economics: F. TRENERY DOLBEAR, PH.D.
  History: E. BLACK, PH.D.
  Politics: D. HINDLEY, PH.D.
  Psychology: JAMES R. LACKNER, PH.D.
  Sociology: IRVING ZOLA, PH.D.
  Physical Education: NICHOLAS RODIS, ED.M.

## BRIDGEWATER STATE COLLEGE
### BRIDGEWATER, MASSACHUSETTS 02324

Telephone: 697-8321.

Founded 1840.

President: ADRIAN RONDILEAU.
Academic Dean: WALLACE L. ANDERSON.
Librarian: O. T. P. MCGOWAN.

The library contains 160,000 vols.
Number of teachers: 243.
Number of students: 4,261 full-time, 3,014 part-time.

## CLARK UNIVERSITY
### 950 MAIN STREET, WORCESTER, MASSACHUSETTS 01610

Telephone: (617) 793-7711.

Founded by Jonas Gilman Clark; Chartered 1887.

President: MORTIMER H. APPLEY.
Vice-President for Business and Finance: JAMES E. COLLINS.
Provost: LAURENCE BERLOWITZ.
Dean of College: WALTER E. WRIGHT.
Dean of Graduate School: ROGER C. VAN TASSEL.
Dean of the College of Professional and Continuing Education: DOUGLAS ASTOLFI.
Dean of Admissions: RICHARD W. PIERSON, M.A.
Dean of Students: JOYCE T. GIBSON.
Registrar: G. T. CORCORAN, M.A.
Librarian: ALBERT G. ANDERSON, Jr., M.S.L.S.

The library contains 370,000 vols.
Number of teachers: 130 full-time, 65 part-time.
Number of students: 1,900 undergraduates, 400 graduates, 650 professional and continuing-education students.

Publications: catalogs, Dissertations and Theses, Clark University News, Economic Geography, President's Report, Clark Now, Idealistic Studies, Journal of Family History.

## COLLEGE OF OUR LADY OF THE ELMS
### 291 SPRINGFIELD STREET, CHICOPEE, MASSACHUSETTS 01013

Telephone: (413) 598-8351.

Founded 1928.

Liberal arts college for women.

President: Sister MARY DOOLEY, S.S.J.
Vice-President: NORA T. HARRINGTON, S.S.J.

*Academic Dean:* MARY F. HONNEN, S.S.J.
*Dean of Students:* MAUREEN KERVICK, S.S.J.
*Librarian:* Sister EDITH MCALICE, S.S.J.

The library contains 72,057 vols.
Number of teachers: 50.
Number of students: 600.

### COLLEGE OF THE HOLY CROSS
WORCESTER, MASSACHUSETTS 01610

Founded 1843.

*President:* Rev. JOHN E. BROOKS, S.J.
*Vice-President:* Rev. PAUL F. HARMAN, S.J.
*Dean of the College:* Rev. JOSEPH R. FAHEY, S.J.
*Dean of Students:* Rev. EARLE L. MARKEY, S.J.
*Librarian:* JAMES M. MAHONEY, B.L.S.

The library contains 360,000 vols.
Number of teachers: 188.
Number of students: 2,513.

### EASTERN NAZARENE COLLEGE
23 EAST ELM AVENUE, QUINCY, MASSACHUSETTS 02170

Telephone: (617) 773-6350.

Founded 1900.

*President:* STEPHEN W. NEASE.
*Dean:* D. L. YOUNG.
*Registrar:* BARBARA FINCH.
*Dean of Students:* R. W. HELFRICH.
*Director of Admissions:* DONALD YERXA.
*Librarian:* SUSAN WATKINS.

The library contains 78,000 vols.
Number of teachers: 52.
Number of students: 835.

### EMERSON COLLEGE
148 BEACON STREET, BOSTON, MASSACHUSETTS 02116

Telephone: 262-2010.

Founded 1880.

*President:* Dr. ALLEN KOENIG.
*Vice-President of Business and Finance:* GEORGE BROADBENT.
*Registrar:* GERD P. BOND.
*Librarian:* DONNA TRIPP.

The library contains 84,000 vols.
Number of teachers: 135.
Number of students: 1,500.

### EMMANUEL COLLEGE
400 THE FENWAY, BOSTON, MASSACHUSETTS 02115

Telephone: (617) 277-9340.

Founded 1919.

*President:* Sister JANET EISNER, S.N.D., PH.D.
*Vice-President for Business and Finance:* THOMAS D. GOLDRICK.
*Director of Admissions:* TINA SEGALLA.
*Academic Dean:* MARION KILSON, PH.D.
*Dean of Continuing Education:* Sister MARY ELLEN O'KEEFE, S.N.D., PH.D.
*Librarian:* Sister MAURA MEADE, S.N.D., M.S.

The library contains 121,600 vols.
Number of teachers: 100.
Number of students: 1,100.

### FITCHBURG STATE COLLEGE
FITCHBURG, MASSACHUSETTS 01420

Telephone: (617) 345-2151.

Founded 1894.

*President:* VINCENT J. MARA.
*Vice-President for Academic Affairs:* PATRICK F. DELANEY.
*Vice-President for Student Affairs:* WILLIAM R. DONOHUE.
*Vice-President for Finance and Administration:* JOHN J. BOURSY.
*Librarian:* W. T. CASEY.

The library contains 160,000 vols.
Number of teachers: 215.
Number of students: c. 6,900.

### FRAMINGHAM STATE COLLEGE
FRAMINGHAM CENTRE, MASSACHUSETTS 01701

Telephone: (617) 620-1220.

Founded 1839.

*President:* D. JUSTIN MCCARTHY.
*Director of Admissions:* JOSEPH LOPES (acting).
*Librarian:* STANLEY MCDONALD.

The library contains 344,185 holdings.
Number of teachers: 152.
Number of students: 3,125 day, 2,127 evening.

### GORDON COLLEGE
255 GRAPEVINE ROAD, WENHAM, MASSACHUSETTS 01984

Telephone: (617) 927-2300.

Founded 1889.

*President:* RICHARD F. GROSS, PH.D.
*Dean of Faculty:* R. JUDSON CARLBERG.
*Registrar:* Miss FLORENCE WINSOR.
*Dean of Admissions and Financial Aid:* DAVID MACMILLAN.
*Librarian:* JOHN BEAUREGARD.

The library contains 156,000 vols.
Number of teachers: 56.
Number of students: 1,057.

### HARVARD UNIVERSITY
CAMBRIDGE, MASSACHUSETTS 02138

Telephone: 495-1000.

Founded October 1636; Charter signed May 1650.

*President:* D. C. BOK, A.M., J.D.
*Vice-President for Administration:* JOE B. WYATT, M.A.
*Vice-President for Financial Affairs:* THOMAS O'BRIEN, PH.D.
*Vice-President for Government and Community Affairs:* ROBIN SCHMIDT, A.B.
*Vice-President for Alumni Affairs and Development:* FRED GLIMP.
*Director of University Library:* OSCAR HANDLIN.

Number of teachers: 5,170.
Number of students: 19,322.

DEANS:

*Harvard College:* J. B. FOX, Jr.
*Divinity School:* G. E. RUPP, PH.D.
*Faculty of Arts and Sciences:* H. ROSOVSKY, PH.D.
*Graduate School of Design:* G. M. MCCUE, A.M.
*Law School:* A. M. SACKS, LL.D.
*Medical School:* D. C. TOSTESON, M.D.
*Graduate School of Public Health:* H. H. HIATT, M.D.
*Graduate School of Business Administration:* J. H. MCARTHUR, D.B.A.
*Graduate School of Education:* P. N. YLVISAKER, PH.D.
*J. F. Kennedy School of Government:* G. T. ALLISON, Jr., PH.D.
*Graduate School of Arts and Sciences:* E. L. KEENAN, PH.D.
*School of Dental Medicine:* P. GOLDHABER, S.B., D.D.S.
*Harvard-M.I.T. Division of Health Sciences and Technology:* I. M. LONDON.

PROFESSORS:

*Divinity School:*
CARMAN, J. B., Comparative Religion
COOGAN, M., Old Testament
COX, H. G., Divinity
CROSS, F., Hebrew
DYCK, A., Divinity
GEORGI, D., Biblical Students
GOMES, P. J., Christian Morals
HANSON, P. D., Old Testament
HUTCHISON, W. R., History of Religion
KAUFMAN, G. D., Theology
KOESTER, H. H., New Testament Studies
LAZZARO, R., Church History
MCGILL, A. C., Theology
MACRAE, G. W., Roman Catholic Theological Studies
NIEBUHR, R. R., Divinity
POTTER, R. B., Social Ethics
SMITH, W. C., Comparative History of Religion
STENDHAL, K., Biblical Studies
STRUGNELL, J., Christian Origins
WILLIAMS, P. N., Theology
WRIGHT, C. C., American Church History

*Faculty of Arts and Sciences:*
AARON, D. B., English and American Literature
ACKERMAN, J. S., Fine Arts
ALAZRAKI, J., Romance Languages and Literatures
ALFRED, W., English
BADIAN, E., History
BAILYN, B., History
BAKER, H. C., English
BALES, R. F., Social Relations
BANFIELD, E., Government

Barghoorn, E. S., Botany
Barnes, L. B., Organizational Behaviour
Bate, W. J., Humanities
Beer, S. H., Government
Bell, D., Sociology
Benson, L. D., English
Bergson, A., Economics
Berthoff, W. B., English
Birkhoff, G., Applied Mathematics
Bloch, H., Greek and Latin
Bloch, K. E., Biochemistry
Bloomfield, M. W., English
Bogorad, L., Biology
Bond, W. H., Bibliography
Boss, K. J., Biology
Bott, R., Mathematics
Branton, D., Biology
Brewer, J., History and Literature
Brody, J., Romance Languages and Literatures
Brown, R. W., Social Psychology
Brustein, R. S., English
Buckley, J. H., English
Bullitt, J. M., English
Burnham, C. W., Mineralogy
Cameron, A., Astronomy
Cavell, S. L., Aesthetics
Caves, R. E., Economics
Chandra, P., Indian and South Asian Art
Chang, K.-C., Anthropology
Chapman, R. H., English
Clark, T. J., Fine Arts
Clausen, W. V., Greek and Latin
Clive, J. L., History
Cohen, I. B., History of Science
Cohn, D., German
Coleman, S., Physics
Constable, G., Medieval History
Coolidge, J. P., Fine Arts
Corey, E. J., Chemistry
Craig, A. M., Japanese History
Cranston, E. A., Japanese Literature
Crompton, A. W., Biology
Cross, F. M., Hebrew
Dalgarno, A., Astronomy
Davis, J. A., Sociology
Della Terza, D., Romance Languages
Dempster, A. P., Theoretical Statistics
Deutsch, K. W., Government
Devore, B. I., Anthropology
Dike, K. O., Botany
Doering, W. von E., Chemistry
Dominguez, J. I., Government
Donald, D. H., American History and Civilization
Dorfman, R., Economics
Doty, P., Chemistry
Dowling, J., Biology
Dreben, B. S., Philosophy
Duesenberry, J., Economics
Dunn, C. W., Celtic Languages
Dziewonski, A. M., Geology
Eckstein, O., Economics
Estes, W. K., Psychology
Evans, G. B., English
Fanger, D., Comparative Literature
Feldstein, M., Economics
Field, G. B., Practical Astronomy
Firth, R., Philosophy
Fitzgerald, R. S., Rhetoric and Oratory
Fleming, D. H., History
Fletcher, J. F., Chinese and Central Asian History
Fogel, R. W., Political Economy and History
Forbes, E., Music
Ford, F. L., History
Freedberg, S.J., Fine Arts
Freidel, F. B., History
Friedman, B. M., Economics
Frye, R. N., Iranian
Georgi, H. M., Physics
Giacconi, R., Astronomy
Gilbert, W., Biophysics

Gilman, S., Romance Languages
Gingerich, O., Astronomy and History of Science
Glashow, S. L., Physics
Glauber, R. J., Physics
Gleason, A. M., Mathematics
Gordon, R. G., Chemistry
Gould, S. J., Geology
Grabar, O., Fine Arts
Green, D. M., Psychophysics
Green, J. R., Economics
Griffiths, P. A., Mathematics
Griliches, Z., Economics
Guidotti, G., Biochemistry
Guillen, C., Comparative Literature and Romance Languages and Literatures
Gursky, H., X-Ray Astronomy
Guthke, K. S., German
Guzzetti, A., Visual Studies
Haller, J., Geology
Halperin, B., Social Studies
Hanan, P. D., Chinese Literature
Handlin, O., History
Hanfmann, G. M. A., Archaeology
Harrison, S. C., Biochemistry and Molecular Biology
Hastings, J., Biology
Hatfield, H. C., German Art and Culture
Hays, J. F., Geology
Heclo, H. H., Government
Heimert, A. E., American Literature
Heinrichs, W. P., Arabic
Henrichs, A. M., Greek and Latin
Herlihy, D. J., History
Herrnstein, R. J., Psychology
Herschbach, D. R., Chemistry
Hibbett, H. S., Japanese Literature
Hiebert, E. N., History of Science
Hightower, J. R., Chinese Literature
Higonnet, P. L.-R., History
Hironaka, H., Mathematics
Hoffmann, S. H., Civilization of France
Hofheinz, R. M., Government
Holland, H. D., Geology
Holldobler, B. K., Biology
Holton, G., Physics
Holzman, P. S., Psychology
Horowitz, P., Physics
Houthakker, H. S., Economics
Howard, R. A., Botany
Hubbard, R., Biology
Huber, P. J., Statistics
Hughes, D. G., Music
Huntington, S. P., Government
Iliescu, N., Romance Languages
Ingalls, D. H. H., Sanskrit
Jaffe, A. M., Physics
Jenkins, F., Biology
Jorgenson, D. W., Economics
Kafatos, F. C., Biology
Kain, J. F., Economics
Kaiser, W. J., English and Comparative Literature
Karplus, M., Chemistry
Kazhdan, D., Mathematics
Kelleher, J. V., Irish Studies
Kelman, H. C., Social Ethics
Keyfitz, N., Sociology
Kiely, R. J., English
Kilson, M. L., Government
Kim, E., Music
Kirchner, L., Music
Kishi, Y., Chemistry
Klemperer, W. A., Chemistry
Knox, B. M. W., Greek
Kuhn, P. A., History and East Asian Languages and Civilizations
Kuno, S., Linguistics
Lambdin, T. O., Semitic Philology
Lamberg-Karlovsky, C. C., Anthropology
Landes, D. S., History
Layzer, D. R., Astronomy

Leibenstein, H., Economics and Population
Levi, H. W., Biology
Levin, H. T., Comparative Literature
Levine, R. A., Fine Arts
Lewontin, R. C., Biology
Liem, K., Ichthyology
Liller, W., Applied Astronomy
Lilley, A. W., Astronomy
Lintner, J. V., Economics and Business Administration
Lipscomb, W. N., Chemistry
Lockwood, L. H., Music
Loomis, L. H., Mathematics
Lord, A. B., Slavic and Comparative Literature
Luce, R., Psychology
Lunt, H. G., Slavonic Languages and Literature
Maass, A., Government
MacCaffrey, W. T., History
Mackey, G. W., Mathematics
Mahdi, M. S., Arabic
Maher, B. A., Psychology
Mansfield, H. C., Government
Marglin, S. A., Economics
Marichal, J., Romance Languages
Marquez, F., Romance Languages and Literature
May, E. R., History
Maybury-Lewis, D. H., Anthropology
Mazur, H. C., Mathematics
McClelland, D. C., Psychology
Mendelsohn, E. I., History of Science
Meselson, M. S., Biology
Meyer, A. J., Middle East Studies
Mitten, D. G., Classical Art and Archaeology
Moran, W. L., Assyriology
Mosteller, C. F., Mathematical Statistics
Mumford, D. B., Mathematics
Murdoch, J. E., History of Science
Musgrave, R. A., Economics
Nagatomi, M., Buddhist Studies
Nagy, G. J., Greek and Latin
Nash, L. K., Chemistry
Nelson, D. R., Physics
Neustadt, R. E., Government
Noyes, R. W., Astronomy
Nozick, R., Philosophy
Nye, J. S., Government
Nykrog, P., Romance Languages and Literatures
O'Connell, R. J., Geophysics
Ozment, S. E., History
Papaliolios, C. D., Physics
Parry, J. H., Oceanic History
Patterson, O., Sociology
Pelzel, J. C., Anthropology
Perkins, D. D., Literature
Perkins, D. H., Modern China Studies
Petersen, U., Mining
Pettigrew, T. F., Social Psychology
Pian, R. C., East Asian Languages and Civilizations
Pipes, R. E., History
Pipkin, F. M., Physics
Pizzorno, A. D., European Studies
Porte, J. M., English
Pound, R., Physics
Press, W., Astronomy
Price, H. D., Government
Pritsak, O., Linguistics
Ptashne, M. S., Biochemistry
Putnam, H. W., Philosophy
Raiffa, H., Managerial Economics
Rainwater, L., Sociology
Ramsey, N. F., Physics
Rawls, J., Philosophy
Reischauer, E. O., Japanese
Rivers, W., Romance Literature
Rogers, F. M., Portuguese Language and Literature
Rollins, R. C., Systematic Biology

ROSEN, C. W., Poetry
ROSENFIELD, J. M., Fine Arts
ROSENKRANTZ, B., History of Science
ROSENTHAL, R., Social Psychology
RUBBIA, C., Physics
RYBICKI, C. B., Practice of Astronomy
SABRA, A. I., History of Arabic Science
SACKS, G. E., Mathematical Logic
SAFRAN, N., Government
SCHAMA, S. M., History
SCHELLING, T. C., Economics
SCHIMMEL, A., Indo-Muslim Culture
SCHINDLER, H. J., Linguistics
SCHMID, W., Mathematics
SCHULTES, R. E., Biology
SCHWARTZ, B. I., History and Political Science
SCHWITTERS, R. F., Physics
SEKLER, E. F., Architecture
SETCHKAREV, V., Slavic Languages and Literatures
SHACKLETON BAILEY, D. R., Greek and Latin
SHIVELY, D. H., Japanese History and Literature
SHKLAR, J. N., Government
SIEVER, R., Geology
SIMON, E., German
SLIVE, S., Fine Arts
SMYTH, C., Fine Arts
SOLBRIG, O. T., Biology
SOLOMON, A. K., Biophysics
SOUTHERN, E., Afro-American Studies
SPENCE, A., Economics
STERNBERG, S. Z., Mathematics
STEWART, Z., Greek and Latin
STONE, D. A., Romance Languages and Literatures
STONE, P. J., Social Relations
STRAUCH, K., Physics
STRIEDTER, J., Slavic Languages and Literatures
STROMINGER, J. L., Biochemistry
TAMBIAH, S., Anthropology
TARANOVSKY, K., Slavic Languages and Literatures
TATAR, M. M., German
TATE, J. T., Mathematics
TAYLOR, C. R., Zoology
TEETER, K. VAN D., Linguistics
THERNSTROM, S., History
THOMPSON, J. B., Mineralogy
THOMSON, R. W., Armenian Studies
TOMLINSON, P. B., Botany
TORREY, J. G., Botany
TRYON, R. M., Biology
TURNER, R. D., Biology
TWERSKY, I., Hebrew Literature and Philosophy
ULAM, A. B., History and Political Science
VERBA, S., Government
VERMEULE, E., Classics
VERNON, R., International Trade and Investment
VOGEL, E. F., Sociology
VOGT, E. Z., Social Anthropology
VOSGERCHIAN, L., Music
WANG, J. C., Biochemistry
WARD, J. M., Music
WATKINS, C. W., Linguistics and Classics
WEINBERG, S., Physics
WESTHEIMER, F. H., Chemistry
WHITE, H. C., Sociology
WHITE, S. H., Psychology
WHITNEY, C. A., Astronomy
WILEY, D. C., Biochemistry and Biophysics
WILLEY, G. R., Central American and Mexican Archaeology
WILLIAMS, C. M., Biology
WILLIAMS, E. E., Biology
WILLIAMS, S., Anthropology
WILSON, E. O., Zoology
WILSON, J. Q., Government
WILSON, R., Physics
WOLFF, C., Music
WOLFF, R. L., History
WOMACK, J., History
WOOD, C., Biology
WOOD, J., Geology
WOOLLACOTT, R. M., Biology
YALMAN, N. O., Anthropology
ZERNER, H. T., Fine Arts
ZIMMERMANN, M. H., Forestry

*Division of Engineering and Applied Physics:*
ABERNATHY, F. H., Mechanical Engineering
ANDERSON, D. G. M., Applied Mathematics
ANDERSON, J. G., Atmospheric Chemistry
BARTEE, T. C., Computer Engineering
BIRKHOFF, G., Pure and Applied Mathematics
BLOEMBERGEN, N., Physics
BOSSERT, W. H., Applied Mathematics
BROCKETT, R. W., Applied Mathematics
BROOKS, H., Technology and Public Policy
BUDIANSKY, B., Structural Mechanics
BUTLER, J. N., Applied Chemistry
CARRIER, G. F., Applied Mathematics
CHEATHAM, T. E., Computer Science
EHRENREICH, H., Applied Physics
EMMONS, H. W., Mechanical Engineering
FERRIS, B. G., Environmental Health and Safety
FIERING, M. B., Engineering and Applied Mathematics
FIRST, M. W., Environmental Health Engineering
FOFONOFF, N. P., Physical Oceanography
GAGLIARDI, U. O., Computer Engineering
GOODY, R. M., Planetary Physics
HARRINGTON, J. J., Environmental Engineering
HO, Y. C., Engineering and Applied Mathematics
HUTCHINSON, J. W., Applied Mechanics
JONES, R. V., Applied Physics
KRONAUER, R. E., Mechanical Engineering
KROOK, M., Astrophysics
KUNO, S., Linguistics
LINDZEN, R. S., Dynamic Meteorology
MARTIN, P. C., Physics
McELROY, M. B., Atmospheric Science
McMAHON, T. A., Applied Mechanics
MEYER, R. F., Business Administration
MITCHELL, R., Applied Biology
MORRIS, J. C., Sanitary Chemistry
OETTINGER, A. G., Applied Mathematics
PAUL, W., Applied Physics
PERSHAN, P. S., Applied Physics
ROBINSON, A. R., Geophysical Fluid Dynamics
ROGERS, P. P., Environmental Engineering
SANDERS, J. L., Structural Mechanics
THOMAS, H. A., Civil and Sanitary Engineering
TINKHAM, M., Applied Physics
TURNBULL, D., Applied Physics
WU, T. T., Applied Physics

*Graduate School of Design:*
BAKANOWSKY, L., Architecture
BERRY, B., City/Regional Planning
COBB, H., Architecture and Urban Design
DOEBELE, W., Advanced Environmental Studies
HARRIS, C., Landscape Architecture
KALLMANN, G. M., Architecture
KILBRIDGE, M. D., Urban Systems
KOETTER, A. H., Architecture
McKINNELL, N. M., Architecture
NEWMAN, R. B., Architectural Technology
SAFDIE, M., Architecture and Urban Design
SANTOS, A. N., Architecture
SMITH, F. E., Advanced Environmental Studies
STEINITZ, C., Landscape Arichtecture
SZABO, A., Architecture, Visual and Environmental Studies
VIGIER, F. C., City and Regional Planning

*Law School:*
ANDREWS, W. D.
AREEDA, P. E.
BATOR, P. M.
BELL, D. A.
BELLOW, G.
BERMAN, H. J.
BREYER, S. G.
BRUDNEY, V.
BYSE, C.
CHAYES, A. J.
CLARK, R. C.
COHEN, J. A.
COHEN, M. L.
COUNTRYMAN, V.
COX, A.
DERSHOWITZ, A. M.
DONAHUE, C.
FERGUSON, C. C.
FISHER, R. D.
FRIED, C.
HAAR, C. M.
HERWITZ, D. R.
HORWITZ, M. J.
KAUFMAN, A. L.
KENNEDY, D. M.
LIEBMAN, L. M.
LOSS, L.
MANSFIELD, J. H.
MICHELMAN, F. I.
MILLER, A. R.
NESSON, C. R.
OHLIN, L. E.
OLDMAN, O.
OWENS, E. A.
PARKER, R. D.
SANDER, F. E. A.
SARGENTICH, L. D.
SCOTT, H. S.
SHAPIRO, D. L.
SOHN, L. R.
STEINER, H. J.
STEWART, R. B.
STONE, A. A.
SURREY, S. S.
TAYLOR VON MEHREN, A.
TRAUTMAN, D. T.
TRIBE, L. H.
TURNER, D. F.
UNGER, R. M.
VAGTS, D. F.
VORENBERG, J.
WARREN, A. C.
WEINREB, L. L.
WESTFALL, D.
WOLFMAN, B.

*Medical School:*
ABELMAN, W., Medicine
ABRAMS, H. L., Radiology
ALBERT, D., Ophthalmology
ALLEN, H. F., Ophthalmology
ALPER, C., Paediatrics
ALPER, M. H., Anaesthesia
AMES, A., Physiology
AMOS, H., Microbiology
ANDERSON, E., Anatomy
ARKY, R., Medicine
AUSTEN, K. F., Medicine

Austen, W. G., Surgery
Avery, M., Paediatrics
Baden, H., Dermatology
Baldessarini, R. J., Psychiatry
Barger, A. C., Physiology
Barlow, C. F., Neurology
Beckwith, J. R., Microbiology
Benacerraf, B., Comparative Pathology
Berenberg, W., Paediatrics
Bernhard, W., Surgery
Bethune, J., Radiology
Biggers, J., Physiology
Braunwald, E., Medicine
Brenner, B., Medicine
Brooks, J., Surgery
Brown, T., Orthopaedic Surgery
Buckley, M. J., Surgery
Bunn, H. F., Medicine
Burke, J., Surgery
Cahill, G., Medicine
Castaneda, A., Surgery
Clowes, G. H. A., Surgery
Cohen, R. B., Pathology
Cone, T., Paediatrics
Cotran, R., Pathology
David, J. R., Medicine
Davis, B. D., Bacteriology
Densen, P. M., Community Health
Desanctis, R. W., Medicine
Dohlman, C., Ophthalmology
Driscoll, S., Pathology
Eisenberg, L., Psychiatry
Epp, E. R., Radiation Therapy
Epstein, F., Medicine
Fisher, C., Neurology
Fitzpatrick, T. B., Dermatology
Folkman, M. J., Paediatric Surgery
Fraenkel, D. G., Microbiology
Frank, H., Surgery
Frazier, H. S., Medicine
Frazier, S. H., Psychiatry
Frei, E., Medicine
Friedman, E., Obstetrics and Gynaecology
Furshpan, E. J., Neurobiology
Gerald, P. S., Paediatrics
Gissen, A., Anaesthesia
Gittes, R., Surgery
Glimcher, M., Orthopaedic Surgery
Goldberg, A. L., Psyhiology
Goldberg, I. H., Medicine
Goldman, H., Pathology
Goldman, P., Clinical Pharmacology
Grant, W. M., Ophthalmology
Grillo, H. C., Surgery
Haber, E., Medicine
Hackett, T., Psychiatry
Hall, J. E., Orthopaedic Surgery
Harris, W., Orthopedic Surgery
Havens, L., Psychiatry
Hay, L. D., Embryology
Hedley-Whyte, J., Anaesthesiology
Hellman, S., Radiation Therapy
Hendren, W., Surgery
Henneman, E., Physiology
Hiatt, H. H., Medicine
Hipona, F., Radiology
Hollenberg, N., Radiology
Hubel, D. H., Neurophysiology
Ingbar, S. H., Medicine
Isselbacher, K. J., Medicine
Jones, T. C., Comparative Pathology
Karnovsky, M. J., Pathology
Kelleher, R., Psychiatry
Kirkpatrick, J., Radiology
Kitz, R., Anaesthesia
Knapp, R., Obstetrics and Gynaecology
Knox, W. E., Biological Chemistry
Kravitz, E., Neurobiology
Kuffler, S. W., Neurobiology
Latt, S. A., Paediatrics
Leaf, A., Clinical Medicine
Linenthal, A., Medicine
Lombroso, C., Neurology

London, I., Medicine
Mack, J. E., Psychiatry
Malt, R., Surgery
Mankin, H., Orthopaedic Surgery
Mannick, J., Surgery
McArthur, J., Obstetrics and Gynaecology
McCluskey, R., Pathology
McDermott, W. V., Surgery
Mendelson, J. H., Psychiatry
Mishler, E., Psychiatry
Montgomery, W. W., Otolaryngology
Moore, F. D., Surgery
Morse, W., Psychiatry
Murray, J. E., Surgery
Nardi, G. L., Surgery
Nathan, D. G., Paediatrics
Nelson, M., Gynaecology
Nemiah, J. C., Psychiatry
Nichols, G., Medicine
Palay, S. L., Neuroanatomy
Pardee, A. B., Pharmacology
Paulin, S. J. K., Radiology
Pontoppidan, H., Anaesthesia
Pope, A., Neuropathology
Potter, D. D., Neurobiology
Potts, J. T., Medicine
Raviola, E., Human Anatomy
Reid, L., Pathology
Richardson, C. C., Biological Chemistry
Richardson, E. P., Neuropathology
Rosen, F. S., Paediatrics
Rossier, A., Orthopaedic Surgery
Rumbaugh, C. L., Radiology
Russell, P. S., Surgery
Ryan, K. J., Obstetrics and Gynaecology
Sager, R., Microbiology
Salhanick, H. A., Obstetrics and Gynaecology
Sasahara, A., Medicine
Scannell, J. G., Surgery
Schildkraut, J. J., Psychiatry
Schuknecht, H. F., Otology and Laryngology
Scully, R. E., Pathology
Shore, M., Psychiatry
Sidman, R. L., Neuropathology
Sifneos, P. E., Psychiatry
Silen, W., Surgery
Simon, M., Radiology
Sledge, C. B., Orthopaedic Surgery
Smith, T. W., Medicine
Suit, H. D., Radiation Therapy
Swartz, M. N., Medicine
Taveras, J. M., Radiology
Trier, J., Medicine
Tullis, J. L., Medicine
Tyler, H. R., Neurology
Unanue, E. R., Immunopathology
Vallee, B. L., Biological Chemistry
Vandam, L. D., Anaesthesia
Vanpraagh, D. R. M., Pathology
Vawter, G. F., Pathology
Vickery, A. L., Pathology
Villee, C. A., Biological Chemistry
Wacker, W. E. C., Hygiene
Wang, C. C., Radiation Therapy
Webster, E., Radiology Physics
Weinberg, A., Medicine
Welch, W., Surgery
Wiesel, T. N., Physiology
Wilson, R., Surgery
Wilson, J. D. H., Physiology
Wolff, P. H., Psychiatry
Yunis, E., Pathology

*Graduate School of Public Health:*
Alonso, W., Population Sciences
Bloch, K. E., Nutrition
Chernin, E., Tropical Public Health
Drolette, M. E., Biostatistics
Dyck, A. J., Population Ethics
Essex, M. E., Microbiology
Geyer, R. P., Nutrition

Harrington, J. J., Environmental Engineering
Hornig, D. F., Chemistry
Hutchison, G. B., Epidemiology
Levins, R., Population Sciences
Little, J., Physiology
Lown, B., Cardiology in Nutrition
MacMahon, B., Epidemiology
Miettinen, O. S., Epidemiology and Biostatistics
Moeller, D., Engineering in Environmental Health
Morris, J. C., Sanitary Chemistry
Nichols, R. L., Microbiology
Peters, J. M., Physiology
Reed, R. B., Biostatistics
Roberts, M., Politics, Economics and Health Policy
Thomas, H. A., Civil and Sanitary Engineering
Weller, T. H., Tropical Public Health
Whittenberger, J. L., Public Health and Physiology
Yerby, A. S., Health Services Administration

*Graduate School of Education:*
Argyris, C., Education and Organizational Behaviour
Bolster, J. S.
Cazden, C. B.
Chall, J.
Cohen, D. K., Education and Social Policy
Glazer, N., Education and Social Structure
Graham, P. A., History of American Education
Kagan, J., Psychology
Kohlberg, L.
Lesser, G. S., Education and Developmental Psychology
Light, R. J., Education
Oliver, D. W.
Pierce. C. M., Education and Psychiatry
Scheffler, I., Education and Philosophy
Shlien, J. M., Education and Counselling Psychology
White, S. H., Educational Psychology
Willie, C. V., Education and Urban Studies

*Graduate School of Business Administration:*
Aguilar, F. J.
Andrews, K. R.
Anthony, R. N., Management Control
Athos, A. G., Organizational Behaviour
Baughman, J., Business History
Berg, N. A.
Bishop, J. E.
Bower, J. L.
Brown, M. P., Retailing
Bruns, W.
Butters, J. K.
Buzzell, R. D., Marketing
Chandler, A., Business History
Christensen, C. R.
Christenson, C. J.
Corey, E. R., Marketing
Crane, D., Business Administration
Crum, M. C., Investment Management
Dearden, J.
Donaldson, G., Corporate Finance
Dooley, A. R., Manufacturing
Dunlop, J. T., Political Economy
Fouraker, L. E.
Glauber, R. R.
Goldberg, R. A., Agriculture and Business
Greyser, S. A.
Hawkins, D. F.
Hayes, R. H.
Hayes, S., Investment Banking

## UNIVERSITIES AND COLLEGES—MASSACHUSETTS

HEALY, J. J., Industrial Relations
HESKETT, J. L., Business Logistics
LAW, W. A., Finance and Banking
LEVITT, T.
LINTNER, J. V., Economics and Business Administration
LODGE, G. C., Business Administration
LORSCH, J. W., Organizational Behaviour
MARKHAM, J. W.
MARSHALL, M. V.
MATTHEWS, J. B.
MCARTHUR, J., Financial Management
MCCRAW, T. K.
MCFARLAN, F., Business Administration
MCKENNEY, J. L.
MEYER, J. R., Transportation, Logistics and Distribution
MEYER, R. F.
MILLS, D. Q., Business Administration
PRATT, J. W.
RAYMOND, T. C.
REILING, H., Business Administration
ROSENBLOOM, R. S.
SALMON, W. J., Marketing
SALTER, M., Business Administration
SCHLAIFER, R. O.
SCHLEIFER, A. J.
SCOTT, B. R.
SKINNER, W.
STOBAUGH, R. B.
TAGIURI, R., Social Sciences
THURSTON, P. H.
TIMMER, C. P., Agriculture and Business
TURNER, A. N.
UYTERHOEVEN, H. E. R.
VANCIL, R. F.
VATTER, P. A.
WALTON, R. E.
WELLS, L., Business Administration
WHITE, W., Business Administration
WILLIAMS, C. M., Commercial Banking
WYCKOFF, D. D., Transportation
YOSHINO, M. Y.
ZALEZNIK, A., Social Psychology of Management

*J. F. Kennedy School of Government:*
ALLISON, G., Politics
BATOR, F. M., Political Economy
LYNN, L. E., Public Policy
MONTGOMERY, J. D., Public Administration
MOORE, M. H., Criminal Justice Policy and Management
NEUSTADT, R. E., Public Administration
RAIFFA, H., Managerial Economics
ZECKHAUSER, R. J., Political Economy

## HEBREW COLLEGE
43 HAWES STREET,
BROOKLINE,
MASSACHUSETTS 02146
Telephone: 232-8710.

Founded 1921.

*President:* E. GRAD.
*Associate Dean:* MICHAEL LIBENSON.
*Registrar:* JAY J. KROOPNICK.
*Librarian:* M. TUCHMAN.

The library contains 75,000 vols.
Number of teachers: 39.
Number of students: 640.
Publication: *Hebrew College Bulletin*† (quarterly).

## MASSACHUSETTS COLLEGE OF ART
364 BROOKLINE AVENUE,
BOSTON, MASSACHUSETTS 02215
Telephone: (617) 731-2340.

Founded 1873.

*President:* J. NOLAN.
*Vice-President of Academic Affairs:* DON LETTIS.
*Vice-President of Administration:* M. GODINE.
*Vice-President of Students:* D. MCGAVERN.
*Librarian:* B. HOPKINS.

The library contains 65,000 vols.
Number of teachers: 66.
Number of students: 1,041.

## MASSACHUSETTS INSTITUTE OF TECHNOLOGY
CAMBRIDGE,
MASSACHUSETTS 02139
Telephone: 253-1000.

Founded 1861.

*President:* PAUL E. GRAY, SC.D.
*Provost:* FRANCIS E. LOW, PH.D.
*Associate Provosts:* F. E. PERKINS, SC.D., K. A. SMITH, SC.D.
*Treasurer:* G. P. STREHLE, M.S.
*Vice-President, Research:* (vacant).
*Vice-President, Operations:* W. R. DICKSON, S.B.
*Vice-President, Financial Operations:* S. H. COWEN, S.B., M.B.A.
*Vice-President, Resource Development:* S. A. GOLDBLITH, PH.D.
*Vice-President and Dean of the Graduate School:* K. R. WADLEIGH, SC.D.
*Vice-President:* C. B. SIMONIDES, A.B., M.B.A.
*Chairman of the Corporation:* H. W. JOHNSON, LL.D., L.H.D., SC.D.
*Secretary of the Corporation:* V. A. FULMER, S.M., LL.D.
*Secretary of the Institute:* V. A. FULMER, S.M., LL.D.
*Comptroller:* P. J. KEOHAN, B.S., M.B.A.
*Director of Libraries:* J. K. LUCKER, M.L.S.
*Registrar:* W. D. WELLS, S.B.

Teaching staff: 1,730, including 1,015 professors.
Number of students: 9,365.
Publications: *M.I.T. Bulletin* (quarterly), *Technology Review* (8 a year).

### DEANS:
*Engineering:* G. L. WILSON, SC.D.
*Science:* R. A. ALBERTY, PH.D., SC.D.
*Architecture and Planning:* J. P. DE MONCHAUX, M.ARCH.
*Alfred P. Sloan School of Management:* ABRAHAM J. SIEGEL, PH.D.
*Humanities and Social Science:* H. J. HANHAM, PH.D.
*Graduate School:* K. R. WADLEIGH, SC.D.

### HEADS OF DEPARTMENTS:
*Aeronautics and Astronautics:* J. W. MAR, SC.D.
*Architecture:* J. BEINART, M.C.P., M.ARCH.
*Athletics:* R. N. FLIPPIN, Jr., M.B.A.
*Biology:* G. M. BROWN, PH.D.
*Chemical Engineering:* J. WEI, SC.D.
*Chemistry:* J. L. KINSEY, PH.D.
*Civil Engineering:* J. M. SUSSMAN, PH.D.
*Earth and Planetary Sciences:* W. F. BRACE, PH.D.
*Economics:* E. C. BROWN, PH.D.
*Electrical Engineering and Computer Science:* J. MOSES, PH.D.
*Humanities:* P. H. SMITH, PH.D.
*Linguistics and Philosophy:* S. J. KEYSER, PH.D.
*Mathematics:* D. J. KLEITMAN, PH.D.
*Mechanical Engineering:* H. H. RICHARDSON, SC.D.
*Materials Science and Engineering:* W. S. OWEN, PH.D., D.ENG.
*Meteorology and Physical Oceanography:* P. H. STONE, PH.D.
*Nuclear Engineering:* N. E. TODREAS, PH.D.
*Nutrition and Food Science:* G. N. WOGAN, PH.D.
*Ocean Engineering:* C. CHRYSSOSTOMIDIS, PH.D. (acting).
*Physics:* H. FESHBACH, PH.D.
*Political Science:* A. A. ALTSHULER, PH.D.
*Psychology:* R. HELD, PH.D.
*Urban Studies and Planning:* L. E. SUSSKIND, PH.D.

### HEADS OF OTHER ACADEMIC ACTIVITIES:
*Arteriosclerosis Center:* R. S. LEES, M.D.
*Artificial Intelligence Laboratory:* P. H. WINSTON, PH.D.
*Bates Linear Accelerator:* P. T. DEMOS, PH.D.
*Cell Culture Center:* P. W. ROBBINS, PH.D.
*Center for Advanced Engineering Study:* M. TRIBUS, PH.D.
*Center for Advanced Visual Studies:* O. PIENE, M.A.
*Center for Cancer Research:* S. E. LURIA, M.D., D.SC.
*Center for Cognitive Science:* S. J. KEYSER, PH.D.
*Center for Computational Research in Economics and Management Science:* E. KUH, PH.D.
*Center for International Studies:* E. B. SKOLNIKOFF, PH.D.
*Center for Materials Research in Archaeology and Ethnology:* H. N. LECHTMAN, M.A.
*Center for Materials Science and Engineering:* M. S. DRESSLEHAUS, PH.D.
*Center for Policy Alternatives:* J. H. HOLLOMON, SC.D.
*Center for Space Research:* H. S. BRIDGE, PH.D.
*Center for Transportation Studies:* D. ROOS, PH.D.
*Clinical Research Center:* N. S. SCRIMSHAW, PH.D.

*Division for Study and Research in Education:* B. R. SNYDER, M.D.
*Electric Power Systems Engineering Laboratory:* G. L. WILSON, SC.D.
*Energy Laboratory:* D. C. WHITE, PH.D.
*Francis Bitter National Magnet Laboratory:* P. A. WOLFF, PH.D.
*Harvard—M.I.T. Division of Health Sciences and Technology:* I. M. LONDON, M.D.
*Joint Center for Urban Studies:* D. T. KRESGE, PH.D.
*Music:* J. HARBISON, M.F.A.
*Laboratory of Architecture and Planning:* M. L. JOROFF, M.C.P.
*Laboratory for Computer Science:* M. L. DERTOUZOS, PH.D.
*Laboratory for Information and Decision Systems:* S. K. MITTER, PH.D.
*Laboratory for Manufacturing and Productivity:* N. P. SUH, PH.D.
*Laboratory for Nuclear Science:* J. I. FRIEDMAN, PH.D.
*Law-related Studies:* J. D. NYHART, J.D.
*Lincoln Laboratory:* W. E. MORROW, Jr., M.S.
*Lowell Institute School:* B. D. WEDLOCK, SC.D.
*Materials Processing Center:* M. C. FLEMINGS, SC.D.
*Neurosciences Research Program:* F. G. WORDEN, M.D.
*Nuclear Reactor Laboratory:* O. K. HARLING, PH.D.
*Operations Research Center:* R. C. LARSON, PH.D. and J. F. SHAPIRO, PH.D.
*Plasma Fusion Center:* R. C. DAVIDSON, PH.D.
*Program in Science, Technology and Society:* C. KAYSEN, PH.D.
*Research Laboratory of Electronics:* J. ALLEN, SC.D.
*Sea Grant Program:* D. A. HORN, NAV.E.
*Spectroscopy Laboratory:* M. S. FELD, PH.D.
*Summer Session:* J. M. AUSTIN, SC.D.
*Technology and Policy Program:* R. L. DENEUFVILLE, PH.D.
*Undergraduate Research Opportunities Program:* M. L. A. MACVICAR, SC.D.
*Wallace Astrophysical Observatory:* J. L. ELLIOT, PH.D.
*Wallace Geophysical Observatory:* M. NAFI TOKSÖZ, PH.D.
*Whitaker College of Health Sciences, Technology and Management:* I. M. LONDON, M.D.

### PROFESSORS:

*Department of Architecture:*
ANDERSEN, W. V., History of Art
ANDERSON, S., History of Architecture
BEINART, J., Architecture
CAMINOS, H., Architecture
DE MONCHAUX, J.P., Architecture and Planning
GROISSER, L. B., Structures
HABRAKEN, N. J., Architecture
HALASZ, I., Architecture
LEACOCK, R., Cinema
MYER, J. R., Architecture
NEGROPONTE, N. P., Computer Graphics
PIENE, O., Visual Design
PORTER, W. L., Architecture and Urban Planning
PREUSSER, R. O., Visual Design
SMITH, M. K., Architecture
ZALEWSKI, W. P., Structures

*Department of Urban Studies and Planning:*
FLEISHER, A., Urban and Regional Studies
FOGELSON, R. M., History and Urban Studies
FRIEDEN, B. J., City Planning
GAKENHEIMER, R. A., Urban Studies and Planning and Civil Engineering
JONES, F. S., Urban Affairs
KEYES, L. C., City and Regional Planning
LARSON, R. C., Electrical Engineering and Urban Studies
MARX, G. T., Sociology
PEATTIE, L. R., Urban Anthropology
PORTER, W. L., Architecture and Urban Planning
REIN, M., Sociology
RODWIN, L., Urban and Regional Studies
SCHON, D. A., Urban Studies and Education
SUSSKIND, L. E., Urban Studies and Planning

*Department of Aeronautics and Astronautics:*
BARON, J. R.
COVERT, E. E.
DUGUNDJI, J.
FINSTON, M.
HALFMAN, R. H.,
HAM, N. D.
HARRIS, W. L., Sr.
INGARD, K. U., Aeronautics and Astronautics and Physics
KERREBROCK, J. L.
LANDAHL, M. T.
LOUIS, J. F.
MAR, J. W., Aerospace Education
MARKEY, W. R.
MCCARTHY, J. F., Jr.
MCCUNE, J. E.
MILLER, R. H., Flight Transportation
MURMAN, E. M.
ODONI, A. R., Aeronautics and Astronautics and Civil Engineering
PIAN, T. H.-H.
SIMPSON, R. W.
TRILLING, L.
VANDER VELDE, W. E.
WACHMAN, H. Y.
WHITAKER, H. P.
WIDNALL, S. E.
WITMER, E. A.
YOUNG, L. R.

*Department of Chemical Engineering:*
BADDOUR, R. F.
BEÉR, J. M., Chemical and Fuel Engineering
COLTON, C. K.
EVANS, L. B.
HOWARD, J. B.
LONGWELL, J. P.
MERRILL, E. W.
REID, R. C.
SAROFIM, A. F.
SATTERFIELD, C. N.
SMITH, K. A.
WEI, J.
WILLIAMS, G. C.

*Department of Civil Engineering:*
BIGGS, J. M.
CONNOR, J. J., Jr.
CORNELL, C. A.
DE NEUFVILLE, R. L.
EAGLESON, P. S.
FRIEDLAENDER, A. F., Civil Engineering and Economics
HARLEMAN, D. R. F.
LADD, C. C.
LOGCHER, R. D.
MANHEIM, M. L.
MARKS, D. H.
MCGARRY, F. J., Civil and Polymer Engineering
MEI, C. C.
MOAVENZADEH, F.
MOREL, F. M. M.
PERKINS, F. E.
ROBERTS, P. O.
ROOS, D.
SUSSMAN, J. M.
VANMARCKE, E. H.
WHITMAN, R. R. VAN D.

*Department of Electrical Engineering and Computer Science:*
ADLER, D., Electrical Engineering
ADLER, R. B., Electrical Engineering
ALLEN, J., Electrical Engineering
ATHANS, M., Systems Science and Engineering
BERS, A., Electrical Engineering
BOSE, A. G., Electrical Engineering
BOWEN, H. K., Electrical Engineering and Ceramics
BRAIDA, L. B. D., Electrical Engineering
BRUCE, J. D., Electrical Engineering
CORBATÓ, F. J., Computer Science and Engineering
DAVENPORT, W. B., Jr., Communications Science and Engineering
DENNIS, J. B., Computer Science and Engineering
DERTOUZOS, M. L., Computer Science and Electrical Engineering
DINNEEN, G. P., Electrical Engineering
DRAKE, A. W., Systems Science and Engineering
DRESSELHAUS, M. S., Electrical Engineering
ELIAS, P., Electrical Engineering
EPSTEIN, D. J., Electrical Engineering
EZEKIEL, S., Electrical Engineering and Aeronautics and Astronautics
FANO, R. M., Engineering
FREDKIN, E., Computer Science and Engineering
FRISHKOPF, L. S., Electrical and Bioengineering
GALLAGER, R. G., Electrical Engineering
GATOS, H. C., Molecular Engineering and Electronic Materials
GOULD, L. A., Electrical Engineering
HAUS, H. A., Electrical Engineering
HENNIE, F. C., III, Computer Science and Engineering
IPPEN, E. P., Electrical Engineering
KENNEDY, R. S., Electrical Engineering
KHYL, R. L., Electrical Engineering
KONG, J. A., Electrical Engineering
LEE, F. F., Electrical Engineering and Computer Science
LEE, T. H., Electrical Engineering
LETTVIN, J. Y., Electrical and Bioengineering and Communications Physiology
LICKLIDER, J. C. R., Electrical Engineering
LISKOV, B. H., Computer Science and Engineering
MCWHORTER, A. L., Electrical Engineering
MELCHER, J. R., Electrical Engineering and Physics
MEYER, A. R., Computer Science and Engineering
MINSKY, M. L., Science
MITTER, S. K., Electrical Engineering
MORGENTHALER, F. R., Electrical Engineering
MORROW, W. E., Jr., Electrical Engineering
MOSES, J., Computer Science and Engineering

OPPENHEIM, A. V., Electrical Engineering
PARKER, R. R., Electrical Engineering
PEAKE, W. T., Electrical and Bioengineering
PENFIELD, P. L., Jr., Electrical Engineering
PRATT, G. W., Jr., Electrical Engineering
ROBERGE, J. K., Electrical Engineering
ROSENBLITH, W. A., Communications Biophysics
RUINA, J. P., Electrical Engineering
SALTZER, J. H., Computer Science and Engineering
SCHREIBER, W. F., Electrical Engineering
SCHWEPPE, F. C., Electrical Engineering
SEARLE, C. L., Electrical Engineering
SENTURIA, S. D., Electrical Engineering
SIEBERT, W. M., Electrical Engineering
SMITH, A. C., Electrical Engineering
SMITH, H. I., Electrical Engineering
SMULLIN, L. D., Electrical Engineering
STAELIN, D. H., Electrical Engineering
STEVENS, K. N., Electrical Engineering
THORNTON, R. D., Electrical Engineering
WEISS, T. F., Electrical and Bioengineering
WEIZENBAUM, J., Computer Science and Engineering
WHITE, D. C., Engineering
WILSON, G. L., Electrical and Mechanical Engineering
ZIMMERMAN, H. J., Electrical Engineering

*Department of Materials Science and Engineering:*
AVERBACH, B. L., Materials Science
BALLUFFI, Physical Metallurgy
BOWEN, H. K., Ceramic Engineering and Electrical Engineering
COBLE, R. L., Ceramics
ELLIOTT, J. F., Metallurgy
FLEMINGS, M. C., Engineering
GATOS, H. C., Electronic Materials and Molecular Engineering
GRANT, N. J., Metallurgy
JOHNSON, K. H., Materials Science
KAPLOW, R., Materials Science and Education
KING, T. B., Metallurgy
KINGERY, W. D., Ceramics
LATANISION, R. M., Materials Science and Engineering
MASUBUCHI, K., Materials Science and Ocean Engineering
McGARRY, F. J., Polymer Engineering and Civil Engineering
OGILVIE, R. E., Metallurgy
OWEN, W. S., Materials Science and Engineering
PELLOUX, R. M. N., Materials Engineering
ROSE, R. M., Materials Science and Engineering
RUSSELL, K. C., Metallurgy and Nuclear Engineering
SZEKELY, J., Materials Engineering
UHLMANN, D. R., Glass and Polymer Science
VANDER SANDE, J. B., Materials Science
WITT, A. F., Materials Science
WUENSCH, B. J., Ceramics

*Department of Mechanical Engineering:*
ARGON, A. S.
BACKER, S.
COOK, N. H.
CRANDALL, S. H., Engineering
CRAVALHO, E. G., Mechanical Engineering in Medicine
DEWEY, C. F., Jr.

FAY, J. A.
GRIFFITH, P.
HEYWOOD, J. B.
KECK, J. C., Engineering
LEEHEY, P., Naval Architecture and Applied Mechanics
LELE, P. P., Experimental Medicine
LYON, R. H.
MANN, R. W., Biomedical Engineering
McCLINTOCK, F. A.
MIKIC, B. B.
PAYNTER, H. M.
PROBSTEIN, R. F.
RABINOWICZ, E.
RICHARDSON, H. H.
ROHSENOW, W. M.
SHAPIRO, A. H.
SHERIDAN, T. B., Engineering and Applied Psychology
SMITH, J. L., Jr.
SONIN, A. A.
SUH, N. P.
TOONG, T.-Y.
WADLEIGH, K. R.
WILLIAMS, J. H., Jr.
WILSON, D. G.
WORMLEY, D. N.
YANNAS, I. V., Polymer Science and Engineering

*Department of Nuclear Engineering:*
BROWNELL, G. L.
CHEN, S.-H.
DRISCOLL, M. J.
FREIDBERG, J. P.
GYFTOPOULOS, E. P.
HANSEN, K. F.
HARLING, O. K.
HENRY, A. F.
LANNING, D. D.
LIDSKY, L. M.
MEYER, J. E.
RASMUSSEN, N. C.
ROSE, D. J.
TODREAS, N. E.
YIP, S.

*Department of Ocean Engineering:*
ABKOWITZ, M. A., Ocean Engineering
BAGGEROER, A. B., Ocean and Electrical Engineering
CARMICHAEL, A. D., Power Engineering
CHRYSSOSTOMIDIS, C., Naval Architecture
FRANKEL, E. G., Marine Systems
JONES, N., Ocean Engineering
KERWIN, J. E., Naval Architecture
MILGRAM, J. H., Naval Architecture
NEWMAN, J. N., Naval Architecture
NYHART, J. D., Ocean Engineering and Management

*Program in Science, Technology and Society:*
BLACKMER, D. L. M., Political Science
GRAHAM, S. L. R., History of Science
KAYSEN, C., Political Economy
KENISTON, K., Human Development
KUHN, T. S., Philosophy and History of Science
MARX, L., American Cultural History
SMITH, M. R., History of Technology
WEINER, C., History of Science and Technology

*Department of Economics:*
ADELMAN, M. A.
ALEXANDER, S. S., Economics and Management
BISHOP, R. L.
BROWN, E. C.
DIAMOND, P. A.
DOMAR, E. D.
DORNBUSCH, R.
ECKAUS, R. S.

FISCHER, S.
FISHER, F. M.
HAUSMAN, J. A.
JOSKOW, P. L.
KINDLEBERGER, C. P.
KUH, E., Economics and Finance
MASKIN, E. S.
McFADDEN, D. L.
MODIGLIANI, F., Economics and Finance
PIORE, M. J.
ROTHENBERG, J.
SAMUELSON, P. A.
SOLOW, R. M.
TAYLOR, L. J., Nutritional Economics
TEMIN, P.
THUROW, L. C., Economics and Management
WEITZMAN, M. L.

*Department of Humanities:*
DOUGLAS, R. M., History
DYCK, M., German and Literature
EPSTEIN, D. M., Music
FOGELSON, R. M., History and Urban Studies
GRAHAM LOREN, History of Science
GURNEY, A. R., Jr., Literature
HANHAM, H. J., History and Political Science
HARBISON, J., Music
HARRIS, J. W., Spanish and Linguistics
JONES, R. E., French and Humanities
KAMPF, L., Literature
KIBEL, A. C., Literature
LECHTMAN, H. N., Archaeology and Ancient Technology
MACMASTER, R. E., History and Literature
MAHONEY, T. H. D., History
MAIER, P. R., History
MAZLISH, B., History
O'NEIL, W., Literature
POMORSKA, K., Russian and Literature
RATHBONE, R. R., Technical Communication
REICHE, H. A. T. O., Classics and Philosophy
ROTBERG, R. I., History and Political Science
SMITH, M. R., History of Technology
SMITH, P. H., History and Political Science
SPACKS, B. B., Literature
WOLFF, C. G., Literature

*Department of Linguistics and Philosophy:*
BOOLOS, G. S., Philosophy
BRESNAN, J. W., Linguisitics
BROMBERGER, S., Philosophy
CARTWRIGHT, R. L., Philosophy
CHOMSKY, N. A., Linguistics
FODOR, J. A., Philosophy and Psycholinguistics
HALE, K. L., Linguistics
HALLE, M., Linguisitics
KEYSER, S. J., Linguistics
KIPARSKY, R. P. V., Linguistics
O'NEIL, W., Linguistics
ROSS, J. R., Linguistics
SINGER, I., Philosophy
THOMSON, J. F., Philosophy
THOMSON, J. J., Philosophy

*Department of Political Science:*
ALKER, H. R.
ALTSHULER, A. A., Political Science and Urban Studies and Planning
BERGER, S.
BLOOMFIELD, L. P.
BURNHAM, W. D.
FIELD, N. C.
GRIFFITH, W. E.
JOHNSON, W. R.
KAUFMANN, W. W.
LIPSKY, M.

MORTON, D. L.
POOL, I. DE S.
PYE, L. W.
RATHJENS, G. W.
SAPOLSKY, H. M., Public Policy and Organization
SKOLNIKOFF, E. B.
WEINER, M.

*Department of Psychology:*
BIZZI, E., Brain Sciences and Human Behaviour
CHOROVER, S. L., Psychology
GARRETT, M. F., Psychology
GESCHWIND, M. D., Psychology
GRAYBIEL, A. M., Neuroanatomy
HEIN, A., Psychology
HELD, R. M., Experimental Psychology
NAUTA, W. J. H., Neuroanatomy
RICHARDS, W. A., Psychophysics
SCHILLER, P. H., Psychology
SCHNEIDER, G. E., Psychology and Brain Science

*Sloan School of Management:*
ALEXANDER, S. S., Management and Economics
ALLEN, T. J., Jr., Organizational Psychology and Management
BAILYN, L. L., Organizational Psychology and Management
BERNDT, E. R., Applied Economics
BLACK, F., Finance
BOWMAN, E. H., Management
FORRESTER, J. W., Management
HAX, A. C., Management Science
HOLLAND, D. M., Finance
JACOBY, H. D., Management
KAUFMAN, G. M., Operations Research and Management
KOCHAN, T. A., Industrial Relations
LITTLE, J. D. C., Operations Research and Management
MAGNANTI, T. L., Operations Research and Management
McKERSIE, R. B., Industrial Relations
MERTON, R. C., Finance
MOORE, L. B., Management
MORTON, M. S. S., Management
MYERS, S. C., Finance
PINDYCK, R. S., Applied Economics
POUNDS, W. F., Management
ROBERTS, E. B., Management of Technology
ROBINSON, R. D., Management
SCHEIN, E. H., Management
SCHMALENSEE, R. L., Applied Economics
SHAPIRO, E., Management
SHAPIRO, J. F., Operations Research and Management
SIEGEL, A. J., Industrial Relations
SILK, A. J., Management Science
THUROW, L. C., Management and Economics
URBAN, G. L., Management Science
VAN MAANEN, J. E., Organizational Psychology and Management
WALLACE, P. A., Management
WELSCH, R. E., Management Science and Statistics
ZANNETOS, Z. S., Management

*Department of Biology:*
BALTIMORE, D., Microbiology
BEEL, E., Biology
BOTSTEIN, D., Genetics
BROWN, G. M., Biochemistry
BUCHANAN, J. M., Biochemistry
EISEN, H. N., Immunology
FOX, M. S., Genetics
GEFTER, M. L., Biochemistry
HOLT, C. E., III, Biology
INGRAM, V. M., Biochemistry
KHORANA, H. G., Biology and Chemistry
KING, J. A., Biology
LETTVIN, J. Y., Communications Psychology
LODISH, H. F., Biology
LONDON, I. M., Biology
MAGASANIK, B., Microbiology
PARDUE, M. L., Biology
PENMAN, S., Cell Biology
RAJBHANDARY, U. L., Biochemistry
RICH, A., Biophysics
ROBBINS, P. W., Biochemistry
ROSENBERG, R. D., Medicine and Biology
SCHIMMEL, P. R., Biochemistry and Biophysics
SHARP, P. A., Biology
SIGNER, E. R., Biology
STEINER, L. A., Immunology
TONEGAWA, S., Immunology and Cell Biology
TORRIANI, A., Biology
WALSH, C., Chemistry and Biology
WAUGH, D. F., Biophysics

*Department of Chemistry:*
ALBERTY, R. A.
BERCHTOLD, G. A.
BIEMANN, K.
BÜCHI, G. H.
DAVISON, A.
DEUTCH, J. M.
GARLAND, C. W.
GREENE, F. D., II
KEMP, D. S.
KINSEY, J. L.
MASAMUNE, S.
OPPENHEIM, I.
ORME-JOHNSON, W. H.
SCHROCK, R. R.
SEYFERTH, D.
SHARPLESS, K. B.
SILBEY, R. J.
SOLOMON, E. I.
STEINFELD, J. I.
SWAIN, C. G.
WAUGH, J. S.
WHITESIDES, G. M.
WRIGHTON, M. S.

*Department of Earth and Planetary Sciences:*
AKI, K., Geophysics
BRACE, W. F., Geology
BURCHFIEL, B. C., Geology
BURNS, R. G., Geochemistry
EDMOND, J. M., Oceanography
FREY, F. A., Geochemistry
HART, S. R., Geology and Geochemistry
LEWIS, J. S., Geochemistry
MADDEN, T. R., Geophysics
PETTENGILL, G. H., Planetary Physics
SCLATER, J. G., Marine Geophysics
SHAPIRO, I. I., Geophysics and Physics
SIMMONS, M. G., Geophysics
TOKSÖZ, M. N., Geophysics
WUNSCH, C. I., Physical Oceanography

*Department of Mathematics:*
AMBROSE, W., Mathematics
ANKENY, N. C., Mathematics
ARTIN, M., Mathematics
BENNEY, D. J., Applied Mathematics
CHENG, H., Applied Mathematics
CHERNOFF, H., Applied Mathematics
DUDLEY, R. M., Mathematics
FREEDMAN, D. Z., Applied Mathematics
GREENSPAN, H. P., Applied Mathematics
GUILLEMIN, V. W., Mathematics
HELGASON, S., Mathematics
HILDEBRAND, F. B., Mathematics
HOFFMAN, K. M., Mathematics
HOWARD, L. N., Mathematics
KAČ, V., Mathematics
KAN, D. M., Mathematics
KLEIMAN, S., Mathematics
KLEITMAN, D. J., Applied Mathematics
KOSTANT, B., Mathematics
LIN, C.-C., Applied Mathematics
LUSZTIG, G., Mathematics
MALKUS, W. VAN R., Applied Mathematics
MATTUCK, A. P., Mathematics
MELROSE, R. B., Mathematics
MUNKRES, J. R., Mathematics
ORSZAG, S. A., Applied Mathematics
PAPERT, S. A., Mathematics
PETERSON, F. P., Mathematics
QUILLEN, D. G., Mathematics
RAY, D. B., Mathematics
ROGERS, H., Jr., Mathematics
ROTA, G.-C., Applied Mathematics and Philosophy
SACKS, G. E., Mathematical Logic
SCHAFER, R. D., Mathematics
SEGAL, I. E., Mathematics
SHANNON, C. E., Science
STANLEY, R. P., Applied Mathematics
STARK, H. M., Mathematics
STRANG, W. G., Mathematics
TOOMRE, A., Applied Mathematics
VERGNE, M. F., Mathematics
WHITEHEAD, G. W., Mathematics

*Department of Meteorology and Physical Oceanography:*
EVANS, J. V.
LORENZ, E. N.
MOLLO-CHRISTENSEN, E. L., Oceanography
NEWELL, R. E.
SANDERS, F.
STONE, P. H.

*Department of Nutrition and Food Science:*
DEMAIN, A. L., Industrial Microbiology
GOLDBLITH, S. A., Food Science
KAREL, M., Food Engineering
LEES, R. S., Cardiovascular Disease
MILLER, S. A., Nutritional Biochemistry
MUNRO, H. N., Physiological Chemistry
NEWBERNE, P. M., Nutritional Pathology
SCRIMSHAW, N. S., Nutrition and Food Science
SINSKEY, A. J., Applied Microbiology
TANNENBAUM, S. R., Food Chemistry
TAYLOR, L. J., Nutritional Economics
WANG, D. I. C., Biochemical Engineering
WOGAN, G. N., Toxicology
WOLF, G., Physiological Chemistry
WURTMAN, R. J., Neuroendocrine Regulation
YOUNG, V. R., Nutritional Biochemistry

*Department of Physics:*
BARANGER, M.
BARBER, W. C.
BARRETT, A. H.
BECKER, U. J.
BEKEFI, G.
BENEDEK, G. B.
BERNSTEIN, A. M.
BERTOZZI, W.
BIRGENEAU, R. J.
BRADT, H. VAN D.
BRIDGE, H. S.
BURKE, B. F.
BUSZA, W.
CLARK, G. W.
COPPI, B.
COSMAN, E. R.
DAVIDSON, R. C.
DEMOS, P. T.
DEUTSCH, M.
DUPREE, T. H., Physics and Nuclear Engineering
ENGE, H. A.
FELD, B. T.
FELD, M. S.
FESHBACH, H.
FRENCH, A. P.

UNIVERSITIES AND COLLEGES—MASSACHUSETTS

FRIEDMAN, J. I.
FRISCH, D. H.
GOLDSTONE, J.
GREYTAK, T. J.
GRODZINS, L.
HUANG, K.
HULSIZER, R. I., Jr.
JACKIW, R. W.
JAVAN, A.
JOHNSON, K. A.
KENDALL, H. W.
KERMAN, A. K.
KING, J. G.
KISTIAKOWSKY, V.
KLEPPNER, D.
KOSTER, G. F.
LAX, B.
LEWIN, W. H. G.
LITSTER, J. D.
LOMON, E. L.
LOW, F. E.
MORRISON, P.
NEGELE, J. W.
OLBERT, S.
OSBORNE, L. S.
PLESS, I. A.
PORKOLAB, M.
PRITCHARD, D. E.
RAPPAPORT, S. A.
ROSENSON, L.
SHULL, C. G.
STRANDBERG, M. W. P.
TING, S. C. C.
VILLARS, F. M. H.
WEISS, R.
WOLFF, P. A.
YAMAMOTO, R. K.
YOUNG, J. E.

## MERRIMACK COLLEGE
TURNPIKE STREET,
NORTH ANDOVER,
MASSACHUSETTS 01845
Telephone: (617) 683-7111.

Founded 1947.

*President:* Rev. JOHN E. DEEGAN, O.S.A.
*Registrar:* Rev. PAUL C. THABAULT, O.S.A.
*Librarian:* STEPHEN A. BAHRE.
The library contains 93,000 vols.
Number of teachers: 117 full-time, 16 part-time.
Number of students: 3,759.

## MOUNT HOLYOKE COLLEGE
SOUTH HADLEY,
MASSACHUSETTS 01075
Founded 1837.

*President:* ELIZABETH TOPHAM KENNAN, PH.D.
*Treasurer and Business Manager:* MERRILL EWING, M.B.A.
*Dean of Faculty:* JOSEPH J.-M. ELLIS III, PH.D.
*Dean of Students:* RUTH E. WARFEL, M.S.
*Director of Admissions:* CLARA R. LUDWIG, A.B., B.S.
*Registrar:* FLORENCE S. KIMBALL, A.B.
*Librarian:* ANNE C. EDMONDS, M.S.L.S., A.M.
The library contains 449,000 volumes.

Number of teachers: 200.
Number of students: 1,850 women.
Publications: *Directory, Catalogue, Mount Holyoke Now Newsletter, Alumnae Quarterly.*

## NEW ENGLAND CONSERVATORY OF MUSIC
290 HUNTINGTON AVE.,
BOSTON, MASSACHUSETTS 02115
Telephone: (617) 262-1120.

Founded 1867.

*President:* J. STANLEY BALLINGER.
The Spaulding Library contains 47,000 vols. (books, scores, periodicals); the Firestone Library contains 14,000 records and tapes.
Number of teachers: c. 162.
Number of students: 751.
Publication: *Conservatory Notes.*

## NICHOLS COLLEGE
DUDLEY, MASSACHUSETTS 01570
Telephone: 943-1560.

Founded 1815.

*President:* LOWELL C. SMITH.
*Dean of Academic Affairs:* EDWARD G. WARREN (acting).
*Registrar:* PETER M. ENGH.
*Librarian:* WILLIAM L. COHN.
The library contains 45,000 vols.
Number of teachers: 40.
Number of students: 1,076.

## NORTH ADAMS STATE COLLEGE
375 CHURCH ST., NORTH ADAMS,
MASSACHUSETTS 01247
Founded 1894.

Programmes in Education, Business Administration, Liberal Arts, Computer Science and Medical Technology.

*President:* Dr. WILLIAM P. HAAS.
*Executive Vice-President:* ANTHONY F. CEDDIA.
*Vice-President of Academic Affairs:* JAMES R. ROACH.
*Vice-President of Student Services:* RAYMOND C. SULLIVAN.
*Director of Placement:* LAURA CORY.
*Director of Financial Aid:* DONALD HONEMAN.
*Vice-President of Administration and Finance:* THOMAS M. JONES.
The library contains 150,000 vols.
Number of full-time students: 2,100.

## NORTHEASTERN UNIVERSITY
360 HUNTINGTON AVE.,
BOSTON, MASSACHUSETTS 02115
Founded 1898.

*President:* KENNETH G. RYDER.

*Senior Vice-President and Treasurer:* D. J. ROBERTS, Jr.
*Senior Vice-President for Academic Affairs and Provost:* MELVIN MARK.
*Senior Vice-President for Administration:* JOHN A. CURRY.
*Dean of Admissions:* PHILIP R. McCABE.
*Dean of Students:* EDWARD R. ROBINSON.
*Librarian:* R. H. MOODY.
The library contains 1,123,572 vols., including 503,372 vols. on microfilm.
Number of teachers: 779 full-time, 2,270 part-time.
Number of students: 20,934 full-time, 22,250 part-time.

DEANS:
*College of Business Administration:* DAVID H. BLAKE.
*College of Criminal Justice:* N. R. ROSENBLATT.
*College of Engineering:* HAROLD LURIE.
*College of Arts and Sciences:* RICHARD ASTRO.
*School of Law:* MICHAEL C. MELTSNER.
*College of Pharmacy and Allied Health Professions:* GERALD E. SCHUMACHER.
*College of Nursing:* JUANITA LONG.
*Boston Bouvé College of Professional Studies and Education:* PAUL M. LEPLEY.
*University College:* JOHN W. JORDAN.
*College of Co-operative Education:* PAUL PRATT.

## RADCLIFFE COLLEGE
10 GARDEN ST.,
CAMBRIDGE,
MASSACHUSETTS 02138
Founded 1879; Chartered 1894.

Instruction is provided by the Faculty of Arts and Sciences of Harvard University.

*President:* MATINA S. HORNER.
Library of 20,000 vols.
Number of students: 2,474 women.
Publications: *Radcliffe Quarterly, Second Century* (3 a year).

## REGIS COLLEGE
235 WELLESLEY ST., WESTON,
MASSACHUSETTS 02193.
Telephone: (617) 893-1820.

Founded 1927.

*President:* Sister THERESE HIGGINS, C.S.J.
*Registrar:* Sister PATRICIA McDONOUGH, C.S.J.
*Director of Finance and Business Affairs:* THOMAS E. DE WITT.
*Director of Development:* CLOTILDE ZANNETOS.
*Academic Dean:* EDWARD MULHOLLAND.

*Dean of Students:* Sister ZITA FLEMING, C.S.J.
*Librarian:* Sister OLIVIA KIDNEY.

The library contains 122,350 vols.
**Number of teachers:** 102.
**Number of students:** 1,225.

Publications: *Our Times, Regis Today, Hemetera, Alumnae Bulletin.*

### SALEM STATE COLLEGE
321 LAFAYETTE ST., SALEM, MASSACHUSETTS 01970
Telephone: 617-745-0556.
Founded 1854.

*President:* Dr. JAMES T. AMSLER.
*Executive Vice-President:* Dr. ADEL ABU MOUSTAFA.
*Vice-Presidents:* Dr. WILLIAM MAHANEY (Academic Affairs), Dr. WINSTON THOMPSON (Student Services), RICHARD MARRS (Administration and Finance).
*Director of Admissions:* Dr. DAVID SARTWELL.
*Director of Library:* NEIL OLSON.

Library of 180,000 vols.
**Number of teachers:** 300.
**Number of students:** 8,400.

### SIMMONS COLLEGE
300 THE FENWAY, BOSTON, MASSACHUSETTS 02115
Founded 1899.

*President:* WILLIAM J. HOLMES, PH.D.
*Administrative Vice-President:* PRISCILLA L. MCKEE.
*Treasurer:* MICHAEL D. WEST, B.A.
*Registrar:* S. A. BARROW, A.B.
*Director of Libraries:* ARTEMIS KIRK, M.S.

**Number of teachers:** 156 full-time, 152 part-time.
**Number of students:** 2,720.

Publications: *Simmons Review, Now, Janus, Essays and Studies.*

#### DEANS:
*College:* CHARLOTTE M. MOROCCO, M.ED.
*Graduate Studies:* JOHN A. ROBINSON, ED.D.
*Sciences:* ANNE E. COGHLAN, PH.D.
*Humanities:* CHARLES R. MACKEY, PH.D.
*Library Science:* ROBERT STUEART, PH.D.
*Social Work:* DIANA WALDFOGEL, M.S.W.

### SMITH COLLEGE
NORTHAMPTON, MASSACHUSETTS 01063
Founded 1871.

*President:* JILL K. CONWAY, PH.D.
*Treasurer:* R. L. ELLIS, M.B.A.
*Secretary:* MARY E. MCDOUGLE, A.M.
*Registrar:* YVONNE J. FRECCERO, B.A.
*Librarian:* BILLIE BOZONE, M A.L.S.
*Dean of Faculty:* KENNETH H. MCCARTNEY, PH.D.
*Dean of College:* WENDY G. WINTERS, PH.D.

The library contains 866,224 vols.
**Number of teachers:** 260.
**Number of students:** 2,660 undergraduate women, 101 men and women graduates.

Publications: *Smith College Studies* (4 series) in: *Modern Languages, History, Classical Languages, Social Work.* Bulletin and exhibition catalogues of the Museum of Art, *New Valley Music Press,* Land Prize essays (undergraduate), *Smith College Pamphlets, Alumnae Quarterly.*

### SOUTHEASTERN MASSACHUSETTS UNIVERSITY
NORTH DARTMOUTH, MASSACHUSETTS 02747
Telephone: (617) 999-8000.
Founded 1895.

*President:* Dr. DONALD E. WALKER.
*Registrar:* P. FISTORI.
*Director of Admissions:* B. G. PHELPS.
*Dean of Continuing Studies and Special Programs:* Dr. ROBERT L. PIPER.
*Dean of Faculty:* Dr. RICHARD M. FONTERA.
*Dean of Students:* CELESTINO D. MACEDO.
*Dean of Library Services:* JANET FREEDMAN.

The library contains 245,000 vols.
**Number of teachers:** 309.
**Number of students:** 5,308.

#### DEANS:
*Administration:* Dr. WILLIAM C. WILD, Jr.
*College of Arts and Sciences:* Dr. TISH DACE.
*College of Engineering:* Dr. L. BRYCE ANDERSEN.
*College of Nursing:* Dr. JOYCE PASSOS.
*College of Visual and Performing Arts:* Dr. BARBARA NOEL.
*College of Business and Industry:* Dr. RICHARD J. WARD.

### SPRINGFIELD COLLEGE
263 ALDEN ST., SPRINGFIELD, MASSACHUSETTS 01109
Founded 1885.

*President:* WILBERT E. LOCKLIN.
*Registrar:* D. W. WUERTHELE, Jr.
*Librarian:* GERALD F. DAVIS.

The library contains 105,632 vols. and 184,500 microfilms.
**Number of teachers:** 129.
**Number of full-time students:** 2,327.

Publications: *Catalogue, Alumni Bulletin, Presidential Newsletter, YMCA Update.*

#### DEANS:
*College:* Dr. P. U. CONGDON.
*Students:* Dr. J. J. COSTELLO.
*Admissions:* ROBERT B. PALMER.

### STONEHILL COLLEGE
NORTH EASTON, MASSACHUSETTS 02356
Telephone: (617) 238-1081. 696-0400 (Boston Line).
Founded 1948.

*President:* Rev. BARTLEY MACPHAÍDÍN, C.S.C.
*Academic Dean:* ROBERT J. KRUSE, C.S.C.
*Director of Admissions:* FRANCIS DILLON.

The library contains 120,000 vols.
**Number of teachers:** 140.
**Number of students:** 2,200.

### SUFFOLK UNIVERSITY
41 TEMPLE ST., BOSTON, MASSACHUSETTS 02114
Telephone: (617) 723-4700.
Founded 1906.

*President:* Dr. THOMAS A. FULHAM.
*Vice-President and Treasurer:* FRANCIS X. FLANNERY.
*Dean of Students:* Dr. D. B. SULLIVAN.
*Director of Admissions—Colleges:* W. F. COUGHLIN.
*Director of Admissions—Law School:* MARJORIE A. CELLAR.
*Registrar of College Departments:* MARY A. HEFRON.
*Registrar of Law School:* LORRAINE COVE.
*Director of Libraries:* EDMUND HAMANN.

**Number of teachers:** 277.
**Number of students:** 6,163.

Publications: *Suffolk Journal, Suffolk Law Review, The Advocate, The Venture.*

#### DEANS:
*Colleges of Liberal Arts and Sciences:* Dr. MICHAEL R. RONAYNE.
*College of Business Administration and Graduate School of Administration:* Dr. RICHARD L. MCDOWELL.
*Law School:* DAVID J. SARGENT.
*Associate Dean in charge of Evening Div. and Dir. of Summer Sessions:* Dr. J. H. STRAIN.

### TUFTS UNIVERSITY
MEDFORD, MASSACHUSETTS 02155
Telephone: 628-5000.
Chartered 1852.

*President:* JEAN MAYER, PH.D., D.SC.
*Executive Vice-President:* S. S. MANOS.

*Vice-Presidents:* T. W. MURNANE, PH.D., D.M.D., J. A. DUNN, Jr., M.ED., W. R. DURGIN, M.B.A., D. MOFFATT, M.B.A.
*Treasurer:* C. R. DE BURLO, Jr., D.B.A.
*Provost:* SOL GITTLEMAN, PH.D.
*Dean of Undergraduate Admissions:* MICHAEL BEHNKE, M.A.
*Registrar:* MILDRED EASTWOOD, B.A.
*Librarian:* J. S. KOMIDAR, B.S.L.S., M.A.

The library contains 377,940 vols.
**Number of teachers:** 447 full-time, 543 part-time.
Number of students: 4,350.

Publications: *Tufts Journal, Tufts-New England Medical Center News Digest, Tufts Health Science News, Tufts Medical Alumni Bulletin, Tufts Criterion.*

### DEANS:

*Arts and Sciences:* FRANK C. COLCORD, PH.D.
*Dentistry (Boston):* ERLING JOHANSEN, PH.D., D.M.D.
*Medicine (Boston):* ROBERT I. LEVY, M.D.
*Engineering:* FREDERICK C. NELSON, PH.D.
*Veterinary Science (Boston):* ROBERT COOK, D.V.M. (acting).
*Graduate:* G. S. MUMFORD, PH.D.
*Liberal Arts:* N. S. MILBURN, PH.D.
*Dean of Students:* BOBBIE M. KNABLE, M.A.
*Undergraduate Studies and Academic Affairs:* H. M. SOLOMON, PH.D.
*Fletcher School of Law and Diplomacy* (f. 1933): THEODORE L. ELIOT, Jr., M.P.A.
*Summer School:* R. L. H. MILLER, TH.D. (Director).

## UNIVERSITY OF LOWELL
ONE UNIVERSITY AVE.,
LOWELL, MASSACHUSETTS 01854
Telephone: (617) 452-5000.

Founded 1975 by merger of Lowell State College and Lowell Technological Institute.

*President:* WILLIAM T. HOGAN.
*Vice-Presidents:* ROBERT J. FOY (Academic Affairs), RAYMOND I. RIGNEY (Business Affairs), Dr. MARY MCGAUVRAN (Student Affairs).
*Librarian:* WILLIAM MCGRATH.

The library contains 325,000 vols.
Number of teachers: 420.
Number of students: 12,000.

## UNIVERSITY OF MASSACHUSETTS AT AMHERST
AMHERST,
MASSACHUSETTS 01003
Telephone: (413) 545-0111.

**Chartered as Massachusetts Agricultural College 1863; name changed to Massachusetts State College 1931, to University 1947.**

Academic year: September to June.
*Chancellor:* HENRY KOFFLER.
*Vice-Chancellor for Academic Affairs and Provost:* LOREN BARITZ.
*Vice-Chancellor for Student Affairs:* DENNIS MADSON.
*Treasurer:* ROBERT H. BRAND.
*Director of Libraries:* RICHARD J. TALBOT.

The library contains 1,200,000 vols.
Number of teachers: 1,400.
Number of students: 24,000.

Publication: *The Massachusetts Review* (quarterly).

### DEANS:

*College of Arts and Sciences:*
  *Humanities and Fine Arts:* J. M. ALLEN.
  *Social and Behavioral Sciences:* T. O. WILKINSON.
  *Natural Sciences and Mathematics:* FREDERICK BYRON.
*College of Food and Natural Resources:* DANIEL PADBURG.
*School of Business Administration:* HARRY ALLAN.
*School of Health Sciences:* WILLIAM DARITY.
*School of Engineering:* RUSSEL C. JONES.
*School of Education:* MARIO FANTINI.
*School of Physical Education:* DAVID BISCHOFF.
*Graduate School:* SAMUEL CONTI.

### ASSOCIATED INSTITUTE:

**Stockbridge School of Agriculture:** Amherst, Mass. 01003; Tel. (413) 545-2222; est. 1918.
*Director:* JOHN W. DENISON.

## UNIVERSITY OF MASSACHUSETTS AT BOSTON
HARBOR CAMPUS, BOSTON,
MASSACHUSETTS 02125
Founded 1964.

*Chancellor:* ROBERT CORRIGAN.
The library contains 380,000 vols.
Number of teachers: 550.
Number of students: 8,400.

## WELLESLEY COLLEGE
WELLESLEY,
MASSACHUSETTS 02181
Chartered 1870; Opened 1875.

*President:* NANNERL OVERHOLSER KEOHANE.
*Vice-President, College Relations:* ALLA O'BRIEN.
*Vice-President for Business Affairs:* JOHN W. HARTLEY.
*Vice-President for Resources:* PETER M. BUCHANAN.
*Treasurer:* HORACE S. NICHOLS.

*Dean of the College:* MAUD H. CHAPLIN.
*Dean of Students:* FLORENCE C. LADD.
*Director of Admission:* MARY ELLEN AMES.
*Librarian:* ELEANOR GUSTAFSON.

The library contains over 600,000 vols.
**Number of teachers:** 227 full-time, 65 part-time.
Number of students: 2,096 women.

## WESTERN NEW ENGLAND COLLEGE
1215 WILBRAHAM RD.,
SPRINGFIELD,
MASSACHUSETTS 01119
Founded 1919.

Schools of Arts and Sciences, Engineering, Business Administration, and Law.

*President:* BEVERLY W. MILLER.
*Academic Vice-President:* ALLAN W. BOSCH.
*Vice-President for Administration and Finance:* ROBERT W. GAILEY.

The library contains 241,223 vols.
**Number of teachers:** 115 full-time, 208 part-time.
Number of students: 5,378.

## WESTFIELD STATE COLLEGE
WESTFIELD,
MASSACHUSETTS 01086
Founded 1838.

Co-educational College of Liberal Arts.

*President:* FRANCIS J. PILECKI.
*Academic Dean:* JOHN F. NEVINS.

The library contains 122,000 vols.
Number of teachers: 155.
Number of students: 2,900.

## WHEATON COLLEGE
NORTON,
MASSACHUSETTS 02766
Founded 1834.

*President:* ALICE F. EMERSON, PH.D.
*Vice-President for Finance and Operations:* DAVID L. WAGNER, M.B.A.
*Provost:* RUTH A. SCHMIDT, PH.D.
*Dean:* DARLENE L. BOROVIAK.
*Director of Admissions:* ANDRONIKE JANUS.
*Librarian:* SHERRIE BERGMAN, B.S.

The library contains 220,000 vols.
**Number of teachers:** 134, including 37 professors.
Number of students: 1,328.

Publication: *Bulletin.*

## WHEELOCK COLLEGE
200 THE RIVERWAY, BOSTON, MASSACHUSETTS 02215
Telephone: (617) 734-5200.
Founded 1888.

*President:* Dr. GORDON L. MARSHALL.
*Academic Dean:* Dr. ELIZABETH ANN LIDDLE.

The library contains 63,500 vols.
Number of teachers: 55 (full-time).
Number of students: 1,001.
Publications: *Bulletin, Wheelock College Catalogue.*

## WILLIAMS COLLEGE
WILLIAMSTOWN, MASSACHUSETTS 01267

Chartered as Free School 1791; College Charter granted 1793.

*President:* JOHN W. CHANDLER, PH.D., L.H.D., LL.D.
*Secretary of Faculty:* FRED STOCKING, PH.D.
*Vice-President and Treasurer:* F. A. DEWEY III.
*Provost:* NEIL R. GRABOIS, PH.D.
*Dean of Faculty:* FRANCIS C. OAKLEY, PH.D.
*Dean:* DANIEL D. O'CONNOR, PH.D.
*Director of Admissions:* P. H. SMITH, M.A.T.
*Registrar:* G. C. HOWARD, LL.B., M.A.
*Librarian:* L. E. WIKANDER, M.A.

The library contains 475,000 vols.
Number of teachers: 150.
Number of students: 1,110 men and 837 women.

## WORCESTER POLYTECHNIC INSTITUTE
WORCESTER, MASSACHUSETTS 01609
Founded 1865.

*President:* Dr. EDMUND T. CRANCH.
*Vice-President and Dean of Faculty:* Dr. RAY E. BOLZ.
*Vice-President for Student Affairs:* ROBERT F. REEVES.
*Registrar:* Prof. ROBERT LONG II.
*Librarian:* A. G. ANDERSON, Jr.

The library contains 110,000 vols.
Number of students: 2,500.

## WORCESTER STATE COLLEGE
486 CHANDLER ST., WORCESTER, MASSACHUSETTS 01602
Telephone: (617) 793-8000.
Founded 1874.

*President:* Dr. JOSEPH J. ORZE.
*Vice-Presidents:* Dr. BARBARA LEONDAR (Academic Affairs), Dr. O. CLAYTON JOHNSON (Student Services), Dr. ANGELO R. SCOLA (Administration and Finance).

The library contains 148,278 vols.
Number of full-time teachers: 178.
Number of students: 6,318.
Publications: *The New Student Voice* (weekly), *Yearbook, The Agora* (annual).

# MICHIGAN

## ADRIAN COLLEGE
ADRIAN, MICHIGAN 49221
Telephone: 265-5161.
Founded 1859.

*President:* DONALD S. STANTON.
*Vice-President and Dean, Academic Affairs:* JAMES F. TRAER.
*Vice-President, Business Affairs:* RONALD L. BLEECKER.
*Vice-President, Development:* WILLIAM H. LIKINS.
*Admissions Director:* R. DANA PAUL.
*Registrar:* O. IOAN STEPP.
*Librarian:* J. DODD.

The library contains 115,006 vols.
Number of teachers: 62.
Number of students: 1,116.

## ALBION COLLEGE
ALBION, MICHIGAN 49224
Telephone: 629-5511.
Founded 1835.

*President:* BERNARD T. LOMAS.
*Dean of Admissions:* F. BONTA.
*Librarian:* C. H. HELD.

The library contains 190,000 vols.
Number of teachers: 109.
Number of students: 1,715.

## ALMA COLLEGE
ALMA, MICHIGAN 48801
Telephone: (517) 463-2141.
Founded 1886.

*President:* OSCAR E. REMICK.
*Registrar:* WILLIAM P. POTTER.
*Director of Admissions:* TED ROWLAND.
*Librarian:* PETER DOLLARD.

The library contains 142,000 vols.
Number of teachers: 71 full-time, 21 part-time.
Number of students: 1,200.

## ANDREWS UNIVERSITY
BERRIEN SPRINGS, MICHIGAN 49104
Telephone: (616) 471-7771.
Founded 1874.

*President:* JOSEPH G. SMOOT.
*Registrar:* DOUGLAS K. BROWN.
*Librarian:* MARLEY H. SOPER.

The library contains 616,361 vols.
Number of teachers: 228.
Number of students: 3,018.

Publication: *Andrews University Seminary Studies* (2 a year).

DEANS:
*College of Arts and Sciences:* MERLENE A. OGDEN.
*College of Technology:* WILLIAM W. DAVIDSON.
*Graduate Studies:* ROBERT A. WILLIAMS.
*School of Business:* DALE E. TWOMLEY.
*S.D.A. Theological Seminary:* THOMAS H. BLINCOE.

## AQUINAS COLLEGE
1607 ROBINSON RD., GRAND RAPIDS, MICHIGAN 49506
Telephone: 459-8281.
Founded 1922.

*President:* Dr. NORBERT J. HRUBY.
*Vice-Presidents:* Sister BARBARA HANSEN (Academic), JOHN P. O'CONNOR (Business and Finance), JAMES L. SCHULTZ (Student Affairs), THOMAS M. MONAGHAN (Development).
*Registrar:* LOIS B. KALMAN.
*Learning Resource Center Director:* LARRY W. ZYSK.

Library of 110,000 vols., 700 periodicals and over 16,000 non-print items.
Number of teachers: 115.
Number of students: 2,000.
Publication: *Aquinas College* (quarterly).

## CALVIN COLLEGE
3201 BURTON, S.E., GRAND RAPIDS, MICHIGAN 49506
Telephone: 949-4000.
Founded 1876.

*President:* ANTHONY J. DIEKEMA, PH.D.
*Vice-Presidents:* JOHN VANDEN BERG, PH.D. (Academic Administration), HENRY DE WIT, M.B.A. (Business and Finance), PETER VANDE GUCHTE, M.B.A., ED.D. (College Advancement), BERNARD PEKELDER, B.D., M.A. (Student Affairs).
*Dean of Faculty:* PETER A. DE VOS, PH.D.
*Registrar:* ERNEST VAN VUGT, M.A.
*Director of the Library:* M. MONSMA, M.A., M.A.L.S.

The library contains 300,000 vols.
Number of teachers: 199 full-time, 49 part-time.
Number of students: 3,973.

## CENTRAL MICHIGAN UNIVERSITY
MOUNT PLEASANT, MICHIGAN 48859
Telephone: (517) 774-3151.
Founded 1892.

*President:* HAROLD ABEL, M.A., PH.D.

## UNIVERSITIES AND COLLEGES—MICHIGAN — U.S.A.

*Provost and Vice-President for Academic Affairs:* JOHN E. CANTELON, D.PHIL.
*Vice-Presidents:* TERRENCE J. CAREY, PH.D. (University Relations), ARTHUR E. ELLIS, M.A. (Public Affairs), JAMES L. HILL, M.S. (Student Affairs), JERRY R. TUBBS, M.A. (Business and Finance).
*Registrar:* ALICE N. ST. CLAIR, M.A.
*Director of Libraries:* J. L. WEATHERFORD, A.M.L.S.

Number of teachers: 770.
Number of students: 16,900.

DEANS:
*School of Arts and Sciences:* MYRON S. HENRY, PH.D.
*School of Business Administration:* LEONARD E. PLACHTA, M.B.A., PH.D.
*School of Education:* C. E. NASH, ED.M., ED.D.
*School of Fine and Applied Arts:* FRANK S. STILLINGS, M.M., PH.D.
*School of Health and Physical Education:* W. V. THEUNISSEN, A.M., P.E.D.
*School of Graduate Studies:* JANICE M. REYNOLDS, M.A., PH.D. (acting).
*School of Continuing Education and Community Services:* ALAN F. QUICK, M.A., ED.D.

### CRANBROOK ACADEMY OF ART
500 LONE PINE ROAD
P.O.B. 801, BLOOMFIELD HILLS, MICHIGAN 48013
Telephone: 645-3300.
Founded 1932.

*President:* ROY SLADE.
*Registrar:* LUCILLE HARPER.
*Librarian:* DIANE VOGT-O'CONNOR.

The library contains 17,000 volumes.
Number of teachers: 10 full-time.
Number of students: 150.

### DETROIT INSTITUTE OF TECHNOLOGY
2727 SECOND AVE., DETROIT, MICHIGAN 48201
Telephone: 962-0830.
Founded 1891.

*President:* Dr. ROBERT W. ELLIS, Jr.
*Co-ordinator of Co-operative Education:* CHERYL TERMAAT.
*Director of Admissions:* GORDON OSTROWSKI.
*Business Manager:* ROBERT JONES.
*Registrar:* MARY LOU BAKER.
*Personnel Director:* PAUL D. WALKER.
*Librarian:* LINDA SIMS.

Number of teachers: 27 (full-time).
Number of students: 893.
Publications: *The Technonian, Detroit Institute of Technology Newsletter.*

DEANS:
*General Studies:* Dr. PHELPS TRIX.
*Business and Organizational Science:* Dr. JIYA JAIN.

*Technology and Applied Science:* Dr. S. B. SEHGAL.

### EASTERN MICHIGAN UNIVERSITY
YPSILANTI, MICHIGAN 48197
Telephone: (313) 487-1849.
Founded 1849.

*President:* JOHN W. PORTER.
*Vice-President for Academic Affairs:* ANTHONY H. EVANS.
*Vice-President for Administration:* CAROLYN D. SPATTA.
*Vice-President for Student Affairs:* LAURENCE SMITH.
*Vice-President for Business and Finance:* ROBERT ROMKEMA.
*Vice-President for University Relations:* GARY D. HAWKS.
*Registrar:* GEORGE LINN.
*Librarian:* MORELL BOONE.

The library contains 580,341 vols.
Number of teachers: 780.
Number of students: 18,274.
Publication: *The Journal of Narrative Technique.*

DEANS:
*Business:* J. KENT KERBY.
*Education:* W. SCOTT WESTERMAN, Jr.
*Graduate School:* GARY K. KELLER.
*Arts and Sciences:* DONALD F. DRUMMOND.
*Human Services:* PETER DUAL.
*Student Affairs:* BETTE C. WHITE.
*Technology:* ALVIN RUDISILL.
*Continuing Education:* GEORGE P. MELICAN.

### FERRIS STATE COLLEGE
901 SOUTH STATE ST., BIG RAPIDS, MICHIGAN 49307
Telephone: (616) 796-0461.
Founded 1884.

*President:* R. L. EWIGLEBEN.
*Director of Admissions:* K. S. WALKER.
*Director of the Library:* MARY M. BOWER.

The library contains 240,000 vols.
Number of teachers: 540.
Number of students: 11,000.

### GENERAL MOTORS INSTITUTE
1700 WEST THIRD AVE., FLINT, MICHIGAN 48502
Telephone: (313) 762-9500.
Founded 1919.

Degree courses in Electrical, Mechanical and Industrial Engineering and Industrial Administration.

*President:* WILLIAM B. COTTINGHAM, PH.D.
*Dean of Academic Affairs:* ROGER A. HOLMES, PH.D.

*Dean of Student Affairs:* RICHARD R. WARMBOLD, PH.D.
*Librarian:* W. R. ELGOOD.

The library contains 80,000 vols.
Number of teachers: 143.
Number of students: 2,200.

### HILLSDALE COLLEGE
HILLSDALE, MICHIGAN 49242
Telephone: (517) 437-7341.
Founded 1844.

*President:* Dr. GEORGE C. ROCHE III.
*Vice-President for Student Affairs and Director of Admissions:* Dr. RUSSELL L. NICHOLS.
*Academic Dean:* Dr. JOHN B. MULLER.
*Registrar:* KAY COSGROVE.
*Librarian:* DANIEL JOLDERSMA.

The library contains 76,132 vols.
Number of teachers: 65.
Number of students: 1,000.

### HOPE COLLEGE
HOLLAND, MICHIGAN 49423
Telephone: (616) 392-5111.
Founded 1851.

*President:* Dr. GORDON J. VAN WYLEN.
*Provost:* Dr. DAVID MARKER.
*Director of Admissions:* Dr. JAMES A. BEKKERING.
*Librarian:* Dr. HARRY BOONSTRA.

The library contains 192,710 vols.
Number of teachers: 144.
Number of students: 2,400.

### KALAMAZOO COLLEGE
KALAMAZOO, MICHIGAN 49007
Chartered 1833 as Michigan and Huron Institute; name changed to Kalamazoo Literary Institute 1837, to Kalamazoo College 1855.

*President:* GEORGE N. RAINSFORD.
*Provost:* WARREN L. BOARD.
*Vice-President for Finance and Business:* ROGER J. FECHER.
*Vice-President for Student Services:* ROBERT N. MAUST.
*Vice-President for Development:* ALFRED BLUM.

Library of 232,510 vols.
Number of teachers: 92.
Number of students: 1,451.

### MADONNA COLLEGE
36600 SCHOOLCRAFT ROAD, LIVONIA, MICHIGAN 48150
Telephone: (313) 591-1200.
Founded 1947.

*President:* Sister MARY FRANCILENE, C.S.S.F.
*Academic Dean:* Sister ROSE MARIE, C.S.S.F.

*Director of Student Development:* Sister EMELINE BASH.
*Director of Admissions:* LOUIS BROHL, I.I.I.
*Director of Financial Aid:* CHRIS ZIEGLER.
*Registrar:* Sister MARY ANGELIS, C.S.S.F.
*Librarian:* Sister MARY LYDIA, C.S.S.F.
The library contains 100,000 vols.
Number of teachers: 152.
Number of students: 3,000.

## MARYGROVE COLLEGE
8425 WEST McNICHOLS,
DETROIT, MICHIGAN 48221
Telephone: (313) 862-8000.
Founded 1910.

Liberal Arts College; two- and four-year master's degrees; continuing education programme.

*President:* Dr. JOHN E. SHAY, Jr.
*Academic Dean:* Sister JOHN CLEMENT HUNGERMAN, I.H.M.
*Registrar:* Sister MARGARET DONOGHUE, I.H.M.
*Director of Admissions:* CHARLES D. DONALDSON.
*Librarian:* Sister ANNA MARY WAICKMAN, I.H.M.
The library contains 171,500 vols.
Number of teachers: 50.
Number of students: 1,059.

## MICHIGAN STATE UNIVERSITY
EAST LANSING, MICHIGAN 48824
Telephone: 355-1855.

Founded 1855; the first college for teaching scientific agriculture, and the forerunner of the American system of land-grant colleges.

State control; Academic year: September to June (three terms).

*President:* CECIL MACKEY, PH.D.
*Provost:* CLARENCE L. WINDER, PH.D.
*Vice-President for Finance and Operations:* KENNETH W. THOMPSON.
*Vice-President for University Development:* JOSEPH DICKINSON.
*Vice-President for Research and Graduate Studies:* J. E. CANTLON, PH.D.
*Vice-President for University Relations:* CONNIE STEWART.
*Vice-President for Student Affairs and Services:* MOSES TURNER, PH.D.
*Vice-President:* J. BRESLIN, M.A.
*Registrar:* H. C. KING, PH.D.
*Director of Libraries:* R. E. CHAPIN, PH.D.

Library: *see* Libraries.
Number of teachers: 2,781.
Number of students: 44,211.
Publications: *M.S.U. Magazine, Centennial Review Business Topics, College of Education Quarterly, Agricultural Experiment Station Quarterly, University Catalog, Michigan Economic Record.*

DEANS:
*University College:* W. G. WARRINGTON, ED.D.
*Agriculture and Natural Resources:* J. H. ANDERSON, PH.D.
*Arts and Letters:* ALAN HOLLINGSWORTH, PH.D.
*Business:* R. J. LEWIS, D.B.A.
*Communication Arts and Sciences:* E. BETTINGHAUS, PH.D.
*Education:* JUDITH E. LANIER, PH.D. (acting).
*Engineering:* L. W. VON TERSCH. PH.D.
*Graduate Studies:* H. J. OYER, PH.D.
*Human Ecology:* L. A. LUND, PH.D.
*Human Medicine:* W. C. WESTON, M.D.
*James Madison College:* JOHN E. PAYNTER, PH.D. (acting).
*Lyman Briggs College:* M. J. HARRISON, PH.D.
*Natural Science:* R. H. BYERRUM, PH.D.
*Osteopathic Medicine:* M. S. MAGEN, D.O.
*Social Science:* G. H. ANDREW, PH.D.
*Urban Development:* R. L. GREEN, PH.D.
*Veterinary Medicine:* J. R. WELSER, D.V.M., PH.D.

## MICHIGAN TECHNOLOGICAL UNIVERSITY
HOUGHTON, MICHIGAN 49931
Telephone: (906) 487-1885.

Founded 1885; formerly Michigan College of Mining and Technology.

*President:* Dr. DALE F. STEIN.
*Vice-President of Academic Affairs:* Dr. E. H. TIMOTHY WHITTEN.
*Vice-President for Administrative Services and Secretary, Board of Control:* W. G. LUCIER.
Number of teachers: 374 full-time, 33 part-time.
Number of students: 7,710.
Publication: *Catalog.*

DEANS:
*Engineering:* Dr. GORDON P. KRUEGER.
*Sciences and Arts:* W. POWERS.
*Graduate School:* (vacant).
*Forestry and Wood Products:* Dr. E. A. BOURDO.
*School of Business:* Prof. G. ROBERT BUTLER.
*School of Technology:* GERALD J CASPARY.
*Director of Library:* Prof. LEROY J. LEBBIN.

HEADS OF DEPARTMENTS:
*Metallurgical Engineering:* Dr. L. A. HELDT.
*Mining Engineering:* Dr. RUDOLF E. GREUER.
*Physical Education:* Prof. T. H. KEARLY.
*Mathematics and Computer Sciences:* Dr. RICHARD S. MILLMAN.
*Electrical Engineering:* Dr. E. KEITH STANEK.
*Mechanical Engineering:* Dr. HAROLD W. LORD.
*Humanities:* Dr. ARTHUR P. YOUNG.
*Social Sciences:* Dr. JOHN H. WINSLOW.
*Chemistry and Chemical Engineering:* Dr. ANTHONY B. PONTER.
*Forestry:* (vacant).
*Geology and Geological Engineering:* Dr. G. E. FRANTTI (acting).
*Biological Sciences:* Dr. B. K. WHITTEN.
*Physics:* Dr. ROLLAND O. KEELING.
*Civil Engineering:* Dr. VERNON B. WATWOOD.

HEADS OF RESEARCH AGENCIES:
*Director of Research:* Dr. FREDERIC ERBISCH (acting).
*Institute of Mineral Research:* Dr. CLIFFORD W. SCHULTZ.
*Institute of Wood Research:* Dr. ANDERS LUND.
*Ford Forestry Center:* Dr. E. A. BOURDO.
*Institute of Accounting Research:* Prof. S. TIDWELL.

## NAZARETH COLLEGE
NAZARETH, MICHIGAN 49074
Telephone: (616) 349-7783.
Founded 1924.
Professions and Liberal Arts.

*President:* JOHN HOPKINS, PH.D.
*Registrar:* JOAN NOTEBOOM.
*Dean of Academic Affairs:* LYNN W. LINDEMAN, PH.D.
*Director of Admissions:* VIRGINIA JONES, S.S.J., PH.D.
*Executive Vice-President:* MITCHELL WESOLOWSKI.
*Dean of Student Life:* MARY FITZGERALD.
*Library Director:* MARTHA HALLOCK, S.S.J.
The library contains 86,000 vols.
Number of teachers: 74.

## NORTHERN MICHIGAN UNIVERSITY
MARQUETTE, MICHIGAN 49855
Telephone: (906) 227-2242.
Founded 1899.

*President:* JOHN X. JAMRICH.
*Director of Admissions:* JOHN M. KUNKEL.
*Library Director:* Prof. JON D. DRABENSTOTT.
The library contains 361,346 vols.
Number of teachers: 347.
Number of students: 9,376.

## OAKLAND UNIVERSITY
ROCHESTER, MICHIGAN 48063
Telephone: (313) 377-2100.
Founded 1957.

State control; Academic year: September to August (three semesters).

*President:* JOSEPH E. CHAMPAGNE.
*Vice-Presidents:* JOHN H. DE CARLO (Governmental Relations and General Counsel), KEITH R. KLECKNER (Academic Affairs) (acting), ROBERT J. MCGARRY (Administrative Affairs), WILMA H. RAY-BLEDSOE (Student and Urban Affairs), ROBERT W. SWANSON (Development).

Number of teachers: 467.
Number of students: 12,006.

Publications: *Oakland University Undergraduate Catalog* (every 2 years), *Oakland University Graduate Catalog* (every 2 years), *Oakland University Alumni Quarterly*, *Oakland University News* (fortnightly).

### DEANS:
*School of Economics and Management:* RONALD C. HORWITZ.
*School of Education:* GERALD PINE.
*School of Engineering:* M. S. GHAUSI.
*School of Nursing:* ANDREA LINDELL.
*School of Performing Arts:* L. J. HETENYI.
*College of Arts and Sciences:* BRIAN COPENHAVER.
*Graduate Study:* LEWIS N. PINO (acting).
*Graduate Study:* G. P. JOHNSON.
*Division of Continuing Education:* L. R. EKLUND.
*Kresge Library:* GEORGE L. GARDINER.

## OLIVET COLLEGE
OLIVET, MICHIGAN 49076
Telephone: (616) 749-7000.
Founded 1844.

*President:* DONALD A. MORRIS.
*Vice-President and Dean of Students:* JOHN O. MCCANDLESS.
*Academic Vice-President:* DAVID K. ADAMS.
*Vice-President (Finance):* RICHARD PÉWÉ.
*Vice-President (Development):* ROBERT F. PRATHER.
*Director of Student Records:* KATHLEEN A. HALL.
*Director of Admissions:* RONALD LYNCH.
*Director of Libraries:* JOHN KONDELIK.
Number of students: 680.

## SIENA HEIGHTS COLLEGE
ADRIAN, MICHIGAN 49221
Telephone: 263-0731.
Founded 1919.

*President:* Dr. LOUIS C. VACCARO.
*Academic Dean:* JAMES EBBEN.
*Graduate Dean:* Dr. MIRIAM STIMSON.
*Registrar:* ROBERT PARKER.
*Librarian:* MARK DOMBROWSKI.
The library contains 104,500 vols.
Number of teachers: 101.
Number of students: 1,800.

## SPRING ARBOR COLLEGE
SPRING ARBOR, MICHIGAN 49283
Telephone: (517) 750-1200.
Founded 1873.

*President:* Dr. KENNETH H. COFFMAN.
*Vice-Presidents:* DAVID GINES (Development), Dr. ALTON R. KURTZ (Academic Affairs), KENNETH R. BEARDSLEE (Business Affairs), DAVID KLOPFENSTEIN (Student Development).

The library contains 64,050 vols.

## UNIVERSITY OF DETROIT
4001 W. McNICHOLS RD.,
DETROIT, MICHIGAN 48221
Telephone: (313) 927-1000.

Founded 1877 as Detroit College and Chartered as such 1881. Chartered as a University 1911.

*President:* ROBERT A. MITCHELL, S.J.
*Vice-President for Academic Affairs:* NORMAN MCKENDRICK, S.J.
*Director of Admissions:* JAMES MASUGA.
*Registrar:* J. A. BERKOWSKI, PH.B.
*Librarian:* GARY DENUE.

The library contains 508,000 vols.
Number of full-time teachers: 259.
Number of students: 6,650.

Publication: *Bulletin* (monthly, Dec. to Aug.).

### DEANS:
*College of Liberal Arts:* Fr. GERARD ALBRIGHT, S.J.
*College of Business and Administration:* Dr. SAM BARONE.
*College of Engineering and Science:* Dr. JAMES KENT.
*School of Architecture:* B. LEON, B.ARCH.
*School of Law:* CARL M. SELINGER.
*School of Dentistry:* Dr. JAMES SMUDSKI.
*School of Education and Human Services:* Dr. ARLENE NOWAK.

## UNIVERSITY OF MICHIGAN
ANN ARBOR, MICHIGAN 48109
Telephone: (313) 764-1817.
Telegraphic Address: Univ. of Mich., Ann Arbor, Mich.
Founded 1817.

*President:* HAROLD T. SHAPIRO, PH.D.
*Vice-President and Chief Financial Officer:* JAMES F. BRINKERHOFF, M.B.A.
*Vice-President for Student Services:* HENRY JOHNSON, B.A., M.S.W.
*Vice-President for Research:* CHARLES G. OVERBERGER, M.S., PH.D.
*Vice-President for University Relations and Development:* M. RADOCK, M.S.J., LITT.D.
*Vice-President for State Relations and Secretary of the University:* R. L. KENNEDY, B.A.
*Associate Registrars:* H. D. OLSON, M.S., D. R. WOOLLEY, M.A.
*Director of Admissions:* CLIFFORD F. SJOGREN, M.A., PH.D.
*Director of the University Libraries:* RICHARD M. DOUGHERTY, M.L.S., PH.D.
*Library: see Libraries.*

Number of teachers: 4,462.
Number of resident students: 35,824 (excluding extensions).

Publications: *Michigan Quarterly Review*, *The University of Michigan Today* (quarterly), *Research News* (monthly), *Michigan Alumnus*, *Extension Service News* (both monthly during academic year).

### DEANS:
*College of Architecture and Urban Planning:* R. C. METCALF, B.ARCH.
*School of Art:* G. V. BAYLISS, M.F.A.
*School of Business Administration:* G. R. WHITAKER, Jr., M.S., PH.D.
*School of Dentistry:* W. R. MANN, D.D.S., M.S.
*School of Education:* J. S. STARK, M.A., ED.D.
*College of Engineering:* DAVID V. RAGONE, S.M., SC.D.
*Horace H. Rackham School of Graduate Studies:* ALFRED S. SUSSMAN, A.M., PH.D.
*Law School:* T. SANDALOW, A.B., J.D.
*School of Library Science:* R. E. BIDLACK, PH.D.
*College of Literature, Science, and the Arts:* B. E. FRYE, M.S., PH.D.
*Medical School:* JOHN A. GRONVALL, M.D.
*School of Music:* PAUL C. BOYLAN, PH.D.
*School of Natural Resources:* W. J. JOHNSON, M.L.A.
*School of Nursing:* MARY LOHR, B.S.N., M.A., ED.D.
*College of Pharmacy:* ARA G. PAUL, M.A., PH.D.
*School of Public Health:* RICHARD D. REMINGTON, M.P.H., PH.D.
*Residential College:* J. MERSEREAU, M.A., PH.D. (Director).
*School of Social Work:* P. A. FELLIN, M.S.W., PH.D.

### PROFESSORS:
*Aerospace:*
ADAMSON, T. C., Jr.
ANDERSON, W. J.
BARTMAN, F. L.
BEUTLER, F. J.
BUNING, H.
EISLEY, J. G.
GILBERT, E. G.

UNITED STATES OF AMERICA

GREENWOOD, D. T.
HAYS, P. B.
HOWE, R. M.
JONES, L. M.
LESHER, E. J.
LIU, V. C.
McCLAMROCH, N H.
MESSITER, A. F.
NICHOLLS, J. A.
ONG, R. S. B.
PHILLIPS, R. L.
POWERS, W. F.
RAUCH, L. L.
ROOT, W. L.
SHERMAN, P. M.
SICHEL, M.
SIKARSKIE, D. L.
TAYLOR, J. E.
VINH, N.
WILLMARTH, W. W

*Anatomy:*
AVERY, J. K.
BAKER, B. L.
BEAUDOIN, A. R.
BURDI, A. R.,
CARLSON, B. M.
CASTELLI, W. A.
CHRISTENSEN, A. K.
HAN, S. S.
HUELKE, D. F.
KAHN, R. H.
MOOSMAN, D. A.
OELRICH, T. M.
SIPPEL, T. O.

*Anaesthesiology:*
COHEN, P. J.
DEKORNFELD, T. J.
FINCH, J. S.
SWEET, R. B.
ZSIGMOND, E. K.

*Anthropology:*
BECKER, A.
BRACE, C. L.
BURLING, R.
CARROLL, V.
DIAMOND, N.
FLANNERY, K. V.
FORD, R. I.
FRISANCHO, A. R.
GARN, S.
KOTTAK, C. P.
LIVINGSTONE, F. B.
MINER, H. M.
PARSONS, J. R.
RAPPAPORT, R. A.
SCHORGER, W. D.
SNYDER, R. G.
SUDARKASA, N.
WHALLON, R. E.
WITHERSPOON, G. J.
WOLPOFF, M. H.
WRIGHT, H. T.
YENGOYAN, A. A.

*Applied Mechanics and Engineering:*
CLARK, S. K.
DAILY, J. W.
DEBLER, W. R.
GRAEBEL, W. P.
HESS, R. L.
JACOBS, S. J.
LOW, R. D.
SCOTT, R. A.
SMITH, H. J.
TAYLOR, J. E.
WINEMAN, A. S.
YANG, W. H.
YIH, C. S.

*Architecture and Urban Planning:*
BARNETT, N. E.
BIRKERTS, G.

BORKIN, H. J.
CLIPSON, C. W.
CRANDALL, J. S.
CRANE, G. E.
DARVAS, R. M.
DUKE, R. D.
EATON, L. K.
FADER, L.
FELDT, A. G.
GORWIC, N. H.
HANDLER, A. B.
HIMES, H. W.
JOHE, H. W.
JOHNSON, C. D.
KING, J.
KOWALEWSKI, H. S.
LEE, J. T. A.
LYTLE, R. B., Jr.
MALCOLMSON, R. F.
MARANS, R. W.
MARZOLF, K.
METCALF, R. C.
OBERDICK, W. A.
OLENCKI, E. V.
OLVING, G.
PASTALAN, L. A.
PAULSEN, G.
WEHRER, J. J.
WERNER, W. A.

*Art:*
ANDREWS, J. W.
BAUM, M.
BAYLISS, G. V.
CARTER, W. T.
CASSARA, F.
CHENG, M. Y.
DAVIES, P. C.
HEERS, W. W.
KAMROWSKI, G.
KERSTEN, D. B.
KORTEN, C. F.
LARKIN, T. J.
LEWIS, W. A.
McCLURE, T. F.
MULLEN, A. P.
RAMSAY, T. K.
REIDER, D. H.
RUSH, J. N.
SEARS, R. L.
STEPHENSON, J. H.
WEBER, A. J.
WILT, R. H.

*Astronomy:*
COWLEY, C. R.
HADDOCK, F. T.
HILTNER, W. A.
MOHLER, O. C.
TESKE, R. G.

*Atmospheric and Oceanic Science:*
AYERS, J. C.
BARTMAN, F. L.
BEETON, A.
DINGLE, A. N.
DONAHUE, T. M.
HAYS, P. B.
JACOBS, S. J.
JONES, L. M.
KUHN, W. R.
NAGY, A. F.
PORTMAN, D. J.

*Biological Chemistry:*
AGRANOFF, B. W.
BERNSTEIN, I. A.
CHRISTENSEN, H. N.
COON, M. J.
DATTA, P. K.
DEKKER, E. E.
DZIEWIATKOWSKI, D. D.
GOLDSTEIN, I. J.
GREENBERG, G. R.
HOCH, F. L.
JOURDIAN, G. W.

WORLD OF LEARNING

KELLEY, W. N.
LANDS, W. E. M.
LUDWIG, M.
MASSEY, V.
ONCLEY, J. L.
OXENDER, D. L.
RADIN, N.
SHAFER, J. A.

*Biostatistics:*
CORNELL, R. G.
JACQUEZ, J. A.
KALTON, G.
KSHIRSAGAR, A. M.
MOORE, F. E.
SCHORK, M. A.

*Biological Sciences:*
ALEXANDER, R. D.
ALLEN, J. M.
ALLEN, S. L.
BAILEY, R. M.
BECK, C. B.
BENNINGHOFF, W. S.
BEYER, R. E.
BURCH, J. B.
CATHER, J. N.
CRUM, H. A.
DAWSON, W. R.
EVANS, F. C.
FOSTER, M.
FRYE, B. E.
GANS, C.
GATES, D. M.
GAY, H.
GRANT, P. R.
GUTHE, K. F.
HAMILTON, W. D.
HOOPER, E. T.
IKUMA, H.
KAUFMAN, P. B.
KEMP, N. E.
KLEINSMITH, L. J.
KLUGE, A. G.
LOWRY, R. J.
McVAUGH, R.
MARTIN, M. M.
MILLER, R. R.
MOORE, T. E.
NACE, G. W.
NOODEN, L. D.
NORTHCUTT, R. G.
OAKLEY, B.
RIZKI, T. M.
SHAFFER, R. L.
SHAPPIRIO, D. G.
STEINER, E. E.
STORER, R. W.
SUSSMAN, A. S.
TINKLE, D. W.
VOSS, E. G.
WAGNER, W. H., Jr.
YOCUM, C. S.

*Business Administration:*
ADAMS, R. W.
ARNETT, H. E.
BOND, F. A.
CAMERON, G. D., III
CRAWFORD, C. M.
DANIELSON, L. E.
DAVISSON, C. N.
DUFEY, G.
EDWARDS, A. L.
FILGAS, J. F.
GIES, T. G.
HALL, W. K.
HAYES, D. A.
HILDEBRANDT, H. W.
HOSMER, L. T.
JONES, D. L.
KELL, W. G.
LEABO, D. A.
LEWIS, D. L.
LONGE, P. G. S.
McCRACKEN, P. W.

UNIVERSITIES AND COLLEGES—MICHIGAN (UNIVERSITY OF)  U.S.A.

MacDonald, D. L.
Martin, C. R., Jr.
Miller, E. L.
Mitchell, E. J.
**Pearson, K. G.**
**Pierpont, W. K.**
**Pilcher, C. J.**
Reece, J. S.
**Rewoldt, S. H.**
Schriber, T. J.
Skadden, D. H.
**Southwick, A.**
**Spivey, W. A.**
**Swinyard, A. W.**
Taylor, J. R.
Terpstra, V.
**Warshaw, M. R.**
Wheeler, J. E.
Wilhelm, R. J.
Wrobleski, W. J.

*Chemical Engineering:*
Carnahan, B.
Curl, R. L.
Fogler, H. S.
**Kadlec, R. H.**
Kempe, L. L.
Martin, J. J.
Powers, J. E.
Schultz, J. S.
Sinnott, M. J.
Tek, M. R.
Wilkes, J. O.
**Williams, G. B.**
Yeh, G. S. Y.
Young, E. H.

*Chemistry:*
Ashe, A.
**Bartell, L. S.**
Blinder, S. M.
Dunn, T. M.
Elving, P. J.
Gordus, A. A.
Kopelman, R.
Kuczkowski, R. L.
Lawton, R. G.
Lohr, L. L.
Longone, D. T.
Martin, M. M.
Nordman, C.
Oncley, J. L.
**Overberger, C. G.**
Rudolph, R. W.
Rulfs, C. L.
**Smith, P. A. S.**
Stiles, R. M.
Tamres, M.
Taylor, R. C.
Westrum, E. F.
Wiseman, J. R.

*Civil Engineering:*
Berg, G. V.
**Borchardt, J. A.**
**Brater, E. F.**
Buckley, J. W.
Canale, R. P.
Carr, R. I.
**Cleveland, D. E.**
Cortright, D. N.
Glysson, E. A.
Gray, D. H.
Hanson, R. D.
**Harris, R. B.**
Kaldjian, M. J.
**Richart, F. E., Jr.**
Rumman, W. S.
Tons, E.
Weber, W. J., Jr.
Woods, R. D.
**Wylie, E. B.**

*Classical Studies:*
**Buttrey, T. V.**
Cameron, H. D.
D'Arms, J. H.

Koenen, L.
**Pedley, J. G.**
Pulgram, E.
Seligson, G. M.
**Sweet, W. E.**
Witke, C.

*Community Health Programs:*
Arthur, B.
Bagramian, R. A.
Baler, L. A.
Block, W. D.
Corsa, L.
Cruickshank, W. M.
Eliot, J. W.
Garn, S. M.
Margolis, P. M.
Owen, G. M.
Rhodes, W. C.
Smith, D. C.
Striffler, D. F.

*Community Mental Health Services:*
Arthur, B.
Baler, L. A.
Margolis, P. M.
Rhodes, W. C.
Smith, D. C.

*Computer and Communication Services:*
Burks, A. W.
Friedman, J. B.
Holland, J.
Kaplan, S.
Meyer, J.
Reitman, W.

*Dentistry:*
Anderson, J. R.
Asgar, K.
Ash, M. M., Jr.
Avery, J. K.
Baer, M. J.
Burgett, F. G.
Bonnette, G. H.
Buchholz, R. E.
Caffesse, R. G.
Cartwright, C. B.
Charbeneau, G. T.
Cheney, E. A.
Clayton, J. A.
Clewell, D. B.
Comstock, F. W.
Corpron, R. E.
Courtney, R. M.
Craig, R. G.
Dennison, J.
Doerr, R. E.
Dowson, J.
Dziewiatkowski, D. D.
Godwin, W. C.
Han, S. S.
Harris, J. E.
Hartsook, J. T.
Hayes, R. L.
Hayward, J. R.
Higuchi, W. I.
Jaslow, C.
Kahler, F. W., Jr.
Kelsey, C. C.
Koran, A.
Kotowicz, W. E.
Kowalski, C. J.
Lang, B. R.
Loesche, W. J.
Lorey, R. E.
Mann, W. R.
McPhee, E. R.
Millard, H. D.
Moyers, R. E.
Myers, G. E.
Nanda, S. K.
Nissle, R. R.
O'Brien, W. J.
**Ramfjord, S. P.**
Richards, A. G.

Robinson, E.
Rowe, N. H., Jr.
Sawusch, R. H.
Schield, H. W., Jr.
Smith, F. N.
Smith, F. W.
Snyder, D. T.
**Steele P., F.**
Strachan, D. S.
**Striffler, D. F.**
Upton, L.

*Dermatology:*
Dubin, H. V.
**Harrell, E. R.**
Headington, J. T.
Krull, E. A.
Livingood, C.
Taylor, W. B.
Voorhees, J. J.

*Economics:*
Ackley, G.
Anderson, W. H. L.
Barlow, R.
Berg, E. J.
Bergstrom, T. C.
Bornstein, M.
Brazer, H. E.
Cross, J. G.
Dernberger, R. F
Feldstein, P.
Fusfeld, D. R
Gramlich, E. M.
Holbrook, R. S.
Howrey, E. P.
Hymans, S. H.
Johnson, G. E.
Juster, T. F.
Kmenta, J.
Lee, R.
Levinson, H. M.
Morgan, J. N.
Mueller, E. L.
Neenan, W. B.
Shapiro, H. T.
Shepherd, W. G.
Stafford, F.
Steiner, P. O.
Stern, R. M.
Stolper, W. F.
Teigen, R. L.
Varian, H.
Wright, G.

*Education:*
Angus, D. L.
Barritt, L. S.
Bates, P.
Beach, L. W.
Berger, C. F.
**Bertolaet, F. W.**
Blackburn, R. T.
Bobroff, A.
Byrn, D. K.
Cash, W. L.
Cave, W. M.
Cohen, J.
Cohen, W. J.
Collet, L. S.
Cooper, S.
Cosand, J. D.
Coxford, A. F.
Cruickshank, W. M.
Davis, C.
Dixon, W. R.
Dunning, A. S.
Dyer, C. O.
Edington, D. W.
Eggertsen, C. A.
Gamson, Z. F.
Goodman, F. L.
Gordon, M.
Grambeau, R. J.
Gurin, G.
Harris, R. W.

HUGHES, L. H.
HUNGERMAN, A. D.
JENSEN, G. E.
JOHNSON, M. C.
JONES, P. S.
KEHOE, R. E.
LEACH, K. W.
LEHMANN, C. F.
LEHSTEN, N. G.
LOWTHER, M. A.
MCCLENDON, E. J.
MCMAHON, G. G.
MEDLIN, W. K.
MENLO, A.
MERHAB, W. G.
MILLER, J. L., Jr.
MILLS, W. H.
MORRISON, B.
MORSE, W. C.
PAYNE, J. N.
PENIX, F. C.
PETERSON, M. W.
POFFENBERGER, T.
REIFF, G. G.
RUPP, R.
SCHOLL, G. T.
SCHWERTFEGER, J.
SHARF, D.
SMITH, A.
SMITH, D. E. P.
STARK, J. S.
SWEET, W. E.
TO, C.
TRIPPE, M. J.
VAN VOORHEES, C.
VANCE, K. E.
VOSS, B. E.
WAGAW, T.
WADZ, G. R.
WILEY, J.
WINGO, G. M.
WOMER, F. B.
ZANDER, A. F.

*Electrical and Computer Engineering:*
BARTON, B. F.
BEMENT, S. L.
BIRDSALL, T. G.
BROWN, R. K.
CALAHAN, D. A.
CHEN, K.
CHU, C. M.
CHUANG, K.
ENNS, M. K.
FARRIS, H. W.
GETTY, W. D.
GREEN, D.G.
HADDAD, G. I.
HIATT, R. E.
IRANI, K. B.
KAZDA, L. F.
LEITH, E. N.
LOMAX, R. J.
LYON, J. A. M.
MACNEE, A. B.
MASNARI, N. A.
MCMULLEN, C. W.
MEYER, J. F.
NAGY, A. F.
NAYLOR, A. W.
OLTE, A.
SCOTT, N. R.
SENIOR, T. B. A.
SHARPE, C. B.
TAI, C. T.
VOLZ, R. A.
WEIL, H.
WILLIAMS, W. J.
YEH, C.

*Engineering Humanities:*
HUGHES, D. Y.
LOOMIS, R. A.
MARTIN, R. A.
MATHES, J. C.
SAWYER, T. M.

SHAFTER, E. M., Jr.
SKOLIMOWSKI, H.
STANTON, S. S.
STEVENSON, D. W.
WEEKS, R. P.

*English Language and Literatures:*
ALDRIDGE, J. W.
ARTHOS, J.
BAILEY, R. W.
BAKER, S. W.
BARROWS, H. C.
BLOTNER, J. L.
BORNSTEIN, G.
COLES, W. A.
CREETH, E. H.
DOWNER, J. W.
DUNNING, S. A.
EBY, C. D.
ENGLISH, H. M.
FADER, D. N.
FRASER, R. A.
GARBATY, T. J.
GINDIN, J. J.
GREENHUT, M.
HAUGH, R. F.
HAYDEN, R. E.
HILL, D. L.
HORNBACK, B. G
HOWES, A. B.
INGRAM, W. H.
KING, H. V.
KNOTT, J. R.
KONIGSBERG, I.
KUHN, S. M.
LENAGHAN, R. T.
PATRIDES, C. A.
POWERS, L. H.
RABKIN, E. S.
REIDY, J.
ROBERTSON, J.
ROBINSON, J. L.
SANDS, D. B.
SQUIRES, J. R.
STEINHOFF, W. R.
SUPER, R. H.

*Environmental Education/Outdoor Recreation:*
STAPP, W. B.
TOCHER, S. R.

*Environmental and Industrial Health:*
BERNSTEIN, I. A.
BOETTNER, E. A.
BYERS, D. H.
CORNISH, H. H.
DEININGER, R. A.
GANNON, J. J.
HARTUNG, R.
HILBERT, M. S.
MANCY, K. H.
PLATO, P. A.
SMITH, R. G.
WHIPPLE, G. H.

*Epidemiology:*
ACKERMANN, W. W.
COCHRAN, K. W.
ECKERT, E. A.
HAWTHORNE, V. M.
HENNESSY, A. V.
HIGGINS, I. T. T.
HIGGINS, M. W.
MAASSAB, H. F.
MONTO, A. S.
PAYNE, F. E.

*Far Eastern Languages and Literature:*
BROWER, R. H.
CRUMP, J. I.
HUCKER, C. O.
MILLS, H. C.

*Fisheries, Forestry and Wildlife:*
BARNES, B. V.
BASSETT, J. R.

CAROW, J.
MCCULLOUGH, D. R.
MACKINNON, D. A.
OLSON, C. E., Jr.
PATTERSON, R. L.
TOCHER, S. R.

*Geography:*
GOSLING, L. A. P.
KISH, G.
KOLARS, J. F.
LARIMORE, A. E.
MURPHEY, R.
NYSTUEN, J. D.

*Geology and Mineralogy:*
BRIGGS, L. I.
CLOKE, P. L.
DORR, J. A., Jr.
ESCHMAN, D. F.
FARRAND, W. R.
HEINRICH, E. W.
KELLY, W. C.
KESLER, S. E.
KESLING, R. V.
PEACOR, D. R.
POLLACK, H. N.
WILSON, J. L.

*Germanic Languages and Literatures:*
COTTRELL, A. P.
COWEN, R. C.
DUNNHAUPT, G.
GEORGE, E. E.
HUBBS, V. C.
KYES, R. L.
MARKEY, T. L.
SCHOLLER, H.
SEIDLER, I. E.

*History:*
BECKER, M. B.
BERKHOFER, R. F.
BIEN, D. D.
BOWDITCH, J.
BROOMFIELD, J. H.
BROWN, G. S.
CHANG, C. S.
CLUBB, J. M.
CRUSE, H.
DEWEY, H. W.
EADIE, J. W.
EHRENKREUTZ, A. S.
EISENSTEIN, E.
FEUERWERKER, A.
FINE, S.
GIBSON, C.
GREW, R.
HACKETT, R. F.
HOLLINGER, D. A.
HUCKER, C. O.
LIVERMORE, S.
LOCKRIDGE, K. A.
MENDEL, A. P.
MITCHELL, R. P.
PERKINS, B.
PRICE, J. M.
ROSENBERG, W. G.
SHY, J. W.
STARR, C. G.
SZPORLUK, R.
TENTLER, T. N.
TILLY, C.
TONSOR, S. J.
TRAUTMANN, T. R.
TRINKAUS, C.
UZOIGWE, G. N.
WARNER, R. M.
YOUNG, E. P.

*History of Art:*
EDWARDS, R.
EISENBERG, M.
FORSYTH, I. H.
HUNTINGTON, D. C.
MIESEL, V.
SPINK, W. M.
WHITMAN, N. T.

## UNIVERSITIES AND COLLEGES—MICHIGAN (UNIVERSITY OF) — U.S.A.

*Human Genetics:*
BREWER, G. J.
CHU, E. H.
GELEHRTER, T. D.
GERSHOWITZ, H.
LEVINE, M.
NEEL, J. V.
RUCKNAGEL, D. L
SING, C. F.
TASHIAN, R. E.

*Industrial and Operations Engineering:*
BAKKER, W.
CHAFFIN, D. B.
GALLIHER, H. P.
HANCOCK, W. M.
POLLOCK, S.
TEICHROEW, D.
WILSON, R. C.

*Internal Medicine:*
ABBRECHT, P. H.
BAUER, J. M.
BEIERWALTES, W. H.
BISHOP, R. C.
BOLE, G. G.
BREWER, G. J.
BULL, F. E.
CARPENTER, R. R.
CASSIDY, J. T.
CASTOR, C. W.
CONN, J. W.
DUFF, I. F.
ERTEL, I. J.
FAJANS, S. S.
FEKETY, F. R., Jr.
FLOYD, J. C., Jr.
FOX, I. H.
FRENCH, A. B.
GELEHRTER, T. D.
GREEN, R. A.
GREEN, W.
HARLAN, W. R.
HENLEY, K. S.
HOCH, F. L.
JOHNSON, R. D.
JOSEPH, R.
JOURDIAN, G. W.
JULIUS, S.
KELLEY, W. N.
KEYES, J. W.
KNOPF, R. F.
LO BUGLIO, A.
MCLEAN, J. A.
MATHEWS, K. P.
MATOVINOVIC, J.
MEYERS, M. C.
MIKKELSEN, W. M.
NEEL, J. V.
OSTRANDER, L. D.
PENNER, J. A.
PITT, B.
POLLARD, H. M.
ROBINSON, W. D.
RUCKNAGEL, D. L.
SCHTEINGART, D.
SISSON, J.
SOLOMAN, W. R.
TANNEN, R.
THOMPSON, G. R.
WEG, J. G.
WELLER, J. M.
WILLIS, P. W., III
ZARAFONETIS, C. J. D
ZWEIFLER, A. J.

*Journalism:*
BAKER, D. C.
CANNELL, C. F.
CLARKE, P.
FIELD, J. V.
PORTER, W. E.
STEVENS, J. D.
YABLONKY, B. L.

*Landscape Architecture:*
CARES, C. W.

JOHNSON, C. D.
JOHNSON, W. J.
POLAKOWSKI, K. J.

*Law:*
ALLEN, F. A.
ALLEN, L. E.
BLASI, V. A.
BOLLINGER, L. C.
BROWDER, O. L., Jr.
CHAMBERS, D. L.
CONARD, A. F.
COOPER, E. H.
COOPERRIDER, L. K.
CUNNINGHAM, R. A.
DONAHUE, C.
EDWARDS, H. T.
ESTEP, S. D.
GRAY, W.
GREEN, T. A.
ISRAEL, J. H.
JACKSON, J. H.
KAHN, D. A.
KAMISAR, Y.
KAUPER, T. E.
KENNEDY, F. R.
LEMPERT, R. O.
MARTIN, J. A.
PEARCE, J. R.
PIERCE, W. J.
PLANT, M. L.
POOLEY, B. J.
PROFFITT, R. F.
REED, J. W.
REGAN, D. H.
ST. ANTOINE, T. J
SANDALOW, T.
SAX, J. L.
SMITH, A. F.
SOPER, E. P.
STEIN, E.
STEINER, P.
VINING, G. J.
WAGGONER, L. W.
WATSON, A. S.
WESTON, P.
WHITE, J. J.
WRIGHT, L. H.

*Library Science:*
BIDLACK, R. E.
BONK, W. J.
DOUGHERTY, R. M.
HESSLER, D. W.
LLOYD, H. D.
MAGRILL, R. M.
RINEHART, C.
SLAVENS, T. P.
VAINSTEIN, R.
VANCE, K. E.
WARNER, R. M.
WEICHLEIN, W. J.

*Linguistics:*
BECKER, A. L.
BURLING, R.
CATFORD, J. C.
GEDNEY, W. J.
MARKEY, T. L.
SCHRAMM, G. M.
SELINKER, L.

*Materials and Metallurgical Engineering:*
BIGELOW, W. C.
FLINN, R. A.
HOSFORD, W. F.
HUCKE, E. E.
LESLIE, W. C.
PEHLKE, R. D.
RAGONE, D. V.
SINNOTT, M. J.
TIEN, T. Y.
VANVLACK, L. H.
YEH, G. S. Y.
YOUNG, E. H.

*Mathematics:*
BROWN, M.
BRUMFIEL, C. F.
CESARI, L.
DICKSON, D. G.
DOLPH, C. L.
DUREN, P. L.
FEDERBUSH, P. G.
GEHRING, F. W.
HARARY, F.
HAY, G. E.
HEINS, A. E.
HIGMAN, D. G.
HOCHSTER, M.
JONES, P. S.
KAPLAN, W.
KINCAID, W. M.
KISTER, J. M.
KRAUSE, E. F.
LEWIS, D. J
LYNDON, R. C.
MCLAUGHLIN, J. E.
MILNE, J. S.
MONTGOMERY, H. L.
NESBITT, C. J.
PEARCY, C. M.
PIRANIAN, G.
RAMANUJAN, M. S.
RAYMOND, F. A.
READE, M. O.
SHIELDS, A. L.
SMOLLER, J. A.
TAYLOR, B. A.
TITUS, C. J.
ULLMAN, J. L.
WENDEL, J. G.
WINTER, D. J.
WOODROOFE, M. B.

*Mechanical Engineering:*
ALVORD, H. H.
ARPACI, V. S.
BOLT, J. A.
CADDELL, R. M.
CHACE, M. A.
CLARK, J. A.
COLWELL, L. V.
DATSKO, J.
EVALDSON, R. L.
FELBECK, D. K.
FREDERICK, J. R.
HAMMITT, F. G.
JUVINALL, R. C.
LADY, E. R.
LUDEMA, K. C.
MERTE, H.
MIRSKY, W.
PEARSON, J. R.
PRATT, D. T.
QUACKENBUSH, L. J.
SEGEL, L.
SMITH, G. E.
SONNTAG, R. E.
SPRINGER, G. S.
VEST, C. M.
YANG, W. J.

*Medical Care Organization:*
BASHSHUR, R. L.
BERKI, S. E.
DARSKY, B. J.
DONABEDIAN, A.
FEINGOLD, E. N.
METZNER, C. A.
PENCHANSKY, R.

*Microbiology:*
CLEWELL, D. B.
COOPER, S.
FRETER, R.
FRIEDMAN, D. I.
JUNI, E.
KEMPE, L. L.
LOESCHE, W. J.
MURPHY, W. H.
NEIDHARDT, F. C.

Olsen, R. H.
Savageau, M. A.
Wheeler, A. H.

*Music:*
Bassett, L. R.
Bossart, R. E.
Boylan, P.
Britton, A. P.
Browne, R.
Bryan, K.
Bundra, F.
Cavender, G. R.
Chudacoff, E. M.
Clark, R.
Clark, R.
Clough, J.
Cooper, L. H.
Crawford, D.
Crawford, R.
Derr, E.
Dexter, B. W.
Fisher, C. R.
Froseth, J.
Glasgow, R.
Herbert, R.
Hilbish, T.
Hord, R. W.
Hurst, L.
Jacobi, R. E.
Jelinek, J. M.
Krachmalnick, J. M.
Lehman, P.
Lettvin, T.
Lewis, R.
Likova, E. M.
Lillya, C. P.
Makanowitzky, P.
McCollum, J. M.
McPeek, G. S.
Malm, W. P.
Mariotti, A.
Mason, M.
Mayes, S.
Meier, G.
Mohler, J.
Owen, C.
Patterson, W. C.
Reyes, A.
Reynolds, R.
Rosseels, G. A.
Sandor, G.
Sinta, D. J.
Smith, G. P.
Standifer, J.
Stout, L. J.
Torchinsky, A.
Tyler, V.
Wallace, J. B.
Warner, R. A.
Watkins, G. E.
Weichlein, W. J.
Wilson, G. B.

*Naval Architecture and Marine Engineering:*
Benford, H. B.
Couch, R. B.
D'Arcangelo, A. M.
Kaldjian, M. J.
Ogilvie, T. F.
Woodward, J. B.
Yagle, R. A.

*Natural Resources:*
Barnes, B. V.
Bassett, J. R.
Bulkley, J. W.
Cares, C. W.
Carow, J.
Drake, W. D.
Feldt, A. G.
Gregory, G. R.
Hooper, F. F.
Johnson, C. D.
Johnson, W. J.
Kaplan, R.
Lagler, K. F.

MacKinnon, D. A.
McCullough, D. R.
Michael, D. N.
Morton, H. L.
Olson, C. E.
Patterson, R. L.
Polakowski, K. J.
Preston, S. B.
Schramm, G.
Stapp, W. B.
Smith, S.
Suits, G. H.
Tocher, S. R.

*Near Eastern Languages and Literatures:*
Abdel-Massih, E. T.
Bellamy, J. A.
Ehrenkreutz, A. S.
Freedman, D. N.
Krahmalkov, C. R.
LeGassick, T. J.
Luther, K. A.
McCarus, E. N.
Mendenhall, G. E.
Orlin, L. L.
Rammuny, R. M.
Schramm, G. M.
Stewart-Robinson, J. M. L.
Windfuhr, G. L.

*Neurology:*
Casey, K. L.
Feringa, E. R.
Gilman, S.
Kooi, K. A.
Magee, K. R.
Siegel, G. J.
Westerberg, M. R

*Nuclear Engineering:*
Akcasu, Z.
Bach, D. R.
Duderstadt, J. J.
Kammash, T.
Kerr, W.
Kikuchi, C.
King, J. S.
Knoll, G. F.
Osborn, R. K.
Summerfield, G. C.
Vincent, D. H.

*Nursing:*
Davis, C. K.
Donabedian, D.
Gage, L. E.
Hansen, B.
Horsley, J.
Judd, J. M.
Kalisch, B. J.
Kalisch, P.
Lohr, M.
Loomis, M. E.
McCain, R. F.
Marshall, N. E.
Murphy, M. M.
Reynolds, M.
Sana, J. M.
Schultz, S.
Shryock, A.
Strang, R.
Swain, M. A.

*Obstetrics and Gynaecology:*
Morley, G. W.
Willson, J. R.

*Ophthalmology:*
Alpern, M.
Green, D. G.
Henderson, J. W.
Lichter, P. R.
Wolter, J. R.

*Otorhinolaryngology:*
Gross, N.
Hawkins, J. E.
Krause, C. J.

Lawrence, M.
Stebbins, W.
Work, W. P.

*Pathology:*
Abell, M. R.
Abrams, G. D.
Appelman, H. D.
Batsakis, J. G.
Baublis, J. V.
Feringa, E. R.
French, A. J.
Gronvall, J. A.
Hart, W. R.
Headington, J. T.
Hendrix, R. C.
Hicks, S. P.
Hinerman, D. L.
Midgeley, A. R.
Naylor, B.
Nishiyama, R. H.
Oberman, H. A.
Rowe, N. H.
Schmidt, R. W.
Schnitzer, B.
Wolter, J. R.

*Paediatrics and Communicable Diseases:*
Allen, R.
Bacon, G.
Baublis, J.
Cassidy, J.
DeMuth, G.
Dickinson, D.
Ertel, I.
Gibson, R.
Hartsook, J.
Hennessy, A.
Heyn, R.
Howatt, W.
Kelch, R. P.
Kelsch, R. C.
Oliver, W.
Owen, G.
Rosenthal, A.
Schmickel, R.
Smith, D.
Stern, A.
Strang, R.
Sullivan, D.
Wegman, M.

*Pharmacology:*
Counsell, R. E.
La Du, B. N., Jr.
Domino, E. F.
Lucchesi, B. R.
Smith, C. B.
Swain, H. H.
Weber, W. W.
Zannoni, V. G.

*Pharmacy:*
Burckhalter, J. H.
Counsell, R. E.
Flynn, G. L.
Higuchi, W. I.
Ho, N. F. H.
Paul, A. G.
Richards, J. W.
Rowe, T. D.
Sinsheimer, J. E.
Townsend, L. B.
Wagner, J. G.
Weiner, N. D.

*Philosophy:*
Bergmann, F.
Brandt, R. B.
Burks, A. W.
Fine, K.
Frankena, W. K.
Gibbard, A. F.
Goldman, A. I.
Kim, J.
Mavrodes, G. I.

MEILAND, J. W.
MUNRO, D. J.
SKLAR, L.

**Physical Medicine and Rehabilitation:**
COLE, T.
RAE, J. W.

**Physics:**
AKERLOF, C.
CHAPMAN, J. W.
COFFIN, C. T.
FORD, G. W.
HAZEN, W. E.
HECHT, K. T.
HENDEL, A. Z.
JANECKE, J. W.
JONES, L. W.
KANE, G. L.
KATZ, E.
KRIMM, S.
KRISCH, A. D.
LEWIS, R. R.
LONGO, M. J.
MEYER, D. I.
OVERSETH, O. E.
PARKINSON, W. C.
PETERS, C. W.
RICH, A.
ROE, B. P.
ROSS, M. H.
SANDERS, T. M., Jr.
SANDS, R. H.
SINCLAIR, D. A.
TERWILLIGER, K. M.
TICKLE, R. S.
TOMOZAWA, Y.
VANDERVELDE, J. C.
WARD, J. F.
WEINREICH, G.
WIEDENBECK, M. L.
WILLIAMS, W. L.
YAO, Y. P. E.
ZORN, J. C.

**Physiology:**
ABBRECHT, P. H.
ALPERN, M.
BEAN, J.
BOHR, D.
CASEY, K. L.
DAVENPORT, H. W.
FAULKNER, J.
JACQUEZ, J.
JOCHIM, K. E.
MALVIN, P.
RUTLEDGE, L. T.
SPARKS, H.
VANDER, A. J.

**Political Science:**
ABERBACH, J. D.
ANTON, T. J.
BARNES, S. H.
CONVERSE, P. E.
ELDERSVELD, S. J.
FIFIELD, R. H.
GRACE, F.
GRASSMUCK, G. L.
INGLEHART, R. F.
JACOBSON, H. K.
JENNINGS, M. K.
KINGDON, J. W.
MAZRUI, A. A.
MEYER, A. G.
MILLER, W. E.
MOHR, L. M.
ORGANSKI, A. F. K.
OKSENBERG, M. C.
PARK, R. L.
PIERCE, R.
PUTNAM, R. D.
REHMUS, C. M.
SINGER, J. D.
TANTER, R.
WALKER, J. L.
WHITING, A. S.
ZIMMERMAN, W.

*Postgraduate Medicine and Health Professions Education:*
DE KORNFELD, T. J.
HARLAN, W. R.
HISS, R. G.
HODGE, G. P.
JOHNSON, R. D.

*Psychiatry:*
AGRANOFF, B. W.
ARTHUR, B.
BLUMENTHAL, M.
CARROLL, B.
CURTIS, G.
HARRISON, S. I.
HEINE, R.
HENDRICKSON, W. J.
HORVATH, W.
KOCHEN, M.
KOOI, K. A.
KORNBLUM, S.
MARGOLIS, P. M.
MARSDEN, K. G.
NAGERA, H.
POZNANSKI, E.
QUARTON, G. C.
RADIN, N.
SELZER, M. L.
SHEVRIN, H.
SILVERMAN, A. J.
WATSON, A. S.

*Psychology:*
ADELSON, J.
ALPERN, M.
ANDREWS, F.
ARTHUR, B.
ATKINSON, J.
BALER, L. A.
BARDWICK, J.
BORDIN, E.
BROWN, D. R.
BURNSTEIN, E.
BUTTER, C.
CAIN, A.
CAMPBELL, A.
COOMBS, C.
CRUICKSHANK, W.
DAVIS, R.
DOUVAN, E.
ERICKSEN, S.
FAST, I.
FRENCH, J.
GEORGOPOULOS, B.
GORDON, J.
GREEN, D.
GUIORA, A.
GURIN, P.
HAGEN, J.
HOFFMAN, L.
HOFFMAN, M.
KAHN, R.
KAPLAN, S.
KRANTZ, D. H.
LAWLER, E.
LAWRENCE, M.
LINGOES, J.
MANIS, M.
MANN, R. D.
MARSDEN, G.
MAYMAN, M.
MCCONNELL, J.
MCKEACHIE, W. J.
MICHAEL, D.
MORSE, W. C.
NISBETT, R.
NORMAN, W. T.
PELZ, D.
POLLACK, I.
PRICE, R.
REITMAN, W. R.
RHODES, W.
ROSENWALD, G. C.
SEASHORE, S. E.
SHEVRIN, H.
SMITH, J. E. K.

STEBBINS, W. C.
STEVENSON, H. W.
TANNENBAUM, A. S.
THOMAS, E. J., Jr.
UTTAL, W. R.
VALENSTEIN, E. S.
VEROFF, J.
WEINTRAUB, D.
WITHEY, S. B.
WOLOWITZ, H.
ZAJONC, R. B.
ZANDER, A. F.

*Radiology:*
BRINKER, R.
FAYOS, J. V.
GABRIELSON, T. O.
HOLT, J. F.
KEYES, J.
MARTEL, W.
POZNANSKI, A. K.
THORNBURY, J. R.
TUCKER, A.

*Resource Ecology:*
BARNES, B. V.
HOOPER, F. F.
LAGLER, K. F.
MCCULLOUGH, D. R.

*Resource Policy and Management:*
ANDREWS, R. N.
BULKLEY, J. W.
DRAKE, W. D.
FELDT, A. G.
GREGORY, G. R.
LAGLER, K. F.
MICHAEL, D. N.
OLSON, C. E., Jr.
PRESTON, S. B.

*Romance Languages and Literatures:*
BÜDEL, O.
CARDUNER, J. R.
CASA, F. P.
CHAMBERS, L. R.
FRAKER, C. F.
GOIC, C.
GRAY, F. F.
HAFTER, M. Z.
ILIE, P.
LOPEZ-GRIGERA, L.
MERHAB, W. G.
MORGAN, R., Jr.
MULLER, M.
NELSON, R. J.
O'NEILL, J. C.
PULGRAM, E.
WYERS, F.

*Slavic Languages and Literatures:*
BROWN, D. B.
DEWEY, H. W.
HUMESKY, A. K.
MATEJKA, L.
MERSEREAU, J., Jr.
PROFFER, C.
STOLZ, B. A.
TITUNIK, I. R.
WELSH, D.

*Social Work:*
BERNARD, S. E.
BERTCHER, H. J.
CHURCHILL, S. R.
COOK, L. M.
COSTABILE, J. E.
CROXTON, T. A.
DINSMORE, M. L.
EPSTEIN, I.
FELD, S. C.
FELLIN, P. A.
FERMAN, L. A.
GARVIN, C. D.
GOMBERG, E. S.
GORDON, J. E.
HARTMAN, L. A.

Hasenfeld, Y.
Johnson, H. R.
Kilpatrick, D. M.
Lauffer, A. A.
Maple, F. F.
Neenan, W. B.
Radin, N.
Robinson, D.
Rothman, J.
Sarri, R. C.
Thomas, E. J.
Tripodi, T.
Tropman, J. E.
Vinter, R. D.
Wolfson, C. S.

*Sociology:*
Campbell, A. A.
Cole, R. E.
Converse, P. E.
Farley, R.
Freedman, R.
Gamson, W. A.
Goldberg, D.
Hermalin, A.
Kish, L.
Landecker, W. S.
Miner, H. M.
Ness, G. D.
Schuman, H. D.
Tilly, C.
Zald, M.

*Speech:*
Austin, H. R.
Bender, J. E.
Billings, A. G.
Hildebrandt, H. W.
Martin, H. H.
Meyer, R. D.
Okey, L. L.
Rupp, R. R.
Sharf, D. J.
Smith, A.
Weisfeld, Z. H.
Wiley, J. H.
Willis, E. E.

*Statistics:*
Ericson, W. A.
Hill, B. M.
Howry, P.
Hymans, S.
Kmenta, J.
Smith, J. K. E.
Starr, N.
Woodroofe, M.

*Surgery:*
Bailey, R. W.
Behrendt, D.
Bonnette, G. H.
Coon, W. W.
Coran, A. G.
Dent, T. L.
Grabb, W. C.
Hayward, J. R.
Kaufer, H.
Kindt, G. W.
Kirsh, M. M.
Lapides, J.
Lindenauer, S. M.
Schneider, R. C.
Sloan, H. E., Jr.
Smith, W. S.
Taren, J. A.
Thompson, N. W.
Turcotte, J. G.
Vinik, A. I.

*Wildlife and Fisheries:*
Bassett, J. R.
Hooper, F. F.
Lagler, K. F.
Patterson, R. L.

Selected Institutions Attached to the University:

English Language Institute, Kresge Hearing Research Institute, Simpson Memorial Institute, Mental Health Research Institute, Institute for Human Adjustment, Institute for Social Research, Institute for the Study of Mental Retardation, Institute of Gerontology, Institute of Labor and Industrial Relations, Institute of Public Policy Studies, Institute of Environmental and Industrial Health, Institute of Science and Technology, Highway Safety Research Institute, Center for Chinese Studies, Center for Japanese Studies, Center for Near Eastern and North African Studies, Center for Russian Studies, Center for South and Southeast Asian Studies, Lawrence D. Buhl Genetics Research Center for Human Genetics, Urban Planning, Center for Human Growth and Development, Center for Research on Language and Language Behavior, Center for the Study of Higher Education, Center for Research on Learning and Teaching, Computing Center, Biological Station, Botanical Gardens, University Herbarium, Museum of Anthropology, Museum of Paleontology, Museum of Zoology, University Observatories, Program in Ecology, Middle English Dictionary, Clinical Research Unit, Nuclear Medicine Unit, Bureau of Hospital Administration, Center for Continuing Education of Women, Bureau of Public Health Economics, Rackham Arthritis Research Unit, Michigan Memorial Phoenix Project, Center for Population Planning and Population Studies, Hypersonic Wind Tunnel, Cyclotron Laboratory, Cooley Electronics Laboratory, High-Altitude Engineering Laboratory, Electron Physics Laboratory, Radiation Laboratory, Systems Engineering Laboratory, Ship Hydrodynamic Laboratory.

There are more than one hundred other research units attached to the schools, colleges and departments.

## University of Michigan—Dearborn
Dearborn, Michigan 48128

*Chancellor:* William A. Jenkins, M.S., Ph.D.

Number of students: 6,360.

## University of Michigan—Flint
Flint, Michigan 48503
Telephone: (313) 762-3300.

Founded 1956.

State control; Academic year: September to April.

*Chancellor:* Conny E. Nelson.
*Provost and Vice-Chancellor for Academic Affairs:* Margarette F. Eby.
*Vice-Chancellor for Budget and Finance:* James L. Murdock.
*Vice-Chancellor for University Services:* Marvin J. Roberson.

*Registrar:* Mogens F. Jensen.
*Librarian:* David W. Palmer.

The library contains 106,000 vols.
Number of teachers: 209.
Number of students: 4,410.

Deans and Directors:
*College of Arts and Sciences:* (vacant).
*School of Management:* Richard W. Fortner.
*Nursing:* Ellen A. Woodman.
*Graduate and Special Programs:* Gregory L. Waters.

## WAYNE STATE UNIVERSITY
Detroit, Michigan 48202
Telephone: (313) 577-2424.

Oldest antecedent college founded 1868, University 1933.

*President:* Thomas N. Bonner, Ph.D.
*Senior Vice-President and Treasurer:* Charles F. Sturtz, M.A.
*Provost:* Guy Stern, Ph.D.
*Vice-President for State and Congressional Relations:* Norman J. Schlafmann, Ph.D.
*Vice-Presidnt for Human Resources:* Ross E. Taylor, M.B.A.
*Vice-President for Student Affairs:* W. Markus, Ph.D.
*Vice-President for University Relations:* Arthur L. Johnson, M.A.
*Vice-President and Secretary to the Board:* Martin Barr, Ph.D.
*Registrar:* J. Richard Thorderson, Ph.D.
*Librarian:* Vern M. Pings, Ph.D.

Number of teachers: 2,310.
Number of students: 17,663 men, 515,81 women, total 33,524.

Deans:
*College of Education:* J. Edward Simpkins, Ed.D.
*College of Engineering:* Stanley K. Stynes, Ph.D.
*College of Liberal Arts:* M. Stearns, Ph.D.
*College of Nursing:* Lorene R. Fischer, M.A., R.N.
*College of Pharmacy and Allied Health Professions:* Eberhard F. Mammen, M.D.
*School of Social Work:* S. Dillick, Ph.D.
*School of Medicine:* Robert D. Coye, M.D.
*Law School:* Donald H. Gordon, LL.M.
*School of Business Administration:* Victor Doherty, Ph.D.
*College of Lifelong Learning:* Robert Hubbard, Ph.D.
*Graduate Studies:* Albert Bharuchua-Reid, A.B.
*Director of Health and Physical Education:* Chalmer G. Hixson, Ph.D.
*Director of University Clinics and Health Care Institute:* H. H. Gardner, M.D.

## PROFESSORS:

### School of Business Administration:

**Accounting:**
ALVIN, G.
ROBERTS. A.

**General Business:**
FORSYTHE, E. J.
HOUGH, L.
SPENCER, M.

**Management:**
DESPELDER, B.
DOHERTY, V.
FORSYTHE, E. J.

**Marketing:**
JOHNSON, H. W.

### College of Education:

**Academic Services:**
REILLY, H.
McCORMICK, C. A.

**Educational Leadership:**
BOICOURT, G.
CHILDS, J.
CLUTE, M.
DEMONT, R.
ELLSWORTH, R.
ESTVAN, F.
HAGMAN, H.
HAMILTON, J.
HILLMAN, L.
HOTH, W.
HOUGH, W.
PETERSON, R. D.
RISLOV, S.
SIMPKINS, E. J.
SMITH, M.
VRICK, R.

**Library Science:**
BOOTH, R.
CASEY, G.
GRAZIER, M.

**Teacher Education:**
BATESON, W.
BISSETT, D.
COLEMAN, T. W., Jr.
COLVIN, C.
COOK, F.
DOUGLAS, M.
FAIR, J.
HARRINGTON, F.
HUGHES, P.
KAPLAN, L.
LANHAM, F.
MIKELSON, S.
SANDERS, P.
SMITH, E. B., Jr.
SMITH, E. P.
SMITH, G.
STONE, S.
SUCHARA, H.
VANDERLINDE, L.
WEILEY, E.
YOUKSTETTER, F. O.

**Theoretical and Behavioural Foundations:**
ADAMEK, E. G., Jr.
AMBINDER, W.
BARAHAL, G.
BROWN, A.
CANTONI, L.
CAMPBELL, J. F.
CHAMPLIN, N.
CITRON, A.
COLLIER, J.
DEWITT, J.
DOYLE, G. T.
IRWIN, C.
KERBER, A.
KOUNIN, J.
LEONARD, G. E.

MARCOTTE, D.
NEFF, F.
OFCHUS, L.
PIETROTESA, J.
SPLETE, H.
VRIEND, J.
WATTENBERG, W.
WURTZ, R.

### College of Engineering:

**Chemical Engineering:**
COREY, C. L.
DONNELLY, H. G.
FISHER, E. R.
KUMMLER, R.
MARRIOTT, R.
ROTHE, E. W.
STYNES, S. K.

**Civil:**
CHENEY, L. T.
PAULSON, J. M.

**Electrical and Computer Engineering:**
BARNARD, R. D.
BRAMMER, F. E.
FENG, T.
DELLA TORRE, E.
MEISEL, J.
SATHER, R. O.
SCHERBA, M. B.
SHAW, M. P.
WANG, E. Y.
YU, F. T.

**Graphics:**
DeSILVA, C. N.

**Industrial Engineering and Operations Research:**
CHRISTENSEN, J.
JONES, A. W.
KNAPPENBERGER, H. A.
KROEMER, K.

**Mechanical Engineering:**
CARMI, S.
DeSILVA, C. N.
HENEIN, N. A
HOWELL, G. H.
KING, A. I.
KLINE, K.
LEE, J. P.
PICCIRELLI, A. R.
RABINS, M. J.
SACHS, H. K.

**Metallurgical Engineering:**
COREY, C. L.
HIMMEL, L.
ROL, P.

### Law School:
ADELMAN, M.
BARTKE, R. W.
BARTOSIC, F.
BORMAN, P. D.
CALLAHAN, K. R.
DOLAN, J. F.
FRIEDMAN, JANE M.
GLAVIN, J. E.
GLENNON, R. J., Jr.
GORDON, D.
GRANO, J.
HARBRECHT, P. P.
HETZEL, O.
KELMAN, M.
LAMBORN, L.
LANNING, G. J.
LITTLEJOHN, E.
LOMBARD, A. J.
LOMBARD, F. K.
McINTYRE, M. J.
MOGK, J E.
PLATER, Z.
SCHENK, A.
SCHULMAN, S. H.
SEDLER, R. A.

SHUMAN, S. I.
SLOVENKO, R.
STRICHARTZ, R.
TIERNEY, K.
WISE, E. M.

### College of Liberal Arts:

**Anthropology:**
CHRISTENSEN, J. B.
MOSS, L. W.
PILLING, A. R.

**Art and Art History:**
ALLEN, W. A.
ANDREWS, W.
BECKER, W. C.
CONSTANTINE, OLGA
FIKE, P. G.
GILLERAN, P. J.
GOLDMAN, B.
GUTMANN, J.
MILLER, L. A.
MITCHELL, D. A.
NOBILI, L. J.
SMITH, G. ALDEN
WILBERT, R. J.
WOODWARD, W. T.

**Biology:**
CHAVIN, W.
COOK, D. R.
COSGRIFF, J. W., Jr.
DeGIUSTI, D. L.
FOOR, E.
GANGWERE, S. K.
IZAWA, S.
JAY, J. M.
LEVINE, L.
MATTMAN, H.
MAYEDA, K.
MIZUKAMI, H.
PRYCHODKO, W.
ROGERS, C. M.
ROSSMOORE, H. W.
SIEGEL, A. E.
TAYLOR, J.
THOMPSON, W. L.

**Chemistry:**
BACH, R.
EBBING, D. D.
ENDICOTT, J. F.
GAYER, K. H.
GLICK, M. D.
HAHN, R. B.
JOHNSON. C. R.
KEVAN, L.
KIMURA, T.
KIRSCHNER, S.
LeBEL, N. A.
LIM, E.
LINTVELDT, R.
McCLAIN, W. H.
OLIVER, J. P.
POWERS, W. H.
RABAN, M.
RECK, G.
RORABACHER, D.
SCHENK, G. H., Jr.
STEVENS, C. L.
TCHEN, T. T.
TRIVICH, D.

**Computer Science Education:**
WESTERVELDT, F. H.

**Economics:**
FAND, D.
FINN, T. J., Jr.
GOODMAN, I. B.
KAHN, M. L.
LEVIN, J. H.
MATTILA, J. M.
OWEN, J. D.
PAAUW, D. S.

ROSKAMP, K. W.
SMYTH, D.
THOMPSON, W. R.

*English:*
GOLDEN, S. A.
GOLDSMITH, A. L.
HAFNER, C. Y.
HERNLUND, P.
HUGHES, D. J.
NASH, R. L.
PRESCOTT, J.
REED, J. R.
RUMBLE, T. C.
SCHWARZ, A.
WAGNER, V.
WILLIAMSON, M. L.
YU, B.

*Family and Consumer Resources:*
CALLARD, E. D.
BOSTICK, M.
WILLIAMS, W. T.

*Geography:*
DOHRS, F. E.
GOODMAN, R. J.
SINCLAIR, R.

*Geology:*
DRISCOLL, E. G.
MOZOLA, A. J.
RONCA, L. B.

*Greek and Latin:*
MINADEO, R. W.

*History:*
BONNER, T. N.
BRAZILL, W. J., Jr.
BURKS, R. V.
COVENSKY, M.
GILB, C.
GUICE, C. N.
HALL, E. C.
HOOPER, F. A.
MAGOULIAS, H.
MASON, P.
MILES, R. D.
SMALL, M.
SMITH, G. A.
ZIEGER, R.

*Humanities:*
GOLDMAN, B.
HERMAN, M.
LEOPOLD, S.
MCCOY, A.
VOGELBAUM, J.

*Mathematics:*
BHARUCHA-REID, R.
BROWN, L.
CHOW, P.-L.
EISENSTADT, B. J.
HANDEL, D.
HOUH, C.-S.
IRWIN, J. M.
ITO, T.
LAURENT, A. G.
NISHIURA, T.
OWENS, O. G.
SCHREIBER, B. H.
TSAO, C. K.
WECHSLER, M. T.

*Music:*
ARNOLDI, H.
CUCCI, A.
DELEONARD, M. F.
FAVA, J.
FERGUSON, R. P.
JOHNS, M. M.
LABUTA, J.
LANGSFORD, H. M.
LAWSON, R. F.
TICKTON, J. H.
YOUNG, C. W.

*Near Eastern and Asian Studies:*
LASSNER, J.

*Philosophy:*
ANGELL, R.
STERN, A.

*Physics:*
BEARD, G. B.
BERES, W.
BOHM, H. V.
DEGRAAF, A.
DENMAN, H. H.
FAVRO, L.
FRADKIN, D.
GUPTA, S. N.
GUSTAFSON, D. R.
KIM, Y. W.
SAPERSTEIN, A. M.
STEARNS, M.
STEWART, M. G., Jr.
THOMAS, R.

*Political Science:*
CHEN, P.-C.
CUSHMAN, E. L.
DOWNING, R. G.
FEINSTEIN, O.
FLEMING, T.
FRIEDLAND, L. L.
GOULD, W.
MARK, M.
PARRISH, C. J.
PRATT, H. J.
SEIDLER, M. B.
VINYARD, C. D.
WATERS, M.

*Psychology:*
AGER, J.
ALEXANDER, S.
ANDERSON, L. R.
ASDOURIAN, D.
BASS, A.
ELLIOTT, D. N.
GARDNER, L. H.
LACHMAN, S. J.
LEVENTHAL, G.
LEVY, S.
ROSEN, H.
ROSENBAUM, G.
SALTZ, E.
SHANTZ, C. A.
SOLLEY, C. M., Jr.
STAGNER, R.
STETTNER, L.
TEAHAN, J.

*Romance and Germanic Languages:*
ALMAZAN, V. C.
BASSAN, F.
BERSHAS, H. N.
CIRRE, M. M.
DAEMMRICH, H. S.
GOFF, P.
KAPUSTIN, M.
SCHINDLER, M.
SMITH, E. B.

*Slavic and Eastern European Languages:*
CIZEVSKA, T.
ORDON, E.

*Sociology:*
ALBINI, J.
ESHLEMAN, J. R.
KAHANA, E.
RAVITZ, M. J.
SAFILIOS-ROTHSCHILD, C.
WARSHAY, L.
WOLF, ELEANOR

*Speech and Mass Communication Arts:*
BROCK, B.
HAZZARD, R. T.
LEITH, W.
LEONE, L.
PAPPAS, E.
ROSS, R. S.

SMITH, R. E.
TINTERA, J. B.
ZIEGELMUELLER, G. W.

*Urban Planning:*
HONZATKO, G.
RAVITZ, M. J.

*Health and Physical Education:*
HIXSON, C.
MULHAUSER, F. A.
WASSON W. N.

School of Medicine:

*Anatomy:*
BERNSTEIN, M. H.
BOVING, B.
GOODMAN, M.
LASKER, G. W.
MAISEL, H.
MEYER, D. B.
MIZERES, N. J.

*Audiology:*
LYNN, G.

*Biochemistry:*
BROOKS, S.
BROWN, R. K.
LEE, C. P.
TSERNOGLOV, D.
VINOGRADOV, S.

*Immunology and Microbiology:*
BERK, R.
JEFFRIES, C.
KONG, Y.-C.
LEON, M.
RICH, M. A.
ROSE, N.
SWANBERG, R. H.
WEINER, L. M.

*Physiology:*
BAECHLER, C. A.
BARNHART, MARION I.
HENRY, R. L.
MAMMEN, E. F.
SEEGERS, W. H.
SHEPARD, R. S.

*Anaesthesiology:*
BROWN, E.
DALSANTO, G.

*Dermatology and Syphilology:*
BIRMINGHAM, D. J.
BOTVINICK, I.

*Internal Medicine:*
AXELROD, A.
BRENNAN, M.
CARTER, B.
CLAPPER, I. M.
EICHENHOLTZ, A.
HULL, F.
JONES, D.
LERNER, A. M.
LEWIS, B. M.
LUCAS, C.
MCDONALD, F.
MACK, R.
MADRID, F.
POWER, L. H.
PRASAD, A. S.
PURI, P.
SCHLESS, J.
TALMERS, F.
WEISSLER, A.

*Neurology:*
BAUER, R. B.
CHURCHILL, J. A.
GILROY, J.
MAULSBY, R.
REDDING, F.
RODIN, E.

*Neurosurgery:*
HODGSON, V. R.
**THOMAS, L. M.**

*Gynaecology and Obstetrics:*
BEHRMAN, S. J.
BOVING, B. G.
EVANS, T. N.
HAFEZ, E.
MOGHISSI, K.
SHERMAN, A.
SMITH, J. P.

*Occupational and Environmental:*
REEVES, A. L.

*Oncology:*
HORWITZ, J. P.
KESSEL, D. H.
SIMPSON, W.
VAITKEVICIUS, V. K.

*Community Medicine:*
GOLDBERG, T.

*Family Medicine:*
HESS, J. W.

*Comparative Medicine:*
DE GIUSTI, D.
EDWARDS, A. G.

*Ophthalmology:*
ESSNER, E.
HARDING, C.
**JAMPEL, R. S.**

*Orthopaedic Surgery:*
**PEDERSEN, H. E.**

*Otolaryngology:*
**BEEKHUIS, G. J.**
HAUSER, I. J.
PROCTOR, B.
WAGGONER, L.

*Paediatrics:*
COHEN, F.
COHEN, S.
DAJANI, A. S.
DONE, A. K.
GREEN, E.
KRIEGER, I.
LUSHER, J.
PENSLER, L.
POLGAR, G.
WHITTEN, C.
WOLLEY, P. V.

*Pathology:*
COYE, R. D.
GIACOMELI, F. E.
KALDORE, G.
MAMMEN, E.
THIBERT, R.
WIENER, J.
ZAK, B.

*Pharmacology:*
ANDERSON, G.
DONE, A.
DUTTA, S.
GOODMAN, H.
KESSEL, D.
MARKS, B.

*Physical Medicine and Rehabilitation:*
BENDER, L.
HONET, J. C.
SCHAEFFER, J. N.

*Physiology:*
BARNHART, M.
FOA, P.
GALA, R.
HENRY, N.
MAMMEN, F.
SEEGERS, W.
SHEPARD, R.

*Psychiatry:*
FISCHHOFF, J.
LUBY, E.
ROZENZWEIG, N.
SCHORER, C. E.

*Radiology:*
CHAVIN, W.
**KRABBENHUFT, K. C.**
**KURTZMAN, R. S.**
WOLLSCHLAEGER, G.
WOLLSCHLAEGER, P. B.

*Urology:*
PERLMUTTER, A. D.
**PIERCE, J. M., Jr.**

*Surgery:*
KANTROWITZ, A.
KROME, R. L.
LUCAS, C.
NICKEL, W.
ROSENBERG, I. K.
ROSENBERG, J. C.
**WALT, A. J.**
WILSON, R. F.

*College of Nursing:*
CLELAND, V.
FISCHER, L.
GOTTDANK, M.
JOHNSON, J.
McARTHUR, B.
REILLY, D.

*College of Pharmacy and Allied Health Professions:*
ABRAMSON, H. N.
BARR, M.
**DAUPHINAIS, R. J.**
**DUNKER, M. F.**
LOUIS-FERDINAND, R.
MAMMEN, E.
MOORE, W.
NAGWEKAR, J.
SCHNEBLY, M.
WORMSER, H.

*School of Social Work:*
DILLICK, S.
HOURIHAN, J. P.
**HURWITZ, J. I.**
**LEBEAUX, C.**
LUCAS, L.
MAHAFFEY, M.
RUSNACK, B.
SPITZER, K.
WINEMAN, D.

*College of Lifelong Learning:*
BAILS, J. C.
JACKSON, H. M.
MAIER, C.
THOMAS, R.
WRIGHT, R.

*Department of Mortuary Science:*
POOL, W. D.
ROSE, G. W.

## WESTERN MICHIGAN UNIVERSITY
KALAMAZOO, MICHIGAN 49008

*President:* JOHN T. BERNHARD.
*Vice-President for Academic Affairs:* E. B. EHRLE.
*Vice-President for Finance:* R. B. WETNIGHT.
*Vice-President for Student Affairs:* T. E. COYNE.
*Controller:* J. SCHWEMMIN.
*Registrar:* D. BOYLE.

*Librarian:* C. H. SACHTLEBEN.
Number of students: 20,689.

DEANS:

*Business:* D. E. JONES.
*Applied Sciences:* C. W. FITCH.
*Arts and Sciences:* A. B. CLARKE.
*Education:* J. E. SANDBERG.
*Graduate:* L. GROTZINGER.
*General Studies:* N. C. GREENBERG.
*Fine Arts:* R. LUSCOMBE.
*Continuing Education:* R. BURKE.

# MINNESOTA

## AUGSBURG COLLEGE
731 21ST AVENUE SOUTH,
MINNEAPOLIS,
MINNESOTA 55454

Telephone: (612) 330-1000.

Founded 1869.

*President:* CHARLES S. ANDERSON, PH.D.
*Registrar:* JOHN A. HILL.
*Librarian:* MARGARET ANDERSON.

The library contains 158,000 vols.
Number of teachers: 110.
Number of students: 1,428 full-time, 73 part-time.

Publication: *Augsburg College Now* (quarterly).

## BEMIDJI STATE UNIVERSITY
BEMIDJI, MINNESOTA 56601

Telephone: (218) 755-2000.

Founded 1919.

*President:* Dr. REBECCA STAFFORD.
*Director of Admissions and Advising:* Dr. JON QUISTGAARD.
*Librarian:* Dr. JUDITH J. McDONALD.

The library contains 204,500 vols.
Number of teachers: 195 full-time.
Number of students: 4,374.

## BETHEL COLLEGE AND SEMINARY
3900 BETHEL DRIVE,
ST. PAUL, MINNESOTA 55112

Founded 1871.

School of the Baptist General Conference.

Four year liberal arts co-educational Christian College and graduate Theological Seminary.

*President:* CARL H. LUNDQUIST, TH.D., D.D.
*Dean of Seminary:* G. G. JOHNSON, TH.D.
*Dean of College:* G. BRUSHABER, PH.D.
*College Librarian:* ROBERT C. SUDERMAN.
*Seminary Librarian:* NORRIS A. MAGNUSON, PH.D.

The Seminary library contains 59,000 vols., 1,020 periodicals, and the College library 130,000 vols., 600 periodicals.
Number of Seminary teachers: 23 full-time, 7 part-time.
Number of College teachers: 105 full-time, 47 part-time.
Number of Seminary students: 345 men, 38 women.
Number of College students: 913 men, 1,152 women.
Publications: *College Catalog, Theological Seminary Catalog, Bethel, Coeval, Passages* (annually), *The Clarion* (weekly), *Focus, The Seminarian.*

### CARLETON COLLEGE
NORTHFIELD, MINNESOTA 55057

Founded 1866 by Board of Trustees appointed by the Minnesota Conference of Congregational Churches; Independent.

*President:* ROBERT H. EDWARDS, M.A., LL.B.
*Vice-President and Treasurer:* F. I. WRIGHT, B.A.
*Dean of the College:* PETER W. STANLEY, PH.D.
*Dean of Students:* DAVID F. APPLEYARD, PH.D.
*Registrar:* DAVID L. BRODIGAN, PH.D.
The library contains 430,000 vols.
Number of teachers: 189.
Number of students: 1,726.

### COLLEGE OF SAINT BENEDICT
SAINT JOSEPH, MINNESOTA 56374
Telephone: (612) 363-5511.
Founded 1913.

A Catholic Liberal Arts College for Women with extensive academic exchange with nearby St. John's University, a Liberal Arts College for Men.

*President:* Sister EMMANUEL RENNER.
*Director of Admissions:* RICHARD MANDERFELD.
*Librarian:* MICHAEL KATHMAN.
The library contains 150,000 vols.
Number of teachers: 124.
Number of students: 1,713.
Publications: *Cable, St. Benedict's Today, Diotima.*

### COLLEGE OF ST. CATHERINE
2004 RANDOLPH AVENUE, ST. PAUL, MINNESOTA 55105
Telephone: (612) 690-6000.
Founded 1905.

Roman Catholic Liberal Arts College for Women.

*President:* Sister CATHERINE MCNAMEE.
*Vice-President and Academic Dean:* ANITA PAMPUSCH, C.S.J.
*Vice-President for Institutional Advancement:* SHARON TOLBERT.
*Registrar:* PAMELA MARSH.
*Librarian:* Sister ELIZABETH DELMORE.
The library contains 215,000 vols.
Number of teachers: c. 160.
Number of students: c. 2,400.

### COLLEGE OF SAINT TERESA
WINONA, MINNESOTA 55987
Telephone: (507) 454-2930.
Founded 1907.

*President:* Dr. THOMAS J. HAMILTON.
*Dean of Admissions and Registrar:* Sister KATARINA SCHUTH.
*Dean of Students:* Dr. PATRICIA VOLP.
*Director of Residence:* Sister M. FRANCHON PIRKL.
*Librarian:* Sister AVILA SCHURB.
The library contains 133,152 volumes.
Number of teachers: 73.
Number of students: 600.

### COLLEGE OF ST. THOMAS
2115 SUMMIT AVENUE, ST. PAUL, MINNESOTA 55105
Telephone: 647-5000.
Founded 1885.

*President:* Mgr. TERRENCE J. MURPHY.
*Director of Admissions:* CHARLES E. MURPHY.
*Librarian:* Dr. KARL OZOLINS.
The library contains 205,220 vols.
Number of teachers: 194.
Number of students: 4,236.

### CONCORDIA COLLEGE
MOORHEAD, MINNESOTA 56560
Telephone: 299-4321.
Founded 1891.

Four-year liberal arts college, granting bachelor of arts and bachelor of music degrees.

*President:* Dr. PAUL J. DOVRE.
*Vice-President for Academic Affairs:* Dr. DAVID M. GRING.
*Registrar:* D. E. DALE.
*Dean of Admissions:* JAMES L. HAUSMANN.
*Librarian:* V. ANDERSON.
The library contains 251,000 vols.
Number of teachers: 190.
Number of students: 2,625.

### CONCORDIA COLLEGE
ST. PAUL, MINNESOTA 55104
Telephone: (612) 641-8278.
Founded 1893.

*President:* Dr. GERHARDT W. HYATT.
*Dean of the Faculty:* LUTHER MUELLER.
*Director of Admissions:* Mrs. MYRTLE SHIRA.
*Librarian:* G. OFFERMANN.
The library contains 85,000 vols.
Number of teachers: 55.
Number of students: 700.

### GUSTAVUS ADOLPHUS COLLEGE
ST. PETER, MINNESOTA 56082
Telephone: (507) 931-4300.
Founded 1862.

*President:* EDWARD A. LINDELL.
*Registrar:* DAVID WICKLUND.
*Librarian:* KARL L. OZOLINS.
The library contains 190,000 vols.
Number of teachers: 154.
Number of students: 2,400.

### HAMLINE UNIVERSITY
ST. PAUL, MINNESOTA 55104
Founded 1854.
(Related to the United Methodist Church.)
Chartered 1854.

*President:* CHARLES J. GRAHAM.
*Vice-Presidents:* THOMAS J. RUDDY (Development), JOHN BRUEMMER (Finance).
*Registrar:* STEWART A. SHAW.
*Director of Admissions:* DANIEL MURRAY.
*Librarians:* JACK B. KING (Liberal Arts College), ELIZABETH KELLEY (School of Law).
The library contains 230,000 vols.
Number of teachers: 140.
Number of students: 1,750.

DEANS:
*College of Liberal Arts:* K. L. JANZEN.
*School of Law:* STEPHEN B. YOUNG.
*Students:* JOHN C. VINTON.

### MACALESTER COLLEGE
ST. PAUL, MINNESOTA 55105
Telephone: (612) 696-6000.
Founded 1874.
Liberal arts college.

*President:* JOHN B. DAVIS, Jr.
*Vice-Presidents:* JACK ROSSMANN (Academic Affairs), PAUL ASLANIAN (Finance), ALEXANDER HILL (Development).
*Dean of Admissions:* WILLIAM SHAIN.
*Dean of Students:* MARY LUNDBLAD.
*Director of Library:* JEAN K. ARCHIBALD.
The library contains 288,000 vols.
Number of teachers: 129 full-time.
Number of students: 1,750.
Publications: *College Catalog, Prospectus, MacToday*†.

## MANKATO STATE UNIVERSITY
MANKATO, MINNESOTA 56001

Telephone: (507) 389-2463.

Founded 1867.

*President:* Dr. MARGARET PRESKA.
*Academic Vice-President:* Dr. PHILIP KENDALL.
*Vice-President for Fiscal Affairs:* Dr. THOMAS STARK.
*Vice-President for Student Affairs:* Dr. RICHARD FISHER.
*Registrar:* VICTOR SWENSON.
*Librarian:* D. CARRISON.

The library contains 540,000 vols.
Number of teachers: 590.
Number of students: 10,500.
Publication: *M.S.U. Today.*

## MINNEAPOLIS COLLEGE OF ART AND DESIGN
133 EAST 25TH STREET,
MINNEAPOLIS, MINNESOTA 55404

Telephone: (612) 870-3346.

Founded 1886.

*President:* Dr. JEROME J. HAUSMAN.
*Librarian:* RICHARD KRONSTEDT.

The library contains 49,000 vols.
Number of teachers: 46.
Number of students: 540.

## MOORHEAD STATE UNIVERSITY
1100 9TH AVENUE SOUTH,
MOORHEAD, MINNESOTA 56560

Telephone: (218) 236-2011.

Founded 1887.

*President:* Dr. ROLAND DILLE.
*Vice-President for Academic Affairs:* WILLIAM M. JONES.
*Registrar:* D. ENGBERG.
*Dean of Instructional Resources:* DARREL MEINKE.

The library contains 250,000 vols.
Number of teachers: 340.
Number of students: 8,002.

## ST. CLOUD STATE UNIVERSITY
ST. CLOUD, MINNESOTA 56301

Telephone: (612) 255-0121.

Founded 1869.

*President:* LOWELL (TED) GILLETT.
*Vice-President for Academic Affairs:* DAVID C. JOHNSON.
*Dean of Learning Resources:* JOHN G. BERLING.

The library contains 477,305 vols.
Number of teachers: 500 (full-time).
Number of students: 12,511.

## SAINT JOHN'S UNIVERSITY
COLLEGEVILLE,
MINNESOTA 56321

Telephone: (612) 363-2011.
(St. Joseph, Minnesota).

Founded 1857. Private liberal arts college for men.

*President:* Rev. MICHAEL BLECKER O.S.B.
*Director of Admissions:* ROGER YOUNG.
*Librarian:* MICHAEL KATHMAN.

The library contains 280,000 vols., 14,000 microforms, 82,000 government documents, over 1,000 periodicals.

Number of teachers: 150.
Number of students: 1,970.

## SAINT MARY'S COLLEGE
WINONA, MINNESOTA 55987

Telephone: (507) 452-4430.

Founded 1912.

*President:* PETER CLIFFORD, F.S.C.
*Vice-President for Student Development:* PHILIP SCHUMACHER.
*Vice-President for Administration:* Bro. PAUL GRASS, F.S.C.
*Vice-President for Academic Affairs:* JOHN JOHNSON, PH.D.
*Librarian:* MARIANN ALSUM (acting).

The library contains 150,000 vols.
Number of teachers: 102.
Number of students: 1,374.

## SAINT OLAF COLLEGE
NORTHFIELD,
MINNESOTA 55057

Founded 1874.

*President:* Dr. HARLAN F. FOSS.
*Vice-Presidents:* K. ANDERSON, D. JOHNSON, S. L. NESS, H. HELGEN.
*Librarian:* F. BROWN.

The library contains 322,564 vols.
Number of teachers: 225.
Number of students: 3,148.
Publications: *Bulletin, St. Olaf.*

DEANS:

*Faculty:* K. ANDERSON.
*Students:* H. HELGEN.
*Men:* B. ROBERTS.
*Women:* CAROL JOHNSON.

## UNIVERSITY OF MINNESOTA
MINNEAPOLIS,
MINNESOTA 55455

Telephone: (612) 373-2851.

Founded 1851.

State controlled; Academic year: September to June.

*President:* C. PETER MAGRATH, PH.D.
*Vice-Presidents:*
*Academic Affairs:* K. KELLER, PH.D.
*Finance:* F. BOHEN, M.P.A.
*Student Affairs:* FRANK B. WILDERSON, JR., PH.D.
*Administration and Planning:* N. HASSELMO, PH.D.
*Health Sciences:* LYLE A. FRENCH, M.D., PH.D.
*Institutional Relations:* STANLEY B. KEGLER, PH.D.
*Director of Libraries:* ELDRED SMITH, M.L.S.
*Director of University Relations:* RUSSELL D. TALL, B.S.
*Director of Summer Session:* WILLARD L. THOMPSON, PH.D.
*Library: see Libraries.*

Number of teachers: 4,644 full-time, 1,837 part-time.

Number of college level students: 58,705.

Publications: *Brief, Report, Update, Bulletin* series, *Minnesota Magazine, Minnesota Daily* (student newspaper).

### Twin Cities (Minneapolis and St. Paul) Campus
MINNEAPOLIS,
MINNESOTA 55455

Telephone: (612) 373-2851.

DEANS:

*College of Agriculture:* JAMES F. TAMMEN, PH.D.
*Institute of Agriculture, Forestry, and Home Economics:* WILLIAM F. HUEG, Jr., PH.D.
*College of Biological Sciences:* RICHARD S. CALDECOTT, PH.D.
*School of Management:* DAVID LILLY, B.A.
*Continuing Education and Extension:* HAROLD A. MILLER, PH.D.
*School of Dentistry:* RICHARD C. OLIVER, D.D.S., M.S.
*College of Education:* WILLIAM GARDNER, PD.H.
*College of Forestry:* RICHARD A. SKOK, PH.D.
*General College:* JEANNE T. LUPTON, PH.D.
*Graduate School:* WARREN E. IBELE, PH.D.
*College of Home Economics:* KEITH N. McFARLAND, PH.D.
*Law School:* ROBERT A. STEIN, J.D.
*College of Liberal Arts:* FRED LUKERMANN, M.A.
*Medical School:* N. L. GAULT, Jr., M.D.
*School of Nursing:* E. T. FAHY, ED.D.
*College of Pharmacy:* LAWRENCE C. WEAVER, PH.D.
*School of Public Health:* LEE D. STAUFFER, M.P.H.
*Institute of Technology:* ROGER STAEHLE, PH.D.
*University College:* S. SCHOMBERG, PH.D. (acting).
*College of Veterinary Medicine:* ROBERT DUNLOP.

PROFESSORS:

*Aerospace Engineering and Mechanics:*
BEAVERS, G. S., PH.D.
BERMAN, A. S., PH.D.
FOSDICK, R. L., PH.D.
HODGE, P. G., PH.D.
HSIAO, C. C., PH.D.
JOSEPH, D. D., PH.D.
LUNDGREN, T. S., PH.D.
PLUNKETT, R., SC.D.
SETHNA, P. R., PH.D.
WARNER, W. H., PH.D.
WILSON, T. A., PH.D.

*Aerospace Studies:*
PARICK, R. B., PH.D., M.B.A.

*Afro-American Studies:*
  KING, G. D., PH.D.
  SOUTHALL, G. H., PH.D.
  WARD, J. P., LL.B.

*Agricultural and Applied Economics:*
  ANTHONY, W., PH.D.
  BLACKMORE, J., PH.D.
  BLANK, O. U., PH.D.
  BUXTON, B. M., PH.D.
  CHRISTIANSEN, M. K., PH.D.
  COCHRANE, W. W., PH.D., LL.D.
  DAHL, D. C., PH.D.
  DAHL, R. P., PH.D.
  EASTER, K. W., PH.D.
  EGERTSON, K. E., M.S.
  EIDMAN, V. R., PH.D.
  FULLER, E. I., PH.D.
  GREGERSEN, H. M., PH.D.
  HAMMOND, J. W., PH.D.
  HASBARGEN, P. R., PH.D.
  HAWKINS, R. O., M.S.
  HELMBERGER, J. D., PH.D.
  HILDRETH, C. G., PH.D.
  HOUCK, J. P., PH.D.
  HOYT, J. S., Jr., PH.D.
  JENSEN, H. R., PH.D.
  MAKI, W. R., PH.D.
  MARTIN, L. R., PH.D.
  PETERSON, W. L., PH.D.
  PURVIS, M. J., PH.D.
  RAUP, P. M., PH.D.
  ROE, T. L., PH.D.
  ROSE, G. D., PH.D.
  RUTTAN, V. W., PH.D.
  SCHUH, G. E., PH.D.
  SMITH, F. J., PH.D.
  SUNDQUIST, W. B., PH.D.
  THOMAS, K. H., PH.D.
  WAELTI, J. J., PH.D.
  WALDO, A. D., PH.D.
  WELSCH, D. E., PH.D.

*Agricultural Engineering:*
  ALLRED, E. R., M.S.
  BATES, D. W., M.S.
  BEAR, W. F., PH.D.
  BERGSRUD, F. G., M.S.
  CLOUD, H. A., PH.D.
  FLIKKE, A. M., PH.D.
  JORDAN, K. A., PH.D.
  LARSON, C. L., PH.D.
  MACHMEIER, R. E., PH.D.
  MOREY, R. V., PH.D.
  SCHERTZ, C. E., PH.D.
  STRAIT, J., M.S.
  THOMPSON, D. R., PH.D.
  TRUE, J. A., M.S.

*Agronomy and Plant Genetics:*
  ANDERSEN, R. N., PH.D.
  BARNES, D. K., PH.D.
  BEHRENS, R., PH.D.
  BRUN, W. A., PH.D.
  BUSCH, R. H., PH.D.
  CARDWELL, V. B., PH.D.
  COMSTOCK, V. C., PH.D.
  ELLING, L. J., PH.D.
  GEADELMANN, J. L., PH.D.
  GENGENBACH, B. G., PH.D.
  GREEN, C. E., PH.D.
  GOODING, J. A., PH.D.
  HEICHEL, G. H., PH.D.
  HICKS, D. R., PH.D.
  JOHNSON, H. W., PH.D.
  LAMBERT, J. W., PH.D.
  MARTEN, G. C., PH.D.
  MILLER, R. J., PH.D.
  OELKE, E. A., PH.D.
  PHILLIPS, R. L., PH.D.
  RASMUSSON, D. C., PH.D.
  ROBINSON, R. G., PH.D.
  SMITH, L. H., PH.D.
  STRAND, O. E., PH.D.
  STUCKER, R. E., PH.D.
  STUTHMAN, D. D., PH.D.

*American Studies:*
  DELATTRE, R. A., PH.D., Religion and Ethics

*Anatomy:*
  BAUER, G. E., PH.D.
  CARPENTER, A.-M., PH.D., M.D.
  DIXIT, P. K., PH.D.
  ERLANDSEN, S. L., PH.D.
  HAMILTON, D. W., PH.D.
  HEGGESTAD, C. B., M.D., PH.D.
  SHERIDAN, L., PH.D.
  SMITHBERG, M., PH.D.
  SUNDBERG, R. D., M.D., PH.D.

*Anesthesiology:*
  BUCKLEY, J. J., M.D., M.S.
  GORDON, J. R., M.D., M.S.

*Animal Science:*
  ALLEN, C. E., PH.D.
  APPLEMAN, R. D., PH.D.
  ARTHAUD, R. L., PH.D.
  BERG, R. W., PH.D.
  BOYLAN, W. J., PH.D.
  BURKE, W. H., PH.D.
  CHRISTIANS, C. J., PH.D.
  CONLIN, B. J., PH.D.
  CRABO, B. G., PH.D.
  DONKER, J. D., PH.D.
  EPLEY, R. J., PH.D.
  GOODRICH, R. D., PH.D.
  GRAHAM, E. F., PH.D.
  HAMRE, M. L., PH.D.
  HANSON, L. E., PH.D.
  HAWTON, J. D., PH.D.
  HUNTER, A. G., PH.D.
  JACOBS, R. E., M.S.
  JORDAN, R. M., PH.D.
  MEADE, R. J., PH.D.
  MEISKE, J. C., PH.D.
  MUDGE, J. W., PH.D.
  OTTERBY, D. E., PH.D.
  PHILLIPS, R. E., PH.D.
  REMPEL, W. E., PH.D.
  SHOFFNER, R. N., PH.D.
  TOUCHBERRY, R. W., PH.D.
  WAIBEL, P. E., PH.D.
  WILLIAMS, J. B., PH.D.
  YOUNG, C. W., PH.D.

*Anthropology:*
  GERLACH, L. P., PH.D.
  GUDEMAN, S., PH.D.
  HOEBEL, E. A., PH.D.
  KISTE, R., PH.D.
  MILLER, F. C., PH.D.
  MURRILL, R. I., PH.D.
  ROWE, W. L., PH.D.
  SPENCER, R. F., PH.D.

*Architecture and Landscape Architecture:*
  CLEMENCE, R. D., M.ARCH.
  GRAFFUNDER, C., M.ARCH.
  GREBNER, D., M.ARCH.
  HODNE, T. H., M.ARCH.
  MARTIN, R. B., M.L.A.
  MICHELSON, V. L., M.S.ARCH.
  MYERS, J. S., M.ARCH.
  PARKER, L. S., M.ARCH.
  RAPSON, R., B.ARCH.
  RAUMA, J. G., M.ARCH.
  STAGEBERG, J. E., M.ARCH.
  THOMPSON, M. H., M.ARCH.
  WINTEROWD, G. C., M.S.ARCH.

*Art History:*
  CANEDY, N. W., PH.D.
  COOPER, F. A., PH.D.
  MCNALLY, S. J., PH.D.
  NELSON, M. J., PH.D.
  SHEPPARD, C. D., PH.D.
  SIMON, S., PH.D.
  STONES, M. A., PH.D.
  WALDFOGEL, M., PH.D.

*Astronomy:*
  NEY, E. P., PH.D.
  STEIN, W. A., PH.D.

*Biochemistry:*
  BODLEY, J. W., PH.D.
  CARR, C. W., PH.D.
  DEMPSEY, M. E., PH.D.
  FRANTZ, I. D., M.D., PH.D.
  GUTMANN, H. R., M.D., PH.D.
  HOGENKAMP, H. P. C., PH.D.
  HOLMAN, R. T., PH.D.
  KOERNER, J. F., PH.D.
  ROSENBERG, A., FIL.DR.
  SINGER, L., PH.D.
  UNGAR, F., PH.D.
  VAN PILSUM, J. F., PH.D.

*Biological Sciences:*
  ANDERSON, V. E., PH.D., Genetics and Cell Biology
  BLOOMFIELD, V., PH.D., Biochemistry
  CALDECOTT, R., PH.D., Genetics and Cell Biology
  CHAPMAN, P. J., PH.D., Biochemistry
  CUNNINGHAM, W. P., PH.D., Genetics and Cell Biology
  CUSHING, E. J., PH.D., Ecology and Behavioural Biology
  DAGLEY, S., PH.D., Biochemistry
  DAVIS, MARGARET, PH.D., Ecology and Behavioural Biology
  ENFIELD, F. D., PH.D., Genetics and Cell Biology
  FAN, D. P., PH.D., Genetics and Cell Biology
  FORRO, F., Jr., M.D., Genetics and Cell Biology
  FRENKEL, A. W., PH.D., Botany
  GANDER, J. E., PH.D., Biochemistry
  GLASS, R. L., PH.D., Biochemistry
  GORHAM, E., PH.D., Ecology and Behavioural Biology
  HALL, J. W., PH.D., Botany
  HENDERSON, L. M., PH.D., Biochemistry
  HERMAN, R. K., PH.D., Genetics and Cell Biology
  HERMAN, W. S., PH.D., Genetics and Cell Biology
  HOOPER, A. B., PH.D., Genetics and Cell Biology
  JENNESS, R., PH.D., Biochemistry
  JOHNSON, R. G., PH.D., Genetics and Cell Biology
  JONAS, H., PH.D., Botany
  KERR, N., PH.D., Genetics and Cell Biology
  KIRKWOOD, S., PH.D., Biochemistry
  KOUKKARI, W. L., PH.D., Botany
  LIENER, I. E., PH.D., Biochemistry
  LOVRIEN, R. E., PH.D., Biochemistry
  MANN, K. G., PH.D., Biochemistry
  MCKINNELL, R., PH.D., Genetics and Cell Biology
  MCKINNEY, D. F., PH.D., Bell Museum of Natural History
  MCLAUGHLIN, D. J., PH.D., Botany
  MCNAUGHT, D., PH.D., Ecology and Behavioural Biology
  MERRELL, D. J., PH.D., Ecology and Behavioural Biology
  MORLEY, T., PH.D., Botany
  MUENCK, E., PH.D., Gray Freshwater Biological Institute
  NELSESTUEN, G. L., PH.D., Biochemistry
  OWNBEY, G. B., PH.D., Botany
  PARMELEE, D. F., PH.D., Bell Museum of Natural History
  PHILLIPS, R. E., PH.D., Ecology and Behavioural Biology
  PRATT, D. C., PH.D., Botany
  REGAL, F., PH.D., Ecology and Behavioural Biology
  ROGERS, P., PH.D., Biochemistry

## UNIVERSITIES AND COLLEGES—MINNESOTA (UNIVERSITY OF) — U.S.A.

ROSENBERG, M. D., PH.D., M.D., Genetics and Cell Biology
RUBENSTEIN, I., PH.D., Genetics and Cell Biology
SAUERBIER, W., PH.D., Genetics and Cell Biology
SCHMID, W. D., PH.D., Ecology and Behavioural Biology
SEAL, U. S., PH.D., Biochemistry
SHAPIRO, J., PH.D., Ecology and Behavioural Biology
SHEPPARD, J. R., PH.D., Genetics and Cell Biology
SHERIDAN, J. D., PH.D., Genetics and Cell Biology
SINIFF, D. P., PH.D., Ecology and Behavioural Biology
SNUSTAD, D. P., PH.D., Genetics and Cell Biology
SNYDER, L. A., PH.D., Genetics and Cell Biology
TESTER, J. R., PH.D., Ecology and Behavioural Biology
TORDOFF, H. B., PH.D., Bell Museum of Natural History
UNDERHILL, J. C., PH.D., Ecology and Behavioural Biology
WARNER, D. W., PH.D., Bell Museum of Natural History
WARNER, H. R., PH.D., Biochemistry
WOLD, F., PH.D., Biochemistry
WOOD, J. M., PH.D., Gray Freshwater Biological Institute
WOODWARD, V. W., PH.D., Genetics and Cell Biology
WRIGHT, H. E., PH.D., Ecology and Behavioural Biology

*Management:*
ADAMS, C. R., PH.D.
BAILEY, A. D., PH.D.
BEIER, F. J., PH.D.
BERRYMAN, R., G. PH.D.
BOGNANNO, M. F., PH.D.
CARDOZO, R. N., PH.D.
CHERVANY, N. L., D.B.A.
COOKE, B. M., PH.D.
DAVIS, G. B., PH.D.
DICKSON, G. W., D.B.A.
ERICKSON, W. B., PH.D.
FLAGLER, J. J., M.S.
FOSTER, E., PH.D.
GAUMNITZ, R. K., PH.D.
GRAMBSCH, P. V., D.B.A.
GRAY, J. C., PH.D.
HARPER, D. V., PH.D.
HASTINGS, D. C., PH.D.
HOFFMAN, T. R., PH.D.
HOLLOWAY, R. J., PH.D.
JESSUP, P. F., PH.D.
JOHNSON, P., PH.D.
KAREKEN, J. H., PH.D.
LILLY, D. M., B.A.
MCCONNELL, J. J., PH.D.
MAHONEY, T., PH.D.
ROERING, K., PH.D.
ROSS, I., PH.D.
RUDELIUS, C. W., PH.D.
SCHROEDER, R. G., PH.D.
SCOVILLE, J. G., PH.D.
SELTZER, G., PH.D.
UPSON, R. B., PH.D.
VAN DE VEN, A., PH.D.
WALKER, O. C., PH.D.
WHITMAN, A. F., PH.D.
WICKESBERG, A. K., PH.D.
WILLIAMS, C. A., PH.D.
WILLIS, R. E., PH.D.
ZAIDI, M. A., PH.D.
ZIMMER, R. K., PH.D.

*Chemical Engineering and Materials Science:*
ARIS, R., D.SC.
CARR, R. W., PH.D.
CUSSLER, E. L., PH.D.
DAHLER, J. S., PH.D.
DAVIS, H. T., PH.D.
EVANS, D. F., PH.D.
FREDRICKSON, A. G., PH.D.
GERBERICH, W. W., PH.D.
ISBIN, H. S., SC.D.
KELLER, K. H., PH.D.
MACOSKO, C. W., PH.D.
NICHOLSON, M. E., SC.D.
ORIANI, R. A., PH.D.
RANZ, W. E., PH.D.
SCHMIDT, L. D., PH.D.
SCRIVEN, L. E., PH.D.
STEPHANOUPOULOS, G., PH.D.
TOTH, L. E., PH.D.
TSUCHIYA, H. M., PH.D.

*Chemistry:*
BLOOMFIELD, V. A., PH.D.
BRASTED, R. C., PH.D.
BRITTON, J. D., PH.D.
BRYANT, R. G., PH.D.
CRAWFORD, B. L., Jr., PH.D.
DAHLER, J. S., PH.D.
DAVIS, H. T., PH.D.
DODSON, R. M., PH.D.
FENTON, S. W., PH.D.
GASSMAN, P. G., PH.D.
GENTRY, W. R., PH.D.
HEXTER, R. M., PH.D.
KREEVOY, M. M., PH.D.
LEETE, E., PH.D.
LIPSKY, S., PH.D.
LUMRY, R. W., PH.D.
MEAD, C. A., PH.D.
MEEHAN, E. J., PH.D.
MILLER, L., PH.D.
MILLER, W. G., PH.D.
MOSCOWITZ, A. J., PH.D.
NOLAND, W. E., PH.D.
OVEREND, J., PH.D.
PRAGER, S., PH.D.
REYNOLDS, W. L., PH.D.
SWOFFORD, H. S., PH.D.
TRUHLAR, D. G., PH.D.
WERTZ, J. E., PH.D.
WILSON, A. S., PH.D.

*Child Development:*
CHARLESWORTH, W. R., PH.D.
COLLINS, W. A., PH.D.
HARTUP, W. W., ED.D.
MARATSOS, M. P., PH.D.
MOORE, S. G., PH.D.
PICK, A. D., PH.D.
PICK, H. L., Jr., PH.D.
ROFF, M. F., PH.D.
SALAPATEK, P. H., PH.D.
SROUFE, L. A., PH.D.
TAPP, J. L., PH.D.
TEMPLIN, M. C., PH.D.
YONAS, A., PH.D.

*Civil and Mineral Engineering:*
ARNDT, R. E. A., PH.D.
BITSIANES, G., PH.D.
BOWERS, C. E., M.S.
BREZONIK, P. L., PH.D.
CROUCK, S. L., PH.D.
FAIRHURST, C., PH.D.
FANT, J. E., M.S.
GALAMBOS, T. V., PH.D.
GOODMAN, L. E., PH.D.
IWASAKI, I., D.ENG.
MAIER, W. J., PH.D.
REID, K. J., PH.D.
SILBERMAN, E., M.S.
SONG, C. C. S., PH.D.
STARFIELD, A. M., PH.D.
STEFAN, H., DR.ING.
YARDLEY, D. H., PH.D.

*Classics:*
HERSHBELL, J. P., PH.D.
KEULS, E. C., PH.D.
SONKOWSKY, R. P., PH.D.

*Communications Disorders:*
BROOKSHIRE, R. H., PH.D.
DARLEY, F. L., PH.D.
LASSMAN, F. M., PH.D.
MARTIN, R. R., PH.D.
MCDERMOTT, R. P., PH.D.
SIEGEL, G. M., PH.D.
SPEAKS, C. E., PH.D.
STARR, C. D., PH.D.
WARD, W. D., PH.D.

*Computer Science:*
FRANTA, W. R., PH.D.
IBARRA, O. H., PH.D.
MUNRO, W. D., PH.D.
ROSEN, J. B., PH.D.
SAHNI, S. K., PH.D.
STEIN, M. L., PH.D.

*Criminal Justice Studies:*
KNUDSON, BARBARA, PH.D., Community Corrections
MALMQUIST, C., M.D., M.S., Criminal and Juvenile Psychopathology
SAMAHA, J., PH.D., J.D., Criminal Law and Procedure
TAPP, JUNE L., PH.D., Legal Socialization
WARD, D. A., PH.D., Criminology and Penology

*Curriculum and Instruction:*
AHLGREN, A., ED.D.
CASWELL, A. F., ED.D.
COGAN, J., PH.D.
DYKSTRA, R., PH.D.
ELLIS, A. K., ED.D.
GARDNER, W. E., PH.D.
GLENN, A., PH.D.
GRAVES, M., PH.D.
HANSEN, H. S., PH.D.
HOPKINS, C. R., PH.D.
HOWEY, K., PH.D.
JACKSON, R. L., PH.D.
JOHNSON, R., ED.D.
KELLER, R. J., PH.D.
LAMBERT, R., PH.D.
LANGE, D. L., PH.D.
LEWIS, D. R., PH.D.
MANNING, J. C., ED.D.
ODLAND, N., PH.D.
PICHE, G. L., PH.D.
POST, T., PH.D.
SCHREINER, R. L., PH.D.
SCHUESSLER, R. A., M.M.
STOCHL, J. E., PH.D.
TENNYSON, R., PH.D.
TURRENTINE, E. M., PH.D.
ULTAN, L., PH.D.
WILLIAMS, H. Y., PH.D.

*Dentistry:*
ANDERSON, D. L., PH.D.
BANDT, C. L., D.D.S., M.S.
BEVIS, R. R., PH.D.
BORN, D. O., PH.D.
CERVENKA, J., M.D.
COLMAN H. L., D.D.S., M.S.D.
GOODKIND, R. J., D.M.D., M.S.
GORLIN, R. J., D.D.S., M.S.
HAMPEL, A. T., D.D.S., M.S.
HOLLAND, M. R., D.D.S., M.S.D.
HOLTE, N. O., D.D.S., M.S.
JENSEN, J. R., D.D.S., M.S.
JERONIMUS, R. D., D.D.S., M.S.D.
LEGLER, D. W., PH.D.
LITTLE, J. W., D.M.D., M.S.
MARTENS, L. V., M.P.H.
MESKIN, L. H., PH.D.
MESSER, E. B., M.D.SC.
MEYER, M. W., PH.D.
MORSTAD, A. T., D.D.S., M.S.
NOBLE, F. W., D.D.S.
OLIVER, R. C., D.D.S., M.S.
SAUK, J. J., M.S.
SCHACHTELE, C. F., PH.D.
SCHAFFER, E. M., D.D.S., M.S.D.

SEDANO, H. O., DR. ODONT.
SERR, H. H., D.D.S.
SHAPIRO, B. L., PH.D.
SINGER, L., PH.D.
SMITH, Q. T., PH.D.
SPEIDEL, T. M., D.D.S., M.S.D.
TILL, M. J., PH.D.
VICKERS, R. A., D.D.S., M.S.D.
WAITE, D. E., D.D.S., M.S.
WITKOP, C. J., Jr., D.D.S., M.S.
WORMS, F. W., D.D.S., M.S.D.
YOCK, D. H., D.D.S., M.S.

*Dermatology:*
GOLTZ, R. W., M.D.
MANICK, K. P., M.D.

*Earth Sciences:*
BANERJEE, S. K., PH.D.
HOOKE, R. L., PH.D.
MOONEY, H. M., PH.D.
MURTHY, V. R., PH.D.
SAWKINS, F. J., PH.D.
SHAPIRO, J., PH.D.
SLOAN, R. E., PH.D.
SWAIN, F. M., PH.D.
WALTON, M. S., PH.D.
WEIBLEN, P., PH.D.
WRIGHT, H. E., PH.D.
ZOLTAI, T., PH.D.

*East Asian Languages:*
COPELAND, E., M.A.
LIU, C. J., PH.D.
MATHER, R., PH.D.
SHOHARA, H., PH.D.
WANG, S., PH.D.

*Economics:*
BROWNLEE, O. H., PH.D.
CHIPMAN, J. S., PH.D.
COEN, E., PH.D.
HELLER, W. W., PH.D.
HENDERSON, J. M., PH.D.
HILDRETH, C., PH.D.
HURWICZ, L., LL.M.
KAREKEN, J. H., PH.D.
KRUEGER, A. O., PH.D.
MOHRING, H. D., PH.D.
RICHTER, M. K., PH.D.
SARGENT, T. J., PH.D.
SIMLER, N. J., PH.D.
SIMS, C., PH.D.
SMITH, H. M., PH.D.
TURNBULL, J. G., PH.D.
WALLACE, N., PH.D.

*Educational Administration:*
AMMENTORP, W. M., PH.D.
CORCORAN, M. E., PH..D.
HENDRIX, V. L., PH.D.
HOOKER, C. P., ED.D.
KELLER, R. J., PH.D.
KELLOGG, T. E., PH.D.
LAMBERT, R. T., PH.D.
LEWIS, D. R., PH.D.
MUELLER, V. D., ED.D.
NICKERSON, N. C., ED.D.
POPPER, S. H., PH.D.
SEDERBERG, C. H., PH.D.
WEATHERMAN, R. F., PH.D.

*Electrical Engineering:*
ALBERTSON, V. D., PH.D.
ANDERSON, L. T., M.S.
BROWN, W. F., PH.D.
CARRUTHERS, J. A., PH.D.
CARTWRIGHT, P., M.S.
CHAMPLIN, K. S., PH.D.
CHANIN, L. M., PH.D.
COLLINS, R. J., PH.D.
HOEFFLINGER, B., PH.D.
JUDY, J. H., PH.D.
KAIN, R. Y., PH.D.
KUMAR, K. S. P., PH.D.
LAMBERT, R. F., PH.D.
LEE, F. B., PH.D.

MUELLER, R. K., PH.D.
NUSSBAUM, A., PH.D.
OSKAM, H. J., PH.D.
PERIA, W. T., PH.D.
RIAZ, M., PH.D.
ROBINSON, G. Y., PH.D.
SCHMITT, O. H., PH.D.
SHENOI, B. A., PH.D.
VAN DER ZIEL, A., PH.D.
WARNER, R. M., Jr., PH.D.
WEHNER, G. K., PH.D.

*English:*
ANDERSON, C. G., PH.D.
CLAYTON, T., PH.D.
FIRCHOW, P. E., PH.D.
FRUMAN, N., PH.D.
GRIFFIN, E. M., PH.D.
HURRELL, J. D., PH.D.
KWIAT, J. J., PH.D.
MACLEISH, A., PH.D.
MADDEN, W. A., PH.D.
MOORE, R. E., PH.D.
O'BRIEN, G. W., PH.D.
REED, P. J., PH.D.
ROSENDAHL, W. A., PH.D.
ROTH, M., PH.D.
STEKERT, ELLEN J., PH.D.
UNGER, L., PH.D.
WRIGHT, G. T., PH.D.

*Entomology, Fisheries and Wildlife:*
BROOKS-WALLACE, M. A., PH.D.
CHIANG, H. C., PH.D.
COOK, E. F., PH.D.
CUTKOMP, L. K., PH.D.
FRENZEL, L. D., PH.D.
FURGALA, B., PH.D.
GULLION, G. W., M.A.
HAREIN, P. K., PH.D.
KULMAN, H. M., PH.D.
LOFGREN, J. A., M.S.
PRICE, R. D., PH.D.
RADCLIFFE, E. B., PH.D.
WATERS, T. F., PH.D.
WELLER, M. W., PH.D.

*Family Practice and Community Health:*
BERGLUND, E. B., M.D., Family Practice
CIRIACY, E. W., M.D., Family Practice
KELLY, J. T., M.D., Psychiatry
O'LEARY, J. B., M.D., Rural Health
VERBY, J. E., M.D., Rural Health
WECKWERTH, V. E., PH.D., Biostatistics

*Food Science and Nutrition:*
ADDIS, P. B., PH.D.
ALLEN, C. E., PH.D.
BREENE, W. M., PH.D.
BUSTA, F. F., PH.D.
CALDWELL, E. F., PH.D.
CSALLANY, A. S., D.SC.
EPLEY, R. J., PH.D.
GORDON, J., PH.D.
HEGARTY, P. V. J., PH.D.
LABUZA, T. P., PH.D.
MCKAY, L. L., PH.D.
MORRIS, H. A., PH.D.
MORSE, L. M., PH.D.
PACKARD, V. S., Jr., PH.D.
PFLUG, I. J., PH.D.
SWAN, P. B., PH.D.
TATINI, S. R., PH.D.
ZOTTOLA, E. A., PH.D.

*Forestry:*
BAKUZIS, E. V., PH.D., Ecology
BROWN, B. A., PH.D., Silviculture (Soils)
BROWN, G. N., D.F., Physiology
EK, A. R., PH.D., Inventory and Biometrics
ERICKSON, R. W., PH.D., Drying (Mechanical Properties)
GERTJEJANSEN, R. O., PH.D., Fibre Products
GREGERSEN, H. M., PH.D., Economics

HALLGREN, A. A., PH.D., Harvesting (Management)
HANSEN, H. L., PH.D., Silviculture (Ecology)
HAYGREEN, J. G., PH.D., Mechanical-Physical Properties
HENDRICKS, L. T., PH.D., Forest Products
IRVING, F. D., PH.D., Administration (Fire)
KURMIS, V., PH.D., Ecology
LILLESAND, T., PH.D., Silviculture, Extension
MERRIAM, L. C., PH.D., Recreation
MEYER, M.P., PH.D., Remote Sensing
MOHN, C. A., PH.D., Genetics
ROSE, D., PH.D., Economics
SCHOLTEN, H., PH.D., Silviculture, Extension
SKOK, R. A., PH.D., Economics and Policy
SUCOFF, E. I., PH.D., Physiology
WINSNESS, K. E., M.S., Education Administration

*French and Italian:*
CONLEY, T., PH.D.
LOCK, P. W., PH.D.
PIPA, A., PH.D.
RENAUD, A. A., PH.D.
SCHNEIDER, M., PH.D.
WALDAUER, J. L., PH.D.

*General College:*
AMRAM, F. A., M.A.
BENSON, F. T., PH.D.
BOROW, H., PH.D.
DEARDEN, D. M., PH.D.
GATES, J., M.A.
GIESE, D. L., PH.D.
HANSEN, E. U., M.A.
HARRIS, F. J., M.A.
HATHAWAY, W., PH.D.
KING, L. A., PH.D.
KINGSLEY, G. G., ED.D.
KURAK, A., PH.D.
LARSON, R. A., PH.D.
LUPTON, J. T., PH.D.
MACINNES, M. J., PH.D.
MOEN, N. W., PH.D.
RATHBUN, R. C., PH.D.
SAFER, L. T., M.A.
SCHWABACHER, W. B., PH.D.
STEINHAUSER, F. R., PH.D.
STOCKDALE, W. A., M.A.
ZANONI, C., PH.D.

*Geography:*
ADAMS, J. S., PH.D.
BARRETT, W. J., PH.D.
BORCHERT, J. R., PH.D.
HART, J. F., PH.D.
HSU, M. L., PH.D.
LUKERMANN, F. E., M.A.
MATHER, E. C., PH.D.
PORTER, P. W., PH.D.
RICE, J. G., PH.D.
SCHWARTZBERG, J. E., PH.D.
SKAGGS, R. H., PH.D.
TUAN, Y. F., PH.D.

*German:*
FIRCHOW, E. S., PH.D.
HIRSCHBACH, F. D., PH.D.
LIBERMAN, A., PH.D.
SCHULTE-SASSE, J., PH.D.
TARABA, W. F., PH.D.
WEISS, G. H., PH.D.

*History:*
ALTHOLZ, J. L., PH.D.
BACHRACH, B. S., PH.D.
BAMFORD, P. W., PH.D.
BERMAN, H., PH.D.
BRAUER, K. J., PH.D.
CHAMBERS, C. A., PH.D.

FARMER, E. L., PH.D.
HOWE, J. R., PH.D.
ISAACMAN, A. F., PH.D.
KABA, L., PH.D.
KOPF, D., PH.D.
LEHMBERG, S. E., PH.D.
MARSHALL, B. K., PH.D.
MODELL, J., PH.D.
MUNHOLLAND, J. K., PH.D.
MURPHY, P. L., PH.D.
NOBLE, D. W., PH.D.
NOONAN, T. S., PH.D.
RATH, J., PH.D.
RUDOLPH, R. L., PH.D.
SAMAHA, J., PH.D.
SCHWARTZ, S. B., PH.D.
STAVROU, T. G., PH.D.
TAYLOR, R., PH.D.
THAYER, J. A., PH.D.
TRACY, J. D., PH.D.
VECOLI, R. J., PH.D.
WRIGHT, W. E., PH.D.

*History of Medicine:*
WILSON, L. G., PH.D.

*History of Science and Technology:*
LAYTON, E. T., PH.D.
STUEWER, R. H., PH.D.

*Home Economics:*
BAGLEY, M. O., M.A.T., Design
BAIZERMAN, M. L., PH.D.
BEKER, J., PH.D.
BETSINGER, S. T., PH.D., Administration
EICHER, J. B., PH.D., Textiles and Clothing
GAGE, G. M., PH.D., Family Social Science
GRINDERENG, M. P., PH.D., Textiles and Clothing
HEY, R. N., PH.D., Family Social Science
JOHNSON, R. F., PH.D., Textiles and Clothing
JORDAHL, E. K., M.S., Family Social Science
LARKIN, E. D., M.A., Design
McCUBBIN, H. I., PH.D., Family Social Science
McFARLAND, K. N., PH.D., Administration
NEUBECK, G., ED.D., Family Social Science
OLSON, D. H., PH.D., Family Social Science
ROSENBLATT, P. C., PH.D., Family Social Science
STIEGLITZ, M. G., PH.D., Design

*Hormel Institute:*
BAUMANN, W. J., PH.D.
BROCKMAN, H. L., PH.D.
HOLMAN, R. T., PH.D.
JENKIN, H. M., PH.D.
PRIVETT, O. S., PH.D.
SCHLENK, H., PH.D.
SCHMID, H. H. O., PH.D.

*Horticultural Science and Landscape Architecture:*
ASCHER, P. D., PH.D.
BRENNER, M. L., PH.D.
DAVIS, D. W., PH.D.
DEVOS, F., PH.D.
HARD, C. G., PH.D.
HERTZ, L. B., PH.D.
KALLIO, A., PH.D.
LASHEEN, A., PH.D.
LAUER, F. I., PH.D.
LI, P. H., PH.D.
McKINNON, J. P., M.S.
MULLIN, R., PH.D.
OZBUN, J. L., PH.D.
PELLETT, H. M., PH.D.
READ, P. E., PH.D.

STADELMANN, E. J., FH.D.
WHITE, D. B., PH.D.
WIDMER, R. E., PH.D.
WILKINS, H. F., PH.D.

*Humanities:*
AMES, R. J., PH.D.
BRYAN, D. V., PH.D.
D'ANDREA, P., PH.D.
HERSHBELL, J. P., PH.D.
KWIAT, J. J., PH.D.
ROSHWALD, M., PH.D.
TAPP, R. B., PH.D.

*Agricultural Journalism:*
SWANSON, H. B., PH.D.
WELLS, D. E., PH.D.

*Journalism and Mass Communication:*
BROVALD, W., M.A.
CARTER, R. E., Jr., PH.D.
EMERY, W. E., PH.D.
FANG, I. E., PH.D.
GILLMOR, D. M., PH.D.
HAGE, G. S., PH.D.
JONES, R. L., PH.D.
KLINE, F. G., PH.D.
LINDSAY, R. G., PH.D.
THOMPSON, W. L., PH.D.
TICHENOR, P. J., PH.D.
WACKMAN, D. B., PH.D.
WILSON, H. W., M.A.

*Laboratory Medicine and Pathology:*
ACKERMAN, E., PH.D.
AHMED, K., PH.D.
ANDERSON, W. R., M.D.
AZAR, M. M., M.D., PH.D.
BENSON, E. S., M.D.
BLAZEVIC, D. J., M.P.H.
BROWN, D. M., M.D.
BRUNNING, R. D., M.D.
COE, J. I., M.D.
DALMASSO, A. P., M.D., PH.D.
DEHNER, L., M.D.
EDERER, G. M., M.P.H.
EDSON, J. R., M.D.
EDWARDS, J., M.D.
ESTENSEN, R. D., M.D.
FREIER, E. F., M.S.
GREENBERG, L. J., PH.D.
HALBERG, F., M.D.
HOVDE, R. F., M.S.
KERSEY, J. H., M.D.
LOBER, P. H., M.D., PH.D.
McCULLOUGH, J. J., M.D.
OSTERBERG, K. A., M.D.
POLESKY, H. F., M.D.
RATLIFF, N. B., M.D.
RAUSCH, V. L., M.S.
ROSAI, J., M.D.
ROSENBERG, A., PH.D.
SUNDBERG, R. D., M.D., PH.D.
WATTENBERG, L. W., M.D.
YUNIG, J. J., M.D., PH.D.

*Law:*
AUERBACH, C. A., LL.B.
BRYDEN, D. P., LL.B.
COUND, J. J., LL.B.
FELD, B. C., J.D., PH.D.
FREEMAN, A. D., LL.B.
GIFFORD, D. J., LL.B.
GRABB, R. F., LL.B.
HUDEC, R. E., M.A., LL.B.
KILBOURN, W. D., LL.B.
KOEPPEN, B., LL.B.
LEVY, R. J., LL.B.
MARSHALL, D. P., LL.B.
McCLURE, R. C., LL.B.
MORRIS, C. R., LL.B.
MORRISON, F. L., J.D., PH.D.
PARK, R. C., J.D.
RASKIND, L. J., LL.B., PH.D.
SCALLEN, S. B., J.D.
SCHOETTLE, F., LL.B.

STEIN, R. A., J.D.
WATERBURY, T. L., J.D., LL.M.
WEISSBRODT, D. S., J.D.
WOLFRAM, C. W., LL.B.

*Library School:*
BERNINGHAUSEN, D. K., M.A.
SIMONTON, W., PH.D.

*Linguistics:*
ROBINETT, B. W., PH.D.
SANDERS, G. A., PH.D.

*Mathematics:*
AEPPLI, A., PH.D.
ARONSON, D., PH.D.
BERGER, T., PH.D.
CAFFARELLI, L., PH.D.
EAGON, J., PH.D.
ELLIS, R., PH.D.
FABES, E., PH.D.
GAAL, S., PH.D.
GIL DE LAMADRID, J., PH.D.
GOLDMAN, J., PH.D.
HARDT, R., PH.D.
HARRIS, M., PH.D.
HEJHAL, D., PH.D.
JAIN, N., PH.D.
KEYNES, H., PH.D.
KINDERLEHRER, D., PH.D.
LITTMAN, W., PH.D.
LOUD, W., PH.D.
McCARTHY, C., PH.D.
McGEHEE, R., PH.D.
MARDEN, A., PH.D.
MARKUS, L., PH.D.
MESSING, W., PH.D.
MEYERS, N., PH.D.
MILLER, W., PH.D.
NITSCHE, J., PH.D.
OREY, S., PH.D.
PEDOE, D., PH.D.
POHL, W., PH.D.
POUR-EL, MARIAN, PH.D.
PRIKAY, K., PH.D.
PRUITT, W., PH.D.
REICH, E., PH.D.
REJTO, P., PH.D.
RICHARDS, J., PH.D.
ROBERTS, J., PH.D.
SATTINGER, D., PH.D.
SELL, G., PH.D.
SERRIN, J., PH.D.
SIBUYA, Y., PH.D.
SIMON, L., PH.D.
STORVICK, D., PH.D.
WEINBERGER, H., PH.D.

*Mayo Medical School:*
AARO, L. A., M.D., Obstetrics and Gynaecology
ADSON, M. A., M.D., Surgery
AHMANN, D. L., M.D., Oncology
ANDERSEN, H. A., M.D., Medicine
ANDERSON, M. W., M.D., Medicine
ARONSON, A. E., PH.D., Speech Pathology
ATASSI, M. Z., PH.D., D.SC., Biochemistry
BAHN, R. C., M.D., PH.D., Pathology
BAKER, H. L., Jr., M.D., Radiology
BARTHOLOMEW, L. G., M.D., Medicine
BAYRD, E. D., M.D., Medicine
BERGE, K. G., M.D., Medicine
BERNATZ, P. E., M.D., Surgery
BIANCO, A. J., Jr., M.D., Orthopaedics
BISEL, H. F., M.D., Oncology
BLACK, L. F., M.D., Medicine
BLINKS, J. R., M.D., Pharmacology
BOVE, A. A., M.D., PH.D., Medicine
BOWIE, E. J. W., B.M., B.CH., Medicine and Laboratory Medicine
BRANDENBURG, R. O., M.D., Medicine
BRIMIJOIN, W. S., PH.D., Pharmacology
BRUBAKER, R. F., M.D., Ophthalmology
BRYAN, R. S., M.D., Orthopaedics
BURGERT, E. O., Jr., M.D., Paediatrics

BURKE, E. C., M.D., PH.D., Paediatrics
CARLSON, H. C., M.D., PH.D., Radiology
CARTER, E. T., M.D., PH.D., Preventive Medicine
CHAO, E. Y. S., PH.D., Bioengineering
CHILDS, D. S., Jr., M.D., Oncology
CODY, D. T. R., M.D., PH.D., Otolaryngology
CONNOLLY, D. C., M.D., PH.D., Medicine
COVENTRY, M. B., M.D., Orthopaedics
DAHLIN, D. C., M.D., Pathology
DANIELSON, G. K., Jr., M.D., Surgery
DARLEY, F. L., PH.D., Speech Pathology
DAUGHERTY, G. W., M.D., Medicine
DAVID, C. S., PH.D., Immunology
DECKER, D. G., M.D., Obstetrics and Gynaecology
DE SANTO, L. W., M.D., Otolaryngology
DICKSON, E. R., M.D., Medicine
DIDISHEIM, P., M.D., Laboratory Medicine
DIMAGNO, E. P., M.D., Medicine
DINES, D. E., M.D., Medicine
DIVERTIE, M. B., M.D., Medicine
DONADIO, J. V., Jr., M.D., Medicine
DONALD, D. E., PH.D., Physiology
DOUSA, T. P., M.D., PH.D., Medicine and Physiology
DYCK, P. J., M.D., Neurology
DYER, J. A., M.D., Ophthalmology
EARLE, J. D., M.D., Oncology
ELVEBACK, LILLIAN R., PH.D., Biostatistics
ENGEL, A. G., M.D., Neurology
FAIRBANKS, V. F., M.D., Medicine and Laboratory Medicine
FARROW, G. M., M.D., Pathology
FELDT, R. H., M.D., Paediatrics
FERGUSON, R. H., M.D., Medicine
FONTANA, R. S., M.D., Medicine
FOULK, W. T., Jr., M.D., Medicine
FRYE, R. L., M.D., Medicine
FURLOW, W. L., M.D., Urology
FUSTER, V., M.D., Medicine
GASTINEAU, C. F., M.D., PH.D., Medicine
GERACI, J. E., M.D., Medicine
GERICH, J. E., M.D., Medicine and Physiology
GIBILISCO, J. A., D.D.S., Dentistry
GILCHRIST, G. S., M.B., B.CH., Paediatrics
GIULIANI, E. R., M.D., Medicine
GLEICH, G. J., M.D., Medicine and Immunology
GO, V. L. W., M.D., Medicine
GOLDSTEIN, N. P., M.D., Neurology
GOMEZ, M. R., M.D., Paediatric Neurology
GORDON, H., M.D., Medical Genetics
GORMAN, C. A., M.B., B.CH., PH.D., Medicine
GRONERT, G. A., M.D., Anaesthesiology
GROSS, J. B., M.D., Medicine
HAGEDORN, A. B., M.D., Medicine
HAHN, R. G., M.D., Oncology
HARRISON, C. E., Jr., M.D., PH.D., Medicine
HARTMAN, G. W., M.D., Radiology
HAYLES, A. B., M.D., Paediatrics and Medicine
HENDERSON, E. D., M.D., Orthopaedics
HEPPER, N. G. G., M.D., Medicine
HERMANS, P. E., M.D., Medicine
HOFFMAN, H. N., II, M.D., Medicine
HOLLEY, K. E., M.D., Pathology
HOLMAN, R. T., PH.D., Biochemistry
HOWARD, F. M., Jr., M.D., Neurology
HUNDER, G. G., M.D., Medicine
HUIZENGA, K. A., M.D., Medicine
HYATT, R. E., M.D., Medicine and Physiology
JACKSON, I., M.B., CH.B., Plastic Surgery
JIANG, N., PH.D., Laboratory Medicine
JOHNSON, E. W., Jr., M.D., Orthopaedics
JOHNSON, W. J., M.D., Medicine

JONES, J. D., PH.D., Laboratory Medicine
JUERGENS, J. L., M.D., Medicine
KAYE, M. P., Surgery
KEARNS, T. P., M.D., Ophthalmology
KELALIS, P. P., M.D., Urology
KELLY, K. A., M.D., Surgery
KELLY, P. J., M.D., Orthopaedics
KEMPERS, R. D., M.D., Obstetrics and Gynaecology
KERN, E. B., M.D., Otolaryngology
KERR, F. W. L., M.D., Neuroanatomy and Neurosurgery
KIELY, J. M., M.D., Medicine
KINCAID, O. W., M.D., D.SC., Radiology
KLASS, D. W., M.D., Neurology
KNOX, F. G., M.D., PH.D., Physiology and Medicine
KOTTKE, B. A., M.D., PH.D., Medicine
KOVACH, J. S., M.D., Oncology
KURLAND, L. T., M.D., Epidemiology and Biostatistics
KYLE, R. A., M.D., Medicine
LAMBERT, E. H., M.D., PH.D., Physiology and Neurology
LANEY, W. R., D.M.D., Dentistry
LAWS, E. R., M.D., Neurosurgery
LEE, R. A., M.D., Obstetrics and Gynaecology
LIE, J. T., M.D., Pathology
LINSCHEID, R. L., M.D., Orthopaedics
LOFGREN, K. A., M.D., Surgery
LUDWIG, J., M.D., Pathology
MACCARTY, C. S., M.D., Neurosurgery
MCCALL, J. T., PH.D., Laboratory Medicine
MCCONAHEY, W. M., M.D., Medicine
MCGILL, D. B., M.D., Medicine
MCGOON, D. C., M.D., Surgery
MCILRATH, D. C., M.D., Surgery
MCPHERSON, J. R., M.D., Medicine
MAIR, D. D., M.D., Paediatrics
MALAGELADA, J. R., M.D., Medicine
MALKASIAN, G. D., Jr., M.D., Obstetrics and Gynaecology
MANN, K. G., PH.D., Biochemistry
MARTIN, M. J., M.D., Psychiatry
MATTOX, V. R., PH.D., Biochemistry
MAYBERRY, W. E., M.D., Laboratory Medicine
MICHENFELDER, J. D., M.D., Anaesthesiology
MILLER, R. D., M.D., Medicine
MILLER, R. H., M.D., Neurosurgery
MILLER, W. E., M.D., Radiology
MOERTEL, C. G., M.D., Oncology
MOSES, H. L., M.D., Pathology
MULDER, D. W., M.D., Neurology
MULLER, S. A., M.D., Dermatology
NEEDHAM, G. M., PH.D., Microbiology
NEWCOMER, A. D., M.D., Medicine
ONOFRIO, B. M., M.D., Neurosurgery
PALUMBO, P. J., M.D., Medicine
PAYNE, W. S., M.D., Surgery
PEARSON, G. R., PH.D., Microbiology
PENNISTON, J. T., PH.D., Biochemistry
PERRY, H. O., M.D., Dermatology
PETERSON, L. F. A., M.D., Orthopaedics
PHILLIPS, S. F., M.D., Medicine
PIERRE, R. V., M.D., Laboratory Medicine and Medicine
POLLEY, H. F., M.D., D.SC., Medicine
RANDALL, R. V., M.D., Medicine
REED, C. E., M.D., Medicine
REHDER, K., M.D., Anaesthesiology and Physiology
REITEMEIER, R. J., M.D., Medicine
REMINE, W. H., Jr., M.D., D.SC., Surgery
RICHELSON, E., M.D., Psychiatry and Pharmacology
RIGGS, B. L., Jr., M.D., Medicine
RITMAN, E. L., M.B., B.S., PH.D., Physiology and Medicine
RITTER, D. G., M.D., Paediatrics

RITTS, R. E., Jr., M.D., Microbiology and Oncology
ROBERTSON, D. M., M.D., Ophthalmology
ROBERTSON, J. S., M.D., PH.D., Laboratory Medicine
RODARTE, J. R., M.D., Medicine and Physiology
ROMERO, J. C., M.D., Physiology
ROSENBLATT, J. E., M.D., Microbiology and Medicine
ROSENOW, E. C., M.D., Medicine
RYAN, R. J., M.D., Medicine
SALASSA, R. M., M.D., Medicine
SANDOK, B. M., M.D., Neurology
SCANLON, P. W., M.D., Radiology
SCHOLZ, D. A., M.D., Medicine
SCOTT, R. E., M.D., Pathology
SESSLER, A. D., M.D., Anaesthesiology
SHEPHERD, J. T., M.D., D.SC., Physiology
SHEPS, S. G., M.D., Medicine
SHORTER, R. G., M.D., Pathology and Medicine
SIEKERT, R. G., M.D., Neurology
SILVERSTEIN, M. N., M.D., PH.D., Medicine
SMITH, L. H., M.D., Medicine
SMITH, R. E., M.D., Medicine
SPELSBERG, T. C., PH.D., Biochemistry
SPITTELL, J. A., Jr., M.D., Medicine
STEINMULLER, D., PH.D., Immunology
STICKLER, G. B., M.D., PH.D., Paediatrics
STILLWELL, G. K., M.D., PH.D., Physical Medicine and Rehabilitation
STRONG, C. G., M.D., Medicine
SUNDT, T. M., Jr., M.D., Neurosurgery
SWANSON, D. W., M.D., Psychiatry
SWENSON, W. M., PH.D., Psychology
SYMMONDS, R. E., M.D., Obstetrics and Gynaecology
SZURSZEWSKI, J. H., PH.D., Physiology
TAJIK, A. J., M.B., B.S., Medicine
TARHAN, S., M.D., Anaesthesiology
TASWELL, H. F., M.D., Laboratory Medicine
TAYLOR, S. R., PH.D., Physiology and Pharmacology
TAYLOR, W. F., PH.D., Biostatistics
THISTLE, J. L., M.D., Medicine
THOMAS, J. E., M.D., Neurology
THOMPSON, J. H., Jr., PH.D., Laboratory Medicine
TOFT, D. O., PH.D., Biochemistry
TOMASI, T. B., M.D., PH.D., Immunology and Medicine
TYCE, F. A. J., M.D., Psychiatry
TYCE, G. M., PH.D., Physiology
UTZ, D. C., M.D., Urology
VAN DYKE, R. A., PH.D., Anaesthesiology and Biochemistry
VANHOUTTE, P. M., M.D., PH.D., Physiology and Pharmacology
VENEZIALE, C. M., M.D., PH.D., Biochemistry and Medicine
VETTER, R. J., PH.D., Biophysics
WAHNER, H. W., M.D., Laboratory Medicine
WALLER, R. R., M.D., Ophthalmology
WARD, L. E., M.D., Medicine
WASHINGTON, J. A., II, M.D., Microbiology and Laboratory Medicine
WEEKS, R. E., M.D., Medicine
WEIDMAN, W. H., M.D., Paediatrics
WEINSHILBOUM, R. M., M.D., Pharmacology and Medicine
WELCH, J. S., M.D., Surgery
WHISNANT, J. P., M.D., Neurology
WILLIAMS, TIFFANY J., M.D., Obstetrics and Gynaecology
WINKELMANN, R. K., M.D., PH.D., Anatomy and Dermatology
WOOD, E. H., M.D., PH.D., D.SC., Physiology and Medicine
WOODS, J. E., M.D., PH.D.
YANAGIHARA, T., M.D., Neurology
YOSS, R. E., M.D., PH.D., Neurology

YOUNG, D. S., M.B., CH.B., Laboratory Medicine

*Mechanical Engineering:*
ANDERSON, J. E., PH.D.
ARORA, S. R., PH.D.
BLACKSHEAR, P. L., PH.D.
ECKERT, E. R. G., PH.D.
FLETCHER, E. A., PH.D.
FROHRIB, D. A., PH.D.
GOLDSTEIN, R. J., PH.D.
IBELE, W. E., PH.D.
JORDAN, R. C., PH.D.
KLEINHENZ, W. A., PH.D.
LAYTON, E. T.,
LIU, B. Y. H., PH.D.
MURPHY, T. E., M.S.
OGATA, K., PH.D.
PATANKAR, S. V., PH.D.
PFENDER, E., PH.D.
SPARROW, E. M., PH.D.
WHITBY, K. T., PH.D.
WHITE, J. S., PH.D.

*Medicine:*
ALLEN, D. W., M.D.
ANDERSON, V. E., M.D.
BACHE, R.
BLACKBURN, H. W., M.D.
BLOOMER, J., M.D.
BLOOMFIELD, C., M.D.
BOND, J., M.D.
CERVENKA, J., M.D.
CHESTER, E., M.D.
COHN, J. N., M.D.
DOE, R. P., M.D.
DRAGE, C. W., M.D.
FERRIS, T. F., M.D.
FRANTZ, I. D., Jr., M.D.
GAULT, N. L., Jr., M.D.
GOETZ, F. C., M.D.
HALL, W. H., M.D.
HANSON, R., M.D.
HOWARD, R. B., M.D.
HOWE, R., M.D.
JACOB, H. S., M.D.
JACOBSON, M. E., M.D.
KAPLAN, M. E., M.D.
KENNEDY, B. J., M.D.
KJELLSTRAND, C. M., M.D.
KRONENBERG, R., M.D.
LABREE, J., M.D.
LEVITT, M. D., M.D.
MESSNER, R., M.D.
MULHAUSEN, R. O., M.D.
MURRAY, M. J., M.D.
NUTTALL, F. O., M.D.
OPPENHEIMER, J. H., M.D.
PRINEAS, R., M.D.
SABATH, L. D., M.D.
SAROSI, G. A., M.D.
SCHULTZ, A. L., M.D.
SCHWARTZ, S., M.D.
SHAPIRO, F. L., M.D.
SHEPPARD, J., M.D.
SILVIS, S., M.D.
TADDEINI, L., M.D.
TAYLOR, H., M.D.
THEOLOGIDES, A., M.D.
TOBIAN, L., Jr., M.D.
TUNA, N., M.D.
VENNES, J. A., M.D.
WANG, Y., M.D.
WILSON, I. D., M.D.
WILSON, L., M.D.
WINCHELL, C. P., M.D.
ZANJANI, E. D., M.D.
ZIEVE, L., M.D.

*Microbiology:*
BRAND, K. G., M.D.
DWORKIN, M., PH.D.
FARAS, A. J., PH.D.
JOHNSON, R. C., PH.D.
PLAGEMANN, P. G. W., PH.D.
ROGERS, P., PH.D.

SCHMIDT, E. L., PH.D.
WATSON, D. W., PH.D.

*Mortuary Science:*
SLATER, R. C., B.S.

*Music:*
ARGENTO, D., PH.D.
BENCRISCUTTO, F., D.M.A.
CASWELL, A., ED.D.
FETLER, P., PH.D.
FLEISCHER, H., PH.D.
FREED, P., M.M.
JACKSON, D., PH.D.
LAUDON, R., PH.D.
MASSMANN, R., PH.D.
RIEDEL, J., PH.D.
STOKES, E., PH.D.
SUTTON, E., PH.D.
TURRENTINE, E., PH.D.
ULTAN, L., PH.D.
WEISER, B., M.A.

*Naval Science:*
MENIKHEIM, D. K., M.S.

*Near and Middle Eastern Studies:*
FARAH, C., PH.D.

*Neurology:*
BERRY, J. F., PH.D.
ETTINGER, M. G., M.D.
GUMNIT, R. J., M.D.
KENNEDY, W. R., M.D.
KLASSEN, A. C., M.D.
RESCH, J. A., M.D.
SUNG, J. H., M.D.
SWAIMAN, K. F., M.D.
TORRES, F., M.D.
WEBSTER, D., M.D.
WIRTSCHAFTER, J., M.D.
WRIGHT, F. S., M.D.

*Neurosurgery:*
BLOEDEL, J. R., PH.D., M.D.
CHOU, S. N., PH.D., M.D.
FRENCH, L. A., PH.D., M.D.
MEIER, M. I., PH.D.
SELJESKOG, E. L., PH.D., M.D.

*Nursing:*
DUXBURY, M. L., PH.D.
FAHY, E. T., ED.D.
HARRIS, M. ISABEL, PH.D.
HINSVARK, I. G., ED.D.
KING, FLORIS E., PH.D.
MANSFIELD, ELAINE R., D.N.S.
MARTINSON, IDA M., PH.D.
NORRIS, C., ED.D.

*Obstetrics and Gynaecology:*
FOREMAN, H., PH.D., M.D.
FREEMAN, D., M.D.
HAKANSON, E. Y., M.D., M.SC.
OKAGAKI, T., M.D., PH.D.
PREM, K. A., M.D.
TAGATZ, G. E., M.D.

*Ophthalmology:*
DOUGHMAN, D. I., M.D.
KNOBLOCH, W. H., M.D.
WIRTSCHAFTER, J. D., M.D.

*Orthopaedic Surgery:*
BRADFORD, D. S., M.D.
HOUSE, J. H., M.D.
THOMPSON, R. C., M.D.
WINTER, R. B., M.D.

*Otolaryngology:*
DUVALL, A. J., III, M.D.
HARFORD, E. R., PH.D.
JUHN, S. K., M.D.
LASSMAN, F., PH.D.
MEYERHOFF, W. L., M.D., PH.D.
PAPARELLA, M. M., M.D.
WARD, W. D., PH.D.

*Paediatrics:*
ANDERSON, R. C., PH.D.
BALFOUR, H., M.D.
BERGLUND, E., M.D.
BROWN, D. M., M.D.
CLAWSON, C. C., M.D.
FERRIERI, P., M.D.
FISCH, R. O., M.D.
FISH, A., M.D.
KAPLAN, E., M.D.
KERSEY, J., M.D.
KRIVIT, W., PH.D.
LUCAS, R., M.D.
MAUER, S. M., M.D.
MICHAEL, A., M.D.
MIRKIN, B., PH.D.
MOLLER, J., M.D.
NESBIT, M., M.D.
PAGE, A., M.D.
QUIE, P., M.D.
RAILE, R., M.D.
SHARP, H., M.D.
SWAIMAN, K., M.D.
tenBENSEL, R., M.D.
ULSTROM, R., M.D.
VENTERS, H., M.D.
VERNIER, R., M.D.
WANNAMAKER, L., M.D.
WARWICK, W., M.D.
WHITE, J., M.D.
WRIGHT, F., M.D.

*Pharmacology:*
ANDERS, M. W., PH.D., D.V.M.
GOLDBERG, N. D., PH.D.
MANNERING, G. J., PH.D.
MILLER, J. W., PH.D.
MIRKIN, B. L., PH.D., M.D.
SHIDEMAN, F. E., PH.D., M.D.
SLADEK, N. E., PH.D.
SPARBER, S. B., PH.D.
TAKEMORI, A. E., PH.D.
ZIMMERMAN, B. G., PH.D.

*Pharmacy:*
ABDEL-MONEM, M. M., PH.D., Medicinal Chemistry
ABUL-HAJJ, Y. J., PH.D., Pharmacognosy
DiGANGI, F. E., PH.D., Medicinal Chemistry
KABAT, H. F., PH.D., Hospital Pharmacy and Pharmacy Administration
NAGASAWA, H. T., PH.D., Medicinal Chemistry
PORTOGHESE, P. S., PH.D., Medicinal Chemistry
RIPPIE, E. G., PH.D., Pharmaceutics
STABA, E. J., PH.D., Pharmacognosy
VINCE, R., PH.D., Medicinal Chemistry
WEAVER, L. C., PH.D., Pharmacology
WERTHEIMER, A. I., PH.D., Social and Administrative Pharmacy

*Philosophy:*
EARMAN, J. S., PH.D.
EATON, M. M., PH.D.
GUNDERSON, K., PH.D.
HANSON, W. H., PH.D.
HOPKINS, J. S., PH.D.
LEWIS, D., PH.D.
MASON, H. E., PH.D.
SARTORIUS, R. E., PH.D.
SAVAGE, C. W., PH.D.
TERRELL, D. B., PH.D.
WALLACE, J. R., PH.D.

*Physical Education, Recreation, and School Health Education:*
ALEXANDER, J. F., PH.D.
CHAPMAN, F. M., RE.D.
COBB, R. S., PH.D.
JAEGER, E. M., PH.D.
STULL, G. A., ED.D.

*Physical Medicine and Rehabilitation:*
ANDERSON, T., M.D.

ATHELSTAN, G., PH.D.
GULLICKSON, G., M.D.
KOTTKE, F., M.D., PH.D.
KUBICEK, W., PH.D.
LASSMAN, F., PH.D.

*Physics:*
BAYMAN, B. F., PH.D.
BLAIR, J. M., PH.D.
BROADHURST, J. H., PH.D.
CAHILL, L. J., PH.D.
CAMPBELL, C. E., PH.D.
COURANT, H. W. J., PH.D.
DEHNHARD, D., PH.D.
FREIER, G. D., PH.D.
FREIER, P. S., PH.D.
GASIOROWICZ, S. G., PH.D.
GEFFEN, D. A., PH.D.
GIESE, C. F., PH.D.
GOLDMAN, A. M., PH.D.
GREENLEES, G. W., PH.D.
HALLEY, J. W., PH.D.
HAMERMESH, M., PH.D.
HINTZ, N. M., PH.D.
HOBBIE, R. K., PH.D.
JOHNSON, W. H., PH.D.
KELLOGG, P. J., PH.D.
MANTIS, H. T., PH.D.
PEPIN, R. O., PH.D.
ROSNER, J. L., PH.D.
RUDDICK, K., PH.D.
STUEWER, R. H., PH.D.
SUURA, H., D.SC.
TANG, Y. C., PH.D.
WADDINGTON, C. J., PH.D.
WEYHMANN, W. V., PH.D.
WINCKLER, J. R., PH.D.
ZIMMERMANN, W., PH.D.

*Plant Pathology:*
ANDERSON, N. A., PH.D.
BANTTARI, E. E., PH.D.
BISSONNETTE, H. L., PH.D.
BRAMBL, R., PH.D.
BUSHNELL, W. R., PH.D.
EIDE, C. J., PH.D.
FRENCH, D. W., PH.D.
FROSHEISER, F. I., PH.D.
KENNEDY, B. W., PH.D.
KOMMEDAHL, T., PH.D.
MACDONALD, D. H., PH.D.
MIROCHA, C. J., PH.D.
ROWELL, J. B., PH.D.
STIENSTRA, W. C., PH.D.
WILCOXSON, R. D., PH.D.

*Political Science:*
BACKSTROM, C. H., PH.D., Parties and Elections
BENJAMIN, R. W., PH.D., Political Development (Japan and China)
CHASE, H. W., PH.D., Public Law and Defence Policy
FLANIGAN, W. H., PH.D., Political Behaviour
FOGELMAN, E., PH.D., Empirical Theory
HOLT, R. T., PH.D., Comparative Political Systems
HOPMANN, P. T., PH.D., International Relations
KRISLOV, S., PH.D., Judicial Behaviour
SCOTT, T. M., PH.D., Community Politics
SHIVELY, W. P., PH.D., Comparative Politics (Western Europe)
SIBLEY, M. Q., PH.D., Development of Political Theory and American Political Thought
SORAUF, F. J., PH.D., Political Parties and Judicial Behaviour
TURNER, J. E., PH.D., Comparative Politics (Britain, China, Russia)
WYNIA, G. W., PH.D., Comparative Politics (Latin America)

*Psychiatry:*
BRANTNER, J. P., PH.D.
CLAYTON, P. J., M.D.

GARETZ, F. K., M.D.
GREENBERG, L. M., M.D.
HAUSMAN, W., M.D.
HEISTAD, G., PH.D.
HESTON, L. L., M.D.
KIRESUK, T. J., PH.D.
LYKKEN, D. T., PH.D.
MAGRAW, R., M.D.
MEEHL, P. E., PH.D.
PICKENS, R., PH.D.
SCHOFIELD, W., PH.D.
SINES, L. K., PH.D.
TUASON, V., M.D.
WESTERMEYER, J., M.D., PH.D.

*Psychoeducational Studies:*
BALOW, B., PH.D.
BRUININKS, R., PH.D.
DENO, S., PH.D.
EDSON, W., PH.D.
EGELAND, B., PH.D.
FORCE, D., Jr., PH.D.
GLOTZBACH, C., PH.D.
HAGENAH, T., PH.D.
HANSEN, L. S., PH.D.
HUMMEL, T., PH.D.
PARKER, C., PH.D.
RAYGOR, A., PH.D.
REYNOLDS, M., PH.D.
RYNDERS, J., PH.D.
SNOKE, M., PH.D.
SPRINTHALL, N., ED.D.
TENNYSON, W. W., ED.D.
TURNURE, J., PH.D.
WEATHERMAN, R., ED.D.
WEINBERG, R., PH.D.
WILDERSON, F., PH.D.
WOOD, F., PH.D.
YSSELDYKE, J., PH.D.

*Psychology:*
BERSCHEID, E. S., PH.D.
BOUCHARD, T. J., PH.D.
BURKHARDT, D. A., PH.D.
BUTCHER, J. N., PH.D.
CAMPBELL, J. P., PH.D.
DAWIS, R. V., PH.D.
DEPUE, R. A., PH.D.
DUNNETTE, M. D., PH.D.
FOX, P. W., PH.D.
GARMEZY, N., PH.D.
JENKINS, J. J., PH.D.
LABERGE, D. L., PH.D.
LOFQUIST, L. H., PH.D.
MEEHL, P. E., PH.D.
OVERMIER, J. B., PH.D.
ROBERTS, W. W., PH.D.
SNYDER, M., PH.D.
TELLEGEN, A., PH.D.
THOMPSON, T. I., PH.D.
VIEMEISTER, N. F., PH.D.
WEISS, D. J., PH.D.

*Hubert H. Humphrey Institute of Public Affairs:*
ABRAHAMSON, D. A., M.D., PH.D.
ADAMS, J., S. PH.D.
BOHEN, F. M., M.P.A.
BRANDL, J. E., PH.D.
CLEVELAND, H., A.B.
EINSWEILER, R. C., M.S.
GEESAMAN, D. P., M.A.
HOENACK, S. A., PH.D.
JERNBERG, J. E., PH.D.
NAFTALIN, A., PH.D.
WARP, G., J.D., M.A.I.A.

*Public Health:*
ANDERSON, R. K., D.V.M., Veterinary Public Health
BARBER, D. E., PH.D., Environmental Health
BLACKBURN, H. W., M.D., Physiological Hygiene
BOEN, J. R., PH.D., M.P.H., Biometry
DORNBLASER, B. M., M.H.A., Hospital and Health Care Administration

GREENE, V. W., PH.D., Interdisciplinary Studies and Environmental Health
HAFNER, J. A., PH.D., Health Care Psychology
JOHNSON, E. A., PH.D., Biometry
KJELSBERG, M. O., PH.D., Biometry
KRALEWSKI, J. E., PH.D., Health Services Research
LEON, A. S., M.D., Physiological Hygiene
LITMAN, T. J., PH.D., Hospital and Health Care Administration
McHUGH, R. B., PH.D., Biometry
PRINEAS, R. J., M.B.B.D., PH.D., Physiological Hygiene
QUAST, W., PH.D., Health Care Psychology
SCHUMAN, L. M., M.D., Epidemiology
TAYLOR, H. L., PH.D., Physiological Hygiene
TEN BENSEL, R. W., Maternal and Child Health
VESLEY, D., PH.D., Environmental Health
WECKWERTH, V. E., PH.D., Hospital and Health Care Administration

*Radiology:*
AMPLATZ, K., M.D.
FEINBERG, S. B., M.D.
GEDGAUDAS, E., M.D.
LOKEN, MERLE K., PH.D., M.D.

*Rhetoric:*
CONNOLLY, J. E., PH.D.
MARCHAND, W. M., PH.D.
PEARSALL, T. E., PH.D.
SAVAGE, E. B., PH.D.
SCHUELKE, L. D., PH.D.
WRIGHT, E. S., PH.D.

*Scandinavian:*
HASSELMO, N., PH.D.
LIBERMAN, A., PH.D.
SIMPSON, J. A., PH.D.
STOCKENSTRÖM, G., PH.D.

*Social, Psychological, and Philosophical Foundations of Education:*
BAGLEY, A. L., PH.D.
BART, W. M., PH.D.
BECK, R. H., PH.D.
BURRIS, R. W., PH.D.
COLLIER, R. O., Jr., PH.D.
CORCORAN, M. E., PH.D.
JOHNSON, D. W., ED.D.
KELLOGG, T. E., PH.D.
MERWIN, J. C., ED.D.
PARKER, C. A., PH.D.
REST, J. R., PH.D.
SAMUELS, S. J., ED.D.
STECKLEIN, J. E., PH.D.
TERWILLIGER, J. S., PH.D.
WELCH, W. W., PH.D.

*Sociology:*
ANDERSON, T. R., PH.D.
CARTER, R. E., PH.D.
CLARK, J. P., PH.D.
COOPERMAN, D., PH.D.
DONOHUE, G. A., PH.D.
ELLENBOGEN, B. L., PH.D.
FINESTONE, H., PH.D.
FULTON, R. L., PH.D.
HILL, R. L., PH.D.
JOHNSON, A. L., PH.D.
LEIK, R. K., PH.D.
MALMQUIST, C., PH.D.
MARTINDALE, D. A., PH.D.
McTAVISH, D. G., PH.D.
NELSON, J. I., PH.D.
REISS, I. L., PH.D.
REYNOLDS, P. D., PH.D.
SIMMONS, R. G., PH.D.
THORNTON, R. G., PH.D.
WARD, D. A., PH.D.

## UNIVERSITIES AND COLLEGES—MINNESOTA (UNIVERSITY OF) — U.S.A.

*Soil Science:*
ADAMS, R. S., PH.D.
BAKER, D. G., PH.D.
BLAKE, G. R., PH.D.
DOWDY, R. H., PH.D.
FARNHAM, R. S., PH.D.
FENSTER, W. E., PH.D.
GRAVA, J., PH.D.
HANSON, L., PH.D.
LARSON, W. E., PH.D.
MARTIN, W. P., PH.D.
OLSON, T., PH.D.
OVERDAHL, C. J., PH.D.
RUST, R. H., PH.D.
SCHMIDT, E. L., PH.D.
SIMKINS, C. A., PH.D.
SWAN, J. B., PH.D.

*South Asian Studies:*
BARKER, M. A. R., PH.D., South Asian Languages
KOPF, D., PH.D., History
SCHOLBERG, H., M.A., Library Science
SCHWARTZBERG, J., PH.D., Geography
TAPP, R., PH.D., Humanities and Religious Studies

*Spanish and Portuguese:*
CHEJNE, A., PH.D.
HAMILTON, R. G., PH.D.
NARVAEZ, R. A., PH.D.
RAMOS-GASCON, A., PH.D.
SPADACCINI, N., PH.D.
VIDAL, H., PH.D.
ZAHAREAS, A. N., PH.D.

*Speech-Communication:*
BORMANN, E. B., PH.D.
BROWNE, D. R., PH.D.
CASHMAN, P., PH.D.
GOLDSTEIN, S., M.A.
HOWELL, W. S., PH.D.
JENSEN, J. V., PH.D.
SCOTT, R. L., PH.D.
SHAPIRO, G. L., PH.D.

*Statistics:*
BERRY, D. A., PH.D.
BINGHAM, C., PH.D., Applied Statistics
BUEHLER, R. J., PH.D., Theoretical Statistics
COLLIER, R. O., PH.D., Applied Statistics
DASGUPTA, S., PH.D., Theoretical Statistics
EATON, M. L., PH.D., Theoretical Statistics
GEISSER, S., PH.D., Theoretical and Applied Statistics
HILDRETH, C., PH.D., Applied Statistics
HINKLEY, D. V., PH.D., Applied and Theoretical Statistics
LINDGREN, B. W., PH.D., Theoretical Statistics
SUDDERTH, W. D., PH.D., Theoretical Statistics

*Studio Arts:*
BETHKE, K. E., M.F.A.
BUSA, P.
HENDLER, R.
HOARD, C. C., M.F.A.
MACKENZIE, W.
MORRISON, J. G.
MYERS, M. H., M.F.A.
ROWAN, H. T., M.F.A.
SOMBERG, H.

*Surgery:*
ANDERSON, R. W., M.D.
BACH, F. H., M.D.
BUCHWALD, H., M.D.
DELANEY, J. P., M.D.
EISENBERG, M. M., M.D.
HAGLIN, J. J., M.D.
HITCHCOCK, C. R., M.D.
HUMPHREY, E. W., M.D.
LEONARD, A. S., M.D.
MCQUARRIE, D. G., M.D.
NAJARIAN, J. S., M.D.
PERRY, J. F., Jr., M.D.
SAKO, Y., M.D.
SIMMONS, R. L., M.D.

*Theatre Arts:*
ADEY, H. L., M.A.
BALLET, A. H., PH.D.
FREDRICKS, V., PH.D.
JOSAL, W., PH.D.
MOULTON, R. D., PH.D.
NOLTE, C. M., PH.D.
THOMPSON, D. W., PH.D.

*Therapeutic Radiology:*
LEVITT, S. H., M.D.
SONG, C. W., PH.D.

*Urologic Surgery:*
FRALEY, E. E., M.D.
LANGE, P. H., M.D.

*Veterinary Medicine:*
ANDERSON, J. F., D.V.M., M.S.
BARNES, D. M., D.V.M., PH.D.
BEMRICK, W. J., M.S., PH.D.
BRASMER, T. H., D.V.M., PH.D.
CZARNECKI, CAROLINE, M.A., PH.D.
DIESCH, S. L., D.V.M., M.P.H.
DUKE, G. E., M.S., PH.D.
DZIUK, H. E., D.V.M., M.S., PH.D.
FLETCHER, T. F., D.V.M., PH.D.
GOOD, A. L., V.M.D., M.S., PH.D.
HANLON, GRISELDA, D.V.M., M.S., PH.D.
HANSON, J. O., D.V.M.
HIGBEE, J. M., D.V.M.
JESSEN, C. R., D.V.M., PH.D.
JOHNSON, D. W., D.V.M., PH.D.
JOHNSON, K. H., D.V.M., PH.D.
KURTZ, H. J., M.S., D.V.M., PH.D.
LARSON, V. L., D.V.M., PH.D.
LOKEN, K. I., D.V.M., PH.D.
NELSON, G. H., D.V.M.
OSBORNE, C. A., D.V.M., PH.D.
PERMAN, V., D.V.M., PH.D.
POMEROY, B. S., D.V.M., M.S., PH.D.
SAUTTER, J. H., D.V.M., PH.D.
SORENSEN, D. K., D.V.M., M.S., PH.D.
SPURRELL, F. A., D.V.M., PH.D.
STEVENS, J. B., D.V.M., PH.D.
STOWE, C. M., D.V.M.
USENIK, E. A., D.V.M., PH.D.
WALLACE, L. J., D.V.M., M.S.
WEBER, A. F., D.V.M., M.S., PH.D.
WHITMORE, H. C., D.V.M., M.S., PH.D.
ZEMJANIS, R., D.V.M., PH.D.

*Vocational and Technical Education:*
ASHMUN, R. D., PH.D.
BEAR, W. F., PH.D.
BJORKQUIST, D. C., PH.D.
BROWN, M. M., ED.D.
COPA, G. H., PH.D.
HOPKINS, C. R., PH.D.
KAVANAUGH, W., PH.D.
KLAURENS, M. K., PH.D.
MCLEAN, G. N., PH.D.
MARVIN, R. P., PH.D.
MOSS, J., ED.D.
NORENBERG, C. D., PH.D.
PERSONS, E. A., PH.D.
PUCEL, D. J., PH.D.
SWANSON, G. I., PH.D.
SWANSON, R. A., ED.D.
TENNYSON, W. W., ED.D.
WHITEFORD, E. B., ED.D.

### University of Minnesota, Duluth

DULUTH, MINNESOTA 55812
Telephone: (218) 726-8000

*Provost:* ROBERT L. HELLER, PH.D.

*Vice-Provosts:*
Academic Administration: PAUL E. JUNK, PH.D.
Business Affairs: ROBERT BRIDGES.
Student Affairs: BRUCE GILDSETH, PH.D.
Director of Campus Relations: JULIAN B. HOSHAL, M.A.

DEANS:
School of Business and Economics: DAVID A. VOSE, PH.D.
College of Education: JOHN E. VERRILL, PH.D. (acting).
School of Fine Arts: PHILLIP H. COFFMAN, PH.D.
College of Letters and Science: GEORGE R. RAPP, Jr., PH.D.
School of Medicine: JOHN W. LABREE, M.D.
School of Social Development: IRL E. CARTER, PH.D.

PROFESSORS:
ANDERSON, P. M., PH.D., Medicine
AUFDERHEIDE, A. C., M.D., Medicine
BAEUMLER, W. L., PH.D., Sociology-Anthropology
BECK, L., PH.D., Medicine
BOMAN, T. G., PH.D., Secondary Education
BOYCE, W. G., M.ED., Art
BRISSETT, D. D., PH.D., Medicine
BURGSTAHLER, S. D., PH.D., Mathematical Science
BYDALEK, T. J., PH.D., Chemistry
CAPLE, R., PH.D., Chemistry
CARLSON, J. B., PH.D., Biology
CARLSON, R. M., PH.D., Chemistry
CHAMBERLAIN, T. W., PH.D., Geography
COWLES, E. J., PH.D., Chemistry
CRAWFORD, D. A., PH.D., Secondary Education
CROCKETT, W. M., PH.D., English
DETTMANN, J. A., PH.D., Accounting
DIMIAN, F. G., PH.D., Accounting
DUNCAN, J. E., PH.D., English
GLICK, W. P., PH.D., English
GRANT, J. A., PH.D., Geology
GREEN, J. C., PH.D., Geology
GUM, M. F., PH.D., Psychology
HAMILTON, T. R., M.D., Medicine
HANCOCK, R. S., PH.D., Business Administration
HANSON, H. G., PH.D., Physics
HARRISS, D. K., PH.D., Chemistry
HART, R. C., PH.D., English
HATTEN, J. T., PH.D., Communicative Disorders
HELLER, R. L., PH.D., Administration
HENDRICKSON, A. D., PH.D., Secondary Education
HOAG, L. P., PH.D., Geography
HOFSLUND, P. B., PH.D., Biology
HOLLISTER, C. D., PH.D., Social Development
JOHNSON, A. G., PH.D., Medicine
JOHNSON, J. M., PH.D., Health, Physical Education, and Recreation
JORDAN, T. F., PH.D., Physics
KAUPS, M. E., PH.D., Geography
KIM, H. K., PH.D., Business Administration
KROGSTAD, B. O., PH.D., Biology
LABREE, J. W., M.D., Medicine
LEASE, M. H., Jr., PH.D., Political Science
LEPPI, T. J., PH.D., Medicine
LEVANG, L. D., PH.D., English
LIVINGSTON, E. N., PH.D., History

Maclear, J. F., ph.d., History
Marsden, R. W., ph.d., Geology
McEwen, W. R., ph.d., Mathematical Science
Monson, P. H., ph.d., Biology
Murphy, J. R., m.mu.ed., Music
Nichol, J. C., ph.d., Chemistry
Ojakangas, R. W., ph.d., Geology
Ollenburger, A. W., ph.d., Secondary Education
Olsen, D. W., ph.d., Political Science
Olson, D. E., m.s., Physics
Owens, R. R., ph.d., English
Pandey, R. S., ph.d., Social Development
Pearson, A. N., ph.d., Sociology-Anthropology
Pierce, R. F., ph.d., Communicative Disorders
Rapp, G. R., Jr., ph.d., Letters and Science
Schauer, R. I., m.s., Art
Schroeder, F. E. H., ph.d., English
Severson, A. R., ph.d., Biomedical Anatomy
Sielaff, R. O., ph.d., Business Administration
Simula, V. L., ed.d., Special Education
Smith, A. E., ed.d., Art
Stensland, A. L., ph.d., English
Sydor, M., ph.d., Physics
Tamminen, A. W., ph.d., Psychology
Tezla, A., ph.d., English
Thompson, L. C., ph.d., Chemistry
Van Appledorn, E. R., m.m., Music
Verrill, J. E., ph.d., Secondary Education
Witzig, F. T., ph.d., Geography
Wolff, J. F., Jr., ph.d., Political Science

### University of Minnesota, Morris

Morris, Minnesota 56267
Telephone (612) 589-2211.

Provost: John Q. Imholte, ph.d.
Academic Dean: Elizabeth S. Blake, ph.d.
Director of University Relations: Margo L. Warner, m.a.

PROFESSORS:
Abbott, R. S., ph.d., Biology
Ahern, W. H., ph.d., History
Barber, L. H., ph.d., English
Driggs, O. T., ph.d., History
Farrell, C. F., ph.d., French
Granger, S. G., ph.d., Psychology
Gumpel, L., ph.d., German
Hart, N. I., ph.d., English
Hirsh, M. N., ph.d., Physics
Imholte, J. Q., ph.d., History
Johnson, C. E., ph.d., Music
Kemble, E. D., ph.d., Psychology
Klinger, E., ph.d., Psychology
Lammers, R. J., ph.d., Speech and Theatre
Latterell, J. J., ph.d., Chemistry
Lee, J., ph.d., Political Science
Peterson, F. W., ph.d., Art
Roshal, J. Y., ph.d., Biology
Rottier, J. J., ph.d., Education
Spring, W. D., m.a., English
Uehling, T. E., ph.d., Philosophy
Underwood, T. L., ph.d., History

### University of Minnesota Technical College, Crookston

Crookston, Minnesota 56716
Telephone: (218) 281-6510

Provost: Stanley D. Sahlstrom, ph.d.

Assistant Provosts:
Academic Affairs: Donald Sargeant, ph.d.
Student Affairs: Anthony Kuznik, ph.d.
Director of Institutional Advancement: Lowell Larson.

PROFESSORS:
McVey, G., ph.d., Agriculture Division
Sahlstrom, S. D., ph.d., Administration
Sargeant, D. G., ph.d., Administration

### University of Minnesota Technical College, Waseca

Waseca, Minnesota 56093
Telephone: (507) 835-1000

Provost: Edward C. Frederick, ph.d.
Assistant Provosts:
Academic Affairs: James Gibson, ph.d.
Administration: Robert Collins, ph.d.
Student Affairs: Gary Sheldon, ph.d.
Director of University Relations: Tom Yuzer, m.a.

PROFESSORS:
Collins, R., ph.d.
Cullen, W. C., d.v.m.
Frederick, E. C., ph.d.

### WINONA STATE UNIVERSITY

Winona, Minnesota 55987
Telephone: (507) 457-2110.
Founded 1858.

President: Dr. Robert A. Hanson.
Vice-Presidents: Dr. Helen Popovich (Academic), Dr. John Kane (Student), Norman Decker (Administration).
Librarian: E. Jacobsen.

The library contains 177,885 vols., 7,974 reels of microfilm, 568,605 microfiche and films.

Number of teachers: 253.
Number of students: 5,130.

## MISSISSIPPI

### ALCORN STATE UNIVERSITY

Lorman, Mississippi 39096
Telephone: (601) 877-3711.
Founded 1871.

President: Dr. Walter Washington.
Vice-President: Dr. R. E. Waters.
Dean of Academic Affairs: Dr. Malvin Williams.
Business Manager: O. W. Moses.
Dean of Students: Dr. Frederick Harris.
Registrar: Alice Gill.
Librarian: Dr. Epsy Hendricks.

Publication: *The Alcorn State University Catalogue* (biannually).

The library contains 131,715 vols.

Number of teachers: 152.
Number of students: 2,341.

### BELHAVEN COLLEGE

Jackson, Mississippi 39202
Telephone: 352-0013.
Founded 1883.

President: Verne R. Kennedy.
Vice-President, Academic Affairs: S. D. Buckley.
Director of Admissions: Doug Mickey.
Librarian: Hope R. Huebner.

The library contains 60,229 vols.
Number of teachers: 59.
Number of students: 929.

### BLUE MOUNTAIN COLLEGE

Box 338, Blue Mountain, Mississippi 38610
Telephone: (601) 685-5711.
Founded 1873.
Liberal Arts College for Women.

President: E. Harold Fisher.
Academic Dean: William N. Washburn.
Director of Admissions: Gerald Fowler.
Dean of Students: Rebecca Briscoe.
Registrar: Annie Hendricks.
Librarian: Carolyn Mounce.

The library contains 44,000 vols.
Number of teachers: 33.
Number of students: 371.

### DELTA STATE UNIVERSITY

Cleveland, Mississippi 38733
Telephone: (601) 846-6664.
Founded 1924.

President: Forest Kent Wyatt.
Registrar: James Donald Cooper.
Librarian: Dr. Rush Glenn Miller, Jr.

The library contains 350,000 vols.
Number of teachers: 190.
Number of students: 3,350.

### JACKSON STATE UNIVERSITY

1400 J.R. Lynch St., Jackson, Mississippi 39217
Founded 1877.

President: Dr. John A. Peoples, Jr.
Vice-President for Academic Affairs: Dr. Estus Smith.
Vice-President for Administration: (vacant).
Vice-President for Fiscal Affairs: Dr. Paul W. Purdy.
Vice-President for Student Affairs: Dr. G. A. Johnson.
Director of Admissions: (vacant).
Dean of School of Education: Dr. Beatrice Mosley.

Dean, Graduate School: Dr. OSCAR ROGERS.
Dean of Liberal Studies: Dr. R. H. SMITH.
Dean, School of Business and Economics: Dr. WILLIAM M. COOLEY.
Dean, School of Industrial and Technical Studies: Dr. J. T. SMITH.
Director of Records: Mrs. MILDRED KELLY.
Director of the Library: Dr. LELIA G. RHODES.

The library contains 339,234 vols.
Number of students: 7,832.
Publications: Blue and White Flash (quarterly), Alumni Newsletter (quarterly).

## MILLSAPS COLLEGE
JACKSON, MISSISSIPPI 39210
Telephone: (601) 354-5201.
Founded 1892.
President: Dr. GEORGE M. HARMON.
Dean of Faculty: Dr. HARRY GILMER.
Librarian: J. F. PARKS, Jr.

The library contains 130,000 vols.
Number of teachers: 63.
Number of students: 955.

## MISSISSIPPI COLLEGE
CLINTON, MISSISSIPPI 39058
Telephone: 924-5131.
Founded: 1826.
President: Dr. LEWIS NOBLES.
Vice-President for Academic Affairs: Dr. CHARLES MARTIN.
Vice-President for Graduate Studies and Special Programs: Dr. EDWARD L. MCMILLAN.
Vice-President for Business Affairs: JOE H. BARBER, Jr.
Vice-President for Student Personnel: Dr. VAN D. QUICK.
Dean of Admissions: RORY LEE.

The library contains 260,000 vols.
Number of teachers: 177 (including 46 part-time).
Number of students: 4,489.

## MISSISSIPPI STATE UNIVERSITY
MISSISSIPPI 39762
Telephone: (601) 325-2323.
Founded 1878.
President: J. D. MCCOMAS.
Vice-President: T. K. MARTIN.
Vice-President for Academic Affairs: R. E. WOLVERTON.
Vice-President for Agriculture, Forestry and Veterinary Medicine: L. N. WISE.
Vice-President for Business Affairs: G. L. VERRALL.
Vice-President for Student Affairs: R. L. JONES.
Vice-President for Graduate Studies and Research: M. T. LOFTIN.
Registrar: L. D. FURGERSON.

Librarian: G. R. LEWIS.
Number of teachers: 750.
Number of students: 12,225.

DEANS:
Agriculture: C. E. LINDLEY.
Architecture: W. G. MCMINN.
Arts and Sciences: E. L. MCGLONE.
Business and Industry: G. M. ROGERS.
Education: A. J. MOORE.
Engineering: WILLIE L. MCDANIEL.
Forestry: J. CHARLES LEE.
Veterinary Medicine: J. G. MILLER.

## MISSISSIPPI UNIVERSITY FOR WOMEN
COLUMBUS, MISSISSIPPI 39701
Founded 1884; first State-supported college exclusively for women to be founded in the U.S.
President: JAMES W. STROBEL, PH.D.
Vice-President for Academic Affairs: H. CRAFT, M.A., PH.D. (acting).
Vice-President for Student Affairs: GLORIA RAINES, M.A., PH.D.
Vice-President for Financial Affairs: DELENE W. LEE, M.ED., ED.D.
Vice-President for External Affairs: O. WENDELL SMITH, M.B.A., PH.D
Director of Library: DAVID L. PAYNE, M.A., M.S., M.L.S., PH.D.

Library of 304,054 vols.
Number of teachers: 160.
Number of students: 2,307.
Publication: Catalogue (annual).

DEANS:
School of Arts and Sciences: JAMES T. MURRELL, Jr., PH.D.
School of Education: MAUDE D. YOW, ED.D.
School of Home Economics: THRATH COBB CURRY, ED.D.
School of Nursing: ANNETTE K. BARRAR, M.N.
Graduate School: (vacant).

## MISSISSIPPI VALLEY STATE UNIVERSITY
ITTA BENA, MISSISSIPPI 38941
Telephone: 254-9041.
Founded 1950.
President: E. A. BOYKINS.
Dean: SILAS PEYTON.
Registrar: LAWRENCE M. SUTTON.
Librarian: ROBBYE R. HENDERSON.

The library contains 84,315 volumes.
Number of teachers: 150.
Number of students: 3,228.

## TOUGALOO COLLEGE
TOUGALOO, MISSISSIPPI 39174
Telephone: (601) 956-4941.
Founded 1869.
Private liberal arts college, affiliated with Disciples of Christ and United Church of Christ.

President: Dr. GEORGE A. OWENS.
Academic Dean: Dr. VAN S. ALLEN.
Dean of Students: ERNESTINE HOLLOWAY.
Director of Development and Public Relations: Dr. LAWRENCE DURGIN.

The library contains 88,000 vols.
Number of teachers: 67.
Number of students: 886.

Publication: Tougaloo News† (six a year).

## UNIVERSITY OF MISSISSIPPI
UNIVERSITY, LAFAYETTE CO., MISSISSIPPI 38677
Telephone: (601) 232-7111.
Chartered 1844.
The School of Medicine, the School of Dentistry, the School of Nursing and the School of Health Related Professions are situated at Jackson, Mississippi.
Chancellor: PORTER L. FORTUNE, Jr., PH.D.
Executive Vice-Chancellor: HARVEY S. LEWIS, PH.D.
Vice-Chancellor for Health Affairs: NORMAN NELSON, M.D. (Jackson Campus).
Registrar: Dr. MAMIE B. FRANKS, ED.D.
Director of Libraries: (vacant).

The library contains 613,230 documents (Oxford Campus).
Number of teachers: 494 (Oxford Campus).
Number of students: 9,635 (Oxford Campus).
Publications: Space Law Journal, Mississippi Law Journal, Catalogues: Graduate School, Law Medical Center, Summer Session, Undergraduate.

DEANS:
Business Administration: M. LYNN SPRUILL, PH.D.
Education: S. A. MOORHEAD, PH.D.
Engineering: ALLIE M. SMITH, PH.D.
Graduate: JOSEPH SAM, PH.D.
Law: PARHAM H. WILLIAMS, Jr., LL.M.
Liberal Arts: GERALD W. WALTON, PH.D.
Pharmacy: WALLACE L. GUESS, PH.D
Dentistry: W. V. MANN, D.M.D. (Jackson Campus).
Health Related Professions: THOMAS E. FREELAND, PH.D. (Jackson Campus).
Medicine: NORMAN NELSON, M.D. (Jackson Campus).
Nursing: EDRIE JEAN GEORGE, ED.D. (Jackson Campus).

## UNIVERSITY OF SOUTHERN MISSISSIPPI
SOUTHERN STATION, BOX 1, HATTIESBURG, MISSISSIPPI 39401
Telephone: (601) 266-7101.
Founded 1910.

President: AUBREY K. LUCAS, PH.D.
Executive Administrative Assistant: ROGER B. JOHNSON, M.S.
Vice-President of Academic Affairs: CHARLES W. MOORMAN, PH.D.
Vice-President of Administration: SHELBY F. THAMES, PH.D.
Vice-President of Business and Finance: THOMAS G. ESTES, Jr., PH.D.
Vice-President of Student Affairs: PETER E. DURKEE, PH.D.
Registrar: DANNY W. MONTGOMERY, M.ED.
Director of Institutional Research: SIDNEY E. L. WEATHERFORD, Jr., ED.D.
Librarian: GROVER C. ASHLEY, M.S.

The library contains 750,000 vols.
Number of teachers: 612.
Number of students: 12,750.
Publications: *The Southern Quarterly*†, *Journal of Educational Research*† (both quarterly).

### DEANS:

Education and Psychology: BOBBY D. ANDERSON, ED.D.
Liberal Arts: JAMES H. SIMS, PH.D.
Science and Technology: GARY C. WILDMAN, PH.D.
Business Administration: JOSEPH A. GREENE, PH.D.
Fine Arts: JOHN E. GREEN, ED.D.
Home Economics: SARAH W. GIBBS, PH.D.
Nursing: M. ELIZABETH HARKINS, PH.D.
Health, Physical Education, Recreation: WALTER E. COOPER, ED.D.
Students: W. RADER GRANTHAM, M.A.
Social Work: SHIRLEY JONES, D.S.W.
Honors: WALLACE G. KAY, PH.D.
Library Services: O. K. BOSHEARS, PH.D.
Admissions: GENE D. SAUCIER, ED.D.
Graduate School: ROBERT T. VAN ALLER, PH.D.

## WILLIAM CAREY COLLEGE
HATTIESBURG, MISSISSIPPI 39401
Telephone: 582-5051.
Founded 1906.

President: J. RALPH NOONKESTER, PH.D., LL.D.
Academic Vice-President: Dr. HUGH L. DICKENS.
Registrar: Mrs. SARA EMERSON, B.S.
Director of Admissions: ANTONIO PASCALE, M.ED.
Librarian: Y. LEE, M.L.S.

The library contains 105,084 vols.
Number of teachers: 126.
Number of students: 2,710.

## MISSOURI

## AVILA COLLEGE
11901 WORNALL ROAD,
KANSAS CITY, MISSOURI 64145
Telephone: (816) 942-8400.
Founded 1916.

President: Sister OLIVE LOUISE DALLAVIS, C.S.J.
Registrar: Sister JEAN BINK, C.S.J.
Librarian: Sister UNA MARIA BRUMBACK, C.S.J.

The library contains 68,000 vols.
Number of teachers: 198 (full- and part-time).
Number of students: 2,125.
Publication: *Avila College Catalog*†.

## CARDINAL GLENNON COLLEGE
5200 GLENNON DRIVE,
ST. LOUIS, MISSOURI 63119
Telephone: 644-0266.

Founded 1900. Liberal Arts College exclusively for candidates for Roman Catholic priesthood.

President: Rev. FRANCIS A. GAYDOS, C.M.
Registrar: Mrs. CELESTE BRANDHORST.
Librarian: Mrs. MARY BETH GLADIEUX.

The library contains 61,564 volumes.
Number of teachers: 24.
Number of students: 105.

## CENTRAL METHODIST COLLEGE
FAYETTE, MISSOURI 65248
Founded 1854.

President: JOE A. HOWELL, PH.D.
Dean of the College: RONDAL BELL, PH.D.
Librarian: R. SHIELDS, M.A.

The library contains 100,000 vols.
Number of teachers: 59, including 12 professors.
Number of students: 600.
Publication: *Bulletin*.

## CENTRAL MISSOURI STATE UNIVERSITY
WARRENSBURG, MISSOURI 64093
Telephone: 429-4111.
Founded 1871.

President: JAMES M. HORNER.
Provost: CATHERINE TISINGER.
Vice-Presidents: TOM EDMUNDS (Finance and Administration), WILLIAM STUCKER (University Advancement), STEPHEN PETERSEN (Student Affairs).
Dean of Admissions: A. LOUIE SOSEBEE.
Registrar: R. BOYD.
Director of Library Services: EDWARD HARRIS.

The library contains 300,000 vols.
Number of teachers: 450.
Number of students: 10,000.

### DEANS:

School of Arts and Sciences: JOSEPH HATFIELD.
School of Applied Science and Technology: RAWLEIGH GAINES.
School of Business and Economics: ROBERT PIERCE.
School of Education: ROBERT GARD.
School of Public Services: ROBERT MARSHAL.

## CULVER-STOCKTON COLLEGE
CANTON, MISSOURI 63435
Telephone: Canton 288-5221.
Founded 1853.

President: ROBERT W. BROWN.
Registrar: Miss OLGA BAYS.
Vice-President for Academic Affairs: Dr. WALTER S. REULING.
Vice-President for College Relations: (vacant).
Vice-President for Business Affairs: RICHARD L. VOSS, Jr.
Vice-President for Student Services and Admissions: JOHN T. HOHMAN.
Librarian: SHARON UPCHURCH.

The library contains 100,000 vols.
Number of teachers: 40.
Number of students: 600.

Publications: *Catalog*, *View*, *Alumnews* (bi-monthly), *Megaphone* (student newspapers, bi-weekly).

## DRURY COLLEGE
SPRINGFIELD, MISSOURI 65802
Telephone: (417) 865-8731.
Founded 1873.

President: Dr. NORMAN C. CRAWFORD, Jr.
Dean of the College: Dr. JORGE PADRON.
Registrar: GALE BOUTWELL.
Librarian: JUDITH ARMSTRONG.

The library contains 160,000 vols.
Number of teachers: 74 full-time equivalent.
Number of students: 1,926 full-time equivalent.

## EVANGEL COLLEGE OF THE ASSEMBLIES OF GOD
1111 N. GLENSTONE,
SPRINGFIELD, MISSOURI 65802
Telephone: 865-2811.
Founded 1955.

President: Dr. ROBERT H. SPENCE.
Academic Dean: Dr. ZENAS BICKET.
Business Manager: GEORGE CRAWFORD.
Dean of Students: Dr. THURMAN VANZANT.
Director of Development: NEIL J. ESKELIN.

UNIVERSITIES AND COLLEGES—MISSOURI  U.S.A.

The library contains 87,000 vols.
Number of students: 1,460.
Publication: *Vision* (College magazine, six times a year).

### FONTBONNE COLLEGE
6800 WYDOWN BLVD.,
ST. LOUIS, MISSOURI 63105
Telephone: (314) 862-3456.
Founded 1917.

*President*: Sister JANE HASSETT, C.S.J., PH.D.
*Academic Dean*: Sister MARIE DAMIEN ADAMS, C.S.J., PH.D.
*Dean of Students*: BARRY MCARDLE, M.S.
*Registrar*: SUZANNE PROSSER.
*Librarian*: Sister ALBERTA A. RUYS, C.S.J., A.M.
*Director of Development*: THOMAS N. EHLMAN, M.B.A.
*Director of Admissions*: CHARLES BEECH, B.A.

The library contains 86,889 vols.
Number of teachers: 61 full-time, 24 part-time.
Number of students: 878.
Publications: *Fontbonne College Magazine*† (3 a year).

### HARRIS-STOWE STATE COLLEGE
3026 LACLEDE AVENUE,
ST. LOUIS, MISSOURI 63103
Telephone: 533-3366.
Founded 1857.

*President*: Dr. HENRY GIVENS, Jr.
*Director of Admissions*: Mrs. VALERIE BEESON.
*Vice-President for Administration and Academic Affairs*: Dr. GEORGE HYRAM.
*Vice-President for Student Affairs*: RONALD DIEDERICHS.
*Registrar*: Mrs. MARY K. JONES.
*Librarian*: MARTIN KNORR.

The library contains 59,000 vols.
Number of teachers: 50.
Number of students: 1,100.

### KANSAS CITY ART INSTITUTE
4415 WARWICK BLVD.,
KANSAS CITY, MISSOURI 64111
Founded 1885. Four-year college of art and design.

*President*: JOHN W. LOTTES.

The library contains 31,000 vols. and 45,000 slides.
Number of students: 575.

### LINCOLN UNIVERSITY
JEFFERSON CITY, MISSOURI 65101
Founded 1966.

*President*: JAMES FRANK.
*Vice-President*: JOHN CHAVIS.

*Dean of Students*: JESSE JOHNSON.
*Chairman, Graduate Division*: JOE L. SIMMONS.
*Librarian*: Mrs. FREDDYE ASHFORD.

Number of teachers: 145, including 101 professors.
Number of students: 2,225.
Publications: *Lincoln Clarion* (2 a month), *Archives* (annual review), *Lincoln's Page*, *University Relations News Letter*, *Alumni Bulletin*.

### LINDENWOOD COLLEGES, THE
ST. CHARLES, MISSOURI 63301

*President*: ROBERT JOHNS.
*Dean of Faculty*: AARON MILLER.
*Dean of Students*: LARRY JOSEPH.
*Registrar*: JERRY MONTAG.
*Librarian*: VICTORIA FROWINE.

The library contains 100,000 books and pamphlets.
Number of teachers: 100.
Number of students: 1,950.
Publications: *The Lindenwood College Bulletin*, *The Griffin* (annual).

### MARYVILLE COLLEGE
13550 CONWAY ROAD,
ST. LOUIS, MISSOURI 63141
Telephone: (314) 576-9300.
Founded 1872.

*President*: Dr. CLAUDIUS PRITCHARD.
*Vice-President, Academic Dean*: Dr. JOHN BURD.
*Vice-President for Development*: DONALD J. MCLAIN.
*Director of Admissions*: MICHAEL J. GILLICK.
*Registrar*: Dr. ROBERT ADAMS.
*Librarian*: Mrs. PEPPER COIL.

The library contains 90,000 vols.
Number of teachers: 122.
Number of students: 1,450.

### MISSOURI VALLEY COLLEGE
500 EAST COLLEGE,
MARSHALL, MISSOURI 65340
Telephone: (816) 886-6924.
Founded 1889.

*President*: ROBERT J. GLASS.
*Registrar*: BYRON B. BANTA.
*Director of Admissions*: KEN SIBERT.
*Academic Dean*: W. H. BEARCE.
*Dean of Students*: WILLIAM J. PETZ.
*Librarian*: ALAN C. DOOLITTLE.

The library contains 85,654 vols.
Number of teachers: 38.
Number of students: 502.

### NORTHEAST MISSOURI STATE UNIVERSITY
KIRKSVILLE, MISSOURI 63501
Founded 1867.

*President*: Dr. CHARLES J. MCCLAIN.

*Dean of Instruction*: Dr. DARRELL KRUEGER.
*Director of Admissions*: TERRY TAYLOR.
*Registrar*: Mrs. LEE MYERS.

The library contains over 260,000 vols.
Number of teachers: 344.
Number of students: 6,366.
Publications: Official Bulletins (monthly), *Nemoscope* (quarterly), *Index* (weekly student newspaper), *Baldwin Lecture* (yearly), *Echo* (student yearbook), *Northeast Today* (weekly during academic year).

### NORTHWEST MISSOURI STATE UNIVERSITY
MARYVILLE, MISSOURI 64468
Telephone: (816) 582-7141.
Founded 1905.

*President*: Dr. B. D. OWENS.
*Assistant to the President*: CHARLES W. VEATCH.
*Vice-President for Environmental Development*: Dr. ROBERT E. BUSH.
*Vice-President for Student Development*: Dr. J. P. MEES.
*Vice-President for Academic Affairs*: Dr. GEORGE W. ENGLISH.
*Dean of Graduate School*: Dr. LEON F. MILLER.
*Dean of Students*: Dr. PHIL HAYES.
*Librarian*: Dr. C. W. KOCK.

The library contains 219,722 vols.
Number of teachers: 222.
Number of students: 4,916.
Publications: *N.M.S.U. Studies*† (quarterly), *Northwest Missourian* (weekly newspaper), *Tower* (student yearbook).

### PARK COLLEGE
PARKVILLE, MISSOURI 64152
Telephone: Sh 1-2000.
Founded 1875.

*President*: HAROLD CONDIT.
*Registrar*: EILEEN WEST.
*Director of Admissions and Student Services*: JOSEPH HOLST.
*Librarian*: H. SMITH.

The library contains 93,000 vols.
Number of teachers: 32 (Parkville Campus).
Number of students: 471 (Parkville Campus).
Publications: *The Park Alumniad*, *The Park Record* (both quarterly).

### ROCKHURST COLLEGE
5225 TROOST AVENUE,
KANSAS CITY, MISSOURI 64110
Telephone: (816) 926-4000.
Founded 1910.

*President*: Rev. ROBERT F. WEISS, S.J.

*Chancellor:* Rev. MAURICE E. VAN ACKEREN, S.J.
*Vice-President:* Rev. EDWARD FAVILLA, S.J.
*Registrar:* PAUL D. AREND.
*Librarian:* GERALD B. HUBBLE.

The library contains 104,487 vols.
**Number of teachers:** 200.
Number of students: 3,206.

## SAINT LOUIS UNIVERSITY
221 NORTH GRAND BLVD.,
SAINT LOUIS, MISSOURI 63103
Telephone: (314) 658-2222.

**Founded 1818; Chartered 1832.**
Private control; Academic year: September to May (two terms).
*President:* Rev. THOMAS R. FITZGERALD, S.J., M.A., S.T.L., PH.D.
*Chancellor:* Rev. PAUL C. REINERT, S.J., A.M., S.T.L., PH.D., LL.D., PED.D., L.H.D., ED.ADM.D.
*Academic Vice-President:* Rev. JOHN H. GRAY, S.J., M.A., S.T.L., PH.D.
*Vice-President for the Medical Center:* GEORGE E. THOMA, JR., M.D.
*Vice-President for Business and Finance:* JON PRIMES, B.S., M.ED.
*Vice-President for Student Development:* CHARLES C. SCHROEDER, M.A., ED.D.
*Vice-President for Parks College:* PAUL A. WHELAN, M.S., PH.D.
*Director of Campus Ministries:* Rev. NEAL MCDERMOTT, O.P., PH.B., PH.L., S.T.LR., M.A.
*Registrar:* HELEN CANADA, M.S., PH.D.
*Secretary-Treasurer:* Rev. J. J. MARCHETTI, S.J., A.M., S.T.L., PH.D.
*Dean of Admissions:* L. A. MENARD, M.ED.
*Controller:* C. R. PEABODY, B.S. in C.
*Director of University Libraries:* W. P. COLE, A.M.L.S.

Library: see Libraries.
Number of teachers: 1,812.
Number of students: 10,393.

Publications: *The Classical Bulletin, The Modern Schoolman, Review for Religious, Theology Digest, Saint Louis University Law Journal, Seismological Bulletin, Manuscripta, Universitas, Chart, Eads Bridge Review, Challenge, Horizon, Conservator, This Week at Saint Louis University, Institute of Jesuit Sources, Studies in the Spirituality of Jesuits, Symposium, International Legal Education Newsletter, BALSA Reports, Parks Today, Law and Tactics in Juvenile Cases, The University News.*

### DEANS:
*College of Arts and Sciences:* ROLANDO E. BONACHEA, PH.D.
*Graduate School:* Rev. WILLIAM V. STAUDER, S.J., M.S., S.T.L., PH.D.
*School of Medicine:* DAVID R. CHALLONER, B.S., M.D.
*School of Law:* RUDOLPH C. HASL, J.D., LL.M.
*College of Philosophy and Letters:* Rev. JOHN L. TRELOAR, S.J., M.A., PH.L., S.T.L., PH.D.
*School of Business and Administration:* JOHN P. KEITHLEY, A.M., PH.D.
*School of Nursing and Allied Health Professions:* Sister MARY T. NOTH, S.S.M., ED.D.
*School of Social Service:* MURRAY B. MELD, M.S.W.
*Metropolitan College:* CARL L. HARSHMAN, M.S., PH.D.

### PROFESSORS:
ABELL, B. F., M.S., Aeronautical Administration
ACETO, T., Jr., M.D., Paediatrics
ANDRES, R. M., M.S., PH.D., Aerospace Engineering
ARKIN, I. M., M.DIV., PH.D., Theological Studies
ASPINWALL, N. A., M.S., PH.D., Biology
AUSTRIN, H. R., A.M., PH.D., Psychology
AYRES, S. M., B.A., M.D., Internal Medicine
BANVILLE, G. R., M.S.C., PH.D., Marketing
BARMANN, Rev. L. F., S.J., M.A., S.T.L., PH.D., History
BARNER, H. B., B.S., M.D., Surgery
BARTH, Rev. L. A., S.J., A.M., S.T.L., PH.D., Philosophy
BARTLETT, S. J., M.A., PH.D., Philosophy
BECVAR, R. J., M.S., PH.D., Education
**BEDEL, D. P.**, M.S., M.B.A., PH.D., Accounting
BENDER, A. E., M.LITT., PH.D., Education
BENOIT, R. P., PH.D., English
**BHAGAT, B. D.**, PH.D., Physiology
BLACKMAR, C. B., J.D., Law
BLACKWELL, R. J., A.M., PH.D., Philosophy
BOLL, R. W., M.S., Mathematics
BONDI, R. J., Jr., B.A.E.E., M.S.A.E., Aerospace Engineering
BONWICH, W. T., M.S., D.B.A., PH.D., Marketing
BOSE, S. K., M.SC., PH.D., Microbiology
**BRECKWOLDT, G. H.**, PH.D., Communication Disorders
BRENNAN, W. C., M.S.W., PH.D., Social Work
BRINLEY, J. F., A.M., PH.D., Psychology
**BRODEUR, A. E.**, M.D., M.RD., Radiology
BROUN, G. O., Jr., M.D., Internal Medicine
BRUEGGEMANN, I. A., R.T., Orthodontics
BRYER, J. W., B.S. IN AE., M.B.A., Aircraft Maintenance Engineering
BUTLER, R. O., A.M., Theatre Arts
CANTWELL, J. C., PH.D., Mathematics
CHALLONER, D. R., B.S., M.D., Internal Medicine
CHARRON, W. C., A.M., PH.D., Philosophy
**CHIASSON, E. J.**, M.A., PH.D., English
CHILDRESS, MARIANNE, A. M., PH.D., Philosophy
CODD, J. E., B.A., M.D., Surgery
COE, R., A.M., PH.D., Community Medicine
COLLINS, H. A., A.M., PH.D., Psychology
COLLINS, J. D., A.M., PH.D., Philosophy
CORET, I. A., A.B., M.D., Pharmacology
COSCIA, C. J., M.S., PH.D., Biochemistry
DALY, Rev. J. F., S.J., M.S., S.T.L., PH.D., Mathematics
DALY, Rev. L. F., S.J., A.M., S.T.L., PH.D., History
DAVENPORT, D. G., A.M., PH.D., Psychology
DAVIS, B. B., Jr., M.D., Internal Medicine
DE CASTRO, F. J., M.D., M.P.H., Paediatrics
DE MORET, ANNE-MARIE J., D.D'UNIV., Modern Languages
DELANEY, R. M., PH.D., Physics

DONATI, R. M., B.S., M.D., Internal Medicine
DONNELLY, P. R., M.S.H.A., PH.D., Hospital and Health Care Administration
DOYLE, A. M., A.M., PH.D., Education
DOYLE, J. P., A.M., PH.D., Philosophy
DOYLE, R. E., D.V.M., M.S., Comparative Medicine
DREBES, C. B., M.A., D.SC., Management Sciences
DUNNE, G. T., B.S., LL.B., Law
DUNSFORD, J. E., B.S., J.D., LL.M., Law
DWYER, J. D., M.S., PH.D., Biology
ELICEIRI, G. L., M.D., PH.D., Pathology
**ELLIOTT, W. H.**, M.S., PH.D., Biochemistry
**ERMATINGER, C. J.**, A.M., PH.D., Philosophy
ESLICK, L. J., A.M., PH.D., Philosophy
FAHERTY, Rev. W. B., S.J., A.M., PH.D., History
FARRIS, B. E., Jr., A.M., M.S.S.W., PH.D., Social Work
FEIR, DOROTHY J., M.S., PH.D., Biology
FITCH, C. D., M.S., M.D., Internal Medicine
FLANAGAN, E. J., M.B.A., Engineering Sciences
FOLEY, Rev. R. L., M.A., S.T.B., S.T.L., PH.D., Theological Studies
FORSBERG, J. H., M.S., PH.D., Chemistry
FOX, R. T., M.A., PH.D., Hospital and Health Care Administration
**FREESE, R. W.**, A.M., PH.D., Mathematics
FRIEDMAN, W. H., M.D., Otolaryngology
GAFFNEY, Rev. J. P., S.M.M., S.T.L., S.T.D., Theological Studies
GALLAGHER, N. I., A.M., M.D., Internal Medicine
GAMMEL, J. L., M.A., PH.D., Physics
GANTNER, G., Jr., M.D., Forensic and Environmental Pathology
GARCIA, P. G., M.A., PH.D., Modern Languages
GEORGE, J. A., M.S., PH.D., Aerospace Engineering
GILNER, F. H., A.M., PH.D., Psychology
GOLD, A. H., A.M., PH.D., Pharmacology
GOLDMAN, R. L., J.D., Law
GOLDNER, J. A., M.A., J.D., Law
GRANDGENETT, D. P., M.S., PH.D., Molecular Virology
GREEN, M., M.S., PH.D., Microbiology
GREGORY, J. G., M.D., Urology
GROBMAN, HULDA, A.B., M.P.A., ED.D., Health Education
GROSSMAN, L. J., B.S.B.A., PH.D., Economics
GRUENBERG, GLADYS W., A.M., PH.D., Economics
GUENTNER, F. J., S.J., A.M., Music
GUERRA, F. J., M.B.A., C.P.A., Accounting
GUITHUES, H. J., M.B.A., PH.D., Finance
HANDAL, P. J., M.A., PH.D., Psychology
HANSON, A. B., A.M., Theatre Arts
HARRINGTON, J. T., B.S., M.B.A., Aircraft Maintenance Engineering
HARSHMAN, C. L., M.S., PH.D., Education
HASL, R. C., J.D., LL.M., Law
**HAWORTH, Rev. M. A.**, S.J., A.M., S.T.L., PH.D., Classical Languages
HENLE, Rev. R. J., S.J., A.M., PH.L., S.T.L., PH.D., Justice in American Society
HERRON, R. D., M.A., PH.D., Modern Languages
HERTELENDY, F., PH.D., Internal Medicine
HITCHCOCK, J. F., A.M., PH.D., History
HOHNSTEDT, L. F., PH.D., Chemistry
IMMEL, V. C., B.S. IN ED., J.D., Law
JANSEN, Rev. L. F., S.J., A.M., S.T.L., Classical Languages
JENNINGS, J. P., B.SC., M.S.B.A., PH.D., Accounting
JOHNSTON, L. E., Jr., D.D.S., M.S., PH.D., Orthodontics
**KAHLER, CAROL**, B.S. IN C., A.M. IN ED., ED.D., Education

KAISER, G. C., A.B., M.D., Surgery
KAMINSKI, D. L., B.S., M.D., Surgery
KEEFE, Rev. D. J., S.J., J.D., S.T.L., S.T.D., Theological Studies
KEITHLEY, J. P., A.M., PH.D., Accounting
KELLY, Rev. E. E., A.M., PH.D., S.T.L., English
KELTNER, R. M., Jr., A.M., M.D., Surgery
KIM, S. H., M.B.A., PH.D., Finance
KIM, YEE SIK, M.S., PH.D., Pharmacology
KING, D. B., J.D., LL.M., Law
KINSELLA, R. A., Jr., A.B., M.D., Internal Medicine
KNAPP, Rev. J. G., S.J., A.M., PH.D., English
KNIPP, T. R., M.A., PH.D., English
KOLMER, Sr. E., M.A., PH.D., History
KORN, J. H., M.S., PH.D., Psychology
KRAMER, T. J., M.A., PH.D., Psychology
KUSTURA, J. J., M.S., Aeronautical Administration
KWAK, N. K., A.M., PH.D., Management Science
KWON, IK-WHAN, A.M., PH.D., Management Sciences
LAGUNOFF, D., B.S., M.D., Pathology
LASKOWSKI, L. F., Jr., M.S., PH.D., Pathology
LAY, Rev. T. N., M.S., PH.D., S.T.L., Communication Disorders
LEE, S., PH.D., Physics
MOUZY, P. F., C.A.P.E.S., Modern Languages
LIN, YEONG-JER, M.S., PH.D., Meteorology
LIND, A. R., D.PHIL., D.SC., Physiology
LONGMORE, W. J., PH.D., Biochemistry
LOUI, W. A., A.M., Theatre Arts
MCAVOY, W. C., A.M., PH.D., English
MCGEE, J. F., M.S., PH.D., Physics
MCGOWAN, Sister M. NOREEN, S.S.M., M.S. IN NR.ED., Nursing
MCPARTLAND, T. S., PH.D., Sociology
MCSWEENEY, MARYELLEN, A.B., PH.D., Research Methodology
MAGUIRE, E. J., B.S., PH.D., History
MAHER, Rev. T. P., S.J., A.M., PH.D., Education
MALONE, L. J., Jr., M.S., PH.D., Chemistry
MARR, J. J., M.D., M.S., Internal Medicine
MARRS, B. L., PH.D., Biochemistry
MARSH, J. L., M.A., PH.D., Philosophy
MAZZA, Rev. R. R., S.J., M.A., PH.D., Modern Languages
MERZ, P. E., A.M., PH.D., Economics
MEYERS, A. C., Jr., M.S. IN C., PH.D., Economics
MIKHAIL, G., M.D., Obstetrics and Gynaecology
MILL, W. B., Jr., M.D., Radiation Oncology
MILLER, C. H., A.M., PH.D., English
MILLER, E. L., M.S.C., PH.D., Accounting
MITCHELL, B. J., M.S., PH.D., Geophysics
MONTELEONE, J. A., M.D., Paediatrics
MONTELEONE, PATRICIA L., M.D., Paediatrics
MOON, MARGARETE W., M.A., PH.D., Modern Languages
MONTESI, A. J., A.M., PH.D., English
MUDD, J. F. G., B.S., M.D., Internal Medicine
MUELHEIMS, G. H., M.D., Internal Medicine
MUELLER, HILTRUD S., M.D., Internal Medicine
MUNZ, D. C., M.S, PH.D., Psychology
MURRAY, RUTH B., R.N., M.S.N., Nursing
NAPOLI, J. G. M.S., PH.D., Psychology
NEIDLINGER, R. J., M.S., ED.D., Music
NEVINS, F. M., Jr., J.D., Law
NICHOLAS, H. J., PH.D., Biochemistry
NICKESON, R. C., M.S., PH.D., Psychology
NIKOLAI, R. J., M.S., PH.D., Orthodontics
NOTH, Sister M. TERESA, S.S.M., R.N., M.S. IN NR.ED., ED.D., Nursing
NUTTLI, O. W., B.S. IN PET. GPH., M.S., PH.D., Geophysics

O'BRIEN, J. C., B.A., J.D., Law
O'BRIEN, J. J., A.M., PH.D., Education
OLSON, R. E., A.B., M.D., PH.D., Biochemistry
ONG, Rev. W. J., S.J., A.M., S.T.L., PH.D., English
O'REILLY, D. E., M.D., M.OR.SR., Orthopaedic Surgery
OSTAPOWICZ, F., M.D., Obstetrics/Gynaecology
PADBERG, W. H., M.S.W., D.S.W., Social Work
PALLMANN, A. J., DR.RER.NAT., Meteorology
PEDEN, VIRGINIA H., M.D., Paediatrics
PEPPER, A. G., M.S.S., M.P.H., PH.D., Nursing
PEPPER, M. P., M.D., M.P.H., Community Medicine
PETRU, Rev. F. A., A.M., S.T.L., Theological Studies
POGELL, B. M., PH.D., Microbiology
POWER, R. W., A.B., J.D., Law
PUNZO, V. C., A.M., PH.D., Philosophy
RAW, C. J. G., M.SC., PH.D., Chemistry
REAGAN, J. T., A.M., PH.D., Philosophy
RHODES, J. L., M.S. IN M.E., Aerospace Engineering
RICE, B., B.S., PH.D., Chemistry
RICHEY, MARJORIE H., PH.D., Psychology
RIDDLE, IRENE E., R.N., M.S. IN NR.ED., PH.D., Nursing
RILES, J. B., PH.D., Mathematics
ROACH, R. C., A.M., PH.D., Modern Languages
ROHLIK, J., JU.DR., LL.M., Law
ROUGH, R. H., M.A., PH.D., Art and Art History
RUBIN, MARILYN B., M.S., PH.D., Nursing
RUBLE, R. A., A.M., ED.D., Education
SABHARWAL, C. L., M.S., PH.D., Mathematics
SALSICH, P. W., Jr., A.B., J.D., Law
SANCHEZ, J. M., A.M., PH.D., History
SARASOHN, S. E., B.S. IN ECON., J.D., Law
SATA, L. S., M.D., M.S., Psychiatry
SCHULTE, Rev. B. C., S.J., A.M., S.T.L., Modern Languages
SCHULTZ, G. P., LL.B., Law
SCHULZE, I. T., PH.D., Microbiology
SCHWEISS, J. F., M.D., Surgery
SCOTT, J. F., A.M., PH.D., English
SEARLS, EILEEN H., A.B., J.D., M.S., Law
SECKER-WALKER, R. H., M.B., B.CHIR., Internal Medicine
SENAY, L. C., Jr., PH.D., Physiology
SHIELDS, J. B., M.D., Radiology
SIMEONE, J. J., B.S., J.D., Law
SKELLY, MADGE, M.A., PH.D., Communication Disorders
SLAVIN, R. G., A.B., M.D., M.S., Internal Medicine
SMITH, JOAN M., B.A., M.S.W., Social Work
SMITH, K. R., Jr., M.D., Surgery
SOBKOWSKI, F. J., D.D.S., M.S., PH.D., Orthodontics
SPRENGEL, D. P., A.M., PH.D., Urban Affairs
STANGER, K. E., M.S., Aircraft Maintenance Engineering
STANTON, C. M., M.B.A., PH.D., Education
STAUDER, Rev. W. V., S.J., M.S., S.T.L., PH.D., Geophysics
STEVENSON, T. M., A.M., PH.D., Economics
STOEBERL, P. A., M.B.A., PH.D., Management Sciences
STRETCH, J. J., M.S.W., PH.D., Social Work
SULLIVAN, Rev. R. L., S.J., M.S., PH.D., Modern Languages
TAUB, ALICE M., A.M., PH.D., Modern Languages
TISTHAMMER, DANA J.B., A., B.S. IN L.S., Pius XII Library
TONER, T. F. N., M.F.A., Art and Art History

TUCHLER, D. J., J.D., Law
TYREE, D. A., M.B.A., PH.D., Finance
ULRICH, B. H., Jr., M.S.A.E., Aerospace Engineering
VAGO, S., A.M., PH.D., Sociology
VASQUEZ, S. W., M.B.A., C.P.A., Accounting
VINCENZ, S. A., A.R.C.S., D.I.C., PH.D., Geophysics
WAGNER, J. W., M.A., PH.D., Accounting
WALSH, J. J., S.J., A.M., PH.D., Theatre Arts
WALSH, R. R., PH.D., Biology
WEBER, M. M., B.S., SC.D., Microbiology
WEIDLE, CATHERINE E., M.A., M.S. IN L.S., Pius XII Library
WENDEL, G. D., PH.D., Political Science
WESTFALL, T. C., PH.D., Pharmacology
WILLMAN, V. L., M.D., Surgery
WOOLSEY, R. M., B.S., M.D., Neurology
WULLER, C. E., PH.D., Accounting
YEAGER, F. C., M.B.A., PH.D., Finance
YEAGER, V. L., PH.D., Anatomy
YOUNG, P. A., M.S., PH.D., Anatomy
ZEIS, DOLORES M., R.N., M.P.H., Nursing
ZIMNY, G. H., PH.D., Psychiatry

## SCHOOL OF THE OZARKS
POINT LOOKOUT, MISSOURI 65726
Telephone: (417) 334-6411.

Founded 1906.

*President:* Dr. JAMES I. SPAINHOWER.

*Executive Vice-President:* Dr. HOWELL KEETER.

*Vice-President for Work Program*: Dr. MAYBURN DAVIDSON.

*Vice-President for Finance and Comptroller:* Col. CHARLES HACKETT.

*Vice-President for Academic Affairs:* Dr. WAYNE HUDDLESTON.

*Vice-President for Administration:* Dr. WILLIAM D. TODD.

*Vice-President for Public Relations, Vice-President for Development:* Dr. JOHN MOAD.

The library contains 90,000 vols.
Number of teachers: 87.
Number of students: 1,258.

Publication: *Ozark Visitor* (every 2 months.)

## SOUTHEAST MISSOURI STATE UNIVERSITY
CAPE GIRARDEAU, MISSOURI 63701
Telephone: (314) 651-2000.

Founded 1873.

*President:* BILL W. STACY.
*Registrar:* ALTON BRAY.
*Director of Admissions:* JOHN A. BEHRENS.
*Librarian:* JAMES ZINK.

The library contains 441,000 vols. (incl. 170,000 vols. in government documents), 232,000 microforms.

Number of teachers: 422.
Number of students: 9,172 (on campus).

## SOUTHWEST MISSOURI STATE UNIVERSITY
901 SOUTH NATIONAL, SPRINGFIELD, MISSOURI 65802
Telephone: 836-5000.
Founded 1905.

*President:* DUANE G. MEYER.
*Director of Admissions:* EDWARD PIERCE.
*Librarian:* R. HARVEY.

The library contains 348,652 vols., 301,132 government documents, 248,043 books on microform, 5,128 audio-visual titles, 4,500 periodicals.
Number of teachers: 552 full-time, 166 part-time.
Number of students: 15,137.

## STEPHENS COLLEGE
COLUMBIA, MISSOURI 65201
Telephone: (314) 442-2211.
Founded 1833.

*President:* ARLAND F. CHRIST-JANER.
*Executive Vice-President:* BETTY LITTLETON.
*Dean of Faculty:* EUGENE SCHMIDTLEIN.
*Dean of Admissions and Financial Aid:* MARTHA G. WADE.
*Librarian:* WILLIS HUBBARD.

The library contains 120,000 vols.
Number of full-time teachers: 125.
Number of students: 1,400.

## TARKIO COLLEGE
TARKIO, MISSOURI 64491
Telephone: (816) 736-4131.
Founded 1883.
Church-related liberal arts college.

*President:* FRANK H. BRETZ.
*Registrar:* NANCY DOUGHERTY.
*Librarian:* WENDY HARTWIG NOBLE.

The library contains 55,000 volumes.
Number of teachers: 31.
Number of students: 270.

## UNIVERSITY OF MISSOURI SYSTEM
COLUMBIA, MISSOURI
Founded 1839.

*President:* JAMES C. OLSON, PH.D., LL.D.
*Executive Assistant to the President:* PHIL E. CONNELL, M.S.
*Vice-President for Academic Affairs:* MELVIN D. GEORGE, PH.D.
*Vice-President for Administrative Affairs:* JAMES R. BUCHHOLZ, B.S.
*Director, University Relations:* GUY M. HORTON, PH.D.

## University of Missouri—Columbia
COLUMBIA, MISSOURI 65201
Telephone: (314) 882-2121.
Founded 1839.
State control; Academic year: August to July (three semesters).

*Chancellor:* BARBARA S. UEHLING, PH.D.
*Provost:* RONALD F. BUNN, PH.D.
*Vice-Chancellor for Student Services:* NORMAN F. MOORE, M.S.
*Vice-Chancellor for Administrative Services:* RIA C. FRIJTERS, PH.D.
*Vice-Chancellor for Alumni Relations and Development:* GUY H. ENTSMINGER, M.ED.
*Registrar and Director of Admissions:* G. L. SMITH, ED.D.

Number of teachers: 2,822.
Number of students: 24,579.

DEANS AND DIRECTORS:
*College of Agriculture:* A. MAX LENNON (includes School of Forestry, Fisheries and Wildlife).
*College of Arts and Science:* A. F. YANDERS, PH.D.
*College of Business and Public Administration:* STANLEY HILLE, PH.D.
*College of Education:* B. G. WOODS, PH.D.
*College of Engineering:* W. R. KIMEL, PH.D.
*College of Public and Community Services:* GEORGE F. NICKOLAUS, J.D.
*Graduate School:* DON H. BLOUNT, PH.D.
*School of Journalism:* R. FISHER, B.S.
*School of Law:* JAMES E. WESTBROOK, J.D. (acting).
*School of Library and Information Science:* EDWARD P. MILLER, PH.D.
*School of Medicine:* Dr. CHARLES C. LOBECK, Jr., M.D.
*School of Social Work:* RICHARD E. BOETTCHER, PH.D.
*School of Home Economics:* BEATRICE B. LITHERLAND, PH.D.
*School of Nursing:* DONALD T. BROUDER (acting).
*School of Veterinary Medicine:* WILLARD EYESTONE (acting).

## University of Missouri—Kansas City
5100 ROCKHILL ROAD, KANSAS CITY, MISSOURI 64110
Telephone: (816) 276-1000.
Founded 1929.
Academic year: August to May.

*Chancellor:* GEORGE A. RUSSELL, PH.D.
*Director of Admissions and Registrar:* LEO J. SWEENEY, B.A.
*Vice-Chancellor for Academic Affairs:* EUGENE P. TRANI.
*Vice-Chancellor for Administrative Affairs:* J. JOSEPH DOERR.
*Vice-Chancellor for Development:* WILLIAM J. FRENCH (acting).
*Vice-Chancellor for Student Affairs:* Dr. GARY E. WIDMAR.
*Director, University Libraries:* Dr. KENNETH J. LABUDDE.

The library contains 602,630 vols., 14,857 microfilms and 511,896 units of other microtext.
Number of teachers: 650 full-time, 400 part-time.
Number of students: 11,000.

DEANS:
*College of Arts and Sciences:* ELDON J. PARIZEK.
*School of Administration:* ELEANOR B. SCHWARTZ.
*School of Dentistry:* Dr. MARVIN E. REVZIN.
*School of Education:* EUGENE E. EUBANKS.
*School of Graduate Studies:* Dr. HERWIG G. ZAUCHENBERGER.
*School of Law:* PASCO M. BOWMAN.
*Conservatory of Music:* Dr. E. LINDSEY MERRILL.
*School of Pharmacy:* Dr. DONALD L. SORBY.
*School of Nursing:* Dr. KATHLEEN GOLDBLATT.
*School of Medicine:* HARRY S. JONAS.

## University of Missouri—Rolla
ROLLA, MISSOURI 65401
Telephone: (314) 341-4111.
Founded 1870.

*Chancellor:* JOSEPH M. MARCHELLO, PH.D.
*Provost:* TOMLINSON FORT, Jr., PH.D.
*Executive Director of Administrative Services:* J. D. WOLLARD, B.S.
*Registrar:* P. E. PONDER, M.ED.
*Director of Admissions:* R. B. LEWIS, M.ED.
*Librarian:* RONALD BOHLEY.

Number of teachers: 328.
Number of students: 5,633.

DEANS:
*School of Engineering:* ROBERT L. DAVIS, PH.D.
*School of Mines and Metallurgy:* (vacant).
*College of Arts and Sciences:* MARVIN W. BARKER, PH.D.
*Graduate School:* ADRIAN H. DAANE, PH.D.
*Continuing Education and Public Service:* G. E. LOREY, PH.D.

## University of Missouri—St. Louis
8001 NATURAL BRIDGE RD., ST. LOUIS, MISSOURI 63121
Telephone: (314) 553-0111.
Founded 1963.

*Chancellor:* ARNOLD B. GROBMAN, PH.D.
*Vice-Chancellor for Academic Affairs:* A. C. MACKINNEY, PH.D.
*Vice-Chancellor for Administrative Services:* J. P. PERRY, M.S.
*Registrar and Director of Admissions:* H. E. MUELLER, ED.D.

Number of teachers: 426.
Number of students: 11,400.

DEANS:

*Student Affairs:* (vacant).
*College of Arts and Sciences:* R. S. BADER, PH.D.
*School of Business Administration:* D. DRIEMEIER, D.B.A.
*School of Education:* WILLIAM L. FRANZEN, PH.D.
*Division of Continuing Education:* WENDELL SMITH, PH.D.
*Evening College:* JOY WHITENER, ED.D.
*Graduate School:* THOMAS JORDAN, ED.D.
*School of Optometry:* JERRY L. CHRISTIANSEN, PH.D.
*School of Nursing:* SHIRLEY MARTIN, PH.D.

### WASHINGTON UNIVERSITY
SAINT LOUIS, MISSOURI 63130
Telephone: 889-5000.

Chartered 1853 as Eliot Seminary. Charter altered to Washington University 1857.

Private control; Academic year: September to May.

*Chancellor:* WILLIAM H. DANFORTH, A.B., M.D.
*Provost and Executive Vice-Chancellor:* M. KLING, PH.D.
*Vice-Chancellor and Associate Provost:* JAMES W. DAVIS, M.P.A., PH.D.
*Vice-Chancellor for Administration and Finance:* J. H. BIGGS, A.B.
*Vice-Chancellor for Medical Affairs:* SAMUEL B. GUZE, M.D.
*Director of Student Records:* RICHARD F. YOUNG, B.S.
*Librarian:* CHARLES CHURCHWELL, PH.D.

Number of teachers: 2,309.
Number of students: 10,804.

Publications: *Student Life, Quadrangles, Washington University Magazine, Alumni News.*

DEANS:

*Faculty of Arts and Sciences:* RALPH E. MORROW, PH.D.
  *College of Arts and Sciences:* LINDA SALAMON, PH.D.
  *Graduate School of Arts and Sciences:* LUTHER S. WILLIAMS, PH.D.
*School of Architecture:* C. MICHAELIDES, DR.ARCH.
*School of Business and Public Administration:* R. L. VIRGIL, D.B.A.
*School of Dentistry:* G. D. SELFRIDGE, D.D.S.
*School of Engineering and Applied Science:* J. M. MCKELVEY, M.S., PH.D. (includes the *Sever Institute of Graduate Engineering*).
*School of Fine Arts:* R. I. DES ROSIERS, M.A.
*School of Law:* F. HODGE O'NEAL, J.D., S.J.D.

*School of Medicine:* M. K. KING, B.A., M.D.
*George Warren Brown School of Social Work:* SHANTI K. KHINDUKA, PH.D.

### WEBSTER COLLEGE
470 EAST LOCKWOOD AVENUE
ST. LOUIS, MISSOURI 63119
Telephone: (314) 968-6900.
Founded 1915.

*President:* Dr. LEIGH GERDINE.
*Registrar:* Sister LUCY R. RAWE.
*Librarian:* Mrs. K. LUEBBERT.

The library contains 162,000 vols.
Number of teachers: 80 full-time, 512 part-time.
Number of students: 4,442.

### WESTMINSTER COLLEGE
FULTON, MISSOURI 65251
Telephone: (314) 642-3361.
Founded 1851.

*President:* Dr. J. HARVEY SAUNDERS.
*Librarian:* W. E. MARQUARDT.

The library contains 73,521 vols.
Number of teachers: 56.
Number of students: 680.

### WILLIAM JEWELL COLLEGE
LIBERTY, MISSOURI 64068
Telephone: 781-3806.
Founded 1849.

*President:* J. GORDON KINGSLEY.
*Registrar:* Mrs. DEOLA GAIRRETT.
*Director of Admissions:* H. WYATT, JR.
*Librarian:* J. P. YOUNG.

The library contains 121,000 vols.
Number of teachers: 85.
Number of students: 1,700.

### WILLIAM WOODS COLLEGE
FULTON, MISSOURI 65251
Founded 1870.

*President:* RANDALL B. CUTLIP, M.A., ED.D., LL.D., L.H.D., SC.D.
*Vice-President and Dean of Academic Affairs:* C. M. SHIPP, M.A., PH.D.
*Dean of Student Services:* NANCY L. WERST, M.S.
*Vice-President and Dean of Promotional Affairs:* L. D. MILLER, A.B., M.ED., LITT.D.

The library contains 145,000 vols.
Number of teachers: 72 full-time, 43 part-time.

Publications: *Green Owl* (campus newspaper), *Woods Echoes* (alumnae magazine).

## MONTANA

### CARROLL COLLEGE
HELENA, MONTANA 59625
Telephone: 442-3450.
Founded 1909.

*President:* Dr. FRANCIS J. KERINS.
*Registrar:* DANNETTE M. SULLIVAN.
*Librarian:* LOIS FITZPATRICK.

The library contains 94,000 volumes.
Number of teachers: 75.
Number of students: 1,300.

### COLLEGE OF GREAT FALLS
1301 20TH STREET SOUTH,
GREAT FALLS, MONTANA 59405
Telephone: (406) 761-8210.
Founded 1932.

Liberal arts college: 4-year and 2-year degree courses.

*President:* Dr. WILLIAM A. SHIELDS.
*Academic Vice-President:* Dr. CHARLES M. HEPBURN.
*Registrar:* CHARLES NELSON.
*Librarian:* RANDALL COLLVER.

The library contains 84,210 vols.
Number of teachers: 80.
Number of students: 1,200.

### EASTERN MONTANA COLLEGE
BILLINGS, MONTANA 59101
Telephone: (406) 657-2011.
Founded 1927.

*President:* WILLIAM A. JOHNSTONE (acting).
*Registrar:* CHARLES E. KITTOCK.
*Librarian:* EDWARD NERODA.

The library contains 287,187 vols.
Number of teachers: 168.
Number of students: 3,142.

### MONTANA COLLEGE OF MINERAL SCIENCE AND TECHNOLOGY
BUTTE, MONTANA 59701
Founded 1893.

*President:* FRED W. DEMONEY.
*Vice-President of Academic Affairs and Dean:* ROY H. TURLEY.
*Registrar:* JOSEPH KASPERICK.
*Director of Admissions:* RICHARD MEREDITH.
*Director of Fiscal Affairs:* VICTOR BURT.
*Director of Communications:* DAVID EDELMAN.
*Librarian:* ELIZABETH MORRISSETT.

Number of teachers: 85.
Number of students: 1,732.

Publications: *Catalog, The Magma, The Technocrat.*

## MONTANA STATE UNIVERSITY
BOZEMAN, MONTANA 59717

Founded 1893.

*President:* WILLIAM J. TIETZ.
*Director of Administration:* THOMAS E. NOPPER.
*Vice-President for Academic Affairs:* STUART KNAPP.
*Vice-President for Research:* JOHN JUTILA.
*Vice-President for Extension:* CARL J. HOFFMAN.
*Registrar and Director of Admissions:* J. E. FRAZIER.

Number of students: 10,100.

### DEANS OF COLLEGES:
*Letters and Science:* WILLIAM H. KELLY.
*Agriculture:* JAMES R. WELSH.
*Education:* JOHN KOHL.
*Engineering:* B. J. BENNETT.
*Arts and Architecture:* EDWARD GROENHOUT.
*Graduate Studies:* MICHAEL P. MALONE.
*School of Nursing:* ANNA M. SHANNON.
*School of Business:* HARVEY M. LARSON.

## NORTHERN MONTANA COLLEGE
HAVRE, MONTANA 59501

Telephone: (406) 265-7821.

Founded 1929.

Baccalaureate courses in arts and sciences, teacher education, technology.

*President:* Dr. JAMES H. M. ERICKSON.
*Registrar:* RALPH A. BRIGHAM.
*Librarian:* TERRENCE A. THOMPSON.

The library contains 84,000 vols.
Number of teachers: 90.
Number of students: 1,500.

## ROCKY MOUNTAIN COLLEGE
1511 POLY DRIVE,
BILLINGS, MONTANA 59102

Telephone: 245-6151.

Founded 1878.

*President:* Dr. BRUCE T. ALTON.
*Academic Dean:* Dr. R. DEAN BOSWELL, Jr.
*Librarian:* SUE WALKER.

The library contains 60,000 volumes.
Number of teachers: 40.
Number of students: 440.

## UNIVERSITY OF MONTANA
MISSOULA, MONTANA 59812

Telephone: 243-0211.

Founded 1893.

*President:* NEIL S. BUCKLEW, PH.D.
*Academic Vice-President:* DONALD HABBE, PH.D.
*Fiscal Affairs Vice-President:* PATRICIA P. DOUGLAS, PH.D., C.P.A.
*Associate Vice-President for Research:* RAYMOND C. MURRAY, PH.D.
*Registrar:* PHILIP T. BAIN, PH.D.
*Director of Student Affairs:* FRED WELDON, PH.D.
*Dean of Library Service:* E. C. THOMPSON, M.L.S.

The library contains 626,700 vols., plus 77,600 U.S. Government documents.
Number of teachers: 400.
Number of students: 8,800.

### DEANS:
*College of Arts and Sciences:* R. SOLBERG, PH.D.
*School of Fine Arts:* KATHRYN MARTIN, M.A.
*School of Business Administration:* PAUL B. BLOMGREN, D.B.A.
*Graduate School:* RAYMOND C. MURRAY, PH.D.
*School of Education:* ALBERT H. YEE, ED.D.
*School of Forestry:* BENJAMIN B. STOUT, PH.D.
*School of Journalism:* W. BRIER, PH.D.
*School of Law:* JOHN O. MUDD, J.D.
*School of Pharmacy:* PHILIP CATALFOMO, PH.D.

ASSOCIATED INSTITUTIONS (*q.v.*):
Eastern Montana College.
Montana College of Mineral Science and Technology.
Montana State University.
Northern Montana College.
Western Montana College.

## WESTERN MONTANA COLLEGE
DILLON, MONTANA 59725

Telephone: (406) 683-7011.

Founded 1893.

State control; Academic year: September to June.

*President:* ROBERT H. THOMAS.
*Registrar:* LARRY HICKETHIER.
*Academic Dean:* D. TASH.
*Dean of Education:* ALAN ZETLER.
*Librarian:* K. CORY.

Number of teachers: 38.
Number of students: 828.

# NEBRASKA

## CHADRON STATE COLLEGE
CHADRON, NEBRASKA 69337

Telephone: 432-4451.

Founded 1911.

*President:* EDWIN C. NELSON.
*Registrar:* MEREDITH GRAVES.
*Librarian:* TERRENCE BRENNAN.

The library contains 140,000 vols.
Number of teachers: 88.
Number of students: 2,110.

## CONCORDIA TEACHERS COLLEGE
800 NORTH COLUMBIA AVENUE,
SEWARD, NEBRASKA 68434

Telephone: (402) 643-3651.

Founded 1894.

*President:* M. J. STELMACHOWICZ.
*Registrar:* LEEROY HOLTZEN.
*Director of Admissions:* Dr. E. DUENSING.
*Librarian:* VIVIAN PETERSON.

The library contains 75,000 vols.
Number of teachers: 100.
Number of students: 1,150.

## CREIGHTON UNIVERSITY
OMAHA, NEBRASKA 68178

Telephone: 449-2700.

Founded 1878; Chartered 1879.

Private-Independent, associated with the Society of Jesus.

*President:* Rev. MATTHEW E. CREIGHTON, S.J., M.A., S.T.L., PH.D.
*Vice-President Academic Affairs:* Rev. MICHAEL G. MORRISON, S.J., PH.D.
*Vice-President for Health Sciences:* R. P. HEANEY, M.D.
*Vice-President for Finance:* W. R. JAHN, A.M., C.P.A.
*Vice-President for Administration:* ROBERT J. GERRAUGHTY, PH.D.
*Vice-President for University Relations:* Rev. JOHN J. CALLAHAN, S.J., M.A., PH.L.
*Vice-President for Student Personnel:* JAMES R. DOYLE, M.S.
*Business Manager:* EDWARD D. MURPHY, B.S.C.
*Registrar:* JACK N. WILLIAMS, B.S.
*Director of Alumni Library:* RAYMOND B. MEANS, M.A.

The library contains 457,519 vols.
Number of teachers: 964.
Number of students: 5,614.

Publications: *The Creighton University Bulletin, The Creightonian, Bluejay, Creighton Law Review, Alumnews.*

### DEANS:
*Arts and Sciences:* WILLIAM F. CUNNINGHAM, Jr., M.A.
*Business Administration:* J. L. CARRICA, J. D., M.B.A., PH.D.
*Dentistry:* R. V. VINING, D.D.S.
*Graduate:* R. V. ANDREWS, PH.D.
*Law:* R. SHKOLNICK, J.D.
*Medicine:* Rev. J. E. HOFF, PH.D.
*Nursing:* SHEILA A. RYAN, PH.D.
*Pharmacy:* L. K. BENEDICT, PH.D.
*Summer Session:* ANNE E. SCHEERER, M.S., PH.D.
*Students:* JAMES R. DOYLE, M.S.
*Women:* EILEEN B. LIEBEN, A.M.

## DANA COLLEGE
BLAIR, NEBRASKA 68008

Telephone: (402) 426-4101.

Founded 1884.

*President:* Dr. JAMES KALLAS.

# UNIVERSITIES AND COLLEGES—NEBRASKA

*Registrar:* Dr. VERLAN J. HANSON.
*Dean:* Dr. CLIFFORD T. HANSON (acting).
*Librarian:* RONALD D. JOHNSON.

The library contains 100,000 vols.
Number of teachers: 34.
Number of students: 435.

## DOANE COLLEGE
CRETE, NEBRASKA 68333
Telephone: (402) 826-2161.
Founded 1872.

*President:* PHILIP HECKMAN.
*Registrar:* BETTY BURKLUND.
*Librarian:* MARGARET B. SMITH.

The library contains 127,254 vols.
Number of teachers: 47.
Number of students: 650.

## HASTINGS COLLEGE
HASTINGS, NEBRASKA 68901
Telephone: (402) 463-2402.
Founded 1882.

*President:* Dr. CLYDE B. MATTERS.
*Academic Dean:* Dr. JAMES S. WALKER.
*Registrar:* Dr. DWAYNE STRASHEIM.
*Librarian:* CHARLES GARDNER.

The library contains 100,000 vols.
Number of teachers: 54.
Number of students: 832.
Publication: *Hastings College Bulletin†* (quarterly).

## KEARNEY STATE COLLEGE
KEARNEY, NEBRASKA 68847
Telephone: 236-4141.
Founded 1905.

*President:* BRENDAN J. MCDONALD, PH.D.
*Director of Records and Statistics:* LILA WILLIAMS (acting).
*Director of Libraries:* JOHN MAYESKI.

The library contains 367,917 volumes.
Number of teachers: 258.
Number of students: 6,838.

## MIDLAND LUTHERAN COLLEGE
720 E. 9TH STREET,
FREMONT, NEBRASKA 68025
Telephone: (402) 721-5480.
Founded 1883.

*President:* L. DALE LUND.
*Vice-President for Finance and Treasurer:* ELMER B. SASSE.
*Vice-President for College Relations and Development:* ARNOLD E. LACK.
*Vice-President for Academic Affairs:* DONALD L. KAHNK.
*Vice-President for Student Affairs:* C. A. STEYER.
*Registrar:* L. P. MITCHELL.
*Librarian:* THOMAS E. BOYLE.

The library contains 79,000 vols.
Number of teachers: 60.
Number of students: 894.

## NEBRASKA WESLEYAN UNIVERSITY
50TH AND ST. PAUL,
LINCOLN, NEBRASKA 68504
Telephone: (402) 466-2371.
Founded 1887.

*President:* Dr. JOHN W. WHITE, Jr.
*Dean of the College:* Dr. PAUL H. LAURSEN.
*Registrar:* BETTE OLSON.
*Director of Admissions:* KEN SIEG.

The library contains 185,000 vols.
Number of teachers: 83.
Number of students: 1,200.

## PERU STATE COLLEGE
PERU, NEBRASKA 68421
Telephone: (402) 872-3815.
Founded 1867.

*President:* LARRY A. TANGEMAN.
*Vice-President for Administration:* MICHAEL O. STEWART.
*Registrar:* KELLY LIEWER.
*Librarian:* FAYE BRANDT.
*Vice-President for Academic Affairs:* CLYDE J. BARRETT.
*Admissions:* RICHARD C. MUTH.

The library contains 85,000 volumes.
Number of teachers: 48.
Number of students: 736.

## UNION COLLEGE
3800 SOUTH 48TH STREET,
LINCOLN, NEBRASKA 68506
Telephone: 488-2331.
Founded 1891.

*President:* DEAN L. HUBBARD.
*Academic Dean:* JOHN H. WAGNER.
*Business Manager:* S. O. VARTIJA.
*Registrar:* ANITA KIDWILER.
*Director of College Relations:* JIM GALLAGHER.
*Librarian:* LARRY ONSOGER.

The library contains 130,000 vols.
Number of teachers: 53.
Number of students: 923.

## UNIVERSITY OF NEBRASKA
LINCOLN, NEBRASKA 68588
Telephone: (402) 472-2111.

*President:* R. W. ROSKENS, PH.D.
*Executive Vice-President for Academic Affairs:* S. B. SAMPLE, PH.D.
*Executive Vice-President for Administration:* ALAN SEAGREN, M.A., PH.D. (acting).
*Vice-President for Governmental Relations and Corporation Secretary:* W. F. SWANSON, B.S.

## University of Nebraska—Lincoln
LINCOLN, NEBRASKA 68588
Telephone: 472-7211.
Founded 1869.

*Chancellor:* MARTIN MASSENGALE, M.S., PH.D.
*Vice-Chancellor for Academic Affairs:* JOHN W. STRONG, J.D.
*Vice-Chancellor for Business and Finance:* RONALD W WRIGHT, M.A., PH.D.
*Vice-Chancellor for Student Affairs:* RICHARD C. ARMSTRONG, ED.D.
*Vice-Chancellor for Agriculture and Natural Resources:* HOWARD OTTOSON, M.S., PH.D. (acting).
*Vice-Chancellor for Research and Graduate Studies:* ROBERT H. RUTFORD, M.A., PH.D.
*Director of Admissions:* AL PAPIK, M.ED.
*Dean of Libraries:* GERALD A. RUDOLPH, PH.D.
*Library: see* Libraries.

Number of teachers: 1,250 (full-time).
Number of students: 22,477.
Publications: *Nebraska Law Review, University of Nebraska Studies, Nebraska Journal of Economics and Business, Prairie Schooner, University of Nebraska—Lincoln News.*

DEANS:
*College of Agriculture:* T. E. HARTUNG, PH.D.
*College of Architecture:* W. C. STEWARD, B.ARCH., M.S.
*College of Arts and Sciences:* MAX D. LARSEN, M.A., PH.D.
*College of Business Administration:* GARY SCHWENDIMAN, M.S., PH.D.
*College of Engineering and Technology:* STANLEY LIBERTY, M.S., PH.D.
*College of Home Economics:* H. M. ANTHONY, M.S., ED.D.
*Graduate Studies:* HENRY F. HOLTZCLAW, Jr., M.S., PH.D.
*College of Law:* DONALD L. SHANEYFELT, J.D.
*Teachers' College:* R. L. EGBERT, M.S., PH.D.
*Continuing Studies:* QUENTIN H. GESSNER, PH.D.

## University of Nebraska at Omaha
OMAHA, NEBRASKA 68182
Telephone: (402) 554-2200.
Founded 1908.

*Chancellor:* Dr. DEL WEBER.
*Vice-Chancellor for Academic Affairs:* OTTO BAUER, PH.D.
*Vice-Chancellor for Business and Finance:* GARY CARRICO, M.B.A.
*Registrar and Admissions:* GARDNER VAN DYKE, PH.D.
*Vice-Chancellor for Educational and Student Services:* RICHARD HOOVER PH.D.
*Librarian:* ROBERT S. RUNYON, M.L.S.

## UNITED STATES OF AMERICA

The library contains 363,000 volumes and 698,000 micro materials.
Number of teachers: 425.
Number of students: 15,000.

Publications: *Gateway* (weekly), *Catalog* (annually).

DEANS:

*College of Arts and Sciences:* JOHN M. NEWTON, PH.D.
*College of Business Administration:* LARRY TRUSSELL, PH.D.
*College of Education:* DONALD A. MYERS, PH.D.
*College of Engineering and Technology:* HAROLD L. DAVIS, ED.D. (Assoc. Dean).
*College of Continuing Studies:* ALAN S. HACKEL, PH.D.
*College of Home Economics:* NILA MAGDANZ, M.S.
*College of Public Affairs and Community Service:* JOHN E. KERRIGAN, PH.D.
*College of Fine Arts:* MARY WILLIAMSON, PH.D. (acting).
*Graduate Studies and Research:* MARGARET P. GESSAMAN, PH.D.

### WAYNE STATE COLLEGE
WAYNE, NEBRASKA 68787

Telephone: (402) 375-2200.
Founded 1910.

*President:* LYLE E. SEYMOUR.
*Registrar:* VIRGINIA WRIGHT.
*Librarian:* JACK L. MIDDENDORF.

The library contains 272,000 vols.
Number of teachers: 104.
Number of students: 2,168.

## NEVADA

### UNIVERSITY OF NEVADA, RENO
RENO, NEVADA 89557

Telephone: (702) 784-4805.
Founded 1874.

*President:* JOSEPH N. CROWLEY, PH.D.
*Vice-President for Business:* KENNETH D. JESSUP, M.S.
*Vice-President for Academic Affairs:* RICHARD O. DAVIES, PH.D.
*Vice-President for Public Affairs:* RICHARD T. DANKWORTH, ED.D.
*Registrar:* J. H. SHIRLEY, D.ED.
*Librarian:* H. G. MOREHOUSE, M.L.S.

The library contains 680,000 vols.
Number of teachers: 331.
Number of students: 7,039.

Publications: *University Catalogue, Summer Sessions Bulletin, Independent Studies Bulletin, Scholarships and Prizes.*

DEANS:

*College of Agriculture:* DALE W. BOHMONT, PH.D.
*College of Arts and Science:* PAUL A. PAGE, PH.D.
*Extended Programs and Continuing Education:* N. A. FERGUSON, PH.D.
*College of Education:* E. J. CAIN, ED.D.
*College of Engineering:* CHARLES R. BREESE, M.S., P.E.
*Graduate School:* J. E. NELLOR, PH.D.
*School of Home Economics:* DONNA BETH DOWNER, PH.D.
*Mackay School of Mines:* JOSEPH LINTZ, Jr., PH.D.
*School of Medicine:* R. M. DAUGHERTY, Jr., M.D., PH.D.
*Student Affairs:* ROBERTA J. BARNES, PH.D.
*College of Business Administration:* RICHARD E. HUGHS, PH.D.
*Orvis School of Nursing:* MARION M. SCHRUM, ED.D.

### UNIVERSITY OF NEVADA, LAS VEGAS
4505 MARYLAND PARKWAY, LAS VEGAS, NEVADA 89154

Telephone: (702) 739-3011.
Founded 1957.

*President:* Dr. LEONARD GOODALL.
*Vice-President for Administration:* Dr. BROCK DIXON.
*Vice-President for Academic Affairs:* Dr. DALE F. NITZSCHKE.
*Vice-President for Business Affairs:* HERMAN WESTFALL.
*Registrar:* JEFF HALVERSON.
*Director of Admissions:* Dr. ROBERT STEPHENS.
*Director of Libraries:* H. H. J. ERICKSON.

The library contains 350,000 vols. (approx.).

Number of teachers: 295 (full-time), 86 (part-time).
Number of students: 9,200.

DEANS:

*College of Business and Economics:* Dr. G. W. HARDBECK.
*College of Hotel Administration:* Dr. J. J. VALLEN.
*College of Education:* Dr. RICHARD KUNKEL.
*College of Allied Health Professions:* Dr. MARY ANN MICHEL.
*College of Arts and Letters:* Dr. JOHN UNRUE.
*College of Science and Mathematics:* Dr. ROBERT B. SMITH.
*Continuing Education:* DWIGHT A. MARSHALL.
*College of Graduate Studies:* Dr. JAMES S. ADAMS.
*University College:* Dr. SHAREE SCHRADER (Director).

PROFESSORS:

ABBEY, R. D., Art
ADAMS, C. L., Jr., English
AIZLEY, P., Mathematics
ANDERSON, R. C., Education
BABERO, B. B., Zoology
BALEY, V., Music
BASILE, R. E., Hotel Administration
BEALS, M. G., Special Education
BIGLER, R. M., Political Science
BILLINGHAM, E. J., Jr., Chemistry
BOORD, R. O., Education
BORSENIK, F. D., Hotel Administration
BRADLEY, W. G., Jr., Biology
BROOKS, R., Anthropology
BROOKS, S. T., Anthropology
BYRNS, R. H., English
CARNS, D. E., Sociology
CASSESE, T., Education
CLARY, D. A., Accounting
CRAWFORD, J. L., Theatre Arts
DEACON, J. E., Biology
DECOCK, J., French
DETTRE, JOHN, Education
DETTRE, JUDITH, Education
DIXON, B., Political Science
DRAKULICH, M., Physical Education
FIERO, G. W., Jr., Geology
FINOCCHIARO, M., Philosophy
GOLBERG, M. A., Mathematics
GOLDING, L. A., Physical Education
GOLDMAN, A. S., Mathematics
GRAHAM, M., Mathematics
HARDBECK, G. W., Economics
HARRIS, P. C., Jr., Theatre Arts
HESS, H. F., Psychology
HILGAR, M-F., French
HONSA, V., Spanish
HUNT, H. M., Radiologic Technology
IRSFELD, J., English
KELLY, E. J., Special Education
KIRSCHNER, F., Education
KOESTER, R. A., German
KUHL, L. W., Theatre Arts
KUNKEL, R., Curriculum and Instruction
LINDBERG, J. D., Foreign Languages
LOVEDAY, P. N., Management
LOVINGER, E., Psychology
LYNEIS, M., Philosophy
MALAMUD, B., Economics
McCULLOUGH, J., English
MICHEL, M. A., Nursing
MURVOSH, C. M., Biology
NEUMANN, R., Accounting
RAE, C., Physical Education
ROSKE, R. J., History
SAMSON, G. J., Education
SAVILLE, A., Education
SEIDMAN, L., Business Law
SIMMONS, A., Economics
SKAGGS, R. L., Engineering
SMITH, R. B., Chemistry
STEVENS, A. W., Humanities
TARKANIAN, J., Education
TARTE, R. D., Psychology
TITUS, R. L., Chemistry
TRIONE, V., Education
TRYON, J. G., Engineering
UNRUE, J. C., English
VALLEN, J., Hotel Administration
VERGIELS, J., Education
VERMA, S., Mathematics
WAGONSELLER, B., Special Education
WALTON, D. C., Philosophy
WARREN, C. N., Anthropology
WEINSTEIN, M. A., English
WHITE, W. T., Economics
YOUSEF, M. K., Biology
ZORN, R. J., History

ATTACHED INSTITUTE:

**Desert Research Institute:** 4582 Maryland Parkway, Las Vegas, Nevada 89109; offices and laboratories in Reno, Stead, Las Vegas and Boulder City; research in energy, atmospheric environment, water resources,

UNIVERSITIES AND COLLEGES—NEVADA, NEW HAMPSHIRE U.S.A.

ecology, anthropology, socio-economics and demography; Research Administrator Dr. NATE COOPER.

## NEW HAMPSHIRE

### DARTMOUTH COLLEGE
HANOVER,
NEW HAMPSHIRE 03755
Founded 1769.

*President:* Dr. DAVID MCLAUGHLIN.
*Provost:* L. M. RIESER, Jr., PH.D.
*Secretary:* J. M. MCGEAN, A.B.
*Registrar:* D. M. BOWEN, PH.D.
*Director of Admissions:* ALFRED T. QUIRK, M.ED.
*Librarian:* MARGARET A. OTTO, M.A.

Number of teachers: 430.
Number of students: 4,700.

DEANS:

*College:* RALPH N. MANUEL, PH.D.
*Faculty:* HANS H. PENNER, PH.D.
*Students:* JOHN E. HANSON, ED.D.
*Freshmen:* KAREN J. BLANK, M.S.
*Medical School:* JAMES C. STRICKLER, M.D.
*Thayer School of Engineering:* CARL F. LONG, D.ENG.
*Amos Tuck School of Business Administration:* RICHARD R. WEST, PH.D.

PROFESSORS:

ALEXANDER, R., Drama
ALLEN, R. D., Biology
ALMY, T. P., Medicine
APPLETON, J. H., Music
ARKOWITZ, M., Mathematics
ARNDT, W. W., Russian Language and Literature
BAIRD, J. C., Psychology
BAKER, K. R., Business Administration
BALDWIN, D. A., Government
BALDWIN, W. L., Economics
BARTLETT, D., Jr., Physiology
BEACH, W. B., Clinical Psychiatry
BERGEN, B. J., Psychiatry
BERNIER, G. M., Jr., Medicine
BERTHOLD, F., Religion
BIEN, P., English
BLATMAN, S., Maternal and Child Health
BOGHOSIAN, V., Art
BOLEY, F. I., Physics
BOND, H. L., English
BORISON, H. L., Pharmacology and Toxicology
BOULDING, E. M., Sociology
BOWEN, D. M., Chemistry
BOWER, R. S., Business Economics
BRADLEY, E. M., Classics
BRAUN, C. L., Chemistry
BROEHL, W. D., Administration
BROWN, E. M., Mathematics
BURNETT, J. B., Clinical Medicine
CAMPBELL, C. D., Economics
CHAMBERS, W. F., Anatomy
CHRISTY, R. W., Physics
CLELAND, R. L., Chemistry
CLEMENT, M. O., Economics
CLENDENNING, W. E., Clinical Medicine
COLTON, T., Biostatistics
CONVERSE, A. O., Engineering
COPENHAVER, J. H., Jr., Biology
COX, J. M., English
CRICHLOW, R. W., Surgery
CROWELL, R. H., Mathematics

CULVER, C. M., Psychiatry
DANIELL, J. R., II, History
DAVIS, K. R., Marketing
DAVIS, W. P., Jr., Physics
DEMAGGIO, A. E., Biology
DENNISON, D. S., Biology
DOENEGES, N. A., Classics
DONEY, W. F., Jr., Philosophy
DOYLE, W. T., Physics
DRAKE, C. L., Earth Sciences
DUGGAN, T. J., Philosophy
ELLIOTT, R., Psychology
ERDMAN, H. L., Government
FERM, V. H., Anatomy and Embryology
GALTON, V. A., Physiology
GAUDIN, C. L., Romance Languages and Literatures
GAYLORD, A. T., English
GELFANT, B. H., English
GERT, B., Philosophy
GILBERT, J. J., Biology
GOLDSMITH, H. S., Surgery
GOSSELIN, R. E., Pharmacology
GRAY, C. T., Microbiology
GRETHLEIN, H. E., Engineering
GUEST, R. H., Organizational Behaviour
HAMM, C. E., Music
HARBURY, H. A., Biochemistry
HARRIS, E. D., Jr., Medicine
HARRIS, J. D., Physics
HART, J. P., English
HARVEY, L. E., Romance Languages and Literatures
HAURI, P. J., Psychiatry
HEAD, J. M., Clinical Surgery
HEFFERNAN, J. A., English
HENNESSEY, J. W., Jr., Management
HILL, E. G., Drama
HINES, L. G., Economics
HOEFNAGEL, D., Maternal and Child Health
HOFFMEISTER, W., German and Comparative Literature
HOLMES, R. T., Biology
HOOVEM, F. J., Engineering
HORNIG, J. F., Chemistry
HUGGINS, E. R., Physics
HUKE, R. E., Geography
JACKSON, W. T., Biology
JACOBS, N. J., Microbiology
JACOBUS, J., Art
JAMES, H. L., Speech
JOHNSON, N. M., Earth Sciences
KARL, R. C., Surgery
KELLEY, M. L., Jr., Clinical Medicine
KEMENY, J. G., Mathematics
KIDDER, J. N., Physics
KING, F. W., Psychiatry
KLECK, R. E., Psychology
KLEIN, R. Z., Maternal and Child Health
KREIDER, D. L., Mathematics
KURTZ, T. E., Mathematics
LAASPERE, T., Engineering
LAMPERTI, J. W., Mathematics
LANE, F. W., Jr., Clinical Medicine
LANZETTA, J. T., Psychology
LAYTON, W. M., Anatomy
LEATON, R. N., Psychology
LEMAL, D. M., Chemistry
LIENHARD, G. E., Biochemistry
LIPOWSKI, Z. J., Psychiatry
LONG, C. F., Engineering
LONGNECKER, D. S., Pathology
LOOMIS, C. C., Jr., English
LUBIN, M., Microbiology
LYONS, G. M., Government
LYONS, J. B., Geology
MCCANN, F. M., Physiology
MACDONALD, R. M., Business Economics
MCGEE, V. E., Applied Statistics
MCGRATH, R. I., Art
MCINTYRE, O. R., Medicine
MCLANE, C. B., Government
MCMULLAN, B. W., Drama
MALMSTROM, V., Geography

MANSELL, D. L., Jr., English
MARIN-PADILLA, M., Pathology
MASTERS, R. D., Government
MEADOWS, D. L., Engineering
MENGE, J. A., Economics
MILLER, N., Community Medicine
MORRISSEY, L. E., Jr., Accounting
MOSENTHAL, W. T., Clinical Surgery
MUNCK, A. U., Physiology
NAVARRO, M. N., History
NICHOLS, S. G., Jr., Romance Languages and Literature
NODA, L. H., Biochemistry
NORMAN, R. Z., Mathematics
NYE, R. E., Jr., Physiology
OXENHANDLER, N., Romance Languages and Literatures
PAYSON, H. E., Clinical Psychiatry
PENNER, H. H., Religion
PERRIN, E. N., English
PFEFFERKORN, E. R., Jr., Microbiology
PROSSER, R. T., Mathematics
PYTTE, A., Physics
QUENEAU, P. E., Engineering
QUINN, J. B., Business Administration
RADWAY, L. I., Government
RASSIAS, J. A., Romance Languages and Literatures
RAWNSLEY, H. M., Pathology
REINERS, W. A., Biology
REYNOLDS, R. C., Earth Sciences
RIESER, L. M., Physics
ROBERTS, F. D., History
ROLETT, E. I., Medicine
ROOS, T. B., Biology
RUECKERT, F., Clinical Surgery
RUSSELL, R. H., Romance Languages and Literatures
SACCIO, P., English
SCHER, S. P., German Language and Literature
SCOTT, W. C., Classics
SEGAL, B. E., Sociology
SEGAL, M., Economics
SHAFER, P. R., Chemistry
SHELDON, R. R., Russian Language and Literature
SHEWMAKER, K. E., History
SICES, D., Romance Languages and Literatures
SLESNICK, W. B., Mathematics
SMALLWOOD, F., Government
SMITH, R. P., Toxicology
SMITH, W. M., Psychology
SNELL, J. L., Mathematics
SODERBERG, R. H., Chemistry
SOKOL, R., Sociology
SOLOW, C., Clinical Psychiatry
SONNERUP, B. U. O., Engineering
SORENSON, G. D., Jr., Pathology
SPENCER, T. A., Chemistry
SPIEGEL, M., Biology
STARZINGER, V. E., Government
STERLING, R. W., Government
STICKNEY, C. P., Business Administration
STRICKLER, J. C., Medicine
STROHBEHN, J. W., Engineering
SULLIVAN, D. G., Government
TENNEY, S. M., Physiology
TERRIE, H. L., Jr., English
TIGHE, T., Psychology
TUCKER, G. J., Psychiatry
UDY, S. H., Sociology
VALTIN, H., Physiology-Renology
VANDERLINDE, R. J., Clinical Medicine
VARGISH, T., English
VARNUM, J. W., Hospital Administration
WALLIS, G. V., Engineering
WEBSTER, F. E., Jr., Business Administration
WENDLANDT, D. W., Music
WEST, R. R., Business Administration
WHYBROW, P. C., Psychiatry
WIENECKE, M. I., Classics

1795

WILLIAMSON, J. P., Business Administration
WILLIAMSON, R. E., Mathematics
WOLFF, C., Music
WOOD, C. T., History
WYSOCKI, M., Art
ZUBKOFF, M., Community Medicine

### KEENE STATE COLLEGE
229 MAIN STREET, KEENE,
NEW HAMPSHIRE 03431
Telephone: 352-1909.
Founded 1909.

*President:* BARBARA J. SEELYE.
*Dean of College:* RICHARD A. GUSTAFSON (acting).
*Dean of Student Affairs:* RONALD D. HERRON.
*Director of Physical Plant:* R. MALLAT.
*Director of Administration:* (vacant).
*Librarian:* CLIFFORD MEAD (acting).

The library contains 150,000 vols.
Number of teachers: 164.
Number of students: 3,265.

### NEW ENGLAND COLLEGE
HENNIKER,
NEW HAMPSHIRE 03242
Telephone: (603) 428-2211.
Founded 1946.

*President:* Dr. J. K. CUMMISKEY.
*Dean of Academic Affairs:* Dr. GEORGE L. FEARNLEY, Jr. (acting).
*Registrar:* PERCY A. WILSON.
*Director of Records:* MARY A. BALL.
*Director of Finance and Administration:* ARNOLD C. CODA.
*Dean, School of Graduate and Continuing Studies:* Dr. E. F. RUTLEDGE.
*Dean of Admissions:* JOHN J. BEAULIEU, Jr.
*Librarian:* MARY K. WIRTH.

The library contains 73,000 vols.
Number of teachers: 108.
Number of students: 1,491.

BRANCH CAMPUS:
Arundel, Sussex, England
Telephone: Arundel 882259.
Founded 1971.
*Vice-President:* Dr. FRANCIS H. HORN.

The library contains 13,000 vols.
Number of teachers: 33.
Number of students: 279.

### PLYMOUTH STATE COLLEGE
PLYMOUTH,
NEW HAMPSHIRE 03264
Telephone: (603) 536-1550.
Founded 1871.

*President:* KASPER C. MARKING.
*Director of Admissions:* C. W. BAILEY, Jr.
*Librarian:* JANICE GALLINGER.

The library contains 225,000 vols.
Number of teachers: 138.
Number of students: 3,351.

### RIVIER COLLEGE
NASHUA,
NEW HAMPSHIRE 03060
Telephone: 888-1311.
Founded 1933.

*President:* Sister JEANNE PERREAULT, P.M., M.S.
*Academic Dean:* Sister JACQUELINE LANDRY, P.M. PH.D.
*Director of Student Services:* MARY FRAMPTOM.
*Treasurer:* Sister ADRIENNE, P.M., B.A.
*Director of Development:* Mrs. TRACY SCHIER, M.A.
*Dean of Graduate School:* MICHAEL QUIGLEY, M.A.
*Librarian:* Sister ALBINA-MARIE, P.M., M.S. IN L.S.

The library contains 88,000 vols.
Number of teachers: 43 full-time, 77 part-time.
Number of students: 568 full-time, 1,143 part-time.

### SAINT ANSELM'S COLLEGE
MANCHESTER,
NEW HAMPSHIRE 03102
Telephone: (603) 669-1030.
Founded 1889.

A Liberal Arts College with Baccalaureate programs in Nursing and Criminal Justice.

*President:* Bro. JOACHIM W. FROEHLICH, O.S.B.
*Dean of the College:* Rev. PETER J. GUERIN, O.S.B.
*Registrar:* Bro. EDWARD ENGLUND, O.S.B.
*Librarian:* Mrs. NORMA CREAGHE.

The library contains 135,000 vols.
Number of teachers: 101 full-time, 35 part-time.
Number of students: 1,932.

### UNIVERSITY OF NEW HAMPSHIRE
DURHAM,
NEW HAMPSHIRE 03824
Telephone: (603) 862-1234.

Founded 1866 as New Hampshire College of Agriculture and the Mechanic Arts; became university in 1923. In 1963, the State Colleges at Plymouth and Keene were added as separate campuses of the University System of New Hampshire.

*President:* EVELYN E. HANDLER, M.S., PH.D.
*Vice-President for Academic Affairs:* GORDON A. HAALAND, PH.D.
*Vice-President of Financial Affairs and Administration:* FRANK J. BACHICH, B.S.
*Vice-President for Student Affairs:* J. GREGG SANBORN, M.A. (acting).
*Vice-President for University Relations:* EUGENE A. SAVAGE, M.ED.
*Registrar:* STEPHANIE THOMAS, M.A.
*Librarian:* DONALD E. VINCENT, A.M.L.S., A.M., PH.D.

The library contains 794,343 vols.
Number of teachers: 538.
Number of students: 5,284 men, 5,675 women, total 10,959.

Publications: *Catalog, Bulletin, The Alumnus, UNH Magazine.*

DEANS:
*College of Life Sciences and Agriculture:* KURT C. FELTNER, M.S., PH.D.
*College of Liberal Arts:* ROLAND B. KIMBALL, M.ED., ED.D. (acting).
*College of Engineering and Physical Sciences:* A. AMELL, PH.D. (acting).
*Graduate School:* RAYMOND L. ERICKSON, M.A., PH.D.
*School of Health Studies:* BASIL J. F. MOTT, M.P.A., PH.D.
*The Whittemore School of Business and Economics:* DWIGHT R. LADD, M.B.A., PH.D.

## NEW JERSEY

### CALDWELL COLLEGE
CALDWELL,
NEW JERSEY 07006.
Telephone: (201) 228-4424.
Founded 1939.

*President:* Sister EDITH MAGDALEN VISIC, O.P.
*Academic Dean:* Sister RITA MARGARET CHAMBERS, O.P.
*Registrar:* Sister SUZANNE McCAFFREY, O.P.
*Librarian:* Sister ANN BYRNE, O.P.

The library contains 100,000 volumes.
Number of teachers: 77.
Number of students: 705.

### COLLEGE OF SAINT ELIZABETH
CONVENT STATION,
NEW JERSEY 07961
Telephone: (201) 539-1600.
Founded 1899.

*President:* Sister JACQUELINE BURNS.
*Director of Admissions:* Sister MAUREEN SULLIVAN.
*Librarian:* Sister MARIE ROUSEK.

The library contains 149,602 vols.
Number of teachers: 92.
Number of students: 851.

### DON BOSCO COLLEGE
SWARTSWOOD RD., NEWTON,
NEW JERSEY 07860
Telephone: (201) 383-3900.
Founded 1928; primarily for students studying for the priesthood

UNIVERSITIES AND COLLEGES—NEW JERSEY
U.S.A.

*President:* Rev. Francis J. Klauder, ph.d.
*Dean of the College:* Rev. Thomas L. Gwozdz.
*Treasurer:* Rev. Emil Allue, ph.d.
*Librarian:* Rev. P. J. Pascucci, m.l.s.

The library contains over 50,000 vols.
Number of teachers: 22.
Number of students: 65.

## DREW UNIVERSITY
MADISON, NEW JERSEY 07940
Telephone: (201) 377-3000.
Founded 1866.

*President:* Paul Hardin.
*Vice-President and Treasurer:* W. Scott McDonald.
*Vice-President for Development and University Relations:* William G. Wehner.
*Vice-President for Admissions and Student Life:* David F. Lasher.
*Registrar:* B. S. Johnson.
*Librarian:* A. E. Jones, Jr.

Number of teachers: 228.
Number of students: 2,220.

Publications: *The Drew Gateway, Dissonance.*

Deans:

*College of Liberal Arts:* Robert K. Ackerman.
*Theological School:* Thomas W. Ogletree.
*Graduate School:* B. Thompson.

## FAIRLEIGH DICKINSON UNIVERSITY
RUTHERFORD, NEW JERSEY 07070
Founded 1941.

*President:* Dr. Jerome M. Pollack.
*Vice-President for Financial Affairs:* Dr. Lowell W. Herron.
*Vice-President for Academic Affairs:* Dr. Harry A. Marmion.
*Vice-President for Administration:* Dr. Richard W. Powers.
*Vice-President for Development and P.R.:* Paul D. Newland.

Number of teachers: 1,478.
Number of students: 19,686.

Publications: *The Business Review, The Clearing House, The Dialog, The Literary Review, Teaching English Today, Magazine.*

Deans:

*College of Arts and Sciences (Florham-Madison Campus):* Dr. Frederick H. Gaige.
*College of Arts and Sciences (Rutherford Campus):* Dr. Antoinette M. Anastasia.
*College of Business Administration:* Dr. Robert C. Sedwick.
*School of Dentistry:* Dr. Ralph S. Kaslick.

*College of Education:* Dr. Lewis Jacobs (acting).
*College of Liberal Arts (Teaneck-Hackensack Campus:)* Dr. Joan P. Bean.
*College of Science and Engineering:* Dr Wallace Arthur.

The University has campuses at Madison, N.J. 07940; Rutherford, N.J. 07070; Teaneck, N.J. 07666; St. Croix, U.S. Virgin Islands; and Wroxton, Oxon., England.

## GLASSBORO STATE COLLEGE
GLASSBORO, NEW JERSEY 08028
Telephone: 445-5000
Founded 1923.

*President:* Mark M. Chamberlain.
*Vice-President for Academic Affairs:* Lawson J. Brown.
*Registrar:* Rudolph Salati.
*Librarian:* Dr. Sandor Szilassy.

The library contains 300,000 vols.
Number of teachers: 380.
Number of students: 6,486 full-time, 4,024 part-time.

## INSTITUTE FOR ADVANCED STUDY
OLDEN LANE, PRINCETON, NEW JERSEY 08540
Telephone: (609) 734-8000.

Founded 1930 for post-doctoral research in the fields of mathematics, theoretical physics, historical studies and social sciences.

Private control; Academic year: September to April (two terms).

*President of the Corporation:* (vacant).
*Chairman of the Board of Trustees:* J. Richardson Dilworth.
*Director:* H. Woolf, ph.d.
*Secretary:* John Hunt.
*Librarians:* Lily B. Agar, Virginia Radway.

The library contains 100,000 vols.
Number of professors: 23.
Number of visitors: approx. 160.

Faculty:

*School of Historical Studies:*
Bowersock, G.
Clagett, M.
Elliott, J.
Gilliam, J. F.
Habicht, C.
Lavin, I.
Setton, K.
White, M. G.

*School of Mathematics:*
Bombieri, E.
Borel, A.
Harish-Chandra, f.r.s.
Langlands, R.
Milnor, J. H.
Selberg, A.
Yau, S.-T.

*School of Natural Sciences:*
Adler, S.
Bahcall, J. N.
Dashen, R.
Dyson, F. J.
Rosenbluth, M.

*School of Social Science:*
Geertz, C.
Hirschman, A. O.
Walzer, M.

## JERSEY CITY STATE COLLEGE
2039 KENNEDY BOULEVARD, JERSEY CITY, NEW JERSEY 07305
Telephone: (201) 547-6000.
Founded 1927.

*President:* William J. Maxwell.
*Registrar:* P. La Roche.
*Director of Admissions:* W. J. Henry, *Chairman of Department of Library Services:* R. Nugent.

The library contains 150,000 volumes.
Number of teachers: 345.
Number of students: 10,372 (*c.* 5,000 full-time).

## KEAN COLLEGE OF NEW JERSEY
MORRIS AVE., UNION, NEW JERSEY 07083
Telephone: (201) 527-2000.

Founded 1855, present name 1973; College of Liberal Arts and Sciences offering baccalaureate and masters degrees in applied disciplines, professional education and liberal arts.

*President:* Dr. Nathan Weiss.
*Academic Vice-President:* Dr. Vera King Farris.
*Dean of Administrative Services:* Charles J. Longacre, Jr.
*Dean of Students:* Patrick Ippolito.

The library contains 251,783 vols.
Number of teachers: 775.
Number of students: 13,748.

## MONMOUTH COLLEGE
WEST LONG BRANCH NEW JERSEY 07764
Telephone (201) 222-6600.

Founded 1933. An independent, co-educational, non-sectarian, comprehensive college.

*President:* Samuel Hays Magill.
*Vice-President for Academic Affairs and Dean of Faculty:* Robert S. Rouse.
*Director of Admissions:* Robert Cristadoro.
*Librarian:* R. F. Van Benthuysen.

The library contains over 210,000 vols.
Number of teachers: over 200 full-time and part-time.
Number of students: 3,950 undergraduate, graduate.

## MONTCLAIR STATE COLLEGE
UPPER MONTCLAIR, NEW JERSEY 07043
Telephone: (201) 893-4000.

Founded 1908. Liberal arts and professional studies.

*President:* Dr. DAVID W. D. DICKSON.
*Vice-President for Academic Affairs:* Dr. IRWIN H. GAWLEY, Jr.
*Vice-President, Administration and Finance:* Dr. ELLIOT I. MININBERG.
*Librarian:* Mrs. BLANCHE W. HALLER.

The library contains 600,000 vols. and microfilms.

Number of teachers: 500.
Number of students: 15,000.

## NEW JERSEY INSTITUTE OF TECHNOLOGY
323 HIGH STREET,
NEWARK, NEW JERSEY 07102
Founded 1881.

*President:* SAUL FENSTER, M.S., PH.D.

Library of 130,000 vols.

Number of teachers: 268; part-time 125.
Number of students: 6,021.
Publications: *Bulletins, Programmes*

HEADS OF DEPARTMENTS:
*Industrial and Management Engineering:* J. L. RIGASSIO, M.ENG.
*Organizational and Social Sciences:* R. B. HELFGOTT, M.A., PH.D.
*Civil and Environmental Engineering:* E. B. GOLUB, M.S., PH.D.
*Chemical Engineering and Chemistry:* D. HANESIAN, M.S., PH.D.
*Electrical Engineering:* J. J. STRANO, M.S., PH.D.
*Mechanical Engineering:* E. MILLER (acting).
*Computer Science:* G. MOSHOS, M.S., PH.D.
*Humanities:* J. P. PATTINSON, M.A., PH.D.
*Mathematics:* H. ZATZKIS, M.S., PH.D.
*Physics:* LEON D. LANDSMAN, M.A. (acting).
*Aerospace Studies:* Col. HEIKI ELLERMETS, M.S.
*Architecture:* B. JACKSON, M.ARCH. (acting).

## PRINCETON UNIVERSITY
PRINCETON,
NEW JERSEY 08540

Telephone: 452-3000.
Telegraphic Address: Princeton, N.J.
Founded 1746 as the College of New Jersey, became Princeton University 1896.

Academic year: September to May.

*President:* WILLIAM G. BOWEN, PH.D.
*Provost:* N. L. RUDENSTINE, PH.D.
*Financial Vice-President and Treasurer:* C. W. SCHAFER, B.A.
*Vice-President for Development:* VAN ZANDT WILLIAMS, Jr., PH.D.
*Vice-President for Public Affairs:* ROBERT K. DURKEE, M.A.T.
*Vice-President for Administrative Affairs:* A. J. MARUCA, A.B.
*Secretary:* T. H. WRIGHT, Jr., A.B., J.D.
*Controller:* R. J. CLARK, B.B.A.

*Registrar:* B. FINNIE, PH.D.
*Librarian:* D. W. KOEPP.

Library: *see* Libraries.
Number of teachers: 695 full-time.
Number of students: 4,452 undergraduates and 1,487 graduates.

Publications: *Annals of Mathematics* (6 a year), *Library Chronicle, Population Index* (quarterly), *Princeton Weekly Bulletin, Record of the Art Museum*† (2 a year), *University Magazine, World Politics* (quarterly). Publ. by Princeton University Press: *Philosophy and Public Affairs* (quarterly), *Princeton Alumni Weekly*).

DEANS:
*Faculty:* A. LEMONICK, PH.D.
*College:* J. S. GIRGUS, PH.D.
*Student Affairs:* J. A. BROWN, ED.M.
*Graduate School:* T. J. ZIOLKOWSKI, PH.D.
*School of Engineering and Applied Science:* R. G. JAHN, PH.D.
*Director of Admission:* J. A. WICKENDEN, ED.D.
*Woodrow Wilson School of Public and International Affairs:* D. E. STOKES, PH.D.
*School of Architecture and Urban Planning:* R. L. GEDDES, M.ARCH.

DIRECTORS:
*Observatory:* J. OSTRIKER, PH.D.
*Industrial Relations Section:* O. ASHENFELTER, PH.D.
*Art Museum:* P. C. BUNNELL, M.F.A.
*Plasma Physics Laboratory:* M. B. GOTTLIEB, PH.D.
*Index of Christian Art:* ROSALIE B. GREEN, PH.D.
*International Finance Section:* P. B. KENEN, PH.D.
*Shelby Cullom Davis Center for Historical Studies:* L. STONE, M.A.
*Center of International Studies:* C. E. BLACK, PH.D.
*Research Center for Urban and Environmental Planning:* J. WOLPERT, PH.D.
*University Research Board:* R. M. MAY, PH.D.
*University Health Services:* L. A. PYLE, M.D.
*Office of Population Research:* C. W. WESTOFF, PH.D.
*Econometric Research Program:* G. C. CHOW, PH.D.
*Center for Energy and Environmental Studies:* R. H. SOCOLOW, PH.D.
*Financial Research Center:* B. G. MALKIEL, PH.D.
*Princeton Urban and Regional Research Center:* R. P. NATHAN, PH.D.

PROFESSORS:
AARSLEFF, H. C., PH.D., English
ALLEN, L. C., PH.D., Chemistry
ALMGREN, F. J., PH.D., Mathematics
ANDERSON, P. W., PH.D., Physics
ANDRES, R. P., PH.D., Chemical Engineering
ANGRESS, R. K., PH.D., Germanic Languages and Literatures
ARDEN, B., PH.D., Electrical Engineering
ASHBY, P. H., PH.D., Religion
ASHENFLETER, O. C., PH.D., Economics
ATKINS, S. D., PH.D., Classics
AXTMANN, R. C., PH.D., Chemical Engineering
BABBITT, M. B., M.F.A., Music
BATES, B. W., PH.D., Romance Languages and Literatures
BAUMOL, W. J., PH.D., Economics
BENACERRAF, P., PH.D., Philosophy
BERGER, M., PH.D., Sociology
BERRY, C. H., PH.D., Economics and Public Affairs
BIENEN, H. S., PH.D., Politics and International Affairs
BIENKOWSKI, G. K., PH.D., Mechanical and Aerospace Engineering
BILLINGTON, D. P., B.SE., Civil Engineering
BLACK, C. E., PH.D., History
BLINDER, A. S., PH.D., Economics
BLOOMFIELD, P., PH.D., Statistics
BLUM, J., PH.D., History
BOGDONOFF, S. M., M.S.E., Aeronautical Engineering
BONINI, W. E., PH.D., Geophysics and Geological Engineering
BONNER, J. T., PH.D., Biology
BOURNE, F. C., PH.D., Latin
BOWEN, W. G., PH.D., Economics and Public Affairs
BRADFORD, D. F., PH.D., Economics and Public Affairs
BRANSON, W. H., PH.D., Economics and International Affairs
BRESSLER, M., PH.D., Sociology
BROMBERT, V. H., PH.D., Romance Languages and Literatures and Comparative Literature
BROWDER, W., PH.D., Mathematics
BROWN, C. F., Jr., PH.D., Comparative Literature
BROWN, L. C., PH.D., Near Eastern Studies
BURGI, R. T., PH.D., Slavic Languages and Literatures
CAKMAK, A. S., PH.D., Civil Engineering
CALAPRICE, F. P., PH.D., Physics
CALLAN, C. G., Jr., PH.D., Physics
CAMPBELL, B. A., PH.D., Psychology
CARVER, T. R., PH.D., Physics
CHALLENER, R. D., PH.D., History
CH'EN, T.-T., PH.D., East Asian Studies
CHENG, S. I., PH.D., Aeronautical Engineering
CHOW, G. C., PH.D., Economics
COALE, A. J., PH.D., Economics and Public Affairs
COFFIN, D. R., M.F.A., PH.D., Art and Archæology
COHEN, S. F., PH.D., Politics
CONE, E T., M.F.A., Music
CONNOR, W. R., PH.D., Classics
COOPER, J., PH.D., Psychology
COX, E. C., PH.D., Biology
CURSCHMANN, M. J. H., DR.PHIL., Germanic Languages
CURTISS, H. C., Jr., PH.D., Mechanical and Aerospace Engineering
DAHLEN, F. A., PH.D., Geological and Geophysical Sciences
DANIELSON, M. N., PH.D., Politics and Public Affairs
DANSON, L. N., PH.D., English
DARLEY, J. M., PH.D., Psychology
DARNTON, R. C., D.PHIL., History
DAVIES, H. M., PH.D., D.D., Religion
DAVIS, N. Z., PH.D., History
DEFFEYES, K. S., PH.D., Geological and Geophysical Sciences
DIAMOND, M. L., PH.D., Religion
DICKE, R. H., PH.D., Physics
DICKSON, M. B., PH.D., Near Eastern Studies
DOIG, J. W., PH.D., Politics and Public Affairs
DOODY, M. A., PH.D., English

## UNIVERSITIES AND COLLEGES—NEW JERSEY

DOWELL, E. H., D.SC., Mechanical and Aerospace Engineering
**DREWRY, H. N.**, M.A., **History**
DURBIN, E. J., M.S., Mechanical and Aerospace Engineering
**DWORK, B. M.**, PH.D., **Mathematics**
ERINGEN, A. C., PH.D., Civil Engineering
**ERMOLAEV, H.**, PH.D., **Slavic Languages and Literatures**
FAGLES, R., PH.D., Comparative Literature and Humanities
FALK, R. A., J.S.D., International Law, Politics, and International Affairs
FEFFERMAN, C., PH.D., Mathematics
FERNANDEZ, J. W., PH.D., Anthropology
FISCHER, A. G., PH.D., Geology
FITCH, V. L., PH.D., Physics
FLEMING, J. V., PH.D., English and Comparative Literature
FONG, W. C., PH.D., Art History
**FORCIONE, A. K.**, PH.D., **Romance Languages and Literatures and Comparative Literature**
**FRANK, J. N.**, PH.D., **Comparative Literature**
FREDE, M., PH.D., Philosophy
**FREEDMAN, R. W. B.**, PH.D., **Comparative Literature**
FRESCO, J. R., PH.D., Life Sciences
**FRIEMAN, E. A.**, PH.D., **Astrophysical Sciences**
FURLEY, D. J., M.A., Greek Language and Literature
**FURTH, H. P.**, PH.D., **Astrophysical Sciences**
GAGER, J. G., Jr., PH.D., Religion
GARVEY, G., PH.D., Politics
**GEDDES, R. L.**, M.ARCH., **Architecture and Urban Planning**
GEERTZ, H., PH.D., Anthropology
**GILLHAM, J. J.**, PH.D., **Chemical Engineering**
GILLISPIE, C. C., PH.D., History
GILPIN, R. G., PH.D., Politics and International Affairs
GILVARG, C., PH.D., Biochemical Sciences
GIRGUS, J. S., PH.D., Psychology
GLASSMAN, I., D.ENG., Mechanical and Aerospace Engineering
**GLUCKSBERG, S.**, PH.D., **Psychology**
**GOLDFELD, S. M.**, PH.D., **Economics**
**GOLDMAN, E. F.**, PH.D., **History**
**GOLDMAN, M. P.**, PH.D., **English**
**GORDENKER, L.**, PH.D., **Politics**
GOSSMAN, J. L., D.PHIL., Romance Languages and Literatures
**GOTTLIEB, M. B.**, PH.D., **Astrophysical Sciences**
GRAVES, M., M.ARCH., Architecture and Urban Planning
GREEN, R. B., PH.D., Art and Archaeology
GREENSTEIN, F. I., PH.D., Politics
GROSS, C. G., PH.D., Psychology
GROSS, D. J., PH.D., Physics
GUNNING, R. C., PH.D., Mathematics
**HALPERN, M.**, PH.D., **Politics**
HAMA, F. R., D.SC., Mechanical and Aerospace Engineering
**HANSON, J. A.**, PH.D., **Classics and Comparative Literature**
**HARGRAVES, R. B.**, PH.D., **Geological and Geophysical Sciences**
HARMAN, G. H., PH.D., Philosophy
HAYES, W. D., PH.D., Mechanical and Aerospace Engineering
HAZEN, D. C., M.S.E., Mechanical and Aerospace Engineering
HAZONY, Y., PH.D., Civil Engineering
HINDERER, W., D.PHIL., Germanic Languages and Literatures
**HOEBEL, B. G.**, PH.D., **Psychology**
HOFFMANN, L-F., PH.D., Romance Languages
HOLLANDER, R. B., Jr., PH.D., European and Comparative Literature

HOLLISTER, L. S., PH.D., Geological and Geophysical Sciences
HOOG, A., AG. DE L'UNIV., French Literature
HORN, H. S., PH.D., Biology
HSIANG, W.-C., PH.D., Mathematics
HUNT, G. A., PH.D., Mathematics
HUNTER, J. S., PH.D., Civil Engineering
**HUNTER, S.**, A.B., **Art and Archaeology**
HYNES, S., PH.D., Literature
IRBY, J. E., PH.D., Romance Languages and Literatures
ISSAWI, C., M.A., Near Eastern Studies
ITZKOWITZ, N., PH.D., Near Eastern Studies
IWASAWA, K., D.SC., Mathematics
JACOBS, W. P., PH.D., Biology
JAFFEE, D. M., PH.D., Economics
**JAHN, R. G.**, PH.D., **Aerospace Sciences**
JAMESON, A., PH.D., Mechanical and Aerospace Engineering
JANSEN, M. B., PH.D., History and East Asian Studies
JEFFREY, R., PH.D., Philosophy
JOHNSON, E. F., PH.D., Chemical Engineering
JOHNSON, W. C., E.E., Electrical Engineering
JONES, E. E., PH.D., Psychology
JONES, M., PH.D., Chemistry
JUDSON, S., PH.D., Geography
**KAMIN, L. J.**, PH.D., **Psychology**
KAO, Y. K., PH.D., East Asian Studies
KATZ, N. M., PH.D., Mathematics
KATZ, S. N., PH.D., History
KAUFMANN, W., PH.D., Philosophy
KAUZMANN, W. J., PH.D., Chemistry
KAW, P. K., PH.D., Astrophysical Sciences
KEANEY, J. J., PH.D., Classics
KEELEY, E. L., PH.D., English and Creative Arts
**KELLER, S.**, PH.D., **Sociology**
**KELLEY, S.**, PH.D., **Politics**
**KENEN, P. B.**, PH.D., **Economics and International Finance**
KERNAN, A. B., PH.D., English
**KINCHLA, R. A.**, PH.D., **Psychology**
**KING, E. L.**, PH.D., **Spanish**
KNAPP, J. M., M.A., Music
KNORR, K., LL.B., PH.D., Public Affairs
KOCH, R. A., PH.D., Art and Archaeology
KOCHEN, S. B., PH.D., Mathematics
**KOHN, J. J.**, PH.D., **Mathematics**
KORNHAUSER, A. L., PH.D., Civil Engineering
KOSTIN, M. D., PH.D., Chemical Engineering
KRIPKE, S., B.A., Philosophy
KRUSKAL, M. D., PH.D., Mathematics and Astrophysical Sciences
**KUENNE, R. E.**, B.J., PH.D., **Economics**
KUHN, H. W., PH.D., Mathematical Economics
KULSRUD, R. M., PH.D., Astrophysical Sciences
LAM, S.-H., PH.D., Mechanical and Aerospace Engineering
LAMPERT, M. A., PH.D., Electrical Engineering
LEE, P. C. Y., PH.D., Civil Engineering
LEMONICK, A., PH.D., Physics
**LEVY, K.**, PH.D., **Music**
LEVY, M. J., Jr., PH.D., Sociology and International Affairs
LEWIS, B., PH.D., Near Eastern Studies
LEWIS, D. K., PH.D., Philosophy
**LEWIS, J. P.**, M.P.A., PH.D., **Economics and International Affairs**
**LEWIS, W. A.**, PH.D., LITT.D., L.H.D., LL.D., **Economics and International Affairs**
LICKLIDER, H., M.F.A., Architecture and Urban Planning
LIEB, E. H., PH.D., Mathematical Physics
LINK, A. S., PH.D., American History
LISK, R. D., PH.D., Biology

LITZ, A. W., Jr., D.PHIL., Belles-Lettres
**LIU, B.**, D.E.E., **Electrical Engineering**
**LIU, J. T. C.**, PH.D., **East Asian Studies and History**
**LO, A. W.**, PH.D., **Electrical Engineering**
LOCKARD, W. D., PH.D., Politics
LUCE, T. J., Jr., PH.D., Latin Language and Literature
LUCHAK, G., PH.D., Civil Engineering
LUDWIG, R. M., PH.D., English
MAHONEY, M. S., PH.D., History
**MALKIEL, B. G.**, PH.D., **Economics**
MAMAN, A., PH.D., French
MARK, P., PH.D., Electrical Engineering
MARKS, S. H., PH.D., Near Eastern Studies
MARTIN, J. R., M.F.A., PH.D., Art and Archaeology
MATHER, J. N., PH.D., Mathematics
MATHER, N. W., M.S.E., Electrical Engineering
MAXWELL, B., M.S.E., Chemical Engineering for Polymer Studies
MAY, R. M., PH.D., Biology
MAYER, A. J., PH.D., History
**McCLURE, D. S.**, PH.D., **Chemistry**
McFARLAND, T., PH.D., English
McPHERSON, J. M., PH.D., History
**MELLOR, G. L.**, SC.D., **Mechanics**
MENKEN, J. A., PH.D., Sociology
MILLER, G. A., PH.D., Psychology
**MILLER, H. K.**, PH.D., **English**
MILLS, E. S., PH.D., Economics
MILLS, R. G., PH.D., Chemical Engineering
MINER, E., PH.D., English and Comparative Literature
MISLOW, K., PH.D., Chemistry
MOORE, J. C., PH.D., Mathematics
MORGAN, W. J., PH.D., Geophysics
MOTE, F. W., PH.D., East Asian Studies
MURKIN, J. M., PH.D., History
MURPHY, W. F., PH.D., Jurisprudence
NATHAN, R. P., PH.D., Public and International Affairs
NAUMANN, R. A., PH.D., Chemistry and Physics
NELSON, E., PH.D., Mathematics
NEWTON, W. A., PH.D., Biology
NOLLNER, W. L., M.A., F.T.C.L., Music
NOTTERMAN, J. M., PH.D., Psychology
OBERMAN, C. R., PH.D., Astrophysical Sciences
OBEPESEKERE, G., PH.D., Anthropology
O'NEILL, G. K., PH.D., Physics
OSTRIKER, J. P., PH.D., Astrophysical Sciences
PEEBLES, P. J. E., PH.D., Physics
PERKINS, F. W., Jr., PH.D., Astrophysical Sciences
PHINNEY, R. A., PH.D., Geological and Geophysical Sciences
PINDER, G. F., PH.D., Civil Engineering
PIROUÉ, P. A., PH.D., Physics
PITCHER, G. W., PH.D., Philosophy
PLAKS, A. H., PH.D., East Asian Studies
PLUMMER, J. H., PH.D., Art and Archaeology
**QUANDT, R. E.**, PH.D., **Economics**
RABB, T. K., PH.D., History
RABITZ, H. A., PH.D., Chemistry
**RAMSEY, R. P.**, PH.D., **Religion**
RANDALL, J. K., M.F.A., Music
RAPKIN, C., H.D., Architecture and Urban Planning
REINHARDT, U. E., PH.D., Economics and Public Affairs
RIGOLOT, F., PH.D., Romance Languages and Literatures
REYNOLDS, G. T., PH.D., Physics
ROCHE, T. P., Jr., PH.D., English
**ROGERSON, J. B., Jr.**, PH.D., **Astrophysical Sciences**
RORTY, R. M., PH.D., Philosophy
ROSEN, L., J.D., PH.D., Anthropology

ROYCE, B. S. H., PH.D., Mechanical and Aerospace Engineering
ROZMAN, G. F., PH.D., Sociology
RUDENSTINE, N. L., PH.D., English
RUTHERFORD, P. H., PH.D., Astrophysical Sciences
RYDER, N. B., PH.D., Sociology
RYSKAMP, C. A., PH.D., English
SAVILLE, D. A., PH.D., Chemical Engineering
SCANLAN, R., PH.D., DR. ès SCI., Civil Engineering
SCANLON, T. M., Jr., PH.D., Philosophy
SCHOWALTER, W. R., PH.D., Chemical Engineering
SCHWARTZ, J., PH.D., Chemistry
SCHWARTZ, S. C., PH.D., Electrical Engineering
SCOTT, R. A., PH.D., Sociology
SEIGEL, J. E., PH.D., History
SEMMELHACK, M. F., PH.D., Chemistry
SHEAR, T. L., Jr., PH.D., Classical Archaeology
SHEARMAN, J. E., PH.D., Art and Archaeology
SHELLMAN, W. F., Jr., M.F.A., Architecture and Urban Planning
SHERR, R., PH.D., Physics
SHIMURA, G., SC.D., Mathematics
SHOEMAKER, F. C., PH.D., Physics
SIGMUND, P. E., PH.D., Politics
SIMON, B. M., PH.D., Physics
SMITH, A. J., PH.D., Physics
SMITH, J. W., PH.D., Philosophy
SMOLUCHOWSKI, R., PH.D., Solid State Sciences
SOCOLOW, R. H., PH.D., Mechanical and Aerospace Engineering
SOLLENBERGER, N. J., M.SC.E., Civil Engineering
SOMERS, H. M., PH.D., Politics and Public Affairs
SONNENFELD, A., PH.D., French Literature and Comparative Literature
SONNENSCHEIN, H., PH.D., Economics
SOOS, Z. G., PH.D., Chemistry
SPENCER, D. C., SC.D., Mathematics
SPIES, C. C., M.A., Music
SPIRO, T. G., PH.D., Chemistry
SPITZER, L., Jr., PH.D., Astrophysical Sciences
STEIGLITZ, K., D.SC., Electrical Engineering
STEIN, E. M., PH.D., Mathematics
STEIN, S. J., PH.D., History
STEINBERG, M., PH.D., Biology
STIGLITZ, J. E., PH.D., Economics
STIX, T. H., PH.D., Astrophysical Sciences
STOKES, D. E., PH.D., Politics and Public Affairs
STONE, L., M.A., History
SULLIVAN, E. D., PH.D., French and Comparative Literature
SUPPE, J. E., PH.D., Geological and Geophysical Sciences
SURBER, W. H., Jr., PH.D., Electrical Engineering
SZATHMARY, A., PH.D., Philosophy
TANG, W. M., PH.D., Astrophysical Sciences
TAYLOR, E. C., PH.D., Chemistry
TAYLOR, H. F., PH.D., Sociology
TAYLOR, J. B., PH.D., Economics and Public Affairs
TAYLOR, J. H., PH.D., Physics
TERBORGH, J. W., PH.D., Biology
THOMAS, J. B., PH.D., Electrical Engineering
THOMPSON, D. F., PH.D., Politics
THURSTON, W. P., PH.D., Mathematics
TIGNOR, R. L., PH.D., History
TONER, R. K., PH.D., Chemical Engineering
TOWNSEND, C. E., PH.D., Slavic Languages and Literatures
TREIMAN, S. B., PH.D., Theoretical Physics
TROTTER, H. F., PH.D., Mathematics

TUCKER, R. C., PH.D., Politics
TUKEY, J. W., PH.D., Statistics
TUMIN, M. M., PH.D., Sociology and Anthropology
TWITCHETT, D., PH.D., East Asian Studies
UDOVITCH, A. L., PH.D., Near Eastern Studies
UITTI, K. D., PH.D., Modern Languages
ULLMAN, J. D., PH.D., Electrical Engineering
ULLMAN, R., D.PHIL., International Affairs
VALLHONRAT, C. E., M.ARCH., Architecture and Urban Planning
VAN DE VELDE, R. W., PH.D., Public and International Affairs
VAN HOUTEN, F. B., PH.D., Geology
VON GOELER, S. E., DR.RER.NAT., Astrophysical Sciences
WAGNER, S., PH.D., Electrical Engineering
WALLACE, W. L., PH.D., Sociology
WASHNITZER, G., PH.D., Mathematics
WATSON, G. S., PH.D., D.SC., Statistics
WEISS, T. R., M.A., LITT.D., English and Creative Writing
WESTERGAARD, P. T., M.F.A., Music
WESTOFF, C. F., PH.D., Sociology
WIGHTMAN, A. S., PH.D., Mathematical Physics
WILCZEK, F., PH.D., Physics
WILKINSON, D. T., PH.D., Physics
WILLIAMS, F. A., PH.D., Mechanical and Aerospace Engineering
WILLIG, R. D., PH.D., Economics
WILSON, J. F., TH.D., Religion
WILSON, M. D., PH.D., Philosophy
WITTEN, E., PH.D., Physics
WOLIN, S. S., PH.D., Politics
WOLPERT, J., PH.D., Geography, Public Affairs and Urban Planning
WORCEL, A., M.D., Biochemical Sciences
WORTMAN, R. S., PH.D., History
ZIOLKOWSKI, T. J., PH.D., Germanic Languages and Literatures and Comparative Literature

### RIDER COLLEGE
P.O. BOX 6400,
LAWRENCEVILLE,
NEW JERSEY 08648

Telephone: (609) 896-5000.

Founded 1865.

President: Dr. FRANK N. ELLIOTT.
Vice-President for Academic Affairs and Provost: Dr. JERRY WAYNE BROWN.
Vice-President for Business and Finance and Treasurer: ROBERT FORSCHNER.
Director of Admissions: EARL L. DAVIS.
Librarian: R. STEPHEN.

The library contains 327,000 vols.
Number of teachers: 203.
Number of students: 3,453.

### RUTGERS UNIVERSITY
NEW BRUNSWICK,
NEW JERSEY 08903

Founded as Queen's College by Royal Charter 1766, name changed to Rutgers College 1825, Rutgers University 1924. Designated by legislature as State University of New Jersey 1945.

Academic year: September-June.

President: EDWARD J. BLOUSTEIN, PH.D.
Executive Vice-President: NATHANIEL J. PALLONE, PH.D. (acting).
Senior Vice-President and Treasurer: JOSEPH C. O'CONNELL, B.S.
Secretary: JEAN W. SIDAR, A.M.
New Brunswick Area Provost: KENNETH W. WHEELER, PH.D.
Newark Campus Provost: JAMES E. YOUNG, PH.D.
Camden Campus Provost: WALTER K. GORDON, PH.D.
Library: see Libraries.

Number of teachers: 2,500.
Number of students: 50,003.

Publications: *Rutgers Law Review, Alcohol Treatment Digest, Quarterly Journal of Studies on Alcohol, Library Journal, Museum Bulletin, Matrix, Soil Science, Trans-Action.*

DEANS:

#### New Brunswick Campus
Rutgers College: JOHN YOLTON.
Cook College: G. F. WALTON.
Douglass College: JEWEL COBB.
Education: IRENE ATHEY.
Engineering: ELLIS H. DILL.
Graduate School: K. G. WOLFSON.
Livingston College: W. R. JENKINS.
Pharmacy: JOHN COLAIZZI.
Social Work: HAROLD DEMONE.
University College: JACQUELINE K. LEWIS.
Summer Session: A. A. AUSTEN.
Library Service: T. MOTT.
Applied Professional Psychology: D. R. PETERSON.
Creative and Performing Arts: J. BETTENBENDER.

#### Camden Campus
Arts and Sciences: W. K. GORDON.
Law: J. C. PITTENGER.

#### Newark Campus
Arts and Sciences: N. SAMUELS.
Graduate School of Management: H. J. DE-PODWIN.
Law: P. SIMMONS.
Nursing: DOROTHY DE MAIO.
Criminal Justice: D. M. GOTTFREDSON.
Graduate School: M. B. NATHANSON.

### SAINT PETER'S COLLEGE
2641 KENNEDY BLVD.,
JERSEY CITY,
NEW JERSEY 07306

Telephone: (201) 333-4400.

Founded 1872.

Undergraduate courses in the Humanities, Sciences, and Business Studies; Master's degree course in Education.

President: EDWARD GLYNN, S.J.
Academic Vice-President: EDWARD W. BRANDE, S.J.

*Academic Dean:* JAMES J. GRANT, Jr., PH.D. (acting).
*Dean of Admissions:* ROBERT J. NILAN, M.A.
*Registrar:* RONALD J. WELTON, M.S.
*Library Director:* RICHARD D. TETREAU, PH.D., M.L.S.

The library contains 240,000 vols.
Number of teachers: 122 full-time, 234 part-time.
Number of students: 2,646 full-time, 1,349 part-time.

### SETON HALL UNIVERSITY
SOUTH ORANGE,
NEW JERSEY 07079
Founded 1856.

*President:* Rev. LAURENCE T. MURPHY.
*Vice-Presidents:* R. J. DE VALUE, B.S. (Business Affairs), P. MITCHELL, PH.D. (Academic Affairs).
*University Librarian:* Rev. Mgr. W. N. FIELD, M.L.S.

Number of teachers: 343 full-time, 225 part-time.
Number of students: 5,764 men, 4,138 women, total 9,902.
Publications: *Chimaera, Spirit, Journal of the School of Business, The Setonian, The Galleon* (year book), *The Hallmark, News* (Alumni), *Setonotes.*

#### DEANS:
*College of Arts and Sciences:* N. DE PROSPO, PH.D.
*School of Education:* J. H. CALLAN, D.ED.
*College of Nursing:* Sister AGNES REINKEMEYER, S.S.M., PH.D.
*School of Business Administration:* EDWARD MAZZE, PH.D.
*School of Law:* J. X. IRVING, LL.B.
*Graduate Division:* PAUL BUONAGURO, PH.D.

### STEVENS INSTITUTE OF TECHNOLOGY
HOBOKEN, NEW JERSEY 07030
Founded 1870.

*President:* KENNETH C. ROGERS.
*Secretary:* DAVID N. BARUS.
*Treasurer:* R. A. HAND.
*Provost:* R. F. COTELLESSA.
*Dean of the College:* E. A. FRIEDMAN.
*Dean of Graduate Studies:* J. FAJANS.
*Dean for Student Affairs:* R. E. EVERSEN.
*Dean for Research:* I. R. EHRLICH.
*Librarian:* RICHARD P. WIDDICOMBE.

The library contains 90,000 vols.
Number of teachers: 130.
Number of students: 2,800.
Publication: *The Indicator.*

### TRENTON STATE COLLEGE
TRENTON, NEW JERSEY 08625
Founded 1855.

*President:* HAROLD W. EICKHOFF, PH.D.
*Provost:* GORDON I. GOEWEY, MUS.A.D.
*Vice-President for College Planning and Research:* SHELDON HALPERN, PH.D.
*Vice-President for Administration and Finance:* P. L. MILLS, B.A.
*Registrar:* M. W. HUTTON, M.A.
*Librarian:* PAUL Z. DUBOIS, PH.D.

The library contains 300,000 vols.
Number of teachers: 395.
Number of students: 7,000 full-time, 4,000 part-time.

#### DEANS:
*Students:* J. PADDACK, PH.D.
*Arts and Sciences:* W. C. CURRY, PH.D.
*Education:* P. A. OLLIO, ED.D.
*Graduate Studies:* DANIEL R. HALL, ED.D.
*School of Business:* ANTHONY HANTJIS, ED.D.
*School of Industrial Education and Engineering Technology:* ROBERT THROWER, PH.D.
*School of Nursing:* SANDRA D. MCDOUGAL, PH.D.

### UPSALA COLLEGE
EAST ORANGE,
NEW JERSEY 07019
Telephone: (201) 266-7000.
Founded 1893.

*President:* RODNEY FELDER, ED.D.
*Dean of College:* H. EDWIN TITUS, PH.D.
*Vice-President for Finance and Treasurer:* WILLIAM H. WALTON, C.P.A.
*Vice-President for College Relations:* GEORGE A. FENWICK, A.B.
*Dean of Students:* BARBARA E. BENDER, ED.D.
*Dean of Enrolment Services:* BARRY E. ABRAMS, ED.D.
*Librarian:* RAYMOND L. MURRAY, M.A.

The library contains 175,400 vols.
Number of teachers: 71 full-time.
Number of students: 1,383.

### WESTMINSTER CHOIR COLLEGE
PRINCETON, NEW JERSEY 08540
Telephone: (609) 921-7100.
Founded 1926.

*President:* Dr. RAY E. ROBINSON.
*Dean of College:* Dr. CHARLES SCHISLER
*Registrar:* Dr. PETER D. WRIGHT.
*Librarian:* JOHN PECK.

The library contains 35,000 vols.; there is also a choral library with 3,000 titles and 300,000 copies.

Number of teachers: 65.
Number of students: 450.

### WILLIAM PATERSON COLLEGE OF NEW JERSEY
300 POMPTON ROAD,
WAYNE, NEW JERSEY 07470
Telephone: (201) 595-2000.
Founded 1855.

*President:* Dr. SEYMOUR C. HYMAN.
*Vice-President for Academic Affairs:* Dr. ARNOLD SPEERT.
*Vice-President for Administration and Finance:* PETER SPIRIDON.
*Registrar:* MARK EVANGELISTA.
*Librarian:* Dr. ROBERT GOLDBERG.

The library contains 270,726 vols.
Number of teachers: 393 (full-time).
Number of students: 11,997.
Publications: *WPC Report* (5 a year).

#### DEANS:
*Science:* Dr. A. SHINN.
*Humanities:* Dr. R. ATNALLY.
*Fine and Performing Arts:* Dr. J. LUDWIG.
*Education and Community Services:* Dr. T. PROVO.
*Social Science:* Dr. M. WEIL.
*Management:* Dr. B. HAROIAN.
*Nursing and Allied Health:* Dr. S. HAWES.
*Freshman Studies:* Dr. CECILE HANLEY.
*Educational Services:* D. BACCOLLO.
*Student Services:* Dr. S. SILAS.
*Graduate Studies:* (vacant).

## NEW MEXICO

### COLLEGE OF SANTA FE
ST. MICHAEL'S DRIVE,
SANTA FE, NEW MEXICO 87501
Telephone: (505) 473-6011.
Founded 1947.

*President:* Bro. CYPRIAN LUKE, F.S.C.
*Registrar:* Bro. J. M. MILLER, F.S.C.
*Librarian:* Bro. BRENDAN, F.S.C.

The library contains 70,000 volumes.
Number of teachers: 75.
Number of students: 1,150.

### EASTERN NEW MEXICO UNIVERSITY
PORTALES, NEW MEXICO 88130
Telephone: 562-1011.
Founded 1934.

*President:* WARREN B. ARMSTRONG.
*Executive Vice-President for Academic Affairs and Administration:* GORDON R. BOPP.
*Registrar:* JOE GARCIA.
*Dean of Admissions and Records:* ELDON WALKER.
*Librarian:* PEGGY TOZER.

The library contains 285,000 vols.
Number of teachers: 175.
Number of students: 5,600.

## NEW MEXICO HIGHLANDS UNIVERSITY
LAS VEGAS, NEW MEXICO 87701

Telephone: (505) 425-7511.

Founded 1893.

*President:* Dr. JOHN ARAGÓN.
*Chief Fiscal Officer:* A. DENNIS MARQUEZ.
*Academic Dean:* Dr. JESSIE F. QUERRY.
*Registrar and Director of Admissions:* Dr. E. ELOY MARTÍNEZ.
*Librarian:* Dr. RAUL C. HERRERA.

Number of teachers: 132, including 30 professors.
Number of students: 2,200.

DEANS:

*Student Affairs:* Dr. MATTHEW PADILLA.
*Graduate School:* Dr. JOHN PACHECO.


## NEW MEXICO INSTITUTE OF MINING AND TECHNOLOGY
SOCORRO, NEW MEXICO 87801

Founded 1889.

*President:* KENNETH W. FORD.
*Vice-President for Academic Affairs:* GORDON R. BOPP.
*Vice-President for Administration and Finance:* (vacant).
*Librarian:* BETTY REYNOLDS.

The library contains 80,000 vols.
Number of students: 1,334.

DIRECTORS:

*New Mexico Bureau of Mines and Mineral Resources:* FRANK E. KOTTLOWSKI.
*New Mexico Petroleum Recovery Research Centre:* J. J. TABER.
*Research and Development Division:* MARX BROOK.


## NEW MEXICO STATE UNIVERSITY
LAS CRUCES
NEW MEXICO 88003

Telephone: (505) 646-0111.

Founded in 1888 as Las Cruces College; became in 1889 the New Mexico College of Agriculture and Mechanic Arts and in 1960 the State University.

*President:* GERALD W. THOMAS, PH.D.
*Executive Vice-President:* DONALD C. ROUSH, ED.D.
*Vice-President—Finance:* ROBERT KIRKPATRICK, B.S., C.P.A.
*Vice-President—Student Affairs:* PEGGY ELDER, ED.D.
*Vice-President—Development:* STEELE JONES, M.A.
*Librarian:* J. P. DYKE, PH.D.

The library contains 520,000 vols., plus 275,000 bound and unbound government documents and 285,000 microforms.

Number of teachers: 565.
Number of students: 12,000.

Publications: Agricultural Experiment Station: *Annual Report, Bulletin, Circular,* etc.; Physical Science Laboratory: classified publications; Agricultural Extension Service: bulletins; Engineering Experiment Station: bulletins; Solar Energy Institute: bulletins.

DEANS:

*Graduate School:* W. H. MATCHETT, PH.D.
*College of Agriculture and Home Economics:* L. S. POPE, PH.D.
*College of Arts and Sciences:* T. M. GALE, PH.D.
*College of Business Administration and Economics:* CURTIS C. GRAHAM, PH.D.
*College of Education:* DAVID R. BYRNE, ED.D.
*College of Engineering:* JOSEPH GENIN.

ATTACHED RESEARCH INSTITUTES:

**Agricultural Experiment Station:** Dir. L. S. POPE, PH.D.
**Arts and Science Research Center:** Dir. T. M. GALE, PH.D.
**Business Research and Services:** Dir. ORMAN PAANANEN.
**Educational Research Center:** Dir. DARRELL S. WILLEY.
**Engineering Experiment Station:** Dir. NARENDRA N. GUNAJI.
**Physical Science Laboratory:** Dir. H. R. LAWRENCE, M.S.
**New Mexico Solar Energy Institute:** Dir. HARRY ZWIBEL.
**Water Resources Research Institute:** Dir. THOMAS G. BAHR, PH.D.


## ST. JOHN'S COLLEGE
SANTA FE, NEW MEXICO 87501

Telephone: (505) 982-3691.

Founded 1964.

*President:* EDWIN J. DELATTRE.
*Provost:* J. BURCHENAL AULT.
*Dean:* ROBERT BART.
*Registrar:* Miss ELLEN GANT.
*Librarian:* JAMES M. BENEFIEL (acting).

The library contains 40,000 vols.

Number of teachers: 42.
Number of students: 325.

For Annapolis branch *see under* Maryland.


## UNIVERSITY OF ALBUQUERQUE
ST. JOSEPH PLACE N.W.,
ALBUQUERQUE,
NEW MEXICO 87140

Telephone: 831-1111.

Founded 1920.

*President:* J. B. CRANSTON, Jr.
*Academic Dean:* Dr. ANDREW IMRIK.
*Admissions:* MARY GUSTAS.
*Librarian:* ELEANOR NOBLE.

The library contains 78,000 volumes.
Number of teachers: 80.
Number of students: 2,100.


## UNIVERSITY OF NEW MEXICO
ALBUQUERQUE,
NEW MEXICO 87131

Telephone: 277-0111.

Created by act of territorial legislation 1889. Opened 1892.

*President:* Dr. WILLIAM E. DAVIS.
*Provost:* MCALLISTER HULL, PH.D.
**Vice-President for Business and Finance:** J. PEROVICH, M.B.A.
*Director of the Medical Centre:* L. NAPOLITANO, PH.D.
*Associate Provost for Research:* JOSEPH V. SCALETTI, PH.D.
*Associate Provost for Academic Affairs:* JOEL M. JONES. PH.D.
*Associate Provost for Community Education:* ALEX A. SANCHEZ, ED.D.
*Administrative Vice-President for Student Affairs, Alumni Relations and Development:* M. D. JOHNSON.
*Dean of Admissions and Records:* R. W. WEAVER, M.A.
*Dean of Continuing Education:* RUPERT TRUJILLO, ED.D.
*Secretary of the University:* ANNE J. BROWN, B.U.S., M.A.P.A.
*Dean of Library Services:* PAUL VASSALLO, M.L.S.

The library contains 1,000,000 vols.
Number of teachers: 990.
Number of students: 23,500.

Publications: *Journal of Anthropological Research, Natural Resources Journal†, New Mexico Business†, New Mexico Historical Review†.*

DEANS:

*Graduate School:* CHARLENE MCDERMOTT, PH.D.
*School of Architecture and Planning:* GEORGE ANSELEVICIUS.
**Students:** KAREN M. GLASER, M.S.ED.
*College of Arts and Sciences:* F. CHRIS GARCIA, PH.D.
*College of Education:* D. W. DARLING, ED.D.
*College of Engineering:* G. W. MAY, PH.D.
*College of Fine Arts:* D. C. MCRAE, M.A.
*School of Law:* ROBERT DESIDERIO, J.D.
*Anderson Schools of Management:* EDWIN CAPLAN, PH.D. (acting).
*School of Medicine:* L. M. NAPOLITANO, PH.D.
*College of Nursing:* CARMEN WESTWICK, PH.D.
*College of Pharmacy:* C. A. BLISS, PH.D.
*University College:* W. H. HUBER, Jr., J.D.
*Division of Public Administration:* T. ZANE REEVES, PH.D.

PROFESSORS:

ADAMSON, G. W., ED.D., Special Education
AHLUWALIA, H. S., PH.D., Physics

## UNIVERSITIES AND COLLEGES—NEW MEXICO     U.S.A.

ALBRECHT, B., C.E., M.S., PH.D., **Mechanical Engineering**
ALPERT, S. S., PH.D., Physics
ANDERSON, D. E., PH.D., Guidance and Counselling
**ANDERSON, R. E., M.D., Pathology**
ANDERSON, R. Y., M.S., Geology
ANGEL, E. S. PH.D., Electrical and Computer Engineering
**ANTREASIAN, G. Z., B.F.A., Art**
APPENZELLER, O., M.B., M.D., PH.D., **Neurology and Medicine**
AUGER, K. F., ED.D., Elementary Education
BAKER, W. E., PH.D., Mechanical Engineering
BARRETT, E. M., PH.D., Geography
**BATCHELLER, J. M., M.A., ED.M., PH.D., Music**
BELL, S., PH.D., Computer Science
**BECKEL, C. L., PH.D., Physics**
BEN-DAVID, S., PH.D., Economics
**BENEDETTI, D. T., M.A., PH.D., Psychology**
BENNETT, I. V., M.A., PH.D., Geography
BERLIN, I. I., M.D., Psychiatry and Pediatrics
BICKNELL, J. M., M.D., Neurology
BILLS, G., PH.D., Linguistics
BINFORD, L. R., PH.D., Anthropology
BLISS, C. A., M.S., PH.D., Pharmacy
BLOOD, R. E., PH.D., Education Administration
BOATWRIGHT, L., PH.D., Electrical and Computer Engineering
BOCK, P. K., M.A., PH.D., Anthropology
BOLIE, V. W., M.S., PH.D., Electrical and Computer Engineering
BORDEN, T. A., M.D., Surgery
BOWEN, F., M.M., Music
**BOYLE, G. J., M.A. PH.D., Economics**
BRADSHAW, M. D., PH.D., Electrical and Computer Engineering
BRODY, J. J., PH.D., Anthropology
BROOKINS, D. G., PH.D., Geology
BRYANT, H. C., M.S., PH.D., Physics
BURNESS, S. H., PH.D., Economics
BYATT, W. J., M.S., PH.D., Electrical and Computer Engineering
**CAMPBELL, J. M., PH.D., Anthropology**
CAPLAN, E. H., M.B.A., PH.D., Management
CARASSO, A. S., PH.D., Mathematics
CARNEY, J. B., Jr., PH.D., Civil Engineering
CATON, R. D., PH.D., Chemistry
CHANDLER, C., PH.D., Physics
CHENG, C., PH.D., Chemical and Nuclear Engineering
CHOU, D., PH.D., Mechanical Engineering
CHUNG, PHAM, PH.D., Economics
CIKOVSKY, N., Jr., PH.D., Art
CIURCZAK, P. L., PH.D., Music
**CLOUGH, R. H., M.S., SC.D., Civil Engineering**
COGBURN, R. F., PH.D., Mathematics
COHEN, S., M.A., PH.D., Economics
COHLMEYER, R. C., B.S., Architecture
COTTRELL, M. M., M.S., Civil Engineering
COX, K. E., PH.D., Chemical and Nuclear Engineering
CRAWFORD, C. S., PH.D., Biology
CUMMINGS, R. G., PH.D., Economics
CUSHING, A. H., M.D., Paediatrics
CUTTER, D. C., M.A., PH.D., History
**DABNEY, W M., M.A., PH.D., History**
DAHMEN, L. A., PH.D., Guidance and Counselling
DARLING, D. W., M.S., ED.D., Elementary Education
**DAUB, G. H., M.S., PH.D., Chemistry**
DAVID, P. R., PH.D., Sociology
DEGENHARDT, W. G., PH.D., Biology
DEMARR, R. E., PH.D., Mathematics
DEVRIES, R. C., PH.D., Electrical and Computer Engineering
DIETERLE, B., PH.D., Physics

DOBERNECK, R. C., M.D., PH.D., Surgery
DORATO, P., PH.D., Electrical and Computer Engineering
**DUBOIS, D. W., M.A., PH.D., Mathematics**
DUMARS, C., J.D., Law
DUSZYNSKI, D. W., PH.D., Biology
EATON, R. P., M.D., Medicine
EDWARDS, W. S., M.D., Surgery
EFROYMSON, G., PH.D., Mathematics
ELLIS, H. C., M.A., PH.D., Psychology
ELLIS, R. N., PH.D., History
ELLIS, W. H., J.D., Law
ELSTON, W. E., M.A., PH.D., Geology
ENTRINGER, R. C., PH.D., Mathematics
**EPSTEIN, B., M.S., PH.D., Mathematics**
ERTEZA, A., M.S.E.E., PH.D., Electrical and Computer Engineering
ETULAIN, R., PH.D., History
EVANS, R., PH.D., English
EWING, R., PH.D., Geology
FEENEY, D., PH.D., Psychology
FELDBERG, L., M.A., Music
FERNANDEZ, P. H., PH.D., Modern and Classical Languages
FERRARO, D. P., PH.D., Psychology
**FIEDLER, W. C., M.S., PH.D., Pharmacy**
FINDLEY, J. S., PH.D., Biology
FINK, M., M.A., Law Library
FINLEY, J., PH.D., Physics
**FINSTON, H. V., M.A., PH.D., Business and Administrative Sciences**
FISHBURN, W. R., ED.D., Guidance and Counselling
FLEMING, R. E., PH.D., English
FLICKINGER, W. G., J.D., Law
FRANDSEN, K. D., PH.D., Speech Communication
GAFFORD, W. R., M.S., Civil Engineering
GARDNER, K. D., M.D., Medicine
GIBSON, A. G., PH.D., Mathematics
GILBERT, E. J., PH.D., Computer Science
GIRGUS, S., PH.D., American Studies
GISSER, M., PH.D., Economics
GOLDBERG, J., LL.B., Law
GONZALES, A., M.A., Modern and Classical Languages
**GRANNEMANN. W. W., M.A., PH.D., Electrical and Computer Engineering**
GREENBERG, R. E., M.D., Paediatrics
GREGORY, P., PH.D., Economics
GRICE, G. R., M.A., PH.D., Psychology
GRIEGO, R. J., PH.D., Mathematics
GRIFFIN, L. E., PH.D., Health, Physical Education and Recreation
GURBAXANI, S., PH.D., Electrical and Computer Engineering
HALL, J., PH.D., Civil Engineering
**HAMILTON, D. B., Jr., M.A., PH.D., Economics**
HANSEN, B., PH.D., Theatre Arts
HARDY, W., M.D., Medicine
HARPENDING, H., M.A., PH.D., Anthropology
HARRIS, F., J.D., Political Science
HARRIS, M., PH.D., Educational Foundations
HARTUNG, C. R., M.F.A., Theatre Arts
HAWKINS, C., PH.D., Electrical and Computer Engineering
HERSH, R., M.S., PH.D., Mathematics
HILL, H. L., Jr., PH.D., English
HILLERMAN, A. G., M.A., Journalism
**HILLMAN A. P., M.A., PH.D. Mathematics**
HOLLSTEIN, U., PH.D., Chemistry
HOLZOFFEL, T., PH.D., Modern and Classical Languages
**HOUGHTON, A. V., III, M.S., PH.D., Mechanical Engineering**
HUACO, G. A., M.A., PH.D., Sociology
HUBER, W. H., Jr., J.D., Management
**HULSBOS, C. L., M.S., PH.D., Civil Engineering**
HURWITZ, L., PH.D., Pharmacology
**IKLE, F. W., PH.D., History**

JAMSHIDI, M., PH.D., Electrical and Computer Engineering
JOHNSON, P. J., PH.D., Psychology
JOHNSON, R. L., Jr., PH.D., Civil Engineering
JOHN-STEINER, VERA P., PH.D., Educational Foundations
JONAS, P., PH.D., Economics
JONES, J. M., PH.D., American Studies
JU, F. D., M.S., PH.D., **Mechanical Engineering**
**KARNI. S., M.ENG., PH.D., Electrical and Computer Engineering**
KEIL, K., M.S., PH.D., Geology
KELLEY, R. O., PH.D., Anatomy and Biology
KELLNER, R., M.D., PH.D., Psychiatry
KELLY, D. E., ED.D., Elementary Education
KELLY, R. D., M.S., PH.D., Electrical and Computer Engineering
KELSEY, C. A., PH.D., Radiology
KERN, R. W., PH.D., History
KIDD, D. E., PH.D., Biology
KING, D., PH.D., Astronomy
KLINE, R. D., PH.D., Instructional Media
KNUDSEN, H. K., PH.D., Electrical and Computer Engineering
KOOPMANS, L. H., PH.D., Mathematics
KORNFELD, M., M.D., Pathology
KOVNAT, R., LL.B., Law
KROTH, R. L., PH.D., Special Education
KYNER, W. T., M.A., PH.D., Mathematics
LAMB, L. E., PH.D., Communicative Disorders
LAW, D. H., M.D., Medicine
**LAWRENCE, R. E., M.A., ED.D., Educational Administration**
LAWRENCE, R. H., M.A., Journalism
LEAVITT, C. P., PH.D., Physics
LEBARON, F. N. M.A., PH.D., Biochemistry
LEBECK, A., PH.D., Mechanical Engineering
LENBERG, R. A., PH.D., Management
LEVY, J., PH.D., Psychiatry
LEWIS, R. W., M.A., Art
LIBO, L. M., M.A., PH.D., Psychiatry and Psychology
LIEUWEN, E., M.A., PH.D., History
LIGON, J. D., PH.D., Biology
**LOFTFIELD, R. B., M.A., PH.D., Biochemistry**
**LOGAN, F. A. M.A., PH.D., Psychology**
LOUGHLIN, CATHERINE E., ED.D., Elementary Education
McCONEGHEY, H. W., ED.D., Art Education
McDOWELL, R. L., PH.D., Special Education
McGILL, F., PH.D., Health, Physical Education and Recreation
**McLAREN, L. C., M.A., PH.D.. Microbiology**
McPHERSON, D., PH.D., English
McRAE, D. C., M.A., Music and Fine Arts
MAES, W. R., PH.D., Guidance and Counselling
MANN, M., ED.D., Elementary Education
MARTIN, W. C., M.A., PH.D., Biology
**MARTINEZ, J. E., M.S., Civil Engineering**
MESSER, R. H., M.D., Obstetrics and Gynaecology
MICALI, R., ED.D., Guidance and Counselling
MINZNER, P., LL.B., Law
**MITCHELL, MERLE, M.A., PH.D., Mathematics**
MOELLENBERG, W. P., ED.D., Education Foundations
MOLER, C. B., PH.D., Mathematics
MOORE, J. C., PH.D., Educational Foundations
MORI, P. T., M.B.A., J.D., Management
MORRISON, D. R., M.S., PH.D., Mathematics and Computing Science
MOSELEY, R. D., Jr., M.D., Radiology
MUIR, H. B., J.D., Law

Murphy, R. E., m.a., ph.d., Geography
Murray, Beatrice Louise, m.n., ed.d., Nursing
Napolitano, L. M., m.s., ph.d., Anatomy
Nash, G. D., m.a. ph.d., History
Nason, M. R., m.a., ph.d., Modern and Classical Languages
Needler, M. C., ph.d., Political Science
Nesbitt, R. D., Jr., m.a., Secondary Education
Norton, R., ph.d., Economics
Occhialino, M., j.d., Law
Oller, J., ph.d., Linguistics
Omer, G. E., Jr., m.d., m.s., Orthopaedics and Anatomy
Onneweer, C., ph.d., Mathematics
Ortiz, A. A., ph.d., Anthropology
Owen, G. M., m.d., Paediatrics
Paak, C. E., m.a., Art
Palmer, D. L., m.d., Medicine
Panton, D. B., ph.d., Management
Papcsy, F. E., ph.d., Health, Physical Education and Recreation
Parker, A. L., ph.d., Economics
Parnall, T., j.d., Law
Pathak, P. T., ph.d., Mathematics
Peters, W. S., m.b.a., ph.d., Management
Peterson, A. W., ph.d., Physics and Astronomy
Pitcher, J. L., m.d., Medicine
Pohland, P., ph.d., Educational Administration
Potter, L. D., m.a., ph.d., Biology
Price, R., ph.d., Physics and Astronomy
Priola, D. V., ph.d., Physiology
Qualls, C., ph.d., Mathematics
Radosevich, H. R., ph.d., Management
Rehder, R. R., m.b.a., ph.d., Management
Resta, P. E., ph.d., Education and Education Foundations
Rhodes, B. A., ph.d., Pharmacy
Rhodes, J. M., m.a., ph.d., Psychology
Richards, C. G., ph.d., Mechanical Engineering
Riedesel, M. L., m.s., ph.d., Biology
Robert, G., Music
Robertson, J. C., ph.d., Chemical and Nuclear Engineering
Rodriguez, A., ph.d., Modern and Classical Languages
Roebuck, J., ph.d., History
Roll, S., ph.d., Psychology
Romero, L. M., ll.m., Law
Rosasco, L. A., m.a., ed.d., Educational Foundations
Rosenblum, S., m.a., ph.d., Psychology
Rosenfeld, L. B., ph.d., Speech Communication
Ruebush, B. K., ph.d., Psychiatry
Sabloff, J., ph.d., Anthropology
Saiki, J. H., m.d., Medicine
Sala, J. M., m.d., Radiology
Sanchez, D. A, ph.d., Mathematics
Scaletti. J. V., m.s., ph.d. Microbiology
Scallen. T. J., m.d., ph.d., Biochemistry
Schaeffer, R., ph.d., Chemistry
Schlegel, D. P., m.a., Architecture
Schoenfeld, M. G., m.mus., Music
Scholer, E. A., m.s., Recreation
Schwerin, K. H., ph.d., Anthropology
Scully, M. O., ph.d., Physics
Sears, G. A., ph.d., Civil Engineering
Seidler, A. H., m.s., ph.d., Physical Education
Senescu, R., m.d., Psychiatry
Senninger, C. M., ph.d., Modern and Classical Languages
Shelton, M. N., ph.d., Special Education
Sickels, R. J., ph.d., Political Science
Slate, D. M., m.a., ph.d., Management
Slavik, M., m.d., Medicine
Smith, D. E., m.d., Surgery
Smith, R., ed.d., Home Economics
Smith, S. D., Art

Smithburg, D. W., ph.d., Public Administration
Snead, R. E., m.a., ph.d., Geography
Snell, Ednell Margaret, m.a., ed.d, Home Economics
Snyder, R. D., m.d., Neurology
Solomon, S., m.d., Physiology
Southward, H. D., m.a., ph.d., Electrical and Computer Engineering
Spuhler, J. N., m.a., ph.d., Anthropology
Srubek, J., ph.d., Art Education
Stahl, K. H., m.s., ph.d., Pharmacy
Steger, A., m.a., ph.d., Mathematics
Stitelman, L., ph.d., Public Administration
Stone, A. P., ph.d., Mathematics
Stoumbis, G. C., ph.d., Secondary Education
Strickland, R. G., m.d., ph.d., Medicine
Stumpf, H. P., ph.d., Political Science
Sturm, F. G., ph.d., Philosophy
Swinson, D., ph.d., Physics
Tapscott, R., ph.d., Chemistry
Taylor, A., ph.d., Art Education and Architecture
Teitelbaum, L. E., ll.m., Law
Thornbury, J., m.d., Radiology
Tokuda, Sej, ph.d., Microbiology
Tomasson, R. F., m.a., ph.d., Sociology
Tomlins, J. E., m.a., ph.d., Modern and Classical Languages
Tonigan, R. F., m.s., ed.d., Educational Administration
Triandafilidis, G. E., m.s., ph.d., Civil Engineering
Tung, K., m.d., Pathology
Tuttle, H., ph.d., Philosophy
Tweeten, P. W., ph.d., Secondary Education
Ulibarri, H., ed.d., Education Administration
Ulibarri, S. R., m.a., ph.d., Modern and Classical Languages
Ulrich, J. A., ph.d., Microbiology and Pathology
Utton, A. E., m.a. (juris)., Law
Vanderjagt, D., ph.d., Biochemistry
Vassallo, P., m.a., General Library
Vogel, A. W., ed.d., Education Foundations
Vorherr, H. W., m.d., Obstetrics and Gynaecology
Wagoner, R. L., ed.d., Secondary Education
Waterman, E., ph.d., Anatomy and Biology
Watson, B. L., ph.d., Special Education
Weber, E. J., ph.d., Secondary Education
Weston, J. T., m.d., Pathology
Whan, G. A., m.s., ph.d., Nuclear Engineering
White, J. E., Jr., m.a., ph.d., Modern and Classical Languages
White, R. H., ph.d., Secondary Education
Wiens, J., ph.d., Biology
Wiese, W., m.d., Family, Community and Emergency Medicine
Wildin, M. W., ph.d., Mechanical Engineering
Williams, R. C., Jr., m.d., Medicine
Williams, R. H., ph.d., Electrical and Computer Engineering
Winograd, P., j.d., Law
Winslow, W. W., m.d., Psychiatry
Winter, L. G., m.a., ph.d., Management
Witemeyer, H., ph.d., English
Wolfe, D. M., ph.d., Physics
Woodall, D., ph.d., Chemical and Nuclear Engineering
Woodward, L. A., ph.d., Geology
Zepper, J. T., m.ed., ed.d., Educational Foundations
Zimmer, W. J., ph.d., Mathematics

## WESTERN NEW MEXICO UNIVERSITY

BOX 680, SILVER CITY, NEW MEXICO 88062

Telephone: 538-6011.

Founded 1893.

*President:* Dr. Robert E. Glennen.
*Vice-President for Academic Affairs:* Dr. John L. Butler.
*Vice-President for Student Affairs:* Dr. Phillip J. Farren.
*Vice-President for Fiscal Affairs:* James Graff.
*Registrar:* Ramon Carrillo.
*Librarian:* J. Essick.

The library contains 388,19 3vols.
Number of teachers: 72.
Number of students: 1,600.

# NEW YORK

## ADELPHI UNIVERSITY

GARDEN CITY, NEW YORK 11530

Telephone: (516) 663-1120.

Founded 1896.

*President:* Timothy W. Costello.
*Vice-President:* James Campbell.
*Registrar:* Don Ketcham.
*Librarian:* D. Nora Gallagher.

The library contains 333,226 vols.
Number of teachers: c. 4000.
Number of students: 11,500.

### Deans:

*Academic Affairs:* Clifford T. Stewart.
*Arts and Sciences, Graduate and Undergraduate:* Howard S. Grob.
*School of Social Work:* J. L. Vigilante.
*School of Nursing:* June S. Rothberg.
*School of Business:* Robert O. Carlson.
*School of Banking and Money Management:* James Patchias.
*Institute of Advanced Psychological Studies:* Gordon F. Derner.
*University College:* Gerald A. Heeger.

## ALFRED UNIVERSITY

ALFRED, NEW YORK 14802

Founded 1836.

*President:* (vacant).
*Provost:* S. G. Odle, ed.d.
*Vice-President for Business and Finance:* R. E. Heywood, m.s.
*Executive Director of University Relations:* H. Martin Moore, ed.m.
*Dean for Student Affairs:* Donald H. King, m.ed.
*Director of Admissions:* Paul Priggon, m.ed.
*Head Librarian:* June Brown, m.l.s.

The library contains 225,000 vols.
Number of teachers: 186.
Number of students: 2,265.

Publications: *Fiat Lux, Alfred Reporter, Kanakadea, University Catalogue.*

DEANS:
*College of Liberal Arts and Sciences:* JOHN FOXEN, PH.D.
*College of Ceramics:* W. RICHARD OTT, PH.D.
*Graduate School:* L. C. BUTLER, PH.D.
*College of Nursing:* JOELLA M. RAND, R.N., PH.D.
*College of Business and Administration:* (vacant).

## BANK STREET COLLEGE OF EDUCATION
610 WEST 112TH ST.,
NEW YORK, N.Y. 10025
Telephone: (212) 663-7200.
Founded 1916.

*President:* Dr. RICHARD RUOPP.
*Vice-President and Dean for School and Community Services:* Dr. CORINNE J. H. RIEDER.
*Vice-President and Dean for Graduate and Children's Programs:* Dr. GWENDOLYN C. BAKER.
*Dean of Center for Leadership Development:* Dr. GORDON J. KLOPF.
*Associate Dean for Graduate Programs:* ANNE M. SMITH.
*Registrar:* Mrs. PRISCILLA PEMBERTON.
*Director of Admissions:* Mrs. PHYLLIS HALDEMAN.
*Director of Library:* ELEANOR KULLESEID (acting).

The library contains 80,000 vols.
Number of teachers: 51.
Number of students: 1,118.

## BARD COLLEGE
ANNANDALE-ON-HUDSON,
N.Y. 12504
Founded 1860.

*President:* LEON BOTSTEIN.
*Business Manager:* SUSAN L. BARICH.
*Registrar:* ANNYS N. WILSON.
*Dean:* STUART LEVINE.
*Director of Admissions:* KAREN WILCOX.
*Librarian:* THOMAS GAUGHAN.

The library contains 150,000 vols.
Number of teachers: 92.
Number of students: 775.

## CANISIUS COLLEGE
2001 MAIN STREET,
BUFFALO, N.Y. 14208
Telephone: (716) 883-7000.
Founded 1870.

*President:* Very Rev. JAMES M. DEMSKE, S.J., PH.D.
*Exec. Vice-President (Academic):* Rev. EDMUND G. RYAN, S.J., PH.D.
*Exec. Vice-President (Administrative)* GEORGE M. MARTIN, J.D.

*Vice-President for Business and Finance:* LAURENCE W. FRANZ, PH.D.
*Vice-President for Student Affairs:* Mrs. LILIAN LEVEY, M.S.
*Director of Planning and Research:* PHYLLIS A. SHOLTYS, PH.D.
*Librarian:* P. J. LAUX, M.A., M.S.L.S.

The library contains 211,600 vols.
Number of teachers: 150 full-time, 101 part-time, total 251.
Number of students: 4,272.

## CITY UNIVERSITY OF NEW YORK
535 EAST 80TH ST.,
NEW YORK, N.Y. 10021
Founded 1847.

The City University of New York is a public institution comprising nine senior colleges, listed below, a Graduate School and University Center, and an affiliated medical school, Mount Sinai School of Medicine, and seven community colleges: Borough of Manhattan Community College, Bronx Community College, Medgar Evers College, Hostos Community College, Kingsborough Community College, Fiorello H. La Guardia Community College, Queensborough Community College; and New York City Technical College.

*Chancellor:* ROBERT J. KIBBEE.

The combined libraries contain 5,000,000 vols.

### Graduate School and University Center
33 WEST 42ND ST.,
NEW YORK, N.Y. 10036
Telephone: (212) 790-4395.
Established 1961.

*President:* HAROLD H. PROSHANSKY.
Number of teachers: 200 (full-time).
Number of students: 2,840.

### The Bernard M. Baruch College
17 LEXINGTON AVE.,
NEW YORK, N.Y. 10010
Telephone: (212) 725-3000.
Established 1919.

*President:* JOEL SEGALL.
Number of teachers 400 (full-time).
Number of students: 14,890.

### Brooklyn College
BEDFORD AVE. and AVE. H,
BROOKLYN, N.Y. 11210
Telephone: (212) 780-5485.
Established 1930 by combining Brooklyn Centres of City College and Hunter College.

*President:* ROBERT L. HESS.
Number of teachers: 885 (full-time).
Number of students: 18,067.

### City College
CONVENT AVE. AND 138TH ST.,
NEW YORK, N.Y. 10031
Telephone: (212) 690-6741.
Founded 1847.

*President:* ARTHUR E. TIEDEMANN (acting).
Number of teachers: 708 (full-time).
Number of students: 13,161.

### Hunter College
695 PARK AVE.,
NEW YORK, N.Y. 10021
Telephone: 570-5566.
Founded 1870.

*President:* DONNA SHALALA.
Number of teachers: 637 (full-time).
Number of students: 17,989.

### John Jay College of Criminal Justice
444 WEST 56TH ST.,
NEW YORK, N.Y. 10019
Telephone: (212) 489-5184.
Founded 1964.

*President:* GERALD W. LYNCH.
Number of teachers: 240 (full-time).
Number of students: 6,394.

### Herbert H. Lehman College
BEDFORD PARK BLVD. WEST,
BRONX, N.Y. 10468
Telephone: (212) 960-8881.
Founded 1931.

*President:* LEONARD LIEF.
Number of teachers: 438 (full-time).
Number of students: 9,341.

### Queens College
65-30 KISSENA BLVD.,
FLUSHING, N.Y. 11367
Telephone: (212) 520-7000.
Founded 1937.

*President:* SAUL B. COHEN.
Number of teachers: 774 (full-time).
Number of students: 18,807.

### College of Staten Island
130 STUYVESANT PLACE,
STATEN ISLAND, N.Y. 10301.
Telephone: (212) 390-7733.

*President:* EDMOND L. VOLPE.
Number of teachers: 344 (full-time).
Number of students: 3,027.

### York College
150-14 JAMAICA AVE.,
JAMAICA, N.Y. 11432
Telephone: (212) 969-4040.
Founded 1966.

*President:* MILTON G. BASSIN.
Number of teachers: 165 (full-time).
Number of students: 3,855.

UNITED STATES OF AMERICA

## CLARKSON COLLEGE OF TECHNOLOGY
POTSDAM, N.Y. 13676

Founded 1896.

*President:* R. A. PLANE, A.B., S.M., PH.D., D.SC.
*Provost:* H. L. SHULMAN, B.CH.E., M.S., PH.D.
*Vice-President:* W. M. DEMPSEY, B.S., M.B.A.
*Treasurer:* E. J. WIXTED, B.A.MATH., B.B.A.ACCTG.
*Vice-Provost (Admissions, Placement, Student Records):* J. D. CHAPPLE, M.A.
*Director, Institutional Relations:* S. R. MARTIN, M.A.
*Registrar:* R. M. SHURTLEFF, M.DIV.
*Librarian:* Mrs. OTTILIE H. ROLLINS, M.S.

The library contains 131,813 vols., separate government document collection 748, microfilms 99,312.
Number of teachers: 243, including 48 full professors.
Number of students: 3,830.
Publication: *Clarkson.*

DEANS:

*Graduate School:* R. J. NUNGE, M.CH.E., PH.D., CH.E.
*School of Engineering:* H. L. SHULMAN, B.CHEM.ENG., M.S., PH.D.
*School of Arts and Sciences:* M. KERKER, M.A., PH.D.
*School of Management:* E. E. KACZKA, M.S., PH.D.
*Summer Session and Special Programmes:* E. McHUGH, B.S.
*Student Life:* C. N. SMALLING, B.ED.
*Liberal Studies:* O. E. BRADY, M.A., PH.D.


## COLGATE UNIVERSITY
HAMILTON, N.Y. 13346
Telephone: (315) 824-1000.

First Charter 1819; Chartered as Madison University 1846, name changed to Colgate University 1890.

*President:* GEORGE D. LANGDON, Jr.
*Vice-President for Business and Finance:* R. M. KREHEL.
*Controller:* G. B. HITCHCOCK.
*Registrar:* WILLIAM A. KESSLER.
*Secretary:* B. S. RYDER.
*Vice-President for Public Affairs:* STANLEY E. HALL.
*Dean of Students:* WILLIAM MOYNIHAN.
*Dean of Faculty:* CHARLES H. TROUT.
*Director of Graduate Programs:* CAROL WITHERELL.
*Librarian:* GEORGE R. PARKS.

The library contains 320,000 vols.
Number of teachers: 198 full-time, 41 part-time.
Number of students: 2,500.

## COLLEGE OF MOUNT SAINT VINCENT
263RD ST. AND RIVERDALE AVE., RIVERDALE, N.Y. 10471
Telephone: (212) 549-8000.

Founded 1847.

*President:* Sister DORIS SMITH.
*Academic Dean:* Mrs. KATHLEEN KNOWLES.
*Librarian:* Mrs. MARY F. HERNANDEZ.

The library contains 120,000 vols.
Number of teachers: 72.
Number of students: 1,100.


## COLLEGE OF NEW ROCHELLE
NEW ROCHELLE, N.Y. 10801

Founded 1904.

*President:* Sister DOROTHY ANN KELLY, O.S.U., PH.D.
*Vice-President for Academic Affairs:* STEPHEN SWEENY (acting).
*Registrar:* STANLEY CROSS.
*Librarian:* GLORIA GRECO.

The library contains 161,718 vols.
Number of teachers: 509.
Number of students: 5,417.

DEANS:

*School of Arts and Sciences:* Sister BRIDGET PUZON.
*School of New Resources:* NEIL CRONIN.
*Graduate School:* EVELYN BLUSTEIN.
*School of Nursing:* ARLYNE FRIESNER.


## COLLEGE OF SAINT ROSE
432 WESTERN AVENUE, ALBANY, N.Y. 12203
Telephone: (518) 454-5111.

Founded 1920.

*President:* THOMAS A. MANION, PH.D.
*Registrar:* DIANE C. RICH.
*Comptroller:* PETER J. GEORGE.
*Vice-President for Administration and Finance:* PATRICIA HAYES.
*Director of Admissions:* GENE ANN FLAHERTY.
*Vice-President for Academic Affairs:* DONALD W. TAPPA.
*Dean of Graduate and Continuing Studies:* RICHARD OGNIBENE.
*Librarian:* AUDREY GRAHAM.

The library contains 130,826 vols.
Number of teachers: 182.
Number of students: 2,916.


## COLUMBIA UNIVERSITY
MORNINGSIDE HEIGHTS, NEW YORK, N.Y. 10027
Telephone: 280-1754
Telegraphic Address: Columuni.

Founded as King's College 1754; incorporated in 1784 and name changed to Columbia College. By order of the Supreme Court of State of New York,

WORLD OF LEARNING

in 1912, title changed to Columbia University.
Private control; Academic Year: September to May.

*President:* MICHAEL I. SOVERN.
*Provosts:* PETER W. LIKINS, FRITZ R. STERN.
*Executive Vice-President for Administration:* PAUL D. CARTER.
*Vice-Presidents:*
  *Senior Vice-President:* NORMAN N. MINTZ.
  *Facilities Management:* ROBERT M. BROBERG.
  *Finance:* ANTHONY D. KNERR.
  *Government Relations and Community Affairs:* GREGORY FUSCO.
  *Vice-President and University Librarian:* PATRICIA M. BATTIN.
  *Health Sciences:* (vacant).
  *Personnel Management:* ROBERT S. EARLY.
*Student Services:* ROBERT J. COOPER.
*Secretary:* MARION E. JEMMOTT.

Library: see Libraries.

Number of teachers: 4,000.
Number of students: undergraduate 5,033, graduate and professional 8,316, non-degree candidates 1,962, total 15,311 (excluding Barnard College and Teachers' College).

Publications: *Journal of the Ancient Near Eastern Society, The Astronomical Journal, Current Musicology, Germanic Review†, Columbia Human Rights Law Review, Journal of International Affairs†, Johnsonian News Letter, Columbia Journalism Review†, Columbia Journal of Law and Social Problems, Columbia Law Review, Journal of Philosophy†, Public Opinion Quarterly, Renaissance Quarterly, Revista Hispánica Moderna, Romanic Review, Columbia Journal of Trans-national Law, Columbia Journal of World Business.*

DEANS:

*Columbia College:* ARNOLD COLLERY.
*Graduate School of Arts and Sciences:* GEORGE K. FRAENKEL.
*School of Law:* ALBERT J. ROSENTHAL.
*Faculty of Medicine:* DONALD F. TAPLEY.
*School of Engineering and Applied Science:* RALPH J. SCHWARZ (acting).
*Graduate School of Architecture and Planning:* JAMES POLSHEK.
*Graduate School of Journalism:* OSBORN ELLIOTT.
*Graduate School of Business:* BORIS YAVITZ.
*School of Library Service:* RICHARD L. DARLING.
*School of Dental and Oral Surgery:* ALLAN J. FORMICOLA.
*General Studies:* WARD H. DENNIS.
*School of International Affairs:* HARVEY PICKER.
*School of Social Work:* MITCHELL I. GINSBERG.
*School of the Arts:* SCHUYLER G. CHAPIN.

# UNIVERSITIES AND COLLEGES—NEW YORK (COLUMBIA UNIVERSITY)  U.S.A.

*Parker School of Foreign and Comparative Law:* HANS SMIT.

### PROFESSORS:

*Anatomy:*
APRIL, E. W.
BRANDT, P.
ELY, C. L.
GERSHON, M. D.
MOSS, M. L.
NOBACK, C. R.
NUNEZ, E.
PFENNINGER, C.
TENNYSON, V.

*Anaesthesiology:*
BENDIXEN, H. H.
BLANCATO, L. S.
BRAND, L.
EPSTEIN, R. A.
FINSTER, M.
HANKS, E. C.
HYMAN, A. I.
MARK, L. C.
MORISHIMA, H. O.
NAHAS, G. G.
NGAI, S. H.
PANTUCK, E. J.
SALANITRE, E.
TRINER, L.

*Anthropology:*
ALLAND, A., Jr.
COHEN, M. L.
FRIED, M. H.
HOLLOWAY, R. L.
MURPHY. R. F.
PITKIN, H.
SKINNER, E. P.
SOLECKI, R. S.

*Applied Physics and Nuclear Engineering:*
CHU C. K.
GOLDSTEIN, H.
GROSS, R. A.
HAVENS, W.
LIDOFSKY, L. J.
MARSHALL, T. C.
MELKONIAN, E.

*Architecture:*
BOND, J. M., Jr.
COLLINS, G. R.
FRAMPTON, K.
GIURGOLA, R.
GRAVA, S.
HARRIS, C. M.
HERDEG, K.
KOUZMANOFF, A.
MARCUSE, P.
PLUNZ, R.
POKORNY, J. H.
POLSHEK, J. S.
ROHDENBURG, T. K.
STERN, R. A. M.

*Art, History and Archaeology:*
BECK, J. H.
BRILLIANT, R.
COLLINS, G. R.
DAVIS, H. McP.
FRASER, D.
FRAZER, A.
HIBBARD, H.
MURASE, M. C.
PORADA, E.
REFF, T.
ROSAND, D.
STALEY, A.

*The Arts:*
*Division of Film:*
SHARFF, S.
*Division of Music:*
BEESON, J.
CHOU, W.-C.
*Division of Painting and Sculpture:*
RACZ, A.
GOLDIN, L.

*Division of Theatre Arts:*
BECKERMAN, B.
*Writing Division:*
MACSHANE, F.

*Astronomy:*
BAKER, N.
EPSTEIN, I.
LUCY, L. B.
PRENDERGAST, K. H.
SPIEGEL, E. A.

*Biochemistry:*
AXEL, R.
BENESCH, R.
BENESCH, R. E.
EDELMAN, I. S.
EISENBERG, M. A
FEIGELSON, P.
GOLD, A. M.
GRUNBERGER, D.
KARLIN, A.
KRASNA, A. I.
LIEBERMAN, S.
LOW, B. W.
RAPPORT, M. M.
SRINIVASAN, P. R.

*Biological Sciences:*
BEYCHOK, S.
BOCK, W. J.
CHASIN, L. A.
CORPE, W. A.
HILDEBRAND, J.
HOLTZMAN, E.
LEVENE, H.
LEVINTHAL, C.
MANCINELLI, A.
POLLACK, R.
TZAGOLOFF, A.
ZUBAY, G. L.

*Business:*
ADLER, M.
ANSHEN, M.
ARZAC, E. R.
BASTABLE, C. W
BRADY, G.
BURTON, J. C.
CARSON, D.
CHAMBERLAIN, N.
CHANDLER, M.
EDWARDS, F.
FARLEY, J. U.
HIESTAND, D. L.
HORTON, R.
HOWARD, J.
HULBERT, J. M.
KOLESAR, P.
KUHN, J.
LEFF, N.
LEHMANN, D.
LEWIN, D.
MCNULTY, P. J.
MILLER, D.
MORRISON, D.
O'SHAUGHNESSY, J.
OWENS, G. C.
OXENFELDT, A.
PONTECORVO, G.
ROBOCK, S. H.
SAYLES, L.
SCOTT, J.
SEXTON, D.
SHAY, R.
SHILLINGLAW, G.
STARR, M.
STEWART, C.
TENNANT, R.
THOMPSON, G.
WARREN, E. K.
WERNER, W.
WILKINSON, M.
WILLIAMS, E., Jr.
WOLF, C.
YAVITZ, B.

*Chemical Engineering and Applied Chemistry:*
CHEH, H. Y.
GREGOR, H. P.
GRYTE, C.
LEONARD, E. F.
SPENCER, J.

*Chemistry:*
BERNE, B. J.
BERNSTEIN, R.
BERSOHN, R.
BRESLOW, R.
CANTOR, C. R.
DAILEY, B. P.
DODSON, R. W.
EISENTHAL, K. B.
FLYNN, G. W.
FRAENKEL, G. K.
KATZ, T. J.
KLEMPERER, W.
LIPPARD, S. J.
NAKANISHI, K.
PECHUKAS, P.
REINMUTH, W. H.
STORK, G. J.
TURRO, N. J.

*Civil Engineering and Engineering Mechanics:*
BIENIEK, M. P.
DIMAGGIO, F. L.
FRIEDMAN, M. B.
GJELSVIK, A.
SHINOZUKA, M.
SKALAK, R.
STOLL, R. D.
TESTA, R. B.
VAICAITIS, R.
VREELAND, H. W.

*Computer Science:*
BASHKOW, T.
GROSS, J. L.
TRAUB, J. F.
UNGER, S.

*Dental and Oral Surgery:*
CAIN, E. A., Jr.
DISALVO, N. A.
ELLISON, S. A.
FINE, D. H.
GOTTSEGEN, R.
HOROWITZ, S. L.
KAHN, N.
KAPLAN, D.
KUTSCHER, A. H.
LUCCA, J. J.
MANDEL, I. D.
MOSS, M. L.
MOSS-SALENTIJN, L.
NAHOUM, H. I.
UCCELLANI, E. L.
WAYMAN, D. E.
WOTMAN, S.

*Dermatology:*
HARBER, L. C.
SILVA-HUTNER, M.

*East Asian Languages and Cultures:*
BIELENSTEIN, H.
DE BARY, W. T.
HAKEDA, Y. S.
HSIA, C. T.
KEENE, D.
LEDYARD, G. K.
SEIDENSTICKER, E.
VARLEY, H. P.
WEBB, H. F.

*Economics:*
BHAGWATI, J.
CAGAN, P.
CALVO, G.
DESAI, P.
CHICHILNISKY, G.
DEWEY, D. J.

DHRYMES, P.
ERLICH, A.
FINDLAY, R.
HARRISS, C. L.
LANCASTER, K.
MINCER, J.
MUNDELL, R.
NAKAMURA, J.
PHELPS, E.
TAYLOR, J. B.
VICKREY, W. S.
WATTS, H.
WELLISZ, S. H.
ZUPNICK, E.

*Electrical Engineering:*
DIAMENT, P.
HARRIS, C. M.
MEADOWS, H. E.
SCHLESINGER, S. P.
SCHWARTZ, M.
SCHWARZ, R. J.
SEN, A. K.
STERN, T. E.
TEICH, M. C.
WING, O.
YANG, E. S.

*English and Comparative Literature:*
ANDERSON, Q.
BECKERMAN, B.
BERCOVITCH, S.
DONNO, E.
DOUGLAS, A.
FERRANTE, J.
FREDMAN, A.
GRAY, W. A.
HANNING, R.
HEILBRUN, C.
HOVDE, C. F.
JOHNSON, S. F.
KOCH, J. K.
KROEBER, K.
MARCUS, S.
MAZZEO, J. A.
MEISEL, M.
MIDDENDORF, J. H.
MIROLLO, J. V.
RIDGELY, J. V.
ROSENBERG, J. D.
SAID, E.
SCHLESS, H. H.
SCHMITTER, D. M.
SEIDEL, M.
STADE, G.
TAYLER, E. W.
WOODRING, C. R.

*French and Romance Philology:*
GROSS, N.
KATZ, P. A.
LOTRINGER, S.
MAY, G.
PENHAM, D. F.
RIFFATERRE, M.
ROUDIEZ, L. S.
SAREIL, J.

*Geography:*
HANCE, W. A.
LEWIS, R. A.
WEBB, K.

*Geological Sciences:*
BROECKER, W. S.
DALZIEL, I. W. D.
FAIRBRIDGE, R. W.
GORDON, A. L.
HAYES, D. E.
HAYS, J. O.
RICHARDS, P. G.
SCHOLZ, C.
SCHWEICKERT, R.
SIMPSON, H. J.
SYKES, L. R.
TALWANI, M.

*Germanic Languages:*
BAUKE, J. P.
HALPERT, I. D.
JACKSON, W. T. H.

*Greek and Latin:*
BAGNALL, R. S.
CAMERON, A.
COMMAGER, S.
COULTER, J. A.
POUNCEY, P. R.
TARÁN, L.

*History:*
BEAN, J. M. W.
BRUCHEY, S. W.
BULLIET, R.
DEAK, I.
EMBREE, A. T.
GARRATY, J. A.
GARSOIAN, N. G.
GRAFF, H. F.
HAIMSON, L.
HARRIS, W. V.
HUGGINS, N.
IRWIN, G. W.
JACKSON, K. T.
KLEIN, H. S.
KOSS, S.
LEDYARD, G. K.
LEUCHTENBERG, W. E.
LYNCH, H. R.
MALEFAKIS, E. E.
McKITRICK, E. L.
METZGER, W. P.
MUNDY, J. H.
NISBET, R. A.
PAXTON, R.
RAEFF, M.
RICE, E. F.
ROFF, W. R.
ROTHMAN, D.
SHENTON, J. P.
SMIT, J. W.
SMITH, M.
STERN, F.
VAUGHAN, A.
WEBB, H.
WOLOCH, I.
WRIGHT, M.

*Human Genetics and Development:*
ATWOOD, K. C.
BANK, A.
BLOOM, A. D.
JAGIELLO, G.
KABAT, E. A.
MARKS, P. A.
MILLER, O. J.
RIFKIND, R. A.
SPIEGELMAN, S.

*Industrial Engineering and Operations Research:*
COHEN, L. B.
DERMAN, C.
IGNALL, E. J.
KLEIN, M.
MELMAN, S.

*Italian:*
NELSON, J. C.
RAGUSA, O. M.
REBAY, L.

*Journalism:*
BAKER, R. T.
DAVISON, W. P.
GOLDSTEIN, K. K.
JACKSON, L.
KIMBALL, P. T.
MENCHER, M.
OSBORN, E.
SHANOR, D.
YU, F. T. C.

*Law:*
BERGER, C. J.
BERMANN, G.

BLAKE, H. M.
COOPER, G.
EDGAR, H. S. H.
EDWARDS, R.
FARNSWORTH, E. A.
GARDNER, R.
GATES, F.
GOLDSCHMID, H. J.
GRAD, F. P.
GREENAWALT, R. K.
HELLAWELL, R.
HENKIN, L.
HILL, A.
JONES, W. K.
KADEN, L.
KERNOCHAN, J. M.
KORN, H. L.
LUSKY, L.
MURPHY, A. W.
PARKER, K. E.
REESE, W.
ROSENBERG, M.
ROSENTHAL, A.
SCHACHTER, O.
SCHMIDT, B. C., Jr
SMIT, H.
SMITH, J. H.
SOVERN, M.
STONE, R.
STRAUSS, P. L.
UVILLER, H. R.
WERNER, W.
YOUNG, W. F., Jr.

*Library Service:*
DAIN, P. S.
DARLING, R. L.
HANNIGAN, J. A.
MOLZ, R. K.
THOMPSON, S. O.

*Linguistics:*
AUSTERLITZ, R.
DIVER, W.
HERZOG, M. I.

*Mathematical Statistics:*
CHOW, Y. S.
LAI, T. L.
LEVENE, H.
ROBBINS, H. E.
SINGER, B. H.

*Mathematics:*
BASS, H.
BERS, L.
EILENBERG, S.
GALLAGHER, P. X.
JACQUET, H. M.
KOLCHIN, E. R.
KURANISHI, M.
MOISHEZON, B.
MORGAN, J.

*Mechanical Engineering:*
DERESIEWICZ, H.
DOMOTO, G. A.
ELROD, H. G.
FREUDENSTEIN, F.
FULLER, D. D.
LONGMAN, R. W.
SANDERS, W. T.

*Medicine:*
BAER, L. R.
BANK, A.
BERTLES, J. F.
BIGGER, J. T.
BUTLER, V. P.
CALDWELL, P.
CANFIELD, R. E.
CANNON, P. J.
CASE, R. B.
CHESS, L.
DWYER, E. M.
ELLISON, R.
ENSON, Y.
FELTON, C.

Frantz, A. G.
Glickman, R. M.
Goodman, D. S.
Grieco, M. H.
Harvey, R. M.
Hembree, W. C.
Holt, P. R.
Jameson, A. G.
Legato, M. J.
Lindenbaum, J.
Loeb, J.
Morris, T. Q.
Neu, C.
Nossel, H. L.
Osserman, E. F.
Pernis, B.
Peterson, A. S.
Phillips, G. B.
Pi-Sunyer, F. X.
Rifkind, R. A.
Rosner, W.
Smith, F. R.
Taggart, J. V.
Tapley, D. F.
Thomson, G. E.
Turino, G. M.
Van Itallie, T. B.
Weinstein, I. B.
Weiss, H. J.
Weiss, R. J.
Wertheim, A. R.

*Microbiology:*
Ellner, P. D.
Erlanger, B. F.
Ginsberg, H. S.
Godman, G. C.
Kabat E. A.
Manski, W.
Pernis, B.
Vogel, H. J.

*Middle East Languages and Cultures:*
Allworth, E.
Barzilay, I.
Burrill, K. R. F.
Cachia, P. J.
Garsoian, N.
Halasi-Kun, T.
Held, M.
Madina, M.
Riccardi, T.
Wayman, A.
Yarshater, E.

*Mining, Metallurgical and Mineral Engineering:*
Beshers, D. N.
Boshkov, S. H.
Duby, P. F.
Harris, C. C.
Kellogg, H. H.
Kuo, J. T. F.
Machlin, E. S.
Nowick, A. S.
Paul, D. I.
Somasundaran, P.
Tien, J. K.
Wane, M. T.
Yegulalp, T. M.

*Music:*
Beeson, J.
Chou, W.-c.
Christensen, D.
Lippman, E.
Newman, J.
Perkins, L.
Sanders, E.
Shanet H.

*Neurological Surgery:*
Stein, B. M.

*Neurology:*
Brust, J. C. M.
Cote, L. J.
Deviyo, D. C.

Dimauro, S.
Fahn, S.
Goldensohn, E. S.
Kabat, E.
Karlin, A.
Lovelace, R. E.
Penn, A. S.
Reuben, J. P.
Rowland, L. P.
Schwarz, J.
Zimmerman, E. A.

*Nursing:*
Cleary, C. P.
Crawford, M. I.
Earle, A. M.
Kelly, L. S.
Pettit, H. F.

*Obstetrics and Gynaecology:*
Bowe, E. T.
Chao, S.
Dillon, T. F.
Ferin, M.
Finster, M.
Hembree, W. C.
Jagiello, G.
James, L. S.
Jewelewicz, S.
Mandl, I.
Miller, O. J.
Neuwirth, R. S.
Rosenfield, A. G.
Vande Wiele, R. L
Williamson, S. W.

*Ophthalmology:*
Balazs, E. A.
Bito, L.
Campbell, C. J.
Eakins, K. E.
Fischbarg, J.
Gouras, P.
Manski, W.
Spector, A.

*Orthopaedic Surgery:*
Bassett, C. A. L.
Garcia, A., Jr.
Shelton, M. L.

*Oto-Laryngology:*
Abramson, M.
Khanna, M.
Tonndorf, J.

*Pathology:*
Axel, R.
Blanc, W. A.
Branwood, A. W.
Duffy, P.
Ellner, P.
Gambino, S.
Geller, L. M.
Godman, G.
Grey, R. M.
Hagstrom, J. W. C.
King, D. W.
Nicholson, J. R.
Pirani, C.
Richart, R. M.
Roizin, L.
Tennyson, V.
Vogel, H. J.

*Paediatrics:*
Bloom, A. D.
Chutorian, A.
Cooper, L. Z.
Dell, R. B.
Driscoll, J. M.
Dunton, H. D.
Gersony, W. M.
Gold, A.
Griffiths, S. P.
Hammill, J. F.
Heagarty, M.
Heird, W. C.
Hyman, A. I.

James, L. S.
Kahn, E. J.
Katz, M.
Krongrad, E.
LeBlanc, W.
Mellin, G. W.
Mellins, R. B.
Morishima, A.
Nicholson, J. F.
Piomelli, S.
Rosen, M. R.
Rush, D.
Sitarz, A.
Sprunt, K.
Steeg, C. N.
Winick, M.
Wethers, D. L.
Winters, R. W.
Wolff, J. A.

*Pharmacology:*
Bigger, J. T.
Eakins, K.
Hoffman, B. F.
Hoffmann, F. G.
Kahn, N.
Neu, H. C.
Ngai, S.-H.
Rosen, M. R.
Sawyer, W. H.
Wang, H.-H.
Wit, A. L.

*Philosophy:*
Berofsky, B.
Cumming, R. D.
Danto, A. C.
Kuhns, R. F., Jr.
Levi, I.
Morgenbesser, S.
Parsons, C. D.
Sidorsky, D.
Stein, H.
Walsh, J. J.

*Physical Education and Intercollegiate Athletics:*
Rohan, J. P.

*Physics:*
Baltay, C.
Christ, N. H.
Devons, S.
Feinberg, G.
Foley, H. M.
Franzini, P.
Hartmann, S.
Lederman, L. M.
Lee, T. D.
Lee, W.
Luttinger, J. M.
Mueller, A.
Novick, R.
Rainwater, J.
Ruderman, M. A.
Sachs, A. M.

*Physiology:*
Blank, M.
Chien, S.
Cizek, L. J.
Emmers, R.
Ferin, M.
Fischbarg, J.
Kandel, E. R.
Kupferman, I.
Nastuk, W. L.
Nocenti, M.
Reuben, J. P.
Schachter, D.
Schwartz, J. H.
Taggart, J. V.

*Political Science:*
Bernstein, T. P.
Bialer, L.
Brzezinski, Z.

CHALMERS, D. A.
CURTIS, G. L.
DEANE, H. A.
EDINGER, L. J.
FRANKLIN, J. H.
HAMILTON, C. V.
HENKIN, L.
HILSMAN, R.
HUREWITZ, J. C.
KESSELMAN, M. J.
MORLEY, J. W.
NATHAN, A. N.
PUCHALA, D. J.
ROTHSCHILD, J.
RUGGIE, J.
SARTORI, G.
SCHILLING, W. R.
SHULMAN, M. D.
SMITH, B. L. R.
WESTIN, A. F.
WRIGGINS, H.

*Psychiatry:*
DOHRENWEND, B.
FOLEY, A. R.
KANDEL, D.
KANDEL, E. R.
KLEIN, D. F.
KUPFERMANN, I.
KUTSCHER, A. H.
MALITZ, S.
SACHAR, E. J.
SPITZER, R.
WEISS, R. J.
WILKING, V. N.

*Psychology:*
BEVER, T.
CHRISTIE, R.
GALANTER, E. H.
GRAHAM, N.
HOCHBERG, J.
HOOD, D. C.
KRAUSS, R.
MATIN, L.
SCHACHTER, S.
TERRACE, H. S.

*Public Health:*
BENNETT, R. B.
BERGER, A. P.
BRYANT, J. H.
CHALLENOR, B. D.
COLOMBOTOS, J. L.
DESPOMMIER, D. D.
DOHRENWEND, B. S.
ELINSON, J.
FLEISS, J. L.
GRUNBERGER, D.
HASHIM, S. A.
KATZ, M.
KELLY, L. S.
ROSENFIELD, A. G.
RUSH, D.
STEIN, Z. A.
STRUENING, E. L.
SUSSER, M. W.
VAN DYKE, F. W.
VAN RYZIN, J.
WEINSTEIN, I. B.
WILLIAMS, R. W.
WOLFE, S.

*Radiology:*
ASCH, T.
BAKER, D.
BERDON, W.
CHANG, C.
ELLIS, K.
FELDMAN, F.
HALL, E. J.
HILAL, S.
JOHNSON, P.
KING, D. L.
ROSSI, H.
SCHLAEGER, R.
SEAMAN, W. B.
TRETTER, P. K.

*Rehabilitation Medicine:*
ANDERSON, A.
COTE, L. J.
DICKINSON, R.
DOWNEY, J. A.
FRANCISCUS, M.-L.
JONES, A. M.
MYERS, S. J.
THORNHILL, H.

*Religion:*
HAKEDA, Y. S.
LINDT, G. O.
MARTIN, J. A., Jr.
PROUDFOOT, W.
SOMERVILLE, R.
WAYMAN, A.

*Slavic Languages:*
BELKNAP, R. L.
HARKINS, W. E.
LENCEK, R. L.
MAGUIRE, R. A.
MALMSTAD, J. E.
SEGEL, H. B.

*Social Work:*
AKABAS, S.
ALCABES, A.
BRAGER, G.
CHERNESKY, R.
CLOWARD, R. A.
FANSHEL, D.
GINSBERG, M. I.
GITTERMAN, A.
GOLDSON, M. F.
GROSSER, C. F.
HACKSHAW, J. O. F.
HELLENBRAND, S.
JENKINS, S.
JONES, J. A.
KAHN, A. J.
KOHN, R. E.
LITWAK, E.
LOUARD, A. A.
LUKOFF, I. F.
McGOWAN, B.
MEYER, C. H.
MILLER, I.
MILLER, R. S.
MILLER, S. O.
MONK, A.
POLSKY, H.
ROSEN, S.
ROSENBERG, B. N.
SOBEY, F. R.
SOLOMON, R.
WEINER, H. J.
WHITEMAN, M.

*Sociology:*
BARTON, A. H.
BLAU, P.
COLE, J.
DAVISON, W. P.
DIAMOND, S.
GANS, H.
LITWAK, E.
PASSIN, H.
SILVER, A. A.
SPILERMAN, S.
ZUCKERMAN, H.

*Spanish and Portuguese:*
BARRENECHEA, A. M.
REDONDO, S.
SELIG, K.-L.
SILVER, P. W.
TUDISCO, A.

*Surgery:*
BREGMAN, D.
COOPERMAN, A. M.
GUMP, F. E.
HABIF, D. V.
HARDY, M. A.
HERTER, F. P.
HIATT, R. B.

KING, T. C.
KINNEY, J. M.
KRIZEK, T. J.
LO GERFO, P.
PRICE, J. B.
RANDALL, F. R.
REEMTSMA, K.
SANTULLI, T. V.
SPOTNITZ, H. M.
VOORHEES, A. B.
WICHERN, W.
ZIKRIA, B. Z.

*Urology:*
LATTIMER, J. K.
OLSSON, C. A.
VEENEMA, R. J.

AFFILIATED COLLEGES:

**Barnard College.**
*President:* ELLEN F. FUTTER (acting).

**Teachers College.**
*President:* LAWRENCE A. CREMIN.

INSTITUTES AND CENTRES:

**Institute of African Studies.**
*Director:* GRAHAM W. IRWIN.

**Center for the Social Sciences.**
*Director:* JONATHAN R. COLE.

**Institute of Cancer Research.**
*Director:* SOL SPIEGELMAN.

**Research Institute on International Change.**
*Director:* SEWERYN BIALER (acting).

**Program on Comparative National Leadership.**
*Director:* (vacant).

**Columbia University Computer Center.**
*Director of Computing Activities:* BRUCE GILCHRIST.

**Project Double Discovery.**
*Director:* LARRY DAIS.

**East Asian Institute.**
*Director:* GERALD L. CURTIS.

**Institute on East Central Europe.**
*Director:* HAROLD SEGAL.

**Foreign Student Services, Office of.**
*Director:* JOEL B. SLOCUM.

**Institute of Human Nutrition.**
*Director:* MYRON WINICK.

**Bio-Engineering Institute.**
*Director:* RICHARD SKALAK.

**International Institute for the Study of Human Reproduction.**
*Director:* RAYMOND L. VANDE WIELE.

**International Fellows Program.**
*Director:* ROBERT F. RANDLE.

**Center for Israel and Jewish Studies.**
*Director:* MARVIN L. HERZOG (acting).

**Lamont-Doherty Geological Observatory.**
*Director:* MANIK TALWANI.

**Institute of Latin American and Iberian Studies.**
*Director:* LAMBROS COMITAS.

**Inter-American Law Center.**
*Director:* HENRY P. DE VRIES.

**Legislative Drafting Research Fund.**
*Director:* FRANK P. GRAD.

**Middle East Institute.**
*Director:* Jacob C. Hurewitz.

**Center for Research and Demonstration (Social Work).**
*Director:* David Fanshel.

**Russian Institute.**
*Director:* Robert Belknap.

**Southern Asian Institute.**
*Director:* Ainslie T. Embree.

**Program on Soviet Nationality Problems.**
*Director:* Edward A. Allworth.

**Institute of War and Peace Studies.**
*Director:* Warner R. Schilling.

**Institute on Western Europe.**
*Director:* Donald J. Puchala.

## COOPER UNION FOR THE ADVANCEMENT OF SCIENCE AND ART
COOPER SQUARE,
NEW YORK, N.Y. 10003
Founded 1859.

*President:* B. N. Lacy.
*Chairman:* C. F. Michalis.
*Registrar:* H. Liebeskind.
*Vice-President and Provost:* L. Kaplan.
*Vice-President for Business Affairs:* G. J. Cahill.
*Library Co-ordinator:* E. Vajda.

The library contains 88,900 vols.
Number of teachers: 143.
Number of students: 857.

Publication: *At Cooper Union.*

### DEANS:

*School of Art:* G. Sadek.
*School of Architecture:* J. Hejduk.
*School of Engineering:* C. W. Tan.
*Admissions and Records:* H. Liebeskind.
*Students:* M. Gore.
*Continuing Education:* H. C. Alter.

## CORNELL UNIVERSITY
ITHACA, N.Y. 14853
Telephone: (607) 256-1000.
Founded 1865.
State and private control; Academic year: September to May.

*President:* Frank H. T. Rhodes, B.SC., PH.D.
*Provost:* W. Keith Kennedy.
*Provost for Medical Affairs:* Thomas Meikle, Jr.
*Senior Vice-President:* William G. Herbster.
*Vice-President, Treasurer, and Chief Investment Officer:* Robert T. Horn.
*Vice-President for Facilities and Business Operations:* Robert M. Matyas, PH.D.
*Vice-President for Campus Affairs:* W. D. Gurowitz, PH.D.
*Vice-President for Research:* W. D. Cooke.
*Vice-President for Public Affairs:* R. M. Ramin.
*Librarian:* Louis E. Martin.
Library: see Libraries.
Number of teachers: 2,125.
Number of students: 17,273.

Publications: *Cornell Reports, Cornell Chronicle, Cornell Alumni News, Administrative Science Quarterly, Cornell Law Review, Cornell Plantations, Cornell Veterinarian Quarterly, Cornell Engineering Quarterly, Cornell Hotel and Restaurant Administration Quarterly, Graduate School of Nutrition News, Industrial and Labor Relations Review, Library Journal Quarterly, Philosophical Review, Cornell Countryman, Campus Guide, Campus Walks, Cornell Desk Book, Cornell in Perspective, Cornellian, Cornell Daily Sun, Epox, Facts About Cornell, Farm Research Quarterly, Food Topics, Human Ecology Forum, Introduction to Cornell, Music at Cornell, Sapsucker Woods,* 22 annual catalogues.

### DEANS:

*University Faculty:* Kenneth I. Greisen.
*Graduate School:* Alison P. Casarett.
*Law School:* Peter W. Martin.
*Medical College:* Thomas H. Meikle, Jr.
*Graduate School of Medical Sciences:* Julian Rachele.
*College of Architecture, Art and Planning:* Jason L. Seley.
*College of Arts and Sciences:* Alain Seznec.
*College of Engineering:* Thomas E. Everhart.
*Division of Summer Session, Extramural Courses and Related Programs:* Robert D. Macdougall.
*New York State College of Veterinary Medicine:* Edward C. Melby, Jr.
*New York State College of Agriculture and Life Sciences:* David L. Call.
*New York State College of Human Ecology:* Jerome M. Ziegler.
*Graduate School of Business and Public Administration:* David A. Thomas (acting).
*School of Hotel Administration:* John J. Clark.
*New York State School of Industrial and Labor Relations:* Charles M. Rehmus.
*Cornell University—New York Hospital School of Nursing:* Eleanor C. Lambertsen, R.N., ED.D.

### DIRECTORS:

*Africana Studies and Research Center:* J. E. Turner, M.A.
*Center for International Studies:* Milton J. Esman.
*Center for Radiophysics and Space Research:* Prof. T. Gold, M.A.
*Center for Applied Mathematics:* James H. Bramble.
*National Astronomy and Ionosphere Center:* Frank D. Drake.
*Center for Environmental Research:* Gilbert Levine.
*Materials Science Center:* Herbert H. Johnson.
*Graduate Teaching and Research Center:* R. H. Crawford, M.A., PH.D.
*Program in Urban and Regional Studies:* Barclay Jones, Gordon F. Fisher.
*Society for the Humanities:* Michael G. Kammen.
*Center for Religion, Ethics and Social Policy:* Philip Snyder.
*Northeast Regional Center for Regional Development:* Lee M. Day.
*Laboratory of Ornithology:* Douglas A. Lancaster.
*Program on Science, Technology and Society:* Raymond Bowers.
*Agricultural Experiment Stations:* Donald W. Barton, Noland L. Vandemark.

### PROFESSORS:

*Law School:*
Barceló, J. J.
Clermont, K. M.
Cramton, R. C.
Curtiss, W. D.
Dean, W. T.
Gunn, A.
Hammond, Jane L.
Hanslowe, K. L.
Hay, G. A.
Henn, H. G.
Hogan, W. E.
Lyons, D. B.
Martin, P. W.
Palmer, L. I.
Penney, N.
Ratner, D. L.
Roberts, E. F.
Rossi, F. F.
Simson, G. J.
Summers, R. S.
Thoron, G.
Younger, I.
Younger, Judith T.

*Medical College:*
Ahrens, E. H., Jr., Medicine
Armstrong, D., Medicine
Artusio, J. F., Jr., Anaesthesiology
Asch, S. S., Psychiatry
Auld, P. A., Paediatrics
Barber, H. R. K., Obstetrics and Gynaecology
Barnes, W. A., Surgery
Barondess, J. A., Medicine
Bearn, A. G., Medicine
Beattie, E. J., Jr., Surgery
Becker, C. G., Pathology
Becker, D. V., Radiology
Becker, E. L., Medicine
Bedford, J. M., Anatomy and Reproductive Biology
Behrman, S. J., Oral Surgery
Birnbaum, S. J., Obstetrics and Gynaecology
Black, I. B., Neurology
Blass, J. P., Medicine and Neurology
Bogdonoff, M. D., Medicine
Breslow, E. M., Biochemistry
Brierley, J. B., Pathology and Neurology
Briscoe, W. A., Medicine
Brooks, D. C., Anatomy
Burns, J. J., Pharmacology
Burstein, A. H., Applied Biomechanics
Cahan, W. G., Surgery
Carlson, E. T., Psychiatry
Chan, W. W. Y., Pharmacology
Christian, C. L., Medicine
Chu, F. C.-H., Radiology
Clarkson, B. D., Medicine

COOPER, A. M., Psychiatry
DANIELS, F., Jr., Medicine
DAVIS, E. W., Obstetrics and Gynaecology
DINEEN, P., Surgery
DOUGHERTY, J. W., Dermatology
EHLERS, K. H., Paediatrics
ELLIS, J. T., Pathology
ENGLE, M. A., Paediatrics
ENGLE, R. L., Jr., Medicine
FITZGERALD, P. J., Pathology
FORTNER, J. G., Surgery
FREIBERGER, R. H., Radiology
FROSCH, W. A., Psychiatry
FUCHS, F. F., Obstetrics and Gynaecology
GAY, W. A., Surgery
GAZZANIGA, M. S., Neuropsychology
GILMAN, S. L., History in Psychiatry
GIVEN, W. P., Obstetrics and Gynaecology
GLICK, I., Psychiatry
GOLDSMITH, E. I., Surgery
GOLDSTONE, S., Psychology
GOOD, R. A., Paediatrics
GOSS, M. E. W., Sociology in Public Health
GOULIAN, D., Jr., Plastic Surgery
GRABER, E. A., Obstetrics and Gynaecology
GRABSTALD, H., Surgery (Urology)
GRAFE, W., Surgery
GRAFSTEIN, B., Physiology
GREIF, R. L., Physiology
HADLEY, S. J., Medicine
HAGAMEN, W. D., Jr., Anatomy
HARPEL, P. C., Medicine
HASCHEMEYER, R. H., Biochemistry
HAWKS, G. G., Obstetrics and Gynaecology
HEINZ, E., Physiology and Biophysics
HILARIS, B. S., Radiology
HILGARTNER, M. W., Paediatrics
HINKLE, L. E., Medicine in Psychiatry
HOLLAND, J. C. B., Psychiatry
HORWITH, M., Medicine
HOWLAND, W. S., Anaesthesiology
INGLIS, A. E., Anatomy and Orthopaedic Surgery
JACOBS, B., Clinical Surgery
JAVITT, N. B., Medicine
KAGEN, L. J., Medicine
KAPPAS, A., Pharmacology
KELLNER, A., Pathology
KERNBERG, O. F., Psychiatry
KIRKMAN, F. T., Medicine
KOCHEN, J., Paediatrics
KOHL, R. N., Psychiatry
KRAMER, E. E., Obstetrics and Gynaecology
KROOK, L., Pathology
LANDESMAN, R., Obstetrics and Gynaecology
LEDGER, W. J., Obstetrics and Gynaecology
LEVI, R., Pharmacology
LEVIN, A. R., Paediatrics
LEWIS, J. L., Jr., Obstetrics and Gynaecology
LEY, A. B., Medicine
LHAMON, W. T., Psychiatry
LIFSHITZ, F., Paediatrics
LIPKIN, M., Medicine
LITWIN, S. D., Medicine
LUCKEY, E. H., Medicine
MAACK, T. M., Physiology
MARCUS, A. J., Medicine
MARSHALL, V. F., Urology
MARTINI, N., Surgery
MASTERSON, J. F., Psychiatry
MCCRORY, W. W., Paediatrics
MCDOWELL, F. H., Neurology
MCGOVERN, J. H., Urology
MEISTER, A., Biochemistry
MELLORS, R. C., Pathology

MICHELS, R., Psychiatry
MILLER, D. R., Paediatrics
MINICK, C. R., Pathology
MISHKIN, M., Radiology
MUECKE, E. C., Surgery
MURPHY, G. E., Pathology
MURPHY, M. L., Paediatrics
MYERS, W. P. L., Medicine
NACHMAN, R. L., Medicine
NEW, M. I., Paediatrics
OETTGEN, H. F., Medicine
OKAMOTO, M., Pharmacology
O'LEARY, W. M., Microbiology
PATTERSON, R. H., Jr., Neurosurgery
PERRY, M. O., Surgery
PETERSON, R. E., Medicine
PLUM, F., Neurology
POPPENSIEK, G. C., Comparative Pathology
POSNER, A. S., Biochemistry
POSNER, J. B., Neurology
POTTS, D. G., Radiology
PRITCHETT, B. A. R., Clinical Medicine
QUEN, J. M., Clinical Psychiatry
RANAWAT, C. S., Clinical Surgery
READER, G. G., Medicine
REDO, S. F., Surgery
REIDENBERG, M. M., Pharmacology
REIS, D. J., Neurology
RIKER, W. F., Jr., Pharmacology
RIVLIN, R. S., Medicine
ROBERTS, R. B., Medicine
RUBIN, A. L., Biochemistry
RUSKIN, R. A., Obstetrics and Gynaecology
SANTOS-BUCH, C. A., Pathology
SAXENA, B. B., Endocrinology
SCHERER, W. F., Microbiology
SCHERR, L., Medicine
SCHOTTENFELD, D., Public Health
SHAFER, D. M., Ophthalmology
SHAPIRO, T., Psychiatry
SHAPIRO, W. R., Neurology
SHERLOCK, P., Medicine
SHIRES, G. T., Surgery
SILAGI, S., Genetics in Obstetrics and Gynaecology
SILVERBERG, M., Paediatrics
SIRLIN, J. L., Anatomy
SISKIND, G. W., Medicine
SMITH, G. P., Psychiatry
SOFFER, R. L., Biochemistry
SONENBERG, M., Medicine
STEIN, H. L., Radiology
STEINBERG, H., Medicine
STENZEL, K. H., Biochemistry
STRONG, E. W., Surgery
SWAN, R. C., Anatomy
SWEENEY, W. J., III, Obstetrics and Gynaecology
TALBOTT, J. A., Psychiatry
TAN, C. T. C., Paediatrics
TATUM, H. J., Obstetrics and Gynaecology
THOMAS, L., Medicine and Pathology
THOMPSON, D. D., Medicine
THORBJARNSON, B., Surgery
TOPKINS, M. J., Anaesthesiology
TORRE, D. P., Dermatology
VACIRCA, S. J., Clinical Radiology
VAN POZNAK, A., Anaesthesiology
VAUGHAN, E. D., Urology
WATSON, R. C., Radiology
WHALEN, J. P., Radiology
WHITMORE, W. F., Urology
WHITSELL, J. C., III, Surgery
WILLIAMS, H. E., Medicine
WILLIAMS, J. R., Oto-Rhino-Laryngology
WILSON, P. D., Orthopaedics
WINDHAGER, E. H., Physiology

*College of Architecture, Art and Planning:*
*Architecture:*
CRUMP, R. W.

GREENBERG, D. P.
KIRA, A.
PEARMAN, C. W.
ROWE, C.
SCHACK, M.
SHAW, J. P.
STEIN, S. W.
UNGERS, O. M.

*Art:*
BLUM, Z.
COLBY, V.
SELEY, J.
SINGER, A.
SQUIER, J. L.

*City and Regional Planning:*
CZAMANSKI, S.
JONES, B.
PARSONS, K. C.
REPS, J. W.
SALTZMAN, S.
STEIN, S. W.

*College of Arts and Sciences:*
ABRAMS, M. H., English
ADAMS, B. B., English
AHL, F. M., Classics
ALBRECHT, A. C., Chemistry
AMBEGAOKAR, V., Physics
AMMONS, A. R., Poetry
ANDERSON, B. R., Government
ARROYO, C. M., Spanish Literature
ASCHER, R., Anthropology and Archaeology
ASHCROFT, N. W., Physics
ASHFORD, D., Government, Public and International Affairs
AUSTIN, W. W., Musicology, Music
BEM, D. J., Psychology
BÉREAUD, J., Romance Studies
BERKELMAN, K., Physics, Nuclear Studies
BERSTEIN, I., Mathematics
BISHOP, J. P., English
BLACKALL, E. A., German Literature
BLACKALL, J. F., English
BLACKLER, A. W. C., Zoology, Genetics, Development and Physiology, Biological Sciences
BRAMBLE, J. H., Mathematics
BRAZELL, K. W., Japanese Literature
BROWN, L. D., Mathematics
BROWN, S. M., Philosophy
BROWN, T. M., History of Art
CALKINS, R. G., History of Art
CAPUTI, A., English
CARDEN, P. J., Russian Literature
CHASE, S. U., Mathematics
CHESTER, G. V., Physics, Atomic and Solid State Physics
CLARDY, J. C., Chemistry
COLBY, A. M., Romance Studies
COOKE, W. D., Chemistry
COTTS, R. M., Physics, Atomic and Solid State Physics
CULLER, J. D., English, Comparative Literature
DANNHAUSER, W. J., Government
DARLINGTON, R. B., Psychology
DAVIS, T. E., Economics
DEWIRE, J. W., Physics
DOTSON, A. T., Government
DRAKE, F. D., Astronomy
DYNKIN, E. B., Mathematics
EARLE, C. J., Mathematics
ELIAS, R. H., English Literature and American Studies
ELLEDGE, S. B., English
FARRELL, R. H., Mathematics
FAY, R. C., Chemistry
FISHER, M. E., Chemistry, Physics and Mathematics
FITCHEN, D B., Physics
FOGEL, E. G., English
FREED, J. H., Chemistry

# UNIVERSITIES AND COLLEGES—NEW YORK (CORNELL UNIVERSITY) U.S.A.

Fuchs, W. H., Mathematics
Gair, J. W., Linguistics
Gelbart, S. S., Mathematics
Gibian, G., Russian Literature
Gibson, Q. H., Biochemistry, Biochemistry and Molecular Biology, Biological Sciences
Gilbert, C. E., History of Art
Ginet, C. A., Philosophy
Gittelman, B., Physics
Golay, F. W., Economics and Asian Studies
Gold, T., Astronomy
Goldsen, R. K., Sociology
Goldstein, M. J., Chemistry
Gottfried, K., Physics
Greisen, K. I., Physics
Grimes, J. E., Modern Languages
Gross, L., Mathematics
Grossvogel, D. I., Comparative Literature and Romance Studies
Halpern, B. P., Psychology
Hammes, G. G., Chemistry and Biochemistry
Hand, L. N., Physics
Hartman, P. L., Physics and Applied Physics
Hartwit, M. O., Astronomy
Hay, G. A., Economics, Law
Heppel, L. A., Biochemistry, Biochemistry and Molecular Biology, Biological Sciences
Hertz, N. H., English
Hess, G. P., Biochemistry, Biochemistry and Molecular Biology, Biological Sciences
Hildebrand, G. H., Economics
Hockett, C. F., Linguistics and Anthropology
Hoffman, R., Physical Science
Hohendahl, P. U., German
Holcomb, D. F., Physics
Holdheim, W. W., Comparative Literature
Hsu, J. T. H., Music
Hughes, R. E., Chemistry
Husa, K., Music
John, J. J., Palaeography, Medieval History
Jones, R. B., Jr., Linguistics
Jorden, E. H., Linguistics
Kahin, G. McT., International Studies
Kahl, J. A., Sociology
Kahn, A. E., Economics
Kahn, H. P., Fine Arts
Kammen, M. G., American History, History
Kaske, R. E., English
Kelley, G. B., Linguistics
Kesten, H., Mathematics
Kinoshita, T., Physics, Nuclear Studies
Kirkwood, G. M., Classics
Knapp, A. W., Mathematics
Kramnick, I., Government
Kretzmann, N., Philosophy
Kronik, J. W., Romance Studies
Krumhansl, J. A., Physics, Atomic and Solid State Physics
Kufner, H. L., Linguistics, Modern Languages
LaFeber, W. F., American History, History
Lambert, W. W., Sociology, Psychology, Anthropology
Leavitt, T. W., History of Art
Lee, D. M., Physics
Leed, R. L., Linguistics
Levin, H., Psychology
Levy, C. S., English
Lichtenbaum, S., Mathematics
Likens, G. E., Ecology, Ecology and Systematics, Biological Sciences
Littauer, R. M., Physics
Livesay, G. R., Mathematics

Lowi, T. J., American Institutions
Lynch, T. F., Anthropology
Lyons, D. B., Philosophy
Maas, J. B., Psychology
Mahr, H., Physics
McConkey, J. R., English
McGinnis, R., Sociology
McLafferty, F. W., Chemistry
Meinwald, J., Chemistry
Mermin, N. D., Physics
Messing, G. M., Classics and Linguistics
Moore, R. L., History
Morley, M. D., Mathematics
Morris, E. P., Romance Studies
Morrison, G. S., Chemistry
Mozingo, D. P., Government
Murra, J. V., Anthropology
Neisser, U., Psychology
Nelkin, M. S., Applied Physics
Nerode, A., Mathematics
Newhall, H. F., Physics
Noblitt, J. S., Modern Languages
Novarr, D., English
O'Connor, S. J., History of Art
Orear, J., Physics
Parrish, S. M., English
Payne, L. E., Mathematics
Pohl, R. O., Physics, Atomic and Solid State Physics
Polenberg, R., American History
Porter, R. F., Chemistry
Pucci, P., Classics
Quester, G. H., Government
Racker, E., Biochemistry, Molecular and Cell Biology, Biological Sciences
Radzinowicz, M. A., English
Randel, D. M., Music
Reppy, J. D., Physics, Atomic and Solid State Physics
Richardson, R. C., Physics
Roe, A. S., History of Art
Rosecrance, R., International and Comparative Politics
Rosen, B. C., Sociology
Rosenberg, A., Mathematics
Rosenberg, R., English
Rothaus, O. S., Mathematics
Rush, M., Government
Sagan, C. E., Astronomy
Salpeter, M. M., Applied Physics, Neurobiology and Behaviour, Physical Sciences
Salpeter, E. E., Physics, Astrophysics, Nuclear Studies
Scheinman, L., Government
Scheraga, H. A., Chemistry
Schwarz, D. R., English
Seznec, A., Romance Studies
Shoemaker, S. S., Philosophy
Siegel, B. M., Applied Physics
Sienko, M. J., Chemistry
Sievers, A. J., Physics
Silsbee, R. H., Physics, Atomic and Solid State Physics
Silverman, A., Physics
Slatoff, W. J., English
Smith, R. J., Anthropology
Sokol, T. A., Music
Sola, D. F., Linguistics
Spitzer, F. L., Mathematics
Staller, G. J., Economics
Stallworthy, J., English
Stein, P. C., Physcs
Strout, C., English
Stycos, J. M., Sociology
Sweedler, M. E., Mathematics
Talman, R. M., Physics, Nuclear Studies
Tarrow, S. G., Government
Thorbecke, E., Economics
Tierney, B., Medieval History
Tsiang, S-C., Economics
Van Coetsem, F. C., Linguistics
Wan, H. Y., Economics
Weick, K. E., Psychology

White, D. H., Physics
Whittaker, R. H., Biology, Ecology and Systematics, Biological Sciences
Widom, B., Chemistry
Wilcox, C. F., Chemistry
Wilkins, J. W., Physics
Williams, L. P., History
Wilson, K. G., Physics
Wimsatt, W. A., Zoology, Genetics, Development and Physiology, Biological Sciences
Wolff, J. U., Modern Languages
Wolters, O. W., Southeast Asian History, History
Wood, A. W., Philosophy
Wu, R., Biochemistry
Wyatt, D. K., Southeast Asian History
Yennie, D. R., Physics
Young, M. W., History of Art

*College of Engineering:*
Ankrum, P. D., Electrical Engineering
Auer, P. L., Aerospace Engineering
Ballantyne, J. M., Electrical Engineering
Batterman, B. W., Materials Science and Engineering and Applied Physics
Bechhofer, R. E., Operations Research
Berger, T., Electrical Engineering
Bird, J. M., Geological Sciences
Blakeley, J. M., Materials Science
Bloom, A. L., Geology
Bolgiano, R., Jr., Electrical Engineering
Booker, J. F., Mechanical and Aerospace Engineering
Brutsaert, W. H., Civil Engineering
Bryant, N. H., Electrical Engineering
Burton, M. S., Materials Science and Engineering
Capranica, R. R., Electrical Engineering
Carlin, H. J., Electrical Engineering
Clark, D. D., Nuclear Science and Engineering
Constable, R. L., Computer Science
Conta, B. J., Mechanical Engineering
Conway, H. D., Theoretical and Applied Mechanics
Conway, R. W., Computer Science and Operations Research
Cool, T. A., Applied and Engineering Physics
Dalman, G. C., Electrical Engineering
De Boer, P. C. T., Mechanical and Aerospace Engineering
Dick, R. I., Civil and Environmental Engineering
Dworsky, L. B., Civil and Environmental Engineering
Eastman, L. F., Electrical Engineering
Erickson, W. H., Electrical Engineering
Everhart, T. E., Electrical Engineering
Farley, D. T., Jr., Electrical Engineering
Fine, T. L., Electrical Engineering
Finn, R. F., Chemical Engineering
Fisher, G. P., Civil Engineering
Frey, J., Electrical Engineering
Furry, R. B., Agricultural Engineering
George, A. R., Mechanical and Aerospace Engineering
Gergely, P., Civil and Environmental Engineering
Gries, D. J., Computer Science
Gubbins, K. E., Chemical Engineering
Harriott, P., Chemical Engineering
Hartman, P. L., Applied and Engineering Physics
Hartmanis, J., Computer Science
Isacks, B. L., Geology
Johnson, H. H., Materials Science and Engineering
Kim, M., Electrical Engineering

1813

Kramer, E. J., Materials Science and Technology
Lee, C. A., Electrical Engineering
Leibovich, S., Mechanical and Aerospace Engineering
Li, C.-Y., Materials Science and Engineering
Liang, T., Civil Engineering
Liboff, R. L., Electrical Engineering and Applied Physics
Linke, S., Electrical Engineering
Loehr, R. C., Agricultural Engineering
Loucks, D. P., Civil and Environmental Engineering
Lucas, W. F., Operations Research and Applied Mathematics
Ludford, G. S. S., Theoretical and Applied Mechanics
Lumley, J. L., Mechanical and Aerospace Engineering
Lynn, W. R., Environmental Engineering
Maxwell, W. L., Operations Research
Mayer, J. W., Materials Science and Engineering
McGaughan, H. S., Electrical Engineering
McGuire, W., Structural Engineering
McIsaac, P., Electrical Engineering
Merrill, R. P., Industrial Chemistry
Millier, W. F., Agricultural Engineering
Moore, F. K., Mechanical Engineering
Nation, J. A., Electrical Engineering
Nelkin, M. S., Applied and Engineering Physics
Nemhauser, G. L., Operations Research
Nichols, B., Electrical Engineering
Nilson, A. H., Structural Engineering
Oliver, J. E., Engineering
Ott, E., Electrical Engineering
Pao, Y-H., Theoretical and Applied Mechanics
Phelan, R. M., Mechanical and Aerospace Engineering
Prabhu, N. U., Operations Research
Rehkugler, G. E., Agricultural Engineering
Resler, E. L., Jr., Mechanical and Aerospace Engineering
Rhodes, F. H. T., Geology
Rodriguez, F. Chemical Engineering
Rosson, J. L., Electrical Engineering
Ruoff, A. L., Materials Science and Engineering
Salton, G., Computer Science
Sass, S. L., Materials Science and Engineering
Scott, N. R., Agricultural Engineering
Seidman, D. N., Materials Science and Engineering
Shen, S.-F., Mechanical and Aerospace Engineering
Slate, F. O., Civil Engineering
Smith, J. C., Chemical Engineering
Spencer, J. W., Agricultural Engineering
Sudan, R. N., Applied Physics, Electrical Engineering
Tang, C. L., Electrical Engineering
Taylor, H. M., Operations Research and Industrial Engineering
Thorpe, J. S., Electrical Engineering
Torng, H-C., Electrical Engineering
Turcotte, D. L., Aerospace Engineering
Von Berg, R. L., Chemical Engineering
Vrana, N. M., Electrical Engineering
Wang, K. K., Mechanical and Aerospace Engineering
Webb, W. W., Applied and Engineering Physics
Weiss, L. I., Operations Research and Industrial Engineering
Wharton, C. B., Electrical Engineering
White, R. N., Civil and Environmental Engineering
Wiegandt, H. F., Chemical Engineering
Wolf, E. D., Electrical Engineering
Wolga, G. J., Electrical Engineering and Applied Physics

*New York State College of Veterinary Medicine:*
Appel, M. J., Microbiology
Bentinck-Smith, J., Clinical Pathology
Bergman, E. N., Veterinary Physiology
Calnek, B. W., Avian and Aquatic Animal Medicine
Campbell, S. G., Microbiology
Carmichael, L. E., Virology
Coggins, L., Veterinary Virology
Cummings, J. F., Anatomy
De Lahunta, A., Veterinary Anatomy
Dobson, A., Veterinary Physiology
Evans, H. E., Veterinary Anatomy
Fabricant, J., Avian and Aquatic Animal Medicine
Fox, F. H., Veterinary Obstetrics
Gasteiger, E. L., Physical Biology
Georgi, J. R., Veterinary Parasitology
Gillespie, J. H., Veterinary Microbiology
Hansel, W., Physical Biology
Hitchner, S. B., Avian and Aquatic Animal Medicine
Houpt, T. R., Veterinary Physiology
Kallfelz, F. A., Clinical Sciences
Kirk, R. W., Small Animal Medicine
Krook, L. P., Veterinary Pathology
Lee, K. M., Virology
Lengemann, F. W., Radiation Biology
Lewis, R. M., Veterinary Pathology
McEntee, K., Veterinary Pathology
McGregor, D. D., Microbiology
Melby, E. C., Veterinary Medicine
Norcross, N. L., Immuno-chemistry
Noronha, F. M., Veterinary Virology
Peckham, M. C., Avian and Aquatic Animal Medicine
Poppensiek, G. C., Comparative Medicine
Rickard, C. G., Veterinary Pathology
Sack, W. O., Veterinary Anatomy
Scott, F. W., Microbiology
Sellers, A. F., Veterinary Physiology
Sheffy, B. E., Nutrition
Short, C. E., Clinical Sciences
Tapper, D. N., Physical Biology
Tennant, B. C., Comparative Gastroenterology
Wasserman, R. H., Radiation Biology
Whitlock, J. H., Veterinary Parasitology
Winter, A. J., Veterinary Microbiology
Wootton, J. F., Physiology Biochemistry and Pharmacology

*New York State College of Agriculture and Life Sciences:*
Ainslie, H. R., Animal Science
Alexander, M., Soil Science
Allee, D. J., Resource Economics
Andrus, H. G., Guidance and Personnel Administration
Aplin, R. D., Marketing, Agricultural Economics
Bail, J. P., Agricultural Education, Education
Baker, R. C., Poultry Science
Barker, R., Agricultural Economics
Barkley, P. W., Agricultural Economics
Barnett, M. L., Rural Sociology
Bing, A., Floriculture and Ornamental Horticulture
Blanpied, G. D., Pomology
Boodley, J. W., Floriculture
Boothroyd, C. W., Plant Pathology
Bouldin, D. R., Soil Science
Brown, W. L., Jr., Entomology
Bruce, R. L., Extension Education
Brunk, M. E., Marketing, Agricultural Economics
Bugliari, J. B., Agricultural Economics
Call, D. L., Agricultural Economics
Capener, H. R., Rural Sociology
Conklin, H. E., Land Economics, Agricultural Economics
Conneman, G. J., Agricultural Economics
Cooke, J. R., Agricultural Engineering
Creasy, L. L., Pomology
Cummings, G. J., Rural Sociology
Cushman, H. R., Agricultural Education, Education
Day, L. M., Agricultural Economics
Delwiche, E. A., Microbiology, Biological Science
Dethier, B. E., Agricultural Climatology
Dewey, J. E., Insect Toxicology
Dickey, R. S., Plant Pathology
Dondero, N. C., Applied Microbiology
Drake, W. E., Education
Dunn, J. A., Education
Eickwort, G. C., Entomology
Elliot, J. M., Animal Science
Everhart, W. A., Natural Resources
Ewing, E. E., Vegetable Crops
Federer, W. T., Biological Statistics, Biometrics Unit, Plant Breeding and Biometry
Fischer, R. B., Environmental Education
Foote, R. H., Animal Science
Forker, O. D., Marketing
Furry, R. B., Agricultural Engineering
Goodrich, D. C., Jr., Marketing
Gunkel, W. W., Agricultural Engineering
Gyrisco, G. G., Entomology
Hamilton, L. S., Forestry
Hogue, D. E., Animal Science
How, R. B., Agricultural Economics
Johnson, W. T., Entomology and Plant Pathology
Jones, E. D., Plant Pathology
Jordan, W. K., Food Engineering, Food Science
Korf, R. P., Plant Pathology
Kosikowski, F. V., Food Science
Langhans, R. W., Floriculture
Lathwell, D. J., Soil Science, Agronomy
Lemon, E. R., Soil Science, Agronomy
Levine, G., Agricultural Engineering
Lisk, D. J., Entomology and Limnology
Lorbeer, J. W., Plant Pathology
Lowe, C. C., Plant Breeding
Lucey, R. F., Field Crops
Mai, W. F., Plant Pathology
Markwardt, E. D., Agricultural Engineering
Martin, R. D., Communication Arts
McDowell, R. E., International Animal Science
Millar, R. L., Plant Pathology
Miller, R. D., Soil Physics
Miller, W. F., Agricultural Engineering
Millman, J., Educational Research Methodology
Morrow, R. R., Natural Resources
Morse, R. A., Apiculture
Mortlock, R. P., Microbiology
Mount, T. D., Agricultural Economics
Muka, A. A., Entomology and Limnology
Munger, H. M., Plant Breeding and Vegetable Crops
Novak, J. D., Science Education, Education
Obendorf, R. L., Agronomy
Ostrander, C. E., Poultry Science
Pardee, W. D., Plant Breeding and Crop Science
Pechuman, L. L., Entomology
Pimentel, D., Entomology and Limnology

PLAISTED, R. LeRoy, Plant Breeding and Biometry
POTTER, N. N., Food Science
POWELL, L. E., Pomology
REID, J. T., Animal Science
RIPPLE, R. E., Psychological Foundations
ROBINSON, K. L., Agricultural Economics
ROBSON, D. S., Biological Statistics
ROCHOW, W. F., Plant Pathology
ROCKCASTLE, V. N., Science and Environmental Education
RUSSELL, C. C., Communication Arts
SCHANO, E. A., Poultry Science
SCOTT, T. W., Soil Science
SEANEY, R. R., Crop Science and Plant Breeding
SEARLE, S. R., Biological Statistics
SEELEY, J. G., Floriculture and Ornamental Horticulture
SHERF, A. F., Plant Pathology
SHIPE, W. F., Food Science
SINCLAIR, W. A., Plant Pathology
SISLER, D. G., Agricultural Economics
SLACK, S. T., Animal Science
SMITH, E. H., Entomology
SMITH, R. S., Labour Economics and Income Security Farm Finance, Agricultural Economics
SPENCER, J. W., Agricultural Engineering
STANTON, B. F., Farm Management
STOUFER, J. R., Animal Science
STORY, R. P. Marketing
SWEET, R. D., Vegetable Crops
THURSTON, H. D., Plant Pathology
TOMEK, W. G., Prices
TUKEY, H. B., Jr., Ornamental Horticulture
VAN DEMARK, P. J., Microbiology
VAN SOEST, P. J., Animal Nutrition
van TIENHOVEN, A., Animal Physiology
VAN VLECK, L. D., Animal Science
VAN WAMBEKE, A. R., Agronomy
WALLACE, D. H., Vegetable Crops and Plant Breeding
WARDEBERG, Miss H. L., Elementary Education and Supervision
WARNER, R. G., Animal Science
WEBSTER, D. A., Fishery Biology
WRIGHT, M. J., Agronomy
YOUNG, F. W., Rural Sociology
YOUNG, R. J., Animal Science
ZAITLIN, M., Plant Pathology

*New York State College of Human Ecology:*
*Community Service Education:*
BLACKWELL, SARA
LAZAR, I.
NELSON, HELEN Y.

*Consumer Economics and Public Policy:*
BRYANT, W. K.
WIEGAND, ELIZABETH

*Design and Environmental Analysis:*
PURCHASE, MARY
STEIDL, ROSE
STRAIGHT, CLARA

*Human Development and Family Studies:*
BAYER, HELEN T. M.
BRITTAIN, W. L.
BRONFENBRENNER, U.
DORIS, J. L.
FELDMAN, H.
RICCIUTI, H. N.
SUCI, G.

*Division of Nutritional Sciences:*
CAMPBELL, T. C.
DEVINE, M. M.
LATHAM, M. C.

MORRISON, MARY A.
RIVERS, J. M.
ROE, D. A.
THORBECKE, E.
ZILVERSMIT, D. B.

*Graduate School of Business and Public Administration:*
BIERMAN, H., Jr.
BROOKS, E.
BUGLIARI, J. B.
DYCKMAN, T. R.
HASS, J. E.
LIND, R. C.
LODAHL, T. M.
RAO, V. R.
SMIDT, S.
THOMAS, D. A.
THOMAS, L. J.
WEICK, K. E.

*School of Hotel Administration:*
BECK, R. A.
CHRISTIAN, V. A.
CLARK, J. J.
DAVIS, S. W.
DERMODY, D. A.
GAURNIER, P. L.
KAVEN, W. H.
WHITE, J. C.

*New York State School of Industrial and Labor Relations:*
*Collective Bargaining, Labor Law, and Labor History:*
BURTON, J. F.
CULLEN, D. E.
DOHERTY, R. E.
DONOVAN, R.
GROSS, J. A.
HANSLOWE, K. L.
KELLY, M. A.
LIPSKY, D. B.
MORRIS, J. O.
REHMUS, C. M.
WINDMULLER, J. P.

*Economic and Social Statistics:*
BLUMEN, I.
McCARTHY, P. J.

*Organizational Behavior:*
ALDRICH, H. E.
GRUENFELD, L. W.
ROSEN, N. A.
TRICE, H. M.
WHYTE, W. F.
WILLIAMS, L. K.

*Labor Economics and Income Security:*
ARONSON, R. L.
CLARK, M. G.
EHRENBERG, R.
GALENSON, W.

*Personnel and Human Resource Management:*
BRIGGS, V. M.
FOLTMAN, F. F.
FRANK, W. W.
MILKOVICH, G.
MILLER, F. B.
RISLEY, R. F.
WASMUTH, W. J.

*New York State Agricultural Experiment Station at Geneva, New York:*
BOURNE, M. C., Insect Physiology
BOWERS, W. S., Entomology
DAVIS, A. C., Entomology
DOWNING, D. L., Food Science and Technology
FORSHEY, C. G., Pomology
GLASS, E. H., Entomology
KENDER, W. J., Pomology and Viticulture

KHAN, A. A., Seed and Vegetable Sciences
LABELLE, R. L., Food Science and Technology
LIENK, S. E., Entomology
MARX, G. A., Vegetable Crops
MASSEY, L. M., Jr., Biochemistry
MATTICK, L. R., Food Science
MOYER, J. C., Chemistry
NITTLER, LeR. W., Seed Investigation
PECK, N. H., Vegetable Crops
ROBINSON, R. W., Seed and Vegetable Sciences
ROBINSON, W. B., Food Science and Technology
SCHAEFERS, G. E., Entomology
SHALLENBERGER, R. S., Biochemistry
SPLITTSTOESSER, D. F., Microbiology
STAMER, J. R., Food Science and Technology
STEINKRAUS, K. H., Bacteriology
SZKOLNIK, M., Plant Pathology
TASCHENBERG, E. F., Entomology
TASHIRO, H., Entomology
VAN BUREN, J. P., Biochemistry
VITTUM, M. T., Vegetable Crops
WAY R. D., Pomology

## DAEMEN COLLEGE
4380 MAIN ST.,
AMHERST, N.Y. 14226
Telephone: (716) 839-3600,
1-800-462-7652.

Founded 1947 as Rosary Hill College; name changed 1976.
Liberal arts and sciences.

*President:* ROBERT S. MARSHALL, PH.D.
*Vice-President for Admissions:* PETER W. STEVENS.

The library contains 100,000 vols.
**Number of teachers: 120.**
**Number of students: 1,400.**

## D'YOUVILLE COLLEGE
320 PORTER AVENUE,
BUFFALO, N.Y. 14201
Telephone: 886-8100.

Founded 1908 by the Grey Nuns of the **Sacred Heart.**

*President:* Sister DENISE A. ROCHE, G.N.S.H.
*Executive Vice-President:* Dr. THOMAS K. CRAINE.
*Dean of Faculty:* Dr. DAVID RICE.
*Registrar:* Sister RITA MARGRAFF.
*Admissions:* LINDA NISSEN-McQUEEN.
*Development:* ROBERT F. BEECHLER.
*Dean of Students:* Dr. LORRAINE A. SIBBET.
*Librarian:* Mrs. ELLEN H. SMITH.

The library contains 107,260 vols.
**Number of teachers: 90.**
**Number of students: 1,500.**

First degree courses in business, education, gerontology, humanities, natural sciences, nursing, pre-professional programs, social sciences.

## ELMIRA COLLEGE
ELMIRA, N.Y. 14901
Founded 1855.

*President:* Dr. LEONARD T. GRANT.
*Academic Dean:* Dr. MARIE V. TARPEY.
*Dean of Student Services:* THOMAS R. WALTON.
*Director of Admissions:* JOHN H. ZELLER.
*Dean, Center for Personal and Professional Development:* Dr. FRANCIS X. BRADY.
*Director of Development and Advancement:* Dr. REED STEWART.

The library contains 137,955 vols.
Number of students: 1,174 full-time, 1,535 part-time, total 2,709.

## FORDHAM UNIVERSITY
FORDHAM RD.,
BRONX, N.Y. 10458
and at
LINCOLN CENTER,
NEW YORK, N.Y. 10023
Telephone: (212) 933-2233

Founded by Rt. Rev. John Hughes, first Roman Catholic Archbishop of New York, in 1841 as St. John's College. Incorporated as a university 1846. Name changed to Fordham University 1907.

*President:* Rev. JAMES C. FINLAY, S.J., PH.D.
*Executive Vice-President:* PAUL J. REISS.
*Vice-President for Academic Affairs:* JOSEPH F. X. MCCARTHY, PH.D.
*Financial Vice-President and Treasurer:* Bro. JAMES M. KENNY, S.J.
*Vice-President for Administration:* GEORGE J. MCMAHON, S.J., PH.D.
*Provost:* Rev. FRANCIS C. MACKIN, S.J.
*Director of Admissions:* RICHARD T. WALDRON, M.A.
*Registrar:* JOHN P. CLOHESSY, M.A.
*Director of Libraries:* Miss ANNE M. MURPHY, M.L.S.

The library contains 1,278,541 volumes.
Number of teachers: 986.
Number of students: 14,990.
Publications: *Thought* (quarterly), *International Philosophical Quarterly*, *Traditio* (annual).

DEANS:

*Fordham College:* Rev. JAMES LOUGHRAN, S.J., PH.D.
*Graduate School of Arts and Sciences:* Rev. RICHARD DOYLE, S.J., PH.D.
*Graduate School of Business Administration:* BENEDICT HARTER, J.D.
*Graduate Institute of Religious Education:* Rev. VINCENT M. NOVAK, S.J., S.T.D.
*College of Business Administration:* BENEDICT HARTER, J.D.
*Graduate School of Education:* MAX WEINER, PH.D.
*School of Law:* JOSEPH M. MCLAUGHLIN, LL.M.
*College of Liberal Arts:* GEORGE W. SHEA, PH.D.
*Graduate School of Social Service:* (vacant).
*School of General Studies:* CLARA RODRIGUEZ, PH.D.
*Summer Session:* GARY FELLOWS, ED.D.

## HAMILTON COLLEGE
CLINTON, N.Y. 13323

Founded 1793 as Hamilton-Oneida Academy; Chartered as Hamilton College 1812.

*President:* J. MARTIN CAROVANO.
*Dean:* C. DUNCAN RICE.

The library contains 353,779 vols.
Number of teachers: 135.
Number of students: 1,660.

## HARTWICK COLLEGE
ONEONTA, N.Y. 13820
Telephone: (607) 432-4200.
Founded 1928.

Private Liberal Arts College; Academic year: September to June (three terms).

*President:* Dr. PHILIP S. WILDER, Jr.
*Vice-President and Dean of the College:* Dr. BRYANT CURETON.
*Vice-President for Development:* DONALD E. BROWN.
*Vice-President for Financial Affairs:* WALTER R. KUHN.
*Registrar:* D. C. MARSH.
*Director of Libraries:* E. VON BROCKDORFF.

The library contains 162,000 vols.
Number of teachers: 114.
Number of students: 1,450.

## HOBART AND WILLIAM SMITH COLLEGES
GENEVA, N.Y. 14456

Hobart founded 1822, William Smith founded 1908.

*President:* A. A. KUUSISTO.
*Provost:* H. C. DUNATHAN.
*Treasurer:* W. P. VAN ARSDALE.
*Librarian:* P. W. CRUMLISH.

Number of teachers: 120 including 33 professors.
Number of students: Hobart: 1,050 men; William Smith: 700 women.
Publications: *Catalogue*, *Course Book†*, *Prospectus†*, bulletins.

DEANS:

*Hobart:* Dr. C. E. LOVE, Jr.
*William Smith:* Dr. M. R. DUNANT.

## HOFSTRA UNIVERSITY
1000 FULTON AVENUE,
HEMPSTEAD, LONG ISLAND,
N.Y. 11550
Telephone: (516) 560-0500.
Founded 1935.

*President:* Dr. JAMES M. SHUART.
*Provost:* Dr. HAROLD E. YUKER.
*Vice-President and Treasurer:* A. T. PROCELLI.
*Director of University Relations:* HAROLD A. KLEIN.
*Executive Dean of Student Services:* Dr. SANFORD HAMMER.
*Executive Director of Research and Resource Development:* Dr. J. RICHARD BLOCK.
*Director of Development:* ROCHELLE LOWENFELD.
*Registrar:* GERARD COTÉ.
*Director of Admissions:* MARC DION.
*Dean of Library Services:* Dr. CHARLES R. ANDREWS.

The library contains 900,000 vols.
Number of teachers: 620.
Number of students: 11,110.

DEANS:

*School of Business:* Dr. H. A. BERLINER (acting).
*School of Education:* Dr. J. VAN BUREN.
*College of Liberal Arts and Sciences:* Dr. ROBERT C. VOGT.
*School of Law:* JOHN J. REGAN.
*Dean of New College:* DAVID C. CHRISTMAN.
*Director of Alumni College:* RICHARD T. BENNETT.
*Dean of Continuing Education:* Dr. LEONA SELDOW.
*Dean of Students:* Dr. PATRICIA GIARDINI.

## HOUGHTON COLLEGE
HOUGHTON, N.Y. 14744
Telephone: (716) 567-2211.
Founded 1883.

*President:* D. R. CHAMBERLAIN.
*Academic Dean:* F. D. SHANNON.
*Registrar:* R. J. ALDERMAN.
*Librarian:* Mrs. JOYCE MOORE.

The library contains 150,400 vols.
Number of teachers: 74.
Number of students: 1,200.

## IONA COLLEGE
NEW ROCHELLE,
NEW YORK, N.Y. 10801

*President:* Bro. JOHN G. DRISCOLL.
*Vice-President for Academic Affairs:* Dr. RICHARD D. BRESLIN.
*Vice-President for Finance and Administration:* VINCENT J. DOUGHERTY.

*Registrar:* MICHAEL CHRISTY.
*Librarian:* PATRICK J. LARKIN.
Number of students: 6,200.

DEANS:

*School of Arts and Sciences:* Dr. ROBERT R. BEARDSLEY.
*School of Business Administration:* Dr. CHARLES F. O'DONNELL.
*School of General Studies:* Dr. JOHN W. HEALEY.
*Graduate Studies:* Dr. MATTHEW J. QUINN.

## ITHACA COLLEGE
ITHACA, N.Y. 14850
Telephone: (607) 274-3011.
Founded 1892.

*President:* JAMES J. WHALEN.
*Registrar:* J. STANTON
*Director of Admissions:* M. WALL.
*Librarian:* ROBERT WOERNER.

The library contains 270,000 vols.
Number of teachers: 282 full-time, 109 part-time.
Number of students: 4,224.
Publications: *Bulletin for Admissions†, Undergraduate Announcements†, Graduate and Continuing Education Announcements, Ithaca College Outlook, Ithaca Horizon.*

## JUILLIARD SCHOOL
LINCOLN CENTER,
NEW YORK, N.Y. 10023
Founded 1905.

*President:* PETER MENNIN.
*Dean:* G. WALDROP.
*Registrar:* MARY H. SMITH.

The library contains 38,000 music scores and 12,000 books; the record library contains 8,000 long-playing records and tapes.
Number of instructors: 150.
Number of students: 1,000.

## KEUKA COLLEGE
KEUKA PARK, N.Y. 14478
Telephone: (315) 536-4411.
Founded 1890.

*President:* ELIZABETH WOODS SHAW.
*Registrar:* EARL W. BLOOMQUIST.
*Librarian:* DOROTHY C. MANNING.

The library contains 92,382 vols.
Number of teachers: 52.
Number of students: 544.

## LE MOYNE COLLEGE
LE MOYNE HEIGHTS,
SYRACUSE, N.Y. 13214
Telephone: 446-2882.
Founded 1946.

*President:* FRANK HAIG.

*Academic Dean:* Rev. J. A. DINNEEN, S.J.
*Director of Admissions:* E. J. GORMAN.
*Librarian:* Dr. T. J. NIEMI.
The library contains 100,000 volumes.
Number of teachers: 131.
Number of students: 1,918.

## LONG ISLAND UNIVERSITY
GREENVALE,
LONG ISLAND, N.Y. 11548
Telephone: (516) 299-2501
Founded 1926.

*Chancellor:* ALBERT BUSH-BROWN.
*Vice-Chancellor:* HOWARD S. IRWIN.
*The Brooklyn Center:*
  *President:* EDWARD CLARK.
  *Dean, Richard L. Conolly College:* RICHARD SAWYER.
  *Dean, College of Business:* ALBERT JOHNSON.
  *Dean, Arnold and Marie Schwartz College of Pharmacy and Health Sciences:* JOHN SCIARRA.
  *Librarian:* (vacant).
*C. W. Post Center:*
  *President:* EDWARD COOK.
  *Dean, C. W. Post College:* MAITHILI SCHMIDT.
  *Dean, School of Business:* BENJAMIN PERLES.
  *Dean, School of Fine Arts:* JULIAN MATES.
  *Dean, School of Professional Accountancy:* WILLIAM GIFFORD.
  *Dean, Graduate and Undergraduate Schools of Education:* HELEN GREENE.
  *Dean, Palmer Graduate Library School:* JOHN GILLESPIE (acting).
  *Librarian:* DONALD UNGARELLI.
*Southampton Center:*
  *President:* DONALD WILSON.
  *Dean:* JOHN AGRIA.
  *Librarian:* R. GERBEREUX.

The libraries contain 600,000 vols.
Number of teachers: 1,400 (approx.).
Number of students: 23,300.

## MANHATTAN COLLEGE
RIVERDALE, BRONX, N.Y. 10471
Telephone: (212) 548-1400.

Founded as Academy of the Holy Infancy 1853; Chartered as Manhattan College 1863 (Private: co-educational).

*President and Treasurer:* Bro. J. STEPHEN SULLIVAN, F.S.C., S.T.D.
*Provost:* Bro. FRANCIS BOWERS, F.S.C, PH.D.
*Vice-President for Student Services:* JEROME P. CASHMAN, PH.D.
*Vice-President for Administrative Services:* THOMAS S. LENNON, M.A., J.D.
*Controller:* W. B. AUSTIN, B.B.A.
*Bursar:* T. P. O'CONNOR, B.B.A.

*Vice-President for College Relations, Alumni and Development:* Bro. MALCOLM O'SULLIVAN, F.S.C., ED.D.
*Registrar:* E. B. TEIFELD, B.A.
*Director of Library:* Bro. PHILIP M. DOWD, F.S.C., M.S. in L.S., PH.D.

The library contains 228,458 vols.
Number of teachers: 329.
Number of students: 4,750.
Publications: *Scientist, Humanist* (annually), *Engineer, Chalk Dust, Journal of Business* (2 a year).

DEANS:

*Arts and Sciences:* ALBERT J. HAMILTON, PH.D.
*Engineering:* PASQUALE A. MARINO, PH.D.
*Business:* R. F. VIZZA, PH.D.
*Teacher Preparation:* Bro. A. J. NORTON, F.S.C., PH.D.
*General Studies:* T. E. CHAMBERS, M.B.A.
*Graduate Division:* Bro. A. L. GARRAVIGLIA, F.S.C., LITT.D.

## MANHATTAN SCHOOL OF MUSIC
120 CLAREMONT AVE.,
NEW YORK, N.Y. 10027
Telephone: (212) 749-2802.
Founded 1917.

Professional School of Music Performance, Composition, Theory.

*President:* JOHN O. CROSBY.
*Vice-President for Administration:* PEGGY TUELLER.
*Dean of Faculty and Students:* JOSEPH POLISI.
*Dean of Performance Activities:* DANIEL RICE.

The libraries contain over 70,000 vols.
Number of teachers: 179.
Number of students: 711.

## MANHATTANVILLE COLLEGE
PURCHASE, N.Y. 10577
Telephone: (914) 946-9600.
Founded 1841.

*President:* Dr. BARBARA KNOWLES DEBS.
*Dean of Faculty:* CATHERINE MYERS.

The library contains over 300,000 volumes.
Number of teachers: 75 (full-time).
Number of students: 2,073.

## MARIST COLLEGE
NORTH RD., POUGHKEEPSIE,
N.Y. 12601
Telephone: (914) 471-3240.
Founded 1946.

*President:* DENNIS J. MURRAY.
*Vice-President for Special Programs:* EDWARD WATERS.

*Academic Vice-President:* ANDREW A. MOLLOY.
*Registrar:* DANNY MA.
*Dean of Admissions:* JAMES E. DALY.
*Librarian:* BARBARA BRENNER.
The library contains 80,000 vols.
Number of teachers: 122.
Number of students: 1,832.

## MARYMOUNT COLLEGE
TARRYTOWN, N.Y. 10591
Telephone: (914) 631-3200.
Founded 1907.

*President:* Sister BRIGID DRISCOLL, R.S.H.M.
*Director of Admissions:* MICHEILEEN DORAN.
*Librarian:* Sister VIRGINIA McKENNA, R.S.H.M.
The library contains 102,000 volumes.
Number of teachers: 83.
Number of students: 1,112.

## MARYMOUNT MANHATTAN COLLEGE
221 EAST 71ST STREET, NEW YORK, N.Y. 10021
Telephone: (212) 472-3800.
Founded 1936, chartered 1961.

*President:* COLETTE MAHONEY, R.S.H.M.
*Vice-Presidents:* RITA ARTHUR (Planning), EILENE BERTSCH (Academic Affairs), SARA ARTHUR (Student Affairs), WILLIAM E. MAHER (Business), HELEN LOWE (Development).
*Dean of Students:* SARA ARTHUR.
The library contains 63,664 vols.
Number of teachers: 160.
Number of students: 916 full-time, 1,335 part-time.

## NAZARETH COLLEGE OF ROCHESTER
4245 EAST AVE., ROCHESTER, N.Y. 14610
Founded 1924.

*President:* ROBERT A. KIDERA, M.A., L.H.D.
*Provost:* Sr. MARION A. HOCTOR, S.S.J., PH.D.
*Dean of Faculty:* RICHARD DEL-VECCHIO, PH.D.
*Registrar and Director of Academic Services:* ROBERT H. COOK, B.A.
*Librarian:* RICHARD A. MATZEK, M.A.L.S.
Library of 196,967 vols., 1,295 serials.
Number of students: 1,787.
Publications: *Gleaner, Verity, Sigillum.*

## NEW SCHOOL FOR SOCIAL RESEARCH
66 WEST 12TH STREET, NEW YORK, N.Y. 10011
Founded 1919.
*President:* JOHN R. EVERETT.

The library contains 175,000 vols.
Number of teachers: c. 1,500.
Number of students: 27,000.
Publications: *Social Research* (quarterly), *City Almanac* (2 a month), *Fiscal Observer* (2 a week).

DEANS:

*Graduate Faculty of Political and Social Science:* J. J. GREENBAUM.
*New School Adult Division:* A. AUSTILL.
*Undergraduate Division:* E. COLEMAN.
*Center for New York City Affairs:* HENRY COHEN.
*Parsons School of Design:* DAVID C. LEVY.

## NEW YORK UNIVERSITY
WASHINGTON SQUARE, NEW YORK, N.Y. 10003
Telephone: 598-1212.
Founded 1831.

*President:* JOHN BRADEMAS.
*Provost and Executive Vice-President for Academic Affairs:* L. JAY OLIVA.
*Executive Vice-President for Health Affairs:* IVAN L. BENNETT, Jr.
*Vice-Chancellor:* ARNOLD L. GOREN.
*Vice-President and General Counsel, Secretary of the University:* S. ANDREW SCHAFFER.
*Vice-President for Administrative and Student Services:* ANN L. MARCUS (acting).
*Vice-President for External Affairs:* NAOMI B. LEVINE.
*Vice-President for Finance:* ALLEN E. CLAXTON.
*Vice-President for Institutional Facilities:* JOHN M. O'MARA.
Library: see Libraries.
Number of teachers: 6,000.
Number of students: 45,000.

Publications: *Report* (fortnightly), *Alumni News* (9 a year), *Medical Quarterly, Drama Review* (quarterly), *Education Quarterly, Educational Administration Quarterly, Law Review* (6 a year), *Washington Square News* (2 a week), *The Courier* (fortnightly), *Minetta Review* (annually), *Romanica*† (annually), *Historian*† (annually), *Commentator*† (fortnightly), *The Explorer* (monthly), *Opportunity* (6 a year).

DEANS:

*Faculty of Arts and Science and Acting Dean Graduate School of Arts and Science:* LEWIS LEVINE (acting).
*School of Law:* NORMAN REDLICH.
*School of Medicine and Post-Graduate Medical School:* IVAN L. BENNETT, Jr.
*College of Dentistry:* RICHARD D. MUMMA, Jr.
*School of Education, Health, Nursing and Arts Profession:* DANIEL E. GRIFFITHS.
*College of Business and Public Administration:* ABRAHAM L. GITLOW.

*Washington Square and University College of Arts and Science:* JILL CLASTER.
*Faculty of Business Administration and Graduate School of Business Administration:* WILLIAM F. MAY.
*Courant Institute of Mathematical Sciences:* PETER D. LAX.
*School of Continuing Education and Extension Services:* L. STEVEN ZWERLING (acting).
*Graduate School of Public Administration:* DICK NETZER.
*School of Social Work:* SHIRLEY M. EHRENKRANZ.
*School of the Arts:* DAVID J. OPPENHEIM.
*Gallatin Division:* HERBERT I. LONDON.
*University Libraries:* CARLTON C. ROCHELL.

## NIAGARA UNIVERSITY
N.Y. 14109
Telephone: (716) 285-1212.
Founded 1856.

*President:* JOHN G. NUGENT, C.M.
*Academic Vice-President:* Dr. JOHN B. STRANGES.
*Registrar:* DAVID L. SYMES, C.M.
*Librarian:* GEORGE M. TELATNIK.
The library contains 166,506 vols.
Number of teachers: 243.
Number of students: 3,477.
Publications: *Index* (weekly), *Niagaran* (annually), *Aquila* (twice yearly).

DEANS:

*College of Arts and Sciences, Director Graduate School of Arts and Sciences:* Rev. JOSEPH L. LEVESQUE, C.M.
*College of Business Administration:* ROBERT G. ALLYN.
*School of Education, Director of Graduate School of Education:* J. A. PRINCE.
*College of Nursing:* Dr. KATHLEEN SMYTH.
*Students:* FRANCIS X. PRIOR, C.M.
*Special Programmes, Summer and Evening Divisions:* Rev. DANIEL F. O'LEARY, O.M.I.

## NYACK COLLEGE
NYACK, N.Y. 10960
Telephone: (914) 358-1710.
Founded 1882.

*President:* Dr. THOMAS P. BAILEY.
*Vice-President and Dean of the College:* Dr. PAUL D. COLLORD.
*Vice-President and Dean of Students:* Mrs. ELIZABETH C. JACKSON.
*Vice-President and Treasurer:* JAMES M. MITCHELL, Jr.
*Vice-President and Executive Director of Graduate School:* Dr. WENDELL W. PRICE.
*Registrar:* Rev. JAY MAPSTONE.
*Librarian:* Miss MAY K. LEO.
The library contains 66,000 vols.
Number of teachers: 68.
Number of students: 853.

## PACE UNIVERSITY
PACE PLAZA,
NEW YORK, N.Y. 10038
Telephone: 285-3000.
Founded 1906.

Branch campuses at Pleasantville, White Plains (formerly College of White Plains), and Briarcliff (formerly Briarcliff College).

*President:* Dr. EDWARD J. MORTOLA.
*University Registrar:* MARCIA JACQUES.
*University Librarian:* H. BIRNBAUM.

The library contains 679,650 vols. and 4,396 periodicals.

Number of teachers: 1,249.
Number of students: 25,753.

## POLYTECHNIC INSTITUTE OF NEW YORK
333 JAY ST.,
BROOKLYN, N.Y. 11201
Telephone: (212) 643-5000.
Founded 1854.

*President:* GEORGE BUGLIARELLO.
*Vice-President for Administration and Finance:* SEYMOUR SCHER.
*Provost:* (vacant).
*Registrar:* JANYCE WOLF.
*Librarian:* L. COHAN.

Number of teachers: 217.
Number of students: 4,700.

### DEANS:
*Arts and Sciences:* BERNARD J. BULKIN.
*Engineering:* HAROLD LURIE.
*Graduate Studies:* A. B. GIORDANO.

## PRATT INSTITUTE
200 WILLOUGHBY AVE.,
BROOKLYN, N.Y. 11205
Founded 1887.

*President:* RICHARDSON PRATT, JR.
*Provost:* Dr. STEPHEN S. KAAGAN.
*Registrar:* W. J. NOVAK, M.A.
*Librarian:* Dr. GEORGE LOWY.

Library of 215,000 vols.
Number of teachers: 420.
Number of students: 4,200.

Publications: *Pratt Institute Catalogue, Pratt Reports†* (quarterly), *Pratt Campus†* (every 2 weeks), *Annual Report.*

### DEANS:
*School of Art and Design:* BRUCE SHARPE, B.F.A., M.B.A.
*School of Architecture:* PAUL HEYER, M.A.ARCH. (acting).
*School of Engineering:* WILLIAM STACK-STAIKIDIS, PH.D.
*School of Liberal Arts and Sciences:* BETTY T. BENNETT, B.A., M.A., PH.D.
*School of Library and Information Science:* N. SHARIFY, LIC. ès L., M.S., D.L.S.
*Continuing and Independent Programs:* NINA T. KURTIS, M.A.

## RENSSELAER POLYTECHNIC INSTITUTE
110 8TH STREET, TROY,
N.Y. 12181
Telephone: 270-6000.
Founded 1824.

*President:* GEORGE M. LOW, M.AERO.E.
*Provost:* HARRISON SHULL.
*Vice-President for Finance and Administration:* JAMES E. MORLEY, JR., M.S.
*Director, Office of Contracts and Grants:* JOSEPH M. LoGIUDICE, M.S.
*Registrar:* J. ROGERS O'NEILL, D.ED.
*Librarian:* JAMES C. ANDREWS, M.S.L.S.

Library of 276,609 vols.
Number of teachers: 344.
Number of students: 5,097 full-time, 603 part-time.

Publications: *Graduate Catalogue, Undergraduate Catalogue* (annually).

### DEANS AND DIRECTORS:
*Science:* SAMUEL C. WAIT, JR., PH.D. (acting).
*Engineering:* GEORGE S. ANSELL, PH.D.
*Humanities and Social Sciences:* THOMAS PHELAN, S.T L.
*Architecture:* PATRICK J. QUINN, M.ARCH.
*Graduate School:* STEPHEN E. WIBERLEY, PH.D.
*Management:* JOSEPH A. STEGER, PH.D.
*Students:* CARL A. WESTERDAHL, B.A.
*Director of Continuing Studies:* RICHARD J. TEICH, M.S.

## ROBERTS WESLEYAN COLLEGE
ROCHESTER, N.Y. 14624
Telephone: (716) 594-9471.
Founded 1866.

*President:* WILLIAM C. CROTHERS.
*Executive Vice-President:* WILLIAM F. BRUNK.
*Academic Dean:* OSCAR T. LENNING.
*Dean of Students:* DAVID C. MORROW.
*Registrar:* DONALD F. MOHNKERN.
*Director of Admissions:* KARL G. SOMERVILLE.
*Librarian:* A. C. KROBER.

Library of 80,561 vols.
Number of teachers: 54.
Number of students: 625.

Publication: *PRISM* (6 a year).

## ROCHESTER INSTITUTE OF TECHNOLOGY
ONE LOMB MEMORIAL DRIVE,
ROCHESTER, N.Y. 14623
Telephone: (716) 475-2411.
Founded in 1829 as the Rochester Athenaeum.

*President:* M. RICHARD ROSE, M.S., PH.D.
*Vice-President:* ALFRED L. DAVIS.
*Vice-President for Academic Affairs:* ROBERT G. QUINN, PH.D.
*Senior Vice-President for Institutional Advancement:* D. R. FRISINA, PH.D.
*Vice-President for Finance and Administration:* H. DONALD SCOTT.
*Vice-President for Student Affairs:* F. W. SMITH, PH.D.
*Director, National Technical Institute for the Deaf:* WILLIAM E. CASTLE, PH.D.
*Librarian:* G. D. MACMILLAN.

Library of 180,890 vols.
Number of teachers: 560 full-time, 433 part-time.
Number of students: 13,265.

Publication: *Graphic Arts Literature Abstracts* (monthly).

### DEANS:
*College of Business:* Dr. WALTER F. MCCANNA.
*College of Fine and Applied Arts:* Dr. R. H. JOHNSTON.
*College of Graphic Arts and Photography:* Dr. MARK GULDIN (acting).
*College of Engineering:* Dr. R. A. KENYON.
*College of Science:* JOHN D. PALIOURAS.
*College of General Studies:* Dr. M. SULLIVAN.
*National Technical Institute for the Deaf:* Dr. KATHLEEN CRANDALL.
*College of Continuing Education:* ROBERT A. CLARK.
*College of Applied Science and Technology:* Dr. DENNIS C. NYSTROM.
*Eisenhower College:* Dr. THOMAS R. PLOUGH.

## THE ROCKEFELLER UNIVERSITY
NEW YORK, N.Y. 10021
Telephone: (212) 360-1000.

Founded 1901; became a graduate university in 1954; name changed from Rockefeller Institute to The Rockefeller University in 1965.

*President:* JOSHUA LEDERBERG, PH.D.
*Vice-Presidents:* RODNEY W. NICHOLS, A.B. (Executive), DAVID J. LYONS, M.B.A. (Controller), RICHARD S. YOUNG, PH.D.
*Dean of Graduate Studies:* CLARENCE M. CONNELLY, PH.D.
*Librarian:* SONYA W. MIRSKY, M.S.

Library of 196,000 vols.
Number of teachers: 214.
Number of graduate students: 113.

Publications: *Journal of Experimental Medicine, Journal of General Physiology, Journal of Cell Biology, Biophysical Journal, Journal of Clinical Investigation,* and occasional publications.

### PROFESSORS:
AGOSTA, W. C., PH.D., Organic Chemistry and Physical Biochemistry
AHRENS, E. H., JR., M.D., Arteriosclerosis
ALLFREY, V. G., PH.D., Cell Biology
ASANUMA, H., M.D., D.MED.SCI., Neurophysiology

BÉG, M. A. B., PH.D., Theoretical Physics
BLOBEL, G., M.D., PH.D., Cell Biology
CASE, K. M., PH.D., Theoretical Physics
CHOPPIN, P. W., M.D., Virology and Medicine
COHEN, E. G. D., PH.D., Theoretical Physics
COHEN, J. E., PH.D., DR.P.H., Populations
COHN, Z. A., M.D., Cellular Physiology and Immunology
COOL, R. L., PH.D., Experimental High Energy Physics
CRANEFIELD, P. F., M.D., PH.D., Cardiac Physiology; History of Medicine and Science
CUNNINGHAM, B. A., PH.D., Biochemistry
DARNELL, J. E., Jr. M.D., Molecular Cell Biology
DE DUVE, C. R., M.D., M.SC., Biochemical Cytology
DOLE, V. P., M.D., Medicine
EDELMAN, G. M., M.D., PH.D., Developmental and Molecular Biology
FIELD, F. H., PH.D., Mass Spectrometry and Gaseous Ionic Chemistry
FISHMAN, J., PH.D., Endocrinology
GLIMM, J., PH.D., Mathematical Physics
GOTSCHLICH, E., M.D., Bacteriology and Immunology
GRIFFIN, D. R., PH.D., Animal Behaviour
HANAFUSA, H., PH.D., Viral Oncology
HIRSCH, J. G., M.D., Cellular Physiology and Immunology
HOTCHKISS, R. D., PH.D., D.SC., Genetics
KAC, M., PH.D., D.SC., Mathematics
KAPPAS, A., M.D., Metabolism-Pharmacology
KHURI, N. N., PH.D., Theoretical Physics
KUNKEL, H. G., M.D., Immunology
LUCK, D. J. L., M.D., PH.D., Cell Biology
MARLER, P. R., PH.D., Animal Behaviour
MAURO, A., PH.D., Biophysics
MAUZERALL, D., PH.D., Biophysics
MERRIFIELD, R. B., PH.D., D.SC., Biochemistry
MOORE, S., PH.D., Biochemistry
NOTTEBOHM, F., PH.D., Animal Behaviour
PAIS, A., PH.D., Theoretical Physics
PFAFF, D. W., PH.D., Neurobiology and Behaviour
PFAFFMANN, C., PH.D., D.SC., Physiological Psychology
RATLIFF, F., PH.D., Biophysics
REICH, E., M.D., PH.D., Chemical Biology
SIEKEVITZ, P., PH.D., Cell Biology
TAMM, I., M.D., Virology
TOMASZ, A., PH.D., Microbiology
WANG, H., PH.D., Logic
WILSON, V. J., PH.D., Neurophysiology
ZINDER, N. D., PH.D., Genetics

## RUSSELL SAGE COLLEGE
TROY, N.Y. 12180
Founded 1916.

*President:* WILLIAM F. KAHL.
*Vice-Presidents:*
   *Fiscal Affairs:* LINDA ANDERSON.
   *Public Affairs:* JOSEPH CURTIN.
   *Student Affairs:* Miss PHYLLIS HOYT.
*Director of Admissions:* BARBARA EDLER.
*Librarian:* DONALD RYAN.

Number of teachers: 165.
Number of students: 1,470 women.

## SAINT BONAVENTURE UNIVERSITY
SAINT BONAVENTURE,
N.Y. 14778
Telephone: (716) 375-2000.
Founded 1859.

*Chairman, Board of Trustees:* Dr. JAMES L. HAYES.
*Vice-Chairman, Board of Trustees:* Very Rev. ALBAN MAGUIRE, O.F.M.
*President:* Very Rev. MATHIAS DOYLE, O.F.M., PH.D.
*Executive Vice-President:* Rev. JAMES TOAL, O.F.M., PH.D.
*Vice-President for Academic Affairs:* Dr. AL H. NOTHEM.
*Registrar:* Rev. FRANCIS STORMS, O.F.M.
*Librarian:* JOHN MACIK.

Number of teachers: 160.
Number of students: 2,590.

Publications: *Cithara, Laurel, Bonadieu, Bonaventure, Cord, Franciscan Studies, The Works of William of Ockham.*

### DEANS:
*School of Arts and Sciences:* Dr. WILLIAM WEHMEYER.
*School of Business:* Dr. JOHN WATSON.
*School of Education:* Dr. PAUL SCHAFER.
*School of Graduate Studies:* Dr. RONALD HARTMAN.
*Franciscan Institute:* Rev. CONRAD HARKINS, O.F.M., PH.D.

## ST. FRANCIS COLLEGE
180 REMSEN ST.,
BROOKLYN, N.Y. 11201
Telephone: JAckson 2-2300.
Chartered 1884.

*President:* Bro. DONALD SULLIVAN, O.S.F., PH.D.
*Registrar:* Bro. R. SCHAEFER, O.S.F.
*Librarian:* Bro. L. DROWNE, O.S.F.

The library contains 118,756 vols.
Number of teachers: 196.
Number of students: 3,972 full- and part-time.

## ST. JOHN'S UNIVERSITY, NEW YORK
GRAND CENTRAL AND
UTOPIA PARKWAYS,
JAMAICA, N.Y. 11439
Telephone: (212) 990-6161.

Opened 1870; Chartered 1871; re-Chartered by Regents of the University of the State of New York 1906; Campuses at Staten Island and Queens.

*President:* Very Rev. JOSEPH T. CAHILL, C.M.
*Executive Vice-President:* C. CARL ROBUSTO.
*Vice-President for Academic Planning:* BARBARA L. MORRIS.
*Administrative Vice-President:* PATRICK E. McGEE.
*Vice-President for Alumni Affairs and Auxiliary Services and Special Assistant to President:* Rev. JOHN V. NEWMAN, C.M.
*Vice-President for Communications and Public Affairs and Director of Public Relations:* MARTIN J. HEALY.

*Vice-President for University Relations and Secretary of the University:* Rev. JOSEPH I. DIRVIN, C.M.
*Vice-President for Business and Career-Oriented Programs:* JOHN C. ALEXION.
*Vice-President for Health Professions:* ANDREW J. BARTILUCCI.
*Vice-President for Campus Ministry:* Rev. JOSEPH V. DALY, C.M.
*Vice-President for Student Affairs:* Rev. RICHARD J. DEVINE, C.M.
*Vice-President for Business Affairs and Treasurer:* Rev. WALTER F. GRAHAM, C.M.
*Vice-President for Liberal Arts and Sciences, Education and Human Services:* Rev. THOMAS F. HOAR, C.M.
*Director of Libraries:* Rev. LAWRENCE A. LONERGAN, C.M.

Library of 996,870 vols.
Number of teachers: 851.
Number of students: 17,945.

### DEANS:
*Admissions and Registrar:* HENRY F. ROSSI.
*Student Development:* DONALD Z. SCHEIBER.
*Graduate School of Arts and Sciences:* PAUL T. MEDICI.
*Institute for Advanced Studies in Catholic Doctrine:* Msgr. GEORGE A. KELLY (Director).
*St. John's College of Liberal Arts and Sciences:* Rev. THOMAS F. HOAR, C.M.
*St. Vincent's College:* CATHERINE J. RUGGIERI.
*School of Education and Human Services:* PAUL T. MEDICI (acting).
*School of Law:* PATRICK ROHAN.
*Notre Dame College:* Rev. JOSEPH BREEN, C.M.
*Evening Division and Weekend College:* PATRICK J. BASILICE.
*Summer Sessions and Director Institute of Criminal Justice:* GEORGE ANSALONE.
*Government and Research Grants:* Rev. JOHN E. COLMAN (Director).

### Staten Island Campus
300 HOWARD AVE., STATEN ISLAND 10301

*Academic Vice-President:* Rev. KENNETH F. SLATTERY, C.M.
*Administrative Vice-President, Vice-President for Campus Ministry and Director of Student Affairs:* Rev. THOMAS CONCAGH, C.M.
*Dean of Admissions and Registrar:* PATRICIA K. PALERMO.
*Dean of Students:* MARGARET I. LANE.

## ST. LAWRENCE UNIVERSITY
CANTON, N.Y. 13617
Telephone: (315) 379-5011.
Founded 1856.

*President:* W. LAWRENCE GULICK, PH.D.

*Vice-President and Dean:* Dr. GEORGE H. GIBSON.
*Vice-President for Academic Planning:* A. P. SPLETE, PH.D.
*Vice-President for Development:* H. S. WHITTIER.
*Vice-President for Business Affairs:* C. B. RANDALL.
*Vice-President for Student Affairs:* P. E. VAN DE WATER, PH.D.
*Secretary:* A. M. KRAY.
*Registrar:* JANET J. FLIGHT.
*Librarian:* M. N. PETERSON.

The library contains over 250,000 vols.

Number of teachers: 155.
Number of students: 1,100 men, 1,100 women, total 2,200.
Publications: *Bulletin* (5 a year), *Hill News* (weekly), *Laurentian* (annually), *Gridiron* (annually).

DEANS:
*College of Letters and Science:* Dr. GEORGE H. GIBSON.
*Student Services:* L. F. SALTRELLI.

## SARAH LAWRENCE COLLEGE
BRONXVILLE, N.Y. 10708
Provisional Charter 1926; Absolute Charter 1931.

*President:* CHARLES R. DE CARLO.
*Dean of the College:* ILJA WACHS.
*Dean of Studies:* BARBARA KAPLAN.
*Dean of Administration and Communications:* ELIZABETH LINDSEY.
*Director of Admissions:* DUDLEY BLODGET.
*Director of Public Relations:* JANE KLANG.
*Treasurer:* RAY PILKONIS.
*Recorder:* MARY DRISCOLL.
*General Secretary for Development:* JAMES BAKER.

The library contains 150,000 vols.
Number of teachers: 100.
Number of students: 850.
Publication: *Sarah Lawrence Bulletin.*

## SIENA COLLEGE
LOUDONVILLE, N.Y. 12211
Telephone: (518) 783-2300.
Founded 1937. Independent Liberal Arts College.

*President:* Rev. HUGH F. HINES, O.F.M.
*Vice-President for Academic Affairs:* Rev. JOHN C. MURPHY, O.F.M.
*Vice-President for Business Affairs:* ANTHONY G. PONDILLO.
*Vice-President for Development:* DELL N. THOMPSON.
*Dean of Students:* TERRY J. REYNOLDS.
*Director of Admissions:* HARRY W. WOOD.
*Librarian:* BASIL MITCHELL.

Library of 165,000 vols., 27,000 other items.
Number of teachers: 128.
Number of students: 2,300 full-time, 700 part-time.

## SKIDMORE COLLEGE
SARATOGA SPRINGS, N.Y. 12866
Telephone: (518) 584-5000.
Founded 1903, chartered 1922.

*President:* JOSEPH C. PALAMOUNTAIN, Jr.
*Provost and Vice-President for Academic Affairs:* DAVID W. MARCELL.
*Vice-President for Business Affairs and Treasurer:* KARL W. BROEKHUIZEN.
*Vice-President for External Affairs:* DAVID E. LONG.
*Dean of the Faculty:* ERIC WELLER.
*Dean of Student Affairs:* FRANCES HOFFMANN.
*Dean of Special Programs:* MARK I. GELBER.
*Director of Admissions:* LOUISE WISE.
*Librarian:* ALVIN SKIPSNA.

The library contains 280,000 vols.
Number of teachers: 177.
Number of students: 2,100.

## STATE UNIVERSITY OF NEW YORK
CENTRAL ADMINISTRATION, STATE UNIVERSITY PLAZA, ALBANY, N.Y. 12246
Telephone: (518) 473-1011.

*Chancellor:* CLIFTON R. WHARTON, Jr.
*Executive Vice-Chancellor:* DONALD D. O'DOWD.
*University Counsel and Vice-Chancellor for Legal Affairs:* SANFORD H. LEVINE.
*Associate Chancellor for Community Colleges:* CORNELIUS V. ROBBINS.
*Associate Chancellor for Health Sciences:* ALDEN N. HAFFNER.
*Deputy to the Chancellor for Campus Liaison:* MURRAY H. BLOCK.
*Deputy to the Chancellor for Governmental Relations:* HERBERT B. GORDON.
*Vice-Chancellor for Academic Programs, Policy and Planning:* JEROME B. KOMISAR (acting).
*Vice-Chancellor for Capital Facilities and General Manager, State University Construction Fund:* OSCAR E. LANFORD.
*Vice-Chancellor for Finance and Business:* HARRY K. SPINDLER.
*Vice-Chancellor for Faculty and Staff Relations:* JEROME B. KOMISAR.
*Vice-Chancellor for University Affairs:* ROBERT PERRIN.
*Vice-Chancellor for Educational Services:* JAMES S. SMOOT.
*Secretary of the University:* MARTHA J. DOWNEY.

Number of teachers: c. 15,000 full-time.
Number of students: 356,708.

### State University of New York at Albany
ALBANY, N.Y. 12203
*President:* VINCENT O'LEARY.
*Vice-President for Academic Affairs:* DAVID W. MARTIN.
*Vice-President for Finance and Business:* JOHN A. HARTIGAN.
*Vice-President for Research:* WARREN ILCHMAN.
*Vice-President for University Affairs:* LEWIS P. WELCH.

### State University of New York at Binghamton
BINGHAMTON, N.Y. 13901
*President:* CLIFFORD D. CLARK.
*Vice-President for Academic Affairs:* GEORGE H. STEIN.
*Vice-President for Finance and Management:* EDWARD J. DEMSKE.
*Vice-President for Student Services:* DUDLEY B. WOODARD.

### State University of New York at Buffalo
AMHERST, N.Y. 14260
*President:* ROBERT L. KETTER.
*Vice-President for Academic Affairs:* ROBERT H. ROSSBERG.
*Vice-President for Research:* DONALD RENNIE.
*Vice-President for Student Affairs:* RICHARD A. SIGGELKOW.
*Vice-President for Facilities Planning:* JOHN NEAL.
*Vice-President for Health Sciences:* F. CARTER PANNILL.
*Vice-President for Finance and Management:* EDWARD W. DOTY.

### State University of New York at Stony Brook
STONY BROOK, N.Y. 11790
*President:* JOHN H. MARBURGER III.
*Academic Vice-President:* SIDNEY GELBER.
*Vice-President for Student Affairs:* ELIZABETH WADSWORTH.
*Vice-President for Finance and Business:* CARL E. HANES, Jr.
*Vice-President for Health Science Center:* J. HOWARD OAKS.
*Vice-President for Research:* ROBERT SOKAL (acting).
*Vice-President for University Affairs:* JAMES D. BLACK.
*Vice-President for Hospital Affairs:* MICHAEL S. ELLIOTT.

### MEDICAL CENTRES
**Downstate Medical Center at Brooklyn (New York City).**
*President:* DONALD J. SCHERL.

**Upstate Medical Center at Syracuse.**
*President:* RICHARD P. SCHMIDT.

### COLLEGES OF ARTS AND SCIENCE
**College at Brockport.**
*President:* JOHN E. VAN DE WETERING.

**College at Buffalo.**
President: D. Bruce Johnstone.

**College at Cortland.**
President: James M. Clark.

**Empire State College.**
President: John H. Jacobson (acting).

**College at Fredonia.**
President: Dallas K. Beal.

**College at Geneseo.**
President: Edward B. Jakubauskas.

**College at New Paltz.**
President: Alice Chandler.

**College at Old Westbury.**
President: James H. Hall (acting).

**College at Oneonta.**
President: Clifford J. Craven.

**College at Oswego.**
President: Virginia Radley.

**College at Plattsburgh.**
President: Joseph C. Burke.

**College at Potsdam.**
President: James H. Young.

**College at Purchase.**
President: Sheldon N. Grebstein.

SPECIALIZED COLLEGES

**College of Environmental Science and Forestry (Syracuse).**
President: Edward E. Palmer.

**College of Optometry (New York City).**
President: Edward Johnson.

**College of Technology at Utica/Rome.**
President: William R. Kunsela.

**Maritime College (Fort Schuyler, Bronx).**
President: Sheldon H. Kinney.

## SYRACUSE UNIVERSITY

SYRACUSE, N.Y. 13210
Telephone: (315) 423-1870.

Chartered as Syracuse University in 1870.

Chancellor and President: Dr. Melvin A. Eggers.
Vice-Chancellor for Academic Affairs: Dr. John James Prucha.
Vice-Chancellor and Executive Assistant to the Chancellor: Dr. Michael O. Sawyer.
Vice-Chancellor for Administrative Operations: Dr. Clifford L. Winters, Jr.
Vice-President for Institutional Services: Carol H. Heagerty.
Vice-President for Development and Planning: Harry E. Yeiser, Jr.
Vice-President for Public Affairs: Dr. Joseph V. Julian.
Vice-President for Governmental Affairs: Molly Corbet Broad.
Vice-President for Facilities Administration: Dr. Harvey H. Kaiser.
Vice-President for Research and Graduate Affairs: Dr. Volker Weiss.
Vice-President for Student Affairs: Dr. Paul E. Eickmann.
Vice-President for Admissions and Records: Harry W. Peter III.
Dean of Admissions and Financial Aid: Thomas F. Cummings, Jr.
Registrar: Carole A. Barone.
Director of Libraries: Donald C. Anthony.

Library: see Libraries.
Number of teachers: 872.
Number of students: 18,600.

Publications: *Syracuse Scholar* (quarterly), *Symposium* (quarterly on foreign languages and literature), *Syracuse Law Review* (quarterly), *Syracuse University Record* (weekly).

DEANS:

School of Architecture: Prof. Werner Seligmann.
College of Arts and Sciences: Dr. Gershon Vincow.
Maxwell Graduate School of Citizenship and Public Affairs: Dr. Guthrie S. Birkhead.
School of Computer and Information Science: Dr. Warren L. Semon.
School of Education: Dr. Burton Blatt.
College of Engineering: Dr. Bradley J. Strait.
State University of New York College of Environmental Science and Forestry: Dr. Edward E. Palmer (President).
Graduate School: Dr. Volker Weiss.
Hendricks Memorial Chapel: Dr. Richard L. Phillips.
College for Human Development: Dr. Jane Brush Lillestol.
School of Information Studies: Dr. Evelyn Daniel.
College of Law: Prof. Craig W. Christensen.
School of Management: Dr. L. Richard Oliker.
School of Nursing: Dr. Thetis M. Group.
S. I. Newhouse School of Public Communications: Prof. Edward C. Stephens.
School of Social Work: Dr. Kermit K. Schooler.
Summer Sessions: Dr. James R. Manwaring.
University College: Dr. Frank E. Funk.
Utica College: Dr. Thomas D. Sheldon (President).
College of Visual and Performing Arts: Dr. August L. Freundlich.

AFFILIATED INSTITUTIONS:

**Center of Hispanic Studies:** f. 1945.

The Center co-operates closely with the faculties of Geography and History.

**Center on Human Policy.**

**Communications Research Center.**

**Institute for Energy Research.**

**All-University Gerontology Center.**

## UNION UNIVERSITY

Chancellor: John S. Morris, ph.d., ll.d.

The University is made up of the following colleges:

### Union College

SCHENECTADY, NEW YORK 12308
Telephone: (518) 370-6000.

Founded 1795; oldest non-denominational college in U.S.; formerly Union College and University, status changed 1969.

President: John S. Morris, ph.d., ll.d.
Registrar: C. G. Schmidt.
Librarian: Jean Pelletiere, m.a., m.l.s.

The library contains 310,700 vols.
Number of teachers: 144 (full-time).
Number of students: 1,975 (full-time day).

Publications: *Catalogue*, *Concordiensis* (weekly newspaper), *Union College* (Alumni), *Union Book* (Senior Year Book), *Idol* (student literary magazine).

DEANS:

Faculty: Thomas D'Andrea, ph.d.
Graduate and Special Programs: Aaron Feinsot, m.a., ph.d.
Students: Donald E. Spring, m.a., ph.d.

### Albany College of Pharmacy

106 New Scotland Ave.,
Albany, New York 12208
Telephone: (518) 445-7211.

Founded 1881.

Dean: Walter Singer.
Director of Admissions: Mrs. Janice L. Fisher.
Librarian: Mrs. L. Brown.

Number of teachers: 40.
Number of students: 550.

### Albany Law School

80 New Scotland Ave.,
Albany, New York 12208
Telephone: (518) 445-2311.

Founded 1851.

President of Board of Trustees: J. Vanderbilt Straub.
Dean: Richard J. Bartlett.
Registrar: Helen T. Wilkinson.
Libarian: Henry Tseng.

The library contains 127,898 vols.
Number of teachers: 27 full-time, 13 adjunct.
Number of students: 675.

### Albany Medical College

47 New Scotland Ave.,
Albany, New York 12208
Telephone: (518) 445-5544.

Founded 1839.

President: Robert L. Friedlander, m.d.

UNIVERSITIES AND COLLEGES—NEW YORK U.S.A.

*Dean of Admissions:* RICHARD H. EDMONDS, PH.D.
*Librarian:* Mrs. URSULA POLAND.

The library contains 80,000 vols.

Number of teachers: 256.
Number of students: 512.

## U.S. MERCHANT MARINE ACADEMY
### KINGS POINT, NEW YORK 11024
Telephone: (516) 482-8200.

### Founded 1943.

*Superintendent:* Rear-Admiral THOMAS A. KING, U.S.M.S., B.S.
*Deputy Superintendent:* Cdre. HOWARD P. CASEY, U.S.M.S., M.B.A., C.P.A.
*Academic Dean:* Capt. P. L. KRINSKY, U.S.M.S., B.S., M.A., M.B.A.
*Commandant of Midshipmen:* Capt. ROBERT T. MADDEN, U.S.M.S., M.S.M.E.
*Director, Office of External Affairs:* Capt. C. M. RENICK, U.S.M.S., M.S.
*Library:* Cmdr. ELIZABETH A. FUSELER, U.S.M.S., A.B., M.S., M.L.S.

Number of instructors: 80.
Number of midshipmen: 1,100.

HEADS OF ACADEMIC DEPARTMENTS:
*Nautical Science:* Capt. WILLIAM T. MCMULLEN, U.S.M.S., B.S., M.B.A.
*Engineering:* Capt. EVERETT HUNT, U.S.M.S., M.M.E.
*Maritime Law and Economics:* Capt. L. JARETT, U.S.M.S., B.S.(SS), LL.B., M.A., LL.M., J.S.D.
*Humanities:* Capt. ROBERT ANCHOR, U.S.M.S., PH.D.
*Mathematics and Science:* Capt. ALBERT SWERTKA, U.S.M.S., PH.D.
*Naval Science:* Capt. ROBERT MARSHALL, U.S.N., M.S.
*Physical Education and Athletics:* Capt. W. T. LAI, Jr., M.A.

## UNITED STATES MILITARY ACADEMY
### WEST POINT, NEW YORK 10996
### Founded 1802.

*Superintendent:* Lt.-Gen. WILLARD W. SCOTT, Jr.
*Commandant of Cadets:* Brig.-Gen. JOSEPH P. FRANKLIN, M.S.N.E., M.S.C.E.
*Dean of the Academic Board:* Brig.-Gen. F. A. SMITH, Jr., PH.D.
*Director of Admissions:* Col. MANLEY E. ROGERS, M.S.
*Librarian:* E. A. WEISS, M.A., M.S.L.S.

The library contains 400,000 vols.

Number of instructors: 550.
Number of cadets: 4,492.

HEADS OF DEPARTMENTS:
*Behavioral Science and Leadership:* Col. HOWARD PRINCE, PH.D.
*Chemistry:* Col. WILFORD J. HOFF, PH.D.
*Engineering:* Col. A. F. GRUM, M.S., PH.D. (acting).
*Mechanics:* Col. R. M. WILSON, PH.D.
*Mathematics:* Col. J. M. POLLIN, PH.D.
*Geography and Computer Science:* Col. G. W. KIRBY, Jr., PH.D.
*Foreign Languages:* Col. J. COSTA, M.A.
*Law:* Col. R. BERRY, J.D.
*English:* Col. J. CAPPS, PH.D.
*Social Sciences:* Col. L. D. OLVEY, PH.D.
*Physics:* Col. E. A. SAUNDERS, M.S., PH.D.
*Electrical Engineering:* Col. S. E. REINHART, Jr., PH.D.
*History:* Col. T. E. GRIESS, M.S., PH.D
*Military Instruction:* Col. F. G. WALTON, M.A.
*Physical Education:* Col. J. L. ANDERSON, PH.D.

## UNIVERSITY OF ROCHESTER
### WILSON BLVD., ROCHESTER, NEW YORK 14627
Telephone: (716) 275-2121.

### Founded 1850.

Private control; Academic year: September to May (two terms).

*President:* R. L. SPROULL, PH.D.
*Provost:* RICHARD D. O'BRIEN, PH.D.
*Senior Vice-President and Treasurer:* LaR. B. THOMPSON, B.S.
*Vice-President for Planning and Director of Budgets:* R. R. FRANCE, PH.D
*Vice-President for Public Affairs:* G. M. ANGLE, M.A.
*Vice-President for Investments:* S. P. HORSLEY, M.B.A.
*Vice-President for Student Affairs:* BERNARD R. GIFFORD, PH.D.
*Vice-President for Campus Affairs:* D. K. HESS, M.A.
*Registrar:* JEROME D. DIVER.
*Director of Libraries:* JAMES WYATT.
*Library:* see Libraries.

Number of teachers: 1,024.
Number of students: 8,320.

DEANS:
*College of Arts and Science:* J. PAUL HUNTER, PH.D.
*Graduate Studies:* WILLIAM H. RIKER, PH.D.
*School of Medicine and Dentistry:* FRANK E. YOUNG, M.D.
*University College of Liberal and Applied Studies:* R. G. KOCH, PH.D
*Eastman School of Music:* R. FREEMAN, PH.D.
*School of Nursing:* L. C. FORD, R.N., ED.D.
*Graduate School of Management:* W. H. MECKLING, M.B.A.
*Graduate School of Education and Human Development:* WALTER I. GARMS, PH.D.
*College of Engineering and Applied Science:* B. J. THOMPSON, PH.D.
*Memorial Art Gallery:* A. BRET WALLER, M.F.A.

CHAIRMEN OF DEPARTMENTS:
*Psychiatry:* H. BABIGIAN, M.D.
*Health Services:* J. BARTLETT, M.D.
*Foreign Languages, Literatures and Linguistics:* A. BENSTON.
*Preventive Medicine and Community Health:* R. L. BERG, M.D.
*Chemical Engineering:* J. FRIEDLY, PH.D.
*Keyboard:* D. BURGE, D.M.A. (Co-Chair.).
*English:* B. JOHNSON, PH.D.
*Cancer Center:* R. COOPER, Jr., M.D.
*Keyboard:* D. CRAIGHEAD, MUS.DOC., B.M. (Co-Chair.).
*Surgery:* W. DRUCKER, M.D.
*Orthopaedics:* C. McC. EVARTS, M.D.
*Computer Science:* J. A. FELDMAN, PH.D.
*Radiology:* H. W. FISCHER, M.D.
*Theory:* R. GAULDIN, M.M., PH.D.
*Medical Education and Communication:* R. H. GEERTSMA, PH.D.
*Optics:* N. GEORGE., PH.D.
*Anaesthesiology:* A. J. GILLIES, M.B., CH.B.
*Physics and Astronomy:* H. VAN HORN, PH.D.
*Musicology:* J. GRAUE, M.M., PH.D.
*Statistics:* W. J. HALL, PH.D.
*Anthropology:* G. HARRIS, PH.D.
*History:* W. HAUSER, PH.D.
*Brain Research and Co-Chair of Anatomy:* R. HERNDON, M.D.
*Biology:* G. HOCH, PH.D.
*Conducting and Ensembles:* S. HODKINSON, M.M., D.M.A. (Co-Chair.).
*Medicine:* R. HORNICK, M.D.
*Physiology:* P. HOROWICZ, PH.D.
*Psychology:* J. R. ISON, PH.D.
*Neurology and Anatomy:* R. J. JOYNT, M.D., PH.D.
*Chemistry:* A. KENDE, PH.D.
*Laboratory Animal Medicine:* A. KRAUS, D.V.M.
*Philosophy:* H. KYBURG, PH.D.
*Radiation Biology, Biophysics:* P. L. LACELLE, M.D.
*Pharmacology and Toxicology:* L. C. LASAGNA, M.D.
*String Department:* A. LOFT, PH.D.
*Geological Sciences:* L. W. LUNDGREN, Jr., PH.D.
*Voice:* J. MALOY, B.M.
*Biochemistry:* R. HILF, PH.D. (acting).
*Microbiology:* R. MARQUIS, PH.D. (acting).
*Electrical Engineering:* S. SHAPIRO, PH.D.
*Naval Science:* R. MESLER, M.S.
*Ophthalmology:* H. METZ, M.D.
*Fine Arts:* D. DOHANIAN, PH.D.
*Political Science:* R. G. NIEMI, PH.D.
*Biostatistics:* C. ODOROFF, PH.D.
*Economics:* W. Y. OI, PH.D.
*Pathology:* S. F. PATTEN, M.D., PH.D.
*Genetics:* P. T. ROWLEY, M.D. (acting).
*Composition:* J. SCHWANTNER, DOC. MUS.
*Mathematics:* S. SEGAL, PH.D.
*Humanities (Eastman School of Music):* A. SEN, PH.D.
*Music Education:* R. ERNST, ED.D.
*Mechanical Engineering:* A. SIMON, PH.D.

*Paediatrics:* D. H. SMITH, M.D.
*Sociology:* T. SMITH, PH.D.
*Obstetrics and Gynaecology:* H. THIEDE, M.D.
*Woodwind, Brass and Percussion:* K. D. VAN HOESEN, B.M.
*Music:* R. WILHELM, D.M.A.
*Conducting and Ensembles, Jazz and Contemporary Media:* R. WRIGHT, M.A. (Co-Chair.).
*Dental Research:* H. ZANDER, D.D.S.

## VASSAR COLLEGE
POUGHKEEPSIE,
NEW YORK 12601
Chartered 1861

*President:* VIRGINIA B. SMITH, M.A., J.D.
*Vice-President for Administrative and Student Services:* NATALIE J. MARSHALL, PH.D.
*Executive Director for Development:* JUDITH LEWITTES.
*Dean of the College:* H. PATRICK SULLIVAN, PH.D.
*Dean of Studies:* COLTON JOHNSON, PH.D.
*Librarian:* BARBARA LAMONT, M.A., M.L.S.

Library of over 500,000 vols.
Number of teachers: 228.
Number of students: 2,250 men and women.

## WAGNER COLLEGE
GRYMES HILL, STATEN ISLAND, NEW YORK 10301
Telephone: (212) 390-3000.
Founded 1883.

*President:* JOHN SATTERFIELD.
*Dean of Admissions:* Dr. JAMES M. KEATING.
*Librarian:* Y. JOHN AUH.

The library contains 260,000 vols.
Number of teachers: 80 full-time, 70 part-time, total 150.
Number of students: 2,451.

## WEBB INSTITUTE OF NAVAL ARCHITECTURE
GLEN COVE, LONG ISLAND, NEW YORK 11542
Founded 1889.

*President:* Rear-Admiral CHARLES N. PAYNE, U.S.N. (Retd.).
*Registrar:* WILLIAM G. MURRAY.
*Dean:* Dr. JOSEPH URBAN.
*Librarian:* F. H. FORREST.

Library of 30,000 vols.
Number of teachers: 14.
Number of students: 80.

## WELLS COLLEGE
AURORA, NEW YORK 13026
Founded 1868.

*President:* PATTI M. PETERSON, PH.D.

*Vice-President for Development:* ADRIENNE LYBARGER, B.A.
*Vice-President and Treasurer:* LUTHER VAN UMMERSEN, C.P.A.
*Dean of the College:* NENAH FRY, PH.D.
*Dean of Students:* DOROTHY SLATER-BROWN, PH.D.
*Registrar:* CHARLES SNYDER, M.A.
*Director of Admissions:* JOAN IRVING, B.A.
*Librarian:* MARIE DELANEY, M.L.S.

The library contains 198,193 vols.
Number of teachers: 63.
Number of students: 500.
Publication: *Wells College Express.*

## YESHIVA UNIVERSITY
500 WEST 185TH ST.,
NEW YORK, N.Y. 10033
Telephone: (212) 960-5400.
Founded 1886.

Private control; Languages of instruction: English and Hebrew.

*President:* NORMAN LAMM, PH.D.
*Senior Vice-President:* I. MILLER, D.D.
*Executive Vice-President:* E. BRENNER, D.E.E.
*Vice-President for Medical Affairs:* E. FRIEDMAN, M.D.
*Vice-President for Business Affairs:* S. E. SOCOL, J.D.
*Director of Libraries:* F. S. BAUM, J.D.

Seven libraries of *c.* 850,000 vols.
Number of teachers: 2,500.
Number of students: 7,000.

Publications: *Report, Alumni Review, Inside Yeshiva University.*

### DEANS:

*Humanities:* R. A. ACKERMAN, PH.D.
*Behavioral and Social Sciences:* M. BERGER, PH.D.
*Natural Sciences and Mathematics:* E. M. LOBEL, PH.D.
*Undergraduate Jewish Studies and Jewish Education:* J. M. RABINOWITZ, M.S.
*Yeshiva College:* N. ROSENFELD, PH.D.
*Stern College for Women:* K. BACON, PH.D.
*Teachers Institute for Women:* W. ORFENSTEIN, D.H.L.
*Graduate Jewish Studies:* S. Z. LEIMAN, PH.D.
*Benjamin N. Cardozo School of Law:* L. BRICKMAN, J.D. (acting).
*Albert Einstein College of Medicine:* E. FRIEDMAN, M.D.
*Wurzweiler School of Social Work:* L. SETLEIS, D.S.W.

### DIRECTORS:

*James Striar School of General Jewish Studies:* M. J. BESDIN, B.A.
*Mazer Yeshiva Program:* Z. CHARLOP, M.A.
*Sue Golding Graduate Division of Medical Sciences:* J. R. WARNER, PH.D.

ATTACHED RESEARCH INSTITUTES:
Yeshiva University Research Institute.
Irwin S. and Sylvia Chanin Institute for Cancer Research.
Center for Social Research in Rehabilitation Medicine.
Rose F. Kennedy Center for Research in Mental Retardation and Human Development.
Jack and Pearl Resnick Gerontology Center.
Maxwell R. Maybaum Institute of Material Sciences and Quantum Electronics.

## NORTH CAROLINA

### APPALACHIAN STATE UNIVERSITY
BOONE, NORTH CAROLINA 28607
Telephone: (704) 262-2000.

Founded 1899. Linked to the University of North Carolina.

*Chancellor:* JOHN E. THOMAS.
*Registrar:* C. DAVID SMITH.
*Dean of Learning Resources (and Library):* Dr. A. CORUM.

Library of 360,000 vols.
Number of teachers: 550.
Number of students: 9,034.

### ATLANTIC CHRISTIAN COLLEGE
WILSON, NORTH CAROLINA 27893
Telephone: 919-237-3161.

Founded 1902 (Disciples of Christ).

*President:* Dr. HAROLD C. DOSTER.
*Registrar:* BETHANY R. JOYNER.
*Academic Dean:* F. MARK DAVIS.

Library of 96,721 vols.
Number of teachers: 111.
Number of students: 1,620.

### BARBER-SCOTIA COLLEGE
145 CABARRUS AVENUE,
CONCORD, NORTH CAROLINA 28025
Telephone: 786-5171.

Founded 1867.

*President:* Dr. MABLE P. MCLEAN.
*Vice-President for Academic Affairs:* Dr. JAMES E. LYONS.
*Registrar:* OLA STRINGER.
*Librarian:* PERLEE COEFIELD.

The library contains 63,500 vols.
Number of teachers: 38.
Number of students: 451.

### BELMONT ABBEY COLLEGE
BELMONT,
NORTH CAROLINA 28012
Telephone: (704) 825-3711.

Founded 1876.

*President:* Dr. ROBERT M. HOWARD.
*Vice-President for Academic Affairs:* Dr. GEORGE C. HERNDL.

UNIVERSITIES AND COLLEGES—NORTH CAROLINA U.S.A.

*Vice-President for Business Affairs:* J. RAY STARR.
*Vice-President for Institutional Advancement:* HARRY P. CREEMERS.
*Vice-President for Student Affairs:* Rev. MAURICIO W. WEST, O.S.B.

The library contains 73,509 vols.
Number of teachers: 56.
Number of students: 850.

Publications: *Agora†*, *Crossroads†*, *Free Lance†*, *Around Our Campus*.

### BENNETT COLLEGE
GREENSBORO,
NORTH CAROLINA 27420
Telephone: (919) 273-4431.
Founded 1873 (reorganized 1926).

*President:* ISAAC H. MILLER, Jr.
*Director of Admissions:* PHYLLIS JOHNSON.
*Dean of the College:* CHELSEA TIPTON.
*Librarian:* EDNITA W. BULLOCK.

The library contains 76,000 vols.
Number of teachers: 54.
Number of students: 625.

### CAMPBELL UNIVERSITY
BUIE'S CREEK,
NORTH CAROLINA 27506
Telephone: (919) 893-4111.
Founded 1887.

*President:* Dr. NORMAN A. WIGGINS.
*Vice-President and Provost:* FRED McCALL.
*Academic Dean:* JERRY WALLACE.
*Registrar:* J. DAVID McGIRT.
*Director of Admissions:* (vacant).
*Librarian:* J. D. SISTRUNK.

Library of 170,000 vols.
Number of teachers: 100 full-time, 12 part-time.

Publications: *Prospect* (Alumni bulletin), *Creek Pebbles* (newspaper), *Pine Burr* (year book).

### CATAWBA COLLEGE
SALISBURY,
NORTH CAROLINA 28144
Telephone: (704) 637-4111.
Founded 1851.

*President:* Dr. STEPHEN H. WURSTER.
*Registrar:* M. M. RICHARDS.
*Director of Admissions:* J. W. HALL.
*Librarian:* BETTY SELL.

Library of 180,000 vols.
Number of teachers: 57.
Number of students: 988.

### DAVIDSON COLLEGE
DAVIDSON,
NORTH CAROLINA 28036
Founded 1837.

*President:* SAMUEL R. SPENCER, Jr., PH.D., LL.D.
*Vice-President for Academic Affairs:* T. C. PRICE ZIMMERMANN, PH.D.
*Vice-President for Development:* (vacant).
*Dean of Students:* W. H. TERRY, B.D.
*Business Manager:* R. A. CURRIE, M.B.A.
*Director of Communications:* JOHN W. SLATER, M.A.
*Director of Alumni Relations:* ZACHARY F. LONG, Jr., M.B.A.
*Director of the Living Endowment:* E. LEE WILLINGHAM III, M.DIV.
*Director of Admissions and Financial Aid:* JOHN V. GRIFFITH, PH.D.
*Registrar:* R. C. BURTS, Jr., ED.D.
*Director of Library:* LELAND M. PARK, PH.D.

Library of 270,000 vols.
Number of teachers: 112, including 39 professors.
Number of students: 1,350.

Publications: *Davidson College Update* (monthly), *The Davidsonian* (weekly student newspaper), *Quips and Cranks* (year book), *The Miscellany* (Literary Quarterly).

### DUKE UNIVERSITY
DURHAM,
NORTH CAROLINA 27706
Telephone: (919) 684-8111.

Union Institute Society founded in 1838 in Randolph County, North Carolina. In 1851 the Institute was reorganised as Trinity College, and in 1892 the College was removed to Durham. A new Charter was issued in 1924, when, under the Duke Endowment, it became Duke University.

*President:* TERRY SANFORD, J.D., LL.D., D.H., L.H.D., D.P.A.
*Chancellor:* A. KENNETH PYE, LL.M.
*Provost:* WILLIAM BEVAN, PH.D., LL.D., SC.D.
*Vice-President for Business and Finance:* C. B. HUESTIS.
*Vice-President for Health Affairs:* WILLIAM G. ANLYAN, M.D.
*Vice-President for Student Affairs:* WILLIAM J. GRIFFITH, A.B.
*Vice-President for Government Relations and University Counsel:* E. J. McDONALD, A.M.P., J.D., LL.M.
*Treasurer:* S. C. HARVARD, C.P.A.
*Vice-Provosts:* CRAUFURD GOODWIN, PH.D. (Research), COLIN BLAYDON, PH.D. (Academic Policy and Planning).
*Secretary:* ROGER MARSHALL, A.B.
*Librarian:* ELVIN STROWD, A.M.L.S. (acting).

Number of teachers: 1,415 full-time, 307 part-time.
Number of students: 9,325.

DEANS:
*Dean of Trinity College and Dean of Arts and Sciences:* ERNESTINE FRIEDL, PH.D.
*Divinity School:* JAMESON JONES, B.D., PH.D.
*Medical School:* EWALD W. BUSSE, M.D.
*School of Engineering:* ALEKSANDAR S. VESIC, D.SC.
*School of Forestry:* BENJAMIN A. JAYNE, PH.D.
*School of Law:* PAUL D. CARRINGTON, LL.B.
*School of Nursing:* RUBY L. WILSON, M.S.N., ED.D.
*Graduate School:* CRAUFURD GOODWIN, PH.D.
*Graduate School of Business Administration:* THOMAS F. KELLER, PH.D.
*Summer Session:* CALVIN WARD, PH.D.

PROFESSORS:
*Aerospace Studies:*
HAMILTON, J. G., PH.D.

*Anatomy:*
CARTMILL, M., PH.D.
HYLANDER, W. L., PH.D.
MOSES, M. J., PH.D.
NICKLAS, S. C., PH.D.
ROBERTSON, J. D., M.D., PH.D.

*Anaesthesiology:*
BENNETT, P. B., PH.D.
BROMAGE, P. R., M.D.
DAVIS, D. A., M.D.
DENT, SARA J., M.D.
HALL, K. D., M.D.
HARMEL, M. H., M.D.
KARIS, J. H., M.D.
MURRAY, W. J., PH.D.
REDICK, L. F., M.D.
URBAN, B. J., M.D.
VARTANIAN, V., M.D.
WEITZNER, S. W., M.D.

*Anthropology:*
FOX, R., PH.D.
FRIEDL, ERNESTINE, PH.D.
O'BARR, W. M., PH.D.
SIMONS, E. L., PH.D., D.PHIL.

*Art:*
KINKEAD, D. T., PH.D.
SPENCER, J. R., PH.D.

*Biochemistry:*
FRIDOVICH, I., PH.D., Biochemistry
GROSS, S. R., PH.D., Genetics and Biochemistry
GUILD, W. R., PH.D., Biophysics
HANDLER, P., PH.D., Biochemistry and Nutrition
HILL, R. L., PH.D., Biochemistry
KAMIN, H., PH.D., Biochemistry
McCARTY, K. S., PH.D., Biochemistry
RAJAGOPALAN, K. V., PH.D., Biochemistry
WEBSTER, R. E. PH.D.,

*Botany:*
ANDERSON, L. E., PH.D.
ANTONOVICS, J., PH.D.
BOYNTON, J. E., PH.D.
CULBERSON, W. L., PH.D.
HELLMERS, H., PH.D.
JOHNSON, T. W., PH.D.
NAYLOR, A. W., PH.D.
PHILPOTT, JANE, PH.D.
STRAIN, B. R., PH.D.
STONE, D. E., PH.D.
WHITE, R. A., PH.D.
WILBUR, R. L., PH.D.

*Business Administration:*
BALIGH, H. H., PH.D.
COHEN, K. J., PH.D.
DICKENS, R. L., M.S., C.P.A., LL.D., Accounting, Management Sciences

Forsyth, J. D., D.B.A.
Hamner, C., D.B.A.
Keller, T. F., PH.D.
Laughhunn, D. D., PH.D.
Lewin, A. Y., PH.D.
Morey, R. C., PH.D., Management Sciences
Peterson, D. W., PH.D., Management Sciences

*Chemistry:*
Arnett, E. M., PH.D.
Bonk, J., PH.D.
Chesnut, D. B., PH.D.
Jeffs, P. W., PH.D.
Krigbaum, W., PH.D.
Lochmuller, C. H., PH.D.
McPhail, A. T., PH.D.
Palmer, R. A., PH.D.
Poirier, J. C., PH.D.
Porter, N. A., PH.D.
Quin, L. D., PH.D.
Smith, P., PH.D.
Strobel, H. A., PH.D.
Wells, R. L., PH.D.
Wilder, P., Jr., PH.D.

*Classical Studies:*
Newton, F., PH.D., Latin
Oates, J. F., PH.D., Classical Studies
Richardson, L., PH.D., Latin
Willis, W. H., PH.D., Greek

*Community and Family Medicine:*
Estes, E. H., Jr., M.D.
Hammond, W. E., PH.D.
Heyden, S., M.D.
Salber, Eva J., M.D.
Woodbury, M. A., PH.D., Biomathematics, Computer Science

*Computer Science:*
Gallie, T. M., PH.D.
Loveland, D. W., PH.D.
Patrick, M. L., PH.D.
Starmer, C. F., PH.D.

*Divinity:*
Beach, W., B.D., PH.D., Christian Ethics
Farris, D. M., M.DIV., Theological Bibliography
Goodling, R. A., PH.D., Pastoral Psychology
Henry, S. C., PH.D., American Christianity
Herzog, F., TH.D., Systematic Theology
Ingram, O. K., B.D., Parish Ministry
Lacy, C., B.D., PH.D., World Christianity
Langford, T. A., B.D., PH.D., Systematic Theology
Murphy, R. E., S.T.D., Old Testament
Richey, M. S., B.D., PH.D., Theology and Christian Nurture
Smith, D. M., Jr., PH.D., New Testament Interpretation
Smith, H. L., Jr., PH.D., Moral Theology, Community Health Sciences
Steinmetz, D., TH.D., Church History and Doctrine
Westerhoff, J. H., ED.D., Religion and Education
Wilson, R. L., PH.D., Church and Society
Young, F. W., PH.D., New Testament and Patristic Studies

*Economics:*
Blackburn, J. O., PH.D.
Bronfenbrenner, M., PH.D.
Davies, D. G., PH.D.
Goodwin, C., PH.D.
Grabowski, H. G., PH.D.
Graham, D. A., PH.D.
Havrilesky, T. M., PH.D.
Kelley, A. C., PH.D.
Kreps, Juanita, PH.D.
Lewis, H. G., PH.D.
Naylor, T. H., PH.D.

Tower, E., PH.D.
Treml, V. G., PH.D.
Vernon, J. M., PH.D.
Wallace, T. D., PH.D.
Weintraub, E. R., PH.D.
Yohe, W. P., PH.D.

*Education:*
Cartwright, W., PH.D.
Gehman, W. S., PH.D.
Page, E. B., PH.D.

*Biomedical Engineering:*
Barr, R. C., PH.D.
Clark, H. G., III, PH.D.
Evans, E. A., PH.D.
Hochmuth, R. M., PH.D.
McElhaney, J. H., PH.D.
Pilkington, T., PH.D.
Thurstone, F. L., PH.D.

*Civil Engineering:*
Brown, E. I., II, PH.D.
Melosh, R. J., PH.D.
Muga, B. J., PH.D.
Utku, S., SC.D.
Vesic, A., D.SC.
Vesilind, P. A., PH.D.
Wilson, J. F., PH.D.

*Electrical Engineering:*
Artley, J. L., D.ENG.
Casey, H. C., Jr., PH.D.
Kerr, R. B., PH.D.
Marinos, P. N., PH.D.
Nolte, L. W., PH.D.
Owen, H. A., Jr., PH.D.
Wang, P. P., PH.D.
Wilson, T. G., SC.D.

*Mechanical Engineering:*
Chaddock, J. B., SC.D.
Cocks, F. H., PH.D.
Garg, D. P., PH.D.
Harman, C. M., PH.D.
Pearsall, G. W., SC.D.
Shepard, M. L., PH.D.

*English:*
Anderson, C. L., PH.D.
Budd, L. J., PH.D.
Cady, E. H., PH.D.
Duffey, B. I., PH.D.
Ferguson, O. W., PH.D.
Gleckner, R. F., PH.D.
Nygard, H. O., PH.D.
Price, R., B.LITT.
Randall, D. B. J., PH.D.
Reiss, E. A., PH.D.
Ryals, C. D. L., PH.D.
Smith, G. C., PH.D.
Williams, G. W., PH.D.
Williams, K. J., PH.D.

*Forestry and Environmental Studies:*
Barnes, R. L., PH.D., Forest Biochemistry
Jayne, B., PH.D.
Knoerr, K. R., PH.D., Forest Meteorology
Ralston, C., PH.D., Forest Soils
Stairs, G. R., PH.D., Forestry and Environmental Studies
Stambaugh, W., PH.D., Forest Pathology

*Geology:*
Heron, S., Jr., PH.D.
Perkins, R., PH.D.
Pilkey, O. H., PH.D.

*Health Administration:*
Jaeger, B. J., PH.D.
Warren, D. G., J.D.

*Health, Physical Education and Recreation:*
Buehler, A., M.A.
Falcone, C. M., M.A.
Friedrich, J. A., PH.D.

*History:*
Cahow, C., PH.D.
Chafe, W. H., PH.D.

Colton, J. G., PH.D.
Davis, C. D., PH.D.
Durden, R. F., PH.D.
Ferguson, A. B., PH.D.
Holley, I. B., PH.D.
Hollyday, F., PH.D.
Lerner, W., PH.D.
Maier, C. S., PH.D.,
Mauskopf, S., PH.D.
Richards, J. F., PH.D.
Scott, Anne Firor, PH.D.
Scott, W. E., PH.D.
Tepaske, J. J., PH.D.
Watson, R. L., Jr., PH.D.
Witt, R. G., PH.D.
Young, C. R., PH.D.

*Germanic Languages:*
Phelps, L. R., PH.D.

*Romance Languages:*
Cordle, T. H., PH.D.
Fein, J. M., PH.D.
Osuna, R., PH.D.
Stewart, P., PH.D.
Tetel, M., PH.D.
Wardropper, B., PH.D.

*Slavic Languages:*
Krynski, M. J., PH.D.

*Law:*
Carrington, P. D., LL.B.
Christie, G. C., S.J.D.
Cox, J. D., J.D.
Dellinger, W. E., III, LL.B.
Everett, R. O., LL.M.
Fleishman, J. L., LL.M.
Havighurst, C. C., J.D.
Horowitz, D. L., PH.D.
Lange, D. L., LL.B.
Paschal, J. F., LL.B., PH.D.
Pye, A. K., LL.M.
Reppy, W. A., J.D.
Robertson, H. B., J.D.
Rowe, T. D., Jr., J.D.
Shimm, M. G., LL.B.
Sparks, B. M., S.J.D.
Van Alstyne, W. W., LL.B.
Weistart, J. C., J.D.

*Mathematics:*
Allard, W. K., PH.D.
Reed, M. C., PH.D.
Schaefer, D. G., PH.D.
Shoenfield, J. R., PH.D.
Warner, S. L., PH.D.
Weisfeld, M., PH.D.

*Medicine and Neurology:*
Behar, V. S., M.D.
Buckley, C. E., III, M.D.
Callaway, J. L., M.D.
Clapp, J. R., M.D.
Cohen, H. J., M.D.
Davis, J. N., M.D.
Floyd, W. L., M.D.
Gallagher, J. J., M.D.
Goldsmith, L., M.D.
Greenfield, J. C., Jr., M.D.
Gunnells, J. C., M.D.
Heyman, A., M.D.
Kong, Y. H., M.D.
Kredich, M. M., M.D.
Kylstra, J., M.D., PH.D.
Laszlo, J., M.D.
Lazarus, G. S., M.D.
Lebovitz, H. E., M.D.
Lefkowitz, R. J., M.D.
Lynn, W. S., Jr., M.D.
McKee, P. A., M.D.
McPherson, H. T., M.D.
Morris, J. J., Jr., M.D.
Peter, R. H., M.D.
Pfeiffer, J. B., M.D.
Pinnell, S. R., M.D.
Roses, A. D., M.D.
Rosse, W. F., M.D.

# UNIVERSITIES AND COLLEGES—NORTH CAROLINA — U.S.A.

Rundles, W., M.D., PH.D.
Saltzman, H. A., M.D.
Sieker, H. O., M.D.
Silberman, H. R., M.D.
Snyderman, R., M.D.
Sokal, J. E., M.D.
Tyor, M. P., M.D.
Wallace, A. G., M.D.
Whalen, R. E., M.D.
Wyngaarden, J. B., M.D.

*Microbiology and Immunology:*
Amos, D. E., M.D., Immunology and Experimental Medicine
Burns, R. O., PH.D., Microbiology
Day, E. D., PH.D., Immunology, Experimental Surgery
Joklik, W. K., PH.D., Microbiology and Immunology
Metzgar, R. S., PH.D., Immunology
Osterhout, S., M.D., PH.D., Microbiology, Medicine
Scott, D. W., PH.D.
Smith, R. E., PH.D.
Vanaman, T. C., PH.D.
Ward, F. E., PH.D.
Wheat, R. W., PH.D., Microbiology
Willett, Hilda P., PH.D., Bacteriology

*Music:*
Bone, A. H., M.M.
Bryan, P. R., PH.D.
Douglass, F., M.MUS.
Hanks, J. K., M.A.
Kirkendale, W., DR.PHIL.
Withers, L. R., M.S.

*Naval Science:*
Peek, R. E., M.S.

*Nursing:*
Gratz, Pauline, ED.D.
Hall, Joanne, M.S.N.
Minniear, Wilma A., M.S.N.
Wilson, Ruby L., ED.D.

*Obstetrics and Gynaecology:*
Christakos, A., M.D.
Creaseman, W. T., M.D.
Gall, S. A., M.D.
Hammond, C. B., M.D.
Parker, R. T., M.D.
Peete, C., Jr., M.D.

*Ophthalmology:*
Anderson, W. B., M.D.
Landers, M. B., M.D.
Machemer, R. E., M.D.
Wadsworth, J. A. C., M.D.
Wolbarsht, M. L., PH.D.

*Pathology:*
Bigner, D. D., M.D., PH.D.
Bossen, E. H., M.D.
Fetter, B. F., M.D.
Hackel, D. B., M.D.
Jennings, R., M.D.
Johnston, W. W., M.D.
Klintworth, G., M.B., PH.D.
Koepke, J. A., M.D.
Pratt, P. C., M.D.
Schneider, K., M.D.
Sommer, J. R., M.D.
Vogel, F. S., M.D.
Wittels, B., M.D.

*Paediatrics:*
Buckley, Rebecca H., M.D.
Frothingham, T. E., M.D.
Katz, S. L., M.D.
Sidbury, J. B., Jr., M.D.
Spach, M. S., M.D.
Spock, A., M.D.
Wilfert, Catherine, M.D.

*Pharmacology:*
Kirshner, N., PH.D.
Lack, L., PH.D.

Menzel, D. B., PH.D.
Ottolenghi, A., M.D.
Schanberg, S. M., M.D., PH.D.
Shand, D. G., M.B., PH.D.
Slotkin, T. A., PH.D.

*Philosophy:*
Golding, M. P., PH.D.
Mahoney, E. P., PH.D.
Peach, W. B., PH.D.
Sanford, D. H., PH.D.

*Physical Therapy:*
Bartlett, R. C., M.A.

*Physics:*
Biedenharn, L. C., Jr., PH.D.
Bilpuch, E. G., PH.D.
Cusson, R. Y., PH.D.
Evans, L., PH.D.
Fairbank, H., PH.D.
Han, M. Y., PH.D.
Lewis, H. W., PH.D.
Meyer, H., PH.D.
Roberson, N., Jr., PH.D.
Robinson, H., PH.D.
Walker, W. D., PH.D.
Walter, R. L., PH.D.

*Physiology:*
Blum, J. J., PH.D.
Gutnecht, J. W., PH.D.
Jobsis, F. F., PH.D.
Johnson, E. A., M.D.
Lauf, P. K., M.D.
Lieberman, M., PH.D.
Moore, J. W., PH.D.
Reynolds, S. J., PH.D.
Salzano, J. V., PH.D.
Somjen, G. G., M.D.
Tanford, C., PH.D.

*Political Science:*
Barber, J. D., PH.D.
Braibanti, R., PH.D.
Cleaveland, F. N., PH.D.
Fish, P. G., PH.D.
Hall, H. M., Jr., PH.D.
Hallowell, J., PH.D., LITT.D.
Holsti, O. R., PH.D.
Hough, J. F., PH.D.
Kornberg, A., PH.D.
Leach, R. H., PH.D.
Rogowski, R. L., PH.D.

*Psychiatry and Medical Psychology:*
Brodie, H. K. H., M.D., Psychiatry
Busse, E. W., M.D., Psychiatry
Cavenar, J. O., M.D.
Clifford, E., PH.D., Medical Psychology
Crovitz, H. F., PH.D., Medical Psychology
Ellinwood, E. H., M.D., Psychiatry
Fowler, J. A., M.D., Psychiatry
Gianturco, D. T., M.D., Psychiatry
Green, R. L., Jr., M.D., Psychiatry
Hine, F., M.D., Psychiatry
Melges, F., M.D.
Palmore, E. B., PH.D., Medical Sociology
Parker, J. B., Jr., M.D., Psychiatry
Rhoads, J. M., M.D., Psychiatry
Verwoerdt, A., M.D., Psychiatry
Wang, H., M.B., Psychiatry
Werman, D. S., M.D., Psychiatry
Williams, R. B., M.D.
Wilson, W. P., M.D., Psychiatry
Zung, W. W., M.D., Psychiatry

*Psychology:*
Alexander, I., PH.D.
Bevan, W., PH.D.
Borstelmann, L., PH.D.
Carson, R. C., PH.D.
Costanzo, P. R., M.D.
Diamond, I. T., PH.D.
Erickson, C., PH.D.
Erickson, R. P., PH.D.

Guttman, N., PH.D.
Kimble, G. A., PH.D.
Lakin, M., PH.D.
Lockhead, G., PH.D.
Schiffman, H., PH.D.
Staddon, J., PH.D.
Wallach, M. A., PH.D.
Wing, C. W., Jr., PH.D.

*Public Policy Studies:*
Blaydon, C. C., PH.D.

*Radiology:*
Baylin, G. J., M.D.
Chen, J. T. T., M.D.
Coleman, R. E., M.D.
Grossman, H., M.D.
Heinz, E. R., M.D.
Korobkin, M., M.D.
O'Foghludha, F., PH.D.
Putman, C. E., M.D.
Rice, R. P., M.D.
Sanders, A. P., PH.D.

*Religion:*
Bradley, D. G., PH.D.
Jones, B. L., PH.D.
Kort, W., PH.D.
Lawrence, B. B., PH.D.
Lincoln, C. E., PH.D.
Long, C. H., PH.D.
Meyers, E. M., PH.D.
Osborn, R. T., PH.D.
Poteat, W. H., B.D., PH.D.
Price, J. L., Jr., PH.D.
Wintermute, O. S., PH.D.

*Sociology:*
Back, K. W., PH.D.
Kerckhoff, A. C., PH.D.
Maddox, G. L., PH.D.
McKinney, J. C., PH.D.
Myers, G. C., PH.D.
Preiss, J., PH.D.
Smith, J., PH.D.
Tiryakian, E. A., PH.D.

*Surgery:*
Anderson, E. E., M.D., Urology
Anlyan, W. G., M.D., Surgery
Bassett, F. H., III, M.D., Orthopaedics
Bolognesi, D. P., PH.D.
Clippinger, F. W., M.D., Orthopaedic Surgery
Fuchs, J. C. A., M.D.
Georgiade, N., D.D.S., M.D., Plastic, Maxillofacial and Oral Surgery
Goldner, J. L., M.D., Orthopaedic Surgery
Hudson, W. R., M.D., Otolaryngology
Jones, R. S., M.D.
Kunze, L. H., PH.D., Hearing and Speech Pathology
McCollum, D. E., M.D., Orthopaedic Surgery
Moylan, J. A., M.D.
Nashold, B. S., M.D., Neurosurgery
Oldham, H. N., Jr., M.D.
Paulson, D. F., M.D.
Peete, W. P., M.D., Surgery
Postlethwait, R., M.D., Surgery
Quinn, G. W., D.D.S., Orthodontics
Sabiston, D. C., M.D., Surgery
Sealy, W. C., M.D., Thoracic Surgery
Seigler, H. F., M.D.
Shingleton, W. W., M.D., Surgery
Stickel, D. L., M.D., Surgery
Urbaniak, J. R., M.D.
Wechsler, A. S., M.D.
Wells, S. A., M.D.
Wilkins, R. H., M.D.
Wolfe, W. G., M.D.
Young, W. G., Jr., Surgery

*Zoology:*
Bailey, J. R., PH.D.
Barber, R. T., PH.D.

Costlow, J. D., PH.D.
Fluke, D. J., PH.D.
Gillham, N. W., PH.D.
Gregg, J. R., PH.D.
Klopfer, P. H., PH.D.
Livingstone, D., PH.D.
Nicklas, R. B., PH.D.
Schmidt-Nielsen, K., PH.D.
Tucker, V. A., PH.D.
Vogel, S., PH.D.
Wainwright, S. A., PH.D.
Ward, C. L., PH.D.
Wilbur, K. M., PH.D.

### EAST CAROLINA UNIVERSITY
GREENVILLE,
NORTH CAROLINA 27834

Telephone: 757-6131.

Founded 1907. Linked to the University of North Carolina.

Chancellor: Thomas B. Brewer.
Registrar: J. Gilbert Moore.
Dean of Admissions: Walter M. Bortz.
Librarian: Eugene Brunelle.

The library contains 800,000 volumes.
Number of teachers: 800.
Number of students: 13,000.

### ELIZABETH CITY STATE UNIVERSITY
ELIZABETH CITY,
NORTH CAROLINA 27909

Telephone: (919) 335-0551.

Founded 1891. Linked to the University of North Carolina.

Chancellor: Marion D. Thorpe, PH.D.
Registrar: Tommy M. Foust, M.S.
Librarian: Claude W. Green, M.L.S.

The library contains 83,960 vols.
Number of teachers: 117 full-time, 17 part-time.
Number of students: 1,620.

### ELON COLLEGE
NORTH CAROLINA 27244

Telephone: (919) 584-9711.

Founded 1889.

Related to the United Church of Christ.
President: James Fred Young.
Vice-President for Academic and Student Affairs: James A. Moncure.
Dean of Academic Affairs: M. Christopher White.
Librarian: Charles B. Lowry.

The library contains 150,000 vols.
Number of teachers: 99 full-time, 37 part-time.
Number of students: 2,501.

### FAYETTEVILLE STATE UNIVERSITY
NEWBOLD STATION,
FAYETTEVILLE,
NORTH CAROLINA 28301

Telephone: 486-1141.

Founded 1867 as College, attained University status 1969. Part of University of North Carolina System.

Chancellor: Dr. Charles A. Lyons, Jr.
Registrar: Frank Barreca.
Librarian: Richard Griffin.

Library of 134,014 vols.
Number of teachers: 148.
Number of students: 2,465.

### GREENSBORO COLLEGE
COLLEGE BOX 971,
GREENSBORO,
NORTH CAROLINA 27420

Telephone: (919) 272-7102.

Founded 1838.

President: James S. Barrett.
Academic Dean: Y. L. Medlin.
Director of Admissions: James M. Tucker, Jr.
Librarian: Michael LaCroix.

The library contains 75,000 vols.
Number of teachers: 60.
Number of students: 650.

### GUILFORD COLLEGE
GREENSBORO,
NORTH CAROLINA 27410

Telephone: Greensboro 292-5511.

Founded 1837.

President: William R. Rogers.
Provost: B. Stewart.
Dean: S. Schuman.
Library Director: H. Poole.

The library contains 189,645 vols.
Number of teachers: 84.
Number of students: 1,675.
Publication: *Journal of Undergraduate Mathematics*†.

### HIGH POINT COLLEGE
HIGH POINT,
NORTH CAROLINA 27262

Telephone: (919) 885-5101.

Founded 1924.

President: Dr. Wendell M. Patton.
Dean: Dr. D. W. Cole.
Registrar: David H. Holt.
Director of Admissions: Alfred S. Hassell.
Librarian: Larry B. Keesee.

Library of 102,624 vols.
Number of teachers: 61.
Number of students: 1,037.

### JOHNSON C. SMITH UNIVERSITY
100–152 BEATTIES FORD RD.,
CHARLOTTE,
NORTH CAROLINA 28216

Founded 1867.

President: Wilbert Greenfield, PH.D.
Vice-President for Academic Affairs: Limone C. Collins, PH.D.
Vice-President for Business and Financial Affairs: Mack L. Davidson.
Vice-President for Student Affairs: Joseph A. Gaston, PH.D.
Vice-President for Development: Ray Davis.
Director of Admissions: Moses Jones.
Director of Development: Ray Davis.
Registrar: Mary H. Byuarm.
Librarian: Shirley P. Wilkins (acting).

The library contains 95,000 vols.
Number of teachers: 78, including 15 professors.
Number of students: 1,446.

### LENOIR-RHYNE COLLEGE
HICKORY,
NORTH CAROLINA 28601

Telephone: (704) 328-1741.

Founded 1891.

President: Albert B. Anderson, PH.D.
Academic Dean: Arthur E. Puotinen, PH.D.
Dean of Students: C. Lee Dubs, PH.D.
Admissions Director: R. P. Thompson.

Library of 100,000 vols.
Number of teachers: 92.
Number of students: 1,325.

### LIVINGSTONE COLLEGE
SALISBURY,
NORTH CAROLINA 28144

Telephone: (704) 633-7960.

Founded 1879.

President: D. F. George Shipman.
Registrar/Director of Admissions: Mrs. Emily H. Harper.
Librarian: Louise M. Rountree.

The library contains 76,504 vols.
Number of teachers: 59.
Number of students: 909.

### MEREDITH COLLEGE
RALEIGH,
NORTH CAROLINA 27611

Telephone: 833-6461.

Founded 1891.

President: John E. Weems.
Registrar: C. A. Davis.
Dean: C. A. Burris.
Director of Admissions: Mary B. Josey.
Librarian: Jonathan L. Lindsey.

Library of 94,000 vols.
Number of teachers: 80.
Number of students: 1,550.

### METHODIST COLLEGE
FAYETTEVILLE,
NORTH CAROLINA 28301

Chartered 1956; Opened 1960.

President: Dr. Richard W. Pearce.

*Dean:* Dr. Fred Clark.
*Business Manager:* Roy Whitmire.
*Secretary to the Board of Trustees:* R. Dillard Teer.

The library contains 63,386 vols.
Number of students: 802 full-time, 74 part-time.

### NORTH CAROLINA AGRICULTURAL AND TECHNICAL STATE UNIVERSITY
312 NORTH DUDLEY ST.,
GREENSBORO,
NORTH CAROLINA 27411
Telephone: (919) 379-7500.

Founded 1891. Linked to the University of North Carolina.

*Chancellor:* Dr. Cleon Thompson (acting).
*Registrar:* Dr. Rudolh Artis.
*Librarian:* Dr. Myrtle Bennett.

The library contains 294,484 vols.
Number of teachers: 342.
Number of students: 5,467.

### NORTH CAROLINA CENTRAL UNIVERSITY
DURHAM,
NORTH CAROLINA 27707
Telephone: 682-2171.

Founded 1910. Linked to the University of North Carolina.

State control.

*Chancellor:* Dr. Albert N. Whiting.
*Vice-Chancellor for Financial Affairs:* G. Thorne.
*Vice-Chancellor for Academic Affairs:* Dr. Cecil L. Patterson.
*Registrar:* B. T. McMillon.
*Librarian:* Pennie E. Perry.

Library of 532,134 vols.
Number of teachers: 328.
Number of students: 4,810.

Publications: *Varia, Ex Umbra, Bulletins.*

DEANS:

*Undergraduate School:* Dr. Walter H. Pattillo.
*Graduate School:* Dr. Mary M. Townes.
*Library School:* Dr. Annette L. Phinazee.
*Law School:* Charles E. Daye.
*School of Business:* Dr. Tyronza Richmond.

### NORTH CAROLINA WESLEYAN COLLEGE
WESLEYAN COLLEGE STATION,
ROCKY MOUNT,
NORTH CAROLINA 27801
Telephone: (919) 442-7121.

Founded 1956; co-educational, church-related liberal arts college.

*President:* Dr. S. Bruce Petteway.
*Dean:* Dr. F. H. G. Holck.

The library contains 60,000 vols.
Number of teachers: 48.
Number of students: 850.

Publication: *Bulletin* (six times yearly).

### PEMBROKE STATE UNIVERSITY
PEMBROKE,
NORTH CAROLINA 28372
Telephone: (919) 521-4214.

Founded 1887 as College, attained University status 1969. Part of the University of North Carolina System.

*Chancellor:* Dr. Paul R. Givens.
*Vice-Chancellor:* Dr. Leon Rand.
*Vice-Chancellor for Student Affairs:* Dr. James B. Chavis.
*Director of Graduate Studies:* W. Howard Dean.
*Registrar:* Mrs. Joyce S. Singletary.
*Dean of Admissions:* Dr. Norma J. Thompson.
*Vice-Chancellor for Business:* William S. Mason, Jr.
*Librarian:* Dr. Robert Hersch.

The library contains 155,000 vols.
Number of teachers: 119.
Number of students: 2,158.

### PFEIFFER COLLEGE
MISENHEIMER,
NORTH CAROLINA 28109
Telephone: (704) 463-7343.

Founded 1885.

Private (Methodist) control.

*President:* Dr. Cameron West.
*Registrar:* K. D. Holshouser.
*Dean of the College:* Dr. Daniel N. Moury.
*Librarian:* N. B. Wilson.

Library of 98,314 vols.
Number of teachers: 56.
Number of students: 800.

### QUEENS COLLEGE
1900 SELWYN AVE.,
CHARLOTTE,
NORTH CAROLINA 28274
Telephone: (704) 332-7121.

Founded 1857; liberal arts college for women.

*President:* Dr. Billy O. Wireman.
*Vice-President for Academic Affairs and Dean of College:* Dr. Cynthia H. Tyson.
*Dean of Students:* Sidney Kerr.
*Vice-President for Development and College Relations:* Alan W. Lee.
*Admissions Director:* Miss Gene Burton.
*Vice-President for Finance and Planning:* Dennis W. Frodsham.

*Librarian:* Stewart Lillard.

Library of 100,219 vols.
Number of teachers: 55.
Number of students: 600.

Publications: *Queens College Bulletin* (quarterly), *Queens College Close Up.*

### ST. ANDREWS PRESBYTERIAN COLLEGE
LAURINBURG,
NORTH CAROLINA 28352
Telephone: (919) 276-3652.

Founded 1858.

Private control; Academic year: September to June.

*President:* Alvin Perkinson.
*Vice-President for Development:* J. Bruce Frye.
*Registrar:* Dr. James F. Stephens.
*Dean of the College:* Dr. Ronald C. Crossley.
*Librarian:* Elizabeth Holmes.

The library contains 91,000 vols.
Number of teachers: 51.
Number of students: 568.

Publication: *St. Andrew's Review* (twice a year).

### SALEM ACADEMY AND COLLEGE
BOX 10548, SALEM STATION,
WINSTON-SALEM,
NORTH CAROLINA 27108
Telephone: 721-2600.

Founded 1772.

Private control.

*President:* Dr. Richard L. Morrill.
*Director of Admissions:* Jeannie Dorsey (acting).
*Academic Dean:* Dr. Patricia Sullivan.
*Dean, School of Music:* Clemens Sandresky.
*Librarian:* Rose Simon.

Library of 107,992 vols.
Number of teachers: 70.
Number of students: 570.

### SHAW UNIVERSITY
RALEIGH,
NORTH CAROLINA 27611
Telephone: (919) 755-4800.

Founded 1865.

*President:* Stanley H. Smith.
*Vice-President of Academic Affairs and Research:* Wilmoth A. Williams.
*Registrar:* Rudolph A. Williams.
*Librarian:* Mildred H. Mallette.

Library of 82,554 vols.
Number of teachers: 58.
Number of students: 1,400.

# UNITED STATES OF AMERICA

## UNIVERSITY OF NORTH CAROLINA
CHAPEL HILL,
NORTH CAROLINA 27514
Telephone: 933-6981.

*President:* WILLIAM C. FRIDAY, B.S., LL.D., D.C.L.
*Vice-President—Academic Affairs:* RAYMOND H. DAWSON, M.A., PH.D.
*Vice-President—Finance:* L. FELIX JOYNER, A.B.
*Vice-President—Planning:* ROY C. CARROLL, PH.D.
*Vice-President—Student Services and Special Programs:* CLEON F. THOMPSON, Jr., M.S., PH.D.
*Vice-President—Research:* E. WALTON JONES, PH.D.

The University of North Carolina is a multi-campus university composed of sixteen institutions: the University of North Carolina at Asheville, the University of North Carolina at Chapel Hill, the University of North Carolina at Greenboro, the University of North Carolina at Charlotte, the University of North Carolina at Wilmington, and North Carolina State University at Raleigh. Also the Appalachian State University, East Carolina University, Elizabeth City State University, Fayetteville State University, North Carolina Agricultural and Technical State University, North Carolina Central University, North Carolina School of the Arts, Pembroke State University, Western Carolina University, Winston-Salem State University (*q.v.*).

## University of North Carolina at Asheville:
University Heights, Asheville, North Carolina 28814; established as Buncombe County Junior College 1927; later as Asheville-Biltmore College; made a unit of the University in 1969; Telephone: 704-258-6600.

*Chancellor:* WILLIAM E. HIGHSMITH, M.A., PH.D.
*Vice-Chancellor for Academic Affairs:* LAURENCE A. DORR, PH.D.
*Vice-Chancellor for Finance:* W. H. POTT, B.A., C.P.A.
*Vice-Chancellor for Student Affairs:* ERIC IOVACCHINI, PH.D.
*Director of Admissions:* JAMES C. BLACKBURN, ED.D.
*Registrar:* Mrs. JO D. CADLE, B.A.
*Librarian:* M. E. BLOWERS, M.A., M.S. IN L.S.

Number of teachers: 83.
Number of students: 2,100.
Publication: *Images*.

PROFESSORS AND CHAIRMEN OF DEPARTMENTS:

BERGEMANN, V. E., Education
BOLAND, W. R., Sociology
BROWNING, S., Economics
COLE, R., Physics
COOKE, S. T., Art and Music
COOPER, G. L., Classics
DAUGHTON, R., Physical Education
GILLUM, M., Humanities
GULLICKSON, C. D., Foreign Languages
HOWARD, D., Philosophy
JOHNSTON, H. H., Biology
KRONUS, S. J., Sociology
LANG, W. W., Computer Science
PERRY, J., Biology
RACKHAM, J., Literature
RAINEY, G. E., Political Science
READY, M., History
REMINGTON, L. D., Chemistry
RUIZ, M., Physics
SEITZ, T. L., Psychology
SHORB, E., Literature
SQUIBB, S. D., Chemistry
STOUGHTON, J., Mathematics
STERN, H. R., Foreign Languages
STEVENS, J. G., Chemistry
THURMAN, W. S., Classics
WALKER, P. A., History
WENGROW, A. K., Drama
WILLIAMS, R., Management

## University of North Carolina at Chapel Hill:
Chapel Hill, N.C. 27514; Chartered 1789, opened 1795; since 1931 a unit of the University of North Carolina; Telephone (919) 962-2211. Academic year: August to May.

*Chancellor:* CHRISTOPHER C. FORDHAM III, M.D.
*Provost:* J. C. MORROW, PH.D.
*Vice-Chancellor, Business and Finance:* JOHN L. TEMPLE.
*Vice-Chancellor, University Relations:* ROLLIE TILLMAN, Jr., D.B.A.
*Vice-Chancellor, Student Affairs:* DONALD A. BOULTON, ED.D.
*Vice-Chancellor, Graduate School:* G. PHILLIP MANIRE, PH.D.
*Vice-Chancellor, University Affairs:* HAROLD D. WALLACE, M.DIV.
*Registrar and Director of Institutional Research:* LILLIAN Y. LEHMAN, PH.D.
*Secretary of the Faculty:* H. C. BOREN PH.D.
*Director of Undergraduate Admissions:* RICHARD G. CASHWELL.
*University Librarian:* JAMES F. GOVAN, PH.D.

Library: see Libraries.

Number of teachers: 1,887.
Number of students: 21,465.

Publications: *Chapel Hill Workshop Reports* (3 a year), *The High School Journal* (monthly, except summer), *Hispanófila* (3 a year), *UNC Newsletter* (irregular), *Popular Government* (quarterly), *Romance Notes* (3 a year), *Social Forces* (quarterly), *Southern Economic Journal* (quarterly), *Studies in Philology* (5 a year).

### DEANS:
*College of Arts and Sciences and General College:* SAMUEL R. WILLIAMSON, Jr., PH.D.
*School of Business Administration:* JOHN P. EVANS, PH.D.
*School of Education:* WILLIAM C. SELF, ED.D.
*School of Law:* KENNETH S. BROUN, J.D.
*School of Medicine:* STUART BONDURANT, M.D.
*School of Pharmacy:* TOM S. MIYA, PH.D.
*School of Public Health:* BERNARD G. GREENBERG, PH.D.
*School of Library Science:* EDWARD G. HOLLEY, PH.D.
*School of Dentistry:* BEN D. BARKER, D.D.S.
*School of Journalism:* RICHARD C. COLE, PH.D.
*School of Nursing:* LAUREL A. COPP, PH.D.
*School of Social Work:* JOHN B. TURNER, D.S.W.
*Research Administration:* G. R. HOLCOMB, PH.D.

### PROFESSORS:
*Allied Medical Programs:*
MITCHELL, M. M., PH.D.
MITCHELL, R. U., PH.D.
PETERS, R. W., PH.D.
SINGLETON, M. C., PH.D.

*Anaesthesiology:*
BROWN, D. R., M.D.
KLEIN, E. F., Jr., M.D.
LEVIN, K. J., M.D.
MUELLER, R. A., PH.D.
SUGIOKA, K., M.D.

*Anatomy:*
BENNETT, H. S., M.D.
HACKENBROCK, C. R., PH.D.
HENSON, O. W., Jr., PH.D.
HOOKER, C. W., PH.D.
KOCH, W. E., PH.D.
MACRAE, E. K., PH.D.
POLLITZER, W. S., PH.D.
STUMPF, W. E., PH.D.

*Anthropology:*
BROCKINGTON, D. L., PH.D.
COE, J. L., M.A.
CRANE, J. G., PH.D.
GULICK, J., PH.D.
HOLCOMB, G. R., PH.D.
PEACOCK, J. L., III, PH.D.
YARNELL, R. A., PH.D.

*Art:*
BARNARD, R. J., M.A.
FOLDA, J. T., III, PH.D.
HOWARD, R. A., M.A.
HUEMER, F., PH.D.
JUDSON, J. R., PH.D.
KINNAIRD, R. W., M.F.A.
PLAGENS, P. L., M.F.A.
SALTZMAN, M., M.F.A.

*Bacteriology:*
BOTT, K. F., PH.D.
CROMARTIE, W. J., M.D
EDGELL, M. H., PH.D.
GOODER, H., PH.D.
HAUGHTON, G., PH.D.
HUTCHINSON, C. A., III, PH.D.
MANIRE, G. P., PH.D.
SCHWAB, J. H., PH.D.
SPARLING, P. F., M.D.

*Biochemistry:*
BERKUT, M. K., PH.D.
CAPLOW, M., PH.D.
GLASSMAN, E. B., PH.D.
HERMANS, J., PH.D.
IRVIN, J. L., PH.D.
JONES, M. E., PH.D.
MORELL, P., PH.D.
PENNIALL, R., PH.D.
SUMMER, G. K., M.D.
WHITE, J. R., PH.D.
WILSON, J. E., PH.D.
WOLFENDEN, R. V., PH.D.

*Biostatistics:*
ABERNATHY, J. R., PH.D.
COULTER, E. J., PH.D.
GRIZZLE, J. E., PH.D.

# UNIVERSITIES AND COLLEGES—NORTH CAROLINA (UNIVERSITY OF) U.S.A.

JOHNSON, R. C., PH.D.
KOCH, G. G., PH.D.
QUADE, D. E., PH.D.
SEN, P. K., PH.D.
SCHACHTMAN, R. H., PH.D.

Botany:
BARRY, E. G., PH.D.
BELL, C. R., PH.D.
BROWN, R. M., Jr., PH.D.
DOMNAS, A. J., PH.D.
HOMMERSAND, M. H., PH.D.
KOCH, W. J., PH.D.
OLIVE, L. S., PH.D.
RADFORD, A. E., PH.D.
SCOTT, T. K., PH.D.

Business Administration:
ADAMS, J. S., PH.D.
BEHRMAN, J. N., PH.D.
BELL, G. B., PH.D.
BRUMMET, R. L., PH.D.
CARLETON, W. T., PH.D.
DEARBORN, D. C., D.S.
EVANS, J. P., PH.D.
HEADEN, R. S., D.B.A.
HUGHES, G. D., PH.D.
JERDEE, T. H., PH.D.
LANGENDERFER, H. Q., D.B.A.
LEE, J. F., Jr., PH.D.
LEE, M. W., PH.D.
LEVIN, R. I., PH.D.
LITTLEFIELD, J. E., PH.D.
MCENALLY, R. W., PH.D.
MCLAUGHLIN, C. P., D.B.A.
PRINGLE, J. J., PH.D.
REYNOLDS, I, N., PH.D.
ROSEN, B., PH.D.
RUBIN, D., PH.D.
RUSS, F. A., PH.D.
STEWART, W. S., J.D.
TERRELL, J. H., PH.D.
TILLMAN, R., D.B.A.
WAGNER, H. M., PH.D.

Chemistry:
BAER, T., PH.D.
BROOKHART, M. S., PH.D.
BUCK, R. P., PH.D.
BURSEY, M. M., PH.D.
COKE, J. L., PH.D.
COLLIER, F. N., Jr., PH.D.
DEARMAN, H. H., PH.D.
ELIEL, E. L., PH.D.
HARRISON, J. H., IV, PH.D.
HATFIELD, W. E., PH.D.
HISKEY, R. G., PH.D.
HODGSON, D. J., PH.D.
ISENHOUR, T. L., PH.D.
JARNAGIN, R. C., PH.D.
JOHNSON, C. S., Jr., PH.D.
KROPP, P. J., PH.D.
LITTLE, W. F., PH.D.
MCKEE, R. L., PH.D.
MEYER, T. J., PH.D.
MORROW, J. C., III, PH.D.
MURRAY, R. W., PH.D.
PARR, R. G., PH.D.
PEDERSEN, L. G., PH.D.
REILLY, C. N., PH.D.
WHITTEN, D. G., PH.D.

Child Development Center:
GALLAGHER, J. J., PH.D.

City and Regional Planning:
GODSCHALK, D. R., PH.D.
KAISER, E. J., PH.D.
MOREAU, D. H., PH.D.
MORONEY, R. M., PH.D.
STEGMAN, M. A., PH.D.
WEISS, S. F., PH.D.

Classics:
BROWN, E. L., PH.D.
KENNEDY, G. A., PH.D.
LINDERSKI, J., PH.D.
RECKFORD, K. J., PH.D.
STADTER, P. A., PH.D.

Computer Science:
BROOKS, F. P., Jr., PH.D.
CALINGAERT, P., PH.D.
PARNAS, D. L., PH.D.

Curriculum, Humanities:
FALK, E. H., PH.D., Comparative Literature

Curriculum, Natural Sciences:
FISHMAN, G. S., PH.D., Operations Research and Systems Analysis
FRANKENBERG, D., PH.D., Marine Sciences
NEUMANN, A. C., PH.D., Marine Sciences
TOLLE, J. W., PH.D., Operations Research and Systems Analysis

Curriculum, Social Sciences:
PALMER, C. A., PH.D.
SESSOMS, H. D., PH.D., Recreation Administration
STEIN, T. A., PH.D., Recreation Administration

Dentistry:
BAKER, R. D., D.D.S.
BARTON, R. E., D.D.S.
BAWDEN, J. W., PH.D.
BURKES, E. J., D.D.S.
CRANDELL, C. E., D.D.S.
CRAWFORD, J. J., PH.D.
CRENSHAW, M. A., PH.D.
DOBSON, D. P., D.D.S.
FORBES, E. A., B.S.
GREGG, J. M., PH.D.
HANKER, J. S., PH.D.
HERSHEY, H. G., Jr., D.D.S.
HOWELL, R. M., M.S.D.
HUTCHENS, L. H., Jr., D.D.S.
JOHNSTON, M. C., PH.D.
LEINFELDER, K. F., M.S.
LINDAHL, R. L., M.S.
LUNDBLAD, R. L., PH.D.
LUPTON, C., D.D.S.
MCCRACKEN, F. W., III, D.D.S.
MCFALL, W. T., Jr., D.D.S.
MACHEN, J. B., PH.D.
MARKS, S. C., M.S.
MECHANIC, G. L., PH.D.
MURRAY, H. V., Jr., D.D.S.
OLDENBURG, T. R., M.S.
PROFFIT, W. R., D.D.S.
SHANKLE, R. J., D.D.S.
SILVERMAN, M. S., PH.D.
SLUDER, T. B., D.D.S.
SMALL, E. W., D.D.S.
SOCKWELL, C. L., D.D.S.
STRICKLAND, W. D., D.D.S.
TAYLOR, D. F., PH.D.
TERRY, B. C., D.D.S.
TURNER, D. T., PH.D.
VIG, P. S., PH.D.
WARREN, D. W., PH.D.
WEBSTER, W. P., M.S.
WHITE, R. P., Jr., PH.D.
WOOD, M. T., M.S.

Dermatology:
BRIGGAMAN, R. A., M.D.
WHEELER, C. E., Jr., M.D.

Dramatic Art:
GRAVES, R. B., Jr., PH.D.
HOUSMAN, A. L., PH.D.
REZZUTO, T. A., M.A.

Economics:
BENAVIE, A., PH.D.
GALLMAN, R. E., PH.D.
INGRAM, J. C., PH.D.
KORTANEK, K. O., PH.D.
LOVELL, C. K., PH.D.
MCFARLAND, D., PH.D.
MOUZON, O. T., PH.D.
MURPHY, J. L., PH.D.
PFOUTS, R. W., PH.D.
SMITH, U. K., PH.D.

TARASCIO, V. J., PH.D.
WAUD, R. N., PH.D.

Education:
BALLEW, J. H., PH.D.
BROWN, D., PH.D.
COOP, R. H., D.ED.
DAY, B. D., PH.D.
HENNIS, R. S., PH.D.
HOLTON, S. M., PH.D.
LILLIE, D. L., D.ED.
MORRISON, J. L., PH.D.
PALMER, W., PH.D.
PAUL, J. L., D.ED.
PHILLIPS, R. C., PH.D.
SCHLECHTY, P. C., PH.D.
SELF, W. C., D.ED.
STEDMAN, D. J., PH.D.
TARBET, D. G., D.ED.
TRACY, N. H., D.ED.
WARE, W. B., PH.D.
WASIK, B. H., PH.D.
WHITE, K. P., PH.D.
WIEGERINK, R., PH.D.

English:
AVERY, L. G., PH.D.
BAIN, R. A., PH.D.
BETTS, D. W.
DESSEN, A. C., PH.D.
EDGE, C. E., PH.D.
FLORA, J. M., PH.D.
HAIG, R. I., PH.D.
HARMON, W. R., PH.D.
JACKSON, B., PH.D.
KANE, G. J., PH.D.
LUDINGTON, C. T., Jr., PH.D.
PATTERSON, D. W., PH.D.
PHIALAS, P. G., PH.D.
REED, M. L., III, PH.D.
RUBIN, L. D., Jr., PH.D.
RUST, R. D., PH.D.
SEELYE, J. D., PH.D.
SHAPIRO, H. I., PH.D.
STEELE, H. M., B.A.
STRAUSS, A. B., PH.D.
THOMSON, F. C., PH.D.
THORNTON, W. E., PH.D.
VOITLE, R. B., PH.D.

Environmental Science and Engineering:
ANDREWS, R. N., PH.D.
CHANLETT, E. T., M.PH.
CHRISTMAN, R. F., PH.D.
FRASER, D. A., D.S.
HARRIS, R. L., PH.D.
JOHNSON, J. D., PH.D.
KUENZLER, E. J., PH.D.
LAMB, J. C., III, D.S.
LAURIA, D. T., PH.D.
OKUN, D. A., D.S.
REIST, P. C., D.S.
SHIFFMAN, M. A., PH.D.
SHUMAN, M. S., PH.D.
SINGER, P. C., PH.D.
WEISS, C. M., PH.D.

Epidemiology:
HULKA, B., M.P.H.
IBRAHIM, M. A., PH.D.
KAPLAN, B. H., PH.D.
OMRAN, A. R., D.PH.
SHY, C. M., D.PH.
SLOME, C., D.PHIL.
TYROLER, H. A., M.D.

Family Medicine:
MAYER, E. S., M.D.
SHAHADY, E. J., M.D.
WALTON, R. F., M.D.

Geography:
BASILE, D. G., PH.D.
BIRDSALL, S. S., PH.D.
BROWNING, C. E., PH.D.
DODD, A. V., PH.D.
EYRE, J. D., PH.D.

Kopec, R. J., PH.D.
Moriarty, B. M., PH.D.

*Geology:*
Butler, J. R., PH.D.
Dennison, J. M., PH.D.
Fullagar, P. D., PH.D.
Ingram, R. L., PH.D.
Rogers, J. J., PH.D.
St. Jean, J., Jr., PH.D.
Textoris, D. A., PH.D.
Wheeler, W. H., PH.D.

*German:*
Lawson, R. H., PH.D.
Mews, S. E., PH.D.
Schweitzer, C. E., PH.D.
Smith, S. R., Jr., PH.D.
Stambaugh, R. S., PH.D.
Tax, P. W., PH.D.

*History:*
Anderle, J., PH.D.
Baron, S. H., PH.D.
Baxter, S. B., PH.D.
Behrends, F. O., PH.D.
Bodman, H. L., PH.D.
Boren, H. C., PH.D.
Cecil, L. R., Jr., PH.D.
Cell, G. T., PH.D.
Douglass, E. P., PH.D.
Filene, P. G., PH.D.
Graham, O. L., PH.D.
Headley, J. M., PH.D.
Higginbotham, R. D., PH.D.
Klingberg, F. W., PH.D.
Leutze, J. R., PH.D.
Lotchin, R. W., PH.D.
Mathews, D. G., PH.D.
McVaugh, M. R., PH.D.
Miller, R. M., PH.D.
Nelson, J. K., PH.D.
Painter, N. I., PH.D.
Pfaff, R. W., PH.D.
Powell, W. S., M.A.
Ryan, F. W., Jr., PH.D.
Semonche, J. E., PH.D.
Sitterson, J. C., PH.D.
Soloway, R. A., PH.D.
Taylor, G. V., PH.D.
Tindall, G. B., PH.D.
Tulchin, J. S., PH.D.
Walker, P. F., PH.D.
Weinberg, G. L., PH.D.
Williamson, J. R., PH.D.
Williamson, S. R., PH.D.

*Institute of Government:*
Campbell, W. A., LL.B.
Crowell, J. M., PH.D.
Ferrell, J. S., LL.M.
Green, P. P., Jr., J.D.
Hayman, D. B., PH.D.
Heath, M. S., Jr., LL.B.
Hinsdale, C. E., J.D.
Lawrence, D. M., LL.B.
Loeb, B. F., Jr., LL.B.
Phay, R. F., J.D.
Sanders J. L., J.D.
Thomas, M. P., Jr., J.D.
Watts, L. P., Jr., J.D.
Wicker, W. J., M.A.

*Journalism:*
Adams, J. B., PH.D.
Bowers, T. A., PH.D.
Cole, R. R., PH.D.
Mullen, J. J., PH.D.
Shaw, D. S., PH.D.

*Law:*
Aycock, W. B., J.D.
Bilder, R. B., J.D.
Billings, R. B., J.D.
Broun, K. S., LL.B.
Byrd, R. G., J.D.
Clifford, D. F., Jr., LL.B.
Coggins, G. C., J.D.
Gressman, E., J.D.
Haskell, P. G., LL.B.
Hazen, T. L., J.D.
Kalo, J. J., J.D.
Lefstein, N., LL.M.
Link, R. C., J.D.
Loewy, A. H., LL.B.
Louis, M. B., LL.B.
Martin, J. H., J.D.
Murphy, W. P., J.D.
Nakell, B., LL.D.
Oliver, M. W., J.D.
Pollitt, D. H., LL.B.
Scott, J. W., LL.M.
Taylor, N. F., LL.B.
Turnier, W. J., LL.B.

*Library Science:*
Asheim, L. E., PH.D.
Broadus, R. N., PH.D.
Gambee, B. L., PH.D.
Govan, J. F., PH.D.
Holley, E. G., PH.D.
McMullen, H., PH.D.

*Linguistics and non-Western Languages:*
Howren, R., PH.D.
Seaton, J., PH.D.
Tsiapera, M., PH.D.

*Marine Sciences:*
Chestnut, A. F., PH.D.
Fahy, W. E., PH.D.
Kohlmeyer, J. J., PH.D.
Schwartz, F. J., PH.D.

*Maternal and Child Health Care:*
Bauman, K. E., PH.D.
Miller, C. A., M.D.
Schaefer, E., PH.D.
Schorr, L. B., B.A.
Siegel, E., M.PH.
Watkins, E. L., D.SC.

*Mathematics:*
Cima, J. A., PH.D.
Davis, R. L., PH.D.
Gardner, R. B., PH.D.
Geissinger, L. D., PH.D.
Graves, W. H., PH.D.
Gross, K. I., PH.D.
Heyneman, R. G., PH.D.
Mann, W. R., PH.D.
Mewborn, A. C., PH.D.
Newhouse, S. E., PH.D.
Pfaltzgraff, J. A., PH.D.
Schlessinger, M., PH.D.
Smith, W. W., PH.D.
Sonner, J., PH.D.
Stasheff, J. D., PH.D.
Wright, F. B., PH.D.

*Medicine:*
Barnett, T. B., M.D.
Battigelli, M. C., M.D.
Beck, P., M.D.
Blythe, W. B., M.D.
Bozymski, E. M., M.D.
Bromberg, P. A., M.D.
Bryan, J. A., II, M.D.
Capizzi, R. L., M.D.
Craige, E., M.D.
Dascomb, H. E., M.D.
Eldridge, F. L., M.D.
Finn, A. L., M.D.
Fischer, J. J., M.D.
Fordham, C. C., III, M.D.
Gettes, L. S., M.D.
Gitelman, H. J., M.D.
Gottschalk, C. W., M.D.
Gray, T. K., M.D.
Heizer, W. D., M.D.
Herion, J. C., M.D.
Herring, W. B., M.D.
Lassiter, W. E., M.D.
Lyle, C. B., Jr., M.D.
Ontjes, D. A., M.D.
Pagano, J. S., M.D.
Palmer, J. G., M.D.
Parker, J. C., M.D.
Powell, D. W., M.D.
Roberts, H. R., M.D.
Sessions, J. T., Jr., M.D.
Sorrow, J. M., Jr., M.D.
Swift, M., M.D.
Utiger, R. D., M.D.
Walker, R. I., M.D.
Werk, E. E., Jr., M.D.
Woods, J. W., M.D.
Young, D. T., M.D.
Yount, W. J., M.D.

*Medicine (General):*
Bondurant, S., M.D.
Sheps, C. G., M.D.
Wilson, I. G., M.A.

*Music:*
Bower, C. M., PH.D.
Haar, J., PH.D.
Hannay, R. D., PH.D.
Kremer, R. J., PH.D.
Pruett, J. W., PH.D.
Serrins, D., M.A.
Smither, H. E., PH.D.

*Neurology:*
Farmer, T. W., M.D.
Hayward, J. N., M.D.
Johnson, R. N., D.SC.

*Nursing:*
Copp, L. A., PH.D.
Duffey, M. A., PH.D.
Milio, N., PH.D.
Nuckolls, K. B., PH.D.

*Obstetrics and Gynaecology:*
Bishop, E. H., M.D.
Brenner, W. E., M.D.
Cefalo, R. C., M.D.
Easterling, W. E., Jr., M.D.
Hendricks, C. H., M.D.
Hulka, J. F., M.D.
Talbert, L. M., M.D.

*Ophthalmology:*
Eifrig, D. E., M.D.

*Paediatrics:*
Chamberlin, H. R., M.D.
Clyde, W. A., Jr., M.D.
Denny, F. W., Jr., M.D.
Dunphy, D., M.D.
Fernald, G. W., M.D.
French, F. S., M.D.
Harned, H. S., Jr., M.D.
Kirkman, H. N., Jr., M.D.
Loda, F. A., M.D.
McMillan, C. W., M.D.
Underwood, L. E., M.D.
VanWyk, J. J., M.D.

*Parasitology:*
Goulson, H. T., PH.D.
Larsh, J. E., Jr., D.S.
Weatherly, N. F., PH.D.

*Pathology:*
Benson, W. R., M.D.
Clark, E. S., PH.D.
Dalldorf, F. G., M.D.
Forman, D. T., PH.D.
Geratz, J. D., M.D.
Graham, J. B., M.D.
Grisham, J. W., M.D.
Huffines, W. D., M.D.
Kaufman, D. G., PH.D.
Krigman, M. R., M.D.
Kuhns, W. J., M.D.
Langdell, R. D., M.D.
McLendon, W. W., M.D.
Wagner, R. H., PH.D.

*Pharmacology:*
Cheng, Y., PH.D.
Cooper, C. W., PH.D.

Dudley, K. H., ph.d.
Hirsch, P. F., ph.d.
Munson, P. L., ph.d.
Pearlman, W. H., ph.d.
Perkins, J. P., ph.d.
Stover, B. J., ph.d.
Toverud, S. U., d.s.d.

*Pharmacy:*
Chambers, M. A., ph.d.
Cocolas, G. H., ph.d.
Eckel, F. M., m.s.
Gagnon, J. P., ph.d.
Hager, G. P., ph.d.
Lee, K. H., ph.d.
Loeffler, L. J., ph.d.
Miya, T. S., ph.d.
Piantadosi, C., ph.d.

*Philosophy:*
Adams, E. M., ph.d.
Long, D. C., ph.d.
Munsat, S. M., ph.d.
Resnik, M. D., ph.d.
Rosenberg, J. F., ph.d.
Schlesinger, G., ph.d.
Smyth, R. A., ph.d.
Ziff, R. P., ph.d.

*Physical Education:*
Billing, J. E., ph.d.
Blyth, C. S., ph.d.
Earey, P. F., ph.d.
Hyatt, R. W., ph.d.
Mueller, F. O., ph.d.
Pleasants, F., Jr., d.ed.

*Physics:*
Bowers, W. A., ph.d.
Briscoe, C. V., ph.d.
Choi, S., ph.d.
Clegg, T. B., ph.d.
Crawford, J. H., Jr., ph.d.
Davis, M. S., ph.d.
Hernandez, J. P., ph.d.
Hubbard, P. S., Jr., ph.d.
Ludwig, E. J., ph.d.
MacDonald, J. R., d.s.
Merzbacher, E., ph.d.
Mitchell, E. N., ph.d.
Palmatier, E. D., ph.d.
Peters, P. B., ph.d.
Roberts, L. D., ph.d.
Schroeer, D., ph.d.
Shafroth, S. M., ph.d.
Silver, M. N., ph.d.
Slifkin, L. M., ph.d.
Thompson, W. J., ph.d.
Van Dam, H., ph.d.
York, J. W., Jr., ph.d.

*Physiology:*
Faust, R. G., ph.d.
Kuno, M., ph.d.
Miller, A. T., Jr., m.d.
Perl, E. R., m.d.
Perlmutt, J. H., ph.d.
Whitsel, B. L., ph.d.

*Political Science:*
Azar, E. E., ph.d.
Beyle, T. L., ph.d.
Bounds, V. L., ll.b.
Cleveland, G. B., ph.d.
Daland, R. T., ph.d.
Gil, F. G., ph.d.
Keech, W., ph.d.
Kress, P. F., ph.d.
Lipsitz, L., ph.d.
MacRae, D., Jr., ph.d.
Preyer, R., ll.b.
Prothro, J. W., ph.d.
Richardson, R. J., ph.d.
Rupen, R. A., ph.d.
Schwartz, J., ph.d.
Scott, A. M., ph.d.
Searing, D. D., ph.d.

Steiner, J., ph.d.
Wallace, E., ph.d.
White, J. W., ph.d.
Wright, D. S., ph.d.

*Population Program:*
Udry, J. R., ph.d.

*Psychiatry:*
Bakewell, W. E., Jr., m.d.
Breese, G. R., Jr., ph.d.
Curtis, T. E., m.d.
Edgerton, J. W., ph.d.
Ewing, J. A., m.d.
Halleck, S., m.d.
Lipton, M. A., m.d.
Myers, R. D., ph.d.
Obrist, P. A., ph.d.
Prange, A. J., Jr., ph.d.
Schopler, E., ph.d.
Schroeder, S. R., ph.d.
Smith, C. E., m.d.
Spencer, R. F., m.d.

*Psychology:*
Appelbaum, M. I., ph.d.
Cairns, R. B., ph.d.
Carroll, J. B., ph.d.
Cramer, E. M., ph.d.
Dahlstrom, W. G., ph.d.
Eichman, W. J., ph.d.
Fillenbaum, S., ph.d.
Galinsky, M. D., ph.d.
Insko, C. A., ph.d.
Jones, L. V., ph.d.
King, R. A., ph.d.
Long, E. R., Jr., ph.d.
Martin, B., ph.d.
Ornstein, P., ph.d.
Schopler, J. H., ph.d.
Shinkman, P. G., ph.d.
Thibaut, J. W., ph.d.
Waller, M. B., ph.d.
Welsh, G. S., ph.d.
Young, F. W., ph.d.

*Public Health:*
  *Administration:*
Freymann, M. W., ph.d.
Hughes, J. T., d.ph.
Jain, S., ph.d.
Kaluzny, A. D., ph.d.
Phillips, H. T., m.d.
Rosenfeld, L. S., m.ph.
Schaefer, M., d.p.a.
Veney, J. E., ph.d.

  *Education:*
Hochbaum, G., ph.d.
Steuart, G. W., ph.d.

  *General:*
Greenberg, B. G., ph.d.

  *Nursing:*
Talbot, D. M., ph.d.

  *Nutrition:*
Anderson, J. J., ph.d.
Edozien, J. C., m.d.

*Radiology:*
Bream, C. A., m.d.
Montana, G. S., m.d.
Scatliff, J. H., m.d.
Staab, E. V., m.d.

*Radio, Television and Motion Pictures:*
Bittner, J. R., ph.d.
Bliss, E. L., Jr., b.a.
Elam, A. R., ph.d.
Hardy, W. M., m.a.
Nickel, J. P., m.a.

*Religion:*
Dixon, J. W., Jr., ph.d.
Gunn, G. B., ph.d.
Long, C. H., ph.d.

Peck, W. J., ph.d.
Sasson, J. M., ph.d.
Schutz, J. H., ph.d.
Van Seters, J., ph.d.

*Romance Languages:*
Avalle-Arce, J. B., ph.d.
Clark, F. M., ph.d.
Daniel, G. B., Jr., ph.d.
Duffey, F. M., ph.d.
Ebersole, A. V., Jr., ph.d.
Haig, I. R. S., II, ph.d.
Masters, G. M., ph.d.
Morot-Sir, E., ph.d.
Salgado, M. A., ph.d.
Scaglione, A. D., ph.d.
Sharpe, L. A., ph.d.
Vogler, F. W., ph.d.

*Slavic Languages:*
Debreczeny, P., ph.d.
Levine, M. G., ph.d.
Mihailovich, V. D., ph.d.
Vickery, W. N., ph.d.

*Social Health Research:*
Boatman, R. H., Jr., ph.d.
Seipp, C., ph.d.
Smith, H. L., ph.d.

*Social Work:*
Cooke, P. W., ph.d.
Dobelstein, A., ph.d.
Galinsky, M. J., ph.d.
Pfouts, J., ph.d.
Teicher, M. I., ph.d.
Turner, J. B., d.s.w.

*Sociology:*
Eckland, B. K., ph.d.
Heise, D. R., ph.d.
Kasarda, T. D., ph.d.
Landsberger, H., ph.d.
Lenski, G. E., ph.d.
Namboodiri, N. K., ph.d.
Obershall, A. R., ph.d.
Reed, J. S., Jr., ph.d.
Simpson, R. L., ph.d.
Wilson, R. N., ph.d.

*Speech Communication:*
Brandes, P. D., ph.d.
Long, B. W., ph.d.

*Statistics:*
Baker, C. R., ph.d.
Chakravarti, I. M., ph.d.
Johnson, N. L., ph.d.
Kallianpur, G., ph.d.
Leadbetter, M. R., ph.d.
Simons, G. D., ph.d.
Smith, W. L., ph.d.

*Surgery:*
Bevin, A. G., Jr., m.d.
Biggers, W. P., m.d.
Brashear, H. R., Jr., m.d.
Buckwalter, J. A., m.d.
Bunce, P. L., m.d.
Coulter, N. A., Jr., m.d.
Fischer, N. D., m.d.
Fried, F. A., m.d.
Johnson, G., Jr., m.d.
Mahaley, M. S., Jr., ph.d.
Mandel, S. R., m.d.
Murray, G. F., m.d.
Newsome, J. F., m.d.
Proctor, H. J., m.d.
Starek, P. J., m.d.
Talmage, R. V., ph.d.
Thomas, C. G., m.d.
Trier, W. C., m.d.
Wilcox, B. R., m.d.
Wilson, F. C., Jr., m.d.

*Zoology:*
Feduccia, J. A., ph.d.
Gilbert, L. I., ph.d.

Hagadorn, I. R., ph.d.
Hairston, N. G., ph.d.
Humm, D. G., ph.d.
Jenner, C., ph.d.
Lehman, H. E., ph.d.
Lucchesi, J. C., ph.d.
McMahan, E. A., ph.d.
Mueller, H. C., ph.d.
Stafford, D. W., ph.d.
Stiven, A. E., ph.d.

**University of North Carolina at Charlotte:** U.N.C.C. Station, Charlotte, North Carolina 28223; established as an extension centre of the University of North Carolina 1946; later Charlotte College; made a unit of the University in 1965; Telephone: (704) 597-2000. Academic year: August to May.

*Chancellor:* E. K. Fretwell, Jr., m.a., ph.d.
*Vice-Chancellor, Academic Affairs:* James H. Werntz, Jr., m.s., ph.d.
*Vice-Chancellor, Student Affairs:* Robert L. Albright, m.a., ph.d.
*Vice-Chancellor for Research and Public Service:* Douglas M. Orr, Jr., m.b.s., ph.d.
*Vice-Chancellor for Development:* William M. Britt, ed.d.
*Vice-Chancellor, Business Affairs:* Leo E. Ells, b.s., m.b.a.
*Dean of Admissions and Registrar:* Robert A. Gwaltney, m.a.
*Librarian:* Richard B. Eggleton, ph.d. (acting).

Library of 302,981 vols., 4,932 periodicals.

Number of teachers: 424.
Number of students: 9,383.

### DEANS:

*College of Architecture:* Charles C. Hight, b.arch.
*College of Business Administration:* R. E. Neel, m.s., ph.d.
*College of Engineering:* Robert D. Snyder, ph.d.
*College of Human Development and Learning:* H. William Heller, m.s., ed.d.
*College of Nursing:* Louise C. Schlachter, r.n., m.a., ph.d.
*College of Arts and Sciences:* S. L. Burson, Jr. ph.d.

**University of North Carolina at Greensboro:** Greensboro, North Carolina 27412; established as a Normal College 1891; since 1931 a unit of the University of North Carolina; 1963 name changed to the University of North Carolina at Greensboro; Telephone: 379-5000.

*Chancellor:* William E. Moran, ph.d.
*Vice-Chancellor for Business Affairs:* F. L. Drake, b.s.
*Vice-Chancellor for Academic Affairs:* S. L. Jones, ph.d.
*Vice-Chancellor for Graduate Studies:* J. W. Kennedy, ph.d.

*Vice-Chancellor for Administration and Planning:* A. L. Fincher, ph.d.
*Vice-Chancellor for Development:* C. W. Patterson, b.a.
*Vice-Chancellor for Student Affairs:* J. H. Allen, m.d.i.v.
*Registrar:* H. H. Price, m.a.
*Library:* J. H. Thompson, ph.d.

Library of 824,864 vols.
Number of teachers: 550 full-time, 83 part-time.
Number of students: 10,201.

### DEANS:

*Academic Advising:* B. A. Goldman, ed.d.
*College of Arts and Sciences:* R. L. Miller, ph.d.
*School of Business and Economics:* D. H. Shelton, ph.d.
*School of Education:* D. H. Reilly, ph.d.
*School of Health, Physical Education and Recreation:* R. A. Swanson, ph.d.
*School of Home Economics:* Naomi G. Albanese, ph.d.
*School of Music:* R. L. Blocker, d.m.a.
*School of Nursing:* Eloise R. Lewis, ed.d.

### PROFESSORS:

Agostini, P., Art
Albanese, Naomi G., ph.d., Home Economics
Allen, R. J., ed.d., Business and Economics
Anderton, Laura G., ph.d., Biology
Ashby, W. D., ph.d., Religious Studies
Atkinson, J., ph.d., Romance Languages
Baecker, Anne F., ph.d., German and Russian
Baer, J. T., ph.d., German and Russian
Barborak, J. C., ph.d., Chemistry
Bardon, J. I., ph.d., Education
Barnes, Ruby G., ed.d., Nursing
Barrett, Kate R., ph.d., Health, Physical Education and Recreation
Batcheller, D. R., ph.d., Communication and Theatre
Bates, W. K., ph.d., Biology
Beeler, J. H., ph.d., History
Berlin, Pearl, ph.d., Health, Physical Education and Recreation
Brownstein, A. J., ph.d., Psychology
Brubaker, D. C., ph.d., Education
Bryson, J. E., ed.d., Education
Buchert, Jean R., ph.d., English
Burgess, Elaine, ph.d., Sociology
Calhoon, R. M., ph.d., History
Canaday, Helen, ed.d., Home Economics
Carpenter, G. F., b.a., Art
Chappell, F. D., m.a., English
Charles, Amy M., ph.d., English
Cheney, Gay E., ph.d., Health, Physical Education and Recreation
Clark, C. B., ph.d., Physics
Clawson, B. N., ph.d., Home Economics
Cline, R. S., ph.d., Business and Economics
Clotfelter, J., ph.d., Political Science
Cox, R., ph.d., Music
Crews, J. W., ed.d., Business and Economics
Crow, Jane H., ph.d., Home Economics
Current, R. N., ph.d., History

Darnell, D. G., ph.d., English
Dixon, R. F., ph.d., Communication and Theatre
Dozier, C. L., ph.d., Geography
Eason, R. G., ph.d., Psychology
Eberhart, B. M., ph.d., Biology
Edinger, L., ph.d., Education
Ellis, J. N., ph.d., English
Farrow, N., m.a., Music
Ferguson, J. S., ph.d., History
Fitzgerald, T. K., ph.d., Anthropology
Formby, J. P., ph.d., Business and Economics
Franklin, Marian P., ed.d., Education
Gariglio, R. J., m.m., Music
Garlington, A. S., ph.d., Music
Gentry, D. L., ph.d., Business and Economics
Gochberg, H. S., ph.d., Romance Languages
Goldman, B. A., ed.d., Education
Goldstein, C., ph.d., Art
Gregory, Joan, ed.d., Art
Grill, G. P., ed.d., Business and Economics
Hageseth, G. T., ph.d., Physics
Hart, L. E., d.m.a., Music
Harter, M. R., ph.d., Psychology
Helms, Mary W., ph.d., Anthropology
Hennis, Gail M., ph.d., Health, Physical Education and Recreation
Herman, H. B., ph.d., Chemistry
Hershey, G. L., ph.d., Business and Economics
Hidore, J. J., ph.d., Geography
Hildebrandt, T., ph.d., Mathematics
Hines, T. C., ph.d., Education
Hounshell, C. D., ph.d., Political Science
Hurwitz, M. D., ph.d., Home Economics
Jaeger, R. M., ph.d., Education
Jellicorse, J. L., ph.d., Communication and Theatre
Johnson, J. E., d.b.a., Business and Economics
Johnson, Mildred B., ph.d., Home Economics
Jones, S. L., ph.d., History
Jud, G. D., ph.d., Business and Economics
Karmel, L. J., ph.d., Education
Kennedy, J. W., ph.d., Business and Economics
Kiorpes, G. A., d.m.a., Music
Kupferer, Harriet J., ph.d., Anthropology
Lagos, R., ph.d., Romance Languages
Lane, W. G., ph.d., English
Levison, A. B., ph.d., Philosophy
Lewis, Eloise R., ed.d., Nursing
Lucas, S. R., ph.d., Business and Economics
Lumsden, E. A., ph.d., Psychology
Lutz, P. E., ph.d., Biology
Lynam, C. A., m.a., Music
MacDonald, J. B., ph.d., Education
Mackenzie, D., ph.d., History
McCormack, F. J., ph.d., Physics
McGee, Rosemary, ph.d., Health, Physical Education and Recreation
McKinney, E. Doris, ed.d., Health, Physical Education and Recreation
Magee, A. C., ph.d., Home Economics
Mathews, Jane D., ph.d., History
Mecimore, C. D., ph.d., Business and Economics
Middleton, H. D., ph.d., Drama and Speech
Miles, B. E., ph.d., Business and Economics
Miller, R. L., ph.d., Chemistry
Moran, W. E., ph.d., Business and Economics
Moskowitz, D. H., d.m.a., Music
Mountjoy, J. B., ph.d., Anthropology
Nelson, Rosemary D., ph.d., Psychology

UNIVERSITIES AND COLLEGES—NORTH CAROLINA (UNIVERSITY OF) U.S.A.

NELSON, R. H., ED.D., Education
NEWTON, R. P., PH.D., German and Russian
NOMIKOS, A. C., PH.D., Communication and Theatre
O'KANE, R. M., D.ED., Education
OLSON, D. M., PH.D., Political Science
PARKER, F. D., PH.D., History
PETIT, T. A., PH.D., Business and Economics
POSEY, E. E., PH.D., Mathematics
PRICE, D. K., PH.D., Sociology
PURKEY, W. W., ED.D., Education
PURPEL, D. E., ED.D., Education
PUTERBAUGH, W. H., PH.D., Chemistry
REILLY, D. H., ED.D., Education
RODMAN, H., PH.D., Home Economics
ROSTHAL, R. B., PH.D., Philosophy
RUSSELL, D., ED D., Education
SAAB, ANN P., PH.D., History
SCANZONI, J. H., PH.D., Home Economics
SCULLION, T. B., PH.D., Social Work
SELLERS, J. R., ED.D., Health, Physical Education and Recreation
SHARMA, C. L., PH.D., Education
SHELTON, D. H., PH.D., Business and Economics
SHER, R. B., PH.D., Mathematics
SHULL, R. L., PH.D., Psychology
SMITH, K. R., PH.D., Psychology
SMITH, REBECCA M., PH.D., Home Economics
SOLLEDER, MARIAN, PH.D., Health, Physical Education and Recreation
SPENCER, C., PH.D., English
STEPHENS, R. O., PH.D., English
SWANSON, R. A., PH.D., Health, Physical Education and Recreation
TITTLE, CAROL K., PH.D., Education
TRELEASE, A. W., PH.D., History
VACC, N. A., ED.D., Education
VAUGHAN, J. E., PH.D., Mathematics
WAKEFIELD, LUCILLE M., PH.D., Home Economics
WATSON, J. A., PH.D., Home Economics
WATSON, R. W., PH.D., English
WEBSTER, PHYLLIS A., PH.D., Business and Economics
WEHNER, W., ED.D., Music
WELLS, H., PH.D., Psychology
WILSON, J. F., PH.D., Biology
WOELFEL, C. J., PH.D., Business and Economics
WRIGHT, K. C., PH.D., Education

### North Carolina State University at Raleigh:
Raleigh, North Carolina 27650; f. 1887 as North Carolina State College of Agriculture and Mechanic Arts; assumed present title 1965; since 1931 a unit of the University of North Carolina; Telephone 737-2011.

*Chancellor:* N. N. WINSTEAD, PH.D. (acting).
*Vice-Chancellor and Provost:* N. N. WINSTEAD, PH.D.
*Vice-Chancellor for Finance and Business:* G. L. WORSLEY, B.S.
*Vice-Chancellor for Extension and Public Service:* W. L. TURNER, D.P.A.
*Vice-Provost and Dean for Research:* H. B. SMITH, PH.D.
*Vice-Chancellor for Student Affairs:* B. C. TALLEY, Jr., PH.D.
*Director of Admissions:* A. P. KELLER, B.S.

Library of 1,000,000 vols.
Number of teachers: 1,090.
Number of students: 21,500.

DEANS:
*Agriculture and Life Sciences:* J. E. LEGATES, PH.D.
*Design:* C. E. MCKINNEY, B.A.
*Education:* C. J. DOLCE, ED.D.
*Engineering:* L. K. MONTEITH, PH.D.
*Forest Resources:* E. L. ELLWOOD, PH.D.
*Humanities and Social Sciences:* R. O. TILMAN, PH.D.
*Physical and Mathematical Sciences:* G. BRIGGS, PH.D.
*Textiles:* D. S. HAMBY, B.S.
*Graduate:* V. T. STANNETT, PH.D.
*Veterinary Medicine:* T. M. CURTIN, PH.D.

PROFESSORS:
*School of Agriculture and Life Sciences:*
ANDERSON, C. E., PH.D., Botany
APPLE, J. L., PH.D., Plant Pathology
ARMSTRONG, F. B., PH.D., Biochemistry
AURAND, L. W., PH.D., Food Science
AVERRE, C. W., PH.D., Plant Pathology
AXTELL, R. C., PH.D., Entomology
AYCOCK, Robert, PH.D., Plant Pathology
BAIRD, J. C., PH.D., Soil Science
BALLINGER, W. E., PH.D., Horticultural Science
BARKER, K. R., PH.D., Plant Pathology
BATEMAN, D. F., PH.D., Plant Pathology
BEASLEY, E. O., M.S., Biological and Agricultural Engineering
BEHLOW, R. F., D.V.M., Animal Science
BEUTE, M. K., PH.D., Plant Pathology
BLAKE, C. T., PH.D., Crop Science
BLALOCK, T. C., PH.D., Animal Science
BLUM, G. B., M.S., Biological and Agricultural Engineering
BLUM, U., PH.D., Botany
BOONE, E. J., PH.D., Adult Education
BOWEN, H. D., PH.D., Biological and Agricultural Engineering
BRADBURY, P. C., PH.D., Zoology
BRADLEY, J. R., Jr., PH.D., Entomology
BROOKS, J. F., M.S., Horticultural Science
BROOKS, R. C., PH.D., Economics and Business
BROOKS, W. M., PH.D., Entomology
BROWN, M. M., M.S., Adult and Community College Education
BUOL, S. W., PH.D., Soil Science
CALDWELL, B. E., PH.D., Crop Science
CAMPBELL, W. V., PH.D., Entomology
CARLSON, G. A., PH.D., Economics and Business
CARPENTER, W. L., ED.D., Agricultural Communications
CARTER, T. A., PH.D., Poultry Science
CASSEL, D. K., PH.D., Soil Science
CHAMBLEE, D. S., PH.D., Crop Science
CLAWSON, A. J., PH.D., Animal Science
COBLE, H. D., PH.D., Crop Science
COLLINS, J. N., M.AGRI., Sociology and Anthropology
COLLINS, W. K., PH.D., Crop Science
COOK, M. G., PH.D., Soil Science
COOK, R. E., PH.D., Poultry Science
COOPER, A. W., PH.D., Forestry
COPELAND, B. J., PH.D., Zoology
CORBIN, F. T., PH.D., Crop Science
COUTU, A. J., PH.D., Economics and Business
COWLING, E. B., PH.D., Plant Pathology
COX, F. R., PH.D., Soil Science
CRAIG, H. B., PH.D., Food Science
CUMMINGS, G. A., PH.D., Soil Science
DAHLE, R. D., PH.D., Economics and Business
DALLA POZZA, ADA B., M.S., Agriculture Extension
DAUTERMAN, W. C., PH.D., Entomology

DAVENPORT, D. G., PH.D., Animal Science
DAVEY, C. B., PH.D., Soil Science and Forestry and Plant Pathology
DEHERTOGH, A. A., PH.D., Horticultural Science
DOBROGOSZ, W. J., PH.D., Microbiology
DONALDSON, W. E., PH.D., Poultry Science
DONNELLY, MARJORIE M., M.S., Agriculture Extension
DOWNS, R. J., PH.D., Botany
DRIGGERS, L. B., M.S., Biological and Agricultural Engineering
DUNCAN, H. E., PH.D., Plant Pathology
ECHANDI, E., PH.D., Plant Pathology
EISEN, E. J., PH.D., Animal Science
ELKAN, G. H., PH.D., Microbiology
EMERY, D A., PH.D., Crop Science
EVANS, J. B., PH.D., Microbiology
FARRIER, M. H., PH.D., Entomology
FIKE, W. T., Jr., PH.D., Crop Science
FITES, R. C., PH.D., Botany
GEORGE, J. D., PH.D., Sociology and Anthropology
GILBERT, W. B., PH.D., Crop Science
GILLIAM, J. W., PH.D., Soil Science
GLAZENER, E. W., PH.D., Poultry Science
GOODE, L., PH.D., Animal Science
GOODING, G. V., Jr., PH.D., Plant Pathology
GRAND, L. F., PH.D., Plant Pathology
GREGORY, M. E., PH.D., Food Science
GROSCH, D. S., PH.D., Genetics
GROSS, H. D., PH.D., Crop Science
GUTHRIE, F. E., PH.D., Entomology
HAMANN, D. D., PH.D., Food Science
HAMILTON, P. B., PH.D., Poultry Science
HANSON, W., PH.D., Genetics
HARDIN, J. W., PH.D., Botany
HARRIS, J. R., D.V.M., Poultry Science
HARVEY, R. W., PH.D., Animal Science
HARWOOD, D. G., Jr., M.S., Economics and Business
HASSLER, F. J., PH.D., Biological and Agricultural Engineering
HASSLER, W. W., PH.D. Zoology
HAYNES, F. L., Jr., PH.D., Horticultural Science
HILL, C. H., PH.D., Poultry Science and Animal Science
HOBGOOD, T. N., PH.D., Agricultural Extension
HODGSON, E., PH.D., Entomology
HOOVER, D. M., PH.D., Economics and Business
HOOVER, M., PH.D., Food Science
HORTON, H. R., PH.D., Biochemistry
HOWELL, E. L., M.ED., Biological and Agricultural Engineering
HUANG, B. K., PH.D., Biological and Agricultural Engineering
HUGHES, G. R., M.S., Horticultural Science
HUMENIK, F. J., PH.D., Biological and Agricultural Engineering
HUMPHRIES, E. G., PH.D., Biological and Agricultural Engineering
IHNEN, L. A., PH.D., Economics and Business
JACKSON, W. A., PH.D., Soil Science
JENKINS, S. F., PH.D., Plant Pathology
JOHNSON, P. R., PH.D., Economics and Business
JOHNSON, T., PH.D., Economics and Business
JOHNSON, W. H., PH.D., Biological and Agricultural Engineering
JONES, E. E., PH.D., Animal Science
JONES, E. W., PH.D., Economics and Business
JONES, G. L., PH.D., Crop Science
JONES, J. C., M.S., Agricultural Extension
JONES, J. R., PH.D., Animal Science
JONES, V. A., PH.D., Food Science

KAHN, J. S., PH.D., Biochemistry
KAMPRATH, E. J., PH.D., Soil Science
KING, R. A., PH.D., Economics and Business
KLOOS, W. E., PH.D., Genetics
KNOTT, F. N., PH.D., Animal Science
KOLBE, M. H., M.S., Horticultural Science
KONSLER, T. R., PH.D., Horticultural Science
KRIZ, G. J., PH.D., Biological and Agricultural Engineering
KUHR, R. J., PH.D., Entomology
LARSON, R. A., PH.D., Horticultural Science
LASSITER, C. A., PH.D., Animal Science
LEATHERWOOD, J. M., PH.D., Animal Science
LEAVIS, C. E., PH.D., Agricultural Extension
LECCE, J. G., PH.D., Animal Science
LEGATES, J. E., PH.D., Animal Science
LEONARD, K. J., PH.D., Plant Pathology
LEVINGS, C. S., III, PH.D., Genetics
LEWIS, W. M., PH.D., Crop Science
LINEBACK, D. R., PH.D., Food Science
LINER, H. L., PH.D., Economics and Business
LONGMUIR, I. S., M.B.B.CH., Biochemistry
LOVE, J. W., PH.D., Horticultural Science
LUCAS, L. T., PH.D., Plant Pathology
LYTLE, C. F., PH.D., Zoology
McCANN, G. C., PH.D., Sociology and Anthropology
McCANTS, C. B., PH.D., Soil Science
McCLURE, W. F., PH.D., Biological and Agricultural Engineering
McDANIEL, B. T., PH.D., Animal Science
McLAUGHLIN, F. W., M.S., Crop Science
MAIN, A. R., PH.D., Biochemistry
MAIN, C. E., PH.D., Plant Pathology
MAINLAND, C. M., PH.D., Horticultural Science
MANN, T. J., PH.D., Genetics
MARTIN, G. A., PH.D., Poultry Science
MARTZINGER, D. F., PH.D., Genetics
MIKSCHE, J. P., PH.D., Botany
MILHOLLAND, R. D., PH.D., Plant Pathology
MILLER, C. H., PH.D., Horticultural Science
MILLER, G. C., PH.D., Zoology
MILLER, N. C., Jr., M.S., Food Science
MOCHRIE, R. D., PH.D., Animal Science
MOLL, ROBERT H., PH.D., Genetics
MONACO, T. J., PH.D., Horticultural Science
MOORE, H. B., Jr., PH.D., Entomology
MOTT, R. L., PH.D., Botany
MURPHY, C. F., PH.D., Crop Science
MYERS, R. M., M.S., Animal Science
NELSON, P. V., PH.D., Horticultural Science
NESBIT, W. B., PH.D., Horticultural Science
NEUNZIG, H. H., PH.D., Entomology
NICHOLS, T. E., PH.D., Economics and Business
PARKHURST, C. R., PH.D., Poultry Science
PARSONS, G. S., M.S., Animal Science
PASOUR, E. C., PH.D., Economics and Business
PATTERSON, J. W., PH.D., Animal Science
PATTERSON, R. P., PH.D., Crop Science
PEELER, R. J., PH.D., Economics and Business
PERRIN, R. K., PH.D., Economics and Business
PERRY, J. J., PH.D., Microbiology
PHILLIPS, J. A., PH.D., Soil Science
PHILLIPS, L. L., PH.D., Crop Science

PORTERFIELD, IRA D., PH.D., Animal Science
POWELL, N. T., PH.D., Plant Pathology
PUGH, C. R., PH.D., Economics and Business
RABB, R. L., PH.D., Entomology
RAKES, A. H., PH.D., Animal Science
RAMSEY, H. A., PH.D., Animal Science
RAULSTON, J. C., Horticultural Science
ROBERTS, J. F., PH.D., Zoology
ROBERTSON, R. L., M.S., Entomology
ROBISON, O. W., PH.D., Animal Science
ROCK, G. C., PH.D., Entomology
ROHRBACH, R. P., PH.D., Biological and Agricultural Engineering
ROZIER, J. J., PH.D., Agricultural Extension
SANCHEZ, P., PH.D., Soil Science
SARGENT, F. D., PH.D., Animal Science
SASSER, J. N., PH.D., Plant Pathology
SCANDALIOS, J. G., PH.D., Genetics
SCHAFFER, H. F., PH.D., Genetics
SCHRIMPER, R. A., PH.D., Economics and Business
SEAGRAVES, J. A., PH.D., Economics and Business
SENECA, E. D., PH.D., Botany and Soil Science
SHEETS, T. J., PH.D., Entomology
SIMMONS, R. L., PH.D., Economics and Business
SKAGGS, R. W., PH.D., Biological and Agricultural Engineering
SKROCH, W. A., PH.D., Horticultural Science
SMITH, D. E., PH.D., Zoology
SNEED, R. E., PH.D., Biological and Agricultural Engineering
SOWELL, R. S., PH.D., Biological and Agricultural Engineering
STANISLAW, C. S., PH.D., Animal Science
STORMER, D. L., ED.D., Agricultural Extension
STRIDER, D. L., PH.D., Plant Pathology
SUGGS, C. W., PH.D., Biological and Agricultural Engineering
SWAISGOOD, H. E., PH.D., Food Science
THAXTON, J. P., Jr., PH.D., Poultry Science
THEIL, E. C., PH.D., Biochemistry
TRAVER, F. R., PH.D., Food Science
THOMAS, F. B., PH.D., Food Science
TIMOTHY, D. H., PH.D., Crop Science
TOUSSANT, W. D., PH.D., Economics and Business
TOVE, S., PH.D., Biochemistry
TRIANTAPHYLLOU, A. C., PH.D., Genetics
TRIANTAPHYLLOU, H. H., PH.D., Plant Pathology
TROYER, J. R., PH.D., Botany
TURINSKY, P. J., PH.D., Nuclear Engineering
ULBERG, L. C., PH.D., Animal Science
VANDENBERGH, J. G., PH.D., Zoology
VOLAND, M. E., PH.D., Sociology and Anthropology
VOLK, R. J., PH.D., Soil Science
WARD, J. B., PH.D., Poultry Science
WATKINS, R. W., M.S., Biological and Agricultural Engineering
WEATHERS, C. R., M.S., Economics and Business
WEBER, J. B., PH.D., Crop Science
WEED, S. B., PH.D., Soil Science
WEEKMAN, G., PH.D., Entomology
WELLS, R. C., PH.D., Economics and Business
WERNSMAN, E. A., PH.D., Crop Science
WESEN, D. P., PH.D., Animal Science
WILK, J. C., PH.D., Animal Science
WILSON, L. G., PH.D., Horticultural Science
WISER, E. H., PH.D., Biological and Agricultural Engineering
WOLLUM, A. G., PH.D., Soil Science

WORSHAM, A. D., PH.D., Crop Science
WRIGHT, C. G., PH.D., Entomology
YOUNG, C. T., PH.D., Food Science
YOUNG, J. H., PH.D., Biological and Agricultural Engineering

*School of Design:*
BATCHELOR, P., M.ARCH., Design
BIRELINE, G. L., Jr., M.ARCH., Design
BURNS, R. P., M.ARCH., Architecture
CLARK, R. H., M.ARCH., Design
FOOTE, V. M., B.S., Design
McKINNEY, C. E., B.A., Design
SANOFF, H., M.ARCH., Architecture
SHOGREN, V. F., M.ARCH., Architecture
STIPE, R. E., M.R.P., Design
WILKINSON, R. R., M.L.A., Landscape Architecture

*School of Education:*
ANDERSON, N. D., PH.D., Mathematics and Science Education
BOONE, E. J., PH.D., Adult and Community College Education
BURT, M. P., PH.D., Adult and Community College Education
CARTER, G. L., PH.D., Adult and Community College Education
CLARK, L. M., ED.D., Mathematics and Science Education
COSTER, J. K., PH.D., Occupational Education
CUNNINGHAM, J. W., PH.D., Psychology
DOLICE, C. J., PH.D., Education
DREWES, D. W., PH.D., Psychology
LEVERE, T. E., PH.D., Psychology
NEWMAN, S. E., PH.D., Psychology
PARRAMORE, B. M., ED.D., Curriculum and Instruction
PEARSON, R. G., PH.D., Psychology
SHEARON, R. W., ED.D., Adult and Community College Education
SIMPSON, R. D., ED.D., Mathematics and Science Education
STORMER, D. L., ED.D., Adult and Community College Education
THAYER, D. W., PH.D., Psychology
TRENT, C., PH.D., Adult and Community College Education
WESTBROOK, B. W., ED.D., Psychology

*School of Engineering:*
AMEIN, M., PH.D., Civil Engineering
AYOUB, M. A., PH.D., Industrial Engineering
BABCOCK, W. F., M.S., Civil Engineering
BAILEY, J. A., PH.D., Mechanical and Aerospace Engineering
BEELER, J. R., PH.D., Nuclear Engineering
BENSON, R. B., Jr., PH.D., Materials Engineering
BERNHARD, R. H., PH.D., Industrial Engineering
BURTON, R. A., PH.D., Mechanical and Aerospace Engineering
CANADA, J. R., PH.D., Industrial Engineering
CONRAD, H., D.ENG., Materials Engineering
CRIBBINS, P. D., PH.D., Civil Engineering
DAVIS, R. F., PH.D., Materials Engineering
DE JARNETTE, F. R., PH.D., Mechanical and Aerospace Engineering
DOUGLAS, R. A., PH.D., Civil Engineering
ECKELS, A. R., PH.D., Electrical Engineering
EDWARDS, J. A., PH.D., Mechanical and Aerospace Engineering
ELMAGHRABY, S. E., PH.D., Industrial Engineering
ELY, J. F., PH.D., Civil Engineering
FAHMY, A. A., PH.D., Mineral Industries
FELDER, R. M., PH.D., Chemical Engineering

UNIVERSITIES AND COLLEGES—NORTH CAROLINA (UNIVERSITY OF) U.S.A.

Ferrell. J., ph.d., Chemical Engineering
Flood, W. A., ph.d., Electrical Engineering
Galler, W. S., ph.d., Civil Engineering
Garcia, B. H., m.s., Mechanical and Aerospace Engineering
Gardner, R. P., ph.d., Nuclear Engineering
Griffith, W. C., ph.d., Mechanical and Aerospace Engineering
Grigg, N. S., ph.d., Civil Engineering
Hale, F. J., sc.d., Mechanical and Aerospace Engineering
Hart, F. D., m.s., Mechanical and Aerospace Engineering
Hassan, H. A., ph.d., Mechanical and Aerospace Engineering
Hauser, J. R., ph.d., Electrical Engineering
Havner, K. S., ph.d., Civil Engineering
**Heimbach, C. L., ph.d., Civil Engineering**
Hodgson, T. H., ph.d., Mechanical and Aerospace Engineering
Hopfenberg, H. B., ph.d., Chemical Engineering
Horie, Y., ph.d., Civil Engineering
Horn, J. W., m.s.c.e., Civil Engineering
Littlejohn, M. A., ph.d., Electrical Engineering
McDonald, P. H., Jr., ph.d., Civil Engineering
**Magor, J. K., ph.d., Mineral Industries**
Manning, C. R., ph.d., Materials Engineering
Masnari, N. A., ph.d., Electrical Engineering
Matthews, N. F., ph.d., Electrical Engineering
**Moazed, K. L., ph.d., Mineral Industries**
Monteith, L. K., ph.d., Electrical Engineering
**Mullen, W. G., ph.d., Civil Engineering**
Mulligan, J. C., ph.d., Mechanical and Aerospace Engineering
**Murray, R. L., ph.d., Nuclear Engineering**
Nunnally, S. W., ph.d., Civil Engineering
O'Neal, J. B., Jr., ph.d., Electrical Engineering
**Ozisik, M. N., ph.d., Mechanical and Aerospace Engineering**
Palmour, H., III, ph.d., Ceramic Engineering
Perkins, J. N., ph.d., Mechanical and Aerospace Engineering
Prak, A. L., ph.d., Industrial Engineering
Rhodes, D. R., ph.d., Electrical Engineering
Rousseau, R. W., ph.d., Chemical Engineering
Royster, L. H., ph.d., Mechanical and Aerospace Engineering
**Saxe, R. F., ph.d., Nuclear Engineering**
**Seely, J. F., m.ch.e., Chemical Engineering**
Siewert, C. E., ph.d., Nuclear Engineering
Smallwood, C., Jr., m.s., Civil Engineering
**Smetana, F. O., ph.d., Mechanical and Aerospace Engineering**
**Smith, H. B., ph.d., Chemical Engineering**
Smith, W. A., Jr., d.eng.sc., Industrial Engineering
Sorrell, F. Y., ph.d., Mechanical and Aerospace Engineering
**Stadelmaier, H. H., Engineering Research**
Stahel, E. P., ph.d., Chemical Engineering

**Stannett, V. T., ph.d., Chemical Engineering**
Stauldhammer, J., ph.d., Electrical Engineering
Stidham, S., Jr., ph.d., Industrial Engineering
Stoops, R. F., ph.d., Engineering Research
Uyanik, M. E., ph.d., Civil Engineering
Verahese, K., ph.d., Nuclear Engineering
**Wahls, H. E., ph.d., Civil Engineering**
Whitfield, J. K., ph.d., Mechanical and Aerospace Engineering
Williams, J. C., III, ph.d., Mechanical and Aerospace Engineering
Wortman, J. J., ph.d., Electrical Engineering
Zia, P. Z., ph.d., Civil Engineering
Zorowski, C. F., ph.d., Mechanical and Aerospace Engineering

*School of Forest Resources:*
**Barefoot, A. C., d.f., Wood and Paper Science**
Chang, H., ph.d., Wood and Paper Science
Cooper, A. W., ph.d., Forestry
Ellwood, E L., ph.d., Wood and Paper Science
Franklin, E. C., ph.d., Forestry
Goldstein, I. S., ph.d., Wood and Paper Science
Gratzl, J. S., ph.d., Wood and Paper Science
Hafley, W. L., ph.d., Forestry
**Hart, C. A., ph.d., Wood and Paper Science**
Hassan, A. E., ph.d., Forestry
**Hitchings, R. G., ph.d., Wood and Paper Science**
Huxter, W. T., m.w.t., Forestry
Johnson, J. W., ph.d., Forestry
Kellison, R. C., ph.d., Forestry
Lammi, J. O., ph.d., Forestry
Levi, M. P., ph.d., Wood and Paper Science
Pearson, R. G., m.e., Wood and Paper Science
Perry, T. O., ph.d., Forestry
**Saylor, L. C., ph.d., Forestry**
Sternloff, R. E., ph.d., Recreation Resources Administration
Thomas, R. J., ph.d., Wood and Paper Science
Warren, M. R., dr. of rec., Recreation Resources Administration

*School of Humanities and Social Sciences:*
**Beers, B. F., ph.d., History**
Blank, P. E., ph.d., English
**Block, W. J., ph.d., History and Political Science**
**Bredenberg, P. A., ph.d., Philosophy and Religion**
**Brown, M. L., ph.d., History and Political Science**
Bryan, R. S., ph.d., Philosophy and Religion
**Cahill, F. V., Jr., ph.d., Political Science and Public Administration**
Carter, W. R., ph.d., Philosophy and Religion
**Champion, L. S., ph.d., English**
Clifford, W. B., II, ph.d., Sociology and Anthropology
Downs, M. S., ph.d., History
**Drabick, L. W., ph.d., Sociology and Anthropology**
**Drews, F. R., ph.d., Physical Education**
Durant, J. D., ph.d., English
Erickson, E. W., ph.d., Economics and Business
Fearn, R. M., ph.d., Economics and Business

Fisher, D., ph.d., Economics and Business
Franklin, W. G., ph.d., Speech Communication
Gallant, A. R., ph.d., Economics and Business Statistics
Gonzalez, A. A., ph.d., Foreign Languages and Literature
**Greenlaw, Ralph, ph.d., History**
Halperen, M., ph.d., English
Harris, W. C., ph.d., History
Hobbs, J. P., ph.d., History
Holthausen, D. M., ph.d., Economics and Business
**Holtzman, A., ph.d., History and Political Science and Public Administration**
Hyman, D. N., ph.d., Economics and Business
Jeffers, L. F., m.a., English
Jones, C. P., ph.d., Economics and Business
King, D. E., ph.d., History and Education
Knowles, A. S., m.a., English
Koonce, B. G., Jr., ph.d., English
**Marsh, C. P., m.s., Sociology and Anthropology**
Messere, C. J., ph.d., Economics and Business
Meyers, W. E., ph.d., English
Mustian, R. D., ph.d., Sociology and Anthropology
Neuman, D. F., ph.d., Economics and Business
Olsen, B. M., ph.d., Economics and Business
**Owen, G., ph.d., English**
**Parker, C. A., ph.d., English**
Regan, T. H., ph.d., Philosophy and Religion
Reynolds, M. S., ph.d., English
Riddle, J. M., ph.d., History
Sawhney, M. M., ph.d., Sociology and Anthropology
Smith, W. E., ed.d., Physical Education
Stack, E. M., ph.d., Foreign Languages and Literatures
Suval, E. M., ph.d., Sociology and Anthropology
Suval, S., ph.d., History
Sylla, R. E., ph.d., Economics and Business
Tilman, R. O., ph.d., Political Science and Public Administration
**Toole, W. B., ph.d., English**
Turner, C. B., ph.d., Economics and Business
Van De Veer, A. D., ph.d., Philosophy and Religion
Wheeler, M. E., ph.d., History
Williams, J. O., ph.d., Political Science and Public Administration
Williams, M. C., ph.d., English
Williams, P., Jr., m.a., English
Wishy, B., ph.d., History
Young, J. N., ph.d., Sociology and Anthropology

*School of Physical Sciences and Applied Mathematics:*
Bachman, K. J., ph.d., Chemistry
**Bent, H. A., ph.d., Chemistry**
Bereman, R. D., ph.d., Chemistry
Bhattacharyya, Bibhuti, ph.d., Statistics
**Bishir, J. W., ph.d., Mathematics**
Bordner, J., ph.d., Chemistry
Bowen, L. H., ph.d., Chemistry
Brown, H. S., ph.d., Marine, Earth and Atmospheric Sciences
**Bumgardner, C. L., ph.d., Chemistry**
Burniston, E. E., ph.d., Mathematics
Carmichael, H. H., ph.d., Chemistry
Cavaroc, V. V., Jr., ph.d., Marine, Earth, and Atmospheric Sciences

CHANDLER, R. E., PH.D., Mathematics
CHOU, W., PH.D., Computer Science
COCKERHAM, C. C., PH.D., Statistics
**DANBY, J. M., PH.D., Mathematics**
**DAVIS, W. R., PH.D., Physics**
DEARMOND, M. K., PH.D., Chemistry
DOGGETT, W. O., PH.D., Physics
DOTSON, W. G., PH.D., Mathematics
DUNN, J. C., PH.D., Mathematics
FREEDMAN, L. D., PH.D., Chemistry
FULP, R. O., PH.D., Mathematics
GERIG, T. M., PH.D., Statistics
GETZEN, F. W., PH.D., Chemistry
GIESBRECHT, F. G., PH.D., Statistics
GOLD, H. J., PH.D., Statistics
GOODMAN, M. M., PH.D., Statistics
GRANDAGE, A., PH.D., Statistics
HADER, R. J., PH.D., Statistics
**HALL, S. P., PH.D., Physics**
HANCK, K. W., PH.D., Chemistry
HARRINGTON, W. J., PH.D., Mathematics
HARTWIG, R. E., PH.D., Mathematics
HENTZ, F. C., Jr., PH.D., Chemistry
**HUGUS, Z. Z., PH.D., Chemistry**
JANOWITZ, G. S., PH.D., Marine, Earth, and Atmospheric Sciences
**JENKINS, A. W., PH.D., Physics**
JENKINS, A. W., Jr., PH.D., Physics
KATZIN, G. H., PH.D., Physics
**KOH, K., PH.D., Mathematics**
KOLB, J. R., PH.D., Mathematics
LANGFELDER, L. J., PH.D., Marine, Earth, and Atmospheric Sciences
LEVINE, S. G., PH.D., Chemistry
LOEPPERT, R. H., PH.D., Chemistry
LONG, G. G., PH.D., Chemistry
LONGMUIR, I. S., M.A., Biochemistry
LUCOVSKY, G. I., PH.D., Physics
LUH, J. PH.D., Mathematics
McVAY, F. E., PH.D., Statistics
**MAIN, A. R., PH.D., Biochemistry**
**MANRING, E. R., PH.D., Physics**
MANSON, A. R., PH.D., Statistics
MARLIN, J. A., PH.D., Mathematics
MARTIN, D. C., PH.D., Computer Science
MARTIN, E. R., PH.D., Computer Science
MARTIN, R. H., PH.D., Mathematics
**MEMORY, J. D., PH.D., Physics**
MEYER, C. D., PH.D., Mathematics
MITCHELL, G. E., PH.D., Physics
MONROE, R. J., PH.D., Statistics
MORELAND, C. G., PH.D., Chemistry
**NELSON, L. A., PH.D., Statistics**
**NICKEL, P. A., PH.D., Mathematics**
PAO, C.-V., PH.D., Mathematics
PARK, J. Y., PH.D., Physics
PATTY, R. R., PH.D., Physics
PETERSON, E. L., PH.D., Mathematics
PROCTOR, C. H., PH.D., Statistics
QUESENBERRY, C. P., PH.D., Statistics
RAWLINGS, J. D., PH.D., Statistics
RIDGEWAY, D. L., PH.D., Statistics
ROSE, N., PH.D., Mathematics
ROULIER, J. A., PH.D., Mathematics
**SAGAN, H., PH.D., Mathematics**
SAUCIER, W. J., PH.D., Marine, Earth, and Atmospheric Sciences
SCHREINER, A. F., PH.D., Chemistry
**SEAGONDOLLAR, L. W., PH.D., Physics**
STEEL, R. G. D., PH.D., Statistics
STITZINGER, E. L., PH.D., Mathematics
**STRUBLE, R. A., PH.D., Mathematics**
THARP, A. L., PH.D., Computer Science
TILLEY, D. R., PH.D., Physics
THEIL, E. C., PH.D., Biochemistry
TUCKER, W. P., PH.D., Chemistry
VAN DER VAART, H. R., PH.D., Statistics
WAHL, G. H., Jr., PH.D., Chemistry
WALTNER, A. W., PH.D., Physics
WASIK, J. L., ED.D., Statistics
WELBY, C. W., PH.D., Marine, Earth, and Atmospheric Sciences
WESLER, O., PH.D., Statistics and Mathematics
WILSON, J. B., PH.D., Mathematics

*School of Textiles:*
BUCHANAN, D. R., PH.D., Textile Material and Management
CATES, D. M., PH.D., Textile Chemistry
CULCULO, J. A., PH.D., Textile Chemistry
ELSHIEKH, A. H., D.S., Textile Material and Management
EMERSON, P. D., B.S., Textile Machine Design and Development
FORNES, R. E., PH.D., Textile Material and Management
GEORGE, T. W., M.A., Textile Material and Management
GILBERT, R. D., PH.D., Textile Chemistry
GUPTA, B. S., PH.D., Textile Material and Management
HAMBY, D. S., B.S., Textile Material and Management
HERSH, S. P., PH.D., Textiles
LORD, P. R., PH.D., Textile Material and Management
McGREGOR, R., PH.D., Textile Chemistry
MOHAMED, M. H., PH.D., Textile Material and Management
WALSH, W. K., PH.D., Textile Chemistry
WHALEY, W. M., PH.D., Textile Chemistry

*School of Veterinary Medicine:*
ADAMS, W. M., M.D., Food, Animal and Equine Medicine
ARONSON, A. L., M.D., Anatomy, Physiological Sciences, Radiology
BATTE, E. G., D.V.M., Microbiology, Pathology and Parasitology
BERKHOFF, G. A., PH.D., Microbiology, Pathology and Parasitology
COGGINS, L., M.S., Microbiology, Pathology and Parasitology
CRANE, S. W., D.V.M., Companion Animal and Special Species Medicine
CURTIN, T. M., PH.D., Veterinary Medicine
DAVIS, D. E., M.S., Food, Animal and Equine Medicine
DILLMAN, R. C., PH.D., Microbiology, Pathology and Parasitology
HARRINGTON, B. D., D.V.M., Food, Animal and Equine Medicine
HOWARD, D. R., PH.D., Companion Animal and Special Species Medicine
McPHERSON, C. W., D.V.M., Companion Animal and Special Species Medicine
MONCOL, D. J., D.V.M., Microbiology, Pathology and Parasitology
OXENDER, W. D., PH.D., Food, Animal and Equine Medicine
SIMMONS, D. G., PH.D., Microbiology, Pathology and Parasitology
SMALLWOOD, J. E., D.V.M., Anatomy, Physiological Sciences
STEVENS, C. E., PH.D., Anatomy, Physiological Sciences
TENG, C. S., PH.D., Anatomy, Physiological Sciences

*Division of University Studies:*
HUISINGH, D., PH.D., University Studies
LAMBERT, J. R., Jr., PH.D., University Studies
TURNER, W. L., D.R.P.A., University Extension and Continuing Education
WALLACE, J. C., J.D., University Studies

**University of North Carolina at Wilmington:** Wilmington, North Carolina 28401; established under the direction of the North Carolina College Conference and under the administration of the Directorate of Extension of the University of North Carolina in 1946; later organized as a county institution under the control of the New Hanover County Board of Education, known as Wilmington College; in 1969 made a unit of the University. Telephone: 791-4330.
*Chancellor:* WILLIAM H. WAGONER, M.A., PH.D.
*Vice-Chancellor for Academic Affairs:* CHARLES L. CAHILL, M.S., PH.D.
*Vice-Chancellor for Student Affairs:* WILLIAM M. MALLOY, M.ED., PH.D.
*Academic Dean:* DANIEL B. PLYLER, M.A., PH.D.
*Librarian:* EUGENE W. HUGUELET, M.A., M.S.

Number of teachers: 187.
Number of students: 3,375.

## WAKE FOREST UNIVERSITY
BOX 7226, WINSTON-SALEM, NORTH CAROLINA 27109

Telephone: 761-5000.

Founded 1834.

*President:* JAMES R. SCALES.
*Registrar:* MARGARET R. PERRY.
*Director of Admissions:* W. G. STARLING.
*Librarian:* M. G. BERTHRONG.

Library of 798,269 vols.
Number of teachers: 601 full-time, 775 part-time.
Number of students: 4,787.

## WESTERN CAROLINA UNIVERSITY
CULLOWHEE, NORTH CAROLINA 28723

Telephone: 227-7211.

Founded 1889. Linked to the University of North Carolina.

*Chancellor:* H. F. ROBINSON.
*Vice-Chancellors:* ROBERT E. STOLTZ (Academic Affairs), C. JOSEPH CARTER (Business Affairs), JAMES E. DOOLEY (Development and Special Services), GLENN W. STILLION (Student Development).
*Director of Academic Services:* JOSEPH D. CREECH.
*Director of Admissions:* TYREE H. KISER.
*Registrar:* HARRIET PARKER.
*Librarian:* WILLIAM J. KIRWAN.

Library of 310,257 vols.
Number of teachers: 322.
Number of students: 6,459.

## WINSTON-SALEM STATE UNIVERSITY
WINSTON-SALEM, NORTH CAROLINA 27102

Telephone: (919) 761-2011.

Founded 1892. Linked to the University of North Carolina.

*Chancellor:* DOUGLAS COVINGTON.
*Registrar:* Dr. BERNELL JONES.
*Director of Admissions:* Mrs. FANNIE M. WILLIAMS.
*Librarian:* Mrs. LUCY L. BRADSHAW.

The library contains 107,493 vols.
Number of teachers: 200.
Number of students: 2,094.

# NORTH DAKOTA

## DICKINSON STATE COLLEGE
DICKINSON,
NORTH DAKOTA 58601
Telephone: 227-2326.

Founded 1918.

*President:* Albert A. Watrel.
*Registrar:* N. Ableidinger.
*Librarian:* B. Reinke.

The library contains 70,000 volumes.
Number of teachers: 87.
Number of students: 1,200.

Publications: *College Catalog*† (biannual), *Prospective Student View Book*† (annual), *Western Concept*† (student newspaper), *Prairie Smoke*† (student yearbook), *Voices*† (student creative writing), *Alumni News*† (quarterly), Departmental brochures† (annual).

## JAMESTOWN COLLEGE
JAMESTOWN,
NORTH DAKOTA 58401
Telephone: (701) 253-2333.

Founded 1884.
Private control.

*President:* J. N. Anderson.
*Provost:* Dr. M. W. Andresen.
*Director of Admissions:* Clayton Ketterling.
*Librarian:* Dan Paquette.

The library contains 55,000 vols.
Number of teachers: 48.
Number of students: 582.

## MAYVILLE STATE COLLEGE
MAYVILLE,
NORTH DAKOTA 58257
Telephone: (701) 786-2301.

Founded 1889.

*President:* J. A. Schobel.
*Registrar:* K. Eastman.
*Dean of College:* Dr. R. Schwieso.
*Librarian:* Richard Van Wye.

The library contains 70,041 volumes.
Number of teachers: 45.
Number of students: 650.

## MINOT STATE COLLEGE
MINOT,
NORTH DAKOTA 58701
Telephone: 852-3100.

Founded 1913.

*President:* Dr. Gordon B. Olson.
*Registrar:* A. Peterson.
*Librarian:* G. Clark.

The library contains 73,430 volumes.
Number of teachers: 160.
Number of students: 2,700.

## NORTH DAKOTA STATE UNIVERSITY
FARGO, NORTH DAKOTA 58105
Telephone: 237-8011.

Founded 1890.

*President:* Dr. L. D. Loftsgard, ph.d
*Vice-President of Academic Affairs:* David G. Worden, ph.d.
*Vice-President for Business and Finance:* H. D. Stockman, m.s.
*Vice-President for Agriculture:* K. A. Gilles, ph.d.
*Vice-President for Student Affairs:* F. L. Pavek, ed.d.
*Registrar:* B. B. Brandrud, b.s.
*Librarian:* K. L. Janecek, m.a.

The library contains 344,663 volumes.
Number of teachers: 573.
Number of students: 6,700.

Publication: *The Bulletin*†.

Deans:

*Dean of Women:* Ellen Kilander, m.s
*Dean of Men:* B. C. Bentson, m.s.
*Faculty of Agriculture:* A. G. Hazen, m.s.
*Faculty of Humanities and Social Sciences:* A. Jones, ph.d.
*Faculty of Science and Mathematics:* John B. Gruber, ph.d.
*Faculty of Engineering and Architecture:* Joseph Stanislao, ph.d.
*Faculty of Home Economics:* Katherine Burgum, m.a.
*Faculty of Pharmacy:* P. N. Haakenson, ph.d.
*Faculty of Continuing Studies:* Virgil D. Gehring, m.s.
*Faculty of Graduate School:* J. M. Sugihara, ph.d.
*Faculty of University Studies:* N. S. Jacobsen, ph.d.

## UNIVERSITY OF NORTH DAKOTA
GRAND FORKS,
NORTH DAKOTA 58201
Telephone: University 777-2121.

Chartered 1883.

*President:* Thomas J. Clifford, m.b.a., j.d.
*Vice-President (Academic Affairs):* Alice T. Clark, ph.d.
*Vice-President (Finance):* G. Skogley, m.a.
*Vice-President (Student Affairs):* Bill Bryan, m.s., ed.d.
*Registrar:* Donald J. Wermers, ed.d.
*Librarian:* Edward S. Warner, a.m.l.s.

Library of 425,000 vols.
Number of teachers: 501.
Number of students: 10,217.

Deans:

*University College:* George Schubert, m.s., ph.d.
*Graduate:* A. W. Johnson, ph.d.
*Arts and Sciences:* B. O'Kelly, p h.d.
*Business:* Clair D. Rowe, ph.d.
*Centre for Teaching and Learning:* V. Perrone, ph.d.
*College for Human Resources Development:* Henry J. Tomasek, ph.d.
*Engineering:* A. G. Fletcher, ph.d.
*Fine Arts:* Bruce C. Jacobsen, ph.d.
*Law:* Karl P. Warden, l.l.m.
*Medicine:* Tom Johnson, b.a., m.d.
*Nursing:* Elizabeth Zinser, m.s., ph.d.
*Extension:* Orlo A. Sundre.

## VALLEY CITY STATE COLLEGE
VALLEY CITY,
NORTH DAKOTA 58072
Telephone: (701) 845-7100.

Founded 1890.

*President:* Dr. Ted D. DeVries.
*Vice-President for Academic Affairs:* Dr. Samuel H. Rankin, Jr.
*Vice-President for Business Affairs:* Nathan E. Crosby.
*Vice-President for Student Services:* Dr. David Nelson.
*Librarian:* Richard C. Holmes.

Library of 71,000 vols.
Number of teachers: 65.
Number of students: 1,150.

Publication: *The Bulletin*.

# OHIO

## ANTIOCH UNIVERSITY
YELLOW SPRINGS, OHIO 45387
Telephone: (513) 767-1424.

Founded 1852.

*President:* William M. Birenbaum.
*Senior Vice-President:* David Warren.
*Financial Vice-President:* James Wallace.
Number of teachers: 75.
Number of students: 4,000.

Publications: *Antioch Review* (quarterly), *The Record* (weekly), *The Antiochian* (monthly).

Directors:

*Antioch College:* William Birenbaum.
*Antioch New England:* Lewis Feldstein.
*Antioch Philadelphia:* David A. Frisby III.
*Antioch International:* Connie Bauer.
*School of Law:* Ronald F. Pollack.
*Antioch West:* Linda Dunne.

## ASHLAND COLLEGE
ASHLAND, OHIO 44805
Telephone: (419) 289-4142.

Founded 1878.

*President:* Joseph R. Shultz.
*Chairman of the Dean's Council:* Gene A. Telego.
*Registrar:* Richard J. Obrecht.
*Director of Libraries:* Dwight W. Robinson.

## ATHENAEUM OF OHIO
6616 BEECHMONT AVE.,
CINCINNATI, OHIO 45230

Founded 1829.

Private control (Roman Catholic); Academic year: September to June (three terms).

*Chancellor:* Archbishop JOSEPH L. BERNARDIN.
*President:* Mgr. LAWRENCE K. BRESLIN.
*Academic Dean:* Rev. MICHAEL D. PLACE.
*Registrar:* Rev. JOHN J. JENNINGS.
*Librarian:* Sister DEBORAH HARMELING.

The library contains 70,000 volumes.
Number of teachers: 33.
Number of students: 110.

## BALDWIN-WALLACE COLLEGE
275 EASTLAND RD.,
BEREA, OHIO 44017
Telephone: 826-2900.

Founded 1845.

*President:* Dr. NEAL MALICKY.
*Registrar and Director of Admissions:* J. T. AMY.
*Librarian:* Dr. PATRICK SCANLAN.

The library contains 160,000 vols.
Number of teachers: 133 full-time.
Number of students: 3,313.

## BLUFFTON COLLEGE
BLUFFTON, OHIO 45817
Telephone: 358-8015.

Founded 1900.

Private control; Academic year: September to May.

*President:* ELMER NEUFELD.
*Provost and Dean:* DONALD L. PANNABECKER.
*Librarian:* DELBERT GRATZ.

The library contains 90,000 vols.; the Mennonite Historical Library contains 15,000 vols.
Number of teachers: 55.
Number of students: 650.

## BORROMEO COLLEGE OF OHIO
28700 EUCLID AVENUE,
WICKLIFFE, OHIO 44092
Telephone: (216) 585-5900.

Founded 1954.

*President:* Very Rev. A. EDWARD PEVEC.
*Vice-President:* Rev. EDWARD MEHOK.
*Academic Dean:* Rev. MARTIN AMOS.
*Registrar:* Rev. JOHN A. VALLEY.

*Librarian:* Mrs. HEIDI MESIC.
The library contains 57,000 vols.
Number of teachers: 29.
Number of students: 90.

## BOWLING GREEN STATE UNIVERSITY
BOWLING GREEN, OHIO 43403
Telephone: (419) 372-2531.

Founded 1910.

Academic year: September to June.

*President:* HOLLIS A. MOORE.
*Provost and Executive Vice-President:* MICHAEL R. FERRARI.
*Vice-President for Operations:* G. POSTICH.
*Vice-President for Development and Alumni Affairs:* JAMES E. HOF.
*Secretary to the Board of Trustees:* RICHARD EDWARDS.

Library of 635,484 vols., 340,728 government documents.
Number of teachers: 723.
Number of students: 16,907.

Publications: Bulletins, Handbooks, *Philosopher's Index* (quarterly), *Alumni News Magazine* (6 a year), *Key* (annually), *Journal of Popular Culture* (quarterly).

DEANS:

*Arts and Sciences:* J. G. ERIKSEN.
*Education:* D. G. ELSASS.
*Business Administration:* K. E. VOGT.
*Graduate College:* G. HEBERLEIN.
*Health and Community Services:* (vacant).
*Musical Arts:* K. WENDRICH.
*Firelands:* ALGALEE ADAMS.

## CAPITAL UNIVERSITY
COLUMBUS, OHIO 43209
Telephone: 236-6011.

Founded 1850.

A Lutheran foundation; Academic year: August to May (two terms).

*President:* Dr. HARVEY A. STEGEMOELLER.
*Provost:* WALLER B. WISER, PH.D.
*Vice-President for University Relations:* JAMES TELFER.
*Vice-President for Financial Affairs:* HUGH R. HIGGINS.
*Registrar:* R. PATTERSON.
*Director of Admissions:* DIANE KOHLMEYER.
*Librarian:* ALBERT MAAG.
Library of 286,000 vols.
Number of teachers: 160.
Number of students: 2,625.

Publications: *Chimes* (newspaper), *Capitalian* (yearbook), *Capital Literary Arts Magazine* (bi-annually), *Alumni Magazine* (4 a year).

DEANS:

*Arts and Sciences:* HARRY JEBSEN, Jr.
*Music:* LARRY CHRISTOPHERSON.

*College of Nursing:* LILLIAN PIERCE (acting).
*Capital Law School:* JOSIAH BLACKMORE II, J.D.
*Graduate School of Administration:* R. PINKERTON, PH.D.
*Student Affairs:* KERMIT ALMOS, PH.D.

## CASE WESTERN RESERVE UNIVERSITY
UNIVERSITY CIRCLE,
CLEVELAND, OHIO 44106

Founded 1967 from the Western Reserve University (f. 1826 as College) and the Case Institute of Technology (f. 1880 as Case School of Applied Science). The University consists of 10 undergraduate, graduate and professional schools, and 14 specialized research centres, institutes and services.

*President:* DAVID V. RAGONE, SC.D.
*University Vice-President:* PETER R. MUSSELMAN, J.D.
*Secretary:* PATRICIA B. KILPATRICK.
*Registrar:* HELEN M. STANKARD.

DEANS:

*Graduate Studies:* LUCILLE S. MAYNE, PH.D.
*School of Dentistry:* THOMAS J. DEMARCO, D.D.S.
*School of Medicine:* RICHARD E. BEHRMAN, M.D.
*School of Law:* LINDSEY COWEN, LL.M.
*Frances Payne Bolton School of Nursing:* JANETTA MACPHAIL, PH.D.
*School of Library Science:* EDWARD T. O'NEILL, PH.D.
*School of Applied Social Sciences:* MERL C. HOKENSTAD, JR., PH.D.
*School of Management:* THEODORE M. ALFRED, PH.D.
*Case Institute of Technology:* ERIC BAER, PH.D.
*Western Reserve College:* T. DIXON LONG, PH.D.

PROFESSORS:

ABELS, P. A., PH.D., Social Sciences
ABRAMS, R., J.D., Law
ADELSON, L., M.D., Pathology
ADLER, R. J., PH.D., Engineering
AGLE, D., M.D., Psychiatry
AIKAWA, M., M.D., Pathology
ALFIDI, R., M.D., Radiology
ALFRED, T. M., PH.D., Management
ALTSCHUL, M., PH.D., History
ANDERSON, R. M., PH.D., Nursing
ANGUS, J. C., PH.D., Engineering
ANKENEY, J. L., M.D., Thoracic Surgery
ANTON, A. H., PH.D., Anesthesiology
AUSTIN, ARTHUR D., II, LL.B., Law
BAER, E., PH.D., Engineering
BALLOU, R., PH.D., Management
BANKER, BETTY Q., M.D., Pathology
BARTELMEZ, E. H., PH.D., German
BEHRMAN, R. E., M.D., Paediatrics
BENADE, A. H., PH.D., Physics
BERK, J. L., M.D., Surgery
BERRETTONI, J. N., PH.D., Statistics
BICKERS, D., M.D., Medicine
BIDELMAN, W. P., PH.D., Astronomy
BILLIAR, R., M.D., Reproductive Biology
BISSADA, N., D.D.S., Periodontics
BLACKWELL, J., Engineering
BLOCH, E. H., PH.D., M.D., Anatomy

BLUM, A., D.S.W., Social Sciences
BODANSZKY, M., D.SC., Chemistry
BOWERS, D. J., PH.D., Banking and Finance
BRADEN, A. C., Accounting
BRODKEY, J., M.D., Neurosurgery
BROSILOW, C., PH.D., Engineering
BROWN, R., PH.D., Physics
BUCHANAN, H., PH.D., History
CAPLAN, A., PH.D., Biology
CARPENTER, C., M.D., Medicine
CARTER, JAMES R., Jr., M.D., Medicine
CARTER, JOHN R., M.D., Pathology
CASCORBI, H. F., PH.D., M.D., Anaesthesiology
CASTON, J. D., PH.D., Anatomy
CHANDRASEKHAR, B. S., D.PHIL., Physics
CHATTERJEE, P., PH.D., Social Sciences
CHERNIAK, N., Medicine
CHESTER, E. H., M.D., Medicine
CHESTER, E. M., M.D., Medicine
CLARK, J. P. H., D.D.S., Dentistry
CLARK, R. A., PH.D., Mathematics
COFFEY, R. J., LL.M., Law
COHEN, K. S., LL.B., Law
COLLIN, R. E., PH.D., Engineering
COOPER, A. R., Jr., SC.D., Engineering
COOPER, C., PH.D., Biochemistry
COWEN, L., LL.M., Law
COX, R. P., M.D., Medicine
CROUCH, M. F., PH.D., Physics
DAHM, A., PH.D., Physics
DANIEL, T., M.D., Medicine
DANNLEY, R. L., PH.D., Chemistry
DAROFF, R., M.D., Neurology
DEAN, B. V., PH.D., Operations Research
DELL OSSO, L., M.D., Neurology
DE MARCO, T. J., D.D.S., Dentistry
DENHAM, J., PH.D., Chemistry
DERR, R. L., ED.D., Education
DOBYNS, B. M., M.D., PH.D., Surgery
DOERSHUK, C. F., M.D., Paediatrics
DROTNING, J. E., PH.D., Management
DUNBAR, R. C., PH.D., Chemistry
DUNN, M., Medicine
DURCHSLAG, M. R., J.D., Law
DYBBS, A., PH.D., Engineering
EASTWOOD, D. W., M.D., Anaesthesia
EBERT, L. J., Jr., PH.D., Engineering
ECK, T. G., PH.D., Physics
EDWARDS, R. V., PH.D., Engineering
ELLIS, ROSEMARY, PH.D., Nursing
ELWELL, K. R., D.D.S., Dentistry
ENLOW, D. H., D.D.S., Dentistry
EPP, E. J., PH.D., Religion
ERNST, G. W., PH.D., Engineering
EVANS, H. M., PH.D., Radiology
FACKLER, J. P., PH.D., Chemistry
FAGAN, J., PH.D., Psychology
FANAROFF, A., M.D., Paediatrics
FARRELL, D., PH.D., Physics
FICKINGER, W. J., PH.D., Physics
FLETCHER, B., M.D., Radiology
FOLDY, L. L., PH.D., Physics
FOLEY, J. M., M.D., Neurology
FORD, A. B., M.D., Medicine
FREEHAFER, A., M.D., Orthopaedics
FRIEDELL, H. L., M.D., PH.D., Radiology
FRIEDLANDER, F., PH.D., Organizational Behaviour
FRYE, G. M., Jr., PH.D., Physics
FU YAO SHI, M.D., Pathology
GABINET, L., J.D., Law
GAMBETTI, P., M.D., Pathology
GIANELLI, P. C., J.D., Law
GIANETTI, L. D., PH.D., English
GIBALA, R., PH.D., Engineering
GIBBONS, D. F., PH.D., Engineering
GIBSON, W. S., PH.D., Art
GOFFMAN, W., PH.D., Library Science
GOLD, B. R., PH.D., Economics
GOLDMAN, M., M.D., Medicine
GOLDSTEIN, H., PH.D., Social Sciences
GOLDSTEIN, M., PH.D., Anthropology
GOLDTHWAIT, D. A., M.D., Biochemistry

GOLDWYN, A. J., M.A., Library Science
GOODRIDGE, A. D., Pharmacology
GORDON, W. L., PH.D., Physics
GRAHAM, R. C., M.D., Medicine
GREBER, I., PH.D., Engineering
GREEN, L. J., PH.D., Mathematics
GREGG, E. C., PH.D., Radiology
GRICE, J. W., PH.D., Physical Education
GRIGGS, R. C., Medicine
GROSS, S., M.D., Paediatrics
GRUBER, S., SC.D., Engineering
GRUMMITT, O. J., PH.D., Chemistry
GRUNDSTEIN, N., PH.D., Organizational Behaviour
GRUNDY, K. W., PH.D., Political Science
HAIMES, Y. Y., PH.D., Engineering
HAJEK, O., DR.RER.NAT., Mathematics
HALL, P., M.D., Medicine
HANSON, R., PH.D., Biochemistry
HARMON, L., B.S.E.E., Engineering
HARRIS, J. W., M.D., Medicine
HAUG, M. R., PH.D., Sociology
HAYMAN, J. M., Jr., M.D., Medicine
HAZONY, D., PH.D., Engineering
HEALD, M., PH.D., History
HEHEMANN, R. F., PH.D., Engineering
HEIPLE, K. G., M.D., Surgery
HELLERSTEIN, H. K., M.D., Medicine
HERNDON, C. H., M.D., Orthopaedic Surgery
HEUER, A. H., PH.D., Engineering
HILTON, P. J., PH.D., Mathematics
HINES, J. D., M.D., Medicine
HIRSCHMANN, H., M.D., Medicine
HLAVACEK, J., PH.D., Management
HOFFMAN, R. W., PH.D., Physics
HOKENSTAD, M. C., Jr., PH.D., Social Sciences
HOLDEN, W. D., M.D., Surgery
HOLLAND, T. P., Social Science
HOPFINGER, A., PH.D., Macrobiotic Sciences
HORTON, B., PH.D., Engineering
HOSHIKO, T., PH.D., Physiology
HOUSER, H. B., M.D., Epidemiology
HRONES, J. A., SC.D., Engineering
HUBAY, C. A., M.D., Surgery
ILAN, J., PH.D., Anatomy
INKLEY, S., M.D., Medicine
IZANT, R. J., Jr., Surgery
JENKINS, T. L., PH.D., Physics
JONES, J. V., M.S., Library Science
JUNGER, P. D., LL.B., Law
KADISH, M. R., PH.D., Philosophy
KAHNE, S. J., PH.D., Engineering
KARIPIDES, K., PH.D., Theatre
KASS, L., M.D., Pathology
KATZ, L. R., J.D., Law
KAUFMAN, B., Radiology
KEAN, E., PH.D., Research
KELLERMEYER, R. W., Medicine
KENNELL, J. H., Paediatrics
KENNEY, M. E., PH.D., Chemistry
KESSLER, JANE W., PH.D., Psychology
KICHER, T., PH.D., Engineering
KLAUS, M. H., Paediatrics
KLEIN, L., M.D., Biochemistry
KLOPMAN, G., D.SC., Chemistry
KO, W.-H., PH.D., Engineering
KOENIG, J. L., PH.D., Engineering
KOHN, R. R., M.D., Pathology
KOLB, D. A., PH.D., Management
KOWAL, J., M.D., Pharmacology
KOWALSKI, K. L., PH.D., Physics
KRAMPITZ, L. O., PH.D., D.SC., Microbiology
KRETCHMER, H. E., M.SC., M.D., Anesthesiology
KRIEGER, H., M.D., Surgery
KURTH, H., Dramatic Arts
KUSHNER, I., M.D., Medicine
LANDAU, B. R., M.D., PH.D., Medicine
LANDO, J. B., PH.D., Engineering
LASEK, R., M.D., Anatomy
LAWRY, R. P., J.D., Law
LEATHERBERRY, W. G., J.D., Law

LEFKOWITZ, I., PH.D., Engineering
LEFTON, M., PH.D., Sociology
LEITMAN, M., PH.D., Mathematics
LENKOSKI, L. D., M.D., Psychiatry
LIEBMAN, J., M.D., Biomedical Engineering
LITT, M. H., PH.D., Engineering
LITTLE, A. B., M.D., Reproductive Biology
LIU, C., PH.D., Engineering
LONG, H., PH.D., Classics
LOWHATER, A. J., PH.D., Mathematics
LYTLE, N. A., ED.D., Nursing
MACINTYRE, M. N., PH.D., Anatomy
MACPHAIL, JANNETTA, PH.D., Nursing
MCCOLLOM, W. G., PH.D., English
MCGERVEY, J. D., PH.D., Physics
MCMILLAN, G. R., PH.D., Chemistry
MAHMOUD, A., M.D., Medicine
MAIN, MARJORIE W., PH.D., Social Sciences
MALONE, C. A., M.A., Psychiatry
MANN, J. A., PH.D., Engineering
MANSON, S. S., M.S., Engineering
MARSH, FLORENCE G., PH.D., English
MARTIN, B., PH.D., Religion
MATT, M. M., D.D.S., Oral Pathology
MATTHEWS, L. W., M.D., Paediatrics
MAWARDI, O. K., PH.D., Engineering
MAYNE, L., PH.D., Banking
MEARNS, E. A., Jr., LL.B., Law
MEDALIE, J. H., M.D., Family Medicine
MEDAERIS, D. N., Jr., M.D., Paediatrics
MENDELSOHN, H. J., Surgery
MENDELSON, A., Engineering
MERGLER, H. W., PH.D., Engineering
MERKATZ, I., M.D., Reproductive Biology
MESAROVIC, M. D., PH.D., Engineering
MILLER, S., M.D., Psychiatry
MIRALDI, F. D., M.D., Biomedical Engineering
MITCHELL, T., PH.D., Engineering
MOIR, T., M.D., Medicine
MORRISEY, T., PH.D., Management
MORTIMER, E. A., Jr., M.D., Community Health
MOSES, F., PH.D., Engineering
MOSKOWITZ, R. W., M.D., Medicine
NAFF, G., M.D., Medicine
NARA, H. R., PH.D., Engineering
NATION, J. E., PH.D., Speech
NEET, K., M.D., Biochemistry
NELSON, R. J., PH.D., Philosophy
NETH, S., LL.M., Law
NEUHAUSER, D. B., M.D., Community Health
NEVILLE, J., PH.D., Nutrition
NORDLANDER, J., E., PH.D., Chemistry
NULSEN, F. E., M.D., Neurosurgery
NYGAARD, O. F., Radiology
OCCHINERO, R. L., D.D.S., Dentistry
ORNSTEIN, R., PH.D., English
OSTRACH, S., PH.D., Engineering
PAO, Y.-H., PH.D., Engineering
PARKER, R. F., M.D., Microbiology
PAYNE, D., D.M.A., Music
PEARSON, O. H., M.D., Medicine
PERNELL, RUBY B., PH.D., Social Sciences
PERSKY, H., M.D., Surgery
PESCH, P., PH.D., Astronomy
PHILLIPS, L., PH.D., Accounting
PHIPPS, WILMA, A.M., Nursing
PICKER, S. I., Jr., LL.M., Law
PREVITS, G., PH.D., Accounting
PRITCHARD, W. H., M.D., Medicine
PTACEK, P. H., PH.D., Speech Communication
PURNELL, E. W., M.D., Surgery
RAKITA, L., M.D., Medicine
RAMMELKAMP, C. H., Jr., M.D., Medicine
RATCHESON, R., M.D., Neurosurgery
RATNOFF, O. D., M.D., Medicine
RAWSKI, C. H., PH.D., Library Science
REAGAN, J. W., M.D., Pathology
RECKNAGEL, R. O., PH.D., Physiology
REES, A. M., M.S., Library Science
REEVES, C. H., PH.D., Classics
REICHART, S., ED.D., Education

REISMAN, A., PH.D., Operations Research
RESHOTKO, E., PH.D., Engineering
RICH, R., PH.D., Nursing
RICHMOND, P., A. PH.D., Library Science
RITCHEY, W. M., PH.D., Chemistry
ROBBINS, F. C., M.D., D.SC., Community Health
ROBERTSON, A. L., M.D., Pathology
ROBINSON, D., PH.D., Physics
ROGERS, C. E., PH.D., Engineering
ROSE, F. A., M.D., Radiology
ROSENBERG, G., PH.D., Sociology
ROSENBLATT, J., PH.D., Biometry
ROSENKRANZ, H., M.D., Community Health
ROSS, H. A., LL.B., Law
ROTH, J. J., PH.D., History
ROTHCHILD, I., M.D., PH.D., Reproductive Biology
ROTTMAN, F., M.D., Microbiology
ROWELL, J. A., PH.D., Library Science
ROWLAND, V., M.D., Psychiatry
RUSHFORTH, N. B., PH.D., Biology
SAADA, A. S., PH.D., Engineering
SABLE, H. Z., M.D., PH.D., Biochemistry
SAIDEL, G., PH.D., Biomedical Engineering
SAKAMI, W., PH.D., Biochemistry
SALKIN, H., PH.D., Operations Research
SALM, P., PH.D., German
SALOMON, R. B., PH.D., English
SARACEVIC, T., PH.D., Library Science
SAVIN, S. M., PH.D., Earth Sciences
SAYERS, G., PH.D., Physiology
SCALETTA, L., D.D.S., Oral Biology
SCHAFER, I. A., M.D., Paediatrics
SCHLOTFELDT, R. M., PH.D., Nursing
SCHORR, A. L., PH.D., Social Work
SCHROEDER, O. C., Jr., LL.B., Law
SCHUELE, P., PH.D., Physics
SEGALL, B., PH.D., Physics
SHANKER, M. G., J.D., Law
SHOLANDER, M. C., PH.D., Mathematics
SHUCK, J., M.D., Surgery
SILVERS, J. B., PH.D., Finance
SIMHA, R., PH.D., Engineering
SINCLAIR, D. M., PH.D., Library Science
SINEY, M. C., PH.D., History
SINGER, M., PH.D., Anatomy
SKEGGS. L. T., PH.D., Biochemistry
SOKOL, R., M.D., Reproductive Biology
SPREY, J., PH.D., Sociology
SRIVASTA, S., PH.D., Organizational Behaviour
STAVITSKY, A. B., PH.D., Microbiology
STEIN, M., D.D.S., Dentistry
STEINBERG, A. G., PH.D., Biology
STEPHENSON, C. B., PH.D., Astronomy
STORAASLI, J. P., M.D., Radiology
STRAUSS, W., PH.D., German
STUEHR, J. R., PH.D., Chemistry
SUESS, J. G., PH.D., Music
SWIFT, T. J., PH.D., Chemistry
TAAFFE, J. G., PH.D., English
TAIT, M., PH.D., Music
TAKACS, L., PH.D., Mathematics
TANDLER, B., D.D.S., Oral Biology
TAVILL, A. S., M.D., Medicine
TAYLOR, P. J., PH.D., Physics
THALER, R. M., PH.D., Physics
THOMPSON, E. D., PH.D., Engineering
TOBOCMAN, W., PH.D., Physics
TROIANO, A. R., SC.D., Engineering
TROOST, B., M.D., Neurology
URBACH, F., PH.D., Chemistry
UBBELOHDE, C. W., PH.D., History
UTTER, M. F., PH.D., Biochemistry
UYEKI, E., PH.D., Special Interdisciplinary Studies
VAN TASSEL, D. D., PH.D., History
VERTES, V., M.D., Medicine
VICTOR, M., M.D., Neurology
VIGNOS, P., M.D., Medicine
WALLACE, J. F., S.M., Engineering
WALLACE, R. A., M.A., English
WALTON, A. G., PH.D., Engineering
WAY, F. III, B.S., Engineering
WEBSTER, L., M.D., Pharmacology
WECKESSER, E. C., M.D., Surgery
WEISMAN, R., M.D., Medicine
WELKER, R., PH.D., Inderdisciplinary Studies
WELLS, C., PH.D., Mathematics
WENTZ, W. B., PH.D., Reproductive Biology
WERNER, RUTH M., PH.D., Social Sciences
WHITE, R. J., M.D., PH.D., Neurosurgery
WHITMAN, D. R., PH.D., Chemistry
WILCOTT, R. C., PH.D., Psychology
WILLARD, H. B., PH.D., Physics
WISOTZKY, J., D.D.S., Dentistry
WOLFE, D. M., PH.D., Organizational Behaviour
WOLINSKY, E., M.D., Pathology
WOOLF, R. B., M.D., Reproductive Biology
WOOD, H. G., PH.D., D.SC., Biochemistry
WRIGHT, D. K., Jr., M.S., Engineering
WU, T.-S., PH.D., Mathematics
YEAGER, E. B., PH.D., Chemistry
YOUNG, D. M., PH.D., Labour Relations
YOUNG, G. S., PH.D., Mathematics
ZUBIZARRETA, A., PH.D., Spanish
ZULL, J., PH.D., Biology

## CENTRAL STATE UNIVERSITY
WILBERFORCE, OHIO 45384
Telephone: 376-6011.
Founded 1887.

*President:* LIONEL H. NEWSOM.
*Registrar:* Dr. HOWARD F. SWONIGAN (acting).
*Director of Admissions:* EDITH JOHNSON.
*Librarian:* GEORGE T. JOHNSON.

The library contains 130,000 vols.
**Number of teachers:** 109.
**Number of students:** 2,594.

Publications: *Annual Catalog*, *Alumni Journal* (quarterly), *Alumni Newsletter* (quarterly).

DEANS:
*College of Arts and Sciences:* Dr. D. W. HAZEL.
*College of Business Administration:* Mrs. URCELLE C. WILLIS (acting).
*College of Education:* Dr. E. L. WINGARD.

## CLEVELAND STATE UNIVERSITY
EUCLID AVE. AT 24TH STREET, CLEVELAND, OHIO 44115
Telephone: (216) 687-2000
Founded 1964.

*President:* WALTER B. WAETJEN, ED.D
*Provost and Vice-President for Academic Affairs:* JOHN A. FLOWER, PH.D.
*Vice-President for Business and Finance:* G. L. HANSEN, B.S.E., M.B.A
*Vice-President for Student Services:* A. G. TEW, PH.D.
*Vice-President for University Relations:* C. R. SMITH, ED.D.
*Director of Libraries:* DUNCAN H. WALL.

Library of 480,654 vols., 6,200 periodicals, 360,579 microforms.
**Number of teachers:** 524 full-time, 190 part-time.
**Number of students:** 19,250.

DEANS:
*College of Business Administration:* E. P. SMITH, PH.D.
*College of Engineering:* Dr. ROBERT COMPARIN.
*College of Arts and Sciences:* J. A. SOULES, M.S., PH.D.
*College of Education:* R. J. MCARDLE, PH.D.
*Cleveland-Marshall College of Law:* Dr. ROBERT BOGOMOLNY.
*Continuing Education:* Dr. FERRIS F. ANTHONY.
*Graduate Studies:* RONALD G. SCHULTZ, PH.D.
*Special Studies:* R. L. PRUITT, PH.D.

## COLLEGE OF MOUNT ST. JOSEPH ON THE OHIO
5700 DELHI ROAD, MOUNT ST. JOSEPH, OHIO 45051
Telephone: (513) 244-4200.
Founded 1920.

*President:* JEAN PATRICE HARRINGTON, PH.D., S.C.
*Executive Assistant to President:* WILLIAM J. SHUSTOWSKI, Jr., PH.D.
*Registrar:* Sister RITA SCHMUTTE, M.A., S.C.
*Academic Dean:* HARRY A. BLANTON, PH.D.
*Comptroller:* RICHARD DAGENBACH, M.B.A.
*Director of Admissions:* DOMENIC TETI, M.A.
*Dean of Student Affairs:* TERESA LOGAN, PH.D.
*Librarian:* Sister ELIZABETH BROWN, M.S.L.S., S.C.

Library of 105,973 vols.
**Number of teachers:** 80 full-time equivalent.
**Number of students:** 1,480.

Publications: *Catalog†*, *Mountings†* (quarterly).

## COLLEGE OF WOOSTER
WOOSTER, OHIO 44691
Founded 1866.

Independent, founded by the United Presbyterian Church in the U.S.A.

*President:* HENRY J. COPELAND, PH.D.
*Vice-President for Academic Affairs:* WILLIAM M. BAIRD, PH.D.
*Vice-President for Development:* SARA L. PATTON, M.A.
*Vice-President for Finance and Business:* HANS H. JENNY, DR.RER.POL.
*Secretary:* DEBORAH P. HILTY, PH.D.
*Registrar:* W. L. CULP, B.A.
*Director of Admissions:* B. E. MORRIS, M.A.
*Librarian:* MICHAEL S. FREEMAN.

Library of over 279,000 vols.
**Number of teachers:** 130.
**Number of students:** 1,805.

Publications: *Voice* (student newspaper), *Wooster Alumni Magazine*, *Wooster Reports*.

DEANS:
*Faculty:* VIVIAN L. HOLLIDAY, PH.D.
*Students:* K. R. PLUSQUELLEC.

## DEFIANCE COLLEGE
DEFIANCE, OHIO 43512
Telephone: (419) 784-4010.

Founded 1850.

*President:* M. J. LUDWIG.
*Dean of the College:* CLIFFORD V. BARR.
*Librarian:* M. J. LAMBRIGHT.
Library of 88,000 vols.
Number of teachers: 50.
Number of students: 699.

## DENISON UNIVERSITY
GRANVILLE, OHIO 43023
Telephone: (614) 587-0810.

Founded 1831.

Private control; Academic year: September to June.

*President:* ROBERT C. GOOD.
*Provost:* L. F. BRAKEMAN.
*Vice-President for Finance and Management:* J. L. HICKS, Jr.
*Registrar:* LARRY R. MURDOCK.
*Director of Admissions:* RICHARD F. BOYDEN.
*Director of the Library:* CHARLES B. MAURER.
Number of teachers: 160 full-time equivalent, including 58 professors.
Number of students: 2,075.

DEANS:
*College:* ANTHONY J. LISSKA.
*Dean of Students:* ALEXANDER F. SMITH.

## FINDLAY COLLEGE
1000 NORTH MAIN ST.,
FINDLAY, OHIO 45840
Telephone: 422-8313.

Founded 1882.

*President:* GLEN R. RASMUSSEN.
*Registrar:* Mrs. MYRA BUSCH-GOETZ.
*Director of Admissions:* J. MICHAEL TURNBULL.
*Librarian:* CHARLES NEWMAN.
The library contains 95,000 vols.
Number of teachers: 80.
Number of students: 1,140.

## HEBREW UNION COLLEGE—JEWISH INSTITUTE OF RELIGION
3101 CLIFTON AVENUE,
CINCINNATI, OHIO 45220
Telephone: (513) 221-1875.

Founded 1875.

*President:* Dr. ALFRED GOTTSCHALK.
*Dean:* Rabbi KENNETH E. EHRLICH.
*Librarian:* H. ZAFREN.
The library contains 500,000 volumes and 6,000 ancient manuscripts.
Number of teachers: 150.
Number of students: 1,100.
Publications: *American Jewish Archives*, *Hebrew Union College Annual*, *Studies in Bibliography and Booklore*, *Bibliographica Judaica*, *The Chronicle*.

## HEIDELBERG COLLEGE
TIFFIN, OHIO 44883
Telephone: 419-448-2202.

Founded 1850.

*President:* WILLIAM C. CASSELL.
*Vice-President and Dean of College:* PRESTON W. FORBES.
*Vice-President for Administration:* WILLIAM F. GOODWIN.
*Registrar:* M. VAN DYKE.
*Director of Admissions:* STEVEN W. POCHARD.
*Librarian:* JANICE STRICKLAND.
The library contains 130,777 vols.
Number of teachers: 71 full-time, 29 part-time.
Number of students: 806.
Publications: *Heidelberg Alumni Magazine†*, *Heidelberg College Catalogue*.

## HIRAM COLLEGE
HIRAM, OHIO 44234
Telephone: (216) 569-3211.

Founded 1850.

*President:* ELMER JAGOW.
*Registrar:* JUDITH ISMAIL.
*Librarian:* BARBARA SNEAD.
The library contains 152,000 vols.
Number of teachers: 95.
Number of students: 1,114.

## JOHN CARROLL UNIVERSITY
CLEVELAND, OHIO 44118
Telephone: (216) 491-4911.

Founded 1886.

Private control (Roman Catholic affiliated); academic year: September to December, January to May, plus two five-week summer terms.

*President:* T. P. O'MALLEY, S.J., S.T.L., LITT.D.
*Academic Vice-President:* A. J. NOETZEL, M.B.A., PH.D.
*Dean of College of Arts and Sciences:* THEODORE W. WALTERS, S.J., PH.D.
*Dean of School of Business:* V. RAY ALFORD, PH.D.
*Dean of Graduate School:* LOUIS G. PECEK, PH.D.
*Dean of Admissions:* (vacant).
*Registrar:* J. F. HUDDLESTON, A.B., J.D.
*Director of Library:* JOHN S. PIETY, M.L.S.
Library of 347,106 vols.
Number of teachers: 271.
Number of students: 4,000.

## KENT STATE UNIVERSITY
KENT, OHIO 44242
Telephone: 672-2121.

Founded 1910.

*President:* Dr. BRAGE GOLDING.
*Vice-President for Business Affairs and Treasurer:* RICHARD E. DUNN.
*Provost and Vice-President for Academic and Student Affairs:* Dr. MICHAEL SCHWARTZ.
*Vice-President for University Affairs:* CHARLES W. INGLER, Jr.
*Vice-President (and Executive Assistant):* Dr. ROBERT MCCOY.
*Associate Vice-President for Extended University:* Dr. GORDON W. KELLER.
*Director of Admissions:* BRUCE L. RIDDLE.
*Librarian:* H. W. KRITZER.
The library contains 1,500,000 vols.
Number of teachers: 800.
Number of students: 25,000.
Publications: College catalogues, monthly bulletins, *Kent* (quarterly).

DEANS AND DIRECTORS:
*Education:* (vacant).
*Arts and Sciences:* R. O. BUTTLAR.
*Business and Administration:* (vacant).
*Fine and Professional Arts:* HARRY AUSPRICH.
*Honors and Experimental College:* OTTAVIO CASALE.
*Graduate College:* ROBERT E. POWELL.
*Library Science:* A. R. ROGERS.
*School of Physical Education, Recreation and Dance:* BETTY HARTMAN.
*School of Nursing:* L. HENDERSON.
*Research and Sponsored Programs:* E. P. WENNINGER.
*Liquid Crystals Institute:* G. BROWN.

## KENYON COLLEGE
GAMBIER, OHIO 43022

Founded 1824.

*President:* P. H. JORDAN, Jr., PH.D.
*Provost:* JERRY A. IRISH, PH.D.
*Director of Admissions:* J. D. KUSHAN, A.B., M.ED.
*Dean of Students:* T. J. EDWARDS, M.A.
*Dean for Academic Advising:* MARGARET E. TOWNSEND, M.A.
*Librarian:* WILLIAM T. DAMERON, M.A.L.S.
The library contains 275,816 vols.
Number of teachers: 116.
Number of students: 1,450.

## LAKE ERIE COLLEGE
PAINESVILLE, OHIO 44077
Telephone: (216) 352-3361.
Founded 1856.

Private control; Academic year: September to June (three terms and one summer session); includes a four-year residential college for women with an academic term abroad, and Garfield Senior College, a non-residential co-educational college serving primarily students in the last two years.

*President:* CHARLES E. P. SIMMONS, PH.D.
*Dean of College:* LESLIE VAN MARTER, PH.D.
*Registrar:* MARGERY AINSWORTH, A.B.
*Director of Admissions:* FRAN COOK, PH.D.

The library contains 1,055 vols.
Number of teachers: 75.
Number of students: 1,055.

Publications: *Lake Erie College Studies* (irregular), *Nota Bene* (annual), *Bulletin, Cymbal.*

## MALONE COLLEGE
515 25TH STREET, N.W.,
CANTON, OHIO 44709
Founded 1892.

*President:* (vacant).
*Executive Vice-President:* RONALD G. JOHNSON.

Library of 97,600 vols.
Number of teachers: 43.
Number of students: 776.
Publication: *The Messenger†.*

## MARIETTA COLLEGE
MARIETTA, OHIO 45750
Telephone: (614) 373-4643.
Chartered 1835.

Private control; liberal arts, fine arts and petroleum engineering.

*President:* SHERRILL CLELAND, PH.D.
*Dean:* DWIGHT L. LING, PH.D.
*Dean of Students:* STEPHEN E. MARKWOOD.
*Librarian:* R. F. CAYTON, PH.D.

Library of 241,912 vols.
Number of teachers: 102, including 36 professors.
Number of students: 860 men, 460 women.

Publications: *Bulletin, Marietta's World, The Blue and White.*

## MIAMI UNIVERSITY
OXFORD, OHIO 45056
Telephone: (513) 529-2161.
Founded 1809.
State control.

*President:* PAUL G. PEARSON, PH.D.
*Executive Vice-President for Academic Affairs and Provost:* D. G. BROWN, PH.D.
*Vice-President for Student Affairs:* R. F. ETHERIDGE, ED.D.
*Vice-President for Finance and Business Affairs:* L. GOGGIN, M.B.A.
*Vice-President for Development and Alumni Affairs:* J. E. DOLIBOIS, A.B.
*Vice-President for University Relations:* JOHN E. DOLIBOIS, A.B.
*Registrar:* K. H. BOGARD, Jr., M.S.
*Director of Libraries:* D. E. OEHLERTS, PH.D.

Number of teachers: 762.
Number of students: 17,865.

DEANS:

*Arts and Science:* C. K. WILLIAMSON, PH.D.
*Business:* B. R. MOECKEL, PH.D.
*Education:* J. S. BRANCH, PH.D.
*Fine Arts:* C. L. SPOHN, PH.D.
*Applied Science:* G. BOWERS, M.S.
*Interdisciplinary Studies (Western College Program):* C. W. ELLISON, PH.D.
*Graduate School:* S. PETERSON, PH.D.

## MOUNT UNION COLLEGE
ALLIANCE, OHIO 44601
Founded 1846.

*President:* G. BENJAMIN LANTZ, Jr., PH.D.
*Dean:* JOHN F. FLEISCHAUER, PH.D.
*Registrar:* PAUL E. FROMAN, M.A.
*Librarian:* N. Y. OSBORNE, LITT.M., B.L.S.

Number of teachers: 73, including 21 full professors.
Number of students: 1,074.
Publications: *Alumni Bulletin, Catalogues.*

## MUSKINGUM COLLEGE
NEW CONCORD, OHIO 43762
Founded 1837.

Church related, liberal arts college.

*President:* ARTHUR J. DE JONG.
*Vice-President of Academic Affairs:* DANIEL E. VAN TASSEL.
*Vice-President of Resources and Public Affairs:* PAUL MORRIS.
*Dean of Student Life:* DAVID R. SKEEN.
*Executive Director of Planning and Development:* RONALD A. MULDER.
*Director of Admissions:* JAY LEIENDECKER.
*Librarian:* H. SAFFORD.

Library of 170,000 vols.
Number of professors: 67.
Number of students: 930.

Publications: *Catalog, Alumni Bulletin, The Muskie Handbook, View Book†.*

## NOTRE DAME COLLEGE OF OHIO
4545 COLLEGE ROAD,
CLEVELAND, OHIO 44121
Telephone: (216) 381-1680.
Founded 1922.

*President:* Sister MARY MARTHE REINHARD, S.N.D.
*Academic Dean:* Sister MARY DONALD DUNHAM, S.N.D.
*Librarian:* ANITA JOHNSON.

Library of 86,178 vols.
Number of teachers: 33 full-time, 31 part-time.
Number of students: 690.

## OBERLIN COLLEGE
OBERLIN, OHIO 44074
Founded 1833

*President:* EMIL C. DANENBERG, MUS.D.
*Vice-President and Provost:* JAMES L. POWELL, PH.D.
*Vice-President for Business and Finance:* DAYTON E. LIVINGSTON, M.B.A.
*Vice-President for External Affairs:* DAVID W. CLARK, M.DIV.
*Director of Admissions:* CARL W. BEWIG, M.A.
*Treasurer:* R. S. COOPER, M.A.
*Secretary:* ROBERT A. HASLUN, B.A.
*Director of Libraries:* WILLIAM A. MOFFETT, M.L.S.

Library of *c.* 825,000 vols.
Number of teachers: 226.
Number of students: 2,750.

DEANS:

*College of Arts and Sciences:* ROBERT M. LONGSWORTH, PH.D.
*Conservatory of Music:* DAVID S. BOE, M.A.

## OHIO DOMINICAN COLLEGE
1216 SUNBURY ROAD,
COLUMBUS, OHIO 43219
Telephone: 253-2741.

Four-year co-educational liberal arts college; founded 1911 as College of St. Mary of the Springs; name changed 1968.

Academic year: August to May (two terms and one 7-week summer session.

*President:* Sister MARY ANDREW MATESICH, O.P.
*Registrar:* Mrs. MARIE TAYLOR.
*Director of Admissions:* WILLIAM ANDERSON.
*Librarian:* Sister THOMAS AQUIN KELLY.

The library contains 74,055 vols.
Number of teachers: 69.
Number of students: 1,000.

## OHIO NORTHERN UNIVERSITY
### ADA, OHIO 45810
Telephone: (419) 634-9921.

Founded 1871.

Private (United Methodist); Academic year: September to May (summer sessions, June to August).

*President:* Dr. DeBow Freed.
*Registrar:* J. L. Moorf.
*Librarian:* J. W. Baker.

The library contains 320,600 vols.
Number of teachers: 183.
Number of students: 2,700.

### Deans:
*Arts and Sciences:* Dr. D. P. Peltier.
*Engineering:* L. H. Archer.
*Pharmacy:* Dr. L. D. Beltz.
*Law:* Dr. D. Guy.
*Business Administration:* Dr. C. A. Painter.

## OHIO STATE UNIVERSITY
### 190 NORTH OVAL MALL, COLUMBUS, OHIO 43210
Telephone: (614) 422-6446.

Founded 1870; campuses at Lima, Mansfield, Marion and Newark.

*President:* Harold L. Enarson, ph.d.
*Provost:* W. Ann Reynolds, ph.d.
*Vice-President for Business and Administration:* Richard D. Jackson, b.s.c.e.
*Vice-President for Educational Services:* Kathryn T. Schoen, ph.d.
*Vice-President for Regional Campuses and Dean of the University College:* J. T. Mount, m.s.
*Vice-President for Student Services:* William R. Nester, ph.d.
*Vice-President for University Development:* Richard O. Buxton, b.a.
*Vice-President for Finance and Planning:* William E. Vandament, ph.d.
*Vice-President for Medical Affairs:* Henry G. Cramblett, m.d. (acting).
*Vice-President for Public Affairs:* Edwin M. Crawford, b.s.
*Vice-President for Personnel Services and Secretary to the Board of Trustees:* Madison H. Scott, b.a.
*Assistant Vice-President for Registration Services:* James F. Loucks, ph.d.

Library: see Libraries.
Number of teachers: 3,681.
Number of students: 57,938.

Publications: *Bulletin of Business Research* (monthly), *College of Medicine Journal* (quarterly), *News in Engineering* (monthly), *Ohio Biological Survey Bulletin* (every 2 months), *Journal of Higher Education* (monthly), *Ohio Journal of Science* (every 2 months), *Journal of Money, Credit and Banking* (quarterly), *Ohio State Engineer* (student quarterly), *Ohio Theatre Collection Bulletin* (annually), *Speculum* (Veterinary Medicine, quarterly), *Theory into Practice* (5 a year), etc.

### Deans.
*College of Administrative Science:* H. Justin Davidson, m.s.
*College of Agriculture and Home Economics:* R. M. Kottman, ph.d.
*College of the Arts:* Andrew J. Broekema, ph.d.
*College of Biological Sciences:* Patrick R. Dugan.
*College of Dentistry:* William R. Wallace, d.d.s. (acting).
*College of Education:* Robert A. Burnham, ph.d.
*College of Engineering:* Donald D. Glower, ph.d.
*College of Humanities:* Diether H. Haenicke, ph.d.
*College of Law:* James E. Meeks.
*College of Mathematical and Physical Sciences:* Colin B. B. Bull, ph.d.
*College of Medicine:* H. G. Cramblett, m.d.
*College of Optometry:* F. W. Hebbard, ph.d., o.d.
*College of Pharmacy:* Albert H. Soloway, ph.d.
*College of Social and Behavioural Sciences:* S. Earl Brown, ph.d.
*College of Veterinary Medicine:* Ronald A. Wright, d.v.m., m.s.
*College of Social Work:* Robert O. Washington, ph.d.
*Graduate School:* Jules P. Lapidus, ph.d.
*University College:* J. T. Mount, m.s.

### Full Professors:
*College of the Arts:*

Art:
Baughman, J. W.
Black, D. E.
Chafetz, S.
Freeman, J. B.
Friley, E. B.
Hebner, E. F., Jr.
King, R. D.
Ruzicka, F. A.

Art Education:
Csuri, C.A.
Efland, A. D.
Severino, D. A.

Design:
Butter, F. F. H.
Konelik, J. A.
Megert, P.
Wallschlaeger, A. C.
Wood, D. G.
Zimmer, F. A., Jr.

History of Art:
Ludden, F. N.
Melnikas, A.

Dance:
Alkire, Helen P.
Blaine, V. J.
Venable, L. D.

Music:
Barnes, M. H.
Burkart, R. E.
Casey, M. T.
Cooper, I. M.
Costanza, P.
Haddad, G. R.
Hare, R. Y.
Kuehefuhs, Gertrude C.
Livingston, H. S.
Main, A. M.
Meeker, D. L.

Mixter, K. E.
Poland, B. W., III
Ramsey, H. W.
Sexton, A. J.
Tetleykardos, R.
Tolbert, Mary R.
Wilson, G. J.
Wink, R. L.

Theatre:
Crepeau, G. P.
Golding, A. S.
Lewis, G. L.
Ritter, C. C.
Walker, J. A.

*College of Biological Sciences:*

Biochemistry:
Barber, G. A.
Behrman, E. J.
Deatherage, F. E.
Doskotch, R. W.
Harper, W. J.
Ives, D. H.
Marzluff, G. A.
Moore, R. O.
Moxon, A. L.
Scott, R. A.
Serif, G. S.
Snell, J. F.
Vanwinkle, Q.

Biophysics:
Blackwell, H. R.
Corson, S. A.
Hill, R. M.
Hollander, P. B.
Lipetz, L. E.
Rothstein, J.
Smith, S. W.
Snell, J. F.
Stow, R. W.
Vanwinkle, Q.

Entomology:
Blair, B. D.
Borror, D. J.
Briggs, J. D.
Britt, N. W.
Collins, W. J.
Goleman, D. L.
Holdsworth, R. Jr.
Johnston, D. E.
Krueger, H. R.
Miller, R. L.
Niemczyk, H. D.
Rings, R. W.
Rothenbuhler, W.
Shambaugh, G. F.
Treece, R. E.
Triplehorn, C. A.
Waldron, A. C.
Wharton, G. W., Jr.

Genetics:
Birky, C. W.
Fechheimer, N. S.
Griffing, J. B.
Harvey, W. R.
House, V. L.
Kriebel, H. B.
Paddock, E. F.
Plaine, H. L.
Rothenbuhler, W.
Swiger, L. A.
Weaver, C. R.
Young, S. S. Y.

Microbiology:
Banwart, G. J.
Bohl, E. H.
Chorpenning, F. W.
Dodd, M. C.
Dugan, P. R.
Ferguson, L. C.
Frea, T. F.
Kreier, J. P.

MILLER, R. H.
PFISTER, R. M.
RANDLES, C. I.
RHEINS, M. S.
ROSEN, S.
SNELL, J. F.
ST. PIERRE, R L.
SUIE, T.
WILSON, G. P., III
WOLFF, D. A.
YOHN, S. D.

*Botany:*
BOHNING, R. H.
POPHAM, R. A.
RUDOLPH, E. D.
SCHMITT, J. A., Jr.
SCHOPF, J. M.
SWANSON, C. A.
TAFT, C. E.
TAYLOR, T. N.

*Zoology:*
COLINVAUX, P. A.
CRITES, J. L.
GILTZ, M. L.
GOOD, E. E.
MITCHELL, R. O.
MYERS, T. B.
MYSER, W. C.
PETERLE, T. J.
PUTNAM, L. S.
ROTHENSBUHLER, W.
STANSBERY, D. H.
STEVENS, B. C.
VALENTINE, B. C.

College of Humanities:
*Black Studies:*
GOUKE, C. G.
NELSON, W. E.
STULL, R. L.

*Classics:*
BABCOCK, C. L.
HAHM, D. E.
LENARDON, R. J.
MORFORD, M. P. O.
TRACY, S. V.

*Comparative Studies:*
BJORNSON, R. W.

*East Asian Languages and Literatures:*
CHING, E.
LI, T.
LIGHT, T.

*English:*
ALTICK, R. D.
BEJA, M.
CANZONERI, R. W.
CORBETT, E. B.
COX, L. S.
GABEL, J. B.
KAHRL, S. J.
KUHN, A. J.
LOCKRIDGE, E. H.
MARKELS, J. H.
MARSHALL, C. L.
MAURER, A. E. W.
MUSTE, J. M.
O'HARE, F.
ROBBINS, E. W.
SOELLNER, R. H.
WHEELER, C. B.
WOODSON, T. M.

*German:*
BEKKER, H.
BELKIN, J. S.
BENSLER, D. P.
HAAS, W.
HAENICKE, D. H.
HOFFMAN, C. W.
SCHMIDT, H. J.

*History:*
ADAMS, A. E.
BALCER, J. M.
BURNHAM, J. C.
CHANG, HAO
CHAPIN, B.
CHU, S. C.
COLES, H. L., Jr.
COOPER, D. B.
DILLON, M. L.
DORPALEN, A.
FULLMER, JUNE Z.
LI, T. Y.
MILLETT, A. R.
MORLEY, C.
PEGUES, F. J.
ROBERTS, C.
ROTHNEY, J. A.
RULE, J. C.
WILDMAN, A. K.
ZAHNISER, M. R.

*Judaic and Near Eastern Languages and Literatures:*
HAYON, Y.

*Linguistics:*
LEHISTE, I.
ZWICKY, A. M., Jr.

*Philosophy:*
BOH, I.
GARNER, R. T.
HAUSMAN, A. M.
HINSHAM, V. G., Jr.
KIELKOPF, C. F.
LYCAN, W. G.
OLDENQUIST, A. G.
SCANLAN, J. P.
SWAIN, M. W.
TURNBULL, R. G.

*Romance Languages and Literature:*
ASTIER, P. A. G.
CARLUT, C. E.
COTTRELL, R. D.
GARCIA, S.
GRIFFIN, D.
KELLER, H. E.
LEVISI, M.
MANCINI, A.
ROSBOTTOM, R. C.

*Slavic and Eastern European Languages and Literatures:*
KRZYZANOWSKI, JERZY R.
MATEJIC, M.
NAYLOR, K. E.
OULANOFF, H.
SILBAJORIS, F. R.
TWAROG, L. I.

College of Mathematical and Physical Sciences:
*Astronomy:*
CAPRIOTTI, E. R.
COLLINS, G. W.
CZYZAK, S. J.
KELLER, G.
MITCHELL, W. E., Jr.
PROTHEROE, W. M.
ROARK, T. P.
SLETTEBAK, A. E.
WING, R. F.

*Chemistry:*
BUSCH, D. H.
CALVERT, J. G.
DORFMAN, L. M.
FIRESTONE, R.
FRAENKEL, G.
FREY, P. A.
GERKIN, R. E.
HINE, J.
HORTON, D.

KERN, W. C.
KUWANA, T.
LEUSSING, D. L., Jr.
MEEK, D. W.
OULLETTE, R. J.
PITZER, R. M.
RUBIN, T. R.
SHECHTER, H.
SHORE, S. G.
SWEET, T. R.
SWENTON, J. S.
TAYLOR, W. J.
WOJCICKI, A.

*Geodetic Science:*
MERCHANT, D. C.
MINTZER, O. W.
RAPP, R. H.
UOTILA, U. A.

*Geology and Mineralogy:*
BERGSTROM, S. M.
BULL, C. B.
CORBATO, C. E.
EHLERS, E. G.
ELLIOT, D. H.
FAURE, G.
FULLER, J. O.
MOORE, G. E., Jr.
NOLTIMIER, H. C.
SUMMERSON, C. H.
SWEET, W. C.
TETTENHORST, R. T.
WEBB, P. N.
WENDEN, H. E.
WHITE, S. E.

*Mathematics:*
BAISHANSKI, B. M.
BOJANIC, R.
BURGHELEA, D.
CARROLL, F. W.
COLSON, H. D.
DAVIS, W. J.
DEAN, D. W.
DROBOT, S.
FERRAR, J. C.
FRIEDMAN, H.
HARADA, K.
HSIA, J. S.
JOHNSON, W. B.
LEVINE, N.
MADAN, M. L.
MITYAGIN, B.
RAYCHAUDHURI, D. K.
RINER, J. W.
SALTZER, C.
SUCHESTON, L.
WOODS, A. C.
YAQUB, J.
ZASSENHAUS, H. J.

*Physics:*
BLATT, S. L.
BROWN, L. C.
DICKEY, F. P.
DONOGHUE, T. R.
EBNER, C. A.
EDWARDS, D. O.
GAINES, J. R.
GARLAND, J. C.
HAUSMAN, M. J.
HEER, C. V.
JASTRAM, P. S.
JOSSEM, E. L.
MILLS, R. L.
MULLIGAN, B.
NIELSEN, C. E.
PALMER, W. F.
RAO, K. N.
REAY, N. W.
REIBEL, K.
ROMANOWSKI, T. A.
SAAM, W. F.
SCOTT, D. M.
SHAW, J. H.

1846

Tanaka, K.
Tough, J. T.
Wada, W. W.
Wigen, P. E.
Yang, C. P.
Yaqub, M.

### Statistics:
Dudewicz, E. J.
Rustagi, J. S.
Srivasteva, R. C.
Whitney, D. R.
Willke, T. A.
Wolfe, D. A.

## College of Social and Behavioural Science:
### Anthropology:
Arewa, E. O.
Bourguignon, Erika E.
Hughes, D.
Messenger, J. C.
Poirier, T. E.

### Economics:
Cunnyngham, J. S.
Dewald, W. G.
Eason, W. W.
Fleisher, B. M.
Gouke, C. G.
Kane, E. J.
Kelley, S. C.
Lesperance, W. L.
Lynn, A. D., Jr.
Oster, C. V., Sr.
Parnes, H. S.
Parsons, D. O.
Quantius, Frances W.
Ray, E. J.
Sandberg, L. G.
Sherman, R. U., Jr.
Stocker, F. D.
Tybout, R. A.

### Geography:
Brown, L. A.
Brown, S. E.
Casetti, E.
Cox, K. R.
Demko, G. J.
Gauthier, H. L., Jr.
Hunker, H. L.
Patten, G. P.
Rayner, J. N.
Taaffe, E. J.

### Journalism:
Berquist, G.
Bunge, W. K.
Clarke, J.
Hall, W. E.
Halsinger, G. R.
Peterson, P. V.
Seifert, W. W.
Toran, W. B.
Underwood, P. S.

### Political Science:
Alger, C.
Asher, H. B.
Clausen, A.
Harf, J. E.
Hermann, C.
Herson, L. J. R.
Kessel, J. H.
Liddle, R. W.
Nelson, W. E.
Richardson, B.
Ripley, R. B.
Sani, G. A.
Stewart, P.
Weisberg, H. F.

### Psychology:
Angelino, H. R.
Brock, T. C.
Clark, P. M.
Greenwald, A. G.
Hakel, M. D.

Horrocks, J. E.
Hothersall, D.
Johnson, N. F.
Jones, M. R.
Krueger, L. E.
Latane, B.
Leland, H.
Meyer, D. R.
Meyer, P. M.
Mirels, H. L.
Nolan, J. D.
Osipow, S. H.
Ostron, F. M.
Pepinsky, H. B.
Schmidt, L. D.
Schwebel, A. I.
Walsh, W. B.
Wenar, C.

### Sociology:
Clarke, A. C.
Corwin, R. G.
Dinitz, S.
Helfirch, M. L.
Hinkle, R. C.
Li, W. L.
McDonagh, E. C.
Nagi, S. Z.
Quarantelli, E. L.
Richardson, L. W.
Schwirian, K. P.
Tien, H. Y.
VanderZanden, J. W.

### Communication:
Berquist, G., Jr.
Brooks, K.
Brown, W.
Douglas, J. E.
Golden, J. L.
Hale, F.
Hardick, E. J.
Monaghan, R.
Peterson, P. V.
Schoen, K.
Wagner, R. W.

## College of Administration Sciences:
### Accounting:
Burns, T. J.
Davidson, H. J.
Greenball, M. N.
Jensen, D. L.
Kindig, F. E.
Kollaritsch, F. P.
McCollough, E. V., Jr.
Shank, J. K.
Stanley, C. H.

### Finance:
Bickelhaupt, D. L.
Blythe, H.
Chen, A. H. Y.
Cole, D. W.
Gibson, F. F.
Kane, E. J.
Racster, R. L.
Rapp, W. A.
Sturdivant, F.

### Labour and Human Resources:
Borus, M. E.
Kelley, S. C.
Miljus, R. C.

### Management Science:
Behling, O. C.
Bobbitt, H. R.
Howland, D.
Hurley, W. E.
Krajewski, L. J.
Ritzman, L. P.
Shapero, A.

### Marketing:
Blackwell, R. D.
Cullman, W. A.
LaLonde, B. J.

Leavitt, C.
Mathews, H. L.
Robeson, J. F.
Talarzyk, W. W.

### Public Administration:
Craig, P. G.
Enarson, H. L.
Lundstedt, S. B.
Lynn, A. D., Jr.
Oster, C. V., Sr.
Ripley, R. B.
Rutledge, I. C.
Snyder, R. C.
Stocker, F. D.

### Continuing Education:
Carroll, P. M.
Slanicka, C. J.

## College of Social Work:
Allen, H. E.
Medhurst, R. R.
Parnicky, J. J.
Rosner, M. S.
Schneiderman, L.

## College of Agriculture and Home Economics:
### Agricultural Economics and Rural Sociology:
Adams, D. W.
Baker, R. L.
Barr, W., Jr.
Baumer, E. F.
Boyne, D. H.
Cravens, M. E.
Dougan, R. S.
Hadley, H. H.
Himes, G. C.
Mitchell, J. B.
Phillips, G. H.
Rask, M.
Sharp, J. W.
Shaudys, E. T.
Smith, M. G.
Stout, T. T.
Walker, F. E.

### Agricultural Education:
Adams, D. A.
Boucher, L. W.
Bruny, S. P.
Cunningham, C. J.
Guiler, G. S.
Hull, W. L.
Jenkins, D. D.
Krill, M. K.
Lifer, C. W.
McCracken, J. D.
Magisos, J. H.
Miller, L. E.
Ritchie, A. E.
Starling, J. T.
Taylor, R. E.
Warmbrod, J. R.

### Agricultural Engineering:
Blaisdell, J. L.
Bondurant, B. L.
Curry, R. B.
Drew, L. O.
Hamdy, M. Y.
Herum, F. L.
Holmes, R. G.
Huber, S. G.
Nelson, G. L.
Nolte, B. H.
Palmer, M. L.
Roller, W. L.
Schwab, G. O.

### Agronomy:
Arscott, T. G.
Bendixen, L. E.
Bone, S. W.
Dollinger, E. J.

Everett, K. R.
Friday, D. T.
Gist, G. R., Jr.
Haghiri, F.
Hall, G. F.
Henderlong, P. R.
Herr, D. E.
Himes, F. L.
Hoff, D. J.
Lafever, H. N.
McLean, E. O.
Mederski, H. J.
Miller, R. H.
Parsons, J. L.
Ray, D. A.
Schmidt, B. L.
Shepherd, L. N.
Streeter, J. G.
Stroube, E. W.
Sutton, P.
Taylor, G. S.
Triplette, G. B., Jr.
VanDoren, D. M., Jr.
Vankeuren, R. W.
Waldron, A. C.

*Animal Science:*
Cahill, V. R.
Cline, J. H.
Dehority, B. A.
Harvey, W. R.
Johnson, G. R.
Johnston, C.
Judy, J. K.
Klosterman, E. W.
Kottman, R. M.
Ludwick, T. M.
Martin, C. M.
Newland, H. W.
Ockerman, H. W.
Parker, C. F.
Plimpton, R. F.
Reed, R. R.
Tyznik, W. J.
Vanstavern, B. D.
Wilson, G. R.
Wilson, R. F.

*Dairy Science:*
Barr, H. L.
Conrad, H. R.
Fechheimer, N. S.
Gomes, W. R.
Harvey, W. R.
Heider, L.
Hibbs, J. W.
Hines, H. C.
Ludwick, T. M.
Porter, R. M.
Porterfield, R. A.
Staubus, J. R.

*Food Science and Nutrition:*
Allred, J. B.
Blaisdell, J. L.
Hansen, P. M. T.
Harper, W. J.
Kristoffersen, T.
Mikolajcik, E. M.
Naber, E. C.
Vivian, V. M.

*Home Economics:*
Bailey, L.
Bowers, J. S.
Dickerscheid, J. D.
Dickey, L.
Firebaugh, Francille
Gritzmacher, J. E.
Hubbard, Rachel M.
Hunt, F. E.
Lapitsky, Mary
McCormick, Anita R.
McCormick, N. R.
Meacham, E.
Vivian, Virginia M.

*Horticulture:*
Berry, S. Z.
Brooks, W. M.
Busher, F. K.
Cahoon, G. A.
Caldwell, J. L.
Donoho, C. W.
Gallander, J. F.
Geisman, Jean R.
Gould, W. A.
Hartman, F. O.
Hill, R. G., Jr.
Kawase, M.
Kretchman, D. W.
Peng, A. C.
Reisch, K. W.
Rollins, H. A., Jr.
Smith, E. M.
Staby, G. L.
Tayama, H. K.
Utzinger, J. D.
Wittmeyer, E. C.

*Natural Resources:*
Bookout, T. A.
Brown, J. H.
Cole, C. F.
Cowen, W. F., Jr.
Dissinger, J. F.
Douglass, R. W.
Gatherum, G. E.
Good, E. E.
Johnson, C. S.
Kriebel, H. B.
Larson, M. M.
Mintzer, O. W.
Murphy, E. F.
Roth, R. E.
Schwab, G. O.
Stairs, G. R.
Stockdale, T. M.
Teater, R. W.
Touse, R. D.
Vogt, A. R.
Weidensaul, T. C.
Whitmore, F.

*Plant Pathology:*
Bradfute, O. E.
Deep, I. W.
Ellett, C. W.
Garraway, M. O.
Gordon, D. T.
Herr, L. J.
Hoitink, H. A. J.
Leben, C.
Schmitthenner, A.
Weidensaul, T. C.
Williams, L. E.

*Poultry Science:*
Allred, J. B.
Brown, K. I.
Clayton, P. C.
Fechheimer, N. S.
Harvey, W. R.
Johnston, C.
Marquand, J. W.
Marsh, G. A.
Naber, E. C.
Nestor, K. E.
Stephens, J. F.

College of Education:
*Education:*
Adams, D.
Alberty, Elsie J.
Allen, E. D.
Anderson, D. P.
Bateman, D. R.
Blanke, V. E.
Blosser, P.
Buffer, J.
Burnham, R.
Cook, D. L.
Cooper, J.

Crosswhite, F. J.
Cruickshank, D. R.
Cunningham, L. L.
Cunningham, R.
Cyphert, F. R.
DeStefano, J.
Dowling, W. D.
Duncan, J. K.
Frymier, J. R.
Galloway, C. M.
Gilliom, M. E.
Hack, W. G.
Helgeson, S.
Higgins, J.
Holloway, W. J.
Hough, J. B.
Howe, R.
Huck, Charlotte S.
Jarvis, G.
Jewett, R. E.
Kaplan, R.
Kennedy, J.
Kerber, J. E.
King, Martha L.
Languis, M. L.
Larmee, R. A.
Lewis, G. L.
Lux, D. G.
Mayer, V. J.
Mehl, B.
Miller, A.
Moore, W.
Muessig, R. H.
Osborne, A.
Peters, H. J.
Porecca, A.
Pratt, R.
Reagan, G.
Quaranta, J. J., Jr.
Ray, W. E.
Rentel, V. M.
Riccio, A. C.
Ryan, K.
Sanders, D. P.
Severino, D. A.
Shumway, R.
Silverman, R.
Staub, W. F.
Stephens, T.
Sutton, R. B.
Tosi, D.
Trimble, H. C.
Trzebiatowski, G.
Wagstaff, L. H.
Wayson, W. W.
White, A.
White, T.
Wigtil, J.
Williams, C. R.
Wohlers, A. E.
Zidonis, F. J.

*Health, Physical Education, and Recreation:*
Bartels, R. L.
Bennett, B. L.
Beyrer, M. K.
Ersing, W. F.
Fox, E. L.
Kleinman, S.
Mand, C. L.
Mathews, D. K.
Rupert, Evelyn A.
Seidentop, D. L.
Yost, Mary M.

College of Engineering:
*Aeronautical and Astronautical Engineering:*
Bailey, C. D.
Burggraf, O. R.
Edse, R.
Gregorek, G.
Lee, J. D.
Li, T. Y.
Petrie, S. L.

## UNIVERSITIES AND COLLEGES—OHIO (STATE UNIVERSITY) U.S.A.

### Architecture:
BORCHERS, P. E.
BREWER, C. H.
CLARK, G. M.
KINOSHITA, M.
KORDA, P. E.
WHITAKER, E. L.
YOUNG, P. E.

### Landscape Architecture:
CARPENTER, J. D.
TOBEY, G. B.
WALQUIST, L. W.

### City and Regional Planning:
BERTSCH, D. F.
FISCH, O.
GERCKENS, L. C.
ROSNER, M. S.
SIMS, W.
VOSS, J. R.

### Aviation:
GILSON, R. D.

### Ceramic Engineering:
READY, D. W.
SHOOK, W. B.

### Chemical Engineering:
BRODKEY, R. S.
GEANKOPLIS, CHRISTIE
HERSHEY, H. C.
LYNN, R. E.
SKIDMORE, D. R.
SLIDER, H. C.
SMITH, E. E.
SWEENEY, T. L.
ZAKIN, J. L.

### Civil Engineering:
BISHARA, A. G.
CHEN, T. Y.
MAJIDZADEH, K.
MINTZER, O. W.
MOORE, C. A.
OJALVO, M.
RICCA, V. T.
RUBIN, A. J.
SANDHU, R. S.
SMITH, C. B.
SPROUL, O. J.
STIEFEL, R. C.
TREITERER, J.
WHITEHURST, E. A.
WU, T. H.

### Computer and Information Science:
BOJANIC, R.
BREEDING, K. J.
CHANDRASEKARAN, B.
CSURI, C. A.
HSIAO, D. K.
LIU, M. T.
SALTZER, C.
WHITE, L. J.

### Electrical Engineering:
BREEDING, K. J.
COLLINS, S. A.
COMPTON, R. T.
CORNETET, W., Jr.
COWAN, J. D., Jr.
DAVIS, D. T.
DAVIS, W. C.
FENTON, R. E.
GOTTLING, J. G.
HEMAMI, H.
HODGE, D. B.
HSU, H.
KO, H. C.
KOOZEKANANI, S. H.
KOUYOUMJIAN, R. G.
KSIENSKI, A. A.
LEVIS, C. A.
LONG, R. K.
MCGHEE, R. B.

MATHIS, H. F.
MIDDLETON, A. E.
PEAKE, W. H.
PETERS, L., Jr.
RICHMOND, J. H.
RUDDUCK, R. C.
SEBO, S. A.
SELIGA, T. A.
SMITH, N. A.
THURSTON, M. O.
WALTER, C. H.
WARREN, C. E.
WEED, H. R.
WEIMER, F. C.

### Engineering Graphics:
DEMEL, J.
HANG, R. I.
KEARNS, C. H., Jr.
LARUE, R. D.
PARKINSON, R. W.
REED, E. O., Jr.
ROMEO, A.

### Engineering Mechanics:
ADVANI, S. H.
ENGIN, A. E.
LEISSA, A. W.
POPELAR, C. H.

### Industrial Engineering:
BISHOP, A. B.
BLACK, J. T.
CLARK, G. M.
GIFFIN, W. C.
MILLER, R. A.
NEUHARDT, J. B.
ROCKWELL, T. H.
SMITH, G. L.

### Mechanical Engineering:
COLLINS, J. A.
DOEBELIN, E. O.
ESSENHIGH, R. H.
HAN, L. S.
JOHN, J. E. A.
JONES, C. D.
KULACKI, F. A.
MILLER, D. W.
MORAN, M. J.
SEPSY, C. F.
VELKOFF, H. R.

### Metallurgical Engineering:
BECK, H. F.
HIRTH, J. P.
MACDONALD, D.
MEYRICK, G.
POWELL, G. W.
RAPP, R. A.
RIGNEY, D. A.
SHEWMON, P. G.
SPEISER, R.
ST PIERRE, G. R.

### Photography and Cinema:
DRVOTA, M.
GREEN, J. R.
WAGNER, R. W.

### Welding Engineering:
GRAFF, K. F.
MCCAULEY, R. B., Jr.

### College of Pharmacy:
BEAL, J. L.
BOPE, F. W.
BURKMAN, A. M.
DOSKOTCH, R. W.
FELLER, D. R.
GERALD, M. C.
LATIOLAIS, C. J.
MALSPEIS, L.
MILLER, D. D.
NOTARI, R. E.
OLSON, N. S.
PATIL, P. N.
REUNING, R. H.

RUCKER, T. D.
SOKOLOSKI, T. D.
SOLOWAY, A. H.
WITIAK, D. T.

### College of Dentistry:
#### Dentistry:
ALLISON, M.
APP, G. R.
BLOZIS, G. G.
BOWERS, D. F.
BRUCE, W. A.
CAVALARIS, C. J.
CHANDLER, H. H.
CONROY, C. W.
DEW, W. C.
DIORIO, L. P.
FOREMAN, D. W.
HALL, A. W.
HUFFMAN, R. W.
LONG, A. C.
MELFI, R. C.
MEYERS, W. J.
OBRIEN, R. C.
PORTER, M. R.
ROSEN, S.
RUSSELL, O E.
SOLT, C. W.
WALLACE, W. R.
WILLIAMS, B. H.
WOELFEL, J. B.
ZACHERL, W. A.

#### Dental Hygiene:
GOOREY-REYNOLDS, NANCY M.

### College of Law:
CLOVIS, A. L.
ERICKSON, N. S.
FINK, H. P.
GERHART, P. M.
GOLDBERGER, D. A.
GREENBAUM, A. F.
HERMAN, L.
HOWARD, L. G.
JACOBS, L. A.
KINDRED, M. J.
KOZYRIS, P. J.
LAUGHLIN, S., Jr.
LYNN, R. J.
MEEKS, J. E.
MODJESKA, L. M.
MURPHY, E. F.
PERNELL, L.
PERRY, M. J.
QUIGLEY, J. B.
REICHMAN, J. H.
RIVERA, R. R.
ROSE, M. D.
SAMANSKY
SHIPMAN, M. E.
SORENSEN, P. C.
SOWLE, C. R.
SOWLE, K. D.
THOMPSON, C. A.
TRAVALIO, G. M.
UPHAM, F. K.
WHALEY, D. J.
WILLS, R. L.

### College of Medicine:
#### Allied Medical Professions:
ATWELL, R. J.

#### Anatomy:
ACKERMAN, G. A.
GAUGHRAN, G. R.
MARTIN, G. F.
ST. PIERRE, R. L.

#### Anaesthesiology:
MCDONALD, J. S.

#### Family Medicine:
WILLIAMS, P. T.

#### Medical Microbiology:
BOWMAN, B.
GLASER, M. R.

Kapral, F. A.
Lang, R. W.
Ottolenghi, A. C.
Somerson, N. L.

*Medicine:*
Balcerzak, S. P.
Beman, F. M.
Bouroncle, B. A.
Cataland, S.
Fass, R. J.
Fry, D. L.
George, J. M.
Kunin, C, M
Lewis, R. P.
Lowney, E. D.
Malarkey, W. B.
McCoy, F. W.
Mekhjian, H.
Mendell, J. R.
Metz, E. M.
Perkins, R. L.
Prior, J. A.
Ryan, J. M.
Sagone, A. L., Jr.
Skillman, T. G.
Wall, R. L.
Warren, J. V.
Whitcomb, M. E.
Wilson, H. E., Jr.
Wooley, C. F.

*Nursing:*
Fritz, E. L.
Sills, G. M.
Stevenson, J. S.

*Obstetrics and Gynaecology:*
Copeland, W., Sr.
Kim, M. H.
Stevens, V. C.
Teteris, N. J.

*Ophthalmology:*
Havener, W. H.
Keates, R. H.
Lubow, M.
Makley, T. A., Jr.
Suie, T.

*Otolaryngology:*
Lim, D. J.
Saunders, W. H.

*Pathology:*
Baba, N.
Barth, R. F.
Liss, L.
Lott, J. A.
Newman, H. A.
Sharma, H. M.
Speicher, C. E.
Stevenson, T. D.

*Paediatrics:*
Cordero, L.
Graham, B. D.
Hamparian, V. V.
Haynes, R. E.
Helper, M.
Hosier, D. M.
Kontras, Stella B.
Meites, S. M.
Sotos, J. F.
Turner, E. V.

*Pharmacology:*
Bianchine, J. R.
Couri, D.
Gerber, N.
Hollander, P. B.

*Physical Medicine:*
Johnson, E. W.
Stow, R. W.

*Physiological Chemistry:*
Alben, J. D.
Brierley, G. P.
Cornwell, D. G.
Horrocks, L. A.
Kruger, F. A.

Merola, A. J.
Milo, G. E.
Richardson, K. E.
Rieske, J. S.
Sprecher, H. W.
Webb, T. E.

*Physiology:*
Hanson, K. M.
Kunz, A. L.
Lebrie, S. J.
Lessler, M. A.
Lipsky, J. A.
Nishikawara, M. T.
Pieper, H. P.
Smith, C. W.
Weiss, H. S.

*Preventive Medicine:*
Chirikos, T. N., Jr.
Keller, M. D.
Lanese, R. R.

*Psychiatry:*
Arnold, L. E.
Gregory, I. W. D
Kangas, J. O.
Knopp, W.
Marks, P. A.
Monroe, L. J.

*Radiology:*
Batley, F.
Freimanis, A. K.
Hart, R. W.
Molnar, W.
Mueller, C.

*Surgery:*
Berggren, R. B.
Boles, E. T., Jr.
Carey, L. C.
Cerilli, E. J.
Clatworthy, H. Wm., Jr.
Hunt, W. E.
Keith, L. M.
Kilman, J. W.
King, J. S.
Meckstroth, C. V.
Minton, J. P.
Vasko, J. S.
Winter, C. C.
Yashon, D.

*College of Optometry:*
Blackwell, H. R.
Fry, G. A.
Hebbard, F. W.
Hill, R. M.
King-Smith, P. E.

*College of Veterinary Medicine:*
*Veterinary Anatomy:*
Anderson, W.
DeWet, P. D.
Diesem, C. D.
Meyer, H.

*Veterinary Clinical Sciences:*
Andreas, J. E.
Burt, J. K.
Capen, C. C.
Donham, J. C.
Donovan, E. F.
Gabel, A. A.
Gardner, H. M.
Hoffsis, G.
Hohn. R. B.
Murdick, P. W.
Ray, R. S.
Rudy, R. L., Sr.
Sams, R.
Tharp, V. L.
Wearly, W. K.
Whiteus, R. G.
Wilson, G. P., III
Wright, R.
Wyman, M.

*Veterinary Pathobiology:*
Capen, C. C.
Cole, C.
Hoover, E.
Koestner, A.
Marsh, G. A.
Olsen, R.
Yohn, D. S.

*Veterinary Physiology and Pharmacology:*
Hamlin, R. L.
Powers, T. E.
Saiduddin, S.
Yeary, R. A.

*Veterinary Preventive Medicine:*
Bohl, E. H.
Dorn, C. R.
Heider, L. E.
Heuschele, W.
Ingalls, W.
Jones, D. O.

*Office of Educational Services:*
*Military Science:*
Plant, R. A.

*Air Force Studies:*
Steen, F.

*Naval Science:*
Semple, W. C.

Attached School:

**Agricultural Technical Institute:** Wooster; f. 1972; 717 students.

## OHIO UNIVERSITY

ATHENS, OHIO 45701
Telephone: 594-5511.

Founded 1804; the first land-grant college in the U.S.

*President:* Charles J. Ping, ph.d.
*Provost:* James L. Bruning, ph.d. (acting).
*Director of Admissions:* James C. Walters, ed.d.
*Librarian:* Hwa-wei Lee, ph.d.

Library of 1,200,000 vols.
Number of teachers: 863.
Number of students: 14,149.
Publications: *Ohio Review†*, *Milton Quarterly*.

Deans:

*Engineering and Technology:* T. Richard Robe, ph.d.
*Arts and Sciences:* William Dorrill, ph.d.
*Business Administration:* Gerald Silver, ed.d.
*Education:* Allen Myers, ph.d.
*Fine Arts:* H. H. Lin, m.f.a.
*University College:* Samuel R. Crowl, ph.d. (acting).
*Graduate College:* Ronald Barr, ph.d.
*Health and Human Services:* Hilda Richards, ed.d.
*Communication:* Paul E. Nelson, ph.d.
*Osteopathic Medicine:* Frank W. Myers, d.o.

## OHIO WESLEYAN UNIVERSITY

DELAWARE, OHIO 43015
Telephone: Delaware 369-4431.

Founded by Methodist Episcopal Church 1841; Chartered 1842.

# UNIVERSITIES AND COLLEGES—OHIO

*President:* THOMAS E. WENZLAU.
*Treasurer:* ALBERT C. WEIDENBUSCH.
*Provost:* KENNETH P. GOODRICH.
*Vice-President (Business Affairs):* R. W. MEYER.
*Vice-President (University Relations):* R. A. JONES.
*Dean of Academic Affairs:* LAUREN R. WILSON.
*Dean of Educational Services:* Dr. VIOLET MEEK.
*Registrar:* M. J. ROACH.
*Librarian:* B. LEWIS.

Number of teachers: 159.
Number of students: 2,241.
Publications: *OWU Bulletin* (yearly), *Focus* (5 a year), *Alumni Magazine* (quarterly).

## OTTERBEIN COLLEGE
WESTERVILLE, OHIO 43081
Telephone: (614) 890-3000.
Founded 1847.
Private control; Academic year: September to August.

*President:* THOMAS J. KERR IV.
*Registrar:* DANIEL THOMPSON.
*Dean of Admissions and Records:* MORRIS BRIGGS.
*Academic Dean:* DONALD BULTHAUP.
*Librarian:* J. BECKER.

The library contains 133,000 vols.
Number of teachers: 90.
Number of students: 1,600.
Publications: *Otterbein Miscellany*, *Quiz and Quill*.

## UNIVERSITY OF AKRON
302 E. BUCHTEL AVENUE,
AKRON, OHIO 44325
Telephone: (216) 375-7111.

Founded 1870 by Ohio Universalist Convention; became Municipal University of Akron 1913; present title 1926; became State University 1967.

*President:* D. J. GUZZETTA, ED.M., ED.D., LL.D., D.S.SC., L.H.D.
*Senior Vice-President and Provost:* NOEL L. LEATHERS, PH.D.
*Vice-President for Business and Finance:* R. W. DUFF, LL.B.
*Vice-President for Planning:* I. R. MACGREGOR, PH.D.
*Vice-President and Dean of Student Services:* RICHARD L. HANSFORD, M.A.ED.
*Executive Director of Personnel:* WILLIAM D. JONES, M.A.
*Registrar:* H. BALDWIN, M.ED.
*Librarian:* P. FRANKS, B.S.L.S.

Library of 1,300,000 vols.
Number of teachers: 1,225.
Number of students: 24,642.
Publications: *Bulletin* (annually), *From the Hilltop* (monthly).

### DEANS:
*Graduate Studies and Research:* ALAN N. GENT, PH.D.
*Buchtel College of Arts and Sciences:* C. E. GRIFFIN, PH.D.
*College of Education:* H. K. BARKER, PH.D.
*College of Engineering:* LOUIS A. HILL, Jr., PH.D.
*College of Business Administration:* J. W. DUNLAP, PH.D.
*College of Fine and Applied Arts:* GERARD L. KNIETER, E.D.
*School of Law:* DONALD M. JENKINS, LL.M.
*College of Nursing:* L. DEYOUNG, PH.D.
*University College:* MARION A. RUEBEL, PH.D.
*Community and Technical College:* ROBERT WEYRICK, M.S.
*Evening College and Summer Sessions:* CAESAR CARRINO, PH.D.
*Executive Dean of Continuing Education and Public Services:* W. A. ROGERS, ED.D.
*Wayne General and Technical College:* TYRONE M. TURNING, ED.D.

## UNIVERSITY OF CINCINNATI
CINCINNATI, OHIO 45221
Telephone: 475-8000.

Chartered as Cincinnati College 1819; as University of Cincinnati and as a municipal institution 1870; became a municipally-sponsored state-affiliated institution in 1968; joined Ohio State University system 1977.

Academic year: September to June.

*President:* HENRY R. WINKLER, PH.D., LITT.D.
*Senior Vice-President for Administration and Secretary to the Board of Trustees:* LAWRENCE C. HAWKINS, ED.D.
*Senior Vice-President and Director of Medical Center:* STANLEY B. TROUP, M.D.
*Senior Vice-President and Provost:* JOHN P. MCCALL, PH.D.
*Vice-President and Dean for Graduate Studies and Research:* EULA BINGHAM.
*Vice-President for Finance and Treasurer:* SIGMUND G. GINSBURG, M.P.A.
*Vice-President for Business Affairs:* MYRON E. ULLMAN III, B.S.I.M.
*Vice-President for Public Affairs:* MARY JEANNE KLYN, B.S.
*University Registrar:* LYNN M. BARBER, M.B.A.
*Director of Admissions:* ROBERT W. NEEL, M.A.
*Director of Libraries:* (vacant).
*Library: see Libraries.*

Number of teachers: 1,862 full-time, 789 part-time.
Number of students: 5,354 graduate, 32,276 undergraduate.

Publications: *Horizon* (7 a year), *U.C. This Week* (weekly during term), *News Record* (2 a week during term), *College Bulletins* (annually).

### DEANS:
*McMicken College of Arts and Sciences:* WILLIAM N. DEMBER, PH.D.
*College of Engineering:* KIRK C. VALANIS, PH.D.
*College of Education:* HENDRIK D. GIDEONSE, ED.D.
*College of Business Administration:* ALBERT J. SIMONE, PH.D.
*College of Medicine:* ROBERT S. DANIELS, B.S., M.D.
*College of Law:* GORDON A. CHRISTENSON, S.J.D.
*College of Nursing and Health:* JEANNETTE R. SPERO, M.P.H., PH.D.
*College of Design, Architecture and Art:* BERTRAM BERENSON, PH.D.
*College of Pharmacy:* ARTHUR C. GLASSER, PH.D.
*College-Conservatory of Music:* NORMAN DINERSTEIN, PH.D.
*University College:* RONALD TEMPLE, M.A.
*College of Community Services:* STEPHEN C. SUNDERLAND, PH.D.
*Evening College:* GAIL A. NELCAMP, PH.D.
*Raymond Walters General and Technical College:* ERNEST G. MUNTZ, PH.D.
*OMI College of Applied Science:* J. C. SPILLE, ED.M.
*Clermont General and Technical College:* ROBERT W. FLINCHBAUGH, PH.D.

### PROFESSORS:
*College of Arts and Sciences:*
ABBOUSHI, W. F., PH.D., Political Science
AESCHBACHER, W. D., PH.D., History
AGNELLO, J. G., PH.D., Speech Pathology
ALEXANDER, J. J., PH.D., Chemistry
ALLINSMITH, W., PH.D., Psychology
ARNER, R., PH.D., English
BANTA, T. J., PH.D., Psychology
BEATLEY, J., PH.D., Biological Sciences
BEAVER, D. R., PH.D., History
BELL, H., PH.D., Mathematics
BENISON, S., PH.D., History
BENT, A., PH.D., Political Science
BLEZNICK, D. W., PH.D., Romance Languages and Literatures
BLUESTEIN, V., ED.D., Psychology
BOBST, A. M., PH.D., Chemistry
BOTCHWAY, F., PH.D., Afro-American Studies
BOULTER, C. G., PH.D., Classics
CARROLL, R. L., PH.D., Sociology
CARUSO, J., PH.D., Chemistry
CHALKEY, R., PH.D., Mathematics
CHANG, T. C., PH.D., Mathematics
CHARD, L., PH.D., English
CHOW, W., PH.D., Physics
CROCKETT, C., PH.D., Philosophy
DANIELS, R., PH.D., History
DAY, R. A., PH.D., Chemistry
DEDDENS, J. A., PH.D., Mathematics
DEMBER, W., PH.D., Psychology
DEUTSCH, E., PH.D., Chemistry
DILLER, V., PH.D., Biophysics
DONNELLY, K., PH.D., Communications, Speech, and Theatre
DURRELL, R., B.S., Geology
DUX, D., PH.D., Political Science
ELDER, R., PH.D., Chemistry

ENGBERG, G. B., PH.D., History
ETGES, F. J., PH.D., Zoology
FENICHEL, H., PH.D., Physics
FENIK, B., PH.D., Classics
FISHBEIN, H., PH.D., Psychology
FISHER, J. W., PH.D., Mathematics
FRANKE, E. K., DR.ING., Biophysics
FRASER, A. S., PH.D., Biological Sciences
FRIEDRICHMEYER, E., PH.D., Germanic Languages and Literatures
GILBERT, T., PH.D., Chemistry
GLENN, J. H., Germanic Languages
GODSHALK, W. L., PH.D., English
GOODMAN, B., PH.D., Physics
GOTTSCHANG, J. L., PH.D., Zoology
GRASHA, A. F., PH.D., Psychology
GÜNTHER, M., PH.D., Physics
GUSTAFSON, D., PH.D., Philosophy
HALPERN, H. P., PH.D., Mathematics
HARRIS, E., PH.D., Germanic Languages
HARVEY, N., PH.D., English
HEINEMAN, W., PH.D., Chemistry
HERMAN, E. E., PH.D., Economics
HONECK, R. P., PH.D., Psychology
HUVOS, K. L., PH.D., Romance Languages
JAFFE, H., PH.D., Chemistry
JHA, S., PH.D., Physics
JOHNSON, A., PH.D., Geology
JOINER, W. C. H., PH.D., Physics
JONES, D. R., PH.D., Physics
KAFKER, F. A., PH.D., History
KAPLAN, F., PH.D., Chemistry
KAROLY, P., PH.D., Psychology
KILINC, A. I., PH.D., Geology
KIM, H.-K., PH.D., Political Science
KLEIN, E., PH.D., Psychology
KRETSCHMER, L. W., ED.D., Communications, Speech and Theatre
KUHN, A., PH.D., Economics
LANSKY, L. M., PH.D., Psychology
LARSEN, L. H., PH.D., Geology
LAUX, J. M., PH.D., History
LAZER, A. C., PH.D., Mathematics
LEAKE, H., PH.D., Mathematics
LECLAIR, T. E., PH.D., English
LEWIS, G., PH.D., History
LIPSICH, H. D., PH.D., Mathematics
LUNDGREN, D., PH.D., Sociology
MACOMBER, R. S., PH.D., Chemistry
MARK, H. B., Jr., PH.D., Chemistry
MARK, J., PH.D., Chemistry
MAYER, W., DR.JUR., PH.D., Economics
McCARTHY, J. T., PH.D., Physics
McDANIEL, D. H., PH.D., Chemistry
McDONALD, C. O., PH.D., English
McNEE, R., PH.D., Geography
MEEKS, F., PH.D., Chemistry
MERKES, E., PH.D., Mathematics
MELTON, R. S., PH.D., Psychology
MEYER, K. R., PH.D., Mathematics
MEYER, R. R., PH.D., Biological Sciences
MEYERS, W., PH.D., Psychology
MILLER, A., PH.D., Political Science
MILLER, W. C., PH.D., English
MILLER, Z., PH.D., History
MITCHELL, O., PH.D., History
MUKKADA, A. J., PH.D., Biological Sciences
MULLANE, H., PH.D., Philosophy
NUSSBAUM, M. M., PH.D., Physics
O'CONNOR, PATRICIA W., PH.D. Romance Languages and Literatures
ORCHIN, M., PH.D., Chemistry
ORVIETO, ENZO, PH.D., Romance Languages and Literatures
OSEAS, L., PH.D., Psychology
PADGETT, E., PH.D., Political Science
PAUL, J., PH.D., Mathematics
PAULS, J. P., PH.D., Russian Languages and Literature
PORTE, M., PH.D., Speech
POTTER, P. E., PH.D., Geology

POWER, P. F., PH.D., Political Science
PRYOR, W. A., PH.D., Geology
RAMUSACK, B. N., PH.D., History
RAWLINGS, E. I., PH.D., Psychology
RICHERT, H., PH.D., Germanic Languages and Literatures
RICKS, D., PH.D., Psychology
ROBINSON, J. K., PH.D., English
RODER, W., PH.D., Geography
RUSSELL, J., PH.D., Physics
RUTLEDGE, F. P., M.A., Speech
RYAN, K., PH.D., Geography
SCHRIER, A., PH.D., History
SCHUMSKY, D. A., PH.D., Psychology
SCHWARTZ, M., PH.D., Psychology
SEEMAN, W., PH.D., Psychology
SENTER, R. J., PH.D., Psychology
SHAPIRO, M. D., PH.D., History
SHEPHERD, C. R., PH.D., Sociology
SIMONS, L., PH.D., Philosophy
SKINNER, G., PH.D., Economics
SLESSAREV, H., PH.D., German
SMITH, P. M., ED.D., Afro-American Studies and Psychology
SMITH, W. D., PH.D., Afro-American Studies and Psychology
STAFFORD, H., PH.D., Geography
STAPLES, H., PH.D., English
STEPHENS, M., PH.D., English
STEWART, J. K., PH.D., English
STROUD, R. V., PH.D., Communications, Speech and Theatre
STUBBINS, W. F., PH.D., Physics
STUTZ, R. M., Psychology
SUAGEE, F. F., PH.D., Economics
SURANYI, P., PH.D., Physics
THOMAS, N., PH.D., Political Science
TODD, W., PH.D., Philosophy
TRAHMAN, C., PH.D., Latin and Romance Palaeography
TUAN, T.-F., PH.D., Physics
UMMINGER, B., PH.D., Biological Sciences
UNGAR, G. S., PH.D., Mathematics
VALENCIA, J., PH.D., Romance Languages and Literatures
VALENTINE, L. M., PH.D., Economics
VERDERBER, R., PH.D., Communications
WAGNER, F. J., PH.D., Mathematics
WARM, J., PH.D., Psychology
WEISE, E., PH.D., Political Science
WESSEL, R. H., PH.D., Economics
WIEBE, D., PH.D., English
WILSON, R. M., PH.D., Chemistry
WINGET, D., PH.D., Biological Sciences
WINGET, J. A., PH.D., Sociology
WINTER, J. F., PH.D., Romance Languages and Literature
WITTEN, L., PH.D., Physics
WOHL, T., PH.D., Psychology
WORKMAN, R., PH.D., Philosophy
WRIGHT, A., PH.D., English
WRIGHT, W., PH.D., Physics
ZIMMER, H., PH.D., Chemistry
ZINAM, O., PH.D., Economics

*College of Engineering:*
ANNO, J. N., PH.D., Nuclear Engineering
ANTOLOVICH, S. D., PH.D., Materials Science
ARMSTRONG, N. A., D.ENG., SC.D., Aerospace Engineering
BERESKIN, A. B., E.E., M.S. IN ENG., P.E., Electrical Engineering
BOERIO, F. J., PH.D., Materials Science
BOYD, J. T., PH.D., Aerospace Engineering and Applied Mechanics
BROWN, M. L., PH.D., Mechanical Engineering
COOK, J. P., M.C.E., D.ENG.SC., Engineering Construction
DAVIES, R. T., PH.D., P.E., Aerospace Engineering
DELCAMP, R. M., PH.D., Chemical Engineering
ELNAN, O., PH.D., Aerospace Engineering

ENGELMAN, R. H., M.S., P.E., Electrical Engineering
ENGLISH, M., M.S., Mechanical Engineering
EYE, D., B.S. IN C.E., SC.D., Environmental Engineering
FOPMA, R. J., B.A., Operations Research
GHIA, K. N., PH.D., Aerospace Engineering and Applied Mechanics
GREENBERG, D. B., PH.D., P.E., Chemical Engineering
HAMED, A., PH.D., Aerospace and Applied Mechanics
HENDERSON, H. T., PH.D., Electrical Engineering
HERSHEY, D., PH.D., Chemical Engineering
HOCH, M., SC.D., Material Science
HOWE, R., C.E., PH.D., P.E., Civil Engineering
HULLEY, C. M., M.E., Engineering and Computer Graphic Science
HUSTON, R. L., PH.D., Engineering Analysis
KINMAN, R. N., PH.D., P.E., Civil Engineering
KROLL, R. J., PH.D., Aerospace Engineering
LAUSHEY, L. McN., SC.D., P.E., Civil Engineering
LEMLICH, R., PH.D., P.E., Chemical Engineering
LICHT, W., PH.D., Chemical Engineering
McDONOUGH, J. F., PH.D., Civil Engineering
MIDDENDORF, W., B.E.E., PH.D., P.E. Electrical Engineering
MORAND, J. M., PH.D., P.E., Civil Engineering
MORSE, I. E., Jr., PH.D., Mechanical Engineering
MOTEFF, J., PH.D., Materials Science
NAYFEH, A. H., PH.D., Aerospace Engineering and Applied Mechanics
OSTERBROCK, C. H., PH.D., Electrical Engineering
PATTISON, J. N., PH.D., Environmental Engineering
POLAK, A., PH.D., Aerospace Engineering and Applied Mechanics
POOL, M. J., PH.D., Metallurgical Engineering
PREUL, H. C., PH.D., P.E., Civil and Environmental Engineering
RAIBLE, PH.D., P.E., Electrical Engineering
RESTEMEYER, W., E.E., A.M., P.E., Applied Mathematics
RINGO, B., B.S. IN ARCH. ENG., M.S. IN C.E., PH.D., P.E., Civil Engineering
ROE, R.-J., PH.D., Materials Science and Metallurgy
SCARPINO, P. V., PH.D., Environmental Engineering
SCHLEEF, D. J., PH.D., Mechanical Engineering
SHAPIRO, A., PH.D., Nuclear Engineering
SHELL, R. L., PH.D., Industrial Engineering
SHUPE, D. S., SC.D., Mechanical Engineering
STOUFFER, D. C., PH.D., Aerospace Engineering and Applied Mechanics
STRAUSS, A. M., PH.D., Engineering Analysis
TABAKOFF, W., DIPL. ING. IN M.E. AND A.E., PH.D., Aerospace Engineering
TAYLOR, F. J., PH.D., Electrical Engineering
THORPE, J. F., PH.D., P.E., Mechanical Engineering
TSE, F. S., M.S. IN M.E., M.B.A., PH.D., Mechanical Engineering

TSUEI, Y. G., PH.D., Mechanical Engineering
WANDMACHER, C., D.ENG., Engineering Education
WANG, I.-C., PH.D., Mechanical Engineering
WEE, W. G., PH.D., Electrical and Computer Engineering
WEISMAN, J., PH.D., Nuclear Engineering
WESTERMANN, F. E., PH.D., P.E., Metallurgical Engineering
ZERKLE, R. D., PH.D., Mechanical Engineering

*College of Education and Home Economics:*
GARVIN, A. D., PH.D., Education
GIDEONSE, H. D., PH.D., Education and Policy Science
HELMS, W., PH.D., Health, Physical Education and Recreation
HINTON, M., ED.D., Education
JONES, W., ED.D., Education
KRETSCHMER, R., ED.D., Education
LAPLANT, J. C., PH.D., Education
MANNEY, AGNES, PH.D., Education
PHILLIPS, J., PH.D., Education
SCHNITZER, W. J., ED.D., Health, Physical Education and Recreation
SCHWARBERG, ED.D., Health, Physical Education and Recreation
SMITH, C., PH.D., Education
SPRING, J., PH.D., Education
STANTON, W. A., ED.D., Education
WEILBAKER, C. R., ED.D., Education
WOLVERTON, MARY, ED.D., Education
ZEMANEK, D., ED.D., Education

*College of Business Administration:*
ANDERSON, D. R., PH.D., Quantitative Analysis
AUMEND, C. L., M.B.A., Finance
BAKER, H. G., B.S. IN COM., ED.D., Management
BAKER, N. R., PH.D., Quantitative Analysis
BALL, R. E., PH.D., Finance
BARNGROVER, C. L., PH.D., Finance
BURNS, D., D.B.A., Accounting
DILLON, R. E., PH.D., Marketing
DORNOFF, R. J., PH.D., Marketing
GORE, G. J., PH.D., Management
GRAEN, G. B., PH.D., Management
HARTMAN, G. E., PH.D., Marketing
KAHLER, R. C., PH.D., Marketing
KARAS, M. R., PH.D., Marketing
KERNAN, J. B., PH.D., Behavioural Analysis
KIEFER, D., PH.D., C.P.A., Accounting
KILEY, W. A., B.SC., LL.M., C.P.A., Business Law
LELIEVRE, C. C., PH.D., Accounting
MANTEL, S., Jr., PH.D., Quantitative Analysis and Management
MARTIN, D. D., D.B.A., Management
MARVIN, P., D.B.A., LL.B., Professional Development and Business Administration
McDOWELL, W. J., PH.D., Marketing
MELNYK, Z. L., PH.D., Finance
RICKETTS, D. E., D.B.A., Accounting
SALE, T., PH.D., Accounting
SIMONE, A. J., PH.D., Quantitative Analysis
SWEENEY, D. J., D.B.A., Quantitative Analysis
YOUSRI, A., PH.D., Insurance

*College of Medicine:*
ADOLPH, R. J., PH.D., M.B. Medicine
ALEXANDER, J. W., M.D., Surgery
ALTEMEIER, W., D.SC., Surgery
ARON, B. S., M.D., Radiation Therapy and Obstetrics
AYER, H., M.S., Environmental Health
BARDEN, T. P., M.D., Obstetrics and Gynaecology
BENISON, S., PH.D., Environmental Health
BENZING, G., III, M.D., Paediatrics
BERMAN, J. R., M.D., Internal Medicine
BERRY, H. K., M.A., Research Paediatrics
BIEHL, J. P., M.D., Neurology
BINGHAM, E., PH.D., Environmental Health
BLAHA, G. C., PH.D., Anatomy
BLOCK, S., PH.D., Psychiatry
BLOOMFIELD, S. S., M.D., Medicine and Pharmacology
BONVENTRE, P. F., PH.D., Microbiology
BOZIAN, R. C., B.S., M.D., Medicine
BRIDENBAUGH, P. O., M.P., Anaesthesia
BROOKS, S. M., M.D., Medicine and Environmental Health
BRYANT, S. H., PH.D., Pharmacology
BUBEL, H.C., PH.D., Microbiology
BULLOCK, W. E., Internal Medicine
BUNCHER, C. R., Environmental Health
CARDELL, R. R., PH.D., Anatomy
CHOU, T.-C., M.D., Medicine
CLARK, L. C., PH.D., Research Paediatrics
CONWAY, G. F., M.D., Medicine
COOPER, G. P., PH.D., Environmental Health
COTTON, R., M.D., Otolaryngology and Maxillofacial Surgery
CRAFTS, R. C., PH.D., Anatomy
CULBERTSON, W. R., B.A., M.D., Surgery
DANIELS, R. S., M.D., Psychiatry
DAVIS, N. C., PH.D., Research Paediatrics
DIGNAN, P. ST. J., M.B., CH.B., Paediatrics
DiSALVO, J., PH.D., Physiology
DONALDSON, VIRGINIA H., M.D., Medicine and Paediatrics
DUNBAR, J. S., M.D., Paediatrics and Radiology
FELSON, B., M.D., Radiology
FISCHER, J. E., M.D., Surgery
FLESSA, H. C., Internal Medicine
FOULKES, E. C., D.PHIL., Environmental Health
FOWLER, N. O., M.D., Medicine
FRANKLIN, D., Pharmacology and Cell Biophysics and Experimental Medicine
FREDERICK, K. A., M.D., Family Medicine
FREISHEIM, J. H., PH.D., Biological Chemistry
GANSCHOW, R. E., PH.D., Paediatrics
GIANNELLA, R. A., Internal Medicine
GLUECK, C. J., M.D., Internal Medicine
GOLDBERG, M., M.D., Internal Medicine
GRUPP, G., M.D., PH.D., Biomedical Communications, Physiology and Internal Medicine
HALL, J., PH.D., Anatomy
HAMBRICK, G. W., M.D., Dermatology
HAMMOND, P. B., D.V.M., PH.D., Environmental Health
HANENSON, I. B., M.D., Internal Medicine
HELM, R. A., M.D., Internal Medicine
HELMSWORTH, J. A., M.D., Surgery
HERMAN, J. H., M.D., Medicine
HESS, E., M.D., Internal Medicine
HIATT, H., M.D., Psychiatry
HOLDER, I. A., PH.D., Microbiology
HOLMES, J. C., Internal Medicine
HORNSTEIN, L., M.D., Paediatrics
HORWITZ, H., M.D., Radiology
HUG, G., M.D., Paediatrics
HUMMEL, R. P., M.D., Surgery
JACKSON, R. L., PH.D., Pharmacology and Cell Biophysics
JAMES, F. W., M.D., Paediatrics
JOYCE, T. H., M.D., Anaesthesia
KALTER, H., PH.D., Research Paediatrics
KAPLAN, S. M., B.S., M.D., Psychiatry
KAPP, F. T., M.D., Psychiatry
KEITH, R. W., PH.D., Otolaryngology and Maxillofacial Surgery
KEITH, T. A., III, M.D., Internal Medicine
KEREIAKES, J. G., PH.D., Radiology
KHODADAD, G., M.D., Surgery (Neurosurgery)
KIELY, C. E., M.D., Internal Medicine
KLEINMAN, L. I., M.D., Environmental Health and Paediatrics, Physiology
KLINE, D. L., PH.D., Physiology
KNOWLES, H. C., Jr., B.S., M.D., Medicine
KRAMER, M., Psychiatry
KRUG, O. M., M.D., Psychiatry
LAMPKIN, B. C., M.D., Paediatrics
LANGSLEY, D. G., M.D., Psychiatry
LEVINSON, J. E., Internal Medicine
LICHSTEIN, H. C., A.B., M.S.P.H., D.SC., Microbiology
LIGHT, I. J., Paediatrics
LINDNER, J., Jr., M.D., Internal Medicine
LINGREL, J. B., PH.D., Biological Chemistry
LIPICKY, R. J., M.D., Internal Medicine
LOGGIE, J., M.B., B.CH., Paediatrics, Pharmacology
LOPER, J. C., PH.D., Microbiology
LOUDON, R. G., M.D., Internal Medicine
MACGEE, J., PH.D., Experimental Medicine
MACMILLAN, B. G., M.D., Surgery
MACPHERSON, C. R., M.D., Pathology
McADAMS, J., M.D., Pathology and Paediatrics
McLAIN, C. R., Jr., M.D., Obstetrics and Gynaecology
McLAURIN, R. L., M.D., Surgery
MARGOLIN, E. G., M.D., Medicine
MARTELO, O. J., M.D., Medicine
MARTIN, L. W., M.D., Surgery
MATHIEU, A., M.D., Anaesthesia
MATTINGLY, S. F., D.V.M., Laboratory Animal Medicine
MEINEKE, H., PH.D., Anatomy
MICHAEL, J. G., PH.D., Microbiology
MICHAELSON, I. A., PH.D., Environmental Health
MILLER, E. H., M.D., Orthopaedic Surgery
MOSKOWITZ, M., M.D., Radiology
NATHAN, P., PH.D., Physiology
NEWMAN, J. C., M.D., Child Psychiatry
OLINGER, C. P., M.D., Neurology
ORNSTEIN, A., M.D., Child Psychiatry
ORNSTEIN, P. H., M.D., Psychiatry
PERLSTEIN, P. H., M.D., Paediatrics, Obstetrics and Gynaecology
POLLAK, V. E., Internal Medicine
PRATT, E. L., M.D., Paediatrics
RAJ, P. P., M.D., Paediatrics and Medicine
ROSENDRANTZ, J. G., M.D., Surgery and Research Paediatrics
ROSS, W. D., B.S., M.D., Psychiatry
RUBENSTEIN, J. H., M.D., Paediatrics
RUDNEY, H., PH.D., Biological Chemistry
SACKS, J. G., M.D., Ophthalmology
SAENGER, E. L., A.B., M.D., Radiology
SALTZMAN, B. E., PH.D., Environmental Health
SAMAHA, F. J., M.D., Neurology
SAPADIN, A., M.D., Medicine
SCHIFF, G. M., M.D., Internal Medicine
SCHNEIDER, H. J., M.D., Radiology
SCHREINER, A. W., B.S., M.D., Medicine
SCHWARTZ, A., PH.D., Pharmacology
SCHWARTZ, D. C., M.D., Paediatrics
SCOTT, R. C., M.D., Medicine
SEEDS, A. E., M.D., Obstetrics and Gynaecology
SHEPHERD, C. R., PH.D., Biomedical Communications

SHOLITON, L. J., Internal Medicine
SHUMRICK, D. A., M.D., Otolaryngology
SILBERSTEIN, E. B., M.D., Radiology
SMITH, C. C., PH.D., Environmental Health
SMITH, J. C., PH.D., Environmental Health
SMITH, R., M.D., Family Medicine
SMITH, R. D., M.D., Pathology
SMITSON, W. S., D.S.W., Psychiatric Social Work
SODD, V. J., PH.D., Radiology
SPITZ, H. B., M.D., Radiology
SRIVASTAVA, L. S., D.V.M., PH.D., Experimental Medicine
STONE, W. N., M.D., Psychiatry
STRIKER, T. W., M.D., Anaesthesia and Paediatrics
SUSKIND, R. R., M.D., Environmental Health, Internal Medicine
SUTHERLAND, J. M., M.D., Paediatrics
TITCHENER, J. L., B.A., M.D., Psychiatry
VAN MAANEN, E. F., PH.D., Pharmacology
VESTER, J. W., M.D., Medicine
VILTER, R. W., M.D., Internal Medicine
WEIHL, C., M.D., Paediatrics
WEST, C. D., A.B., M.D., Paediatrics
WHITMAN, R. M., M.D., Psychiatry
WILL, J. J., M.D., Internal Medicine
WIOT, J. F., M.D., Radiology
WOLF, R., M.D., Paediatrics
WRIGHT, T., Internal Medicine
WULSIN, J. H., PH.D., Surgery
ZELLNER, D. C., M.D., Internal Medicine
ZIMMERMAN, E. F., PH.D., Research Paediatrics

*College of Law:*
APLIN, K. L., B.A., S.J.D., Law
CHRISTENSON, G. A., S.J.D., Law
COOK, R. N., B.A., LL.B., Law
HARPER, S. E., Jr., B.A., LL.B., LL.M., Law
JEFFREY, W., Jr., B.A., B.L.S., LL.B., Law
LAUERMAN, N., J.D., Law
LESTER, W. R., B.A., J.D., LL.M., Constitutional Law
MURPHY, J. J., J.D., LL.M., Law
SQUILLANTE, A. M., A.B., M.S.L.S., LL.M., Law
WEISSENBERGER, G., J.D., Law
WILSON, S., J.D., Law

*College of Nursing and Health:*
BUNYAN, R. M., D.ED., Nursing and Health
SPERO, J. R., PH.D., Nursing

*College of Design, Architecture and Art:*
ALEXANDER, J. M., Jr., B.S.ARCH., Industrial Design
BEAVAN, R. E., B.F.A., Fine Arts
BERENSON, B., M.A. ARCH., Architecture
CHATTERJEE, J., M.R.P., M.ARCH., Urban Planning and Design
DESHON, R. A., M.ARCH., Architecture
FABE, R., Fine Arts
FOSTER, P., Fine Arts
HECK, B. J., B.S.ED., Fashion Design
HOERMAN, E. R., M.ARCH., Urban Planning and Design
KNIPSCHILD, R., B.A., M.F.A., Fine Arts
MERKEL, K., B.S.ARCH., Architecture
MEUNIER, J. C., M.ARCH., M.A., Architecture
MRAS, G. P., PH.D., Art History
NILAND, D. L., M.ARCH., Architecture
NOE, S. V., Jr., M.ARCH., Urban Planning and Design
PETERSON, J. M., M.ARCH., Architecture
QUAYLE, E. J., B.F.A., Fine Arts
ROCKWOOD, L. G., M.A., Film
RUDD, J. W., M.A., Architecture
SALCHOW, G. R., M.F.A., Fine Arts
STEVENS, R. H., M.A., Architecture
STRICEVIC, G., PH.D., Art History
WESSEL, HELEN M., ED.D., Art Education
WHEELER, R. H., B.A., B.ARCH., Architecture
WOLFLEY, E. L., Jr., M.F.A., Fine Arts
WOODMAN, D., A.R.C.A., Art
WYGANT, F. L., M.A., ED.D., Art Education

*College of Pharmacy:*
GLASSER, A. C., PH.D., Pharmaceutical Chemistry
LICHTIN, J. L., PH.D, Pharmacy
OGZEWALLA, C. W., PH.D., Pharmacognosy
RITSCHEL, W. A., M.PHARM., D.UNIV., D.PHIL., Biopharmaceutics

*College-Conservatory of Music:*
ALEXANDER, J., B.MUS., Voice and Opera
ANDERSON, S. V., PH.D., Music Education
BAR-ILLAN, D., Piano
DELAY, D., B.A., Violin
DINERSTEIN, N., PH.D., Composition and Theory
EVANS, R. K., PH.D., Music
FOSTER, D., PH.D., Composition, Theory, History and Literature
GARY, R., D.M.A., Organ
GEORGE, W. E., D.M.E., Music Education
HASHIMOTO, E., M.MUS., M.A., Harpsichord
HORNYAK, R. R., D.M.ED., Music Education
HUSTON, S., PH.D., Composition
KAMNITZER, P., Viola
KIRSTEIN, J., Piano
KIRSTEIN, J., M.A., Violoncello
LEVIN, W., Violin
MALFATTI, L. A., B.MUS., Voice and Opera
MCINNES, D. M., M.MUS., Viola
MCLAIN, D., B.S.ED., M.A., Dance
MEYER, H. W., Violin
MORRIS, R., M.M., Piano
MULBURY, D., D.M.A., Performance Studies (Organ)
OJEDA, S., M.S., Piano
PAGE, C. L., PH.D., Music Education
POGUE, S. F., PH.D., Musicology
PRIDNOFF, E. A., Music
RILEY, J., PH.D., Musicology
SAMUEL, G., M.MUS., Music
SHORTT, P., M.F.A., Opera and Musical Theatre
SIKI, B., Music
TAJO, I., Voice and Opera
THOMAS, E. R., D.M.A., Choral Music
WHITE, A. B., M.MUS., Music and Voice

*College of Community Services:*
DEGROOT, I., B.A., M.P.H., Community Health
HAWKINS, L. C., ED.D., Education and Community Services
MILLS, R. B., PH.D., Psychology
MYERS, J. S., PH.D., Psychology
STRAUSS, M. D., M.P.H., M.C.P., Community Health
SUNDERLAND, S. C., PH.D., Community Services

*OMI College of Applied Science:*
DORSEY, R. W., M.C.P., Architectural Technology
GARRETT, P. H., PH.D., Electrical Engineering Technology
MCMAHAN, R. T., ED.D., Mechanical Engineering Technology

*Raymond Walters General and Technical College:*
DEJONG, D. C. D., PH.D., Botany
LEAKE, J. A., PH.D., History
MATTINGLY, S. F., D.V.M., Laboratory Animal Medicine
MONTERA, A. P., ED.D., Biology
OESCHLER, D. A., M.S.N., Nursing

*University College:*
BETTMAN, E., M.A., English
HART, W. S., M.A., Secretarial Studies
MCGINNIS, J. W., M.A., English
SUTTON, P. W., Jr., PH.D., Philosophy
VORIS, C. A., PH.D., Management

## UNIVERSITY OF DAYTON
DAYTON, OHIO 45469
Telephone: (513) 229-0123.
Founded 1850.

*President:* Bro. RAYMOND L. FITZ, S.M.
*Vice-President for Academic Affairs:* Bro. JOSEPH W. STANDER, S.M.
*Registrar:* Bro. PAUL B. BOECKERMAN, S.M.
*Vice-President for Development and Alumni Relations:* THOMAS T. MONTIEGEL.
*Vice-President for Financial Affairs:* GERALD W. VONDER BRINK.
*Vice-President for Student Development:* MARGARET M. HOLLAND.
*Vice-President for University Relations:* THOMAS J. FRERICKS.
*Librarian:* RAYMOND H. NARTKER.

Library of 693,000 vols.

Number of teachers: 575.

Number of students: 10,785.

Publications: *University of Dayton Review*† (quarterly), *Alumnus-Focus*† (quarterly), *Law Review*.

### DEANS:

*Students:* Rev. FRANCIS J. KENNEY, S.M. (Assoc. Dean).
*Arts and Sciences:* Dr. FRANCIS M. LAZARUS.
*Graduate Studies and Research:* Dr. GEORGE B. NOLAND.
*School of Engineering:* Dr. RUSSELL A. PRIMROSE.
*School of Business:* WILLIAM J. HOBEN.
*School of Education:* Dr. ELLIS A. JOSEPH.
*School of Law:* Prof. FREDERICK B. DAVIS.

### DIRECTORS:

*Continuing Education:* Miss NORA DUFFY.
*Special Sessions:* NORA DUFFY.
*Research Institute:* JOHN R. WESTERHEIDE.

## UNIVERSITY OF STEUBENVILLE
COLLEGE HEIGHTS,
STEUBENVILLE, OHIO 43952
Telephone: (614) 283-3771.
Founded 1946.

*President:* Rev. MICHAEL SCANLAN, T.O.R.
*Registrar:* Mrs. AUDREY KORZI.
*Director of Admissions:* DAVID SKIVIAT.
*Librarian:* Miss JEANNINE KREYENBUHL.

Library of 188,000 vols.

Number of teachers: 42 full-time.

Number of students: 721 full-time, 282 part-time.

## UNIVERSITY OF TOLEDO
TOLEDO, OHIO 43606
Telephone: (419) 537-4242.

Founded 1872 as Toledo University of Arts and Trades; became Municipal University 1884, State University 1967.

*President:* GLEN R. DRISCOLL, PH.D.
*Executive Vice-President:* ROBERT S. SULLIVANT, PH.D.
*Vice-President for Academic Affairs:* WILLIAM N. FREE, PH.D.
*Vice-President for Business Affairs:* WILLARD W. SMITH, M.S.
*Vice-President for Student Affairs:* L. C. A. THOMPSON, PH.D.
*Treasurer:* PAUL E. RIEGER, B.A., C.P.A.
*Director of Student Records:* DEAN BERKEY, B.S.
*Director of Libraries:* LESLIE W. SHERIDAN, M.L.S.

The library contains over 1,000,000 vols.

Number of teachers: 615 full-time, 127 part-time.

Number of students: 20,257.

Publications: *The Alumnus* (6 a year), *The Collegian*, and various departmental newsletters and journals.

### DEANS:
*College of Arts and Sciences:* A. A. CAVE, PH.D.
*College of Business Administration:* R. P. SNOW, M.B.A., C.P.A.
*College of Education:* G. E. DICKSON, ED.D.
*College of Engineering:* L. LAHTI, PH.D.
*College of Law:* F. X. BEYTAGH, J.D.
*College of Pharmacy:* N. F. BILLUPS, PH.D.
*University College:* M. A. HEINRICHS, PH.D.
*Graduate School:* H. ALLEN, PH.D.
*University Community and Technical College:* T. HORST, B.E. (acting).
*Continuing Education:* T. C. CLAPP, PH.D.

### PROFESSORS:
*College of Arts and Sciences:*
   *Anthropology:*
METRESS, S., PH.D.
   *Astronomy:*
DELSEMME, A. H., PH.D.
WITT, A. N., PH.D.
   *Biology:*
ALLEN, H. L., PH.D.
GOLDMAN, S. L., PH.D.
JYUNG, W. H., PH.D.
LEE, H. H., PH.D.
NASATIR, M., PH.D.
PRIBOR, D. B., PH.D.
SHAFFER, H. C., M.S.
SMITH, C. J., PH.D.
TRAMER, E. J., PH.D.

   *Chemistry:*
BLACK, A. H., M.S.CHEM.
BRADY, L., PH.D.
BUROW, D. F., PH.D.
CHRYSOCHOOS, J., PH.D.
EDWARDS, J. G., PH.D.
FOSTER, A. F., PH.D.
FRY, J. L., PH.D.
GANO, J. E., PH.D.
KROHN, A., PH.D.
NIEDZIELSKI, R. J., PH.D.
THOMPSON, H. B., PH.D.
THOMPSON, L. C. A., PH.D.
WALMSLEY, F., PH.D.
   *Communications:*
HARVEY, I. G., PH.D.
RUSSELL, C. G., PH.D.
   *Economics:*
BIGGS, R., PH.D.
GLEASON, A. H., PH.D.
GYLYS, J., PH.D.
ROY, R., PH.D.
SHAPIRO, E., PH.D.
SOPIARZ, E., PH.D.
WINEGARDEN, C. R., PH.D.
   *English:*
BOENNING, J., PH.D.
BOTTORFF, W. K., PH.D.
CHENEY, D. R., PH.D.
DESSNER, L. J., PH.D.
FRAIBERG, L., PH.D.
FREE, W. N., PH.D.
GREGORY, E. R., PH.D.
MANHEIM, M., PH.D.
MARTIN, W. D., PH.D.
McDONALD, W. U., PH.D.
STOCK, N. J.
SZUBERLA, G. A., PH.D.
   *Foreign Languages:*
FEUSTLE, J. A., PH.D.
KRILL, R. M., PH.D.
MORENO, E. E., PH.D.
O'NEAL, W. J., PH.D.
PULLEYN, J. W., PH.D.
SCANLAN, T. M., PH.D.
   *Geography:*
EMERY, B. E., PH.D.
HOFFMAN, L. A., PH.D.
LEWIS, D. W., PH.D.
MURACO, W. A., PH.D.
   *Geology:*
DEAN, S. L., PH.D.
HATFIELD, C., PH.D.
KNELLER, W. A., PH.D.
RUEDISILI, L. C., PH.D.
   *History:*
BOYER, R. E., PH.D.
CARY, L. L., PH.D.
CAVE, A. A., PH.D.
CROFTS, R. A., PH.D.
DeBENEDETTI, C. L., PH.D.
DRISCOLL, G. R., PH.D.
GLAAB, C. N., PH.D.
KAY, M. L., PH.D.
LAPP, L. B., M.A.
LORA, R. G., PH.D.
NOVAK, B. C., PH.D.
RAY, R. D., PH.D.
SCOTT, I. C., PH.D.
SMITH, R. F., PH.D.
   *Mathematics:*
BAILEY, J. L., PH.D.
BENTLEY, H. L., PH.D.
BLAKNEY, S. S., PH.D.
CHIDAMBARASWAMY, J., PH.D.
DAVIS, B., PH.D.
JOHANSON, A. A., PH.D.
KERTZ, G. J., PH.D.
KUMMER, M., PH.D.
RAJAGOPALAN, M., PH.D.

SHIELDS, P. C., PH.D.
SHOEMAKER, R., PH.D.
STEINBERG, S. A., PH.D.
THOMSON, C. W., PH.D.
VAYO, H. W., PH.D.
WENTE, H. C, PH.D.
WOLFF, H. E., PH.D.
   *Music:*
BROWN, M. E., PH.D.
CHAMBERS, V. A., PH.D.
SANCHEZ, B. R., M.M.
SCHOENFIELD, P. E., M.A.
WEBSTER, R. M., M.M.
WINSOR, A. S., PH.D.
   *Nursing:*
CHICKADONZ, G. H., PH.D.
   *Philosophy:*
DALEY, J. W., PH.D.
DEWEY, E. W., PH.D.
GUTHRIE, G., PH.D.
MAYBERRY, T. C., PH.D.
PULIGANDLA, R., PH.D.
TIGNER, S. S., PH.D.
   *Physics:*
BOHN, R. G., PH.D.
CURTIS, L. J., PH.D.
DECK, R. T., PH.D.
ELLIS, D. G., PH.D.
MONTGOMERY, C., PH.D.
SCHECTMAN, R. M., PH.D.
SIMON, H. J., PH.D.
WILLIAMSON, W., PH.D.
   *Political Science:*
AL-MARAYATI, A. A., PH.D.
BLUME, N., PH.D.
GILLESPIE, J., PH.D.
JAN, G., PH.D.
LEWIS, F., PH.D.
LINDEEN, J. W., PH.D.
RANDALL, R. R., PH.D.
SULLIVANT, R., PH.D.
VEZNER, K. O., PH.D.
WILLIS, G., PH.D.
   *Psychology:*
ARMUS, H., PH.D.
BURNS, R., PH.D.
DEL CASTILLO, PH.D.
DOLINSKY, R., PH.D.
GUMENIK, W., PH.D.
HAAF, R. A., PH.D.
HOROWITZ, I. A., PH.D.
KITTERLE, F. L., PH.D.
PALMER, A. B., PH.D.
SLAK, S., PH.D.
WOHL, J., PH.D.
   *Sociology:*
BARDIS, P., PH.D.
BITAR, N., PH.D.
FORMAN, R. E., PH.D.
KAPLAN, S. J., PH.D.
KART, C. S., PH.D.
KING, J. A., PH.D.
MOYER, L. N., PH.D.
PALMER, N., PH.D.
SEARLES, R., PH.D.
   *Theater:*
COYNE, B. A.
OLF, J. M., PH.D.
PENTZELL, R., PH.D.
VICINUS, C. H., PH.D.

*College of Business Administration:*
   *Accounting:*
GIBSON, C. H., D.B.A.
HANSEN, R. E., D.B.A.
KONRATH, L. F., PH.D.
NESS, H. L., J.D., C.P.A.
RIED, G. E., M.B.A., C.P.A.
SNOW, R. P., J.D., B.S.

Computer Systems and Production Management:
ELICANO, R. V., PH.D.
SASS, C. J., M.B.A.

Finance:
AGGARWAL, R., D.B.A.
AUSTIN, D., PH.D., J.D.
CONWAY, L. A., PH.D.

Management:
BHATT, B. J., PH.D.
DEJUTE, A. M., J.D.
KASSEM, M. S., PH.D.
RUDDUCK, R. T., PH.D.
SEIFER, D. M., PH.D.
SIMONETTI, J. L., D.B.A.

Marketing:
BARDI, E. J., PH.D.
BRUNNER, G. A., PH.D.
BRUNNER, J., PH.D.
JUTILA, S. T., PH.D.
KLEIN, T. A., PH.D.
TAOKA, G. M., PH.D.
WEEKLY, J. K., D.B.A.

College of Education:
Educational Administration and Supervision:
BECK, W., ED.D.
DICKSON, G. E., ED.D.
MERRITT, D. L., PH.D.
ROSENBERGER, D., PH.D.
SAXE, R. W., PH.D.
SOMMERVILLE, J. C., PH.D.
SPIESS, J. A., PH.D.

Educational Psychology:
DAVISON, D. C., PH.D.
DUNN, T. G., PH.D.
GRAY, W. M., ED.D.
MEINKE, D. L., PH.D.

Educational Research and Measurement:
BAUMANN, R., PH.D.
JURS, S. G., PH.D.
WIERSMA, W., Jr., PH.D.

Educational Technology and Media:
ELSIE, L. J., ED.D.

Educational Theory and Social Foundations:
HURST, J. B., PH.D.
LOPEZ, T. R., PH.D.
NUSSEL, E. J., ED.D.
TAVEL, D. Z., ED.D.
UTZ., R., PH.D.
WILHOYTE, R., PH.D.

Elementary and Early Childhood:
AHERN, J., D.ED.
BALZER, D. M., PH.D.
COOKE, G. E., D.ED.
DEBRUIN, J. E., PH.D.
DEWITZ, P. A., PH.D.
GIBNEY, T. C., PH.D.
INGLIS, J. D., PH.D.
MOIR, L. H., ED.D.
SANDBERG, H. H., ED.D.
SHIRK, G. B., PH.D.
UNDERFER, J., PH.D.
YORKE, D. B., ED.D.

Guidance and Counselor Education:
HIGGINS, R. E., ED.D.
WYSONG, H. E., PH.D.

Health Education:
FULTON, G. B., PH.D.
MILLER, D. F., HS.D.
PRICE, J. H., PH.D.

Higher Education:
PERRY, R. E., ED.D.
ROCHTE, N. D., PH.D.
WHITE, R. E., PH.D.

Exercise Science and Physical Education:
DROWATZKY, J., ED.D.
GRENINGER, L. O., PH.D.

JOHNSON, P., PH.D.
RANCK, S. L., PH.D.
STOLBERG, D. C., PH.D.

Secondary Education:
DILLEY, C. A., PH.D.
HENNING, M. J., PH.D.
JOHNSON, J. R., PH.D.
SCHAFF, J. F., ED.D.
SINGLETON, H. W., PH.D.
SMALL, D. D., ED.D.

Special Education:
HODGSON, L. N., PH.D.

College of Engineering:
Chemical Engineering:
BENNETT, G. F., PH.D.
DEWITT, K. J., PH.D.
JONES, M. L., PH.D.
LAHTI, L., PH.D.
RENGSTORFF, G., SC.D.
STOOPS, C. E., PH.D.
ZMESKAL, O., SC.D.

Civil Engineering:
ARDIS, C. V., PH.D.
COLONY, D. C., PH.D.
FU, K. C., PH.D.
KOO, B., PH.D.

Electrical Engineering:
ELTIMSAHY, A. H., PH.D.
EWING, D. J., PH.D.
FARISON, J. B., PH.D.

Environmental Engineering:
WEAVER, E. W., M.S.E.

Industrial Engineering:
GLEN, T. M., PH.D.
HANSELL, J. D., M.S.I.E.
MCNICHOLS, R. J., PH.D.
NETTER, M., PH.D.
WOLFE, R. K., PH.D.

Mechanical Engineering:
HEATH, G. L., M.S.M.E.
JENG, D., PH.D.
KEITH, T. G., PH.D.
MILLER, W. R., PH.D.
RAFTOPOULOS, D., PH.D.

College of Law:
BEYTAGH, F., J.D.
BOURGUIGNON, H. J., J.D., PH.D.
EAGLE, S. J., LL.B.
EDWARDS, R., J.D.
FRIEDMAN, H., J.D., LL.M.
HOPPERTON, R. J., J.D.
KADENS, M. G., J.D.
KLEIN, J. M., J.D.
LAWRENCE, W. H., J.D.
MORAN, G. P., J.D., LL.M.
MORANO, A., LL.B.
STOEPLER, J., J.D., LL.M.
VANCE, J. T., LL.B.
WALLIN, J., LL.B.

Library:
Library Administration:
HOGAN, A. D., M.S.L.S.
SHERIDAN, L., M.L.S.
WEIS, I. J., M.S.L.S.

Technological Media:
KALMBACH, J. A., ED.D.
KENNEDY, R. G., M.ED.
KOONTZ, F. R., Jr., M.A.
SHERK, D., PH.D.

College of Pharmacy:
BACHMANN, K. A., PH.D.
BILLUPS, N., F., PH.D.
JUDIS, J., PH.D.
ROLL, W. D., PH.D.
SCHLEMBACH, R. J., PH.D.
SHERMAN, G. P., PH.D.

University Community and Technical College:
General Studies:
ALLRED, M., M.ED.
BELLG, M., ED.S.
GERLACH, J. F., ED.S.
GLEN, M., ED.D.
HANNEKEN, J., PH.D.
HEINRICHS, M. A., PH.D.
HENRY, R., PH.D.
NEUSOM, D. B., ED.D.
NICHOLAS, E. A., ED.D.
SOMOGYE, R. J., ED.D.
WILSON, Th., PH.D.

Technical Science and Mathematics:
KAGY, J. F., ED.S.
LANGE, W. H., ED.S.
QUICK, C. L., ED.D.
ROUSOS, T. G., ED.D.
SHINAVAR, E. E., ED.S.
WELLS, F. D., M.A.

Business Technologies:
BARR, M., M.SC.
DETTINGER, J. F., M.B.A., J.D.
EDGINGTON, M. J., Jr., M.A.
HARTLEY, B. H., ED.D.
LEHMANN, G. D., M.B.A.
MANG, D. J., M.ED.
PAJELLA, F., M.B.A.
POPLAWSKY, G. D., M.B.A.
ROBON, N. C., PH.D.
SIDDENS, R. A., M.S.
SINCLAIR, P. A., M.SC.

Engineering Technologies:
BLANCHARD, D. R., B.S.ARCH.
DRAHEIM, E. H., Jr., ED.S.
HASKINS, W., M.ED.
MINTER, T. J., PH.D.
ZIEGLER, C., PH.D.

Health Technologies:
GYLYS, B. A., M.ED.

Public Service Technologies:
CARTER, C. W., M.A.
MAZAN, J., M.S.
TELB, J. A., PH.D.
THOMPSON, J. R., M.A.

## URSULINE COLLEGE
2550 LANDER RD.,
CLEVELAND, OHIO 44124

Telephone: 449-4200.

Founded 1871.

*President:* Sister M. KENAN, O.S.U.

*Director of Admissions:* AUGUST NAPOLI.

*Vice-President for Academic Affairs:* Rev. THOMAS E. CHAMBERS, C.S.C.

*Vice-President for Student Affairs:* Sr. M. JAMES FRANCIS, O.S.U.

*Vice-President for Financial Affairs:* SAM CHIEFFALO.

*Registrar:* Sr. M. GENEVIEVE, O.S.U.

*Librarian:* Sister MARY HOWARD, O.S.U.

The library contains 72,000 vols.
Number of teachers: 86.
Number of students: 970.

## WILBERFORCE UNIVERSITY
WILBERFORCE, OHIO 45384

Telephone: 376-2911.

Founded 1856.

President: CHARLES E. TAYLOR.
Academic Dean: YVONNE W. TAYLOR.
Registrar: MAISIE G. RIDGEWAY.
Director, Learning Resources Center: SHARON SIMS (acting).
Library of 54,278 vols.
Number of teachers: 65.
Number of students: 1,026.

## WILMINGTON COLLEGE
WILMINGTON, OHIO 45177
Telephone: (513) 382-6661.
Founded 1870.
Private control.

President: ROBERT E. LUCAS.
Assistants to the President: ROBERT DOLPHIN, JR., CAMPBELL GRAF.
Dean of the College: ARTHUR L. BUELL.
Director of Finance: F. B. THOMAS III.
Dean of Student Services: KENNETH W. SCHERER.
Director of Admissions: LESLIE S. CLARK.
Director of Academic Records: SUE BROWN.
Librarian: LARRY A. KROAH.

The library contains 105,000 vols.
Number of teachers: 54 full-time.
Number of students: 750.
Publication: *The Link*.

## WITTENBERG UNIVERSITY
NORTH WITTENBERG AVENUE,
SPRINGFIELD, OHIO 45501
Telephone: (513) 327-6231.
Founded 1845.
Private control. Academic year: September to June.

President: W. A. KINNISON, PH.D.
Provost: WILLIAM M. WIEBENGA, PH.D.
Director of Business Affairs: PETER G. GEIL, M.E.
Director of Admissions: KENNETH G. BENNE, M.DIV.
Registrar: F. E. ROLLER, A.B.
Librarian: B. L. MOWERY, M.A.

The library contains 300,000 vols.
Number of teachers: 140 full-time, 116 part-time.
Number of students: 2,300.
Publications: *The Wittenberg Bulletin, Wittenberg Today*.

DEANS:

School of Music: F. F. JACKISCH PH.D.
School of Community Education: (vacant).

## XAVIER UNIVERSITY
VICTORY PARKWAY,
CINCINNATI, OHIO 45207
Telephone: (513) 745-3000.
Founded 1831.
President: ROBERT W. MULLIGAN, S.J.

Vice-President, Student Affairs: R. C. SHEARER.
Vice-President for Academic Affairs: Rev. F. C. BRENNAN, S.J.
Vice-President, Business and Finance: I. F. BEUMER.
Vice-President, Development and Public Relations: J. W. SASSEN.
Vice-President, Special Projects: Rev. E. J. O'BRIEN, S.J.
Dean of Admissions: R. A. DURAND.
Comptroller: PAUL L. BURKHART.
Registrar: JAMES KAISER.
Librarian: Dr. MARY ANN GRIFFIN.

The library contains 208,000 vols.
Number of teachers: 200.
Number of students: 7,336.

Publications: *Xavier University News, Xavier Athenaeum* (quarterly), *The Alumni Newsletter, The Athletic Review, The Xavier Communiqué*.

DEANS:

College of Arts and Sciences: Dr. CHARLES CUSICK.
College of Continuing Education: Dr. R. H. HELMES.
Edgecliff College: Dr. ROGER FORTIN.
Graduate School: Dr. D. C. FLASPOHLER.
School of Business Administration: Dr. T. H. HAILSTONES.

## YOUNGSTOWN STATE UNIVERSITY
410 WICK AVENUE,
YOUNGSTOWN, OHIO 44555
Telephone: 742-3000.
Founded 1908.
State control; academic year: October to September (four terms).

President: Dr. JOHN J. COFFELT.
Academic Vice-President: Dr. BERNARD T. GILLIS.
Dean of Administrative Affairs: EDMUND J. SALATA.
Executive Vice-President for Financial Affairs: Dr. NEIL D. HUMPHREY.
Dean of Admissions and Records: Dr. JAMES A. SCRIVEN.
Librarian: Dr. D. GENAWAY.

The library contains 433,960 vols.
Number of teachers: 926.
Number of students: 15,652.

DEANS:

College of Arts and Sciences: Dr. B. J. YOZWIAK.
School of Business Administration: Dr. H. ROBERT DODGE.
School of Education: Dr. DAVID P. RUGGLES.
William Rayen School of Engineering: GEORGE E. SUTTON.
College of Fine and Performing Arts: Dr. WILLIAM R. MCGRAW.
College of Applied Science and Technology: Dr. N. PARASKA.
Graduate School: Dr. LEON RAND.

# OKLAHOMA

## BETHANY NAZARENE COLLEGE
6729 N.W. 39TH EXPRESSWAY,
BETHANY, OKLAHOMA 73008
Telephone: (405) 789-6400.
Founded 1899.
Church control; Academic year: August to June (two summer sessions and two terms).

President: Dr. JOHN A. KNIGHT.
Academic Dean: Dr. W. DON BEAVER.
Registrar: Dr. VERNON SNOWBARGER.
Librarian: Mrs. ALFREDA HANNA.

Number of teachers: 70.
Number of students: 1,378.
Publication: *The Perspective*.

## CENTRAL STATE UNIVERSITY
EDMOND, OKLAHOMA 73034
Founded 1890.

President: BILL J. LILLARD.
Vice-President for Academic Affairs: NORMAN RUSSELL.
Vice-President for Administration: A. ALCORN.
Vice-President for Student Services: (vacant).
Director of Public Relations: JOE PARK.
Director of Library Services: ADA INGRAM (acting).

Number of teachers: 415.
Number of students: 12,763.

Publications: *Alumni Newsletter*, (quarterly), *Central-ly Yours* (monthly), *Vista Newspaper* (twice weekly), *Bronze Catalog* (every two years).

DEANS:

Graduate School: B. FISHER.
School of Business: J. PERRY.
School of Education: D. MULLINS.
School of Liberal Arts: F. FINNEY.
School of Mathematics and Science: DAVID M. HART.
School of Special Arts and Sciences: Dr. LUCILLE PATTON.

## EAST CENTRAL OKLAHOMA STATE UNIVERSITY
ADA, OKLAHOMA 74820
Telephone: 332-8000.
Founded 1909.

President: S. P. WAGNER.
Registrar: MERLE BOATWRIGHT.
Librarian: JOHN WALKER.

Library of 275,000 vols.
Number of teachers: 147.
Number of students: 3,882.

## LANGSTON UNIVERSITY
LANGSTON, OKLAHOMA 73050

President: ERNEST L. HOLLOWAY, ED.D.
Vice-President for Academic Affairs: REUBEN MANNING, ED.D.

*Vice-President for Administrative and Fiscal Affairs:* BRYAN KINNEY, B.S.
*Vice-President for Student Affairs:* ELBERT JONES, ED.D.
*Director of Co-operative Extension:* GILBERT TAMPKINS, M.S.
*Director of Co-operative Research:* STEVE B. LATIMER, PH.D.
*Director of Institutional Support:* JAMES A. SIMPSON, M.S.

DIRECTORS AND CHAIRMEN:
*Division of Arts and Sciences:* MAURICE LOVE, ED.D.
*Department of Art:* REUBEN D. MANNING, ED.D.
*Department of Biology:* SARAH THOMAS, PH.D.
*Department of English and Foreign Languages:* E. B. WELCH, ED.D.
*Department of Mathematics:* MAURICE LOVE, ED.D.
*Department of Music:* LEMUEL BERRY, PH.D.
*Department of Social Science:* ADA LOIS FISHER, J.D.
*Department of Physical Science:* REUBEN D. MANNING, ED.D.
*Division of Business Administration and Management:* A. C. PARKER, M.S.
*Division of Education and Behavioral Sciences:* ELBERT L. JONES, ED.D.
*Department of Elementary Education:* ALTA WATSON, PH.D.
*Department of Health, Physical Education and Recreation:* HERESE CARTER, M.S.
*Division of Applied Sciences:* R. C. JOHNSON, ED.D.
*Department of Agriculture:* R. E. KINNARD, M.S.
*Department of Home Economics:* WILLA COMBS, ED.D.
*Department of Technology:* R. C. JOHNSON, ED.D.
*Department of Nursing:* M. M. SMITH, M.S.

## NORTHEASTERN OKLAHOMA STATE UNIVERSITY
TAHLEQUAH, OKLAHOMA 74464
Telephone: (918) 456-5551.
Founded 1846.

*President:* Dr. W. ROGER WEBB.
*Vice-President:* Dr. RONALD SELTZER.
*Registrar:* JAMES A. WATKINS.
*Librarian:* (vacant).

Library of 186,858 vols.
**Number of teachers:** 284.
**Number of students:** 5,558.

## NORTHWESTERN OKLAHOMA STATE UNIVERSITY
ALVA, OKLAHOMA 73717
Telephone: (405) 327-1700.
Founded 1897.

*President:* Dr. JOE J. STRUCKLE.
*Registrar:* Mrs. DORIS BLUE.
*Librarian:* RAY D. LAU.

The library contains 302,559 vols. (including microforms).
**Number of teachers:** 71.
**Number of students:** 1,875.

## OKLAHOMA BAPTIST UNIVERSITY
SHAWNEE, OKLAHOMA 74801
Telephone: (405) 275-2850.
Founded 1910.

*President:* Dr. E. EUGENE HALL.
*Executive Vice-President:* Dr. PAUL R. CORTS.
*Vice-President for Student Development:* DONALD G. OSBORN.
*Vice-President for Business Affairs and Treasurer:* J. THOMAS TERRY.
*Registrar:* Mrs. PEGGY ASKINS.
*Librarian:* Dr. STANLEY BENSON.

Library of 158,000 vols.
**Number of teachers:** 110.
**Number of students:** 1,525.

DEANS:
*Arts and Sciences:* Dr. PAUL BEASLEY.
*Fine Arts:* JAMES D. WOODWARD.
*Business and Administration:* Mrs. MANOI ADAIR (acting).
*Christian Service:* Dr. JOHN TRESCH.
*Nursing:* Mrs. JUANITA MILLSAP (acting).

## OKLAHOMA CITY UNIVERSITY
2501 NORTH BLACKWELDER, OKLAHOMA CITY, OKLAHOMA 73106
Telephone: 521-5000.
Founded 1904.

*President:* JERALD C. WALKER.
*Vice-President for Academic Affairs:* WILLIAM J. COFFIA.
*Registrar:* ADELYN WINDERS.
*Librarian:* SUSAN MCVEY.

The library contains 339,402 vols.
**Number of teachers:** 185.
**Number of students:** 2,800.

## OKLAHOMA PANHANDLE STATE UNIVERSITY
GOODWELL, OKLAHOMA 73939
Telephone: (405) 349-2611.
Founded 1909.

*President:* THOMAS L. PALMER.
*Registrar:* JACK V. BEGLEY.
*Dean of Instruction:* R. H. BOWERS.
*Business Manager:* IRVIN HOPSON.
*Librarian:* EDWARD BRYAN.

The library contains 80,000 vols.
**Number of teachers:** 63.
**Number of students:** 1,255.

## OKLAHOMA STATE UNIVERSITY
STILLWATER, OKLAHOMA 74078
Telephone: 624-5000.
Founded 1890.

*President:* L. L. BOGER, PH.D.
*Vice-President for Academic Affairs (Instruction and Research):* J. H. BOGGS, PH.D.
*Vice-President for Business and Finance:* E. E. DAVIDSON, PH.D.
*Vice-President for University Relations, Development, and Extension:* Dr. R. W. POOLE, PH.D.
*Vice-President for Student Services:* RONALD S. BEER, PH.D.
*Business Officer:* E. E. DAVIDSON, PH.D.
*Registrar:* R. GIROD, M.S.
*Librarian:* R. ROUSE, PH.D.

**Number of teachers:** 1,140.
**Number of students:** 22,486.

DEANS:
*College of Education:* D. W. ROBINSON, PH.D.
*College of Agriculture:* C. BROWNING, PH.D.
*Graduate School:* N. DURHAM, PH.D.
*College of Veterinary Medicine:* P. M. MORGAN, D.V.M., PH.D.
*Division of Home Economics:* BEVERLY CRABTREE, PH.D.
*College of Arts and Sciences:* S. HOLT, PH.D.
*College of Engineering:* K. A. MCCOLLOM, PH.D.
*College of Business Administration:* R. L. SANDMEYER, PH.D.

## ORAL ROBERTS UNIVERSITY
7777 SOUTH LEWIS, TULSA, OKLAHOMA 74171
Telephone: (918) 492-6161.
Founded 1965.

*President:* Dr. ORAL ROBERTS.
*Provost:* Dr. CARL H. HAMILTON.
*Director of Learning Resources and Instruction:* Dr. WILLIAM JERNIGAN.

The library contains 1,000,000 items.
**Number of teachers:** 375.
**Number of students:** 4,170.

DEANS:
*School of Arts and Sciences:* Dr. ROBERT VOIGHT.
*School of Business:* Dr. HENRY MIGLIORE.
*School of Dentistry:* Dr. ROBERT HANSEN.
*School of Law:* CHARLES KOTHE.
*School of Medicine:* Dr. SYDNEY GARRETT.
*School of Nursing:* Dr. TOMINE TJELTA.
*School of Theology:* Dr. JAMES BUSKIRK.

## PHILLIPS UNIVERSITY
ENID, OKLAHOMA 73701
Telephone: 237-4433.

*President:* JOE R. JONES.
*Registrar:* RICHARD ANDERSON.
*Librarian:* JOHN L. SAYRE.

**Number of teachers:** 93.
**Number of students:** 1,299.

Publications: *Haymaker, Venture, This Month at Phillips.*

## SOUTHEASTERN OKLAHOMA STATE UNIVERSITY
DURANT, OKLAHOMA 74701

Founded 1909, refounded under present name 1974.

Academic year: September to May (and summer session).

*President:* LEON HIBBS.

The library contains 140,000 vols.
Number of students: 4,700.

## SOUTHWESTERN OKLAHOMA STATE UNIVERSITY
WEATHERFORD, OKLAHOMA 73096

Telephone: 772-6611.

Founded 1901.
*President:* L. G. CAMPBELL.
*Registrar:* W. W. WILMETH.
*Librarian:* Mrs. SHEILA HOKE.

Library of 204,554 vols.
Number of teachers: 212.
Number of students: 4,800.

## UNIVERSITY OF OKLAHOMA
660 PARRINGTON OVAL, NORMAN, OKLAHOMA 73019

Telephone: (405) 325-0311.

Founded 1890; opened 1892. Campuses at Norman, Oklahoma City and Tulsa.

State control; Academic year: August to May (summer session June and July).

*President:* WILLIAM S. BANOWSKY, PH.D.
*Vice-President for Administrative Affairs:* ARTHUR J. ELBERT, PH.D.
*Vice-President for University Affairs:* DAVID A. BURR, B.A.
*Executive Assistant to the President:* R. GERALD TURNER, PH.D.

Number of teachers: 1,335.
Number of students: 24,638.

Publications: *University of Oklahoma Bulletins* (2 a month), *World Literature Today* (quarterly), *Oklahoma Law Review* (quarterly), *Oklahoma Business Bulletin* (monthly), *American Indian Law Review* (2 a year), *Genre* (quarterly), *Papers on Anthropology* (2 a year), *Comparative Frontiers Studies: An Interdisciplinary Newsletter* (4 a year).

### Norman Campus
*Provost:* JOHN R. MORRIS, Jr., PH.D.
*Registrar:* MILFORD D. MESSER, PH.D.
*Librarian:* SUL-LEE, M.A.L.S.

Number of teachers: c. 780.
Number of students: c. 22,000.

### DEANS:
*College of Arts and Sciences:* JAMES R. BURWELL, PH.D.
*College of Business Administration:* LAWRENCE E. MCKIBBIN, PH.D.
*College of Education:* RICHARD WISNIEWSKI, ED.D.
*College of Engineering:* MARTIN C. JISCHKE, PH.D.
*College of Environmental Design:* MURLIN R. HODGELL, PH.D.
*College of Fine Arts:* NATHANIEL S. EEK, PH.D.
*Graduate College:* KENNETH L. HOVING, PH.D.
*College of Law:* WAYNE ALLEY.
*College of Liberal Studies:* WILLIAM H. MAEHL, Jr., PH.D.
*University College:* JEROME C. WEBER, PH.D.

PROFESSORS:
*College of Arts and Sciences:*

*Anthropology:*
BITTLE, W. E.
WHITECOTTON, J. W.

*Botany and Microbiology:*
BEEVERS, L.
BOKE, N. H.
CLARK, J. B.
COZAD, G. C.
LARSH, H. W.
RICE, E. L.
RISSER, P.
SKVARLA, J. J.

*Chemistry:*
ATKINSON, G.
BURR, J. G.
CHRISTIAN, S. D.
CIERESZKO, L. S.
DRYHURST, G.
FOGEL, N.
FRECH, R. E.
FUNG, B. M.
KRAYNAK, M. E.
LEHR, R. E.
MARCHAND, A. P.
MURPHY, G. W.
SCHMITZ, F. J.
SMITH, E. C.
VAN DER HELM, D.
WENDER, S. H.
ZUCKERMAN, J. J.

*Classics:*
NOLAN, P. J.

*Communication:*
BANOWSKY, W.
BROOKS, W. D.
CARMACK, W. R., Jr.
HIGGINBOTHAM, D. C.
HILL, L. B.
NUTTALL, E. C.
WISPE, L. G.

*English:*
BAMBAS, R. C.
DAVIS, R. M.
FRENCH, D. P.
GRANGER, B. I.
KENDALL, J. L.
MALE, R. R.
MCCARTER, P. K.
PEARCY, R. J.
RUGGIERS, P. G.
YOCH, J. J., Jr.

*Geography:*
SALISBURY, N. E.

*Geology and Geophysics:*
BLATT, H.
DUBOIS, R. L.
HARPER, C. W., Jr.
HUFFMAN, G. G.
KITTS, D. B.
MANKIN, C. J.
MYERS, A. J.
STEARNS, D. W.
SUTHERLAND, P. K.
THOMPSON, T. L.
WICKHAM, J. S.

*Health, Physical Education and Recreation:*
EICK, W. F.
WEBER, J. C.

*History:*
BROWN, S. D.
BUHITE, R. D.
CROCKETT, N. L.
EZELL, J. S.
GIBSON, A. M.
GLAD, P. W.
MAEHL, W. H., Jr.
MORGAN, H. W.
SHALHOPE, R. E.
SHARP, P. F.
TOBIAS, H. J.

*History of Science:*
KITTS, D. B.
ROLLER, D. H. D.
SMITH, T. M.

*Home Economics:*
CRIM, S. R.
DUMAS, C. S.
KRAYNAK, M. E.

*Human Relations:*
GATCH, V. M.
HENDERSON, G.

*Journalism and Mass Communication:*
BICKHAM, J. M.
BRYSON, R. L., Jr.
CARRELL, B., Jr.
HOCKMAN, C. N.
HOLLAND, C. J.
LARKIN, E. F.
MOORADIAN, K. A.
PALMER, M. R.

*Library Science:*
CARROLL, F. L.
HEALEY, J. S.
LAUGHLIN, M. K.
TOMBERLIN, I. R.

*Mathematics:*
ANDREE, R. V.
HILL, T. J.
HUFF, W. N.
HUNEKE, H. V.
KAY, D. C.
LEVY, G.
MAGID, A. R.
MARX, M. L.
MCDONALD, B. R.
RUBIN, L. R.

*Medical Technology:*
COZAD, G. C.

*Modern Languages:*
ABBOTT, J. H.
ARTMAN, J. P.
DUNHAM, L.
EICHHOLZ, E. H.
FEILER, S.
IVASK, I.
MILIVOJEVIC, D. D.
TOLSON, M. B., Jr.

*Philosophy:*
FEAVER, J. C.
HOROSZ, W.
KOVACH, F. J.

MERRILL, K. R.
MOHANTY, J. N.
SHAHAN, R. W.

*Physics and Astronomy:*
BABB, S. E., Jr.
BROERSMA, S.
BURWELL, J. R.
CHINCARINI, G.
COHN, J.
FISCHBECK, H. J.
GOLDEN, D.
HERCZEG, T. J.
KALBFLEISCH, G. R.
PETRY, R. F.
ST. JOHN, R. M.

*Political Science:*
BAKER, R. D.
CHAPMAN, S. G.
HALL, R. G., Jr.
HEBERT, F. T.
HILL, L. B.
HOLLOWAY, H. A.
KASH, D. E.
MAC NIVEN, H. G.
MORGAN, D. R.
PRAY, J. C.
SCHEFFER, W. F.
SLOAN, S.
VARDYS, V. S.
WELLS, R. S.
WHITE, I. L., Jr.
WOOD, J. W.

*Psychology:*
FOUTS, R. S.
GETTYS, C. F.
HOVING, K. L.
KANAK, N. J.
LEMMON, W. B.
MELLGREN, R. L.
MORRIS, J. R.
NICEWANDER, W. A.
TOOTHAKER, L. E.
WEISS, R. F.
WISPE, L. G.

*Regional and City Planning:*
LEHR, R. L.

*Social Work:*
CHESS, W. A.
HO, M. K.
KAGAN, M.
PEIRCE, F. J.
RICHEK, H. G.
TOLLIVER, L. P.

*Sociology:*
HILBERT, R. E.
SILBERSTEIN, F. B.
STEGLICH, W. G.
WATSON, W.

*Zoology:*
BRAVER, G.
BROWN, H. P.
CARPENTER, C. C.
CLEMENS, H. P.
FARMER, J. N.
HAINES, H. B.
HILL, L. G.
HOPLA, C. E.
HUTCHISON, V. H.

College of Business Administration:
*Accounting:*
BROWN, H. A., Jr.
GOGGANS, T. P.
HERRICK, T. P., Jr.
KLINGSTEDT, J. P.
MCGREW, W. C.
SCOTT, G. M.

*Economics:*
BRINKER, P. A.
CRIM, E. F. Jr.
HIBDON, J. E.
KONDONASSIS, A. J.
MURRAY, D. A.
PEACH, W. N.
STEPHENS, J. K.
TAYLOR, B. J.

*Environmental Analysis and Policy:*
LIS, A. S.

*Finance:*
CHILDRESS, D. R.
FORD, R. A.
MURPHY, N. B.

*Management:*
ALONSO, R. C.
ATHERTON, R. M., Jr.
BISHOP, L. D.
ENGLAND, G. W.
MCKIBBIN, L. E.
PHILLIPS, M. C.
SCANLAN, B. K.
SCHUMACHER, B. G.
TERSINE, R. J.
WEITZEL, W. F.
WREN, D. A.

*Marketing:*
BROWN, H. B., Jr.
CONSTANTIN, J. A.
CRITES, D. M.
EVANS, R. E.
MCCAMMON, B. C., Jr.
MORRIS, M. L.

College of Education:
BIBENS, R. F.
CURRY, R. L.
HENDERSON, G.
HENGST, H. R.
HOLCOMB, B. D.
KING, C. R.
KOWITZ, G. T.
PARKER, J. F.
PRICKETT, L. E.
PULLIAM, J. D.
RENNER, J. W.
RUPIPER, O. J.
SHARP, P. F.
SHEPHERD, G. D.
SMOUSE, A. D.
WIGGINS, T. W.
WILLIAMS, L. P.
WILLIAMS, R. P.
WISNIEWSKI, R.

College of Engineering:
*Aerospace, Mechanical and Nuclear Engineering:*
BERGEY, K. H.
BERT, C. W., III.
BLICK, E. F.
EGLE, D. M.
EMANUEL, G.
FRANCIS, J. E.
JISCHKE, M. C.
LOVE, T. J., Jr.
PURCUPILE, J. C.
RASMUSSEN, M. L.
REDDY, J. N.
TERRELL, C. W.
TURKINGTON, D. B.
UPTHEGROVE, W. R.

*Chemical Engineering and Materials Science:*
BLOCK, R. J.
DANIELS, R. D.
SLIEPCEVICH, C. M.
SOFER, S. S.

STARLING, K. E.
TOWNSEND, F. M.
UPTHEGROVE, W. R.

*Civil Engineering and Environmental Science:*
CANTER, L. W.
HARP, J. F.
KLEHR, E. H.
LAGUROS, J. G.
MURRAY, T. M.
REID, G. W.
STREEBIN, L. E.

*Electrical Engineering and Computing Sciences:*
ANDREE, R. V.
BREDESON, J. G.
COUNCIL, M. E.
HADEN, C. R.
KAHNG, S. K.
KURIGER, W. L.
LEE, S. C.
TUMA, G.
WALKER, G. B.
ZELBY, L. W.

*Industrial Engineering:*
DEVINE, M. D.
FOOTE, B. L.
PURSWELL, J. L.
SHAPIRO, R. A.

*Meteorology:*
DUCHON, C. E.
EDDY, G. A.
INMAN, R. L.
SASAKI, Y.

*Petroleum and Geological Engineering:*
MCCRAY, A. W.
MENZIE, D. E.

College of Environmental Design:
CALVERT, F. O.
HENDERSON, A. G.
HESS, R. E.
HODGELL, M. R.
KUHLMAN, R. N.
SHELLABARGER, F. D.
SOREY, T. L., Jr.
WILSON, W. H.

College of Fine Arts:
*Art:*
BOGART, G. A., Jr.
HENKLE, J. L.
HOBBS, J. F.
LEE, C. E.
OLKINETZKY, S.

*Drama:*
EEK, N. S.
HERSTAND, T.
KUNESH, G. D.
LARSON, R. D.
SUGGS, C. C.
TEREKHOV, M.

*Music:*
BELL, D. B.
BIRKHEAD, J.
BRAUGHT, E. A.
CAREY, T. D.
DE STWOLINSKI, G. B.
HENNAGIN, M.
KAISERMAN, D. N.
MATHIS, G. R.
PLATT, M. C.
SMITH, J. N.
TRUMBLE, E. L.
WAGNER, I. L.

College of Law:
COX, M. P.
ELKOURI, F.
FRASER, G. B.
GASAWAY, L. N.

## UNIVERSITIES AND COLLEGES—OKLAHOMA (UNIVERSITY OF) — U.S.A.

Gibbens, D. G.
Kershen, D. L.
Kuntz, E. O.
Long, J. C.
McNichols, W. J.
Miller, F. H.
Million, E. M.
Morgan, E. D.
Phelps, E. D.
Rarick, J. F.
Reynolds, O. M.
Richardson, R. E. L.
Swank, D.
Te Selle, J.
Vliet, R. D.
Westbrook, J. E.
Whinery, L. H.
Young, H. W.

*College of Liberal Studies:*
Artman, J. P.
Bergey, K. H.
Block, R. J.
Brinker, P. A.
Burkett, J. E.
Childress, D. R.
Cohn, J.
Constantin, J. A.
Crim, S. R.
Crockett, N. L.
DeStwolinski, G.
Eddy, G. A.
Eick, W. F.
Ezell, J.
Feaver, J. C.
Fogel, N.
Gibson, A. M.
Hall, R. G.
Henderson, A.
Hibdon, J. E.
Hilbert, R. E.
Holland, C. J.
Horosz, W.
Huffman, G.
Jischke, M.
Kanak, N. J.
Kendall, J.
Kitts, D. B.
Lee, C.
Levy, G.
MacNiven, H. G.
Maehl, W. H., Jr.
Nolan, P. J.
Olson, R. E.
Phillips, M. C.
Ruggiers, P. G.
Shahan, R. W.
Smith, E. C.
Smith, T. M.
Suggs, C. C.
Tobias, H. J.
Tolson, M. B., Jr.
Walker, G. B.
Weber, J. C.
Wells, R. S.
Wiggins, T. W.
Zelby, L. W.

### Oklahoma City Campus

The University of Oklahoma Health Sciences Center,
P.O.B. 26901, Oklahoma City, Oklahoma 73190

*Provost, Health Sciences:* Clayton Rich, M.D.
*Director of Admissions:* Norman Goodwin, B.A.
*Librarian:* Clinton M. Thompson, M.L.S.

DEANS:
*College of Dentistry:* William E. Brown, D.D.S.
*Graduate College-Health Science Center:* Kenneth L. Hoving, Ph.D.
*College of Health:* Philip E. Smith, Sc.D.
*College of Medicine:* Thomas N. Lynn, M.D.
*College of Nursing:* Gloria R. Smith, Ph.D.
*College of Pharmacy:* Rodney D. Ice, Ph.D.

PROFESSORS:
*College of Dentistry:*
  *Biochemistry and Molecular Biology:*
Johnson, B. C.

  *Community Dentistry:*
Shapiro, S.
Sullens, R. H.

  *Family Practice and Community Medicine and Dentistry:*
Lynn, T. N.
Steen, W. D.

  *Fixed Prosthodontics:*
Shillingburg, H.

  *Microbiology and Immunology:*
Hyde, R. M.
Ivey, M. H.
Patnode, R. A.
Sokatch, J. R.

  *Occlusion:*
Whitsett, L.

  *Operative Dentistry:*
Collard, E. W.
Dilts, W. E.

  *Oral Diagnosis-Oral Radiology:*
Reynolds, R. L.

  *Oral Pathology:*
Glass, R. T.

  *Oral Surgery:*
Staples, A. F.

  *Orthodontics:*
Nanda, R. S.

  *Pathology:*
Coalson, J. J.

  *Pedodontics:*
Brown, W. E., Jr.
Mathewson, R. J.

  *Periodontics:*
Tow, H. D.

  *Pharmacology:*
Hornbrook, R.
Moore, J. I.

  *Physiology and Biophysics:*
Staples, A. F.

  *Restorative Dentistry:*
Welk, D. A.

*College of Health:*
  *Biostatistics and Epidemiology:*
Anderson, P. S., Jr.
Asal, N. R.
Deal, R. B., Jr.
Parker, D. E.
Silberg, S. L.
West, K. M.

  *Clinical Laboratory Sciences:*
Smith, P. E.

  *Communication Disorders:*
Barry, S. J.
Counihan, D. T.
Cullinan, W. L.
Emanuel, F. W.
Mencke, E. O.
Ochsner, G. J.

  *Environmental Health:*
Coleman, R. L.
Lawrence, C. H.
Mill, R. A.

  *Health Administration:*
Amidon, R. L.
Hanson, I. R.

  *Medical Library Science:*
Rucker, L. A.
Wender, R. W.

  *Occupational Therapy:*
Reed, K.

  *Radiologic Technology:*
Curcio, B. M.
Sullivan, C. A.

  *Social Sciences and Health Behaviour:*
Jones, B. L.
Ketner, R. W.
McGowan, T. R.
Owens, M. V.

*College of Medicine:*
  *Anatomical Sciences:*
Allison, J. E.
Coalson, R.
Faulkner, K. K.
Felts, W. J. L.
Lee, J. C.
Lhotka, J. F.

  *Anaesthesiology:*
Carmack, C. A.
Deutsch, S.
Massion, W. H.
Sears, B. E.

  *Biochemistry and Molecular Biology:*
Chandler, A. M.
Delaney, R.
Johnson, B. C.
Rabinovitch, B.
Unger, L.

  *Clinical Laboratory Science:*
McClellan, B. J.

  *Dental Surgery:*
Staples, A. F.

  *Dermatology:*
Everett, M. A.
Weigand, D. A.

  *Family Practice and Community Medicine and Dentistry:*
Lynn, T. N.
Parrish, J.
Steen, W. D.

  *Gynaecology-Obstetrics:*
Crosby, W. M.
McMaster, A. J.
Merrill, J. A.

  *History of Medicine:*
Howard, R. P.

  *Medicine:*
Bottomley, R.
Bottomley, S. S.
Clark, M. L.
Coussons, R. T.
Czerwinski, A.
Dubowski, K. M.
Eichner, E. R.
Frew, A. L.
Gunn, C. G.
Howard, R. P.
Kem, D. C.
Lazzara, R.
McCall, C. B.
Mock, D. C.
Mohr, J. A.

MUCHMORE, H. G.
PAPPER, S.
RHOADES, E.
SCHECHTER, E.
SCHERLAG, B. J.
SCHNEIDER, R. A.
SCHULTZ, R. T.
SMITH, W. O.
TRACHEWSKY, D.
WELSH, J. D.
WHANG, R.
WHITSETT, T. L.
WILSON, M. F.

*Microbiology and Immunology:*
BULMER, G. S.
FERRETTI, J. J.
HYDE, R. M.
IVEY, M. H.
PATNODE, R. A.
SCOTT, L. V.
SOKATCH, J. R.

*Neurology:*
NELSON, J. W.

*Ophthalmology:*
ACERS, T. E.

*Orthopaedic Surgery:*
KOPTA, J. A.

*Pathology:*
ALTSHULER, G. P.
BRITZ, W. E., Jr.
FAHMY, A.
MCCLELLAN, B. J.
TAYLOR, F. B.

*Paediatrics:*
HUMPHREY, G. B.
MARKS, M. I.
RENNERT, O. M.
RILEY, H. D., Jr.
THOMAS, E. D.
THOMPSON, W. M.
TORRES-PINEDO, R. B.
WENZL, J. E.

*Pharmacology:*
HORNBROOK, R.
MOORE, J. I.

*Physiology and Biophysics:*
HINSHAW, L.
KEYL, J.
STONE, H. L.
WEISS, K. A.

*Psychiatry and Behavioural Sciences:*
DECKERT, G. H.
GATHMAN, L. T.
HOLLOWAY, F. A.
KRUG, R.
LOPEZ, A.
PARSONS, O.
PISHKIN, V.
SHURLEY, J. T.
TAPIA, F.
TOUSSIENG, P. W.
VON BRAUCHITSCH, H.
WALKER, C. E.
WATKINS, J. T.
WEITZENHOFFER, A.
WILLIAMS, H.
ZEINER, A. R.

*Pulmonary Diseases:*
MUCHMORE, H. G.

*Radiological Sciences:*
ACKER, S. E.
ADAMS, G. D.
ANDERSON, D. W.
BOGARDUS, C. R.
EATON, B. G.
HABERMAN, J. D.
JOHNSON, T. H.
KOLLMORGEN, M.

LEMON, W. E.
RAESIDE, D. E.
TRAUB, S. P.
VAN HOUTTE, J. J.
WIZENBERG, M. J.

*Surgery:*
ELKINS, R. C.
KAPLAN, R. J.
POLLAY, M.
SMITH, E. I.
TUNELL, W. P.
WILDER, R. J.
WILLIAMS, G. R.

*Urology:*
GEYER, J. R.
PARRY, W. L.

*College of Nursing:*
BAKER, C. M.
BIRCHER, A. U.
SMITH, G. R.

*College of Pharmacy:*
DANIELS, R.
ICE, R. D.
KAUL, P. N.
SOMMERS, E. B.

## Tulsa Campus

THE UNIVERSITY OF OKLAHOMA
TULSA MEDICAL COLLEGE,
2727 EAST 21ST ST., TULSA,
OKLAHOMA 74105

*Dean:* EDWARD J. TOMSOVIC, M.D.

PROFESSORS:
*Family Practice:*
GOOD, R. C.
GREENSHER, A.

*Gynaecology-Obstetrics:*
BETHEA, R. C.
KICKHOFER, W. H.
NETTLES, J. B.
PUFTY, F. P.

*Medicine:*
FITZPATRICK, M. J.
GIBBS, R. M.
GREENE, J. N.
NICHOLS, N.

*Paediatrics:*
PLUNKET, D.

*Psychiatry:*
ALLEN, J. R.

*Surgery:*
CLINGAN, F. A.
GUERNSEY, J. M.

## UNIVERSITY OF SCIENCE AND ARTS OF OKLAHOMA
CHICKASHA, OKLAHOMA 73018

Founded 1908.

State-supported college.

*President:* Dr. ROY TROUTT.
*Vice-President for Academic Affairs:* Dr. FLOYD COPPEDGE.
*Vice-President for Fiscal Affairs:* Dr. CLYDE SPRUELL.
*Vice-President for the University Community:* BILL SMITH.
*Librarian:* W. MARTIN, Jr.

Library of 78,000 vols.
Number of teachers: 60.
Number of students: 1,350.

Publication: *Trend.*

## UNIVERSITY OF TULSA
600 SOUTH COLLEGE AVENUE,
TULSA, OKLAHOMA 74104

Telephone: (918) 939-6351.

Founded as Henry Kendall College under Presbyterian control 1894, reorganized and name changed to University of Tulsa 1920; became non-denominational 1928.

*President:* J. PASCHAL TWYMAN.
*Vice-Presidents:* J. HAYES, J. DOWGRAY, E. C. TURNER.
*Dean of Admissions and Records:* C. E. MALONE.
*Librarian:* R. H. PATTERSON.

Number of teachers: 315.
Number of students: 6,200.

Publications: *James Joyce Quarterly, University of Tulsa Magazine†.*

DEANS:
*Arts and Sciences:* THOMAS F. STALEY.
*Business Adminitsration:* ROBERT J. MONROE.
*Education:* B. HOWELL.
*Engineering:* NICHOLAS D. SYLVESTER.
*Nursing:* IRA TRAIL ADAMS.
*Law:* FRANK WALWER.
*Graduate:* ALLEN R. SOLTOW.

PROFESSORS:
ALWORTH, P., PH.D., English
BRILL, J. P., PH.D., Petroleum Engineering
BROWN, K. E., PH.D., Petroleum Engineering
BROWN, P. L., TH.D., Philosophy
BUCKLEY, T. H., PH.D., History
BUTHOD, P., M.S., Chemical Engineering
CADENHEAD, I. E., Jr., PH.D., History
CAIRNS, T. W., PH.D., Mathematics
CLARK, D. S., J.S.M., Law
COKER, C., M.A., Art
DAILEY, D., M.M., Music
DOWGRAY, J. L., PH.D., History
DRATZ, J. P., PH.D., Physical Education
ELLINGSWORTH, H. W., PH.D., Communications
FRANKS, P., PH.D., Engineering
FREY, MARTIN A., LL.M., Law
FRIZZELL, KENT, J.D., Law
GRIFFITH, P. M., PH.D., English
GUERRERO, E. T., PH.D., Petroleum Engineering
GUP, B. E., PH.D., Banking and Finance
HAGER, J. W., LL.M., Law
HALL, R. L., ED.D., Education
HENDERSON, R. W., PH.D., Religion
HICKS, J. F., LL.M., Law
HIPSHER, W. L., Jr., ED., Education
HOLLINGSWORTH, W. G., J.D., Law
HORNBOSTEL, V. O., PH.D., Education
HOWELL, BRUCE, PH.D., Education
HUTTON, C. E., PH.D., Accounting
JOHNSON, M., PH.D., English
JONES, H. R., PH.D., Speech
KINSEY, B., PH.D., Sociology
LINDSAY, H. L., PH.D., Zoology
LOGSDON, G. W., ED.D., American Culture
LUCE, T. S., PH.D., Education
MCKAY, E. S., PH.D., Chemistry
MCKEE, W. E., PH.D., History of Music
MANNING, F. S., PH.D., Chemical Engineering
MARDER, D., PH.D., English
MERRELL, H. B., PH.D., Communicative Disorders
MONROE, R. J., PH.D., Business
O'BRIEN, D., PH.D., Modern Letters
OLIVER, B. C., ED.D., Education
PLACE, B. E., B.S., Art

REEVES, E., PH.D., Political Science
SARGENT, E. A., ED.D., Education
STALEY, T. F., PH.D., English
STRICKLAND, RENNARD, S.J.D., Law
SYLVESTER, N. D., PH.D., Petroleum Engineering
TAYLOR, G., PH.D., English
THOMAS, J. C., LL.M., Law
THOMAS, R. C., LL.M., Law
THOMPSON, R. E., PH.D., Chemical Engineering
TIDROW, J., ED.D.. Education
TRAIL ADAMS, IRA, PH.D., Nursing
TRUEBLOOD, L. R., D.B., Management
TURNER, EMERY C., D.B.A., Accounting
TWYMAN, J. P., PH.D., Education
VUNOVICH, N., PH.D., Theatre
WEATHERS, W., PH.D., English
WEBER, C. E., PH.D., German
WESTERLUND, S., ED.D., Education
WINCHESTER, O. W., PH.D., English
ZUSNE, L., PH.D., Psychology

## OREGON

### EASTERN OREGON STATE COLLEGE
LA GRANDE, OREGON 97850

Telephone: (503) 963-2171.

Founded 1929.

*President:* RODNEY A. BRIGGS.
*Dean of Academic Affairs:* DAVID GILBERT.
*Director of Student Affairs:* WILLIAM WELLS.
*Director of Business Affairs:* JAMES LUNDY.
*Director of College Relations:* JACK SCHUT.
*Director of Regional Services Institute:* TERRY EDVALSON.
*Director of Continuing Education and Regional Programmes:* DOUGLAS TREADWAY.
*Director of Information:* SUSAN JONES.
*Librarian:* J. W. EVANS.

The library contains 25,000 vols.
Number of teachers: 205.
Number of students: 1,770.

DEANS:

*School of Professional Studies:* HARVEY BENNETT.
*School of Arts and Sciences:* GERALD YOUNG.

### GEORGE FOX COLLEGE
NEWBERG, OREGON 97132

Telephone: (503) 538-8383.

Founded 1891.

*President:* Dr. DAVID C. LESHANA.
*Director of Admissions:* J. SETTLE.
*Librarian:* Miss GENETTE MCNICHOLS.

The library contains 65,000 vols.
Number of teachers: 75.
Number of students: 775.
Publication: *Life*† (every 2 months).

### LEWIS AND CLARK COLLEGE
PORTLAND, OREGON 97219

Founded 1867.

*President:* JAMES A. GARDNER.
*Registrar:* R. WILKIN.
*Provost and Dean of Faculty:* JOHN E. BROWN.
*Vice-President for Student Affairs:* RICHARD A. SORENSON.
*Vice-President for Development:* GLENN H. GREGG.
*Vice-President for Business and Finance:* WILLIAM T. MALLINSON.
*Dean of Law School:* STEPHEN KANTER (acting).
*Librarian:* LEONOOR SWETS INGRAHAM.

Library of 340,914 vols.
Number of teachers: 144 full-time, 61 part-time.
Number of students: 3,224.
Publication: *Journal*†.

### LINFIELD COLLEGE
MCMINNVILLE, OREGON 97128

Telephone: (503) 472-4121.

Founded 1849.

*President:* Dr. C. U. WALKER.
*Registrar:* Dr. K. C. WILLIAMS.

Library of 105,163 vols.
Number of teachers: 81.
Number of students: 1,242.

### NORTHWEST CHRISTIAN COLLEGE
ELEVENTH AND ALDER STREETS, EUGENE, OREGON 97401

Telephone: (503) 343-1641.

Founded 1895.

*President:* WILLIAM E. HAYS.
*Registrar:* DORIS BOKOVOY.
*Librarian:* MARGARET W. HEWITT.

Library of 51,000 vols.
Number of teachers: 15.
Number of students: 300.

### OREGON STATE UNIVERSITY
CORVALLIS, OREGON 97331

Telephone: (503) 754-0123.

Founded 1868.

State control; Academic year: September to June.

*President:* R. W. MACVICAR, PH.D.
*Vice-President for Administration:* CLIFFORD V. SMITH, Jr., PH.D.
*Vice-President for Student Services:* ROBERT W. CHICK, ED.D.
*Dean of Faculty:* D. B. NICODEMUS, PH.D.
*Dean of Research:* (vacant).
*Registrar:* W. E. GIBBS, ED.M.
*Director of Business Affairs:* HUGH F. JEFFREY, Jr., B.S.
*Librarian:* R. K. WALDRON, M.A.

Library of 842,200 vols., 668,000 microfilms.
Number of teachers: 1,582.
Number of students: 17,500.

Publications: *Oregon Stater*, *Yearbook of Asscn. of Pacific Coast Geographers*, *Biology Colloquium Proceedings*, *Genetics Lecture Series* (annually), etc., occasional publs., monographs.

DEANS

*Graduate School:* (vacant).
*School of Agriculture:* ERNEST J. BRISKEY, PH.D.
*School of Business:* E. E. GODDARD, D.B.A.
*School of Education:* SYLVIA TUCKER, ED.D.
*School of Engineering:* F. J. BURGESS, M.S.
*School of Forestry:* C. H. STOLTENBERG, PH.D.
*School of Health and Physical Education:* MICHAEL G. MAKSUD, PH.D.
*School of Home Economics:* BETTY E. HAWTHORNE, PH.D.
*College of Liberal Arts:* DAVID J. KING, PH.D.
*School of Oceanography:* G. ROSS HEATH, PH.D.
*School of Pharmacy:* RICHARD A. OHVALL, PH.D.
*College of Science:* THOMAS D. SUGIHARA, PH.D.
*School of Veterinary Medicine:* E. EDWARD WEDMAN, PH.D.

### PACIFIC UNIVERSITY
COLLEGE WAY, FOREST GROVE, OREGON 97116

Telephone: (503) 357-6151.

Founded 1849.

*President:* JAMES V. MILLER.
*Registrar:* Mrs. GLORIA WULF.
*Director of Admissions:* PAUL B. RANSLOW.
*Librarian:* JAN FORTIER.

Library of 127,212 vols., 136,657 U.S. documents, 6,970 Oregon documents.
Number of teachers: 80 full-time.
Number of students: 1,100.

### PORTLAND STATE UNIVERSITY
P.O. BOX 751, PORTLAND, OREGON 97207

Telephone: (503) 229-4411.

Founded 1955.

Academic year: September to June (and Summer Session).

*Chancellor:* R. E. LIEUALLEN.
*Vice-Chancellor for Academic Affairs:* CLARETHEL KHAANANUI (acting).
*Vice-Chancellor for Administration:* W. T. LEMMAN.
*Vice-Chancellor for Facilities Planning:* J. I. HUNDERUP.

*Vice-Chancellor for Educational Systems:* REX KRUEGER.
*President:* Dr. JOSEPH C. BLUMEL.
*Vice-President for Finance and Administration:* JAMES E. TODD.
*Vice-President for Academic Affairs:* JOHN GRUBER.
*Vice-President for Student Affairs:* ORCILIA FORBES.
*Assistant to the President for University Relations:* PETER VAN'T SLOT.
*Director of Budget:* J. KENNETH HARRIS.
*Director of Admissions:* EILEEN ROSE.
*Librarian:* TOM PFINGSTEN.

Library of 600,479 vols.
Number of teachers: 699.
Number of students: 16,730.

Publications: *Choosing Portland State, Graduate Bulletin, PSU Profile, This is Portland State, General Catalogue, Summer Catalogue, Transferring to PSU* (all annually).

DEANS:

*College of Arts and Letters:* JOHN TRUDEAU.
*College of Science:* GARY GARD (acting).
*College of Social Science:* GEORGE C. HOFFMANN.
*School of Business Administration:* DONALD D. PARKER.
*School of Social Work:* BERNARD ROSS.
*School of Education:* DONALD LEU.
*School of Health and Physical Education:* JACK SCHENDEL.
*School of Urban Affairs:* NOHAD TOULAN.
*Graduate Studies and Research:* STANLEY RAUCH.
*Division of Continuing Education:* ROBERT NICHOLAS.
*Division of Engineering and Applied Science:* HACIK ERZURUMLU.

## REED COLLEGE
3203 S.E. WOODSTOCK BLVD., PORTLAND, OREGON 97202

Founded 1909.

*President:* PAUL E. BRAGDON.
*Executive Vice-President:* GEORGE A. HAY.
*Vice-President-Provost:* G. FRANK GWILLIAM.
*Vice-President for External Affairs:* DEBORAH S. MARTSON.
*Vice-President and Treasurer:* EDWIN McFARLANE.
*Registrar:* ELLEN K. JOHNSON.
*Deans of Students:* JOHN A. DUDMAN, PRISCILLA HANAWALT.
*Librarian:* LUELLA R. POLLOCK.

Library of 280,000 vols.
Number of teachers: 116.
Number of students: 1,155.

## SOUTHERN OREGON STATE COLLEGE
ASHLAND, OREGON 97520

Telephone: (503) 482-3311.

Founded 1926.

*President:* NATALE A. SICURO.
*Registrar:* R. DAVIDSON.
*Librarian:* R. E. MOORE.

The library contains 185,000 vols., 250,000 items on microfilm.
Number of teachers: 242.
Number of students: 4,500.

## UNIVERSITY OF OREGON
EUGENE, OREGON 97403

Telephone: (503) 686-3111.

Established 1872; opened 1876.

State controlled; Academic year: September to June.

*President:* PAUL OLUM, PH.D.
*Vice-President for Administration and Finance:* R. HAWK, D.ED.
*Vice-President for Academic Affairs:* RICHARD J. HILL, PH.D. (acting).
*Vice-President for Public Services:* CURTIS R. SIMIC, B.S.
*Registrar:* WANDA JOHNSON, M.S.
*Director of Business Affairs:* W. N. McLAUGHLIN, B.S., C.P.A.
*Librarian:* GEORGE W. SHIPMAN, A.M.L.S., M.A.
*Library: see* Libraries.
Number of teachers: 1,000.
Number of students: 17,400.

Publications: *University of Oregon Bulletins, University of Oregon Books, Comparative Literature, Oregon Law Review, Oregon Business Review* (quarterly), *Physical Education Microcards, Governmental Research Bulletins, Imprint Oregon, Northwest Review, Bulletin of the Museum of Natural History.*

DEANS:

*Graduate School:* RICHARD H. HERSH, ED.D.
*College of Liberal Arts:* ROBERT M. BERDAHL, PH.D.
*School of Architecture and Allied Arts:* WILMOT G. GILLAND, M.F.A. (acting).
*College of Business Administration:* JAMES REINMUTH, PH.D.
*School of Community Service and Public Affairs:* KENNETH C. TOLLENAAR, M.A. (acting).
*College of Education:* R. GILBERTS, PH.D.
*College of Health, Physical Education and Recreation:* CELESTE ULRICH, PH.D.
*School of Journalism:* EVERETTE E. DENNIS, PH.D.
*School of Law:* DERRICK A. BELL, Jr., LL.B.
*School of Music:* MORETTE RIDER, PH.D.
*Honors College:* R. A. KIMBALL, PH.D. (Director).

PROFESSORS:

ABBOTT, M. G., PH.D., Education
ACKER, M. H., M.A., PH.D., Education
AIKENS, C. M., PH.D., Anthropology
ALBAUM, G. S., PH.D., Marketing
ALBRECHT, R. C., PH.D., English
ALEF, G., M.A., PH.D., History
ANDERSON, F. W., PH.D., Mathematics
ANDREWS, F. C., PH.D., Mathematics
ANDRUS, R. R., PH.D., Marketing
ANTHONY, H. G., Maj., M.S., Military Science
ATTNEAVE, F., III, PH.D., Psychology
BAILEY, EXINE A., M.A., Music
BAJER, A. S., M.A., D.SC., Biology
BAKER, B. M., PH.D., Geology
BALDWIN, J. E., PH.D., Chemistry
BALL, R. C., PH.D., English
BARNES, B. A., PH.D., Mathematics
BARRAR, R. B., M.S., PH.D., Mathematics
BARTEL, R., PH.D., English
BASYE, W. M., A.B., LL.B., Law
BATEMAN, BARBARA, M.A., PH.D., Education
BECK, J., PH.D., Psychology
BECKER, W. C., PH.D., Education
BELL, D. A., LL.B., Law
BERGQUIST, P., PH.D., Music
BERNHARD, S. A., PH.D., Chemistry
BIERWAG, G. O., PH.D., Economics
BINGHAM, E. R., PH.D., History
BIRN, R., PH.D., History
BIRN, R. M., PH.D., Romance Languages
BOEKELHEIDE, V. C., PH.D., Chemistry
BOGEN, G. K., D.ED., Education
BOGGS, S., Jr., PH.D., Geology
BONNETT, HOWARD T., PH.D., Biology
BOWERS, C. A., PH.D., Education
BRADY, T. A., PH.D., History
BREIDENTHAL, L., A.MUS.DOC., Music
BRICKER, D. D., PH.D., Special Education
BRISCOE, J. L., B.ARCH. ENG., Architecture
BRODIE, D. W., LL.B., Law
BROEKHOFF, J., PH.D., Physical Education
BROWN, RICHARD M., PH.D., History
BROWN, W. B., PH.D., Management
BROWNING, P. L., PH.D., Education
BRYAN, S. W., M.ARCH., Architecture
BUCKNER, P. E., M.F.A., Sculpture
BURGNER, J. W., M.A., Art
CADBURY, W. E., PH.D., Film Studies
CALIN, W. C., PH.D., French
CAMPBELL, P., PH.D., Economics
CARLSON, R. O., ED.D., Education
CASTENHOLZ, R. W., PH.D., Biology
CHARTERS, W. W., Jr., PH.D., Education
CHRISTENSEN, N. J., PH.D., Education
CLARK, C. D., LL.M., Law
CONANT, E. H., PH.D., Management
COOK, S. A., PH.D., Biology
CRASEMAN, B., PH.D., Physics
CSONKA, P. L., PH.D., Physics
CURTIS, C. W., PH.D., Mathematics
DASSO, J. J., PH.D., Finance
DAVIES, J. C., PH.D., Political Science
DAVIS, R. M., PH.D., Economics
DAWES, R. M., PH.D., Psychology
DeCHAINE, F. B., PH.D., Theatre
DEJUNG, J. E. S., ED.D., Education
DEUTSCH, S. E., PH.D., Sociology
DIETHELM, J., M.L.ARCH., Landscape Architecture
DILLER, E., D.M.L., German
DIZNEY, H. F., PH.D., Education
DOLBY, L. J., PH.D., Chemistry
DOLE, P. H., M.S., Architecture
DONNELLY, M., PH.D., Art History
DONNELLY, R. J., PH.D., Physics
DORJAHN, V. R., PH.D., Anthropology
DOWNES, B. T., PH.D., Community Service
DUMOND, D. E., PH.D., Anthropology
DYER, MICHEAL D., PH.D., Mathematics
ELLIS, M. J., PHD., Physical Education
ENGELMANN, S. E., B.A., Education
EVONUK, E., PH.D., Physical Education

FAGOT, R. F., PH.D., Psychology
FERENS, R. R., M.ARCH., Architecture
FISZMAN, J. R., PH.D., Political Science
FORD, P. M., RE.D., Recreation Management
FOSMIRE, F. R., PH.D., Psychology
FOSTER, D. G., M.F.A., Art
FRANK, P. W., PH.D., Biology
FRIEDMAN, R. P., PH.D., Speech
GALL, M., PH.D., Education
GILBERTS, R. D., PH.D., Educational Administration
GILLAND, W. G., M.F.A., Architecture
GIRARDEAU, M. D., PH.D., Physics
GOLDBERG, L. R., PH.D., Psychology
GOLDRICH, D., PH.D., Political Science
GOLDSTEIN, H. N., PH.D., Economics
GOLES, G. G., PH.D., Chemistry/Geology
GONTRUM, P., PH.D., German
GORDON-LICKEY, B., PH.D., Psychology
GORDON-LICKEY, M., PH.D., Psychology
GOSWAMI, AMIT, PH.D., Physics
GRANT, P., PH.D., Biology
GRAY, J., PH.D., Biology
GREENFIELD, S. B., PH.D., English
GREENFIELD, T. C., PH.D., English
GRIFFITH, C., PH.D., English
GRIFFITH, O. H., PH.D., Chemistry
GROVE, M. A., PH.D., Economics
HAHN, W. L., PH.D., German
HAISLIP, J. A., PH.D., English
HALPERN, A. S., PH.D., Education
HAMILTON, J., D.M.A., Music
HANDY, W. J., PH.D., English
HANHARDT, A. M., PH.D., Political Science
HARRISON, D. K., Mathematics
HART, T. R., PH.D., Romance Languages
HATZANTONIS, E. S., PH.D., Romance Languages
HAWK, R., D.ED., Education
HAWKINS, D. I., PH.D., Marketing
HEDETNIEMI, S., PH.D., Computer Science
HERBERT, E., PH.D., Chemistry
HERSH, R. H., ED.D., Education
HIGGINS, R. J., PH.D., Physics
HILDRETH, R. G., J.D., Law
HILL, R. J., PH.D., Sociology
HINTZMAN, D. L., PH.D., Psychology
HLADKY, J. R., A.MUS.D., Music
HODGE, G. M., Jr., PH.D., Architecture
HOFFER, A. R., PH.D., Mathematics
HOLBO, P. S., PH.D., History
HOLSER, W. T., PH.D., Geology
HOVET, T., PH.D., Political Science
HOYLE, G., D.SC., Biology
HWA, R. C., PH.D., Physics
HYMAN, R., PH.D., Psychology
HYNES, J. A., Jr., PH.D., English
JACOBSON, J. L., J.D., Law
JAMES, R. C., M.F.A., Art
JOHANNESSEN, C. L., PH.D., Geography
JOHNSON, G. B., PH.D., Sociology
JOHNSON, L. T., M.A., Interior Architecture
JONES, H. R., M.A., Library
JUNG, A., PH.D., Chinese
KANTOR, W. M., PH.D., Mathematics
KAYS, M. A., PH.D., Geology
KEANA, JOHN F. W., PH.D., Chemistry
KEELE, S., PH.D., Psychology
KELLY, J. G., PH.D., C.S.P.A., Psychology
KEMP, E. C., M.L.S., Library
KEMP, J. C., PH.D., Physics
KENSLER, G. L., ED.D., Art Education
KERLINGER, F. N., PH.D., Education
KEZER, J., PH.D., Biology
KHANG, CHULSOON, PH.D., Economics
KIMBLE, D. P., PH.D., Psychology
KIME, R. E., PH.D., Health Education
KIRKPATRICK, L. C., J.D., Law
KLEINSASSER, T. W., M.F.A., Architecture
KLEMM, L. H., PH.D., Chemistry
KLONOSKI, J. R., PH.D., Political Science
KOENIG, T. W., PH.D., Chemistry
KOPLIN, H. T., PH.D., Economics
KRANZLER, G. D., ED.D., Education

KRAUSE, L., B.S., Fine and Applied Arts
KRETSINGER, E. A., PH.D., Speech
LACY, F. R., J.D., LL.M., Law
LAING, E. J., PH.D., Art History
LALLAS, J. E., ED.D., Education
LANCE, W. D., ED.D., Special Education
LANIER, V., ED.D., Art Education
LARUSSO, D. A., PH.D., Speech
LEAHY, J. V., PH.D., Mathematics
LEFEVRE, H. W., PH.D., Physics
LEMERT, J. B., PH.D., Journalism
LEISTNER, C. A., PH.D., Speech
LEPPMANN, W. A., PH.D., Germanic Languages
LEWINSOHN, P. M., PH.D., Psychology
LICHTENSTEIN, E., PH.D., Psychology
LINDERSKI, J., PH.D., History
LITTMAN, R. A., PH.D., Psychology
LOEB, H. L., PH.D., Mathematics
LOUGHARY, J. W., PH.D., Education
LOVE, G. A., PH.D., English
LOVELL, L. L., PH.D., Education
LOVINGER, R. J., M.L.A., Landscape Architecture
LOWE, R. N., ED.D., Education
LOY, W. G., PH.D., Geography
LYONS, R. M., M.F.A., English
MALARKEY, S., PH.D., English
MARTIN, R. P., PH.D., Music
MATTHEWS, B. W., PH.D., Physics
MATTIS, J. M., J.D., Public Affairs
MATTSON, R. H., D.ED., Special Education
MAVEETY, S. R., PH.D., English
MAZO, R. M., PH.D., Chemistry
MCBIRNEY, A. R., PH.D., Geology
MCCLURE, J. W., PH.D., Physics
MCCOLLOUGH, R. R., M.S., Library
MCCONNAUGHEY, B. H., PH.D., Biology
MCDANIELS, D. K., PH.D., Physics
MCFEE, J. K., ED.D., Art Education
MCKENZIE, A. D., PH.D., Art History
MCMANUS, J. C., M.A., Music
MENAKER, M., PH.D., Zoology
MERRILL, F. R., J.D., Law
METZLER, K. T., M.S.J., Journalism
MIKESELL, R. E., PH.D., Economics
MILLER, J. A., A.MUS.D., Music
MITCHELL, JOYCE, PH.D., Political Science
MITCHELL, W. C., PH.D., Political Science
MITTMAN, A., PH.D., Education
MORAVCSIK, M. J., PH.D., Physics
MORRIS, R. W., PH.D., Biology
MORRISON, P. D., D.L.S., Librarianship
MOURSUND, D. G., PH.D., Computer Science
MOURSUND, E. E., M.ARCH., Architecture
MUNZ, F. W., PH.D., Biology
NELSON, R. P., M.S., Journalism
NICHOLLS, R. A., PH.D., Germanic Languages
NOVICK, A., PH.D., Biology
NOVITSKI, E., PH.D., Biology
NOYES, R. M., PH.D., Chemistry
OKADA, F. S., B.F.A., Fine Arts
OLUM, P., PH.D., Mathematics
ORBELL, J. M., PH.D., Political Science
OWEN, H. J., D.M.A., Music
PALMER, T. W., PH.D., Mathematics
PASCAL, C. B., PH.D., Classics
PATTERSON, G. R., PH.D., Education
PATTON, C. P., PH.D., Geography
PETICOLAS, W. L., PH.D., Chemistry
PIELE, P. K., PH.D., Education
PIERCE, L. C., PH.D., Political Science
PIERSON, S. A., PH.D., History
PLATT, G. M., LL.B., Law
POLK, K., PH.D., Sociology
POSNER, M. I., PH.D., Psychology
POWERS, P. J., PH.D., Romance Languages
RAGATZ, R. L., PH.D., Urban Planning
RANDOLPH, W. D., J.D., Law
RANKIN, R. J., PH.D., Education
RARICK, G. R., PH.D., Journalism
RAY, M. L., J.D., Law

REINMUTH, J. E., PH.D., Quantitative Methods
REYNOLDS, J. S., M.ARCH., Architecture
RICH, S. U., D.B.A., Industrial Marketing
RIDER, M. L., D.ED., Music
ROBECK, M. C., PH.D., Education
ROBERT, W. J., LL.M., Business Law
ROSS, K. A., PH.D., Mathematics
ROTHBART, M., PH.D., Psychology
ROUSSEVE, R. J., PH.D., Education
RUDY, P. R., PH.D., Biology
RUSCH, C. W., M.ARCH., Architecture
RUNKEL, P. J., PH.D., Psychology
SALISBURY, R. J., M.F.A., English
SALTZMAN, H. R., D.M.A., Music
SANDERS, J. T., PH.D., Religious Studies
SAVAGE, N. M., PH.D., Geology
SCHAAF, O. F., PH.D., Education
SCHELLMAN, J. A., PH.D., Chemistry
SCHLAADT, R. G., ED.D., Health Education
SCHMINKE, C. W., PH.D., Education
SCHMUCK, R. A., PH.D., Education
SCHWARZ, R. H., PH.D., Education
SCOLES, E. F., J.S.D., Law
SCOTT, F. G., PH.D., Gerontology
SEITZ, G. M., PH.D., Mathematics
SHEPERD, GEORGE, ED.D., Education
SHEPHERD, J. R., PH.D., Speech
SHERRIFFS, R. E., PH.D., Telecommunication
SHERWOOD, J. C., PH.D., English
SIEGEL, B. N., PH.D., Economics
SIERADSKI, A. J., PH.D., Mathematics
SIMMONS, J. A., PH.D., Biology
SIMONDS, P. E., PH.D., Anthropology
SISTROM, W. R., PH.D., Biology
SMITH, E. G., Jr., PH.D., Geography
SMITH, R. E., PH.D., Economics
SMITH, R. W., PH.D., History
SMITH, W. E., ED.D., Health Education
SORENSON, L. R., PH.D., History
STAHL, F. W., PH.D., Biology
STERN, T., PH.D., Anthropology
STRANGE, W. C., PH.D., English
STRATON, G. D., PH.D., Religious Studies
STREISINGER, G., PH.D., Biology
SUNDBERG, N. D., PH.D., Psychology
SUTTLE, J. E., ED.D., Education
SWAN, P., LL.B., Law
SWINEHART, D. F., PH.D., Chemistry
SYLWESTER, R. A., ED.D., Education
TANG, S. J. Y., M.S., Architecture
TATE, R. F., PH.D., Mathematics
TATTERSALL, J. N., PH.D., Economics
TAYLOR, D. S., PH.D., English
TEPFER, S. S., PH.D., Biology
TERWILLIGER, R. C., PH.D., Biology
THATCHER, E. P., M.A., Library
THURBER, C. E., PH.D., International and Public Affairs
TOELKEN, J. B., PH.D., English
TOLLENAAR, K., M.A., Public Affairs
TROTTER, R. M., PH.D., Music
TRUAX, D. R., PH.D., Mathematics
TULL, D. S., PH.D., Marketing
ULRICH, A. C., PH.D., Physical Education
URQUHART, A. W., PH.D., Geography
VETRI, D. R., J.D., Law
VIA, E. F., PH.D.
VON HIPPEL, P. H., PH.D., Chemistry
WALKER, H. M., PH.D., Special Education
WARD, L. E., Jr., PH.D., Mathematics
WATSON, D. A., PH.D., Finance
WEATHERHEAD, A. K., PH.D., English
WEILL, D. F., PH.D., Geology
WEISS, R. L., PH.D., Psychology
WESTON, J. A., PH.D., Biology
WICKELGREN, W. A., PH.D., Psychology
WICKES, G. A., PH.D., English
WILSON, N. E., PH.D., Music
WIMBER, D. E., PH.D., Biology
WINTER, W. L., PH.D., Journalism

Wolcott, H. F., ph.d., Education and Anthropology
Wolfe, R. G., Jr., ph.d., Chemistry
Woods, Wm. C., m.mus., Music
Wooten-Kolan, Edna P., ph.d., Physical Education
Wright, C. R. B., ph.d., Mathematics
Zaninovich, M. G., ph.d., Political Science
Zeigler, L. H., ph.d., Political Science
Zweig, A., ph.d., Philosophy

Attached Institutes:

**Institute for Community Art Studies:** Dir. Gordon L. Kensler.

**Institute for Industrial and Labor Relations:** Dir. Eaton H. Conant.

**Institute for Social Science Research:** Dir. John Orbell, ph.d.

**Institute of Molecular Biology:** Dir. Brian W. Matthews, ph.d.

**Institute of Theoretical Science:** Dir. Rudolph Hwa, ph.d.

**Oregon Institute of Marine Biology:** Dir. Paul P. Rudy, ph.d.

**Solar Energy Center:** Dir. John S. Reynolds, m.arch.

**Center for Environmental Research:** Dir. Charles Rusch.

## UNIVERSITY OF OREGON HEALTH SCIENCES CENTER
PORTLAND, OREGON 97201

*President:* Leonard Laster, m.d.
*Vice-President for Hospital Affairs:* Donald Kassebaum, m.d.
*Dean, School of Dentistry:* Louis Terkla, d.m.d.
*Dean School of Medicine:* Ransom Arthur, m.d.
*Dean, School of Nursing:* Carol Lindeman, ph.d.
*Director, Crippled Children's Division:* Victor Menashe, m.d.

## UNIVERSITY OF PORTLAND
5000 N. WILLAMETTE BLVD., PORTLAND, OREGON 97203

Telephone: 283-7911.

Founded 1901.

Private control; language of instruction: English; academic year: September to May (two terms and summer session).

*President:* Raphael Wilson, c.s.c.
*Executive and Financial Vice-President:* Arthur A. Schulte.
*Academic Vice-President:* George C. Bernard.
*Registrar:* Francis G. Morgan.
*Librarian:* Joseph P. Browne, c.s.c.

The library contains 185,000 vols.
Number of teachers: 155, including 22 full professors.
Number of students: 2,746.

Publications: *The Bulletin, The Log, The Beacon†, The Dedalus†, The Review†.*

Deans:

*Graduate School:* Rev. James Anderson, c.s.c.
*College of Arts and Sciences:* Richard F. Berg.
*School of Business Administration:* Kent Collings.
*School of Nursing:* Miss Patricia Chadwick.
*School of Engineering:* Thomas J. Nelson.
*School of Education:* Leo Leonard.
*Continuing Education:* Hal Westby.

Professors:

Albright, R. J., Engineering
Anderson, J. G., Chemistry
Becker, H., Business Administration
Bonhorst, C. W., Chemistry
Chou, G. T., Business Administration
Collings, K., Business Administration
Covert, J. T., History
Danner, D. G., Theology
De La Mare, P. R., Music
Faller, T., Philosophy
Gritta, P. R., Business Administration
Leonard, L., Education
Kehoe, J. A., Economics
Macias, M. J., Spanish
Mayr, F. K., Philosophy
McCoy, J. W., Chemistry
Pereyra, L. A., History
Robinson, M. D., Psychology
Schulte, A. A., Business Administration
Wack, P. E., Physics
Wetzel, K. J., Physics
Wilson, R., Biology

## WARNER PACIFIC COLLEGE
2219 S.E. 68TH AVENUE, PORTLAND, OREGON 97215

Telephone: 775-4366.

Founded 1937.

*President:* Marshall K. Christensen.
*Registrar:* Dale W. Mark.
*Director of Admissions:* Arthur Kelly.
*General Library Administrator:* William Orr.

The library contains 52,811 vols.
Number of teachers: 35.
Number of students: 500.

## WILLAMETTE UNIVERSITY
SALEM, OREGON 97301

Telephone: (503) 370-6300.

*President:* Jerry E. Hudson.
*Registrar:* R. A. Yocom.
*Librarian:* Charles Weyant.

Number of teachers: 114 (full-time).
Number of students: 1,886.

Publications: *Willamette University Bulletin, College of Law Bulletin, Willamette Scene, Willamette College of Law Journal.*

Deans:

*College of Liberal Arts:* William G. Berberet.
*College of Law:* Leroy Tornquist.
*George H. Atkinson Graduate School of Management:* D. Jay Doubleday.

# PENNSYLVANIA

## ALBRIGHT COLLEGE
READING, PENNSYLVANIA 19603

Telephone: (215) 921-2381.

Founded 1856.

*President:* Dr. David G. Ruffer.
*Director of Admissions:* Dale H. Reinhart.
*Librarian:* Dr. Mary E. Stillman.

The library contains 142,000 vols.
Number of teachers: 95.
Number of students: 1,450.

## ALLEGHENY COLLEGE
MEADVILLE, PENNSYLVANIA 16335

Founded 1815.

*President:* David Baily Harned, ph.d.
*Vice-President for Development:* Sebastian C. Sommer.
*Treasurer:* Larry J. Yartz, m.a.
*Registrar:* Elizabeth R. Allen, m.ed.
*Secretary:* Richard E. Madtes, ph.d.
*Librarian:* Margaret L. Moser, m.s., m.a.

The library contains 276,500 vols.
Number of teachers: 126, including 36 professors.
Number of students: 1,800.

Publications: *Campus, Bulletin, Kaldron, Literary Magazine.*

Deans:

*Dean of the College:* Andrew T. Ford, ph.d.
*Students:* Don Colvill Skinner, d.s.s.
*Associate Students:* Susan C. Rumsey, a.b., Charles Woodard, m.s.

## ALLIANCE COLLEGE
CAMBRIDGE SPRINGS, PENNSYLVANIA 16403

Telephone: (814) 398-4611.

Founded 1912.

*President:* Arthur H. Auten.
*Registrar:* Rhoda Bernstein.
*Librarian:* Stanley S. Kozaczka.

The library contains 100,000 vols.
Number of teachers: 21.
Number of students: 218.

## AMERICAN COLLEGE, THE
270 BRYN MAWR AVE., BRYN MAWR, PENNSYLVANIA 19010

Telephone: (215) 896-4500.

Founded 1927. Independent professional college, following open university mode of operation.

*President:* Davis W. Gregg.
*Senior Vice-President:* Robert M. Crowe.
*Vice-President for Academic Affairs:* Charles E. Hughes.

## UNIVERSITIES AND COLLEGES—PENNSYLVANIA U.S.A.

*Vice-President and Treasurer:* CHARLES S. DiLULLO.
*Director of Admissions and Records:* WILLIAM J. McCOUCH.
*Librarian:* MAUREEN E. STRAZDON.

Library of 12,500 vols.
Number of teachers: 35.
Number of students: 60,000 (part-time and non-resident).

DEANS:

*Huebner School of CLU Studies:* ROBERT W. COOPER.
*School of Advanced Career Studies:* HERBERT CHASMAN.
*Graduate School of Financial Sciences:* ROBERT T. LeCLAIR.

### BEAVER COLLEGE
GLENSIDE, PENNSYLVANIA 19038
Founded 1853.

*President:* EDWARD D. GATES, B.D., PH.D., LL.D.
*Vice-Presidents:* D. M. GRAY, PH.D., FRANCES H. LEWIS, B.A., BETTE E. LANDMAN, PH.D., WILLIAM E. JAMES, B.S., T. EDWARDS TOWNSLEY, B.S.
*Registrar:* HAROLD W. STEWART, M.A.
*Treasurer:* WILLIAM E. JAMES, B.S.
*Librarian:* R. McWHINNEY, M.S.L.S.

The library contains 121,000 vols., 6,547 microforms.
Number of teachers: 153.
Number of students: 2,597.

Publications: *Beaver Bulletins*, *Beaver College Herald*, *Undergraduate Studies Catalog*, *Graduate Studies Catalog*, catalogues for Evening/Weekend College and Center abroad.

DEANS:

*Admissions:* T. EDWARDS TOWNSLEY.
*College:* BETTE E. LANDMAN, PH.D.
*Graduate Studies:* A RICHARD POLIS, ED.D.
*Students:* GALE DiGIORGIO, M.ED.

### BLOOMSBURG STATE COLLEGE
BLOOMSBURG, PENNSYLVANIA 17815
Telephone: (717) 389-0111.
Founded 1839.

Courses in Arts and Sciences, Business, Teacher Education, Nursing and Medical Technology.

*President:* J. H. McCORMICK.
*Registrar:* R. L. BUNGE.
*Librarian:* W. O. RYAN.

The library contains 298,839 vols.
Number of teachers: 325.
Number of students: 6,503.

### BRYN MAWR COLLEGE
BRYN MAWR, PENNSYLVANIA 19010
Incorporated 1885.

*President:* MARY PATTERSON McPHERSON, PH.D.
*Director of Admissions:* ELIZABETH VERMEY, M.A.
*Business Manager:* P. W. KLUG, C.P.A., B.S.
*Librarian:* JAMES R. TANIS, D.TH.
*Administrator of Records and Financial Aid:* JULIE E. PAINTER, A.B.

The library contains 561,860 vols.
Number of students: 1,062 undergraduate, 660 graduates, total 1,722.

DEANS:

*Graduate School of Arts and Sciences:* BARBARA McLAUGHLIN KREUTZ, PH.D.
*School of Social Work and Social Research:* ROBERT R. MAYER, PH.D.

### BUCKNELL UNIVERSITY
LEWISBURG, PENNSYLVANIA 17837
Telephone: (717) 523-1271.
Founded 1846.

*President:* Dr. G. DENNIS O'BRIEN.
*Provost:* Dr. W. I. SMITH.
*Vice-President for Administration and Finance:* J. F. ZELLER.
*Vice-President for Development:* C. W. WOLFE.
*Librarian:* A. M. DE KLERK.

The library contains 410,000 volumes.
Number of teachers: 223 full-time, 28 part-time, 75 professors.
Number of full-time students: 3,300.

Publications: *Catalogue*, *Bucknellian*, *L'Agenda*, *Handbook*, *Tristram*, *Bucknell Engineer*, *Bucknell Review*, *Bucknell World*.

DEANS:

*College of Arts and Sciences:* Dr. R. H. CHAMBERS, III.
*College of Engineering:* Dr. B. A. MAXWELL.
*Student Affairs:* Dr. J. P. DUNLOP.

### CABRINI COLLEGE
KING OF PRUSSIA RD., RADNOR, PA. 19087

Founded 1957 by the Missionary Sisters of the Sacred Heart; four-year co-educational liberal arts and sciences college.

*President:* Sr. MARY LOUISE SULLIVAN.
*Vice-President for Academic Affairs:* Dr. JOSEPH ROMANO.
*Business Manager:* WILLIAM EICHNER.
*Dean of Students:* Sr. EILEEN CURRIE.
*Admissions Director:* Mrs. ESTELLE ORISTAGLIO.
*Library Director:* CLAIRE SKERETT.

Library of 66,000 vols.
Number of teachers: 31 full-time, 29 part-time.
Number of students: 750.

### CALIFORNIA STATE COLLEGE
CALIFORNIA, PENNSYLVANIA 15419
Telephone: (412) 938-4000.
Founded 1852.

*President:* JOHN PIERCE WATKINS.
*Dean of Admissions and Academic Records:* NORMAN HASBROUCK.
*Director of Library Services:* WILLIAM L. BECK.

The library contains 434,000 vols. (211,000 microform).
Number of teachers: 286.
Number of students: 4,606.

Publications: *Contribution to Scholarship*† (annual), *Undergraduate Catalog*† (2 a year), *Graduate Catalog*† (2 a year).

DEANS:

*School of Arts and Sciences:* PHILIP Y. COLEMAN.
*School of Continuing Education:* WILLARD McCARTNEY.
*School of Education:* WILLIAM R. BENEDETTI.
*School of Graduate Studies:* HOMER PANKEY.
*School of Science and Technology:* RICHARD HART.

### CARLOW COLLEGE
3333 FIFTH AVE., PITTSBURGH, PENNSYLVANIA 15213
Telephone: (412) 578-6000.
Founded 1929.

*President:* Sister JANE SCULLY, R.S.M.
*Director of Admissions:* JOHN HINE.
*Director of Continuing Education:* MARY CAY CONROY.
*Dean of the Faculty:* Dr. T. A. HOPKINS.
*Librarian:* JOAN M. MITCHELL.

The library contains 102,062 vols.
Number of teachers: 90.
Number of students: 871.

### CARNEGIE-MELLON UNIVERSITY
5000 FORBES AVENUE, PITTSBURGH, PENNSYLVANIA 15213
Telephone: (412) 578-2000.
Founded 1900.

Private control; Academic year: September to May.

*President:* R. M. CYERT, PH.D.
*Provost:* D. BERG, PH.D.
*Senior Vice-President:* E. R. SCHATZ, M.S., D.SC.
*Director of University Libraries:* J. MICHALAK, M.A., M.S.

The library contains 604,128 vols.
Number of teachers: 431.
Number of students: 5,634.

UNITED STATES OF AMERICA

**DEANS AND DIRECTORS:**
*Carnegie Institute of Technology:* A. JORDAN, PH.D.
*College of Fine Arts:* A. MIDANI, M.A.
*College of Humanities and Social Sciences:* C. KIESLER, PH.D. (acting).
*Graduate School of Industrial Administration:* R. S. KAPLAN, PH.D.
*Mellon College of Science:* GUY C. BERRY, PH.D. (acting).
*School of Urban and Public Affairs:* BRIAN J. L. BERRY, PH.D.
*Dean of Student Affairs:* E. R. SWANK, M.A.
*Hunt Institute for Botanical Documentation:* ROBERT W. KIGER, PH.D. (Dir.).

**FULL PROFESSORS:**
*Mellon College of Science:*
ANDREWS, P. B., PH.D., Mathematics
ARTMAN, J. O., A.M., PH.D., Physics and Electrical Engineering
ASKHIN, J., PH.D., Physics
BERGER, L., PH.D., Physics
BERRY, G. C., PH.D., Polymer Science
BLANK, A. A., PH.D., Mathematics
BOTHNER-BY, A. A., PH.D., Chemistry
CARETTO, A. A., PH.D., Chemistry
CARLIN, R. B., PH.D., Chemistry
CASSASSA, E. F., PH.D., Chemistry
CASTELLANO, S. M., Biophysical Chemistry
COFFMAN, C. V., PH.D., Mathematics
COLEMAN, B. D., M.A., PH.D., Mathematics
CONROY, H., PH.D., Chemistry
CUTKOSKY, R. E., M.S., PH.D., Physics
DADOK, J., M.SC., PH.D., Chemistry
DUFFIN, R. J., PH.D., Mathematics
EDELSTEIN, R. M., PH.D., Physics
ENGLER, A., PH.D., Physics
FETKOVICH, J. G., PH.D., Physics
FIX, G. J., M.S., PH.D., Mathematics
FRIEDBERG, S. A., M.S., D.SC., Physics
GOLDMAN, R. D., PH.D., Biological Sciences
GRIFFITHS, R. B., PH.D., Physics
GURTIN, M. E., PH.D., Mathematics
HABERMANN, A. N., PH.D., Computer Science
HO, C., PH.D., Biological Sciences
KAPLAN, M., PH.D., Chemistry
KAY, R. L., PH.D., Chemistry
KISSLINGER, L., PH.D., Physics
KOHMAN, T. P., PH.D., Chemistry
KOLODNER, I. I., PH.D., Mathematics
KRAEMER, R. W., PH.D., Physics
LANGER, J. S., PH.D., Physics
LEVINE, M. J., PH.D., Physics
MACCAMY, R. C., PH.D., Mathematics
MARKOVITZ, H., M.A., PH.D., Chemical Physics
MIZEL, V. J., PH.D., Mathematics
MOORE, R. A., A.M., PH.D., Mathematics
MURPHY, A. T., M.S., PH.D., Mechanical Engineering
NAGLE, J. F., PH.D., Physics
NEWELL, A., PH.D., Systems and Communication Sciences
NOLL, W., PH.D., Mathematics
OWEN, D. R., PH.D., Mathematics
PEDERSON, R. N., PH.D., Mathematics
POPLE, J. A., M.A., PH.D., Chemical Physics
RAYNE, J. A., PH.D., Physics
REDDY, D. R., PH.D., Computer Science
RICE, R. V., M.S., PH.D., Biochemistry
RUSS, J., PH.D., Physics
SCHAFFER, J. J., PH.D., Mathematics
SCHUMACHER, R. T., M.S., PH.D., Physics
SORENSEN, R. A., PH.D., Physics
SOUTHWICK, P. L., M.A., PH.D., Chemistry
STEWART, R. F., PH.D., Chemistry
SUTTON, R. B., M.A., PH.D., Physics
VAN DER VEN, N. S., PH.D., Physics
WILLIAMS, J. F., M.A., PH.D., Biological Sciences
WOLFENSTEIN, L., M.S., PH.D., Physics
WOLKEN, J. J., M.S., PH.D., Biophysics
WORTHINGTON, C. R., PH.D., Physics and Chemistry
WULF, W. A., M.S., D.SC., Computer Science
WYLER, O., D.SC., Mathematics
ZENER, C., PH.D., Engineering

*Carnegie Institute of Technology:*
AARONSON, H. I., PH.D., Metallurgy and Materials Science
ANDERSON, J. L., PH.D., Chemical Engineering
ANGRIST, S. W., PH.D., Mechanical Engineering
AU, TUNG, PH.D., Civil Engineering
AYRES, R. U., PH.D., Physics
BAUER, C. L., PH.D., Metallurgy and Materials Science
BAUMANN, D. M. B., D.SC., Mechanical Engineering
BERNSTEIN, I. M., M.S., PH.D., Metallurgy and Materials Science
CASASENT, D., M.S. PH.D., Electrical Engineering
CHARAP, S. H., PH.D., Electrical Engineering
DIRECTOR, S. W., PH.D., Electrical Engineering
FENVES, S. J., PH.D., Civil Engineering
HUMPHREY, F. B., PH.D., Chemistry
JORDAN, A. G., PH.D., Electrical Engineering
KOZAK, W., PH.D., Biotechnology
KROKOSKY, E. M., PH.D., Civil Engineering
KRYDER, M. H., PH.D., Electrical Engineering
LAVI, A., PH.D., Electrical Engineering
LI, K., D.SC., Chemical Engineering
MASSALSKI, T. B., PH.D., D.SC., Mechanics and Polymer Science
MCMICHAEL, F. C., M.S., PH.D., Engineering and Public Affairs
MILLER, C. A., PH.D., Chemical Engineering
MILNES, A. G., D.SC., Electrical Engineering
MORGAN, M. G., PH.D., Electrical Engineering
MULLINS, W. W., PH.D., Metallurgy and Materials Science
MURPHY, A. T., M.S., PH.D., Mechanical Engineering
NEUMAN, C. P., PH.D., Electrical Engineering
OSTERLE, J. F., D.SC., Mechanical Engineering
PHILBROOK, W. O., B.S., Metallurgy and Materials Science
PIEHLER, H. R., S.M., SC.D., Metallurgy and Materials Science
RICE, R. A., B.A., Transportation Engineering
ROMUALDI, J. P., PH.D., Civil Engineering
ROSEN, S. L., PH.D., Chemical Engineering
ROTHFUS, R. R., D.SC., Chemical Engineering
ROULEAU, W. T., PH.D., Mechanical Engineering
RUBIN, E. S., PH.D., Mechanical Engineering
SANGREY, D. A., PH.D., Civil Engineering
SCHATZ, E. R., D.SC., Electrical Engineering
SEKERKA, R. R., PH.D., Metallurgy and Materials Science
SHAW, M. C., PH.D., Mechanical Engineering

WORLD OF LEARNING

SIEWIOREK, D. P., PH.D., Electrical Engineering
SIRIGNANO, W. A., PH.D., Mechanical Engineering
SWEDLOW, J. L., PH.D., Mechanical Engineering
THOMPSON, A. W., PH.D., Metallurgy and Materials Science
TOOR, H. L., PH.D., Chemical Engineering
WEINSTEIN, A. S., PH.D., Mechanical Engineering
WILLIAMS, J. C., PH.D., Metallurgy and Materials Science
WOHL, M., PH.D., Civil Engineering and School of Urban and Public Affairs

*College of Fine Arts:*
ANDERSON, B. J., M.F.A., Drama
BALADA, L. I., Music
BRELAND, B., M.A., Painting and Sculpture
CARTER, C. B., PH.D., Painting and Sculpture
EASTMAN, C. M., B.ARCH., Architecture, Computer Science, Urban Planning
FRANKLIN, H., Music
GROER, W. F., M.ED., PH.D., Art
HIGHLANDS, D., M.ARCH., Architecture
LIBBY, W. C., B.A., Painting and Sculpture
NELSON, W. A., M.F.A., Drama
PICKERING, D., M.S., Painting and Sculpture
ROSENBERG, J. L., M.A., PH.D., Drama
SAALMAN, H., PH.D., Architecture
SANCHEZ, M., PH.D., Music
SAUER, L., M.ARCH., Architecture
TAYLOR, R. S., M.F.A., Architecture
WILKINS, D., M.A., Music
WINSAND, O. M., PH.D., Painting

*College of Humanities and Social Sciences:*
ANDERSON, J. R., PH.D., Psychology
CHASE, W. G., M.A., PH.D., Psychology
COTTRELL, B. W., PH.D., English
CRECINE, J. P., M.S., PH.D., Political Economy
CYERT, R. M., PH.D., Economics
FENTON, E., M.A., PH.D., History
FIENBERG, S. E., PH.D., Statistics
FOWLER, D. H., PH.D., History
FOWLER, L., PH.D., English
HAYES, A. L., M.A., English
HAYES, J. R., A.B., PH.D., Psychology
JONAS, I. B., M.A., Modern Languages
KIESLER, C., PH.D., Social Sciences
KIESLER, S., PH.D., Social Sciences
KLAHR, D., M.S., PH.D., Psychology
MELTZER, A. H., PH.D., Economics and Industrial Administration
MILLER, D. W., PH.D., History
MOYER, K. E., M.A., PH.D., Psychology and Education
RESNICK, D. P., PH.D., History
SCHAEFER, L., PH.D., History
SCHOENWALD, R. L., PH.D., History
SILENIEKS, J., PH.D., Modern Languages
SLACK, R. C., PH.D., English
STEARNS, P. W., PH.D., History
STEINBERG, E. R., M.S., PH.D., English
TARR, J. A., PH.D., History and School of Urban and Public Affairs
YOUNG, R. E., PH.D., English

*Graduate School of Industrial Administration:*
BALAS, E., PH.D., Industrial Administration and Mathematics
CYERT, R. M., PH.D., Economics and Industrial Administration
DEGROOT, M. H., PH.D., Statistics
GOODMAN, P. S., PH.D., Industrial Administration
IJIRI, Y., PH.D., Industrial Administration

KADANE, J. B., PH.D., Statistics
KAPLAN, R. S., PH.D., Industrial Administration
KRIEBEL, C. H., PH.D., Industrial Administration
LAVE, L. B. PH.D., Economics
MELTZER, A. H., PH.D., Economics and Industrial Administration
MORTON, T. E., PH.D., Industrial Administration
NEWELL, A., PH.D., Systems and Communication Sciences
PRESCOTT, E. C., M.S., PH.D., Economics
ROSENTHAL, H. L., PH.D., Political Science
SIMON, H. A., PH.D., Administration and Psychology
STAELIN, R., PH.D., Industrial Administration
THOMPSON, G. L., PH.D., Industrial Administration and Mathematics
TOWNSEND, R. M., PH.D., Economics

*School of Urban and Public Affairs:*
BLUMSTEIN, A., PH.D., Operations Research
DAVIS, O. A., M.A., PH.D., Economics
JOHNSON, N. J., PH.D., Social Policy
KORTANEK, K. O., PH.D., Operations Research
LEINHARDT, S., PH.D., Sociology
MANSKI, C. F., PH.D., Economics
ORDESHOOK, P., PH.D., Political Science
STRAUSS, R. P., PH.D., Economics

## CEDAR CREST COLLEGE
ALLENTOWN,
PENNSYLVANIA 18104
Telephone: (215) 437-4471
Founded 1867.

*President:* Dr. GENE S. CESARI.
*Director of Admissions:* DANA L. LACIS.
*Librarian:* P. A. SACKS.

The library contains 108,000 vols.
Number of teachers: 65.
Number of students: 871.
Publications: *Alumnae Magazine*†, *Commentary*† (4 times a year), *Catalog and Information Brochure*†.

## CHATHAM COLLEGE
PITTSBURGH,
PENNSYLVANIA 15232
Telephone: (412) 441-8200
Founded 1869.

Liberal arts college for women.

*President:* ALBERTA ARTHURS.
*Director of Admissions:* MARILYN KIMBALL.
*Librarian:* PEGGY PORTER.

The library contains 119,000 vols.
Number of teachers: 62.
Number of students: 600.

## CHESTNUT HILL COLLEGE
PHILADELPHIA,
PENNSYLVANIA 19118
Telephone: (215) 248-7000.
Founded 1871.

*President:* Sister MATTHEW ANITA, S.S.J.

*Academic Dean:* Sister KATHRYN MILLER, S.S.J.
*Librarian:* Sister REGINA MARIA, S.S.J

The library contains 92,000 vols
Number of teachers: 94.
Number of students: 660

## CHEYNEY STATE COLLEGE
CHEYNEY, PENNSYLVANIA 19319
Telephone: (215) 758-2000.
Founded 1837.

*President:* Dr. WADE WILSON.
*Director of Admissions:* C. M. ROULHAC.
*Librarian:* VIOLET R. SMITH.

The library contains 170,156 vols.
Number of teachers: 235.
Number of students: 2,508.

## CLARION STATE COLLEGE
CLARION, PENNSYLVANIA 16214
Telephone: (814) 226-2000
Founded 1867.

*President:* THOMAS A. BOND.
*Director of Admissions:* JOHN SHROPSHIRE.
*Librarian:* D. GRAVES.

The library contains 320,000 vols.
Number of teachers: 302.
Number of students: 4,600.

## THE CURTIS INSTITUTE OF MUSIC
1726 LOCUST ST.,
PHILADELPHIA,
PENNSYLVANIA 19103
Founded 1924.

*President:* A. MARGARET BOK.
*Director:* JOHN DE LANCIE.
*Vice-President:* WILLIAM C. BODINE.
*Treasurer:* SAMUEL R. SHIPLEY III.
*Secretary:* ROBERT S. SOMMER.
*Registrar:* JULIAN PLYS.
*Librarian:* ELIZABETH WALKER.
Library of *c.* 40,000 vols., musical items and recordings.

Number of students: 150.

## DELAWARE VALLEY COLLEGE OF SCIENCE AND AGRICULTURE
DOYLESTOWN,
PENNSYLVANIA 18901
Telephone: (215) 345-1500.
Founded 1896.

*President:* JOSHUA FELDSTEIN.
*Vice-President for Planning and Financial Affairs:* Dr. ARTHUR E. WOLF.
*Vice-President and Assistant to the President:* JEAN H. WORK.
*Registrar:* OSKAR LARSSON.
*Director of Admissions:* H. WILLIAM CRAVER.
*Librarian:* CONSTANCE SHOOK.
*Dean:* Dr. CLINTON R. BLACKMON.

The library contains 81,457 vols.
Number of teachers: 80.
Number of students: 1,506.

## DICKINSON COLLEGE
CARLISLE,
PENNSYLVANIA 17013
Founded 1773.

*President:* SAM A. BANKS, PH.D.
*Treasurer:* JAMES M. NICHOLSON, B.A.
*Registrar:* RONALD E. DOERNBACH, B.A.
*Librarian:* (vacant).
Number of teachers: 120.
Number of students: 1,685.
Publications: *Catalogue*, *The Dickinson Alumnus*.

DEANS:

*Faculty:* GEORGE J. ALLAN, PH.D.
*Students:* LEONARD S. GOLDBERG, PH.D.
*Residential Services:* R. BRUCE WALL, M.A.
*Special Programs:* MARY WATSON CARSON, M.A.

## DREXEL UNIVERSITY
32ND AND CHESTNUT STS.,
PHILADELPHIA,
PENNSYLVANIA 19104
Founded 1891 as Institute of Technology.

*President:* WILLIAM W HAGERTY, M.S., PH.D., SC D.
*Assistant to the President:* M. JERRY KENIG, M.A., M.S., PH.D.
*Registrar:* J. W. NEAL, Jr., B.S. IN M E.
*Librarian:* R. L. SNYDER, M.A.
*Curator:* GERALDINE P. STAUB.

The library contains 425,000 vols.
Number of teachers: 353 full-time.
Number of students: 13,714.

DEANS:

*Business and Administration College:* P. E. DASCHER, PH.D.
*Engineering College:* R. WOODRING, PH.D.
*Nesbitt College:* MARJORIE E. RANKIN, M.S.
*School of Library and Information Science:* G. G. GARRISON, PH.D.
*Evening College:* S. J. GWIAZDA, M.S. IN M.E.
*College of Science:* F. K. DAVIS, PH.D.
*College of Humanities and Social Science:* THOMAS L. CANAVAN, PH.D.

## DROPSIE UNIVERSITY
BROAD AND YORK STREETS,
PHILADELPHIA,
PENNSYLVANIA 19132
Telephone: 229-0110.
Founded 1907 as College, attained University status 1969.

*President:* JOSEPH RAPPAPORT.
*Registrar:* RUTH H. ROBBINS.

Librarian: HAYIM Y. SHEYNIN.
The library contains 140,000 volumes
Number of teachers: 12.
Number of students: 75.

Publications: *Jewish Quarterly Review*, *Apocrypha* (series).

### DUQUESNE UNIVERSITY
600 FORBES AVE.,
PITTSBURGH,
PENNSYLVANIA 15282
Telephone: (412) 434-6000.

Founded 1878; Chartered 1911.
Private control.

President: Rev. DONALD S. NESTI, S.T.D., C.S.SP.
Chancellor: Rev. HENRY J. MCANULTY, D.ED., C.S.SP.
Vice-President for Finance: Rev. JOSEPH A. DUCHENE, C.S.SP.
Academic Vice-President: Rev. EDWARD L. MURRAY, PH.D., C.S.SP.
Director of University Relations: REGIS J. EBNER, B.A.
University Secretary: Rev. CHARLES J. FENNER, PH.D., C.S.SP.
Registrar: THOMAS F. BAILEY.
Librarian: PAUL J. PUGLIESE, M.L.S.

The library contains 330,383 vols. (law library 64,165 vols.).
Number of teachers: 296 full-time, 166 part-time.
Number of students: 7,124.

#### DEANS:
College of Liberal Arts and Sciences: J. A. MCCULLOCH, PH.D.
Graduate School: OSCAR GAWRON, PH.D.
School of Business Administration: B. J. KOLASA, PH.D.
School of Education: DOROTHY FRAYER, PH.D.
School of Law: R. R. DAVENPORT, LL.M.
School of Music: R. F. EGAN, PH.D.
School of Nursing: CAROL SMITH, PH.D.
School of Pharmacy: DOUGLAS KAY, PH.D.
Institute of Formative Spirituality: SUSAN MUTO, PH.D. (Director).

### EASTERN COLLEGE
ST. DAVIDS,
PENNSYLVANIA 19087
Telephone: (215) 688-3300.

Founded 1952.

President: DANIEL E. WEISS.
Vice-President and Academic Dean: JEAN B. KIM.
Vice-President and Dean of Student Affairs: THEODORE J. CHAMBERLAIN.
Dean of Admissions: WILLIAM A. ZULKER.
Director of Alumni and College Relations: DAVID R. MCINTIRE.
Registrar and Director of Institutional Research: MAJORIE A. WILY.
Librarian: JAMES L. SAUER.

The library contains 100,000 vols.
Number of teachers: 80.
Number of students: 700.

### EDINBORO STATE COLLEGE
MEADVILLE STREET,
EDINBORO,
PENNSYLVANIA 16444
Telephone: (814) 732-2000.

Founded 1857.

President: FOSTER F. DIEBOLD.
Vice-President for Academic Affairs: J. E. MCKINLEY.
Vice-President for Administration and Student Personnel Services: ROBERT CAROTHERS.
Dean of Admissions: HAROLD UMBARGER.
Director of Libraries: SAUL WEINSTEIN.

The library contains 337,000 volumes
Number of teachers: 396.
Number of students: 5,600.

### ELIZABETHTOWN COLLEGE
ELIZABETHTOWN,
PENNSYLVANIA 17022
Telephone: (717) 367-1151.

Founded 1899.

President: MARK C. EBERSOLE, PH.D., LL.D.
Dean of Faculty: BRUCE L. WILSON, PH.D.
Treasurer: THOMAS J. KINGSTON, Jr., M.ED.

The library contains 160,000 vols.
Number of teachers: 95.
Number of students: 1,416.

### FRANKLIN AND MARSHALL COLLEGE
P.O.B. 3003, LANCASTER,
PENNSYLVANIA 17604

Franklin College founded in 1787, Marshall College founded in 1836; merged in 1853.

President: KEITH SPALDING, A.B., LL.D
Dean: RICHARD P. TRAINA, PH.D.
Vice-President, Administration: RICHARD KNEEDLER, PH.D.
Vice-President, Development: JOHN A. SYNODINOS, M.A.
Treasurer: JAMES R. WETZEL.
Librarian: (vacant).

The library contains 190,000 vols.
Number of teachers: 132.
Number of students: 1,996.

### GANNON UNIVERSITY
109 WEST SIXTH ST., ERIE,
PENNSYLVANIA 16541
Telephone: (814) 871-7000.

Founded 1944.

President: JOSEPH P. SCOTTINO, PH.D.
Academic Vice-President: PAUL WARD PETERSON, PH.D.
Registrar: WARD MCCRACKEN.
Librarian: Rev. Dr. L. THOMAS SNYDERWINE.

The library contains 161,855 vols.
Number of teachers: 124 full-time, 130 part-time.
Number of students: 3,973.

### GENEVA COLLEGE
COLLEGE AVENUE AND
32ND STREET, BEAVER FALLS,
PENNSYLVANIA 15010
Telephone: (412) 846-5100.

Founded 1848.

President: Dr. DONALD W. FELKER.
Dean: Dr. WILLIAM H. RUSSELL.
Registrar: Miss B. BURROWS.
Librarian: GERALD MORAN.

The library contains 100,000 vols.
Number of teachers: 76.
Number of students: 1,285.

### GETTYSBURG COLLEGE
GETTYSBURG,
PENNSYLVANIA 17325
Telephone: (717) 334-3131.

Chartered 1832 as Pennsylvania College; name changed 1921.

President: CHARLES E. GLASSICK.
Dean: DAVID B. POTTS.
Dean of Students: F. B. WILLIAMS.
Director of Admissions: D. K. GUSTAFSON.

The library contains 235,000 vols.
Number of teachers: 146.
Number of students: 1,850.

### HAVERFORD COLLEGE
HAVERFORD,
PENNSYLVANIA 19041

An independent liberal arts college for men, founded in 1833 as the first American college established by the Society of Friends.

President: ROBERT B. STEVENS, M.A., LL.M.
Vice-President for Institutional Advancement: G. HOLGER HANSEN.
Treasurer and Vice-President for Planning: EDWARD T. REWOLINSKI.
Director of Admissions: W. W. AMBLER, B.A.
Provost and Dean of Faculty: ROBERT M. GAVIN, Jr.
Dean of College: DAVID POTTER, B.A., ED.M.
Librarian: E. B. BRONNER, PH.D.

The library contains 320,000 vols.
Number of teachers: 57 full-time, 46 part-time.
Number of students: 990.

Publications: *Bulletin* (quarterly), *Haverford Horizons* (quarterly).

## HOLY FAMILY COLLEGE
GRANT AND FRANKFORD AVENUES, PHILADELPHIA, PENNSYLVANIA 19114
Telephone: 637-7700.

Founded 1954.

Degree programs in the liberal arts, business, child care, education, medical technology, nursing; interdisciplinary programs.

*President:* Sister M. FRANCESCA, C.S.F.N.
*Director of Admissions and Financial Aid:* ANGELA A. GODSHALL.
*Librarian:* Sister M. KATHRYN, C.S.F.N.

The library contains 91,049 vols.
Number of teachers: 124.
Number of students: 1,281.

Publications: *College Catalog†, Familogue* (annual), *Tri-Lite, Logos Journal†, Folio†, College Newsletter.*

## IMMACULATA COLLEGE
IMMACULATA, PENNSYLVANIA 19345
Telephone: (215) 647-4400.

Founded 1920.

*President:* Sister MARIE ANTOINE.
*Registrar:* Sister DOROTHY REGINA.
*Director of Admissions:* Sister MARIA CLAUDIA.
*Librarian:* Sister FLORENCE MARIE.

The library contains 120,000 vols.
Number of teachers: 57.
Number of students: 1,377.

## INDIANA UNIVERSITY OF PENNSYLVANIA
INDIANA, PENNSYLVANIA 15705
Telephone: (412) 357-2100.

Founded 1875, as Indiana State Normal School.

State control; Academic year: September to May.

*President:* Dr. JOHN E. WORTHEN.
*Provost and Vice-President for Academic Affairs:* Dr. NORMAN J. NORTON.
*Vice-President for Administration:* C. EDWARD RECESKI.
*Vice-President for Development and Finance:* I. R. LENGLET.
*Vice-President for Student Affairs:* Dr. JOHN D. WELTY.
*Associate Provost and Dean of Graduate School:* R. O. WARREN.
*Dean of Admissions:* Dr. F. DAKAK.
*Director of Libraries and Media Resources:* W. E. LAFRANCHI.

The library contains c. 500,000 vols.
Number of teachers: 673.
Number of students: 12,278.

DEANS:
*School of Business:* Dr. C. A. ALTIMUS.
*School of Continuing and Non-Resident Education:* Dr. J. T. ICE.
*School of Education:* Dr. C. M. KOFOID.
*School of Fine Arts:* Dr. J. C. BENZ.
*School of Health Services:* Dr. J. CHELLMAN.
*School of Home Economics:* Dr. M. KATHLEEN JONES.
*School of Natural Sciences and Mathematics:* Dr. C. R. FUGET.
*School of Humanities and Social Sciences:* OLIVER FORD.

## KING'S COLLEGE
WILKES-BARRE, PENNSYLVANIA 18711
Telephone: (717) 826-5900.

Founded 1946.

*President:* Rev. JAMES LACKENMIER, C.S.C.
*Registrar:* STEVEN SEITCHIK.
*Director of Admissions:* G. J. MACHINCHICK.
*Librarian:* PAUL CHAO.

The library contains 154,000 vols.
Number of teachers: 100 (full-time).
Number of students: 2,173.

## KUTZTOWN STATE COLLEGE
KUTZTOWN, PENNSYLVANIA 19530
Telephone: (215) 683-4000.

Founded 1866.

*President:* LAWRENCE M. STRATTON.
*Vice-President for Academic Affairs:* R. J. WITTMAN.
*Vice-President for Student Affairs:* F. A. BUCCI.
*Director of Admissions:* GEORGE MCKINLEY.
*Registrar:* J. ERDMANN.
*Librarian:* J. AMRHEIN.

The library contains 300,000 vols.
Number of teachers: 303.
Number of students: 5,154.

DEANS:
*School of Art:* EVAN KERN.
*Arts and Sciences:* WALTER WARZESKI.
*Teacher Education:* HENRY RYAN.
*Graduate Studies:* PAUL R. DRUMM.
*Academic Services and Director of Summer Sessions:* J. G. GUTEKUNST.

## LAFAYETTE COLLEGE
EASTON, PENNSYLVANIA 18042
Founded 1826.

*President:* DAVID W. ELLIS, PH.D.
*Provost and Dean of the Faculty:* G. G. SAUSE, Jr., PH.D.
*Dean of the College:* W. A. JEFFERS, PH.D.
*Secretary, Board of Trustees:* G. C. LAUB, LL.B.
*Registrar:* C. S. FLECK, Jr., M.B.A.
*Clerk of the Faculty:* W. KECK, M.A., PH.D.
*Librarian:* DOROTHY L. CIESLICKI, M.L.S.

The library contains 376,521 vols.
Number of teachers: 159.
Number of students: 2,000.

Publications: *Catalogue* (annual), *Mélange* (annual), *The Lafayette* (weekly), *The Alumnus* (quarterly), *The Alumni News* (quarterly).

## LA SALLE COLLEGE
20TH AND OLNEY AVENUE, PHILADELPHIA, PENNSYLVANIA 19141
Telephone: (215) 951-1000.

Founded 1863.

Undergraduate Liberal Arts and Sciences, Business Administration; Master's degree in Religious Education and Business Administration.

*President:* Bro. PATRICK ELLIS, F.S.C.
*Director of Admissions:* Bro. LEWIS MULLIN, F.S.C.
*Librarian:* Bro. T. WARNER, F.SC.

The library contains 272,864 vols.
Number of teachers: 363.
Number of students: Day Division 3,850, Evening Division 2,534, Graduate Division 780.

## LEBANON VALLEY COLLEGE
ANNVILLE, PENNSYLVANIA 17003
Telephone: (717) 867-4411.

Founded 1866.

*President:* Dr. FREDERICK P. SAMPLE.
*Registrar:* Dr. R. SHAY.
*Dean of Admissions:* GREGORY G. STANSON.
*Dean of Faculty:* Dr. RICHARD A. REED.
*Librarian:* W. E. HOUGH.

The library contains 105,000 vols.
Number of teachers: 95.
Number of students: 1,250.

## LEHIGH UNIVERSITY
BETHLEHEM, PENNSYLVANIA 18015
Founded 1865.

*President:* W. D. LEWIS, A.M., PH.D., M.A., LL.D., L.H.D.
*Provost and Vice-President:* A. E. HUMPHREY, PH.D.
*Vice-President for Administration and Planning:* E. V. OTTERVIK, PH.D.
*Vice-President for Student Affairs:* P. PARR, M.S.
*Vice-President for Research:* J. F. LIBSCH, PH.D.
*Dean of Students:* WILLIAM L. QUAY, PH.D.
*Vice-President and Treasurer:* JOHN W. WOLTJEN, B.S.
*Registrar:* J. H. WAGNER, M.A.
*Director of Libraries:* BERRY G. RICHARDS, M.L.S.

The library contains 730,000 volumes.
Number of teachers: 388.
Number of students: 5,500.

Publications: *Graduate Catalogue, University Catalogue, Annual Report,* etc.

DEANS:
*College of Arts and Science:* JOHN W. HUNT, PH.D.
*College of Business and Economics:* RICHARD W. BARSNESS, PH.D.
*College of Engineering:* D. M. BOLLE, PH.D.
*Graduate School:* J. P. KING, PH.D.
*School of Education:* PERRY A. ZIRKEL, PH.D., J.D.

## LINCOLN UNIVERSITY
PENNSYLVANIA 19352

Telephone: (215) 932-8300.

Founded 1854.

*President:* Dr. HERMAN R. BRANSON.
*Executive Vice-President/Provost:* Dr. BERNARD R. WOODSON, Jr.
*Vice-President for Fiscal Affairs:* DONALD L. MULLETT.
*Vice-President for Development:* Dr. EARLE D. WINDERMAN.
*Vice-President for Student Affairs:* Dr. LEONARD K. LOCKLEY.
*Dean of Student Services:* Dr. BERNARD M. GROSS.
*Librarian:* EMERY WIMBISH, Jr.

The library contains 130,000 vols.
Number of teachers: 89 (full-time).
Number of students: 1,105.

## LOCK HAVEN STATE COLLEGE
LOCK HAVEN,
PENNSYLVANIA 17745

Telephone: (717) 893-2000.

Founded 1870.

*President:* F. N. HAMBLIN.
*Director of Admissions:* JOSEPH COLDREN.
*Librarian:* R. S. BRAVARD.

The library contains 295,973 vols.
Number of teachers: 163.
Number of students: 2,394.

## LYCOMING COLLEGE
WILLIAMSPORT,
PENNSYLVANIA 17701

Telephone: 326-1951.

Founded 1812.

*President:* Dr. FREDERICK E. BLUMER.
*Dean:* SHIRLEY VAN MARTER.
*Registrar:* ROBERT J. GLUNK.
*Librarian:* CHARLES E. WEYANT.

The library contains 132,000 vols.
Number of teachers: 76.
Number of students: 1,159.

## MANSFIELD STATE COLLEGE
MANSFIELD,
PENNSYLVANIA 16933

Telephone: (717) 662-4046.

Founded 1857.

*President:* Dr. JANET L. TRAVIS.
*Registrar:* JOHN J. MONOSKI.
*Dean of Admissions:* JOHN ABPLANALP (acting).
*Librarian:* Dr. ELAINE DiBIASE (acting).

The library contains 182,206 vols.
Number of teachers: 196.
Number of students: 2,327 undergraduate, 254 graduate.

## MARYWOOD COLLEGE
2300 ADAMS AVENUE, SCRANTON, PENNSYLVANIA 18509

Telephone: (717) 343-6521.

Founded 1915.

*President:* Sister M. COLEMAN NEE, I.H.M.
*Academic Vice-President:* Sister ESPIRITU DEMPSEY, I.H.M.
*Registrar:* Sister PAULETTE FURNESS.
*Director of Admissions:* Sister M. GABRIEL KANE, I.H.M.
*Director of Library:* J. P. CLARKE.

The library contains 157,796 vols.
Number of teachers: 232.
Number of students: 3,202.

## MESSIAH COLLEGE
GRANTHAM,
PENNSYLVANIA 17027

Telephone: (717) 766-2511.

Founded 1909.

Private control; Academic year: September to May.

*President:* Dr. D. RAY HOSTETTER.
*Director of Business and Finance:* Dr. R. E. HAMILTON.
*Dean:* Dr. H. DAVID BRANDT.
*Dean of Student Development:* Dr. JAMES H. BARNES.
*Registrar:* Dr. D. WAYNE CASSEL.
*Director of Learning Resources Center:* ROGER C. MILLER.

The library contains 110,000 vols.
Number of teachers: 89.
Number of students: 1,350.
Publications: *Messiah College Catalog, Messiah College Bulletin.*

## MILLERSVILLE STATE COLLEGE
MILLERSVILLE,
PENNSYLVANIA 17551

Telephone: 872-5411.

Founded 1855.

*President:* Dr. WILLIAM H. DUNCAN.
*Registrar:* G. W. BURKHARDT.
*Director of Admissions:* BLAIR TREASURE.
*Librarian:* J. S. MAINE.

The library contains 310,147 vols.
Number of teachers: 310.
Number of students: 6,025.

## MORAVIAN COLLEGE
BETHLEHEM,
PENNSYLVANIA 18018

Telephone: 861-1300.

Founded 1742; men first admitted 1807.

*President:* HERMAN E. COLLIER, Jr., PH.D.
*Vice-President and Dean of Academic Affairs:* J. J. HELLER, PH.D.
*Senior Vice-President:* R. P. SNYDER.
*Director of Development:* TOM A. TENGES.
*Vice-President for Seminary Affairs and Dean:* WILLIAM W. MATZ, TH.M.

The library contains 141,000 vols.
Number of teachers: 85.
Number of students: 1,494.

## MUHLENBERG COLLEGE
24TH AND CHEW STREETS, ALLENTOWN,
PENNSYLVANIA 18104

Telephone: 433-3191.

Founded 1848.

*President:* Dr. JOHN H. MOREY.
*Vice-President and Dean of the College:* Dr. HAROLD L. STENGER.

The library contains 176,000 volumes.
Number of teachers: 100.
Number of students: 1,529.

## PENNSYLVANIA COLLEGE OF OPTOMETRY
1200 WEST GODFREY AVE., PHILADELPHIA,
PENNSYLVANIA 19141

Telephone: (215) 424-5900.

Founded 1919.

*President:* MELVIN D. WOLFBERG, O.D.
*Dean of Academic Affairs:* THOMAS L. LEWIS, O.D., PH.D.
*Dean of Student Affairs and Director of Admissions:* JOHN J. CROZIER, O.D.
*Director of Continuing and Post-Graduate Education:* LOUIS J. CATANIA, O.D.
*Librarian:* MARITA KRIVDA, B.A., M.S.

The library contains 12,000 volumes.
Number of teachers: 55.
Number of students: 585.

## PENNSYLVANIA STATE UNIVERSITY
UNIVERSITY PARK,
PENNSYLVANIA 16802

Telephone: (814) 865-4700.

Established 1855 by Act of the State legislature of Pennsylvania. Undergraduate, Master's and Doctor's degrees; associate degrees at 17 regional campuses.

*President:* JOHN W. OSWALD, PH.D., LL.D., D.SC., D.H.L.

## UNIVERSITIES AND COLLEGES—PENNSYLVANIA (STATE UNIVERSITY) U.S.A.

*Provost:* EDWARD D. EDDY, PH.D., LL.D., LITT.D., L.H.D., LET.D.
*Senior Vice-President for Administration:* RICHARD E. GRUBB, D.ED.
*Senior Vice-President for Finance and Operations:* ROBERT A. PATTERSON, M.B.A.
*Vice-President for Research and Graduate Studies:* RICHARD G. CUNNINGHAM, PH.D.
*Vice-President for Undergraduate Studies:* ROBERT E. DUNHAM, PH.D.
*Vice-President for Continuing Education and Commonwealth Campuses:* ROBERT J. SCANNELL, PH.D.
*Vice-President for Administrative Services:* RICHARD E. GRUBB, D.ED.
*Vice-President for Business:* RALPH E. ZILLY, M.A.
*Vice-President for Student Affairs:* RAYMOND O. MURPHY, D.ED.
*Special Assistant to President for Government Affairs:* FREDERICK M. CILLETTI, M.A.
*Dean of Libraries:* STUART FORTH, PH.D.

Number of teachers: 3,465.
Number of students: 62,571.

### DEANS:

*College of Agriculture:* SAMUEL H. SMITH, PH.D.
*College of Business Administration:* EUGENE J. KELLEY, PH.D.
*College of Science:* T. WARTIK, PH.D.
*College of Education:* HENRY J. HERMANOWICZ, ED.D.
*College of Engineering:* N. J. PALLADINO, D.ENG.
*College of Human Development:* EVAN G. PATTISHALL, Jr., M.D.
*College of the Liberal Arts:* S. F. PAULSON, PH.D.
*College of Earth and Mineral Sciences:* C. L. HOSLER, PH.D.
*College of Health, Physical Education and Recreation:* KARL G. STOEDEFALKE, PH.D. (acting).
*College of Arts and Architecture:* W. H WALTERS, PH.D.
*College of Medicine:* HARRY PRYSTOWSKY, M.D.
*Graduate School:* J. B. BARTOO, PH.D.
*Behrend College:* JOHN M. LILLEY, D.M.A. (Director)..
*Capitol Campus:* THEODORE L. GROSS, PH.D.
*Division of Instructional Services:* DONALD W. JOHNSON, ED.D. (Director).
*Office of Foreign Studies:* W. LAMARR KOPP, PH.D. (Director).
*Military Services Co-ordinator:* Capt. M. C. RITZ, M.S.

### PROFESSORS:

*College of Agriculture:*

*Agricultural Economics and Rural Sociology:*
BEALER, R. C., PH.D., Rural Sociology
BIRTH, A. K., M.S., Agricultural Economics Extension
BROWN, E. J., PH.D., Rural Sociology
CARDENUTO, J. R., ED.B., M.S., Rural Sociology Extension
CARROLL, W. M., M.S., Agricultural Economics Extension
CRAWFORD, C. O., M.S., PH.D., Rural Sociology
CROWLEY, V. E., PH.D., Farm Management Extension
DUM, S. A., PH.D., Farm Management Extension
FREY, J. C., PH.D., Land Economics
GAMBLE, H. B., M.S., PH.D., Agricultural Economics
HALLBERG, M. C., M.S., PH.D., Agricultural Economics
HERMANN, R. O., PH.D., Agricultural Economics
HOLT, J. S., PH.D., Agricultural Economics
HUGHES, F. A., M.S., Farm Management Extension
HUTTON, R. F., PH.D., Farm Management
JANSMA, J. D., M.S., PH.D., Agricultural Economics
JOHNSTONE, W. F., M.S., Agricultural Economics Extension
KELLY, B. W., M.S., Farm Management Extension
McALEXANDER, R. H., PH.D., Farm Management
MADDEN, J. P., PH.D., Agricultural Economics
MOORE, H. L., M.S., Agricultural Economics Extension
PARTENHEIMER, E. J., PH.D., Agricultural Economics
PASTO, J. K., PH.D., Agricultural Economics
SCHUTJER, W. A., M.S., PH.D., Agricultural Economics
STEMBERGER, A. P., PH.D., Agricultural Economics
VOIGT, A. O., M.S., Agricultural Economics Extension
WARLAND, R. H., M.S., PH.D., Rural Sociology
WILKINSON, K. P., M.A., PH.D., Rural Sociology
WILLITS, F. K., PH.D., Rural Sociology

*Agricultural Education:*
LOVE, G. M., M.S., PH.D.
STINSON, R. F., PH.D.

*Agricultural Engineering:*
ALDRICH, R. A., PH.D.
BARTLETT, H. D., M.S.
DAUM, D. R., M.S.
GROUT, A. R., M.S.
McCURDY, J. A., M.S.
MOHSENIN, N. N., PH.D.
PERSSON, S. P. E., PH.D.
SCHROEDER, M. E., PH.D.
STEPHENSON, K. Q., M.S.
WALTON, H. V., M.S., PH.D., P.E.
WOODING, N. H., M.S.

*Agronomy:*
BAKER, D. E., PH.D., Soil Chemistry
BAYLOR, J. E., PH.D., Agronomy Extension
BOLLAG, J. M., PH.D., Soil Microbiology
CLEVELAND, R. W., PH.D., Plant Breeding
CUNNINGHAM, R. L., M.S., PH.D., Social Genesis and Morphology
DUICH, J. M., PH.D., Turfgrass Science
FORTMANN, H. R., PH.D., Agronomy
HARPER, J. C., II, PH.D., Agronomy Extension
HARRINGTON, J. D., PH.D., Agronomy
HEDDLESON, M. R., PH.D., Agronomy Extension
HINISH, W. W., PH.D., Agronomy Extension
McCLELLAN, W. L., PH.D., Agronomy Extension
McKEE, G. W., PH.D., Agronomy
PETERSEN, G. W., PH.D., Soil Genesis and Morphology
RISIUS, M. L., PH.D., Plant Breeding
STARLING, J. L., PH.D., Agronomy
THOMAS, W. I., PH.D., Agronomy
WADDINGTON, D. V., M.S., PH.D., Soil Science

*Dairy and Animal Science:*
ACE, D. L., M.S., Dairy Science Extension
ADAMS, R. S., PH.D., Dairy Science Extension
ALMQUIST, J. O., PH.D., Dairy Physiology
AMANN, R. P., PH.D., Dairy Physiology
BAUMGARDT, B. R., PH.D., Animal Nutrition
BURDETTE, L. A., PH.D., Animal Science Extension
COWAN, R. L., PH.D., Animal Nutrition
FLIPSE, R. J., PH.D., Dairy Science Extension
GILMORE, H. C., M.S., Dairy Science Extension
HARTSOOK, E. W., PH.D., Animal Nutrition
KEAN, G. R., M.S., Animal Science
KESLER, E. M., PH.D., Dairy Science
KING, T. B., PH.D., Animal Science
MERRITT, T. L., PH.D., Animal Science
PUTNAM, D. N., M.S., Dairy Science Extension
SHAFFER, H. E., M.S., Dairy Science Extension
SHELLENBERGER, P. R., PH.D., Dairy Science
SINK, J. D., PH.D., Meat Science
SPECHT, L. W., PH.D., Dairy Science Extension
SPENCER, S. B., M.AGR., Dairy Science Extension
WILSON, L. L., PH.D., Animal Science
YOUNKIN, D. E., M.S., Animal Science Extension
ZIEGLER, J. H., PH.D., Meat Science

*Entomology:*
BEATTY, A. F., M.S., PH.D., Biology and Entomology
BENTON, A. W., PH.D., Apiculture
GESELL, S. G., M.S., Entomology Extension
MUMMA, R. O., PH.D., Chemical Pesticides
PITTS, C. W., PH.D., Entomology
RUTSCHKY, C. W., PH.D., Entomology
SMYTH, THOMAS, Jr., PH.D., Entomology
SNETSINGER, R. J., PH.D., Entomology
YENDOL, W. G., PH.D., Entomology

*Food Science:*
BARNARD, S. E., M.S., Food Science Extension
DIMICK, P. S., PH.D., Food Science
HAMILTON, L. W., M.S., Foods and Nutrition Extension
KEENEY, P. G., PH.D., Food Science
MacNEIL, J. H., PH.D., Food Science
McCARTHY, R. D., PH.D., Food Science
PATTON, S., PH.D., Agriculture

*Horticulture:*
BEATTIE, J. M., PH.D., Horticulture
BERGMAN, E. L., PH.D., Plant Nutrition
GRUN, P., PH.D., Cytology and Cytogenetics
HAESELER, C. W., PH.D., Pomology

HARAMAKI, C., PH.D., Ornamental Horticulture
KUHN, G. D., PH.D., Food Science
MARTSOLF, J. D., PH.D., Agricultural Microclimatology
MASTALERZ, J. W., PH.D., Floriculture
MCARDLE, F. J., M.S., PH.D., Food Science
OLIVER, C. S., PH.D., Ornamental Horticulture Extension
RATHMELL, J. K., Jr., M.S., Floriculture Extension
RICHARDSON, R. W., PH.D., Environmental Science
RITTER, C. M., PH.D., Pomology
SHANNON, J. C., PH.D., Horticultural Physiology
SMITH, C. B., PH.D., Plant Nutrition
STINSON, R. F., PH.D., Horticulture
TUKEY, L. D., PH.D., Pomology
WHITE, J. W., M.S., PH.D., Floriculture

*Plant Pathology:*
BLOOM, J. R., PH.D.
BOYLE, J. S., PH.D.
COLE, H., Jr., PH.D.
HICKEY, K. D., PH.D.
LUKEZIC, F. L., PH.D.
MERRILL, W., Jr., M.S., PH.D.
NELSON, P. E., PH.D.
NELSON, R. R., PH.D.
NICHOLS, L. P., M.S.
OSWALD, J. W., PH.D.
PETERSON, D. H., PH.D.
SCHEIN, R. D., PH.D.
SCHISLER, L. C., M.S., PH.D.
STOUFFER, R. F., PH.D.
WUEST, P. J., PH.D.

*Poultry Science:*
BUSS, E. G., PH.D., Poultry Science
GOODWIN, K., PH.D., Poultry Science
HICKS, F. W., PH.D., Poultry Science Extension
LEACH, R. M., Jr., PH.D., Poultry Science
MACNEIL, J. H., PH.D., Food Science
MUELLER, W. J., DR.SC.TECH., Poultry Science

*Veterinary Science:*
CARD, C. S., D.V.M., PH.D.
EBERHART, R. J., D.V.M., PH.D.
GENTRY, R. F., PH.D.
GLANTZ, P. J., PH.D.
HOKANSON, J. F., D.V.M.
KAVANAUGH, J. F., D.V.M.
MASSARO, E. J., PH.D.
ROTHENBACHER, H., D.V.M., M.S., PH.D.
SCHWARTZ, L. D., M.S.
SWOPE, R. E., V.M.D.
ZARKOWER, A., PH.D.

*School of Forest Resources:*
BOND, R. S., PH.D., Forestry and Wildlife Management
GEORGE, J. L., M.S., PH.D., Wildlife Management
GERHOLD, H. D., PH.D., Forest Genetics
HUTNIK, R. J., PH.D., Forest Ecology
MCDERMOTT, R. E., PH.D., Forestry
MELTON, R. E., M.F., Forestry
SHIPMAN, R. D., M.F., PH.D., Forest Ecology
SOPPER, W. E., PH.D., Forest Hydrology
WARD, W. W., D.FOR., Silviculture
WINGARD, R. G., M.S., Wildlife Management Extension

*Pesticide Research Laboratory:*
BARRON, G. P., Jr., PH.D., Nutrition and Food Safety

*Home Economics and Family Living:*
BELL, H. E., PH.D., Home Management Extension

*College of Arts and Architecture:*
*Architecture:*
CORBELLETTI, R., M.S., Architecture
GOLANY, G., PH.D., Urban and Regional Planning
HALLOCK, P. F., M.S., Architecture

*Art:*
COOK, J. A., M.F.A.
FROST, S. H., B.A.
MCCOY, W. V., M.F.A.
SHIPLEY, J. R., M.A.
SHOBAKEN, B., M.F.A.
ZORETICH, G. S., M.A.

*Art Education:*
BEITTEL, K. R., D.ED.
CHOMICKY, Y. G., M.S.
HOFFA, H., D.ED.
SCHWARTZ, A., D.ED.
VAN DOMMELEN, D. B., M.A.

*Art History:*
BATTISTI, E., PH.D.
CUTLER, A., PH.D.
FLEISCHER, R., PHD.
HAGER, H., DR.PHIL.
MAUNER, G. L., PH.D.

*Landscape Architecture:*
YOUNG, D. L., M.L.A.

*Music:*
BAISLEY, R. W., M.A.
BROWN, R. H., B.S.
FENNER, B. L., M.A.
TREHY, R. F., B.A.

*Music Education:*
DIEHL, N. C., D.ED.

*Theatre and Film:*
ALLISON, W. H., M.F.A.
COOK, D. N., M.A.
MANFULL, L. L.
WALTERS, W. H., PH.D.

*College of Business Administration:*
*Accounting and Management Information Systems:*
FERRARA, W. L., PH.D.
MALCOLM, R. E., PH.D.
NELSON, G. K., PH.D.
PHILIPS, G. E., PH.D.
SCHRADER, W. J., PH.D.

*Business Logistics:*
CARROLL, J. L., D.B.A., Business Administration
COYLE, J. J., Jr., D.B.A., Business Administration
DANIELS, J. D., M.B.A., PH.D., Business Administration
PASHEK, R. D., PH.D., Business Administration
PHALAN, R. T., J.D., Business Law
SPYCHALSKI, J. C., D.B.A., Business Administration

*Finance:*
BRADLEY, J. F., PH.D.
CURLEY, A. J., M.B.A., PH.D.
PHILIPPATOS, G. C., PH.D.

*Insurance and Real Estate:*
HAMMOND, J. D., PH.D., Business Administration
WILLIAMS, A. L., PH.D., Insurance

*Management Science and Organizational Behaviour:*
AGGARWALL, S. C., PH.D., Management Science
HAYAA, J. C., PH.D., Management Science
HEITMANN, G., PH.D., Management Science
HOTTENSTEIN, M. P., D.B.A., Management
KOCHENBERGER, G. A., D.B.A., Management Science
KOOT, R. S., PH.D., Management Science
MELANDER, E. R., PH.D., Quantitive Business Analysis
RIGBY, P. H., PH.D., Business Administration
SHILLING, N., PH.D., Quantitive Business Analysis

*Marketing:*
BEIK, L. L., PH.D., Marketing
BENNETT, P. D., PH.D., Marketing
BITHER, S. W., D.B.A., Marketing
KELLEY, E. J., PH.D., Business Administration
WILSON, D. T., PH.D., Marketing

*Business Administration Continuing Education:*
MARLOW, H. L., ED.D., Management Development

*College of Earth and Mineral Sciences:*
*Geography:*
ABLER, R. F., PH.D.
GOULD, P. R., PH.D.
LEWIS, P. F., PH.D.
MILLER, E. W., PH.D.
RODGERS, A. L., PH.D.
SIMKINS, P. D., PH.D.
WERNSTEDT, F. L., PH.D.
ZELINSKY, W., PH.D.

*Geosciences:*
ALEXANDER, S. S., PH.D.
BARNES, H. L., PH.D., Geochemistry
BURNHAM, C. W., PH.D., Geochemistry
DACHILLE, F., PH.D., Geochemistry
GOLD, D. P., M.SC., PH.D., Geology
HOWELL, B. F., Jr., PH.D.
MUAN, A., PH.D., Mineral Sciences
NEWNHAM, R. E., PH.D., Solid State Science
OHMOTO, H., PH.D., Geochemistry
PARIZEK, R. R., PH.D., Geology
ROSE, A. W., PH.D., Geochemistry
ROY, R., PH.D., Solid State Science
SCHMALZ, R. F., PH.D., Geology
SCHOLTEN, R., PH.D., Petroleum Geology
SMITH, D. K., PH.D., Mineralogy
SPACKMAN, W., Jr., PH.D., Palaeobotany
THORNTON, C. P., PH.D., Petrology
TRAVERSE, A., PH.D., Palynology
VOIGHT, B., PH.D., Geology
WHITE, W. B., PH.D., Geochemistry
WILLIAMS, E. G., PH.D., Geology
WRIGHT, L. A., PH.D., Geology

*Polymer Science:*
KLINE, D. E., PH.D., Materials Science

*Ceramic Science:*
BRADT, R. C., M.S., PH.D., Ceramic Science
HUMMEL, F. A., M.S., Ceramic Science
NEWNHAM, R. E., PH.D., Solid State Science
RINDONE, G. E., PH.D., Ceramic Science
STUBICAN, V. S., D.SC., Ceramic Science

*Fuel Science:*
AUSTIN, L. G., PH.D.
GIVEN, P. H., D.PHIL.
PALMER, H. B., PH.D.
VASTOLA, F. J., PH.D.
WALKER, P. L., Jr., PH.D.

*Metallurgy:*
APLAN, F. F., SC.D., Metallurgy and Mineral Processing
BITLER, W. R., PH.D., Metallurgy
MUAN, A., PH.D., Mineral Sciences
PICKERING, H. W., PH.D., Metallurgy
SIMKOVICH, G., PH.D., Metallurgy

## UNIVERSITIES AND COLLEGES—PENNSYLVANIA (STATE UNIVERSITY) U.S.A.

### Meteorology:
Anthes, R. A., ph.d.
Blackadar, A. K., ph.d.
DePena, R. G., ph.d.
Dutton, J. A., ph.d.
Hosler, C. L., ph.d.
Panofsky, H. A., ph.d., Atmospheric Science
Thompson, D. W., ph.d.

### Mineral Economics:
Gordon, R. L., ph.d., Mineral Economics
Tilton, J. E., ph.d.
Vogely, W. A., ph.d., Mineral Economics

### Mineral Engineering:
Aplan, F. F., sc.d.
Austin, L. G., ph.d.
Bieniawski, Z. T., ph.d.
Frantz, R. L., p.e.
Hardy, H. R., Jr., ph.d.
Lovell, H. L., ph.d.
Ramini, R. V., ph.d.
Saperstein, L. W., d.phil., p.e.
Stefanko, R., ph.d.

### Petroleum and Natural Gas:
Burcik, E. J., ph.d.
Farouq-Ali, S. M., ph.d.
Stahl, C. D., ph.d.

### Mineral Conservation:
Parizek, R. R., ph.d., Geology
Rose, A. W., ph.d., Geochemistry
Williams, E. G., ph.d., Geology

### Ore Deposits:
Barnes, H. L., ph.d., Geochemistry
Burnham, C. W., ph.d., Geochemistry

## College of Education:
### Curriculum and Instruction:
Alessandro, J. V., d.ed.
Bliesmer, E. P., ph.d.
Brewer, M., ed.d.
DuPuis, V. L., ph.d.
Fagan, E. R., ed.d.
Fowler, H. S., ph.d.
Golub, L. S., ph.d.
Heimer, R. T., ed.d.
Hermanowicz, H. J., ed.d.
Searles, J. E., ed.d.
Trueblood, C., d.ed.
Welliver, P. W., ph.d.
Withall, J., ph.d.
Wood, F. H., ed.d.
Zafforoni, J., ed.d.

### Counselor Education:
Britton, J. O., m.a., ph.d., Educational Psychology
Herr, E. L., m.a., ed.d., Counselor Education
Hudson, G. R., m.a., ed.d., Education
Keat, D. B., II, ph.d.
Kelz, J. W., m.ed., ph.d., Education
Swisher, J. D., ph.d.

### Educational Psychology:
Di Vesta, F. J., m.s., ph.d.
French, J. L., m.s., ed.d.
Games, P. A., m.a., ph.d.
Mitzel, H. E., m.a., ph.d.
Rabinowitz, W., m.a., ph.d.
Thevaos, D. G., m.a., ph.d.
Withall, J., m.ed., ph.d.

### Education Policy Studies:
Alessandro, J. V., d.ed.
Best, J. H., ph.d.
Eddy, E. D., ph.d.
Godbey, G. C., m.a., ed.d.
Johnson, H. C., Jr., ph.d.
Lutz, F. W., m.s., ed.d.

Lynch, P. D., m.a., ph.d.
Martorana, S. V., m.a., ph.d.
Mortimer, K. P., ph.d.
Sweitzer, R. E., m.a., ph.d.
Willower, D. J., m.a., ed.d.

### Occupational and Vocational Studies:
East, M., m.a., ed.d., Home Economics Education
Ray, E. M., m.ed., ph.d., Home Economics Education
Shear, T. M., m.s., ed.d., Home Economics Education
Thal, H. M., m.a., ed.d., Home Economics Education

### Special Education:
Berlin, A. J., ph.d., Speech Pathology
Cartwright, G. P., ph.d.
French, J. L., m.s., ed.d.
Heilman, A. W., ph.d.
McDonald, E. T., d.ed.
Michael, P., m.s., ph.d.
Siegenthaler, B. M., m.a., ph.d.
Smith, R. J., m.ed., ed.d.

## College of Science:
### Astronomy:
Hagen, J. P., ph.d.
Matsushima, S., ph.d., d.sc.
Sampson, D. H., m.s., ph.d.
Weedman, D. W., ph.d.

### Biochemistry:
Bernlohr, R. W., ph.d.
Mallette, M. F., m.s., ph.d.
McCarl, R. L., ph.d.
Pazur, J. H., m.sc., ph.d.
Phillips, A. T., ph.d.
Schraer, R., m.a., ph.d.
Shigley, J. W., m.s., ph.d.

### Biophysics:
Deering, R. A., ph.d.
Hymer, W. C., ph.d.
Keith, A., ph.d.
Person, S. R., ph.d.
Schraer, H., m.a., ph.d.
Snipes, W. C., ph.d.
Strother, G. K., m.s., ph.d.
Taylor, W. D., ph.d.
Todd, P. W., ph.d.

### Biology (including Botany, Genetics, and Zoology):
Anthony, A., m.s., ph.d., Zoology
Beatty, A. F., ph.d., Biology
Bellis, E. D., m.s., ph.d., Biology
Butler, R. L., m.s., ph.d., Biology
Cooper, E. L., m.s., ph.d., Zoology
Dunson, W. A., m.s., ph.d., Biology
Fergus, C. L., m.a., ph.d., Botany
Grove, A. R., m.s., ph.d., Botany
Grove, M. O., ph.d., Biology
Grun, P., ph.d., Cytology
Hamilton, R. H., m.s., ph.d., Biology
Hibbard, E., ph.d., Biology
Hillson, C. J., m.s., ph.d., Botany
Lindstrom, E. S., ph.d., Bacteriology
Pursell, R. A., ph.d., Botany
Schein, R. D., ph.d., Botany
Spackman, W., m.s., ph.d., Palaeobotany
Traverse, A., a.m., ph.d., Palynology
Wooldridge, D. P., ph.d., Biology
Wright, J. E., Jr., ph.d., Genetics

### Chemistry:
Allcock, H. R., ph.d.
Anderson, J. B., ph.d.
Benkovic, S. J., ph.d.
Bernheim, R. A., m.a., ph.d.
Bernoff, R. A., m.a., ph.d.
Deno, N. C., m.s., ph.d.
Dixon, J. A., m.s., ph.d.
Fritz, J. J., m.s., ph.d.

Haas, C. G., m.sc., ph.d.
Hamilton, G. A., m.a., ph.d.
Heicklen, J. P., ph.d.
Hisatune, I. C., ph.d.
Horrocks, W. de W., ph.d.
Jackman, L. M., ph.d.
Jordan, J., m.sc., ph.d.
Jurs, P. C., ph.d.
Lampe, F. W., a.m., ph.d.
Moore, G. G., ph.d.
Olofson, R. A., m.s., ph.d.
Richey, H. G., Jr., m.a., ph.d.
Rosenblatt, G. M., ph.d.
Shamma, M., ph.d.
Skell, P. S., m.a., ph.d.
Steele, W. A., ph.d.
Wartik, T., ph.d.
Zook, H. D., m.s., ph.d.

### Mathematics:
Andrews, G. E., m.a., ph.d.
Armentrout, S., ph.d.
Axt, P., m.sc., ph.d.
Ayoub, C. W., a.m., ph.d.
Ayoub, R. G. D., m.sc., ph.d.
Farrell, F. T., ph.d.
Fine, N. J., a.m., ph.d.
Glaser, A., d.ed.
Hahn, K. T., ph.d.
Hunter, R. P., m.s., ph.d.
James, D. G., ph.d.
Jech, T. J., ph.d.
Kanwal, R. P., m.a., ph.d.
Krall, A. M., m.a., ph.d.
Lallement, G. J., ph.d.
Overdeer, P. M., m.s.
Rung, D. C., m.s., ph.d.
Yood, B., m.s., ph.d.

### Microbiology:
Casida, L. E., m.s., ph.d.
Lindstrom, E. S., m.s., ph.d., Bacteriology
Ludwig, E., m.s., ph.d.
Zimmerman, L. N., m.s., ph.d., Bacteriology

### Physics:
Barsch, G. R., dipl.ing., dr.rer.nat.
Bleuler, E., m.s., d.sc.nat.
Cutler, P. H., m.s., ph.d.
Feuchtwang, T. E., m.s., ph.d.
Fleming, G. N., ph.d.
Frankl, D. R., ph.d.
Good, R. H., Jr., ph.d.
Grotch, H., ph.d.
Henisch, H. K., ph.d.
Herman, R. W., ph.d.
Kazes, E., m.s., ph.d.
Kendall, B. R. F., ph.d.
Lang, I. G., m.s., ph.d.
McCubbin, T. K., Jr., ph.d.
Plíva, J., ing. chem., dr.tech.
Polo, S. R., m.s., ph.d.
Pratt, W. W., ph.d.
Skudrzyk, E., ph.d.
Strother, G. K., ph.d.
Tsong, T. T., m.s., ph.d.
Vedam, K., m.sc., ph.d.
Wiggins, T. A., m.s., ph.d.

### Computer Science:
Culik, K., ph.d.
DeMaine, P. A. D., ph.d.
Fischer, C. F., ph.d.
Fischer, P. C., ph.d.
Goldstein, J., ph.d.

### Statistics:
Antle, C. E., m.a., ph.d.
Bartoo, J. B., m.s., ph.d.
Haight, F. A., m.sc., ph.d.
Harkness, W. L., m.a., ph.d.
Hettmansperger, T. P., ph.d.
Hultquist, R. A., m.s., ph.d.
Patil, G. P., m.sc., m.s., ph.d.

### College of Engineering:

#### Aerospace Engineering:
HOLL, J. W., M.S., PH.D.
KAPLAN, M. H., PH.D.
LAKSHMINARAYANA, B., PH.D.
MCCORMICK, B. W., M.S., PH.D., P.E.
PARKIN, B. R., M.S., PH.D.
PHILLIPS, W. M., D.SC.
TENNEKES, H., DR.TECH.SC.

#### Agricultural Engineering:
ALDRICH, R. A., M.S., PH.D., P.E.
BARTLETT, H. D., M.S., P.E.
MOHSENIN, N. N., M.S., PH.D.
PERSSON, S. P. E., M.S., PH.D.
SCHROEDER, M. E., M.S., PH.D.
STEPHENSON, K. Q., M.S., P.E.
WALTON, H. V., PH.D., P.E.

#### Architectural Engineering:
ALBRIGHT, G. H., M.S.
FLYNN, J. E., B.ARCH.
GILMAN, S. F., M.S., PH.D.
TICHY, J., M.SC, D.SC.
WHEELER, C. H., Jr., M.S., R.A.

#### Chemical Engineering:
BRAUN, W. G., M.S., PH.D.
DANNER, R. P., PH.D.
DAUBERT, T. E., M.SC., PH.D.
DUDA, J. L., M.CH.E., PH.D.
EAGLETON, L. C., M.S., D.ENG.
ENGEL, A. J., PH.D.
JONES, J. H., M.S., PH.D.
KABEL, R. L., PH.D., P.E.
KLAUS, E. E., M.S., PH.D.
MCCORMICK, R. H., M.S.

#### Civil Engineering:
BARNOFF, R. M., M.S., PH.D., P.E.
CADY, P. D., M.S., PH.D., P.E.
CROWLEY, K. W., PH.D., P.E.
GOTOLSKI, W. H., M.S., PH.D., P.E.
LARSON, T. D., M.S., PH.D., P.E.
MCDONNELL, A. J., M.S., PH.D.
NESBITT, J. B., S.M., SC.D.
UNTRAUER, R., M.S., PH.D., P.E.

#### Electrical Engineering:
ADAMS, W. S., M.S., PH.D.
BROWN, J. L., PH.D.
CROSS, L. E., PH.D.
FERRARO, A. J., M.S., PH.D.
HALE, L. C., M.S., PH.D.
LACHS, G. PH.D.
LEE, HAI-SUP, M.S., PH.D.
LEWIS, J. B., M.S., PH.D.
MCMURTRY, G. J., PH.D.
NISBET, J. S., M.S., PH.D.
ROSS, W. J., M.SC., PH.D.

#### Engineering Science and Mechanics:
FONASH, S. J., PH.D., Engineering Sciences
HAYEK, S. I., D.ENG.SC., Engineering Mechanics
HAYTHORNTHWAITE, R. M., M.S., PH.D., P.E., Engineering Mechanics
HU, L. W., M.S., PH.D., Engineering Mechanics
KIUSALAAS, J., M.S., PH.D., Engineering Mechanics
LLORENS, R. E., PH.D., Engineering Sciences
MENTZER, J. R., M.S., PH.D., Engineering Sciences
NEUBERT, V. H., M.S., D.ENG., Engineering Mechanics
SHARMA, M. G., D.I.I.S., PH.D., Engineering Mechanics
ZAMRIK, S. Y., PH.D., Engineering Mechanics

#### General Engineering:
BARTOWIAK, R. A., P.E.
CHAPIN, J. F., M.S.
GRENIER, G. S., M.S.E.E., PH.D., P.E.
KRAYBILL, E. K., M.S.E., E.E., PH.D., P.E.
KOLESAR, J., B.S., R.S.
MCCLUNG, A. R., M.S., P.E.
PROSSER, D. R., M.S., P.E.
QUINN, R. G., M.S., PH.D.
SOWA, W. A., M.S.
TAYLOR, C. H., M.S., P.E.
WEIDHAAS, E. R., M.E., P.E.

#### Industrial and Management Systems Engineering:
BILES, W. E., PH.D., P.E.
DRAPER, A. B., PH.D.
HAM, I., M.S., PH.D.
RAPHAEL, D. L., M.A
ROSENSHINE, M., PH.D.
THUERING, G. L., M.S., M.E., P.E.
ZINDLER, R. E., M.S., PH.D.

#### Mechanical Engineering:
BRICKMAN, A. D., M.S., MECH.E., PH.D.
CUNNINGHAM, R. G., M.S., PH.D., P.E.
FAETH, G. M., PH.D.
HEINSOHN, R. J., PH.D.
LESTZ, S. S., M.S., PH.D.
OLSON, D. R., M.ENG., D.ENG., P.E
REETHOF, G., M.S., D.SC.
SCHMIDT, F. W., M.S., PH.D.
SHEARER, J. L., M.S., M.E., SC.D., P.E.
WEBER, H. E., M.S., D.SC.
WOGELMUTH, C. H., PH.D.

#### Nuclear Engineering:
DIETHORN, W. S., M.S., PH.D.
FODERARO, A. H., PH.D.
JACOBS, A. M., M.S., PH.D.
KENNEY, E. S., PH.D.
KLEVANS, E. H., PH.D.
LEVINE, S. H., M.S., PH.D.
PALLADINO, N. J., M.S., D.ENG., P.E.
REMICK, F. J., PH.D.
SCHULTZ, M. A., B.S.
WITZIG, W. F., M.S., PH.D., P.E.

### College of Human Development:

#### Biological Health:
COLEMAN, M. C., M.S., PH.D., Experimental Foods
GUNTER, L. M., M.A., PH.D., Nursing
GUTHRIE, H. A., M.S., PH.D., Nutrition
MAYERS, S. P., M.P.H., M.D., Health Care Planning
NEWMAN, M. A., PH.D., Nursing
RAFFEL, M. W., PH.D., Health Planning
WALCHER, D. N., M.D., Health Planning and Administration
WOOLEY, P. O., Jr., M.D., M.P.H., Health Planning and Administration

#### Man-Environment Relations:
COHN, S., M.S., PH.D., Urban Design
MANN, S. H., PH.D., Operations Research
POWERS, T. F., M.B.A., PH.D., Organizational Behaviour
STUDER, R. G., M.ARCH., Environmental Design
VALLANCE, T. R., M.A., PH.D., Human Development
WOHLWILL, J. F., PH.D., Man-Environment Relations and Psychology

#### Community Development:
FREEMAN, W. E., M.A., PH.D., Human Development
GUTTENPLAN, H. L., M.S., D.P.A., Law Enforcement
RITTI, R. R., M.S., PH.D., Organizational Behaviour

#### Individual and Family Studies:
BALTES, P. B., M.A., PH.D.
BRITTON, J. H., M.A., PH.D.
BURGESS, R. L., M.A., PH.D.
DELISSOVOY, V., M.A., PH.D.
FORD, D. H., M.S., PH.D.
GENTRY, L., M.S., PH.D.
GUERNEY, B. G., Jr., M.S., PH.D.
KNOLL, M. M., M.A., PH.D.
NESSELROADE, J. R., M.A., PH.D.
SEWARD, D. M., M.A., PH.D.
STEIN, A. H., M.A., PH.D.
TAYLOR, C., PH.D.
URBAN, H. B., M.S., PH.D.
WALCHER, D. N., M.D.

### College of the Liberal Arts:

#### Anthropology:
BAKER, P. T., PH.D.
CHAGNON, N. A., PH.D.
HUNT, E. E., A.M., PH.D.
MICHELS, J. W., M.A., PH.D.
MORRILL, W. T., M.A., PH.D.
SANDERS, W. T., M.A., PH.D.

#### Classics:
CARRUBBA, R. W., M.A., PH.D.

#### Economics:
BUDD, E. C., A.A., PH.D.
FARR, G. N., M.B.A., PH.D.
FELLER, I., PH.D.
FOX, T. G., M.A., PH.D.
HERENDEEN, J. B., M.S., PH.D.
HU, T.-W., M.A., PH.D.
KLEIN, P. A., M.A., PH.D.
NELSON, J. P., PH.D.
NEWMAN, M., M.A., PH.D.
PRYBYLA, J. S., M.ECON.SC., PH.D.
RIEW, J. H., M.A., PH.D.
ROBINSON, W. C., M.A., PH.D.
RODGERS, J. D., PH.D.
ROZEN, M. E., PH.D.
SMITH, J. D., M.A., PH.D.

#### English:
AUSTIN, D. S., M.A., PH.D.
BEGNAL, M. H., PH.D.
BURNS, L., M.A., PH.D.
CONDEE, R. W., A.M., PH.D.
DAMERST, W. A., M.A.
EBBITT, W. R., M.A., PH.D.
HUME, R. D., PH.D.
KLASS, P., M.A.
LEWIS, A. O., Jr., A.M., PH.D.
MANN, C. W., M.A., M.L.S.
MESEROLE, H. T., M.A., PH.D.
PRICE, J. G., M.A., PH.D.
ROGERS, T. H., M.A., PH.D.
RUBINSTEIN, S. L., M.F.A.
TRAUTMANN, J., PH.D.
WALDEN, D., PH.D.
WEAVER, R. G., M.A.
WEINTRAUB, S., M.A., PH.D.
WEST, P. N., M.A.
YOUNG, P., PH.D.

#### French:
BELASCO, S., A.M., PH.D., Romance Linguistics
BRAULT, G. J., M.A., PH.D.
CHAPMAN, H. H., Jr., M.A., PH.D., Romance Languages
FRAUTSCHI, R. L., M.A., PH.D.

#### German:
EBBINGHAUS, E. A., PH.D.
KOPP, W. L., M.A., PH.D.
PREISNER, R., PH.D.
SCHURER, E., PH.D.

#### History:
AMERINGER, C. D., M.A., PH.D., Latin American History
BROWN, I. V., A.M., PH.D., American History
DUIKER, W. J., III., PH.D., East Asian History
EGGERT, G. G., M.A., PH.D., American History
FORSTER, K., A.M., PH.D., European History
GREEN, R. W., A.M., PH.D., European History

HASSLER, W. W., A.M., PH.D., American History
MADDOX, R. J., M.S., PH.D, American History
MURRAY, R. K., M.A., PH.D., American History
SUN, E.-T. Z., M.A., PH.D., Chinese History
UTECHIN, S. V., PH.D., Russian History

*Labour Studies:*
GOLATZ, H. J., M.A.

*Philosophy:*
ANDERSON, J. M., M.A., PH.D.
GINSBERG, R., PH.D.
HAUSMAN, C. R., M.A., PH.D.
JOHNSTONE, H. W., Jr., A.M., PH.D
KOCKELMANS, J. J., PH.D.
ROSEN, S. H., M.A., PH.D.
SEEBOHM, T. M., DR.PHIL.HABIL.

*Political Science:*
ALBINSKI, H. S., M.A., PH.D.
ASPATURIAN, V. V., PH.D.
BROWN, J. C., M.A., PH.D.
CHANG, P. H., PH.D.
EISENSTEIN, J., PH.D.
FRIEDMAN, R. S., M.A., PH.D.
GILBERG, T., PH.D.
KEYES, E., PH.D.
KOCHANEK, S. A., M.A., PH.D.
MARTZ, J. D., PH.D.

*Psychology:*
BORKOVEC, T. D., PH.D.
DIVESTA, F. J., M.S., PH.D.
DRAGUNS, J. G., PH.D.
DUBIN, S. S., M.A., PH.D.
GORLOW, L., M.A., PH.D.
GUTHRIE, G. M., PH.D.
HALL, J. F., M.A., PH.D.
KAZDIN, A. E., PH.D.
LEIBOWITZ, H. W., M.A., PH.D.
LUNDY, R. M., M.S., PH.D.
MAHONEY, M. J., PH.D.
MITZEL, H. E., M.A., PH.D.
NICHOLS, J. R., M.S., PH.D. (Capitol Campus)
NOBLE, M. E., PH.D.
PALERMO, D. S., M.S., PH.D.
SHERIF, C., M.A., PH.D.
SMITH, J. L., M.A., PH.D.
STERN, R., M.A., PH.D.
TAYLOR, C., PH.D.
THOMAS, H., PH.D.
URBAN, H. B., M.S., PH.D.
WARREN, J. M., M.S., PH.D.

*Public Administration:*
LA PORTE, R., Jr., M.A., PH.D.
LEE, R. D., Jr., PH.D.
MOWITZ, R. J., PH.D.

*Religious Studies:*
CHANG, C.-C.
CHERRY, C. C., PH.D.
FUKUYAMA, Y., B.D., PH.D.
HARRISON, P. M., PH.D.
HARSHBARGER, L. H., D.D.
VASTYAN, A. E., B.D.

*Slavic Languages and Literatures:*
BIRKENMAYER, S. S., M.A., PH.D.
MAGNER, T. F., M.A., PH.D.
PATERNOST, J., PH.D.
SCHMALSTIEG, W. R., M.A., PH.D.

*Sociology:*
BUCK, R. C., M.S., PH.D.
DE JONG, G. F., M.A., PH.D.
PELLEGRIN, R. J., M.A., PH.D.
SIMIRENKO, A., M.A., PH.D.
SNYDER, E. C., M.A., PH.D.
THEODORSON, G. A., M.A., PH.D.

*Spanish, Italian and Portuguese:*
DALBOR, J. B., M.A., PH.D., Romance Languages
LIMA, R. F., Jr., M.A., PH.D., Spanish
LYDAY, L. F., III, PH.D., Spanish
PÉREZ, L. C., M.A., PH.D., Spanish
STABB, M. S., M.A., PH.D., Spanish
STURCKEN, H. T., M.A., PH.D., Romance Languages

*Speech Communication:*
BENSON, T. W., M.A., PH.D.
BRUBAKER, R. S., M.A., PH.D.
COHEN, H., M.A., PH.D.
DUNHAM, R. E., M.A., PH.D.
FRANDSEN, K. D., M.A., PH.D.
GREGG, R. B., M.A., PH.D.
HOLTZMAN, P. D., M.A., PH.D.
PAULSON, S. F., M.A., PH.D.
PHILLIPS, G. M., M.A., PH.D.
ROSENFIELD, L. W., PH.D.
WHITE, E. E., M.A., PH.D.

*School of Journalism:*
BLANCHARD, R. O., PH.D.
DULANEY, W. L., M.S., PH.D.
FARSON, R. H., M.A.
FROKE, M. D., M.S.
GOODWIN, H. E., M.A.

*College of Health, Physical Education and Recreation:*
ADAMS, M. A., M.A., Physical Education
BUSKIRK, E. R., M.A., PH.D., Applied Physiology
HARRIS, D. V., M.ED., PH.D., Physical Education
HUNT, E. E., A.M., PH.D., Health Education
KAMON, E., M.SC., PH.D., Applied Physiology
LUCAS, J. A., M.A., M.S. D.ED., Physical Education
LUNDEGREN, H. M., M.ED., PH.D., Physical Education
MAGNUSSON, L. I., M.A., PH.D., Physical Education
MENDEZ, J., M.S., PH.D., Health and Applied Physiology
MOREHOUSE, C. A., M.S., PH.D., Physical Education
NELSON, R. C., M.ED., PH.D., Physical Education
PATERNO, J. V., B.S., Physical Education
SCANNELL, R. J., M.S., PH.D., Physical Education
STOEDEFALKE, K. G., M.S., PH.D., Physical Education

*Department of Military Science:*
ROSE, Col. R. S., M.P.A., B.A.

*Department of Naval Science:*
RITZ, Capt. M. C., M.S., B.S.

*Department of Air Force Aerospace Studies:*
DUCKWORTH, Col. R. D., PH.D., M.S.E.

ATTACHED RESEARCH INSTITUTES:
**Applied Research Laboratory.**
**Center for Air Environment Studies.**
**Center for Study of Environmental Policy.**
**Computation Center.**
**Institute for the Arts and Humanistic Studies.**
**Institute for Policy Research and Evaluation.**
**Institute for Research on Land and Water Resources.**
**Laboratory Animal Resources.**
**Laboratory for Human Performance Research.**
**Laboratory for Research on Animal Behavior.**
**Materials Research Laboratory.**
**Pennsylvania Transportation Institute.**

## PHILADELPHIA COLLEGE OF ART

BROAD AND SPRUCE STREETS,
PHILADELPHIA,
PENNSYLVANIA 19102

Telephone: 893-3100.
Founded 1876.

*President:* THOMAS F. SCHUTTE.
*Dean of Academic Affairs:* NATHAN KNOBLER.
*Dean of Students:* VICTOR S. ZARZYCKI.
*Director of Admissions:* CAROLINE KELSEY.
*Librarian:* Mrs. HAZEL GUSTOW.

Number of teachers: 90 full-time, 65 evrt-time.
Number of students: 1,200 day, 1,000 paening.

## PHILADELPHIA COLLEGE OF PHARMACY AND SCIENCE

43RD ST. AND KINGSESSING MALL,
PHILADELPHIA,
PENNSYLVANIA 19104

Founded 1821.

*President:* WILLIAM A. THAWLEY, B.S. (acting).
*Dean of Faculty:* DANIEL A. HUSSAR, PH.D.
*Associate Dean for Research and Graduate Studies:* G. VICTOR ROSSI, PH.D.
*Associate Dean for Science:* ALFONSO R. GENNARO, PH.D.
*Dean of Students:* NATHAN RUBIN, PH.D.
*Financial Aid Officer:* BEVERLY S. TRIESTMAN, B.A.
*Registrar:* RICHARD C. KENT, ED.M.
*Comptroller:* JOHN J. GULLA, C.P.A.
*Librarian:* CAROL H. FENICHEL, PH.D.

The library contains 80,000 vols.
Number of students: 1,155.

DIRECTORS:
*Biological Sciences:* G. VICTOR ROSSI, PH.D.
*Chemistry:* ALFONSO R. GENNARO, PH.D.
*Clinical Programs:* JOHN A. GANS, PHARM.D.
*Languages and Social Sciences:* BEAUVEAU BORIE IV, PH.D.
*Mathematics and Physics:* BERNARD J. BRUNNER, PH.D.
*Medical Technology:* ARA DER MARDEROSIAN, PH.D.
*Pharmacy:* MAVEN J. MYERS, PH.D.

### PHILADELPHIA COLLEGE OF TEXTILES AND SCIENCE
PHILADELPHIA, PENNSYLVANIA 19144
Telephone: VI 3-9700.
Founded 1884.

*President:* Donald B. Partridge, B.S., ED.M.
*Assistant to the President:* George R. Spann, M.A., PH.D.
*Director of Admissions:* M. R. Linn, B.A., M.S., ED.D.
*Registrar:* P. H. Kerstetter, M.S.
  Number of teachers: 92.
  Number of students: 2,064.
  Publication: *Textile Engineer.*

### ROSEMONT COLLEGE
ROSEMONT, PENNSYLVANIA 19010
Telephone: (215) 527-0200.
Founded 1921.

Catholic liberal arts college for women.
*President:* Dorothy M. Brown, ED.D.
*Registrar:* Lynne Dalla.
*Director of Admissions:* Miss Jane Maloney.
*Librarian:* Sister Mary Dennis Lynch, S.H.C.J.
  The library contains 129,220 vols.
  Number of teachers: 84.
  Number of students: 424 full-time, 123 part-time.

### SAINT FRANCIS COLLEGE
LORETTO, PENNSYLVANIA 15940
Telephone: (814) 472-7000.
Founded 1847.

*President:* Rev. Christian Oravec, T.O.R.
*Executive Vice-President:* Rev. Gervase Cain, T.O.R.
*Vice-President for College Relations:* Rev. Vincent Negherbon, T.O.R.
*Vice-President for Academic Affairs:* Dr. John Willoughby.
*Vice-President for Community Educational Services:* Dr. Richard Crawford.
*Vice-President for Finance:* Frank Kuzemchak.
*Vice-President for Student Affairs:* (vacant).
*Librarian:* Margaret Tobin.
  The library contains 147,362 vols.
  Number of teachers: 85.
  Number of students: 1,600.

### SAINT JOSEPH'S UNIVERSITY
5600 CITY AVE., PHILADELPHIA, PENNSYLVANIA 19131
Telephone: (215) 879-7300.
Founded 1851.

Degree courses in the Liberal Arts Science, Business Administration and Military Management Studies.
*President:* Rev. Donald I. MacLean, S.J.
*Director of Admissions:* Dennis P. Farrell.
*Academic Vice-President:* Dr. Richard H. Passon.
*Registrar:* William P. Lyons.
*Librarian:* Josephine Savaro.
  The library contains 180,000 vols.
  Number of teachers: 180 full-time, 152 part-time.
  Number of students: 2,300 day, 2,400 evening, 900 graduate.

### SAINT VINCENT COLLEGE
LATROBE, PENNSYLVANIA 15650
Telephone: (412) 539-9761.
Founded 1846.

*President:* Rev. Cecil G. Diethrich.
*Academic Dean:* Rev. Campion Gavaler.
*Registrar:* Miss Mary Ellen Bayuk.
*Librarian:* Rev. F. R. Shoniker.
  The library contains 299,979 vols.
  Number of teachers: 79.
  Number of students: 896.

### SETON HILL COLLEGE
GREENSBURG, PENNSYLVANIA 15601
Telephone: (412) 834-2200.
Founded 1883.

*President:* Miss Eileen Farrell.
*Director of Admissions:* Sister Jean Boggs.
*Director of Library:* Sister Mary Ronald Madden.
  The library contains 70,000 vols.
  Number of teachers: 47 full-time, 34 part-time.
  Number of students: 951.

### SHIPPENSBURG STATE COLLEGE
SHIPPENSBURG, PENNSYLVANIA 17257
Telephone: (717) 532-9121.
Founded 1871.

*President:* Anthony F. Ceddia, D.ED.
*Vice-President (Academic Affairs):* H. Erik Shaar, PH.D.
*Vice-President (Administrative and Student Affairs):* John E. Hubley, ED.D.
*Dean of Admission:* A. Drachbar, M.ED.
*Librarian:* (vacant).
  The library contains 463,789 items.
  Number of teachers: 267.
  Number of students: 5,959.

DEANS:
*School of Arts and Sciences:* Benjamin S. Nispel, PH.D.
*School of Business:* Joseph W. Hunt.
*School of Education and Professional Studies:* Wilbur O. Carthey, ED.D.
*School of Graduate Studies and Continuing Education:* Harry M. Bobonich, PH.D.

### SLIPPERY ROCK STATE COLLEGE
SLIPPERY ROCK, PENNSYLVANIA 16057
Telephone: (412) 794-2510.
Founded 1889.

*President:* Dr. Herb F. Reinhard.
*Vice-President for Academic Affairs:* Dr. Robert N. Aebersold.
*Vice-President for Administrative Affairs:* Dr. Stephen Hulbert.
*Vice-President for Student Affairs:* Dr. C. R. Storch.
*Registrar:* Joseph C. Marks.
*Director of Admissions:* Eliott Baker.
*Director of Public Information Services:* Pamela J. W. Shingler.
*Director of Library Services:* William W. Garton.
  The library contains 406,750 vols.
  Number of teachers: 343.
  Number of students: 5,600.

DEANS:
*Faculty of Arts and Sciences:* Dr. Charles Zuzak.
*Faculty of Professional Studies:* Dr. B. W. Walker.
*Graduate and Special Programs:* Dr. William Meise.

### SUSQUEHANNA UNIVERSITY
SELINSGROVE, PENNSYLVANIA 17870
Telephone: (717) 374-0101.
Founded 1858.

*President:* Dr. Jonathan C. Messerli.
*Dean of Admissions:* Paul W. Beardslee.
*Librarian:* J. B. Smillie.
  The library contains 110,000 vols.
  Number of teachers: 110.
  Number of students: 1,473.
  Publication: *Susquehanna University Studies†.*

### SWARTHMORE COLLEGE
SWARTHMORE, PENNSYLVANIA 19081
Founded 1864 by members of the Religious Society of Friends.

*President:* Theodore W. Friend III, PH.D.
*Vice-Presidents:* Kendall Landis, M.A., Lawrence L. Landry, M.B.A.
*Registrar:* Jane H. Mullins, B.A.
*Provost:* Harrison M. Wright, PH.D.
*Librarian:* Michael Durkan, DIP. IN LIB. TRAINING.

UNIVERSITIES AND COLLEGES—PENNSYLVANIA                              U.S.A.

The library contains 579,907 vols.
Number of teachers: 133.
Number of students: 710 men, 606 women.

Publication: *Bulletin*.


## TEMPLE UNIVERSITY
BROAD ST. AND MONTGOMERY AVE., PHILADELPHIA, PENNSYLVANIA 19122

Telephone: 787-7000.

Founded 1884.

*President:* MARVIN WACHMAN, PH.D., LL.D., D.H.L.
*Director of Admissions:* R. KENNETH HALDEMAN, M.S.
*Librarian:* ARTHUR T. HAMLIN, B.S.L.S.

Library of c. 1,000,000 vols.
Number of teachers: c. 3,000.
Number of students: 33,000.

Publications: *Law Quarterly*, *The American Journal of Legal History*, *Alumni Review*, *Journal of Economics and Business*, etc.


## THIEL COLLEGE
GREENVILLE, PENNSYLVANIA 16125

Telephone: (412) 588-7700.

Founded 1866.

*President:* LOUIS T. ALMÉN, PH.D.
*Vice-President for Academic Services:* OMRO M. TODD, PH.D.
*Vice-President for Student Development and Services:* JAMES R. JUDY.
*Vice-President for Development:* GERALD R. WICKERHAM.
*Vice-President for Administrative Services:* HENRY H. HEIL.
*Director of Admissions and Financial Aid:* JOHN R. HAUSER.
*Librarian:* DOUGLAS J. CERRONI.

The library contains 108,275 vols.
Number of teachers: 64.
Number of students: 920.


## UNIVERSITY OF PENNSYLVANIA
PHILADELPHIA, PENNSYLVANIA 19104

Telephone: (215) 243-5000.

Founded 1740.

Private control; Academic year: September to May, and two six-week summer terms.

*President:* F. S. HACKNEY, M.A., PH.D.
*Provost:* T. EHRLICH, B.A., LL.B.
*Vice-Presidents:* T. W. LANGFITT, B.A., M.D., W. G. OWEN, M.S.ED.

*Associate Provost:* (vacant).
*Vice-Provost for University Life:* JANIS I. SOMERVILLE, M.B.A.
*Vice-Provost for Research:* (vacant).
*Secretary:* MARY ANN MEYERS, M.A., PH.D.
*Treasurer:* JOHN PYNE.
*Registrar:* JOHN SMOLEN, Jr., M.B.A.
*Librarian:* R. DE GENNARO, A.M., M.S.L.S.
Library: *see* Libraries.

Number of teachers: 4,722.
Number of students: 22,000.

Publications: *American Journal of Anatomy* (monthly), *American Journal of Physical Anthropology* (bi-monthly), *American Quarterly*, *Biological Abstracts* (bi-monthly), *Expedition* (quarterly), *Hispanic Review* (quarterly), *Journal of Anatomical Record* (monthly), *Journal of Cellular Physiology* (bi-monthly), *Journal of Comparative Neurology* (monthly), *Journal of Experimental Zoology* (monthly), *Journal of Morphology* (monthly), *Journal of Nutrition* (monthly), *Journal of Social Work* (annually), *Library Chronicle* (bi-annually), *Morris Arboretum Bulletin* (quarterly), *Orbis* (quarterly), *Penn Dental Journal* (monthly), *Pennsylvania Gazette* (8 issues yearly), *Pennsylvania Triangle* (monthly), *Teratology* (quarterly), *University Bulletin* (19 issues yearly), *U.P. Law Alumni Journal* (quarterly), *Veterinary Extension Quarterly*, *Wharton Quarterly*.


DEANS AND DIRECTORS:

*Faculty of Arts and Sciences:* V. GREGORIAN, PH.D.
*Wharton School:* D. C. CARROLL, M.S., PH.D.
*Wharton Graduate Division:* S. R. SAPIENZA, PH.D. (Director).
*School of Medicine:* E. J. STEMMLER, M.D.
*School of Veterinary Medicine:* R. R. MARSHAK, D.V.M.
*School of Nursing:* D. A. MERENESS, ED.D.
*School of Allied Medical Professions:* E. MICHELS, M.A.
*College of Engineering and Applied Science:* A. E. HUMPHREY, M.S., PH.D.
*Law School:* L. POLLAK, A.B., LL.B.
*Graduate School of Fine Arts:* P. F. SHEPHEARD, B.ARCH.
*Graduate School of Education:* D. H. HYMES, PH.D.
*School of Social Work:* L. T. SHOEMAKER, D.S.W.
*Annenberg School of Communications:* G. M. GERBNER, PH.D.
*School of Public and Urban Policy:* ALMARIN PHILLIPS, PH.D.
*College of General Studies:* (vacant).
*Evening School of Accounts and Finance:* R. L. MACDONALD, B.S.ECON., M.B.A. (Director).

*Summer Sessions:* (vacant).
*Dean of Admissions and Student Financial Aid:* STANLEY E. JOHNSON, A.B., TH.B.


DEPARTMENT HEADS:

ASBURY, A. K., M.D., Neurology
AUSTRIAN, R., M.D., Research Medicine
BALTZELL, G. D., PH.D., Sociology
BAUM, S., M.D., Radiology
BEDROSIAN, S. D., PH.D., Systems Engineering
BERNSTEIN, L. F., PH.D., Music
BRADY, J. P., M.D., Psychiatry
BREEDIS, C., M.D., Pathology
BRIGHT, H. J., PH.D., Biochemistry and Biophysics (acting)
BROWN, R., PH.D., Medical Technology
CARLIN, E. J., M.S., SC.D., Physical Therapy
CHANCE, B., PH.D., Biophysics in Medicine
COLANTONI, C. S., PH.D., M.S., Accounting
CONARROE, J., PH.D., English
CORTNER, J. A., M.D., Paediatrics
DALY, L. W., PH.D., Classical Archaeology
DECANI, J. S., PH.D., Statistics
DETWEILER, D. K., V.M.D., Comparative Medical Sciences
EISENBERG, L., PH.D., Energy Management and Policy
FRAYER, W., M.D., Ophthalmology
FREY, F. W., PH.D., International Relations
GINSBERG, R., PH.D., Public Policy Analysis
GLASSIE, H. H., III, M.A., PH.D., Folklore and Folklife
GOODENOUGH, W. H., PH.D., Anthropology
GOODMAN, C. S., PH.D., Marketing
GOTS, J. S., PH.D., Microbiology in Medicine
GURNSEY, L., D.D.S., Oral Surgery
HAMMOND, B. F., D.D.S., PH.D., Microbiology in Dentistry
HARKER, R. I., PH.D., Geology
HURST, G. E., PH.D., Decision Sciences
ISAACSON, D., D.D.S., Restorative Dentistry
ISARD, W., PH.D., Peace Science
JERGE, C., D.D.S., PH.D., Dental Care Systems
JOSHI, A. K., PH.D., Computer and Information Science
KAHN, C. H., PH.D., Philosophy
KATZ, S., D.D.S., Paediatric Dentistry
KEMPIN, F. G., Jr., J.D., Business Law
KOELLE, G. B., M.D., PH.D., Pharmacology
KRITCHEVSKY, D., PH.D., Molecular Biology
LAIRD, C., PH.D., Metallurgy and Materials Science
LISKER, L., PH.D., Linguistics
LLOYD, A. L., PH.D., Germanic Languages
LUBIN, J. F., M.S., PH.D., Management
MACKDISI, G., PH.D., Oriental Sciences
MANSON, L. A., PH.D., Immunology
MASTROIANNI, L., M.D., Obstetrics and Gynaecology
MCCLEARY, P., B.SC., Architecture
MCGILL, D. M., PH.D., Business and Applied Economics
MCHARG, I. L., M.L.A., M.C.P., Landscape Architecture
MELLMAN, W. J., M.D., Human Genetics
MILLER, L. D., M.D., Surgery
MOSSMAN, E. D., J.D., PH.D., Slavic Languages
MUHLY, J., PH.D., Ancient History
MURPHEY, M. G., PH.D., American Civilization
MYERS, A. L., PH.D., Chemical Engineering
NACHMIAS, J., PH.D., Psychology
NOORDERGRAAF, A., PH.D., Bioengineering
OLIET, S., D.D.S., Endodontics

PALMER, R. E. A., PH.D., Classical Studies
PAUL, B., PH.D., Mechanical Engineering and Applied Mechanics
PERLMUTTER, D. D., D.ENG., Chemical and Biochemical Engineering
PERLMUTTER, H. V., PH.D., Multinational Enterprise
RALSTON, E. L., M.D., Orthopaedic Surgery
RELMAN, A. S., M.D., Medicine
RIM, D. S., PH.D., Mathematics
ROCHER, L., PH.D., South Asian Regional Studies
ROSENBERG, C. E., PH.D., History
ROSENBLOOM, J., D.D.S., Histology and Embryology in Dentistry
ROWLANDS, D. T., M.D., Pathology
SEBOLD, R. P., PH.D., Romance Languages
SHAPIRO, I. M., L.D.S.R.C.S., M.S., PH.D., Biochemistry in Dentistry
SHELLEY, W. B., M.D., M.B., Dermatology
SHEN, B. S. P., PH.D., Astronomy
SHIP, I. I., D.D.M., Oral Medicine
SHORE, S., PH.D., Civil and Urban Engineering
SMITH, P., PH.D., Business and Applied Economics
SNOW, J. B., M.D., Oto-Rhino-Laryngology
SOULSBY, E. J. L., M.A., D.V.S.M., PH.D., M.R.C.V.S., Parasitology
SPRAGUE, J. M., PH.D., Anatomy
TAICHMAN, N. S., D.D.S., PH.D., Pathology in Dentistry
TELFER, W. H., PH.D., Biology
TEUNE, H., M.A., PH.D., Political Science
THACKRAY, A. W., PH.D., History and Sociology of Science
VALENTINE, R., M.S., Oral Hygiene
VAN DE WALLE, E., PH.D., Biochemistry and Biophysics
VANARSDALL, R., D.D.S., Periodontics (acting)
WALES, W. D., PH.D., Physics
WALTER, J. C., PH.D., Finance
WATSON, P. F., PH.D., History of Art
WEISS, L., PH.D., Animal Biology
WELLIVER, N. G., M.F.A., Fine Arts
WHITE, D., PH.D., Chemistry
WILCOX, W. C., PH.D., Microbiology
WILLIAMSON, O. E., PH.D., Economics
WINGO, L., PH.D., City and Regional Planning
WOLLMAN, H., M.D., Anaesthesia
WRIGHT, C. R., PH.D., Communications
ZEMEL, J. M., PH.D., Electrical Engineering and Science

### ATTACHED INSTITUTIONS:

**American Institute of Indian Studies.**
**Anspach Institute for Diplomacy and Foreign Affairs.**
**Bockus Research Institute.**
**Busch Center.**
**Center for Urban Research and Experiment.**
**Center for Studies in Criminology and Criminal Law.**
**Center for the Study of Financial Institutions.**
**G. S. Cox Medical Research Institute.**
**W. H. Donner Center for Radiology.**
**Econometric Forecasting Unit.**
**Economic Research Unit.**
**Fels Center for Government.**
**Foreign Policy Research Institute.**
**Henry Phipps Institute of Genetics and Community Diseases.**
**Huebner Foundation for Insurance.**
**Industrial Research Unit.**
**Institute for Direct Energy Conversion.**
**Institute for Environmental Medicine.**
**Institute for Environmental Studies.**
**Institute for International Studies of Values in Politics.**
**Institute for Medieval Japanese Studies.**
**Institute of Contemporary Art.**
**Institute of Electrical and Electronics Engineers.**
**Institute of Gastroenterology.**
**Institute of Gynecologic Research.**
**Institute for Neurological Sciences.**
**Laboratory for Research on the Structure of Matter.**
**Leonard Davis Institute of Health Economics.**
**Management and Behavioral Science Center.**
**Monell Chemical Senses Center.**
**Morris Arboretum.**
**National Center for Energy Management and Power.**
**Near East Center.**
**Oral Health Research Center.**
**Philadelphia Center for Research in Child Growth.**
**Population Studies Center.**
**Prison Research Council.**
**Valley Forge Research and Education Center.**
**Wharton Entrepreneurial Center.**

## UNIVERSITY OF PITTSBURGH
PITTSBURGH, PENNSYLVANIA 15260
Telephone: (412) 624-4141.
Telex: 81-2466.

Founded 1787 as Pittsburgh Academy; in 1819 became Western University of Pennsylvania, and in 1908 University of Pittsburgh.

Private control, State-related; Academic year: September to August (three terms).

*Chancellor:* W. W. POSVAR, PH.D.
*Assistant Chancellor:* EDWARD E. BOZIK.
*Senior Vice-Chancellor and Provost:* R. A. SMITH, PH.D.
*Senior Vice-Chancellor for Health Sciences:* EDISON MONTGOMERY, B.A.
*Senior Vice-Chancellor for Administration:* JACK E. FREEMAN, PH.D.
*Vice-Chancellor (Public Affairs):* B. J. KOBOSKY, PH.D.
*Vice-Chancellor (Business and Finance):* J. A. DUTTON, Jr., B.S.
*Vice-Chancellor, Student Affairs:* CONNEY M. KIMBO, PH.D.
*Secretary of the Board of Trustees:* JOHN R. QUATROCHE, PH.D.
*Registrar:* FRANK F. REED, B.S.
*Director, University Libraries:* G. E. ROSSELL.

Number of teachers: 2,285 full-time, 560 part-time.

Number of students: 17,066 full-time, 11,715 part-time.

### DEANS:

*College of Arts and Sciences:* I. J. SCHULMAN.
*Faculty of Arts and Sciences:* J. L. ROSENBERG.
*Graduate Studies:* E. BARANGER.
*Graduate School of Business:* H. J. ZOFFER.
*Graduate School of Public and International Affairs:* J. FUNARI.
*Graduate School of Public Health:* H. E. GRIFFIN.
*Graduate School of Social Work:* D. E. EPPERSON.
*School of Dental Medicine:* E. J. FORREST.
*School of Education:* J. KELLY, Jr.
*School of Engineering:* M. L. WILLIAMS, Jr.
*School of General Studies:* J. S. GOW, Jr.
*School of Health Related Professions:* A. PASCASIO.
*School of Law:* J. E. MURRAY, Jr.
*School of Library and Information Science:* T. J. GALVIN.
*School of Medicine:* D. F. LEON.
*School of Nursing:* E. GOLDBERG.
*School of Pharmacy:* L. DITTERT.

### CHAIRMEN OF DEPARTMENTS:

*Arts and Sciences:*
*Anthropology:* J. RICHARDSON III.
*Biological Sciences:* M. SUSSMAN.
*Black Studies:* R. PENNY.
*Chemistry:* D. M. HERCULES.
*Classics:* H. AVERY.
*Computer Science:* O. TAULBEE.
*Crystallography:* G. A. JEFFREY.
*East Asian Language and Literature:* D. MILLS.
*Economics:* J. CHAPMAN.
*English:* M. L. BRISCO.
*Fine Arts:* J. W. WILLIAMS.
*French and Italian Language and Literature:* W. ALBERT.
*Geography:* H. V. B. KLINE.
*Geology and Planetary Sciences:* E. G. LIDIAK.
*Germanic Language and Literature:* D. ASHLIMAN.
*Hispanic Language and Literature:* K. A. McDUFFIE.
*History:* S. DRESCHER.
*History and Philosophy of Science:* P. MACHAMER.
*Linguistics:* C. PAULSTON.
*Mathematics and Statistics:* W. DESKINS.
*Music:* D. FRANKLIN.
*Philosophy:* N. RESCHER.
*Physics and Astronomy:* M. GARFUNKEL.
*Political Science:* M. S. OGUL.
*Psychology:* F. B. COLVITA.
*Religious Studies:* F. CLOTHEY.
*Slavic Language and Literature:* J. G. HARRIS.
*Sociology:* T. J. FERRARO.
*Speech and Theatre Arts:* J. MATTHEWS.
*Studio Arts:* V. CANTINI.

*Engineering:*
*Chemical and Petroleum:* T. Y. SHAH.
*Civil:* J. I. ABRAMS.
*Electrical:* R. C. COLCLASER.
*Industrial:* A. G. HOLZMAN.
*Mechanical:* C. C. YATES.
*Metallurgy and Materials:* F. S. PETTIT.

*Education:*
*Educational Development and Service:* W. B. SMITH.
*Teacher Development:* H. SOUTHWORTH.
*Educational Studies Specialized Professional Development:* F. HAMMERMEISTER.
*Educational Studies:* N. MULGRAVE.

*Dental Medicine:*
*Anatomy:* R. MUNDELL.
*Anaesthesiology:* C. R. BENNETT.
*Behavioural Sciences:* D. C. KRUPER.
*Biochemistry:* F. DRAUS.
*Cleft Palate Center:* B. J. McWILLIAMS.
*Microbiology:* D. PLATT.
*Oral Hygiene and Dental Assisting:* R. FRIEDMAN.
*Oral Surgery:* S. S. SPATZ.
*Orthodontics:* V. SASSOUNI.
*Diagnostic Services:* R. S. VERBIN.
*Pedodontics:* R. RAPP.
*Periodontics:* J. C. CONWAY.
*Pharmacology, Physiology:* J. GILBERTSON.
*Prosthodontics:* Y. H. ISMAIL.
*Community Dentistry:* M. E. NICHOLSON.

*Pharmacy:*
*Medical Chemistry:* D. J. ABRAHAM.
*Pharmacognosy:* P. J. SCHIFF.
*Pharmaceutics:* T. R. BATES.
*Pharmacy Practice:* R. P. JUHL.

*Graduate School of Public Health:*
*Biostatistics:* P. ENTERLINE.
*Epidemiology:* L. H. KULLER.
*Health Services Administration:* G. K. MACLEOD.
*Industrial Environmental Health Sciences:* Y. ALARIE.
*Microbiology:* M. HO.
*Radiation Health:* N. WALD.

*School of Health Related Professions:*
*Child Development and Child Care:* N. E. CURRY.
*Health Records Administration:* E. B. ANDERSON.
*Medical Technology:* A. C. ALBERS.
*Interdisciplinary Programmes:* F. GEIGEL-BENTZ.

ATTACHED RESEARCH CENTERS:

**Learning Research and Development Center:** Dirs. ROBERT GLASER, LAUREN B. RESNICK.

**Knowledge Availability Systems Center:** Dir. ALLEN KENT.

**Space Research Co-ordination Center:** Dir. FREDERICK KAUFMAN.

**University Center for International Studies:** Dir. BURKART HOLZNER.

**History and Philosophy of Science Center:** Dir. LAURENS L. LAUDEN.

**University Center for Social and Urban Research:** Dir. VIJAI P. SINGH.

## UNIVERSITY OF SCRANTON
SCRANTON,
PENNSYLVANIA 18510

Telephone: (717) 961-7400.

Founded 1888.

*President:* Rev. WILLIAM J. BYRON, S.J.
*Academic Vice-President:* VINCENT PONKO, PH.D.
*Executive Vice-President:* Rev. HENRY J. BUTLER, S.J.
*Treasurer:* ROBERT T. RYDER.
*Registrar:* Z. E. LAWHON.
*Librarian:* KENNETH OBEREMBT, PH.D.
Number of teachers: 180.
Number of students: 4,900.

Publications: *Best Sellers*, *The Scranton Journal* (quarterly), *Windhover* (yearbook), *Esprit* (literary magazine), *Aquinas* (student newspaper).

DEANS:

*College of Arts and Sciences:* Dr. W. PARENTE.
*Graduate School:* Dr. H. B. STRICKLAND.
*Dexter Hanley College:* CHARLES J. BUCKLEY.
*School of Management:* Dr. HENRY A. AMATO.

## URSINUS COLLEGE
COLLEGEVILLE,
PENNSYLVANIA 19426

Telephone: (215) 489-4111.

Founded 1869.

*President:* R. P. RICHTER.
*Dean of Admissions:* K. L. SCHAEFER.
*Librarian:* H. E. BROADBENT.
The library contains 161,000 vols.
Number of teachers: 90.
Number of students: 1,128 day, 800 evening.

## VILLA MARIA COLLEGE
2551 WEST LAKE RD.,
ERIE, PENNSYLVANIA 16505

Telephone: 838-1966.

Founded 1925.

*President:* Sister M. LAWREACE ANTOUN.
*Vice-President for Academic Affairs and Academic Dean:* Sister MARY MARK DOUBET.
*Dean, Erie Institute for Nursing:* Dr. DOROTHY J. NOVELLO.

*Vice-President for External Affairs:* DENNIS STEFANACCI.
*Vice-President for Finance and Planning:* Sister JEAN BAPTISTE DILUZIO.
*Vice-President for Student Affairs:* Dr. JOANN D. PAINTER.
*Registrar:* Sister JOAN THOMAS.
*Librarian:* Sister MARY THOMAS DOWNING.
The library contains 52,000 vols.
Number of teachers: 78.
Number of students: 652.

Publication: *Villécrit*.

## VILLANOVA UNIVERSITY
VILLANOVA,
PENNSYLVANIA 19085

Founded 1842.

*President:* Rev. JOHN M. DRISCOLL, O.S.A.
*Vice-President for Academic Affairs:* Dr. JAMES J. CLEARY.
*Vice-President for Financial Affairs:* Rev. GEORGE F. BURNELL, O.S.A.
*Vice-President for Student Life:* Rev. JOHN E. DEEGAN, O.S.A.
*Vice-President for University Relations:* Rev. GEORGE F. RILEY, O.S.A.
*Vice-President, Administration:* Rev. PATRICK RICE, O.S.A.
*Librarian:* Rev. L. A. RONGIONE, O.S.A.
Number of teachers: 454 full-time, 88 part-time, total 542.
Number of students: 9,300.

Publications: *Villanova University Bulletin*, *Religion and the Public Order*, *Villanova Law Review*, *Spires*.

DEANS:

*Engineering:* Dr. ROBERT D. LYNCH.
*Arts and Science:* Rev. JOHN O'MALLEY, O.S.A.
*Commerce and Finance:* ALVIN A. CLAY.
*Nursing:* M. LOUISE FITZPATRICK.
*Law:* J. WILLARD O'BRIEN.

## WASHINGTON AND JEFFERSON COLLEGE
WASHINGTON,
PENNSYLVANIA 15301

Washington Academy chartered 1787, rechartered as Washington College 1806; Jefferson Academy (Canonsburg) chartered 1794, rechartered as Jefferson College 1802; Colleges united 1865.

*President:* H. J. BURNETT, PH.D.
*Dean of College:* H. E. WYLEN, PH.D.
*Dean of Institutional Planning:* F. J. FRANK, PH.D.
*Registrar:* A. J. AMENDOLA, B.A.
*Dean of Students:* D. K. SCARBOROUGH, PH.D.
*Librarian:* R. E. CONNELL, M.L.S.
The library contains 171,677 vols.
Number of teachers: 95.
Number of students: 1,000.

Publications: *Topic*†, *W & J News*, *Catalogue*.

## WAYNESBURG COLLEGE
WAYNESBURG, PENNSYLVANIA 15370
Telephone: (412) 627-8191.

Founded 1849. Liberal Arts and Sciences.

*President:* Joseph F. Marsh.
*Vice-President for Academic Affairs:* G. W. Smith.
*Vice-President for Business and Finance:* C. B. Stoy.
*Vice-President for Development:* Jerry L. Beasley.
*Vice-President for Student Life:* R. W. Cahn.
*Registrar:* Robert J. Hurd.
*Director of Admissions and Financial Aid:* Ronald L. Shunk.
*Librarian:* Miss T. Viarengo.

The library contains 117,000 vols.
Number of teachers: 54 full-time, 19 part-time.
Number of students: 882.

## WEST CHESTER STATE COLLEGE
WEST CHESTER, PENNSYLVANIA 19380
Telephone: (215) 436-2471.

Founded 1871.

*President:* Dr. Charles G. Mayo.
*Director of Admissions:* William E. Kipp.
*Librarian:* F. Q. Helms.

The library contains 385,000 vols.
Number of teachers: 512.
Number of students: 8.600.

Publications: *Serpentine*, *College Literature*.

## WESTMINSTER COLLEGE
NEW WILMINGTON, PENNSYLVANIA 16142
Founded 1852.
(Related to United Presbyterian Church in the U.S.A.)

*President:* Earland I. Carlson, PH.D.
*Dean:* P. A. Lewis, PH.D.
*Dean of Students:* William McK. Wright, ED.D.
*Director of Admissions:* Edwin G. Tobin, ED.D.
*Registrar:* D. L. McLaughlin, M.ED.
*Librarian:* F. E. Smith, M.L.S.

The library contains 190,000 vols.
Number of teachers: 111.
Number of students: 1,610 undergraduates, 174 graduates.

Publications: *Holcad* (newspaper), *Scrawl* (literary), *Argo* (yearbook).

## WIDENER UNIVERSITY
CHESTER, PENNSYLVANIA 19013
Telephone: (215) 499-4000.
Founded 1821; formerly PMC Colleges.

*President:* Robert J. Bruce.
*Chancellor:* Dr. Clarence R. Moll.
*Provost:* Dr. Norman P. Auburn.
*Dean:* Dr. Joel M. Rodney.
*Librarian:* Theresa Taborsky.

The library contains 327,000 vols.
Number of teachers: 198 full-time, 245 part-time.
Number of students: 3,649 full-time, 3,109 part-time.
Publications: *Bulletin*†, *Summer Sessions Bulletin*†, *Alumni Magazines*†.

### Deans:
*Center of Arts and Science:* Dr. Lawrence P. Buck.
*Center of Engineering:* Dr. Thomas G. McWilliams, Jr.
*Center of Management and Applied Economics:* Dr. John T. Meli.
*Center of Nursing:* Dr. Janette L. Packer.
*University College:* Dr. Peter K. Mills.
*Delaware Law School:* J. Kirkland Grant.
*Brandywine College:* Dr. Andrew A. Bushko.
*School of Hotel and Restaurant Management:* Nicholas J. Hadgis.

## WILKES COLLEGE
WILKES-BARRE, PENNSYLVANIA 18766
Telephone: (717) 824-4651.

Founded 1933.

*President:* Robert S. Capin.
*Dean of Academic Affairs:* Gerald E. Hartdagen.
*Dean of Health Sciences:* Ralph B. Rozelle.
*Dean of Admissions:* Gerald K. Wuori.
*Registrar:* Doris Barker.
*Librarian:* Dale Buehler.

The library contains 278,050 vols.
Number of teachers: 156 full-time.
Number of students: 2,100 full-time.

## WILSON COLLEGE
CHAMBERSBURG, PENNSYLVANIA 17201
Founded 1869.

*President* Dr. Mary-Linda Merriam.
*Director of Admissions:* Frank J. Kamus.
*Librarian:* Alice Ingraham.

The library contains 155,349 vols.
Number of teachers: 34.
Number of students: 225.

Publication: *View Book and Catalogue*.

# RHODE ISLAND

## BARRINGTON COLLEGE
MIDDLE HIGHWAY, BARRINGTON, RHODE ISLAND 02806
Telephone: (401) 246-1200.

Founded 1900.

Liberal Arts, Education, Business and Computer Science, Biblical Studies, Music, Biology, Chemistry, Marine Biology, Mathematics and Computer Science, Philosophy, Psychology, Social Work, Youth Ministries and American Studies.

*President:* David G. Horner.
*Academic Dean:* Dr. Muriel Radke.
*Registrar:* Mrs. Lucille Wooding.
*Librarian:* Miss Eleanor Wilson.

The library contains 62,000 vols.
Number of teachers: 61.
Number of students: c. 500.

## BROWN UNIVERSITY
PROVIDENCE, RHODE ISLAND 02912
Telephone: (401) 863-1000.

Founded 1764.

Academic year: September to May.

*President:* H. R. Swearer, PH.D., LL.D.
*Chancellor:* R. Salmon, PH.B., LL.D.
*Vice-Chancellor:* T. J. Watson, Jr., A.B., L.H.D., LL.D.
*Secretary:* A. H. D. Joslin, A.B., LL.B.
*Treasurer:* A. M. Hunt.
*Provost:* M. Glicksman, PH.D.
*Vice-President for Biology and Medicine:* Pierre M. Galletti, M.D., PH.D.
*Vice-President for Administration and Finance:* R. J. Ramsden, M.B.A.
*Vice-President for University Relations:* R. A. Reichley, M.A.
*Registrar of the University:* M. E. Noble, A.B.
*Librarian:* C. J. Schmidt, PH.D.

Number of teaching and research faculty: 965.
Number of students: 6,784.

Publications: *Quarterly of Applied Mathematics*, *Brown University Studies*, *Colver Lectures*, *American History Research Center Publications*, *Brown Egyptological Studies*, *Brown University Slavic Reprint Series*, *Novel A Forum on Fiction*.

### Deans:
*Faculty:* M. Glicksman, PH.D.
*Graduate School:* E. S. Frerichs, PH.D.
*College:* H. W. Sheridan, PH.D.
*Admission:* J. H. Rogers, ED.M.
*Medicine:* S. M. Aronson, M.D.
*Biological Sciences:* R. J. Goss, PH.D.

### Professors:
Accola .R. D. M., PH.D., Mathematics
Adamsons, K., M.D., PH.D., Obstetrics and Gynaecology

AHLBERG, J. H., PH.D., Applied Mathematics
AMOR Y VAZQUEZ, J., PH.D., Hispanic Studies
ARANT, P. M., PH.D., Slavic Languages
ARCHAMBAULT, R. D., ED.D., Education
ARONSON, S. M., M.D., Medical Science
AVERY, D. H., SC.D., Engineering
BAIRD, J. C., Jr., PH.D., Chemistry and Physics
BALDINI, M. G., M.D., Medical Science
BANCHOFF, T. F., PH.D., Mathematics
BANKS, H. T., PH.D., Applied Mathematics
BARLOW, D. H., PH.D., Psychiatry and Human Behaviour
BARNHILL, J. O., A.M., M.F.A., Theatre Arts
BAUER, C., PH.D., French
BAUM, P. F., PH.D., Mathematics
BECKMANN, M. J., DR.RER.POL., Economics
BEISER, E. N., PH.D., Political Science
BEYER, R. T., PH.D., Physics
BIGGINS, J., PH.D., Biology
BLISTEIN, E. M., PH.D., English
BLOUGH, D. S., Psychology
BOEGEHOLD, A. L., PH.D., Classics
BOLLE, D. M., PH.D., Engineering
BORTS, G. H., PH.D., Economics
BOULGER, J. D., PH.D., English
BRAY, P. J., PH.D., Physics
BROWDER, A., PH.D., Mathematics
CALABRESI, P., M.D., Medical Science
CAMINOS, R. A., PH.D., Egyptology
CARLETON, R. A., M.D., Medicine
CARPENTER, G. B., PH.D., Chemistry
CASSILL, R. V., M.A., English
CASWELL, B., PH.D., Engineering
CHA, S., M.D., PH.D., Medical Science
CHAMPA, K., PH.D., Art
CHAPPLE, W. M., PH.D., Geological Science
CHISHOLM, R. M., PH.D., Philosophy
CHURCH, R. M., PH.D., Psychology
CLAPP, L. B., PH.D., PD.D., Chemistry
CLARKE, J. H., PH.D., Engineering
CLIFTON, R. J., PH.D., Engineering
COBB, S., M.D., Medical Science
COLE, R. H., PH.D., Chemistry
COLEMAN, J. R., PH.D., Biology
COOK, A., M.A., Comparative Literature
COOPER, D. B., PH.D., Engineering
COOPER, L. N., PH.D., Physics
CORBIT, J. D., PH.D., Psychology
CORNWELL, E. E., Jr., PH.D., Political Science
CURTIS, L. P., Jr., PH.D., History
CZECH, M. P., PH.D., Medical Science
DAFERMOS, C., PH.D., Applied Mathematics
DAVIDS, A., PH.D., Psychology
DAVIS, P. J., PH.D., Applied Mathematics
DAVIS, R. P., M.D., Medical Science
DIETRICH, W. S., PH.D., Religious Studies
DINNEEN, W., A.M., Music
DOBBINS, R. A., PH.D., Engineering
DONOVAN, B. E., PH.D., Classics
DUFFY, J. W., PH.D., Engineering
DUPREE, A. H., PH.D., History
DURAND, F., PH.D., Hispanic and Italian Studies
EBNER, F. F., PH.D., Medical Science
EDWARDS, J. O., PH.D., Chemistry
EIMAS, P. D., Psychology
ELBAUM, C., PH.D., Physics
ELLIS, R. A., PH.D., Biology
ENGEN, T., PH.D., Psychology
ERIKSON, G. E., PH.D., Medical Science
ESCHENBACHER, H. F., ED.D., Education
ESTRUP, P. J. Z., PH.D., Physics and Chemistry
FAIN, J. N., PH.D., Medical Science
FALB, P. L., PH.D., Applied Mathematics
FALLIEROS, S., PH.D., Physics
FANGER, H., M.D., Medical Science
FAUSTO, N., M.D., Medical Science
FEDERER, H., PH.D., Mathematics
FELDMAN, D., PH.D., Physics
FELDMAN, W. S., M.F.A., Art

FENTON, P. F., PH.D., Biology
FIDO, F., DOTT.LITT., Italian Studies
FINDLEY, W. N., SC.M. IN ENG., A.M., Engineering
FISCHER, G. A., PH.D., Biochemical Pharmacology
FISHMAN, R., M.F.A., Art
FLEMING, W. H., PH.D., Mathematics and Applied Mathematics
FORNARA, C. W., PH.D., Classics and History
FREIBERGER, W., PH.D., Applied Mathematics
FRERICHS, E. S., PH.D., Religious Studies
FREUND, L. B., PH.D., Engineering
FRIED, H. M., PH.D., Physics
FULTON, W. E., PH.D., Mathematics
GALLETTI, P. M., M.D., PH.D., Medical Science
GANN, D. S., M.D., Surgery
GERRITSEN, H. J., PH.D., Physics
GILETTI, B. J., PH.D., Geological Sciences
GLEASON, A., PH.D., History
GLICKSMAN, A. S., M.D., Medical Science
GLICKSMAN, M., PH.D., Engineering
GLICKSTEIN, M., PH.D., Psychology
GOLD, E., M.D., Obstetrics and Gynaecology
GOLDSTEIN, L., PH.D., Medical Science
GOLDSTEIN, S., PH.D., Sociology
GOODMAN, E. R., PH.D., Political Science
GOSS, R. J., PH.D., Biology
GRANGER, C. V., M.D., Community Health
GRAUBARD, S. R., PH.D., History
GREENE, E. F., PH.D., Chemistry
GREER, D. S., M.D., Community Health
GRENANDER, U., PH.D., Probability and Statistics
GRIEDER, J. B., PH.D., History
GROSSMAN, H., PH.D., Economics
GURALNIK, J. S., PH.D., Physics
GURLAND, J., SC.D., Engineering
HAGY, G. W., PH.D., Biology
HALE, J. K., PH.D., Applied Mathematics
HAMOLSKY, M. W., M.D., Medical Science
HARPER, M. S., M.A., English
HARRIS, B., PH.D., Mathematics
HARROWER, H. W., M.D., Surgery
HAWKES, J., A.B., English
HAZELTINE, B., PH.D., Engineering
HEATH, D. B., PH.D., Anthropology
HELLER, G. S., PH.D., Engineering
HERNDON, J. H., M.D., Orthopaedic Surgery
HIRSCH, D. W., PH.D., English
HOLLOWAY, R. R., PH.D., Classical Archaeology
HONIG, E., A.M., English and Comparative Literature
HOPKINS, R. W., PH.D., Medical Science
HOUGHTON, A., PH.D., Physics
HSIEH, D. Y., PH.D., Applied Mathematics
IMBRIE, J., PH.D., Geological Sciences
INFANTE, E., PH.D., Applied Mathematics
JAY, R. R., PH.D., Anthropology
JAYNE, S., PH.D., English and Comparative Literature
JONES, F., PH.D., Psychology
JORDY, W. H., PH.D., Art
KANG, K., PH.D., Physics
KARLSON, K. E., M.D., Medical Science
KARLSSON, S. K. F., PH.D., Engineering
KAU, Y. M., PH.D., Political Science
KESTIN, J., PH.D., D.I.C., D.SC., Engineering
KIDWELL, J. F., PH.D., Biology
KING, M. T., PH.D., Chemistry
KIRKPATRICK, L. B., Political Science
KLING, J. W., PH.D., Psychology
KNOPF, P. N., PH.D., Medical Science
KOLSKY, H., PH.D., D.SC., Applied Physics
KORNHAUSER, E. T., PH.D., Engineering
KOSSOFF, A. D., PH.D., Hispanic Studies
KOSTERLITZ, J. M., PH.D., Physics
KRAUSE, D., PH.D., English

KUCERA, H., PH.D., Slavic Languages and Linguistics
KUHN, R., PH.D., French Studies and Comparative Literature
KUSHNER, H. J., PH.D., Applied Mathematics and Engineering
LADD, J., PH.D., Philosophy
LANDOW, G. P., PH.D., English
LANDY, A., PH.D., Medical Science
LANOU, R. E., PH.D., Physics
LASALLE, J. P., PH.D., Applied Mathematics
LAURENT, D., Music
LAWLER, R. G., PH.D., Chemistry
LEDERBERG, S., PH.D., Biology
LEDUC, E. H., PH.D., Biology
LEIS, P. E., PH.D., Anthropology
LENZ, J. W., PH.D., Philosophy
LEONE, L. A., M.A., Medicine
LEVIN, F. S., PH.D., Physics
LEWALSKI, B. K., PH.D., English
LIEBERMAN, P., PH.D., Linguistics
LIPSITT, L. P., PH.D., Psychology and Medical Science
LITCHMAN, H. C., M.D., Medical Science
LIU, J. T., PH.D., Engineering
LOFERSKI, J. J., PH.D., Engineering
LONGABAUGH, R., A.M.T., ED.D., Psychiatry and Human Behaviour
LUBIN, J. D., PH.D., Mathematics
LYON, B., PH.D., History
McDONALD, C. J., M.D., Medical Science
McENANY, M. T., M.D., Surgery
McILWAIN, J. T., M.D., Medical Science
McLOUGHLIN, W. G., Jr., PH.D., History
MACPHERSON, R. D., PH.D., Mathematics
MAEDER, P. F., PH.D., Engineering
MAJEWSKI, H., PH.D., French Studies
MARIS, H. J., PH.D., Physics
MARSH, R. M., PH.D., Sociology
MARSHALL, J. M., PH.D., Medical Science
MARTEL, M. U., PH.D., Sociology
MASON, E. A., PH.D., Chemistry and Engineering
MASON, R. G., M.D., Medical Science
MASSIMO, J. T., PH.D., Physics
MATTHEWS, R. K., PH.D., Geological Sciences
MAXSON, D. R., PH.D., Physics
MAYFIELD, D. G., M.D., Psychiatry and Human Behaviour
MILHAVEN, J. G., PH.D., Religious Studies
MILLWARD, R. B., PH.D., Psychology
MOEHRING, H. R., PH.D., Religious Studies
MOLHO, A., PH.D., History
MONTEIRO, G., PH.D., English, Portuguese and Brazilian Studies
MORGAN, G. W., PH.D., University Course
MORSE, D. H., PH.D., Biology
MORSE, T. F., PH.D., Engineering
MUSLINER, T., M.D., Medicine
MUTCH, T. A., PH.D., Geological Sciences
MYLONAS, C., PH.D., Engineering
NACE, H. R., PH.D., Chemistry
NELSON, R., D.MUS., Music
NEU, C., PH.D., History
NEUSNER, J., PH.D., Religious Studies
NICHOLS, C. H., PH.D., English
NOMIZU, K., PH.D., SC.D., Mathematics
NORDLINGER, E. A., PH.D., Political Science
OH, W., M.D., Medical Science
PADDEN, R. C., PH.D., History
PARKS, R. E., Jr., M.D., PH.D., Medical Science
PATTERSON, J. T., PH.D., History
PEARSON, A. E., PH.D., Engineering
PECK, R. A., Jr., PH.D., Physics
PERKINS, W. T., PH.D., Political Science
PFAUTZ, H. W., PH.D., Sociology
PINGREE, D. E., PH.D., History of Mathematics
PIPKIN, A. C., PH.D., Applied Mathematics
POOLE, W., PH.D., Economics
POTTER, R. G., Jr., PH.D., Sociology
POVAR, M. I., M.D., Medical Sciences
PUTNAM, M. C. J., PH.D., Classics

QUEVEDO, W. C., Jr., PH.D., Biology
QUINN, J. J., PH.D., Physics
QUINN, P. L., PH.D., Philosophy
REEDER, J. P., PH.D., Religious Studies
RIBBANS, G., PH.D., Hispanic Studies
RICE, J. R., PH.D., Engineering
RICH, N., PH.D., History
RICHARDSON, P. D., PH.D., Engineering
RICHMAN, M. H., SC.D., Engineering
RIDGELY, B. S., PH.D., French Studies
RIEGER, P. H., PH.D., Chemistry
RISEN, W. M., Jr., PH.D., Chemistry
ROESSLER, B., SC.D., Engineering
ROHR, D. G., PH.D., History
ROSEN, M. I., PH.D., Mathematics
ROSENBERG, B. A., PH.D., English and American Civilization
ROTHMAN, F. G., PH.D., Biology
ROTMAN, M. B., PH.D., Medical Science
RUESCHEMEYER, D., DR.RER.POL., Sociology
RYDER, H. E., PH.D., Economics
SABOL, A. J., PH.D., English
SACHS, A. J., PH.D., History of Mathematics
ST. ARMAND, B. L., PH.D., English
SAKODA, J. M., PH.D., Sociology
SATO, R., PH.D., Economics
SAVAGE, J. E., PH.D., Computer Science and Engineering
SCHEVILL, J. E., SC.B., English
SCHMITT, A. E., PH.D., German
SCHMITT, R. G., PH.D., Philosophy
SCHNERR, W. J., PH.-., Hispanic and Italian Studies
SCHOLES, R. E., PH.D., English and Comparative Literature
SCHRIER, A. M., PH.D., Psychology
SCHULZ, J., PH.D., Art
SCHUPACK, M. B., PH.D., Economics
SCHWARTZ, R. A., M.D., Medical Science
SEGAL, C. P., PH.D., Classics and Comparative Literature
SEIDEL, G. M., PH.D., Physics
SENFT, A. W., M.D., Medical Sciences
SHAPIRO, A. M., PH.D., Physics
SHEPP, B. E., PH.D., Psychology
SHERMAN, S. C., LITT.D., Bibliography
SHROEDER, J. W., PH.D., English
SIBULKIN, M., M.S. IN M.E., AE.E., A.M., Engineering
SINGER, D. B., M.D., Pathology
SIROVICH, L., PH.D., Applied Mathematics
SLABY, A., M.D., PH.D., Psychiatry and Human Behaviour
SORRENTINO, R., PH.D., Psychology
SOSA, E., PH.D., Philosophy
SPILKA, M., PH.D., English and Comparative Literature
STEIM, J. M., PH.D., Chemistry
STEIN, J. L., PH.D., Economics
STEINER, M., M.D., Medicine
STERN, L., M.D., Medical Sciences
STEWART, F. M., PH.D., Mathematics
STEWART, P. A., PH.D., Medical Science
STILES, P. J., PH.D., Physics
STRAUSS, W. A., PH.D., Mathematics
STULTZ, N. M., PH.D., Political Science
STURNER, W. Q., M.D., Pathology
SU, C. H., PH.D., Applied Mathematics
SYMONDS, P. S., PH.D., Engineering
TAUC, J., ING.DR., Engineering and Physics
TEFFT, M., M.D., Radiation Medicine
TERRAS, V., PH.D., Slavic Languages and Comparative Literature
THAYER, W. R., Jr., Medical Science
THOMAS, J. L., PH.D., History
TOMAS, V. A., PH.D., Philosophy
TOOMER, G. J., M.A., History of Mathematics
TOWNLEY, H., A.M., Art
TRUEBLOOD, A. S., PH.D., Hispanic Studies and Comparative Literature
TURNER, M., M.D., Medicine
UNDERDOWN, D. E., A.M., History

VAN DAM, A., PH.D., Computer Science and Applied Mathematics
VAN NOSTRAND, A. D., PH.D., English
VARGAS, L. L., M.D., Medical Science
WARD, H. R., PH.D., Chemistry
WEGNER, P., PH.D., Computer Science and Applied Mathematics
WEIMAR, K. S., PH.D., German
WEINER, J. H., PH.D., Engineering and Physics
WEINSTEIN, A., PH.D., Comparative Literature and French Studies
WEISZ, P. B., PH.D., PED.D., Biology
WERMER, J., PH.D., Mathematics
WESSEN, A. F., PH.D., Sociology and Medical Science
WESTERVELT, P. J., PH.D., Physics
WILLIAMS, L. E., PH.D., History
WILMETH, D. B., PH.D., Theatre Arts and English
WINNER, T. G., PH.D., Slavic Languages and Comparative Literature
WOLD, A., PH.D., Chemistry and Engineering
WOLOVICH, W. A., PH.D., Engineering
WOOD, G. S., PH.D., History
WORKMAN, J. R., PH.D., Classics
WRENN, J. J., PH.D., Linguistics
WYATT, W. F., Jr., PH.D., Classics
YUND, R. A., PH.D., Geological Sciences
ZACKS, S. I., M.D., Pathology
ZIMMER, B. G., PH.D., Sociology and Urban Studies
ZIMMERING, S., PH.D., Biology

## BRYANT COLLEGE
SMITHFIELD,
RHODE ISLAND 02917

Founded 1863.

*President:* WILLIAM T. O'HARA.
*Vice-President for Academic Affairs:* WALLACE A. WOOD.
*Vice-President for Institutional Development:* DENNIS MACRO.
*Vice-President for Student Affairs:* LESLIE L. LaFOND.
*Vice-President for Business Affairs:* ALTON MOTT.
*Dean of Admissions:* ROY A. NELSON.
*Dean of Undergraduate Faculty:* STANLEY KOZIKOWSKI.
*Dean of Graduate School:* GEORGE DE TARNOWSKY.
*Dean of Academic Administration and Registrar:* RICHARD F. ALBERG.
*Director of Library Services:* J. P. HANNON.

The library contains over 100,000 vols.

Number of students: 4,990.

Publications: *Bulletin of Bryant College, Catalog, Alumni Bulletin, Career Bulletin, Introducing Bryant.*

## NEWPORT COLLEGE-SALVE REGINA
NEWPORT, RHODE ISLAND 02840

Telephone: (401) 847-6650.

Founded 1947.

Private control (Religious Sisters of Mercy).

*President:* Dr. LUCILLE MCKILLOP, R.S.M.

*Vice-President/Academic Dean and Provost:* Dr. SHEILA MEGLEY, R.S.M.
*Treasurer:* JAMES C. COLTON.
*Vice-President/Institutional Advancement:* Dr. THERESE ANTONE, R.S.M.
*Vice-President/Dean of Faculty:* Dr. WILLIAM BURRELL.
*Dean of Admissions:* CHRISTOPHER KIERNAN.
*Dean of Campus Ministry:* KAREN DOBSON.
*Dean of Student Development:* BARBARA SYLVIA.

The library contains 86,000 vols.
Number of teachers: 170.
Number of students: 1,700.

## PROVIDENCE COLLEGE
PROVIDENCE,
RHODE ISLAND 02918

Telephone: (401) 865-1000.

Founded 1917.

*Chancellor:* Very Rev. VINCENT C. DORE, O.P.
*President:* Very Rev. T. R. PETERSON, O.P., PH.D.
*Director of Admissions:* M. G. BACKES.
*Registrar:* Dr. L. GOUSIE.
*Librarian:* JOSEPH H. DOHERTY.

The library contains 23,5568 vols.
Number of teachers: 238.
Number of students: 3,500.

## RHODE ISLAND COLLEGE
600 MOUNT PLEASANT AVE.,
PROVIDENCE,
RHODE ISLAND 02908

Telephone: 456-8000.

Founded 1854.

*President:* DAVID E. SWEET.
*Vice-President for Academic Affairs:* E. M. McMAHON.
*Vice-President for Student Affairs:* GARY M. PENFIELD.
*Vice-President for Administrative Services:* JOHN NAZARIAN.
*Executive Director of College Budget and Management:* JOHN SPEER.
*Director of Records:* BURT D. CROSS.
*Director of Admissions:* JAMES COLMAN.
*Executive Director for Advancement and Support:* JOHN FOLEY.
*Librarian:* R. A. OLSEN.

The library contains 205,000 vols.
Number of teachers: 364.
Number of students: 5,200 full-time, 3,500 part-time.

DEANS:

*Arts and Sciences:* JAMES V. KOCH.
*Graduate Studies:* WILLIAM A. SMALL (acting).
*Educational Studies:* ROGER BENNETT.

## RHODE ISLAND SCHOOL OF DESIGN
PROVIDENCE,
RHODE ISLAND 02903

Founded 1877.

*President:* Dr. LEE HALL.

*Vice-Presidents:* FRIEDRICH ST. FLORIAN (acting, Academic Affairs), DONALD E. PEARSON (Budget and Control), MURRAY S. DANFORTH, Jr. (Financial Affairs), JOAN PATOTA (Public Affairs), Dr. FRANKLIN ROBINSON (Director, Museum).
*Librarian:* Mrs. JEANNE BORDEN.

The library contains 60,000 vols.

Number of teachers: 98 full-time.
Number of students: 1,360.

Publications: *Annual Catalogue†, Alumni Bulletin†, Portfolio†* (Student Year Book), *Bulletin of Rhode Island School of Design†, Museum Notes†.*

## UNIVERSITY OF RHODE ISLAND
KINGSTON, RHODE ISLAND 02881

Telephone: (401) 792-1000.

Founded 1892 as Rhode Island College of Agriculture and Mechanic Arts; attained university status 1951.

*President:* FRANK NEWMAN, M.S.
*Vice-President for Academic Affairs:* W. R. FERRANTE, PH.D.
*Vice-President for Business Affairs and Finance:* A. W. PETROCELLI, PH.D.
*Vice-President for Student Affairs:* A. ROBERT RAINVILLE (acting).
*Vice-President for Development and University Relations:* J. W. LESLIE, M.S.
*Registrar:* J. F. DEMITROFF, M.A.
*Librarian:* ARTHUR P. YOUNG, PH.D.

The library contains 695,000 volumes.
Number of teachers: 705.
Number of students: 14,543.

Publications: *URI Commercial Fisheries Newsletter†, URI Reporter* (Newsletter), etc.

DEANS:

*College of Arts and Sciences:* BARRY A. MARKS, PH.D.
*College of Business Administration:* R. R. WEEKS, PH.D.
*College of Continuing Education:* THOMAS R. PEZZULLO, PH.D. (acting).
*College of Engineering:* JAMES W. DALLY, PH.D.
*College of Human Science and Services:* ROBERT W. MACMILLAN, PH.D.
*University College:* DIANE W. STROMMER, PH.D.
*College of Pharmacy:* LOUIS A. LUZZI, PH.D.
*College of Resource Development:* G. A. DONOVAN, PH.D.
*School of Nursing:* BARBARA TATE, ED.D.
*Graduate School of Oceanography:* J. A. KNAUSS, PH.D.
*Graduate School:* ALOYS A. MICHEL, PH.D.
*Graduate Library School:* BERNARD S. SCHLESSINGER, PH.D., M.L.S.

ATTACHED RESEARCH PROGRAMS:
Academic Computer Center.
Agricultural Experiment Station.
Bureau of Government Research.
Center for Energy Study.
Center for Ocean Management Studies.
Coastal Resources Center.
Consortium for the Development of Technology.
Co-operative Extension Service.
Curriculum Research and Development Center.
Laboratories for Scientific Criminal Investigation.
Marine Experiment Station.
Marine Advisory Service.
Research Center in Business and Economics.
International Center for Marine Resource Development.
National Sea Grant Depository.
Division of Engineering Research and Development.
Rhode Island Teachers' Center.
R.I. Water Resources Center.

# SOUTH CAROLINA

## THE CITADEL
(Military College of South Carolina)
CHARLESTON,
SOUTH CAROLINA 29409

Founded 1842.

Controlled by State of South Carolina.

*President:* Maj.-Gen. JAMES A. GRIMSLEY, Jr. (ret.).
*Vice-President for Academic Affairs and Dean of the College:* Brig.-Gen. GEORGE F. MEENAGHAN.
*Commandant of Cadets:* Col. FLOYD W. BROWN, U.S.A.F.
*Vice-President for Development:* Col. D. D. NICHOLSON, Jr.
*Director of Libraries:* Col. JAMES M. HILLARD.
*Registrar and Director of Admissions:* Lt.-Col. JOSEPH P. CAMERON.

The library contains 367,000 vols.

Number of teachers: 159, including 38 professors.
Number of students: 3,435.

Publications: *Sphinx, Brigadier, Guidon, Shako.*

## CLEMSON UNIVERSITY
CLEMSON,
SOUTH CAROLINA 29631

Founded 1893 as Clemson Agricultural College.

*President:* BILL L. ATCHLEY.
*Provost and Vice-President for Academic Affairs:* W. DAVID MAXWELL, PH.D.
*Vice-Provost:* JEROME V. REEL, Jr., PH.D.
*Vice-President for Business and Finance:* M. E. BARNETTE, M.S.
*Executive Officer:* J. B. MC DEVITT, B.A., J.D.
*Vice-President for Student Affairs:* W. T. COX, B.S.
*Librarian:* J. F. BOYKIN, M.S.

Library of 944,618 vols.

Number of teachers: 915, including 874 full-time.
Number of students: 11,579.

DEANS:

*Vice-Provost and Dean of Graduate School:* A. E. SCHWARTZ, PH.D.
*College of Agricultural Sciences:* L. P. ANDERSON, PH.D.
*College of Architecture:* H. E. MCCLURE, M.ARCH., F.A.I.A.
*College of Education:* H. F. LANDRITH, ED.D.
*College of Engineering:* J. C. JENNETT, PH.D.
*College of Forest and Recreation Resources:* B. H. BOX, D.F.
*College of Industrial Management and Textile Science:* R. C. AMACHER, PH.D.
*College of Liberal Arts:* R. A. WALLER, PH.D.
*College of Nursing:* MARY LOHR, ED.D.
*College of Sciences:* H. E. VOGEL, PH.D.

HEADS OF DEPARTMENTS:

*College of Agricultural Sciences:*
*Agricultural Economics and Rural Sociology:* J. E. FARIS, PH.D.
*Agricultural Education:* J. H. ROGERS, PH.D.
*Agricultural Engineering:* B. K. WEBB, PH.D.
*Agronomy and Soils:* G. R. CRADDOCK, PH.D.
*Animal Science:* L. T. FROBISH, PH.D.
*Dairy Science:* J. H. MARTIN, PH.D.
*Entomology and Economic Zoology:* S. B. HAYS, PH.D.
*Food Science:* W. P. WILLIAMS, PH.D.
*Horticulture:* E. T. SIMS, PH.D. (acting).
*Plant Pathology and Physiology:* O. J. DICKERSON, PH.D.
*Poultry Science:* B. D. BARNETT, PH.D.

*College of Architecture:*
*Architectural Studies:* G. B. WITHERSPOON, M.S.ARCH.
*Building Science:* R. E. KNOWLAND, M.B.A.
*History and Visual Studies:* J. T. ACORN, M.F.A.
*Planning Studies:* E. L. FALK, D.P.A.

*College of Education:*
*Aerospace Studies:* Col. L. E. JORDAN, M.B.A., M.S.
*Agricultural Education:* J. H. ROGERS, PH.D.
*Elementary and Secondary Education:* ERNEST J. KOZMA, ED.D.
*Industrial Education:* A. F. NEWTON, ED.D.
*Military Science:* Lt.-Col. R. B. POWELL, M.S.

*College of Engineering:*
*Ceramic Engineering:* G. C. ROBINSON, SC.D.
*Chemical Engineering:* W. B. BARLAGE, Jr., PH.D.
*Civil Engineering:* H. W. BUSCHING, PH.D.
*Electrical and Computer Engineering:* A. WAYNE BENNETT, PH.D.
*Engineering Technology:* R. M. ROBERDS, PH.D.

*Environment Systems Engineering:* T. M. Keinath, Ph.D.
*Interdisciplinary Studies:* F. W. Cooke, Ph.D.
*Mechanical Engineering:* Christian E. G. Przirembel, Ph.D.

College of Forest and Recreation Resources:
*Forestry:* R. M. Allen, Ph.D.
*Recreation and Park Administration:* H. Brantley, Ph.D.

College of Industrial Management and Textile Science:
*Accounting and Finance:* James R. Davis, Ph.D.
*Economics:* Rex L. Cottle, Ph.D.
*Industrial Management:* B. J. Todd, Ph.D.
*Textiles:* E. A. Vaughn, Ph.D.

College of Liberal Arts:
*English:* M. T. Inge, Ph.D.
*History:* A. G. Schaffer, Ph.D.
*Languages:* H. E. Stewart, Ph.D.
*Music:* J. H. Butler, Ed.D.
*Political Science:* C. W. Dunn, Ph.D.
*Psychology:* J. D. Davenport, Ph.D.
*Sociology:* R. F. Larson, Ph.D.

College of Nursing:
*Assoc. Degree Program:* Leon Roswal, M.S.
*BACC. Degree Program:* M. J. Wilhite, Ed.D.
*Continuing Education:* J. J. Chodil, Ph.D.

College of Sciences:
*Biochemistry:* J. M. Shively, Ph.D.
*Biology Program:* Doris R. Helms, Ph.D.
*Botany:* C. R. Dillon, Ph.D.
*Chemistry and Geology:* R. A. Abramovitch, Ph.D.
*Computer Science:* A. J. Turner, Ph.D.
*Mathematical Sciences:* J. D. Fulton, Ph.D.
*Microbiology:* M. J. B. Paynter, Ph.D.
*Physics and Astronomy:* J. P. McKelvey, Ph.D.
*Zoology:* C. W. Helms, Ph.D.

## COKER COLLEGE
HARTSVILLE,
SOUTH CAROLINA 29550

Telephone: (803) 332-1381.

Founded 1908.

*President:* James D. Daniels.
*Dean of the College:* Malcolm C. Doubles.
*Director of Admissions:* Charles F. Geren.
*Librarian:* David M. Bowles.
The library contains 60,000 vols.
**Number of teachers:** 40.
**Number of students:** 350.

## COLLEGE OF CHARLESTON
CHARLESTON,
SOUTH CAROLINA 29401

Telephone: (803) 722-0181.

Founded 1770; Chartered 1785.

*President:* Edward M. Collins, Jr., Ph.D.
*Academic Vice-President:* John M. Bevan.
*Registrar:* Calvin W. Jackson.
*Librarian:* Ralph Melnick (acting).
**Number of teachers:** 208.
**Number of students:** 5,289.

## COLUMBIA COLLEGE
COLUMBIA,
SOUTH CAROLINA 29203

Telephone: (803) 786-3012.

Founded 1854.

*President:* Ralph T. Mirse.
*Registrar:* Frances S. Owens.
*Librarian:* Miss Helen Jordan.
The library contains 107,871 volumes.
**Number of teachers:** 68.
**Number of students:** 1,040.

## CONVERSE COLLEGE
SPARTANBURG,
SOUTH CAROLINA 29301

Telephone: 585-6421.

Founded 1889.

*President:* Robert T. Coleman, Jr.
*Director of Admissions:* Margaret A. Printz.
*Librarian:* Dr. James G. Harrison, Jr.
The library contains 110,000 vols.
**Number of teachers:** 90.
**Number of students:** 973.

## ERSKINE COLLEGE
DUE WEST,
SOUTH CAROLINA 29639

Telephone: (803) 379-8833.

Founded 1839.

*President:* M. Stanyarne Bell.
*Director of Admissions:* W. W. Lesesne.
*Librarian:* John Wilde.
The library contains 85,000 volumes.
**Number of teachers:** 55.
**Number of students:** 668.

## FURMAN UNIVERSITY
GREENVILLE,
SOUTH CAROLINA 29613

Telephone: 294-2000.

Founded 1826.

*President:* John E. Johns, Ph.D.
*Vice-President:* F. W. Bonner, Ph.D.
*Registrar:* Paul H. Anderson.
*Librarian:* Rachel Martin.
The library contains 250,000 vols.
**Number of teachers:** 154.
**Number of students:** 2,631.
Publications: *Studies* (semi-annual), *Paladin* (weekly), *The Echo* (literary, semi-annual), *Furman Magazine* (quarterly), *Furman Reports* (quarterly).

DEANS:
*Academic:* John H. Crabtree, Jr., Ph.D.
*Graduate Studies:* Hazel W. Harris, Ed.D.
*Continuing Education:* L. Phillips, Ed.D.

## LANDER COLLEGE
GREENWOOD,
SOUTH CAROLINA 29646

Telephone: 229-5521.

Founded 1872.

*President:* Larry A. Jackson.
*Vice-President for Academic Affairs:* Oscar C. Page.
*Vice-President for Business and Administration:* W. E. Troublefield, Jr.
*Vice-President for College Relations:* Charles Dunn.
*Vice-President for Student Affairs:* Randy Bouknight.
*Registrar:* Earl Hendricks.
*Librarian:* Mrs. Ann T. Hare.
The library contains 132,856 vols.
**Number of teachers:** 90.
**Number of students:** 1,762.

## LIMESTONE COLLEGE
GAFFNEY,
SOUTH CAROLINA 29340

Telephone: (803) 489-7151.

Founded 1845.

*President:* Dr. William J. Briggs.
*Executive Vice-President and Dean of the College:* Dr. S. Wallace Taylor.
*Librarian:* Judy Abner.
The library contains 61,000 vols.
**Number of teachers:** 33 (full-time).
**Number of students:** 1,200.

## NEWBERRY COLLEGE
NEWBERRY,
SOUTH CAROLINA 29108

Telephone: (803) 276-5010.

Founded 1856.

Private control (Lutheran Church in America: South Carolina, Southeastern and Florida Synods).

*President:* Glenn E. Whitesides, Ph.D.
*Librarian:* John Sukovich.
The library contains 80,000 vols.
**Number of teachers:** 53.
**Number of students:** 850.

Publications: *Dimensions, Studies in Short Fiction* (quarterly), *The Indian* (weekly), *Kinnikinnick* (annually), *The Newberrian* (annually).

### PRESBYTERIAN COLLEGE
CLINTON,
SOUTH CAROLINA 29325
Telephone: (803) 833-2820.

Founded 1880.

*President:* Dr. KENNETH B. ORR.
*Academic Dean:* Dr. DONALD A. KING.
*Dean of Students:* JOSEPH O. NIXON.
*Director of Admissions:* WILLIAM K. JACKSON.
*Librarian:* Dr. L. PEARSON.

The library contains 115,000 vols.
Number of teachers: 56.
Number of students: 975.

### SOUTH CAROLINA STATE COLLEGE
ORANGEBURG,
SOUTH CAROLINA 29117
Telephone: 536-7000.

Founded 1896.

*President:* M. MACEO NANCE, Jr.
*Director, Admissions and Records:* T. J. CRAWFORD.
*Registrar:* Mrs. EDITH VAUGHN.
*Librarian:* Miss BARBARA J. WILLIAMS.

The library contains 132,673 volumes.
Number of teachers: 162.
Number of students: 3,519.

### UNIVERSITY OF SOUTH CAROLINA
COLUMBIA,
SOUTH CAROLINA 29208
Telephone: 777-5266.

Chartered 1801; Opened 1805.

*President:* JAMES B. HOLDERMAN, PH.D.
*Senior Vice-President for Academic Affairs:* FRANCIS T. BORKOWSKI, PH.D.
*Senior Vice-President for University Relations and Public Affairs:* CHRISTOPHER VLAHOPLUS, B.A.
*Senior Vice-President for Business Affairs:* B. A. DAETWYLER, B.A.
*Vice-President for Two-Year Campuses and Continuing Education:* JOHN J. DUFFY, PH.D.
*System Vice-President for Physical Facilities:* DAVID P. RINKER, M.A.
*System Vice-President for Computer Services:* ROBERT E. ROBERSON, B.A.
*System Vice-President for Personnel:* M. D. TAVENNER, B.S.
*System Vice-President for Fiscal Affairs:* R. W. DENTON, PH.D.
*Registrar:* T. LUKE GUNTER.
*Librarian:* KENNETH E. TOOMBS.

The library contains over 1,000,000 vols.

Number of teachers: 1,937 (9 campuses).
Number of students: 36,058 (9 campuses).
Publications: Annual Bulletins.

DEANS:

*College of Science, Mathematics and Statistics:* JAMES R. DURIG, PH.D.
*College of Business Administration:* JAMES F. KANE, D.B.A.
*College of Education:* JOHN D. MULHERN, PH.D.
*College of Engineering:* J. D. WAUGH, M.S.
*College of Humanities and Social Science:* CHESTER W. BAIN, PH.D.
*College of Journalism:* A. SCROGGINS, PH.D.
*College of Pharmacy:* JULIAN H. FINCHER, PH.D.
*School of Law:* HARRY M. LIGHTSEY, Jr.
*College of Nursing:* CONSTANCE BAKER, PH.D.
*College of General Studies:* HARRY E. VARNEY, ED.D.
*College of Social Work:* FRANK B. RAYMOND, III, D.S.W.
*College of Librarianship:* F. WILLIAM SUMMERS, PH.D.
*College of Criminal Justice:* WILLIAM J. MATHIAS, ED.D.
*Graduate School:* GEORGE M. REEVES, D.U.
*School of Medicine:* RODERICK MACDONALD, M.D.
*College of Health:* W. B. VERNBERG, PH.D.

### WINTHROP COLLEGE
ROCK HILL,
SOUTH CAROLINA 29733
Telephone: (803) 323-2211.

Founded 1886.

College of Arts and Sciences, School of Business Administration, School of Education, School of Consumer Science and Allied Professions, School of Music.

*President:* CHARLES B. VAIL.
*Provost:* GLENN G. THOMAS.
*Director of Records and Registration:* JANE TUCKER.
*Director of Admissions:* MARGARET WILLIAMSON (acting).

The library contains over 270,000 vols.
Number of teachers: 317.
Number of students: 5,040.
Publications: *The Johnsonian†* (weekly), *Winthrop College News†* (quarterly), *The Tatler, The Anthology* (annually).

DEANS:

*Arts and Sciences:* ALBERT M. LYLES.
*Business Administration:* J. H. PADGETT.
*Education:* JAMES H. REX.
*Consumer Science:* JUNE F. MOHLER.
*Music:* J. T. CASEY.

### WOFFORD COLLEGE
SPARTANBURG,
SOUTH CAROLINA 29301
Telephone: 585-4821.

Founded 1854.

*President:* JOAB M. LESESNE, Jr.
*Registrar:* E. B. SYDNOR.
*Dean of the College:* DAN B. MAULTSBY.
*Director of Admissions:* CHARLES GRAY.
*Director of Development:* RUSSELL R. PICTON.
*Director of Finance:* EDWARD E. GREENE.
*Vice-President for Student Affairs:* J. MICHAEL PRESTON.
*Librarian:* F. J. ANDERSON.

The library contains 170,000 vols.
Number of teachers: 59 full-time, 16 part-time.
Number of students: 1,020.
Publications: *Wofford Today†* (newspaper), *Wofford Bulletin*.

## SOUTH DAKOTA

### AUGUSTANA COLLEGE
29TH AND SUMMIT, SIOUX FALLS,
SOUTH DAKOTA 57102
Telephone: 336-0770.

Founded 1860.

*President:* Dr. WILLIAM NELSEN.
*Executive Vice-President:* Dr. T. KILIAN.
*Provost:* Dr. ARTHUR OLSEN.
*Vice-President for Business Affairs:* Dr. DONALD SCOTT.
*Vice-President for Development:* (vacant).
*Registrar:* Mrs. SHARON NEISH.
*Director of Admissions:* DEAN SCHUELER.
*Librarian:* RAYMOND DUNMIRE.

The library contains 150,000 vols.
Number of teachers: 136.
Number of students: 2,200.

### BLACK HILLS STATE COLLEGE
SPEARFISH,
SOUTH DAKOTA 57783
Telephone: (605) 642-6111.

Founded 1883.

*President:* J. GILBERT HAUSE.
*Registrar:* MARGARET SAGER.
*Director of Admissions:* G. BAUER.
*Director of Library—Learning Center:* Dr. EDWIN ERICKSON.

The library contains 102,784 vols.
Number of teachers: 97.
Number of students: 2,054.

### DAKOTA STATE COLLEGE
MADISON,
SOUTH DAKOTA 57042
Telephone: 256-3551.

Founded 1881.

*President:* Dr. CARLETON OPGAARD.

*Dean of Instruction:* Dr. RICHARD KONKEL.
*Dean of Student Services:* TERRENCE RYAN.
*Director of Admissions:* KATHY SCHNEIDER.
*Registrar:* HELEN SIMMONS.
*Librarian:* JOSEPH PAULUKONIS.

The library contains 83,320 vols.
Number of teachers: 50.
Number of students: 1,000.

Courses in teacher training, business management, respiratory therapy, medical records, travel, real estate and liberal arts.

### DAKOTA WESLEYAN UNIVERSITY
MITCHELL,
SOUTH DAKOTA 57301
Telephone: 996-6511.
Founded 1885.

*President:* Dr. JAMES B. BEDDOW.
*Registrar:* SYLVIA WEDMORE.
*Business Manager:* DENNIS BOLEN.
*Vice-President for Academic Affairs:* Dr. HELEN M. TRIMBLE.
*Director of Learning Resources:* MICHAEL WRIGHT.

The library contains c. 77,000 vols.
Number of teachers: 58.
Number of students: 567.

### HURON COLLEGE
HURON, SOUTH DAKOTA 57350
Telephone: (605) 352-8721.
Founded 1883.

*President:* Dr. W. L. JAHNKE.
*Dean of the College:* Dr. JAMES LAWRENCE.
*Registrar:* ELIZABETH VAN BUREN.
*Director of Admissions:* DOUGLAS ALMOND.
*Librarian:* JAMES HEMESATH.

The library contains 59,941 volumes.
Number of teachers: 26.
Number of students: 318.

### MOUNT MARTY COLLEGE
1100 WEST 5TH, YANKTON,
SOUTH DAKOTA 57078
Telephone: 668-1011.
Founded 1936.

*President:* Dr. WILLIAM V. TUCKER.
*Registrar:* Sister PIERRE ROBERTS.
*Librarian:* GLENN SUNDVOLD.

The library contains 71,500 vols.
Number of teachers: c. 53.
Number of students: c. 570.

### NORTHERN STATE COLLEGE
12TH AVE. AND JAY ST.,
ABERDEEN,
SOUTH DAKOTA 57401
Telephone: 622-3011.
Founded 1901.

*President:* JOSEPH M. MCFADDEN.

*Director of Admissions and Records:* R. VAN BEEK.
*Librarian:* E. GARTEN.

The library contains 175,000 vols.
Number of teachers: 114.
Number of students: 2,600.

### SIOUX FALLS COLLEGE
SIOUX FALLS,
SOUTH DAKOTA 57101
Telephone: (605) 331-5000.
Founded 1883.

Pre-professional Liberal Arts College.

*President:* OWEN P. HALLEEN.
*Registrar:* PHYLLIS THOMPSON.
*Librarian:* JANE KOLBE.

The library contains 79,000 vols.
Number of teachers: 40 full-time, 17 part-time.
Number of students: 849.

### SOUTH DAKOTA SCHOOL OF MINES AND TECHNOLOGY
RAPID CITY,
SOUTH DAKOTA 57701
Telephone: (605) 394-2411.
Founded 1885.

*President:* R. A. SCHLEUSENER.
*Vice-President and Dean of Engineering:* RICHARD J. GOWEN.
*Dean of Graduate Division and Director of Research:* R. NORMAN ORAVA.
*Dean of Students:* H. C. PETERSON.
*Registrar:* R. H. MOORE.
*Director of Library:* HARRY F. WELSH.

The library contains 180,000 vols.
Number of teachers: 118.
Number of students: 2,393.

### SOUTH DAKOTA STATE UNIVERSITY
COLLEGE STATION,
BROOKINGS,
SOUTH DAKOTA 57007

Founded as Dakota Agricultural College 1881, University 1964.

*President:* SHERWOOD BERG, M.S., PH.D.
*Vice-President for Administration:* GARY A. THIBODEAU, PH.D.
*Director of Finance:* W. A. BUGG.
*Dean of Student Services:* J. PEDERSEN, PH.D.
*Vice-President for Academic Affairs:* H. S. BAILEY, PH.D.
*Director of Library:* A. L. RANEY.

The library contains 325,000 vols.
Number of teachers: 453 full-time.
Number of students: 6,464.

### UNIVERSITY OF SOUTH DAKOTA
VERMILLION,
SOUTH DAKOTA 57069
Telephone: (605) 677-5011.
Founded 1862.

*President:* CHARLES D. LEIN, ED.D.

The library contains 349,972 vols.
Number of teachers: 375.
Number of students: 6,100.

DEANS:

*College of Arts and Sciences:* JOSEPH CASH, PH.D.
*School of Business:* DALE CLEMENT, PH.D.
*School of Education:* ROBERTA ANDERSON, PH.D.
*College of Fine Arts:* JOHN DAY.
*School of Law:* (vacant).
*School of Medicine:* CHARLES HOLLERMAN, M.D.
*School of Nursing:* B. SUGA, M.A.
*Graduate School:* CHARLES KAUFMAN, D.B.A.

### UNIVERSITY OF SOUTH DAKOTA AT SPRINGFIELD
SPRINGFIELD,
SOUTH DAKOTA 57062
Telephone: 369-2201.
Founded 1881.

*President:* Dr. CHARLES D. LEIN.
*Dean:* Dr. THOMAS C. STONE.
*Registrar:* R. E. HOWE.
*Librarian:* JOEL HANSON.

The library contains 93,000 vols.
Number of teachers: 65.
Number of students: 853.

DEANS:

*Business Education and Office Administration:* Dr. MARVIN SCHAMBER.
*Construction Technology:* H. NICHELSON.
*Electronics Engineering Technology:* J. SORENSEN.
*Health, Physical Education and Recreation:* DELBERT W. BARHAM (acting).
*Humanities:* V. PETRIK.
*Mechanical Technology:* C. BRYAN.
*Physical and Natural Sciences:* M. FOSS.
*Social and Behavioral Sciences:* DELBERT W. BARHAM (acting).

### YANKTON COLLEGE
YANKTON, SOUTH DAKOTA 57078
Telephone: (605) 665-3661.
Founded 1881.

*President:* ORLAN E. MITCHELL, PH.D.
*Dean of the College:* JOHN NIES, PH.D.
*Vice-President for Development:* JIM GILLIHAN.
*Business Manager:* OSCAR JENSEN (acting).
*Director of Financial Aid and Placement:* JEAN BARKLEY (acting).
*Director of Admissions:* JAMES FRED.
*Registrar:* BERNETTA VOLLMER, LITT.B.
*Librarian:* PATRICIA MCDONALD, M.A.

The library contains 65,000 volumes.
Number of teachers: 43.
Number of students: 300.

Courses in the humanities, fine arts, natural and social sciences, physical education; professional and pre-professional training.

## TENNESSEE

### AUSTIN PEAY STATE UNIVERSITY
CLARKSVILLE, TENNESSEE 37040
Telephone: (615) 648-7566.
Founded 1927.

*President:* ROBERT O. RIGGS.
*Vice-President for Academic Affairs:* JAMES SAWREY.
*Vice-President for Student Affairs:* C. BOEHMS.
*Vice-President for Administration and Finance:* FRED WILLIAMS.
*Business Manager:* SANDRA BRIGHT.
*Registrar:* G. S. GENTRY.
*Librarian:* ROBERT SIMMONS.

The library contains 206,144 vols.
Number of teachers: 195.
Number of students: 5,200.

### BELMONT COLLEGE
NASHVILLE, TENNESSEE 37203
Telephone: (615) 383-7001.
Founded 1951.

*President:* HERBERT C. GABHART.
*Registrar:* R. E. UNDERWOOD.
*Librarian:* ERNEST W. HEARD.

The library contains 87,500 vols.
Number of teachers: 107.
Number of students: 1,706.

Publications: *The Tower* (annually), *Vision* (monthly), *Belmont Circle* (quarterly).

DEANS:
*Academic:* JAMES C. STAMPER.
*Students:* K. B. SIDWELL.
*Women:* LUCILE P. WARDIN.

### BETHEL COLLEGE
McKENZIE, TENNESSEE 38201
Telephone: 352-5321.
Founded 1842.

*President:* WILLIAM L. ODOM.
*Dean:* JOHN N. LANGFITT.
*Registrar:* SHIRLEY MARTIN.
*Director of Development:* ROBERT RUTLEDGE.
*Librarian:* BOBBYE McCARTER.

The library contains 68,754 vols.
Number of teachers: 23.
Number of students: 360.

Publications: *Bethel Beacon* (monthly), *Log Cabin* (annually), *Alumni Bulletin* (bi-monthly).

### CARSON-NEWMAN COLLEGE
SOUTH RUSSELL AVE.,
JEFFERSON CITY,
TENNESSEE 37760
Founded 1851.

*President:* J. CORDELL MADDOX.
*Treasurer:* ROBERT DRINNEN.
The library contains 140,469 vols.
Number of teachers: 102.
Number of students: 1,737.

Publications: *Today*, *Orange and Blue*, *The Eagle's Quill*, *Faculty Studies†*, *College Catalog†*.

### CHRISTIAN BROTHERS COLLEGE
650 EAST PARKWAY SOUTH,
MEMPHIS, TENNESSEE 38104
Telephone: (901) 278-0100.
Founded 1871.
Private (Roman Catholic) control.

*President:* Bro. THEODORE DRAHMANN, F.S.C.
*Registrar:* Bro. J. WEGENER, F.S.C.
*Librarian:* Dr. A. WAYNE DENTON, PH.D., M.L.S.

The library contains 85,000 vols.
Number of teachers: 120.
Number of students: 1,436.

### DAVID LIPSCOMB COLLEGE
NASHVILLE, TENNESSEE 37203
Telephone: (615) 385-3855.
Founded 1891.

*President:* WILLARD COLLINS.
*Vice-Presidents:* CARL McKELVEY (Campus Affairs), MACK WAYNE CRAIG (Institutional Planning), EDSEL F. HOLMAN (Business Affairs), EARL DENNIS (Academic Affairs and Dean of the Faculty).
*Librarian:* J. E. WARD.

The library contains 130,576 vols.
Number of teachers: 98.
Number of students: 2,196.

### EAST TENNESSEE STATE UNIVERSITY
JOHNSON CITY,
TENNESSEE 37614
Telephone: 929-4112.
Founded 1911.

*President:* Dr. RONALD E. BELLER.
*Dean of Admissions:* J. W. LOYD.
*Vice-President for Academic Affairs:* (vacant).
*Vice-President for Administration:* Dr. RICHARD MANAHAN.
*Librarian:* Dr. FRED BORCHUK.

The library contains 537,155 vols.
Number of teachers: 480 full-time, 83 part-time.
Number of students: 10,252.

DEANS:
*Arts and Sciences:* ROBERT BOTKIN.
*Education:* L. SCOTT HONAKER.
*Business:* JAMES McLEAN.
*School of Public and Allied Health:* J. P. LAMB.
*Graduate Studies:* ELIZABETH McMAHAN.
*Extended Services:* Dr. BENJAMIN CARMICHAEL.
*School of Applied Science and Technology:* ROLLIN WILLIAMS.
*School of Nursing:* EDITH SUMMERLIN.
*College of Medicine:* JACK MOBLEY.

### FISK UNIVERSITY
17TH AVE. NORTH, NASHVILLE,
TENNESSEE 37203
Opened as Fisk School 1866; Chartered as University 1867.

*President:* Dr. WALTER J. LEONARD.
*Vice-President, Dean of University and Provost:* Dr. SHERMAN JONES (acting).
*Vice-President for Administration:* Dr. WAYNE M. WORMLEY (acting).
*Dean of Student Affairs:* JOHN S. HARWELL.

The library contains 189,174 vols.
Number of teachers: 71 full-time, 20 part-time.
Number of students: 1,100.

Publications: *Bulletin* (annually), *Fisk Magazine* (quarterly).

### KING COLLEGE
BRISTOL, TENNESSEE 37620
Founded 1867.

*President:* DONALD R. MITCHELL.
*Dean:* JOHN S. GAINES.
*Business Manager:* J. E. DILLOW.
The library contains 81,000 vols.
Number of students: 277.
Publication: *Bulletin*.

### KNOXVILLE COLLEGE
901 COLLEGE ST., KNOXVILLE,
TENNESSEE 37921
Telephone: (615) 524-6500.
Founded 1875.
Liberal Arts College.

*President:* Dr. RUTHERFORD H. ADKINS.
*Dean:* Dr. JESSE JAMES.
*Registrar:* CHARLES W. WILLIAMSON.
*Librarian:* Mrs. LOIS CLARK.

The library contains 78,445 vols.
Number of teachers: 45.
Number of students: 700.

### LAMBUTH COLLEGE
JACKSON, TENNESSEE 38301
Telephone: (901) 427-6743.
Founded 1843.

*President:* HARRY W. GILMER.
*Chancellor:* JAMES S. WILDER, Jr.
*Vice-President and Dean of the College:* K. BRUCE SHERBINE.
*Vice-President for External Affairs:* WILLIAM H. NACE.
*Vice-President for Business Affairs:* JAMES C. MITCHELL.
*Librarian:* Mrs. JUDITH HAZLEWOOD.

## LANE COLLEGE
545 LANE AVE., JACKSON, TENNESSEE 38301
Telephone: 424-4600.
Founded 1882.

*President:* HERMAN STONE, Jr.
*Executive Vice-President:* EARNEST B. CAMPBELL.
*Registrar:* G. L. THACKER.
*Dean:* ARTHUR L. DAVID.
*Business Manager:* R. D. MERRIWEATHER.
*Director of Development:* MORRIS P. FAIR.
*Librarian:* Mrs. ANNA L. COOKE.

The library contains 82,487 vols.
Number of teachers: 42.
Number of students: 757.

## LE MOYNE-OWEN COLLEGE
807 WALKER AVENUE, MEMPHIS, TENNESSEE 38126
Telephone: (901) 774-9090.
Founded 1870.

*President:* WALTER L. WALKER.
*Registrar:* Mrs. NELLIE POWELL.
*Librarian:* MAE I. FITZGERALD.

The library contains 80,000 vols.
Number of teachers: 60.
Number of students: 1,000.

## LINCOLN MEMORIAL UNIVERSITY
HARROGATE, TENNESSEE 37752
Telephone: (615) 869-3611.
Founded 1897.

*President:* FRANK W. WELCH.
*Executive Vice-President:* G. J. BURCHETT.
*Vice-President for Academic Affairs:* DAVID DU BOSE.
*Director of Admissions:* CONRAD DANIELS.
*Librarian:* ELIZABETH GRAVES.

The library contains 60,000 vols.
Number of teachers: 55.
Number of students: 1,200.
Publication: *The Lincoln Herald* (quarterly).

## MARYVILLE COLLEGE
MARYVILLE, TENNESSEE 37801
Telephone: (615) 982-6412.
Founded 1819.

*President:* Dr. WAYNE W. ANDERSON.
*Academic Vice-President:* Dr. ALFRED PERKINS.
*Vice-President for Administration:* (vacant).
*Vice-President for Development:* R. ARCHIBALD ELLIS, Jr.
*Vice-President for Student Affairs:* WILLIAM STRICKLAND.
*Director of Admissions:* LARRY WEST.
*Librarian:* Mrs. EXIR BRENNAN.

The library contains 108,233 vols.
Number of teachers: 50.
Number of students: 650.

## MEMPHIS ACADEMY OF ARTS
OVERTON PARK, MEMPHIS, TENNESSEE 38112
Telephone: (901) 726-4085.
Founded 1936.

*President:* WILLIAM C. COLLINS.
*Registrar:* KAY BETTS.
*Librarian:* ROBERT SCARLETT.

The library contains 15,000 vols.
Number of teachers: 17 full-time, 10 part-time.
Number of students: 210 full-time, 500 part-time.

## MEMPHIS STATE UNIVERSITY
MEMPHIS, TENNESSEE 38152
Founded 1912.

*President:* THOMAS CARPENTER.
*Vice-President for Academic Affairs:* JERRY BOONE.
*Vice-President for Business and Finance:* R. EUGENE SMITH.
*Vice-President for Student Educational Services:* DONALD CARSON.
*Vice-President for Continuing Education and Special Programs:* JOHN RHODES.
*Librarian:* LESTER J. POURCIAU, Jr.

The library contains 867,770 vols.
Number of teachers: 781.
Number of students: 20,784.

Publications: *The Southern Journal of Philosophy* (quarterly), *Educational Quest, Law Review, The Columns, Memphis State University Bulletin, Mid-South Business Journal, Memphis Economy, Memphis Housing Market Area Report.*

## MIDDLE TENNESSEE STATE UNIVERSITY
MURFREESBORO, TENNESSEE 37132
Telephone: (615) 898-2300.
Founded 1911.
Academic year: mid-August to mid-May.

*President:* S. H. INGRAM.
*Vice-President for Finance and Administration:* MORRIS F. BASS.
*Vice-President for Academic Affairs:* Dr. H. KIRKSEY.
*Vice-President for Student Affairs:* Dr. H. WAGNER.
*Dean of Admissions:* Dr. F. GLASS.
*Librarian:* J. D. MARSHALL.

The library contains 320,175 vols.
Number of teachers: 470.
Number of students: 10,514.

DEANS:
*School of Business and Economics:* Dr. A. SIMON.
*School of Basic and Applied Sciences:* Dr. E. S. VOORHIES.
*School of Education:* Dr. D. POCKAT.
*School of Liberal Arts:* Dr. H. C. TUCKER.
*Graduate School:* Dr. R. ADEN.

## MILLIGAN COLLEGE
TENNESSEE 37682
Telephone: (615) 929-0116.
Founded 1866 (reorganized 1881).

*Chancellor:* JESS W. JOHNSON.
*President:* (vacant).
*Academic Dean:* KENNETH W. OOSTING.
*Library Director:* STEVEN L. PRESTON.

The library contains c. 108,500 vols.
Number of teachers: 60.
Number of students: 755.

## SCARRITT COLLEGE
NASHVILLE, TENNESSEE 37203
Telephone: (615) 327-2700.
Founded 1892.

Private Methodist control; Graduate school specializing in Christian education and church music.

*President:* DONALD J. WELCH.
*Dean of Students:* LAWRENCE HAY.
*Registrar:* NATHALIE PENNINGTON, M.A.
*Librarian:* Dr. LEO RIPPY, Jr.

The library contains 48,000 vols.
Number of teachers: 18 full-time, 9 part-time.
Number of students: 110.
Publication: *The Scarritt Bulletin.*

## SOUTHERN MISSIONARY COLLEGE
COLLEGEDALE, TENNESSEE 37315
Telephone: 396-2111.
Founded 1892.

*President:* Dr. F. KNITTEL.
*Registrar:* MARY ELAM.
*Librarian:* C. DAVIS.

The library contains 120,000 vols.
Number of teachers: 125.
Number of students: 2,000.

## SOUTHWESTERN AT MEMPHIS
2000 NORTH PARKWAY, MEMPHIS, TENNESSEE 38112
Telephone: (901) 274-1800.
Founded 1848.
Liberal Arts College.

*President:* JAMES H. DAUGHDRILL, Jr.

Vice-President and Dean of College: GERALD DUFF.
Registrar: J. TURPIN.
Director of Admissions: MARY JO MILLER.
Dean of Students: C. V. SCARBOROUGH.
Dean of Enrollment: LLOYD C. TEMPLETON, Jr.
Dean of Development: DONALD LINEBACK.
Librarian: LYNNE M. BLAIR.

The library contains 182,000 vols.
Number of teachers: 89 full-time.
Number of students: 1,050.

## TENNESSEE STATE UNIVERSITY
3500 CENTENNIAL BOULEVARD, NASHVILLE, TENNESSEE 37203

Founded 1912.

President: FREDERICK S. HUMPHRIES
Vice-President: Dr. BERNARD CROWELL
Registrar: CASS F. TEAGUE.
Librarian: Dr. EVELYN FANCHER.

The library contains 445,053 vols.
Number of teachers: 302.
Number of students: 5,698.

## TENNESSEE TECHNOLOGICAL UNIVERSITY
COOKEVILLE, TENNESSEE 38501
Telephone: 526-9541.

Founded 1915.

President: ARLISS L. ROADEN.
Dean of Admissions: H. LAWSON
Provost and Academic Vice-President: W. S. PRESCOTT.
Director of Business and Fiscal Affairs: ROY RUFFNER.
Director of Library Services: DUDLEY V. YATES.

The library contains 943,985 vols.
Number of teachers: 316.
Number of students: 7,849.

## TENNESSEE WESLEYAN COLLEGE
P.O.B. 40, ATHENS, TENNESSEE 37303
Telephone: (615) 745-9523.

Founded 1857.

President: Dr. GEORGE E. NAFF, Jr.
Dean: Dr. M. ALBERT DIMMITT.
Director of Admissions: JAMES E. CHEEK, II.

The library contains c. 64,745 vols.
Number of teachers: 30.
Number of students: 447.

## TUSCULUM COLLEGE
GREENEVILLE, TENNESSEE 37743
Telephone: (615) 639-2661.

Founded 1794.

President: EARL R. MEZOFF.
Registrar: ESTEL C. HURLEY.

The library contains 61,000 volumes.
Number of teachers: 30.
Number of students: 356.

## UNION UNIVERSITY
JACKSON, TENNESSEE 38301
Telephone: (901) 668-1818.

Founded 1825.

President: Dr. ROBERT E. CRAIG.
Director of Student Enlistment: JOE S. LAYMAN.
Vice-President for Academic Affairs: Dr. HYRAN E. BAREFOOT.
Librarian: HAROLD BASS.

The library contains 77,347 vols.
Number of teachers: 80.
Number of students: 1,345.

## UNIVERSITY OF TENNESSEE SYSTEM
KNOXVILLE, TENNESSEE 37016
Telephone: (615) 974-2591.

Chartered 1794 as Blount College. Name changed by legislature 1840 to East Tennessee University, and in 1879 to The University of Tennessee. Major campuses at Chattanooga, Knoxville, Martin and Memphis.

State control; Academic year: September to August (four terms, except Chattanooga and UTK Law School—three terms).

President: EDWARD J. BOLING, M.S., ED.D.
Executive Vice-President, Vice-President for Development: JOSEPH E. JOHNSON, A.M., ED.D.
Vice-President for Academic Affairs: JOHN W. PRADOS, M.S., PH.D.
Vice-President for Agriculture: WILLIS W. ARMISTEAD, D.V.M., PH.D.
Vice-President for Continuing Education: CHARLES H. WEAVER, M.S., PH.D.
Vice-President for Health Affairs: Dr. JAMES C. HUNT, M.S., M.D.
Vice-President for Public Service: ROBERT S. HUTCHINSON.
Vice-President for Business and Finance: EMERSON H. FLY, B.S., C.P.A.
Libraries: see Libraries.
Number of teachers: 3,392.
Number of students: 45,402.

Publications: *The University Record*, Extension Series (4 to 6 a year), *Tennessee Alumnus*, *Horizons* (both quarterly).

### University of Tennessee at Chattanooga
CHATTANOOGA, TENNESSEE 37401
Chancellor: FERDERICK W. OBEAR, PH.D.
Vice-Chancellor for Academic Affairs: JANE W. HARBAUGH, PH.D.
Executive Vice-Chancellor: C. TEMPLE, M.A., ED.D.
Vice-Chancellor for Business and Finance: D. LARSON, M.B.A.
Vice-Chancellor for Development: IAN T. STURROCK, PH.D.

DEANS:

Admissions and Records: R. FOX, ED.D.
College of Arts and Sciences: JOHN E. TRIMPEY, PH.D.
Graduate Studies and Research: C. HYDER, M.A., ED.D.
Students: C. RENNEISEN, M.S., ED.D.
Continuing Education: RON G AREA, PH.D.
School of Business Administration: KERMIT G. CUDD, PH.D.
School of Education: ROY L. STINNET, ED.D.
Division of Human Services: KENNETH R. VENTERS, M.S., PH.D.
School of Engineering: RONALD B. COX, PH.D.
Department of Nursing: MARJORIE SCZEKAN, PH.D.

### University of Tennessee at Knoxville
Chancellor: JACK REESE, A.M., PH.D.
Vice-Chancellor for Academic Affairs: WALTER HERNDON, M.S., PH.D.
Vice-Chancellor for Business and Finance: HOMER S. FISHER, M.B.A.
Vice-Chancellor for Graduate Studies and Research: L. EVANS ROTH, B.A., M.S., PH.D.
Vice-Chancellor for Planning and Administration: Dr. LUKE EBERSOLE, A.M., PH.D.
Vice-Chancellor for Student Affairs: HOWARD F. ALDMON, A.M., ED.D.

DEANS:

Admissions and Records: J. McDOW, M.S., PH.D.
College of Agriculture: O. G. HALL, M.S., PH.D.
School of Architecture: ROY F. KNIGHT, M.ARCH.
College of Business Administration: C. WARREN NEEL, PH.D.
College of Communications: D. G. HILEMAN, M.S., PH.D.
College of Education: WILLIAM H. COFFIELD, PH.D.
College of Engineering: ROBERT WEAVER, M.S., PH.D.
College of Home Economics: NANCY H. BELCK, PH.D.
College of Law: K. L. PENEGAR, J.D., LL.M.
College of Liberal Arts: ROBERT G. LANDEN, M.A., PH.D.
College of Veterinary Medicine: HYRAM KITCHEN, D.V.M., PH.D.
Division of Continuing Education: J. GODDARD, M.S., ED.D.
Graduate School of Social Work: B. GRANGER, M.P.A., M.S.S.W., PH.D.
Graduate Studies: CLARENCE W. MINKEL, PH.D.
Research: C. THOMAS, PH.D.
College of Nursing: SYLVIA HART, M.S.N., PH.D.

*Oak Ridge Graduate School of Biomedical Sciences:* W. E. BARNETT, M.S., PH.D.

*School of Health, Physical Education and Recreation:* MADGE PHILLIPS, PH.D. (Director).

*School of Library and Information Science:* ANN PRENTICE, D.L.S. (Director).

*School of Planning:* DAVID A. JOHNSON, M.C.P., PH.D. (Director).

*Space Institute:* C. WEAVER, PH.D.

PROFESSORS:

*College of Liberal Arts:*
ABEL, J. H., Jr., Zoology
ADAMS, P. G., English
ADLER, SOL, Audiology and Speech Pathology
AIKEN, C. S., Geography
ALLEN, R. G., Speech and Theatre
AQUILA, R. E., Philosophy
ASP, C. W., Audiology and Speech Pathology
BAGBY, R. M., Zoology
BARRETTE, P., Romance Languages
BASS, W. M., Anthropology
BECK, R. W., Microbiology
BECKER, J. M., Microbiology
BERGERON, P. H., History
BINGHAM, C. R., Physics
BIRKHOFF, R. D., Physics
BLACK, J. A., Sociology
BOWMAN, N. S., Chemistry
BRADLEY, J. S., Mathematics
BRATTON, E. W., English
BREAZEALE, M. A., Physics
BROWN, A., Microbiology
BUGG, W. M., Physics
BULL, W. E., Chemistry
BUNTING, D. L., II, Zoology
BURGHARDT, G. M., Psychology
BYRNE, J. F., Psychological Clinical Training
CALHOUN, W. H., Psychology
CALLCOTT, T. A., Physics
CARLISLE, D. H., Political Science
CARNEY, P. J., Audiology and Speech Pathology
CARRUTH, J. H., Mathematics
CARTER, W. P., Music
CHAMBERS, J. Q., Chemistry
CHAMPION, D. J., Sociology
CHMIELEWSKI, E. V., History
CHRISTOPHOROU, L. G., Physics
CHURCHICH, J. E., Biochemistry
CLARKE, R. A., Arts
CLEAVER, D. G., Arts
CLEBSCH, E. E., Botany
COBB, C. W., Romance Languages
COHEN, C. P., Psychological Clinical Training
CONDO, G. T., Physics
COOKE, T. P., Speech and Theatre
COTHRAN, R. M., Jr., Speech and Theatre
DANIEL, J. C., Jr., Zoology
DAVERMAN, R. J., Mathematics
DAVIS, J .W., Philosophy
DEAN, J. A., Chemistry
DEEDS, W. E., Physics
DESELM, H. R., Botany
DEVINE, G. F., Music
DOBBS, D. E., Mathematics
DORN, W. J., Music
DRAKE, R. Y., Jr., English
DUNCAN, R. E., History
DUNGAN, D. L., Religious Studies
EASTHAM, J. F., Chemistry
EDWARDS, R. B., Philosophy
ENSOR, ALLISON R., English
ETNIER, D. A., Zoology
EVANS, A. M., Botany
FALEN, J. E., Germanic and Slavic Languages
FAULKNER, C. H., Anthropology
FALSETTI, J. S., Arts
FINE, H. J., Psychological Clinical Training
FISHER, J. H., English
FLETCHER, W. H., Chemistry
FOWLER, J. L., Physics
FOX, K., Physics
FRANDSEN, H., Mathematics
FRASER, R. C., Zoology
FRAUENDORF, S. G., Physics
FRED, H. W., Music
FULLER, H. W., Germanic and Slavic Languages
GAILAR, N. M., Physics
GARDINER, D. A., Mathematics
GRAF, L. P., History
GREGORY, R. T., Computer Science
GUTHE, A. K., Anthropology
HAAS, A.G., History
HALLAM, T. G., Mathematics
HANDEL, S. J., Psychology
HAMMOND, E. H., Geography
HANDLER, L., Psychological Clinical Training
HAO, YEN-PING, History
HARRIS, E. G., Physics
HART, E. L., English
HASKINS, R. W., History
HENSHAW, W., Speech and Theatre
HILLER, R. L., Germanic and Slavic Languages
HINTON, D. B., Mathematics
HOCHMAN, B., Zoology
HOLTON, R. W., Botany
HUBER, C. R., Music
HURAY, P. G., Physics
HUSCH, L. S., Mathematics
IREDELL, V. R., Political Science
JACKSON, R. L., Romance Languages
JANTZ, R. L., Anthropology
JEON, KWANG W., Zoology
JONES, L. W., Botany
JUMPER, S. R., Geography
KEENAN, C. W., Chemistry
KELLY, R. M., English
KENNEDY, J. R., Zoology
KING, D. T., Physics
KLATT, L. N., Chemistry
KLEIN, M. M., History
KLEINFELTER, D. C., Chemistry
KOPP, O. C., Geology
KRATZ, H., Germanic and Slavic Languages
KURKA, D. F., Arts
LARSEN, J. W., Chemistry
LEGGETT, B. J., English
LEWALD, H. E., Romance Languages
LIETZKE, M. H., Chemistry
LILES, J. N., Zoology
LIPSCOMB, D. M., Audiology and Speech Pathology
LIVINGSTON, P. R., Arts
LORION, R. P., Psychology
LOVELL, R. J., Physics
LOY, W. F., Arts
LUBAR, S., Psychology
LUPER, H. L., Audiology and Speech Pathology
LUSBY, F. S., Religious Studies
MCCALL, W. G., Political Science
MCCONNEL, R. M., Mathematics
MCCORMICK, J. F., Ecology
MCKEEBY, B. G., Arts
MCLAUGHLIN, R. E., Geology
MAMANTOV, G., Chemistry
MARTINSON, F. H., Arts
MATHEWS, H. T., Mathematics
MAURINO, F. D., Romance Languages
MEACHAM, J. J., Music
MONTIE, T. C., Microbiology
MONTY, K. J., Biology Co-ordination
MUNDT, J. O., Microbiology
NABELEK, I. V., Audiology and Speech Pathology
NEUEN, D. L., Music
NEWTON, K. R., Psychological Clinical Training
NICHOLS, P. G., Arts
NIMMO, D. D., Political Science
OBENSHEIN, F. E., Physics
O'KELLEY, G. D., Chemistry
OLSON, J. S., Botany
OSBORNE, J. C., Germanic and Slavic Languages
PEDERSON, D. M., Music
PEGG, D. J., Physics
PETERSEN, R. H., Botany
PETERSON, H. A., Audiology and Speech Pathology
PETERSON, J. R., Chemistry
PLAAS, H., Political Science
PLEMMONS, R. J., Computer Science
PLOCH, D. R., Sociology
POLLIO, H. R., Psychology
PRESENT, R. D., Physics
RASCH, N. L., Psychological Clinical Training
REYNOLDS, C. H., Religious Studies
RICE, M. P., Germanic and Slavic Languages
RIEDINGER, L. L., Physics
RIGGSBY, W. S., Microbiology
ROBINSON, N. M., Political Science
RUTLEDGE, H. C., Classics
SALO, T. P., Biochemistry
SAMEJIMA, F., Psychology
SANDERS, N. J., English
SCHAEFER, P. W., Mathematics
SCHMUDDE, T. H., Geography
SCHNEIDER, D. J., English
SCHWEINLER, H. C., Physics
SCHWEITZER, G. K., Chemistry
SELLIN, I. A., Physics
SHIVERS, C. A., Zoology
SHRADER, R. R., Psychology
SILVERSTEIN, B., Audiology and Speech Pathology
SPEJEWSKI, E. H., Physics
STALLMANN, F. W., Mathematics
STARR, W. J., Music
STELSON, P. H., Physics
STEPHENS, O. H., Jr., Political Science
STEWART, B. T., English
SUBLETT, C. C., Arts
TAYLOR, L. A., Geology
THOMSON, J. D., Physics
TRAHERN, J. B., Jr., English
TURNER, J. E., Physics
UNGS, T. D., Political Science
VAN DE VATE, D., Jr., Philosophy
VANHOOK, A., Chemistry
VAZQUEZ-BIGI, A. M., Romance Languages
VERPLANCK, W. S., Psychology
WADE, W. R., Mathematics
WAHLER, R. G., Psychology
WALKER, K. R., Geology
WALKER, R. H., English
WALLACE, A. H., Romance Languages
WALLACE, S. E., Sociology
WALNE, P. L., Botany
WEHRY, E. L., Chemistry
WELBORN, D. M., Political Science
WHEELER, T. V., English
WHITE, J. M., English
WHITE, J. W., Physics
WHITSON, G. L., Zoology
WIBERLEY, J. A., Psychology
WICKS, W. D., Biochemistry
WILLIAMS, T. F., Chemistry
WOODWARD, J. M., Microbiology
WRIGHT, NATHALIA, English
WUST, C. J., Microbiology
YEOMANS, G. A., Speech and Theatre
ZAMBARA, E. H., Music

## UNIVERSITIES AND COLLEGES—TENNESSEE (UNIVERSITY OF) — U.S.A.

*College of Home Economics:*
- BEACH, BETTY L., Nutrition and Food Sciences
- BEAUCHENE, R. E., Food Science, Nutrition and Food Systems Administration
- BLAKEMORE, R. G., Crafts, Interior Design Housing
- GOERTZ, GRAYCE E., Nutrition and Food Sciences
- GOSWAMI, B. C., Textiles Merchandising and Design
- HIGHBERGER, R. L., Child and Family Studies
- HITCHCOCK, M. J., Food Science, Nutrition and Food Systems Administration
- ODLAND, L. M., Food Science, Nutrition and Food Systems Administration
- ORLANDO, JACQUELYN Y., Textiles Merchandising and Design
- SAVAGE, J. R., Food Science, Nutrition and Food Systems Administration
- SMITH, J. T., Food Science, Nutrition and Food Systems Administration

*College of Engineering:*
- AKIN, J. E., Engineering Science and Mechanics
- ALEXEFF, I., Electrical Engineering
- BAILEY, J. F., Mechanical and Aerospace Engineering
- BAILEY, J. M., Electrical Engineering
- BAKER, A. J., Engineering Science and Mechanics
- BEARD, O. S., Civil Engineering
- BLALOCK, T. V., Electrical Engineering
- BODENHEIMER, R. E., Electrical Engineering
- BOGUE, D. C., Chemical and Metallurgical Engineering
- BORIE, B. S., Chemical and Metallurgical Engineering
- BROOKS, C. R., Jr., Chemical and Metallurgical Engineering
- BURDETTE, E. G., Civil Engineering
- CARLEY, T. G., Engineering Science and Mechanics
- CLARK, E. S., Chemical and Metallurgical Engineering
- CULBERSON, O. L., Chemical and Metallurgical Engineering
- DEWEY, B. R., Engineering Science and Mechanics
- EDMONDSON, A. J., Mechanical and Aerospace Engineering
- ERASLAN, A. H., Engineering Science and Mechanics
- FELLERS, J. F., Chemical and Metallurgical Engineering
- FORRESTER, J. H., Engineering Science and Mechanics
- FRAZIER, G. C., Chemical and Metallurgical Engineering
- FUSSELL, J. B., Nuclear Engineering
- GONZALEZ, R. C., Electrical Engineering
- GOODPASTURE, D. W., Civil Engineering
- GOOGE, J. M., Electrical Engineering
- GRECCO, W., Civil Engineering
- GREEN, W. L., Electrical Engineering
- HALL, E. L., Electrical Engineering
- HODGSON, J. W., Mechanical and Aerospace Engineering
- HOFFMAN, G. W., Electrical Engineering
- HOLLAND, R. W., Mechanical and Aerospace Engineering
- HSU, HSIEN-WEN, Chemical and Metallurgical Engineering
- HUMPHREYS, J. B., Civil Engineering
- HUNG, J. C., Electrical Engineering
- JOHNSON, H. F., Jr., Chemical and Metallurgical Engineering
- JOHNSON, H. L., Civil Engineering
- KENNEDY, E. J., Electrical Engineering
- KERLIN, T. W., Jr., Nuclear Engineering
- KESHOCK, E. G., Mechanical and Aerospace Engineering
- LEE, CHING-WEN, Engineering Science and Mechanics
- LOVELESS, H. L., Industrial Engineering
- LUNDIN, C. D., Chemical and Metallurgical Engineering
- MCHARGUE, C. J., Chemical and Metallurgical Engineering
- MAXWELL, R. L., Mechanical and Aerospace Engineering
- MIHALCZO, J. T., Nuclear Engineering
- MILLIGAN, M. W., Mechanical and Aerospace Engineering
- MOORE, C. F., Chemical and Metallurgical Engineering
- NAUMAN, E. B., Chemical and Metallurgical Engineering
- NEFF, H. P., Jr., Electrical Engineering
- OLIVER, B. F., Chemical and Metallurgical Engineering
- PACE, M. O., Electrical Engineering
- PASQUA, P. F., Nuclear Engineering
- PEEBLES, P. Z., Electrical Engineering
- PEREZ, R. B., Nuclear Engineering
- PERONA, J. J., Chemical and Metallurgical Engineering
- PIERCE, J. F., Electrical Engineering
- PIH, HUI, Engineering Science and Mechanics
- REID, R. L., Mechanical and Aerospace Engineering
- REMENYIK, C. J., Engineering Science and Mechanics
- ROBINSON, J. C., Nuclear Engineering
- ROCHELLE, R. W., Electrical Engineering
- ROLAND, H. C., Nuclear Engineering
- ROTH, J. R., Electrical Engineering
- SNIDER, J. N., Industrial Engineering
- SNYDER, W. T., Engineering Science and Mechanics
- SPECKHART, F. H., Mechanical and Aerospace Engineering
- SPRUIELL, J. E., Chemical and Metallurgical Engineering
- STANSBURY, E. E., Chemical and Metallurgical Engineering
- STEVENS, P. N., Nuclear Engineering
- STONEKING, J. E., Engineering Science and Mechanics
- SULLIVAN, W. G., Industrial Engineering
- SYMONDS, F. W., Electrical Engineering
- THOMAS, L. C., Mechanical and Aerospace Engineering
- TILLMAN, J. D., Jr., Electrical Engineering
- TSCHANTZ, B. A., Civil Engineering
- VANDERMEER, R. A., Chemical and Metallurgical Engineering
- WATSON, J. S., Chemical and Metallurgical Engineering
- WEGMANN, F. J., Civil Engineering
- WHITE, J. L., Chemical and Metallurgical Engineering
- WILKERSON, H. J., Mechanical and Aerospace Engineering

*College of Business Administration:*
- ANDERSON, L. P., Finance
- BOHM, R. A., Finance
- BOLING, R. W., Industrial Management
- BOWLBY, R. L., Economics
- CARROLL, S. L., Economics
- COLE, W. E., Economics
- CRAVENS, D. W., Marketing and Transportation
- DAVIS, F. W., Jr., Marketing and Transportation
- DEWHIRST, H. D., Industrial Management
- DICER, G. N., Marketing and Transportation
- DITTRICH, N. E., Accounting
- DOTTERWEICH, W. W., Jr., Finance
- DUVALL, R. M., Finance
- FEIWEL, G. R., Economics
- FISHER, B. D., Accounting
- FRYE, J. L., Marketing and Transportation
- GARFINKEL, R. S., Management Science
- GARRISON, C. B., Economics
- GORDON, M. E., Industrial Management
- HENDRIX, F. L., Marketing and Transportation
- HENRY, H. W., Industrial Management
- HINES, MARY A., Finance
- JENSEN, H. E., Economics
- KIGER, J. E., Accounting
- LAMBERT, E. W., Jr., Finance
- LARSEN, J. M., Jr., Industrial Management
- LEE, FENG-YAO, Economics
- MCLEAN, R. A., Statistics
- MORSE, W. J., Accounting
- NEALE, W. C., Economics
- PATTON, E. P., Marketing and Transportation
- PHILPOT, J. W., Statistics
- QUALLS, P. D., Economics
- REED, S. K., Industrial Management
- REESE, D., Office Administration
- SMITH, E. R., Office Administration
- SPIVA, G. A., Jr., Economics
- THIGPEN, C. C., Statistics
- TOWNSEND, M. L., Accounting
- WHITLOCK, G. H., Industrial Management
- WILLIAMS, J. R., Accounting
- WOODRUFF, R. B., Marketing and Transportation

*College of Education:*
- ACHILLES, C. M., Bureau of Educational Research and Service
- ALEXANDER, J. E., Curriculum and Instruction
- ALLISON, C. B., Curriculum and Instruction
- BALL, C. H., Arts and Music Education
- BELLON, J. J., Curriculum and Instruction
- BLANK, K. J., Curriculum and Instruction
- BROMAN, B. L., Curriculum and Instruction
- BURNS, P. C., Curriculum and Instruction
- BUTEFISH, W. L., Student Teaching Operations
- CHRISTIANSEN, M. A., Curriculum and Instruction
- COAKLEY, C. B., Vocational and Technical Education, Administration
- CRAIG, D. G., Vocational and Technical Education
- DAVIS, A. R., Curriculum and Instruction
- DE RIDDER, L. M., Educational Psychology and Guidance
- DESSART, D. J., Curriculum and Instruction
- DIETZ, S. C., Educational Psychology and Guidance
- DOAK, E. D., Curriculum and Instruction
- DOLL, E. E., Special Education and Rehabilitation
- FRANKS, B. D., School of Health, P.E. and Recreation
- FREY, R. M., Special Education and Rehabilitation
- HAABY, L. O., Curriculum and Instruction
- HARGIS, C. H., Special Education and Rehabilitation
- HASKELL, R. W., Vocational and Technical Education, Administration
- HOLBERT, W. M., Special Education and Rehabilitation

HOWARD, R., Curriculum and Instruction
HUCK, S. W., Educational Psychology and Guidance
HUFFMAN, W. J., School of Health, P.E. and Recreation
JOHNSTON, A. M., Curriculum and Instruction
JOST, K. J., Curriculum and Instruction
JULIAN, W. J., Arts and Music Education
KIRK, R. H., School of Health, P.E. and Recreation
KNIGHT, L. N., Curriculum and Instruction
LIEMOHN, W. P., School of Health, P.E. and Recreation
LOGAN, N. P., Vocational and Technical Education, Administration
LOVELL, J. T., Educational Administration
McCLAIN, E. W., Educational Psychology and Guidance
MALIK, A., Curriculum and Instruction
MATTHEWS, J. I., Vocational and Technical Education
MILLER, J. H., Special Education and Rehabilitation
MURPHY, W. C., Curriculum and Instruction
PETERS, J. M., Continuing and Higher Education
PETERS, MARTHA L., School of Health, P.E. and Recreation
PHILLIPS, M. M., School of Health, P.E. and Recreation
POPPEN, W. A., Educational Psychology and Guidance
RAY, J. R., Curriculum and Instruction
REED, J. L., Vocational and Technical Education, Administration
ROBERTSON, J. W., Arts and Music Education
ROESKE, C. E., Curriculum and Instruction
RONEY, R. K., Educational Administration and Supervision
SHAPIRO, A., Educational Administration
STOLLAR, D. H., Educational Administration
TANNER, C. K., Educational Administration
THOMPSON, C. L., Educational Psychology and Guidance
THURMAN, R. S., Curriculum and Instruction
TRUSTY, F. M., Educational Administration
TURNER, T. N., Curriculum and Instruction
UBBEN, G. C., Educational Administration
VENDITTI, F. P., Educational Administration
WALLACE, B. C., School of Health, P.E. and Recreation
WELCH, H., School of Health, P.E. and Recreation
WIEGERS, G. W., Jr., Vocational and Technical Education, Administration
WILLIAMS, R. L., Educational Psychology and Guidance
WISHART, A. P., Curriculum and Instruction
WOODRICK, W. F., School of Health, P.E. and Recreation
WYATT, W. W., Curriculum and Instruction

*College of Communications:*
CROOK, J. A., Journalism
FLETCHER, A. D., Advertising
HASKINS, J., Journalism
HOLT, D. W., Broadcasting
HOWARD, H. H., Broadcasting
JOEL, R., Advertising
LEITER, B. K., Journalism
LYNN, J. R., Advertising

*College of Agriculture:*
BADENHOP, M. B., Agricultural Economics
BARTH, K. M., Animal Science
BELL, F. F., Plant and Soil Science
BELL, M. C., Animal Science
BROOKER, J. R., Agricultural Economics
BROWN, D. W., Agricultural Economics
CALLAHAN, L. M., Ornamental Horticulture and Landscape Design
CHAMBERLAIN, C. C., Animal Science
COLLINS, J. L., Food Technology and Science
CONGER, B. V., Plant and Soil Science
CONSTANTIN, M. J., Animal Research Laboratory
DARDEN, E. B., Animal Research Laboratory
DIMMICK, R. W., Forestry
DUBOV, I., Agricultural Economics
ERICKSON, B. H., Animal Research Laboratory
FRIBOURG, H. A., Plant and Soil Science
HILTY, J. W., Agricultural Biology
JAYNES, H. O., Food Technology and Science
JOHNSON, L. F., Agricultural Biology
JOHNSON, R. R., Animal Science
KELLER, L. H., Agricultural Economics
LEUTHOLD, F. O., Agricultural Economics
LIDVALL, E. R., Jr., Animal Science
McCLAREN, J. B., Animal Science
McFEE, A. F., Animal Research Laboratory
McMANUS, B. R., Agricultural Economics
MARTIN, J. A., Agricultural Economics
MELTON, C. C., Food Technology and Science
MILES, J. T., Food Technology and Science
MONTGOMERY, M. J., Animal Science
MRAZ, F. R., Animal Research Laboratory
MURPHREE, R. L., Animal Science
PARKS, W. L., Plant and Soil Science
PELTON, M. R., Forestry
PLESS, C. D., Entomology and Plant Pathology
REYNOLDS, J. H., Plant and Soil Science
RICHARDSON, D. O., Animal Science
SAPPINGTON, C. B., Agricultural Economics
SCHNEIDER, G., Forestry
SCHNEIDER, M. D., Animal Research Laboratory
SEATZ, L. F., Plant and Soil Science
SHIRLEY, H. V., Jr., Animal Science
SHRODE, R. R., Animal Science
SKOLD, L. N., Plant and Soil Science
SOUTHARDS, C. J., Agricultural Biology
SWANSON, E. W., Animal Science
THOR, E., Forestry
WOODS, F. W., Forestry

*College of Veterinary Medicine:*
BARRON, H. T., Rural Practice
GAGE, E. D., Urban Practice
JONES, J. B., Environmental Practice
KRAHWINKEL, D. J., Jr., Urban Practice
McGAVIN, M. D., Pathobiology
MICHEL, R. L., Pathobiology
POTGIETER, L. N. D., Pathobiology
ROUSE, B. T., Microbiology and Veterinary Medicine

*College of Law:*
COOK, J. G.
COVEN, G.
GOBERT, J. J.
JONES, D. S.
KING, J. H., Jr.
LACEY, F. W.
LECLERQ, F. S.
PHILLIPS, J. J.
SEBERT, J. A.
SOBIESKI, J. L., Jr.
SEWELL, T. H.
THOMFORDE, F. H.
WICKHAM, D. Q.

*School of Architecture:*
ANDERSON, G.
CONLEY, C.
DELONG, A. J.
FORTEY, J. W.
GRIEGER, F.
KERSAVAGE, J. A.
RUTH, D. K.
SHELL, W. S.
WODEHOUSE, L. M.

*Graduate School of Social Work:*
BLOCH, M. H.
BONOVICH, R. C.
FRYER, G. W.
McLARNAN, GEORGIANA
MULLINS, M. K.

*Graduate School of Bio-medical Sciences:*
BILLEN, D.
COOK, J. S.
DUMONT, J. N.
JACOBSON, K. B.
LEVY, H. A.
OLINS, D. E.
STULBERG, M. P.

*Graduate School of Planning:*
JOHNSON, D. A.
KENNEY, K. B.
PROCHASKA, J. M.
SHOUSE, W. L.
SPENCER, J. A.

*Graduate School of Library Sciences:*
MAULDIN, E. E.
PURCELL, G. R.

*Space Institute:*
CRAWFORD, L. W.
DAVIS, M. G.
DICKS, J. B.
DONALDSON, F. W.
FROST, W.
HARWELL, K. E.
HUEBSCHMANN, E. C.
JACOBS, W. F.
KEEFER, D. R.
KUROSAKA, M.
LEWIS, J. W.
MAUS, J. R., Jr.
PETERS, C. E.
REDDY, K. C.
SHAHROKHI, F.
WRIGHT, M. A.
WU, J. M.
WU, YING-CHU
YOUNG, R. L.

*Transportation Center:*
HEATHINGTON, K. W.

*Nashville Graduate Engineering Program:*
WESTBROOK, J. D. (Director)

*Library:*
BASSETT, R. J.
BRANCH, O. H.
DOBSON, J. H.

*Computer Center:*
CLINE, R. E.

## University of Tennessee Center for Health Sciences

MEMPHIS, TENNESSEE 38103
*Chancellor:* Dr. JAMES C. HUNT.
*Executive Assistant to the Chancellor:* Dr. SAMUEL R. BOZEMAN.

# UNIVERSITIES AND COLLEGES—TENNESSEE (UNIVERSITY OF) — U.S.A.

*Vice-Chancellor for Academic Affairs:* Dr. JOHN A. SHIVELY.
*Vice-Chancellor for Administration:* T. EARL BOWEN.
*Vice-Chancellor for Business and Finance:* ROBERT L. BLACKWELL.
*Vice-Chancellor for Knoxville Unit:* Dr. ALBERT W. BIGGS.
*Registrar:* LEON HESS.

### DEANS:

*College of Basic Medical Sciences and Graduate School:* (vacant).
*College of Community and Allied Health Professions:* L. HOLDER, M.PH., PH.D.
*College of Medicine:* ROBERT L. SUMMITT, M.D.
*College of Dentistry:* WILLIAM A. SLAGLE (acting).
*College of Pharmacy:* J. AUTIAN, PH.D.
*College of Nursing:* (vacant).
*Director, Interdisciplinary Programs:* JOHN A. SHIVELY, M.D.

### DEPARTMENT CHAIRMEN:

*College of Basic Medical Sciences:*
  *Anatomy:* SIDNEY A. COHN.
  *Biochemistry:* WILLIAM E. JEFFERSON.
  *Medical Biology, Knoxville Unit:* ROBERT D. LANGE.
  *Microbiology:* BOB A. FREEMAN.
  *Pharmacology:* MURRAY HEIMBERG.
  *Physiology and Biophysics:* LEONARD SHARE.

*College of Medicine:*
  *Anaesthesiology:* WILLIAM C. NORTH.
  *Family Medicine:* THORNTON E. BRYAN.
  *Neurology:* ALBERT F. HECK.
  *Obstetrics and Gynaecology:* PRESTON V. DILTS.
  *Paediatrics:* JOHN F. GRIFFITH.
  *Community Medicine:* JOHN W. RUNYAN.
  *Psychiatry:* WILLIAM WEBB.
  *Radiology:* BARRY E. GERALD.
  *General Surgery:* JAMES W. PATE.
  *Urology:* CLAIR E. COX.
  *Neurosurgery:* JAMES T. ROBERTSON.
  *Ophthalmology:* ROGER L. HIATT.
  *Orthopaedic Surgery:* R. A. CALANBRUCCIO.
  *Otolaryngology:* WINSOR V. MORRISON.
  *Pathology:* ERIC MUIRHEAD.
  *Medicine:* GENE H. STOLLERMAN.
  *Medicine—Haematology:* ALFRED P. KRAUS.
  *Medicine—Oncology:* CHARLES L. NEELY.
  *Family Practice Resident Program:* GEORGE E. SHACKLETT.

*College of Dentistry:*
  *Biomaterials:* LOYS NUNEZ (acting).
  *Fixed Prosthodontics:* FRED A. SHAW, Jr.
  *Operative Dentistry:* JAMES T. ANDREWS.
  *Oral Diagnosis:* ROY M. SMITH.
  *Oral Surgery:* JOE H. MORRIS.
  *Orthodontics:* ROBERT F. TAYLOR.
  *Pedodontics:* JAMES P. MCKNIGHT.
  *Periodontics:* BERNARD L. RAINEY.
  *Removable Prosthodontics:* GIRD A. MCCARTY.
  *Oral Pathology:* JAMES E. TURNER.
  *Behavioral Sciences:* VICTOR M. COURY.
  *Preventive and Community Dentistry:* W. THOMAS FIELDS.
  *General Dentistry:* WILLIAM A. SLAGLE.

*College of Pharmacy:*
  *Drug and Material Toxicology:* GEORGE C. WOOD.
  *Pharmaceutics:* D. C. HUFFMAN, Jr.
  *Medicinal Chemistry:* ANDREW LASSLO.
  *Pharmacy Practice:* WILLIAM A. MILLER.

*College of Nursing:*
  *Basic Nursing Concepts:* ELINOR F. REED (acting).
  *Community Mental Health:* SHIRLEY F. BURD.
  *Community Health Family Nursing:* ELINOR F. REED (acting).
  *Medical Surgical Nursing:* ELIZABETH N. STOKES (acting).
  *Primary and Long-Term Care:* E. DIANNE GREENHILL.
  *Secondary Care:* ELIZABETH N. STOKES (acting).

## University of Tennessee at Martin

MARTIN, TENNESSEE 38328

*Chancellor:* CHARLES SMITH, PH.D.
*Vice-Chancellor for Academic Affairs:* MILTON D. SIMMONS, PH.D.
*Vice-Chancellor for Business and Finance:* F. GROSS, M.S., ED.D.
*Vice-Chancellor for Student Affairs:* P. WATKINS, M.S., PH.D.
*Librarian:* JOEL A. STOWERS.

### DEANS:

*Admissions and Records:* R. W. O'BRYAN, M.C.M., ED.D.
*School of Agriculture:* H. J. SMITH, M.S., PH.D.
*School of Business Administration:* W. H. BAKER, M.S., PH.D.
*School of Education:* GEORGE M. DREW, M.A., PH.D.
*School of Home Economics:* RONALD FANNIN.
*School of Arts and Sciences:* DARYL KREILING, M.A., PH.D.
*School of Engineering:* JAMES J. JOHNSON, M.S., PH.D. (acting).
*Graduate Studies and Research:* RONALD SATZ.

## UNIVERSITY OF THE SOUTH
### (Protestant Episcopal Church)
SEWANEE, TENNESSEE 37375
Telephone: (615) 598-5931.
Chartered 1858.

*Chancellor:* Rt. Rev. FURMAN C. STOUGH.
*Vice-Chancellor:* ROBERT M. AYERS, D.C.L.
*Provost:* ARTHUR M. SCHAEFER, PH.D.
*Director of Summer College:* FREDERICK H. CROOM, PH.D.
*Director of Graduate School of Theology:* Rev. DONALD S. ARMENTROUT, TH.D.
*Registrar:* J. B. RANSOM.
*Librarian:* T. G. WATSON, M.S.L.S.

The library contains 329,017 vols.
Number of teachers: College 99, Seminary 13.
Number of students: College 1,063, Seminary 75.

Publications: *Sewanee Review*, *St. Luke's Journal of Theology*.

### DEANS:

*College of Arts and Sciences:* W. BROWN PATTERSON, PH.D.
*Dean of Men:* J. DOUGLAS SEITERS, PH.D.
*Dean of Women:* MARY S. CUSHMAN, M.ED.
*School of Theology:* Very Rev. U. T. HOLMES, S.T.M., PH.D., D.D.

## VANDERBILT UNIVERSITY
NASHVILLE, TENNESSEE 37240
Telephone: (615) 322-7311.
Founded 1873.

*Chancellor:* ALEXANDER HEARD, PH.D.
*President:* EMMETT B. FIELDS, PH.D.
*Provost:* W. G. HOLLADAY, PH.D.
*Vice-Presidents:* R. R. ROBINSON, M.D., J. R. CARR, J.D.
*Treasurer:* CHARLES J. KANE, Jr.
*Secretary:* J. R. CARR, J.D.
*Registrar:* W. O. BATTS, Jr., PH.D.
*Librarian:* F. P. GRISHAM, M.L.S.

Number of teachers: 2,182.
Number of students: 8,911.

### DEANS:

*Graduate School:* E. Q. CAMPBELL, PH.D.
*College of Arts and Science:* V. J. VOEGELI, PH.D.
*School of Engineering:* PAUL HARRAWOOD, PH.D.
*Divinity School:* H. JACKSON FORSTMAN, B.D., TH.D.
*School of Law:* C. DENT BOSTICK, J.D.
*Owen Graduate School of Management:* S. B. RICHMOND, PH.D.
*School of Medicine:* J. E. CHAPMAN, M.D.
*School of Nursing:* S. K ARCHER, ED.D.
*George Peabody College for Teachers:* W. D. HAWLEY, PH.D.

### PROFESSORS:

ABERNETHY, V. D., PH.D., Psychiatry
ADEN, J. M., PH.D., English
ALAM, D., ED.D., Education
ALBRIDGE, R. G., PH.D., Physics
ALFORD, R. H., M.D., Medicine
ALLEN, J. H., Jr., M.D., Radiology
ALTEMEIER, W. A., III, M.D., Paediatrics
ANABTAWI, S. N., PH.D., Political Science

ANDREWS, J. R., PH.D., Spanish and Portuguese
ARCHER, S. K., ED.D., Nursing
ARENSTORF, R. F., PH.D., Mathematics
ASHCROFT, S. C., ED.D., Special Education
AUBREY, R. F., ED.D., Psychology and Education
BAN, T. A., PH.D., Psychiatry
BARACH, J. P., PH.D., Physics
BARTEE, E. M., PH.D., Engineering Management
BASSLER, O. C., PH.D., Mathematics Education
BATSON, R., M.D., Paediatrics
BAUCH, J. P., ED.D., Education
BAUMEISTER, A. A., PH.D., Psychology
BAYUZICK, R. J., PH.D., Materials Science and Engineering
BENDER, H. W., Jr., M.D., Surgery
BENNETT, G. N., PH.D., English
BEN-PORAT, T., PH.D., Microbiology
BERMAN, M. L., PH.D., M.D., Anaesthesiology
BESS, F. H., PH.D., Audiology
BIGLER, H. F., D.N.SC., Psychiatric Nursing
BJORK, R. M., PH.D., Education
BLACK, S. W., PH.D., Economics
BLANTON, R. L., PH.D., Psychology
BLITZ, R. C., PH.D., Economics
BLOCH, I., PH.D., Physics
BLUMSTEIN, J. F., LL.B., Law
BÖER, G., PH.D., Management
BOGITSH, B. J., PH.D., Biology
BOLCH, B. W., PH.D., Economics
BOORMAN, H. L., B.A., History
BOSTICK, C. D., LL.B., Law
BOURNE, J. R., PH.D., Electrical Engineering and Biomedical Engineering
BRANSFORD, J. D., PH.D., Psychology
BRIGHAM, K. L., M.D., Medicine
BRITTINGHAM, T. E., M.D., Medicine
BRODERSEN, A. J., Electrical Engineering
BROOKS, A. L., Orthopaedics and Rehabilitation
BROOKS, P. H., PH.D., Psychology
BROOKS, R. C., Jr., PH.D., Business Administration
BROQUIST, H. P., PH.D., Biochemistry
BRUMBAUGH, T. B., PH.D., Fine Arts
BRYANT, B. F., PH.D., Mathematics
BURNETT, L. S., M.D., Obstetrics and Gynaecology
BURR, I. M., M.D., Paediatrics
BURT, A. M., III, PH.D., Anatomy
CALVANI, T., J.D., Law
CAMPBELL, E. Q., PH.D., Sociology
CANNON, R. O., M.D., Medical Administration
CASTELNUOVO-TEDESCO, P., M.D., Psychiatry
CAUL, W. F., PH.D., Psychology
CHANNELL, R. B., PH.D., Biology
CHAPMAN, J. E., M.D., Pharmacology, Medical Administration
CHARNEY, J. I., J.D., Law
CHYTIL, F., C.SC., Biochemistry
CLAYTON, K. N., PH.D., Psychology
COHEN, S., PH.D., Biochemistry
COLEMAN, R., PH.D., Hearing and Speech Sciences
COLLEY, D. G., PH.D., Microbiology
COLLINS, R. D., PH.D., Pathology
COLOWICK, S. P., PH.D., Microbiology
COMPTON, J. J., PH.D., Philosophy
CONIGLIO, J. G., PH.D., Biochemistry
CONKIN, P. K., PH.D., History
COOK, G. E., Electrical Engineering
CORBIN, J. D., PH.D., Physiology
COVINGTON, R. N., J.D., Law
CRENSHAW, J. L., PH.D., Old Testament
CRIST, L. S., PH.D., French
CROFFORD, O. B., Jr., M.D., Medicine
CUNNINGHAM, L. W., PH.D., Biochemistry
DAANE, J. D., D.P.A., Banking

DAVIE, D. A., PH.D., Humanities and English
DAVIES, J., M.D., Anatomy
DELZELL, C. F., PH.D., History
DENNIS, H. F., Jr., J.D., Special Education
DES PREZ, R. M., M.D., Medicine
DETTBARN, W., M.D., Pharmacology
DOKECKI, P., PH.D., Psychology and Special Education
DONALDSON, M. L., PH.D., Nursing
DONALDSON, R. H., PH.D., Political Science
DORE, C., PH.D., Philosophy
DORSEY, J. T., Jr., PH.D., Political Science
DREWS, R., PH.D., Classics
ECKENFELDER, W. W., M.CHEM.ENG., Environmental and Water Resources
ELLEDGE, W. P., PH.D., English
ELLIOTT, J. H., M.D., Ophthalmology
ELY, J. W., Jr., LL.B., PH.D., Law
ENGEL, J. E., Germanic Languages and Literatures
ENGEL, W. V.R., PH.D., Linguistics
EXTON, J. H., M.B., CH.B., PH.D., Physiology
FARLEY, E., PH.D., Theology
FARRAR, D. F., Jr., Mechanical Engineering
FEDERSPIEL, C. F., PH.D., Biostatistics
FELS, R. T., PH.D., Economics
FENICHEL, G. M., M.D., Neurology and Paediatrics
FIELD, L., PH.D., Chemistry
FIELDS, E. B., PH.D., History
FINEGAN, T. A., PH.D., Economics
FISCHER, C. F., PH.D., Computer Science and Mathematics
FISCHER, P. C., PH.D., Computer Science
FLANAGAN, W. F., SC.D., Materials Science, Technology and Public Policy
FLEISCHER, S., PH.D., Molecular Biology
FORCE, W. W., ED.D., Education
FORD, C. V., M.D., Psychiatry
FORSTMAN, H. J., TH.D., Theology
FOX, R., PH.D., Psychology and Biomedical Engineering
FREEMAN, J. A., M.D., PH.D., Anatomy and Ophthalmology
FREEMAN, J. L., PH.D., Political Science
FREEMON, F. R., M.D., Neurology
FRIESINGER, G. C., II, M.D., Medicine
FURTWENGLER, W. J., PH.D., Education
GARDNER, W. A., M.D., Pathology
GIBBS, J. P., PH.D., Sociology
GINN, H. E., M.D., Medicine
GLEAVES, E. S., Jr., PH.D., Library Science
GOBBEL, W. G., M.D., Surgery
GOLDBERG, R. R., PH.D., Mathematics
GOODWIN, R. A., M.D., Medicine
GORSTEIN, F., M.D., Pathology
GOSHEN, C. E., M.D., Engineering Management and Psychiatry
GOVE, W. R., PH.D., Sociology
GRAHAM, G. J., Jr., PH.D., Political Science
GRAHAM, T. P., Jr., M.D., Paediatrics
GRANTHAM, D. W., Jr., PH.D., History
GREENE, H. L., M.D., Paediatrics
GRIFFIN, P. P., M.D., Orthopaedics and Rehabilitation
HAHN, G. T., SC.D., Metallurgical Engineering
HALL, D. J., J.D., Law
HALL, D. S., PH.D., Physics and Astronomy
HALL, H. D., D.M.D., Oral Surgery
HAMILTON, J. H., PH.D., Physics
HANCOCK, M. D., PH.D., Political Science
HARDACRE, P. H., PH.D., History
HARDIE, R. H., PH.D., Physics and Astronomy
HARDMAN, J. G., PH.D., Pharmacology
HARGROVE, E. C., PH.D., Political Science
HARLEY, R., PH.D., Special Education
HARRAWOOD, P., PH.D., Civil Engineering
HARRELSON, W., TH.D., Old Testament
HARRIS, T. M., PH.D., Chemistry

HARRIS, T. R., PH.D., M.D., Biomedical Engineering and Chemical Engineering
HARSHMAN, S., D.SC., Microbiology
HARTMANN, W. H., M.D., Pathology
HASH, J. H., PH.D., Microbiology
HAVARD, W. C., Jr., PH.D., Political Science
HAWIGER, J., D.M.SC., Pathology and Medicine
HAWLEY, W. D., PH.D., Education and Political Science
HAYES, W. J., Jr., PH.D., Biochemistry
HAYWOOD, H. C., Psychology and Neurology
HAZLEHURST, F. H., PH.D., Fine Arts
HEARD, A., PH.D., Political Science
HELGUERA, J. L., PH.D., History
HELLER, R. M., Jr., M.D., Radiology
HEMMINGER, R. C., PH.D., Mathematics
HESS, B. A., Jr., PH.D., Chemistry
HNILICA, L., PH.D., Cancer Research, Biochemistry, Pathology
HOADLEY, P. G., PH.D., Civil Engineering
HODGSON, P. C., PH.D., Theology
HOGGE, J., PH.D., Psychology
HOLADAY, D. A., M.D., Anaesthesiology
HOLLADAY, W. G., PH.D., Physics
HOLLENDER, M. H., M.D., Psychiatry
HORN, R. G., Pathology
HOUSE, R. W., PH.D., Technology and Public Policy
HUNTER, R. G., PH.D., English
INAGAMI, T., PH.D., D.SC., Biochemistry
JAMES, A. E., M.D., Radiology and Medical Administration
JENKINS, D. E., Jr., Medicine and Pathology
JOESTEN, M. D., PH.D., Chemistry
JOHNSON, L. E., PH.D., Electrical Engineering and Biomedical Engineering
JONES, C. D., PH.D., Drama
JONES, E. A., PH.D., Physics
JONES, M. M., PH.D., Chemistry
JONSSON, B., PH.D., Mathematics
KAAS, J. H., PH.D., Psychology
KAMENSHIRE, R. D., LL.M., Law
KAPLAN, A. S., PH.D., Microbiology
KARZON, D. T., M.D., Paediatrics
KATAHN, M., PH.D., Psychology
KAVASS, I. I., LL.B., Law
KEEDY, H. F., PH.D., Engineering Science
KILLAM, A. P., M.D., Obstetrics and Gynaecology
KILLINGER, J. L., PH.D., S.T.B., TH.D., Preaching
KILROY, J. F., PH.D., English
KINSER, D. L., PH.D., Materials Science
KIRKMAN, R. E., ED.D., Higher Education
KNAUSS, R. L., J.D., Law
KONO, T., PH.D., Physiology
KRAL, R., PH.D., Biology
KRANTZ, S. B., M.D., Medicine
LABEN, J. K., J.D., Nursing
LACHS, J., PH.D., Philosophy
LAWTON, A. R., M.D., Paediatrics and Microbiology
LEACH, D. E., PH.D., History
LEBLON, J., PH.D., French
LEFKOWITZ, L. B., Jr., M.D., Preventive Medicine and Public Health
LENT, J. R., ED.D., Special Education
LEQUIRE, V. S., M.D., Anatomy and Experimental Pathology
LEVINSON, L. H., J.S.D., Law
LICHTER, B. D., SC.D., Materials Science
LIDDLE, G. W., M.D., Medicine
LOVE, R., PH.D., Hearing and Speech Sciences
LUCAS, F. V., M.D., Pathology
LUKENS, J. M., M.D., Paediatrics
LYNCH, J. B., Plastic Surgery
MCCOY, T. R., J.D., Law
MCFAGUE, S., PH.D., Theology
MCGEE, Z. A., M.D., Medicine
MAIER, H. G., LL.M., Law

UNIVERSITIES AND COLLEGES—TENNESSEE, TEXAS                                                                U.S.A.

MARTIN, T. W., PH.D., Chemistry
MASTERS, J. C., PH.D., Psychology
MAUKSCH, I. G., PH.D., Nursing
MEADOR, C., M.D., Medicine
MEGIBBEN, C. K., PH.D., Mathematics
MENG, H. C., PH.D., Physiology and Surgery
MILLER, F. A., PH.D., History
MILLER, J. W., ED.D., Education
MILLS, L. O., TH.D., Pastoral Theology and Counseling
MITCHELL, W. M., PH.D., Pathology
MORLEY, S. A., PH.D., Economics
MOSIG, G., M.D., Molecular Biology
MYERS, C. B., PH.D., Social Studies Education
NEAL, R. A., PH.D., Biochemistry
NETSKY, M. G., M.D. Pathology
NEWBROUGH, J. R., PH.D., Psychology and Education
NORRIS, R. C., PH.D., Psychology
NORTON, H. A., M.A., PH.D., Church History
NUNNALLY, J. C., PH.D., Psychology
OATES, J. A., M.D., Medicine and Pharmacology
O'DAY, D. M., M.D., Ophthalmology
ODOM, R. D., PH.D., Psychology
OGLETREE, T. W., PH.D., Theological Ethics
O'LEARY, J. P., M.D., Surgery
O'NEILL, J. A., M.D., Paediatric Surgery
ORGEBIN-CRIST, M.-C., Reproductive Biology and Family Planning, Anatomy
ORTH, D. N., M.D., Medicine
PAGE, D. L., M.D., Pathology
PAINE, T. F., Jr., M.D., Medicine
PALMER, R. E., Jr., PH.D., English
PARK, C. R., M.D., Physiology
PARK, J. H., PH.D., Physiology
PARKER, F. L., PH.D., Environmental and Water Resources Engineering
PATE, J.E., ED.D., Psychiatry (Educational Psychology)
PATTE, D. M., PH.D., Religious Studies
PATTY, J. S., PH.D., French
PEARSON, D. E., PH.D., Chemistry
PENDERGRASS, H., M.D., Radiology
PETERKIN, G., ED.D., Education
PETERSON, R. A., PH.D., Sociology
PHILLIPS, L., PH.D., Psychology
PICHOIS, C., D. ès L., French
PINCUS, T., M.D., Medicine and Microbiology
PINKSTON, W. T., PH.D., Physics
PLUMMER, M. D., PH.D., Mathematics
POGGENBURG, R. P., PH.D., French
POST, R. L., M.D., Physiology
PUETT, J. D., PH.D., Biochemistry
PUPO-WALKER, E., PH.D., Spanish
RABIN, D., M.D., Obstetrics and Gynaecology
RADOS, D. L., PH.D., Management
RAMAYYA, A. V., PH.D., Physics
RAMSEY, L. H., M.D., Medicine
RANDLES, H. E., PH.D., Education
RANSOM, H. H., PH.D., Political Science
RAY, O. S., PH.D., Psychology
REGEN, D. M., PH.D., Physiology
RHAMY, R. K., M.D., Urology
RHEIN, P. H., PH.D., Comparative Literature and German
RICHMOND, S. B., PH.D., Management
ROBACK, H. B., PH.D., Psychiatry and Psychology
ROGERS, I. L., PH.D., Higher Education
ROLLO, F. D., M.D., Radiology
ROOS, C. E., PH.D., Physics
ROTH, J. A., PH.D., Chemical Engineering and Environmental Engineering
ROWAN, W. H., Jr., PH.D., Computer Science
ROWE, R. S., D.ENG., Civil Engineering and Environmental and Water Resources Engineering
RUSHING, W. A., PH.D., Sociology

SAHOTA, G. S., PH.D., Economics
SALMON, W. D., Jr., M.D., Medicine
SANDERS, J., PH.D., Audiology
SANDERS-BUSH, E., PH.D., Pharmacology
SASTRY, B. V. R., D.SC., PH.D., Pharmacology
SAWYERS, J. L., M.D., Surgery
SCHAAD, L. J., PH.D., Chemistry
SCHAFFNER, W., M.D., Medicine and Public Health
SCHENKER, S., M.D., Medicine
SCHNEIDER, F. D., PH.D., History
SCHNELLE, K. B., Jr., PH.D., Chemical and Environmental Engineering
SCOTT, C. E., PH.D., Philosophy
SCOTT, H. W., Jr., M.D., Surgery
SEEMAN, J., PH.D., Psychology
SEVERINO, A. E., PH.D., Portuguese
SHAPIRO, A., PH.D., Education
SHAVER, L., PH.D., Physical Education
SHERBURNE, D. W., PH.D., Philosophy
SHORES, R. E., ED.D., Special Education
SIEGEL, E., PH.D., Radiology and Physics
SINCLAIR-SMITH, B., M.B.B.S., Medicine
SKEEL, D. J., D.ED., Social Studies Education
SLOAN, F. A., PH.D., Economics
SMITH, B. E., M.D., Anaesthesiology
SMITH, H. E., PH.D., Chemistry
SMITH, W. P., PH.D., Psychology
SNELL, J. D., Jr., M.D., Medicine
SOUPART, P., PH.D., Obstetrics and Gynaecology (Research)
SPICKARD, W. H., Jr., M.D., Medicine
SPORES, R., PH.D., Anthropology
STAHLMAN, M., M.D., Pediatrics
STEARNS, R. G., PH.D., Geology
STEPHENSON, C. V., PH.D., Electrical Engineering
STOLL, H. R., PH.D., Finance
STOVALL, T. F., PH.D., Education
STRUPP, H. H., PH.D., Psychology
STUMPF, S. E., PH.D., Law
SULLIVAN, W. L., M.F.A., English
SULSER, F., M.D., Pharmacology
SURFACE, J. R., D.C.S., Management
TANG, A. M., PH.D., Economics
TARBELL, D. S., PH.D., Chemistry
TeSELLE, E. A., Jr., PH.D., Church History and Theology
THACKSTON, E. L., PH.D., Civil and Environmental Engineering
THEIL, G. B., M.D., Medicine
THISTLEWAITE, D. L., PH.D., Psychology
THREADGILL, W. D., PH.D., Chemical Engineering
THWEATT, W. O., B.PHIL., Economics
TITUS, W. I., PH.D., English Education
TOUSTER, O., PH.D., Biochemistry, Molecular Biology
TOWNSEND, M. A., PH.D., Mechanical Engineering
ULLRICH, R. A., D.B.A., Management
VANCE, C. M., M.A., Spanish
VAN WAZER, J. R., PH.D., Chemistry
VOEGELI, V. J., PH.D., History
WACHS, M., PH.D., French
WADE, J. W., S.J.D., Law
WAGNER, C., PH.D., Biochemistry
WALTER, B., PH.D., Political Science
WARDEN, K. P., LL.M., Law
WEATHERBY, H. L., Jr., PH.D., English
WEBB, G. F., PH.D., Mathematics
WEBB, W. W., PH.D., Psychiatry and Psychology
WEBSTER, M. S., PH.D., Physics
WEINGARTNER, H. M., PH.D., Finance
WELLS, C. E., M.D., Psychiatry and Neurology
WERT, J. J., PH.D., Metallurgy
WESSON, J. R., M.A., PH.D., Mathematics
WESTFIELD, F. M., PH.D., Economics
WHITLOCK, J. W., ED.D., Education
WHITTIER, D. P., PH.D., Biology
WILCOXON, H. C., PH.D., Psychology

WILKINSON, G. R., PH.D., Pharmacology
WILLERS, J. C., PH.D., Education
WILLIAMS, H. E., PH.D., Mathematics
WILLIAMSON, J. W., PH.D., Mechanical Engineering
WILLIAMSON, M. A., PH.D., Engineering Management
WILSON, B. J., PH.D., Biochemistry
WILSON, D. J., PH.D., Chemistry and Environmental Chemistry
WILSON, L. K., PH.D., Electrical Engineering
WILSON, V. E., M.D., Medical Administration, Preventive Medicine and Public Health
WINTERS, D. L., PH.D., History
WOLF, F. T., M.A., PH.D., Biology
WORLEY, J. S., PH.D., Economics and Business Administration
WRIGHT, J. E., M.A., Drama and Speech
WRIGHT, W. F., M.S., Mechanical Engineering
YOUNG, T. D., PH.D., English


# TEXAS

## ABILENE CHRISTIAN UNIVERSITY
ACU STATION,
ABILENE, TEXAS 79699

Founded 1906.

Private (Church of Christ) liberal arts.

*President:* JOHN C. STEVENS.
*Vice-President:* ROBERT D. HUNTER.
*Vice-President for Academic Affairs:* EDWARD M. BROWN.
*Dean:* EDWARD M. BROWN.
*Dean of Research and Graduate School:* FLOYD W. DUNN.

The library contains c. 354,152 vols.
Number of teachers: 208.
Number of students: 4,372.

Publication: *ACU Today.*


## ANGELO STATE UNIVERSITY
ASU STATION,
SAN ANGELO, TEXAS 76901
Telephone: (915) 942-2131.

Founded 1928.

*President:* Dr. LLOYD D. VINCENT.
*Vice-President for Academic Affairs:* Dr. HUGH E. MEREDITH.
*Vice-President for University Affairs:* Dr. OLLIE S. CAUTHEN.
*Vice-President for Fiscal Affairs:* ROBERT L. KRUPALA.
*Registrar:* Dr. WARREN L. GRIFFIN.
*Librarian:* JOE B. LEE.

The library contains 200,000 vols.
Number of teachers: 162.
Number of students: 5,637.


## AUSTIN COLLEGE
SHERMAN, TEXAS 75090

Founded 1849.

Four-year Liberal Arts Co-educational Christian College.

*President:* HARRY E. SMITH.

*Assistant President and Vice-President for Institutional Advancement:* J. SCOTT BUCHANAN.
*Executive Vice-President and Dean of the Faculty:* DAN T. BEDSOLE.
*Treasurer and Vice-President for Business Affairs:* GEORGE ROWLAND.
*Vice-President for Development:* W. R. WILSON.
*Vice-President for College Relations:* HOWARD A. STARR.

The library contains 179,000 vols.
Number of teachers: full-time 100, part-time 14.
Number of students: full-time 1,120, part-time 70.

### BAYLOR UNIVERSITY
WACO, TEXAS 76706

Telephone: (817) 755-1011.

Chartered 1845 under Republic of Texas by Texas Baptist Educational Society at Independence, Texas; consolidated 1886 with Waco University and came under control of Baptist General Convention of Texas.

*President:* ABNER V. MCCALL, LL.M., LL.D.
*Executive Vice-President and Chief Operating Officer:* H. H. REYNOLDS, PH.D.
*Vice-President of Baylor University in Dallas:* B. POWELL, LL.D.
*Secretary:* B. FANNING.
*Director of Admissions:* H. D. THOMAS.
*Librarian:* J. H. ROGERS, M.LIB.SC.

Number of teachers: 400.
Number of students: 9,000.

Publications: *Bulletin* (quarterly), *Law Review*, *Business Studies* (quarterly), *Baylor Line*, *Baylor Geological Studies*, *Journal of Church and State*.

### BISHOP COLLEGE
3837 SIMPSON-STUART RD.,
DALLAS, TEXAS 75241

Telephone: 372-8000.

Founded 1881.

*President:* Dr. HARRY S. WRIGHT (acting).
*Registrar:* J. D. HURD.
*Librarian:* Dr. HARRY ROBINSON, Jr.

Number of teachers: 53.
Number of students: 926.

Publications: *The Bishop Herald*, *The Caretaker*.

### CORPUS CHRISTI STATE UNIVERSITY
P.O.B. 6010, CORPUS CHRISTI, TEXAS 78411

Founded 1971.

*President:* B. ALAN SUGG, M.ED., PH.D.
*Registrar:* WILLIAM C. MARTIN, B.M.E., M.M., ED.D.

*Business Manager:* J. A. GARCIA, Jr., B.A.
*Librarian:* CARL R. WROTENBERY, B.D., TH.D.

DEANS:
*Arts and Humanities:* MIRIAM WAGENSCHFIN, M.A., ED.D.
*Science and Technology:* RALPH GILCHRIST, M.S., PH.D.
*Teacher Education:* WALLACE DAVIS, M.S., PH.D.
*Business Administration:* JOHN M. RICHARDS, M.S., PH.D.

### EAST TEXAS BAPTIST COLLEGE
1209 N. GROVE STREET,
MARSHALL, TEXAS 75670

Telephone: (214) 935-7963.

Founded 1912.

*President:* Dr. JERRY F. DAWSON.
*Registrar:* MARGARET FROMM.
*Librarian:* E. M. ADAMS, Jr.

The library contains 85,000 vols.
Number of teachers: 42.
Number of students: 900.

### EAST TEXAS STATE UNIVERSITY
COMMERCE, TEXAS 75428

Telephone: (214) 886-5014.

Founded 1889.

*President:* F. H. MCDOWELL.
*Vice-President for Administration:* CHARLES MORROW.
*Vice-President for Academic Affairs:* Dr. BARRY B. THOMPSON.
*Vice-President for Student Affairs:* Dr. RUTH A. WHITE.
*Director of Admissions and Records:* Mrs. JEAN SMITH.

The library contains 527,689 vols. and microfilms.
Number of teachers: 365 full-time.
Number of students: 8,752.

### HARDIN-SIMMONS UNIVERSITY
DRAWER A, H-SU STATION,
ABILENE, TEXAS 79698

Telephone: (915) 677-7281.

Founded 1891.

*President:* Dr. JESSE C. FLETCHER.
*Registrar:* Mrs. CHARLENE ARCHER.
*Director of Admissions:* ED JACKSON.
*Dean:* Dr. RONALD A. SMITH.
*Librarian:* JOE F. DAHLSTROM.

The library contains 294,400 vols.
Number of teachers: 121.
Number of students: 1,969.

### HOWARD PAYNE UNIVERSITY
BROWNWOOD, TEXAS 76801

Telephone: 646-2502.

Founded 1889.

*President:* Dr. RALPH A. PHELPS, Jr.

*Registrar:* BENNETT RAGSDALE.
*Librarian:* CORRINE SHIELDS.

The library contains 123,000 vols.
Number of teachers: 75.
Number of students: 1,121.

### HUSTON-TILLOTSON COLLEGE
1820 EAST 8TH STREET,
AUSTIN, TEXAS 78702

Telephone: 476-7421.

Founded 1876.

*President:* JOHN Q. TAYLOR KING.
*Dean:* E. A. DELCO, Jr.
*Registrar:* Mrs. VIRGINIA L. LEWIS.
*Librarian:* Mrs. VIVIAN L. DORN.

The library contains 62,650 vols.
Number of teachers: 50.
Number of students: 793.

### INCARNATE WORD COLLEGE
4301 BROADWAY,
SAN ANTONIO, TEXAS 78209

Telephone: 828-1261.

Chartered 1881.

*President:* Sister MARGARET PATRICE SLATTERY.
*Registrar:* Sister M. ANTONINUS BUCKLEY.
*Librarian:* MENDELL MORGAN.

The library contains 123,686 vols.
Number of teachers: 112.
Number of students: 1,573.

### LAMAR UNIVERSITY
LAMAR UNIVERSITY STATION,
P.O. BOX 10001, BEAUMONT,
TEXAS 77710

Telephone: 838-7011.

Founded 1923 as South Park Junior College.

*President:* Dr. C. ROBERT KEMBLE.
*Vice-President for Finance:* OSCAR K. BAXLEY.
*Vice-President for Academic Affairs:* Dr. DAVID D. GEDDES.
*Vice-President for Administration:* Dr. A. J. JOHNSON.
*Vice-President for Student Affairs:* Dr. G. E. MCLAUGHLIN.
*Vice-President for University Relations:* W. S. LEONARD.
*Dean of Admissions and Registrar:* ELMER G. RODE.
*Librarian:* MAXINE JOHNSTON.

The library contains 430,000 vols.
Number of teachers: 496.
Number of students: 12,800.

DEANS:
*Graduate Studies:* Dr. R. E. YERICK.
*College of Education:* Dr. JAMES SCHNUR.
*College of Sciences:* Dr. R. E. YERICK.
*College of Business:* Dr. JOHN A. RYAN.

*College of Fine and Applied Arts:* Dr. W. B. Brentlinger.
*College of Engineering:* Dr. Fred M. Young.
*College of Liberal Arts:* Dr. P. B. Williams.
*College of Technical Arts:* Dr. Kenneth E. Shipper.
*College of Health Sciences:* Dr. Edna Lee Neumann.

## LAREDO STATE UNIVERSITY
WEST END WASHINGTON ST., LAREDO, TEXAS 78040

Founded 1969 as part of Texas A & I University, name changed 1977.

Upper Level College; Junior, Senior and Graduate Courses.

*President:* Billy F. Cowart, M.A., Ph.D.
*Dean:* Leo Sayavedra, M.Ed., Ph.D.
*Director of Admissions and Advisement:* Mary Trevino.
*Director of Administrative Services:* David E. VerMilyea, M.S.
*Librarian:* Mayellen Bresie, M.L.S., M.A.

## McMURRY COLLEGE
ABILENE, TEXAS 79697
Telephone: 692-4130.
Founded 1923.

*President:* Thomas K. Kim, Ph.D.
*Vice-President for Academic Affairs and Dean of the College:* Dr. Paul Jungmeyer, Ph.D.
*Vice-President for Financial Affairs and Director of Financial Aid:* Donald F. Scales.
*Vice-President for Development:* Jack Holden.
*Director of Library:* Joe W. Specht.

The library contains 14,394 vols.
Number of teachers: 118.
Number of students: 1,494.

## MIDWESTERN STATE UNIVERSITY
WICHITA FALLS, TEXAS 76308
Founded 1922.

*President:* Dr. Louis J. Rodriguez.
*Vice-President for Academic Affairs:* Dr. Jesse W. Rogers.
*Director of University Affairs:* Stephen A. Holland.
*Vice-President for Business Affairs:* Joe Hooper.
*Vice-President for Student Affairs:* James Stewart.
*Registrar:* Betty Bullock.
*Librarian:* Melba S. Harvill.

Number of teachers: 144.
Number of students: 4,400.

Publications: *The Wichitan†* (weekly), *The Wai-Kun* (annually), *M.U. News and Views†* (quarterly), *Voices* (annually), *Faculty Forum Papers* (annually).

## NORTH TEXAS STATE UNIVERSITY
DENTON, TEXAS 76203
Telephone: (817) 788-2122.
Founded 1890.

*President:* Frank E. Vandiver, Ph.D.
*Vice-President for Academic Affairs:* Howard W. Smith, Jr., Ph.D.
*Vice-President for Fiscal Affairs:* Eddie J. Davis.
*Vice-President for External Affairs:* Frederick R. Pole.
*Vice-President for University Relations:* Dr. Roy K. Busby, Ph.D.
*Vice-President for Administrative Affairs:* Alfred F. Hurley, Ph.D.
*Dean of Admissions and Records:* E. D. Norton, Jr., Ph.D.
*Librarian:* Dr. Edward R. Johnson, Ph.D.

The library contains 1,316,854 vols.
Number of teachers: 710 full-time, 102 part-time, 340 teaching fellows.
Number of students: 17,158.

### Deans:
*Students:* Dr. Joe G. Stewart, Ph.D.
*Graduate School:* Dr. R. B. Toulouse, Ph.D.
*Education:* Dr. James J. Muro, Ph.D.
*Arts and Sciences:* Dr. Hugh Ayer, Ph.D. (acting).
*Music:* Dr. Marceau Myers, Ph.D.
*Business Administration:* Dr. Marvin Berkeley, Ph.D.
*Library Science:* Dr. Dewey E. Carroll, Ph.D.
*Community Service:* Dr. Hiram Friedsam, Ph.D.

## OUR LADY OF THE LAKE UNIVERSITY OF SAN ANTONIO
411 S.W. 24TH STREET, SAN ANTONIO, TEXAS 78285
Telephone: (512) 434-6711.
Founded 1896.

*President:* Sr. Elizabeth Anne Sueltenfuss, C.D.P.
*Vice-President and Dean of Academic Affairs:* Albert J. Griffith.
*Vice-President for Finance and Facilities:* Robert F. Smith.
*Vice-President for University Relations:* Antonio Rigual.
*Registrar and Director of Admissions:* Loretta A. Schlegel.
*Planning Officer:* Marilyn Molloy, C.D.P.

The library contains 300,000 vols.
Number of teachers: 158.
Number of students: 1,900.

## PAN AMERICAN UNIVERSITY
EDINBURG, TEXAS 78539
Telephone: (512) 381-2101.
Founded 1927, reorganized 1952.

*President:* Dr. Miguel A. Nevarez.
*Director of Admissions:* David Zuniga.
*Director of Financial Aid:* Clementine Cantu.
*Librarian:* Leslie Gower.

The library contains 205,664 vols.
Number of teachers: 441.
Number of students: 9,500.

## RICE UNIVERSITY
P.O. BOX 1892, HOUSTON, TEXAS 77001
Telephone: (713) 527-8101.
Founded 1891.
Private control.

*President:* Norman Hackerman, Ph.D.
*Provost and Vice-President:* W. E. Gordon, Ph.D.
*Director of Admissions and Academic Records:* R. N. Stabell.
*Vice-President for Administration:* William W. Akers, Ph.D.
*Vice-President for Advanced Studies and Research:* J. L. Margrave.
*Registrar:* James Williamson, Ph.D.
*Librarian:* Samuel M. Carrington, Jr.

Library of over 1,000,000 vols.
Number of teachers: 410.
Number of students: 3,600.

Publications: *Journal of Southern History, Studies in English Literature 1500–1900, Rice University Studies* (quarterly).

### Deans:
*Humanities:* V. Topazio, Ph.D.
*Natural Sciences:* G. K. Watters, Ph.D.
*Social Sciences:* Joseph Cooper.
*Undergraduate Affairs:* Katherine T. Brown, M.F.A.
*Architecture:* O. Jack Mitchell, A.I.A., A.I.P.
*Music:* A. Ross, Ph.D.
*George R. Brown School of Engineering:* J. D. Hellums, Ph.D.
*Jesse H. Jones School of Administration:* D. Tuggle, Ph.D. (acting).

### Professors:
Adams, J. A. S., Ph.D., Geology
Akers, W. W., Ph.D., Chemical and Environmental Engineering
Ambler, J. S., Ph.D., Political Science
Anderson, H. R., Ph.D., Space Physics and Astronomy
Apple, Max, Ph.D., English
Armeniades, C. D., Ph.D., Chemical Engineering
Austin, W. J., Ph.D., Civil Engineering
Awapara, J., Ph.D., Biochemistry
Baker, D. R., Ph.D., Geology
Baker, S. D., Ph.D., Physics
Bearden, F. W., Ed.D., Health and Physical Education
Beckmann, H. W. K., Dr.Ing., Mechanical Engineering

BELL, P. W., PH.D., Administrative Science
BERRY, M. J., PH.D., Chemistry
BESEN, S. M., PH.D., Economics
BOCHNER, S., PH.D., Mathematics
BOWEN, R. M., PH.D., Mechanical Engineering and Mathematical Sciences
BRADY, P., D.U.P., French
BRELSFORD, J. W., PH.D., Psychology
BRODY, B. A., PH.D., Philosophy
BROOKS, P. R., PH.D., Chemistry
BROTZEN, F. R., PH.D., Materials Science
BROWN, KATHERINE T., M.F.A., Fine Arts
BURRUS, C. S., PH.D., Electrical Engineering
CAMFIELD, W. A., PH.D., Fine Arts
CAMPBELL, J. W., PH.D., Biology
CANNADY, W. T., M.ARCH., Architecture
CARRINGTON, S. M., Jr., PH.D., French
CASBARIAN, J. J., B.ARCH., Architecture
CASTAÑEDA, J. A., PH.D., Spanish
CHAMBERLAIN, J. W., PH.D., Space Physics and Astronomy
CHAPMAN, A. J., PH.D., Mechanical and Aerospace Engineering
CHEATHAM, J. B., PH.D., Mechanical and Aerospace Engineering
CLARK, J. W., Jr., PH.D., Electrical Engineering
CLASS, C. M., PH.D., Physics
CLAYTON, D. D., PH.D., Space Physics, Astronomy, Physics
CLOUTIER, P. A., PH.D., Physics, Astronomy
COOPER, J., PH.D., Political Science
COOPER, P., D.M.A., Music
CURL, R. F., Jr., PH.D., Chemistry
CURTIS, M. L., PH.D., Mathematics
CUTHBERTSON, G. M., PH.D., Political Science
DAVIS, S. H., Jr., SC.D., Chemical Engineering
DEANS, H. A., PH.D., Chemical Engineering
DEBREMAECKER, J.-C., PH.D., Geology
DE FIGUEIREDO, R. J. P., PH.D., Electrical Engineering
DENNIS, J. E., PH.D., Mathematical Sciences
DESSLER, A. J., PH.D., Space Physics and Astronomy
DIX, R. H., PH.D., Political Science
DOWDEN, W. S., PH.D., English
DREW, KATHERINE F., PH.D., History
DUCK, I., PH.D., Physics
DYSON, D. C., PH.D., Chemical Engineering
EDWARDS, E. O., PH.D., Political Economy
ENGEL, P. S., PH.D., Chemistry
ESTLE, T. L., PH.D., Physics
EVANS, ELINOR, M.F.A., Architecture
FISHER, F. M., PH.D. Biology
FREEMAN, J. W., PH.D., Space Science
GARSIDE, C., Jr., PH.D., History
GORDON, C., PH.D., Sociology
GORDON, W. E., PH.D., Electrical Engineering and Space Science
GRANDY, R. E., PH.D., Philosophy
GROB, A., PH.D., English
GRUBER, I. D., PH.D., History
HACKERMAN, N., PH.D., Chemistry
HANNON, J. P., PH.D., Physics
HARCOMBE, P. A., PH.D., Biology
HARVEY, F. R., PH.D., Mathematics
HAVENS, N., M.A., Drama
HAYMES, R. C., PH.D., Space Science
HELLUMS, J. D., PH.D., Chemical Engineering
HEMPEL, J., PH.D., Mathematics
HEYMANN, D., PH.D., Geology and Space Science
HIGGINBOTHAM, S. W., PH.D., History
HIGHTOWER, J. W., PH.D., Chemical Engineering
HOLLOWAY, C., PH.D., Music
HOWELL, W. C., PH.D., Psychology
HUDDLE, D. L., PH.D., Economics
HUSTON, J. D., PH.D., English
HYMAN, H. M., PH.D., History
ISLE, W., PH.D., English
JACO, W. H., PH.D., Mathematics
JONES, B. F., PH.D., Mathematics
JONES, S., PH.D., Music
JUMP, J. R., PH.D., Electrical Engineering
KENNEDY, K. W., PH.D., Mathematics
KILPATRICK, J. E., PH.D., Chemistry
KIM, D. M., PH.D., Electrical Engineering
KOBAYASHI, R., PH.D., Chemical Engineering
KOLENDA, K., PH.D., Philosophy
KRAHL, N. W., PH.D., Civil Engineering and Architecture
KRZYZANIAK, M., PH.D., Economics
LANE, N. F., PH.D., Physics
LEAL DE MARTINEZ, M. T., PH.D., Spanish
LEEDS, J. V., PH.D., Electrical and Environmental Engineering
LELAND, T. W., PH.D., Chemical Engineering
LEVIN, D. N., PH.D., Classics
LEWIS, E. S., PH.D., Chemistry
LOEWENHEIM, F. L., PH.D., History
LUTES, L., PH.D., Civil Engineering and Mathematics
McINTIRE, L. V., PH.D., Chemical Engineering
McLELLAN, R. B., PH.D., Materials Science
MARGRAVE, J. L., PH.D., Chemistry
MARTIN, W. C., PH.D., Sociology
MATUSOW, A. J., PH.D., History
MEIXNER, J., PH.D., English
MERWIN, J. E., PH.D., Civil Engineering
MICHEL, F. C., PH.D., Space Science
MIELE, A., Dr., Astronautics and Mathematical Sciences
MINTER, D. L., PH.D., English
MITCHELL, O. J., M.C.P., Architecture
MORRIS, W. A., PH.D., English
NIELSEN, N. C., PH.D., Philosophy and Religious Thought
NITZSCHE, J. C., PH.D., English
NORBECK, E., PH.D., Anthropology
O'NIEL, J., M.F.A., Fine Arts
OLIVER, C. T., LL.D., Public Affairs
OLIVER-SMITH, P., PH.D., Fine Arts
PALMER, G. A., PH.D., Biochemistry
PARISH, J. E., PH.D., English
PARKS, T. W., PH.D., Electrical Engineering
PARSONS, D. G., M.S., Fine Arts
PATTEN, R. L., PH.D., English
PEARSON, J. B., PH.D., Electrical Engineering
PFEIFFER, P. E., PH.D., Mathematical Sciences and Electrical Engineering
PHILLIPS, G. C., PH.D., Physics
PHILPOTT, C. W., PH.D., Biology
PIPER, W. B., PH.D., English
POINDEXTER, H. B., PH.D., Health and Physical Education
POLKING, J. C., PH.D., Mathematics
RAAPHORST, MADELEINE, PH.D., French
RABSON, T. A., PH.D., Electrical Engineering
RACHFORD, H. H., SC.D., Mathematics and Mathematical Sciences
RANSOM, H. S., M.ARCH., Architecture
RIMLINGER, G. V., PH.D., Economics
RISSER, J. R., PH.D., Physics
ROBERTS, J. M., PH.D., Materials Science
RORSCHACH, H. E., Jr., PH.D., Physics
ROSS, A., PH.D., Music
SANTOS, A. P. DE S., M.C.P., Architecture
SASS, R. L., PH.D., Chemistry
SCHNOEBELEN, A. M., PH.D., Music
SCHROEPFER, G. J., PH.D., Biochemistry
SCHUM, D. A., PH.D., Psychology
SELLERS, J., PH.D., Ethics
SHAPIRO, E., Music
SIMS, J. R., PH.D., Civil Engineering
SOLIGO, R., PH.D., Economics
SPEARS, M. K., PH.D., English
SPENCE, D. W., PH.D., Health and Physical Education
STEBBINGS, R. F., PH.D., Space Science
STOKES, G., PH.D., History
STORCK, R., PH.D., Biology
SUBTELNY, S., PH.D., Biology
TAPIA, R. A., PH.D., Mathematical Sciences
TAYLOR, M. E., PH.D., Mathematics
THOMPSON, E. M., PH.D., Russian
THOMPSON, J. R., PH.D., Mathematical Sciences
THRALL, R. M., PH.D., H.SC.D., Mathematical Sciences
TIPTON, A. N., M.M., Music
TITTEL, F., PH.D., Electrical Engineering
TODD, A., M.F.A., Architecture
TOPAZIO, V. W., PH.D., French
TRAMMELL, G. T., PH.D., Physics
TROELSTRA, A., PH.D., Electrical Engineering
TUGGLE, F. D., PH.D., Administrative Science
TYLER, S. A., PH.D., Anthropology and Linguistics
VEECH, W. A., PH.D., Mathematics
VELETSOS, A. S., PH.D., Engineering
VON DER MEHDEN, F., PH.D., Political Science
WALKER, J. B., PH.D., Biochemistry
WALKER, W. F., PH.D., Mechanical Engineering
WALTERS, G. K., PH.D., Physics and Space Science
WANG, CHAO-CHENG, PH.D., Mathematical Sciences
WARD, C. H., PH.D., Biology and Environmental Science
WARD, J. A., PH.D., English
WEISSENBERGER, K. H., PH.D., German
WELLS, R. O., PH.D., Mathematics
WIENER, M. J., PH.D., History
WIERUM, F. A., PH.D., Mechanical and Aerospace Engineering
WILHOIT, J. C., Jr., PH.D., Mechanical Engineering
WILLIAMS, E. E., PH.D., Administrative Science
WINKLER, M., PH.D., German
WINNINGHAM, G. L., M.S., Art
WOLF, R. A., PH.D., Space Physics
WOOD, D. I., PH.D., Education
YOUNG, R. D., PH.D., Economics
ZEFF, S. A., PH.D., Accounting

## ST. EDWARDS UNIVERSITY

3001 SOUTH CONGRESS AVE.,
AUSTIN, TEXAS 78704

Telephone: 444-2621.

Founded 1885.

Private, co-educational; four-year liberal arts courses.

*President:* Bro. STEPHEN WALSH, C.S.C.
*Vice-President for Fiscal Affairs:* DAVID A. DICKSON, Jr.
*Vice-President for University Relations:* JOHN KNUDSEN.
*Director of Admissions and Records:* JOHN LUCAS.
*Executive Vice-President and Academic Dean:* Bro. HENRY ALTMILLER, C.S.C.
*Librarian:* JOSEPH SPRUG.

The library contains 70,000 vols.
Number of teachers: 160.
Number of students: 2,300.

## SAINT MARY'S UNIVERSITY OF SAN ANTONIO
SAN ANTONIO, TEXAS 78284

Founded 1852.

*President:* Rev. DAVID J. PAUL.
*Academic Vice-President:* Rev. JOHN A. LEIES, S.M.
*Vice-President for Student Services:* Dr. DANIEL J. CAREY.
*Vice-President for Development:* DONALD K. RYCKMAN.
*Registrar:* PAUL RYAN, S.M.
*Librarian:* H. PALMER HALL.

The library contains 185,000 volumes.
Number of students: 3,381.

DEANS:

*School of Arts and Sciences:* Dr. JEROME MATZ, S.M.
*Graduate School:* Dr. ANTHONY KAUFMANN.
*Law School:* JAMES CASTLEBERRY.
*School of Business Administration:* Dr. GEORGE PETRELLO.

## SAM HOUSTON STATE UNIVERSITY
HUNTSVILLE, TEXAS 77341

Telephone: (713) 294-1111.

Founded 1879 as Sam Houston Normal Institute.

Academic year: August to May, with two summer sessions.

*President:* ELLIOTT T. BOWERS, ED.D.
*Vice-President for Academic Affairs:* JACK W. HUMPHRIES, PH.D.
*Vice-President for Business and Operations:* FRANK P. LEATHERS, PH.D.
*Vice-President for University Affairs:* FEROL ROBINSON, ED.D.
*Registrar:* EUNICE M. EVANS, M.B.A.
*Director of Libraries:* J. P. NUNELEE, PH.D.

The library contains 616,944 books, 15,796 microfilms and 385,727 other microforms.

Number of teachers: 337 full-time.
Number of students: 9,532 full-time.

Publication: *The Alumnus.*

DEANS:

*College of Arts and Sciences:* RICHARD A. CORDING, PH.D.
*College of Business Administration:* B. K. MARKS, PH.D.
*College of Education and Applied Science:* S. E. RYAN, ED.D.
*College of Criminal Justice:* VICTOR G. STRECHER, PH.D.
*School of Library Science:* C. EDWIN DOWLIN, PH.D. (Director.)

DIRECTORS OF DIVISIONS:

*English, Foreign Languages and Journalism:* J. E. GOODWIN, PH.D.
*Dance, Drama, Radio, Television, Film and Speech Communication:* MARY E. MANTAGUE, PH.D.

*Life Science, Geoscience and Geography:* D. D. HALL, PH.D.
*Chemistry and Physics:* JACK M. WILSON, PH.D.
*Mathematical and Information Sciences:* G. MATTINGLY, PH.D.
*Teacher Education:* J. N. MERCHANT, PH.D.
*Career Education and Human Resources:* M. B. MEDFORD, PH.D.
*Psychology and Philosophy:* A. J. BRUCE, PH.D.

DIRECTORS OF DEPARTMENTS:

*Art:* DARRYL L. PATRICK, PH.D.
*Music:* F. A. TULL, PH.D.
*Political Science:* R. H. PAYNE, PH.D.
*Sociology:* W. H. BENNETT, PH.D.
*Accounting:* R. B. HUFF, ED.D.
*General Business and Finance:* J. E. GILMORE, ED.D.
*Economics and Business Analysis:* V. E. SWEENEY, PH.D.
*Management and Marketing:* R. W. LOVELL, PH.D.
*Physical Education:* N. HATTLESTAD, ED.D.
*Industrial Technology:* N. C. MUNS, ED.D.
*Agriculture and Natural Resources:* D. G. MOORMAN, PH.D.

## SOUTHERN METHODIST UNIVERSITY
DALLAS, TEXAS 75275

Telephone: (214) 692-2000.

Chartered 1911.

*President:* Dr. L. DONALD SHIELDS.
*Provost:* Dr. HANS J. HILLERBRAND.
*Vice-President for Student Affairs:* WALTER A. SNICKENBERGER.
*Vice-President for Administration:* DAN HUDSON (acting).
*Vice-President for Development and University Relations:* DONALD E. SMITH.
*Registrar:* JOHN A. HALL.

The library contains 1,700,000 vols.
Number of teachers: 433 full-time, 156 part-time.
Number of students: 9,112.

Publications: *Southwest Review* (quarterly), *Journal of Air Law and Commerce*† (quarterly), *Southwest Law Journal*† (5 a year), *Perkins School of Theology Journal*† (quarterly).

DEANS:

*University College:* Dr. R. HAL WILLIAMS.
*Arts:* Dr. EUGENE BONELLI.
*Business:* Dr. EUGENE T. BYRNE (acting).
*Continuing Education:* Mrs. MARY E. MILLER.
*Engineering and Applied Science:* Dr. WILLIAM F. LEONARD (acting).
*Law:* JESWALD W. SALACUSE.
*Student Life:* Dr. JAMES E. CASWELL.
*Theology:* Dr. JAMES E. KIRBY.

## SOUTHWEST TEXAS STATE UNIVERSITY
SAN MARCOS, TEXAS 78666

Telephone: (512) 245-2111.

Founded 1899.

*President:* Dr. LEE H. SMITH.
*Vice-President for Academic Affairs:* Dr. RICHARD I. MILLER.
*Vice-President for Finance and Management:* Dr. EUGENE E. PAYNE.
*Vice-President for University Affairs:* Dr. B. ALLAN WATSON.
*Vice-President for Institutional Advancement:* W. C. BOURLAND.
*Librarian:* Dr. L. MOLONEY.

The library contains 564,807 vols., 542,888 microfilms and 113,034 other items.

Number of teachers: 682.
Number of students: 15,400.

DEANS:

*School of Liberal Arts:* (vacant).
*School of Science:* Dr. W. YOUNG.
*School of Health Professions:* Dr. D. GREEN.
*School of Education:* Dr. J. GARLAND.
*School of Business:* Dr. E. D. ROACH.
*School of Applied Arts:* Dr. R. GRATZ.
*School of Creative Arts:* Dr. J. HARREL.
*Graduate School:* Dr. SUSAN WITTIG.
*Student and Academic Services:* Dr. F. WAYNE SIGLER.

## SOUTHWESTERN UNIVERSITY
GEORGETOWN, TEXAS 78626

Opened 1873 by merging of Rutersville College (Chartered 1840), Wesleyan College (1844), McKenzie College (1848), and Soule University (1856).

*President:* Dr. ROY B. SHILLING, Jr.
*Administrative Vice-President and Provost:* WILLIAM B. JONES.
*Vice-President for Fiscal Affairs:* KIRK TREIBLE.
*Vice-President for Admissions and Student Development:* W. D. SWIFT.
*Registrar:* GEORGE BRIGHTWELL.
*Librarian:* Dr. JON SWARTZ.

The library contains 132,552 vols.
Number of teachers: 75.
Number of students: 1,029.

Publications: *Bulletin* (monthly), *The Megaphone* (weekly), *Southwestern Magazine* (quarterly), *The Sou' Wester* (annual).

DEANS:

*College of Arts and Sciences:* G. BENJAMIN OLIVER.
*Fine Arts:* THEODORE LUCAS.
*Students:* BARBARA BRIGHTWELL.

## STEPHEN F. AUSTIN STATE UNIVERSITY
NACOGDOCHES, TEXAS 75962

Telephone: 569-2011.

Founded 1923.

*President:* WILLIAM R. JOHNSON.

*Vice-President for Academic Affairs:* BILL J. FRANKLIN.
*Vice-President for Fiscal Affairs:* C. G. HAAS.
*Vice-President for Student Affairs:* BAKER PATILLO.
*Library Director:* ALVIN CAGE.

The library contains 254,000 vols.
Number of teachers: 435.
Number of students: 10,300.

DEANS:

*School of Applied Arts and Sciences:* JAMES STANDLEY.
*School of Business Administration:* F. LAUDERDALE.
*School of Education:* LANGSTON KERR.
*School of Fine Arts:* ROBERT SIDNELL.
*School of Forestry:* KENT T. ADAIR.
*School of Liberal Arts:* JAMES REESE.
*School of Sciences and Mathematics:* GLEN T. CLAYTON.
*Graduate School:* EDWIN GASTON.

## SUL ROSS STATE UNIVERSITY
ALPINE, TEXAS 79830

Telephone: (915) 837-8011.

Founded 1917.

*President:* C. R. RICHARDSON.
*Registrar:* Mrs. DOROTHY LEAVITT.
*Librarian:* NORMAN SPEARS.

The library contains 192,225 vols., 29,417 microforms.

Number of teachers: 90.
Number of students: 2,140.

## TEXAS A & I UNIVERSITY
KINGSVILLE, TEXAS 78363

Founded 1917.

Established as South Texas Normal School; name changed to South Texas State Teachers' College by law in 1923, to Texas College of Arts and Industries by law in 1929, and to Texas A & I University by law in 1967.

*President:* BILL J. FRANKLIN, M.A., PH.D.
*Vice-President for Academic Affairs:* RICHARD MEYER, M.S., ED.D.
*Vice-President for University Affairs:* MANUEL SALINAS, Jr., M.S., PH.D.
*Director of Research:* ALBERTO M. OLIVARES, B.S., PH.D.
*Director of Continuing Education:* ELISEO S. TORRES, B.S., M.A., ED.D.
*Registrar:* GUSTAVO DELEON, M.S.
*Librarian:* PAUL GOODE, M.S.L.S.

The library contains 633,541 vols. and receives 2,122 periodicals.

Number of teachers: 217.
Number of students: 5,357.

DEANS:

*Agriculture:* CHARLES A. DEYOUNG, M.S., PH.D.
*Arts and Sciences:* JOHN TALMER PEACOCK, M.S., PH.D.
*Business Administration:* ROBERT T. NASH, PH.D.
*Engineering:* DONALD P. KEDZIE, M.S., PH.D.
*Teacher Education:* JERRY D. BOGENER, M.A., D.ED.
*Graduate Studies:* ALBERTO M. OLIVARES, B.S., PH.D.

ATTACHED INSTITUTE:

**Texas A & I University Citrus and Vegetable Training Center:** Weslaco, Texas; Dir. RICHARD A. HENSZ, M.S., PH.D.

## TEXAS A & M UNIVERSITY SYSTEM
COLLEGE STATION, TEXAS 77843

Telephone: (713) 845-4331.

Founded 1876.

Academic year: September to August.

*Chancellor:* FRANK W. R. HUBERT, PH.D.
*Deputy Chancellor for Agriculture:* PERRY L. ADKISSON, PH.D.
*Deputy Chancellor for Engineering:* JOHN C. CALHOUN, Jr., PH.D.
*Executive Vice-Chancellor for Administration:* W. C. FREEMAN.
*Executive Vice-Chancellor for Programs:* DON HELLRIEGEL, PH.D. (acting).
*Vice-Chancellor for Legal Affairs and General Counsel:* JAMES B. BOND.
*Vice-Chancellor for Facilities Planning and Construction:* W. E. PEEL.

The System covers the following senior institutions:

### Texas A & M University
COLLEGE STATION, TEXAS 77843

Telephone: (713) 845-3211.

Founded 1876, University 1963.

*President:* CHARLES H. SAMSON, PH.D. (acting).
*Vice-Presidents:* J. M. PRESCOTT, PH.D. (Academic Affairs), HOWARD L. VESTAL (Business Affairs), ROBERT L. WALKER (Development), JOHN J. KOLDUS, PH.D. (Student Services), T. R. GREATHOUSE, PH.D. (International Affairs).
*Dean of Admissions and Records:* EDWIN H. COOPER, B.S.
*Director of Library:* IRENE B. HOADLEY, PH.D.

The library contains 1,150,000 vols.
Number of teachers: 1,700.
Number of students: 35,000.

DEANS:

*College of Engineering:* R. H. PAGE, PH.D.
*College of Agriculture:* H. O. KUNKEL, PH.D.
*College of Veterinary Medicine:* GEORGE C. SHELTON, D.V.M.
*Graduate College:* G. W. KUNZE, PH.D.
*College of Education:* D. C. CORRIGAN, PH.D.
*College of Geosciences:* GORDON EATON, PH.D.
*College of Science:* T. T. SUGIHARA, PH.D.
*College of Liberal Arts:* K. L. BRYANT, PH.D.
*College of Business Administration:* W. V. MUSE, PH.D.
*College of Architecture and Environmental Design:* CHARLES M. HIX.
*College of Medicine:* ROBERT S. STONE, M.D.

### Texas A & M University at Galveston
P.O.B. 1675, GALVESTON, TEXAS 77553

Telephone: (713) 766-3200.

Founded 1971 as Moody College.

*President:* WILLIAM H. CLAYTON, PH.D.

Library of 36,000 vols.
Number of teachers: 69.
Number of students: 650.

Consists of the Moody College of Marine Technology, the Texas Maritime College and the Coastal Zone Laboratory (marine research).

### Prairie View A & M University
PRAIRIE VIEW, TEXAS 77445

Telephone: (713) 857-3311.

Founded 1876, University 1973.

*President:* A. I. THOMAS, PH.D.
*Registrar:* C. A. THOMAS.
*Vice-President for Fiscal Affairs:* GRIFF W. KENDRICK.
*Vice-President for Physical Planning and Engineering:* DECATUR B. ROGERS, PH.D.
*Vice-President for Research and Special Programs:* IVORY V. NELSON, PH.D.
*Vice-President for Academic Affairs:* (vacant).
*Director of Library:* FRANK FRANCIS, M.S.

The library contains 90,000 vols.
Number of teachers: 292.
Number of students: 5,229.

DEANS:

*College of Agriculture:* FREDDIE RICHARDS.
*College of Arts and Sciences:* (vacant).
*College of Engineering:* AUSTIN E. GREAUX.
*College of Home Economics:* FLOSSIE M. BYRD, PH.D.
*College of Industrial Education:* S. R. COLLINS, ED.D.
*College of Nursing Education:* JEWEL-LEAN MANGAROO, PH.D.
*College of Business:* BERNICE R. ROLLINS (acting).
*College of Education:* HARRY HENDRICKS, PH.D.
*Graduate School:* WAYMAN WEBSTER, PH.D.
*Men:* L. MARION, B.S.
*Women:* Mrs. R. L. BLAND EVANS, M.S.

### Tarleton State University
STEPHENVILLE, TEXAS 76402
Telephone: (817) 968-9000.

Founded 1899, University 1973.

*President:* W. O. TROGDON, PH.D.
*Vice-President for Academic Affairs:* ROBERT C. FAIN, PH.D.
*Vice-President for Student Services:* MIKE LEESE.
*Vice-President for Business Affairs:* JERRY W. GRAHAM.
*Vice-President for Physical Facilities:* W. S. NORRIS, Jr.
*Director of Admissions:* CONLEY JENKINS, PH.D.
*Registrar:* J. M. WHITING, M.S.
*Librarian:* KENNETH W. JONES, PH.D.
The library contains 160,000 vols.
Number of teachers: 150.
Number of students: 3,590.

DEANS:

*School of Arts and Sciences:* LAMAR JOHANSON, PH.D.
*School of Education:* DON M. BEACH, PH.D.
*School of Agriculture and Business:* JESSE L. TACKETT, PH.D.
*School of Graduate Studies:* ROBERT WALKER, PH.D.
*Men* (vacant).
*Women:* Mrs. ALICE D. MATTHEWS.

### TEXAS CHRISTIAN UNIVERSITY
FORT WORTH, TEXAS 76129
Telephone: (817) 921-7000.

Founded 1873.

*Chancellor:* WILLIAM E. TUCKER, PH.D.
*Vice-Chancellor for Finance and Planning:* E. LEIGH SECREST, PH.D.
*Vice-Chancellor for Academic Affairs:* WILLIAM H. KOEHLER, PH.D. (acting).
*Vice-Chancellor for Student and Administrative Services:* H. G. WIBLE, ED.D.
*Vice-Chancellor for University Relations and Development:* PAUL W. HARTMAN, PH.D.
*Registrar:* C. A. CUMBIE, M.ED., M.A.
*Librarian:* P. M. PARHAM, PH.D.
The library contains one million vols.
Number of teachers: 374.
Number of students: 6,283.
Publications: *Bulletins.*

DEANS:

*Add Ran College of Arts and Sciences:* MICHAEL D. McCRACKEN, PH.D. (acting).
*Brite Divinity School:* M. JACK SUGGS, PH.D.
*Harris College of Nursing:* PATRICIA D. SCEARSE, D.N.SC.
*M. J. Neeley School of Business:* Dr. EDWARD A. JOHNSON, PH.D.
*School of Education:* H. F. LAGRONE, ED.D.
*School of Fine Arts:* G. T. TADE, PH.D.

### TEXAS LUTHERAN COLLEGE
SEGUIN, TEXAS 78155
Telephone: (512) 379-4161.

Founded 1891.

Liberal arts college which aims to provide a disciplined process of self-education within the context of academic freedom.

*President:* Dr. C. H. OESTREICH.
*Registrar:* M. R. JAROSZEWSKI.
*Librarian:* W. LUSSKY.
Number of teachers: 64.
Number of students: 1,100.

### TEXAS SOUTHERN UNIVERSITY
3100 CLEBURNE AVE.,
HOUSTON, TEXAS 77004
Telephone: (713) 527-7011.

Founded 1947.
State control.

*President:* LEONARD H. O. SPEARMAN, M.A., PH.D.
*Vice-President for University Development:* WAYNE M. CARLE, M.E., PH.D.
*Vice-President for Academic Affairs:* R. J. TERRY, M.S., PH.D.
*Vice-President for Administrative Services:* JOSHUA HILL, M.S., ED.D.
*Vice-President for Fiscal Affairs:* PLUMMER ALSTON, M.B.A.
*Vice-President for Student Affairs:* JAMES RACE, Jr., M.S., PH.D.
*Registrar and Director of Admissions:* J. E. WESTBERRY, M.S., M.A.
*Director of Libraries:* S. W. MOTHERSHED, M.S.
Libraries contain 572,986 vols.
Number of teachers: 390.
Number of students: 8,102.

Publications: *Ex-Press* (quarterly), *Inside T.S.U.* (monthly), *Urban Notebook†* (quarterly).

DEANS:

*College of Arts and Sciences:* L. L. CLARKSON, M.S., PH.D.
*School of Communications:* CARLTON W. MOLLETTE, M.S.A., PH.D.
*School of Law:* CALIPH JOHNSON, LL.M. (acting).
*School of Pharmacy:* P. R. WELLS, M.S., PH.D. (acting).
*School of Technology:* R. L. PRATER, M.S., DE.D.
*Graduate School:* JOSEPH JONES, Jr., M.S.C., PH.D.
*School of Business:* HERBERT N. WATKINS, M.B.A., PH.D.
*School of Education:* CHARLES E. MOSLEY, M.A. M.ED., PH.D. (acting).
*School of Public Affairs:* TANDY TOLLERSON, M.A., PH.D. (acting).

### TEXAS TECH UNIVERSITY
LUBBOCK, TEXAS 79409
Telephone: (806) 742-2011.

Founded by Texas Legislature 1923.

*President:* LAURO F. CAVAZOS, PH.D.

*Registrar:* DON WICKARD.
*Dean of Library Services:* R. C. JANEWAY, M.S.
The library contains 2,500,000 vols.
Number of teachers: 1,386.
Number of students: 23,129.

DEANS:

*College of Agricultural Sciences:* SAMUEL E. CURL, PH.D.
*College of Arts and Sciences:* L. L. GRAVES, PH.D.
*College of Business Administration:* CARL H. STEM, PH.D.
*College of Education:* ROBERT ANDERSON, PH.D.
*College of Engineering:* J. R. BRADFORD, PH.D.
*College of Home Economics:* DONALD LONGWORTH, PH.D.
*Graduate School:* J. KNOX-JONES, PH.D.
*School of Law:* RICHARD M. HEMINGWAY, J.D.

**Texas Tech University Health Sciences Center:** Tel. (806) 743-3111.
*President:* LAURO F. CAVAZOS, PH.D.
*Dean, School of Medicine:* GEORGE TYNER, M.D.
*Dean, School of Nursing:* TEDDY LANGFORD, PH.D.

ATTACHED INSTITUTE:

**International Center for Arid and Semi-Arid Land Studies.**
*Director:* H. E. DREGNE, PH.D.

ATTACHED CENTERS:

Textile Research Center.
Center for Professional Development.
Research and Training Center in Mental Retardation.
Disaster Research Center.
Center for Public Service.
Center for Energy Research.
Natural Science Laboratory.
Institute for Studies in Pragmaticism.
Museum of Texas Tech University.
Texas Tech University Water Resources Center.

### TEXAS WESLEYAN COLLEGE
FORT WORTH, TEXAS 76105
Telephone: (817) 534-0251.

Founded 1891.

*President:* JON H. FLEMING.
*Provost:* W. L. HAILEY.
*Vice-Presidents:* JAKE B. SCHRUM, THOMAS D. McSKIMMING, JERRY G. BAWCOM.
*Registrar:* D. E. CARTER.
*Librarian:* Mrs. NELL ORNEE.
The library contains 131,375 vols.
Number of teachers: 85.
Number of students: 1,500.

### TEXAS WOMAN'S UNIVERSITY
DENTON, TEXAS 76204
Telephone: 387-1322

Founded 1901.

*President:* Dr. MARY EVELYN BLAGG HUEY.

*Vice-President for Academic Affairs:* Dr. PHYLLIS BRIDGES.
*Vice-President for Fiscal Affairs:* ROBERT O. BENFIELD.
*Vice-President for Student Life:* RUTH M. CRARY (acting).
*Provost for the Institute of Health Sciences:* Dr. CAROLYN K. ROZIER.
*Provost of the Graduate School:* Dr. ROBERT S. PAWLOWSKI.
*Librarian:* ELIZABETH SNAPP.

The library contains 847,062 vols.
**Number of teachers:** 552.
**Number of students:** 7,935.
**Publication:** *Daedalian* (quarterly).

### TRINITY UNIVERSITY
715 STADIUM DRIVE,
SAN ANTONIO, TEXAS 78284
Telephone: 736-7011.
Founded 1869.

*President:* RONALD CALGAARD.
*Vice-President for Academic Affairs:* Dr. J. NORMAN PARMER.
*Registrar:* RICHARD C. ELLIOTT.
*Librarian:* R. A. HOUZE.

**Number of teachers:** 228, including 74 professors.
**Number of students:** 3,255.
**Publications:** *Trinitonian, Mirage.*

#### DEANS:
*Faculty of Humanities and Arts:* Dr. GEORGE BOYD.
*Faculty of Science, Mathematics and Engineering:* Dr. JOHN A. BURKE, Jr.
*Faculty of Business and Management Studies:* Dr. ROGER SPENCER.
*Faculty of Behavioural Sciences:* Dr. THOMAS C. GREAVES.

### UNIVERSITY OF DALLAS
IRVING, TEXAS 75061
Telephone: 579-5000.
Founded 1956.

*President:* ROBERT F. SASSEEN.
*Registrar:* Mrs. SYBIL NOVINSKI.
*Librarian:* Mrs. NETTIE BAKER.

The library contains 218,800 vols.
**Number of teachers:** 181.
**Number of students:** 2,688.

### UNIVERSITY OF HOUSTON
4800 CALHOUN BLVD.,
HOUSTON, TEXAS 77004
Founded 1927.

*President:* CHARLES BISHOP.
*Vice-President for Administration and Finance:* GEORGE H. HUXEL.
*Senior Vice-President for Academic Affairs:* ROBERT C. MAXSON.
*Chancellor:* BARRY MUNITZ.
*Provost:* GEORGE MAGNER.

*Library Director:* ROBIN N. DOWNES.

The library contains 1,100,000 vols.
**Number of teachers:** 1,000 full-time, 800 part-time.
**Number of students:** 29,000.
**Publications:** *Forum* (literary quarterly), *Houston Law Review* (Bates College of Law Publication), *South Central Language Association Bulletin, The Staffer* (staff monthly), numerous student periodicals.

#### DEANS:
*College of Architecture:* W. R. JENKINS.
*College of Business Administration:* A. B. COCANOUGHER.
*College of Education:* W. GEORGIADES.
*Hilton College of Hotel Restaurant Management:* D. C. KEISTER.
*Cullen College of Engineering:* A. E. DUKLER.
*Continuing Education:* L. TRANSIER.
*College of Humanities and Fine Arts:* J. H. PICKERING.
*Bates College of Law:* R. L. KNAUSS.
*College of Natural Sciences and Mathematics:* R. H. WALKER.
*College of Optometry:* W. BALDWIN.
*College of Pharmacy:* J. P. BUCKLEY.
*College of Social Sciences:* G. DALY.
*College of Technology:* L. WOLF.
*Graduate School of Social Work:* D. E. JENNINGS.

#### ATTACHED INSTITUTIONS:
Computing Center: Dir. W. J. ROWLEY.
Center for Open Learning: Dir. F. S. HOWARD.
Energy Institute: Dir. A. F. HILDEBRANDT.
Institute for Urban Studies: Dir. L. STERN.
Institute for Labor and Industrial Relations: Dir. J. E. WILLIAMS.
Blaffer Gallery: Dir. W. A. ROBINSON.

### UNIVERSITY OF MARY HARDIN-BAYLOR
BELTON, TEXAS 76513
Telephone: (817) 939-5811.
Founded 1845.

*President:* Dr. BOBBY E. PARKER.
*Vice-President for Academic Affairs:* Dr. KENNETH W. JOHNSON.
*Registrar:* R. W. MONTGOMERY.
*Director of Admissions:* CARLA PRICE.
*Librarian:* Mrs. JUANITA JONES.

The library contains 106,918 vols.
**Number of teachers:** 65.
**Number of students:** 1,100.

### UNIVERSITY OF ST. THOMAS
3812 MONTROSE BLVD.,
HOUSTON, TEXAS 77006
Telephone: 522-7911.
Founded 1947.
Private control.

*President:* Rev. WILLIAM J. YOUNG, C.S.B.
*Vice-President for Community Services:* Rev. FRANCIS E. MONAGHAN, C.S.B.
*Vice-President for University Affairs:* Dr. JAMES T. SULLIVAN.
*Vice-President for Academic Affairs:* Rev. P. WALLACE PLATT, C.S.B.
*Vice-President for Development:* MICHAEL C. FRICK.
*Registrar:* Dr. G. A. KNAGGS.
*Librarian:* PETER KUPERSMITH.

The library contains 120,000 vols.
**Number of teachers:** 172.
**Number of students:** 1,765.
**Publications:** *Cauldron, Dimension.*

#### DEANS:
*Dean of Student Affairs:* PATRICK B. MULVEY.
*Dean of Studies:* D. W. HOGAN.
*School of Theology:* Rev. RICHARD J. SCHIEFEN, C.S.B.
*School of Nursing:* Dr. HELEN GAEVERT.
*School of Business:* Dr. YHI-MIN HO.
*School of Education:* ANNA DEWALD.

ATTACHED INSTITUTE:
**Institute for Storm Research.**

### UNIVERSITY OF TEXAS SYSTEM
AUSTIN, TEXAS 78701
Telephone: (512) 471-4227.
Founded 1881.

*Chancellor:* E. DON WALKER, M.B.A., C.P.A., LL.D.
*Vice-Chancellor for Academic Affairs:* ERNEST T. SMERDON, PH.D.
*Vice-Chancellor for Health Affairs:* (vacant).
*Vice-Chancellor for Administration:* ROBERT L. HARDESTY, B.A.
*Vice-Chancellor for Lands Management:* (vacant).
*Vice-Chancellor for Business Affairs:* JOE E. BOYD, Jr., B.S., M.B.A., C.P.A.
*Vice-Chancellor and General Counsel:* JAMES L. CROWSON, B.A., LL.B.
*Assistant Chancellor for Planning:* HERMAN ADAMS, B.S., M.ED.

#### University of Texas at Austin
AUSTIN, TEXAS 78712
Telephone: 471-1232.

Founded 1881; formerly University of Texas, Main University.
State control; Academic year: September to May (two terms) with two summer sessions.

*President:* PETER T. FLAWN.
*Vice-President for Student Affairs:* RONALD M. BROWN.
*Senior Vice-President:* JAMES H. COLVIN.
*Vice-President for Academic Affairs and Research:* GERHARD J. FONKEN.

## UNIVERSITIES AND COLLEGES—TEXAS

*Vice-President for Business Affairs:* G. CHARLES FRANKLIN.
*Vice-President and Dean of Graduate Studies:* WILLIAM S. LIVINGSTON.
*Vice-President for Administration:* ROBERT D. METTLEN.
*Vice-President and Co-ordinator of Centennial Programs:* SHIRLEY BIRD PERRY.
*Librarian:* HAROLD BILLINGS.
Library: see Libraries.
Number of teachers: 2,362.
Number of students: 44,102.

### DEANS:

*College of Business Administration:* G. KOZMETSKY, D.C.S.
*School of Communications:* ROBERT C. JEFFREY, PH.D.
*College of Education:* L. G. KENNAMER, PH.D.
*College of Engineering:* E. F. GLOYNA, D.ENG.
*College of Fine Arts:* J. ROBERT WILLS, PH.D.
*College of Liberal Arts:* ROBERT D. KING, PH.D.
*College of Natural Sciences:* ROBERT E. BOYER, PH.D.
*College of Pharmacy:* JAMES T. DOLUISIO, PH.D.
*School of Law:* JOHN F. SUTTON, Jr., PH.D.
*Graduate School of Library Science:* C. G. SPARKS, PH.D.
*School of Architecture:* HAROLD BOX.
*Graduate School of Social Work:* MARTHA WILLIAMS, PH.D.
*LBJ School of Public Affairs:* ELSPETH ROSTOW.
*Continuing Education:* THOMAS HATFIELD, PH.D.
*School of Nursing:* BILLYE J. BROWN, ED.D., R.N.

### PROFESSORS:

*College of Liberal Arts:*
ADAMS, R. N., PH.D., Anthropology
ALLAIRE, E. B., Philosophy
AMSEL, A., Psychology
ANGELELLI, I., PH.D., Philosophy
AROCENA, L. A., PH.D., Spanish and Portuguese
ASKARI, H. G., PH.D., Center for Middle Eastern Studies and Marketing Administration
BAKER, C. L., PH.D., Linguistics
BAR-ADON, A., Linguistics, Oriental and African Languages
BARKER, N. N., PH.D., History
BARNES, W. J., PH.D., English
BAUMAN, R., PH.D., Anthropology
BEAN, F. D., PH.D., Sociology
BENSON, N. L., PH.D., History
BIERI, J., Psychology
BILL, J. A., PH.D., Government
BONJEAN, C. M., Sociology
BOWDEN, E. T., English
BOWLT, J. E., PH.D., Slavic Languages
BOYER, M. V., Spanish and Portuguese
BRAISTED, W. R., History
BROWNING, G. D., PH.D., Philosophy
BROWNING, H. L., PH.D., Sociology
BRUELL, J., Psychology
BUCHLER, I. R., PH.D., Anthropology
BULHOF, F., PH.D., Germanic Languages
BUSS, A., Psychology
CABLE, T. M., PH.D., English
CANTARINO, V., Middle Eastern Studies
CAUSEY, R. L., PH.D., Philosophy
CNUDDE, C. F., PH.D., Government
COHEN, L. B., PH.D., Psychology
CORNELL, J. B., PH.D., Anthropology
CROSBY, A. W., PH.D., American Studies and Geography
CRUNDEN, R. M., PH.D., American Studies and History
DACY, D. C., PH.D., Economics
DASSONVILLE, M., PH.D., French
DAVIS, E. M., PH.D., Anthropology
DIVINE, R. A., PH.D., History
DULLES, J. W. F., Comparative Studies
EDWARDS, D. V., PH.D., Government
ELLISON, F. P., PH.D., Spanish and Portuguese
ENGLISH, P. W., Geography, Middle Eastern Studies
EPSTEIN, J. F., Anthropology
FEAGIN, J., PH.D., Sociology
FERNEA, R. A., Anthropology
FIREY, W. I., Jr., PH.D., Sociology
FITZPATRICK, SHEILA, D.PHIL., History
FORSTER, M. H., PH.D., Spanish and Portuguese
FOSS, D. J., PH.D., Psychology
FRIEDMAN, A. W., PH.D., English
GALINSKY, G. K., PH.D., Classics
GLADE, W. P., Jr., PH.D., Economics
GLENN, N. D., Sociology
GOETZMANN, W. H., PH.D., American Studies and History
GORDON, A., Jr., PH.D., English
GORDON, W., PH.D., Economics
GOUGH, P., Psychology
GOULD, L. L., PH.D., History
GRAHAM, L. S., PH.D., Government
GRAHAM, R., PH.D., History
GRANT, R. B., PH.D., French
GREEN, P. M., PH.D., Classics
GRONOUSKI, J. A., Economics
GRUBBS, C. M., PH.D., Economics
HAKES, D. T., PH.D., Psychology
HALL, M. G., History
HANSEN, N. M., PH.D., Economics
HARDGRAVE, R. L., Government
HARMS, R. T., Linguistics
HAYS, W. L., PH.D., Psychology
HELMREICH, R. L., PH.D., Psychology
HILL, F. G., PH.D., Economics
HOCHBERG, H. I., PH.D., Philosophy
HOFFMAN, G. W., PH.D., Geography
HOLTZMAN, W. H., PH.D., Psychology
HOLZ, R. K., PH.D., Geography
HUFF, D. L., Geography
ISCOE, I., PH.D., Psychology
JANNUZI, F. T., PH.D., Economics
JAZAYERY, M. A., Oriental and African Languages
KARTTUNEN, L. J., PH.D., Linguistics
KAUFMANN, R. J., English and Comparative Studies
KENDRICK, D. A., PH.D., Economics
KENNAMER, L., PH.D., Geography
KING, R. D., PH.D., Linguistics
KINNEAVY, J. L., PH.D., English
LANGFORD, G., PH.D., English
LASBY, C. G., PH.D., History
LEHMANN, W. P., PH.D., Germanic Languages, Linguistics
LEIDEN, C., PH.D., Government
LIEB, I. C., PH.D., Philosophy
LIEBHAFSKY, H. H., PH.D., Economics
LINDFORS, B. O., PH.D., English and Oriental and African Languages and Literature
LIVINGSTON, W. S., PH.D., Government
LOEHLIN, J. C., PH.D., Psychology, Computer Science
LOPEZ-MORILLAS, J., PH.D., Spanish and Portuguese
LOPREATO, J., Sociology
LOUIS, W. R., D.PHIL., History
MACDONALD, H. M., PH.D., Government
McDONALD, S. L., Economics
McFADDEN, D., PH.D., Psychology
McGANN, T. F., History
MACKEY, L. H., PH.D., Philosophy
McKIE, J. W., PH.D., Economics
McLEMORE, S. D., Sociology
MACNEILAGE, P. F., PH.D., Linguistics and Psychology
MALINA, R. M., PH.D., Anthropology
MALOF, J. F., PH.D., English
MANOSEVITZ, M., PH.D., Psychology
MARSHALL, F. R., PH.D., Economics
MARTIN, N., Philosophy, Computer Science
MATLUCK, J. H., PH.D., Spanish and Portuguese
MEACHAM, S., History
MEGAW, R. N. E., English
MENDELSON, W., PH.D., Government
MICHAEL, W. F., PH.D., Germanic Languages
MIDDLETON, J. C., Germanic Languages
MOLDENHAUER, J. J., PH.D., English
MONAS, S., PH.D., Slavic Languages and History
MORGAN, D. C., PH.D., Economics
MORGAN, G., Classics and History
MORGAN, M. G., PH.D., Classics
MOURELATOS, A. P. D., PH.D., Philosophy
NETHERCUT, W. R., PH.D., Classics
NEWCOMB, W. W., Jr., PH.D., Anthropology
OLIVER, S. C., PH.D., Anthropology
ORTEGA, J., PH.D., Spanish and Portuguese
ORUM, A. M., PH.D., Sociology
OTIS, J., PH.D., Sociology
PALTER, R., History, Philosophy
PAREDES, A., PH.D., English, Anthropology
PARKER, D. S., Classics
PETERS, P. S., Linguistics
PINCOFFS, E., Philosophy
POLOMÉ, E. G. C., PH.D., Germanic Languages, Linguistics, Oriental and African Languages
POSTON, D. L., Jr., PH.D., Sociology
POTTER, JOY M., PH.D., French and Italian
PRENTICE, N. M., Psychology
RAMIREZ, M., III, PH.D., Psychology
ROACH, J. R., PH.D., Government
ROSS, S. R., History
ROSTOW, E. D., Government
ROSTOW, W. W., History, Economics
SCHADE, G. D., Jr., Spanish and Portuguese
SCHAEDEL, R. P., Anthropology
SCHEIK, W. J., PH.D., English
SCHMITT, K. M., Government
SCHULZ-BEHREND, G., PH.D., Germanic Languages
SCHWARTZ, T., PH.D., Government
SELBY, H. A., Anthropology
SELLSTROM, A. D., French and Italian
SEUNG, T. K., PH.D., Philosophy
SHERZER, J., PH.D., Anthropology
SIMMONS, R. F., Computer Science, Psychology
SJOBERG, G. A., Sociology
SLEDD, J. H., PH.D., Linguistics, English
SMITH, A. G., PH.D., Anthropology and Speech Communication
SMITH, CARLOTA S., PH.D., Linguistics
SOLOMON, R. C., PH.D., Philosophy
SPENCE, J. T., Psychology and Educational Psychology
SPIVAK, G. C., English
STEPHENS, J. M., Jr., French and Italian
STORY, D. A., Anthropology
STOTT, W., PH.D., English
SUNDER, J. E., History
SUSSMAN, H., PH.D., Linguistics
SUTHERLAND, W. O., PH.D., English
TABORSKY, E., DR. OF STATE SCI., Government

Teele, R. E., Asian Studies
Thieleman, L. J., ph.d., French and Italian
Thiessen, D. D., ph.d., Psychology
Thompson, C. C., ph.d., Economics
Todd, W. B., ph.d., English
Velz, J. W., English
Wadlington, W. P., ph.d., English
Walter, J. A., English
Werbow, S. N., ph.d., Germanic Languages
Westbrook, M. R., ph.d., English
Whitbread, T. B., ph.d., English
White, P. L., ph.d., History
Wicklund, R. A., ph.d., Psychology
Willerman, L., ph.d., Psychology
Willson, A. L., Germanic Languages
Wimsatt, J. I., ph.d., English
Wolitz, S. L., ph.d., French and Italian
Young, R. K., Psychology
Zimic, S., ph.d., Spanish and Portuguese

*College of Natural Sciences:*
Aggarwal, J. K., ph.d., Computer Sciences and Electrical Engineering
Armendariz, E. P., ph.d., Mathematics
Backus, M. M., ph.d., Geology
Bailey, P. S., Chemistry
Bard, A. J., Chemistry
Barker, D. S., ph.d., Geology
Bash, F. N., ph.d., Astronomy
Bauld, N. L., ph.d., Chemistry
Bengston, R. D., ph.d., Physics
Berberian, S. K., Mathematics
Berk, H., ph.d., Physics
Bernau, S. J., ph.d., Mathematics
Berry, L. J., ph.d., Microbiology
Bing, R. H., ph.d., Mathematics
Blair, W. F., ph.d., Zoology
Bledsoe, W. W., ph.d., Mathematics, Computer Science
Bloch, D. P., Botany
Boggs, J. E., Chemistry
Bohm, A. R., ph.d., Physics
Bose, H. R., ph.d., Microbiology
Boyer, R. E., Geology
Breland, O. P., ph.d., Zoology
Bronson, F. H., ph.d., Zoology
Brown, D. T., ph.d., Microbiology
Brown, L. F., Jr., ph.d., Geology
Browne, J. C., Computer Science, Physics
Cannon, J. R., Mathematics
Carry, L. R., ph.d., Mathematics and Curriculum and Instruction
Chandy, K. M., ph.d., Computer Sciences
Charnes, A., ph.d., Computer Science, Mathematics
Cheney, E. W., Mathematics
Chiu, C. B., ph.d., Physics
Coker, W. R., ph.d., Physics
Cowley, A. H., Chemistry
Dale, A. G., ph.d., Computer Sciences
Daniel, J. W., ph.d., Computer Science and Mathematics
Danielson, W. A., ph.d., Computer Sciences and Journalism
Davis, R. E., ph.d., Chemistry
Delevoryas, T., ph.d., Botany
Desjardins, C., ph.d., Zoology
De Vaucouleurs, G., d.sc., Astronomy
Dewar, M. J. S., ph.d., Chemistry
De Wette, F. W., ph.d., Physics
Dewitt, B. S., ph.d., Physics
Dewitt, C. M., ph.d., Astronomy
Dollard, J. D., ph.d., Mathematics
Douglas, J. N., ph.d., Astronomy
Drummond, W. E., ph.d., Physics
Duggan, M. A., Computer Sciences and Business Law
Durbin, J. R., ph.d., Mathematics
Durrett, Mary E., ph.d., Home Economics
Eaton, W. T., ph.d., Mathematics
Edmonds, F. N., ph.d., Astronomy
Edmondson, D. E., ph.d., Mathematics
Eppwright, Margaret A., ph.d., Home Economics
Evans, D. S., Astronomy
Fink, M., ph.d., Physics
Fisher, W. L., Geology
Flawn, P. T., ph.d., Geology
Folk, R. L., ph.d., Geology
Folkers, K., Chemistry and Pharmacy
Fonken, G. J., ph.d., Chemistry
Forrest, H. S., ph.d., Zoology
Freeman, G. L., ph.d., Zoology
Frommhold, L. W., Physics
Gardiner, W. C., Jr., ph.d., Chemistry
Gardner, C. S., Mathematics
Gavenda, J. D., Physics
Gentle, K. W., ph.d., Physics
Gibb, Glenadine, ph.d., Mathematics
Gibson, D. T., ph.d., Microbiology
Gilbert, J. E., ph.d., Mathematics
Gillman, L., Mathematics
Gleeson, A. M., ph.d., Physics
Gottlieb, P. D., ph.d., Microbiology
Grant, Verne, ph.d., Botany
Greenwood, R. E., ph.d., Mathematics
Griffy, T. A., Physics
Guy, W. T., Jr., ph.d., Mathematics
Hamilton. T., Zoology
Hardesty, B. A., ph.d., Chemistry
Haskell, B. E., ph.d., Home Economics
Herman, R., ph.d., Physics
Hiraizumi, Y., dr.sci., Zoology
Hinton, F. L., ph.d., Physics
Hubbs, C., ph.d., Zoology
Hudspeth, E. L., ph.d., Physics
Ivash, E. V., Physics
Jacobson, A. G., Zoology
Jefferys, W. H., ph.d., Astronomy
John, P. W. M., Mathematics
Johnston, M. C., ph.d., Botany
Jonas, E. C., Geology
Kitto, G. B., ph.d., Chemistry
Kleinman, L., Physics
Klingman, D., ph.d., Computer Sciences
Kolthoff, K. O., ph.d., Zoology
Kozmetsky, G., d.c.s., Computer Sciences and Business Administration
Lagow, R. J., ph.d., Chemistry
Lagowski, J. J., Chemistry
Lambert, D. L., ph.d., Astronomy
Land, L. S., ph.d., Geological Sciences
Langston, W., ph.d., Geology
Larimer, J. L., Zoology
Levin, D. A., ph.d., Botany
Little, R. N., Jr., ph.d., Physics
Loehlin, J. C., ph.d., Psychology, Computer Science
Long, L. E., ph.d., Geology
Longnecker, J. B., ph.d., Home Economics
Lundelius, E. L., Jr., Geology
Mabry, T. J., Botany
McBride, E. F., Geology
McMillan, C., ph.d., Botany
Maguire, B., ph.d., Zoology
Maguire, Marjorie, ph.d., Zoology
Mandy, W. J., ph.d., Microbiology
Martin, N. M., ph.d., Philosophy, Computer Sciences and Electrical Engineering
Matsen, F. A., ph.d., Chemistry and Physics
Matsumoto, T., ph.d., Marine Studies
Matzner, R. A., Physics
Maxwell, J. C., Geology
Millett, W. E., ph.d., Physics
Monti, S. A., ph.d., Chemistry
Moore, C. F., ph.d., Physics
Moore, J. R., ph.d., Marine Studies
Morgan, L. O., ph.d., Chemistry
Morris, C. N., ph.d., Mathematics
Muelberger, W. R., ph.d., Geology
Nakamura, Y., ph.d., Marine Studies
Nather, R. E., ph.d., Astronomy
Ne'eman, Y., ph.d., Physics
Nicol, J. A. C., d.phil., Marine Studies
Nolle, A. W., ph.d., Physics
Oakes, M. E. L., ph.d., Physics
Oppenheimer, C. H., Microbiology
Osborn, R. C., Mathematics
Parker, P. T., ph.d., Chemistry and Marine Studies
Pettit, R., ph.d., Chemistry
Pianka, E. R., ph.d., Zoology
Powers, E. L., ph.d., Zoology
Prigogine, Ilya, Physics
Ravel, J. M., ph.d., Chemistry
Reed, L. J., ph.d., Chemistry
Reeder, W. G., ph.d., Zoology
Richards, Phyllis L., ph.d., Home Economics
Richardson, R. H., ph.d., Zoology
Riggs, A. F., ph.d., Zoology
Riley, P. J., ph.d., Physics
Roberts, R. M., ph.d., Chemistry
Robertson, W. W., ph.d., Physics
Roels, O. C., ph.d., Marine Science
Rosenbluth, M. N., ph.d., Physics
Rosenthal, H. P., ph.d., Mathematics
Salvador, A., ph.d., Geological Sciences
Sanders, B., ph.d., Zoology
Schaefer, H. F., ph.d., Chemistry
Scherr, C. W., Physics
Schieve, W. C., ph.d., Physics
Schrank, A. R., ph.d., Zoology
Sciama, D. W., ph.d., Physics
Scott, A. J., Geology
Shive, W., ph.d., Chemistry
Showalter, R. E., ph.d., Mathematics
Simmons, R. F., Computer Science, Psychology
Simonsen, S. H., ph.d., Chemistry
Simpson, B. B., ph.d., Botany
Smith, H. J., ph.d., Astronomy
Smoluchowski, R., ph.d., Astronomy
Snell, E., ph.d., Chemistry and Microbiology
Spear, I., Botany
Spurr, S. H., ph.d., Botany and Public Affairs
Starr, R. C., ph.d., Botany
Sudarsham, E. C. G., Physics
Sutton, H. E., ph.d., Zoology
Swinney, H. L., ph.d., Physics
Szaniszlo, P. J., ph.d., Microbiology
Szygenda, S. A., ph.d., Computer Sciences
Tamura, T., Physics
Thompson, Guy A., ph.d., Botany
Thompson, J. C., Physics
Turner, B. L., ph.d., Botany
Van Baalen, C., ph.d., Botany
Vanden Bout, P. A., ph.d., Astronomy
Vankensburgh, W. C. J., ph.d., Geological Sciences
Wade, W. H., ph.d., Chemistry
Walker, J. R., ph.d., Microbiology
Whaley, W. G., ph.d., Botany
Wheeler, J. C., ph.d., Astronomy
White, J. M., ph.d., Chemistry
Wohlschlag, D. E., ph.d., Marine Studies
Wyatt, R. F., ph.d., Chemistry
Wyss, O., ph.d., Microbiology
Yeh, R. T., ph.d., Computer Science and Electrical Engineering
York, C. W., ph.d., Home Economics
Young, D. M., Jr., Computer Science, Mathematics
Young, K. P., ph.d., Geology
Ziegler, D. M., Chemistry

*College of Business Administration:*
Allison, J. R., j.d., General Business
Alpert, M. I., d.b.a., Marketing Administration
Blair, C. P., ph.d., Marketing Administration
Brandt, F. S., Management

# UNIVERSITIES AND COLLEGES—TEXAS (UNIVERSITY OF)

**Charnes, A.**, General Business
**Clark**, C. T., ph.d., General Business
Cooper, W. W., d.s., Management
**Crum, L. L.**, Finance
Cunningham, W. H., ph.d., Marketing Administration
Deakin, E. B., ph.d., Accounting
Doenges, R. C., d.b.a., Finance
**Duggan, M. A.**, m.p.l., General Business
**Dyer, J.**, ph.d., Management
Fitzsimmons, J. A., ph.d., Management
Granof, M. H., ph.d., Accounting
Graydon, F. D., m.b.a., Accounting
Harmon, E. G., ph.d., General Business
Harris, R. D., ph.d., General Business
Helburn, I. B., ph.d., Management
Henion, K. E., ph.d., Marketing Administration
Holt, C. C., ph.d., Management
**Huff, D. J.**, Marketing Administration
**Jentz, G.**, General Business
Klingman, D. D., ph.d., General Business and Computer Sciences
Knight, K. E., ph.d., Management
Konecci, E. B., Management
Kozmetsky, G., Management
**Larson, K. D.**, d.b.a., Accounting
Lasdon, L. S., ph.d., General Business
**Lord, W. J.**, Jr., General Business
McDaniel, R. R., ph.d., Management
Magee, S. P., ph.d., Finance
May, F. B., ph.d., General Business
May, R. G., ph.d., Accounting
Mettlen, R. D., d.b.a., Finance
Moore, B. E., ph.d., Management
Nelson, E. W., ph.d., General Business
Peterson, R. A., ph.d., Marketing Administration
Robertson, J. C., ph.d., Accounting
Ruefli, T. W., ph.d., Management
**Sommerfeld, R. M.**, Accounting
**Sord, B. H.**, ph.d., Management
Summers, E. L., ph.d., Accounting
**Walker, E. W.**, d.b.a., Finance
**Welsch, G. A.**, ph.d., c.p.a., Accounting
Williamson, R. B., ph.d., Finance
Witt, R. C., ph.d., Finance
Witt, R. E., ph.d., Marketing Administration
**Wolf, H. A.**, Finance
Woodward, N. P., ph.d., General Business
**Zlatkovich, C. T., ph.d., c.p.a.,** Accounting

*School of Communications:*
**Ashmore, L. L., ph.d.,** Speech
Brooks, R. D., ph.d., Radio-Television-Films
Cunningham, Isabella, C. M., ph.d., Advertising
**Danielson, W. A.**, Journalism
Gibson, M. L., ph.d., Journalism
Gray, P. H., ph.d., Speech Communication
**Jeffrey, R. C.**, Speech
**King, C. R.**, Journalism
**Kopra, L. L.**, ph.d., Speech
Davis, R. E., ph.d., Radio-Television-Films
Hanson, G. H., Speech Communication
Hart, R. P., ph.d., Speech Communication
Hooper, R. W., ph.d., Speech Communication
MacFadden, D., ph.d., Speech Communication
Martin, F. N., ph.d., Speech Communication
Meyer, T. P., ph.d., Radio-Television-Films
Neal, J. W., Speech
Powers, G. R., ph.d., Speech Communication
Ruben, L., ph.d., Advertising

Scott, A., Journalism
Sharpe, E. A., ph.d., Journalism and Advertising
Smith, Alfred G., ph.d., Speech Communication
Sussman, H. H., ph.d., Speech Communication
Teeter, D. L., ph.d., Journalism
Villarreal, J. J., ph.d., Speech

*College of Education:*
Ashbaugh, C. R., ph.d., Educational Administration
**Barraga, Natalie C., ed.d.**, Special Education
**Bennie, W. A.**, Curriculum and Instruction
**Bessent, E. W.**, Educational Administration
Bordie, J. G., ph.d., Curriculum and Instruction
Borich, G. D., Educational Psychology
Bown, O. H., Educational Psychology
Brown, R. M., ph.d., Educational Administration
Carry, L. R., ph.d., Curriculum and Instruction; Mathematics
Cleland, C. C., Educational Psychology, Special Education
Davis, O. L., Jr., Curriculum and Instruction
Duncan, J. P., ph.d., Educational Administration
Dunham, J. L., ph.d., Educational Psychology
Emmer, E. T., ph.d. Educational Psychology
Estes, N., ph.d., Educational Administration
Farrell, E. J., ph.d., Curriculum and Instruction
Flournoy, **Mary F.**, Curriculum and Instruction
Frost, J. L., ph.d., Curriculum and Instruction
Fruchter, B., ph.d., Educational Psychology
Gallessich, J. M., ph.d., Educational Psychology
**Gibb, E. Glenadine**, Curriculum and Instruction
Guszak, F. J., ph.d., Curriculum and Instruction
Hall, S., Physical Education, Health and Recreation
Hansen, C. E., ph.d., Special Education
Harmer, W. R., ph.d., Curriculum and Instruction
**Harris, B. M.**, Educational Administration
Hays, W. L., ph.d., Educational Psychology
**Hereford, C. F.**, Educational Psychology
**Horn, T. D.**, ph.d., Curriculum and Instruction
Jennings, E. E., ph.d., Educational Psychology
Jensen, Julie M., ph.d., Curriculum and Instruction
Kelley, H. P., Educational Psychology
**Kennamer, L. G., ph.d.**, Curriculum and Instruction
King, J. D., ph.d., Special Education and Educational Administration
**Kinneavy, J. L., ph.d.**, Curriculum and Instruction
Klein, K. K., Physical Education, Health and Recreation
**Koile, E. A., ed.d.**, Educational Psychology
Larsen, S. C., ph.d., Special Education
Laska, J. A., ph.d., Curriculum and Instruction

McCraw, L. W., ed.d., Physical Education, Recreation and Health
**McIntyre, K. E., ph.d.,** Educational Administration
Malina, R. M., ph.d., Physical and Health Education
Manaster, G. J., ph.d., Educational Psychology
Montague, E. J., Curriculum and Instruction
Oakland, T. D., ph.d., Educational Psychology
Parker, R. M., ph.d., Special Education
Peck, R. F., ph.d., Educational Psychology
Phillips, B. N., Educational Psychology
**Pilgrim, Geneva H., ph.d.**, Curriculum and Instruction
Prentice, N., Educational Psychology
Reid, J. B., ph.d., Educational Psychology
Rich, J. M., Cultural Foundations of Education
Rippey, D. T., ph.d., Educational Administration
Roueche, J. E., Educational Administration
Royal, D. K., Health, Physical Education and Recreation
Sikes, M. P., Educational Psychology
**Spence, Janet T.**, Educational Psychology and Psychology
Spirduso, W. W., ph.d., Health, Physical Education and Recreation
Thomas, M. P., Jr., ph.d., Educational Administration
Thompson, B. A., Physical Instruction
Veldman, D. J., Educational Psychology
Wicker, F. W., ph.d., Educational Psychology
**Wolfe, W. G., ph.d.,** Educational Psychology and Special Education
Yates, J. R., ph.d., Educational Administration

*College of Engineering:*
Aggarwal, J. K., ph.d., Electrical Engineering
Amstead, B. H., ph.d., Mechanical Engineering
Armstrong, N. E., ph.d., Civil Engineering
Baker, L. E., ph.d., Electrical Engineering
Becker, E. B., ph.d., Aerospace Engineering and Engineering Mechanics
Bedford, A., ph.d., Aerospace Engineering and Engineering Mechanics
Beightler, C. S., Mechanical Engineering
Bene, R. W., ph.d., Electrical Engineering
Bertin, J. J., ph.d., Aerospace Engineering and Engineering Mechanics
Bostick, F. X., Jr., ph.d., Electrical Engineering
Breen, J. E., Civil Engineering
Brock, J. R., Chemical Engineering
**Brons, F.**, Petroleum Engineering
Burns, N. H., ph.d., Civil Engineering
Caudle, B. H., ph.d., Petroleum Engineering
Chandy, K. M., ph.d., Electrical Engineering
Clark, L. G., Jr., ph.d., Aerospace Engineering
Collins, R. E., ph.d., Petroleum Engineering
Craig, R. R., ph.d., Aerospace Engineering and Engineering Mechanics
Dorfman, M. H., ph.d., Petroleum Engineering

DOUGAL, A. A., PH.D., Electrical Engineering
DUESTERHOEFT, W. C., Jr., PH.D., Electrical Engineering
DUNCOMBE, R. L., PH.D., Aerospace Engineering and Engineering Mechanics
EDGAG, T. F., PH.D., Chemical Engineering
FAIR, J. R., PH.D., Chemical Engineering
FANNIN, B. H., PH.D., Electrical Engineering
FLAKE, R. H., D.SCI., Electrical Engineering
FOWLER, DAVID W., PH.D., Architectural Engineering and Civil Engineering
FOWLER, W. T., PH.D., Aerospace Engineering and Engineering Mechanics
FURLONG, R. W., PH.D., Civil Engineering
GLOYNA, E. F., D.ENG, Civil Engineering
GRAY, K. E., PH.D., Petroleum Engineering
HARTWIG, W. H., PH.D., Electrical Engineering
HEALEY, A. J., PH.D., Mechanical Engineering
HERMAN, R., PH.D., Civil Engineering
HIMMELBLAU, D. M., PH.D., Chemical Engineering
HIXON, E. L., Electrical Engineering
HOLLEY, E. R., PH.D., Civil Engineering
HOWELL, J. R., PH.D., Mechanical Engineering
HUDSON, W. R., PH.D., Civil Engineering
HULL, D. G., PH.D., Aerospace Engineering and Engineering Mechanics
ITOH, T., PH.D., Electrical Engineering
JENSEN, P. A., PH.D., Mechanical Engineering
JIRSA, J. O., PH.D., Civil Engineering
JOHNSON, F. B., PH.D., Civil Engineering
JURICIC, D., PH.D., Mechanical Engineering
KENNEDY, T. W., PH.D., Civil Engineering
KREISLE, L. F., Mechanical Engineering
LAGRONE, A. H., PH.D., Electrical Engineering
LAMB, J. P., Mechanical Engineering
LASDON, L. S., PH.D., Mechanical Engineering
LEDBETTER, J. O., PH.D., Civil Engineering
LEE, C. E., Civil Engineering
LESSO, W. G., PH.D., Mechanical Engineering
MCCULLOUGH, B. J., D.ENGR., Civil Engineering
MCKETTA, J. J., Jr., PH.D., Chemical Engineering
MALINA, J. F. Jr., Civil Engineering
MARCUS, H. L., PH.D., Mechanical Engineering
MARTIN, N. M., PH.D., Electrical Engineering
MOORE, W. L., PH.D., Civil Engineering
MORGAN, C. W., P.E., PH.D., Civil Engineering
NACOZY, P. E., PH.D., Aerospace Engineering and Engineering Mechanics
ODEN, J. T., PH.D., Aerospace Engineering and Engineering Mechanics
OLSON, R. E., PH.D., Civil Engineering
PANTON, R. L., PH.D., Mechanical Engineering
PAUL, D. R., PH.D., Chemical Engineering
PODIO, A. L., PH.D., Petroleum Engineering
POPOVICH, R. P., PH.D., Chemical Engineering
POWERS, E. J., PH.D., Electrical Engineering

PRIGOGINE, I., Chemical Engineering
RALLS, K. W., PH.D., Mechanical Engineering
RASE, H. F., PH.D., Chemical Engineering
REESE, L. C., PH.D. IN C.E., Civil Engineering
RICHARDSON, P. C., M.D., Electrical Engineering
RIPPERGER, E. A., PH.D., Aerospace Engineering
ROESSET, J. M., PH.D., Civil Engineering
ROHLICH, G., PH.D., Civil Engineering and LBJ School of Public Affairs
ROTH, C. H., Jr., PH.D., Electrical Engineering
RUNGE, T. M., M.D., Electrical, Biomedical and Aerospace Engineering
RYLANDER, H. G., Jr., Mechanical Engineering
SCHECHTER, R. S., PH.D., Chemical Engineering
SCHMIDT, P. S., PH.D., Mechanical Engineering
SCHUTZ, B. E., PH.D., Aerospace Engineering and Engineering Mechanics
SMITH, H. W., PH.D., Electrical Engineering
SPEYER, J. L., PH.D., Aerospace Engineering and Engineering Mechanics
STARK, J. P., PH.D., Mechanical Engineering
STEARMAN, R. O., PH.D., Aerospace Engineering and Engineering Mechanics
STEINFINK, H., PH.D., Chemical Engineering
STERN, M., PH.D., Aerospace Engineering and Engineering Mechanics
STICE, J. R., PH.D., Engineering Education
STRAITON, A. W., PH.D., Electrical Engineering
SZEBEHELY, V. G., D.SC., Aerospace Engineering
TAPLEY, B. D., PH.D., Aerospace Engineering
THOMPSON, J. N., PH.D., Civil Engineering
THURSTON, G. B., Electrical, Biomedical, Mechanical Engineering
TUCKER, R. L., PH.D., Civil Engineering
VLIET, G. C., PH.D., Mechanical Engineering
WAGNER, T. J., PH.D., Electrical Engineering
WALLS, H. A., PH.D., Mechanical Engineering
WALSER, R. M., PH.D., Electrical Engineering
WELCH, A. J., PH.D., Electrical Engineering
WISSLER, E. H., Chemical Engineering
WOMACK, B. F., PH.D., Electrical Engineering
WOODSON, H. H., Electrical Engineering
YEH, R. T., PH.D., Electrical Engineering
YEW, C., PH.D., Aerospace Engineering and Engineering Mechanics
YURA, J. A., PH.D., Civil Engineering

*College of Fine Arts:*
ALEXANDER, S. M., PH.D., Art
BARRINGTON, W. R., Music
BEACHY, M. J., Music
BEHAGUE, G. H., PH.D., Music
BLAIR, R. D., M.MUS., Music
CONTINO, F. C., PH.D., Music
CRISARA, R. D., Music
DEATHERAGE, MARTHA, M.M., Music
DENNEY, R. R., M.S., Drama
DIETZ, H. B., PH.D., Music
DININO, V. R., Music
DUCLOUX, W., Music
ENGEL, B. B., PH.D., Drama

FEARING, K., M.F.A., Art
FISKE, K. B., M.A., Art
FRANCIS, B. D., Art
FRARY, M. G., Art
GARVEY, D. W., Music
GREEN, D. M., PH.D., Music
GRIEDER, T., PH.D., Art
GREENHILL, E. S., PH.D., Art
HALL, S., Drama and Physical and Health Education
HATGIL, P. P., M.A., Art
HICKS, J. H., Music
HUNTER, F. J., PH.D., Drama
JENNINGS, C. A., ED.D., Drama
JORDAN, B., PH.D., System Professor of Music
KANABLE, BETTY, PH.D., Music
KENNAN, K. W., B.MUS., Music
KNAUB, D. L., Music
KORTE, K., Music
LETHCO, AMANDA V., M.MUS., Music
LEVERS, R. L., M.F.A., Art
MANNION, E. B., Music
MARIANI, V. A., Art
MCGAUGHEY, J., M.MUS., Music
NICKEL, A. A., M.A.E., Art
OLEFSKY, PAUL, Music
PRESCOTT, K. W., PH.D., Art
POSNER, L., Music
RACE, W., D.M.A., Music
REINHARDT, P. D., PH.D., Drama
ROTHGEB, J. R., Drama
SANKEY, S. M., M.S., Music
SMALLEY, W. D., PH.D., Drama
SNOW, R. J., Music
STEIN, H., PH.D., Drama
STEWART, W., Music
WALTERS, J., Music
WHITE, R. E., Jr., Art
WILLIAMS, J. A., PH.D., Art and Center of Middle Eastern Studies
YOUNG, P. C., Music
YOUSKEVITCH, I., Drama

*College of Pharmacy:*
DELGADO, J., PH.D.
DOLUISIO, J. T., PH.D.
ERICKSON, C. K., PH.D.
FINEG, J., D.V.M., Physiology and Pharmacology
FOLKERS, K., D.PHARM., Pharmacy and Chemistry
MARTIN, A., PH.D.
SMITH, R. V., PH.D.
WALTON, C. A., PH.D.
YANCHICK, V. A., PH.D.

*School of Law:*
ALDAVE, B. B., J.D.
ANDERSON, D. A., J.D.
BAADE, H. W., LL.M.
BARNDT, R. V., LL.B.
BOBBITT, P. C., J.D.
CAIN, P. A., J.D.
CHURGIN, M. J., J.D.
COHEN, E. R., LL.B.
DAWSON, R. O., S.J.D.
DIX, G. E., J.D.
DODGE, J. M., L.L.M.
FIELDER, P. C., LL.B.
FILVAROFF, D. B., LL.B.
GIBSON, W. W.
GRAGLIA, L. A.
HAMILTON, R. W.
HUIE, W. O., S.J.D.
JOHANSON, S. M.
JOHNSON, C. W., J.D.
LEBOWITZ, L., LL.M.
LEVINSON, S. V., PH.D.
MCGARITY, T. O., J.D.
MARKOVITS, INGA, J.D.
MARKOVITS, R. S., PH.D.
MEANS, R. C., LL.B.
MERSKY, R. M., M.S., Library
POWE, L. A., J.D.
POWERS, W. C., J.D.

UNIVERSITIES AND COLLEGES—TEXAS (UNIVERSITY OF) U.S.A.

Rau, A. S., LL.B.
Rosenthal, M. P.
Rudd, M. H., LL.B.
Sampson, J. J., LL.B.
Sharlot, M. M., LL.B.
Sherman, E. F., J.D.
Smith, E. E., III
Sutton, J. F., Jr., LL.B.
Treece, J. M.
Ward, B. J.
Weinberg, Louise, LL.M.
Weintraub, R. J., LL.B.
Wellborn, O. G., J.D.
Witherspoon, J. B., LL.B.
Woodward, M. K., M.A.
Wright, C. A., LL.B.
Yudof, M. G., LL.B.

*Graduate School of Library Science:*
Harmon, E. G., PH.D.
Jackson, E. B., M.A.
Jackson, W. V., PH.D.
Reagan, A. G., PH.D.
Sparks, C. G., PH.D.

*School of Architecture:*
Alexander, D. B.
Arumi, F. N., PH.D.
Bell, M. W., B.ARCH.
Bergquist C. O., M.S.
Black, J. S., M.ARCH.
Bowman, J. A., M.ARCH.
Coote, R. J., M.A.
Dodge, R. L., M.ARCH.
Kermacy, M. S., M.ARCH.
McClure, E. E., PH.D.
Mather, R. G.
Roessner, R. G., M.ARCH.
Swallow, R. P.

*School of Social Work:*
Austin, D. M., PH.D.
Bounous, R. C., PH.D.
Heffernan, W. J.
Hess, D., PH.D.
Hill, W. G., D.S.W.
Otis, J., PH.D.
Williams, M. S., PH.D.
Zurcher, L., PH.D.

*LBJ School of Public Affairs:*
Anderson, L. F., M.A.
Blissett, Marlin, PH.D.
Cohen, W. J., PH.D.
Flawn, P. T., PH.D.
Gronouski, J. A., PH.D.
Hansen, R. D., PH.D.
Jordan, B. C., LL.B.
Redford, E., PH.D.
Rohlich, G., PH.D.
Rostow, E. D., M.A.
Schmandt, J., PH.D.
Spurr, S. H., PH.D.
Tolo, K. W., PH.D.
Warner, D. C., PH.D.
Weintraub, S., PH.D.

*School of Nursing:*
Brown, Billye J., ED.D.
Field, W. E., PH.D.
Walker, L. O., ED.D.
Wandelt, M. A., PH.D.

Attached Research Organizations:
Animal Resources Center: Dir. Jerry Fineg.
Applied Research Laboratories: Dir. C. M. McKinney.
Institute for Biomedical Research: Dir. Karl Folkers.
Computation Center: Dir. C. H. Warlick.
Institute for Computer Sciences and Computer Applications: Dir. J. C. Browne.
Bureau of Economic Geology: Dir. W. L. Fisher.
Center for Energy Studies: Dir. H. H. Woodson.
Center for Fusion Research: Dir. W. E. Drummond.
Institute for Human Development: Dir. Ira Iscoe.
Humanities Research Center: Dir. Dechard Turner.
Institute for Latin American Studies: Dir. W. Glade.
Marine Science Institute: Dir. J. R. Moore.
Mining and Mineral Resources Research Institute: Dir. W. C. J. van Rensburg.
McDonald Observatory: Dir. H. J. Smith.
Radio Astronomy Project: Dir. J. N. Douglas.
Texas Memorial Museum: Dir. W. G. Reeder.
Radiocarbon Laboratory: Dir. E. M. Davis.
Vertebrate Paleontology Laboratory: Dir. Wann Langstron.

Attached to the College of Business Administration:
Bureau of Business Research: Dir. Charles C. Holt.
Institute for Constructive Capitalism: Dir. George Kozmetsky.

Attached to the College of Education:
Research and Development Center for Teacher Education: Dir. O. H. Bown.

Attached to the College of Engineering:
Center for Transportation Research: Dir. B. F. McCullough.
Center for Building Research: Dir. Richard Tucker (acting).
Center for Earth Sciences and Engineering: Dir. K. E. Gray.
Electrical Engineering Research Laboratory: Dir. H. W. Smith.
Center for Electromechanics: Dir. H. G. Rylander, Jr.
Electronics Research Center: Dir. E. J Powers.
Bureau of Engineering Research: Dir. E. F. Gloyna.
Environmental Health Engineering Laboratory: Dir. Neal E. Armstrong.
Texas Institute for Computational Mechanics: Dir. J. T. Oden.
Center for Research in Water Resources: Dir. Leo Beard.

Attached to the Division of General and Comparative Studies:
Center for Intercultural Studies in Folklore and Ethnomusicology: Dir. Gerhard Behague.

Attached to the College of Natural Sciences:
Laboratory of Algal Physiology: Dir. Jack Myers.
Brackenridge Field Laboratory: Dir. W. F. Blair.
Cell Research Institute: Dir. Dennis Brown.
Clayton Foundation Biochemical Institute: Dir. Lester J. Reed.
Center for Fast Kinetics Research: Dir. E. L. Powers.
Genetics Institute: Dir. Burk Judd.
Research in Microbiology: Dir. Orville Wyss.
Center for Numerical Analysis: Dir. David M. Young.
Center for Particle Theory: Co-Dirs. E. C. J. Sudarshan and Y. N'eman.
Plant Resources Center: Dir. B. L. Turner.
Ilya Prigogine Center for the Study of Statistical Mechanics: Dir. Ilya Prigogine.
Laboratory for Radiation Biology: Dir. E. L. Powers.
Center for Relativity Theory: Dir. B. S. DeWitt.
Laboratory of Reproductive Biology: Dir. F. H. Bronson.
Research Instruments Laboratory: Dir. W. H. Wade.
Center for Structural Studies: Dir. James E. Boggs.
Center for Theoretical Chemistry: Dir. J. E. Boggs.
Center for Theoretical Physics: Dir. John Wheeler.

Attached to the School of Nursing:
Center for Health Care Research and Evaluation: Dir. Mabel Wandelt.

Attached to the School of Pharmacy:
Drug Dynamics Institute: Dir. R. V. Smith.

Attached to the College of Social and Behavioral Studies:
Center for Economic Research: Dir. Ed Hewett.
Center for Study of Human Resources: Dir. R. W. Glover.
Institute for Classical Archaeology: Dir. J. C. Carter.
Center for Cognitive Science: Dirs. Philip Gough, Stanley Peters.
Linguistics Research Center: Dir. Winfred P. Lehmann.
Phonetics Laboratory: Dir. P. F. MacNeilage.
Population Research Center: Dir. Omer Galle.
Texas Archaeological Research Laboratory: Dir. Dee Ann Story.
Research in Texas History: Dir. L. Tuffly Ellis.

Attached to the School of Social Work:
Center for Social Work Research: Dir. David M. Austin.

**University of Texas at Arlington**
Arlington, Texas 76019
Telephone: (817) 273-2011.

Founded 1895 as Arlington College,

reorganized as a campus of the University of Texas 1967.
*President:* Dr. W. H. NEDDERMAN.
*Vice-President for Business Affairs:* J. D. WETSEL.
*Vice-President for Academic Affairs:* Dr. W. A. BAKER.
*Vice-President for Student Affairs:* Dr. B. WAYNE DUKE.
*Librarian:* J. HUDSON.
The library contains 753,000 vols.
Number of teachers: 883.
Number of students: 20,166.

DEANS:

*Liberal Arts:* THOMAS E. PORTER.
*Science:* H. ARNOTT.
*Business:* W. E. MULLENDORE.
*Engineering:* JOHN ROUSE, Jr.
*Graduate School:* BOB F. PERKINS.
*Graduate School of Social Work:* PAUL H. GLASSER.
*Architecture and Environmental Design:* GEORGE WRIGHT.
*Nursing:* MYRNA PICKARD.
*Institute of Urban Studies:* Dir. RICHARD L. COLE.
*Center for Professional Teacher Education:* CHARLES FUNKHOUSER.

### University of Texas at El Paso
EL PASO, TEXAS 79968
Telephone: (915) 747-5000.

Founded 1913 as Texas School of Mines and Metallurgy; name changed to Texas Western College 1949; current name adopted 1967.

*President:* HASKELL M. MONROE, Jr.
*Vice-President for Academic Affairs:* JOSEPH D. OLANDER.
*Vice-President for Business Affairs:* WILLIAM C. ERSKINE.
*Director of Admissions:* WILLIAM P. NELSEN.
*Librarian:* FRED W. HANES.

Library: see Libraries.
Number of teachers: 663.
Number of students: 15,750.

Publications: *El Paso Economic Review* (monthly), *Nova* (quarterly), *Southwestern Studies* (quarterly), *El Burro* (twice a year), *The Flowsheet* (annual), *Accounting Trends* (quarterly), *The Amphora Review* (quarterly), *The Prospector* (2 a week).

DEANS:

*Students:* JOSE F. AVILA.
*Education:* (vacant).
*Engineering:* JACK SMITH.
*Liberal Arts:* DIANA NATALICIO.
*Sciences:* CHOO-SENG GIAM.
*Business Administration:* WELDON C. NEILL.
*Graduate School:* MICHAEL AUSTIN.
*Nursing:* EILEEN M. JACOBI.

### University of Texas Medical Branch at Galveston
GALVESTON, TEXAS 77550
Telephone: (713) 765-1011.

Founded 1891; Formerly Medical Branch, Galveston.

*President:* WILLIAM C. LEVIN, M.D.
*Executive Vice-President for Administration and Business Affairs:* VERNON E. THOMPSON.
*Director of Library:* EMIL FREY.

Number of teachers: 603.
Number of students: 1,525.

Publications: *Texas Reports on Biology and Medicine*†.

DEANS:

*Medicine:* GEORGE T. BRYAN, M.D.
*Graduate School of Biomedical Sciences:* J. PALMER SAUNDERS, PH.D.
*School of Allied Health Sciences:* JOHN G. BRUHN, PH.D.
*School of Nursing:* DOROTHY DAMEWOOD, ED.D.

### University of Texas Health Science Center at Dallas
5323 HARRY HINES BLVD., DALLAS, TEXAS 75235
Telephone: (214) 688-3111.

Founded 1949; formerly Southwestern Medical School founded 1943.

*President:* CHARLES C. SPRAGUE, M.D.
*Vice-President for Administration:* JACK D. WHEELER.
*Vice-President for Business Affairs:* J. E. WEEKS, LL.B.
*Dean, Southwestern Medical School:* FREDERICK J. BONTE, M.D.
*Dean, Graduate School of Biomedical Sciences:* KERN WILDENTHAL, M.D., PH.D.
*Dean, School of Allied Health Sciences:* JOHN W. SCHERMERHORN, PH.D.
*Associate Dean for Clinical Programs:* ALBERT D. ROBERTS, M.D.
*Associate Dean for Student Affairs:* BRYAN WILLIAMS, M.D.
*Associate Dean for Continuing Education:* GEORGE G. RACE, M.D., PH.D.
*Registrar and Director of Student Services:* J. WESLEY NORRED, B.A.
*Librarian:* JEAN MILLER, PH.D.

Number of teachers: 512.
Number of students: 760 medical, 190 graduate, 200 Allied Health.

Publications: *Spectrum* (annually), *Newsletter* (monthly).

### University of Texas Health Science Center at San Antonio
7703 FLOYD CURL DRIVE, SAN ANTONIO, TEXAS 78284

Founded 1959 as South Texas Medical School, a part of The University of Texas System, name changed to University of Texas Medical School at San Antonio 1967, present name 1972.

*President:* FRANK HARRISON, M.D., PH.D.
*Executive Vice-President for Administration and Business Affairs:* ROBERT B. PRICE.
*Assistant to the President:* MARTHA W. WOOD, PH.D.
*Director of Continuing Education Services:* GEORGE B. VAUGHAN, PH.D.
*Executive Director, Bexar County Hospital:* CHARLES E. GIBBS, M.D. (acting).
*Director of Student Services:* DAVID M. SHAPIRO, PH.D.

The library contains 100,000 vols.

DEANS:

*Medical School:* TIMOTHY N. CARIS, M.D. (acting).
*Dental School:* JOHN J. SHARRY, D.M.D.
*Graduate School of Biomedical Sciences:* ARMAND J. GUARINO, PH.D.
*School of Allied Health Sciences:* JAMES F. WITTMER (acting).
*School of Nursing:* PATTY L. HAWKEN, PH.D.

### University of Texas Health Science Center at Houston School of Public Health
P.O.B. 20186, HOUSTON, TEXAS 77025
Founded 1967.

*Dean:* R. A. STALLONES, M.D., M.P.H.
Number of teachers: 66.
Number of students: 555.

### University of Texas of the Permian Basin
ODESSA, TEXAS 79762

Founded 1969. Liberal arts, sciences, engineering, business, teacher education.

*President:* V. R. CARDOZIER.
*Vice-President, Business Affairs:* W. A. WATTS.
*Assistant to the President:* THOMAS WOLFF.

The library contains c. 375,000 vols.
Number of students: 1,588.

DEANS:

*College of Management:* J. E. BECHT.
*College of Arts and Education:* W. R. TANKSLEY.
*College of Science and Engineering:* R. G. REEVES.

### WAYLAND BAPTIST COLLEGE
PLAINVIEW, TEXAS 79072
Telephone: (806) 296-5521.
Founded 1908.

*President:* Dr. ROY C. MCCLUNG.
*Vice-President for Academic Affairs:* Dr. PAUL BUTLER (acting).
*Registrar:* Mrs. AUDREY H. BOLES.
*Librarian:* Miss FLORRIE CONWAY.

The library contains 78,000 vols.
Number of teachers: 62.
Number of students: 1,126.

## WEST TEXAS STATE UNIVERSITY
WEST TEXAS STATION,
CANYON, TEXAS 79016

Founded 1909.

*President:* MAX R. SHERMAN.
*Executive Vice-President:* Dr. GAIL SHANNON.

The library contains 686,597 vols.
Number of teachers: 263.
Number of students: 6,469.

Publications: *The Prairie* (newspaper), *Le Mirage* (annual).

## WILEY COLLEGE
MARSHALL, TEXAS 75670
Telephone: (214) 938-8341.

Founded 1873.

*President:* Dr. ROBERT E. HAYES, Sr.
*Dean of Faculty:* Dr. DAVID R. HOUSTON.
*Vice-President for Student Affairs:* Dr. STEVE FAVORS.
*Vice-President of Academic Affairs:* Dr. DAVID R. HOUSTON.
*Librarian:* RODNEY ATKINS.

The library contains 84,434 vols.
Number of teachers: 36.
Number of students: 615.

# UTAH

## BRIGHAM YOUNG UNIVERSITY
PROVO, UTAH 84602
Telephone: (801) 378-1211.

Founded 1875 by President Brigham Young of the Church of Jesus Christ of Latter-Day Saints.

*President:* JEFFREY R. HOLLAND, PH.D.
*Provost and Academic Vice-President:* JAE R. BALLIF, PH.D.
*Executive Vice-President:* W. ROLFE KERR.
*Financial Vice-President:* R. J. SMITH, PH.D.
*Support Services Vice-President:* FRED A. SCHWENDIMAN.
*General Counsel:* H. HAL VISICK, B.A., J.D.
*Dean of Admissions and Records:* R. W. SPENCER, M.S., ED.D.
*Director of Libraries:* STERLING J. ALBRECHT, M.L.S.

The library contains over 2 million volumes, pamphlets and bulletins.

Number of teachers: 1,237 full-time, 515 part-time; does not include graduate assistants.
Number of students: 26,000.

DEANS:

*School of Law:* CARL S. HAWKINS.
*College of Biological and Agricultural Sciences:* A. LESTER ALLEN, PH.D.
*School of Management:* W. G. DYER, PH.D.
*College of Education:* CURTIS VAN ALFEN, M.S., ED.D.
*College of Family, Home and Social Sciences:* MARTIN B. HICKMAN, PH.D.
*College of Fine Arts and Communications:* L. J. WOODBURY, M.A., PH.D.
*College of Humanities:* RICHARD H. CRACROFT, PH.D.
*College of Engineering Sciences and Technology:* L. DOUGLAS SMOOT, M.S., PH.D.
*College of Nursing:* ELAINE D. DYER, M.S., PH.D.
*College of Physical and Mathematical Sciences:* J. REX GOATES, PH.D.
*College of Physical Education:* C. R. JENSEN, M.S., P.E.D.
*Department of Religious Instruction:* ROBERT J. MATTHEWS, PH.D.
*Student Life:* DAVID M. SORENSON, ED.D.
*Continuing Education:* WILLIAM R. SIDDOWAY, M.B.A.

## UNIVERSITY OF UTAH
SALT LAKE CITY, UTAH 84112
Telephone: (801) 322-7211.

Incorporated 1850 as University of Deseret; Chartered 1892 as University of Utah.

*President:* DAVID P. GARDNER, PH.D.
*Vice-Presidents:* R. J. SNOW, PH.D. (University Relations), CEDRIC I. DAVERN, PH.D. (Academic Affairs), CHASE PETERSON, M.D. (Health Sciences), WALT GNEMI, M.A. (Administrative Services), JAMES BROPHY, PH.D. (Research).
*Registrar:* KAY HARWARD, M.A.
*Librarian:* ROGER K. HANSON, M.A.L.S.

Number of teachers: 1,350.
Number of students: 21,880.

DEANS:

*Dean, Admissions and Registration:* F. L. McKEAN, M.A.
*Dean of Liberal Education:* L. JACKSON NEWELL, PH.D.
*Dean of Humanities:* MALCOLM O. SILLARS, PH.D.
*Dean for Science:* DAVID M. GRANT, M.S., PH.D.
*Graduate School of Social Work:* E. SCHATZ, PH.D.
*College of Engineering:* L. M. LATTMAN, PH.D.
*College of Business:* (vacant).
*Graduate School:* JAMES L. CLAYTON, PH.D.
*College of Mines and Mineral Industries:* LAURENCE H. LATTMANN, PH.D.
*College of Health:* O. N. HUNTER, PH.D.
*College of Law:* WALTER E. OBERER, J.D.
*College of Medicine:* GLENN R. LEE, M.D.
*College of Pharmacy:* HAROLD H. WOLF, PH.D.
*College of Nursing:* (vacant).
*College of Fine Arts:* E. D. MARYON, PH.D.
*Graduate School of Architecture:* ROBERT L. BLISS, B.ARCH.
*Graduate School of Education:* ROBERT L. ERDMAN, PH.D.
*Division of Continuing Education:* OAKLEY J. GORDON, PH.D.

PROFESSORS:

AARON, I. R., LL.D., Law
ABBEY, J. C., PH.D., Nursing
ABILDSKOV, J. A., M.D., Internal Medicine
ADIX, V., M.A., Theatre
AGGELER, G. N., PH.D., English
AILION, D. C., PH.D., Physics
AJAX, E. T., M.D., Neurology
ALLEY, C. L., M.S., Electrical Engineering
ALLRED, E. L., PH.D., Chemistry
ALTMAN, I., PH.D., Psychology
ANDERSEN, J. R., J.D., Law
ANDERSON, J. A., PH.D., Communication
ANDERSON, L. R., Mining and Fuels Engineering
ANDERSON, R., PH.D., Anthropology
ANDRADE, J. D., PH.D., Materials Science and Engineering
ANSTALL, H. B., M.D., Pathology and Medical Technology
ATHENS, J. W., M.D., Internal Medicine
ATIYA, A. S., PH.D., Languages
ATWOOD, K. W., PH.D., Electrical Engineering
BAER, A. D., PH.D., Chemical Engineering
BAGLEY, R. N., PH.D., Accounting
BAIRD, B. F., PH.D., Management Science
BAKER, W. K., PH.D., Biology
BALL, J. S., PH.D., Physics
BANHAM, P. B., D.PHIL., Music
BARNETT, A. M. L., PH.D., Languages
BARNHILL, R. E., PH.D., Mathematics
BARTON, D. K., PH.D. Languages
BEAN, L., PH.D., Sociology
BEARNSON, D., PH.D., Art
BECK, E. C., PH.D., Neurology
BEIER, E. G., PH.D., Psychology
BELL, T. H., ED.D., Educational Administration
BENNETT, D. W., PH.D., Philosophy
BENNETT, W. R., LL.M., J.D., Law
BENTRUDE, W. G., PH.D., Chemistry
BERCHAN, R., PH.D., Languages
BERGESON, H. E., PH.D., Physics
BITTON, D., PH.D., History
BLISS, E. L., M.D., Psychiatry
BLISS, R. L., B.ARCH., Architecture
BODILY, D. M., PH.D., Fuels Engineering
BOEHM, R. F., PH.D., Mechanical and Industrial Engineering
BOYCE, R. N., J.D., Law
BOYD, R. H., PH.D., Chemical Engineering
BRAGG, D. S., M.D., Radiology
BRANDLE, K., DR.ING., Architecture
BRAY, P. K., M.D., Paediatrics and Neurology
BROOKS, R. M., PH.D., Mathematics
BROOM, A. N., PH.D., Medical Chemistry
BROWN, E. G., PH.D., Social Work
BROWN, H. M., Jr., PH.D., Physiology
BROWN, W. S., PH.D., Mechanical Engineering
BRUMBAUGH, W. D., ED.D., Educational Systems and Learning Resources
BRUNVAND, J. H., PH.D., English
BRYNER, C. G., M.S., Civil Engineering
BURGESS, C. E., PH.D., Mathematics
BURGESS, M. J., PH.D., Cardiology
BURGESS, P. R., PH.D., Physiology
BUTERBAUGH, J. G., ED.D., Education
BYRNE, J. G., PH.D., Materials Science and Engineering
CAGLE, F. W., PH.D., Chemistry
CALDER, G. H., D.B.A., Management
CANNING, R. R., PH.D., Sociology

CAPECCHI, M. R., PH.D., Biology
CARAVAGLIA, A. T. C., Art
CARRUTH, M. L., PH.D., Sociology
CARTWRIGHT, G. E., M.D., Internal Medicine
CASE, J. H., PH.D., Mathematics
CASTLE, C. H., M.D., Community and Family Medicine
CATHEY, W. J., M.D., Pathology
CHAMBERLIN, R. E., PH.D., Mathematics
CHEMERS, M. M., PH.D., Psychology
CHOPYK, D. B., PH.D., Languages
CLARK, A. O., D.B.A., Management
CLARK, L. D., M.D., Psychiatry
CLAYTON, J. L., PH.D., History
CLIFFORD, J. A., M.S., Modern Dance
CLEMENS, H. C., PH.D., Mathematics
COHEN, M. F., PH.D., Philosophy
COLEMAN, S. S., M.D., Surgery
COLES, W. J., PH.D., Mathematics
COOK, K. L., PH.D., Geophysics
COOLEY, E. L., PH.D., Library Science and History
CRAWLEY, S. W., M.ARCH., Architecture
CUSHING, B., PH.D., Accounting
DAVERN, C. I., M.D., PH.D., Biology and Microbiology
DAVIS, E. A., PH.D., Mathematics
DAVISON, N. J., PH.D., Languages
DEA, KAY L., D.S.W., Social Work
DELLA-PIANA, G. M., PH.D., Educational Psychology
DENEVERS, N. H., PH.D., Chemical Engineering
DETHLEFSEN, L. A., PH.D., Radiology
DEVRIES, K. L., PH.D., Mechanical Engineering
DEWITT, C., PH.D., Pathology, Surgery and Medical Technology
DICK, B. G., PH.D., Physics
DICKMAN, S. R., PH.D., Biological Chemistry
DIXON, J. A., M.D., Surgery
DONNER, M., PH.D., English
DREW, C. J., PH.D., Special Education
DURNEY, C. H., PH.D., Electrical Engineering
DURHAM, L. M., PH.D., Music
DVORAK, C. J., PH.D., Engineering
DYER, B. K., J.D., Law
EBLE, KENNETH E., PH.D., English
EDMINSTER, R. R., PH.D., Economics
EDMUNDS, G. F., Jr., PH.D., Biology
EDMUNDSON, A. B., PH.D., Microbiology and Biology
EICHWALD, E. J., M.D., Pathology, Surgery and Medical Technology
ELTRINGHAM, J. R., M.D., Radiology
EMERY, A. C., J.D., Law
ENGAR, K. M., PH.D., Theatre
ENGLERT, E., Jr., M.D., Internal Medicine
EPSTEIN, W. W., PH.D., Chemistry
ERDMAN, R. L., ED.D., Special Education
EVANS, D. C., PH.D., Computer Science
EVANS, F. R., PH.D., Biology
EYRING, E. M., PH.D., Chemistry
EYRING, H., PH.D., Chemistry and Metallurgical Engineering
EYZAGUIRRE, C., M.D., Physiology
FADLEY, C. S., PH.D., Chemistry
FARLEY, O. W., PH.D., Social Work
FARRAR, D. E., PH.D., Finance
FAULES, D. F., PH.D., Communication
FAUST, A. F., PH.D., Educational Administration
FIFE, J., PH.D., English
FINGL, E., PH.D., Pharmacology
FIRMAGE, E. B., S.J.D., Law
FISHER, A., PH.D., Geography
FISHER, A., PH.D., Communication
FLANDRO, G. A., PH.D., Mechanical Engineering
FLYNN, J. J., S.J.D., Law
FOLIAS, E. S., PH.D., Civil Engineering and Mathematics
FORDHAM, J. B., J.S.D., Law

FOWLES, G. R., PH.D., Physics
FRANKEL, L. H., LL.M., Law
FRESTON, J. W., M.D., Internal Medicine, Pharmacology
FUKUTA, N., PH.D., Meteorology
FUTRELL, J. H., PH.D., Chemistry
GAHIN, F. S., PH.D., Finance
GANDER, J. P., PH.D., Economics
GANDHI, O. P., SC.D., Electrical Engineering
GARDNER, D. P., ED.D., Education
GARDNER, J. H., PH.D., Management
GARDNER, P. D., PH.D., Chemistry
GARDNER, W. W., PH.D., Management
GARLINGTON, J., PH.D., English
GAVERS, M., Ballet
GEHMLICH, D. K., P.D.D., Electrical Engineering
GELFAND, DONNA M., PH.D., Psychology
GERLACH, S. L., PH.D., History
GERSTEN, S. M., PH.D., Mathematics
GIBB, J. W., PH.D., Pharmacology
GIBBS, P., PH.D., Physics
GIRTON, L., PH.D., Economics
GIDDINGS, J. C., PH.D., Chemistry
GILMORE, F. C., M.S., Naval Science
GITTINS, A. L., B.A., Art
GLASER, L. C., PH.D., Mathematics
GLASGOW, L. A., M.D., Microbiology
GORDON, O. J., PH.D., Psychology
GORDON, R. S., SC.D., Materials Science and Engineering
GRANT, C. W., PH.D., Educational Psychology
GRANT, D. M., PH.D., Chemistry
GRANZIN, K. L., PH.D., Marketing
GRAY, R. M., PH.D., Sociology
GRAY, W. R., PH.D., Biology and Chemistry
GRESSETH, G. K., PH.D., Languages
GRIFFITHS, F. A., ED.D., Social Work
GROSS, F. I., PH.D., Mathematics
GROSSER, B. I., M.D., Psychiatry
GROW, R. W., PH.D., Electrical Engineering
GRUNDMANN, A. W., PH.D., Biology
GUILLORY, W. A., PH.D., Chemistry
HAGEN, F. W., PH.D., Philosophy
HAHN, WALTER, PH.D., Education
HAIGH, R. M., PH.D., History
HAIR, MARY JANE, PH.D., Library
HALES, B. W., ED.D., Music
HAMMOND, P. C., PH.D., Anthropology
HANKS, J. W., PH.D., Economics
HANLY, E. W., PH.D., Biology
HANSEN, P. J., PH.D., Education
HANSON, D. W., PH.D., Political Science
HANSON, M. L., PH.D., Communication
HARMER, E., PH.D., Education
HARRIS, F. E., PH.D., Physics
HARRY, S., ED.D., Education
HARTMANN, D. P., Psychology
HARVEY, J. E., PH.D., Languages
HARVEY, S., PH.D., Pharmacology
HASHIMOTO, E. I., M.D., Anatomy
HAYES, ELIZABETH R., ED.D., Modern Dance
HEARN, A. C., PH.D., Physics and Computer Science
HELBLING, R. E., PH.D., Languages
HENCLEY, S. P., PH.D., Educational Administration
HEPWORTH, D. H., PH.D., Social Work
HESS, O. L., PH.D., Education
HESS, W. H., PH.D., Languages
HILL, A. C., PH.D., Biology
HILL, G. R., PH.D., Chemical Engineering
HIRTH, H. F., PH.D., Biology
HOLLSTEIN, M. C., PH.D., Communication
HOPPENSTEADT, F. C., PH.D., Mathematics
HUBER, R. J., PH.D., Electrical Engineering
HUGHES, C., PH.D., Community and Family Medicine
HUNT, E. K., PH.D., Economics
HUNTER, O. N., ED.D., Health, P.E. and Leisure Studies

HUNTSMAN, A. B., PH.D., Finance
ISAACSON, L. K., PH.D., Mechanical Engineering
JABUSCH, D. M., PH.D., Communication
JACOBS, H. R., PH.D., Mechanical and Industrial Engineering
JACOBSEN, G. S., ED.D., Educational Administration
JACOBSON, M., PH.D., Anatomy
JARCHO, L. W., M.D., Neurology
JARVIS, J. B., PH.D., Communication
JEE, W. S. S., PH.D., Anatomy
JENNINGS, J. D., PH.D., Anthropology
JENSEN, M. L., PH.D., Geology
JEX, F. B., PH.D., Educational Psychology
JOHNSON, A. F., PH.D., Mechanical Engineering
JOHNSON, A. H., PH.D., Accounting
JOHNSON, D. G., M.D., Surgery
JOHNSON, F., PH.D., Marketing
JOHNSON, O., PH.D., Physics
JOHNSON, R. E., PH.D., Finance
JOHNSTON, W. A., PH.D., Psychology
JONES, C. E., PH.D., Languages
JONES, D. E., PH.D., Theatre
JORGENSEN, J. L., PH.D., Finance
KADESCH, R. R., PH.D., Physics
KAO, S.-K., PH.D., Meteorology
KARLF, R., PH.D., Pharmacology
KASS, T. B., PH.D., Architecture
KNOWLTON, C. S., PH.D., Sociology
KOEHLER, P. R., M.D., Radiology
KOLFF, W. J., PH.D., Surgery
KRANES, D. A., D.F.A., English
KUBY, S. A., PH.D., Biochemistry
KUCHAR, K. V., Physics
KUIDA, H., M.D., Internal Medicine and Physiology
LAHEY, M. E., M.D., Paediatrics
LANDAU, E. D., PH.D., Education
LARK, K. G., PH.D., Biology
LATTMAN, L. H., PH.D., Geology and Geophysics
LAZOWSKI, N. Y., PH.D., Ballet
LEE, G. R., M.D., Internal Medicine
LEGLER, J. M., PH.D., Biology
LEININGER, M. M., PH.D., Nursing
LIEBERMAN, S., PH.D., Economics
LINTON, M., PH.D., Psychology
LOGAN, D. R., ED.D., Special Education
LOH, E. C., PH.D., Physics
LORDS, J. L., PH.D., Biology
LORENZO-RIVERA, L., PH.D., Languages
LUCKEY, E. B., PH.D., Family and Consumer Studies
LUEDERS, E. G., PH.D., English
LÜTY, F., DOZENT, Physics
LYMAN, D. J., PH.D., Materials Science and Engineering
McCANDLESS, G. A., PH.D., Communication
McCARTER, M. K., PH.D., Mining and Fuels Engineering
McCLEARY, L. E., ED.D., Educational Administration
McCLOSKEY, J. A., PH.D., Biomedical Chemistry
McCORMACK, W., LL.D., Law
McCOY, R. M., PH.D., Psychology
McMAHON, J., PH.D., Pharmacy
McMURRIN, S. M., PH.D., History and Philosophy of Education
McNULTY, I. B., PH.D., Biology
McPHIE, W. E., ED.D., Education
MADSEN, B. D., PH.D., History
MADSEN, J. A., M.D., Paediatrics
MAGLEBY, F. L., PH.D., Social Work
MALOUF, P. J., PH.D., Educational Psychology
MANGUM, G. L., PH.D., Economics and Management
MARCUS, S., PH.D., Microbiology and Medical Technology
MARYON, E. D., M.F.A., Art
MASON, R. C., PH.D., Medicinal Chemistry
MASON, R. G., M.D., Medicine

Massoth, F. E., ph.d., Mining, Metallurgy and Fuels Engineering
Matsen, J. M., m.d., Pathology and Paediatrics
Matthews, M. P., ph.d., Marketing
Mayfield, J. B., ph.d., Political Science
Mecham, G. D., j.d., m.s.w., Social Work
Mecham, M. J., ph.d., Communication
Merrill, R. M., ph.d., Educational Psychology
Michl, J., ph.d., Chemistry
Miles, C. B., m.d., Pathology
Miller, G., ph.d., Sociology
Miller, G. R., ph.d., Materials Science
Miller, J. D., ph.d., Metallurgical Engineering
Miller, W. R., ph.d., Anthropology
Millikan, C. N., m.d., Neurology
Moody, F. G., m.d., Surgery
Moore, H. E., ph.d., English
Morrill, W. K., ph.d., Educational Psychology
Mostofi, K., ph.d., Political Science
Nabers, L., ph.d., Economics
Nackowski, M. P., ph.d., Geology and Geophysics
Nash, W. P., ph.d., Geology and Geophysics
Negus, N. C., ph.d., Biology
Nelson, A. T., ph.d., Accounting
Nelson, C. E., ph.d., Economics
Nelson, D. H., m.d., Internal Medicine
Nelson, J. A., ph.d., Radiology
Nelson, R. H., ed.d., Management
Nicholes, P. S., ph.d., Microbiology
Nielson, H. C., ph.d., Psychology
Nielsen, L. T., ph.d., Biology
Nutting, W. C., ed.d., Education
Oberer, W. E., j.d., Law
Oblad, A. S., ph.d., Metallurgy and Fuels Engineering
Ohlsen, W., ph.d., Physics
Olivera, B. M., ph.d., Biology
Olpen, R. S., ph.d., Art
Olson, F. A., ph.d., Metallurgical Engineering
Organick, E. J., ph.d., Computer Science
Oviatt, B. E., d.s.w., Social Work
Painter, J. J., ph.d., Marketing
Pappas, J. P., ph.d., Educational Psychology
Pariseau, W. G., ph.d., Mining Engineering
Parker, S., ph.d., Anthropology
Parry, R. W., ph.d., Chemistry
Parry, W. T., ph.d., Geology and Geophysics
Partee, M. H., ph.d., English
Patton, M. J., ph.d., Educational Psychology
Paxman, D. G., Ballet
Peery, J. S., ph.d., Economics and Finance
Pendleton, R. C., ph.d., Biology
Petajan, J. H., ph.d., Neurology
Petersen, R. V., ph.d., Pharmacy
Pettit, Lynne A., ph.d., Foods and Nutrition
Picard, M. D., ph.d., Geology and Geophysics
Pitt, C. A., ph.d., Metallurgy and Metallurgical Engineering
Porter, P. B., ph.d., Psychology
Pratt, R. T., ph.d., Finance
Prokasy, W. F., ph.d., Psychology
Ragsdale, R. O., m.s., Chemistry
Rahde, F. H., ph.d., Languages
Randa, E. W., ph.d., Economics
Raskin, D. C., ph.d., Psychology
Redford, H. E. D., ph.d., Theatre
Renzetti, A. D., m.d., Internal Medicine
Rich, S. G., Jr., ph.d., Political Science
Richards, R. C., m.d., Surgery
Richardson, R. C., ph.d., Economics and Management

Ridd, M. K., ph.d., Geography
Rieke, R. N., ph.d., Communication
Rilling, H. C., ph.d., Biochemistry
Ririe, S. R., m.a., Modern Dance
Roberts, T., m.d., Surgery
Robson, R. T., ph.d., Management
Rockwood, L. R., ed.d., Leisure Studies
Rogers, L. M., ph.d., Philosophy
Roll, D. B., ph.d., Medicinal Chemistry
Rosenberg, G., Music
Rossi, H., ph.d., Mathematics
Roth, J. R., ph.d., Biology
Rushforth, C. K., ph.d., Electrical Engineering
Ryan, N. W., sc.d., Chemical Engineering
Salt, D. L., ph.d., Chemical Engineering
Sandberg, L. B., m.d., Pathology
Sandquist, G. M., ph.d., Mechanical and Industrial Engineering
Schmid, R. L., j.d., Law
Schmitt, K., ph.d., Mathematics
Schramm, R., ph.d., English
Scott, J. R., ph.d., Mathematics
Scott, W. R., ph.d., Mathematics
Seader, J. D., ph.d., Chemical Engineering
Shabtai, J., ph.d., Mining and Fuels Engineering
Shand, D. A., ph.d., Music
Shaw, R. T., ph.d., Marketing
Shimp, C. P., ph.d., Psychology
Sievers, A., ph.d., Economics
Sill, W. R., ph.d., Geology and Geophysics
Sillars, M. O., ph.d., Communication
Simons, J., ph.d., Chemistry
Skidmore, R. A., ph.d., Social Work
Slager, W. R., ph.d., English
Sloane, H. N., ph.d., Educational Psychology
Smart, M. N., ph.d., Communications
Smith, C. B., m.d., Internal Medicine
Smith, R. B., ph.d., Geology
Smith, T. C., ph.d., Sociology
Smith, V. G., m.s.w., Social Work
Snow, V. D., m.f.a., Art
Snyder, C. C., m.d., Surgery
Snyder, G., m.s.w., Social Work
Sorensen, P. D., m.s., Communication
Sorenson, J. A., ph.d., Radiology
Sosin, A., ph.d., Materials Science and Engineering
Spicer, L., ph.d., Chemistry
Spikes, J. D., ph.d., Biology
Steensma, R. C., ph.d., English
Stenger, F., ph.d., Mathematics
Stephenson, R. E., ph.d., Electrical Engineering
Stevens, W., Jr., ph.d., Anatomy
Stewart, J. R., m.d., Radiology
Stockham, T. S., Jr., sc.d., Electrical Engineering and Computer Science
Stokes, W. L., ph.d., Geology and Geophysics
Stoll, F. D., ph.d., Music
Stone, J. B., ph.d., Educational Psychology
Strachan, K., ll.d., Law
Streadbeck, A. L., ph.d., Languages
Stuart, R. B., Social Work
Sturges, P. C., ph.d., History
Sugden, J., ph.d., Archaeology
Sullivan, P. E., ph.d., English
Summers, R. W., m.d., Microbiology
Symco, O. G., ph.d., Physics
Tapscott, B. L., ph.d., Philosophy
Taylor, J. L., ph.d., Mathematics
Thackeray, M. G., ph.d., Social Work
Thurman, S. D., ll.b., Law
Tiemens, R. K., ph.d., Communication
Tierney, P. L., m.a., Art
Tikoff, G., m.d., Internal Medicine
Tompson, R. S., ph.d., History
Treshow, M., ph.d., Biology
Tsagaris, T. J., m.d., Internal Medicine
Tucker, D. H., ph.d., Mathematics

Tyler, F. H., m.d., Medicine
Tyler, S. L., ph.d., History
Uhl, C. R., ph.d., Psychology
Ussachevsky, V., ph.d., Music
Ure, R. W., Jr., ph.d., Materials Science and Engineering and Electrical Engineering
Van Alstyne, A., ll.b., Law
Van Norman, R. W., ph.d., Biology
Van Strien, D. O., m.s., Civil Engineering
Veasy, L. G., m.d., Paediatrics
Velick, S. F., ph.d., Biochemistry
Vernon, G. M., ph.d., Sociology
Viavant, W., ph.d., Computer Science
Vickery, R. K., ph.d., Biology
Voigt, M., ph.d., English
Vonschmidt, W. A., ph.d., Languages
Wadsworth, M. E., ph.d., Metallurgical Engineering
Wahrhaftig, A. L., ph.d., Chemistry
Walker, J. L., Jr., Physiology
Walling, C., ph.d., Chemistry
Wang, Chen-hsien, ph.d., Chemistry
Wann, A. J., ph.d., Political Science
Ward, J. R., m.d., Internal Medicine
Ward, S. H., ph.d., Geological and Geographical Sciences
Warner, H. R., m.d., ph.d., Biophysics and Bioengineering
Watts, A. W., m.m., Music
Webb, H. J., ph.d., English
Weight, N. B., d.m.a., Music
Welch, J. E., ph.d., Music
Wender, P. H., m.d., Psychiatry
West, Barbara H., ed.d., Physical Education
West, C. D., m.d., ph.d., Internal Medicine
Westlund, C. D., ph.d., Electrical Engineering
Whelan, J. A., ph.d., Geology and Geophysics
White, B. J., ph.d., Psychology
Wiens, D., ph.d., Biology
Wiest, J. D., ph.d., Management
Wilcox, C. H., ph.d., Mathematics
Wilkins, Ruth W., ll.b., Law
Willett, D. W., ph.d., Mathematics
Williams, G. A., ph.d., Physics
Williams, J. D., ph.d., Political Science
Willson, J. E., e.m., Mining Engineering
Wilson, R. H., m.a., Theatre
Wintrobe, M. M., m.d., Internal Medicine
Wiser, W. H., ph.d., Fuels Engineering
Wolcott, M., m.d., Surgery
Wolf, H. H., ph.d., Pharmacology
Wolfe, J. H., ph.d., Mathematics
Wolfer, J., Nursing
Wolstenholme, D. R., ph.d., Biology
Wong, K. C., ph.d., Anæsthesiology
Woodbury, D. M., ph.d., Pharmacology
Woodbury, Joan, m.s., Modern Dance
Woodbury, J. W., ph.d., Physiology
Wormuth, F. D., ph.d., Political Science
Yu, J. C., ph.d., Civil Engineering
Young, E. R., ph.d., Accounting
Zillman, D. N., ll.d., Law

## UTAH STATE UNIVERSITY
### of Agriculture and Applied Science
LOGAN, UTAH 84322

Telephone: (801) 750-1000.

Chartered 1888.

Academic year: September to June (and Summer Session).

*President:* Stanford Cazier.

*Provost:* R. Gaurth Hansen.

*Vice-Provost:* Richard M. Swenson.

*Vice-President, Research:* Bartell C. Jensen.

Vice-President, Business: EVAN N. STEVENSON.
Vice-President, Extension and Continuing Education: J. C. BALLARD.
Vice-President, Student Services: VAL R. CHRISTENSEN.
Vice-President, University Relations: GERALD R. SHERRATT.
Librarian and Director of Learning Resources Program: M. C. ABRAMS.
Number of teachers: 750.
Number of students: 9,939.

Publications: *Outlook* (monthly), *Outreach* (monthly), *Utah Science* (quarterly), *Western Historical Quarterly*, *Western Literary Journal* (quarterly).

### DEANS:

College of Graduate Studies: ALAN HOFMEISTER.
College of Agriculture: D. MATHEWS.
College of Business: RICHARD L. SMITH.
College of Education: O. L. BALLAM.
College of Engineering: EDDIE JOE MIDDLEBROOKS.
College of Family Life: JOAN R. MCFADDEN.
College of Humanities, Arts and Social Sciences: WILLIAM F. LYE.
College of Natural Resources: T. W. BOX.
College of Science: R. M. JOHNSON.

### HEADS OF DEPARTMENTS:

College of Agriculture:
  Plant Science: K. R. ALLRED.
  Agricultural Economics: J. C. ANDERSON.
  Nutrition and Food Sciences: C. A. ERNSTROM.
  Animal, Dairy and Veterinary Science: S. J. KLEINSCHUSTER.
  Agricultural Education: G. A. LONG.

College of Business:
  Business Education and Office Administration: LLOYD W. BARTHOLOME.
  Business Administration: H. CARLISLE.
  Accounting: L. G. HALE.

College of Education:
  Elementary Education: A. JACKSON.
  Communicative Disorders: T. S. JOHNSON.
  Special Education: D. P. MORGAN.
  Secondary Education: W. L. SAUNDERS.
  Instructional Media: D. C. SMELLIE.
  Health, Physical Education and Recreation: R. E. SORENSON.
  Psychology: B. R. WORTHEN.

College of Engineering:
  Electrical Engineering: D. J. BAKER.
  Civil and Environmental Engineering: W. J. GRENNEY.
  Agricultural and Irrigation Engineering: JACK KELLER.
  Industrial and Technical Education: REED M. NIELSEN (acting).
  Mechanical Engineering: A. P. MOSER.

College of Family Life:
  Family and Human Development: G. R. ADAMS.
  Home Economics and Consumer Education: CAROL BOCAN.

College of Humanities, Arts and Social Sciences:
  Music: W. L. BURTON.
  Theatre Arts: W. V. CALL.
  Art: R. T. CLARK (acting).
  Landscape Architecture and Environmental Planning: RICHARD E. TOTH.
  Political Science: R. HOOVER.
  English: K. HUNSAKER.
  Sociology, Social Work and Anthropology: WILLIAM F. STINNER (acting).
  Communication: H. J. KINZER.
  History and Geography: F. R. PETERSON.
  Languages and Philosophy: KENT E. ROBSON.

College of Natural Resources:
  Forestry and Outdoor Recreation: L. S. DAVIS.
  Range Science: D. D. DWYER.
  Wildlife Science: G. S. INNIS.

College of Science:
  Physics: P. M. BANKS.
  Mathematics: L. DUANE LOVELAND.
  Geology: C. T. HARDY.
  Applied Statistics and Computer Science: R. HURST.
  Biology: G. MILLER.
  Chemistry and Biochemistry: KAREN W. MORSE.

## WEBER STATE COLLEGE
OGDEN, UTAH 84408
Telephone: (801) 626-6000.
Founded 1889.

Liberal Arts, Vocational, Technical 4-year college.

President: Dr. RODNEY H. BRADY.
Registrar: M. C. MECHAM.
Director of Library: CRAIGE HALL.

The library contains 315,000 vols.
Number of teachers: 361.
Number of students: 10,000.

Publications: *Annual Catalog†*, *Comment†*, *Viewbook†*.

## WESTMINSTER COLLEGE
1840 SOUTH 13 EAST STREET, SALT LAKE CITY, UTAH 84105
Telephone: (801) 484-7651.
Founded 1875.

President: C. DAVID CORNELL.
Academic Vice-President and Dean: Dr. DOUGLAS W. STEEPLES.
Dean of Student Affairs: Mrs. DEBORAH M. JENKINS (acting).
Dean of Admissions: Mrs. SHELIA HERRIOTT.
Librarian: R. WUNDER.

The library contains 59,949 vols.
Number of teachers: 57.
Number of students: 1,249.

# VERMONT

## BENNINGTON COLLEGE
BENNINGTON, VERMONT 05201
Chartered 1925.

President: JOSEPH S. MURPHY.
Director of Admissions and Financial Aid: JOHN NISSEN.
Dean of Faculty: DONALD R. BROWN.
Dean of Studies: R. ARNOLD RICKS.
Vice-President for Finance and Administration: JAMES VANDERPOL.
Director of Development: DONALD G. MEYERS.
Director of Student Services: ALICE T. MILLER.
Librarian: TONI PETERSON.

The library contains c. 80,000 vols.
Number of teachers: 65.
Number of students: 600.

Publications: *Quadrille†*, *Bennington Review* (3 a year).

## CASTLETON STATE COLLEGE
CASTLETON, VERMONT 05735
Telephone: (802) 468-5611.
Founded 1787.

Liberal Arts, Career Education.

President: Dr. THOMAS K. MEIER.
Dean for Academic Affairs: Dr. ROSE MARIE BESTON.
Director of Admissions: GARY FALLIS.
Registrar: J. GILBERT.
Librarian: E. SCOTT.

The library contains 60,000 vols.
Number of teachers: 88.
Number of students: 1,500.

## GODDARD COLLEGE
PLAINFIELD, VERMONT 05667
Telephone: (802) 454-8311.
Founded 1938.

President: JOHN HALL.
Registrar: CORINNE ELLIOTT.
Dean of Administration: RONALD PITKIN.
Librarian: DICK WALTON.

The library contains 66,800 vols.
Number of teachers: 49 full-time, 30 part-time.
Number of students: 525 resident, 1,269 external.

## JOHNSON STATE COLLEGE
JOHNSON, VERMONT 05656
Telephone: (802) 635-2356.
Founded 1828, re-founded 1867.

President: EDWARD M. ELMENDORF.
Registrar: WILL EICK.
Librarian: PAUL GALLAGHER.

The library contains 60,800 vols.
Number of teachers: 80.
Number of students: 1,100.

# UNIVERSITIES AND COLLEGES—VERMONT, VIRGINIA

DIVISION CHAIRMEN:
*Humanities:* Dr. P. ALLEN.
*Education and Social Sciences:* Dr. F. STAHUBER.
*Environmental and Scientific Studies:* Dr. J. KNAPCZYK.

## LYNDON STATE COLLEGE
LYNDONVILLE, VERMONT 05851
Telephone: (802) 626-9371.
Founded 1911.
*President:* Dr. JANET GORMAN MURPHY.
*Comptroller:* A. R. BOERA.
*Dean of Students:* WILLIAM A. LARAMEE.
*Dean of Administration:* JAMES J. MCCARTHY.
*Dean of Academic Affairs:* RAY C. DETHY.
*Director of Admissions:* RUSSELL S. POWDEN.
*Librarian:* SUZANNE GALLAGHER.

The library contains 55,000 vols. and 6,700 periodicals.
Number of teachers: 60 (full-time).
Number of students: 1,100.

## MARLBORO COLLEGE
MARLBORO, VERMONT 05344
Telephone: (802) 257-4333.
Founded 1946.
*President:* RODERICK M. GANDER.
*Dean of Faculty:* JAMES E. THOMAS.
*Dean of the College:* R. E. SKEELE.
*Librarian:* J. P. NEVINS.

The library contains 45,000 vols.
Number of teachers: 35.
Number of students: 210.

## MIDDLEBURY COLLEGE
MIDDLEBURY, VERMONT 05753
Founded 1800.
*President:* OLIN C. ROBISON.
*Vice-President for Academic Affairs:* NICHOLAS R. CLIFFORD.
*Vice-President for Development:* W. E. BROOKER.
*Vice-President for Foreign Languages:* H. MIYAJI.
*Dean of Students:* E. WONNACOTT.
*Dean of College:* S. C. ROCKEFELLER.
*Treasurer:* C. RIKERT, Jr.

The library contains 325,000 vols.
Number of teachers: 154.
Number of students: 1,832.

## NORWICH UNIVERSITY
NORTHFIELD, VERMONT 05663
Telephone: 485-5011.
Founded 1819.
*President:* Dr. L. E. HART.
*Dean of Admissions:* MELVIN C. SOMERS.
*Librarian:* A. B. TURNER.

The library contains 187,500 vols.
Number of teachers: 168.
Number of students: 2,046.

## ST. MICHAEL'S COLLEGE
WINOOSKI, VERMONT 05404
Telephone: (802) 655-2000.
Founded 1903.
*President:* EDWARD L. HENRY, PH.D.
*Registrar:* M. MCNAMARA.
*Dean:* RONALD H. PROVOST, PH.D.
*Director of Admissions:* JERRY E. FLANAGAN.
*Librarian:* J. POPECKI.

The library contains 102,825 vols., 2,917 microfilm, 15,088 microfiche, and 1,001 periodicals.
Number of teachers: 90.
Number of students: 1,640.

## TRINITY COLLEGE
COLCHESTER AVENUE,
BURLINGTON, VERMONT 05401
Telephone: (802) 658-0337.
Founded 1925.
*President:* JANICE RYAN, R.S.M.
*Registrar:* (vacant).
*Academic Dean:* Dr. MICHAEL DONNELLAN.
*Director of Admissions:* JESSICA MESERVE.
*Director of Development:* SUZANNE J. VILLANTI.
*Director of the Annual Fund:* BROOKE MILLER TORSETH.
*Director of Public Relations:* INGE SCHAEFER.
*Library Director:* PATRICIA HODGE, R.S.M.

The library contains 94,468 vols.
Number of teachers: 54.
Number of students: 783.

## UNIVERSITY OF VERMONT
BURLINGTON, VERMONT 05401
Telephone: (802) 656-3480.
Founded 1791.
*President:* L. F. COOR, PH.D.
*Vice-President for Academic Affairs:* R. G. ARNS, PH.D.
*Vice-President for Development and External Affairs:* B. W. SNELLING.
*Vice-President for Administration:* B. R. FORSYTH.
*Registrar:* C. C. HOWE.
*Librarian:* P. B. KEBABIAN, B.A., B.S.L.S.
*Curator:* W. C. LIPKE, PH.D.

The library contains 920,000 vols.
Number of teachers: 1,145.
Number of students: 9,239.
Publication: *Annual Bulletin*.

DEANS:
*Graduate College:* R. B. LAWSON, PH.D.
*College of Arts and Sciences:* J. G. JEWETT.
*College of Agriculture:* R. O. SINCLAIR.
*Division of Engineering, Mathematics and Business Administration:* G. P. FRANCIS.
*College of Medicine:* W. H. LUGINBUHL.
*School of Nursing:* JEAN B. MILLIGAN.
*School of Allied Health Sciences:* H. L. MCCROREY.
*College of Education and Social Services:* C. A. TESCONI, Jr.
*School of Natural Resources:* H. H. JOHN.
*School of Business Administration:* A. L. THIMM.

# VIRGINIA

## BRIDGEWATER COLLEGE
BRIDGEWATER, VIRGINIA 22812
Telephone: 828-2501.
Founded 1880.
*President:* Dr. WAYNE F. GEISERT.
*Dean:* Dr. D. V. ULRICH.
*Registrar:* C. BESS.
*Director of Admissions:* L. GLOVER.
*Librarian:* O. WAGES.

The library contains 115,000 vols.
Number of teachers: 58.
Number of students: 900.

## COLLEGE OF WILLIAM AND MARY IN VIRGINIA
WILLIAMSBURG, VIRGINIA 23185
Founded 1693.
*President:* T. A. GRAVES, Jr., M.B.A., D.B.A.
*Vice-President for Academic Affairs:* G. R. HEALY, M.A., PH.D.
*Vice-President for Business Affairs:* W. J. CARTER, M.S.
*Vice-President for University Advancement:* DUANE A. DITTMAN, A.B.
*Registrar:* CHARLES R. TOOMAJIAN, M.A., PH.D.
*Librarian:* CLIFFORD CURRIE, M.A., LL.B., B.C.L.

The libraries contain 1,000,000 vols.
Number of teachers: 359 (full-time).
Number of students: 6,300.

Publications: *The William and Mary Quarterly, Studies in Third World Societies*.

DEANS:
*Faculty of Arts and Sciences:* ZEDDIE P. BOWEN, PH.D.
*Graduate Studies:* J. E. SELBY, M.A., PH.D.
*School of Education:* JAMES YANKOVICH, M.ED., ED.D.
*School of Marine Science:* FRANK O. PERKINS, PH.D.
*School of Business Administration:* C. L. QUITTMEYER, M.B.A., PH.D.
*Marshall-Wythe School of Law:* W. B. SPONG, LL.B.
*Virginia Associated Research Campus:* H. C. VON BAEYER, PH.D.
*Students:* W. S. SADLER, M.ED.
*Undergraduate Program:* LINDA COLLINS REILLY, PH.D.

### EASTERN MENNONITE COLLEGE
HARRISONBURG, VIRGINIA 22801

Telephone: (703) 433-2771.

Founded 1917.

*President:* Dr. MYRON S. AUGSBURGER.
*Director of Admissions and Records:* J. DAVID YODER.
*Librarian:* JAMES O. LEHMAN.

The library contains 96,000 vols.
**Number of teachers: 64.**
**Number of students: 1,140.**

### GEORGE MASON UNIVERSITY
FAIRFAX, VIRGINIA 22030

Founded 1957.

*President:* GEORGE W. JOHNSON.
*Vice-President for Business and Finance:* MAURICE W. SCHERRENS.
*Vice-President for Students:* DONALD J. MASH.
*Vice-President for Academic Affairs:* DAVID R. POWERS.
*Vice-President for Development:* JOAN M. BRISKIN.
*Vice-President for Public Affairs:* MARTHA A. TURNAGE.

The library contains 205,000 vols.
**Number of teachers:** 420 full-time, 299 part-time.
**Number of students: 13,293.**

### HAMPDEN-SYDNEY COLLEGE
HAMPDEN-SYDNEY, VIRGINIA 23943

Telephone: (804) 223-4381.

Founded 1776.

**Men's college of the Liberal Arts and Sciences.**

*President:* JOSIAH BUNTING III.
*Dean of the Faculty:* DANIEL P. POTEET II.
*Registrar:* MERRILL A. ESPIGH.
*Librarian:* JOHN A. RYLAND.

The library contains 131,474 vols.
**Number of teachers: 68.**
**Number of students: 780.**

### HAMPTON INSTITUTE
HAMPTON, VIRGINIA 23668

Founded 1868.

*President:* Dr. WILLIAM R. HARVEY.
*Vice-President for Academic Affairs:* Dr. MARTHA DAWSON.
*Vice-President for Business Affairs:* L. C. WYATT.
*Vice-President for Administrative Services:* Dr. OSCAR L. PRATER.
*Dean of Admissions:* Dr. OLLIE M. BOWMAN.
*Registrar:* Dr. EDWARD B. HANRAHAN.
*Director of Student Affairs:* ALEXANDER E. STRAWN.
*Director of Development:* LARON J. CLARK.
*Secretary of the College and Administrative Assistant to the President:* Mrs. M. B. PLEASANT.

The library contains 269,000 vols.
**Number of students: 3,100.**

### HOLLINS COLLEGE
VIRGINIA 24020

Founded 1842.

*President:* PAULA P. BROWNLEE.
*Dean of the College:* ROBERTA A. STEWART.
*Director of Admissions:* SANDRA J. LOVINGUTH.
*Registrar:* MARGARET L. ELDRIDGE.
*Librarian:* R. E. KIRKWOOD.

The library contains 205,000 vols.
**Number of teachers:** 76, including 22 professors.
**Number of students:** 950; graduate students 100 (of total number).
**Publications:** *Alumnae Bulletin Hollins Herald, Hollins Bulletin, Hollins Critic.*

### JAMES MADISON UNIVERSITY
HARRISONBURG, VIRGINIA 22807

Telephone: Harrisonburg 433-6211.

Founded 1908, name changed from Madison College 1977.

*President:* Dr. RONALD E. CARRIER.
*Vice-President for Academic Affairs:* Dr. THOMAS C. STANTON.
*Vice-President for Student Affairs:* Dr. HAROLD J. MCGEE.
*Dean of Admissions and Records:* Dr. FAY J. REUBUSH.
*Dean of Libraries and Learning Resources:* Dr. MARY F. HABAN.

Schools of Letters and Sciences, Fine Arts and Communication, Business, Education and Human Services, and Graduate Studies.

The library contains 350,000 vols.
**Number of teachers: 510.**
**Number of students: 8,800.**

### LONGWOOD COLLEGE
FARMVILLE, VIRGINIA 23901

Telephone: (804) 392-9251.

Founded 1839 as Comprehensive College.

*President:* JANET D. GREENWOOD.
*Registrar:* SANDRA BOLLINGER.
*Admissions:* GARY C. GRONEWIEG.

The library contains 176,850 vols.
**Number of teachers: 170.**
**Number of students: 2,500.**

### LYNCHBURG COLLEGE
LYNCHBURG, VIRGINIA 24501

Telephone: 845-9071.

Founded 1903.

*President:* Dr. CAREY BREWER.
*Registrar:* JAY WEBB.

*Director of Admissions:* E. CHADDERTON.
*Librarian:* Mrs. M. SCUDDER.

The library contains 152,000 vols.
**Number of teachers: 152.**
**Number of students: 2,486.**

### MARY BALDWIN COLLEGE
STAUNTON, VIRGINIA 24401

Telephone: 885-0811.

Founded 1842.

*President:* VIRGINIA L. LESTER.
*Dean:* MICHAEL S. PINCUS.
*Registrar:* A. L. BOOTH.
*Librarian:* WILLIAM C. POLLARD.

The library contains 140,000 items.
**Number of teachers: 66.**
**Number of students: 929.**

### MARY WASHINGTON COLLEGE
FREDERICKSBURG, VIRGINIA 22401

Founded 1908.

*President:* PRINCE B. WOODARD, M.A., ED.D., L.L.D.

**Number of teachers:** c. 145.
**Number of students:** c. 2,700.

### OLD DOMINION UNIVERSITY
NORFOLK, VIRGINIA 23508.

Telephone: (804) 440-3000.

Founded 1930 as a college.

*President:* ALFRED B. ROLLINS, Jr.
*Registrar:* M. MARCELINE STAPLES.
*Director of Admissions:* J. R. VAILLANCOURT.
*Librarian:* CYNTHIA B. DUNCAN.

The library contains 638,085 vols.
**Number of teachers: 646.**
**Number of students: 15,139.**

### PRESBYTERIAN SCHOOL OF CHRISTIAN EDUCATION
1205 PALMYRA AVENUE, RICHMOND, VIRGINIA 23227

Telephone: (804) 359-5031.

Founded 1914.

*President:* HEATH K. RADA.
*Registrar:* VIRGINIA CALDWELL.
*Librarian:* J. TROTTI.

The library contains 218,942 vols.
**Number of teachers: 16.**
**Number of students: 106.**

### RADFORD UNIVERSITY
RADFORD, VIRGINIA 24142

Founded 1910.

*President:* DONALD N. DEDMON.

## UNIVERSITIES AND COLLEGES—VIRGINIA — U.S.A.

*Vice-President for Academic Affairs:* DAVID J. MOORE.
*Vice-President for Student Affairs:* JAMES S. HARTMAN.
*Vice-President for Business Affairs:* JANE SMILEY (acting).
*Treasurer:* W. SCOTT WEAVER.
*Registrar:* EDWARD L. GIBBON.
*Director of Admissions:* DRUMONT BOWMAN.

Number of students: 5,757.

### RANDOLPH-MACON COLLEGE
ASHLAND, VIRGINIA 23005
Telephone: (804) 798-8372.
Founded 1830.

*President:* LADELL PAYNE.
*Registrar:* R. L. HOPKINS.
*Director of Admissions:* CHARLES F. NELSON, Jr.
*Librarian:* Mrs. FLAVIA R. OWEN.

The library contains 105,000 vols.
Number of teachers: 66 full-time.
Number of students: 950.

### RANDOLPH-MACON WOMAN'S COLLEGE
LYNCHBURG, VIRGINIA 24503
Founded 1891.

*President:* ROBERT A. SPIVEY.
*Director of Admissions:* ROBERT T. MERRITT.
*Director of Business Affairs and Treasurer:* DONALD C. ANDERSON.
*Librarian:* RUTH A. EDWARDS.

The library contains 144,803 vols.
Number of professors: 84, including 26 full professors.
Number of students: 750.

Publications: *Catalogue, Student's Handbook, Pictorial Bulletin, R-MWC Today, Randolph-Macon Alumnae Bulletin.*

### ROANOKE COLLEGE
SALEM, VIRGINIA 24153
Telephone: (703) 389-2351.
Founded 1842.

*President:* NORMAN D. FINTEL.
*Vice-President and Dean:* Dr. C. FREEMAN SLEEPER.
*Vice-President for Finance:* C. P. CALDWELL, Jr.
*Vice-President for Resource Development:* JOHN M. HILLS.
*Dean of Students:* MCMILLAN JOHNSON.
*Director of Admissions:* WILLIAM C. SCHAAF.
*Librarian:* Dr. GEORGE CRADDOCK.

The library contains 127,000 vols.
Number of teachers: 66.
Number of students: 1,250.

### SWEET BRIAR COLLEGE
SWEET BRIAR, VIRGINIA 24595
Chartered 1901.
Liberal Arts and Sciences College.

*President:* Dr. H. B. WHITEMAN, Jr.
*Dean:* Dr. BEATRICE P. PATT.
*Director of Admissions:* TERRY SCARBOROUGH.
*Registrar:* MARY R. LINN.
*Librarian:* HENRY JAMES.

The library contains 178,000 vols.
Number of teachers: 78.
Number of students: 680 women.

Publications: *Catalog*† (annual). *Newsletter, Alumnae News*†.

### UNIVERSITY OF RICHMOND
RICHMOND, VIRGINIA 23173
Chartered as Richmond College 1830; as University of Richmond 1920.

*President:* E. B. HEILMAN, PH.D., LL.D., D.HUM.
*Chancellor:* G. M. MODLIN, PH.D., LL.D.
*Vice-President for Business and Finance:* L. W. MOELCHERT.
*Vice-President and Provost:* M. L. VULGAMORE, PH.D.
*Vice-President for University Relations:* H. G. QUIGG, B.A.
*Vice-President for Student Affairs:* WILLIAM H. LEFTWICH, PH.D.
*Registrar:* W. VON KLEIN, M.A.
*Librarian:* D. E. ROBISON, B.S., M.S., M.A.

The library contains 282,428 vols.
Number of teachers: 198 full-time, 127 part-time.
Number of students: 3,036 full-time, 1,596 part-time.

Student Publications: *The Messenger* (magazine), *The Richmond Collegian* (weekly newspaper), *The Web* (annual).

DEANS:
*Faculty of Arts and Sciences:* (vacant).
*Richmond College (Men):* R. A. MATEER, PH.D.
*Westhampton College (Women):* S. L. M. BENNETT, PH.D.
*Business Administration:* T. L. REUSCHLING, PH.D.
*Law:* T. A. EDMONDS, J.S.D.
*Graduate:* JOHN L. GORDON, Jr., PH.D.
*University College, Summer School, Continuing Education:* M. C. GRAEBER, M.A., PH.D.

### UNIVERSITY OF VIRGINIA
CHARLOTTESVILLE, VIRGINIA 22903
Telephone: 924-0311.
Founded by act of General Assembly of Virginia, 1819.
Academic year: September to May (two semesters).

*President:* FRANK L. HEREFORD, Jr., PH.D.
*Vice-President and Provost:* DAVID A. SHANNON, PH.D.
*Dean of Students:* R. T. CANEVARI, M.ED.
*Dean of Admissions:* JOHN T. CASTEEN, M.A., PH.D.
*Librarian:* R. W. FRANTZ, Jr., M.S. IN L.S., M.A., PH.D.
Library: see Libraries.

Number of teachers: 1,534.
Number of students: 16,400.

Publications: *Virginia Quarterly Review, Virginia Law Review*†, *Virginia Law Weekly*†, *News Letter*†, *Alumni News*†, *Register*†, *University Topics*†.

DEANS:
*Faculty of Arts and Sciences:* EDWIN E. FLOYD, PH.D.
*College of Arts and Sciences:* ROBERT L. KELLOGG, A.M., PH.D.
*School of Architecture:* JACQUELIN ROBERTSON.
*School of Education:* RICHARD M. BRANDT, M.A., PH.D.
*School of Engineering and Applied Science:* JOHN E. GIBSON, PH.D.
*The Graduate School of Arts and Science:* W. DEXTER WHITEHEAD, PH.D.
*The Graduate School of Business Administration:* C. STEWART SHEPPARD, PH.D.
*School of Law:* RICHARD A. MERRILL.
*School of Medicine:* NORMAN J. KNORR, M.D.
*School of Nursing:* ROSE MARIE CHIONI, M.A., PH.D.
*McIntire School of Commerce:* WILLIAM G. SKENKIR, PH.D.
*Division of Continuing Education:* ADELLE F. ROBERTSON, ED.D.

PROFESSORS:
*College of Arts and Sciences:*
ABBOT, W. W., M.A., PH.D., History
ABRAHAM, H. J., PH.D., Government
AINSWORTH, M. D., PH.D., Psychology
ALDEN, D. W., A.M., PH.D., French
ANDREWS, W. L., PH.D., Chemistry
ARNHOFF, F. N., M.A., PH.D., Sociology
BATTESTIN, M. C., PH.D., English
BEAURLINE, L. A., M.A., PH.D., English
BELL, R. Q., M.A., PH.D., Psychology
BEST, P. J., PH.D., Psychology
BICE, R. C., PH.D., Psychology
BIERSTEDT, R., PH.D., Sociology and Anthropology
BREIT, W. L., PH.D., Economics
BREWER, J. W., PH.D., Mathematics
BRILL, A. S., PH.D., Physics
BURMEISTER, E., PH.D., Economics
CAPLOW, T., Sociology
CAUTHEN, I. B., Jr., M.A., PH.D., English
CELLI, V., PH.D., Physics
CLAUDE, I. L., M.A., PH.D., Government and Foreign Affairs
COHEN, R., M.A., PH.D., English
COLEMAN, R. V., PH.D., Physics
COLKER, M. L., PH.D., Classics
COUGHLIN, R. J., M.A., PH.D., Sociology
CROSS, R. D., PH.D., History
DAMROSCH, L., PH.D., English
DAVIDSON, H. M., PH.D., French
DAY, D. T., III, M.A., English
DEAVER, B. S., M.A., PH.D., Physics
DEESE, J. E., PH.D., Psychology
DELL, H. J., M.A., PH.D., History

Denommé, R. T., French
Dent, J. N., PH.D., Biology
Dolan, R., M.S., PH.D., Environmental Sciences
Ehrenpreis, I., M.A., PH.D., English
Elzinga, K. G., M.A., PH.D., Economics
Ern, E. H., M.S., PH.D., Environmental Sciences
Evans, R. H., M.A., PH.D., Government and Foreign Affairs
Fenigstein, A., PH.D., Psychology
Fernbach, A. P., PH.D., Government and Foreign Affairs
Feuer, Katherine B., PH.D., Slavic Languages
Feuer, L. S., PH.D., University Professor
Floyd, E. E., PH.D., Mathematics
Fowler, M., PH.D., Physics
Frantz, R. W., M.S. IN L.S., M.A., PH.D., Library Science
Fredrick, L. W., M.A., PH.D., Astronomy
Garnett, J. C., M.SC., Government and Foreign Affairs
Garrard, J. G., PH.D., Slavic Languages
Garstang, R. H., Environmental Sciences
Gaston, P. M., PH.D., History
Goodell, H. G., Environmental Sciences
Goodman, F. O., PH.D., D.SC., Physics
Germino, D. L., M.A., PH.D., Government and Foreign Affairs
Graebner, N. A., M.A., PH.D., American History
Grimes, R. N., PH.D., Chemistry
Gugelot, P. C., PH.D., Physics
Hadden, J. K., PH.D., Sociology and Anthropology
Hahn, J. F., PH.D., Psychology
Hamilton, H. L., M.A., PH.D., Biology
Hammond, T. T., M.A., PH.D., History
Harbaugh, W. H., M.A., PH.D., History
Harrison, W. W., A.M., PH.D., Chemistry
Hartt, F., M.A., PH.D., History of Art
Hartt, J. N., PH.D., Religious Studies
Havran, M. J., PH.D., History
Heath, P. L., B.A., Philosophy
Hereford, F. L., PH.D., Physics
Hetherington, E. M., PH.D., Psychology
Hirsch, E. D., M.A., PH.D., English
Howland, J. S., M.S., PH.D., Mathematics
Hutchinson, C. A., PH.D., History
Johnston, S. G., PH.D., Government and Foreign Affairs
Jordan, D. C., PH.D., Government
Kabir, P. K., PH.D., Physics
Kellogg, R. L., A.M., PH.D., English
Kelly, H. P., PH.D., Physics
Kett, J. F., PH.D., History
Khare, R. S., PH.D., Anthropology
Kirsch, A. C., PH.D., English
Kolve, V. A., PH.D., English
Konigsberg, I. R., PH.D., Biology
Kraehe, E. E., History
Kretsinger, R. H., PH.D., Biology
Lang, C. Y., M.A., PH.D., English
Langbaum, R. W., M.A., PH.D., English and American Literature
Lashoff, R. K., PH.D., Mathematics
Leng, Shao Chuan, M.A., PH.D., Government and Foreign Affairs
Levenson, J. C., PH.D., English
Levin, D., PH.D., English
Little, D., PH.D., Religious Studies
Little, W. A., M.A., L.T.C.L. PH.D., German
McCallum, B. T., M.B.A., PH.D., Economics
McClellan, W. D., PH.D., History
McCrimmon, K. M., PH.D., Mathematics
McDonald, O. J., A.M., Biology
McGrady, D. L., PH.D., Spanish

McKean, R. N., A.M., PH.D., Economics
Martin, R. B., PH.D., Chemistry
Miller, O. L., M.S., PH.D., Biology
Mitchell, J. W., M.S., D.PHIL., F.R.S., Physics.
Mitchell, R. S., M.S., PH.D., Environmental Sciences
Mook, D. G., M.A., PH.D., Psychology
Morgan, R. J., PH.D., Government and Foreign Affairs
Mosher, F. C., M.S., D.P.A., Government and Foreign Affairs
Murray, J. J., M.A., D.PHIL., Biology
Nelson, B. W., PH.D., Geology
Paige, E. C., Jr., PH.D., Mathematics
Perkowski, J. L., PH.D., Slavic Languages
Peterson, M. D., PH.D., History
Pitts, L. D., PH.D., Mathematics
Prosser, M. H., PH.D., Speech
Ramazani, R., LL.M., S.J.D., Government and Foreign Affairs
Ramos Gil, C., PH.D., Spanish
Rao, K. S., PH.D., Religious Studies
Rebhun, L. I., M.S., PH.D., Biology
Reese, G. H., M.A., PH.D., Humanistic Sources
Reppucci, N. D., M.S., PH.D., Psychology
Richardson, F. L., PH.D., Anthropology
Richardson, F. S., PH.D., Chemistry
Ritter, R. C., Physics
Rosenblum, M., M.A., PH.D., Mathematics
Rovnyak, J. L., M.A., PH.D., Mathematics
Rutland, R. A., PH.D., History
Ruvalds, J., PH.D., Physics
Ryder, F. G., PH.D., German
Saslaw, W. C., PH.D., Astronomy
Schatz, P. N., PH.D., Chemistry
Schmitt, H. A., PH.D., History
Schnatterly, S. E., PH.D., Physics
Schroeder, Gertrude E., PH.D., Economics
Scott, L. L., M.A., PH.D., Mathematics
Scott, N. A., PH.D., Religious Studies
Sebo, S., M.A., Physical Education
Sedgwick, A., PH.D., History
Selden, R. T., M.A., PH.D., Economics
Shannon, D. A., M.S., PH.D., History
Shannon, E. F., A.M., D.PHIL., LITT.D., LL.D., D.HUM., English
Shattuck, R. W., B.A., French
Shea, V., M.S., Government
Sherman, R., PH.D., Economics
Simpson, J., PH.D., Environmental Sciences
Singer, S. F., PH.D., Environmental Sciences
Sobottka, S. E., PH.D., Physics
Sokel, W. H., M.A., PH.D., German
Stein, H., PH.D., Economics
Stong, R. E., PH.D., Mathematics
Stocker, A. F., A.M., PH.D., Classics
Sundberg, R. J., PH.D., Chemistry
Sykes, G. M., PH.D., Sociology
Taylor, P. H., B.A., English
Thompson, K. W., PH.D., LL.D., Government and Foreign Affairs
Trefil, J. S., M.A., M.S., PH.D., Physics
Turner, V., PH.D., Anthropology
Velimirovic, M. M., PH.D., Music
Via, D. O., PH.D., Religious Studies
Wagner, Roy, PH.D., Anthropology
Weber, H., M.S., PH.D., Physics
Weiss, D. W., PH.D., Drama
Whitaker, J. K., M.A., PH.D., Economics
Whitehead, W. D., Jr., M.S., PH.D., Physics
Wilmsen, E. N., M.A., PH.D., Anthropology
Wilsdorf, Doris K., M.SC., PH.D., D.SC., Physics and Materials Science
Winter, E. H., PH.D., Anthropology
Woozley, A. D., Philosophy

Worchel, S., PH.D., Psychology
Wright, T. R., M.A., PH.D., Biology
Yeager, L. B., M.A., PH.D., Economics
Younger, E. E., M.A., PH.D., History
Ziock, K. O., PH.D., Physics

*School of Architecture:*
Bosserman, J. N., B.S. IN ARCH., M.F.A.
Collins, R. C., PH.D., Public Administration, City Planning
Cox, J. A., Architectural History
Graham, R. E., M.A., Architectural History
Hoppner, P. J., M.ARCH., Architecture
Howland, B. C., B.S., Landscape Architecture
Kayhoe, M. E., M. OF ARCH., Architecture
Massey, J. C., B.ARCH., Architectural History
Nichols, F. D., B.F.A., Architecture
Pelliccia, C., DR. IN ARCH., Architecture
Porter, H. W., Jr., M.L.A., Landscape Architecture
Tuley, J. S., B.ARCH., Architecture
Vickery, R. L., Jr., B.ARCH., Architecture
White, H. K., B.S., Architecture
Wiebenson, D., M.ARCH., M.A., PH.D., Architectural History
Zuk, W., M.S.E., PH.D., Architecture

*School of Education:*
Abidin, R. R., ED.D., Education
Bash, J. H., M.ED., ED.D., Education
Beard, R. L., M.A., PH.D., Education
Brandt, R. M., M.A., ED.D., Education
Burr, Helen G., M.A., PH.D., Speech Pathology
Busse, B. W., M.MUS., PH.D., Music Education
Carriker, W. R., M.A., ED.D., Special Education
Henderson, E. H., PH.D., Education
Holmes, G. W., III, A.M., PH.D., Education
Horner, J. S., PH.D., Speech Pathology
Jacobson, M. D., Education
Leahy, J. F., Jr., M.A., PH.D., Education
Lowry, W. C., M.ED., PH.D., Education
MacDougall, M. A., ED.D., Research Methodology
Meade, R. A., M.A., PH.D., Education
Medley, D. M., PH.D., Education
Mesinger, J. F., PH.D., Special Education
Mosher, Edith, PH.D., Education
Seawell, W. H., M.A., ED.D., Education
Shoemaker, D. H., ED.D., Education
Short, J. G., PH.D., Education
Taylor, A. L., ED.D., Education
Thompson, E., PH.D., Curriculum and Instruction
Vanhoose, W. H., PH.D., Education
Walter, P. B., M.A., PH.D., Guidance and Counselor
Ward, V. S., M.ED., PH.D., Education

*School of Engineering and Applied Science:*
Attinger, E. O., M.D., M.S., PH.D., Biomedical Engineering
Barton, F. W., PH.D., P.E., Civil Engineering
Batson, A. P., PH.D., Computer Science
Boring, J. W., PH.D., Aerospace Engineering
Bouloucon, P., M.CH.E., PH.D., Chemical Engineering
Catlin, A., M.A., PH.D., Materials Science
Chartres, B. A., M.SC., PH.D., Applied Mathematics and Computer Science
Cook, G., M.S.E.E., SC.D., Electrical Engineering
Fletcher, L. S., M.S., PH.D., Mechanical Engineering
Fornes, G. S., M.S. IN M.E., Mechanical Engineering

## UNIVERSITIES AND COLLEGES—VIRGINIA (UNIVERSITY OF) — U.S.A.

FOSTER, M. G., PH.D., Electrical Engineering
GADEN, E. L., Chemical Engineering
GIBSON, J. E., M.ENG., PH.D., Electrical Engineering
GUNTER, E. J., M.E., M.S.E.M., PH.D., Mechanical Engineering
HAVILAND, J. K., PH.D., Aerospace Engineering
HEREFORD, T. G., Jr., PH.D., General Engineering
HOEL, L. A., D.ENG., Civil Engineering
HUDSON, J. L., M.S.E., PH.D., Chemical Engineering
JESSER, W. A., PH.D., Materials Science
JOHNSON, R. A., PH.D., Materials Science
JOHNSON, W. R., D.SC., Nuclear Engineering
KAUZLARICH, J. J., M.S.M.E., PH.D., Mechanical Engineering
KELLY, J. L., PH.D., Nuclear Engineering
KINNIER, H. L., M.S.E., Civil Engineering
KUHLTHAU, A. R., M.S., PH.D., Aerospace Engineering
LAREW, H. G., M.S.C.E., PH.D., Civil Engineering
LATTA, G. E., PH.D., Applied Mathematics
LAWLESS, K. R., PH.D., Materials Science
LEWIS, D. W., Mechanical Engineering
LONGLEY, J. L., Jr., M.A., PH.D., Humanities
LOONEY, W. B., M.D., PH.D., Biomedical Engineering
LOWRY, R. A., PH.D., Aerospace Engineering
McCORMICK, F. C., PH.D., Civil Engineering
McVEY, E. S., M.S.ENGR., PH.D., Electrical Engineering
MATTAUCH, R. J., M.E., PH.D., Electrical Engineering
MATTHEWS, G. B., Aerospace Engineering
MEEM, J. L., Jr., M.S., PH.D., Nuclear Engineering
MOORE, J. W., M.S.M.E., PH.D., P.E., Mechanical Engineering
OWENS, R. H., M.A., PH.D., Applied Mathematics and Computer Science
PARRISH, E. A., M.E.E., D.SC., Electrical Engineering
PILKEY, W. D., M.S., PH.D., Mechanical Engineering
RADER, L. T., M.S., PH.D., Electrical Engineering, Business Administration
RAMEY, R. L., M.S.E.E., PH.D., Electrical Engineering
SAGE, A. P., PH.D., Electrical Engineering
SCOTT, J. E., Jr., M.S., M.A., PH.D., Aerospace Engineering
SIEGEL, C. M., M.S.E.E., PH.D., Electrical Engineering
SIMMONDS, J. G., PH.D., Applied Mathematics and Computer Science
UHL, V. W., M.S.CH.E., PH.D., P.E., Chemical Engineering
UPDIKE, O. T., PH.D., P.E., Chemical and Biomedical Engineering
WARFIELD, J. N., B.S., PH.D., Electrical Engineering
WILLIAMSON, T. G., PH.D., Nuclear Engineering
WILSDORF, D. K., PH.D., D.SC., Materials Science
WILSDORF, H. G., PH.D., D.SC., Materials Science

*Graduate School of Business Administration:*
ALLEN, B. R., M.B.A., D.B.A.
BAUMAN, W. S., D.B.A.
BORDEN, N. H., D.B.A.
COLLEY, J. L., M.S., D.B.A.
FAIR, R. R., M.B.A.
FELTON, E. L., D.B.A.
GRAYSON, L. E., A.M., PH.D., International Business Economics
HAIGH, R. W., PH.D.
HORNIMAN, A. B., D.B.A.
JOHNSTON, L. R., M.B.A., D.C.S.
LANDELL, R. D., M.S., PH.D.
MORTON, F. S., III, M.B.A., D.C.S.
NEWTON, D. A., D.B.A.
RADER, L. T., M.S., PH.D.
RICHARDSON, F. L. W., PH.D.
ROTCH, W., D.B.A.
SARGENT, C. F., M.S., M.B.A.
SHEPPARD, C. S., M.B.A., PH.D.
SIHLER, W. W., D.B.A.
SMITH, C. R., M.B.A., C.P.A.
SNOOK, J. L., J.D.
VANDELL, R. F., D.B.A.

*School of Law:*
ALFORD, N. H., B.A., LL.B., J.S.D.
BEVIER, L. R., J.D.
BONNIE, R. J., B.A., LL.B.
BERGIN, T. F., B.A., LL.B.
COHEN, E. S., B.A., LL.B.
DAVISON, C. M., Jr., B.A., LL.B.
DOOLEY, M. P., B.A., J.D.
FOLK, E. L., III, M.A., LL.B.
GOETZ, C., PH.D.
GRAETZ, M. J., B.B.A., LL.B.
HENDERSON, S. D., J.D.
HETHERINGTON, J. A. C., A.B., LL.M.
HOFFMAN, P. B., M.D.
HOWARD, A. E. D., M.A., LL.B.
KITCHIN, L. C., P.M.D., M.A.
KNEEDLER, H. L., LL.B.
LESLIE, D. L., J.D.
LILLICH, R. B., A.B., LL.M., J.S.D.
LILLY, G. C., B.S., LL.B.
LOW, P. W., A.B., LL.B.
McCOID, J. C., II, B.A., LL.B.
McKEE, W. S., J.D.
MANSON, P. C., B.A., LL.B.
MERRILL, R. A., M.A., LL.B.
MOORE, J. N., A.B., LL.M.
PAULSEN, M. G., A.B., J.D.
PERLMAN, H. S., J.D.
REDDEN, K. R., LL.B.
RITCHIE, J., III, B.S., LL.B., J.S.D.
ROBINSON, G. O., A.B., LL.B.
SALTZBURG, S. A., J.D.
SCHWARTZ, W. F., A.B., LL.B.
SCOTT, R. E., J.D., LL.M.
SHAPO, M., A.M., LL.B.
SPIES, E. G., A.B., B.A., B.C.L., LL.D.
THOMPSON, S. C., M.A., J.D., LL.M.
TURNBULL, A. R., A.B., LL.B.
WADLINGTON, W. J., III, A.B., LL.B.
WALKER, W. L., J.D., S.J.D.
WARD, B. J., LL.M.
WHITE, G. E., J.D., PH.D.
WHITE, T. R., III, B.A., LL.B.
WHITEBREAD, C. H., A.B., LL.B., Law
WOLTZ, C. K., B.A., LL.B.
WOODARD, C., PH.D.

*School of Medicine:*
ABSE, D. W., M.D., Psychiatry
ALDRICH, C. K., M.D., Psychiatry
ALLEN, M. S., M.D., Pathology
ALRICH, E. M., M.D., Surgery
ARDIS, M. B., M.D., Clinical Services
ATTINGER, E. O., PH.D., Biomedical
AYERS, C. R., M.D., Internal Medicine
BARNETT, B. L., M.D., Family Health
BASS, N. H., M.D., Neurology
BECKWITH, J. R., M.D., Internal Medicine
BELLER, G. A., M.D., Internal Medicine
BERN, R. M., M.D., Physiology
BERRY, F. A., M.D., Anaesthesiology
BILTONEN, R. L., M.D., Pharmacology
BITHELL, T. C., M.D., Pathology
BLIZZARD, R. M., M.D., Paediatrics
BOBBITT, O., M.D., Pathology
BROCHU, F. L., M.D., Clinical Services
BROOKER, G., PH.D., Pharmacology
BUCKMAN, J., M.D., Psychiatry
CANTRELL, R. W., M.D., Otolaryngology
CARDELL, R. R., M.D., Anatomy
CARRON, H., M.D., Anaesthesiology
CAWLEY, E. P., M.D., Dermatology
COHEN, D. H., PH.D., Physiology
CRADDOCK, W. E., M.D., Radiology
CRAIG, J. W., M.D., Internal Medicine
CRAMPTON, R. S., M.D., Internal Medicine
CONSTABLE, W. C., M.D., Radiology
COOPER, G., M.D., Radiology
CROCKETT, C. L., M.D., Family Health
CRUISE, M. O., M.D., Paediatrics
DAMMANN, J. F., M.D., Paediatrics
DIFAZIO, C. A., M.D., Anaesthesiology
DULING, B. R., PH.D., Physiology
DUNN, J. T., M.D., Internal Medicine
EDGERTON, M. T., M.D., Plastic Surgery
EDLICH, R. F., M.D., Plastic Surgery
EPSTEIN, R. M., M.D., Anaesthesiology
FRANKEL, C. J., M.D., Orthopaedics
GILLENWATER, J. Y., M.D., Urology
GILMAN, A. G., PH.D., Pharmacology
GOLDSTEIN, G., M.D., Internal Medicine
GWALTNEY, J. M., M.D., Internal Medicine
GUERRANT, J. L., M.D., Internal Medicine
HALEY, H. B., M.D., Surgery
HANNA, G. R., M.D., Neurology
HARBERT, G. M., M.D., Obstetrics and Gynaecology
HAWKINS, D. R., M.D., Psychiatry
HAYNES, R. C., PH.D., Pharmacology
HOOK, E. W., M.D., Internal Medicine
HOWARDS, S. S., M.D., Urology
HUANG, C.-H. H., PH.D., Biochemistry
HUMPHRIES, M. K., M.D., Ophthalmology
HUNTER, T. H., M.D., Internal Medicine
JANE, J. A., M.C., Neurosurgery
JOHANSON, A. J., M.C., Paediatrics
JOHNS, T. I., M.D., Neurology
KEATS, T. E., M.D., Radiology
KITAY, J. I., M.D., Internal Medicine
KOMP, DIANE M., M.D., Paediatrics
KROVETZ, L. J., PH.D., Paediatrics
KUPKE, D. W., PH.D., Biochemistry
LANGDON, R. G., PH.D., Biochemistry
LANGMAN, J., PH.D., Anatomy
LARNER J., PH.D., Pharmacology
LOONEY, W. B., M.D., Biomedical
MACLEOD, R. M., M.D., Internal Medicine
McCUE, F. C., M.D., Orthopaedics
MANDELL, J., M.D., Internal Medicine
McGILVERY, R. W., PH.D., Biochemistry
McGOVERN, F. H., M.D., Otolaryngology
McGUIRE, L. B., M.D., Internal Medicine
McLAUGHLIN, R. E., M.D., Orthopaedics
McLAURIN, C. A., M.D., Orthopaedics
MILLER, J. Q., M.D., Neurology
MILLER, S. E., M.D., Family Health
MINOR, G. R., M.D., Surgery
MOHLER, D. N., M.D., Internal Medicine
MOON, G. N., M.D., Otolaryngology
MORRIS, J. L., M.D., Radiology
MURAD, F., PH.D., Internal Medicine
MURPHY, R. A., PH.D., Physiology
NOLAN, S. P., M.D., Surgery
O'BRIEN, W. M., M.D., Internal Medicine
OWEN, J. A., M.D., Internal Medicine
PEACH, M. J., PH.D., Pharmacology
PRATT, J. G., PH.D., Psychology
PULLEN, E. W., M.D., Anatomy
RALL, T. W., PH.D., Pharmacology
REEFE, W. E., M.D., Clinical Services
RESPESS, J. C., M.D., Internal Medicine
RITCHIE, W. P., M.D., Surgery
ROBINOW, M., M.D., Paediatrics
ROCHESTER, D. F., M.D., Internal Medicine
RUBIO, R., PH.D., Physiology
RUDOLF, L. E., M.D., Surgery

SAVORY, J., PH.D., Pathology
SCHNAITMAN, C. A., PH.D., Microbiology
SHAW, A., M.D., Surgery
SPERELAKIS, N., PH.D., Physiology
STAMP, W. G., M.D., Orthopaedics
STEVENSON, I. P., M.D., Psychiatry
STONE, D. D., M.D., Internal Medicine
STURGILL, B. C., M.D., Pathology
THOMPSON, T. E., PH.D., Biochemistry
THORNTON, W. N., M.D., Obstetrics and Gynaecology
TILLACK, T. W., M.D., Pathology
VANDECASTLE, R. L., PH.D., Psychiatry
VILLAR PALASI, C., PH.D., Pharmacology
VOLKAN, V. D., M.D., Psychiatry
VOLK, W. A., PH.D., Microbiology
WAGNER, R. R., M.D., Microbiology
WANEBO, H. J., M.D., Surgery
WEARY, P. E., M.D., Dermatology
WESTERVELT, F. B., M.D., Internal Medicine
WESTFALL, T. G., PH.D., Pharmacology
WHEBY, M. S., M.D., Internal Medicine
WILLS, M. R., M.D., Pathology and Internal Medicine
WILSON, L. A., M.D., Obstetrics and Gynaecology
WYKER, A. W., M.D., Urology

*School of Nursing:*
BRODIE, B., M.S.N., PH.D., Nursing
CHIONI, R. M., M.A., PH.D., Nursing
CROSBY, MARIAN H., R.N., B.S.N., M.S.ED., ED.D., Nursing
PARSONS, L. C., M.S., PH.D., Nursing

*McIntire School of Commerce:*
BERRY, L. L., D.B.A.
GIBSON, J. E., LL.B., Commerce
HUNT, R. C., PH.D.
KAULBACK, F. S., Jr., M.A., PH.D., Accountancy
MORIN, B. A., M.B.A.
PARTAIN, R. T., PH.D.
SCOTT, C. H., M.B.A.
THOMPSON, D. W., M.S.
TRENT, R. H., PH.D.
WHEELEN, T. L., D.B.A., Business Administration

AFFILIATED COLLEGE:
**Clinch Valley College:** Wise, Virginia 24293.
*Chancellor:* JOSEPH C. SMIDDY, M.A., LH.D.
*Dean:* EMMET F. LOW, Jr., PH.D.

Number of teachers: 60.
Number of students: 1,096.

# VIRGINIA COMMONWEALTH UNIVERSITY
910 WEST FRANKLIN ST., RICHMOND, VIRGINIA 23284

Telephone: (804) 257-0100.

Founded 1838 as the medical department of Hamden-Sydney College. Richmond Professional Institute and Medical College of Virginia merged in 1968 to form this University.
State control.

*President:* Dr. EDMUND F. ACKELL.
*Provost and Vice-President, Academic Affairs:* WAYNE C. HALL, PH.D.
*Vice-President, Administration:* DONALD C. BRUEGMAN.
*Vice-President, Finance:* J. G. GUERDON.
*Vice-President, Student Affairs:* R. I. WILSON, PH.D.

*Directors of Admission:* J. J. JOHNSON, PH.D., W. A. ROBERTSON.
*Vice-President, Health Sciences:* L. A. WOODS, M.D., PH.D.
*Vice-President, Research and Graduate Affairs:* JOHN J. SALLEY, D.D.S., PH.D.
*Librarian:* G. B. MCCABE.

The library contains 550,000 vols.
Number of teachers: 1,607 full-time, 662 part-time.
Number of students: 19,000.

DEANS:
*Academic Division:*
School of the Arts: M. N. DEPILLARS.
School of Arts and Sciences: ELSKE SMITH.
School of Business: J. C. HALL.
School of Community Services: LAURIN L. HENRY.
School of Education: C. P. RUCH.
School of Social Work: ELAINE Z. ROTHENBERG.
Evening College and Summer School: ROZANNE EPPS.

*Health Sciences Division:*
School of Allied Health Professions: T. C. BARKER.
School of Basic Sciences: D. T. WATTS.
School of Dentistry: J. E. KENNEDY.
School of Medicine: J. L. STEINFELD.
School of Nursing: DORIS B. YINGLING.
School of Pharmacy: W. E. WEAVER.

# VIRGINIA MILITARY INSTITUTE
LEXINGTON, VIRGINIA 24450
Founded 1839.

*Superintendent:* Gen. SAM S. WALKER.
*Deputy Superintendent:* Brig.-Gen. GEORGE H. RIPLEY.
*Dean of Faculty:* Brig.-Gen. J. M. MORGAN, Jr.
*Commandant:* Col. HAROLD B. SNYDER, Jr.
*Treasurer:* Col. R. M. HARPER.
*Librarian:* Lt.-Col. JAMES E. GAINES, Jr.

The library contains 261,045 vols.
Number of teachers: 91 academic (of whom 48 are professors), 28 military.
Number of students: 1,300 men.
Publication: *Catalogue.*

# VIRGINIA POLYTECHNIC INSTITUTE AND STATE UNIVERSITY
BLACKSBURG, VIRGINIA 24061

Telephone: (703) 961-6000.

Established 1872; opened to women 1921.
State control; Academic year: September to June.

*President:* Dr. W. E. LAVERY.

*Provost:* J. D. WILSON.
*Vice-President, Administration:* (vacant).
*Vice-President, Finance:* M. E. RIDENOUR.
*Vice-President, Development:* C. M. FORBES.
*Vice-President, Student Affairs:* J. W. DEAN.
*Dean of Admissions:* A. G. PHLEGAR.
*Librarian:* H. G. BECHANAN.

Number of teachers: 1,861.
Number of students: 21,069.

Publications: *The Techgram, Virginia Tech Magazine, Extension Division Series, Research Division Series.*

DEANS:
*Agriculture:* J. R. NICHOLS.
*Architecture:* C. W. STEGER (acting).
*Arts and Sciences:* H. H. BAUER.
*Business:* (vacant).
*Education:* R. M. SMITH.
*Engineering:* P. E. TORGERSEN.
*Home Economics:* S. J. RITCHEY.
*Graduate:* D. P. ROSELLE.
*Veterinary Medicine:* R. B. TALBOT.
*Extension:* W. R. VAN DRESSER.
*Research:* W. J. FABRYCKY.

# VIRGINIA STATE UNIVERSITY
PETERSBURG, VIRGINIA 23803

Founded by State of Virginia as Virginia Normal and Collegiate Institute 1882; opened 1883; name changed to Virginia Normal and Industrial Institute 1902; to Virginia State College for Negroes 1930; to Virginia State College 1946; to Virginia State University 1979.

*President:* Dr. THOMAS M. LAW.
*Executive Vice-President:* Dr. CURTIS E. BRYAN.
*Vice-President for Academic Affairs:* Dr. ARNOLD R. HENDERSON, Jr.
*Vice-President for Research and Human Services:* Dr. HUEY J. BATTLE.
*Vice-President for Business and Finance:* Dr. JOHN W. MCCLUSKEY (acting).
*Vice-President for Student Affairs:* Dr. SAMUEL L. CREIGHTON.
*Director of Admissions:* EDWARD L. SMITH.
*Registrar:* Mrs. MABEL M. WASHINGTON.

The library contains 207,924 vols.
Number of teachers: 200.
Number of students: 4,097.

DEANS:
School of Agriculture and Applied Sciences: Dr. BEVERLY B. ARCHER.
School of Business: HELMUTH H. BODE.
School of Graduate Studies: Dr. EDGAR TOPPIN.
School of Natural Sciences: Dr. WALTER ELIAS.
School of Education: Dr. ILA MARTIN.
School of Continuing Education: Dr. ALVIN L. HALL.

## VIRGINIA UNION UNIVERSITY
1500 NORTH LOMBARDY ST., RICHMOND, VIRGINIA 23220

Telephone: 359-9331.

Founded 1865.

*President:* Dr. DAVID T. SHANNON.
*Registrar:* Mrs. JANICE D. BAILEY.
*Dean of the College:* Dr. SAMUEL K. ROBERTS.
*Chief Fiscal and Personnel Officer:* L. D. SMITH.
*Librarian:* Mrs. VERDELLE V. BRADLEY.

The library contains 131,122 vols.
Number of teachers: 96.
Number of students: 1,423.

## WASHINGTON AND LEE UNIVERSITY
LEXINGTON, VIRGINIA 24450

Telephone: (703) 463-9111.

Founded as Augusta Academy 1749, chartered as Liberty Hall Academy 1782, name changed to Washington Academy 1798, to Washington College 1813, and to present name 1871.

*President:* ROBERT E. R. HUNTLEY, LL.M., LL.D.
*Treasurer:* E. STEWART EPLEY, B.S.
*Registrar:* H. S. HEAD, A.M.
*Librarian:* M. D. LEACH, A.B., B.L.

The undergraduate library contains 360,000 vols.; the Law library 200,000 vols.

Number of teachers: 147.
Number of students: 1,721.

Publications: *Shenandoah* (literary quarterly), *Washington and Lee Law Review*.

DEANS:

*Arts and Sciences:* W. J. WATT, PH.D.
*Commerce, Economics, and Politics:* E. C. ATWOOD, PH.D.
*Law:* R. L. STEINHEIMER, A.B., J.D.

# WASHINGTON

## CENTRAL WASHINGTON UNIVERSITY
ELLENSBURG, WASHINGTON 98926

Telephone: (509) 963-1111.

Founded 1891.

*President:* DONALD L. GARRITY.
*Registrar:* LOUIS BOVOS.
*Librarian:* FRANK A. SCHNEIDER.
*Vice-President for Academic Affairs:* EDWARD J. HARRINGTON.
*Vice-President for Business Affairs:* COURTNEY JONES.
*Dean of Admissions and Records:* JAMES PAPPAS.
*Dean of Students:* DONALD GUY.

The library contains 314,195 vols.
Number of teachers: 311.
Number of students: 7,551.

## EASTERN WASHINGTON UNIVERSITY
CHENEY, WASHINGTON 99004

Telephone: 235-6221.

Founded 1890.

*President:* H. GEORGE FREDERICKSON.
*Registrar:* MELANIE BELL (acting).
*Director of the Library:* C. H. BAUMANN.

The library contains 354,000 volumes.
Number of teachers: 373.
Number of students: 7,469.

## FORT WRIGHT COLLEGE
SPOKANE, WASHINGTON 99204

Telephone: (509) 328-2970.

Founded 1907.
Liberal Arts College.

*President:* SHEILA MCEVOY, S.N.J.M.
*Academic Vice-President:* KATHLEEN ROSS, S.N.J.M.
*Business Manager:* WILLIAM SEMMLER.
*Director of Student Services:* KATHLEEN NEWBURY.
*Dean of Admissions and Registrar:* MARY FALKENRECK.
*Dean of Graduate and Special Programs:* ANIS QUIDWAI.
*Librarian:* M. KATHRYN LERITZ.

The library contains 80,000 vols.
Number of teachers: 35.
Number of students: 425.

## GONZAGA UNIVERSITY
SPOKANE, WASHINGTON 99258

Telephone: (509) 328-4220.

Founded 1887.

Private control; Academic year: September to May, and Summer Session.

*President:* Rev. BERNARD J. COUGHLIN, S.J.
*Academic Vice-President:* Rev. PETER ELY, S.J.
*Vice-President for University Relations:* WILLIAM WAGNER.
*Vice-President of the University:* Rev. A. L. DUSSAULT, S.J.
*Vice-President:* Rev. CLEMENT H. REGIMBAL, S.J.
*Vice-President, Student Life:* JOHN R. HALSTEAD.
*Vice-President, Business and Finance:* STANLEY FAIRHURST.
*Vice-President, Administration and Planning:* Rev. MARTIN D. O'KEEFE, S.J.
*Registrar:* B. COLE.
*Director (Admissions):* J. MANSFIELD.
*Librarian:* ROBERT BURR.

The library contains 365,000 vols.
Number of teachers: 203.
Number of students: 3,421.

Publications: *Signum* (10 issues yearly), *Gonzaga Bulletin* (weekly), *Charter* (annually), *Reflections* (annually).

DEANS:

*Arts and Sciences:* JAMES ARENZ, S.J.
*Law:* THEODORE CLEMENTS.
*Engineering:* W. P. ILGEN.
*Graduate School:* J. E. BYRNE.
*Continuing Education:* HARRY HAZEL.
*Education:* J. WARDIAN.
*Business Administration:* CLARENCE BARNES.

## PACIFIC LUTHERAN UNIVERSITY
TACOMA, WASHINGTON 98447

Telephone: (206) 531-6900.

Founded 1890.

*President:* W. O. RIEKE.
*Provost:* R. JUNGKUNTZ.
*Librarian:* JOHN HEUSSMAN.

The library contains 269,861 vols.
Number of teachers: 204.
Number of students: 3,475.

## SAINT MARTIN'S COLLEGE
LACEY, WASHINGTON 98503

Telephone: (206) 491-4700.

Founded 1895.

*President:* Dr. JOHN D. ISHII.
*Registrar:* Mrs. MARY LAW.
*Librarian:* Mrs. JOAN MCINTYRE.

The library contains 80,000 volumes.
Number of teachers: 48.
Number of students: 750.

## SEATTLE PACIFIC UNIVERSITY
3307 THIRD AVE. WEST, SEATTLE, WASHINGTON 98119

Telephone: 281-2111.

Founded 1891.

*President:* DAVID L. MCKENNA.
*Vice-President for Academic Affairs:* DAVID O. DICKERSON.
*Senior Vice-President:* CURTIS A. MARTIN.
*Vice-President for Finance and Planning:* LAWRENCE W. WRIGHT.
*Vice-President for Student Affairs:* ALVIN O. AUSTIN.
*Director of Registration and Records:* WAYNE BALCH.
*Director of Learning Resources:* GEORGE MCDONOUGH.

The library contains 108,000 vols.
Number of teachers: 196.
Number of students: 2,700.

## SEATTLE UNIVERSITY
SEATTLE, WASHINGTON 98122

Telephone: (206) 626-6200.

Founded 1891.

*President:* WILLIAM J. SULLIVAN, S.J.
*Registrar:* MARY A. LEE.
*Vice-President for Academic Affairs:* Dr. GARY A. ZIMMERMAN.
*Controller:* NEIL SULLIVAN.

*Librarian:* LAWRENCE THOMAS.

The library contains 176,000 vols.
Number of teachers: 175.
Number of students: 4,000.
Publication: *Bulletin of Information.*

DEANS:

*College of Arts and Sciences:* Fr. WILLIAM F. LeROUX, S.J.
*School of Business:* Dr. JOHN D. ESHELMAN.
*School of Education:* Dr. GARY H. ZARTER (acting).
*School of Science and Engineering:* Dr. TERRY J. VAN DER WERFF.
*School of Nursing:* Dr. PATRICIA FERRIS.
*Graduate School:* Dr. MARYLOU WYSE.

## UNIVERSITY OF PUGET SOUND
TACOMA, WASHINGTON 98416

Telephone: 756-3100.

Founded 1888.

Private control.

*President:* PHILIP M. PHIBBS.
*Dean of University:* THOMAS A. DAVIS
*Vice-Presidents:* SHIRLEY BUSHNELL, R. BELL.
*Registrar:* JOHN FINNEY.
*Librarian:* DESMOND TAYLOR.

Number of teachers: 165.
Number of students: 2,800 full-time.

DIRECTORS:

*School of Business and Public Administration:* (vacant).
*School of Education:* R. HODGES.
*School of Music:* JAMES SORENSON.
*School of Physical Therapy:* SUZANNE OLSEN.
*School of Occupational Therapy:* STEVE MORELAN.
*School of Law:* FREDRIC TAUSEND.

## UNIVERSITY OF WASHINGTON
SEATTLE, WASHINGTON 98195

Telephone: 543-2100.

Established by legislature 1861.

*President:* WILLIAM P. GERBERDING, PH.D.
*Provost:* G. M. BECKMANN, PH.D.
*Vice-President for Business and Finance:* J. F. RYAN, B.S.
*Vice-President for Health Sciences:* J. T. GRAYSTON, M.S., M.D.
*Vice-President for Minority Affairs:* H. D. LUJAN, PH.D.
*Vice-President for Student Affairs:* A. E. ULBRICKSON, M.S., M.P.A.
*Vice-President for University Relations:* M. E. CHISHOLM, PH.D.
*Executive Director, Admissions and Records:* W. W. WASHBURN, B.A.
*Director of Libraries:* MERLE N. BOYLAN, M.L.S.

Library: see Libraries.

Number of teachers: 2,593, full-time faculty.
Number of students: 35,000.

Publications: *American Journal of Human Genetics, Biochemistry, Journal of Limnology and Oceanography, Modern Language Quarterly, Pacific Northwest Quarterly, Poetry Northwest, Trends in Engineering, Washington Law Review, Journal of Financial and Quantitative Analysis, Papers of Regional Science Association.*

DEANS:

*Graduate School:* R. GEBALLE, PH.D.
*College of Architecture and Urban Planning:* M. WOLFE, M.R.P.
*College of Arts and Sciences:* E. M. HENLEY, PH.D.
*School of Business Administration:* K. O. HANSON, M.S., PH.D.
*College of Education:* J. I. DOI, M.A., PH.D.
*College of Engineering:* D. A. CARLSON, M.S.C.E., PH.D.
*College of Fisheries:* D. BEVAN, PH.D.
*College of Forest Resources:* J. S. BETHEL, M.F., D.F.
*Continuing Education:* R. G. WALDO, D.P.A.
*School of Pharmacy:* M. GIBALDI, PH.D.
*School of Dentistry:* R. RIEDEL, D.D.S. (acting)
*School of Law:* G. SCHATZKI, LL.M.
*School of Librarianship:* P. HIATT, PH.D. (Director).
*School of Medicine:* R. L. vanCITTERS, M.D.
*School of Nursing:* R. DE TORNYAY, ED.D.
*School of Social Work:* S. BRIAR, D.S.W.
*School of Public Health and Community Medicine:* R. W. DAY, M.P.H., PH.D.
*Graduate School of Public Affairs:* J. HAZLETON, PH.D.

DIRECTORS:

*Alcoholism and Drug Abuse Institute:* R. E. LITTLE, SC.D.
*Applied Physics Laboratory:* S. MURPHY, PH.D.
*Center for Bioengineering:* L. HUNTSMAN, PH.D.
*Center for Inherited Diseases:* A. G. MOTULSKY, M.D.
*Center for Research in Oral Biology:* R. C. PAGE, PH.D.
*Friday Harbor Laboratories:* A. O. D. WILLOWS, PH.D.
*Center for Law and Justice:* J. G. WEIS, D.CRIM.
*Center for Studies in Demography and Ecology:* T. W. PULLUM, PH.D.
*Institute on Aging:* M. HENDERSON, D.P.H.
*Institute for Environmental Studies:* G. H. ORIANS, PH.D.
*Institute of Governmental Research:* R. H. PEALY, PH.D.
*Institute for Marine Studies:* W. WOOSTER, PH.D. (acting).
*Quaternary Research Center:* E. B. LEOPOLD, PH.D.
*Child Development and Mental Retardation Center:* I. EMANUEL, M.A., M.D.

*Fisheries Research Institute:* R. L. BURGNER, PH.D.
*Institute of Forest Products:* J. S. BETHEL, D.F.
*Regional Primate Center:* O. A. SMITH, Jr., PH.D.

PROFESSORS:

*College of Architecture and Urban Planning:*
AMOSS, H. L., M.A., PH.D., Urban Planning
BELL, E. J., PH.D., Urban Planning
BONSTEEL, D. L., M.ARCH., Architecture
BOSWORTH, T. L., M.A., Architecture
BUCHANAN, R. T., M.L.A., Landscape Architecture
GREY, A. L., Jr., PH.D., Urban Planning
HAAG, R., M.L.A., Landscape Architecture
HANCOCK, J. L., PH.D., Urban Planning
HILDEBRAND, G., M.ARCH., Architecture and Art History
HORWOOD, E. M., PH.D., Urban Planning and Civil Engineering
JACOBSON, P. L., M.ARCH., Architecture
JOHNSTON, N. J., B.A., B.ARCH., PH.D., Architecture and Urban Planning
KELLEY, C. M., M.ARCH., Architecture
LOVETT, W. H., M.ARCH., Architecture
MILLER, D. H., PH.D., Urban Planning
MITHUN, O. L., B.ARCH., Architecture
PUNDT, H. G., PH.D., Architecture and Art History
RABINOWITZ, A., PH.D., Urban Planning
SCHNEIDER, J. B., PH.D., Urban Planning and Civil Engineering
SCHNEIDER, R. C., ED.D., Architecture
SEYFRIED, W. R., Jr., D.B.A., Urban Planning and Business, Government and Society
SHINN, R. D., PH.D., Urban Planning
SMALL, R. E., M.ARCH., Architecture and Landscape Architecture
STREISSGUTH, D. M., M.ARCH., Architecture
THIEL, P., B.ARCH., Architecture
VAREY, G. B., M.ARCH., Architecture and Building Construction
WOLFE, M. R., B.S. IN ARCH., M.R.P., Urban Planning
ZARINA, A., M.ARCH., Architecture

*College of Arts and Sciences:*
ADAMS, H. S., PH.D., English
ADAMS, J. B., PH.D., Geological Sciences and Astronomy
**ADAMS, R. P., PH.D., English**
ADELBERGER, E. D., PH.D., Physics
ALDEN, D., M.A., PH.D., History and International Studies
**ALEXANDER, E., M.A., PH.D., English**
ALPS, G. E., M.F.A., School of Art
ALTIERI, C. F., PH.D., English
AMES, W. E., PH.D., Communications
ANDERSEN, N. H., PH.D., Chemistry
**ANDERSON, A. G., Jr., M.S., PH.D., Chemistry**
ANDERSON, F. N., B.A., M.F.A., Art
ANDERSON, G. C., PH.D., Oceanography
ARNOLD, R. R., M.F.A., Art
**ARONS, A. B., M.S., PH.D., Physics**
**ARSOVE, M. G., M.S., PH.D., Mathematics**
ATTNEAVE, C. L., PH.D., Psychology
**BADGLEY, F. I., M.S., PH.D., Atmospheric Sciences**
BAER, J.-L., PH.D., Computer Science
BAKER, D. J., PH.D., Oceanography
**BAKER, M., PH.D., Physics**
**BANSE, K., PH.D., Oceanography**
BANTA, M., PH.D., English
BARASH, D. P., PH.D., Psychology
BARDEEN, J. M., PH.D., Physics
**BARTH, E. A., M.A., PH.D., Sociology**

## UNIVERSITIES AND COLLEGES—WASHINGTON (UNIVERSITY OF) — U.S.A.

BARZEL, Y., PH.D., Economics
BEACH, L. R., PH.D., Psychology
BEALE, J. M., M.MUS., Music
BEAUMONT, R. A., M.S., PH.D., Mathematics
BECKER, J., M.A., PH.D., Psychiatry and Psychology
BECKMANN, G. M., PH.D., School of International Studies
BEHLER, E., PH.D., Germanics and Comparative Literature
BERGSMA, W., M.M., School of Music
BLALOCK, H. M., Jr., PH.D., Sociology
BLAIR, J. S., M.S., PH.D., Physics
BLESSING, R. A., PH.D., English
BLISS, L. C., PH.D., Botany
BLUMENTHAL, R. M., PH.D., Mathematics
BOBA, I., PH.D., School of International Studies and History
BODANSKY, D., M.A., PH.D., Physics
BOHM, K.-H., PH.D., Astronomy
BOHM-VITENSE, ERIKA, PH.D., Astronomy
BOLER, J. F., PH.D., Philosophy
BOLLES, R. C., M.S., PH.D., Psychology
BORDEN, W. T., PH.D., Chemistry
BORIS, R., Music
BOSMAJIAN, H. A., PH.D., Speech
BOSTROM, R. C., M.A., PH.D., Geological Sciences and Geophysics
BOULWARE, D. G., PH.D., Physics
BRASS, P. R., PH.D., Political Science and Asian Studies in School of International Studies
BRAVMANN, R. A., PH.D., Art History
BROWN, G. M., PH.D., Economics
BROWN, L. S., PH.D., Physics
BROWNELL, F. H., III, M.S., PH.D., Mathematics
BURKE, R., M.A., PH.D., History
BUSINGER, J., PH.D., Atmospheric Sciences and Geophysics
BUTOW, R. J. C., PH.D., School of International Studies and History
CARLSEN, J. C., M.A., PH.D., Music
CARR, J. E., PH.D., Psychology and Psychiatry
CARRAHER, R. G., M.A., Art
CARTER, R. F., M.A., PH.D., Communications
CARTWRIGHT, P. W., M.A., PH.D., Economics
CASSINELLI, C. W., A.M., PH.D., Political Science
CELENTANO, F., M.A., Art
CHAN, H.-L., PH.D., International Studies
CHAPMAN, D. G., M.A., PH.D., Mathematics, Fisheries, Forest Resources
CHARLSON, R. F., PH.D., Environmental Studies, Civil Engineering and Geophysics
CHEUNG, S. N. S., PH.D., Economics
CHILTON, W. S., PH.D., Chemistry
CHIROT, D., PH.D., Sociology
CHRISTIAN, G. D., PH.D., Chemistry
CHRISTENSEN, N. I., PH.D., Geological Sciences and Geophysics
CHRISTOFIDES, C. G., M.A. PH.D., Romance Languages and Literature and Comparative Literature
CLARK, K. C., A.M., PH.D., Physics and Geophysics
CLELAND, R. E., PH.D., Botany
CLONEY, R. A., PH.D., Zoology
COACHMAN, L. K., PH.D., Oceanography
COBURN, R. C., PH.D., Philosophy
COHEN, S. M., PH.D., Philosophy
CONCHA, J. H., DR., Romance Languages and Literatures
CONTRERAS, H., PH.D., Linguistics
COOK, V., PH.D., Physics
CORSON, H. H., M.A., PH.D., Mathematics

COSTNER, H. L., PH.D., Sociology
CRAMER, J. G., Jr., PH.D., Physics
CREAGER, J. S., PH.D., Oceanography
CRIDER, J. R., M.A., Drama
CRIMINALE, W. O., Jr., PH.D., Oceanography, Geophysics
CRUTCHFIELD, J. A., Jr., A.M., PH.D., Economics, Public Affairs, and Marine Studies
CURJEL, C. R., D.SC., Mathematics
CURTIS, E. B., PH.D., Mathematics
CURTIS-VERNA, MARY, A.B., Music
DAHN, R. F., M.F.A., Art
DAILEY, M. D., M.F.A., Art
DASH, J. G., M.A., PH.D., Physics
DAVIDSON, E. R., PH.D., Chemistry
DEHMELT, H. G., M.S., PH.D., Physics
DEYRUP-OLSEN, INGRITH J., PH.D., Zoology
DIETRICHSON, P., PH.D., Philosophy
DOERMANN, A. H., M.A., PH.D., Genetics
DOUGLAS, H. C., PH.D., Genetics and Microbiology
DUBISCH, R., M.S., PH.D., Mathematics
DUNNE, T., PH.D., Geological Sciences
DUNNELL, R. C., PH.D., Anthropology
DU PEN, E. G., B.F.A., Art
EASTMAN, C. M., PH.D., Anthropology
EDELSTEIN, A. S., PH.D., Communications
EDMONDSON, W. T., PH.D., Zoology
EDWARDS, A. L., M.A., PH.D., Psychology
EDWARDS, J. S., PH.D., Zoology
EGGERS, D. F., Jr., PH.D., Chemistry
EICHINGER, B. E., PH.D., Chemistry
ELLISON, H. J., M.A., PH.D., School of International Studies and History
EMONDS, J., PH.D., Linguistics
EMERSON, R. M., PH.D., Sociology
ERICKSON, J. W., M.F.A., Art
EVANS, B. W., PH.D., Geological Sciences
FAIN, S. C., PH.D., Physics
FAIRHALL, A. W., PH.D., Chemistry, Physics and Geophysics
FANGMAN, W. L., PH.D., Genetics
FARNER, D. S., M.A., PH.D., Zoology
FARWELL, G. W., PH.D., Physics
FELSENSTEIN, J., PH.D., Genetics
FERRILL, A. L., PH.D., History
FIEDLER, F. E., A.M., PH.D., Psychology
FISCHER, M. J., PH.D., Computer Science
FLEAGLE, R. G., M.S., PH.D., Atmospheric Sciences
FLEMING, R. H., M.A., PH.D., Oceanography
FOLLAND, G. B., PH.D., Mathematics
FORTSON, E. N., II, PH.D., Physics
FOWLER, D., M.A., PH.D., English
FOWLER, W. B., PH.D., History
FRIEDMAN, L. J., M.A., PH.D., Romance Languages and Literature
FROST, B. W., PH.D., Oceanography
GALLANT, J. A., PH.D., Genetics
GANGOLLI, R. A., PH.D., Mathematics
GARFIAS, R. A., PH.D., Music
GARTLER, S., PH.D., Genetics and Medicine
GEBALLE, R., M.A., PH.D., Physics
GERBERDING, W. P., PH.D., Political Science
GERHART, J. B., M.A., PH.D., Physics
GERSTENBERGER, DONNA L., PH.D., English
GHOSE, S., PH.D., Geological Sciences
GLICKSBERG, I. L., PH.D., Mathematics
GOLDE, H., PH.D., Computer Science
GOLDSTEIN, A. A., M.A., PH.D., Mathematics
GORBMAN, A., M.S., PH.D., Zoology
GORE, W. J., PH.D. Political Science
GOUTERMAN, M. P., M.S., PH.D., Chemistry
GREGORY, N. W., M.S., PH.D., Chemistry
GRIFFITHS, G., PH.D., History

GROSS, E., M.A., PH.D., Sociology
GROSSMAN, A. J., Music
GRUMMEL, W. C., PH.D., Classics and Comparative Literature
GRUNBAUM, B., PH.D., Mathematics
HALL, B. D., PH.D., Genetics and Biochemistry
HALPERN, I., PH.D., Physics
HALSEY, G. D., Jr., PH.D., Chemistry
HANEY, J. V., PH.D, Slavic Languages and Literatures
HANKINS, T. L., PH.D., History
HARMAN, A., B.MUS., Music
HARTWELL, L. H., PH.D., Genetics
HAWTHORNE, D. G., PH.D., Genetics
HEER, N. L., PH.D., Near Eastern Languages and Literature
HELLMANN, D. C., PH.D., Political Science and School of International Studies
HENLEY, E. M., PH.D., Physics
HERTLING, G. H., PH.D., Germanics
HEWITT, E., M.A., PH.D., Mathematics
HIGGS, R. L., PH.D., Economics
HILDEBRAND, G., M.ARCH., Art History and Architecture
HITCHNER, D. G., M.A., PH.D., Political Science
HIXSON, W. J., M.F.A., Art
HOBBS, P. V., PH.D., Atmospheric Sciences
HOBBS, R. L., PH.D., Drama
HODGE, P. W., B.S., PH.D., Astronomy and Geophysics
HOKANSON, R., Music
HOLM, B., M.F.A., Art History
HOLTON, J. R., PH.D., Atmospheric Sciences
HOSTETLER, P. S., PH.D., Drama
HRUBY, A. F. PH.D., Germanic Languages and Literature and Comparative Literature
HUGHES, E. L., M.S., D.ED., Kinesiology
HUNT, E. B., PH.D., Psychology
ILLG, P. L., M.A., PH.D., Zoology
INGALLS, R. L., PH.D., Physics
IRMSCHER, W. F., PH.D., English
JACKSON, W. A. D., M.A., PH.D., L.T.C.M., Geography and School of International Studies
JANS, J. P., M.A., PH.D., Mathematics
JOHNSON, MARY L., M.S., D.SC., Nutritional Sciences and Textiles
JONES, R. C., M.S., Art
KAPETANIC, D., PH.D., Slavic Languages and Literature, and International Studies
KAPLAN, A., Music
KARTIGANER, D. M., PH.D., English
KATZ, S., PH.D., History
KECHLEY, G. R., M.A., Music
KEHL, T. H., PH.D., Computer Science and Physiology and Biophysics
KELLER, A. C., M.A., PH.D., Romance Languages and Literature
KEYES, C. F., PH.D., Anthropology and International Studies
KEYT, D., M.A., PH.D., Philosophy
KLEE, V. M., Jr., PH.D., Mathematics
KOHN, A. J., PH.D., Zoology
KORG, J., PH.D., English
KOTTLER, H. W., M.F.A., Art
KOWALSKI, B. R., PH.D., Chemistry
KOZLOFF, E. N., M.A., PH.D., Zoology
KROLL, M., PH.D., Political Science and Public Affairs
KRUCKEBERG, A. R., PH.D., Botany
KRUME, G., PH.D., Geography
KWIRAM, A. L., PH.D., Chemistry
LaCHAPELLE, E. R., D.SC., Geophysics and Atmospheric Sciences
LAIRD, C. D., PH.D., Zoology
LARSEN, O. J., M.A., PH.D., Sociology
LAWRENCE, J. A., Art

1923

LEGTERS, L. H., M.A., PH.D., School of International Studies
LEINER, J. Dr., Romance Languages and Literature and Comparative Literature
LEINER, W., PH.D., Comparative Literature
LEOPOLD, E. B., PH.D., Botany
LEOVY, C. B., PH.D., Atmospheric Sciences and Geophysics
LEV, D. S., PH.D., Political Science
LEVY, F. J., PH.D., History
LINGAFELTER, E. C., Jr., PH.D., Chemistry
LISTER, C. R. B., PH.D., Geophysics and Oceanography
LOCKWOOD, T. F., PH.D., English
LOCKARD, J. S., PH.D., Psychology and Neurology
LOFTUS, E. J., PH.D., Psychology
LOPER, R. B., M.A., PH.D., Drama
LORD, J. J., M.A., PH.D., Physics
LUBATTI, H. J., PH.D., Physics
LUJAN, H. D., PH.D., Political Science
LUMSDAINE, A. A., PH.D., Psychology, Education
LUNDIN, N. K., M.F.A., Art
LUNNEBORG, P. W., PH.D., Psychology
MACKAY, P. A., PH.D., Classics, Comparative Literature and Near Eastern Language and Literature
McCAFFREE, K. M., M.A., PH.D., Economics
McCRACKEN, J. D., PH.D., English
McCRONE, D. J., PH.D., Political Science
McDERMOTT, M. N., PH.D., Physics
McDIARMID, J. B., PH.D., Classics
McGEE, J. S., PH.D., Economics
McINNES, D. M., M.M., Music
McKINNON, R. N., PH.D., Asian Languages and Literature, International Studies and Comparative Literature
McMANUS, D. A., PH.D., Oceanography
MAH, F. H., PH.D., Economics and International Studies
MAKIN, J. H., PH.D., Economics
MAKOUS, W., PH.D., Psychology
MALLORY, V. S., M.A., PH.D., Geological Sciences
MAR, B. W., PH.D., Environmental Studies and Civil Engineering
MARKS, C. E., PH.D., Philosophy
MARLATT, G. A., PH.D., Psychology
MARSHALL, J. C., M.F.A., Art
MARTIN, A. W., Jr., PH.D., Zoology
MARTS, MARION E., M.A., PH.D., Geography
MASON, A. C., M.F.A., Art
MATCHETT, W. H., PH.D., English
MATHEWS, B. P., D.PH.H., Kinesiology
MATTHEWS, D. R., PH.D., Political Science
MATTHEWS, W., M.A., English
MEEUSE, B. J., DR., Botany
MERRILL, R. T., PH.D., Oceanography and Geophysics
MEYER, C. B., PH.D., Chemistry
MICHAEL, E. A., M.A., PH.D., Mathematics
MICKLESEN, L. R., PH.D., Slavic Languages and Literature, Linguistics and International Studies
MILLER, R. A., PH.D., Asian Languages and Literature
MINIFIE, F. D., PH.D., Speech and Hearing Sciences
MISCH, P. H., D.SC., Geological Sciences
MITCHELL, T. R., PH.D., Management and Organization and Psychology
MIYAMOTO, S. F., M.A., PH.D., Sociology
MODELSKI, G., PH.D., Political Science
MONSEN, E. R., PH.D., Nutritional Sciences and Textiles
MOORE, J. T., M.MUS., Music
MOREL, A. C., PH.D., Mathematics
MORRILL, R. L., M.A., PH.D., Geography and Environmental Studies
MORRIS, M. D., PH.D., Economics

MORROW, J. A., PH.D., Mathematics
MOSELEY, S., M.F.A., Art
MOTULSKY, A., B.S., M.D., Genetics and Medicine
MURPHY, S. R., PH.D., Oceanography, Mechanical Engineering
NAMIOKA, I., M.A., PH.D., Mathematics
NELSON, C. R., PH.D., Economics
NILSEN, T. R., PH.D., Speech
NOE, J. D., PH.D., Computer Science
NORMAN, J. L., PH.D., Asian Languages and Literatures
NORRIS, R. E., PH.D., Botany
NORTH, D. C., PH.D., Economics
NOSTRAND, H. L., A.M., PH.D., Romance Languages and Literature
NUNKE, R. J., M.S.. PH.D., Mathematics
O'DOAN, N. D., M.M., Music
OLSON, D. J., PH.D., Political Science
ORIANS, G. H., PH.D., Zoology and Environmental Studies
OTTENBERG, S., PH.D., Anthropology
PACE, A., M.A., PH.D., Romance Languages and Literature
PAINE, R. T., Jr., PH.D., Zoology
PALKA, J. M., PH.D., Zoology
PALMER, J. M., PH.D., Prosthodontics and Speech and Hearing Sciences
PALUMBO, P. M., PH.D., Music
PARKS, G. K., PH.D., Geophysics
PARKS, R. W., PH.D., Economics
PASCAL, PAUL, PH.D., Classics
PEASE, O. A., PH.D., History
PEMBER, D. R., PH.D., Communication
PENUELAS, M. C., M.ED., M.A., PH.D., Romance Languages and Literature
PERLMAN, M. D., PH.D., Statistics
PETERS, P. C., PH.D., Physics
PHELPS, R. R., PH.D., Mathematics
PINKNEY, D. H., PH.D., History
PIZZUTO, E., M.F.A., Art
POCKER, Y., M.SC., PH.D., D.SC., Chemistry
PORTER, S. C., PH.D., Geological Sciences
POTTER, K. H., PH.D., International Studies and Philosophy
PREDMORE, M. P., PH.D., Romance Languages and Literature
PRESSLY, T. J., A.M., PH.D., History
PRINS, D., PH.D., Speech and Hearing Sciences
PUFF, R. D., PH.D., Physics
PUNDT, G. H., PH.D., Art History and Architecture
PYKE, R., PH.D., Mathematics
PYLE, K. B., PH.D., International Studies and History
QUIMBY, G. I., M.A., Anthropology
RABINOVITCH, S., PH.D., Chemistry
RATTRAY, M., Jr., M.S., PH.D., Oceanography
RAYMOND, C. F., PH.D., Geophysics
READ, K. E., M.A., PH.D., Anthropology
REED, R., SC.D., Atmospheric Sciences
REINERT, O., PH.D., English and Comparative Literature
RESHETAR, J. S., Jr., M.A., PH.D., Political Science
REY, W. H., PH.D., Germanics
RICHARDS, F. A., M.S., PH.D., Oceanography
RICHMAN, R. J., PH.D., Philosophy
RIDDIFORD, L. M., PH.D., Zoology
RIEDEL, E. K., DR., Physics
RITCHIE, R. W., PH.D., Computer Science
RITCHIE, W. H., M.A., Art
ROBINSON, H. B., M.A., PH.D., Psychology
ROCKAFELLAR, R. T., PH.D., Mathematics
ROGERS, M., PH.D., History
ROMAN, H. L., PH.D., Genetics
ROSE, N. J., PH.D., Chemistry
ROSSEL, S. H., MAG., Scandinavian Languages and Literatures

ROTH, G., PH.D., Sociology
ROTHBERG, J E., PH.D., Physics
RUEGG, D. S., D.LITT., Asian Languages and Literature
SACKETT, G. P., PH.D., Psychology
SALE, R. H., M.A., PH.D., English
SANDLER, L. M., PH.D., Genetics
SAPORTA, S., M.A., PH.D., Linguistics and Romance Languages
SARASON, I. G., M.A., PH.D., Psychology
SARASON, L., PH.D., Mathematics
SAUM, L. O., PH.D., History
SAX, G., PH.D., Psychology and Education
SCHEIDEL, T. M., PH.D., Speech
SCHEINGOLD, S. A., PH.D., Political Science
SCHICK, M., PH.D., Physics
SCHIFFMAN, H. F., PH.D., Asian Languages and Literatures
SCHMIDT, F. H., M.A., PH.D., Physics
SCHMITT, D. R., PH.D., Sociology
SCHOENER, T. W., PH.D., Zoology
SCHOMAKER, V., M.SC., PH.D., Chemistry
SCHRAG, C. C., M.A., PH.D., Sociology
SCHUBERT, W. M., PH.D., Chemistry
SEGAL, J., PH.D., Mathematics
SERRUYS, P. L., PH.D., Asian Languages and Literature and International Studies
SHAW, A. C., PH.D., Computer Science
SHERMAN, J. C., M.A., PH.D., Geography
SHORACK, G. R., PH.D., Mathematics
SILBERBERG, E., PH.D., Economics
SIMONSON, H. P., M.A., PH.D., English
SKOWRONEK, F. E., B.M., Music
SLUTSKY, L. J., PH.D., Chemistry
SMITH, C. W., M.F.A., Art
SMITH, J. D., PH.D., Oceanography and Geophysics
SMITH, M. H., M.A., PH.D., Psychology
SMITH, R. E., PH.D., Psychology
SMITH, S. W., PH.D., Geophysics
SMITH, W. O., M.A., Music
SNYDER, R., A.M. PH.D., Zoology
SOKOL, V., M.MUS., Music
SOLBERG, C. E., PH.D., History and International Studies
SOLBERG, R. L., M.F.A., Art
SPAFFORD, M. C., M.A., Art
SPERRY, R. H., M.F.A., Art
STADLER, D. R., M.A., PH.D., Genetics
STARK, R., PH.D., Sociology
STEENE, BIRGITTA, PH.D., Scandinavian Languages and Literature
STERN, E. A., PH.D., Physics
STERNBERG, R. W., PH.D., Oceanography
STEVICK, R. D., M.A., PH.D., English
STORCH, L., B.A., Music
STOTLAND. E., M.A., PH.D.. Psychology
STOUT, E. L., PH.D., Mathematics
STREIB, J. F., PH.D., Physics
STUIVER, M., PH.D., Geological Sciences, Zoology
SUGAR, P. F., M.A., PH.D., History and International Studies
SWINDLER, D. R., M.A., PH.D., Anthropology
SYDOW, J. D., Jr., M.F.A., Drama
TELLER, D. Y., PH.D., Psychology
THOMAS, M. D., PH.D., Geography
THORNTON, J., PH.D., Economics
TIFFANY, W. R., M.A., PH.D., Speech and Hearing Sciences
TOWNSEND, J. R., PH.D., International Studies and Political Science
TREADGOLD, D. W., M.A., D.PHIL., Institute for Foreign Area and Comparative Studies and History
TRUMAN, J. W., PH.D., Zoology
TSUKADA, M., PH.D., Botany
TUFTS, P. D., M.A., Music
ULLMAN, J., PH.D., History
UNTERSTEINER, N., PH.D., Atmospheric Sciences and Geophysics

## UNIVERSITIES AND COLLEGES—WASHINGTON (UNIVERSITY OF)     U.S.A.

VANDENBOSCH, R., PH.D., Chemistry
VAN DEN BERGHE, P. L., M.D., PH.D., Sociology
VELIKONJA, J., PH.D., Geography and International Studies
VILCHES, O. E., PH.D., Physics
VOYLES, J. B., PH.D., Economics
WAGER, L. W., PH.D., Sociology
WAGONER, D. R., M.A., English
WALKER, R. B., PH.D., Botany
WALLACE, J. M., PH.D., Atmospheric Sciences
WALLERSTEIN, G., PH.D., Astronomy
WARASHINA, P. B., M.F.A., Art
WARFIELD, R. B., PH.D., Mathematics
WARNER, G. W., Jr., PH.D., Mathematics
WATSON, J. B., A.M., PH.D., Anthropology
WEBB, E., PH.D., International Studies and Comparative Literature
WELANDER, P. L., PH.D., Oceanography
WEINSTEIN, B., PH.D., Chemistry
WHETTEN, J. T., PH.D., Geological Sciences
WHISLER, H. C., PH.D., Botany
WHITELEY, A. H., M.A., PH.D., Zoology
WILETS, L., M.A., PH.D., Physics
WILLIAMS, R. W., M.A., PH.D., Physics
WILLOWS, A. O. D., PH.D., Zoology
WILSON, W. R., PH.D., Speech and Hearing Sciences
WINANS, E. V., PH.D., Anthropology
WINTER, D. F., PH.D., Oceanography
WOODS, S. C., PH.D., Psychology
WORCESTER, D. A., PH.D. Economics
WORTHINGTON-ROBERTS, B. S., PH.D., Nutritional Sciences and Textiles
WYLIE, T. V., PH.D., Asian Languages and Literature and International Studies
YAMAMURA, K., PH.D., International Studies
YANTIS, P. A., M.A., PH.D., Speech and Hearing Sciences
YERXA, F. W., A.B., Communications
YOUNG, K. K., PH.D., Physics
ZIADEH, F. J., LL.D., Near Eastern Languages and Literature
ZSIGMONDY-LIEDEMANN, D., Baccalaureate, Music

*School of Business Administration:*

ALBERTS, W. W., M.A., PH.D., Finance, Business Economics and Quantitative Methods
BERG, K., M.S., PH.D., C.P.A., Accounting
BOURQE, P. J., M.A., PH.D., Finance, Business Economics and Quantitative Methods
CHIU, J. S. Y., M.S., PH.D., Finance, Business Economics and Quantitative Methods
D'AMBROSIO, C. A., PH.D., Finance, Business Economics
DECOSTER, D. T., PH.D., Accounting
ETCHESON, W. W., M.A., PH.D., Marketing
FELIX, W. L., PH.D., Accounting
FENN, M. P., D.B.A., Management and Organization
FIEDLER, F. E., PH.D., Management and Organization, Psychology
FRENCH, W. L., M.P.S., D.ED., Management and Organization
FROST, P. A., PH.D., Finance, Business Economics and Quantitative Methods
GOLDBERG, L. D., J.D., Business, Government and Society
HALEY, C. W., PH.D., Finance, Business Economics and Quantitative Methods
HANSON, K. O., M.S., PH.D., Accounting
HARDER, V. E., M.A., PH.D., Marketing
HART, D. K., PH.D., Business, Government and Society
HEATH, L. C., PH.D., Accounting

HENNING, C. N., M.A., PH.D., Finance, Business Economics and Quantitative Methods
HENNING, D. A., M.B.A., FH.D., Management and Organization
HESS, A. C., PH.D., Finance, Business Economics and Quantitative Methods
HIGGINS, R. C., PH.D., Finance, Business Economics and Quantitative Methods
JOHNSON, D. W., PH.D., Finance, Business Economics and Quantitative Methods
JOHNSON, R. A., M.B.A., D.B.A., Management and Organization
KAST, F. E., M.B.A., D.B.A., Management and Organization
KING, B. F., Jr., M.B.A., PH.D., Finance, Business Economics and Quantitative Methods
KNUDSON, H. R., M.B.A., D.B.A., Management and Organization
KOLDE, E. J., D.H.S., M.A., D.B.A., Marketing, Transportation and International Business
LE BRETON, P. P., M.B.A., PH.D., Management and Organization
LESSINGER, J., PH.D., Business, Government and Society
MACLACHLAN, D. L., PH.D., Marketing
MITCHELL, T. R., PH.D., Management and Organization
MONSEN, R. J., PH.D., Business, Government and Society
MUELLER, F. J., M.A., PH.D., Accounting
MUELLER, G. G., M.B.A., PH.D., Accounting
NARVER, J. C., PH.D., Marketing, Transportation and International Business
NEWELL, W. T., M.B.A., PH.D., Management and Organization
PAGE, A. N., M.B.A., PH.D., Finance, Business Economics and Quantitative Methods
PETERSON, R. B., PH.D., Finance, Business Economics and Quantitative Methods
RAMANATHAN, K. V., PH.D., Accounting
ROSENZWEIG, J. E., M.B.A., PH.D., Management and Organization
SCHALL, L. D., PH.D., Finance, Business Economics and Quantitative Methods
SCHRIEBER, A. N., M.B.A., Management and Organization
SAXBERG, B. O., M.S., PH.D., Management and Organization
SCOTT, R. H., M.A., PH.D., Finance, Business Economics and Quantitative Methods
SCOTT, W. G., M.S.I.R., D.B.A., Management and Organization
SEYFRIED, W. R., Jr., D.B.A., Business, Government and Society, Urban Planning
SPRATLEN, T. H., PH.D., Marketing, Transportation and International Business
SUMMER, C. E., M.B.A., PH.D., Management and Organization
SUNDEM, G. L., PH.D., Accounting
VESPER, K. H., M.B.A., PH.D., Management and Organization and Mechanical Engineering
WAGNER, L. C., B.B.A., M.A., Marketing, Transportation and International Business
WALKER, L. M., M.B.A., C.P.A., Accounting
WHEATLEY, J. J., PH.D., Marketing, Transportation and International Business

*College of Education:*

ABBOTT, R. D., PH.D.
AFFLECK, J. Q., M.A., ED.D.

ANDERSON, R. A., PH.D.
BANKS, J. A., M.A., PH.D.
BOLTON, D. L., M.S., PH.D.
BRAMMER, L. M., PH.D.
BROWN, F. A., M.A.
BURGESS, C. O., M.S., PH.D.
DOI, J. I., PH.D.
DRISCOLL, J. P., M.S., PH.D.
EDGAR, E. B., PH.D.
EVANS, E. D., ED.D.
FOSTER, C. D., M.A., PH.D.
FREEHILL, M. F., M.A., ED.D.
GILES, F. T., M.A., ED.D.
HARING, N. G., M.A., ED.D.
HAWK, R. L., ED.D.
HUNKINS, F. P., M.ED., PH.D.
JAROLIMEK, J., M.A., PH.D.
JENKINS, J. R., PH.D.
KALTSOUNIS, T., PH.D.
KERR, D. H., PH.D.
LOVITT, T. C., M.ME., ED.D.
LOWENBRAUN, S., PH.D.
LUMSDAINE, A. A., PH.D., Psychology and Education
MADSEN, D. L., PH.D.
MCCARTIN, R. E., PH.D.
MEACHAM, M. L., M.S., ED.D.
MONSON, D. L., M.A., PH.D.
ODEGAARD, C. E., A.M., PH.D
OLSTAD, R. G., PH.D.
PECKHAM, P. D., PH.D.
REITAN, H. M., PH.D.
SAX, G., PH.D.
SCHILL, W. J., ED.D.
SEBESTA, S. L., ED.D.
TORKELSON, G. M., PH.D., ED.D.
TOSTBERG, R. E., M.A., PH.D.

*College of Engineering:*

ALBRECHT, R. W., PH.D., Nuclear Engineering
ALLAN, G. G., PH.D., D.SC., Forest Resources and Chemical Engineering
ANDERSEN, J., PH.D., Electrical Engineering
ANDERSON, D. L., B.SC., B.S., Metallurgical and Ceramic Engineering
ARCHBOLD, T. F., M.S., PH.D., Mining, Metallurgical and Ceramic Engineering
AUTH, D. C., PH.D., Electrical Engineering
BABB, A. L., M.S., PH.D., Chemical and Nuclear Engineering
BALISE, P. L., S.M., Mechanical Engineering
BERG, J. C., PH.D., Chemical Engineering
BERGSETH, F. R., S.M. IN E.E., Electrical Engineering
BJORKSTAM, J. L., M.S. IN E.E., PH.D., Electrical Engineering
BOGAN, R. H., M.S., SC.D., Civil Engineering
BOLLARD, R. J. H., M.E., PH.D., Aeronautics and Astronautics
BROWN, C. B., PH.D., Civil Engineering
BURGES, S. J., PH.D., Civil Engineering
CARLSON, D. A., M.S.C.E., Civil Engineering
CARLSON, F. P., PH.D., Electrical Engineering
CHALUPNIK, J. D., PH.D., Mechanical Engineering
CHARLSON, R. J., M.S., PH.D., Civil Engineering and Geophysics and Environmental Studies
CHILDS, M. E., M.S., PH.D., Mechanical Engineering
CHRISTIANSEN, W. H., M.S.A.E., PH.D., Aeronautics and Astronautics
CLARK, R. N., M.S., Electrical Engineering
COLCORD, J. E., M.S., Civil Engineering
CORLETT, R. C., PH.D., Mechanical Engineering

1925

DALEY, C. H., PH.D., Mechanical Engineering
DAY, E. E., B.S., M.S., Mechanical Engineering
DEPEW, C. A., M.S., PH.D., Mechanical Engineering
DOW, D. G., M.S., PH.D., Electrical Engineering
DUNN, W. L., M.P.H., Civil Engineering
ELIAS, Z. M., SC.D., Civil Engineering
EMERY, A. F., M.S. PH.D., Mechanical Engineering
EVANS, R. J., PH.D., Civil Engineering
FERGUSON, J. F., PH.D., Civil Engineering
FINLAYSON, B. A., PH.D., Chemical Engineering
FYFE, I. M., M.ME., PH.D., Aeronautics and Astronautics
GALLE, K. R., PH.D., Mechanical Engineering
GARLID, K. L., PH.D., Chemical and Nuclear Engineering
GESSNER, F., PH.D., Mechanical Engineering
GUILFORD, E. C., M.A., PH.D., Electrical Engineering
HAMMER, V. B., B.S. IN C.E., M.S., Civil Engineering
HARTZ, B. J., M.S., PH.D., Civil Engineering
HAWKINS, N. M., M.S., PH.D., Civil Engineering
HEIDEGER, W. J., PH.D., Chemical Engineering
HERTZBERG, A., M.A., Aeronautics and Astronautics
HOFFMAN, A. S., M.S., SC.D., Chemical Engineering and Bioengineering
HOLDEN, A., PH.D., Electrical Engineering
HORWOOD, E. M., M.S., PH.D., Civil Engineering and Urban Planning
HSU, C.-C., PH.D., Electrical Engineering
HUTCHINSON, T. E., PH.D., Bioengineering and Chemical Engineering
ISHIMARU, AKIRA PH.D., Electrical Engineering
JOHANSON, L. N., M.S., PH.D., Chemical Engineering
JOHNSON, D. L., PH.D., Electrical Engineering
JOPPA, R. G., M.S., Aeronautics and Astronautics
JORGENSEN, J. E., SC.D., Mechanical Engineering
KEVORKIAN, J. K., PH.D., Aeronautics and Astronautics
KIPPENHAM, C. J., M.S.M.E., PH.D., Mechanical Engineering
KOBAYASHI, A. S., M.S., PH.D., Mechanical Engineering
LAURITZEN, P. O., M.S., PH.D., Electrical Engineering
LEAHY, J. T., M.A., Humanistic-Social Studies
LOVE, W. J., PH.D., Mechanical Engineering
LYTLE, D. W., M.S., PH.D., Electrical Engineering
MCCARTHY, J. L., M.S., PH.D., Chemical Engineering and Forestry Resources
MCCORMICK, N J., PH.D., Nuclear Engineering
MCFERON, D. E., M.S. IN M.E., PH.D., Mechanical Engineering
MAR, B. W., M.S., PH.D., Civil Engineering and Environmental Studies
MARTIN, R. D., PH.D., Electrical Engineering
MATTOCK, A. H., M.SC., PH.D., Civil Engineering
MEDITCH, J. S., PH.D., Electrical Engineering
MEESE, R. H., S.M., Civil Engineering
MERCHANT, H. C., S.M., PH.D., Mechanical Engineering
MORRISON, J. B., M.S. IN M.E., Mechanical Engineering
MUELLER, J. I., PH.D., Mining, Metallurgical and Ceramic Engineering
MURPHY, S. R., B.A., PH.D., Mechanical Engineering, Oceanography
NECE, R. E., M.S., SC.D., Civil Engineering
NOGES, E., M.S., PH.D., Electrical Engineering
OATES, G. C., PH.D., Aeronautics and Astronautics
PARMETER, R. R., PH.D., Aeronautics and Astronautics
PEARSON, C. E., PH.D., Mathematics, Aeronautics and Astronautics
PEDEN, IRENE, PH.D., Electrical Engineering
PILAT, M. J., PH.D., Civil Engineering
POLONIS, D. H., M.ASC., PH.D., Mining, Metallurgical and Ceramic Engineering
RAO, Y. K., PH.D., Mining, Metallurgical and Ceramics Engineering
REYNOLDS, D. K., M.A., PH.D., Electrical Engineering
RIBE, F. L., PH.D., Nuclear Engineering
RICHEY, E. P., M.S., PH.D., Civil Engineering
ROBKIN, M. A., PH.D., Nuclear Engineering
ROSSANO, A. T., Jr., D.SC., S.M., Civil Engineering
RUSSELL, D. A., M.SC., PH.D., Aeronautics and Astronautics
SARKANEN, K., M.SC., PH.D., Chemical Engineering and Forest Resources
SAWHILL, R. B., M.E., Civil Engineering
SCHNEIDER, J. B., PH.D., Urban Planning and Civil Engineering
SCOTT, W. D., PH.D., Mining, Metallurgical and Ceramic Engineering
SEABLOOM, R. W., M.S.C.E., Civil Engineering
SHERIF, M.A., PH.D., Civil Engineering
SIGELMANN, R. A., PH.D., Electrical Engineering
SKEELS, D. R., M.A., PH.D., Humanistic Social Studies
SLEICHER, C. A., Jr., PH.D., Chemical Engineering
SOUTHER, J. W., M.A., Humanistic Social Studies
STOEBE, T. G., PH.D., Mining, Metallurgical and Ceramic Engineering
STREET, R. E., A.M., PH.D., Aeronautics and Astronautics
SWARM, H. M., M.S. IN E.E., PH.D., Electrical Engineering and Geophysics
TAGGART, R., PH.D., Mechanical Engineering
TERREL, R. L., PH.D., Civil Engineering
TRIMBLE, L. P., ED.M., Humanistic-Social Studies
VAGNERS, J., PH.D., Aeronautics and Astronautics
VASARHELYI, D. D., DR.ING., Civil Engineering
VENKATA, S. S., PH.D., Electrical Engineering
VERESS, S. A., M.S., Civil Engineering
VESPER, K. H., PH.D., Mechanical Engineering and Management and Organization
VLASES, G. C., M.S., PH.D., Nuclear Engineering
WAIBLER, P. J., M.S. IN M.E., PH.D., Mechanical Engineering
WELCH, E. B, M.S., PH.D., Civil Engineering
WENK, E., Jr., PH.D., Engineering and Public Affairs
WHITE, M. L., PH.D., Humanistic-Social Studies
WHITTEMORE, O. J., M.S., Mining, Metallurgical and Ceramic Engineering
WOODRUFF, G. L., PH.D., Nuclear Engineering
YEE, S. S., M.S., PH.D., Electrical Engineering
ZERBE, R. O., PH.D., Engineering

*College of Fisheries:*
BEVAN, D. E., PH.D.
BROWN, G. W., PH.D.
BURGNER, R. L., PH.D., Fisheries Research Institute
CHAPMAN, D. G., PH.D., Fisheries, Forest Resources and Mathematics
CHEW, K. K., PH.D.
HALVER, J. D., PH.D.
LISTON, J., PH.D.
MATCHES, J. R., PH.D.
MATHISEN, O. A., PH.D.
NAKATANI, R. E., PH.D.
PIGOTT, G. M., M.S., PH.D.
ROYCE, W. F., PH.D.
SALO, E. O., PH.D.
SCHELL, W. R., PH.D.
SEYMOUR, A. H., PH.D.
SMITH, L. S., M.S., PH.D.
TAUB, FRIEDA, PH.D.
WHITNEY, R. R., M.S., PH.D.
WOOSTER, W. S., PH.D., Fisheries and Marine Studies

*College of Forest Resources:*
ALLAN, G. G., PH.D., Forest Resources and Chemical Engineering
BETHEL, J. S., M.F., D.F.
BRYANT, B. S., M.S.F., D.F.
CHAPMAN, D. G., PH.D., Forest Resources, Fisheries and Mathematics
COLE, D. W., M.S., PH.D.
DOWDLE, B., M.F., PH.D.
DRIVER, C. H., M.S.F., PH.D.
FIELD, D. R., PH.D.
FRITSCHEN, L. J., M.S., PH.D.
GARA, R. I., M.S., PH.D.
GESSEL, S. P., PH.D.
HATHEWAY, W. H., PH.D.
HRUTFIORD, B. F., PH.D.
LEOPOLD, E. B., PH.D., Forest Resources and Botany
MCCARTHY, J. L., PH.D., Forest Resources and Chemical Engineering
MCKEAN, W. T., PH.D.
SARKENEN, K., M.SC., PH.D., Forest Resources and Chemical Engineering
SCHREUDER, G. F., PH.D.
SHARPE, G. W., M.F., PH.D.
SCOTT, D. R. M., M.F., PH.D.
STETTLER, R. F., PH.D.
TABER, R. D., M.S., PH.D.
THOMAS, D. P., M.F.
TURNBULL, K. J., PH.D.
UGOLINI, F. C., PH.D.
WAGGENER, T. R., PH.D.

*Graduate School:*
BENNE, M. M., M.S.L.S., Librarianship
CHISHOLM, M. E., PH.D.
HIATT, P., M.L.S., PH.D., Librarianship
LIEBERMAN, I., M.A., ED.D., School of Librarianship
SHAW, S. G., B.L.S.

*Graduate School of Public Affairs:*
CRUTCHFIELD, J. A., Jr., A.M., PH.D., Public Affairs and Economics
DENNY, B. C., M.A., PH.D., Public Affairs
KROLL, M., PH.D., Public Affairs and Political Science
LOCKE, H. G., M.A.
LYDEN, F. J., PH.D.

## UNIVERSITIES AND COLLEGES—WASHINGTON (UNIVERSITY OF)   U.S.A.

Miles, E. L., ph.d., Public Affairs and Marine Studies
Pealy, R. H., m.p.a., ph.d., Public Affairs
Wenk, E., Jr., ph.d., Public Affairs and Engineering
Williams, W., ph.d., Public Affairs

### School of Dentistry:
Beder, O. E., d.d.s., Prosthodontics
Bolender, C. L., m.s., d.d.s., Prosthodontics
Canfield, R. C., d.d.s., Restorative Dentistry
Cohen, M. M., m.s.d., ph.d., Oral Surgery
Dworkin, S. F., d.d.s., ph.d., Oral Surgery
Fales, M. H., m.a., ph.d., Dental Hygiene
Frank, R. P., d.d.s., Prosthodontics
Gehrig, J. D., d.d.s., m.d.s., Oral Surgery
Guild, R. E., m.s., ph.d., Community Dentistry
Hamilton, A. I., m.a., ph.d., Restorative Dentistry
Harrington, G. W., d.d.s., m.s.d., Endodontics
Hodson, Jean, m.s., Restorative Dentistry
Hooley, J. R., d.d.s., Oral Surgery
Keller, Patricia J., ph.d., Oral Biology
Law, D. B., d.d.s., m.s., Pedodontics
Lewis, T. M., d.d.s., m.s.d., Restorative Dentistry
Luschei, E. S., ph.d., Orthodontics, Physiology and Biophysics
Moffett, B. C., a.b., ph.d., Orthodontics
Morrison, K. N., d.d.s., m.s., Restorative Dentistry
Natkin, E., d.d.s., m.s.d., Endodontics
Nicholls, J. I., ph.d., Restorative Dentistry
Page, R. C., d.d.s., ph.d., Pathology and Periodontics
Palmer, J. M., ph.d., Speech and Hearing Sciences and Prosthodontics
Riedel, R. A., d.d.s., m.s.d., Orthodontics
Robinovitch, M. R., d.d.s., Oral Biology
Siegel, I. A., m.s., ph.d., Oral Biology
Smith, D. E., d.d.s., Prosthodontics
Swoope, C. C., d.d.s., m.s.d., Prosthodontics
Tamarin, A., d.d.s., Oral Biology
Truelove, E. L., d.d.s., Oral Diagnosis
Warnick, M. E., d.d.s., Restorative Dentistry
Yuodelis, R. A., d.d.s., m.s.d., Restorative Dentistry

### School of Law:
Andersen, W. R., ll.m.
Burke, W. T., j.d., j.s.d.
Chisum, D. S., a.b., ll.b.
Corker, C. E., a.b., ll.b.
Cosway, P. R., a.b., ll.b.
Cross, H. M., b.a., ll.b.
Fletcher, R. L., a.b., ll.b.
Gallagher, Marian G., b.a., ll.b., b.a. in lib.sc.
Haley, J. O., ll.m.
Hardisty, J. H., a.b., ll.b.
Henderson, D. F., ph.d.
Hjorth, R. L., a.b., ll.b.
Hume, L. S., j.d.
Hunt, R. S., a.m., s.j.d.
Huston, J. C., ll.m.
Johnson, R. W., b.a., ll.b.
Junker, J. M., j.d.
Kummert, R. O., m.b.a.
Loh, W. D., j.d., ph.d.
Meisenholder, R., j.d., s.j.d.
Morris, A., m.a., ll.m., j.d.
Peck, C. J., b.s., ll.b.
Price, J. R., a.b., ll.b.
Prosterman, R. L., ll.b.
Rieke, L. V., ll.d.
Roddis, R. S., b.a., j.d.
Rodgers, W. H., j.d.
Rombauer, Marjorie, j.d.
Schatzki, G., ll.m.
Smith, C. Z., b.s., ll.b.
Stoebuck, W. B., ll.b., m.a.
Trautman, P. A., b.a., ll.b.
Tunks, L. K., j.d., j.s.d.
Whitman, D. A., ll.b.

### School of Medicine:
Aagaard, G. N., b.s., m.d., Medicine, Pharmacology
Adamson, J. W., m.d., Medicine
Alvord, E. C., b.s., m.d., Pathology
Ansell, J. S., b.a., m.d., ph.d., Urology
Bakker, C. B., b.s., m.d., Psychiatry
Barnes, G. W., ph.d., Urology
Bassingthwaighte, J. B., ph.d., Bioengineering
Baylink, D. J., m.d., Medicine
Becker, J., m.a., ph.d., Psychiatry, Psychology
Beckwith, J. B., b.a., m.d., Pathology and Paediatrics
Benditt, E. P., b.a., m.d., Pathology
Bergman, A. B., m.d., Paediatrics and Health Services
Bierman, E. L., m.d., Medicine
Blackmon, J. R., m.d., Medicine
Blagg, C. R., m.d., Medicine
Blandau, R. J., a.b., ph.d., m.d., Biological Structure
Bodemer, C. W., m.a., ph.d., Biomedical History
Bonica, J. J., m.d., Anaesthesiology
Bornstein, P., a.b., m.d., Medicine and Biochemistry
Bowden, D. M., m.d., Psychiatry
Brengelmann, G., ph.d., Physiology and Biophysics
Bruce, R. A., m.s., m.d., Medicine
Brunzell, J. D., m.d., Medicine
Buchanan, T. M., m.d., Medicine and Pathobiology
Buckner, C. D., m.d., Medicine
Butler, J., ch.b., m.d., Medicine
Carr, J. E., ph.d., Psychiatry and Psychology
Carrico, C. J., m.d., Surgery
Chapman, C. R., ph.d., Anaesthesiology and Psychiatry
Chapman, W. H., b.s., m.d., Urology
Chase, J. D., m.d., Medicine
Chatrian, G. E., m.d., Laboratory Medicine and Neurological Surgery
Cheney, F. W., b.s., m.d., Anaesthesiology
Cobb, L. A., m.d., Medicine
Crill, W. E., m.d., Medicine, Physiology and Biophysics
Croake, J. S., ph.d., Psychiatry
Cummings, C. W., m.d., Otolaryngology
Cutler, R. E., m.d., Medicine
Dale, D. C., m.d., Medicine
Davie, E. W., ph.d., Biochemistry
Deisher, R. W., a.b., m.d., Paediatrics
Delateur, B. J., m.d., Rehabilitation Medicine
Dillard, D. H., m.d., Surgery
Dodge, H. T., m.d., Medicine
Donaldson, J. A., b.a., m.d., Otolaryngology
Dudley, D. L., m.d., Psychiatry
Eisdorfer, C., m.a., ph.d., m.d., Psychiatry
Eliel, L. P., m.d., Medicine
Emanuel, I., m.d., Epidemiology and International Health and Paediatrics
Ensinck, J. W., b.sc., m.d., c.m., Medicine
Evans, C. A., m.d., ph.d., Microbiology
Falkow, S., m.s., ph.d., Microbiology
Fefer, A., m.d., Medicine
Feigl, E., b.a., m.d., Physiology and Biophysics
Fellner, C. H., m.d., Psychiatry
Fetz, E. E., ph.d., Physiology and Biophysics
Fialkow, P. J., a.b., m.d., Medicine and Genetics
Figge, D. C., m.d., Obstetrics and Gynaecology
Figley, M. M., m.d., Radiology
Finch, C. A., b.s., m.d., Medicine
Fink, B. R., b.s., b.sc., m.d., Anaesthesiology
Fischer, E. H., ph.d., Biochemistry
Fletcher, T. L., m.a., ph.d., Surgery
Fordyce, W. E., ph.d., Rehabilitation Medicine
Fowler, R. S., ph.d., Rehabilitation Medicine
Frankel, V. H., m.d., Orthopaedics
Freund, F. G., m.d., Anaesthesiology
Fuchs, A., ph.d., Physiology and Biophysics
Gale, C. C., ph.d., Physiology and Biophysics
Gartler, S. M., b.s., ph.d., Medicine, Genetics
Geyman, J. P., m.d., Family Medicine
Gilliland, B., m.d., Laboratory Medicine and Medicine
Glomset, J. A., m.d., Medicine
Goodner, C. J., b.a., m.d., Medicine
Gordon, A. M., ph.d., Physiology and Biophysics
Gordon, M., ph.d., Biochemistry
Graham, C. B., b.a., m.d., Radiology and Paediatrics
Green, W. L., m.d., Medicine
Groman, N. B., s.b., ph.d., Microbiology
Guntheroth, W. G., m.d., Paediatrics
Guy, A., m.s.e.e., ph.d., Rehabilitation Medicine
Hakomori, S., dr.med.sci., Pathobiology and Microbiology
Hall, J. G., m.d., Medicine and Paediatrics
Hammarsten, J. F., m.d., Medicine
Hamilton, G., m.d., Medicine
Hampson, J. L., m.d., Psychiatry
Hansen, S., m.d., Orthopaedics
Harker, L. A., m.d., Medicine
Hazzard, W. R., m.d., Medicine
Hellstrom, I. E., m.d., Microbiology and Nursing
Hellstrom, K. E., dr.med., Pathology
Henderson, M., d.p.h., Medicine and Health Services
Henney, C. S., ph.d., d.sc., Microbiology
Herman, C. M., m.d., Surgery
Hille, B., b.s., ph.d., Physiology and Biophysics
Hillman, R. S., m.d., Medicine
Hodson, W. A., m.d., m.m.sc., Paediatrics
Hoffman, A. S., sc.d., Bioengineering and Chemical Engineering
Holmes, K. K., m.d., Medicine
Holmes, T. H., III, a.b., m.d., Psychiatry
Horita, A., m.s., ph.d., Pharmacology
Hornbein, T. F., m.d., Anaesthesiology, Physiology and Biophysics
Hutchinson, T. E., ph.d., Bioengineering and Chemical Engineering
Jensen, L. H., b.a., ph.d., Biological Structure and Biochemistry
Johnson, M. H., m.d., Psychiatry
Jones, R. F., m.d., Surgery

Juchau, M. R., ph.d., Pharmacology
Kalina, R. E., b.a., b.s., m.d., Ophthalmology
Kehl, T. H., ph.d., Physiology, Biophysics and Computer Science
Kelley, V. C., b.a., m.b., m.s., m.d., ph.d., Paediatrics
Kelly, W. A., m.d., Neurological Surgery
Kennedy, J. W., m.d., Medicine
Kennedy, T. T., m.s., ph.d., Physiology and Biophysics
Kennedy, W. F., Jr., b.s., m.d., Anaesthesiology
Kirby, W. M. M., b.s., m.d., Medicine
Klebanoff, S. J., ph.d., m.d., Medicine
Kleinman, A. M., m.d., Psychiatry
Koehler, J. K., ph.d., Biological Structure
Kraft, G. H., m.d., Rehabilitation Medicine
Kraus, R. F., m.d., Psychiatry
Krebs, E. G., m.d., Pharmacology
Labbe, R. F., m.s., ph.d., Laboratory Medicine
Lehmann, J. F., m.d., Rehabilitation Medicine
Lein, J. N., m.d., Obstetrics and Gynaecology
Lemire, R. J., m.d., Paediatrics
Lockard, J. S., ph.d., Neurological Surgery
Loeb, L. A., m.d., ph.d., Pathology
Loomis, T. A., m.s., ph.d., m.d., Pharmacology
Loop, J. W., m.d., Radiology
Luft, J. H., b.s., m.d., Biological Structure
Luschei, E. S., ph.d., Physiology and Biophysics
Mackler, B., m.d., Paediatrics
Mannik, M., b.a., m.d., Medicine
Marchioro, T. L., m.d., Surgery
Martin, G. M., b.s., m.d., Pathology
Martin, J. C., ph.d., Psychiatry
McArthur, J. R., m.d., Medicine
Merendino, K. A., b.a., m.d., ph.d., Surgery
Miller, J. M., ph.d., Otolaryngology, Physiology and Biophysics
Morgan, B. C., m.d., Paediatrics
Morris, D. R., ph.d., Biochemistry
Mottet, N. K., b.s., m.d., Pathology
Motulsky, A., b.s., m.d., Genetics and Medicine
Neiman, P. E., m.d., Medicine
Nelp, W. B., m.d., Medicine and Radiology
Nester, E. W., b.s., ph.d., Microbiology
Nishimura, E. T., m.d., Pathology
Norris, H. T., m.d., Pathology
Novack, A. H., m.d., Paediatrics
Ochs, H. D., m.d., Paediatrics
Odland, G. F., m.d., Medicine, Biological Structure
Ojemann, G. A., m.d., Neurological Surgery
Omenn, G. S., m.d., ph.d., Medicine
Page, R. C., d.d.s., ph.d., Pathology and Periodontics
Parson, W. W., ph.d., Biochemistry
Patton, H. D., b.a., ph.d., m.d., Physiology and Biophysics
Paulsen, C. A., m.d., Medicine
Phillips, T. J., b.a., m.d., Family Medicine
Pious, D. A., m.d., Paediatrics
Plorde, J. J., m.d., Laboratory Medicine
Pollack, G. H., ph.d., Anaesthesiology
Pope, C. E., m.d., Medicine
Porte, D. A., b.a., m.d., Medicine
Reichenbach, D. D., m.d., Pathology
Reichler, R. J., m.d., Psychiatry
Ripley, H. S., a.b., m.d., Psychiatry

Robertson, R. P., m.d., Medicine and Pharmacology
Robertson, W. O., b.a., m.d., Paediatrics
Rodieck, R. W., ph.d., Ophthalmology
Roosen-Runge, E. R. C., m.d., Biological Structure
Ross, R., d.d.s., ph.d., Pathology
Rosse, C., m.b.ch.b., m.d., Biological Structure
Rothenberg, M. B., a.b., m.d., Psychiatry and Paediatrics
Rowell, L. B., ph.d., Physiology, Biophysics and Medicine
Rubin, C. E., a.b., m.d., Medicine
Rushmer, R. F., b.s., m.d., Bioengineering
Ruvalcaba, R., m.d., Paediatrics
Saunders, D. R., m.d., Medicine
Schaller, J., m.d., Paediatrics
Scher, A. M., b.a., ph.d., Physiology and Biophysics
Schilling, J. A., a.b., m.d., Surgery
Schmer, G., m.d., Laboratory Medicine
Scott, C. R., m.d., Paediatrics
Scribner, B. H., a.b., m.d., m.s., Medicine
Shapiro, B. M., m.d., Biochemistry
Sherrard, D. J., m.d., Medicine
Shaw, C., m.d., Pathology
Shepard, T. H., b.a., m.d., Paediatrics
Sherris, J. C., b.s., m.d., Microbiology
Shurtleff, D. B., m.d., Paediatrics
Smith, A. L., m.d., Paediatrics
Smith, D. W., a.b., m.d., Paediatrics
Smith, N. J., b.a., m.d., Paediatrics and Orthopaedics
Smith, O. A., Jr., m.a., ph.d., Physiology and Biophysics
Spadoni, L. R., b.s., m.d., Obstetrics and Gynaecology
Staheli, L. T., m.d., Orthopaedics
Stahl, W., ph.d., Medicine, Physiology and Biophysics
Stamatoyannopoulos G., Dr., Medicine
Stenchever, M. A., m.d., Obstetrics and Gynaecology
Stevenson, J. K., m.d., Surgery
Stolov, W. C., m.d., Rehabilitation Medicine
Storb, R., m.d., Medicine
Strandjord, P. E., m.a., m.d., Laboratory Medicine
Strandness, D. E., m.d., Surgery
Streissguth, A. P., ph.d., Psychiatry
Striker, G. E., m.d., Pathology
Sumi, S. M., m.d., Medicine and Pathology
Swanson, P. D., b.s., m.d., Medicine
Teller, D. C., ph.d., Biochemistry
Thomas, E. D., m.a., m.d., Medicine
Towe, A. L., ph.d., Physiology and Biophysics
Turck, M., m.d., Medicine
VanArsdel, P. P., b.s., m.d., Medicine
VanCitters, R. L., m.d., Physiology and Biophysics, Medicine
Van Hoosier, G. L., d.v.m., Pathology
Vincenzi, F. F., ph.d., Pharmacology
Volwiler, W., a.b., m.d., Medicine
Vracko, R., m.d., Pathology
Wallace, J. F., m.d., Medicine
Walsh, K. A., m.s., ph.d., Biochemistry
Ward, A. A., b.a., m.d., Neurological Surgery
Ward, R. J., m.d., Anaesthesiology
Wedgwood, R. J., m.d., Paediatrics
Whiteley, Helen R., m.a., ph.d., Microbiology
Wiederhielm, C., ph.d., Physiology and Biophysics
Winterscheid, L. C., b.a., m.d., Surgery
Wootton, P., Radiation Oncology

*School of Nursing:*
Barnard, K. E., m.s., ph.d., Maternal and Child Nursing
Batey, Marjorie V., m.s., ph.d., Community Health Care Systems
Benoliel, J. Q., d.n.s., Community Health Care Systems
Crowley, D. M., ph.d., Physiological Nursing
deTornyay, R., ed.d., Community Health Care Systems
Disbrow, M. A., m.s., ph.d., Maternal and Child Nursing
Giblin, Elizabeth, C., m.d., ed.d., Physiological Nursing
Heinemann, E., m.n., Psychosocial Nursing
Horn, B. J., ph.d., Community Health Care Systems
Little, Delores E., m.n., Community Health Care Systems
Murillo-Rohde, I., ph.d., Community Health Care Systems
Nakagawa, H., ph.d., Psychosocial Nursing
O'Neil, S. M., ph.d., Maternal and Child Nursing
Osborne, O. H., m.a., ph.d., Psychosocial Nursing
Patrick, M. I., m.n., d.p.h., Physiological Nursing

*School of Pharmacy:*
Brady, L. R., m.s., ph.d.
Campbell, W. H., ph.d.
Gibaldi, M., ph.d.
Hall, N. A., b.s., ph.d.
Hammarlund, E. R., m.s., ph.d.
Krupski, E., m.s., ph.d.
Levy, R. H., ph.d.
McCarthy, W. C., ph.d.
Nelson, W. L., ph.d.
Orr, J. E., ph.d.
Plein, J. B., ph.d.
Romano, J. A., pharm.d.
Trager, W. F., ph.d.

*School of Social Work:*
Austin, M. J., ph.d.
Briar, S., d.s.w.
Farber, A. S., m.s.
Gottlieb, N. R., d.s.w.
Jaffee, B., d.s.w.
Maier, H. W., m.s.sc., ph.d.
Nash, K. B., d.s.w.
Northwood, K. K., ph.d.
Patti, R. J., d.s.w.
Resnick, H., ph.d.
Stier, Florence, m.s.
Takagi, C. Y., m.s.w., ph.d.
Whittaker, J. K., ph.d.

*School of Public Health and Community Medicine:*
Alexander, E. R., s.b., m.d., Epidemiology
Bell, C. B., ph.d., Biostatistics
Bergman, A. B., m.d., Health Services
Bice, T. W., ph.d., Health Services
Boatman, E. S., ph.d., Environmental Health
Breslow, N. E., ph.d., Biostatistics
Buchanan, T. L., m.d., Pathobiology and Medicine
Cooney, M. K., ph.d., Pathobiology
Day, R. W., ph.d., Health Services
Dowling, W. L., ph.d., Health Services
Emanuel, I., m.d., Epidemiology and Paediatrics
Feigl, P., ph.d., Biostatistics
Fisher, L. D., m.a., ph.d., Biostatistisc
Foy, H. M., m.d., Epidemiology
Frank, N. R., a.b., m.d., Environmental Health
Gale, J. L., m.d., Epidemiology

Gilson, B. S., M.D., Health Services
Grayston, J. T., M.S., M.D., Epidemiology
Hakomori, S., M.D., Pathobiology and Microbiology
Henderson, M. M., D.P.H., Health Services
Jackson, K. L., PH.D., Environmental Health
Kenny, G. E., PH.D., Pathobiology
Kronmal, R. A., PH.D., Biostatistics
Kuo, C.-C., PH.D., Pathobiology
Lee, J. A., M.D., Epidemiology and Environmental Health
McCaffree, K. M., PH.D., Health Services
Martin, D. C., PH.D., Biostatistics
Perrin, E. B., PH.D., Health Services
Peterson, D. R., M.D., Epidemiology
Prentice, R. L., PH.D., Biostatistics
Rausch, R. L., D.V.M., PH.D., Pathobiology
Richardson, W. C., PH.D., Health Services
Riedel, D. C., PH.D., Health Services
Shortell, S. M., PH.D., Health Services
Thompson, D. J., PH.D., Biostatistics
Van Belle, G., PH.D., Biostatistics
Wang, S., M.PH.D., Pathobiology
Weiss, N. S., M.D., D.P.H., Epidemiology
Wilson, J. T., M.D., SC.D., Environmental Health

## WALLA WALLA COLLEGE
COLLEGE PLACE, WASHINGTON 99324

Telephone: (509) 527-2121.

Founded 1892.

*President:* N. Clifford Sorensen.
*Vice-President for Academic Affairs:* D. Malcolm Maxwell.
*Vice-President for Student Affairs:* D. D. Lake.
*Vice-President for Financial Affairs:* Richard A. Beck.
*Vice-President for Recruitment and Public Relations:* Verne Wehtje.
*Vice-President for Development:* Robert Spies.
*Director of Admissions and Records:* Orpha Osborne.
*Librarian:* E. L. Mabley.

The library contains 135,100 vols.
Number of teachers: 150.
Number of students: 2,000.

## WASHINGTON STATE UNIVERSITY
PULLMAN, WASHINGTON 99164

Telephone: 335-3564.

Founded (as College) 1890; University 1959.

Academic year: September to June.

*President:* Glenn Terrell, PH.D.
*Academic Vice-President and Provost:* Albert C. Yates, PH.D.
*Vice-President for Business and Finance:* George A. Hartford, Jr., M.S.
*Dean of Student Affairs:* Arthur E. McCartan, M.S.

*Registrar:* C. J. Quann, D.ED.
*Librarian:* Allene F. Schnaitter, PH.D.

The library contains 1,189,899 volumes.

Number of teachers: 1,108, including 361 professors.
Number of students: 17,468.

DEANS:

*College of Agriculture:* John S. Robins, PH.D.
*College of Economics and Business:* Rom J. Markin, Jr., D.B.A.
*College of Education:* G. B. Brain, ED.D.
*College of Engineering:* C. W. Hall, PH.D.
*Graduate School:* C. J. Nyman, Jr., PH.D.
*College of Home Economics:* Alberta D. Hill, ED.D.
*Intercollegiate Center for Nursing Education, Spokane:* Laura C. Dustan, ED.D.
*College of Pharmacy:* Larry M. Simonsmeier, J.D. (acting).
*College of Sciences and Arts:* R. A. Nilan, PH.D. (Natural Sciences), Lois B. DeFleur, PH.D. (Humanities and Social Sciences).
*College of Veterinary Medicine:* Leo K. Bustad, D.V.M., PH.D.

## WESTERN WASHINGTON UNIVERSITY
BELLINGHAM, WASHINGTON 98225

Telephone: 676-3000.

Founded 1893 as Bellingham Normal School, name changed to Western Washington College of Education 1937, finally Western Washington University 1977.

*President:* Paul J. Olscamp.
*Vice-President for Academic Affairs and Provost:* James L. Talbot.
*Vice-President for Business and Financial Affairs:* Donald H. Cole.
*Vice-President for Student Affairs:* Thomas E. Quinlan.
*Librarian:* Dr. W. R. Lawyer.

Library of 470,000 vols.
Number of teachers: 495.
Number of students: 10,016.

## WHITMAN COLLEGE
BOYER AVE., WALLA WALLA, WASHINGTON 99362

Telephone: (509) 527-5111.

Founded 1859.

*President:* Robert A. Skotheim.
*Registrar:* R. Polzin.
*Librarian:* A. D. Jonish.

The library contains 272,724 vols.

Number of teachers: 85 full-time.
Number of students: 1,140.

## WHITWORTH COLLEGE
SPOKANE, WASHINGTON 99251

Telephone: (509) 466-1000.

Founded 1890.

*President:* Dr. Duncan S. Ferguson (acting).
*Vice-President, Academic Affairs:* (vacant).
*Librarian:* Dr. Ralph W. Franklin.

The library contains 75,500 vols.
Number of teachers: 69.
Number of students: 1,350.

# WEST VIRGINIA

## ALDERSON-BROADDUS COLLEGE
PHILIPPI, WEST VIRGINIA 26416

Telephone: (304) 457-1700.

Founded 1871.

Academic year: September to July (four terms).

*President:* Dr. Richard E. Shearer, M.A., ED.D., D.D., LL.D., H.H.D.
*Vice-President for Academic and Related Affairs:* W. C. Johnson.
*Vice-President of College Relations and Development:* Donald A. Smith.
*Dean of Instruction:* Robert V. Digman.
*Dean of Students:* I. Jean Fenstermacher.
*Business Manager:* L. V. Lobello.
*Registrar:* Martha Rose Roy.
*Director of Admissions:* Kenneth H. Yount.
*Librarian:* William B. Wartman III.

The library contains 89,000 vols.
Number of teachers: 63 full-time, 30 part-time.
Number of students: 878.

## BETHANY COLLEGE
BETHANY, WEST VIRGINIA 26032

Founded 1840.

*President:* Todd H. Bullard.
*Vice-President and Provost for College Advancement:* R. A. Sandercox.
*Dean of Faculty:* W. Daniel Cobb III.
*Dean of Students:* John S. Cunningham.
*Treasurer and Business Manager:* J. A. Graham.
*Registrar:* J. M. Kurey.
*Librarian:* Nancy Sandercox.

The library contains 141,847 vols.
Number of teachers: 60.
Number of students: 900.

Publications: *The Harbinger*, *The Bethanian* (annually), *Tower* (weekly), *Bethany College Bulletin*† (quarterly).

### BLUEFIELD STATE COLLEGE
BLUEFIELD,
WEST VIRGINIA 24701
Telephone: 325-7102.
Founded 1895.

*President:* Jerold O. Dugger, ed.d.
*Registrar:* Richard H. Snow, m.s.
*Library Director:* Michael B. Pate, m.a.l.

The library contains 100,000 vols.
Number of teachers: 72.
Number of students: 2,723.

### CONCORD COLLEGE
ATHENS, WEST VIRGINIA 24712
Telephone: (304) 384-3115.
Founded 1872.

*President:* Dr. M. N. Freeman, ed.d.
*Vice-President and Academic Dean:* Craig D. Willis.
*Registrar:* N. Price.
*Librarian:* Michael B. Pate.

The library contains 172,000 vols.
Number of teachers: 81.
Number of students: c. 2,081.

### DAVIS AND ELKINS COLLEGE
ELKINS,
WEST VIRGINIA 26241
Telephone: 636-1900.
Founded 1904.

*President:* Gordon E. Hermanson.
*Vice-President and Dean of the Faculty:* Margaret P. Goddin.
*Vice-President for Business Affairs:* Harry Thompson.
*Vice-President for Development:* Nevin E. Kendell.
*Vice-President for Student Affairs:* Guy Sievert.
*Director of Admissions:* Blaine Steensland.
*Registrar:* John Neill.
*Director of the Library:* Douglas D. Oleson.

The library contains 80,000 vols.
Number of teachers: 53 full-time, 29 part-time.
Number of students: 1,098.

### FAIRMONT STATE COLLEGE*
FAIRMONT,
WEST VIRGINIA 26554
Telephone: Fairmont 367-4000.
Founded 1867.

*President:* Wendell G. Hardway.
*Registrar:* Otis H. Milam, Jr.
*Librarian:* Mrs. Josephine L. Rosier.

The library contains 72,000 volumes.
Number of teachers: 150.
Number of students: 5,072.

* No reply received to our questionnaire this year.

### GLENVILLE STATE COLLEGE
GLENVILLE, WEST VIRGINIA 26351
Telephone: (304) 462-7361.
Founded 1872.

*President:* Dr. William K. Simmons.
*Dean of Academic Affairs:* Dr. James W. Peterson.
*Librarian:* David M. Gillespie.

The library contains 96,000 vols.
Number of teachers: 89.
Number of students: 1,777.

### MARSHALL UNIVERSITY
HUNTINGTON,
WEST VIRGINIA 25701
Telephone: (304) 696-3170.
Founded 1837.

*President:* Dr. Robert B. Hayes.
*Provost:* Dr. Olen E. Jones, Jr.
*Vice-President, Administration:* Karl J. Egnatoff.
*Vice-President, Financial Affairs:* Michael F. Thomas.
*Vice-President, Medical School:* Dr. Robert W. Coon.
*Vice-President, Community College:* Dr. Paul Hines.
*Dean of Student Affairs:* Dr. Nell Bailey.
*Director, Athletics:* Lynn J. Snyder.
*Director, Development:* Dr. Bernard Queen.
*Director of Libraries:* Dr. Kenneth T. Slack.
*Director of University Relations:* C. T. Mitchell.

DEANS:
*College of Education:* Dr. Philip J. Rusche.
*College of Liberal Arts:* Dr. Alan B. Gould.
*College of Business:* Dr. Sara Anderson.
*College of Science:* Dr. E. S. Hanrahan.
*Graduate School:* Dr. Paul Stewart.

The library contains 350,000 vols.
Number of teachers: 400 full-time.
Number of students: 11,500.

### SALEM COLLEGE
SALEM, WEST VIRGINIA 26426
Telephone: (304) 782-5011.
Founded 1888.

*President:* James C. Stam.
*Dean of the College:* Ronald O. Champagne.
*Registrar:* D. K. Zwiebel.
*Librarian:* Myron J. Smith.

The library contains 100,000 vols.
Number of teachers: 55 full-time and 12 part-time.
Number of students: 900.

### SHEPHERD COLLEGE
SHEPHERDSTOWN,
WEST VIRGINIA 25443
Telephone: (304) 876-2511.
Founded 1871.

*President:* Dr. James A. Butcher.
*Dean:* (vacant).
*Librarian:* George Gaumond.

The library contains 157,990 vols.
Number of teachers: 107.
Number of students: 3,001.

### UNIVERSITY OF CHARLESTON
2300 MacCorkle Ave. S.E.,
CHARLESTON,
WEST VIRGINIA 25304
Telephone: 346-9471.

Founded 1888 as Morris Harvey College, present name 1980.

*President:* Thomas G. Voss.
*Provost:* Sally M. Horner.
*Vice-President and Dean of Admissions:* E. Norman Jones.
*Vice-President for Finance and Administration:* Neil McDade.
*Librarian:* Frank W. Badger.

Library of 85,000 vols.
Number of teachers: 75.
Number of students: 1,856.

DEANS:
*College of Arts and Sciences:* Sally M. Horner.
*College of Health Sciences:* Leslie W. Melton.
*College of Business:* Robert Hieronymus (acting).
*Student Life:* John H. Taylor.

### WEST LIBERTY STATE COLLEGE
WEST LIBERTY,
WEST VIRGINIA 26074
Telephone: (304) 336-5000.
Founded 1837.

*President:* Dr. James L. Chapman.
*Director of College Relations and Alumni Affairs:* C. F. Beall.
*Registrar and Director of Admissions:* E. N. Cain.
*Librarian:* D. R. Strong.

The library contains 160,000 vols.
Number of teachers: 150.
Number of students: 2,708.

### WEST VIRGINIA INSTITUTE OF TECHNOLOGY
MONTGOMERY,
WEST VIRGINIA 25136
Telephone: (304) 442-3071.
Founded 1895.

*President:* Dr. Leonard C. Nelson.
*Registrar:* Elvin E. Dillon.

*Director of Admissions:* ROBERT P. SCHOLL, Jr.
*Librarian:* V. C. YOUNG.

The library contains 134,708 vols.
Number of teachers: 190.
Number of students: 3,343.

## WEST VIRGINIA STATE COLLEGE
INSTITUTE,
WEST VIRGINIA 25112

Founded 1891 as a land-grant college by West Virginia Legislature.

*President:* FLOYDELH ANDERSON, D.ED. (acting).
*Provost for Academic Affairs:* ANCELLA BICKLEY, ED.D.
*Director of Fiscal Affairs:* JAMES GERMAN.
*Co-ordinator of Recruitment:* SHARON ZITZELSBURGER.
*Director of Registration and Records:* JOHN L. FULLER.
*Director of Planning and Research:* GARY W. GRAFF, PH.D.
*Librarian:* J. E. SCOTT.

The library contains 210,000 vols.
Number of teachers: 132 full-time, 98 part-time.
Number of students: 4,366.

## WEST VIRGINIA UNIVERSITY
MORGANTOWN,
WEST VIRGINIA 26506

Founded 1867.

*President:* HARRY B. HEFLIN, PH.D.
*Vice-President and Provost for Academic Affairs:* B. A. NUGENT, PH.D.
*Vice-President for Administration:* R. M. HAAS, D.B.A.
*Vice-President for Energy Studies, Research and Graduate Programs:* R. KOPPELMAN, PH.D.
*Vice-President for Health Sciences:* W. ROBERT BIDDINGTON, D.D.S. (acting).
*Dean of Admissions and Records:* J. BRISBANE, ED.D.
*Dean of Library Services:* R. F. MUNN, PH.D.
*Vice-President for Student Affairs:* GEORGE D. TAYLOR, ED.D.

Library: see Libraries.
Number of faculty: 2,043.
Number of students: 21,220.

Publications: *Victorian Poetry, West Virginia Agriculture and Forestry, Small Business Management Journal.*

DEANS:

*College of Agriculture and Forestry:* DALE W. ZINN, PH.D.
*Center for Extension and Continuing Education:* RONALD L. STUMP, M.S.
*College of Arts and Sciences:* WILLIAM E. COLLINS, PH.D.
*College of Business and Economics:* J. T. TURNER, D.B.A.
*Creative Arts Center:* WAYNE M. SHELEY, D.M.A.

*School of Dentistry:* JAMES E. OVERBERGER, D.D.S. (acting).
*College of Engineering:* CURTIS J. TOMPKINS, PH.D.
*Graduate School:* S. WEARDEN, PH.D.
*College of Human Resources and Education:* W. G. MONAHAN, ED.D.
*School of Journalism:* G. H. STEWART, PH.D.
*College of Law:* E. GORDON GEE, J.D., ED.D.
*School of Medicine:* J. E. JONES, M.D.
*College of Mineral and Energy Resources:* GEORGE W. FUMICH, L.L.D.
*School of Pharmacy:* SIDNEY A. ROSENBLUTH, PH.D.
*School of Nursing:* LORITA D. JENAR, ED.D.
*School of Physical Education:* J. WILLIAM DOUGLAS, PH.D.
*School of Social Work:* JOHN J. MILLER, ED.D.

## WEST VIRGINIA WESLEYAN COLLEGE
BUCKHANNON,
WEST VIRGINIA 26201

Founded 1890.

*President:* HUGH A. LATIMER.
*Chairman of the Board of Trustees:* JAMES R. THOMAS II.
*Secretary of the Board of Trustees:* Rev. ROBERT A. CHANDLER.
*Vice-President for Academic Affairs and Dean of the College:* KENNETH B. WELLIVER.
*Vice-President for Administrative Affairs:* PATTON L. NICKELL, Jr.
*Vice-President for College Advancement:* DAVID G. PUDDINGTON.

The library contains 124,000 vols.
Number of teachers: 124.
Number of students: 1,800.

Publications: *College Bulletin, Sundial, Murmurmontis.*

## WHEELING COLLEGE
WHEELING,
WEST VIRGINIA 26003

Founded 1954.

*President:* Rev. CHARLES L. CURRIE, S.J.
*Academic Vice-President:* Dr. JEANNE H. KAMMER (acting).
*Vice-President of Student Affairs:* FREDERICK LAMBERT.
*Vice-President of Development:* PATRICK M. JOYCE.
*Dean of Instruction:* Dr. RICHARD MULLIN.
*Director of Financial Administration:* (vacant).
*Director of Admissions:* KENNETH J. RUDZKI.
*Director of Public Relations:* ARLENE H. HOUSER.
*Registrar:* KATHERINE L. MCCREADY.
*Librarian:* EILEEN R. CARPINO.

Library of 108,000 vols.
Number of students: 1,026.

# WISCONSIN

## ALVERNO COLLEGE
3401 SOUTH 39 STREET,
MILWAUKEE, WISCONSIN 53215

Telephone: 647-3999.

Founded 1887.

*President:* Sister JOEL READ.
*Registrar:* Sister MADELINE MEYER.
*Dean:* Sister AUSTIN DOHERTY.
*Director of Admissions:* STEPHANIE CHAPKO.
*Director of Development:* ROSE O'ROURKE.
*Director of Library/Media Center:* CATHLEEN KRZYMINSKI.

The library contains 175,000 vols.
Number of teachers: 74 full-time, 34 part-time.
Number of students: 682 full-time, 704 part-time.

## BELOIT COLLEGE
BELOIT, WISCONSIN 53511

Chartered 1846.

*President:* ROGER H. HULL, S.J.D.
*Vice-President for Academic Affairs:* FRANK WONG, PH.D.
*Vice-President for Administration:* ERWIN F. ZUEHLKE.
*Dean of Students:* LINDA LEE.

The library contains 225,000 vols.
Number of teachers: 80.
Number of students: 1,000

Publications: *The Round Table* (weekly), *Avatar* (annual), *Beloit Magazine* (3 a year).

## CARDINAL STRITCH COLLEGE
6801 N. YATES ROAD,
MILWAUKEE, WISCONSIN 53217

Telephone: (414) 352-5400.

Founded 1937.

*President:* Sister M. CAMILLE KLIEBHAN, O.S.F.
*Registrar:* Sister FRANCES MARIE DELANY, O.S.F.
*Librarian:* Sister COLETTE ZIRBES, O.S.F.

The library contains 94,000 vols.
Number of teachers: 101.
Number of students: 1,190.

## CARROLL COLLEGE
WAUKESHA, WISCONSIN 53186

Telephone: (414) 547-1211.

Founded 1846

*President:* R. V. CRAMER, PH.D.
*Vice-President and Provost:* MORRIS N. SPENCER, PH.D.
*Vice-President for Administration:* JON GROTELUSCHEN.

The library contains 160,000 vols.

Number of teachers: 100.
Number of students: 1,150.
Publications: Carroll College Catalog†, The Quarterly Report†.

### EDGEWOOD COLLEGE
855 WOODROW ST., MADISON, WISCONSIN 53711
Telephone: (608) 257-4861.
Founded 1927.

Four-year liberal arts college; co-educational.

President: Sister ALICE O'ROURKE, O.P.
Registrar: Sister DOLORES GRASSE.
Academic Dean: Sister JEAN MCSWEENEY, O.P.
Librarian: Sister MARY JEROME HEYMAN, O.P.

The library contains 83,000 vols.
Number of teachers: 72.
Number of students: 625.

### LAKELAND COLLEGE
SHEBOYGAN, WISCONSIN 53081
Telephone: (414) 565-2111.
Founded 1862.

President: Dr. RICHARD E. HILL.
Dean: Dr. KEITH STRIGGOW.
Librarian: CHARLOTTE WELLS.

The library contains 70,000 vols.
Number of teachers: 35.
Number of students: 600.

### LAWRENCE UNIVERSITY
APPLETON, WISCONSIN 54912
Telephone: (414) 735-6500.

Founded 1847 as Lawrence College; University 1964.

President: RICHARD WARCH.
Dean of the University Faculty: J. MICHAEL HITTLE.
Dean of Campus Life: RICHARD AGNESS.
Registrar: DONALD C. ROSENTHAL.
Librarian: D. N. RIBBENS.

Number of teachers: 103, including 36 professors.
Number of students: 1,158.
Publications: Bulletin, Annual Report, etc.

DEANS:
Conservatory: COLIN MURDOCH.
Dean of Student Affairs: C. F. LAUTER.

### MARIAN COLLEGE OF FOND DU LAC
45 SOUTH NATIONAL AVE., FOND DU LAC, WISCONSIN 54935
Telephone: (414) 921-3900.
Founded 1936.

President: Dr. LEO KRZYWKOWSKI.
Dean of Admissions: JEROME WIEDMEYER.

Librarian: Sister MARY PATRICK, C.S.A.
The library contains 74,000 volumes.
Number of teachers: 75.
Number of students: 500.

### MARQUETTE UNIVERSITY
MILWAUKEE, WISCONSIN 53233
Telephone: (414) 224-7302.

Founded 1864 as Marquette College; chartered as a university in 1907.

President: Rev. JOHN P. RAYNOR, S.J., M.A., PH.D.
Executive Vice-President: QUENTIN L. QUADE, M.A., PH.D.
Vice-Presidents: Rev. BRUCE BIEVER, S.J., M.A., PH.L., S.T.L., PH.D., R. O. KALLENBERGER, M.S., EDWARD D. SIMMONS, M.A., PH.D., J. L. SANKOVITZ, M.S., J. H. SCOTT, M.A., ED.D.
Registrar: R. S. GAWKOSKI, M.A., PH.D.

Number of books in library: 700,000.
Number of teachers: 850.
Number of students: 13,932.

Publications: Marquette News and Views (monthly), Medieval Philosophical Texts and Translations (irregularly), Aquinas Lectures (annually), The Marquette Law Review (quarterly), The Marquette Journal (6 times a year), The Marquette Tribune (twice weekly), Renascence Magazine (quarterly), Marquette Today (quarterly), The Marquette Engineer (quarterly).

DEANS AND DIRECTORS:
College of Business Administration: THOMAS A. BAUSCH, D.B.A.
School of Dentistry: R. V. BROWN, D.D.S., M.S.
Dental Hygiene Program: TILLIE D. GINSBERG, D.H., B.A., M.ED.
School of Education: Rev. THOMAS C. HENNESSY, S.J., M.A., PH.D.
College of Engineering: R. J. KIPP, M.S., PH.D.
Graduate School: JOHN K. C. OH, PH.D.
College of Journalism: JAMES F. SCOTTON, PH.D.
Law School: R. F. BODEN, J.D.
College of Liberal Arts: Rev. FREDERICK J. DILLEMUTH, S.J., M.S., S.T.L., PH.D.
Medical Technology Program: ALICE M. SEMRAD, M.S.
Physical Therapy Program: RICHARD JENSEN, M.S., PH.D.
College of Nursing: Sister M. ROSALIE KLEIN, O.S.F., D.SC.
School of Speech: MICHAEL J. PRICE, M.A.
Summer Session and Continuing Education: ROBERT L. HASENSTAB, M.ED., PH.D.

### MOUNT MARY COLLEGE
2900 NORTH MENOMONEE RIVER PARKWAY, MILWAUKEE, WISCONSIN 53222
Telephone: (414) 258-4810.
Founded 1913.

President: Sister ELLEN LORENZ, ED.D.

Academic Dean: Sister LUETTA WOLF, PH.D.
Co-ordinator of Admissions: Mrs. MARY JANE REILLY.
Librarian: Sister ANNE LUCY HOFFMAN, M.A.

The library contains 100,000 vols.
Number of teachers: 115.
Number of students: 1,170.

### NORTHLAND COLLEGE
ASHLAND, WISCONSIN 54806
Telephone: 682-4531.
Founded 1892.

President: MALCOLM MCLEAN.
Director of Admissions and Records: R. P. MACKEY.
Librarian: T. T. SURPRENANT.

The library contains 60,000 volumes.
Number of teachers: 50.
Number of students: 748.

### RIPON COLLEGE
P.O.B. 248,
RIPON, WISCONSIN 54971
Founded 1851.

President: BERNARD S. ADAMS, PH.D., LL.D.
Vice-President and Dean of Faculty: DOUGLAS A. NORTHROP, PH.D.
Vice-President and Dean of Students: ROBERT H. YOUNG, PH.D.
Director of Libraries: SARAH M. MCGOWAN, M.L.S.

The library contains 114,000 vols.
Number of teachers: 81, including 29 full professors.
Number of students: 526 men, 404 women, total 930.

DEANS:
Admissions: JOHN C. CORSO, A.B.
Men: D. L. HARRIS, M.A., LITT.M.
Women: HELEN I. TUTTLE, ED.D.

### ST. NORBERT COLLEGE
DE PERE, WISCONSIN 54115
Telephone: (414) 337-3181.
Founded 1898.

President: N. J. WEBB.
Dean of the College: ROBERT L. HORN.
Registrar: JON CURTIS.
Librarian: EUGENE BUNKER.

The library contains 119,000 vols.
Number of teachers: 86 full-time, 17 part-time.
Number of students: 1,625.

### SILVER LAKE COLLEGE OF THE HOLY FAMILY
MANITOWOC, WISCONSIN 54220
Telephone: 684-6691.
Founded 1935.

President: Sister ANNE KENNEDY.
Registrar: Sister JANICE STINGLE.
Librarian: Sister MARY JOHN WOOD.

UNIVERSITIES AND COLLEGES—WISCONSIN

The library contains 60,820 volumes (approx.).
Number of teachers: 44 full-time.
Number of students: 346.

## UNIVERSITY OF WISCONSIN SYSTEM
MADISON, WISCONSIN 53706
Founded 1848.

In 1971 the University of Wisconsin system merged with the Wisconsin State University system. There are 13 four-year institutions (see below).

*President:* ROBERT M. O'NEIL.
*Executive Vice-President:* JOSEPH F. KAUFFMAN.
*Vice-President and Trust Officer:* REUBEN LORENZ.
*Vice-President for General Services:* ROBERT W. WINTER, JR.
Number of students (26 campuses): c. 155,499.

### University Center System
*Chancellor:* ROBERT R. POLK (acting).
Provides lower-division programmes (2-year) at 13 campuses.
Number of students: 8,700.

DEANS:
*Baraboo-Sauk County Campus:* AURAL UMHOEFER.
*Barron County Campus:* JOHN MEGGERS.
*Fond du Lac County Campus:* W. HENKEN.
*Fox Valley County Campus:* R. JOHNSON.
*Manitowoc County Campus:* C. NATUNEWICZ.
*Marathon County Campus:* STEPHEN PORTCH.
*Marinette County Campus:* W. A. SCHMIDTKE.
*Marshfield-Wood County Campus:* N. E. KOOPMAN.
*Richland County Campus:* D. GRAY.
*Rock County Campus:* THOMAS WALTERMAN.
*Sheboygan County Campus:* K. BAILEY.
*Washington County Campus:* R. THOMPSON.
*Waukesha County Campus:* MARY KNUDTEN.

## UNIVERSITY OF WISCONSIN—EAU CLAIRE
EAU CLAIRE, WISCONSIN 54701
Telephone: 836-2326.
Founded 1916.

*Chancellor:* Dr. M. EMILY HANNAH.
*Assistant Chancellor for Administrative Services:* J. BOLLINGER.
*Assistant Chancellor for Budget and Development:* C. BAUER.
*Assistant Chancellor for Student Affairs:* Dr. O. L. HARRY.
*Registrar:* Dr. LAWRENCE S. BUNDY.
*Librarian:* Dr. STEVE R. MARQUARDT.

The library contains 643,647 vols.
Number of teachers: 670.
Number of students: 11,054.

DEANS:
*School of Arts and Sciences:* Dr. LEE E. GRUGEL.
*School of Graduate Studies:* R. D. DICK.
*School of Business:* J. F. WENNER.
*School of Education:* R. H. JOHNSON.
*School of Nursing:* SUZANNE VAN ORT.

## UNIVERSITY OF WISCONSIN EXTENSION
MADISON, WISCONSIN 53706
*Chancellor:* J. C. EVANS, PH.D.

DEANS:
*Professional and Human Development:* H. W. MONTROSS, PH.D.
*Economic and Environmental Development:* ROBERT E. RIECK, PH.D.
*Educational Communications:* L. F. LAMB, PH.D.
*Urban Outreach:* M. HABERMAN, PH.D.
*Community Programs:* MARVIN T. BEATTY, PH.D.

## UNIVERSITY OF WISCONSIN—GREEN BAY
GREEN BAY, WISCONSIN 54302
Founded 1968.

*Chancellor:* Dr. EDWARD W. WEIDNER.
*Associate Chancellor:* Dr. DONALD F. HARDEN.
*Vice-Chancellor for Academic Affairs:* Dr. WILLIAM G. KUEPPER.

The library contains 350,896 vols., regional depository for Wisconsin and U.S. government documents, etc.
Number of students: 4,000.

Publications: *UWGB Undergraduate Catalog* (every 2 years), *Inside UWGB* (2 a year), *UWGB Graduate Catalog* (every 2 years).

## UNIVERSITY OF WISCONSIN—LA CROSSE
1725 STATE STREET,
LA CROSSE, WISCONSIN 54601
Telephone: (608) 785-8000.
Founded 1909.

*Chancellor:* NOEL J. RICHARDS.
*Vice-Chancellor:* W. CARL WIMBERLY.
*Assistant Chancellor:* DAVID R. WITMER.
*Registrar:* R. O. LEROY.
*Director of Admissions:* G. GRIMSLID.
*Librarian:* D. GRESSETH.

The library contains 491,000 vols.
Number of teachers: 440.
Number of students: 8,896.
Publication: *Voyages to the Inland Sea* (annually).

## UNIVERSITY OF WISCONSIN—MADISON
MADISON, WISCONSIN 53706
*Chancellor:* IRVING SHAIN.

*Vice-Chancellor for Academic Affairs:* BRYANT KEARL.
*Vice-Chancellor for Health Sciences:* DAVID A. KINDIG.
*Vice-Chancellor for Administration:* LEN VAN ESS.
*Registrar:* T. H. HOOVER.
*Director of Admissions:* D. E. VINSON.
*Director of Libraries:* J. TREYZ.
*Secretary of the Faculty:* PETER BUNN.
Library: *see* Libraries.
Number of teachers: 2,116.
Number of students: 40,233.

DEANS:
*College of Letters and Science:* E. DAVID CRONON
*College of Engineering:* J. G. BOLLINGER.
*College of Agriculture and Life Sciences:* LEO M. WALSH.
*School of Education:* JOHN R. PALMER.
*School of Business:* ROBERT H. BOCK.
*School of Pharmacy:* A. P. LEMBERGER.
*Law School:* ORRIN HELSTAD.
*Medical School:* ARNOLD L. BROWN.
*School of Nursing:* VALENCIA PROCK.
*Graduate School:* R. M. BOCK.
*School of Veterinary Medicine:* B. C. EASTERDAY.
*School of Allied Health Professions:* ISABEL J. BARNES (acting).
*School of Family Resources and Consumer Sciences:* ELIZABETH J. SIMPSON.
*Institute for Environmental Studies:* REID A. BRYSON (Director).
*Summer Sessions:* C. A. SCHOENFELD (Director).

## UNIVERSITY OF WISCONSIN—MILWAUKEE
MILWAUKEE, WISCONSIN 53201.

*Chancellor:* FRANK E. HORTON, PH.D.
*Vice-Chancellor:* NORMAN LASCA, PH.D. (acting).
*Assistant Chancellors:* CARL MUELLER, GILBERT L. LEE, Jr., DONALD HARDY.

Number of teachers: 835 full-time, 300 part-time.
Number of students: 25,933.

DEANS AND DIRECTORS:
*Graduate School:* GEORGE W. KEULKS, PH.D.
*College of Letters and Science:* WILLIAM F. HALLORAN, PH.D.
*School of Allied Health Professions:* WARD GATES (acting).
*School of Architecture and Urban Planning:* ANTHONY J. CATANESE, PH.D.
*School of Education:* MICHAEL STOLEE.
*School of Fine Arts:* ROBERT W. CORRIGAN, PH.D.
*College of Engineering and Applied Science:* FRED LANDIS, PH.D.
*School of Social Welfare:* FRED M. COX, PH.D.
*School of Business Administration:* ERIC SCHENKER, PH.D.

*School of Nursing:* NORMA LANG, PH.D.
*School of Library and Information Science:* MOHAMMED M'AMAN.
*Division of Urban Outreach:* MARTIN HABERMAN.
*Director of Libraries:* W. C. ROSELLE, M.S.
*Student Affairs:* DONALD HARDY.
*Director of Admissions, Records and Registration:* FREDERICK E. SPERRY.

PROFESSORS:

ADERMAN, R. M., PH.D., English
BACON, V. W., B.S., Civil Engineering
BAGEMIHL, F., M.A., Mathematics
BAHE, L. W., PH.D., Chemistry
BAKER, G., PH.D., Materials Engineering
BALMER, R. T., SC.D., Mechanical Engineering
BARNOUW, V., PH.D., Anthropology
BARON, A., PH.D., Psychology
BASILE, A., B.M., Music
BAUMANN, CAROL, PH.D., Political Science
BAXTER, J. W., PH.D., Botany
BECK, C., PH.D., Education
BECKER, A. P., PH.D., Economics
BECKLEY, R. M., M.ARCH., Architecture
BEIMBORN, E., PH.D., Transportation
BERMAN, F., M.S., Applied Art
BESAG, F. P., PH.D., Education, Cultural Foundations
BESEL, M., M.ED., Engineering, Systems Design
BIBBY, J. F., PH.D., Political Science
BLAIR, F. X., PH.D., Exceptional Education
BLUM, J. L., PH.D., Botany
BLUM, R. J., PH.D., Mathematics
BLUM, L. P., PH.D., Educational Psychology
BOETTCHER, H. P., PH.D., Electrical Engineering
BONTLY, T. J., PH.D., English
BOROWIECKI, B. Z., PH.D., Geography
BOWKER, L. H., PH.D., Social Welfare
BOYSEN, J. H., M.S., Military Science
BRATANOW, T., PH.D., Engineering Mechanics
BROWN, A. T., PH.D., History and Urban Affairs
BRUNDAGE, J. A., PH.D., History
BURKERT, R., M.S., Art
CALLAWAY, R. L., ED.D., Education
CAROZZA, D. A., PH.D., Comparative Literature
CATANESE, A. J., Urban Planning
CHAN, A., PH.D., Educational Psychology
CHANG, Y. A., PH.D., Materials Engineering
CHILMAN, C., PH.D., Social Welfare
CHOW, Y., PH.D., Physics
COLT, J., M.S., Art
COOK, B. B., PH.D., Political Science
COOK, W., M.S., Music
CORRE, A., PH.D., Hebrew Studies
CORRIGAN, R. W., PH.D., Theatre
COSTELLO, R. L., PH.D., Botany
COTTER, C., PH.D., Political Science
CRANE, W., PH.D., Political Science
CUMMINGS, R., PH.D., Education, Cultural Foundations
CUTLER, V., PH.D., Engineering Mechanics
DAVIDA, G. I., PH.D., Electrical Engineering and Computer Science
DAVIS, J. L., PH.D., Educational Psychology
DE LAURETIS, T. M., D.L.M., French and Italian
DENNIS, E., M.A., Theatre Arts
DOWNEY, J. W., PH.D., Music
DESALVO, J. S., PH.D., Economics
DUNLEAVY, G. W., PH.D., English

EDWARDS, C., PH.D., Geography
EIDT, R., PH.D., Geography
EISMAN, E., PH.D., Psychology
ELLIOTT, G. W., D.B.A., Economics
EARNEST, J., M.F.A., Art
ERNST, D. J., PH.D., History
FELLER, E., PH.D., Mathematics
FENSKE, R., PH.D., Business Administration
FICKEN, M., PH.D., Zoology
FILIPS-JUSWIGG, K. P., PH.D., Slavic Languages
FISCHER, P. M., PH.D., Business Administration
FLYNN, G., PH.D., Spanish and Portuguese
FOWLER, M. L., PH.D., Anthropology
FRIEDMAN, M. J., PH.D., Comparative Literature and English
GERWIN, D., PH.D., Business Administration
GLEASON, G. T., PH.D., Educational Psychology
GLICKMAN, D. H., M.S., Architecture
GORTON, R. A., ED.D., Education, Administrative Leadership
GREENBAUM, S., PH.D., English
GREENE, V. R., PH.D., English
GREENFIELD, S., PH.D., Sociology
GREENLER, R., PH.D., Physics
GREER, S., PH.D., Sociology and Urban Affairs
GRISKEY, R. G., PH.D., Energetics
GROSSFELD, B. J., PH.D., Hebrew Studies
GUERINOT, J., PH.D., English
GUNDERSEN, R. M., PH.D., Mathematics
HABERMAN, M., ED.D., Education
HABERSTROH, C., PH.D., Political Science
HAGEN, W. W., LL.B., Business Administration
HAGENSICK, C., PH.D., Political Science
HALL, N., PH.D., Sociology
HALLORAN, W. F., PH.D., English
HAMDANI, A. H., PH.D., History
HANDELMAN, H., PH.D., Political Science
HANEY, R. E., PH.D., Education
HASSAN, I., PH.D., English and Comparative Literature
HAWKINS, B., PH.D., Political Science
HAY, J. C., PH.D., Psychology
HAZARD, J. A., M.A., English
HEALY, D. F., PH.D., History
HEDLUND, R. D., PH.D., Political Science
HELTON, T., PH.D., English
HERNANDEZ, J., PH.D., Sociology
HICKMAN, R., M.ED., Art
HILL, E. A., PH.D., Chemistry
HILL, R., PH.D., Mass Communication
HOLLANDER, J., D.M.A., Music
HOLZNER, L., PH.D., Geography
HORSMAN, R., PH.D., History
HORTON, F. E., PH.D., Geography
HUBER, C., PH.D., Chemistry
HUBER, M., PH.D., Urban Affairs
HULL, D. L., PH.D., Philosophy
HUNT, W., ED.D., Education, Curriculum and Instruction
HUTCHINSON, G. K., PH.D., Business Administration
HUYSSEN, A. A., PH.D., German
INGLE, R. B., PH.D., Education
JAMES, B. J., PH.D., Anthropology
JAYADEV, T. S., PH.D., Electrical Engineering
JOHNSON, B. S., Social Welfare
JOHNSON, K. G., PH.D., Mass Communication
KARADI, G., PH.D., Civil Engineering
KAUFMAN, A., PH.D., Psychology
KEULKS, G. W., PH.D., Chemistry
KHATCHADOURIAN, H., PH.D., Philosophy
KHAVARI, K. A., PH.D., Psychology
KOCH, G. H., PH.D., Chemistry
KOVACIC, P, PH.D., Chemistry
KRAMER, P., M.M., Music

KURZ, M., M.A., Social Welfare
LACKTMAN, M., M.F.A., Art
LANDIS, F., SC.D., Energetics
LANG, N. M., PH.D., Nursing
LARSON, R. G., PH.D., Education
LASCA, N. P., PH.D., Geology
LEE, T. H., PH.D., Economics
LEER, J. A., M.B.A., Commerce, Accounting
LEUTENEGGER, R., PH.D., Speech Pathology and Audiology
LEVINE, L., PH.D., Electrical Engineering
LEVY, M., PH.D., Physics
LICHTMAN, D., PH.D., Physics
LINDEMANN, A. J., M.S.I.E., Business Administration
LINGREN, R., PH.D., Educational Psychology
LOEWENBERG, J. R., PH.D., Botany
LURIE, M., PH.D., Economics
LYDOLPH, P. E., PH.D., Geography
McGAFFEY, R. S., PH.D., Communications
McLAUGHLIN, T. J., PH.D., Communication
McMILLAN, J. E., PH.D., Mathematics
McQUISTAN, R. B., PH.D., Physics
MADISON, H. L., PH.D., Psychology
MAMALAKIS, M., PH.D., Economics
MANGIAMELE, J. F., PH.D., Urban Affairs
MARTIN, J. M., PH.D., Physics
MAYER, H. M., PH.D., Geography
MEYER, A., PH.D., Educational Psychology
MEYER, M. D., PH.D., French and Italian
MILLER, D., PH.D., Geography
MILLER, M. E., PH.D., Psychology
MILLER, M. H., PH.D., Communication
MILLER, N., PH.D., History
MOORE, J., PH.D., Sociology
MURSKY, G., PH.D., Geological Sciences
MURVAR, V., PH.D., Religious Studies, Sociology
MUSKATEVC, L., M.M., Music
MYERS, O., PH.D., Spanish and Portuguese
NACHMIAS, D., PH.D., Urban Affairs, Political Science
NELSON, KATHERINE, PH.D., Geology
NOEL, D. L., PH.D., Sociology
NORDEN, C. R., PH.D., Zoology
OLSON, F. I., PH.D., History
OLSON, J. L., ED.D., Exceptional Education
ONG, J., Jr., PH.D., Materials Engineering
PALEN, J. J., PH.D., Sociology
PARKER, L. E., PH.D., Physics
PATRICK, J. M., PH.D., English
PAULL, R. A., PH.D., Geology
PERLMAN, R. W., PH.D., Economics
PESEK, B., PH.D., Economics
PHILLABAUM, C. E., PH.D., Theatre Arts
PINCUS, H., PH.D., Geological Sciences
PIRIE, R. G., PH.D., Geology
PORTER, J. J., PH.D., Psychology
PRESS, N., PH.D., Zoology
RAPOPORT, A., PH.D., Architecture and Anthropology
RATHSACK, L., B.S., Art
RAUSCHER, G., PH.D., German
RAYMS, W., PH.D., Management Research
REPLOGLE, J., PH.D., English
ROBINSON, R., PH.D., Education
ROSE, H., PH.D., Geography and Urban Affairs
SABLE, M. H., Library and Information Science
SAHIN, I., PH.D., Business Administration
SALAMUN, P. J., PH.D., Botany
SALOTTI, C. A., PH.D., Geological Science
SAMORE, T., Library and Information Science
SANKAR, U., PH.D., Economics
SCHENK, Q. F., PH.D., Social Work
SCHENKER, E., PH.D., Economics
SCHMANDT, H. J., PH.D., Political Science
SCHOELLER, A. W., PH.D., Elementary Education
SCHROEDTER, H., M.S., Art

SCHUR, L. M., PH.D., Economics and Education
SCREVEN, C. G., PH.D., Psychology
SHAH, V. L., PH.D., Energetics
SHAIKH, A. F., PH.D., Civil Engineering
**SHEA, D. R., PH.D., Political Science**
SHERMAN, D., PH.D., Civil Engineering
**SHURMAN, M. M., PH.D., Physics**
SIDKAR, D. N., PH.D., Geological Sciences
**SIEBRING, B. R., PH.D., Chemistry**
**SILVERBERG, J., PH.D., Anthropology**
SKOLLER, D., PH.D., Film
SLESINGER, J., PH.D., Social Work
SMITH, D. K., PH.D., Communication
SMITH, W. H., PH.D., Art
SNAVELY, J., M.M., Music
SOSNOVSKY, G., PH.D., Chemistry
SPAIGHTS, E., PH.D., Education
**SPITZBART, A., PH.D., Mathematics**
STAATS, G. W., PH.D., Electrical Engineering
STAGAKIS, G., PH.D., History
**STAMPFL, T., PH.D., Psychology**
STARBUCK, W. H., PH.D., Business Administration
STEARNS, F., PH.D., Botany
STEWIG, J., PH.D., Education
**STILLMAN, D., PH.D., Art History**
STOEVEKEN, A. C., M.S., Art
STOLEE, M. J., PH.D., Education
STONE, R. K., PH.D., English
**STROMBERG, R., PH.D., History**
SUAREZ-MURIAS, M. C., PH.D., Spanish and Portuguese
**SUCHY, G., M.M., Music**
SUMMERS, M., PH.D., Political Science
SUSARLA, V., PH.D., Mathematical Sciences
SWANSON, R., PH.D., Classics
**TAPPEN, N. C., PH.D., Anthropology**
TESSLER, M. A., PH.D., Political Science
THOMPSON, R. K., Jr., B.M., Music
TONG, S. Y., PH.D., Physics
TRATTNER, W. I., PH.D., History
TSAO, K. C., PH.D., Energetics
**TURNER, R. K., Jr., PH.D., English**
ULLMAN, P., PH.D., Spanish and Portuguese
VAIRAVAN, K., PH.D., Electrical Engineering
VAN ATTA, R. E., PH.D., Education
VANSELOW, R. W., PH.D., Chemistry
**WADE, J. W., M.ARCH., Architecture**
WALDHEIM, J., B.S., Art
WALKER, J. H., Theatre
WALTER, G. G., PH.D., Mathematics
**WALTERS, W. L., PH.D., Physics**
WALTON, T., PH.D., Education
WARREN, R., PH.D., Zoology
WARREN, R. M., PH.D., Psychology
**WEBER, C. E., PH.D., Business Administration**
**WEISE, C. M., PH.D., Zoology**
**WELLIN, E., PH.D., Anthropology**
**WHITFORD, P. B., PH.D., Botany**
WILLIS, D. E., PH.D., Geological Sciences
ZAHORIK, J. A., PH.D., Education
ZIPES, J. D., PH.D., German

## UNIVERSITY OF WISCONSIN—OSHKOSH

800 ALGOMA BLVD., OSHKOSH, WISCONSIN 54901

Telephone: 424-1234.

Founded 1871.

*Chancellor:* EDWARD M. PENSON.
*Vice-Chancellor:* WALTER T. JAMES.
*Registrar:* A. LEHMAN.
*Librarian:* J. DANIEL VANN.

The library contains 624,925 vols.
Number of teachers: 544.
Number of students: 10,800.

### DEANS:

*Graduate School:* LAURINE E. FITZGERALD.
*College of Education and Human Services:* ROGER V. BENNETT.
*College of Business Administration:* CLIFFORD E. LARSON.
*College of Letters and Science:* WILLIAM J. LEFFIN.
*College of Nursing:* DIXALENE C. BAHLEDA.
*Students:* EDWIN B. SMITH.


## UNIVERSITY OF WISCONSIN-PARKSIDE

KENOSHA, WISCONSIN 53141

Founded 1966.

*Chancellor:* ALAN E. GUSKIN.
*Vice-Chancellor:* LORMAN A. RATNER.
*Assistant Chancellor for Educational Services:* CARLA STOFFLE.
*Assistant Chancellor for Administration and Fiscal Affairs:* GARY G. GOETZ.

The library contains 260,000 vols.
Number of students: 5,300.


## UNIVERSITY OF WISCONSIN—PLATTEVILLE

PLATTEVILLE, WISCONSIN 53818

Telephone: 342-1100.

Founded 1866.

*Chancellor:* WARREN CARRIER.
*Vice-Chancellor for Academic Affairs:* MERVYN CADWALLADER.
*Assistant Chancellor for Business Affairs:* F. DUNN.
*Assistant Vice-Chancellor:* RALPH CURTIS.
*Registrar:* CAROL KIES.
*Director of Library:* JEROME DANIELS.

The library contains 195,000 vols.
Number of teachers: 354.
Number of students: 4,510 undergraduate, 203 graduate.

### DEANS:

*College of Engineering:* E. O. BUSBY.
*College of Arts and Sciences:* DALE FATZINGER.
*College of Agriculture:* CHARLES DE NURE.
*College of Business, Industry and Communications:* KAHTAN AL YASIRI.
*College of Education:* JAMES STOLTENBURG.
*Dean of Students:* L. LINDEN.
*Associate Dean of Students:* NICK JOHANSEN.

## UNIVERSITY OF WISCONSIN—RIVER FALLS

RIVER FALLS, WISCONSIN 54022

Telephone: 425-6701.

Founded 1874.

State control.

*Chancellor:* Dr. GEORGE R. FIELD.
*Vice-Chancellor:* R. J. DELORIT.
*Assistant Chancellor:* WAYNE WOLFE.
*Dean of Students:* W. MUNNS.
*Registrar:* M. GERMANSON.
*Librarian:* R. COOKLOCK.

The library contains 166,959 vols.
Number of teachers: 291.
Number of students: 5,022.

### DEANS:

*College of Agriculture:* J. C. DOLLAHON.
*College of Arts and Sciences:* R. D. SWENSON.
*College of Education:* D. BROWN.
*Graduate School:* P. ANDERSON.


## UNIVERSITY OF WISCONSIN—STEVENS POINT

2100 MAIN ST., STEVENS POINT, WISCONSIN 54481

Telephone: (715) 346-0123

Founded 1894.

*Chancellor:* PHILIP R. MARSHALL.
*Vice-Chancellor:* PATRICK MCDONOUGH.
*Assistant Chancellor, University Services:* DAVID L. COKER.

The library contains 550,000 vols.
Number of teachers: 550.
Number of students: 8,853.


## UNIVERSITY OF WISCONSIN—STOUT

MENOMONIE, WISCONSIN 54751

Telephone: (715) 232-1123.

Founded 1893.

State control; Academic year: August to May.

*Chancellor:* Dr. ROBERT STERLING SWANSON.
*Vice-Chancellor:* Dr. WESLEY FACE.
*Dean of Students:* SAMUEL WOOD.
*Assistant Chancellor for Administrative Services:* Dr. WESLEY SOMMERS.
*Dean of Learning Resources:* Dr. DAVID BARNARD.
*Librarian:* J. JAX.

The library contains 180,000 volumes.
Number of teachers: 450.
Number of students: 7,200.

### DEANS:

*School of Liberal Studies:* Dr. GERANE DOUGHERTY.
*School of Industry and Technology:* Dr. M. JAMES BENSEN.
*School of Home Economics:* Dr. SAMENFINK.
*School of Education:* Dr. HOFFMAN (acting).

*Dean of Curriculum, Research and Graduate Studies:* Dr. N. RUNNALLS.

### UNIVERSITY OF WISCONSIN—SUPERIOR
SUPERIOR, WISCONSIN 54880
Telephone: (715) 392-8101.
Founded 1893.

*Chancellor:* K. W. MEYER.
*Director of Admissions:* L. BANKS.
*Librarian:* JOSEPH PRITCHARD.

The library contains 220,000 vols.
**Number of teachers:** 160.
**Number of students:** 2,323.

### UNIVERSITY OF WISCONSIN—WHITEWATER
WHITEWATER, WISCONSIN 53190
Founded 1868.

*Chancellor:* JAMES R. CONNOR.
*Vice-Chancellor and Dean of Faculties:* H. GAYLON GREENHILL.
*Assistant Chancellor for Administrative Services:* JAMES W. COLMEY.
*Assistant Chancellor for Student Affairs:* WILLIAM L. RILEY.
*Assistant to the Chancellor:* DOROTHY M. TIEDE.
*Dean of Library and Learning Resources:* RONALD L. FINGERSON.

The library contains 287,000 vols.
**Number of teachers:** 527.
**Number of students:** 10,006.

### VITERBO COLLEGE
815 SOUTH 9TH STREET,
LA CROSSE, WISCONSIN 54601
Telephone: (608) 784-0040.
Founded 1931.
Liberal arts college, coeducational.

*President:* Dr. ROBERT E. GIBBONS.
*Director of Admissions:* RAY DUVALL.
*Academic Dean:* Sister HELEN ELSBERND, F.S.P.A.
*Dean of Students:* Sister ALICE KAISER, F.S.P.A.
*Librarian:* Sister M. FRANCES CLAIRE MEZERA, F.S.P.A.

The library contains 68,000 vols.
**Number of teachers:** 85.
**Number of students:** 1,100.

## WYOMING

### UNIVERSITY OF WYOMING
LARAMIE, WYOMING 82071
Founded 1886.

*President:* DONALD L. VEAL (acting).
*Registrar:* A. L. GROVER.
*Vice-President, Academic Affairs:* ALLAN SPITZ.
*Vice-President, Finance:* E. G. HAYS.
*Vice-President, Research:* DONALD VEAL.
*Librarian:* WALTER F. EGGERS (acting).

The library contains 700,000 vols.
**Number of teachers:** 825.
**Number of students:** 8,600.

Publications: *University Bulletin*† (4 annually), *Agricultural Experimental Station Bulletin*† (12 to 20 annually), *Geological Survey Bulletins*, *Natural Resources Research Institute Bulletins*†.

#### DEANS:
*College of Agriculture:* H. J. TUMA.
*College of Commerce and Industry:* EDWARD A. DYL.
*College of Education:* JOHN DOLLY.
*College of Engineering:* S. D. HAKES.
*College of Law:* P. C. MAXFIELD.
*College of Arts and Sciences:* JOAN K. WADLOW.
*College of Health Sciences:* J. N. BONE.
*Graduate School:* R. J. MCCOLLOCH.
*Summer School:* W. N. SMITH.

## UNITED STATES EXTERNAL TERRITORIES

### UNIVERSITY OF GUAM
P.O.B. EK, AGANA,
GUAM 96910
Telephone: 734-2177.
Founded 1952; formerly the College of Guam; the only American university in the Western Pacific.

*President:* ROSA ROBERTO CARTER, PH.D.
*Director of Admissions and Registration:* FORREST GENE ROGERS.
*Academic Vice-President:* Dr. RUSSELL G. PECKENS.

The library contains 255,000 vols.
**Number of teachers:** 190.
**Number of students:** 3,168.

Publication: *Micronesica* (twice yearly), *Guam Recorder* (annually).

#### DEANS:
*College of Agriculture and Life Sciences:* W. L. GUERRERO.
*College of Arts and Sciences:* E. MCGINNIES.
*College of Education:* A. KALLINGAL (acting).
*College of Business and Public Administration:* A. LEADER.
*Graduate School and Research:* ROY TSUDA.
*Student Affairs:* A. RIOS (acting).
*Library Services:* Dr. K. L. CARRIVEAU.

### COLLEGE OF THE VIRGIN ISLANDS
ST. THOMAS,
VIRGIN ISLANDS 00801
Telephone: (809) 774-9200.
Founded 1962.

Four-year Liberal Arts College. (Two-year branch at St. Croix.)

*President:* Dr. ARTHUR A. RICHARDS.
*Vice-President for Academic Affairs:* Dr. GEORGE A. COUDUN.
*Vice-President for Business and Financial Affairs:* MALCOLM C. KIRNAN.
*Dean of Instruction:* Dr. ORVILLE KEAN.
*Director of Admissions:* MARIO A. WATLINGTON.
*Librarian:* ERNEST C. WAGNER.

The library contains 70,000 vols.
**Number of teachers:** 75.
**Number of students:** 2,000 (515 full-time).

# UPPER VOLTA
**Population 6,728,000**

## RESEARCH INSTITUTES

**Bureau de Recherches Géologiques et Minières:** B.P. 86, Bobo-Dioulasso; Dir. M. RIEDEZ.

**Centre Culturel Américain/U.S. International Communication Agency:** B.P. 539, Ave. Binger, Ouagadougou.

**Centre Technique Forestier Tropical:** Centre de Haute-Volta, B.P. 303, Ouagadougou; f. 1963; research in silviculture and soil erosion; Dir. J. PIOT ICGREF.

**Centre Voltaïque de la Recherche Scientifique:** B.P. 7047, Ouagadougou; f. 1950; 1968 incorporated into Ministère de L'Education Nationale; basic and applied research in humanities and natural sciences; library of 6,000 vols.; Dir. MARCEL POUSSI; publs. *Notes et Documents Voltaïques†* (quarterly), *Recherches Voltaïques* (irregular), *Rapport d'Activités* (annually), *Travaux et Mémoires du CVRS* (irregular).

**Compagnie Française pour le Développement des Fibres Textiles (C.F.D.T.):** B.P. 317, Ouagadougou; br. at Bobo-Dioulasso.

**Direction de la Géologie et des Mines (D.G.M.):** B.P. 601, Ouagadougou; f. 1960; 67 mems.; library of 2,480 vols.; Dir. P. TAPSOBA; publ. *Rapport Annuel*.

**Institut de Recherches Agronomiques Tropicales (I.R.A.T.):** B.P. 596, Ouagadougou; f. 1924; research on cereals and general agronomy; stations at Saria and Farako-Ba; Dir. M. POULAIN; publ. *Rapport Annuel*.

**Institut de Recherches du Coton et des Textiles Exotiques (I.R.C.T.):** B.P. 208, Bobo-Dioulasso; f. 1961; Dir. H. CORRE.

**Institut de Recherches pour les Huiles et Oléagineux (I.R.H.O.):** Niangoloko, par Bobo-Dioulasso; f. 1949; research into oil-bearing plants and their selection; Head Office in Paris, France (*q.v.*); research station also at Saria; Dir. for Upper Volta M. DHÉRY (Saria); Dir. Niangoloko Station A. GIARD.

**Institut National d'Education (INE):** B.P. 7043, Ouagadougou; f. 1976 by the Ministry of National Education and Culture as an instrument of educational reform to ease the transfer to a new system of education; library of 10,209 vols.; 66 staff; Dir. Gen. IGNACE SANWIDI; publ. *Action, Réflexion et Culture†* (8 a year).

**Office de la Recherche Scientifique et Technique Outre-Mer Mission O.R.S.T.O.M. auprès de l'O.C.C.G.E., Centre Muraz:** B.P. 171, Bobo-Dioulasso; f. 1947; medical entomology and parasitology; staff of 4 researchers, 4 technicians, 4 assistant technicians; library of 862 vols., 44 current periodicals, 4,100 reprints and many other documents; Dir. J. P. HERVY. (*See* main entry under France.)

**Office de la Recherche Scientifique et Technique Outre-Mer Centre O.R.S.T.O.M. à Ouagadougou:** B.P. 182, Ouagadougou; hydrology, geography, agronomy, botany, medical entomology, economics, demography, archaeology, geology; library; Dir. J. CLAUDE.

**Organisation de Coordination et de Coopération pour la lutte contre les Grandes Endémies (OCCGE):** B.P. 153, Bobo-Dioulasso; f. 1960 to combat endemic and transmitted diseases and malnutrition; conducts research and trains medical workers; mem. states: Benin, Ivory Coast, France, Upper Volta, Mali, Mauritania, Niger, Senegal and Togo; library of 1,450 vols., 175 current periodicals, 7,600 technical documents; Exec. Pres. Dr. YOUSSOUF DIAGANA; Vice-Pres. Dr. JEAN MARIE KYELEM; Sec. Gen. Dr. CHEICK SOW; publs. *Bulletin OCCGE Informations†* (monthly), *Communiqué Bibliographique†* (monthly), *Rapport Final des Conférences Techniques†* (annually), *Rapport Final des Conférences Ministérielles* (annually), monographs, technical reports.

## UNIVERSITY AND COLLEGES

### UNIVERSITÉ DE OUAGADOUGOU
B.P. 7021, OUAGADOUGOU

Telephone: 329-44, 45.
Telex: 5270 UNIOUAGA.

Founded 1969; university status 1974.
Academic year: October to June.

*Rector:* YEMBILA ABDOULAYE TOGUYENI.
*Secretary-General:* SIGUIGNA AMADOU OUIMINGA.
*Librarian:* BOUREIMA ZOROME.

Number of books in library: 30,000.
Number of teachers: 87.
Number of students: 1,226.

CONSTITUENT INSTITUTES:

**Ecole Supérieure des Lettres et des Sciences Humaines (E.S.L.S.H.):** Dir. BAKARY COULIBALY.

**Institut Universitaire de Technologie (I.U.T.):** Dir. JOSEPH BELDA.

**Institut Supérieur Polytechnique (I.S.P.):** Dir. SITA GUINKO.

**Institut de Mathématiques et de Sciences Physiques (I.M.P.):** Dir. SIÉ FAUSTIN SIB.

**Ecole Supérieure des Sciences Economiques (E.S.S.EC.):** Dir. LOUIS NOËL LE GOAER (acting).

**Institut Africain d'Education Cinématographique (IN. AF. E.C.):** Dir. Mme. ODILE GERMAINE NACOULMA.

**Ecole Supérieure de Droit (E.S.D.):** Dir. LARBA YARGA (acting).

**Ecole Supérieure des Sciences de la Santé (E.S.S.SA.).**

---

**Centre d'Etudes Economiques et Sociales d'Afrique Occidentale:** B.P. 305, Bobo-Dioulasso; f. 1960; courses include hygiene, the mother and child, development projects, the promotion of women and world progress, promotion of villages, agricultural progress, self-promotion within zones, credit unions and management; library of 6,000 vols. and 120 periodicals; Dir. P. BUIJSROGGE; publ. *Construire Ensemble* (6 a year).

# URUGUAY
Population 2,878,000

## LEARNED SOCIETIES
Montevideo

**Academia Nacional de Letras:** 25 de Mayo 376 (Palacio Taranco); f. 1946.
President: ARTURO SERGIO VISCA.
First Vice-President: (vacant).
Second Vice-President: JULIO C. DA ROSA.
Secretary: FERNANDO GARCÍA ESTÉBAN.
Treasurer: RODOLFO V. TÁLICE.
Librarian: ANÍBAL BARRIOS PINTOS.
Publication: Boletín† (2 a year).

MEMBERS:

CARLOS SABAT ERCASTY
CARLOS RODRÍGUEZ PINTOS
MIGUEL ANTONIO BARRIOLA
DOMINGO L. BORDOLI
JUAN E. PIVEL DEVOTO
ARTURO SERGIO VISCA
CELIA MIERES
JULIO C. DA ROSA
ROLANDO LAGUARDA TRÍAS
ANÍBAL BARBAGELATA
FERNANDO GARCÍA ESTEBAN
MARÍA DE MONTSERRAT
ILDEFONSO PEREDA VALDÉS
ANÍBAL BARRIOS PINTOS
ELIDA MIRANDA
LUIS BAUSERO
RODOLFO V. TÁLICE
ANGEL CUROTTO

**Academia Nacional de Ingeniería:** Avda. Libertador Brigadier Gral. Lavalleja 1464, piso 14, Montevideo; f. 1965; 30 full mems., 2 hon. mems.; Pres. Ing. HECTOR FERNANDEZ GUIDO; Sec. Ing. ALBERTO PONCE DELGADO.

**Agrupación Bibliotecológica del Uruguay** (Library Association): Cerro Largo 1666; activities include library science, archives, documentation, bibliography, history and numismatics; Pres. LUIS ALBERTO MUSSO; publs. Bibliografía uruguaya sobre Brasil†, Aportes para la historia de la bibliotecología en el Uruguay†, Bibliografía y documentación en el Uruguay†, La estrella del sur—Indice†, Bibliografía bibliográfica y bibliotecología†, etc.

**Alliance Française:** Soriano 1180; f. 1923; 865 mems.; 7,600 students; library of 15,000 vols.; Pres. J. PRAT; Dir.-Gen. R. ARBELOT; publ. Bulletin Pédagogique.

**Asociación de Bibliotecologos y Afines del Uruguay** (Library Science Association of Uruguay): Entre Rios 1118; f. 1978; 182 mems.; Pres. MA. TERESA MORAS PONS; publ. Actualidades (every 2 months).

**Asociación de Ingenieros del Uruguay** (Association of Uruguayan Engineers): Avda. Libertador Brigadier Gral. Lavalleja 1464, piso 14; f. 1950; 800 mems., also hon. and corresp. abroad; Pres. Ing. EDUARDO CRISPO AYALA; Sec. Ing. PONCIANO J. TORRADO; affiliated to the Unión Panamericana de Asociaciones de Ingenieros; library of 2,000 vols.; publ. Ingeniería.

**Asociación de Química y Farmacia del Uruguay** (Chemical and Pharmaceutical Association): Av. Libertador Brigadier Gral. Lavalleja 1464, piso 14; f. 1888; 600 mems.; Pres. BLANCA CERDEIRAS; Sec.-Gen. HUGO LARRAMENDI; publs. Anales (occasional), Química y Farmacia (quarterly).

**Asociación Odontológica Uruguaya** (Odontological Association): Avda. Libertador Brigadier Gral. Lavalleja 1464, piso 13; f. 1946; 2,551 mems.; comprises 8 depts. and 6 sections; museum; library of 2,200 vols.; Pres. Dr. VARTAN BEHSNILIAN; Sec. Dr. MARTHA BAGNASCO; publs. Odontología Uruguaya (annually), Organo Informativo (every 2 months).

**Asociación Rural del Uruguay** (Rural Association): Avda. Uruguay 864; f. 1871; Pres. CONRADO FERBER AROCENA; Vice-Pres. LUIS ARTAGAVEYTIA; publs. Revista (monthly), Boletín; library of 15,000 vols.

**Ateneo de Clínica Quirúrgica** (Athenaeum of Clinical Surgery): f. 1934; Dir. Prof. Dr. EDUARDO BLANCO ACEVEDO; publ. Anales.

**Centro de Estadísticas Nacionales y Comercio Internacional del Uruguay (CENCI Uruguay):** Misiones 1361, Casilla de Correo 1510; f. 1956; non-commercial organization, sponsored by the Uruguayan Government, to provide economic and statistical information on all American countries; 1,200 mems.; library of over 550 vols.; Sec.-Gen. LADISLAO VERTESI; Sec. KENNETH BRUNNER; publs. Boletines: Noticias Latinoamericanas, Industrias por sectores de actividad, Anuario estadístico sobre el intercambio comercial, Manuales prácticos del Importador, del Exportador, Aduanero y del Contribuyente, Notas Explicativas de NCCA y su Indice Alfabético, Estudios de Mercado.

**Centro Nacional de Información y Documentación** (National Information and Documentation Centre): Avda. Libertador Brigadier Lavalleja 2025; f. 1961; primary, secondary and technical education; part of National Education Council; Dir. Sra. MERCEDES FITZ-PATRICK.

**Comisión Nacional de Energía Atómica:** Calle Soriano 1014, piso 1, Montevideo; f. 1955; 7 permanent mems. (representatives of Ministries); for the study and utilization of nuclear technology for peaceful purposes; Pres. Ing. PABLO BAÑALES; Technical Sec. Dr. JORGE L. SERVIAN.

**Consejo Nacional de Higiene** (National Health Council): Av. 8 de Julio 1892, Ministerio de Salud Pública; Minister Dr. CARLOS STAJANO; publ. Memoria Anual.

**Goethe Institut:** Río Branco 1494, Casilla de Correo 1257; f. 1962; Dir. H. U. MÜHLSCHLEGEL.

**Instituto Cultural Anglo-Uruguayo** (Anglo-Uruguayan Cultural Institute): San José 1426; f. 1934; library: see Libraries; theatre, exhibition hall; English language courses, teacher training courses, lectures, films, musical, dramatic and social activities; 8,250 students; 2 suburban annexes and 25 regional institutes throughout the country; Dir. R. A. COWLEY, M.A.

**Instituto Histórico y Geográfico:** Hospital Maciel, Montevideo; f. 1843; 32 mems.; Pres. Prof. ALBERTO REYES THEVENET; publ. Revista.

**Istituto Italiano di Cultura:** Calle Paraguay 1177; f. 1950; 350 mems.; runs courses in Italian language and culture; library of 11,324 vols.; Dir. Dra. RENATA GERONE.

**Sociedad de Amigos de Arqueología** (*Archaeological Society*): Buenos Aires 652, Casilla 399; f. 1926; 70 mems., 16 foreign mems.; publ. *Revista*.

**Sociedad de Arquitectos del Uruguay** (*Society of Architects*): Av. Libertador Brigadier Gral. Lavalleja 1464, Piso 14; f. 1914; Pres. Arq. Gustavo Nicolich; publs. *Boletín, Revista*.

**Sociedad de Cirugía del Uruguay** (*Surgical Society*): Av. Libertador Gral. Brig. Lavalleja 1464, piso 13; f. 1920; 426 mems.; library of over 3,300 vols.; Pres. Dr. Raul Praderi; Sec.-Gen. Dr. Jorge Bermudez; publ. *Cirugía del Uruguay†* (every 2 months).

**Sociedad de Radiología del Uruguay:** Avda. Libertador Brigadier Gral. Lavalleja 1464, piso 13, Montevideo; f. 1923; holds conferences and seminars; 60 mems.; Pres. Dr. José Alejandro Glausiuss.

**Gremial Uruguaya de Médicos Radiólogos:** f. 1972; 70 mems.; Pres. Dr. Ernesto H. Cibils.

**Sociedad Malacológica del Uruguay** (*Malacological Society*): Casilla 1401; f. 1957; 210 mems.; Pres. José Gatti; Sec. Jorge Pita; publs. *Comunicaciones* (2 a year) and specialized articles.

**Sociedad Uruguaya de Patología Clínica:** Hospital de Clínicas Dr. Manuel Quintela, Avda. Italia s/n, Montevideo; f. 1954; publ. *Revista*.

**Sociedad Uruguaya de Pediatría** (*Paediatrics Society*): Av. Libertador Brigadier Gral. Lavalleja 1464, piso 13; f. 1915; 360 mems., affiliated to the Asociación Latino Americana de Pediatría; library of 4,800 vols.; Pres. Prof. Dr. Walter Taibo-Canale; Sec. Prof. Agr. Dr. Mauricio Gajer; publ. *Archivos de Pediatría del Uruguay†* (quarterly).

**Sociedad Zoológica del Uruguay:** Casilla 399; f. 1961; Pres. Prof. Miguel A. Klappenbach; publ. *Boletín*.

# RESEARCH INSTITUTES
## Montevideo

**Consejo Nacional de Investigaciones Científicas y Técnicas:** Sarandí 450 P4, Montevideo; f. 1961; to stimulate research in all branches of knowledge; 9 mems.; Pres. Dr. Alvarez Olloniego; Sec. Téc. Arq. José Austt.

**Dirección General de Estadística y Censos** (*Statistical Office*): Cuareim 2052; f. 1829; library of 5,000 vols.; Dir.-Gen. Horacio H. Parodi; publs. *De los Precios del Consumo* (monthly), *Del Costo de la Construcción* (monthly), *Medio de Salarios* (quarterly), *De Precios al Por Mayor de Productos Importados, De Precios Minoristas* (annually).

**Dirección Nacional de Meteorología del Uruguay** (*National Meteorological Directorate*): Javier Barrios Amorín No. 1488, Casilla de Correo 64; f. 1895; library of 6,000 vols., 13,800 documents; Dir.-Gen. Col. Fernando J. Arbe; publs. *Boletín Agrometeorológico, Anuario Climatológico, Notas Técnicas*.

**Instituto Artigas del Servicio Exterior** (*Artigas Foreign Service Institute*): Avda. 18 de Julio 1205; organizes professional courses for diplomatic staff; library of 12,850 vols., 1,486 maps, 83 atlases; Dir. José Luis Bruno.

**Instituto de Endocrinología "Profesor Dr. Juan C. Mussio Fournier"** (*Institute of Endocrinology*): Hospital Pasteur, Calle Larravide 74; f. 1937; under Ministry of Health; Dir. Prof. Dr. Alfredo Navarro; publs. *Archivos* and learned treatises and articles.

**Instituto de Investigaciones Biológicas Clemente Estable:** Avda. Italia 3318; f. 1927; 11 divisions, 3 depts.; 42 research staff; library of 10,000 vols.; Dir. Prof. J. Roberto Sotelo.

**Instituto de Oncología:** Avda. 8 de Octubre 3265, Montevideo; f. 1960; Dir. Prof. Dr. Alfonso Frangella.

**Instituto de Tecnología y Química:** (*see* under Universidad de la República).

**Instituto Geológico del Uruguay:** Calle Hervidero 2853; f. 1912; library of 14,200 vols.; Dir. Mario E. Latorre; publs. *Boletín*, geological maps.

**Instituto Interamericano del Niño** (*Inter-American Child Institute*): Avenida 8 de Octubre 2904; f. 1927 by Prof. Dr. Luis Morquio; all the States of the Americas are members; specialized library of 46,000 vols.; open to the public; Pres. Dr. Florencio Varela; Sec. and Dir.-Gen. Dr. Rafael Sajón; publs. *Boletín* and specialized books and pamphlets.

**Instituto Nacional de Pesca** (*National Fishery Institute*): Constituyente 1497; Dir. Capt. Ulises W. Pérez.

**Instituto Uruguayo de Normas Técnicas** (*Uruguayan Standards Institution*): Avda. Libertador Brigadier Gral. Lavalleja 1464; f. 1939; 400 mems.; oversees the normalization and control of weights and measures; library of 120,000 vols.; Pres. Ing. Pedro Ponsetí; Dir. Eng. Pablo Benia; publ. *Normas UNIT*.

**Jardín Botánico:** 19 de Abril 1181, Montevideo; f. 1940; Dir. Ing. Agr. Pablo B. Ross.

**Liga Uruguaya contra la Tuberculosis** (*Anti-Tuberculosis League*): Magallanes 1320; f. 1902; owns an Observation Hospital for 400 child patients, a Dispensary Preventive and Dental Centres; Pres. Dr. Carlos Morató Manaro; Dir.-Gen. Dr. Ruben Gorlero Bacigalupi; Sec. Daniel G. Armandugon.

**Observatorio Astronómico** (*Astronomical Observatory*): Casilla de Correo 867; f. 1928; Dir. Prof. Carlos A. Etchecopar.

**Oficina Regional de Ciencia y Tecnología de la Unesco para América Latina y el Caribe** (*Unesco Regional Office for Science and Technology in Latin America and the Caribbean*): Bulevar Artigas 1320, Casilla 859; f. 1949; co-ordinates Unesco's programme in the region; main activities in the fields of engineering and teaching of engineering, science policy, marine sciences, hydrology, earth sciences, ecology, science teaching, scientific information and natural resources; organizes meetings, conferences, etc.; collection of over 1,000 Latin American scientific periodicals and card index of *c*. 60,000 scientific institutions and scientists in the region; Dir. Dr. Gustavo Malek; publs. *Boletín†, Boletín Internacional de Ciencias del Mar†*.

**Servicio Geográfico Militar** (*Military Geographical Institute*): Avda. 8 de Octubre 3255; f. 1913; geodesy, photogrammetry, geophysics and cartography; library of 3,000 vols.; Dir. Col. Ivho R. Acuña; publs. *Boletín*, scale aeronautic and aerial maps.

## La Estanzuela, Dpto. Colonia

**Centro de Investigaciones Agrícolas "Alberto Boerger"** (*Agricultural Research Centre*): f. 1914; library of 6,100 vols.; Dir. Mario Allegri; publs. *Boletines de Divulgación†, Boletines Técnicos†, Misceláneas†, Memoria Anual*.

# LIBRARIES
## Montevideo

**Archivo General de la Nación** (*National Archives*): Calle Convención 1474; f. 1926; 14,000 vols.; Dir. Prof. Juan E. Pivel Devoto; publ. *Revista*.

**Biblioteca Central y Publicaciones del Consejo de Educación Secundaria, Básica y Superior:** Eduardo Acevedo 1419, piso 1; f. 1885; 100,000 vols.; Librarian Aída Elcarte de Carrió.

URUGUAY — WORLD OF LEARNING

**Biblioteca del Palacio Legislativo:** Avda. Agraciada y Avda. Gral. Flores; f. 1929; legal deposit library in conjunction with National Library; 300,000 vols.; specializes in jurisprudence; Dir. Ruben A. Bulla; publ. *Bibliografia Nacional* (monthly, with quadrennial accumulation, etc.).

**Biblioteca Municipal "Dr. Francisco Alberto Schinca":** 8 de Octubre 3362/64, Montevideo; f. 1929; 20,000 vols.; Dir. Carlos Pappa.

**Biblioteca Municipal "Dr. Joaquín de Salterain":** Ciudadela 1225; 36,000 vols.; includes a slide library; Librarian Rolando Brianes.

**Biblioteca Nacional del Uruguay** (*National Library*): 18 de Julio 1790; f. 1816; 900,000 vols.; comprises departments of children's and students' books, documentation, bibliography, administration, Uruguayan and special materials, restoration of printed works; Dir.-Gen. Arturo Sergio Visca; publs. *Anuario Bibliográfico Uruguayo, Revista*, etc.

**Centro Nacional de Documentación Científica, Técnica y Económica:** 18 de Julio 1790; f. 1953; part of National Library; Dir. Elena Castro de Blengini; publs. *Boletín Informativo, Directorio de Servicios de Información y Documentación en el Uruguay.*

**Biblioteca Artigas-Washington/U.S. International Communication Agency:** Calle Paraguay 1217; f. 1943; 11,517 vols., mainly by modern United States authors; 1,412 musical scores, 2,068 records, 2,537 pamphlets, 124 periodical subscriptions; cassettes, videotapes, videocassettes, etc.; Dir. Francis William Lowrey.

**Biblioteca del Instituto Cultural Anglo-Uruguayo:** San José 1426; 19,000 books and 50 periodicals in English; 600 records of English music, prose, poetry and plays.

**Biblioteca del Museo Histórico Nacional** (*Library of the National Historical Museum*): Casa Lavalleja Zabala 1469, Casa de Rivera, Rincón 437, Museo Romántico (library), 25 de mayo 428, and Casa de Giró, Cerrito 584; f. 1940; 150,000 vols., 4,000 vols. of MSS.; iconography, engravings, maps, numismatics; the entire library and Uruguayan collections of Dr. Pablo Blanco Acevedo; Dir. Juan E. Pivel Devoto.

**Biblioteca Pedagógica Central** (*Pedagogic Library*): Plaza Cagancha 1175; f. 1888; library of 139,305 vols.; Dir. Nilda A. Barbagelata de Ritter; publs. *Información Bibliográfica*† (bi-monthly), *Cuadernos*†, *Temas*†, *Traducciones*†, *Bibliografía Uruguaya sobre Educación*†.

Florida

**Biblioteca Pública Municipal:** f. 1889; 42,000 vols.; Dir. José Alberto Dibarbourie.

## MUSEUMS

### Montevideo

**Museo Histórico Nacional** (*National Historical Museum*): Casa Rivera, Calle Rincón 437; f. 1900; sectional collections of local Indian cultures (prehistoric, colonial epoch, development and political history of the country); portraits, relics, arms, documents, coins, medals, etc., relating to the Wars of Independence, British invasion, early revolutions, etc. *Casa Lavalleja:* Independence period, 1825-28; donated collections; *Casa de Garibaldi*, 25 de Mayo 314: José Garibaldi in Uruguay 1837-1848; *Museo Romántico* 1830-1890; social history and musicology; newspaper and periodicals library; *Casa Quinta del Dr. Luis Alberto de Herrera*, Av. Luis Alberto de Herrera 3760-62: general history of Uruguay from 1897 to 1959; *Casa Quinta de D. José Batlle y Ordóñez*, Calle Teniente Rinaldi 3870: general history of Uruguay from 1886 to 1929; *Casa de Manuel Ximénez y Gómez*, Calle 25 de Agosto 580: evokes the tradition of Montevideo as a fortress and sea-port; *Casa del Presidente Juan Francisco Giró*, Calle Cerrito 584; general history of Uruguayan culture, iconographic and cartographic sections; Dir. Juan E. Pivel Devoto; publs. *Revista Historica*†, catalogues, related leaflets.

**Museo Municipal de Bellas Artes:** Ave. Millan 4015; f. 1928; paintings, drawings, wood-carvings, sculptures; Dir. Juan Carlos Weigle.

**Museo Nacional de Artes Plásticas** (*National Museum of Fine Arts*): Tomás Giribaldi 2283, Parque Rodó; f. 1911; 4,217 paintings, engravings, drawings, sculptures, ceramics; Dir. Angel Kalenberg.

**Museo Nacional de Historia Natural** (*Natural History Museum*): Casilla 399; f. 1837 as National Museum; zoology, botany, palaeontology, archaeology; 32 mems.; library of 90,000 vols.; Dir. Miguel A. Klappenbach; Sub-Dir. Héctor S. Osorio; publs. *Anales*†, *Comunicaciones Zoológicas*†, *Comunicaciones Botánicas*†, *Comunicaciones Antropológicas*†, *Comunicaciones Paleontológicas*†, *Flora del Uruguay*†.

**Museo Pedagógico** (*Pedagogic Museum*): Plaza Cagancha 1175; f. 1888; Dir. Sra. Nilda Barbagelata de Ritter; publ. *Boletín* (weekly).

**Museo y Archivo Histórico Municipal:** Palacio del Cabildo, Calle Juan Carlos Gómez 1362; f. 1915; permanent exhibition of the history of Montevideo from 1726; furniture, icons, paintings, jewellery and maps; library of 2,000 vols.; Hon. Dir. Dr. Armando D. Pirotto; publ. *Anales*†.

**Museo y Jardín Botánico de Montevideo:** Avda. 19 de Abril 1179; f. 1940; Chief Botanist Atilio Lombardo.

**Museo Zoológico "Dámaso Antonio Larrañaga":** Rambla República de Chile 4215; f. 1956; instruction on national and exotic fauna; library of 2,000 specialized vols.; 2,000 species of fauna and molluscs, etc.; Dir. Juan Pablo Cuello; publs. monographs on national fauna†.

### San José de Mayo

**Museo Departamental de San José:** Calle Dr. Julián Becerro de Bengoa 493, paintings, drawings, sculptures, ceramics; Dir. Horacio Delgado Larriera.

### Tacuarembó

**Museo del Indio y del Gaucho:** Calle 25 de Mayo 315; affiliated to the Museo Histórico de Montevideo; large collection representing ancient native crafts, weapons and other implements of the aboriginal Indians and gauchos; Founder and Dir. Washington Escobar.

## UNIVERSITY

### UNIVERSIDAD DE LA REPÚBLICA
AV. 18 DE JULIO 1968,
MONTEVIDEO

Telephone: 40-92-01/05.

Founded 1849.

State control; Language of instruction: Spanish; Academic year: March to December.

*Rector:* Cr. Jorge Anselmi.
*Secretary-General:* Esc. Juan A. Tróccoli.

Number of teachers: 3,906.
Number of students: 34,044.
Publications: faculty bulletins.

UNIVERSITY, COLLEGES                                                                                           URUGUAY

DEANS:
*Faculty of Agronomy:* Ing. Agr. DANIEL H. FAGGI.
*Faculty of Architecture:* Arq. RECLUS AMENEDO.
*Faculty of Economics and Administration:* Cr. NILO BERCHESI.
*Faculty of Law and Social Sciences:* Dr. MANUEL A. VIEIRA.
*Faculty of Humanities and Sciences:* Lic. MIGUEL KLAPPENBACH.
*Faculty of Engineering:* Ing. NORBERTO FAROPPA.

*Faculty of Medicine:* Dr. EDUARDO ANAVITARTE.
*Faculty of Dentistry:* Dr. HUGO AMORÍN.
*Faculty of Chemistry:* Dra. RAQUEL LOMBARDO DE DE BETOLAZA.
*Faculty of Veterinary Medicine:* Dr. HÉCTOR LAZANEO.

DIRECTORS:
*School of Librarianship and Related Sciences:* see below.
*School of Social Service:* Dr. ALBERTO LEIZAGOYEN.
*School of Psychology:* Dr. MARIO BERTA.

## COLLEGES

**Escuela Universitaria de Bibliotecología y Ciencias Afines "Ing. Federico E. Capurro":** Tristán Narvaja 1427, Montevideo; f. 1945; attached to Universidad de la Republica; 3-year course in librarianship; 30 teachers; 150 students; postgraduate course: 50 students; library of 7,000 vols.; Dir. Profa. ERMELINDA ACERENZA.

**Instituto de Enseñanza de Mecánica y Electrotecnia "Prof. Dr. José F. Arias":** Joaquín Requena 1931, Montevideo.

**Instituto de Estudios Superiores** (*Institute of Higher Studies*): Constituyente 1711, Montevideo; f. 1928; Pres. Dr. CARLOS M. FEIN; Sec. Prof. LEONARDO TUSO; Music, Phonetics, Experimental Philology, Geography and Geomorphology, Palaeontology, Spanish-American Literature, Biological Climatology, Mathematics, Oriental Culture; publs. *Boletines Revista*.

**Universidad del Trabajo del Uruguay:** Calle San Salvador 1674, Montevideo; f. 1878; offers 220 different courses at 81 colleges in agriculture, handicrafts, industry and commerce; lower- and intermediate-level education and training; 4,500 full-time teachers; 50,000 students; Dir. Dr. HÉCTOR G. LÓPEZ ESTREMADOURO; publs. *U.T.U. Visión†, Anales†*.

# VATICAN CITY STATE

## ACADEMIES

**Pontificia Academia Scientiarum** (*Pontifical Academy of Sciences*): Casina Pio IV, Vatican Gardens; f. 1603 as *Linceorum Academia*; reorganized by Pope Pius IX in 1847 as *Pontificia Accademia dei Nuovi Lincei*; reconstituted with present title by Pius XI, 1936. The Academy is composed of seventy Pontifical Academicians, nominated by the Holy Father himself, proposed by the Academic Body and chosen from experts in mathematical and experimental sciences in all countries. The Academy holds plenary sessions and organizes study groups to further scientific research and promote scientific investigations.

*President:* Prof. CARLOS CHAGAS.
*Director:* Rev. ENRICO DI ROVASENDA.
Publications. *Commentarii, Scripta varia*.

PONTIFICAL ACADEMICIANS:

ABRAGAM, ANATOLE (France).
ANFINSEN, CHRISTIAN (U.S.A.)
ARBER, WERNER (Switzerland).
BALTIMORE, DAVID (U.S.A.).
BLANC-LAPIERRE, ANDRÉ (France).
BOHR, AAGE (Denmark).
BONINO, GIOVANNI BATTISTA (Italy).
BRÜCK, HERMANN ALEXANDER (United Kingdom).
CHAGAS-FILHO, CARLOS (Brazil).
CROXATTO, HECTOR R. (Chile).
DE ALMEIDA, ANTONIO (Portugal).
DE BROGLIE, Prince LOUIS (France).
DE DUVE, CHRISTIAN (Belgium).
DE GIORGI, ENNIO (Italy).
DIRAC, PAUL ADRIEN MAURICE (United Kingdom).
DÖBEREINER, JOHANNA (Brazil).
DOISY, EDWARD ADELBERT (U.S.A.).
ECCLES, Sir JOHN CAREW (Switzerland).
EIGEN, MANFRED (Germany).
GARNHAM, PERCY C. C. (United Kingdom).
GIUSTI, MARTINO (Vatican).
HERZBERG, GERHARD (Canada).
HODGKIN, Sir ALAN LLOYD (United Kingdom).
HÖRSTADIUS, SVEN (Sweden).
HURTADO, ALBERTO (Peru).
KHORANA, HAR GOBIND (U.S.A.).
LAMBO, THOMAS (Switzerland).
LEJEUNE, JÉRÔME (France).
LELOIR, LUIS FEDERICO (Argentina).
LÉPINE, PIERRE RAPHAËL (France).
LEPRINCE-RINGUET, LOUIS (France).
LEVI-MONTALCINI, RITA (Italy).
LICHNEROWICZ, ANDRÉ (France).
LILEY, ALBERT WILLIAM (New Zealand).
LORA TOMAYO, MANUEL (Spain).
MARINI BETTOLO, G. B. (Italy).
MENON, MAMBILLIKALATHIL (India).
MIZUSHIMA, SANICHIRO PAUL (Japan).
MORGAN, WILLIAM WILSON (U.S.A.).
MORUZZI, GIUSEPPE (Italy).
MÖSSBAUER, RUDOLF L. (Germany).
NIRENBERG, MARSHALL (U.S.A.).
OCHOA, SEVERO (U.S.A.).
O'CONNELL, DANIEL J. K. (Vatican City State).
ODHIAMBO, THOMAS (Kenya).
OORT, JAN HENDRIK (Holland).
PALADE, GEORGE E. (U.S.A.).
PAVAN, CRODOWALDO (Brazil).
PERUTZ, MAX (U.K.).
PORTER, Sir GEORGE (U.K.).
PULLMAN, BERNARD (France).
PUPPI, GIAMPIETRO (Italy).
RASETTI, FRANCO (Belgium).
ROCHE, MARCEL (Venezuela).
RYLE, Sir MARTIN (United Kingdom).
SALAM, ABDUS (Italy).
SELA, MICHAEL (Israel).
SIDDIQUI, SALIMUZZAMAN (Pakistan).
SPERI SPERTI, GEORGE (U.S.A.).
SPERRY, ROGER W. (U.S.A.).
STICKLER, ALFONS M. (Vatican).
STRÖMGREN, BENGT (Denmark).
SZENTÁGOTHAI, JANOS (Hungary).
SZENT-GYÖRGYI, ALBERT (U.S.A.).
TUPPY, HANS (Austria).
UBBELOHDE, ALFRED (United Kingdom).
WEISSKOPF, VICTOR (U.S.A.).
WIESNER, KAREL (U.S.A.).
YUKAWA, YDEKI (Japan).

HONORARY PONTIFICAL ACADEMICIAN:
RANZI, SILVIO (Italy).

**Accademia Romana di S. Tommaso d'Aquino e di Religione Cattolica** (*Roman Academy of St. Thomas Aquinas*): 1 Piazza della Cancelleria, 00186 Rome; f. 1879; 70 mems.; theological, philosophical and juridico-economic sections; Pres. Cardinal MARIO LUIGI CIAPPI; Vice-Pres. Mgr. ANTONIO PIOLANTI; Sec. D. LUIGI BOGLIOLO, S.D.B.

**Pontificia Accademia dell' Immacolata** (*Academy of the Immaculate Conception*): 51 Piazza SS. Apostoli, 00187 Rome; f. 1835; 26 mems.; Sec. and Archivist Fr. LORENZO DI FONZO, O.F.M.CONV.

**Pontificia Academia Mariana Internationalis** (*Pontifical International Marian Academy*): via Merulana 124, 00185 Rome (Telephone 755-25-05); f. 1946, Pontifical since 1959; 80 mems., 40 corresp. mems., 188 hon. mems.; Pres. PAVAO MELADA, O.F.M.; Sec. DINKO ARAČIĆ, O.F.M.; publs. *Acta*, Scientific collections.

**Pontificia Accademia Romana di Archeologia** (*Pontifical Roman Academy of Archaeology*): Palazzo della Cancelleria Apostolica; f. 1810; 116 mems.; Pres. CARLO PIETRANGELI; Sec. GEORG DALTROP; publs. *Rendiconti, Memorie*.

**Pontificia Insigne Accademia Artistica dei Virtuosi al Pantheon:** Palazzo della Cancelleria Apostolica, Piazza della Cancelleria 1, Rome; f. 1543; Protector (vacant); Pres. Prof. BRUNO MOLAJOLI; Sec. Prof. GIULIO R. ANSALDI.

**Pontificia Accademia Teologica Romana:** attached to the Pontifical University of the Lateran; 4 Piazza S. Giovanni in Laterano, 00184 Rome; f. 1718; 34 hon. mems., 40 ordinary mems., 20 being normally resident in Rome, 10 from the rest of Italy and 10 from other countries, and 12 corresp. mems.; Protector Cardinal GABRIELE GARRONE; Sec. Rt. Rev. Mgr. ANTONIO PIOLANTI; publ. *Divinitas*.

**Collegium Cultorum Martyrum:** 1 via Napoleone III, 00185 Rome; f. 1879; c. 750 mems.; Sec. Ing. PIETRO POZZI.

**Römisches Institut der Görres-Gesellschaft** (*Roman Institute of the Society of Goerres*): via della Sagrestia 17, Vatican City; Dir. Rev. Prof. Dott. ERWIN GATZ.

**The Vatican Observatory:** I-00120 Vatican City State; f. 1889; 11 staff; galactic structure, relativistic astrophysics; library of 33,000 vols.; Dir. GEORGE V. COYNE; publ. *Vatican Observatory Publications*.

## LIBRARIES

**Archivio Segreto Vaticano** (*Papal Archives*): estab. by Pope Paul V in 1611; opened to students in 1880; Prefect MARTINO GIUSTI; Vice-Prefect TERZO NATALINI; publ. *Collectanea Archivi Vaticani*. The *Scuola di Paleografia, Diplomatica e Archivistica* is attached to the Archives.

**Biblioteca Apostolica Vaticana** (*Vatican Apostolic Library*): Over the centuries, the Papal Library was several times dispersed and reconstructed; the present library was founded by Pope Sixtus IV in 1475; at the present time it contains some 65,000 MSS., 130,000 archival files, 100,000 engravings, 7,000 incunabula, and 900,000 other vols.; among famous collections which have helped to build up the Library are those of the Dukes of Urbino (1657), of Queen Christina of Sweden (1690), of the Florentine Marquis Capponi (1745), of Barberini (1902), of Chigi (1923), and the Borghese collection, which included many items housed in the Papal Library at Avignon; the Sistine Chapel collection is of the greatest importance to historians of music; among the many rare and precious MSS. in the Library are a Greek Bible of the 4th century, Vergils of the 4th and 6th centuries, a 4th–5th-century palimpsest of Cicero's *Republic*, autographs of St. Thomas Aquinas, Tasso, Petrarch, Boccaccio, Poliziano, Michaelangelo, and Luther; Cardinal Protector ANTONIO SAMORE; Prefect Dr. ALFONS STICKLER, S.D.B.; Vice-Prefect Mgr. JOSÉ RUYSSCHAERT; publs. *Studi e Testi, Edizioni Illustrate, Cataloghi*. Includes:

**Gabinetto Numismatico:** f. 1738; Curator Dr. LUIGI MICHELINI TOCCI;

**Museo Sacro:** *see below.*

**Museo Profano:** *see below.*

ATTACHED INSTITUTE:

**Scuola Vaticana di Biblioteconomia** (*Vatican Library School*): c. 100 students a year; Dir. Prof. NICCOLÓ DEL RE.

## MUSEUMS

*Dir.-General of the Pontifical Monuments, Museums and Galleries:* Dott. Gr. Uff. DEOCLECIO REDIG DE CAMPOS.

**The Vatican Museums and Galleries:** Dir. Gen. Prof. CARLO PIETRANGELI; Sec. WALTER PERSEGATI; contain the following sections:

**Museo Pio Clementino:** f. by Pope Clement XIV (1770–74), and enlarged by his successor, Pius VI; exhibits include the Apollo of Belvedere, the Apoxyomenos by Lysippus, the Laocoon Group, the Meleager of Skopas, the Apollo Sauroktonous by Praxiteles; the original Vatican Museum was begun with the Apollo—already in possession of Pope Julius II when he was still a Cardinal, at the end of the 15th century—and the Laocoon Group, found in 1506; Curator Dott. GEORG DALTROP.

**Museo Sacro:** f. 1756 by Pope Benedict XIV; administered by the Apostolic Vatican Library; contains objects of liturgical art, historical relics and curios from the Lateran, objects of palaeolithic, medieval and Renaissance minor arts, paintings of the Roman era; Curator Prof. LUIGI MICHELINI-TOCCI.

**Museo Profano:** f. 1767 by Pope Clement XIII; administered by the Apostolic Vatican Library; bronze sculptures and minor arts of the classical era; Prof. LUIGI MICHELINI-TOCCI.

**Museo Chiaramonti e Braccio Nuovo:** f. by Pope Pius VII at the beginning of the 19th century, to house the many new findings excavated in that period; exhibits include the statues of the Nile, of Demosthenes and of the Augustus "of Primaporta", Curator Dott. GEORG DALTROP.

**Museo Gregoriano Etrusco:** f. by Pope Gregory XVI in 1837; contains objects from the Tomba Regolini Galassi of Cerveteri, the Mars of Todi, bronzes, terracottas and jewellery, and Greek vases from Etruscan tombs; Curator Prof. FRANCESCO RONCALLI.

**Museo Gregoriano Egizio:** inaugurated by Pope Gregory XVI in 1839; contains Egyptian papyri, mummies, sarcophagi and statues, including statue of Queen Tuia (1300 B.C.); Curator Mgr. Prof. GIANFRANCO NOLLI.

**Museo Gregoriano Profano:** f. by Gregory XVI in 1844 and housed in the Lateran Palace, it was transferred to a new building in the Vatican and opened to the public in 1970; Roman sculptures from the Pontifical States; portrait-statue of Sophocles, the Marsyas of the Myronian group of Athena and Marsyas, the Flavian reliefs from the Palace of the Apostolic Chancery; Curator Dott. GEORG DALTROP.

**Museo Pio Cristiano:** f. by Pius IX in 1854 and housed in the Lateran Palace; transferred to a new building in the Vatican and opened to the public in 1970; large collection of sarcophagi; Latin and Greek inscriptions from Christian cemeteries and basilicas; the Good Shepherd; Curator (vacant).

**Museo Missionario Etnologico:** f. by Pius XI in 1926 and housed in the Lateran Palace; transferred to a new building in the Vatican and opened to the public in 1973; ethnographical collections from all over the world; Curator Rev. P. J. PENKOWSKI; publ. *Annali*.

**Pinacoteca Vaticana:** inaugurated by Pope Pius XI in 1932; includes paintings by Fra Angelico, Raphael, Leonardo da Vinci, Titian and Caravaggio, and the Raphael Tapestries; Curator Dott. FABRIZIO MANCINELLI.

**Collezione d'Arte Religiosa Moderna:** inaugurated 1973; paintings, sculptures and drawings offered to the Pope by over 200 artists and donors; Curator Dott. MARIO FERRAZZA.

**Cappelle, Sale e Gallerie Affrescate:** Chapel of Beato Angelico (or Niccolo V, 1448-1450); Sistine Chapel constructed for Sixtus IV (1471-1484); Borgia Apartment: decorated by Pinturicchio; Chapel of Urbano VIII (1625-1644); rooms and loggias decorated by Raphael; Gallery of the Maps (1580-83), etc.; Curator Dott. FABRIZIO MANCINELLI.

Publs. for all except the Missionary Museum: *Bollettino dei Monumenti, Musei, Gallerie Pontificie*.

## UNIVERSITIES AND COLLEGES

### PONTIFICIA UNIVERSITAS GREGORIANA
### (Pontifical Gregorian University)
4 PIAZZA DELLA PILOTTA,
00187 ROME
Telephone: (06) 6701.

Founded by St. Ignatius Loyola and St. Francis Borgia, and constituted by Pope Julius III in 1553; confirmed and established by Pope Gregory XIII in 1582

The central university for ecclesiastical studies under the direction of the Jesuit Order; Pontificium Institutum Biblicum and Pontificium Institutum Orientalium Studiorum are autonomous colleges associated with the University (see below); Languages of instruction: Italian, Latin and English; Academic year: October to June (two terms).

*Grand Chancellor:* Cardinal WILLIAM WAKEFIELD BAUM.
*Vice-Grand Chancellor:* Most Rev. Father P. ARRUPE.
*Rector Magnificus:* Most Rev. Father URBANO NAVARRETE.
*Vice-Rector:* Rev. Fr. E. HAMEL.
*Secretary-General:* C. GONZÁLEZ JIMÉNEZ.
*Librarian:* J. GALLÁN DIESTE.
Library of 800,000 vols.
Number of teachers: 218.
Number of students: 2,352.

Publications: *Gregorianum, Periodica de re morali canonica liturgica, Studia Missionalia, Archivum Historiae Pontificiae, Analecta Gregoriana, Miscellanea Historiae Pontificiae, Saggi I.S.R., Studia Spiritualia, Documenta Missionalia, Studia Socialia, Acta Nuntiaturae Gallicae, Studi Critici sulle Scienze.*

#### DEANS:
*Faculty of Theology:* G. PELLAND.
*Faculty of Canon Law:* J. B. BEYER.
*Faculty of Philosophy:* F. SELVAGGI.
*Faculty of Ecclesiastical History:* M. FOIS.
*Faculty of Missionary Work:* A. ROEST CROLLIUS.
*Faculty of Social Sciences:* J. SCHASCHING.
*Institute of Psychology:* F. IMODA.
*Institute of Spirituality:* G. DUMEIGE.
*Institute of Religious Sciences:* S. BIOLO.
*School of Advanced Latin Studies:* J. GALLÁN DIESTE.

#### PROFESSORS:
*Faculty of Theology:*
ADNÈS, P., Dogmatic Theology
ALFARO, J. B., Dogmatic Theology
ALSZEGHY, Z., Dogmatic Theology
ANTÓN, A., Dogmatic Theology
BECKER, K. J., Dogmatic Theology
CABA, J., Fundamental Theology
CARTECHINI, S., Dogmatic Theology
CONROY, C., Exegesis
COX, D., Exegesis
DEMMER, K., Moral Theology
FUCHS, J., Moral Theology
GALOT, J., Dogmatic Theology
GRASSO, D., Pastoral Theology
HAMEL, E., Moral Theology
LATOURELLE, R., Fundamental Theology
LIGIER, L., Dogmatic Theology
MARTINA, G., Church History
MRUK, A., Moral Theology
NEUFELD, K., Fundamental Theology
O'COLLINS, G., Fundamental Theology
ORBE, A., Patrology and Patristic Theology
PASTOR, F., Dogmatic Theology
PELLAND, G., Dogmatic Theology
PRATO, G., Exegesis
RASCO, E., Introduction to Scripture and Exegesis
ROCHA, R. P., Liturgy
ROSATO, P., Dogmatic Theology
SULLIVAN, F., Dogmatic Theology
VANNI, U., Exegesis
VAN ROO, W., Dogmatic Theology
VERCRUYSSE, J., Church History and Ecumenical Theology
WICKS, J., Fundamental Theology
ZITNIK, M., Dogmatic Theology

*Faculty of Law:*
BEYER, J. B., Text of Canon Law
DE PAOLIS, V., Text of Canon Law
GHIRLANDA, G., Canon Law and Theology of Church Law
GORDON, I., Text of Canon Law
NAVARRETE, U., Text of Canon Law
URRUTIA, F., Canon Law and Mission Law

*Faculty of Philosophy:*
BIOLO, S., Natural Theology and Philosophy of Religion
EVAIN, F., Metaphysics and History of Contemporary Philosophy
GONZÁLEZ CAMINERO, N., History of Greek Philosophy
HENRICI, P., History of Modern Philosophy
HUBER, C., Introduction to Philosophy, Philosophy of Knowledge
HUBER, E., Marxist Philosophy
MAGNANI, G., Phenomenology and Philosophy of Religion
NOWLAN, E., Experimental and Social Psychology
O'FARRELL, F., Metaphysics
SELVAGGI, F., Cosmology and Philosophy of Science
SPROKEL, N., History of Christian Philosophy
SZASZKIEWICZ, J., Philosophical Anthropology and Philosophy of Human Culture
VALORI, P., General Ethics and History of Modern Philosophy
WELTEN, W., Philosophy of Sciences
WETTER, G. A., Marxist Philosophy

*Faculty of Ecclesiastical History:*
BLET, P., Historical Methodology and Modern Church History
DÍAZ DE CERIO, F., Philosophy of History
FOIS, M., Modern Church History and Historical Synthesis
GROTZ, H. B., Medieval Church History
MARTÍNEZ-FAZIO, L., Christian Archaeology
PFEIFFER, H., Christian Art
RABIKAUSKAS, P., Palaeography and Diplomacy

*Faculty of Missionary Work:*
DHAVAMONY, M., Hinduism and History of Religions
LÓPEZ-GAY, J., Missiology and Japanese Buddhism
ROEST CROLLIUS, A., Islamic Studies
SHIH, J., Mission Catechetics and Chinese Religions
WOLANIN, A., Mission Dogmatics

*Faculty of Social Sciences:*
BELDA F., Economic Ethics and Church Social Doctrine
BELTRÃO, P., Introduction to Social Sciences, Demography
CARRIER, H., Sociology
CARROLL, J. J., Sociology
CERECEDA, R., International and Political Law, Political Ethics
MACHA, J., Soviet Sociology and History of Sociology
MULDER, TH., Economics
SCARVAGLIERI, G., General Religious Sociology
SCHASCHING, J., Urban Sociology
STEIDL-MEIER, P., Economics

*Institute of Spirituality:*
ARVESÚ, F., Pastoral Psychology
BERNARD, C. A., Spiritual Theology
DEBLAERE, A., History of Spirituality
DE JAEGER, J.-F., Spiritual Psychology
DUMEIGE, G., History of Spirituality
FARICY, R., Spiritual Theology
GUMPEL, K., Spiritual Theology
MARUCA, D., Pastoral Theology
MOLINARI, P., Spiritual Theology
NAVONE, J., Biblical Spirituality
QUERALT, A., Spiritual Theology
RUIZ-JURADO, M., Spiritual Theology
SECONDIN, B., Pastoral Theology

*Institute of Psychology:*
AHERN, B., Holy Scripture
CUSSON, G., Spiritual Theology
IMODA, F., Psychology
KIELY, B., Psychopathology
RIDICK, J., Psychology and Statistics
RULLA, L. M., Psychology
ZADRA, D., Religious Psychology

*Institute of Religious Sciences:*
BIOLO, S., Natural Theology
DELMIRANI, M., Dogmatic Theology
GALOT, J., Dogmatic Theology
HENRICI, P., Philosophy
HUBER, C., Philosophy
MAGNANI, G., Fundamental Theology
MARTINA, G., Church History
MOLINARO, A., Moral Theology
VALORI, P., Philosophy
VANNI, U., Old Testament Introduction and Theology

*School of Advanced Latin Studies:*
FOSTER, R., Stylistics
GORDON, I., Canonical Latin
MACKOWSKI, R., Latin Languages
SANCHEZ VALLEJO, F., Stylistics

#### AFFILIATED INSTITUTES:
**Centro di Ricerche Sociologiche (CIRIS):** Piazza della Pilotta 3, 00187 Rome.

**Institut de Philosophie St. Pierre Canisius:** Kimwenza, B.P. 3724, Kinshasa, Gombe, Zaire.

# UNIVERSITIES AND COLLEGES

*Rector:* R. Mejia.
*Secretary:* E. Dirven.

**Instituto Teologico del Uruguay:** Av. 8 de Octubre 3060, Montevideo, Uruguay.
*Rector:* E. Rodríguez.

**Pontificio Istituto Regina Mundi:** Lungotevere Tor di Nona 7, 00186 Rome.
*Director:* R. M. I. Breslin.
*Secretary:* S. Alphandery.

**Studio Teologico Fiorentino:** Lungarno Soderini 19, 50124 Florence, Italy.
*Director:* Mgr. V. Mannucci.
*Secretary:* Rev. P. Kuo.

## PONTIFICIUM INSTITUTUM ALTIORIS LATINITATIS
(Faculty of Classical and Christian Letters)

PIAZZA ATENEO SALESIANO 1, 00139 ROME

Telephone: 8184641.

Founded 1964.

*President:* Sergio Felici.
*Registrar:* Remo Bracchi.
*Librarian:* Guiseppe Zver.

The library contains 21,500 vols.
Number of teachers: 10.
Number of students: 25.

## PONTIFICIUM INSTITUTUM BIBLICUM DE URBE
(Pontifical Biblical Institute)

25 VIA DELLA PILOTTA, 00187 ROME

Telephone: (06) 679.64.53.

Founded 1909 by Pope Pius X for scriptural studies; Faculty of Ancient Oriental Studies added 1932; Pontifical Biblical Institute of Jerusalem f. 1927 (branch of Roman Institute).

*Rector:* Rev. M. Gilbert.
*Director, Institute of Jerusalem:* Rev. W. Dalton.
*Secretary:* Rev. W. A. Ryan.
*Librarian:* Rev. S. Corradino.

Number of teachers: 40.
Number of students: 281.

Publications: *Biblica* (quarterly), *Orientalia* (quarterly), *Elenchus Bibliographicus* (annual), *Acta Pont. Inst. Biblici* (annual), *Analecta Biblica*, *Analecta Orientalia*, *Biblica et Orientalia*, *Monumenta Biblica et Ecclesiastica*, *Studia Pohl*.

### Deans:

*Biblical Faculty:* Rev. L. Alonso Schökel.
*Faculty of Ancient Oriental Studies:* Rev. R. Caplice.

### Professors:

*Faculty of Biblical Studies:*
Aletti, J.-N., New Testament Exegesis
Alonso Schökel, L., Hermeneutics, Old Testament Introduction and Theology
Boccaccio, P., Hebrew and Aramaic
Foresti, F., Hebrew
Gilbert, M., Old Testament Exegesis
La Potterie, I. de, New Testament Exegesis
Le Déaut, R., Targumic Literature
Lentzen-Deis, F., Judaism and The New Testament
Lyonnet, S., Exegesis, New Testament Theology
McCarthy, D., Old Testament Exegesis
McCool, F., New Testament Introduction
Mínguez, D., New Testament Exegesis
Neudecker, R., Rabbinic Literature
North, R., Archaeology and Geography
O'Callaghan, J., Greek Palaeography and Papyrology, Textual Criticism
Pavlovský, W., History of Israel
Places, E. des, History of Greek Religion and Philosophy
Proulx, P., History of Exegesis
Swetnam, J., Biblical Greek
Simian Yofre, H., Old Testament Exegesis
Vanhoye, A., New Testament Exegesis
Welch, J., Biblical Greek, Linguistics

*Faculty of Ancient Oriental Studies:*
Arnold, L., Arabic Language
Caplice, R., Accadian Language and Literature
Dahood, M., Ugaritic and Phoenician Language and Literature
Franxman, T., Mishnaic and Intertestamentary Literature
Kammenhuber, A., Hittite Language and Literature
Köbert, R., Syriac and Arabic Languages and Literature
Lavenant, R., Syriac Language
Massart, A., Egyptian Language and Literature
Mayer, W., Accadian Language and Literature
Pavlovský, W., Syriac Language and Literature
Quecke, H., Coptic, Armenian and Georgian Language and Literature
van Dijk, J., Sumerian Language and Literature

Affiliated Institute:

**Pontifical Biblical Institute:** Jerusalem. (*See* under Israel.)

## PONTIFICIUM INSTITUTUM ORIENTALIUM STUDIORUM
(Pontifical Institute of Oriental Studies)

7 PIAZZA SANTA MARIA MAGGIORE, 00185 ROME

Telephone: 731.22.54

Founded 1917 by Pope Benedict XV for the benefit of Eastern and Western scholars both Catholic and non-Catholic, interested in Oriental ecclesiastical questions.

*President:* Rev. Eduard Huber.
*Secretary:* Rev. J. Řezáč.
*Librarian:* Rev. R. Taft.
Library of 117,000 vols.

Number of professors: 36.
Number of students: 230.

Publications: *Orientalia Christiana Periodica*, *Orientalia Christiana Analecta*, *Concilium Florentinum* (*Documenta et Scriptores*), *Anaphorae Syriacae*.

# VATICAN CITY STATE

### Deans:

*Faculty of Oriental Ecclesiastical Studies:* Rev. C. Capizzi.
*Faculty of Oriental Canon Law:* Rev. J. Řezáč.

### Professors:

Amato, P., Iconography
Arranz, L. M., Oriental Liturgy
Berger, M., Iconography
Capizzi, C., Byzantine Church History and Greek Palaeography
Crouzel, H., Oriental Patrology
Dejaive, G., Dogmatic Theology
Dominic, L., Russian
Garjano, J., Oriental Patrology
Hitti, J., Oriental Canon Law
Krajcar, J., Slav Church History
Lacko, M., Balkan Church History
Lavenant, R., Syriac Patrology
Leskovec, P., Dogmatic Theology
Mateos, J., Oriental Liturgy
Mudry, S., Oriental Canon Law
Nadal, J., Dogmatic Theology
Murray, R., Oriental Patrology
Nedungatt, G., Oriental Canon Law
Obolensky, S., Russian
Olšr, J., Slav Church History and Old Slav Language
Passarelli, Byzantine Church History
Poggi, V., Church History of the Near East
Poliakova, L., Russian
Prader, J., Oriental Canon Law
Řezáč, J., Oriental Canon Law
Samir, K., Christian Arabic Literature
Senyk, S., Slavic Church History
Špidlík, T., Mystical and Ascetic Theology
Stephanou, P., Byzantine Church History
Świerkosz, S., Dogmatic Theology
Taft, R., Oriental Liturgy
Toniolo, H., Dogmatic Theology
Urumpackal, A., Malabarian Canon Law
Van Esbroeck, M., Armenian and Georgian History
Van de Paverd, F., Oriental Liturgy
Vries, W. de, Church History in the Near East, Dogmatic Theology
Wetter, A. G., History of Russian Philosophy
Žužek, J., Oriental Canon Law
Žužek, R., Dogmatic Theology

## PONTIFICIA UNIVERSITAS LATERANENSIS

4 PIAZZA S. GIOVANNI IN LATERANO, 00184 ROME

Telephone: Rome 754385, 754704.

Founded 1824.

Languages of instruction: Latin, Italian and French.

*Grand Chancellor:* H.E. Mgr. Ugo Poletti.
*Rector Magnificus:* Mgr. F. Biffi.
*Secretary:* Rev. Dr. A. Ciani.
*Librarian:* Mgr. Dr. J. V. Polc.

The library contains 300,000 vols.
Number of teachers: 144.
Number of students: 1,190.

Publications: *Apollinaris*, *Aquinas*, *Lateranum*, *Studia et Documenta Historiae et Juris*.

DEANS:
*Faculty of Theology:* Rev. Fr. B. HONINGS.
*Faculty of Canon Law:* Rev. Fr. S. OCHOA.
*Faculty of Civil Law:* Prof. P. CIPROTTI.
*Faculty of Philosophy:* Mgr. A. MOLINARO.

INSTITUTES:

**Pontificium Institutum Pastorale.**
*President:* Rev. Fr. S. RIVA.

**Institutum Theologiae Moralis** (*Academia Alfonsiana*).
*President:* Rev. Fr. D. CAPONE.

**Institutum "Augustinianum".**
*President:* Rev. Fr. A. TRAPE.

**Institutum Theologiae Vitae Religiosiae "Claretianum".**
*President:* Rev. Fr. M. AUGÉ.

**Institutum "Ecclesia Mater".**
*President:* Rev. Dr. F. MARINELLI.

AFFILIATED INSTITUTES:

**Studio Teologico del Seminario Regionale:** Via di Barbiano, 40136 Bologna; Rector Mgr. P. RABITTI.

**Istituto Teologico "Don Orione":** Via della Camilluccia 120, 00135 Rome; Dir. Rev. I. TERZI.

**Istituto di Teologia del Seminario Regionale:** 66100 Chieti; Rector Mgr. E. DI NINO.

**Istituto Teologico de Assisi:** Basilica S. Francesco, 06082 Assisi; Praeses Rev. O. BATTAGLIA.

**Istituto Teologico Marchigiano:** Via Posatora 47, 60100 Ancona; Praeses Very Rev. Mgr. O. FUSI PECCI.

**Seminario Patriarcale di Gerusalemme:** P.O.B. 14151, Beit Jal, Jerusalem; Rector P. J. MIRANDE.

**Istituto Teologico del Seminario Maggiore:** Chelmo, Poland; Rector F. ZNANIECKI.

**Istituto di Teologia a Distanza, Centro "Ut Unum Sint":** Piazza S. Giovanni in Laterano 4, 00184 Rome; Pres. Mgr. Cardinal P. PALAZZINI.

## UNIVERSITÀ PONTIFICIA SALESIANA
(Salesian Pontifical University)
PIAZZA ATENEO SALESIANO 1, 00139 ROME

Telephone: 818.46.41.

Founded by the Holy See 1940; University status granted 1973 by Pope Paul VI.

*Chancellor:* Very Rev. EGIDIO VIGANÒ.
*Rector:* Rev. RAFFAELE FARINA.
*Vice-Rector:* Very Rev. ROBERTO GIANNATELLI.
*Secretary-General:* Very Rev. MARIO MORRA.
*Librarian:* Very Rev. MARIO SIMONCELLI.

Library of 250,000 vols.
Number of teachers: 115.
Number of students: 540.

Publications: *Salesianum* (quarterly), *Orientamenti Pedagogici* (every 2 months).

DEANS:
*Faculty of Canon Law:* Very Rev. TARCISIO BERTONE.
*Faculty of Theology:* Very Rev. ANGELO AMATO.
*Faculty of Philosophy:* Very Rev. GIUSEPPE GEMMELLARO.
*Faculty of Education:* Very Rev. GUGLIELMO MALIZIA.
*Faculty of Letters (Classics and Christian):* Very Rev. S. FELICI.

ATTACHED RESEARCH INSTITUTES:

**Gratian Studies Centre.**

**Medieval Studies Centre.**

**Studies on Don Bosco Centre.**

**Psychopedagogical Research Centre.**

**Counselling Centre.**

**Scholastic and Professional Guidance Centre.**

**Electronic Computation Centre.**

ATTACHED INSTITUTES:

**Don Bosco International Institute:** Section of Faculty of Theology, Via Caboto 27, 10129 Turin.
*Vice-Dean:* Very Rev. G. CAVIGLIA.

**Philosophisch-Theologische Hochschule der Salesianer:** 8174 Benediktbeuern, Federal Germany.
*Rector:* Very Rev. O. WAHL.

**Salesian House Philosophical Studies:** 10A Avda. 36-73, Zona 11, Guatemala, C.A.
*Dean:* DANIEL MORALES.

**Salesian House Philosophical Studies:** Avda. El Liceo, Apdo. 43, Los Teques, Venezuela.
*Dean:* CORRADO PASTORE.

**Salesian House Theological Studies:** Calle Torelló 8, Barcelona 32, Spain.
*Dean:* José R. ALBERDI.

**Salesian House Theological Studies:** P.O.B. 160, Bethlehem-Cremisan, Israel.
*Dean:* GIOVANNI CAPUTA.

**Salesian House Theological Studies:** 20 Avenida 13-45, Zona 11, Guatemala, Guatemala, C.A.
*Dean:* ANGEL RONCERO MARCOS.

**Salesian House Theological Studies:** Via del Pozzo, C.P. 256, 98100 Messina, Italy.
*Dean:* FRANCIS VARAGONA.

**Salesian House Theological Studies:** Paseo de Delicias 20, Madrid 5, Spain.
*Dean:* ANTONIO QUINTANA.

**Salesian House Theological Studies:** Rua Pio XI 1100 (Lapa), St. Paul, Brazil.
*Dean:* GERALDO LOPES.

**Salesian House Theological Studies:** Kristu Jyoti College, Bangalore 560036, India.
*Dean:* THOMAS KALATHUVEETTIL.

**Salesian House Theological Studies:** Mawlai Shillong 793008, Meghalaya, India.
*Dean:* SEBASTIAN KAROTTEMPRAIL.

## PONTIFICIA UNIVERSITAS URBANIANA
16 VIA URBANO VIII, 00165 ROME

Telephone: 655-992, 65-68-640.

Founded 1627 by Pope Urban VIII.

*Rector Magnificus:* Rev. Fr. J. SARAIVA MARTINS, C.M.F.
*Vice-Rector:* Rev. Fr. EMMANUELE TESTA, O.F.M.
*Secretary-General:* Rev. Fr. F. S. CUMAN, O.F.M.CAP.
*Librarian:* Rev. Fr. W. HENKEL, O.M.I.

Number of teachers: 102.
Number of students: 811.

Publications: *Euntes Docete†, Bibliotheca Missionaria†, Annales†*.

DEANS:
*Faculty of Theology:* Rev. Fr. P. CHIOCCHETTA, M.C.C.J.
*Faculty of Philosophy:* Rev. Fr. G. MONDIN, S.X.
*Missiology:* Mgr. P. TCHAO YU-KOEN.
*Canon Law:* Mgr. V. CHE CHEN-TAO.

PROFESSORS:
*Faculty of Theology:*
DI GIORGI, S.
ERBETTA, M.
FEDERICI, T.
NIGRO, F.
PUCCINELLI, M.
SARAIVA MARTINS, J.
SCHMID, E.
TESTA, E.
VIRGULIN, S.
VISSER, J.
VODOPIVEC, J.

*Faculty of Philosophy:*
GRUMELLI, A.
MICCOLI, P.
MONDIN, G. B.
VIGLINO, U.

*Faculty of Missiology:*
ESQUERDA BIFET, J.
FILESI, T.
GROTTANELLI VINIGI, L.
SEUMOIS, A.

# UNIVERSITIES AND COLLEGES

## VATICAN CITY STATE

Faculty of Canon Law:
  ABATE, A.
  COMPOSTA, D.
  FUERTES, J.

HEADS:

Department of Languages: Rev. Fr. MARIO ERBETTA.

Institute for the Study of Atheism: Rev. P. MICCOLI.

Institute for Missionary Catechesis: Rev. Fr. PAOLO GIGLIONI.

Archivistic Centre: Rev. J. METZLER.

Institute for Missionary Research: Rev. P. PANG (Chinese Section); Mgr. C. BALDUCCI (Evangelization Section).

Attached Foreign Seminaries: Mgr. M. JEZERNIK.

## PONTIFICIA UNIVERSITÀ S. TOMMASO D'AQUINO
1 LARGO ANGELICUM,
00184 ROME
Telephone: 6790818.

College founded 1580; became University 1909; present title conferred 1963

Grand Chancellor: Rev. V. DE COUESNONGLE, O.P., Master General.

Rector Magnificus: Very Rev. P. G. SALGUERO.

Secretary-General: Rev. F. JIMENEZ.

Librarian: Rev. F. VON GUNTEN.

The library contains 140,000 vols.

Number of students: 751.

Publications: Angelicum, Rassegna di Letteratura Tomistica.

DEANS:

Faculty of Theology: Rev. E. KACZYNSKI.

Faculty of Canon Law: Rev. B. GANGOITI.

Faculty of Philosophy: Rev. A. WILDER.

Faculty of Social Sciences: Rev. C. SORIA.

ATTACHED INSTITUTES:

**Institute of Spirituality.**
Director: Rev. J. AUMANN, O.P.

**"Mater Ecclesiae" Institute.**
Director: Rev. J. CASTAÑO.

## PONTIFICIO ATENEO S. ANSELMO
5 PIAZZA CAVALIERI DI MALTA,
00153 ROME
Telephone: Rome 573569.
Telegraphic Address:
Santanselmo Aventino, Rome.
Founded 1687.

Language of instruction: Italian.

Faculties of Philosophy and Theology, Pontifical Liturgical Institute.

Grand Chancellor: Most Rev. Father VICTOR DAMMERTZ, O.S.B., I.C.D., S.TH.L.

Rector Magnificus: Rev. Father M. LOHRER, O.S.B., S.TH.D.

Secretary: Rev. Father P. D. SPOTORNO.

Librarian: Rev. Father G. FARNEDI.

Treasurer: Rev. Father P. PICAS.

The library contains 56,900 vols.

Number of professors: 55.

Number of students: 230.

Publications: Studia Anselmiana†, Rerum Ecclesiasticarum Documenta (Critical Editions of Liturgical Texts), Corpus Consuetudinum Monasticarum.

## PONTIFICIO ATENEO ANTONIANUM
124 VIA MERULANA, 00185 ROME
Telephone: Rome 779749.
Founded 1933.

Franciscan International University.

Grand Chancellor: Most Rev. Father G. VAUGHN.

Rector Magnificus: Rev. Father G. CARDAROPOLI.

Vice-Rector: Rev. Father A. SOUSA COSTA.

Secretary-General: Rev. Father C. STANZIONE.

Librarian: Rev. Father D. GUIDARINI.

The library contains 200,000 vols.

Number of professors: 85.

Publication: Antonianum.

DEANS:

Faculty of Theology: Rev. Father M. CONTI.

Faculty of Canon Law: Rev. Father A. BONI.

Faculty of Philosophy: Rev. Father E. MARIANI.

Director of Biblical Studies: Rev. Father S. LOFFREDA.

Director of Apostolic Institute: Rev. Father P. G. PESCE.

Director of Institute of Spirituality: Rev. Father O. VAN ASSELDONK.

Director of Pedagogical Institute: Rev. Father B. GIORDANI.

## PONTIFICIA FACOLTÀ TEOLOGICA DI S. BONAVENTURA DEI FRATI MINORI CONVENTUALI
VIA DEL SERAFICO 1,
00142 ROME
Telephone: Rome 5911651.
Founded 1587, re-founded 1905.

Grand Chancellor: Most Rev. Father VITALE BOMMARCO.

President: Most Rev. Father ALFONSO POMPEI.

Secretary: Father LUIGI NOLÈ.

Librarian: Rev. Father P. BONAVENTURA DANZA.

The library contains 120,000 vols.

Number of professors: 33.

Number of students: 54.

Publication: Miscellanea Francescana† (annually).

## PONTIFICIA FACOLTÀ TEOLOGICA DEI SS. TERESA DI GESU E GIOVANNI DELLA CROCE
5A PIAZZA SAN PANCRAZIO,
00152 ROME
Telephone: Rome 582362.
Founded 1935.

Academic year: October to June.

Grand Chancellor: Most Rev. Father FELIPE SAINZ DE BARANDA.

President: Very Rev. Father ERMANNO ANCILLI.

Secretary: Rev. Father ISIDORE D'SILVA.

Librarian: Rev. Father SEAN CONLON.

Library of 140,000 volumes (open to the public).

Number of teachers: 30.

Number of students: 80.

Publications: Ephemerides Carmeliticae† (specialist review twice yearly), Archivum Bibliographicum Carmelitanum (bibliographical supplement to Ephemerides Carmeliticae; annual), Bibliotheca Carmelitica (textus-studia—subsidial), Bibliographia Internationalis Spiritualitatis, Rivista di Vita Spirituale.

**Pontificio Istituto di Spiritualità:** Founded 1957; 30 teachers, 300 students; centre for bibliographical research in field of spiritual theology.

Moderator: Very Rev. Father EULOGIO PACHO.

Secretary: Rev. Father ISIDORE D'SILVA.

## PONTIFICIO ISTITUTO DI ARCHEOLOGIA CRISTIANA
(Pontifical Institute of Christian Archaeology)
1 VIA NAPOLEONE III,
00185 ROME

Founded 1925 by Pope Pius XI.

Grand Chancellor: Cardinal GABRIEL MARIE GARRONE.

Rector: R. P. UMBERTO M. FASOLA, B.

Secretary: R. P. P. SAINT-ROCH.

Librarian and Prefect of Collections: Dr. PHILIPPE PERGOLA.

Library of 35,000 vols.

Publication: Rivista di Archeologia Cristiana†.

PROFESSORS:

FASOLA, U., Christian Cemeteries and Topography of Ancient Rome
MAZZOLENI, D., Classical and Christian Epigraphy
NESTORI, A., Ancient Sacred Architecture
RECIO VEZANGONES, A., O.F.M., Christian Iconography
SAXER, V., Hagiography and Liturgy of the Early Church
TESTINI, P., General Introduction to Christian Archaeology

## PONTIFICIO ISTITUTO DI MUSICA SACRA

20A PIAZZA S. AGOSTINO, ROME
Founded 1911 by Pope Pius X.

*Grand Chancellor:* Cardinal WILLIAM WAKEFIELD BAUM.
*President:* Most Rev. Dr. FERDINAND HABERL.
*Prefect of Studies:* Father EGIDIO CIRCELLI, O.F.M.
*Secretary:* Rag. Cav. ALDO. BARTOCCI.

Number of teachers: 19.
Number of students: 112.

Publication: *Calendar.*

## PONTIFICIO ISTITUTO DI STUDI ARABI E ISLAMICI

PIAZZA DI S. APOLLINARE 49, 00186 ROME
Telephone: 656-11-31/656-15-92.
Founded 1949.

*Director:* Father ANDRÉ FERRE.
*Librarian:* Father ALBERT MULLER.

The library contains 10,000 vols.

Number of teachers: 11.
Number of students: 80.

Publications: *Islamochristiana*† (annual), *Etudes Arabes*† (quarterly), *Encounter* (*Documents for Christian-Muslim Understanding*) (10 a year).

# VENEZUELA
## Population 13,913,000

## ACADEMIES

### Caracas

**Academia Venezolana de la Lengua** (*Venezuelan Academy of Language*): Bolsa a San Francisco; f. 1882; correspondent of the Real Academia Española, Madrid; library (*see* under Libraries); publ. *Boletín* (quarterly).
*Director:* RENÉ DE SOLA.
*Secretary:* LUIS BELTRÁN GUERRERO.
*Librarian:* FRAY CESÁREO DE ARMELLADA.

**Academia Nacional de la Historia** (*National Academy of History*): Bolsa a San Francisco, Palacio de las Academias; f. 1888; library (*see* under Libraries); publs. *Boletín, Memorias, Anuario*.
*Director:* Dr. BLAS BRUNI CELLI.
*First Vice-Director:* Dr. RAMÓN J. VELÁSQUEZ.
*Second Vice-Director:* Dr. OSCAR BEAUJON.
*Secretary:* Dr. CARLOS FELICE CARDOT.
*Librarian:* Dr. MARIO BRICEÑO PEROZO.

**Academia Nacional de Medicina** (*National Academy of Medicine*): Bolsa a San Francisco, Apdo. Postal 804; f. 1904; 40 mems.; library (*see* under Libraries); publ. *Gaceta Médica de Caracas*.
*President:* Dr. RAFAEL RÍSQUEZ IRIBARREN.
*Vice-President:* Dr. GABRIEL BRICEÑO ROMERO.
*Secretary:* Dr. LEOPOLDO BRICEÑO IRAGORRY.
*Treasurer:* Dr. ERNESTO VIZCARRONDO.
**Librarian:** Dr. RICARDO ARCHILA.

**MEMBERS (by seniority):**
BRICEÑO ROMERO, G.
GARCÍA GALINDO, G.
BAQUERO GONZÁLEZ, RICARDO (elected)
ARCHILA, RICARDO
BEAUJÓN, OSCAR
BRICEÑO MAAZ, TULIO
MÁRQUEZ REVERÓN, VICTORINO
OROPEZA, PASTOR
LEÓN, AUGUSTO
GABALDÓN, ARNOLDO
RODRÍGUEZ DÍAZ, LUIS H.
ZÚÑIGA CISNEROS, MIGUEL
TOLEDO TRUJILLO, H.
PAZ, OTTO
BRUNI CELLI, BLAS
IZAGUIRRE, PABLO
LAYRISSE, MIGUEL (elected)
AGÜERO, OSCAR (elected)
CASTILLO, RAFAEL
CORONIL FERNANDO, RUBÉN
VIZCARRONDO, ERNESTO
ALVAREZ, PEDRO J.
ANZOLA CARRILLO, A. J.
KERDEL VEGAS, FRANCISCO
RODRÍGUEZ, CÉSAR
GUERRA MAS, JOSÉ B. (elected)
VALENCIA PARPACÉN, JOEL
JIMÉNEZ ARRÁIZ, J. T.
CASTRO, PEDRO B.
PIFANO, FÉLIX
CONVIT, JACINTO (elected)
MORALES ROCHA, J.
O'DALY, JOSÉ A.
RÍSQUEZ IRIBARREN, RAFAEL
DE ARMAS, JULIO
IRIARTE, DAVID R.
BRICEÑO IRAGORRY, LEOPOLDO
GONZÁLEZ CÉLIS, JORGE
VEGAS, MARTÍN
GRANIER, MARCEL

**Academia de Ciencias Exactas, Físicas e Matemáticas** (*Academy of Sciences*): Bolsa a San Francisco, Apdo. 1421; f. 1917; 30 Venezuelan, 20 foreign mems.; Permanent Commissions: Mathematics; Applied Mathematics; Astronomy, Geography, Hydrography and Navigation; Physical Science; Chemistry; Natural Science and Resources of the Country; Study of Educational Textbooks; Geology and Minerals; Agronomy; Meteorology; publs. *Boletín* (quarterly), collections of works.
*President:* Dr. GUSTAVO RIVAS MIJARES.
*First Vice-President:* EDGARD PARDO STOLK.
*Second Vice-President:* VICTOR SARDI SOCORRO.
*Secretary:* JOSÉ LORENZO PRADO C.
*Treasurer:* LUIS WANNONI LANDER.
*Librarian:* ALBERTO E. OLIVARES.

MEMBERS:
Drs.:
ANDUZE, PABLO J.
ARISTAGUIETA, LEANDRO
AZPURUA, PEDRO PABLO
BAEZ DUARTE, LUIS (elected)
BELLARD PIETRI, EUGENIO DE
BERTI, ARTURO LUIS
BRICEÑO-IRAGORRY, LEOPOLDO
BRUNI CELLI, BLAS
CARRILLO, JOSÉ MARÍA
FERNÁNDEZ MORÁN, HUMBERTO
GRANIER D., MARCEL
KERDEL VEGAS, FRANCISCO
LASSER, TOBÍAS
LÓPEZ, VÍCTOR M.
LUSTGARTEN, PAUL (elected)
MICHALUP, ERICH
O'DALY, JOSÉ A.
OLIVARES, ALBERTO E.
PARDO STOLK, EDGARD
PARRA LEÓN, MIGUEL
PHELPS, WILLIAM H.
PRADO, JOSÉ LORENZO
RAVARD, RAFAEL ALFONZO (elected)
RIVAS MIJARES, GUSTAVO
ROMERO, ADOLFO C.
SARDI SOCORRO, VÍCTOR
VEGAS, LUIS FELIPE
VERA-IZQUIERDO, SANTIAGO
WANNONI LANDER, LUIS
ZULOAGA, GUILLERMO

**Academia de Ciencias Políticas y Sociales** (*Academy of Political and Social Sciences*): Palacio de las Academias, Antigua Universidad Central; f. 1917; publ. *Boletín*.
*President:* Dr. OSCAR GARCÍA VELUTINI.
*First Vice-President:* Dr. TOMÁS ENRIQUE CARRILLO BATALLA.
*Second Vice-President:* Dr. NUMA QUEVEDO.

*Secretary:* Dr. Víctor M. Alvarez.
*Treasurer:* Dr. Alejandro Urbaneja Achelpohl.
*Librarian:* Dr. Jesús Leopoldo Sánchez.

Members (by seniority):

Schacht Aristeguieta, Efrain
Caldera Rodríguez, Rafael
Urbaneja Blanco, Luis Felipe
Muci-Abraham, José
Uslar Pietri, Arturo
Díez, Julio
Lara Peña, Pedro José
López Herrera, Francisco
Mármol, Francisco Manuel
Carrillo Batalla, Tomás Enrique
Monsalve Casado, Ezequiel
Guzmán, Pedro P.
Venegas Filardo, Pascual
Urbaneja Achelpohl, Alejandro
Leopoldo Sánchez, Jesús
Arismendi, José Loreto
Sanabria, Edgard
de Sola, René
Alvarez, Víctor M.
Escovar Salom, R.
Chiossone, Tulio
Mijares, Augusto
García Velutini, Oscar
Montiel Molero, Carlos
Parra Aranguren, Gonzalo
Parra, Darío
Lares Martínez, Eloy
Loreto, Luis
González Gorrondona, José Joaquin
Villalba Villalba, Luis
Quevedo, Numa
Aguilar Mawdsley, Andrés (elected)
Brewer Carías, Allan Randolph
Mendoza Goiticoa, Carlos (elected)
Duque Sánchez, José Román

# LEARNED SOCIETIES

### Architecture and Town Planning

**Asociación de Agrimensores de Venezuela** (*Surveyors' Association*): c/o Colegio de Ingenieros de Venezuela, Caracas; Pres. Agm. Germán Añez Otero; Sec. Agm. Rafael Elster Noda.

**Colegio de Arquitectos de Venezuela** (*Venezuela Architects' Association*): Apdo. 5262, Caracas; f. 1945 as Sociedad Venezolana de Arquitectos; 478 mems.; Pres. Arq. Carlos Guinard Baldó; Sec. Arq. José Guerrero Alvarez; publ. *Revista del CAV*.

**Junta Nacional Protectora y Conservadora del Patrimonio Histórico y Artístico de la Nación** (*Commission for the Protection and Preservation of the Historical and Artistic Heritage of the Nation*): Caracas; there is a subsidiary office in each State; authorizes exploration and excavation of sites; mems. are nominated by the Government for five-year terms, and may be re-elected.

### The Arts

**Asociación Venezolana Amigos del Arte Colonial** (*Venezuelan Association of Friends of Colonial Art*): Museo de Arte Colonial, Quinta de "Anauco", Avda. Panteón y Calle Gamboa, San Bernardino, Caracas; preservation and collection of period furniture, paintings, architectural forms, music, silver, etc. up to 1810; Pres. Dr. Lucas Guillermo Castillo Lara; Vice-Pres. Carlos F. Duarte; publ. *Revista*.

**Consejo Nacional de la Cultura (CONAC)** (*National Cultural Council*): Avda. Principal de Chuao, Edificio Los Roques, Apdo. 50995, Caracas; f. 1975; for the planning, promotion, dissemination and formation of human resources in the fields of music, theatre, dancing, plastic arts, literature, libraries, historic and artistic resources, museums, cinema and folklore; Pres. Dr. José Luis Alvarenga; Sec. Dr. José Vicente Torres; publs. *Revista Nacional de Cultura* (every 2 months)†, *Revista "IMAGEN"*† (monthly), *Revista de Teatro "ESCENA"* (weekly), *Revista Nacional de Folklore*† (weekly).

**Instituto Interamericano de Etnomusicologia y Folklore** (*Interamerican Institute for Ethnomusicology and Folklore*): Apdo. Postal 81015, Caracas; f. 1970; attached to CONAC (see above); multi-national centre for the OAS Regional Development Programme; aims to preserve and protect the American cultural heritage; specialized library of 1,300 vols., 164 periodicals; Dir. Dra. Isabel Aretz; publs. *Revista INIDEF, Cuadernos INIDEF*.

**Instituto Zuliano de la Cultura "Andrés E. Blanco"**: Gobernación del Estado Zulia, Academia de Bellas Artes, "Neptali Rincón", Maracaibo; f. 1972; administers all the cultural institutes in the state; Dir. Carmen Delgado Peña; Administrator Domingo Guzmán Ramos.

**Sociedad Amigos del Museo de Bellas Artes** (*Society of the Friends of the Museum of Fine Arts*): Museo de Bellas Artes, Parque los Caobos, Caracas; f. 1957; 250 mems.; Pres. Mimi de Herrera Uslar; Exec. Sec. Ana de Besson.

### Bibliography

**Colegio de Bibliotecologos y Archivologos de Venezuela** (*Venezuelan Library and Archives Association*): Apdo. 6283, Caracas; f. 1962; 340 mems.; Pres. Florencia Fuentes Z.; Sec. Aida Espinoza Biord; publ. *Boletín Informativo*.

### Economics, Law and Politics

**Colegio de Abogados del Distrito Federal** (*Lawyers' Association*): Apdo. 347, Caracas; f. 1788; 2,000 mems.; Pres. Dr. Luis González Berti; Sec. Dr. Adán Febres Cordero; publ. *Revista*.

### Education

**Centro Regional para la Educación Superior en América Latina y el Caribe/Regional Centre for Higher Education in Latin America and the Caribbean:** Apdo. postal 62090, Caracas 1060; f. 1978 by UNESCO; promotes co-operation in the field of higher education among the countries of the region; exchange of personnel, information and experience; serves as secretariat of regional cttee. for validation of courses and diplomas; library of 2,000 vols., 300 periodicals; Dir. Enrique Oteiza; publs. *Educación Superior, Boletín de Adquisiciones, Boletín de Resúmenes*.

**Consejo Nacional de Universidades** (*National University Council*): Avda. Urdaneta, Edif. Bco. Italo, piso 4, Caracas; f. 1946; consists of staff and student representatives of all universities and representatives from the Ministry of Finance and the Science Council; library of 2,000 vols.; Pres. The Minister of Education; Perm. Sec. Alberto Drayer B.; publ. *Boletín Informativo* (quarterly).

**Grupo Universitario Latinoamericano para la Reforma y Perfeccionamiento de la Educación** (*Latin American University Group for Reform and Improvement in Education*): Calle Occidente, Edif. IESA, San Bernardino, Caracas; f. 1958; higher education, research, and educational planning; Pres. Dr. Luis M. Peñalver; Dir. Dr. Miguel Escotet; publs. *Universitas 2000*† (quarterly), *Newsletter*† (monthly).

## LEARNED SOCIETIES

### History, Geography and Archaeology

**Academia de Historia del Zulia:** Academia de Bellas Artes, Maracaibo; f. 1940; 12 mems.; Pres. Abrahán Belloso; Sec.-Gen. Aniceto Ramírez y Astier; Librarian José A. Butrón Olivares; publ. *Boletín*.

**Centro de Historia del Táchira** (*Historical Centre*): Avda. 19 Abril 9-111, San Cristóbal; f. 1942; Dir. Ing. Xuan Tomás García-Tamayo; Sec. Lic. Nerio Leal-Chacón; publ. *Boletín†*.

**Centro de Historia Larense** (*Lara Historical Centre*): Casa Colonial, Calle 22, diagonal a Plaza Lara, Apdo. 406, Barquisimeto, Distrito Iribarren; f. 1941; 12 mems.; publ. *Boletín*; library of c. 1,000 vols.

**Centro Histórico Sucrense** (*Historical Centre*): Cumaná; f. 1945; 24 national and 14 foreign corresp. mems.; Dir. R. P. Fray Cayetano de Carrocera; Sec.-Gen. Br. Alberto Sanabria; publ. *Boletín*.

**Sociedad Bolivariana de Venezuela** (*Bolivar Society*): Apartado 874, Caracas; to promote by all available media the knowledge of Simón Bolívar's life and works, as well as his political, cultural and social ideas and publishes about 15,000 volumes of historical works per year; 180 mems.; library of 3,000 vols.; Pres. Dr. Luis Villalba-Villalba; Sec. J. A. Escalona-Escalona; publ. *Revista de la Sociedad Bolivariana*.

### International Cultural Institutes

**Alianza Francesa en Venezuela:** Apdo. 61000, Chacao, Caracas 106; f. 1976 to promote French language and culture; brs. in Valencia and Maracaibo; 142 mems.; library of 2,000 vols.; Pres. Dr. Marcel Granier Doyeux; Sec. Dr. Nelson Socorro; publs. *Bulletins* (annually).

**Asociación Cultural Humboldt** (*Venezuelan Cultural Institute*): Edif. Pigalle, 1° piso, Av. L. da Vinci, Colinas de Bello Monte, Caracas; f. 1949; affiliated to the Goethe-Institut; library of 7,000 vols.; German and Spanish classes, concerts, lectures, films and exhibitions; 450 mems. including branches in Maracaibo and Mérida; Dir. Dr. Egon Graf von Westerholt; Pres. Dr. Pedro Trebbau M.; publ. *Annual Bulletin*.

**British Council:** Edificio Los Frailes, Piso 4°, Calle La Guairita, Chuao (Apdo. 1246), Caracas 101; Representative J. Mallon, O.B.E.

**Centro Venezolano-Americano** (*Venezuelan-American Centre*): Avda. Ppl. Las Mercedes, Edificio C.V.A., Caracas 1060; f. 1941; English and Spanish classes; library of 13,000 vols.; cultural programme of art and music; Pres. Dr. Carlos E. Bullos; Dir.-Gen. Dr. Lorenzo Monroy.

**Instituto Cultural Venezolano-Británico** (*Venezuelan-British Cultural Institute*): Apdo. 51055, Caracas 105; f. 1941; English classes given; lectures, concerts and films; centre for British academic examinations; library of 9,500 vols.; 200 mems.; Pres. Dr. T. Lasser; Dir. Thomas P. Gale.

**Instituto Venezolano-Francés** (*French-Venezuelan Institute*): Avda. Buenos Aires, Los Caobos, Apdo. 62324, Caracas; French classes, language laboratory, library of 7,000 vols.; theatre, cinema; Dir. Robert Boucher; Sec.-Gen. Gabriel Geneix.

**Instituto Venezolano-Italiano de Cultura** (*Italian-Venezuelan Cultural Institute*): Avda. Monte Sacro, Colinas de Bello Monte, P.O.B. 51-947, Caracas; f. 1954; Italian language and culture; library of 7,000 vols.; Dir. Prof. Dr. Giorgio Valli.

### Language and Literature

**Asociación de Lingüística y Filología de América Latina (ALFAL)** (*Latin American Association of Linguistics and Philology*): Avda. Río Orinoco 12-41, Cumbres de Curumo, Caracas 108; f. 1962; c. 500 mems.; Pres. Juan M. Lope Blanch; Sec. Luis Quiroga; publs. *Boletín Informativo*, *Cuadernos de Lingüística*, *Actas*.

**Asociación Nacional de Escritores Venezolanos** (*Venezuelan Writers' Association*): Velázquez a Miseria 22, Apdo. 429, Caracas; f. 1935; Pres. José Ramón Medina; Gen. Sec. Angel Mancera Galetti; publ. *Cuadernos*.

### Medicine

**Colegio de Farmacéuticos del Distrito Federal y Estado Miranda** (*Association of Pharmacists*): Apdo. 224, Carmelitas 60688, Chacao; Calle Chivacoa, Sector Román, Urbanización Las Mercedes; deals with all aspects of the pharmaceutical industry; 1,200 mems.; library of 600 vols.; Pres. Dr. Pedro Rodríguez Murillo; Sec. Dra. Esther Valera de Pérez B.; Librarian Dra. Carmen Elena Garcia; publ. *Revista "Colfar"*.

**Colegio de Médicos del Distrito Federal** (*Doctors' Association*): Plaza de Bellas Artes, Avenida Bellas Artes, Los Chaguaramos, Caracas; f. 1942; 2,800 mems.; Pres. Dr. Néstor Bracho Semprún; Sec. Dr. Hernán Valero Díaz; publ. *Acta Médica Venezolana*.

**Colegio de Médicos del Estado Miranda** (*Doctors' Association*): Av. El Golf, Qta. La Setentiseis, El Bosque, Caracas; f. 1944; 3,100 mems.; professional and scientific association; Pres. Dr. Hernán Vásquez Rigual, m.d.; Gen. Sec. Dr. Ruben Hernández Serrano, m.d.; publ. *Cuadernos Medicos†*.

**Instituto J. I. Baldó:** El Algodonal, Antímano, Caracas; f. 1937; lung diseases; Pres. Dr. Manuel Adrianza.

**Sociedad de Obstetricia y Ginecología de Venezuela** (*Society of Obstetrics and Gynaecology*): Maternidad Concepción Palacios, Av. San Martín, Apdo. 20081, Caracas 1020 A.; Pres. Otto Rodríguez Armas; publ. *Revista de Obstetricia y Ginecología de Venezuela*.

**Sociedad Latinoamericana de Farmacología** (*Latin American Society of Pharmacology*): Apartado de Correo 2455, Caracas; f. 1964 to promote pharmacological teaching and research; 250 mems.; Pres. Dr. J. Cato-David; Sec. Dr. A. Jacir.

**Sociedad Médico-Quirúrgica del Zulia** (*Medical and Surgical Society*): Apdo. 170, Maracaibo; f. 1917; 51 mems.; Pres. Dr. Jorge Hómez Chacín; Sec. Dr. Franz Weiser; publ. *Revista*.

**Sociedad Venezolana de Anestesiología** (*Society of Anaesthesiology*): Colegio de Médicos, Apto. 40 217, Caracas; Pres. Oscar Loynaz-Reverón.

**Sociedad Venezolana de Angiología** (*Society of Angiology*): Colegio de Médicos del D.F., Caracas; Pres. Dr. Julián Morales Rocha.

**Sociedad Venezolana de Cardiología** (*Society of Cardiology*): Torre del Colegio, 15°, Oficina B-1, Avda. José María Vargas, Urb. Santa Fé, Apdo. 80.917 (Prados del Este), Caracas 1080; 196 mems.; Pres. Dr. Simón Muñoz Armas; Sec. Dr. Domingo Navarro Dona.

**Sociedad Venezolana de Cirugía** (*Society of Surgery*): Torre del Colegio, 15°, Oficina "A", Avda. José María Vargas, Urb. Santa Fé, Caracas 1080; f. 1945; Pres. Dr. Augusto Diez; Sec.-Gen. Dr. Ismael J. Salas M.

**Sociedad Venezolana de Dermatología** (*Society of Dermatology*): Colegios de Médicos del D.F., 2° piso, Caracas; Pres. Dr. Mauricio Goihman-Yahr.

**Sociedad Venezolana de Cirugía Ortopédica y Traumatología** (*Society of Orthopaedics and Traumatological Surgery*): Colegio de Médicos del D.F., Plaza Las Tres Gracias, Los Chaguaramos, Caracas; f. 1949; 197 mems.; Pres. Dr. Alberto J. Jacir S.; publ. *Boletín de Ortopedia y Traumatología* (quarterly).

**Sociedad Venezolana de Gastroenterología** (*Society of Gastroenterology*): 3 Avda. de los Palos Grandes, entre 8 y 9 transversales, No. 211/11-12, Caracas 106; f. 1945; Dir. Dr. Vicente Lecuna Torres; publ. *GEN* (quarterly).

**Sociedad Venezolana de Hematología** (*Society of Haematology*): Hospital Vargas, San José, Caracas; Pres. Dr. TULIO VILLALOBOS CAPRILES.

**Sociedad Venezolana de Historia de la Medicina** (*History of Medicine Society*): Palacio de las Academias, Bolsa a San Francisco, Caracas 101; Pres. Dr. TULIO BRICEÑO MAAZ.

**Sociedad Venezolana de Medicina Interna** (*Society of Internal Medicine*): Hospital Universitaria, Ciudad Universitaria, Caracas; Pres. Dr. ADOLFO STAROSTA.

**Sociedad Venezolana de Oftalmología** (*Society of Ophthalmology*): Apdo. 50. 150A, Caracas 1050; f. 1953; 300 mems.; Pres. Dr. OSCAR BEAUJÓN-RUBIN; Sec.-Gen. Dr. STANISLAO ARONOWICZ; publ. *Revista Oftalmológica Venezolana*† (quarterly).

**Sociedad Venezolana de Oncología** (*Society of Oncology*): Centro Médico de Caracas, San Bernardino, Caracas; Pres. Dr. VÍCTOR BRITO.

**Sociedad Venezolana de Otorinolaringología** (*Society of Oto-Rhino-Laryngology*): Apdo. postal 40174, Caracas 104; Pres. Dr. FRANÇOIS CONDE JAHN; Sec. Dr. GERMÁN TOVAR BUSTAMANTE; publ. *Acta Venezolana de O.R.L.* (annually).

**Sociedad Venezolana de Psiquiatría y Neurología** (*Society of Psychiatry and Neurology*): P.O.B. 3380, Caracas; Pres. Dr. ABEL SÁNCHEZ PELAEZ.

**Sociedad Venezolana de Puericultura y Pediatría** (*Society of Puericulture and Paediatrics*): Avda. Libertador, Edif. La Linea, Piso 9, Ofc. 93-A, Caracas 105; Pres. Dr. NAHEM SEGUIAS SALAZAR.

**Sociedad Venezolana de Radiología** (*Society of Radiology*): Policlínica Méndez Gimón, Av. Andrés Bello, Caracas; Pres. Dr. SEBASTIÁN NUÑEZ MIER Y TERÁN.

**Sociedad Venezolana de Urología** (*Society of Urology*): Apdo. 75.988, Caracas 1071; Pres. Dr. DARÍO PISANI; Sec. Dr. FELIPE PULIDO BUENO; publ. *Revista Venezolana de Urología*.

### NATURAL SCIENCES

**Asociación Venezolana para el Avance de la Ciencia (ASOVAC)** (*Venezuelan Association for the Advancement of Science*): Apdo. del Este 61843, Caracas 107; f. 1950; 3,000 mems.; publ. *Acta Cientifica Venezolana*† (6 a year).

**Consejo de Desarrollo Científico y Humanístico** (*Council of Scientific and Humanistic Development*): Universidad Central de Venezuela, Caracas; f. 1958; promotes research, finances publications, invites foreign scientists, sends representatives to International Congresses, awards scholarships; Pres. Dr. MIGUEL LAYRISSE; publs. *Bibliografía de Ciencia y Tecnología y de Humanidades y Ciencias Sociales del Profesorado de la UCV* (quarterly).

**Fundación La Salle de Ciencias Naturales** (*La Salle Foundation for Natural Sciences*): Edificio Fundación La Salle, Avda. Boyacá, Apdo. Postal 1930, Caracas; f. 1957; library (*see* under Libraries); 190 mems.; oceanography, anthropology and education; runs stations for marine and hydrobiological research, the *Instituto Universitario de Tecnología del Mar* on the island of Margarita, and various technical schools; Pres. Hno. GINÉS; Exec. Dir.-Gen. Dr. JUAN J. CAMACARO; publs. *Monografías*† (irregular), *Antropológica*† (quarterly review) and reports on oceanological studies.

**Instituto de Ciencias Naturales del Estado Zulia:** Centro de Bellas Artes, Maracaibo; f. 1954 to promote cultural activities; administered by the Instituto Zuliano de la Cultura (*q.v.*); Dir. MATILDE PIERREFEU; publ. *Boletín*.

**Sociedad de Ciencias Naturales "La Salle"** (*"La Salle" Society of Natural Sciences*): Edificio Fundación La Salle, Avenida Boyacá, PB3, Apdo. 1930, Caracas 101; f. 1940; 504 mems.; 17 hon., 42 national and 30 foreign corresps., 350 associates; comprises three depts.: Botany, Zoology and Publications; the Museum contains more than 100,000 exhibits; other museums in Barquisimeto; Dirs. Rev. Hno. GINÉS, Lic. JESÚS HOYOS; Pres. Dr. JUAN GUEVARA B.; Sec. Lic. FRANCISCO DELASCIO; publs. *Memoria* (3 a year), *Natura* (every 3 months).

**Sociedad Venezolana de Ciencias Naturales** (*Venezuelan Society of Natural Sciences*): Calle Arichuna y Cumaco, El Marqués, Apdo. 1521, Caracas; f. 1931; 770 mems.; library of 12,000 vols., 4,000 periodicals; annual exhibitions, lectures, films on nature conservation; department of speleology for study and exploration of caves throughout the country; biological station for research on flora and fauna, soil science and crop studies; department for the study of tropical orchids; studies in environmental pollution; Pres. R. AVELEDO HOSTOS; Gen. Sec. Dr. RICARDO MUÑOZ TÉBAR; publs. *Boletín de la SVCN*, *Ciencia al Día* (quarterly).

**Sociedad Venezolana de Geólogos** (*Society of Geologists*): Apartado 2006, Caracas 101; Pres. GUSTAVO CORONEL.

### PSYCHOLOGY

**Asociación Latinoamericana de Análisis y Modificación del Comportamiento** (*Latin American Asscn. of Analysis and Behavioural Modification*): Apdo. 66126, Caracas 1061A; f. 1974; professional society for psychology in research and teaching on experimental analysis of behaviour; 1,583 mems.; Pres. MIGUEL A. ESCOTET, PH.D.; Vice-Pres. CARLOS M. QUIRCE; publs. *Learning and Behavior*† (2 a year), *Alamoc Newsletter*† (quarterly).

### TECHNOLOGY

**Asociación Venezolana de Ingeniería Eléctrica y Mecánica (AVIEM)** (*Electrical and Mechanical Engineering Association*): c/o Apdo. 6255, Caracas 105; f. 1955; 3,100 mems.; Pres. GASTÓN TOZZI; Vice-Pres. DEMÓCRITO CRESPO; publs. *Energía e Industria* (every 2 months), *Boletín Informativo* (monthly).

**Asociación Venezolana de Ingeniería Sanitaria y Ambiental** (*Sanitary and Environmental Engineering Association*): c/o Colegio de Ingenieros de Venezuela, Apdo. 2006, Caracas 1050; Pres. EDUARDO GENATIOS G.

**Colegio de Ingenieros de Venezuela** (*Engineers' Association*): Apdo. 2006, Bosque Los Caobos, Caracas 101; f. 1861; 7,000 mems.; library of 4,000 vols.; Pres. DARÍO BRILLEMBOURG; Sec. JULIO URBINA; publ. *Boletín* (monthly).

**Sociedad Venezolana de Ingeniería Hidráulica** (*Society of Hydraulic Engineering*): c/o Colegio de Ingenieros de Venezuela, Apdo. 2006, Caracas; f. 1960; Pres. FEDERICO LOVERA.

**Sociedad Venezolana de Ingeniería Vial** (*Society of Transportation Engineering*): Apdo. 5669, Caracas 101; f. 1962; 347 mems.; Pres. JOSÉ MARTÍNEZ ESCARBASSIERE.

**Sociedad Venezolana de Ingenieros Agrónomos** (*Society of Agricultural Engineers*): c/o Colegio de Ingenieros de Venezuela, Apdo. 2006, Caracas; f. 1944; Pres. Ing. Agr. HUMBERTO FONTANA.

**Sociedad Venezolana de Ingenieros Civiles** (*Society of Civil Engineers*): c/o Colegio de Ingenieros de Venezuela, Apdo. 2006, Caracas; Pres. MANUEL FERNANDO MEJÍAS.

**Sociedad Venezolana de Ingenieros de Minas y Metalúrgicos** (*Society of Mining Engineers and Metallurgists*): Apdo. 18223, Caracas 1010 A; f. 1958; c. 400 mems.; Pres LUIS FRANCISCO RIVERA INFANTE; publ. *Fusión*† (every 2 months).

LEARNED SOCIETIES, RESEARCH INSTITUTES

**Sociedad Venezolana de Ingenieros de Petróleo** (*Society of Petroleum Engineers*): c/o Colegio de Ingenieros de Venezuela, Apdo. 2006, Caracas; Pres. RUBÉN A. CARLO.

**Sociedad Venezolana de Ingenieros Forestales** (*Society of Forestry Engineers*): c/o Colegio de Ingenieros de Venezuela, Apdo. 2006, Caracas; f. 1960; 360 mems.; library of 5,000 vols.; Pres. SIXTO J. PERICCHI; Sec. GERARDO ARELLANO P.; publ. *Boletín de la SVIF*† (quarterly).

**Sociedad Venezolana de Ingenieros Quimicos** (*Society of Chemical Engineers*): c/o Colegio de Ingenieros de Venezuela; Apdo. 2006, Caracas; f. 1958.

# RESEARCH INSTITUTES

### AGRICULTURE AND VETERINARY SCIENCE

**Centro Nacional de Investigaciones Agropecuarias** (*Agricultural Research Centre*): Apdo. 4653, Maracay 200, Estado Aragua; f. 1937; attached to the National Foundation for Agricultural Research; Dir. Dr. SIMÓN ANTICH; publ. *Agronomía tropical* (2 a month).

**Consejo Nacional de Investigaciones Agrícolas** (*National Council for Agricultural Research*): Torre Norte, Piso 14, Centro Simón Bolívar, Apdo. 5662, Caracas; f. 1959; functions include administration of the National Foundation for Agricultural Research; Pres. Dr. RAFAEL ISIDRO QUEVEDO; Sec. Dr. LUIS V. FRÓMETA BELLO.

**Estación Experimental de Café** (*Experimental Coffee Station*): Rubio, Bramón, Táchira; f. 1954; library of 1,100 vols.; Dir. Ing. ALFREDO RIVAS VÁZQUEZ; publ. Annual Report.

**Instituto Agrario Nacional** (*Agrarian Institute*): Quinta Barrancas, Av. San Carlos, Vista Alegre, Caracas 102; f. 1949; concerned with agrarian reform activities; Pres. ANTONIO MERCHAN; publ. *Memoria y Cuenta*†.

**Instituto de Investigaciones Veterinarias** (*Veterinary Research Institute*): Apdo. 70, Maracay, Estado Aragua; f. 1940; small specialized library; 55 mems.; Dir. Dr. MANUEL VARGAS DÍAZ.

### ARCHITECTURE AND TOWN PLANNING

**Dirección General de Desarrollo Urbanistico del Ministerio del Desarrollo Urbano** (*Bureau of Urban Development of the Ministry of Urban Development*): Edificio Banco de Venezuela, 5° piso, Caracas; f. 1946; 350 mems.; library of 20,000 vols.; Dir. Arq. DANIEL BARREIRO DELGADO.

### ECONOMICS, LAW AND POLITICS

**Centro de Estudios del Desarrollo (CENDES)** (*Centre for Development Studies*): P.O.B. 6622, Edificio Fundavec-Asovac, Avda. Neverí, Colinas de Bello Monte, Caracas; f. 1960; centre for research, teaching and planning of problems relating to economic, social and administrative aspects of Venezuelan development; under the patronage of the Central University; Dir. Dr. LUIS LANDER.

**Instituto Iberoamericano de Derecho Agrario y Reforma Agraria:** Facultad de Derecho, Universidad de los Andes, Mérida; f. 1973; training and research in agrarian law, agricultural economics, rural sociology, etc.; postgraduate and doctoral courses; Pres. RAMÓN VICENTE CASANOVA.

**Instituto Venezolano de Análisis Económico y Social** (*Institute of Economic and Social Analysis*): Apdo. 6320, Caracas; f. 1960; private institution for the study and diffusion of economic and financial problems; Pres. NICOMEDES ZULOAGA, Jr.; publ. *Orientación Económica*.

**Oficina Central de Estadística e Informática** (*Central Statistical and Information Office*): Apdo. 4593 (San Martin), Caracas 1010; f. 1978; Dir. Ing. HECTOR MARTINEZ; publs. *Anuario Estadístico de Venezuela, División Político-Territorial, Encuesta de Hogares por Muestreo, Encuesta Industrial, Estadísticas del Comercio Exterior de Venezuela, Resumen anual, Indicadores de Coyuntura, Censo de Población, Censo de Vivienda, Censo Agropecuario*.

### EDUCATION

**Instituto Latinoamericano de Investigaciones Científicas en Educación a Distancia** (*Latin American Institute of Scientific Research on Distance Education*): Calle California, Qta. Las Churrucas, Apdo. 69680, Las Mercedes 1060A, Caracas; f. 1980; research, teaching and planning in distance and open education; library of 8,000 vols.; Pres. MIGUEL A. ESCOTET, PH.D.; publ. *ILICED Newsletter* (quarterly).

### HISTORY, GEOGRAPHY AND ARCHAEOLOGY

**Centro de Historia del Estado Carabobo:** Valencia, Edo. de Carabobo; f. 1979 to conduct research into national and regional history, preserve and improve regional archives, conserve monuments, encourage and publicize celebrations of national historic events, and establish cultural relations with similar Venezuelan and foreign organizations; 24 mems.; Pres. Dr. ADOLFO BLONVAL LÓPEZ; Sec. Prof. CARLOS VICCI OBERTO; publ. *Boletín*.

**Dirección de Cartografía Nacional del Ministerio de Obras Públicas** (*Department of Cartography of the Ministry of Public Works*): Avda. Este 6, Esquina de Camejo, Edificio Camejo 1° piso, Of. 113, Centro Simón Bolívar, Caracas; f. 1935; Dir. Ing. ADOLFO C. ROMERO M.

**Instituto de Geografía y Conservación de Recursos Naturales** (*Institute of Geography and Conservation of Natural Resources*): Los Chorros de Milla, Mérida; f. 1959; library of 34,938 vols.; research in theoretical geography, applied geography and geographical techniques; committees for research and teaching technical co-ordination; documentation and information; 18 mems.; Dir. Dr. CARLOS FERRER OROPEZA; publs. *Revista Geográfica*† (2 a year), *Cuadernos Geográficos*† (irregular), *Colección Humboldt*† (irregular).

### MEDICINE

**Instituto de Medicina Experimental** (*Institute of Experimental Medicine*): P.O.B. 50.587, Sabana Grande, Ciudad Universitaria, Caracas 1051; f. 1940; research in biochemistry, pharmacology, physiology, neurology, general and applied pathology; 130 mems.; library of 23,254 vols., 1,000 periodical titles; Dir. Dr. FORTUNATO ROSA; Librarian Lic. ALECIA FREITES DE ACOSTA; publ. *Boletín Informativo Sistema Nacional de Documentación e Información Biomédica*†. (*See* also under the Universidad Central de Venezuela.)

**Instituto Nacional de Nutrición** (*Institute of Nutrition*): Apdo. 2049, Caracas; f. 1949; library of 10,000 vols.; Dir. Dr. LUIS BERMÚDEZ CHAURIO; publ. *Archivos Latinoamericanos de Nutrición*.

### NATURAL SCIENCES

**Consejo Nacional de Investigaciones Científicas y Tecnológicas (CONICIT)** (*National Council for Scientific and Technological Research*): Apartado 70617 Los Ruices, Caracas; f. 1967 for the promotion of research in the fields of physical, mathematical, natural, human and

VENEZUELA

social sciences and in technology; Pres. PEDRO OBREGON; Vice-Pres. IGNACIO IRIBARREN; Exec. Sec. LUIS ENRIQUE ALCALA.

**Dirección de Geología del Ministerio de Energía y Minas** (*Department of Geology of the Ministry of Energy and Mines*): Torre Norte Centro Simón Bolívar, Piso 19, Caracas; f. 1936; conducts national geological surveys, and research in geotechnics, marine geology and mineralogy; Dir. A. BELLIZZIA; publs. *Boletín de Geología* (2 a year), *Boletín Informativo del Centro de Análisis de Información Geológica-Minera (CAIGEOMIN)* (2 a year), research bulletins, statistical and other data (annually).

**Dirección de Minas del Ministerio de Minas e Hidrocarburos** (*Department of Mining of the Ministry of Mines and Hydrocarbons*): Torre Norte, Piso 20, Caracas 101; f. 1936; Dir. BRÍGIDO R. NATERA.

**Estación Biológica de los Llanos** (*Biological Station*): Calabozo, Estado Guárico; f. 1961; library of 3,200 vols.; Dirs. F. TAMAYO, R. A. HOSTOS, L. ARISTEGUIETA.

**Estación de Investigaciones Marinas de Margarita:** Punta de Piedras, Edo. Nueva Esparta; affiliated to the Fundación La Salle de Ciencias Naturales (*see* under Learned Societies); f. 1960; fisheries, oceanography, marine geology, aquaculture, marine food processing; publ. *Contribuciones*† (irregular).

**Estación Meteorológica** (*Meteorological Station*): Ciudad Bolívar; f. 1940; undertakes meteorological research and hydrographical surveys of the River Orinoco and its tributaries; Dir. E. SIFONTES; numerous publications on meteorology and climatology of Venezuela.

**Instituto Botánico** (*Botanical Institute*): Apdo. 2156, Ministerio de Agricultura y Cría, Caracas; f. 1920; library of 2,500 vols.; Dir. Dr. TOBÍAS LASSER; publ. *Acta Botánica Venezuelica* (annual).

**Instituto Venezolano de Investigaciones Científicas (IVIC)** (*Scientific Research Institute*): Apdo. 1827, Caracas; f. 1959; research in biology, medicine, chemistry, physics, mathematics and technology, atomic research; postgraduate studies; M.Sc. and Ph.D.; library of c. 400,000 vols. and 4,200 periodicals; Dir. MIGUEL LAYRISSE.

**Instituto Venezolano de Petroquímica** (*Venezuelan Institute of Petro-chemistry*): Edificio Norte, Piso 18, Centro Simón Bolívar, Caracas; f. 1956; official institute in charge of the government petro-chemical industry; Sec. ALFREDO CABRERA ALEMÁN.

**Liceo Náutico Pesquero:** Punta de Piedras, Edo. Nueva Esparta, Caracas; affiliated to the Fundación La Salle de Ciencias Naturales (*see* under Learned Societies); Dir. YVAN J. RAMÍREZ ROMERO.

**Observatorio Naval "Juan Manuel Cagigal"** (*Juan Manuel Cagigal Naval Observatory*): Colina del Calvario, Apdo. 6745, Caracas; f. 1890; astronomy, geophysics, seismology, meteorology, oceanography, hydrography, geomagnetism, planetarium; Dir. Capt. SAÚL CHACÍN SÁNCHEZ; publs. monthly bulletins.

**Office de la Recherche Scientifique et Technique Outre-Mer Mission Venezuela:** Apdo. 68.183, Caracas 1062-A; f. 1974; pedology, economics, demography, oceanography; 8 mems.; Dir. MICHEL R. PICOUET. (See main entry under France.)

RELIGION, SOCIOLOGY AND ANTHROPOLOGY

**Centro de Estudios Venezolanos Indígenas** (*Centre for Indigenous Venezuelan Studies*): Apdo. 261, Caracas; f. 1943; 50 mems.; affiliated to the Institute of Historical Research, Universidad Católica Andrés Bello; Pres. P. CESÁREO DE ARMELLADA; Sec. P. VINCENTE LÓPEZ; publs. *Venezuela Misionera* (monthly), irregular publs.

**Fundación "Lisandro Alvarado":** Frente a la Plaza Girardot, Apdo. 4518, Maracay 2101-A, Estado Aragua; f. 1964 (fmr. *Instituto de Antropología e Historia*); archaeological research; 38 mems. and representatives in the states of Aragua and Carabobo; Dir. HENRIQUETA PEÑALVER GÓMEZ; publ. *Boletín*†.

**Instituto Caribe de Antropología y Sociología:** Apdo. Postal 1930, Caracas 1010-A; affiliated to the Fundación La Salle de Ciencias Naturales (*see* under Learned Societies); f. 1962; anthropological research and development programmes among Indian populations of Venezuela; 6 mems.; library of 3,000 vols.; Dir. W. COPPENS; publ. *Antropológica*† (2 a year).

TECHNOLOGY

**Consejo Nacional para el Desarrollo de la Industria Nuclear:** Apdo. 68233, Caracas 106; f. 1975; Exec. Sec. Lieut. Col. JUAN A. TORRES SERRANO.

## LIBRARIES AND ARCHIVES

### Caracas

**Archivo de Música Colonial Venezolano** (*Archives of Colonial Music*): Escuela Superior de Música, Veroes a Santa Capilla; Librarian GARCÍA LAZO.

**Archivo General de la Nación** (*National Archives*): Santa Capilla a Carmelitas 5; f. 1910; Sections: La Colonia (1498-1810), La Revolución (1810-21), La Gran Colombia (1821-30), La República (1830 to present day); comprises Seminario de Investigación Archivística and courses on palaeography; Dir. Dr. MARIO BRICEÑO PEROZO; publ. *Boletín* (2 a year).

**Biblioteca Central de la Universidad Católica "Andrés Bello"** (*Central Library of the "Andrés Bello" Catholic University*): Urb. Montalbán, La Vega, Apt. 29068; f. 1953; 111,558 vols.; Librarian ANA DE FERNÁNDEZ; publ. *Montalbán*†.

**Biblioteca Central de la Universidad Central de Venezuela** (*Central University Library*): Ciudad Universitaria; f. 1850; sections on social science, the humanities, pure science and technology; official publications; reference section; 146,716 vols., 3,500 periodicals; Dir. ERMILA ELÍES DE PÉREZ PERAZZO.

**Biblioteca de la Academia Venezolana de la Lengua** (*Library of the Venezuelan Academy of Language*): Palacio de las Academias, Bolsa a San Francisco; f. 1883; 15,500 vols.; Librarian RAMÓN DÍAZ SÁNCHEZ.

**Biblioteca de la Academia Nacional de la Historia** (*Library of the National Academy of History*): Palacio de las Academias; f. 1888; 40,000 vols.; Librarian MARIO BRICEÑO PEROZO.

**Biblioteca Médica Venezolana de la Academia Nacional de Medicina** (*Venezuelan Medical Library*): Palacio de las Academias; f. 1904; 8,000 vols.; Librarian RICARDO ARCHILA; publ. *Gaceta Médica de Caracas*.

**Biblioteca de la Corte Suprema de Justicia** (*Law Courts Library*): Esquina de la Bolsa, Caracas; f. 1942; 4,500 vols.; Dir. Br. FERNANDO ARAUJO M.

**Biblioteca de la Sociedad de Ciencias Naturales "La Salle"** (*Library of the "La Salle" Society of Natural Sciences*): Av. Cota Mil., Edif. Fundación La Salle, Planta Baja 2; f. 1942; 30,800 vols.; Librarian MARÍA AUXILIADORA RAMOS; publs. *Memoria*† (3 a year), *Natura*† (quarterly).

**Biblioteca del Congreso** (*Congress Library*): Plaza del Capitolio; f. 1915; 9,000 vols.; Librarian LOURDES GARCÍA.

## LIBRARIES AND ARCHIVES — VENEZUELA

**Biblioteca "Marcel Roche" del Instituto Venezolano de Investigaciones Científicas** (*Library of the Venezuelan Institute for Scientific Research*): Altos de Pipe, Km. 11, Carretera Panamericana, Apdo. 1827; f. 1955; c. 400,000 vols., 4,200 periodicals; Librarian Hana M. de David.

**Biblioteca de los Tribunales del D.F. "Fundación Rojas Astudillo"** (*Law Library*): Apt. 344, Edificio Gradillas, 4° piso letra B; f. 1950; bibliographical services and studies; 33,000 vols.; Librarian Gert Kummerow; publ. *Boletín*.

**Biblioteca "Dr. M. A. Sánchez Carvajal" de la Sociedad de Obstetricia y Ginecología de Venezuela:** Maternidad Concepción Palacios, Avda. San Martín, Apdo. 20081, Caracas 101; f. 1940; over 8,000 vols.; also MSS. and medical history collection; Librarian Dra. Livia Escalona de Ayala.

**Biblioteca "Ernesto Peltzer" del Banco Central de Venezuela:** Torre Financiera, Piso 16, Esq. de Santa Capilla, Avda. Urdaneta; f. 1940; 73,511 vols.; Librarian Asta de Moore.

**Biblioteca Nacional** (*National Library*): Bolsa a San Francisco; f. 1833; the library now constitutes, by Act of Congress, the nucleus of the recently formed *Instituto Autónomo Biblioteca Nacional y Servicios de Bibliotecas*, following the NATIS (UNESCO) system; over 400,000 vols.; Dir. Lic. Virginia Betancourt; publs. include *Anuario Bibliográfico Venezolano*, *Catálogo General*, *Indice Bibliográfico*, *Boletín de la Biblioteca Nacional*, etc.

**Biblioteca Pública "Mariano Picón Salas"** (*Public Library*): Parque Arístides Rojas, Avda. Andrés Bello; f. 1965; 23,689 vols.; Dir. Lic. Romulo Navea Soto.

*Government Libraries:*

**Biblioteca Central del Ministerio de Agricultura y Cría** (*Library of the Ministry of Agriculture*): Centro Simón Bolívar, Torre Norte, Piso 15; f. 1936; 40,000 vols.; Librarian Luisa Bustillos García.

**Biblioteca del Ministerio de Hacienda** (*Library of the Ministry of Finance*): Centro Simón Bolívar, Edificio Norte, 4° piso, Oficina 421; f. 1937; 10,600 vols.; Librarian Olga de Giorgi.

**Biblioteca del Ministerio de Fomento** (*Library of the Ministry of Development*): Centro Simón Bolívar, Edificio Sur, 5° piso, Oficina 535; f. 1953; 6,000 vols.; Librarian Rosario Barnola.

**Biblioteca y Archivo General, Ministerio de Energía y Minas** (*Library and General Archives of the Ministry of Energy and Mines*): Centro Simón Bolívar, Torre Norte, piso 24; f. 1950; specializes in mines, petroleum, gas, energy, hydrocarbons; 8,287 vols.; Librarian Libia Hernández; publs. *Boletín de Geología†*, *Memoria del Ministerio de Energía y Minas†*, *Petróleo y otros Datos Estadísticos†*, *Carta Semanal†*, *Hierro y Otros Datos Estadísticos†*.

**Biblioteca del Ministerio de Obras Públicas** (*Library of the Ministry of Public Works*): Central Library: Centro Simón Bolívar, Edificio Camejo, Mezzanina; f. 1948; 4,312 vols.; Dir. Carlos A. Arreaza F.

**Biblioteca del Ministerio de Relaciones Exteriores** (*Library of the Ministry of Foreign Affairs*): 5,000 vols.; specializes in international law; Librarian Alicia Curiel.

**Biblioteca del Ministerio de Relaciones Interiores** (*Library of the Ministry of the Interior*): Esquina de Carmelitas, 2° piso; 3,585 vols.; Librarian Dr. Ruiz Lander.

**Biblioteca del Ministerio de Sanidad y Asistencia Social** (*Library of the Ministry of Health*): Instituto Nacional de Higiene, Ciudad Universitaria, Apdo. 61.153, Correos del Este; f. 1936; 9,411 vols.; Librarian Esperanza Reyes Baena; publs. *Revista Venezolana de Sanidad y Asistencia Social*, *Memorias del M.S.A.S.*

**Biblioteca del Ministerio del Trabajo** (*Library of the Ministry of Labour*): Centro Simón Bolívar, Edificio Sur, 5° piso; 1,000 vols.; Librarian Africa Valero Zerpa.

### Barquisimeto

**Biblioteca Pública "Pío Tamayo"** (*Public Library*): Calle 26, entre Carreras 20 y 21; f. 1911; 21,943 vols.; Librarian Germán Hurtado Reyes.

**Biblioteca Técnica Científica Centralizada** (*Central Scientific and Technical Library*): Apdo. 254; f. 1966; specializes in social sciences and technology; 15,550 vols. and 1,261 periodicals; Librarian Lic. Celmira Tirado E.; publs. *Boletín Bibliográfico†*, *Catálogo Colectivo de Publicaciones Periódicas†*, *Indice Bibliográfico de los estudios de FUDECO†*.

### Cumaná

**Biblioteca General de la Universidad de Oriente** (*General Library of the Universidad de Oriente*): Apdo. Postal 245, Cerro Colorado; 42,672 vols.; Librarian Lic. Rosa González de López.

### Maracaibo

**Biblioteca "Baralt"** (*Public Library*): Avda. 3 E No. 71-15, Apdo. 1340; f. 1961; founded and maintained by Fundación Belloso; 35,000 vols.; Librarian Mercedes Bermúdez de Belloso.

**Biblioteca Pública del Estado Zulia:** administered by the Instituto Zuliano de la Cultura (*q.v.*); Dir. Fernando Guerrero Matheus.

**Biblioteca de la Universidad de Zulia:** Apdo. de Correos 526; f. 1946; 19,000 vols.; Librarian Margarita Alvarez González.

### Maracay

**Biblioteca del Centro Nacional de Investigaciones Agropecuarias** (*Library of the National Agricultural Research Centre*): Apdo. Postal 4653, Maracay 2101, Edo. Aragua; Librarian Orfila Márquez M.

### Mérida

**Biblioteca Central "Tulio Febres Cordero"** (*Los Andes University Main Library*): Edificio Administrativo de la Universidad de los Andes; f. 1889; c. 114,000 vols.; reference books for all subjects taught in the University; large collection of 16th- and 17th-century books; Dir. Dra. Francisca Rodríguez Cruz; publs. *Boletín Bibliográfico*, *Catálogo de Publicaciones Periódicas*, *Catálogo de Tesis de Grado*, *Catálogo de Trabajos de Ascenso*.

### Trujillo

**Biblioteca "24 de Julio"** (*Public Library*): f. 1930; 12,000 vols.; Librarian Itala Briceño Rumbos.

### Valencia

**Biblioteca Central de la Universidad de Carabobo:** 11,000 vols.; Librarian Antonieta Pinto de Katz.

## MUSEUMS

### Caracas

**Casa de Simón Bolívar** (*Bolívar's House*): San Jacinto a Traposos; murals by Tito Salas depicting events of the Independence Movement; contains the correspondence and official documents written by Bolívar during the Wars of Independence; Curator Dr. VICENTE LECUNA.

**Colección Ornitológica Phelps** (*Phelps Ornithological Collection*): Sur 4, Dolores a Pte. Soublette, Apdo. 2009; f. 1938; 4 mems. of staff; Dir. WILLIAM H. PHELPS; Curator R. AVELEDO HOSTOS; occasional papers published in scientific journals.

**Galería de Arte Nacional:** Plaza Morelos, Los Caobos, Apdo. 6729, Caracas 101; f. 1976; visual art from prehispanic time to the present; 4,700 items; Dir. MANUEL ESPINOZA; publ. *Boletín* (quarterly).

**Museo de Arte Colonial** (*Museum of Colonial Art*): Quinta de Anauco, Avda. Panteón y Calle Gamboa, San Bernardino; f. 1942; Pres. Dr. LUCAS GUILLERMO CASTILLO LARA; under the supervision of the Asociación Venezolana de Amigos del Arte Colonial (*q.v.*).

**Museo de Bellas Artes de Caracas** (*Museum of Fine Arts*): Los Caobos, Caracas 105; f. 1938, enlarged 1957, 1963, 1974; paintings and sculpture by national and foreign artists; library of 3,100 vols.; Dir. MIGUEL G. ARROYO C.

**Museo Bolivariano** (*Bolívar Museum*): San Jacinto a Traposos; f. 1911 and inaugurated in present building 1960; contains 1,546 exhibits; mementos, portraits, personal relics and historical paintings of Simón Bolívar and his fellow-workers in the Independence Movement; library of 834 vols.; Dir. Dr. LINO IRIBARREN-CELIS; Sec. FLOR ZAMBRANO DE GENTILE.

**Museo de Ciencias Naturales** (*Natural Sciences Museum*): Apdo. 8011; formerly Museo de Arqueología e Historia Natural; inaugurated under present name 1940; c. 20,500 archaeological, ethnological, geological, zoological and palaeontological exhibits, with special reference to Venezuela; important herpetological collection (reptiles and amphibians); gold "guará" (funeral treasure) of the Tairona culture, artificially deformed prehistoric crania, etc.; Dir. ABDEM RAMÓN LANCINI V.; occasional publs.

### Ciudad Bolívar

**Museo "Talavera":** Calle Bolívar 103; f. 1940; pre-Columbian and Colonial period exhibits, religious art, natural science, numismatics; Dir. Dr. J. GABRIEL MACHADO; publ. *Museo Talavera*.

### Ciudad de El Tocuyo

**Museo Colonial** (*Historical Museum*): f. 1945.

### Maracaibo

**Museo Histórico Gral. "Rafael Urdaneta":** administered by the Instituto Zuliano de la Cultura (*q.v.*); Dir. EVARISTO FERNÁNDEZ OCANDO.

**Museo "Urdaneta" Histórico Militar** (*Museum of Military History*): Calle 91A No. 7A-70; f. 1936; Dir. Prof. J. C. BORGES ROSALES.

### Trujillo

**Museo "Cristóbal Mendoza"** (*Historical Museum*).

## UNIVERSITIES

### UNIVERSIDAD DE CARABOBO
AVDA. BOLÍVAR 125-39,
APDO. POSTAL 129, VALENCIA

Telephone: 215044.

Founded 1852.

State control.

*Rector:* Dr. PABLO BOLAÑOS.
*Academic Vice-Rector:* Dr. LUIS CARRILLO ROMERO.
*Administrative Vice-Rector:* Dr. LUIS DELGADO FILARDO.
*Secretary:* Dr. EZEQUIEL VIVAS TERÁN.
*Librarian:* ANTONIETA PINTO DE KATZ.

Library: see Libraries.

Number of teachers: *c.* 500.

Number of students: 40,000.

Publications: *Boletín Universitario, Revista de la Facultad de Ciencias Económicas y Sociales, Revista de la Facultad de Derecho.*

DEANS:

*Faculty of Economics and Social Sciences:* Econ. GUSTAVO HIDALGO VITALE.
*Faculty of Engineering:* Ing. FRANCISCO MANZANILLA.
*Faculty of Law:* Dr. JOAQUÍN ALVARADO.
*Faculty of Medicine:* Dr. JACOBO DIVO.

### UNIVERSIDAD CATÓLICA ANDRÉS BELLO
URB. MONTALBÁN, LA VEGA
APT. 29068, CARACAS 1021

Telephone: 47-51-10/19.

Founded 1953.

Private control: Academic year: October to July.

*Chancellor:* Excmo. Mons. JOSÉ ALÍ LEBRÚN.
*Rector:* Ing. GUIDO ARNAL ARROYO.
*Vice-Rector:* R.P. LUIS AZAGRA, S.J.
*Secretary-General:* R. P. GUSTAVO SUCRE, S.J.
*Librarian:* Lic. ANA DE FERNÁNDEZ.

Library: see under Libraries.

Number of professors: 600.

Number of students: 8,200.

Publications: *Revista Montalbán†, Revista de la Facultad de Derecho†.*

DEANS:

*Faculty of Law:* R. P. LUIS OLASO, S.J.
*Faculty of Social and Economic Sciences:* R. P. GUSTAVO SUCRE, S.J.
*Faculty of Humanities and Education:* R. P. FRANCISCO ARRUZA, S.J.
*Faculty of Engineering:* Ing. GUILLERMO VIDAL G.

DIRECTORS:

*School of Law:* Abog. MARÍA HELENA FERNÁNDEZ V.
*School of Economics:* Econ. RAFAEL LÓPEZ CASUSO.
*School of Business Administration and Accounting:* Lic. DOMINGO ACOSTA VIERA.
*School of Philosophy:* R.P. FRANCISCO ARRUZA, S.J.
*School of Letters:* Dra. LYLL BARCELÓ S.
*School of Social Communication:* Lic. CARMEN DE GRIJALVA.
*School of Education:* Lic. ADOLFO OSTOS B.
*School of Psychology:* Lic. MIGUEL ANGEL GÓMEZ.
*School of Civil Engineering:* Ing. JOSÉ ASAPCHI, S.J.
*School of Industrial Engineering:* Ing. JAVIER ARADAS.
*School of Basic Engineering:* R.P. ADOLFO HERNÁNDEZ, S.J.
*School of Social Sciences:* Dr. MARCOS BRITO.
*Centre of Indigenous Languages:* R. P. CESÁREO DE ARMELLADA.
*Institute of Historical Research:* R.P. CESÁREO DE ARMELLADA.
*Institute of Economics Research:* Dr. CHI-YI-CHEN.
*Centre of Legal Research:* Dra. CEDILIA SOSA.

## UNIVERSIDAD CENTRAL DE VENEZUELA
### (Central University of Venezuela)
CIUDAD UNIVERSITARIA
LOS CHAGUARAMOS,
CARACAS,
APDO. POSTAL 104
Telephone: 61 98 11 AL 30.

Founded 1725.

State control; Language of instruction: Spanish.

*Rector:* Dr. MIGUEL LAYRISSE.
*Academic Vice-Rector:* Dr. ERNESTO DÍAZ MONTES.
*Administrative Vice-Rector:* Dr. ALBERTO ESCOBAR FERNÁNDEZ.
*Secretary:* Dr. GUSTAVO DÍAZ SOLIS.
*Registrar:* Srta. GLADYS FERNANDEZ.
*Librarian:* Dra. ERMILA ELÍES DE PÉREZ PERAZZO.
Number of teachers: 6,477.
Number of students: 51,169.

Publications: *Memoria y cuenta, Anales, Gaceta,* faculty bulletins etc.

### DEANS:
*Faculty of Agriculture:* Dr. JOSE RAFAEL RODRÍGUEZ BRITO.
*Faculty of Architecture and Town Planning:* Dr. EDUARDO CASTILLO CASTILLO.
*Faculty of Science:* NILO GUILLÉN.
*Faculty of Engineering:* Dr. PIAR SOSA.
*Faculty of Medicine:* Dr. MIGUEL YABER.
*Faculty of Dentistry:* Dr. VÍCTOR RODRÍGUEZ URDANETA.
*Faculty of Veterinary Science:* Dr. JOSÉ LUIS LEAL MEDINA.
*Faculty of Law and Political Science:* Dr. PEDRO NIKKEN.
*Faculty of Economic and Social Sciences:* Dr. HÉCTOR SILVA MICHELENA.
*Faculty of Pharmacy:* Dr. MIGUEL ANGEL LÓPEZ.
*Faculty of Humanities and Education:* Dr. RAFAEL DI PRISCO.

There are faculties of agriculture and veterinary science at Maracay, and a faculty of engineering at Cagua.

## UNIVERSIDAD CENTRO-OCCIDENTAL "LISANDRO ALVARADO"
APDO. 400,
BARQUISIMETO, LARA
Telephone: 510-011/210/410/610.

Founded 1963 as Experimental Centre of Higher Education; University status 1968.

State control; Language of instruction: Spanish.

*Rector:* Ing. Agr. HÉCTOR OCHOA ZULETA.
*Vice-Rector:* Dr. MARIO BAPTISTA.
*Administrative Vice-Rector:* Dr. FRANCISCO DIAMONT.
*Secretary-General:* Dr. CARMEN ALICIA CARMONA DE GARCIA.
*Librarian:* Lic. PILAR DE GIMÉNEZ.
Number of teachers: 791.
Number of students: 10,631.

Publications: *Memoria y Cuenta* (annually), *Tarea Común* (quarterly), *Boletín Técnico Informativo Escuela de Agronomía, Boletín del Centro de Investigaciones de la Escuela de Administración y Contaduría, Boletín El Veterinario* (every 2 months), *Enfoques* (monthly).

### DEANS:
*Faculty of Administration and Accountancy:* Lic. FLORENCIO SÁNCHEZ.
*Faculty of Agronomy:* Ing. OMAR GIMÉNEZ.
*Faculty of Sciences:* Lic. FRANCISCO GUÉDEZ.
*Faculty of Medicine:* Dr. RAFAEL MARANTE.
*Faculty of Civil Engineering:* Ing. LUIS MARTURET.
*Faculty of Veterinary Medicine:* Dr. JORGE RAMIREZ.

### ATTACHED INSTITUTES:
*Consejo Asesor de Investigación y Servicios* (Advisory Council on Research and Services): assessment and consultation on the planning of research; Pres. Dr. H. MOUSSATCHE.
*Instituto de la Uva* (Institute for Research on Grapes): research on grape cultivation and advisory service to wine growers; Dir. HERNÁN RÍOS OHEP.

## UNIVERSIDAD DE LOS ANDES
AVDA. 3, INDEPENDENCIA, EDIF. CENTRAL, ZONA POSTAL 802, MÉRIDA
Telephone: 23201-23205.

Founded 1785 as the Real Colegio Seminario de San Buenaventura de Mérida, became University 1810. Campuses at Trujillo and San Cristóbal.

State control; Academic year: January to June, August to December.

*Rector:* Dr. JOSÉ MENDOZA ANGULO.
*Academic Vice-Rector:* Dr. ALFONSO OSUNA CEBALLOS.
*Administrative Vice-Rector:* Dr. HERBERT SIRA RAMÍREZ.
*Secretary:* Dr. ANTONIO VAN GRIEKEN MOLINA.
*Librarian:* FRANCISCA RODRÍGUEZ CRUZ.
Library: see Libraries.
Number of teachers: 2,301.
Number of students: 24,185.

Publications: *Revista Forestal, Revista de Farmacia, Revista de Derecho, Humanidades,* Faculty yearbooks.

### DEANS:
*Faculty of Law:* MILTON GRANADOS P.
*Faculty of Humanities and Education:* LUBIO CARDOZO.
*Faculty of Pharmacy:* ALONSO UZCATEGUI.
*Faculty of Odontology:* JOSÉ L. COVA N.
*Faculty of Medicine:* ROBERTO RONDÓN N.
*Faculty of Engineering:* GERMÁN MORA C.
*Faculty of Economics:* MANUEL MENDOZA ANGULO.
*Faculty of Forestry:* JOSÉ ROLANDO CORREDOR T.
*Faculty of Architecture:* VÍCTOR A. BLANCO GINEAU.
*Faculty of Sciences:* WILBERTO OMAÑA.

## UNIVERSIDAD METROPOLITANA
APDO. 76.819, CARACAS 107
Telephone: 38.71.21.

Founded 1970.

Private control; Academic year: October to March, March to July.

*Rector:* Ing. RODOLFO MOLEIRO.
*Academic Vice-Rector:* (vacant).
*Administrative Vice-Rector:* Ing. JOSÉ ABDALA.
*Chief Administrative Officer:* GINO COLPI.
*Dean of Science:* Dra. FRANCESCA PENSIERI.
*Dean of Engineering:* Dr. JUAN TORREALBA MORALES.
*Librarian:* Lic. M. ANTONIETA DE MOLLER.

### HEADS OF DEPARTMENTS:
*Physics:* Prof. VINCENSO GIAMBERNARDINO.
*Humanities:* Prof. MICHELE MARCOTRIGIANO.
*Modern Languages:* Prof. SUZY SZIDON.
*Pre-School Education:* Prof. RAQUEL ARMAS.
*Mathematics:* Prof. AUGUSTO ANSALONI.
*Chemistry:* Prof. AQUIBA MIZRACHI.
*Administration:* Prof. ALBERTO GENATIO.
*Chemical Engineering:* Prof. RUGGIERO LUGARESI.
*Mechanical Engineering:* Prof. SIMÓN HERNÁNDEZ.
*Electrical Engineering:* Prof. RAÚL ARREAZA.
*Systems Engineering:* Prof. ELÍAS LOPATA.

## UNIVERSIDAD NACIONAL EXPERIMENTAL FRANCISCO DE MIRANDA
CALLE NORTE,
CORO, ESTADO FALCÓN
Telephone: 59.335-2733.

Founded 1977.

*Rector:* Dr. Tulio Arends.
*Academic Vice-Rector:* Dr. Pedro Borregales.
*Administrative Vice-Rector:* Dr. Douglas Játem.
*Librarian:* Lic. Tusnelda Crespo.

Number of teachers: 109.
Number of students: 1,000.

Publications: *Gaceta* (quarterly), *Hoja Universitaria* (monthly), *Boletín* (weekly), *Cultura Falconiana* (quarterly), etc.

Faculties of civil and industrial engineering, medicine, veterinary science, agronomy.

### UNIVERSIDAD NACIONAL EXPERIMENTAL DE LOS LLANOS CENTRALES "ROMULO GALLEGOS"
APDO. POSTAL 102, SAN JUAN DE LOS MORROS 2301-A, ESTADO GUARICO
Telephone: (043) 2613-3250.

Founded 1977.

*Rector:* Ing. Agr. José J. González Matheus.
*Academic Vice-Rector:* Econ. Agr. César Cano Alfonzo.
*Administrative Vice-Rector:* Econ. Eduardo Carreño Llamozas.
*Librarian:* Lic. Mariela de Valero.

Number of teachers: 65.
Number of students: 340.

Faculties of agriculture and health sciences.

### UNIVERSIDAD NACIONAL EXPERIMENTAL DE LOS LLANOS OCCIDENTALES "EZEQUIEL ZAMORA"
APDO. POSTAL 19, BARINAS
Telephone: 073-41201/09.
Telex: 73171 UENEZ-V.

Founded 1975.

Language of instruction: Spanish.

An autonomous government-sponsored institute of higher education, serving the Los Llanos Occidentales region, and the States of Apure, Barinas, Cojedes and Portuguesa. Courses in agriculture and mechanization, economics, social development, regional planning, human ecology.

*Rector:* Dr. Felipe Gómez Alvarez.
*Vice-Rector (Services):* Dr. Humberto Jiménez Gonzáles.
*Area Vice-Rectors:* Dr. Martín Ramírez Blanco, Dr. Israel Tineo Gamboa, Dr. Pedro Urriola Muñoz, Dr. Juan Rivera Galvis.
*Librarian:* Lic. Zarabeth Molina.

Number of teachers: 250.
Number of students: 1,987.

### UNIVERSIDAD NACIONAL EXPERIMENTAL SIMÓN RODRÍGUEZ
APDO. POSTAL 3690, SAN MARTÍN, CARACAS
Telephone: 92.20.22.

Founded 1974.

*Rector:* Dr. Felix Adam.
*Academic Vice-Rector:* Dr. Pedro Tomás Vásquez.
*Administrative Vice-Rector:* Dr. David Bentolila.
*Secretary:* Dr. Ramón Lizardo G.

Number of teachers: 369.
Number of students: 13,607.

Publications: *Memoria y Cuenta de la Universidad* (annually), *Gaceta Universitaria* (quarterly), *Revista*.

Faculties of education and administration.

### UNIVERSIDAD NACIONAL EXPERIMENTAL DEL TÁCHIRA
AVDA. UNIVERSIDAD, PARAMILLO, SAN CRISTÓBAL, TÁCHIRA, P.O.B. 436
Telephone: (076) 59578, 59678, 59292
Telex 76196.

Founded 1974.

State control; Language of instruction: Spanish; Academic year: February to June, August to December.

*Rector:* Dr. Jorge Francisco Rad Rached.
*Academic Vice-Rector:* Ing. Quim. Francisco Mijares Santana.
*Secretary and Vice-Rector:* Lic. Pedro Rosales Acero.
*Dean of Teaching:* Ing. Agr. Alfredo Rivas Vásquez.
*Dean of Research:* Ing. Mec. Luis Ramírez.
*Dean of Extension:* Ing. Agr. Humberto Acosta Rivas.
*Dean of Studies:* Lic. Leopoldo Coronel Ocanto.
*Librarian:* Lic. Maritza Villegas de Moros.

Number of teachers: 240.
Number of students: 1,751.

Publications: *Gaceta*†, *UNET vocero Universitario*†, *Boletín*†, *Aleph sub cero*†, student guides, etc.

Heads of Departments:
*Agricultural Engineering:* Ing. Agr. Rafael Useche.
*Animal Husbandry:* Zoot. Orlando Ramírez.
*Industrial Engineering:* Ing. Ind. Alejandro López.
*Mechanical Engineering:* Ing. Mec. Trino Muñoz.
*Physics:* Ing. Elect. José Luis Peña-Dugarte.
*Biochemistry:* Med. Vet. Joaquín Vega-Coronado.
*Mathematics and Systems:* Ramón Mirabal, Ph.D.
*Social Sciences and Economics:* Lic. Heriberto Delgado Colmenares, M.A.
*Earth and Environment:* Ing. Agr. Juan José Pacheo Guerra.
*Laboratories and Projects:* Ing. Mech. José Antonio Duque-Duque.
*Process of Teaching and Learning:* Lic. Carmen Teresa Alcalde de Rosales.

Attached Centres:
*Centro de Estudios Regionales* (Centre for Regional Studies): Edificio Lisbey, Barrio Ambrosio Plaza, San Cristóbal; social and economic studies for regional development; Dir. Manuel Perez Rodriguez.
*Centro de Informacion Regional* (Centre for Regional Information): Edificio Lisbey, Barrio Ambrosio Plaza, San Cristóbal; documentation centre for information on agriculture, animal husbandry, industry, mechanics, etc. in the area; Dir. Ing. Agr. Xuan Tomas Garcia-Tamayo.

### UNIVERSIDAD DE ORIENTE
EDIFICIO RECTORADO, APARTADO POSTAL 094, CUMANÁ, ESTADO SUCRE
Telephone: 23366.

Founded 1958.

State control; Academic year: March to December.

*Rector:* Dr. Hugo Sánchez Medina.
*Academic Vice-Rector:* Dr. Alberto Ochoa Domínguez.
*Administrative Vice-Rector:* Dr. Francisco Vilacha Barreto.
*Secretary-General:* Dr. Luis Geronimo D'Lacoste.
*Director of the Libraries:* Prof. Eudes Hernández B.

Library: see Libraries.
Number of teachers: 1,181.
Number of students: 16,436.

Publications: *Oriente Universitario* (monthly bulletin), *Boletín del Instituto Oceanográfico*, *Lagena*, *Oriente Agropecuario*, *La UDO Investiga*.

Directors:
*School of Sciences:* Prof. Emir Milano.
*School of Administration:* Prof. Ibrahin González.
*School of Agricultural Sciences:* Prof. José Jesús Gamboa.
*School of Humanities and Education:* Prof. Ronald Rojas.

Attached Institute:
**Instituto Oceanográfico:** Dir. Prof. Amado Acuña.

**Nucleo Anzoátegui**
(*Anzoátegui Campus*)
Puerto La Cruz, Anzoátegui
Founded 1965.

*Dean:* Dr. Andres Pastrana.

UNIVERSITIES VENEZUELA

HEADS OF SCHOOLS:
*School of Engineering and Applied Science:* Prof. SERGIO VÁSQUEZ.
*School of Administrative Sciences:* Prof. BENJAMIN FRIAS.

ATTACHED INSTITUTE:
**Centro de Investigaciones Tecnológicas:** Dir. Prof. ROJAS BOCCALANDRO.

### Nucleo Monagas
(*Monagas Campus*)
MATURIN Y JUSEPÍN, MONAGAS
Founded 1961.

*Dean:* Dr. PEDRO A. BEAUPERTHUY.

HEADS OF SCHOOLS:
*School of Agriculture:* Prof. CÉSAR A. BOADA S.
*School of Animal Husbandry:* Prof. CARLOS ACUÑA.

ATTACHED INSTITUTE:
**Instituto de Investigaciones Agropecuarias:** Dir. Dr. HERMÓGENES FLORES.

### Nucleo Bolívar
(*Bolívar Campus*)
CIUDAD BOLÍVAR, BOLÍVAR
Founded 1961.

*Dean:* Eng. LEON GENARO CARRASCO.

HEADS OF SCHOOLS:
*School of Medicine:* Dr. FREDDY MEJIAS.
*School of Geology and Mines:* Eng. LUIS HERNANDO PEREZ (acting).

### Nucleo Nueva Esparta
(*Nueva Esparta Campus*)
PORLAMAR, NUEVA ESPARTA
Founded 1969.

*Dean:* Dr. PABLO GONZÁLEZ.
School of Biology.

ATTACHED INSTITUTE:
**Centro de Investigaciones:** Dir. Prof. MAXIMILIANO PADRÓN.

## UNIVERSIDAD RAFAEL URDANETA
APDO. 614, MARACAIBO
Telephone: 71601, 71605.
Founded 1973.

*Rector:* Dr. ELOY PÁRRAGA VILLAMARÍN.
*General Secretary:* Lic. BINGEN DE ARBELOA.
*Academic Vice-Rector:* Dr. JOSÉ LEÓN GARCÍA DÍAZ.
*Vice-Rector for Research and Postgraduate Studies:* Dr. VINICIO CASA RINCÓN.
*Administrative Vice-Rector:* Eco. JORGE SÁNCHEZ MELEAN.
*Librarian:* Lic. ANGELINA OROPEZA DE GÓMEZ.

DEANS:
*Faculty of Political and Administrative Sciences:* Dr. CARLOS ALTIMARI.
*Faculty of Stockbreeding:* Dr. GUSTAVO GARCÍA RINCÓN.
*Faculty of Engineering:* Dr. WILBERTO HERNANDEZ.

## UNIVERSIDAD DE SANTA MARIA*
FRENTE PLAZA MADARIAGA,
EL PARAISO. CARACAS
Founded 1953; Private control.

*Rector:* Dr. JOSÉ RAFAEL MENDOZA.
*Secretary:* Dr. JUAN BAUTISTA FUENMAYOR RIVERA.
*Vice-Rector:* Dr. JOSÉ RAMÓN BERRIZBEITIA.
Number of teachers: c. 300.
Number of students: c. 4,500.

DEANS:
*Faculty of Economics:* Dr. CÉSAR BALESTRINI.
*Director, School of Economics:* Dr. ALBERTO GENATIOS.
*Director, School of Administration:* Lic. LUIS F. VARELA.
*Faculty of Engineering:* Dr. HUMBERTO ACHE RAMOS.
*Faculty of Law:* Dr. HUMBERTO BELLO LOZANO.
*Faculty of Pharmacy:* Dr. RAÚL SOJO BIANCO.

* No reply received to our questionnaire this year.

## UNIVERSIDAD SIMÓN BOLÍVAR
80659 PRADOS DEL ESTE, CARACAS
Telephone: 962-11-01.
Founded 1970.

State control; Language of instruction: Spanish; Academic year: September to July.

*Rector:* Dr. ANTONIO JOSÉ VILLEGAS DELGADO.
*Academic Vice-Rector:* Dr. IGNACIO IRIBARREN TERRERO.
*Administrative Vice-Rector:* Dr. FREDDY ARREAZA LEÁÑEZ.
*Librarian:* Prof. PEDRO REIXACH.
Number of teachers: 860.
Number of students: 7,800.
Publications: *Boletin Universitario*† (fortnightly), *Revista Atlántida*†, *Revista Tiempo Real*†.

DEANS:
*General Studies:* Dr. JOSÉ SANTOS URRIOLA.
*Professional Studies:* Dr. SIMÓN SPÓSITO.
*Postgraduate Studies:* Dr. SIMÓN LAMAR.
*Liberal Studies:* Dr. JOSÉ GIMÉNEZ ROMERO.
*Research:* Dr. JULIÁN CHELA FLORES.

DIVISION DIRECTORS:
*Physics and Mathematics:* Dr. JUAN LECUNA.

*Humanities and Social Sciences:* Dr. DINO GARBER.
*Biological Sciences:* Dr. FELIPE MARTÍN SALAZAR.

ATTACHED RESEARCH INSTITUTES:
**Instituto del Petróleo:** Dr. JUAN JONES PARRA.
**Instituto de Tecnología y Ciencias Marinas:** Dr. JOSÉ ANTONIO GALAVÍS.
**Instituto de Investigaciones Educativas:** Dr. GERARDO TÁLAMO BUSTILLOS.
**Instituto de Altos Estudios de América Latina:** Dr. MIGUEL ANGEL BURELLI RIVAS.
**Instituto de Recursos Naturales Renovables:** Dr. ANTONIO JOSÉ VILLEGAS DELGADO (acting).
**Instituto de Estudios Regionales y Urbanos:** Dr. OMER LARES.
**Instituto de Investigaciones Metalúrgicas:** Dr. JOAQUÍN LIRA OLIVARES.
**Instituto de Energía Eléctrica:** Dr. MANUEL ACOSTA.
**Instituto de Investigación y Desarrollo Industrial:** Dr. ESTEBAN BERTHA.

## UNIVERSIDAD DE TÁCHIRA
CARRERA 14 CON CALLE 14, APT. 366, SAN CRISTÓBAL, EDO. TÁCHIRA
Telephone: 31-3-90.

Founded 1962; fmrly. campus of Universidad Católica Andrés Bello.

*Vice-Rector:* R.P. CÉSAR HUMBERTO NIÑO, S.J.
*Vice-Rector:* Dr. CARLOS REYNA, S.J.
Number of teachers: 110.
Number of students: 2,035.
Publication: *Revista U.C.A.B.E.T.* (twice yearly).

DIRECTORS:
*School of Law:* Dr. JULIO SUÁREZ LOZADA.
*School of Business and Administration:* Lic. CONRADO CONTRERAS PULIDO.
*School of Education:* R.P. CÉSAR HUMBERTO NIÑO, S.J.
*School of Basic Engineering:* Dr. JOSÉ ANTONIO BAUIRS.

## UNIVERSIDAD DEL ZULIA
APDO. DE CORREOS 526,
MARACAIBO 4011, EDO. ZULIA
Telephone: 515077-81 and 512077-81.

Founded 1891, closed 1904, reopened 1946.

State control; Academic year: February to December.

*Rector:* (vacant).
*Academic Vice-Rector:* Ing. RICARDO A. CARRILLO M.
*Administrative Vice-Rector:* Dr. ARMANDO SOTO ESCALONA.

Secretary: Dr. Rafael Acosta Martínez.

Librarian: Lic. Sofía González.

Number of teachers: 1,415.
Number of students: 26,882.
Library: see under Libraries.

Publications: *Memoria y Cuenta de L.U.Z.*, *Periodico de L.U.Z.* (fortnightly), *Revista de L.U.Z.*, *Boletín Estadístico*, faculty reviews and information bulletins.

### Deans:

Faculty of Law: Dr. Ricardo Hernández Ibarra.

Faculty of Humanities and Education: Lic. Imelda Rincón de Maldonaldo.

Faculty of Economic and Social Sciences: Lic. Antonio Matheus Colina.

Faculty of Medicine: Dr. Gilberto Olivares Romero.

Faculty of Engineering: Ing. Antonio Cova Ríos.

Faculty of Agriculture: Ing. Agr. Edmundo Rubio Espina.

Faculty of Dentistry: Dr. Fernando Barrios Carvajal.

Faculty of Architecture: Arq. Aquiles Asprino Perozo.

Faculty of Veterinary Sciences: Dr. José Ch. Montilla.

Faculty of Experimental Sciences: Lic. Antonio Castejón.

### Directors:

School of Law: Dr. Jan Van Den Berg de Urdaneta.

School of Medicine: Dr. Ricardo Cárdenas.

School of Dentistry: Dr. Luis Barrios Carvajal.

School of Nutrition and Dietetics: Lic. Miriam de Costabella.

School of Nursing: Lic. Ligia Palazzi.

School of Economics: Econ. Iris Moreno de Villasmil.

School of Business Administration and Accountancy: Lic. Emercio Cacique.

School of Agricultural Engineering: Ing. Agr. Enio Wilhelm Rubio.

School of Petroleum Engineering: Ing. Nelson Cardozo.

School of Civil Engineering: Ing. Antonio Cova.

School of Geodetic Engineering: Ing. Jesús Morón.

School of Chemical Engineering: Ing. Pierre Lichaa.

School of Mechanical Engineering: Ing. Rafael Hoiro.

School of Journalism: (vacant).

School of Education: Lic. Yolanda Avila de Pirela.

School of Letters: Lic. Carlos Sánchez.

School of Philosophy: Dr. Antonio Pérez Estevez.

School of Architecture: Arq. Avelino Casado Parrondo.

School of Veterinary Science: Dr. Angel Rafael Chirinos.

School of Bio-Analysis: Dr. Pedro Mármol.

School of Sociology: Soc. Elsa Romero de Baptista.

Department of General Studies (Maracaibo): Rubén Prieto.

Department of General Studies (Punto Fijó): Lic. Jacinto Lugo.

Department of General Studies (Cabimas): Lic. Pedro Mavarez.

Department of Basic Engineering: Dr. Jesús Ortega González.

### Attached Research Institutes:

**Centro de Investigaciones Criminológicas** (*Research Centre of Criminology*): Dir. Dra. Lola Aniyar de Castro.

**Instituto de Medicina del Trabajo** (*Institute of Labour Medicine*): Dir. Dr. Rafael Quevedo.

**Instituto de Investigaciones Clínicas** (*Institute of Clinical Research*): Dir. Dra. Elena Ryder.

**Instituto de Cálculo Aplicado** (*Institute of Applied Calculus*): Dir. Juan Simón Márquez.

**Instituto de Investigaciones Odontológicas** (*Research Institute of Dentistry*): Dir. Dr. Gustavo Jiménez Maggiolo.

**Centro de Investigaciones Económicas** (*Institute of Economic Research*): Dir. Econ. Ángel Felipe Díaz.

**Centro de Investigaciones Humanísticas** (*Humanities Research Centre*): Dir. Lic. Noemí de Pérez.

**Centro de Estudios Literarios** (*Centre for Literary Studies*): Dir. Dr. José A. Castro.

**Centro de Documentación e Información Pedagógica** (*Centre for Educational Documentation and Information*): Dir. Lic. Inés Laredo.

**Centro de Estudios Matemáticos** (*Centre for Mathematical Studies*): Dir. Lic. Wiliberto Díaz.

**Unidad de Investigación Biológica** (*Biological Research Unit*): Co-ordinator Dr. Orlando Castejón.

**Centro de Orientación:** Dir. Lic. Edelmira Duarte de Aquaviva.

**Centro de Investigaciones Urbanas y Regionales** (*Centre for Urban and Regional Research*): Dir. Arq. Ramón Pérez Rodríguez.

**Instituto de Filosofía del Derecho** (*Institute of Legal Philosophy*): Dir. Dr. José Manuel Delgado O.

**Unidad de Genética Médica** (*Unit for Medical Genetics*): Dir. Dra. Sandra de Mena.

**Centro de Cirugía Experimental** (*Centre for Experimental Surgery*): Dir. Dr. José L. García Díaz.

**Centro Estación Biológica "Kasmera"** (*"Kasmera" Biological Station*): Dir. Dr. Adolfo Pons.

**Instituto de Investigaciones Petroleras** (*Centre for Petroleum Research*): Dir. Ing. Rolando López.

**Centro de Estudios de la Empresa** (*Centre for Business Studies*): Lic. Juan Laya Baquero.

**Centro de Investigaciones Biológicas** (*Centre for Biological Research*): Lic. Lope García Pinto.

**Centro Audiovisual** (*Audiovisual Centre*): (vacant).

**Centro de Estudios para Graduados, Facultad de Economía** (*Centre for Graduate Studies, Faculty of Economics*): Econ. Benildo Gómez Bonilla.

**Centro de Estudios Filosóficos** (*Centre for Philosophical Studies*): Lic. Angel Bustillos.

**Instituto de Investigaciones Agronómicas** (*Institute of Agricultural Research*): Ing. Agr. Publio Santiago.

**Centro Experimental de Producción Animal** (*Experimental Centre for Animal Production*): Dr. Freddy Perozo Gory.

# COLLEGE

## INSTITUTO UNIVERSITARIO POLITÉCNICO

APDO. POSTAL 539, BARQUISIMETO, ESTADO LARA

Telephone: 051-41-10-01/05.

Founded 1962.

Mechanical, Electrical, Chemical, Metallurgical and Electronic Engineering; Mechanical and Electrical Technology.

Director: Ing. Matías Pérez.

Academic Sub-director: Ing. José Mariano Navarro.

Administrative Sub-director: Econ. Edgar Urbaez.

Number of teachers: 160.

Number of students: 2,600.

Publication: *Catálogo*† (annually).

# SCHOOLS OF ART AND MUSIC

**Academia de Bellas Artes "Neptali Rincón"** (*School of Plastic Arts*): Centro Vocacional Dr. O. Hernández, Avenida El Milagro, Maracaibo; f. 1957; courses in painting, sculpture, ceramics, etc.; 12 teachers, 300 students; Dir. Prof. I. Rossi.

SCHOOLS OF ART AND MUSIC / VENEZUELA

**Academia de Música "Padre Sojo"** (*Padre Sojo Academy of Music*): Avenida Los Granados, La Castellana; P.O.B. 60479 Este, Caracas; Dir. Prof. José Antonio Calcaño.

**Academia de Música Fischer** (*Fischer Academy of Music*): Edif. Léon de San Marco, Avda. Ciencias y Calle Risquez, Los Chaguaramos, Caracas; Dir. Carmen de Fischer.

**Conservatorio de Música "José Luis Paz":** Maracaibo; administered by the Instituto Zuliano de la Cultura (q.v.); Dir. Prof. Luis Soto Villalobos.

**Conservatorio Italiano de Música** (*Italian Conservatoire of Music*): Edif. Centro Venezolano-Italiano de Cultura, Avda. Anauco, Colinas de Bello Monte, Caracas; Dir. C. Galzio.

**Escuela de Artes Visuales "Cristóbal Rojas"** (*Cristóbal Rojas School of Visual Arts*): Avda. Lecuna-Este 10 bis, El Conde, Caracas; f. 1936; Dir. Carmen Julia Negrón de Valery.

**Escuela Nacional de Opera** (*National School of Opera*): Dirección de Cultura y Bellas Artes del Ministerio de Educación, Este 2 con Sur 25, El Conde, Los Caobos, Caracas; Dir. Primo Casale.

**Escuela Superior de Música "José Angel Lamas"** (*Lamas High School of Music*): Veroes a Santa Capilla, Caracas; f. 1887; Dir. Vicente Emilio Sojo.

# VIET-NAM
Population 52,741,000

## LEARNED SOCIETIES
### Hanoi

**Union of Scientific and Technical Associations:** 39 Tran Hung Dao St.; includes the following:
- Agriculture Association.
- Architects Association.
- Biology Association.
- Cast and Metallurgy Association.
- Chemistry Association.
- Engineering Association.
- Forestry Association.
- Geography Association.
- Geology Association.
- Mathematics Association.
- Mining Association.
- Physics Association.
- Radio-Electronics Association.

**General Association of Medicine:** 68 Ba Trieu St.; includes the following:
- Acupuncture Association.
- Anaesthesiology Association.
- Anti-Contagious Diseases Association.
- Anti-Tuberculosis and Lung Diseases Association.
- Dentists Association.
- Dermatology Association.
- Forensic Scientists Association.
- Internal Medicine Association.
- Medical Biochemistry Association.
- Morphology Association.
- Neurology, Psychiatry and Neurosurgery Association.
- Obstetrics, Gynaecology and Family Planning Association.
- Odonto-Maxillo-Facial Association.
- Oto-Rhino-Laryngology Association.
- Paediatrics Association.
- Pharmacists Association.
- Physiology Association.
- Prophylactic Hygiene Association.
- Radiology Association.
- Serum and Blood Transfusion Association.
- Surgery Association.

**Eastern Medicine Association:** 19 Tong Dan St.
**Viet-Nam Journalists Association:** 59 Ly Thai To St.
**Writers and Artists Union:** 51 Tran Hung Dao St.; f. 1957; includes the following:
- Viet-Nam Cinema Workers Association.
- Viet-Nam Fine Arts Association.
- Viet-Nam Musicians' Association.
- Viet-Nam Photographers Association.
- Viet-Nam Stage Arts Association.
- Viet-Nam Writers' Association.

## RESEARCH INSTITUTES
### Hanoi

**State Commission for Science and Technology:** organizes research at the universities and the institutes attached to the Ministry of Higher Education.

**Institute of Sciences:** f. 1975; organizes the research carried out by institutes and laboratories.

---

**Institute for Research on Communications Technology:** attached to the Ministry of Communications and Transport.

**Institute of Building Materials Research:** attached to the Ministry of Construction.

**Institute of Traditional Medicine Research:** attached to the Ministry of Public Health.

**Institute of Forestry Science and Technology:** attached to the Ministry of Forestry.

**Institute of Hygiene and Epidemiology:** attached to the Ministry of Public Health.

**Institute of Malariology, Parasitology and Entomology:** attached to the Ministry of Public Health.

**Pharmaceutical Material Institute:** attached to the Ministry of Public Health.

**Central Institute of Ophthalmology:** attached to the Ministry of Public Health.

**Central Institute of Tuberculosis:** attached to the Ministry of Public Health.

### Dalat

**Centre for Nuclear Research:** P.O.B. 60, Dalat; f. 1962; devoted to the peaceful uses of atomic energy, particularly in agriculture and medicine; 250 kW. Triga Mk. 2 Reactor; library of 10,000 vols., 25,000 microfilms; 30 technicians.

**Pasteur Research Institute:** Dalat.

### Ho Chi Minh City

**Institute of Agricultural Research:** 121 Ngugen-binh-Khiem; f. 1965; attached to the Ministry of Agriculture; research into agricultural methods, improvement and applications, etc.

**Institute of Chemistry:** f. 1975; attached to the Institute of Sciences.

### Nha-Trang

**Viên Nghiên Cuu Biên Viet-Nam** (*Oceanographic Institute of Viet-Nam*): Nha-Trang; f. 1922; biological, chemical, physical and geological oceanography; seismographic station; biological museum; reference library of 55,000 vols.; 200 staff; Dir. Dr. Lê Trong Phán (acting); publ. *Collection of Marine Research Works*†.

## LIBRARIES

**Viet-Nam National Library:** 31 Tràng Thi, Hanoi; f. 1919; attached to Ministry of Culture; 1,200,000 vols., 70,000 bound vols. of periodicals; Dir. Trinh Giem; publs. *National Bibliography* (monthly and annually), *Biblio-*

*graphy of Periodical Articles, Bibliography of Newspaper Articles* (monthly), *Information on Culture and Arts, Library and Bibliographical Work* (quarterly).

**Central Institute of Information and Library for Medical Sciences:** 13 Lê Thánh Tông, Hanoi; f. 1979 to succeed fmr. Central Library for Medical Sciences; attached to Ministry of Health; 50,000 vols.; Dir. Dr. DINH DUC TIEN; publs. *Vietnam Medical Information* (quarterly, in English), *Bibliography of Vietnamese Medical Literature* (annually, in Vietnamese).

**Central Library for Science and Technology:** 26 Lý Thuòng Kiêt, Hanoi; f. 1960; attached to the State Commission for Science and Technology; 200,000 vols., 5,000 periodicals; Dir. Mrs. NGUYEN NHU VAN.

**General Scientific Library of Ho Chi Minh City:** 69 Lý Tú Trong, Ho Chi Minh City; f. 1976; fmrly National Library II; attached to Ho Chi Minh City Cultural Office; 600,000 vols.; Dir. THANH NGHI.

**Institute of Social Sciences Information—Central Social Sciences Library:** 26 Lý Thuòng Kiêt, Hanoi; f. 1975 by amalgamation of Dept. of Social Sciences Information and Central Social Sciences Library; attached to the Cttee. for Social Sciences; 300,000 vols., 1,200 periodicals; Dir. HOÀNG VI NAM; publs. *Review of Social Sciences Information* (monthly), *Bibliography of Social Sciences* (annually).

**Social Sciences Library:** 34 Ly-Tú-Trong, Ho Chi Minh City; f. 1975; the collections of the fmr. Archaeological Research Institute have been added to the library; provides facilities for research in philosophy, sociology, literature, linguistics, archaeology, ethnology, history, economics, law; Dir. PHAN GIA BEN.

## MUSEUMS

**Haiphong Museum:** Haiphong; f. 1959; local history.

**Historical Museum:** 1 Pham Ngu Lao, Hanoi; f. 1958; research, studies and conservation; history of Vietnam from palaeolithic period to 1945; library of 35,000 vols.; Dir. Prof. DINH NGOC THUY; publs. *Bulletin*† (2 a year), monographs†.

**Ho Chi Minh City Museum:** P.O.B. 2512, Botanical Gardens, Ho Chi Minh City; f. 1977; two sections: one devoted to the revolution, the other to ancient arts.

**Ho Chi Minh Museum:** Hanoi; f. 1977; study of the President's life and work.

**Hué Museum:** Hué; history of the old capital.

**National Art Gallery:** 66 Nguyen Thái Hoc St., Hanoi; f. 1966; Dir. NGUYEN VAN Y.

**Nghe-Tinh Museum:** Vinh, Nghe Tinh province.

**People's Army Museum:** Dien Bien Phu St., Hanoi; f. 1959.

**Revolution Museum:** 25 Tong Dan St., Hanoi; f. 1959; study of revolutionary history.

**Viet Bac Museum:** Thai-Nguyen, Bac Thai province; f. 1965; history of the revolution.

## UNIVERSITY AND COLLEGES

### TRUONG DAI-HOC TONG-HO'P
(Hanoi University)

19 LE THANH TONG ST., HANOI

Re-founded 1956.

Academic year: September to July.

Number of teachers: *c.* 150.
Number of students: *c.* 1,500.
Library: *c.* 62,000 vols.

The University engages in research and practical work in factories and co-operative farms, and participates in the scientific research of the State Commission for Science and Technology.

Publication: *Tâp-san Dar-Hoe* (University Review).

Faculties of natural sciences, geology and geography, literature and philology, history, and Vietnamese language for foreign students).

**Hanoi Polytechnic:** Kim Lien St., Hanoi; f. 1955.

**College of Economics and Planning:** Kim Lien St., Hanoi; f. 1956.

**Hanoi Medical College:** 13 Le Thanh Tong St., Hanoi; f. 1955.

**Hanoi College of Pharmacy:** 13 Le Thanh Tong St., Hanoi; f. 1964.

**College of Road and Rail Transport:** Cau Giay St., Hanoi; f. 1968.

**College of Mining and Geology:** Pho Yen township, Bac Thai province; f. 1966.

**College of Telecommunications:** Dong Da, Hanoi; f. 1969.

**College of Water Conservation:** Tay Son St., Hanoi; f. 1959.

**Industrial Decorative Arts College:** O Cho Dua, Hanoi; f. 1965.

**Tay Nguyen College:** Buon Me Thuot, Daclac province; f. 1977; for ethnic minorities; comprises faculties of agriculture, forestry, medicine, and pedagogy.

# WESTERN SAMOA
**Population 155,000**

## LIBRARIES

**Nelson Memorial Public Library:** P.O.B. 598, Apia; f. 1959; 36,000 vols.; 2 bookmobiles with a film projector operate on Upolu and Savaii with an organized programme for schools; Senior Librarian Miss MATAINA TUATAGALOA TE'O.

**Avele College Library:** P.O.B. 45, Apia; 5,000 vols. serving 260 students.

## COLLEGES

### AVELE COLLEGE
P.O.B. 45, APIA

Founded 1924, under Education Department from 1966. Provides four-year courses.

*Principal:* P. B. BOAG, B.SC.

Number of students: 260, including students from the Tokelau Islands.

**University of the South Pacific School of Agriculture:** Alafua Campus, P.O.B. 890, Apia; f. 1966; academic year: February to December; library of c. 16,000 vols.; diploma and degree courses; 35 staff; 117 (full-time) students; publ. *Alafua Agricultural Bulletin†* (quarterly). (*See* also under Fiji.)

*Head of School and Dean of Campus:* Prof. FELIX WENDT, PH.D.

# YEMEN ARAB REPUBLIC
### Population 6,471,000

**British Council:** P.O.B. 2157, Beit Al-Mattahar, Harat Handhal, Sana'a; f. 1974; library of 5,701 vols., 15 periodicals; Rep. Dr. P. J. A. CLARK; Regional Librarian S. ROMAN (based in Sudan).

**Library of the Great Mosque of Sana'a:** Sana'a; f. 1925; the collection of 10,000 MSS. and printed vols. is not at present accessible to the public; Librarian ZAID BIN ALI ENAN.

### SANA'A UNIVERSITY
P.O.B. 1247, SANA'A
Telephone: 3443.
Founded 1970.

State control; financial support from Kuwait; Languages of instruction: Arabic and English; Academic year: October to June.

*President:* Dr. ABDUL KARIM EL-ERYANI.
*Vice-President:* Dr. MOHAMED MOTAHER.
*Secretary-General:* SALEM M. AL-SAQQAF.

*Librarian:* FATHI AL-SHAFEI.

Number of teachers: 89.
Number of students: 3,139.

Publications: *University News* (monthly, Arabic), *Research Journal of the Department of English*.

#### DEANS:
*Faculty of Arts:* Dr. M. MANDOUR.
*Faculty of Law and Sharia:* Dr. H. AL-MARSAFAWI.
*Faculty of Commerce and Economics:* Dr. SAMA'AN BUTROSS.
*Faculty of Science:* Dr. A. MUHSIN AL-ABBADY.
*Faculty of Education:* Dr. M. ABDO GHANEM.

**Kulliat Asshari'a Wa Alqanun** (*Faculty of Islamic Law*): Sana'a; f. 1970.

There are also six vocational schools, a Military Academy, a College of Aviation, a College for Radio Telecommunications and an Agricultural School.

# PEOPLE'S DEMOCRATIC REPUBLIC OF YEMEN
### Population 1,853,000

## LIBRARIES AND MUSEUMS

**Miswat Library:** previously called Lake Library; administered by Aden Municipality; c. 30,000 vols., in English, Arabic and Urdu.

**Teachers' Club Library:** over 2,000 vols.

**Travelling Library:** ancillary to Miswat Library; administered by Aden Municipality; c. 9,500 vols., in English and Arabic.

**Department of Antiquities and Museums:** P.O.B. 473, Ministry of Culture and Guidance, Aden; f. 1948 for the protection of antiquities and archaeological sites, the supervision of museums, investigation and survey of sites and application of the Antiquities and Museums Ordinance; Dir. MUHAMMAD ABDULWAHED; publs. Reports and Bulletins.

There are two museums, one in Crater and the other in Steamer Point, both displaying archaeological material.

## UNIVERSITY
### UNIVERSITY OF ADEN
AIRPORT RD., KHORMAKSAR, ADEN
Founded 1975; in process of formation.

Faculties of education, agriculture, economics, commerce, law, medicine, engineering and technology.

# YUGOSLAVIA
Population 22,299,000

## ACADEMIES

**Akademia e Shkencave dhe e Arteve e Kosovës/Akademija Nauka i Umetnosti Kosova** (*Academy of Sciences and Arts of Kosovo*): 38000 Priština, Milladin Popoviqi 10; f. 1976 as Society for Sciences and Arts, reorganized 1978; sections of Social Sciences, Natural Sciences, and Linguistics, Literature and Arts; activities carried out in Albanian and Serbocroatian; publs. *Vjetari/Godisnjak* (Annual Report), *Kërkime/Istraživanja* (Research), *Libërshënuesi/Spomenica* (Diary), *Studime/Studije* (Studies), *Botime të veçanta/Posebna izdanja* (monographs), *Bibliografia/Bibliografija, Acta Biologiae et Medicinae Experimentalis*.

PRESIDIUM:

*President:* IDRIZ AJETI.

*Vice-President:* DERVISH ROZHAJA.

*Chief Scientific Secretary:* SYRJA PUPOVCI.

*Secretaries:* ALI HADRI (Social Sciences), LJUBISA RAKIC (Natural Sciences), REZHEP QOSJA (Linguistics, Literature and Arts).

MEMBERS:
AJETI, IDRIZ, philologist
DUSHI, MINIR, mineralogist
FILIPOVIĆ, VUKASIN, writer
HADRI, ALI, historian
HAXHIU, MUSA, pathophysiologist
HOXHA, HAJREDIN, sociologist
HRABAK, BOGUMILJ, historian
IMAMI, OSMAN, epidemiologist
KARAMAN, MLADEN, zoologist
KRASNIQI, MARK, ethnographer
MEKULI, ESAD, writer
MULLIQI, MUSLIM, painter
PUPOVCI, SYRJA, jurist
QOSJA, REXHEP, writer
RAKIC, LJUBISA, biochemist
REXHEPAGIQ, JASHAR, educationist
ROZHAJA, DERVISH, physiologist
VUKOVIQ, VLADETA, writer
ZAJMI, GAZMEND, jurist, political scientist

**Crnogorska Akademija Nauka i Umjetnosti** (*Montenegrin Academy of Sciences and Arts*): 81000 Titograd, Rista Stijovića 5; library of 35,000 vols.; publs. *Godišnjak CANU* (annually), *Glasnik* (Review), *Posebna izdanja* (special editions).

PRESIDIUM:

*President:* BRANKO PAVIĆEVIĆ.

*Vice-Presidents:* MIHAILO LALIĆ, MILORAD MIJUŠKOVIĆ.

*Secretary-General:* Dr. DRAGUTIN VUKOTIĆ.

*Members:* DRAGIŠA IVANOVIĆ, LJUBOMIR RAŠOVIĆ, MARKO ULIĆEVIĆ, DIMITRIJE VUJOVIĆ, ČEDO VUKOVIĆ.

MEMBERS:

*Natural Sciences Department:*
BEŠIĆ, ZARIJA
BLEČIĆ, VILOTIJE
IVANOVIĆ, BOŽINA
IVANOVIĆ, DRAGIŠA
LEPETIĆ, VLADIMIR
MIJUŠKOVIĆ, MILORAD
PAVIĆEVIĆ, LJUBO
POPOVIĆ, IVO DJANI
RAŠOVIĆ, LJUBOMIR
ULIĆEVIĆ, MARKO
VLAHOVIĆ, VLADISLAV
VUKOTIĆ, DRAGUTIN

*Social Sciences Department:*
DJUROVIĆ, MIRČETA
MIJUŠKOVIĆ, SLAVKO
PAVIĆEVIĆ, BRANKO
PEJOVIĆ, DJOKO
SOŠKIĆ, BRANISLAV
STRUGAR, VLADO
VUJOVIĆ, DIMITRIJE

*Arts Department:*
DJONOVIĆ, JANKO
KOSTIĆ, DUŠAN
LALIĆ, MIHAILO
RADOVIĆ, DJUZA
STANIĆ, VOJO
TOMANOVIĆ, LUKA
VEŠOVIĆ, RADONJA
VUKOTIĆ, DUŠAN
VUKOVIĆ, ČEDO
ZOGOVIĆ, RADOVAN

**Jugoslavenska akademija znanosti i umjetnosti** (*Yugoslav Academy of Sciences and Arts*): Zagreb 1, Zrinski trg 11; f. 1867; comprises 17 Institutes for History, Language and Literature, Biology, Chemistry, Research and Art; library: see Libraries; publs. *Rad* (Memoirs), *Ljetopis* (annual), *Bulletin International Starine*, and material dedicated to the history of Croatian Literature.

*President:* Dr. JAKOV SIROTKOVIĆ.

*Vice-Presidents:* Dr. ANDRE MOHOROVIČIĆ, Dr. BRANKO KESIĆ.

*General Secretary:* Dr. HRVOJE POŽAR.

*Director of Library:* Dr. ALEKSANDAR STIPČEVIĆ.

MEMBERS:

*Social Sciences:*
BAKARIĆ, Dr. VLADIMIR.
BRAJKOVIĆ, Dr. VLADISLAV.
ČALIĆ, Dr. DUŠAN.
GUNJAČA. Dr. STJEPAN.
KATIČIĆ, Dr. NATKO.
RENDIĆ-MIOČEVIĆ, Dr. DUJE.
SIROTKOVIĆ, Dr. JAKOV.
STIPETIĆ, Dr. VLADIMIR.
SUIĆ, Dr. MATE.
VRANICKI, Dr. PREDRAG.

*Mathematical Sciences and Physics:*
BALENOVIĆ, Dr. KREŠIMIR.
**BLANUŠA, Dr. Ing. DANILO.**
GRDENIĆ, Dr. Ing. DRAGO.
**IVEKOVIĆ, Dr. Ing. HRVOJE.**
JANKOVIĆ, Dr. ZLATKO.
KARŠULIN, Dr. Ing. MIROSLAV.
NIČE, Dr. VILIM.
**PAIĆ, Dr. Ing. MLADEN.**
POŽAR, Dr. HRVOJE.
**SUPEK, Dr. IVAN.**

*Natural Sciences:*
BUJAS, Dr. ZORAN.
HERAK, Dr. MILAN.
JURKOVIĆ, Dr. IVAN.
KOCHANSKY-DEVIDÉ, Dr. VANDA.
LORKOVIĆ, Dr. ZDENKO.
MALEZ, Dr. MIRKO.
**ROGLIĆ, Dr. JOSIP.**
ŠKREB, Dr. NIKOLA.
**TAJDER, Dr. MIROSLAV.**
VIDAKOVIĆ, Dr. MIRKO.

*Medical Sciences:*
**ALLEGRETTI, Dr. NIKŠA.**
ČUPAR, Dr. IVO.
**FORENBACHER, Dr. SERGIJE.**
IKIĆ, Dr. DRAGO.
**KESIĆ, Dr. BRANKO.**

## ACADEMIES

KOGOJ, Dr. FRANJO.
OKLJEŠA, Dr. BOŽIDAR.
TOMAŠEC, Dr. IVO.
TOPOLNIK, Dr. EUGEN.

*Philology:*
DEANOVIĆ, Dr. MIRKO.
FILIPOVIĆ, Dr. RUDOLF.
GORTAN, Dr. VELJKO.
GUBERINA, Dr. PETAR.
HAMM, Dr. JOSIP.
ŠKREB, Dr. ZDENKO.
TORBARINA, Dr. JOSIP.

*Modern Literature:*
BOŽIĆ, MIRKO.
FRANGEŠ, Dr. IVO.
FRANIČEVIĆ, Dr. MARIN.
KALEB, VJEKOSLAV.
KAŠTELAN, JURE.
KRLEŽA, MIROSLAV.
MATKOVIĆ, MARIJAN.
ŠEGEDIN, PETAR.
TADIJANOVIĆ, DRAGUTIN.

*Art:*
FISKOVIĆ, Dr. CVITO.
GALIĆ, DRAGO.
HORVAT, LAVOSLAV.
KRŠINIĆ, FRAN.
MOHOROVIČIĆ, ANDRE.
PARAĆ, VJEKOSLAV.
SEISSEL, JOSIP.
ŠIMUNOVIĆ, FRANO.
TARTAGLIA, MARINO.

*Music:*
ANDREIS, JOSIP.
GOTOVAC, JAKOV.
PAPANDOPULO, BORIS.
ŠULEK, STJEPAN.

**Makedonska akademija na naukite i umetnostite** (*Macedonian Academy of Sciences and Arts*): 91000 Skopje, P.O.B. 428; f. 1967; publs. *Letopis* (annual), *Prilozi na Oddelenieto za opštestveni nauki* (Contributions of the Dept. of Social Sciences), *Prilozi za lingvistika i literaturna nauka* (Dept. of Linguistics and Literary Sciences), *Prilozi na Oddelenieto za biološki i medicinski nauki* (Contributions of the Dept. of Biological and Medical Sciences), *Prilozi na Oddelenieto za matematičko-tehnički nauki* (Contributions of the Dept. of Mathematical and Technical Sciences), *Posebni izdanija* (Special Editions), *Povremeni izdanija* (Non-serial Editions).

The library contains 70,000 vols.

PRESIDIUM:
*President:* Acad. MIHAILO APOSTOLSKI.
*Vice-President:* Acad. BLAGOJ S. POPOV.
*Chief Scientific Secretary:* Assoc. mem. EVGENI DIMITROV.
*Secretaries:* HARALAMPIE POLENAKOVIĆ (Linguistics and Literary Science), KIRIL MILJOVSKI (Social Sciences), KIRIL MICEVSKI (Biological and Medical Sciences), TODOR SKALOVSKI (Arts), KRUM TOMOVSKI (Mathematical and Technical Sciences).

MEMBERS:
*Social Sciences Department:*
APOSTOLSKI, MIHAILO
BOGOEV, KSENTE
KOCO, DIMČE
LAPE, LJUBEN
MILJOVSKI, KIRIL
PETRUŠEVSKI, MIHAIL

*Mathematical and Technical Sciences Department:*
POP JORDANOV, JORDAN
POPOV, BLAGOJ
SERAFIMOV, PETAR
TOMOVSKI, KRUM

*Surgical and Medical Sciences Department:*
EM, HANS
FILIPOVSKI, DJORDJI
MICEVSKI, KIRIL
TADŽER, ISAK

*Arts Department:*
ILJOVSKI, VASIL
JANEVSKI, SLAVKO
SKALOVSKI, TODOR
ŠOPOV, ACO
TODOROVSKI, DIMO

*Linguistics and Literary Science Department:*
KONESKI, BLAŽE
POLENAKOVIĆ, HARALAMPIE
SPASOV, ALEKSANDAR
VIDOESKI, BOŽIDAR

ASSOCIATE MEMBERS:
*Social Sciences Department:*
ANTOLJAK, STJEPAN
BOŠKOVIĆ, DJURDJE
DIMITROV, EVGENI
DJURDJEV, BRANISLAV
HRISTOV, ALEKSANDAR
MOŠIN, ALEKSANDAR
NEDELJKOVIĆ, DUŠAN
PANDEVSKI, MANOL
UZUNOV, NIKOLA

*Mathematical and Technical Sciences Department:*
ČUPONA, DJORDJI
KARŠULIN, MIROSLAV
SAVIĆ, PAVLE

*Biological and Medical Sciences Department:*
ANDREEVSKI, ALEKSANDAR
EFREMOV, DJORDJI
ČAMO, EDHEM
MILČINSKI, JANEZ

*Arts Department:*
KODŽOMAN, VANGEL
KREFT, BRATKO
MATEVSKI, MATEJA
NIKOLOVSKI, VLASTIMIR
VIDMAR, JOSIP

*Linguistics and Literary Science Department:*
ILIEVSKI, PETAR
JAŠAR-NASTEVA, OLIVERA

FOREIGN MEMBERS:
BATOWSKI, HENRYK
BERNŠTEJN, SAMUIL BORISOVIČ
DOROVSKI, IVAN
HAMM, JOSIP
HENSEL, WITOLD
GOLAB, ZBIGNIEW
LUNT, HORACE G.
MAREŠ, FRANTIŠEK
MINISI, NULLO
PEUKERT, HERBERT
TOLSTOJ, NIKITA I.
TOPOLIŃSKA, ZUZANA
USIKOVA, RINA P.

**Slovenska akademija znanosti in umetnosti** (*Slovene Academy of Sciences and Arts*): 61000 Ljubljana, Novi trg 3; f. 1921 as Scientific Society for Humanistic Researches; reorganized 1938 as Slovene Academy of Sciences and Arts; comprises Institutes for Marxism, General and National History, History of Art, Archaeology, Oriental Studies, the Slovene Language, Slovene Ethnography, Literature, Musicology, Terminology, Biology, Palaeontology, Geography, Karst Research, Medicine; publs.† *Annual Report, Slovene Biographical Lexicon, Dissertationes, Opera, Acta archaeologica, Acta geographica, Acta Carsologica, Fontes rerum Slovenicarum, Traditiones,* etc.

The Library contains 300,000 vols.

*President:* JANEZ MILČINSKI.
*Vice-Presidents:* BRATKO KREFT, ROBERT BLINC.
*Secretary-General:* JOŽE GORIČAR.

MEMBERS:
BAJEC, ANTON
BERKOPEC, OTON
BEZLAJ, FRANCE
BRECELJ, BOGDAN
BRODAR, SREČKO
BRZIN, MIROSLAV
ČOP, BOJAN
CVETKO, DRAGOTIN
DOLAR, DAVORIN
FETTICH, JANEZ
FINŽGAR, ALOJZIJ
GASPARI, MAKSIM
GOSAR, PETER
GRAFENAUER, BOGO
GRAFENAUER, STANKO
HADŽI, DUŠAN
ILEŠIČ, SVETOZAR
INGOLIČ, ANTON
JAKAC, BOŽIDAR
JURANČIČ, JANKO
KALIN, ZDENKO
KOROŠEC, VIKTOR
KRANJEC, MIŠKO
KRAŠOVEC, STANE
KUŠEJ, GORAZD
KYOVSKY, RUDI
LOGAR, VALENTIN
MAJER, BORIS
MIHELIČ, FRANCE
MORAVEC, DUŠAN
MUŠIČ, MARJAN
NOVAK, FRANC
PAVŠIČ, VLADIMIR
PEKLENIK, JANEZ
PETERLIN, ANTON
PRETNAR, STOJAN
RAKOVEC, IVAN
RAVNIKAR, EDO
SLODNJAK, ANTON
ŠUKLJE, LUJO
TIŠLER, MIHA
VAVPETIČ, LADO
VIDAV, IVAN
VIDMAR, JOSIP
ZWITTER, FRAN
ŽUPANČIČ, ANDREJ

**Srpska akademija nauka i umetnosti** (*Serbian Academy of Sciences and Arts*): 11000 Belgrade, Knez Mihailova ulica 35; f. 1886.

*President:* (vacant).
*Vice-Presidents:* DUŠAN KANAZIR, VOJISLAV DJURIĆ.
*Secretary:* MILUTIN GARAŠANIN.

Comprises the following Sections: Natural Sciences and Mathematics, Medical Sciences, Technical Sciences, Language and Literature, Social Sciences, Historical Sciences, Fine Arts (painting and music).

Publications: *Godišnjak* (annually), *Glas* (Review), *Posebna izdanja* (monographs), *Spomenik* (Monument), *Srpski etnografski zbornik* (Serbian Ethnographic Collection), *Zbornik za istoriju, jezik i književnost srpskog naroda* (Anthology of the History, Language and Literature of the Serbian People), *Naučni skupovi* (Scientific Anthology), *Musička izdanja* (Musical Editions), *Spomenice* (Memoirs), *Bulletin* (in French and English), *Izdanja van serija* (Non-serial editions).

FULL MEMBERS:

ALJANČIĆ, SLOBODAN, mathematician.
ANDJELIĆ, TATOMIR, mathematician.
ANDJUS, RADOSLAV, physiologist.
ARNOVLJEVIĆ, VOJISLAV, cardiologist.
BEGOVIĆ, MEHMED, jurist.
BELIĆ, JOVAN, biologist.
BLAGOJEVIĆ, OBREN, economist.
BOŽOVIĆ, BORISLAV, physician.
BUKUROV, BRANISLAV, geographer.
ČELEBONOVIĆ, MARKO, painter.
ĆIRKOVIĆ, SIMA, historian.
ĆOPIĆ, BRANKO, writer.
ĆOSIĆ, DOBRICA, writer.
ČUBRILOVIĆ, VASA, historian.
DANILOVIĆ, VOJISLAV, physician.
DEDIJER, VLADIMIR, historian.
DEROKO, ALEKSANDAR, architect.
DESPIĆ, ALEKSANDAR, chemist (technologist).
DJORDJEVIĆ, BOŽIDAR, cardiologist.
DJORDJEVIĆ, JOVAN, jurist.
DJURIĆ, MILAN, engineer.
DJURIĆ, VOJISLAV J., art historian.
DJURIĆ, VOJISLAV, literary historian.
DJURIŠIĆ, MILUTIN, bacteriologist.
GARAŠANIN, MILUTIN, archaeologist.
GVOZDENOVIĆ, NEDELJKO, painter.
HAJDIN, NIKOLA, engineer.
ISAKOVIĆ, ANTONIJE, writer.
IVIĆ, PAVLE, philologist.
JOSIFOVIĆ, MLADEN, phytopathologist.
KANAZIR, DUŠAN, biologist.
KAŠANIN, RADIVOJE, mathematician.
KOJIĆ, BRANISLAV, architect.
KOSTIĆ, SLOBODAN, neurosurgeon.
KOŠ, ERIH, writer.
KRLEŽA, MIROSLAV, writer.
LALIĆ, MIHAILO, writer.
LAZAREVIĆ, DJORDJE, engineer.
LESKOVAC, MLADEN, literary historian.
LUKIĆ, RADOMIR, philosophy jurist and sociologist.
LUTOVAC, MILISAV, geographer and ethnologist.
MACURA, MILOŠ, economist.
MAKSIMOVIĆ, DESANKA, writer.
MARIĆ, LJUBICA, composer.
MARTINOVIĆ, PETAR, biologist.
MEDAKOVIĆ, DEJAN, art historian.
MIHAILOVIĆ, MIHAILO, chemist.
MILIN, RADIVOJ, physician.
MILOSAVLJEVIĆ, PREDRAG, painter.
MILJANIĆ, PETAR, engineer.
MITROVIĆ, MITAR, surgeon.
MOKRANJAC, VASILIJE, composer.
NEDELJKOVIĆ, DUŠAN, philosopher.
NENADOVIĆ, MIROSLAV, engineer.
NIKOLIŠ, GOJKO, physician.
OBRADOVIĆ, ILIJA, engineer.
OBRADOVIĆ, NIKOLA, engineer.
PANTIĆ, MIROSLAV, literary historian.
PANTIĆ, VLADIMIR, physiologist.
PAPO, ISIDOR, surgeon.
PAVLOVIĆ, STOJAN, mineralogist.
PETKOVIĆ, KOSTA V., geologist.
PETKOVIĆ, SAVA, surgeon.
PETROVIĆ, BOŠKO, writer.
PIVKO, SVETOPOLK, engineer.
POPOVIĆ, PETAR, historian.
RAIČKOVIĆ, STEVAN, writer.
RAJIČIĆ, STANOJLO, composer.
RISTIĆ, JOVAN, neuro-psychiatrist.
RISTIĆ, MILAN, composer.
SAVIĆ, PAVLE, physicist.
SELIMOVIĆ, MEŠA, writer.
SOKIĆ, LJUBICA, painter.
SPUŽIĆ, VLADIMIR, physician.
STANKOVIĆ, BOGOLJUB, mathematician.
STEFANOVIĆ, DJORDJE, chemist.
STEFANOVIĆ, MILUTIN, chemist.
STEFANOVIĆ, STANOJE, physician.
STEVANOVIĆ, MIHAILO, philologist.
STEVANOVIĆ, PETAR, geologist.
TERZIN, ALEKSANDAR, virologist.
TEŠIĆ, ŽIVOJIN, microbiologist.
TOMIĆ, MIODRAG, mathematician.
UROŠEVIĆ, ATANASJE, anthropo-geographer.
VUKDRAGOVIĆ, MIHAILO, composer.
ŽEŽELJ, BRANKO, engineer.

## LEARNED SOCIETIES

### FEDERAL

**Association of the Mathematicians', Physicists' and Astronomers' Societies of the F.S.R. of Yugoslavia:** Belgrade, Knez Mihailova 35, P.O.B. 791; f. 1950; Dir. Dr. BLAGOJ POPOV; publs. *Topologija, Matematica balkanica, Matematički list za učenike osnovnih škola, Fizika, Matematičko-fizički list za učenike srednjih škola, Bilten* (Astronomy).

**Jugoslovenski centar za tehničku i naučnu dokumentaciju** (*Yugoslav Centre for Technical and Scientific Documentation*): Belgrade, S. Penezića-Krcuna 29-31, P.O.B. 724; f. 1952; information retrieval, translation, reproduction and editorial activities; library of over 770,000 vols.; Dir. ALEXSIĆ MIODRAG; publs. *Bulletin of Documentation*† (24 series, abstracts from technical literature), *Informatika*† (theory and practice of documentation and information), *Bibliography on Automatic Data Processing*†, *Scientific and Professional Meetings in Yugoslavia and foreign countries*†, *UDC—Editions (FID)*†, *Microfilm techniques*†.

**Pedagogical Society of the F.S.R. of Yugoslavia:** Belgrade, Moše Pijade 12; f. 1952; Pres. Dr. RADULE SEKULIĆ; publs. *Pedagogija, Predškolsko dete*.

**Savez društava bibliotekara Jugoslavije** (*Federation of Library Associations*): 71000 Sarajevo, Obala 42.

**Savez Muzejskih društava Jugoslavije** (*Federation of Museums Associations*): Belgrade, Vuka Karaclžića 18; publ. *Muzeji*.

**Union of Engineers and Technicians of Yugoslavia:** Belgrade, Kneza Miloša 9/11, P.O.B. 187; f. 1841; social, scientific-professional organization; eight territorial sub-divisions, eleven professional sub-divisions and four specialized societies; Chair. Ing. RADOJE KONTIĆ; Sec. Dr. Ing. PETAR RADIČEVIĆ; publs. *Tehnika*† (monthly), *It Novine*† (every 2 weeks).

Comprises the following federations, etc.:

*Territorial:*
**Union of Engineers and Technicians of Serbia.**
**Union of Engineers and Technicians of Croatia.**
**Union of Engineers and Technicians of Slovenia.**
**Union of Engineers and Technicians of Bosnia and Herzegovina.**
**Union of Engineers and Technicians of Macedonia.**
**Union of Engineers and Technicians of Montenegro.**
**Union of Engineers and Technicians of Vojvodina.**
**Union of Engineers and Technicians of Kosovo.**

*Professional:*
**Union of Architects of Yugoslavia.**
**Union of Surveyors and Geometers of Yugoslavia.**
**Union of Civil Engineers and Technicians of Yugoslavia.**
**Union of Engineers and Technicians for Protection of Materials of Yugoslavia.**
**Union of Mechanical and Electrical Engineers and Technicians of Yugoslavia.**
**Union of Agricultural Engineers and Technicians of Yugoslavia.**
**Union of Mining, Geological and Metallurgical Engineers and Technicians of Yugoslavia.**
**Union of Transportation and Communications Engineers and Technicians of Yugoslavia.**
**Union of Textile Engineers and Technicians of Yugoslavia.**
**Union of Chemists and Technologists of Yugoslavia.**
**Union of Forestry and Wood Processing Engineers and Technicians of Yugoslavia.**

*Specialized Societies:*
**Yugoslav Union of Organizations for Quality Control and Reliability.**
**Yugoslav Society for Soil Mechanics and Subterranean Works.**
**Yugoslav Society for Mechanics.**
**Union of Societies for the Advancement of Standardization.**

**Union of Jurists' Associations of Yugoslavia:** Belgrade, Proleterskih brigada 74, P.O.B. 179; f. 1947; aims include: the study and elaboration of the principles of socialist democracy and law of the Republic, and co-operation with the foreign and international legal organizations; 30,000 mems.; Pres. Dr. ASEN GRUPČE; Sec.-Gen. Dr. MIODRAG ORLIĆ; publs. include *The New Yugoslav Law*.

**Yugoslav Economists' Association:** 11000 Belgrade, Nušićeva 6/III; f. 1945; Pres. Prof. Dr. NEDA ANDRIĆ; publ. *Ekonomist* (quarterly).

**Zajednica Univerzitéta Jugoslavije** (*Association of Yugoslav Universities*): Palmotićeva 22, Belgrade 11000; Pres. Dr. MOMČILO DIMITRIJEVIĆ; Sec.-Gen. Dr. SULEJMAN RESULOVIĆ.

### SERBIA

**Association of Jurists of the S.R. of Serbia:** Belgrade, Proleterskih brigada 74; f. 1946; Pres. ČEDA MILOŠEVIĆ; publ. *Pravni život*.

**Association of Pharmacists of the S.R. of Serbia:** Belgrade, Terazíje 12; f. 1946; Pres. LJUBOMIR ŠAROVIĆ; publs. *Arhiv za farmaciju*, *Bilten*.

**British Council:** Generala Ždanova 34, 11001 Belgrade; Rep. O. D. ELLIOTT; libraries: see Libraries.

**Centre Culturel Français:** Zmaj Jovina 11, 11000 Belgrade; f. 1950; library of 10,000 vols.; Dir. O. MANESSE.

**Oruštvo za Srpski Jezik i Književnost** (*Society of Serbian Language and Literature*): Belgrade University; f. 1910; Pres. P. STEVANOVIĆ; Sec. D. PAVLOVIĆ; publ. *Pritozi za knjizevnost, jezik, istorija i folklor*.

**Economists' Society of the S.R. of Serbia:** Belgrade, Nusićeva 6-III, P.O.B. 490; f. 1944; Pres. BOGOLJUB STOJANOVIĆ; publ. *Ekonomika preduzeća* (monthly).

**Historical Society of the S.R. of Serbia:** Belgrade, Faculty of Philosophy, Čika Ljubina 18-20; f. 1948; 1,500 mems.; Pres. Prof. Dr. LJUBOMIR MAKSIMOVIĆ; publ. *Istoriski glasnik* (2 a year).

**Matica srpska** (*Serbian Society*): Novi Sad; f. 1826; literary, scientific and publishing society; Sec. DUŠAN POPOV; publs. *Letopis Matice srpske* and *Proceedings* (in the following series: natural sciences, history, social sciences, literature and language, philology and linguistics, art, Slavonic studies).

**"Nikola Tesla" Association of Societies for Promotion of Technical Sciences in Yugoslavia:** Belgrade, P.O.B. 359; organizes an international festival of scientific and technical films, held every two years.

**Savez Bibliotečkih Radnika Srbije** (*Union of Serbian Library Workers*): Belgrade, Skerlićeva 1; f. 1947; library of 1,000 vols.; Pres. MILAN JANKOVIĆ; publ. *Bibliotekar*† (The Librarian, every 2 months).

**Savez pedagoških društava S.R. Srbije** (*Federation of Pedagogical Societies of the S.R. of Serbia*): Belgrade, Terazije 26; fmrly. *Pedagogical Society of the S.R. of Serbia*, f. 1923, reorganized 1950; name changed and reorganized 1977; 11 units; 800 mems.; library of 8,000 vols.; Pres. Dr. VLADETA TEŠIĆ; Sec. ZEMIRA PTIČEK; publs. *Nastava i va spitanje*† (Teaching and Education, 5 a year), *Pedagoška Biblioteka*† (Pedagogical Library, occasionally).

**Serbian Chemical Society:** 11000 Belgrade, Karnegijeva 4, P.O.B. 462; f. 1897 to promote chemical research and education; 2,200 mems.; Pres. Prof. Dr. DRAGOMIR VITOROVIĆ; Sec. Prof. Dr. LJUBICA VRHOVAC; publs. *Glasnik hemijskog društva Beograd* (11 a year), *Hemijski pregled* (6 a year).

**Serbian Geographical Society:** Belgrade, Studentski trg 3/III; f. 1910; 1,350 mems.; library of 2,100 vols.; Chair. Prof. Dr. D. Ž. DUKIĆ; Sec. BORKA RADOVANOVIĆ; publs. *Bulletin*† (2 a year), *Terre et Hommes* (annually), *Globus* (annually), *Editions Spéciales*† (1 to 3 a year), *Mémoires*.

**Serbian Geological Society:** Belgrade, Kamenička 6, P.O.B. 227; f. 1891; 500 mems.; library of c. 2,000 vols.; Pres. Dr. ALEKSANDER GRUBIĆ; publ. *Zapisnici zborova*† (Reports, annually).

**Society of Mathematicians, Physicists and Astronomers of Serbia:** Belgrade, Knez Mihailova 35; f. 1948; Pres. Dr. DJORDJE KARAPANDŽIĆ; publ. *Vesnik*.

**Society for Research and Prevention of Cancer:** Belgrade, Knez Mihailova 2; f. 1967; Pres. Dr. VLADETA POPOVIĆ.

**Srpsko biološko društvo** (*Serbian Biological Society*): 11000 Belgrade, Nemanjina 26; f. 1947; 780 mems.; Pres. Prof. Dr. MILOJE KRUNIĆ; Sec. Dr. LJUBINKA ĆULAFIĆ; publs. *Arhiv bioloških nauka* (Archives of Biological Sciences), *Savremena biologija* (Contemporary Biology), *Bios*.

**Union of Engineers and Technicians of the S.R. of Serbia:** Belgrade, 7a Kneza Miloša; f. 1945; 8,014 mems.; Pres. M. STEFANOVIĆ; Sec. S. PANTOVIĆ; publ. *Tehnika* (monthly).

## CROATIA

**British Council:** Ilica 12/I, 41001 Zagreb; Regional Dir. P. L. ELBORN; library: *see* Libraries.

**Croatian Library Association:** National and University Library, 41000 Zagreb, Marulićev trg 21; f. 1948; 850 mems.; Pres. MIRA MIKAČIĆ; Sec. IRINA PAŽAMETA; publs. *Vjesnik bibliotekara Hrvatske†* (quarterly), *Knjiga i čitaoci†* (every 2 months).

**Economists' Society of Croatia:** Zagreb, Berislavićeva 6.

**Geographical Society of Croatia:** Zagreb, Marulićev Trg. 19; f. 1947; 425 mems.; library of 2,600 vols.; Pres. Prof. Dr. VELJKO ROGIĆ; publs. *Geografski glasnik†* (annually), *Geografski horizont†* (quarterly).

**Hrvatsko numizmatičko društvo** (*Croatian Numismatic Society*): 41000 Zagreb, Habdeliceva 2; f. 1928; Pres. Dr. IVO MEIXNER; Sec. Prof. DRAGUTIN HORKIĆ; publs. *Numizmatičke vijesti, Numizmatika Hrvatskog numizmatičkog Društva Obol.*

**Hrvatsko Prirodoslovno Društvo** (*Croatian Society of Natural Sciences*): Zagreb, Ilica 16/III; f. 1885; Pres. Dr. MARIJAN STRABAŠIĆ; Secs. Dr. BOJAN BENKO, Dr. MLADEN ILLE; publs. *Priroda* (Nature), *Periodicum Biologorum†* (scientific journal with papers on biomedicine and biochemistry).

The Society has the following three sub-sections:
*Section for the Protection of Nature.*
*Group for the History of Science.*
*"Popular Science" publications.*

**League of Jurists' Associations of the S.R. of Croatia:** Zagreb, Zrinski trg 3.

**Matica Hrvatska** (*Croatian Society*): Zagreb, Matičina ul. 2; f. 1842; literary and publishing society.

**Pedagoško-književni zbor, Pedagoško društvo S.R. Hrvatske** (*Pedagogical and Literary Union of Croatia*): Zagreb, Trg. Maršala Tita 4; member of the Union of Pedagogical Societies of Yugoslavia, Belgrade.

**Pharmacists' Society of the S.R. of Croatia:** 41000 Zagreb, Masarykova 2; f. 1945; 2,500 mems.; library of 3,500 vols.; Chair. IVAN GRGIĆ; publ. *Farmaceutski glasnik†* (monthly).

**Physicians' Association of Croatia:** Zagreb, Šubićeva ul. 9.

**Savez Muzejskih društava Hrvatske** (*Federation of Museums Associations of Croatia*): 41000 Zagreb, Savska cesta 18; f. 1945; 385 mems.; Pres. VLADIMIR GALEKOVIĆ; Sec. MILAN KRUHEK; publ. *News of Museum Custodians and Conservator Scientists of Croatia* (every 2 months).

**Society for Promoting the Activities of the Technical Museum of Croatia:** 41000 Zagreb, Savska c.18; f. 1955; Pres. Ing. HERMAN MATTES; Sec. PREDRAG GRDENIĆ.

**Union of the Societies of Engineers and Technicians of the S.R. of Croatia:** 41000 Zagreb, Berislavićeva 6; f. 1970; 3,017 mems.; library of 5,000 vols.; Chief Officer Prof. Dr. Ing. ERVIN NONVEILLER; publ. *Gradevinar.*

## SLOVENIA

**Association of Engineers and Technicians of Slovenia:** Erjavčeva 15, Ljubljana; f. 1953; organizes conferences, lectures, exhibitions; 60 affiliated unions, library of 95,000 vols.; Dir. TONE TRIBUŠON; publ. *Nova proizvodnja†* (2 a month).

**Društvo matematikov, fizikov in astronomov S.R.S.** (*Association of Mathematicians, Physicists and Astronomers of Slovenia*): Ljubljana, P.O.B. 227; f. 1949; Chair. JANEZ STEPIŠNIK; publs. *Obzornik mat. fiz.†* (every 2 months), *Presek†, Knjižnica SIGMA.*

**Društvo Slovenskih skladateljev** (*Society of Slovene Composers*): Ljubljana, Trg francoske revolucije 6; f. 1946; 97 mems.; Pres. BOJAN ADAMIČ; Sec. PAVEL MIHELČIČ; publs. *Concert atelier* (contemporary music), *Edicije DSS* (printed scores, etc., of its mems.).

**Geografsko društvo Slovenije** (*Geographical Society of Slovenia*): Ljubljana, University Edvard Kardelj of Ljubljana, Aškerčeva 12; f. 1922; 450 mems.; Pres. Prof. Dr. VLADIMIR KLEMENČIC; Sec. Mgr. DUŠAN PLUT; publs. *Geografski Vestnik†, Geografski Obzornik†.*

**Institut za raziskovanje krasa** (*Institute for Karst Research*): 66230 Postojna, Titov trg 2; f. 1947; Pres. Dr. PETER HABIČ; publ. *Acta carsologica* (annual).

**Jamarska zveza Slovenije** (*Speleological Association of Slovenia*): 61000 Ljubljana, Aškerčeva 12; f. 1889; 26 caving societies and research groups with a total of c. 750 mems.; Pres. Prof. Dr. BORIS SKET; Sec. Ing. DUŠAN NOVAK; publ. *Naše jame†* (2 a year).

**Pedagogical Society of the S.R. of Slovenia:** Ljubljana, Gosposka ulica 3; f. 1920; active participation in social roles of education, organization of discussions of educators, continuing education of teachers; Pres. MILOJKO VIDMAR; Vice-Pres. RESMAN METOD; publ. *Sodobna pedagogika* (monthly).

**Raziskovalna skupnost Slovenije** (*Interdisciplinary Slovene Research Community*): Jadranska 21, Ljubljana; f. 1953; awards prizes for the best scientific works written by Slovene authors, and prizes for technological inventions; also grants university scholarships and finances scientific research and publications; Pres. TONE ZIMŠEK; Sec.-Gen. JOŽE KORBER; publ. *Raziskovalec†* (Researcher) (monthly).

**Skupnost študentov LVZ** (*Students' Society for Scientific Work*): Trg revolucije 1, 61000 Ljubljana.

**Slavistično društvo Slovenije** (*Society for Slavonic Studies in Slovenia*): Aškerčeva 12, 61000 Ljubljana; f. 1935; a forum for professional Slavists, to bring research to bear on practice, to nurture cultural values regarding Slovene language and literature and awareness of Slovene history; to organize, support and publish Slavic research in academic and popular books and periodicals; 700 mems.; Chair. Dr. JANEZ ROTAR; publs. *Slavistična revija* (Slavonic Review; quarterly), *Jezik in slovstvo* (Language and Literature; 8 a year).

**Slovenska Matica** (*Slovenian Society*): Ljubljana, Trg osvoboditve 7; f. 1864; literary and publishing society; 2,500 mems.; 10,000 vols.; Pres. Akad. Prof. Dr. BOGO GRAFENAUER; Sec. DRAGO JANČAR.

**Slovensko Umetnostnozgodovinsko društvo** (*Slovenian Society of Historians of Art*): Aškerčeva 12/III, Ljubljana; f. 1921; Chair. STANE BERNIK; publs. *Archives d'Histoire de l'Art, Zbornik za umetnostno zgodovino.*

**Society for Natural Sciences of Slovenia:** 61000 Ljubljana, Novi trg 4/IV; f. 1934; 3,000 mems.; Pres. R. KAVČIČ; Vice-Pres. A. VADNAL, M. KALIŠNIK; Sec. T. WRABER; publ. *Proteus†* (10 a year).

**Society of Jurists of the S.R. of Slovenia:** Ljubljana, Dalmati-nova 4; f. 1947; 1,073 mems.; Pres. JOŽE PAVLIČIČ; publ. *Jurist.*

**Zgodovinsko društvo za Slovenijo** (*Slovenian Historical Society*): Ljubljana, Aškerčeva 12; f. 1839, reorganized 1946; 610 mems.; library of 4,488 vols.; Pres. Dr. IGNACIJ VOJE; publs. *Zgodovinski časopis†* (Historical Review, quarterly); *Kronika†* (3 a year), *Časopis za zgodovino in narodopisje†* (2 a year).

## BOSNIA AND HERZEGOVINA

**Društvo Bibliotekara BiH** (*Librarians' Society of Bosnia and Herzegovina*): 71000 Sarajevo, Obala 42.

**Društvo Istoričara BiH** (*Historical Society of Bosnia and Herzegovina*): Filozofski fakultet, 71000 Sarajevo, Račkog 1.

**Društvo Ljekara BiH** (*Physicians' Society of Bosnia and Herzegovina*): Zavod za zdravstvenu zaštitu BiH, 71000 Sarajevo, Maršala Tita 7.

**Društvo Matematičara, Fizičara i Astronoma BiH** (*Society of Mathematicians, Physicists and Astronomers of Bosnia and Herzegovina*): Prirodnomatematički fakultet, 71000 Sarajevo, Vojvode Putnika 43.

**Geografsko Društvo BiH** (*Geographical Society of Bosnia and Herzegovina*): Prirodnomatematički fakultet, 71000 Sarajevo, Vojvode Putnika 43A; f. 1947; 1,541 mems.; Pres. Dr. MILOŠ BJELOVITIĆ; Vice-Pres. Dr. KREŠIMIR PAPIĆ; publs. *Geografski pregled†*, *Nastava geografije†* (annually), *Geografski list* (5 a year).

**Muzička Omladina BiH** (*Bosnia and Herzegovina Society of Music Lovers and Young Musicians*): Muzička akademija, 71000 Sarajevo, Svetozara Markovića 1.

**Pedagoško Društvo BiH** (*Pedagogical Society of Bosnia and Herzegovina*): 71000 Sarajevo, Djure Djakovića 4.

**Savez Inženjera i Tehničara BiH** (*Union of Engineers and Technicians of Bosnia and Herzegovina*): 71000 Sarajevo, Obala 21.

**Savez Organizacija Fizičke Kulture BiH** (*Union of Organizations for Physical Culture of Bosnia and Herzegovina*): 71000 Sarajevo, Mahmuta Bušatlije 2.

**Savez Organizacija Tehničke Kulture BiH** (*Union of Organizations for Technical Culture of Bosnia and Herzegovina*): 71000 Sarajevo, Vojvode Putnika 21.

**Savez Udruženja Pravnika BiH** (*Union of Jurists' Associations of Bosnia and Herzegovina*): 71000 Sarajevo, Valtera Perića 11.

**Savez Za Esperanto BiH** (*Union for Esperanto of Bosnia and Herzegovina*): 71000 Sarajevo, Vase Pelagića 8.

**Savez Zdravstvenih Radnika BiH** (*Medical Society of Bosnia and Herzegovina*): 71000 Sarajevo, Moše Pijade 25; promotes medical science, assists Government in medical education of people; Sec. Gen. NEVENKA KOVAČEVIĆ.

**Udruženje Književnika BiH** (*Association of Writers of Bosnia and Herzegovina*): 71000 Sarajevo, Preradovićeva 3; f. 1945; organizes annual international library exhibition; 220 mems.; Principal Officer MIROSLAV JANČIĆ; Sec. DŽEMALUDIN ALIĆ.

**Udruženje Književnih Prevodilaca BiH** (*Association of Literary Translators of Bosnia and Herzegovina*): 71000 Sarajevo, Kralja Tvrtka 11.

**Udruženje Kompozitora BiH** (*Association of Composers of Bosnia and Herzegovina*): 71000 Sarajevo, Radićeva 15.

**Udruženje Muzičkih Umjetnika BiH** (*Association of Musicians of Bosnia and Herzegovina*): Muzička akademija, 71000 Sarajevo, Sv. Markovića 1.

## MACEDONIA

**Arheološko Društvo na Makedonija** (*Archaeological Society of Macedonia*): 97500 Prilep, Moša Pijade 138; f. 1970; 50 mems.; Pres. BOŠKO BABIĆ; Sec. VOISLAV SANEV; publ. *Acta archaeologica macedonica*.

**Društvo na Istoričarite na Umetnosta od S.R.M.** (*Society of Art Historians of Macedonia*): Arheološki muzej na Makedonija, 91000 Skopje, Kurčiska b.b.; f. 1970; 40 mems.; Pres. PETAR MILJKOVIĆ; Sec. V. POPOVSKA-KOROBAR; publ. *Likovna umetnost* (Plastic Arts).

**Društvo na Kompozitorite na S.R. Makedonija** (*Society of Macedonian Composers*): 91000 Skopje, Maksim Gorki 18; f. 1950; 40 mems.; Pres. VLASTIMIR NIKOLOVSKI; Sec. SOTIR GOLABOSKI; publ. *Bilten* (Bulletin).

**Društvo na Likovnite Umetnici na Makedonija** (*Society of Plastic Arts of Macedonia*): Umetnička galerija, 91000 Skopje, 10110; f. 1944; 150 mems.; Pres. BORO MITRIKESKI; Sec. NASO BEKAROSKI.

**Društvo na Literaturnite Preveduvači na S.R.M.** (*Society of Literary Translators of Macedonia*): 91000 Skopje, P.F. 3; f. 1955; 102 mems.; Pres. Prof. Dr. BOŽIDAR NASTEV; Sec. TAŠKO ŠIRILOV.

**Društvo na Matematičarite i Fizičarite od S.R.M.** (*Society of Mathematicians and Physicists of Macedonia*): Matematički institut na Prirodo-matematički fakultet, 91000 Skopje, P.F. 146; publ. *Bilten* (Bulletin).

**Društvo na Muzejskite Rabotnici na Makedonija** (*Museum Society of Macedonia*): Muzej na grad Skopje, 91000 Skopje, Mito Hadži-Vasilev-Jasmin b.b.; f. 1951; 100 mems.; Pres. KUZMAN GEOGRIEVSKI; Sec. GALENA KUCULOVSKA.

**Društvo na Pisatelite na S.R.M.** (*Society of Writers of Macedonia*): 91000 Skopje, Maksim Gorki 18; f. 1951; 159 mems.; Pres. BLAGOJA IVANOV; Secs. ADEM GAJTANI, EFTIM MANEV.

**Društvo za Filozofija, Sociologija i Politikologija na S.R.M.** (*Society for Philosophy, Sociology and Politics of Macedonia*): Institut za sociološki i poliličko-pravni istraživanja, 91000 Skopje, Bul. Partizanski odredi b.b.; f. 1960; 170 mems.; Pres. Dr. DRAGAN TAŠKOVSKI; Sec. SVETA ŠKARIĆ; publ. *Zbornik* (Collected Papers).

**Farmaceutsko Društvo na Makedonija** (*Pharmacological Society of Macedonia*): 91000 Skopje, Ivo Ribar Lola MI/6; Pres. LAZAR TOLOV; Sec. GALABA SRBINOVSKA; publ. *Bilten* (Bulletin).

**Geografsko Društvo na S.R.M.** (*Geographical Society of Macedonia*): Geografski institut pri Prirodomatematički fakultet, 91000 Skopje, P.F. 146; f. 1949; 600 mems.; Pres. Prof. Dr. MITKO PANOV; Sec. Ass. TOME ANDONOVSKI; publs. *Geografski razgledi* (Geographical surveys), *Geografski vidik* (Geographical look).

**Makedonsko Geološko Društvo** (*Macedonian Geological Society*): Geološki zavod, P.O.B. 28, 91001 Skopje; f. 1951; 150 mems.; Pres. Dipl. Ing. VLADIMIR PASKALEV; Sec. Dipl. Ing. BRANKO PAVLOVSKI.

**Makedonsko Lekarsko Društvo** (*Medical Society of Macedonia*): 91000 Skopje, Gradski zid blok 11/6; f. 1946; 2,000 mems.; publ. *Makedonski medicinski pregled* (Macedonian Medical Review).

**Republički Zavod za Zaštita na Spomenicite na Kulturata** (*Institute for the Protection of Cultural Monuments of Macedonia*): 91000 Skopje, Maršal Tito b.b., Gorče Petrov; f. 1949; Dir. DIMITAR KORNAKOV; publ. *Kulturno-istorisko nasledstvo na S.R.M.* (The Cultural and Historical Heritage of the S.R. of Macedonia).

**Sojuz na društvata na arhivskite rabotnici na Makedonija** (*Union of Societies of Archivists of Macedonia*): 91000 Skopje, Kej Dimitar Vlahov bb; f. 1954; 128 mems.; publ. *Makedonski arhivist* (annually).

**Sojuz na Društvata na Bibliotekarite na Makedonija** (*Union of Librarians' Associations of Macedonia*): Narodna i univerzitetska biblioteka "Kliment Ohridski", 91000 Skopje, Bul. Goce Delčev, br. 6; f. 1949; 320 mems.; Pres. Mgr. KIRO DOJČINOVSKI; Sec. ZORKA KORKALEVA; publ. *Bibliotekarska iskra*.

**Sojuz na Društvata na Ekonomistite na Makedonija** (*Union of Economists' Societies of Macedonia*): 91000 Skopje, Ivan Milutinović b.b., Tavtalidže I. baraka 6; f. 1950; 2,700 mems.; Pres. Prof. Dr MITRA ŠAROSKA; Sec. Mag. DIMITRIJE NOVAČEVSKI; publ. *Stopanski pregled* (Economic review).

**Sojuz na Društvata na Veterinarnite Lekari i Tehničari na Makedonija** (*Union of Associations of Veterinary Surgeons and Technicians of Macedonia*): Veterinaren institut, 91000 Skopje, Lazar Pop-Trajkov 5; f. 1950; 400 mems.; Pres. Dipl. Vet. SILJAN ZAHARIEVSKI; Sec. Dipl. Vet. NIKOLA POPOVSKI; publ. *Makedonski veterinaren pregled* (Macedonian Veterinary review).

**Sojuz na Društvata za Makedonski Jazik i Literatura** (*Union of Associations for Macedonian Language and Literature*): Institut za makedonski jazik "Krste Misirkov", 91000 Skopje, Grigor Prličev 5; f. 1954; 700 mems.; Pres. Vasil Čipov; Sec. Olga Ivanova; publ. *Literaturen zbor* (Literary word).

**Sojuz na Hemičarite i Tehnolozite na Makedonija** (*Union of Chemists and Technologists of Macedonia*): Tehnološko-metalurški fakultet, 91000 Skopje, Karpos II; f. 1950; 1,200 mems.; Pres. Prof. Boro Ladinski; Sec. Todor Todorovski; publ. *Glasnik* (Review).

**Sojuz na Inženeri i Tehničari na Makedonija** (*Society of Engineers and Technicians of Macedonia*): 91000 Skopje, Nikola Vapcarov b.b.; f. 1945; 27,000 mems.; Pres. Prof. Dr. Ing. Dime Lazarov; Sec. Boro Ravnjanski.

**Sojuz na Inženeri i Tehničari po Sumarstvo il ndustrija za Prerabotka na Drvo na S.R.M.** (*Union of Forestry Engineers and Technicians of Macedonia*): Šumarski institut, 91000 Skopje, Engelsova 2; f. 1952; 500 mems.; Pres. Dipl. Ing. Živko Minčev; Sec. Dipl. Ing. Mile Stamenkov; publ. *Sumarski pregled* (Forester's review).

**Sojuz na Istoriskite Društva na S.R. Makedonija** (*Union of Historical Societies of Macedonia*): Institut za nacionalna istorija, 91000 Skopje, Boris Kidrič b.b.; f. 1952; 1,000 mems.; Pres. Dr. Petar Stojanovski; Sec. Gligor Nikolov; publ. *Istorija* (History).

**Sojuz na Združenijata na Pravnicite na Makedonija** (*Union of Associations of Jurists of Macedonia*): Ustaven sud na Makedonija, 91000 Skopje, XII udarna brigada 2; f. 1946; 4,000 mems.; Pres. Boro Dogandžiski; Sec. Petar Golubovski; publ. *Pravna misla* (Law's opinion).

**Sojuz na Zemjodelskite Inženeri i Tehničari na S.R.M.** (*Union of Agricultural Engineers and Technicians of Macedonia*): Zemjodelskošumarski fakultet, 91000 Skopje; f. 1945; 5,000 mems.; Pres. Prof. Dr. Risto Lozanovski; Sec. Doc. Dr. Risto Ilkovski; publ. *Socijalističko zemjodelstvo* (Socialist agriculture).

**Združenie na Folkloristite na Makedonija** (*Association of Folklorists of Macedonia*): Institut za folklor, 91000 Skopje, Ruzveltova 3; f. 1952; 60 mems.; Pres. Gorgi Georgiev; Sec. Tatjana Žeželj-Kaličanin.

## RESEARCH INSTITUTES

### Federal

**Drustvo za Proučavanje i Unapredenje Pomorstva Jugoslavije** (*Yugoslav Society for Research and Promotion of Maritime Sciences*): Rijeka, Rade Končara 44/V, P.O.B. 391; f. 1962; research divided into 9 sections: economics, history, law, technology, natural sciences, nautical sciences, literature, ethnology, medicine; 323 elected mems.; Pres. Adm. Bogdan Pecotić; Sec. Dr. Drago Crnković; publ. *Pomorski Zbornik* (Maritime Annals, annually).

**Institut "Jožef Stefan"** (*Jožef Stefan Institute*): Jamova 39, 61000 Ljubljana; f. 1949; 670 mems.; attached to Ljubljana University; library of 50,000 vols.; Dir. Prof. Dr. Boris Frlec.

**Institut Prometnih Znanosti** (*Institute of Transport Sciences*): 40000 Zagreb, Gruška 20; f. 1965; attached to Zagreb University; library of 8,000 vols.; Dir. Prof. Ing. Stjepan Lamer; publs. *Zbirka radova*† (Collection of Scientific Papers) (every 2 years), *Suvremeni Prometi* (Modern Transport) (every 2 months).

**Institut "Rudjer Bošković"** (*Rudjer Bošković Institute*): Bijenička cesta 54, P.O.B. 1016, 41001 Zagreb; f. 1950 as branch of the Yugoslav Academy of Sciences and Arts, became independent in 1955; research in physics (theoretical, nuclear and atomic, health), electronics, chemistry (physical, organic, and biochemistry), biology, medicine; marine research centre (laboratories in Zagreb and Rovinj); 703 mems.; library of 32,500 books and 600 periodicals; Dir. Vojno Kundić; publs. *Thalassia Jugoslavica*† (annually).

**Institut za nuklearne nauke "Boris Kidrič"** (*Boris Kidrič Institute of Nuclear Sciences*): 11000 Belgrade, Vinča, P.O.B. 522; f. 1948; low energy nuclear physics, solid state physics, radio chemistry and radiation chemistry, nucleic acid metabolism and radiogenetics, nuclear power problems, reactor physics, heat transfer, reactor engineering and reactor electronics, systems science and information, production and application of radio isotopes; library of 26,000 vols.; Dir. Gen. Dr. Djordje Jović.

**Institute for Agricultural Mechanization:** Belgrade; Zemun, P.O.B. 41; f. 1947; 30 mems.; library of 6,000 vols.; Dir. Radmilo Orović; publ. *Poljoprivredna Tehnika*† (Agricultural Engineering, annually).

**Institute for the Philosophy of Science and Peace of the Yugoslav Academy of Sciences and Arts:** Zagreb, Marulićev trg 19, P.O.B. 187; f. 1965 at the suggestion of Academician Ivan Supek, Chairman of the Yugoslav Pugwash Group; concerns itself with the synthesis and social ethics of sciences and arts; 6 mems.; Pres. Ivan Supek; publ. *Encyclopaedia Moderna* (quarterly).

**Institute for Plant Protection:** 11000 Belgrade, T. Drajzera 9; f. 1945; depts. of Entomology, Phytopathology, Weed Control, Phytopharmacy, Biological Control; 20 research staff; 60 mems.; library of 6,025 books and 12,000 periodicals; Dir. Dr. Ljubiša Vasiljević; publ. *Zaštita bilja*† (Plant Protection; quarterly).

**Institute for Scientific and Technical Documentation and Information:** Belgrade, Katanićeva 15; publ. *Yugoslav Research Guide*.

**Institute of International Politics and Economics:** Belgrade, P.O.B. 750; Dir. Božidar Frangeš.

**Jadranski Institut:** 41000 Zagreb, Opatička 18; f. 1945; research in maritime law and shipping; library of 16,200 vols.; Dir. Dr. Branko Kojić; publs. *Zbornik za pomorsko pravo*†, *Anali*, *Uporedno pomorsko pravo i pomorska kupoprodaja*.

**Jugoslovenski Bibliografski Institut** (*Yugoslav Bibliographic Institute*): Belgrade, Terazije 26, P.O.B. 20; f. 1949; publishes the Bibliography of Yugoslavia, which includes books, pamphlets, music scores and articles of literary, scientific interest, philology, art and sport; exchange of publications with other countries; Dir. Dr. Venceslav Glišić.

**Jugoslovenski Institut za zaštitu spomenika kulture** (*Yugoslav Institute for the Preservation of Historical Monuments*): Belgrade, Božidara Adžije 11; f. 1950; research into and preservation of cultural possessions (paintings, museum objects, murals, architecture, etc.); Dir. Ivan Zdravković; Head, Architecture Dept. Ivan Zdravković; Head, Paintings Dept. (Vacant); Head, Physical and Chemical Laboratory Mihailo Vunjak; Dept. of History of Art, Ethnology and Archaeology; Depts. of Law, Documentation, Photographic Laboratory; 24 mems.; library of 16,000 vols.; publs. *Zbornik zaštite spomenika kulture*, annuals, summaries in French, special reports.

**Poljoprivredni Institut** (*Agricultural Institute*): 54000 Osijek, Tenjska c. b.b.; f. 1916; agricultural and scientific research; 41 mems.; library of 9,317 vols.; Dir. Antun Novoselović; publ. *Zbornik radova Poljoprivrednog instituta u Osijeku*† (annually).

**Restauratorski Zavod** (*Conservation Department of the Institute of Fine Arts, Yugoslav Academy of Sciences and Arts*): Zagreb, Brače Kavurića 1: f. 1948, under the control of the Section for Fine Arts of the Yugoslav Academy of Sciences and Arts; Chief Restorer LELA ČERMAK.

**Zavod za Pomorsko-društvene Nauke Jugoslavenske Akademije Znanosti i Umjetnosti** (*Institute for Maritime Sciences of the Yugoslav Academy of Sciences and Arts*): Split, Trg Braće Radića 7, P.O.B. 100; f. 1925 as Maritime Museum, re-constituted 1965; research in maritime economics and history; Dir. Dr. Capt. OLIVER FIO; Librarian MARICA RISMONDO; publ. *Contributiones Studiis Scientiarum Maritimarum*.

**Zavod za povijest prirodnih, matematičkih i medicinskih znanosti Istraživačkog centra Jugoslavenske akademije znanosti i umjetnosti** (*Institute for the History of Natural, Mathematical and Medical Sciences of Research Centre of Yugoslav Academy of Sciences and Arts*): Demetrova 18 and Opatička 18, 41000 Zagreb; f. 1960 by the Yugoslav Academy of Sciences and Arts; incorporates Department of the History of Medicine of the Yugoslav Academy, Institute of the History of Pharmacy of the Pharmaceutical Society of Croatia, Cabinet of the History of Medicine of the University of Zagreb, Cabinet for the History of Veterinary Medicine, Museum of the Society of Physicians of Croatia and the Bošković Museum; scientific institution to foster research into the history of science, especially that of southern Slavs; plans to study problems of methodology, to organize at Zagreb higher education for the study of the history of science, to collaborate with analogous institutes at home and abroad; library of 8,000 vols.; Dir. Acad. BRANKO KESIĆ; publ. *Rasprave i Gradja za Povijest Nauka* (annually).

SERBIA

**Astronomska Opservatorija u Beogradu** (*Astronomical Observatory of Belgrade*): Belgrade, Volgina 7; f. 1887, re-formed 1932; library of 9,750 vols.; Dir. M. B. PROTITCH; publ. *Bulletin*.

**Botanical Institute and Garden of the University:** Belgrade, Takovska 43; Dir. Prof. V. BLEČIĆ; publ. *Bulletin*.

**Hidrometeorološki Zavod S. R. Srbije** (*Hydro-Meteorological Institute of the S. R. of Serbia*): Belgrade, Bačvanska 21; Dir. IGOR DELIJANIĆ.

**Meteorološka opservatorija Beograd** (*Belgrade Meteorological Observatory*): Belgrade, Bul. Jugoslovenske narodne armije 8; f. 1887; Dir. KATARINA MILOSAVLJEVIĆ; publ. *Observations Météorologiques à Beograd*.

**Seismological Institute:** Belgrade, Tašmajdan, P.O.B. 351; f. 1906; Dirs. Dr. B. A. SIKOŠEK, Dr. M. N. VUKAŠINOVIČ; 12 mems.; publs. *Annuaire macroséismique et microséismique, Bulletin mensuel, Studies*.

**Zavod za Zdravstvenu Zaštitu S.R. Srbije** (*Institute of Health Protection of S.R. Serbia*) (formerly Institute of Hygiene): Belgrade, Dr. Subotića 12; f. 1924; library of 40,000 vols.; Dir. Prof. Dr. JOVAN CEKIĆ; publs. *Glasnik* and series of monographs.

CROATIA

**Hidrometeorološki Zavod S.R. Hrvatske** (*Hydro-Meteorological Institute of the S.R. of Croatia*): Žagreb, Grič 3; f. 1947; Dir. Ing. M. ŠIKIĆ; publs. *Annual Report of the Meteorological Mountain Observatory Sljeme, near Zagreb, Material for the Climate of Croatia, Memoirs, Annual Report of the Meteorological Observatory Marjan-Split*.

**Institut za oceanografiju i ribarstvo** (*Institute of Oceanography and Fisheries*): Split, Moše Pijade 63; f. 1930; research in oceanography, hydrography, geology, marine biology, marine fisheries, ichthyology, and fishery technology; has 3 laboratories and a staff of 33 naturalists; Dir. Capt. RADE STIJELJA; library of c. 15,000 vols.; publs. *Acta Adriatica†, Notes†, Collected Reprints†*.

**Institute for Folklore Research:** Zagreb, Socialističke revolucije 17; f. 1948; fmrly. Institute for Folk Arts; branch of the Institute of Philology and Folkloristics; there are the following sections: Dance, Music, Folk Literature, Theatre and Customs; 18 mems.; library of 14,000 vols.; Dir. DUNJA RIHTMAN-AUGUŠTIN; publ. *Narodna Umjetnost†* (annually).

**Institute for Medical Research and Occupational Health:** 41000 Zagreb, Moše Pijade 158, P.O.B. 291; f. 1949 to study the influence of ecological factors upon health; 240 mems.; library of 6,400 vols.; Dir. Prof. MARKO ŠARIĆ; publ. *Archives of Industrial Hygiene and Toxicology* (quarterly).

**Institute for Nature Preservation of the S. R. of Croatia:** 41000 Zagreb, Ilica 44/II; f. 1961; 19 mems.; library of 3,535 vols.; photo collection of 123,000 negatives and 3,800 colour transparencies; Dir. IVAN BRALIĆ.

**Institute for the Preservation of Historical and Cultural Monuments:** Zagreb, Ilica 44; f. 1910; library of 6,975 vols.; photo collection of c. 36,000 negatives, 9,000 charts; Dir. Prof. STJEPAN HUMEL; publs. *Spomenici kulture i likovnih umjetnosti u Medjumurju†, Spomenici u SR Hrvatskoj njihova rasprostranjenost i opca valorizacija†, Kako narod gradi†, Gradja za proučavanje starih kamenih mostova i akvedukata u Hravatskoj†, Godišnjak zaštite spomenika Kulture Hrvatske†* (Yearbook of Protection of Croation Cultural Monuments).

**Institute for the Preservation and Scientific Study of Historical Monuments in Dalmatia:** Split, Zrinjsko-Frankopanska ul. 25/I; f. 1854; Dir. Dr. CVITO FISKOVIĆ; Sec. NEIRA STOJANAC; publ. *Prilozi povijesti umjetnosti u Dalmaciji*.

**Zavod za Arhitekturu i Urbanizam** (*Institute of Architecture and Town Planning*): 41000 Zagreb, Ulica braće Kavurića 1; f. 1952 for the scientific study of the history of architecture and town planning and of methods of protection, conservation and presentation of monuments; 5 mems.; library of 2,000 vols., 30 periodicals; Dir. ANA DEANOVIĆ; publs. *Rad JAZU†* (irregular), *Bulletin Razreda za likovne umjetnosti†* (2 a year), *Monographs†* (irregular).

SLOVENIA

**Geološki Zavod** (*Geological Institute*): 61000 Ljubljana, Dimičeva 16; f. 1946; library of 8,500 vols., 835 periodicals; Dir. SLAVKO PAPLER; publ. *Geologija-razprave poročila* (annually).

**Zavod SR Slovenije za varstvo naravne in kulturne dediščine** (*Institute of the SR of Slovenia for the Preservation of Natural and Historical Patrimony*): 61000 Ljubljana, Plečnikov trg 2; f. 1913, reorganized 1919, refounded 1945; to preserve and study historical, archaeological and natural monuments, and sites of historical, artistic, scientific, ethnological, natural and sociological interest; a complete register of historical monuments in Slovenia; 41 mems.; library of 8,000 books; Pres. KOLARIČ MARJAN; publs. *Varstvo spomenikov†* (Preservation of Monuments), *Varstvo narave†* (Nature Conservation), Series *Kulturni in naravni spomeniki Slovenije* (guides to the historical and natural monuments of Slovenia).

BOSNIA AND HERZEGOVINA

**Institute for Modern Serbo-Croatian:** Sarajevo.

**Institute of Meteorology:** Hadži Loje 4, Sarajevo; f. 1891; Dir. M. V. VEMIĆ.

**Institute for the Preservation of Historical Monuments:** 71001 Sarajevo, Obala 27 Jula 11A, P.O.B. 650; f. 1947; Dir. DŽEMAL CELIĆ; publ. *Naše starine* (Our Antiquities, annual).

## MACEDONIA

**Ekonomski Institut na Univerzitetet "Kiril i Metodij"** (*Institute of Economics of the Cyril and Methodius University*): 91000 Skopje, Njudelhiska b.b.; f. 1952; Dir. Dr. LAZAR SOKOLOVSKI.

**Geološki Zavod** (*Geology Institute*): 91001 Skopje, P.O.B. 28; f. 1944; geological mapping, exploration of mineral deposits, drilling, mining, grouting; c. 700 mems.; library of c. 10,000 vols.; Gen. Dir. DRAGAN ANGELESKY; publs. *Trudovi*† (Transactions), *Posebni Izdanija*† (Special issues).

**Institut za Folklor** (*Institute of Folklore*): 91000 Skopje, Ruzveltova 3; f. 1950; Dir. Dr. CVETANKA ORGANDŽIEVA; publ. *Makedonski folklor*.

**Institut za Makedonski Jazik "Krste Misirkov"** (*The Krste Misirkov Institute of Macedonian*): 91000 Skopje, Grigor Prličev 5; f. 1953; Dir. TRAJKO STAMATOVSKI; publs. *Makedonski jazik* (The Macedonian Language), *Povremeni izdanija* (non-serial editions).

**Institut za Nacionalna Istorija** (*Institute of National History*): 91000 Skopje, Boris Kidrič b.b.; f. 1948; history of Macedonian peoples; 50 mems.; library of 200,000 vols.; Dir. ORDE IVANOSKI; publ. *Glasnik*† (Journal).

**Institut za Pamuk** (*Cotton Institute*): 92400 Strumica, Goce Delčev 27; f. 1956; Dir. HRISTO HRISTOMANOV; publ. *Zbornik* (Collected Papers).

**Institut za Tutun** (*Tobacco Institute*): 97500 Prilep, Kičevsko Džade; Dir. Dr. JOSIF MICKOVSKI; publ. *Tutun* (Tobacco).

**Veterinaren Institut na S.R. Makedonija** (*Veterinary Institute of Macedonia*): 91000 Skopje, XVI makedonska brigada 5; f. 1927; Dir. GORGI GRAMATIKOVSKI; Sec. DIMITAR ANASTASOV.

**Zavod za Ovoštarstvo na S.R. Makedonija** (*Institute of Pomology of Macedonia*): 91000 Skopje, Pat za Dračevo 5; f. 1953; Dir. Dr. JANKO LAZAREVSKI; publ. *Godišnjak* (Yearbook).

**Zavod za Ribarstvo na S.R. Makedonija** (*Institute of Fisheries of Macedonia*): 91000 Skopje, Gradski park; f. 1951; Dir. NIKOLA PETROVSKI; Sec. TIMKO TRAJKOV; publs. *Izdanija* (Publications), *Folia Balcanica*, *Godišen izveštaj* (Annual Report).

**Zavod za Unapreduvanje na Lozarstvoto i Vinarstvoto na S.R. Makedonija** (*Institute for the Advancement of Viticulture of Macedonia*): 91000 Skopje, Naselba Butel 1; f. 1952; Dir. Dr. DIME PEMOVSKI; publs. *Lozarstvo i vinarstvo* (Viticulture), *Godišen izveštaj* (Annual Report).

**Zavod za Unapreduvanje na Stočarstvoto na S.R. Makedonija** (*Institute for the Advancement of Animal Husbandry of Macedonia*): 91000 Skopje, Avtokomanda; f. 1952; Dir. Prof. Dr. BLAGOJ VASKOV.

**Zavod za vodostopanstvo na S.R. Makedonija** (*Institute for Water Resources of Macedonia*)· 91000 Skopje, Apostol Guslarot 1; f. 1952; Dir. Dr.-Ing. MOMČILO ANDREJEVIČ; Sec. PREDRAG JOVČEVSKI; publ. *Vodostopanski problemi* (Water Resources).

## MONTENEGRO

**Istoriski Institut S.R. Crne Gore** (*Historical Institute*): Naselje Kruševac, Titograd.

# LIBRARIES AND ARCHIVES

## SERBIA

**Arhiv Srbije:** Karnedžijeva 2, 11000 Belgrade; f. 1900; history of Serbia; 65,000 vols.; Dir. MIRJANA DAJIĆ; publ. *Arhivski pregled*† (2 a year).

**Arhiv Vojvodine:** Trg Branka Radičevića 8, 21205 Sremski Karlovci; f. 1926; library of 11,000 vols.; Dir. Dr. KALMAN ČEHAK; publs. *Naučno-informativna sredstva o arhivskoj gradji u arhivima Vojvodine* (Scientific information on the Vojvodina archives), *Izveštaji o naučno-istraživačkom radu u inostranstvu* (Research reports from archives abroad).

**Narodna biblioteka Socijalističke Republike Srbije** (*National Library (Central Library for the Socialist Republic of Serbia)*): Belgrade, Skerličeva 1; f. 1832; 729,172 vols., 130,843 vols. of periodicals, 61,634 vols. of newspapers, 204 old MSS., 1,108 MSS., and 712,208 rare books, prints, maps, reviews, scores, etc.; federal copyright and deposit library; Dir. SVETISLAV DJURIĆ.

**Univerzitetska biblioteka "Svetozar Markovič"** (*University Library "Svetozar Markovič"*): Bulevar revolucije 71, Belgrade; its forerunner was the library of the Serbian Lyceum (1844); it receives editors' copies of scientific publications printed in Serbia; about 1,200,000 vols. (books, periodicals, newspapers), 15 incunabula, 71 Serbian MSS. 13th–18th centuries, over 300 Oriental codices, 4,040 other MSS.; Head Mrs. STANIJA GLIGORIJEVIĆ; publs. *Pregled doktorskih disertacija odbranjenih u S.R. Srbiji* (every 2 years), *Popis radova nastavnika Beogradskog univerziteta* (annually).

**Biblioteka Srpske akademije nauka i umetnosti** (*Library of the Serbian Academy of Sciences and Arts*): Knez Mihailova 35, 11000 Belgrade; f. 1842 by the Serbian Learned Society; information service, inter-library loan scheme; prepares bibliographies and edits special publications; c. 700,000 vols.; Dir. MILE ŽEGARAC; publs. numerous publications of the Academy and its attached Institutes†.

**Biblioteka grada Beograda** (*Belgrade Town Library*): Zmaj Jovina 1, Belgrade; f. 1929; 200,000 vols., 399 MSS.; Head BRANKO DJURDJULOV.

**Biblioteka Matice srpske** (*Library of the Serbian Society*): Ul. Matice srpske 1, 21000 Novi Sad; f. 1826 in Budapest, opened 1838 and transferred to Novi Sad in 1864; c. 629,900 vols.; 125,790 vols. of periodicals, 16 incunabula, 320 Serbian manuscript books, 124 Serbian palestipe, 9,000 rare Yugoslav books; copyright and deposit library for the Vojvodina S.A.P.; Dir. JOVANKA TODOROVIĆ; publs. *Bibliotekarske novosti* (quarterly), *Godišnjak Biblioteke Matice srpske*.

**British Council Library:** Belgrade, Knez Mihailova 45; f. 1946; 19,868 vols., 142 periodicals; Librarian Mrs. V. RAKIC.

**Narodna biblioteka "Žika Popovič"** (*Public Library "Zika Popovič"*): Sabac; f. 1847; over 60,000 vols.

**Narodna biblioteka** (*Public Library*): Požarevac; f. 1847; about 30,000 vols.

**Narodna biblioteka** (*Public Library*): Niš; f. 1903; about 90,000 vols.

**Narodna biblioteka** (*Public Library*): Kragujevac; f. 1866; about 50,000 vols.

## CROATIA

**Arhiv Hrvatske** (*Archives of Croatia*): 41000 Zagreb, Marulićev trg 21; f. 1643; documents dating from 10th century, concerning mainly the history of Northern Croatia and Slavonia; Croatia film archive; library of

40,000 vols., collection of microfilms; Dir. PETAR STRČIĆ; publs. *Arhivski vjesnik* (Archives Bulletin), *Zaključci Hrvatskog sabora* (Acts of the Croatian Parliament).

**British Council Library:** Zagreb, Ilica 12/I; f. 1946; reference; 3,195 vols., 56 periodicals; Librarian Mrs. Z. VDOVIČIĆ.

**Gradska knjižnica** (*Town Library*): Rooseveltov trg 4, Zagreb; f. 1907; 183,259 vols.; Dir. VERA MUDRI-ŠKUNCA.

**Gradska knjižnica i čitaonica "Sloboda"** (*Town Library and Reading Club "Sloboda"*): Varaždin, Trg Slobode 8A; f. 1838; 5,000 mems.; library of 67,000 vols.; Dir. WANDA MILČETIĆ.

**Knjižnica Jugoslavenske akademije znanosti i umjetnosti** (*Library of the Yugoslav Academy of Sciences and Arts*): Zrinski trg 11, Zagreb; f. 1868; c. 208,000 vols.; Dir. ALEKSANDAR STIPČEVIĆ.

**Nacionalna i sveučilišna biblioteka** (*National and University Library*): Marulićev trg 21, Zagreb; its beginnings reach back as far as the first years of the 17th century; 1,069,471 vols. (including books, periodicals and newspapers), 186 incunabula, about 4,754 rare and precious Yugoslav books; 5,184 MSS., 7,393 prints, 15,097 maps, 13,602 scores, 5,457 records, 3,500 microfilms; Federal copyright and deposit library; Head MATKO ROJNIĆ.

**Naučna biblioteka** (*Research Library*): Knežev dvor, Dubrovnik; f. 1936; 140,426 vols., 76 incunabula, 919 MSS.

**Naučna biblioteka** (*Research Library*): Trg Oslobodenja 1, Pula; f. 1930; about 180,000 vols.

**Naučna biblioteka** (*Research Library*): Dolac 1, Rijeka; f. 1627; special collection of material on the Istria, Hrvatsko primorje and Gorski kotar regions; 400,000 vols., 23 incunabula; Head Dr. VANDA EKL; publ. *Informacije o novim knjigama* (3 a year).

**Naučna biblioteka** (*Scientific Library*): Zagrebačka 2, Split; f. 1903; 300,000 vols., 13,000 periodicals; Dir. Prof. LALIE AUTICE.

**Naučna biblioteka** (*Research Library*): Žrtava fašizma bb., Zadar; f. 1850; about 300,000 vols.

**Radnička biblioteka Zagreb** (*Workers' Library*): Lenjinov trg 2, Zagreb; f. 1927; 114,173 vols.; Dir. MARIJA PICHLER.

## SLOVENIA

**Arhiv S.R. Slovenije** (*Archives of P.R. of Slovenia*): Zvezdarska 1, 61000 Ljubljana; f. 1945; collection of important archives, especially those connected with the territory populated by Slovenes from the 13th century onwards; Chief MARIJA OBLAK-ČARNI.

**Biblioteka Slovenske akademije znanosti in umetnosti** (*Library of the Slovene Academy of Sciences and Arts*): Novi trg 4-5, 61001 Ljubljana; f. 1938; over 300,000 vols.; Librarian PRIMOŽ RAMOVŠ; publs. *Seznam prejetih knjig†* (monthly), *Letni seznam periodik†* (annual), *Poročilo o delu biblioteke†* (annual), *Objave†* (irregular).

**Centralna ekonomska knjižnica** (*Central Economic Library*): Ljubljana, Kardeljeva ploščad 17; f. 1948; 112,300 vols., 1,714 periodicals; Librarian TOMAŽ KOBE; publ. *Mesečni pregled novih knjig†*.

**Centralna medicinska knjižnica** (*Central Medical Library*): 61000 Ljubljana, Vrazov trg 2; f. 1945; central library for all institutes and clinics attached to the Faculty of Medicine, Ljubljana; literature of biomedicine and cognate sciences; 121,761 books and periodicals, 1,345 current periodicals; Librarian SONJA GOREC.

**Centralna tehniška knjižnica Univerze Edvarda Kardelja v Ljubljani** (*Central Technical Library of the Edvard Kardelj University of Ljubljana*): Tomšičeva 7, 61000 Ljubljana; f. 1949; literature of pure and applied sciences; central library of the technological faculties of the university of Ljubljana and centre for all technical and industrial libraries in Slovenia; information and referral centre for science and technology; 129,464 vols.; Chief Librarian Mrs. Prof. MARA ŠLAJPAH; publs. *Annual Report, New Books Accession List, New Industrial Standards Accession List and Literature about Standards, Information about Energetics, Information about Environmental Protection* (included in the review *Naše okolje*) (every 2 months).

**Knjižnica Narodnega Muzeja** (*National Museum Library*): Prešernova 20, Ljubljana; f. 1821; over 100,000 vols.; Librarian BRANKO REISP.

**Knjižnica Pravne fakultete** (*Library of the Faculty of Law*): Ljubljana, Trg revolucije 11; f. 1920; 84,000 vols.; Librarian DANICA LOVREČIČ.

**Narodna in univerzitetna knjižnica** (*National and University Library*): Turjaška 1, 61001 Ljubljana; f. 1774; about 1,300,000 vols.; Federal copyright and deposit library; Dir. TOMO MARTELANC; publs. *Slovenska bibliografija†* (annual), *Obvestila republiške matične službe* (irregular).

**Osrednja knjižnica, Oddelek za študij** (*Central Library, Dept. of Study and Research*): Celje, Muzejski trg 1; f. 1946; 140,692 vols.; Librarian IVAN SENIČAR.

**Slovanska knjižnica** (*Slavonic Library*): Gosposka 15/I, Ljubljana; f. 1901, re-founded 1946; language, literature and history of the Slavs; 81,153 vols.; Dir. Dr. ŠTEFAN BARBARIČ.

**Študijska knjižnica** (*Regional Library*): Koper, Trg revolucije 1; f. 1956; 100,000 vols.; Librarian SREČKO VILHAR.

**Študijska knjižnica Mirana Jarca** (*"Milan Jarc" Regional Library*): Novo Mesto, C. Kom. Staneta 26/28; f. 1945; 154,545 vols.; Librarian NATAŠA PETROV.

**Univerzitetna knjižnica Maribor** (*University of Maribor Library*): Prešernova 1, 62000 Maribor; f. 1903; general scientific library with special regard to the needs of the University; 385,637 vols.; Chief Librarian Dr. BRUNO HARTMAN; publs. *Časopis za zgodovino in narodopisje†, Slavistična revija†*.

## BOSNIA AND HERZEGOVINA

**Biblioteka Zemaljskog muzeja** (*National Museum Library*): V. Putnika 7, Sarajevo; f. 1888; archaeology, ethnology and natural sciences; 5 mems.; about 100,000 vols.; Dir. DOBRILA BOKAN; publs. *Glasnik Zemaljskog muzeja†, Wissenschaftliche Mitteilungen†*.

**Gazi Husrevbegova biblioteka** (*Gazi Husrevbeg Library*): Obala Pariške komune 4, Sarajevo; f. 1537; the most important oriental library in Yugoslavia; c. 34,000 vols., 11,000 Islamic MSS., 4,500 documents.

**Narodna i univerzitetska biblioteka Bosne i Hercegovine** (*National and University Library of Bosnia and Herzegovina*): 71000 Sarajevo, P.O.B. 337, Obala Vojvode Stepe 42; f. 1945; 670,000 vols.; Federal copyright and deposit library; Head DRAGIŠA IVKOVIĆ.

## MACEDONIA

**American Center Library:** P.O.B. 296, Gradski Zid, Blok IV, 91000 Skopje.

**Arhiv na Skopje** (*Archives of Skopje*): Moskovska 1, reon 45, 91000 Skopje; f. 1954; 3,000 vols.; Dir. Dr. MILOŠ KONSTANTINOV; publs. *Dokumenti za istorijata na Skopje†* (irregular), *Special editions* (irregular).

## YUGOSLAVIA

**Arhiv na S.R. Makedonija:** Kej Dimitar Vlahov b.b., Skopje; f. 1951; over 10,000 vols., 872 periodicals; Dir. ALEKSANDER BLAGOJA ALEKSIEV; publs. Series of Turkish, French, British documentation on Macedonia.

**Istoriski arhiv na Bitola** (*Historical Archives of Bitola*): 97000 Bitola, 1 May 171; f. 1954; conservation, collection and printing of archive materials; 3,946 vols.; Dir. JOVAN KOCHANKOVSKY.

**Istoriski Arhiv na Ohrid** (*Historical Archives of Ohrid*): 97300 Ohrid, Kosta abraševic 8; f. 1953; Dir. NAUM CELAKOVSKI.

**Narodna i univerzitetska biblioteka "Kliment Ohridski"** (*National and University Library "Kliment Ohridski"*): Bul. Goce Delčev b.b., 91000 Skopje, P.O.B. 566; f. 1944; 1,150,000 vols.; copyright and deposit library of the S.F.R. Yugoslavia; Head DIMITAR SOLEV.

**Biblioteka "Braka Miladinovci"** (*District of Skopje Public Library*): Partizanski odredi b.b., Skopje; f. 1935; about 120,000 vols.; Dir. LAZO STRAČKOV.

**Gradska biblioteka** (*Town Library*): Maršala Titoa 89, Bitola; f. 1945; 27,000 vols.

### MONTENEGRO

**Biblioteka Državnog muzeja NR Crne Gore** (*Library of the National Museum of the P.R. of Montenegro*): Titov trg 7, Cetinje; f. 1926; over 20,000 vols.

**Biblioteka Istorijskog Instituta NR Crne Gore** (*Library of the Historical Institute of the P.R. of Montenegro*): Naselje Kruševac, Titograd; f. 1948, over 38,000 vols.

**Centralna narodna biblioteka SR Crne Gore** (*Central National Library of the S.R. of Montenegro*): Bulevar Lenjina 159, Cetinje; f. 1946; about 1,000,000 vols.; Federal copyright and deposit library; Head Dr. DUŠAN MARTINOVIĆ; publs. *Bibliografski vjesnik†, Geološki glasnik†, Glasnik Etnografskog muzeja na Cetinju†, Glasnik cetinjskih muzeja†, Godišnjak geografskog društva Crne Gore†, Zbornik Više pomorske škole u Kotoru†, Istorijski zapisi†, Poljoprivreda i šumarstvo†, Pravni zbornik†, Praksa†, Starine Crne Gore†, Stvaranje†.*

## MUSEUMS AND ART GALLERIES

### Belgrade

**Etnografski muzej** (*Ethnographical Museum*): Studentski trg. 13, p.p. 357; f. 1901, reorganized 1967; departments: Costumes and Textiles, Economy, Social Life, Houses and other buildings, Customs, Documentation, Conservation; library of 30,000 vols.; Dir. GVOZDEN JOVANIĆ; publ. *Glasnik* (annually).

**Museum of Modern Art:** 11070 Belgrade, Ušće Save b.b.; f. 1958, opened 1965; exhibitions of Yugoslav and foreign art; library of over 2,800 vols.; Dir. MARIJA PUŠIĆ; publs. 25 exhibition calatogues a year†.

**Muzej grada Beograda** (*Belgrade City Museum*): Zmaj Jovina St. 1, P.O.B. 87; f. 1903; Dir. TODOROVIC D'JOVAN.

**Muzej Nikole Tesle** (*Nikola Tesla Museum*): Proleterskih brigada 51; f. 1952; Dir. KORAĆ VELJKO.

**Muzej Pozorišne Umetnosti** (*Museum of Theatre Art*): Gospodar Jevremova 19; f. 1950; Dir. DRAGOVAN JOVANOVIĆ.

**Muzej primenjene umetnosti** (*Museum of Applied Arts*): Belgrade, Vuka Karadžića 18; f. 1950; library of 12,500 vols.; Dir. Dr. BOJANA RADOJKOVIĆ; publ. *Muzej primenjene umetnosti-Zbornik†* (annually).

**Narodni muzej** (*National Museum*): Trg Republike 1 A; f. 1844; archaeological collections and an art gallery (Yugoslav and foreign collections); library of 45,000 vols.; Dir. JEVTA JEVTOVIĆ; publs. *Zbornik, Numizmatičar,* various catalogues.

**Prirodnjački muzej u Beogradu** (*Belgrade Natural History Museum*): Njegoševa 51; f. 1895; botanical, geological, mineralogical, palaeontological, petrological and zoological collections; library of 54,706 vols.; Dir. ŽIVOMIR VASIĆ; publ. *Glasnik Prirodnjačkog muzej u Beogradu* (Report).

**Vojni Muzej** (*Military Museum*): Belgrade-Kalemegdan; f. 1878, refounded 1934, and again 1945-47; new exhibition was opened in 1961. There are five sections:(1) The military history of the Yugoslav peoples up till 1918; (2) The military history of the Yugoslav peoples after 1918; (3) Conservation; (4) Pedagogical; (5) Photo archives; library of 15,000 vols.; Dir. ERNEST MEZGA; publ. *Vesnik* (annually).

**Zeljeznicki Muzej** (*Railway Museum of F.S.R. of Yugoslavia*): 6 Nemanjina ul., Belgrade; f. 1950; there are five depts.; library of 15,000 vols.; archives section being formed; Dir. Dr. M. H. RISTIĆ; publ. *History of Yugoslavian Railway in Pictures.*

### Banja Luka

**Muzej Bosanske Krajine** (*Museum of Basanska Krajina Region*): Regional museum for north-west Bosnia; f. 1930; Departments of Archaeology, History, Ethnography, National Revolution; Dir. BRANKO SURUČIĆ.

### Brežice

**Posavski muzej** (*Regional Museum*): f. 1940; collection of archæological exhibits from Neolithic times to the early Middle Ages; also ethnographical collection; historical section: Slovene-Croat peasants' revolt 1573 and Slovene national struggle for liberation 1941-45; Baroque painting and frescoes; Dir. MARJAN GREGORIČ.

### Celje

**Pokrajinski muzej** (*Local Museum*): 63000 Celje, Muzejski trg 1; f. 1882; collections of archaeology, art and cultural history, ethnography and history; library of 5,868 vols.; Dir. VERA KOLŠEK.

### Cetinje

**Državni muzej** (*State Museum*): Titov trg; depts. of history, ethnography, archaeology, arts; 34 mems.; library of 28,000 vols.; Dir. STANISLAV-RAKO VUJOŠEVIĆ; publ. *Glasnik Cetinjskih Muzeja†*.

**Njegošev muzej** (*Njegoš's Museum*): local exhibits; Dir. JANKO LEPIČIČ.

### Dubrovnik

**Muzej Srpske Pravoslavne Crkve** (*Museum of the Serbian Orthodox Church*): Od Puća 2; f. 1953; collection of portraits, and over 170 icons from Serbia, Crete, Corfu, Venice, Russia, Greece, Dubrovnik, Boka-Kotorska; the palace which houses the collection is also of historical interest and there is a library of 25,000 vols.

**Pomorski muzej** (*Maritime Museum*): St. John's Fortress, f. 1872; since 1949 under the administration of the Yugoslav Academy of Arts and Sciences; collecting and exhibiting items illustrating Dubrovnik's maritime past; library of 8,000 vols.; Dir. Dr. JOSIP LUETIĆ; publ. *Materials Concerning the Maritime History of Dubrovnik.*

**Umjetnička Galerija Dubrovnik:** Frana Supila 45; f. 1945; modern paintings and sculptures; library of 2,418 vols.; Dir. Prof. ANTUN KARAMAN; publs. catalogues†.

### Kotor

**Pomorski muzej** (*Maritime Museum*): Kotor; f. 1900; 10,000 vols.; Dir. JOVAN MARTINOVIĆ; publ. *Godišnjak Pomorskog Muzeja u Kotoru* (Yearbook).

## Ljubljana

**Mestni muzej** (*Municipal Museum*): Gosposka 15; f. 1935; cultural history museum of Ljubljana; collections include furniture from the Gothic period to the Biedermeierzeit, arts and crafts and topography; archaeological dept., containing articles from lake dwellings of the chalcolithic period, cemetery of the Illyrian-Celtic period and of Roman domination (Emona); Dir. ANDREJ UJČIČ; publs. various guides.

**Moderna galerija** (*Modern Art Gallery*): Tomšičeva 14; f. 1947; permanent collection of contemporary Slovene (Yugoslav) art from the Impressionists to the present day; organizes regular art exhibitions and the International Biennial of Prints; photography department; art library of 17,498 vols.; Dir. Prof. ZORAN KRŽIŠNIK; publs. *Monographs, Catalogues.*

**Muzej ljudske revolucije Slovenije** (*Museum of the Slovene People's Revolution*): Celovška c. 23; f. 1944 to collect all important archives, museum objects and library material from the War of Liberation, 1941–45; a permanent exhibition opened in 1955, depicting the struggle of the Slovene people for liberation; Dir. STANE MRVIČ.

**Narodna galerija** (*National Art Gallery*): 61000 Ljubljana, Prežihova 1; f. 1918, reorganized 1933, nationalized 1946; collection of Gothic sculptural arts, mediaeval frescoes and imitations of Gothic frescoes from Slovenia; collection of Renaissance, Baroque and 19th-century paintings and sculptures; paintings by Slovenian impressionists; collection of Slovenian graphic arts from the 18th to the beginning of the 20th century; collection of photographs, negatives and prints; photo-documentation of works of art from Slovenia; library of 9,436 vols.; Dir. Dr. ANICA CEVC; publs. manuals, catalogues.

**Narodni muzej** (*National Museum*): Prešernova ul. 20, P.O.B. 529-X; f. 1821; Departments of archaeology and prehistory; history of applied arts; coins and medals; graphic arts; library of 100,000 vols.; branch: Museum of Bled (Medieval Castle, Exhibition rooms "Arkade", and in Ljutomer the Exhibition of Tabori in Slovenia); Dir. Dr. PETER PETRU; publs. *Situla†, Catalogi et Monographiae†, Argo†.*

**Prirodoslovni muzej Slovenije** (*Slovenian Natural History Museum*): Prešernova 20; first founded 1821, became separate institution 1944; studies and gives its protection to natural phenomena; exhibits are displayed according to an ecological classification; the exhibition is composed of 115 dioramas with mixed zoological, botanical, palaeontological samples; library of 8,000 vols.; Dir. MARKO ALJANČIČ; publs. *Scopolia†* (2 a year), guides.

**Slovenski etnografski muzej** (*Ethnographical Museum*): 61000 Ljubljana, Prešernova cesta 20; f. 1923; reorganized 1963; Slovene and non-European ethnographic collection; library of 20,000 vols.; Dir. Dr. BORIS KUHAR; publ. *Slovenski etnograf* (annual).

**Slovenski šolski muzej** (*Slovenian School Museum*): Poljanska c. 28; f. 1898 to collect school documents and pedagogic books from the 12th century onwards; collection of records of cultural workers killed during the 1941–45 war; over 36,701 exhibits; library of 43,734 vols.; 487 fascicules; permanent exhibitions of development of schools in Slovenia; Dir. SLAVICA PAVLIČ.

**Zemljepisni muzej Slovenije** (*Geographical Museum of Slovenia*): Trg francoske revolucije 7; f. 1946; maps of Slovenia, geographical collections, and exhibitions; library; Dir. Prof. Dr. VLADIMIR KLEMENČIČ.

## Maribor

**Pokrajinski muzej** (*Regional Museum*): Grajska ul. 2; f. 1903 from collections of the Maribor Museum, the historical societies and the Episcopal Museum; archaeological, ethnographical, historical, topographical, and art exhibits; library of 7,862 vols.; Dir. Dr. SERGEJ VRIŠER.

## Novi Sad

**Art Gallery of Matica Srpska:** Trg Proleterskih brigada 1; f. 1847; collection of Serbian art from 18th century; Dir. RADIVOJ M. KOVAČEVIĆ (acting).

**Vojvodjanski muzej** (*Museum of Vojvodina*): 21000 Novi Sad, Dunavska 35; f. 1947; sections: archaeology, ethnology, history, applied art; library of 40,000 vols.; Dir. Dr. LJUBIVOJE ĆEROVIĆ; publs. *Rad vojvodjanskih muzeja†* (annually), *Posebna izdanja†* (occasional).

## Ptuj

**Pokrajinski muzej** (*Regional Museum*): Muzejski trg 1; f. 1945 from collections at the historic Ptuj castle, and the Ptuj Museum Society (f. 1893); archaeological, art, historical and ethnographic departments covering prehistoric, Roman, Old Slavic and Feudal periods; ecclesiastical art, folklore, three temples of Mithras; local history.

## Rijeka

**Moderna Galerija** (*Museum of Modern Art*): Dolac 1; f. 1948; paintings, sculpture and graphics from Yugoslavia and other countries; library of 1,854 vols.; Dir. Dr. BORIS VIŽINTIN; publs. catalogues.

**Prirodoslovni muzej** (*Natural Science Museum*): Setalište Vladimira Nazora 3; f. 1946; Dir. Dr. CRNKOVIĆ DRAGO.

## Sarajevo

**Umjetnička galerija Bosne i Hercegovine:** JNA 38; f. 1946; collections of modern art from Yugoslavia and Bosnia and Herzegovina; also ancient icons and art; library of 3,000 vols.; Dir. ARFAN HOZIĆ; publs. catalogues.

**Zemaljski Muzej Bosne i Hercegovine** (*Bosnian and Herzegovinian Museum*): f. 1888; prehistoric, Roman, Greek and Medieval periods, ethnological, botanical, zoological, geological sections; botanical garden; library of c. 100,000 vols.; Dir. Dr. ŽELJKA BJELČIĆ (Mrs.); publs. *Glasnik Zemaljskog muzeja†* (annual), *Wissenschaftliche Mitteilungen des Bosnisch-Herzegowinischen Landes-museums* (annual), *Novitates Musei Sarajevoensis* (occasional), *Srednjovjekovni nadgrobni spomenici Bosne i Hercegovina* (occasional), *Posebna izdanjai* (occasional), *Katalog prehistorijske zbirke* (occasional).

## Škofja Loka

**Loški Muzej:** 64220 Škofja Loka, p.p. 9; f. 1936 by the museum club of Škofja Loka; special collection of exhibits relating to the Freising dominion (973–1803); ethnographic, topographic, natural history and historical exhibits; records of altars from 17th century, exhibits of medieval guilds; relics of the struggle for national liberation; art gallery; open air museum; museum; Pres. JANEZ ERJAVEC.

## Skopje

**Arheološki muzej na Makedonija** (*Archaeological Museum of Macedonia*): 91000 Skopje, Kuršumli An; f. 1924; library of 5,000 vols.; Dir. SARŽO SARŽOSKI; publ. *Zbornik†* (Collected Papers, annually).

**Art Gallery:** P.O.B. 278, 91000 Skopje; f. 1948; Yugoslav medieval and modern art; Dir. NIKOLA MARTINOSKI; publs. catalogues.

**Etnološki muzej na Makedonija** (*Ethnological Museum*): Evlija Čelebija b.b.; f. 1949; Dir. MARIJA HADŽI PECEVA.

**Prirodonaučen muzej na Makedonija** (*Natural History Museum of Macedonia*): 91000 Skopje, 55 Bulevar Ilinden b.b.; f. 1926; library of 19,000 vols.; Dir. OGNJANKA POPOVSKA-STANKOVIĆ; publs. *Acta†, Fragmenta Balcanica†, Posebni izdanija†* (special publications), *Fauna na Makedonija†*.

## Slavonski Brod

**Brlić House (Ivana Brlić-Mažuranić Memorial):** Titov trg 8; private family house containing archives, furniture, library (8,000 vols.) showing the evolution over 250 years of a Croatian middle-class family; Ivana Brlic (1874-1938) was a writer and first woman mem. of the Yugoslav Acad. of Sciences and Arts; Curator Mrs. ZDENKA BENČEVIĆ-BRLIĆ.

## Split

**Arheološki muzej u Splitu** (*Archaeological Museum*): Zrinjsko-Frankopanska 25; f. 1820; prehistoric collections, relics from the Greek colonies on the east shore of the Adriatic Sea, Roman and Christian relics from Salonae and Dalmatia; Croatian medieval monuments from 9th to 13th century; library of 28,500 vols.; Dir. Prof. Dr. NENAD CAMBI; publ. *Vjesnik zu arheologiju i historiju dalmatinsku*† (Bulletin of Dalmatian Archaeology and History).

**Etnografski muzej** (*Ethnographical Museum*): Narodni trg 1; f. 1910; national costumes, jewels, weapons, and technological objects from Dalmatia; illustrations section and textbook library; Dir. ILDA VIDOVIĆ-BEGONJA.

**Galerija Meštrović** (*Meštrović Gallery*): 58000 Split, Moše Pijade 46; f. 1952; permanent exhibition of sculptures of Ivan Meštrović (1883-1962); Dir. DUŠKO KEČKEMET; publs. catalogues.

**Galerija umjetnina** (*Art Gallery*): Lovretska 11; f. 1931; 2,300 paintings and sculptures (ancient and modern); library of 10,000 vols.; Dir. Prof. MILAN IVANIŠEVIĆ.

**Muzej grada Splita** (*City Museum of Split*): Papaličeva 1; f. 1946; political and cultural history of Split; library of 10,000 vols.; Dir. Dr. DUSKO KEČKEMET; publ. *Editions*.

**Prirodoslovni muzej** (*Museum of Natural Sciences*): f. 1924; contains more than 100,000 exhibits of mineralogical, palaeontological and zoological specimens from Dalmatia and the Adriatic Sea; collections of coleoptera, shells and birds (mostly Dalmatian); library of 3,500 vols.; zoological garden (Vrh Marjana 1); Dir. Prof. ANTUN CVITANIĆ.

## Subotica

**Gradski muzej:** f. 1892; sections: archaeology, local history, art and ethnology (Slav and Hungarian), coins; library of 8,000 vols.; Dir. TIBOR SEKELJ.

## Zagreb

**Arheoloski muzej** (*Archaeological Museum*): Zrinjski trg 19; f. 1846; museum of Croatian history from neolithic times until the 13th century; 30,000 vols.; Dir. Univ. Prof. Dr. DUJE RENDIĆ-MIOČEVIĆ; publ. *Vjesnik Arheološkog Muzeja u Zagrebu*†.

**Etnografski muzej** (*Ethnographical Museum*): Mažuranićev trg 14; f. 1919; cultural traditions of the three ethnographic regions of Croatia: Pannonic, Dinaric, Adriatic; department of Non-European cultures; library of 12,430 vols.; Dir. Dr. MARIO PETRIĆ.

**Galerije Grada Zagreba:** Habdelićeva 2; f. 1961; library; Dir. Dr. BORIS KELEMEN; publ. *Dokumenti* (Documents); controls:

**Galerija Suvremene Umjetnosti** (*Gallery of Contemporary Art*): Katarinin trg 2; f. 1954; Chief Curator BOŽO BEK.

**Galerija "Benko Horvat":** Habdelićeva 2; f. 1946; private collection of antique and renaissance art; Chief Curator ŽELIMIR KOŠČEVIĆ.

**Galerija Primitivne Umjetnosti** (*Gallery of Primitive Art*): Cirilometodska 3; f. 1952; Chief Curator Dr. BORIS KELEMEN.

**Atelje Meštrović:** Mletačka 8; f. 1952; memorial collection of the sculptor Ivan Meštrović; Curator VESNA BARBIĆ.

**Centar za Fotografiju, Film i Televiziju** (*Centre for Photography, Film and Television*): Habdelićeva 2; f. 1973; Chief Curator Dr. DIMITRIJE BAŠIČEVIĆ.

**Memorijalna Galerija "Jozo Kljaković"** (*Jozo Kljaković Memorial Gallery*): Rokov perivoj 4; f. 1974; Chief Curator ŽELIMIR KOŠČEVIĆ.

**Geološko-paleontološki muzej** (*Geological and Palaeontological Museum*): Demetrova 1, 41.000 Zagreb; f. 1846; library of 5,850 vols.; Curator Prof. IVAN CRNOLATAC, MR.GEOL.

**Glyptothèque:** Yugoslav Academy of Sciences and Arts, Medvedgradska 2; f. 1937; collection of medieval frescos and plaster casts of ancient, medieval and recent sculptures and architecture; originals of sculptures of the 19th and 20th centuries in the S.R. of Croatia; Dir. MONTANI MIRO.

**Hrvatski školski muzej** (*Croatian Schools' Museum*): Trg maršala Tita 4; f. 1901; Dir. Prof. BRANKO PLEŠE; library of 32,896 vols. on the history of schools and education in Croatia; publ. *Zbornik za istoriju školstva i prosvjete* (Collected papers on History of Education).

**Kabinet Grafike** (*Print Room*): Braće Kavurića 1; f. 1951; more than 7,500 prints, drawings, and about 1,800 posters; sponsored by the Yugoslav Academy of Sciences and Arts; Dir. Prof. RENATA GOTTHARDI-ŠKILJAN.

**Mineraloško-petrografski muzej** (*Museum of Mineralogy and Petrography*): Demetrova ul. 1; f. 1846; Dir. Prof. Dr. LJUDEVIT BARIĆ.

**Moderna Galerija** (*Gallery of Modern Arts*): Braće Kavurića 1; f. 1909; Dir. Prof. ZELJKO GRUM.

**Muzej grada Zagreba** (*City Museum of Zagreb*): Opatička 20; f. 1907; arranged so as to depict Zagreb from prehistoric times to 20th century; library of 7,000 vols.; Dir. Prof. ZDENKO KUZMIĆ; Librarian AGNEZA SZABO; publ. *Iz starog i novog Zagreba* (From Old and New Zagreb, irregular).

**Muzej Narodne Revolicije** (*The People's Revolution Museum*): Zagreb, Trg Žrtava Fašizma; f. 1945; library of 4,500 vols.; Dir. MANE TRBOJEVIĆ.

**Muzej za umjetnost i obrt** (*Museum of Applied Arts*): Trg maršala Tita 10; f. 1880; applied arts from the 14th to the 20th century: furniture, tapestries, textiles, ceramics, glass, gold and silver work, sculpture, paintings, miniatures, costume, samples of industrial design, clocks and watches, toys, prints and posters; art library of 23,917 vols.; Dir. Prof. RADOSLAV PUTAR; publs. *Muzej za umjetnost i obrt—Monografija* (Museum monograph), *Minijatura u Jugoslaviji* (Miniature in Yugoslavia, catalogue/monograph), Catalogues of temporary exhibitions.

**Povijesni muzej Hrvatske** (*Historical Museum of Croatia*): Matoševa 9; f. 1846; history of Croatia with collections of different historical objects, arms, paintings, icons, prints, stone monuments, etc.; library of 24,500 vols.; Dir. Prof. IVAN BARBARIĆ; Librarian Prof. ZORA GAJSKI; publs. Catalogues†.

**Strossmayerova galerija starih majstora** (*Strossmayer's Gallery of Old Masters*): Zrinski trg 11/II; f. 1884; 13th to 19th centuries; Dir. Prof. VINKO ZLAMALIK; under the control of the Yugoslav Academy of Sciences and Fine Arts.

**Tehnički muzej** (*Technical Museum*): Savska c. 18; f. 1954; Dir. VLADIMIR GALEKOVIĆ.

**Zoološki muzej** (*Zoological Museum*): Demetrova 1/II; f. 1846; library of 16,000 vols.; Dir. MARIJA STOŠIĆ; publ. *Periodicum biologorum*†.

# UNIVERSITIES

## UNIVERZITET "DURO PUCAR STARI" U BANJA LUCI
(University of Banja Luka)

TRG. PALIH BORACA 2/11,
78000 BANJA LUKA

Telephone: (078) 35-018, 35-034.
Founded 1975.
State control; Language of instruction: Serbo-Croat; Academic year: September to July.

*Rector:* Prof. IBRAHIM TABAKOVIĆ.
*Chief Administrative Officer:* DRAGO TOJČIĆ.
*Librarian:* IRFAN NURUDINOVIĆ.
Number of teachers 158.
Number of students: 10,489 (5,940 external).
Publications: *Collections of Papers* (Faculty of Economics, Faculty of Law, annually; Pedagogical Academy (3 a year).

### DEANS:

*Faculty of Economics:* Dr. VOJISLAV OTAŠEVIĆ.
*Faculty of Electrical Engineering:* Dr. SADAT ŠIRBEGOVIĆ.
*Faculty of Mechanical Engineering:* MILAN JURKOVIĆ.
*Faculty of Law:* RADOVAN HRNJAZ.
*Faculty of Chemical Engineering:* Dr. MLADEN TRKOVNIK.
*Pedagogical Academy:* RIFAT MEHMEDBEGOVIĆ.
*Undergraduate School of Economics and Commerce:* KJAZIM KRAJIŠNIK.
*Undergraduate Technical School:* JUSUF ČAUŠEVIĆ.

### PROFESSORS:

MALIĆ, D., Thermodynamics
MIHAJLOVIĆ, B., Mathematics
OTAŠEVIĆ, V., Organization and Economic Production
PAVLOVIĆ, Z., Analytical Chemistry
ROZGAJ, S., Operational Units
TRKOVNIK, M., Organic Chemistry
VASIĆ, P., Organizations of Associated Work Theory

## UNIVERZITET U BEOGRADU
(University of Belgrade)

STUDENTSKI TRG 1, BELGRADE
Telephone 635-153.
Founded 1863; reorganized 1905 and 1954.
Language of instruction: Serbo-Croat; Academic year: October to September.

*Rector:* Dr. VOJISLAV PETROVIĆ.
*Vice-Rectors:* Dr. ALEKSANDAR DJOKIĆ, Dr. ALEKSA PIŠČEVIĆ, Dr. DJORDJE JOVIĆ, Dr. SLOBODAN UNKOVIĆ, STEVAN MAROŠAN.
*General Secretary:* DRAGIŠA STIJOVIĆ.
*Librarian:* Mrs. STANIJA GLIGORIJEVIĆ.
Library: See Libraries.
Number of teachers: 3,702.
Number of students: 57,200.

Publication: *List of Professors* (annually).

### DEANS:
*Faculty of Agriculture:* D. VELIČKOVIĆ.
*Faculty of Architecture:* V. DAMJANOVIĆ.
*Faculty of Civil Engineering:* M. SEKULOVIĆ.
*Faculty of Defectology:* LJ. SAVIĆ.
*Faculty of Economics:* V. KOLARIĆ.
*Faculty of Electrical Engineering:* P. PRAVICA.
*Faculty of Forestry:* N. JOVIĆ.
*Faculty of Law:* M. DJORDJEVIĆ.
*Faculty of Mechanical Engineering:* V. NOVAKOVIĆ.
*Faculty of Medicine:* LJ. RAKIĆ.
*Faculty of Mining and Geology:* D. SALATIĆ.
*Faculty of Organizational Sciences:* B. LAZAREVIĆ.
*Faculty of Pharmacy:* M. MIRIĆ.
*Faculty of Philology:* J. DERETIĆ.
*Faculty of Philosophy:* R. SREJOVIĆ.
*Faculty of Physical Education:* J. PETROVIĆ.
*Faculty of Political Sciences:* J. MARJANOVIĆ.
*Faculty of Sciences:* B. TATIĆ.
*Faculty of Stomatology:* B. JOJIĆ.
*Faculty of Technical Engineering, Bor:* V. VESELINOVIĆ.
*Faculty of Technology and Metallurgy:* D. VUČUROVIĆ.
*Faculty of Transport:* M. ČIČAK.
*Faculty of Veterinary Medicine:* N. ŠEVKOVIĆ.

### PROFESSORS:

*Faculty of Agriculture:*
AVRAMOV, L., Viticulture
BABOVIĆ, M., Phytopathology
BAJČETIĆ, B., Farm Management
BOGOJEVIĆ, J., Zoology and Ecology
BULATOVIĆ, S., Special Pomology
DANIČIĆ, M., Wine Technology
DOBRIVOJEVIĆ, K., Entomology
DŽAMIĆ, M., Biochemistry
DŽAMIĆ, R., Plant Physiology and Agrochemistry
DJAJA, Č., Mathematics
DJOKIĆ, A., Plant Genetics
DJORDJEVIĆ, J., Dairy Technology
DJURIČIĆ, M., Chemistry
ERDELJAN, V., Statistics
GLIGORIĆ, M., Mechanics
GUGUŠEVIĆ-DJAKOVIĆ, M., Technology of Precooked Food
ILIĆ, B., Entomology
JAKŠIĆ, M., Physical and Colloidal Chemistry
JELENIĆ, DJ., Plant Physiology and Agricultural Chemistry
JOKIĆ, A., Organic Chemistry
JORGOVIĆ-KREMZER, J., Analytical Chemistry
JOKSIMOVIĆ, J., Meat Technology
JOVANOVIĆ, B., Plant Breeding
JOVAŠEVIĆ, V., Political Economy
KAMENOVIĆ, S., Geodesy
KARAN-DJURDJIĆ, S., Technology of By-Products of the Meat Industry
KILIBARDA, K., Sociology
KLJAJIĆ, R., Phytopharmacy
KOJIĆ, M., Botany
KOLJAJIĆ, V., Feed Science and Technology
KONSTANTINOVIĆ, B., Apiculture
KORUNOVIĆ, R., Pedology
KRNJAJIĆ, S., Entomology
LOVIĆ, R., Viticulture
LJESOV, D., Statistics
MARIĆ, M., Genetics and Plant-Breeding Methods
MARKOVIĆ, P., Agricultural Economics
MARKOVIĆ, R., Hydraulics and Hydrology
MIĆIĆ, J., Agricultural Machinery
MIJATOVIĆ, M., Forage Crops Production
MILOJIĆ, B., Field Crops
MILOJIĆ, M., Animal Husbandry
MILOSAVLJEVIĆ, M., General Viticulture
MILOŠEVIĆ, P., Agricultural Machinery
MILUTINOVIĆ, M., Fruit and Vine Breeding Selection
MITIĆ, N., Animal Science
MIŠIĆ, D., Technology of Milk By-Products
MOŠORINSKI, N., Chemistry
NIKETIĆ-ALEKSIĆ, G., Fruit and Vegetable Technology
NENIĆ, P., Agricultural Machinery
OSTOJIĆ, N., Plant Protection
OTAŠEVIĆ, S., Farm Work Organization
PANIĆ, M., Bacteriology
PANTOVIĆ, M., Agricultural Chemistry Soil Fertility and Fertilizers
PAUNOVIĆ, R., Alcoholic Beverage Technology
PAVASOVIĆ, V., Unit Operations
PAVLOVIĆ, M., Engineering Materials, Fuels and Lubricants
PEJIN, D., Farm Organization
PEJKIĆ, B., Fruit and Vine Selection
PETROVIĆ, M., Book-keeping and Financial Operation
PETROVIĆ, MIL., Agricultural Chemistry
PETROVIĆ, V., Livestock Breeding
POPOVIĆ, Ž., Plant Physiology, Agricultural Chemistry, Soil Fertility and Fertilizers
RADOVANOVIĆ, B., Agricultural Economics
RADULOVIĆ, J., Physiology of Domestic Animals
RAHOVIĆ, D., Fruticulture
RODIĆ, J., Financial Analysis
SIMOVA-TOŠIĆ, D., Entomology
SIMOVIĆ, B., Animal Breeding and Genetics
STANKOVIĆ, LJ., Agricultural Calculations
STANOJEVIĆ, D., Physics
STANOJEVIĆ, S., Meteorology and Climatology
STEFANOVIĆ, R., Dairy Technology
STOJANOVIĆ, M., Agroecology
STOJANOVIĆ, S., Pedology
STOJIĆEVIĆ, D., Irrigation and Drainage
ŠESTOVIĆ, M., Special Phytopharmacy
SINŽAR, D., Pedology
ŠLJIVOVAČKI, K., Animal Nutrition
ŠUPUT, M., Field Crop Production
ŠUTIĆ, D., Phytopathology
ŠUTIĆ, M., Microbiology
TANASIJEVIĆ, N., Entomology
TODOROVIĆ, M., Thermodynamics
TODOROVIĆ, MIL., Microbiology
TOMIN, A., Marketing
TOŠIĆ, M., Agricultural Machinery
TOŠIĆ, MAL., Mycology
VITOROVIĆ, S., Agricultural Toxicology
ZEREMSKI, D., Animal Nutrition
ŽIVANOVIĆ, Ž., Botany and Plant Ecology
ŽIVKOVIĆ, M., Pedology

*Faculty of Architecture:*
ALEKSIĆ, B., Housing

ANTIĆ, I., Building Design
BELAJČIĆ, D., Mathematics
BJELIKOV, V., Town Planning
BOGDANOVIĆ, B., Memorial Architecture
DAMJANOVIĆ, V., Industrial Buildings, Architectural Physics
DIMITRIJEVIĆ, M., Foundation Systems
DJOKIĆ, M., Building Design
GRUJIĆ, N., Descriptive Geometry
ILIĆ, D., Graphics and Painting
IVKOVIĆ, V., Architectural Constructions
JOVANOVIĆ, J., Building Installations
JOVANOVIĆ, P., Theory of Construction
MARTINOVIĆ, U., Building Design
MILENKOVIĆ, B., Architectural Analysis
NOVAKOVIĆ, B., Town Planning
PETROVIĆ, B., Mechanics and Strength of Materials
PETROVIĆ, M., Architectural Construction
PETROVIĆ, Z., Interior Design
PJANIĆ, LJ., Spatial Economy and Environment
RADOJEVIĆ, A., Architectural Drawing
RADOVIĆ, R., Modern Architecture
SIMONOVIĆ, DJ., Rural Planning
STOJAKOVIĆ, A., History of Art
TRBOJEVIĆ, R., Architectural Construction
ZLOKOVIĆ, D., Structural Systems

*Faculty of Civil Engineering:*
AĆIMOVIĆ, M., Earthwork and Tunnelling
BOGUNOVIĆ, V., Engineering Mechanics
BORELI, M., Hydraulics and Hydrology
BOŽANOVIĆ, A., Construction Materials
BRČIĆ, V., Engineering Mechanics
CVETKOVIĆ, Č., Applied Geodesy
DJURIĆ, M., Theory of Structures
HAJDIN, G., Fluid Mechanics
HAJDIN, N., Theory of Structures
ILIĆ-DAJOVIĆ, M., Mathematics
IVKOVIĆ, P., Engineering Structures
JANJIĆ, S., Railway Track Construction and Railway Stations
JELISAVČIĆ, I., Construction Materials
JOVANOVIĆ, M., Mathematic Cartography
JOVANOVIĆ, S., Plan Surveying
KONTIĆ, S., Plan Surveying
KOSTIĆ, V., Foundation
LAZAREVIĆ, D., Concrete Structures
MARKOVIĆ, M., Highway Design and Construction
MILOJEVIĆ, M., Water Supply and Waste Water Disposal
MILOSAVLJEVIĆ, M., Steel Structures and Steel Bridges
MRKŠIĆ, D., Theory of Structures
PAVLOVIĆ, Z., Steel Structures and Steel Bridges
PEŠIĆ, B., Building Construction
POPADIĆ, M., Mathematics
RADOJKOVIĆ, M., Testing of Structures, Welding
SBUTEGA, V., Descriptive Geometry
STIPANIĆ, E., Mathematics
STOJADINOVIĆ, R., Soil Mechanics
TRBOJEVIĆ, B., Work Methods in Civil Engineering and Construction
VERČON, M., Water Power
VLADISAVLJEVIĆ, Ž., Irrigation and Drainage
ZARIĆ, B., Steel Structures and Steel Bridges

*Faculty of Defectology:*
BIGA, S., Pleoptics and Orthoptics
BOJANIN, S., Neuropsychology with Reeducative Methods
BRAJOVIĆ, Ć., Methods of Logopaedic Work, Rehabilitation of Children with Developmental Disorders
BRAJOVIĆ, LJ., Anatomy, Physiology and Pathology of Hearing, Speech and Voice
BUKELIĆ, J., Social Psychiatry
ĆORDIĆ, A., Pedagogy of the Mentally Retarded
COTIĆ, D., Basis of Penal Law
CVEJIĆ, D., Phoniatry
CVETKOVIĆ, S., Geometrical Optics
DAVIDOVIĆ, D., Social Self Protection, Penology
DJORDJEVIĆ, D., Pedagogical Psychology
DJURIČIĆ, Z., Sociology
GOJKOVIĆ, G., Social Politics
GRUBETIĆ, V., Russian Language
HRNJICA, S., General Psychology
JAKULIĆ, S., Professional Rehabilitation of the Mentally Retarded
JAŠOVIĆ, Ž., Criminology
KERAMITČIJEVSKI, S., Special Pedagogy
KOKALOVIĆ, M., Processing of Materials
KOSTIĆ, S., Clinical Pathology of Chronic Physical Disablement
KRAJINČANIĆ, B., Clinical Genetics
KRSTIĆ, S., Neurology
LEKIĆ, D., General Education with Didactics
LUKIĆ, M., Ethics
MARKOVIĆ, D., Sociology
MAŠOVIĆ, S., Professional Rehabilitation of the Deaf
MITROVIĆ, MŽ., Orthopaedics
MRAOVIĆ, M., Basis of General National Defence and Social Self Protection
NIKOLIĆ-SIMONČIĆ, C., Introduction to Marxism
PECO, A., Phonetics, Study of Language
PEJIĆ, Z., English Language
PIŠTELJIĆ, D., Ophthalmology
PRAVICA, P., Electronics with Electroacoustics
RADENKOVIĆ, S., German Language
SAMARDŽIJA, S., Methodology of Resocialization of Persons with Behavioural Disturbances
SAVIĆ, LJ., Methods of Work with the Deaf
SIMIĆ, J., Economic System of Yugoslavia
SIMONOVIĆ, M., Audiology
SIMONOVIĆ, J., Physics, Acoustics
SMILJANIĆ, V., Developmental Psychology
STANOJČIĆ, I., Methodology of Scientific Research
ŠTEFANOVIĆ, B., Clinical Refraction
STEFANOVIĆ, N., French Language
STOŠLJEVIĆ, L., Methods of Work with Physically Disabled Children
ŠKEROVIĆ, DJ., Medical Physiology
ŠPADIJER-DŽINIĆ, J., Social Pathology
TADIĆ, N., Child Psychiatry
VLADISAVLJEVIĆ, S., Logopaedics
ZEC, Ž., Basis of Physical Medicine and Rehabilitation
ZLATKOVIĆ, V., Basis of General National Defence and Self Protection
ŽIVKOVIĆ, M., Psychology of the Deaf, the Hard of Hearing and of Persons with Speech Disorders

*Faculty of Economics:*
ADAMOVIĆ, LJ., International Economic Relations I
BARALIĆ, Ž., Cost Accounting and Analysis in Commerce
ĆIROVIĆ, M., Monetary Economy
ČOBELJIĆ, D., Theory and Systems Planning
CVIJETIĆ, L., Economic History
DRAGIŠIĆ, D., Political Economy
DRAŠKIĆ, M., International Economic Law
EREMIĆ, G., National Accounts
JANKOV, S., Contemporary Economic Systems
KOLARIĆ, V., Organization and Working of Transportation
KONSTANTINOVIĆ, G., Microeconomic Analysis
KOSTIĆ, Ž., Business Administration I
KOVAČ, O., International Economic Relations III
KOVAČEVIĆ, M., Accounting II
KOVAČEVIĆ, ML., International Economic Relations II
KRASULJA, D., Business Finance and Financial Analysis
MARIČIĆ, B., Marketing
MARSENIĆ, D., Economics of Yugoslavia
MIHALJEVIĆ, G., Communal Economics
MILISAVLJEVIĆ, M., Business Administration II
MLADENOVIĆ, D., Economic Statistics
NIKOLAJEVIĆ, R., Accounting I
NJEGIĆ, R., Statistics I
NOVAKOVIĆ, S., Economics of Transport
PERIĆ, A., Finance II
PERIŠIĆ, R., Technology in Transportation
PETKOVIĆ, M., Organization of Associated Labour
PETROVIĆ, P., Econometrics
PILIĆ, V., Political Economy II
PJANIĆ, Z., Theory and Policy of Prices
POPOVIĆ, B., Accounting IV
POPOVIĆ, BOJAN, Cybernetics
POPOVIĆ, M., Economic Geography
RADIĆ, M., Agricultural Economics
RADUNOVIĆ, D., Economics of Trade
RAKOČEVIĆ, K., Mathematics I
RALEVIĆ, R., Financial and Actuarial Mathematics
RANKOVIĆ, J., Accounting III
RAŠKOVIĆ, V., Sociology
RISTIĆ, S., Information Systems in Transportation
ŠOŠKIĆ, B., Economic Doctrines
STOJANOVIĆ, D., Economic Mathematical Methods and Models
STOJANOVIĆ, R., Theory and Policy of Economic Development
SUBOTIĆ, N., Commercial Law I
TASIĆ, A., Insurance
TRIČKOVIĆ, V., Market Research
UNKOVIĆ, S., Economics of Tourism
UROŠEVIĆ, S., Technology
VUČENOVIĆ, V., Theory and Methodology of Self-Managing Decision-making
VULIĆEVIĆ, B., Linear Algebra
ZEČEVIĆ, T., Statistics III and Operational Research
ZEKOVIĆ, V., Economics of Industry

*Faculty of Electrical Engineering:*
ALEKSIĆ, T., Data Processing
BORELI, F., Nuclear Physics
ĆALOVIĆ, M., Transmission and Distribution Systems
CVETKOVIĆ, D., Mathematics
DRAJIĆ, D., Telecommunications
DUDUKOVIĆ, P., Electrical Measurements
HORVAT, R., Electric Circuit Theory
IČEVIĆ, D., Marxism
IVANOVIĆ, D., Theoretical Physics
JANIĆ, R., Mathematics
JOVANOVIĆ, M., Electrothermal Plants
JOVANOVIĆ, V., Telecommunications Systems
JOVIČIĆ, J., Physics
KURTOVIĆ, H., Electro-acoustics
LUKATELA, G., Telecommunications Theory
MARINČIĆ, A., Telecommunications
MARJANOVIĆ, S., Electronics
MILANOVIĆ, D., Microwaves
MILANKOVIĆ, LJ., High Voltage Engineering

# UNIVERSITIES (UNIVERSITY OF BELGRADE) — YUGOSLAVIA

Milić, M., Electric Circuit Theory
Mitraković, B., Electrical Machines
Muždeka, G., Electrical Power Transmission
Nahman, J., Electrical Energy Transmission
Nastić, B., Television
Nikolić, P., Mechanical and Electronic Elements
Pop-Jordanov, J., Physics
Popović, B., Electromagnetic Theory
Popović, D., Physics of Reactors
Popović, V., Telecommunication Measurements
Popović, Ž., Telephony and Telegraphy
Pravica, P., Technical Acoustics
Rabrenović, D., Electronics
Radojković, B., Electro-motive Plants and Electric Traction
Rakić, M., Automatic Control
Raković, B., Electronics
Stanić, B., Physics
Stojanović, I., Fundamentals of Telecommunications
Stojić, M., Automation
Surutka, J., Electromagnetics Theory
Tešić, S., Electronics
Tjapkin, D., Solid State Physics, Mechanical and Electronic Components
Todorović, S. M., Atomic Physics
Tomović, R., Computers
Tošić, D., Numerical Analysis
Vasić, P., Mathematical Methods in Electrical Engineering
Volčkov, I., Electrical Machines

Faculty of Forestry:
Aleksov, I., Organization of Production
Avdalović, V., Pedology
Dimitrijević, M., Principles of Arts
Djorović, M., Agricultural Land Reclamation
Gajić, M., Botany
Gvozdenović, R., Machines and Industrial Energetics
Janković, A., Final Processing of Wood
Jevtić, Lj., Flood Control and Forest Reclamation
Jovanović, B., Dendrology and Plant Communities
Jovanović, B., Descriptive Geometry
Jovanović, N., Chemical Wood Processing
Jović, D., Wildlife Management
Jović, N., Forest Pedology
Jovičić, D., Geodesy
Kolić, B., Meteorology and Climatology
Lalić, M., Forest Transportation Vehicles
Lukić-Simonović, N., Wood Properties
Malešević, J., Mathematics
Marković, Z., Marxism and Self-Management
Marinković, P., Phytopathology
Mijanović, O., Floriculture
Milin, Ž., Forest Management
Miščević, M., Dendrometry
Nikolić, M., Saw-mill Wood Processing
Nikolić, M., Veneer and Veneer Boards
Nikolić, S., Forest Utilization
Pekić, M., Foreign Languages
Perović, B., Planning of Woods Processing Enterprises
Petković, S., Hydraulics with Hydrology
Petrović, Lj., Forest Economics
Petrović, M., Building Construction and Roads
Petrović, M., Wood Protection
Pjević, V., Chemistry
Potrebić, M., Wood Constructions
Rakić, V., Foreign Languages
Redžić, A., Economics of Wood Industry
Sakić, M., Fundamentals of National Defence
Senić, R., Technology of Auxiliary Materials
Simić, N., History of Arts and Horticulture
Stamenković, V., Increment Study
Stefanović, S., Timber Trade
Stilinović, S., Seed Production
Teržan, N., Chemistry
Tomanić, L., Forest Management
Tomić, D., Forest Entomology
Tonić, A., Foreign Languages
Trifunović, M., Mathematics
Tucović, A., Genetics and Plant Breeding
Velašević, V., Water Resources Management
Veselinović, M., Organization of Buildings and Mechanization
Vukičević, E., Decorative Dendrology
Zaplotnik, R., Technical Mechanics
Živojinović, D., Forest Protection

Faculty of Law:
Avramov, S., International Public Law
Antonijević, Z., Economic Law
Aleksić, Z., Criminology
Atanacković, D., Criminal Law
Bakić, V., Family Law
Brajić, V., Labour Law
Danilović, J., Roman Law
Despotović, M., Labour Law and Labour Sociology
Dimitrijević, D., Criminal Procedure
Dimitrijević, P., Administrative Law and Science of Management
Dimitrijević, V., International Relations
Djordjević, M., Criminal Law
Djordjević, Ž., Law of Intellectual and Industrial Property
Djukić-Veljović, Z., Constitutional Law
Djurović, R., International Business Law
Jovanović, V., Economic Law
Kandić, Lj., General Law History
Kavran, D., Administrative Law, Theory of Organization
Lazarević, Lj., Criminal Law
Lukić, M., Forensic Medicine
Lukić, R., Philosophy of Law, Introduction to Law and Legal Sciences
Maksimović, I., Political Economy
Milojević, M., International Organizations
Milutinović, M., Criminology and Penology
Mladenović, M., Family Law and Sociology
Nikolić, P., Constitutional Law
Pak, M., International Private Law
Pavićević, R., Political Sociology
Pečujlić, M., General Sociology, Marxism and Contemporary Society
Perović, S., Obligation Law
Petrović, M., Public Finance
Poznić, B., Civil Procedure
Rajović, V., Civil Procedure
Ristić, P., Social and Political System of Yugoslavia
Simić, M., National Defence
Simović, V., Constitutional Law
Srnić, I., Social and Political Systems
Stanković, J., Sociology
Stanković, O., Civil Law Introduction
Stanković, V., Obligation Law
Stanković, V., Economic System of Yugoslavia
Stanojević, O., Roman Law
Šoškić, D., Political Economy
Šulejić, P., Insurance Law
Trajković, M., Transportation Law
Vacić, A., Economic Policy
Vasić, V., Economic Policy
Vidaković, Z., Marxism and Contemporary Society
Zlatić, M., Criminal Procedure

Faculty of Mechanical Engineering:
Antić, M., Theory of Traction, Industrial Furnaces, Drying Plants, Locomotives
Banić, M., Strength of Materials and Structures
Borisavljević, M., Utilization of Motor Vehicles
Bulat, V., Scientific Labour Management
Deijer, S., Material Handling Machinery
Djaković, B., Chemical Engineering Equipment
Djordjević, V., Dynamics of Gases
Dragović, T., High-Speed Aerodynamics, Computer Technology
Džordžo, B., Ship Installations
Gajić, D., Aerodynamics Structure
Grujić, L., Discrete and Nonlinear Systems
Janićijević, N., Motor Vehicle Design
Jankov, R., Piston Compressors
Janković, D., Calculation of Motor Vehicles
Janković, S., Dynamics of Projectile Flight
Jojić, K., Strength of Materials
Josifović, M., Theory of Elasticity Aero-elasticity
Jovanović, D., Scientific Labour Management
Jovanović, S., Engineering Economics
Jovanović, T., Quantitative Analysis Methods
Jovičić, M., Descriptive Geometry
Jovičić, M., Tools and Tooling
Kolendić, I., Internal Combustion Engines
Krsmanović, Lj., Turbomachines, Hydraulic Transmissions
Lovrić, D., National Defence
Mamuzić, Ž., Mathematics
Manojlović, B., Engineering Materials
Marcikić, N., Aircraft Equipment
Marković, S., Railway Vehicles
Milačić, V., Machine Tools
Milinčić, D., Heat and Mass Transfer
Miljanić, P., Electrical Engineering
Milojković, B., Automatic Control, Linear Systems
Milović, P., Building and Mining Machinery
Novaković, V., Agricultural Machinery
Ostrić, D., Metal Structures
Pantelić, T., Theory of Mechanisms
Pejović, S., Hydraulic Installations
Pilić, B., Sociology and Economics
Pivko, S., Engineering Mechanics
Popović, D., Factory Layout, Processing Apparatus, Operations Equipment
Protić, Z., Hydraulic Machinery
Radosavljević, L., Engineering Mechanics, Theory of Oscillations
Radovanović, M., Fuels and Lubricants
Ristić, M., Nuclear Engineering
Saljnikov, V., Hydromechanics, Fluid Mechanics
Šašić, M., Pipe Conveyance
Šolaja, V., Machine Tools
Stanić, J., Engineering Metrology, Metal Working Processes
Stanojević, D., Aircraft Design and Construction
Stojanović, D., Steam Turbines, Power Plant Installations
Stojanović, Ž., Pumps, Compressors and Fans
Todorović, B., Heating and Air Conditioning
Todorović, J., Calculation and Testing of Motor Vehicles

Trifunović, T., Internal Combustion Engine Testing
Urošević, M., Heating and Ventilating
Verčon, J., Lubrication Techniques
**Veriga, S., Machine Elements**
**Vesović, M., Railway Engineering**
Voronjec, D., Basic Industrial Processes
Vujić, M., Jet and Rocket Engines, Jet Propulsion
**Vujić, S., Refrigeration Engineering, Design of Air-Conditioning Equipment**
Vušković, I., Hydraulic Machines, Engineering Metrology
Zarić, S., Automation of Production Processes
**Živković, C. M., Internal Combustion Engines**
**Živković, S. M., Aircraft Design and Construction**
Živojinov, J., Engineering Physics
Zrnić, N., Design and Construction of Ships

*Faculty of Medicine:*
Antić, R., Internal Medicine
Arambašić, M., Pathological Anatomy
Beleslin, D., Pharmacology
**Blagojević, M., Ophthalmology**
Budisavljević, M., Phthisiology
Bugarski, O., Chemistry
Bumbaširević, Ž., Orthopaedic Surgery
Conić, Z., Physical Medicine and Rehabilitation
Cvetković, M., Biochemistry
Čalić-Perišić, N., Paediatrics
Davidović, M., Biology
Durić, D., Internal Medicine
Drndarski, K., Bacteriology
Funtek, M., Military Education
Gerzić, Z., Surgery
Glidžić, V., Surgery
Gospavić, J., Neuropsychiatry
Išvaneski, M., Pathological Anatomy
Japundžić, I., Biochemistry
**Jokanović, D., Forensic Medicine**
Jokanović, R., Paediatrics
**Josipović, V., Internal Medicine**
**Jovanović, S., Anatomy**
Kilibarda, M., Professional Diseases
Korać, D., Paediatrics
**Kostić-Simonović, J., Physics**
**Krajinović, S., Epidemiology**
Lalević, P., Surgery
**Lambić, I., Internal Medicine**
Marković, A., Surgery
Mićović, P., Social Medicine
Milanović, V., Sociology
**Milosević, M., Pharmacology**
**Mladenović, D., Gynaecology**
Morić-Petrović, S., Neuropsychiatry
Mršević, D., Histology
Najdanović, B., Internal Medicine
Nikolić, M., Neuropsychiatry
Pavlović, D., Surgery
Perišić, S., Dermatology
**Perišić, V., Internal Medicine**
Petrović, F., Medical Statistics
Popović, S., Child Surgery
Radmanović, B., Pharmacology
Radojičić, B., Neuropsychiatry
**Radulović, B., Orthopaedic Surgery**
Rakić, C., Orthopaedic Surgery
Rakić, Lj., Biochemistry
**Savić, D., Oto-Rhino-Laryngology**
**Savićević, M.**, Hygiene
**Simić, B.**, Hygiene
Škerović, D., Physiology
Stefanović, B., Oto-Rhino-Laryngology
Stefanović, D., Dermatology
Stefanović, P., Oto-Rhino-Laryngology
Šulović, V., Gynaecology
Šuvaković, V., Infectious Diseases
Tomić, M., Gynaecology

Varagić, V., Pharmacology
Vujadinović, B., Surgery

*Faculty of Mining and Geology:*
Andjelković, M., Historical Geology
Cvetićanin, R., Coal Deposits
Dimitrijević, M., Geological Mapping
Djordjević, V., Petrography
Draškić, D., Ore Processing
Eremija, M., Palaeogeography
Filipović, B., Hydrogeology
Genčić, B., Underground Methods applied to Bedded Deposits
Grubić, A., Historical Geology
Janjić, M., Engineering Geology
Janković, S., Prospecting of Ore Deposits
Jovanović, P., Mine Development
Jovičić, V., Safety in Mines
Kačkin, D., Mine Fans, Pumps and Compressors
Karamata, S., Petrogenesis
Krstanović, I., Crystallography
Maksimović, Z., Geochemistry
Manojlović-Gifing, M., Elements of Ore Dressing
Marković, S., Geotectonics
Milosavljević, R., Mineral Dressing
Milovanović, D., Economic Geology
Mitrović, J., Palaeozoology
Nikolić, P., General Geology
Obradović, J., Sedimentology
Pantić, N., Palaeobotany
Paradanin, Lj., Oil and Gas Field Development
Pavlović, M., Palaeogeology
Petković, M., Prospecting of Ore Deposits
Petrović, B., Structural Geology
Protić, M., Petrology of Sedimentary Rocks
Simonović, M., Open-pit Mining Equipment
Spajić, O., Historical Geology
Stefanović, D., Geophysical Prospecting
Sutić, J., Elements of Civil Engineering
Terzić, M., Petrology of Magmatic Rocks
Topolac, Ž., Physics
Vakanjac, B., Non-metallic Ore Deposits
Vuković, M., Hydraulics

*Faculty of Engineering—Bor:*
Aćić, R., Flotation of Concentration
Andjelković, H., Descriptive Geometry
Angelov, C., Mathematics II
Antić, M., Pyrometallurgical Process Theory
Bogosavljević, M., Automation of Technological Processes
Budić, I., Ore Dressing Raw Minerals
Čolović, N., Chemical Kinetics
Čikara, D., Physical Metallurgy
Dimitrijević, D., Caustobioliths
Djordjević, G., Mineralogy
Dostanić, Č., Industrial Plant in Processing Metallurgy
Gajić, S., Petrography, Mineral Deposits of Metals and Non-metals
Grbović, M., Technology of Ore Dressing and Concentration, Machines and Equipment in Ore Dressing
Grujić, V., Electrical Engineering
Ignjatović, R., Physical Methods of Mineral Concentration
Ilić, P., Chemical Thermodynamics, Inorganic Chemistry II
Janjić, S., Mineralogy
Jeftić, D., Mining Machine Design
Jovanović, D., Business Economics
Kalčić, S., Thermodynamics
Knežević, Č., Heavy Non-ferrous Metallurgy

Kočovski, B., Theory of Casting, Metallurgy of Cast Iron and Steel, Alloys and Non-ferrous Metals
Konstantinović, Z., Material Resistivity
Kovačević, M., Rock and Soil Mechanics
Kovačević, P., Elements of Mechanical Engineering
Krotin, E., Machines in Metallurgy
Ljubić, J., Surface Mining
Magdalinović, N., Ore Reduction in Minerals Processing
Marjanović, R., Technical Mechanics, Matter Resistivity
Milanović, R., Methods and Machinery for Transport and Haulage
Milićević, Ž., Elements of Exploitation of Ore Deposits
Miljkovic, M., Accident Prevention (Labour Protection)
Ničić, D., Elements of Sociology
Nikolić, H., Foreign Languages
Nikolić, M., Hydro and Electrometallurgical Operation
Nikolić, P., Elements of Geology, Geological Documentation
Nikolić, V., Civil Engineering in Mining
Nikolić, Ž., Mine Ventilation, Underground Mine Drainage
Pacović, N., Metallurgy of Rare Metals, Light Metals Metallurgy, Chemical Methods in Concentration
Pajić, T., Elements of General Protection
Pavlović, D., Mathematics I
Pavlović, G., Thermal Technology and Furnaces in Metallurgy, Design in Chemical Industry
Pelemiš, J., Russian
Protić, Ž., Pumps, Compressors and Ventilators
Ristić, B., General and Inorganic Chemistry, Technology of Fuels, Lubricants and Waters
Savić B., Unit Operations and Equipment in Pyrometallurgy
Spasojević, D., Fluid Mechanics and Transport
Stanković, D., Fundamental Foundry
Stanković, R., Mine Projecting
Stanković, R., Transport in Ore Dressing
Stanković, Z., Physical Chemistry
Stanojević, B., Heat Treatment of Metals
Stefanović, Ž., Iron and Steel Metallurgy, Engineering in Extractive Metallurgy
Stevanović, J., Mining Surveying
Stoiljković, V., Mechanical Processing
Stojadinović, S., Plastic Deformation of Metals
Stolić, R., Heat Engines and Device in Processing Metallurgy
Tolić, A., Unit Operations
Tomašević, M., Machine Maintenance
Topolac, Ž., Physics
Traparić, U., Technical Drawing
Trifunović, D., Sinter Metallurgy
Veselinović, V., Drilling and Blasting
Vidojković, T., Analytical Chemistry
Živković, M., Underground Building
Žikvović, Ž., Extractive Metallurgy
Živković, M., Internal-Combustion Engines
Žlatković, V., Theory of Hydro and Electrometallurgical Processes

*Faculty of Organizational Sciences:*
Bingulac, S., Automation of Production Processes
Bogić, V., Organization and Management of Business Systems
Bošković, D., Organization of Research and Development

Božić, V., Economics of Organization of Associated Labour
Ćamilović, S., Follow-up System of Staff Development
Ćirić, V., Computers, Programming and Application
Dajović, S., Mathematics I
Drulović, M., Theory of Decision Making
Džinović, M., Organization of Associated Labour
Filipović, D., Andragogy
Grujić, M., Staff Function in Associated Labour
Jovanović, Lj., Organization of Energy Systems in Production
Karadžić, R., Foundations of National Defence
Kozić, P., Marxism and Self-Management
Kratina, H., Self-management Relations in Associated Labour
Krčevinac, S., Econometric Methods
Lazarević, B., Information Systems
Mileusnić, N., Organization of the Production Process
Milićević, D., Political Economy
Mitrović, Ž., Organization of Quality Control
Olbina, Ž., Economic Structure of Yugoslavia
Pejović, P., Numerical Analysis
Perić, A., German and English Language
Petrić, J., Operations Research
Rajkov, M., Systems Theory
Roglić, V., French Language
Šuković, F., Psychophysiology of Labour
Terzić, B., Russian Language
Todorović, J., Construction Systems
Zeremski, V., Economic Organization of Associated Labour

*Faculty of Pharmacy:*
Arsenijević, V., Organic Chemistry
Blagojević, Z., Pharmaceutical Chemistry
Burić, I., Physics
Draškoci, M., Pharmacodynamics with Fundamentals of Pathological Physiology
Dugandžić, M., Analytical Chemistry
Janković, B., Microbiology
Kapetanović, B., Biochemistry
Kečkić, J., Mathematics
Lukić, O., Pharmacognosy
Nikolić, K., Physical Chemistry
Pavlović, S., Botany
Popović, A., Physiology with Fundamentals of Anatomy
Soldatović, D., Toxicological Chemistry
Stanimirović, S., Bromatology
Stefanović-Djukanović, Neo-organic Chemistry
Tufegdžić, N., Pharmaceutical Technology

*Faculty of Philology:*
Babović, M., Russian 19th-century Literature
Bandić, M., 20th-century Serbian Literature
Bogdanović, I., Theory of Expression in 20th-century Literature
Bugarski, R., Theory of Translation, English Language
Čolak, T., Croatian Literature
Dimić, I., Proust and Contemporary Novel
Dimitrijević, N., Methodology of English Language Teaching
Djukanović, M., Turkish Language and Literature
Drašković, V., French Language
Flora, R., Romanian Language and Literature
Ilić, M., Fundamentals of Social Science
Ilić, V., Macedonian Language
Jović, D., General Linguistics
Josimović, R., Theory of Literature
Kostić, V., English Literature
Košutić, V., English Literature
Marinković, R., Medieval Literature
Marković, S., Serbian Literature
Milinčević, V., 19th-century Serbian Drama
Mihailović, Lj., English Language
Milošević, N., Literary Criticism
Mojašević, M., German Literature
Naumov, N., English Literature
Nedeljković, D., Realism
Pantić, M., History of Yugoslav Literature from the Renaissance to the Age of Enlightenment
Pavlović, M., French Literature
Peco, A., History of Serbo-Croat and Dialectology
Perišić, D., Survey of German Literature
Pešić, R., Folk Studies on Marko Kraljevic
Petrović, S., Introduction to Literature
Polovina, P., French Language
Savić, M., Italian Grammar
Stanojčić, Ž., Contemporary Serbo-Croatian
Stipčević, N., Italian Literature
Stojnić, M., 20th-century Russian Literature
Tartalja, I., Theory of Literature
Vitanović, S., French Literature

*Faculty of Philosophy:*
Arandjelović, J., General Methodology
Bandić, D., Ethnology of Yugoslavia
Berger, J., Methods of Clinical Psychology
Bojanović, R., Psychology of Interpersonal Relations
Bukvić, A., Psychometrics
Bulatović, R., Special Andragogy
Cermanović-Kuzmanović, A., Classical Archaeology
Ćirković, S., Medieval National History
Crepajac, Lj., Greek Language
Cvetković, Z., Mathematics Teaching
Djordjević, J., Didactics
Djurić, V., History of Medieval Art
Dragićević, Č., Statistics in Psychology
Ferjančić, B., Byzantology
Flašar, M., Classical Literature
Garašanin, M., Prehistoric Archaeology
Gavela, B., Classical Archaeology
Guzina, M., Industrial Psychology
Havelka, N., Social Psychology
Ivić, I., Developmental Psychology
Kalić, J., General Medieval History
Knjazev-Adamović, S., Theory of Cognisance
Korać, Voj., History of Architecture
Kovačević, J., Medieval Archaeology
Krestić, V., Modern History of Yugoslavia
Kvaščev, R., Educational Psychology
Maksimović, J., History of Medieval Art
Marjanović, S., Pre-School Education
Medaković, D., History of Modern Art
Mihailović, R., History of Art of the New Era
Mirković, M., Ancient History
Munišić, Z., History and Theory of Marxism
Ognjenović, P., General Psychology
Petranović, B., History of Yugoslavia
Petrović, Dj., Ethnology of Yugoslavia
Petrović, V., Psychotherapy and Counselling
Popović, B., Psychology of Personality
Potkonjak, N., General Education Science
Radonjić, S., General Psychology
Ranković, M., General Sociology
Roter, M., General Psychology
Šalabalić, R., Latin Language
Samardžić, R., General History of the New Era
Savićević, D., Andragogy
Smiljanić, V., Psychology of Development
Srejović, D., Prehistoric Archaeology
Stajnberger, I., Engineering Psychology, Ergonomics
Tešić, V., Educational Theory of Adults
Trifunović, L., Modern Art
Vlahović, P., Ethnology of the Yugoslav People
Vučić, L., Educational Psychology

*Faculty of Physical Education:*
Aleksić, I., Hygiene
Djordjević, D., Field Activities, Psychomotor Studies
Gluščević, M., Marxism
Horvatić, F., Handball, Basket-ball
Ivančević, S., Methodology of School Physical Education
Janković, R., Boxing, Wrestling and Judo
Koturović, B., Dance
Koturović, Lj., Kinestherapeutics
Kurelić, N., Track and Field Athletics, History of Physical Culture
Leskošek, J., Pedagogy, Methodology of Recreation
Lukić, B., Common National Defence
Mrvaljević, D., Anatomy
Nišavić, M., Games and Sports
Opavski, P., Biomechanics
Petrović, A., Sports, Gymnastics (Women)
Petrović, J., Gymnastics (Men)
Rajnović, V., Association Football
Stevanović, V., Swimming and Water Polo
Stojanović, M., Human Developmental Biology and Introduction to Sports Medicine
Todorović, B., Physiology
Tomić, D., Games and Sports

*Faculty of Political Sciences:*
Bezdanov, S., Educational Policy
Blagoev, B., Labour Relations
Bogetić, Lj., Modern Political History
Božović, R., Sociology of Culture and Cultural Policy
Bulat, S., Political Economy
Četković, V., General Sociology
Damjanović, M., Organization and Administration in Self-Management Society
Djokanović, T., International Economic Relations
Djordjević, J., Political System and Political Life
Djordjević, M., Recent Political History; History of Journalism
Djordjević, T., Public Opinion and Mass Communication
Franković, D., Elements of Education with Methodology of Social Sciences
Gavranov, V., International Relations
Gligorijević, S., Political Economics
Grozdanić, S., Methodology of Social Research
Grličkov, A., International Economic Relations
Gudac, Ž., Contemporary Political History
Jakovljević, Dj., Social Medicine and Health Protection
Jakšić, S., Sociology of the Family
Janković, B., International Law
Lakićević, D., Doctrines and Comparative Systems in Social Policy
Lazin, S., Social Psychology and Psychology of Political Behaviour

LUKAČ, D., Cybernetics
LUKAČ, S., Journalism
MALOBABIĆ, P., Elements of National Defence
MARINKOVIĆ, R., Sociology of Local Communities
MARJANOVIĆ, J., Introduction to Political Science
MARKOVIĆ, D., Sociology of Work
MARKOVIĆ, LJ., Yugoslav Economic System
MATIĆ, M., Political Systems and Political Life
MATIĆ, V., Methodology of Social Work
MILOSAVLJEVIĆ, S., Methodology
MITROVIĆ, D., International Business Relations
NAJMAN, V., Social Pathology
NEDELJKOVIĆ, I., Theory of Social Work
PAŠIĆ, N., Yugoslav Political System and Political Life
PAVLOVIĆ, V., Political Sociology of Contemporary Society
PEJANOVIĆ, O., Contemporary Philosophy
PETROVIĆ, D., Mental Hygiene, Methodology of Social Work
PEŠIĆ, M., General Sociology
PODUNAVAC, M., Theory of Political Systems
PRIBIĆEVIĆ, B., Contemporary Socialism
PRNJAT, B., Sociology of Culture and Cultural Policy
RAČIĆ, O., Diplomacy and International Organizations
RAKOČEVIĆ, Ž., Political Economics
RATKOVIĆ, R., Introduction to Political Sciences
SMILJKOVIĆ, R., Political Sociology
STANOJČIĆ, I., Contemporary Sociology
STANOVČIĆ, V., History of Political Theories
STOJILJKOVIĆ, D., Information and Propaganda
STOJKOVIĆ, M., Yugoslav Foreign Policy
STRAHINJIĆ, Č., Theory and Practice of Self-Government
ŠEFER, B., Yugoslav Social Policy and Development
ŠEŠIĆ, B., Methodology of Social Research
ŠPADIJER, B., Socio-political System
TARTALJA, S., History of Political Theories
VAJS, E., International Social Policy
VASOVIĆ, V., Contemporary Political Systems
VRATUŠA, A., Self-Government in Theory and Practice
VUKMIRICA, V., Contemporary Economic Systems
ZEČEVIĆ, M., Normative Legal Proceedings
ZORIĆ, D., General Sociology
ŽIVANOV, S., Contemporary Socialism

*Faculty of Sciences:*
ADNADJEVIĆ, D., Topology
ALJANČIĆ, S., Theory of Function
ANDJUS, R., Physiology
ČADEŽ, M., Dynamic Meteorology
ĆELAP, M., Inorganic Chemistry
DJURIĆ, V., Economic Geography
DUKIĆ, D., Hydrology
GRUJIĆ-INJAC, B., Chemistry of Natural Products
JANJIĆ, T., Analytical Chemistry
JANKOVIĆ, M., Plant Ecology and Plant Geography
JURIĆ, M., Atomic Physics
KANAZIR, D., Biochemistry
KUREPA, DJ., Mathematical Analysis
MARKOVIĆ, J., Geography of Yugoslavia
MIHAILOVIĆ, M., Theoretical Organic Chemistry
MILOJEVIĆ, A., General Physics
MUŠICKI, DJ., Theoretcial Physics
ORLOV, K., Numerical Mathematics
PETROVIĆ, D., Geomorphology
PETROVIĆ, V., Comparative Physiology, Endocrinology
RAKIEVIĆ, T., Physical Geography
RAŠAJSKI, B., Analytical Geometry
RIBNIKAR, S., Radiochemistry
RISTIĆ, S., Spectrochemistry
RODIĆ, D., Economic Geography of Yugoslavia
STEFANOVIĆ, M., Organic Chemistry
ŠEVARLIĆ, B., Astronomy
ŠUŠIĆ, M., Electrochemistry
VAJGAND, V., Analytical Chemistry
VASOVIĆ, M., Regional Geography
VELJKOVIC, S., Chemical Kinetics
VITOROVIĆ, D., Applied Chemistry
VUJIČIĆ, V., Statistics
VUKANOVIĆ, V., Atomistics

*Faculty of Stomatology:*
ANDJIĆ, J., Physiology and Biochemistry
DERGENC, S., Ophthalmology
DIMITRIJEVIĆ-LEGRADIĆ, K., Pathophysiology
DJAJIĆ, D., Diseases of the Mouth
GAVRILOVIĆ, V., History of Stomatology
ILIĆ, Č., Oto-Rhino-Laryngology
IVANKOVIĆ, D., Internal Medicine
JOJIĆ, B., Oral Surgery
KARAPANDŽIĆ, M., Maxillo-Facial Surgery
KOSOVČEVIĆ, M., Prosthetics
LEKOVIĆ, B., Dermatovenerology
LUKIĆ, V., Children's and Preventive Dentistry
MARKOVIĆ, D., Diseases of the Teeth
MARKOVIĆ, D., Roentgenology
MARKOVIĆ, M., Orthodontics
NEDELJKOVIĆ, D., Surgery
PALJM, A., Pathological Anatomy
PAVLOVIĆ, V., Chemistry
PEROVIĆ, J., Oral Surgery
PIŠČEVIĆ, A., Maxillo–Facial Surgery
POPOV, S., Physics
STOŠIĆ, P., Children's and Preventive Dentistry
ŠĆEPAN, V., Microbiology
TERZIĆ, M., Pharmacology
VOLF, N., Neuropsychiatry
VUKOVIĆ, I., Fundamentals of Marxism

*Faculty of Technology and Metallurgy:*
AST, T., Spectrometric Identification of Organic Compounds
BARAS, J., Technology of Brewing
BASTIĆ, B., Organic Chemistry I
BOGOSAVLJEV, P., Blast Furnace Preparation, Iron Ore Agglomeration, Research and Control Techniques in Iron and Steel Making
BULATOVIĆ, Z., Mathematical Treatment of Experimental Data, Mathematical Introduction to Mechanics
DESPIĆ, A., Physical Chemistry, Chemical Kinetics
DRAGOJEVIĆ, M., General Chemistry
DRAŽIĆ, D., Kinetics of Electrode Processes, Electro-Chemical Double Layer and Absorption, Electro-Chemical Kinetics, Physical Chemistry
DROBNJAK, D., Physical Metallurgy
DJORDJEVIĆ, B., Chemical Engineering Thermodynamics
DJORDJEVIĆ, S., Physical Chemistry, Electro-Metallurgy, Electroplating
DJOKIĆ, D., Technology of Fertilizers
DJURKOVIĆ, B., Metallurgy of Rare Metals
DJURKOVIĆ, O., Textile Organic Chemistry
GAKOVIĆ, N., Metallurgy of Iron and Steel Making, Continuous Processes
GOLUBOVIĆ, V., Analytical Chemistry, Organic Reagents in Analytical Chemistry
ILIĆ, I., Theory of Metallurgical Processes
JAĆOVIĆ, M., Chemistry of Macromolecules
JANAĆKOVIĆ, T., Chemistry and Technology of Building Materials
JANČIĆ, M., Materials Science
JOKSIMOVIĆ-TJAPKIN, S., Combustion and Industrial Furnaces
JOVANOVIĆ, J., Physical Methods in Organic Chemistry
JOVANOVIĆ, M., Methods of Electroanalytical Chemistry
JOVANOVIĆ, M., Glass Technology
JOVANOVIĆ, M., Energy of Metallurgical Furnaces, Furnaces and Design in Metallurgy
JOVANOVIĆ, R., Textile Fibres
JOVANOVIĆ, S., Colloidal Chemistry
KENDEREŠKI, S., Industrial Microbiology
KRSMANOVIĆ, M., Mathematics
MAJDANAC, LJ., Pulp and Paper Technology
MIĆIĆ, J., Organic Chemical Technology, Chemical Reaction Engineering
MIHAJLOVIĆ, D., Metallography
MIJOVIĆ, V., Textile Testing (with Statistics)
MILENKOVIĆ, V., Mechanical Working—Extrusion, Cold Drawing Forging
MIŠIĆ-VUKOVIĆ, M., Geography of Organic Molecules
MIŠKOVIĆ, B., Mechanical Working—Rolling
MIŠKOVIĆ, N., Theory of Plastic Deformation
MIŠOVIĆ, J., Instrumental Methods of Chemical Analysis, Physical and Chemical Methods of Separation
MLADENOVIĆ, S., Industrial Electro-Chemistry, Corrosion, Corrosion Protection
MUŠKATIROVIĆ, M., Physical Organic Chemistry
NEDELJKOVIĆ, LJ., Metallurgy of Alloyed and Clean Steel Making, Physical Chemistry of Iron and Steel Making
PAVLOVIĆ, B., Physics
RADOJKOVIĆ-VELIČKOVIĆ, M., Heterocyclic Chemistry
RADOSAVLJEVIĆ, S., Inorganic Chemistry
RADOVANOVIĆ, D., Principles of Inorganic Chemical Technology, Chemical Thermodynamics
RAJKOVIĆ, V., Technology of Food Preservation
RAKIĆ, O., Selected Topics in Mathematical Analysis
REKALIĆ, V., Analytical Methods of Industrial Products Analysis
ROGULIĆ, M., Physical Metallurgy, Electron Microscopy, X-ray Diffraction of Metals
SINADINOVIĆ, D., Non-ferrous Metallurgy
SPASIĆ, M., Non-ferrous Metallurgy
STANKOVIĆ, S., Chemical Technology of Cellulose
STEVANČEVIĆ, D., Chemical Technology of Primary Petrochemical Products, Chemical Technology of Secondary Technological Products
STOJANOVIĆ, O., Organic Chemistry II
ŠAPER, R., Process Control
ŠĆEPANOVIĆ, V., General Chemistry
ŠUŠIĆ, S., Technology of Carbohydrates
TADIĆ, Z., Mechanism and Structure in Organic Chemistry
TATIĆ-JANJIĆ, O., Electrochemistry
TECILAZIĆ-STEVANOVIĆ, M., Ceramic Technology
TRAJKOVIĆ, J., Biochemistry of Food

TRAJKOVIĆ, R., Technology of Dyeing, Technology and Technical Preparation of Printing
TRIFUNOVIĆ, D., Material Science
UŠĆUMLIĆ, M., Mathematics
VALČIĆ, A., Material Science
VELIČKOVIĆ, J., Chemical Technology of Synthetic Resins
VIDOJEVIĆ, N., Heat Treatment of Metals
VITOROVIĆ, O., Qualitative Analysis
VRAČAR, R., Non-Ferrous Metallurgy, Light Metals
VRHOVAC, LJ., Organic Chemical Technology
VUČUROVIĆ, D., Non-Ferrous Metallurgy, Theory of Metallurgical Processes

*Faculty of Transport:*
ADAMOVIĆ, M., Transport Economics and Geography
BANKOVIĆ, R., Public Transit Systems
ČIČAK, M., Railway Transport and Traffic Management
ČUČUZ, N., Dynamics of Vehicles
DINIĆ, D., Railway Vehicles, Train Traction Organization
JOVANOVIĆ, B., Political Economy, Basics of Marxist Philosophy and Sociology
JOVANOVIĆ, D., Telecommunications, Process Control Automation
JOVANOVIĆ, N., Transport Planning, Regulation and Safety in Road and City Traffic
KRECULJ, D., Shipping and Power Drive Systems, Resistance and Ship Propulsion
KUZOVIĆ, LJ., Traffic Flow Theory
LAZOVIĆ, S., Telecommunication Systems
LUKIĆ, M., Airports
MACURA, D., Highway Design
MILIĆEVIĆ, M., Railway Signals, Safety Systems
MILOŠEVIĆ, B., Railway Tracks and Stations
PERIŠIĆ, R., Containers, Special Transport
RADOVANOVIĆ, V., Vehicle Maintenance
VUKADINOVIĆ, S., Mathematical Statistics and Operations Research
VUKIĆEVIĆ, S., Internal Transport
ZORIĆ, D., Aircraft, Propulsion and Mechanics of Flight

*Faculty of Veterinary Medicine:*
ANTIĆ, S., Economics and Statistics
BERKEŠ, P., Chemistry
DANON, J., Botany
DIMITRIJEVIĆ, B., Pharmacology and Toxicology
DJUKIĆ, B., Forensic Veterinary Medicine
DJURDJEVIĆ, D., Pathological Physiology
GLIGORIJEVIĆ, J., Physical Therapy
JANKOVIĆ, Ž., Anatomy of Domestic Animals
JOVANČEVIĆ, V., Physics
JOVANOVIĆ, M., Physiology
KNEŽEVIĆ, N., Pathological Anatomy
KOZIĆ, LJ., Diseases of Poultry
MIHAJLOVIĆ, B., Virology
MILJKOVIĆ, V., Obstetrics of Domestic Animals
MILJKOVIĆ, VIŠESLAVA, Hygiene and Technology of Milk Production
PANJEVIĆ, DJ., Infectious Diseases of Domestic Animals
PETROVIĆ, M., Diseases of Ungulates and Carnivores
PETROVIĆ, Z., Parasitology
POPESKOVIĆ, D., Biology
PUHAČ, I., Veterinary Hygiene
RAŠETA, J., Meat Inspection, Hygiene and Technology of Meat
SAVIĆ, I., Meat Hygiene and Technology
STAMATOVIĆ, S., Internal Diseases of Ruminants and Pigs
ŠEVKOVIĆ, N., Nutrition of Domestic Animals
ŠIBALIĆ, S., Parasitic Diseases
ŠOVLJANSKI, B., Animal Husbandry
TADIĆ, M., Surgery and Ophthalmology
TEŠIĆ, D., Pharmacology
TRBIĆ, B., Microbiology, Serology, Immunology

## UNIVERZITET UMETNOSTI U BEOGRADU
(Belgrade Arts University)
VUKA KARADŽIĆA 12,
11000 BELGRADE
Telephone: 624-020.

Founded 1957 as Academy of Arts; became University 1973.

Language of instruction: Serbo-Croat; Academic year: October to September.

*Rector:* Prof. ALEKSANDAR OBRADOVIĆ.
*Vice-Rectors:* Prof. DEJAN KOSANOVIĆ, Prof. VOJISLAV TODORIĆ, Prof. BOGDAN KRŠIĆ, RADIVOJ MARINKOVIĆ (student).
*Secretary-General:* Mrs. DOBRILA ŠOŠKIĆ-PETROVIĆ.

Number of teachers: 284.
Number of students: 1,566.
Publication: *4F†* (2 a year).

DEANS:

*Faculty of Musical Art:* Prof. RADOMIR PETROVIĆ.
*Faculty of Fine Arts:* Prof. RUDOLF GABERC.
*Faculty of Applied Arts:* Prof. STJEPAN FILEKI.
*Faculty of Dramatic Arts:* SLOBODAN SELENIĆ.


## UNIVERZITET BITOLJ
(Bitola University)
97000 BITOLA
Telephone: (38-97) 23788.
Founded 1979.

*Rector:* Dr. STEVAN GABER.


## UNIVERZITET "SVETOZAR MARKOVIĆ" U KRAGUJEVCU
(Kragujevac "Svetozar Markovic" University)
TRG AVNOJA 1,
34000 KRAGUJEVAC
Telephone: (034) 65-424; foreign calls: 68-232.
Founded 1976.

State control; Language of instruction: Serbo-Croat.

*Rector:* Prof. Dr. DUŠAN SIMIĆ.
*Vice-Rectors:* Prof. Dr. VLADO VODINELIĆ, Prof. Dr. RADE DJORDJEVIĆ.
*General Secretary:* MIROSLAV MIJAILOVIĆ.

*Librarian:* MILAN STANKOVIĆ.

Number of teachers: 280.
Number of students: 10,000 full time, 6,000 part-time.
Publication: *Bulletin* (every 2 months).

DEANS:

*Faculty of Mechanical Engineering:* Prof. Ing. MILIVOJ BOŽIN.
*Faculty of Economics:* Prof. Dr. ŽIVADIN STEFANOVIĆ.
*Faculty of Law:* Prof. Dr. DRAGOLJUB STOJANOVIĆ.
*Faculty of Sciences:* Prof. Dr. STANIMIR KONSTANTINOVIĆ.
*Teachers' Technical Faculty at Čačak:* Prof. Dr. VUKOLA STEVANOVIĆ.
*Faculty of Agriculture, Čačak:* Prof. Dr. PETAR MAKSIMOVIĆ.

ATTACHED INSTITUTES:

**Institute for Fruit Research at Čačak:** 32000 Čačak; Dir. Dipl. Ing. Dr. VOJIN BUGARČIĆ.

**Institute for Crops Research at Kragujevac:** 34000 Kragujevac, Jovanovački put b.b.; Dir. Dipl. Ing. Dr. ŽIVORAD JESTROVIĆ.


## UNIVERZA EDVARDA KARDELJA V LJUBLJANI
(Edvard Kardelj University of Ljubljana)
TRG OSVOBODITVE 11,
LJUBLJANA
Telephone: 22-052, 23-721.

Founded 1595, reconstituted 1809, reopened 1919.

Academic year: September to August (two terms); Language of instruction: Slovene.

*Rector:* Prof. Dr. IVO FABINC.
*Vice-Rectors:* Prof. Dr. FRANC BUČAR, Prof. Dr. VINCENC ČIŽMAN, Prof. Dr. FRANCE VREG.
*Secretary-General:* ZVONIMIR ZALAR.

Number of teachers: 2,178.
Number of students: 19,201.

Publications: *Objave, Poročilo, Vestnik, Seznam predavanj Univerze v Ljubljani, Bibliografija doktorskih disertacij univerze in drugih visokošolskih in znanstvenih ustanov, Biografije in bibliografije univerzitetnih učiteljev in sodelavcev.*

DEANS:

*Faculty of Philosophy:* Prof. Dr. MIRKO JURAK.
*Faculty of Law:* Prof. Dr. IVAN KRISTAN.
*Faculty of Economics:* Prof. Dr. VLADIMIR FRANKOVIČ.
*Faculty of Natural Science and Technology:* Prof. Dr. BOGOMIR DOBOVIŠEK.
*Faculty of Architecture, Civil Engineering and Geodesy:* Doc. PETER ŠIVIC.

*Faculty of Electrical Engineering:* Prof. Dr. SLAVKO HODŽAR.
*Faculty of Mechanical Engineering:* Prof. Dr. VIKTOR PROSENC.
*Faculty of Medicine:* Prof. Dr. MILOŠ KOBAL.
*Faculty of Biotechnics:* Prof. Dr. SRDJAN BAVDEK.
*Faculty of Sociology, Political Science and Journalism:* Prof. Dr. ZDENKO ROTER.
*Academy of Music:* Prof. DANIJEL ŠKERL.
*Academy of Theatre, Radio, Film and Television:* Prof. MIRAN HERZOG.
*Academy of Fine Arts:* Prof. SLAVKO TIHEC.
*Higher School of Physical Culture:* Doc. RAJKO ŠUGMAN.
*Higher School of Pedagogy:* Prof. IVAN ŠKOFLEK.
*Higher School of Maritime Engineering:* IVAN SMERDU.
*Higher School for Social Workers:* Prof. BLAŽ MESEC.
*Higher School for Sanitary Workers:* MIRO LUBEJ.
*Higher School of Safety Engineering:* Mag. VLADIMIR DRUSANY.
*Higher School of Public Administration:* Prof. RUDOLF KOCJANČIČ.

### UNIVERZA V MARIBORU
(University of Maribor)
62000 MARIBOR,
KREKOVA ULICA 2
Telephone: (062) 22-281.

Founded 1975.

State control; Language of instruction: Slovene; Academic year: September to August.

*Rector:* Dr. DALI DJONLAGIĆ.
*Vice-Rectors:* Dr. MAJDA ŠKERBIC, Dr. STOJAN VRABL, ALENKA VINDIŠ (student).
*Secretary-General:* DARIN HASL.
*Librarian:* Dr. BRUNO HARTMAN.

Number of teachers: 297 full-time, 193 part-time.
Number of students: 5,161 full-time, 4,142 external.

Publications: *Naše gospodarstvo* (published by the School of Economics and Commerce, every 2 months), *Organizacija in Kadri* (published by the School of Organizational Sciences, 10 a year), *Časopis za zgodovino in narodopisje.*

DEANS:

*School of Economics and Commerce:* Dr. DANE MELAVC.
*School of Technical Sciences:* Dr. ADOLF ŠOSTAR.
*School of Organizational Sciences:* Dr. JOŽE FLORJANČIČ.
*Pedagogical Academy:* Mag. ALOJZ FRIDL.

*Law School:* Dr. ŠIME IVANJKO.
*School of Agriculture:* Mag. ALEKSANDER KRAVOS.

ATTACHED INSTITUTES:

**Computer Centre:** Visoka tehniška škola Maribor, Smetanova 17; Dir. MARJAN PIVKA.

**Marxist Centre of the University of Maribor:** Koroška cesta 160, 62000 Maribor; Dir. FRANCI PIVEC.

### UNIVERZITET "DŽEMAL BIJEDIC" U MOSTARU
(University of Mostar)
TRG. "14 FEBRUAR" B.B.,
79000 MOSTAR
Telephone: (088) 39-140.

Founded 1977.

Number of teachers: 125.
Number of students: 5,200.

Language of instruction: Serbo-Croat; Academic year: September to August.

*Rector:* Prof. EMIR HUMO.
*Pro-Rector:* Prof. DUŠAN PETROVIĆ.
*General Secretary:* EDIN ŠEMIĆ.
*Librarian:* Prof. SALIH LEHO.
Publication: *Bilten* (quarterly).

DEANS:

*Law:* Prof. Dr. KASIM TRNKA.
*Economics:* Prof. Dr. ZORAN TRPUTEC.
*Mechanical Engineering:* BOŽIDAR ĆORIĆ.
*Pedagogical Academy:* (vacant).

ATTACHED INSTITUTES:

**"HEPOK"—Istraživačko-razvojni centar:** 79000 Mostar; agricultural research and development; Dir. VLADO TRNINIĆ.

**Duvanski Institut:** 79000 Mostar, Put za Glavicu 8; tobacco research institute; Dir. SLAVKO JELČIĆ.

### UNIVERZITET U NIŠU
(University of Niš)
MIKE PALIGORIĆA 2, 18000 NIŠ
Telephone: 25722, 25544.

Founded 1965.

State control; Language of instruction: Serbo-Croat.

*Rector:* Prof. MOMČILO DIMITRIJEVIĆ.
*Vice-Rectors:* Dr. SLOBODAN LAZOVIĆ, Dr. ŽIVOTA ŽIVKOVIĆ.
*General Secretary:* BULATOVIĆ DRAGOMIR.

Number of teachers: 825.
Number of students: 21,061.

Publications: *Pregled predavanja* (Prospectus, annual), *Glasnik Univerziteta u Nišu* (Review, irregular), *Bilten referata za izbor nastavnika i fakultetskih saradnika* (Bulletin of Academic Titles, irregular).

DEANS:

*Faculty of Medicine:* MILAN MILANOVIĆ.
*Faculty of Electronic Engineering:* RADOSAV DJORDJEVIĆ.
*Faculty of Civil Engineering:* LAZAR IGNJATOVIĆ.
*Faculty of Mechanical Engineering:* ZORAN BORIČIĆ.
*Faculty of Law:* (vacant).
*Faculty of Economics:* GAVRILO VIDANOVIĆ.
*Faculty of Safety at Work:* TEOFILO POPOVIĆ.
*Faculty of Philosophy:* Dr. ŽELJKO KUČER.

ATTACHED INSTITUTES:

There are 13 institutes attached to or associated with the Faculty of Medicine, one attached to the Faculty of Mechanical Engineering, one attached to the Faculty of Civil Engineering and one to the Faculty of Economics.

### UNIVERZITET U NOVOM SADU
(University of Novi Sad)
21000 NOVI SAD,
VELJKA VLAHOVIĆA 3,
POŠT. FAH 7
Telephone: 55-621, 55-629.

Founded 1960.

State control; Language of instruction: Serbo-Croat; Academic year: October to June.

*Rector:* Prof. Dr. DUŠAN JAKŠIĆ.
*Pro-Rectors:* Prof. Dr. STEVAN MEZEI, Prof. Dr. MILIVOJE NAUMOVIĆ, Prof. Dr. DRAGIŠA POPOVIĆ.
*Student Pro-Rector:* ŽARKO PUTNIK.
*General Secretary:* PETAR MIŠIĆ.

Number of teachers: 1,342.
Number of students: 26,871.

Publications: *Glasnik* (Review, irregular), *Bilten* (Bulletin, irregular).

DEANS:

*Faculty of Economics:* Prof. Dr. MILENA VLAŠKALIĆ.
*Faculty of Agriculture:* Prof. Dr. ZORAN STOJANOVIĆ.
*Faculty of Law:* Prof. Dr. MOMČILO GRUBAČ.
*Faculty of Technical Sciences:* Prof. Dr. VASILIJE KELIĆ.
*Faculty of Medicine:* Prof. Dr. DUŠAN POPOVIĆ.
*Faculty of Natural Sciences and Mathematics:* Prof. Dr. JEVREM JANCIĆ.
*Faculty of Philosophy:* Prof. Dr. ČEDOMIR POPOV.
*Faculty of Technology:* Prof. Dr. LJUBOMIR JAZIĆ.
*Faculty of Physical Culture:* Prof. ALEKSIJE BER.
*Faculty of Civil Engineering:* Prof. Dr. DRAGOSLAV BRANKOVIĆ.
*Academy of Fine Arts:* Prof. Dr. BOŽIDAR KOVAČEK.
*Pedagogical-Technical Faculty:* Prof. Dr. MILISAV JOKSIMOVIĆ.

**PROFESSORS:**

*Faculty of Agriculture:*
ARSENIJEVIĆ, M., Fruit and Vine Protection
BELIĆ, B., General Farming
**BOROJEVIĆ, S., Genetics**
**BURIĆ, D., Fruit and Vine Growing**
ČAMPRAG, D., Special Entomology, Plant Protection
DJURKIĆ, J., General Entomology
**DREZGIĆ, P., Special Field Crops**
**HADŽIVUKOVIĆ, S., Statistics**
JEVTIĆ, S., Farming
JOVANOVIĆ, V., Veterinary Science and Zoohygiene
KATIĆ, P., Meteorology and Climatology
**KONČAR, L., Domestic Animal Breeding**
KUKIN, A., Hydrology
MANČIĆ, D., Special Cattle Raising
MANOJLOVIĆ, S., Agrochemistry
MARIĆ, A., Phytopathology
MARKO, J., Book-keeping and Accountancy
MARKOVIĆ, Ž., Special Farming
MEKINDA, M., Agricultural Machinery
**MEZEI, S., Political Economy**
MILENKOVIĆ, P., Economic Policy in Agriculture
MILJKOVIĆ, N., Pedology
MILOVANKIĆ, M., Pomology
MIŠKOVIĆ, M., Reproduction of Domestic Animals
**NIKOLIĆ, V., Phytopathology**
RAJKOV, B., Organization of Agricultural Production
RELJIN, S., Marketing
RUDIĆ, M., Fruit Growing
SARIĆ, Z., Microbiology
SAVIĆ, R., General Field Crops
ŠIJAČKI, N., Anatomy and Histology
**SLOVIĆ, D., Fruit Growing**
STANAĆEV, S., Special Farming
**STANKOVIĆ, A., Phytopharmacy**
STOJANOVIĆ, T., Special Entomology
STOJANOVIĆ, Z., Veterinary Science and Zoohygiene
STOJŠIĆ, M., Melioration and Fishponds
ŠIJAČKI, N., Anatomy and Histology
VAPA, M., Physiology of Domestic Animals
VREBALOV, T., Special Farming
VUČIĆ, N., Irrigation
VUJIČIĆ, I., Dairy Technology
ŽIVKOVIĆ, S., Domestic Animal Breeding

*Faculty of Economics:*
BANDIN, T., Economics of BSMO*
DOHČEVIĆ, S., Economic Analysis of Industrial BSMO*
DUNDJEROV, M., Business Policy and Planning of Agricultural BSMO* Development
JANČURIĆ M., Statistics
KUN, L., Technological Systems in Industry
RAKOVAČKI, M., Theory and Methodology of Accountancy
REHAK, L., Sociology
**TASIĆ, A., International Economic Relations**
VLAŠKALIĆ, M., Yugoslavian Economy
* Basic Self-Management Organization

*Faculty of Law:*
CARIĆ, S., Economic Law
**DJETVAI, K., Introduction to Civil Law, Real Law**
KOVAČEVIĆ, M., Administrative Law
MILOŠEVIĆ, LJ., Law of Obligation
PUPIĆ, B., Introduction to Law
STEFANOV, M., Family Law, Law of Inheritance
ŽARKOVIĆ, D., Political Economy

*Faculty of Technical Sciences:*
**ĆULUM, Z., Physics**
**ČUPIĆ, E., Industrial Engineering**

CVEKIĆ, V., Electronics
FLAŠAR, A., Technology and Production Organization
**GULIĆ, M., Boilers and Installations**
JAKŠIĆ, D., Regulation and Automation
KELIĆ, V., Land Reclamation Machinery
KRIŽNAR, M., Motor Vehicles and Equipment
**MANDIĆ, J., Mechanical Resistance**
MARIĆ, V., Mathematics
NENADIĆ, G., Metal Construction
OLJACA, M., Refrigerators
PANTELIĆ, I., Technology of Metals
REKECKI, J., Machine Tools Automatic Control
SEKULIĆ, S., Metal Cutting Processing
SOVILJ, R., Mechanics of Fluids
VUJANOVIĆ, B., Mechanics II, Dynamics
ZELENOVIĆ, D., Production Systems

*Faculty of Medicine:*
BERIĆ, B., Gynaecology
BRANOVAČKI, D., Stomatology
**DIMKOVIĆ, D., Surgery with War Surgery**
GOLDMAN, S., Internal Medicine with Phthisiology
KRAGUJEVIĆ, M., Microbiology
MARINKOV, S., Medical Biochemistry
MILIN, R., Histology and Embryology
RADOVANOVIĆ, M., Hygiene and Industrial Medicine
SAVIĆ, D., Social Medicine
SLANKAMENAC, S., Stomatological Prosthetics
STANULOVIĆ, D., Internal Medicine with Phthisiology
SVIRČEVIĆ, A., Internal Medicine with Pneumophthisiology
VURDELJA, N., Neuro-Psychiatry with Medical Psychology

*Faculty of Natural Sciences and Mathematics:*
BOROJEVIĆ, K., Genetics
CANIĆ, V., General and Inorganic Chemistry
CARIĆ, N., Geography of Settlements
CARIĆ, S., Solid State Physics
GAVRILOVIĆ, Ž., General Biology
GAĆEŠA, N., General History, History of Yugoslavia
GLUMAC, S., Morphology and Systematics of Invertebrates, Organic Evolution
JANIĆ, I., Atomic Physics
JANKOVIĆ, D., Physics
MARIĆ, D., General Physiology
MARINKOV, J., Nuclear Physics
NIKOLIĆ, M., General Physics
OBRADOVIĆ, M., Phytogeography, Practical Botany, Biogeography
OKILJEVIĆ, B., Mathematics I
PELICARIĆ, Š., Biology
PETROVIĆ, J., Geology, Hydrology, Geomorphology
PRVANOVANIĆ, M., Geometry
PUJIN, V., Zoology with Ecology
RANČIĆ, D., Physical Chemistry, Electro-Chemistry
SARIĆ, M., Plant Physiology
STANKOVIĆ, B., Introduction to Functional Analysis
SEFANOVIĆ, O., Chemistry

*Faculty of Philosophy:*
BORI, I., Hungarian Literature
ČURIĆ, R., Fundamentals of Pedagogy
GAVRILOVIĆ, S., National History
IVIĆ, M., Modern Serbo-Croatian Language, General Linguistics
KOSTIĆ, S., German Literature, History of German-Yugoslav Literary Relations
MIRNIĆ, J., National Liberation War and Socialistic Revolution

MLADENOVIĆ, A., History of Serbian Language and Dialectology
NAUMOVIĆ, M., Sociology
PENAVIN, O., General and Hungarian Linguistics
PERVAZ, D., History of English Language and Literature
POGAČNIK, J., Slovenian Language and Literature
RAKIĆ, B., Pedagogical Methodology and Psychology
SELI, I., History of 19th-century Hungarian Literature
VULETIĆ, V., 19th- and 20th-century Russian Literature
ŽIVKOVIĆ, D., 19th-century Serbian Literature
ZIVANČEVIĆ, M., Modern Croatian Literature

*Faculty of Technology:*
BEĆAREVIĆ, A., Biochemistry
BOGOSLAVLJEVIĆ, M., Technological Operations
DJAKOVIĆ, L. J., Colloidal Chemistry
MATIJAŠEVIĆ, B., Oils and Fats Technology
NOVAKOVIĆ, M., Technical Thermodynamics
PILETIĆ, M., Organic Chemistry
PUTANOV, P., Physical Chemistry
RAHELIĆ, S., Meat Technology
STEVANČEVIĆ, D., Technology of Secondary Petrochemical Products
**ŠULC, D., Fruit and Vegetable Technology**
**ŽAKULA, R., Food Microbiology with Hygiene of Production**

*Faculty of Civil Engineering:*
MILOVIĆ, D., Soil Mechanics

*Academy of Fine Arts:*
BRUČI, R., Composition, Orchestration
DRAŠKOVIĆ, B., Conducting
JAŠVILI, M., Violin
KARLAVARIS, B., Fine Arts Teaching Methods
NIKOLAJEVIĆ, M., Drawing
PATAKI, L., Drama
TIMAKIN, E., Piano

*Pedagogical-Technical Faculty:*
CIJAN, B., Technical Mechanics
LEKIĆ, DJ., Experimental Didactics

There are research institutes attached to each faculty.

## SVEUČILIŠTE U OSIJEKU
(University of Osijek)
OSIJEK

Founded 1975; in process of formation
Number of teachers: 212.
Number of students: 4,701.

## UNIVERZITET U KOSOVO*
(University of Kosovo)
RRUGA E MARËSHALIT
TITO P.N., 38000-PRIŠTINA
Telephone: 24-970.

Founded 1970 as University of Priština, amalgamated 1980 with seven higher education institutes to form University of Kosovo.

State control; Languages of instruction: Serbo-Croat and Albanian; Academic year: September to June.

*Rector:* Dr. MINIR DUSI.
*Vice-Rectors:* Dr. ALI DIDA, Dr. DRAGOSLAV PEJCINOVIC.
*General Secretary:* SHEHU ZEQ.
*Librarian:* BEDRI HYSA.

Number of teachers: c. 1,000.
Number of students: 26,000.

DEANS:

*Faculty of Agriculture:* MUHARREM SHALA.
*Faculty of Philosophy:* Dr. JELKA MATJASEVIĆ.
*Faculty of Law:* Dr. PETAR STANIŠIĆ.
*Faculty of Economics:* Dr. NURI BASHOTA.
*Faculty of Engineering:* Ing. NEXHAT ORANA.
*Faculty of Medicine:* Dr. IZEDIN OSMANI.
*Faculty of Natural Sciences and Mathematics:* Dr. RIZA ÇAVOLLI.
*Academy of Art:* SVETOMIR ARSIĆ.

There is also a faculty of mining at Kosovska Mitrovica.

*No reply received to our questionnaire this year.

## SVEUČILIŠTE U RIJECI
### (University of Rijeka)

TRG. RIJEČKE REZOLUCIJE
7/1, 51000 RIJEKA

Telephone: (38-51) 25-682.

Founded 1973

Academic year: September to August; Language of instruction: Croatian literary language.

*Rector:* Dr. SLOBODAN MARIN.
*Pro-Rectors:* Dr. BOGOSAV KOVAČEVIĆ, Dr. EDGAR ŠKROBONJA.
*Secretary-General:* VELJKO SRDOČ.

Number of teachers: 720, including 96 professors.
Number of students: 7,800 full-time, 5,420 part-time.

DEANS:

*Faculty of Medicine:* (vacant).
*Faculty of Engineering:* Dr. ZLATKO ŠVERER.
*Faculty of Law:* Dr. ZORAN KOMPANJET.
*Faculty of Seamanship and Transportation:* Dr. BORIS PRIKRIL.
*Maritime College:* ALEKSANDAR DOLINAR.
*College of Economics (Pula):* EDUARD KVATERNIK.
*Teacher Training School (Rijeka):* Dr. MILAN CRNKOVIĆ.
*Teacher Training School (Pula):* ALDO MACINIĆ.
*Teacher Training School (Gospić):* STIPE JOSIPOVIĆ.
*University Centre of Economics and Organizational Sciences:* Dr. ŽARKO POPOVIĆ.
*Faculty of Economics:* Dr. IVO ŽUVELA.
*Faculty of Hotel Management:* Dr. DUŠAN JAGODIĆ.
*Faculty of Education:* SREĆKO MRAMOR.
*Faculty of Industrial Education:* Dr. VESNA TOMAŠIĆ.

PROFESSORS:

*Faculty of Medicine:*
ANTONIN, B., Clinical Propaedeutics
ATANACKOVIĆ, D., Pharmacology, Pathological Physiology
BAČIĆ, V., Histology and Embryology
BEZJAK, V., Microbiology
BLEČIĆ, K., Hygiene and Public Health
CEZNER, M., Infectious Diseases
ĆUK, S., Neuropsychiatry
FRANCIŠKOVIĆ, V., War Surgery
GALL-PALLA, V., Chemistry
GLIGO, D., Ophthalmology
JURETIĆ, M., Paediatrics
KOGOJ-BAKIĆ, V., Gynaecology and Obstetrics
KOPAJTIĆ, B., Internal Medicine
KORIN, N., History of Medicine
KRIŽAN, Z., Anatomy
LEDIĆ, P., Neuropsychiatry
LENKOVIĆ, M., Surgery
LONGHINO, A., Surgery
MARIN, S., Phthisiology
MATEJČIĆ, M., Roentgenology
MATUTINOVIĆ, T., Otolaryngology
MOHOROVIČIĆ, D., Pathology and Pathological Anatomy
PAVEŠIĆ, D., Gynaecology and Obstetrics
PAVLOVIĆ, P., Clinical Radiology and Oncology
PEROVIĆ, D., Gynaecology and Obstetrics
PREMUŽIĆ-LAMPIĆ, M., Internal Medicine
RUKAVINA, D., Physiology
ŠUSTIĆ, V., Surgery
TAVČAR, R., Dental Surgery
URBAN, S., Biology
VOLARIĆ, B., Legal Medicine
VRBANIĆ, D., Gynaecology and Obstetrics
WOLF, A., Dermato-venerology

*Faculty of Engineering:*
BARIĆ, J., Electrical Engineering
EREN, R., Technological Planning of Production Procedure
GRUBIŠA, O., Technology of Ship Building and Construction
KATAVIĆ, I., Metal Forming
KRPAN, M., Mechanics
KULJANIĆ, E., Metal Cutting, Optimization of Machine Processes
MARGIĆ, S., Tools and Work Devices
MILOŠEVIĆ, Š., Steam Boilers, Ships' Auxiliary Engines
OBSIGER, J., Machine Elements
OBSIGER, V., Thermodynamics of Binary Mixtures
OSTOJIĆ, B., Automation and Regulation of Control
PEČORNIK, M., Mechanics of Fluids, Hydraulic Machines
PIRŠ, J., Testing of Materials, Heat Treatment of Metals
RUMAN, R., Theory of Oscillation, Strength of Materials
SAPUNAR, Z., Mechanics
SELAKOVIĆ, M., Factory Economics and Organizations
ŠKROBONJA, E., Thermodynamics
ŠVERER, Z., Transport Equipment, Internal Transport
VUČINIĆ, A., Ship Propulsion
WINKLER, Z., Shipyard Organization, Business Economics and Organization

*Faculty of Economics:*
DEŽELJIN, J., Political Economy
DVORNIK, I., Financing
KRALJIĆ, I., Banking
MRKUŠIĆ, Ž., Foreign Trade and Exchange Systems
NEMARNIK, I., Marketing
POPOVIĆ, Z., Business Development Policy
ŠABAN, S., Basic Organization of Associated Labour
ŠIŠUL, N., Contemporary Economic Theories and Theory of Self-management
ŽUVELA, I., International Economic Relations, Scientific Research Study

*Faculty of Hotel Management:*
ANDRIĆ, N., Tourism, Tourist Trade Economics
ANTUNAC, I., Organization and Economics of Travel Agencies
JAGODIĆ, D., Economics of Yugoslavia
JAKOVLIĆ, V., Commodity Economics and Nutrition
ŠTAMBUK, M., Law, Hotel Organization and Management, Catering Economics

*Faculty of Law:*
ČAVAL, J., Statistics
DWORSKI, E., Maritime and Transport Law
KOMPANJET, Z., Commercial Law
MARGETIĆ, L., Roman Law
MILOVIĆ, Dj., General History of State and Law, History of State and Law of Peoples of Yugoslavia

*Faculty of Civil Engineering:*
EKL, B., Regulations and Meliorations
MAGAŠ, B., High Constructions
REISER, I., Geodesy
SABLJAK, Z., Concrete and Reinforced Concrete
SAMARDŽIJA, V., Mathematics
SILA, Z., Town Planning

*Faculty of Education:*
KOVAČEVIĆ, B., Didactics
POLIĆ, V., Economics of Education
RADIĆ, M., Mathematics, Algebra and Methodology
SALAMON, T., Industrial Education
SREMEC, B., Psychology
ŠVAJCER, V., Didactics
TOMAŠIĆ, V., Geometry, Topology, Theory of Sets

*Faculty of Seamanship and Transportation:*
BONEFAČIĆ, B., Technics and Economics of Ship Employment
PRIKRIL, B., Integral Transportation Systems
RUBINIĆ, I., Marine Economics and Organization, Means of Sea Traffic
SOKOLIĆ, D., International Forwarding, Tariffs and Tariff Policy
STANKOVIĆ, P., Insurance of Goods in Transportation, Maritime Property Law, Surface and Air Traffic Law
ZOROVIĆ, D., Ship Navigation Equipment, Basis of Computer Application, Corrosion and Ship Protection, Cybernetics in Transport

## UNIVERZITET U SARAJEVU
### (University of Sarajevo)

71000 SARAJEVO, V.S. OBALA 7/11, POST. FAH 186

Telephone: 23-891, 23-875.

Founded 1946.

Academic year: October to September;

Language of instruction: Serbo-Croat.
*Rector:* Prof. Dr. Arif Tanović.
*Pro-Rectors:* Dr. Petar Drinić, Dr. Zdravko Pujić.
*Student Pro-Rector:* Drago Milošević.
*General Secretary:* Branimir Ljubičić.

Number of teachers: 1,550.
Number of students: 25,913

Publication: *Bilten Univerziteta u Sarajevu* (quarterly).

### DEANS:

*Faculty of Law:* Prof. Dr. Mihajlo Velimirović.
*Faculty of Economics:* Prof. Dr. Hasan Hadžiomerović.
*Faculty of Medicine:* Prof. Dr. Aleksandar Nikulin.
*Faculty of Veterinary Sciences:* Prof. Dr. Dmitar Varenika.
*Faculty of Philosophy:* Prof. Dr. Kasim Prohić.
*Faculty of Sciences:* Prof. Dr. Muso Dizdarević.
*Faculty of Agriculture:* Prof. Dr. Mitar Bašović.
*Faculty of Forestry:* Prof. Dr. Sead Izetbegović.
*Faculty of Building:* Prof. Faruk Filipović.
*Faculty of Architecture:* Prof. Džemal Celić.
*Faculty of Mechanical Engineering:* Prof. Dr. Vlatko Doleček.
*Faculty of Mechanical Engineering in Zenica:* Prof. Vladimir Savić.
*Electro-Technical Faculty:* Prof. Branko Knežević.
*Faculty of Metallurgy in Zenica:* Prof. Dr. Kemal Kapetanović.
*Faculty of Political Sciences:* Prof. Dr. Vladimir Degan.
*Faculty for Physical Culture:* Prof. Dr. Djordje Najšteter.
*Faculty of Pharmacy:* Prof. Dr. Branko Nikolin.
*Faculty of Communications:* Prof. Dr. Mihajlo Galić.
*Faculty of Dentistry:* Prof. Dr. Osman Ceribašić.
*Academy for Plastic Arts:* Prof. Dr. Muhamed Karamehmedović.
*Academy for Music:* Prof. Zdravko Verunica.
*Academy for Pedagogics:* Prof. Dr. Razija Lagumdžija.
*High School for Economics:* Prof. Nedžib Žerić.
*High School for Medicine:* Prof. Dr. Fadil Čengić.
*High School for Administration:* Prof. Sulejman Hrle.
*High School for Social Workers:* Prof. Vahid Kljajić.

## UNIVERZITET "KIRIL I METÓDIJ" VO SKOPJE
### (University of Skopje)
BULEVAR "KRSTE MISIRKOV" B.B., 91000 SKOPJE

Telephone: 37-712; 30-334; 30-915.
Founded 1949.
*Rector:* Prof. Dr. Jovan Stojanovski.
*Pro-Rectors:* Prof. Dr. Borislav Karanfilski, Prof. Anatoli Damjanovski.
*Secretary-General:* Trajan Bendevski.

Number of teachers: 1,500.
Number of students: 40,000 (full- and part-time).

Publications: *Univerzitetski bilten, Pregled predavanja.*

### DEANS:

*Faculty of Law:* Prof. Dr. Ivo Puhan.
*Faculty of Economics:* Prof. Dr. Krume Mihajlov.
*Faculty of Philology:* Prof. Dr. Božidar Nastev.
*Faculty of Philosophy:* Prof. Dr. Giorgi Stardelov.
*Faculty of Architecture:* Prof. Dr. Krum Tomovski.
*Faculty of Civil Engineering:* Prof. Dr. Dragi Miladinov.
*Faculty of Agriculture:* Prof. Dr. Risto Lozanovski.
*Faculty of Forestry:* Prof. Dr. Strahil Todorovski.
*Faculty of Medicine:* Prof. Dr. Savo Mironski.
*Faculty of Electrotechnics:* Prof. Ing. Todor Jakimov.
*Faculty of Mechanical Engineering:* Prof. Ing. Tlija Cherepnalkoski.
*Faculty of Technology:* Prof. Ing. Zdravko Kovachevski.
*Faculty of Metallurgy:* Prof. Ing. Giorgi Orovchanov.
*Faculty of Biology:* Prof. Dr. Ljupcho Grupche.
*Faculty of Geography:* Prof. Dr. Dushko Manakovich.
*Faculty of Mathematics:* Prof. Dr. Blagoj Popov.
*Faculty of Physics:* Prof. Dr. Ordan Pechijare.
*Faculty of Chemistry:* Prof. Dr. Dimche Toshev.

## SVEUČILIŠTE U SPLITU
### (University of Split)
58000 SPLIT, LIVANJSKA 5/1

Telephone: (058) 49966.
Founded 1974.
State control; Language of instruction: Croatian; Academic year: September to August.

*Rector:* Dr. Anton Afrić.
*Pro-Rectors:* Dr. Ivo Gančević, Dr. Ivo Petricioli.
*Secretary-General:* (vacant).

Libraries are in the course of formation.

Number of teachers: 618.
Number of students: 11,646.

Publication: *Red predavanja.*

### DEANS:

*Faculty of Law:* Dr. Vjekoslav Šmid.
*Faculty of Electrical, Mechanical and Marine Engineering:* Dr. Martin Jadrić.
*Faculty of Philosophy (Zadar):* Dr. Tomislav Grgin.
*Faculty of Economics:* Dr. Marin Buble.
*Faculty of Technology:* Dr. Stjepan Lipanović.
*Faculty of Civil Engineering:* Jakša Miličić, B.Sc.
*Faculty of Tourism and Foreign Trade (Dubrovnik):* Dr. Donko Mirković.

### PROFESSORS:

*Faculty of Law:*
Anzulović, Ž., Introduction to Law
Borković, I., Administrative Law
Cvitanić, A., State and Legal History
Dujić, A., Theory of State and Comparative Political Systems
Grabovac, I., Maritime and General Transport Law
Komazec, S., Financial Studies
Petrinović, I., Political Theory
Rudolf, D., International Public Law
Vrcan, S., Sociology

*Faculty of Electrical, Mechanical and Marine Engineering:*
Afrić, A., Electrical Networks, Information Theory
Čišić, M., Electric Machines and Devices
Gugić, P., Automatic Regulation, Biocybernetics
Petković, I., Mechanics, Ship Stability, Theory of Mechanisms
Pilić, Lj., Hydromechanics
Slapničar, P., Pulse and Digital Circuits, Computer Aided Design

*Faculty of Technology:*
Krstulović, R., Processes of Inorganic Chemistry
Roje, U., Processes of Organic Industry
Zglav, M., Technological Operations in Chemical Industries

*Faculty of Philosophy (Zadar):*
Brida, Marija, History of Philosophy
Brozović, D., Croato-Serbian Language
Čimić, E., Systematic Sociology
Festini, H., Systematic Philosophy
Festini, M., Italian Language
Foretić, D., 20th-Century History of the Yugoslav People
Franić, A., Modern Croatian Literature
Glavičić, B., Greek Language and Literature
Ivanišin, Nikola, Recent Croatian Literature
Kolumbić, N., Old Croatian Literature
Košutić-Brozović, N., World Literature
Krstulović, A., Sculpture
Marasović, T., Medieval Art in Yugoslavia and Europe
Petricioli, I., Yugoslav Art History
Prijatelj, K., Renaissance and Baroque Art
Rabac-Čondrić, Glorija, Italian Literature
Zaninović, M., History of Pedagogy

## YUGOSLAVIA

*Faculty of Economics:*
DOMANČIĆ, P., Finance
PETRIĆ, I., Economic System of Yugoslavia

*Faculty of Tourism and Foreign Trade:*
KOBAŠIĆ, A., Marketing
MARKOVIĆ, S., Tourist Economy and Planning

### UNIVERZITET "VELJKO VLAHOVIĆ" U TITOGRADU
**(University of Titograd)**

P.O.B. 105, 81000 TITOGRAD

Telephone: (081) 52981.

Founded 1974 from existing faculties and high schools in Titograd, Nikšić and Kotor.

Academic year: October to July.

Language of instruction: Serbo-Croat.

*Rector:* Prof. MILJAN RADOVIĆ.
*Vice-Rector for Teaching:* Prof. MILENKO PASINOVIĆ.
*Vice-Rector for Finance:* Prof. LUKA VUJOŠEVIĆ.
*Vice-Rector for Research Work:* Prof. ŽARKO KALEZIĆ.
*Registrar:* DRAGIŠA IVANOVIĆ.
*Librarian:* VASO JOVOVIĆ.

Number of teachers: 540.
Number of students: c. 18,000.

DEANS:

*Law:* Prof. BRANISLAV IVANOVIĆ.
*Economics:* Prof. MIRKO PETRANOVIĆ.
*Electrical Engineering:* Prof. SVETOZAR JOVIĆEVIĆ.
*Metallurgy:* Prof. BOŠKO PEROVIĆ.
*Mechanical Engineering:* Prof. BOŽIDAR NIKOLIĆ.
*Education:* Prof. SLOBODAN VUKIĆEVIĆ.
*Higher Marine School, Kotor:* Prof. BORISLAV IVOŠEVIĆ.

ATTACHED RESEARCH INSTITUTES:

**Institute for Biological and Medical Research:** Dir. Dr. GORDON KARAMAN.

**History Institute:** Dir. Dr. JOVAN BOJEVIĆ.

**Agricultural Institute:** Dir. Dr. ŽARKO KALEZIĆ.

### UNIVERZITET U TUZLI*
**(University of Tuzla)**

RUDARSKA 71, 75000 TUZLA, BOSNIA-HERZEGOVINA

Founded 1976; in process of formation.

Telephone: (38-75) 34-650.

*Rector:* Prof. T. MARKOVIĆ.

Number of teachers: 465.
Number of students: 15,000.

Faculties of technology, mining and geology, education, commerce, electrical engineering, medicine.

* No reply received to our questionnaire this year.

### SVEUČILIŠTE U ZAGREBU
**(University of Zagreb)**

TRG MARŠALA TITA 14,
P.O.B. 815, 41001 ZAGREB

Telephone: (041) 32451.

Founded 1669.

Academic year: September to August; Language of instruction: Croatian literary language.

*Rector:* Dr. IVAN JURKOVIĆ.
*Pro-Rectors:* Dr. BOŠIDAR JELČIC, Dr. KREŠIMIR ČUPAK, Dr. BOŠKO BJELAJAC.
*Secretary-General:* DAVOR DELIĆ.

Number of teaching staff: 2,872.
Number of students: 35,886.

Publications: *Sveučilišni vjesnik* (University Herald), *Red predavanja* (Syllabus).

DEANS OF FACULTIES:

*Philosophy:* Dr. M. SUIĆ.
*Law:* Dr. Ž. MATIĆ.
*Economic Sciences:* Dr. V. FRANC.
*Natural Sciences and Mathematics:* Dr. I. CRKVENČIĆ.
*Medicine:* Dr. M. SEKSO.
*Stomatology:* Dr. I. MIŠE.
*Veterinary Medicine:* Dr. V. MITIN.
*Pharmacy and Biochemistry:* Dr. A. GERTNER.
*Architecture:* Dr. S. GVOZDANOVIĆ.
*Civil Engineering:* Dr. A. SOLC.
*Geodesy:* V. PETKOVIĆ.
*Mechanical and Marine Engineering:* Dr. F. DUSMAN.
*Electrical Engineering:* Dr. A. ŠANTIĆ.
*Technology:* Dr. M. BRAVAR.
*Mining Engineering, Geology and Petroleum:* Dr. I. STEINER.
*Agriculture:* Dr. J. GOTLIN.
*Forestry:* Dr. I. DEKANIĆ.
*Political Sciences:* Dr. P. NOVOSEL.
*Defectology:* Dr. V. KOVAČEVIĆ.
*Metallurgy (Sisak):* Dr. Y. LOGOMERAC.
*Physical Education:* Dr. V. JURAS.
*Foreign Trade:* Dr. M. CEROVAC.
*Organization and Informatics (Varaždin):* Dr. F. RUŽA.
*University Interfaculty Studies:* Dr. B. EMAN, Dr. D. SREMAC, Dr. S. KLJAIĆ.

PROFESSORS:

*Faculty of Philosophy:*
ANIĆ, A., Contemporary Croatian Literary Language
BABIĆ, S., Contemporary Croatian Literary Language
BEKER, B., Theory and Methodology of Literary Research
BOBAN, B., History of Yugoslav Peoples
BOGIŠIĆ, R., Old Croatian Literature
BOŠNJAK, B., History of Philosophy
BRANDT, M., General Medieval History
BRATANIĆ, B., Ethnology
BUJAS, Z., Fundamentals of Psychological Statistics, Physiological Bases of Psychological Phenomena
BUJAS, Ž., English Language
ČALE, F., Italian Literature
ČUBELIĆ, T., National Literature
CVJETIČANIN, V., Political Sociology

DIMITRIJEVIĆ, S., Prehistoric Archaeology
FILIPOVIĆ, R., English Language
FLAKER, A., Russian Literature
FRANGEŠ, I., Modern Croatian Literature
GRLIĆ, D., Aesthetics
GROSS, M., Croatian History
GUBERINA, P., Phonetics
HERCIGONJA, E., Old Slavic Language
HORVAT-PINTARIĆ, V., Visual Communications and Design, Theory of Plastic Art
IVANČEVIĆ, R., Art History of Yugoslav Nations
JERNEJ, J., Italian Language
KANGRGA, M., Ethics and Aesthetics
KARAMAN, I., Economics of History
KAŠTELAN, J., Theory of Literature
KLAIĆ, N., Croatian History
KUVAČIĆ, I., Introduction to Methodology, Theoretical Elements of Sociology
MATVEJEVIĆ, P., French Literature
MENAC, A., Russian Language
MILIĆEVIĆ, N., Modern Croatian Literature
MOGUŠ, M., History and Dialectology of Croatian Language
MUŽIĆ, V., Theoretical Education
OGRIZOVIĆ, M., History of Education
PEJOVIĆ, D., History of Philosophy
PETROVIĆ, G., Theoretical Philosophy
PETZ, B., Industrial Psychology
POLJAK, V., Didactics and Methodics
PRANJIĆ, K., Contemporary Croatian Literary Language
PRELOG, M., History of Medieval Art, History and Theory of Town Planning
RENDIĆ-MIOČEVIĆ, D., Archaeology
ROSANDIĆ, D., Methodology of Croatian Language
SIRONIĆ, M., Greek Language and Literature
SOLAR, M., World Literature
SPALATIN, L., English Language
SUIĆ, M., General Ancient History
ŠICEL, M., Modern Croatian Literature
TEKAVČIĆ, P., Italian Language
VIDAN, I., English and American Literature
VINJA, V., Roman Linguistics
VONČINA, J., History of Croatian Literary Language
VRATOVIĆ, V., Latin Language and Literature
VUKASOVIĆ, A., Theoretical Education
ZANINOVIĆ, M., Archaeology
ZORIĆ, M., Italian Literature
ŽMEGAČ, V., German Literature

*Faculty of Law:*
BAČIĆ, F., Criminal Law
BAKOTIĆ, B., International Law
BAYER, V., Criminal Procedure Law
BEUC, I., History of State and Civil Rights in Yugoslavia
BOSANAC, M., Sociology
DRAGIČEVIĆ, A., Political Economics
GOLDŠTAJN, A., Commercial Law
IBLER, V., International Public Law
IVANČEVIĆ, V., Administrative Law
JAKAŠA, B., Maritime and General Transport Law
JELČIĆ, B., Finance and Financial Law
KRIZMAN, B., General History of State and Law
LANG, R., Political Economy
MATIĆ, Ž., International Private Law
PERIĆ, B., Principles of Theory of State and Law
PULIŠELIĆ, S., Sociology
PUSIĆ, E., Theory of Management
ROMAC, A., Roman Law
SEJKO, K., International Private Law

SIROTKOVIĆ, H., History of State and Civil Rights of Yugoslavia
TINTIĆ, N., Labour and Social Security Law
TRIVA, S., Civil Procedure Rights
VEDRIŠ, M., Civil Rights

*Faculty of Economic Science:*
ALFIER, D., Economics of Tourism
BAZALA, A., Market Analysis, Marketing
ĆOSIĆ, B., Political Economy
JELEN, I., Economic Geography
JURIN, S., Political Economy
KRAL, V., Accountancy, Financial Control
MARTIĆ, LJ., Mathematical Methods in Economic Analysis
MEDARIĆ, J., Economic Geography, Ecology
MEDVEŠČEK, I., Marketing
NOVAK, M., Organization of Work in Socialism, Business Organization
OBRAZ, R., Marketing
PERTOT, V., Economy of International Exchange
ROCCO, F., Market Sales Research, Marketing
VRANČIĆ, I., Political Economy
WERTHEIMER-BALETIĆ, A., Demography, Political Economy

*Faculty of Natural Sciences and Mathematics:*
ALAGA, G., Electrodynamics
BALENOVIĆ, K., Organic Chemistry
BARIŠIĆ, S., Solid State Physics
BONEFAČIĆ, A., Physics
CRKVENČIĆ, I., Geography
DEVIDÉ, Z., Plant Physiology and Cell Biology
DJULIĆ, B., Vertebrate Zoology
DOMAC, R., Botany
FRIGANOVIĆ, M., Geography
GAMULIN-BRIDA, H., Zoogeography, Marine Biology
GRDENIĆ, D., Inorganic Chemistry
HERAK, MARKO, Analytical Chemistry
HERAK, MILAN, Geology
ILAKOVAC, K., Physics
ILIJANIĆ, LJ., Geobotany and Plant Ecology
JANKOVIĆ, Z., Theoretical Mechanics
KAMENAR, B., Inorganic Chemistry
KAŠTELAN, A., Animal Physiology
KOCHANSKY-DEVIDÉ, V., Palaeobotany, Palaeobiology
KRANJC, K., Physics
KUREPA, S., Functional and Mathematical Analysis
LEONTIĆ, B., Physics
MAKJANIĆ, B., Dynamic Meteorology
MARDEŠIĆ, S., Topology
MARUŠIĆ, A., Elements of Marxism, Sociology of Knowledge
MATONIČKIN, I., Zoology
MEŠTROV, M., Biology, Animal Ecology
MILIČIĆ, D., General Botany
MIRNIK, M., Physical Chemistry
PALMAN, D., Geometry
PAPIĆ, P., Mathematics
PAVLETIĆ, Z., Microbiology, Thallophyta
POLŠAK, A., Geology
RIDJANOVIĆ, J., Hydrogeography
RODÈ, B., Animal Histology, Embryology
ROGIĆ, V., Geography of Yugoslavia
SOUČEK, B., Computers
SUNKO, D., Organic Chemistry
SUPEK, I., Modern Physics and Philosophy
ŠĆAVNIČAR, S., Mineralogy
ŠEGOTA, T., Climatology
ŠTEFANAC, Z., Analytic Chemistry
TADIĆ, D., Quantum Physics
WOLF, R., Physical Chemistry

*Faculty of Medicine:*
ALLEGRETTI, N., Physiology
BAGOVIĆ, P., Gynaecology and Obstetrics
BAKRAN, I., Surgery
BARAC, B., Neurology
BAŠIĆ, M., Radiology
BENČIĆ, S., General Epidemiology
BEZJAK, B., Infectious Diseases
BLAŽEVIĆ, D., Medical Psychology
BOHAČEK, N., Psychiatry
BOŽOVIĆ, LJ., Physiology
BRADIĆ, I., Surgery
BRUDNJAK, Z., Microbiology
BUNAREVIĆ, A., General Pathology, Pathological Anatomy
ČEČUK, L., Urology
ČERLEK, S., Internal Medicine
ČIČIN-SAIN, Š., Radiology
ČUPAK, K., Ophthalmology
DEŽELIĆ, D., Hygiene, Application of Electronic Counters
DROBNJAK, P., Gynaecology and Obstetrics
DÜRRIGL, T., Physical Medicine and Rehabilitation
FALIŠEVAC, J., Infectology
FEMENIĆ, B., Oto-Rhino-Laryngology
FIŠTER, V., Physiology
GALINOVIĆ-WEISGLASS, M., Microbiology
GRČEVIĆ, N., General Pathology, Pathological Anatomy
GRGUREVIĆ, M., Gynaecology and Obstetrics
HAJNŠEK, F., Neurology
HANČEVIĆ, J., Surgery
HAUPTMAN, E., Internal Medicine
HIRTZLER, R., General Pathology, Pathological Anatomy
IVANČIĆ, R., Internal Medicine
IVANIŠEVIĆ, B., Surgery
JAKŠIĆ, Z., Social Medicine
JUŠIĆ, A., Neurology
KALAFATIĆ-VLATKOVIĆ, Z., Paediatrics
KALLAI, L., Internal Medicine
KARAS-GAŠPARAC, V., Chemistry
KEROS, P., Human Anatomy
KNEŽEVIĆ, S., Internal Medicine
KOSANOVIĆ, F., Oto-laryngology
KRAJINA, Z., Oto-Rhino-Laryngology
KRMPOTIĆ, J., Human Anatomy
KRSTULOVIĆ, B., General Pathology, Pathological Anatomy
KUBOVIĆ, M., General Clinical Oncology
LUETIĆ, V., Surgery
LUKOVIĆ, G., Statistics
LJUŠTINA, N., Ophthalmology
MANDIĆ, V., Physical Medicine and Rehabilitation
MARK, B., Radiology
MATASOVIĆ, T., Orthopaedics
MENIGA, A., Hygiene
MILIĆ, N., Internal Medicine
MILKOVIĆ, K., Biology
NIKOLIĆ, V., Human Anatomy
OBERMAN, B., General Pathology, Pathological Anatomy
OREŠKOVIĆ, M., Oto-Rhino-Laryngology
PADOVAN, I., Oto-Rhino-Laryngology
PALMOVIĆ, V., Forensic Medicine
PASINI, M., Surgery
PERŠIĆ, N., Psychiatry
PETROKOV, V., Surgery
POPOVIĆ, B., Sociol Medicine
POPOVIĆ, M., Biochemistry
POSINOVEC, J., Histology and Embryology
PROŠTENIK, M., Biochemistry
PRPIĆ, I., Surgery
RADONIĆ, M., Internal Medicine
RADOŠEVIĆ, Z., Internal Medicine
RAJHVAJN, B., Gynaecology and Obstetrics
RICHTER, B., Microbiology
RUDEŽ, V., Human Anatomy
RUSZKOVSKI, I., Orthopaedics

SEKSO, M., Internal Medicine
SKALOVA, R., Hygiene
SKURIĆ, Z., Hygiene
SUPEK, Z., Pharmacology
ŠIK, T., Paediatrics
ŠIMONOVIĆ, I., Clinical Propaedeutics
ŠKRABALO, Z., Clinical Propaedeutics
ŠKRBIĆ, M., Marxism
ŠKREB, N., Biology
ŠRENGER, Ž., Ophthalmology
ŠTAJDUHAR-CARIĆ, Z., Forensic Medicine
ŠTAMPAR-PLASAJ, B., Paediatrics
STANČIĆ-ROKOTOV, F., Surgery
TIEFENBACH, A., Paediatrics
URBANKE, A., General Pathology, Pathological Anatomy
VALIĆ, F., Hygiene, Social Medicine
VIDOVIĆ, M., Surgery
VLATKOVIĆ, G., Paediatrics
VUKADINOVIĆ, S., Paediatrics
WINTERHALTER, D., Physics
ZERGOLLEN-ČUPAK, LJ., Paediatrics
ŽEŠKOV, P., Paediatrics
ZIMOLO, A., General Pathology and Pathological Anatomy

*Faculty of Stomatology:*
AURE-KOŽELJ, J., Oral Pathology
BARIĆ, LJ., Internal Medicine
DOBRENIĆ, M., Oral Pathology
GABRIĆ, D., Physiology, Biochemistry
HUDOLIN, V., Neurology
KATUNARIĆ, Roentgenology
KNEŽEVIĆ, M., Pathology
KOSOVEL, Z., Fixed Prosthetics
LAPTER, V., Orthodontics
MIŠE, I., Oral Surgery
NIKŠIĆ, D., Mobile Prosthetics
NJEMIROVSKIJ, Z., Dental Pathology
OBERHOFER, B., General Surgery
TOMIĆ, D., Pharmacology
ZELINEK, E., Juvenile and Preventive Stomatology
ŽMEGAČ, Z., Dermato-Venerology

*Faculty of Veterinary Medicine:*
ASAJ, A., Zoohygiene
CVETNIĆ, S., Microbiology and Immunology
ČERMAK, K., Surgery
DELAK, M., Pharmacology and Toxicology
EHRLICH, I., Biology
FIJAN, N., Biology and Pathology of Fish and Bees
FINDRIK, M., Nutrition of Domestic Animals
FORENBACHER, S., Internal Diseases of Domestic Animals
FRANK, A., Anatomy, Histology and Embryology
HERAK, M., Obstetrics, Sterility and Artificial Insemination
ILIJAŠ, B., Radiology and Physical Therapy
IVOŠ, J., Zoohygiene
KALIVODA, M., Nutrition of Domestic Animals
KRALJ, M., Pathology of Poultry
KRVAVICA, S., Pathological Physiology
LJUBIĆ, I., Hygiene and Technology of Animal Victuals
MAŘAN, B., Pathological Anatomy
MARTINČIĆ, T., Pathological Physiology
MITIN, V., Physiology, Radiobiology
RAKO, A., Animal Husbandry
SREBOČAN, V., Pharmacology and Toxicology
SVIBEN, M., Applied Biology in Nutrition of Domestic Animals
TIMET, D., Physiology
TOPOLNIK, E., Microbiology, Immunology
VALPOTIĆ, I., Physiology

WIKERHAUSER, T., Parasitology and Invading Diseases
ŽUKOVIĆ, M., Parasitology and Invading Diseases

*Faculty of Pharmacy and Biochemistry:*
AŠPERGER, S., Physical Chemistry
BEZJAK, A., General and Inorganic Chemistry
BORČIĆ, S., Organic Chemistry
GERTNER, A., Analytical Chemistry, Water and Atmosphere
HERAK, J., Physics
**KOLBAH, D., Organic Chemistry**
MALNAR, M., Biochemistry, Organic Chemistry
**MILKOVIĆ, S., Pharmacology**
MOVRIN, M., Pharmaceutical Chemistry and Biochemistry of Medicaments
PAVLOVIĆ, D., Physical Chemistry
PETRIĆEVIĆ, V., Pharmaceutical Technology
**PETRIČIĆ, J., Pharmacognosy**
ŠTIVIĆ, I., Pharmaceutical Technology
ŠTRAUS, B., Medical Biochemistry

*Faculty of Architecture:*
BOLTAR, D., Town Planning
GVOZDANOVIĆ, S., Historical Development of Architecture
KORAĆ, V., Analysis of Materials, Basic Civil Engineering
MARINOVIĆ-UZELAC, A., Spacial Planning, Town Planning
**MILIĆ, B., Town Planning**
**MOHOROVIČIĆ, A., History of Art, Theory of Architecture**
RAŠICA, B., Architecture of Public Buildings, Architectural Design
ROSMAN, R., Theory of Construction, Constructive Project
ŠEGVIĆ, N., Modern Architecture, Architecture of Yugoslav Nations, Architectural Design

*Faculty of Civil Engineering:*
BRITVEC, S., Dynamics of Constructions
IVANČIĆ, M., Steel Construction, Theory of Stability
KOSTRENČIĆ, Z., Analysis of Materials and Constructions
NIKŠIĆ, R., Building Construction
NONWEILLER, E., Geomechanics, Foundation Laying
SIMOVIĆ, V., Structural Statics
ŠOLC, A., Roads
SVETLIČIĆ, E., Regulations, Hydrology
TONKOVIĆ, K., Large-Scale Bridges
ŽUGAJ, N., Use of Water Power

*Faculty of Geodesy:*
**BRAUM, F., Photogrammetry**
DOČKAL, M., Descriptive Geometry
KLAK, S., Geophysics, Gravimetry
MACAROL, S., Lower Geodesy
MIŠIĆ, R., Theoretical Mechanics
RANDIĆ, L., Spherical Astronomy
SREBRENOVIĆ, D., Hydraulics, Melioration, Hydrology and Hydrometry

*Faculty of Mechanical and Naval Engineering:*
BRLEK, V., Cooling Technique, Thermodynamics, Thermal Processes and Equipment
**DEVIDÉ, V., Mathematics**
ESIH, J., Physical Chemistry, Materials Protection
JAEGER, H., Organization of Production
KREUH, L., Steam Boilers, Thermoenergetic Machinery
MAJCEN, M., Thermoturbines, Turbocompressors
OBERŠMIT, E., Machine Elements, Mechanical Constructions

ŠAVAR, Š., Surveying
**SERDAR, J., Sprocket Wheels, Locomotives and Cranes**
TABORŠAK, D., Work Study
TURK, I., Thermodynamics
URŠIĆ, J., Theory of Ships, Strength of Ships
VUČETIĆ, A., Mechanics, Theory of Vibration
ZDENKOVIĆ, R., Tool Machinery
ZGAGA, R., Metals

*Faculty of Electrical Engineering:*
BABIĆ, H., Theory of Linear Systems and Signalling, Design of Active and Passive Filters
BEGO, V., Electrotechnical Measuring, Measuring Technique
BOSANAC, T., Physical Basis of Electrical Engineering, Electric Fields and Circuits, Energy Conversion
GREGURIĆ, M., Receivers, Tone Frequency and Magnetic Registering
HAZNADAR, Z., Electrical Engineering, Theoretical Electrical Engineering
JURKOVIĆ, B., Electromotor Operations, Motor Operations, Electric Machines
KNAPP, V., Physics, Elements and Application of Over Conductibility
KVIZ, B., Radiotelemetrics, Radiocommunications
**LOPAŠIĆ, V., Physics**
MATKOVIĆ, V., Information Theories
MULJEVIĆ, V., Theory of Automatic Regulation, Automatic Regulation, Industrial Measuring
PADELIN, M., High Frequency Technique,
PERUŠKO, U., Electronic Concatenation, Impulsive and Digital Electronics, Digital Computers
POŽAR, H., Electric Plants and Instruments, Elements of Electroenergetics, Distribution of Charge in Electroenergesic System
SIROTIĆ, Z., Electric Machines, Constructions of Electric Rotating Machines
SMILJANIĆ, G., Electronic and Digital Computers
SMRKIĆ, Z., High Frequency Technique, Radio Relay System, Radiocommunications
STEFANINI, B., Electrical Engineering
ŠANTIĆ, A., Electronic Instrumentation, Biomedical Electronics
TURK, S., Computers
VUKOVIĆ, Z., Multiplex Systems, Efficacy of Information Systems, Digital Transmitting Systems, Transmission of Data, Economy of Electrical Systems
WOLF, R., Electric Machines, Electric Machines Laboratory, Electric Motors
ZENTNER, E., Radiocommunications
ŽUPAN, J., Logical Algebra, Commutation Systems

*Faculty of Technology:*
ALAČEVIĆ, M., Microbe Genetics, Industrial Microbiology
BAKOVIĆ, D., Dairy Technology
BAN, S., Technology of Fermentation, Technological Design
BAUMAN, E., Chemical Engineering
BRAVAR, M., Macromolecular Processes, Technological Processes, Technology of Chemical Industries
ČAVLEK, B., Meat and Fish Technology
FILAJDIĆ, M., Food Analysis
FILIPOVIĆ, I., Inorganic Chemistry
GRÜNER, M., Food Analysis
JAKOPČIĆ, K., Organic Chemistry
JOHANIDES, V., Industrial Microbiology

JOVANOVIĆ-KOLAR, J., Chemistry of Paints, Technological and Chemical Industry Processing
**JURILJ, A., Biology with Technical Microscopy**
KOLIN, I., Thermodynamics
KUNST, B., Physical Macromolecular Chemistry
LAĆAN, M., Organic Chemistry
LOVREČEK, B., Electrochemistry, Eelctrical Engineering
LOVREČEK, I., Chemical Engineering
LOVRIĆ, T., Nutritional Engineering
MIHELIĆ, F., Food Analysis
MILDNER, P., Biochemistry, Molecular Biology
**MITROVIĆ, D., Higher Mathematics**
PETRIČIĆ, A., Milk Technology
PILJAC, I., General and Inorganic Chemistry, Instrumental Analysis
SOLJAČIĆ, I., Textile Cleaning and Finishing

*Faculty of Mining Engineering, Geology and Petroleum:*
CRNKOVIĆ, B., Petrography
JURKOVIĆ, I., Science of Mine Location, Mining Microscopy
KRANJEC, V., Geological Map-making, Structural Geology
MAGDALENIĆ, A., Hydrogeology, Engineering Geology
MAJER, V., Petrology, Sedimentology
MARUŠIĆ, R., Mineral Grading and Metallurgy
MILETIĆ, P., Engineering Geology and Hydrogeology
PROTIĆ, R., Economy of Naphtha Enterprises
ŠARC-LAHODNY, O., Physical Chemistry
ŠINKOVEC, B., Mineralogy
VIJEC, S., Mechanics of Rocks, Ventilation and Mine Drainage
VRAGOVIĆ, M., Mineralogy and Petrology, Geochemistry
ZAGORAC, Ž., Geophysical Exploration

*Faculty of Agriculture:*
ANIĆ, J., Plant Nutrition, Basic Agriculture
BARIĆ, S., Statistical Methods, Research Technique in Cattle Breeding
BRČIĆ, J., Agricultural Machinery, Storage
CAR, M., Cattle-Raising and Horse-Breeding
ČIŽEK, J., Fodder Production
DOKMANOVIĆ, D., Organization and Management of Agricultural Enterprises
GAŽI, V., Agricultural Botany
GLIHA, R., Special Fruit Cultivation
GOTLIN, J., Industrial Plants, Agricultural Cultures, Bases of Special Agriculture
HORGAS, D., Chemistry, Biochemistry
JANČIĆ, S., Pig and Sheep Breeding
KIŠPATIĆ, J., Phytopathology
KOMUNJER, J., Agricultural Machinery
KOVAČEVIĆ, J., Agricultural Phytocenology
KUMP, M., Genetics, Research Technique
LICUL, R., Vine-Growing
MACELJSKI, M., Entomology, Plant Protection
MIHALIĆ, V., General Plant Production
MILATOVIĆ, I., Phytopathology, Plant Protection
MILETIĆ, S., Dairy Manufacturing
PAVLEK, P., Vegetable Cultivation
PLAVŠIĆ, N., Agricultural Botany
PREMUŽIĆ, D., Viticulture
PRŠA, M., Microbiology
RACZ, Z., Pedology
SABADOŠ, D., Technology of Milk and Milk Products

SCHMIDT, L., Zoology for Cattle Breeders, Beekeeping
STILINOVIĆ, Ž., Physiology, Embryology and Anatomy of Domestic Animals
ŠARIĆ, A., Bases of Biology
ŠIKIĆ, D., Agricultural Architecture
ŠKORIĆ, A., Pedology, Bases of Agriculture
STANCL, B., Agricultural Economics
VINCEK, Z., Organization and Management of Agricultural Enterprises
ZLATIĆ, H., Nutrition of Domestic Animals, Cattle-Breeding and Nutrition

*Faculty of Forestry:*
ANDROIĆ, M., Forest Entomology
BENIĆ, R., **Forest Exploitation and Rationalization of Work in Timber Industry**
BOJANIN, S., Forest Exploitation
BREŽNJAK, M., Saw-milling
DEKANIĆ, I., Forest Cultivation Technique
HAMM, D., **Electrotechnics, Wood Machinery**
KLEPAC, D., **Forest Management**
KRALJIĆ, B., Organization and Economics of Forestry
OPAČIĆ, I., Chemical Wood Processing
SPAIĆ, I., Wood Protection
TOMAŠEGOVIĆ, Z., **Forest Photogrammetry, Descriptive Geometry**
VIDAKOVIĆ, M., Forest Genetics, Dendrology

*Faculty of Political Sciences:*
BILANDŽIĆ, D., Political System of Yugoslavia
KLAUZER, J., Statistics
NOVOSEL, P., Theory of Information and Communication
PAŽANIN, A., Philosophy of Politics, Law and History
RENDULIĆ, N., Economy of Yugoslavia
RODIN, D., History of Marxism
SUTLIĆ, V., Political Anthropology

VUKADINOVIĆ, R., International Political Relations
ŽUPANOV, J., Sociology of Work Organization

*Faculty of Physical Education:*
HORVAT, V., Kinesiological Physiology
LANC, M., Biomechanics
MEDVED, R., Sport Medicine
MRAKOVIĆ, M., Systematic Kinesiology
PAVIŠIĆ-MEDVED, V., Foundations of Biological Anthropology
RADAN, Ž., Sport History
RELAC, M., Kinesiological Recreation

*Faculty of Defectology:*
JURAS, Z., Education of the Handicapped
KOVAČEVIĆ, V., Special Psychology, Professional Rehabilitation
STANČIĆ, V., Special Psychology
TONKOVIĆ, F., Education of Blind People, Peripathology
ZOVKO, G., Special Education, Education of the Partially-Sighted

*Faculty of Foreign Trade:*
CEROVAC, M., Political Economy
HORVAT, B., Economic Analysis
KATUNARIĆ, A., Banking Transactions and Bank Policies
KURTEK, P., International and Regional Markets of Goods and Services
MATIĆ, S., Theory and Practice of Socialistic Self-Management
VRSALJKO, K., Regional and International Trade

*Faculty of Metallurgy (Sisak):*
LOGOMERAC, V., Metallurgy of Non-Ferrous Metals and Ferro-alloys
PAVLOVIĆ, P., Theory of Metallurgic Processes

ATTACHED INSTITUTES:

**Institute of Physics:** Zagreb, Bijenička 46; Dir. Dr. V. VUJNOVIĆ.

**Institute of Traffic Science:** Zagreb, Gruška 22; Dir. S. LAMER.

**Institute of Medical Research and Labour Medicine:** Zagreb, Moše Pijade 158; Dir. Dr. M. ŠARIĆ.

**Institute of Social Research:** Zagreb, Tomislavov trg 21; Dir. A. PETAK.

**Institute of Historical Sciences:** Zagreb, Krčka 1; Dir. Dr. M. PRELOG.

**Documentation Centre:** Zagreb, Trg maršala Tita 3; Dir. Dr. N. PRELOG.

**Interuniversity Postgraduate Centre:** Dubrovnik; Dir. Dr. S. KORNINGER.

**University Centre for Pedagogical Education and Research:** Zagreb, Dure Salaja 3; Dir. Dr. A. VUKASOVIĆ.

**University Electronic Computer Centre:** Zagreb, Engelsova b.b.; Dir. Dr. B. STEFANINI.

## FACULTY OF THEOLOGY IN LJUBLJANA

POLJANSKA 4,
61000 LJUBLJANA

Founded 1919 (1952). (Formerly attached to Ljubljana University.)

*Dean:* Prof. Dr. Š. STEINER.

*Pro-Deans:* Dr. M. BENEDIK, Dr. ST. JANEŽIĆ.

The library contains 29,000 vols.

Number of professors: 43.

Publication: *Bogoslovni Vestnik†* (quarterly).

## SCHOOLS AND COLLEGES

**Academy of Fine Arts:** Zagreb, Ilica 85; f. 1907; 33 professors, 118 students; painting, sculpture, graphic art and pedagogy; Dean Prof. OMER MUVADŽIĆ.

**Academy of Applied Arts:** Zagreb; departments of graphic art, ceramics, painting, architecture, sculpture, metals, textiles, printing; 45 professors, 360 students; Dir. Prof. BELIZAR BAHORIĆ.

**Academy of Theatre, Film and Television:** Zagreb, Trg M. Tita 5; depts. of acting, directing, editing, camera and dramaturgy; library of 7,000 vols.; Dean Prof. Dr. NIKOLA BATUŠIĆ.

**Academy of Theatre, Radio, Film and Television:** Ljubljana; f. 1945; attached to Edvard Kardelj University; 29 professors, 65 students; library of 15,403 vols.; Dean Prof. Dr. PRIMOŽ KOZAK; publs. *List Akademije, Informations et Recherches*.

**Akademija za Likovno Umetnost** (*Academy of Fine Arts*): Ljubljana, Erjavčeva ul. 23; f. 1945; attached to Edvard Kardelj University; 19 professors, 119 students; Dean Prof. SLAVKO TIHEC.

**Faculty of Dramatic Arts:** Belgrade, Ho Ši Minova 20; f. 1949; 73 professors and assistants, 395 students; eight main branches: acting, theatre and radio direction and management, dramaturgy, film and TV direction, camera, editing, management; four-year course leading to B.A. and two-year graduate course leading to M.A.; library of 13,000 vols.; Dean Prof. VLADAN SLIJEPČEVIĆ.

**Higher School of Economics:** Belgrade; f. 1956; two-year course leading to a Diploma in Economics, Finance and Commerce; 64 professors, 1,630 students; library of 10,066 vols.; Dir. Prof. N. POTKONJAK.

**Institute of Musicology of the Serbian Academy of Sciences and Arts:** Belgrade, Knez Mihailova 35; f. 1948; music theory and aesthetics, history of Yugoslav music, ethnomusicology of the Balkans; 9 mems.; library of 5,000 vols., recorded Yugoslav folk music and Serbian Orthodox Church music; Dir. DIMITRIJE STEFANOVIĆ.

**Inter-University Centre of Postgraduate Studies:** Frana Bulića 4, 50000 Dubrovnik; f. 1972; an independent institution for international co-operation in teaching and research; library of c. 5,000 vols.; c. 150 staff, 250 students a year; Dir.-Gen. Prof. SIEGFRIED KORNINGER; publ. *Newsletter*.

**Musical Academy:** Belgrade, Maršala Tito 50; f. 1937; 100 professors, 539 students; library of 53,000 scores; Dean VLADIMIR MARKOVIĆ.

**Akademija za glasbo** (*Musical Academy*): Ljubljana, Gosposka 8; f.

1939; 29 professors, 192 students; classes for composition, conducting, voice, piano, string, wind and brass instruments, and department for training music teachers; library of 10,590 vols.; Dean Prof. DANIJEL ŠKERL; publs. *Anthology*, various articles.

**Muzička Akademija** (*Musical Academy*): Sarajevo; depts. of composing, conducting, singing, piano, string and wind instruments, history and folklore, theoretical teaching; Dean MATUSJA BLUM.

**Musical Academy:** 41001 Zagreb, Gundulićeva 6, P.O.B. 528; f. 1827; library of 55,654 vols.; 51 professors, 320 students; Dean Prof. STANKO HORVAT; publs. *Arti Musices* (Yearbook, in Croatian with English summaries), *The International Review of the Aesthetics and Sociology of Music* (in English, French, German and Italian with summaries in English and Croatian, 2 a year).

# ZAIRE
Population 27,869,000

## LEARNED SOCIETIES AND RESEARCH INSTITUTES

**Alliance Française (Délégation Générale):** B.P. 5237, Kinshasa; branches in 13 towns.

**Association Zaïroise des Archivistes, Bibliothécaires et Documentalistes:** B.P. 805, Kinshasa XI; f. 1973; to assist the Government in the planning and organization of archives, libraries and documentation centres; professional training and seminars.

**Bureau de Recherches Géologiques et Minières (B.R.G.M.):** B.P. 1974, Kinshasa I; copper mining; Dir. G. VINCENT. (See main entry under France.)

**Centre Culturel Américain:** coin des Avenues Commerce et Kasavubu, Kinshasa; br. at Lubumbashi.

**Centre d'Exécution de Programmes Sociaux et Economiques (C.E.P.S.E.):** 208 ave. Kasa-Vubu, B.P. 1873, Lubumbashi; f. 1946; aims at social development and the improvement of rural life (Shaba district), and undertakes to educate unemployed young people in farm schools and craft classes; 30 mems.; library of 9,000 vols.; Pres. KAFITWE WA PABOA; Dir. N'KASHAMA KADIMA; Sec.-Gen. NAWEJ YAV; publ. *Problèmes Sociaux Zaïrois* (quarterly).

**Commissariat Général à l'Energie Atomique:** B.P. 868-184, Kinshasa XI; f. 1959; part of Dept. of Energy; scientific research in peaceful applications of atomic energy; 80 staff; library of 2,400 vols.; Commissary Gen. Prof. MALU WA KALENGA; publs. *Revue Zaïroise des Sciences Nucléaires*† (2 a year), *Rapport de Recherche*† (annually), *Bulletin d'information Scientifique et Technique*† (quarterly).

**Goethe-Institut:** B.P. 7465, Kinshasa I; f. 1962; Dir. Dr. CLAUS VON SCHOELER.

**Institut Géographique du Zaïre:** 106 blvd. du 30 Juin, B.P. 3086, Kinshasa-Gombe; f. 1949; geodetic, topographical, photogrammetric and cartographic studies; small library; Dir.-Gen. PUNGU BEYA MULI; Technical Advisor LUMINGU-NDONA.

**Institut de Médecine Tropicale:** B.P. 1697, Kinshasa; f. 1899; clinical laboratory serving Hôpital Mama Yemo with reference laboratory functions for other medical services in Kinshasa; Dir. Dr. DARLY JEANTY, M.D.

**Institut National pour l'Etude et la Recherche Agronomique (INERA):** B.P. 1513, Kisangani; f. 1933 to promote the scientific development of agriculture; 6,010 staff; library of 41,000 vols.; Dir.-Gen. NGONDO-MOJUNGWO; publs. *Rapport Annuel*†, *Programme d'Activités*† (annual).

**Institut de Recherche Scientifique (I.R.S.):** B.P. 3474, Kinshasa/Gombe; f. 1975 by fusion of I.R.S.A.C., O.N.R.D. and C.R.I.A.C.; economics, law, administration, medicine, geology, biology, entomology, geophysics, education, psychology, history, energy and technology, food sciences; 96 research mems.; 8 research centres; library of 11,786 vols. and 2,243 periodicals; Dir.-Gen. Dr. KANKWENDA M'BAYA (acting); publs. *Revue de Recherche Scientifique* (quarterly), *Rapport annuel*.

**Institut de la Conservation de la Nature:** B.P. 4019, Kinshasa II; name changed 1969 from *Institut des Parcs Nationaux*; protection of national parks and conservation of the environment; Dir. Dr.Sc. J. VERSCHUREN.

**Service Géologique:** B.P. 898, 44 avenue des Huileries, Kinshasa I; f. 1939; staff of 250 undertake mineral exploration and geological mapping; library of 7,000 vols.; Dir. GABRIEL DEMBE; publ. *Bulletin et Mémoire*.

**Société des Historiens Zairois:** Campus Universitaire, Lubumbashi; f. 1974; to bring about a better understanding of the nation's past; to organize meetings, etc. for historians; to preserve the national archives, works of art, and archaeological remains; Pres. Prof. NDAYWEL E NZIEM; Sec.-Gen. LUMENGA NESO.

## LIBRARIES AND ARCHIVES

**Archives de Zaïre:** B.P. 3428, 42 ave. de la Justice, Kinshasa; f. 1949.

**Bibliothèque Centrale de l'Université Nationale du Zaïre, Campus de Kinshasa:** B.P. 125, Kinshasa XI; f. 1954; 300,000 vols.; Chief Librarian (vacant); publs. *Annales de la Faculté de Droit*†, *Annales de la Faculté de Médecine et de Pharmacie*†, *Annales de la Faculté des Sciences*, *Annales des Facultés Polytechniques*, *Cahiers Economiques et Sociaux*† (quarterly), *Lettre mensuelle de l'I.R.E.S.*, *Liste des Acquisitions*, *Nouvelles du Mont Amba*† (weekly).

**Bibliothèque Centrale de l'Université Nationale, Campus de Kisangani:** B.P. 2022, Kisangani; 26,000 vols.; Chief Librarian LELO MAMOSI; publ. *Revue Zaïroise de Psychologie et de Pédagogie*†.

**Bibliothèque Centrale de l'Université Nationale, Campus de Lubumbashi:** P.O.B. 2896, Lubumbashi; f. 1955; 92,235 vols.; Librarian H. KAPIPASEKA; publs. *Revue de l'Université Nationale du Zaïre, Séries A, Lettres, Cahiers Philosophiques Africains* (every 2 months), *Likundoli* (irregular).

**Bibliothèque Publique:** B.P. 410, Kinshasa; f. 1932; 24,000 vols.; Librarian B. MONGU.

## MUSEUMS

**Institut des Musées Nationaux:** B.P. 4249, Kinshasa 2; f. 1970; art, archaeology, traditional music and contemporary art; Pres.-Dél.-Gen. J. CORNET; publ. *Rapport Annuel*.

**Musée National de Kananga:** B.P. 612.

**Musée National de Lubumbashi:** B.P. 2375; Curator, GUY DE PLAEN.

## UNIVERSITY

### UNIVERSITÉ NATIONALE DU ZAIRE
B.P. 13.399, KINSHASA I
Telephone: 31-147.

State control; Academic year: October to July (2 terms).

*Rector:* Mgr. Tshibangu Tshishiku.
*General Administrator:* Mpeye Nyango.
*Director of International Relations:* Akwesi Ngobaasu.

Number of teachers: c. 2,450.
Number of students: 28,000.

#### Campus de Kinshasa
B.P. 127, Kinshasa XI
Telephone: 77-920.

Founded 1954.

Founded as the Université Lovanium by the Université Catholique de Louvain in collaboration with the Government; reorganized 1971.

Language of instruction: French; Academic year: October to July.

*Vice-Rector:* Prof. Léon de Saint Moulin.
*Secretary-General:* Kapeta Nzovu.
*Librarian:* (vacant).

Library: see Libraries.
Number of teachers: 536.
Number of students: 5,858.
Publications: *Cahiers Economiques et Sociaux* (quarterly), *Cahiers des Religions Africaines* (weekly).

Faculties of law, medicine, pharmacy, sciences, economics, engineering.

ATTACHED RESEARCH INSTITUTES:

**Institut de recherches économiques et sociales (I.R.E.S.):** B.P. 257, Kinshasa XI; Dir. B. Luemba.

**Centre de Coordination des Recherches et de la Documentation en Sciences Sociales en Afrique Sud-Saharienne (C.E.R.D.A.S.).**

**Centre de Criminologie.**

**Centre Interdisciplinaire d'Etudes et de Documentation Politiques (C.I.E.-D.O.P.).**

**Centre Universitaire d'Orientation (C.U.O.).**

#### Campus de Kisangani
B.P. 2012, Kisangani
Telephone: 2837.

Founded 1963; reorganized 1971 (formerly Université Libre du Congo).

State control; Language of instruction: French; Academic year: October to July (three terms).

*Vice-Rector:* Buka Eka Ngoy.
*Administrative Secretary:* Imbata Bosumbe.
*Academic Secretary:* Tshimanga Wa Tshibangu.

*Librarian:* Lelo Mamosi.
Library: see Libraries.
Number of teachers: 149.
Number of students: 1,275.
Publications: *Revue Zaïroise de Psychologie et de Pédagogie* (2 a year), *Annales de la Faculté d'Agronomie (Yangambi).*

DEANS:
*Faculty of Education:* Lumeka Yansenga.
*Faculty of Science:* Wawa Molamba.
*Faculty of Medicine:* Alamita Gheorge.

ATTACHED RESEARCH INSTITUTES:
**Bureau Africain des Sciences de l'Education (B.A.S.E.):** B.P. 14, Kisangani.
**Centre Interdisciplinaire pour le Développement de l'Education (C.R.I.-D.E.):** Dir. Abemba Bulaimu.

#### Campus de Lubumbashi
B.P. 1.825, Lubumbashi (Shaba)
Telephone: 5403-7.

Founded 1955; reorganized 1971.

Language of instruction: French; State control; Academic year: October to July (October–February, March–July).

*Vice-Rector:* Vundwawe Te Pemako.
*Secretary-General (Academic):* Musa Mundedi.
*Secretary-General (Administrative):* Rubuz Difang.

Number of teachers: 403.
Number of students: 4,370.
Publications: various scientific reviews.

DEANS:
*Faculty of Letters:* (vacant).
*Faculty of Social Sciences:* Malela Mwabila.
*Faculty of Sciences:* J. P. Carron.
*Polytechnic Faculty:* (vacant).
*Faculty of Veterinary Medicine:* Kurek Czeslaw.

AFFILIATED RESEARCH INSTITUTES:
**Centre d'Etudes Politiques en Afrique Centrale (C.E.P.A.C.).**
**Centre de Linguistique Théorique et Appliquée (C.E.L.T.A.).**
**Centre d'Etudes de Littérature Africaine (C.E.L.A.).**
**Centre d'Etudes et de Recherches Documentaires pour l'Afrique Centrale (C.E.R.D.A.C.).**

UNIVERSITY INSTITUTES:
**Institut facultaire des sciences agronomiques (I.F.A.):** B.P.28, Yangambi (Haut-Zaïre); first degrees and doctorates in agriculture; 52 staff, 638 students; Dir.-Gen. Pierre Antoine.

**Institut supérieur de techniques appliquées (I.S.T.A.):** B.P. 7.999, Kinshasa I; 87 staff, 833 students; Dir.-Gen. Prof. Makiese.

**Institut des bâtiments et travaux publics (I.B.T.P.):** B.P. 4.731, Kinshasa II; 83 staff, 916 students; Dir.-Gen. Prof. Sabiti Soku.

**Institut supérieur des techniques médicales (I.S.T.M.):** B.P. 774, Kinshasa XI; 80 staff, 1,005 students; Dir.-Gen. Mbendi Nsukimi.

**Institut supérieur de commerce (I.S.C.), Kinshasa:** B.P. 16.596, Kinshasa I; 37 staff, 600 students; Dir.-Gen. Prof. Musenga Tshimpangila.

**Institut supérieur de commerce (I.S.C.), Kisangani:** B.P. 2.012, Kisangani (Haut-Zaïre); Dir. Rutazibwa Iyeze.

**Institut des sciences et techniques de l'information (I.S.T.I.):** B.P. 14.998, Kinshasa I; first degrees and doctorates; 15 staff, 103 students; Dir.-Gen. Malembe Tamandiak.

**Institut supérieur d'études agronomiques (I.S.E.A.) de Bengamisa:** B.P. 202, Kisangani (Haut-Zaïre); 31 staff, 328 students; Dir.-Gen. Nabindi Dena.

**Institut supérieur d'études agronomiques (I.S.E.A.) de Mondongo:** B.P. 22, Lisala (Equateur); 6 staff, 60 students; Dir. Nguba.

**Institut supérieur d'arts et métiers (I.S.A.M.):** B.P. 15.198, Kinshasa I; 16 staff, 101 students; Dir. Omonga Okoka.

**Institut supérieur de développement rural (I.S.D.R.) de Bukavu:** B.P. 2.849, Bukavu (Kivu); 19 staff, 182 students; Dir. Mukuna.

**Institut supérieur d'études sociales (I.S.E.S.) de Lubumbashi:** B.P. 1.575, Lubumbashi (Shaba); 8 staff, 124 students; Dir. Mangala.

**Institut supérieur de statistique (I.S.S.):** B.P. 2.471, Lubumbashi (Shaba); 6 staff, 240 students; Dir.-Gen. Martin de Housse.

**Institut national des arts (I.N.A.):** B.P. 8.332, Kinshasa I; 41 staff, 201 students; Dir. Mbuyamba Lupwishi.

**Académie des beaux-arts (A.B.A.):** B.P. 8.349, Kinshasa I; 44 staff, 248 students; Dir. Pululu.

**Centre interdisciplinaire pour le développement et l'éducation permanente (C.I.D.E.P.):** B.P. 2.307, Kinshasa I; 4-year degree courses studied at evening classes; branches at Kisangani and Lubumbashi; politics and administration, commerce, social sciences, applied education, applied technology; 1,785 students.

# ZAMBIA
Population 5,834,000

## LEARNED SOCIETIES

**British Council:** P.O.B. 34571, Heroes Place, Cairo Rd., Lusaka; Rep. G. A. TINDALE; libraries: see Libraries.

**Commission for the Preservation of Natural and Historical Monuments and Relics:** P.O.B. 124, Livingstone; f. 1948; administers antiquities legislation, records and investigates archaeological sites, controls national monuments; Sec./Inspector JOHN H. ROBERTSON; publs. *Annual Report, Research Publications, Newsletter*.

**Engineering Institution of Zambia, The:** P.O.B. 34730, Lusaka; f. 1955; 700 mems.; Pres. A. MKANDAWIRE; Vice-Pres. J. E. HARPER; publs. *Journal* (quarterly).

**Institution of Mining and Metallurgy:** P.O.B. 450, Kitwe; f. 1950; local section of Institution of Mining and Metallurgy, London; 310 mems.; Chair. J. HOATSON; Hon. Sec. W. G. WATTS.

**Wildlife Conservation Society of Zambia:** P.O.B. 30255, Lusaka; f. 1953; 1,500 mems.; Pres. P. T. S. MILLER, O.B.E.; Exec. Officer R. C. V. JEFFREY; publ. *Black Lechwe* (2 a year).

**Zambia Library Association:** P.O.B. 32839, Lusaka; Chair. Mrs. C. ZULU; Hon. Sec. W. C. MULALAMI; publs. *Journal* (quarterly), *Newsletter* (every 2 months).

**Zambia Medical Association:** P.O.B. RW 148, Lusaka; Chair. Dr. S. SIKANETA, M.D.; Sec. Dr. D. LEVITT, F.C.P.(S.A.); publ. *Medical Journal of Zambia* (every 2 months).

## RESEARCH INSTITUTES

**Central Fisheries Research Institute:** P.O.B. 100, Chilanga; f. 1965; hydrobiological research directed towards increasing fish production; library of 4,000 vols.; Project Man. L. S. JOERIS; publs. *Puku, Fisheries Research Bulletin, Fisheries Statistics, Annual Report*.

**Central Veterinary Research Station:** P.O.B. 50, Mazabuka; f. 1926; directed by the Ministry of Lands and Agriculture; general veterinary diagnosis and research; Asst. Dir., Veterinary Research Dr. M. A. Q. AWAN, PH.D.

**Division of Forest Products Research:** P.O.B. 388, Kitwe; f. 1963; controls research into timber properties and utilization; responsible for product development and dissemination of information; 60 staff; Chief Officer I. E. O. MUSOKOTWANE; publs. *Bulletin, Records* (irregular).

**Division of Forest Research:** P.O.B. 22099, Kitwe; f. 1956; ecological and botanical studies; soil and site assessment investigations; silvicultural research, exotic plantations and indigenous forests and woodlands; mensurational studies of plantation growth; tree breeding and selection; forest pathology and entomology; seed collection, processing, testing and low-temperature storage; staff of 24; library of 1,644 vols., 118 periodicals and 87 serials; Chief Forest Research Officer C. MEKI; publs. *Research Notes, Research Pamphlets, Research Bulletins*.

**Geological Survey of Zambia (Ministry of Mines):** P.O.B. 50135, Ridgeway, Lusaka; f. 1951; statutory depository for mining and prospecting reports; library of c. 39,000 vols.; Dir. E. H. B. MWANANG'ONZE; qualified staff of 40; publs. *Annual Report†, Records†, Bulletins†, Memoirs†, Reports†, Occasional Papers†, Economic Reports†, Annotated Bibliography and Index of the Geology of Zambia†*, and maps.

**Institute for African Studies, University of Zambia:** P.O.B. 30900, Lusaka; f. 1937; there are five current research units: Arts and Communication Studies, Manpower, Community Health, Technology and Industry, Urban Community; 11 research fellows; Dir. ROBERT SERPELL; publs. *African Social Research†, Journal†* (2 a year), *Zambian Papers and Communications†* (annually), *Monographs†* (irregular).

**International Red Locust Control Organisation for Central and Southern Africa:** P.O.B. 37, Mbala; f. 1970; to prevent plagues of Red Locust by controlling incipient outbreaks and to carry out research; member countries: Botswana, Kenya, Lesotho, Malawi, Swaziland, Tanzania, Uganda, Zambia; Dir. M. E. A. MATERU, PH.D.; publs. *Annual Report, Scientific Papers*.

**Mount Makulu Agricultural Research Station:** Private Bag 7, Chilanga; f. 1952; Headquarters of Research Branch of Department of Agriculture, Ministry of Agriculture and Water Development, and 11 regional and specialist research stations; research on soils, soil classification, vegetation types and land classification; agronomy; chemistry; ecology; entomology; pasture research; phytosanitary services; plant breeding; plant pathology; seeds services; stored products entomology; cotton entomology; main crops under investigation: maize, groundnuts, cotton, tobacco, pastures and pasture legumes, beans, etc.; library of 10,000 vols., 10,000 reports, 10,000 reprints; Dir. of Agriculture N. E. MUMBA; publs. *Accessions List* (every 2 months), *Research Branch Memoranda* (occasional), *Farming in Zambia†, Annual Report†, Reprints of Articles by Staff Members†*.

**National Council for Scientific Research:** P.O.B. CH. 158, Chelston, Lusaka; f. 1967; statutory body to advise the government on scientific research policy, to promote and co-ordinate research and to collect and disseminate scientific information; Chair. Hon. D. LISULO, M.P., Prime Minister; Sec.-Gen. Dr. S. M. SILANGWA.

**National Food and Nutrition Commission:** P.O.B. 2669, Lusaka; f. 1967; statutory body to improve the nutritional status of the people of Zambia; 98 mems.; Chair. Hon. J. MUMPANSHYA, M.P.; Exec. Sec. A. P. VAMOER.

**Pneumoconiosis Medical and Research Bureau:** Independence Ave., P.O.B. 205, Kitwe; f. 1950; research on pneumoconiosis and related chest diseases; library of c. 300 vols.; Dir. (vacant).

## LIBRARIES AND MUSEUMS

**British Council Library:** P.O.B. 34571, Lusaka; f. 1973; 9,450 vols., 97 periodicals; Librarian Mrs. DIANA SIMONS; also at P.O.B. 415, Ndola; f. 1951; 11,550 vols., 86 periodicals; Librarian Mrs. V. KAY.

**Hammarskjöld Memorial Library:** P.O.B. 21493, Kitwe; f. 1963; 20,000 vols.; collection of films, filmstrips, tape-recordings on local history; rare book collection on the history of central Africa; specializes in social sciences; resource library and archives of the Mindolo Ecumenical Foundation; Librarian NYAMBE NAMUSHI.

**Kitwe Public Library:** P.O.B. 70, Kitwe.

**Lusaka City Library:** P.O.B. 31304, Katondo Rd., Lusaka; f. 1943; 3 br. libraries and a mobile library; 140,000 vols., 300 periodicals, 420 maps; City Librarian P. C. KULLEEN, M.LIB.SC.; publs. *Library Bulletin*† (quarterly), *Annual Report*.

**National Archives of Zambia:** P.O.B. RW 10, Ridgeway, Lusaka; f. 1947; covers national literature from earliest times to the present day in the forms of national archives, historical MSS., microfilms, cartographic, philatelic, currency, pictorial and printed publication collections; 4,202 linear metres of records; depository and lending library of about 11,500 vols. and 1,000 periodicals; the National Archives Library is a reference and legal deposit library for all printed publications published in Zambia; Dir. P. M. MUKULA, B.A.; Archivist M. P. K. NHANDU, B.A.; Librarian Mrs. K. A. REHMAN, M.A.; publs. *National Bibliography, Guide to the Public Archives*, National Archives occasional papers, descriptive lists, calendars.

**Ndola Public Library:** P.O.B. 70388, Independence Way, Ndola; central library and 5 brs., school library service; 68,000 vols., 50 periodicals; 1,200 special collection; Librarian K. MUMBA CHISAKA.

**Zambia Library Service:** P.O.B. 802, Lusaka; f. 1962; maintains 904 library centres, 6 regional libraries, 3 branch libraries and a central library with 400,000 vols.; aims to provide a countrywide free public library service; Librarian M. WALUBITA; publs. *Bulletin* (quarterly), *Directory of Library Centres* (annually), *Buyers' Guide to Library Equipment* (2 a year).

---

**National Museums Board:** P.O.B. 30198, Lusaka.

**The Livingstone Museum:** Mosi-oa-Tunya Rd., P.O.B. 60498, Livingstone; f. 1934; ethnology of the peoples of Zambia; archaeology, history and natural history of Zambia; autograph, letters and relics of David Livingstone; early maps of Africa; library specializing in archaeology, history, ethnography and Africana; publs. *Zambia Museum Journal, Zambia Museum Papers*, Robins Series of Monographs.

**Copperbelt Museum:** P.O.B. 1444, Ndola.

**Moto Moto Museum:** P.O.B. 55, Mbala.

## UNIVERSITY

### UNIVERSITY OF ZAMBIA

P.O.B. 31338, LUSAKA
Telephone: Lusaka 213221.

Founded 1965; federal system established 1979.

Academic year: October to June (three terms).

*Chancellor:* Dr. KENNETH KAUNDA.
*Vice-Chancellor:* JACOB MWANZA, M.A., PH.D.
*Deputy Vice-Chancellor:* M. J. KELLY, M.A., L.PH., S.T.L.
*Chairman of the Council:* J. M. MWANAKATWE, B.A., LL.B.
*Secretary:* V. G. NYIRENDA, M.S.W., PH.D.
*Librarian:* E. T. K. LWANGA, B.SC., A.L.A.

Library of c. 300,000 vols.

Number of teachers: 445.
Number of students: 3,177.

Publications: *African Social Research, Zambian Papers, Communications, Bulletin.*

#### DEANS:

*Natural Sciences:* Prof. M. SIAMWIZA, PH.D.
*Humanities and Social Sciences:* J. NGWISHA, PH.D. (acting).
*Education:* Prof. T. A. COOMBE, ED.M., PH.D.
*Law:* Prof. MUNA B. NDULO, LL.M., PH.D.
*Engineering:* Prof. D. WHITTAKER, PH.D., C.ENG., F.I.E.E.
*Medicine:* Prof. C. CHINTU, M.D., A.B.D., F.R.C.P., A.INST.P.
*Agriculture:* (vacant).
*Mines:* E. H. JERE, PH.D.

#### ATTACHED INSTITUTES:

**Centre for Continuing Education:** Dir. M. M. KAUNDA, M.S.
**Institute for African Studies:** see Research Institutes.
**Rural Development Studies Bureau:** Dir. (vacant).
**Educational Research Bureau:** Dir. Prof. L. P. TEMBO, M.A., ED.D.
**Institute for Human Relations:** Dir. Prof. J. HATCH.

#### Lusaka Campus

P.O.B. 32379, LUSAKA
*Principal:* Prof. K. MWAULUKA, PH.D.
*Registrar:* J. D. ZULU, M.A.

#### Ndola Campus

P.O.B. 1692, KITWE
Telephone: 210841, 215526.
*Principal:* Prof. M. E. KASHOKI, M.A.
*Registrar:* C. M. MUYANGANA, M.A.
Number of teachers: 13.
Number of students: 380.

#### DEAN:

*Business and Industrial Studies:* Prof. S. NEELAMEGMAN, PH.D.

## COLLEGES

**Evelyn Hone College of Applied Arts and Commerce:** P.O.B. 30029, Lusaka; f. 1963.
*Principal:* A. E. C. MULEMENA, B.A.
*Vice-Principal:* A. W. HODGES, B.A. (ED.).
*Senior Registrar:* E. S. TEMBO (acting).
*Librarian:* E. C. KONDOWE, B.L.S.

The library contains 17,000 vols.

Number of students: 1,200 full-time, 1,500 part-time.

Publications: *Beacon Newspaper* (quarterly), *College Prospectus* (annual).

**National Institute of Public Administration:** P.O.B. 1990, Lusaka; f. 1963; trains government administrators and accounting personnel for central and local government.
*Principal:* A. K. MUKELA.
*Registrar:* M. M. CHISANGA.
*Librarian:* Mrs. B. C. KALENGA.

The library contains 20,000 vols.

Number of teachers: 50.

Number of students: 1,270 (including some on in-training courses).

Publications: *Administration for Rural Development*† (research papers), teaching pamphlets.

## COLLEGES

**Natural Resources Development College:** P.O.B. CH 99, Chelston, Lusaka; f. 1964; 3-year diploma course in agriculture, agricultural education and engineering, fisheries, nutrition, water development.
*Principal:* F. M. MBEWE.
*Vice-Principal:* J. P. ARMITAGE.
*Farm Director:* H. M. NGWIRA.
*Librarian:* (vacant).
 Library of 32,000 vols.
 Number of teachers: 40.
 Number of students: 400.

**Northern Technical College:** P.O.B. KJ 93, Ndola; f. 1964.
*Principal:* S. S. SANGHERA, M.A., C.ENG., M.I.MECH.E., M.E.I.Z.
*Registrar:* ALFRED M. BANDA.
*Librarian:* N. N. CHISOWA, B.A. IN L.S.
 The library contains 12,500 vols.
 Number of students 550 full-time, 600 part-time.

**United Nations Institute for Namibia:** Sadzu Rd., P.O.B. 33811, Lusaka; f. 1976; provides training for Namibians to equip them for organization and administration of government departments and public services in an independent Namibia.
*Director:* HAGE G. GEINGOB.
*Chief Administration Officer:* P. D. LOMBE.
*Registrar:* STAN C. SHANA.
 Number of students: c. 400.

Publications: *UNIN News* (quarterly), *Prospectus* (annually).

**Zambia College of Agriculture:** P.O.B. 53, Monze; f. 1947; 2-year certificate course; 42 staff, 240 students; library of 3,000 vols.; Principal D. H. MCCLEERY.

**Zambia Institute of Technology:** P.O.B. 21993, Kitwe; f. 1970.
*Principal:* M. K. DE BEER, M.SC.(ELEC. ENG.), M.I.E.E.
*Vice-Principal:* E. NGOMA, B.A.(ED.).
*Senior Registrar:* M. J. MUMBATI.
*Student Affairs Officer:* P. N. CHELELWA.
*Librarian:* M. C. BANDA (acting).
 Library of 22,000 vols.
 Number of teachers: 200.
 Number of students: 3,500.

### HEADS OF DEPARTMENT:

*Academic and Industrial Science:* J. S. CHAUDHRY, M.SC., LL.B.
*Business Studies:* A. S. N. PILAI, B.COM.
*Construction:* A. M. CUMARASWAMY, B.SC.
*Electrical Engineering, Electronics, Instrumentation and Telecommunications:* L. D. SIMPITO.
*Instruction Resources:* M. C. BANDA.
*Mining:* S. H. MAJID, B.SC., C.ENG., M.I.M.M., M.I.MIN.E.
*Secretarial and Extension Studies:* R. B. MATHUR, M.A. (COM.).

# ZIMBABWE
Population 7,360,000

## LEARNED SOCIETIES

### Agriculture and Veterinary Science
**Crop Science Society of Zimbabwe:** P.O.B. UA 409, Union Ave., Salisbury; Pres. Prof. M. A. Schweppenhauser.

**Zimbabwe Agricultural and Horticultural Society:** P.O.B. 442, Salisbury; Gen. Man. A. J. Dawkins.

**Zimbabwe Veterinary Association:** P.O.B. 8387, Causeway, Salisbury; Pres. Dr. B. H. Wells; Sec. Dr. D. M. McNerney; publ. *Zimbabwe Veterinary Journal*†.

### Arts
**Salisbury Arts Council:** P.O.B. 4011, Salisbury; f. 1968; Chair. Harold Marsh; Sec. Mrs. Margaret Weare.

### History, Geography and Archaeology
**Geographical Association of Zimbabwe:** c/o Hughes, Mount Pleasant School, P.O.B. MP90, Mount Pleasant, Salisbury; Chair. W. D. Michie; Sec. T. A. Hughes.

**Prehistory Society of Zimbabwe:** P.O.B. 876, Salisbury; f. 1958; promotion of the study of early history, prehistory and archaeology in Africa, with particular reference to Zimbabwe; Chair. C. L. Gale; Sec. Mrs. B. Boaler; publ. *Zimbabwean Prehistory*† (annually).

### International Cultural Institutes
**British Council:** P.O.B. 664, Salisbury; f. 1980; Rep. C. W. Perchard.

### Language and Literature
**The Literature Bureau, Zimbabwe:** P.O.B. 8137, Causeway, Salisbury; f. 1954; a br. of Ministry of Education and Culture; encourages, advises and sponsors African authors, finds publishers for their work and establishes markets for their books; also active in language studies, etc.; Matabeleland branch: P.O.B. 555, Bulawayo; Dir. E. W. Krog; publ. *Bureau Bulletin* (quarterly).

### Medicine
**Cancer Association of Zimbabwe:** P.O.B. 3388, Bulawayo; f. 1959; 423 mems.

**Dental Association of Zimbabwe:** P.O.B. 3303, Salisbury; Pres. Dr. J. Ritchie; Sec. Dr. J. M. Stubbs; publ. *Journal* (2 a year).

**Pharmaceutical Society of Zimbabwe:** P.O.B. 351, Bulawayo; Pres. Mrs. T. Feigenbaum; Sec. A. Cormack.

**Zimbabwe Medical Association:** P.O.B. 3671, Salisbury; Pres. Dr. M. Chiware; Sec. Mrs. R. D. Martin.

### Natural Sciences
#### General
**Zimbabwe Scientific Association:** P.O.B. 978, Salisbury; f. 1899; 350 mems.; Pres. Dr. G. Vale; Hon. Sec. R. Törnbohm; publs. *Proceedings and Transactions*, *Zimbabwe Science News*.

#### Biological Sciences
**Botanical Society of Zimbabwe:** P.O.B. 461, Salisbury; f. 1934; Hon. Sec. J. R. James.

**Kirk Biological Society:** Division of Biological Sciences, University of Zimbabwe, P.O.B. MP167, Mount Pleasant, Salisbury.

**Low Veld Natural History Society:** P.O.B. 112, Chiredzi; Chair. Dr. C. Saunders.

**Ornithological Association of Zimbabwe:** P.O.B. 8382, Causeway, Salisbury; Pres. A. J. Tree; Membership Sec. S. Perrett; publ. *The Honeyguide*†.

**Wildlife Society of Zimbabwe:** P.O.B. 3497, Salisbury; f. 1927; all aspects of wild life conservation; 1,500 mems.; Pres. W. P. Brookes Ball; Vice-Pres. A. C. Pakenham; Hon. Sec. N. Butler; publ. *Zimbabwe Wildlife* (quarterly).

#### Physical Sciences
**Geological Society of Zimbabwe:** P.O.B. 8427, Causeway, Salisbury; Chair. J. G. Lurie; Sec. Dr. R. P. Foster.

**Mennel Society:** Dept. of Geology, University of Zimbabwe, P.O.B. MP 167, Mount Pleasant, Salisbury; f. 1964; to promote the understanding of earth sciences through lectures, films, field trips; 30 mems.; Pres. Prof. G. Bond, PH.D., A.R.C.S., C.ENG., F.I.M.M., F.G.S.; Sec. J. F. Wilson, D.SC., PH.D., F.G.S.; publ. *Detritus*†.

### Technology
**Institution of Mining and Metallurgy (Zimbabwe Section):** P.O.B. 405, Salisbury; f. 1931; Chair. Prof. K. A. Viewing; Hon. Sec. J. H. E. Seear.

**Survey Institute of Zimbabwe:** P.O.B. 3869, Salisbury; f. 1967; 120 mems.; Pres. R. E. Hockey; Hon. Sec. R. Marsden.

**Zimbabwe Institution of Engineers:** P.O.B. 660, Salisbury; f. 1944; 1,200 mems.; Pres. Eng. K. D. Elliott; Sec. Mrs. E. Dudley; publs. *The Zimbabwe Engineer* (every 2 months), *Year Book*.

## RESEARCH INSTITUTES
(see also under University)

**Agricultural Research Council of Zimbabwe:** P.O.B. 8108, Causeway, Salisbury; f. 1970; advises on agricultural research policy and programmes in Zimbabwe; administers 14 regional research institutes and stations through the Department of Research and Specialist Services; Chair. K. D. Kirkman; Exec. Sec. R. C. Smith; publs. *Annual Report*†, *Technical Reports*.

*Department of Research and Specialist Services:* P.O.B. 8108, Causeway, Salisbury; under the Ministry of Agriculture; f. 1948; responsible for research and education in agriculture; Dir. (vacant); Asst. Dir. Crop Research Division W. R. Mills; Asst. Dir. Livestock and Pasture Division Dr. P. Chigaru; Asst. Dir. Research Services Division Dr. P. M. Grant; Head, Education and Executive Branch J. W. Walsh; publs. *Zimbabwe Agricultural Journal*† (every 2 months), technical handbooks† (occasional), *Zimbabwe Journal of Agriculture Research*† (2 a year), *Kirkia*† (annually), annual reports of Institutes and Stations†.

*Research Institutes:*

**Agronomy Institute:** P.O.B. 8100, Causeway; f. 1976; formerly Salisbury Research Station; research into crop agronomy, weed research, crop ecology and crop production; Head (vacant).

**Chemistry and Soil Research Institute:** P.O.B. 8100, Causeway; f. 1909; research and advisory work on soils and agricultural chemistry; registration and regulation of fertilizers and foodstuffs; crop nutrition, chemistry, pedology, soil physics and soil productivity research sections; Head R. J. FENNER.

**Cotton Research Institute:** P.O.B. 530, Gatooma; f. 1925; all aspects of cotton agronomy, breeding and pest research; Head J. A. GLEDHILL.

**Crop Breeding Institute:** P.O.B. 8100, Causeway; f. 1976; formerly Salisbury Research Station; responsible for breeding programmes on maize, soya beans, groundnuts, wheat, barley and potatoes; Head J. R. TATTERSFIELD.

**Horticulture and Coffee Research Institute:** Private Bag 701, Marandellas; Head M. O. DALE.

**Plant Protection Research Institute:** P.O.B. 8108, Causeway; f. 1964; research and advisory work on plant pests; entomology, pathology and nematology sections; Head Miss N. MUGABE.

**Biometrics Bureau:** P.O.B. 8108, Causeway; f. 1968; undertakes applied biometrical research; provides professional advice and a computer service to other research workers; Principal Biometrician in Charge (vacant).

*Research Stations:*

**Grasslands Research Station:** Private Bag 701, Marandellas; f. 1929; research on pasture, animal and crop production for the high-rainfall sandveld area; selection and testing of Rhizobium strains and commercial production of legume inoculants; Head (vacant).

**Henderson Research Station:** Private Bag 222A, Salisbury; f. 1949; pasture work on the introduction and screening of grasses and legumes for suitability as fertilized pastures; research in ruminant nutrition; herbicide and weed control research; Head Dr. M. G. W. RODEL.

**Lowveld Research Station:** P.O.B. 97, Chiredzi; f. 1967; research in irrigation agronomy in South-Eastern Lowveld; sub-tropical horticulture and vegetable crops; Head (vacant).

**Matopos Research Station:** Private Bag K5137, Bulawayo; f. 1903; research in veld management, ecology of regional soil types, bush encroachment, cattle breeding, and beef production; Head H. K. WARD.

**Makoholi Experiment Station:** Private Bag 9182, Fort Victoria; f. 1942; research into problems of animal and crop production for sandveld and medium rainfall districts of Zimbabwe; crop agronomy, cattle production (indigenous breeds) and natural grazing management; Officer-in-Charge (vacant).

**Horticultural Research Centre:** located on Grasslands Research Station, Private Bag 701, Marandellas; f. 1968; responsible for all aspects of horticultural research; Officer-in-Charge M. O. DALE.

**Coffee Research Station:** P.O.B. 61, Chipinga; f. 1964; research into all aspects of coffee management, growth, pest and disease control; tea research projects; Officer-in-Charge (vacant).

**Rhodes-Inyanga Experiment Station:** Private Bag 8044, Rusape; f. 1910; Pome fruit research; Officer-in-Charge C. B. PAYNE.

**National Herbarium and Botanic Garden:** P.O.B. 8100, Causeway; f. 1909; maintains a comprehensive collection of c. 250,000 specimens, provides an identification service for workers in agriculture and related fields and contributes to knowledge of the flora of South-Central Africa; botanical and ecological research, and research on medicinal and poisonous plants; Officer-in-Charge (Botanic Garden) T. MULLER; Keeper R. B. DRUMMOND (Herbarium).

*Agricultural Services:*

**Dairy Services:** P.O.B. 8108, Causeway, Salisbury; f. 1924; regulatory and advisory services to ensure high standards of hygiene and quality in dairy products; also operates milk recording scheme; Chief Dairy Officer H. L. DAVIES.

**Meat Grading:** P.O.B. 8108, Causeway, Salisbury; f. 1945; responsible for grading all cattle, sheep and pig carcasses for consumption in prescribed areas and for export; Chief Meat Grader (vacant).

**Seed Services:** P.O.B. 8100, Causeway, Salisbury; f. 1950; laboratory service for routine testing of seed purity and germination; responsible for administering the Seeds Act and for issuing international seed and phytosanitary certificates; controls National Seed Certification Scheme and administers Plant Breeders' Rights Act; Principal Research Officer in Charge K. B. HANSSEN.

There are four attached agricultural colleges: *see* under Colleges.

---

**Blair Research Laboratory:** P.O.B. 8105, Causeway, Salisbury; Dir. Dr. V. DE V. CLARKE.

**Central Statistical Office:** P.O.B. 8063, Causeway, Salisbury; f. 1927; co-ordinated statistical service for the Government; staff of 143; Dir. C. A. L. MYBURGH, C.L.M., M.COMM., PH.D., F.S.S.

**Department of Metallurgy:** Ministry of Mines, P.O.B. 8340, Causeway, Salisbury; f. 1920; conducts investigations on methods of economic extraction from precious, base-metal and non-metallic ores.

**Department of Veterinary Services; Tsetse and Trypanosomiasis Control Branch:** P.O.B. 8283, Causeway, Salisbury; under the Ministry of Agriculture; f. 1909; for the control of trypanosomiasis and tsetse fly and the investigation of methods of control; laboratory at Salisbury and two research stations in Zambezi Valley; Asst. Dir. R. D. PILSON.

**Veterinary Research Laboratory:** P.O.B. 8101, Causeway, Salisbury; f. 1906; diagnostic centre and research institute for animal diseases; 30 mems.; library of 1,200 vols.; Dir. J. A. LAWRENCE; Chief Research Officer R. SWANEPOEL.

**Forestry Commission:** P.O.B. 8111, Causeway, Salisbury; f. 1954; state forest authority, responsible for formulating forest policy in Zimbabwe; engaged in large-scale plantation operations; research and advisory services.

**Forest Research Centre:** P.O.B. HG 595, Highlands, Salisbury; conducts research into many aspects of forestry, principally high-yielding plantations, with special emphasis on tree genetics and the production of progressively improved pine and eucalypt seed, wood quality, general plantation management and fertilizer research.

**Geological Survey of Zimbabwe:** P.O.B. 8039, Causeway, Salisbury; f. 1910; geological mapping and survey of mineral resources; library of 780 vols., 700 symposia, 11,500 periodicals, 2,500 technical files; museum displaying Zimbabwean geology and economic minerals;

Dir. E. R. MORRISON; publs. *Annual Reports†, Bulletins†, Mineral Resources Series†* (irregular), short reports and maps.

**Institute of Mining Research:** P.O.B. MP 167, Mt. Pleasant Salisbury; f. 1969; multidisciplinary research for the benefit of the mining industry; 35 full-time staff; Dir. Prof. K. A. VIEWING.

**Meteorological Service:** P.O.B. BE 150, Belvedere, Salisbury; f. 1897; Dir. J. E. STEVENS; publs. *Monthly Meteorological Summaries†, Rainfall Handbook Supplements†, Climate Handbook Supplements†*, daily weather reports and forecasts†, weekly rainfall maps during rainy season Nov.-Mar.†.

*Affiliated Institute:*
**Goetz Observatory:** P.O.B. A C 65, Ascot, Bulawayo; also seismology; publ. *Seismological Bulletin†*.

**Public Health Laboratory:** P.O.B. 8079, Causeway, Salisbury; f. 1909; Dir. Dr. P. G. DAVIES; Pathologist Dr. R. F. LOWE; Chief Medical Technologist D. A. MVERE.

**Scientific Council of Zimbabwe:** P.O.B. 8510, Causeway, Salisbury; f. 1964; advisory body to the Government on general scientific policy and official channel for exchange of national and international scientific and technical information; Chair. Prof. W. R. MACKECHNIE; Sec. R. TORNBOHM; publs. *Directory of Organizations concerned with Scientific Research and Services in Zimbabwe* (every 3 years), *Zimbabwe Research Index* (annually).

**Standards Association of Central Africa:** Coventry Rd., Salisbury; f. 1957; encourages high standards; has laboratory facilities for testing and operates certification marking schemes; 191 mems.; Chair. B. H. WATTS (acting); publ. *Standards Bulletin†* (quarterly).

**Tobacco Research Board:** P.O.B. 1909, Salisbury; a statutory body est. 1950 by Tobacco Research Act; board represents growers, buyers, and Ministry of Agriculture; conducts research into all types of tobacco, agronomy, breeding and pest control; operates three research stations; library of 9,500 vols., 560 periodicals; Chair. J. W. FIELD; Dir. I. MCDONALD, O.L.M., M.A., PH.D., C.CHEM., M.R.S.C.; publs. *Handbooks of Recommendations, Bulletins†* and *Interim Reports†*.

## LIBRARIES AND ARCHIVES

**Library of Parliament:** P.O.B. 8055, Causeway, Salisbury; f. 1899; 100,000 vols.; wide range of parliamentary and government material from many countries; general collection specializing in political science, history, biography, economics, sociology; separate law collection; Librarian W. C. HOPE GURURE, B.A.

**National Archives:** Private Bag 7729, Causeway, Salisbury; f. 1935 as the Government Archives of Southern Rhodesia; incorp. archives of Northern Rhodesia and Nyasaland and designated the Central African Archives 1947; became National Archives of Rhodesia and Nyasaland 1958–63; reverted January 1964 to Rhodesian Government and responsibility for Northern Rhodesia and Nyasaland archives ceased; also serves Zimbabwean municipalities and holds archives of late Federation of Rhodesia and Nyasaland; comprises divisions of Public Archives, Records Management, Historical Manuscripts, Oral History, National Library (legal deposit library) including Pictorial, Sound Recordings and Map Collections; photo-copying services available; document restoration; H.Q. Govt. Library Services; Dir. ANGELINE S. KAMBA, B.A., M.L.S.; publs. *Oppenheimer Series, Bibliographical Series, Occasional Papers, Zimbabwe National Bibliography†* (annual), *Guide to the Public Archives of Rhodesia, Vol. 1, 1890–1923†, Guide to the Historical Manuscripts in the National Archives†, Report of the Director†* (annually), *Current Periodicals†, Directory of Libraries*, various histories and monographs.

**National Free Library of Zimbabwe:** P.O.B. 1773, Bulawayo; f. 1943 as national lending library for educational, scientific and technical books and national centre for inter-library loans; 76,000 vols.; Librarian N. JOHNSON, A.L.A.

**Public Library:** P.O.B. 586, Bulawayo; f. 1896; reference, lending, junior library; mobile library; postal service to rural readers; African and Zimbabwe collections; Zimbabwe map collection; legal deposit library for Zimbabwe; brs. at Ascot and Waterford; 65,000 vols.; Librarian R. W. DOUST, A.L.A.; publ. *Spectrum†* (quarterly).

**Queen Victoria Memorial Library:** P.O.B. 1087, Salisbury; f. 1902; 60,000 vols.; Librarian and Sec. Mrs. M. ROSS-SMITH, F.L.A.

**Turner Memorial Library:** Umtali; f. 1902; 25,000 vols.; Librarian Mrs. P. JARVIS.

**University of Zimbabwe Library:** P.O.B. MP45, Mount Pleasant, Salisbury; f. 1956; 302,000 vols.; 4,730 periodicals; Medical library; Law library; Education library; Map library; Africana collection; collection of African languages; photo-copying facilities; Librarian S. M. MADE, M.A., F.L.A.

## MUSEUMS AND ART GALLERIES

**National Museums and Monuments of Zimbabwe:** P.O.B. 8540, Causeway, Salisbury; administered by a Board of Trustees appointed by the Minister of Home Affairs; Exec. Dir. H. D. JACKSON; includes the following:

**Great Zimbabwe National Monument:** P.B. 9158, Fort Victoria; ruins of medieval dry stone buildings representing the Zimbabwe culture; history and development of Great Zimbabwe shown in site museum; archaeological research in south-eastern region of Zimbabwe; Dir. C. K. COOKE.

**National Museum:** Selborne Ave., P.O.B. 240, Bulawayo; f. 1901; geological, palaeontological, entomological and zoological exhibits; study collections covering Ethiopian region, with special reference to southern Africa; historical, ethnographical and prehistorical exhibits and study collections appertaining to Zimbabwe and adjacent regions; Dir. (vacant); Curator of Mammals M. P. S. IRWIN; Curator of Invertebrate Zoology D. L. HANCOCK, M.SC.; Curator of Ornithology B. G. DONNELLY, B.SC.; Curator of Herpetology D. G. BROADLEY, PH.D.; Curator of Palaeontology M. R. COOPER, PH.D.; publs. *Arnoldia Zimbabwe, Smithersia*, occasional natural history papers.

**Midlands Museum:** Lobengula Ave., P.O.B. 1300, Gwelo; f. 1972; history of Zimbabwe Midlands and military history of Zimbabwe; Dir. W. S. REES.

**Queen Victoria Museum:** Civic Centre, P.O.B. 8006, Causeway, Salisbury; f. 1902; zoological, ethnographical, archaeological and historical exhibits, study collections of archaeological, ethnographical, rock art appertaining to Zimbabwe and adjacent areas; Dir. J. MINSHULL, M.SC.; publs. *Zimbabwea, Cookeia*, occasional human science papers.

**Umtali Museum:** Victory Ave., P.O.B. 920, Umtali; f. 1954; geological, zoological, ethnographical, archaeological and historical exhibits, appertaining to the Eastern Districts in particular; Dir. P. G. LOCKE, B.SC.

**National Gallery of Zimbabwe:** P.O.B. 8155, Causeway, Salisbury; f. 1957; permanent collection includes works by Reynolds, Gainsborough, Morland, Murillo, Ribera, Bellini, Pannini, Mantegna, Caracciolo, Rodin and traditional and contemporary African art; library and reading room; Dir. C. M. TILL, M.F.A.; publ. *Insight*† (3 a year), exhibition catalogues†.

# UNIVERSITY

## UNIVERSITY OF ZIMBABWE

P.O.B. MP167, MOUNT PLEASANT, SALISBURY

Telephone: Salisbury 303211.

Telegraphic Address: University, Salisbury

Academic year: March to December.

In February 1955 a Royal Charter was granted to the University College of Rhodesia and Nyasaland. The College became the University of Rhodesia under revised statutes adopted in 1970 and in 1980 became the University of Zimbabwe, but the Charter was preserved as the basic constitutional instrument of the University.

*Principal and Vice-Chancellor:* Prof. W. J. KAMBA, B.A., LL.M.

*Vice-Principal and Deputy Vice-Chancellor:* P. M. MAKHURANE, M.SC., PH.D.

*Registrar:* R. D. D. BLAIR, B.A., F.C.I.S.

*Librarian:* S. M. MADE, M.A., F.L.A.

Number of teachers: 324 full-time, 72 part-time.
Number of students: 2,525.
Publication: *Prospectus.*

### DEANS:

*Faculty of Agriculture:* Prof. M. A. SCHWEPPENHAUSER, D.SC.

*Faculty of Arts:* G. P. KAHARI, M.A.

*Faculty of Commerce and Law:* Prof. F. S. BARDO, B.L., C.A., F.C.I.S., D.A.E.

*Faculty of Education:* Prof. N. D. ATKINSON, M.LITT., PH.D.

*Faculty of Engineering:* (vacant).

*Faculty of Medicine:* Prof. I. M. BROWN, M.B., B.S., M.R.C.O.G.

*Faculty of Science:* Prof. A. G. R. STEWART, M.SC., PH.D.

*Faculty of Social Studies:* R. MURAPA, M.A., PH.D.

### PROFESSORS AND HEADS OF DEPARTMENTS:

*Faculty of Agriculture:*
BLACKIE, M. J., M.S., PH.D., Land Management
OLIVER, J., PH.D., Animal Science
SCHWEPPENHAUSER, M. A., D.SC., Crop Science

*Faculty of Arts:*
ANNAN, B., M.A., Linguistics
DAVIES, D. H., M.A., PH.D., F.R.G.S., Geography
FEIN, P. L.-M., B.A., Modern Languages
KAHARI, G. P., M.A., African Languages
MANDIVENGA, E. C., M.PHIL., Theology and Philosophy
MCLOUGHLIN, T. O., M.A., PH.D., English
ROBERTS, R. S., PH.D., F.R.HIST.S., History
SADDINGTON, D. B., M.A., PH.D., Classics

*Faculty of Commerce and Law:*
BARDO, F. S., B.L., F.C.I.S., D.A.E., Accountancy
HACKWILL, G. R. J., M.A., PH.D., Law
HAWKINS, A. M., B.A., B.LITT., Business Studies

*Faculty of Education:*
HENRIKZ, ELIZABETH, M.A., PH.D., Education
ORBELL, S. F. W., M.PHIL., PH.D., Institute of Education
RUSSELL, D. D., B.SC., Institute of Adult Education

*Faculty of Engineering:*
HARLEN, M. A., PH.D., M.I.E.E., C.ENG., M.ZIM.I.E., Electronic and Power Engineering
LAMB, J. F., PH.D., C.ENG., Mechanical Engineering
MACKECHNIE, W. R., M.SC., D.I.C., C.ENG., Civil Engineering

*Faculty of Medicine:*
AXTON, J. H. M., M.B., B.S., Paediatrics and Child Health
BROWN, I. McL., M.B.B.S., M.R.C.O.G., Obstetrics and Gynaecology
BUCHAN, T., M.A., M.B., B.CHIR., F.F.PSYCH., F.R.C.PSYCH., D.T.M. & H., Psychiatry
CMELIK, S. H. W., M.SC., PH.D., Chemical Pathology
DUTHIE, A. M., M.B., CH.B., D.A., Anaesthetics
LEVY, L. F., M.B., M.SC., F.R.C.S., Surgery
LYONS, N. F., M.PHIL., Medical Microbiology
PETROPOULOS, E. A., M.D., PH.D., Physiology
RILEY, M. J., M.B., CH.B., M.R.C.P., Clinical Pharmacology
ROSS, W. F., B.SC., M.B., CH.B., Community Medicine
RYAN, P. M., M.B., CH.B., M.R.C.S., L.R.C.P., Anatomy (acting)
SUMMERS, R. S., M.SC., PH.D., M.P.S., Pharmacy
THOMAS, J. E. P., M.B., CH.B., F.R.C.P.ED., F.R.C.P., Medicine

*Faculty of Science:*
COTTRELL, C. B., PH.D., Zoology
JONES, D. L., PH.D., Physics
RIDLER, P. F., B.E., C.ENG., F.I.E.E., Computer Science
SHEPPARD, J. G., PH.D., D.I.C., Chemistry
STEWART, A. G. R., PH.D., Mathematics
SWIFT, M. J., M.A., PH.D., Botany
WILSON, J. F., PH.D., P.G.S.S.A., F.G.S., Geology
WOOD, T., PH.D., D.SC., A.R.C.S., D.I.C., Biochemistry

*Faculty of Social Studies:*
CHAVUNDUKA, G. L., M.A., PH.D., Sociology
MUNRO, D., M.A., PH.D., Psychology
MURPHREE, M. A., PH.D., Applied Social Sciences
PATEL, H. H., B.SC., M.A., C.PHIL., Political Science
SEIDMAN, A., M.S., PH.D., Economics

### ATTACHED INSTITUTES:

**Centre for Applied Social Sciences.**
*Director:* M. A. MURPHREE, M.A., PH.D.

**Computing Centre.**
*Director:* P. F. RIDLER, B.E., C.ENG., F.I.E.E., F.Z.I.E., M.R.C.S.

**Institute of Adult Education.**
*Director:* D. D. RUSSELL, B.SC.

**Institute of Education.**
*Director:* S. F. W. ORBELL, M.PHIL., PH.D.

**Institute of Mining Research.**
*Director:* K. A. VIEWING, B.SC., PH.D., D.I.C., C.ENG., A.I.M.M., F.G.S.

**Institute for Social Research.**
*Director:* G. L. CHAVUNDUKA, M.A., PH.D.

**Nuffield Lake Kariba Research Station.**
*Director:* R. J. PHELPS, PH.D. (acting).

**Regional and Urban Planning Centre:** P. VAN HOFFEN, B.SC.

**Science Education Centre.**
*Director:* P. G. S. GILBERT, B.SC.

# COLLEGES

**Bulawayo Technical College:** Main Centre, Twelfth Avenue Extension, P.O.B. 1392, Bulawayo; f. 1927, regional college 1961; further education in technical, commercial and management subjects; teachers: 172 full-time, 87 part-time; 3,435 students; library of 13,000 vols.; Principal J. H. BOWMAN, C.ENG., M.I.MECH.E., M.ZIM.I.E.; Registrar I. F. BECKER.

## ZIMBABWE

**Chibero College of Agriculture:** Private Bag 901, Norton; f. 1961; Three-year Diploma in Agriculture for Africans.
*Principal:* L. TENGENDU.
Library of 1,150 vols.
Number of teachers: 16.
Number of students: 80.
Publication: *Agricultural Education.*

**Gwebi College of Agriculture:** Private Bag 376B, Salisbury; f. 1950; 2-year Diploma in Agriculture.
*Principal:* H. J. McLEAN.
Library of 2,000 vols.
Number of teachers: 17.
Number of students: 88.

**Esigodini Agricultural Institute:** Private Bag 5808, Essexvale; f. 1921; 3-year certificate course for African students.
*Principal:* (vacant).

**Kwanongoma College of Music:** Private Bag T5392, Bulawayo; research into African music and musicology, results applied to music education at teacher training and primary education levels; manufacture of musical instruments; Dir. O. E. ALEXSSON, M.A.

**Mlezu Agricultural Institute:** P.O.B. 311, Que Que; f. 1959; 3-year course for African students.
*Principal:* M. P. PSWARAYI.

**Salisbury School of Art:** Corner Rhodes Avenue/Eighth-Street, Salisbury.

**Salisbury Polytechnic:** P.O.B. 8074, Causeway, Salisbury; f. 1927; 327 teachers (incl. 180 part-time); c. 5,000 students; full-time and sandwich courses for technicians and craftsmen; courses in printing and adult education; full-time and part-time courses in commercial subjects to B.Com. level; library of 30,000 vols.; Principal L. STACK.

**Zimbabwe College of Music:** Civic Centre, Rotten Row, Salisbury C.3; f. 1948.
*Chairman:* R. P. LANDER, M.A.
*Director:* NEIL CHAPMAN, L.R.A.M.
*Registrar:* Mrs. E. M. WAY.

# INDEX OF INSTITUTIONS

## A

19 Mayis Üniversitesi, Samsun, 1308
Aalborg Historiske Museum, 395
— Universitetscenter, 396
Aargauer Kunsthaus Aarau, 1261
Aarhus Kunstmuseum, 395
— Universitet, 396
Abadan Institute of Technology, 724
Abashiri Kyodo Hakubutsukan, 822
Abastumani Astrophysical Observatory, Kanobili Mountain, 1327
Abbas Kattan Library, Mecca, 1142
Abbasid Palace Museum, Baghdad, 726
Abbeydale Industrial Hamlet, Sheffield, 1471
Abbot Hall Art Gallery and Museum of Lakeland Life and Industry, Kendal, 1469
Abdul Kalam Azad Oriental Research Institute, Hyderabad, 668
Abdullaev, K. M., Institute of Geology and Geophysics, Tashkent, 1335
Abe Bailey Centre for Intergroup Studies, Rondebosch, 1167
Abegyan, M. A., Institute of Literature, Erevan, 1324
Aberdeen Art Gallery and Museums, 1472
— College of Commerce, 1552
Abgusswerkstatt, Dresden, 509
Abilene Christian University, 1897
Abisko naturvetenskapliga station, 1238
Abkhazian D. I. Gulia Institute of Linguistics, Literature and History, Sukhumi, 1328
Åbo Akademi, 434
— Akademis Bibliotek, 431
— Swedish University School of Economics, 440
Abteilung für Struktur- und Regionalforschung, Saarbrucken, 603
— Wirtschaftswissenschaft im Osteuropa Instituts an der Freien Universität Berlin, 528
Academi Gymreig, Cardiff, 1426
Academia Amazonense de Letras, 178
— Antioqueña de Historia, 346
— Argentina de Cirugía, 64
— — Letras, 62
— Belgica, Rome, 758
— Boliviana, 173
— Boyacense de Historia, Tunja, 346
— Brasileira de Ciência da Administração, Rio de Janeiro, 178
— — — Ciências, 178
— — — Letras, 178
— Brasiliense de Letras, Brasília, 178
— Cachoeirense de Letras, Cachoeiro de Itapemerim, 178
— Catarinense de Letras, 178
— Cearense de Letras, Fortaleza, 178
— Chilena de Ciencias Naturales, 323
— — — la Historia, 322
— — — Lengua, Santiago, 322
— Colombiana de Ciencias Exactas, Fisicas y Naturales, 346
— — — Historia, 346
— — — Jurisprudencia, 346
— — — la Lengua, 346
— Costarricense de la Lengua, 359
— — — Periodoncia, San José, 359
— Cubana de la Lengua, Havana, 362
— das Ciências de Lisboa, 1097
— de Bellas Artes, Santiago, 322
— — — — "Neptali Rincón", Maracaibo, 1960

— — — — "Remigio Crespo Toral", Cuenca, 412
— — Buenas Letras de Barcelona, 1187
— — Ciencias, Santiago, 322
— — — de Cuba, Havana, 362
— — — — Biblioteca Central, 364
— — — Exactas, Fisicas e Matemáticas, Caracas, 1949
— — — Fisico-Químicas y Naturales, Zaragoza, 1188
— — — Históricas de Monterrey, 926
— — — Médicas de Bilbao, 1187
— — — Fisicas y Naturales de Guatemala, Guatemala City, 624
— — — Políticas y Sociales, Caracas, 1949
— — — Sociales, Politicas y Morales, Santiago, 322
— — Cirugía de Madrid, 1186
— — Estomatología del Perú, 1037
— — Geografia e Historia de Costa Rica, San José, 359
— — — — — Guatemala, Guatemala City, 624
— — — — — Nicaragua, 988
— — Historia de Cartagena de Indias, 346
— — — del Zulia, Maracaibo, 1951
— — la Investigación Científica, Mexico City, 929
— — — Lengua Maya Quiché, Quezaltenango, 624
— — — — y Cultura Guarani, 1034
— — Letras da Bahia, 178
— — — de Piauí, 178
— — — e Artes do Planalto, Luziania, 178
— — — "Humberto de Campos", Vila Velha, 179
— — Medicina, Santiago, 322
— — — de São Paulo, 178
— — Musica Fischer, Caracas, 1961
— — — "Padre Sojo", Caracas, 1961
— — Științe Agricole și Silvice, Bucharest, 1116
— — — Medicale, Bucharest, 1118
— — — Sociale și Politice, Bucharest, 1120
— — — Studii Economice, Bucharest, 1139
— — Dominicana de Historia, 403
— — — Lengua, 403
— — Ecuatoriana de la Lengua, 407
— — — de Medicina, Quito, 407
— — Española de Bellas Artes, Rome, 756
— — — — Dermatología y Sifiliografía, 1186
— — Faeroensis, Tórshavn, 402
— — Feminina Espírito Santense de Letras, Vitória, 179
— — Filipina, 1047
— — Guatemalteca de la Lengua, 624
— — Historica, Taipei, 340
— — Hondureña, Tegucigalpa, 630
— — — de Geografía e Historia, Tegucigalpa, 630
— — Iberoamericana y Filipina de Historia Postal, 1186
— — Matogrossense de Letras, 178
— — Médico-Quirúrgica Española, 1186
— — Mexicana de Cirugía, Mexico City, 927
— — — Dermatología, Mexico City, 927
— — — la Historia, Mexico City, 925
— — — — Lengua, Mexico City, 925
— — Mineira de Letras, 178
— — Nacional de Agronomia y Veterinaria, Buenos Aires, 62
— — — Belas Artes, Lisbon, 1097
— — — Bellas Artes, Buenos Aires, 62
— — — Ciencias, Buenos Aires, 62
— — — — Mexico City, 925

— — — — Panama, 1030
— — — — de Bolivia, La Paz, 173
— — — — Córdoba, 62
— — — — Económicas, Buenos Aires, 63
— — — — Exactas, Fisicas y Naturales, Buenos Aires, 62
— — — — — y Naturales de Lima, 1036
— — — Derecho y Ciencias Sociales, Buenos Aires, 62
— — — — — Sociales, Córdoba, 62
— — — Farmacia, Rio de Janeiro, 178
— — — Filosofía, Managua, 988
— — — Geografia, San Martin, 62
— — — Historia y Geografía, Mexico City, 925
— — — Ingeriería, Montevideo, 1938
— — — la Historia, Buenos Aires, 62
— — — — Caracas, 1949
— — — — La Paz, 173
— — — Letras, Montevideo, 1938
— — — Medicina, Bogotá, 346
— — — — Buenos Aires, 62
— — — — Caracas, 1949
— — — — Lima, 1036
— — — — Rio de Janeiro, 178
— — — — de México, 925
— — Nicaragüense de la Lengua, 988
— — Norteamericana de la Lengua Española, New York, 1607
— — Panameña de la Historia, 1030
— — — Lengua, 1030
— — Paraguaya, 1034
— — Paraibana de Letras, João Pessoa, 178
— — Paulista de Letras, São Paulo, 178
— — Pernambucana de Letras, 178
— — Peruana, 1036
— — — de Cirugía, Lima, 1037
— — Portena del Lunfardo, Buenos Aires, 63
— — Portuguesa de História, 1097
— — Puertorriqueña de la Historia, Santurce, 1109
— — — — Lengua Española, San Juan, 1109
— — Republicii Socialiste România, 1115
— — Riograndense de Letras, 178
— — Salvadoreña, 422
— — — de la Historia, 422
— — Sinica, Taipei, 340
— — "Stefan Gheorghiu" pentru Pregatirea și Perfectionarea Cadrelor de Conducere, Bucharest, 1140
— — Venezolana de la Lengua, 1949
Acadèmia de Ciencies Mediques de Catalunya i de Balears, Barcelona, 1187
Academias de Música, Santo Domingo, 406
Academic Circle of Tel Aviv, 738
Academician Bakulev Institute of Cardiac and Vascular Surgery, Moscow, 1342
— N. N. Burdenko Institute of Neurosurgery, Moscow, 1342
— F. N. Chernyschev Central Scientific Geological and Prospecting Museum, Leningrad, 1358
— A. F. Joffe Institute of Physics and Technology, Leningrad, 1318
— E. N. Pavlovsky Institute of Zoology and Parasitology, Dushanbe, 1332
— A. N. Zavaritsskovo Institute of Geology and Geochemistry, Sverdlovsk, 1322
Academie van Beeldende Kunsten Rotterdam, 973
— — Bouwkunst Rotterdam, 973

# INDEX OF INSTITUTIONS

Academie voor Beeldende Kunsten St. Joost, Breda, 973
Académie Canadienne Française, 241
— d'Agriculture de France, 444
— d'Architecture, 444
— de Chirurgie, 444
— — la Langue Basque, Bayonne, 445
— — — Réunion, Saint-Denis, 500
— — Marine, Antwerp, 169
— — — Paris, 444
— — Musique, Geneva, 1276
— — — Prince Rainier III, Monaco, 946
— — Nîmes, 444
— — Philatélie, Paris, 445
— des Beaux-Arts, 443
— — — Kinshasa, 1996
— — Inscriptions et Belles-Lettres, 442
— — Jeux Floraux, 444
— — Lettres et des Arts, 444
— — Sciences, 443
— — — Agriculture, Arts et Belles-Lettres d'Aix, 444
— — — Arts et Belles-Lettres de Dijon, 444
— — — Belles-Lettres et Arts de Lyon, 444
— — — d'Outre-mer, 445
— — — Morales et Politiques, 444
— Diplomatique et des Affaires internationales, Cologne, 23
— du Monde Latin, Paris, 445
— française, Paris, 442
— Goncourt, 445
— Internationale d'Astronautique, Paris, 46
— — de médecine légale et de médecine sociale, Munich, 37
— — — Science Politique et d'Histoire Constitutionelle, Paris, 24, 496
— — des Sciences Sociales et Morales, des Arts et des Lettres, Cologne, 24
— Malgache, Antananarivo, 910
— Mallarmé, Paris, 445
— Mauricienne de Langue et de Littérature, Curepipe, 923
— Montaigne, 445
— Nationale de Médecine, 445
— — — Pharmacie de Paris, 445
— Royale d'Archéologie de Belgique, Brussels, 149
— — de Langue et de Littérature Françaises, 148
— — — Médecine de Belgique, 149
— — — des Beaux-Arts de Bruxelles, 170
— — — Sciences d'Outre-Mer, Brussels, 149
— — — — des Lettres et des Beaux-Arts de Belgique, 147
— Scientifique Internationale pour la Protection de la Vie, l'Environnement et la Biopolitique, Luxembourg, 908
— Suisse des Sciences Médicales, Basel, 1255
— Vétérinaire de France (CSSF), 445
Academy of Agricultural and Forest Sciences, Bucharest, 1116
— — Science, Pyongyang, 883
— — Agronomy and Veterinary Science, Buenos Aires, 62
— — Applied Arts, Zagreb, 1993
— — Architecture, Bombay, 707
— — Arts, Berlin (West), 517
— — — Giza, 421
— — — of the U.S.S.R., 1338
— — — Athens, 615
— — Diplomacy and International Affairs (ADIA), Cologne, 23
— — Ecuador, Quito, 407
— — Fine Arts, Copenhagen, 388
— — — Helsinki, 441
— — — Santiago, 322
— — — Vienna, 138
— — — Zagreb, 1993
— — — Finland, Helsinki, 427
— — Fisheries, Pyongyang, 883
— — Forestry Science, Pyongyang, 883
— — Industrial and Art Design, Linz, 138
— — Light Industry Science, Pyongyang, 883
— — Medical, Physical and Natural Sciences, Guatemala City, 624
— — — Sciences, Bucharest, 1118
— — — — Pyongyang, 882
— — — — of the U.S.S.R., 1339
— — Medicine, Santiago, 322
— — — Singapore, 1150
— — — Sofia, 217
— — — Toronto, 241
— — Natural Sciences of Philadelphia, 1597
— — Pedagogical Sciences of the U.S.S.R, 1342
— — Political and Social Sciences, Caracas, 1949
— — — Science, New York, 1602
— — Railway Sciences, Pyongyang, 883
— — Sciences, Caracas, 1949
— — — Pyongyang, 882
— — — Tiranë, 54
— — — Ulan Bator, 947
— — — and Arts of Kosovo, Pristina, 1966
— — — — Literature, Mainz, 516
— — — Museum of Zoology, Leningrad, 1358
— — — of the U.S.S.R., 1313
— — Scientific Research and Technology, Cairo, 414
— — Social and Political Sciences, Bucharest, 1120
— — — Political and Moral Sciences, Santiago, 322
— — — Sciences, Moscow, 1388
— — — — Pyongyang, 882
— — Technical Sciences, Lyngby, 388
— — the Arabic Language, 413
— — — Guarani Language and Culture, Asunción, 1034
— — — Hebrew Language, 738
— — — Social Sciences in Australia, Canberra, 84
— — — Socialist Republic of Romania, Bucharest, 1115
— — Theatre, Film and Television, Zagreb, 1993
— — — Radio, Film and Television, Ljubljana, 1993
— — Zoology, Agra, 659
Acadia Divinity College, Nova Scotia, 252
— University, 252
Accademia Albertina di Belle Arti, Turin, 796
— Americana, Rome, 758
— de la Cultura, Mogadishu, 1153
— dei Filedoni, Perugia, 755
— della Crusca, 755
— delle Scienze, Ferrara, 755
— — di Torino, 755
— — dell'Istituto di Bologna, 755
— — Mediche di Palermo, 755
— di Agricoltura di Torino, 755
— Belle Arti, Florence, 796
— — Milan, 796
— — Palermo, 797
— — Perugia, 796
— — Ravenna, 796
— — Venice, 797
— — e Liceo Artistico, Bologna, 796
— — — Artistico, Carrara, 797
— — — Artistico, Lecce, 797
— — — Artistico, Naples, 797
— — — Artistico, Rome, 797
— — Danimarca, Rome, 758
— — Francia, Rome, 758
— — Medicina di Torino, 755
— — Scienze, Lettere, Arti, Milan, 755
— — — ed Arti, Palermo, 755
— — Economico-Agraria dei Georgofili, 755
— — Etrusca, Cortona-Arezzo, 755
— — Filarmonica Romana, 755
— — Gioenia di Scienze Naturali, Catania, 755
— — Italiana di Economia Aziendale, Bologna, 755

# WORLD OF LEARNING

— — — Scienze Forestali, Florence, 755
— Ligure di Scienze e Lettere, 755
— — Medica di Roma, 755
— — Musicale Chigiana, Siena, 755
— — Nazionale dei Lincei, 754
— — — Sartori, Rome, 755
— — — delle Scienze, detta dei XL, Rome, 755
— — — di Agricoltura, Bologna, 755
— — — Arte Drammatica "Silvio d'Amico", Rome, 797
— — — Danza, Rome, 797
— — — Marina Mercantile, Genoa, 755
— — — San Luca, Rome, 754
— — — Santa Cecilia, Rome, 755
— — — Scienze, Lettere e Arti, Modena, 755
— Petrarca di Lettere, Arti, e Scienze, 755
— Romana di S. Tommaso d'Aquino e di Religione Cattolica, 1942
— Spoletina, Spoleto, 755
— Tedesca, Rome, 758
— Tiberina, Rome, 755
— Toscana di Scienze e Lettere la Colombaria, 756
— Virgiliana di Scienze, Lettere e Arti di Mantova, 756
Accra Central Library, 612
— Polytechnic, 614
— Technical Training Centre, 614
Acharya Narendra Dev Pustakalaya, Lucknow, 673
Acharyan, P., Institute of Linguistics, Erevan, 1324
Acoustical Society of America, 1613
Acoustics Institute, Beijing, 331
— — Moscow, 1318
Acropolis Museum, 618
Acton Society Trust, London, 1416
ACUM Ltd. (Authors', Composers' and Publishers' Society), Tel Aviv, 737
Acupuncture Association, Hanoi, 1962
— Moxibustion Institute, Beijing, 333
Adam Mickiewicz Museum of Literature, Warsaw, 1075
— — University in Poznań, 1081
Adams National Historic Site, 1635
— State College of Colorado, 1675
Adamson University, Manila, 1050
Adana Bölge Müzesi, 1301
Addis Ababa University, 425
— — Library, 424
Adelaide College of the Arts and Education, 114
Adelphi University, Garden City, N.Y., 1804
Adler Museum of the History of Medicine, Johannesburg, 1165
— Planetarium, 1635
Administratieve Bibliotheek, 963
Administrative Bibliothek und Österreichische Rechtsdokumentation in Bundeskanzleramt, Vienna, 127
— Staff College, Henley-on-Thames, 1552
— — — of India, Bella Vista, 706
Admiralty Marine Technology Establishment, Teddington, 1448
— Surface Weapons Establishment, Portsmouth, 1448
— Underwater Weapons Establishment, Portland, 1448
Adnan Malki Museum, Damascus, 1277
Adrian College, Michigan, 1760
Adult Education and Extension Services Unit, Zaria, 995
— — Association of the U.S.A., 1603
Advanced Institute of Accounting, Seoul, 894
Advisory Centre for Education (ACE) Ltd., London, 1418
Adyar Library and Research Centre, Madras, 673
Aegean University, Izmir, 1305
— Faculty and School of Engineering and Architecture, Izmir, 1309
Aeronautical Engineering College, Beijing, 335

— Society of India, The, New Delhi, 664
Aeroplane and Armament Experimental Establishment, Boscombe Down, 1448
Aerospace Medical Association, Washington, 1608
Afghanistan Academy of Sciences, 52
Africa Institute, Moscow, 1321
— — of South Africa, Pretoria, 1154
African and Malagasy Council on Higher Education, Ouagadougou, 26
— Cultural Institute, Dakar, 18
— Society, Cairo, 413
— Studies Association, Los Angeles, 1614
— — — of the United Kingdom, Birmingham, 1434
— — Institute, Johannesburg, 1182
— Training and Research Centre in Administration for Development, Tangier, 23
Africana Museum in Progress, Johannesburg, 1165
— — Monrovia, 904
Afro-Asiatisches Institut in Wien, 121
Afyon Mali Bilimler Fakültesi, Eskişehir, 1309
Agnes Scott College, 1698
Agra University, 676
Agrarian Institute of Nicaragua, 988
— Research and Training Institute, Colombo, 1224
— — — — — Library, Colombo, 1225
— Society, Valletta, 921
Agrarsoziale Gesellschaft (ASG), Göttingen, 517
Agrártudományi Egyetem, Gödöllő, 651
— Keszthely, 651
— — Központi Könyvtára, Gödöllő, 640
— — Keszthely, 640
Agrarwirtschaftliches Institut des Bundesministeriums für Land- und Forstwirtschaft, Vienna, 124
Agricultural Association of China, Taipei, 340
— Business Research Institute, Armidale, N.S.W., 106
— Department Library, Zanzibar, 1280
— Economics Research Unit, Canterbury, N.Z., 984
— — Institute, Beijing, 332
— — Society, Aberdeen, 1410
— Economy Research Institute, Giza, 414
— Experiment Station, Las Cruces, 1802
— Experimental Station, Kuwait, 897
— Extension and Research Liaison Services, Zaria, 993
— Guidance Research Institute, Dokki, 414
— History Society, Washington, 1599
— Institute, Titograd, 1990
— West Bank, Jordan, 877
— — of Canada, Ottawa, 239
— Machinery College, Zhenjiang, 339
— Museum, Damascus, 1277
— — Dokki, 417
— Research Centre, Aleppo, 1278
— — — Baghdad, 725
— — — Ministry of Agriculture, Giza, 414
— — Library, Tripoli, 906
— — Corporation, Ministry of Agriculture, Wadi Medani, 1229
— — — Library, Wadi Medani, 1229
— — Council, London, 1440
— — — of Zimbabwe, Salisbury, 2000
— — Institute, Washington, D.C., 1617
— — — of Northern Ireland, Hillsborough, 1554
— — Organisation, Bet-Dagan, 739
— School, Ulan Bator, 948
— Schools, Mongolia, 948
— Scientific Services, Edinburgh, 1440
— Society of Kenya, Nairobi, 878
— — — Trinidad and Tobago, 1293
— Technical Institute, Wooster, 1850
— University, Vienna, 137
— — Wageningen, 971
— — of Warsaw, 1093

Agriculture and Home Economics Experiment Station, Ames, 1728
— Association, Hanoi, 1962
— Institute, Beijing, 333
— Science Service, Harpenden Laboratory, 1440
Agri-Horticultural Society of India, Calcutta, 659
— — — Madras, 659
Agro-Economic Research Centre, West Bengal, 666
Agronomy Institute, Salisbury, Zimbabwe, 2001
Agrophysical Research Institute, Leningrad, 1338
Agrupación Bibliotecológica del Uruguay, Montevideo, 1938
Ägyptisches Museum und Papyrus-Sammlung, Berlin (East), 508
— — — (West), 541
Ahfad University College for Women, Omdurman, 1231
Ahmadu Bello University, Zaria, 995
Ahmedabad Textile Industry's Research Association, 672
Ain Shams University, Cairo, 417
Air Pollution Research Group (CSIR), Pretoria, 1159
Airlangga University, Surabaja, 712
Ajia Keizai Kenkyusho, Tokyo, 813
— Seikai Gakkai, Tokyo, 804
Akademi Akunting Trisakti, Jakarta, 720
— Angkutan Udara Niaga Trisakti, Jakarta, 720
— Teknologi Kulit, Yogjakarta, 710
Akademia e Shkencave dhe e Arteve e Kosovës, Pristina, 1966
— Ekonomiczna w Krakowie, Cracow, 1094
— — State Museum, 1094
— — Poznań, 1094
— — im O. Langego, Wrocław, 1094
— — Górniczo-Hutnicza im. Stanislawa staszica, 1086
— Medyczna, Białystok, 1095
— — Gdańsk, 1095
— — Łódź, 1095
— — Lublin, 1095
— — Poznań, 1095
— — Warsaw, 1095
— — Wrocław, 1095
— — im Mikolaya Kopernika, Cracow, 1095
— Muzyczna, Katowice, 1095
— — im. Fryderyka Chopina, Warsaw, 1095
— — w Krakowie, 1095
— Rolnicza, Lublin, 1094
— — w Poznaniu, 1094
— — Szczecin, 1094
— — Wrocław, 1094
— — im. Hugona Kollątaja, Cracow, 1094
— — w Warszawie, 1093
— Rolniczo-Techniczna, Kortowo, 1094
— Sztuk Pieknych, Cracow, 1095
— — Warsaw, 1096
— Teologii Katolickiej, Warsaw, 1095
Akademie der bildenden Künste, Munich, 608
— — — — Nuremberg, 608
— — — — Vienna, 138
— — Künste, Berlin (West), 517
— — — der Deutschen Demokratischen Republik, Berlin (East), 505
— — Landwirtschaftswissenschaften der DDR, Berlin (East), 505
— — Pädagogischen Wissenschaften der DDR, Berlin (East), 506
— — Wissenschaften der DDR, Berlin (East), 503
— — — in Göttingen, 515
— — — und der Literatur, Mainz, 516
— für Fernstudium, Bad Harzburg, 519
— — Fremdsprachen GmbH, Berlin (West), 608
— — Führungskräfte der Wirtschaft, Bad Harzburg, 509
— — Raumforschung und Landesplanung, Hanover, 528

— — Staats- und Rechtswissenschaft der DDR, Potsdam-Babelsberg, 513
— Industriële Vormgeving Eindhoven, 973
— múzických umění, Prague, 387
— van Bouwkunst, Amsterdam, 973
— — — Arnhem, 973
— — — Groningen, 973
— — — Maastricht, 973
— — — Tilburg, 973
— voor Beeldende Kunst Enschede, 973
— — Kunsten, Arnhem, 973
— — — — "Akademie Minerva", Groningen, 973
— vytvarných umění, Prague, 387
Akademiet for de Skønne Kunster, Copenhagen, 388
— — — Tekniske Videnskaber, Copenhagen, 388
Akademija Nauka i Umetnosti Kosova, Pristina, 1966
— za glasbo, Ljubljana, 1963
— — Likovno Umetnost, Ljubljana, 1963
Akademisk Arkitektforening, Copenhagen, 389
Akadimia Athinon, 615
Akhundov (M.F.) State Public Library of the Azerbaijan S.S.R., 1348
Akita Prefectural Library, 819
— University, 824
Akko Municipal Museum, Akko, 743
Akron-Summit County Public Library, 1627
Aktiubinsk State Medical Institute, 1382
Alabama State University, Montgomery, 1643
Ålands Museum, Mariehamn, 433
— Sjofartsmuseum, Mariehamn, 433
Alaska Historical Library, 1628
— Pacific University, 1645
— — State Museum, 1635
Al-Awqaf Central Library, Baghdad, 725
Al-Azhar University, Cairo, 418
— — — Library, 416
Al-Baath University, Homs, 1278
Albanian Folk Culture Museum, Tiranë, 55
Albany College of Pharmacy, 1822
— Law School, 1822
— Medical College, 1822
— Museum, Grahamstown, 1164
— State College, Georgia, 1699
Albert-Ludwigs-Universität, Freiburg, 569
Alberta College of Art, Calgary, 319
— — — Institute of Pedology, Edmonton, 257
— Research Council, Edmonton, 244
Albertus Magnus College, New Haven, 1677
— — -Institut, Bonn, 524
Albion College, Michigan, 1760
Albrecht-Dürer Haus, Nuremberg, 545
Albright College, Reading, Pa., 1866
Alcázar de Diego Colón, Santo Domingo, 404
— — Sevilla, 1201
Alcorn State University, Lorman, Miss., 1784
Alderson-Broaddus College, Philippi, 1929
Aleppo Institute of Music, 1279
— National Museum, 1277
Alexander Stambolisky Museum, Sofia, 221
— Turnbull Library, Wellington, 981
— von Humboldt Stiftung, Bonn, 520
Alexandria Institute of Oceanography and Fisheries, 415
— Medical Association, 414
— Municipal Library, 416
Alfateh University, Tripoli, 906
Alfred North Whitehead Center for Lifelong Learning, Redlands, 1673
— P. Sloan Foundation, Inc., 1603
— University, Garden City, N.Y., 1804
Algantighe Art Gallery, Timaru, 982
Al-Gawhara Palace Museum, Cairo, 417
Algemeen Rijksarchief te 's Gravenhage, 963
Algemene Nederlandse Vereniging voor Sociale Geneeskunde, 958
— — — Wijsbegeerte, Uithoorn, 959
Algoma College, Sault Ste. Marie, 270

# INDEX OF INSTITUTIONS

Algonquin Radio Observatory, Lake Traverse, 245
Aliança Francesa, Rio de Janeiro, 180
Alianza Colombo-Francesa, Bogotá, 346
— Francesa, Buenos Aires, 63
— — La Paz, 173
— — Lima, 1037
— — San Salvador, 422
— — en Venezuela, Caracas, 1951
Aligarh Muslim University, 677
Al-Imam Al-A'dham College, Baghdad, 728
Alipore Observatory and Meteorological Office, 670
Alisher Navoi State Public Library of the Uzbek S.S.R., Tashkent, 1349
Allahabad Mathematical Society, 663
— Public Library, 673
Allama Iqbal Open University, Islamabad, 1025
Állami Gorkij Könyvtár, Budapest, 640
Allan Memorial Institute of Psychiatry, Montreal, 277
Állategészségügyi Főiskolai Kar, Hódmezővásárhely, 652
Állatorvostudományi Egyetem, Budapest, 651
Állattenyésztési es Takarmányozási Kutatóközpont, Gödöllő, 636
— Kutatóintézet, Gödöllő, 636
Allegheny College, 1866
Allen County Public Library, Fort Wayne, 1626
Allgemeine Bibliotheken der Gesellschaft für das Gute und Gemeinnützige, Basel, 1259
— Geschichtforschende Gesellschaft der Schweiz, Bern, 1254
— Gesellschaft für Philosophie in Deutschland e.V., 524
Alliance Agricole Belge, Brussels, 150
— College, Cambridge Springs, 1866
— Française, Accra, 611
— — Bangkok, 1283
— — Canberra, 89
— — Chittagong, 142
— — Colombo, 1224
— — Copenhagen, 390
— — Dakar, 1145
— — Dar es Salaam, 1280
— — Delhi, 661
— — Dublin, 730
— — Kingston, Jamaica, 800
— — Kuala Lumpur, 914
— — Lisbon, 1098
— — Lomé, 1292
— — Montevideo, 1938
— — New York, 1607
— — Ottawa, 241
— — Paris, 448
— — Port-au-Prince, 629
— — Quito, 407
— — Reykjavik, 656
— — San José, 359
— — Santo Domingo, 403
— — Singapore, 1150
— — du Maroc, Rabat, 949
— — (Délégation Générale), Kinshasa, 1995
— Médicale Internationale—A.M.I., Paris, 41
All-India Fine Arts and Crafts Society, New Delhi, 660
— Institute of Hygiene and Public Health, 707
— — — Medical Sciences, New Delhi, 707
— Ophthalmological Society, Bombay, 662
— Oriental Conference, 668
All-Pakistan Educational Conference, Nazimabad, 1019
— Homeopathic Association, 1020
All Saviour's Cathedral Museum, Isfahan, 722
All Souls College, Oxford, 1524
All-Union Antileprosy Research Institute, Saratov, 1346

— Astronomical and Geodesical Society, 1318
— Biochemical Society, Moscow, 1319
— Botanical Society, Leningrad, 1320
— Cardiological Research Centre, Moscow, 1342
— Council of Scientific and Engineering Societies, Moscow, 1344
— Entomological Society, 1320
— Extra-Mural Agricultural Institute, 1369
— — Civil Engineering Institute, Moscow, 1379
— — Finance Institute, Moscow, 1373
— — Institute of Food Industry, Moscow, 1381
— — — Railway Engineers, Moscow, 1388
— — — Soviet Trade, Moscow, 1373
— — — the Textile and Light Industries, Moscow, 1380
— — Law Institute, 1382
— — Mechanical Engineering Institute, Moscow, 1377
— — Polytechnic Institute, 1374
— — Telecommunications Institute, Moscow, 1377
— Flax Research Institute, Torzhok, 1345
— Geological Library, Leningrad, 1348
— — Oil Prospecting Research Institute, Moscow, 1346
— — Research Institute, Leningrad, 1346
— Hydrobiological Society, Moscow, 1320
— Institute for Designing of Scientific Buildings, Moscow, 1323
— — — Nature Protection and Reserves, Moscow, 1345
— — of Experimental Veterinary Science, Moscow, 1338
— — — Medical Polymers, Moscow, 1346
— Labour-Protection Research Institute of the Central Council of Trade Unions, 1386
— Legumes and Pulse Crops Research Institute, Orel, 1338
— V. I. Lenin Academy of Agricultural Sciences, Moscow, 1335
— Maize Research Institute, Dnepropetrovsk, 1338
— I. I. Mechnikov Scientific Medical Society of Microbiologists, Epidemiologists and Infectionists, Moscow, 1344
— Microbiological Society, Moscow, 1319
— Mineralogical Society, Leningrad, 1320
— Palaeontological Society, Leningrad, 1320
— Patent and Technical Library, Moscow, 1348
— Permanent Exhibition of Labour Protection, Moscow, 1359
— Pharmaceutical Society, Moscow, 1345
— Plant Breeding and Genetics Institute, Odessa, 1338
— Pushkin Museum, Pushkin Town, 1358
— Research and Project Institute of Man-made Fibres, Moscow, 1347
— Institute for Electrification of Agriculture, Moscow, 1338
— — — Mechanization of Agriculture, Moscow, 1338
— — of Agricultural Forest Reclamation, Volgograd, 1338
— — — Microbiology, Moscow, 1338
— — — Animal Husbandry, Moscow, 1338
— — — Applied Molecular Biology and Genetics, Moscow, 1338
— — — Astrakhan Raising, Samarkand, 1345
— — — Biological Methods of Plant Protection, Kishinev, 1338
— — — Chemical Reagents and Substances of High Purity, Moscow, 1346
— — — Economics in Agriculture, Moscow, 1338

— — — Electromechanics, Moscow, 1346
— — — Farm Animal Physiology and Biochemistry, Borovsk, 1338
— — — Forestry Reclamation, Volgograd, 1345
— — — Gastroenterology, Moscow, 1346
— — — Geophysical Prospecting Methods, Moscow, 1346
— — — Gold and Rare Metals, Magadan, 1346
— — — Grain Farming, Shortandy, 1338
— — — — Tselinograd, 1345
— — — Hydraulic Engineering and Land Reclamation, Moscow, 1347
— — — Hydrogeology and Geological Engineering, Moscow, 1347
— — — Livestock Breeding and Genetics, Leningrad, 1338
— — — Marine Fishing Industry and Oceanography, Moscow, 1347
— — — Meat Industry, Moscow, 1347
— — — Metallurgical Machine Building, Moscow, 1347
— — — Monocrystals, Kharkov, 1346
— — — Nonferrous Metals, Ust-Kamenogorsk, 1347
— — — Obstetrics and Gynaecology, Moscow, 1384
— — — Oil Refineries, Baku, 1347
— — — Pharmaceutical Chemistry, Moscow, 1346
— — — — Plants, Moscow, 1346
— — — Plant Protection, Leningrad, 1338
— — — Soil Erosion Control, Koursk, 1338
— — — Submarine Geology and Geophysics, Riga, 1346
— — — Tea and Subtropical Plants, Makharadze, 1345
— — — the Cellulose and Paper Industry, Leningrad, 1346
— — — Tobacco and Makhorka, Krasnodar, 1347
— — — Veterinary Entomology and Arachnology, Tumen, 1338
— — — Water Supply, Drainage, Hydro-Engineering Works and Engineering Hydrogeology, 1377
— — — Winegrowing and Wine Production, Novocherkassk, 1345
— Rice Research Institute, Krasnodar, 1338
— Scientific Medical Society of Anatomists, Histologists and Embryologists, Moscow, 1344
— — — — Anatomists-Pathologists, Moscow, 1344
— — — — Cardiologists, Moscow, 1344
— — — — Endocrinologists, Moscow, 1344
— — — — Forensic Medical Officers, Moscow, 1344
— — — — Gerontologists and Geriatrists, Kiev, 1344
— — — — Hygienists, Moscow, 1344
— — — — Neuropathologists and Psychiatrists, Moscow, 1345
— — — — Neurosurgeons, Moscow, 1345
— — — — Obstetricians and Gynaecologists, Moscow, 1345
— — — — Oncologists, Moscow, 1345
— — — — Ophthalmologists, Moscow, 1345
— — — — Oto-Rhino-Laryngologists, Moscow, 1345
— — — — Pathophysiologists, Leningrad, 1345
— — — — Pediatricians, Moscow, 1345
— — — — Pharmacologists, Moscow, 1345

— — — — Phthisiologists, Moscow, 1345
— — — — Physical Therapists and Health Resort Physicians, Moscow, 1345
— — — — Physicians-Analysts, Moscow, 1344
— — — — Roentgenologists and Radiologists, Moscow, 1345
— — — — Specialists in Medical Control and Exercise Medicine, Moscow, 1344
— — — — Stomatologists, Moscow, 1345
— — — — Surgeons, Moscow, 1345
— — — — Therapists, Moscow, 1345
— — — — Traumatic Surgeons and Orthopaedists, Moscow, 1345
— — — — Urological Surgeons, Moscow, 1345
— — — — Venereologists and Dermatologists, Moscow, 1345
— — Research Institute for the Investigation of New Antibiotics, Moscow, 1341
— — — of Cybernetics, Moscow, 1321
— — — — Economics of Mineralogical Raw Materials and Prospecting, Moscow, 1320
— — Society of History of Medicine, Moscow, 1344
— Society of Geneticists and Breeders, Moscow, 1320
— — — Helminthologists, 1320
— — — Mammalogists, Moscow, 1320
— — — Protozoologists, Leningrad, 1320
— — "Znanie", Moscow, 1345
— Soil Science Society, Moscow, 1319
— State Institute of Cinematography, Moscow, 1388
— — Library of Foreign Literature, Moscow, 1348
— Sugar Research Institute, Kiev, 1345
— Toxicological Institute, Leningrad, 1346
All-University Gerontology Center, Syracuse, N.Y., 1822
Alma-Ata Institute of National Economy, 1373
— Medical Institute, 1382
— Pedagogical Institute of Foreign Languages, 1382
— Zootechnical and Veterinary Institute, 1372
Alma College, Michigan, 1760
Al Maktabah Al Wataniah, 1277
Almindelige Danske Lægeforening, Copenhagen, 391
Al-Mustansiriya University, Baghdad, 727
— — Library, Baghdad, 725
Alphabet Museum, Tel-Aviv, 743
Alpine Forschungsstelle der Universität Innsbruck in Obergurgl, 134
Alšova Jihočeská galerie, 378
Altai Agricultural Institute, 1369
— Medical Institute, Barnaul, 1382
— I. I. Polzunov Polytechnic Institute, Barnaul, 1374
— State Museum of Applied Arts, Barnaul, 1353
— — University, Barnaul, 1360
Altonaer Museum in Hamburg, 543
Alupka Palace Museum, 1353
Alushta S.M. Sergeyev-Tsensky Literary Museum, 1357
Alverno College, Wisconsin, 1931
Al Zahiriah, Damascus, 1277
Amaldus Nielsen malerisamling, Oslo, 1012
Amasya Müzesi, 1301
American Academy and Institute of Arts and Letters, New York, 1597
— — of Allergy, 1608
— — — Arts and Sciences, 1597
— — — Family Physicians, Kansas City, 1608
— — — Ophthalmology, 1608
— — — Otolaryngology, Rochester, 1608

— — — — Pediatrics, 1608
— — — — Periodontology, Chicago, 1608
— — — — Political and Social Science, 1602
— — — — Religion, Chico, Calif., 1614
— — Accounting Association, 1602
— — Anthropological Association, 1614
— — Antiquarian Society, 1605
— — — Library, 1629
— — Arbitration Association, 1602
— — Association for Cancer Research Inc., New York, 1618
— — — — Higher Education, Washington, D.C., 1604
— — — — State and Local History, 1605
— — — — the Advancement of Science, 1611
— — — — — the Humanities, Washington, D.C., 1607
— — — of Anatomists, 1608
— — — — Immunologists, Bethesda, Md., 1608
— — — — Law Libraries, 1601
— — — — Museums, Washington, 1610
— — — — Pathologists, 1608
— — — — Petroleum Geologists, 1613
— — — — State Colleges and Universities, Washington, D.C., 1604
— — — — University Professors, 1604
— — Astronomical Society, 1613
— — Bar Association, 1602
— — Cancer Society, Inc., 1608
— — Catholic Historical Association, 1605
— — Center, Amman, 875
— — — Barton, A.C.T., 89
— — — Cairo, 413
— — — Colombo, 1224
— — — Helsinki, 428
— — — Karachi, 1020
— — — Port of Spain, 1293
— — — Stockholm, 1236
— — — in Japan, Tokyo, 806
— — — Libraries, New Delhi, 673
— — — Library, Dar es Salaam, 1280
— — — — Skopje, 1975
— — — of PEN, New York, 1607
— — Ceramic Society, Inc., 1615
— — Chemical Society, 1613
— — Classical League, 1607
— — College, Bryn Mawr, Pa., 1866
— — — in Jerusalem, 752
— — — of Obstetricians and Gynecologists, Washington, D.C., 1608
— — — — Physicians, 1608
— — — — Surgeons, 1608
— — Comparative Literature Association, Binghamton, N.Y., 1607
— — Consulting Engineers Council, Washington, D.C., 1615
— — Council for the Arts, New York, 1600
— — — of Learned Societies, 1598
— — — on Education, 1604
— — Crystallographic Association, 1613
— — Cultural Center, Antananarivo, 910
— — — — Dakar, 1145
— — — — Khartoum, 1229
— — — — (USIS), Lomé, 1292
— — — — Rabat, 949
— — — — Taipei, 340
— — — — Yaoundé, 231
— — — — and Library, Kathmandu, 954
— — — — Library, Dacca, 143
— — — — — Nairobi, 879
— — — — — Seoul, 886
— — Dairy Science Association, 1599
— — Dental Association, 1608
— — Dialect Society, London, Ont., 1607
— — Dietetic Association, Chicago, 1608
— — Economic Association, 1602
— — Educational Research Association, 1617
— — Federation for Clinical Research, Thorofare, N.J., 1618
— — — of Arts, New York, 1600
— — Finance Association, New York University, 1602
— — Folklore Society, Inc., 1614
— — Forestry Association, 1599
— — Genetic Association, 1611

— — Geographical Society, 1606
— — — Collection of the University of Wisconsin-Milwaukee Library, 1630
— — Geological Institute, Falls Church, Va., 1613
— — Geophysical Union (of the National Academy of Sciences—National Research Council), Washington, 1613
— — Geriatrics Society, New York, 1608
— — Gynecological and Obstetrical Society, 1608
— — Heart Association, Dallas, 1608
— — Historical Association, 1605
— — Hospital Association, Chicago, 1608
— — Institute for Research in the Behavioural Sciences, Pittsburgh, 1622
— — — in Taiwan, Taipei, 1622
— — — of Aeronautics and Astronautics, New York, 1615
— — — — Architects, 1600
— — — — Biological Sciences, 1611
— — — — Chemical Engineers, 1615
— — — — Chemists, 1613
— — — — Indian Studies, Philadelphia, 1880
— — — — Industrial Engineers, Inc., Norcross, Ga., 1615
— — — — Mining, Metallurgical and Petroleum Engineers, Inc., New York, 1615
— — — — Nutrition, 1608
— — — — Physics, 1613
— — International College, Springfield, Mass., 1747
— — Irish Historical Society, 1605
— — Iron and Steel Institute, 1615
— — -Jewish Historical Society, 1605
— — Judicature Society, 1602
— — Laryngological, Rhinological and Otological Society, Inc. (Triological Society), 1608
— — Law Institute, 1602
— — — -American Bar Association Committee on Continuing Professional Education, Philadelphia, 1602
— — Library, Athens, 618
— — — Brussels, 155
— — — Paris, 461
— — — Association, 1601
— — — Resource Centre, Singapore, 1150
— — Lung Association, New York, 1608
— — Malacological Union, Houston, 1611
— — Mathematical Society, 1612
— — Medical Association, 1609
— — — Division of Library and Archival Services, Chicago, 1628
— — — Technologists, 1609
— — — Women's Association, Inc., 1609
— — Meteorological Society, 1613
— — Microscopical Society, 1613
— — Museum in Britain, near Bath, 1467
— — — of Natural History, 1635
— — — — Library, 1629
— — — — Science and Energy, Oak Ridge, Tenn., 1635
— — Musicological Society, 1600
— — National Standards Institute, New York, 1615
— — Neurological Association, 1609
— — Nuclear Society, 1613
— — Numismatic Society, 1605
— — Occupational Therapy Association, 1609
— — Optometric Association Inc., 1609
— — Oriental Society, 1614
— — Ornithologists' Union, 1611
— — Peace Society, 1602
— — Pediatric Society, 1609
— — Personnel and Guidance Association, Falls Church, Va., 1614
— — Pharmaceutical Association, Inc., 1613
— — Philological Association, 1607
— — Philosophical Association, 1614
— — — Society, 1598

## INDEX OF INSTITUTIONS

American Philosophical Society Library, Philadelphia, 1630
— Physical Society, 1613
— — Therapy Association, 1609
— Physiological Society, 1609
— Phytopathological Society, 1611
— Planning Association, Washington, 1600
— Political Science Association, 1602
— Psychiatric Association, 1609
— Psychological Association, 1614
— Public Health Association, 1609
— Rheumatism Association, Atlanta, Ga., 1609
— Roentgen Ray Society, 1609
— School of Classical Studies at Athens, 622
— Schools of Oriental Research, Cambridge, Mass., 1622
— Society for Aesthetics, 1600
— — — Clinical Investigation, 1609
— — — Eighteenth-Century Studies, Columbus, 1605
— — — Engineering Education, 1615
— — — Ethnohistory, Wichita Falls, Tex, 1614
— — — Horticultural Science, 1599
— — — Information Science, Washington, D.C., 1601
— — — Medical Technology, 1609
— — — Metals, 1616
— — — Microbiology, Washington, 1609
— — — Pharmacology and Experimental Therapeutics, Inc., 1609
— — — Photobiology, Bethesda, 1612
— — — Political and Legal Philosophy, Durham, N.C., 1602
— — — Physical Research, Inc., New York, 1622
— — — Public Administration, 1602
— — — Testing and Materials, 1616
— — — Theatre Research, Flushing, N.Y., 1600
— — of Agricultural Engineers, 1599
— — — Agronomy, 1599
— — — Animal Science, 1599
— — — Biological Chemists, Inc., 1613
— — — Church History, 1605
— — — Civil Engineers, 1616
— — — Clinical Hypnosis, Des Plaines, Ill., 1609
— — — — Pathologists, 1609
— — — Composers, Authors and Publishers (ASCAP), New York, 1600
— — — Heating, Refrigerating and Air-Conditioning Engineers, 1616
— — — Human Genetics, Richmond, Va., 1609
— — — Ichthyologists and Herpetologists, 1611
— — — International Law, 1602
— — — Landscape Architects, Inc., 1600
— — — Limnology and Oceanography, 1606
— — — Mammalogists, 1611
— — — Mechanical Engineers, 1616
— — — Naturalists, 1612
— — — Naval Engineers, Inc., 1616
— — — Parasitologists, 1612
— — — Photogrammetry, Falls Church, 1616
— — — Tropical Medicine and Hygiene, 1609
— — — Zoologists, 1612
— Sociological Association, 1614
— Speech-Language-Hearing Association, Rockville, Md., 1609
— Statistical Association, 1602
— Studies Association, Philadelphia, 1615
— Surgical Association, 1610
— Swedish Historical Foundation and Museum, 1605
— Theological Library Association, 1601
— University, Washington, 1688
— — in Cairo, 418
— — — Library, 416
— — — of Beirut, 900
— — — — Library, 899

— Urological Association, Inc., Baltimore, 1610
— Veterinary Medical Association, 1599
— Vocational Association, Inc., 1604
— Welding Society, Miami, 1616
Amerika-Gedenkbibliothek, 534
Amerika Haus Berlin, 521
— — Library, Vienna, 127
Ames Research Center, Moffett Field, 1623
Amherst College, 1747
Amigos de la Ciudad, La Paz, 173
A.M.L.I. Central Library for Music and Dance, Tel-Aviv, 741
Amstelkring Museum, Amsterdam, 966
Amsterdams Historisch Museum, 966
Amt für Wissenschaft und Forschung des Eidgenössischen Departement des Innern, Bern, 1258
Amtliche Materialprufanstalt für das Bauwesen, Brunswick, 556
Anadolu Medeniyetieri Müzesi, Ankara, 1301
— Üniversitesi, Eskişehir, 1302
Anaemia and Malnutrition Research Centre, Chiangmai, 1285
Anaesthesiology Association, Hanoi, 1962
Anambra State Library Board, Enugu, 994
Anatolian University, Eskişehir, 1302
Anatomical Society of Great Britain and Ireland, 1427
Anatomische Gesellschaft, Aachen, 521
Ancient Iran Cultural Society, Teheran, 721
— Monuments Society, London, 1421
Andalas University, Padang, 712
Andersens, H. C., Barndomshjem, Odense, 395
— Hus, Odense, 395
Anderson College, Indiana, 1716
— Museum, Cairo, 417
— Park Art Gallery, Invercargill, 982
Andhra Pradesh Agricultural University, Hyderabad, 677
— — State Museum, Hyderabad, 674
— — University, 677
Andijan Medical Institute, 1382
— Pedagogical Institute of Languages, 1382
Andrews University, Berrien Springs, 1760
"Angel Kancev" Technical University, Ruse, 224
Angeles University Foundation, Angeles City, 1050
Angelo State University, San Angelo, 1897
Anglia, Reykjavik, 656
Anglo-Bolivian Cultural Institute, 173
— -Chinese Educational Institute, London, 1424
Angus L. Macdonald Library, Antigonish, 247
Anhui Library, Hefei, 335
Animal Breeding Research Organisation (A.R.C.), Edinburgh, 1440
— Diseases Research Association, 1440
— Genetics and Breeding Unit, Armidale, N.S.W., 106
— Health Research Centre, Entebbe, 1311
— — Institute, Dokki, 414
— — Trust, Newmarket, 1419
— Husbandry and Dairy Research Institute, Pretoria, 1159
— — Research Institute, Comila, 142
— Production Corporation, Research Division, Khartoum, 1229
— — Research and Training Institute, Dodoma, 1280
— — — Institute, Dokki, 414
— Research Institute, Achimota, 611
— Virus Research Institute, Woking, 1440
Anit-Kabir Müzesi, 1301
Anjuman Taraqqi-e-Urdu Pakistan, 1020
Anjuman-i-Islam Urdu Research Institute, Bombay, 668
Ankara Nükleer Araştırma ve Eğitim Merkezi, Ankara, 1299
— Üniversitesi, 1301
— University Library, 1300
Anna Maria College, 1747

Annamalai University, 678
Année de Formation aux Ministères, Paris, 494
Anotati Biomichaniki Scholi Pireos, Piraeus, 623
— Geoponiki Scholi Athinon, Athens, 622
— Scholi Economikon Kai Emborikon Epistimon, Athens, 622
— Kalon Technon, 622
— Viomichaniki Scholi Thessalonikis, Thessaloniki, 623
Anspach Institute for Diplomacy and Foreign Affairs, Philadelphia, 1880
Antalya Bölge Müzesi, 1301
Antarctic Research Centre, Wellington, N.Z., 986
Anthropological Society of Bombay, 663
— — New South Wales, Sydney, 91
— Survey of India, Calcutta, 671
Anthropologische Gesellschaft in Wien, 123
— Staatssammlung, Munich, 544
Anti-Contagious Diseases Association, Hanoi, 1962
Antikenmuseum Basel und Sammlung Ludwig, 1261
— Berlin (West), 541
Antiken-Sammlung, Berlin (East), 508
Antikvarisk-topografiska arkivet, Stockholm, 1242
Antioch University, Yellow Springs, 1839
Antiquarian and Numismatic Society of Montreal, 241
Antiquarische Gesellschaft, 1254
Antiquities Service, Khartoum, 1229
— — Library, Khartoum, 1229
Anti-Tuberculosis and Lung Diseases Association, Hanoi, 1962
Antonio A. Roig Public Library, Humaçao, 1110
Antwerp State University Centre, 166
Anuchin (D. N.) Anthropological Institute and Museum, 1358
Anuradhapura Folk Museum, 1226
Aoyama Gakuin University, Tokyo, 861
Apollonia Museum, Marsa Sousa, 906
Apothecaries' Hall, Dublin, 731
— of London, Worshipful Society of, 1427
Appalachian State University, Boone, N.C., 1824
Appartamenti Monumentali, Florence, 770
Applied Chemistry Unit (CSIR), Pretoria, 1157
— Economics Research Centre, Karachi, 1021
— Psychology Unit (M.R.C), Cambridge, 1440
— Research Institute, Research and Development Authority, Ben-Gurion University of the Negev, Beersheva, 740
— — Laboratory, University Park, Pa., 1877
— Science Research Institute, Kyoto, 816
— Scientific Research Corporation of Thailand, Bangkok, 1283
Apsley House, London, 1467
Aquinas College, Grand Rapids, 1760
— — Inc., North Adelaide, 99
— — of Higher Studies, Colombo, 1228
— University, Legazpi City, 1050
Aquincumi Múzeum, Budapest, 643
Arab Academy of Damascus, 1227
— Archivists Institute, Baghdad, 725
— Bureau of Education for the Gulf States, Riyadh, 1142
— Center for Educational Research, Kuwait, 1142
— — — the Studies of Arid Zones and Dry Lands (ACSAD), Damascus, 1277
— Centre for Educational Research, Safat, 897
— League Educational, Cultural and Scientific Organization (ALECSO), Tunis, 1295
— — Information Centre (Library), Cairo, 416

— Library, Boutilimit, 922
— — Chinguetti, 922
— — Kaédi, 922
— — Oualata, 922
— — Tidjika, 922
— Planning Institute, Kuwait, 897
— Regional Branch of the International Council on Archives (ARBICA), Baghdad, 725
— Research Centre, London, 1434
— States Regional Centre for Functional Literacy in Rural Areas (ASFEC), Menoufia, 421
Arany János Múzeum, 644
Araştirma Fen Heyeti Müdürlüğü, Ankara, 1299
Arbeitsgemeinschaft der Altphilologen Österreichs, 121
— — Spezialbibliotheken, Frankfurt, 518
— deutscher wirtschaftswissenschaftlicher Forschunginstitute, 528
— für Kunst und Wissenschaft, Vienna, 119
— Historischer Kommissionen und Landesgeschichtlicher Institute, Münster, 520
— industrieller Forschungsvereinigungen e.V., 533
— Schweizer Grafiker, Zürich, 1253
— Sozialwissenschaftlicher Institute, 530
Arbeitsstelle für Robert-Musil-Forschung, Saarbrücken, 531
Arbil Museum, 726
Arbuzov, A. E. Institute of Organic and Physical Chemistry, Kazan, 1323
Archaeological Department, Ministry of Culture, Rangoon, 228
— Institute of America, 1606
— Library, Taxila, 1023
— Museum, Al Ain, 1391
— — Bodh Gaya, 674
— — Corinth, 619
— — Crete, 619
— — Delphi, 619
— — Durrës, 55
— — Fier, 55
— — Göteborg, 1242
— — Harappa, 1024
— — Mathura, 674
— — Mohenjodaro, 1024
— — Nagarjunakonda, 674
— — Nalanda, 674
— — Olympia, 619
— — Rhodes, 619
— — Taxila, 1024
— Natural History, Epigraphy, Prehistory and Ethnography Museums, Tripoli, 906
— Reasearch Unit, Johannesburg, 1182
— (Rockefeller) Museum, East Jerusalem, 743
— Survey of India, New Delhi, 667
Archaeologiki Hetairia, Athens, 616
Archaeology Institute, Beijing, 332
Archief der Gemeente Leeuwarden en Stedelijke Bibliotheek, 963
— en Museum voor het Vlaamse Cultuurleven, 155
— — Stadsbibliotheek, Malines, 156
Archipelago Research Institute, Turku, 439
Architects Association, Hanoi, 1962
Architectural Association (Inc.), London, 1411
— — of Ireland, 730
— — — Israel, Tel-Aviv, 737
Architecture Museum, Berat, 55
Architektenraad, Amsterdam, 956
Archiv der Hansestadt Lübeck, 539
— — sozialen Demokratie (Friedrich-Ebert-Stiftung), Bonn, 538
— — Universität Wien, Vienna, 127
— des Stiftes Schotten, Vienna, 127
— für Schweizerische Kunstgeschichte, Basel, 1259
— hlavného mesta SSR Bratislavy, Regionálna knižnica, 376
— University Karlovy, Prague, 375

Archival Museum, Peshawar, 1024
Archivberatungsstelle Rheinland, Cologne, 539
Archives d'Etat, Geneva, 1259
— de l'Archevêché, Malines, 156
— — l'Etat, Arlon, 155
— — — Bruges, 155
— — — Liège, 156
— — — Luxembourg, 908
— — — Mons, 157
— — — Namur, 157
— — — Neuchâtel, 1260
— — — la Guerre, 156
— — — République du Niger, 990
— — — Ville de Bruxelles, 155
— — — Sénégal, Dakar, 1146
— — — Zaire, Kinshasa, 1995
— Départementales, Sainte-Clotilde, 500
— — de la Guadeloupe, Basse-Terre, 499
— — — — Martinique, Fort de France, 499
— du Centre public d'aide sociale de Bruxelles, 156
— Economiques Suisses, Basel, 1259
— et Bibliothèque du Palais de Monaco, 946
— Générales du Royaume, Brussels, 156
— Nationales, Abidjan, 799
— — Algiers, 58
— — Antananarivo, 910
— — Conakry, 697
— — Nouakchott, 922
— — Paris, 460
— — Tunis, 1295
— — Yaoundé, 231
— — de la République Populaire du Benin, Porto Novo, 172
— — du Mali, Institut des Sciences Humaines, Bamako, 920
— — Québec, Quebec City, 248
— of American Art, New York, 1600
— — the U.S.S.R. Academy of Sciences, Moscow, 1320, 1347
— Office of New South Wales, Sydney, 96
Archivi Istorici della Città di Genoa, 771
Archivio Centrale dello Stato, Rome, 767
— Segreto Vaticano, 1943
Archivo-Biblioteca de la Función Legislativa, Quito, 408
Archivo Capitular de la Santa Iglesia Catedral de Barcelona, 1199
— de la Casa de Medinaceli y Camarasa, Seville, 1201
— — — Corona de Aragón, 1199
— — — Real Chancillería de Granada, 1200
— — Musica Colonial Venezolano, 1954
— del Reino de Mallorca, Palma de Mallorca, 1201
— — — Valencia, 1201
— Diocesano, Barcelona, 1199
— General de Centro América, Guatemala City, 625
— — — Indias, 1201
— — — la Administración Civil del Estado, Madrid, 1199
— — — Musica Nacional, Buenos Aires, 69
— — — Nacíon, Buenos Aires, 69
— — — — Caracas, 1954
— — — — Lima, 1039
— — — — Managua, 988
— — — — Mexico City, 930
— — — — Montevideo, 1939
— — — — San Salvador, 422
— — — — Santo Domingo, 404
— — — Puerto Rico, San Juan, 1110
— — — Simancas, 1201
— — Histórico de la Ciudad, Sabadell, 1200
— — Nacional, Madrid, 1199
— — Provincial, Lérida, 1200
— Nacional, Havana, 364
— — Panama City, 1030
— — Santiago, 326
— — de Colombia, 349
— — — Costa Rica, San José, 360

— — — Historia, Quito, 408
— — — Honduras, 630
— Regional de Galicia, 1200
— y Biblioteca Capitulares, Toledo, 1201
Archivos Históricos y Bibliotecas, Mexico City, 930
Archiwum Akt Nowych, Warsaw, 1072
— Dokumentacji Mechaniccnej, Warsaw, 1072
— Głównej Akt Dawnych, Warsaw, 1072
— Polskiej Akademii Nauk, Warsaw, 1072
Arctic and Antarctic Scientific Research Institute, Leningrad, 1346
— Institute of North America, Calgary, 245
— Station, University of Copenhagen, Godhavn, 393
Arecibo Observatory, P. Rico, 1109, 1621
Arellano University, Manila, 1050
Arendal og Hisøy Bibliotek, 1010
Arentshuis, Bruges, 158
Argentine Academy of Letters, 62
— — — Surgery, Buenos Aires, 64
— University for Lawyers, La Plata, 80
— — of Business Studies, Buenos Aires, 78
Argonne National Laboratory, 1620
Arheološki Muzej na Makedonija, Skopje, 1977
— — Split, 1978
— — Zagreb, 1978
Arheološko Društvo na Makedonija, Prilep, 1971
Arhiv Hrvatske, Zagreb, 1974
— na S.R. Makedonija, Skopje, 1976
— — na Skopje, 1975
— — S.R. Slovenije, Ljubljana, 1975
— Srbije, Belgrade, 1974
— — Vojvodine, Sremski Karlovci, 1974
Arhivele Statului, Bucharest, 1124
Århus Kommunes Biblioteker, 394
— Tandlaegehojskole, 401
Arif Hikmat Library, Medina, 1142
Aristotelian Society, 1434
— University of Thessaloniki, 619
Aristotelion Panepistimion Thessalonikis, 619
Arizona Archaeological and Historical Society, 1607
— Department of Library, Archives and Public Records, Phoenix, 1630
— State Museum, 1635
— — University, Tempe, 1645
Arkansas College, Batesville, 1650
— State University, 1650
— Tech University, Russellville, 1650
Arkeologisk Museum i Stavanger, 1013
Arkhangelsk Institute of Epidemiology, Microbiology and Hygiene, 1384
— V. V. Kuibyshev Forest Engineering Institute, 1381
— Medical Institute, 1382
— State Museum, 1355
— — — of Fine Arts, 1353
Arkitektafélag Íslands, 656
Arkitektøgskolen i Oslo, 1017
Arkitektskolen i Aarhus, 400
Arktisk Institut, Charlottenlund, 390
Arlis (Art Libraries Society), Hull, 1415
Armed Forces Institute of Pathology, Washington, D.C., 1610
Armeemuseum der DDR, Dresden, 509
Armémuseum, Stockholm, 1241
Armenian Agricultural Institute, 1369
— Artistic Union, Cairo, 413
— Biochemical Society, Erevan, 1324
— Botanical Society, Erevan, 1324
— Genetic Society, Erevan, 1324
— Geographical Society, Erevan, 1324
— Gynaecological Institute, Erevan, 1384
— Institute of Spa Treatment and Physiotherapy, 1387
— Physiological Society, Erevan, 1324
— S.S.R. Academy of Sciences, 1324
— State Picture Gallery, Erevan, 1352
Armeria Reale, Turin, 773
Armidale College of Advanced Education, N.S.W., 112

Armoury Museum, Kremlin, Moscow, 1354
Armstrong College, Berkeley, 1651
Army Library, Washington, 1624
— Museum, Brunei, 213
Arnold Bergstraesser Institut für Kulturwissenschaftliche Forschung (ABI), Freiburg, 530
Arquivo Distrital, Vizeu, 1102
— — Biblioteca e Museu Regional Abade de Baçal, 1102
— — do Funchal, Madeira, 1102
— — — Porto, 1102
— e Museu de Arte da Universidade de Coímbra, 1102
— Histórico de Angola, Luanda, 61
— — — Moçambique, 952
— — do Estado do Rio Grande do Sul, Pôrto Alegre, 187
— — Ministério das Finanças, 1101
— — Militar, Lisbon, 1101
— Nacional, Rio de Janeiro, 187
— — da Torre do Tombo, 1101
— Público e Museu Histórico do Estado do Ceará, 189
Arsip Nasional Republik Indonesia, Jakarta, 711
Art Association of the Philippines, Manila, 1047
— Center College of Design, Pasadena, 1651
— Galleries and Museums Association of New Zealand, Auckland, 978
— Gallery, Plovdiv, 221
— — Skopje, 1977
— — "De Volle Maan", Delft, 966
— — of Hamilton, Ont., 250
— — — Matica Srpska, 1977
— — — New South Wales, Sydney, 97
— — — Nova Scotia, Halifax, 250
— — — Ontario, Toronto, 250
— — — South Australia, Adelaide, 97
— — — Western Australia, 98
— Institute of Chicago, 1635
— Libraries Society of North America (ARLIS/NA), Tucson, 1601
— School of the National Academy, New York, 1601
— Society of India, Bombay, 660
Arthritis and Rheumatism Council for Research, London, 1444
Arthur J. Dyer Observatory, 1620
Artificial Cells and Organs Research Centre, Montreal, 277
Artists' League of Great Britain, London, 1413
Arts and Crafts School, Tripoli, 907
— — Science Research Centre, Las Cruces, 1802
— — — University, Mandalay, 229
— — — — Rangoon, 229
— — — — Library, Mandalay, 228
— Council of Australia, 87
— — — Dublin, 730
— — — Ghana, Accra, 611
— — — Great Britain, 1412
— — — Northern Ireland, Belfast, 1554
— — — Pakistan, Karachi, 1019
Aruba Public School of Music, 975
Arya Mehr University of Technology, Teheran, 723
Ärztegesellschaft Innsbruck, 121
A/S Bergens Musikkonservatorium, 1018
Asahikawa Kyodo Hakubutsukan, 822
Ascension Historical Society, Georgetown, 1558
Ashanti Regional Library, Kumasi, 612
Ashkhabad Institute of Epidemiology and Hygiene, 1384
Ashland College, Ohio, 1839
Ashmolean Library, Oxford, 1464
— Museum, Oxford, 1470
Asia Foundation, The, Bangkok, 1283
— — — Colombo, 1224
— — — Dacca, 142
— — — Hong Kong, 1559
— — — Islamabad, 1020
— — — Jakarta, 708

— — Kabul, 52
— — Kuala Lumpur, 914
— — Manila, 1047
— — San Francisco, 1607
— — Seoul, 885
— — Taipei, 340
— — Tokyo, 806
— Pacific Association of Japan, Tokyo, 813
— University, Tokyo, 861
Asian Art Museum of San Francisco, The Avery Brundage Collection, 1635
— Cultural Centre for Unesco, Tokyo, 806
— Documentation Centre for UNESCO, Teheran, 721
— Institute of Technology, Bangkok, 1284
— — — Library and Regional Documentation Centre, Bangkok, 1284
— Student's Cultural Association, Tokyo, 806
Asiatic Society, Bombay, 663
— — Calcutta, 663
Âsiyan Museum, Istanbul, 1301
Aslib, London, 1415
— Library, 1455
Asmara Public Library, 424
Asociación Amigos de los Museos, 1188
— Archivista Argentina, Buenos Aires, 63
— Argentina Amigos de la Astronomía, Buenos Aires, 65
— — de Astronomía, La Plata, 65
— — Bibliotecas y Centros de Información Científicos y Técnicos, Santa Fé, 63
— — Biología y Medicina Nuclear, Buenos Aires, 64
— — Ciencias Naturales, 65
— — Ecología, Buenos Aires, 65
— — Farmacia y Bioquímica Industrial, 64
— — Geofísicos y Geodestas, 65
— — la Ciencia del Suelo, Buenos Aires, 62
— — del Frío, Buenos Aires, 65
— — para el Progreso de las Ciencias, Buenos Aires, 65
— Bernardino Rivadavia—Biblioteca Popular, Bahia Blanca, 63
— Chilena de Microbiología, Santiago, 323
— — Sismología e Ingeniería Antisísmica, Santiago, 324
— Colombiana de Bibliotecarios— ASCOLBI, Bogotá, 346
— — — Facultades de Medicina, 346
— — — Fisioterapia, Bogotá, 346
— — — Sociedades Científicas, 346
— — — Universidades, Bogotá, 346
— Costarricense de Bibliotecarios, 359
— — de Cirugía, San José, 359
— — — Pediatria, 359
— Cultural Humboldt, Caracas, 1951
— — Peruano-Alemána, Lima, 1037
— — Peruano-Británica, 1037
— Dante Alighieri, Buenos Aires, 63
— de Agrimensores de Venezuela, 1950
— — Arquitectos de Bolivia, 173
— — Artistas Aficionados, 1036
— — Bibliotecarios Graduados de la República Argentina (ABGRA), 63
— — y Archivistas de Honduras, Tegucigalpa, 630
— — Bibliotecologos y Afines del Uruguay, Montevideo, 1938
— — Cardiología, San José, 359
— — Escritores y Artistas Españoles, 1190
— — Ingenieros Civiles del Perú, 1037
— — — del Uruguay, 1938
— — y Arquitectos de México, 925
— — — Geólogos de Yacimientos Petrolíferos Fiscales Bolivianos, 173
— — Lingüistica y Filología, de América Latina (ALFAL), Caracas, 1951
— — Médicas Mexicanas, A.C., 927
— — Medicina Interna, San José, 359
— — Obstetricia y Ginecologia, San José, 359

— Ortodoncistas de Guatemala, 624
— Química y Farmacia del Uruguay, 1938
— Dominicana de Bibliotecarios, Inc., Santo Domingo, 403
— Electrotécnica Argentina, 65
— — Peruana, Lima, 1037
— Española de Pintores y Escultores de España, Madrid, 1188
— — para el Progreso de la Ciencias, 1191
— Farmacéutica y Bioquímica Argentina, Buenos Aires, 64
— Física Argentina, 65
— Franco-Mexicana de Ingenieros y Técnicos, A.C., Mexico City, 928
— Geológica Argentina, 65
— Guatemalteca de Historia Natural, 624
— Indigenista del Paraguay, 1034
— Inter-americana de Escritores, Buenos Aires, 19
— Judicial de Chile, 322
— Latino-Americana de Sociología (A.L.A.S.), Córdoba, 65
— Latinoamericana de Análisis y Modificación del Comportamiento, Caracas, 1952
— Médica Argentina, 64
— — de Santiago, 403
— — Dominicana, 403
— — Franco-Mexicana, 927
— — Peruana "Daniel A. Carrión", 1037
— Mexicana de Bibliotecarios, A.C., Mexico City, 926
— — Facultades y Escuelas de Medicina, San Luis de Potosí, 927
— — Geólogos Petroleros, 928
— — Ginecología y Obstetricia, Mexico, 927
— — Microbiología, A.C., 927
— Musical Manuel M. Ponce, A.C., Mexico City, 925
— Nacional de Bibliotecarios, Archiveros, Arqueólogos y Documentalistas, Madrid, 1188
— — — y Arqueólogos (Delegación de Cataluña y Baleares), 1188
— — — Escritores y Artistas (ANEA), Lima, 1037
— — — Venezolanos, Caracas, 1951
— — — Químicos de España, 1191
— — — Universidades e Insitutos de Enseñanza Superior, Mexico City, 926
— Odontológica Argentina, 64
— — Uruguaya, 1938
— Paleontológica Argentina, 63
— Pediátrica de Guatemala, 624
— Peruana de Archiveros, Lima, 1036
— — Astronomia, Lima, 1037
— — Bibliotecarios, Lima, 1036
— Química Argentina, 65
— Rural del Uruguay, 1938
— Venezolana Amigos del Arte Colonial, 1950
— — de Ingeniería Eléctrica y Mecánica, Caracas, 1952
— — — Sanitaria y Ambiental, Caracas, 1952
— — para el Avance de la Ciencia (ASOVAC), Caracas, 1952
Asociaţia Cineaştilor din R.S.R., Bucharest, 1121
— de Drept International şi Relaţii Internaţionale din R.S.R., 1121
— Filateliştilor din R.S.R., 1122
— Juriştilor din R.S.R., Bucharest, 1122
— Oamenilor de Arta din Institutele Teatrale şi Muzicale, Bucharest, 1122
— — Ştiinţa din R.S.R., 1122
— Psihologilor din R.S.R., 1122
— Română de Ştiinţe Politice, 1122
Assam Agricultural University, 678
— State Museum, Gauhati, 674
Associação Bahiana de Medicina, 181

— Brasileira de Escolas Superiores Catolicas, Belo Horizonte, 179
— — — Farmacêuticos, 181
— — — Mecánica dos Solos, 179
— — — Metais, São Paulo, 182
— — — Odontologia, 181
— — — Psiquiatria, Rio de Janeiro, 181
— — — Química, 182
— de Educação Catolica do Brasil, 179
— — Engenharia Química, São Paulo, 182
— — Ensino Unificado do Distrito Federal, Brasília, 210
— dos Arqueólogos Portugueses, 1098
— — Arquivistas Brasileiros, 179
— Internacional de Lunologia, São Paulo, 185
— Luso-Britanica do Porto, Oporto, 1098
— Médica Brasileira, São Paulo, 181
— — do Espírito Santo, Vitória, 181
— Nacional de Musica, Rio de Janeiro, 179
— Paulista de Medicina, 181
— Portuguesa de Bibliotecários, Arquivistas e Documentalistas, Lisbon, 1098
— — — Escritores, Lisbon, 1098
— — para o Progresso das Ciências, Lisbon, 1099
— Universal de Escritores, Rio de Janeiro, 181
Associated Scientific and Technical Societies of South Africa, 1156
Association Aéronautique et Astronautique de France (AAAF), Paris, 452
— Africaine de Cartographie, Algiers, 57
— — pour l'avancement des sciences et techniques, Dakar, 1145
— Belge de Documentation, Brussels, 150
— — Photographie et de Cinématographie, Brussels, 150
— — d'Hygiène et de Médecine Sociale, Brussels, 152
— Canadienne de Linguistique, Kingston, Ont., 241
— — — Science politique, Ottawa, 240
— — — des Etudes Africaines, Ottawa, 243
— — — — Latino-Américaines, Vancouver, 243
— — — Physiciens, Ottawa, 243
— — — Vétérinaires, Ottawa, 239
— Canadienne-Française pour l'Avancement des Sciences, Inc., Montreal, 242
— Centrale des Vétérinaires, Paris, 445
— d'éducation comparée en Europe, Brussels, 27
— d'Etudes et d'Informations Politiques Internationales, Paris, 446
— de Géographes Français, 447
— — l'Ecole Nationale Supérieure de Bibliothécaires, Villeurbanne, 446
— — Préhistoire et de Spéléologie, Monaco, 946
— des Amateurs de la Musique Andalouse, Casablanca, 949
— — amis de l'art antique, Basel, 1255
— — Anatomistes, Nancy, 449
— — Anciens Elèves de l'Ecole Nationale Supérieure des Industries Agricoles et Alimentaires, Paris, 453
— — Archivistes et des Bibliothécaires de Belgique, Brussels, 150
— — — Français, Paris, 446
— — Artistes Professionnels de Belgique, Brussels, 150
— — Bibliothécaires Français, 446
— — Chimistes de l'Industrie Textile, Paris, 453
— — — Ingénieurs et Cadres des Industries Agricoles et Alimentaires, Paris, 453
— — Designers Industriels du Canada, 243
— — Ecrivains Belges de Langue Française, Brussels, 151
— — — Combattants, Paris, 449
— — — de langue française (Mer et Outre-Mer,) Paris, 449
— — Etudiants en Droit, Cayenne, 499

— — instituts d'études européennes, Geneva, 27
— — Musées Suisses, Zurich, 1254
— — Musiciens Suisses, Lausanne, 1253
— — Professeurs de Mathématiques de l'Enseignement Public (APMEP), Paris, 451
— — Psychiatres du Canada, Ottawa, 242
— — Sociétés Scientifiques Médicales Belges, Brussels, 152
— — Universités Africaines, Accra, 26
— — — Partiellement ou Entièrement de Langue Française (AUPELF), Montreal, 26
— européenne des enseignants (AEDE), Geneva, 27
— — festivals de musique, Geneva, 43
— — pour l'Echange de la Littérature Technique dans le Domaine de la Sidérurgie, Luxembourg, 45
— for Asian Studies, Ann Arbor, 1615
— — Commonwealth Literature and Language Studies, Guelph, Ont., 18
— — Medical Education in Europe, Edinburgh, 39
— — Research in Nervous and Mental Disease, New York, 1618
— — — Vision and Ophthalmology Inc., New Rochelle, N.Y., 1618
— — Science Education, Hatfield, 1430
— — Teacher Education in Africa, Lagos, 991
— — — — Kampala, 1311
— — the Advancement of Christian Scholarship, Toronto, 243
— — — — Science in Israel, Jerusalem, 738
— — European University Community, Paris, 26
— — Study of Afro-American Life and History, Inc., Washington, D.C., 1615
— — — Animal Behaviour, Durham, 1431
— — — Medical Education, Dundee, 1427
— — — Taxonomic Study of Tropical African Flora, Pretoria, 44
— Française d'Observateurs d'Etoiles Variables, St. Genis Laval, 452
— — d'Urologie, Paris, 449
— — des Arabisants, Paris, 452
— — Ingénieurs, Chimistes et Techniciens des Industries du Cuir, Lyon, 453
— — — Professeurs de Langues Vivantes, Paris, 449
— — du Froid, 453
— — pour l'Avancement des Sciences (AFAS), 451
— — — l'Etude des Eaux, Paris, 459
— — — du Cancer, 449
— — — — Quaternaire, Paris, 452
— — — — Sol, Versailles, 445
— — — la Recherche et la Création Musicales, Paris, 445
— — — le Développement de l'Enseignement Technique, Paris, 447
— France-Amérique, Paris, 448
— France-Grande-Bretagne, Paris, 448
— -Yemen, Paris, 449
— Francophone d'Education, Sèvres, 447
— Générale des Conservateurs des Collections Publiques de France, Paris, 446
— des Médecins de France, 449
— Guillaume Budé, 449
— Historique Internationale de l'Océan Indien, Saint-Clotilde, 500
— Internationale d'Allergologie, Ottawa, 37
— — d'Asthmologie, INTERASMA, Pamplona, 40
— — d'Epidemiologie, Sydney, 37
— — d'Essais de Semences, Zürich, 18

— — d'information scolaire universitaire et professionnelle, Paris, 28
— — d'Orientation Scolaire et Professionnelle—AIOSP, Nuremberg, 28
— — de Bibliophilie, Paris, 21
— — — cybernétique, Namur, 46
— — — droit pénal, Paris, 35
— — — géodésie (AIG), Paris, 46
— — — géomagnétisme et d'aéronomie—AIGA, Tokyo, 46
— — — la Science du Sol, Wageningen, 18
— — — Limnologie Théorique et Appliquée, Hickory Corners, 47
— — — Linguistique Appliquée, Edinburgh, 19
— — — littérature comparée, Paris, 19
— — — Médecine Agricole, Saku, 40
— — — Météorologie et de Physique de l'Atmosphère, Boulder, 46
— — — Pédiatrie, Paris, 38
— — — Phytosociologie, Rinteln, 49
— — — psychiatrie de l'enfant et de l'adolescent et de professions affiliées, London, 39
— — — psychologie appliquée, Nijmegen, 40
— — — recherche pour la paix, Tokyo, 12
— — — Recherches Hydrauliques, Delft, 32
— — — Science Politique, Ottawa, 12
— — — Sociologie, Montreal, 12
— — — Volcanologie et de Chimie de l'Intérieur de la Terre, Nottingham, 47
— — des Anatomistes du Bois, Leiden, 47
— — — arts plastiques, Paris, 19
— — — Bibliothécaires et Documentalistes Agricoles, Southend-on-Sea, 21
— — — bibliothèques, archives et centres de documentation musicaux, Stockholm, 21
— — — d'universités polytechniques, Enschede, 21
— — — de droit, Nashville, Tenn., 21
— — — Critiques d'Art, Paris, 19
— — — Littéraires, Paris, 19
— — — études, et recherches sur l'information, Leicester, 21
— — — Etudiants en Sciences Economiques et Commerciales, Brussels, 28
— — — Femmes Médecins, Vienna, 38
— — — Juristes Démocrates, Brussels, 35
— — — musées d'armes et d'histoire militaire, London, 19
— — — Ponts et Charpentes, Zurich, 32
— — — Producteurs de l'Horticulture, The Hague, 17
— — — sciences économiques, Paris, 12
— — — — juridiques, Paris, 12
— — — — physiques, de l'Océan, San Diego, 46
— — — Sédimentologistes, Liège, 46
— — Permanente des Congrès de la route, Paris, 33
— — — — Navigation, Brussels, 33
— — pour la Culture Française, Paris, 448
— — — — taxonomie végétale, Utrecht, 46
— — — l'histoire des religions, Jerusalem, 10
— — — les mathématiques et Calculateurs en simulation, Brussels, 46
— — — Vétérinaire de Production Animale, Madrid, 18
— Libanaise des Sciences Juridiques, Beirut, 899
— littéraire et artistique internationale, Paris, 20
— Marc Bloch, Paris, 448
— Médicale Mondiale, Ferney-Voltaire, 39
— Mondiale de Psychiatrie, Vienna, 39
— — des Sciences de l'Education, Ghent, 31

2013

# INDEX OF INSTITUTIONS

Association Mondiale des Vétérinaires, Microbiologistes, Immunologistes et Spécialistes des Maladies Infectieuses. Maisons-Alfort, 43
— — pour l'étude de l'opinion publique, Allensbach am Bodensee, 13
— — Vétérinaire, Geneva, 39
— Motessori Internationale, Amsterdam, 30
— Nationale de la Recherche Technique, Paris, 453
— — pour la Protection des Eaux, Paris, 459
— — — — — Villes d'Art, Paris, 445
— of African Universities, Accra-North, 26
— — American Colleges, Inc., 1604
— — — Geographers, 1606
— — — Law Schools, 1602
— — — Library Schools, 1601
— — — Medical Colleges, 1610
— — — Physicians, 1610
— — — Railroads, Economics and Finance Department Library, Washington, D.C., 1628
— — — Universities, 1604
— — Anaesthetists of Great Britain and Ireland, London, 1427
— — Applied Biologists, 1431
— — Arab Universities, Giza, 26
— — Art Museum Directors, Savannah, 1611
— — Arts and Letters, Athens, 617
— — British Neurologists, London, 1427
— — — Science Writers, London, 1426
— — Canadian Community Colleges, 240
— — — Industrial Designers, Ottawa, 243
— — — University Information Bureaux, Montreal, 240
— — Caribbean Universities and Research Institutes, San Juan, P.R., 26
— — Certified Accountants, London, 1416
— — Commonwealth Universities, London, 27
— — Consulting Chemists and Chemical Engineers, Inc., 1616
— — Contemporary Historians, London, 1421
— — Engineers and Architects in Israel, 739
— — — — Technicians of Slovenia, 1970
— — Indian Universities, New Delhi, 660
— — Information Dissemination Centers, Athens, Ga., 44
— — Institutes for European Studies, Geneva, 27
— — International Accountants Ltd. (by guarantee), Bedford, 23
— — — Colleges and Universities, Aix-en-Provence, 27
— — Jurists of the S.R. of Serbia, 1969
— — Pharmacists of the S.R. of Serbia, 1969
— — Public Analysts, London, 1432
— — — Lighting Engineers, 1435
— — Religious Writers, Jerusalem, 738
— — Research Libraries, Washington, 1601
— — Southeast Asian Institutions of Higher Learning, Bangkok, 27
— — Soviet Economic Scientific Institutions, Moscow, 1321
— — Special Libraries in the Philippines, Manila, 1047
— — Surgeons of East Africa, Nairobi, 878
— — — — Great Britain and Ireland, London, 1427
— — — — India, Madras, 662
— — the Bar of the City of New York Library, 1629
— — — Mathematicians', Physicists' and Astronomers' Societies of the F.S.R. of Yugoslavia, 1968
— — Theological Schools in the United States and Canada, Vandalia, 1604
— — Universities and Colleges of Canada, Ottawa, 240

— — — for Research in Astronomy Inc., Tucson, 1620
— — Visual Science Librarians, Boston, Mass., 1601
— pour l'avancement des sciences et des techniques de la documentation, Montreal, 240
— — l'Enseignement des Sciences Anthropologiques, Paris, 452
— — l'Etude de la Neige et des Avalanches (ANENA), Grenoble, 458
— — — Taxonomique de la Flore d'Afrique Tropicale-AETFAT, Pretoria, 44
— — la Communauté Européenne Universitaire, Paris, 26
— — le Développement des Relations Médicales entre la France et les Pays Etrangers, Paris, 449
— professionnelle suisse de psychologie appliquée, Zürich, 1257
— Royale des Demeures Historiques, Brussels, 151
— Scientifique des Médecins Acupuncteurs de France, Paris, 449
— — du Pacifique, Honolulu, 50
— — et Technique pour l'Exploitation des Océans, Paris, 452
— Suisse de Documentation, Bern, 1254
— — — Microtechnique, Zürich, 1257
— — — Politique Etrangère, 1254
— — — Science Politique, Neuchâtel, 1254
— — des ingénieurs agronomes et des ingénieurs en technologie alimentaire, Bern, 1257
— — professeurs d'université, Zürich, 1254
— — pour l'étude de l'antiquité, Zürich, 1255
— Togolaise d'Echanges Culturelles avec l'Etranger, Lomé, 1292
— — pour le développement de la documentation, des bibliothèques, archives et musée, Lomé, 1292
— Tunisienne de Bibliothécaires, documentalistes et Archivistes, Tunis, 1295
— Universitaire pour la Diffusion Internationale de la Recherche, Paris, 447
— Zaïroise des Archivistes, Bibliothécaires et Documentalistes, Kinshasa, 1995
Associazione Archeologica Romana, 757
— Elettrotecnica ed Elettronica Italiana (AEI), Milan, 761
— Filatelica Italiana, Rome, 756
— Forestale Italiana, Rome, 756
— Geofisica Italiana, Rome, 760
— Internazionale Filosofia, Arti e Scienze, Bologna, 761
— Italiana Biblioteche, Rome, 756
— — di Dietetica e Nutrizione Clinica (ADI), Rome, 759
— — — Diritto Marittimo, Rome, 757
— — — Medicina Aeronautica e Spaziale, Rome, 759
— — — Radiologia Medica e Medicina Nucleare (S.I.R.M.N.), Genoa, 759
— — — Ricerca Operativa, Rome, 763
— — per le Scienze Astronautiche, Rome, 761
— Nazionale dei Musei Italiani, Rome, 756
— — di Ingegneria Nucleare, Rome, 761
— — per la Tutela del Patrimonio Storico Artistico e Naturale della Nazione, Rome, 756
Assumption College, Worcester, Mass., 1747
— University, Windsor, Ont., 316
Astaneh Razavy Library, 722
Asthma Research Council, London, 1440
Astrakhan Institute of Fish Industry, 1381
— Medical Institute, 1382
— State Conservatoire, 1387
— — B. M. Kustodiev Gallery, 1353

# WORLD OF LEARNING

Astronautische Gesellschaft der DDR, Berlin (East), 504
Astronomical Association of Indonesia, 708
— Institute, Mexico City, 933
— — Tashkent, 1335
— Observatory, Beijing, 331
— — Calcutta, 670
— — Fenghuangshan, 331
— — Iaşi, 1135
— — Mount John, New Zealand, 979
— — Nanjing, 331
— — Riga, 1364
— — Shaanxi, 331
— — Shanghai, 331
— — of St. Xavier's College, 670
— — — the University of the Punjab, 1022
— — — Warsaw University, 1070
— Society of Australia, Sydney, 90
— — — Bermuda, Hamilton, 1558
— — — India, Hyderabad, 663
— — — South Australia, 90
— — — Southern Africa, Cape Town, 1156
— — — Tasmania, 90
— — — the Republic of China, Taipei, 340
— — — Victoria, Melbourne, 90
— — — Western Australia, Perth, 90
Astronomische Gesellschaft, Tübingen, 523
Astronomischer Verein, Vienna, 123
Astronomisches Institut der Universität Munster und Sternwarte, 532
— — — — Tübingen, 532
— Rechen-Institut, Heidelberg, 532
Astronomisk Institut, Aarhus Universitet, 393
— Selskab, Copenhagen, 391
Astronomska Opservatorija u Beogradu, 1973
Astrophysical Institute, Alma-Ata, 1328
— Observatory, Arosa, 1258
Asutosh Museum of Indian Art, Calcutta, 674
Atatürk Library, Istanbul, 1300
— — Üniversitesi, 1304
Atatürk's Revolution Museum, Istanbul, 1301
Atelier, Alexandria, 413
Atelje Meštrovic, Zagreb, 1978
Ateneo Barcelonés, 1188
— Científico, Literario y Artístico, Mahón, 1188
— y Artístico, Madrid, 1188
— de Ciencias y Artes de Chiapas, Tuxtla Gutiérrez, 927
— Clínica Quirúrgica, 1938
— El Salvador, 422
— la Habana, 362
— Manila University, Quexon City, 1050
— — Libraries, Quezon City, 1049
— Medicina de Sucre, 174
— Ponce, 1109
— Nacional de Ciencias y Artes de México, 927
— Puertorriqueño, San Juan, 1109
— Veracruzano, 925
Athabasca University, Edmonton, Alb., 257
Atheism Museum, Shkodër, 56
Athenaeum of Ohio, 1840
Athens Academy Library, 618
— Centre of Ekistics (ACE), 617
— State College, Alabama, 1643
Athinisin Ethnikon kai Kapodistriakon Panepistimion, 619
Atif Efendi Library, 1300
Atkinson Art Gallery, Southport, 1471
Atlanta Public Library, Georgia, 1626
— University, 1699
Atlantic Christian College, Wilson, N.C., 1824
— Council of the United States, Washington, D.C., 1602
— Industrial Research Institute, Halifax, N.S., 290
— Institute for International Affairs, Paris, 23
— Union College, South Lancaster, Mass., 1747

Atmospheric Environment Service, Downsview, Ont., 245
— Physics Institute, Beijing, 331
— Soundings Institute, Beijing, 333
Atoll Research Unit, Tarawa, 881
Atomic Energy Agricultural Research Centre, Tandojam, 1022
— — — — Tarnab, 1022
— — Commission, Tel-Aviv, 741
— — Council, Taipei, 341
— — Institute, Beijing, 331
— — Medical Centre, Karachi, 1022
— — Minerals Centre, Lahore, 1022
— — — Library, Lahore, 1023
— — of Canada, Ltd., Ottawa, 246
— — Utilization in Agriculture Institute, Beijing, 333
Atominstitut der Österreichischen Universitäten, Vienna, 125
Attila József University, Szeged, 650
Auburn University, Alabama, 1643
Auchi Polytechnic, 1002
Auchmuty Library, Newcastle, N.S.W., 96
Auckland City Art Gallery, 982
— Institute and Museum, 982
— Medical Research Foundation, 979
— Public Library, 981
— Technical Institute, 987
Audio-Visual Aids Unit, Cambridge, 1485
Auezov, M. O., Institute of Literature and Arts, Alma-Ata, 1329
Augsburg College, Minneapolis, 1773
Augustana College, Rock Island, Ill., 1703
— — Sioux Falls, 1887
— Hochschule, Neuendettelsau, 609
Ausgrabungen in Ephesos, Vienna, 119
Aussenstelle Schlossmuseum Gobelsburg, 130
Austin College, Sherman, Tex., 1897
— Peay State University, Clarksville, 1889
Australasian and Pacific Society for Eighteenth-Century Studies, Parkville, 87
— Association of Philosophy, Melbourne, 91
— College of Dermatologists, Glebe, N.S.W., 89
— Institute of Metals, Parkville, 91
— — — Mining and Metallurgy, Parkville, 91
— Political Studies Association, Bedford Park, S.A., 87
Australian Academy of Science, 82
— — — Technological Sciences, Parkville, 85
— — — the Humanities, Canberra, 83
— Administrative Staff College, 117
— Agricultural Council, Canberra, 86
— and New Zealand Association for Medieval and Renaissance Studies, Canberra, 87
— — — — — the Advancement of Science (ANZAAS), 89
— Archives, Dickson, A.C.T., 95
— Association of Adult Education, 88
— — — Neurologists, 89
— Atomic Energy Commission Research Establishment, Sutherland, 93
— Bar Association, Melbourne, 87
— Biochemical Society, Clayton, Vic., 91
— Bureau of Statistics, Canberra, 93
— College of Education, Carlton, 88
— Conference of Principals of Colleges of Advanced Education, Braddon, 88
— Conservation Foundation, 89
— Council for Educational Research, 92
— — of National Trusts, Canberra, 87
— Dental Association, Sydney, 89
— Elizabethan Theatre Trust, 87
— Entomological Society, Sydney, 90
— Graduate School of Management, 117
— Institute of Aboriginal Studies, 94
— — — Agricultural Science, 91
— — — Anatomy, 89
— — — Archaeology, Melbourne, 94
— — — Cartographers, Perth, 88
— — — Credit Management, Melbourne, 87

— — — Food Science and Technology, Castle Hill, N.S.W., 91
— — — International Affairs, Canberra, 87
— — — Management, Melbourne, 87
— — — Marine Science, 93
— — — Physics, Sydney, 91
— — — Political Science, 87
— — — Quantity Surveyors, 87
— Maritime College, Launceston, 115
— Mathematical Society, Murdoch, W.A., 90
— Medical Association, Glebe, N.S.W., 89
— Mineral Devlopment Laboratories, 94
— Museum, 97
— National Radio Astronomy Observatory (C.S.I.R.O.), 93
— — University, 99
— — — Library, 95
— Numismatic Society, Sydney, 88
— Optometrical Association, Carlton, 89
— Patent, Trade Marks and Designs Office Library, Woden, A.C.T., 95
— Physiological and Pharmacological Society, Brisbane, 89
— Physiotherapy Association (N.S.W.), 89
— Psychological Society, Parkville, 91
— Radiation Laboratory, Yallambie, 92
— Research Grants Committee, 88
— Road Research Board, Melbourne, 94
— Rural Adjustment Unit, Armidale, 106
— School of Nuclear Technology, Lucas Heights, 117
— Society for Fish Biology, Sydney, 90
— — — Limnology, Caulfield East, 90
— — — Microbiology, Parkville, 90
— — — Parasitology, Glebe, N.S.W., 90
— — of Dairy Technology Incorporated, Melbourne, Vic., 86
— Veterinary Association, Artarmon, N.S.W., 87
— Vice-Chancellors' Committee, Canberra City, 88
— War Memorial, Canberra City, 97
— Wool Corporation, Parkville, 94
Austria Esperanto Federacio, Vienna, 121
Austrian Academy of Sciences, Vienna, 118
— Institute, London, 1424
— — New York, 1607
Automation Institute, Beijing, 331
Automotive Research Association of India, Pune, 672
Autonomous University of the State of Mexico, Toluca, 934
Avele College, Apia, 1964
— — Library, Apia, 1964
Avila College, Kansas City, Miss., 1786
Avon County Library, Bristol, 1453
Avrupa Elonomik Topuluğu Enstitüsü, Eskişehir, 1309
Awadhesh Pratap Singh University, Madhya Pradesh, 678
Awassa Community Development Training and Demonstration Centre, 425
Awkaf Supreme Council Library, Jerusalem, 741
Awqaf Public Library, Tripoli, 906
Ayasofya (Saint Sophia) Museum, 1301
Aydin Müzesi, 1301
Ayuthaya Agricultural College, 1291
Azabu Veterinary College, Kanagawa, 862
Azerbaijan Agricultural Institute, 1369
— M. F. Akhundov Pedagogical Institute of Languages, Baku, 1382
— M. A. Aliev Dramatic Institute, 1388
— M. Azizbekov Institue of Oil and Chemistry, Baku, 1379
— Biochemical Society, Baku, 1325
— Blood Transfusion Institute, 1385
— Genetics and Selection Society, 1325
— Institute of Epidemiology, Microbiology and Hygiene, Baku, 1384
— — — Medical Parasitology and Tropical Medicine, Baku, 1386
— — — Mother and Child Care, 1384
— — — Orthopaedics and Restorative Surgery, Baku, 1385

— — — Roentgenology, Radiology and Oncology, Baku, 1386
— — — Spa Treatment and Physiotherapy (Kirov Institute), Baku, 1387
— — — Tuberculosis, 1384
— S. M. Kirov State University, 1360
— Mathematics Society, Baku, 1325
— Museum of History, Baku, 1326
— R. Mustafaev State Art Museum, 1352
— N. Narimanov Medical Institute, 1382
— Physical Society, Baku, 1325
— Polytechnic Institute, 1374
— Republic D. Buniat-Zade Institute of National Economy, Baku, 1373
— Research Institute of Ophthalmology, Baku, 1385
— Section of All-Union Chemical Society, Baku, 1325
— S.S.R. Academy of Sciences, 1325
— — U. Gajibekov State Conservatoire, Baku, 1387
Azov-Black Sea Institute of Agricultural Engineering, 1371
Azusa Pacific University, Calif., 1651


B

Babson College, Wellesley, Mass., 1747
Babylon Museum, 726
Bacterial Genetics Research Unit, Pretoria, 1156, 1175
Badische Landesbibliothek, 536
Badisches Landesmuseum, 543
Baendaskólinn á Hvanneyri, 658
Baghdad Museum, 726
Bahamas Historical Society, Nassau, 140
— National Trust, Nassau, 140
Bahamia Museum, Nassau, 140
Bahauddin Zakariya University, Multan, 1025
Bahrain Historical and Archaeological Society, 141
— Museum, 141
— Society of Engineers, Manama, 141
— Writers and Literators Association, Manama, 141
Baikonur Cosmodrome, 1346
Baikov, A. A., Institute of Metallurgy, Moscow, 1319
Baka Agricultural Research Station, Karonga, 912
Baker Medical Research Institute, Prahran, 92
— University, Baldwin City, 1729
Bakh, A. N., Institute of Biochemistry, Moscow, 1319
Bakhchisarai State Museum of History and Archaeology, 1355
Bakht er Ruda Institute of Education Library, Khartoum, 1229
Bakonyi Múzeum, Veszprém, 644
— Természettudományi Múzeum, Zirc, 644
Baku Museum of Education, 1357
Bal Bhavan Society, New Delhi, 660
Balai Besar Penelitian Dan Pengembangan Industri Hasil Pertanian, Bogor, 710
— Fotogrametri, Jakarta, 710
— Penelitian Batik & Kerajinan, Yogjakarta, 710
— — Industri, Jakarta, 710
— — Kulit, Yogjakarta, 710
— — Perkebunan Bogor, 708
— — — Medan, 708
— — Pengetahuan Umum Bandung, 708
— — Penjelidikan Bahan-Bahan, 710
— — — Perusahaan Perkebunan Gula, Pasuruan, 708
Balassa Bálint Múzeum, Esztergom, 644
Balatoni Múzeum, 644
Balda Museum, Dacca, 143
Baldwin-Wallace College, Berea, 1840
Balfour and Newton Library, Cambridge, 1462

# INDEX OF INSTITUTIONS

Ball State University, Muncie, 1716
Ballarat College of Advanced Education, 115
Balliol College, Oxford, 1524
— — Library, Oxford, 1463
Balneoclimatological Institute, Poznań, 1070
Baluchi Academy, Quetta, 1020
Balogh Adám Múzeum, 644
Baltic Commission on Examination of Bird Migration, Tartu, 1327
Baltimore Museum of Art, 1635
Baluchistan University, 723
Bamian Museum, Bamian, 52
Banaras Hindu University, Varanasi, 678
Bandalag Íslenzkra Listamanna, 656
Bandung Institute of Technology, 712
Banff Centre, Alberta, 319
— National History Museum, 249
Bang Phra Agricultural College, 1291
Bangalore State Central Library, 673
— University, 678
Bangla Academy, Dacca, 142
Bangladesh Agricultural University, Mymensingh, 143
— Council of Scientific and Industrial Research, Dacca, 142
— Economic Association, Dacca, 142
— Institute of Development Studies, Dacca, 142
— Jute Research Institute, Dacca, 142
— Medical Association, Dacca, 142
— National Scientific and Technical Documentation Centre (BANSDOC), Dacca, 142
— Textile Institute, Dacca, 145
— University of Engineering and Technology, Dacca, 143
Bank Street College of Education, New York, 1805
Bánki Donát Gépipari Müszaki Foískola, Budapest, 655
Baptist College, Bristol, 1481
— Historical Society, London, 1421
Baptistère Saint-Jean, Poitiers, 470
Bar Association of India, New Delhi, 660
Barbados Astronomical Society, St. Michael, 146
— Community College, St. Michael, 146
— Museum and Historical Society, 146
— Pharmaceutical Society, St. Michael, 146
Barber-Scotia College, Concord, 1824
Bard College, 1805
Bar-Ilan University, Ramat-Gan, 745
— — — Library, 741
Barking and Dagenham Public Libraries, 1453
Barnard College, New York, 1810
Barnes Foundation Collection, Merion, 1635
Barnet Public Libraries, 1452
Barockmuseum, Dresden, 509
Baroda Museum and Picture Gallery, 674
Baron Bliss Institute, Belize, 171
Barra Mexicana, Mexico City, 926
Barrack Street Museum, Dundee, 1472
Barrington College, Rhode Island, 1882
Barry College, Miami, 1692
Bartok Béla Emlékház, Budapest, 643
Base Océanologique pour la Méditerranée, La Seyne-Sur-Mer, 459
Bashkimi i Gazetarëve të Shqipërisë, Tiranë, 54
Bashkir Agricultural Institute, 1369
— Branch, Academy of Sciences of the U.S.S.R., 1322
— State University of the Fortieth Anniversary of the October Revolution, 1360
— 15th Anniversary of the Komsomol Medical Institute, Frunze, 1382
Basic Medicine Institute, Beijing, 332
— Sciences and Humanities Division, Peshawar, 1027
Basque University, Lejona, 1214
Bassein College Library, Bassein, 228
Bataafsch Genootschap der Proefondervindelijke Wijsbegeerte, 959

Bates College, Lewiston, Maine, 1741
Bath Academy of Art, Corsham, 1550
— College of Higher Education, 1481
Báthory István Múzeum, Nyirbator, 644
Battelle-Institut e.V., Forschung, Entwicklung, Innovation, Frankfurt, 533
Battelle Memorial Institute, Columbus, 1619
Battle of Britain Museum, London, 1466
Battlefield Museum, Magersfontein, 1165
Batumi Botanical Garden, 1328
— Research Institute, 1328
Batyrov, S., Institute of History, Ashkhabad, 1332
Bauakademie der DDR, Berlin (East), 505
Baussky Art Museum, 1353
Bavarian Academy of Sciences, Munich, 515
Bayamón Central University, P.R., 1112
Bayerische Akademie der Schönen Künste, 518
— — — Wissenschaften, Munich, 515
— Botanische Gesellschaft, 522
— -Julius-Maximilians-Universität Würzburg, 606
— Staatsbibliothek, 537
— Staatsgemäldesammlungen, 544
— Staatssammlung für allgemeine und angewandte Geologie, Munich, 544
— — Paläontologie und historische Geologie, Munich, 544
Bayerisches Hauptstaatsarchiv, Munich, 540
— Nationalmuseum, Munich, 544
Bayero University, Kano, 996
Baylor University, Waco, 1898
Beaton Institute, Nova Scotia, 265
Beatson Institute for Cancer Research, Glasgow, 1444, 1493
Beaver College, Glenside, Pa., 1867
Beaverbrook Art Gallery, Fredericton, N.B., 250
Bedford College, London, 1509
Bedfordshire County Library, 1453
Bedrosian, K., Erevan Scientific Research Institute of Orthopaedics and Traumatology, 1385
Bees Institute of Jiangxi, 333
Beethoven-Archiv, Bonn, 538
— -Haus, Bonn, 541
Behavioural Science Research Unit, Ibadan, 998
Beijerinstitutet, Stockholm, 1238
Beijing Agricultural University, 335
— Industrial College, 335
— Institute of Foreign Languages, 335
— Medical College, 335
— Teachers University, 335
— Traditional Medicine College, 335
— University, 335
Beirut Arab University, Beirut, 901
— — — Library, 900
— University College, 902
Beit Chaim Sturman House, Gilboa, 743
— Ha'Omanim, 743
— Memorial Fellowships for Medical Research, 1419
Belediye Kütüphanesi, Istanbul, 1300
— Müzesi, Istanbul, 1301
Belfast College of Technology, 1557
— Library and Society for Promoting Knowledge (Linen Hall Library), 1554
— Natural History and Philosophical Society, 1554
— Public Libaries, 1554
Belgian American Educational Foundation Inc., New York, 1607
Belgisch Instituut voor Bestuurswetenschappen, 150
Belgische Vereniging voor Aardrijkskundige Studies, Louvain, 151
— — — Biochemie, Brussels, 152
— — — Documentatie, Brussels, 150
— — — Geologie, 152
— — — Tropische Geneeskunde, 152
Belgorod Civil Engineering Institute, 1379
Belgrade Arts University, 1985

Belhaven College, Jackson, Miss., 1784
Belinsky (V. G.) State Museum, 1357
Belize College of Arts, Science and Technology, Belize City, 171
Bell Institute, Nova Scotia, 265
— R. P., Library, Sackville, 247
Bellairs Research Institute, Barbados, 146, 277
Bellarmine College, 1735
Belmont Abbey College, Belmont, 1824
— College, Nashville, 1889
Beloit College, Wisconsin, 1931
Belotserkovsky Agricultural Institute, Belaya Tserkov, 1369
"Belovezhskaya Pushcha" Museum, 1359
Bemidji State University, Minn., 1773
Benaki Library, Athens, 618
— Museum, 618
Benakion Phytopathologikon Institouton, Kifissia, 617
Bendel State Library Board, Benin City, 994
Bendigo College of Advanced Education, 115
Benedictine College, Atchison, Kansas, 1730
Bengal Ceramic Institute, 672
— Natural History Society, Darjeeling, 663
— Tanning Institute, Calcutta, 672
— Textile Institute, 672
Benghazi Museum, 906
Ben Gurion University of the Negev, Beersheva, 749
— — — — — Library, 741
Benin Museum, Benin, 995
Benjamin Franklin Reference Library, Paris, 462
Bennett College, Greensboro, 1825
Bennington College, Vt., 1914
Bensusan Museum of Photography, Parktown, S.A., 1165
Bentley College, Waltham, Mass., 1747
Benzion Katz Institute for Research in Hebrew Literature, Tel-Aviv, 750
Ben-Zvi Institute for the Study of Jewish Communities in the East, Jerusalem, 741
Berea College, Ky., 1735
Berg- und Hüttenschule Leoben, 139
Bergakademie Freiberg, 513
Bergbau-Forschung G.m.b.H., Forschungsinstitut des Steinkohlbergbauvereins, Essen-Kray, 533
Bergen offentlige Bibliotek, 1010
Bergianska stiftelsen, Stockholm, 1238
Berhampore Textile Institute, 672
Berhampur University, 680
Berkshire County Library, Reading, 1453
Berliner Gesellschaft für Anthropologie, Ethnologie und Urgeschichte, 524
— — — Innere Medizin, 506
— Mathematische Gesellschaft e.V., 523
— Medizinische Gesellschaft, 521
— — Zentralbibliothek, 534
— Stadtbibliothek, 506
— Zentralbibliothek, Berlin (West), 534
Bermuda Aquarium, Museum and Zoo, 1558
— Archives, Hamilton, 1558
— Audubon Society, Hamilton, 1558
— Biological Station for Research, 1558
— College, Devonshire, 1558
— Department of Agriculture and Fisheries, Paget East, 1558
— Historical Society, 1558
— Library, 1558
— Maritime Museum, Somerset, 1558
— National Trust, Hamilton, 1558
— Society of Arts, 1558
— Technical Society, 1558
Bernard M. Baruch College, New York, 1805
— Price Institute for Palaeontological Research, Johannesburg, 1182
— — — of Geophysical Research, Johannesburg, 1182
Bernberg Museum of Costume, Johannesburg, 1165
Bernhard-Nocht-Institut für Schiffs- und Tropenkrankheiten, 531

Bernice P. Bishop Museum, Honolulu, 1636
Bernische Botanische Gesellschaft, 1256
Bernisches Historisches Museum, 1261
Berry College, 1699
Berufsverband Österreichischer Psychologen, Vienna, 123
Beth Gordon Agriculture and Nature Study Institute, Emeq Ha-Yarden, 739
Bethany Bible College, Santa Cruz, 1651
— College, Lindsborg, 1730
— — West Virginia, 1929
— — Nazarene College, Oklahoma, 1857
Bethel College and Seminary, St. Paul, 1773
— — McKenzie, 1889
— — North Newton, 1730
Bethlehem University, 876
Bethnal Green Museum of Childhood, 1467
Bethune-Cookman College, Fla., 1692
Betriebspädagogisches Institut, Basel, 1257
Bexley Public Libraries, 1452
Beyazit Devlet Kütüphanesi, Istanbul, 1300
Bezalel Academy of Arts and Design, Jerusalem, 752
— National Art Museum, Jerusalem, 744
Bhabha Atomic Research Centre (B.A.R.C.), Bombay, 670
Bhagalpur University, 680
Bhandarkar Oriental Research Institute, 668
Bharat Kala Bhavan, Varanasi, 674
Bharata Ganita Parisad, 663
— Itihasa Samshodhaka-Mandala, 661
Bharatiya Vidya Bhavan, 707
Bhavnagar University, 680
Bhopal University, 680
BHRA Fluid Engineering, Bedford, 1448
Bibelausstellung der Württembergischen Bibelanstalt, Stuttgart, 545
Bibliographical Society, London, 1415
— — of America, 1601
— — — Australia and New Zealand, Melbourne, 87
— — — Canada, 240
— — — the University of Virginia, Charlottesville, 1601
Bibliophile (Le), Port-au-Prince, 629
Biblioteca Abel Guerrero Vega, Jamundí, 349
— Academiei Republicii Socialiste România, 1124
— Agropecuaria de Colombia—ICA, 349
— "Álvaro Castro J.", San José, 360
— Amador-Washington, Panama City, 1030
— Ambrosiana, Milan, 766
— Ambulantes, Ministerio de Educación, San Salvador, 422
— Americana, Asunción, 1034
— "Angel Andrés García" de la Universidad Nacional "Vicente Rocafuerte", 408
— Angelica, Rome, 767
— Antoniana, Padua, 767
— Apostolica Vaticana, 1943
— Archivo y Colección Arqueológica Municipal, Jérez de la Frontera, 1200
— Arcivescovile, Naples, 766
— Argentina "Dr. Juan Alvarez" de la Municipalidad de Rosario, 70
— — para Ciegos, 69
— Artigas-Washington, Montevideo, 1940
— Augusta, Perugia, 767
— Balmes, Barcelona, 1200
— "Baralt", Maracaibo, 1955
— Bastos Tigre da Associação Brasileira de Imprensa, Rio de Janeiro, 187
— Batthyaneum, Alba Iulia, 1125
— Benjamin Franklin, Mexico City, 930
— Bio-Médica del Laboratorio Commemorativo Gorgas, Panama City, 1030
— Cantonale: Lugano, Ticino, 1260
— Capitular Colombina, Seville, 1201
— Cardinale Giulio Alberoni, 767
— Carducci, Bologna, 765
— "Carlos Monge Alfaro" de la Universidad de Costa Rica, 360

— Casanatense, Rome, 767
— Central, Chapingo, 931
— da Universidade Federal de Pernambuco, Recife, 187
— — — — do Ceará, 187
— — — — Pará, Belém, 186
— — — — Paraná, Curitiba, 187
— — — — Rio Grande do Sul, 187
— — de la Armada, Buenos Aires, 69
— — — Pontificia Universidad Católica del Perú, 1039
— — — — Javeriana, Bogotá, 349
— — — Universidad Católica "Andrés Bello", Caracas, 1954
— — — — Central de Venezuela, 1954
— — — — de Carabobo, 1955
— — — — Chile, Santiago, 326
— — — — Concepción, 326
— — — — El Salvador, 422
— — — — Oriente, Santiago, 364
— — — — San Carlos, Guatemala City, 625
— — — — del Salvador "Padre Guillermo Furlong, S.J.", Buenos Aires, 69
— — — — Mayor de San Andrés, La Paz, 174
— — — — — de San Francisco Xavier, Sucre, 174
— — — — — de San Simón, Cochabamba, 174
— — — — Nacional Autónoma de México, 931
— — — — — de Colombia, 349
— — — — — de Cuyo, 70
— — — — — de Nicaragua, 988
— — — — — de Tucumán, 70
— — — — — del Sur, Bahia Blanca, 69
— — — — — Mayor de San Marcos, Lima, 1039
— — — — "Federico Santa María, Valparaíso, 326
— — Marina, Madrid, 1199
— — Marinha, Lisbon, 1101
— del Instituto de Investigaciones Agropecuarias, Santiago, 326
— — Ministerio de Agricultura y Cria, Caracas, 1955
— — — — Educación Pública, Lima, 1039
— — — — Hacienda, Madrid, 1199
— — — del Aire, 1199
— do Centro de Ciências da Saude da Universidade Federal do Rio de Janeiro, 187
— — Estado da Bahia, Salvador, 188
— — Militar, Madrid, 1199
— — "Rubén Martínez Villena" de la Universidad de la Habana, 364
— — "Tulio Febres Cordero", Mérida, 1955
— — Universidad de Caldas, 349
— — Pedagógica y Tecnológica de Colombia, Tunja, 349
— — Universidade de Brasília, 186
— — y Publicaciones del Consejo de Educación Secundaria, Básica y Superior, Montevideo, 1939
— Centrală a Academiei de Stiinţe Agricole şi Silvice, Bucharest, 1125
— — Institutului Agronomic "Nicolae Bălcescu", Bucharest, 1125
— — — Universitaţii din Braşov, 1125
— Academia de Studii Economic, Bucharest, 1125
— — de Stat, 1125
— — Medicală, Bucharest, 1125
— — Pedagogică, Bucharest, 1125
— — Universitară, Bucharest, 1125
— — — Cluj-Napoca, 1126
— — — Craiova, 1126
— — — Galaţi, 1126
— — — "M. Eminescu", Iaşi, 1126
— — — Timisoara, 1126
— Centrale del Consiglio Nazionale delle Ricerche, Rome, 767

— — — Politecnico di Milano, 766
— — della Regione Siciliana, Palermo, 767
— — Giuridica presso il Ministero di Grazia e Giustizia, Rome, 767
— Civica, Alessandria, 765
— — Milan, 766
— — Padua, 767
— — Pavia, 767
— — Verona, 769
— — Bertoliana, Vicenza, 769
— — Gambalunga, Rimini, 767
— — "A. Hortis", Trieste, 768
— — A. Mai, Bergamo, 765
— — Queriniana, Brescia, 765
— Comitetului de Stat a Planificarii, Bucharest, 1125
— Comunale, Ascoli Piceno, 765
— — Como, 765
— — Fermo, 765
— — Imola, 766
— — Mantua, 766
— — Palermo, 767
— — Trento, 768
— — Treviso, 768
— — Ariostea, Ferrara, 765
— — "A. Saffi", Forli, 766
— — Classense, Ravenna, 767
— — degli Intronati, Siena, 768
— — dell'Archiginnasio, Bologna, 765
— — Forteguerriana, Pistoia, 767
— — Joppi, Udine, 769
— — Labronica Francesco Domenico Guerrazzi, Leghorn, 766
— — Luciano Benincasa, Ancona, 765
— — Malatestiana, Cesna (Forli), 765
— — Mozzi-Borgetti, Macerata, 766
— — Passerini Landi, Piacenza, 767
— Conservatorului de muzică "Ciprian Porumbescu", Bucharest, 1125
— d'Arte, Milan, 766
— da Academia das Ciências de Lisboa, 1101
— Ajuda, 1101
— — Escola de Minas e Metalurgia da Universidade Federal de Ouro Prêto, 187
— — Sociedade Brasileira de Cultura Inglesa, Rio de Janeiro, 187
— — Humanitária dos Empregados no Comércio, 188
— de Autores Nacionales "Carlos A. Rolando", 408
— — — "Fray Vicente Solano", Cuenca, 408
— — Cataluña y Central de Bibliotecas Populares, Barcelona, 1200
— — Derecho y Legislación de la Secretaría de Hacienda, Mexico City, 930
— — Historia de la Secretaría de Hacienda, 930
— — l'Associació de Enginyers Industrials de Catalunya, Barcelona, 1199
— — la Academia Nacional de la Historia, Caracas, 1954
— — — Venezolana de la Lengua, Caracas, 1954
— — Asamblea Legislativa, San José, 360
— — Asociación Cultural Peruano-Británica, Lima, 1039
— — Cámara de Comercio, Agricultura e Industria del Distrito Nacional, Santo Domingo, 404
— — — Oficial de Comercio Industria y Navegación de Barcelona, 1200
— — Casa de la Cultura Ecuatoriana, Guayaquil, 408
— — — Cultura Ecuatoriana, Quito, 408
— — Comisión Nacional de Energía Atómica, Buenos Aires, 69
— — Corte Suprema de Justicia, Caracas, 1954
— — — — Justicia, Guatemala City, 625

2017

# INDEX OF INSTITUTIONS

Biblioteca de la Delegación Provincial de Barcelona de la Organización Nacional de Ciegos, 1200
— — — Dirección de Estadística y Censo, Panama City, 1030
— — — — General de Cultura, La Paz, 174
— — — Escuela Naval del Perú, 1039
— — — Técnica Superior de Ingenieros de Caminos, Canales y Puertos, 1199
— — — — — de Ingenieros Industriales, Madrid, 1199
— — — Legislatura, La Plata, 70
— — — Oficina de Estudios del Canal Interocéanico, Panama City, 1031
— — — Secretaría de Communicaciones y Transportes, Mexico City, 930
— — — — Estado de Relaciones Exteriores, 404
— — — — — Gobernación, 930
— — — — — Industria y Comercio, Mexico City, 930
— — — — — Relaciones Exteriores, Mexico City, 930
— — — — — Salubridad y Asistencia y de la Escuela de Salud Pública, 930
— — — Sociedad Amantes de la Luz, Santiago de los Caballeros, 404
— — — — Científica del Paraguay, Asunción, 1034
— — — — — de Ciencias Naturales "La Salle", Caracas, 1954
— — — — — Rural Argentina, 69
— — — Tipografía Nacional, Guatemala City, 625
— — — Universidad Autónoma de Santo Domingo, 404
— — — — Católica de Chile, 326
— — — — — — Córdoba, 70
— — — — — — Valparaiso, 326
— — — — Central del Ecuador, 408
— — — — Complutense de Madrid, 1199
— — — — de Panamá, 1030
— — — — — Zulia, Venezuela, 1955
— — — — — las Americas, A.C., Puebla, 931
— — — — Nacional, Tegucigalpa, 630
— — — — — de Ingeniería, Lima, 1039
— — — — — La Plata, 70
— — — — — San Agustín, Arequipa, 1039
— — — — Pontificia Bolivariana, 349
— — — — las Facultades de Filosofía Teología S. I., San Miguel, 70
— — Leprología "Dr. Enrique P. Fidanza", Buenos Aires, 69
— — los Escritores del Perú, 1039
— — — Tribunales del D.F. "Fundación Rojas Astudillo", Caracas, 1955
— — Menéndez Pelayo, 1200
— — México, Mexico City, 931
— degli Istituti Ospedalieri, 766
— del Ateneo de Macoris, 404
— — Banco Central de la República Argentina, Buenos Aires, 69
— — — de Guatemala, 625
— — Bibliotecario, Buenos Aires, 69
— — Centro Cultural Costarricense-Norteamericano, San José, 360
— — Excursionista de Cataluña, Barcelona, 1200
— — — Nacional de Investigaciones Agropecuarios, Maracay, 1955
— — — Nazionale di Studi Manzoniani, Milan, 766
— — Civico Museo Correr, Venice, 769
— — Club Arequipa, Lima, 1039
— — Collegi de Farmacèutics de la Provincia de Barcelona, 1200
— — Colegio de Abogados de Barcelona, 1200
— — — Notarial de Barcelona, 1200
— — Congreso, Caracas, 1954

— — — de la Unión, Mexico City, 930
— — — — Nacional, Guatemala City, 625
— — — — La Paz, 174
— — — — Santiago, 326
— — — Consejo Nacional de Tuberculosis "Paulina Aldina", 364
— — — Conservatorio di Musica G. Verdi, 766
— — — — — S. Pietro a Maiella, 766
— — — Fomento del Trabajo Nacional, 1200
— — — Gabinetto Scientifico Letterario G.B. Vieussieux, Florence, 765
— — — Giardino Botanico, Lucca, 766
— — — Instituto Boliviano de Estudio y Acción Social, La Paz, 174
— — — — Centroamericana de Administración de Empresas, Managua, 988
— — — — Cultural Anglo-Uruguayo, Montevideo, 1940
— — — — de Literatura y Lingüística, Havana, 364
— — — — Municipal de Historia de la Ciudad, 1200
— — — — Nacional del Libro Español (INLE), Mallorca, 1200
— — — — Panamericano de Geografía e Historia, Tacubaya, 931
— — — — Pre-universitario de la Habana, 364
— — — — Tecnológico y de Estudios Superiores de Monterrey, 931
— — — Marco Fidel Suárez, Bello, 349
— — — Ministerio de Asuntos Exteriores, Madrid, 1199
— — — — Economía, Buenos Aires, 69
— — — — San Salvador, 422
— — — — Fomento, Caracas, 1955
— — — — Gobierno de la Provincia de Buenos Aires, 70
— — — — Hacienda, Caracas, 1955
— — — — Información y Turismo, Madrid, 1199
— — — — Obras Públicas, Caracas, 1955
— — — — Relaciones Exteriores, Buenos Aires, 69
— — — — — Caracas, 1955
— — — — — La Paz, 174
— — — — — Lima, 1039
— — — — — San José, 360
— — — — — San Salvador, 422
— — — — — Tegucigalpa, 630
— — — — Interiores, Caracas, 1955
— — — — Sanidad y Asistencia Social, Caracas, 1955
— — — — del Trabajo, Caracas, 1955
— — — Ministero degli Affari Esteri, Rome, 768
— — — — dell' Agricoltura e delle Foreste, Rome, 768
— — — — Interno, 768
— — — — delle Finanze e del Tesoro, 768
— — — Museo Histórico Nacional, Uruguay, 1940
— — — Palacio de Pereleda, 1200
— — — — Legislativo, Montevideo, 1940
— — — — Real, Madrid, 1199
— — — Politecnico di Torino, 768
— — — Popolo, Trieste, 768
— — — Seminario de Química de la Universidad de Barcelona, 1200
— — — Vescovile, Cremona, 765
— — — — Padua, 767
— — — Senato, Rome, 768
— — — Servicio Geológico Nacional, 69
— dell' Accademia dei Concordi, 768
— — — delle Scienze di Torino, 768
— — — Nazionale dei Lincei e Corsiniana, Rome, 767
— — — — Virgiliana, Mantua, 766
— — — Istituto di Entomologia Agraria dell' Università di Napoli, 767
— — — — Giuridico "Antonio Cicu", Bologna, 765
— — — — Italo-Latino Americano, Rome, 768

— — — Lombardo Accademia di Scienze e Lettere, 766
— — — Nazionale d'Archeologia e Storia dell'Arte, Rome, 768
— — — Università, Palermo, 767
— — — — Cattolica del S. Cuore, Milan, 766
— — — — Commerciale Luigi Bocconi, 766
— — — della Camera dei Deputati, 768
— — — — Cassa di Risparmio, Bologna, 765
— — — — Città di Arezzo, 765
— — — — Congregazione dei Mechitaristi, 769
— — — — Facoltà di Agraria, Milan, 766
— — — — — Giurisprudenza, Palermo, 767
— — — — — Lettere e Filosofia dell' Università, Florence, 765
— — — — — Scienze Agrarie dell' Università di Napoli, 767
— — — — Fondazione Marco Besso, 768
— — — — Galleria degli Uffizi, 765
— — — — Nazionale d'Arte Moderna, Rome, 768
— — — — Società Geografica Italiana, 768
— — — — Italiana per Organizzazione Internazionale, Rome, 768
— — — — Napoletana di Storia Patria, 767
— — — delle Facoltà di Giurisprudenza e di Lettere e Filosofia dell' Università, Milan, 766
— — Demonstrativa do Instituto Nacional do Livro, Brasília, 186
— — Departamental de Caldas, Manizáles, 349
— di Castelcapuano, 767
— — Storia Moderna e Contemporanea, 768
— do Banco do Brasil, Rio de Janeiro, 187
— — Centro Brasileiro de Pesquisas Educacionais, Rio de Janeiro, 187
— — Conservatório Dramático e Musical de São Paulo, 188
— — Convento dos Franciscanos, 188
— — Departamento do Arquivo do Estado do São Paulo, 188
— — Exército, Brasília, 186
— — — Lisbon, 1101
— — Gabinete Português de Leitura, 188
— — Grêmio Literário e Comercial Português, Belém, 186
— — Instituto Brasiliero do Café, 187
— — — de Sáude, São Paulo, 188
— — — dos Advogados Brasileiros, 187
— — Ministério da Fazenda no Estado do Rio de Janeiro, 187
— — — Justiça, Brasília, 186
— — — das Relações Exteriores, 186
— — — do Trabalho, Brasília, 186
— — Mosteiro de S. Bento, 187
— — Palácio Nacional de Mafra, 1102
— — Senado Federal, Brasília, 186
— "Dr. M. A. Sánchez Carvajal" de la Sociedad de Obstetricia y Ginecología de Venezuela, Caracas, 1955
— Documentará a Direcţiei Generale a Arhivelor Statului, Bucharest, 1125
— — de Istorie a Medicinii, Bucharest, 1125
— — Năsăud, 1126
— — "Timotei Cipariu", Blaj, 1126
— — Dominicana, Santo Domingo, 404
— — Ducal de Lerma, Madrid, 1199
— — Durazzo Giustiniani, Genoa, 766
— e Archivio, Raccolte Storiche del Comune di Milano, dei Musei del Risorgimento e Storia Contemporanea, Milan, 766
— — Arquivo da Assembleia Nacional, Lisbon, 1101
— — Histórico do Ministerio da Habitação e Obras Públicas, Lisbon, 1101
— — Público de Manaus, 187
— — — do Pará, 186
— — Musei Oliveriani, Pesaro, 767
— — Económica y Financiera, Managua, 988

— Ecuatoriana "Aurelio Espinosa Polit", Quito, 408
— "Eduardo Montealegre", Chinandega, 988
— "El Ateneo", Masaya, 988
— "Ernesto Peltzer" del Banco Central de Venezuela, Caracas, 1955
— Erudita e Arquivo Distrital, 1102
— Estadual, Rio de Janeiro, 187
— — Vitória, 188
— Estense, Modena, 766
— Filialei Cluj-Napoca a Academiei Republicii Socialiste România, 1126
— General de la Universidad Central de las Villas, Santa Clara, 364
— — — — de Oriente, Cumaná, 1955
— — Universidad de Guayaquil, 408
— "George Alexander", 188
— Geral da Fundação Gulbenkian, Lisbon, 1101
— Gustavo Pinto Lopes, Tôrres Novas, 1102
— Hispánica (del Centro Iberoamericano de Cooperación), Madrid, 1199
— Hispano-Americana, 408
— Histórica Cubana y Americana, 364
— — y Archivo Colonial, Guayaquil, 408
— Ibero-Americana y de Bellas Artes, 931
— Institutului de Arte Plastice "N. Grigorescu", Bucharest, 1125
— — Medico-Farmaceutic, Bucharest, 1125
— — — — Cluj-Napoca, 1126
— — — — Iași, 1126
— — National de Informare și Documentare, Bucharest, 1125
— — Politehnic "Gheorge Gheorghiu-Dej" București, 1125
— — — Cluj-Napoca, 1126
— — — Iași, 1126
— "José Antonio Echevarria", Havana, 364
— "Juan Bautista Vázquez" de la Universidad de Cuenca, 408
— Județeană Arad, 1125
— — Bacău, 1125
— — Brașov, 1125
— — Cluj-Napoca, 1126
— — Constanța, 1126
— — Dolj, Craiova, 1126
— — "Duiliu Zamfirescu", Focșani, 1126
— — Mehedinți, Drobeta-Turnu Severin, 1126
— — Bihor, Oradea, 1126
— — Argeș, Pitesti, 1126
— — Suceava, 1126
— — Mureș, Tîrgu-Mureș, 1126
— — Timiș, Timișoara, 1126
— — "Astra" Sibiu, 1126
— — "Gh-Asachi", Iași, 1126
— — "N. Iorga" Ploiești, 1126
— — "V. A. Urechia", Galați, 1126
— Lancisiana, Rome, 768
— "Luis-Angel Arango" del Banco de la República, 349
— Madre Maria Teresa Guevara, Santurce, 1110
— "Manuel Sanguily", Havana, 364
— "Marcel Roche" del Instituto Venezolano de Investigaciones Cientificas, Caracas, 1955
— Marucelliana, 765
— Matematica dell' Università di Torino, 768
— Mayor de la Universidad Nacional de Córdoba, 70
— Médica Venezolana de la Academia Nacional de Medicina, Caracas, 1954
— Medicea-Laurenziana, 765
— "Miguel de Cervantes Saavedra", 931
— "Miguel Lerdo de Tejada" de la Secretaria de Hacienda y Crédito Público, Mexico City, 930
— Moncayo, Zaragoza, 1201
— Morando, 766
— "Morazan", 988
— Moreniana, Florence, 765

— Municipal, Coímbra, 1102
— — León, 988
— — Luanda, 61
— — Maputo, 952
— — Petropolis, 187
— — Quito, 408
— — Santander, 1201
— — Vitória, 188
— — Zelaya, 988
— — Central, Lisbon, 1101
— — da Horta, 1102
— — de Lima, 1039
— — — Santarém, 1102
— — — Santo Domingo, 404
— — del Centenario, Calí, 349
— — do Funchal, Madeira, 1102
— — "Dr. Francisco Alberto Schinca", Montevideo, 1940
— — "Dr. Joaquín de Salteraín", Montevideo, 1940
— — "Gabriel Morillo", Moca, 404
— — Mário de Andrade, São Paulo, 188
— — "Mariscal Andrés de Santa Cruz", 174
— — "Pedro Carbo", Guayaquil, 408
— — "Ricardo Jaimes Freires", Potosí, 174
— Municipală "Mihail Sandovianu", Bucharest, 1125
— Municipale "A. Panizzi," Reggio Emilia, 767
— Museu e Arquivo dos Hospitais Civis de Lisboa, 1101
— Musicale S. Cecilia, 768
— Muzeului Brukenthal, 1126
— Nacional, Buenos Aires, 69
— — Caracas, 1955
— — "José Marti", Havana, 364
— — Lima, 1039
— — Lisbon, 1102
— — Madrid, 1199
— — Managua, 988
— — Panama, 1030
— — Rio de Janeiro, 187
— — San José, 360
— — San Salvador, 422
— — Santo Domingo, 404
— — de Aeronáutica, Buenos Aires, 69
— — — Agricultura, Brasília, 186
— — — Angola, Luanda, 61
— — — Antropologia e Historia "Dr. Eusebio Davalos Hurtado", Mexico City, 931
— — — Chile, 326
— — — Colombia, Bogotá, 349
— — — Educación, Buenos Aires, 69
— — — Guatemala, 625
— — — Honduras, 630
— — — Macau, 1108
— — — Maestros, Buenos Aires, 69
— — — México, 930
— — — Moçambique, Maputo, 952
— — — del Ecuador, Quito, 408
— — — Uruguay, 1940
— — Militar, Buenos Aires, 69
— Nazionale, Braidense, Milan, 766
— — Centrale, Florence, 766
— — — Vittorio Emanuele II, Rome, 768
— — Marciana, 769
— — Pedagogica, Florence, 766
— — Sagarriga-Visconti-Volpi, 765
— — Universitaria, Turin, 768
— — "Vittorio Emanuele II", Naples, 767
— Oratoriana del Monumento Nazionale dei Gerolamini, Naples, 767
— "Padre Billini", Baní, 404
— Palatina, 767
— — -Sezione Musicale Presso Il Conservatorio di Musica "A. Boito", Parma, 767
— Panamericana, Cuenca, 408
— Pedagógica Central, Montevideo, 1940
— Popular, Bahia Blanca, 63
— — Lisboa, 1102
— Provinciale "Elvira Cape", Santiago, 364
— — Melchiorre Delfico, 768
— — "Salvatore Tommasi", L'Aquila, 766

— Scipione e Giulio Capone, 765
— Pública, Vila Real, 1102
— "Cassiano Ricardo", São Paulo, 188
— Central del Estado de Chiapas, Tuxtla Gutierrez, 931
— de Arte, Buenos Aires, 69
— — Minas Gerais, Belo Horizonte, 186
— — — Ponta Delgada, 1102
— — — Quezaltenango, 625
— — del Colegio de Escribanos, 69
— — — Estado, Santander, 1201
— — — — de Jalisco, 931
— — — — — México, Toluca, 931
— — — — "Elias Amador", Zacatecas, 931
— — — Zulia, 1955
— — — Ministerio de Defensa Nacional, Asunción, 1034
— — Departamental, Barranquilla, 349
— — do Ceará, 187
— — — Estado, São Luis, 188
— — — — da Paraíba, 187
— — — — de Pernambuco, 187
— — — — Santa Catarina, 187
— — — — Sergipe, 186
— — — — do Rio de Janeiro, 187
— — — — Grande do Sul, 187
— — — — Paraná, Curitiba, 187
— — — e Arquivo Distrital de Angra do Heroísmo, 1102
— — — — Evora, 1102
— — Española, Tanger, 950
— — "Estanislao S. Zeballos", Rosario, 70
— — General San Martin, Mendoza, 70
— — Mariano Picón Salas", Caracas, 1955
— — Municipal, Cuenca, 408
— — — Florida, Uruguay, 1940
— — — de Arequipa, 1039
— — — do Porto, 1102
— — — "Dr. Joaquín Menéndez", Pergamino, Buenos Aires, 70
— — — Piloto, Callao, 1039
— — Pelotense, 187
— — Piloto de Medellín para la América Latina, Medellín, 349
— — "Pio Tamayo", Venezuela, 1955
— — "Raul Cepero Bonilla", Havana, 364
— — Reale, Turin, 768
— — Regional da Lagoa, Rio de Janeiro, 188
— — — de Copacabana, 188
— — Regionale Universitaria, Catania, 765
— — Riccardiana, 766
— — Rio Grandense, 188
— — Romana A. Sarti, 768
— — "Rubén Martínez Villena", Havana, 364
— — "Segovia", 988
— — Seminario Mayor Arquidiocesano, Bogotá, 349
— — Severin de Valparaiso, 326
— — Sir Robert Ho Tung, Macau, 1108
— — Statale di Lucca, 766
— — — e Libreria Civica, Cremona, 765
— — "Studium" S. Domenico, Bologna, 765
— — Técnica Científica Centralizada, Barquisimeto, 1955
— — Teleki-Bolyai, Tîrgu-Mures, 1126
— — Tornquist, 69
— — Trivulziana, 766
— — "24 de Julio", Trujillo, 1955
— — Universitaria, Bologna, 765
— — — Cagliari, 765
— — — Genoa, 766
— — — Messina, 766
— — — Modena, 766
— — — Padua, 767
— — — Pavia, 767
— — — Pisa, 767
— — — Potosí, 174
— — — Sassari, 768
— — — Urbino, 769
— — — Alessandrina, Rome, 768
— — — di Napoli Statale, Naples, 767
— — — y Provincial, Barcelona, 1200
— — Vallicelliana, 768

# INDEX OF INSTITUTIONS

Biblioteca Washington Irving (Centro Cultural de los Estados Unidos), San Bernardo, 1199
— Weil-Weiss, 766
— "Wilson Popenoe", Tegucigalpa, 630
— y Archivo del Ministerio de Relaciones Exteriores, 1034
— — — General, Ministerio de Energia y Minas, Caracas, 1955
— — — Nacional de Bolivia, 174
— — — Nacionales, Asunción, 1034
— — Museo del Instituto del Teatro, Barcelona, 1202
— — Sala de Lectura de la Sociedad El Porvenir de los Obreros, 625
Bibliotecas de la Universidad de Buenos Aires, 69
Biblioteche Civiche e Raccolte Storiche, 769
— Riunite "Civica e Negroni", Novara, 767
Biblioteka "Braka Miladinovci", Macedonia, 1976
— Državnog muzeja NR Crne Gore, Cetinje, 1976
— Gdańska P.A.N., Gdańsk, 1072
— Główna Akademii Górniczo-Hutniczej w Krakowie im Stanislawa Staszica, Cracow, 1072
— — — Sztuk Pieknych, Cracow, 1072
— — — — Warszawie, 1072
— — i Osrodek Informacji Naukowo-Technicznej Politechniki Wroclawskiej, 1073
— — Politechniki Czestochowskiej, 1072
— — — Gdańskiej, Gdańsk, 1072
— — — Krakowskiej, Cracow, 1072
— — — Łódzkiej, Łódź, 1073
— — — Poznańskiej, Poznań, 1073
— — — Slaskiej, Gliwice, 1073
— — — Szczecińskiej, Szczecin, 1073
— — — Warszawskiej, Warsaw, 1073
— — Slaskiej Akademii Medyczna im. L. Waryńskiego, Katowice, 1073
— — Szkoly Głównej Gospodarstwa Wiejskiego Akademii Rolniczej w Warszawie, Warsaw, 1073
— — Uniwersytetu im. Adama Mickiewicza, Poznań, 1073
— grada Beograda, Belgrade, 1974
— Istorijskog instituta NR. Crne Gore, Titograd, 1976
— Jagiellonska, 1073
— Katolockiego Uniwersytetu Lubelskiego w Lublinie, Lublin, 1073
— Kornicka PAN, Kornik, 1073
— Matice srpske, Novi Sad, 1974
— Narodowa, Warsaw, 1073
— P.A.N. w Krakowie, 1074
— — — Warszawie, 1074
— Poznańskiego Towarzystwa Przyjaciól Nauk, Poznań, 1074
— Publiczna m. st. Warszawie, 1074
— Sejmowa, Warsaw, 1074
— Śląska, Katowice, 1074
— Slovenske akademije znanosti in umetnosti, Ljubljana, 1975
— Srpske akademije nauka i umetnosti, Belgrade, 1974
— Szkoly Glownej Planowania i Statystyki, Warsaw, 1074
— Uniwersytecka w Łódzi, 1074
— — — Toruniu, 1074
— — — Warszawie, 1074
— — — Wrocławiu, 1074
— Uniwersytetu Marii Curie-Skłodowskiej w Lublinie, 1074
— Wyzsza Szkoła Pedagogiczna, Cracow, 1074
— Zakładu Narodowego im. Ossolińskich, 1074
— Zemaljskog muzeja, Sarajevo, 1975
Biblioteket for Vejle by og Amt, 394
Bibliotekscentralen, Ballerup, 389
Bibliotheca Bogoriensis, 711
— Hertziana (Max-Planck-Institut), Rome, 768
— Tilboschensis, Echt, 964

Bibliotheek der Hogeschool te Tilburg, 965
— — Katholieke Leergangen Afdeling Middelbare Akten, Tilburg, 965
— — Koninklijke Nederlandse Akademie van Wetenschappen, 963
— — Landbouwhogeschool, 965
— — Rijksakademie van Beeldende Kunsten, 964
— — Rijksuniversiteit, Groningen, 964
— — Leiden, 965
— — Utrecht, 965
— — Technische Hogeschool, Delft, 964
— — — Eindhoven, 1202
— — — Twente, Enschede, 964
— — Universitaire Faculteiten Sint-Ignatius, Antwerp, 155
— — Vrije universiteit, Amsterdam, 964
— en Documentatiecentrum van de Economische Voorlichtingsdienst, The Hague, 964
— — Documentatiedienst van de Tweede Kamer der Staten-Generaal, The Hague, 964
— — Gemeentelijke Archiefdienst, Delft, 964
— — Katholieke Theologische Hogeschool, Amsterdam, 964
— — Universiteit, Nijmegen, 965
— — Mathematisch Centrum, Amsterdam, 964
— -Rijkuniversitair Centrum, Antwerp, 155
— — Universitaire Instelling Antwerpen, 155
— van de Maatschappij der Nederlandse Letterkunde, 965
— — Rijksuniversiteit te Gent, 156
— — het Centraal Bureau voor de Statistiek, The Hague, 965
— — Koninklijk Nederlands Meteorologisch Instituut, 964
— — Nationaal Hoger Instituut en Koninklijke Academie voor Schone Kunsten, Antwerp, 155
— — Oud Katholiek Seminarie, 963
— — Provinciaal Genootschap van Kunsten en Wetenschappen in Noordbrabant, 965
— — Vredespaleis, 965
— — Teyler's Stichting, 964
— voor Hedendaagse Dokumentatie, Sint Niklaas Waas, 157
Bibliothek Braunschweig der Biologischen Bundesanstalt für Land- und Forstwirtschaft, Brunswick, 535
— der Akademie der Bildenden Künste, Vienna, 127
— — — Wissenschaften, Vienna, 127
— — für Staats- und Rechtswissenschaft der DDR, Potsdam, 508
— — Benediktinerabtei, Admont, 128
— — Seckau, 128
— — Benediktiner-Erzabtei St. Peter, Salzburg, 128
— — Bundesministerien für soziale Verwaltung und für Gesundheit und Umweltschutz, Vienna, 128
— — Deutschen Akademie der Naturforscher Leopoldina, Halle, 507
— — Bundespost, Bonn, 534
— — Generaldirektion der Österreichischen Bundesbahnen, Vienna, 127
— — Handelskammer Hamburg, 536
— — Hansestadt Lübeck, 536
— — Hochschule für Arkitektur und Bauwesen Weimar, 508
— — — Bodenkultur, 127
— — — Musik und darstellende Kunst in Wien, 127
— — — Verkehrswesen, "Friedrich List", Dresden, 507
— — Kammer der Gewerblichen Wirtschaft für Wien, 127
— — Mechitaristenkongregation, Vienna, 127
— — Österrichischen Geographischen Gesellschaft, Vienna, 127
— — Technischen Hochschule, Aachen, 534

— — — — Ilmenau, 507
— — — — Karl-Marx-Stadt, 507
— — — Universität, Vienna, 127
— — — Universität Konstanz, 536
— — — Veterinärmedizinischen Universität Wien, 127
— — — Wirtschaftsuniversität, Vienna, 128
— des Augustiner-Chorherrenstiftes, Klosterneuburg, 129
— — — St. Florian, 129
— — Benediktinerklosters Melk in Niederösterreich, 129
— — Bundesgerichtshofes, Karlsruhe, 536
— — Bundesministeriums für Finanzen, Vienna, 128
— — — Land-u. Forstwirtschaft, Vienna, 128
— — — Unterricht und Kunst, Vienna, 128
— — Deutschen Bundestages, Bonn, 534
— — Museums, Munich, 537
— — Patentamtes, Munich, 537
— — Freien Deutschen Hochstiftes, Frankfurt, 535
— — Germanischen National-Museums, Nuremberg, 537
— — Gesamteuropäischen Studienwerks, Vlotho, 538
— — Instituts für Auslandsbeziehungen, Stuttgart, 537
— — — Österreichische Geschichtsforschung, Vienna, 128
— — Seeverkehrswirtschaft, Bremen, 535
— — Johann-Gottfried-Herder-Instituts, Marburg, 536
— — Konservatoriums für Musik, 1259
— — Kriegsarchivs Wien, 128
— — Max-Planck-Instituts für Ausländisches Öffentliches Recht und Völkerrecht, Heidelberg, 536
— — — Ausländisches und Internationales Privatrecht, Hamburg, 536
— — Museums für Volkerkunde, 1259
— — Oberösterreichische Landesmuseums, Linz/Donau, 129
— — Obersten Gerichts der Deutschen Demokratischen Republik, 506
— — Österreichischen Statistischen Zentralamtes, 128
— — Priesterseminars Trier, 537
— -Dokumentation-Archiv, Statistiches Bundesamt, Wiesbaden, 538
— — für Zeitgeschichte-Weltkriegsbücherie, Stuttgart, 537
— — "Georgius Agricola", Freiberg, 507
— — und Archiv zur Geschichte der Max-Planck-Gesellschaft, Berlin (West), 528
— — Geographisch-Kartographischer Dienst des Auswärtigen Amts, Bonn, 535
— — Wissenschaft und Weisheit, Mönchen Gladbach, 537
Bibliotheksverband des Deutschen Demokratischen Republik, Berlin (East), 506
Bibliothèque Administrative de la Marine, Paris, 461
— Aubert, 58
— Ben Youssef, Marrakech, 950
— Bernheim, Nouméa, 500
— Calvet, Avignon, 462
— Cantonale et Universitaire, Fribourg, 1259
— — — de Lausanne, 1260
— Centrale de l'Ecole Polytechnique, Paris, 461
— — l'Université Nationale de Côte d'Ivoire, Abidjan, 799
— — — du Zaïre, Campus de Kinshasa, 1995
— — — — Campus de Kisangani, 1995
— — — — de Lubumbashi, 1995
— — — — la Côte d'Ivoire, Abidjan, 799

— — — Faculté Polytechnique de Mons, 157
— — — Prêt, Saint-Denis, 500
— — du Ministère de l'Education Nationale, Brussels, 156
— Champlain (Université de Moncton), New Brunswick, 247
— d'Art et d'Archéologie, Geneva, 1259
— — — — (Fondation Jacques-Doucet), Paris, 465
— de Documentation Internationale Contemporaine, Nanterre, 465
— — l'Abbaye de Saint-Benoît, 157
— — l'Académie Nationale de Médecine, Paris, 461
— — Royale des Beaux-Arts, Brussels, 156
— — l'Alliance Française, Dakar, 1146
— — l'Arsenal, Paris, 461
— — l'Assemblée Nationale, 461
— — l'Ecole Biblique et Archéologique Française, Jerusalem, 741
— — — des Langues Orientales, Paris, 461
— — — Nationale Supérieure d'Architecture et des Arts Visuels, 156
— — — — des Mines, 461
— — — Normale Supérieure, 461
— — — Supérieure des Lettres, Beirut, 899
— — l'Hospice du Grand Saint-Bernard, 1260
— — l'Institut Archéologique Liégeois, 156
— — — Catholique, Paris, 461
— — — de France, Paris, 461
— — — — Géographie, Paris, 465
— — — Fondamental d'Afrique Noire, Dakar, 1146
— — — National de la Statistique et des Etudes Economiques, 461
— — — Royal des Sciences Naturelles de Belgique, 156
— — — Scientifique Chérifien, Rabat, 950
— — l'Organisation mondiale de la Santé, Bureau régional de l'Afrique, Brazzaville, 358
— — l'Université, Besançon, 463
— — — Brazzaville, 358
— — — Bujumbura, 230
— — — Dijon, 463
— — — Liège, 156
— — — Limoges, 464
— — — de Haute Alsace, Mulhouse, 464
— — — l'Etat, Mons, 157
— — — Pau et des Pays de l'Adour, Pau, 465
— — — Picardie, Amiens, 463
— — — Reims, 465
— — — Savoie, Chambéry, 463
— — — Toulon et du Var, 465
— — — du Maine, Le Mans, 464
— — — Quaraouyine, Fès, 950
— — la Bourgeoisie de Berne, 1259
— — Communauté Urbaine de Casablanca, 950
— — Cour des Comptes, 461
— — Faculté de Droit, Paris, 465
— — — — Médecine, Paris, 465
— — — — Pharmacie, Paris, 465
— — — des Sciences Agronomiques de l'Etat, Gembloux, 156
— — — Sorbonne, Paris, 465
— — — Ville, Colmar, 462
— — — — Esch-sur-Alzette, 908
— — — — de Montréal, 248
— — — — et du Musée Fabre, Montpellier, 462
— Départementale, Saint-Denis, 500
— des Avocats à la Cour d'Appel, 461
— — Facultés Universitaires Saint-Louis, Brussels, 156
— — Nations Unies, Geneva, 1259
— — Pasteurs, Neuchâtel, 1260
— Documentation, Publications du Ministère de l'Emploi et du Travail, Brussels, 156

— du Barreau de Montréal, 248
— — Centre Culturel "Albert Camus", Antananarivo, 910
— — — Américain, Abidjan, 799
— — — Français, Abidjan, 799
— — — d'Information, Libreville, 502
— — — Universitaire, Avignon, 463
— — Collège de l'Immaculée-Conception, 248
— — Conseil d'Etat, 461
— — Conservatoire National des Arts et Métiers, 461
— — — Supérieur de Musique, 461
— — Ministère de l'Intérieur, Lomé, 1292
— — — des Affaires Etrangères, 461
— — — Armées, Paris, 461
— — — Lomé, 1292
— — Muséum National d'Histoire Naturelle, 461
— — Parlement, Brussels, 156
— — Petit Séminaire, Port-au-Prince, 629
— — Sénat, 461
— — Service d'Information, Abidjan, 799
— Espagnole, Paris, 461
— et Archives du Louvre et des Musées Nationaux, 461
— — Centre de Documentation de la Faculté de Médecine, Lausanne, 1260
— — Musée de la Ville, Haguenau, 462
— Fonds Quetelet, 156
— Forney, 461
— Franconie, Cayenne, 499
— Générale et Archives, Rabat, 950
— — — — Tétouan, 950
— — pour tous, Berne, 1259
— Georges Duhamel, Paris, 461
— Historique de la Marine, 461
— — — — Ville de Paris, 461
— Inguimbertine, 462
— Interuniversitaire, Aix-Marseille, 463, 464
— — Bordeaux, 463
— — Grenoble, 464
— — Lille, 464
— — Lyon, 464
— — Montpellier, 464
— — Nancy, 464
— — Rennes, 465
— — Toulouse, 465
— Louis Notari, Monaco, 946
— Mazarine, 461
— Municipale, Abbeville, 462
— — Abidjan, 799
— — Aix en Provence, 462
— — Albi, 462
— — Amiens, 462
— — Antananarivo, 910
— — Antsirabé, 910
— — Bamako, 920
— — Besançon, 462
— — Bordeaux, 462
— — Boulogne-sur-Mer, 462
— — Caen, 462
— — Châlons-sur-Marne, 462
— — Constantine, 58
— — Dijon, 462
— — Douai, 462
— — Grenoble, 462
— — La Rochelle, 462
— — Le Havre, 462
— — Lille, 462
— — Limoges, 462
— — Lyon, 462
— — Marseille, 462
— — Metz, 462
— — Nancy, 462
— — Nantes, 462
— — Nimes, 463
— — Orléans, 463
— — Pau, 463
— — Périgueux, 463
— — Poitiers, 463
— — Reims, 463
— — Rennes, 463
— — Rouen, 463
— — Saint-Pierre, 500
— — Toulouse, 463
— — Tours, 463

— — Troyes, 463
— — Valence, 463
— — Valenciennes, 463
— — Versailles, 463
— — Classée, Angers, 462
— — — Cambrai, 462
— — d'Etudes, Nice, 462
— — de la Ville de Lausanne, 1260
— — et Universitaire, Clermont-Ferrand, 463
— Musée de l'Opéra, Paris, 461
— Nationale, Abidjan, 799
— — Algiers, 58
— — Antananarivo, 910
— — Conakry, 627
— — Lomé, 1292
— — Luxembourg, 908
— — Nouakchott, 922
— — Paris, 460
— — Porto Novo, 172
— — Vientiane, 898
— — d'Haiti, 629
— — de Tunis, 1296
— — du Cameroun, Yaoundé, 231
— — — Liban, 899
— — — Québec, Montreal, 248
— — et Universitaire, Strasbourg, 465
— — Institut des Sciences Humaines, Bamako, 920
— — Suisse, 1259
— Orientale, Beirut, 899
— Pédagogique, Paris, 461
— Polonaise, 461
— pour tous, Berne, 1259
— Publique, Bujumbura, 230
— — Kinshasa, 1995
— — Centrale, Nouakchott, 922
— — — de la ville de Liège, 156
— — d'Information, Paris, 461
— — de la Ville, Neuchâtel, 1260
— — et Universitaire de Genève, 1259
— — Royale Albert 1er, Brussels, 156
— Saint Louis de Gonzague, Port-au-Prince, 629
— — Sainte-Geneviève, 465
— Schoelcher, Fort-de-France, 499
— — Thiers, 462
— Universitaire, Algiers, 58
— — Angers, 463
— — Antananarivo, 910
— — Antilles-Guyane (Section Guadeloupe), Pointe-à-Pitre, 499
— — — (Section Martinique), Fort de France, 500
— — Brest, 463
— — Caen, 463
— — Metz, 464
— — Nantes, 464
— — Nice, 464
— — Orleans, 464
— — Perpignan, 465
— — Poitiers, 465
— — Rouen, 465
— — St. Clothilde, 500
— — Saint-Etienne, 465
— — Tours, 465
— — Centrale de Dakar, 1146
— — Moretus Plantin, Namur, 157
Bibliothèques de l'Université de Montréal, 248
— — Libre de Bruxelles, 156
— — — St. Joseph, Beirut, 899
— — des Universités de Paris, 465
— — Municipales, Geneva, 1259
— — Publiques, Tunis, 1296
Bicol University, Legazpi City, 1051
Bidhan Chandra Krishi Viswa Vidyalaya, Kalyani, 680
Biennale di Venezia, 773
Bigaku-Kai, Tokyo, 811
Bihar Research Society, 667
Bijutsu-shi Gakkai, Tokyo, 804
Bilharz (Theodor) Research Institute, Giza, 415
Bilharzia Field Research Unit, Tygerberg, 1156

## INDEX OF INSTITUTIONS

Billedkunstfaglig Sentralorganisasjon, 1007
Billy Rose Art Garden, Jerusalem, 744
Biochemical Parasitology Unit (M.R.C.), Cambridge, 1444
— Society, London, 1433
— — of Israel, 738
Biochemistry Institute, Shanghai, 331
Bioengineering Institute, New York, 1810
Biofizikai Intézet, Szeged, 638
Biokémiai Intézet, Szeged, 638
Biokemiallinen Tutkimuslaitos, 431
Biola University, La Mirada, California, 1651
Biological and Geographical Research Institute, Irkutsk, 1362
— Engineering Society, London, 1435
— Experimentation Plant, God, 647
— Research Centre, Baghdad, 725
— — Institute, Kazan, 1363
— Station, Cholpon-Ata, 1329
— — Gdansk, 1078
— — Gorky, 1362
Biologisch Centrum, Haren, 961
Biologische Anstalt Helgoland, 531
— Gesellschaft der DDR, Berlin (East), 504
— Station, Neusiedler See, 125
Biologisk Selskab, Copenhagen, 391
Biology Association, Hanoi, 1962
Biomedical Engineering Institute, Sichuan, 332
Biomembrane Research Unit, Tygerberg, 1156
Biometeorological Research Centre, Wassenaar, 962
Biometric Society, Corvallis, 44
Biometrics Bureau, Salisbury, Zimbabwe, 2001
Biophysical Society, Bethesda, Md., 1612
Biophysics Institute, Beijing, 331
Biostatistics Unit (M.R.C.), Cambridge, 1443
Bir Library, Katmandu, 954
Birbal Sahni Institute of Palaeobotany, 670
Birkbeck College, London, 1510
Birla Industrial and Technological Museum, Calcutta, 674
— Institute of Technology and Science, Pilani, 681
— Research Institute for Applied Sciences, Birlagram-Nagda, 672
Birmingham Museums and Art Gallery, 1467
— Public and Jefferson County Free Library, Birmingham, Alabama, 1625
— Libraries, 1453
— Southern College, Alabama, 1643
Biro Pusat Statistik, 709
Birzeit University, 876
Biscayne College, Miami, 1692
Bischöfliche Zentralbibliothek, Regensburg, 537
Bishop College, Dallas, 1898
— Hooper's Lodging, Gloucester, 1468
Bishop's House, Sheffield, 1471
— University, Lennoxville, 257
Bitola University, 1985
Black Hills State College, S.D., 1887
— Sea Technical University, Trabzon, 1307
Blackburn College, Carlinville, 1703
— Museum and Art Gallery, 1467
Blagoveshchensk Agricultural Institute, 1369
— State Medical Institute, 1383
Blair Research Laboratory, Salisbury, Zimbabwe, 2001
Bloemfontein Regional Library, 1161
Bloemfonteinse Streekbibliotek, 1161
Blood Group Unit (M.R.C.), London, 1443
— Platelet Research Unit, Tygerberg, 1156
— Pressure Unit (M.R.C.), Glasgow, 1443, 1493
— Transfusion Institute, Sichuan, 332
Bloomsburg State College, Pa., 1867
Blue Mountain College, Miss., 1784
Bluefield State College, West Virginia, 1930
Bluffton College, Ohio, 1840
B.M. Institute of Mental Health, Navrangpura, 669

Bockus Research Institute, Philadelphia, 1880
Bodensee-Naturmuseum, Konstanz, 544
Bodleian Library, 1461
Bodrum Sualti Arkeoloji Müzesi, 1301
Boğaziçi Üniversitesi, Istanbul, 1304
— University Library, Istanbul, 1300
Bogomolets, A. A., Institute of Physiology, Kiev, 1334
Bogor Agricultural University, 712
Bogyoke Aung San Museum, Rangoon, 229
Bolivian Academy, La Paz, 173
— National Academy of Sciences, La Paz, 173
Bologna Centre School of Advanced International Studies of The Johns Hopkins University, Bologna, 796
Bolyai János Matematikai Tarsulat, 635
Bombay Art Society, 660
— Medical Union, 662
— Natural History Society, 663
Bond Heemschut, Amsterdam, 956
Bone Metabolism Research Group, Tygerberg, 1156
Bonnefantenmuseum, Maastricht, 968
Booker Washington Institute, Kakata, 905
Boras Stadsbibliotek, 1239
Boreal Institute for Northern Studies, Edmonton, Alberta, 257
Borgarbókasafn Reykjavíkur, Reykjavik, 657
Borgo e Castello Medioevali, Turin, 773
Bőr-, Cipő-, és Bőrfeldolgozóipari Tudományos Egyesület, Budapest, 636
Borochov Library, Haifa, 741
Borodino State Museum-Preserve of Military History, 1355
Borough of Newport Museum and Art Gallery, Mon., 1472
Borromeo College of Ohio, 1840
Borthwick Institute of Historical Research, York, 1539
Bose Institute, 669
Bosra Museum, 1277
Boston College, Chestnut Hill, 1747
— Museum of Fine Arts, 1636
— Public Library and Eastern Massachusetts Regional Public Library System, Boston, 1626
— State College, Mass., 1747
— University, 1748
— — Libraries, 1633
Botanical Garden, Alma-Ata, 1329
— — Ashkhabad, 1332
— — Baku, 1325
— — Donetsk, 1334
— — Frunze, 1329
— — Gorky, 1362
— — Iași, 1135
— — Kaunas, 1331
— — Kishinev, 1331
— — Minsk, 1326
— — Moscow, 1320
— — Riga, 1364
— — Salaspils, Riga District, 1330
— — Singapore, 1150
— — Tallinn, 1327
— — Tashkent, 1335
— — Tbilisi, 1328
— Institute, Cracow, 1067
— — and Garden of the University, Belgrade, 1973
— Research Institute, Pretoria, 1159
— Society of America Inc., 1612
— — — Edinburgh, 1431
— — — Israel, 738
— — — South Africa, 1156
— — — the British Isles, 1431
— — — Zimbabwe, Salisbury, 2000
— Survey of India, 670
Botanische Institute und Botanischer Garten, Bern, 1258
— Staatssammlung, Munich, 544
Botanischer Garten, Munich, 544
— — des Landes Kärnten, Klagenfurt, 131

— — und Botanisches Museum, Berlin-Dahlem, 541
— — — Museum der Universität, Zürich, 1263
Botanisches Institut und Botanischer Garten, Vienna, 125
Botanisk Hage og Museum, Oslo, 1012
— Have, Copenhagen, 395
— Museum Universitetet i Bergen, 1011
Botany Institute, Beijing, 332
Botswana Agricultural College, 177
— National Archives, 177
— — Library Service, Gaborone, 177
Boulder Laboratories Library, Colo., 1625
Bowdoin College, Brunswick, Maine, 1741
Bowes Museum, Barnard Castle, 1467
Bowling Green State University, 1840
Boyana Church National Museum, Sofia, 221
Boyce Thompson Institute for Plant Research Inc., Ithaca, N.Y., 1620
Boyden Observatory, Bloemfontein, 1160
Brace Research Institute, Montreal, 277
Bradford Public Libraries, 1453
Bradley University, Peoria, 1703
Brain Metabolism Research Group, Tygerberg, 1156
— — Unit (M.R.C.), Edinburgh, 1443
Branch of Institute of Mathematics, Minsk, 1326
— — — — Physics, Mogilev, 1326
— — — — Solid State and Semiconductor Physics, Vitebsk, 1326
— — Metabolism Regulation, Grodno, 1326
Brandeis University, Waltham, Mass., 1748
Brandon University, Manitoba, 257
Brasenose College, Oxford, 1524
— Library, Oxford, 1463
Brasília Academy of Letters, 178
Brawidjaja University, Malang, 713
Bray Libraries (SPCK), London, 1456
Brazilian Academy of Administration, Rio de Janeiro, 178
— — Letters, Rio de Janeiro, 178
— — Sciences, Rio de Janeiro, 178
Bremer Ausschuss für Wirtschaftsforschung, 529
Brent Library Service, 1452
Brescia College, London, Ontario, 315
Brest Civil Engineering Institute, 1379
Bridgestone Museum of Art, Tokyo, 820
Bridgewater College, 1915
— State College, Mass., 1748
Brigham Young University, Hawaii Campus, 1702
— — — Provo, Utah, 1911
Brighton Polytechnic, 1540
Bristol Old Vic Theatre School, 1552
— Polytechnic, 1540
— — Faculty of Education, 1481
British Academy, 1407
— — of Forensic Sciences, London, 1416
— Agricultural History Society, Reading, 1411
— and Foreign Bible Society's Library, London, 1456
— Antarctic Survey, London, 1446
— Archaeological Association, 1421
— Architectural Library, London, 1456
— Association for Rheumatology and Rehabilitation, London, 1427
— — — the Advancement of Science, 1430
— Astronomical Association, London, 1433
— Biophysical Society, London, 1431
— Broadcasting Corporation Music Library, London, 1456
— — — Reference Library, London, 1456
— Cartographic Society, Epping, 1421
— Centre, Stockholm, 1236
— Ceramic Research Association, Stoke-on-Trent, 1448
— — Society, Stoke-on-Trent, 1436
— College of Ophthalmic Opticians (Optometrists), London, 1427
— Columbia Provincial Museum, Victoria, 249

— — Research Council, Vancouver, 244
— Computer Society, London, 1432
— Council, Abu Dhabi, 1391
— — Accra, 611
— — Addis Ababa, 424
— — Algiers, 57
— — Amman, 875
— — Amsterdam, 958
— — Ankara, 1298
— — Athens, 617
— — Baghdad, 725
— — Bangkok, 1283
— — Beijing, 334
— — Beirut, 899
— — Belgrade, 1969
— — Bogotá, 347
— — Brasília, 180
— — Brussels, 151
— — Bucharest, 1122
— — Budapest, 635
— — Buenos Aires, 63
— — Cairo, 414
— — Caracas, 1951
— — Cologne, 521
— — Colombo, 1224
— — Copenhagen, 391
— — Dacca, 142
— — Dakar, 1145
— — Damascus, 1277
— — Dar es Salaam, 1280
— — Doha, 1114
— — Dubai, 1391
— — Freetown, 1148
— — Gaborone, 177
— — Helsinki, 428
— — Hong Kong, 1559
— — Islamabad, 1020
— — Jakarta, 708
— — Kathmandu, 954
— — Khartoum, 1229
— — Kuala Lumpur, 914
— — Lagos, 991
— — Lilongwe, 912
— — Lima, 1037
— — Lisbon, 1098
— — London, 1425
— — Lusaka, 1997
— — Madrid, 1190
— — Manama, 141
— — Maseru, 903
— — Mexico City, 926
— — Moscow, 1345
— — Mutrah, 1018
— — Nairobi, 878
— — New Delhi, 661
— — Nicosia, 367
— — Oslo, 1007
— — Ottawa, 241
— — Paris, 448
— — Prague, 374
— — Pretoria, 1155
— — Quezon City, 1047
— — Quito, 407
— — Rabat, 949
— — Rangoon, 228
— — Riyadh, 1142
— — Rome, 758
— — Safat, 897
— — Salisbury, Zimbabwe, 2000
— — Sana'a, 1965
— — Santiago, 323
— — Seoul, 885
— — Singapore, 1150
— — Stockholm, 1236
— — Sydney, 89
— — Tel Aviv, 738
— — Tokyo, 806
— — Tunis, 1295
— — Vienna, 121
— — Warsaw, 1066
— — Washington, D.C., 1607
— — Wellington, N.Z., 978
— — Yaoundé, 231
— — Zagreb, 1970
— — Library, Accra, 612
— — — Addis Ababa, 424

— — Amman, 875
— — Amsterdam, 964
— — Ankara, 1300
— — Asmara, 424
— — Athens, 618
— — Bandung, 710
— — Bangkok, 1284
— — Barcelona, 1200
— — Belgrade, 1974
— — Berlin (West), 534
— — Blantyre, 912
— — Bogotá, 349
— — Bombay, 673
— — Bordeaux, 462
— — Brussels, 156
— — Cairo, 416
— — Calcutta, 673
— — Chittagong, 143
— — Cologne, 535
— — Colombo, 1225
— — Copenhagen, 394
— — Dacca, 143
— — Dar es Salaam, 1280
— — Hamburg, 536
— — Helsinki, 431
— — Hong Kong, 1559
— — Islamabad, 1023
— — Istanbul, 1300
— — Jakarta, 711
— — Karachi, 1023
— — Kata Kinabalu, 915
— — Kathmandu, 954
— — Khartoum, 1229
— — Kisumu, 879
— — Kuala Lumpur, 915
— — Kyoto, 819
— — Lahore, 1023
— — Lille, 462
— — Lilongwe, 912
— — Lisbon, 1102
— — Lusaka, 1997
— — Lyon, 462
— — Madras, 673
— — Madrid, 1199
— — Marseille, 462
— — Maseru, 903
— — Medan, 711
— — Milan, 766
— — Mombasa, 879
— — Munich, 537
— — Nairobi, 879
— — Naples, 767
— — New Delhi, 673
— — Nicosia, 367
— — Paris, 462
— — Penang, 915
— — Peshawar, 1023
— — Quezon City, 1049
— — Rabat, 950
— — Rajshahi, 143
— — Riyadh, 1142
— — Rome, 768
— — Rose Hill, 923
— — Tel-Aviv, 741
— — Thessaloniki, 618
— — Tokyo, 818
— — Toulouse, 463
— — Valencia, 1201
— — Vienna, 128
— — Warsaw, 1074
— — Wellington, N.Z., 981
— — Zagreb, 1975
— Cryogenics Council, Rugby, 1433
— Dental Association, London, 1428
— Diabetic Association, London, 1428
— Dietetic Association, Birmingham, 1428
— Ecological Society, Bangor, 1431
— Educational Management and Administration Society, Edinburgh, 1418
— Federation of Music Festivals, 1414
— Film Institute, London, 1415
— Geriatrics Society, Mitcham, 1428
— Glass Industry Research Association, Sheffield, 1448
— Horological Institute, Newark, 1433

— Institute, Barcelona, 1190
— — Coímbra, 1098
— — Florence, 758
— — Rome, 758
— — in Eastern Africa, Nairobi, 878
— — Paris, 1513
— — South-East Asia, Singapore, 1150
— — of Afghan Studies, Kabul, 52
— — — Archaeology at Ankara, 1299
— — — International and Comparative Law, London, 1416
— — — Management, London, 1436
— — — Persian Studies, Teheran, 721
— — — Radiology, London, 1428
— — — Recorded Sound, London, 1456
— — — Surgical Technologists, London, 1428
— Interplanetary Society, London, 1433
— Library, London, 1449
— of Political and Economic Science, London, 1460
— Lichen Society, London, 1431
— Medical Association, London, 1428
— — — Library, London, 1456
— Museum, London, 1465
— — (Natural History), London, 1465
— — — — Library, London, 1456
— Mycological Society, Ashford, Kent, 1431
— Nuclear Energy Society, London, 1433
— Numismatic Society, Edgware, 1422
— Nutrition Foundation, London, 1428
— Ornithologists' Union, London, 1431
— Orthopaedic Association, London, 1428
— Paediatric Association, London, 1428
— Pharmacological Society, Leeds, 1428
— Postgraduate Medical Federation, London, 1512
— Psychoanalytical Society, London, 1428
— Psychological Society, Leicester, 1434
— Records Association, London, 1422
— School at Athens, 623
— — Rome, 758
— — of Archaeology in Iraq (Gertrude Bell Memorial), London, 725
— — — — Jerusalem, 752
— Senegalese Institute, Dakar, 1145
— Ship Research Association, 1448
— Social Biology Council, London, 1431
— Society for Middle Eastern Studies, Oxford, 1434
— — Research on Ageing, 1444
— — Social Responsibility in Science, London, 1430
— — the History of Mathematics, Enfield, 1432
— — — — Science, Chalfont St. Giles, 1430
— — — Philosophy of Science, Brighton, 1430
— — — Study of Orthodontics, 1428
— — of Aesthetics, London, 1434
— — — Animal Production, 1411
— — — Gastroenterology, London, 1428
— — — Rheology, Newcastle-upon-Tyne, 1436
— — — Soil Science, Loughborough, 1411
— Sociological Association, London, 1434
— Standards Institution, London, 1436
— Theatre Association, London, 1413
— — Library, London, 1456
— Trust for Ornithology, Tring, 1431
— Veterinary Association, London, 1411
Brlić House (Ivana Brlić-Mazuranić Memorial), Slavonski Brod, 1978
Brock University, St. Catherines, 262
Bromley Public Libraries, 1452
Bronfman Biblical and Archaeological Museum, Jerusalem, 744
Brontë Society, Haworth, 1426
Brookhaven National Laboratory, Upton, 1622
Brookings Institution, Washington, 1617
Brooklyn Botanic Garden and Arboretum, 1636
— Children's Museum, 1636
— College, 1805

INDEX OF INSTITUTIONS

Brooklyn Museum, 1636
— Public Library, 1626
Broughty Castle Museum, 1472
Brown University, Providence, R.I., 1882
— — Library, Providence, 1634
Brücke Museum, Berlin (West), 541
Brüder Grimm-Museum, Kassel, 543
Brunei Museum, Kota Baru, 213
Brunel University, Uxbridge, 1481
Bryansk Institute of Transport Engineering, 1377
— State Museum of Soviet Fine Arts, 1353
Bryant College, Smithfield, R.I., 1884
Bryn Mawr College, Pa., 1867
Bu-Ali Sina University, Hamadan, 723
Bücherei der Staatlichen Hochschule für Musik und Darstellende Kunst, Stuttgart, 537
— des Österreichischen Patentamtes, Vienna, 128
Buckinghamshire County Library, Aylesbury, 1453
Bucknell University, Lewisburg, 1867
Budapest Főváros Levétara, 640
Budapesti Muszaki Egyetem, 652
— — — Központi Könyvtara, 640
— Történeti Múzeum, 643
Buddhist Academy of Ceylon, 1224
— Research Centre, Bangkok, 1283
Buena Vista College, Storm Lake, 1722
Buffalo and Erie County Public Library, 1627
— Fine Arts Academy, 1636
— Museum of Science, 1636
— Society of Natural Sciences, 1611
Buhl Planetarium and Institute of Popular Science, Pittsburgh, 1636
Building and Road Research Institute, Kumasi, 611
— Research Advisory Board, Washington, D.C. 1622
— — Centre, Baghdad, 725
— — Establishment, Watford, 1448
— — Institute, Tokyo, 817
— Services Research Unit, Glasgow, 1493
— Trades School, Jalan Muara, 213
Bukkyo University, Kyoto, 862
— Jidó Hakubutsukan, Kyoto, 821
Bulawayo Technical College, 2003
Bulgarian Academy of Sciences, Sofia, 214
— Association for Penal Law, Sofia, 218
— — of International Law, Sofia, 218
— Astronautical Society, Sofia, 218
— Botanical Society, 218
— Geographical Society, 218
— Geological Society, 218
— Historical Society, Sofia, 218
— Philosophical Society, Sofia, 218
— Sociological Society, Sofia, 218
— Soil Society, Sofia, 217
— State Conservatoire, Sofia, 227
Buma Bibliotheek, Leeuwarden, 965
Búnadarfélag Íslands, Reykjavík, 656
Búnadarskólinn á Hólum i Hjaltadal, 658
Bund Schweizer Architekten, 1253
Bunda College of Agriculture, Malawi, 913
Bundesamt für Statistik, Bern, 1254
Bundesanstalt für Geowissenschaften und Rohstoffe, Hannover, 532
— — Materialprüfung, Berlin (West), 533
— — Veterinärmedizinische Untersuchungen, Linz, 124
— — Wasserbauversuche und hydrometrische Prüfung, Vienna, 126
— — Wasserhaushalt von Karstgebieten, Vienna, 125
Bundesarchiv, Coblenz, 539
— -Militärarchiv, Freiburg, 539
Bundesdenkmalamt, Vienna, 119
Bundesforschungsanstalt für Ernährung, Karlsruhe, 533
— — Fischerei, Hamburg, 528
— — Landeskunde und Raumordnung, Bonn, 530
— — Landwirtschaft, Brunswick, 528

Bundesinstitut für Ostwissenschaftliche und Internationale Studien, Cologne, 530
Bundesmobilienverwaltung, Vienna, 129
Bundespostmuseum, Frankfurt, 542
Bundesstaatliche Anstalt für experimentellpharmakologische und balneologische Untersuchungen, Vienna, 125
— Paedagogische Bibliothek beim Landesschulrat für Niederösterreich, Vienna, 128
— Studien-bibliothek, Klagenfurt, 129
— — Linz, 129
Bundesversuchsanstalt für Alpenländische Landwirtschaft, Gumpenstein, 124
Bündner Kunstmuseum, Chur, 1261
Burden Neurological Institute, Bristol, 1445
Bureau Africain des Sciences de l'Education (B.A.S.E.), Kisangani, 1996
— d'Ethnologie, Port-au-Prince, 629
— de Recherches et de Participations Minières (B.R.P.M.), Rabat, 949
— — — Géologiques et Minières (BRGM), Abidjan, 798
— — — — Antananarivo, 910
— — — — Bobo-Dioulasso, 1937
— — — — Dakar, 1145
— — — — Jeddah, 1142
— — — — Kinshasa, 1995
— — — — Libreville, 502
— — — — Niamey, 990
— — — — Orleans, 458
— des Longitudes, Paris, 458
— européen de l'éducation populaire, Amersfoort, 27
— for Continuing Education, Potchefstroom, 1173
— — Higher Education, Johannesburg, 1176
— — Mineral Studies, Johannesburg, 1182
— — Research, Potchefstroom, 1173
— — University Education, Potchefstroom, 1173
— — — Research, Pretoria, 1178
— Intergouvernemental pour l'Informatique, Rome, 45
— international de l'heure, Paris, 50
— — Liaison et de Documentation (BILD), Paris, 448
— — Recherches sur les Oiseaux d'Eau, Slimbridge, 50
— — des Poids et Mesures, Sèvres, 47
— of Hygiene and Tropical Diseases, London, 1445
— — Market Research, Pretoria, 1178
— — Mineral Resources, Geology and Geophysics, Parkes, 93
— — Mines and Geosciences, Manila, 1048
— — Plant Industry, Manila, 1048
— — the Census Library, Washington, D.C., 1624
— pour le Développement de la Production Agricole (BDPA), Brazzaville, 358
— — — — Production Agricole, N'Djamena, 321
— Régional de l'UNESCO pour l'Education en Afrique, Dakar, 1145
Burgenländische Landesbibliothek, Eisenstadt, 129
Burgenländisches Landesarchiv, Eisenstadt, 127
— Landesmuseum, Eisenstadt, 131
Burgerbibliothek Bern, 1259
Burgmannenhaus, Giessen, 542
Burgmuseum, Salzburg, 131
Burma Educational Research Bureau, 228
— Research Society, Rangoon, 228
Burnley Horticultural College, Victoria, 115
Burns Museum, Alloway, Ayrshire, 1472
Bursa Arkeoloji Müzesi, 1301
— Türk ve Islam Eserleri Müzesi, 1301
— Üniversitesi, 1304
Buryat Agricultural Institute, 1369
— — Library, 886

WORLD OF LEARNING

— — Museum, 887
Busch Centre, Philadelphia, 1880
Business History Documentation Center, Tel-Aviv, 750
— — Unit, London, 1510
— Research and Services, Las Cruces, 1802
— Statistics Office Library, Newport, Gwent, 1450
Butler University, Indianapolis, 1716
Butlerov, A. M., Research Institute of Chemistry, Kazan, 1363
Butsuri Tansa Gakkai, Tokyo, 810
Büyük Millet Meclisi Müzesi, Ankara, 1301
Bvumbwe Agricultural Research Station, Limbe, 912
Byarbókasavnid, Tórshavn, 402
Bydgoskie Towarzystwo Naukowe, Bydgoszcz, 1066
Byelorussian Agricultural Academy, Gorki, 1369
— Blood Transfusion Institute, Minsk, 1385
— Institute of Agricultural Engineering, Minsk, 1371
— — — Microbiology, Epidemiology and Hygiene, Minsk, 1385
— — — Neurology, Neuro-Surgery and Physiotherapy, Minsk, 1386
— — — Railway Engineers, 1389
— — — Tuberculosis, 1384
— S. M. Kirov Technological Institute, Minsk, 1381
— V. V. Kuibyshev State Institute of National Economy, Minsk, 1373
— V. I. Lenin State University, 1361
— Maternity and Child Welfare Institute, Minsk, 1384
— Polytechnic Institute, Minsk, 1374
— S.S.R. Academy of Sciences, Minsk, 1326
— State Art Museum, Minsk, 1352
— — Conservatoire, Minsk, 1387
— — Museum of History of World War II, Minsk, 1356
— — Theatrical and Art Institute, Minsk, 1388
Byggecentrum, Copenhagen, 392
Byurakan Astro-Physical Observatory, Ashtarak, 1324
— Optical and Mechanical Laboratory, Ashtarak, 1324
Byzantine Museum, Athens, 618


C

Ca' Rezzonico, Venice, 773
Cabinet des estampes, Geneva, 1261
— Library, Tokyo, 818
— Office Library, Entebbe, 1311
Cabrini College, Radnor, Pa., 1867
Caesarea Museum, Kibbutz Sedot Yam, 743
Cagayan Valley Institute of Technology, Isabela, 1060
Cairo Geological Museum, 417
— Museum of Hygiene, 417
— Odontological Society, 414
— Polytechnic Institute, 421
— University, Khartoum Branch, 1230
Calcutta Mathematical Society, 663
Caldwell College, N.J., 1796
Calgary Public Library, 246
California Academy of Sciences, San Francisco, 1597
— Baptist College, Riverside, 1651
— College of Arts and Crafts, Oakland, 1651
— — — Podiatric Medicine, San Francisco, 1651
— Historical Society, 1605
— Institute of Asian Studies, San Francisco, 1651
— — — Integral Studies, San Francisco, 1651
— — — Technology, Pasadena, 1651
— — — the Arts, Valencia, 1653
— Library Association, Sacramento, 1601
— Lutheran College, 1653

VORLD OF LEARNING

— Media and Library Educators Association, Burlingame, 1601
— Palace of the Legion of Honor, San Francisco, 1636
— Polytechnic State University, San Luis Obispo, 1653
— State College, Bakersfield, 1653
— — — Pennsylvania, 1867
— — — San Bernardino, 1653
— — — Stanislaus, Turlock, 1653
— — Library, Sacramento, 1630
— — Polytechnic University, Pomona, 1653
— — University, Chico, 1653
— — — Dominguez Hills, 1654
— — — Fresno, 1654
— — — Fullerton, 1654
— — — Hayward, 1654
— — — Long Beach, 1654
— — — Los Angeles, 1654
— — — Northridge, 1654
— — — Sacramento, 1654
— — — and Colleges, Golden Shore, 1653
Calouste Gulbenkian Foundation, London, 1419
Calumet College, Hammond, Ind., 1716
Calvin College, Grand Rapids, Mich., 1760
Cama (K.R.) Oriental Institute and Library, Bombay, 668
Camberwell School of Arts and Crafts, 1550
Camborne School of Mines, 1553
Cambrian Archaeological Association, 1422
Cambridge Bibliographical Society, 1415
— Philosophical Society, 1430
Cambridgeshire Libraries, Huntingdon, 1453
Camden Public Libraries, London, 1452
Campbell University, Buie's Creek, 1825
Campbellsville College, 1735
Camperdown House, Dundee, 1472
Campion College, Regina, 299
— Hall, Oxford, 1524
Campo Agricola Experimental, Rio Bravo, 925
Camrose Lutheran College, Alberta, 257
Canada Centre for Inland Waters, Burlington, Ont., 246
— Council, 239
— Institute for Scientific and Technical Information (CISTI), Ottawa, 247
Canadian Aeronautics and Space Institute, Ottawa, 243
— Association for Adult Education, 241
— — of African Studies, Ottawa, 243
— — — Anatomists, Winnipeg, 241
— — — Geographers, Montreal, 241
— — — Latin American Studies, Vancouver, 243
— — — Optometrists, 241
— — — Physicists, 243
— Authors' Association, 241
— Bar Association, Ottawa, 240
— Biochemical Society, Saskatoon, 243
— Council for International Co-operation, Ottawa, 241
— — of Professional Engineers, Ottawa, 243
— Cultural Institute in Rome, 758
— Dental Association, 241
— — Research Foundation, 244
— Economics Association, Ottawa, 240
— Education Association, 241
— Electrical Association, 243
— Federation for the Humanities, Ottawa, 245
— — of Biological Societies, Saskatoon, 242
— Film Institute, Ottawa, 240
— Forestry Association, Ottawa, 239
— — Service, Ottawa, 244
— Geotechnical Society, Montreal, 244
— Historical Association, 241
— Institute of Chartered Accountants, Toronto, 240
— — — International Affairs, 240
— — — Mining and Metallurgy, 244
— — — Planners, Ottawa, 239
— — — Ukrainian Studies, Edmonton, Alb., 257

— Library Association, 240
— Linguistic Association, Kingston, 241
— Lung Association, Ottawa, 242
— Mathematical Society, Ottawa, 243
— Medical Association, 242
— Museums Association, Ottawa, 240
— Music Centre, Toronto, 240
— — Council, Ottawa, 240
— Paediatric Society, Quebec, 242
— Pharmaceutical Association, 242
— Philosophical Association, Ottawa, 243
— Physiological Society, Edmonton, Alb., 242
— Phytopathological Society, 242
— Plains Research Centre, Regina, 297
— Political Science Association, 240
— Psychiatric Association, Ottawa, 242
— Psychological Association, 243
— Public Health Association, 242
— Research Centre for Anthropology, Ottawa, 245
— Society for Cell Biology, Downsview, 242
— — — Civil Engineering, Montreal, 244
— — — Electrical Engineering, Montreal, 244
— — — Immunology, Winnipeg, 242
— — — Mechanical Engineering, Montreal, 244
— — of Animal Science, Ottawa, 239
— — — Biblical Studies, Toronto, 243
— — — Landscape Artists, Ottawa, 239
— — — Microbiologists, Ottawa, 242
— — — Painters in Watercolour, 240
— — — Petroleum Geologists, Calgary, 243
— Union College, College Heights, 257
— Veterinary Medical Association, Ottawa, 239
— 220 MHz NMR Centre, Toronto, 245
Canal Zone Library and Museum, Panama, 1031
Canberra College of Advanced Education, 112
— School of Music, 112
Cancer Association of Zimbabwe, Bulawayo, 2000
— Institute, Japanese Foundation for Cancer Research, Tokyo, 815
— Research Campaign, London, 1428
— — Centre, Moscow, 1342
— — Institute, Bombay, 669
— — — Durban, 1168
— — — Kanazawa City, 831
— — — Karachi, 1021
— — — Sapporo City, 860
— Society of Finland, Helsinki, 429
Canisius College, Buffalo, 1805
Canning House Library, London, 1456
Canterbury and York Society, 1422
— Cathedral Archives and Library and City Record Office, 1458
— College, Windsor, Ont., 316
— Medical Research Foundation, Christchurch, 979
— Museum, N.Z., 982
— Public Library, N.Z., 981
Cape Education Department Library Service, Cape Town, 1161
— Provincial Library Service, Cape Town, 1161
— Technikon, Cape Town, 1183
— Town City Libraries, 1161
Capital University, Columbus, 1840
Cappella degli Scrovegni, Padua, 772
Cappelle, Sale e Gallerie Affrescate, 1943
Capricornia Institute of Advanced Education, Rockhampton, 114
Carabaisch Marien-Biologisch Instituut, Curaçao, 975
Cardiff Central Library, 1455
Cardinal Glennon College, St. Louis, 1786
— Stritch College, Wisconsin, 1931
Cardiothoracic Insitute, London, 1512
Cardiovascular Diseases Institute, Beijing, 332
— Institute, Tokyo, 815

INDEX OF INSTITUTIONS

— Research Unit, Johannesburg, 1182
— — — Turku, 439
Carey Hall, Vancouver, 261
Caribbean Agricultural Research and Development Institute, Bridgetown, 146
— — — — — Kingston, Jamaica, 801
— — — — — Trinidad, 1294
— Food and Nutrition Institute, Kingston, Jamaica, 800
— Regional Library, San Juan, P.R., 1110
Carl Duisberg-Gesellschaft e.V., Cologne, 520
— Nielsens Barndomshjem, Nr. Søby, 395
Carleton College, Northfield, 1774
— University, Ottawa, 265
— — Library, Ottawa, 247
Carlow College, Pittsburgh, 1867
Carlsbergfondet, 391
Carlyle's House, 1465
Carnegie Corporation of New York, 1604
— Endowment for International Peace, 1603
— Foundation for the Advancement of Teaching, 1604
— Free Library, Kota Bharu, 916
— — — San Fernando, 1293
— Institution of Washington, 1619
— Library, Curepipe, 923
— — of Pittsburgh, 1627
— -Mellon University, Pittsburgh, 1867
— Public Library, San Juan, P.R., 1110
— Trust for the Universities of Scotland, 1420
— United Kingdom Trust, 1420
Carroll College, Helena, 1791
— — Waukesha, 1931
Carson-Newman College, Jefferson City, 1889
Carter Observatory, N.Z., 979
Casa de Cervantes, Bologna, 758
— — — Valladolid, 1204
— — — la Cultura, Arequipa, 1039
— — — — Checoslovaca, Vedado, 363
— — — — de Occidente, Quezaltenango, 624
— — — — Ecuatoriana, Quito, 407
— — — — Independencia, Asunción, 1034
— — — — Sucre, 175
— — — las Americas, Havana, 363
— — — Simón Bolívar, Caracas, 1956
— — — Velázquez, Madrid, 1190
— — degli Italiani, Somalia, 1153
— — del Greco: Fundaciones Vega Inclán, Toledo, 1204
— — Libro, San Juan, P.R., 1110
— — do Brasil, London, 1424
— — Goldoni, Venice, 773
— — Thomas Jefferson, Brasília, 180
Casa-Fuerte de Ponce de León, Santo Domingo, 404
Case Center, Tel-Aviv, 750
— Western Reserve University, Cleveland, Ohio, 1840
— — — Libraries, Cleveland, 1633
Cassel Educational Trust, 1420
Cast and Metallurgy Association, Hanoi, 1962
Castello Sforzesco, Milan, 771
— Visconteo, Pavia, 772
— Visconti, Locarno, 1262
Castillo de Bellver, Majorca, 1201
Casting Research Laboratory, Tokyo, 873
Castle Museum, York, 1471
Castleton State College, Vt., 1914
Catawba College, Salisbury, N.C., 1825
Cátedra Francisco Suárez, Granada, 1210
— "Ramiro de Maeztu", Madrid, 1223
Catholic Library Association, 1601
— Medical College, Seoul, 896
— Record Society, London, 1422
— University, Nijmegen, 970
— — of America, 1688
— — — Chile, Santiago, 328
— — — Cuyo, 79
— — — La Plata, 80

Catholic University of Louvain, 162, 163
— — — Lublin, 1080
— — — Puerto Rico, Ponce, P.R., 1111
— — — — Law Library, Ponce, 1110
— — — — Library, Ponce, 1110
— — — Salta, 81
— — — Santa Fé, 81
— — — the Sacred Heart, Milan, 792
Caulfield Institute of Technology, 115
Cawthron Institute, Nelson, 979
Çay Araştırma Enstitüsü, Rize, 1299
Čebuano Studies Center, Cebu City, 1049
Cedar Crest College, Allentown, 1869
CEDIAS Musée Social, Paris, 466
Cell Biology Institute, Shanghai, 332
— Biophysics Unit (M.R.C.), London, 1444
— Mutation Unit (M.R.C.), Brighton, 1444, 1534
Cellular Immunology Unit (M.R.C.), Oxford, 1443
Cement och Betonginstitutet, Stockholm, 1238
— Research Institute of India, New Delhi, 672
Cenacolo Triestino, 757
"Cenov, D.A." Higher Institute of Economics and Finance, Svištov, 226
Centar za Fotografiju, Film i Televizju, Zagreb, 1978
Centenary College of Louisiana, Shreveport, 1737
Center for Advanced Studies, Tel-Aviv, 750
— — — Study in the Behavioural Sciences, Stanford, 1622
— — Agricultural and Rural Development, Ames, 1728
— — Air Environment Studies, University Park, 1877
— — Bio-Technology, Tel-Aviv, 750
— — Business History Studies, New Orleans, 1741
— — Chicano Studies, Santa Barbara, 1673
— — Creative Photography, Tucson, 1600
— — Energy and Environment Research, San Juan, P.R., 1109
— — Environmental Research, Eugene, 1866
— — Industrial Research, Haifa, 740
— — — and Service, Ames, 1728
— — Israel and Jewish Studies, New York, 1810
— — Latin American Studies, New Orleans, 1741
— — Nuclear Research, Nahal Soreq, Tel-Aviv, 750
— — Public Policy Studies, New Orleans, 1741
— — Reformation Research, St. Louis, Mo., 1618
— — Research and Demonstration (Social Work), New York, 1811
— — — in the Biology of Cancer, Tel-Aviv, 750
— — Short-Lived Phenomena, Cambridge, Mass., 1619
— — Social Research in Rehabilitation Medicine, New York, 1824
— — Strategic Studies, Tel-Aviv, 750
— — Studies in Criminology and Criminal Law, Philadelphia, 1880
— — Study of Environmental Policy, University Park, Pa., 1877
— — Technological Education, Tel-Aviv, 750
— — the Social Sciences, New York, 1810
— — — Study of Aging and Human Development, Durham, N.C., 1610
— — — — Financial Institutions, Philadelphia, 1880
— — — — Polish Jewry, Tel-Aviv, 750
— — Udviklingsforskning, Copenhagen, 393
— — University Studies, Hamburgo, 934
— — Urban and Regional Studies, Tel-Aviv, 750

— — — Research and Experiment, Philadelphia, 1880
— of Hispanic Studies, Syracuse, N.Y., 1822
— — Occupational Therapy, Hygiene and Health, Tel-Aviv, 750
— on Human Policy, Syracuse, N.Y., 1822
Centraal Bureau voor de Statistiek, Voorburg, 960
— — — Genealogie, The Hague, 957
— Museum, Utrecht, 969
— — der Gemeente, Utrecht, 969
Central Acoustics Laboratory, Cape Town, 1167
— Aerological Observatory, 1346
— Agricultural Experiment Station, Saitama, 813
— — Library, Pretoria, 1163
— — — Sofia, 220
— — — Tel-Aviv, 741
— — Research Institute, Peradeniya, 1224
— Agriculture Experimental Station, Suakoko, 904
— American Technical Institute, Santa Tecla, 423
— and West Asian Institute, Karachi, 1026
— Apothecary Research Institute, Moscow, 1346
— Archives for the History of the Jewish People, Jerusalem, 741
— Arid Zone Research Institute, Jodhpur, 666
— Artificial Limb Research Institute, Moscow, 1385
— Asian Institute of Microbiology and Virology, 1385
— Astronomical Observatory, Leningrad, 1318
— A. A. Bakhrushin State Theatrical Museum, Moscow, 1360
— Biological Station, Arzni, 1324
— Botanical Garden, Kiev, 1334
— Building Research Institute, Roorkee, 664
— Bureau for Educational Visits and Exchanges, 1418
— Catholic Library, Dublin, 731
— — — Melbourne, 96
— China Engineering College, Wuhan, 338
— — Mining and Metallurgy College, Wuhan, 338
— College, Pella, Iowa, 1723
— — of Commerce, Glasgow, 1552
— — Connecticut State College, 1677
— Council of Physical Recreation, 1428
— — — Scientific and Technical Unions, Sofia, 218
— Documentation and Library of the Ministry of Information, Jakarta, 711
— Drug Research Institute, Lucknow, 664
— Economic Mathematical Institute, Moscow, 1321
— Electrochemical Research Institute, Karaikudi, Madras, 664
— Electronics Engineering Research Institute, Pilani, 664
— Fisheries Research Institute, Chilanga, 1997
— Food Technological Research Institute, Mysore, 664
— Fuel Research Institute, Bihar, 664
— Geological Survey, Taipei, 341
— Glass and Ceramic Research Institute, Calcutta, 664
— Government Archives, Nairobi, 879
— Hindi Directorate, Delhi, 662
— Historical State Archives, Sofia, 220
— Inland Fisheries Research Institute, West Bengal, 666
— Institute for Cultural Relations between Israel, Ibero-America, Spain and Portugal, Jerusalem, 738
— — — Labour Protection, Warsaw, 1070
— — — Leprosy Research, Jakarta, 709
— — — Scientific Research in Health Education, Moscow, 1387

— — — — and Technical Information, Sofia, 220
— — of Dermatology and Venereal Diseases, Moscow, 1385
— — — English and Foreign Languages, Hyderabad, 705
— — — Haematology and Blood Transfusion, Moscow, 1385
— — — Indian Languages, Mysore, 706
— — — Information and Library for Medical Sciences, Hanoi, 1963
— — — Medicinal and Aromatic Plants, Lucknow, 664
— — — Ophthalmology, Hanoi, 1962
— — — Roentgenology and Radiology, Moscow, 1386
— — — Traumatology and Orthopaedics, Moscow, 1385
— — — Tuberculosis, Hanoi, 1962
— Jalma Institute for Leprosy, Agra, 669
— Laboratory for Design and Statistical Analysis Research, Giza, 414
— Leather Research Institute, Madras, 665
— Lenin Museum, 1354
— Leprosy Teaching and Research Institute, Chingleput, 669
— Library, Baroda, 673
— — Pyongyang, 883
— — Sofia, 220
— — and Documentation Centre of Teheran University, 722
— — — — University of Tabriz, 722
— — for Science and Technology, Hanoi, 1963
— — of Agricultural Science, Rehovot, 741
— — — the Academy of Medical Sciences, Moscow, 1349
— — — — — Sciences of the Armenian S.S.R., Erevan, 1349
— — — — — Sciences of the Azerbaijan S.S.R., Baku, 1349
— — — — — Sciences of the Estonian S.S.R., Tallinn, 1349
— — — — — Sciences of the Georgian S.S.R., Tbilisi, 1349
— — — — — Sciences of the Kazakh S.S.R., Alma-Ata, 1328, 1349
— — — — — Sciences of the Kirghiz S.S.R., Frunze, 1349
— — — — — Sciences of the Latvian S.S.R., Riga, 1349
— — — — — Sciences of the Lithuanian S.S.R., Vilnius, 1330, 1349
— — — — — Sciences of the Moldavian S.S.R., Kishinev, 1349
— — — — — Sciences of the Tajik S.S.R., Dushanbe, 1349
— — — — — Sciences of the Turkmen S.S.R., Ashkhabad, 1349
— — — — — Sciences of the Ukrainian S.S.R., Kiev, 1334, 1349
— — — — — Sciences of the Uzbek S.S.R., Tashkent, 1349
— — — Azerbaijan S. M. Kirov State University, Baku, 1350
— — — Far Eastern State University, Vladivostock, 1350
— — — Gorky N. I. Lobachevsky State University, Gorky, 1350
— — — Higher Technical Institutes, Sofia, 220
— — — Kazakh S. M. Kirov State University, Alma-Ata, 1350
— — — Perm A. M. Gorky State University, 1351
— — — Petrozavodsk University, 1351
— — — Samarkand Alisher Navei State University, 1351
— — — Tashkent V. I. Lenin State University, 1351
— — — Voronezh State University, 1351
— — — Trinidad and Tobago, 1293
— Luzon Agricultural Research Center, CLSU, Munoz, 1051

— — Polytechnic College, Cabanatuan City, 1060
— — State University, Nueva Ecija, 1051
— Mechanical Engineering Research Institute, Durgapur, 665
— Medical Library, Islamabad, 1023
— — — Lagos, 994
— — — Sofia, 220
— Metallurgical Research and Development Institute, Cairo, 416
— Meteorological Bureau, Beijing, 334
— — Office, Seoul, 886
— Methodist College, Fayette, 1786
— Michigan University, 1760
— Mindanao University, Bukidnon, 1051
— Mining Research Station, CSIR, Bihar, 665
— Missouri State University, 1786
— Museum, Nagpur, 674
— of Aviation and Cosmonautics, Moscow, 1354
— — — the Armed Forces of the U.S.S.R., Moscow, 1354
— — — — Revolution of the U.S.S.R., Moscow, 1354
— — — — Revolutionary Movement, Ulan Bator, 947
— Music College, Beijing, 336
— — Library, Leningrad, 1349
— National Library, Seoul, 886
— Nationalities Institute, Beijing, 336
— Naval Museum, Leningrad, 1354
— Paper Research Institute, Moscow, 1347
— Philippine University, Ilo-Ilo City, 1052
— Public Health Laboratory, London, 1445
— — — Research Institute, New Delhi, 669
— — Library, Dacca, 143
— Rabbinical Library of Israel, 741
— Records Office, Khartoum, 1229
— Reference and Research Library (C.S.I.R.), Accra, 612
— Research and Design Institute for Dwellings, Moscow, 1346
— — Design and Technology Institute of Mechanization and Electrification of Livestock Production in the Southern Zone of the U.S.S.R., Zaporozhye, 1338
— — Institute, Kasauli, 669
— — — for Evaluation of Working Capacity and Vocational Assistance to Disabled Persons, Moscow, 1386
— — — Geodesy, Aerial Photography and Cartography, 1346
— — — of Automobile Engineering, Moscow, 1347
— — — — Epidemiology, Moscow, 1346
— — — — Nonferrous Metallurgy, Moscow, 1347
— — — — Roentgenology and Radiology, Leningrad, 1386
— — Organization, Rangoon, 228
— Rice Breeding Station, Batalagoda, 1225
— — Research Institute, Cuttack, 666
— Road Research Institute, New Delhi, 665
— Salt and Marine Chemicals Research Institute, Bhavnagar, 665
— School of Art and Design, London, 1550
— — — Speech and Drama, London, 1552
— Scientific Agricultural Library of the All-Union Lenin Academy of Agricultural Sciences, Moscow, 1349
— — Instruments Organisation, Chandigarh, 665
— — Library of the Kharkov A. M. Gorky State University, 1350
— — Research and Design Institute of Wood Chemical Industry, Gorky, 1347
— — — Institute of Health Resorts and Physical Therapy, Moscow, 1387
— — — — Prosthetics and Artificial Limbs, Moscow, 1385

— — Technical Library, Sofia, 220
— Sechenov Research Institutes, Yalta, 1386
— Secretariat Library, Karachi, 1023
— — — New Delhi, 673
— Seismological Observatory, Shillong, 670
— Siberian Botanical Garden, Novosibirsk, 1322
— Social Sciences Library, Hanoi, 1963
— State Archives of Ancient Arts, Moscow, 1347
— — — Documentary Films and Photographs of the U.S.S.R., Moscow, 1347
— — — — the October Revolution and Higher State Bodies, Moscow, 1347
— — — People's Republic of Bulgaria, Sofia, 220
— — — — R.S.F.S.R., Moscow, 1347
— — — — Soviet Army, Moscow, 1347
— — — — U.S.S.R. National Economy, Moscow, 1347
— — — — Navy, Leningrad, 1347
— — Historical Archives of U.S.S.R., Leningrad, 1347
— — Literature and Art Archives of the U.S.S.R., Moscow, 1347
— — Military Historical Archives of the U.S.S.R., Moscow, 1347
— — Museum of the Kazakh S.S.R., Alma-Ata, 1355
— — — — Turkmen S.S.R., Ashkhabad, 1355
— — University, Edmond, 1857
— — — Wilberforce, Ohio, 1842
— — Statistical Office, Karachi, 1021
— — — Salisbury, Zimbabwe, 2001
— Tobacco Research Institute, Rajahmundry, 666
— University of Venezuela, Caracas, 1957
— Urdu Development Board, Lahore, 1020
— Veterinary Institute, Sofia, 219
— — Laboratory, Lilongwe, 912
— — — (Ministry of Agriculture, Fisheries and Food), Weybridge, 1440
— — Research Station, Mazabuka, 1997
— Washington University, 1921
— Water and Power Research Station, Pune, 672
— Zionist Archives, Jerusalem, 741
Centralbiblioteket for Sydvestjylland, 394
Centrale Bibliotheek, Faculteit Landbouwwetenschappen, Ghent, 156
— — Fraters, Tilburg, 965
— — van het Koninklijk Instituut voor de Tropen, Amsterdam, 964
— — — — Ministerie van Nationale Opvoeding en Nederlandse Cultuur, Brussels, 156
Centralna Biblioteka Rolnicza, 1074
— — Statystyczna, Warsaw, 1074
— — ekonomska knjižnica, Ljubljana, 1975
— — medicinska knjižnica, Ljubljana, 1975
— — narodna biblioteka SR Crne Gore, Cetinje, 1976
— — tehniška knjižnica Univerze Edvarda Kardelja v Ljubljana, 1975
Centralne Archiwum Wojskowe, Warsaw, 1072
— Muzeum Morskie, Gdansk, 1076
— — Włókiennictwa, Łódź, 1076
Centre Africain de Formation et de Recherches Administratives pour le Développement—CAFRAD, Tangier, 23
— Armoricain d'etude structurale des socles, Rennes, 455
— Beaubourg, Paris, 466
— Belge de Traduction, Brussels, 154
— Canadien de Recherches en Anthropologie, Ottawa, 245
— — des Recherches Généalogiques, Haute-Ville, 248
— College of Kentucky, 1735

— Culturel Allemand, Yaoundé, 231
— — Américain, Kinshasa, 1995
— — — N'Djamena, 321
— — — Niamey, 990
— — — Ouagadougou, 1937
— — Français, Baghdad, 725
— — — Belgrade, 1969
— — — Brazzaville, 358
— — — Bujumbura, 230
— — — Jakarta, 708
— — — Khartoum, 1229
— — — Milan, 758
— — — Nicosia, 367
— — — Palermo, 758
— — — Rome, 758
— — — Tripoli, 906
— — — Yaoundé, 231
— — Franco-Italien Galliera, Genoa, 758
— — Hispanique, Beirut, 899
— d'Actualisation des Connaissances et de l'Etude des Matériaux Industriels, Paris, 493
— d'Archives et de Documentation Politiques et Sociales, Paris, 446
— d'Art, Port-au-Prince, 629
— — Dramatique (Etudes Théâtrales), Hammamet, 1296
— d'Ecologie de Camargue, Le Sambuc, 456
— d'Edition et de Production de Manuels Scolaires de l'UNESCO, Yaoundé, 231
— d'Enseignement du Management, Paris, 497
— et de Recherche de Statistique Appliquée, Paris, 496
— — Supérieur des Affaires, Jouy-en-Josas, 496
— d'Epidémiologie, Lyon, 456
— d'Etude de l'Expression, Paris, 449
— — Prospective et d'Informations Internationales, Paris, 457
— d'Etudes Administratives et Techniques Supérieures, Brazzaville, 358
— — Bioclimatiques, Strasbourg, 455
— — Biologiques des Animaux Sauvages, Villiers en Bois, 455, 472
— d'Océanographie et de Biologie Marine, 455
— de Chimie Métallurgique, Vitry, 454
— — — Documentation et d'Information Economiques et Sociales, Casablanca, 949
— — — Géographie Tropicale, Talence, 456
— — l'Energie Nucléaire (CEN), Brussels, 154
— — la Socio-Economie, Paris, 446
— — Littérature Africaine (C.E.L.A.), Lubumbashi, 1996
— — Madrid, 495
— des Sciences et Techniques de l'Information, Dakar-Fann, 1146
— — du Milieu Naturel, Lyon, 480
— — Système Nerveux, Gif-sur-Yvette, 456
— — Economiques et Sociales d'Afrique Occidentale, Bobo-Dioulasso, 1937
— — et d'Expérimentation du Machinisme Agricole et Tropical (C.E.E.M.A.T.), Antony, 457
— — de Réalisations cartographiques géographiques, Paris, 456
— — — Recherche sur le Développement Régional (CERDA), Annaba, 58
— — — — le Développement Régional (CERDO), Oran, 58
— — — — Recherches de Chimie Organique Appliquée, 454
— — — — — Documentaires pour l'Afrique Centrale, Lubumbashi, 1996
— — — — — Economiques et Sociales (CERES), Tunis, 1296
— — — — — en Biologie Humaine et Animale (CERBHA), Algiers, 58

Centre d'Etudes et de Recherches Ibéro-Americaines, Paris, 494
— — Mathématiques et Physiques (Université de Lyon), Beirut, 902
— — — sur les Energies renouvelables "Henri Masson", Dakar-Fann, 1146
— — Géologiques et Minières, Paris, 458
— — Industrielles, Geneva, 1268
— — Juridiques de l'Ain, Lyon, 480
— — Marines Avancées, Marseille, 458
— — Nordiques, Quebec, 273
— — Nucléaires de Cadarache, 459
— — — Fontenay-aux-Roses, 459
— — — Saclay, Gif-sur-Yvette, 460
— — Orthodoxes, Lyon, 480
— — Phytosociologiques et Ecologiques Louis-Emberger, Montpellier, 455
— — Politiques en Afrique Centrale (C.E.P.A.C.), Lubumbashi, 1996
— — Romaines et Gallo-Romaines, Lyon, 480
— — Sociologiques, Paris, 456
— — Supérieures de la Renaissance, Tours, 458
— — — Mécanique, St. Cloud, 493
— — — du Marketing (CESMA), Lyon, 496
— — sur l'Humanisme et la Communication, Lyon, 480
— — — la Trypanosomiase Animale, Bouar, 320
— — universitaires d'Abitibi-Témiscamingue, Rouyn, 294
— d'Exécution de Programmes Sociaux et Economiques (C.E.P.S.E.), Lubumbashi, 1995
— d'Expérimentations d'Hydraulique Agricole, Rabat, 949
— d'Hydrobiologie et d'Hydrologie, Besançon, 475
— d'Immunologie, Marseille, 456
— d'Informations Scientifiques et Techniques de Transferts Technologiques (CISTT), Algiers, 57
— de Biochemie et de Biologie Moléculaire (CNRS), Marseille, 455
— — Biophysique Moléculaire, Orleans, 454
— — Calcul, Strasbourg, 456
— — de l'INAG, Meudon, 456
— — — Physique Nucléaire de l'IN2P3, Paris, 456
— — du Pharo, Marseille, 456
— — et d'Informatique, Mons, 163
— — Coordination des Etudes et des Recherches sur les Infrastructures, les Equipements du Ministère de l'Enseignement et de la Recherche Scientifique, Algiers, 58
— — — Recherches et de la Documentation en Sciences Sociales en Afrique Sud-Saharienne (C.E.R.D.A.S.), Kinshasa, 1996
— — Criminologie, Kinshasa, 1996
— — Cytologie Expérimentale, Ivry, 456
— — Documentation, Niamey, 990
— — Benjamin Franklin, Paris, 462
— — Economique de la Chambre de Commerce et d'Industrie de Paris, 462
— — — sur le Proche-Orient, Beirut, 899
— — et de Bibliographie Philosophiques, Besançon, 475
— — — — Recherche Européenne, Lyon, 480
— — — — Recherches Historiques "Ahmed Baba" (CEDRAB), Timbuktu, 920
— — — Nationale, Tunis, 1295
— — — Pédagogique, N'Djamena, 321
— — — — Nouakchott, 922

— — — Sciences Humaines, Paris, 456
— — — scientifique et technique, Paris, 456
— — Formation de Formateurs d'Adultes, Paris, 493
— — — des Psychologues Scolaires, Besançon, 471
— — — et de Recherches Psycho-Pédagogiques, Besançon, 475
— — — Pédagogique pour l'Enseignement Spécialisé, Paris, 494
— — — permanente, Rueil Malmaison, 497
— — — Professionnelle Agricole de Tove, Kpalime, 1292
— — Génétique des Virus, Gif-sur-Yvette, 455
— — — Moléculaire, Gif-sur-Yvette, 455
— — Géomorphologie, Caen, 456
— — Hautes Etudes sur l'Afrique et l'Asie Modernes, Paris, 492
— — la Recherche Archéologique et Historique, Tunis, 1295
— — Linguistique Appliquée, Besançon, 475
— — — Dakar, 1146
— — — et Comparée et de Néo-Dialectologie, Lyon, 480
— — — Théorique et Appliquée, Lubumbashi, 1996
— — Mécanique Ondulatoire Appliquée, Paris, 454
— — Morphologie Expérimentale, Talence, 455
— — Neurochimie, Strasbourg, 455
— — Pédologie biologique, Vandoeuvre-les-Nancy, 455
— — Perfectionnement dans l'Administration des Affaires, 496
— — Physique Théorique, Marseille, 453
— — Préparation au Diplôme d'Etat d'Audioprothésiste, Paris, 493
— — Recherche en Aménagement et en Développement, Quebec, 273
— — — nutrition, Quebec, 273
— — — sociologie religieuse, Quebec, 273
— — — et d'Etude des Populations, Bangui, 320
— — — Science, Technologie et Société, Paris, 493
— — Recherches Agricoles de Richard-Toll, 1145
— — — Agronomiques de Gembloux, 153
— — — — Rennes, 492
— — — Anthropologiques, Préhistoriques et Ethnographiques (CRAPE), Algiers, 57
— — — Archéologiques, Valbonne, 456
— — — Atmosphériques Henri Dessens, Lannemezan, 459
— — — Biologiques sur la Lèpre, Dakar-Fann, 1146
— — — d'Etudes et de Documentation sur les Institutions et la Législation Africaines, Dakar, 1146
— — — d'Histoire Religieuse, Paris, 495
— — — de Biochimie et de Génétique Cellulaires, Toulouse, 455
— — — — — macromoléculaire, Montpellier, 455
— — — — Chimie Structurale "Paul Pascal", Talence, 454
— — — — Microcalorimétrie et de Thermochimie, Marseille, 454
— — — — Economiques Appliquées, Dakar-Fann, 1146
— — — — Sociologiques et de Gestion, Lille, 495
— — — en Architecture et Urbanisme, Algiers (CRAU), 57
— — — — Economie Appliquées (CREA), Algiers, 57
— — — — Physique de l'Environnement terrestre et planétaire, Orleans, 455

— — et d'Application en Ergonomie, Lyon, 480
— — — d'Etudes Océanographiques, Boulogne, 459
— — — de Documentation de Sénégal (CRDS), Saint-Louis, 1145
— — — Géophysiques, Garchy-Suilly, 455
— — — Historiques, Paris, 458
— — — Nucléaires de Strasbourg Cronenbourg (I.N2P3.), 453
— — — Océanographiques, Abidjan, 798
— — — — de Dakar-Thiaroye, 1145
— — — — et des Pêches, Algiers, 57
— — — Pétrographiques et Géochimiques, Vandoeuvre-les-Nancy, 455
— — — pour l'Utilisation de l'Eau Salée en Irrigation, Ariana, 1295
— — — psychopathologiques, Dakar-Fann, 1146
— — — Rizicoles, Kankan, 627, 920
— — — — de Djibelor, Ziguinchor, 1145
— — — Robert Musil, Saarbrucken, 531
— — — Socio-Economiques et d'Initiation aux Responsabilités dans les Entreprises Publiques ou Privées, Besançon, 475
— — — Spécialisées en Histoire Ancienne, Besançon, 475
— — — — Littérature Française, Besançon, 475
— — — l'eau, Quebec, 273
— — — l'U.R.S.S. et les Pays de l'Est, Strasbourg, 457
— — — la Chimie de la Combustion et des Hautes Températures, Orleans, 454
— — — — Nutrition, Meudon, 455
— — — — Physicochimie des Surfaces Solides, Mulhouse, 464
— — — — Physique des Hautes Températures, Orleans, 464
— — — — Synthèse et la Chimie des Minéraux, Orleans, 455
— — — les Macromolécules, Strasbourg, 454
— — — — Végétales, Grenoble, 454
— — — — Mécanismes de la Croissance Cristalline, Marseille, 454
— — — — Monuments Historiques, Paris, 458
— — — — Ressources Biologiques Terrestres (CRBT), Algiers, 57
— — — — Solides à Organisation Cristalline Imparfaite, Orleans, 454
— — — — très basses Températures, Grenoble, 454
— — — Zootechniques, Bouaké, 798
— — — — Dahra-Djoloff, 1145
— — — — de Kolda, 1145
— — Sédimentologie et de Géochimie de la Surface, Strasbourg, 455
— — Sélection et d'Elevage des Animaux de Laboratoire, 455
— — Sociologie des Organisations, Paris, 456
— — Spectrométrie Nucléaire et de Spectrométrie de Masse (1. N2. P3), Orsay, 453
— — Télé-Enseignement Universitaire, Besançon, 475
— des Arts et Traditions Populaires, Tunis, 1295
— — Cultures Vivrières et Fruitières, Njombé, 231
— — Etudes Hispano-Andalouses, Tunis, 1295
— — Faibles Radioactivités, Gif-sur-Yvette, 455
— — Hautes Etudes Afro-Ibéro-Américaines, Dakar-Fann, 1146
— — Recherches Forestières, Douala, 231
— — Sciences et de la Technologie nucléaires (CSTN), Algiers, 57
— — — Humaines, Abidjan, 798

— Emile Bernheim pour l'Etude des Affaires, Brussels, 159
— Européen d'Education Permanente, Fontainebleau, 496
— — d'Études de Population, The Hague, 23
— — de Coordination de Recherche et de Documentation en Sciences Sociales, Vienna, 13
— — pour l'enseignement supérieur (CEPES), Bucharest, 31
— for Advanced International Studies, Coral Gables, 1698
— — — Study in Theoretical Psychology, Edmonton, Alb., 257
— — Advancement of Postgraduate Science Studies, Alexandria, 418
— — African Studies, Rondebosch, 1167
— — Agricultural Research in Suriname, Paramaribo, 1231
— — American Studies, Nagoya, 866
— — Applied Legal Studies, Johannesburg, 1182
— — — Social and Survey Research, Bedford Park, S.A., 101
— — — — Sciences, Durban, 1179
— — — — Salisbury, 2003
— — Arab Gulf Studies, Exeter, 1491
— — Archaeological Operations, Kyoto, 836
— — Area Study of North America, Latin America and Africa, Islamabad, 1028
— — Byzantine Research, Thessaloniki, 621
— — Cold Ocean Resources Engineering, St. Johns, 285
— — Computing Services (CSIR), Pretoria, 1158
— — Continuing Education, Johannesburg, 1182
— — — — Kampala, 1312
— — — — Lusaka, 1998
— — Cultural Studies, Lagos, 1000
— — Data Processing, Namur, 165
— — Development Studies, Bedford Park, S.A., 101
— — — — Salford, 1527
— — Documentation and Research, Abu Dhabi, 1391
— — Economic and Administrative Research, Baghdad, 727
— — Educational and Psychological Research, Baghdad, 725, 727
— — — Research and Innovation, Paris, 27
— — — Technology, Cardiff, 1536
— — Energy Studies, Halifax, N.S., 290
— — European Agricultural Studies, London, 1511
— — Extension Studies, Loughborough, 1514
— — Foreign Languages Teaching, Mexico City, 933
— — Forestry Research, Cracow, 1069
— — Industrial Innovation, Glasgow, 1531
— — — Studies, Loughborough, 1514
— — International Peace Studies, Seoul, 893
— — — Politics, Potchefstroom, 1173
— — — Studies, London, 1510
— — — — Sydney, N.S., 265
— — Iranian Anthropology, Ministry of Culture and Arts, Teheran, 721
— — Islamic Legal Studies, Zaria, 995
— — Japanese Studies, Nagoya, 866
— — Journalism Studies, Cardiff, 1536
— — Labour Economics, London, 1510
— — Leisure Studies, Salford, 1527
— — Lexicography, Ramat-Gan, 745
— — Medical Research, Baghdad, 727
— — Medieval Studies, York, 1539
— — Micro-engineering and Metrology, Coventry, 1539
— — Neuroscience, Bedford Park, S.A., 101
— — Nigerian Cultural Studies, Zaria, 995
— — Nuclear Research, Dalat, 1962

— — — Namur, 165
— — — Studies, Mexico City, 933
— — Operations Research and Statistics, Pretoria, 1178
— — Overseas Educational Development, Manchester, 1518
— — — Pest Research, London, 1440
— — Palestinian Studies Research, Baghdad, 727
— — Petroleum and Mineral Law Studies, Dundee, 1486
— — Postgraduate Hebrew Studies, Oxford, 1525
— — Pre-Historic Research in Israel, Jerusalem, 739
— — Public Libraries, Jerusalem, 737
— — Research and Training in Physical Culture and Sports, Sofia, 220
— — — in Biology, Sofia, 216
— — — — Chemistry, Sofia, 215
— — — — Earth Sciences, Sofia, 216
— — — — Experimental Space Science, Downsview, Ont., 318
— — — — History, Sofia, 216
— — — — Industry, Business and Administration, Coventry, 1539
— — — — Labrador, St. Johns, 285
— — — — Latin America and the Carribean, Downsview, 318
— — — — Linguistics and Literature, Sofia, 216
— — — — Mathematics and Mechanics, Sofia, 215
— — — — Philosophy and Sociology, Sofia, 216
— — — — Physics, Sofia, 215
— — — — State and Legal Sciences, Sofia, 216
— — — — The New Literatures in English, Bedford Park, S.A., 101
— — — — on Environmental Quality, Downsview, Ont., 318
— — Resource and Environmental Studies, Canberra, 100
— — Science and Research Policy, Teheran, 721
— — Scientific and Educational Planning, Teheran, 721
— — — Information, Central Library and Scientific Archives of the Bulgarian Academy of Sciences, Sofia, 220
— — — Technical and Economic Information (at the National Agro-Industrial Union), Sofia, 220
— — Socio-Legal Studies, Oxford, 1525
— — Solid State Physics, Lahore, 1028
— — South Asian Studies, Lahore, 1021
— — Southeast Asian Studies, Kyoto, 836
— — Southern African Studies, York, 1539
— — Tax Law, Pretoria, 1178
— — the Advancement of Mathematical Education in Technology, Loughborough, 1514
— — Reconstruction of Human Society, Seoul, 893
— — Study of Australian-Asian Relations, Nathan, Qd., 101
— — — — Industrial Innovation, Bourne End, 1448
— — — — International Relations, Stockholm, 1235
— — — — Mental Retardation, Edmonton, Alb., 257
— — — — Public Policy (Dept. of Politics), Glasgow, 1531
— — — — Social History, Coventry, 1538
— — Theoretical Studies, Coral Gables, 1698
— — Transport Economic Research, Pretoria, 1178
— — — Engineering Practice, Loughborough, 1514
— — — Studies, Salford, 1527
— — Tribological Studies, Salford, 1527

— Underwater Science and Technology, Salford, 1527
— Urban and Regional Planning (Graduate Studies), Baghdad, 727
— — — — Research, Manchester, 1518
— — Youth Studies, Manchester, 1518
— Français, Stockholm, 1236
— — de Documentation, Bamako, 920
— — — — Odonto-Stomatologique, Paris, 497
— — — Droit Comparé, Paris, 492
— Général de Documentation de l'Université Catholique de Louvain, 156
— Géologique et Géophysique, Montpellier, 455
— INRA Antilles Guyane, Petit-Bourg, 499
— Interdisciplinaire d'Etudes et de Documentation Politiques (C.I.E.D.O.P.), Kinshasa, 1996
— — pour le Développement de l'Education (C.R.I.D.E.), Kisangani, 1996
— — — — et l'éducation permanente (C.I.D.E.P.), Kinshasa, 1996
— international d'études des relations entre groupes ethniques, Paris, 13
— — Pédagogiques de Sèvres, 458
— — Romanes, Paris, 448
— — de Documentation Concernant les Expressions Plastiques (CIDEP), Paris, 21
— — la Tapisserie Ancienne et Moderne, Lausanne, 19
— — perfectionnement professionel et technique, Turin, 24
— — recherche sur le Cancer, Lyon, 39
— — recherches sur le bilinguisme, Quebec, 245
— — Synthèse, Paris, 451
— — du Film pour l'Enfance et la Jeunesse, Paris, 19
— Inter-Régional d'Informatique et d'Automatique "El Khawarezmi", Tunis, 1296
— — de Calcul Electronique, Orsay, 456
— Interuniversitaire de Droit Comparé, Brussels, 154
— Limousin Associé au Conservatoire des Arts et Métiers, Limoges, 478
— — d'Administration des Entreprises, Limoges, 478
— Lyonnais d'Études de Sécurité Internationale et de Défense, Lyon, 480
— National d'Art et de Culture Georges-Pompidou, Paris, 466
— — d'Astronomie, Astrophysique et de Géophysique, Algiers, 58
— — d'Etudes et de Recherche en Energie Renouvelable, Algiers, 58
— — — — pour l'Aménagement du Territoire (CNERAT), Algiers, 58
— — — Historiques, Algiers, 57
— — — Spatiales, Paris, 460
— — d'Hydrométéorologie, Bujumbura, 230
— — de Coordination des Etudes et Recherches sur la Nutrition et l'Alimentation, Paris, 455
— — — Documentation, Rabat, 950
— — — et de Recherche en Pédagogie, Algiers, 58
— — — Scientifique et Technique, Brussels, 154
— — la Recherche Scientifique (CNRS), Paris, 453
— — Recherche Appliquée au Développement Rural, Antananarivo (CENRADERU), 910
— — Recherches Agronomiques, Versailles, 456
— — — — de Bambey, 1145
— — — — de Logique, Brussels, 155
— — — — et d'Application des Géosciences, Algiers, 57

# INDEX OF INSTITUTIONS

Centre National de Recherches et Expérimentations Forestières (CNREF), Algiers, 57
— — — — Forestières, Dakar-Hann, 1145
— — — — Seichamps, 457
— — — Fruitières, Bamako, 920
— — — "Primitifs Flamands", Brussels, 154
— — — sur les Zones Arides, Beni-Abbes (CNRZA), 57
— — — Zootechniques, Bamako, 920
— — — — Jouy-en-Josas, 457
— — — Traduction et de Terminologie Arabe, Algiers, 58
— — des Académies et Associations Littéraires et Savantes des Provinces Françaises, Paris, 449
— — — Hautes Etudes Juives, Brussels, 155
— — — Lettres, Paris, 449
— — — pour l'Exploitation des Océans, Paris, 459
— Océanologique de Bretagne, Brest, 459
— — pour le Pacifique, Taravao, Tahiti, 459
— of African Studies, Cambridge, 1485
— — Atmospherical Sciences, Mexico City, 933
— — Documentation and Studies on Ancient Egypt, Cairo, 416
— — International and European economic law, Thessaloniki, 617
— — Studies, Cambridge, 1485
— — Latin American Studies, Cambridge, 1485
— — Marine Sciences and Limnology, Mexico City, 933
— — Materials Research, Mexico City, 933
— — Nuclear Studies, Mexico City, 933
— — Planning and Economic Research, Athens, 617
— — Rural Economy, Edinburgh, 1490
— — Scientific and Humanities Research, Mexico City, 933
— — South Asian Studies, Cambridge, 1485
— Parisien de Management, 496
— Pédagogique de Documentation de l'Ecole nationale des Ponts et Chaussées, Paris, 462
— — Supérieur, Bamako, 920
— Polynésien des Sciences Humaines Te Anavaharau, Tahiti, 501
— pour l'Etude des Problèmes du Monde Musulman Contemporain, Brussels, 153
— — — le Développement de l'Horticulture, Dakar, 1145
— Régional d'Elevage et de Production d'Animaux de Laboratoire, Le Rousset, 445
— — de Recherche et de Documentation pour la Tradition Orale, Niamey, 990
— — — — — Documentation pour le Développement Culturel, Dakar, 1145
— Scientifique de Monaco, 946
— Social et Educatif, Bujumbura, 230
— Suisse de Documentation en Matière d'Enseignement et d'Education, Geneva, 1254
— Technique du Génie Rural, Des Eaux et des Forêts, Antony, 457
— — et du Matériel de la Météorologie Nationale, Paris, 459
— — Forestier Tropical, Abidjan, 798
— — — — Antananarivo, 910
— — — — Libreville, 502
— — — — Nogent-sur-Marne, 457
— — — — Ouagadougou, 1937
— — — — Pointe Noire, 358
— — — — Richard-Toll, 1145
— Universitaire Antilles-Guyane, Cayenne, 499
— — — — Fort de France, 500
— — — — Pointe-à-Pitre, 499
— — d'Avignon, 471
— — d'Education et de Formation des Adultes, Saint-Martin-d'Hères, 491
— — d'Environnement et d'Urbanisme, Besançon, 475
— — d'Etudes Oecuméniques, Céligny, 1268
— — — Régionales, Besançon, 475
— — d'Orientation (C.U.O.), Kinshasa, 1996
— — de Batna, 59
— — — la Réunion, Saint-Denis, 500
— — — Luxembourg, 908
— — — Recherche sur la Pharmacopée et la Médecine Traditionnelle, Butare, 1141
— — — Recherches, d'études et de réalisations, Constantine, 57, 59
— — — Tiaret, 59
— — — Tizi-Ouzou, 59
— — — Tlemcen, 59
— — — des Sciences de la Santé, Yaoundé, 232
— — Méditerranéen, Nice, 482
— Voltaïque de la Recherche Scientifique, Ouagadougou, 1937
Centro Agronómico Tropical de Investigación y Enseñanza (CATIE), Turrialba, 359
— Argentino de Ingenieros, 65
— Audiovisual, Zulia, 1960
— Brasileiro de Cultura, Bogotá, 347
— — — Pesquisas Educacionais, Rio de Janeiro, 183
— — — — Fisicas, 185
— Camuno di Studi Preistorici, Valcamonica, 763
— Científico y Técnico Francés en México, Mexico City, 927
— Colombo-Americano, Bogotá, 347
— Cultural Americano, Lisbon, 1098
— — Costarricense-Norteamericano, San Jose, 359
— — Español, Rabat, 949
— — Hispánico, Alexandria, 414
— — — Damascus, 1277
— — Panameño-Norte-Americano, Panama City, 1030
— — Paraguayo-Americano, Asunción, 1034
— — Culturale Tedesco, Palermo, 759
— de Altos Estudios en Ciencias Exactas, Buenos Aires, 81
— — Análise Conjuntura Econômica, Rio de Janeiro, 183
— — Artes UNI-RIO, Rio de Janeiro, 212
— — Cálculo, San Sebastian, 1213
— — Ciências, Letras e Artes, Campinas, 184
— — Cirugía Experimental, Zulia, 1960
— — Desenvolvimento e Planejamento Regional, Minas Gerais, 198
— — Documentação Científica e Técnica, Lisbon, 1099
— — — e Informação da Câmara dos Deputados, Brasília, 186
— — Documentación Bibliotecológica, Bahia Blanca, 66
— — — e Información Pedagógica, Zulia, 1960
— — — Internacional, Buenos Aires, 69
— — Energia Nuclear na Agricultura (CENA), Piracicaba, 182
— — Enseñanza Técnica y Superior, Baja California, 944
— — Enseñanzas Integradas (Universidad Laboral) de Alcalá de Henares, Madrid, 1221
— — — — de Eibar, 1221
— — — — de la Coruña, 1221
— — — — de Sevilla, 1222
— — — — de Zaragoza, 1221
— — — — "Francisco Franco", Tarragona, 1222
— — — — — "José Antonio Girón", Asturias, 1222
— — — — — Onésimo Redondo de Córdoba, 1222
— — Ensino Unificado de Brasília, 210
— — Estadísticas Nacionales y Comercio Internacional del Uruguay (CENCI Uruguay), 1938
— — Estudios Antropológicos de la Universidad Católica, Asunción, 1034
— — — Constitucionales, Madrid, 1189
— — — de Ecología Urbana, Pamplona, 1213
— — — Historia y Organización de la Ciencia, Havana, 362
— — — — la Empresa, Zulia, 1960
— — — del Desarrollo, Caracas, 1953
— — — Económicos Sociales, Buenos Aires, 66
— — — Educativos, Mexico City, 928
— — — Filosóficos, Havana, 362
— — — — Zulia, 1960
— — — Histórico-Militares del Perú, Lima, 1036
— — — Literarios, Zulia, 1960
— — — Matemáticos, Zulia, 1960
— — — Médicos Ricardo Moreno Cañas, San José, 359
— — — para Graduados, Facultad de Economía, Zulia, 1960
— — — sobre Desarrollo Económico, Bogotá, 347
— — — — la Responsabilidad de la Iniciativa Privada, Pamplona, 1213
— — — Sociales y de Población, San José, 360
— — — Urbanos y Regionales, Buenos Aires, 66
— — — Venezolanos Indígenas, Caracas, 1954
— — Estudos de Arte e Museologia, Lisbon, 1097
— — — Historicos Ultramarinos, Lisbon, 1098
— — Higiene y Estación de Adiestramiento en Enfermedades Tropicales, Boca del Río, 929
— — Historia del Estado Carabobo, Valencia, 1953
— — — Tachira, 1951
— — — Larense, Barquisimento, 1951
— — Información Científica y Humanística, Mexico City, 926
— — — de Drogas, Santo Domingo, 405
— — — Educativa, Mendoza, 70
— — — Geo-Biológica NOA, San Miguel de Tucumán, 67
— — — y Documentación Agropecuaria (CIDA-INRA), Havana, 363
— — — — — del Instituto para la Formación y Approvechamiento de Recursos Humanos, Panama, 1030
— — Investigação Científica Algodeira, Angola, 61
— — Investigações Florestais, Lisbon, 1100
— — Investigación de Biología Marina, Buenos Aires, 68
— — — Recursos Naturales, Lima, 1043
— — — y de Estudios Avanzados del Instituto Politécnico Nacional, Mexico City, 929
— — — Desarrollo "Ing. Juan C. Van Wyk", Santa Fé, 68
— — — — Restauración de Bienes Monumentales del Instituto Nacional de Cultura, Lima, 1036
— — Investigaciones, Nueva Esparta, 1959
— — — Santo Domingo, 405
— — — Agrícolas "Alberto Boerger", La Estanzuela, 1939
— — — Agropecuarias, Panama City, 1031

2030

— — — Antropológicas, Panama City, 1031
— — — Bella Vista, Corrientes, 67
— — — Biológicas, Zulia, 1960
— — — Criminológicas, Zulia, 1960
— — — de la Universidad Católica, Asuncion, 1034
— — — — Recursos Naturales, Buenos Aires, 66
— — — Económicas, Buenos Aires, 66
— — — — Zulia, 1960
— — — Geotécnicas, San Salvador, 422
— — — Históricas, Guayaquil, 408
— — — Humanísticas, Zulia, 1960
— — — Jurídicas, Panama City, 1031
— — — para la Industria Minero Metalúrgica, Havana, 363
— — — Pesqueras, Havana, 363
— — — Técnicas de Guipúzcoa, San Sebastián, 1213
— — — Tecnológicas, Anzoátegui, 1959
— — — Urbanas y Regionales, Zulia, 1960
— — — y Capacitación Forestal del INDAF, Havana, 363
— — — — Ediciones Musicales, San Juan, P.R., 1109
— — Orientación, Zulia, 1960
— — Pesquisa Agropecuária do Trópico Úmido (EMBRAPA), Pará, 180
— — Pesquisas de Geografia do Brasil, Rio de Janeiro, 183
— — — e Desenvolvimento (CEPED), Salvador, 185
— — — — Leopoldo A. Miguez de Mello (PETROBRAS), Rio de Janeiro, 185
— — — Folclóricas, Rio de Janeiro, 212
— — Preclasificación Oceánica de México, Mexico City, 929
— — Relaciones Internacionales, Mexico City, 928
— — Tecnologia Agrícola e Alimentar da EMBRAPA, Rio de Janeiro, 185
— del PEN Internacional, Lima, 1037
— Di, Florence, 756
— di Giuscibernetica, Turin, 790
— — Ricerche Sociologiche (CIRIS), Vatican City, 1944
— — Studi e Ricerche di Medicina Aeronautica e Spaziale dell' Aeronautica Militare, Rome, 759
— — — Italiani in Turchia, Istanbul, 1298
— — Didattico Nazionale di Studi e Documentazione, Florence, 757
— Ecuatoriano-Norteamericano, Guayaquil, 408
— Escolar University, Manila, 1052
— Espacial San Miguel, 68
— — Vicente Lopez, 68
— Estación Biológica "Kasmera", Zulia, 1960
— Europeo dell'Educazione, Frascati, 763
— Experimental de Ingenieria, Panama City, 1031
— — — Producción Animal, Zulia, 1960
— Filosófico-Literario, Manizales, 348
— Fusione e Applicationi Laser, Rome, 764
— Histórico Sucrense, 1951
— Iberoamericano de Cooperación, Madrid, 1190
— Informazioni Studi Esperienze (C.I.S.E.), Milan, 764
— Internacional de escritores, La Paz, 174
— — — Estudios Pedagógicos de Buenos Aires, 67
— — — — Superiores de Comunicación para América Latina, Quito, 412
— — — la Asociación PEN, Buenos Aires, 64
— — — Mejoramiento de Maiz y Trigo, Mexico City, 928
— Internazionale delle Arti e del Costume, Milan, 756
— — di Studi di Architettura "Andrea Palladio", Vicenza, 756
— Italiano Studi Containers, Genoa, 755

— Latinoamericano de Demografía, San José, 360
— — — Estudios para la Conservación y Restauración de Bienes Culturales, Mexico City, 929
— — — Pesquisas em Ciências Sociais, Rio de Janeiro, 185
— Meteorológico de Baleares, 1198
— Mexicano de Escritores, Mexico, 927
— Nacional de Cálculo, Mexico City, 928
— — — Ciencias y Tecnologías Marinas, Veracruz, 929
— — — Conservación de Obras Artísticas, Mexico City, 926
— — — Documentacão, Maputo, 952
— — — e Investigação Histórica, Luanda, 61
— — — Documentación Científica y Tecnologia, La Paz, 173
— — — — Técnica y Económica, Montevideo, 1940
— — — e Información Educativa, Buenos Aires, 67
— — — — — Educativa, La Paz, 173
— — — — Pedagógica y Museo Pedagógico Nacional, Mexico City, 926
— — — Información de Ciencias Médicas, Havana, 363
— — — — y Documentación, Montevideo, 1938
— — — — — Santiago, 326
— — — Investigaciones Agropecuarias, Maracay, 1953
— — — — Científicas, Havana, 363
— — — Pesquisa de Mandioca e Fruticultura da EMBRAPA, Bahia, 182
— — — — Milho e Sorgo, Sete Lagoas, 182
— — — Tecnología Agropecuaria (CENTA), San Salvador, 422
— para el Desarrollo de la Capacidad Nacional de Investigación, Panama, 1030
— Paraguayo de Estudios de Desarrollo Económico y Social, Asunción, 1034
— — — Ingenieros, Asunción, 1034
— per lo Sviluppo dei Trasporti Aerei, Rome, 764
— Radioelettrico Sperimentale "Guglielmo Marconi", Rome, 764
— Regional de Alfabetización Funcional en las Zonas Rurales de América, Michoacán, 30
— — — Educación de Adultos y Alfabetización Funcional para América Latina, Pátzcuaro, 928
— — — Pesquisas Educacionais do Sul, Porto Alegre, 183
— — para el Fomento del Libro en America Latina, Bogotá, 347
— — — la Educación Superior en América Latina y el Caribe, Caracas, 1950
— Ricerche sulle Attività Umane Superiori, Ferrara, 763
— Siciliano di Fisica Nucleare e di Struttura della Materia, Catania, 763
— Sperimentale di Cinematografia, Rome, 763
— — Metallurgico (S.p.A.), Rome, 764
— Superiore di Logica e Scienze Comparate, Bologna, 764
— Universitario de Holguín, 366
— — — Matanzas, 366
— — — Pinar del Rio, 366
— Venezolano-Americano, Caracas, 1951
Centrul de Cercetări Biologice Cluj-Napoca, 1123
— — — — Iași, 1123
— — — Medicale, Tîrgu-Mureș, 1119
— — — Sociologice, Bucharest, 1121
— — — Fizică Tehnică Iași, 1123
— — — Igienă și Sănătate Publică, Timișoara, 1119

— — — Științe Sociale, Cluj-Napoca, 1121
— — — — Craiova, 1121
— — — — Iași, 1121
— — — — Sibiu, 1121
— — — — Timișoara, 1121
— — — — Tîrgu-Mures, 1121
— — — Studii și Cercetări de Istorie și Teorie Militara, Bucharest, 1123
— National de Fono-Audiologie și Chirurgie Functionala O.R.L., Bucharest, 1119
Centrum Informacji Naukowej, Technicznej i Ekonomicznej, Warsaw, 1074
— Medyczne Ksztacenia Podyplomowego, Warsaw, 1095
— voor Agrobiologisch Onderzoek, Wageningen, 960
— — de Studie van de Mens, Antwerp, 153
— — — het Onderwijs in Ontwikkelingslanden, The Hague, 957
— — Interdisciplinair Antropologisch Onderzoek, Leuven, 155
Ceramics Museum, Tel-Aviv, 743
Cercle Culturel Français, Kabul, 52
— Germano-Malagasy, Antananarivo, 910
Cercles des Jeunes Naturalistes, Montreal, 242
Česká společnost pro estetiku, Prague, 370
— — — mezinárodni právo, Prague, 370
České Vysoké Učení Technické v Praze, 382
Československá Akademie Věd, 369
— — Slezský ústav, Vědecká knihovna, Opava, 376
— — Zemědělska, Prague, 373
— — astronomická společnost, Prague, 370
— — biologická společnost, Brno, 370
— — botanická společnost, Prague, 370
— — chirurgická společnost, Prague, 371
— — demografická společnost, Prague, 371
— — geografická společnost, 371
— — historická společnost, Prague, 371
— — kybernetická společnost, Prague, 371
— — lékařská společnost J. E. Purkyně, Prague, 371
— — limnologická společnost, Prague, 371
— — meteorologická společnost, Prague, 371
— — pedagogická společnost, Prague, 371
— — sociologická společnost, Prague, 371
— — spektroskopická společnost, Prague, 371
— — společnost antropologická, Brno, 371
— — — archeologická, Prague, 371
— — — biochemická, Prague, 371
— — — bioklimatologická, Prague, 371
— — — chemická, Prague, 371
— — — ekonomická, Prague, 371
— — — entomologická, Prague, 371
— — — histo- a cytochemická, Prague, 371
— — — mikrobiologická, Prague, 371
— — — orientalistická, Prague, 371
— — — parasitologická, Prague, 371
— — — pro dějiny věd a techniky, Prague, 371
— — — mechaniku, Prague, 371
— — — mineralogii a geologii, Prague, 371
— — — nauku o kovech, Prague, 371
— — — politicke vedy, Prague, 371
— — — vědeckou kinematografii, Brno, 371
— — — vědy zemědělské, lesnické, veterinárni a potravinářské, Prague, 371
— — — zoologicka, Prague, 371
— — vědecká společnost pro mykologii, Prague, 371
— — — — psychologii, Prague, 371
Ceský spolek pro komorní hudbu, Prague, 374
Ceylon College of Physicians, 1228
— Gemmologists Association, 1224
— Geographical Society, Colombo, 1224
— Humanist Society, Colombo, 1224
— Institute of Scientific and Industrial Research, 1225
— — — — Research Library, 1225
— — — World Affairs, Colombo, 1224

# INDEX OF INSTITUTIONS

Ceylon Palaeological Society, 1224
— Society of Arts, 1224
Chacra Experimental de Barrow, 66
Chadron State College, Nebraska, 1792
Chadwick Trust, London, 1420
Chagang Provincial Library, Kangge, 883
Chaim Weizmann Zionist Research Institute, Tel-Aviv, 750
Chalk River Nuclear Laboratories, Ont., 246
Challenger Society, 1422
Chalmers Tekniska Högskola, 1243
— — — Bibliotek, 1240
— University of Technology, Göteborg, 1243
Chamber of Architects and Civil Engineers, St. Julians, 921
— — Mines Precambrian Research Unit, Cape Town, 1167
Chaminade University of Honolulu, 1702
Chancellor College, Zomba, 913
Changsha Engineering College, 336
Chapman College, Orange, 1654
Charing Cross Hospital Medical School, 1511
Charles Darwin Foundation for the Galapagos Isles, Ongar, 44
— — Research Station, Galapagos Islands, 408
— Lamb Society, 1426
— University, Prague, 381
Chartered Institute of Building, London, 1436
— — — Patent Agents, London, 1436
— — — Transport, London, 1436
— — — in Australia, Templestowe, 91
— Institution of Building Services, London, 1436
— Insurance Institute, 1416
— Society of Physiotherapy, 1428
Chashma Nuclear Power Project (Chasnupp), Islamabad, 1022
Château d'Azay-le-Ferron, 470
— de Langeais, 468
— Plessis-les Tours, 470
— Le, Vevey, 1263
Chatham College, Pittsburgh, 1869
Chebotarev, N. G., Research Institute of Mathematics and Mechanics, Kazan, 1363
Checheno Ingush Museum of Fine Arts, Grozny, 1353
— — University, Grozny, 1361
Chehel Sotun Museum, Isfahan, 722
Cheju College, Cheju City, 896
Chekhov (A.P.) House-Museum, Moscow, 1357
— Memorial Museum, Melikhovo, 1358
— Museum, Taganrog, 1358
Chelsea College, University of London, 1510
— School of Art, 1550
Chelyabinsk Institute of Agricultural Engineering, 1371
— Polytechnic Institute, 1374
— State Institute of Culture, 1382
— — Medical Institute, 1383
— — Picture Gallery, 1353
Chemical Defence Establishment, Salisbury, 1448
— Economy Research Institute, Tokyo, 815
— Engineering and Metallurgy Institute, Beijing, 332
— — College, Beijing, 336
— — Research Group (CSIR), Pretoria, 1159
— Institute, Gorky, 1362
— — of Canada, 243
— Metallurgical Institute, Karaganda, 1329
— Physics Institute, Luda, 332
— Research Institute of Non-Aqueous Solutions, Sendai, 851
Chemisch-Physikalische Gesellschaft in Wien, 123
Chemische Gesellschaft der DDR, 504
Chemistry and Soil Research Institute, Salisbury, Zimbabwe, 2001
— Association, Hanoi, 1962

— Institute, Beijing, 332
— — Jinan, 332
— — of Guangdong, Guangzhou, 332
Chemotherapeutic Institute, Chiba, 815
Chemotherapeutisches Forschungsinstitut Georg-Speyer-Haus, Frankfurt, 531
Chengdu Institute of Geology and Mineral Resources, Sichuan, 333
— Telecommunications Engineering College, 336
Chernigov M. M. Kotsyubinsky Literary Museum, 1357
Chernovtsy Y. Fedkovicha Memorial Museum, 1357
— State Medical Institute, 1383
— — University, 1361
Chernyshevsky Memorial Museum, Saratov, 1358
— (N.G.) State Public Library of the Kirghiz S.S.R., Frunze, 1348
Cheshire Libraries and Museums, Chester, 1453
Chest Disease Research Institute, Kyoto, 836
— Heart and Stroke Association, London, 1428
Chester Beatty Library and Gallery of Oriental Art, Dublin, 731
Chestnut Hill College, Philadelphia, 1869
Chetham's Library, 1458
Cheyney State College, Pennsylvania, 1869
Chiangmai University, 1285
Chiba Prefectural Central Library, 819
— University, 824
Chibero College of Agriculture, Norton, 2004
Chicago Academy of Sciences, 1597
— Public Library, 1626
— State University, 1703
Chief Astronomical Observatory, Kiev, 1333
Chigaku Dantai Kenkyu-Kai, 810
Child Guidance and Research Centre, Durban, 1168
— — Institute, Pretoria, 1175
— Malnutrition Unit, Kampala, 1311
Chilean Academy of History, Santiago, 322
— — — Sciences, Santiago, 322
Chimkent State Institute of Culture, 1382
China Academy, Yang Ming Shan, 340
— Acoustics Society, 334
— Aeronautics and Astronautics Society, Beijing, 334
— Agricultural Crops Society, 334
— — Economy Society, 334
— — Machinery Society, 334
— Agronomy Society, 334
— Animal Husbandry and Veterinary Society, 334
— Anti-Tuberculosis Society, 334
— Aquatic Products Society, 334
— Architectural Society, 334
— Astronomical Society, 334
— Automation Society, 334
— Automotive Engineering Society, 334
— Biochemistry Society, 334
— Botany Society, 334
— Chemical Engineering Society, 334
— — Society, 334
— Civil Engineeering Society, 334
— Coal Mining Society, 334
— Education Association, 334
— Electrical Engineering Society, 334
— Electronics Society, 334
— Engineering Thermophysics Society, 334
— Environmental Science Society, 334
— Fishery Society, 334
— Forestry Society, 334
— Future Society, 334
— Genetics Society, 334
— Geography Society, 334
— Geological Society, 334
— Geophysics Society, 334
— Historical Society, 334
— Hydraulic Engineering Society, 334
— Light Industry Society, 334
— Mathematics Society, 334
— Mechanical Engineering Society, 334

# WORLD OF LEARNING

— Mechanics and Automation Society, 334
— Mechanics Society, 334
— Medical College, Taichung City, 345
— — Society, 334
— Metals Society, 334
— Meteorology Society, 334
— Metrology Society, 334
— Microbiology Society, 334
— Mineralogical, Petrological and Geochemical Society, 334
— National Association of Literature and the Arts, Taipei, 340
— Navigation Society, 334
— Nuclear Society, 334
— Nurses Society, 334
— Palaeopalynological Society, 334
— Pedology Society, 334
— Petroleum Society, 334
— Pharmacology Society, 334
— Photography Society, 334
— Physics Society, 334
— Physiology Society, 334
— Precision Machinery Society, 334
— Psychology Society, 334
— Pulp and Paper Engineering Society, 334
— Railway Society, 335
— Research Institute, Tokyo, 813
— Society for Modernization of Management, 335
— Scientific and Technical Association, Beijing, 334
— — — Technological Information Society, 335
— Sericulture Society, 335
— Silicates Society, 335
— Society, London, 1434
— — Singapore, 1150
— — Taipei, 340
— — of Naval Architecture and Marine Engineering, Beijing, 334
— Sociological Research Society, 335
— Space Flight Society, 335
— Study of Religion Society, 335
— Technical Economy Research Society, 335
— Textile and Engineering Society, 335
— Traditional Medicine Society, 335
— West European Economy Society, 335
Chinese Academy of Agricultural Sciences, Beijing, 333
— — — Coal Mining Sciences, Beijing, 333
— — — Forestry Sciences, Beijing, 333
— — — Geological Sciences, Beijing, 333
— — — Medical Sciences, Beijing, 332
— — — Meteorological Sciences, Beijing, 333
— — — Sciences, Beijing, 331
— — — — Library, Beijing, 335
— — — Social Sciences, Beijing, 332
— — — Space Technology, 333
— — — Traditional Medicine, Beijing, 333
— Association for Folklore, Taipei, 340
— — — the Advancement of Science, Taipei, 340
— Chemical Society, Taipei, 340
— Classical Music Association, Taipei, 340
— Culture University, Taipei, 345
— Forestry Association, Taipei, 340
— Institute of Civil Engineering, Taipei, 340
— — — Engineers, Taipei, 340
— Language and Research Centre, Singapore, 1152
— — Society, Taipei, 341
— Mathematical Society, Taipei, 341
— Medical Association, Taipei, 341
— National Foreign Relations Association, Taipei, 341
— People's University, Beijing, 336
— Statistical Association, Taipei, 341
— University of Hong Kong, 1560
— — — — Library System, 1559
Chingyi (Providence) College of Arts and Sciences, Taichung, 345
Chishakuin, Kyoto City, 821
Chita State Medical Institute, 1383

Chitala Agricultural Research Station, Salima, 912
Chitedze Agricultural Research Station, Lilongwe, 912
Chittagong Polytechnic Institute, 145
— Public Library, 143
Chongjin City Library, 883
— Historical Library, 884
Chongqing Construction Engineering College, 336
— University, 336
Chonnam National University, 887
Chosun University, 888
Christ Church, Oxford, 1524
— — Library, Oxford, 1463
Christchurch Industrial Development Division, Department of Scientific and Industrial Research, 979
— Polytechnic, N.Z., 987
Christian-Albrechts-Universität, Kiel, 582
— Brothers College, Memphis, 1889
— Institute for the Study of Religion and Society, Chunnakam, 1228
— University of Indonesia, Jakarta, 718
Christ's College, Cambridge, 1484
— — Library, Cambridge, 1461
Chrzeščijanska Akademia Teologiczna, Warsaw, 1095
Chubu Institute of Technology, Nagoya, 862
Chulalongkorn University, Bangkok, 1285
— Library, 1284
Chungbuk National University, 889
Chung Chi College, Hong Kong, 1561
— Yuan Christian University, Chung Li, 345
Chungang University, Seoul, 888
— Library, 886
Chungnam National University, 889
Chuo University, Tokyo, 862
— Library, 818
Church Education Society, Dublin, 730
— Missionary Society Library, 1456
— Museum, Przemysl, 1077
Churchill College, Cambridge, 1484
— — Library, Cambridge, 1461
— Memorial Museum, Brunei, 213
Chuson-ji Sanko-zo, Nishi-Iwai-gun, 822
Chuto Chosakai, Tokyo, 813
Chuvash Agricultural Institute, 1369
— Eye Diseases Research Institute, 1385
— Picture Gallery, Cheboksary, 1353
— I. N. Ulyanov State University, Cheboksary, 1361
Ciba Foundation, London, 1420
Cincinnati Art Museum, 1636
Cinémathèque Scientifique Internationale, Brussels, 22
Circulation Research Unit, Johannesburg, 1182
— — — Tygerberg, 1156
Circulo de Bellas Artes, La Paz, 173
— — Cultura Musical, Macau, 1108
Circum-Pacific Council for Energy and Mineral Resources, Menlo Park, 44
Citadel, The, Charleston, 1885
Citrus and Subtropical Fruit Research Institute, Nelspruit, 1160
— Fruit Research Institute, Chongqing, 333
City and Guilds of London Art School, 1550
— — — — Institute, 1418
— Business Library, London, 1456
— College, New York, 1805
— Library, Port Louis, 923
— of Sofia, 220
— Museum and Art Gallery, Gloucester, 1468
— of Birmingham Polytechnic, 1539
— — Bristol Museum and Art Gallery, 1468
— — Canterbury College of Art, 1550
— — Edmonton Archives, Alberta, 246
— — London Polytechnic, 1543
— — Phoenix Public Library, 1626
— — Sydney Public Library, 96
— University, London, 1485

— — of New York, 1805
Civic Museum, Dublin, 732
— Trust, London, 1411
Civiche Raccolte Archeologiche e Numismatiche, Milan, 771
Civici Musei, Pavia, 772
— — e Gallerie di Storia ed Arte, Udine, 773
— — Veneziani d'Arte e di Storia, Venice, 773
Civico Museo del Castello di S. Giusto, 773
— — — Risorgimento e Sacrario Oberdan, Trieste, 773
— — della Risiera di S. Sabba, Trieste, 773
— — di Storia ed Arte e Orto Lapidario Trieste, 773
— — — Patria, Trieste, 773
— — Sartorio, Trieste, 773
— — Teatrale di Fondazione Carlo Schmid, Trieste, 773
Civil Engineering Research Institute, Sapporo-city, 817
Clare College, Cambridge, 1484
— — Library, Cambridge, 1461
— — Hall Cambridge, 1485
Claremont Graduate School, 1654
— Teachers College, W.A., 117
Clarion State College, Pennsylvania, 1869
Clark College, Atlanta, 1699
— University, Worcester, Mass., 1748
Clarke College, Dubuque, 1723
Clarkson College of Technology, 1806
Classical Association, Cardiff, 1426
— — of Ceylon, The, 1224
— — — Ghana, 611
— — — South Africa, 1155
Clean Air Society of Australia and New Zealand (N.Z. Branch), 977
Clemson University, 1885
Cleveland County Libraries, Middlesbrough, 1453
— Health Education Museum, 1636
— Museum of Art, 1637
— — — Natural History, 1637
— Public Library, 1627
— State University, Ohio, 1842
Clinch Valley College of the University of Virginia, Wise, 1920
Clinica Universitaria, Pamplona, 1213
Clinical Cytology Research Group, Tygerberg, 1156
— Genetics Unit (M.R.C.), London, 1443
— Medicine Institute, Beijing, 333
— Oncology and Radiotherapeutics Unit (M.R.C.), Cambridge, 1443
— Pharmacology Unit (M.R.C.), Oxford, 1444
— Population Cytogenetics Unit (M.R.C.), Edinburgh, 1444
— Psychiatry Unit (M.R.C.), Chichester, 1444
— Research Centre, Harrow, 1443
Cloisters, The (Metropolitan Museum of Art), Fort Tryon Park, 1639
Clwyd Library Service, Mold, 1455
Coal Chemistry Institute, Beijing, 333
— Mining College, Fuxin, 336
Coastal Marine Study Center, Santa Cruz, 1673
Cocoa Research Institute, Ghana, Tafo, 611
— — of Nigeria, Ibadan, 992
Coconut Research Institute, Ceylon, 1225
Çocuk Sağilği Enstitüsü, Ankara, 1299
Codrington College, Barbados, 1487
— Library (All Souls College), Oxford, 1463
Coe College, Cedar Rapids, 1723
Coffee Research Foundation, Ruiru, 878
— Station, Chipinga, 2001
Cografya Enstitüsü, Istanbul, 1299
Coker College, Hartsville, 1886
Colby College, Waterville, 1741
Colchester and Essex Museum, 1468
Cold Spring Harbor Laboratory, 1620
Colección Carlos Alberto Pusineri Scala, Asunción, 1034
— "Gill Aguínaga", Asunción, 1035

— Ornitológica Phelps, 1956
Colectia "Ion Minulescu", Bucharest, 1126
Colegio de Abogados de Barcelona, 1189
— — — Buenos Aires, 63
— — — Mexico City, 926
— — — del Distrito Federal, Caracas, 1950
— — Arquitectos de Chile, Santiago de Chile, 322
— — — Venezuela, 1950
— — — del Perú, Lima, 1036
— — Bibliotecarios de Chile, Santiago, 322
— — Bibliotecologos y Archivologos de Venezuela, Caracas, 1950
— — Farmacéuticos del Distrito Federal y Estado Miranda, Caracas, 1951
— — Graduados en Ciencias Económicas, Buenos Aires, 63
— — Ingenieros de Guatemala, 624
— — — Venezuela, 1952
— — Médicos del Distrito Federal, Caracas, 1951
— — — Estado Miranda, 1951
— — — y Cirujanos de Nicaragua, 989
— — México, 944
— — Quimico-Farmacéuticos de Chile, Santiago, 323
— Mayor de Nuestra Señora del Rosario, Bogotá, 357
— Médico de El Salvador, 422
— — Farmacéutico de Filipinas, Inc., Quezon City, 1047
— Nacional, Mexico City, 925
— — de Agricultura "Luis A. Martínez", Ambato, 412
— — — Buenos Aires, 72
— — "24 de Mayo", Quito, 412
— — "Rafael Hernández", La Plata, 75
— Notarial, Barcelona, 1189
— Oficial de Arquitectos de Cataluña, Barcelona, 1188
— — Ingenieros Industriales, de Cataluña, Barcelona, 1190
— Técnico Industrial (Campinas), 193
— — (Limeira), 193
Colgate University, 1806
Collection Oskar Reinhart am Römerholz, Winterthur, 1263
Collections Baur, Geneva, 1261
College Art Association of America, New York, 1600
— of Agriculture, Nitra, 385
— — Arms, London, 1456
— — Arts, Science and Technology, Kingston, Jamaica, 801
— — Basic Sciences and Foreign Languages, Erzurum, 1304
— — Business Education, Dar es Salaam, 1281
— — Cape Breton, 265
— — Charleston, S.C., 1886
— — Chemical Engineers, Barton, A.C.T., 91
— — Technology in Pardubice, 384
— — Chinese Medicine and Pharmacy, Taipei, 345
— — Civil Engineers, Barton, A.C.T., 91
— — Economics and Planning, Hanoi, 1963
— — — Social Science, Babolsar, 724
— — Education, Peshawar, 1027
— — Electrical Engineers, Barton, A.C.T., 91
— — Environmental Science and Forestry, Syracuse, 1822
— — Estate Management, Reading, 1552
— — Europe, Bruges, 167
— — Fine and Applied Art, Khartoum, 1231
— — Forestry and Wood Technology, Zvolen, 385
— — Great Falls, Montana, 1791
— — Health, Diyarbakir, 1305
— — Sciences and Hospital (Kansas City and Wichita), 1734
— — — Hospital, Okinawa, 848
— — Home Economics, Peshawar, 1027
— — Idaho, 1702

College of Mechanical and Electrical Engineering in Plzeń, 385
—— —— —— Textile Engineering in Liberec, 385
—— —— Engineers, Barton, A.C.T., 91
—— —— Medical Technology, Kyoto, 837
—— —— Medicine, Lagos, 1000
—— —— of South Africa, Rondebosch, 1160
—— —— Mining and Geology, Hanoi, 1963
—— —— Mount St. Joseph-on-the-Ohio, 1842
—— —— Mount Saint Vincent, Riverdale, 1806
—— —— National Education, Korogwe, 1281
—— —— New Rochelle, N.Y., 1806
—— —— Notre Dame, Belmont, 1655
—— —— Nursing, Australia, Melbourne, 89
—— —— Optometry, New York City, 1822
—— —— Our Lady of the Elms, Chicopee, 1748
—— —— Physicians and Surgeons, Pakistan, Karachi, 1020
—— —— of Philadelphia, 1610
—— —— Political Studies, Central Committee of the Czechoslovak Communist Party, Prague, 380
—— —— Preceptors, London, 1418
—— —— Production Technology and School of Business Administration, Ashford, 1552
—— —— Ripon and York St. John, York, 1498
—— —— Road and Rail Transport, Hanoi, 1963
—— —— Saint Benedict, St. Joseph, 1774
—— —— Catherine, St. Paul, 1774
—— —— Elizabeth, Convent Station, 1796
—— —— Francis, Joliet, 1703
—— —— Hild and St. Bede, Durham, 1487
—— —— Paul and St. Mary, Bristol, 1481
—— —— Rose, Albany, 1806
—— —— Teresa, Winona, 1774
—— —— Thomas, St. Paul, 1774
—— —— Santa Fé, New Mexico, 1801
—— —— Staten Island, 1805
—— —— Surveying, Teheran, 724
—— —— Technology, Calabar, 1002
—— —— Owerri, 1003
—— —— Utica/Rome, 1822
—— —— Telecommunications, Hanoi, 1963
—— —— the Bahamas, Nassau, 140
—— —— Holy Cross, Worcester, Mass., 1749
—— —— —— Spirit, Manila, 1060
—— —— Ozarks, Clarksville, 1650
—— —— Resurrection, Mirfield, 1498
—— —— Virgin Islands, St. Thomas, 1936
—— —— Veterinary Medicine, Helsinki, 440
—— —— Košice, 386
—— —— —— Science, Lahore, 1025
—— —— Water Conservation, Hanoi, 1963
—— —— William and Mary in Virginia, 1915
—— —— Wooster, 1842
Collège d'Enseignement Technique, Papeete, 501
—— —— —— Agricole, Sibiti, 358
—— de France, Paris, 491
—— Hearst, Ontario, 270
—— Dominicain de Philosophie et de Théologie, Ottawa, 268
—— International de Chirurgiens, Chicago, 37
—— —— pour l'étude scientifique des techniques de production mécanique, Paris, 33
—— Libre des Sciences Sociales et Economiques, Paris, 497
—— Médical, Luxembourg, 908
—— Militaire Royal de St.-Jean, Sherbrooke, 302
—— Rural d'Ambatolbe, Antananarivo, 911
—— Technique Commercial et Industriel de Brazzaville (et centre d'Apprentissage), 358
Collegium Cultorum Martyrum, Rome, 1942
—— Internationale Allergologicum, Basel, 39
—— Romanicum, Yverdon, 1255
Collezione d'Arte Religiosa Moderna, Vatican City, 1943

Collezioni artistiche Stavropulos, Trieste, 773
Collingwood College, Durham, 1487
—— Museum, Ontario, 250
Colombian Academy, Bogotá, 346
—— —— of Exact, Physical and Natural Sciences, Bogotá, 346
—— —— —— History, Bogotá, 346
—— —— —— Jurisprudence, Bogotá, 346
Colombo National Museum, 1226
—— —— Library, 1225
—— Observatory, 1225
Colonial Williamsburg Foundation, 1637
Colorado College, Colorado Springs, 1675
—— School of Mines, 1675
—— State University, Fort Collins, 1675
—— Women's College, Denver, 1675
Columbia College, Columbia, S.C., 1886
—— Union College, Takoma Park, Md., 1742
—— University, Morningside Heights, 1806
—— —— Computer Center, New York, 1810
—— —— Libraries, 1633
Combustion Institute, Pittsburgh, 1622
Comenius Museum, Naarden, 968
—— University of Bratislava, 380
Comeniusbücherei, Leipzig, 507
Comisia de Istorie a Economiei și a Gindirii Economice, Bucharest, 1121
Comisión Asesora de Teatro, San Juan, 1109
—— Boliviana de Energía Nuclear, 173
—— Chilena de Energía Nuclear, 324
—— de Energía Atómica de Costa Rica, 359
—— Investigaciones Científicas de la Provincia de Buenos Aires, 67
—— Ecuatoriana de Energía Atómica, Quito, 407
—— Nacional de Arqueología y Monumentos Históricos, Panama City, 1030
—— Energía Atómica, Buenos Aires, 68
—— —— —— Montevideo, 1938
—— —— Investigación Científica y Tecnológica (CONICT), Santiago, 325
—— —— Investigaciones Espaciales, Buenos Aires, 68
—— —— Museos y de Monumentos y Lugares Históricos, 63
—— Protectora de Bibliotecas Populares, 63
—— Provincial de Monumentos Históricos y Artísticos de Barcelona, 1189
—— Salvadoreña de Energía Nuclear, San Salvador, 422
Comissão de Historia Militar, Lisbon, 1101
—— Nacional de Energia Nuclear (CNEN), Rio de Janeiro, 185
—— —— Folclore, Rio de Janeiro, 182
Comitato Elettrotecnico Italiano (C.E.I.), Milan, 761
—— Glaciologico Italiano, Turin, 763
—— Italiano per lo Studio dei Problemi della Popolazione, Rome, 761
—— Nazionale per l'Energia Nucleare (C.N.E.N.), 764
—— Termotecnico Italiano (C.T.I.), Turin, 761
Comité Belge d'Histoire des Sciences, Brussels, 152
—— Culturel National, Tunis, 1295
—— International d'histoire de l'art, Paris, 10
—— —— de Médecine et de Pharmacie Militaires, Liège, 39
—— —— des Associations Techniques de Fonderie, Zurich, 32
—— —— —— sciences historiques, Lausanne, 10
—— —— Permanent des Congrès de Pathologie Comparée, Paris, 43
—— —— —— —— linguistes, Leiden, 11
—— —— pour la documentation des sciences sociales, Paris, 22
—— maritime international, Antwerp, 36
—— Nacional de Geografía, Geodesia y Geofísica, Santiago, 325
—— —— —— la Federación Dental International, Lima, 1037
—— Español del Consejo Internacional de la Música, Madrid, 1188

—— National contre les Maladies Respiratoires et la Tuberculose, Paris, 449
—— —— de Géographie du Maroc, Rabat, 949
—— —— des Musées, Tunis, 1295
—— —— Français de Géodésie et Géophysique, Paris, 452
—— —— —— Géographie, Paris, 447
—— —— —— Mathématiciens, 451
—— —— des Recherches Antarctiques, Paris, 451
—— Oceanografico Nacional, Valparaiso, 324
—— permanent des congrès internationaux de génétique, Kyoto, 51
—— —— du congrès international d'entomologie, London, 50
—— —— international du Congrès de physiologie et pathologie de la reproduction animale et la fécondation artificielle, Potters Bar, 18
—— Scientifique du Club Alpin Français, 447
—— Technique de la Recherche Archéologique en France, Paris, 458
Comitetul National al Geologilor din R.S.R., Bucharest, 1122
—— —— Istoricilor Din Romania, Bucharest, 1122
—— pentru Literatură Comparăta, Bucharest, 1121
Commerzbibliothek, 536
Commissariat à l'Energie Atomique (CEA), Paris, 459
—— Général à l'Energie Atomique, Kinshasa, 1995
Commission Belge de Bibliographie, Brussels, 150
—— des Musées Archéologiques et Historiques, Tunis, 1295
—— Electrotechnique Internationale, Geneva, 34
—— for Multilateral Co-operation of Academies of Science of Socialist Countries "Neurophysiology and Higher Nervous Activity" (Intermozg), Moscow, 1319
—— the Preservation of Natural and Historical Monuments and Relics, Livingstone, 1997
—— grand-ducale d'Instruction, Luxembourg, 908
—— Internationale d'Optique, Delft, 47
—— de juristes, Geneva, 35
—— l'éclairage, Paris, 34
—— nomenclature zoologique, London, 48
—— numismatique, Oslo, 25
—— des grands barrages, Paris, 32
—— industries agricoles et alimentaires, Paris, 17
—— irrigations et du drainage, New Delhi, 32
—— du Génie Rural, Paris, 17
—— verre—CIV, Prague, 33
—— pour l'Exploration Scientifique de la Mer Méditerranée, Monaco, 47
—— l'histoire des assemblées d'états, Brighton, 24
—— océanographique Intergouvernementale, Paris, 45
—— on Exhibitions, Tbilisi, 1327
—— Instillation of Science Achievements in National Economy, Tbilisi, 1327
—— International Scientific Contacts, Baku, 1326
—— —— —— Erevan, 1325
—— —— —— Tbilisi, 1327
—— Mining, Baku, 1325
—— Mountain Mud Flows, Baku, 1325
—— National Problems, Moscow, 1320
—— Nature Conservation, Ashkhabad, 1332
—— —— —— Baku, 1325
—— —— —— Kishinev, 1331

— — — — Tartu, 1327
— — — — Tbilisi, 1327
— — — Regional Studies, Tallinn, 1327
— — — Science Equipment, Riga, 1330
— — — Scientific Information, Tbilisi, 1327
— — — Space Exploration, Moscow, 1323
— — — Speleology, Tbilisi, 1327
— — — Terminology, Frunze, 1329
— — — the Caspian Sea, Baku, 1325
— — — — History of Natural Sciences and Technology, Ashkhabad, 1332
— — — — — Science Technology, Kishinev, 1331
— — — Orthography and Terminology of the Turkmen Language, Ashkhabad, 1332
— — — Study of Cancer Tumours, Tbilisi, 1328
— Permanente et Association Internationale pour la Médecine du Travail, London, 43
— pour l'Encouragement des Recherches Scientifiques, Bern, 1258
— Royale d'Histoire, Brussels, 148
Committee for Economic Development of Australia—CEDA, Melbourne, 87
— of Directors of Polytechnics, London, 1418
— — Vice-Chancellors and Principals of the Universities of the United Kingdom, 1418
— on Co-ordinating Studies in Malignant Tumours, Tbilisi, 1328
— — Data for Science and Technology (CODATA), Paris, 9
— — International Scientific Contacts, Kishinev, 1331
— — Petrography, Moscow, 1320
— — Promotion of the Peaceful Uses of Atomic Energy, Taipei, 341
— — Science and Technology for the Developing Countries (COSTED), Madras, 9
— — Space Research (COSPAR), Paris, 9
— — the Teaching of Science (CTS), Malvern, 9
Commons, Open Spaces and Footpaths Preservation Society, 1411
Commonwealth Agricultural Bureaux, Slough, 15
— Association of Museums, London, 18
— Bureau of Agricultural Economics, Oxford, 15
— — — Animal Breeding and Genetics, Edinburgh, 15
— — — — Health, Weybridge, 16
— — — Dairy Science and Technology, Reading, 16
— — — Horticulture and Plantation Crops, East Malling, 16
— — — Nutrition, Aberdeen, 16
— — — Pastures and Field Crops, Maidenhead, 16
— — — Plant Breeding and Genetics, Cambridge, 16
— — — Soils, Harpenden, 16
— Council for Educational Administration, Armidale, N.S.W., 106
— Forestry and Timber Bureau, 91
— — Association, Oxford, 1411
— — Bureau, Oxford, 16
— — Institute, Oxford, 1524
— Fund, New York, 1610
— Geographical Bureau, London, 44
— Institute, London, 1424
— — of Biological Control, Curepe, 15, 1293
— — — Entomology, London, 15
— — — Health, Townsville, 110
— — — Helminthology, St. Albans, 15
— — — Valuers, Sydney, 88
— Library Association, London, 21
— Mycological Institute, Richmond, 15
— of Australia Bureau of Meteorology, 93
— — Puerto Rico, Department of Justice Library, San Juan, 1110

— Scientific and Industrial Research Organisation (CSIRO), Canberra, 92
— — — — — Libraries, East Melbourne, 96
— Secretariat, Education Division, London, 1418
— Serum Laboratories Commission, 92
Communication Research Center, Seoul, 893
Communications Museum Library, Chiyoda-ku, 818
— Media Research, Durban, 1168
— Research Center, Syracuse, N.Y., 1822
— School, Ulan Bator, 948
Community and Organisation Research Institute, Santa Barbara, 1673
Compagnie des Experts Architectes, Paris, 445
— Française pour le Développement des Fibres Textiles (CFDT), Douala, 231
— — — — — Fibres Textiles, Niamey, 990
— — — — — Fibres Textiles, Ouagadougou, 1937
Comparative Education Society in Europe, Brussels, 27
— — Study and Adaptation Centre, Lagos, 1000
Complex Experimental Station, Kishinev, 1331
— Institute for Research and Design "Glavproekt", Sofia, 219
— — of Natural Sciences, Nukus, 1335
— Research and Design Institute of Regional and Town Planning and Architecture, Sofia, 219
Complexul Muzeal de Stinte ale Naturu, Constanta, 1128
— — Goleşti, Arges, 1128
— Muzeistic Iasi, 1128
Composers, Authors and Publishers Association of Canada Ltd., Toronto, 240
— Guild of Great Britain, London, 1414
Computation Center, Ames, 1728
— — University Park, 1877
— Science Centre, Alexandria, 418
Computer Aided Design Centre, Cambridge, 1448
— Centre, Cracow, 1090
— — Johannesburg, 1182
— — Lausanne, 1273
— — Loughborough, 1514
— — Maribor, 1986
— — Turku, 439
— Services Centre, Canberra, 100
— Systems Laboratory, Santa Barbara, 1673
— Technology Institute, Beijing, 332
— — — Shanghai, 332
— — — Shenyang, 332
Computing Centre, Cardiff, 1536
— — Erevan, 1324
— — Iaşi, 1135
— — Jyväskylä, 436
— — Krasnoyarsk, 1321
— — Moscow, 1318
— — Novosibirsk, 1321
— — Salisbury, Zimbabwe, 2003
— — Tbilisi, 1327
— Laboratory, Canterbury, 1496
— Services Centre, Mexico City, 933
Concepción University, 329
Concervatoire municipal, Istanbul, 1310
Concord Antiquarian Society, 1605
— College, Athens, West Virginia, 1930
Concordia College, Moorhead, Minn., 1774
— — St. Paul, 1774
— Lutheran College, Edmonton, Alberta, 257
— Teachers College, Seward, 1792
— University, Montreal, 265
— — Libraries, Montreal, 248
Confederación Universitaria Centroamericana, San José, 27
Confederate Museum, Bermuda, 1558

Confederation Centre Library, Charlottetown, 248
— of British Industry, London, 1436
— — the Universities of Central America, San José, 27
Confédération des Sociétés Scientifiques Françaises (CSSF), 451
— — Syndicats Médicaux Français, 449
— Européenne de l'Agriculture, Aargau, 16
— internationale des ingénieurs agronomes, Rome, 17
— — — sociétés d'auteurs et compositeurs, Paris, 35
Conférence de La Haye de droit international privé, The Hague, 35
— des Présidents d'Université, Paris, 447
— — Recteurs des Universités Belges, Brussels, 151
— internationale des économistes agricoles, Oak Brook, 16
— — — Grands Réseaux Electriques à Haute Tension, Paris, 32
— permanente des recteurs et vice-chanceliers des universités européennes—CRE, Geneva, 31
— Universitaire Suisse, Bern, 1254
Confucius-Mencius Society of the Republic of China, Taipei, 341
Congregational Library, 1456
Congrès géologique international, Paris, 48
— International de Botanique, Sydney, 47
— — — Médecine Tropicale et de Paludisme, Manila, 39
— — des Africanistes, Lubumbashi, 11
— — Ornithologique, Berlin (West), 49
Connecticut Academy of Arts and Sciences, New Haven, 1597
— College, New London, 1677
— State Library, Hartford, 1630
Connemara (State Central) Public Library, Madras, 673
Conrad Grebel College, Waterloo, Ont., 311
Conradh na Gaeilge, Dublin, 730
Conseil Administratif de la Réunion des Musées Nationaux, Paris, 466
— africain et malgache de l'enseignement supérieur, Ouagadougou, 26
— Artistique de la Réunion des Musées Nationaux, Paris, 466
— de recherches en sciences humaines du Canada, 245
— des Arts, Ottawa, 239
— — organisations internationales des sciences médicales, Geneva, 37
— — Sciences du Canada, Ottawa, 242
— international de l'action sociale, Vienna, 24
— — — la musique, Paris, 43
— — — — populaire, New York, 43
— — — — philosophie et des sciences humaines, Paris, 10
— des archives, Paris, 22
— — — Associations de Bibliothèques de Théologie, Köln, 22
— — — monuments et des sites, Paris, 19
— — — sciences sociales—CISS, Paris, 11
— — unions scientifiques, Paris, 7
— du bâtiment pour la recherche, l'étude et la documentation, Rotterdam, 34
— — Cinéma et de la Télévision (et tout autre Moyen Audiovisuel de Communication), Paris, 20
— pour l'Exploration de la Mer—CIEM, Copenhagen, 48
— Mondial de Management, The Hague, 26
— National de la Recherche Scientifique, Beirut, 899
— — — — et Technique, Brazzaville, 358
— — — recherches Canada, Ottawa, 244
— — des Recherches Scientifiques, Port-au-Prince, 629
— scientifique international de recherches sur les trypanosomiases et leur controle, Lagos, 41

Conseil Supérieur de statistique, Brussels, 152
— Suisse de la Musique, Basel, 1253
— — — Science, Bern, 1256
Consejo de Desarrollo Científico y Humanístico, Caracas, 1952
— — Rectores de Universidades Chilenas, Santiago, 322
— General de Colegios Médicos de España, Madrid, 1190
— — — — Oficiales de Farmacéuticos, Madrid, 1190
— — — — — Ingenieros Técnicos Agrícolas de España, Madrid, 1188
— Nacional de Ciencia y Tecnología—CONACYT, Mexico City, 930
— — — Colegios Oficiales de Doctores y Licenciados en Filosofía y Letras y en Ciencias, 1189
— — — Higiene, Montevideo, 1938
— — — Investigaciones Agrícolas, Caracas, 1953
— — — — Cientificas y Tecnicas, Buenos Aires, 67
— — — — — Tecnicas, Montevideo, 1939
— — — — — Tecnológicas (CONICIT), Caracas, 1953
— — — la Cultura (CONAC), Caracas, 1950
— — — — Universidad Peruana, 1036
— — — Universidades, Caracas, 1950
— — — Havana, 363
— — — para el Desarrollo de la Industria Nuclear, Caracas, 1954
— Peruano de la Federación Odontológica Latino-Americana, 1037
— Superior de Investigaciones Científicas (C.S.I.C.), Madrid, 1193
Conselho de Reitores das Universidades Brasileiras, Brasília, 179
— Federal de Biblioteconomia—CFB, Brasília, 179
— Nacional de Desenvolvimento Científico e Technológico, Rio de Janeiro, 184
Conservation des Musées de Poitiers, 470
— du Patrimoine Archéologique et Historique, Tunis, 1193
Conservatoire de musique, Agadir, 951
— — — Chefchaouen, 951
— — — Esch sur Alzette, 908
— — — Fès, 951
— — — Geneva, 1276
— — — Kebir, 951
— — — Larache, 951
— — — Lausanne, 1276
— — — Marrakech, 951
— — — Montreal, 319
— — — Neuchâtel, 1276
— — — Quebec, 319
— — — Safi, 951
— — — Taza, 951
— — — Tétouan, 951
— — — de la Ville de Luxembourg, 908
— — — et de Déclamation, Algiers, 59
— Tanger, Tangiers, 951
— et Académie de Musique, Fribourg, 1276
— — Jardin botanique de la Ville de Genève, 1258
— Municipal de Musique et de Déclamation, Oran, 59
— National d'Art Dramatique, Paris, 498
— — de Musique, de Danse, et d'Arts Populaires, Tunis, 1296
— — — — — et d'Art Dramatique, Rabat, 951
— — des Arts et Métiers, Paris, 493
— — — — — Nouméa, 500
— — Supérieur de Musique de Lyon, 498
— — — — Paris, 498
— of Music, Potchefstroom, 1173
— Royal de Musique d'Anvers, 170
— — — — de Bruxelles, 170
— — — — Gand, 170
— — — — Liège, 170

— — — — Mons, 170
Conservatorio Alejandro Garcia Caturla, Havana, 366
— Brasileiro de Música, 212
— de Música Amadeo Roldán, Havana, 366
— — — de la Universidad del Atlántico, Barranquilla, 357
— — — "José Luís Paz", Maracaibo, 1961
— — — "José María Rodriguez", 412
— — — del Tolima, 357
— — — "Manuel de Falla", Cadiz, 1223
— di Musica A. Boito, Parma, 796
— — — Gioacchino Rossini, Pesaro, 796
— — — Giuseppe Tartini, Trieste, 796
— — — G. Verdi, Milan, 796
— — — L. Cherubini, Florence, 796
— — — Niccoló Piccinni, Bari, 796
— — — S. Pietro a Maiella, Naples, 796
— — — "Santa Cecilia, Rome, 796
— — — V. Bellini, Palermo, 796
— Dramático e Musical de São Paulo, 212
— Italiano de Musica, Caracas, 1961
— Municipal de Musica "Manuel de Falla", Buenos Aires, 81
— Nacional, Lisbon, 1108
— — de Canto Orfeônico, Rio de Janeiro, 212
— — Música, Bogotá, 357
— — — — Guatemala City, 626
— — — — La Paz, 176
— — — — Lima, 1046
— — — — Mexico City, 946
— — — — Quito, 412
— — — — Santo Domingo, 406
— — — "Carlos López Buchardo", Buenos Aires, 81
— Nazionale di Musica "Benedetto Marcello", Venice, 796
— Professional de Musica y Escuela de Arte Dramático, Málaga, 1223
— — Municipal de Música, San Sebastian, 1203
— Statale di Musica, "C. Monteverdi", Bolzano, 796
— — — — G. B. Martini, 796
— — — — Giuseppe Verdi, 796
— — — — "P. L. da Palestrina", 796
— Superior de Música de Barcelona, 1223
— — — y Escuela de Arte Dramático y Danza, Córdoba, 1223
— — — — — de Arte Dramático, Murcia, 1223
— — — — — de Arte Dramático, Seville, 1223
— — — — — de arte Dramático y Danza de Valencia, 1223
Conservatorium voor Muziek-Nederland, Maastricht, 973
Conservatorul de Muzica "Ciprian Porumbescu", Bucharest, 1139
— "George Dima", Cluj, 1139
— "George Enescu", Iasi, 1139
Conservatory of Music, Holon, 753
— — — of Puerto Rico, Santurce, 1113
Consiglio Nazionale delle Ricerche (C.N.R.), Rome, 762
— per i Beni Culturali e Ambientali, Rome, 756
Consiliul National al Inginerilor și Tehnicienilor din R.S.R., Bucharest, 1122
— Ziariștilor din Uniunea Sindicatelor din Presă, Poligrafie și Edituri, Bucharest, 1122
Construction Industry Research and Information Association, London, 1448
— School, Darhan, 948
— Ulan Bator, 948
Contemporary Art Society, London, 1413
— — of Australia, 87
— China Institute, London, 1511
Continuing Education Centre, Lagos, 1000
Control Engineering Institute, Beijing, 333
— Theory Centre, Coventry, 1539
Converse College, Spartanburg, 1886

Cook County Law Library, Chicago, 1628
Cooper Union for the Advancement of Science and Art, 1811
— -Hewitt Museum, Smithsonian Institution's National Museum of Design, New York, 1637
Co-operative College of Malaysia, 919
— League of the Republic of China, Taipei, 341
Copernicus Astronomical Centre, Warsaw, 1068
Copperbelt Museum, Ndola, 1998
Coppin State College, Baltimore, 1742
Coptic Museum, Cairo, 417
Corinium Museum, Cirencester, 1468
Cork Historical and Archaeological Society, 730
— Public Museum, 732
Cornell College, Mount Vernon, Iowa, 1723
— University, 1811
— — Libraries, 1633
Cornwall County Library, Truro, 1453
Corpus Christi College, Cambridge, 1484
— — — Library, Cambridge, 1461
— — — Oxford, 1524
— — — Library, Oxford, 1463
— — State University, Texas, 1898
Cosmic Ray Research Institute, Tokyo, 856
Cotswold Countryside Collection, Northleach, 1468
Cotton Museum, Cairo, 417
— Research Corporation Library, Kampala, 1311
— — Institute, Gatooma, 2001
— — Giza, 414
— — Station (Namulonge), Kampala, 1311
— — Kibos, 878
— — Technological Research Laboratory (I.C.A.R.), Bombay, 672
Council for Agricultural Planning and Development, Taipei, 341
— — — Science and Technology, Ames, Iowa, 1599
— — Basic Education, Washington, D.C., 1604
— — British Archaeology, London, 1422
— — Co-ordination of Natural and Social Sciences, Vilnius, 1330
— — Cultural Co-operation, Strasbourg, 27
— — Studies, New Delhi, 661
— — Education in World Citizenship, London, 1418
— — Educational Technology for the United Kingdom, London, 1418
— — Environmental Conservation, London, 1430
— — European Studies, New York, 1603
— — International Organisations of Medical Sciences (CIOMS), Geneva, 37
— — National Academic Awards, London, 1419
— — Scientific and Industrial Research, Accra, 611
— — — — — (CSIR), Pretoria, 1157
— — — — — Library, Pretoria, 1163
— — Study of Productive Forces, Alma-Ata, 1328
— — the Accreditation of Correspondence Colleges, London, 1418
— — — Care of Churches, London, 1411
— — — Protection of Rural England, London, 1411
— of Adult Education, Melbourne, 88
— — Legal Education, London, 1416
— — National Library and Information Associations, 1601
— — Scientific and Industrial Research, New Delhi, 664
— — — Centre of Biological Research of the USSR Academy of Sciences, Moscow region, 1319
— — State Governments, Lexington, 1603
— — the U.S.S.R. Scientific Medical Societies, Moscow, 1344

— on Conservation and Restoration of Cultural Monuments, Baku, 1325
— — — — — Cultural Monuments, Erevan, 1324
— — — of Nature, Erevan, 1324
— — Co-ordination of Economy, Erevan, 1324
— — — — Science Investigations, Ashkhabad, 1332
— — — Scientific Activities of Academies of the Union Republics, Moscow, 1323, 1324
— — — — of Research and Higher Educational Institutions in the Armenian S.S.R., Erevan, 1324
— — — Research, Baku, 1325
— — Cybernetics, Erevan, 1324
— — — Riga, 1330
— — Exploitation of Scientific Equipment, Baku, 1325
— — Foreign Relations, Inc., New York, 1603
— — International Collaboration on Space, Moscow, 1323
— — Libraries, Moscow, 1323
— — — Riga, 1330
— — Library Resources, Washington, D.C., 1601
— — Museums, Moscow, 1323
— — Problems of Machine-Building, Erevan, 1324
— — Scientific Instrument-Making, Moscow, 1323
— — Semiconductors, Erevan, 1324
— — the History of Natural Sciences and Technology, Erevan, 1324
— — — — — Sciences and Technology, Tbilisi, 1327
— — — Preservation of Cultural Monuments, Tbilisi, 1327
Counselling Centre, Vatican City, 1946
County Museum, Armagh, 1554
Cours Universitaires d'Été, Paris, 495
Courtauld Institute Galleries, London, 1465
— — of Art, 1551
Coventry Public Library, 1453
— (Lanchester) Polytechnic, 1540
Cox, G. S., Medical Research Institute, Philadelphia, 1880
Cracow Technical University, 1089
Crafts Council, London, 1412
— — of Western India, Bombay, 660
— Museum, New Delhi, 674
Craigflower Manor Historic Museum, Victoria, B.C., 249
Cranbrook Academy of Art, Bloomfield Hills, 1761
— Institute of Science, 1611
Cranfield Institute of Technology, 1553
Creative Arts Centre, Kingston, Jamaica, 801
Creighton University, Omaha, Neb., 1792
Crimean Astro-Physical Observatory, 1318
— M. I. Kalinin Agricultural Institute, 1369
— State Medical Institute, Simferopol, 1383
Crnogorska Akademija Nauka I Umjetnosti, Titograd, 1966
Croatian Library Association, Zagreb, 1970
Cromwell College, Brisbane, 109
Crop Breeding and Cultivation Institute, Beijing, 333
— — Institute, Salisbury, Zimbabwe, 2001
— Science Society of the Philippines, Laguna, 1047
— — — Zimbabwe, Salisbury, 2000
Crops Institute, Beijing, 333
— Research Institute, Kumasi, 611
Croydon Public Libraries, 1452
Csontváry Múzeum, Pecs, 644
Çukurova Üniversitesi, Adana, 1304
Culgoora Solar Observatory (C.S.I.R.O.), New South Wales, 93
Cultural Institute, Malta, 921
— — Rangoon, 228
Culver-Stockton College, Canton, Mo., 1786
Cumberland College, Williamsburg, 1735

— — of Health Sciences, Lidcombe, N.S.W., 112
Cumhuriyet Universitesi, Sivas, 1305
Cuming Museum (Borough of Southwark), London, 1465
Curaçao Museum, Curaçao, 975
— Public School of Music, Curaçao, 975
Curriculum Development and Instructional Materials Centre, Nsukka, 1001
— Research and Development Center, Gifu-ken, 826
Currier Gallery of Art, Manchester, N.H., 1637
Curso de Biblioteconomia e Documentação, Rio de Janeiro, 210
Curtis Institute of Music, Philadelphia, 1869
Cusanuswerk Bischöfliche Studienförder-ung, Bonn, 520
Cuttington University College, Liberia, 905
Cyclotron Unit (M.R.C.), London, 1443
Cyprus College of Art, 368
— Forestry College, Prodromos, 368
— Geographical Association, Nicosia, 367
— Historical Museum and Archives, Nicosia, 367
— Museum, 367
— Research Centre, Nicosia, 367
Cyrene Museum (Shatat), 906
Cyril and Methodius University of Veliho Tărnovo, Sofia, 223
Czartoryski Collection, Cracow, 1076
— Library and Archives, Cracow, 1076
Czechoslovak Academy of Agriculture, Prague, 373
— — — Sciences, Prague, 369
Czestochowa Technical University, 1087
Czóbel Múzeum, Szentendre, 644

D

Dacca Museum, 143
— Polytechnic Institute, Dacca, 145
Daching Petroleum College, Anda, 335
Dachverband Wissenschaftlicher Gesellschaften der Agrar-, Forst-, Ernährungs-, Veterinär- und Umweltforschung e.V., Munich, 517
Daemen College, Amherst, N.Y., 1815
Dag Hammarskjöld Foundation, Stockholm, 1236
— — Library, New York, 1630
Daghestan Agricultural Institute, 1369
— Branch of the U.S.S.R. Academy of Science, Makhach-kala, 1322
— V.I. Lenin State University, 1361
— Museum of Fine Arts, 1353
— State Medical Institute, 1383
Daheshite Museum and Library, Beirut, 900
Daigoji Reihoden, Kyoto, 821
Dairy Society International (DSI), Washington, D.C., 16
Daito Bunka University, Tokyo, 862
Dakota State College, Madison, 1887
— Wesleyan University, 1888
Dal Research Farm for Fur-Bearing Animals, Oslo, 1018
Dalhousie University, Halifax, N.S., 266
— — Library System, Halifax, N.S., 247
Dallas Historical Society, 1605
— Public Library, 1627
Damanhour Municipal Library, 416
Damascus Institute of Technology, 1279
— Oriental Institute of Music, 1279
Damat Ibrahim Paşa Library, 1300
Damjanich János Múzeum, 644
Dana College, Blair, 1792
Danchi-Nogaku, Kenkyu-Kai, 803
DANDOK, Copenhagen, 392
Danish Institute, Edinburgh, 1424
Dänisches Institut, Dortmund, 521
— — für Information und kulturen Austausch, Zürich, 1255
Dan Kook University, Seoul, 889

Danmarks Biblioteksforening, Copenhagen, 390
— Biblioteksskole, Copenhagen, 401
— Biblioteksskoles Aalborgafdeling, 401
— Farmaceutiske Højskole, Copenhagen, 401
— — Hojskoles Bibliotek, 394
— — Selskab, Copenhagen, 391
— Fiskeri- og Havundersøgelser, Charlottenlund, 393
— Forskningsbiblioteksforening, Copenhagen, 390
— Geologiske Undersøgelse, Copenhagen, 393
— Ingeniørakademi, Copenhagen, 400
— Journalisthøjskole, Århus, 400
— Jurist-og Økonomforbund, Copenhagen, 390
— Laererhøjskole, Copenhagen, 401
— Laererhøjskoles Bibliotek, 394
— Naturfredningsforening, Copenhagen, 391
— Naturvidenskabelige Samfund, Lyngby, 391
— Paedagogiske Bibliotek, Copenhagen, 394
— — Institut, Copenhagen, 393
— Statistik, Copenhagen, 393
— Tekniske Bibliotek, Lyngby, 394
— — Museum, Elsinore, 395
— Veterinaer- og Jordbrugsbibliotek, Copenhagen, 394
Dansk Agronomforening, Copenhagen, 389
— Billedhuggersamfund, 389
— Botanisk Forening, Copenhagen, 391
— Byplanlaboratorium, Copenhagen, 389
— Farmaceutforening, Copenhagen, 391
— Forening for Hjem og Skole, Copenhagen, 390
— Forfatterforening, Copenhagen, 391
— Geologisk Forening, Copenhagen, 391
— Huflidsselskab, Copenhagen, 392
— Ingeniørforening, Copenhagen, 392
— Komponist-Forening, Copenhagen, 389
— Korforening, Copenhagen, 389
— Kriminalistforening, Copenhagen, 390
— Kulturhistorisk Museumforening, Copenhagen, 390
— Medicinsk Selskab, Hellerup, 391
— Mejeristforening, Odense, 389
— Naturhistorisk Forening, Copenhagen, 391
— Ornithologisk Forening, Copenhagen, 391
— Psykologforening, Copenhagen, 392
— Selskab for Oldtids- og Middelalderforskning, 390
— Skovforening, Copenhagen, 389
— Tandlægeforening, Copenhagen, 391
— Tonekunster Forening, Copenhagen, 389
— Veterinaerhistorisk Samfund, Birkerød, 389
Danske Arkitekters Landsforbund, Copenhagen, 389
— Bibelselskab, Copenhagen, 392
— Historiske Forening, Copenhagen, 390
— Komité for Historikernes Internationale Samarbejde, Aarhus, 393
— Kunsthåndvaerkeres Landssammenslutning, Copenhagen, 389
— Meteorologiske Institut, Charlottenlund, 393
— Selskab, Copenhagen, 391
— — i Reykjavík, 656
— Sprog- og Litteraturselskab, Copenhagen, 391
Dar al-Kutub al-Wataniah, Homs, 1277
— — al-Wataniya, Riyadh, 1142
Dar es Salaam Technical College, 1282
Daresbury Laboratory, Lancs., 1446
Darling Downs Institute of Advanced Education, Toowoomba, 114
Dartington Hall Trust, 1420
Dartmouth College, Hanover, N.H., 1795
Darwin College, Cambridge, 1485
— Community College, Casuarina, N.T., 113
Data Processing Centre, Kyoto, 836

INDEX OF INSTITUTIONS

Dates and Palm Research Centre, Baghdad, 725
David Davies Memorial Institute of International Studies, London, 1416
— Dunlap Observatory of the University of Toronto, 245
— Horowitz Research Institute for Developing Countries, Tel-Aviv, 750
— Lipscomb College, Nashville, Tenn., 1889
— Livingstone Institute of Overseas Development Studies, Glasgow, 1531
— Owen Centre for Population Growth Studies, Cardiff, 1536
Davidson College, N.C., 1825
Davis and Elkins College, Elkins, 1930
Dawood College of Engineering and Technology, Karachi, 1029
Dayton and Montgomery County Public Library, Dayton, 1627
Dazhai Agricultural College, Xiyang, 339
De La Salle University, Manila, 1052
— Young (M. H.) Memorial Museum, San Francisco, 1639
Deakin University, Geelong, 100
Dean Savage Reference Library, Lichfield, 1459
Debrecen University of Agrarian Sciences, 653
— — — Medicine, 649
Debreceni Agrártudományi Egyetem, 653
— — — Kutató Intézet, Debrecen, 653
— Orvostudományi Egyetem, 649
Deccan College Postgraduate and Research Institute, 668
Defence Ministry's Science Research Institute, Seoul, 886
— Services Academy, Maymyo, 229
Defiance College, Ohio, 1843
Deichmanske Bibliotek, Oslo, 1010
Deir ez-Zor Museum, 1277
Delaware State College, Dover, 1686
— Valley College of Science and Agriculture, Doylestown, Penn., 1869
Delegationen för vetenskaplig och teknisk informationsförsörjning, Stockholm, 1235
Delft University of Technology, 972
Delhi Fort Museum, Red Fort, 674
— Public Library, 677
Delta Regional Primate Research Center, New Orleans, 1741
— State University, Cleveland, Miss., 1784
Demeure Historique, Paris, 448
"Democritus" Nuclear Research Centre, Athens, 617
Denison University, Granville, Ohio, 1843
Denki Gakkai, Tokyo, 812
Denshi Tsushin Gakkai, Tokyo, 812
Dental Association of Zimbabwe, Salisbury, 2000
— Board, Dublin, 731
— Research Institute, Johannesburg, 1182
— — Tygerberg, 1156
— Unit (M.R.C.), Bristol, 1443
Dentists Association, Hanoi, 1962
Denver Art Museum, 1637
— Museum of Natural History, 1637
— Public Library, 1626
— Research Institute, 1677
Departamento Administrativo Nacional de Estadística, Bogotá, 348
— de Antropología e Historia de Nayarit, 926
— — Bibliotecas, Universidad de Antioquia, Medellín, 349
— — — — Cartagena, 349
— — — — del Cauca, Popayán, 349
— — y Publicaciones, Mexico City, 931
— — Conservação Ambiental, Rio de Janeiro, 184
— — Estudios Etnográficos y Coloniales, Santa Fé, 68

— — — Históricos Navales, Buenos Aires, 67
— — Música del Centro Nacional de Artes, San Salvador, 423
— — Papirología, Madrid, 1208
— — Perfeccionamiento y Prospección Educativa, Madrid, 1198
— — Pesquisas e Experimentação Agropecuárias, Rio de Janeiro, 182
— — Nacional da Produção Mineral, Brasília, 185
— — de Meteorologia, Rio de Janeiro, 185
— — — Museus e Monumentos, Luanda, 61
— — — Protección Vegetal, Madrid, 1198
Département d'Economie Appliquée, Brussels, 159
— de Géologie et Mines du Burundi, Bujumbura, 230
Department of Agricultural and Scientific Research and Extension, Amman, 875
— Agriculture Research Sections, Brunei, 213
— — Antiquities, Amman, 875
— — — Fezzan, 906
— — — Tripoli, 906
— — — and Museums, Aden, 1965
— — — — Jerusalem, 738
— — — — Kuwait City, 897
— — — — Riyadh, 1142
— — — Eastern Region, Beida, 906
— — Archaeology, Colombo, 1225
— — Biogenic Amines, Łódz, 1069
— — Commerce Library, Washington, 1624
— — Cultural Affairs, Colombo, 1225
— — Culture and Arts, Amman, 875
— — Defence: Defence Science and Technology Organisation, Canberra, 94
— — Education and Science Library, London, 1451
— — — Library, Hato Rey, 1110
— — — — Woden, A.C.T., 95
— — Embryology, Baltimore, 1619
— — Energy Library, London, 1450
— — Ethnography and Art, Kishinev, 1331
— — Extra-Mural Studies, Hong Kong, 1561
— — — Kingston, Jamaica, 801
— — Fine Arts, Rangoon, 228
— — Foreign Languages, Kishinev, 1331
— — Geology Museum, University of Alberta, 249
— — Health and Human Services Libraries, Washington, D.C., 1625
— — — Social Security Library, London, 1625
— — Historical Research, Rangoon, 228
— — Industry Ashdown House Library, London, 1450
— — Justice Library, Washington, 1625
— — Labor Library, Washington, 1625
— — Marine Biology, Bergen, 1014
— — Medical Research, Rangoon, 228
— — Metallurgy, Ministry of Mines, Salisbury, Zimbabwe, 2001
— — Mineral Resources, Bangkok, 1283
— — Mines and Geology, Kabul, 52
— — National Archives, Colombo, 1226
— — — Education Library, Pretoria, 1163
— — Philosophy, Kishinev, 1331
— — — and Law, Kishinev, 1331
— — Plant Biology, Stanford, 1619
— — — Physiology, Cracow, 1069
— — — Protection, Karachi, 1022
— — Psychology and Educational Science, Coímbra, 1105
— — Religious Affairs, Rangoon, 228
— — Science, Bangkok, 1283
— — — Information, Kishinev, 1331
— — Scientific and Industrial Research, Baghdad, 725
— — — — Wellington, N.Z., 979
— — — — — Central Library, Wellington, 981

— — Information, Ulan Bator, 947
— — State Library, Washington, D.C., 1625
— — Teaching Technology, Jyväskylä, 436
— — Terrestrial Magnetism, Washington, D.C., 1619
— — the Interior Libraries, Washington, 1625
— — Treasury Library, Washington, 1625
— — Trade Library, London, 1450
— — — Marine Library, London, 1450
— — — Statistics and Market Intelligence Library, London, 1450
— — Veterinary Services: Tsetse and Trypanosomiasis Control Branch, Salisbury, 2001
— — Wild Life Conservation, Colombo, 1225
Departments of Industry and Trade, Common Services: Libraries, London, 1450
— — the Environment and Transport Library, London, 1451
DePaul University, Chicago, 1703
DePauw University, Greencastle, 1716
Deprem Arastirma Enstitüsü, Ankara, 1299
Derbyshire County Library, Matlock, 1453
Deree College, Athens, 623
Déri Múzeum, Debrecen, 644
Dermatology Association, Hanoi, 1962
— Institute, Jiangsu, 333
Desai Memorial Library, Nairobi, 879
Desert Ecological Research Unit of the Council for Scientific and Industrial Research, Walvis Bay, 953
— Institute, Ashkhabad, 1332
— Locust Control Organization for Eastern Africa, Addis Ababa, 424
— — — — — Africa, Nairobi, 878
— Research Institute, Cairo, 414
— — — Las Vegas, 1794
Design Council, London, 1413
Detroit Institute of Arts, 1637
— — Technology, 1761
— Public Library, 1626
Deutsch-Mexikanisches Kultur-Institut Alexander von Humboldt, Mexico City, 926
-Paraguayisches Kulturinstitut, Asunción, 1034
-Schweizerisches PEN-Zentrum, Basel, 1255
Deutsche Akademie der Naturforscher Leopoldina, Halle/Sale, 505
— für Städtebau und Landesplanung, Hannover, 528
— Bibliothek, Frankfurt, 535
— Botanische Gesellschaft, Göttingen, 523
— Bücherei, Leipzig, 507
— Bunsen-Gesellschaft für physikalische Chemie e.V., Frankfurt, 523
— Dermatologische Gesellschaft, Cologne, 521
— Film- und Fernsehakademie, Berlin (West), 608
— Forschungsanstalt für Lebensmittelchemie, Munich, 533
— Forschungsgemeinschaft, Bonn, 526
— Forschungs- und Versuchsanstalt für Luft und Raumfahrt e.V. (DFVLR), Cologne, 533
— Gemmologische Gesellschaft e.V., 525
— Geologische Gesellschaft, Hanover, 523
— Geophysikalische Gesellschaft, Clausthal, 523
— Gesellschaft für Allergieforschung, Tübingen, 531
— — allgemeine und angewandte Entomologie e.V., Kiel, 523
— — Anästhesiologie und Intensivmedizin, 521
— — angewandte Optik, Wetzlar, 521
— — Anthropologie und Humangenetik, Göttingen, 524
— — Arbeitsschutz e.V., Frankfurt, 521

— — — Asienkunde e.V., Hamburg, 524
— — — Auswärtige Politik, Bonn, 519
— — — Bauingenieurwesen, Karlsruhe, 525
— — — Betriebswirtschaft e.V., Berlin (West), 519, 529
— — — Bevölkerungswissenschaft e.V., Wiesbaden, 524
— — — Biophysik e.V., Frankfurt, 523
— — — chemisches Apparatewesen e.V. (DECHEMA), Frankfurt, 525
— — — Chirurgie, Munich, 521
— — — Dokumentation e.V., Frankfurt, 518
— — — Elektronenmikroskopie e.V., 523
— — — Endokrinologie, Hannover, 521
— — — Ernährung e.V., Frankfurt, 521
— — — Friedens- und Konfliktforschung, Bonn, 530
— — — Geschichte der Medizin, Naturwissenschaft und Technik e.V., Berlin, 521
— — — Gynäkologie und Geburtshilfe, Frankfurt, 522
— — — Hals-Nasen-Ohren-Heilkunde, Kopf-und Hals-Chirurgie, Bonn, 522
— — — Herz- und Kreislaufforschung, Bad Nauheim, 531
— — — Holzforschung, Munich, 528
— — — Hopfenforschung, Wolnzach, 528
— — — Hygiene und Mikrobiologie, Lübeck, 522
— — — Innere Medizin, Wiesbaden, 522
— — — Kartographie e.V., Dortmund, 520
— — — Kinderheilkunde, Essen, 522
— — — Kulturmorphologie, Frankfurt, 524
— — — Kybernetik, Seeweisen, 523
— — — Luft- und Raumfahrt e.V. (DGLR), Cologne, 525
— — — Metallkunde, Oberrursel/Taunus, 525
— — — Mineralölwissenschaft und Kohlchemie e.V., Hamburg, 525
— — — Moor- und Torfkunde, Hannover-Buchholz, 532
— — — Neurochirurgie, Essen, 522
— — — Nuklearmedizin, Hannover, 522
— — — Operations Research—DGOR, Henstedt-Ulzberg, 523
— — — Orthopädie und Traumatologie, Kassel, 522
— — — Ortung und Navigation e.V., Düsseldorf, 520
— — — Osteuropakunde e.V., Berlin (West), 519
— — — Pathologie, 522
— — — Photogrammetrie, Hanover, 525
— — — Photographie, Cologne, 518
— — — Physikalische Medizin und Rehabilitation, Sendenhorst, 522
— — — Plastische und Wiederherstellungs-Chirurgie, Berlin (West), 522
— — — Psychiatrie und Nervenheilkunde, München, 522
— — — Psychologie, Trier, 524
— — — Psychotherapie, Psychosomatik und Tiefenpsychologie, Hamburg, 522
— — — Rechtsmedizin, Mainz, 522
— — — Rheumatologie, Bad Bramstedt, 522
— — — Sexualforschung e.V., Frankfurt, 531
— — — Sozialmedizin, Heidelberg, 522
— — — Soziologie, Munich, 524
— — — Sprachwissenschaft, Köln, 521
— — — Versicherungsmathematik, Cologne (Deutscher Aktuar Verein), 525
— — — Völkerrecht, Heidelburg, 519
— — — Volkskunde e.V., Tubingen, 524
— — — Zahn-, Mund- und Kieferheilkunde, Düsseldorf, 522
— — — Zerstorungsfreie Prüfung e.V., Berlin (West), 525
— — — Züchtungskunde e.V., Bonn, 523
— — zur Förderung der Rehabilitation, Aachen, 522
— Glastechnische Gesellschaft, Frankfurt, 525
— Keramische Gesellschaft, 525
— Krebsgesellschaft e.V., Essen, 531
— Landwirtschafts-Gesellschaft, Frankfurt, 517
— Malakozoologische Gesellschaft, Frankfurt, 523
— Mathematikervereinigung e.V., Freiburg, 523
— Meteorologische Gesellschaft, Munich, 524
— Mineralogische Gesellschaft, Regensburg, 524
— Morgenländische Gesellschaft, Berlin (West), 524
— Mozart Gesellschaft e.V., Augsburg, 518
— Ophthalmologische Gesellschaft, Heidelberg, 522
— Orient-Gesellschaft, Berlin (West), 524
— Ornithologen-Gesellschaft, Möggingen, 523
— Pharmakologische Gesellschaft, Munich, 524
— Pharmazeutische Gesellschaft, Darmstadt, 524
— Physikalische Gesellschaft e.V., Bad Honnef, 524
— Physiologische Gesellschaft, Munich, 522
— Phytomedizinische Gesellschaft e.V., Göttingen, 523
— Psychoanalytische Gesellschaft, Munich, 522
— — Vereinigung, Berlin (West), 522
— Quartärvereinigung, Hannover, 520
— Röntgengesellschaft für Medizinische Radiologie, Strahlenbiologie und Nuklearmedizin e.V., Munich, 522
— Shakespeare-Gesellschaft West, Bochum, 521
— Staatsbibliothek, Berlin (East), 506
— Statistische Gesellschaft, Cologne, 519
— Tropenmedizinische Gesellschaft, Wuppertal, 522
— Vereinigung für Politische Wissenschaft, Hamburg, 519
— Veterinärmedizinische Gesellschaft, Giessen, 518
— Volkswirtschaftliche Gesellschaft e.V., 519
— Zoologische Gesellschaft, 523
Deutscher Akademischer Austauschdienst (DAAD), 522
— Architekten- und Ingenieur-Verband e.V., 518
— Beton-Verein, 525
— Forstwirtschaftsrat e.V., 518
— Juristentag e.V., 519
— Kälte- und Klimatechnischer Verein, Stuttgart, 525
— Komponisten-Verband, Berlin (West), 518
— Markscheider Verein, 525
— Museumsbund, e.V., Frankfurt, 518
— Nautischer Verein von 1868, Hamburg, 520
— Verband für Materialprüfung, Berlin (West), 525
— — Schweisstechnik e.V., 525
— — Wohnungswesen, Städtebau und Raumplanung e.V., Köln-Mülheim, 518
— technisch-wissenschaftlicher Vereine, 525
— Verein des Gas- und Wasserfaches e.V., 525
— — für Kunstwissenschaft, 518
— — Vermessungswesen, 525
— Volkschochschulverband, Bonn, 519
— Wasser- Wirtschafts- und Wasserkraft-Verband, 520

— Wetterdienst, 532
— Zentralausschuss für Chemie, 524
Deutsches Adelsarchiv, Marburg, 539
— Archäologisches Institut, Abteilung Athen, 623
— — — Berlin (West), 530
— — — Cairo, 415
— — — Istanbul, 1299
— — — Madrid, 1189
— — — Rome, 757
— Atomforum e.V., Bonn, 524
— Bibel-Archiv, Hamburg, 539
— Bibliotheksinstitut, Berlin (West), 518
— Buch- und Schriftmuseum der Deutschen Bücherei, Leipzig, 510
— Bucharchiv München (Institut für Buchwissenschaften), Munich, 540
— Historisches Institut, Paris, 448
— Hyderographisches Institut, 532
— Institut, Lisbon, 1098
— — für Fernstudien, Tübingen, 606
— — — Internationale Pädagogische Forschung, Frankfurt, 530
— — — Normung e.V., Berlin (West), 525
— — — Wirtschaftsforschung (Institut für Konjunkturforschung), Berlin (West), 528
— — zur Förderung des industriellen Führungsnachwuchses, Cologne, 529
— Krankenhausinstitut, Düsseldorf, 563
— Kultur-Institut, Alexandria, 414
— — Copenhagen, 391
— — Naples, 759
— — Tokyo, 806
— — Tunis, 1295
— Literaturarchiv, Marbach a. Neckar, 536
— Museum, Munich, 544
— Orient-Institut, Hamburg, 524
— Spracharchiv im Institut für deutsche Sprache, Mannheim, 539
— Textilforschungszentrum Nord-West e.V., Krefeld, 533
— Volksliedarchiv, Freiburg i. Br., 539
— Wirtschaftswissenschaftliches Institut für Fremdenverkehr an der Universität München, Munich, 529
— Wollforschungsinstitut, Aachen, 548
— Zentrum, Göteborg, 1236
Development Economics Research Centre, Coventry, 1539
— Psychology Unit (M.R.C.), London, 1444
— Research Institute, Sapporo, 863
— — Tilburg, 973
Developmental Neurobiology Unit (M.R.C.), London, 1444
Devlet Sulşleri Araştırma Dairesi, Ankara, 1299
Devon Library Services, Exeter, 1453
Dewan Bahasa dan Pustaka, Kuala Lumpur, 914
Diabetes-Forschungsinstitut an der Universität Düsseldorf, 563
Diaspora Research Institute, Tel-Aviv, 750
Dibrugarh University, Assam, 684
Dickens Fellowship, 1426
Dickinson College, 1869
— State College, North Dakota, 1839
Dillard University, 1737
"Dimitr Blagoev" Higher Institute of National Economy, Varna, 227
— — Museum, Sofia, 221
Dimokriteio Panepistimio Thrakis, Komotini, 621
Dinas Geodesi Jawatan Topografi T.N.I.-A.D., Bandung, 710
— Inteijen Medan & Geografi Jawatan Topografi T.N.I.-A.D., 709
Diocesan College of Montreal, 277
Diözesanarchiv Wien, Vienna, 127
Diplomatische Akademie, Vienna, 124
Direcção dos Serviços de Geologia e Minas, Maputo, 952
— Geral de Geologia e Minas, Lisbon, 1101

Direcção Provincial dos Serviços de Geologie e Minas de Angola, Luanda, 61
Dirección de Bibliotecas Municipales, 69
—— Cartografía Nacional del Ministerio de Obras Públicas, 1953
—— Geología del Ministerio de Energía y Minas, Caracas, 1954
—— Minas del Ministerio de Minas e Hidrocarburos, Caracas, 1954
— General de Arquitectura y Tecnología de la Edificación, Madrid, 1188
—— Bellas Artes, Santo Domingo, 406
—— Bibliotecas, Archivos y Museos, Santiago, 326
—— Desarrollo Urbanístico del Ministerio del Desarrollo Urbano, Caracas, 1953
—— Energía Nuclear, Guatemala City, 624
—— Estadística, Mexico City, 926
—— — y Censos, Montevideo, 1939
—— — — San José, 359
—— — — San Salvador, 422
—— Geología, Minas y Petróleo, San José, 359
—— — y Minas, Quito, 407
—— Hidrocarburos, Quito, 407
—— Meteorología del Peru, 1038
—— Relaciones Culturales. Madrid, 1190
—— — Educativas, Científicas y Culturales, Mexico City, 926
—— del Servicio Meteorológico Nacional, Tacubaya, 926
— Nacional de Meteorología del Uruguay, Montevideo, 1939
—— del Patrimonio Histórico, Panama, 1031
Direction de l'Action Culturelle et de la Jeunesse et des Sports, Paris, 466
—— la Géologie, Rabat, 949
—— — — et de la Prospection Minière, Abidjan, 798
—— — — des Mines (D.G.M.) Ouagadougou, 1937
—— — Recherche Agronomique, Rabat, 949
— des Archives de France, 460
—— Mines, de la Géologie et des Hydrocarbures, Cotonou, 172
—— — et de l'Industrie, Nouakchott, 922
—— — — la Géologie, Sous-Direction de la Géologie, Algiers, 57
—— Musées de France, 466
—— — l'Archéologie et des Monuments et Sites Historiques, Algiers, 58
—— — Nice, 469
—— — Services d'Archives de Paris, 462
—— — Techniques, Rabat, 949
— du Livre, Paris, 460
— Nationale de la Météorologie, Bamako, 920
Directorate of Agricultural Research (Pretoria), 1159
—— Archives and Libraries, Dacca, 143
—— Museums of Koprivština, 221
—— the Omani Heritage, Muscat, 1018
Direktion Bau und Denkmalpflege, Weimar, 510
— Gärten und Parke, Weimar, 510
— Öffentlichkeitsarbeit, Weimar, 510
— Verwaltung und Werkstätten, Weimar, 510
Direktorat Meteorologi dan Geofisik, Jakarta, 710
— Penyelidikan Masalah Air, Bandung, 710
—— — Bangunan, Bandung, 709
—— Perlindungan dan Pembinaan Peninggalan Sejarah dan Purbakala, Jakarta, 709
Direzione Belle Arti e Storia, Genoa, 770
— Civici Musei d'Arte e Storia, Brescia, 769
— delle Attività del Comitato Nazionale per l'Energia Nucleare a Ispra, Rome, 764

— Musei Civici d'Arte Moderna, Ferrara, 770
Diş Hekimliği Yüksek Okulu, Istanbul, 1309
Disaster Prevention Research Institute, Kyoto, 836
Discoteca di Stato, Rome, 768
Disraeli Museum, High Wycombe, 1469
District Historical Museum, Berat, 55
—— — Fier, 55
—— — Përmet, 56
—— — Shkodër, 56
—— — Vlorë, 56
—— Museums, Cyprus, 368
Divadelní ústav, Prague, 374
Divine Word University, Tacloban City, 1052
Divisão de Biblioteca e Documentação da Universidade de São Paulo, 188
—— Discoteca e Biblioteca de Música de São Paulo, 188
—— Fitotecnia do D.P.E.A., São Paulo, 182
Division de l'Agriculture, Bern, 1258
—— l'inventaire du patrimoine culturel, Rabat, 949
— des Musées, des Sites, de l'Archéologie et des Monuments Historiques, Rabat, 950
— du Théâtre, da la Musique et du Folklore, Rabat, 949
— of Agricultural and Livestock Services Training, Zaria, 995
—— Agriculture, Kuala Lumpur, 914
—— Forest Products Research, Kitwe, 1997
—— — Research, Kitwe, 1997
—— Logic, Methodology and Philosophy of Science, International Union of the History and Philosophy of Science, Oxford, 9
—— Research, Institute of Economics, Rangoon, 228
—— the History of Science, International Union of the History and Philosophy of Science, Edinburgh, 8
División de Documentación e Información Educativa, Ministerio de Educación Nacional, Bogotá, 349
Diyarbakir Universitesi, 1305
Djambul Institute of Irrigation, Land Reclamation and Construction, 1372
Djanashiya, S.N., State Museum of Georgia, Tbilisi, 1327
Dneprodzerzhinsk Arsenichev Institute of Metallurgy, 1378
— Museum of Town History, 1355
Dnepropetrovsk Agricultural Institute, 1369
— Artem Mining Institute, 1379
— Civil Engineering Institute, 1379
— F. E. Dzerzhinsky Institute of Chemical Technology, 1378
— Historical Museum, 1355
— Institute of Epidemiology, Microbiology and Hygiene (Gamaley Institute), 1385
—— — Railway Engineers, 1389
— Metallurgical Institute, 1379
— State Art Museum, 1353
—— Medical Institute, 1383
— University of the Three Hundredth Anniversary of the Union of Russia and the Ukraine, 1361
Doane College, Crete, Nebraska, 1793
Dobó István Vármuzeum, Eger, 644
Doboku Gakkai, 812
— Kenkyujo, Tokyo, 817
Dr. Alidina Memorial Library and Ismaili Archives, Karachi, 1023
— Bhau Daji Lad Museum, Bombay, 675
— Friedrich Tessmann-Sammlung, Vienna, 119
— Mahmud Hussain Library, University of Karachi, 1023
— Veeger Institute, Nijmegen, 970

— Williams's Library, London, 1456
Documentatiecentrum Zeeuws Deltagebied, Middelburg, 965
Documentation Centre, Zagreb, 1993
— Research and Training Centre, Bangalore, 667
Dokuchayev Central Soil Museum, Leningrad, 1358
— V. V., Institute of Soil Science, Moscow, 1388
Dokumentationsabteilung und Bibliothek der Westdeutschen Rektorenkonferenz, Bonn-Bad Godesberg, 538
Dolmetsch Foundation, Godalming, 1414
Dom Jana Matejki, Cracow, 1076
Dominican Academy, Santo Domingo, 403
—— of History, Santo Domingo, 403
Dominion Astrophysical Observatory, Victoria, B.C., 245
Don Agricultural Institute, Rostov Region, 1369
— Bosco College, Newton, N.J., 1796
—— International Institute, Turin, 1946
—— Severino Agricultural College, Cavite, 1060
Doncaster Museum and Art Gallery, 1468
Donetsk A. M. Gorky Medical Institute, 1383
— Institute of Industrial Physiology, 1386
—— — Soviet Trade, 1373
— Museum of Art, 1353
— Musical-Pedagogical Institute, 1387
— Physical Engineering Institute, 1333
— Polytechnic Institute, 1374
— Scientific Research Institute of Traumatology and Orthopaedics, 1385
— State University, 1361
Dong A University, Busan, 889
Dongguk University, Seoul, 889
—— Library, Seoul, 886
Dongsaphangmeuk Library, Vientiane, 898
Donish Institute of History, Dushanbe, 1332
Donner, W. H., Center for Radiology, Philadelphia, 1880
Dookie Agricultural College, 115
Dordt College, Sioux Center, 1723
Dorset County Library, Dorchester, 1453
—— Museum and Natural History and Archaeological Society, 1468
Doshisha University, Kyoto, 862
— Women's University, Kyoto, 862
Doshitsu Kogakkai, Tokyo, 812
Dostoyevsky House-Museum, Leningrad, 1357
— (F.) Museum, Moscow, 1357
Dove Cottage and Wordsworth Museum (The Dove Cottage Trust), Grasmere, 1468
Downing College, Cambridge, 1485
—— Library, Cambridge, 1461
Downstate Medical Center at Brooklyn (New York City), 1821
Dozenal Society of America, Garden City, N.Y., 1612
Drake University, 1723
Dramatiki Scholi, 623
Drammen Folkebibliotek, 1010
Drammens Museum, 1011
Drew University, Madison, N.J., 1797
Drexel University, Philadelphia, 1869
Dropsie University, Philadelphia, 1869
Drury College, Springfield, Mo., 1786
Društvo Bibliotekara BiH, Sarajevo, 1970
— Istoričara BiH, Sarajevo, 1970
— Ljekara BiH, Sarajevo, 1971
— Matematičara, Fizičara i Astronoma BiH, Sarajevo, 1971
— Matematikov, Fizikov in Astronomov S.R.S., Ljubljana, 1970
— na Istoričarite na Umetnosta od S.R. Makedonija, Skopje, 1971
— Kompozitorite na S.R. Makedonija, Skopje, 1971

— — Likovnite Umetnici na Makedonija, Skopje, 1971
— — Literaturnite Preveducači na S.R. Makedonija, Skopje, 1971
— — Matematičarite i Fizičarite od S.R. Makedonija, Skopje, 1971
— — Muzejskite Rabotnici na Makedonija, Skopje, 1971
— — Pisatelite na S.R. Makedonija, Skopje, 1971
— Slovenski Skladateljev, Ljubljana, 1970
— za Filozofija, Sociologija i Politikologija na S.R. Makedonija, Skopje, 1971
— — Proučavanje i Unapredenje Pomorstva Jugoslavije, Rijeka, 1972
— — Srpski Jezik i Književnost, 1969
Državni Muzej, Cetinje, 1976
Dubai Public Library, 1391
"Dubbelde Palmboom", Rotterdam, 968
Dublin Institute for Advanced Studies, 735
— Public Libraries, 731
— University Biological Association, 731
Duchesne College, Brisbane, 109
Dugdale Society for the Publication of Warwickshire Records, 1422
Duke University, Durham, N.C., 1825
— — Library, 1633
Duksung Women's College, Seoul, 896
Dulwich Picture Gallery, 1465
Dumbarton Oaks Research Library and Collection, 1628
Dumfries Museum, 1472
Dunant-Museum, Heiden, 1262
Dunboyne Institute, Maynooth, 736
Duncan of Jordanstone College of Art, Dundee, 1551
Dundee City Art Gallery and Museum, 1472
— College of Commerce, 1552
— — Technology, 1541
— District Libraries, 1455
Dundurn Castle, 250
Dunedin Public Art Gallery, 982
— Library, 981
Dunn Nutrition Unit (M.R.C.), Cambridge, 1443
Duquesne University, 1870
Durban Municipal Library, 1162
— Museum and Art Gallery, 1164
Durham County Library, 1454
Durrës Public Library, 55
Dushanbe Branch of the All-Union Astronomical and Geodesical Society, 1332
Duvanski Institute, Mostar, 1986
"Dvir-Bialik" Municipal Central Public Library, Ramat-Gan, 742
Dwight D. Eisenhower Library, Abilene, 1629
Dyal Singh College Library, 1023
Dyfed County Library, Carmarthen, 1455
D'Youville College, Buffalo, N.Y., 1815
Dzhambul Technological Institute of Food and Light Industries, 1381
Dzhavakhishvili, I. A., Institute of History, Archaeology and Ethnography, Tbilisi, 1328
Dzhordania, I., Research Institute of Physiology and Pathology of Woman, Tbilisi, 1346

E

Ealing Public Libraries, 1452
Earlham College, Richmond, Ind., 1716
Early English Text Society, 1426
Earth Physics Branch, Department of Energy, Mines and Resources, Ottawa, 245
Earthquake Research Institute, Tokyo, 856
East Africa Natural History Society, Nairobi, 878
— African Institute for Medical Research, Mwanza, 1280

— — — of Malaria and Vector-Borne Disease, Tanga, 1280
— — Literature Bureau, Dar es Salaam, 1280
— — School of Librarianship, Kampala, 1312
— — Wild Life Society, Nairobi, 878
— Asian History of Science Library, Cambridge, 1459
— — Institute, New York, 1810
— Carolina University, Greenville, 1828
— Central Oklahoma State University, Ada, 1857
— China Engineering College, Shanghai, 337
— — Petroleum College, 337
— — Technical University of Water Resources, Nanjing, 337
— London Museum (S.A.), 1164
— — Municipal Library Service (S.A.), 1162
— Malling Research Station, 1440
— of Scotland College of Agriculture, Edinburgh, 1550
— Sussex County Library, Lewes, 1455
— Tennessee State University, Johnson City, 1889
— Texas Baptist College, 1898
— — State University, 1898
East-West Center, Honolulu, 1617
— Medical Research Institute, Seoul, 893
Eastern and Southern African Management Institute, Arusha, 1282
— College, St. Davids, Pa., 1870
— Connecticut State College, Pa., 1678
— Illinois University, Charleston, 1703
— Kentucky University, 1735
— Medicine Association, Hanoi, 1962
— Mennonite College, Harrisonburg, 1916
— Michigan University, Ypsilanti, 1761
— Montana College, Billings, 1791
— Nazarene College, Quincy, 1749
— New Mexico University, 1801
— Oregon State College, 1863
— Pennsylvania Psychiatric Institute, 1622
— Siberian State Institute of Culture, Ulan-Ude, 1382
— Washington University, Cheney, 1921
Eberhard-Karls-Universität, Tübingen, 604
Ecclesiastical History Society, London, 1422
Ecclesiological Society, 1435
Ecole Africaine et Mauricienne d'Architecture et d'Urbanisme, Lomé, 1292
— Biblique et Ecole Archéologique Française, Jerusalem, 753
— Cantonale des Beaux-Arts et d'Art appliqué, Lausanne, 1276
— Catholique des Arts et Métiers, Lyon, 497
— Centrale d'Agriculture, Boukoku, 320
— — de Lyon, 497
— — des Arts et Manufactures, Chatenay-Malabry, 493
— d'Anthropologie, Paris, 497
— d'Application du Service de Santé des Armées, Paris, 493
— d'Education Physique et de Sport, Geneva, 1268
— d'Electricité et de Mécanique Industrielles (Ecole Violet), Paris, 497
— d'Ergologie, Brussels, 169
— d'Infirmières Annexée à l'Université, Brussels, 159
— — et de Puéricultrices, Lille, 495
— d'Interprètes Internationaux, Mons, 163
— de Bibliothécaires-Documentalistes, Paris, 495
— — Biochimie Pratique, Lyon, 495
— — Chirurgie Dentaire et de Stomatologie de Paris, 497
— — Droit, Cap Haitien, 629
— — — de Cayes, 629
— — — Gonaïves, 629
— — — Jérémie, 629

— — Formation d'Animateurs Sociaux, Lille, 495
— — Psycho-Pédagogique, Paris, 494
— — Hautes Etudes Commerciales du Nord (E.D.H.E.C.), 495
— — — Internationales, Paris, 497
— — — Sociales, Paris, 497
— — l'Aviation Civile et de la Météorologie, Tunis, 1297
— — langue et civilisation françaises, Geneva, 1268
— — Masso-Kinésitherapie et de Pedicurie, Lille, 495
— — Médecine et de Dentisterie, Bamako, 920
— — Musique Vincent-D'Indy, Montreal, 302
— — Notariat d'Amiens, 497
— — — de Bordeaux, 497
— — — Clermont-Ferrand, 497
— — — Paris, 497
— — Professeurs (E.D.P.), Lille, 495
— — Psychologues-Praticiens, Paris, 494
— — Secrétariat Bilingue et Trilingue, Lille, 495
— — Service Social de la Région Nord, Lille, 495
— — Statistique d'Abidjan, 799
— — Technologie Supérieure, Montreal, 294
— — Thermique, Paris, 497
— — Traduction et d'Interprétation, Geneva, 1267
— Dentaire Française, 497
— des Affaires de Paris, 496
— — arts décoratifs, Geneva, 1276
— — — et Métiers, Luxembourg, 909
— — Bibliothécaires, Archivistes et Documentalistes, Dakar, 1146
— — Hautes Etudes Commerciales, Liège, 167
— — — — en Sciences Sociales, Paris, 492
— — — Pratiques, Bamako, 920
— — Métiers d'Art, Tétouan, 951
— — Postes et des Télécommunications, Tunis, 1297
— — Sciences Criminologiques Léon Cornil, Brussels, 159
— — de l'Information, Rabat-Agdal, 951
— — — Philosophiques et Religieuses, Brussels, 166
— — Secrétaires et Attachées de Direction, Lille, 495
— du Chef d'Entreprise—E.C.E., Paris, 496
— — Louvre, Paris, 498
— Française d'Athènes, 623
— — de Papeterie, Grenoble, 491
— — — Radioélectricité, d'Electronique et d'Informatique, Paris, 497
— — — — Rome, 757
— Industrielle, Mogadishu, 1153
— Inter-Etats Vétérinaires, Dakar, 1147
— Nationale Arts et Métiers, Paris, 493
— — d'Administration, Abidjan, 799
— — — Bamako, 920
— — — N'Djamena, 321
— — — Lomé, 1292
— — — Nouakchott, 922
— — — Paris, 492
— — — Tunis, 1297
— — — du Niger, Niamey, 990
— — — — Sénégal, Dakar, 1147
— — — et de Magistrature, Yaoundé, 232
— — — Publique, Quebec, 294
— — — — Rabat, 951
— — d'Assurances, Paris, 493
— — d'Ingénieurs, Bamako, 920
— — — de Belfort, 493
— — — — Gabès, 1296
— — — — Tunis, 1296
— — de l'Aviation Civile, Aéroport d'Orly, 493
— — — — Toulouse, 493
— — — — la Marine Marchande, Algiers, 59

# INDEX OF INSTITUTIONS

Ecole Nationale de la Marine Marchande, Paimpol, 493
— — — — Météorologie, Paris, 493
— — — — Santé Publique, Paris, 493
— — — — Statistique, Tunis, 1297
— — — — — et d'Administration Economique, Malakoff, 492
— — — — Médecine Vétérinaire, Medjez El Bab, 1297
— — — — musique, Casablanca, 951
— — — — Meknès, 951
— — des Arts, Bangui, 320
— — — et Métiers, Conakry, 627
— — — Beaux-Arts, Algiers, 59
— — — Tétouan, 951
— — — Ingénieurs des Travaux des Eaux et Forêts, Nogent-sur-Vernisson, 493
— — — Ponts et Chaussées, 493
— — — Postes et Télécommunications, Abidjan, 799
— — — Sciences Géographiques, Saint-Mandé, 492
— — — Télécommunications, Sarh, 321
— — du Génie Rural et des Eaux et Forêts, Nancy, 492
— — Polytechnique, Algiers, 59
— — Supérieure Agronomique, Abidjan, 799
— — — — de Montpellier, 492
— — — — Yaoundé, 232
— — — d'Arts et Métiers, Lille, 494
— — — d'Horticulture de Versailles, 492
— — — de Céramique Industrielle de Limoges, 494
— — — — l'Aéronautique et de l'Espace, Toulouse, 493
— — — — l'Electronique et de ses Applications (ENSEA), Cergy, 494
— — — — Meunerie et des Industries Céréalières, Paris, 497
— — — — Techniques Avancées, Paris, 494
— — des Arts Décoratifs, 498
— — — — — des Industries Textiles de Roubaix, 493
— — — — — Visuels de la Cambre, Brussels, 170
— — — — Beaux-Arts, 498
— — — — Bibliothèques, Villeurbanne, 493
— — — Industries Agricoles et Alimentaires, Massy, 492
— — — Mines de Paris, 494
— — — Télécommunications, 494
— — — Travaux Publics, Abidjan, 799
— — — du Pétrole et des Moteurs à Combustion Interne, Rueil-Malmaison, 494
— — — Féminine d'Agronomie, Rennes, 492
— — — Polytechnique, Yaoundé, 232
— — — Vétérinaire, Algiers, 59
— — — d'Alfort, 492
— — — de Lyon, 492
— — — Nantes, 492
— — — Toulouse, 492
— — Normale d'Education Physique Féminine et Institut Libre d'Education Physique Supérieure, Paris, 495
— — Supérieure, Bamako, 920
— — — Le Bardo, 1296
— — — Paris, 492
— — — Yaoundé, 232
— — — de Jeunes Filles, Paris, 492
— — — — l'Enseignement Technique, Cachan, 494
— — — — Tunis, 1296
— — Nouvelle d'Organisation Economique et Sociale (E.N.O.E.S.), Paris, 496
— Polytechnique, Palaiseau, 494
— — d'Architecture et d'Urbanisme, El Harrach, 59
— — d'Haïti, 629
— — de Thiès, 1147
— — Fédérale de Lausanne, 1272
— — Féminine, 498
— Pratique des Hautes Etudes, Paris, 491
— Professionnelle de l'Etat, Esch-sur-Alzette, 909
— Régionale des Beaux-Arts de Lille, 498
— — — et des Arts Industriels de Clermont-Ferrand, 498
— Royale du Service de Santé, Brussels, 169
— — Militaire, Brussels, 169
— Scientia, Paris, 498
— Spéciale d'Architecture, 498
— — de Mécanique et d'Electricité A.-M.-Ampère, 498
— — des Travaux Aéronautiques, Paris, 498
— — — Publics, du Bâtiment et de l'Industrie, 498
— Supérieure Africaine des Cadres des Chemins de Fer, Brazzaville, 358
— — d'Administration, Conakry, 627
— — d'Agronomie Tropicale, Nogent-sur-Marne, 492
— — d'art visuel, Geneva, 1276
— — d'Electricité, 498
— — d'Electronique de l'Ouest, Angers, 496
— — d'Ingénieurs en Electrotechnique et d'Electronique, Paris, 498
— — de Marseille, 498
— — — et Techniciens pour l'Agriculture, Le Vaudreuil, 496
— — d'Interprétariat, Algiers, 59
— — d'Optométrie, 497
— — de Biochimie et de Biologie, 497
— — Chimie Organique et Minérale, Paris, 495
— — Commerce d'Alger, Algiers, 59
— — — de Lyon, 496
— — — Paris, 496
— — — et d'Administration des Entreprises, Clermont-Ferrand, 492
— — — — des Entreprises du Havre, 488
— — — — des Entreprises de Lille, 496
— — — — des Entreprises de Marseille, 496
— — — — des Entreprises, Montpellier, 496
— — — — des Entreprises, Mont-Saint-Aignan, 488
— — — — des Entreprises de Poitiers, 496
— — Cuir et des Peintures, Ancres et Adhésifs, Lyon, 498
— — Droit, Ouagadougou, 1937
— — Fonderie, 498
— — Journalisme, Paris, 497
— — Physique et de Chimie Industrielle de la Ville de Paris, 494
— — Secrétaires-Traducteurs, Lyon, 495
— — Soudure Autogène, 498
— — Traducteurs, Interprètes, et de Cadres du Commerce Extérieur (E.S.T.I.C.E.), Lille, 495
— — des Industries du Caoutchouc, Montrouge, 498
— — — Vêtement, Paris, 498
— — — Textiles d'Epinal, 498
— — Lettres de Beyrouth, Beirut, 902
— — — et des Sciences Humaines, Ouagadougou, 1937
— — Sciences Commerciales d'Angers, 496
— — — de la Santé, Ouagadougou, 1937
— — — Economiques, Ouagadougou, 1937
— — — — et Commerciales, Cergy, 496
— — — Infirmières, Butare, 1141
— — — Techniques Aéronautiques et de Construction Automobile, Levallois-Perret, 498
— — du Bois, Paris, 498
— — Interafricaine de l'Electricité, Bingerville, 799
— — Internationale de Journalisme (E.S.I.J.Y.), Yaoundé, 232
— — Libre de Chimie de Paris, 497
— — Professionnelle OZANAM, Lille, 495
— — Textile, Lyon, 498
— — Technique Officielle Don Bosco, Kigali, 1141
— — Supérieure de Chimie de l'Ouest, Angers, 496
— — du Laboratoire, Paris, 498
— — Territoriale d'Agriculture, Grimari, 320
— Ecoles d'Art de Genève, 1276
— Polytechniques de Notariat, de Droit, et d'Assurances, Paris, 497
Ecological Society of America, 1612
— — Australia, Inc., Canberra, 90
— — Nigeria, Ile-Ife, 991
Econometric Forecasting Unit, Philadelphia, 1880
— Society, Evanston, 23
Economic and Administrative Research Centre, Baghdad, 725
— — Social Research Institute, Dublin, 730
— Development Administration Library, Santurce, 1110
— — Institute, Nsukka, 1001
— Geology Research Unit, Johannesburg, 1182
— History Association, Wilmington, Del., 1603
— — Society, London, 1422
— Institute Tilburg, 973
— Research Centre, Iaşi, 1135
— — — Singapore, 1152
— — Council, 1442
— — Unit, Colombo, 1225
— — — Philadelphia, 1880
— Society of Australia and New Zealand, 88
— — — Ghana, Legon, 611
— — — South Africa, Pretoria, 1155
Economics Association, Sutton, 1416
— Institute, Beijing, 332
— Research Institute, Yokohama, 861
Economisch-Historische Bibliotheek Amsterdam, 964
Economische Hogeschool Limburg, Diepenbeek, 169
Economists' Society of Croatia, 1970
— — — the S.R. of Serbia, Belgrade, 1969
Ecothèque Méditerranéenne du CNRS, Montpellier, 456
Ecuadorian Academy of Medicine, 407
Ecumenical Patriarchate Library, Istanbul, 1300
Eczacilik Yüksek Okulu, Istanbul, 1309
EDB-senteret, Bergen, 1014
Edgewood College, Madison, 1932
Edinboro State College, Pa., 1870
Edinburgh Bibliographical Society, 1415
— City Libraries, 1455
— Museums and Art Galleries, 1472
— College of Art, 1551
Edison Electric Institute, Washington D.C., 1616
— Institute, Dearborn, Mich., 1637
Edmonton Art Gallery, Alberta, 249
— Public Library, Alberta, 246
Educational Centre for Information Processing, Kyoto, 836
— Documentation and Research Centre, Khartoum, 1229
— Library, Baghdad, 726
— Foundation for Visual Aids, 1420
— Institute of Design, Craft and Technology, Bristol, 1419
— — — Scotland, Edinburgh, 1419
— Library, Jeddah, 1142
— Management Centre, Manila, 1052
— Research Bureau, Lusaka, 1998
— — Centre, Las Cruces, 1802
— Technology Centre, Zaria, 995
Eduskunnan Kirjasto, 431

# INDEX OF INSTITUTIONS

Edvard Kardelj University of Ljubljana, 1985
Edwardian Studies Association, Dagenham, 1426
Efes Müzesi Müdürlügü, Selsuk, Izmir, 1301
Ege Universitesi, Izmir, 1305
— — Mühendislik Bilimleri Fakültesi Mühendislik ve Mimarlik Yüksek Okulu, Izmir, 1309
Egerton College, Njoro, 880
Egry Jozsef Emlékmúzeum, Badacsony, 644
Egypt Exploration Society, London, 1422
Egyptian Association for Archives, Librarianship and Information Sciences, Cairo, 413
— — — Mental Health, Cairo, 414
— — — Psychological Studies, Cairo, 414
— Atomic Energy Establishment, Cairo, 416
— Botanical Society, Cairo, 414
— Cultural Centre, Mogadishu, 1153
— — Library, Tripoli, 906
— Geographical Society, 413
— Library, Cairo, 416
— Medical Association, 414
— — National Library, Cairo, 416
— — Museum, 417
— Organization for Biological Products and Vaccines, Giza, 415
— Society of Dairy Science, Cairo, 413
— — — Engineers, 414
— — — International Law, 413
— — — Medicine and Tropical Hygiene, Alexandria, 414
— — — Political Economy, Statistics and Legislation, 413
Ehime University, Matsuyama, 825
Eidgenössische Anstalt für das forstliche Versuchswesen, Birmensdorf, 1274
— — Wasserversorgung, Abwasserreinigung und Gewässerchutz, Dübendorf, 1274
— Materialprüfungs- und Versuchsanstalt für Industrie, Bauwesen, und Gewerbe, Dübendorf, 1274
— Parlaments- und Zentralbibliothek, Bern, 1259
— Technische Hochschule, Zurich, 1273
Eidgenössisches Institut für Reaktorforschung, Wurenlingen, 1274
— — — Schnee- und Lawinenforschung, Weissfluhjoch/Davos, 1258
Eindhoven University of Technology, 972
Ekonomi Fakultesi, Eskişehir, 1309
Ekonomisk-geografiska Institutionen, Åbo, 440
Ekonomiska Forskningsinstitutet vid Handelshögskolan i Stockholm, 1251
— Samfundet i Finland, 428
Ekonomiski institut na Univerzitet "Kiril i Metodij", Skopje, 1974
Eläinlääketieteellinen Korkeakoulu, Helsinki, 440
Elbasan Public Library, 55
El-Djazaira El-Mosilla, Algiers, 57
Electoral Reform Society of Great Britain and Ireland Ltd., London, 1416
Electrical Engineering Institute, Beijing, 332
Electrochemical Society, Inc., 1613
— — of India, Bangalore, 663
Electron Microscope Unit, Johannesburg, 1182
— — — Rondebosch, 1167
— Microscopy Society of America, Oak Ridge, 1613
— Optics Institute, Shanghai, 332
Electronic Computation Centre, Tokyo, 874
— — — Vatican City, 1946
— Computer Centre, Vladivostock, 1362
— Computing Centre, Irkutsk, 1362
— — — Perm, 1366
— — — Riga, 1364
Electronics Institute, Beijing, 332
— Research and Service Organization, Hsinchu, 341

Elektrisitetsforsyningens forskningsinstitutt, Trondheim, 1009
Elektroteknisk Forening, Copenhagen, 392
Elizabeth City State University, North Carolina, 1828
— University of Music, Hiroshima, 874
Elizabethan Exhibition Gallery, Wakefield, 1471
Elizabethtown College, Pa., 1870
Elmhurst College, Ill., 1704
Elmira College, N.Y., 1816
Elon College, N.C., 1828
El Salvador Academy, San Salvador, 422
— — — of History, San Salvador, 422
Emei Institute of Multi-purpose Utilization of Mineral Resources, Sichuan, 333
Emerson College, Boston, 1749
Emeryk Hutten-Czapski Department, Cracow, 1076
Emmanuel College, Boston, 1749
— — Brisbane, 109
— — Cambridge, 1485
— — Toronto, 310
— — Library, Cambridge, 1461
Emory University, Atlanta, Ga., 1699
Emporia State University, Kansas, 1730
Empresa Brasileira de Pesquisa Agropecuária (EMBRAPA), 182
— de Pesquisa Agropecuária da Bahia, 183
— — — — de Minas Gerais, Belo Horizonte, 183
— Pernambucana de Pesquisa Agropecuária, 183
Encyclopaedia Africana Secretariat, Accra, 610
Endüstri Bilimleri Fakültesi, Eskişehir, 1309
Energiagazdálkodási Tudományos Egyesület, 636
Energiewirtschaftliches Institut an der Universität Köln, 529
Energy and Mineral Resources Research Institute, Ames, 1728
— Research Institute, Regina, 297
— — Unit, Rondebosch, 1167
Enfield Public Libraries, 1452
Engei Gakkai, 803
Engineering Academy of Denmark, Bygning, 400
— and Scientific Association of Ireland, 731
— Association, Hanoi, 1962
— Design Centre, Loughborough, 1514
— Experiment Station, Atlanta, 1700
— — Las Cruces, 1802
— Foundation, New York, 1617
— Institute of Canada, 244
— Institution of Zambia, Lusaka, 1997
— Mechanics Institute, Harbin, 332
— Research Institute, Ames, 1728
— — Tokyo, 817
— Societies' Library, 1629
English Academy of Southern Africa, Johannesburg, 1155
— Association, 1426
— — (Sydney Branch), 89
— — Folk Dance and Song Society, 1414
— Language Institute, Wellington, N.Z., 986
— — Teaching Institute, Riyadh, 1144
— Place-Name Society, Nottingham, 1422
— Speaking Board (International), Ltd., Southport, 1426
— -Speaking Union (of the Commonwealth), London, 1424
— — — United States, New York, 1607
Enoch Pratt Free Library, Baltimore, 1626
Enosis Ellinon Chimikon, Athens, 617
— Hellinon Bibliothekarion, Athens, 616
— — Mousourgon, Athens, 616
Ente Nazionale Italiano di Unificazione (U.N.I.), Milan, 761
Entebbe Botanic Gardens, Uganda, 1311
Entomological Museum of Fujikyu, 823
— Society of America, 1613
— — — Canada, Ottawa, 242
— — — New South Wales, Sydney, 90

— — — Zealand, Upper Hutt, 977
— — — Nigeria, Ibadan, 991
— — — Queensland, Brisbane, 90
Entomologisk Forening, Copenhagen, 391
Entomology Institute, Shanghai, 332
Environment Preservation Centre, Kyoto, 836
Environmental Chemistry Institute, Beijing, 332
— Engineering Research Institute, Nanjing, 337
— Epidemiology Unit (M.R.C.), Southampton, 1443
— Institute, Salford, 1527
— Mutagen Society, Bethesda, Md., 1612
— Pollution Research Centre, Jadiriyah, 725
— Resources Center, Atlanta, 1700
Enzimológiai Intézet, Budapest, 638
Eötvös Loránd Fizikai Társulat, 635
— — Tudományegyetem, Budapest, 647
— — — Állam- és Jogtudományi Kar Könyvtára, Budapest, 640
— — — Egyetemi Könyvtar, Budapest, 640
— — University, Budapest, 647
Epidemiology and Medical Care Unit (M.R.C./D.H.S.S.), Harrow, 1444
— Institute, Beijing, 333
— Unit South Wales (M.R.C.), Cardiff, 1443
Epítöiperi Tudományos Egyesület, 634
Equipe de Recherche Associée au C.N.R.S. de Neurobiologie des Hormones et Comportement, Bordeaux, 472
— — — — "Laboratoire de Génétique", Talence, 472
— — C.N.R.S. "Laboratoires d'Enzymologie", Talence, 472
"Eranos Vindobonensis", 121
Erasmus Universiteit Rotterdam, 970
Érc és Ásványbányászati Múzeum, Rudabánya, 644
Erdészeti és Faipari Egyetem, Sopron, 653
— — — Központi Könyvtára, Sopron, 640
— Talajmikrobiológiai Kutatócosport, Sopron, 653
Erevan Children's Picture Gallery, 1353
— Institute of Fine Arts and Theatre, 1374
— — — National Economy, 1373
— K. Marx Polytechnic Institute, 1375
— Komitas State Conservatoire, 1387
— State Medical Institute, 1383
— — University, 1361
— Zootechnical and Veterinary Institute, 1372
Ergonomics Society, Hockley, 1436
Erhvervsarkivet. Statens Erhvervshistoriske Arkiv, Århus, 394
Erich-Schmid-Institut für Festkörperphysik, Leoben, 119
Erindale College, 309
Erkel Ferenc Múzeum, 644
Ernest Oppenheimer Institute of Portuguese Studies, Johannesburg, 1182
Ernst-Haeckel-Haus, Jena, 511
Ernst-Moritz-Arndt-Universität, Greifswald, 511
Erskine College, Due West, S.C., 1886
Ersman Health Research Institute, 1387
Erzbischöfliche Diözesan- und Dombibliothek, Cologne, 535
Erzbischöfliches Dom- und Diözesanmuseum, Vienna, 129
Escola de Administração de Emprêsas de São Paulo da Fundação Getúlio Vargas, São Paulo, 210
— Arte-Fundação Armando Alvares Penteado, São Paulo, 212
— — Artes Visuais, Rio de Janeiro, 212
— — Biblioteconomia e Documentação, São Carlos, 210
— — Comunicações e Artes, São Paulo, 212
— — Engenharia de Lins, 211
— — — Taubaté, 211
— — Farmacia, Ouro Prêto, 199

# INDEX OF INSTITUTIONS

Escola de Farmacia e Odontologia de Alfenas, 211
— — Minas, Ouro Préto, 199
— — Música da Universidade Federal do Rio de Janeiro, 212
— — — e Belas Artes do Paraná, 212
— Federal de Engenharia, Itajuba, 211
— Paulista de Medicina, São Paulo, 211
— Superior de Belas Artes, Lisbon, 1108
— — — Oporto, 1108
— — — Desenho Industrial, Rio de Janeiro, 212
Escuela Agricola "El Vergel", Angol, 330
— — Panamericana, Tegucigalpa, 631
— Argentina de Periodismo, Buenos Aires, 81
— Centroamericana de Geografia, San José, 360
— de Administración de Negocios para Graduados, Lima, 1046
— — — y Finanzas y Tecnologías, Medellín, 357
— — Agricultura, Daule, 412
— — — Ibarra, 412
— — Arte Dramático, Madrid, 1223
— — — Escén co, Santo Domingo, 406
— — Artes Plá ticas, Santiago, 406
— — — Visua s "Cristóbal Rojas", Caracas, 1961
— — Ciencias de la Administración, Entre Rios, 81
— — Estado Mayor, Madrid, 1223
— — Estudios Arabes, Granada, 1210
— — Ingeniería Aeronautica, Córdoba, 78
— — Musica, Nariño, 357
— — — y Artes Representativas, Medellín, 357
— — Pintura y Artes Plásticas, Barranquila, 357
— — Trabajo Social de El Salvador, 423
— Graduada "Joaquin V. González", La Plata, 75
— Interamericana de Bibliotecología de la Universidad de Antioquía, Medellin, 350
— Militar de Ingenieros, Mexico City, 944
— — "General Bernardo O'Higgins", Santiago, 330
— Nacional de Agricultura "Mariscal Estigarriba", Asunción, 1035
— — — "Roberto Quiñonez", La Libertad, 423
— — — y Ganaderia, Managua, 989
— — Antropología e Historia, 944
— — Arte Dramático, Buenos Aires, 81
— — Artes Gráficas, Madrid, 1223
— — — Plásticas, Guatemala City, 626
— — — — Panama, 1031
— — — Bellas Artes, Santo Domingo, 406
— — — — "Manuel Belgrano", Buenos Aires, 81
— — — — "Prilidiano Pueyrredón", Buenos Aires, 81
— — — — "San Alejandro", Havana, 366
— — Bibliotecarios, Lima, 1046
— — Biblioteconomía y Archivonomía, Mexico, 944
— — Danzas, Panama City, 1031
— — Educación Técnica, Buenos Aires, 81
— — — — Neuquen, 81
— — Música, Panama, 1031
— — — Tegucigalpa, 631
— — Opera, Caracas, 1961
— — Teatro, Panama, 1031
— — Superior de Bellas Artes, Lima, 1046
— Náutica de Panamá, 1031
— Politécnica Nacional, Quito, 411
— Práctica de Agricultura y Ganadería "Maria Cruz y Manuel L. Inchausti", La Plata, 75
— Professional de Medicina Interna, Pamplona, 1213
— Regional de Artes Plásticas, Quetzaltenango, 626

— — Bellas Artes, Arequipa, 1046
— — — — "Diego Quispe Tito", Cuzco, 1046
— — Música de Arequipa, 1046
— — — — Ayacucho, 1046
— — — — Cusco, 1046
— — — — Huanuco, 1046
— — — — Piura, 1046
— — — — Trujillo, 1046
— Superior de Administración Pública, Bogotá, 354
— — — y Dirección de Empresas (ESADE), Barcelona, 1222
— — Bellas Artes "Ernesto de la Cárcova", 81
— — — — La Paz, 176
— — — — de Madrid, 1223
— — — — — San Carlos, 1223
— — — — — San Jorge, 1223
— — — — — Santa Isabel de Hungria de Sevilla, 1223
— — Comercio "Carlos Pellegrini", Buenos Aires, 72
— — Filosofia, Ciencias y Educación, Asunción, 1035
— — Música "Jose Angel Lamas", Caracas, 1961
— — — Sagrada y de Pedagogía Musical, Madrid, 1223
— — Periodismo y Communicación Social, La Plata, 75
— — Técnica Empresarial Agrícola, Cordoba, 1222
— — Politecnica de Chimborazo, Riobamba, 411
— — — del Litoral, Guayaquil, 412
— — Tecnica Superior de Arquitectura, Seville, 1223
— — — — Ingenieros Industriales, Madrid, 1222
— Universitaria de Bibliotecología y Ciencias Afines "Ing. Federico E. Capurro", Montevideo, 1941
Escuelas de Bellas Artes, Dominican Republic, 406
Esie Museum, Kwara State, 995
Esigodini Agricultural Institute, Essexvale, 2004
Eskilstuna Stadsbibliotek, Eskilstuna, 1239
Eskişehir Academy of Economic and Commercial Sciences, 1309
— Arkeoloji Müzesi, 1301
— Iktisadî Ve Ticarî Ilímler Akademisi, Eskişehir, 1309
Essex County Library, Chelmsford, 1454
Estacão Agronomica Nacional, 1100
— Aqüicola (Divisão de Produção Pisícola do Norte), Villa do Conde, 1101
— Experimental de Biología e Piscicultura, 184
— — — Campos, 183
— — — Cana de Açúcar do Curado, Pernambuco, 183
— — — Itaguaí, São Paulo, 183
— — — Itapirema, Pernambuco, 182
— — — Rio Grande, 183
— — — Fitotécnica de Taquari, 183
Estación Altoandina de Biología y Reserva Zoo-Botánica de Checayani, 1038
— Biológica de los Llanos, Calabozo, 1954
— de Biología Pesquera, San Antonio, 325
— — Investigaciones Marinas de Margarita, Caracas, 1954
— Experimental Agricola del Norte, Lambayeque, 1038
— Agro-Industrial, San Miguel de Tucumán, 66
— Agropecuaria de Salta (I.N.T.A.), 66
— — — Tulumayo, Huánuco, 1038
— — — Mendoza, 66
— — de Café, Bramón, Táchira, 1953
— — — Pastos y Forrajes "Indio Hatuey", Havana, 365
— — del Zaidin, Granada, 1210
— "Las Vegas" de la Sociedad Nacional de Agricultura, Santiago, 324

— — Regional Agropecuaria, Pergamino, 66
— Hidrobiológica, Buenos Aires, 68
— Meteorológica, Ciudad Bolívar, 1954
Estonian Agricultural Academy, 1369
— Geographical Society, Tallinn, 1327
— S.S.R. Academy of Sciences, Tallinn, 1327
— — State Arts Institute, Tallinn, 1374
— State Open Air Museum, Tallinn, 1352
Estudios Universitarios y Técnicos de Guipuzcoa, San Sebastian, 1222
Établissement d'Etudes et de Recherches Météorologiques, 459
Etaireia Kypriakon Spoudon, 367
ETH-Bibliothek, Zürich, 1260
Ethiopian Library Association, Addis Ababa, 424
— Mapping Agency, Addis Ababa, 424
— Medical Association, 424
Ethnikon Idryma Erevnon, Athens, 617
— Metsovion Polytechneion, 621
Ethnographic and Folk Culture Society, 671
— Museum, Berat, 55
— — Durrës, 55
— — Gjirokastër, 55
Ethnographical Museum, Ankara, 1301
— — Göteborg, 1242
— — Khartoum, 1230
Ethnographisches Museum Schloss Kittsee, 130
Ethnological Museum and Folklore Archives, Haifa, 743
Etnografický ústav, Martin, 379
Etnografisch Museum, Antwerp, 157
Etnografiska Museet, Stockholm, 1241
Etnografski musej, Belgrade, 1976
— — Split, 1978
— — Zagreb, 1978
Etnoloski muzej na Makedonija, 1977
Etz Hayim, General Talmud Torah and Grand Yeshivah, 753
Eugenics Society, London, 1435
Euphrates University, Elazig, 1305
Euratom, Brussels, 44
Eureka College, Illinois, 1704
Europa-Institut, Mannheim, 590
Europa Nostra, London, 18
European Association for the Exchange of Technical Literature in the Field of Metallurgy, Luxembourg, 45
— — of Music Festivals, Geneva, 43
— — — Teachers, Geneva, 27
— Atomic Energy Community, Brussels, 44
— Bureau of Adult Education, Amersfoort, 27
— Centre for Population Studies, The Hague, 23
— Confederation of Agriculture, Aargau, 16
— Co-ordination Centre for Research and Documentation in Social Sciences, Vienna, 13
— Cultural Foundation, Amsterdam, 18
— Foundation for Management Development (EFMD), Brussels, 28
— Institute of Business Administration, Fontainebleau, 496
— — Environmental Cybernetics, Athens, 45
— Molecular Biology Organization (EMBO), Heidelberg, 45
— Movement (British Council), London, 1417
— Organisation for Civil Aviation Electronics (EUROCAE), Paris, 33
— Organization for Nuclear Research (CERN), Geneva, 45
— Science Foundation, Strasbourg, 45
— Society of Culture, Venice, 18
— Southern Observatory, Munich, 45
— — Santiago, 325
— Space Agency, Paris, 45
— University Institute, Florence, 792
Euskaltzaindia, Bayonne, 445
— Bilbao, 1187

2044

Evangel College of the Assemblies of God, Springfield, Miss., 1786
Evangelische Akademie in Wien, Vienna, 123
Everyman's University, Tel-Aviv, 745
Evlyn Hone College of Applied Arts and Commerce, Lusaka, 1998
Ewha Women's University, Seoul, 890
— — — Library, Seoul, 886
Ewing Memorial Library, Lahore, 1023
Exeter Cathedral Library, 1459
— College, Oxford, 1524
— — Library, Oxford, 1463
— — of Art and Design, 1551
Experimental Medicine Institute, Beijing, 333
— Psychology Society, York, 1434
Explosives Research and Development Establishment, Waltham Abbey, 1488
Exposition Permanente du Débarquement, Arromanches, 468
Extra-Mural Division, University of Liberia, Monrovia, 905
— Studies Centre, Cardiff, 1536
Eye Research Institute of the Retina Foundation, Boston, Mass., 1618

F

Fabian Society, 1417
Fabrique Nationale Museum of Industrial Archaeology, Herstal, 158
Faculdade Católica de Ciências Humanas, Brasília, 210
— — — Tecnologia, Brasília, 210
— de Arquitetura e Urbanismo "Elmano Ferreira Veloso", São José dos Campos, 210
— — Belas Artes de São Paulo, 212
— — Ciências Agrárias do Pará, 212
— — — Contábeis de Santa Cruz do Sul, 211
— — — Econômicas de Marília, 211
— — — — do Sul de Minas, 211
— — — — e Administrativas de Santo-André, 211
— — — — — de Taubaté, 211
— — — — — — do Vale do Paraíba, 210
— — — — Médicas de Pernambuco, 211
— — — — Politicas e Econômicas de Cruz Alta, 211
— — — — — de Rio Grande, 211
— — Direito Candido Mendes, Rio de Janeiro, 211
— — — de Caruaru, 211
— — — — São Bernardo do Campo, 211
— — — — Soracabana, Sorocaba, 211
— — — — do Vale do Paraíba, 210
— — Engenharia, São José dos Campos, 210
— — Filosofia, Ciências e Letras, Ouro Fino, 211
— — — — — São José dos Campos, 210
— — — — — de Santos, 211
— — — Música e Enfermagem do Sagrado Coração de Jesus, Bauru, 211
— — Medicina do Triângulo Mineiro, Uberaba, 211
— — Musica Mãe de Deus, Londrina, Paraná, 212
— — — Pio XII, Bauru, 212
— — — "Sagrado Coração de Jesus", São Paulo, 212
— — — Odontologia de Lins, São Paulo, 211
— — — — Passo Fundo, 211
— — — Pernambuco, 211
— — — do Triângulo Mineiro, 211
— — Serviço Social "Ministro Tarso Dutra", São José dos Campos, 210
— Estadual de Ciências Econômicas de Apucarana, Paraná, 211

— — — Filosofia, Ciências e Lêtras, Paraná, 211
— Municipal de Ciências Econômicas e Administrativas de Osasco, 211
— — Salesiana de Filosofia, Ciências e Lêtras, São Paulo, 211
— — Santa Marcelina, São Paulo, 212
Faculdades de Tecnologia e de Ciências, Barretos, 212
— Unidas Católicas de Mato Grosso, 210
Facultad de Ciencias Aplicadas a la Industria, Mendoza, 81
— — Teología, Granada, 1208
— Latinoamericana de Ciencias Sociales, Chile, 330
Facultades S. Francisco de Borja, Barcelona, 1208
Faculté des Lettres et Sciences Sociales, Brest, 497
— — Sciences Agronomiques de l'Etat, Gembloux, 164
— Libre de Théologie Protestante de Paris, 497
— Polytechnique de Mons, 164
— Universitaire Catholique de Mons, 164
— — de Théologie Protestante de Bruxelles, 164
Faculteit voor Vergelijkende Godsdienstwetenschappen, Antwerp, 167
Facultés Catholiques de Lyon, 495
— de Théologie et de Philosophie de la Compagnie de Jésus, Montreal, 248
— Universitaires Notre-Dame de la Paix, Namur, 164
— — Saint-Louis, Brussels, 165
Faculties, The, Canberra, 100
Faculty of Actuaries in Scotland, Edinburgh, 1417
— — Advocates, Edinburgh, 1417
— — Agriculture, Forestry and Irrigation, Vientiane, 898
— — Architects and Surveyors, Chippenham, 1412
— — Art, Vientiane, 898
— — Classical and Christian Letters, Vatican City, 1945
— — Dramatic Arts, Belgrade, 1993
— — Education, Vientiane, 898
— — Medicine, Trondheim, 1017
— — — Vientiane, 898
— — Royal Designers for Industry, 1413
— — Theology in Ljubljana, 1993
Failaka Island Ethnographical Museum, 897
— Museum, 897
Faipari Tudomanyos Egyesület, 636
Fairbairn, Esmee, Research Centre, Edinburgh, 1494
Fairfax County Public Library, Springfield, Va., 1627
Fairfield University, Conn., 1678
Fairleigh Dickinson University, Rutherford, N.J., 1797
Fairmont State College, W. Va., 1930
Fakultätsbibliothek für Rechtswissenschaften, Vienna, 128
Falmouth School of Art, 1551
Fa-Ngum College, Vientiane, 898
Far East Institute, Moscow, 1321
— Eastern Institute of Geology, Vladivostock, 1322
— — — — Soviet Trade, Vladivostock, 1373
— — — the Fish Industry, 1381
— V. V. Kuibyshev Polytechnic Institute, 1375
— — Pedagogical Institute of Arts, Vladivostock, 1387
— — Scientific Centre, Vladivostock, 1322
— — State University, Vladivostock, 1362
— — University, Manila, 1053
— — — Library, Manila, 1049
Farabi University, Teheran, 723
Farmaceutsko Društvo na Makedonija, Skopje, 1971

Fauna and Flora Preservation Society, London, 1431
Fayetteville State University, N.C., 1828
Fazenda Regional de Criação, Barbacena, 183
Fazi-i-Omar Research Institute, 1022
Feati University, Manila, 1053
Federação Brasileira de Associações de Bibliotecários, São Paulo, 179
— de Escolas Superiores, Belo Horizonte, Minas Gerais, 210
Federación Argentina de Asociaciones de Anestesiología, Buenos Aires, 64
— de Alianzas Francesas de México, A.C., México, 926
— del Patronato del Enfermo de Lepra de la Republica Argentina, 64
— Española de Religiosos de Enseñanza (FERE), 1191
— Lanera Argentina, Buenos Aires, 65
— Médica Peruana, Lima, 1037
— Mundial de Sociedades de Anestesiologos, Bristol, 38
— Nacional de Médicos del Ecuador, Quito, 407
Federal Bar Association, 1603
— Council on the Arts and the Humanities, Washington, D.C., 1598
— Department of Antiquities, Lagos, 994
— Institute of Industrial Research, Ikeja, 994
— Polytechnic, Akure, 1001
— — Bida, 1002
— — Idah, 1002
— School of Dental Hygiene, Lagos, 1003
— Trust for Education and Research, London, 1417
Federální statistický uřad, Prague, 375
Federasie Van Afrikaanse Kultuurvereniginge (F.A.K.), Auckland Park, 1155
— — Rapportryekorpse, Johannesburg, 1155
Federatie van Organisaties van Bibliotheek-, Informatie-, Dokumentatiewezen (FOBID), The Hague, 956
Federation of American Societies for Experimental Biology, 1612
— — Astronomical and Geophysical Services (FAGS), St. Mandé, 9
— — British Artists, London, 1413
— — French Alliances in the United States, New York, 1607
— — International Music Competitions, Geneva, 43
— — Obstetric & Gynaecological Societies of India, Bombay, 662
Fédération Belge des Alliances Françaises et Institutions Associées, 151
— Britannique des Comités de l'Alliance Française, 1424
— Dentaire Internationale, London, 37
— des Alliances Françaises du Mexique, A.C., México, 926
— — Architectes Suisse, Bern, 1253
— — Concours Internationaux de Musique, Geneva, 43
— — Gynécologues et Obstétriciens de Langue Française, Paris, 450
— — Notaires de Suisse, Lausanne, 1254
— — Sociétés d'Agriculture de la Suisse Romande, Lausanne, 1253
— Française de Spéléologie, Paris, 447
— — des Sociétés de Sciences Naturelles, Paris, 451
— Internationale d'Astronautique, Paris, 47
— — d'Education Physique—FIEP, Arreau, 41
— — d'Electronique Médicale et des Techniques Biologiques, Ottawa, 40
— — de Biologie Cellulaire, London, 48
— — — documentation, The Hague, 22
— — gynécologie et d'obstétrique (FIGO), London, 40
— — — la Précontrainte, Slough, 32

INDEX OF INSTITUTIONS

Fédération Internationale de laiterie, Brussels, 17
— — — l'Automatique, Laxenburg, 32
— — — des archives du film, Brussels, 22
— — — associations d'anatomistes, Paris, 40
— — — — d'études classiques, Geneva, 11
— — — — de bibliothécaires et des bibliothèques, Hague, 22
— — — — Collèges de Chirurgie, Edinburgh, 41
— — — — Femmes de Carrières Libérales et Commerciales, London, 24
— — — — diplômées des universités, Geneva, 29
— — — — géomètres, Thun, 32
— — — — hôpitaux, London, 41
— — — — jeunesses musicales, Brussels, 43
— — — — langues et litératures modernes, Aix-en-Provence, 11
— — — — mouvements d'école moderne, Sèvres, 29
— — — — musiciens, Zurich, 43
— — — — organisations de correspondence et d'échanges scolaires—FIOCES, Paris, 29
— — — — — science social, Copenhagen, 12
— — — — Professeurs de Français, Sèvres, 28
— — — — Sociétés d'Electro-encéphalographie et de Neurophysiologie clinique, Vancouver, 37
— — — — — d'ingénieurs des techniques de l'automobile, Paris, 34
— — — — — d'Ophtalmologie, Nijmegen, 40
— — — — — de Microscopie Electronique, Berkeley, 8
— — — — — — philosophie, Fribourg, 11
— — — — — oto-rhino-laryngologiques, Mexico, 37
— — — — Universités Catholiques—FIUC, Paris, 29
— — — du diabète, London, 37
— — — — Thermalisme et du Climatisme—FITEC, Bad Ragaz, 41
— — — pour l'habitation, l'urbanisme et l'aménagement des territoires, The Hague, 34
— — — — la recherche théâtrale, Lancaster, 20
— Mondiale de Neurologie, Aarhus, 38
— des Sociétés de Neurochirurgie, Oegstgeest, 43
— pour la Santé Mentale, Vancouver, 13
— Nationale des Costumes Suisses, Zürich, 1257
— — — Syndicats Départementaux de Médecins Electro-Radiologistes Qualifiés, Paris, 450
— Royale des Sociétés d'Architectes de Belgique, Brussels, 150
— Universelle des Associations Chrétiennes d'Etudiants—FUACE, Grand Saconnex, 31
— Universitaire et Polytechnique de Lille, 495
Félag Islenzkra Kvikmyndagerdarmanna, Reykjavik, 656
— — Leikara, Reykjavik, 656
— — Listdansara, 656
— — Myndlistarmanna, Reykjavik, 656
— — Tónistarmanna, Reykjavik, 656
Felagid "Vardin", Tórshavn, 402
Fellowship of Australian Writers, 89
Fels Center for Government, Philadelphia, 1880
— Planetarium of the Franklin Institute, 1637
— Research Institute, Yellow Springs, 1618
Felsőfokú Épitőgépészeti Technikum, Debrecen, 655
— Vegyipari Gépészeti Technikum, Esztergom, 655

Feng Chia University, Taichung, 345
Ferenczy Múzeum, Szentendre, 644
Ferghana Polytechnic Institute, Uzbek, S.S.R., 1375
Fermentation Research Institute, Chiba, 817
— Unit, Jerusalem, 740
Fernuniversität, Hagen, 546
Ferris State College, Big Rapids, 1761
Fersman, A. E., Mineralogical Museum of the U.S.S.R. Academy of Sciences, Moscow, 1320, 1358
Festival Casals, San Juan, 1109
Field Crops Research Institute, Giza, 414
— Museum of Natural History, Chicago, 1637
— Naturalists' Club of Victoria, 90
— Studies Council, Shrewsbury, 1430
Figl, L., Observatorium für Astrophysik, Vienna, 126
Fiji College of Agriculture, 426
— Institute of Technology, Samabula, 426
— Law Society, Suva, 426
— Medical Association, Suva, 426
— Museum, The, 426
— School of Medicine, Suva, 426
— Society, The, 426
Filharmonisk Selskap, Oslo, 1007
Filologisk-Historiske Samfund, 391
Finance and Economics School, Ulan Bator, 948
Financial Management Research Centre, Armidale, N.S.W., 106
Findlay College, 1843
Fine Arts Gallery, Korcë, 56
— — — Tiranë, 55
— — — Museum, Ulan Bator, 947
Finlands Museiförbund, Helsinki, 428
— Svenska Författareförening, 428
Finseninstitutet, Copenhagen, 393
Finska Fornminnesföreningen, Helsinki, 428
— Kemistsamfundet, 429
— Läkaresällskapet, 429
— Vetenskaps-Societeten, Helsinki, 427
Firat Üniversitesi, Elazig, 1305
Firdousi State Public Library of the Tajik S.S.R., Dushanbe, 1348
Fire Research Institute, Tokyo, 817
Fiscal Institute Tilburg, 973
Fisheries Laboratory (Ministry of Agriculture, Fisheries and Food), Lowestoft, 1488
— Museum of the Pacific Scientific Research Institute of Fisheries and Oceanography, Vladivostock, 1359
— Research and Technology Laboratory, Halifax, N.S., 290
— — Station, Negombo, 1225
— — — Department of Fisheries, Colombo, 1225
— — Unit, Monkey Bay, 912
— Society of Nigeria, Lagos, 991
— Technology Section, Bangkok, 1283
Fishing Industry Research Institute, Rondebosch, 1167
Fisk University, Nashville, 1889
Fiskeridirektoratets Havforskningsinstitutt, Bergen, 1009
Fiskirannsóknarstovan, Tórshavn, 402
Fitchburg State College, Mass., 1749
Fitzwilliam College, Cambridge, 1485
— — Library, 1461
— Museum, Cambridge, 1468
Five Associated University Libraries, U.S.A., 1633
Fletcher College, Corozal, 171
Flinders Institute for Atmospheric and Marine Sciences, Bedford Park, S.A., 101
— Petrie Library, Khartoum, 1229
— University of South Australia, Bedford Park, 100
— — Library, 96
Florence and George S. Wise Observatory, Tel-Aviv, 750

Florida Agricultural and Mechanical University, 1692
— Atlantic University, Boca Raton, 1692
— Institute of Technology, Melbourne, Florida, 1692
— Memorial College, 1693
— Southern College, 1693
— State University, Tallahassee, 1693
— — — Library, 1632
Flygtekniska Försöksanstalten FFA, 1238
Fockemuseum, Bremen, 541
Foerder Institute for Economic Research, Tel-Aviv, 750
Fogg Art Museum, Cambridge, Mass., 1637
Folger Shakespeare Library, 1628
Folk Art Museum, Moscow, 1352
— — — Nicosia, 368
— Museum, Holywood, N.I., 1555
Folkeuniversitetsudvalget, Copenhagen, 390
Folklore and Language Archive, St. John's, Newfoundland, 284
— Museum, Amman, 875
— of Ireland Society, 730
— Society, London, 1435
— Studies Centre, Giza, 421
FOM-Instituut voor Atoom- en Molecuulfysica, Amsterdam, 962
— — — Plasma-Fysica, Rijnhuizen, 962
Fondation Archéologique, Brussels, 159
— Biermans-Lapôtre, Paris, 447
— Born-Bunge pour la Recherche, Antwerp, 154
— Calouste Gulbenkian, Paris, 447
— Egyptologique Reine Elisabeth, Brussels, 151
— Européenne de la Culture, Amsterdam, 18
— Fernand Lazard, Brussels, 151
— Francqui, Brussels, 151
— Hindemith, Vevey, 1253
— internationale des stations scientifiques du Jungfraujoch et du Gornergrat, Berne, 48
— Maeght, St. Paul-de-Vence, 470
— Médicale Reine Elisabeth, Brussels, 154
— Nationale des Sciences Politiques, Paris, 446
— pour la Recherche Sociale, Paris, 457
— "pour la science", Centre international de Synthèse, Paris, 45
— Saint-John Perse, Aix-en-Provence, 449
— Schiller Suisse, 1255
— suisse pour la psychologie appliquée, Zürich, 1257
— Universitaire, Brussels, 151
Fondazione "Centro di Studi di Patologia Molecolare Applicata alla Clinica", Milan, 759
— Giangiacomo Feltrinelli, Milan, 757
— Internazionale Premio E. Balzan, Milan, 761
— Marco Besso, Milan, 761
— Querini-Stampalia, Venice, 769
Fondo Colombiano de Investigaciones Cientificas y Proyectos Especiales "Francisco José de Caldas", 348
— Nacional de las Artes, Buenos Aires, 63
Fonds de la Recherche Fondamentale Collective, Brussels, 154
— — — Scientifique Médicale, Brussels, 154
— National de la Recherche Scientifique, Brussels, 154
— — suisse de la recherche scientifique, Bern, 1256
— zur Förderung der wissenschaftlichen Forschung, Vienna, 125
Fontbonne College, St. Louis, 1787
Food and Agriculture Organization of the United Nations (FAO), Rome, 15
— Research Institute, Accra, 611
— — — (A.R.C.), Norwich, 1440, 1488
Footscray Institute of Technology, Victoria, 115
Ford Foundation, 1604
Fordham University, Bronx, N.Y., 1816

Foreign Affairs Association of Japan, 805
— and Commonwealth Office Library, London, 1451
— Language College, Shanghai, 337
— — Publications and Distribution Bureau, Beijing, 334
— Literature Institute, Beijing, 332
— Policy Association, Inc., 1603
— — Research Institute, Philadelphia, 1880
— Student Services, Office of, New York, 1810
— Trade College, Beijing, 336
— Institute, Tel-Aviv, 750
Foreningen af Danske Kunstmuseer, Roskilde, 390
— — — Museumsmaend, Copenhagen, 390
— for National Kunst, Copenhagen, 389
— Norden, Copenhagen, 391
— Svensk Form, Stockholm, 1235
— Svenska Tonsättare, Stockholm, 1235
— til norske Fortidsminnesmerkers Bevaring, 1007
Forensic Scientists Association, Hanoi, 1962
Forest and Forest Products Research Institute, Ibaraki, 813
— Chemical Industry Institute, Beijing, 333
— Department Library and Herbarium, Entebbe, 1312
— Division Headquarters, Dar es Salaam, 1280
— Museum, Peshawar, 1024
— Pest Management Institute, Sault Ste. Marie, Ont., 244
— Products Research and Industries Development Research Commission (FORPRIDECOM), Laguna, 1049
— — — Division, Bangkok, 1283
— — — Institute, Kumasi, 611
— — — Society, Madison, 1617
— Rangers College, Khartoum, 1231
— Research and Education Institute, Khartoum, 1229
— — Centre, Salisbury, Zimbabwe, 2001
— — Institute, Bogor, 708
— — — Kepong, 914
— — — Rotorua, 979
— — — and Colleges, Dehra Dun, 666
— — — of Malawi, Zomba, 912
— — Station, Farnham, 1440
Forestry and Pedology Institute, Shenyang, 332
— Range College, Gorgan, 724
— Association, Hanoi, 1962
— of Nigeria, Ibadan, 991
— Commission, Salisbury, Zimbabwe, 2001
— — Research and Development Division, U.K., 1440
— — Institute, Beijing, 333
— — Research Centre and Museum, Kampala, 1312
— — Institute, Addis Ababa, 424
— — — of Nigeria, Ibadan, 992
— School, Hyalganat, 948
Foretagsekonomiska Institutionen, Åbo, 440
Forhistorisk Museum, Moesgård, 395
Foro Romano e Palatino, Rome, 773
Føroya Búnadarfelag, Tórshavn, 402
— Forngripafelag, Tórshavn, 402
— Fornminnissavn, Tórshavn, 402
— Fróðskaparfelag, Tórshavn, 402
— Landsbókasavn, Tórshavn, 402
— Náttúra—Føroya Skúli, Tórshavn, 402
— Náttúrugripasavn, Tórshavn, 402
— Verfrøðingafelag, Tórshavn, 402
Føroyskt-Bretskt Felag, Tórshavn, 402
Forschungsbereich Denkendorf, 533, 534
— Reutlingen, 534
Forschungsbibliothek Gotha, 507
Forschungsgemeinschaft Bauen und Wohnen, Stuttgart, 533
— Explorations-Geophysik e.V., Gehrden, 532
Forschungsgesellschaft für Agrarpolitik und Agrarsoziologie, Bonn, 528

Forschungsinstitut Borstel, Institut für Experimentelle Biologie und Medizin, Borstel, 532
— der Friedrich-Ebert-Stiftung, Bonn, 529
— für Aufbereitung, Freiburg, 504
— — Edelmetalle und Metallchemie, Schwäbisch-Gmünd, 533
— — Internationale Technisch-Wirtschaftliche Zusammenarbeit der RWTH, Aachen, 533
— — Rationalisierung, Aachen, 548
— — Technikgeschichte am Technischen Museum für Industrie und Gewerbe in Wien, 126
— — Wärmeschutz e.V., München, 533
— — Wirtschaftspolitik an der Universität, Mainz, 529, 590
— und Natur-Museum Senckenberg, Frankfurt, 531
Forschungsstelle für Akademiegeschichte, Berlin (East), 504
— — allgemeine und textile Marktwirtschaft an der Universität Münster, 529
— — chemische Toxikologie, Leipzig, 504
— — Psychopathologie und Psychotherapie in der Max-Planck-Gesellschaft z.F.d.W., Munich, 527
— — Wirbeltierforschung im Berliner Tierpark, 504
— Vennessland, Berlin (West), 527
Forschungsvereinigung Feinmechanik und Optik e.V., Cologne, 531
Forskningsinstitutet för Atomfysik, Stockholm, 1238
Forskningssekretariatet, Copenhagen, 392
Forskningsstationen för astrofysik på La Palma, Saltsjöbaden, 1238
Forsøgsanlæg, Roskilde, 393
Forstliche Bundesversuchsanstalt, Vienna, 124
Forsvarsmuseet, Oslo, 1012
Fort Anne National Historic Park and Museum, 250
— Beauséjour National Historic Park and Museum, 250
— Hays State University, 1730
— Hayes Museum, Georgetown, 1558
— Jesus Museum, Mombasa, 879
— Lewis College, Colorado, 1676
— Museum, Madras, 675
— Valley State College, Georgia, 1699
— Worth Public Library, 1627
— Wright College, Spokane, 1921
Fortress of Louisbourg National Historic Park, 250
Foster Radiation Laboratory, Montreal, 277
Főszékesegyházi Könyvtár, 640
Foundation Center, New York, 1604
— for Business Responsibilities, London, 1449
— — Education, Science and Technology, Pretoria, 1165
— — International Scientific Co-ordination, Paris, 45
— — Scientific Research, Baghdad, 725
— — Technical Institutes, Baghdad, 728
— University, Dumaguete City, 1053
Fourah Bay College, 1148
— — Library, 1148
Fővárosi Szabó Ervin Könyvtár, Budapest, 640
Framingham State College, Mass., 1749
Francis A. Countway Library of Medicine, Boston, 1629
— Bacon Society, London, 1426
Franeker (Fr.) Friesmunt- en penningkabinet, Leeuwarden, 967
Frankfurter Goethemuseum (Goethes Elterhaus), Frankfurt, 542
Fränkische Geographische Gesellschaft, Erlangen, 520
Franklin and Marshall College, Pa., 1870
— College, Indiana, 1716
— D. Roosevelt Library, New York, 1629
— Institute, Philadelphia, 1611

— — Science Museum and Planetarium, 1637
— — Research Centre, Philadelphia, 1621
Frans Halsmuseum, 967
Franz Joseph Dolger Institut, Bonn, 556
— Lehár-Gesellschaft, Vienna, 120
Fraser of Allander Institute for Research on the Scottish Economy (Dept. of Economics), Glasgow, 1531
— Valley Regional Library, 246
— -Hickson Institute, Montreal (Free Library), 248
Frashëri Brothers Museum, Përmet, 56
Fraunhofer-Gesellschaft zur Förderung der angewandten Forschung e.V., 531
— Institut für Bauphysik, 532
— — — Holzforschung, Brunswick, 556
— — — Lebensmitteltechnologie und Verpackung, Munich, 533
Fred and Eleanor Schonell Educational Research Centre, St. Lucia, Qd., 109
Frederic Chopin Museum, Warsaw, 1077
Frederiksberg Kommunes Biblioteker, 394
Fredrikstad Bibliotek, 1010
— Museum, 1011
Free Library of Philadelphia, 1627
— State Provincial Library Service, Bloemfontein, 1161
— University, Amsterdam, 969
— — Bogotá, 355
— — of Brussels, 159
— — — Iran, Teheran, 723
Freer Gallery of Art, 1637
Freie Universität Berlin, 550
Freies Deutsches Hochstift, Frankfurt, 542
French Cultural Centre, Kathmandu, 954
— Institute in the United States, New York, 1607
Freshwater Aquaculture Center, CLSU, Munoz, 1051
— Biological Association, Ambleside, 1431
— Fisheries Research Station, Malacca, 914
Fresno Pacific College, Calif., 1655
Frick Collection, New York, 1638
Friedrich-Alexander-Universität, Erlangen-Nürnberg, 564
— -Ebert-Stiftung e.V., Bonn, 520
— -Miescher-Laboratorium in der Max-Planck Gesellschaft, Tübingen, 527
— -Schiller-Universität, Jena, 512
Friends Historical Society, London, 1422
— Library, 1456
— of the National Collections of Ireland, 730
— — — Libraries, London, 1415
— University, Wichita, 1730
Friendship Museum, Darhan, 947
Fries Genootschap van Geschied-, Oudheid-en Taalkunde Leeuwarden, 957
— Museum, 967
Fritz-Haber-Institut der Max-Planck-Gesellschaft, Berlin (West), 527
— -Thyssen Stiftung, Cologne, 520
Frobenius-Gesellschaft e.V., Frankfurt, 524
Frøðskaparsetur Føroya, Tórshavn, 402
Frostburg State College, Maryland, 1742
Frühchristlich-Byzantinische Sammlung, Berlin (East), 508
Fruit and Food Technology Research Institute, Stellenbosch, 1160
— Tree Research Station, Kanagawa, 813
Frunze Polytechnic Institute, 1375
Fryske Akademy, Ljouwert/Leeuwarden, 959
Fudan University, Shanghai, 337
Fu Jen Catholic University, Taipei, 343
Fuel and Leather Research Centre, Karachi, 1022
Fujian Library, Fuzhou, 335
Fukada Geological Institute, Tokyo, 815
Fukuoka University, 863
Fukushima Medical College, 859
Fulmer Research Institute, Ltd., Stoke Poges, 1446

# INDEX OF INSTITUTIONS

Fundação Calouste Gulbenkian, Lisbon, 1098
— Casa de Rui Barbosa, Rio de Janeiro, 188
— Centro de Pesquisas e Estudos, Bahia, 181
— Educacional de Fortaleza, Ceará, 179
— Faculdade Católica de Medicina, Pôrto Alegre, 211
— "Getúlio Vargas", Rio de Janeiro, 179
— Instituto Brasileiro de Geografia e Estatística, Rio de Janeiro, 182
— — Tecnológico do Estado de Pernambuco (ITEP), Recife, 185
— Joaquim Nabuco, Apipucos, 185
— Moinho Santista, São Paulo, 181
— Norte Mineira de Ensino Superior, Minas Gerais, 199
— Universidade do Rio Grande, 203
— Valparaibana de Ensino, São Paulo, 210
Fundación Charles Darwin para las Islas Galápagos, Ongar, 44
— Cossio, Buenos Aires, 67
— Gildemeister, Santiago, 324
— Juan March, Madrid, 1189
— La Salle de Ciencias Naturales, Caracas, 1952
— "Lisandro Alvarado", Maracay, 1954
— Miguel Lillo, San Miguel de Tucuman, 67
— Universidad Central, Bogotá, 351
— — de Bogotá "Jorge Tadeo Lozano", Bogota, 354
— Universitaria "Simon I. Patiño", La Paz, 173
Fundamental Library of the Academy of Social Science, Pyongyang, 883
Fung Ping Shan Library, Hong Kong, 1559
Furman University, Greenville, S.C., 1886
Fuyo Research Institute, Tokyo, 817
Fylkesmuseet for Telemark og Grenland, Skien, 1013
Fylkesmuseum for Buskerud, Drammen, 1011
Fylkingen, Stockholm, 1235
Fyns Kunstmuseum, Odense, 395
— Stiftsmuseum, Odense, 395
Fynske Landsby, Hjallese, 395
— Musikkonservatorium, Odense, 401

## G

Gabinete Numismático de Lérida, 1203
Gabinetto delle Stampe e Disegni, Venice, 773
— Disegni e Stampe, Florence, 770
— Nazionale delle Stampe, Rome, 772
— Numismatico, Vatican City, 1943
— — di Brera e Civiche Raccolte Numismatiche, Milan, 771
Gabonatermesztési Kutató Intézet, Szeged, 636
Gadjah Mada University, Jogjakarta, 713
Gakujutsu Bunken Fukyukai, Tokyo, 804
Gakushuin Toyo Bunka Kenkyu-Jo, Tokyo, 863
— University, Tokyo, 863
Galeria de Arte Moderna, Santo Domingo, 404
Galería de Arte Nacional, Caracas, 1956
— Facultad de Bellas Artes, San José, 360
— la Casa del Artista, San José, 360
— Nacional de Bellas Artes, 404
— Teatro Nacional, San José, 360
Galéria hlavného mesta Slovenskej socialistikej republiky Bratislavy, 378
Galerie d'Art Contemporain, Nice, 469
— der Stadt Stuttgart, 545
— des Ponchettes, Nice, 469
— du Jeu de Paume, Paris, 466
— Graf Czernin, Vienna, 129
Galerija "Benko Horvat", Zagreb, 1978
— Meštrovic, Split, 1978
— Primitivne Umjetnosti, Zagreb, 1978

— Suvremene Umjetnosti, Zagreb, 1978
— umjetnina, Split, 1978
Galerije Grada Zagreba, 1978
Gallaudet College, Washington, D.C., 1688
Galleria Borghese, Rome, 772
— Civica d'Arte Moderna, Turin, 773
— d'Arte Moderna, Brescia, 769
— — Florence, 770
— — e Padiglione d'Arte Contemporanea, Milan, 771
— degli Uffizi, Florence, 770
— dell' Accademia, Florence, 770
— — Carrara, Bergamo, 769
— di Arte Moderna, Genoa, 770
— — Palazzo Bianco, Genoa, 770
— e Museo di Palazzo Ducale, Mantua, 771
— — Mediovale e Moderno, Arezzo, 769
— "G. Franchetti", Venice, 773
— Museo e Medagliere Estense, Modena, 771
— Nazionale, Parma, 772
— d'Arte Antica, Rome, 772
— — Moderna-Arte Contemporanea, Rome, 772
— dell' Umbria, 772
— delle Marche, Urbino, 773
— di Palazzo Spinola, Genoa, 771
— Palatina, Florence, 770
— Querini-Stampalia, Venice, 773
— Sabauda, Turin, 773
Gallerie dell' Accademia, Venice, 773
Gallery of Polish Painting and Sculpture of the XIV-XVIII Centuries, Cracow, 1076
— — — — — of the XVIII–XIX Centuries, 1076
— — — — — of the XX Century, 1076
Gamalei, N. F., Institute of Epidemiology and Microbiology, Moscow, 1342
Game and Fisheries Museum, Zoo, Aquarium and Library, Entebbe, 1312
Gandhi National Museum and Library, New Delhi, 675
Ganganatha Jha Kendriya Sanskrit Vidyapeetha, Allahabad, 668
Gannon University, Erie, Pa., 1870
Gansu Library, Lanzhou, 335
Garching Instrumente Gesellschaft zur Industriellen Nutzung von forschungsergebnissen m.b.H., 528
Garhwal University, Srinigar, 684
Gattegno, B., Research Institute of Human Reproduction and Fetal Development, Tel-Aviv, 750
Gauhati University, Assam, 684
Gävie Stadsbibliotek, 1239
**Gazetecilik Halkla Ilişkiler Yüksek Okulu, Istanbul, 1309**
Gazi Husrevbegova biblioteka, Sarajevo, 1975
Gdańsk Technical University, 1088
Gdańskie Towarzystwo Naukowe, 1063
Gedenkstätte: Gothaer Parteitag 1875, Gotha, 509
Gedik Ahmed Paşa Library, 1300
Geffrye Museum, 1465
Geh. Staatsarchiv Preuss. Kulturbesitz, Berlin, 538
Gemäldegalerie Alte Meister, Dresden, 509
Gemälde-Galerie, Berlin (East), 508
— — (West), 541
— der Akademie der Bildenden Kunste, Vienna, 129
— Neue Meister, Dresden, 509
Gemeenschappelijk Instituut voor toegepaste psychologie, Nijmegen, 970
Gemeenschappelijke Openbare Bibliotheek, Eindhoven, 964
Gemeente-Archief, Alkmaar, 963
— Deventer, 963
— Dordrecht, 963
— Kampen, 963
Gemeentebibliotheek, Rotterdam, 965
Gemeentelijk Museum het Princessehof, Leeuwarden, 967

# WORLD OF LEARNING

— Museum, Roermond, 968
Gemeentelijke Archiefdienst, Maastricht, 963
— — Rotterdam, 963
Gemeentemusea van Deventer, 966
Gemeentemuseum Arnhem, 966
— The Hague, 967
Gemmological Association of Great Britain, Inc., 1436
Genealogical Office, Dublin, 730
— Society of South Africa, Cape Town, 1155
Genealogiska Samfundet i Finland, Helsinki, 428
General Archives of the City of Tel-Aviv-Yafo, 742
— Assembly Library, Wellington, 981
— Association of Medicine, Hanoi, 1962
— Bureau of Economic Research, Potchefstroom, 1173
— College of Engineering, Barton, A.C.T., 91
— Department of Agricultural Research Stations, Giza, 414
— — — Audio Visual Aids, Ministry of Science, Culture and Arts, Teheran, 722
— Library of Izmir, 1300
— Motors Institute, 1761
— Organization for Housing, Building and Planning Research, Cairo, 415
— People's Committee for Information Libraries, Tripoli, 906
— Scientific Library of Ho Chi Minh City, 1963
— Soedirman University, Purwokerto, 715
Generaldirektion der Staatlichen Naturwissenschaftlichen Sammlungen Bayerns, Munich, 544
Generallandesarchiv Karlsruhe, 539
Genetical Society, Edinburgh, 1431
Genetics Institute, Beijing, 332
— Izmir, 1305
— Society of America, Austin, Texas, 1612
— — —, Nigeria, Ibadan, 991
Genetikai Intézet, Szeged, 638
Geneva College, Beaver Falls, Pa., 1870
Gengo Bunka Kenkyujo, Tokyo, 814
Gennadius Library, Athens, 618
Genootschap Architectura et Amicitia (A. et A.), 956
— tot bevordering van Natur-Genees- en Heelkunde, 958
— voor Wetenschappelijke Filosofie, Paterswolde, 959
Gentofte Kommunebibliotek, 394
Geochemical Society, Blacksburg, Va., 1613
Geochemistry Institute, Guiyang, 332
Geodeettinen Laitos, 431
Geodetic and Research Branch, Survey of India, Dehra Dun, 670
— Institute, Copenhagen, 393
Geodéziai és Kartográfiai Egyesület, Budapest, 634
Geofysiske Kommisjon, 1009
Geografiska Sällskapet i Finland, Helsinki, 428
Geografsko Društvo BiH, Sarajevo, 1971
— — na S.R. Makedonija, Skopje, 1971
— — Slovenije, 1970
Geographical Association, 1422
— — of Zimbabwe, Salisbury, 2000
— Society of Croatia, 1970
— — — India, Calcutta, 661
— — — New South Wales, 88
— — — the Azerbaijan S.S.R., 1325
— Survey Institute, Ibaraki, 814
Geographisch-Ethnographische Gesellschaft, Zurich, 1254
— -Ethnologische Gesellschaft, Basel, 1254
— Kartographische Gesellschaft, Rendsburg, 520
Geographische Gesellschaft, Bern, 1254
— — der DDR, Leipzig, 505
Geography Association, Hanoi, 1962
— Institute, Beijing, 332

2048

Geological and Mining Museum, Sydney, 97
— Association of Canada, Waterloo, Ont., 243
— Institute, Tbilisi, 1327
— — of Israel, Jerusalem, 740
— Mining and Metallurgical Society of India, 664
— — — — — Liberia, 904
— Museum, Beijing, 333
— — Johannesburg, 1165
— — London, 1465
— Society, London, 1433
— — Library, London, 1456
— — of America Inc., 1613
— — — Australia, Sydney, 91
— — — New Zealand, 977
— — — South Africa, Marshalltown, 1157
— — — Zimbabwe, Salisbury, 2000
— Survey and Mines Department, Entebbe, 1311
— — — — — Mbabane, 1232
— — Mining Authority, Cairo, 415
— — Department, Colombo, 1225
— — — Khartoum, 1229
— — — Maseru, 903
— — — Mogadishu, 1153
— — Division, Freetown, 1148
— — Library, Khartoum, 1229
— — — Reston, Va., 1625
— Museum and Library, Entebbe, 1312
— — of Canada, 245
— — — — Library, Ottawa, 247
— — — Ethiopia, Addis Ababa, 424
— — — Ghana, Accra, 612
— — — India, 670
— — — Japan, Ibaraki, 815
— — — Malawi, Zomba, 912
— — — Malaysia, Perak, 914
— — — — Sabah, 914
— — — — Sarawak, 914
— — — New South Wales, 93
— — — Nigeria, Kaduna South, 991
— — — Queensland, 94
— — — South Africa, Pretoria, 1160
— — — Western Australia, 94
— — — Zambia (Ministry of Mines), Lusaka, 1997
— — — Zimbabwe, Salisbury, 2001
Geologinen Tutkimislaitos, 431
Geologisch Bureau, 962
— Mijnbouwkundige Dienst, 1231
— Paläontologisches Institut, Hamburg, 532
Geologische Bundesanstalt, Vienna, 125
— Vereinigung, Mendig, 524
Geologisk Museum, Copenhagen, 395
— — Universitetet i Bergen, 1011
Geologiska Föreningen, Stockholm, 1236
Geologists' Association, London, 1433
Geology and Mines Division, Dodoma, 1280
— — — Palaeontology Institute, Nanjing, 332
— Association, Hanoi, 1962
— Institute, Beijing, 332
Geološki Zavod, Ljubljana, 1973
— — Skopje, 1974
Geolosko-paleontološki muzej, 1978
Geomechanical Comprehensive Research Brigade, Hebei, 333
Geomedizinische Forschungsstelle der Heidelberger Akademie der Wissenschaften, 531
Geophysical Laboratory, Washington, D.C., 1619
— Observatory, Addis Ababa, 424
— — Tihany, 638
Geophysics Institute, Beijing, 332
Georg-Agricola Gesellschaft zur Förderung der Geschichte der Naturwissenschaften und der Technik e.V., Essen, 522
Georg-August-Universität zu Göttingen, 572
George Fox College, Newberg, Ore., 1863
— C. Marshall Space Flight Center, Alabama, 1623
— Mason University, Fairfax, Va., 1916
— Washington University, Washington, D.C., 1688

— Williams College, Downers Grove, 1704
Georgetown Center for Strategy and International Studies, Washington, D.C., 1691
— College, Kentucky, 1736
— University, Washington, D.C., 1691
Georgi Dimitroff Museum, Leipzig, 510
— Dimitrov Higher Institute of Physical Culture, Sofia, 224
— — National Museum, Sofia, 221
Georgia College, Milledgeville, 1699
— Institute of Technology, Atlanta, 1699
— — — Traumatology and Orthopaedics, Tbilisi, 1385
— Southern College, 1700
— State University, 1700
— Tech Research Institute, Atlanta, 1700
Georgian Agricultural Institute, 1369
— Biochemical Society, Tbilisi, 1328
— Botanical Society, Tbilisi, 1328
— Commission on Archaeology, 1327
— — Clay Studies, Tbilisi, 1327
— Geographical Society, Tbilisi, 1327
— Geological Society, Tbilisi, 1327
— Institute of Industrial Hygiene and Occupational Diseases, Tbilisi, 1386
— — Psychiatry, Tbilisi, 1386
— — Subtropical Cultivation, Sukhumi, Kelasuri, 1369
— V. I. Lenin Polytechnic Institute, Tbilisi, 1375
— S. Rustaveli State Institute of Dramatic Art, 1388
— Society for History, Archaeology, Ethnography and Folklore, 1328
— — of Helminthologists, Tbilisi, 1328
— — Patho-Anatomists, Tbilisi, 1328
— — Physiologists, Tbilisi, 1328
— — Psychologists, Tbilisi, 1328
— S.S.R. Academy of Sciences, 1327
— State Art Museum, Tbilisi, 1352
— — Museum of Oriental Art, 1352
— — Picture Gallery, Tbilisi, 1352
— Zoological Society, Tbilisi, 1328
— Zootechnical and Veterinary Institute, 1372
Geotechnical Research Centre, Montreal, 277
Geotectonic Institute, Changsha, 332
Gépipari és Automatizálási Műszaki Főiskola, Kecskemét, 655
— Tudományos Egyesület, 636
Germa Museum (Fezean), 906
German Cultural Center, New York, 1607
— — Tel-Aviv, 738
— — Institute, Colombo, 1224
— — — Dacca, 142
— — — Lagos, 991
— Democratic Republic Academy of Sciences, Berlin (East), 503
— Historical Institute, London, 1422
Germanisches Nationalmuseum, 545
Gerontological Society of America, 1610
Gesamthochschule Paderborn, 599
Gesamtverein der Deutschen Geschichts- und Altertumsvereine, 520
Geschichtsverein für Kärnten, 121
Gesellschaft der Ärzte, Vienna, 122
— der Chirurgen in Wien, 122
— — Musikfreunde in Wien, 120
— des Bauwesens e.V., Frankfurt, 518
— Deutscher Chemiker, Frankfurt, 524
— — Naturforscher und Ärzte, Wuppertal, 522
— für angewandte Mathematik und Mechanik, Frankfurt, 523
— — Anthropologie und Humangenetik, Hamburg, 524
— — Biologische Chemie, Berlin (West), 523
— — Deutsche Sprache e.V., Wiesbaden, 521
— — — und Literatur in Zürich, 1255
— — Deutschlandforschung e.V., Berlin (West), 530

— — die Geschichte des Protestantismus in Österreich, 123
— — Erd- und Völkerkunde, 520
— — Erdkunde zu Berlin (West), 520
— — Ethische Kultur, Vienna, 123
— — Evangelische Theologie, Göttingen, 525
— — Geistesgeschichte e.V., Erlangen, 524
— — Geologische Wissenschaften der DDR, Berlin (East), 505
— — Gerontologie der DDR, Berlin (East), 506
— — Jugendkriminologie und Psychogogik, Vienna, 123
— — Klassiche Philologie in Innsbruck, 121
— — Landeskunde, Linz, 120
— — Mathematik und Datenverarbeitung m.b.H. Bonn (GMD), St. Augustin, 523
— — Medizinische Radiologie und Nuklearmedizin, Vienna, 122
— — Musikforschung, Kassel, 528
— — Naturkunde in Württemberg, Stuttgart, 523
— — Neue Musik e.V., Mannheim, 518
— — Öffentliche Wirtschaft und Gemeinwirtschaft e.V., Berlin (West), 519
— — physikalische und mathematische Biologie der DDR, Berlin (East), 504
— — Programmierte Instruktion und Mediendidaktik e.V., Lahn/Giessen, 523
— — Psychologie der DDR, Berlin (East), 505
— — Rechtsvergleichung, Freiburg, 519
— — Schweizerische Kunstgeschichte, Basel, 1253
— — Schwerionenforschung m.b.H., Darmstadt, 533
— — Sozial- und Wirtschaftsgeschichte, Bonn, 519
— — Strahlen- und Umweltsforschung mbH, Neuherberg, 531
— — Übernationale Zusammenarbeit e.V., Cologne, 521
— — Vergleichende Kunstforschung, 124
— — Wirtschafts- und Sozialwissenschaften (Verein für Sozialpolitik), Göttingen, 519
— — wissenschaftliche Datenverarbeitung m.b.H., Göttingen, 528
— Schweizerischer Landwirte, 1253
— — Maler, Bildhauer und Architekten, Muttenz, 1253
— — Tierärzte, Bern, 1253
— zur Förderung Pädagogischer Forschung e.V., Frankfurt, 530
Gettysburg College, Pa., 1870
Gewerbemuseum, Basel, 1261
— und Gewerbebibliothek, Bern, 1261
Gezira Research Station Library, Wadi Medani, 1229
G.f.K.—Nürnberg, Gesellschaft für Konsum-, Markt- und Absatzforschung e.V., Nuremberg, 529
Ghana Academy of Arts and Sciences, Accra, 610
— Association of Writers, Accra, 611
— Bar Association, Accra, 611
— Geographical Association, 611
— Institute of Architects, Accra, 610
— Institution of Engineers, Accra, 610
— Library Association, Accra, 611
— — Board, Accra, 612
— Medical Association, Accra, 610
— Meteorological Services Department, Legon, 612
— National Museum, Accra, 612
— — — of Science and Technology, Accra, 612
— Science Association, Legon, 611
— Sociological Association, Legon, 611
— Theological Association, Accra, 610

Ghaqda Bibljotekarji, Valletta, 921
Ghazni Museum, 52
Gibraltar Garrison Library, 1559
— Library Service, 1559
— Museum, 1559
— Ornithological Society, 1558
— Society, 1558
Gida, Tarim ve Hayvancilik Bakanliği Bölge Zirai Mücadele Araştirma Enstitüsü, Ankara, 1299
Gidan Makama Museum, Kano, 995
Gifu University, 825
Gilchrist Educational Trust, 1420
Ginkakuji, Kyoto, 821
Gippsland Institute of Advanced Education, Churchill, Victoria, 115
Girton College, Cambridge, 1485
— — Library, Cambridge, 1461
Gisborne Museum and Arts Centre, 982
Gjirokastër Public Library, 55
Glasgow College of Building and Printing, 1553
— — — Technology, 1541
— District Libraries, 1455
— Institute of Radiotherapeutics, 1493
— Museums and Art Galleries, 1472
— School of Art, 1551
Glass Museum, Tel-Aviv, 743
Glassboro State College, New Jersey, 1797
Glasshouse Crops Research Institute, Sussex, 1440
Glaxo Institute for Clinical Pharmacology, Pretoria, 1175
Glenbow Museum, 249
— -Alberta Library and Archives, 246
Glenville State College, West Virginia, 1930
Glicenstein Museum, Safad, 743
"Glinka, M.I.", State Central Museum of Musical Culture, Moscow, 1360
Global Co-operation Society International, Seoul, 893
Gloucester Museums, 1468
Gloucestershire College of Art and Design, Cheltenham, 1551
— County Library, Gloucester, 1454
Główna Biblioteka Lekarska, Warsaw, 1075
Główny Instytut Górnictwa, Katowice, 1070
Glyptothek, Munich, 544
Glyptothèque, Zagreb, 1978
Gmelin-Institut für anorganische Chemie und Grenzgebiete in der Max-Planck-Institut, Frankfurt, 527
Gnessiny State Musical and Pedagogical Institute, Moscow, 1387
Göcseji Múzeum, 644
Goddard College, Plainfield, Vt., 1914
— Institute for Space Studies, New York, 1621
— Space Flight Center, Greenbelt, 1623
Goethe Gesellschaft in Weimar, 506
— House, New York, 1607
— Institut, Accra, 611
— — Addis Ababa, 424
— — Alexandria, 414
— — Algiers, 57
— — Amman, 875
— — Amsterdam, 958
— — Athens, 617
— — Bangkok, 1283
— — Beirut, 899
— — Brussels, 151
— — Casablanca, 949
— — Copenhagen, 391
— — Dar es Salaam, 1280
— — Dublin, 730
— — Genoa, 759
— — Helsinki, 428
— — Hong Kong, 1559
— — Kabul, 52
— — Karachi, 1020
— — Kinshasa, 1995
— — Kuala Lumpur, 914
— — Lagos, 991
— — Lahore, 1020
— — Lomé, 1292
— — London, 1424

— — Manila, 1047
— — Mendoza, 63
— — Milan, 759
— — Montevideo, 1938
— — Montreal, 241
— — Munich, 521
— — Nairobi, 878
— — New Delhi, 661
— — Nicosia, 367
— — Oporto, 1098
— — Oslo, 1007
— — Palermo, 759
— — Paris, 448
— — Rabat, 949
— — Rio de Janeiro, 180
— — Rome, 759
— — San Francisco, 1607
— — Seoul, 885
— — Stockholm, 1236
— — Teheran, 721
— — Tel-Aviv, 738
— — Toronto, 241
— — Trieste, 759
— — Viña del Mar, 323
— -Gedenkstätte (im Inspektorhaus des Botanischen Gartens), Jena, 510
— -Nationalmuseum, Weimar, 510
— -und Schiller-Archiv, Weimar, 510
— -Wörterbuch, Tubingen, 606
Goetz Observatory, Bulawayo, 2002
Gogaku Kyoiku Kenkyuio, 814
Gogol, N.V., House Museum, Suvorosky, 1357
Gőkay, F. K., Library, Istanbul, 1300
Gokhale Institute of Politics and Economics, Poona, 667
Golden Gate University, San Francisco, 1655
Goldsmith's College, London, 1513
Golestan Palace Museum, 722
Gollwitzer-Meier-Institut, Bad Oeynhausen, 531
Goltziusmuseum, Venlo, 969
Gomal University, D.I. Khan, 1025
Gomel State University, 1362
Gonville and Caius College, Cambridge, 1485
— — — Library, Cambridge, 1461
Gonzaga University, Spokane, 1921
Gorakhpur University, 685
Gordion Museum, Ankara, 1301
Gordon College, Wenham, 1749
Gorgas Memorial Institute of Tropical and Preventive Medicine Inc., Washington, D.C., 1610
— — Laboratory of Tropical and Preventive Medicine, Panama City, 1030
Gorky Agricultural Institute, 1369
— A. M., Archives, Moscow, 1347
— V. P. Chkalov Civil Engineering Institute, 1379
— M. I. Glinka State Conservatoire, 1387
— Historical Museum, 1355
— Institute for Skin and Venereal Diseases, 1385
— — of Epidemiology and Microbiology, 1385
— — — Industrial Hygiene and Occupational Diseases, 1386
— — — Restorative Surgery, Orthopaedics and Traumatology, 1385
— — — Water Transport Engineers, 1389
— — — World Literature, Moscow, 1321
— — S. M. Kirov Medical Institute, 1383
— N. I. Lobachevsky State University, 1362
— Memorial Museum, Moscow, 1357
— Museum, Kirov, 1358
— Region Institute of Mother and Child Care, 1384
— Research Institute of Vaccines and Sera, 1386
— Radiophysical Institute, 1362
— State Art Museum, 1353
— A. A. Zhdanov Polytechnic Institute, 1375
Görres-Gesellschaft zur Pflege der Wissenschaft, Cologne, 520

Gorsium Szabadtéri Muzeum, Tác, 645
Gorsky Agricultural Institute, Orjonikidze, 1369
Gorzow Museum, 1077
Goshen College, Ind., 1716
Göteborgs Konstmuseum, 1242
— Museer, 1242
— stads bibliotek, 1239
— Universitet, 1243
— Universitetsbibliotek, 1240
Gothenburg University, 1243
Gotoh Art Museum, Tokyo, 820
Gottfried-Wilhelm-Leibniz Gesellschaft, Hanover, 524
Göttingen Academy of Sciences, 515
Gottlieb Duttweiler Institute for Economic and Social Studies, Rüschlikon/Zürich, 1254
Goucher College, Towson, Md., 1742
Government Archives Service, Pretoria, 1163
— — Windhoek, 953
— Chemist Department, Kampala, 1311
— College Library, Lahore, 1023
— — of Technology, Karachi, 1027
— Library, Tripoli, 906
— Mechanical Laboratory, Tokyo, 817
— Museum, Karnataka, 675
— — Rajasthan, 675
— — and National Art Gallery, Madras, 675
— Observatory, Sydney, 94
— Oriental Manuscripts Library, Tarnaka, 674
— Public Library, Monrovia, 904
— Research Departments, Colombo, 1225
— Technical Institute, Sunyani, 614
Govind Ballabh Pant University of Agriculture and Technology, Uttar Pradesh, 685
Gowthami Library, Rahamhundry, 673
Gozo Public Library, 921
Grace College, Brisbane, 109
Graceland College, Lamoni, Iowa, 1723
Gradska biblioteka, Bitola, 1976
— Knjižnica, Zagreb, 1975
— i čitaonica "Sloboda", Varaždin, 1975
Gradski Muzejs Subotica, 1978
Graduate House, University of Melbourne, Parkville, Vic., 104
— School, Shatin, 1561
— — and University Centre, New York, 1805
— — of Business, Lima, 1046
— — — Surveying, Holon, 753
— — Society, Durham, 1487
Grahamstown Public Library, 1162
Grambling State University, La., 1737
Grand National Assembly Library, Ankara, 1300
Grantham Museum, 1468
Graphic Arts Technical Foundation, Inc., Pittsburgh, 1600
Graphische Sammlung Albertina, 129
— — der Eidgenössischen Technischen Hochschule, 1263
Graphisches Kabinet Stift Göttweig, 131
Grassland Research Institute, Berkshire, 1441
— — Station, Molo, 878
Grasslands Research Station, Marandellas, 2001
Gratian Studies Centre, Vatican City, 1946
Graves Art Gallery, Sheffield, 1471
Gray's Inn Library, 1456
Graz Technical University, 136
— University, 132
Great Lakes Forest Research Centre, Sault Ste. Marie, Ont., 244
— Zimbabwe National Monument, Fort Victoria, 2002
Greater London Group, London, 1510
Grebenshchikov, I. V., Institute of Chemistry of Silicates, Leningrad, 1319
Greco-Roman Museum, Alexandria, 417
Greek Institute, London, 1424

— National Committee for Astronomy, Athens, 616
— — — — Space Research, Athens, 616
— — — — the Quiet Sun International Years, Athens, 616
Green College, Oxford, 1524
Greensboro College, N.C., 1828
Greenville College, Ill., 1704
Greenwich Public Libraries, 1452
Gregorio Araneta University Foundation, Manila, 1054
Gremial Uruguaya de Médicos Radiólogos, Montevideo, 1939
Grey College, Durham, 1487
Greyfriars, Oxford, 1524
Griffith Observatory and Planetarium, 1638
— University, Nathan, Qd., 101
Grinnell College, Iowa, 1723
Grocers' Company, 1420
Grodno Agricultural Institute, 1369
— State Historical Museum, 1355
— — Medical Institute, 1383
— — University, 1362
Groeninge Museum, Bruges, 158
Groninger Museum voor Stad en Lande, Groningen, 966
Grønlandske Selskab, Charlottenlund, 392
Grossherzogliche Porzellansammlung, Darmstadt, 542
Grosvenor House, Stellenbosch, 1165
Grotian Society, London, 1417
Groupe d'Etude et de Synthèses des Microstructures, Paris, 455
— Rhône-Alpes de Recherche et d'Etudes en Gestion, Lyon, 480
Groupement d'Etudes et de Recherches pour le Développement de l'Agronomie Tropicale (G.E.R.D.A.T.), Paris, 457
Grozny Oil Institute, 1379
Grünes Gewölbe, Dresden, 509
Grupo Hidráulico de Desarrollo Agropecuario del Pais, Havana, 363
— Nacional de Radiologia, Havana, 363
— Universitario Latinoamericano para la Reforma y Perfeccionamiento de la Educación, Caracas, 1950
Gruppo Italiano di Storia della Scienza, Florence, 760
Gruuthusemuseum, Bruges, 158
Guangdong Zhong-shan Library, Guangzhou, 335
Guangxi First Library, Guilin, 335
— Second Library, Nanning, 335
Guatemala Academy of Languages, 624
Gubkin, I. M., Institute of Geology, Baku, 1325
Guernsey Museum and Art Gallery, 1467
Guggenheim Museum, New York, 1638
Guildhall Library, London, 1456
— School of Music and Drama, 1552
Guilford College, Greensboro, 1828
Guilin Institute of Karst Geology, Guangxi, 333
Guizhou Library, Guiyang, 335
Gujarat Agricultural University, 685
— Ayurved University, 685
— Research Society, Bombay, 668
— University, 685
— Vidyapith, 686
— — Granthalaya Library, 673
Guk Min University, Seoul, 896
Gulbenkian Foundation, London, 1468
— Library, Jerusalem, 742
— Museum of Oriental Art and Archaeology, Durham, 1468
Gulf Technical College, Isa Town, 141
Gunma University, 826
Guru Nanak Dev University, Amritsar, 686
Gustavus Adolphus College, St. Peter, 1774
Gustinus Ambrosi-Museum, Vienna, 130
Gutenberg-Gesellschaft, Mainz, 528
Gutenbergmuseum, 544
Guyana Institute of International Affairs, Georgetown, 628

— Medical Science Library, Georgetown, 628
— Museum, Georgetown, 628
— School of Agriculture Corporation, East Coast Demerara, 628
— Society, Georgetown, 628
— Zoo, Georgetown, 628
Guybau Technical Training Complex, Mackenzie, Guyana, 628
Guy's Hospital Dental School, 1511
— — Medical School, 1511
— — — — The Wills Library, 1460
Gwebi College of Agriculture, Salisbury, Zimbabwe, 2004
Gwent County Library, Newport, 1455
Gwynedd Library Service, Caernarvon, 1455
Gymnastik- och Idrottshögskolan, Örebro, 1252
— — — Stockholm, 1252
Gyogyo Keizai Gakkai, Tokyo, 803
Gyöngyös Historic Library, 642
Győrffy István Nagykun Múzeum, Karcag, 645
Gyungbok Art Gallery, 887


H

Haaretz Museum, Tel-Aviv, 743
Hacettepe Üniversitesi, Ankara, 1305
Hackney Public Libraries, London, 1452
Hadtudományi Könyvtár, Budapest, 640
Haeju Historical Museum, 884
Haematology Institute, Sichuan, 333
Haffkine Institute, 669
Hafrannsóknastofnunin, Reykjavik, 656
Hagstofa Islands (Statistical Bureau), 657
Hague Academy of International Law, 957
— Conference on Private International Law, 35
Hahn-Meitner-Institut für Kernforschung, Berlin (West), 532
Haifa Museum of Modern Art, 744
— University, Haifa, 745
— — Library, 743
Haigazian College, Beirut, 902
Hailey College of Commerce, Lahore, 1028
Haiphong Museum, 1963
Hajdúsági Múzeum, 645
Hakluyt Society, 1422
Hakodate City Library, 819
— — Museum, 822
Hakutsuru Bijitsukan, 822
Halil Hamit Paşa Library, Isparta, 1300
— Nuri Bey Library, Bor, 1300
Halkevi Library, 1300
Hall of State, Dallas, 1638
Halmstads Stadsbibliotek, 1239
Ham House, Richmond, 1467
Hama Museum, 1277
Hamburger Kunsthalle, Hamburg, 543
— Sternwarte, 532
Hamburgisches Museum für Völkerkunde, 543
Hamdard Foundation, Karachi, 1021
Hämeen Museo, Tampere, 433
Hamhung Historical Museum, 884
Hamilton College, Clinton, 1816
— Kerr Institute, Cambridge, 1551
— Public Library, Ont., 247
Hamline University, St. Paul, Minn., 1774
Hammarskjöld Memorial Library, Kitwe, 1998
Hammersmith and Fulham Public Libraries, 1452
Hampden-Sydney College, Va., 1916
Hampshire County Library, 1454
Hampton Court Palace, 1465
— Institute, Va., 1916
Hancock Museum, Newcastle upon Tyne, 1470
Handels- og Söfartsmuseet, Elsinore, 395
Handelshogeschool, Antwerp, 167
Handelshögskolan i Stockholm, 1251
— Vid Åbo Akademi, Åbo, 440

Handelshögskolans Bibliotek, Stockholm, 1240
Handelshøjskolen i Århus, 400
— — Kobenhavn, 400
Handelshøjskolens Bibliotek, Copenhagen, 394
Handelsinstitut, Saarbrucken, 602
Hangzhou University, 336
Hankuk University of Foreign Studies, Seoul, 890
Hannah Research Institute, Ayr, 1441
Hanoi College of Pharmacy, 1963
— Medical College, 1963
— Polytechnic, 1963
— University, 1963
Hanover College, Indiana, 1716
— School of Veterinary Medicine, 578
— University of Medicine, 576
Hans-Erni-Museum, Lucerne, 1262
— Snyckers Institute, Pretoria, 1175
Hansági Múzeum, Hungary, 645
Hansard Society for Parliamentary Government, 1417
Hanyang University, Seoul, 890
Harbin Shipbuilding Engineering College, 336
— University of Science and Technology, 336
Hardin-Simmons University, Abilene, Tex., 1898
Harding University, Searcy, 1650
Haringey Libraries, 1452
Harkness Fellowships of the Commonwealth Fund of New York, London, 1420
Harleian Society, 1422
Harold Campbell Vaughan Memorial Library, Acadia University, Wolfville, 247
Harper Adams Agricultural College, Newport, Shropshire, 1550
Harriet Irving Library, Fredericton, 247
Harris Museum and Art Gallery, 1470
— -Stowe State College, St. Louis, Mo., 1787
Harrow Public Library Service, 1452
Harry Fischel Institute for Research in Talmud and Jewish Law, Jerusalem, 740
— S. Truman Library, Independence, 1629
Hartford Graduate Center, 1678
Hartwick College, Oneonta, N.Y., 1816
Harvard University, Cambridge, Mass., 1749
— Library, 1633
— Center for Italian Renaissance Studies, Florence, 763
Harveian Society of London, 1428
Harvey Mudd College, Calif., 1655
Haryana Agricultural University, Hissar, 686
Háskólabókasafn, Reykjavík, 656
Háskóli Islands, 656
Hasanuddin University, Makassar (Ujungpandang), 714
Hassei Seibutsu Gakkai, Kyoto, 809
Hastings College, Neb., 1793
Hatay Museum, 1301
Hatfield College, Durham, 1487
— Polytechnic, 1541
— — Observatory, 1541
Hauptbibliothek Berlin (East), 507
Hauptstaatsarchiv, Düsseldorf, 539
— Stuttgart, 540
Haus der Natur, Salzburg, 131
— — Technik e.V., Essen, 548
Haverford College, Pa., 1870
Havering Public Libraries, 1452
Hawaii State Library, 1630
Hawke's Bay Art Gallery and Museum, Napier, 982
— — Medical Research Foundation, Napier, 979
Hawkesbury Agricultural College, Richmond, N.S.W., 112
Hayden Planetarium, New York, 1635
Health College, Budapest, 649
— Education Council, London, 1428
— Laboratory Services, Accra, 612

INDEX OF INSTITUTIONS

**Health Research Project, Canberra**, 100
— Schools, Mongolian P.R., 948
— Systems Research Center, Atlanta, 1700
Hearing and Balance Unit (M.R.C.),
   London, 1444
Hebei Electric Power College, 338
— Library, Baoding, 335
Heberden Society, London, 1429
Hebrew College, Brookline, Mass., 1753
— Union College Cincinnati, 1843
— — Jerusalem, 753
— University of Jerusalem, 746
— Writers Association in Israel, Tel-Aviv,
   730
Hechal Shlomo, Jerusalem, 739
Hedeselskabet, Copenhagen, 393
Hedmarksmuseet og Domkirkeodden,
   Hamar, 1011
Heeresgeschichtliches Museum, Vienna, 129
Hefei Industrial University, 337
Heidelberg Academy of Sciences, 516
— College, Tiffin, 1843
Heidelberger Akademie der Wissenschaften,
   516
Heilongjiang Library, Harbin, 335
Heilsufrødiliga Starvsstovan, Tórshavn, 402
Heinrich-Heine-Institut, Düsseldorf, 535
Helders Marinemuseum, 967
Helikon Kastélymúzeum, Keszthely, 645
Hellenic Association of University Women,
   Athens, 616
— Geographical Society, 616
— Institute of International and Foreign
   Law, 617
— Society of Ptolemaic Egypt, 413
Hellenikon Kentron Paragochikotitos,
   Athens, 617
Helliniki Epitropi Atomikis Energhias,
   Athens, 617
— Mathimatiki Eteria, Athens, 617
Helmcken House Museum, 249
Helmholtz-Institut für Biomedizinische
   Technik, Aachen, 548
Helminthological Society of India, Mathura,
   669
— — Baku, 1325
Helsingfors Universitet, 434
Helsingin Kauppakorkeakoulu, Helsinki, 440
— — Kirjasto, Helsinki, 431
— Kaupunginarkisto, Helsinki, 432
— Kaupunginkirjasto, 431
— Teknillinen Oppilaitos, Helsinki, 441
— Yliopisto, 434
— Yliopiston Eläinmuseo, Helsinki, 433
— — Historiallis-Kielitieteellinen Kirjasto,
   Helsinki, 431
— — Kirjasto, 431
— — Maatalouskirjasto, Helsinki, 432
— — Metsäkirjasto, Helsinki, 432
— — Oikeustieteellisen Tiedekunnan
   Kirjasto, Helsinki, 432
— — Valtiotieteellinen Tiedekunnan
   Kirjasto, Helsinki, 432
Helsinki City Museum, 433
— College of Technology, 441
— School of Economics, 440
— University of Technology, 438
Helwan Observatory Library, 416
— University, Cairo, 419
Helytörténeti Múzeum, Pápa, 645
Hemeroteca Municipal de Madrid, 1199
— Nacional de México, 931
Henan Library, Kaifeng, 335
Henderson Research Station, Salisbury,
   Zimbabwe, 2001
— State University, Arkadelphia, 1650
Hendrix College, 1650
Henley Centre for Forecasting, London, 1442
— **The Management College, Henley-on-
   Thames**, 1552
Henrietta Szold Institute, Jerusalem, 739
Henry and Grete Abrahams Library of Life
   Sciences and Medicine, Tel-Aviv
   University, 742
— Francis du Pont Winterthur Museum,
   1638

— Phipps Institute of Genetics and
   Community Diseases,
   Philadelphia, 1880
"HEPOK"—Istraživačko-razvojni centar,
   Mostar, 1986
Heraldisch-Genealogisch Gesellschaft
   "Adler", 121
Heraldry Society, London, 1422
— — of Southern Africa, Cape Town, 1155
Herat Museum, D, 72
Herbario "Barbosa Rodrigues", 184
Herbarium Bogoriense, Bogor, 710
— Hausknecht, Jena, 512
— Universitatis Florentinae, Florence, 760
Herbert H. Lehman College, Bronx, 1805
— Hoover Presidential Library and
   Museum, 1629
Hereford and Worcester County Libraries,
   Worcester, 1454
Heriot-Watt University, Edinburgh, 1493
— — Cameron Smail Library, 1464
Herman Ottó Múzeum, 645
Herpetological Association of Africa,
   Humewood, 1156
Hertford College, Oxford, 1524
— — Library, Oxford, 1463
Hertfordshire Library Service, Hertford,
   1454
Herty Foundation, Savannah, 1622
Herzen, P. A., State Research Institute of
   Oncology, Moscow, 1386
Herzog Anton Ulrich-Museum, 541
— -August Bibliothek, 538
— World Academy of Jewish Studies,
   Jerusalem, 739
Hessische Landes- und Hochschulbibliothek,
   Darmstadt, 535
— Landesbibliothek, Fulda, 536
— — Wiesbaden, 538
Hessisches Hauptstaatsarchiv, Wiesbaden,
   540
— Landesmuseum, Darmstadt, 542
— — Kassel, 543
— Staatsarchiv, Darmstadt, 539
— — Marburg, 539
Hester Adrian Research Centre for the
   Study of Learning Processes in
   the Mentally Handicapped,
   Manchester, 1518
Hetairia Hellinon Logotechnon, 617
— — Theatricon Syngrapheon, 617
Heythrop College, London, 1512
Hidrometeorološki Zavod S.R. Hrvatske,
   1973
— — Srbije, Belgrade, 1973
High Council of Arts and Literature, Cairo,
   413
— Court of Australia Library, Parkes, 96
— — Kenya Library, Nairobi, 879
— Energy Physics Institute, Beijing, 332
— Point College, N.C., 1828
Higher Council for Promotion of Arts and
   Letters, Riyadh, 1142
— Industrial Institute, Aswan, 421
— — School, Damascus, 1279
— Institute for Administration and
   Commerce, Brussels, 168
— — Technical and Vocational
   Education, Wemmel, 169
— — Translators and Interpreters,
   Antwerp, 166
— — of Arab Music, Giza, 421
— — Architecture and Civil
   Engineering, Sofia, 224
— — Artistic Criticism, Giza, 421
— — Ballet, Giza, 421
— — Chemical Technology, Burgas, 223
— — — Sofia, 224
— — Cinema, Giza, 421
— — Dramatic Art, Giza, 421
— — Electrical and Mechanical
   Engineering, Varna, 227
— — Electronics, Tripoli, 907
— — Food and Flavour Industries,
   Plovdiv, 223
— — Forestry, Sofia, 225

WORLD OF LEARNING

— — — Mining and Geology, Sofia, 225
— — — Music (Conservatoire), Giza, 421
— — — Public Health, Alexandria, 421
— — — Statistics, Khartoum, 1230
— — — Technology, Tripoli, 907
— — — Telecommunications Training,
   Ministry of Posts, Telegraphs and
   Telephones, Teheran, 724
— — — the Islam Faith, Istanbul, 1310
— — — Konya, 1310
— — — Zootechnics and Veterinary
   Medicine, Stara Zagora, 226
— Mechanical Electrotechnical Institute,
   Gabrovo, 223
— Medical Institute (Pleven), 217
— — — (Plovdiv), 217
— — — (Sofia), 217
— — — (Varna), 217
— Pedagogical Institute of Music, Plovdiv,
   227
— Polytechnic Institute, Ulan Bator, 948
— Russian Language School, Ulan Bator,
   948
— School of Economics, Belgrade, 1993
— — Navigation, Istanbul, 1309
— Technical Institute, Nicosia, 368
Hikaku-ho Gakkai, Tokyo, 805
Hill Farming Research Organisation,
   Penicuik, 1441
Hillingdon Borough Libraries, 1452
Hillsdale College, Mich., 1761
Himachal Pradesh Agricultural University,
   Palampur, 686
— — Krishi Vishva Vidyalaya, Palampur,
   686
— — University, Simla, 686
Himeji Institute of Technology, Hyogo, 859
Hiradástechnikai Tudományos Egyesulet,
   636
Hiram College, Ohio, 1843
Hirosaki University, 827
Hiroshima Jogakuin College, 863
— Prefectural Library, 819
— University, 827
Hirsch Music Library, 1456
Hirshhorn Museum and Sculpture Garden,
   Washington, D.C., 1638
Hirszfeld (L.) Institute of Immunology and
   Experimental Therapy, 1069
Hisar Salepcioğlu Library, 1300
Hispanic and Luso-Brazilian Council,
   London, 1435
— Society of America, New York, 1600
— — Library, 1629
— — Museum, 1638
Historian Ystäväin Liitto, Helsinki, 428
Historical and Ethnological Society, Athens,
   616
— Association, London, 1422
— of Kenya, Nairobi, 878
— — Oman, Muscat, 1018
— — Tanzania, Dar es Salaam, 1280
— Museum, Göteborg, 1242
— — Hanoi, 1963
— — Mahebourg, 923
— — of Tel-Aviv-Yafo, 743
— — Warsaw, 1075
— Society of Ghana, 611
— — Israel, Jerusalem, 738
— — Nigeria, Lagos, 991
— — Pennsylvania, 1605
— — — Library, 1630
— — Sierra Leone, 1148
— — the S.R. of Serbia, 1969
— — Trinidad and Tobago, 1293
Historické muzeum Slavkové, Slavkov u
   Brna-zámek, 378
Historico-Ethnographic Museum of the
   Lithuanian S.S.R., Vilnius, 1356
Historiker Gesellschaft der DDR, Berlin
   (East), 505
Historiographical Institute, Tokyo, 856
Historisch-Antiquarischer Verein Heiden,
   1254
— Genootschap "de Maze", 957
— Museum der Stad Rotterdam, 968

Historische Kommission, Vienna, 118
— Landeskommission für Steiermark, 121
— und Antiquarische Gesellschaft zu Basel, 1255
Historischer Verein des Kantons Bern, 1255
— — für Steiermark, 121
Historisches Archiv, Cologne, 539
— Museum, Basel, 1261
— — Dresden, 509
— — Frankfurt, 542
— — Lucerne, 1262
— — St. Gallen, 1262
— — am Hohen Ufer, Hanover, 543
— — der Pfalz, Speyer, 545
— — — Stadt Wien, 129
Historisk Museum, Universitetet i Bergen, 1011
History and Art Museum at Zagorsk, 1357
— — Philosophy of Science Center, Pittsburgh, 1881
— Institute, Titograd, 1990
— — (Ancient History), Beijing, 332
— — (Modern History), Beijing, 332
— — (World), Beijing, 332
— Museum of the City of Cracow, 1076
— of Science Society, 1611
Hitotsubashi University, 828
— — Library, 818
Hittudományi Akadémia Könyvtára, Budapest, 640
H.M. Customs and Excise Library, London, 1456
Ho Chi Minh City Museum, 1963
— — — Museum, 1963
— Phakeo, Vientiane, 898
— Technical Institute, 614
Hobart and William Smith Colleges, Geneva, N.Y., 1816
Hochschulbibliothek der Pädagogische Hochschule Ruhr, Dortmund, 535
Hochschule der Künste Berlin (West), 608
— für Angewandte Kunst in Wien, 138
— — Architektur und Bauwesen Weimar, 513
— — Bildende Künste, Brunswick, 608
— — — Dresden, 513
— — — Hamburg, 608
— — Film und Fernsehen der DDR, Potsdam, 513
— — Grafik und Buchkunst in Leipzig, 513
— — Industrielle Formgestaltung, Halle, 513
— — Künstlerische und Industrielle Gestaltung, Linz, 138
— — Landwirtschaft und Nahrungsgüterwirtschaft, Bernberg/Saale, 513
— — Landwirtschaftliche Produktionsgenossenschaften, Meissen, 513
— — Musik, Munich, 608
— — — Würzburg, 608
— — — "Carl Maria V. Weber", Dresden, 513
— — — "Felix Mendelssohn Bartholdy", Leipzig, 513
— — — "Franz Liszt", Weimar, 513
— — — "Hanns Eisler", Berlin (East), 513
— — und Darstellende Kunst, Frankfurt, 608
— — — — Graz, 138
— — — — — Hamburg, 608
— — — — "Mozarteum" in Salzburg, 139
— — — — — Vienna, 138
— — — — — Theater Hannover, 608
— — Ökonomie "Bruno Leuschner", Berlin (East), 513
— — Philosophie, Munich, 609
— — Politik, Munich, 608
— — Verkehrswesen "Friedrich List", Dresden, 513
— — Verwaltungswissenschaften, Speyer, 608
— Hildesheim, 580

— St. Gallen für Wirtschafts- und Sozialwissenschaften, 1275
Hofburg, Innsbruck, 131
Hofstra University, Long Island, 1816
Hog Culture Institute, Beijing, 333
Hogaku Kyokai, Tokyo, 805
Hoger Instituut voor Bestuurs-en Handelswetenschappen, Brussels, 168
— — — Lichamelijke Opvoeding, Brussels, 159
— Rijksinstituut voor Technisch Onderwijs met Normaalafdelingen, Wemmel, 169
Hogeschool te Tilburg, 972
Högskolan i Borås, 1251
— — Karlstad, 1244
— — Luleå, 1245
— — Örebro, 1247
— — Växjo, 1251
Höhere Bundeslehr- und Versuchanstalt für Textilindustrie, Vienna, 139
— — — — Wein- und Obstbau, Klosterneuburg, 139
— — — — Technologisches Gewerbemuseum, Vienna, 139
— Graphische Bundeslehr- und Versuchsanstalt, Vienna, 139
— Technische Bundeslehranstalt, Graz, 139
— — — Krems, 139
— — — Salzburg, 139
— — — Steyr, 139
— — — für Waffentechnik, Werkzeug-und Vorrichtungsbau, Ferlach, 139
— Bundeslehr- und Versuchsanstalt, Graz, 139
— — — — Innsbruck, 139
— — — — Vienna, 139
— — — — Waidhofen an der Ybbs, 139
Hokkai Gakuen University, Sapporo, 863
Hokkaido University, 828
— — Library, 819
Holburne of Menstrie Museum, Bath, 1467
Hölderlin-Gesellschaft e.V., Tübingen, 521
Hollanda Tarih ve Arkeoloji Enstitüsü, Istanbul, 1299
Hollandsche Maatschappij der Wetenschappen, Haarlem, 956
— — van Landbouw, The Hague, 956
Hollins College, Va., 1916
Holy Family College, Philadelphia, 1871
— Names College, Oakland, 1655
— Redeemer College, Windsor, Ont., 316
Home Economics Research Institute, Ames, 1728
— Office Library, London, 1451
Homerton College, Cambridge, 1485
Homs Museum, 1277
Honduran Academy, Tegucigalpa, 630
Hong-ik University, Seoul, 890
Hong Kong Chinese PEN Centre, 1552
— — Junior Chamber of Commerce Libraries, 1559
— — Library Association, 1559
— — Medical Association, 1559
— — Museum of Art, 1560
— — — History, 1560
— — Polytechnic, 1561
— — — Library 1559
— — Surgical Society, 1559
Honiara Technical Institute, 1152
Honolulu Academy of Arts, 1638
Honourable Society of Cymmrodorion, 1422
— — King's Inns, Dublin, 730
Hood College, Frederick, 1742
Hoogveld-institute, Nijmegen, 970
Hoover Institution on War, Revolution and Peace, 1628
Hope College, Holland, Mich., 1761
Hopkins Society, London, 1426
Hopp Ferenc Keletázsiai Muvészeti Múzeum, Budapest, 643
Horniman Museum and Library, 1466
Horticultural Research Centre, Marandellas, 2001

— — Institute, Giza, 414
— — — Pretoria, 1160
Horticulture and Coffee Research Institute, Salisbury, Zimbabwe, 2001
Hortus Botanicus, Haren, 961
Horyuji, Ikoma-gun, 823
Hosei University, Tokyo, 863
— Library, 818
Hosei-shi Gakkai, Tokyo, 805
Hosokai, Tokyo, 805
Houghton College, N.Y., 1816
— Poultry Research Station, 1441
Hounslow Library Services, 1452
House of Commons Library, 1451
— — Lords Library, 1451
— — Representatives Library, Washington, D.C., 1625
Houston Public Library, 1627
Hovedkomiteen for Norsk Forskning, Oslo, 1008
Howard Payne University, Brownwood, Texas, 1898
— University, Washington, D.C., 1691
Hrdličkovo muzeum Človeka, Prague, 377
Hristo Botev Museum, Kalofer, 221
Hrvatski školski musej, Zagred, 1978
Hrvatsko Numizmatičko Društvo, Zagreb, 1970
— Prirodoslovno Drustvo, 1970
Hubei Construction Industry College, 338
— Library, Wuhan, 335
Hubrecht Laboratory, Utrecht, 961
Huddersfield Polytechnic, 1541
Hué Museum, 1963
Huebner Foundation for Insurance, Philadelphia, 1880
Hugh Lane Municipal Gallery of Modern Art, Dublin, 732
Hughes Hall, Cambridge, 1485
Huguenot Memorial Museum, Franschhoek, 1164
— Society of London, 1422
Human Biochemical Genetics Unit, (M.R.C.), London, 1443
— Biochemistry Research Unit, Tygerberg, 1156
— Ecogenetics Research Unit, Tygerberg, 1156
— Genetics Centre, Montreal, 277
— Sciences Research Council (H.S.R.C.), Pretoria, 1161
— — — Library, Pretoria, 1163
Humanistisk-samhällsvetenskapliga forskningsrådet, Stockholm, 1238
Humanities Research Centre, Canberra, 100
Humberside County Libraries, Hull, 1454
Humboldt Gesellschaft für Wissenschaft, Kunst und Bildung e.V., Mannheim, 520
— State University, Arcata, Calif., 1655
— -Universität zu Berlin (East), 511
Hunan Library, Changsha, 335
— University, Changsha, 336
Hungarian Academy of Sciences, Budapest, 632
Hunter College of the City University of New York, 1805
Hunterian Art Gallery, Glasgow, 1472
— Museum, Glasgow, 1472
— Society, 1429
Huntingdon College, Montgomery, 1643
Huntington College, Indiana, 1717
— Library, Art Gallery and Botanical Gardens, San Marino, 1628, 1638
— University, Sudbury, 270
Huntsman Marine Laboratory, St. Andrews, N.B., 245
Huron College, Huron, 1888
— — London, Ontario, 315
Hus-Museum, Konstanz, 543
Husein Ibrahim Jamal Postgraduate Institute of Chemistry, Karachi, 1026
Hüsrev Pasa Library, 1300
Huston-Tillotson College, Austin, 1898
Hwa Kang Museum, Tapei, 342

2053

HWWA-Institut für Wirtschaftsforschung, Hamburg, 529
Hyderabad Educational Conference, Deccan, 660
Hydraulic Engineering Research Institute, Nanjing, 337
Hydraulics and Sediment Research Institute, Delta Barrage, Egypt, 416
Hydrobiology Institute, Wuhan, 332
Hydrocarbon Development Institute of Pakistan, Islamabad, 1023
Hydro-Geological Society "Tukan", Tashkent, 1335
Hydrographisches Zentralbüro, Vienna, 125
Hydrological Research Unit, Johannesburg, 1182
Hydrometeorologický ústav, Prague, 375
Hygiene Institute, Beijing, 333
Hyo Seong Women's College, Taegu, 896
Hypogée des Dunes, Poitiers, 470
Hysni Kapo House-Museum, Tërbac, 56

I

Ibaraki University, Mito, 830
Ibero-American Bureau of Education, Madrid, 28
— — Institute, Göteborg, 1236
— Amerikanisches Institut Preussischer Kulturbesitz, Berlin (West), 534
Ibragimov, G., Institute of Language, Literature and History, Kazan, 1323
Iceland Glaciological Society, Reykjavik, 656
ICSU Abstracting Board, Paris, 9
— -UATI Co-ordinating Committee on Water Research, Paris, 9
Idaho State University, 1702
Idarah-i-Yadgar-i-Ghalib, Karachi, 1020
Iðntaeknistofnun Íslands, Reykjavík, 656
Ife Museum, 995
IFO-Institut für Wirtschaftsforschung, Munich, 529
Iga Bunka Sangyó Kyokai, 823
IIT Research Institute, Chicago, 1704
Ikatan Dokler Indonesia, Jakarta, 708
Ikomasan Tenmon Kyokai, 810
Ikonenmuseum, Recklinghausen, 545
Iktisat ve Ticaret Yüksek Okulu, Istanbul, 1309
Il Halk Kütüphanesi, Balikeşir, 1300
Illinois Benedictine College, Lisle, 1704
— College, Jacksonville, 1704
— Institute of Technology, 1704
— State Historical Library, 1628
— — Library, Springfield, 1630
— — Museum, Dickson Mounds, 1638
— — University, Normal, 1704
— Wesleyan University, 1704
Illuminating Engineering Society of North America, New York, 1616
Ilmatieteen laitos, Helsinki, 431
Ilmen Mineral Preserve Museum, Cheliabinsk, Region, 1359
Immaculata College, Pa., 1871
Immunochemistry Unit (M.R.C.), Oxford, 1443
Imperial Cancer Research Fund, London, 1445
— College Libraries, London, 1460
— — of Science and Technology, 1510
— Household Agency Library, Tokyo, 818
— War Museum, London, 1466
Incarnate Word College, San Antonio, Texas, 1898
Incorporated Association of Architects and Surveyors, 1412
— — — Organists, 1415
— Guild of Church Musicians, 1415
— Law Society of Ireland, 730
— Society of Musicians, 1415
Independence Hall, Tel-Aviv, 743
— Museum, Vlorë, 56

Independent International University of Social Studies in Rome, 795
India International Centre, New Delhi, 661
— Meteorological Department, New Delhi, 670
— Office Library, London, 1451
— — Records, London, 1451
Indian Academy of International Law and Diplomacy, Delhi, 707
— — — Sciences, 659
— Adult Education Association, New Delhi, 661
— Agricultural Research Institute, 705
— Anthropological Association, Delhi, 663
— Association for the Cultivation of Science (I.A.C.S.), 669
— — — of Biological Sciences, Calcutta, 663
— — — Geohydrologists, Calcutta, 664
— — — Parasitologists, Calcutta, 662
— — — Special Libraries and Information Centres (IASLIC), 660
— — — Systematic Zoologists, 670
— Biophysical Society, Calcutta, 663
— Botanical Society, 663
— Brain Research Association, Calcutta, 669
— Bureau of Mines, Delhi, 671
— Cancer Society, Bombay, 662
— Ceramic Society, 660
— Chemical Society, 663
— Council for Cultural Relations, New Delhi, 661
— — of Agricultural Research, 666
— — — Historical Research, New Delhi, 667
— — — Medical Research, 669
— — — Social Science Research, New Delhi, 671
— — — World Affairs, New Delhi, 660
— — — — Library, 673
— Dairy Association, 659
— Economic Association, Delhi, 660
— Institute for Population Studies, Gandhinagar, 671
— — Library, Oxford, 1459
— — of Advanced Study, Simla, 667
— — — Architects, Bombay, 659
— — — Astrophysics, Kodaikanal, 671
— — — Experimental Medicine, Calcutta, 665
— — — Geomagnetism, Bombay, 671
— — — Management, Ahmedabad, 706
— — — — Calcutta, 706
— — — Metals, 664
— — — Petroleum, Dehra Dun, 665
— — — Philosophy, 671
— — — Public Administration, 667
— — — Radio Physics and Electronics, Calcutta, 671
— — — Science, Bangalore, 705
— — — Technology, Bombay, 705
— — — — Kanpur, 705
— — — — Kharagpur, 705
— — — — Madras, 706
— — — — New Delhi, 705
— — — — Central Library, Madras, 673
— — — World Culture, Bangalore, 661
— Lac Research Institute, 672
— Law Institute, 660
— Library Association, 660
— Mathematical Society, 663
— Medical Association, 662
— Museum, 675
— National Science Academy, New Delhi, 659
— — Scientific Documentation Centre (INSDOC), Delhi, 673
— Pharmaceutical Association, 662
— Phytopathological Society, New Delhi, 663
— Plywood Industries Research Institute, Bangalore, 666
— Psychometric and Educational Research Association, Patna, 667
— Public Health Association, Calcutta, 662

— Rubber Manufacturers Research Association, Maharashtra, 672
— School of Mines, Dhanbad, 706
— Science Congress Association, 662
— Society of Agricultural Economics, 659
— — — Engineers, Calcutta, 664
— — — Genetics and Plant Breeding, New Delhi, 663
— — — Mechanical Engineers, New Delhi, 664
— — — Oriental Art (Calcutta), 660
— Space Research Organization (ISRO), Bangalore, 671
— Standards Institution, New Delhi, 672
— Statistical Institute, 670
— Veterinary Research Institute, Izatnagar, 666
Indiana Central University, 1717
— Institute of Technology, 1717
— State Library, Indianapolis, 1630
— — University, 1717
— University, Bloomington, 1717
— — Library System, Bloomington, 1632
— — of Pennsylvania, 1871
Indianapolis-Marion County Public Library, Indianapolis, 1626
Indira Kala Sangit University, 687
Indo-Iransk Institutt, 1007
Indonesian Institute of Science, Jakarta, 708
— — — World Affairs, 708
Industrial and Commercial Museum, Lahore, 1024
— Centre for Design and Manufacturing Engineering, Salford, 1527
— Consultancy Corporation, Khartoum, 1229
— Decorative Arts College, Hanoi, 1963
— Designers Society of America Inc., McLean, Va., 1616
— Development Board of Sri Lanka, Moratuwa, 1225
— — Unit, Bangor, 1535
— Economics Centre of Northern Thailand, Chiangmai, 1285
— Economy Institute, Beijing, 332
— Exhibition at the House for Dissemination of Scientific and Technical Propaganda, Leningrad, 1359
— Health Foundation Inc., Pittsburgh, 1610
— Injuries and Burns Unit (M.R.C.), Birmingham, 1443
— Mathematics Society, Roseville, Mich., 1612
— Relations, Center, Ames, 1728
— — Centre, Montreal, 277
— — — Wellington, 986
— Research Institute, Accra, 611
— — Institute, Inc., New York, 1622
— — — Japan, Tokyo, 817
— — Unit, Philadelphia, 1880
— Studies and Development Centre, Riyadh, 1142
— Technology Research Institute, Taiwan, 341
— University of Santander, 352
Industrie- und Gewerbemuseum mit Textil- und Modeschule, 1262
Industriens Utredningsinstitut, 1237
Information and Computing Centre of the Ministry of Public Health, Sofia, 220
— Resources Research, Ghent, 154
Informations- und Dokumentationsstelle, Hamburg, 528
Informationszentrum Sozialwissenschaftlichen, Bonn, 530
Informationsverbundzentrum Raum und Bau der Fraunhofer-Gesellschaft, Stuttgart, 518
Ingenieurhochschule Cottbus, 514
Ingenjörsvetenskapsakademien, 1235
Inha University, Incheon City, 890
Inner London Education Authority Library, 1456

— Temple Library, London, 1456
Innis College, Toronto, 309
Inns of Court Bar Library and Probate Library, London, 1457
Innsbruck University, 133
Inokashira Onshi Kōen Shizen Bunkaen, 820
Inönü Universitesi, Malatya, 1306
Insas, Brussels, 170
In-Service Training Institute and Central Research Station, Peradeniya, 1228
Institouton Geologikon kai Metalleutikon Ereunion, Athens, 617
Instituição "Moura Lacerda", Ribeirão Prêto, 210
Institución Cultural Argentino-Germana, Buenos Aires, 63
— "Fernando e Católico" de la Excma. Diputación Provincial, Zaragoza, 1192
Institut Africain, Mouyondzi, 358
— — d'Education Cinématographique (IN.AF.EC.), Ouagadougou, 1937
— — de Développement Economique et de Planification, Dakar, 1147
— — et Mauricien de Statistique et d'Economie Appliquée, Kigali, 1141
— — international, London, 24
— — pour le Développement Economique et Social, Abidjan, 798
— Agricola Catala de Sant Isidre, Barcelona, 1188
— Agronomique et Vétérinaire Hassan II, Rabat-Agdal, 951
— Alfred-Fournier, Paris, 458
— Archéologique du Luxembourg, 151
— — Liégeois, 151
— Armand Frappier, Laval-les-Rapides, 294
— Artoing, Tunis, 1295
— Atlantique des Affaires Internationales, Paris, 23
— Autrichien, Paris, 448
— Belge d'Information et de Documentation, Brussels, 150
— — de Droit Comparé, 150
— — — Normalisation, Brussels, 153
— — des Hautes Etudes Bouddiques, Brussels, 153
— — — — Chinoises, Brussels, 153
— — — Sciences Administratives, Brussels, 150
— Berlin (West), 534
— Botànic de Barcelona, 1191
— Bourguiba des Langues Vivantes, Tunis, 1296
— Canadien des Urbanistes, Ottawa, 239
— — Français d'Ottawa, 241
— Cardiovasculaire, Lyon, 479
— Catholique d'Arts et Métiers, Lille, 495
— — de Paris, 494
— — — Toulouse, 495
— — des Hautes Etudes Commerciales, Brussels, 168
— Collégial Européen, dit de Royaumont, 448
— Culturel Africain, Dakar, 18
— — et Social, Mogadishu, 1153
— — Franco-Chilien, Concepción, 323
— Curie, Paris, 459
— Danois, Brussels, 151
— d'Administration des Entreprises, Yaoundé, 232
— d'Aéronomie Spatiale de Belgique, Brussels, 358
— d'Archéologie, Addis Ababa, 424
— d'Astrophysique, 455
— d'Audiophonologie, Lyon, 479
— d'Economie d'Entreprise et de Formation Sociale pour Ingénieurs (I.E.F.S.I.), Lille, 495
— — Quantitative Ali-Bach-Hamba, Tunis, 1297
— — Scientifique et de Gestion (I.E.S.E.G.), Lille, 495
— d'Education Permanente, Lille, 477

— d'Egypte, 413
— d'Elevage et de Médecine Vétérinaire des Pays Tropicaux, Antananarivo, 910
— — — — des Pays Tropicaux, Bouaké, 798
— — — — des Pays Tropicaux, N'Djamena, 321
— — — — des Pays Tropicaux, Maisons-Alfort, 457
— d'Embryologie, Nogent-sur-Marne, 455
— d'Enseignement Supérieur Lucien Cooremans, Brussels, 168
— d'Estudis Catalans, 1192
— — Europeus, Barcelona, 1222
— d'Ethnologie, Paris, 459
— d'Etude et de Recherche pour l'Arabisation, Rabat, 951
— d'Etudes Administratives, Lyon, 480
— — Agronomiques d'Afrique Centrale, Wakombo, 320
— — Comtoises et Jurassiennes, Besançon, 476
— — de la Population et des Relations Internationales, Lyon, 480
— — et de Recherches Interethniques et Interculturelles, Nice, 482
— — Judiciaires, Lyon, 480
— — Politiques de Paris, 492
— — Rhodaniennes, Lyon, 480
— — Religieuses, Paris, 494
— — Scientifiques de Cargese (Corsica), Nice, 482
— — Sociales, Paris, 494
— — Supérieures des Techniques d'Organisation, Paris, 493
— d'Expertise Comptable (I.E.C.), Lille, 495
— d'histoire de l'Amérique Française, Montreal, 1295
— — du Christianisme, Lyon, 480
— — Sociale, Paris, 446
— d'Hydrologie et de Climatologie, Paris, 460
— — — — Lyon, 479
— d'Hygiène, Abidjan, 798
— — et de Santé Publique, Luxembourg, 900
— — Sociale, Dakar, 1145
— d'Informatique d'Entreprise, Paris, 493
— — et de Management de l'Information, Compiègne, 473
— d'Ontologie et de Stomatologie, Dakar-Fann, 1146
— d'Ophtalmologie Tropicale de l'Afrique de l'Ouest Francophone, Bamako, 920
— d'Optique, Oran, 60
— — Théorique et Appliquée, Orsay, 497
— de Bibliothéconomie et des Sciences Documentaires, Algiers, 57
— — Biologie moléculaire et cellulaire, Strasbourg-Cronenbourg, 455
— — — Physico-chimique, Paris, 458
— — — Sociale et d'Hygiène Mentale, Paris, 497
— — Chimie des Substances Naturelles, Gif-sur-Yvette, 454
— — — et Physique Industrielles, Lyon, 495
— — — Pharmaceutique, Lille, 477
— — Développement Rural (IDR), Brazzaville, 358
— — Droit et d'Economie des Affaires, Lyon, 480
— — — international, Brussels, 35
— — Formation d'Animateurs Conseillers d'Entreprises, Paris, 496
— — — en Education Physique et Sportive, Angers, 496
— — — et de Recherches Démographiques, Yaoundé, 231
— — Français pour les Etudiants étrangers, Dakar-Fann, 1146

— — France, 442
— — Géographie, Algiers, 60
— — — du Proche et Moyen Orient, Beirut, 899
— — Hautes Etudes Industrielles, Lille, 495
— — l'Unesco pour l'Education, Hamburg, 31
— — la Conservation de la Nature, Kinshasa, 1995
— — — Construction, de l'Environnement et de l'Urbanisme, Lille, 477
— — — — et de l'Habitation, Paris, 493
— — — Langue Française, Nancy, 456
— — — Recherche Agronomique, Yaoundé-Messa, 231
— — Langue et Culture Françaises, Paris, 495
— — Mathématiques appliquées "Souleymane Fall", Dakar-Fann, 1146
— — — et de Sciences Physiques, Ouagadougou, 1937
— — Médecine du Travail, Lyon, 479
— — — et d'Hygiène Tropicales, Lyon, 479
— — — Légale et Sociale, Lille, 477
— — — Tropicale, Kinshasa, 1995
— — — — Appliquée, Dakar, 1146
— — — Prince Léopold, Antwerp, 168
— — Météorologie et Sciences Climatiques, Villeurbanne, 479
— — Neurophysiologie et Psychophysiologie, Marseille, 455
— — Paléontologie Humaine, Paris, 497
— — Pédiatrie Sociale, Dakar, 1146
— — Pharmacie Industrielle, Lyon, 479
— — Philosophie St. Pierre Canisius, Kinshasa, 1944
— — Presse et des Sciences de l'Information, Tunis, 1296
— — Psychologie Appliquée, Algiers, 60
— — Recherche en Pédagogie de l'Economie et en Audiovisuel pour la Communication dans les Sciences sociales, Ecully, 456
— — — et d'Histoire des Textes, Paris, 456
— — — Scientifique (I.R.S.), Kinshasa/Gombe, 1995
— — — du Mali, Bamako, 920
— — — et Technique, Tunis, 1296
— — — sur l'Enseignement des Mathématiques, Besançon, 475
— — — — Mathématiques, Nice, 482
— — — — Mathématiques (I.R.E.M.), Villeurbanne, 479
— — — — la Catalyse, Villeurbanne, 454
— — — — le Cadre de Vie et l'Economie, Lyon, 480
— — Recherches Agronomiques de Boukoko, 320
— — — — la République Malgache, 910
— — — Tropicales (I.R.A.T.), Ouagadougou, 1937
— — — et des Cultures Vivrières (IRAT) Awassa, 424
— — — — des Cultures Vivrières, Bamako, 920
— — — — des Cultures Vivrières, Cotonou, 172
— — — — des Cultures Vivrières, Fort de France, 499
— — — — des Cultures Vivrières, Libreville, 502
— — — — des Cultures Vivrières, Lomé, 1292
— — — — des Cultures Vivrières, Paris, 457
— — — — des Cultures Vivrières, Saint-Denis, 500
— — — — Appliquées, Porto-Novo, 172
— — — — Chimiques, Tervuren, 155

## INDEX OF INSTITUTIONS

Institut de Recherches d'Economie
  Appliquée, Beirut, 899
— — — du Coton et des Textiles
  Exotiques (IRCT), Bobo-
  Dioulasso, 1937
— — — — — des Textiles Exotiques,
  Bouaké, 798
— — — — — des Textiles Exotiques,
  Cotonou, 172
— — — — — des Textiles Exotiques,
  Lomé 1292
— — — — — des Textiles Exotiques,
  Maroua, 231
— — — — — des Textiles Exotiques,
  N'Djamena, 321
— — — — — des Textiles Exotiques,
  Paris, 460
— — — économiques et sociales (I.R.E.S.),
  Kinshasa, 1996
— — — en Biologie Moléculaire, Paris,
  455
— — — Sciences Humaines de
  l'Université de Niamey, 990
— — — et de Biologie Appliquée Pastoria,
  Kindia, 627
— — — Fruitières, Kindia, 627
— — — Médicales "Louis Malardé",
  Papeete, 501
— — — pour les Huiles et Oléagineux
  (IRHO), Bambey, 1145
— — — — et Oléagineux,
  Bingerville, 798
— — — — — et Oléagineux, Bobo-
  Dioulasso, 1937
— — — — — et Oléagineux, Douala,
  231
— — — — — et Oléagineux, Paris,
  457
— — — — — et Oléagineux, Sibiti,
  358
— — — Scientifiques et Techniques,
  Tunis-Carthage, 1295
— — — — sur le Cancer, 455
— — — — sur l'Enseignement de la
  Mathématique, de la Physique et
  de la Technologie, Dakar-Fann,
  1146
— — — — — la Lèpre, Bamako, 920
— — — — — Trypanosomiase et
  l'Onchocercose, Bouaké, 798
— — — — le Caoutchouc, Paris, 460
— — — — — — en Afrique, Abidjan,
  798
— — — — — — en Afrique (IRCA),
  Paris, 457
— — — — — les Fruits et Agrumes (IRFA),
  Abidjan, 798
— — — — — et Agrumes, Fort de
  France, 499
— — — — — et Agrumes, Niamey,
  990
— — — — — et Agrumes,
  Nouakchott, 922
— — — — — et Agrumes, Paris, 457
— — — — — et Agrumes, Sainte
  Marie, 499
— — — — — et Agrumes, Saint-
  Pierre, 500
— — — Science Financière et d'Assurance,
  Villeurbanne, 479
— — — — Politique, Brussels, 150
— — — Sciences Mathématiques et
  Economiques Appliquées, Paris,
  457
— — — Sociologie, Brussels, 159
— — — Stomatologie, Lyon, 479
— — — Technologie des Surfaces Actives,
  Biologiques et Chimiques,
  Compiègne, 473
— — — — nucléaire appliquée, Dakar-Fann,
  1146
— — — Théologie Orthodoxe, 497
— — — Topométrie et Ecole Supérieure des
  Géometres et Topographes, Paris,
  493
— del Teatre, Barcelona, 1188

— der Deutschen Wirtschaft, Cologne, 529
— des Actuaires Français, 446
— — Assurances de Lyon, 480
— — bâtiments et travaux publics
  (I.B.T.P.), Kinshasa, 1996
— — Belles Lettres Arabes, Tunis, 1295
— — Etudes Augustiniennes, Paris, 459
— — Hautes Etudes Commerciales, Tunis,
  1296
— — — — de Belgique, 168
— — Industries de Fermentation, Brussels,
  155
— — Musées Nationaux, Kinshasa, 1995
— — Nations Unies pour la formation et la
  recherche, New York, 26
— — Relations Internationales du
  Cameroun (IRIC), Yaoundé, 231
— — Savanes, Département des Cultures
  Vivrières (IRAT), Bouaké, 798
— — Sciences Agronomiques du Burundi
  (ISABU), Bujumbura, 230
— — — — Rwanda (I.S.A.R.), Butare,
  1141
— — — de l'Environnement, Dakar-Fann,
  1146
— — — — la Famille, Lyon, 495
— — — — Santé, Brazzaville, 358
— — — et Techniques de l'Information,
  Kinshasa, 1996
— — — Historiques, Paris, 448
— — — Politiques et de l'Information,
  Algiers, 60
— — — sociales appliquées, Lyon, 495
— — — Techniques de Planification, Algiers, 60
— — — Télécommunications, Oran, 60
— Dominicain d'Etudes Orientales, Cairo,
  414
— du Droit Comparé, Lyon, 480
— — — de l'Environnement, Lyon, 480
— — Economique Agricole, Brussels, 153
— — et Musée Voltaire, Geneva, 1255
— — Observatoire de Physique du Globe
  du Puy de Dôme, 459
— Européen des Hautes Etudes
  Internationales, Nice, 497
— facultaire des sciences agronomiques
  (I.F.A.), Yangambi, 1996
— Finanzen und Steuern e.V., 530
— Fondamental d'Afrique Noire, Dakar, 1145
— Français, Amsterdam, 958
— — Bonn, 521
— — Budapest, 635
— — Copenhagen, 391
— — Madrid, 1190
— — Stockholm, 1236
— — Tel-Aviv, 738
— — Vienna, 121
— d'Archéologie, Beirut, 899
— — Orientale, Cairo, 415
— d'Athènes, 617
— d'Etudes Anatoliennes d'Istanbul,
  1299
— — Arabes, Damascus, 1277
— — Byzantines, Paris, 448
— — d'Haiti, Port-au-Prince, 629
— — d'Histoire Sociale, Paris, 448
— — d'Ingénierie, Paris, 493
— — d'Iranologie de Téhéran, 721
— — de l'Energie, 453
— — — Lisbonne, 1098
— — — Porto, 1098
— — Pétrole, Rueil Malmaison, 460
— — des Relations Internationales, Paris,
  446
— — du Café, du Cacao et autres plantes
  stimulantes (I.F.C.C.), Paris, 457
— — — — et du Cacao (I.F.C.C.),
  Abidjan, 798
— — — — — Cacao, Boukoko, 320
— — — Froid Industriel, Paris, 493
— — — Royaume-Uni, 1424
— Franco-Japonais de Tokyo, 806
— für Afrika-Kunde, Hamburg, 530
— — Allgemeine Botanik und Botanischer
  Garten der Universität, Hamburg,
  532

— — Mikrobiologie, Bern, 1258
— — Überseeforschung der Stiftung
  "Deutsches Übersee-Institut",
  Hamburg, 529
— — Angewandte Botanik, Hamburg, 532
— — Pflanzensoziologie, Klagenfurt,
  125
— — Sozial- und Wirtschaftsforschung,
  Vienna, 124
— — Wirtschaftsforschung, Tübingen,
  529
— — Arbeits- und Baubetriebswissen-
  schaft, Vienna, 126
— — Arbeitsmarkt- und Berufsforschung
  der Bundesanstalt für Arbeit,
  Nurnberg, 529
— — Arbeitsphysiologie, Dortmund, 561
— — Asienkunde, Hamburg, 525
— — Astronomie, Zurich, 1258
— — der Universität Innsbruck, 126
— — — — Wien, 126
— — und Astrophysik der Universität
  Wurzburg, 532
— — — und Sonnenobservatorium
  Wendelstein, Munich, 533
— — Aufbaustudien, Mannheim, 590
— — Auslandsbeziehungen, Stuttgart, 519
— — Bauforschung, Hanover, 533
— — Bibliothekarausbildung, Berlin (West),
  551
— — Biochemie der Pflanzen, Halle, 504
— — — und Technologie, Hamburg, 528
— — Biotechnologie an der
  Kernforschungsanlage Jülich
  G.m.b.H., Düsseldorf, 563
— — das Recht der Wasserwirtschaft,
  Bonn, 556
— — Spar-, Giro- und Kreditwesen,
  Bonn, 556
— — Demographie, Vienna, 119
— — den Wissenschaftlichen Film,
  Göttingen, 518
— — deutsche Sprache, Mannheim, 531
— — die Pädagogik der Naturwissen-
  schaften an der Universität Kiel,
  584
— — Empirische Wirtschaftsforschung,
  Mannheim, 590
— — — Saarbrucken, 602
— — Entwicklungshilfe, Saarbrucken, 602
— — Erdölforschung, Hanover, 534
— — Ernährung und Diätetik, Düsseldorf,
  563
— — Europäische Geschichte, Mainz, 530
— — Fangtechnik, Hamburg, 528
— — Festkörperphysik und Elektronen-
  mikroskopie, Halle, 504
— — Gegenwartsvolkskunde, Vienna, 119
— — Geographie und Geoökologie, Leipzig,
  504
— — — — der Akademie der
  Wissenschaften der DDR:
  Arbeitsgruppe Geographische
  Zentralbibliothek, 506
— — Gerichtspsychologie, Bochum, 533
— — Gewerbeforschung, Vienna, 126
— — gewerbliche Wasserwirtschaft und
  Luftreinhaltung, Cologne, 526
— — Handelsforschung an der Universität
  zu Köln, 529
— — Hirnforschung, Vienna, 119
— — Hochenergiephysik, Vienna, 119
— — — Zeuthen, 504
— — höhere Studien und wissenschaftliche
  Forschung, Vienna, 124
— — Immunologie, Basel, 1258
— — Informationsverarbeitung, Vienna,
  119
— — International Vergleichende
  Wirtschafts- und Sozialstatistik
  an der Universität Heidelberg, 530
— — Internationale Beziehungen an der
  Akademie für Staats- und
  Rechtswissenschaft der DDR,
  Potsdam-Babelsberg, 513
— — Kartographie, Vienna, 119

— — Kirchliche Sozialforschung, Vienna, 126
— — — Zeitgeschichte, Salzburg, 126
— — klassische deutscher Literatur, Weimar, 510
— — Kunststoffverarbeitung in Industrie und Handwerk, Aachen, 548
— — Küsten- und Binnenfischerei, Hamburg, 528
— — landwirtschaftliche Marktforschung der Bundesforschungsanstalt für Landwirtschaft Braunschweig-Völkenrode (FAL), Brunswick, 529
— — — Technologie und Zuckerindustrie, Brunswick, 556
— — Limnologie, Vienna, 119
— — Literatur "Johannes R. Becher", Leipzig, 506
— — Medizin an der Kernforschungsanlage Jülich GmbH, Düsseldorf, 563
— — Meeresforschung, Bremerhaven, 532
— — Meereskunde, Rostock, 504
— — — an der Christian-Albrechts-Universität Kiel, 584
— — Mittelalterliche Realienkunde Österreichs, Krems, 119
— — Molekularbiologie, Vienna, 119
— — Neurobiologie, Magdeburg, 504
— — nichtnumerische Informationsverarbeitung, Rorschach, 1259
— — Österreichische Kunstforschung, Vienna, 124
— — Physik der Werkstoffbearbeitung, Berlin (East), 504
— — Politische Wissenschaft, Salzburg, 124
— — Polymerenchemie, Teltow-Seehof, 504
— — Publikumsforschung, Vienna, 119
— — Radiumforschung und Kernphysik, Vienna, 119
— — Raumforschung, Berlin-Adlershof, 504
— — Religionswissenschaft und Theologie, 126
— — Röntgenfeinstrukturforschung analyse, Graz, 119
— — Seefischerei, Hamburg, 528
— — Seeverkehrswirtschaft, Bremen, 530
— — Sozialpolitik und Sozialreform, Vienna, 124
— — Sozialwissenschaften, Mannheim, 590
— — Sozio-Ökonomische Entwicklungsforschung, Vienna, 119
— — Spektrochemie und angewandte Spektroskopie, Dortmund, 532
— — Technische Chemie, Leipzig, 504
— — Technologie der Fasern, Dresden, 504
— — textile Messtechnik M'Gladbach, 533
— — Textiltechnik der Institute für Textil- und Faserforschung Stuttgart, 534
— — Theorie des Staates und des Rechts, Berlin (East), 504
— — — Geschichte und Organisation der Wissenschaft, Berlin (East), 504
— — Umweltschutz und Umweltgüteplanung, Dortmund, 561
— — Umweltwissenschaften und Naturschutz, Vienna, 119
— — Vergleichende Verhaltensforschung, Vienna, 119
— — Vogelforschung "Vogelwarte Helgoland", Wilhelmshaven, 532
— — Volkswirtschaftslehre und Statistik, Mannheim, 590
— — Wasserchemie und Chemische Balneologie der Technischen Universität, Munich, 531
— — Weltraumforschung, Bochum, 533
— — — Graz, 119
— — Weltwirtschaft an der Universität Kiel, 584
— — Werkstoffkunde der Technischen Hochschule Darmstadt, 534
— — Wirkstofforschung, Berlin (East), 504
— — Wirtschafts- und Gesellschaftspolitik, Bonn, 529

— — Wirtschaftsgeschichte, Berlin (East), 504
— — Wirtschaftsinformatik, Saarbrücken, 603
— — Wirtschaftspolitik an der Universität zu Köln, 529
— — Wissenschaft und Kunst, Vienna, 125
— — Wissenschaftstheorie, Salzburg, 125
— — Zeitgeschichte, Munich, 531
— Géographique du Zaire, Kinshasa-Gombe, 1995
— — National, Brussels, 151
— — — Paris, 447
— — — Yaoundé, 231
— — — (Agence de Dakar), Dakar, 1145
— Géologique Albert-de-Lapparent, Paris, 495
— Gramme Liège, 168
— Grand-Ducal, Luxembourg, 908
— Haïtiano-Américain, 629
— Hydrométéorologique de Formation et de Recherche, Gambetta-Oran, 60
— hygieny a epidemiologie, Prague, 375
— International d'Administration Publique, Paris, 492
— — de Droit de l'Espace, Paris, 35
— — — la soudure, London, 33
— — — Littérature pour Enfants et de Recherches sur la Lecture, Vienna, 22
— — — philosophie—IIP, Paris, 25
— — — Sociologie—IIS, Rome, 24
— — — statistique, Voorburg, 49
— — des Droits de l'Homme, Strasbourg, 497
— — sciences administratives, Brussels, 12
— — du fer et de l'acier, Brussels, 34
— — — froid, Paris, 34
— — — théâtre, Paris, 20
— — pour l'unification du droit privé, Rome, 35
— — — la Conservation des Objets d'Art et d'Histoire, London, 20
— Interuniversitaire des Sciences Nucléaires, Brussels, 154
— "Jožef Stefan", Ljubljana, 1972
— Jules Bordet, Brussels, 159
— juridique international, The Hague, 36
— Malgache des Arts Dramatiques et Folkloriques (Imadefolk), Antananarivo, 910
— Max von Laue-Paul Langevin (ILL), Grenoble, 460
— Meurice Chimie, Brussels, 155
— Michel-Pacha, Lyon, 479
— National Agronomique, Algiers, 60
— — — de Paris-Grignon, 492
— — — Tunisie, Tunis, 1297
— — d'Administration de Gestion et des Hautes Etudes Internationales (INAGHEI), Port-au-Prince, 629
— — d'Archéologie et Art, Tunis, 1295
— — d'Astronomie et de Géophysique (INAG), Paris, 456
— — d'Education (INE) Ouagadougou, 1937
— — d'Etude du Travail et d'Orientation Professionnelle, 459, 493
— — d'Etudes Démographiques, 457
— — d'Hygiène, Rabat, 949
— — — et de Sécurité, Algiers, 57
— — de Cartographie, Algiers, 57
— — — Formation des Cadres Supérieurs de la Vente, Paris, 493
— — — Géodésie et Cartographie, Antananarivo, 910
— — — la Recherche Agronomique, Algiers, 57
— — — — Paris, 457
— — — — de Tunisie, Ariana, 1295
— — — — Scientifique, Lomé, 1292
— — — Quebec, 294
— — — Santé et de la Recherche Médicale, Paris, 458

— — — Statistique et des Etudes Economiques, Paris, 457
— — — Métrologie, Paris, 493
— — — musique et de danse, Kenitra, 951
— — — Nutrition et de Technologie Alimentaire, Tunis, 1297
— — — Physique Nucléaire et de Physique des Particules, (I.N2. P3), Paris, 456
— — — Recherche en Informatique et en Automatique, Le Chesnay, 460
— — — — Pédagogique, Paris, 458
— — — — Scientifique, Butare, 1141
— — — recherches agronomiques du Niger, Niamey, 990
— — — et Documentation, Conakry, 627
— — — — Forestières de Tunisie, Ariana, 1295
— — — — Textiles et Cultures Vivrières, Bangui, 320
— — — — Vétérinaires, Brussels, 153
— — — — Tunis, 1295
— — — Service Social, Tunis, 1297
— — — Statistique, Brussels, 154
— — — et d'Economie Appliquée, Rabat, 951
— — — des Arts (I.N.A.), Kinshasa, 1996
— — — hautes études islamiques, Boutilimit, 922
— — — Industries Extractives (INIEX), Liège, 155
— — — Sciences Appliquées de Lyon, 493
— — — — Rennes, 493
— — — — de l'Education, Tunis, 1295
— — — — et Techniques Nucléaires—INSTN, Gif-sur-Yvette, 460
— — — — Humaines, N'Djamena, 321
— — — Techniques de la Documentation, Paris, 493
— — — — Economiques et Comptables, Paris, 493
— — Genevois, 1256
— — Polytechnique, Grenoble, 491
— — — de Lorraine, Nancy, 491
— — — — Toulouse, 491
— — pour l'Etude et la Recherche Agronomique (INERA), Kisangani, 1995
— — Scientifique et Technique d'Océanographie et de Pêche, Salammbô, 1295
— — Supérieur de Chimie, Mont-Saint-Aignan, 488
— — — — l'Enseignement Technique, Abidjan, 799
— Néerlandais, Paris, 448
— Néo-Hellénique, Lyon, 480
— Neurologique Belge, Brussels, 154
— Océanographique, Paris, 497
— Orthodoxe Français de Paris (Saint-Denis), 497
— Pan-Africain pour le Développement, Geneva, 25
— Pasteur, Antananarivo, 910
— — Bangui, 320
— — Casablanca, 949
— — Cayenne, 499
— — Dakar, 1145
— — d'Algérie, 57
— — Hellénique, 617
— — Paris, 458
— — Tanger, 949
— — Teheran, 721
— — Tunis, 1295
— — de Côte d'Ivoire, Abidjan, 798
— — — la Guadeloupe, 499
— — — Nouméa, 500
— — du Brabant, Brussels, 154
— — — Cameroun, Yaoundé, 231
— Pédagogique National, Rabat, 951
— Pertanian Bogor, 712
— Polytechnique Gamal Abdul Nasser de Conakry, 627
— — Rural de Katibougou, Koulikoro, 920

INDEX OF INSTITUTIONS

Institut pour l'Encouragement de la
   Recherche Scientifique dans
   l'Industrie et l'Agriculture,
   Brussels, 155
— — l'Etude des Méthodes de Direction de
   l'Entreprise (I.M.E.D.E.),
   Lausanne, 1275
— — le Redressement de l'Art Complet,
   Ghent, 150
— Prometnih Znanosti, Zagreb, 1972
— Prophylactique, 458
— Romand de Recherches et de
   Documentation Pédagogiques,
   Neuchâtel, 1254
— Royal des Relations Internationales,
   Brussels, 154
— — Sciences Naturelles de Belgique,
   154
— — Météorologique de Belgique, 155
— "Rudjer Bošković", Zagreb, 1972
— Scientifique, Rabat, 949
— — des Pêches Maritimes, Casablanca,
   950
— — et Technique de l'Alimentation, Paris,
   493
— Sénégalais de Recherches Agricoles,
   Dakar, 1145
— Sérothérapique et Vaccinal, Suisse, 1258
— Sparchlabor, Mannheim, 590
— Suisse de recherche sur les Pays de l'Est,
   Bern, 1258
— — recherches expérimentales sur le
   cancer, Lausanne, 1258
— — pour l'Etude de l'Art, Zürich, 1253
— Supérieur Agricole de Beauvais, 495
— — d'Agriculture, Lille, 495
— — — Rhône-Alpes, Lyon, 495
— — d'Architecture Victor Horta de la
   Ville de Bruxelles, 168
— — d'arts et métiers (I.S.A.M.), Kinshasa,
   1996
— — d'Education Physique et Sportive,
   Brazzaville, 358
— — d'Electronique de Paris, 495
— — — du Nord, Lille, 495
— — d'Études agronomiques (I.S.E.A.) de
   Bengamisa, Kisangani, 1996
— — — — Mondongo, Lisala, 1996
— — sociales de Lubumbashi, 1996
— — d'Interprétariat et de Traduction,
   Paris, 495
— — de commerce (I.S.C.), Kinshasa, 1996
— — — — Kisangani, 1996
— — — Saint-Louis, Brussels, 168
— — développement rural de Bukavu,
   1996
— — Gestion des Entreprises, Tunis,
   1296
— — l'État de Traducteurs et
   Interprètes, Brussels, 168
— — Pédagogie, Paris, 494
— — statistique (I.S.S.), Lubumbashi,
   1996
— — techniques appliquées (I.S.T.A.),
   Kinshasa, 1996
— — Technologie, Kirchberg-
   Luxembourg, 909
— — des Matériaux et de la Construction
   Mécanique, 494
— — Sciences de l'Education
   (INSSED), Brazzaville, 358
— — — Economiques, Juridiques,
   Administratives et de Gestion,
   Brazzaville, 358
— — — Humaines, Quebec, 273
— — techniques médicales (I.S.T.M.),
   Kinshasa, 1996
— — du Béton Armé, Marseille, 494
— — Industriel, Brussels, 155
— — Polytechnique, Ouagadougou, 1937
— — Technique d'Haiti, Port-au-Prince,
   629
— — — de Gabès, 1296
— Technique de Banque, Paris, 493
— — Prévision Economique et Sociale,
   Paris, 493

— — du Bâtiment et des Travaux Publics,
   Paris, 460
— — Roubaisien, Roubaix, 495
— — Technologique d'Art, d'Architecture et
   d'Urbanisme de Tunis, 1297
— Teknologi, Bandung, 712
— — Tekstil, Bandung, 710
— — 10 Nopember, Surabaja, 717
— Textile de France, Boulogne, 498
— Togolais des Sciences Humaines, Lomé,
   1292
— Universitaire d'Etudes du Développe-
   ment, Geneva, 1268
— — — Européennes, Geneva, 1268
— — — — Turin, 795
— — de Formation Continue, Besançon,
   475
— — — Hautes Etudes Internationales,
   Geneva, 1268
— — — la Recherche Scientifique, Rabat,
   951
— — — Technologie, Ouagadougou, 1937
— — — International de Luxembourg, 908
— — za Folklor, Skopje, 1974
— — Makedonski Jazik "Krste Misirkov",
   Skopje, 1974
— — Nacionalna Istorija, Skopje, 1974
— — Nuckearne Nauke "Boris Kidric",
   Belgrade, 1972
— — Oceanografiju i Ribarstvo, Split, 1973
— — Pamuk, Strumica, 1974
— — raziskovanje krasa, Postojna, 1970
— — Tutun, Prilep, 1974
Institute for Accountancy Research, Ramat-
   Gan, 745
— — Administration Studies, Antwerp, 166
— — Advanced Studies in the Humanities,
   Edinburgh, 1490
— — Study, Princeton, 1797
— — Torah Studies, Ramat-Gan, 745
— — Areospace Studies, Downsview, Ont.,
   246
— — African Studies, University of
   Zambia, Lusaka, 1997
— — Afrikaans Culture and Folklore,
   Potchefstoom, 1173
— — Agrarian Economy and Sociology,
   Antwerp, 166
— — Agricultural and Biological Sciences,
   Okayama, 844
— — — Mechanization, Belgrade, 1972
— — — Policy and Law, St. Gallen, 1275
— — — Research, Sendai, 851
— — — Zaria, 993
— — American Studies, Johannesburg,
   1176
— — Applied Research on Natural
   Resources, Jadiriyah, Baghdad,
   725
— — Archaeological Research, Tel-Aviv,
   750
— — Asian Studies, Tokyo, 862
— — Atomic Studies, Bedford Park, S.A.,
   101
— — Australasian Geodynamics, Bedford
   Park, S.A., 101
— — Automation and Operations Research,
   Fribourg, 1266
— — Balkan Studies, Thessaloniki, 617
— — Banking, St. Gallen, 1275
— — Behavioural Research, Downsview,
   Ont., 318
— — Sciences, Pretoria, 1178
— — Biological and Medical Research,
   Titograd, 1990
— — Biostatistics, Tygerberg, 1155
— — Business Administration Research,
   Tokyo, 874
— — Cancer Research, Philadelphia, 1618
— — Cardio-Angiological Research,
   Fribourg, 1266
— — Cereal Crops Improvement, Tel-Aviv
   750
— — Chemical Research, Kyoto, 836
— — Child and Adult Guidance,
   Johannesburg, 1176

WORLD OF LEARNING

— — — Guidance, Bellville, S.A., 1180
— — Chromatography, Pretoria, 1175
— — Community Art Studies, Eugene,
   1866
— — Computer Sciences, Pretoria, 1178
— — — — and Technology, Washington,
   D.C., 1623
— — Consumer Ergonomics,
   Loughborough, 1514
— — Contemporary History, Bloemfontein,
   1172
— — Criminology, Pretoria, 1178
— — Crops Research at Kragujevac, 1985
— — Cultural Research, Tunbridge Wells,
   1442
— — Data Retrieval, Ramat-Gan, 745
— — Defence Studies and Analyses, New
   Delhi, 667
— — Demography, Padang, 712
— — Dental Research, Sydney, 110
— — Developing Countries, Antwerp, 166
— — Development Studies, Johannesburg,
   1176
— — — — Nairobi, 880
— — Direct Energy Conversion,
   Philadephia, 1880
— — East European Studies, Fribourg,
   1266
— — Economics Research, St. Gallen, 1275
— — Ecumenical Studies, Fribourg, 1266
— — Educational Research, Jyväskylä,
   436
— — — — Warsaw, 1070
— — — — and Development, St. Johns,
   285
— — — Technology, Guildford, 1532
— — — Pretoria, 1178
— — Electron Microscopy, Tygerberg, 1155
— — Employment Research, Coventry,
   1539
— — Energy Research Syracuse, N.Y.,
   1822
— — — Studies, Bedford Park, S.A., 101
— — — Johannesburg, 1176
— — Environmental Medicine,
   Philadelphia, 1880
— — — Studies, Philadelphia, 1880
— — Fermentation, Osaka, 817
— — Fibres and Forest Products,
   Jerusalem, 740
— — Folklore Research, Zagreb, 1973
— — Fruit Reasearch at Čačak, 1985
— — Future Technology, Tokyo, 817
— — Geological Research on the Bushveld
   Complex, Pretoria, 1175
— — German History, Tel-Aviv, 750
— — Groundwater Studies, Bloemfontein,
   1172
— — Higher Education, Armidale, 106
— — Historical Research, Bellville, S.A.,
   1180
— — Human Relations, Lusaka, 1998
— — Industrial and Labor Relations,
   Eugene, 1866
— — — Research and Standards, Dublin,
   731
— — International Co-operation, Ottawa,
   293
— — — Sociological Research, Cologne, 23
— — — Studies of Values in Politics,
   Philadelphia, 1880
— — Islamic Studies, Johannesburg, 1176
— — Journalism, Fribourg, 1266
— — Labour and Management, Seoul, 894
— — — Social Studies, Tel-Aviv, 750
— — — Relations, Pretoria, 1178
— — Latin-American Research and for
   Development Co-operation, Saint-
   Gallen, 1275
— — Management, Padang, 712
— — Marine Environmental Research,
   Plymouth, 1445
— — Materials Research, Hamilton, Ont.,
   280
— — Medical Literature, Tygerberg, 1155
— — — Research, Kuala Lumpur, 914

— — — and Occupational Health, Zagreb, 1973
— — — — Training, Nairobi, 878
— — Medieval Japanese Studies, Philadelphia, 1880
— — Mediterranean Affairs, New York, 1603
— — Microstructures (Epitaxy, Thin Layers, Electro-Optics, Mos and other structures), Pretoria, 1175
— — Missiological Research, Pretoria, 1175
— — Missions and the Study of Religions, Fribourg, 1266
— — Modern Biography, Nathan, Qd., 101
— — — Greek Studies, Thessaloniki, 621
— — — Serbo-Croatian, Sarajevo, 1973
— — Molecular and Cellular Evolution, Coral Gables, 1698
— — Nature Preservation of the S.R. of Croatia, Zagreb, 1973
— — — — Research, Tel-Aviv, 750
— — Neurological Sciences, Philadelphia, 1880
— — Nuclear Study, Tokyo, 856
— — Oaxacan Studies, Oaxaca, 934
— — Operations Research, Saint-Gallen, 1275
— — Palestine Studies, Beirut, 899
— — Pedology, Potchefstroom, 1173
— — Petroleum Research and Geophysics, Holon, 740
— — Philosophical Research, Chicago, 1622
— — Plant Protection, Belgrade, 1972
— — Policy Research and Evaluation, University Park, Pa., 1877
— — Practical English, Fribourg, 1266
— — — French, Fribourg, 1266
— — — German, Fribourg, 1266
— — Protein Research, Suita City, 847
— — Public Health, Tilburg, 973
— — Regional Economic Research, Padang, 712
— — Religion and Culture, Nagoya, 866
— — Research and Planning in Science and Education, Teheran, 721
— — — in Children's Literature, Potchefstroom, 1173
— — — — Contemporary Political and Economic Affairs, Tokyo, 874
— — — — Human Abilities, St. John's, Newfoundland, 284
— — — into Religious Zionism, Ramat-Gan, 745
— — — of Eretz-Israel, Jerusalem, 741
— — — on Animal Diseases (A.R.C.), Newbury, 1440
— — — — Land and Water Resources, University Park, 1877
— — — — Technology of Communications, Hanoi, 1962
— — Sacred Music, New Haven, 1686
— — Scientific and Technical Documentation and Information, Belgrade, 1972
— — — Information, Philadelphia, 1617
— — — — on the Social Sciences of the U.S.S.R. Academy of Sciences, Moscow, 1349
— — Social and Economic Research, Durban, 1168
— — — Development, Bellville, S.A., 1180
— — — Research, Salisbury, Zimbabwe, 2003
— — — — Tel-Aviv, 750
— — — — Tilburg, 973
— — — Science Research, Eugene, 1866
— — Solid State Physics, Tokyo, 856
— — Soviet and East European Studies, Tel-Aviv, 750
— — State Control of Drugs, Sofia, 220
— — Stomatology and Bone Biology, Pretoria, 1175
— — Storm Research, Houston, 1904
— — Strategic Studies, Pretoria, 1175
— — Studies in Higher Education, Copenhagen, 398

— — Study of Okinawa Culture, Tokyo, 863
— — the Advancement of Calvinism, 1173
— — — Arts and Humanistic Studies, University Park, 1877
— — — Control of Foot and Mouth Disease and Dangerous Infections, Sofia, 219
— — — — Swine Diseases, Vraca, 219
— — — Development of Educational Administrators, Cagayan de Oro City, 1060
— — — — Mountain Regions, Gifa-ken, 826
— — — History and Philosophy of Sciences, Tel-Aviv, 750
— — — — of Arabic Science, Aleppo, 1278
— — — Interdisciplinary Applications of Algebra and Combinatorics, Santa Barbara, 1673
— — — Meat, Oil and Margarine Industry, Warsaw, 1070
— — — Oil-bearing Rose, Ethereal Oil Plants and Medicinal Plants, Kazanlak, 219
— — — Philosophy of Science and Peace of the Yugoslav Academy of Sciences and Arts, Zagreb, 1972
— — — Preparation of Serums and Vaccines, Mogadishu, 1153
— — — Preservation and Scientific Study of Historical Monuments in Dalmatia, Split, 1973
— — — — of Historical and Cultural Monuments, Zagreb, 1973
— — — — — Monuments, Sarajevo, 1973
— — — Study and Treatment of Delinquency, London, 1447
— — — — of Christianity and Culture, Tokyo, 864
— — — — — Conflict, London, 1442
— — — — — English in Africa (I.S.E.A.), Grahamstown, 1176
— — — — — Jews in Diaspora, Ramat-Gan, 745
— — — — — in Islamic Lands, Ramat-Gan, 745
— — — — — Languages and Cultures of Asia and Africa, Tokyo, 857
— — — — — Man in Africa, 1161
— — — — — Natural Resources from Space, Baku, 1325
— — — — — Plural Societies, Pretoria, 1175
— — — Teaching of Economics, St. Gallen, 1275
— — — Theological Research, Pretoria, 1178
— — — — Seoul, 894
— — — Thermal Spring Research, Tottoriken, 844
— — — Tourism and Transport Economy, St. Gallen, 1275
— — — Urban Studies, Johannesburg, 1176
— — — Virus Research, Kyoto, 837
— — für Chemie und Pharmazie, Hamburg, 532
— of Actuaries, London, 1417
— — Administration, Baghdad, 728
— — — Karkh (Baghdad), 728
— — — Zaria, 995
— — Administrative Automation, Potchefstroom, 1173
— — Adult Education, Legon, 613
— — — Salisbury, Zimbabwe, 2003
— — — Studies, Nairobi, 880
— — Advanced Architectural Studies, York, 1539
— — — Legal Studies, 1513
— — — — Library, London, 1460
— — — Studies, Canberra, 99
— — Aesthetics Research, Mexico City, 933
— — African and Bantu Studies, Potchefstroom, 1173
— — — Studies, Freetown, 1148

— — — Ibadan, 998
— — — Legon, 613
— — — Monrovia, 905
— — — Nairobi, 880
— — — New York, 1810
— — — Nsukka, 1001
— — Agricultural History and Museum of English Rural Life, Reading, 1471
— — — Machine-Building, Ruse, 220
— — — Research, Addis Ababa, 424
— — — — Ho Chi Minh City, 1962
— — — — and Training, Ibadan, 993
— — Agriculture, Pyinmana, 229
— — — Library, Pyinmana, 228
— — Agro-Chemical Problems and Hydroponics, Erevan, 1324
— — Agrochemistry and Soil Science, Moscow, 1319
— — Air and Space Law, Montreal, 277
— — American Culture, Taipei, 340
— — Anaerobic Bacteriology, Gifu-ken, 826
— — Animal Husbandry, Kostinbrod, 219
— — — — and Veterinary Science, Ulan Bator, 947
— — — — — — Science Library, Insein, 228
— — — Physiology (A.R.C.), Cambridge, 1440
— — — — and Nutrition, Jablonna, Warsaw, 1069
— — Anthropological Research, Mexico City, 933
— — — Studies, Moscow, 1365
— — Anthropology, Nagoya, 866
— — — Wroclaw, 1067
— — Applied Arts, Baghdad, 728
— — — Electricity and Magnetism, Tokyo, 815
— — — Manpower Research, New Delhi, 671
— — — Mathematics, Moscow, 1318
— — — — Tbilisi, 1367
— — — — and Cybernetics, Gorky, 1362
— — — — — Mechanics, Donetsk, 1333
— — — — Systems Research, Mexico City, 933
— — — Mechanics and Mathematics, Lvov, 1333
— — — Microbiology, Tokyo, 856
— — — Physics, Kishinev, 1331
— — — — Minsk, 1326
— — — Social and Economic Research, Boroko, 1032
— — — — Research, Nathan, Qd., 101
— — Aquaculture, Stirling, 1530
— — Aquatic Biology, Achimota, 611
— — Arab Music, Alexandria, 413
— — — Cairo, 413
— — — Research and Studies, Cairo, 415
— — Arabic and Religious Study, Kabul, 53
— — Archaeology, Kiev, 1334
— — — London, 1513
— — — Moscow, 1320
— — — Samarkand, 1335
— — — and Ethnography, Erevan, 1324
— — Architecture, Ulan Bator, 947
— — — and Arts, Baku, 1326
— — — — Urban Studies, Seoul, 893
— — Art, Ethnography and Folklore, Minsk, 1326
— — — Research, Tokyo, 813
— — Arts, Erevan, 1324
— — Asian Cultural Studies, Tokyo, 864
— — Astronomy, Moscow, 1365
— — — and Geophysics: Egyptian Observatories, Cairo, 415
— — Astrophysics, Dushanbe, 1332
— — — and Atmospheric Physics, Tartu, 1327
— — Atmospheric Physics, Moscow, 1320
— — Atomic Energy, Kyoto, 836
— — Australian Geographers, Sydney, 88
— — Automation, Frunze, 1329
— — — and Control Processes with Computer Centre, Vladivostok, 1322

Institute of Automation and Electrical Measurements, Novosibirsk, 1321
— — Bangladesh Studies, Rajshahi, 145
— — Bankers, London, 1417
— — — in Scotland, 1417
— — — South Africa, 1155
— — Barley Crops, Karnobat, 219
— — Basic Medical Sciences, London, 1512
— — Bibliographical Research, Mexico City, 933
— — Biochemistry, Erevan, 1324
— — — Tashkent, 1335
— — — Vilnius, 1330
— — — and Biophysics, Warsaw, 1067
— — — — Physiology, Frunze, 1329
— — — — of Micro-organisms, Moscow, 1319
— — — of Plants, Tbilisi, 1328
— — — Plant and Micro-organism Physiology, Saratov, 1322
— — Biological and Medical Chemistry, Moscow, 1342
— — — Chemistry, Taipei, 340
— — — Physics, Moscow, 1319
— — — Problems of the North, Magadan, 1322
— — Biology, Frunze, 1329
— — — London, 1431
— — — Mexico City, 933
— — — Novosibirsk, 1321
— — — Petrozavodsk, 1322
— — — Riga, 1330
— — — Syktyvkar, 1323
— — — Ufa, 1322
— — — and Soil Science, Vladivostok, 1322
— — — of Southern Seas, Sevastopol, 1334
— — Biomedical Research, Mexico City, 933
— — Bio-organic Chemistry, Minsk, 1326
— — Biophysics, Moscow, 1346
— — Botanic Research, Potchefstroom, 1173
— — Botanical Chemistry, Tashkent, 1335
— — Botany, Alma-Ata, 1329
— — — Ashkhabad, 1332
— — — Dushanbe, 1332
— — — Erevan, 1324
— — — Taipei, 340
— — — Tashkent, 1335
— — — Tbilisi, 1328
— — — Ulan Bator, 947
— — — Vilnius, 1330
— — Brain and Blood Vessels, Gumma, 815
— — — Research, Moscow, 1342
— — Brazilian Studies, Seoul, 893
— — British Geographers, 1423
— — Buddhist Culture, Kyoto, 868
— — Building Materials Research, Hanoi, 1962
— — Business Administration, St. Gallen, 1275
— — — — and Commerce, Karachi, 1026
— — Cancer Research, London, 1445
— — — — Royal Cancer Hospital, London, 1512
— — — — New York, 1810
— — Canning Industry, Plovdiv, 219
— — Cardio-Vascular Diseases, Sofia, 219
— — Cartography, Kabul, 52
— — Catalysis, Novosibirsk, 1321
— — Catholic Education, Melbourne, 115
— — Cattle and Sheep Breeding, Stara Zagora, 219
— — Cellular Physiology, Pretoria, 1175
— — Ceramics, Stoke-on-Trent, 1436
— — Cereals and Fodder Industry, Sofia, 219
— — Chartered Accountants in England and Wales, 1417
— — — — — Ireland, 730
— — — — — of India, 660
— — — — — Scotland, Edinburgh, 1417

— — — Secretaries and Administrators, London, 1417
— — Chemical Additives, Baku, 1325
— — — and Biological Physics, Tallinn, 1327
— — — Engineering and Technology, Lahore, 1028
— — — Fibres, Łódź, 1070
— — — Kinetics and Combustion, Novosibirsk, 1322
— — — Physics, Erevan, 1324
— — — — Moscow, 1319
— — — Sciences, Alma-Ata, 1329
— — Chemistry, Ashkhabad, 1332
— — — Dushanbe, 1332
— — — Gorky, 1319
— — — Ho Chi Minh City, 1962
— — — Kishinev, 1331
— — — Lahore, 1028
— — — Mexico City, 933
— — — Sverdlovsk, 1322
— — — Taipei, 340
— — — Tallinn, 1327
— — — Tashkent, 1335
— — — Ufa, 1322
— — — Ulan Bator, 947
— — — Vladivostok, 1322
— — — and Chemical Technology, Krasnoyarsk, 1321
— — — — — Vilnius, 1330
— — — — Technology of Rare Elements and Minerals, Murmansk, 1323
— — — of Ireland, 731
— — Child Health, Calcutta, 669
— — — Ibadan, 998
— — — Lagos, 1000
— — — London, 1512
— — — Rondebosch, 1167
— — — Sydney, 110
— — Chile, Santiago, 322
— — Chinese Studies, Hong Kong, 1561
— — Classical Studies, London, 1513
— — Clinical and Experimental Medicine, Novosibirsk, 1342
— — — Science and Research, Dublin, 736
— — Colloidal Chemistry and Chemistry of Water, Kiev, 1333
— — Commonwealth Studies, London, 1513
— — — Oxford, 1524
— — Communal Economy and Services, Ulan Bator, 947
— — Communication Research, Potchefstroom, 1173
— — Community Service, Palembang, 717
— — — Studies, London, 1435
— — Comparative Law, Montreal, 277
— — — — Tokyo, 873
— — Complex Problems of Hygiene and Professional Diseases, Novokuznetsk, 1342
— — — Transportation Problems, Moscow, 1347
— — Computational Mathematics, Uxbridge, 1482
— — Constitutional Medicine, Kumamoto, 834
— — Constructional Mechanics and Seismic Resistance, Tbilisi, 1328
— — Contemporary Arts, London, 1413
— — — History and Wiener Library, London, 1457
— — Control Sciences, Moscow, 1347
— — — Systems, Tbilisi, 1328
— — Cost and Management Accountants, London, 1417
— — — — — — of Pakistan, 1019
— — Cotton Crops, Čirpan, 219
— — Criminology, Rondebosch, 1167
— — — Wellington, N.Z., 986
— — — and Criminal Law, Tel-Aviv, 750
— — Crystallography, 1318
— — Cybernetics, Baku, 1324
— — — Kiev, 1333
— — — Talinn, 1327

— — — Tbilisi, 1327
— — — and Computing Centre, Tashkent, 1335
— — Cytology, Leningrad, 1319
— — — and Genetics, Novosibirsk, 1322
— — Dairy Industry, Vidin, 219
— — Data Processing, Oulu, 437
— — Dental Research, The, Sydney, 92
— — — Surgery, London, 1512
— — Dermatology, 1512
— — — and Venerology, Sofia, 219
— — Development Studies, Brighton, 1534
— — — — Dar es Salaam, 1281
— — — — Georgetown, 628
— — Developmental Biology, Moscow, 1320
— — Early American History and Culture, Williamsburg, 1605
— — Earth and Atmospheric Physics, Ashkhabad, 1332
— — — — Planetary Physics, Edmonton, Alb., 257
— — — Sciences Preparatory Office, Taipei, 340
— — Ecclesiastical Law, Fribourg, 1266
— — Ecology, Łomianki, 1067
— — Economic Affairs, London, 1417
— — — and Social Sciences, Fribourg, 1266
— — — Growth, Research Centre on Social and Economic Development in Asia, Delhi, 671
— — — Research, Bangor, 1535
— — — — Kyoto, 837
— — — — Tokyo, 628
— — — — (Osaka City University), 860
— — Economics, Alma-Ata, 1329
— — — Ashkhabad, 1332
— — — Baku, 1325
— — — Dushanbe, 1332
— — — Erevan, 1324
— — — Frunze, 1330
— — — Kiev, 1334
— — — Kishinev, 1331
— — — Minsk, 1326
— — — Moscow, 1321
— — — Rangoon, 229
— — — Riga, 1330
— — — Sverdlovsk, 1322
— — — Taipei, 340
— — — Tallinn, 1327
— — — Tashkent, 1335
— — — Ulan Bator, 947
— — — Vilnius, 1331
— — — and Organization of Agriculture, Sofia, 219
— — — Library, Rangoon, 228
— — — of the World Socialist System, Moscow, 1321
— — — Research, Mexico City, 933
— — Economy and Law, Tbilisi, 1328
— — Education, Freetown, 1149
— — — Ibadan, 998
— — — Ile-Ife, 998
— — — Lagos, 1000
— — — Lahore, 1028
— — — London, 1513
— — — Nsukka, 1001
— — — Paris, 28
— — — Rangoon, 229
— — — Salisbury, Zimbabwe, 2003
— — — Singapore, 1152
— — — Zaria, 995
— — — and Research, D. I. Khan, 1026
— — — Library, Ankara, 1300
— — — — Rangoon, 228
— — Educational Research and Service, Tokyo, 864
— — Electrical and Electronics Engineers, New York, 1616
— — — — — Philadelphia, 1880
— — — — — — Canadian Regional Office, Thornhill, 244
— — — — Dynamics, Kiev, 1333
— — — — Engineering and Electronics, Damascus, 1278
— — Electro-Chemistry, Moscow, 1319

— — Sverdlovsk, 1322
— Electron Technology, Warsaw, 1068
— Electronics, Minsk, 1326
— — Tashkent, 1335
— — and Computing Equipment, Riga, 1330
— Elementary Organic Compounds, Moscow, 1319
— Endocrinology, Gerontology and Geriatrics, Sofia, 219
— Energy, London, 1436
— — Riga, 1330
— — Auckland, N.Z., 977
— Economics, Tokyo, 817
— Engineering, Mexico City, 933
— — Cybernetics, Minsk, 1326
— — Studies, Moscow, 1347
— — Thermal Physics, Kiev, 1333
— Engineers (Pakistan), Lahore, 1021
— Environmental Research, Bloemfontein, 1171
— — Stress, Santa Barbara, 1673
— Equilibrium Research, Gifu-ken, 826
— Ethiopian Studies, Addis Ababa, 424
— Ethnology, Taipei, 340
— European and International Economic and Social Law, St. Gallen, 1275
— — Finance, Bangor, 1535
— — Studies, Karachi, 1026
— Experimental Biology, Alma-Ata, 1329
— — — Erevan, 1324
— — — Kharku, 1327
— — Botany, Minsk, 1326
— — Endocrinology and Hormone Chemistry, Moscow, 1342
— — Medicine, Leningrad, 1342
— — Meteorology, Obninsk, 1346
— — Pathology, Mosfellssveit, 658
— — and Therapy, Sukhumi, 1342
— — Plant Biology, Tashkent, 1335
— Fish Industry, Burgas, 219
— — Resources, Varna, 219
— Fodder Crops, Pleven, 219
— Folklore, Seoul, 893
— Food Science and Technology of the United Kingdom, London, 1436
— — Technologists, Chicago, 1616
— Foreign and Comparative Law, Pretoria, 1178
— — Countries, Vladivostock, 1322
— Forensic Research, Cracow, 1070
— Foresters, 1411
— Forestry, Chittagong, 144
— — Petrozavodsk, 1322
— — Science and Technology, Hanoi, 1962
— Foundry Problems, Kiev, 1333
— Freshwater Fishery Biology, Cairo, 415
— Fruit-Growing, Kjustendil, 219
— — — Plovdiv, 219
— Gas, Kiev, 1333
— — Technology, Chicago, 1704
— Gastroenterology, Dushanbe, 1332
— — Philadelphia, 1880
— — and Nutrition, Sofia, 219
— General and Experimental Biology, Ulan Bator, 947
— — — Inorganic Chemistry, Erevan, 1324
— — — — Kiev, 1333
— — — — Minsk, 1326
— — Genetics, Moscow, 1319
— — Pathology and Pathological Physiology, Moscow, 1342
— Genetics and Animal Breeding, Warsaw, 1069
— — — Breeding, Warsaw Agriculture Academy, 1070
— — — Cytology, Minsk, 1326
— — — Selection, Baku, 1325
— Geochemistry, Irkutsk, 1321
— — and Geophysics, Minsk, 1326
— — — Physics of Minerals, Kiev, 1333

— — Geodesy and Photogrammetry, 219
— — Geography, Baku, 1325
— — — Mexico City, 933
— — — Moscow, 1320
— — — and Permafrost Studies, Ulan Bator, 947
— — — of Siberia and the Far East, Irkutsk, 1321
— — Geological Information, Beijing, 333
— — — Sciences, London, 1445
— — — — Warsaw, 1069
— — — — Reference Library of Geology, London, 1457
— — Geology, Ashkhabad, 1332
— — — Beijing, 333
— — — Dnepropetrovsk, 1361
— — — Dushanbe, 1332
— — — Erevan, 1324
— — — Frunze, 1329
— — — Kiev, 1333
— — — Makhachkala, 1322
— — — Mexico City, 933
— — — Minsk, 1346
— — — Moscow, 1320
— — — Murmansk, 1323
— — — Petrozavodsk, 1322
— — — Syktyvkar, 1323
— — — Tallinn, 1327
— — — Ufa, 1322
— — — Ulan Bator, 947
— — — and Exploitation of Mineral Fuels, Moscow, 1320
— — — — Geochemistry of Combustible Minerals, Lvov, 1333
— — — — Geophysics, Novosibirsk, 1321
— — — — Precambrian Geochronology, Leningrad, 1320
— — — of Mineral Deposits, Beijing, 333
— — — Oil and Gas Deposits, Tashkent, 1335
— — Geomechanics, Beijing, 333
— — Geophysics, Kiev, 1333
— — — Mexico City, 933
— — — Sverdlovsk, 1322
— — — Tbilisi, 1327
— — — Warsaw, 1069
— — — Wellington, N.Z., 986
— — — and Engineering Seismology, Leninakan, 1324
— — — — Geology, Kishinev, 1331
— — Germanic Studies, London, 1513
— — Gerontology, Kiev, 1342
— — Gynecologic Research, Philadelphia, 1880
— — Haematology and Blood Transfusion, Sofia, 219
— — Health Resort Study, Physiotherapy and Rehabilitation, Sofia, 219
— — — Studies, Infectious Diseases and Bacteriology, Ulan Bator, 947
— — Hearing Research, Nottingham, 1443
— — Heat and Mass Exchange, Minsk, 1326
— — — Engineering, Warsaw, 1069
— — Heraldic and Genealogical Studies, Canterbury, 1423
— — High Energy Physics, Alma-Ata, 1328
— — — — Tbilisi, 1367
— — — Pressure Physics, Akademgorodok, 1318
— — — Speed Mechanics, Sendai, 851
— — — Temperatures, Moscow, 1318
— — Higher Nervous Activity and Neurophysiology, Moscow, 1319
— — Historical Research, London, 1513
— — — Library, London, 1460
— — — Mexico City, 933
— — — Sciences, Zagreb, 1993
— — History, Baku, 1325
— — — Erevan, 1324
— — — Frunze, 1330
— — — Kiev, 1334
— — — Kishinev, 1331
— — — Manila, 1047
— — — Minsk, 1326
— — — Riga, 1330

— — Tallinn, 1327
— — Tashkent, 1335
— — Ulan-Bator, 947
— — Vilnius, 1331
— — and Philology, Taipei, 340
— — — Library, Taipei, 342
— — Archaeology, Ethnography of the Far Eastern Nations, Vladivostok, 1322
— — Language and Literature, Makhachkala, 1322
— — — Ufa, 1322
— — of Arts, Moscow, 1346
— — — Medicine and Medical Research, New Delhi, 669
— — — Natural Science and Engineering, Moscow, 1321
— — — the Georgian Arts, Tbilisi, 1328
— — — U.S.S.R., Moscow, 1320
— — Philology and Philosophy, Novosibirsk, 1321
— — Holy Land Studies, Jerusalem, 753
— — Human Morphology, Moscow, 1342
— — Nutrition, New York, 1810
— — Hydraulics and Hydrology, Tamil Nadu, 672
— — Hydrobiology, Dnepropetrovsk, 1361
— — — Kiev, 1334
— — Hydrodynamics, Novosibirsk, 1321
— — Hydrogeology and Hydrophysics, Alma-Ata, 1329
— — Hydrology, Wallingford, 1446
— — — and Meteorology, Ulan Bator, 947
— — Hydromechanics, Kiev, 1333
— — Hydrotechnics and Improvement, Sofia, 219
— — Hygiene and Epidemiology, Hanoi, 1962
— — — Occupational Health, Sofia, 219
— — Ideological Problems and Medical Pedagogics, Sofia, 220
— — Immunology, Moscow, 1342
— — — Sofia, 219
— — Incorporated Photographers, Ware, 1415
— — Industrial Chemistry, Warsaw, 1070
— — — Economics, Kiev, 1334
— — — Hygiene and Occupational Diseases, Moscow, 1341
— — — Management, Kabul, 53
— — — Seoul, 893
— — — Pharmacy, Potchefstroom, 1173
— — — Science, Tokyo, 856
— — — Training, Uxbridge, 1482
— — Infectious and Parasitic Diseases, Sofia, 220
— — Information Science, Preparatory Office, Taipei, 340
— — — Scientists, London, 1430
— — — Transmission, Moscow, 1318
— — Inland Waters Fisheries, Plovdiv, 219
— — Inorganic and Physical Chemistry, Baku, 1325
— — — — Frunze, 1329
— — — Chemistry, Novosibirsk, 1321
— — — — Riga, 1330
— — — — and Electrical Chemistry, Tbilisi, 1328
— — Insurance Economics, St. Gallen, 1275
— — Internal Medicine and Pharmacology, Sofia, 220
— — International Education, New York, 1604
— — — Labour Movements, Moscow, 1321
— — — Law, Brussels, 35
— — — Politics and Economics, Belgrade, 1972
— — — Relations, Beijing, 336
— — — — Kingston, Jamaica, 801
— — — — St. Augustine, 1294
— — — Introduction and Plant Resources, Sadovo, 219
— — Irish Studies, Belfast, 1557
— — Islamic Culture, Lahore, 1020

Institute of Islamic Studies, Montreal, 277
— — Jamaica, 800
— — — Library, 800
— — — Museum, 800
— — Jewish Affairs, London, 1435
— — Journalism, Tokyo, 856
— — Juridical Research, Mexico City, 933
— — Karstology and Speleology, Perm, 1366
— — Kiswahili Research, Dar es Salaam, 1280
— — Korean Culture, Gyongsan, 896
— — — Seoul, 893
— — — Studies, Seoul, 896
— — Laboratory Technology, Khartoum, 1231
— — Labor-Management Relations, Seoul, 893
— — Lake Conservation, Leningrad, 1320
— — Language and Literature, Kishinev, 1331
— — — — Riga, 1330
— — — — Ulan-Bator, 947
— — — Teaching, Tokyo, 874
— — Languages and Linguistics, Canterbury, 1496
— — Laryngology and Otology, London, 1512
— — Latin American and Iberian Studies, New York, 1810
— — — Studies, London, 1513
— — Law Research and Reform, Edmonton, Alberta, 257
— — Leather Technology, Dacca, 145
— — Legal Studies, Seoul, 893
— — Limnology, Irkutsk, 1321
— — Linguistic and Literary Research, Potchefstroom, 1173
— — — Studies, Moscow, 1321
— — Linguistics, Alma-Ata, 1329
— — — Baku, 1326
— — — Tbilisi, 1328
— — — and Literature, Frunze, 1330
— — — — Tallinn, 1327
— — — Literature and History, Petrozavodsk, 1322
— — — — — Syktyvkar, 1323
— — Linguists, London, 1426
— — Lithuanian Language and Literature, Vilnius, 1331
— — Local Government, Ramat-Gan, 745
— — — Tokyo, 813
— — Low Temperature Science, The, Sapporo-City, 830
— — Macromolecular Chemistry, Kiev, 1333
— — — Compounds, Leningrad, 1319
— — Maize Crops, Kneža, 219
— — Malariology, Parasitology and Entomology, Hanoi, 1962
— — Management and Technology, Enugu, 1002
— — — Sciences, Providence, R.I., 1603
— — — Services, London, 1437
— — Manpower Studies, Brighton, 1534
— — Marine Biochemistry, Aberdeen, 1445
— — — Biology, Karachi, 1022
— — — — and Oceanography, Freetown, 1148
— — — Engineers, London, 1437
— — — Geology, Qingdao, 333
— — — Sciences, Zanzibar, 1281
— — Market Analysis, Cagayan de Oro City, 1060
— — Mathematical Sciences, Madras, 670
— — — — Tel-Aviv, 750
— — — Statistics, Hayward, Calif., 45
— — Mathematics, Cracow, 1090
— — — Dushanbe, 1332
— — — Erevan, 1324
— — — Iași, 1135
— — — Kiev, 1333
— — — Mexico City, 933
— — — Minsk, 1326
— — — Novosibirsk, 1321

— — — Taipei, 340
— — — Ulan Bator, 947
— — — Warsaw, 1068
— — — and Computing Centre, Kishinev, 1331
— — — — its Applications, Southend-on-Sea, 1432
— — — — Mechanics, Alma-Ata, 1328
— — — — — Baku, 1324
— — Measurement and Control, London, 1437
— — Meat Industry, Sofia, 219
— — Mechanics, Kiev, 1333
— — — Moscow, 1365
— — — and Mathematics, Sverdlovsk, 1322
— — — Seismic Resistance of Constructions, Tashkent, 1335
— — — of Geological Engineering, Dnepropetrovsk, 1333
— — — — Machines, Tbilisi, 1328
— — — — Polymer Compounds, Riga, 1330
— — Mechanization and Electrification of Agriculture, Sofia, 219
— — Medical and Veterinary Science, Adelaide, 92
— — — Biological Problems, Pushchinona-Oke, 1346
— — — Genetics, Moscow, 1342
— — — History, Diyarbakir, 1305
— — — Laboratory Sciences, London, 1429
— — — Problems of the North, Krasnoyarsk, 1342
— — — Radiology, Moscow, 1342
— — — Research and Labour Medicine, Zagreb, 1993
— — — Science, Tokyo, 856
— — Medicine, Mandalay, 229
— — — I, Rangoon, 229
— — — II, Rangoon, 229
— — — Library, Mandalay, 228
— — — I Library, Rangoon, 228
— — — II Library, Rangoon, 228
— — — Washington, D.C., 1595
— — Medieval Studies, Fribourg, 1266
— — Mental Health Research and Postgraduate Training, Parkville, Vic., 92
— — Metal Physics, Sverdlovsk, 1322
— — Metallopolymer Systems of Mechanics, Gomel, 1326
— — Metallurgy, Sverdlovsk, 1322
— — — Tbilisi, 1328
— — — and Ore-Dressing, Alma-Ata, 1329
— — Meteorology, Sarajevo, 1973
— — — and Water Management, Warsaw, 1070
— — Microbiology, Alma-Ata, 1329
— — — Erevan, 1324
— — — Minsk, 1326
— — — Moscow, 1319
— — — Riga, 1330
— — Mineralogy, Geochemistry and Crystallochemistry of Rare Elements, Moscow, 1320
— — Mining, Alma-Ata, 1329
— — — Novosibirsk, 1321
— — — Vladivostock, 1322
— — — Research, Salisbury, Zimbabwe, 2002
— — Modern History, Taipei, 340
— — Molecular Biology, Eugene, 1866
— — — Moscow, 1319
— — — and Genetics, Kiev, 1334
— — Moral Theology, Fribourg, 1266
— — Mountain Animal Husbandry and Agriculture, Trojan Lovech District, 219
— — Municipal Administration, Oak Park, Vic., 88
— — Musicology of the Serbian Academy of Sciences and Arts, Belgrade, 1993
— — National Affairs, Port Moresby, 1032

— — — Planning, Cairo, 415
— — Natural Compounds, Ulan Bator, 947
— — — Resources, Pietermaritzburg, 1170
— — — Sciences, Perm, 1366
— — Nephrology, Urology, Haemodialysis and Kidney Transplantation, Sofia, 220
— — Neurology, London, 1512
— — — Moscow, 1342
— — — Psychiatry and Neurosurgery, Sofia, 220
— — Neustonology, Odessa, 1346
— — Normal Physiology, Moscow, 1342
— — Northern Mining, Yakutsk, 1321
— — Nuclear Energy, Minsk, 1326
— — — Physics, Alma-Ata, 1328
— — — — Novosibirsk, 1322
— — — — Tashkent, 1335
— — — Research, Kiev, 1333
— — — — Moscow, 1318
— — — Studies, Moscow, 1365
— — Nutrition, Moscow, 1341
— — Obstetrics and Gynaecology, Leningrad, 1342
— — — — London, 1512
— — — — Sofia, 220
— — Occupational Health, Helsinki, 441
— — — and Safety, Montreal, 277
— — Ocean Economics, Vladivostock, 1322
— — Oceanographic and Fisheries Research, Athens, 617
— — — Sciences, Godalming, 1445
— — Oceanography, Montreal, 277
— — — Rondebosch, 1167
— — — and Fisheries, Cairo, 415
— — Oceanology, Moscow, 1320
— — — Qingdao, 332
— — Offshore Engineering, Edinburgh, 1494
— — Oil Chemistry, Tomsk, 1322
— — Oncology, Sofia, 220
— — — Warsaw, 1070
— — Operating Problems (Automatic and Telemechanic), Moscow, 1318
— — Ophthalmology, London, 1512
— — — Sofia, 220
— — Optics of the Atmosphere, Tomsk, 1321
— — Organic Catalysis and Electro-Chemistry, Alma-Ata, 1329
— — — Chemistry, Erevan, 1324
— — — — Frunze, 1329
— — — — Kiev, 1333
— — — — Novosibirsk, 1321
— — — Industrial Chemistry, Warsaw, 1070
— — — Synthesis, Riga, 1330
— — Organisation and Social Studies, Uxbridge, 1482
— — Oriental Culture, Tokyo, 856
— — — Studies, Erevan, 1324
— — — — Moscow, 1320
— — — — Tbilisi, 1328
— — — — Ulan Bator, 947
— — Orthopaedics, 1512
— — — and Traumatology, Sofia, 220
— — Oto-Rhino-Laryngology, Sofia, 220
— — Pacific Ocean Geography, Vladivostok, 1322
— — Paediatrics, Moscow, 1342
— — — Sofia, 220
— — Paleobiology, Tbilisi, 1327, 1328
— — Papua New Guinea Studies, Boroko, 1032
— — Parasitology, Montreal, 277
— — — Warsaw, 1068
— — Pastoral Theology, Fribourg, 1266
— — Pasture and Fodder, Ulan Bator, 947
— — Pathology, Montreal, 277
— — Peat, Minsk, 1326
— — Pedagogical Sciences, Ulan Bator, 947
— — Pedagogy, Fribourg, 1266
— — Peoples of the Near and Middle East, Baku, 1325
— — Permafrost, Yakutsk, 1321

— — Petrochemical Research, Potchefstroom, 1173
— — Petroleum, London, 1437
— — — Chemistry and Natural Salts, Guryev, 1329
— — — Processing, Cracow, 1070
— — Pharmaceutical Chemistry, Tbilisi, 1328
— — Pharmacology, Cracow, 1069
— — — Moscow, 1342
— — Philippine Culture, Quezon City, 1047
— — Philological Research, Mexico City, 933
— — Philosophical Research, Mexico City, 933
— — Philosophy, Kiev, 1334
— — — Moscow, 1321
— — — Tbilisi, 1328
— — — and Law, Alma-Ata, 1329
— — — — Baku, 1326
— — — — Erevan, 1324
— — — — Frunze, 1330
— — — — Minsk, 1326
— — — Sociology and Public Law, Ulan Bator, 947
— — Photobiology, Minsk, 1326
— — Photosynthesis, Moscow, 1319
— — Physical and Technical Problems of Energetics, Vilnius, 1330
— — — Chemistry, Moscow, 1319
— — — — Odessa, 1333
— — — — Warsaw, 1068
— — — Education, Ile-Ife, 998
— — — — and Sport, Fribourg, 1266
— — — Organic Chemistry and Coal Chemistry, Donetsk, 1334
— — — — Minsk, 1326
— — — Research, Potchefstroom, 1173
— — Physics, Baku, 1324
— — — Cracow, 1090
— — — Erevan, 1324
— — — Kiev, 1333
— — — London, 1433
— — — Makhachkala, 1322
— — — Mexico City, 933
— — — Minsk, 1326
— — — Odessa, 1365
— — — Riga, 1330
— — — Singapore, 1150
— — — Taipei, 340
— — — Tartu, 1327
— — — Tbilisi, 1327
— — — Zagreb, 1993
— — — and Applied Physics, Ulan Bator, 947
— — — — Mathematics, Frunze, 1329
— — — — Vilnius, 1330
— — — — Mechanics of Rocks, Frunze, 1329
— — — in New Zealand, Otago, 977
— — — of Metals, Kiev, 1333
— — Physiological Hygiene, Tel-Aviv, 750
— — — Research, Potchefstroom, 1173
— — Physiology, Alma-Ata, 1329
— — — Baku, 1325
— — — Minsk, 1326
— — — Novosibirsk, 1342
— — — Tashkent, 1335
— — — Tbilisi, 1328
— — — Plant Biochemistry, Tbilisi, 1328
— — — and Animal Ecology, Sverdlovsk, 1322
— — — Genetics, Poznań, 1069
— — — Industry, 670
— — — Physiology, Kiev, 1334
— — — — and Biochemistry, Kishinev, 1331
— — — — — Biophysics, Dushanbe, 1332
— — — Plants and Crops, Ulan Bator, 947
— — Plasma Physics, Nagoya, 842
— — Plastic Surgery, Moscow, 1387
— — Plateau Geology, Chengdu, 333
— — Pneumology and Phthisiology, Sofia, 220
— — Polar Studies, Columbus, 1621

— — Poliomyelitis and Virus Encephalitis, Moscow, 1341
— — Politics and Economy, Tokyo, 813
— — Polymer Chemistry, Zabrze, 1068
— — — Technology, Loughborough, 1514
— — Population Problems, Tokyo, 813
— — — Studies, Exeter, 1491
— — Postgraduate Medicine and Research, Dacca, 145
— — Precision Mechanics and Computing Technology, 1318
— — Problems of Criobiology and Medicine, Kharkov, 1334
— — — — Deep Oil and Gas Deposits, Baku, 1325
— — — — Engineering, Kharkov, 1333
— — — — Materials, Kiev, 1333
— — — — Mechanics, Moscow, 1318
— — — — Oncology, Kiev, 1334
— — Professional Legal Studies, Belfast, 1557
— — Protein, Puschino/Oka, 1319
— — Psychiatry, London, 1512
— — — Moscow, 1342
— — Psychological and Educational Services and Research, Potchefstroom, 1173
— — Psychology, Fribourg, 1266
— — — Moscow, 1321
— — Psychophysical Research, Oxford, 1447
— — Public Administration, Amman, 877
— — — — Khartoum, 1229
— — — — Riyadh, 1144
— — — — Library, Riyadh, 1142
— — — — Affairs, Melbourne, 88
— — — — Finance and Fiscal Law, St. Gallen, 1275
— — — — Health, Kabul, 52
— — — — Tokyo, 815
— — Quarrying, Nottingham, 1437
— — Race Relations, London, 1435
— — Radio Engineering and Electronics, Moscow, 1318
— — — Physics and Electronics, Kharkov, 1333
— — — Technology, Moscow, 1318
— — Radiography and Radiotherapy, Khartoum, 1231
— — Radiology and Radiobiology, Sofia, 220
— — Radiophysical Research, Gorky, 1318
— — Radiophysics and Electronics, Ashtarak, 1324
— — — — Calcutta, 707
— — Radiotherapy and Nuclear Medicine, Peshawar, 1022
— — Refrigeration, Wallington, 1437
— — Regional Medicine, Ashkhabad, 1332
— — — Planning, Potchefstroom, 1173
— — Reliability of Machines, Minsk, 1326
— — Religious Studies, Santa Barbara, 1673
— — Research, Palembang, 717
— — Rheumatism, Moscow, 1342
— — Rock and Mineral Analysis, Beijing, 333
— — Russian Language, Moscow, 1321
— — — Literature (Pushkin House), Leningrad, 1321
— — Science and Technology, Hong Kong, 1561
— — — Technology, London, 1437
— — — Sciences, Hanoi, 1962
— — Scientific and Industrial Research, Suita City, 847
— — — — Technical Communicators Ltd., Hatfield, 1426
— — — — Information of China (ISTIC), Beijing, 335
— — — Atheism, Moscow, 1346
— — — Sea Biology, Vladivostok, 1322
— — — Seismic Resistant Construction and Seismology, Dushanbe, 1332
— — Seismology, Tashkent, 1335
— — Semiconductor Physics, Kiev, 1333

— — — — Novosibirsk, 1322
— — — — Vilnius, 1330
— — Sindhology, Jamshoro, 1022
— — Slavonic and Balkan Studies, Moscow, 1320
— — Social and Economic Problems of Foreign Countries, Kiev, 1334
— — — — — Research, Bloemfontein, 1172
— — — — — Bridgetown, 146
— — — — — Grahamstown, 1176
— — — — — Kingston, Jamaica, 801
— — — — — St. Augustine, 1294
— — — — — St. John's, Newfoundland, 284
— — — — — Suita City, 847
— — — — — York, 1539
— — — — Science, Cracow, 1090
— — — Economic Problems, Leningrad, 1321
— — — Research, Mexico City, 933
— — — — Zagreb, 1993
— — — Science, Kyoto, 868
— — — — Lvov University, 1364
— — — — Tokyo University, 856
— — — Sciences, Lvov, 1334
— — — — Tokyo, 873
— — — — Information, Hanoi, 1963
— — — Studies, The Hague, 972
— — — — and Humanities, Hong Kong, 1561
— — Socio-Economic Problems of the Development of the Agrarian-Industrial Complex, Saratov, 1322
— — Sociological Research, Moscow, 1321
— — Soil Science, Alma-Ata, 1329
— — — — and Agrochemistry, Baku, 1325
— — — — — Novosibirsk, 1321
— — Solar and Terrestrial Communications, Vladivostock, 1322
— — Solid State and Semiconductor Physics, Minsk, 1326
— — — — Physics, Moscow, 1318
— — South African Architects, Johannesburg, 1154
— — — — Music, Potchefstroom, 1173
— — — — Politics, Potchefstroom, 1173
— — — West African Architects, Windhoek, 953
— — Southeast Asian Studies, Singapore, 1150
— — Soviet and East European Studies, Glasgow, 1493
— — Soya Bean Growing, Pavlikeni, 219
— — Space and Planetary Science, Tel-Aviv, 750
— — — Research, Moscow, 1318
— — Spain, London, 1424
— — Spanish American Studies, Saltillo, 944
— — Spectroscopy, Akademgorodok, 1318
— — Spirituality, Vatican City, 1947
— — Stable Isotopes, Tbilisi, 1346
— — State and Law, Kiev, 1334
— — — — — Moscow, 1321
— — Statistical Mathematics, Tokyo, 815
— — — Social and Economic Research, Legon, 613
— — Statisticians, Bury St. Edmunds, 1432
— — Statistics, Lahore, 1028
— — — and Applied Economics, Kampala, 1312
— — — — Operations Research, Wellington, N.Z., 986
— — Strategic Studies, Islamabad, 1021
— — Strength Problems, Kiev, 1333
— — Sugar Industry, Gorna Orjahovica, 219
— — Superhard Materials, Kiev, 1333
— — Surgery and Anaesthesiology, Sofia, 220
— — Survey Technicians, Khartoum, 1231
— — Swine Breeding, Sumen, 219
— — Systematic and Experimental Zoology, Cracow, 1067

Institute of Technical Training, Damascus, 1279
— — Technology, Baghdad, 728
— — — and Higher Education, Monterrey, 943
— — — — Vocational Education, Bangkok Campus, 1291
— — — — — Tak Campus, 1291
— — — Library, Rangoon, 228
— — Tectonic and Geophysics, Khabarovsk, 1322
— — Terrestrial Ecology, Cambridge, 1446
— — Magnetism, Radio Research and the Ionosphere, Akademgorodok, 1318
— — Textile Technology, Charlottesville, 1622
— — the Earth's Crust, Irkutsk, 1321
— — — Economics and Organization of Industrial Production, Novosibirsk, 1322
— — — Fermentation Industry, Warsaw, 1070
— — — Geology of Ore Deposits, Petroleum, Mineralogy and Geochemistry, Moscow, 1320
— — — Physical and Chemical Foundations of Mineral Processing, Novosibirsk, 1322
— — — Sugar Industry, Warsaw, 1070
— — — Three Principles of the People Preparatory Office, Taipei, 340
— — — Theoretical and Applied Mechanics, Novosibirsk, 1321
— — Astronomy, Leningrad, 1318
— — Physics, Kiev, 1333
— — — Problems of Chemical Technology, Baku, 1325
— — — Science, Eugene, 1866
— — Therapeutic Pedagogy and Social Work, Fribourg, 1266
— — Thermal and Electrical Physics, Tallinn, 1327
— — Thermophysics, Novosibirsk, 1322
— — Tobacco and Tobacco Products, Markovo, 219
— — Traditional Medicine Research, Hanoi, 1962
— — Traffic Science, Zagreb, 1993
— — Transport, Johannesburg, 1157
— — Tropical Forestry, Rio Piedras, 1109
— — Turkology Library, Istanbul, 1300
— — United States Studies, London, 1513
— — Urban Studies, Winnipeg, 317
— — Urology, London, 1512
— — U.S.A. and Canada Studies, Moscow, 1321
— — Viticulture and Oenology, Pleven, 219
— — Vulcanology, Petropavlovsk/Kamchatsky, 1322
— — War and Peace Studies, New York, 1811
— — Water Conservation Biology, Borok, 1319
— — — Pollution Control, Maidstone, 1437
— — — Problems, Moscow, 1320
— — Wheat and Sunflower Crops, General Toševo, Tolhubin District, 219
— — Wine Industry, Sofia, 219
— — Wood Chemistry, Riga, 1330
— — World Economics and International Relations, Moscow, 1321
— — — History, Moscow, 1320
— — Zoological Research, Potchefstroom, 1173
— — Zoology, Alma-Ata, 1329
— — — Ashkhabad, 1332
— — — Baku, 1325
— — — Erevan, 1324
— — — Kiev, 1334
— — — Kishinev, 1331
— — — London, 1446
— — — Taipei, 340
— — — Tbilisi, 1328
— — — Warsaw, 1067

— — — and Botany, Tartu, 1327
— — — — Parasitology, Minsk, 1326
— — — — Tashkent, 1335
— — — — Vilnius, 1331
— — Zootechnics, Cracow, 1070
— — on East Central Europe, New York, 1810
— — Western Europe, New York, 1811
Institutes of Medical Sciences, San Francisco, 1618
Institutet för metallforskning, Stockholm, 1238
Instituti i Gjeologjisë, Naftës dhe Gazit, Fier, 54
— Higjenës, Epidemiologjisë dhe i prodhimeve imunobiologjike, Tiranë, 55
— — Kërkimeve Bujqësore, Lushnjë, 54
— — Kimiko-Teknologjike të Industrisë së Lehtë dhe Ushqimore, Tiranë, 55
— — të Blegtorisë, Tiranë, 55
— — Kulturës Fizike "Vojo Kushi", Tiranë, 55
— — Lartë Bujqësor Korcë, 56
— — — Tiranë, 56
— — i Arteve, Tiranë, 56
— — pedagogjik, Shkodër, 56
— — — "Aleksandër Xhuvani", Elbasan, 56
— — — Gjirokastër, 56
— — Mjekësisë Popullore, Tiranë, 55
— — Monumenteve të Kulturës, Tiranë, 55
— — Studimeve dhe Projektimeve Mekanike, Tiranë, 54
— — — të Gjeologjisë dhe Minierave, Tiranë, 54
— — — — Hidrocentraleve (ISP Nr. 3), Tiranë, 55
— — — — Rrugëve te Hekurudhave (ISP Nr. 2), Tiranë, 55
— — — — urbanistikes dhe të Arkitekturës (ISP Nr. 1), Tiranë, 55
— — — Veprave Industriale, Tiranë, 55
— — — Veprave të Kullimit dhe Ujitjes, Tiranë, 55
— — — Teknologjike Minerare, Tiranë, 55
— — — Teknologjisë në Ndërtim (ISTN Nr. 5) Tiranë, 55
— — Marksiste-leniniste pranë KQ të PPSH, Tiranë, 54
— — Pedagogjike, Tiranë, 55
— — Studimit të Tokave, Tiranë, 55
Institution for Social and Policy Studies, New Haven, Conn., 1686
— of Agricultural Engineers, Bedford, 1411
— — Certificated Mechanical and Electrical Engineers, Marshalltown, 1157
— — Chemical Engineers, Rugby, 1437
— — Civil Engineers, London, 1437
— — Electrical Engineers, Dublin, 731
— — — London, 1437
— — — Library, London, 1457
— — — Pakistan, 1021
— — Electronic and Radio Engineers, London, 1437
— — Electronics, Rochdale, 1437
— — Engineering Designers, Westbury, 1437
— — Engineers, Australia, 91
— — — (India), Calcutta, 664
— — — and Shipbuilders in Scotland, 1437
— — — of Ireland, Dublin, 731
— — Environmental Sciences, London, 1430
— — Fire Engineers, 1437
— — Gas Engineers, 1437
— — Highway Engineers, 1438
— — Mechanical and General Technician Engineers, London, 1438
— — — Engineers, 1438

— — Metallurgists, London, 1438
— — Mining and Metallurgy, Kitwe, 1997
— — — — London, 1438
— — — — (Zimbabwe Section), Salisbury, 2000
— — — Engineers, 1438
— — Municipal Engineers, 1438
— — Nuclear Engineers, London, 1433
— — Plant Engineers, London, 1438
— — — Protection, Kostinbrod, 219
— — Production Engineers, 1438
— — Public Health Engineers, London, 1438
— — Radio and Electronics Engineers Australia, Sydney, 91
— — Structural Engineers, 1438
— — Water Engineers and Scientists, London, 1438
— Saint Pierre, Lille, 495
Instituto Açoriano de Cultura, The Azores, 1098
— "Adolfo Lutz", São Paulo, 184
— Agrario Argentino de Cultura Rural, 66
— — de Estudios Económicos (INTAGRO), Santiago, 324
— — Nacional, Caracas, 1953
— Agronômico, Campinas, 183
— Aleman, Barcelona, 1190
— — Madrid, 1190
— Alemão, Oporto, 1098
— — de Coímbra (Casa Alemã), 1098
— Amatiler de Arte Hispánico, 1188
— Americano de Investigaciones Económicas, Jurídicas y Sociales, Buenos Aires, 67
— Anglo-Mexicano de Cultura, 926
— Antártico Argentino, Buenos Aires, 67
— — Chileno, Santiago, 325
— Antituberculosis "Francisco Moragas", 1191
— "António Aurélio de Costa Ferreira", 1100
— Argentino de Racionalización de Materiales, 66
— Arqueológico del Ayuntamiento de Madrid, 1189
— — Histórico e Geográfico Pernambucano, 179
— Artigas del Servicio Exterior, Montevideo, 1939
— Astronómico, Coímbra, 1105
— Aula de "Mediterráneo", 1190
— Azucarero Dominicana, 403
— Bacteriológico de Chile, 324
— J. I. Baldó, Caracas, 1951
— "Benjamin Constant", Urca, 184
— Bibliografico Hispánico, Madrid, 1188
— Bibliotecológico, Buenos Aires, 72
— Biológico, São Paulo, 184
— — Português, Lisbon, 1100
— Birchner-Benner, Lima, 1038
— Boliviano de Cultura, 173
— — Tecnologia Agropecuaria (IBTA), La Paz, 173
— — del Petróleo (I.B.P.), La Paz, 173
— Bonaerense de Numismática y Antigüedades, 63
— Botánico, Caracas, 1954
— Botânico "Dr. Julio Henriques", 1105
— Brasileiro de Desenvolvimento Florestal (IBDF), Rio de Janeiro, 183
— — Economia, 179
— — Educação, Ciência e Cultura, Rio de Janeiro, 179
— — Estudos e Pesquisas de Gastroenterologia, São Paulo, 184
— — — Informação em Ciência e Tecnlogia (IBICT), 179
— — — Petróleo, Rio de Janeiro, 186
— — — Relaçoes Internacionais, 179
— — do Café, Rio de Janeiro, 183
— Brasil-Estados Unidos, Rio de Janeiro, 180
— Butantan, 184
— Cajal, Madrid, 1198

— — Caribe de Antropología y Sociología, Caracas, 1954
— Caro y Cuervo, Bogotá, 347
— Cartográfico Militar de las Fuerzas Armadas, Santo Domingo, 403
— Centroamericano de Administración de Empresas (INCAE), Managua, 989
— — — Pública, San José, 359
— — — y Supervisión de la Educación, Panama City, 1031
— — — Extensión de la Cultura, San José, 359
— — — Investigación y Tecnologia Industrial—ICAITI, Guatemala City, 624
— Chileno-Alemán de Cultura, Santiago, 323
— — — — Viña del Mar, 323
— — -Británico, Viña del Mar, 323
— — -Francés de Cultura, 323
— — -Norteamericano de Cultura, Santiago, 323
— Científico de Lebu, Valparaíso, 325
— Colombiano Agropecuario, Bogotá, 348
— — de Administración, Bogotá, 348
— — — Antropología, 348
— — — Crédito Educativo y Estudios Técnicos en el Exterior, 347
— — — Cultura, Bogotá, 347
— — — — Hispánica, Bogotá, 347
— — — Normas Técnicas, 348
— — — para el Fomento de la Educación Superior, Bogotá, 348
— Comercial Superior de la Nación, La Paz, 173
— — — — — "Federico Alvárez Plate", Cochabamba, 174
— Costarricense de Ciencias Políticas y Sociales, San José, 359
— Cristóbal Colón, Santo Domingo, 403
— Cubano de Investigaciones de los Derivados de la Caña de Azúcar, Havana, 363
— — — Mineras y Metalúrgicas, Havana, 363
— Cultural Anglo-Uruguayo, 1938
— — Argentino Norte-Americano, 63
— — Boliviano-Alemán, La Paz, 173
— — Brasil-Alemanha, Rio de Janeiro, 180
— — -Japão, Rio de Janeiro, 180
— — Colombo-Alemán, Bogotá, 347
— — Dominicano-Americano, Santo Domingo, 403
— — Peruano-Norte Americano, 1037
— — Venezolano-Británico, 1951
— Cuyano de Cultura Alemana, Mendoza, 63
— de Administración, Oriente, 363
— — Alajuela, 359
— — Algodão de Moçambique, Maputo, 952
— — Altos Estudios de América Latina, Caracas, 1959
— — Estudos, Lisbon, 1097
— — Antropología, Coímbra, 1101
— — e Etnologia do Pará, 182
— — — Historia, Guatemala City, 624
— — Arqueologia y Prehistoria, Barcelona, 1207
— — Arte "Diego Velázquez", Madrid, 1188
— — — Peruano, Lima, 1036
— — Artes Plásticas, Medellín, 357
— — Astronomía, Mexico City, 929
— — Asuntos Nucleares, Bogotá, 348
— — Bibliografia del Ministerio de Educación de la Provincia de Buenos Aires, La Plata, 66
— — Biología Andina, Lima, 1038, 1043
— — — e Patologia Médica, Belo Horizonte, 184
— — — Fundamental, Barcelona, 1207
— — — Maritima, Lisbon, 1100
— — — y Medicina Experimental, 67
— — Bioquímica Clínica, Barcelona, 1207
— — — y Nutrición, Lima, 1043

— — Botánica, Havana, 362
— — — "Darwinion", 68
— — — San Miguel de Tucumán, 67
— — — São Paulo, 184
— — — "C. Spegazzini", 68
— — Cálculo Aplicado, Zulia, 1960
— — Cancerología "Cupertino Arteaga", Sucre, 174
— — Capacitación Sindical, León, 988
— — Chile, Santiago, 322
— — Ciencia Animal, Havana, 365
— — Ciencias Agrícolas, Havana, 365
— — — de la Comunicación, Lima, 1038
— — — — Educación (Universidad Autónoma de Barcelona), 1207
— — — — — (Universidad Central de Barcelona), 1207
— — — — — (Universidad Politécnica de Barcelona), 1220
— — — Naturales, Bogotá, 348
— — — — del Estado Zubia, 1952
— — — Nucleares, Quito, 407
— — — Sociales, Durango, 936
— — — — Havana, 362
— — Climatologia e Hidrologia, Coímbra, 1105
— — Coímbra, 1098
— — Criminología, Barcelona, 1207
— — — Panama City, 1031
— — Cultura Dominicano, 403
— — — Puertorriqueña, 1109
— — — e Lingua Portuguesa, Lisbon, 1098
— — — Derecho de Trabajo y de la Seguridad Social, Lima, 1043
— — — Penal y Criminología, Medellín, 356
— — Desarrollo Económico y Social, Buenos Aires, 67
— — Documentación e Información Científica y Técnica, Havana, 362
— — Ecologia, A.C., Mexico City, 929
— — Economia Agricola, São Paulo, 183
— — Educação e Serviço Social de Angola, Luanda, 61
— — Electrotecnia, São Paulo, 208
— — Endocrinología "Professor Dr. Juan C. Mussio Fournier", Montevideo, 1939
— — Energia Eléctrica, Caracas, 1959
— — Engenharia de São Paulo, 182
— — — Nuclear, Rio de Janeiro, 185
— — Enseñanza de Mecanica y Electrotecnia "Prof. Dr. José F. Arias", Montevideo, 1941
— — España, Madrid, 1185
— — — en Lisboa, 1098
— — — Munich, 521
— — Estudios Africanos, Madrid, 1191
— — — Americanos, Buenos Aires, 67
— — — Asturianos, Oviedo, 1192
— — — Biomedicos, Santo Domingo, 405
— — — de Administración Local, Madrid, 1189
— — — — Postgrado e Investigación, Medellín, 356
— — — Etnológicos, Lima, 1037
— — — Fiscales, Madrid, 1198
— — — Ibéricos y Etnología Valenciana, 1192
— — — Iberoamericanos, Saltillo, 944
— — — Interamericanos, Santiago, 323
— — — Islámicos, Lima, 1037
— — — Laborales, Barcelona, 1222
— — — Norteamericano, Barcelona, 1190
— — — Regionales y Urbanos, Caracas, 1959
— — — Superiores, Montevideo, 1941
— — — — Commerciales, Santo Domingo, 406
— — — en Ciencia y Tecnología del Mar, Veracruz, 946
— — — Estudos Sociais, Lisbon, 1107
— — — Filología Experimental, Buenos Aires, 67
— — — — Hispánica, Saltillo, 944
— — Filosofía del Derecho, Zulia, 1960

— — Fomento Pesquero, Santiago, 325
— — Formación Integral, Santo Domingo, 406
— — Geofísica y Astronomía, Havana, 362
— — Geografía, Havana, 362
— — — y Conservación de Recursos Naturales, Mérida, 1953
— — — Geología, San Miguel de Tucumán, 67
— — — y Paleontología, Havana, 362
— — Hematología, Instituto Nacional de la Salud, Buenos Aires, 67
— — Higiene e Medicina Tropical, Lisbon, 1107
— — Ingeniería Cibernética, Barcelona, 1220
— — Ingenieros de Chile, Santiago, 324
— — — y Arquitectos de Honduras, Tegucigalpa, 630
— — Investigação Agronómica de Angola, Huambo, 61
— — — Científica "Bento de Rocha Cabral", 1100
— — — Médica de Angola, 61
— — — Veterinária, Huambo, 61
— — Investigación Aplicada al Automovil, Barcelona, 1220
— — — Científica, Durango, 936
— — — de Zonas Desérticas, San Luis Potosí, 941
— — — Social "Juan XXIII", Managua, 989
— — — Técnica Fundamental, Havana, 362
— — — Textil y Cooperación Industrial, Barcelona, 1220
— — — y Desarrollo Industrial, Caracas, 1959
— — Investigaciones Aeronáuticas y Espaciales, Córdoba, 69
— — — Agropecuarias, Monagas, 1959
— — — — Santiago, 324
— — — Agronómicas, Zulia, 1960
— — — Alérgicas, San Miguel, 1038
— — — Bibliográficas, Mexico City, 928
— — — Biológicas Clemente Estable, Montevideo, 1939
— — — Científicas, Guanajuato, 937
— — — Clínicas, Zulia, 1960
— — — de la Caña de Azúcar, Havana, 362
— — — del Desarrollo, León, 988
— — — Económicas y Sociales, Lima, 1036
— — — Educativas, Caracas, 1959
— — — Folklóricas, Santo Domingo, 405
— — — Fundamentales del Cerebro, Havana, 362
— — — en Agricultura Tropical "Alejandro de Humboldt", Santiago de las Vegas, 362
— — — Geológicas, Santiago, 325
— — — Históricas, Santo Domingo, 403
— — — Jurídicas, Lima, 1046
— — — Marinas de "Punta de Betin", Santa Maria, 349
— — — Médicas, Buenos Aires, 72
— — — — Rosario, 67
— — — Metalúrgicas, Caracas, 1959
— — — Nucleares, Havana, 362
— — — Nutricionales y Médico-Sociales, Quito, 407
— — — Odontológicas, Zulia, 1960
— — — Petroleras, Zulia, 1960
— — — Psicopedagógicas, Guanajuato, 937
— — — Tecnológicas, Bogotá, 348
— — — — Guanajuato, 937
— — — Veterinarias, Maracay, 1953
— — — — del Litoral, Guayaquil, 408
— — — y Ensayos de Materiales, Santiago (IDIEM), 325
— — la Ingeniería de España, Madrid, 1192
— — Letres e Artes, Pelotas, 212
— — Lexicografía Hispanoamericana Augusto Malaret, San Juan, 1109
— — Lingüística, Lisbon, 1100
— — Literatura, La Plata, 64
— — — y Lingüística, Havana, 362

Instituto de Malariología, 1100
— — Matemática, Cibernética y Computación, Havana, 362
— — Matemáticas, Mexico, 929
— — Medicina del Trabajo, Zulia, 1960
— — — Experimental, Caracas, 1953
— — — — del Servicio Nacional de Salud, Santiago, 324
— — — Tropical, Lima, 1043
— — Meteorología, Havana, 362
— — Microbiología e industrias agropecuarias, Castelar, 66
— — Música da Bahia, 212
— — Numismática y Antiguedades del Paraguay, Asunción, 1034
— — Nutrição, Rio de Janeiro, 184
— — Nutrición de Centro América y Panama (INCAP), Guatemala City, 624
— — Oceanología, Cuba, 362
— — Oncología, Montevideo, 1939
— — — "Angel H. Roffo", Buenos Aires, 72
— — — y Radiobiología de La Habana, 363
— — Patología, Lima, 1043
— — Pesquisas do Experimentação Agropecuário do Nordeste, Curado, 183
— — — Energéticas e Nucleares, São Paulo, 185
— — — Espaciais, São José dos Campos, 186
— — — Gonzaga de Gama Filho, Rio de Janeiro, 194
— — — Tecnológicas, São Paulo, 186
— — — Veterinárias Desidério Finamor, Pôrto Alegre, 183
— — Petrolquimia Aplicada, Barcelona, 1220
— — Planeamiento Regional y Urbano, Buenos Aires, 66
— — Política Internacional, Havana, 363
— — Química y Biología Experimental, Havana, 362
— — Radioproteção e Dosimetria, Jacarepaguá, 185
— — Recursos Naturales Renovables, Caracas, 1959
— — Salubridad y Enfermedades Tropicales, Mexico City, 929
— — Saúde, São Paulo, 184
— — — Publica de Moçambique, Maputo, 952
— — Sociología, Buenos Aires, 68
— — — Aplicada, Buenos Aires, 68
— — — Boliviana, 174
— — Suelos, Cuba, 362
— — — y Agrotecnia, Buenos Aires, 66
— — Superación Educacional, Havana, 363
— — Técnicas Energéticas, Barcelona, 1220
— — Tecnologia do Paraná, Curitiba, 184
— — — y Ciencias Marinas, Caracas, 1959
— — — — Química, Montevideo, 1939
— — Tisiología y Pneumología da U.F.R.J., Rio de Janeiro, 184
— — Valencia de Don Juan, 1201
— — Zoología, Havana, 362
— — — San Miguel de Tucumán, 67
— — Zoonosis e Investigación Pecuaria, Lima, 1038
— — Zootecnia, Nova Odessa, 183
— — Zootécnica, Lima, 1043
— del Mar del Peru, Callao, 1038
— — Petróleo, Caracas, 1959
— do Ceará, 180
— dos Advogados Brasileiros, Rio de Janeiro, 179
— Ecuatoriano de Antropología y Geografía, Quito, 407
— — — Ciencias Naturales, 407
— Egipcio de Estudios Islámicos, Madrid, 1190
— Español de Hematología y Hemoterapía, 1191

— — — Oceanografía, 1189
— — — Santiago, Naples, 759
— — — Tánger, Tangier, 951
— Evandro Chagas, Belém, 184
— Experimental de Educación Primaria No. 1, Lima, 1038
— "Ezequiel Dias", Belo Horizonte, 184
— Federico Olóriz, Sección de Anatomia, Granada, 1210
— Florestal Estado de São Paulo, 183
— Forestal, Santiago, 324
— — de Investigacion y Experiencias, Madrid, 1198
— Francés de América Latina, Mexico City, 926
— Genealógico Brasileiro, 180
— Geofísico Coímbra, 1105
— — de los Andes Colombianos, 355
— — del Perú, Lima, 1038
— Geográfico "Augustín Codazzi", 348
— — e Histórico da Bahia, 180
— — — do Amazonas, Manaos, 180
— — Militar, Asunción, 1034
— — — Buenos Aires, 67
— — — Santiago, 323
— — — y de Catastro Nacional, La Paz, 173
— — Nacional, Guatemala City, 624
— — — Lima, 1036
— — — Madrid, 1189
— — — San José, 359
— — — Tegucigalpa, 630
— Geológico, São Paulo, 180
— — del Uruguay, Montevideo, 1939
— — Minero y Metalurgico, Lima, 1038
— — y Minero de España, 1198
— Germano-Español de Investigación, Madrid, 1198
— Goethe, São Paulo, 181
— Gregoriano de Lisboa, 1098
— Guatemalteco-Americano (IGA), Guatemala City, 624
— Hidrográfico, Lisbon, 1101
— — de la Armada, Valparaíso, 324
— Hispano-Arabe de Cultura, Baghdad, 725
— — — — Madrid, 1190
— Histórico Centroamericano, Managua, 989
— — da Ilha Terceira, 1098
— — de Alagoas, 180
— — — Marina, Madrid, 1189
— — do Ceará, Fortaleza, 180
— — — Minho, 1098
— — e Geográfico Brasileiro, 180
— — — de Goias, 180
— — — — Santa Catarina, 180
— — — São Paulo, 180
— — — Sergipe, Aracajú, 180
— — — do Espírito Santo, 180
— — — Maranhão, 180
— — — Pará, 180
— — — Rio Grande do Norte, 180
— — — Rio Grande do Sul, 180
— — — Paraíbano, 180
— — Geográfico e Etnográfico Paranaense, Curitiba, 180
— — y Geográfico, Montevideo, 1938
— Hondureño de Antropología e Historia, 630
— — Cultura Inter-americana, Tegucigalpa, 630
— Iberoamericano de Derecho Agrario y Reforma Agraria, Mérida, 1953
— Indigenista Interamericano, Mexico City, 930
— — Nacional, Guatemala City, 624
— — Peruano, 1037
— Interamericano Agricultural Experimental, Quito, 407
— — de Ciencias Agrícolas de la OEA, San José, 359
— — — Etnomusicologia y Folklore, Caracas, 1950
— — del Niño, Montevideo, 1939
— Latinoamericano de Investigaciones Científicas en Educación a Distancia, Caracas, 1953

— — — Sociales (ILDIS), Quito, 407
— — — la Comunicación Educativa, Mexico City, 30
— — — las Naciones Unidas para la Prevención del Delito y Tratamiento del Delincuente, San José, 359
— — — Planificación Económica y Social, Santiago, 322
— Llorente, 1191
— López Neyra de Parasitología, Granada, 1210
— Martin Azpilcueta, Pamplona, 1213
— Médico Legal, Santiago, 322
— — "Sucre", 174
— Meteorológico Nacional, San José, 359
— Mexicano de Investigaciones Tecnológicas, A.C., Mexico City, 930
— — — Recursos Renovables, A.C., Mexico City, 929
— — del Café, Xalapa, 926
— — — Petroleo, Mexico City, 930
— — -Norte Americano de Relaciones Culturales, Mexico City, 926
— Miles de Terapéutica Experimental, Mexico City, 929
— Modelo de Clínica Médica "Luis Agote", Buenos Aires, 72
— Muley el-Hasan, Tétouan, 949
— Municipal de Administração e Ciencias Contábeis, Belo Horizonte, 179
— — Botánica, Jardín Botánico "Carlos Thays", Buenos Aires, 68
— — Historia de la Ciudad, Barcelona, 1189
— — Musical de Cartagena, 357
— — — São Paulo, 212
— Nacional de Antropología, Buenos Aires, 68
— — e Historia, Mexico City, 930
— — Arqueologia de Bolivia, La Paz, 173
— — Astrofísica, Optica y Electrónica, Puebla, 929
— — Bellas Artes, Mexico City, 925
— — Cancerología, Bogotá, 348
— — Cardiología, Mexico City, 929
— — Cultura, Lima, 1036
— — — Panama, 1030
— — Desarrollo y Aprovechamiento Forestales, Havana, 363
— — Estadística, La Paz, 173
— — — Madrid, 1189
— — y Censos, Buenos Aires, 67
— — — — Quito, 407
— — Estadísticas, Santiago, 324
— — Estatística, Lisbon, 1099
— — Estudios del Teatro, 66
— — — Lingüísticos, La Paz, 173
— — Estudos e Pesquisas Educacionais, Brasilia, 183
— — Geofísica, Madrid, 1198
— — Hidrometeorologia e Geofísica, Luanda, 61
— — Higiene, Havana, 363
— — — Mexico City, 929
— — — y Medicina Tropical "Leopoldo Izquieta Pérez", Guayaquil, 408
— — Investigação Científica, Lisbon, 1100
— — Investigación Agraria, Lima, 1038
— — — de las Ciencias Naturales, Buenos Aires, 70
— — — Recursos Naturales, Santiago, 325
— — — y Desarrollo Pesquero, Mar del Plata, 68
— — Investigaciones Agrarias, Madrid, 1198
— — — Agricolas, Mexico City, 928
— — — Agropecuarios, Quito, 407
— — — Científicas, Asunción, 1034
— — — Forestales, Mexico City, 928
— — — Geológico-Mineras, Bogotá, 348

— — — — Nucleares, México, 929
— — — — Pecuarias, Palo Alto, 928
— — — — sobre Recursos Bióticos, Veracruz, 929
— — — la Reforma Agraria (INRA), Havana, 363
— — — Limnología, Santo Tomé, 68
— — — Medicina Legal, Bogotá, 347
— — — — y Seguridad del Trabajo, Madrid, 1191
— — — Meteorología, Madrid, 1191
— — — — e Geofisica, Lisbon, 1101
— — — — — Hidrologia, Quito, 407
— — — Microbiología, Buenos Aires, 67
— — — Música, Panama, 1030
— — — Neumología, Mexico, 929
— — — Normalización, Santiago, 325
— — — Nutrición, Caracas, 1953
— — — Parasitologia, Asunción, 1034
— — — Pesca, Guayaquil, 408
— — — — Mexico City, 929
— — — — Montevideo, 1939
— — — Pesquisas da Amazonia, 184
— — — Psicología Aplicada y Orientacion Profesional, Madrid, 1191
— — — Reeducación de Inválidos, 1191
— — — Salud, Bogotá, 348
— — —. Sismología, Vulcanología, Meteorología e Hidrología, Guatemala City, 624
— — — Tecnología, Rio de Janeiro, 186
— — — — Agropecuaria, Buenos Aires, 66
— — — — Industrial, Buenos Aires, 69
— — — — Telecomunicações de Santa Rita do Sapucaí, 212
— — — — Vitivinicultura, Mendoza, 66
— — — del Libro Español, Madrid, 1190
— — — Indigenista, Mexico City, 930
— "Nami Jafet" Para o Progreso da Ciencia e Cultura, 179
— Neo-Pitagórico, Curitiba, 185
— Nicaraguense de Cine, Managua, 989
— Oceanográfico, Cumaná, 1958
— — de la Armada, Guayaquil, 408
— "Oscar Freire", São Paulo, 184
— Oswaldo Cruz, Rio de Janeiro, 184
— Panameño de Arte, Panama City, 1030
— Panamericano de Alta Direccion de Empresa, Mexico City, 945
— — — Geografía e Historia, Mexico City, 50
— para la Integración de América Latina, Buenos Aires, 67
— Paranaense de Botânica, Curitiba, 184
— Pasteur, São Paulo, 184
— — de Lisboa, Lisbon, 1100
— Pedagogico, Bogotá, 352
— "Penido Bournier", Campinas, 184
— Peruano de Cultura Hispánica, 1036
— — — Energia Nuclear, 1038
— — — Ingenieros Mecánicos, 1037
— — — Investigaciones Genealógicas, San Isidro, 1038
— — para la Investigación de la Estadística, Lima, 1038
— — — Promoción de la Cultura, 1036
— Politécnico Nacional, Mexico City, 943
— Português da Sociedade Científica de Goerres, Lisbon, 1100
— — de Arqueologia, História e Etnografia, Lisbon, 1098
— Químico de Sarriá, 1222
— Regional de Meteorologia "Coussirat Araújo", 185
— Rio Branco, Brasília, 211
— Riva-Agüero, Lima, 1046
— Salvadoreño de Investigaciones del Café, Santa Tecla, 422
— Superior de Administración y Tecnologia, Lima, 1046
— — — Agricultura, Santiago, 406
— — — Ciencias, Cordoba, 81
— — — — Económicas de Jujuy, 81
— — — Linguas e Administração, Lisbon, 1107

— — del Hogar Agricola "Ing. Agr. Dr. Tomas Amadeo", Bolívar, 81
— Técnico Industrial, Zipaquirá, 352
— — Superior "Otto Krause", Buenos Aires, 81
— Tecnológico Autónomo de Mexico, 945
— — de Aeronáutica, São Paulo, 212
— — — Buenos Aires, 81
— — — Costa Rica, 361
— — — Electrónica "Fernando Aguado Rico", Havana, 363
— — — la Càna de Azucar "Carlos M. de Cespedes", Oriente, 363
— — — Santo Domingo, 406
— — — "Mártires de Girón", Havana, 363
— — Regional de Celaya, 945
— — — — Chihuahua, 945
— — — — Ciudad Juárez, 945
— — — — — Madero, 945
— — — — Durango, 945
— — — — Mérida, 945
— — — — Morelia, 945
— — — — Oaxaca, 946
— — — — Orizaba, 946
— — — — Querétaro, 946
— — — — Saltillo, 946
— — — — Sonora, 946
— — y de Estudios Superiores de Monterrey, 943
— — — — — de Occidente, Guadalajara, 945
— — — Metalúrgico "Emilio Jimeno", Barcelona, 1207
— Teologico del Uruguay, Montevideo, 1945
— Torcuato di Tella, Buenos Aires, 66
— Universitário de Pesquisas do Rio de Janeiro, 211
— — Politécnico, Barquisimeto, 1960
— Uruguayo de Normas Técnicas, 1939
— Vasco de Criminología, San Sebastian, 1219
— Venezolano de Análisis Económico y Social, Caracas, 1953
— — — Investigaciones Científicas (IVIC), Caracas, 1954
— — — — Petroquímica, Caracas, 1954
— — — -Francés, Caracas, 1951
— — — -Italiano de Cultura, Caracas, 1951
— Vizcardo de Estudios Históricos, Lima, 1036
— y Observatorio de Marina, Cádiz, 1198
— Zuliano de la Cultura "Andres E. Blanco", 1950
Institutos Nacionales de Salud, Lima, 1038
Instituts et Jardin Botaniques de l'Université, Bern, 1258
Institutt for energiteknikk, Kjeller, 1009
— — fjellsprengningsteknikk, Oslo, 1009
Instituttet for Sammenlignende Kulturforskning, Oslo, 1009
Institutul Agronomic "N. Balescu" Bucharest, 1139
— — "Dr. Petru Groza", Cluj-Napoca, 1139
— — "Ion Ionescu de la Brad", Iași, 1139
— — Timișoara, 1139
— "V. Babes", Bucharest, 1119
— Cantacuzino, Bucharest, 1119
— Central de Chimie, Oficiul de Informare Documentară pentru Industria Chimică, Bucharest, 1123
— — — Fizică, Bucharest, 1124
— — Perfecționare a Personalului Didactică, Bucharest, 1124
— de Arheologie, Bucharest, 1121
— — Arhitectură "Ion Mincu", Bucharest, 1139
— — Arta Teatrala și Cinematografica "I. L. Caragiale", Bucharest, 1139
— — Arte Plastice "Ion Andrescu", Cluj-Napoca, 1139
— — — "N. Grigorescu", Bucharest, 1139
— Cercetare, Proiectare și Inginerie Tehnologică pentru Mecanizarea Agriculturii, Bucharest, 1117

— — și Producție a Cartofului, Brasov, 1117
— — — Proiectare pentru Sistematizare Locuinte și Gospodărie Comunală, Bucharest, 1123
— — Cercetări Economice, Bucharest, 1121
— — Etnologice și Dialectologice, Bucharest, 1124
— — Juridice, Bucharest, 1121
— — Pedagogice și Psihologice, Bucharest, 1121
— — pentru Apicultură, Bucharest, 1117
— — Cereale și Plante Technice, Fundulea, 1117
— — Chimie și Industrie Alimentară, Bucharest, 1117
— — Creșterea Taurinelor, Corbeanca, 1117
— — Legumicultură și Floricultura, Vidra, 1117
— — Nutritia Animalelor, Balotești, 1117
— — Pedologie și Agrochimie, Bucharest, 1117
— — Protecția Plantelor, Bucharest, 1117
— — Viticultură și Vinificație, Valea Călugărească, 1117
— — Pomicole, Pitești-Marăcineni, 1117
— — și Amenajări Silvice, Bucharest, 1117
— — Inginerie Tehnologica pentru Irigatii și Drenaj, Băneasa-Giurgiu, 1117
— — Proiectări "Delta Dunării", Tulcea, 1118
— — — pentru Gospodărirea Ápelor, Bucharest, 1118
— — — Valorificarea și Industrializarea Legumelor și Fructelor, Bucharest, 1118
— — Stiințifice pentru Protecția Muncii, Bucharest, 1124
— — Veterinare și Biopreparate "Pasteur", Bucharest, 1118
— — Construcții, Bucharest, 1139
— — Economie Agrara, Bucharest, 1117
— — Mondială, Bucharest, 1124
— — Educație Fizică și Sport, Bucharest, 1139
— — Endocrinologie "C. I. Parhon", Bucharest, 1109
— — Filozofie, Bucharest, 1121
— — Fiziologie Normala și Patologica "D. Danielopolu", 1119
— — Geodezie, Fotogrametrie, Cartografie și Organizarea Teritoriului, Bucharest, 1118
— — Geologie și Geofizică, Bucharest, 1124
— — Igienă și Sănătate Publică, Bucharest, 1119
— — — — Cluj-Napoca, 1119
— — — — Iași, 1119
— — Istorie Artei, Bucharest, 1121
— — "Nicolae Iorga", Bucharest, 1121
— — și Arheologie, Cluj-Napoca, 1121
— — — "A. D. Xenopol", Iași, 1121
— — — Teorie Literară "George Calinescu", Bucharest, 1121
— — Medicină, Timișoara, 1139
— — Internă "Nicolae Gh. Lupu", Bucharest, 1119
— — Legală "Prof. Dr. Mina Minovici", Bucharest, 1119
— — și Farmacie, Bucharest, 1139
— — — Cluj-Napoca, 1140
— — — Iași, 1140
— — — Tîrgu Mures, 1140
— — Meteorologie și Hidrologie, Bucharest, 1118
— — Mine Petroșani, 1140
— — Neurologie și Psihiatrie, Bucharest, 1119

# INDEX OF INSTITUTIONS

Institutul de Petrol şi Gaze, Ploieşti, 1140
— — Planificare şi Prognoză, Bucharest, 1124
— — Ştiinţe Politice şi de Studiere a Problemei Naţionale, Bucharest, 1121
— — Studii Istorice şi Social-Politice de pe Linga Comitetul Central al Partidului Comunist Roman, Bucharest, 1124
— — — Sud-Est Europene, Bucharest, 1121
— — Teatreu "Szentgyörgyi Istvan", Tîrgu-Mures, 1140
— — Virusologie "St. S. Nicolau", Bucharest, 1119
— Naţional de Informare şi Documentare, Bucharest, 1123
— — — Metrologie, Bucharest, 1124
— Oncologic, Bucharest, 1119
— pentru Controlu de Stat al Medicamentului şi Cercetării Farmaceutice, Bucharest, 1120
— Politehnic Cluj-Napoca, 1136
— — "Gh. Gheorghiu-Dej", Bucharest, 1135
— — "Gheorghe Asachi" Din Iaşi, 1137
— — "Traian Vuia", Timişoara, 1138
— Român de Cercetări Marine, Constanţa, 1124
— — pentru Relaţiile Culturale cu Strainatatea, Bucharest, 1124
Institutum "Augustinianum", Rome, 1946
— "Ecclesia Mater", Rome, 1946
— Romanum Finlandiae, Rome, 759
— Theologiae Moralis, Vatican City, 1946
— — Vitae Religiosiae "Claretianum", Rome, 1946
Instituut voor Bewaring en Verwerking van Landbouwprodukten, 962
— — de studie van de Renaissance en het Humanisme, Brussels, 159
— — — Veredeling van Tuinbouwgewassen, 960
— — Didactiek en Andragogiek, Antwerp, 167
— — het Redden der Artistieke Constanten (IRAC), Ghent, 150
— — Kernphysisch Onderzoek, Amsterdam, 962
— — Maatschappij Wetenschappelijk Onderzoek in Ontwikkelingslanden, The Hague, 962
— — Mechanisatie, Arbeid en Gebouwen, Wageningen, 962
— — Onderzoek van het Wetenschappelijk Onderwijs, Nijmegen, 970
— — Plantenziektenkundig Onderzoek, 961
— — Postuniversitair Onderwijs, Antwerp, 167
— — toegepastesociologie, Nijmegen, 970
Instrument Society of America, Triangle Park, N.C., 1616
Instruments Centre, Mexico City, 933
Instytut Badán Jadrowych, Świerk, 1070
— — Literackich, Warsaw, 1067
— Badawczy Leśnictwa, Warsaw, 1071
— Bałtycki, Gdansk, 1067
— Budownictwa Wodnego, Gdańsk-Oliwa, 1069
— Chemii Nieorganicznej, Gliwice, 1071
— — Organicznej, Warsaw, 1068
— Cieźkiej Syntezy Organicznej, Blachownia Kędzierzyn-Koźle, 1071
— Dendrologii, PAN, Kornik, 1067
— Ekonomiki Rolnej, Warsaw, 1071
— Filozofii i Socjologii, Warsaw, 1067
— Fizyki, Warsaw, 1068
— — Jądrowej, Cracow, 1071
— Geografii i Przestrzennego Zagospodarowania, Warsaw, 1069
— Geologiczny, Warsaw, 1071
— Górnictwa Naftowego i Gazownicta, Cracow, 1071

— Historii, Warsaw, 1066
— — Kultury Materialnej, Warsaw, 1066
— — Nauki, Oswiaty i Techniki, Warsaw, 1067
— Hodowli i Aklimatyzacji Róslin, Radzików, 1071
— Informacji Naukowo-Technicznej i Ekonomicznej, Warsaw, 1075
— Maszyn Matematycznych, Warsaw, 1068
— — Przeplywowych Gdansk-Wrzeszcz, 1068
— Mechaniki Górotworu, Cracow, 1069
— Morski, Gdańsk, 1071
— Nawozów Sztucznych, Puławy, 1071
— Organizacji i Kierowania, Warsaw, 1068
— Pánstwa i Prawa, Warsaw, 1066
— Podstawowych Problemów Techniki, Warsaw, 1068
— Przemyslu Farmaceutycznego, Warsaw, 1071
— — Gumowego, Piastów, 1071
— — Tworzyw i Farb, Gliwice, 1071
— Rozwoju Wsi i Rolnictwa, Warsaw, 1067
— Sadownictwa i Kwiaciarstwa, Skierniewice, 1071
— Śląski, Opole, 1067
— Słowianoznawsta, Warsaw, 1067
— Sztuki, Warsaw, 1066
— Techniki Budowlanej, Warsaw, 1071
— Technologii Drewna, Poznan, 1071
— Wzornictwa Przemyslowego, Warsaw, 1071
— Zachodni, Poznan, 1067
— Ziemniaka, Bonin, 1069
Integrated Research Centre, Manila, 1052
Intellectual Society of Libya, Tripoli, 906
Inter Nationes, Bonn-Bad Godesberg, 521
Interafrican Bureau for Animal Resources, Nairobi, 878
Inter-American Association of Writers, Buenos Aires, 19
— Bar Association, Washington, 35
— Bibliographical and Library Association, 1601
— Council for Education, Science and Culture, Washington, D.C. 28
— Institute of Agricultural Sciences, San José, 16
— Law Center, New York, 1810
— Statistical Institute (IASI), Washington, 1603
— University of Puerto Rico, 1112
Intercampus Institute for Research of Particle Accelerators, Santa Barbara, 1673
Intercisa Múzeum, Dunaujváros, 645
Interdepartmental Commission on the Study of Antarctica, Moscow, 1320
— Committee on Stratigraphy, Leningrad, 1320
— — — Tectonics, Moscow, 1320
— — Geophysical Committee, Moscow, 1320
— Institute of Metallurgy—Electron Microscopy, Lausanne, 1273
— — — Micro-Electronics, Lausanne, 1273
Interdisciplinary Center for Technological Analysis and Forecasting, Tel-Aviv, 750
— Programmes, Atlanta, 1700
— Research Unit for Electronic Microscopy, Namur, 165
Interfacultair Centrum voor de Studie van Lucht-, Bodem- en Waterverontreiniging, Ghent, 161
— — — Informatica, Ghent, 161
— — — Management, Ghent, 161
— Studie- en Vormingscentrum voor Ontwikkelingssamenwerking, Ghent, 161
Intergovernmental Bureau for Informatics, Rome, 45
— Copyright Committee, Paris, 35
— Oceanographic Commission (IOC), Paris, 45
Intermediate Institute for Agriculture, Aleppo, 1278

— — — Commerce, Aleppo, 1278
— — — Engineeering, Aleppo, 1278
— — — Medicine, Aleppo, 1278
Internal Medicine Association, Hanoi, 1962
Internationaal Instituut voor Sociale Geschiedenis, Amsterdam, 957
— Juridisch Instituut, The Hague, 957
International Academic Union, Brussels, 10
— Academy of Astronautics (IAA), Paris, 46
— — — Indian Culture, New Delhi, 668
— — — Legal and Social Medicine, Munich, 37
— — Political Science and Constitutional History, Paris, 24
— — — Social and Moral Sciences, Arts and Letters, Cologne, 24
— African Institute, London, 24
— Agency for Research on Cancer, Lyon, 39
— — — the Prevention of Blindness, Naestved, 37
— Amateur Theatre Association, Amsterdam, 19
— Association for Biological Oceanography, Kiel, 46
— — — Bridge and Structural Engineering, Zurich, 32
— — — Child and Adolescent Psychiatry and Allied Professions, London, 39
— — — Cybernetics, Namur, 46
— — — Educational and Vocational Guidance, Nuremberg, 28
— — — — Information, Paris, 28
— — — Hydraulic Research, Delft, 32
— — — Mass Communication Research, Leicester, 21
— — — Mathematics and Computers in Simulation, Brussels, 46
— — — Penal Law, Paris, 35
— — — Philosophy of Law and Social Philosophy, Brussels, 35
— — — Plant Physiology (IAPP), North Ryde, N.S.W., 46
— — — — Taxonomy, Utrecht, 46
— — — the Development of Documentation, Libraries and Archives in Africa, Dakar, 21
— — — Exchange of Students for Technical Experience, Athens, 28
— — — — History of Religions, Jerusalem, 10
— — — — Physical Sciences of the Ocean, San Diego, 46
— — — — Prevention of Blindness, Honolulu, 37
— — — — Study of the Liver, Clichy, 37
— — Futuribles, Paris, 24
— — of Agricultural Economists, Oak Brook, 16
— — — Librarians and Documentalists (IAALD), Southend-on-Sea, 21
— — — Medicine and Rural Health, Nagano, 40
— — — Allergology and Clinical Immunology, Ottawa, 37
— — — Applied Linguistics, Edinburgh, 19
— — — Psychology, Nijmegen, 40
— — — Art, Paris, 19
— — — Critics, Paris, 19
— — — Asthmology, Pamplona, 40
— — — Bibliophiles, Paris, 21
— — — Democratic Lawyers (IADL), Brussels, 35
— — — Dental Students, London, 28
— — — Documentalists and Information Officers (IAD), Paris, 21
— — — Geodesy, Paris, 46
— — — Geomagnetism and Aeronomy (IAGA), Tokyo, 46
— — — Gerontology, Rehovot, 37
— — — Horticultural Producers, The Hague, 17
— — — Law Libraries (IALL), Nashville, Tenn., 21
— — — Legal Sciences, Paris, 12

— — — Literary Critics, Paris, 19
— — — Meteorology and Atmospheric Physics, Boulder, 46
— — — Metropolitan City Libraries (INTAMEL), Rotterdam, 21
— — — Museums of Arms and Military History (IAMAM), London, 19
— — — Music Libraries, Archives and Documentation Centres (IAML), Stockholm, 21
— — — Oral Surgeons, Amsterdam, 40
— — — Schools of Social Work, Vienna, 24
— — — Sedimentologists, Liège, 46
— — — Students in Economics and Commercial Sciences, Brussels, 28
— — — Technological University Libraries (IATUL), Enschede, 21
— — — Theoretical and Applied Limnology, Hickory Corners, 47
— — — Traffic and Safety Sciences, Tokyo, 817
— — — Universities, Paris, 14
— — — University Professors and Lecturers, Paris, 28
— — — Volcanology and Chemistry of the Earth's Interior (IAVCEI), Nottingham, 47
— — — Wood Anatomists, Leiden, 47
— — on Water Pollution Research, London, 33
— Astronautical Federation (IAF), Paris, 47
— Astronomical Union, Paris, 7
— Atomic Energy Agency (IAEA), Vienna, 47
— Baccalaureate Office (IBO), Geneva, 29
— Bar Association, London, 35
— Board on Books for Young People, Basel, 21
— Book Exchange Centre, Karachi, 1023
— Botanical Congress, Sydney, 47
— Brain Research Organisation, Los Angeles, 40
— Bureau of Education (IBE), 6
— — — Fiscal Documentation, Amsterdam, 22
— — — Weights and Measures, Sèvres, 47
— Cardiovascular Society, Manchester, Mass., 40
— Cargo Handling Co-ordination Association (ICHCA), London, 33
— Cell Research Organisation, Paris, 40
— Center for Arid and Semi-Arid Land Studies, Lubbock, 1903
— — — Intergroup Relations, Paris, 13
— — — Research on Bilingualism, Sainte-Foy, 245
— — of Information on Antibiotics, Liège, 40
— Centre for Advanced Mediterranean Agronomic Studies, Paris, 17
— — — — Technical and Vocational Training, Turin, 24
— — — Agricultural Education, Berne, 29
— — — Ancient and Modern Tapestry, Lausanne, 19
— — — Classical Research, Athens, 617
— — — Diarrhoeal Disease Research, Bangladesh, 142
— — — Economics and Related Disciplines, London, 1510
— — — Rural Development, Alexandria, 414
— — — Scientific and Technical Information, Moscow, 1346
— — — the Study of the Preservation and Restoration of Cultural Property (ICCROM), Rome, 19
— — — Theoretical Physics, Trieste, 47
— — of Films for Children and Young People, Paris, 19
— — — Insect Physiology and Ecology, Nairobi, 878
— Christian University, Tokyo, 863
— — — Library, Tokyo, 818
— College of Surgeons, Chicago, 37

— Commission for Food Industries, Paris, 17
— — — Optics, Delft, 47
— — — the History of Representative and Parliamentary Institutions, Brighton, 24
— — — — Scientific Exploration of the Mediterranean Sea, Monte Carlo, 47
— — of Agricultural Engineering, Paris, 17
— — — Jurists, Geneva, 35
— — on Glass (ICG), Prague, 33
— — — Illumination, Paris, 34
— — — Irrigation and Drainage, New Delhi, 32
— — — Large Dams, Paris, 32
— — — Zoological Nomenclature, London, 48
— Committee for Social Science Documentation, Paris, 22
— — of Foundry Technical Associations, Zurich, 32
— — — Historical Sciences, Lausanne, 10
— — — Military Medicine and Pharmacy, Liège, 39
— — on the History of Art, Paris, 10
— — — Veterinary Anatomical Nomenclature (ICVAN), Vienna, 17
— Communication Association, Austin, Texas, 1616
— Comparative Literature Association, Paris, 19
— Confederation of Societies of Authors and Composers, Paris, 35
— — — Technical Agriculturists, Rome, 17
— Conference on Large High Voltage Electric Systems, Paris, 32
— Congress of Africanists, Lubumbashi, 11
— — on Tropical Medicine and Malaria, Manila, 39
— Co-ordinating Committee for the Presentation of Science and the Development of Out-of-School Scientific Activities (ICC), Brussels, 29
— Council for Adult Education, Toronto, 29
— — — Bird Preservation, Cambridge, 48
— — — Building Research, Studies and Documentation (CIB), Rotterdam, 34
— — — Philosophy and Humanistic Studies (ICPHS), Paris, 10
— — — the Exploration of the Sea (ICES), Copenhagen, 48
— — of Graphic Design Associations (ICOGRADA), Chislehurst, 19
— — — Museums (ICOM), Paris, 19
— — — Nurses, Geneva, 40
— — — Scientific Unions, Paris, 7
— — — Theological Library Associations, Köln, 22
— — on Archives, Paris, 22
— — — Monuments and Sites (ICOMOS), Paris, 19
— — — Social Welfare, Vienna, 24
— Cultural Society of Korea, Seoul, 885
— Culture Centre, New Delhi, 660
— Cystic Fibrosis Association, New York, 40
— Dairy Federation, Brussels, 17
— Dental Federation, London, 37
— Development Research Centre, Ottawa, 245
— Diabetes Federation, London, 37
— Doll Museum, New Delhi, 675
— Economic Association, Paris, 12
— — Relations, Izmir, 1305
— Electrotechnical Commission, Geneva, 34
— Epidemiological Association, Sydney, 37
— Federation for Cell Biology, London, 48
— — — Documentation, The Hague, 22
— — — European Law (FIDE), Brussels, 35
— — — Housing and Planning, The Hague, 34

— — — Medical and Biological Engineering, Ottawa, 40
— — — Theatre Research, Lancaster, 20
— — of Agricultural Producers, Paris, 17
— — — Anatomists, Paris, 40
— — — Automatic Control (IFAC), Laxenburg, 32
— — — Business and Professional Women, London, 24
— — — Catholic Universities, Paris, 29
— — — "Ecole Moderne" Movements, Sèvres, 29
— — — Film Archives, Brussels, 22
— — — Gynaecology and Obstetrics, London, 40
— — — Library Associations and Institutions (IFLA), 22
— — — Modern Languages and Literatures, 11
— — — Multiple Sclerosis Societies, Vienna, 40
— — — Musicians, Zürich, 43
— — — Operational Research Societies, Lyngby, 34
— — — Ophthalmological Societies, Nijmegen, 40
— — — Organisations for School Correspondence and Exchange, Paris, 29
— — — Oto-Rhino-Laryngological Societies, Mexico, 37
— — — Philosophical Societies, Fribourg, 11
— — — Physical Education, Arreau, 41
— — — — Medicine and Rehabilitation, Stockholm, 37
— — — Social Science Organizations, Copenhagen, 12
— — — Societies for Electroencephalography and Clinical Neurophysiology, Vancouver, 37
— — — — Electron Microscopy, Berkeley, 48
— — — — of Automobile Engineers, Paris, 34
— — — Surgical Colleges, Edinburgh, 41
— — — Surveyors, Thun, 33
— — — Teachers of French, Sèvres, 28
— — — the Societies of Classical Studies, Geneva, 11
— — — Thermalism and Climatism, Bad Ragaz, 41
— — — University Women, Geneva, 29
— — — Workers' Educational Associations, London, 29
— — — Youth and Music, Brussels, 43
— Fellows Program, New York, 1810
— Film and Television Council (and all other Audiovisual Media of Communication), Paris, 20
— Fiscal Association, Rotterdam, 24
— Folk Music Council, New York, 43
— Food Information Service, Reading, 48
— Foundation of the High Altitude Research Stations, Jungfraujoch and Gornergrat, 48
— Gas Union, Paris, 33
— Geographical Union, Freiburg, 7
— Geological Congress, Paris, 48
— Glaciological Society, Cambridge, 48
— Gypsy Committee, Avon, France, 24
— Hospital Federation, London, 41
— House, Brisbane, 109
— — Association, Taipei Chapter, 341
— Hydrographic Organization, Monte Carlo, 48
— Institute for Adult Literacy Methods, Teheran, 29
— — — Applied Systems Analysis, Laxenburg, 48
— — — Audio-Visual Communication and Cultural Development—MEDIACULT, Vienna, 44
— — — Children's Literature and Reading Research, Vienna, 22

## INDEX OF INSTITUTIONS

International Institute for Comparative Music Studies and Documentation, Berlin (West), 43
— — — Conservation of Historic and Artistic Works, London, 20
— — — Development, Co-operation and Labour Studies, Tel-Aviv, 753
— — — Educational Planning (IIEP), Paris, 6
— — — Labour Studies, Geneva, 24
— — — Land Reclamation and Improvement, Wageningen, 960
— — — Ligurian Studies, Bordighera, 24
— — — Sociology, Rome, 24
— — — Strategic Studies, London, 1442
— — — the Study of Human Reproduction, New York, 1810
— — — Unification of Private Law (UNIDROIT), Rome, 35
— — of Administrative Sciences, Brussels, 12
— — — Philosophy (IIP), Paris, 25
— — — Refrigeration, Paris, 34
— — — Seismology and Earthquake Engineering, Tokyo, 49
— — — Social and Political Sciences, Fribourg, 1266
— — — Space Law, Paris, 35
— — — Tropical Agriculture, Ibadan, 17, 993
— — — Welding, London, 33
— Institution for Production Engineering Research, Paris, 33
— Iron and Steel Institute (IISI), Brussels, 34
— Juridical Institute, The Hague, 36
— Labour Office Library, Geneva, 1259
— — Organisation (ILO), Geneva, 23
— Latitude Observatory of Mizusawa, Iwate, 815
— Law Association, London, 12
— — — Danish Branch, Copenhagen, 390
— — — Finnish Branch, Helsinki, 428
— — — Swedish Branch, Stockholm, 1235
— League Against Epilepsy, Bethesda, Md., 41
— — — Rheumatism, Basel, 37
— — for Child and Adult Education, Paris, 29
— — of Societies for Persons with Mental Handicap, Brussels, 41
— Leprosy Association, Sutton, 37
— Literary and Artistic Association, Paris, 20
— Livestock Centre for Africa (ILCA), Addis Ababa, 424
— Maritime Committee, Antwerp, 36
— Mathematical Union, Paris, 7
— Medical Alliance, Paris, 41
— — Sciences Academy (IMSA), New Delhi, 662
— Mineralogical Association, Berlin (West), 49
— Music Centre, Vienna, 44
— — Council, Paris, 43
— Musicological Society, Basel, 11
— Numismatic Commission, Oslo, 25
— Optometric and Optical League, London, 41
— Organisation for the development of concrete, prestressing and related materials and techniques, Slough, 32
— — of Legal Metrology, Paris, 49
— Organization Against Trachoma, Créteil, 41
— — for Biological Control of Noxious Animals and Plants (IOBC), Zurich, 17
— — — Standardization, Geneva, 34
— Ornithological Congress, Berlin (West), 49
— Palaeontological Association, Göttingen, 49
— Peace Academy, New York, 25
— — Research Association, Tokyo, 12

— Pediatric Association, Paris, 38
— PEN Club, Brussels, 151
— — Montreal, 241
— — (Sydney Centre), 89
   *See also* P.E.N.
— Permanent Committee of Linguists, Leiden, 11
— Phonetic Association, London, 30
— Polar Motion Service, Iwate-ken, 49
— Political Science Association (IPSA), Ottawa, 12
— Primatological Society, Providence, R.I., 49
— Psycho-Analytical Association, Baltimore, Md., 41
— Red Locust Control Organisation for Central and Southern Africa, Mbala, 1997
— Reference Centre for Avian Haematozoa, St. Johns, 285
— Robert-Musil Society, Saarbrucken, 20
— School of Hotel Administration, Seoul, 893
— Schools Association (ISA), Geneva, 30
— Scientific Council for Trypanosomiasis Research and Control, Lagos, 41
— — Film Library, Brussels, 22
— — Research Institute, Teheran, 721
— Seed Testing Association, Zürich, 18
— Social Science Council (ISSC), Paris, 11
— Society and Federation of Cardiology, Geneva, 38
— — for Business Education, Le Mont sur Lausanne, 30
— — — Clinical and Experimental Hypnosis (ISCEH), Prague, 41
— — — — Electrophysiology of Vision, Soesterberg, 41
— — — Community Development, New York, 25
— — — Contemporary Music, Geneva, 44
— — — Education through Art, Boulogne, 30
— — — Ethnology and Folklore (SIEF), Bucharest, 25
— — — Human and Animal Mycology (ISHAM), Basle, 49
— — — Music Education, Christchurch, N.Z., 44
— — — Photogrammetry and Remote Sensing, Reston, Va., 34
— — — Rehabilitation of the Disabled, New York, 39
— — — Research on Civilization Diseases and Vital Substances, Hannover-Kirchrode, 42
— — — Soil Mechanics and Foundation Engineering, London, 33
— — — the Study of Medieval Philosophy, Louvain, 25
— — — Tropical Ecology, Varanasi, 49
— — — Vegetation Science, Rinteln, 49
— — of Art and Psychopathology, Paris, 42
— — — Audiology, London, 38
— — — Biometeorology, Zürich, 49
— — — Blood Transfusion, Paris, 42
— — — Criminology, Paris, 38
— — — Cybernetic Medicine, Naples, 42
— — — Developmental Biologists, Hanover, N.H., 49
— — — Electrochemistry (ISE), Lausanne, 49
— — — Geographical Pathology, Zurich, 38
— — — Haematology, México, D.F., 42
— — — Internal Medicine, Lausanne, 38
— — — Lymphology, Freiburg, 42
— — — Orthopaedic Surgery and Traumatology, Brussels, 42
— — — Radiology, Bern, 42
— — — Social Defence, Milan, 25
— — — Soil Science, Wageningen, 18
— — — Surgery, Brussels, 42
— — — the History of Medicine, Montpellier, 38
— Sociological Association, Montreal, 12

— Standing Committee of the Congress on Physiology and Pathology of Animal Reproduction and of Artificial Insemination, Potters Bar, 18
— Statistical Institute, Voorburg, 49
— Tables of Selected Constants, Paris, 50
— Tamil League, Tamil Nadu, 662
— Theatre Institute, Paris, 20
— Time Bureau, Paris, 50
— Training Centre for University Human Rights Teaching, Strasbourg, 497
— Translations Centre, Delft, 22
— Union Against Cancer, Geneva, 38
— — — Tuberculosis, Paris, 38
— — — Venereal Diseases and Treponematoses, Paris, 42
— — for Conservation of Nature and Natural Resources, Gland, 50
— — — Electroheat, Paris, 33
— — — Health Education, Paris, 38
— — — Oriental and Asian Studies, Saint-Maur, 11
— — — Quaternary Research (INQUA), Brussels, 50
— — — the Protection of Literary and Artistic Works, Geneva, 20
— — — Study of Social Insects, Southampton, 50
— — of Amateur Cinema, La Louvière, 20
— — — Angiology, Florence, 38
— — — Anthropological and Ethnological Sciences, Durham, 12
— — — Architects, Paris, 20
— — — Biochemistry, Miami, 7
— — — Biological Sciences, Paris, 7
— — — Crystallography, Chester, 7
— — — Forestry Research Organisations, Vienna, 18
— — — Geodesy and Geophysics, Brussels, 7
— — — Geological Sciences, Paris, 8
— — — Immunological Societies, (IUIS), Oslo, 8
— — — Lawyers, Brussels, 36
— — — Microbiological Societies (IAMS), Marseille, 39
— — — Nutritional Sciences, Rüschlikon, 8
— — — Pharmacology, Heidelberg, 8
— — — Physiological Sciences, Budapest, 8
— — — Prehistoric and Protohistoric Sciences, Højbjerg, 11
— — — Psychological Science, Austin, Texas, 12
— — — Public Transport, Brussels, 33
— — — Pure and Applied Biophysics, Zürich, 8
— — — — — Chemistry (IUPAC), Oxford, 8
— — — — — Physics, Quebec, 8
— — — Radio Science, Brussels, 8
— — — Railway Medical Services, Brussels, 42
— — — Speleology, Vienna, 50
— — — Students, Prague, 30
— — — Testing and Research Laboratories on Materials and Structures (RILEM), Paris, 33
— — — the History and Philosophy of Science, 8
— — — Theoretical and Applied Mechanics, Gothenburg, 9
— — — Therapeutics, Paris, 38
— University—Africa, Nairobi, 1660
— — Europe, Watford, 1660
— Veterinary Association for Animal Production, Madrid, 18
— Waterfowl Research Bureau, Slimbridge, 50
— Young Christian Workers, Brussels, 30
— Youth and Student Movement for the United Nations, Geneva, 30
— — Library, Munich, 23
Internationale Jugendbibliothek, Munich, 23

— Paracelsus-Gesellschaft, Salzburg, 122
— Robert-Musil-Gesellschaft, Saarbrucken, 20
— Vereinigung der Musikbibliotheken, Musikarchive und Musikdokumentationszentren Gruppe BRD, Bremen, 518
— Veterinär-Anatomische Nomenklatur-Kommission (IVANK), Vienna, 17
Internationaler Verband Forstlicher Forschungsanstalten, Vienna, 18
Internationales Forschungsinstitut für Staatssoziologie und Politik, Freiburg, 530
— Institut für Vergleichende Musikstudien und Dokumentation, Berlin (West), 43
— Musikinstitut, Darmstadt, 608
— Musikzentrum (IMZ), Vienna, 44
— Studienzentrum für Landwirtschaftliches Bildungswesen, Bern, 29
— Zeitungsmuseum der Stadt Aachen, 541
Inter-Parliamentary Union, Geneva, 25
Inter-Union Commission on Frequency Allocations for Radio Astronomy and Space Science (IUCAF), Egham, 10
— — — Radio Meteorology (IUCRM), Boulder, Colo., 10
— — — Solar and Terrestrial Physics, (IUCSTP), Washington, D.C., 10
— — — Spectroscopy (IUCS), Ottawa, 10
Interuniversity Centre for European Studies, Montreal, 244
— — of Postgraduate Studies, Dubrovnik, 1993
— Council for East Africa, Kampala, 1311
— Institute of Engineering Control, Bangor, 1535
— — — — Coventry, 1539
— Postgraduate Centre, Dubrovnik, 1993
Iodine Metabolism Research Unit, Tygerberg, 1156
Iona College, New Rochelle, 1816
— — Windsor, Ont., 316
Iowa State University Library, Ames, 1632
— — — of Science and Technology, 1723
— Wesleyan College, 1728
Iparművészeti Múzeum, Budapest, 643
— — Könyvtára, Budapest, 640
Iqbal Academy, 1020
Iran Bastan Museum, Teheran, 722
— College of Science and Technology, Teheran-Narmak, 724
— Cultural Centre, Karachi, 1020
— League, 661
— National Archives, Teheran, 722
— Society, Calcutta, 661
Iranian Academy, 721
— Centre for Archaeological Research, Teheran, 721
— Culture Foundation, Teheran, 721
— — Research Institute, Teheran, 722
— Documentation Center, Teheran, 721
— Library Association, Teheran, 721
— Society for Cultural Relations with the U.S.S.R., Teheran, 721
— — of Microbiology, Teheran, 721
Iranische Kommission, Vienna, 118
Iraq Military Museum, A'dhamiya, 726
— Natural History Research Centre and Museum, Baghdad, 726
Iraqi Academy, 725
— — Library, Baghdad, 726
— Medical Society, Baghdad, 725
— Museum, 726
Irish Academy of Letters, 729
— Astronomical Society, 731
— Central Library for Students, 731
— Manuscripts Commission, 730
— Medical Association, 731
— PEN, Dublin, 730
— Society for Design and Craftwork, Dublin, 730
— — of Arts and Commerce, 730
Irkutsk Agricultural Institute, 1369

— Institute of National Economy, 1373
— — — Organic Chemistry, 1321
— — — Orthopaedics and Traumatology, Irkutsk, 1385
— Museum of Art, 1353
— Polytechnic Institute, 1375
— State Medical Institute, 1383
— A. A. Zhdanov State University, 1362
Iron and Red Cell Metabolism Research Unit, Tygerberg, 1156
— — — — Unit, Johannesburg, 1182
— — Steel College, Beijing, 336
Ironbridge Gorge Museum, Telford, 1469
Irrigation and Power Research Station, Amritsar, 672
— Drainage and Flood Control Research Council, Islamabad, 1023
— Research Institute, Lahore, 1023
Irwin S. and Sylvia Chanin Institute for Cancer Research, New York, 1824
Ischaemic Heart Disease Research Unit, Tygerberg, 1156
Islamia College, Peshawar, 1027
— — Library, Lahore, 1023
— University, Bahawalpur, 1026
Islamic Cultural Centre, London, 1424
— Museum, Tripoli, 906
— Research Association, Bombay, 672
— — Institute, Islamabad, 1023
— University, Islamabad, 1026
— — Medina, 1143
— — Library, Medina Munawarah, 1142
— — of Imam Muhammad ibn Saud, Riyadh, 1143
— — — Indonesia, Yogyakarta, 718
— — — in Cirebon, 719
— — — North Sumatra, Medan, 719
Islamisches Museum, Berlin (East), 508
Íslenzka Bókmenntafélag, Híd, 657
— fornleifafélag, 656
— fraedafélag, Hillerød, 391
— náttúrufraedifélag, 657
İşletme Fakültesi, Eskişehir, 1309
Işletmecilik Yüksek Okulu, Istanbul, 1309
Islington Libraries, London, 1452
Ismail Rahimtulla Trust Library, Nairobi, 879
Isotopenlaboratorium, Hamburg, 528
Israel Academy of Sciences and Humanities, Jerusalem, 737
— Association for Asian Studies, Jerusalem, 740
— — of Archaeologists, Jerusalem, 738
— Bar Association, 737
— Center for Psychobiology, Haifa, 740
— Ceramic and Silicate Institute, 741
— Chemical Society, Tel-Aviv, 738
— Desalination Engineering (Zarchin Process) Ltd., Tel-Aviv, 740
— Exploration Society, 739
— Geographical Society, Jerusalem, 738
— Geological Society, Jerusalem, 738
— Gerontological Society, Tel-Aviv, 738
— Institute for Biological Research, Ness Ziona, 740
— — of Applied Social Research, 740
— — — Business Research, Tel-Aviv, 750
— — — Metals, Haifa, 752
— — — Productivity, Tel-Aviv, 739
— — — Technology, Haifa, 750
— — — Library System, 743
— Library Association, Jerusalem, 737
— Mathematical Union, Jerusalem, 738
— Medical Association, Tel-Aviv, 738
— Meteorological Service, Bet Dagan, 740
— Mining Industries, Haifa, 740
— Museum, Jerusalem, 744
— Music Institute, Tel-Aviv, 737
— Oceanographic and Limnological Research Company, Haifa, 740
— Oriental Society, The, 739
— Physical Society, Jerusalem, 738
— Political Science Association, 737
— Psychological Association, Tel-Aviv, 739
— Society for Biblical Research, Jerusalem, 741

— — of Aeronautics and Astronautics, Tel-Aviv, 739
— — — Allergology, 738
— — — Criminology, Jerusalem, 738
— — — Special Libraries and Information Centers, Tel-Aviv, 737
— State Archives, Jerusalem, 742
— Theater Museum, Tel-Aviv, 743
— Wine Institute, Rehovot, 740
Israeli Centre of the World Union of Jewish Students, 738
— Institute for Poetics and Semiotics, Tel-Aviv, 750
Istanbul Academy of Economics and Commercial Sciences, 1309
— Arkeoloji Müzeleri, 1301
— Belediyesi Kütüphane ve Müzeleri, 1300
— Deniz Müzesi, 1301
— Devlet Güzel Sanatiar Akademisi, 1310
— — Mühendislik ve Mimarlik Akademisi, 1309
— İktisadî ve Ticari Ilimler Akademísi, Istanbul, 1309
— State Academy of Engineering and Architecture, 1309
— Technical University Library, 1300
— Teknik Üniversitesi, 1307
— Universitesi, 1306
— University Central Library, 1300
Istituti Culturali ed Artistici, 770
Istituto Affari Internazionali, Rome, 763
— Agronomico per l'Oltremare, Florence, 756
— Applicazione Calcolo "Mauro Picone", Rome, 762
— Austriaco di Cultura in Roma, 759
— Biochimico Italiano, 760
— Centrale del Restauro, Rome, 797
— — di Patologia del Libro, Rome, 756
— — — Statistica, Rome, 760
— — per il Catalogo Unico delle Biblioteche Italiane e per le Informazioni Bibliografiche, Rome, 765
— — — l'Industrializzazione e la Tecnologia Edilizia, Milan, 762
— "CNUCE", Pisa, 762
— Culturale Italo-Braziliano, Rome, 759
— Danese di Cultura, Milan, 759
— d'Arte Sassari, 797
— del Legno, Florence, 762
— di Acustica "O. M. Corbino", Rome, 762
— — Biologia del Mare, Venice, 762
— — Chimica delle Macromolecole, Milan, 762
— — Diritto Romano e dei Diritti dell' Oriente Mediterraneo, 757
— — Economia Politica, L'Aquila, 757
— — Elaborazione della Informazione, Pisa, 762
— — Ingegneria Nucleare, Centro di Studi Nucleari Enrico Fermi (CESNEF), Milan, 763
— — Metrologia "Gustavo Colonetti", Turin, 762
— — Norvegia in Roma di Archaeologia e Storia dell'Arte, Rome, 757
— — Psicologia, Rome, 762
— — Ricerca per la Protezione Idrogeologica nell'Italia Meridionale ed Insulare, Cosenza, 762
— — — sulle Acque, Rome, 762
— — — — Onde Elettromagnetiche, Florence, 762
— — Storia dell'Arte, Florence, 756
— — Studi Adriatici, Venice, 760
— — e Ricerche Carlo Cattaneo, Bologna, 760
— — Etruschi ed Italici, 757
— — Europei "Alcide de Gasperi", Rome, 763
— — Filosofici, Rome, 764
— — Nucleari per l'Agricultura, Rome, (I.S.N.A.), 761
— — — Romani, Rome, 763

Istituto di Studi sul Lavoro, Rome, 757
— — — sulle Regioni, Rome, 762
— — — Verdiani, Parma, 756
— — Teologia a Distanza, Centro "Ut Unum Sint", Rome, 1946
— — — del Seminario Regionale, Chieti, 1946
— Elettrotecnico Nazionale "Galileo Ferraris", 761
— Ellenico di Studi Bizantini e Postbizantini di Venezia, Venice, 757
— Geografico Militare, Florence, 757
— Giapponese di Cultura, Rome, 759
— Idrografico della Marina, 760
— Internazionale di Genetica e Biofisica, Naples, 762
— — — Studi Liguri, Bordighera, 24
— — — Vulcanologia, Catania, 762
— — — per le Ricerche Geotermiche, Pisa, 762
— Italiano del Marchio di Qualità, Milan, 761
— — della Saldatura, Genoa, 761
— — di Antropologia, 761
— — — Arti Grafiche, S.p.A., 756
— — — Cultura, Algiers, 57
— — — — Athens, 617
— — — — Barcelona, 1190
— — — — Beirut, 899
— — — — Bogotá, 347
— — — — Brussels, 151
— — — — Budapest, 635
— — — — Buenos Aires, 63
— — — — Cairo, 414
— — — — Cologne, 521
— — — — Copenhagen 391
— — — — Dublin, 730
— — — — Helsinki, 428
— — — — Lagos, 991
— — — — Libya, 906
— — — — Lima, 1037
— — — — Lisbon, 1098
— — — — Madrid, 1190
— — — — Melbourne, 89
— — — — Mexico City, 926
— — — — Montevideo, 1938
— — — — Montreal, 241
— — — — Oslo, 1007
— — — — Paris, 448
— — — — Rio de Janeiro, 181
— — — — Santiago, 323
— — — — São Paulo, 181
— — — — Teheran, 721
— — — — Tel-Aviv, 738
— — — — Tokyo, 806
— — — — Tunis, 1295
— — — — Vienna, 121
— — — — "C. M. Lerici", Stockholm, 1236
— — — — per i Paesi Bassi, Amsterdam, 958
— — — Diritto Spaziale, Rome, 757
— — — Idrobiologia "Marco de Marchi", 760
— — — Numismatica, Rome, 757
— — — Paleontologia Umana, Rome, 757
— — — Speleologia, 763
— — — Storia della Chimica, Rome, 760
— — — Studi Germanici, Rome, 759
— — — — Legislativi, Rome, 763
— — per il Medio ed Estremo Oriente (I.S.M.E.O.), Rome, 761
— — — — la Storia Antica, Rome, 757
— — — — della Musica, Rome, 756
— Italo-Africano, Rome, 759
— Italo-Latino Americano, Rome, 759
— Lombardo Accademia di Scienze e Lettere, 755
— Luigi Sturzo, Rome, 764
— Motori, Naples, 762
— Nazionale di Alta Matematica Francesco Severi, Rome, 760
— — — Archeologia e Storia dell'Arte, Rome, 757
— — — Architettura, Rome, 756

— — — Entomologia, Rome, 760
— — — Fisica Nucleare, Rome, 763
— — — Geofisica, Rome, 760
— — — Ottica, Florence, 760
— — — Studi sul Rinascimento, Florence, 758
— — — Urbanistica (I.N.U.), Rome, 756
— — — per la Grafica, Rome, 772
— — — Studi ed Esperienze di Architettura Navale, Rome, 764
— Olandese a Roma, 758
— Papirologico "Girolamo Vitelli", 758
— per gli Studi di Politica Internazionale, Milan, 757
— — — — Micenei e Egeo-anatolici, Rome, 762
— — il Rinnovamento Economico (I.R.E.), Rome, 757
— — — l'Economia Europea, Rome, 757
— — — l'Oriente, Rome, 764
— — — la Cooperazione Universitaria, Rome, 757
— — — Documentazione Giuridica, Florence, 762
— — — Fisica dell'Atmosfera, Rome, 762
— — — Storia del Risorgimento Italiano, Rome, 758
— Siciliano di Studi Bizantini e Neoellenici, Palermo, 763
— Sieroterapico Milanese, 759
— Sperimentale per la Cerealicoltura, Rome, 762
— — — — Zoologia Agraria, Florence, 763
— Statale d'Arte, Urbino, 797
— — — "Enrico e Umberto Nordio", Trieste, 797
— — — per la Ceramica, Faenza, 797
— Storico Germanico, 758
— — Italiano per il Medio Evo, 758
— — — — l'Età Moderna e Contemporanea, Rome, 758
— Superiore di Scienze e Tecniche dell'Opinione Pubblica, Rome, 761
— Svedese di Studi Classici, Rome, 758
— Svizzero di Roma, 759
— Teologico de Assisi, 1946
— — del Seminario Maggiore, Chelmo, Poland, 1946
— — "Don Orione", Rome, 1946
— — Marchigiano, Ancona, 1946
— Universitario di Architettura, 795
— — — Lingue e Letterature Straniere, Bergamo, 795
— — Navale, Naples, 795
— — Olandese di Storia dell'Arte, Florence, 756
— — Orientale, Naples, 795
— — Statale d'Architettura, Reggio Calabria, 795
— Veneto di Scienze, Lettere ed Arti, 761
Istoriski Arhiv na Bitola, 1976
— — — Ohrid, 1976
— — Institut S. R. Crne Gore, Montenegro, 1974
István Király Múzeum, Székesfehérvár, 645
Italia Nostra, Rome, 756
Italian Institute, London, 1424
— School of Archaeology, Athens, 623
Ithaca College, N.Y., 1817
Itsukuishma Jinja Hómotsukan, 822
Ivan Vazov Museum, Sofia, 221
— — Sopot, 222
— — National Library, Plovdiv, 220
Ivano-Frankovsk Institute of Oil and Gas, 1379
— — Medical Institute, 1383
Ivanovo Agricultural Institute, 1369
— M. V. Frunze Textile Institute, 1380
— Institute of Chemical Technology, 1378
— V. I. Lenin Power Institute, 1377
— Museum of Art, 1353
— State Medical Institute, 1383
— University, 1362
Ivanovsky, D. I., Institute of Virology, Moscow, 1341

Iveagh Bequest, 1466
IVITA, Lima, 1043
Iwate Medical University, 864
— University, Morioka, 830
Izhevsk Agricultural Institute, 1369
— Mechanical Engineering Institute, 1377
— State Medical Institute, 1383
Izmir Arkeoloji Müzesi, 1301
— State Conservatoire, 1310


J

Jabalpur University, Madhya Pradesh, 687
Jabotinsky Institute in Israel, Tel-Aviv, 744
Jackson Laboratory, Bar Harbor, 1618
— State University, Miss., 1784
Jacksonville State University, Ala., 1643
— University, Florida, 1695
Jadavpur University, 687
Jadranski Institut, Zagreb, 1972
Jaffna College, Vaddukoddai, 1228
Jagdmuseum, Schloss Kranichstein, Darmstadt, 542
Jagiellonian University, Cracow, 1078
Jagt-og Skovbrugsmuseet, Hørsholm, 395
Jahangirnagar University, Dacca, 145
Jajasan Dana Normalisasi Indonesia, Bandung, 710
— Kerja-Sama Kebudajaan, Bandung, 708
Jamaica Archives, Spanish Town, 800
— Library Service, Kingston, 800
— National Trust Commission, Kingston, 800
Jamaican Association of Sugar Technologists, Mandeville, 800
Jamarska zveva Slovenije, Ljubljana, 1970
Jambi State University, 715
James Cook University of North Queensland, Townsville, 101
— Dun's House, Aberdeen, 1472
— Hall Museum of Transport, Johannesburg, 1165
— Jerome Hill Reference Library, 1629
— Joyce Museum, Sandycove, 732
— Madison University, Harrisonburg, 1916
Jamestown College, 1839
Jamia Millia Islamia, New Delhi, 688
Jamiyatul Falah, Karachi, 1021
Jammu and Kashmir Academy of Arts, Culture and Languages, 659
Jämtlands Iäns Bibliotek, Östersund, 1239
Janáčkova akademie musických umém, Brno, 387
Jane Austen's House, Alton, 1468
Janet Clarke Hall, Parkville, 104
Janus Pannonius Múzeum, Pécs, 645
Japan Academy, Tokyo, 802
— Atomic Energy Research Institute, Tokyo, 816
— Center for International Exchange, Tokyo, 811
— Construction Method and Machinery Research Institute, Shizuoka, 817
— Meteorological Agency Library, Tokyo, 818
— PEN Club, 806
— Weather Association, Tokyo, 810
Japanese American Society for Legal Studies, Tokyo, 805
Japanisches Kulturinstitut, Cologne, 521
Jardim Botânico do Rio de Janeiro, 185
— de Praça da República, 185
Jardin Botanique National de Belgique, Brussels, 154
Jardín Botánico, Guatemala City, 625
— — Montevideo, 1939
— — Nacional de Cuba, Havana, 363
— — y Museo de Historia Natural, 1034
Jász Múzeum, Jászberény, 645
Jawaharlal Nehru Agricultural University, Jabalpur, 688
— Krishi Vishwa Vidyalala, Jabalpur, 688

— — Technological University, Hyderabad, 689
— — University, New Delhi, 689
Jawatan Hidro-Oseanografi, Jakarta, 710
— Pertambangan, Jakarta, 710
**Jayaswal (K.P.) Research Institute, Patna, 667**
Jazykovědné sdruženi, Prague, 372
Jeddah Health Institute, 1144
Jednota československých matematiku a fysiku, Prague, 372
— filosofická, Bratislava, 372
— klasiských filologov, Bratislava, 372
— — filologu, Prague, 373
— slovenska matematikov a fyzikov, Bratislava, 373
Jeffry Bolkiah School of Engineering, Kuala Belait, 213
Jember University, 715
Jeonbug National University, Chonchu, 891
Jersey City State College, N.J., 1797
Jerusalem City (Public) Library, 742
Jesus College, Cambridge, 1485
— — Old Library, Cambridge, 1461
— — Oxford, 1524
— — Library, Oxford, 1463
Jeunesse Belge à l'Etranger, Brussels, 151
— Intellectuelle, Brussels, 151
— ouvrière chrétienne internationale, Brussels, 30
Jeunesses Musicales de France, Paris, 445
Jewish Historical Society of England, London, 1423
— Institute of Religion, Cincinnati, 1843
— — — Jerusalem School, 753
— Museum, New York, 1638
— National and University Library, Jerusalem, 742
— Theological Seminary of America Library, 1629
Jiangxi Communist Labour University, 337
— Library, Nanchang, 335
Jiaotong University, Shanghai, 337
Jihočeské muzeum České Budějovice, Prague, 378
Jihomoravske muzeum, Znojmo, 378
Jikei University School of Medicine, Tokyo, 864
Jilin Geology College, Changchun, 336
— Industrial College, 336
— Library, Changchun, 335
— University, 336
Jimma Agricultural Institute, 425
Jingú Chókokan, 823
— Nogyokan, 823
Jinnah College for Women, Peshawar, 1027
— Postgraduate Medical Centre, Karachi, 1029
Jishoji, Kyoto, 821
Jiwaji University, Gwalior, 689
Joachim-Jungius-Gesellschaft der Wissenschaften e.V., 522
Jôchi University, Tokyo, 869
Joensuun Korkeakoulu, 435
Johann Strauss-Gesellschaft, Vienna, 120
— Wolfgang Goethe Universität Frankfurt-am-Main, 565
— -Gottfried-Herder-Institut, Marburg/Lahn, 530
Johannes Gutenberg Universität, Mainz, 587
— Kepler Universität Linz, 137
Johannesburg Public Library, 1162
John A. Hartford Foundation, Inc., 1610
— and Mary R. Markle Foundation, 1610
— Brown University, Siloam Springs, 1650
— Carroll University, Cleveland, 1843
— Crerar Library, Chicago, 1628
— Curtin School of Medical Research, Canberra, 99
— George Joicey Museum, Newcastle upon Tyne, 1470
— Harvard Lending Library, Freeport, 140
— Innes Institute, 1441, 1488
— Jay College of Criminal Justice, New York, 1805

— F. Kennedy American Center, Beirut, 899
— — -Institut für Nord-amerikastudien, Berlin (West), 551
— — Institute, Tilburg, 973
— — Space Center, Florida, 1623
— Rylands University Library of Manchester, 1462
— G. Shedd Aquarium, Chicago, 1638
— Simon Guggenheim Memorial Foundation, New York, 1604
Johns Hopkins University, 1743
— — Libraries, 1632
Johnson C. Smith University, Charlotte, 1828
— Society of London, 1427
— State College, Vermont, 1914
Johnston Center for Individualized Learning, Redlands, Calif., 1673
Joho Shori Gakkai, Tokyo, 804
Joint Committee for Higher National Certificates and Diplomas in Metallurgy, 1438
— Institute for Nuclear Research, Moscow, 50
Jönköpings Stadsbibliotek, Jönköping, 1239
Jordan Archaeological Museum, Amman, 875
— Historical Museum of the Twenty, 250
— Library Association, Amman, 875
— Research Council, Amman, 875
— Statistical Training Centre, Amman, 877
Jordbrukstekniska Institutet, Uppsala, 1237
Jos Museum, Nigeria, 995
Jósa András Múzeum, 645
José P. Laurel Memorial Museum and Library, Tanauan, 1049
Josefinum, Vienna, 130
Joseph and Rose Kennedy Institute of Ethics, Washington, D.C., 1691
Journalism Institute, Beijing, 332
**József Attila Tudományegyetem, Szeged, 650**
— — Központi Könyvtára, Szeged, 640
Jugoslavenska Akademija Znanosti i Umjetnosti, 1966
Jugoslovenski Bibliografski Institut, Belgrade, 1972
— centar za tehnicku i naucnu dokumentaciju, Belgrade, 1968
— Institut za zastitu spomenika kulture, Belgrade, 1972
Juilliard School, New York, 1817
Julius Kruttschnitt Mineral Research Centre, Indooroopilly, 109
Jundi Shapur University, Ahwaz, 723
Jung-Institut (C.G.), Zürich, 1276
Jungfraujoch and Gornergrat Scientific Stations, Bern, 1258
Junta de Energia Nuclear, Lisbon, 1099
— — — Madrid, 1192
— — — Historia Ecclesiástica Argentina, 63
— — Investigaçoes Cientificas do Ultramar, Lisbon, 1099
— Nacional Protectora y Conservadora del Patrimonio Histórico y Artístico de la Nación, Caracas, 1950
Jura-Museum, Eichstätt, 544
Juridisk Forening, Copenhagen, 390
Juridiska Föreningen i Finland, 428
Jurisics Miklós Múzeum, 645
Justus Liebig-Universität, 570
Jydsk Teknologisk Institut, Århus, 401
— Musikkonservatorium, Århus, 401
Jysk Arkaeologisk Selskab, Mosegård, 390
— Selskab for Historie, Århus, 390
Jyväskylän Yliopisto, Jyväsklkä, 435
— Yliopiston Kirjasto, Jyväskylä, 432

K

Kabarda-Balkar Art Museum, Nalchik, 1353
— — State University, Nalchik, 1362
Kabinet Grafike, Zagreb, 1978

Kabul Art School, 53
— Museum, 52
— Pohantoon, 53
— Polytechnic, 53
— University, 53
— — Library, 52
Kabushikikaisha Mitsubishi Sogo Kenkyusho, Tokyo, 813
Kadman Numismatic Museum, Tel-Aviv, 743
Kaduna Polytechnic, 1002
— State Library Board, Kaduna, 994
Kaesong City Library, 883
— Historical Library, 884
Kaffrarian Museum, Kingwilliamstown, 1165
Kagawa University, 830
Kagoshima Prefectural Library, 819
— University, 830
Kaicab Museum, Gaigab, 906
Kaiji Sangyo Kenkyusho, Tokyo, 814
Kainji Lake Research Insitute, New Bussa, 992
Kaiyoo Kisho Gakkai, Kobe, 810
Kalakshetra, Madras, 707
Kalamazoo College, 1761
Kalinin Art Gallery, 1353
— Polytechnic Institute, 1375
— State Medical Institute, 1383
— (M.I.) State Museum, Moscow, 1354
— University, 1362
Kaliningrad Higher School of Marine Engineering, 1389
— Institute of Fish Industry, 1381
— State University, 1363
Kallitechnikon Epimelitirion, Athens, 616
Kalmar stadsbibliotek, Kalmar, 1239
Kalmyk State University, Elista, 1363
Kaluga Museum of Art, 1353
Kalyani University, 690
Kamakura Kokuhókan, 822
Kamaraj University, Madurai, 690
Kamarupa Anusandhan Samiti, 667
Kamenets-Podolsk Agricultural Institute, 1370
— State Historical Museum-Preserve, 1355
Kameshwar Singh Darbhanga Sanskrit University, Darbhanga, 690
Kamuzu College of Nursing, Lilongwe, 913
Kanagawa Prefectural Library, Yokohama, 819
Kanazawa Bunko Museum, Yokohama City, 822
— City Library, 819
— College of Fine and Industrial Arts, Kanazawa City, 874
— University, 830
Kandahar Museum, 52
Kandó Kálmán Villamosipari Müszaki Föiskola, Budapest, 655
Kandy National Museum, 1226
Kangwon Provincial Library, Wonsan, 883
Kanizsai Dorottya Múzeum, 645
Kano State Institute for Higher Education, 1002
— — Library Board, 994
Kanpur University, Kalyanpur, 690
Kansai University, 864
— — Library, 819
— Zosen Kyokai, Osaka, 804
Kansanperinteen laitos, Tampere, 438
Kansantaloudellinen Yhdistys, 428
Kansas City Art Institute, Missouri, 1787
— — Museum of Regional History, 1638
— — Public Library, 1626
— State Historical Society Library, 1629
— — Library, Topeka, 1630
— — University of Agriculture and Applied Science, 1730
— — — — — Applied Science, Farrell Library, 1632
— Wesleyan University, 1730
Kant-Gesellschaft, Röttgen, 524
Kantonales Amt für Wirtschafts- und Kulturausstellungen, Bern, 1261

Kantons- und Universitätsbibliothek, Fribourg, 1259
Kantonsbibliothek, St. Gallen, 1260
— Vadiana, St. Gallen, 1260
Kaohsiung Medical College, 345
Karachi Nuclear Power Plant, 1022
— Theosophical Society, 1021
Karadeniz Teknik Üniversitesi, Trabzon, 1307
Karaganda Co-operative Institute, 1373
— Polytechnic Institute, 1375
— State Medical Institute, 1383
— University, 1363
Karakalpak Art Museum, Nukus, 1353
— Historical Museum Nukus, 1356
Karelian Branch, U.S.S.R. Academy of Sciences, Petrozavodsk, 1322
— Museum of Fine Arts, Petrozavodsk, 1353
— State Museum of Regional History, Petrozavodsk, 1356
Karikatur Müzesi, Istanbul, 1301
Karjalan Tutkimuslaitos, Joensuu, 435
Karl Marx Higher Institute of Economics, Sofia, 226
— — -Universität, Leipzig, 512
— — University of Economic Sciences, Budapest, 648
Karlovarské muzeum, Karlovy, 378
Karnatak Historical Research Society, Dharwar, 667
— University, 690
Kärntner Landesarchiv, Klagenfurt, 127
— Landeskonservatorium, Klagenfurt, 139
Karol Szymanowski Museum, Cracow, 1076
Karolinska Institutet, Stockholm, 1251
— Institutets Bibliotek och Informationscentral, Stockholm, 1240
Károlyi Mihály Országos Mezőgazdasági Könyvtár, Budapest, 641
Kartografiska Sallskapet, Gavle, 1236
Kasetsart University, Bangkok, 1284
→ Main Library, 1284
Kasinthula Agricultural Research Station, Chikwawa, 912
Kastélymúzeum, Fertőd, 645
Kasugataisha Hómotsuden, 823
Katharinenkirche, Lubeck, 544
Kathleen Lumley College Inc., North Adelaide, 99
Katholiek Documentatiecentrum, Nijmegen, 970
Katholieke Universiteit Leuven, 162
— — Nijmegen, 970
Katholische Universität Eichstätt, 563
Katholischer Akademischer Ausländer-Dienst, Bonn, 520
Katolicki Uniwersytet Lubelski, 1080
Katona József Múzeum, 645
Katsina College of Arts, Science and Technology, Zaria, 1002
Kaunas Antanas Sniechkus Polytechnic Institute, 1375
— M. K. Chiurlenis State Art Museum, 1353
— State Historical Museum, 1355
— Medical Institute, 1383
Kavak ve Hizli Gelisen Orman Ağaçlari Araştirma Enstitüsü, Izmit, 1299
Kawanda Agricultural Research Station, Kampala, 1311
Kayseri Universitesi, 1307
Kazakh Chemical Technology Institute, 1378
— S. M. Kirov State University, 1363
— Polytechnic Institute, Alma-Ata, 1375
— T. G. Shevchenko State Art Gallery, Alma-Ata, 1352
— S.S.R. Academy of Sciences, Alma-Ata, 1328
— — Kurmangazy State Institute of Arts, Alma-Ata, 1387
— State Agricultural Institute, Alma-Ata, 1370

Kazakhstan Institute of Tuberculosis, Alma-Ata, 1384
— Maternity and Child Welfare Institute, Alma-Ata, 1384
— Skin and Venereal Disease Institute, Alma-Ata, 1385
Kazan N.E. Bauman Veterinary Institute, 1372
— Branch of the USSR Academy of Sciences, 1323
— Civil Engineering Institute, 1380
— A. M. Gorky Agricultural Institute, 1370
— Institute of Biology, 1323
— — — Epidemiology, Microbiology and Hygiene, 1385
— S. M. Kirov Institute of Chemical Technology, 1378
— V. V. Kuibyshev Finance and Economics Institute, 1373
— V. I. Lenin State University, 1363
— Physical Technical Institute, 1323
— State Conservatoire, 1387
— — A. M. Gorky Memorial Museum, 1358
— — Institute of Orthopaedics and Traumatology, Kazan, 1385
— — Medical Institute, 1383
— A. N. Tupolev Aviation Institute, 1390
Kean College of New Jersey, Union, 1797
Kearney State College, Nebraska, 1793
Keats-Shelley Memorial Association, Rome, 759
Keble College, Oxford, 1524
— — Library, Oxford, 1463
Kebun Raya Indonesia, Bogor, 709
Keene State College, N.H., 1796
Keidanren Kaikan, Tokyo, 814
Keikinzoku Gakkai, Tokyo, 812
Keimyung University, Daegu, 891
Keio University, Tokyo, 864
— Library and Information Center at Mita, Tokyo, 818
— Medical Library and Information Center, Tokyo, 818
— School of Library and Information Sciences Library, Tokyo, 818
— Science and Engineering Library and Information Center, Yokohama, 818
Keisoku Jidoseigyo Gakkai, Tokyo, 812
Keizai Chiri Gakkai, Tokyo, 806
— Riron Gakkai, Tokyo, 805
Keizai-ho Gakkai, Tokyo, 805
Keizaigaku-shi Gakkai, Nishinomiya City, 805
Kekelidze, K. S., Institute of Manuscripts, Tbilisi, 1328
Kekkaku Yobo Kai Kekkaku Kenkyujo, Tokyo, 815
Kellogg (W. K.) Foundation, Battle Creek, 1605
— Health Sciences Library, Halifax, 247
Kelvin Grove College of Advanced Education, Queensland, 114
Kemerovo State Medical Institute, 1383
— — University, 1363
Kemisk Forening, Copenhagen, 391
Kendeja National Cultural Centre, 904
Kennedy, Mathilda and Terence, Institute of Rheumatology, London, 1445
Kensington and Chelsea Libraries and Art Service, London, 1452
Kent County Library, Maidstone, 1454
— State University, Ohio, 1843
Kentron Ekdoseos Ellinon Syngrafeon, Athens, 616
— Erevnis Ellinikis Laographias, Athens, 617
— — Historias Ellinikou Dikeou, Athens, 616
— — Messeonikou kai Neou Ellinismou, Athens, 616
— — Neoterou Ellinismou, Athens, 616
— Erevon Astronomias kai Ephirmosmenon Mathimatikon tis Akademias Athinon, Athens, 616

— Syntaxeos Historikou Lexikou, Athens, 616
Kentucky Department of Library and Archives, 1630
— State University, Frankfort, 1736
— Wesleyan College, 1736
Kenya Agricultural Research Institute, Nairobi, 878
— — — Library, 879
— Conservatoire of Music, Nairobi, 880
— Industrial Research Organization, Nairobi, 878
— Institute of Administration, Lower Kabete, 880
— Leprosy Research Centre, Busia, 879
— Library Association, Nairobi, 878
— National Academy for Advancement of Arts and Sciences, Nairobi, 878
— — Archives, Nairobi, 879
— — Library Service, Nairobi, 879
— Polytechnic, Nairobi, 880
— School of Law, Nairobi, 880
— Tuberculosis Investigation Centre, Nairobi, 879
Kenyatta University College, Nairobi, 880
Kenyon College, Gambier, Ohio, 1843
Kerala Agricultural University, Trichur, 692
— State Museums, Zoos and Government Gardens, 675
Kerch State Historico-Archaeological Museum, 1355
Kerckhoff-Klinik, Bad Nauheim, 528
Kereskedelmi és Vendéglátóipari Föiskola, Budapest, 655
Keresztény Múzeum, Esztergom, 645
Kerkmuseum Janum, Leeuwarden, 967
Kernforschungszentrum Karlsruhe GmbH, 532
Kertészeti Egyetem, Budapest, 653
— — Könyvtára, Budapest, 640
— — Tangazdaság, Budapest, 653
Kestner-Gesellschaft, Hannover, 518
— -Museum, 543
Keszthely Agricultural University, 651
Keuka College, N.Y., 1817
Kfar Giladi Library, 742
Khabarovsk Complex Research Institute, 1322
— Institute of Epidemiology and Hygiene, 1385
— — — National Economy, 1373
— — — Railway Engineers, 1389
— Polytechnic Institute, 1375
— State Institute of Culture, 1382
— — Medical Institute, 1383
Khalifa's House, Omdurman, 1230
Khalikdina Hall Library Association, Karachi, 1023
Kharkov Aviation Institute, 1390
— Chemical and Pharmaceutical Institute, 1387
— Civil Engineering Institute, 1380
— V. V. Dokuchayev Agricultural Institute, 1370
— A. M. Gorky State University, 1363
— Institute of Agricultural Engineering, 1371
— — — Engineering and Economics, 1382
— — — Food, 1373
— — — Industrial and Applied Arts, 1374
— — — Mining Engineering, Automation and Computing Equipment, 1379
— — — Municipal Engineers, 1380
— — — Radio Electronics, 1377
— S. M. Kirov Institute of Railway Engineers, 1389
— Law Institute, 1382
— V. I. Lenin Polytechnic Institute, 1375
— Motor and Highways Institute, 1389
— Pharmaceutical Institute, 1384
— Psycho-Neurological Research Institute, 1386
— Research Institute of Endocrinology and Hormone Chemistry, 1387
— — — General and Emergency Surgery, 1385

— — — Industrial Hygiene and Occupational Diseases, 1386
— — — Mother and Child Care, 1384
— M. I. Sitenko Research Institute of Orthopaedics and Traumatology, 1385
— State Art Museum, 1353
— — Historical Museum, 1355
— — Institute of Arts, 1387
— — — — Culture, 1382
— — Medical Institute, 1383
— Tuberculosis Research Institute, 1384
— Zootechnical and Veterinary Institute, 1372
Khartoum Nursing College, 1231
— Polytechnic, 1231
— — Library, 1229
Kherson A. D. Tsuryupa Agricultural Institute, 1370
Khersones Museum of History and Archaeology, Sevastopol, 1356
Kholodny, V. M. G., Institute of Botany, Kiev, 1334
Khonkaen University, 1287
Khorezm Historical-Revolutionary Museum, Khiva, 1355
Khuda Bakhsh Oriental Public Library, Bihar, 673
Kieleckie Towarzystwo Naukowe, Kielce, 1066
Kielikeskus, Tampere, 438
Kiepenheuer-Institut für Sonnenphysik, Freiburg i.Br., 533
Kiev Blood Transfusion Research Institute, 1385
— A. A. Bogomolets Medical Institute, 1383
— Civil Engineering Institute, 1380
— Institute of Civil Aviation, 1390
— — — Industrial Hygiene and Occupational Diseases, 1386
— — — National Economy, 1373
— — — Nutritional Hygiene, 1387
— — — Orthopaedics, 1386
— I. K. Karpenko-Kary State Theatrical Institute, 1388
— Lesya Ukrainia State Literature Museum, 1358
— Motor Vehicles Institute, 1390
— -Pechersky State Historical Museum, 1355
— Polytechnic Institute, 1375
— Research Institute of Neurosurgery, 1386
— — — — Roentgenology and Oncology, 1386
— T. G. Shevchenko State Museum, 1358
— — University, 1363
— — State Art Institute, 1374
— — Historical Museum, 1355
— — Institute of Culture, 1382
— — Museum of Russian Art, 1352
— — — — Ukrainian Art, 1352
— — — — Western and Oriental Art, 1352
— — Sofiysky Museum, 1352
— P. I. Tchaikovsky Conservatoire, 1387
— Technological Institute of Food Industry, 1381
— — — — Light Industry, 1380
Kihara Institute for Biological Research, Yokohama-city, 816
Kim Chaek Polytechnic Institute, Pyongyang, 884
— Hyong-chik Normal University, Pyongyang, 884
— Il Sung University, Pyongyang, 884
Kimberley Public Library, 1162
Kimron Veterinary Institute, Tel-Aviv, 750
Kina Múzeum, Budapest, 643
King Abdul-Aziz Military Academy, Riyadh, 1144
— — — Research Centre, Riyadh, 1142
— — — University, Jeddah, 1143
— College, Bristol, Tennessee, 1889
— Faisal University, Dammam, 1144
— George VI Art Gallery, Port Elizabeth, 1165

— Institute of Preventive Medicine, Madras, 669
— Mongkut's Institute of Technology, Bangkok, 1288
King's College, Brisbane, 109
— — Cambridge, 1485
— — London, 1510
— — — Ontario, 315
— — Wilkes-Barre, 1871
— — Hospital Medical School, 1511
— — Library, Cambridge, 1461
— — — London, 1460
Kingston Polytechnic, 1542
— upon Thames Public Libraries, 1452
Kinki University, Osaka, 864
Kinyu Gakkai, Tokyo, 805
Kipling Society, London, 1427
Kirchenvater Kommission, Vienna, 118
Kirchliche Hochschule, Berlin, 609
— — Bethel, 609
— — Wuppertal, 609
Kirensky, L.V., Institute of Physics, Krasnoyarsk, 1322
Kirghiz Agricultural Institute, 1370
— Branch of the Soviet National Association for the History of Natural Sciences and Technology, Frunze, 1329
— — — — U.S.S.R. Biochemical Society, Frunze, 1329
— — — — Genetics and Selection Society, Frunze, 1329
— — — — Microbiological Society, Frunze, 1329
— — — — Mineralogical Society, Frunze, 1329
— — — — Society of Soil Scientists, Frunze, 1329
— Department of All-Union Botanical Garden, Frunze, 1329
— — Society of Helminthology, Frunze, 1329
— Entomological Society, Frunze, 1329
— Geographical Society, Frunze, 1329
— Institute of Epidemiology, Microbiology and Hygiene, 1385
— Southern Forest Station, Dzhalal-Abad, 1329
— S.S.R. Academy of Sciences, Frunze, 1329
— State Institute of Fine Art, Frunze, 1374
— — Medical Institute, 1383
— — Museum of Fine Art, Frunze, 1352
— — University, 1363
Kirjallisuudentutkijain Seura, Helsinki, 428
Kirk Biological Society, Salisbury, Zimbabwe, 2000
Kirkcaldy District Library, 1455
— Museums and Art Gallery, 1472
Kirkehistorisk Samfunn, Oslo, 1007
Kirkeligt Centrum, Hellerup, 392
Kirov Agricultural Institute, 1370
— Polytechnic Institute, 1375
— A. M. Gorky Museum, 1353
— S. M. Kola Branch, U.S.S.R. Academy of Sciences, Murmansk, 1323
Kirovograd Institute of Agricultural Engineering, 1371
Kiscelli Múzeum, Budapest, 643
Kishinev M. V. Frunze Agricultural Institute, 1370
— V. I. Lenin State University, 1363
— G. Musichesku State Conservatoire, 1387
— Polytechnic Institute, 1375
— State Medical Institute, 1383
Kiskun Múzeum, 645
Kitano Temmangu Homotsuden, Kyoto, 821
Kitasato Institute, Tokyo, 816
Kitwe Public Library, 1998
Kivukoni College, Dar es Salaam, 1282
Kizhi State Historical Museum, 1356
Klassillis-filologinen Yhdistys, Helsinki, 428
Klingspor-Museum der Stadt, Offenbach a. M., 545
Knihovna Archeologického ústavu ČSAV, Prague, 375

— Bedřicha Smetany, Prague, 375
— Husova domu, Prague, 375
— Komenského fakulty, Prague, 375
— Moravské galerie, Brno, 376
— Národni galerie, Prague, 375
— Národniho musea, 375
— — technického musea, Prague, 375
— Orientálniho Ustavu Československé Akademie Věd, 375
— Ustředniho ústavu geologického, Prague, 375
— Vaclava Kopeckeho, Liberec, 376
Knihovny fakult a ústavu University Karlovy, Prague, 375
Knjižnica Jugoslavenske akademije znanosti i umjetnosti, Zagreb, 1975
— Narodrega Muzeja, Ljubljana, 1975
— Pravne fakultete, Ljubljana, 1975
Knowledge Availability Systems Center, Pittsburgh, 1881
Knox College, Galesburg, 1705
— — Toronto, 310
Knoxville College, 1889
Kobayasi Institute of Physical Research, Tokyo, 816
Kobe City Library, Kobe, 819
— Gakuin University, 864
— Municipal Museum of Nanban Art, 822
— University, 831
— — Library, 819
Københavns Bymuseum, Copenhagen, 395
— Kommunes Biblioteker, 394
— Stadsarkiv, 394
— Tandlaegehøjskole, 400
— tekniske Skole, 401
— Universitet, 397
Kobunshi Gakkai, Tokyo, 810
Kochi Kóen Kaitokukan, 822
— Prefectural Library, 819
Koforidua Technical Institute, 614
Kogakuin University, Tokyo, 865
Kogyo Kayaku Kyokai, Tokyo, 812
Kohno Clinical Medicine Research Institute, Tokyo, 815
Koizumi-Yakumo Kinenkan, Matsue City, 823
Kokubungaku Kenkyu Siryokan, Tokyo, 814
Kokugakuin University, 865
— Library, 818
Kokugogakkai, Tokyo, 806
Kokuritsu Kagaku Hakubutsukan, Tokyo, 820
— Kobunshokan, Tokyo, 818
— Kokugo Kenkyusho, Tokyo, 815
— Kyoiku Kenyusho Toshokan, Tokyo, 818
— Kyokuchi Kenkyujyo, Tokyo, 816
Kokusai Saibo Gakkai, Tokyo, 809
Kokusaiho Gakkai, Tokyo, 805
Kokushi-Gakkai, Kokugakuin University, 806
Kolas, J., Central Library of the Academy of Sciences of the Byelorussian S.S.R., Minsk, 1349
Kolling Institute of Medical Research, St. Leonards, N.S.W., 92
Kölnisches Stadtmuseum im Zeughaus, Cologne, 542
Kolomya State Museum of Folk Art, 1353
Komarov, V. L., Botanical Institute, Leningrad, 1319
— Institute of Botany, Baku, 1325
Komazawa University, Tokyo, 865
Komi Art Museum, Syktyvkar, 1353
— Branch—U.S.S.R. Academy of Sciences, Skytyvkar, 1323
Komiteti Shqiptar për Marrëdhenie Kulturore me botën e jashtme, Tiranë, 1
Komitia Lumiati Romani, Avon, France, 24
Kommandør Chr. Christensens Hvalfangstmuseum, Sandefjord, 1012
Kommission für Altgermanistik, Vienna, 118
— — Byzantinistik, Vienna, 119
— — das Corpus der Kleinasiatischen Mosaiken, Vienna, 119

# INDEX OF INSTITUTIONS

Kommission für das Corpus Signorum Imperii Romani, Vienna, 119
— — — — Vasorum Antiquorum, Vienna, 118
— — — Lexicon Iconographicum Mythologiae Classicae, Vienna, 119
— — die Archäologische Erforschung Kleinasiens, Vienna, 118
— — — Geschichte der österr.-ungar. Monarchie, Vienna, 119
— — — Herausgabe eines Catalogus Faunae Austriae, Vienna, 118
— — — Tabula Imperii Byzantini, Vienna, 119
— — Europarecht, Vienna, 118
— — Frühchristliche und Ostchristliche Kunst, Vienna, 119
— — Geschichte des Parlamentarismus, und der Politischen Parteien, Bonn, 519
— — — Österreichs, Vienna, 119
— — Hochalpine Forschungen, Vienna, 118
— — Linguistik und Kommunikationsforschung, Vienna, 118
— — Menschenrechte, Vienna, 119
— — Mundartkunde und Namenforschung, Vienna, 118
— — Musikforschung, Vienna, 119
— — Mykenische Forschung, Vienna, 118
— — neuere Geschichte Österreichs, Vienna, 121
— — Ökologie und SCOPE, Vienna, 118
— — Raumforschung, Vienna, 118
— — Schallforschung, Vienna, 118
— — Schrift- und Buchwesen des Mittelalters, Vienna, 118
— — Theatergeschichte Österreichs, Vienna, 119
— — Wirtschafts-, Sozial- und Stadtgeschichte, Vienna, 119
— zur Erforschung des Römischen Limes im Gebiete von Over- und Niederösterreich, Vienna, 118
Kommunarsk Institute of Ore Mining and Metallurgy, 1379
Komsomolsk-on-Amur Polytechnic Institute, 1375
— Museum of Soviet Fine Arts, 1353
Konan University, Kobe City, 865
Kongelige Bibliotek, Copenhagen, 394
— Danske Geografiske Selskab, 390
— — Kunstakademi, Copenhagen, 401
— — Landhusholdningsselskab, Copenhagen, 389
— — Musikkonservatorium, 401
— — Selskab for Faedrelandets Historie, 390
— — Videnskabernes Selskab, 388
— — Garnisonsbibliotek, Copenhagen, 394
— — Nordiske Oldskriftselskab, 390
— — Norske Videnskabers Selskab, 1008
— — — — Museet, 1013
— — — Selskabs Bibliotek, 1010
— Veterinaer- og Landbohøjskole, 398
Koninklijk Aardrijkskundig Genootschap van Antwerpen, 151
— Belgisch Instituut voor Natuurwetenschappen, Brussels, 154
— Conservatorium voor Muziek, 973
— Genootschap voor Landbouwwetenschap, Wageningen, 956
— Instituut van Ingenieurs, The Hague, 960
— — voor de Tropen, 960
— — — Taal-, Land- en Volkenkunde, 960
— Kabinet van Schilderijen (Mauritshuis), 967
— Museum voor Midden-Afrika, Brussels, 158
— — — Schone Kunsten, 157
— Nederlands Aardrijkskundig Genootschap, 957

— — Geologisch Mijnbouwkundig Genootschap, 959
— — Leger- en Wapenmuseum "General Hoefer", Leiden, 967
— — Meteorologisch Instituut, 959
— — Oudheidkundig Genootschap, 957
— — Penningkabinet (Koninklijk Kabinet van Munten, Penningen en Gesneden Stenen), The Hague, 967
— — Sterrenkundig Genootschap van Antwerpen, 152
— — Vlaams Conservatorium Van Antwerpen, 170
Koninklijke Academie van Beeldende Kunsten, The Hague, 973
— — voor Geneeskunde van België, Brussels, 149
— — — Nederlandse Taal- en Letterkunde, Ghent, 148
— — — Wetenschappen, Letteren en Schone Kunsten van Belge, Brussels, 147
— Akademie voor Kunst en Vormgeving, s'Hertogenbosch, 974
— Belgische Vereniging voor Radiologie, Brussels, 152
— Bibliotheek, The Hague, 965
— Commissie voor Geschiedenis, Brussels, 148
— Maatschappij tot Bevordering der Bouwkunst Bond van Nederlandsche Architecten, Amsterdam, 956
— — Tuinbouw en Plantkunde, The Hague, 956
— — voor Dierkunde van Antwerpen, 152
— Militaire School, Brussels, 169
— Nederlandse Maatschappij tot Bevordering der Geneeskunst, 958
— Nederlandse Akademie van Wetenschappen, 955
— — Bosbouw Vereniging, Arnhem, 956
— — Botanische Vereniging, 959
— — Chemische Vereniging, 959
— — Maatschappij ter bevordering der Pharmacie, 958
— — Natuurhistorische Vereniging, Rotterdam, 958
— — Toonkunstenaars-vereniging, 956
— Vlaamse Ingienieursvereniging, Antwerp, 153
Konkan Agricultural University, Ratnagiri, 692
Kon-kuk University, Seoul, 891
Könnyüipari Müszaki Föiskola, Budapest, 655
Konservator v Brně, 387
— — Praze, 387
Konservatorium der Stadt Innsbruck, 139
— — — Wien, 139
— für Musik in Bern, 1276
— und Musikhochschule, Zürich, 1276
Konstantinov, B.P., Leningrad Institute of Nuclear Physics, 1318
Konstfackskolan, Stockholm, 1251
Konsthögskolan, Stockholm, 1251
Konstnärsgillet i Finland, Helsinki, 427
Konya Museums, 1301
Könyvtártudományi és Módszertani Központ, Budapest, 642
Konzervatórium, Bratislava, 387
— Košice, 387
— Žilina, 387
Köprülü Library, Istanbul, 1300
Korçë Public Library, 55
Korea Advanced Energy Research Institute, Seoul, 886
— — Institute of Science, Seoul, 886
— Branch of the Royal Asiatic Society, Seoul, 885
— Institute of Energy and Resources, Seoul, 886
— — — Science and Technology, Seoul, 886
— Merchant Marine College, Busan, 896
— Scientific and Technological Information Centre (KORSTIC), Seoul, 885

— University, 891
— — Library, Seoul, 836
Korean Association of Sinology, Seoul, 885
— Central Historical Museum, Pyongyang, 884
— Chemical Society, Seoul, 885
— Economic Association, Seoul, 885
— Educational Development Institute, Seoul, 886
— Engineers' Association, Seoul, 885
— Ethnographic Museum, Pyongyang, 884
— Fine Arts Museum, Pyongyang, 884
— Forestry Association, Suwon, 885
— Geographical Society, Seoul, 885
— Historical Association, Seoul, 885
— Institute for Research in the Behavioural Sciences, Seoul, 886
— — of Bright Society, Seoul, 893
— — — National Security, Seoul, 893
— — — Ornithological Studies, Seoul, 893
— — — Plant Resources, Seoul, 893
— — — the History of Economics and Business Administration, Seoul, 893
— Library Association, Seoul, 885
— Medical Association, Seoul, 885
— PEN Centre, Seoul, 885
— Pyschological Association, Seoul, 885
— Research Institute of Physical Education, Seoul, 893
— Revolutionary Museum, Pyongyang, 884
— Social Sciences Research Society, Seoul, 886
Koryúji Reihóden, 821
Košice Technical University, 385
Kossuth Lajos Tudományegyetem, Debrecen, 648
— — — Könyvtár, 640
— — Múzeum, 645
Kostroma Agricultural Institute, 1370
— Museum of Fine Arts, 1353
— Technological Institute, 1378
Koszta Jozsef Múzeum, 645
Kotikielen Seura, 429
Kotohira-gü Hakubutsukan, Nakatadogun, 822
Kótsu Hakubutsukan, 820
Kovács Margit Kerámiagüjtemény, Szentendre, 645
Kóyasan Reihókan, 823
Közlekedési és Távközlési Müszaki Föiskola, Budapest, 655
— Múzeum, Budapest, 643
Közlekedéstudományi Egyesület, Budapest, 636
— Kohászati Múzeum, Miskolc-Lillafured, 645
— Statisztikai Hivatal Könyvtár és Dokumentációs Szolgálat, Budapest, 640
Kpandu Technical Institute, 614
Kragujevac "Svetozar Markovic" University, 1985
Krahnletz Museum, 131
Krajská knižnica, Košice, 376
Krajské muzeum Východních Čech, Pardubice, 378
— — v Teplicich, Teplice, 378
— — vlastivédné muzeum, Olomouc, 379
Krasnodar Polytechnic Institute, 1375
— State Institute of Culture, 1382
Krasnoyarsk Agricultural Institute, 1370
— M. I. Kalinin Institute of Non-Ferrous Metals, 1379
— Picture Gallery, 1353
— Polytechnic Institute, 1375
— State Medical Institute, 1383
— University, 1364
"Krastju Sarafov" Higher Institute of Dramatic Art and Cinematography, Sofia, 227
Kratikon Odeion Thessaloniki, 623
Kremlin Cathedrals, Moscow, 1354
— Museums, Moscow, 1354

Kreutzwald, F. R., Literature Museum, Tartu, 1327
— State Public Library of the Estonian S.S.R., Tallinn, 1348
Krigsarkivet, Stockholm, 1240
Kristiansands Folkebibliotek, 1010
**Kristinebergs marinbiologiska station, Fiskebäckskil, 1238**
Kristoforidhi, K., House-Museum, Elbasan, 55
Krivoy Rog Ore Mining Institute, 1379
Kronborg, Elsinore, 395
Kruh modernich filologu, Prague, 372
Krupskaya (N.K.) State Public Library of the Moldavian S.S.R., 1348
Krúžok moderných filologov, Bratislava, 373
Krylov, A. N., Scientific and Engineering Society of the Shipbuilding Industry, Leningrad, 1344
Krzhizhanovsky, G. M., Power Engineering Institute, Moscow, 1347
Książnica Miejska im Kopernika w Toruniu, 1075
Kuala Lumpur Public Library, 916
Kuban Agricultural Institute, 1370
— "Red Army" Medical Institute, 1383
— State University, Krasnodar, 1364
Kubinyi Ferenc Múzeum, Szécsény, 645
Kucherenko, V. A., Central Research Institute of Building Constructions, Moscow, 1346
Kuffner Sternwarte, Vienna, 126
Kuibyshev Agricultural Institute, 1370
— Art Museum, 1353
— Aviation Institute, 1390
— A. M. Gorky Memorial Museum, 1358
— Institute of Epidemiology, Microbiology and Hygiene, 1385
— — — Planning, 1373
— A. I. Mikoyan Civil Engineering Institute, 1380
— Polytechnic Institute, 1375
— State Medical Institute, 1383
— Telecommunications Institute, 1377
— University, 1364
Kuki-Chowa Eisei Kogakkai, Tokyo, 812
Külkereskedelmi Főiskola, Budapest, 655
Kulliat Asshari'a Wa Alqanun, Sana'a, 1965
Kültürel Calışmalar ve Çevre Eğitimi Enstitüsü, Eskişehir, 1309
Kulturhistorisches Museum, Magdeburg, 510
— Stralsund, 510
Kulturhistorisk Museum, Overgade, 395
Kulturhistoriska Museet, Lund, 1242
Kulturinstitut der Bundesrepublik Deutschland, Stockholm, 1236
Kumamoto Museum, 823
— University, 832
Kumaun University, Nainital, 692
Kungl. Akademien för de fria Konsterna, Stockholm, 1234
— Biblioteket, 1240
— Fysiografiska Sällskapet i Lund, 1236
— Gustav Adolfs Akademien, 1235
— Humanistiska Vetenskapssamfundet i Uppsala, 1235
— Krigsvetenskapsakademien, Stockholm, 1235
— Musikaliska Akademien, Stockholm, 1235
— — — bibliotek, 1240
— Myntkabinettet Statens Museum för Mynt Medalj och Penninghistoria, Stockholm, 1242
— Skogs-och Lantbruksakademien, 1234
— Tekniska Högskolan, 1244
— — Högskolans Bibliotek, 1240
— Vetenskaps- och Vitterhets-Samhälle ut i Göteborg, 1235
— — Societeten, 1235, 1237
— Vetenskapsakademien, Stockholm, 1233
— — Bibliotek, Stockholm, 1240
— Vitterhets Historie och Antikvitets Akademiens, 1234
— — — — — Bibliotek, 1240
Kunitachi College of Music, Tokyo, 874

Kunst- und Museumsbibliothek, Cologne, 535
Kunstakademiets Bibliotek, 394
Kunstbibliothek Berlin mit Museum für Architektur, Modebild und Grafik-Design, Berlin (West), 534
Kunstforeningen i København, 389
Kunstgewerbe-Museum, Berlin (East), 508
— Berlin (West), 541
— Cologne, 542
— der Stadt Zürich, **Museum für Gestaltung**, 1263
— — — — Bibliothek, 1260
Kunsthalle Bremen, 541
— Cologne, 542
— Stadt Nürnberg, 545
Kunsthaus, Glarus, 1262
— Zürich, 1263
Kunsthistorische Gesellschaft, Vienna, 120
— Musea, Antwerp, 157
— Sammlungen, Innsbruck, 131
Kunsthistorisches Institut, Florence, 756
— Museum, Vienna, 130
Kunsthochschule Berlin (East), 513
Kunstindustrimuseet, Copenhagen, 395
— i Oslo, 1012
Künstlerhaus (Gesellschaft bildender Künstler Österreichs), Vienna, 120
Kunstmuseum Basel (Öffentliche Kunstsammlung), 1261
— Bern, 1261
— Düsseldorf, 542
— Lucerne, 1262
— Olten, 1262
— St. Gallen, 1262
— Solothurn, 1263
— Winterthur, 1263
Kunstnerforening af 18 de November, 389
Kunstsammlung Nordrhein-Westfalen, 542
Kunstsammlungen zu Weimar, 510
Kunstverein, St. Gallen, 1253
Kunyi Domokos Múzeum, 645
Kuomintang Central Committee Library, Taipei, 342
Kuopion Korkeakoulu, 436
Kupferstichkabinett, Berlin (West), 541
— Dresden, 509
— und Sammlung der Zeichnungen, Berlin (East), 508
— der Akademie der Bildenden Künste, Vienna, 130
Kuppuswami Sastri Research Institute, 668
Kurchatov, I. V., Institute of Atomic Energy, Moscow, 1346
— Mechanical Engineering Institute, 1377
Kürk Hayvanlari Enstitüsü, Erzurum, 1304
Kurgan Agricultural Institute, 1370
Kurnakov (N.S.) Institute of General and Inorganic Chemistry, Moscow, 1319
Kurpfälzisches Museum der Stadt Heidelberg, 543
Kursk Art Gallery, 1353
— Polytechnic Institute, 1375
— Prof. I. Ivanov Agricultural Institute, 1370
Kurukshetra University, Haryana, 692
Kurume University, Fukuoka-Ken, 865
Kushiro-shi Kyódo Hakubutsukan, 822
Kütahya Yönetim Bilimleri Fakültesi, Eskişehir, 1309
Kutaissi State Museum of History and Ethnography, 1355
Kutztown State College, Pa., 1871
Kuwait Central Library, 897
— Institute for Scientific Research, 897
— National Museum, Kuwait City, 897
— University, 897
— — Libraries, 897
Kuzbass Polytechnic Institute, Kemerovo, 1375
Kvenfélagasamband Íslands, 656
Kwanongoma College of Music, Bulawayo, 2004
Kwansei Gakuin University, 865
— — Library, 819

Kwara State College of Technology, Ilorin, 1002
Kyoiku Tetsugakkai, Tokyo, 805
Kyoto City University of Arts, 874
— College of Pharmacy, 865
— Daigaku Bungakubu Chinretsukan, 821
— Kokuritsu Hakubutsukan, 821
— Prefectural University of Medicine, 859
— — Library, 819
— University, 834
— — Library, 820
Kyoto-shi Bijutsukan, 821
Kyung Hee Language Institute, Seoul, 893
— — Research Institute of Oriental Drugs Development, Seoul, 893
— — School of Nursing, Seoul, 893
— — University, Seoul, 892
— — -Pook National University, Daegu, 893
— — — Library, Daegu, 887
Kyungje-Kwahak-Shimuihoeui, Seoul, 886
Kyusei Atami Art Museum, Atami, 823
— Hakone Art Museum, Gora, 822
Kyushu Institute of Technology, Tobata, 837
— University, 837
— — Library, 820

L

Lääketieteellinen Keskuskirjasto, Helsinki, 432
Laboratoire "Aimé Cotton", Paris, 453
— Central de Recherches Vétérinaires, 457
— d'Aérothermique, 454
— d'Analyse par Activation "Pierre Sue", Gif-sur-Yvette, 454
— d'Annecy de Physique des Particules (I.N2.P3), 453
— d'Astronomie de l'Université de Lille I, 459
— Spatiale, Marseille, 455
— d'Automatique et d'Analyse des Systèmes, Toulouse, 454
— d'Ecologie tropicale, Brunoy, 456
— d'Economie et de Sociologie du Travail, Aix-en-Provence, 456
— d'Electrochimie Interfaciale, Bellevue, 454
— d'Electrostatique, Grenoble, 454
— d'Energétique Solaire, Font-Romeu, 454
— d'Enzymologie, Gif-sur-Yvette, 455
— d'Information et de Documentation en Géographie "INGERGEO", Paris, 456
— d'Informatique pour la Mécanique et les Sciences de l'Ingénieur, Orsay, 454
— — — les Sciences de l'Homme, Marseille, 446
— d'Optique Electronique, Toulouse, 454
— — Quantique, Palaiseau, 453
— de Biologie et de Génétique Evolutives, Gif-sur-Yvette, 456
— — — Technologie des Membranes, Villeurbanne, 456
— — Chimie bactérienne, 455
— — — de coordination, Toulouse, 445
— — du Solide, Bordeaux, 454
— — Macromoléculaire sous Rayonnement, Meudon, 454
— — Cristallographie, Grenoble, 454
— — Génétique et Biologie Cellulaire, Marseille, 456
— — — — Physiologie du Développement des Plantes, Gif-sur-Yvette, 456
— — — Moléculaire des Eucaryotes, Strasbourg, 456
— — Géologie du Quaternaire, Meudon, 455
— — Glaciologie, Grenoble, 455
— — Langues et Civilisations à Traditions Orales, Ivry, 456
— — Magnétisme de Bellevue, Meudon, 454
— — Mécanique et d'Acoustique, Marseille, 454

# INDEX OF INSTITUTIONS

**Laboratoire de Météorologie Dynamique, Palaiseau, 455**
455
— — Neurophysiologie Sensorielle, Paris, 456
— — Pharmacologie et Toxicologie fondamentales, Toulouse, 455
— — Photophysique Moléculaire, Orsay, 453
— — Photosynthèse, 455
— — Physiologie Comparée des Régulations, Strasbourg, 455
— — des Organes Végétaux après Récolte, Meudon, 455
— — — du Travail, Paris, 455
— — — Respiratoire, Strasbourg, 455
— — Physique des Matériaux, Meudon, 454
— — — des Solides, Meudon, 454
— — — et de Métrologie des Oscillateurs, Besançon, 454
— — — théorique, Paris, 453
— — Primatologie et d'Ecologie des Forêts Equatoriales, Makokou, 502
— — Recherches sur les Interactions Gaz-Solides "Maurice Letort", Villiers-le-Nancy, 454
— — Spectrochimie Infrarouge et Raman, Thiais, 454
— Départemental d'Hygiène de la Martinique, Fort de France, 499
— des Interactions Moléculaires et de Hautes Pressions, Villetaneuse, 454
— — Matériaux Organiques, Vernaison, 455
— — Propriétés Mécaniques et Thermodynamiques des Matériaux, Villetaneuse, 454
— — Sciences du Génie Chimique, Nancy, 454
— — Signaux et Systèmes "L25", Gif-sur-Yvette, 454
— — Ultra-Réfractaires, Font-Romeu, 454
— — Verres, Montpellier, 454
— du Phytotron, 456
— Interdépartemental, Douala, 231
— "Léon Brillouin", Gif-sur-Yvette, 454
— Louis Néel, Grenoble, 454
— **Médicale, Bujumbura, 230**
— **Peiresc, Valbonne, 456**
— pour l'Utilisation du rayonnement électro-magnétique, Orsay, 454
— Public d'Essais et d'Etudes, Casablanca, 949
— Souterrain de Moulis, 455
— vétérinaire de Niamey, 990
Laboratori Nazionali di Frascati dell'INFN (Istituto Nazionale di Fisica Nucleare), Rome, 764
Laboratório Central Gonçalo Moniz, Salvador, 184
— de Edificación, Pamplona, 1213
— — Isótopos Abilio Lopes do Rego, do Instituto Português de Oncologia de Francisco Gentil, Lisbon, 1100
— di Restauro di Documenti, Libri e Legature, Milan, 766
— Nacional de Análise, Rio de Janeiro, 185
— — — Engenharia Civil, Ministério das Obras Públicas, Lisbon, 1101
Laboratorium Kesehatan Daerah, Medan, 709
— — Pusat Lembaga Eijkman, 709
— voor Ruimteonderzoek, Utrecht, 962
Laboratorul de Cercetări Maşini Hidraulice, Timisoara, 1124
Laboratory Animal Resources, University Park, 1877
— Animals Centre (M.R.C.), Carshalton, 1443
— for Human Performance Research, University Park, Pa., 1877
— — Research on Animal Behaviour, University Park, 1877
— — — — the Structure of Matter, Philadelphia, 1880

— of Enzymology, Moscow, 1342
— — Experimental Biological Models, Moskovskaya oblast, 1342
— — — Immunobiology, Moscow, 1342
— — — Physiology on Reanimation, Moscow, 1342
— — Hygiene and Prophylaxy, Mogadishu, 1153
— — Molecular Biology (M.R.C.), Cambridge, 1443
— — Physiology, Warsaw, 1069
— — the Government Chemist, London, 1448
— — Transplantation of Organs and Tissues, Moscow, 1342
— — Water Biology, Cracow, 1067
Labour Relations Institute, Izmir, 1305
Ladha Maghji Indian Public Library, Mwanza, 1280
Lady Lever Art Gallery, Port Sunlight, 1470
— Margaret Hall, Oxford, 1524
Lafayette College, Easton, Pa., 1871
La Grange College, Ga., 1700
Lagos City Libraries, 994
— State College of Science and Technology, 1003
Lahore Fort Museum, 1024
— Museum, 1024
Laing Art Gallery and Museum, Newcastle upon Tyne, 1470
Lajos Kossuth University, Debrecen, 648
Lake Baikal Biological Station, Irkutsk, 1362
— Chad Research Institute, Malamfatori, 992
— Erie College, Ohio, 1844
— Forest College, Ill., 1705
Lakehead University, Thunder Bay "P", 269
Lakeland College, Sheboygan, Wis., 1932
Lalit Kala Akademi, New Delhi, 659
— Narayan Mithila University, Darbhanga, 693
Lamar University, Beaumont, Texas, 1898
Lambeth Palace Library, 1457
— Public Libraries, London, 1452
Lambuth College, Jackson, Tenn., 1889
Lamont-Doherty Geological Observatory, New York, 1810
Lampung University, Tanjungkarang, 715
Lancashire College of Agriculture and Horticulture, Preston, 1550
— Library, Preston, 1454
Łańcut Museum, 1077
Landau, L. D., Institute of Theoretical Physics, Moscow, 1318
Landbouw-Economisch Instituut, The Hague, 960
Landbouwhogeschool, 971
Landbouwproefstation, Paramaribo, 1231
Landbrugsmuseet, Auning, 395
Lander College, Greenwood, S.C., 1886
Landesanstalt für Immissionsschutz des Landes Nordrhein-Westfalen, Essen, 534
— — Pflanzenzucht und Samenprüfung, Tirol, 124
Landesarchiv Berlin (West), 538
— Saarbrücken, 540
— Salzburg, 127
— Schleswig-Holstein, 540
— Speyer, 540
Landesbibliothek, Coburg, 535
— Oldenburg, 537
Landesgewerbeamt Baden-Württemberg, Bibliothek für Berüfliche Bildung, Stuttgart, 537
Landeshauptarchiv, Koblenz, 539
Landesinstitut Sozialforschungsstelle, Dortmund, 561
Landeskirchliches Archiv, Munich, 540
— der Evangelisch-Lutherischen Kirche in Bayern, Nuremberg, 540
Landesmuseum für Kärnten, Klagenfurt, 131
— — Vorgeschichte, Dresden, 509
— — Halle, 509
Landessammlungen für Naturkunde, 543

## WORLD OF LEARNING

Landessternwarte auf dem Königsthul bei Heidelberg, 533
Landsarkivet for Fyn, 394
— — Nørrejylland, 394
Landsbiblioteket i Växjö, 1239
Landsbókasafn Islands, 657
Landslaget for Bygde-og Byhistorie, Oslo, 1007
Landsskjalasavnid, Tórshavn, 402
Landwirtschaftlich-Chemische Bundesversuchsanstalt in Vienna, 124
— Zentralbibliothek, Berlin (East), 506
Lane College, Jackson, Tenn., 1890
Langley Research Center, Hampton, Va., 1623
Langston University, 1857
Language and Literature Bureau Library, Brunei, 213
— Centre, Jyväskylä, 436
— — Turku, 439
— Institute, Kuala Lumpur, 919
— Laboratory, Johannesburg, 1182
Lanna Thai Social Sciences Research Centre, Chiangmai, 1285
Lanzhou Institute of Glaciology and Cryopedology, 332
— University, 337
Lao Buddhist Fellowship, Vientiane, 898
Laos-China Association, Vientiane, 898
— -Mongolia Association, Vientiane, 898
— -Soviet Association, Vientiane, 898
— -Viet Nam Association, Vientiane, 898
Lappeenrannan Teknillinen Korkeakoulu, 436
Lappeenranta University of Technology, 436
Laredo State University, 1899
La Salle College, Philadelphia, 1871
Lasky Planetarium, Tel-Aviv, 743
Lateinamerika-Institut, Berlin, 551
Latin America Institute, Moscow, 1321
— American Center, Los Angeles, 1668
— — **for Educational Communication, Mexico City, 30**
Latinamerika-Institutet, Stockholm, 1237
La Trobe University, Victoria, 102
— — — Library, Bundoora, 96
Latvian Agricultural Academy, 1370
— Association for the History of Natural Sciences and Technology, Riga, 1330
— Department of All-Union Biochemistry Society, Riga, 1330
— — — — Botanical Society, Riga, 1330
— — — — Entomological Society, 1330
— — — — I.P. Pavlov Physiological Society, Riga, 1330
— — — — N.I. Vavilov Society of Genetics and Selections, Riga, 1330
— Historical Museum, Riga, 1356
— Open-Air Ethnographical Museum, 1355
— S.S.R. Academy of Sciences, Riga, 1330
— — Revolution Museum, Riga, 1356
— — State Academy of Arts, Riga, 1374
— — Yazep Vitol State Conservatoire, Riga, 1387
— State Museum of Foreign Fine Arts, Riga, 1352
— P. Stuchka State University, Riga, 1364
Laurentian Forest Research Centre, St. Foy, P.Q., 244
— University of Sudbury, 269
Laval University Library, Quebec, 248
Law College, Peshawar, 1027
— Council of Australia, Melbourne, 88
— Institute, Beijing, 332
— Library, Colombo, 1226
— — Dublin, 731
— — Hong Kong, 1559
— School, Ulan Bator, 948
— Society, London, 1417
— — Library, 1457
— — of Manitoba Library, 247
— — New South Wales, 88
Lawrence University, Appleton, 1932

League of Jurists' Associations of the S.R. of Croatia, Zagreb, 1970
Learning Research and Development Center, Pittsburgh, 1881
Leather Industries Research Institute, Grahamstown, 1176
— Research Institute of Nigeria, Zaria, 992
Leathersellers of the City of London, Worshipful Company of, 1420
Lebanese Library Association, Beirut, 899
— University, Beirut, 901
Lebanon Valley College, Annville, Pa., 1871
Lebedev (P. N.) Physical Institute, Moscow, 1318
— S. V., All-Union Research Institute of Synthetic Rubber, Leningrad, 1347
Leeds City Art Gallery, 1469
— — Libraries, 1454
— — Museums, 1469
— Philosophical and Literary Society, Ltd., 1434
— Polytechnic, 1542
Legal Research Institute, Coventry, 1539
Legislative Drafting Research Fund, New York, 1810
— Library, Fredericton, 247
— — Victoria, B.C., 246
Legislature Library, Edmonton, Alb., 246
Lehigh University, Bethlehem, Pa., 1871
Leicester Polytechnic, 1542
Leicestershire Libraries and Information Service, Leicester, 1454
— Museums, Art Galleries and Records Service, Leicester, 1469
Leiden Southern Station, 1160
— State University, 970
Leitstelle Politische Dokumentation, Freie Universität Berlin (West), 518
Lembaga Administrasi Negara, Jakarta, 709
— — Perusahaan, Jakarta, 720
— Antropologi, Jakarta, 714
— Archeologi, Jakarta, 714
— Biologi Nasional, Bogor, 709
— Demografi, Jakarta, 714
— Ekonomi dan Penelitian Masjarakat, Jakarta, 714
— Farmasi Nasional, Jakarta, 709
— Ilmu Pengetahuan Indonesia, Jakarta, 708
— Kesusastraan, Jakarta, 714
— Konsultasi Hukum, Jakarta, 720
— — — dan Bantuan Hukum, Jakarta, 714
— Kriminolgi, Jakarta, 714
— Malaria, Jakarta, 709
— Management, Jakarta, 714
— Oseanologi Nasional, Jakarta-Barat, 710
— Pendidikan Perhotelan dan Katering, Jakarta, 720
— Penelitian Hortikultura, Jakarta, 708
— — Ilmu-Ilum Sosial (LPIS), Salatiga, Java, 720
— — Masyarakat, Jakarta, 714
— — Pendidikan, Jakarta, 718
— — Penyakit Hewan, Bogor, 708
— — Pertanian Banjarmasin, 709
— — — Makassar (Ujungpandang), 709
— — — Malang, 709
— — — Padang, 709
— — — Yogjakarta, 709
— — Tanah, Bogor, 709
— Penjelidikan Ilmiah, Bandung, 719
— — Teknologi Makanan, Jakarta, 709
— Pers Dan Pendapat Unum, Jakarta, 709
— Psikologi Terapan, Jakarta, 714
— Publisistik, Jakarta, 714
— Pusat Penelitian Pertanian, Bogor, 709
— Research dan Bantuan Hukum, Jakarta, 718
— — — Pengujian Materiil Angkatan Darat, Bandung, 710
— — Ekonomi, Jakarta, 718
— Sejarah, Jakarta, 714
— Teknologi, Jakarta, 714
Le Moyne College, Syracuse, 1817
— — Owen College, Memphis, 1890

"Lenin, V. I.", Higher Institute of Electrical and Mechanical Engineering, Sofia, 225
— Ilmen State Reservation, Chelyabinsk, 1322
— Museum, Ulan Bator, 947
— State Public Library of the Byelorussian S.S.R., Minsk, 1348
— Stalin Museum, Tiranë, 55
Leningrad Academician V. N. Obraztov Institute of Railway Engineers, 1389
— Academy of Civil Aviation, 1390
— Admiral S. O. Makarov Higher School of Marine Engineering, 1389
— Agricultural Institute, 1370
— Artificial Limb Research Institute, 1386
— Blood Transfusion Institute, 1385
— M. A. Bonch-Bruyevitch Telecommunications Institute, 1377
— Chemical-Pharmaceutical Institute, 1384
— Civil Engineering Institute, 1380
— F. Engels Institute of Soviet Trade, 1373
— Engineering Institute, 1377
— A.M. Gorky House of Scientists, 1323
— Hydro-Meteorological Institute, 1374
— Institute of Aircraft Instrumentation, 1390
— — — Cinematography, 1388
— — — Eye Diseases, 1385
— — — Oto-Rhino-Laryngology, 1387
— — — Precision Engineering and Optics, 1377
— — — Sanitation and Hygiene, 1383
— — — Surgical Tuberculosis and Diseases of the Bones and Joints, 1384
— — — Traumatology and Orthopaedics, 1386
— — — Tuberculosis, 1384
— — — Vaccines and Sera, 1386
— — — Water Transport, 1389
— M. I. Kalinin Polytechnic Institute, 1375
— S. M. Kirov Academy of Wood Technology, 1381
— — Institute of Textile and Light Industry, 1380
— N. K. Krupskaya Institute of Culture, 1382
— V. I. Lenin Institute of Electrical Engineering, 1377
— Lensoviet Technological Institute, 1378
— Medical Paediatrics Institute, 1383
— V. I. Mukhina Higher Industrial Art School, 1374
— Municipal Museum, 1352
— Museum of Railway Transport, 1359
— Pasteur Institute of Epidemiology and Microbiology, 1385
— I. P. Pavlov Medical Institute, 1st, 1383
— G. V. Plekhanov Mining Institute, 1379
— Pulp and Paper Technological Institute, 1378
— I. E. Repin Institute of Arts, 1374
— Research Institute of Antibiotics, 1385
— — — Industrial Hygiene and Occupational Diseases, 1386
— N. A. Rimsky-Korsakov State Conservatoire, 1387
— Shipbuilding Institute, 1389
— State Institute of Theatre, Music and Cinematography, 1388
— Technological Institute of Refrigerating Industry, 1381
— P. Togliatti Institute of Engineering and Economics, 1382
— Veterinary Institute, 1372
— N. A. Voznesensky Finance and Economics Institute, 1373
— A. A. Zhdanov State University, 1364
Lenoir Rhyne College, Hickory, N.C., 1828
Leo Baeck Institute, London, 1442
— — New York, 1618
— Cussen Institute for Continuing Education, Clayton, 105

— Tolstoy Museum Estate, Yasnaya Poliana, Tulskaya Region, 1358
Leonard Davis Institute of Health Economics, Philadelphia, 1880
Leopold-Franzens Universität Innsbruck, 133
— Mozart Konservatorium, Augsburg, 608
Leptis Magna Museum, 906
Lermontov (M. Y.) State Museum, Lermontovo, 1357
Lesotho Agricultural College, Maseru, 903
— Government Archives, Maseru, 903
Letcombe Laboratory (A.R.C.), Wantage, 1440
Leukaemia Unit (M.C.R.), London, 1444
Leverhulme Trust, London, 1420
Lewis and Clark College, Portland, 1863
— Research Center, Cleveland, Ohio, 1623
— University, Romeoville, Ill., 1705
Lewisham Library Service, 1452
Leys Institute Branch, Auckland Public Libraries, N.Z., 981
Leyte Institute of Technology, Tacloban City, 1060
Liaoning Library, Shenyang, 335
Liaquat Hall Library, Karachi, 1023
— Memoriel Library, Karachi, 1023
Libera Università Abruzzese Degli Studi "Gabriele d'Annunzio", Chieti, 795
— — degli Studi di Trento, 795
— — Internazionale degli Studi Sociali in Roma, 795
Liberia Arts and Crafts Association, Monrovia, 904
Liberian Information Service Library, Monrovia, 904
— Institute of the American Foundation for Tropical Medicine, Inc., 904
Libraries Division, Department of Agriculture, Ottawa, 247
Library Association, London, 1416
— — Library (British Library), London, 1457
— — of Australia, Surry Hills, 87
— — Bangladesh, Dacca, 142
— — Barbados, Bridgetown, 146
— — China, Taipei, 341
— — Cyprus, Nicosia, 367
— — Ireland, 730
— — Portland, 1627
— — Singapore, 1150
— — Trinidad and Tobago, Port of Spain, 1293
— — (Valletta), 921
— Board of Western Australia, Perth, 96
— of Alharam, 1142
— — Chamber of Deputies, Athens, 618
— — Congress, Washington, D.C., 1623
— — Hasanuddin University, Makassar (Ujungpandang), 711
— — International Relations, Chicago, 1603
— — National Defence, Ankara, 1300
— — Parliament, Cape Town, 1162
— — Ottawa, 247
— — Salisbury, Zimbabwe, 2002
— — Phaneromeni, 367
— — Political and Social History, Jakarta, 711
— — Supreme Court, Ottawa, 247
— — Tel Hai Regional College, Upper Galilee, 742
— — the Academy of Sciences, Pyongyang, 883
— — — All Union Museum of A. S. Pushkin, Leningrad, 1349
— — — Altai State University, Barnaul, 1350
— — — American Centre, Nicosia, 367
— — — Archbishopric, Nicosia, 367
— — — Association of Engineers and Architects in Israel, 742
— — — Bank Markazi Iran, Teheran, 722
— — — Bashkir State University, Ufa, 1350

## INDEX OF INSTITUTIONS

Library of the Beth Gordon Institute of Agriculture and Nature Study, Emeq Ha Yarden, 742
— — — Boston Athenaeum, Mass., 1629
— — — Byelorussian V. I. Lenin State University, Minsk, 1350
— — — Central Bank of Egypt, Cairo, 416
— — — — Bureau of Statistics, Jerusalem, 742
— — — — Museum of the Revolution of the U.S.S.R., Moscow, 1349
— — — Checheno-Ingush State University, Grozny, 1350
— — — Chuvash State University, Cheboksary, 1350
— — — Commission of the European Communities, Brussels, 156
— — — Cyprus Museum, 367
— — — Daghestan V. I. Lenin State University, 1350
— — — Department of Science, Bangkok, 1284
— — — Donetsk State University, 1350
— — — Faculties of Geography and Regional Studies of Warsaw University, 1075
— — — Famagusta Greek Gymnasium, 367
— — — Food and Agriculture Organization of the United Nations, Rome, 768
— — — Great Mosque of Sana'a, 1965
— — — Greek Orthodox Patriarchate of Alexandria, 416
— — — Institut d'Egypte, 416
— — — Institute of Education, Nicosia, 367
— — — Iran Bastan Museum, Teheran, 722
— — — Iraqi Museum, 726
— — — Israel Department of Antiquities and Museums, Jerusalem, 742
— — — Ivanovo State University, 1350
— — — Jewish Community, Budapest, 640
— — — — Theological Seminary of Hungary, Budapest, 640
— — — Kabardino-Balkar State University, Nalchik, 1350
— — — Kalinin State University, 1350
— — — Kaliningrad State University, 1350
— — — Kalmuck State University, Elista, 1350
— — — Karaganda State University, 1350
— — — Kemerovo State University, 1350
— — — Kirghiz State University, Frunze, 1350
— — — Knesset, 742
— — — Komi State University, Syktyvkar, 1350
— — — Krasnoyarsk State University, 1350
— — — Kuban State University, Krasnodar, 1350
— — — Kuibyshev State University, 1350
— — — Legislature of Quebec, 249
— — — Ministry of Agriculture, Giza-Orman, Cairo, 416
— — — — Education, Cairo, 416
— — — — Foreign Affairs, Jerusalem, 742
— — — — Health, Cairo, 416
— — — — Justice, Cairo, 416
— — — — Jerusalem, 742
— — — — Trade, Cairo, 416
— — — — Waqfs, 416
— — — Monastery of St. Catherine, Mount Sinai, 416
— — — — Saint-Saviour, Saida, 899
— — — Mordovian State University, Saransk, 1351
— — — National Bank, Kabul, 52
— — — — Museum of Wales, Cardiff, 1459
— — — — Polytechnic University of Athens, 618
— — — North-Ossetian State University, Orjonikidze, 1350
— — — Novosibirsk State University, 1351
— — — Omsk State University, 1351
— — — Otago District Law Society, 981
— — — Pontifical Institute of Medieval Studies, 247
— — — Press and Information Department, Kabul, 52
— — — St. John Monastery, 900
— — — Seminar Hakibbutzim, Tel-Aviv, 742
— — — Simferopol M. V. Frunze State University, 1351
— — — State Hermitage Museum, 1349
— — — — Literature Museum, Moscow, 1349
— — — — Museum of Oriental Arts, Moscow, 1349
— — — — A. S. Pushkin Museum of Fine Arts, Moscow, 1349
— — — — Theatrical A. Bakhrushin Museum, Moscow, 1349
— — — Studium Biblicum Franciscanum, Jerusalem, 742
— — — Supreme Court, Jerusalem, 742
— — — Syrian Patriarchal Seminary, 900
— — — Technical Chamber of Greece, 618
— — — Three Hierarchs, Volos, 618
— — — L. N. Tolstoy State Museum, Moscow, 1349
— — — Tyumen State University, 1351
— — — Udmurd State University, Izhevsk, 1351
— — — University of Thessaloniki, 618
— — — U.S.S.R. Academy of Sciences, Leningrad, 1349
— — — Yakutsk State University, 1351
— — — Yaroslavl State University, 1351
— — — Service of Fiji, Lautoka, 426
— — — Western Australia, 94
Liceo Artistico Statale "Mattia Preti", Calabria, 797
— Náutico Pesquero, Caracas, 1954
Lichttechnische Gesellschaft, Berlin (West), 526
Lick Observatory, Mount Hamilton, 1621
— — Santa Cruz, 1673
Lidhja e Shkrimtarëve dhe e Artistëve të Shqipërisë, Tiranë, 54
Lifuwu Agricultural Research Station, Salima, 912
Liga Argentina contra la Tuberculosis, 64
— Marítima de Chile, 324
— Uruguaya contra la Tuberculosis, 1939
Light and Food Industry School, Ulan Bator, 948
Ligue des Bibliothèques Européennes de Recherche (LIBER), Oslo, 23
— internationale contre l'epilepsie, Bethesda, Md., 41
— — le Rhumatisme, Basel, 37
— — de l'Enseignement, de l'Education et de la Culture Populaire, Paris, 29
— — des associations pour les personnes handicapées mentales, Brussels, 41
Liiketaloustieteellinen Tutkimuslaitos, Helsinki, 430
Lillehammer Bys Malerisamling, 1012
Lima Academy of Exact, Physical and Natural Sciences, 1036
Limburgs Universitair Centrum, 166
Limestone College, 1886
Limnological Station, Borucino, 1078
Linacre College, Oxford, 1524
Lincoln City and County Museum, 1469
— College, Canterbury, N.Z., 984
— — Inc., North Adelaide, 99
— — Oxford, 1524
— — Library, Canterbury, N.Z., 981
— — Oxford, 1463
— Institute of Health Sciences, Carlton, Vic., 116
— Memorial University, Harrogate, Tenn., 1890
— Park Zoological Gardens, Chicago, 1638
— University, Jefferson City, 1787
— — Pa., 1872
Lincoln's Inn Library, 1457
Lincolnshire County Library, Lincoln, 1454
Linden-Museum Stuttgart, Staatliches Museum für Völkerkunde, 545
Lindenwood Colleges, St. Charles, Mo., 1787
Linfield College, 1863
Linguistic Society of America, 1607
— — — India, Pune, 662
Linguistics and Philology Institute, Beijing, 332
— Association of Great Britain, York, 1427
Linköping University, 1245
Lingköpings universitetsbibliotek, 1240
Linnean Society of London, 1432
— — — Library, 1457
— — — New South Wales, 90
Lipetsk Polytechnic Institute, 1375
Lipid Metabolism Unit (M.R.C.), London, 1444
Lippische Landesbibliothek, Detmold, 535
Lisbon Academy of Sciences, 1097
Listasafn Einars Jónssonar, 657
Lister Institute of Preventive Medicine, 1512
Listerian Society of King's College Hospital, 1429
Liszt Ferenc Múzeum, 645
— — Társaság, Budapest, 634
— — Zeneművészeti Főiskola, 654
— — — Könyvtára, Budapest, 640
Literárněvědná společnost, Prague, 372
Literary Museum of the Institute of Russian Literature, Leningrad, 1357
Literature Bureau, Zimbabwe, Salisbury, 2000
— Institute, Beijing, 332
Lithuanian Agricultural Academy, 1370
— Republican Institute of Tuberculosis, 1384
— Research Institute of Oncology, Vilnius, 1386
— S.S.R. Academy of Sciences, Vilnius, 1380
— State Arts Institute, Vilnius, 1374
— State Art Museum, Vilnius, 1352
— — Conservatoire, 1388
— — Picture Gallery, Vilnius, 1352
— Veterinary Academy, 1372
Liver Research Group, Tygerberg, 1156
Liverpool City Libraries, 1454
— Polytechnic, 1543
— School of Tropical Medicine, 1445
Livesey Museum (London Borough of Southwark), 1466
Livingston University, Ala., 1643
Livingstone College, Salisbury, N.C., 1828
— Museum, Zambia, 1998
Livrustkammaren, Stockholm, 1241
Löbbecke-Museum und Aquarium, 542
Local History Museum, Durban, 1164
Lock Haven State College, Pa., 1872
Łódzkie Towarzystwo Naukowe, 1063
Loma Linda University, Calif., 1655
London Academy of Music and Dramatic Art (L.A.M.D.A.), 1553
— and Cambridge Economic Service, 1417
— — Middlesex Archaeological Society, London, 1423
— Business School, 1552
— Hospital Medical College, 1511
— — — Library, 1460
— Library, 1457
— Mathematical Society, 1432
— Natural History Society, 1431
— Oratory Library, 1457
— Public Libraries and Museums, Ontario, 248
— Record Society, 1423
— Regional Art Gallery, London, Ont., 250
— School of Economics and Political Science, 1510
— — — Hygiene and Tropical Medicine, 1512
— — — — Medicine Library, London, 1460

— Society, 1412
— Topographical Society, 1423
Long Ashton Research Station (University of Bristol), 1441
— Island Historical Society, Brooklyn, 1606
— — University, 1817
Longerenong Agricultural College, Dooen, 116
Longwood College, Farmville, Va., 1916
Lopez Memorial Museum and Library, Pasay City, 1049
Loras College, Dubuque, 1728
Lord Kitchener National Memorial Fund, 1420
Lorenz-von-Stein-Institut für Verwaltungswissenschaften, Kiel, 584
Loretto Heights College, Denver, 1676
Los Angeles County Law Library, 1628
— — Museum of Natural History, 1638
— — — Public Library System, 1626
— — Public Library, 1626
— Baños Biological Club, 1048
Loški Muzej, Skofja Loka, 1977
Lotherton Hall, Aberford, 1469
Loughborough College of Art and Design, 1551
— University of Technology, 1514
Louisiana, Humlebaek, 395
— College, Pineville, 1737
— State University System, Baton Rouge, 1737
— — — Alexandria, 1738
— — — Eunice, 1738
— — — Library, Baton Rouge, 1632
— — — Medical Center, New Orleans, 1738
— — — Shreveport, 1738
— Technical University, Ruston, 1738
Louisville Free Public Library, 1626
Lovelace Foundation for Medical Education and Research, Albuquerque, 1618
Low Temperature and Vacuum Institute, Lanzhou, 333
Lowell Observatory, Flagstaff, 1621
Lowveld Experiment Station, Big Bend, 1232
— Natural History Society, Chiredzi, 2000
— Research Station, Chiredzi, 2001
Loyola House of Studies Library, Manila, 1049
— Marymount University, Los Angeles, 1655
— University, Chicago, 1705
— — New Orleans, 1738
Lubelskie Towarzystwo Naukowe, Lublin, 1066
Lublin District Museum, 1077
Lucy Cavendish Collegiate Society, Cambridge, 1484
Luda Engineering College, 337
Lüderitz Museum, 953
Ludwig Boltzmann Institut für Festkorperphysik, Vienna, 126
— Institute for Cancer Research, Sydney, 110
— Maximilians-Universität, Munich, 593
Lugansk Mechanical Engineering Institute, 1377
Luigi Gurakuqi House-Museum, Shkodër, 56
Luleå Stadsbibliotek, Luleå, 1239
Lunacharsky, A. V., House Museum, Leningrad, 1357
— — State Theatrical Library, Leningrad, 1349
Lunar and Planetary Institute, Houston, 1621
Lund Wild Life Exhibit, 251
Lunds Matematiska Sällskap, 1237
— Universitet, 1246
Lunyangwa Agricultural Research Station, 912
Lusaka City Library, 1998
Luther College, Decorah, 1728
— — Regina, 297

Lutherhalle, Staatliches Reformationsgeschichtliches Museum, 510
Lutherische Theologische Hochschule, Oberursel, 609
Luxton Museum, Banff, 249
Luzonian University Foundation, Lucena City, 1054
Lvov Agricultural Institute, 1370
— Forest Engineering Institute, 1381
— Historical Museum, 1356
— Institute of Blood Transfusion and Emergency Surgery, 1385
— — — Trade Economics, 1373
— Ivan Franko State University, 1364
— N. V. Lysenko State Conservatoire, 1388
— Museum of Ethnology, 1355
— Polytechnic Institute, 1375
— Research Institute of Mother and Child Care, 1384
— Science Museum, 1334
— State Institute of Applied and Decorative Art, 1374
— — Medical Institute, 1383
— — Museum of Ukrainian Art, 1353
— — Picture Gallery, 1353
— — Tuberculosis Research Institute, 1384
— Zootechnical and Veterinary Institute, 1372
Lycée Technique, Bujumbura, 230
— — agricole, Ettelbruck, 909
— — d'Esch-sur-Alzette, 909
— Vientiane, 898
Lyceum of the Philippines, Manila, 1060
Lycoming College, Williamsport, Pa., 1872
Lyman Entomological Research Laboratory, Montreal, 277
Lynchburg College, Va., 1916
Lyndon B. Johnson Space Center, Houston, 1622
— State College, Lyndonville, Vt., 1915

M

Maatalouden Tutkimuskeskuksen Kirjasto, Jokioinen, 432
— Tutkimuskeskus, Jokioinen, 430
Maatschappij "Arti et Amicitiae", 956
— der Nederlandse Letterkunde, 958
— tot Bevordering der Toonkunst, 956
Ma'ayan Baruch Prehistoric Museum of the Huleh Valley, Upper Galilee, 744
Macalester College, St. Paul, 1774
Macaulay Institute for Soil Research, Aberdeen, 1441
McCord Museum, Montreal, 251
McGill Cancer Centre, Montreal, 277
— Centre for Northern Studies and Research, Montreal, 277
— University, Montreal, 273
— — Libraries, 249
McGregor Museum, Kimberley, S.A., 1165
Macleay Museum, Sydney, 97
McMaster Institute for Energy Studies, Hamilton, Ont., 280
— University, Hamilton, 277
— — Libraries, 248
McMillan Memorial Library, Nairobi, 879
Macmurray College, Jacksonville, Ill., 1705
McMurry College, Abilene, 1899
McNeese State University, Lake Charles, Louisiana, 1738
MacQuarie University, North Ryde, 102
Macedonian Academy of Sciences and Arts, Skopje, 1967
Maden Tetkik ve Arama Enstitütsü (M.T.A.), 1299
Madonna College, Livonia, Mich., 1761
Madras Institute of Development Studies, 667
— Literary Society and Auxiliary of the Royal Asiatic Society, 662
— — — Library, 673
Madrasat Ahl Al Hadith, Mecca, 1144

— — — Library, 1142
Maejo Institute of Agricultural Technology (MIAT), Chiengmai, 1291
Magadh University, Bodhgaya, 693
Magdalen College, Oxford, 1524
— — Library, Oxford, 1463
Magdalene College, Cambridge, 1484
— — Old Library, Cambridge, 1461
Magee University College, 1555
— — Library, 1554
Maghreb Studies Association, Manchester, 1435
Magnetic Observatory of the S.A.C.S.I.R., Hermanus, 1159
Magnitogorsk G. I. Nosov Institute of Ore Mining and Metallurgy, 1379
Magwe College Library, 229
Magyar Agrártudományi Egyesület, 634
— Állami Eötvös Loránd Geofizikai Intézet, 638
— — Földtani Intézet, 638
— Bélyegmúzeum, Budapest, 643
— Biofizikai Társaság, Budapest, 635
— Biokémiai Egyesület, Budapest, 635
— Biológiai Társaság, 635
— Elektrotechnikai Egyesület, 636
— Élelmezéripari Tudományos Egyesület, Budapest, 634
— Építészeti Múzeum, Budapest, 643
— Földrajzi Társaság, 635
— Geofizikusok Egyesülete, 635
— Gyógyszérzeti Társaság, Budapest, 635
— Hidrológiai Társaság, 635
— Iparművészeti Főiskola, 654
— Iparjogvédelmi Egyesület, 636
— Irodalomtörténeti Társaság, 635
— Irok Könyvtára, Budapest, 640
— — Szövetsége, Budapest, 635
— Izraeliták Országos Könyvtára, 640
— Karszt- és Barlangkutató Társulat, Budapest, 635
— Kémikusok Egyesülete, 635
— Képzőművészeti Főiskola, 654
— Kereskedelmi és Vendéglátóipari Múzeum, Budapest, 643
— Könyvtárosok Egyesülete, Budapest, 634
— Külügyi Intézet, Budapest, 634
— Madártani Intézet, 638
— Meteorológiai Társaság, 635
— Mezögazdasági Múzeum, 643
— Munkásmozgalmi Múzeum, Budapest, 643
— Naiv Művészek Múzeuma, Kecskemét, 645
— Nemzeti Galeria, Budapest, 643
— — — Könyvtára, Budapest, 641
— — — Múzeum, 643
— — — Régészeti Könyvtára, Budapest, 641
— Néprajzi Társaság, 636
— Nyelvtudományi Társaság, 635
— Olajipari Múzeum, Zalaegerszeg, 645
— Országos Levéltár, 641
— Orvostudományi Társaságok és Egyesületek Szövetsége, 635
— PEN Club, 635
— Pszichológiai Társaság, Budapest, 636
— Régészeti és Művészettörténeti Társulat, Budapest, 635
— Rovartani Társaság, 635
— Szinházi Intézet, Budapest, 634
— — — Könyvtára, Budapest, 641
— Szocialista Munkáspárt Politikai Főiskolája, 654
— Tejgazdasági Kisérleti Intézet, Mosonmagyaróvár, 637
— Testnevelési Főiskola, 654
— — — Könyvtára, Budapest, 641
— Történelmi Társulat, 635
— Tudományos Akadémia, 632
— — Allam- és Jogtudományi Intézete, 637
— — Allatorvostudományi Kutatóintézete, Budapest, 637
— — — Atommag Kutató Intézete, 639

# INDEX OF INSTITUTIONS

Magyar Tudományos Akadémia Biologiai Kutató Intézete, Tihany, 638
— — — Botanikai Kutató Intézete, Vácrátot, 638
— — — Csillagvizsgáló Intézet, 638
— — — Dunántuli Tudományos Intézete, 637
— — — Filozófiai Intezete, 639
— — — Földrajztudományi Kutató intézete, 638
— — — — — Könyvtára, 641
— — — Geodéziai és Geofizikai Kutató Intézete, Sopron, 639
— — — Ipargazdaságtani Kutatócsoportja, Budapest, 637
— — — Irodalomtodumányi Intézete, Budapest, 638
— — — Izotópintézete, Budapest, 639
— — — Kisérleti Orvostudományi Kutató Intézete, Budapest, 638
— — — Kónyvtára, 641
— — — Közgazdaságtudományi Intézete, 637
— — — Központi Fizikai Kutató Intézete, Budapest, 639
— — — — Kémiai Kutató Intézete, 639
— — — Matematikai Kutató Intézete, 638
— — — Mezögazdasági Kutató Intézete, 637
— — — Mikrobiológiai Kutatócsoportja, Budapest, 638
— — — Müszaki Fizikai Kutató Intézete, 639
— — — — Kémiai Kutató Intézete, 639
— — — Müvészet törteneti Kutatócsoportja, Budapest, 637
— — — Napfizikai Obszervatóriuma, Debrecen, 639
— — — Néprajzi Kutatócosportja, Budapest, 639
— — — Nyelvtudományi Intézete, 638
— — — Olajbányászati Kutatólaboratóriuma, Miskolc, 639
— — — Pedagógiai Kutatócsoportja, Budapest, 637
— — — Pszichólógiai Intézete, 639
— — — Régészeti Intézet, Budapest, 638
— — — Számitástechnikai es Automatizálási Kutató Intézete, 639
— — — Szegedi Biológiai Központja, Szeged, 638
— — — Szociologiai Kutató Intézete, Budapest, 639
— — — Talajtani és Agrokémiai Kutató Intézet, Budapest, 637
— — — Történettudományi Intézete, 638
— — — Világgazdasági Kutató Intézete, Budapest, 637
— — — Zenetudományi Intézete, 637
— Urbanisztikai Társaság, Budapest, 634
— Vizügyi Múzeum, Budapest, 645
— Zenemüvészek Szövetsége, 634
— Zenetörténeti Muzeum, Budapest, 643
Magyarhoni Földtani Társulat, Budapest, 635
Maha Bodhi Society of Ceylon, 1224
Maharaja Sawai Man Singh II Museum, Jaipur, 675
— Sayajirao University of Baroda, 679
Maharshi Dayanand University Rohtak, 694
Mahatma Gandhi Institute, Moka, 924
— Phule Krishi Vidyapeeth, Rahuri, 693
Mahbubeh Motahedin University, Teheran, 723
— — — Libraries, Shiraz, 722
Mahidol University, Bangkok, 1288
Maidstone College of Art, 1551
Maimana Museum, 52
Maison de Balzac, Paris, 466
— — Poésie, 449
— — Victor Hugo, 466
— des Sciences de l'Homme, Paris, 459
— Française d'Oxford, 1426

Makarna Mittag-Lefflers Matematiska Stiftelse, Djursholm, 1238
Makedonska akademija na naukitei umetnostite, Skopje, 1967
Makedonsko Geološko Društvo, Skopje, 1971
— Lekarsko Društvo, Skopje, 1971
Makerere Institute of Social Research, Kampala, 1311
— University, Kampala, 1312
— — Albert Cook Library, 1311
— — Library Service, Kampala, 1311
Makhanga Agricultural Research Station, Chiromo, 912
Makhtumkuli Institute of Linguistics and Literature, Ashkhabad, 1332
Makoholi Experiment Station, Fort Victoria, 2001
Maktab Perguruan Bahasa, Kuala Lumpur, 919
Malacca Public Library Corporation, 916
Malacological Society of Australia, Perth, 90
— — — London, 1432
Malaria Institute, Dacca, 142
Malawi Library Association, Zomba, 912
— National Library Service, Lilongwe, 912
— Polytechnic, Blantyre, 913
Malayan Nature Society, Kuala Lumpur, 914
Malaysian Agricultural Research and Development Institute, Selangor, 914
— Biochemical Society, Kuala Lumpur, 914
— Branch of The Royal Asiatic Society, Petaling Jaya, 914
— Historical Society, Kuala Lumpur, 915
— Institute of Architects, Kuala Lumpur, 915
— — — Management, Kuala Lumpur, 919
— Library Association, Kuala Lumpur, 915
— Medical Association, Kuala Lumpur, 915
— Rubber Producers' Research Association, Hertford, 1449
— — Research and Development Board, 915
— Scientific Association, Kuala Lumpur, 915
— Zoological Society, Kuala Lumpur, 915
Malek Library, Teheran, 722
Malende Kunsteres Sammenslutning, 389
Malkerns Research Station, 1232
Malmö stadsbibliotek, Malmö, 1239
Malone College, Canton, Ohio, 1844
— Society, 1427
Maloyaroslavets Museum of Military History of 1812, 1356
Malta Society of Arts, Manufacturers & Commerce, Valleta, 921
Mamedaliev, Y. G., Institute of Oil Processes, Baku, 1325
Mammal Research Institute, Pretoria, 1175
Mammalian Development Unit (M.R.C.), London, 1444
— Genome Unit (M.R.C.), Edinburgh, 1444
Mammals Research Institute, Białowieźa, 1067
Man and His Work Museum, Tel-Aviv, 743
Manabí Technical University, 411
Management and Behavioral Science Center, Philadelphia, 1880
— Institute, Montreal, 277
Manchester Business School, 1518
— City Art Galleries, 1469
— College, Indiana, 1717
— Geographical Society, 1423
— Literary and Philosophical Society, 1434
— Museum, 1470
— Polytechnic, 1544
— Public Libraries, 1454
— -Sheffield-U.M.I.S.T. School of Probability and Statistics, Manchester, 1518
— University Centre for the Study of Chronic Rheumatism, 1518
Manhattan College, 1817
— School of Music, New York, 1817
Manhattanville College, Purchase, 1817

Manila Central University, 1054
— City Library, 1049
— Medical Society, 1047
Manipur State Museum, 675
Manitoba Museum of Man and Nature, Winnipeg, 249
— Naturalists Society, Winnipeg, 243
Mankato State University, Minn., 1775
Mannix College, Clayton, 105
Mansfield College, Oxford, 1524
— State College, Pennsylvania, 1872
Mansoura Municipal Library, 416
— Polytechnic Institute, 421
— University, 420
Manuel L. Quezon University, Manila, 1057
Manukau Technical Institute, 987
Manyo Gakkai, Osaka, 806
Maori Education Foundation, 979
Mappin Art Gallery, Sheffield, 1471
Mapua Institute of Technology, Manila, 1060
Mara Institute of Technology, Selangor, 919
Marathwada Agricultural University, Parbhani, 694
— University, Maharashtra, 694
Margaret Trowell School of Fine Art, Kampala, 1312
Margaretha Mes Institute of Plant Physiology, Pretoria, 1175
Mari A. M. Gorky Polytechnic Institute, Yoshkar-Ola, 1381
— University, 1364
Maria Mitchell Observatory, Nantucket, 1621
Marian College, Indianapolis, 1717
— — of Fond Du Lac, 1932
Mariano Gálvez University of Guatemala, 626
"Marica" Institute of Vegetable Crops, Plovdiv, 219
Marie Curie Skłodowska University, Lublin, 1080
Marietta College, Ohio, 1844
Marine Academie, Antwerp, 169
— Biological Association of India, Kerala, 663
— — — — the United Kingdom, 1432
— — Laboratory, Falmouth, Mass., 1620
— — — Kanazawa City, 831
— Biology Centre, Bangkok, 1283
— Hydrophysical Institute, Sevastopol, 1333
— Laboratory of the Department of Agriculture and Fisheries for Scotland, 1475
— Museum of Upper Canada, Toronto, 250
— Science Institute, Santa Barbara, 1673
— — Research Laboratory, St. John's, Newfoundland, 284
— Transport College, Luda, 337
Marineland of Florida (Marineland Inc.), St. Augustine, 1638
Marinens Bibliotek, Copenhagen, 394
Mariners' Museum, Va., 1639
Marintekniska institutet, SSPA, Goteborg, 1239
Marion College, Indiana, 1717
Marist College, Poughkeepsie, 1817
Maritiem Museum "Prins Hendrik", Rotterdam, 968
Maritime College (Fort Schuyler, Bronx), 1822
— Conservatory of Music, Halifax, N.S., 319
— History Group, St. Johns, 285
— Museum, Aberdeen, 1472
— — Cape Town, 1164
— Trust, London, 1423
Maritimes Forest Research Centre, Fredericton, N.B., 244
Marketing Science Institute, Cambridge, Mass., 1617
— Survey Research Institute, Seoul, 893
Märkisches Museum kultur-historisches Museum der Stadt Berlin, (East), 508
Marlboro College, Vermont, 1915

Marmara Scientific and Industrial Research Institute, Gebze-Kocaeli, 1299
Marquette University, Milwaukee, Wis., 1932
Marsh's Library, Dublin, 731
Marshall Library of Economics, Cambridge, 1462
— University, Huntington, W. Va., 1930
Martin Luther-Universität, Halle-Wittenberg, 512
Martsinovsky, I. E., Institute of Medical Parasitology and Tropical Medicine, Moscow, 1346
Marx-Engels Museum, Moscow, 1355
Marx, K., State Public Library of the Georgian S.S.R., Tbilisi, 1348
— — — — — the Turkmen S.S.R., Ashkhabad, 1348
— Károly Közgazdaságtudományi Egyetem, Budapest, 648
— — — — Központi Könyvtára, 641
— Memorial Library, London, 1457
Marxist Centre of the University of Maribor, 1986
Mary Baldwin College, Staunton, Va., 1916
— Washington College, Fredericksburg, 1916
Marycrest College, Davenport, Iowa, 1728
Marygrove College, Detroit, 1762
Maryland Academy of Sciences, 1597
— Historical Society, 1606
— Institute, College of Art, Baltimore, 1745
Marymount College of Kansas, Salina, 1730
— — Tarrytown, 1818
— -Manhattan College, New York, 1818
Maryville College, Tenn., 1890
— — St. Louis, Mo., 1787
Marywood College, Scranton, Pa., 1872
Marzeev, A. N., Scientific Research General and Municipal Hygiene Institute, Kiev, 1386
Mashhad Museum, 722
— University, 723
— — Central Library and Documentation Centre, 722
Massachusetts College of Art, Boston, 1753
— Historical Society, Boston, 1606
— — — Library, 1629
— Institute of Technology, 1753
— — — — Libraries, 1633
Massey College, Toronto, 310
— University, Palmerston North, 984
Mataram State University, Lambok, 716
Matematiska Föreningen, Universitetet, Uppsala, 1237
Matenadaran, M. M., Institute of Ancient Armenian Manuscripts, Erevan, 1350
"Mater Ecclesiae" Institute, Rome (Vatican City), 1947
Materia Medica Institute, Beijing, 333
— — — Shanghai, 332
Materials Handling Research Group, Johannesburg, 1181
— Research Laboratory, University Park, 1877
Mathematical Association of America, Inc., Washington, D.C., 1613
Mathematics Association, Hanoi, 1962
— Education Research Centre, Coventry, 1539
— Institute, Beijing, 332
— Research Centre, Coventry, 1538
Mathematisch Centrum, Amsterdam, 962
— Physikalische Gesellschaft in Innsbruck, 122
Mathematische Gesellschaft der DDR, Berlin (East), 505
Mathematisches Forschungsinstitut, 532
Matica Hrvatska, Zagreb, 1970
— slovenská, Martin, 376
— Srpska, Novi Sad, 1969
Matice moravská, Brno, 374
Matopos Research Station, Bulawayo, 2001
Mátra Múzeum, Gyongyos, 645

Matsumoto Kinenkan, 823
Matsuyama University of Commerce, 865
— — — — Library, 820
Mátyás Király Múzeum, Visegrad, 645
— Templom Egyháztörténeti Gyűjteméye, Budapest, 643
Maurice Thorez Moscow Institute of Foreign Languages, 1382
Mauritius Archives, 923
— College of the Air, Moka, 924
— Herbarium, Reduit, 923
— Institute, 923
— — Public Library, 923
Mawson Institute for Antarctic Research, Adelaide, 99
Max Mueller Bhavan, New Delhi, 661
— -Planck-Gesellschaft zur Förderung der Wissenschaften e.V., Munich, 526
— Institut für Limnologie zu Plön, Kiel, 584
— Society for the Advancement of Science, Munich, 526
— -Reger-Archive, Meiningen, 508
— von Pettenkofer Institut, Munich, 531
Maxwell R. Maybaum Institute of Material Sciences and Quantum Electronics, New York, 1824
Mayo Foundation, Rochester, Minn., 1618
Mayville State College, North Dakota, 1839
Mazandaran University, 723
Mazar-i-Sharif Museum, 52
Mbawa Agricultural Research Station, Embangweni, 912
Meat Research Institute (A.R.C.), Langford, Bristol, 1440
Mechanics Institute, Beijing, 332
Mechanisms in Tumour Immunity Unit (M.R.C.), Cambridge, 1444
Medagliere, Turin, 773
Medelhavsmuseet, Stockholm, 1242
Medical and Agricultural Drugs Research Institute, Izmir, 1305
— Association of Jamaica, 800
— — — South Africa, 1155
— — — Thailand, 1283
— Biochemistry Association, Hanoi, 1962
— Biology Institute, Kunming, 333
— Council, Dublin, 731
— — of India, New Delhi, 662
— Information Institute, Beijing, 333
— Library, Hong Kong, 1559
— — Association, Omaha, 1601
— Research Centre, Warsaw, 1069
— — Council, London, 1443
— — — Laboratories, Carshalton, 1444
— — — — Gambia, 1443
— — — — Kingston, Jamaica, 800, 1443
— — — — of Canada, Ottawa, 245
— — — — Ireland, Dublin, 731
— — — — New Zealand, 979
— — Foundation of the Philippines, Inc., San Miguel, Manila, 1047
— — Institute, Colombo, 1225
— — Laboratory (Medical Department, Kenya), Nairobi, 879
— — Library of Brooklyn, 1629
— School, Ulan Bator, 948
— Social Research Project, Lahore, 1022
— Society for the Study of Venereal Diseases, London, 1429
— — of London, 1429
— — — the State of New York, 1610
— — Sociology Unit (M.R.C.), Aberdeen, 1444
— University of Pécs, 649
— — — Southern Africa, Pretoria, 1168
— Women's International Association, Vienna, 38
Medicine Hat College, 265
— — Museum and Art Gallery, 249
Medicinska forskningsrädet, Stockholm, 1238
Medicinske Selskap i Bergen, 1008
— — — København, 391
Medico-Biological Institute, Sofia, 220
— -Legal Society, London, 1429

Medieval Academy of America, Cambridge, Mass, 1606
— Studies Centre, Vatican City, 1946
Medina Awkaf Libraries, 1142
Mediterranean Agronomic Institute of Bari, 17
— — — — Montpellier, 17
— — — — Zaragoza, 17
Medizinhistorische Bibliothek, Basel, 1259
Medizinische Akademie "Carl Gustav Carus", Dresden, 513
— — Erfurt, 513
— — Magdeburg, 513
— — Hochschule, Hanover, 576
— — Lübeck, 587
Medizinisches Institut für Umwelthygiene, Düsseldorf, 531, 563
Meerut University, Uttar Pradesh, 694
Mehmet Paşa Library, 1300
Mehran University of Engineering and Technology, Nawabshah, 1026
Meiji Gakuin University, Tokyo, 866
— Jingu Hómotsuden, 820
— University, 865
— — Library, 818
Meijo University, Nagoya, 866
Meisei University, Tokyo, 866
Mekise Nirdamin Society, 738
Melanesian Mission Museum, Auckland, 982
Melbourne State College, Carlton, Vic., 116
Melikishvili, P. G., Institute of Physical and Organic Chemistry, Tbilisi, 1328
Melitopol Institute of Agricultural Engineering, 1372
Mellemfolkeligt Samvirke, Copenhagen, 390
Mellon Institute, Pittsburgh, 1611
Memling Museum, Bruges, 158
Memorial Institute for Ophthalmic Research, 415
— Museum of the War of Liberation, Pyongyang, 884
— University of Newfoundland, 283
— — — — Library, 247
Memorijalna Galerija "Jozo Kljaković", Zagreb, 1978
Memphis Academy of Arts, 1890
— and Shelby County Public Library and Information Centre, 1627
— State University, 1890
Mendel Art Gallery and Civic Conservatory (Saskatoon Gallery and Conservatory Corporation), Saskatoon, 251
Mendeleyev (D.I.) All-Union Chemical Society, Moscow, 1344
— Institute of Chemical Technology, Moscow, 1378
Menia University, 420
Mennel Society, Salisbury, Zimbabwe, 2000
Menningarsjodur, Reykjavík, 656
Menningarstofnun, Bandarikjanna, Reykjavík, 656
Menninger Foundation, Topeka, 1618
Menntamalaráð, Reykjavík, 656
Menufia University, 420
Mercantile Library Association, New York, 1629
Mercer University, Macon, Ga., 1700
Meredith College, Raleigh, N.C., 1828
Méréstechnikai és Automatizálási Tudományos Egyesület, Budapest, 636
Merowe Museum, Sudan, 1230
Merrimack College, North Andover, Mass., 1757
Merseyside County Museum, Liverpool, 1469
Merton College, Oxford, 1524
— Library, Oxford, 1463
— Public Libraries, 1452
Messiah College, Grantham, Pa., 1872
Mestni muzej, Ljubljana, 1977
Městská knihovna, Prague, 376
— knižnica, Bratislava, 376
Mestké muzeum v Bratislave, 379
Metabolic and Nutrition Research Unit, Johannesburg, 1182

INDEX OF INSTITUTIONS

Metal Industrial Research Laboratories, Hsinchu, 341
Metallurgy Institute, Shanghai, 332
Metals Institute, Shenyang, 332
— Society, London, 1438
— — Library, London, 1457
Metaphysical Society of America, Columbia, S.C., 1614
Meteorological and Geophysical Research Station, Kerguelen Island, 501
— Automatization Institute, Beijing, 333
— Information Institute, Beijing, 333
— Instruments Institute, Changchun, 333
— Museum of the Central Geophysical Observatory, Leningrad, 1359
— Office, Bracknell, Berks., 1447
— Research Institute, Tokyo, 816
— Service, Salisbury, Zimbabwe, 2002
— Station, New Amsterdam, 501
Météorologie Nationale, Boulogne, 459
— — du Cameroun, Douala, 231
Meteorologische Dienst Van de Nederlandse Antillen, 975
— Gesellschaft der DDR, Potsdam, 505
Meteorologischer Dienst der DDR, Potsdam, 506
Meteoroloska opservatorija Beograd, 1973
Methodist College, Fayetteville, 1828
Metrology, Calibration and Correction of Metrological Instruments Institute, Beijing, 333
Metropolitan Museum of Art, 1639
— Research Trust, Canberra City, 91
— Toronto Library, 248
Metsäntutkimuslaitos, Helsinki, 430
Mexican Academy of History, Mexico City, 925
— — — Languages, Mexico City, 925
— National Academy of Medicine, Mexico City, 925
Mezőgazdasági és Elelmezésügyi Minisztérium Információs Központja, Budapest, 641
Miami University, Oxford, Ohio, 1844
— -Dade Public Library, Miami, 1626
Michaelis Collection, Cape Town, 1164
Michigan State Library, Lansing, 1630
— — University, 1762
— — — Libraries, East Lansing, 1633
— Technological University, 1762
Michurin (I.V.) Central Laboratory of Genetics, Michurinsk, 1338
Microbiology Institute, Beijing, 332
Mid Glamorgan County Library, Bridgend, 1455
Middle American Research Institute, New Orleans, 1622
— Asian Research Institute of Natural Gas, **Tashkent, 1346**
— — — — Silk Industry, Dzhar-Aryk, 1347
— East College, Beirut, 902
— — Institute, New York, 1811
— — — Washington, D.C., 1622
— — Technical University, Ankara, 1300
— — — Library, 1300
— Eastern Regional Radioisotope Centre for the Arab Countries, Giza, 416
— Temple Library (The Hon. Society of the), London, 1457
— Tennessee State University, 1890
Middlebury College, Vt., 1915
Middlesex Hospital Medical School, 1511
— — — Boldero Library, London, 1460
— Polytechnic, London, 1544
Midland Lutheran College, Fremont, 1793
Midlands Museum, Salisbury, Zimbabwe, 2002
Midwest Research Institute, Kansas City, 1619
Midwestern State University, Wichita Falls, 1899
Mie Shinto Library, Ujiyamada, 820
— University, 840
Miejska Biblioteka Publiczna w Krakowie, Cracow, 1075

— — — im E. Raczyńskiego w Poznaniu, 1075
— — — L. Waryńskiego w. Łódzi, Łódz, 1075
Migjeni House-Museum, Shkodër, 56
Mikeladze, G. S., Republican Scientific and Technical Library of the Georgian S.S.R., Tbilisi, 1351
Miklukho-Maklaya (N.N.) Institute of Ethnography, Moscow, 1320
Mikolongwe Livestock Improvement Centre, Limbe, 912
Milde Arboretum, Bergen, 1014
Military Academy, Teheran, 724
— College of South Carolina, Charleston, 1885
— Historical Archives, Sofia, 220
— History Society of Ireland, Dublin, 730
— Medical Museum of the U.S.S.R. Ministry of Defence, Leningrad, 1354
— Museum, Cape Town, 1164
— — Damascus, 1277
— — "Kronan", Göteborg, 1242
— — Pretoria, 1165
— School of Engineers, Mexico City, 944
— Vehicles and Engineering Establishment, Chertsey, 1448
Millersville State College, Pa., 1872
Millet Kütüphanesi, Istanbul, 1300
Milletlerarasi Sark Tetkikleri Cemiyeti, 1299
Milli Kütüphane, Ankara, 1300
Milligan College, Tenn., 1890
Millikin University, Ill., 1705
Mill's Observatory, Dundee, 1472
Mills College, Calif., 1655
Millsaps College, Jackson, Miss., 1785
Milton Margai Teachers College, Freetown, 1149
Milwaukee Public Library, 1627
Mimarlik Y. Okulu, Istanbul, 1310
MIND (National Association for Mental Health), London, 1434
Mind Association, Oxford, 1434
**Mindanao State University, Marawi City,** 1055
Mineral Industry Museum, Akita City, 824
— Information Bureau, Delhi, 671
— Metabolism Unit (M.R.C.), Leeds, 1443
— Research and Exploration Institute Library, Ankara, 1300
Mineralogical Society, Baku, 1325
— — of America, 1613
— — — Great Britain and Ireland, 1433
— — — India, Mysore, 664
Mineralogische Staatssammlung, Munich, 544
Mineralogisches Museum, Berlin (East), 509
Mineraloško-petrografski muzej, 1978
Minerva Gesellschaft für die Forschung m.b.H., Munich, 528
Mines and Geological Department, Nairobi, 878
Mining and Metallurgical Institute, Murmansk, 1323
— — — Society of America, 1616
— — Mineral Resources Research Institute, Ames, 1728
— Association, Hanoi, 1962
— Geological and Metallurgical Institute of India, 671
— Museum of the G. V. Plekhanov Mining Institute, Leningrad, 1358
— Research and Service Organization, Hsinchu, 341
Ministère de la Recherche Scientifique, Abidjan, 798
Ministerio de Educación y Ciencia, Gabinete de Documentación, Biblioteca y Archivo, Madrid, 1199
Ministerrat der Deutschen Demokratischen Republik Staatliche Zentralverwaltung für Statistik, Berlin (East), 506
Ministry of Agriculture and Fisheries, Wellington, N.Z., 979

— — — Natural Resources, Lilongwe, 912
— — — Rural Development Library, Kuala Lumpur, 916
— — — Works Library, Islamabad, 1023
— — — Co-operatives and Marketing, Maseru, 903
— — — Fisheries and Food Library, London, 1451
— — Defence (Whitehall) Library, London, 1451
— — Education Library, Kabul, 52
— — — Nicosia, 367
— — — Tokyo, 818
— — Foreign Affairs Library, Tokyo, 818
— — Justice Library, Tokyo, 818
— — Livestock Development, Veterinary Services Division, Kabete, 879
Minji Soshoho Gakkai, Kobe City, 805
Minneapolis College of Art and Design, 1775
— Public Library and Information Centre, 1626
— Society of Fine Arts, 1639
Minnesota Historical Society, 1606
— — Library, 1629
Minobusan Hómotsukan, 823
Minot State College, North Dakota, 1839
Minsk Institute of Orthopaedics and Restorative Surgery, 1386
— — Radio Engineering, 1377
— State Art Museum, 1353
— — Medical Institute, 1383
Mio, V., House-Museum, Korcë, 56
Miramichi Natural History Museum, 250
Mironovsky Research Institute of Wheat Breeding and Seed Production, Mironovka, 1338
Mission I.R.A.T. à Madagascar, Bamako, 910
— I.R.A.T./Guyane, Cayenne, 499
— I.R.C.T. à Mali, Bamako, 920
— ORSTOM au Pérou, Coopération auprès du Ministerio de Energía y Minas, Lima, 1038
— Pédologique, Rabat, 949
— Permanente en Egypte, Cairo, 456
— — Israel, Jerusalem, 456
— Sociologique du Haut-Oubangui, Bangassou, 320
— Universitaire et Culturelle Française au Maroc, Rabat, 949
Mississippi Bureau of Geology, Jackson, 1618
— College, Clinton, 1785
— State University, 1785
— University for Women, Columbus, 1785
— Valley State University, Itta Bena, 1785
Missouri Valley College, 1787
Miswat Library, Aden, 1965
Mitchell College of Advanced Education, Bathurst, 113
— Library, Glasgow, 1455
Mitsubishi Kasei Institute of Life Sciences, 816
Mittelrheinisches Landesmuseum, Mainz, 544
Miyagi Gakuin Women's College, Sendai City, 866
Miyake Medical Institute, Kagawa, 815
Miyazaki University, 840
Miyazakijingu Chókokan, 823
Mlezu Agricultural Institute, Que Que, 2004
Modern Churchmen's Union, 1435
— Humanities Research Association, 1442
— Language Association, London, 1427
— — of America, New York, 1607
Moderna galerija, Ljubljana, 1977
— Rijeka, 1977
— — Zagreb, 1978
— Museet, Stockholm, 1241
Mogilev Mechanical Engineering Institute, 1377
Moldavian Department D. I. Mendeleyev Chemistry Society, Kishinev, 1331

— — of All-Union Botanical Society, Kishinev, 1331
— — — — Entomological Society, 1331
— — — — Hydrobiological Society, Kishinev, 1331
— — — — Society of Genetics, Kishinev, 1331
— Geographical Society, Kishinev, 1331
— Institute of Epidemiology, Microbiology and Hygiene, 1385
— S.S.R. Academy of Sciences, 1331
— State Art Museum, Kishinev, 1353
Molecular and Cellular Cardiology Research Unit, Tygerberg, 1156
— Haematology Unit (M.R.C.), Oxford, 1443
Mombasa Polytechnic, 880
Mommsen Gesellschaft, 521
Monash University, Clayton, 104
— Library, 96
Monasterio de San Lorenzo de El Escorial, 1201
Monell Chemical Senses Center, Philadelphia, 1880
Mongol Ulsyn Ih Surguul', Ulan Bator, 948
Mongolian State University, Ulan Bator, 948
Monmouth College, Illinois, 1706
— — West Long Branch, 1797
Monopolies and Mergers Commission Library, London, 1450
Montana College of Mineral Science and Technology, Butte, 1791
— State University, Bozeman, 1792
Montanuniversität Leoben, 137
Montanwissenschaftlichen Gesellschaft der DDR, Berlin (East), 506
Montclair Art Museum, 1639
— State College, N.J., 1797
Montenegrin Academy of Sciences and Arts, Titograd, 1966
Monterey Institute of International Studies, 1655
Montessori International Association, Amsterdam, 30
Montreal Neurological Institute, 277
Montserrat Public Library, Plymouth, 1561
Monumenta Germaniae Historica, 520
Monumental Brass Society, 1423
Monumentenraad, The Hague, 956
Moorhead State University, Minn., 1775
Morá Ferenc Múzeum, 646
Moralogy Kenkyusho, Chiba, 811
Moravian College, Bethlehem, Pa., 1872
Moravská galerie v Brně, 379
Moravské Museum v Brně, 379
Mordovian Art Gallery, Saransk, 1353
— N. P. Ogorev State University, 1365
Morehead Planetarium, 1639
— State University, Kentucky, 1736
Morehouse College, Atlanta, 1700
Morgan State University, Baltimore, 1745
Morningside College, Sioux City, 1728
Morphology Association, Hanoi, 1962
Morris Arboretum, Philadelphia, 1880
— Brown College, Atlanta, 1700
Morrison Hill Technical Institute, Hong Kong, 1561
Morski Instytut Rybacki, Gdynia, 1071
Mosad Harav Kook, Jerusalem, 753
Mosaic Gallery, Amman, 875
Moscow Academician I. M. Gubkin Institute of the Petrochemical and Gas Industry, Moscow, 1379
— Arts Theatre Museum, 1360
— Automobile and Road Construction Institute, 1390
— N. E. Bauman Technical Institute, 1377
— Co-operative Institute, 1373
— Evening Institute of Metallurgy, 1379
— Finance Institute, 1374
— Forest Engineering Institute, 1381
— V. P. Gorjachkin Institute of Agricultural Engineers, 1372
— Higher School of Industrial Art, 1374
— House of Scientists, 1323
— Institute for Historian-Archivists, 1382

— — of Architecture, 1374
— — — Aviation Technology, 1390
— — — Chemical Engineering, 1378
— — — Economics and Statistics, 1374
— — — Electronic Machine Building, 1377
— — — Engineers, 1389
— — — — for Geodesy, Aerial Photography and Cartography, 1382
— — — Irrigation and Land Reclamation, 1372
— — — Land Exploitation Engineering, 1372
— — — Physical Engineering, 1378
— — — Printing, 1382
— — — Radio Electronics and Automation, 1378
— — — — Engineering and Electronics, 1378
— — — Steel and Alloys, 1379
— — — Vaccines and Sera, 1386
— V. V. Kuibyshev Civil Engineering Institute, 1380
— Literary Institute of the Union of Soviet Writers, 1382
— M. V. Lomonosov Institute of Fine Chemical Technology, 1378
— — State University, 1365
— Machine Tool Engineering Institute, 1377
— Mechnikov Institute of Epidemiology, Microbiology and Hygiene, 1385
— Medical Institute of the Health Ministry of the R.S.F.S.R., 1383
— — — (1st), 1383
— — Stomatological Institute, 1384
— Mining Institute, 1379
— Motor Engineering Institute, 1377
— Municipal Research First Aid Institute, 1387
— S. Orjonikidze Aviation Institute, 1390
— — Institute of Engineering and Economics, 1382
— — — — — Geological Research, 1374
— Physical Engineering Institute, 1377
— N. I. Pirogov State Medical Institute (2nd), 1383
— Region Gynaecological Institute, 1384
— — Tuberculosis Institute, 1384
— Research Institute of Psychiatry, 1346
— K. I. Skryabin Veterinary Academy, 1372
— Society of Naturalists, 1345
— State Art Institute, 1374
— — Institute of International Relations, 1346
— — University Museum of Zoology, 1358
— P. I. Tchaikovsky State Conservatoire, 1388
— Technological Institute of Dairy and Meat Industries, 1381
— — — — Food Industry, 1381
— — — — Light Industry, 1381
— Telecommunications Institute, 1377
— Textile Institute, 1381
— Timiryazev Academy of Agriculture, 1370
Moss Landing Marine Laboratories, 1620
Mosul Museum, 726
Mote Marine Laboratory, Inc., Sarasota, 1620
Mother and Child Research Institute, Warsaw, 1072
Moto Moto Museum, Mbala, 1998
Moulmein College Library, 229
Mount Allison University, 288
— Gravatt College of Advanced Education, Queensland, 114
— Holyoke College, Mass., 1757
— Makulu Agricultural Research Station, Chilanga, 1997
— Marty College, Yankton, S. Dak., 1888
— Mary College, Milwaukee, 1932
— Mercy College, Cedar Rapids, 1728
— Myohyang-san Museum, Hyangsan County, 884
— Nimba National Reserve, Guinea, 627
— Royal College, Calgary, 265

— Saint Mary's College, Emittsburg, 1745
— — — Los Angeles, 1656
— — Vincent University, Halifax, 288
— Stromlo and Siding Spring Observatories, Woden P.O., A.C.T., 94
— Union College, Ohio, 1844
— Wilson and Las Campanas Observatories, Pasadena, Calif., 1619
Mouvement international des jeunes et des étudiants pour les Nations Unies, Geneva, 30
Mozart Museum, Salzburg, 131
Mozarteum, Salzburg, 131
— University of Music and Dramatic Art in Salzburg, 139
Mpisi Cattle Breeding Experimental Station, Swaziland, 1232
MSZMP KB Párttörténeti Intézetének Könyvtár és Dokumentációs Osztálya, Budapest, 641
Mücsarnok, Budapest, 643
Muhlenberg College, Allentown, 1872
Muiderslot Rijksmuseum, 968
Mullard Radio Astronomy Observatory, Cambridge, 1447
— Space Science Laboratory, London, 1513
Multiple Cropping Project, Chiang Mai, 1285
Multnomah County Library, Portland, Oregon, 1627
Mumbai Marathi Granth Sangrahaaya, Bombay, 668
Munch-museet, Ohio, 1012
Münchner Entomologie Gesellschaft e.V., Munich, 523
Mundelein College, Chicago, 1706
Municipal Art Gallery, Johannesburg, 1165
— Botanic Gardens, Durban, 1160
— Library, Famagusta, 367
— — Isfahan, 722
— — Limassol, 367
— — in Memory of William and Chia Boorstein, Nahariva, 742
— Museum, Beit Shean, 744
— — of Antiquities, Tiberias, 744
— van Abbe-Museum in Eindhoven, 966
Munkácsy Mihály Múzeum, 646
Münzkabinett, Berlin (East), 508
— Dresden, 509
Münzsammlung, Mainz, 544
Murat Molla Library, 1300
Murdoch University, W.A., 105
Murhardsche Bibliothek der Stadt Kassel und Landesbibliothek, 536
Murmansk Higher School of Marine Engineering, 1389
— Marine Biological Institute, 1323
Muroran Institute of Technology, Hokkaido, 840
Murray State University, 1736
Murtala Polytechnic, Makurdi, 1003
Musashino College of Music, Tokyo, 874
Muscle Research Unit, Tygerberg, 1156
Musée Adrien Dubouché, 469
— Antiquarium, Utique, 1296
— Archéologique, Addis Ababa, 424
— — Carthage, 1296
— — d'El Djem, Thysdrus, 1296
— — Nîmes, 469
— — Port-au-Prince, 629
— — Strasbourg, 470
— — Tétouan, 950
— — Vaison-la-Romaine, 470
— — de Mactar, 1296
— — — Sfax, 1296
— — — Sousse (Kasbah), 1296
— Ariana, Geneva, 1261
— Astronomique de l'Observatoire de Paris, 466
— Atger, Montpellier, 469
— Basque de Bayonne, 468
— Bernadotte, Pau, 470
— Borély, Marseille, 469
— Calvet, 468
— Cantini, Marseille, 469
— Cantonal des Beaux-Arts, Lausanne, 1262

# INDEX OF INSTITUTIONS

Musée Carnavalet, 466
— Catalan des Arts et Traditions Populaires, Perpignan, 470
— Cernuschi, 466
— Cognacq-Jay, 466
— Constantin Meunier, Brussels, 158
— Curtius, 158
— d'Ansembourg, 158
— d'Anthropologie Préhistorique, Monaco, 946
— d'Archéologie, Nice, 469
— d'Armes de Bordj Nord, Fès, 950
— d'Arras, 468
— d'Art Africain de Dakar, 1146
— — Ancien, Brussels, 158
— — et d'Archéologie de l'Université de Madagascar, Antananarivo, 910
— — — d'Histoire, Fribourg, 1261
— — — Geneva, 1261
— — — Neuchâtel, 1262
— — — d'Industrie, St. Etienne, 470
— — Islamique, Kairiouan, 1296
— — — du Ribat, Monastir, 1296
— — Moderne, Brussels, 158
— — — de la Ville de Paris, 466
— d'Arts Decoratifs, Saumur, 470
— d'Enfidaville, Tunis, 1296
— d'Ennery, 466
— d'Ethnographie, Neuchâtel, 1262
— — de la Ville de Genève, 1261
— d'Histoire au Palais Granville, Besançon, 468
— — des Sciences, Geneva, 1261
— — Naturelle, Neuchâtel, 1262
— d'Instruments Anciens de Musique, Geneva, 1261
— d'Ozé, Alençon, 468
— de Bretagne, 470
— — Cirta, Constantine, 58
— — Dar Batha, Fès, 950
— — — Jamaï, Meknès, 950
— — — si Saïd, Morocco, 950
— — l'Air, Meudon, 466
— — l'Ancien Havre, 469
— — L'Annonciade, St. Tropez, 470
— — l'Armée, Paris, 466
— — l'Art Wallon, 158
— — l'Automobile, Le Mans, 469
— — l'Histoire de France, Paris, 466
— — l'Homme, 466
— — l'Horlogerie, Geneva, 1261
— — l'Hospice de la Potterie, Bruges, 158
— — l'Hôtel de Ville, Amboise, 468
— — l'Ile de France, 470
— — l'Impression sur Etoffes, Mulhouse, 469
— — l'Orangerie, 466
— — la Boverie, Liège, 158
— — — Côte d'Ivoire, Abidjan, 799
— — — Kasbah, Tanger, 950
— — — Marine, Marseille, 469
— — — Paris, 466
— — — Mer, Gorée, 1146
— — — Mode et du Costume, Paris, 466
— — — Poste, Amboise, 468
— — — Reine Bérengère, Le Mans, 469
— — — Révolution 1954–62, Algiers, 58
— — — Société Archéologique de Touraine, 470
— — — Vie Wallonne, Liège, 158
— — Normandie, 468
— — Picardie, 468
— — Richelieu, 470
— — Saint-Malo, 470
— — Setif, 58
— — Skikda, Algeria, 58
— — Tahiti et des Iles, 501
— — Tesse, Le Mans, 469
— — Tlemcen, Oran, 58
— — Village de Moknine, 1296
— Départemental de la Martinique, Fort de France, 500
— des Antiquités, Rabat, 950
— — — Volubilis, 950
— — — Nationales, 466
— — Arts Africains et Océaniens, Paris, 466

— — Décoratifs, 466
— — Traditionnels, Tétouan, 950
— — Augustins, Poitiers, 470
— — Toulouse, 470
— — Beaux-Arts, Agen, 467
— — — Angers, 468
— — — Beirut, 900
— — — Besançon, 468
— — — Bordeaux, 468
— — — Dijon, 468
— — — Ghent, 158
— — — Grenoble, 468
— — — La Chaux-de-Fonds, 1262
— — — Lille, 469
— — — Lyon, 469
— — — Marseille, 469
— — — Montréal, 251
— — — Nancy, 469
— — — Nantes, 469
— — — Nice, 469
— — — Nîmes, 469
— — — Orleans, 469
— — — Pau, 470
— — — Rennes, 470
— — — Tours, 470
— — — Valenciennes, 470
— — — "André Malraux", Le Havre, 468
— — — d'Ixelles, Brussels, 158
— — — et de Céramique, Rouen, 470
— — — — la Dentelle, Alençon, 468
— — deux Guerres Mondiales, 466
— — Docks Romains, Marseille, 469
— — Oudaia, Rabat, 950
— — Plans-Reliefs, Paris, 467
— — Thermes et de l'Hôtel de Cluny, 467
— — Trois Guerres, Diors, 468
— — Vins de Touraine, Tours, 470
— du Château, Maisons-Laffitte, 467
— — Compagnonnage, Tours, 470
— — Fer et du Charbon, Cour des Mineurs, 158
— — Louvre, 466
— — Mont Riant, Algiers, 58
— — Père Pinchon, Fort de France, 500
— — Petit Palais, Avignon, 468
— — — Paris, 466
— — Prieuré de Graville, Le Havre, 469
— — Quebéc, Montreal, 251
— — Verre, Liège, 158
— — Vieux-Logis, Nice, 469
— — Nîmes, 469
— Ducal "Les Amis du Vieux Bouillon", 157
— — et Château de Chantilly (Musée Condé), Chantilly, 468
— Fabre, 469
— Granet, 467
— Guimet, 467
— Gustave Moreau, 467
— Historique, Antananarivo, 910
— — Gorée, 1146
— — Saint-Gilles-les-Hauts, 500
— — de l'ancien Evêché, Lausanne, 1262
— — et Archéologique de l'Orléanais, Orleans, 469
— International d'Horlogerie, La Chaux-de-Fonds, 1262
— — du Long Cours, Saint Malo, 470
— Jacquemart André, 467
— Jenisch, Vevey, 1263
— Khalil Gibran, Besharre, 900
— Lapidaire de l'Abbatiale St.-Paul, Besançon, 468
— Léon-Dierx, Saint-Denis, 500
— Local, Cayenne, 499
— Magnin, 468
— Marmottan, Paris, 467
— Masséna, Nice, 469
— Matisse, Nice, 469
— Monétaire, 467
— Municipal, Limoges, 469
— — Oran, 58
— — Soissons, 470
— — National, Beirut, 900
— — Brazzaville, 358
— — Conakry, 627

— — Cotonou, 172
— — Lomé, 1292
— — Monte Carlo, 946
— — N'Djamena, 321
— — Port-au-Prince, 629
— — d'Abomey, 172
— — de Bois-Préau, Rueil-Malmaison, 467
— — — Carthage, 1296
— — — Céramique, Sèvres, 467
— — — Fontainebleau, 467
— — — Gitega, 230
— — — Kananga, 1995
— — — Lubumbashi, 1995
— — — la Coopération Franco-Américaine, Chauny, 468
— — — — Légion d'Honneur et des Ordres de Chevalerie, Paris, 467
— — — — Voiture et du Tourisme, Compiègne, 468
— — — Malmaison (Musée d'art et d'histoire de l'époque napoléonienne), Rueil-Malmaison, 467
— — — Préhistoire et d'Ethnographie du Bardo, Algiers, 58
— — des Antiquités, Algiers, 58
— — — Arts et Traditions Populaires, 467
— — — Beaux-Arts d'Alger, 58
— — — Granges de Port-Royal, Magny-les-Hameaux, 467
— — — Monuments Français, 467
— — — Techniques, Paris, 467
— — du Bardo, Tunis, 1296
— — — Château de Compiègne, 468
— — — — Pau, 470
— — — — Versailles, 467
— — — Moudjahid, El Biar, 58
— — — Niger, Niamey, 990
— — — Fernand Léger, Paris, 468
— — — Message Biblique Marc Chagall, Nice, 469
— — — Picasso de Vallauris "La Guerre et la Paix", 470
— — Suisse, Zürich, 1263
— Nissim de Camondo, 467
— Océanographique de Monaco, 946
— — Paris, 497
— Paul Gaugin, Tahiti, 501
— Picasso, Antibes, 468
— Populaire Comtois, Besançon, 468
— Régional Béarnais, Pau, 470
— Rodin, 467
— Romain Avenches, 1261
— Royal de l'Afrique Centrale, Brussels, 158
— — l'Armée et d'Histoire Militaire, Brussels, 158
— — et Domaine de Mariemont, 159
— Saint-Denis, Reims, 470
— Saint-Rémi, Reims, 470
— Sainte-Croix, Poitiers, 470
— Schoelcher, Point-à-Pitre, 499
— Stendhal, Grenoble, 468
— Vivant de Bujumbura, 230
— Wiertz, Brussels, 158
Museen der Stadt Gotha, 509
— — Köln, 541
— — Recklinghausen, 545
Musées, Le Mans, 469
— Communaux, Verviers, 159
— d'Archéologie, Marseille, 469
— et des arts Décoratifs de Liège, 158
— d'Art et d'Histoire de Nîmes, 469
— de l'Etat, Luxembourg, 908
— l'Institut Fondamental d'Afrique Noire, 1146
— Pau, 470
— Royaux d'Art et Histoire, 158
— — des Beaux-Arts de Belgique, 158
Museet for Danmarks Frihedskamp, 1940–45, 395
Musei Capitolini, Rome, 772
— Civici, Ferrara, 770
— di Storia ed Arte di Trieste, 773
— — Verona, 774

Museo Agrícola y Exposición Permanente, Havana, 364
— Antropológico de Caldas, Manizales, 350
— — del Banco Central del Ecuador, Guayaquil, 409
— — "Antonio Santiana", Quito, 408
— — Montané, Havana, 364
— Archeologico, Aquileia, 769
— — Arezzo, 769
— — Bari, 769
— — Florence, 770
— — Milan, 771
— — Sarsina, 773
— — Siena, 773
— — Venice, 774
— — al Teatro Romano, Verona, 774
— — e d'Arte della Maremma, Grosseto, 771
— — Nazionale, Cagliari, 769
— — — Cividale, 769
— — — Naples, 771
— — — Parma, 772
— — — di Spina, Ferra, 770
— — — dell'Umbria, Perugia, 772
— — — Regionale, Syracuse, Italy, 773
— — Sigismondo Castromediano, Lecce, 771
— Argentino de Ciencias Naturales "Bernardino Rivadavia", 70
— **Arqueología y Histórico de Comayagua, 630**
— Arqueológico, Arequipa, 1040
— — Cuzco, 1040
— — Valladolid, 1204
— — de Barcelona, 1202
— — — Burgos, 1203
— — — Ibiza, 1203
— — — Iquique, Instituto Profesional de Iquique, 327
— — — La Serena, 327
— — — Mérida, 1203
— — — Ovalle, 327
— — — Teotihuacán, 932
— — del Instituto de Estudios Ilerdenses, Lerida, 1203
— — Etnográfico e Histórico del Estado, Campeche, 932
— — "Federico Gálvez Durand" de la Gran Unidad Escolar "Santa Isabel", Huancayo, 1040
— — Municipal, Cartagena, 1203
— — Nacional, Bogotá, 349
— — — Madrid, 1201
— — Provincial, Seville, 1204
— — — Tarragona, 1204
— — — de Córdoba, 1203
— — "Rafael Larco Herrera", 1039
— — y Galerias de Arte del Banco Central del Ecuador, Quito, 408
— Aurelio Castelli, Siena, 773
— Bardini, Florence, 770
— Barraco, Rome, 772
— -Biblioteca Gabriela Mistral, Vicuña, 327
— — "Leoncio Prado", Huanuco, 1040
— Bodoniano, Parma, 772
— Bolivariano, Bogotá, 349
— — Caracas, 1956
— Botánico, Cordoba, Argentina, 71
— — Florence, 760
— Cabrera, Ica, 1040
— Canario, Las Palmas, 1204
— "Casa de Murillo", La Paz, 175
— Cerralbo, Madrid, 1201
— Charcas, Sucre, 175
— Chiaramonti e Braccio Nuovo, 1943
— Civico, Modena, 771
— — Padua, 772
— — Pesaro, 772
— — Vicenza, 774
— — Viterbo, 774
— — Archeologico, Bologna, 769
— — d'Arte Antica, Turin, 773
— — di Archeologia Ligure, Genoa, 770
— — — Belle Arti, Lugano, 1262
— — — Bolzano, 769
— — — Storia Naturale, Brescia, 769

— — — — Venice, 774
— — — — "G. Doria", Genoa, 771
— — — Torino, Turin, 773
— — — "Gaetano Filangieri", Naples, 771
— — Colonial, Antigua Guatemala, 625
— — Ciudad de El Tocuyo, 1956
— — de la Habana, 364
— — e Histórico "Enrique Udaondo", Luján, 71
— — Histórico y de Bellas Artes, Corrientes, 71
— — Comparativo de Zoología Marina, Viña del Mar, 327
— — Correr, Venice, 773
— — "Cristobal Mendoza", 1956
— — Dali, Figueras, 1203
— — d'Arte Antica, Milan, 771
— — — Moderna, Venice, 774
— — — Orientale, Venice, 774
— — — "Edoardo Chiossone", Genoa, 770
— — de Anatomía Humana "Manuel Villela", 326
— — Antropología de la Universidad Veracruzana, Jalapa, 932
— — Armas de la Nación, Buenos Aires, 70
— — Arqueologia, San Pedro de Atacama, 327
— — — de la Universidad de Trujillo, 1040
— — — y Etnología (del Instituto Ecuatoriano de Antropología y Geografía), Quito, 409
— — Arte, Lima, 1039
— — — Ponce, 1110
— — — Colonial, Bogotá, 349
— — — — Caracas, 1956
— — — — Quito, 409
— — — — de San Francisco, Santiago, 326
— — — Contemporáneo, Santiago, 326
— — — Costarricense, San José, 360
— — — de Cataluña, Barcelona, 1202
— — — e Historia de la Ciudad, Quito, 409
— — — Italiano, Lima, 1039
— — — "José Luis Bello y González", 932
— — — Moderno, Barcelona, 1202
— — — — Mexico City, 931
— — — — de Buenos Aires, 70
— — — — "Jaime Morera", Lérida, 1203
— — — Popular, Toluca, 932
— — — Americano, Santiago, 326
— — — Religioso, San Germán, 1110
— — — — Colonial, Panama, 1031
— — — y Artesania de Linares, 327
— — Artes Decorativas, Vedado, 364
— — — e Industrias Populares, Guatemala City, 625
— — Bellas Artes, Bilbao, 1203
— — — — Caracas, 1956
— — — — Sabadell, Barcelona, 1203
— — — — San Juan, P.R., 1110
— — — — Valencia, 1204
— — — — de la Boca, 70
— — — — "Rosa Galisteo de Rodriguez", Santa Fé, 72
— — Cerámica, Barcelona, 1202
— — — y Bellas Artes "Julián de la Herreira", Asunción, 1035
— — Ciencias Naturales, Caracas, 1956
— — — — Panama, 1031
— — — — Toluca, 932
— — — de la Escuela Militar "Eloy Alfaro", Quito, 409
— — — del Colegio de San José, 350
— — — y Antropológicas de Entre Rios, Paraná, 71
— — — — — "Juan Cornelio Moyano", 71
— — Concepción, 327
— — Entomologia, San José, 360
— — Geología, Barcelona, 1202
— — Historia, Sabadell, Barcelona, 1203
— — — de la Ciudad, Barcelona, 1202
— — — — Panama, 1031
— — — Eclesiastica "Anselmo Liorente y Lafuente", San José, 360

— — — Militar y Naval, San Juan, P.R., 1110
— — — Natural, Bogotá, 348
— — — San Miguel de Tucumán, 67
— — — de la Ciudad de Mexico, 931
— — — — San Pedro Nolasco, 326
— — — — Valparaíso, 327
— — — — "Javier Prado", 1039
— — — Primitiva, Madrid, 1202
— — Hualpen, 327
— — la Cultura Huasteca, Madero, 932
— — Dirección Nacional del Antártico, Buenos Aires, 70
— — — Encarnación, Madrid, 1201
— — — Familia Dominicana Siglo XIX, Santo Domingo, 404
— — — Paherra de Ciudad de Lérida, 1203
— — — Patagonia, Punta Arenas, 327
— — — "Perito Dr. Francisco P. Moreno", San Carlos de Bariloche, 72
— — — Policia Federal Argentina, 70
— — — República, Lima, 1039
— — — Universidad Austral de Chile, Valdivia, 327
— — La Plata, 71
— — las Bellas Artes, Toluca, 932
— — Casas Reales, Santo Domingo, 404
— — Culturas, Mexico City, 931
— — Descalzas Reales, Madrid, 1201
— — Mallorca, Palma de Mallorca, 1204
— — Mineralogía y Geología, 70
— — Música, Barcelona, 1202
— — Oro, Banco Central, San José, 360
— — Pedralbes, Barcelona, 1201
— — Pesca de la Escuela Naval del Mariel, 365
— — Pintura y Salas de Escultura, 1202
— — Pontevedra, 1203
— — Prehistoria y Arqueología, Santander, 1204
— **Remedios "José Maria Espinosa", 365**
— Reproducciones Artisticas, 1202
— San Carlos, Mexico City, 931
— Santa Cruz de Toledo, 1204
— Santiago, Antigua Guatemala, 625
— Transportes, Luján, 71
— Zamora, 1204
— Zoología, Barcelona, 1202
— — San José, 360
— degli Argenti, Florence, 770
— del Automóvil, Luján, 71
— — Carmen de Maipu, Santiago, 326
— — "Cau Ferrat", 1204
— — Ejército, Madrid, 1202
— — Estado de Jalisco, Guadalajara, 932
— — Greco, Toledo, 1204
— — Hombre Argentino, Luján, 71
— — — Dominicano, Santo Domingo, 404
— — — Panameño, Panama, 1031
— — Indio y del Gaucho, Tacuarembó, 1940
— — Libro Antiguo, Antigua Guatemala, 625
— — Oro, Bogotá, 350
— — Prado, 1202
— — Pueblo Español, 1202
— — Risorgimento, Brescia, 769
— — — Venice, 773
— — — e Istituto Mazziniano, Genoa, 770
— — — — Raccolte Storiche del Commune di Milano, 771
— — Tesoro di San Lorenzo, Genoa, 770
— — Virreinato, 1039
— dell' Età Cristiana, Brescia, 769
— — Opera del Duomo, Florence, 770
— della Casa Buonarotti, Florence, 770
— — Fiorentina Antica, Florence, 770
— — Civiltà Romana, Rome, 772
— delle Armi Antiche, Brescia, 769
— — Porcellane, Florence, 770
— Departamental de San José de Mayo, 1940
— di Antichità, Turin, 773

## INDEX OF INSTITUTIONS

**Museo di Architettura e Scultura Ligure, Genoa, 770**
— — Castelvecchio, Verona, 774
— — Palazzo Rosso, Genoa, 770
— — — di Venezia, Rome, 772
— — — Roma, 772
— — — S. Marco o dell' Angelico, 770
— — — Storia della Scienze a Firenze, 770
— — Villa Guinigi, Lucca, 771
— — Dillman S. Bullock, Angol, 327
— — Diocesano, Lérida, 1203
— — d'Arte Sacra, Brescia, 769
— — — — Volterra, 774
— — Doctor Francia, Yaguarón, 1035
— — Don Benito Juárez, Mexico City, 931
— — "Duca di Martina" alla Floridiana, Naples, 772
— — e Gallerie Nazionali di Capodimonte, Naples, 772
— — — Pinacoteca Nazionale di Palazzo Mansi, Lucca, 771
— — Egizio, Turin, 773
— — "Emilio Bacardi Moreau", Santiago, 365
— — Español de Arte Contemporáneo, Madrid, 1202
— — Etnográfico "Andres Barbero", Asunción, 1035
— — — de Esculturas de Cera, Mexico City, 931
— — — del Castello d'Albertis, Genoa, 770
— — — Juan B. Ambrosetti, Buenos Aires, 70
— — — y Arqueológico, Tzintzuntzan, 932
— — Etnológico, Barcelona, 1202
— — Etrusco, Bologna, 769
— — — Volterra, 774
— — Folklórico Araucano de Cañete "Juan A. Rios M.", 327
— — Geológico de la Universidad Nacional de Ingeniería del Perú, 1039
— — Giacomo Manzu, Ardea, 769
— — Giannettino Luxoro, Genoa, 770
— — Gregoriano Egizio, Vatican City, 1943
— — — Etrusco, 1943
— — — Profano, 1943
— — Hemingway, Havana, 364
— — Histórico de Entre Rios "Martiniano Leguizamón", 71
— — — — Guanabacoa, Havana, 365
— — — las Ciencias Médicas "Carlos J. Finlay", Havana, 365
— — — — San Roque, 1203
— — — Gral. "Rafael Urdaneta", Maracaibo, 1956
— — — "Miguel Paz Baraona" Municipio de Quimistan, 630
— — — Militar, Asunción, 1035
— — — — del Perú, Callao, 1040
— — — Nacional, Buenos Aires, 70
— — — — Montevideo, 1940
— — — — Santiago, 326
— — — Provincial de Rosario "Dr. Julio Marc", 71
— — — — — Santa Fé, 72
— — — Regional de Ayacucho, 1040
— — — — — Cuzco, 1040
— — — Sarmiento, Buenos Aires, 70
— — Horne, Florence, 770
— — Ignacio Agramonte, Camagüey, 365
— — Indigeno, San José, 360
— — Internazionale delle Ceramiche, Faenza, 770
— — **Jacinto Jijón y Caamaño de Arqueología e Historia, Quito, 409**
— — "Jorge Eliecer Gaitán", Bogotá, 350
— — José Marti, Havana, 365
— — Lapidario Estense, Modena, 771
— — Lázaro Galdiano, Madrid, 1202
— — Maffeiano, Verona, 774
— — Maritimo de Barcelona, 1202
— — "Martin Gusinde", Magallanes, 327
— — Mediceo, Florence, 770
— — Michoacano, Morelia, 932
— — Misional de Nuestra Señora de Regia, 1203

— Missionario-Etnologico, Vatican City, 1943
— Mitre, Buenos Aires, 71
— Monasterio de las Huelgas, Burgos, 1201
— — Tordesillas, Valladolid, 1201
— Monográfico de Ampurias, Gerona, 1203
— Morpurgo de Nilma, Trieste, 773
— Municipal, Guayaquil, 409
— "Brigadier-General Cornelio de Saavedra", 71
— de Arte Decorativo "Firma y Odilo Estevez", Rosario, 71
— — — Español "Enrique Larreta", Buenos Aires, 71
— — — Hispanoamericano "Isaac Fernández Blanco", 71
— — Bellas Artes, Montevideo, 1940
— — — — de Tandil, 72
— — — — "Juan B. Castagnino", Rosario, 72
— — — Madrid, 1202
— — — Matanzas, 365
— — San Telmo, 1203
— — Numismática y Medallística, Buenos Aires, 71
— — Oscar M. de Rojas, Cárdenas, 365
— Nacional, Bogotá, 349
— — Havana, 364
— — San José, 360
— — Tegucigalpa, 630
— — "David J. Guzmán, San Salvador, 422
— — de Aeronáutica, Buenos Aires, 71
— — Antropología, Bogotá, 350
— — — Mexico City, 931
— — — y Arqueologia, Lima, 1039
— — Arqueología, La Paz, 175
— — y Etnología de Guatemala, 625
— — Arte, La Paz, 175
— — — Decorativo, Buenos Aires, 71
— — — Moderno, Guatemala City, 625
— — — Oriental, Buenos Aires, 71
— — Artes Decorativas, 1202
— — — e Industrias Populares, Mexico City, 931
— — — Plásticas, Montevideo, 1940
— — Bellas Artes, Asunción, 1035
— — — — Buenos Aires, 71
— — — — Santiago, 326
— — Cerámica "Gonzalez Marti", Valencia, 1204
— — Ciencias Naturales, Madrid, 1202
— — Escultura Policromada, Valladolid, 1204
— — Etnología, Madrid, 1202
— — Historia, Guatemala City, 625
— — — Mexico City, 931
— — — Colonial, Cortés, 630
— — — Natural, Guatemala City, 625
— — — — Montevideo, 1940
— — — — Santiago, 326
— — la Campaña de Alfabetización, Havana, 365
— — — Casa de Moneda de Potosi, 175
— — — Cultura Peruana, Lima, 1039
— — Nicaragua, 988
— — del Virreinato, Tepotzotlán, 932
— Napoleónico, Havana, 365
— — di S. Martino, Elba, 772
— Naval, Madrid, 1202
— — de la Nación, Buenos Aires, 71
— — del Peru "C. de N. Julio J. Elias M.", Callao, 1040
— — y Aquarium, 1203
— Navale, Genoa, 770
— Nazionale, Ancona, 769
— — Chieti, 769
— — Messina, 771
— — Reggio Calabria, 772
— — Taranto, 773
— — (Bargello), Florence, 770
— — d'Abruzzo, L'Aquila, 771
— — d'Arte Orientale, Rome, 772
— — della Scienza e della Tecnica "Leonardo da Vinci", Milan, 771
— — — Scuola, Florence, 770

— — delle Arti e Tradizioni Popolari, Rome, 772
— — di Castel Sant' Angelo, Rome, 772
— — — Ravenna, 772
— — — S. Martino, 772
— — — Matteo, Pisa, 772
— — — Villa Giulia, Rome, 772
— — — Preistorico Etnografico Luigi Pigorini, 772
— — D. Ridola, Matera, 771
— — Romano, 773
— — G. A. Sanna, 773
— — Tarquiniense, 773
— — Numantino, Soria, 1204
— — Numismatico, Havana, 365
— — O'Higginiano y de Bellas Artes, Talca, 327
— — Paleocristiano, Aquileia, 769
— — — Tarragona, 1204
— — Pedagógico, Montevideo, 1940
— — — Carlos Stuardo do Ortiz, Santiago, 327
— — Petrográfico de la Dirección General de Geologia y Minas, Quito, 409
— — Picasso, Barcelona, 1203
— — Pietro Micca, Turin, 773
— — Pio Clementino, Vatican City, 1943
— — — Cristiano, Vatican City, 1943
— — Poey, 365
— — Poldi Pezzoli, Milan, 771
— — Popular Juan N. Madero, 71
— — Postal y Filatélico Correo Central de Lima, 1040
— — Profano, Vatican City, 1943
— — Provincial de Arqueologia "Wagner", Santiago del Estero, 72
— — — Bellas Artes, Zaragoza, 1204
— — — — "Emilio A. Caraffa", Córdoba, 71
— — — Ciencias Naturales "Florentino Ameghino", Santa Fe, 72
— — — — "Bartolomé Mitre" de Córdoba, 71
— — Provinciale Campano, Capua, 769
— — — d'Arte, Trento, 773
— — Regional Arqueológico "Bruning", de Lambayeque, 1040
— — — de Actopán, 932
— — — Ancash, 1040
— — — Antropologia e Historia, Guadalajara, 932
— — — — — Tuxtla Gutiérrez, Chiapas, 932
— — — Arqueologia Maya, Honduras, 630
— — — Artes Populares, Patzcuaro, Michoacán, 932
— — — Atacama, Copiapó, 327
— — — Chichicastenango, 625
— — — la Araucania, Temuco, 327
— — — los Padres Salesianos, 327
— — — Nayarit, 932
— — — Nuevo León, 932
— — — Oaxaca, 932
— — — Querétaro, 932
— — — Santa Monica, 932
— — — del Estado de Puebla, Puebla, 932
— — — San Miguel de Azapa, Arica, 327
— — Regionale Archeologico, Palermo, 772
— — Romano, Brescia, 769
— — Romántico, Madrid, 1202
— — Sacro, Vatican City, 1943
— — Social Argentino, Buenos Aires, 71
— — Sorolla, Madrid, 1202
— — Stibbert, Florence, 770
— — Storico Navale, Venice, 774
— — "Talavera", Ciudad Bolívar, 1956
— — -Taller José Clemente Orozco, Guadalajara, 932
— — Tazumal, San Salvador, 422
— — "Tenderi", Masaya, 998
— — Tesoro della Basilica di S. Francesco, Assisi, 769
— — Universitario, Medellin, 350
— — "Urdaneta" Histórico Militar, 1956
— — Vela, Ligornetto, 1262
— — Vetrario di Murano, Venice, 773

— y Archivo Histórico Municipal, Montevideo, 1940
— — — — de la Ciudad de la Habana, 365
— — Jardín Botánico de Montevideo, 1940
— — Necropolis del Puig des Molins, Ibiza, 1203
— Zoológico "Dámaso Antonio Larrañaga, Montevideo, 1940
Museos de la Universidad de Guanajuato, 932
Museovirasto, Helsinki, 431
Museu Arqueològic Artistic Episcopal de Vic, 1204
— Arqueológico, Lisbon, 1103
— — Infante D. Henrique, 1104
— -Biblioteca "Conde Castro Guimarães", 1103
— — da Casa de Bragança, Vila Viçosa, 1104
— Bocage, Lisbon, 1103
— Calouste Gulbenkian, Lisbon, 1103
— Carlos Reis, Tôrres Novas, 1104
— Carpológico do Jardin Botânico de Rio de Janeiro, 189
— da Cidade, Lisbon, 1103
— — Escola Nacional de Minas e Metalurgia, Ouro Preto, 189
— — Fauna, Rio de Janeiro, 189
— — Inconfidência, Ouro Prêto, 189
— — Quinta das Cruzes, Madeira, 1104
— — República, Rio de Janeiro, 189
— — Secção de Tecnologia do Serviço Florestal do Ministério da Agricultura, Rio de Janeiro, 189
— de Alberto Sampaio, Guimarães, 1104
— — Angola, Luanda, 61
— — Angra do Heroismo, The Azores, 1104
— — Arqueologia e Etnologia, São Paulo, 190
— — Arte Antiga: Instituto Femenino da Bahia, Salvador, 190
— — — Contemporanea, São Paulo, 190
— — da Bahia, Salvador, 190
— — de São Paulo, 190
— — do Rio Grande do Sul, 189
— — e História da Universidade Federal do Espírito Santo, Vitória, 190
— — — Moderna do Rio de Janeiro, 189
— — — Popular, Belém, 1103
— — Sacra, Madeira, 1104
— — — São Paulo, 190
— — Congo, Carmona, 190
— — Etnografia e História do Porto, 1104
— — — "Plínio Ayrosa" da Faculdade de Filosofia, Letras e Ciencias Humanas, São Paulo, 190
— — Évora, 1104
— — Francisco Tavares Proença Júnior, Castelo Branco, 1103
— — "Grão Vasco", Viseu, 1104
— — História Natural, Campinas, 189
— — — Coímbra, 1104
— — — Maputo, 952
— — Lamegó, 1104
— — Martins Sarmento, Guimarães, 1104
— — São Roque, Lisbon, 1103
— — Zoologia, Univ. de São Paulo, 190
— — do Departamento Nacional da Produção Mineral, Rio de Janeiro, 189
— — Estado, Recife, 189
— — Indio, Rio de Janeiro, 189
— — Instituto Geográfico e Histórico da Bahia, Salvador, 190
— — — Histórico e Geográfico Brasileiro, Rio de Janeiro, 190
— — Nina Rodrigues, Salvador, 190
— — Ouro, 190
— e Arquivo Histórico do Banco do Brasil, Rio de Janeiro, 190
— — Laboratório Mineralógico e Geológico, Lisbon, 1103
— — — Zoológico de Coímbra, 1104
— — — e Antropológico, Lisbon, 1103

— -Escola de Artes Decorativas, Lisbon, 1103
— Estadual, Goiânia, 189
— Etnográfico da Sociedade de Geografia, Lisbon, 1103
— Etnológico Dr, Leite de Vasconcelos, Lisbon, 1103
— Florestal "Octavio Vecchi", 190
— Freire de Andrade, Maputo, 952
— "Hipolito Cabaço", Alenquer, 1103
— Histórico, Belo Horizonte, 189
— — da Cidade do Rio de Janeiro, 190
— — do Piaui, Casa "Anisio Brito", Terezina, 190
— — Nacional, Rio de Janeiro, 190
— Imperial, Petrópolis, 189
— Instrumental da Escola Superior de Musica de Lisboa, Lisbon, 1103
— "Julio de Castilhos", 189
— Laboratório e Jardim Botanico, Lisbon, 1100
— Luis de Camões, Macau, 1108
— Maritimo "Almirante Ramalho Ortigão", Faro, 1104
— Militar, Lisbon, 1103
— Municipal do Funchal, Madeira, 1104
— — "Dr. Santos Rocha", 1104
— — Nacional, Rio de Janeiro, 190
— — de Arqueologia e Etnologia, Lisbon, 1103
— — — Arte Antiga, Lisbon, 1103
— — — — Contemporânea, Lisbon, 1103
— — — Belas Artes, 190
— — — História Natural, Lisbon, 1103
— — — "Machado de Castro", Coimbra, 1104
— — — Soares dos Reis, 1104
— — — dos Côches, 1103
— Numismático Português, 1103
— Oceanográfico, Rio Grande, 190
— Paranaense, Curitiba, 189
— — Emilio Goeldi, Belem, 189
— Paulista da Universidade de São Paulo, 190
— Rafael Bordalo Pinheiro, Lisbon, 1103
— Regional Abade de Baçal, Bragança, 1103
— — D. Bosco, Campo Grande, 189
— — da Huíla, Lubango, 61
— — de Olinda, Brazil, 189
— — — Uíge, 61
— — do Dundo, 61
— Repúblicano Convenção de Itú, 189
— S. Antonio, Faro, 1104
— Territorial do Amapá, Macapá, 189
Museum and Library of Maryland History, Maryland Historical Society, 1639
— attached to the Institute of Russian Literature of the U.S.S.R. Academy of Sciences, 1357
— Bali, Denpasar, 711
— Behnhaus, Lübeck, 544
— Bellerive, Zürich, 1263
— Boymans-van Beuningen, 968
— Bredius, 967
— Brouwershuis, Antwerp, 157
— Carnuntinum, Bad Deutsch Altenburg, 131
— de Drie Haringen, Deventer, 966
— — Schotze Huizen, 969
— — Waag, Deventer, 966
— — der bildenden Künste, Leipzig, 510
— — Natur, Gotha, 509
— — Stadt Worms, 545
— des Kunsthandwerks Leipzig Grassi- Museum, Leipzig, 510
— 20. Jahrhunderts, Vienna, 130
— Erasmus, Brussels, 158
— Folkwang, Essen, 542
— für Deutsche Geschichte, Berlin (East), 508
— — — Volkskunde, Berlin (West), 541
— — Geschichte der Stadt Dresden, 509
— — — Leipzig, 510
— — Hamburgische Geschichte, 543
— — Indische Kunst, Berlin (West), 541
— — Islamische Kunst, Berlin (West), 541

— — Kunst und Gewerbe, Hamburg, 543
— — — Kulturgeschichte, Dortmund, 542
— — — — Lübeck, 544
— — Kunsthandwerk, Dresden, 509
— — — Frankfurt, 542
— — Naturkunde der Humboldt- Universität, Berlin (East), 508
— — Ostasiatische Kunst, Berlin (West), 541
— — — Cologne, 542
— — Regionalgeschichte und Volkskunde, Gotha, 509
— — Ur- und Frühgeschichte, Berlin (East), 508
— — — Potsdam, 510
— — — (Forschungstelle), Schwerin, 510
— — — Stillfried/March, 131
— — — Thüringens in Weimar, 510
— — Völkerkunde, Berlin (West), 541
— — — Frankfurt, 542
— — — Leipzig, 510
— — — St. Gallen, 1262
— — — Vienna, 130
— — und Schweizerisches Museum für Volkskunde, Basel, 1261
— — Volkskunde, Berlin (East), 508
— — Volkskunst, Dresden, 509
— — Vor- und Frühgeschichte, Berlin (West), 541
— — — Frankfurt, 542
— Historische Landbouwtechniek, Wageningen, 969
— Holstentor, Lübeck, 544
— Kirchoferhaus, St. Gallen, 1262
— Library, Zanzibar, 1280
— Ludwig, Cologne, 542
— Mayer van den Bergh, Antwerp, 157
— mittelalterlicher österreichischer Kunst, 130
— Nasional, Jakarta, 711
— of Albanian Medieval Art, Korcë, 56
— — Ancient Art, Haifa, 744
— — Antiquities of Tel-Aviv-Yafo, 743
— — — the University and the Society of Antiquaries of Newcastle-upon- Tyne, 1470
— — Applied Arts and Crafts, Trojan, 222
— — — Sciences, Sydney, 97
— — Arab Antiquities, Baghdad, 726
— — Arabic Epigraphy, Damascus, 1277
— — Archaeology and Anthropology, Cambridge, 1468
— — — Ethnography, Riyadh, 1142
— — — Tiranë, 55
— — Architecture, Wrocław, 1077
— — Artillery, Signal Corps and Corps of Engineers, Leningrad, 1354
— — Classical Archaeology of the Tartu State University, 1356
— — Decorative Arts, Athens, 618
— — Earth Science of the Moscow State M.V. Lomonosov University, 1359
— — Education, Korcë, 56
— — Ethnography and Folklore, Tel-Aviv, 743
— — Fine Arts, Göteborg, 1242
— — — Houston, 1639
— — Frontier Guards, Moscow, 1355
— — History of the Uzbek People, Tashkent, 1335
— — Islamic Art, Cairo, 417
— — Japanese Art, Haifa, 744
— — Lincolnshire Life, Lincoln, 1469
— — Local Crafts and Industries, Burnley, 1468
— — London, 1466
— — Military History, Pleven, 221
— — Modern art, Belgrade, 1976
— — — Cairo, 417
— — — Kamakura, 822
— — — New York, 1639
— — — Oxford, 1470
— — Natural History, Göteborg, 1242
— — New Mexico, 1639

Museum of Northern British Columbia, 249
— — Prehistory, Sha'ar Ha-golan, 744
— — — of the Institute of Archaeology in the Hebrew University, Jerusalem, 744
— — Religion, Ulan Bator, 947
— — Science and Charles Hayden Planetarium, Boston, 1639
— — — — Engineering, Newcastle upon Tyne, 1470
— — — — Industry, Chicago, 1639
— — — — Technology, Tel-Aviv, 743
— — Sculpture, Leningrad, 1352
— — Sofia's History, Sofia, 221
— — South African Rock Art, Johannesburg, 1165
— — the Academic Maly Theatre of Opera and Ballet, 1359
— — — American Indian, 1640
— — — Arctic and the Antarctic, Leningrad, 1358
— — — City of New York, 1640
— — — Gorky Bolshoi Drama Theatre, 1359
— — — History and Reconstruction of the City of Moscow, 1355
— — — — of Azerbaijan of the Azerbaijan S.S.R. Academy of Sciences, Baku, 1355
— — — — Religion and Atheism, Leningrad, 1354
— — — Institute of Ethiopian Studies, Addis Ababa, 424
— — — Kirov Academic Theatre of Opera and Ballet, Leningrad, 1359
— — — Palaeontological Institute, 1359
— — — Revolution of the Lithuanian S.S.R., Vilnius, 1357
— — — September Uprising, Mihajlovgrad, 221
— — — State Academic Maly Theatre, 1360
— — — Struggle for National Liberation, Durrës, 55
— — — — — — — Liberation, Elbasan, 55
— — — — — — — Liberation, Gjirokastër, 55
— — — — — — — Liberation, Korcë, 56
— — — — — — — Liberation, Tiranë, 55
— — — Studium Biblicum Franciscanum, 744
— — Theatre and Music of the Estonian S.S.R., Tallinn, 1360
— — Transport and Technology of New Zealand Inc. (MOTAT), 982
— — Ukrainian Arts and Crafts, Saskatoon, 251
— — Uzbek History, Culture and Arts, Samarkand, 1356
— — Welsh Antiquities, University College of North Wales, 1472
— — Wood Carving and Mural Paintings, Trjavna, 222
— — Zoology, Riga, 1364
— Palaces and Parks in Pavlovsk, 1352
— — — — — — Petrodvoretz, 1352
— — — — — — Pushkin, 1352
— Plantin-Moretus, Antwerp, 157
— Rietberg, 1263
— Schwab, 1261
— Smidt van Gelder, Antwerp, 157
— van Hedendaagse Kunst, Ghent, 158
— — het Provinciaal Utrechts Genootschap voor Kunsten en Wetenschappen, Utrecht, 969
— Vleeshuis, Antwerp, 157
— voor Land- en Volkenkunde, Rotterdam, 968
— — Mechanisch Speelgoed, Deventer, 966
— Yamato Bunkakan, Nara City, 823
— Zoologicum Bogoriense, 711
— zu Allerheiligen, 1263
Muséum d'Histoire Naturelle, Geneva, 1262
— — — Nice, 469
— — — Saint-Denis, 500

— National d'Histoire Naturelle, Paris, 493
Museums Association, London, 1416
— — of Australia, Sydney, 87
— — — India, 660
— — — Israel, Tel-Aviv, 738
— Department, Valletta, 921
— of Malawi, Blantyre, 912
Museums-Bibliothek, Berlin (East), 508
— — Berlin (West), 541
Museumship "Buffel", Rotterdam, 968
Museumvereniging van de Nederlandse Cultuurgemeenschap in België, 150
Music Academy, Madras, 707
— Association of Ireland, Dublin, 730
— — — Korea, Seoul, 886
— Foundation of Pakistan, Karachi, 1019
— Library Association, Ann Arbor, 1601
— — of the Leningrad Conservatoire, 1350
— — — — State Philharmonic Society, 1350
Musical Academy, Belgrade, 1993
— — Zagreb, 1994
Musicological Society of Australia, Kensington, N.S.W., 87
Musik-Akademie der Stadt Basel, 1276
Musikakademie Zürich, 1276
Musikaliska Konstföreningen, 1235
Musikbibliothek der Stadt Leipzig, 508
Musikhistorisk Museum og Carl Claudius Samling, Copenhagen, 395
Musikhochschule, Lübeck, 608
— des Saarlandes, Saarbrücken, 608
Musikhögskolan i Göteborg, 1252
— — Malmö, 1252
— — Stockholm, 1252
Musikmuseet, Stockholm, 1241
Musikschule und Konservatorium Winterthur, 1276
Musikselskabet "Harmonien", Bergen, 1007
Muskingum College, New Concord, Ohio, 1844
Műszaki és Természettudományi Egyesületek Szövetsége, 634
Művelődési Minisztérium Levéltári Osztály, Budapest, 641
Művelődéskutató Intézet, Budapest, 637
Muzej Bosanske Krajine, Banja Luka, 1976
— grada Beograda, 1976
— — Splita, 1978
— — Zagreba, 1978
— ljudske revolucije SRS, Ljubljana, 1977
— Narodne Revolucije, Zagreb, 1978
— Nikole Tesle, Belgrade, 1976
— Pozjorisne Umetnosti, Belgrade, 1976
— Primenjene Umetnosti, Belgrade, 1976
— Srpske Pravoslavne Crkve, Dubrovnik, 1976
— za umjetnost i obrt, 1978
Muzeul Arheologic "Ulpia Traiana Sarmizegetusa", 1129
— Artei Lemnului, Suceava, 1128
— Banatului, Timişoara, 1129
— Biblioteca şi arhiva istorică a primei şcoli româneşti din Scheii Braşovului, 1127
— Brukenthal, Sibiu, 1129
— Cetatii Bran, 1127
— colectiilor de artă, Bucharest, 1127
— Curtea Veche, Bucharest, 1127
— de Arheologie din Mangalia, 1128
— — Artă, Cluj-Napoca, 1128
— — — Constanţa, 1128
— — — Ploieşti, 1129
— — — al R.S.R., Bucharest, 1126
— — — brîncovenească, 1127
— — — Contemporană Românească, Galaţi, 1128
— — — din Craiova, 1128
— — — — Iaşi, 1128
— — — — Tîrgu-Mureş, 1129
— Feudală D. Minovici, Bucharest, 1127
— Plastică "Fr. Storck şi C. Cuţescu Storck", Bucharest, 1126
— Istorie a Moldovei, Iaşi, 1128

— — — Municipiului Bucureşti, Bucharest, 1127
— — — — Partidului Comunist, a Mişcării Revoluţionare şi Democratice din România, Bucharest, 1127
— — — al Republicii Socialiste Romania, Bucharest, 1127
— — — — Transilvaniei, Cluj-Napoca, 1128
— — — — Aiud, 1127
— — — din Roman, 1129
— — — Etnografie şi Artă, Lugoj, 1128
— — — Gherla, 1128
— — — Naţională şi Arheologie din Constanţa, 1128
— — — Naturală din Sibiu, 1129
— — — "Grigore Antipa", Bucharest, 1127
— — — Sighişoara, 1129
— — — Turda, 1129
— — — Literature a Moldovei, Iaşi, 1128
— — — Ştiinţele Naturii, Aiud, 1127
— — — — Bacău, 1127
— — — — Focşani, 1128
— — — — Galaţi, 1128
— — — — Piatra-Neamţ, 1129
— — — — Ploieşti, 1129
— — — — Roman, 1129
— Deltei Dunarii, Tulcea, 1129
— din Blaj, 1127
— — Brăila, 1127
— — Sebes, 1129
— Etnografic al Moldovei, Iaşi, 1128
— — — Transilvaniei, Cluj-Napoca, 1128
— — — Radauţi, 1129
— — — Reghin, 1129
— "N. Grigorescu", Cîmpina, 1128
— Herbarul şi Grădina botanică, Cluj-Napoca, 1124
— Judeţean Arad, 1127
— — Argeş, Piteşti, 1129
— — Botoşani, 1127
— — Braşov, 1128
— — Bistriţa-Năsăud, 1127
— — Călărasi, 1127
— — Caraş Severin, Reşita, 1129
— — Covasna, Sf. Gheorghe, 1129
— — de Istorie, Alexandria, 1127
— — — Buzău, 1128
— — — Galaţi, 1128
— — — Piatra Neamţ, 1128
— — — Prahova, Ploieşti, 1129
— — Satu Mare, 1129
— — şi Artă, Bacău, 1127
— — — Etnografie din Focşani, 1128
— — Dimbovita, Tîrgovişte, 1129
— — din Tîrgu-Mureş, 1129
— — Gorj, Tîrgu-Jiu, 1129
— — Harghita, 1128
— — Hunedoara-Deva, 1128
— — Maramureş, Baia Mare, 1127
— — Suceava, 1129
— — Vilcea, 1129
— Literaturii Romane, Bucharest, 1127
— Maramureşean, Sighetul Marmaţiei, 1129
— Marinei Române, Constanţa, 1128
— memorial Bojdeuca Ion Creangă, Iaşi, 1128
— — B. P. Hascleu, Cimpina, 1128
— Militar Central, Bucharest, 1127
— Mineritului, Petroşani, 1128
— Olteniei, Craiova, 1128
— Peleş, Sinaia, 1129
— Petrolului, Ploieşti, 1129
— Politehnic, Iaşi, 1128
— "Portile de Fier", Turnu Severin, 1129
— Satului şi de Artă Populară, Bucharest, 1127
— Scriitorilor Tîrgovişteni, 1129
— Sporturilor, Bucharest, 1127
— Stiinţelor Experimentale- Observatorul Astronomic Popular, Bucharest, 1127
— Tării Crişurilor, Oradea, 1128

— Teatrului, Iași, 1128
— — National, Bucharest, 1127
— Tehnic "Prof. Ing. Dimitrie Leonida", Bucharest, 1127
— Theodor Aman, Bucharest, 1126
— Tiparului și Cartii Vechi Romanești, Tîrgoviște, 1129
— Unirii, Alba Julia, 1127
— — Iași, 1128
— Zoologic, Cluj-Napoca, 1128
Muzeum Aloise Jiráska a Mikoláše Alse, Prague-Liboc, 377
— — Archeologiczne, Poznań, 1076
— — i Etnograficzne, Łódź, 1076
— Etnograficzne, Cracow, 1076
— Husitského Revolučniho Hnutí, Zizkove, 379
— hl. m. Prahy, Prague, 377
— in. Leona Wyczólkowskiego, Bydoszcz, 1077
— Klementa Gottwalda, Prague, 377
— J. A. Komenského V. Uherském Brodě, 379
— V. I. Lenina, Prague, 377
— Lenina w Poroninie, Poronin, 1077
— mesta, Brna, 379
— Narodowe w Krakowie, Cracow, 1076
— — Gdańsk, 1077
— — Kielce, 1077
— — Poznań, 1076
— — Szczecin, 1077
— — Warsaw, 1075
— — Wroclaw, 1077
— Okregowe w Przemyslu, 1077
— — — Rzeszowie, 1077
— — — Toruniu, 1077
— skla, Harrachov, 377
— — a biżuterie, Jablonec nád Nisou, 379
— Sztuki, Łódź, 1076
— — Medalierskiej, Wrocław, 1077
— Techniki w Warszawie, Warsaw, 1075
— tělesné výchovy a sportu, Prague, 377
— Ukrajinskej kultúry, Svidnik, 379
— Vysočiny, Jihlava, 379
— Warmii i Mazur, Olsztyn, 1077
— Wojska Polskiego, Warsaw, 1076
Múzeumi Restaurátor- es Módszertani Központ, Budapest, 634
Muzeye Mardomchenassi, Teheran, 722
Muzička Akademija, Sarajevo, 1994
— Omladina BiH, Sarajevo, 1971
Muzium Negara, Kuala Lumpur, 916
Mwimba Tobacco Research Station, Kasungu, 912
Myasnikian (A.F.) State Public Library of the Armenian S.S.R., Erevan, 1348
Myasnikov, A. L., Institute of Cardiology, Moscow, 1342
Mycological Society of America, 1612
Myóhóin, 821
Myong Ji University, Seoul, 893
Mythic Society, Bangalore, 662

N

Nachrichtentechnische Gesellschaft im VDE (NTG), Frankfurt, 526
Nacionalna Sveučilisna Biblioteka, Zagreb, 1975
Naczelna Dyrekcja Archiwów Państwowych, Warsaw, 1072
Nádasdy Ferenc Múzeum, Sárvár, 646
Nafisi Technicom Institute, Teheran, 724
Nagano Prefectural Library, 820
Nagarjuna University, 695
Nagasaki Prefectural Library, 820
— University, 840
Nagoya Castle Donjon, 822
— City University, 859
— Institute of Technology, 840
— University, 840
— — Library, 820
Nagytétényi Kastélymúzeum, Budapest, 643

Naha Cultural Centre Library, 820
Nakorn Sithammarat Agricultural College, 1291
Namdaimoon Library, Seoul, 887
Namei Polytechnic Institute, Manila, 1060
Nanjing Aeronautical Engineering College, 337
— Engineering College, 337
— Institute of Geology and Mineral Resources, Jiangsu, 333
— Library, 335
— Meteorology College, 337
— University, 337
Nankai University, 338
Nanzan University, Nagoya, 866
Napier College, Edinburgh, 1544
Náprstkovo museum asijskych, africkych a americkych kultur, Prague, 377
Nara Art Museum, 823
— Kokoritsu Hakubutsukan, 823
— Medical University, 859
— Prefectural Library, 820
— Women's University, 842
Naritasan Museum, Chiba, 822
Narodna Biblioteka, Kragujevac, 1974
— — Niš, 1974
— — Pozarevac, 1974
— — "Kiril i Metodij", Sofia, 220
— — Socijalističke Republike Srbije, Belgrade, 1974
— — "Zika Popovic", Sabac, 1974
— galerija Ljubljana, 1977
— i univerzitetska biblioteka Bosne i Hercegovine, Sarajevo, 1975
— — — — "Kliment Ohridski", Skopje, 1976
— in studijska Knijžnica v. Trstu, Trieste, 768
— in univerzitetna Knijižnica, 1975
Národní galerie, Prague, 378
— muzej, Belgrade, 1976
— — Ljubljana, 1977
— muzeum, Prague, 378
— — Ustřední muzeologický Kabinet, Prague, 374
— technické Muzeum, Prague, 378
Národopisná společnost československá, 372
Národopisné muzeum horniho Poljizetí, Zeleny Brod, 379
Nasiryah Museum, 727
Nasjonalgalleriet, 1012
Nassau Public Library, 140
Nasson College, Me., 1741
Natal Institute of Immunology, 1160
— Museum, Pietermaritzburg, 1165
— Provincial Library Service, Pietermaritzburg, 1162
— Society Public Library, 1163
Nationaal Centrum voor Navorsingen over de Vlaamse Primitieven, Brussels, 154
— Hoger Instituut en Koninklijke Academie voor Schone Kunsten-Antwerpen, 170
— — voor Bouwkunst en Stedebouw-Antwerpen, 170
— Instituut voor Diergeneeskundig Onderzoek, Brussels, 153
— Lucht- en Ruimtevaartlaboratorium, Amsterdam, 962
— Scheepvaartmuseum (Steen), Steenplein, 157
National Academy of Art, New Delhi, 659
— — — Arts, Seoul, 885
— — — Córdoba, 62
— — — Design, New York, 1600
— — — Education, Washington, D.C., 1596
— — — Engineering, Washington, 1582
— — — Exact, Physical and Natural Sciences, Buenos Aires, 62
— — — Fine Arts, Buenos Aires, 62
— — — — Lisbon, 1097
— — — Geography, Buenos Aires, 62
— — — History, Buenos Aires, 62
— — — — Caracas, 1949

— — — — La Paz, 173
— — — — and Geography, Mexico City, 925
— — — Law and Social Sciences, Buenos Aires, 62
— — — — — Sciences, Córdoba, 62
— — — Letters, New Delhi, 659
— — — Medicine, Bogotá, 346
— — — — Buenos Aires, 62
— — — — Caracas, 1949
— — — — Lima, 1036
— — — — Rio de Janeiro, 178
— — — Pharmacy, Rio de Janeiro, 178
— — — Philosophy, Managua, 988
— — — Science, Mexico City, 925
— — — Sciences, Allahabad, 659
— — — — Buenos Aires, 62
— — — — of Panama, 1030
— — — — Seoul, 885
— — — — Washington, D.C., 1562
— Accelerator Centre, Stellenbosch, 1158
— Aeronautical Laboratory, Bangalore, 665
— Aeronautics and Space Administration (NASA), Florida, 1622
— Aerospace Laboratory, Tokyo, 816
— Agricultural Laboratories, Nairobi, 879
— — Library, Beltsville, 1624
— — Museum, Sofia, 221
— Air and Space Museum, Washington, D.C., 1640
— Animal Production Research Institute, Zaria, 993
— Archaeological Museum, Athens, 618
— — — Sofia, 221
— Archives, Cairo, 416
— — Dar es Salaam, 1280
— — Ibadan, 994
— — Port of Spain, 1293
— — Salisbury, Zimbabwe, 2002
— — Tripoli, 906
— — Wellington, N.Z., 981
— — and Library of Malaysia, 916
— — — Records Centre, Singapore, 1151
— — — Service, Washington, D.C., 1624
— — Division, Bangkok, 1284
— — of Fiji, Suva, 426
— — — Ghana, Accra, 612
— — — India, 673
— — — Malawi, Zomba, 912
— — — Malaysia, Petaling Jaya, 916
— — — Pakistan, Islamabad, 1024
— — — Zambia, Lusaka, 1998
— Army Museum, London, 1466
— Art-Collections Fund, London, 1413
— — Gallery, Hanoi, 1963
— — — Sofia, 221
— — — Wellington, 982
— Arts Centre, Ottawa, 250
— Assembly Library, Cairo, 417
— — — Islamabad, 1024
— — — Republic of Korea, Seoul, 887
— Association for Cultural Relations, Teheran, 721
— — of Power Engineers, Inc., Chicago, 1616
— Astronomy and Ionosphere Center, Ithaca, N.Y., 1621
— Atlas and Thematic Organization, Calcutta, 668
— — Project, Accra, 611
— Audubon Society, New York, 1612
— Autonomous University of Mexico, 933
— **Bank of Pakistan, Head Office Library, Karachi, 1024**
— Bar Association, Taipei, 341
— Biological Institute, Jakarta, 708
— — Standards Laboratories, Canberra, A.C.T., 93
— Book Council of Pakistan, Karachi, 1019
— — League, London, 1416
— — Trust, India, New Delhi, 660
— Botanic Gardens of South Africa, 1160
— Botanical Research Institute, Lucknow, 665

National Building Research Institute (C.S.I.R.), Pretoria, 1158
— Bureau of Economic Research, Cambridge, Mass., 1617
— — — Standards, Taipei, 341
— — — — Washington, D.C., 1623
— — — — Library, Gaithersburg, Md., 1625
— Cancer Centre, Tokyo, 815
— — Institute, Bethesda, Md., 1619
— — — of Canada, 245
— Capodistrian University of Athens, 619
— Cartographic Centre, Teheran, 721
— Center for Atmospheric Research (NCAR), Boulder, 1621
— — — Energy Management and Power, Philadelphia, 1880
— Central Library, Dar es Salaam, 1280
— — Taipei, 342
— — University, Chung-li, 343
— Centre for Educational Research, Cairo, 415
— — — Radiation Research and Technology, Cairo, 416
— — — Training and Education in Prosthetics (Bioengineering Unit), Glasgow, 1531
— — of Archives, Baghdad, 726
— — — Photography, Bath, 1415
— — — Scientific and Technological Information, Tel-Aviv, 739
— — — Social Research (EKKE), Athens, 618
— Cereals Research Institute, Ibadan, 992
— Chemical Institute, Jakarta, 708
— — Laboratory for Industry, 817
— — — of India, 665
— — Research Centre, Cairo, 416
— — — Laboratory (CSIR), Pretoria, 1157
— Chengchi University, Taipei, 343
— Cheng Kung University, Tainan, 343
— Chiao Tung University, Shinchu, 343
— Chung Hsing University, Taichung, 344
— College of Agricultural Engineering, Bedford, 1553
— — — Art and Design, Dublin, 736
— — — Education, Evanston, 1706
— Committee of Soviet Biochemists, Moscow, 1319
— — — — Biologists, Moscow, 1320
— — — — Chemists, Moscow, 1319
— — — — Geographers, 1320
— — — — Geologists, Moscow, 1320
— — — — Historians, Moscow, 1320
— — — — Mathematicians, Moscow, 1320
— — — — Physicists, Moscow, 1318
— — on Thermal and Mass Exchange, Moscow, 1318
— Computing Centre, Manchester, 1447
— Conservatory of Music, Teheran, 724
— Council for Research, Khartoum, 1229
— — — and Development, Jerusalem, 739
— — Scientific Research, Lusaka, 1997
— — of Applied Economic Research, New Delhi, 667
— — — Educational Research and Training, New Delhi, 667
— — on the Arts, Washington, 1598
— — — — Humanities, Washington, D.C., 1598
— Cultural History and Open-Air Museum, Pretoria, 1165
— Dairy Research Institute, Karnal, 666
— Defence Scientific and Technological Commission, Beijing, 334
— Design Council, Ottawa, 240
— Development Association, Dublin, 729
— Diet Library, Tokyo, 818
— Economic and Social Research Institute, Jakarta, 708
— Education Association of the United States, 1604
— — Society of Ceylon, Peradeniya, 1224

— Electrical Engineering Research Institute (CSIR), Pretoria, 1158
— Electrotechnical Institute, Jakarta, 708
— Endowment for the Arts, Washington, D.C., 1598
— — — Humanities, Washington, D.C., 1598
— Engineering Laboratory, Glasgow, 1448
— — — Washington, D.C., 1623
— Environmental Engineering Research Institute, Nagpur Maharashtra, 665
— Ethnographical Museum, Sofia, 221
— Eye Institute, Bethesda, Md., 1619
— Federation of Abstracting and Indexing Services, Philadelphia, 1617
— Film and Television Institute, Accra, 614
— — Archive, London, 1457
— — School, Beaconsfield, 1553
— Fisheries University of Busan, 887
— Food and Nutrition Commission, Lusaka, 1997
— — Research Institute (C.S.I.R.), Pretoria, 1158
— — — Ibarake, 813
— Foundation, New York, 1610
— — for Educational Research in England and Wales, 1442
— — on the Arts and the Humanities, Washington, D.C., 1598
— Free Library of Zimbabwe, Bulawayo, 2002
— Gallery, London, 1466
— — of Art, Washington, 1640
— — — Canada, 250
— — — Ireland, Dublin, 732
— — — Modern Art, New Delhi, 675
— — — Scotland, 1473
— — — Victoria, 97
— — — Zimbabwe, Salisbury, 2003
— Gas Turbine Establishment, Farnborough, 1448
— Geographic Society, Washington, 1606
— Geological Library, Beijing, 333
— Geophysical Research Institute, Hyderabad, 665
— Health and Medical Research Council, Woden, A.C.T., 92
— — Laboratories, Burma, 228
— Heart, Lung and Blood Institute, Bethesda, 1619
— Herbarium and Botanic Garden, Salisbury, Zimbabwe, 2001
— Historical Museum, Sofia, 221
— — — Tirana, 55
— Horticultural Research Institute, Ibadan, 993
— — — Station, Thika, 879
— Housing and Town Planning Council, Inc., London, 1412
— Industrial Research Institute, Seoul, 886
— Information and Documentation Centre, Cairo, 413
— Institute for Aeronautics and Systems Technology (CSIR), Pretoria, 1158
— — — Careers Education and Counselling, Hatfield, 1541
— — — Compilation and Translation, Taipei, 340
— — — Cultural Studies, Jakarta, 708
— — — Educational Research, Tokyo, 814
— — — Higher Education, Dublin, 736
— — — — Limerick, 736
— — — Instrumentation, Jakarta, 708
— — — Leprosy Research, Tokyo, 815
— — — Medical Research, London, 1443
— — — — Nigeria, Lagos, 994
— — — Metallurgy, Randburg, 1161
— — — Personnel Research (C.S.I.R.), Braamfontein, 1158
— — — Research Advancement, Tokyo, 816
— — — — in Dairying, 1525
— — — — Inorganic Materials, Ibaraki, 816

— — — the Behavioural Sciences, Jerusalem, 739
— — — Social Work, London, 1435
— — — Standards, Cairo, 416
— — — Telecommunications Research (C.S.I.R.), Johannesburg, 1158
— — — Transport and Road Research (CSIR), Pretoria, 1158
— — — Water Research (C.S.I.R.), Pretoria, 1158
— — of Adult Education (England and Wales), 1419
— — — Agricultural Botany, Cambridge, 1441
— — — — Engineering, Silsoe, 1441
— — — — Sciences, Ibaraki, 813
— — — Allergy and Infectious Diseases, Bethesda, Md., 1619
— — — Animal Health, Tokyo, 813
— — — — Industry, Chiba-city, 813
— — — Arthritis, Metabolism and Digestive Diseases, Bethesda, 1618
— — — Basic Education, New Delhi, 667
— — — Child Health and Human Development, Bethesda, Md., 1618
— — — Communicable Diseases, Delhi, 669
— — — Dental Research, Bethesda, Md., 1619
— — — Design, Ahmedabad, 666
— — — Development Administration, Bangkok, 1291
— — — — and Cultural Research, Gaborone, 177
— — — Dramatic Art at the University of New South Wales, 113
— — — Economic and Social Research, London, 1442
— — — Education, Kampala, 1312
— — — — Seoul, 886
— — — — Washington, D.C., 1618
— — — — Materials, Taipei, 341
— — — Environmental Health Sciences, Bethesda, Md., 1619
— — — Folk Heritage, Islamabad, 1019
— — — General Medical Sciences, Bethesda, Md., 1619
— — — Genetics, Shizuoka, 815
— — — Geology and Mining, Jakarta, 708
— — — Health, Tokyo, 815
— — — — and Family Welfare, New Delhi, 707
— — — Historical and Cultural Research, Islamabad, 1028
— — — Hospital Administration, Tokyo, 815
— — — Hygienic Sciences, Tokyo, 815
— — — Industrial Health, Kanagawa, 815
— — — — Psychology, London, 1434
— — — Japanese Literature Library, Tokyo, 819
— — — Labour Studies, Bedford Park, S.A. 101
— — — Mental Health, Chiba, 815
— — — Metallurgy, Jakarta, 708
— — — Modern Languages, Islamabad, 1028
— — — Neurological and Communicative Disorders and Stroke, Bethesda, 1619
— — — Nutrition, Hyderabad, 669
— — — — Tokyo, 816
— — — Oceanography (C.S.I.R.), Goa, 665
— — — Oceanology, Jakarta, 708
— — — Pakistan Studies, Islamabad, 1028
— — — Psychology, Islamabad, 1028
— — — Public Administration, Karachi, 1021
— — — — — Lahore, 1021
— — — — — Lusaka, 1998
— — — Radiological Sciences, Chiba, 816
— — — Rural Development, Hyderabad, 672
— — — Science and Technology, Manila, 1048

– – – Social Sciences, New York, 1615
– – on Aging, Bethesda, 1619
– Institutes of Health, Bethesda, 1618
– Kaohsiung Institute of Technology, Kaohsiung, 345
– Labour Institute, New Delhi, 671
– Library, Athens, 618
– – Baghdad, 726
– – Bangkok, 1284
– – Calcutta, 674
– – Georgetown, 628
– – Kathmandu, 954
– – Manila, 1049
– – Ottawa, 248
– – Rangoon, 228
– – Riyadh, 1142
– – Singapore, 1151
– – Teheran, 722
– – Tiranë, 55
– – and Archives, Addis Ababa, 424
– – – Tarawa, 881
– – for the Blind, London, 1459
– – of Australia, Canberra, 95
– – – Beijing, 335
– – – Higher Education and Culture, Mogadishu, 1153
– – – Ireland, 731
– – – Latakia, 1277
– – – Malaysia, Kuala Lumpur, 916
– – – Malta, Valletta, 921
– – – Medicine, Bethesda, 1624
– – – New Zealand, Wellington, 981
– – – Nigeria, Lagos, 994
– – – Pakistan, Karachi, 1023
– – – Scotland, 1450
– – – the Lithuanian S.S.R., 1348
– – – Wales, 1450
– – Service, Belize City, 171
– – – Boroko, 1032
– Malaria Eradication Programme, Delhi, 669
– Maritime Museum, Haifa, 744
– – – London, 1466
– Measurement Laboratory, Washington, D.C., 1623
– Mechanical Engineering Research Institute (C.S.I.R.), Pretoria, 1158
– Memorial Museum, Amman, 875
– Mental Health Association, Arlington, Va., 1610
– Metallurgical Laboratory, Bihar, 665
– Meteorological Library, Bracknell, 1452
– Museum, Bangkok, 1284
– – Bloemfontein, 1164
– – Bulawayo, 2002
– – Damascus, 1277
– – Doha, 1114
– – Kaduna, 995
– – Lagos, 995
– – Mogadishu, 1153
– – Monrovia, 904
– – Seoul, 887
– – Singapore, 1151
– – Tarawa, 881
– – Wellington, N.Z., 982
– – and Art Gallery, Gaborone, 177
– – – – – Port-of-Spain, 1293
– – Library, Wellington, N.Z., 981
– – of American Art, Washington, D.C., 1640
– – – – History, Washington, D.C., 1640
– – – Antiquities of Scotland, 1473
– – – Applied and Decorative Arts, Sofia, 221
– – – Art and Archaeology, Rangoon, 229
– – – Bulgarian Architecture, Veliko Tarnovo, 222
– – – – Literature, Sofia, 221
– – – – -Soviet Friendship, Sofia, 221
– – – Ecclesiastical History and Archaeology, Sofia, 221
– – – History, Taipei, 342
– – – India, 675
– – – Ireland, Dublin, 732

– – – Malaysia, 916
– – – Man, Ottawa, 250
– – – Military History, Sofia, 221
– – – Modern Art, Baghdad, 727
– – – – Kyoto, 821
– – – – Tokyo, 821
– – – Natural History, New Delhi, 675
– – – – – Washington, D.C., 1640
– – – – Sciences, Ottawa, 250
– – – Nepal, Kathmandu, 954
– – – Pakistan, 1024
– – – Science and Education, Taipei, 342
– – – – – Technology, Ottawa, 250
– – – Tanzania, Dar es Salaam, 1281
– – – the Philippines, Manila, 1049
– – – – Revolutionary Movement of Bulgaria, Sofia, 221
– – – Victoria, 98
– – – Wales, 1472
– – – Western Art, Tokyo, 821
– – – Kenya, Kitale, 879
– Museums and Monuments of Zimbabwe, Salisbury, 2002
– – Board, Lusaka, 1998
– – of Canada, Ottawa, 250
– – – Kenya, Nairobi, 879
– – – Sri Lanka, 1226
– Music Council, New York, 1601
– Natural History Museum, Sofia, 221
– Observatory, Athens, 618
– Oceanic and Atmospheric Administration, Environmental Data and Information Service, Environmental Science Information Center, Library and Information Services Division, 1624
– Organisation for the Protection of Historical Monuments, Teheran, 722
– Organization for Drug Control and Research, Giza, 415
– Palace Museum, Taipei, 342
– Park Museum, Mweya, 1312
– – – Paraa, 1312
– Pedagogical University, Bogotá, 352
– Physical Institute, Jakarta, 708
– – Laboratory, Teddington, 1448
– – – of India, New Delhi, 665
– – – – Israel, Jerusalem, 740
– – Research Laboratory (C.S.I.R.), Pretoria, 1157
– Picture Gallery and Alexander Soutzos Museum, Athens, 618
– Planning Agency, Kingston, Jamaica, 800
– Polytechnic Institute, Zacateno, 943
– – Museum, Sofia, 221
– – School, Quito, 411
– Portrait Gallery, London, 1466
– – – Washington, D.C., 1640
– Postal Museum, London, 1466
– – – Ottawa, 250
– Productivity Council, New Delhi, 667
– Radio Astronomy Observatory, Green Bank, 1621
– Railway Museum, York, 1471
– Remote Sensing Centre, Farnborough, 1448
– Renaissance Museum, Gjirokastër, 55
– – Korcë, 56
– Reprographic Centre for Documentation, Hatfield, 1541
– Research Center for Disaster Prevention, Tokyo, 817
– – Centre, Cairo, 414
– – Council, Washington, D.C., 1596
– – – of Canada, Ottawa, 244
– – – – Italy, Rome, 762
– – – – the Philippines, 1048
– – Development Corporation, London, 1449
– – – – of India, New Delhi, 665
– – Institute for Mathematical Sciences (C.S.I.R.), Pretoria, 1158
– – – – – Metals, Tokyo, 816

– – – – Nutritional Diseases, Tygerberg, 1155
– – – – Oceanology (CSIR), Stellenbosch, 1158
– – – – Pollution and Resources, Saitama, 816
– – – of Agricultural Economics, Tokyo, 813
– – – – – Engineering, Ibaraki, 813
– – – – – Brewing, Tokyo, 817
– – Laboratory for Conservation of Cultural Property, Lucknow, 667
– – – of Metrology, Tokyo, 816
– Root Crops Research Institute, Umuahia, 993
– School of Anthropology and History, Mexico, 944
– – – Drama, New Delhi, 707
– – – Librarianship and Archives, Mexico, 944
– – – Music, Addis Ababa, 425
– Science and Technology Development Agency, Lagos, 992
– – – – Library and Documentation Centre, Ibadan, 994
– – – Council of Pakistan, 1022
– – – – Sri Lanka, Colombo, 1225
– – – Taipei, 341
– – – Development Board, Manila, 1048
– – – Foundation (NSF), Washington, D.C., 1611
– – – Museum, Seoul, 887
– – – Teachers Association, Washington, D.C., 1611
– – Scientific Commissions of the State Council (Cabinet), Beijing, 334
– – Research Institute of Tuberculosis, Tbilisi, 1384
– Sculpture Society, New York, 1601
– Society (Church of England), London, 1435
– – for Art Education, Rochdale, 1413
– – – Clean Air, Brighton, 1438
– – – Medical Research, Washington, D.C., 1610
– – – the Study of Education, Chicago, 1604
– – of Mural Painters, Inc., New York, 1601
– – – Printers, Sculptors and Printmakers, London, 1414
– – – Professional Engineers, Washington, D.C., 1616
– Staff College for Educational Planners and Administrators, New Delhi, 706
– Sugar Institute, Kanpur, 666
– Swedish Board of Universities and Colleges, Stockholm, 1243
– Taiwan Academy of Arts, Taipei, 345
– – Arts Center, Taipei, 342
– – Institute of Technology, Taipei, 344
– – Normal University, 344
– – Science Hall, Taipei, 342
– – University, 344
– Technical University of Athens, 621
– Timber Research Institute (CSIR), Pretoria, 1159
– Trust for Historic Preservation in the United States, Washington, D.C., 1600
– – – Places of Historic Interest or Natural Beauty, 1412
– – – Scotland, Edinburgh, 1412
– Tsing Hua University, Hsinchu, 349
– Tuberculosis Institute, Bangalore, 669
– University, Jakarta, 720
– – Manila, 1055
– – of Colombia, Bogota, 351
– – – Engineering, Lima, 1042
– – – Iran, Eveen, 724
– – – Ireland, 733
– – – Lesotho, Roma, 903
– – – Malaysia, Bangi, 916
– – – Singapore, 1151

# INDEX OF INSTITUTIONS

National University of Singapore Library, 1151
— — — the Littoral, Santa Fé, 75
— — — North-East, Corrientes, 76
— — — South, Bahia Blanca, 77
— — — Tucumán, 77
— Vegetable Research Station, Warwick, 1441
— Veterinary Research Institute, Vom, 993
— War College Library, Taipei, 342
— Water Research Institute, Burlington, Ont., 246
— Wildlife Federation, Washington, 1612
— Zoological Gardens of South Africa, 1160
Nationale Forschungs- und Gedenkstätten der klassischen deutschen Literatur in Weimar, 510
— — — — — deutschen Literatur, Zentralbibliothek der deutschen Klassik, 508
— Plantentuin Van België, Meise, 154
— Raad voor Landbouwkundig Onderzoek TNO, The Hague, 961
Nationalekonomisk Forening, Copenhagen, 390
Nationalekonomiska Foreningen, Stockholm, 1236
— Institutionen, Åbo, 440
Nationalgalerie, Berlin (East), 508
Nationalhistoriske Museum paa Frederiksborg, 395
Nationalities Institute, Beijing, 332
Nationalmuseet, Copenhagen, 395
Nationalmuseum, Stockholm, 1241
Nationalökonomische Gesellschaft, Vienna, 120
Natishvili, A. N., Institute of Experimental Morphology, Tbilisi, 1328
Natsagdorj Museum, Ulan Bator, 947
Natturufraedistofnun Íslands, Reykjavik, 657
Natural Environment Research Council (NERC), Swindon, 1445
— — — — Computing Service, Birkenhead, 1446
— — — — Research Vessel Services, Barry, 1446
— — — — Scientific Services, 1446
— History Museum, Iași, 1135
— — of the University of Basrah, 727
— Resources Council of America, Tracy's Landing, Md., 1612
— Development College, Lusaka, 1999
— Library of the U.S. Department of the Interior, Washington, 1625
— — Research Organization, Jerusalem, 740
— Science Museum, Plovdiv, 221
— — Tiranë, 55
— Sciences and Engineering Research Council of Canada, 245
Naturalistes Belges, Brussels, 152
— Parisiens, 451
Nature Conservancy, Arlington, Va., 1612
Naturforschende Gesellschaft, Bamberg, 532
— — Freiburg i. Br., 532
— — Schaffhausen, 1256
— — in Basel, 1256
— — Bern, 1256
— — Zürich, 1256
Naturhistorische Gesellschaft zu Hannover, 523
Naturhistorisches Museum, Bern, 1261
— — Mainz, 544
— — St. Gallen, 1263
— — Vienna, 130
Naturhistorisk Museum, Aarhus, 395
Naturhistoriska Riksmuseet, Stockholm, 1241
Naturkundliches Bildungszentrum, Munich, 544
Naturvetenskapligaforskningsrådet, Stockholm, 1238
Naturwissenschaftliche Gesellschaft Winterthur, 1256

Naturwissenschaftlicher Verein, Hamburg, 523
— — für Kärnten, Klagenfurt, 122
— — zu Bremen, 529
Natuurhistorisch Museum te Maastricht, 968
Naucna biblioteka, Dubrovnik, 1975
— — Pula, 1975
— — Rijeka, 1975
— — Split, 1975
— — Zadar, 1975
Nava Nalanda Pali Mahavihara, 668
Naval Aerospace Medical Institute, Pensacola, 1619
— Historical Library, London, 1451
— Institute of Technology, Philippines, 1060
Navoi Literature Museum, Tashkent, 1335
Navy Department Library, Washington, D.C., 1625
— Records Society, London, 1423
Nazareth College, Michigan, 1762
— — of Rochester, N.Y., 1818
Ndërmarrja e studimeve inxhiniero-gjeologjike e gjeodezike, Tiranë, 55
Ndola Public Library, 1998
Neandertal-Museum, Düsseldorf, 542
Near East Center, Philadelphia, 1880
— — School of Theology, Beirut, 902
— — — Library, Beirut, 900
Nebraska Wesleyan University, 1793
Nechustan Pavilion-Timna Excavation, 743
NED University of Engineering and Technology, Karachi, 1026
Nederlands Agronomisch-Historisch Instituut, 960
— Bibliotheek en Lektuur Centrum, The Hague, 957
— Cultuurhistorisch Instituut, Pretoria, 1155
— Documentatiecentrum voor Ontwikkelingslanden, Amsterdam, 964
— Economisch Instituut, Rotterdam, 957
— Genootschap voor Internationale Zaken, The Hague, 960
— Historisch Genootschap, Utrecht, 957
— Instituut voor Hersenonderzoek, Amsterdam, 961
— — — Onderzoek der Zee, Texel, 962
— — Praeventieve Gezondheidszorg TNO, Leiden, 961
— Interuniversitair Demografisch Instituut, The Hague, 962
— Kostuummuseum, The Hague, 967
— Orgaan voor de Bevordering van de Informatieverzorging-NOBIN, 961
— Postmuseum, 967
— Psychoanalytisch Genootschap, Utrecht, 959
— Theater Instituut, Amsterdam, 956
Nederlands-Zuidafrikaanse Vereniging, Amsterdam, 958
Nederlandsche Centrale Organisatie voor Toegepast-Natuurwetenschappelijk, The Hague, 961
— Vereniging voor Druk- en Boekkunst, 958
Nederlandse Dierkundige Vereniging, Wageningen, 959
— Entomologische Vereniging, Amsterdam, 959
— Kunststichting, Amsterdam, 956
— Museumvereniging, Amsterdam, 957
— Mycologische Vereniging, Amsterdam, 959
— Natuurkundige Vereniging, Utrecht, 959
— Organisatie voor Zuiver-Wetenschappelijk Onderzoek (Z.W.O.), 961
— Ornithologische Unie, Arnhem, 959
— Stichting voor Statistiek, The Hague, 957
— Toonkunstenaarsraad, Amsterdam, 956
— Tuinbouwrand, The Hague, 956

— Vereniging van Bibliothecarissen, Documentalisten en Literatuur Onderzoekers, Middelburg, 957
— — Pedagogen, Onderwijskundigen en Andragologen, Utrecht, 957
— — Specialisten in de Dento-Maxillaire Orthopaedie, Nijmegen, 958
— — voor Heelkunde, Utrecht, 958
— — Internationaal Recht, The Hague, 957
— — Logica en Wijsbegeerte der Exacte Wetenschappen, Amstelveen, 959
— — Microbiologie, Bilthoven, 958
— — Microscopie, Rotterdam, 959
— — Neurologie, Utrecht, 958
— — Orthodontische Studie, Apeldoorn, 958
— — Parasitologie, Amsterdam, 959
— — Psychiatrie, 958
— — Tropische Geneeskunde, Amsterdam, 958
— — Weer- en Sterrenkunde, The Hague, 959
— Zootechnische Vereniging, Voorburg, 959
Nedlands College of Advanced Education, W.A., 117
Negarestan Museum, Teheran, 722
Negev Museum, Israel, 744
Nehézipari Műszaki Egyetem, Miskolc, 653
— — Központi Könyvtára, Miskolc, 641
Nehézvegyipari Kutató Intézet, Budapest, 639
Nehru Memorial Museum and Library, New Delhi, 674
Nei Monggol Library, Hohhot, 325
— — University, Hohhot, 337
Neilson Hays Library, 1284
Nekrasov (N. A.) House-Museum, Leningrad, 1357
Nelson Memorial Public Library, Apia, 1964
— Provincial Museum (N.Z.), 982
Nelson-Atkins Gallery of Art, Washington, D.C., 1640
Nemirovich-Danchenko, V. I., Flat-Museum, Moscow, 1360
— — Studio-School attached to the Moscow Art Theatre, 1388
Nemzetközi Kulturális Intézet, Buadapest, 635
Nencki, M., Institute of Experimental Biology, Warsaw, 1068
Nepal-Bharat Sanskritikt Kendra Pustakalay, Kathmandu, 954
Nepean College of Advanced Education, Kingswood, N.S.W., 113
Népművelési Intézet, Budapest, 634
Néprajzi Múzeum, Budapest, 643
Netherlands-America Institute Library, Amsterdam, 964
— Centre of the International PEN, 958
— Energy Research Foundation (ECN), The Hague, 962
— School of Business, Nijenrode Breukelen, 973
Neue Galerie, Kassel, 543
— — der Stadt Linz, 131
— Nationalgalerie, Berlin (West), 541
— Sammlung, Munich, 544
Neumann János Számítógéptudományi Társaság, Budapest, 636
Neuro- and Electrophysiolcgy Research Unit, Tygerberg, 1156
Neurochemical Pharmacology Unit (M.R.C.), Cambridge, 1444
Neuro Chemistry Research Group, Tygerberg, 1156
Neuroendocrinology Unit (M.R.C.), Newcastle, 1444
Neurological Prostheses Unit (M.R.C.), London, 1444
Neurology, Psychiatry and Neurosurgery Association, Hanoi, 1962
Neuropsychiatric Research Institute, Tokyo, 815

WORLD OF LEARNING

New Amsterdam Technical Institute, Berbice, Guyana, 628
— Asia College, Shatin, 1561
— Brunswick Museum, 250
— College, Edinburgh, 1490
— — Oxford, 1524
— — Library, Oxford, 1463
— — Toronto, 309
— — of the University of South Florida, Sarasota, 1695
— England Aquarium, Boston, 1620
— — College, Henniker, 1796
— — Conservatory of Music, Boston, 1757
— — Institute, Ridgefield, 1620
— English Art Club, 1414
— Hall, Cambridge, 1484
— Hampshire State Library, Concord, 1631
— Jersey Institute of Technology, Newark, 1798
— — State Library, Trenton, 1631
— Mexico Highlands University, 1802
— — Institute of Mining and Technology, Socorro, 1802
— — Solar Energy Institute, Las Cruces, 1802
— — State University, 1802
— Orleans Museum of Art, 1640
— — Public Library, 1626
— Plymouth Astronomical Society Observatory, 980
— School for Social Research, 1818
— South Wales Institute of Technology, Broadway, N.S.W., 113
— — State Conservatorium of Music, Sydney, 113
— Territories Public Libraries, Cultural Services Department, Hong Kong, 1559
— University of Lisbon, 1106
— — Ulster, Coleraine, 1555
— — — Library, 1554
— York Academy of Medicine, 1610
— — — Library, 1630
— — — Sciences, 1597
— — Botanical Garden, 1620
— — Cultural Centre in association with Fairleigh Dickinson University, 1640
— — Historical Society, 1606
— — Law Institute Library, 1630
— — Public Library, 1627
— — State Library, 1631
— — University, 1818
— — Libraries, 1633
— Zealand Academy of Fine Arts, Wellington, 978
— — Agricultural Engineering Institute, Canterbury, 984
— — Archaeological Association, Palmerston North, 977
— — Association of Clinical Biochemists (Inc.), Auckland, 977
— — — — Scientists, Wellington, 978
— — Atomic Energy Committee, Lower Hutt, 978
— — Biochemical Society, Auckland, 977
— — Cartographic Society (Inc.), Wellington, 977
— — Computer Society, Lower Hutt, 977
— — Council for Educational Research, Wellington, 980
— — Dairy Research Institute, Palmerston North, 980
— — Dietetic Association, Wellington, 977
— — Ecological Society, Christchurch, 977
— — Geographical Society, 978
— — Geological Survey, Lower Hutt, 982
— — Hydrological Society, Wellington, 977
— — Institute of Agricultural Sciences, Wellington, 977
— — — Architects (Inc.), 978
— — — — Chemistry, Christchurch, 977
— — — — Economic Research, Wellington, 980
— — — — Food Science and Technology, Auckland, 977

— — — — Foresters (Inc.), Darfield, 977
— — — — International Affairs, Wellington, 978
— — — — Surveyors, Wellington, 977
— — Institution of Engineers, Wellington, 978
— — Law Society, Wellington, 978
— — Library Association Inc., 978
— — Limnological Society, Christchurch, 977
— — Marine Sciences Society, Wellington, 977
— — Mathematical Society, Auckland, 977
— — Medical Association, Wellington, 978
— — Meteorological Society, Wellington, 977
— — Microbiological Society, Palmerston North, 977
— — National Research Advisory Council, Wellington, 978
— — — Society for Earthquake Engineering, Wellington, 978
— — Psychological Society, Christchurch, 977
— — Society for Electron Microscopy (Inc.), Palmerston North, 978
— — — — Parasitology, 977
— — — of Animal Production (Inc.), Hamilton, 977
— — — — Dairy Science and Technology, Palmerston North, 977
— — — — Plant Physiologists, Palmerston North, 977
— — — — Soil Science, Lower Hutt, 977
— — Statistical Association, Wellington, 977
— — Technical Correspondence Institute, Lower Hutt, 987
— — Veterinary Association, Wellington, 977
Newark Public Library, N.J., 1626
Newberry College, S.C., 1886
— Library, 1629
Newcastle College of Advanced Education, Waratah, 113
— Region Public Library, N.S.W., 96
— upon Tyne City Libraries, 1454
— — — Polytechnic, 1545
Newcomen Society for the Study of the History of Engineering and Technology, 1439
Newfoundland Forest Research Centre, St. John's, 244
— Museum, St. John's, 250
Newham Public Libraries, 1452
Newnham College, Cambridge, 1484
— Library, 1461
Newman College, Parkville, 104
Newport College—Salve Regina, R.I., 1884
Neytendasamtokin (The Consumers' Union), Reykjavík, 656
Nezu Art Museum, Tokyo, 821
Ngee Ann Technical College, Singapore, 1152
Nghe-Tinh Museum, Vinh, 1963
NHMRC Social Psychiatry Unit, Canberra, 100
Niagara University, N.Y., 1818
Nicaraguan Academy of Languages, Managua, 988
Nichibei Hogaku Kai, Tokyo, 805
Nicholas Copernicus University of Torun, 1081
— Kopernik Museum, Frombork, 1077
Nichols College, Dudley, Mass., 1757
Nicholls State University, Thibodaux, 1738
Nicholson Museum of Antiquities, 97
Niederösterreichische Landesbibliothek, Vienna, 128
Niederösterreichisches Landesarchiv, Vienna, 127
— Landes-Museum, 130
Niedersächsische Landesbibliothek, 536
— Staats- und Universitäts-bibliothek, Göttingen, 536
Niedersächsisches Hauptstaatsarchiv in Hannover, 539

INDEX OF INSTITUTIONS

— Landesmuseum, Hanover, 543
— Staatsarchiv, Aurich, 538
— — Buckeburg, 538
— — in Oldenburg, 540
— — Osnabruck, 540
— — Wolfenbüttel, 540
Nigeria Educational Research Council, Lagos, 994
— Medical Council, Lagos, 991
Nigerian Academy of Science, Ibadan, 991
— Bar Association, Ibadan, 991
— Economic Society, Ibadan, 991
— Geographical Association, Ibadan, 991
— Institute for Oceanography and Marine Research, Lagos, 993
— — — Oil Palm Research, Benin City, 993
— — — Trypanosomiasis Research, Kaduna, 993
— — of International Affairs, Victoria Island, 991
— — — Management, Lagos, 992
— — — Road and Building Construction, Lagos, 994
— — — Social and Economic Research, Ibadan, 994
— Library Association, Enugu, 992
— Political Science Association, Port Harcourt, 992
— Society for Microbiology, Ibadan, 992
— Stored Products Research Institute, Lagos, 993
— Veterinary Medical Association, Zaria, 992
Nihon Bunseki Kagaku-Kai, Tokyo, 810
— Chiri Gakkai, 806
— Denpun Gakkai, Tokyo, 803
— Dobutsu Gakkai, 809
— Dokubungakkai, 806
— Eibungakkai, 807
— Esperanto Gakkai, 807
— Furanso-go Furansu-bungaku-kai, 807
— Gakko-hoken Gakkai, Tokyo, 805
— Gakujutsu Kaigi, 803
— — Shinko-kai, Tokyo, 809
— Gengogakkai, Tokyo, 807
— Hakko Kogakukai, Osaka, 803
— Hakubutsukan Kyokai, Tokyo, 804
— Hikaku Kyoiku Gakkai, Tokyo, 805
— Ikushi Gakkai, Tokyo, 803
— -Indogaku-Bukkyôgakukai, Tokyo, 811
— Ishi-Kai, Tokyo, 807
— Ju-i Gakkai, 803
— Kakuigakukai, Tokyo, 807
— Kasai Gakkai, Tokyo, 812
— Keizai Kenkyu Center, Tokyo, 814
— Kikai Gakkai, 812
— Koho Gakkai, Tokyo, 805
— Koko Geka Gakkai, Tokyo, 807
— Kokogakkai, Tokyo, 806
— Koku Eisei Gakkai, Tokyo, 807
— Kokuka Gakkai, Tokyo, 807
— Kyoiku Gakkai, Tokyo, 806
— — -shakai Gakkai, Tokyo, 806
— — -shinri Gakkai, Univ. of Tokyo, 806
— Kyosei Shikagakkai, Tokyo, 807
— Masui Gakkai, Tokyo, 807
— Naika Gakkai, 807
— Oyo Shinri-gakkai, 811
— Rinrigakukai, 811
— Ronen Igakukai, Tokyo, 807
— Seishin Shinkei Gakkai, 807
— Seppyo Gakkai, Tokyo, 810
— Shukyo Gakkai, 811
— Syôyakugakkai, Kyoto, 807
— Tokei Gakkai, Tokyo, 805
— Toshokan Kyokai, Tokyo, 804
— University, 866
— Zaisei, Gakkai, 805
— Zoen Gakkai, Tokyo, 804
— Zosen Gakkai, Tokyo, 804
Niigata Prefectural Library, 820
— University, 842
— — Library, 820
Nijmeegs Museum "Commanderie van St. Jan", Nijmegen, 968

2095

# INDEX OF INSTITUTIONS

Nikko Research Center Ltd., Tokyo, 814
"Nikola Tesla" Association of Societies for Promotion of Technical Sciences in Yugoslavia, Belgrade, 1969
"Nikolaj Pavlovic" Higher Institute of Fine Arts, Sofia, 227
Nikolayev Admiral S. O. Makarov Shipbuilding Institute, 1389
Nimba Research Laboratory, 904
Ningxia Library, Yinchuan, 335
Ninnaji Reihóden, 821
Nipissing College, North Bay, 270
Nippon Arerugi Gakkai, Tokyo, 807
— Bitamin Gakkai, Kyoto, 807
— Bungaku Kyokai, Tokyo, 807
— Bunko Gakkai, Tokyo, 810
— Butsuri Gakkai, 810
— — -Kagaku Kenkyu kai, 810
— Byorigakkai, Tokyo, 807
— Chikusan Gakkai, 803
— Chikyu Denki Ziki Gakkai, 810
— Chishitsu Gakkai, 810
— Chô Gakkai, Tokyo, 809
— Dai-Yonki Gakkai, Tokyo, 810
— Densenbyo Gakkai, Tokyo, 807
— Denshi Ken-bikyo Gakkai, Tokyo, 810
— Dental University, Tokyo, 867
— Dobutsu Shinri Gakkai, Tokyo, 811
— Dojyo-Hiryo Gakkai, Tokyo, 803
— Dokumentêsyon Kyokai, Tokyo, 804
— Dokyo Gakkai, Tokyo, 811
— Eisei Gakkai, Tokyo, 807
— — Konchu Gakkai, 809
— Engeki Gakkai, Tokyo, 804
— Gakushin, 802
— Gan Gakkai, Tokyo, 807
— Ganka Gakkai, Tokyo, 808
— Ganseki Kibutsu Kosho Gakkai, 810
— Geka Gakkai, Tokyo, 808
— Genshiryoka Gakkai, Tokyo, 812
— Gyosei Gakkai, Tokyo, 805
— Hifu-ka Gakkai, Tokyo, 808
— Hikaku Bungakukai, Tokyo, 807
— Hinyoki-ka Gakkai, Tokyo, 808
— Hoi Gakkai, Tokyo, 808
— Hoshakai Gakkai, Tokyo, 805
— Hôshasen Eikyo Gakkai, Chiba, 808
— Hotetsu-Gakkai, Kyoto, 805
— — Shika Gakkai, Tokyo, 808
— Iden Gakkai, 809
— Igaku Hoshasen Gakkai, Tokyo, 808
— Institute for Biological Science, Tokyo, 816
— Jibi-Inkoka Gakkai, Tokyo, 808
— Jidoseigyo Gakkai, Kyoto, 812
— Jinrui Iden Gakkai, Tokyo, 809
— Jinruigaku Kai, Tokyo, 811
— Junkan-ki Gakkai, Kyoto, 808
— Junkatsu Gakkai, Tokyo, 812
— Kagaku-Gijutsu Joho Sentah, Tokyo, 804
— Kagaku Kyoiku Gakukai, Tokyo, 806
— Kagakukai, 810
— Kagakushi Gakkai, Tokyo, 809
— Kaibo Gakkai, 808
— Kaiho Gakkai, Chuo University, 805
— Kai-Rui Gakkai, 809
— Kaisui Gakkai, Tokyo, 810
— Kaiyo Gakkai, Tokyo, 810
— Kazan Gakkai, Tokyo, 810
— Keiei Gakkai, Tokyo, 805
— Keiho Gakkai, Tokyo, 805
— Keizai Seisaku Gakkai, Tokyo, 805
— Kekkaku-byo Gakkai, Tokyo, 808
— Kenchiku Bunken Sentah, Tokyo, 804
— — Gakkai, Tokyo, 804
— Kessho Gakkai, Tokyo, 810
— Ketsueki Gakkai, Kyoto, 808
— Kikan-Shokudo-ka Gakkai, Tokyo, 808
— Kin Gakkai, Tokyo, 809
— Kinzoku Gakkai, Tokyo, 812
— Kisei-chu Gakkai, Tokyo, 808
— Kisho Gakkai, Tokyo, 810
— Kogakukai, Tokyo, 812
— Kogyokai, Tokyo, 812
— Kokai Gakkai, Tokyo, 810
— Kokogaku Kyokai, Tokyo, 806
— Koku Gakkai, Tokyo, 812
— Kokusai Seiji Gakkai, Tokyo, 805
— Kontyû Gakkai, 809
— Koseibutsu Gakkai, 810
— Koshu-Eisei Kyokai, Tokyo, 808
— Kyobe Shikkan Gakkai, Tokyo, 808
— Mingei-Kan, Tokyo, 821
— Mokuzai Gakkai, Tokyo, 803
— Naíbumpigaku-Kai Tobu-bakai, Tokyo, 808
— Nendo Gakkai, Tokyo, 811
— Nensho Kenkyu-kai, Tokyo, 811
— Nogakkai, 803
— Nogei Kagaku Kai, 803
— Nogyo Keizai Gakkai, Tokyo, 804
— — -Kisho Gakkai, 811
— No-Shinkei Gek Gakkai, Tokyo, 808
— Onkyo Gakkai, Tokyo, 811
— Onsei Gakkai, Tokyo, 807
— Orient Gakkai, Tokyo, 806
— Oyo-Dobutsu-Konchu Gakkai, Tokyo, 809
— Rai Gakkai, 808
— Research Center Ltd., Tokyo, 814
— Rikusui Gakkai, 809
— Ringakukai, Tokyo, 804
— Rodo-ho Gakkai, Tokyo, 805
— Romazikai, 807
— Rosiya Bungakkai, Tokyo, 807
— Saikingakkai, 808
— Sakumotsu Gakkai, Tokyo, 804
— Sanka Fujinka Gakkai, Tokyo, 808
— Sanshi Gakkai, 804
— Seibutsu Kankyo Chosetsu Kenkyukai, Tokyo, 809
— Seibutsuchiri Gakkai, 806
— Seikagakukai, Tokyo, 809
— Seikei Geka Gakkai, Tokyo, 808
— Seiri Gakkai, Tokyo, 808
— Seitai Gakkai, Sendai, 809
— Seiyo Koten Gakkai, Kyoto, 807
— Seiyoshi Gakkai, Osaka, 806
— Seizi Gakkai, Tokyo, 805
— Shakai Gakkai, 811
— — Shinri Gakkai, Tokyo, 811
— Shashin Gakkai, Tokyo, 812
— — Sokuryo Gakkai, Tokyo, 812
— Shiho Gakkai, Tokyo, 805
— Shika Hôshasen Gakkai, Tokyo, 808
— — Hozon Gakkai, Tokyo, 808
— — Igakkai, Tokyo, 808
— Shimbun Gakkai, Tokyo, 811
— Shinkei Gakkai, Tokyo, 808
— Shinkeikagaku Kyokai, Tokyo, 808
— Shinrigakkai, Tokyo, 811
— Shogyo Gakkai, Tokyo, 805
— Shokaki-byo Gakkai, Tokyo, 808
— Shokubutsu Gakkai, 809
— — Byori Gakkai, 804
— — Seiri Gakkai, Kyoto, 809
— Shoni-ka Gakkai, Tokyo, 809
— Sokuchi Gakkai, Tokyo, 811
— Sugaku Kai, 810
— — Kyoiku Gakkai, 810
— Suisan Gakkai, Tokyo, 804
— Taiiku Gakkai, Tokyo, 806
— Teiinoshujutsu Kenkyukai, Tokyo, 809
— Tekko Kyokai, 812
— Temmon Gakkai, 811
— Tonyo-byo Gakkai, Tokyo, 809
— Toshi Keikaku Gakkai, Tokyo, 804
— Toshokan Gakkai, Tokyo, 804
— Uirusu Gakkai, Tokyo, 809
— Yakugaku-Kai, Tokyo, 809
— Yakuri Gakkai, Tokyo, 809
— Yukagaku Kyokai, Tokyo, 811
— Yuketsu Gakkai, Tokyo, 809
Nizami Institute of Literature, Baku, 1326
— Museum of Literature and Linguistics, Baku, 1325
Nizamiah and Japal-Rangapur Observatories and Centre of Advanced Study in Astronomy, Hyderabad, 671
Njala University College, 1149
Njegošev Muzej, Cetinje, 1976
Nobel Foundation, 1233
Nobelstiftelsen, 1233
Nogami Memorial Noh Drama Research Institute, Tokyo, 863
Nógrádi Sándor Múzeum, Salgótarján, 646
Noguchi Institute, Tokyo, 817
— Memorial Institute for Medical Research, Legon, 613
Nogyo-Doboku Gakkai, Tokyo, 812
— Ho Gakkai, Tokyo, 805
— -Kikai Gakkai, 804
Noordbrabants Museum, s'Hertogenbosch, 967
Norddeutsches Landesmuseum, Hamburg, 543
Nordenfjeldske Kunstindustrimuseum, 1013
Nordisk Byggedag, Copenhagen, 392
— Institut for Teoretisk Atomfysik (NORDITA), Copenhagen, 393
— Kollegium for Marinbiologi, Blomsterdalen, 1009
Nordiska Afrikainstitutet, Uppsala, 1238
— Institutet för samhällsplanering, Stockholm, 1237
— Museet, 1241
— samfundet för Latinamerika-forskning, Stockholm, 1238
Nordjyllands Kunstmuseum, Aalborg, 395
Nordjyske Landsbibliotek, 394
— Musikkonservatorium, Det, Ålborg, 401
Nordland Fylkesmuseum, Bodø, 1010
Norfolk and Norwich Institute for Medical Education, 1488
— County Library, Norwich, 1454
— Museums Service, Norwich, 1470
Norges Almenvitenskapelige Forskningsråd, 1008
— byggforskningsinstitutt, Oslo, 1009
— Fiskeriforskningsråd, Trondheim, 1008
— Geologiske Undersøkelse, 1009
— geotekniske institutt, Oslo, 1009
— Handelshøgskole, 1017
— Kunstnerråd, Oslo, 1007
— Laererhøgskole, Trondheim, 1016
— Landbrukshøgskole, 1018
— Landbrukshøgskoles Bibliotek, 1010
— Landbruksvitenskapelige Forskningsråd, 1008
— Musikkhøgskole, Oslo, 1018
— skipsforskningsinstitutt, Trondheim, 1009
— Teknisk-Naturvitenskapelige Forskningsråd, 1008
— Tekniske Høgskole, Trondheim, 1016
— — — Biblioteket, 1010
— — Vitenskapsakademi, Trondheim, 1008
— Veterinarhøgskole, 1017
Norinsho Toshokan, Tokyo, 819
Norman Mackenzie Art Gallery, Regina, 251
Norraena Félagid, 656
Norrköpings Stadsbibliotek, 1239
Norrøna Felagid í Føroyum, Tórshavn, 402
Norsk Arkeologisk Selskap, Oslo, 1007
— Botanisk Forening, Trondheim, 1008
— Farmaceutisk Selskap, Oslo, 1008
— Folkemuseum, 1012
— Forening for Internasjonal Rett, 1007
— Geologisk Forening, 1008
— Historisk Forening, 1007
— institutt for by- og regionforskning, Oslo, 1009
— — — Luftforskning, Kjeller, 1010
— — — vannforskning, Oslo, 1010
— Kirurgisk Forening, Oslo, 1008
— Kjemisk Selskap, 1008
— Lokalhistorisk Institutt, Oslo, 1007
— Musikk-informasjon, Oslo, 1007
— Polarinstitutt, 1009
— Regnesentral, Oslo, 1007
— Senter for Informatikk, Oslo, 1007, 1010
— Sjøfartsmuseum, Oslo, 1012
— Slektshistorisk Forening, Oslo, 1007
— Teknisk Museum, Oslo, 1012
— Utenrikpolitisk Institutt, Oslo, 1009
Norske Akademi for Sprog og Litteratur, Oslo, 1007
— Architekters Landsforbund, Oslo, 1007

— Forfatterforening, 1008
— Kunst- og Kulturhistoriske Museer, Oslo, 1007
— Laegeforening, Oslo, 1008
— Medicinske Selskab, Oslo, 1008
— Meteorologiske Institutt, Oslo, 1009
— PEN-klubb, Lysaker, 1008
— Sivilingeniørs Forening, Oslo, 1008
— Tannlaegeforening, Den, Oslo, 1008
— Videskaps Akademi i Oslo, 1004
North Adams State College, Mass., 1757
— American Spanish Language Academy, New York, 1607
— Brisbane College of Advanced Education, 114
— Carolina Agricultural and Technical State University, Greensboro, 1829
— — Central University, Durham, 1829
— — State University at Raleigh, 1835
— — Wesleyan College, Rocky Mount, 1829
— Caucasian Institute of Ore Mining and Metallurgy, Orjonikidze, 1379
— Central College, Naperville, 1706
— China Agricultural Mechanization College, Beijing, 336
— — — University, Zhengzhou, 339
— Dakota State University, 1839
— Georgia College, 1701
— Hamgyong Provincial Library, Chongjin, 883
— Hwanghae Provincial Library, Sariwon, 883
— Japan College, Sendai, 869
— of Scotland College of Agriculture, 1550
— -Ossetian K. L. Khetagurov Memorial Museum, Ordjonikidze, 1358
— — — State University, 1365
— — Medical Institute, 1383
— Park College and Theological Seminary, Chicago, 1706
— Pyongan Provincial Library, Shinuiju, 883
— Staffordshire Polytechnic, 1545
— Texas State University, 1899
Northamptonshire Libraries, Northampton, 1454
Northeast College of Technology, Shenyang, 338
— Heavy Machinery College, Fulaerji, 336
— London Polytechnic, 1543
— Louisiana University, Monroe, 1739
— Missouri State University, Kirksville, 1787
Northeastern Complex Scientific Research Institute, Magadan, 1322
— Education and Library Board, Library Service, Ballymena, 1554
— Hill University, Shillong, 696
— Illinois University, Chicago, 1706
— Oklahoma State University, Tahlequah, 1858
— Technical Institute, Korat, 1291
— University, Boston, 1757
Northern Arizona University, Flagstaff, 1645
— Forest Research Centre, Edmonton, Alberta, 244
— Illinois University, 1706
— Jiaotong University, Beijing, 336
— Luzon State College of Agriculture, Cagayan, 1060
— Michigan University, Marquette, 1762
— Montana College, Havre, 1792
— Research Station, Midlothian, 1440
— State College, Aberdeen, S.D., 1888
— Technical College, Ndola, 1999
— — Institute, Chiangmai, 1291
Northland College, Ashland, 1932
Northrop University, Inglewood, Calif., 1656
Northumberland County Library, Morpeth, 1454
Northwest Christian College, Eugene, 1863
— Industrial University, Xian, 339
— Light Industry College, Xian, 339
— Missouri State University, 1787
— Nazarene College, Nampa, 1702

— Telecommunications College, Xian, 339
— University, Xian, 339
Northwestern College, Orange City, 1728
— Extra-Mural Polytechnic Institute, Leningrad, 1376
— Museum of Science and Industry, Manchester, 1470
— Oklahoma State University, Alva, 1858
— State University of Louisiana, 1739
— University, Evanston, 1706
— — Libraries, 1632
Norway-America Association, Oslo, 1007
Norwegian Academy of Science and Letters in Oslo, 1004
— Cultural Council, Oslo, 1007
— Nobel Committee (Nobel Peace Prize), Oslo, 1006
— Nobel Institute, Oslo, 1006
— Seismic Array (NORSAR), Kjeller, 1010
Norwich Cathedral Dean and Chapter Library, 1459
— School of Art, 1551
— University, Northfield, Vt., 1915
Notre Dame College of Ohio, 1844
— — Joshi Daigaku, Kyoto, 867
— — University, Cotabato City, 1056
— — Women's College, Kyoto, 867
Nottingham City Museum and Art Gallery, 1470
— Natural History Museum, 1470
Nottinghamshire County Library, Nottingham, 1454
Nova Scotia Agricultural College, 290
— — College of Art and Design, 290
— — Legislative Library, Halifax, 247
— — Museum, 250
— — Research Foundation Corporation, Dartmouth, 244
— — Scotian Institute of Science, 242
Növényélettani Intézet, Szeged, 638
Növényvédelmi Kutató Intézet, 637
Novocherkassk Institute of Engineering Amelioration, 1372
— Museum of the History of the Don Cossacks, 1356
— S. Orjonikidze Polytechnic Institute, 1376
Novodevichy Monastery Museum, 1356
Novosibirsk Agricultural Institute, 1370
— M. I. Glinka State Conservatoire, 1388
— Institute of Electrical Engineering, 1378
— — Engineers for Geodesy, Aerial Photography and Cartography, 1382
— — — National Economy, 1373
— — — Orthopaedics and Restorative Surgery, 1386
— — — Railway Engineers, 1389
— — — Soviet Co-operative Trade, 1373
— — — Tuberculosis, 1384
— — — Water Transport Engineers, 1389
— V. V. Kuibyshev Civil Engineering Institute, 1380
— State Medical Institute, 1383
— — University, 1365
— Telecommunications Institute, 1378
Nuclear Institute for Agriculture and Biology (NIAB), Faisalabad, 1022
— Physics Institute, Shanghai, 332
— — Research Unit, Johannesburg, 1182
— Research and Education Institute, Izmir, 1305
— — Centre, Bandung, 710
— — — Edmonton, Alberta, 257
— — — Inshas, 416
— — — Świerk, 1070
— — — Żerań, Warsaw, 1070
— — Institute, Baghdad, 725
Nuffield College, Oxford, 1524
— Foundation, London, 1420
— Laboratories of Comparative Medicine, London, 1446
— Lake Kariba Research Station, Johannesburg, 1182
— — — — Salisbury, 2003
— Radio Astronomy Laboratories: Jodrell Bank, 1447

Nukada Institute for Medical and Biological Research, Chiba, 815
Nukus University, 1365
Numismatische Kommission, Vienna, 119
Nuruosmaniye Library, 1300
Nushi Brothers Museum, Vuno, 56
Nutrition Research Institute, Cairo, 415
— Society, London, 1429
— — of Canada, St. Anne de Bellevue, 242
— — — New Zealand, Auckland, 977
— — — Nigeria, Ile-Ife, 992
Ny Carlsberg, Glyptotek, 395
— Carlsbergfondet, Copenhagen, 389
Nyack College, N.Y., 1818


O

Oak Ridge Associated Universities, 1614
Oakland University, Rochester, Mich., 1763
Oakwood College, Huntsville, 1643
Oates Memorial Library and Museum and Gilbert White Museum, Alton, 1471
Oberhessisches Museum und Gailsche Sammlungen der Stadt Giessen, 543
Oberlausitzische Bibliothek der Wissenschaften bei den Städtischen Kunstsammlungen Görlitz, 509
Oberlin College, Ohio, 1844
Oberösterreichischer Museaverein 120
Oberösterreichisches Landesarchiv, Linz, 127
— Landesmuseum, Linz, 131
Oberrheinisches Dichter-Museum, Karlsruhe/Baden, 543
Obihiro University of Agriculture and Veterinary Medicine, Hokkaido, 842
Oblastní muzeum Jihovýchodní Moravy v Gottwaldově, 379
"Obrazcov Čiflik" Institute of Seed Science, Seed Production and Leguminous Crops, Ruse, 219
Obraztsov's Central State Puppet Theatre Museum, 1360
Observatoire, Geneva, 1258
— Cantonal, Neuchâtel, 1258
— d'Antananarivo, 910
— de Haute-Provence, 455
— — l'Université de Bordeaux, 459
— — Lyon, 459
— — Marseille, 459
— — Nice, 459
— — Paris, 459
— — Strasbourg, 459
— National, Besançon, 459
— Royal de Belgique, 155
Observatoires du Pic du Midi et de Toulouse, 459
Observatorio Astrofísico "Manuel Foster", Santiago, 325
— Astronómico, Córdoba, 68
— — La Plata, 75
— — Lisbôa, 1101
— — Montevideo, 1939
— — Quito, 407
— — da Faculdade de Ciências, Lisbon, 1101
— — — Universidad de Coímbra, 1101
— — e Meteorológico Campos Rodrigues, Maputo, 952
— — Meteorológico y Sísmico Fabra, Barcelona, 1187
— — Nacional, Bogotá, 348
— — — Madrid, 1198
— — — Santiago, 325
— de Cartuja, 1198
— del Ebro, 1198
— Interamericano de Cerro Tololo, La Serena, 325
— Nacional de Fisica Cósmica, San Miguel, 68
— — do Brasil, 185

# INDEX OF INSTITUTIONS

Observatorio Naval "Juan Manuel Cagigal", 1954
— San Calixto, La Paz, 173
Observatorium Bosscha, Lembang, 710
Observatory, Armagh, 1554
Obstetrics, Gynaecology and Family Planning Association, Hanoi, 1962
Occidental College, Los Angeles, 1656
Ocean and Coastal Engineering Research Institute, Nanjing, 337
— Research Institute, Tokyo, 856
Oceanographic Research Institute, Durban, 1170
Oceanography of the South Seas Institute, Guangzhou, 332
Ochanomizu University, Tokyo, 842
— — Library, 819
Odeion Athenon, 623
— Ethnikon, Athens, 623
Odense Bys Museer, 395
— Centralbibliotek, 394
— Universitet, 399
— Universitetsbibliotek, 394
Odessa Agricultural Institute, 1370
— Archaeological Museum, 1356
— Civil Engineering Institute, 1380
— Glavche Research Institute of Dermatology and Venereal Diseases, 1385
— Higher School of Marine Engineering, 1389
— Hydro-Meteorological Institute, 1374
— Institute of National Economy, 1374
— — — Water Transport Engineers, 1389
— I. I. Mechnikov State University, 1365
— Museum of Western and Eastern Art, 1353
— A. V. Nezhdaova State Conservatoire, 1388
— N. I. Pirogov Medical Institute, 1383
— Polytechnic Institute, 1376
— State Picture Gallery, 1353
— Technological Institute of Food and Refrigerating Industries, 1381
— Telecommunications Institute, 1378
— Tuberculosis Research Institute, 1384
Odonto-Maxillo-Facial Association, Hanoi, 1962
OECD Nuclear Energy Agency (NEA), Paris, 50
Öffentliche Bibliothek, Aachen, 534
— — der Universität, Basel, 1259
Office Central Universitaire Suisse, Zürich, 1254
— de la Recherche Scientifique et Technique Outre-Mer, Abidjan, 798
— — — — — Technique Outre-Mer, Antananarivo, 910
— — — — — Technique Outre-Mer, Bamako, 920
— — — — — Technique Outre-Mer, Bangui, 320
— — — — — Technique Outre-Mer, Bogotá, 348
— — — — — Technique Outre-Mer, Brasília, 184
— — — — — Technique Outre-Mer, Brazzaville, 358
— — — — — Technique Outre-Mer, Dakar, 1146
— — — — — Technique Outre-Mer, Damascus, 1277
— — — — — Technique Outre-Mer, Hermosillo, 930
— — — — — Technique Outre-Mar, Jakarta, 710
— — — — — Technique Outre-Mer, La Paz, 174
— — — — — Technique Outre-Mer, Lomé, 1292
— — — — — Technique Outre-Mer, Manila, 1049
— — — — — Technique Outre-Mer, Mexico City, 928
— — — — — Technique Outre-Mer, N'Djamena, 321

— — — — — Technique Outre-Mer, Niamey, 990
— — — — — Technique Outre-Mer, Paris, 458
— — — — — Technique Outre-Mer, Pointe-Noire, 358
— — — — — Technique Outre-Mer, Port Louis, 923
— — — — — Technique Outre-Mer, Quito, 408
— — — — — Technique Outre-Mer, Rabat, 950
— — — — — Technique Outre-Mer, San José, 360
— — — — — Technique Outre-Mer, Yaoundé, 231
— — — — — Technique Outre-Mer, Centre ORSTOM à Ouagadougou, 1937
— — — — — Technique Outre-Mer, Centre ORSTOM des Antilles/Bureau des Sols, Pointe-à-Pitre, 499
— — — — — Technique Outre-Mer, Centre ORSTOM de Cayenne, 499
— — — — — Technique Outre-Mer, Centre ORSTOM de Nouméa, 500
— — — — — Technique Outre-Mer, Centre ORSTOM de Papeete, 501
— — — — — Technique Outre-Mer, Centre ORSTOM en Martinique, Fort de France, 499
— — — — — Technique Outre-Mer, Mission Entomologique ORSTOM auprès de l'OCCGE, Centre Muraz, Bobo-Dioulasso, 1937
— — — — — Technique Outre-Mer, Mission ORSTOM auprès du CENAREST, Libreville, 502
— — — — — Technique Outre-Mer, Mission ORSTOM auprès du Ministère de l'Agriculture, Tunis-Belvedere, 1295
— — — — — Technique Outre-Mer, Mission Venezuela, Caracas, 1954
— — — — — Technique Outre-Mer, Station Ecologique ORSTOM de Richard-Toll, 1146
— — — — — Technique Outre-Mer, Station Géophysique, M'Bour, 1146
— science et de la recherche du Département fédéral de l'Intérieur, Bern, 1258
— du Niger, Ségon, 920
— Fédéral de la Statistique, Bern, 1254
— for the Preservation of Arabic Monuments, 413
— Général du Bâtiment et des Travaux Publics, 445
— National d'Etudes et de Recherches Aérospatiales (ONERA), Chatillon-sur-Bagneux, 460
— — d'Information sur les Enseignements et les Professions, Paris, 447
— — de l'Energie Solaire, Niamey, 990
— — la Recherche Scientifique et Technique (ONAREST), Yaoundé, 231
— of Fair Trading Library, London, 1450
— — Rural Development, Suweon, 886
— — the Atomic Energy Commission for Peace, Bangkok, 1283
— — Chief Scientist, Ministry of Industry and Trade, Jerusalem, 740
— on Aging, Hamilton, Ont., 280
— Territorial d'Action Culturelle, Te Fare Tauhiti Nui, 501
Offshore Supplies Office Library, Glasgow, 1450
Oficina Central de Estadística e Informática, Caracas, 1953
— de Educación Iberoamericano, Madrid, 28
— — Patrimonio Cultural, Santo Domingo, 404

# WORLD OF LEARNING

— Internacional de Información y Observación del Español, Madrid, 1190
— Meteorológica de Chile, 325
— Nacional de Estadística, Lima, 1037
— Regional de Ciencia y Tecnología de la Unesco para América Latina y el Caribe, Montevideo, 1939
— — — Cultura de la Unesco para América Latina y el Caribe, Havana, 363
— — — Educación de la Unesco para América Latina y el Caribe, Santiago, 323
Oficiul de Informare, Documentara in Stiintele Sociale și Politice, Bucharest, 1121
— — — pentru Agricultură și Industrie Alimentară, Bucharest, 1118
— — — Construcții, Arhitectură și Sistematizare, Bucharest, 1124
— — — energetică, Bucharest, 1124
— — — și Documentare pentru Invatamint, Bucharest, 1124
Ogata Institute for Medical and Chemical Research, Tokyo, 815
Ogawa Eiichi Collection, Gifu, 822
Oglethorpe University, Atlanta, 1701
Ohara Bijitsukan, 823
— Institute for Social Research, Tokyo, 863
Ohio Academy of Science, Columbus, 1598
— Dominican College, Columbus, 1844
— Northern University, Ada, 1845
— State University, Columbus, 1845
— — — Libraries, 1634
— University, Athens, Ohio, 1850
— Wesleyan University, Delaware, 1850
Oil and Coal Products Research Institute, Irkutsk, 1362
— — — Colour Chemists' Assocation, 1439
Oireachtas Library, Dublin, 732
Okayama University, 843
— — Library, 820
Okinawa University, 867
— — Library, 820
Oklahoma Baptist University, 1858
— City University, 1858
— Panhandle State College, 1858
— State University, 1858
Okura Institute for Spiritual Culture, Yokohama, 816
— Shukokan, 821
Okurayama Bunka Kagaku Kenkyujo, 811
Old Agricultural Hall, Stellenbosch, 1166
— Dominion University, Norfolk, Va., 1916
— Dublin Society, 730
Olivet College, Mich., 1763
— Nazarene College, Ill., 1707
Oman Museum, Qurm, 1018
Omdurman Central Public Library, 1229
— Islamic University, 1230
Omsk Fine Art Museum, 1353
— Institute of Infectious Diseases, 1387
— — Railway Engineers, 1389
— M. I. Kalinin Medical Institute, 1383
— S. M. Kirov Agricultural Institute, 1370
— Polytechnic Institute, 1376
— State University, 1365
— Veterinary Institute, 1372
Oncology Institute, Beijing, 333
Ondo State Library, Akure, 994
Ongaku Gakkai, Tokyo, 804
Onsala Space Observatory, 1243
Ontario Archaeological Society, 241
— Cancer Treatment and Research Foundation, Toronto, 245
— College of Art, 319
— Crafts Council, Toronto, 240
— Historical Society, 241
— Institute for Studies in Education, Toronto, 310
— Legislative Library, Research and Information Services, Toronto, 248
— Research Foundation, 244
— Science Centre, Don Mills, 251

- Society for Education through Art, Toronto, 240
- — of Artists, Toronto, 240
Ontödei Muzeum, Budapest, 643
Open University, Hagen, 546
— — Madrid, 1205
— — Milton Keynes, 1521
— — Library, Milton Keynes, 1463
— — San José, 361
Openbare Bibliotheek, The Hague, 965
— — Hilversum, 965
— — 's Hertogenbosch, 965
— Leeszaal en Bibliothek, Amersfoort, 963
— — — Curaçao, 975
— — — Boekerij, Eilandgebied Aruba, 975
Openluchtmuseum voor Beeldhouwkunst, (Middelheim), Antwerp, 157
Opera Svizzera dei Monumenti d'Arte, Locarno, 1255
Operational Research Society of New Zealand, Wellington, 977
Operations Research Center, Tel-Aviv, 750
Ophthalmological Society of Egypt, 414
— — — the United Kingdom, 1429
Opolskie Towarzystwo Przjaciól Nauk, Opole, 1063
Optical Society of America, Inc., 1614
— — — India, Calcutta, 663
Optics and Precision Instruments Institute, Shanghai, 332
— — — — Xian, 332
Optikai, Akusztikai és Filmtechnikai Egyesület, Budapest, 636
Optisches Museum der Carl-Zeiss-Stiftung, Jena, 510
Oral and Dental Hospital, Johannesburg, 1182
— Health Research Center, Philadelphia, 1880
— Roberts University, Tulsa, 1858
Orange Agricultural College, 113
Orbaeli, L., Institute of Physiology, Erevan, 1324
Ordem dos Engeheiros, 1099
— — Médicos, 1098
Ordre des Architectes, Paris, 445
— — Musiciens, Paris, 445
Ordrupgaardsamlingen, Charlottenlund, 395
Ordzonikidze Mineralogical Museum, Moscow, 1359
Orebro stadsbibliotek, 1239
Oregon Historical Society, Portland, 1606
— Institute of Marine Biology, Eugene, 1866
— State Library, Salem, 1631
— — University, Corvallis, 1863
Orenburg A. A. Andreyev Agricultural Institute, 1370
— Fine Art Museum, 1353
— Polytechnic Institute, 1376
— State Medical Institute, 1383
Organic Chemistry Institute, Shanghai, 332
Organisation de Coordination et de Coopération pour la lutte contre les Grandes Endémies (OCCGE), Bobo-Dioulasso, 1937
— — la Jeunesse Esperantiste Française, Paris, 449
— — — Ligue Arabe pour l'Education, la Culture et la Science, Tunis, 1295
— des Nations Unies pour l'Alimentation et l'Agriculture, Rome, 15
— européenne de biologie moléculaire, Heidelberg, 45
— — pour des recherches astronomiques dans l'hémisphère austral, Munich, 45
— — — l'Equipement Electronique de l'Aviation Civile, Paris, 33
— — — la Recherche nucléaire, Geneva, 45
— for Economic Co-operation and Development (OECD), Paris, 25
— hydrographique internationale, Monte Carlo, 48
— internationale contre le trachome, Créteil, 41
— — de lutte biologique contre les ennemis des cultures (O.I.L.B.), Zürich, 17
— — — métrologie légale, Paris, 49
— — — normalisation, Geneva, 34
— — — Recherche sur la Cellule, Paris, 40
— Météorologique Mondiale, Geneva, 51
— mondiale contre la cécité, Naestved, 37
— — de gastro-entérologie (OMGE), Barcelona, 39
— — la Santé, Geneva, 36
— of the Catholic Universities of Latin America, Buenos Aires, 30
— pour les Museés, les Monuments et les Sites d'Afrique, Accra, 20
Organisme de Recherches sur l'Alimentation et la Nutrition Africaine (ORANA), Dakar, 1146
— National de la Recherche Scientifique, Algiers, 57
Organización de Estudios Tropicales, San José, 360
— — Universidades Católicas de América Latina (ODUCAL), Buenos Aires, 30
Organization for Museums, Monuments and Sites of Africa, Accra, 20
— — Tropical Studies, San José, 360
— of American Historians, Bloomington, 1606
Oriel College, Oxford, 1524
— — Library, Oxford, 1463
Orient-Institut der Deutschen Morgenländischen Gesellschaft, Beirut, 899
Oriental Ceramic Society, London, 1414
— Institute, Baroda, 668
— — of Indian Languages, Bombay, 668
— — — the University of Chicago, 1640
— Library, Tokyo, 819
— Research Institute, Mysore, 668
Orientalische Gesellschaft, Vienna, 121
Orientalisches Institut der Görres-Gesellschaft, Jerusalem, 738
Orientalsk Samfund, Copenhagen, 392
Orissa State Museum, Bhubaneswar, 675
— University of Agriculture and Technology, Bhubaneswar, 696
Orlogsmuseet, Copenhagen, 396
Orlovskaya Art Gallery, Orel, 1353
Ormond College, Parkville, 104
Ornithological Association of Zimbabwe, Salisbury, 2000
— Society of New Zealand, Pinehaven, 977
Oron Museum, Nigeria, 995
Országgyülesi Könyvtár, 641
Országos Allategészségügyi Intézet, 637
— Erdészeti Egyesület, 634
— Hadtörteneti Múzeum, Budapest, 643
— Közegészégügyi Intézet, Budapest, 638
— Magyar Bányászati és Kohászati Egyesület, 636
— — Cecilia Tarsulat, 634
— Müszaki Könyvtar es Dokumentációs Központ, Budapest, 641
— — Múzeum, Budapest, 643
— Onkológiai Intézet, Budapest, 638
— Orvostudományi Információs Intézet és Könyvtár, Budapest, 641
— Pedagógiai Könyvtár és Múzeum, Budapest, 641
— Széchenyi Könyvtár, 642
— Vetömag és Szaporítóanyag Felügyelöseg, Budapest, 637
Orta Doğu Teknik Universitesi, Ankara, 1307
Orthological Institute, London, 1443
Orvostovábbképzö Intézet, Budapest, 648
Osaka City University, 859
— College of Music, 874
— Medical College, 867
— Municipal Electricity Museum 822
— Museum of Fine Arts, 822
— Museum of Natural History, 822
— Prefectural Nakanoshima Library, 820
— Yûhigaoka Library, 820

— University, 844
— — Library, 820
— — of Foreign Studies, 847
Oskar von Miller Institut, Obernach, 534
Osler Library, Montreal, 249
Oslo Kommunes Kunstsamlinger, 1012
Osmania University, 696
Osrednja knjižnica: Oddelek za študij, Celje, 1975
Ośrodek Informacji Naukowej Polskiej Akadameii Nauk, Warsaw, 1075
Osservatorio Astronomico, Padua, 763
— — Trieste, 763
— — di Capodimonte, Naples, 763
— — — Roma, 763
— Geofisico Sperimentale, Trieste, 763
— — Vesuviano, 763
Ostasiatische Sammlung, Berlin (East), 508
Ostasiatiska Museet, Stockholm, 1241
Osterley Park House, 1467
Österreich-Institut, Vienna, 121
Österreichisch-Ungarische Vereinigung zur Pflege kulturelle Beziehungen, 121
Österreichische Akademie der Wissenschaften, 118
— Arbeitsgemeinschaft für Kunde des Slawentums und Osteuropas, 126
— — Ur- und Frühgeschichte, Vienna, 125
— Ärztegesellschaft für Psychotherapie, Vienna, 122
— Biochemische Gesellschaft, Vienna, 123
— Byzantinische Gesellschaft, Vienna, 121
— Dermatologische Gesellschaft, 122
— Ethnologische Gesellschaft, Vienna, 123
— Exlibris-Gesellschaft, 121
— Forschungsstiftung für Entwicklungshilfe, Vienna, 124
— Galerie, Vienna, 130
— — des XIX und XX Jahrhunderts, Vienna, 130
— Geographische Gesellschaft, Vienna, 121
— Geologische Gesellschaft, Vienna, 123
— Gesellschaft der Tierärzte, Vienna, 119
— — für Anästhesiologie, Reanimation und Intensivtherapie, Vienna, 122
— — — Arbeitsmedizin, Vienna, 122
— — — Archäologie, Vienna, 121
— — — Aussenpolitik und Internationale Beziehungen, Vienna, 120
— — — Balneologie und medizinische Klimatologie, Innsbruck, 122
— — — Chirurgie, Vienna, 122
— — — Christliche Kunst, Vienna, 120
— — — Dokumentation und Information, Vienna, 120
— — — Elektroencephalographie und Klinische Neurophysiologie, Vienna, 122
— — — Erdölwissenschaften, Vienna, 123
— — — Filmwissenschaft, Kommunications- und Medien Forschung, Vienna, 120
— — — Geriatrie, Vienna, 122
— — — Hals-Nasen-Ohrenheilkunde, Kopf- und Halschirurgie, Vienna, 122
— — — Innere Medizin, Vienna, 122
— — — Kinderheilkunde, Vienna, 122
— — — Kirchenrecht, Vienna, 120
— — — Klinische Chemie, Vienna, 123
— — — Kommunikationsfragen, Vienna, 120
— — — langfristige Entwicklungsforschung (Zukunftsforschung), Vienna, 125
— — — Literatur, Vienna, 121
— — — Meteorologie, 123
— — — Mikrochemie und Analytische Chemie, Graz, 123
— — — Musik, Vienna, 120
— — — Parapsychologie, Vienna, 123
— — — Psychologie, Vienna, 123
— — — Raumforschung and Raumplanung, Vienna, 124
— — — Sexualforschung, Vienna, 125

Österreichische Gesellschaft für Soziologie, Vienna, 123
— — — Statistik und Informatik, Vienna, 120
— — — Urologie, Vienna, 122
— — — Volkslied- und Volkstanzpflege (Volksgesang-Verein Wien), 120
— — — Weltraumforschung, Innsbruck, 126
— — — Wirtschaftspolitik, Vienna, 120
— — zum Studium der Sterilität und Fertilität, Vienna, 122
— Kommission für Internationale Erdmessung, Vienna, 126
— Mathematische Gesellschaft, 122
— Mykologische (pilzkundliche) Gesellschaft, Vienna, 122
— Nationalbibliothek, 128
— Numismatische Gesellschaft, 121
— Ophthalmologische Gesellschaft, Vienna, 122
— Physikalische Gesellschaft, Vienna, 123
— Rektorenkonferenz, 120
— Röntgengesellschaft, Vienna, 122
— Studiengesellschaft für Kybernetik, Vienna, 126
Österreichischer Ingenieur- und Architektenverein, 119
— Komponistenbund, Vienna, 120
— PEN-Club, Vienna, 121
— Verein für Vermessungswesen und Photogrammetrie, Vienna, 124
Österreichisches Barockmuseum, 130
— Bauzentrum, Vienna, 123
— Biographisches Lexicon, Vienna, 118
— College, 121
— Forschungsinstitut für Wirtschaft und Politik, Salzburg, 125
— Forschungszentrum Seibersdorf G.m.b.H., Vienna, 126
— Gesellschafts- und Wirtschafts-Museum, Vienna, 130
— Giesserei- Institut, Leoben, 126
— Holzforschungsinstitut der Österreichischen Gesellschaft für Holzforschung, Vienna, 126
— Institut für Bauforschung, Vienna, 126
— — — Bibliographie, Vienna, 120
— — — Bibliotheksforschung, Vienna, 124
— — — Entwicklungshilfe und technische Zusammenarbeit mit den Entwicklungsländern, Vienna, 125
— — — Formgebung, Vienna, 124
— — — Raumplanung, Vienna, 124
— — — technische Forschung und Entwicklung, Vienna, 126
— — — Wirtschaftsforschung, Vienna, 125
— Kulturinstitut, Cairo, 414
— — Istanbul, 1298
— — Teheran, 721
— — Warsaw, 1066
— Meinungs- und Marktforschungsinstitut, Vienna, 125
— Museum für Angewandte Kunst, 130
— — — Volkskunde, 130
— Normungsinstitut, Vienna, 126
— Ost- und Südosteuropa-Institut, Vienna, 125
— Staatsarchiv, Vienna, 127
— Statistiches Zentralamt, Vienna, 125
— Textil-Forschungsinstitut, Vienna, 127
Osteuropa-Institut, Berlin, 551
— — München, 529
Ostrovsky, N.A., State Museum, Moscow, 1357
Otago Museum, 982
— Polytechnic, 987
Otis Art Institute of Parsons School of Design, Los Angeles, 1656
Oto-Laryngology Association, Hanoi, 1962
Ottawa City Archives, 248
— Public Library, 248
— University, Kansas, 1730
Otterbein College, Westerville, 1851

Otto-Seiz-Institut für Psychologie und Erziehungswissenschaft, Mannheim, 590
Oudheidkundig Museum van de Stad Gent, 158
Oudheidkundige Musea, Antwerp, 157
Oudheidskamer, 969
Oulun Yliopisto, Oulu, 436
— Yliopiston Kirjasto, Oulu, 432
Our Lady of Holy Cross College, New Orleans, 1739
— — — the Lake University of San Antonio, Tex., 1899
Overseas Development Institute, London, 1442
Owo Museum, 995
Oxford Centre for Management Studies, 1552
— Polytechnic, 1545
— Preservation Trust, 1412
Oxfordshire County Libraries, Oxford, 1454
Oy Keskuslaboratorio-Centrallaboratorium Ab, Helsinki, 431
Oyamazumi Jinja Kóhokan, 822
Oyo-buturi Gakkai, Tokyo, 811


P

Pablo Borbon Memorial Institute of Technology, Batangas City, 1060
Pace University, Brooklyn, 1819
Pacific Forest Research Centre, Victoria, B.C., 244
— Lutheran University, Tacoma, 1921
— Oaks College, Pasadena, 1656
— Ocean Institute, Vladivostok, 1322
— — — of Bio-organic Chemistry, Vladivostok, 1322
— Science Association, Honolulu, 50
— Scientific Research Institute of Fisheries and Oceanography (TINRO), Vladivostock, 1346
— Sociological Association, Tempe, 1615
— Union College, Angwin, Calif., 1656
— University, Forest Grove, 1863Pädagogische Zentralbibliothek, Deutsche Lehrerbücherei, Berlin (East), 506
Paedagogiki Academia, Nicosia, 368
Paediatric Research Institute, Leningrad, 1384
— — — Moscow, 1384
Paediatrics Association, Hanoi, 1962
— Institute, Beijing, 333
Paine College, Ga., 1701
Paint Research Association, Haifa, 740
Paisley College of Technology, 1546
"Paisij Hilendarski" University of Plovdiv, 223
Pajajaran State University, Bandung, 716
Pakistan Academy of Letters, Islamabad, 1019
— — — Sciences, Islamabad, 1019
— Administrative Staff College, Lahore, 1029
— Agricultural Research Council, Islamabad, 1021
— Air Force College of Aeronautical Engineering, Karachi, 1027
— Animal Husbandry Research Institute, Peshawar, 1021
— Arab Cultural Association, Karachi, 1020
— Association for the Advancement of Science, 1020
— Atomic Energy Commission, 1022
— Concrete Institute, Karachi, 1021
— Council of Scientific and Industrial Research, Karachi, 1022
— — — — — Research Laboratories, Karachi, 1022
— Economic Research Institute (PERI), Lahore, 1021
— Forest Institute, Peshawar, 1021
— -German Cultural Centre, Lahore, 1020

— Historical Society, Karachi, 1019
— Institute of Architects, Lahore, 1019
— — — Cotton Research and Technology, Karachi, 1023
— — — Development Economics, Islamabad, 1021
— — — International Affairs, 1019
— — — Management, Karachi, 1023
— — — Nuclear Science and Technology (PINSTECH), Islamabad, 1022
— Library Association, Karachi, 1019
— Medical Association, Karachi, 1020
— — Research Council, Karachi, 1022
— Meteorological Department, 1022
— Museum Association, 1020
— National Centre Library and Culture Centre, Hyderabad, 1024
— Naval Engineering College, Karachi, 1027
— Philosophical Congress, Lahore, 1021
— Scientific and Technological Information Centre (Pastic), Islamabad, 1024
— Standards Institution, 1023
— Writers Guild, Karachi, 1020
Pak-Swiss Precision Mechanics and Instrumentation Training Centre, Karachi, 1022
Palace Museum, Ulan Bator, 947
Palacio de la Granja de San Ildefonso, Segovia, 1201
— — Riofrió, Segovia, 1201
— — Real, Aránjuez, 1201
— — Madrid, 1201
Palacký University, Olomouc, 382
Palaeontographical Society, London, 1433
Palais de Bellevue, Brussels, 158
— la Découverte, 467
Lascaris, Nice, 469
Paläontologische Gesellschaft, Münster, 524
Paläontologisches Institut und Museum der Universität Zürich, 1263
— Museum, Berlin (East), 509
Palawan National Agricultural College, 1060
Palazzo Davanzati, Florence, 770
— Ducale, Urbino, 773
— — Venice, 774
— Mocenigo, Venice, 773
— Vecchio, Florence, 770
Paleontological Institute, Moscow, 1320
— Research Institution, Ithaca, N.Y., 1618
— Society, Baku, 1325
— — Columbus, Ohio, 1614
Palestine Exploration Fund, 1423
Pali Institute, Vientiane, 898
Palladin, O. V., Institute of Biochemistry, Kiev, 1417
Palmerston North Medical Research Foundation, 980
— — Public Library, 981
Palmyra Museum, 1277
Palóc Múzeum, 646
Palompon Institute of Technology, Leyte, 1060
Palynological Society of India, 663
Pamantasan Ng Lungsod Ng Maynila, 1054
Památník národního písemnictví na Strahově, Prague, 378
— Terezín, 379
Pamfilov, K. D. Academy of Municipal Economy, 1380
Pamir Station, Khorog, 1332
Pan Library ("Circle of the Friends of Progress"), Tripolis, 618
Pan-African Institute for Development, Geneva, 25
Pan-American Institute of Geography and History, Mexico, 50
— Medical Association, New York, 42
— University, Edinburg, Texas, 1899
Pan-Hellenic Musical Association, 616
Panama Academy, 1030
— — of History, 1030
Panitya Induk Untuk Meter Dan Kilogram, Bandung, 710
Panjab University, Chandigarh, 697
Pannonhalmi Főapátság Gyüjteménye, Pannonhalma, 646

— Szent-Benedek-Rend Főapátsági Könyvtár, Pannonhalma, 642
Państwowa Wyższa Szkoła Filmowa Telewizyjna i Teatralna im. Leona Schillera, Łódź, 1096
— — — Muzyczna, Gdańsk, 1096
— — — — Wrocław, 1096
— — — — Sztuk Plastycznych, Gdańsk, 1096
— — — — — Wrocław, 1096
— — — Teatralna, Cracow, 1096
Państwowe Muzeum Archeologiczne, Warsaw, 1076
— — Etnograficzne w Warszawie, Warsaw, 1076
— — Oświęcim-Brzezinka, 1077
Państwowy Zakład Higieny, Warsaw, 1072
Panteios School of Political Sciences, Athens, 623
Papír és Nyomdaipari Müszaki Egyesület, 636
Papirindustriens Forskningsinstitutt, Oslo, 1010
Papua New Guinea Institute of Administration, Boroko, 1033
— — — — Medical Research, Goroka, 1032
— — — Library Association, Boroko, 1032
— — — National Museum and Art Gallery, Boroko, 1032
— — — Scientific Society, Boroko, 1032
— — — University of Technology, 1033
Paraguayan Academy, Asunción, 1034
Parasitologische Gesellschaft der DDR, Berlin (East), 505
Parasitologistic Institute, Shanghai, 333
Park College, Parkville, 1787
Parlamentsbibliothek, Vienna, 128
Parliament Library, Melbourne, 96
— Teheran, 722
Parliamentary Library of New South Wales, Sydney, 96
Parque Histórico en las Ruinas de Caparra, San Juan P.R., 1110
— Zoológico Nacional y Jardín Botánico, San Salvador, 422
Pars Museum, 722
Party Museum, Tiranë, 55
Pasadena Foundation for Medical Research, 1619
Pashto Academy, Peshawar, 1020
Pastel Society, London, 1414
Pasteur Institute and Medical Research Institute, Assam, 669
— — of India, 669
— Research Institute, Dalat, 1962
Patent Office Library, Tokyo, 819
— — Scientific Library, Arlington, Va., 1625
Paterson Laboratories, Manchester, 1445
Pathological Society of Great Britain and Ireland, Sheffield, 1429
Patna Museum, Bihar, 675
Paton, E. O., Institute of Electrical Welding, Kiev, 1333
Patriarchal Institute for Patristic Studies, Thessaloniki, 618
"Patrice Lumumba" People's Friendship University, Moscow, 1365
Patrimonio Nacional, Madrid, 1201
Patronato de Biología Animal, Madrid, 1191
Paul-Ehrlich-Institut, Bundesamt für Sera und Impfstoffe, Frankfurt, 531
Paul (J.) Getty Museum, Malibu, 1638
Pavillon Chinois, Brussels, 158
Pavlov, I.P., All-Union Physiological Society, Moscow, 1319
— Institute of Physiology, 1319
— Museum of Geology and Palaeontology, Moscow, 1359
Pax Romana, Fribourg, 30
Pazarlama Enstitüsü, Eskişehir, 1309
Peabody Museum of Archaeology and Ethnology, 1640
— — — Natural History, 1641
— — — Salem, 1641
Pécsi Orvostudományi Egyetem, 649
— — — Könyvtára, Pécs, 642

— Tudományegyetem, 649
— — Könyvtára, 642
Pedagogical and Technological University of Colombia, Boyacá, 353
— Society of the F.S.R. of Yugoslavia, Belgrade, 1968
— — — — S. R. of Slovenia, 1970
Pedagogické muzeum J. A. Komenského, Prague, 378
Pedagogiska Föreningen i Finland r.y., Helsinki, 428
**Pedagogiske seminar, Bergen, 1014**
**Pedagogy and Didactics Unit, Lausanne, 1273**
**Pedagoško Društvo BiH, Sarajevo, 1971**
— -književni zbor, Pedagoško Društvo SR Hrvatske, Zagreb, 1970
Pedology Institute, Nanjing, 332
Peggy Guggenheim Collection (Solomon R. Guggenheim Foundation, New York), Venice, 774
PEL Geophysical Observatory, Christchurch, N.Z., 980
Pembroke College, Cambridge, 1484
— — Library, Cambridge, 1461
— — Oxford, 1524
— — Library, Oxford, 1463
— State University, North Carolina, 1829
PEN All-India Centre, 662
— Club, Amsterdam, 958
— — Bogotá, 347
— — Bombay, 662
— — Brussels, 151
— — Bucharest, 1122
— — Budapest, 635
— — Buenos Aires, 64
— — Cape Town, 1155
— — Darmstadt, 521
— — Dublin, 730
— — Geneva, 1255
— — Hong Kong, 1559
— — Istanbul, 1298
— — Kingston, Jamaica, 800
— — La Paz, 174
— — Lima, 1037
— — London, 20
— — Montreal, 241
— — New York, 1607
— — Oslo, 1008
— — Paris, 449
— — Rio de Janeiro, 181
— — Rome, 759
— — San Juan, P.R., 1109
— — Seoul, 885
— — Sydney, 89
— — Tokyo, 806
— — Vienna, 121
— — Warsaw, 1066
— — Wellington, N.Z., 978
— — Zurich, 1255
— — de Puerto Rico, San Juan, 1109
— — — Suisse Romande, Geneva, 1255
— — of Iran, Teheran, 721
— Internacional de Escritores de Colombia, Bogotá, 347
— International, London, 20
— — Jamaica, 800
— — Centre, Rome, 759
— — (Centre Français), Paris, 449
— — New Zealand Centre, Wellington, 978
— Yazariar Derneği, Istanbul, 1298
— Zentrum Bundesrepublik Deutschland, Darmstadt, 521
See also International P.E.N.
Penang Museum and Art Gallery, 916
— Public Library, 916
Pennklubben, Stockholm, 1236
Pennsylvania Academy of the Fine Arts, 1641
— College of Optometry, 1872
— State University, 1872
— — — Libraries, University Park, 1634
— Transportation Institute, 1877
Penza Agricultural Institute, 1370
— Civil Engineering Institute, 1380
— Picture Gallery, 1353

— Polytechnic Institute, 1376
Pénzügyi és Számviteli Föiskola, Budapest, 655
People's Army Museum, Hanoi, 1963
Pepperdine University, Malibu, 1656
Pepys Library (Magdalene College), Cambridge, 1462
Perak Museum, 916
Perarignar Anna University of Technology, Madras, 919
Perceptual and Cognitive Performance Unit (M.R.C.), Brighton, 1443, 1534
Percy Fitzpatrick Institute of African Ornithology, Rondebosch, 1167
Pereira Technological University, 354
Pergamon Museum, 1302
Perm Academician D. N. Pryanishnikov Agricultural Institute, 1371
— A. M. Gorky State University, 1366
— Pharmaceutical Institute, 1384
— Polytechnic Institute, 1376
— State Art Gallery, 1354
— — Medical Institute, 1383
Permanent Commission and International Association on Occupational Health, London, 43
— Committee of the International Congress of Entomology, London, 50
— Exhibition of Musical Instruments, Leningrad, 1359
— International Association of Navigation Congresses, Brussels, 33
— — — — Road Congresses, Paris, 33
— — Committee for Genetics Congresses, Kyoto, 51
— — — of Congresses of Comparative Pathology, Paris, 43
— Scientific Exhibition, Moscow, 1323
— Tchaikovsky Exhibition in the Tchaikovsky Concert Hall, Moscow, 1360
Perpustakaan Bagian Patologi Klinik R.S. Dr. Tjipto Mangunkusumo, Jakarta, 711
— Balai Penjelidikan Bahan-Bahan, 710
— Biro Pusat Statistik, 711
— Dewan Perwakilan Rakjat Gotong Rojong, Jakarta, 711
— Institut Pertanian, Bogor, 711
— Islam, 711
— Jajasan Hatta, 711
— Kementerian Perekonomian, 711
— Museum Pusat, Direktorat Jendral Kebudajaan, Dept. Pendidikan dan Kebudajaan, Jakarta, 711
— Negara, 711
— Negeri Sabah, 916
— Pusat Institut Teknologi Bandung, 710
— — Penelitian dan Pengembangan Geologi, Bandung, 710
— Sultan Ismail, Johore, 916
— Umum Makassar (Ujungpandang), 711
Persatuan Insinjur Indonesia, 708
Perth Observatory, Bickley, 94
Peru State College, Nebraska, 1793
Perusahaan Negara Bio-Farma, Bandung, 709
Peruvian Academy, Lima, 1036
Peshawar Museum, 1024
Pestalozzi-Fröbel-Haus, Berlin (West), 520
Petawawa National Forestry Institute, Chalk River, Ont., 244
Peter the Great Museum of Anthropology and Ethnography, Leningrad, 1354
Peterborough Cathedral Library, 1459
Peterhouse, Cambridge, 1484
— (Perne) Library, Cambridge, 1462
Petit, J. N., Institute, Bombay, 661
— — — Library, Bombay, 673
Petöfi Irodalmi Múzeum, Budapest, 643
Petone Technical Institute, nr. Wellington, N.Z., 987
Petra Christian University, Surabaya, 720
Petroleum Research Institute, Jadiriyah, 725
— Training Institute, Warri, 1003

Petrozavodsk O. V. Kuuisen State University, 1366
Pevsner Public Library, Haifa, 742
Pfälzische Landesbibliothek, 537
Pfeiffer College, Misenheimer, N.C., 1829
Pflanzenphysiologisches Institut, Bern, 1258
Pharmaceutical Material Institute, Hanoi, 1962
— Museum of the Central Drug Research Institute, Moscow, 1359
— Research Institute, Osaka, 815
— Society of Ghana, 611
— — — Great Britain, London, 1429
— — — Ireland, 731
— — — Trinidad and Tobago, Port-of-Spain, 1293
— — — Zimbabwe, Bulawayo, 2000
Pharmacists Association, Hanoi, 1962
— Society of the S.R. of Croatia, 1970
Pharmacognosy Research Centre, Fudhailiyah, 725
Pharmacological Society of Canada, Montreal, 242
Pharmacy Council of India, New Delhi, 662
Pharmazeutische Zentralbibliothek, Bern, 1259
Philadelphia Center for Research in Child Growth, Philadelphia, 1880
— College of Art, 1877
— — Pharmacy and Science, 1877
— — Textiles and Science, 1878
— Museum of Art, 1641
Philander Smith College, 1650
Philippine Academy, Manila, 1047
— Association of Agriculturists, 1047
— — Mechanical and Electrical Engineers, 1048
— — Nutrition, 1048
— Atomic Energy Commission, Manila, 1049
— Council of Chemists, Manila, 1048
— Economic Society, 1047
— Historical Association, Manila, 1047
— Institute of Architects, 1047
— Library Association Inc., 1047
— Medical Association, 1048
— Normal College, Manila, 1060
— Numismatic and Antiquarian Society, 1047
— Paediatric Society, 1048
— Pharmaceutical Association, 1048
— Society of Civil Engineers, 1048
— — — Mining, Metallurgical and Geological Engineers, 1048
— — — Parasitology, 1048
— Veterinary Medical Association, 1047
— Women's University, 1056
— — — Library, Manila, 1049
Philipps-Universität, Marburg, 591
Phillips University, Enid, Okla., 1858
Philological Society, London, 1427
Philosophical Association of the Philippines, Manila, 1048
— Society, Khartoum, 1229
— — of England, Amesbury, 1434
Philosophisch-Theologische Hochschule Fulda (Päpstlich Errichtete Theologische Fakultät), 609
— — — Sankt Georgen, 609
— — — der Salesianer, Benedikbeuern, 1946
Philosophische Gesellschaft Wien, 123
Philosophy and Humanities Society of Iran, Teheran, 721
— of Education Society, Tallahassee, Fla., 1604
— — Science Association, East Lansing, 1614
— Society of the U.S.S.R., Moscow, 1321
Phoenix Trust, London, 1421
Phonogramm-Archivs-Kommission, Vienna, 118
Photobiology Research Unit, Pretoria, 1156
Photoelectricity Institute of Sichuan, 332
Photogrammetric Society, London, 1439
Photographic Society of Ireland, 730

Photosensitive Chemistry Institute, Beijing, 332
Photosynthetic Nitrogen Metabolism Unit, Johannesburg, 1182
Phuket Community College, Songkla, 1289
Phuthadikobo Museum, Mochudi, 177
Physical and Chemical Research Institute, Irkutsk, 1362
— Culture College, Beijing, 336
— Engineering Institute, Ashkhabad, 1332
— — — Gorky, 1362
— — — Kharkov, 1333
— — — Minsk, 1326
— — — of Low Temperatures, Kharkov, 1333
— -Mechanical Institute, Lvov, 1333
— Research Laboratory, Ahmedabad, 671
— Science Laboratory, Las Cruces, 1802
— Society of China, Taipei, 341
Physicians' Association of Croatia, 1970
Physics Association, Hanoi, 1962
— Institute, Beijing, 332
— — Southwest, Luoshan, 332
Physikalisch-Technische Bundesanstalt, Brunswick, 534
— — Veruschsanstalt für Wärme- und Schalltechnik am Technologischen Gewerbemuseum, Vienna, 127
Physikalische Gesellschaft, Zürich, 1256
— — der DDR, Berlin (East), 505
Physiological Society, 1432
— — of New Zealand, Dunedin, 977
Physiology Association, Hanoi, 1962
— Institute, Shanghai, 332
Piatigorsk Balneological Institute, 1387
— Pharmaceutical Institute, 1384
Piedmont College, Demorest, 1701
Pierpont Morgan Library, 1630
Pikeville College, 1736
Pilgrim Society, The, Plymouth, Mass., 1606
— Trust, 1421
Pilkington Glass Museum, St. Helens, 1471
Pinacoteca Ambrosiana, 771
— di Brera, 771
— do Estado de São Paulo, 190
— e Musei Comunali, Forli, 770
— Manfrediana, Venice, 774
— Nacional de San Diego, Mexico City, 932
— Nazionale, Bologna, 769
— — Ferrara, 770
— — Siena, 773
— — Provinciale, Bari, 769
— — Tosio Martinego, Brescia, 769
— — Vaticana, 1943
Pinchas Sapir International Center for Development, Tel-Aviv, 750
"Pirogov" Emergency Medical Institute, Sofia, 220
Pisarzhevsky, L. V., Institute of Physical Chemistry, Kiev, 1334
Pittsburgh State University, Kansas, 1730
Pitzer College, Claremont, 1656
Plainsong and Mediaeval Music Society, 1415
Planetarium, Johannesburg, 1182
Planlaegningsrådet for Forskningen, Copenhagen, 392
Planning and Special Services, Swindon, 1446
Plant Breeding Institute, Cambridge, 1441
— — Station, Njoro, 879
— Pathology Research Institute, Giza, 415
— Pests and Diseases Research Institute, Teheran, 722
— Physiology Institute, Shanghai, 332
— Protection Institute, Beijing, 333
— — Research Institute, Giza, 415
— — — — Pretoria, 1160
— — — — Salisbury, Zimbabwe, 2001
Plantenziekkentundige Dienst, Wageningen, 960
Plasma Physics Laboratory, Kyoto, 837
— — Research Institute, Durban, 1170
— — — Lausanne, 1273
Plastics and Rubber Institute, London, 1439
Plateau Meteorology Institute, Beijing, 333

Plekhanov, G. V., Institute of National Economy, Moscow, 1373
Plovdivski Universitet "Paisij Hilendarski", Plovdiv, 223
Plunkett Foundation for Co-operative Studies, London, 1421
Plymouth Museum and Art Gallery, 1470
— Polytechnic, 1546
— State College, New Hampshire, 1796
Pneumoconiosis Medical and Research Bureau, Kitwe, 1997
— Unit (M.R.C.), Penarth, 1444
Poetry Society, London, 1427
— of America, 1607
Pohjois-Pohjanmaan Museo, Oulu, 433
— Suomen Tutkimuslaitos, Oulu, 437
Pokrajinski muzej, Celje, 1976
— — Maribor, 1977
— — Ptuj, 1977
Polar Alpine Botanical Garden, Murmansk, 1323
— Institute of Geophysics, Murmansk, 1323
Polding College, Castle Hill, N.S.W., 113
Polemological Institute of the University of Groningen, 961
Polenov, A. L., Neurosurgery Research Institute, Leningrad, 1346
Policy Studies Institute (PSI), London, 1442
Polish Academy of Sciences, 1061
— Cultural Institute, London, 1426
— Dermatological Society, Warsaw, 1072
— Institute of International Affairs, Warsaw, 1072
Politechnika Czestochowska, 1087
— Gdanska, 1088
— Krakowska, 1089
— Łódzka, 1090
— Poznańska, 1090
— Rzeszowska, 1091
— Śląska im W. Pstrowskiego, Silesia, 1091
— Szczecińska, 1091
— Warszawska, 1091
— Wroclawska, 1093
Politecnico di Milano, 791
— — Torino, 791
Politisches Archiv des Auswärtigen Amts, Bonn, 538
Politologisch Instituut, Louvain, 150
Poljoprivredni Institut, Osijek, 1972
Pollution Research Unit, Manchester, 1518
Polska Akademia Nauk, Rome, 759
Polski Klub Literacki PEN, Warsaw, 1066
Polskie Towarzystwo Anatomiczne, Warsaw, 1063
— — Antropologiczne, 1063
— — Archeologiczne i Numizmatyczne, 1063
— — Astronautyczne, Warsaw, 1063
— — Astronomiczne, 1063
— — Biochemiczne, Warsaw, 1064
— — Botaniczne, 1064
— — Chemiczne, 1064
— — Ekonomiczne, 1064
— — Endokrynologiczne, 1064
— — Entomologiczne, Warsaw, 1064
— — Farmaceutyczne, 1064
— — Filologiczne, 1064
— — Filozoficzne, 1064
— — Fizjologiczne, 1064
— — Fizyczne, 1064
— — Geofizyczne, Warsaw, 1064
— — Geograficzne, Warsaw, 1064
— — Geologiczne, 1064
— — Gleboznawcze, 1064
— — Higieny Psychicznej, Warsaw, 1064
— — Historii Medycyny, Warsaw, 1064
— — Historyczne, 1064
— — Immunologiczne, Wrocław, 1064
— — Jezykoznawcze, 1064
— — Leśne, 1064
— — Ludoznawcze, 1064
— — Matematyczne, 1064
— — Mechaniki Teoretycznej i Stosowanej, Warsaw, 1065
— — Mikrobiologów, 1065
— — Miłośników Astronomii, 1065

— — Mineralogiczne, Cracow, 1065
— — Nauk Weterynaryjynch, 1065
— — Orientalistyczne, 1065
— — Parazytologiczne, 1065
— — Patologów, Warsaw, 1065
— — Przyrodników im Kopernika, 1065
— — Psychologiczne, 1065
— — Semiotyczne, Warsaw, 1065
— — Socjologiczne, Warsaw, 1065
— — Zoologiczne, 1065
— — Zootechniczne, 1065
Poltava Agricultural Institute, 1371
— Art Museum, 1354
— Civil Engineering Institute, 1380
— Gravimetric Observatory, 1333
— State Museum, 1358
Polynesian Society, Wellington, N.Z., 978
Polytechnic, Darhan, 948
— Ibadan, 1002
— Vientiane, 898
— Wolverhampton, 1549
— Institute, Bahar-Dar, 425
— — of New York, Brooklyn, 1819
— — of Central London, 1543
— — North London, 1543
— — the South Bank, London, 1548
— — Wales, Pontypridd, 1549
Polytechnical Museum, Moscow, 1359
Polytekniske Forening, 1008
— Laereanstalt, Danmarks Tekniske Højskole, Copenhagen, 399
Pomona College, 1656
Pomorska Akademia Medyczna, 1095
Pomorski Musej, Dubrovnik, 1976
— Kotor, 1976
Ponce Public Library, 1110
Pontefract Museum, 1471
Pontifical Academy of Sciences, Vatican City, 1942
— Biblical Institute, Jerusalem, 753
— — Rome, 1945
— Gregorian University, Rome, 1944
— Institute of Christian Archaeology, Rome, 1947
— — Oriental Studies, Rome, 1945
— University Comillas, Madrid, 1207
Pontificia Academia Mariana Internationalis, Vatican City, 1942
— — Scientiarum, 1942
— Accademia dell' Immacolata, 1942
— Romana di Archeologia, 1942
— Teologica Romana, Vatican City, 1942
— Facoltà Teologica di S. Bonaventura dei Frati Minori Conventuali, 1947
— — dei SS. Teresa di Gesu e Giovanni Della Croce, Rome, 1947
— Insigne Accademia Artistica dei Virtuosi al Pantheon, 1942
— Universidad Católica del Ecuador, Quito, 409
— — — Perú, Lima, 1045
— — Javeriana, 355
— Universidade Católica de Campinas, São Paulo, 192
— — — São Paulo, 209
— — — do Rio de Janeiro, 205
— — — Rio Grande do Sul, Porto Alegre, 204
— Università S. Tommaso d'Aquino, Rome, 1947
— Universitas Gregoriana, 1944
— — Lateranensis, Rome, 1945
— — Urbaniana, 1946
Pontificio Ateneo Antonianum, 1947
— S. Anselmo, 1947
— Istituto di Archeologia Cristiana, 1947
— — Musica Sacra, 1948
— — — Spiritualità, Vatican City, 1947
— — — Studi Arabi e Islamici, Rome, 1948
— — Regina Mundi, Vatican City, 1945
Pontificium Institutum Altioris Latinitatis, Rome, 1945
— — Biblicum de Urbe, Rome, 1945
— — Orientalium Studiorum, 1945

— — Pastorale, Vatican City, 1946
Pope John XXIII Foundation Library, Missouri, 1629
Popov (A. S.) Central Museum of Communications, Leningrad, 1359
— Scientific and Engineering Society of Radio Engineering and Electrical Communications, Moscow, 1344
Popular Life Museum, Amman, 875
— Traditions Museum, Qasr el-Azem, 1277
Population Association of America, Inc., 1615
— Council, Inc., New York, 1615
— Investigation Committee, London, 1510
— Research Laboratory, Edmonton, Alb., 257
— Studies Center, Philadelphia, 1880
Porcelán Múzeum, Herend, 646
Porphyria Research Group, Tygerberg, 1156
Port and Harbour Research Institute, Kanagawa, 817
— Elizabeth City Libraries, 1163
— — Museum, Snake Park and Oceanarium, 1165
— — Technikon, 1183
— Louis Museum, 923
Portland State University, 1863
Portsmouth Polytechnic, 1546
Portuguese Academy of History, 1097
Porzellansammlung, Dresden, 509
Posavski muzej, Brežice, 1976
Posta Múzeum, Budapest, 644
Postal Museum, Taipei, 342
Postgraduate College, Chapingo, 935
— — of Foreign Languages, Budapest, 647
— Institute of Law and Political Science, Budapest, 647
— Medical Foundation, Sydney, 89
— — School, Budapest, 648
Poštovni muzeum, Prague, 378
Posts and Telecommunications College, Beijing, 336
— — Institute, Tripoli, 907
Postuniversitair Centrum Limburg, Diepenbeek, 169
Potchefstroom College of Education, 1173
— University for Christian Higher Education, Transvaal, 1172
— — — — Libraries, 1163
Potebnya, A. A., Institute of Linguistics, Kiev, 1334
Poultry Research Centre (A.R.C.), Edinburgh, 1440
— Science Association, Champaign, 1599
Povijesni musej Hrvatske, Zagreb, 1978
Powys County Library, Llandrindod Wells, 1455
Poznań Technical University, 1090
Poznańskie Towarzystwo Przyjaciół Nauk, 1065
Prague Agricultural University, 386
— Institute of Chemical Technology, 383
Prahran College of Advanced Education, 116
Prähistorische Staatssammlung, Munich, 544
Prairie View A & M University, Texas, 1902
Pratt Institute, Brooklyn, 1819
Preclinical Diagnostic Chemistry Research Group, Tygerberg, 1156
Prehistoric Society, London, 1423
Pre-History Society of Zimbabwe, 2000
Pre-University School, Johannesburg, 1182
Presbyterian College, Clinton, 1887
— — Montreal, 277
— Historical Society, Philadelphia, 1606
— School of Christian Education, 1916
President Henry Tucker House, St. George's, Bermuda, 1558
Press Library, London, 1458
Preston Institute of Technology, Victoria, 116
— Polytechnic, 1547
Pretoria Art Museum, 1165
Primate Behaviour Research Group, Johannesburg, 1182
— Research Institute, Kyoto, 837

Prime Minister's Office, Statistics Bureau Library, Tokyo, 819
Primorye Agricultural Institute, 1371
Prince Albert Heritage Musueum, 251
— Consort's Army Library, 1459
— Edward Island Provincial Library, 248
— of Songkla University, 1288
— — Wales Museum of Western India, Bombay, 675
Princeton University, 1798
— — Library, 1633
Principia College, Elsah, Ill., 1707
Prins Leopold Instituut voor Tropische Geneeskunde, Antwerp, 168
Print and Drawing Council of Canada, Edmonton, 240
Prirodnjački Muzej u Beogradu, 1976
Prirodonaučen muzej na Makedonija, Skopje, 1977
Prirodoslovni muzej Slovenije, Ljubljana, 1977
— — Rijeka, 1977
— — Split, 1976
Prison Research Council, Philadelphia, 1880
Pro Helvetia, Zürich, 1257
Production and Research Institute of Forestry and Hunting, Ulan Bator, 947
— — — — the Ministry of Communications, Ulan Bator, 947
— — — — — Ministry of Geology and Mining Industry, Ulan Bator, 947
— — — — — Trade and Catering, Ulan Bator, 947
— Engineering Research Association (PERA), Melton Mowbray, 1449
Proefstation voor de Rundveehouderij, Wageningen, 960
Professional Communication Unit, Rondebosch, 1167
"Prof. Iv. Ivanov" Science and Production Complex, 219
Program on Comparative National Leadership, New York, 1810
— — Soviet Nationality Problems, New York, 1811
Programme for Research in the Field of Music, Johannesburg, 1182
Project Double Discovery, New York, 1810
— Planning Centre for Developing Countries, Bradford, 1479
Projects Development Institutes, Enugu, 994
Projektgruppe für Laserforschung, Garching bei München, 527
Propellants, Explosives and Rocket Motor Establishment, Waltham Abbey, 1448
Property Services Agency (Dept. of the Environment) Library, Croydon, 1451
Prophylactic Hygiene Association, Hanoi, 1962
Providence College, Rhode Island, 1884
— Public Library, R.I., 1627
Provinciaal Overijssels Museum, Zwolle, 969
Provincial Archives, Victoria, B.C., 246
— — of Alberta, Edmonton, 246
— — — Newfoundland and Labrador, St. John's, 247
— Museum of Alberta, Edmonton, 249
Provinciale Bibliotheek van Friesland, Leeuwarden, 965
— — — Zeeland, Middelburg, 965
Provost Ross's House, Aberdeen, 1472
— Skene's House, Aberdeen, 1472
Pryanishnikov, D.N., All-Union Research Institute of Fertilizers and Agropedology, Moscow, 1338
Przemyslowy Instytut Telekomunikacji, Warsaw, 1072
Psychological Society of Ireland, Dublin, 731
Psychology Clinic, Baghdad, 727
— Institute, Beijing, 332
Psychometric Society, 1614
Psychopedagogical Research Centre, Vatican City, 1946

# INDEX OF INSTITUTIONS

Psychotechnisches Institut, Vienna, 126
Ptolemais Museum, Tolmeitha, 906
Public Archives of Canada, 248
— — — Nova Scotia, 247
— — — Sierra Leone, Freetown, 1148
— Health Laboratories, Cairo, 415
— — Laboratory, Salisbury, Zimbabwe, 2002
— — — Service Centre for Applied Microbiology and Research, Salisbury, 1445
— Libraries Board, Kampala, 1311
— Library, Abu Dhabi, 1391
— — Amman, 875
— — Ankara, 1300
— — Armagh, 1554
— — Benghazi, 906
— — Bloemfontein, 1161
— — Bridgetown, Barbados, 146
— — Bulawayo, 2002
— — Colombo, 1226
— — Irbid, 875
— — Kabul, 52
— — Konya, 1300
— — Nablus, 875
— — Ramallah, 875
— — of Charlotte and Mecklenburg County, Charlotte, N.C., 1627
— — — Cincinnati and Hamilton County, 1627
— — — Columbus and Franklin County, 1627
— — — the District of Columbia, Washington, 1626
— Record Office, London, 1449
— — — of Ireland, Dublin, 732
— — — Victoria, Melbourne, 96
— — Records Office, Nassau, 140
Publication and Information Directorate, New Delhi, 665
Puerto Rican Academy, San Juan, 1109
— Rico Planning Board Library, 1110
Puheopin laitos, Tampere, 438
Pulp and Paper Research Institute of Canada, Pointe Claire, Que., 246
Punjab Agricultural University, Ludhiana, 638
— Bureau of Education, Lahore, 1019
— Government Central Record Office and Archival Museum, Lahore, 1024
— Public Library, Lahore, 1024
— University Extension Library, Ludhiana, 674
— Veterinary Research Institute, 1021
Punjabi Adabi Academy, Lahore, 1020
— University, Patiala, 699
Punjabrao Agriculture University, Maharashtra, 699
Purdue University, 1717
— — Libraries, Lafayette, Ind., 1632
Purkyne University, Brno, 380
Pusat Bahasa, Jakarta, 714
— Dokumentasi Hukum, Jakarta, 714
— — Ilmiah Nasional, Lembaga Ilmu Pengetahuan Indonesia, Jakarta, 711
— Ilmu Komputer, Jakarta, 714
— Meteorologi dan Geofisika, Jakarta, 710
— Pembinaan Dan Pengembangan Bahasa, Jakarta, 709
— Penelitian Arkeologi Nasional, Jakarta, 709
— — Botani, Bogor, 710
— — dan Pengembangan Geologi, Bandung, 710
— — — — Pelayanan Kesehatan, Surabaya, 709
— — — — Peternakan, Bogor, 709
— Perpustakaan Angkatan Darat, Bandung, 710
— Risat dan Pengembangan, Semerang, 713
— Studi Ilmu Lingkungan, Jakarta, 714
Pushkin House Museum, 1357
— Institute of Literature and Linguistics, Tashkent, 1335
— Memorial Committee, Kishinev, 1331

— Museum, Moscow, 1357
— State Public Library of the Kazakh S.S.R., Alma-Ata, 1348
— — Preserve, Pskovskaya Region, 1358
"Puškarov, N.", Institute of Soil Science and Yields Programming, Sofia, 219
Pustovoit, V.S., All-Union Oil-Bearing Crops Research Institute, Krasnodar, 1338
Pyongyang Medical Institute, 884
— Scientific Library, 883
Pyrethrum Bureau, Nakuru, 879

## Q

Qatar National Library, Doha, 1114
Qinghai Library, Xining, 335
Qinghua (Tsinghua) University, 336
Qom Museum, 722
Quaid-i-Azam Academy, Karachi, 1019
— Birthplace, Reading Room, Museum and Library, Karachi, 1024
— College of Commerce, Peshawar, 1027
— University, Islamabad, 1028
Quantum Institute, Santa Barbara, 1673
Quebec Seminary Museum, 251
Queen Elizabeth II Arts Council of New Zealand, Wellington, 978
— — College, London, 1510
— — House, Oxford, 1426
— Mary College, London, 1510
— — — Library, London, 1460
— Victoria Memorial Library, Salisbury, Zimbabwe, 2002
— — Museum and Art Gallery, Launceston, 97
— — — Salisbury, Zimbabwe, 2002
Queen's College, Oxford, 1524
— — Library, Oxford, 1463
— — Parkville, 104
— Theological College, Kingston, Ont., 296
— University, Belfast, 1555
— — Kingston, Ont., 294
— — Library, Belfast, 1554
— — — Kingston, Ont., 248
— — Museums, Kingston, Ont., 251
Queens Borough Public Library, 1627
— College, Charlotte, N.C., 1829
— — of the City University of New York, Flushing, 1805
Queens' College, Cambridge, 1485
— — Library, Cambridge, 1462
Queensland Agricultural College, Lawes, 114
— Art Gallery, Brisbane, 97
— Conservatorium of Music, Brisbane, 114
— Herbarium, Indooroopilly, 97
— Institute of Medical Research, Brisbane, 92
— — — Technology, Brisbane, 114
— Museum, 97
— Parliamentary Library, Brisbane, 96
Quekett Microscopical Club, London, 1433
Quincy College, 1707
Quinnipiac College, Conn., 1678
Qurinna Library, Benghazi, 906

## R

Raad voor Gezondheidsresearch TNO, The Hague, 961
Rabindra Bharati University, Calcutta, 699
— Bhavan Art Gallery, 675
— Bhavana, Santiniketan (Bolpur), 675
Raccolte di Palazzo Tursi, Genoa, 771
Radcliffe College, Cambridge, Mass., 1757
Radford University, 1916
Radiation Biology Centre, Kyoto, 837
— Medicine Institute, Sichuan, 333
— Research Society, Bethesda, 1619
Radio Atmospheric Science Center, Kyoto, 837

— Research Laboratories, Tokyo, 817
— Society of Great Britain, 1439
— Space Research Station, Johannesburg, 1161
— Technique Institute, Xian, 333
— -Astrophysical Observatory, Riga, 1330
Radiobiology Unit (M.R.C.), Didcot, 1444
— -Electronics Association, Hanoi, 1962
Radiological Society of North America, Oak Brook, Ill., 1610
Radiology Association, Hanoi, 1962
Radioisotope Research Centre, Kyoto, 837
Radnicka biblioteka, Zagreb, 1975
Ragib Paṣa Library, 1300
Railway Engineering School, Ulan Bator, 948
— Museum, Cairo, 417
— Technical Research Institute, Tokyo, 818
Rainis, J., Museum of the History of Literature and Arts, Riga, 1358
Rajasthan Academy of Science, Pilani, 659
Rajendra Agricultural University, Samastipur, 700
Rajputana Museum, 675
Rákóczi Múzeum, 646
Raman Research Institute, Bangalore, 670
Rambam Library, Tel-Aviv, 742
Ramkhamhaeng University, Bangkok, 1289
Ramkrishna Mission Library, Nandi, 426
Ranchi University, Bihar, 700
Rand Afrikaans University, Johannesburg, 1175
— Corporation, Santa Monica, Calif., 1620
Randolph-Macon College, Ashland, Va., 1917
— — Woman's College, Lynchburg, Va., 1917
Ranfurly Out Island Library, Nassau, 140
**Rangoon Institute of Technology, Insein, 229**
**Rannsóknaráð Riksins, Reykjavik, 656**
**Rannsóknastofa Háskólans, 657**
**Rannsóknastofnun byggingaidnadarins, Reykjavik, 657**
— fiskidnadarins, Reykjavik, 656
— Landbúnadarins, Reykjavik, 656
Rare Earth Information Center (RIC), Ames, 1621
Rasht University, 724
Rathausbücherei der Stadt Stuttgart, 540
Rationalisierungs-Kuratorium der deutschen Wirtschaft (RKW), 526
Ratnapura National Museum, 1226
Rautenstrauch-Joest-Museum, 542
Ravensberg, Ludwig, Donation, Oslo, 1012
Ravensbourne College of Art and Design, Chislehurst, 1551
Ravishankar University, Raipur, 700
Rawalpindi Government College of Technology, 1029
Ray Society, London, 1431
Razi State Institute, Teheran, 722
— University, Kermanshah, 724
Raziskovalna skupnost Slovenije, Ljubljana, 1970
Reading Museum and Art Gallery, 1470
Real Academia de Bellas Artes de la Purisima Concepción, 1187
— — — — San Fernando, 1185
— — — — San Jorge, 1186
— — — — San Telmo, 1187
— — — — Santa Isabel de Hungría, 1187
— — — y Ciencias Históricas de Toledo, 1187
— — Ciencias, Bellas Letras y Nobles Artes, Córdoba, 1187
— — — Exactas, Fisicas y Naturales, Madrid, 1185
— — — Morales y Políticas, Madrid, 1185
— — — y Artes de Barcelona, 1186
— — Farmacia, Madrid, 1186
— — Jurisprudencia y Legislación, 1186
— — la Historia, Madrid, 1185
— — la Lengua Vasca, Bilbao, 1187

- - - Medicina de Sevilla, 1187
- - - y Cirurgía de Palma de Mallorca, 1188
- - Nobles y Bellas Artes de San Luis, 1187
- - Española, 1185
- - Gallega, 1187
- - Hispano-Americana, 1187
- - Nacional de Medicina, 1186
- - Sevillana de Buenas Letras, 1187
- Biblioteca de San Lorenzo de El Escorial, Madrid, 1200
- Colegio de San Clemente de los Españoles, Bologna, 759
- Universitario "Maria Cristina", Madrid, 1222
- Conservatorio Superior de Música de Madrid, 1223
- Escuela Superior de Arte Dramático, Madrid, 1223
- Jardín Botánico, Madrid, 1198
- Sociedad Arqueológica Tarraconense, 1190
- - Económica de Amigos del Pais de Tenerife, 1189
- - Española de Física y Química, 1191
- - - Historia Natural, 1191
- - Fotográfica Española, 1188
- - Geográfica, 1190
- - Matemática Española, 1191
- - Vascongada de los Amigos del País, 1192
Rechenzentrum, Hagen, 546
- Mannheim, 590
Rechtschreibungskommission, Vienna, 119
Redbridge Public Libraries, 1452
Redpath Museum, Montreal, 251
Reed College, Portland, Ore., 1864
Regent College, Vancouver, 261
Regent's Park College, Oxford, 1524
Regina Public Library, 249
- Water Research Institute, Sask., 297
Regional and Urban Planning Centre, Salisbury, Zimbabwe, 2003
- Centre for Adult Education and Functional Literacy for Latin America (CREFAL), Michoacán, 30
- - Higher Education in Latin America and the Caribbean, Caracas, 1950
- - of Mineral Resources Region 3, Chiangmai, 1285
- Cultural and Historical Heritage Management Board, Blagoevgrad, 221
- Institute for Population Studies, Legon, 613
- - of Higher Education and Development (RIHED), Singapore, 1150
- Library, Burgas, 220
- - Ruse, 220
- - Stara Zagora, 220
- - Šumen, 221
- - Varna, 221
- - Veliko Tărnova, 221
- Museum of Archaeology, Plovdiv, 221
- - Ethnology, Plovdiv, 221
- - History, Burgas, 221
- - - Haskovo, 221
- - - Loveč, 221
- - - Pazardžik, 221
- - - Pernik, 221
- - - Pleven, 221
- - - Ruse, 222
- - - Stara Zagora, 222
- - - Sumen, 222
- - - Tolbuhin, 222
- - - Varna, 222
- - - Veliko Tárnovo, 222
- - - Vidin, 222
- - - Vraca, 222
- - - the Revolutionary Movement, Plovdiv, 221
- Museums, Uganda, 1312

- Research Institutes (Directorate of Agricultural Research), Pretoria, 1160
- - Laboratory, Hyderabad, 666
- - - Jammu-Tawi, 666
- - - Jorhat, 666
- - - Orissa, 665
- - Studies Association, London, 1423
- Sugar Cane Training Centre for Africa, Réduit, 924
- Training Centre, Doha, 1114
- - - for Archivists, Legon, 613
- - Veterinary Institute, Plovdiv, 219
- - - Stara Zagora, 219
- - - V. Tărnovo, 219
Regis College, Weston, 1757
Reguly Antal Historic Library, Zirc, 642
Rehabilitation International, New York, 39
Reinier de Graafstichting, Nijmegen, 970
Reiss-Museum, Mannheim, 544
Rekencentrum, Antwerp, 167
Rektorkollegiet, Copenhagen, 390
Religious Research Association, New York, 1615
Rembrandt-Huis Museum, Amsterdam, 966
Remeis-Sternwarte, 533
Remote Sensing Center, Cairo, 415
Renaissance Society of America, New York, 1606
Rengeoin (Sanjusangendo), Kyoto, 821
Renison College, Waterloo, Ont., 311
Rensselaer Polytechnic Institute, 1819
Repartição do Arquivo e Biblioteca do Ministério dos Negócios Estrangeiros, Lisbon, 1102
Representative Church Body Library, Dublin, 732
Reproductive Biology Unit (M.R.C.), Edinburgh, 1444
Republic University, Sivas, 1305
Republican Archives of Manuscripts, Baku, 1326
- Scientific and Technical Library of the Armenian S.S.R., Erevan, 1351
- - - - - - the Azerbaijan S.S.R., Baku, 1351
- - - - - - The Byelorussian S.S.R., Minsk, 1351
- - - - - - The Estonian S.S.R., Tallinn, 1351
- - - - - - the Kazakh S.S.R., Alma-Ata, 1351
- - - - - - the Kirghiz S.S.R., Frunze, 1351
- - - - - - the Latvian S.S.R., Riga, 1351
- - - - - - the Lithuanian S.S.R., Vilnius, 1351
- - - - - - the Moldavian S.S.R., Kishinev, 1351
- - - - - - the Tajik S.S.R., Dushanbe, 1351
- - - - - - the Turkmen S.S.R., Ashkhabad, 1351
- - - - - - the Uzbek S.S.R., Tashkent, 1351
Republički Zavod za Zaštita na Spomenicite na Kulturata, Skopje, 1971
Research and Design Institute of Health Institutions Construction, Sofia, 220
- - - - the Fuel and Power Industry, Ulan Bator, 947
- - Development Centre, Jeddah, 1144
- - Productivity Council, Fredericton, N.B., 246
- Study Centre for the Protection of Historical Monuments, Teheran, 722
- Archives of the Israel Department of Antiquities and Museums, 742
- Association for the Fine Arts, Sofia, 217
- - on Fundamental Problems of Technical Sciences, Sofia, 216

- Centre for Atomic Energy, Pyongyang, 883
- - - Education, Sofia, 219
- - - Genetics, Skierniweice, 1069
- - - Land Development, Seoul, 893
- - - Medical Polymers and Biomaterials, Kyoto, 837
- - - Sports Science, Kyoto, 837
- - of Chemical Engineering and of Chemical Apparatus Construction, Gliwice, 1069
- - - Linguistics, Literary History and Folklore, Iași, 1135
- - - Social Sciences, Iași, 1135
- - on the Mathematical Modelling of Clinical Tests, Coventry, 1539
- Designs and Standards Organisation, Lucknow, 672
- Group for Dental Epidemiology, Tygerberg, 1156
- - - the Diffuse Obstructive Pulmonary Syndrome, Tygerberg, 1156
- Institute for Catalysis, Sapporo, 830
- - - Chemobiodynamics, Chiba, 816
- - - Diseases in a Tropical Environment, Durban, 1170
- - - - - Tropical Environment, Tygerberg, 1155
- - - Environmental Health, Tel-Aviv, 750
- - - Food Science, Kyoto, 837
- - - Fundamental Physics, Kyoto, 837
- - - Humanistic Studies, Kyoto, 837
- - - - Library, Kyoto, 820
- - - Iron, Steel and Other Metals, Sendai, 851
- - - Marketing and Distribution, St. Gallen, 1275
- - - Mathematical Sciences, Kyoto, 837
- - - Microbial Diseases, Osaka, 847
- - - Mindanao Culture, Cagayan de Oro City, 1060
- - - Natural Resources, Tokyo, 816
- - - Polymers and Textiles, Ibaraki, 818
- - - Production Development, Kyoto, 818
- - - Protection of Mothers and Newborn Children, Ulan Bator, 947
- - - Scientific Measurements, Sendai City, 851
- - - Studies in Education, Ames, 1728
- - - Tropical Medicine, Cairo, 415
- - - Tuberculosis and Cancer, Sendai, 851
- - of Applied Electricity, Sapporo-City, 830
- - - Atmospherics, Nagoya, 842
- - - Atomic Energy, Osaka, 860
- - - - Reactors, Melekess, 1346
- - - Basic Chemistry, Kharkov, 1346
- - - Biological Preparations and Blood, Ulan Bator, 947
- - - Economics and Business, Seoul, 894
- - - Educational Affairs, Seoul, 893
- - - Electrical Communication, Sendai City, 851
- - - Environmental Medicine, Nagoya-city, 842
- - - Fermentation, Kofu, 859
- - - Food Development, Seoul, 893
- - - Forensic Medicine, Moscow, 1346
- - - Fuel Cells, Kofu, 859
- - - Humanities, Seoul, 894
- - - Immunological Science, Sapporo, 830
- - - Industrial Technology, Seoul, 893
- - - Inorganic Synthesis, Kofu, 859
- - - Introscopy, Moscow, 1346
- - - Magnetosphere, Nagoya, 862
- - - Marxism-Leninism, Moscow, 1346

Research Institute of Material and Technical Supply, Ulan Bator, 947
— — — Mathematical Computing Machines, Erevan, 1346
— — — Medicine, Seoul, 893
— — — Medicinal Sources, Tokyo, 815
— — — Mineral Dressing and Metallurgy, Sendai, 851
— — — Prices and Standards, Ulan Bator, 947
— — — Printing Bureau, Tokyo, 818
— — — Science, Seoul, 894
— — — Skin and Venereal Diseases, Tbilisi, 1385
— — — Social Science, Kyung Hee University, Seoul, 893
— — — State Procurator's Office) of Causes of Crime, Ulan Bator, 947
— — — the Ministry of Light and Food Industry, Ulan Bator, 947
— — — — State Planning Commission and Academy of Sciences) of Development and Location of Productivity Forces, Ulan Bator, 947
— — — Underground Resources, Akita City, 824
— — — Water Resources, Ulan Bator, 947
— — — Welding, Tokyo, 818
— — on International Change, New York, 1810
— — — Theory and History of Fine Arts, Moscow, 1339
— Library on African Affairs, Accra, 612
— Museum, Leningrad, 1339
— Reactor Institute, Kyoto, 837
— School of Biological Sciences, Canberra, 99
— — — Chemistry, Canberra, 99
— — — Earth Sciences, Canberra, 99
— — — Pacific Sciences, Canberra, 99
— — — Physical Sciences, Canberra, 99
— — — Social Sciences, Canberra, 99
— Society of Pakistan, Lahore, 1021
— Unit for Chemical Kinetics, Potchefstroom, 1173
— — — Cosmic Rays, Potchefstroom, 1173
— — — Emergent Pathogens, Tygerberg, 1156
— — — Human Cellular Immunology, Tygerberg, 1156
— — — the design of Catecholaminergic Drugs, Tygerberg, 1156
— — — Transplantation, Tygerberg, 1156
— — on Vector Pathology, St. John's, Newfoundland, 284
Resim ve Heykel Müzesi, Istanbul, 1302
Resnick, Jack and Pearl, Gerontology Center, New York, 1824
Restauratorski Zavod, 1972
Reuchlinhaus, Pforzheim, 545
Réunion des Musées Nationaux, Paris, 466
— Internationale des Laboratoires d'Essais et de Recherches sur les Matériaux et les Constructions, Paris, 33
Revolution Museum, Hanoi, 1963
Revolutionary Museum, Ulan Bator, 947
Rheinisch-Westfälische Akademie der Wissenschaften, Düsseldorf, 516
— Technische Hochschule, Aachen, 546
Rheinisch-Westfälisches Institut für Wirtschaftsforschung, Essen, 529
— Wirtschaftsarchiv zu Köln e.V., 539
Rheinische Friedrich-Wilhelms-Universität Bonn, 554
— Vereinigung für Volkskunde, 525
Rheinisches Landesmuseum, Trier, 545
— — in Bonn, 541
Rheinland-Westphalia Academy of Sciences, Düsseldorf, 516
Rhode Island College, 1884
— — Historical Society, 1606
— — School of Design, 1884

Rhodes Institute for Freshwater Studies, Grahamstown, 1176
— -Inyanga Experiment Station, Rusape, 2001
— Memorial Museum and Commonwealth Centre, Bishop's Stortford, 1467
— Trust, Oxford, 1421
— University, Grahamstown, 1176
— — Library, 1162
Rice Research Institute, Dokri, 1021
— University, Houston, 1899
Richard-Strauss Konservatorium, Munich, 608
— Wagner-Museum, Bayreuth, 541
— — — Lucerne-Tribschen, 1262
Richmond-upon-Thames Public Libraries, 1452
Rider College, Lawrenceville, N.J., 1800
Ridley College, Parkville, 104
Riga Institute of Civil Aviation Engineers, 1390
— Polytechnic Institute, 1376
— State Medical Institute, 1383
Rigsarkivet, Copenhagen, 394
Riijks Geologische Dienst, Haarlem, 962
Rijksakademie van Beeldende Kunsten, 974
Rijksarchief in de Provincie Noord-Brabant, 963
— — — Utrecht, 963
— — Drente te Assen, 963
— — Friesland te Leeuwarden, 963
— — Gelderland, 963
— — Groningen, 963
— — Limburg te Maastricht, 963
— — Noord-Holland te Haarlem, 963
— — Overijssel, 963
— — Zeeland, 963
— te Antwerpen, 155
— — Gent, 156
Rijksbureau voor Kunsthistorische Documentatie, 956
Rijksdienst voor de Monumentzorg, Zeist, 956
Rijksherbarium, 961
Rijksinstituut voor het Rassenonderzoek van Cultuurgewassen, Wageningen, 960
— — Natuurbeheer, Arnhem, 960
— — Oorlogsdocumentatie, 963
— — Visscherijonderzoek, 960
Rijksmuseum, Amsterdam, 966
— "Huis Lambert van Meerten" te Delft, 966
— G. M. Kam te Nijmegen, 968
— "Kroller-Muller", Otterlo, 968
— Meermanno-Westreenianum (Museum Van het Boek), The Hague, 967
— Hendrik Willem Mesdag te 's-Gravenhage, 967
— "Nederlands Scheepvaart Museum", Amsterdam, 966
— Paleis Het Loo, Apeldoorn, 966
— Twenthe te Enschede, 966
— van Geologie en Mineralogie, 967
— — Natuurlijke Historie, Leiden, 968
— — Oudheden, 968
— Vincent van Gogh, Amsterdam, 966
— voor de Geschiedenis der Natuurwetenschappen en van de Geneeskunde "Museum Boerhaave", Leiden, 968
— — Volkenkunde, Leiden, 968
— — Volkskunde "Het Nederlands Openluchtmuseum", 966
Rijksproefstation voor Zaadonderzoek, 960
Rijksuniversitair Centrum te Antwerpen, 166
Rijksuniversiteit, Gent, 159
— Groningen, 970
— Leiden, 970
— Limburg, Maastricht, 970
— Utrecht, 971
Rikagaku Kenkyusho, Saitama, 816
Rikkyo University, 867
Riksantikvaren, Oslo, 1010
Riksantikvarieämbetet och Statens Historiska museer, Stockholm, 1242

Riksantikvarieämbetets Gotlandsundersökningar, Visby, 1237
Riksarkivet, Oslo, 1010
— Stockholm, 1239
Riksdagsbiblioteket, Stockholm, 1240
Rila Monastery National Museum, 222
Rimsky-Korsakov House-Museum, 1359
Ring House Gallery, Edmonton, Alb., 249
Ripon Cathedral Library, 1459
— College, Wisconsin, 1932
Rippi-Rónai Muzeum, 646
Riron Keizai Gakkai, 805
Rissho University, 867
Rithöfundasamband Íslands, Reykjavík, 656
Rithøvundafelag Føroya, Tórshavn, 402
Ritsumeikan University, 867
Riverina College of Advanced Education, Wagga Wagga, 113
Rivers State University of Science and Technology, Port Harcourt, 1001
Riverview College Observatory, 94
Rivier College, 1796
Rjukan Bibliotek, 1010
Roanoke College, Salem, 1917
Robens Institute of Industrial and Environmental Health and Safety, Guildford, 1532
Robert Gordon's Institute of Technology, Aberdeen, 1547
— McDougall Art Gallery, Christchurch, N.Z., 982
— Maynard Hutchins Center for the Study of Democratic Institutions, Santa Barbara, Cal., 1617
Roberts Wesleyan College, Rochester, N.Y., 1819
Robinson College, Cambridge, 1485
— W. S. and L. B., University College, Broken Hill, 107
Rochester Institute of Technology, N.Y., 1819
— Museum and Science Center, N.Y., 1641
— Public Library, N.Y., 1627
Rock Soil Mechanics Institute, Wuhan, 332
Rockefeller Foundation, 1604
— University, New York, 1819
Rockford College, Ill., 1707
Rockhurst College, Kansas City, Mo., 1787
Rocky Mountain College, Billings, 1792
Rôdô Kagaku Kenkyusho, 814
Roemer- und Palizaeus-Museum, Hildesheim, 543
Rogoff-Wellcome Medical Research Institute, Tel-Aviv, 740
Rohilkhand University, Bareilly, 700
Röhss Museum of Art and Crafts, Gothenburg, 1242
Rokuonji, Kyoto, 821
Rolf E. Stenersens Donation, Oslo, 1012
Rollins College, Winter Park, 1695
Romanovsky, V. I., Institute of Mathematics, Tashkent, 1335
Römisch-Germanisches Museum, Cologne, 542
— — Zentralmuseum-Forschungsinstitut für Vor- und Frühgeschichte, Mainz, 544
Römisches Institut der Görres-Gesellschaft, Vatican City, 1943
Roosevelt University, Chicago, 1708
Roosevelt's Little White House, Warm Springs, 1641
Rosary College, River Forest, 1708
Rose F. Kennedy Center for Research in Mental Retardation and Human Development, New York, 1824
— -Hulman Institute of Technology, Terre Haute, 1721
Rosemont College, Pa., 1878
Rosenborg Slot, 396
Roseworthy Agricultural College, 114
Rosgarten Museum, Konstanz, 543
Roskilde Universitets Center, 399
Roslavl Historical Museum, 1356

Ross Dependency Research Committee, Wellington, 980
— Institute of Tropical Hygiene, 1445
Rostov Civil Engineering Institute, 1380
— Institute of Agricultural Engineering, 1372
— — — National Economy, 1373
— — — Radiology and Oncology, 1386
— — — Railway Engineers, 1389
— Museum of Fine Art, 1354
— Region Paediatric Research Institute, 1384
— State Institute of Pedagogics and Music, 1388
— — Medical Institute, 1383
— — University, 1366
Rotary International in Great Britain and Ireland, 1421
Rothamsted Experimental Station, 1441
Rotterdams Conservatorium, 974
Rotterdamsch Leeskabinet, 965
Rowett Research Institute, 1441
Royal Academy of Archaeology of Belgium, Brussels, 149
— — — Arts in London, 1406
— — — — Library, 1457
— — — Dramatic Art, London, 1553
— — — Dutch Language and Literature, Ghent, 148
— — — Exact, Physical and Natural Sciences, Madrid, 1185
— — — Fine Arts, Stockholm, 1234
— — — French Language and Literature, Brussels, 148
— — — History, Madrid, 1185
— — — Jurisprudence and Legislation, Madrid, 1186
— — — Letters, History and Antiquities, Stockholm, 1234
— — — Medicine, Dublin, 731
— — — — of Belgium, Brussels, 149
— — — Moral and Political Sciences, Madrid, 1185
— — — Music, London, 1553
— — — — Library, London, 1460
— — — — Stockholm, 1235
— — — Overseas Sciences, Brussels, 149
— — — Pharmacy, Madrid, 1186
— — — Science, Letters and Fine Arts of Belgium, Brussels, 147
— — Schools, 1551
— Aeronautical Society, London, 1439
— — — Auckland, N.Z., 977
— — — (Australian Division), 91
— African Society, 1435
— Agricultural College, Cirencester, Glos., 1550
— — Society of England, 1411
— — — — New Zealand, 978
— Air Force Museum, Hendon, 1466
— Aircraft Establishment, Farnborough, 1448
— Anthropological Institute of Great Britain and Ireland, London, 1435
— Archaeological Institute, 1423
— Architectural Institute of Canada, Ottawa, 239
— Armament Research and Development Establishment, Sevenoaks, 1448
— Art Society of New South Wales, 87
— Asiatic Society, Colombo, 1224
— — — Hong Kong Branch, 1559
— — — of Great Britain and Ireland, London, 1435
— — — Library, London, 1457
— Association for Disability and Rehabilitation, London, 1429
— Astronomical Society, 1433
— — — Library, 1457
— — — of Canada, 243
— — — New Zealand, 978
— Australasian College of Dental Surgeons, Sydney, 89
— — — — Physicians, 89
— — — — Radiologists, Millers Point, 89
— — — — Surgeons, 89

— — Ornithologists' Union, 90
— Australian Chemical Institute, Parkville, 91
— — College of Ophthalmologists, Sydney, 89
— — Historical Society, Sydney, 88
— — Institute of Architects, Red Hill, A.C.T., 87
— Botanic Garden, Edinburgh, 1447
— — — Library, 1459
— — — Gardens, Kew, 1447
— — — Peradeniya, 1225
— — — and National Herbarium of New South Wales, Sydney, 93
— — — — — of Victoria, S. Yarra, 93
— — — Library and Archives Division, Kew, 1457
— Cambrian Academy of Art, 1414
— Canadian Academy of Arts, 239
— — College of Organists, Toronto, 319
— — Geographical Society, 241
— — Institute, 239
— College of Art, 1551
— — — General Practitioners, London, 1429
— — — Music, 1553
— — — — Library, 1460
— — — — Museum of Instruments, London, 1466
— — — Obstetricians and Gynaecologists, 1429
— — — Organists, 1553
— — — Pathologists of Australasia, Sydney, 89
— — — Physicians, London, 1429
— — — — and Surgeons of Canada, Ottawa, 242
— — — — of Glasgow, 1429
— — — — of Glasgow Library, 1459
— — — — Library, 1457
— — — — of Edinburgh, 1429
— — — — — Library, 1459
— — — — Ireland, Dublin, 731
— — — Psychiatrists, London, 1429
— — — Radiologists, London, 1429
— — — Surgeons in Ireland, Dublin, 736
— — — — Library, Dublin, 732
— — — — Museum, Dublin, 732
— — — — Museum, London, 1466
— — — — of Edinburgh, 1429
— — — — England, 1429
— — — — — Library, 1457
— — — Veterinary Surgeons, London, 1411
— — — — Wellcome Library, 1457
— Commission for the Exhibition of 1851, London, 1421
— — on Historical Manuscripts, London, 1423
— Commonwealth Society, London, 1435
— — — Bermuda Branch, 1558
— — — Library, 1457
— Conservatory of Music, Toronto, 319
— Danish Academy of Sciences and Letters, Copenhagen, 388
— Dental Hospital of London, School of Dental Surgery, 1511
— Drawing Society, 1414
— Dublin Society, 729
— — — Library, 732
— Economic Society, 1417
— Entomological Society of London, 1432
— Faculty of Procurators in Glasgow, 1417
— Fine Art Commission, 1413
— — — — for Scotland, 1413
— Forestry Society of England, Wales and Northern Ireland, 1411
— Free Hospital School of Medicine, 1511
— Geographical Society, London, 1423
— — — Library, 1458
— — — of Australasia, Queensland, Inc., 88
— Greenwich Observatory, 1446
— Gustavus Adolphus Academy, Uppsala, 1235

— Hamilton College of Music, 319
— Hibernian Academy of Painting, Sculpture, and Architecture, 729
— Highland and Agricultural Society of Scotland, 1411
— Historical Society, 1423
— — — of Queensland, Brisbane, 88
— — — Victoria, 88
— Holloway College, 1511
— Horticultural Society, London, 1411
— — — of Ireland, 729
— Incorporation of Architects in Scotland, 1412
— Institute, Bangkok, 1283
— — of British Architects, 1412
— — — International Affairs, 1417
— — — — Library, 1458
— — — Oil Painters, 1414
— — — Painters in Water Colours, 1414
— — — Philosophy, 1434
— — — Public Administration, 1418
— — — Health and Hygiene, London, 1429
— — — Technology, Stockholm, 1244
— — — the Architects of Ireland, Dublin, 730
— Institution of Chartered Surveyors, Dublin, 730
— — — — London, 1412
— — — Great Britain, 1410
— — — — Library, London, 1458
— — — Naval Architects, London, 1439
— Irish Academy, 729
— — — of Music, 736
— Jubilee Trusts, London, 1421
— Medical Society, Edinburgh, 1430
— Melbourne Institute of Technology, 116
— Meteorological Society, 1433
— Microscopical Society, 1433
— Military College of Canada, 297
— — — — Science, Swindon, 1553
— — School of Music, 1553
— Musical Association, London, 1415
— National Academy of Medicine, Madrid, 1186
— — Institute for the Deaf Library and Information Services, London, 1458
— Naval College, Greenwich, 1553
— Nepal Academy, Kathmandu, 954
— Netherlands Academy of Arts and Sciences, Amsterdam, 955
— Northern College of Music, Manchester, 1553
— Nova Scotia Historical Society, Halifax, 241
— Numismatic Society, 1423
— Observatory, Edinburgh, 1446
— — Hong Kong, 1559
— Ontario Museum, 251
— Pavilion, Art Gallery and Museums, Brighton, 1467
— Philatelic Society, London, 1413
— Philosophical Society of Glasgow, 1434
— Photographic Society of Great Britain, 1415
— Physical Society of Edinburgh, 1433
— Postgraduate Medical School, London, 1512
— Queensland Art Society, 87
— School of Church Music, 1553
— Scientific Society, Amman, 875
— Scottish Academy, 1406
— — — of Music and Drama, Glasgow, 1553
— — Forestry Society, 1411
— — Geographical Society, 1423
— — Museum, 1473
— Signals and Radar Establishment, Baldock, 1448
— — — — Malvern, 1448
— Society, London, 1392
— — for Asian Affairs, London, 1435
— — — Nature Conservation, Lincoln, 1431
— — — the Protection of Birds, 1432

# INDEX OF INSTITUTIONS

Royal Society Library, London, 1458
— — of Antiquaries of Ireland, 730
— — — Arts, 1413
— — — and Sciences of Mauritius, 923
— — — British Artists, London, 1414
— — — Sculptors, 1414
— — — Canada, 233
— — — Chemistry, London, 1433
— — — Library, London, 1458
— — — Edinburgh, 1398
— — — Library, 1459
— — — Health, London, 1430
— — — Literature of the United Kingdom, 1427
— — — Marine Artists, London, 1414
— — — Medicine, 1430
— — — Library, 1458
— — — Miniature Painters, Sculptors and Gravers, London, 1414
— — — New South Wales, 89
— — — New Zealand, 976
— — — Painters in Water Colours, 1414
— — — Portrait Painters, 1414
— — — Queensland, 90
— — — South Africa, 1154
— — — — Library, Rondebosch, 1162
— — — Australia Inc., 90
— — — Tasmania, 90
— — — Tropical Medicine and Hygiene, 1430
— — — Victoria, 90
— — — Western Australia, 90
— South Australian Society of Arts, Adelaide, 87
— Spanish Academy, Madrid, 1185
— Statistical Society, 1418
— Swedish Academy of Agriculture and Forestry, Stockholm, 1234
— — — Engineering Sciences, Stockholm, 1235
— — — Military Sciences, Stockholm, 1235
— — — Sciences, Stockholm, 1233
— Television Society, London, 1439
— Town Planning Institute, London, 1412
— United Services Institute for Defence Studies Library, London, 1458
— Veterinary College, 1511
— — and Agricultural University, Copenhagen, 398
— Victoria College, Montreal, 277
— Welsh Agricultural Society, Builth-Wells, 1411
— West of England Academy, Bristol, 1414
— Western Australian Historical Society, Nedlands, W.A., 89
— Zoological Society of Ireland, 731
— — — New South Wales, 90
— — — Scotland, 1432
— — — South Australia, 90
R.S.F.S.R. Institute of Medical Parasitology, 1386
Rubber Board and Rubber Research Institute of India, Kottayam, 666
— Research Association Ltd., Haifa, 740
— — Centre, Bangkok, 1283
— — Institute of Malaysia, 915
— — — Library, 916
— — — Nigeria, Benin City, 993
— — — Sri Lanka, Agalawatta, 1225
Rubenianum, Antwerp, 157
Rubenshuis, Antwerp, 157
Rubin Academy of Music, Jerusalem, 753
Rublyov (Andrei) Museum of Ancient Russian Art, Moscow, 1352
Rudaki Institute of Language and Literature, Dushanbe, 1332
Rudolph Tegners Museum og Statuepark, Dronningmøll, 396
Ruhr Universität, Bochum, 551
Ruhuna University College, Matara, 1228
Ruprecht-Karl-Universität, Heidelberg, 578
Rural Development Institute, Monrovia, 905
— — Studies Bureau, Lusaka, 1998
Rusden State College, Clayton, Vic., 116

Ruskin School of Drawing and Fine Art, Oxford, 1551
Russell Sage College, Troy, N.Z., 1820
— — Foundation, 1615
Russian Friendship Cultural Center, Mogadishu, 1153
— Institute, New York, 1811
— Palestine Society, Moscow, 1320
Rutgers University, New Brunswick, N.J., 1800
— — Libraries, 1633
Rutherford Laboratory, Chilton, 1446
Ruusbroecgenootschap, Antwerp, 153
Ryanggang Provincial Library, Hesan, 883
Ryazan Historico-architectural Museum Reservation, 1356
— V. D. Kalmykov Institute of Radio Engineering, 1378
— Professor P. A. Kostychev Agricultural Institute, 1371
— I. P. Pavlov Medical Institute, 1383
— Regional Art Museum, 1354
Ryerson Polytechnical Institute, Toronto, 297
Rylsky, M. F., Institute of Art, Folklore and Ethnography, Kiev, 1334
Ryukoku University, Kyoto, 867
— — Library, Kyoto, 820
Ryukyu Islands Central Library, Okinawa, 820

## S

Sabah Museum, Kota Kinabalu, 916
— State Libraries, 916
Sabratha Museum of Antiquities, 906
Sächsische Akademie der Wissenschaften zu Leipzig, 505
— Landesbibliothek, 507
Sacramento Peak Observatory, Sunspot, 1621
Safárik University, Košice, 382
Saga University, 848
Sağlik Bilimleri Fakültesi, Eskişehir, 1309
Saha Institute of Nuclear Physics, Calcutta, 671
Sahitya Akademi, New Delhi, 659
St. Aidan's College, Durham, 1487
St. Ambrose College, 1729
St. Andrew's College, Winnipeg, 283
— — Hall, Vancouver, 261
— — Presbyterian College, Laurinburg, 1829
St. Annen-Museum, Lubeck, 544
St. Ann's College Inc., North Adelaide, 99
St. Anne's College, Oxford, 1524
Saint Anselm's College, 1796
St. Antony's College, Oxford, 1524
St. Bartholomew's Hospital Medical College, 1512
St. Benet's Hall, Oxford, 1524
St. Bonaventure University, 1820
St. Boniface College, Manitoba, 283
St. Bride Printing Library, London, 1458
St. Catharine's College, Cambridge, 1485
— — — Library, Cambridge, 1462
St. Catherine's College, Oxford, 1524
St. Chad's College, Durham, 1487
St. Cloud State University, 1775
St. Cross College, Oxford University, 1524
St. Cuthbert's Society, Durham, 1487
St. David's University College, 1537
— — — Library, Lampeter, 1465
St. Deiniol's Residential Library, 1459
St. Edmund Hall, Oxford, 1524
— — — Library, Oxford, 1463
St. Edmund's House, Cambridge, 1485
St. Edward's University, 1900
Saint Francis College, Brooklyn, 1820
— — Fort Wayne, 1721
— — Loretto, 1878
— — Xavier University, 298
St. Gallen Graduate School of Economics, Business and Public Administration, 1275

St. George's Historical Society, Bermuda, 1558
— — Hospital Medical School, 1512
— Helena Heritage Society, Jamestown, 1561
St. Hilda's College, Parkville, 104
— — Oxford, 1524
St. Hugh's College, Oxford, 1524
St. John's College, Annapolis, 1745
— — — Brisbane, 109
— — — Camarillo, 1656
— — — Cambridge, 1485
— — — Durham, 1487
— — — Oxford, 1524
— — — Santa Fe, 1802
— — — Winnipeg, 283
— — — Library, Cambridge, 1462
— — — — Oxford, 1463
— — — Hospital Dermatological Society, London, 1430
— — University, Collegeville, 1775
— — — Jamaica, N.Y., 1820
Saint Joseph College, West Hartford, 1678
Saint Joseph's College, Edmonton, Alb., 257
— — — North Windham, 1742
— — — Rensselaer, 1721
— — University, Philadelphia, 1878
St. Lawrence University, Canton, N.Y., 1820
St. Leo College, Fla., 1695
St. Leo's College, Brisbane, 109
St. Louis Art Museum, Missouri, 1641
— — County Library, 1626
— — Public Library, 1626
— — University, Baguio City, 1058
— — — St. Louis, 1788
— — — Libraries, 1633
St. Mark's College, Vancouver, 261
— — Inc., North Adelaide, 99
St. Martin's College, Lacey, Wash., 1921
— — School of Art, London, 1551
Saint Mary College, Leavenworth, 1731
— — of the Plains College, Dodge City, 1731
— — — Woods College, Indiana, 1721
St. Mary's College, Durham, 1487
— — Parkville, 104
— — Notre Dame, Indiana, 1722
— — Winona, 1775
— — of California, 1656
— — Dominican College, New Orleans, 1739
— — Hospital Medical School, London, 1512
— — — Library, London, 1460
— — Seminary and University, Baltimore, 1745
— — Tower, Dundee, 1472
— — University, Halifax, 298
— — — of San Antonio, 1901
St. Michael's College, Winooski, 1915
St. Norbert College, de Pere, 1932
Saint Olaf College, Northfield, Minn., 1775
St. Patrick's College, Maynooth, 736
— — — Library, Maynooth, 732
St. Paul College of Manila, 1060
— — Public Library, Minneapolis, 1626
— — University, Ottawa, 292
St. Paul's Cathedral Library, 1458
— — College, Waterloo, Ontario, 311
— — — Winnipeg, 283
— — University, Tokyo, 867
Saint Peter's College, Jersey City, N.J., 1800
— — — Oxford, 1524
St. Scholastica's College, Manila, 1060
St. Stephen's College, Edmonton, Alb., 257
St. Thomas More College, Saskatoon, 301
— — University, Fredericton, 290
St. Thomas's Hospital Medical School, 1512
Saint Vincent College, Latrobe, Pa., 1878
Saint Xavier College, Chicago, 1708
Saitama University, Urawa City, 848
Sakhalin Complex Scientific Research Institute, 1322
Sala de Arte Prehispánico, Santo Domingo, 404
— — Conciertos Tassara, San José, 360

Salarjung Museum, Hyderabad, 675
Salem Academy and College, 1829
— College, West Virginia, 1930
— State College, Mass., 1758
Salesian House Philosophical Studies, Guatemala, 1946
— — — Los Teques, Venezuela, 1946
— — Theological Studies, Bangalore, 1946
— — — Barcelona, 1946
— — — Bethlehem, 1946
— — — Guatemala, 1946
— — — Madrid, 1946
— — — Meghalaya, 1946
— — — Messina, 1946
— — — St. Paul, Brazil, 1946
— Pontifical University, Rome, 1946
Salford Orthopaedic Appliance Unit, 1527
Salisbury and South Wiltshire Museum, Salisbury, 1471
— Arts Council, Zimbabwe, 2000
— Cathedral Library, 1459
— College of Advanced Education, South Australia, 114
— Polytechnic, Salisbury, Zimbabwe, 2004
— School of Art, Zimbabwe, 2004
— State College, Maryland, 1746
Salk Institute for Biological Studies, San Diego, Calif., 1620
Salmer, Archivo Fotográfico Internacional, Barcelona, 1203
Salt Lakes Institute, Xining, 332
Salters' Institute of Industrial Chemistry, 1421
Saltire Society, 1413
Salzburg University, 134
Salzburger Landessammlungen-Residenzgalerie, Salzburg, 131
— Museum Carolino-Augusteum, 131
Sam Houston State University, Huntsville, 1901
Samarkand Alisher Navoi State University, 1366
— Civil Engineering Institute, 1380
— V. V. Kuibyshev Agricultural Institute, 1371
— — — Co-operative Institute, 1373
— I. P. Pavlov Medical Institute, 1383
Samarra Museum, 727
Sambalpur University, 701
Samford University, Birmingham, Alabama, 1644
Samfund til Udgivelse af Gammel Nordisk Litteratur, Valby, 391
Samfundet de Nio, 1236
— for Dansk Genealogie og Personalhistorie, 390
— — Pedagogisk Forskning, Helsinki, 430
— til Udgivelse af Dansk Musik, Copenhagen, 389
Sammenslutningen af Danske Kunstforeninger, Copenhagen, 389
Sammlung Religiöse Volkskunst, Vienna, 130
Sammlungen der Gesellschaft der Musikfreunde in Wien, 128
Samoylov, Y. V., Research Institute of Fertilisers and Insectofungicides, Moscow, 1345
Sampurnanand Sanskrit University, Varanasi, 701
San Beda College, Manila, 1060
— Carlos University of Guatemala, 625
— Diego Museum of Art, 1641
— — Public Library, 1626
— — Society of Natural History Museum, 1641
— — State University, Calif., 1657
— Fernando Royal Academy of Fine Arts, Madrid, 1185
— Francisco Conservatory of Music, 1657
— — Law Library, 1628
— — Museum of Modern Art, 1641
— — Public Library, 1626
— — State University, 1657
— Jacinto Museum of History Association, 1641

— José State University, Calif., 1657
Sana'a University, 1965
Sandvigske Samlinger (De), 1012
Sangeet Natak Akademi, New Delhi, 659
San-in Rekishikan, 823
Sanno Institute of Business Administration, Tokyo, 868
Sanskrit Academy, Madras, 662
— Institute, Vientiane, 898
Santo Domingo University, 405
— Tomás Museum, 1049
Sapporo Medical College, 860
— Norin Gakkai, 804
— University, 868
Sara Hildénin Taidemuseo, Tampere, 433
Sarah Lawrence College, Bronxville, 1821
Saratov Agricultural Institute, 1371
— N. G. Chernyshevsky State University, 1366
— Institute of Economics, 1373
— — — Restorative Surgery, Traumatology and Orthopaedics, 1386
— M. I. Kalinin Institute of Agricultural Engineering, 1372
— D. I. Kursky Law Institute, 1382
— Polytechnic Institute, 1376
— A. N. Radischev State Art Museum, 1354
— Scientific Centre, 1322
— L. V. Sobinov State Conservatoire, 1388
— State Medical Institute, 1383
— Zootechnical and Veterinary Institute, 1372
Sarawak Museum, 916
— State Library, Kuching, 916
Sarbah Society (Law), Accra, 610
Sardar Patel University, Vallabh Vidyanagar, 701
Sarjeant Gallery, Wanganui, 982
Sarnath Museum, 675
Sarpay Beikman Division, Rangoon, 228
— — Public Library, Rangoon, 229
Saskatchewan Indian Federated College, Regina, 297
— Legislative Reference Library, 249
— Museum of Natural History, 251
— Provincial Library, Regina, 249
— Research Council, Saskatoon, 244
— Western Development Museums, 251
Saskatoon Public Library, 249
Satakunnan Museo, Pori, 433
Säteilyturvall isuuslaitos, Helsinki, 431
Satpaev, K. I., Institute of Geological Sciences, Alma-Ata, 1329
Satya Wacana Christian University, Salatiga, Java, 720
Saudi Arabian Institute for Higher Education, 1144
— Library, Riyadh, 1142
Saurashtra University, Rajkot, 701
Savannah State College, Georgia, 1701
Savaria Múzeum, 646
Savez Bibliotečkih Radnika Srbije, Belgrade, 1969
— Društava Biblotekara Jugoslavije, Sarajevo, 1968
— Inženjera i Tehničara BiH, Sarajevo, 1971
— Muzejskih društava Hrvatske, Zagreb, 1970
— — — Jugoslavije, Belgrade, 1968
— Organizacija Fizičke Kulture BiH, Sarajevo, 1971
— — Tehničke Kulture BiH, Sarajevo, 1971
— pedagoskih društava S.R. Srbije, Belgrade, 1969
— Udruženja Pravnika BiH, Sarajevo, 1971
— za Esperanto BiH, Sarajevo, 1971
— Zdravstvenih Radnika BiH, Sarajevo, 1971
Scandinavian Society of Forensic Odontology, Copenhagen, 1236
Scarborough College, Westhill, 309
Scarritt College, Nashville, 1890
Scavi di Ostia, 772

— — Pompeii e di Ercolano, 772
Schiller International University, Heidelberg, 608
— — — London Campus, 608
— — — Madrid Campus, 608
— — — Paris Campus, 608
— — — Strasbourg Campus, 608
Schiller-Gedenkstätte (Schillerhäusen und-Garten), Jena, 510
— -Nationalmuseum, Marbach a. Neckar, 536
Schleswig-Holsteinische Landesbibliothek, Kiel, 536
Schleswig-Holsteinisches Landesmuseum, 545
— für Vor- und Frühgeschichte, 545
Schloss Friedrichstein, Kassel, 543
— Hellbrunn, 131
— Weesenstein, Dresden, 509
Schlossmuseum, Darmstadt, 542
— Gotha, 509
— Gobelsburg Österreichische Volkskunst, Krems, 131
Schmalenbach-Gesellschaft, Köln, 529
Schmidt, O.Y., Institute of Earth Physics, Moscow, 1320
Schnütgen-Museum, 542
Schocken Library, Jerusalem, 742
Schola Cantorum, Ecole Supérieure de Musique, de Danse et d'Art Dramatique, Paris, 498
Scholastic and Professional Guidance Centre, Vatican City, 1946
Schönnbrunn Palast und Park, Vienna, 130
School of Agriculture, Akure, 1003
— — — Ibadan, 1003
— — — Kabul, 53
— — — Kundasale, 1228
— — — Spanish Town, Jamaica, 801
— — American Research, Santa Fé, 1618
— — Applied Arts, Medina, 1144
— — Architecture, Architectural Association, London, 1551
— — Art and Design, Darlinghurst, 113
— — Basic Studies, Zaria, 995
— — Celtic Studies, Dublin, 736
— — Commerce, Kabul, 53
— — Continuing Education, Canterbury, 1496
— — Cosmic Physics, Dublin, 736
— — Economics, Bratislava, 384
— — — Prague, 385
— — Education, Ramat-Gan, 745
— — — Shatin, 1561
— — Environmental Studies, Rondebosch, 1167
— — Fine Arts, Auckland, 987
— — — — Canterbury, N.Z., 987
— — Forestry, Ibadan, 1003
— — Home Economics, Cardiff, 1536
— — Hygiene, Khartoum, 1231
— — Islamic Disciplines, Mogadishu, 1153
— — Journalism, Nairobi, 880
— — — and Communication, Legon, 613
— — Mechanics, Kabul, 53
— — Nursing, Aleppo, 1278
— — — Erzurum, 1304
— — Oriental and African Studies, London, 1511
— — — — Library, 1460
— — Pharmacy, London, 1511
— — Public Health, Somalia, 1153
— — Seamanship and Fishing, Somalia, 1153
— — Slavonic and East European Studies, London, 1513
— — — — Studies Library, 1460
— — Social Work, Ramat-Gan, 745
— — the Art Institute of Chicago, 1708
— — — Biological Sciences, Cambridge, 1485
— — — Ozarks, Point Lookout, 1789
— — — Physical Sciences, Cambridge, 1485
— — — Theoretical Physics, Dublin, 736
Schreuder House, Stellenbosch, 1166

INDEX OF INSTITUTIONS

Schweizer Heimatschutz, Zürich, 1253
— Musikrat, Basel, 1253
Schweizerische Akademie der Medizinischen Wissenschaften, 1255
— Akademische Gesellschaft der Anglisten, Neuchâtel, 1255
— Amerikanisten-Gesellschaft, Geneva, 1255
— Astronomische Gesellschaft, Lucerne, 1257
— Bibliophilen-Gesellschaft, 1253
— Botanische Gesellschaft, 1256
— Chemische Gesellschaft, Basel, 1257
— Entomologische Gesellschaft, 1256
— Geisteswissenschaftliche Gesellschaft, Bern, 1257
— Geologische Gesellschaft, Basel, 1257
— Gesellschaft für Asienkunde, Zürich, 1255
— — — Aussenpolitik, Lenzburg, 1254
— — — die Rechte der Urheber musikalischer Werke (SUISA), Zürich, 1253
— — — Feintechnik, Zürich, 1257
— — — Geschichte der Medizin und der Naturwissenschaften, 1256
— — — Innere Medizin, Luzern, 1256
— — — Kartographie, Zürich, 1255
— — — Orthopädie, Fribourg, 1256
— — — Psychologie und ihre Anwendungen, Bern, 1257
— — — Skandinavische Studien, Zürich, 1255
— — — Soziologie, Lausanne, 1257
— — — Ur- und Frühgeschichte, Basel, 1255
— — — Volkskunde, Basel, 1257
— Heraldische Gesellschaft, Lucerne, 1255
— Hochschulkonferenz, Bern, 1254
— Landesbibliothek, Bern, 1259
— Mathematische Gesellschaft, Bern, 1256
— Meteorologische Anstalt, 1257
— Musikforschende Gesellschaft, 1253
— Naturforschende Gesellschaft, Bern, 1256
— Neurologische Gesellschaft, Basel, 1256
— Numismatische Gesellschaft, Bern, 1255
— Paläontologische Gesellschaft, Basel, 1257
— Philosophische Gesellschaft, Geneva, 1257
— Physikalische Gesellschaft, Neuchâtel, 1257
— Schillerstiftung, Zumikon, 1255
— Sprachwissenschaftliche Gesellschaft, Neuchâtel, 1255
— Stiftung für Alpine Forschungen, 1256
— — — Angewandte Psychologie, Zürich, 1257
— Theologische Gesellschaft, Bern, 1257
— Trachtenvereinigung, 1257
— Vereinigung für Altertumswissenschaft, Zürich, 1255
— — — Dokumentation, Bern, 1254
— — — Internationales Recht, Zürich, 1254
— Volksbibliothek, Bern, 1259
— Zentralstelle für Hochschulwesen, Zürich, 1254
Schweizerischer Anwaltsverband, Berne, 1254
— Apotheker-Verein, Bern, 1256
— Berufsverband für Angewandte Psychologie, Zürich, 1257
— Juristenverein, Bern, 1254
— Kunstverein, Bettingen, 1253
— Musikverband, 1253
— Nationalfonds zur Förderung der Wissenschaftlichen Forschung, Bern, 1256
— Notaren-Verband, Lausanne, 1254
— Protestantischer Volksbund, Zürich, 1257
— Schriftsteller-Verband, 1255
— Technischer Verband, Zürich, 1257
— Tonkünstlerverein, 1253
— Verband der Ingenieur-Agronomen und der Lebensmittelingenieure, Bern, 1257

— Werkbund, 1253
— Wissenschaftsrat, Bern, 1256
Schweizerisches Bundesarchiv, Bern, 1259
— Institut für Auslandforschung, Zürich, 1258
— — — Experimentelle Krebsforschung, Epalinges, 1258
— — — Kunstwissenschaft, Zürich, 1253
— — — Nuklearforschung, Villigen, 1274
— Landesmuseum, 1263
— Sozialarchiv, 1260
— Tropeninstitut, 1258
— Wirtschaftsarchiv, 1259
Science and Engineering Research Council, Swindon, 1446
— — — — Data Analysis Unit (Natural Philosophy), Glasgow, 1493
— — — — Laboratory, Tokyo, 874
— — — — Humanities Research Institute, Ames, 1728
— — Natural History Museum, Kuwait, 897
— Council of Canada, Ottawa, 242
— — — Japan, (J.S.C.), Tokyo, 803
— — — — Secretariat, Scientific Information Division, Tokyo, 819
— — — Singapore, 1150
— Education Centre, Salisbury, Zimbabwe, 2003
— Institute, Reykjavik, 658
— Museum, London, 1466
— — Library, London, 1458
— — of Minnesota, St. Paul, 1641
— — Victoria, Melbourne, 98
— Policy Research Centre, Nathan, Qd., 101
— — Unit, Brighton, 1534
— Society of Thailand, Bangkok, 1283
— Teachers Association of Singapore, 1150
Scientific and Engineering Society of Agriculture, Moscow, 1344
— — — — Ferrous Metallurgy, Moscow, 1344
— — — — Flour-Grinding and Peeling Industries and Elevator Economy, Moscow, 1344
— — — — Light Industry, Moscow, 1344
— — — — Mining, Moscow, 1344
— — — — Municipal Economy and Motor Transport, Moscow, 1344
— — — — Non-Ferrous Metallurgy, Moscow, 1344
— — — — the Building Industry, Moscow, 1344
— — — — Food Industry, Moscow, 1344
— — — — Instrument Building Industry, Moscow, 1344
— — — — Machine Building Industry, Moscow, 1344
— — — — Oil and Gas Industry, Moscow, 1344
— — — — Paper and Wood-Working Industry, Moscow, 1344
— — — — Power Industry, Leningrad, 1344
— — — — Printing Industry and Publishing Houses, Moscow, 1344
— — — — Railways, Moscow, 1344
— — — — Timber Industry and Forestry, Moscow, 1344
— — — — Water Transport, Moscow, 1344
— Technical Forestry Information Institute, Beijing, 333
— — — Information Institute, Beijing, 332
— — Archives,Sofia, 220
— Centre for Home Trade, Public Utilities and Local Industry, Sofia, 219
— Committee on Antarctic Research (SCAR), Cambridge, 9
— — — Oceanic Research (SCOR), Dartmouth, N.S., 9
— — — Problems of the Environment (SCOPE), Paris, 9

WORLD OF LEARNING

— Council of Zimbabwe, Salisbury, 2002
— — on Biological Reconstruction of Animals, Ashkhabad, 1332
— — — Complex Problems (Cybernetics), Baku, 1325
— — — Cybernetics, Moscow, 1323
— — — Exhibitions, Riga, 1330
— — — of the U.S.S.R. and Union Republics' Academies of Science, Moscow, 1323
— — — Philosophy of Contemporary Natural History, Moscow, 1323
— — — Studying of Deserts of Middle Asia and Kazakhstan, Ashkhabad, 1332
— — — Techniques in Production and Processing of Metals, Kiev, 1323
— — — the History and Theory of Science, Baku, 1325
— Documentation Centre, Baghdad, 725, 726
— A. M. Gorky Library of the Leningrad "A. A. Zhdanov" State University, 1350
— — — — Moscow M. V. Lomonosov State University, Moscow, 1351
— Information Centre, Sofia, 220
— — of the Ministry of Education, Sofia, 220
— — Institute, Beijing, 332
— Instrumentation Centre, 611
— Library and Documentation Division, National Science Development Board, Manila, 1049
— — attached to the State Research Institute of Theatre, Music and Cinematography, Leningrad, 1350
— — of the Academy of Arts of the U.S.S.R., Leningrad, 1349
— — — — Chernovtsky State University, 1350
— — — — Dnepropetrovsk State University, Dnepropetrovsk, 1350
— — — Erevan State University, 1350
— — — Irkutsk A. A. Zhdanov University, 1350
— — — V. Kapsukas State University of Vilnius, 1351
— — — Kiev T. G. Shevchenko State University, 1350
— — — Kishinev State University, 1350
— — — Latvian State University, "Peter Stuchka", Riga, 1350
— — — Lvov Ivan Franko State University, 1351
— — — Odessa I. I. Mechnikov State University, 1351
— — — People's Friendship "Patrice Lumumba" University, Moscow, 1351
— — — Rostov State University, Rostov-on-Don, 1351
— — — Saratov N. G. Chernyshevsky State University, 1351
— — — State Russian Museum, Leningrad, 1350
— — — Tretyakov Gallery, Moscow, 1350
— — — Tajik V. I. Lenin State University, Dushanbe, 1351
— — — Tartu State University, 1351
— — — Tbilisi State University, 1351
— — — Tomsk V. V. Kuibyshev State University, 1351
— — — Turkmen A. M. Gorky State University, Ashkabad, 1351
— — — Urals A. M. Gorky State University, Sverdlovsk, 1351
— — — Uzhgorod State University, Uzhgorod, 1351
— N. I. Lobachevsky Library of the Kazan V. I. Ulyanov (Lenin) State University, 1350
— Research Council, Kingston, Jamaica, 800

– – Institute for the Refrigeration Industry, Moscow, 1347
– – – – of Art Education, Moscow, 1343
– – – – Child and Pre-Adult Physiology, Moscow, 1343
– – – – Defectology, Moscow, 1344
– – – – Educational Methodology and Standards, Moscow, 1343
– – – – General Adult Education, Leningrad, 1344
– – – – and Educational Psychology, Moscow, 1343
– – – – Educational Problems, Moscow, 1343
– – – – Pedagogics, Moscow, 1343
– – – – Labour Education and Vocational Studies, Moscow, 1343
– – – – Pre-School Education, Moscow, 1343
– – – – Professional and Technical Education, Kazan, 1344
– – – – Russian Language Instruction in National Schools, Moscow, 1344
– – – – School Equipment and Technical Aids in Education, Moscow, 1343
– – Laboratory of Allergology, Moscow, 1342
– Society of Pakistan, Karachi, 1020
– S. I. Taneyev Library of the Moscow P. I. Tchaikovsky State Conservatoire, 1350
SCITEC: Association of the Scientific, Engineering and Technological Community of Canada, Ottawa, 242
Scott Polar Research Institute, Cambridge, 1442
Scottish Arts Council, Edinburgh, 1412
– Crop Research Institute, Dundee, 1441
– Field Studies Association, Edinburgh, 1431
– Fisheries Museum, Anstruther, 1473
– History Society, 1423
– Institute of Agricultural Engineering, Penicuik, 1441
– Library Association, Aberdeen, 1416
– Marine Biological Association, 1432
– National Gallery of Modern Art, Edinburgh, 1473
– – Portrait Gallery, 1473
– Record Office, Edinburgh, 1459
– Universities Research and Reactor Centre, Glasgow, 1449
Scripps College, Claremont, 1657
– Foundation for Research in Population Problems, Oxford, Ohio, 1617
Sculptors' Society of Canada, 246
Scuola di Perfezionamento in Studi Europei, Rome, 764
– – – – Politici Internazionali, Florence, 777
– Francese di Roma, 757
– Internazionale Superiore di Studi Avanzati in Trieste, 796
– Normale Superiore di Pisa, 796
– Spagnola di Storia e Archeologia, Rome, 758
– Superiore Enrico Mattei E.N.I., Milan, 796
– Vaticana di Biblioteconomia, Rome, 1943
Sea Fisheries Institute, Rogge Bay, 1161
– Mammal Research Unit, Cambridge, 1446
Seale-Hayne Agricultural College, Newton Abbot, 1550
Seattle Pacific University, 1921
– Public Library, 1627
– University, 1921
Sechenov, I. M., Climatotherapy Institute of Tuberculosis, Yalta, 1384
– Institute of Evolutionary Physiology and Biochemistry, Leningrad, 1319
Secretariat Library, Kampala, 1311
– – Patna, 674

Secrétariat d'Etat à la Recherche Scientifique, Conakry, 627
Secteur Centre Sud-Kaolack (CRS), Kaolack, 1145
Section de Diffusion Scientifique et Technique du Centre Culturel Français d'Alger, Algiers, 57
– of Chemical, Technological and Biological Sciences, U.S.S.R. Academy of Sciences, 1319
– – – – – Sciences, Kiev, 1333
– – Earth Sciences, Academy of Sciences of the U.S.S.R., Moscow, 1320
– – Energy Cybernetics, Kishinev, 1331
– – Geography, Alma-Ata, 1329
– – – Kishinev, 1331
– – Gerontology, Minsk, 1326
– – Microbiology, Baku, 1325
– – – Kishinev, 1331
– – – Tashkent, 1335
– – Oriental Studies and Ancient Scriptures, Dushanbe, 1332
– – Palaeontology and Stratigraphy, Kishinev, 1331
– – Philosophy, Dushanbe, 1332
– – – and Law, Ashkhabad, 1333
– – Physical-Engineering and Mathematical Sciences, Kiev, 1333
– – – -Technical and Mathematical Sciences, Academy of Sciences of the U.S.S.R., Moscow, 1318
– – Plant Genetics, Kishinev, 1331
– – Social Sciences, Academy of Sciences of the U.S.S.R., Moscow, 1320
– – the Ionosphere, Alma-Ata, 1328
– on Technology of Engineering, Erevan, 1324
Seif Bin Salim Public Library, Mombasa, 879
Seijo University, Tokyo, 869
Seikado Bunko Library, 819
Seisaku Kagaku Kenkyu Sho, Tokyo, 814
Seisan Gijitsu Kenkyusho, Tokyo, 812
Seisen Women's College, Tokyo, 869
Seismic Station, Kishinev, 1331
Seismological Institute, Belgrade, 1973
– Society of America, 1614
Sekolah Tinggi Arsitektur Pertamanan Trisakti, Jakarta, 720
Sekondi Regional Library, 612
Selangor Public Library, Kuala Lumpur, 916
Selborne Society, 1432
Selçuk Üniversitesi, Konya, 1308
Selden Society, 1418
Selimiye Library, 1300
Selly Oak Colleges Library, 1464
Selskabet for Dansk Kulturhistorie, 390
– – Historie og Samfundsøkonomi, Copenhagen, 390
– – Naturlaerens Udbredelse, 392
Selskapet til Videnskapenes Fremme, 1008
Selwyn College, Cambridge, 1485
– – Library, Cambridge, 1462
Sem Research Farm for Animal Husbandry, Oslo, 1018
Semiconductors Institute, Beijing, 332
Séminaire Israélite (Ecole Rabbinique) de France, 497
Seminario de Astronomía y Geodesía de la Universidad Complutense de Madrid, 1198
– – Filología Vasca "Julio de Urquijo" San Sebastián, 1190
– Patriarcale di Gerusalémme, Jerusalem, 1946
Seminary of Modern French for Foreigners, Neuchâtel, 1269
Semipalatinsk Institute of Zootechnics and Veterinary Science, 1372
Semmelweis Orvostörténeti Múzeum Könyvtár és Levéltár, Budapest, 644
– Orvostudományi Egyetem, Budapest, 647
– – Könyvtára, Budapest, 642
– University of Medicine, Budapest, 647
Senate Library, Washington, D.C., 1625

– of the Inns of Court and the Bar, London, 1418
Senckenbergische Bibliothek, Frankfurt, 536
Senefelder Group of Artist Lithographers, London, 1414
Sen-i-Gakkai, Tokyo, 811
Senshu University, 869
Sentralinstitutt for industriell forskning, Oslo, 1010
Seoul Agricultural College, Seoul, 896
– National University, 893
– – – Library, 887
– Women's College, 896
Serbian Academy of Sciences and Art, Belgrade, 1968
– Chemical Society, 1969
– Geographical Society, 1969
– Geological Society, 1969
Serbsky Central Scientific Research Institute of Forensic Psychiatry, Moscow, 1346
Seri Begawan Religious Teachers' College, Brunei, 213
Sericultural Experiment Station, Tokyo, 813
Serotherapeutisches Institut Wien, 125
Serum and Blood Transfusion Association, Hanoi, 1962
Service Belge des Echanges Internationaux, Brussels, 150
– Central d'Analyse, Vernaison, 454
– d'Aéronomie, Verrières-le-Buisson, 455
– d'Architecture Antique, Paris, 456
– d'Instrumentation et de Techniques Audio-Visuelles (S.I.T.A.), Mons, 164
– de Calcul en Sciences Humaines, Paris, 456
– – Diffusion de la Technologie des Matériaux, Orsay, 454
– – la Carte de la Végétation, Toulouse, 456
– – Physique du Globe, Rabat, 950
– – Recherches Juridiques Comparatives, Ivry-sur-Seine, 456
– des Bibliothèques, Paris, 460
– – Collections artistiques, Liège, 159
– – Langues, Mons, 163
– – Mines du Togo, Lomé, 1292
– du Cyclotron, Orleans, 454
– Géologique, Antananarivo, 910
– – Kinshasa, 1995
– – Tunis, 1295
– – du Rwanda, Ruhengeri, 1141
– international du Mouvement Polaire, Iwateke, 49
– National des Champs Intenses, Grenoble, 453
– Universitaire de Prestations Informatiques, Besançon, 475
Services Culturels et de Coopération, Algiers, 57
– Généraux du groupe des Laboratoires de Verrières-le-Buisson, 455
Servicio de Documentación y Biblioteca, Santo Domingo, 404
– – Endocrinología y Metabolismo, Buenos Aires, 67
– – Investigación Prehistórica de la Excelentisima Diputación Provincial, 1190
– – Publicaciones del Ministerio de Trabajo, Madrid, 1199
– Geográfico Militar, Montevideo, 1939
– Geológico de Bolivia, La Paz, 174
– – Nacional, Buenos Aires, 68
– – – Managua, 988
– Meteorológico Nacional, Buenos Aires, 68
– – – de El Salvador, 422
– Tecnico Interamericano de Co-operación Agricola, Asunción, 1034
Serviço de Defesa Sanitária Vegetal, Brasília, 183
– – Documentação Geral da Marinha, Rio de Janeiro, 188
– – Pesquisa e Experimentação de Cancer, Rio de Janeiro, 184

Serviço Nacional de Levantamento e Conservação de Solos da EMBRAPA, Rio de Janeiro, 182
Serviços Geologicos de Portugal, 1101
Servizio Geologico d'Italia, 760
Seshasayee Institute of Technology, Tamilnadu, 707
Sesoko Marine Laboratory, Okinawa, 848
Seton Hall University, 1801
— Hill College, Greensburg, 1878
Sevan Hydrobiological Station, 1324
Sevastopol Institute of Instrument Making, 1377
Severočeská galerie výtvarného uměni, Litoměřice, 375
Severoçeské Muzeum v Liberci, 375
Severtsov (A.N.) Institute of Evolutionary Morphology and Animal Ecology, 1320
Shaanxi Library, Xian, 335
Shah Waliullah Academy, Hyderabad, 1020
Shakai Hosho Kenkyusho, Tokyo, 814
— Keisai Kenkyujo, 814
Shakespeare Centre, Stratford-upon-Avon, 1459
Shamsul Ulama Daudpota Sind Government Library, Hyderabad, 1024
Shandong Library, Jinan, 335
— Oceanography College, 337
— University, 337
Shanghai Chemical Engineering College, 337
— College of Textile Technology, 337
— First Medical College, 337
— Library, 335
— Teachers University, 337
Shanxi Library, Taiyuan, 335
Sharkia Provincial Council Library, 417
Shaviana, Dagenham, 1427
Shaw University, Raleigh, 1829
Shchepkin (M.S.) Drama School attached to the Maly Theatre, Moscow, 1388
Shchukin, B.V., Drama School attached to the E.B. Vakhtangov State Theatre, Moscow, 1388
— Museum Room, 1360
Shchusev (A. V.) Architectural Museum of the State Committee of Building and Architecture, Moscow, 1352
Sheffield City Libraries, 1454
— — Museum, 1471
— — Polytechnic, 1547
Sheikan Museum, El Obeid, 1230
Shellac Institute, Beijing, 333
Shellshear (J. L.) Museum of Comparative Anatomy and Physical Anthropology, Sydney, 97
Shemakha Astro-Physical Observatory, Baku, 1325
Shemyakin, M.M., Institute of Bio-organic Chemistry, Moscow, 1319
Shenyang Institute of Geology and Mineral Resources, Liaoning, 333
Shephela Museum, Kibbutz Kefar Menahem, 744
Shepherd College, Shepherdstown, 1930
— Wheel, Whiteley Wood, 1471
Sherman Theatre, Cardiff, 1536
Sheth Maheklal Jethabhai Pustakalaya Library, 674
Shevchenko, T. G., Institute of Literature, Kiev, 1334
— State Memorial Museum, 1358
Shibusawa (K.) Memorial Foundation for Ethnology, Tokyo, 812
Shiga University, 848
Shigaku-kai, 806
Shikiya Memorial Library, Naha, 820
Shiloah Center for Middle Eastern and African Studies, Tel-Aviv, 750
Shimane Prefectural Museum, Matsue City, 823
— University, 848
Shimer College, Waukegan, Ill., 1708
Shinchon Museum, 884
Shinshu University, Matsumoto, 848
Shinuiju Historical Museum, 884

Ship Research Institute, Tokyo, 818
Shippensburg State College, Pa., 1878
Shire Valley Research Programme, Ngabu, 912
Shivaji University, Kolhapur, 702
Shizuoka College of Pharmacy, 860
— Prefectural Library, 820
— University, 848
Shkodër Public Library, 55
Shodó Hakubutsukan, 821
Shokubai Gakkai, Tokyo, 811
Shokubutsu Bunrui Chiri Gakkai, 810
Shomei Gakkai, 812
Shoren-in, Japan, 821
Shorter College, Georgia, 1701
Shota Rustaveli Institute of History of Georgian Literature, Tbilisi, 1328
Shreemati Nathibai Damodar Thackersey Women's University, Bombay, 702
Shrimati Radhika Sinha Institute and Sachchidananda Sinha Library, Patna, 674
Shrine of the Book, Jerusalem, 744
Shropshire County Library, Shrewsbury, 1454
Shuttleworth Agricultural College, Biggleswade, Beds., 1550
Siam Society, Bangkok, 1283
Sibelius Academy, Helsinki, 441
— Akatemia, Helsinki, 441
— -Akatemian Kirjasto, Helsinki, 432
Sibeliusmuseum (Musikvetenskapliga Institutionen vid Åbo Akademi), 433
Siberian Department of the Academy of Sciences, U.S.S.R., 1321
— Energy Institute, Irkutsk, 1322
— Institute of Plant Physiology and Biochemistry, Irkutsk, 1322
— — Terrestrial Magnetism, the Ionosphere and Radio Wave Propagation, Irkutsk, 1321
— V. V. Kuibyshev Motor and Highways Institute, 1390
— S. Orjonikidze Institute of Metallurgy, Novokuznetsk, 1379
— Technological Institute of the Timber Industry, 1381
Sichuan Library, Chengdu, 335
— Medical College, 336
— Mining College, 336
— University, 336
Side Müzesi, 1302
Sidney Sussex College, Cambridge, 1485
— — — Library, Cambridge, 1462
Siena College, Loudonville, 1821
— Heights College, Adrian, 1763
Sierra Leone Library Association, Freetown, 1148
— — — Board, Freetown, 1148
— — National Museum, Freetown, 1148
— — Science Association, Freetown, 1148
Sigma Xi, the Scientific Research Society, New Haven, Conn., 1611
Sigmund Freud-Gesellschaft, Vienna, 123
Signet Library, Edinburgh, 1459
Sikkim Research Institute of Tibetology, Gangtok, 672
Silesia Technical University, Gliwice, 1091
Silesian University, Katowice, 1082
Silk and Art Silk Mills' Research Association, Bombay, 673
Silkeborg Bibliotek, Silkeborg, 394
Silliman University, 1059
— — Library, 1049
Silpakorn University, Bangkok, 1290
Silver Lake College of the Holy Family, Manitowoc, 1932
Silviculture Research Institute, Lushoto, 1280
Simferopol M. V. Frunze State University, 1366
Simmons College, Boston, Mass., 1758
Simon Fraser University, Burnaby, 302
— Stevin Instituut voor Wetenschappelijk Onderzoek, Bruges, 154

— van der Stel Foundation, Pretoria, 1154
Simpson College, Indianola, 1729
Sinagoga del Tránsito, Toledo, 1204
Sind Agriculture University, Tandojam, 1029
— Library Association, Hyderabad, 1019
— University, Jamshoro, 1028
— — Central Library, 1024
Sindhi Adabi Board, Hyderabad, 1020
Singapore Association for the Advancement of Science, 1150
— Institute of Architects, 1150
— — — Biology, 1150
— — — International Affairs, 1151
— Mathematical Society, 1150
— Medical Association, 1151
— National Academy of Sciences, 1150
— — Institute of Chemistry, 1150
— Polytechnic, 1152
Singh Darbar, Kathmandu, 954
Sinha, A. N., Institute of Social Studies, Bihar, 672
Sint-Aloysius Economische Hogeschool, Brussels, 169
Sion College Library, London, 1458
Sioux Falls College, 1888
Sipka-Buzludza National Park Museum, Sipka, 222
Sir James Dunn Law Library, Wolfville, N.S., 247
— John Soane's House and Museum, 1467
— — — — Library, 1458
Siriraj Medical Library, Bangkok, 1284
Sisal Research Station (Millingano), Ngomeni, 1280
Sisavangvong University, Vientiane, 898
Siyasal Bilimler Yüksek Okulu, Istanbul, 1309
Sjofartsmuseet, Göteborg, 1242
Skansen, Stockholm, 1242
Skegness Church Farm Museum, 1469
Skidmore College, Saratoga Springs, 1821
Skipsfartsøkonomist Instituut, Bergen, 1010
Skochinsky, A.A., Institute of Mining, Lyubertsy, 1320
Skogs- och jordbrukets forskningsråd, Stockholm, 1237
Skolen for Klinikassistenter og Tandplajere, Copenhagen, 401
Skryabin (A. N.) Museum, Moscow, 1360
— K.I., All-Union Institute of Helminthology, Moscow, 1338
Skulpturen Sammlung, Berlin (East), 509
Skulpturengalerie, Berlin (West), 541
Skulpturensammlung, Dresden, 508
Skupnost študentov LVZ, Ljubljana, 1970
Slade School of Fine Art, 1551
Śląska Akademia Medyczna im. L. Waryńskiego, Katowice, 1095
Śląski Instytut Naukowy w Katowicach, Katowice, 1072
Slavistično društvo Slovenije, Ljubljana, 1970
Slezské muzeum, Opava, 379
Slippery Rock State College, Pa., 1878
Sloan-Kettering Institute for Cancer Research, New York, 1619
Slough Laboratory (Ministry of Agriculture, Fisheries and Food), 1441
Slovak Academy of Sciences, Bratislava, 372
— Technical University in Bratislava, 383
Slovanská knjiznica, Ljubljana, 1975
Slovene Academy of Sciences and Arts, Ljubljana, 1967
Slovenská Akadémie Vied, Bratislava, 372
— Akademija znanosti in umetnosti, 1967
— antropologická spoločnost, Bratislava, 373
— archeologická spoločnost, Bratislava, 373
— astronomická spoločnost, Bratislava, 373
— biochemická spoločnost, Bratislava, 373
— bioklimatologická spoločnost, Bratislava, 373
— biologická spoločnost, Bratislava, 373
— botanická spoločnost, Bratislava, 373
— chemická spoločnost, Bratislava, 373

— — demograficko-štatistická spoločnost, Bratislava, 373
— — ekonomická spoločnost, Bratislava, 373
— — entomologická spoločnost, Bratislava, 373
— — filozofická spoločnost, Bratislava, 373
— — geografická spoločnost, Bratislava, 373
— — geologická spoločnost, Bratislava, 373
— — historická spoločnost, Bratislava, 373
— — jazykovedná spoločnost, Bratislava, 373
— — kybernetická spoločnost, Bratislava, 373
— — Lekárska Knižnica, Bratislava, 376
— — literárnovedná spoločnost, Bratislava, 373
— — Matica, Ljubljana, 1970
— — meteorologická spoločnost, Bratislava, 373
— — národná galéria, Bratislava, 379
— — národopisná spoločnost, Bratislava, 373
— — orientalistická spoločnost, Bratislava, 373
— — pedagogická knižnica a Ustav Školkých informacii, Bratislava, 377
— — spoločnost, Bratislava, 373
— — psychologická spoločnost, Bratislava, 373
— — sociologická spoločnost, Bratislava, 373
— — spoločnost pre dejiny vied a techniky, Bratislava, 373
— — — mechaniku, Bratislava, 373
— — — medzinárodné právo, Bratislava, 373
— — — vedy polnohospodarn, lesnické, potravinárské, Bratislava, 373
— — technická knižnica, Bratislava, 377
— — Vysoká Škola Technická Bratislava, 383
— — zoologická spoločnost, Bratislava, 373
Slovenské Banské Muzeum, 379
— národné muzeum, Bratislava, 379
— — — Martin, 379
Slovenski Etnografski muzej, Ljubljana, 1977
— školski muzej, 1977
Slovensko Umetnostnozgodovinsko društvo, Ljubljana, 1970
Small Business Advisory Bureau, Potchefstroom, 1173
— Industries Institute, Lahore, 1023
Smith College, Northampton, Mass., 1758
— — Museum of Art, 1641
— J. L. B., Institute of Ichthyology, Grahamstown, 1176
Smithsonian Astrophysical Observatory, Cambridge, Mass., 1621
— Institution, Washington, D.C., 1598
— — Libraries, Washington, D.C., 1628
— Tropical Research Institute, Balboa, 1030
Smolensk State Medical Institute, 1382
Snail Research Unit, Tygerberg, 1156
Snow Entomological Museum, 1641
Sochi Health Research Institute, 1387
Social and Applied Psychology Unit (M.R.C.), Sheffield, 1444
— — Economic Affairs Research Institute, Tokyo, 814
— Paediatric and Obstetric Research Group, Glasgow, 1493
— Process Research Institute, Santa Barbara, 1673
— Psychiatry Unit (M.R.C.), London, 1444
— Science Documentation Centre, New Delhi, 674
— — Federation of Canada, Ottawa, 245
— — Institute, Seoul, 894
— — Research Council, London, 1447
— — — — New York, 1622
— — — — Designated Research Centre in Comparative Structure and Efficiency, London, 1442
— — — — Industrial Relations Research Unit, Coventry, 1539
— — — — Unit on Ethnic Relations, Birmingham, 1475
— — — Institute, Tokyo, 864
— — — Scientific Information Institute, Moscow, 1320
— Sciences and Humanities Research Council of Canada, 245
— — Association of Egypt, Cairo, 414
— — Library, Ho Chi Minh City, 1963
Socialforskningsinstituttet, Copenhagen, 393

Socialstyrelsen, Stockholm, 1236
Sociedad Agronómica de Chile, 322
— — Mexicana, Mexico City, 925
— Amigos del Museo de Bellas Artes, Caracas, 1950
— Antioqueña de Ingenieros y Arquitectos, Medellín, 348
— Argentina de Anatomía Normal y Patológica, Buenos Aires, 64
— — Antropología, 65
— — Biología, 65
— — Ciencias Fisiológicas, 64
— — — Neurológicas, Psiquiátricas y Neuroquirúrgicas, 64
— — Cirujanos, Buenos Aires, 64
— — Criminología, 63
— — Dermatología, Buenos Aires, 64
— — Endocrinología y Metabolismo, Buenos Aires, 64
— — Estudios Geográficos, 63
— — — Lingüísticos, 64
— — Farmacología y Terapéutica, Buenos Aires, 64
— — Fisiología Vegetal, 65
— — Gastroenterología, 64
— — Gerontología y Geriatria, 64
— — Hematología, Buenos Aires, 64
— — Investigación Clínica, 64
— — Leprología, Buenos Aires, 64
— — Micología, Córdoba, 64
— — Minería y Geología, 65
— — Oftalmología, 64
— — Ortopedía y Traumatología, 64
— — Pediatría, 65
— — Psicología, Buenos Aires, 65
— Arqueológica de Bolivia, 174
— Astronómica de México, 928
— — — España y América, 1191
— Bolivariana de Venezuela, 1951
— Boliviana de Cirugía, La Paz, 174
— — — Salud Pública, La Paz, 174
— Botánica de Mexico, A.C., Mexico City, 927
— Central de Arquitectos, Buenos Aires, 62
— Chilena de Cardiología y Cirugía Cardiovascular, Santiago, 323
— — Entomología, 324
— — Física, Santiago, 324
— — Gerontología, Santiago, 323
— — Hematología, Santiago, 323
— — Historia Natural, 323
— — — y Geografía, 323
— — Lingüística, 323
— — Nutrición, Bromatología y Toxicología, Santiago, 323
— — Parasitología, Santiago, 323
— — Química, Concepción, 324
— — Reumatología, Santiago, 323
— Científica Argentina, 65
— — Chilena "Claudio Gay", 323
— — de Chile, 323
— — del Paraguay, 1034
— Colombiana de Cancerología, 347
— — Cardiología, Bogotá, 347
— — Economista, Bogotá, 347
— — Ingenieros, 347
— — Matemáticas, Bogotá, 347
— — Obstetricia y Ginecología, 347
— — Patología, Bogotá, 347
— — Pediatría y Puericultura, 347
— — Psiquiatría, Bogotá, 347
— — Químicos e Ingenieros Químicos, Bogotá, 347
— — Radiología, 347
— Cubana de Historia de la Medicina, 363
— — Ingenieros, 363
— Cubano-Mexicana de Relaciones Culturales, Vedado, 364
— de Agricultores de Colombia, 347
— — Amigos de Arqueología, 1939
— — Anestesiología de El Salvador, San Salvador, 422
— — Arquitectos del Uruguay, 1939
— — Bibliófilos Chilenos, 322
— — Bibliotecarios de Puerto Rico, Río Piedras, 1109

— — Biología de Bogotá, 348
— — — — Chile, Santiago, 324
— — — Bioquímica de Concepción, 324
— — — Ciencias "Aranzadi", San Sebastián, 1191
— — — Letras y Artes, "El Museo Canario", Las Palmas, 1188
— — — — Naturales, Caldas, Medellín, 348
— — — — La Salle, 1952
— — — Cirugía de Buenos Aires, 65
— — — — del Uruguay, 1939
— — — Educación, Mexico, 926
— — — Estudios Geográficos e Históricos, 174
— — — Genética de Chile, Santiago, 324
— — — Ginecología y Obstetricia de El Salvador, San Salvador, 422
— — — Ingenieros del Perú, 1037
— — — Medicina Legal y Toxicología, 65
— — — — Veterinaria de Chile, 322
— — — Obstetricia y Ginecología de Venezuela, Caracas, 1951
— — — Oftalmología de Valparaíso, 323
— — — — Nicaraguense, Managua, 988
— — — Pediatría de Cochabamba, 174
— — — — — Madrid y Región Centro, 1191
— — — — — Valparaíso, 323
— — — — y Puericultura del Paraguay, 1034
— — — Psicología Médica, Psicoanálisis y Medicina Psico-somática, Buenos Aires, 65
— — — Radiología del Uruguay, Montevideo, 1939
— Dominicana de Bibliófilos Inc., Santo Domingo, 403
— Ecuatoriana de Pediatría, 408
— Entomológica Argentina, 65
— — del Peru, Lima, 1037
— Española de Antropología, Etnografía y Prehistoria, Madrid, 1192
— — Cerámica y Vidrio, Madrid, 1193
— — Patología Digestiva y de la Nutrición, 1191
— — Radiología y Electrología Médicas, Madrid, 1191
— Forestal Mexicana, 925
— General de Autores de España, 1190
— — — — la Argentina (Argentores), 64
— Geográfica de Colombia, 348
— — La Paz, 174
— — Lima, 1036
— — "Sucre", 174
— — y de Historia "Potosí", 174
— Geológica Boliviana, La Paz, 174
— — de Chile, Santiago, 324
— — del Peru, 1037
— — Mexicana, 928
— Jurídica de la Universidad Nacional, Bogotá, 348
— Latinamericana de Alergología, Mexico, 927
— — — Farmacología, Caracas, 1951
— Malacológica del Uruguay, Montevideo, 1939
— Matemática Mexicana, 928
— Mayaguezana Pro Bellas Artes, Mayaguez, 1109
— Médica de Concepción, 323
— — — Salud Publica, San Salvador, 422
— — — Santiago, 323
— — — Valparaíso, 323
— Médico-Quirúrgica, Zulia, 1951
— Mexicana de Antropología, 928
— — Bibliografía, 926
— — Biología, 927
— — Cardiología, Mexico City, 927
— — Entomología, Mexico City, 927
— — Estudios Psico-Pedagógicos, 928
— — Eugenesia, 927
— — Fitogenética, Chapingo, 927
— — Fitopatología A.C., 927
— — Geografía y Estadística, 926
— — Historia de la Ciencia y la Tecnología, Mexico City, 926
— — — Natural, 927

# INDEX OF INSTITUTIONS

Sociedad Mexicana de Historia y Filosofía de la Medicina, 927
— — — Ingeniería Sísmica, 928
— — — Micología, Mexico City, 928
— — — Nutrición y Endocrinología, 927
— — — Parasitología A. C., Mexico City, 927
— — — Pediatría, 927
— — — Salud Pública, Mexico City, 927
— — Nacional Agraria, Lima, 1036
— — — de Agricultura, Santiago, 322
— — — Minería, Lima, 1037
— — — — Santiago, 324
— — Nicaraguense de Psiquiatría y Psicología, Managua, 988
— — Nuevoleonesa de Historia, Geografía y Estadística, 926
— — Odontológica Antioqueña, Medellín, 348
— — — de Concepción, 323
— — Peruana de Derecho Internacional, 1036
— — — Espeleología, Lima, 1037
— — — Historia de la Medicina, 1037
— — — Tisiología y Enfermedades Respiratorias, Lima, 1037
— — Pro Arte Musical, Guatemala City, 624
— — Puertorriqueña de Autores, Compositores y Editores Musicales, 1109
— — — Escritores, San Juan, 1109
— — Química de México, Mexico City, 928
— — — del Perú, 1037
— — Rural Argentina, 62
— — — Boliviana, La Paz, 174
— — Uruguaya de Patología Clínica, Montevideo, 1939
— — — Pediatría, 1939
— — Venezolana de Anestesiología, 1951
— — — Angiología, Caracas, 1951
— — — Cardiología, Caracas, 1951
— — — Ciencias Naturales, 1952
— — — Cirugía, Caracas, 1951
— — — — Ortopédica y Traumatología, Caracas, 1951
— — — Dermatología, Caracas, 1951
— — — Gastroenterología, Caracas, 1951
— — — Geólogos, Caracas, 1952
— — — Hematología, Caracas, 1952
— — — Historia de la Medicina, 1952
— — — Ingeniería Hidráulica, 1952
— — — — Vial, Caracas, 1952
— — — Ingenieros Agrónomos, 1952
— — — — Civiles, Caracas, 1952
— — — — de Minas y Metalúrgicas, Caracas, 1952
— — — — — Petróleo, Caracas, 1953
— — — — Forestales, Caracas, 1953
— — — — Químicos, Caracas, 1953
— — — Medicina Interna, Caracas, 1952
— — — Oftalmología, Caracas, 1952
— — — Oncología, Caracas, 1952
— — — Otorrinolaringología, 1952
— — — Psiquiatría y Neurología, 1952
— — — Puericultura y Pediatría, 1952
— — — Radiología, Caracas, 1952
— — — Urología, 1952
— — Veterinaria de Zootecnia de España, 1188
— — Zoológica del Uruguay, Montevideo, 1939
Sociedade Anatómica Luso-Hispano-Americana, 1099
— — Portuguesa, Lisbon, 1099
— — Botánica do Brasil, 182
— — Brasileira de Autores Teatrais, 181
— — — Cartografia, Rio de Janeiro, 180
— — — Cultura Inglesa, Rio de Janeiro, 181
— — — Dermatologia, 181
— — — Entomologia, 182
— — — Filosofia, 182
— — — Geografia, Rio de Janeiro, 180
— — — Para o Progresso do Ciência, 181
— — Broteriana, 1099
— — Cientifica de São Paulo, 181
— — de Biologia do Brasil, Rio de Janeiro, 182
— — — Estudos Açoreanos "Afonso Chaves", 1100

— — — Tecnicos SARL-SETEC, Lisbon, 1099
— — Geografia de Lisboa, 1098
— — Medicina de Alagoas, 181
— — — Legal e Criminologia de São Paulo, 181
— — Pediatria de Bahia, 181
— — Farmacêutica Lusitana, 1099
— — Geológica de Portugal, 1099
— — Martins Sarmento, Guimarães, 1098
— — Nacional de Agricultura, 179
— — — Belas Artes, 1098
— — Portuguesa de Antropologia e Etnologia, 1099
— — — Autores, Lisbon, 1098
— — — Ciencias Naturais, 1099
— — — — Veterinárias, 1097
— — — Especialistas de Pequenos Animais, Lisbon, 1097
— — — Higiene Alimentar, Lisbon, 1097
— — — Nutrição e Alimentação Animal, Lisbon, 1097
— — — Quimica, 1099
— — — Veterinária de Anatomia Comparativa, Lisbon, 1097
— — — — Estudos Sociológicos, Lisbon, 1097
Società Adriatica di Scienze, 760
— Astronomica Italiana, 761
— Botanica Italiana, 760
— Chimica Italiana, 761
— Dante Alighieri, 759
— — Mogadishu, 1153
— Dantesca Italiana, 759
— di Etnografia Italiana, 761
— — Letture e Conversazioni Scientifiche, 761
— — Minerva, 758
— — Studi Geografici, 758
— Entomologica Italiana, 760
— Filologica Romana, 759
— Geografica Italiana, 758
— Geologica Italiana, 761
— Incoraggiamento d'Arti e Mestieri, Milan, 756
— Italiana degli Economisti, Genoa, 757
— — delle Scienze Veterinarie, Pisa, 756
— — di Anestesiologia e Rianimazione, Turin, 759
— — — Cancerologia, Naples, 759
— — — Chirurgia, Rome, 759
— — — Economia Agraria, Florence, 756
— — — Demografia e Statistica, Rome, 757
— — — Epatologia, Rome, 759
— — — Fisica, 761
— — — Medicina del Lavoro e Igiene Industriale, Milan, 760
— — — — Traffico, Rome, 759
— — — — Interna, Rome, 760
— — — Legale e delle Assicurazioni, Rome, 760
— — — Musicologia, Bologna, 756
— — — Neuroradiologia, Naples, 760
— — — Odontostomatologia e Chirurgia Maxillo-Facciale, Rome, 760
— — — Ortopedia e Traumatologia, Rome, 760
— — — Ostetricia e di Ginecologia, Rome, 760
— — — Parapsicologia, Rome, 761
— — — Reumatologia, Milan, 760
— — — Scienze Naturali, 760
— — — — Farmaceutiche, Milan, 760
— — — Sociologia, 761
— — — Statistica, 760
— — Musica Contemporanea, Rome, 756
— — per gli Studi Filosofici e Religiosi, 761
— — — il Progresso delle Scienze, 760
— — — l'Organizzazione Internazionale (S.I.O.I.), Rome, 757
— — — lo Studio delle Sostanze Grasse, Milan, 763
— Letteraria, 759
— Medica Chirurgica di Bologna, 760
— Napoletana di Storia Patria, 758

## WORLD OF LEARNING

— Nazionale di Scienze, Lettere ed Arti, Naples, 761
— Retorumantscha, 1255
— Romana di Storia Patria, Rome, 758
— Storica Locarnese, Locarno, 1255
— — Lombarda, Milan, 758
— ticinese di scienze naturali, Lugano, 1256
— Toscana di Scienze Naturali, 760
Societas Amicorum Naturae Ouluensis, Oulu, 429
— Biochemica, Biophysica et Microbiologica Fenniae, Helsinki, 429
— Biologica Fennica Vanamo, Helsinki, 429
— Entomologica Fennica, Helsinki, 429
— pro Fauna et Flora Fennica, 429
— Scientiarum Faeroensis, Tórshavn, 402
— — Fennica, 427
Societat Arqueologica Lui-liana, Palma de Mallorca, 1190
Societatea de Ştiinţe Biologice din R.S.R., Bucharest, 1122
— — — Filologice din R.S.R., 1122
— — — Fizice şi Chemice, din R.S.R., Bucharest, 1122
— — — Geografie din R.S.R., 1122
— — — Geologice din R.S.R., 1122
— — — Istorice din R.S.R., 1122
— — — Matematice din R.S.R. 1122
— Naţională Română Pentru Ştiinţa Solului, Bucharest, 1122
— Numismatica Română, Bucharest, 1122
— Română de Lingvistica, 1122
Société Archéologique, Namur, 151
— — d'Alexandrie, 413
— — du département de Constantine, 57
— Asiatique, 452
— Astronomique de France (CSSF), 452
— — Liège, 152
— — Suisse, Lucerne, 1257
— Belge d'Etudes Byzantines, Brussels, 151
— — Géographiques, Ghent, 151
— — d'Ophtalmologie, section francophone, Brussels, 152
— — de Biochimie, 152
— — Biologie, 152
— — Géologie, Brussels, 152
— — Logique et de Philosophie des Sciences, Brussels, 153
— — Médecine Tropicale, 152
— — Musicologie, Brussels, 150
— — Philosophie, Brussels, 153
— — Photogrammétrie et de Télédétection, Brussels, 153
— — des Auteurs, Compositeurs et Editeurs (SABAM), Brussels, 151
— — Urbanistes et Architectes Modernistes, Brussels, 150
— Botanique de France (CSSF), 451
— Canadienne d'Immunologie, Winnipeg, 242
— — des Microbiologistes, Ottawa, 242
— Centrale d'Architecture de Belgique, Brussels, 150
— Chimique de Belgique, 152
— — France (CSSF), 452
— d'Anthropologie de Paris (CSSF), 452
— d'Economie et de Sciences Sociales, Paris, 446
— — Politique, Paris, 446
— d'Electroencephalographie et de Neurophysiologie Clinique de Langue Française, Paris, 450
— d'Emulation du Bourbonnais, 448
— d'Encouragement pour l'Industrie Nationale, 453
— d'Ethnographie de Paris, 447
— d'Ethnologie Française, 447
— d'Etude du XVIIe Siècle, Paris, 448
— d'Etudes Dantesques, Nice, 449
— — Economiques, Sociales et Statistiques du Maroc, Rabat, 949
— — et de Documentation Economiques, Industrielles et Sociales (SEDEIS), Paris, 446
— — Hispaniques et de Diffusion de la Culture Française à l'Etranger, Périgueux, 448

— — Jaurésiennes, Paris, 446
— — Latines de Bruxelles, Brussels, 152
— — Océaniennes, Papeete, 501
— — Ornithologiques, 451
— — pour le Développement Economique et Social, Paris, 446
— d'Histoire de la Pharmacie, 450
— — — Suisse Romande, 1255
— — du Droit (CSSF), 446
— — — Théâtre, Paris, 445
— — Ecclésiastique de la France, Paris, 452
— — et d'Archéologie, 1255
— — Générale et d'Histoire Diplomatique, Paris, 448
— — Littéraire de la France (CSSF), 449
— — Moderne (CSSF), 448
— d'Horticulture et d'Acclimatation du Maroc, 949
— d'Ophtalmologie de Paris, 450
— de Biogéographie (CSSF), 447
— — Biologie (CSSF), 451
— — — Chimie Biologique (CSSF), 452
— — — Industrielle (CSSF), 452
— — — Physique (CSSF), 452
— — Chirurgie Thoracique et cardio-vasculaire de Langue Française, 450
— — Dermatologie et Syphilographie, 450
— — Gastronomie Médicale, Paris, 450
— — Géographie, Paris, 447
— — — Commerciale de Paris, 448
— — — de Genève, 1255
— — — du Maroc, 949
— — l'Histoire de France, 448
— — — — l'Art Française (CSSF), 445
— — — — l'Ile Maurice, Port Louis, 923
— — — du Protestantisme Français, Paris, 452
— — Langue et de Littérature Wallonnes, A.S.B.L., Liège, 152
— — Législation Comparée (CSSF), 446
— — Linguistique de Paris (CSSF), 449
— — Médecine de Paris, Boulogne, 450
— — — Strasbourg, 450
— — Légale et de Criminologie de France, 450
— — Mythologie Française, Paris, 452
— — Neuro-Chirurgie de Langue Française, Paris, 450
— — Pathologie Exotique, Paris, 450
— — Végétale et d'Entomologie Agricole de France (CSSF), 451
— — Physique et d'Histoire Naturelle, 1256
— — Préhistoire du Maroc, Casablanca, 949
— — Spectroscopie du Canada, Montreal, 243
— — Stomatologie de France, 450
— — Technologie Agricole et Sucrière de l'Ile Maurice, 923
— des Africanistes (CSSF), 452
— — Américanistes (CSSF), 452
— — Amis de la Revue de Géographie de Lyon, 448
— — — du Louvre, 446
— — — Anciens Textes Français (CSSF), 449
— — — Artistes Décorateurs (SAD), 446
— — — Français, 446
— — — Indépendants, 446
— — — Auteurs, Compositeurs et Editeurs de Musique, Paris, 446
— — — et Compositeurs Dramatiques, Paris, 449
— — — Bollandistes, Brussels, 153
— — — Chirurgiens de Paris, 450
— — — Electriciens, des Electroniciens et des Radio-électriciens (SEE), Paris, 453
— — — Etudes Historiques (CSSF), 448
— — — — Latines, Paris, 449
— — — — Mélanésiennes, Noumea, 500
— — — Experts-Chimistes de France (CSSF), 452
— — — Gens de Lettres, 449

— — Historiens Zairois, Lubumbashi, 1995
— — Ingénieurs Civils de France, 453
— — Naturalistes Luxembourgeois, 908
— — Océanistes, 448
— — Peintres, Sculpteurs et Architectes Suisses, Muttenz, 1253
— — Poètes Français, 449
— — Sciences et Arts, Saint-Denis, 500
— — — Naturelles et Physiques du Maroc, 949
— — Vétérinaires Suisses, Bern, 1253
— du Salon d'Automne, 446
— Entomologique d'Egypte, 414
— — de France, 451
— Européenne de Culture, Venice, 18
— Française d'Allergologie, Paris, 450
— — d'Anesthésie, d'Analgésie et de Réanimation, Paris, 450
— — d'Angéiologie, 450
— — d'Archéocivilisation et de Folklore, Paris, 447
— — d'Archéologie (CSSF), 447
— — d'Economie Rurale, Paris, 445
— — d'Egyptologie, Paris, 447
— — d'Electroradiologie médicale, 450
— — d'Endocrinologie, St.-Germain, 450
— — d'Etude des Phénomènes Psychiques, Paris, 452
— — d'Histoire d'Outre-Mer, Paris, 448
— — — de la Médecine, 450
— — d'Hydrologie et de Climatologie Médicales, Paris, 450
— — d'Hygiène, de Médecine Sociale et de Génie Sanitaire, Paris, 450
— — d'Ichtyologie, 445
— — d'Ophtalmologie, Paris, 450
— — d'Oto-Rhino-Laryngologie et de Pathologie Cervico-Faciale, Paris, 450
— — d'Urologie, 450
— — de Biologie Clinique, 450
— — — Chirurgie Infantile, Paris, 450
— — — Orthopédique et de Traumatologie, Paris, 450
— — — Plastique et Reconstructive, Paris, 450
— — — Gynécologie, 450
— — — la Tuberculose et des Maladies Respiratoires, Paris, 451
— — — Métallurgie, Paris, 453
— — — Microscope Electronique, Paris, 453
— — — Minéralogie et de Cristallographie (CSSF), 452
— — — Musicologie, Paris, 446
— — — Mycologie Médicale, Paris, 450
— — — Neurologie, 450
— — — Numismatique, 447
— — — Pédagogie, 447
— — — Pédiatrie, Paris, 450
— — — Philosophie (CSSF), 452
— — — Phlébologie, Paris, 450
— — — Photographie et Cinématographie, 446
— — — Photogrammetrie et de Télédétection, St. Mandé, 453
— — — Physiologie et de Médecine Aéronautiques et Cosmonautiques, Paris, 450
— — — — Végétale, Paris, 451
— — — Physique (CSSF), 452
— — — Phytiatrie et de Phytopharmacie, Paris, 451
— — — Psychologie (CSSF), 452
— — — Sociologie, Paris, 452
— — — Thérapeutique et de Pharmacodynamie, Paris, 451
— — des Architectes, Paris, 445
— — Généalogique Canadienne-Française, Montreal, 241
— — Générale d'Education et d'Enseignement, Paris, 447
— — — suisse d'histoire, Bern, 1254
— — Géologique de Belgique, Liège, 152
— — — France (CSSF), 452
— — — suisse, Basel, 1257

— Helvétique des Sciences naturelles, Bern, 1256
— Historique Algérienne, 57
— — Archéologique et Littéraire de Lyon, 447
— Hydrotechnique de France, 453
— Internationale Cardiovasculaire, Manchester, Mass., 40
— — contre la lèpre, Sutton, 37
— — d'Audiologie, London, 38
— — d'Electrochimie, Lausanne, 49
— — d'Electrorétinographie Clinique, Soesterberg, 41
— — d'Etudes Historiques Cercle Louis XVII, Paris, 448
— — d'Hématologie, México, D.F., 42
— — d'Histoire de la médecine, Montpellier, 38
— — de Bibliographie Classique, 446
— — — biométrie, Corvallis, 44
— — — chirurgie, Brussels, 42
— — — orthopédique et de traumatologie, Brussels, 42
— — — criminologie, Paris, 38
— — — défense sociale, Milan, 25
— — — mécanique des sols et des travaux de fondations, London, 33
— — — médecine cybernétique (SIMC), Naples, 42
— — — — interne, Lausanne, 38
— — — musicologique, Basle, 11
— — — Mycologie Humaine et Animale, Basle, 49
— — — pathologie géographique, Zürich, 38
— — — Photogrammétrie et de Télédétection, Reston, Va., 34
— — — Psycho-pathologie de l'Expression, Paris, 42
— — — Radiologie, Bern, 42
— — — Transfusion Sanguine, Paris, 42
— — — laitière, Washington, D.C., 16
— — — pour l'Education Artistique, Boulogne, 30
— — — l'enseignement commercial, Le Mont sur Lausanne, 30
— — — l'Etude de la Philosophie Médiévale (SIEPM), Louvain, 25
— — — la musique contemporaine, Geneva, 44
— — — — Réadaptation des Handicapés, New York, 39
— — — — Recherche sur les Maladies de Civilisation et les Substances Vitales, Hannover-Kirchrode, 42
— — — le Développement, Rome, 25
— Linnéenne de Québec, 243
— Mathématique de Belgique, 152
— — France (CSSF), 451
— — du Canada, Ottawa, 243
— — suisse, Bern, 1256
— Médicale des Hôpitaux de Paris, 451
— Médico-Chirurgicale des Hôpitaux et Formations Sanitaires des Arinées, Paris, 450
— — — Libres, 450
— Médico-Psychologique, 451
— Météorologique de France (CSSF), 452
— Mycologique de France (CSSF), 451
— Nationale d'Horticulture de France (SNHF), 445
— de la Protection de la Nature et d'Acclimatation de France, Paris, 451
— — Laiterie, Crainhem, 150
— — Recherches et d'Exploitation des Ressources Minières de Mali (SONAREM), Service de Documentation, Kati, 920
— — des Antiquaires de France (CSSF), 447
— — — Architectes de France, 445
— — — Beaux-Arts, 446
— — Française de Gastro-Entérologie, 451
— Odontologique de Paris, 451

Société Ontarienne d'Education par l'Art, Toronto, 240
— Ornithologique de France, Paris, 451
— Paléontologique Suisse, 1257
— Philosophique de Louvain, 153
— pour la Protection des Paysages, Sites et Monuments, Paris, 445
— — le Développement Minier de la Côte d'Ivoire (SODEMI), Abidjan, 798
— Royale Belge d'Anthropologie et de Préhistoire, 153
— — d'Astronomie, de Météorologie et de Physique du Globe, Brussels, 152
— — — d'Entomologie, Brussels, 152
— — — de Géographie, 151
— — — — Radiologie, Brussels, 152
— — — des Electriciens, 153
— — — — Ingénieurs et des Industriels, 153
— — d'Archéologie de Bruxelles, 151
— — d'Astronomie d'Anvers, 152
— — d'Economie Politique de Belgique, Brussels, 150
— — de Botanique de Belgique, 152
— — — Géographie d'Anvers, Berchen, Antwerp, 151
— — Numismatique de Belgique, 151
— — — Zoologie d'Anvers, Antwerp, 152
— — des Beaux-Arts, 150
— — — Sciences de Liège, 152
— — — — Médicales et Naturelles de Bruxelles, 152
— — Zoologique de Belgique, 152
— Scientifique d'Hygiène Alimentaire (CSSF), 451
— — de Bruxelles, 152
— suisse d'études anglaises, Neuchâtel, 1255
— — — asiatiques, Zürich, 1255
— — d'héraldique, Lucerne, 1255
— — d'Orthopédie, Fribourg, 1256
— — de Chimie, Basel, 1257
— — — Chirurgie, Zürich, 1256
— — — Droit International, Zürich, 1254
— — — linguistique, Neuchâtel, 1255
— — — Médecine Interne, Luzern, 1256
— — — numismatique, Bern, 1255
— — — Pédagogie Musicale, 1253
— — — Pharmacie, 1256
— — — philosophie, Geneva, 1257
— — — Psychologie et de Psychologie appliquée, Bern, 1251
— — — Sociologie, Lausanne, 1257
— — — Théologie, Bern, 1257
— — des Agriculteurs, Zürich, 1253
— — — Américanistes, Geneva, 1255
— — — Beaux-Arts, Bettingen, 1253
— — — Ingénieurs et des Architectes, 1253
— — — Juristes, Bern, 1254
— — — Sciences Humaines, Bern, 1257
— — — traditions populaires, Basel, 1257
— — vaudoise d'histoire et d'archéologie, 1255
— — — des Sciences Naturelles, 1256
— Vétérinaire Pratique de France, 445
— Zoologique de France (CSSF), 451
Sociétés de Statistique de Paris et de France, Paris, 447
Societies for the Promotion of Hellenic and Roman Studies Library, 1458
Society for Anglo-Chinese Understanding, London, 1426
— — Applied Anthropology, Washington, D.C., 1615
— — Army Historical Research, 1423
— — Byzantine Studies, Athens, 616
— — Coptic Archaeology, Cairo, 413
— — Cultural Relations with the U.S.S.R., 1426
— — Developmental Biology, Eliot, Me., 1612
— — Economic Botany, Storrs, Conn., 1612
— — Education through Art, 1413
— — Endocrinology, Bristol, 1430
— — Ethnomusicology, Ann Arbor, 1601
— — Experimental Biology and Medicine, 1620

— — International Development, Rome, 25
— — Medieval Archaeology, London, 1424
— — Natural Sciences of Slovenia, Ljubljana, 1970
— — Nautical Research, 1424
— — Pediatric Research, Albuquerque, N.M., 1619
— — Post-Medieval Archaeology, Bradford, 1424
— — Promoting the Activities of the Technical Museum of Croatia, 1970
— — Psychical Research, London, 1434
— — Range Management, Denver, 1600
— — Renaissance Studies, London, 1413
— — Research and Prevention of Cancer, Belgrade, 1969
— — into Higher Education Ltd., Guildford, 1442
— — the Advancement of Research, Laguna, 1047
— — — — the Vegetable Industry (SAVI), Laguna, 1047
— — — History of Technology, Santa Barbara, Calif., 1616
— — — Promotion of Hellenic Studies, 1427
— — — — New Music, 1415
— — — — Roman Studies, 1427
— — — Protection of Ancient Buildings, 1412
— — — — Culture, Kishinev, 1331
— — — Study of Evolution, Boulder, Colo., 1615
— — — — Medieval Languages and Literature, 1427
— — Theatre Research, London, 1413
— of Actuaries, Chicago, 1603
— — Aesthetes, Art and Literary Critics, Sofia, 218
— — African Culture, Paris, 20
— — American Archivists, 1601
— — Foresters, 1600
— — Historians, New York, 1606
— — Anaesthesiology and Intensive Care, Bucharest, 1122
— — Antiquaries of London, 1424
— — — — Library, 1458
— — — — Scotland, 1424
— — Architectural Historians, 1600
— — Archivists, Sheffield, 1424
— — Arts, Literature and Welfare, Chittagong, 142
— — Australian Genealogists, Sydney, 89
— — Authors, London, 1427
— — Automotive Engineers—Australasia, Parkville, 91
— — — — Inc., Warrendale, Pa., 1617
— — Aviation Artists, London, 1414
— — Biblical Literature, 1608
— — Biological Chemists, Bangalore, 663
— — British Neurological Surgeons, Wimbledon, 1430
— — Bulgarian Physicists, Sofia, 218
— — — Psychologists, Sofia, 218
— — Canadian Artists, Toronto, 240
— — Cardiology, Bucharest, 1122
— — Chemical Industry, 1433
— — — — (Canadian Section), 243
— — Community Medicine, London, 1430
— — Consulting Marine Engineers and Ship Surveyors, 1439
— — Dairy Technology, 1411
— — Dermatology, Bucharest, 1123
— — Designer Craftsmen, London, 1414
— — Dyers and Colourists, 1439
— — Economic Geologists, Lakewood, Colo., 1614
— — Paleontologists and Mineralogists, 1614
— — Endocrinology, Bucharest, 1123
— — Engineers (Inc.), London, 1439
— — Esaff Alkhairia, 1142
— — Foreign Language Teachers, Sofia, 218
— — Forensic Medicine, Bucharest, 1123

— — Gastro-Enterology, Bucharest, 1123
— — Genealogists, 1424
— — General Medicine, Bucharest, 1123
— — Gerontology, Bucharest, 1123
— — Glass Technology, 1439
— — Graphic Artists, 1414
— — Histochemistry and Cytochemistry, Bucharest, 1123
— — Hygiene and Public Health, Bucharest, 1123
— — Industrial Artists and Designers, London, 1414
— — Infectious Diseases, Parasitology and Epidemiology, Bucharest, 1123
— — Internal Medicine, Bucharest, 1123
— — Iranian Clinicians, Teheran, 721
— — Iraqi Artists, Baghdad, 725
— — Jurists of the S.R. of Slovenia, 1970
— — Liberian Authors, Monrovia, 904
— — Licensed Aircraft Engineers and Technologists, Surrey, 1439
— — Malawi, The, Blantyre, 912
— — Mathematicians, Physicists and Astronomers of Serbia, Belgrade, 1969
— — Medical Jurisprudence, New York, 1610
— — Medicine and Tropical Hygiene, Mogadishu, 1153
— — Military Medicine and Pharmacy, Bucharest, 1123
— — Miniaturists, London, 1414
— — Municipal Engineers of Israel, Tel-Aviv, 739
— — Mural Painters, London, 1414
— — Natural Sciences, Sofia, 218
— — Naturalists, Tartu, 1327
— — Naval Architects and Marine Engineers, New York, 1617
— — Neurology and Neurosurgery, Bucharest, 1123
— — Normal and Pathological Morphology, Bucharest, 1123
— — Obstetrics and Gynaecology, Bucharest, 1123
— — Obstetricians and Gynaecologists of Canada, Toronto, 242
— — Occupational Medicine, London, 1430
— — Oncology, Bucharest, 1123
— — Ophthalmology, Bucharest, 1123
— — Orthopaedics and Traumatology, Bucharest, 1123
— — Oto-Rhino-Laryngology, Bucharest, 1123
— — Paediatrics, Bucharest, 1123
— — Pharmacy, Bucharest, 1123
— — Physiologists and Pharmacologists, Baku, 1325
— — Physical Medicine, Balneoclimatology and Medical Rehabilitation, Bucharest, 1123
— — Physiology, Bucharest, 1123
— — Pneumology and Phthisiology, Bucharest, 1123
— — Portrait Sculptors, London, 1414
— — Professional Engineers Ltd., London, 1439
— — Psychiatry, Bucharest, 1123
— — Radiology, Radiobiology and Nuclear Medicine, Bucharest, 1123
— — Rheology, New York, 1617
— — Scribes and Illuminators, London, 1413
— — Soil Scientists, Baku, 1325
— — Sport Medicine, Sofia, 218
— — Sports Medicine, Bucharest, 1123
— — Stomatology, Bucharest, 1123
— — Surgery, Bucharest, 1123
— — the Estonian Language, Tallinn, 1327
— — — History of Medicine and Pharmacy, Bucharest, 1123
— — — Middle Sanitary Staff, Bucharest, 1123
— — Vertebrate Paleontology, 1612
— — Wildlife Artists, London, 1414
— — Woman Geographers, 1606

Sociological Association of Australia and New Zealand, Wollongong, 91
Sofia City and District State Archives, 221
Sofiiski Universitet "Kliment Ohridsky", 222
— — — Biblioteka, Sofia, 221
Sogang University, Seoul, 894
Sögufélagid, Reykjavik, 657
Soil and Water Research Institute, Giza, 415
— Conservation Service of N.S.W., Sydney, 91
— Fertilizer Institute, Beijing, 333
— Research Institute, Kumasi, 611
— — Station, Rodet-al-Farassa, 1114
— Science Society of America, 1600
Soils and Irrigation Research Institute, Pretoria, 1160
Sojuz na društvata na arhivskite rabonici na Makedonija, Skopje, 1971
— — — Bibliotekarite na Makedonija, Skopje, 1971
— — — Ekonomistite na Makedonija, Skopje, 1971
— — — Veterinarnite Lekari i Tehničari na Makedonija, Skopje, 1971
— — — za Makedonski Jazik i Literatura, Skopje, 1972
— — Hermičarite i Tehnolozite na Makedonija, Skopje, 1972
— — Inženeri i Tehnicari na Makedonija, Skopje, 1972
— — — — po Šumarstvo i Industrija za Prerabotka na Drvo na S.R. Makedonija, Skopje, 1972
— — Istoriskite Društva na S.R. Makedonija, Skopje, 1972
— — Združenijata na Pravnicite na Makedonija, Skopje, 1972
— — Zemjodelskite Inženeri i Tehničari na S.R.M., Skopje, 1972
Solar Energy Center, Eugene, 1866
— — Research Centre, St. Lucia, Qd., 109
— — Institute, Seoul, 893
Solid State Physics Research Unit, Johannesburg, 1182
Solomon R. Guggenheim Museum, 1641
— Islands National Archives, 1152
— — — Library, Honiara, 1152
— — — Museum and Cultural Centre, Honiara, 1152
Somali Institute of Public Administration Library, Mogadishu, 1153
— National University, Mogadishu, 1153
Somerset County Library, Bridgwater, 1455
Somerville College, Oxford, 1524
Somogyi Könyvtár, Szeged, 642
Sonnenobservatorium Kanzelhöhe der Universität Graz, 126
Sonoma State University, Rohnert Park, 1657
Soochow University, Shihlin, 345
Sookmyung Women's University, 894
Soong Jun University, Seoul, 894
Sophia University, Tokyo, 869
— — Library, 819
Soprintendenza Archeologica della Liguria, 771
— — di Roma, 773
SORIN Biomedica S.p.A., Vercelli, 764
Sota-arkisto, Helsinki, 432
Sourasky Central Library, Tel-Aviv University, 742
Sous-Direction des Fouilles et Antiquités, Paris, 458
South Africa Foundation, Johannesburg, 1155
— African Archaeological Society, 1155
— — Association for the Advancement of Science, 1156
— — — of Arts (Western Cape Region), Cape Town, 1155
— — Astronomical Observatory, 1158
— — Atomic Energy Board, 1161
— — Biological Society, 1156
— — Bureau of Racial Affairs, 1157
— — — Standards, Pretoria, 1161

— — Chemical Institute, 1157
— — Cultural History Museum, 1164
— — Forestry Research Institute, Pretoria, 1160
— — Geographical Society, 1155
— — Institute for Agricultural Extension, Pretoria, 1175
— — — Librarianship and Information Science, Potchefstroom, 1155
— — — Medical Research, 1160
— — — of Assayers and Analysts, 1157
— — — — Co-operatives, Potchefstroom, 1173
— — — Electrical Engineers, 1157
— — — International Affairs, 1155
— — — Mining and Metallurgy, 1157
— — — Physics, Pretoria, 1157
— — — Race Relations, 1157
— — — — Library, Johannesburg, 1162
— — Institution of Civil Engineering, 1157
— — — Mechanical Engineers, 1157
— — Library, Cape Town, 1162
— — Medical Research Council, Tygerberg, 1155
— — Mining Research Centre for Heart Disease and Organ Transplantation, Cape Town, 1167
— — Missionary Museum, Kingwilliamstown, 1165
— — Museum, Cape Town, 1164
— — National Gallery, 1164
— — Nutrition Society, Tygerberg, 1156
— — P.E.N. Centre, Cape Town, 1155
— — Society of Dairy Technology, Pretoria, 1160
— — Wool and Textile Research Institute, Port Elizabeth, 1159
— Australian Department of Mines and Energy, 94
— — Institute of Technology, Adelaide, 114
— — — — Library, 96
— — Museum, 97
— Carolina State College, 1887
— Dakota School of Mines and Technology, 1888
— — State University, 1888
— Glamorgan County Libraries, Cardiff, 1455
— Gujarat University, 702
— Hamgyong Provincial Library, Hamheung, 883
— Hwanghae Provincial Library, Haeju, 883
— India Society of Painters, Madras, 660
— London Art Gallery, 1467
— Pacific Commission Library, Nouméa, 500
— Pyongan Provincial Library, 883
— Wales Institute of Engineers, 1439
— West African Association of Arts, Windhoek, 953
— — — Scientific Society, Windhoek, 953
Southampton Art Gallery, 1471
Southeast Asian Ministers of Education Organization (SEAMEO), Bangkok, 31
— — — — Regional Center for Educational Innovation and Technology (INNOTECH), Quezon City, 1049
— — — — — Regional Language Centre, Singapore, 1152
— — Rural Social Leadership Institute, Cagayan de Oro City, 1060
— Missouri State University, 1789
South-Eastern Education and Library Board, Library Service, Ballynahinch, 1554
— Louisiana University, 1739
— Massachusetts University, 1758
— Oklahoma State University, Durant, 1859
— Union of Scientific Societies, 1431
— University, Washington, D.C., 1691
Southern African Museums Association, Cape Town, 1155

— — Ornithological Society, Johannesburg, 1156
— — Wildlife Management Association, Pretoria, 1156
— Asian Institute, New York, 1811
— California Academy of Sciences, Los Angeles, 1598
— — College, Costa Mesa, 1657
— — — of Optometry, Fullerton, 1657
— Connecticut State College, 1678
— Education and Library Board, Library Service, Craigavon, 1554
— Illinois University—Carbondale, 1708
— — — Edwardsville, 1708
— Methodist University, Dallas, 1901
— Missionary College, Collegedale, 1890
— Oregon State College, 1864
— Ossetian Research Institute, Tskhinivali, 1328
— Research Institute, Birmingham, Alabama, 1620
— Technical Institute, Songkla, 1291
— Turkmen Complex Archaeological Expedition, Ashkhabad, 1332
— Universities Nuclear Institute, Cape Town, 1167
— University, Baton Rouge, 1739
— — of Chile, Valdivia, 328
Southland Museum and Art Gallery, Invercargill, 982
Southwark Public Libraries, 1452
Southwest Foundation for Research and Education, San Antonio, 1619
— Jiaotong University, 336
— Missouri State University, 1790
— Political Science and Law College, Chongqing, 336
— Texas State University, 1901
Southwestern at Memphis, 1890
— College, Winfield, 1731
— Oklahoma State University, 1859
— University, Cebu City, 1059
— — Georgetown, Texas, 1901
Soviet Association of International Law, Moscow, 1321
— — Political (State) Sciences, Moscow, 1321
— Committee of Finno-Ugric Philologists, Moscow, 1321
— — — Slavonic Philologists, Moscow, 1321
— — — Turkish Philologists, Moscow, 1321
— Cultural Centre, Baghdad, 725
— — — Khartoum, 1229
— National Association of History and Philosophy of Natural Science and Engineering, Moscow, 1321
— — Committee of the International Brain Research Organisation, 1319
— — — — — Scientific Radio Union, Moscow, 1318
— — — — Pacific Ocean Scientific Association, Moscow, 1319
— — — on the International Biological Programme, Moscow, 1320
— Sociological Association, Moscow, 1320
Sozialwissenschaftliche Arbeitsgemeinschaft, Vienna, 123
— Studienbibliothek der Kammer für Arbeiter und Angestellte für Wien, 128
Space Activities Commission, Tokyo, 816
— Physics Institute, Xian, 332
— Research Co-ordination Center, Pittsburgh, Pa., 1881
— — Laboratory, Utrecht, 962
Spalding College, Louisville, 1736
Special Course for Foreign Students, Asia University, Tokyo, 862
— Libraries Association, New York, 1602
— Mathematics Unit, Lausanne, 1273
Specola Solare Ticinese, Locarno-Monti, 1259
Spectroscopy Society of Canada, Montreal, 243

## INDEX OF INSTITUTIONS

Speech and Hearing Clinic, Johannesburg, 1182
— Communication Association, Annandale, Va., 1608
Spelman College, Georgia, 1701
Spencer Museum of Art, University of Kansas, 1641
Spielzeugmuseum, Burgerspital, 131
Sport Bureau, Potchefstroom, 1173
— Research and Training Institute, Pretoria, 1175
Sports Council, London, 1428
Sprenger Instituut, Wageningen, 963
Spring Arbor College, Michigan, 1763
— Hill College, Mobile, 1644
Springfield City Library, Mass., 1626
— College, 1758
Sproul Observatory, Swarthmore, Pa., 1621
Squire Law Library, Cambridge, 1462
Sri Aurobindo Centre, New Delhi, 672
— Chitra Art Gallery, Gallery of Asian Paintings, Kerala, 675
— Lanka Association for the Advancement of Science, Colombo, 1224
— — Law College, Colombo, 1228
— — Library Association, 1224
— — Medical Association, Colombo, 1224
— — National Library Services Board, Colombo, 1226
— — Technical College, Colombo, 1228
— — Water Resources Board, 1225
— Nakharinwirot University, Bangkok, 1290
— — — Library, Bangkok, 1284
— Pratap Singh Museum, Srinagar, 675
— Rallabandi Subbarao Government Museum, Andhra Pradesh, 675
— Varalakshmi Academies of Fine Arts, Mysore, 707
— Venkateswara University, 703
— — — Oriental Research Institute, Tirupati, 668
SRI International, Menlo Park, 1623
Srpska akademija nauka i umetnosti, 1968
Srpsko biolosko Drustvo, 1969
Staatliche Akademie der Bildenden Künste, Karlsruhe, 608
— — — — — Stuttgart, 608
— Antikensammlungen, Munich, 544
— Bibliothek, Passau, 537
— — Regensburg, 537
— Forschungsstelle, Leipzig, 510
— Graphische Sammlung, Munich, 545
— Hochschule für Bildende Künste-Städelschule, Frankfurt, 608
— — — Musik, Freiburg i. Br., 608
— — — — Heidelberg-Mannheim, 609
— — — — Karlsruhe, 609
— — — — Mainz, 608
— — — — Rheinland, Cologne, 609
— — — — — Robert Schumann Institut, Düsseldorf, 609
— — — — und Darstellende Kunst, Stuttgart, 609
— — — — — Westfalen-Lippe (Nordwestdeutsche Musikakademie), Detmold, 608
— Kunstakademie Düsseldorf, Hochschule für bildende Künste, 608
— Kunsthalle, Baden-Baden, 541
— — Karlsruhe, 543
— Kunstsammlungen, Dresden, 509
— — Kassel, 543
— — Stuttgart, 545
— Münzsammlung, Munich, 545
— Museen, Berlin (East), 508
— — Preussischer Kulturbesitz, Berlin (West), 541
— Sammlung Ägyptische Kunst, Munich, 545
Staatlicher Mathematisch-Physikalischer Salon, Dresden, 509
Staatliches Institut für Musikforschung Preussischer Kulturbesitz, Berlin (West), 528
— Museum für Mineralogie und Geologie, Dresden, 509

— — — Naturkunde, Stuttgart, 545
— — — Tierkunde, Dresden, 509
— — — Völkerkunde, Dresden, 509
— — — — Munich, 545
Staatsarchiv Amberg, 538
— Bamberg, 538
— Basel-Stadt, 1259
— Bremen, 538
— Coburg, 539
— Detmold (Personenstandsarchiv), 539
— Dresden, 507
— Graubünden, 1260
— Hamburg, 539
— Landshut, 539
— Ludwigsburg, 539
— Magdeburg, 508
— München, 540
— Münster, 540
— Neuburg a.d. Donau, 540
— Nürnberg, 540
— Potsdam, 508
— Sigmaringen, 540
— Weimar, 508
— Würzburg, 540
— des Kantons Bern, 1259
— — Luzern, 1260
— — Zürich, 1260
Staatsbibliothek Bamberg, 534
— Preussischer Kulturbesitz, Berlin (West), 534
Staatsgalerie, Stuttgart, 545
Staats- und Seminarbibliothek, Eichstätt, 535
— — Stadtbibliothek, Augsburg, 534
— — Universitätsbibliothek, Hamburg, 536
Stacioni i frutikulturës, Vlorë, 55
— mekanizimit të bujqësisë, Tiranë, 55
— pyjeve dhe i kulturave etero-vajore, Tiranë, 55
— Studimeve dhe i Kërkimeve të Peshkimit, Durrës, 55
Städelsches Kunstinstitut, Frankfurt, 542
Stads- of Athenaeumbibliotheek, Deventer, 964
Stadsarchief, Antwerp, 155
Stadsarkivert i Stockholm, 1240
Stadsbibliotheek, Antwerp, 155
— Maastricht, 965
— en Leeszaal, Haarlem, 964
Stadsmuseum, Malines, 159
Stadtarchiv, Brunswick, 538
— Duisburg, 539
— Frankfurt, 539
— Freiburg i. Br., 539
— Leipzig, 508
— Munich, 540
— Nürnberg, 540
— Worms, 540
— und wissenschaftliche Stadtbibliothek, Bonn, 538
Stadtbibliothek, Dessau, 507
— Duisburg, 535
— Essen, 535
— Hanover, 536
— Mainz, 536
— Mönchen Gladbach, 537
— Nuremberg, 537
— Trier, 537
— Ulm, 538
— Winterthur, 1260
— Worms, 538
— Wuppertal-Elberfeld, 538
Stadtbücherei, Bochum, 534
Städtische Bibliotheken, Brunswick, 535
— — Munich, 537
— Büchereien der Gemeinde Wien, 128
— Galerie, Frankfurt, 542
— — im Lenbachhaus, Munich, 545
— Kunsthalle, Düsseldorf, 542
— — Mannheim, 544
— — Reckinghausen, 545
— Museen, Frankfurt, 542
— — Freiburg im Breisgau, 542
Städtisches Kunstmuseum Bonn, 541
— Museum, Brunswick, 541
— — Flensburg, 542

— — Göttingen, 543
Stadtmuseum Fembohaus, Nuremberg, 545
— Jena, 510
Stadt- und Bezirksbibliothek, Dresden, 507
— — — Karl-Marx-Stadt, 507
— — — Leipzig, 508
— — — Magdeburg, 508
— — — Landesbibliothek, Dortmund, 535
— — — Universitätsbibliothek, Bern, 1259
— — — — Frankfurt, 536
Stafa, Q., House-Museum, 55
Staffordshire County Library, Stafford, 1455
Stair Society, Edinburgh, 1418
Stalin Museum, Gori, 1355
Stalsky Memorial Museum of Daghestan A.S.S.R., Ashagastal, 1357
Standards and Industrial Research Institute of Malaysia (SIRIM), 915
— Association of Central Africa, Salisbury, 2002
— Institution of Israel, 741
Standing Commission on Museums and Galleries, London, 1416
— Committee on Agriculture, Canberra, 86
— Conference of National and University Libraries (SCONUL), London, 1416
— — Rectors, Presidents and Vice-Chancellors of the European Universities, Geneva, 31
— — on University Problems, Strasbourg, 31
Stanford University, 1657
— Libraries, 1631
Stanislav Dospevsky Museum, Pazardžik, 221
Stanislavsky, K. S., Flat-Museum, Moscow, 1360
Stanisław Staszic University of Mining and Metallurgy, Cracow, 1086
Starodubtsev, S. V., Physical-Engineering Institute, Tashkent, 1335
Stars' City (Soviet Space Training Centre), 1346
State Aquatic Products Bureau, Beijing, 334
— Archives, Ulan Bator, 947
— Central Library, Enugu, 994
— — — Hyderabad, 674
— — — for the Blind, Moscow, 1348
— — Museum, Ulan-Bator, 947
— — Polytechnic Library, Moscow, 1348
— — Scientific Medical Library, Moscow, 1348
— — Theatrical Library, Moscow, 1348
— Circus Museum, Leningrad, 1359
— College of Mining and Metallurgy, Ostrava, 383
— — — Victoria at Hawthorn, 116
— Commission for Science and Technology, Hanoi, 1962
— Committee for Atomic Energy, Pyongyang, 883
— Conservatoire, Ankara, 1310
— Darwin Museum, Moscow, 1359
— Egishe Charentz Literary and Art Museum, Erevan, 1356
— Ethnographical Museum of the Estonian S.S.R., Tartu, 1356
— — — — Peoples of the U.S.S.R., Leningrad, 1354
— Farm Bureau, Beijing, 334
— Forestry Bureau, Beijing, 334
— Geology Bureau, Beijing, 334
— A. M. Gorky Museum of Literature, Gorky, 1357
— Hermitage Museum, Leningrad, 1352
— Historical Museum, Moscow, 1355
— — — of the Armenian S.S.R., Erevan, 1355
— — — — Estonian S.S.R., Tallinn, 1356
— — — — Kirghiz S.S.R., Frunze, 1355
— — Society of Wisconsin, 1606
— V. I. Lenin Library of the U.S.S.R., Moscow, 1348

2118

— Lermontov Literary Memorial Museum, Piatigorsk, 1358
— Library, Bassein, 229
— — Kyaukpyu, 229
— — Mandalay, 229
— — Moulmein, 229
— — Pretoria, 1163
— — of Massachusetts, Boston, 1630
— — — New South Wales, Sydney, 96
— — — Ohio, Columbus, 1631
— — — Pennsylvania, Harrisburg, 1631
— — — Queensland, Brisbane, 96
— — — South Australia, Adelaide, 96
— — — Tasmania, Hobart, 96
— — — Victoria, Melbourne, 96
— Literary Museum of Georgia, Tbilisi, 1358
— Literature Museum, Moscow, 1357
— A. V. Lunacharsky Institute of Dramatic Art, Moscow, 1388
— V. V. Mayakovsky Museum, Moscow, 1357
— Museum, Kyaukpyu, 229
— — Mandalay, 229
— — Moulmein, 229
— — Windhoek, 953
— — of Azerbaijan Literature, Baku, 1357
— — — Ceramics (country-seat Kuskovo), Moscow, 1352
— — — Ethnography and Art Handicraft, Lvov, 1334
— — — — Arts and Crafts of the Ukrainian Academy of Sciences, Lvov, 1355
— — — — Latvian and Russian Art, Riga, 1353
— — — Oriental Art, Moscow, 1352
— — — Palekh Art, Ivanovsk, 1353
— — — the Abkhasian A.S.S.R., Sukhumi, 1356
— — — — Byelorussian S.S.R., Minsk, 1356
— — — — Defence of Volgograd, 1357
— — — — Great October Socialist Revolution, Leningrad, 1354
— — — — History of Georgia, 1356
— — — — — Leningrad, 1354
— — — — — Riga, 1356
— — — — Tatar A.S.S.R., Kazan, 1355
— Museums and Archaeological Data Bureau (Cultural Relics Administrative Bureau), Beijing, 334
— — Palace of Shirvan-Shakh, Baku, 1353
— Nationality Languages Translation Bureau, Beijing, 334
— Nikitsky Botanical Garden, Yalta, 1338
— Oceanography Bureau, Beijing, 334
— Paper Office, Dublin, 732
— Pharmaceutical Administration, Beijing, 334
— Public Historical Library of the R.S.F.S.R., Moscow, 1348
— — Library, Ulan Bator, 947
— — — of the Ukrainian S.S.R., Kiev, 1348
— — Scientific and Technical Library, Moscow, 1348
— — — — — of the Siberian Department of the Academy of Sciences, Novosibirsk, 1349
— Pushkin Museum of Fine Arts, 1352
— A. N. Radizhchev Memorial Museum, Saratov, 1358
— Republican Scientific and Technical Library of the Ukrainian S.S.R., Kiev, 1351
— Research Institute for Tractors, Moscow, 1347
— — — — of Eye Diseases, Moscow, 1346
— — — — — the Nitrogen Industry, Moscow, 1347
— — — — — Vitaminology, Moscow, 1346
— Russian Museum, 1352
— M. E. Saltykov-Schedrin Public Library, 1348

— School of Fine Arts, Mandalay, 229
— — — — — Rangoon, 229
— — — Music and Drama, Mandalay, 229
— — — — Society —, Rangoon, 229
— Scientific and Technological Commission, Beijing, 334
— Seismological Bureau, China, 334
— Standardization and Metrology Bureau, China, 334
— Surveying and Cartography Bureau, China, 334
— Theatrical Museum, Leningrad, 1359
— Tretyakov Gallery, Moscow, 1352
— University, Teheran, 724
— — of Ghent, 159
— — — Groningen, 970
— — — Limburg, Maastricht, 970
— — — New York, 1821
— — — — at Albany, 1821
— — — — — Binghamton, 1821
— — — — — Buffalo, 1821
— — — — — Stony Brook, 1821
— — — Utrecht, 971
Statens Bibliotektilsyn, Oslo, 1010
— Geotekniska Institut, Stockholm, 1239
— Handverks-og Kunstindustriskole, 1018
— historiska museum, Stockholm, 1242
— Humanistiske Forskningsråd, Copenhagen, 392
— Husdrybrugsforsøg, Copenhagen, 393
— jordbrugs- og veterinaervidenskabelige Forskningsråd, Copenhagen, 392
— kulturråd, Stockholm, 1235
— Kunstakademi, 1018
— laegevidenskabelige Forskningsråd, Copenhagen, 392
— Livsmedelsverk, Stockholm, 1238
— Museum for Kunst, Copenhagen, 396
— naturvidenskabelige Forskningsråd, Copenhagen, 392
— Provingsanstalt, 1239
— Psykologisk-Pedagogiska Bibliotek, Stockholm, 1240
— råd för byggnadsforskning, Stockholm, 1239
— samfundsvidenskabelige Forskningsråd, Copenhagen, 392
— Seruminstitut, Copenhagen, 393
— sjöhistoriska museum, Stockholm, 1242
— teknisk-videnskabelige Forskningsråd, Copenhagen, 392
— Veterinärmedicinska anstalt, 1237
Station Avicole et Centre d'Elevage Caprin, Maradi, 990
— Biologique de Roscoff, Finistère, 458
— d'Oenologie et de Technologie Végétale, Narbonne, 460
— de Physiologie et de Biochimie Végétales (I.N.R.A.), Pont-de-la-Maye, 472
— — Radioastronomie de Nancay, 459
— — recherche Bardai, Tibesti, 321
— — Recherches sur le Cocotier, Seme-Podji, 172
— — — — Palmier à l'huile, Pobe, 172
— Experimentale de Maboké, M'Baiki, 320
— Fédérale de Recherches Agronomiques de Changins, Nyon, 1258
— — — — Zürich-Reckenholz, 1258
— — — d'Economie d'entreprise et de génie rural de Tanikon, 1258
— — — en Arboriculture, Viticulture et Horticulture de Wädenswil, 1258
— — — — Chimie Agricole et sur l'Hygiène de l'Environnement, Bern, 1258
— — — — Laitières de Liebefeld-Berne, 1258
— — — — sur la production animale de Grangeneuve, 1258
— Fruitière du Congo, Loudima, 358
— Géophysique de Lamto, Abidjan, 798
— Sahélienne Expérimentale de Toukounous, 990
Statistical and Social Inquiry Society of Ireland, 730

— Institute for Asia and the Pacific, Tokyo, 26
— Laboratory, Ames, 1728
— Society of Australia, Canberra, 90
Statistics Group (A-R-C-), Cambridge, 1440
Statistisches Bundesamt, Wiesbaden, 529
Statistisk Sentralbyrå, Oslo, 1009
— Sentralbyras Bibliotek, Oslo, 1011
Statistiska Centralbyrån, Stockholm, 1238
— — Bibliotek, 1240
— Föreningen, 1237
Stațiunea centrală de cercetări avicole, Corbeanca, Jud. Ilfov, 1118
— — — — pentru Ameliorares Solurilor Săraturate, Brăila, 1118
— — — — — combaterea eroziunii solului, Perieni, 1118
— — — — — Creșterea Ovinelor, Constanta, 1118
— — — — — porcinelor, Periș, 1118
— — — — — Cultivarea Plantelor de Nisipuri, Dabuleni, 1118
— — — — — Cultura Pajistilor, Magurele, 1118
— — — — — și Industrializarea Tutunului, Bucharest, 1118
— de Cercetări pentru Piscicultură, Nucet, 1118
— — — — Plante Medicinale și Aromatice, Fundulea, 1118
— — — — Sericicultură, Bucharest, 1118
Stațiuni de Cercetare și Producție Pomicolă, Romania, 1118
— Cercetări Agricole, 1118
— — — Legumicole, 1118
— — — pentru Cultura Cartofului, Romania, 1118
— — — și Amenajari Silvice, 1118
— — — Viticole, 1118
— — — Zootehnice, 1118
Státna vedecká knižnica, Košice, 377
— — — Prešov, 377
Státní knihovna České socialistické republiky, Prague, 376
— pedagogická knihovna, Komenského při Ústavu školských informaci ministerstva školstri ČSR, Prague, 376
— technická knihovna, Prague, 376
— ustav pro kontrolu léčiv, Prague, 375
— vědecká knihovna, Brno, 377
— — — České Budějovice, 377
— — — Hradec Králové, 377
— — — Olomouc, 377
— — — Ostrava, 377
— — — Plzen, 377
— — — Maxima Gorkého, Ústí nad Labem, 377
— zidovské muzeum, Prague, 378
Statsarkivet i Hamar, 1011
Statsbiblioteket i Århus, 394
Statsøkonomisk Forening, 1017
Stavanger Bibliotek, 1011
— Museum, 1013
Stavropol Agricultural Institute, 1371
— Institute of Vaccines and Sera, 1386
— Museum of Fine Art, 1354
— Polytechnic Institute, 1376
— Territorial Medical Institute, Stavropol-Kavkaszky, 1383
Stazione Zoologica di Napoli, 763
Stedelijk Museum, Amsterdam, 966
— — "de Lakenhal" te Leiden, 968
— — "de Moriaan", 966
— — "het Catharina Gasthuis", 966
— — "Het Prinsenhof", Delft, 966
— — te Alkmaar, 966
— — Vlissingen, 969
— — voor Volkskunde, Bruges, 158
— Prentenkabinet, Antwerp, 157
Stedelijke Bibliotheek, Ypres, 157
Stefan Banach International Mathematical Center, Warsaw, 1068
Steiermärkische Landesbibliothek, Graz, 129
Steiermärkisches Landesarchiv Graz, 127
— Landesmuseum, Joanneum, 131

Steklov, V. A., Institute of Mathematics, 1318
Stellenbosch Museum, 1165
Stepano-Kert Museum of History of Nagorno-Karabakhskoy, A.O., 1356
Stephen F. Austin State University, Nacogdoches, 1901
— Leacock Memorial Home, Orillia, 251
Stephens College, Columbia, Mo., 1790
Sterling College, Kansas, 1731
Sternwarte Bochum—Institut für Weltraumforschung, 533
— Kremsmünster, 126
Sterrekundig Instituut te Utrecht, 962
Stetson University, 1695
Stevens Institute of Technology, 1801
Stichting Arnhemse Openbare en Gelderse Wetenschappelijke Bibliotheek, 964
— Centrale Raad voor de Academies van Bouwkunst, Amsterdam, 956
— Cultureel Centrum Suriname, 1231
— der Nederlandse Universiteiten en Hogescholen voor Internationale Samenwerking, The Hague, 957
— Economisch Instituut voor de Bouwnijverheid, Amsterdam, 960
— "Het Spaans, Portugees en Ibero-Amerikaans Instituut", Utrecht, 958
— Internationale School voor Wijsbegeerte, Leusden, 959
— Interuniversitair Instituut voor Sociaal-Wetenschappelijk Onderzoek, Amsterdam, 962
— Koninklijk Zoologisch Genootschap "Natura Artis Magistra", Amsterdam, 959
— Limburgs Museum voor Kunst en Oudheden, Maastricht, 968
— Nationaal Glasmuseum, Leerdam, 967
— Natuur en Milieu, Utrecht, 958
— Nederlands Agronomisch Historisch Instituut, Groningen, 956
— Nijenrode Instituut voor Bedrijfskunde, Nijenrode Breukelen, 973
— Planbureau, Suriname, 1231
— Surinaams Museum, Paramaribo, 1231
— Sweelinck Conservatorium Amsterdam, 974
— Utrechtse Openbare Bibliotheken, Utrecht, 965
— Verenigd Nederlands Filminstituut, Hilversum, 956
— voor Bodemkartering, 962
— — Fundamenteel Onderzoek der Materie (FOM), Utrecht, 962
— — Plantenveredeling (S.V.P.), 960
— — Wetenschappelijk Onderzoek van de Tropen (WOTRO), The Hague, 961
— — — — — — Tropen (WOTRO), Paramaribo, 1231
— Wetenschappelijke Bibliotheek, Curaçao, 975
— Wonen, Amsterdam, 960
Stiftelsen for industriell og teknisk forskning ved Norges tekniske høgskole, Trondheim, 1010
.Stifterverband für die Deutsche Wissenschaft, Essen, 517
Stiftsarchiv des Zisterzienserstiftes, Heiligenkreuz bei Baden, 127
Stifts-Bibliothek St. Gallen, 1260
— och landsbiblioteket i Linköping, 1239
— — — — Skara, 1239
Stiftung Kunsthaus Heylshof, 545
— Mitbestimmung, Düsseldorf, 520
— Preussischer Kulturbesitz, Berlin (West), 518
— Volkswagenwerk, Hannover-Döhren, 520
— Wissenschaft und Politik, Forschungsinstitut für Internationale Politik und Sicherheit, Ebenhausen/Isartal, 530

Stoa of Attalos, Athens, 618
Stockbridge School of Agriculture, Amherst, 1759
Stockholm International Peace Research Institute, 25
— universitets bibliotek med Kungl. Vetenskapsakademiens, Bibliotek, 1240
Stockholms Observatorium, 1238
— Stadsbibliotek, 1239
— Stadsmuseum, 1242
— Universitet, 1247
Stoke-on-Trent City Museum and Art Gallery, 1471
Stonehill College, North Easton, 1758
Stortingsbiblioteket, Oslo, 1011
Stourbridge College of Technology and Art, 1552
Stowarzyszenie Architektów Polskich, Warsaw, 1066
— Bibliotekarzy Polskich, Warsaw, 1066
Stradin, P., Historical-Medical Museum, Riga, 1356
Strangeways Research Laboratory, Cambridge, 1445
Strathmore College, Nairobi, 880
Strazhesko, N. D., Research Institute of Clinical Medicine, Kiev, 1387
Středočeská Galerie v Praze, 378
Strossmayerova galerija starih majstora, Zagreb, 1978
Structural Engineering Research Centre, Madras, 666
— — — — Roorkee, 666
Structure of Matter Institute of Fujian, Fuzhou, 332
Studiecentrum voor Kernenergie (S.C.K.), Brussels, 154
Studienstiftung des deutschen Volkes, Bonn, 520
Studies on Don Bosco Centre, Vatican City, 1946
Studijska knjižnica, Koper, 1975
— — Mirana Jarca, Novo Mesto, 1975
Studio Teologico del Seminario Regionale, Bologna, 1946
— — Fiorentino, Florence, 1945
Studium Biblicum Franciscanum, Jerusalem, 753
Studsvik Energiteknik AB Library, Nyköping, 1241
Styrelsen för teknisk utveckling, Stockholm, 1239
Styret for det Industrielle Rettsverns Bibliotek, 1011
Sub-arctic Research Institute Kevo, Turku, 439
Sub-tropical Forestry Institute, Hanzhou, 333
Sudan Medical Research Laboratories, Khartoum, 1229
— — — — Library, Khartoum, 1229
— National Museum, Khartoum, 1230
— Natural History Museum, Khartoum, 1230
Südasien-Institut, Heidelberg, 580
Suermondt-Ludwig-Museum, Aachen, 541
Suez Canal University, 420
Suffolk County Library, Ipswich, 1455
— University, Boston, Mass., 1578
Sugar Industry Research Institute, 923
— — — Library, Reduit, 923
— — — — of the Sugar Industry Authority, Mandeville, 800
— Milling Research Institute, Durban, 1170
— Technologists' Association of Trinidad and Tobago, Port-of-Spain, 1293
Sühbaatar and Choybalsan Museum, Ulan Bator, 947
— Higher Party School, Ulan Bator, 948
— Military School, Ulan Bator, 948
Suid Afrikaanse Akademie vir Wetenskap en Kuns, Pretoria, 1154
— — Biologiese Vereniging, Pretoria, 1156
— — Institut vir Biblioteek en Inligtingwese, Potchefstroom, 1155

— — Instituut, Amsterdam, 958
Sukachev, V.N., Institute of Forestry and Timber, Krasnoyarsk, 1321
Sukhothai Thammathirat Open University, Bangkok, 1290
Sukhumi Botanical Garden, 1328
Sul Ross State University, Texas, 1902
Süleymaniye Library, 1300
Sultan Hassanal Bolkiah Teachers' Training College, Brunei, 213
— (M. L.) Technikon, Durban, 1183
Sultan's Library, Nicosia, 367
Summer Garden and Museum Palace of Peter the Great, Leningrad, 1352
Sumy State Art Museum, U.S.S.R., 1354
Sun Yat-Sen Library, Kowloon, 1559
Sunderland Polytechnic, 1548
Sungkyunkwan University, Seoul, 894
Suomalainen Lääkäriseura Duodecim, 429
— Lakimiesyhdistys, 428
— Teologinen Kirjallisuusseura, Helsinki, 429
— Tiedeakatemia, 427
Suomalais-ugrilainen Seura, 429
Suomalaisen Kirjallisuuden Seura, 429
— — Seuran Kansanrunousarkisto, Helsinki, 432
— — — Kirjallisuusarkisto, Helsinki, 432
— — — Kirjasto, Helsinki, 432
Suomalaisten Kemistien Seura, Helsinki, 429
Suomen Akatemia, 427
— englanninopettajat r.y., Helsinki, 429
— Filosofinen Yhdistys, Helsinki, 429
— Geologinen Seura, Espoo, 429
— Hammaslääkäriseura, Helsinki, 429
— Historiallinen Seura, 428
— Itämainen Seura, 429
— kansallismuseo, Helsinki, 433
— Kasvatusopillinen Yhdistys, Helsinki, 428
— Kasvatustieteellinen Seura r.y., Helsinki, 430
— Kemistiseura, Helsinki, 429
— Kirjailijaliitto, 429
— Kirjastoseura, Helsinki, 427
— Kirkkohistoriallinen seura, 428
— Koulumuseo, Tampere, 433
— Kulttuurirahasto, Helsinki, 428
— Lintutieteellin Yhdistys, Helsinki, 429
— Maantieteellinen Seura, Helsinki, 428
— Maataloustieteellinen Seura, Helsinki, 427
— Metsätieteellinen Seura, 427
— Muinaismuistoyhdistys, 428
— Museoliitto, 428
— Näytelmäkirjailijaliitto, 427
— Säveltäjät ry, Helsinki, 427
— Sukututkimusseura, Helsinki, 428
— Taideakatemia Koulu, Helsinki, 441
— Taideyhdistys, 427
— Taiteilijaseura, 427
— Teknillinen Seura, Helsinki, 429
— Tiedeseura, Helsinki, 427
— Tieteellinen Kirjastoseura, Helsinki, 428
— Väestötieteen Yhdistys, Helsinki, 428
Supreme Court Library, Brisbane, 96
— — — London, 1458
— — — Tokyo, 819
— — — Tripoli, 906
— — of Puerto Rico Library, San Juan, 1110
Surabaya Institute of Technology, 717
Surgery Association, Hanoi, 1962
Surikov Institute, Moscow, 1374
Surin Agricultural College, 1291
Surrey County Library, Esher, 1455
Sursock Museum, Beirut, 900
Surtseyjarfélagid, Reykjavík, 657
Survey and Mapping Department, Mogadishu, 1153
— Institute of Zimbabwe, Salisbury, 2000
— of India, Dehra Dun, 668
— Research Centre, Canberra, 100
Susquehanna University, Selinsgrove, Pa., 1878
Sussex European Research Centre, Brighton, 1534

Suter Art Gallery, Nelson, N.Z., 982
Sutton Libraries and Arts Services, 1452
Suvorov Museum, Novogorodskaya Region, 1355
Svaz architektů ČSR, Prague, 374
— československých dramatických umělců, 374
— — skladatelů, Prague, 374
— českých dramatických umělců, Prague, 374
— — skladetelů, a koncertnich umělců, Prague, 374
— — spisovatelů, Prague, 374
— výtvarných umělců, Prague, 374
Svenska Akademien, Stockholm, 1233
— Akademiens Nobelbibliotek, 1240
— Arkitekters Riksförbund, 1235
— Bibliotekariesamfundet, Uppsala, 1235
— fysikersamfundet, Lund, 1237
— Geofysiska Föreningen, 1237
— Handelshögskolan, 440
— Handelshögskolans Bibliotek, 432
— Institutet, Athens, 623
— — Rome, 759
— — Stockholm, 1236
— Konsulterande Ingenjörers Förening, 1237
— Läkaresällskapet, Stockholm, 1236
— Litteratursällskapet i Finland, 429
— Livsmedelsinstitutet—SIK, Gothenburg, 1239
— Matematikersamfundet, Stockholm, 1237
— Museiföreningen, Stockholm, 1236
— naturskyddsföreningen, Stockholm, 1237
— Sällskapet för Antropologi och Geografi, 1236
— Samfundet för Musikforskning, 1235
— Social- och Kommunalhögskolan, Helsinki, 441
— Tekniska Vetenskapsakademien i Finland, Helsinki, 430
— Textilforskningsinstitutet, 1239
— Träforskninginstitutet, 1237
Svenskt musikhistoriskt arkiv, Stockholm, 1240
Sverdlovsk Agricultural Institute, 1371
— Bazhov Literary Museum, 1358
— Institute of Epidemiology, Microbiology and Hygiene, 1385
— — — National Economy, 1373
— — — Physical Curative Methods and Spa Treatment, 1387
— — — Restorative Surgery, Traumatology and Orthopaedics, 1386
— Law Institute, 1382
— Picture Gallery, 1354
— Region Institute of Dermatology and Venereal Diseases, 1385
— State Medical Institute, 1383
— Tuberculosis Research Institute, 1384
— V. V. Vakhrushev Mining Institute, 1379
Sverdlovsky Maternity and Child Welfare Institute, 1384
Sverige-Amerika Stiftelsen, Stockholm, 1236
Sveriges Allmänna Konstförening, Stockholm, 1235
— Civilingenjörsförbund CT-STF, Stockholm, 1237
— Författarförbund, Stockholm, 1236
— Geologiska Undersökning, 1238
— Lantbruksuniversitet, Uppsala, 1248
— lantbruksuniversitets bibliotek, Uppsala, 1241
— Radio Bibliotek och Arkiv, Stockholm, 1240
Sveučilište u Osijeku, Osijek, 1987
— — Rijeci, 1988
— — Splitu, 1989
— — Zagrebu, 1990
Swakopmund Museum, 953
Swami Satyananda Puri Foundation Library, Bangkok, 1283
Swarthmore College, Pa., 1878
Swaziland Art Society, Mbabane, 1232
— National Archives, Mbabane, 1232

— Library Service, Manzini, 1232
— — Museum, Lobamba, 1232
— Sugar Association, Big Bend, 1232
Swedenborg Society (Inc.), London, 1435
Swedish Academy, Stockholm, 1233
— National Portrait Gallery, Mariefred, 1242
— Pakistani Institute of Technology, Karachi, 1029
— School of Economics and Business Administration, Helsinki, 440
— — — Social Work and Local Administration, Helsinki, 441
— Theological Institute, Jerusalem, 753
— University of Åbo, 434
— — — Agricultural Sciences, Uppsala, 1248
Sweet Briar College, Va., 1917
Sweida Museum, 1277
Swinburne College of Technology, Hawthorn, 116
Swiss Federal Institute of Technology, Zürich, 1273
— Institute for International Economics, Regional Science and Market Research, St. Gallen, 1275
— — of Courses in Public Administration, St. Gallen, 1275
— Research Institute of Small Business, St. Gallen, 1275
Swiss-American Society for Cultural Relations, Zürich, 1255
Sydney Cancer Therapy Unit, 110
— College of Advanced Education, 113
Syktyvkar State University, 1366
Syllogos Pros Diadosin ton Hellenikon Grammaton, 616
Syndicat des Critiques Littéraires, 449
Synoptic Meteorology and Climatology Institute, Beijing, 333
Syöpätautien Tutkimussäätiö, Helsinki, 429
Syracuse University, New York, 1822
— — Library, 1633
Sysin, A. N., Institute of General and Municipal Hygiene, Moscow, 1341
System Development Corporation, Santa Monica, 1623
— Science Institute, Tokyo, 874
Systematics Association, Durham, 1432
Systematisch-Geobotanisches Institut, Bern, 1258
Systems Science Institute, Beijing, 332
Szabadtéri Néprajzi Múzeum, Szentendre, 646
Szatmári Múzeum, Mátészalka, 646
Szczecinskie Towarzystwo Naukowe, Szczecin, 1065
Széchenyi István Emlékmúzeum, Nagycenk, 646
Szeged University of Medicine, 650
Szegedi Elelmiszeripari Főiskola, Szeged, 655
— Orvostudományi Egyetem, Szeged, 650
— — — — Központi Könyvtára, Szeged, 642
Szépmuvészeti Múzeum, Budapest, 644
Szervezési es Vezetési Tudományos Társaság, Budapest, 636
Szilikátipari Központi Kutató és Tervező Intézet, Budapest, 639
— Tudományos Egyesület, Budapest, 636
Szinház és Filmművészeti Főiskola, 654
Szinháztörténeti Múzeum, Budapest, 644
Szkoła Główna Gospodarstwa Wiejskiego, Warsaw, 1093
— — Planowania i Statystyki, 1094
Szőleszeti és Borászati Kutató Intézet, Budapest, 637


T

Tables Internationales de Constantes Sélectionnées, Paris, 50
Tabor College, Hillsboro, 1731
Tabriz Public Library, 722
Taekniskóli Islands, Reykjavík, 658

Taganrog Institute of Radio Engineering, 1378
Taideteollonen Korkeakoulu, Helsinki, 440
Taipei City Library, Taipei, 342
— Institute of Technology, 345
— Medical College, 345
Taiten Kinen Kyoto Shokubutsuen, 822
Taiwan Agricultural Research Institute, Taipei, 341
— Branch Library, National Central Library, Taipei, 342
— Fisheries Research Institute, Keelung, 341
— Forestry Research Institute, Taipei, 341
— Provincial College of Marine and Oceanic Technology, Keelung, 345
— — Museum, Taipei, 342
— — Pingtung Institute of Agriculture, 345
— Sugar Research Institute, Tainan, 342
Tajik Agricultural Institute, Dushanbe, 1371
— Branch of the All-Union Biochemical Society, Dushanbe, 1332
— — — — Entomological Society, Dushanbe, 1332
— — — — Mineralogical Society, Dushanbe, 1332
— — — — Palaeontological Society, Dushanbe, 1332
— — — D. I. Mendeleyev All-Union Chemical Society, Dushanbe, 1332
— Geographical Society, Dushanbe, 1332
— Historical State Museum, Dushanbe, 1355
— Ibn-Cina Abu-Ali (Avicenna) State Medical Institute, Dushanbe, 1383
— V. I. Lenin State University, Dushanbe, 1366
— Polytechnic Institute, Dushanbe, 1376
— S.S.R. Academy of Sciences, Dushanbe, 1331
Takar ányozási Kutatóintézet, Herceghalom, 636
Takoradi Polytechnic, 614
Takushoku University, Tokyo, 869
Talim-ul-Islam College Library, Rabwah, Pakistan, 1024
Tallinn City Museum, 1356
— Polytechnic Institute, 1376
— State Art Museum, 1353
— — Conservatoire, 1388
Talouhistoriallinen Yhdistys, Helsinki, 428
Tama Art University, Tokyo, 874
Tamagawa University, Tokyo, 869
Tamale Technical Institute, 614
Tambov Institute of Chemical Engineering, 1378
— Picture Gallery, 1354
Tamil Association, Tamil Nadu, 662
— Language Society, Kuala Lumpur, 915
— Nadu Agricultural University, 703
— — Government Oriental Manuscripts Library, Madras, 674
— Tamil Development and Research Council, Madras, 662
Tamkang University, Taipei, 345
Tampere University of Technology, 437
Tampereen Kaupungin Museolautakunta, Tampere, 433
— Kaupunginmuseo, Tampere, 433
— Keskussairaalan Laaketieteellinen Kirjasto, Tampere, 432
— Luonnontieteellinen Museo, 433
— Teknillinen Korkeakoulu, 437
— — Museo, Tampere, 433
— Teknillisen Korkeakoulun Kirjasto, 432
— Yliopisto, Tampere, 437
— — Kirjasto, Tampere, 432
Tanta Municipal Library, 417
— University, 420
Tanzania Information Services Library, Dar es Salaam, 1280
— Library Association, Dar es Salaam, 1280
— — Service, Dar es Salaam, 1280
— National Scientific Research Council, Dar es Salaam, 1280
— Society, Dar es Salaam, 1280

Tanzimat Müzesi, Istanbul, 1302
Tarasevich, L. A., State Research Institute for Standardization and Control of Medical Biological Preparations, Moscow, 1386
Tarbiat Library, Tabriz, 722
Tarkio College, Mo., 1790
Tarlac College of Technology, 1060
Tarleton State University, Stephenville, 1903
Tartu Art Museum, 1354
— State University, 1367
Tartus Museum, 1277
Tasavallan Presidentti J. K. Paasikiven Rahsto Syöpätautien Tieteellistä Tutkimustyötä Varten, Helsinki, 429
Tashkent Agricultural Institute, 1371
— Historical Museum of the People of Uzbekistan, 1356
— Institute of Agricultural Engineering, 1372
— — — National Economy, 1373
— — — Railway Engineers, 1389
— — V. I. Lenin State University, 1367
— A. N. Ostrovsky State Theatrical and Art Institute, 1388
— Pharmaceutical Institute, 1384
— Polytechnic Institute, 1376
— State Conservatoire, 1388
— — Medical Institute, 1384
— Telecommunications Institute, 1378
— Textile Institute, 1381
Tasmanian College of Advanced Education, Launceston, 115
— Geological Survey, 94
— Historical Research Association, 92
— Museum and Art Gallery, 97
Tata Institute of Fundamental Research, 670
— — — Social Sciences, Bombay, 706
Tatar Historical Museum (house of V. I. Lenin), Kazan, 1355
— State Museum of Fine Arts, Kazan, 1354
Tate Gallery, 1467
Tatham Art Gallery (Municipal), Pietermaritzburg, 1165
Tatra Museum, 1077
Tatung Institute of Technology, Taipei, 345
Tauchira Museum, Tokra, 906
Tavistock Institute of Human Relations, London, 1444
— — — Medical Psychology, London, 1430
Tax Accounting Research Institute, Seoul, 893
Tay Nguyen College, Hanoi, 1963
Täydennyskoulutuskeskus, Tampere, 438
Taylor Institution Library, Oxford, 1464
— University, Upland, Ind., 1722
Tbilisi Academy of Arts, 1374
— A. M. Razmadze Mathematical Institute, Tbilisi, 1327
— V. Sarjishvili State Conservatoire, 1388
— State Medical Institute, 1384
— — Museum of Anthropology and Ethnography, 1356
— — University, 1367
Tchaikovsky House Museum, Moscow, 1360
Tea Institute, Hangzhou, 333
— Research Foundation of Central Africa, Mulanje, 912
— — Institute of Kenya, 879
— — — Sri Lanka, Talawakelle, 1225
— — — — — Library, 1226
— — Station, Shizuoka, 813
Teachers' Club Library, Aden, 1965
— College, New York, 1810
Teaching Methods Unit, Rondebosch, 1167
Teatermuseet, Copenhagen, 396
Technical Atomic Energy Library, Baghdad, 726
— College, Burgo, 1153
— — Sokodé, 1292
— — Vientiane, 898
— — Institute, Basrah, 728
— — Freetown, 1149

— — Helsinki, 441
— — Kenema, 1149
— — Riyadh, 1144
— — in Arbil, 728
— — — Hilla, 728
— — — Kirkuk, 728
— — — Missan, 728
— — — Mosul, 728
— — — Najaf, 728
— — — Ramadi, 728
— — — Sulaimania, 728
— — — of Agriculture, Abu-Ghraib (Baghdad), 728
— — — — Aski-Kalak (Arbil), 728
— — — — Kumait, 728
— — — — Mussaib-Babylon, 728
— — — — Shatra-Thi Qar, 728
— — — Medicine, Baghdad, 728
— Physics Institute, Shanghai, 332
— University of Brno, 386
— — Budapest, 652
— — Denmark, Copenhagen, 399
— — Heavy Industry, Miskolc-Egyetemváros, 653
— — Łódź, 1090
— — Nova Scotia, Halifax, 290
— — Prague, 382
— — Rzeszów, 1091
— — Szczecin, 1091
— — Warsaw, 1091
Technické muzeum Tatra Kopřivnice, 379
Technicki muzej, Zagreb, 1978
Technion (Israel Institute of Technology), Haifa, 750
— — — — — Library System, 743
— Research and Development Foundation Ltd., Haifa, 739, 752
Technikon Natal, Durban, 1183
— Pretoria, 1183
Technische Akademie e.V., Wuppertal, 548
— Bibliotheek Zeeland, Vlissingen, 965
— Hochschule Darmstadt, 558
— — Ilmenau, 514
— — Karl-Marx-Stadt, 514
— — Karlsruhe, 581
— — Leipzig, 514
— — "Carl Schorlemmer", Leuna-Merseburg, 514
— — "Otto von Guericke", Magdeburg, 514
— Hogeschool te Delft, 972
— — Eindhoven, 972
— — Twente, Enschede, 972
— Universität Berlin (West), 551
— — Carolo Wilhelmina, Brunswick, 556
— — Clausthal, Clausthal-Zellerfeld, 558
— — Dresden, 511
— — Graz, 136
— — München, 595
— — Wien, Vienna, 137
Technisches Museum Dresden, 509
— — für Industrie und Gewerbe in Wien mit Österreichisches Eisenbahnmuseum und Post- und Telegraphen-museum, Vienna, 130
Technological University of Malaysia, Kuala Lumpur, 917
— — — the Philippines, Metro Manila, 1059
Teesside Polytechnic, Middlesbrough, 1548
Tegelmuseum "It Noflik Ste", Otterlo, 968
Teheran Book Processing Centre, 721
— Museum of Contemporary Art, 722
— Polytechnic, 724
Teishin Hakubutsukan, 821
Tekelioğlu Library, 1301
Tekniikan Edistämissäätiö, Helsinki, 430
Teknillinen Korkeakoulu, Espoo, 438
Teknillisen Korkeakoulon Kirjasto, Espoo, 432
Teknillisten Tieteiden Akatemia, Helsinki, 430
Tekniska Föreningen i Finland, Helsinki, 430
— institutionen, Stockholm, 1242
— Läroverket i Helsingfors, Helsinki, 441
— Museet, Stockholm, 1242

Teknologisk Institut, Copenhagen, 401
Tel-Aviv Central Public Library "Shaar Zion", 745
— — Museum, 744
— — University, 749
— Hai Museum, Upper Galilee, 744
— — Regional College, Upper Galilee, 753
Tel-Quasila Excavations, Tel-Aviv, 743
Telecommunications Research Centre, New Delhi, 673
Télé-Université, Quebec City, 294
Temple Newsam House, 1469
— University, Philadelphia, 1879
Tennessee State University, Nashville, 1891
— Technological University, 1891
— Wesleyan College, 1891
Tenri Central Library, 820
— Sankokan Museum, Tenri City, 823
Tensor Society, Chigasaki, 818
Teologiske Menighetsfakultet, Oslo, 1017
Temelésfejlesztési Intézet, Debrecen, 653
Természettudományi Muzeum, Budapest, 644
Terminological Commission, Riga, 1330
— Committee, Baku, 1326
Ternopol State Medical Institute, 1384
Terra Sancta Museum, Nazareth, 744
Tertiary Education Institute, Brisbane, 109
Tessedik Sámuel Múzeum, Szarvas, 646
Testnevelési es Sportmuzeum, Budapest, 644
Tetsugaku-kai, 811
Texas A. & I. University, Kingsville, 1902
— — — — Citrus and Vegetable Training Center, 1902
— A. & M. University System, College Station, 1902
— — — — at Galveston, 1902
— Christian University, 1903
— Lutheran College, 1903
— Memorial Museum, 1642
— Southern University, 1903
— Tech University, Lubbock, 1903
— — Health Sciences Center, Lubbock, 1903
— Wesleyan College, 1903
— Woman's University, 1903
Textil- und Modeschule, St. Gallen, 1275
Textile Consolidation Fund, Alexandria, 416
— Institute, Manchester, 34
— Research Institute, Princeton, 1623
Textilforschungsantalt Krefeld, 533
Textilipari Müszaki es Tudományos Egyesület, 636
— Múzeum, Budapest, 644
Teylers Museum, Haarlem, 967
Thai-Bhara Cultural Lodge, Bangkok, 1283
— -German Technical Institute, Khonkaen, 1291
— Library Association, Bangkok, 1283
— National Documentation Department, Bangkok, 1284
Thames Polytechnic, Woolwich, 1548
Thammasat University, Bangkok, 1291
— — Library, Bangkok, 1284
That Luang, Vientiane, 898
Theaterhochschule "Hans Otto", Leipzig, 513
Theatre Library Association, 1602
— Museum, Göteborg, 1242
Theological College of the Reformed Churches, Kampen, 973
— School of the Reformed Church in South Africa, Potchefstroom, 1173
Theologische Fakultät, Paderborn, 609
— — Trier, 609
— Hogeschool van de Gereformeerde kerken, Kampen, 973
Theomin Gallery (Olveston), Dunedin, 982
Theoretical Physics Institute, Beijing, 332
— — Edmonton, Alb., 257
Theosophical Society, Madras, 663
— — in Ireland, 731
— — of Ceylon, 1224
— — Trinidad, Guaico, 1293
Thermae Museum Heerlen, 967
Thiel College, Greenville, Pa., 1879

## INDEX OF INSTITUTIONS

Thijmgenootschap, Nijmegen, 958
Thjódminjasafn, Reykjavik, 657
Thjódskjalasafn, 657
Thomas Coram Research Unit, London, 1513
— More College, Fort Mitchell, 1736
Thomson Foundation, London, 1421
Thorma János Múzeum, 646
Thorneloe University, Sudbury, 270
Thorvaldsen's Museum, 396
Thurrock Borough Museum, Grays, 1469
— Riverside Museum, Tilbury, 1469
Thury György Múzeum, Nagykanizsa, 646
Tichreen University, Lattakia, 1279
Tianjin Institute of Geology and Mineral Resources, 333
— Municipal Library, 335
— University, 338
Tierärztliche Hochschule, Hanover, 578
Tieteellisen Informoinnin Neuvosto, Helsinki, 428
Tietokonekeskus, Tampere, 438
Tihanyi Múzeum, Tihany, 646
Tilastokeskus, Helsinki, 431
Tilastokirjasto, Helsinki, 432
Tilburg University, 972
Tilraunastod Háskólans í meinafraedi á Keldum, 657
Timiryazev, K. A., Apartment Museum, Moscow, 1359
— Institute of Plant Physiology, Moscow, 1319
— State Museum of Biology, Moscow, 1359
Tiroler Landesarchiv, Innsbruck, 127
— Landeskundliches Museum, 132
— Landes-Museum Ferdinandeum, 132
— Volkskunstmuseum, 132
Tiszáninneni Református Egyházkerület, Nagykönyvtára, Debrecen, 642
Tiszántuli Refomátus Egyházkerület Nagykönyvtára, Sarospatak, 642
Titus Brandsma Institute, Nijmegen, 970
Toa Kumo Gakkai, 810
Tobacco Research Board, Salisbury, Zimbabwe, 2002
— — Institute, Rustenburg, 1160
Tobago District Agricultural Society, 1293
Tobolsk Picture Gallery, 1354
— State Historical Museum, 1356
Tochigi Prefectural Library, Utsunomiya City, 820
Tódaiji, 823
Togliatti Polytechnic Institute, 1376
Toho Gakkai, Tokyo, 812
— Gakuen School of Music, 874
Tohoku Gakuin University, Sendai, 869
— University, Sendai, 849
— — Library, 820
Tøjhusmuseet, Copenhagen, 396
Tokai University, 870
Tokyo Astronomical Observatory, 816
— Biochemical Research Institute, 816
— Chigaku Kyokai, 806
— College of Music, 874
— — — Pharmacy, 870
— Daigaku Keizai Gakkai, 805
— — Rigakubu Fuzoki Shokubutsuen, 821
— Electrical Engineering University, 870
— Geijutsu Daigaku Toshokan, 819
— Institute of Technology, 856
— Keizai University, 870
— Kokuritsu Hakubutsukan, 821
— Medical and Dental University, 856
— Metropolitan Central Library, 819
— — Hibiya Library, 819
— — University, 860
— — Library, 819
— National University of Fine Arts and Music, 857
— — — — — and Music Art Museum, 821
— Science University, 870
— Shina Gakkai, 870
— University of Agriculture, 870
— — — — and Technology, 857
— — — Fisheries, 857

— — — Library, 819
— — — Foreign Studies, 857
— — — — Library, 819
— — — Mercantile Marine, 857
— Women's Medical College, 870
Tokyo-to Bijutsukan, 821
Toledo-Lucas County Public Library, 1627
Tolson Memorial Museum, 1469
Tolstoy Residence Museum, 1357
— State Museum, 1357
Tom Thomson Memorial Art Gallery, Owen Sound, 251
Tompkins Institute of Human Values and Technology, Nova Scotia, 265
Tomsk Civil Engineering Institute, 1380
— Institute of Automatic Control Systems and Radio-electronics, 1378
— — Physiotherapy and Spa Treatment, 1387
— S. M. Kirov Polytechnic Institute, 1376
— V. V. Kuibyshev State University, 1367
— State Medical Institute, 1384
Tongji University, 337
Tónlistarfélagid, Reykjavik, 657
Tónlisttarskólinn i Reykjavik, 658
Tonskáldafélag Islands, 656
Topchiev, A. V., Institute of Oil Chemical Synthesis, Moscow, 1319
Topkapi Palace Museum, Istanbul, 1302
Tornyai János Múzeum, 646
Toronto Public Library, 248
Torry Research Station, Aberdeen, 1475
Tottori Nogakkai, 804
— University, Tottori City, 857
Tougaloo College, Miss., 1785
Towarzystwo im. Fryderyka Chopina, Warsaw, 1066
— Internistów Polskich, Warsaw, 1065
— Literackie im. Adama Mickiewicza, 1065
— Miłosników Historii i Zabytków Krakowa, Cracow, 1065
— — Jezyka Polskiego, 1065
— Naukowe Organizacji i Kierownictwa Warsaw, 1065
— — Płockie, Płock, 1065
— — w Toruniu, 1065
— Przyjaciót Nauk w Przemyslu, 1066
— — Nauki i Sztuki e Rzeszówie, Rzeszów, 1066
Tower Hamlets Public Libraries, 1452
— of London Armouries, 1467
Town and Country Planning Association, London, 1412
— Planning Institute of Canada, Toronto, 239
Towneley Hall Art Gallery and Museums, Burnley, 1468
Towson State University, Baltimore, 1746
Toxicology Unit (M.R.C.), Carshalton, 1444
Toyama University, 857
Toyo Bunka Kenkyusho, Tokyo, 816
— Ongaku Gakkai, Tokyo, 813
— University, Tokyo, 870
Toyokuni Jinja Hómotsuden, 822
Toyoshi Kenkyukai, Kyoto, 806
Trade and Commerce Institute, Beijing, 332
— School, Ulan Bator, 948
— — Uliastay, 948
— Union Education Institute, Kingston, Jamaica, 801
Traditional Pharmacology Institute, Beijing, 333
Trakai Historical Museum, 1356
Transfer of Technology Centre, Jadiriyah, 725
Transplantation Research Unit, Johannesburg, 1182
Transport and Road Research Laboratory, Crowthorne, 1448
— Library, Seoul, 887
— Museum, Holywood, 1555
Transportøkonomisk institutt, Oslo, 1010
Transvaal Education Library and Audio-Visual Ancillary Service, Pretoria, 1163

— Museum, 1165
— Provincial Library Service, Pretoria, 1163
Transylvania University, Lexington, 1736
Trauma Unit (M.R.C.), Manchester, 1444
Travelling Library, Aden, 1965
Treasury and Cabinet Office Library, London, 1451
Trent Polytechnic, Nottingham, 1549
— University,Peterborough, Ont., 310
Trenton State College, N.J., 1801
Trevelyan College, Durham, 1487
Tribal Research Centre, Chiangmai, 1285
Tribhuvan University, Nepal, 954
— — Library, 954
Trinidad Art Society, Port-of-Spain, 1293
— Music Association, 1293
— Public Library, Port-of-Spain, 1293
— and Tobago Law Society, Port-of-Spain, 1293
Trinity College, Burlington, Vermont, 1915
— — Cambridge, 1485
— — Hartford, 1678
— — Oxford, 1524
— — Parkville, 104
— — Washington, D.C., 1691
— — Library, Cambridge, 1462
— — — Dublin, 732
— — — Oxford, 1463
— — of Music, 1553
— Hall, Cambridge, 1485
— — Library, Cambridge, 1462
— University, San Antonio, Tex., 1904
Trivandrum Public Library, 674
Troitsk Veterinary Institute, 1372
Tromsø Museum (Universitet i Tromsø: Institutt for museumsvirksomhet), 1013
Tropenmuseum, Amsterdam, 966
Tropical Agriculture Research Facilities, Okinawa, 848
— Botanic Garden and Research Institute, Trivandrum, 670
— Forestry Institute, Beijing, 333
— Meteorology Institute, Guangzhou, 333
— Pesticides Research Institute, Arusha, 1280
— Plant Research Institute of South China, 332
— — — — Yunnan, Mengla, 332
— Products Institute, London, 1449
— — Library, London, 1451
— Science Centre, San José, 360
Troy State University System, Ala., 1644
Truong Dai-Hoc Tông-Ho'p, Hanoi, 1963
Truva Müzesi, Canakkale, 1302
Tselinograd Agricultural Institute, 1371
— Civil Engineering Institute, 1380
Tsessissky State Historical Museum, 1356
Tsiolkovsky, K.E., State Museum of the History of Cosmonautics, Moscow, 1359
Tsuda College, Tokyo, 870
Tsulukidze, G. A., Institute of Mining Mechanics, Tbilisi, 1328
Tsurumei (Nagoya) Central Library, 820
Tuberculosis and Chest Diseases Unit (M.R.C.), London, 1444
— Research Institute, Tygerberg, 1156
— — — Warsaw, 1072
Tubman, William V.S., College of Technology, Monrovia, 905
Tuborgfondet, Copenhagen, 390
Tudományos Ismeretterjesztö Társulat, Budapest, 635
Tufts University, Medford, Mass., 1758
Tula Art Museum, 1354
— Historical Museum, 1356
— Polytechnic Institute, 1376
Tulane University of Louisiana, 1739
— — — Libraries, 1632
Tun Abdul Razak Library, Selangor, 916
— Razak Library, Perak, 916
Tunghai Christian University, Taichung, 345
Turgenev, I.S., State Museum, Orel, 1358
Türk Biyoloji Derneği, Istanbul, 1298
— Cerrahi Cemiyeti, 1298

# INDEX OF INSTITUTIONS

Türk Dil Kurumu, 1298
— Eczacilari Birliği, Istanbul, 1298
— Halk Bilgisi Derneği, 1298
— Hukuk Kurumu, 1298
— Kültürünü Araştirma Enstitüsü, 1299
— Mikrobiyoloji Cemiyeti, 1298
— Nörö-Psikiyatri Cemiyeti, 1298
— Ortopedi ve Travmatoloji Derneği, 1298
— Oto-Rhino-Laryngoloji Cemiyeti, 1298
— Sirff ve Tatbiki Matematik Derneği, Istanbul, 1298
— Tarih Kurumu, 1298
— Tib Cemiyeti, 1298
— Tibbi Elektro Radyografi Cemiyeti, 1298
— Tip Tarihi Kurumu, Istanbul, 1298
— Tüberküloz Cemiyeti, Istanbul, 1298
— Üniversite Rektörleri Konseyi, Ankara, 1298
— Üroloji Cemiyeti, 1298
— ve Islam Eserleri Muzesi, Istanbul, 1302
— Veteriner Hekimleri Derneği, 1298
Turkish Natural History Museum, Ankara, 1302
— Public Library, Nicosia, 367
Türkiyat Enstitüsü, 1307
Türkiye Akil Sağliği Derneği, Istanbul, 1298
— Askeri Müzesi, 1298
— Bilimsel ve Teknik Araştirma Kurumu, Ankara, 1299
— Ekonomisini Araştirma Enstitüsü, Eskişehir, 1309
— Jeoloji Kurumu, 1298
— Kimya Cemiyeti, 1298
Turkmen Branch of the All-Union Botanical Society, Ashkhabad, 1332
— — — — Entomological Society, Ashkhabad, 1332
— — — — Geographical Society, Ashkhabad, 1332
— Department of All-Union Department of Soil Science, Ashkhabad, 1332
— — — Protozoologists, Ashkhabad, 1332
— Eye Diseases Research Institute, Ashkhabad, 1385
— A. M. Gorky State University, 1367
— Institute of Neurology and Physiotherapy, Ashkhabad, 1386
— M. I. Kalinin Agricultural Institute, Ashkhabad, 1371
— Polytechnic Institute, Ashkhabad, 1376
— Skin and Venereal Diseases Institute, Ashkhabad, 1385
— S.S.R. Academy of Sciences, Ashkhabad, 1332
— State Medical Institute, 1384
— — Museum of Fine Art, 1353
Turku Institute of Technology, 441
— School of Economics, 440
Turner Child Orthopaedics Research Institute, 1384
— Memorial Library, Umtali, 2002
Turr István Muzeum, 646
Turun Kauppakorkeakoulu, Turku, 440
— — Kirjasto, Turku, 432
— Maakuntamuseo, Turku, 433
— Soitannollinen Seura, Turku, 427
— Taidemuseo, Turku, 433
— Teknillinen Oppilaitos, Turku, 441
— Yliopisto, 438
— Yliopiston Kirjasto, 432
Tusculum College, Greeneville, Tenn., 1891
Tuskegee Institute, Ala., 1644
Tussock Grasslands and Mountain Lands Institute, Canterbury, N.Z., 984
Tüzoltó Múzeum, Budapest, 644
TV ile Öğretim ve Eğitim Fakültesi, Eskişehir, 1309
Twente University of Technology, Enschede, 972
Twentieth Century Fund, 1603
Tyan-Shan Physical-Geographical Station, Pokrovka Village, 1329
Tyndale Library, Cambridge, 1459
Tyne and Wear County Council Museums, Newcastle upon Tyne, 1470
Tyoterveyslaitos, Helsinki, 441

Typhoon Studies Institute, Shanghai, 333
Tyumen Agricultural Institute, 1371
— Picture Gallery, 1354
— State Medical Institute, 1384
— — University, 1368

## U

Überseemuseum, Bremen, 541
Uchu Koku Kenkyushu, Tokyo, 818
Udenrigspolitiske Selskab, Copenhagen, 390
Udmurd State University, Izhvsk, 1368
Udruženje Književnih Prevodilaca BiH, Sarajevo, 1971
— Književnika BiH, Sarajevo, 1971
— Kompozitora BiH, Sarajevo, 1971
— Muzičkih Umjetnika BiH, Sarajevo, 1971
Ueno Gakuen College of Music, Tokyo, 874
Ufa Institute of Hygiene and Occupational Diseases, 1386
— Oil Institute, 1379
— S. Orjonikidze Aviation Institute, 1390
— Skin and Venereal Diseases Institute, 1385
— State Institute of Fine Arts, 1388
— Trachoma Institute, Ufa, 1385
Ufficio Centrale di Ecologia Agraria e difesa delle Piante coltivate dalle Avversità Meteoriche, Rome, 761
Uganda Library Association, Kampala, 1311
— Museum, 1312
— Society, Kampala, 1311
— Technical College, Kampala, 1312
Uglich Historical Museum, 1356
Uitz Múzeum, Pecs, 646
Uj Magyar Központi Levéltár, Budapest, 642
Ukraine Experimental Institute for Eye Disease and Tissue Therapy, Odessa, 1385
— Institute of Water Conservation, Rovno, 1372
— Skin and Venereal Diseases Institute, Kharkov, 1385
Ukrainian Agricultural Academy, Kiev, 1371
— Extra-Mural Polytechnic Institute, Kharkov, 1376
— Institute of Epidemiology, Microbiology and Hygiene, 1385
— — — Mother and Child Care, 1384
— — — Printing, 1382
— Museum of Folk and Decorative Art, Kiev, 1353
— Radiological and Oncological Institute, 1386
— Research Institute of Orthopaedics and Traumatology, Kiev, 1386
— S.S.R. Academy of Sciences, Kiev, 1333
— State Museum of Theatrical, Musical and Cinematographic Art, Kiev, 1360
— — Steppe Reservation, Donetsk, 1334
Ukrainische Freie Universität, Munich, 597
Ulan-Bator Museum, 947
Ulmer Museum, Ulm, 545
Ulster Archaeological Society, Belfast, 1554
— Folk and Transport Museum, Holywood, 1554
— Museum, Belfast, 1555
— Polytechnic, Newtownabbey, 1557
Ulucami Library, 1301
Ulyanovsk Agricultural Institute, 1371
— Polytechnic Institute, Ulyanovsk, 1376
Uman A. M. Gorky Agricultural Institute, 1371
Umarov, S. U., Physical Engineering Institute, Dushanbe, 1332
Umeå stadsbibliotek, 1239
— Universitet, 1249
— Universitetsbibliotek, 1241
Uměleckoprůmyslové Muzeum, Prague, 378
Umjetnička galerija Bosne i Hercegovine, Sarajevo, 1977
— — Dubrovnik, 1976
Umm El-Qurah University, Mecca, 1144

Umtali Museum, 2002
UNDP/FAO Assisted Project: Water and Soil Investigations for Agricultural Development, Ras Al Khaimah, 1391
UNESCO, 1
— European Centre for Higher Education, Bucharest, 31
— Institut für Pädagogik, Hamburg, 31
— Institute for Education, Hamburg, 31
— Mission Library, Monrovia, 904
— Regional Office for Book Development in Asia and the Pacific, Karachi, 1019
— — — — Education in Africa, Dakar, 1145
— — — — — Asia and Oceania, Bangkok, 1284
— — — — — the Arab States, Beirut, 899
— — — — Science and Technology for Africa, Nairobi, 878
— — — — — Technology in the Arab States (ROSTAS), Cairo, 416
Ungku Omar Polytechnic, Perak, 919
União Cultural Brasil-Estados Unidos, São Paulo, 181
Unidad de Genética Médica, Zulia, 1960
— — Investigación Biológica, Zulia, 1960
Unidade de Execução de Pesquisa de Âmbito Estadual de Pelotas, 182
Union académique internationale, Brussels, 10
— astronomique internationale, Paris, 7
— Centrale des Arts Décoratifs, 446
— College, Barbourville, 1736
— — Brisbane, 109
— — Lincoln, Nebraska, 1793
— — Schenectady, 1822
— Culturelle et Technique de Langue Française, Paris, 449
— des associations techniques internationales, Paris, 32
— Ecrivains Algériens, Algiers, 57
— — et Artistes Latins, Paris, 449
— — — Tunisiens, Tunis, 1295
— Physiciens (CSSF), 452
— — Professeurs de Spéciales (Mathématiques et Physiques), 447
— — Travailleurs Scientifiques, Paris, 451
— géodésique et géophysique internationale, Brussels, 7
— géographique internationale, Freiburg, 7
— Industrial Research Laboratories, Hsinchu, 341
— internationale contre la tuberculose, Paris, 38
— — — le cancer, Geneva, 38
— — — péril vénérien et les tréponématoses, Paris, 42
— d'Angéiologie, Florence, 38
— d'Education pour la Santé, Paris, 38
— d'Electrothermie, Paris, 33
— de biochimie, Miami, 7
— — chimie pure et appliquée, Oxford, 8
— — — cristallographie, Chester, 7
— — l'Industrie du Gaz, Paris, 33
— — — Pharmacologie, Heidelberg, 8
— — — physique pure et appliquée, Quebec, 8
— — — psychologie scientifique, Austin, 12
— — Spéléologie, Vienna, 50
— des architectes, Paris, 20
— — Avocats, Brussels, 36
— — études orientales et asiatiques, Saint-Maur, 11
— — étudiants, Prague, 30
— — instituts de recherches forestières, Vienna, 18
— — sciences anthropologiques et ethnologiques, Durham, 12
— — — biologiques, Paris, 7
— — — — de la Nutrition, Rüschlikon, 8

— — — — géologiques, Paris, 8
— — — — préhistoriques et protohistoriques, Højbjerg, 11
— — — Services Médicaux des Chemins de Fer, Brussels, 42
— — — Sociétés d'Immunologie, Oslo, 8
— — — — de microbiologie, Marseille, 39
— — — Transports Publics, Brussels, 33
— — du cinéma d'amateurs, La Louvière, 20
— — — mécanique théorique et appliquée, Gothenburg, 9
— — pour l'Etude des Insectes Sociaux, Southampton, 50
— — — — scientifique de la population, Liège, 12
— — — — la Conservation de la Nature et de ses Ressources, Gland, 50
— — — — — protection des oeuvres littéraires et artistiques, Geneva, 20
— Nationale des Arts Plastiques, Tunis, 1295
— of Actors in Bulgaria, Sofia, 217
— — Agricultural Engineers and Technicians of Yugoslavia, 1969
— — Agriculture and Stockbreeding, Sofia, 217
— — Architects in Bulgaria, Sofia, 217
— — — of Yugoslavia, Belgrade, 1969
— — Bulgarian Artists, 217
— — — Composers, Sofia, 217
— — — Economists, Sofia, 218
— — — Film Makers, Sofia, 217
— — — Journalists, Sofia, 218
— — — Musicians, Sofia, 217
— — — Writers, 218
— — Chemistry and the Chemical Industry, Sofia, 218
— — Chemists and Technologists of Yugoslavia, 1969
— — Civil Engineering, Sofia, 218
— — — Engineers and Technicians of Yugoslavia, 1969
— — Energetics, Electrical Engineering and Communications, Sofia, 218
— — Engineers and Technicians for Protection of Materials of Yugoslavia, 1969
— — — — — of the S.R. of Serbia, Belgrade, 1969
— — — — — Yugoslavia, Belgrade, 1968
— — Forest Engineering, Sofia, 218
— — Forestry and Wood Processing Engineers and Technicians of Yugoslavia, 1969
— — International Engineering Organisations (UIEO), Paris, 32
— — Jurists' Associations of Yugoslavia, 1969
— — Mechanical and Electrical Engineers and Technicians of Yugoslavia, 1969
— — — Engineering, Sofia, 218
— — Mining Engineering, Geology and Metallurgy, Sofia, 218
— — Geological and Metallurgical Engineers and Technicians of Yugoslavia, 1969
— — Scientific and Technical Associations, Hanoi, 1962
— — — Medical Societies in Bulgaria, Sofia, 218
— — — Workers in Bulgaria, Sofia, 217
— — Societies for the Advancement of Standardization, Belgrade, 1969
— — Surveyors and Geometers of Yugoslavia, Belgrade, 1969
— — Textile Engineers and Technicians of Yugoslavia, 1969
— — Textiles and Clothing, Sofia, 218
— — the Food Industry, Sofia, 218
— — — Societies of Engineers and Technicians of the S.R. of Croatia, Zagreb, 1970

— — Soviet Societies of Friendship and Cultural Relations with Foreign Countries, Moscow, 1345
— — Universities of Latin America, Mexico, D.F., 31
— — Translators in Bulgaria, Sofia, 218
— — Transport, Sofia, 218
— — Transportation and Communications Engineers and Technicians of Yugoslavia, 1969
— — U.S.S.R. Architects, Moscow, 1345
— — — Artists, Moscow, 1345
— — — Composers, Moscow, 1345
— — — Writers, Moscow, 1345
— — Water Works, Sofia, 218
— radio scientifique internationale, Brussels, 8
— Research Institute, Kowloon, 1559
— Royale Belge pour les Pays d'Outre-mer et l'Europe Unie, 150
— Theological College, Belfast, 1557
— Thérapeutique Internationale, Paris, 38
— — Seminary Library, 1630
— University, Jackson, 1891
— — New York, 1822
Unión de Escritores y Artistas de Cuba, Havana, 364
— — Universidades de América Latina, Mexico City, 31
— — Matemática Argentina, Buenos Aires, 65
— Nacional de Astronomía y Ciencias Afines, 1191
— Sudamericana de Asociaciones de Ingenieros (USAI), Asunción, 1034
Unit Diponegoro, Jakarta, 709
— for Epidemiological Studies in Psychiatry (M.R.C.), Edinburgh, 1444
— — Laboratory Studies of Tuberculosis (M.R.C.), London, 1444
— — Research in Clinical Psychiatry, Tygerberg, 1156
— — the History, Philosophy and Social Relations of Science, Canterbury, 1496
— of Comparative Plant Ecology, Sheffield, 1446
— — Invertebrate Chemistry and Physiology (A.R.C.), Brighton, 1440, 1534
— — Marine Invertebrate Biology, 1446
— — Nitrogen Fixation (A.R.C.), Brighton, 1440, 1534
— — Statistics (A.R.C.), Edinburgh, 1440
— — Virology, Oxford, 1446
— on Development and Integration of Behaviour (M.R.C.), Cambridge, 1444
— — Neural Mechanisms of Behaviour (M.R.C.), London, 1443
— — the Experimental Pathology of the Skin (M.R.C.), Birmingham, 1444
Unité de Recherches de Cardiologie, Bordeaux, 472
— — — — Radiobiologie Experimentale et de Cancerologie, Bordeaux, 472
— — — — sur l'Immunologie des Affections Parasitaires, Bordeaux, 472
— — — — — les Applications Médicales et Biologiques des Isotopes Radio-Actifs, Bordeaux, 472
— Pédagogique d'Architecture de Lille, 498
United Arab Emirates University, Al Ain, 1391
— College of the Chinese University of Hong Kong, 1561
— Engineering Trustees, Inc., New York, 1617
— Kingdom Atomic Energy Authority, London, 1447
— Nations Depository Library, Seoul, 887
— — Economic and Social Commission for Asia and the Pacific Library, Bangkok, 1284
— — Educational, Scientific and Cultural Organization (UNESCO), Paris, 1

— — Information Centre Library, London, 1458
— — Institute for Namibia, Lusaka, 1999
— — — — Training and Research (UNITAR), New York, 26
— — Library: Dag Hammarskjöld Library, New York, 1630
— — Regional Centre for Research on Human Settlements, Bandung, 709
— — University, Tokyo, 6
— Reformed Church History Society, London, 1424
— Society of Artists, London, 1414
— States Coast Guard Academy, New London, Conn., 1678
— — Cultural Center, Berlin (West), 521
— — — — Jerusalem, 738
— — Energy Research and Development Administration Library, Washington, 1625
— — International Communication Agency, Amman, 875
— — — — — Athens, 618
— — — — — Barton, A.C.T., 89
— — — — — Copenhagen, 391
— — — — — Dar es Salaam, 1280
— — — — — Freetown, 1148
— — — — — Georgetown, 628
— — — — — Ibadan, 992
— — — — — Jakarta, 708
— — — — — Jeddah, 1142
— — — — — Kuala Lumpur, 915
— — — — — Manila, 1047
— — — — — Mexico City, 930
— — — — — Montevideo, 1940
— — — — — New Delhi, 673
— — — — — Oslo, 1007
— — — — — Ouagadougou, 1937
— — — — — Rangoon, 228
— — — — — Rome, 759
— — — — — The Hague, 958
— — — — — Library, Bamako, 920
— — — — — — Panama City, 1030
— — — — — — Songkla, 1284
— — — — University, San Diego, 1660
— — Merchant Marine Academy, 1823
— — Military Academy, West Point, New York, 1823
— — — — Library, 1630
— — Naval Academy, 1746
— — — Observatory, Washington, 1621
— — — Postgraduate School, 1660
— — Reference Centre, Oslo, 1011
— Theological College, Montreal, 277
Uniunea Arhitectilor din R.S.R., Bucharest, 1122
— Artistilor Plastici din R.S.R., Bucharest, 1122
— Compozitorilor din R.S.R., 1122
— Scriitorilor din Republica Socialistă Română, Bucharest, 1122
— Societatilor de Ştiinţe Medicale din R.S.R., Bucharest, 1122
Universidad Anáhuac, 934
— Argentina de la Empresa, Buenos Aires, 78
— "John F. Kennedy", Buenos Aires, 78
— Austral de Chile, Valdivia, 328
— Autónoma "Benito Juárez", de Oaxaca, 940
— de Aguascalientes, 934
— — Baja California, 935
— — Barcelona, 1207
— — Chapingo, 935
— — Chiapas, 935
— — Chihuahua, 935
— — Ciudad Juárez, Chihuahua, 938
— — Coahuila, Saltillo, 935
— — Guadalajara, 937
— — Guerrero, 937
— — Hidalgo, 937
— — Madrid, 1212
— — Nayarit, 939
— — Nuevo León, Monterrey, 940
— — Puebla, 940

# INDEX OF INSTITUTIONS

**Universidad Autónoma de Querétaro, 941**
— — — San Luis Potosí, 941
— — — Santo Domingo, 405
— — — Sinaloa, Culiacán, 941
— — — Tamaulipas, 942
— — — Zacatecas, 943
— — del Estado de Mexico, Toluca, 934
— — — — Morelos, 939
— — — Noreste, Coahuila, 940
— — — Juárez de Tabasco, 942
— — — Latinoamericana, Medellín, 354
— — — Metropolitana, Mexico City, 938
— — Boliviana "Mariscal Jose Ballivian", Beni, 176
— — — "Juan Misael Saracho", Tarija, 176
— — — Mayor de "San Andrés", La Paz, 175
— — — "Gabriel René Moreno", Santa Cruz de la Sierra, 175
— — — Real y Pontificia de San Francisco Xavier, Sucre, 175
— — — "Tomás Frías", Potosi, 175
— — Católica Andrés Bello, Caracas, 1956
— — Argentina "Santa Maria de los Buenos Aires", 78
— — Boliviana, La Paz, 176
— — de Chile, Santiago, 328
— — — Córdoba, 79
— — — Cuenca, 409
— — — Cuyo, San Juan, 79
— — — La Plata, 80
— — — Puerto Rico, Ponce, 1110
— — — Salta, 81
— — — Santa Fe, 81
— — — — Maria, Arequipa, 1046
— — — Santiago de Guayaquil, 410
— — — — del Estero, 81
— — — — Valparaíso, 328
— — "Madre y Maestra", Santiago de los Caballeros, 405
— — "Nuestra Señora de la Asunción", Asunción, 1035
— — Central de Barcelona, 1205
— — — Venezuela, 1957
— — del Ecuador, Quito, 409
— — Este, San Pedro de Macoris, 405
— — Centroamericana, Managua, 988
— — "José Simeón Cañas", San Salvador, 423
— Centro-Occidental "Lisandro Alvarado", Lara, 1957
— Complutense de Madrid, 1210
— de Alcalá de Henares, 1205
— — Alicante, 1205
— — Antioquia, Medellín, 350
— — Belgrano, Buenos Aires, 78
— — Bilbao, 1207
— — Buenos Aires, 72
— — Cádiz, 1207
— — Caldas, 350
— — Camagüey, 366
— — Carabobo, 1956
— — Cartagena, 350
— — Chile, Santiago, 329
— — Colima, 936
— — Concepción, 329
— — Córdoba, 1208
— — — Montería, 351
— — Costa Rica, 360
— — Cuenca, 410
— — Deusto, Bilbao, 1209
— — El Salvador, 423
— — Extremadura, Badajoz, 1209
— — Granada, 1209
— — Guadalajara, 936
— — Guanajuato, 937
— — Guayaquil, 410
— — la Habana, 365
— — — Laguna, 1210
— — — República, Montevideo, 1940
— — las Americas, Puebla, 934
— — — Baleares, Palma de Mallorca, 1205
— — — Villas, 366
— — León, 1210
— — Lima, 1041
— — los Andes, Bogotá, 355
— — — — Mérida, 1957
— — Malaga, 1212
— — Medellín, 355
— — Mendoza, 80
— — Montemorelos, Nuevo León, 939
— — Monterrey, 939
— — Morón, 80
— — Murcia, 1213
— — Nariño, 352
— — Navarra, Pamplona, 1213
— — Oriente, Cumana, 1958
— — — Nucleo Anzoátegui, 1958
— — — — Bolívar, 1959
— — — — Monagas, 1959
— — — — Nueva Esparta, 1959
— — — Santiago de Cuba, 365
— — Oviedo, 1214
— — Pamplona, 352
— — Panamá, 1031
— — Puerto Rico, Rio Pedras, 1110
— — Salamanca, 1215
— — San Buenaventura, Bogotá, 356
— — — Carlos de Guatemala, 625
— — — Santa Maria, Caracas, 1959
— — — Santander, 1215
— — Santiago de Chile, 330
— — — — Compostela, 1216
— — — Santo Tomás, Bogotá, 356
— — Sevilla, 1216
— — Sonora, 941
— — Táchira, 1959
— — Valencia, 1217
— — Valladolid, 1218
— — Yucatán, Mérida, 943
— — Zaragoza, 1219
— del Aconcagua, Mendoza, 78
— — Atlántico, Barranquilla, 350
— — Cauca, Popayán, 351
— — Museo Social Argentino, Buenos Aires, 79
— — Norte, Antofagasta, 329
— — — Barranquilla, 356
— — — Nuevo León, 940
— — — Santo Tomás de Aquino, San Miguel de Tucuman, 80
— — Pacífico, Lima, 1044
— — Quindío Armenia, 352
— — Salvador, Buenos Aires, 79
— — Sudeste, Campeche, 941
— — Tolima, Ibagué, 353
— — Trabajo del Uruguay, 1941
— — Valle, Cali, 353
— — — de Guatemala, 625
— — — Mexico, 938
— — — Zulia, 1959
— Distrital "Francisco José de Caldas", Bogotá, 351
— "Dr. José Matias Delgado", San Salvador, 423
— Estatal a Distancia, San José, 361
— Externado de Colombia, Bogotá, 355
— Femenina de México, 934
— — del Sagrado Corazón, Lima, 1040
— Francisco de Paula Santander, Cúcuta, 351
— — Marroquin, Guatemala, 626
— Iberoamericana, Mexico City, 938
— "Inca Garcilaso de la Vega", Lima, 1041
— Industrial de Santander, 352
— Intercontinental, Mexico City, 938
— Internacional de Mexico, 1660
— — Menéndez Pelayo, Santander, 1222
— "Juan Agustín Maza", Mendoza, 80
— "Juarez" del Estado de Durango, 936
— La Gran Colombia, Bogotá, 355
— — Salle de México, 938
— Laica "Vicente Rocafuerte" de Guayaquil, 411
— Libre de Colombia, 355
— Mariano Gálvez de Guatemala, 626
— Mayor de "San Simon", Cochabamba, 175
— Metropolitana, Caracas, 1957
— Michoacana de San Nicolás de Hidalgo, 939
— Motolinia A.C., Mexico City, 939

WORLD OF LEARNING

— Nacional Agraria, Lima, 1040
— — de la Selva, Huánuco, 1040
— — Autónoma de Heredia, 361
— — — Honduras, 630
— — — México, 933
— — — Nicaragua, León, 988
— — "Daniel Alcides Carrión", Cerro de Pasco, 1041
— — de Asunción, 1035
— — — Catamarca, 72
— — — Colombia, 351
— — — Córdoba, 73
— — — Cuyo, 74
— — — Educación a Distancia, Madrid, 1205
— — — "Enrique Guzman y Valle", Lima, 1041
— — — Huánuco "Hermilio Valdizán", Huánuco, 1041
— — — Ingeniería, Lima, 1042
— — — Jujuy, 74
— — — la Amazonia Peruana, Iquitos, 1041
— — — Pampa, 75
— — — Patagonia San Juan Bosco, Chubut, 76
— — — La Plata, 75
— — — Loja, 410
— — — Lomas de Zamora, La Plata, 75
— — — Mar del Plata, 75
— — — Piura, 1044
— — — Río Cuarto, 76
— — — Rosario, 76
— — — Salta, 76
— — — San Agustín, 1043
— — — — Antonio Abad, Cuzco, 1043
— — — — Cristóbal de Huamanga, 1043
— — — Santiago del Estero, 77
— — — Trujillo, 1044
— — — Tucumán, 77
— — — del Centro de la Provincia de Buenos Aires, Tandil, 73
— — — — del Peru, Huáncayo, 1041
— — — Comahue, Neuquén, 73
— — — Litoral, 76
— — — Nordeste, Corrientes, 76
— — — Sur, Bahía Blanca, 77
— — — Experimental de Los Llanos Centrales "Romulo Gallegos", San Juan, 1958
— — — — Occidentales "Ezequiel Zamora", Barinas, 1958
— — — del Táchira, San Cristóbal, 1958
— — — Francisco de Miranda, Coro, 1958
— — — Simón Rodríguez, Caracas, 1958
— — "Federico Villareal", Lima, 1042
— — "José Faustino Sánchez Carrión", Huacho, 1042
— — Mayor de San Marcos de Lima, 1042
— — "Pedro Henríquez Ureña", Santo Domingo, 405
— — Ruíz Gallo, Lambayeque, 1042
— — "San Luis Gonzaga", Ica, 1044
— — Técnica de Cajamarca, 1044
— — — Piura, 1046
— — — del Altiplano, Puno, 1044
— — — Callao, 1046
— Notarial Argentina, La Plata, 80
— Pais Vasco, Lejona, 1214
— Particular Ricardo Palma, Lima, 1046
— — "San Martín de Porres", Lima, 1045
— Pedagógica Nacional, Bogotá, 352
— — y Tecnológica de Colombia, Boyacá, 353
— Peruana "Cayetano Heredia", Lima, 1045
— Politécnica de Barcelona, 1220
— — — las Palmas, 1220
— — — Madrid, 1221
— — — Nicaragua, Managua, 989
— — — Valencia, 1221
— Pontificia Bolivariana, Medellín, 354
— — Comillas, Madrid, 1207
— — de Salamanca, 1214
— Popular Autónoma del Estado de Puebla, 940
— Rafael Landivar, Guatemala City, 626

— — Urdaneta, Maracaibo, 1959
— Regiomontana, Monterrey, 941
— Santa María la Antigua, Panama City, 1031
— Santiago de Cali, 356
— Simón Bolívar, Caracas, 1959
— Social Católica de la Salle, Bogotá, 356
— Técnica de Babahoyo, Los Rios, 410
— — Machala, 411
— — Manabí, 411
— — Oruro, 175
— — "Federico Santa María", 330
— — "Luis Vargas Torres", Esmeraldas, 411
— — Particular de Loja, 410
— Tecnológica de Pereira, Pereira, 354
— — Santiago, 405
— — del Magdalena, Santa Marta, 354
— Nacional, Buenos Aires, 77
— Veracruzana, 942
Universidade Católica de Goiás, 194
— — Minas Gerais, 197
— — Pelotas, 201
— — Pernambuco, Recife, 201
— — Petrópolis, 203
— — do Paraná, Curitiba, 200
— — Salvador, 206
— — Portuguesa, Lisbon, 1105
— de Angola, Luanda, 61
— Asia Oriental, Taipa, 1108
— Aveiro, 1105
— Brasília, 192
— Caxias do Sul, Rio Grande do Sul, 193
— Coímbra, 1105
— — Bibliotecas, 1102
— Évora, 1105
— Fortaleza, Ceará, 194
— Itaúna, Minas Gerais, 195
— Lisboa, 1106
— Mogi das Cruzes, 198
— Passo Fundo, 201
— São Paulo, 207
— do Amazonas, Manáus, 191
— Estado do Rio de Janeiro, 205
— Minho, Braga, 1106
— Porto, 1107
— Vale do Rio dos Sinos, São Leopoldo, 209
— dos Açores, Ponta Delgada, 1105
— Eduardo Mondlane, Maputo, 952
— Estadual de Campinas, São Paulo, 192
— — Londrina, 196
— — Maringá, 197
— — Mato Grosso do Sul, 197
— — Ponta Grossa, 203
— — Paulista "Julio de Mesquita Filho", São Paulo, 208
— Federal da Bahia, Salvador, 191
— — Paraíba, 199
— — de Alagoas, 191
— — Goiás, 194
— — Juiz de Fora, Minas Gerais, 196
— — Mato Grosso, Cuiaba, 197
— — Minas Gerais, 198
— — Ouro Prêto, 199
— — Pelotas, 201
— — Pernambuco, Recife, 202
— — Santa Catarina, 207
— — — Maria, 207
— — São Carlos, 207
— — Sergipe, 209
— — Uberlândia, 209
— — Viçosa, Minas Gerais, 210
— — do Acre, 191
— — Ceará, 193
— — Espírito Santo, 193
— — Maranhão, 196
— — Para, Belem-Pará, 190
— — Paraná, Curitiba, 200
— — Piauí, 203
— — Rio de Janeiro, 206
— — — Grande do Norte, 203
— — — Sul, 204
— — Fluminense, Rio de Janeiro, 194
— — Rural de Pernambuco, Recife, 202

— — do Rio de Janeiro, 206
— Gama Filho, Rio de Janeiro, 194
— Mackenzie, São Paulo, 196
— Mineira de Arte, Belo Horizonte, 198
— Nova de Lisboa, 1106
— Para o Desenvolvimento do Estado de Santa Catarina, 207
— Regional de Blumenau, Santa Catarina, 191
— — do Nordeste, Paraíba, 198
— — Rio Grande do Norte, Mossoró, 204
— Técnica de Lisboa, 1107
Universidat di Aruba, 975
Università Cattolica del Sacro Cuore, 792
— Commerciale Luigi Bocconi, Milan, 792
— degli Studi, Ancona, 774
— — Bari, 774
— — Bologna, 776
— — Ferrara, 777
— — Florence, 777
— — Genova, 777
— — Lecce, 778
— — L'Aquila, 792
— — Macerata, 778
— — Messina, 778
— — Milan, 778
— — Modena, 781
— — Naples, 781
— — Padua, 782
— — Palermo, 782
— — Parma, 782
— — Pavia, 782
— — Perugia, 782
— — Pisa, 783
— — Rome, 785
— — Salerno, 789
— — Sassari, 789
— — Siena, 789
— — Trieste, 790
— — Turin, 790
— — Udine, 791
— — Urbino, 793
— — Venice, 791
— di Cagliari, 775
— — Calabria, Cosenza, 776
— — Camerino, 776
— — Catania, 776
— — Corti, 473
— Italiana per Stranieri, Perugia, 795
— Pontificia Salesiana, Rome, 1946
Universitaire Faculteiten Sint-Aloysius, Brussels, 167
— — Ignatius te Antwerpen, 167
— Instelling Antwerpen, Wilrijk, 167
— Protestantse Theologische Faculteit te Brussel, 164
Universitas Airlangga, Surabaja, 712
— Andalas, 712
— Bogor, 718
— Brawijaja, Malang, 713
— Cenderawasih, Irian Barat, 713
— Diponegoro, Semarang, 713
— Gadjah Mada, Jogjakarta, 713
— Hasanuddin, Ujungpandang, 714
— H.K.B.P. Nomensen, Medan, 720
— Ibnu Chaldun, Bogor, 718
— — Jakarta, 718
— Indonesia, Jakarta, 714
— Islam Indonesia, Yogjakarta, 718
— — Cirebon, 719
— — Jakarta, 718
— — Nusantara, Bandung, 719
— — Sumatera Utara, Medan, 719
— Jajabaja, Jakarta, 718
— Jenderal Soedirman, Purwokerto, 715
— Katolik Indonesia "Atma Jaya", Jakarta, 719
— — Parahyangan, Bandung, 719
— — Krisnadwipajana, Jakarta, 719
— — Kristen Indonesia, Jakarta, 718
— — Satya Wacana, Salatiga, 720
— Lambung Mangkurat, Bandjarmasin, 715
— Lampung, Tanjungkaran, 715
— Muhammadijah, Jakarta, 719
— Mulawarman, Kalimantan, 716

— Nasional, Jakarta, 720
— Negeri Jambi, 715
— — Jember, 715
— — Mataram, Lombok, 716
— — Padjadjaran, Bandung, 716
— Nusa Cendana, Kupang Timor, 716
— Palangka Raya, 716
— Pancasila, Jakarta, 720
— Pattimura Ambon, 716
— Riau, Sumatra, 716
— Sam Ratulangi, Manado, 716
— Sriwijaya, Palembang, 717
— Sumatera Utara, 717
— Syiah Kuala, Banda Aceh, 717
— Tanjungpura, Pontianak, 717
— Tarumanegara, Jakarta, 720
— Tjokroaminoto Surakarta, 720
— Trisakti, Jakarta, 720
— Udayana, Denpasar, 717
— Veteran Republik Indonesia, Ujungpandang, 720
— 17 Augustus 1945, Jakarta, 718
Universität Augsburg, 548
— Bamberg, 549
— Basel, 1263
— Bayreuth, 550
— Bielefeld, 551
— Bern, 1264
— Bremen, 556
— des Saarlandes, 601
— Dortmund, 560
— Duisburg Gesamthochschule, 561
— Düsseldorf, 562
— Essen-Gesamthochschule, 565
— Fridericiana, Karlsruhe, 581
— Graz, 132
— Hamburg, 573
— Hannover, 577
— Hohenheim, Stuttgart-Hohenheim, 580
— Kaiserslautern, 581
— Kassel, 582
— Konstanz, 586
— Mannheim, 590
— Oldenburg, 597
— Osnabrück, 598
— Passau, 599
— Regensburg, 600
— Salzburg, 134
— Stuttgart, 603
— Trier, 604
— Ulm, 606
— Wien, 134
— für Bildungswissenschaften Klagenfurt, 134
— — Bodenkultur Wien, Vienna, 137
— Gesamthochschule Siegen, 603
— zu Wuppertal, 606
— zu Köln, 584
— Zürich, 1270
Universitatea "Al. I. Cuza" din Iași, 1134
— "Babes-Bolyai" Cluj-Napoca, 1131
— București, Bucharest, 1130
— din Brașov, 1132
— — Craiova, 1133
— — Galati, 1133
— — Timișoara, 1135
Universitätsbibliothek, Augsburg, 534
— Bamberg, 534
— Bayreuth, 534
— Berlin (East), 507
— Bochum, 534
— Bonn, 535
— Dortmund, 535
— Düsseldorf, 535
— Erlangen, 535
— -Nürnberg, Wirtschafts- und Sozialwissenschaftliche Zentralbibliothek, Nuremberg, 537
— Freiburg, 536
— Graz, 129
— Greifswald, 507
— Heidelberg, 536
— Hohenheim, Stuttgart, 537
— Innsbruck, 129
— Jena, 507
— Karlsruhe, 536

# INDEX OF INSTITUTIONS

Universitätsbibliothek, Kiel, 536
— Mainz, 536
— **Mannheim, 536**
— Marburg, 537
— Munich, 537
— Münster, 537
— Passau, 537
— Regensburg, 537
— Rostock, 508
— Saarbrücken, 537
— Salzburg, 129
— Stuttgart, 537
— Tübingen, 538
— Vienna, 128
— Würzburg, 538
— der Freien Universität Berlin (West), 534
— — Justus Liebig-Universität, Giessen, 536
— — Karl-Marx-Universität, Leipzig, 508
— — Montanuniversität, Leoben, 129
— — Technischen Universität, Berlin, (West), 534
— — — — Brunswick, 535
— — — — Clausthal-Zellerfeld, 535
— — — — Dresden, 507
— — — — Graz, 129
— — — — Munich, 537
— Hannover und Technische Informationsbibliothek, 536
— (mit Staatsbibliothek), Bremen, 535
Universitätsmuseum für Kunst und Kulturgeschichte, Marburg/Lahn, 544
Universitäts-Sternwarte, Göttingen, 533
— — Jena, 506
— — Munich, 533
— — und Landesbibliothek Sachsen Anhalt, Halle, 507
— — Stadtbibliothek, Cologne, 535
Université Catholique de Louvain, 163
— — — l'Ouest, Angers, 496
— d'Aix Marseille I (Université de Provence), 471
— — — II, 471
— — — III (Université de Droit, d'Economie et des Sciences), 471
— d'Alger, Algiers, 58
— d'Angers, 471
— d'Etat d'Haiti, Port-au-Prince, 629
— d'Oran, 59
— d'Orléans, 482
— de Annaba, 59
— — Bangui, 320
— — Bordeaux I, 472
— — — II, 472
— — — III, 472
— — Boumerdès, 59
— — Bretagne Occidentale, 472
— — Caen, 473
— — Clermont-Ferrand I, 473
— — — — II, 473
— — Constantine, 59
— — Corse, Corte, 473
— — Dakar, 1146
— — Dijon, 473
— — Franche-Comté, Besançon, 474
— — Fribourg, 1265
— — Genève, 1266
— — Grenoble I (Université Scientifique et Médicale), 476
— — — — II (Université des Sciences Sociales), 476
— — — — III (Université des Langues et Lettres), 476
— — Haute-Alsace, Mulhouse, 476
— — Lausanne, 1268
— — l'Etat à Mons, 163
— — Liège, 161
— — Lille I (Université des Sciences et Techniques), 477
— — — — II (Droit et Santé), 477
— — — — III (Sciences Humaines, Lettres et Arts), 477
— — Limoges, 478
— — Lyon I (Université Claude-Bernard), 478

— — — II, 479
— — — III (Université Jean Moulin), 480
— — Madagascar, Antananarivo, 910
— — Metz, 480
— — Moncton, N.B., 285
— — Montpellier I, 481
— — — II (Université des Sciences et Techniques de Languedoc), 481
— — — III (Université Paul Valéry), 481
— — Montréal, 285
— — Nancy I, 481
— — — II, 481
— — Nantes, 482
— — Neuchâtel, 1269
— — Niamey, 990
— — Nice, 482
— — Ouagadougou, 1937
— — Paris I (Panthéon-Sorbonne), 483
— — — II (Université de Droit, d'Economie et des Sciences Sociales), 484
— — — III (Sorbonne-Nouvelle), 484
— — — IV (Paris-Sorbonne), 484
— — — V (René Descartes), 485
— — — VI (Pierre et Marie Curie), 485
— — — VII, 485
— — — VIII (Paris-Vincennes), 485
— — — IX (Paris-Dauphine), 486
— — — X (Paris-Nanterre), 486
— — — XI (Paris-Sud), 486
— — — XII (Paris-Val-de-Marne), 486
— — — XIII (Paris-Nord), 486
— — Pau et des Pays de l'Adour, 486
— — Perpignan, 486
— — Picardie, Amiens, 487
— — Poitiers, 487
— — Reims, 487
— — Rennes I, 487
— — — II (Université de Haute Bretagne), 487
— — Rouen-Haute Normandie, 485
— — Saint-Etienne, 488
— — Savoie (Chambéry), 488
— — Sétif, 59
— — Sherbrooke, Quebec, 301
— — Strasbourg I (Université Louis Pasteur), 488
— — — II, 489
— — — III, 489
— — Technologie de Compiègne, 473
— — Toulon et du Var, La Garde, 490
— — Toulouse I (Sciences Sociales), 490
— — — II (Le Mirail), 490
— — — III (Université Paul Sabatier), 490
— — Tours (François Rabelais), 490
— — Tunis, 1296
— — Valenciennes et du Hainaut-Cambrésis, 490
— — Yaoundé, 231
— des Mutants, Gorée, 1146
— — Sciences et de la Technologie Houari Boumedienne, Algiers, 58
— — — — — Technologie d'Oran, 59
— — du Bénin, Lomé, 1292
— — Burundi, 230
— — Maine, Le Mans, 480
— — Québec à Chicoutimi, 293
— — — — Hull, 293
— — — — Montréal, 293
— — — — Rimouski, 293
— — — — Sainte-Foy, 293
— — — — Trois-Rivières, 293
— — Tchad, N'Djamena, 321
— — Européenne du Travail, Brussels, 169
— — Hassan II, Casablanca, 950
— — Laval, Québec, 270
— — Libanaise, Beirut, 901
— — Libre de Bruxelles, 159
— — Marien-Ngouabi, Brazzaville, 358
— — Mohammed ben Abdellah, Fès, 950
— — — V, Rabat, 950
— — Nationale de Côte d'Ivoire, Abidjan, 799
— — — du Benin, Cotonou, 172
— — — Rwanda, Butare, 1141
— — — Zaire, Kinshasa, 1996
— — Omar Bongo, Libreville, 502

— Quaraouyine, Fez, 951
— Saint-Esprit de Kaslik, Jounieh, 901
— — Joseph, Beirut, 902
— Sainte-Anne, Church Point, N.S., 298
Universiteit van Amsterdam, 969
— — Suriname, Paramaribo, 1231
Universiteitsbibliotheek, Amsterdam, 964
— -K.U. Leuven, Louvain, 156
— **Erasmus Universiteit Rotterdam, 965**
Universitetet i Bergen, 1013
— — Linköping, 1245
— — Oslo, 1014
— — Tromsø, 1015
— — Trondheim, 1015
Universiteti Tiranës, Tiranë, 56
Universitetets Astronomiske Observatorium, Copenhagen, 393
— Etnografiske Museum, Oslo, 1012
— Mineralogisk Geologiske Museum, Oslo, 1012
— Paleontologiske Museum, Oslo, 1012
— Samling av Nordiske Oldsaker, 1012
Universitetsbiblioteket, Copenhagen, 394
— Oslo, 1011
— avd. B. Trondheim, 1011
— i Bergen, 1011
Universitets- och Högskoleämbetet, Stockholm, 1243
Universiti Kebangsaan Malaysia, Selangor, 916
— Malaya, Kuala Lumpur, 918
— Pertanian Malaysia, Selangor, 917
— Sains Malaysia, Penang, 919
— Teknoloji Malaysia, Kuala Lumpur, 917
Universities Administration Office, Rangoon, 229
— Central Library, Rangoon, 229
— Field Staff International-Institute of World Affairs, Salisbury, Conn., 1603
University Art Museum, Berkeley, 1642
— Association for Contemporary European Studies, London, 1419
— Center for International Studies, Pittsburgh, 1881
— — Social and Urban Research, Pittsburgh, 1881
— Centre for Cinematic Studies, Mexico City, 934
— — — Pedagogical Education and Research, Zagreb, 1993
— College, Buckingham, 1482
— — Cardiff, 1535
— — — English Centre for Overseas Students, 1536
— — — Library, 1465
— — Clinical Sciences Library, London, 1460
— — Cork, 734
— — — Library, 732
— — Dublin, 733
— — — Library, 732
— — Durham, 1487
— — Galway, 735
— — — Library, 732
— — London, 1511
— — Oxford, 1524
— — Parkville, 104
— — Sudbury, 270
— — Toronto, 309
— — — Library, London, 1460
— — — Oxford, 1463
— — of Arts, Science and Education, Bahrain, 141
— — — Botswana, Gaborone, 177
— — North Wales, 1535
— — — — Library, Bangor, 1465
— — Swansea, 1536
— — — Library, 1465
— — Swaziland, Kwaluseni, 1232
— — Wales, 1534
— — — Library, Aberystwyth, 1464
— — Zoological Museum, Cork, 732
— Electronic Computer Centre, Zagreb, 1993
— Experimental Farm, Thessaloniki, 621

— — School, Thessaloniki, 621
— — Forests, Thessaloniki, 621
— Grants Commission, New Delhi, 661
— — Committee, London, 1419
— — — Wellington, N.Z., 978
— Hospital, Kanazawa, 831
— — Ōsaka, 860
— Industry Centre, Cardiff, 1536
— Institute of Petroleum and Energy Studies, Tel-Aviv, 750
— Law College, Lahore, 1028
— — — Multan, 1025
— Library, Halifax, N.S., 247
— Marine Biological Station, Millport, 1447
— Museum, Philadelphia, 1642
— of Zoology, Cambridge, 1468
— Observatory, Oxford, 1447
— of Aberdeen, 1474
— — Library, 1464
— — Adelaide, 98
— — — Library, 96
— — Aden, 1965
— — Agricultural Sciences, Bangalore, 676
— — — Gödöllő, 651
— — Agriculture, Brno, 386
— — — Faisalabad, 1024
— — — Selangor, 917
— — Akron, 1851
— — Alabama, University, 1644
— — — in Birmingham, 1644
— — — Huntsville, 1645
— — — Library, 1631
— — — Museum of Natural History, 1642
— — Alaska Statewide System, 1645
— — Alberta, 252
— — — Cancer Research Institute, Edmonton, 257
— — — Library, 246
— — — Surgical-Medical Research Institute, 257
— — Albuquerque, New Mexico, 1802
— — Aleppo, 1278
— — Alexandria, Shatby, 417
— — — Library, Shatby, 417
— — Allahabad, 677
— — Amsterdam, 969
— — Ankara, 1302
— — Applied Art in Vienna, 138
— — Arizona, Tucson, 1645
— — — Library, 1631
— — Arkansas, Fayetteville, 1650
— — — at Little Rock, 1650
— — — — Monticello, 1651
— — — — Pine Bluff, 1651
— — Asmara, 425
— — Assiut, 418
— — — Library, 417
— — Aston in Birmingham, 1475
— — — Library, 1460
— — Auckland, 983
— — — Library, 981
— — Baghdad, 727
— — — Central Library, 726
— — Baguio, 1051
— — Baltimore, 1746
— — Baluchistan, Quetta, 1025
— — Banja Luka, 1979
— — Basrah, 727
— — — Central Library, 726
— — Bath, 1476
— — — Library, 1461
— — Belgrade, 1979
— — Benin, 996
— — Bergen, 1013
— — Bihar, Muzaffarpur, 681
— — Birmingham, 1476
— — — Library, 1461
— — Bombay, 681
— — Bophuthatswana, Montshiwa, 1184
— — Bradford, 1478
— — — Library, 1461
— — — Management Centre, 1479
— — Bridgeport, 1678
— — Bristol, 1479
— — — Library, 1461
— — British Columbia, 258

— — — Library, 247
— — Burdwan, 682
— — Cairo, Giza, 418
— — — Library, 417
— — Calabar, 996
— — Calcutta, 682
— — Calgary, 262
— — — Library, 246
— — Calicut, Kerala, 683
— — California, Berkeley, 1661
— — — Davis, 1661
— — — Irvine, 1661
— — — Los Angeles (UCLA), 1663
— — — Riverside, 1668
— — — San Diego, 1669
— — — San Francisco, 1671
— — — Santa Barbara, 1671
— — — Cruz, 1673
— — — Libraries, Berkeley, 1631
— — Cambridge, 1482
— — — Archives, 1461
— — — Institute of Astronomy, 1446
— — — Library, 1461
— — Canterbury, N.Z., 983
— — — Library, N.Z., 981
— — Cape Coast, Ghana, 613
— — — Town, 1166
— — — Libraries, 1162
— — Charleston, W.Va., 1930
— — Chicago, 1708
— — — Library, 1632
— — Chile, Santiago, 329
— — Chittagong, 144
— — Cincinnati, 1851
— — — Library, 1634
— — Cochin, Kerala, 683
— — Colombo, 1226
— — — Library, 1226
— — Colorado, 1676
— — — at Colorado Springs, 1676
— — — Denver, 1676
— — — Libraries, 1631
— — Connecticut, 1679
— — — Library, 1631
— — Dacca, 144
— — — Library, 143
— — Dakar, 1146
— — Dallas, 1904
— — Damascus, 1278
— — — Library, 1277
— — Dar es Salaam, 1281
— — — Library, 1281
— — Dayton, 1854
— — Delaware, 1686
— — Delhi, 683
— — Denver, 1676
— — Detroit, 1763
— — Dublin, Trinity College, 732
— — Dubuque, 1729
— — Dundee, 1486
— — — Library, 1464
— — Durban-Westville, Durban, 1167
— — Durham, 1486
— — — Library, 1462
— — East Anglia, Norwich, 1487
— — — Library, Norwich, 1462
— — — Asia, Taipa, 1108
— — Eastern Philippines, Northern Samar, 1053
— — Edinburgh, 1488
— — — Library, 1464
— — Electro-Communications, Tokyo, 857
— — Engineering and Technology, Lahore, 1027
— — Essex, Colchester, 1490
— — — Library, 1462
— — Evansville, Indiana, 1722
— — Exeter, 1490
— — — Library, 1462
— — Florida, Gainesville, 1695
— — — Libraries, 1632
— — Forestry and Wood Science, Sopron, 653
— — Fort Hare, 1168
— — — Library, 1162
— — Garyounis, Benghazi, 907

— — — Library, 906
— — Gdańsk, 1078
— — Georgia, 1701
— — Gezira, Wadi Medani, 1230
— — Ghana, Legon, 612
— — — Library (Balme Library), 612
— — Glasgow, 1491
— — — Library, 1464
— — Guam, 1936
— — Guelph, 268
— — Guyana, Georgetown, 628
— — Hartford, 1682
— — Hawaii, Honolulu, 1702
— — — at Manoa, 1702
— — — Hilo, 1702
— — Helsinki, 434
— — Hong Kong, 1560
— — — Main Library, 1559
— — Horticulture, Budapest, 653
— — Houston, 1904
— — Hull, 1494
— — — The Brynmor Jones Library, 1462
— — Hyderabad, 687
— — Ibadan, 996
— — — Library, 994
— — Iceland, Reykjavík, 657
— — Idaho, 1702
— — Ife, Ibadan, 998
— — — Library, 994
— — Illinois at the Medical Center, Chicago, 1715
— — — Chicago Circle, 1715
— — — Urbana-Champaign, 1709
— — — Library, 1632
— — Ilo-Ilo, Rizal, 1054
— — Ilorin, 998
— — Indore, 687
— — Industrial Arts, Helsinki, 440
— — Ioannina, 622
— — Iowa, 1729
— — — Libraries, Iowa City, 1632
— — Isfahan, 723
— — — Library, 722
— — Jaffna, 1227
— — Jammu, 688
— — Jodhpur, 689
— — Joensuu, 435
— — Jordan, Amman, 876
— — — Library, Amman, 875
— — Jos, 999
— — Juba, 1230
— — Jyväskylä, 435
— — Kansas, Lawrence, 1731
— — — Libraries, 1632
— — Karachi, 1026
— — Kashmir, Srinagar, 691
— — Keele, 1495
— — — Library, 1463
— — Kelaniya, 1227
— — Kent at Canterbury, 1495
— — — Library, Canterbury, 1463
— — Kentucky, 1736
— — — Libraries, Lexington, 1632
— — Kerala, 691
— — Kerman, 723
— — Khartoum, 1230
— — — Library, 1229
— — King's College, Halifax, N.S., 269
— — — Library, Halifax, N.S., 247
— — Kosovo, Priština, 1987
— — Kuopio, 436
— — La Verne, 1673
— — Lagos, 999
— — — Library, 994
— — Lancaster, 1496
— — — Library, 1463
— — Leeds, 1497
— — — Library, 1463
— — Leicester, 1498
— — — Library, 1463
— — Lethbridge, 273
— — Liberia, Monrovia, 904
— — — Libraries, Monrovia, 904
— — Liège, 161
— — Liverpool, 1499
— — — Library, 1463

# INDEX OF INSTITUTIONS

University of Łódź, 1078
— — London, 1500
— — — Goldsmiths' College (School of Art and Design), 1552
— — — Library, 1460
— — — Observatory, 1447
— — Louisville, 1737
— — Lowell, Mass., 1759
— — Lucknow, 693
— — Luleå, 1245
— — Lund, 1246
— — — Library, 1241
— — Madras, 693
— — Maiduguri, 1000
— — Maine, Orono, 1742
— — — at Farmington, 1742
— — Malawi, Zomba, 913
— — — Library, Zomba, 912
— — Malaya, Kuala Lumpur, 918
— — — Library, 916
— — Malta, Msida, 921
— — — Library, Msida, 921
— — Manchester Institute of Science and Technology, 1517
— — Manila, 1054
— — — Central Library, 1049
— — Manitoba, Winnipeg, 280
— — — Libraries, 247
— — — Museums, Winnipeg, 249
— — Maribor, 1986
— — Mary Hardin-Baylor, Texas, 1904
— — Maryland, Baltimore, 1746
— — — County, Catonsville, 1746
— — — College Park, 1746
— — — Eastern Shore, Princess Anne, 1746
— — — Libraries, 1632
— — — System, Adelphi, 1746
— — Massachusetts, Amherst, 1759
— — — at Boston, 1759
— — Mauritius, Reduit, 923
— — — Library, Reduit, 923
— — Melbourne, 103
— — — Library, 96
— — Miami, 1698
— — Michigan, Ann Arbor, 1763
— — — — Library, 1633
— — — Dearborn, 1770
— — — Flint, 1770
— — Mindanao, Davao City, 1055
— — Mining and Metallurgy, Leoben, 137
— — Minnesota, Minneapolis, 1775
— — — Library, 1633
— — — Duluth, 1783
— — — Morris, 1784
— — — Technical College, Waseca, 1784
— — — Twin Cities (Minneapolis and St. Paul) Campus, 1775
— — Mississippi, 1785
— — Missouri System, Columbia, 1790
— — — Kansas City, 1790
— — — Rolla, 1790
— — — St. Louis, 1790
— — — Library, 1633
— — Montana, Missoula, 1792
— — Montevallo, 1645
— — Moratuwa, 1227
— — Mostar, 1986
— — Mosul, 728
— — — Central Library, 726
— — Music and Dramatic Art, Graz, 138
— — — — — Vienna, 138
— — Mysore, 695
— — Nagpur, 695
— — Nairobi, 879
— — — Libraries, 879
— — Nangrahar, 53
— — Natal, 1169
— — — Library, Durban, 1162
— — — — Pietermaritzburg, 1163
— — Nebraska, Lincoln, 1793
— — — Omaha, 1793
— — — Libraries, 1633
— — Negros Occidental-Recoletas, 1055
— — Nevada, Las Vegas, 1794
— — — Reno, 1794

— — New Brunswick, 288
— — — England, N.S.W., 105
— — — — Library, 96
— — — Hampshire, 1796
— — — Haven, Conn., 1683
— — — Mexico, 1802
— — — Orleans, 1741
— — — South Wales, Sydney, 106
— — — — — Libraries, Sydney, 96
— — Newcastle, N.S.W., 107
— — — upon Tyne, 1518
— — — — Library, 1463
— — Nigeria, Nsukka, 1000
— — — Libraries, Nsukka, 994
— — Niš, 1986
— — North Alabama, Florence, 1645
— — — Bengal, 696
— — — Carolina at Asheville, 1830
— — — — Chapel Hill, 1830
— — — — Charlotte, 1834
— — — — Greensboro, 1834
— — — — Wilmington, 1838
— — — — Library, 1633
— — — Dakota, 1839
— — — Sumatra, Medan, 717
— — Northern Colorado, 1677
— — — Iowa, Cedar Falls, 1729
— — — Philippines, Vigan, 1055
— — Notre Dame, Indiana, 1722
— — — Libraries, 1632
— — Nottingham, 1519
— — — Library, 1463
— — Novi Sad, 1986
— — Nueva Caceres, 1056
— — October, Lattakia, 1279
— — Oklahoma, Norman, 1859
— — — Oklahoma City, 1861
— — — Tulsa Medical College, 1862
— — — Library, Norman, 1634
— — Örebro, 1247
— — Oregon, 1864
— — — Health Sciences Center, Portland, 1866
— — — Library, Eugene, 1634
— — Osaka Prefecture, 860
— — Osijek, 1987
— — Oslo, 1014
— — Otago, 985
— — — Library, 981
— — Ottawa, 291
— — — Library System, 248
— — Oulu, 436
— — Oxford, 1521
— — — Bodleian Library, 1463
— — Pangasinan, Dagupan City, 1056
— — Papua New Guinea, Port Moresby, 1032
— — — — — Library, Port Moresby, 1032
— — Patna, Bihar, 697
— — Patras, 622
— — Pécs, 649
— — Pennsylvania, 1879
— — — Library, 1634
— — Peradeniya, 1227
— — — Library, 1226
— — Peshawar, 1027
— — Petroleum and Minerals, Dhahran, 1144
— — Pittsburgh, 1880
— — — Libraries, 1634
— — Port Elizabeth, 1172
— — — — Library, 1163
— — — Harcourt, 1001
— — Portland, Ore., 1866
— — Pretoria, 1173
— — — Libraries, 1163
— — Prince Edward Island, 293
— — Puerto Rico, 1110
— — — — General Library, 1110
— — — — Libraries, 1110
— — Puget Sound, Tacoma, 1922
— — Pune, Maharashtra, 698
— — Qatar, Doha, 1114
— — Queensland, 108
— — — Library, 96

— — Rajasthan, 700
— — Rajshahi, 145
— — — Library, 143
— — Reading, 1525
— — — Library, 1464
— — Redlands, 1673
— — Regina, Sask., 296
— — Rhode Island, 1885
— — Richmond, Virginia, 1917
— — Rijeka, 1988
— — Riyadh, 1143
— — — Libraries, 1142
— — Rochester, N.Y., 1823
— — — Libraries, 1633
— — Roorkee, 701
— — St. Andrews, 1525
— — — Library, 1464
— — — Jerome's College, Waterloo, Ont., 311
— — — Michael's College, 310
— — — Thomas, Houston, Tex., 1904
— — Salford, 1526
— — — Library, 1464
— — San Agustin, Ilo-Ilo City, 1058
— — — Carlos, Cebu City, 1058
— — — — Library, Cebu City, 1049
— — — Diego, 1674
— — — Francisco, 1674
— — — Santa Clara, 1674
— — Santo Tomas, Manila, 1058
— — — — Library, Manila, 1049
— — Sarajevo, 1988
— — Saskatchewan, Saskatoon, 298
— — — Biology Museum, Saskatoon, 251
— — — Library, 249
— — Saugar, Sagar, 701
— — Science, Malaysia, Penang, 919
— — — and Arts of Oklahoma, Chickasha, 1862
— — — — Technology, Kumasi, 613
— — — — — Library, Kumasi, 612
— — — — — of China, Hefei, 337
— — Scranton, 1881
— — Sheffield, 1527
— — — Library, 1464
— — Shiraz, 724
— — Sierra Leone, Freetown, 1148
— — Skopje, 1989
— — Sofia, 222
— — Sokoto, 1001
— — South Africa, Pretoria, 1177
— — — — Sanlam Library, 1163
— — — Alabama, Mobile, 1645
— — — Carolina, 1887
— — — Dakota at Springfield, 1888
— — — — Vermillion, 1888
— — — Florida, Tampa, 1698
— — Southampton, 1528
— — — Library, 1464
— — Southern California, Los Angeles, 1674
— — — — Library, Los Angeles, 1631
— — — Colorado, Pueblo, 1677
— — — Maine, Portland, 1742
— — — Mindanao, Kabacan, 1059
— — — Mississippi, 1785
— — — Philippines, Cebu City, 1059
— — Southwestern Louisiana, 1741
— — Split, 1989
— — Sri Jayewardenepura, Gangodawila, 1228
— — Stellenbosch, 1178
— — — Library, 1164
— — Steubenville, 1854
— — Stirling, 1530
— — — Library, 1464
— — Stockholm, 1247
— — Strathclyde, Glasgow, 1530
— — — The Andersonian Library, 1464
— — Sudbury, 270
— — Sulaimaniya, 728
— — — Central Library, 726
— — Suriname, Paramaribo, 1231
— — Surrey, Guildford, 1531
— — — Library, 1464
— — Sussex, Brighton, 1532

— — — Library, Brighton, 1464
— — Sydney, 109
— — — Library, 96
— — Tabriz, 724
— — Tampa, Florida, 1698
— — Tampere, 437
— — Tasmania, 110
— — — Library, 96
— — Technology, Baghdad, 727
— — Teheran, 704
— — Tennessee System, Knoxville, 1891
— — — at Chattanooga, 1891
— — — — Martin, 1895
— — — Center for Health Sciences, Memphis, 1894
— — — Libraries, Knoxville, 1634
— — Texas at Arlington, 1909
— — — — Austin, 1904
— — — — El Paso, 1910
— — — Health Science Center at Dallas, 1910
— — — — — at Houston School of Public Health, 1910
— — — — — at San Antonio, 1910
— — — Medical Branch at Galveston, 1910
— — — of the Permian Basin, Odessa, 1910
— — — System, Austin, 1904
— — — Libraries, 1634
— — the Americas, Puebla, 934
— — — Argentine Museum of Sociology, Buenos Aires, 79
— — — Bosphorus, Istanbul, 1304
— — — City of Manila, 1054
— — — District of Columbia, Washington, D.C., 1692
— — — East, Manila, 1052
— — — Library, Manila, 1049
— — — Netherlands Antilles, Curaçao, 975
— — — North, Pietersburg, 1170
— — — Orange Free State, 1170
— — — — Library, 1161
— — — Pacific, Stockton, 1674
— — — Philippines, 1056
— — — Library, Quezon City, 1049
— — — Punjab, 1027
— — — — Library, 1024
— — — Ryukyus, Okinawa, 847
— — — Sacred Heart, Santurce, P.R., 1113
— — — — Tokyo, 868
— — — Saviour, Buenos Aires, 79
— — — South, Sewanee, Tenn., 1895
— — — — Pacific, Suva, 426
— — — — — Kiribati Extension Centre, Tarawa, 881
— — — — School of Agriculture, Alafua, 1964
— — — — Solomon Islands Centre, Honiara, 1152
— — — Visayas, 1059
— — — West Indies, Barbados, 146
— — — — Jamaica, 800
— — — — Trinidad, 1294
— — — — Extra-Mural Department, Belize City, 171
— — — — — Department, Nassau, 140
— — — — Library, Barbados, 146
— — — — — Jamaica, 800
— — — — — Trinidad, 1293
— — — Western Cape, Bellville, 1180
— — — Witwatersrand, 1180
— — — Library, Johannesburg, 1162
— — Thrace, Komotini, 621
— — Tirana, 56
— — Titograd, 1990
— — Tokushima, 851
— — Tokyo, 852
— — — Library, 819
— — Toledo, 1855
— — Toronto, 303
— — — Libraries, 248
— — — -York University Joint Program in Transportation, 318

— — Transkei, Umtata, 1184
— — Transport and Telecommunications, Zilina, 384
— — Trinity College, Toronto, 310
— — — Library, Toronto, 248
— — Tromsø, 1015
— — Trondheim, 1015
— — Tsukuba, Ibaraki, 857
— — Tulsa, 1862
— — Turku, 438
— — Tuzla, 1990
— — Udaipur, Rajasthan, 703
— — Uppsala, 1249
— — — Library, 1241
— — Utah, 1911
— — — Library, Salt Lake City, 1634
— — Vaasa, 439
— — Vermont, 1915
— — Veterinary Science, Budapest, 651
— — Victoria, B.C., 310
— — Virginia, 1917
— — — Library, 1634
— — Waikato, Hamilton, N.Z., 986
— — Wales, 1534
— — — Institute of Science and Technology (UWIST), Cardiff, 1537
— — — — — and Technology Library, Cardiff, 1465
— — — Libraries, Aberystwyth, 1464
— — Warsaw, 1083
— — Warwick, Coventry, 1538
— — — Library, 1464
— — Washington, Seattle, 1922
— — — Libraries, 1634
— — Waterloo, Ont., 311
— — Western Australia, Nedlands, 111
— — — Library, 97
— — — Ontario, London, Ont., 312
— — — Libraries, 248
— — Windsor, Ontario, 315
— — Winnipeg, 316
— — Wisconsin Center System, 1933
— — — Eau Claire, 1933
— — — Extension, Madison, 1933
— — — Green Bay, 1933
— — — La Crosse, 1933
— — — Madison, 1933
— — — Milwaukee, 1933
— — — Oshkosh, 1935
— — — Parkside, 1935
— — — Platteville, 1935
— — — River Falls, 1935
— — — Stevens Point, 1935
— — — Stout, Menomonie, 1935
— — — Superior, 1936
— — — Whitewater, 1936
— — — Library, 1634
— — Wollongong, 112
— — Wyoming, 1936
— — Yaoundé, 231
— — York, 1539
— — — Library, 1464
— — Zagreb, 1990
— — Zambia, Lusaka, 1998
— — Zimbabwe, Salisbury, 2003
— — — Library, Salisbury, 2002
— — Zululand, Kwa-Dlangezwa, 1182
— Office, Durham, 1487
— Philosophical Society, Dublin, 731
— Planning and Development Board, Palembang, 717
— School of Veterinary Medicine in Brno, 386
Univerza Edvarda Kardelja v Ljubljani, 1985
— v Mariboru, Maribor, 1986
Univerzita Karlova, Prague, 381
— Komenského Bratislava, 380
— Palackého v Olomouci, Olomouc, 382
— Pavla Jozefa Safárika, Košice, 382
— J. E. Purkyně, 380
Univerzitet u Beogradu, Belgrade, 1979
— — Bitolj, Bitola, 1985
— — Kosovo, Priština, 1987
— — Nišu, 1986

— — Novom Sadu, 1986
— — Sarajevu, 1988
— — Tuzli, Tuzla, 1990
— "Duro Pucar Stari" u Banja Luci, 1979
— "Džemal Bijedic" u Mostaru, 1986
— Kiril I Metódij vo Skopje, 1989
— "Svetozar Markovic" u Kragujevcu, Kragujevac, 1985
— Umetnosti u Beogradu, Belgrade, 1985
— Veljko Vlahović u Titogradu, 1990
Univerzitetna knijižnica Maribor, 1975
Univerzitetska biblioteka "Svetozar Markovic", Belgrade, 1974
Univerzitná knižnica, Bratislava, 377
Uniwersytet Gdanski, 1078
— im Adama Mickiewicza w Poznańiu, Poznan, 1081
— Jagiellonski, 1078
— Lódžki, 1075
— Marii Curie Sklodowskiej, 1080
— Mikolaja Kopernika w Toruniu, 1081
— Slaski, Katowice, 1082
— Warszawski, 1083
— Wroclawski im Boleslawa Bieruta, 1086
Upper Canada Village, Morrisburg, 251
— Iowa University, 1729
— Norwood Public Library, 1452
— Silesian Museum, Bytom, 1077
Upplandsmuseet, Uppsala, 1242
Uppsala Stadsbibliotek, Uppsala, 1239
— Universitet, 1249
Upsala College, East Orange, N.J., 1801
Upstate Medical Center at Syracuse, 1821
Úrad pro normalizaci a měřeni, Prague, 375
Urals Electromechanical Institute of Railway Engineers, Sverdlovsk, 1389
— Forest Engineering Institute, Sverdlovsk, 1381
— A. M. Gorky State University, Sverdlovsk, 1368
— S. M. Kirov Polytechnic Institute, Sverdlovsk, 1376
— M. P. Mussorgsky State Conservatoire, 1388
— Scientific Centre, Sverdlovsk region, 1322
Uránia Bemutató Csillagvizsgáló, Budapest, 639
Urban Council Libraries, Hong Kong, 1559
Urdu Academy, Bahawalpur, 1020
— Development Board, Pakistan, 1020
Ursinus College, Collegeville, 1881
Ursuline College, Cleveland, 1856
Usambara Trade School, Lushoto, 1282
Ushaw College, Durham, 1487
Usher Art Gallery, Lincoln, 1469
Ushinsky (K.D.) State Scientific Library of the Academy of Pedagogical Sciences, Moscow, 1349
U.S.S.R. Antibiotics Research Institute, 1387
— Geographical Society, Moscow, 1320
— National Committee on Automatic Control, Moscow, 1319
— — — Theoretical and Applied Mechanics, Moscow, 1319
— — — Welding, Moscow, 1319
— State Academic Bolshoi Theatre Museum, 1360
— — Collection of Antique String Instruments, 1360
Ust-Kamenogorsk Institute of Construction and Road Building, 1380
Ústav mezinárodnich vztahu, Prague, 375
— pro kulturně výchovnou činnost, Prague, 374
— — výzkum, výrobu a využiti radio-isotopu, Prague, 375
— sér a očkovacich látek, Prague, 375
— vědeckých lékařských informaci, Prague, 376
Ústředná Ekonomická Knižnica, Bratislava, 377
— knižnica Slovenskej akademie vied, Bratislava, 377
— lesnicka a drevárska knižnica, Zvolen, 377

# INDEX OF INSTITUTIONS

Ústredná pôdohospodárska knižnica, Študijného a informačného centra Vysoken skoly pol'nohohospodárskej, Nitra, 377
Ústřední knihovna fakulty všeobecného lékařstvi, Universita Karlova, Prague, 376
— — patentové literatury, Prague, 376
— — Pedagogické fakulty Univerzity Karlovy, Oborové informačni stredisko, Prague, 376
— — Vysoké Školy Bańske, Ostrava, 377
— — — veterinární, Brno, 377
— telovychovná knihovna, Prague, 376
— ústav geologicky, 375
— Zemědělská a Lesnická knihovna ČSAZV, 376
Utah State University of Agriculture and Applied Science, 1913
Utenriksdepartementets Bibliotek, Oslo, 1011
Utkal University, Bhubaneswar, India, 704
Utrechts Conservatorium, 974
Utrikesdepartementet, Stockholm, 1240
Utrikespolitiska Institutet, Stockholm, 1236
Utsunomiya University, 858
Uttar Pradesh State Museum, Lucknow, 676
Uusfilologinen Yhdistys, 429
Uygulamali Endüstri Sanatlar Y. Okulu, Istanbul, 1310
Uzbek Anti-Tuberculosis Institute, Tashkent, 1384
— Blood Transfusion Institute, 1385
— Institute of Energy and Electrification, Tashkent, 1335
— — — Malaria and Medical Parasitology, 1386
— — — Orthopaedics and Traumatology, 1386
— — — Sanitation and Hygiene, Tashkent, 1386
— — — Spa Treatment and Physiotherapy (Šemashko Institute), Tashkent, 1387
— Republic Skin and Venereal Diseases Institute, Tashkent, 1385
— S.S.R. Academy of Sciences, Tashkent, 1335
— State Museum of Art, Tashkent, 1353
Uzhgorod Institute of Epidemiology, Microbiology and Hygiene, 1385
— State University, 1368
Uznadze, D. N., Institute of Psychology, Tbilisi, 1328

## V

Vaal Triangle Technikon, Vanderbijlpark, 1184
Vaasan Kauppakorkeakoulu, Raastuvank, 439
Väinö Tuomaalan Museosäätiö, Vasikkaaho, 433
Vák Bottyán Múzeum, 646
Vakhrushev (V. V.) Urals Geological Museum, Sverdlovsk, 1359
Vakhtangov Museum-Room, 1360
— Theatre Museum, 1360
Vakhushti Institute of Geography, Tbilisi, 1327
Valands Konsthogskola, Göteborg, 1252
Valašské muzeum v pirodě, Roznov pod Radhostem, 379
Valdosta State College, Georgia, 1701
Valery Bryusov Erevan Institute of Russian and Foreign Languages, 1382
Valikhanov, C. C., Institute of History, Archaeology and Ethnography, Alma-Ata, 1329
Vallabhbhai Patel Chest Institute, Delhi, 669
Valley City State College, N.D., 1839
— Forge Research and Education Center, Philadelphia, 1880

Valparaiso University, Ind., 1722
Valtion Maatalouskoneiden Tutkimuslaitos, Olkkala, 430
— Teknillinen Tutkimuskeskus, Helsinki, 431
Valtionarkisto, 432
Van der Bijl House, Stellenbosch, 1166
— Mildert College, 1487
— Müzesi, 1302
— Riebeeck Society, Durham, 1155
Vancouver Art Gallery, 249
— Island Regional Library, 247
— Museums and Planetarium, 249
— Natural History Society, 243
— Public Library, 247
— School of Theology, 261
— — — Library, 247
Vanderbilt University, Nashville, 1895
— — Library, Nashville, 1634
Varendra Research Museum, 142
Vármúzeum, Budapest, 646
Vasarely Múzeum, Pécs, 646
"Vasil Kolarov" Higher Institute of Agriculture, Plovdiv, 223
— Levski Museum, Karlovo, 221
Vaso Pascha House-Museum, Shkodër, 56
Vassar College, Poughkeepsie, N.Y., 1824
Västerås stadsbibliotek, 1239
Vatican Museums and Galleries, 1943
— Observatory, 1943
Vavilov, N.I., All Union Research Institute of Plant Industry, Leningrad, 1338
— (S. I.) Institute of Physical Problems, 1318
Växjö University College, 1251
Vedurstofa Islands, 657
Veeartsenijkundige Dienst en Warenkeuring, 975
Veenklooster (Fr.) Fogelsangh State Museum, Leeuwarden, 967
Vegetable Institute, Beijing, 333
Vegyészeti Múzeum, Varpalota, 646
Velikie Luki Agricultural Institute, 1371
Veliko Tarnovski Universitet "Kiril I Metodii", Sofia, 223
Venezuelan Academy of Language, Caracas, 1949
Verband der Akademikerinnen Österreichs, Vienna, 120
— — Historiker Deutschlands, 520
— — Museen der Schweiz, Zürich, 1254
— — Wissenschaftlichen Gesellschaften Österreichs, Vienna, 122
— deutscher Elektrotechniker (VDE) e.V., 526
— — Kunsthistoriker e.V., 518
— — Landwirtschaftlicher Untersuchungs und Forschungsanstalten e.V., Darmstadt, 518
— Jüdischer Lehrer und Kantoren der Schweiz, Zürich, 1257
— Österreichischer Geschichtsvereine, Vienna, 121
— Schweizerischer Abwasserfachleute, Zürich, 1257
— — Vermessungstechniker, Baugy-Montreux, 1257
Verdmont, Hamilton, Bermuda, 1558
Vereeniging der Antwerpsche Bibliophielen, Antwerp, 150
Verein der Zellstoff- und Papier-Chemiker- und Ingenieure, 526
— Deutscher Bibliothekare, e.V., 519
— — Eisenhüttenleute, Düsseldorf, 526
— — Giessereifachleute, 526
— — Ingenieure, 526
— für Geschichte der Stadt Wien, 121
— — Landeskunde von Niederösterreich und Wien, 123
— — Volkskunde, 123
— — Naturschutzpark, e.V., Hamburg, 523
— Österreichischer Chemiker, Vienna, 123
Vereinigung der Freunde antiker Kunst, Basel, 1255
— für angewandte Botanik, Göttingen, 523

— österreichischer Bibliothekare, Vienna, 120
— Schweizerischer Archivare, Bern, 1254
— — Bibliothekare, 1254
— — Hochschuldozenten, Zürich, 1254
— Westdeuscher Hals-, Nasen- und Ohrenärzte, Cologne, 522
— zur Erforschung der Neuren Geschichte e.V., Bonn, 531
Vereniging "Gelre", Arnhem, 958
— Het Nederlands Economisch-Historisch Archief, Amsterdam, 958
— — Kankerinstituut, Amsterdam, 961
— "Sint Lucas", Amsterdam, 956
— tot Behoud van Natuurmonumenten in Nederland, 's-Graveland, 958
— van Archivarissen en Bibliothecarissen, van België, Brussels, 150
— — Religious-Wetenschappelijke Bibliothecarissen, St. Truiden, 150
— voor Agrarisch Recht, Wageningen, 957
— — Arbeidsrecht, The Hague, 957
— — Calvinistische Wijsbegeerte, Amsterdam, 959
— — de Staathuishoudkunde, Delft, 957
— — Filosofie-Onderwijs, Zoetermeer, 959
— — Statistiek, Rotterdam, 959
— — Wijsbegeerte des Rechts, Bussum, 959
— — — te s'-Gravenhage, The Hague, 959
Verkehrshaus der Schweiz, Lucerne, 1262
Verkehrsmuseum, Dresden, 509
Verkfraedingafelag Íslands, Reykjavík, 657
Vermont Historical Society, 1606
Vernadsky (V. I.) Institute of Geochemistry and Analytical Chemistry, 1320
Versuchsanstalt für Binnenschiffbau e.V., Duisburg, 548
— — Wasserbau und Wassermengenwirtschaft, Obernach, 534
Vertebrate Palaeontology and Palaeo-Anthropology Institute, Beijing, 332
Vértesszőllősi Ostelep, 646
Verulam Institute, Chichester, 1434
Verwaltung der Staatlichen Schlösser und Gärten, West Berlin, 541
Vestisches Museum, Recklinghausen, 545
Vestjysk Musikkonservatorium, Esbjerg, 401
Vestlandske Kunstindustrimuseum, Bergen, 1011
Veszprem University of Chemical Engineering, 654
Veszprémi Vegyipari Egyetem, Veszprém, 654
— — — Központi Könyvtára, Veszprém, 642
Veterans Administration Library Division, Washington, D.C., 1625
Veterinaren Institut na S.R. Makedonija, Skopje, 1974
Veterinärmedizinische Universität Wien, Vienna, 138
Veterinary College, Mogadishu, 1153
— Council Dublin, 729
— Medical Diagnostic Laboratory, Ames, 1728
— — Research Institute, Ames, 1728
— Research Department (Muguga), Kikuyu, 878
— — Institute, Peradeniya, 1225
— — — Pretoria, 1160
— — — Pulawy, 1072
— — Laboratories, Belfast, 1554
— — Laboratory, Blantyre, 912
— — — Mzuzu, 912
— — — Salisbury, Zimbabwe, 2001
— Services Council, Wellington, N.Z., 980
— University, Vienna, 138
Victoria and Albert Museum, London, 1467
— — — Library, 1458
— Institute or Philosophical Society of Great Britain, London, 1434
— Memorial Hall, Calcutta, 676
— University, Toronto, 310
— — Library, Toronto, 248

— — of Manchester, 1515
— — — Wellington, N.Z., 986
— — — Library, 981
Victorian Artists' Society, 87
— College of Pharmacy, Parkville, 116
— — the Arts, Melbourne, 116
— Post-Secondary Education Commission, Hawthorn, Vic., 88
— School of Forestry, Creswick, 116
— Society, London, 1412
Vieilles Maisons Françaises, Paris, 448
Vién Nghiên Cuu Bién Viet-Nam, Nha-Trang, 1962
Vienna Institute for Development, 26
— Technical University, 137
— University, 134
— — of Commerce, 137
Viet Bac Museum, Thai-Nguyen, 1963
Viet-Nam Cinema Workers Association, Hanoi, 1962
— Fine Arts Association, Hanoi, 1962
— Journalists' Association, Hanoi, 1962
— Musicians' Association, Hanoi, 1962
— National Library, Hanoi, 1962
— Photographers Association, Hanoi, 1962
— Stage Arts Association, Hanoi, 1962
— Writers' Association, Hanoi, 1962
Vigeland-Museet, Oslo, 1012
— -parken, Oslo, 1012
Vikingeskibshallen i Roskilde, 396
Vikram University, Ujjain, 704
Vilis Lacis State Library of the Latvian S.S.R., Riga, 1348
Vilkovyissky P. I. Bagration Historical Museum, 1356
Villa della Farnesina, Rome, 773
— I Tatti, Florence, 763
— Maria College, Erie, 1881
Villanova University, Pa., 1881
Vilnius Civil Engineering Institute, 1380
— V. Kapsukas State University, 1368
Vinnitsa State Medical Institute, 1384
Virginia Commonwealth University, Richmond, 1920
— Institute for Scientific Research, Richmond, 1620
— Military Institute, 1920
— Museum of Fine Arts, Richmond, 1642
— Polytechnic Institute and State University, 1920
— State Library, Richmond, 1631
— — University, 1920
— Union University, 1921
Virology Institute, Beijing, 333
— Unit (M.R.C.), Glasgow, 1444
Virsaladze Institute of Medical Parasitology and Tropical Medicine of the Georgian S.S.R., Tbilisi, 1386
Vishnevsky, A. V., Institute of Surgery, 1342
Vishveshvaranand Vedic Research Institute, Hoshiarpur, 668
— Vishra Bandhu Institute of Sanskrit and Indological Studies, Hoshiarpur, 668
Visindafélag Islendinga, Reykjavik, 657
Visky Károly Múzeum, Kalocsa, 646
Visual Arts Ontario, Toronto, 240
Visva-Bharati, 705
Visvesvaraya Industrial and Technological Museum, Bangalore, 676
Vitebsk State Medical Institute, 1384
— Technological Institute of Light Industry, 1381
— Veterinary Institute, 1372
Viterbo College, Wisconsin, 1936
Viticultural and Oenological Research Institute, Stellenbosch, 1160
Vizgazdálkodási Tudományos Kutatóközpont, 637
Vlaamse Chemische Vereniging, Brussels, 152
Vladimir Polytechnic Institute, 1376
Vladivostock Higher School of Marine Engineering, 1389
— State Medical Institute, 1384
V.O.C. Kruithuis, Stellenbosch, 1165

Vocational and Industrial Training Board, Singapore, 1151
— Training Centre, Ruwi, 1018
Vogt (C.u.O.) Institut für Hirnforschung, Universität Düsseldorf, 531
Vojenské múzeum, Prague, 378
Vojenský zeměpisný ustav, Prague, 375
Vojni Muzej, Belgrade, 1976
Vojvodjanski muzej, Novi Sad, 1977
Volgograd Agricultural Institute, 1371
— Civil Engineering Institute, 1380
— Polytechnic Institute, 1376
— State Medical Institute, 1384
— University, 1368
Volkenrechtelijk Instituut, Utrecht, 957
Völkerkunde-Sammlung, Lübeck, 544
Volkskundemuseum, Antwerp, 157
— Salzburg, 131
Vologda Dairy Institute, 1372
— Picture Gallery, 1354
Vologodsky Historical Museum, Vologda, 1357
Volta Basin Research Project, 613
Von Karman Institute for Fluid Dynamics, Rhode-St.-Genese, 155
Vorarlberger Landesarchiv, Bregenz, 127
— Landesbibliothek, Bregenz, 129
— Landesmuseum, Bregenz, 132
Vorderasiatisches Museum, 508
Voronezh Agricultural Institute, 1371
— Art Museum, 1354
— Civil Engineering Institute, 1380
— Forest Engineering Institute, 1381
— Polytechnic Institute, 1376
— Region Radiological and Oncological Institute, 1386
— State Medical Institute, 1384
— University, 1368
— Technological Institute, 1378
Voroshilovgrad Agricultural Institute, 1371
Vrije Universiteit, Amsterdam, 969
— — Brussels, 159
Vrystaatse Provinsiale Biblioteekdiens, Bloemfontein, 1161
Vychodoslovenske muzeum, Kosice, 379
Vysoká Škola Bánská, 383
— — Chemicko-Technologická, Pardubíce, 384
— — v Praze, 383
— — Dopravy a Spojov, Žilina, 384
— — Ekonomická, Bratislava, 384
— — Prague, 385
— — Lesnická a Dřevařská, 385
— — musických umění, Bratislava, 387
— — Politická úv KSČ, Prague, 385
— — Polnohospodárska, Nitra, 385
— — Strojní a Textilní v Liberci, Liberec, 385
— — — Electrotechniká, Plzeň, 385
— — Technická V. Košiciach, 385
— — umeleckoprumyslová, 387
— — Veterinární v Brně, 386
— — Veterinárska v Košiciach, Košice, 386
— — výtvarných umění, Bratislava, 387
— — Zemědělská, Brno, 386
— — — Prague, 386
Vysoké Učení Technické v Brně, 386
Výzkumný ústav Geodetický, Topograficý a Kartograficý v Praze, 375
— — Pedagogický, Bratislava, 375
— — Prague, 375
— — vodohospodárský, 375


W

Wabash College, Ind., 1722
Wadham College, Oxford, 1524
— — Library, Oxford, 1464
Wadsworth Atheneum, Hartford, 1642
Wagenburg, Vienna, 130
Wagner College, Staten Island, 1824
Wagnervereeniging, 956
Waikato Geological and Lapidary Society (Inc.), 978

— Technical Institute, 987
Waitangi Treaty House, Waitangi, 982
Waite Agricultural Research Institute, 99
Wakayama Medical College, 861
— University, Wakayamasi, 858
Wake Forest University, Winston-Salem, 1838
Wakefield Art Gallery, 1471
— Museum, 1471
Walker Art Centre, 1642
— — Gallery, Liverpool, 1469
Walla Walla College, Washington, 1929
Wallace Collection, London, 1467
Wallraf-Richartz-Museum, 542
Walter and Eliza Hall Institute of Medical Research, 92
Walters Art Gallery, 1642
Waltham Forest Public Libraries, 1453
Wandsworth Public Libraries, London, 14ɔ3
Wanganui Regional Museum, Wanganui, 982
Wapiti Regional Library, Prince Albert, 249
War Memorial Gallery of Fine Arts, Sydney, 97
— Museum, Cairo, 417
Warburg Institute, 1513
Warner and Swasey Observatory, East Cleveland, Ohio, 1621
— Pacific College, Portland, 1866
Warren Spring Laboratory, Stevenage, Herts., 1448
Warrnambool Institute of Advanced Education, 116
Wartburg College, Waverley, Iowa, 1729
Warwickshire County Library, Warwick, 1455
Wasavarvet, Stockholm, 1242
Wäschereiforschung Krefeld, 533
Waseda Daigaku Tsubouchi Hakase Kinen Engeki Hakubutsukan, 821
— University, 870
— Library, 819
Washburn University of Topeka, Kansas, 1735
Washington and Jefferson College, 1881
— Lee University, 1921
— College, Chestertown, Maryland, 1746
— State Library, Olympia, 1631
— University, Pullman, 1929
— University, Saint Louis, Mo., 1791
Wat Sisaket, Vientiane, 898
Water Research Centre, Stevenage, 1448
— — Foundation of Australia, Ltd., Kingsford, N.S.W., 95
— — Institute, Nagoya, 842
— Resources Research Institute, Ames, 1728
— — — Las Cruces, 1802
— — — Unit, Accra, 611
— Supply School, Ulan Bator, 948
Waterloo Historical Society, Ont., 241
Wattle Research Institute, Pietermaritzburg, 1170
Wawel State Art Collections, Cracow, 1076
Wayland Baptist College, Plainview, Tex., 1910
Wayne State College, Nebraska, 1794
— University, Detroit, 1770
— — Libraries, 1633
Waynesburg College, 1882
Weald and Downland Open Air Museum, Chichester, 1468
Weather Modification Institute, Beijing, 333
Webb Institute of Naval Architecture, 1824
Weber State College, Ogden, Utah, 1914
Webster College, St. Louis, Mo., 1791
Weed Research Organization (A.R.C.) Oxford, 1440
Weizmann Archives, Rehovoth, 743
— Institute of Science, Rehovoth, 752
— — — Libraries, 743
Welding Institute, Cambridge, 1439
— Research Institute, Suita City, 847
Wellcome Chemical Laboratories Library, 1230
— Institute for the History of Medicine Library, London, 1458

2133

# INDEX OF INSTITUTIONS

Wellcome Laboratories of Comparative Physiology, London, 1446
— — — Tropical Medicine, London, 1445
— Museum of Medical Science, London, 1467
— Research Institute, Dunedin, 986
— — Laboratories, Beckenham, 1445
— Surgical Research Institute, Glasgow, 1493
Wellesley College, Mass., 1759
Wellington Medical Research Foundation, N.Z., 980
— Polytechnic, N.Z., 987
— Public Library (N.Z.), 981
Wells, H. G., Society, London, 1427
— College, Aurora, N.Y., 1824
Welsh Agricultural College, Aberystwyth, 1550
— Arts Council, Cardiff, 1412
— National School of Medicine, Cardiff, 1536
— — — — Library, Cardiff, 1465
— Plant Breeding Station (University College of Wales), 1442
Weltliche und Geistliche Schatzkammer, Vienna, 130
Wenner-Gren Center Foundation for Scientific Research, Stockholm, 1237
— — Foundation for Anthropological Research, 1622
Wesley College, Belize, 171
— — Bristol, 1481
— Historical Society, 1424
Wesleyan College, Macon, Ga., 1701
— University, Middletown, Conn., 1683
West African Association of Agricultural Economists, Ibadan, 992
— — Examinations Council, 611
— — Science Association, Legon, 611
— — Historical Museum, Cape Coast, 612
— Chester State College, Pa., 1882
— Coast Historical Museum, Hokitika, 982
— — University, Los Angeles, 1675
— Georgia College, 1701
— Kazakhstan Agricultural Institute, Uralsk, 1371
— Liberty State College, W. Va., 1930
— Midland Institute of Geriatric Medicine and Gerontology, Birmingham, 1445
— of Scotland Agricultural College, 1550
— Surrey College of Art and Design, Farnham, 1552
— Sussex County Council Library Service, Chichester, 1455
— Texas State University, Canyon, 1911
— Virginia Institute of Technology, 1930
— — State College, 1931
— — University, Morgantown, 1931
— — — Library, Morgantown, 1634
— — Wesleyan College, Buckhannon, 1931
Westdeutsche Rektorenkonferenz, 520
Western Australian Institute of Technology, South Bentley, 117
— — Museum, Perth, 98
— Carolina University, Cullowhee, 1838
— Connecticut State College, Danbury, 1683
— Illinois University, Macomb, 1715
— Kentucky University, 1737
— Maryland College, 1747
— Michigan University, Kalamazoo, 1773
— Montana College, Dillon, 1792
— New England College, Springfield, Mass., 1759
— — Mexico University, 1804
— Reserve Historical Society 1606
— State College of Colorado, 1677
— Washington University, Bellingham, 1929
Westfälische Wilhelms-Universität, Münster, 597
— Landesmuseum für Kunst und Kulturgeschichte, Münster, 545
Westfälisches Archivamt Münster im Landschaftsverband Westfalen-Lippe, 540

Westfield College, London, 1511
— State College, Mass., 1759
West-Fries Museum, Hoorn, 967
Westmar College, Le Mars, Iowa, 1729
Westmead Centre, N.S.W., 110
Westminster Chapter Library, 1458
— Choir College, Princeton, 1801
— City Libraries, London, 1453
— College, Fulton, Mo., 1791
— — New Wilmington, 1882
— — Salt Lake City, 1914
— Medical School, London, 1512
Westmont College, Santa Barbara, Calif., 1675
Wetenschapelijk Onderwijs Limburg, Diepenbeek, 169
Wharton Entrepreneurial Centre, Philadelphia, 1880
Wheat Research Institute, Christchurch, N.Z., 980
Wheaton College, Norton, 1759
— — Wheaton, 1716
Wheeling College, W. Va., 1931
Wheelock College, Boston, 1760
Wheelwright Museum, Santa Fé, 1642
Whitechapel Art Gallery, 1467
Whiteshell Nuclear Research Establishment, Pinawa, 246
Whitley College, Parkville, 104
Whitman College, Washington, 1929
Whitney Museum of American Art, New York, 1642
Whittier College, Calif., 1675
Whitworth Art Gallery, Manchester, 1518
— College, Spokane, 1929
Wichita State University, Kansas, 1735
Widener University, Chester, Pa., 1882
Wiener Beethoven Gesellschaft, Vienna, 120
— Entomologische Gesellschaft, Vienna, 122
— Gesellschaft für Theaterforschung, Vienna, 124
— Goethe-Verein, Vienna, 121
— Institut für Entwicklungsfragen, Vienna, 26
— Juristische Gesellschaft, 120
— Katholische Akademie, Vienna, 123
— Konzerthausgessellschaft, 120
— Library, London, 1457
— Männergesangverein, 120
— Medizinische Akademie für Ärztliche Fortbildung, Vienna, 122
— Philharmoniker, 120
— Psychoanalytische Vereinigung, 123
— Secession, 120
— Sprachgesellschaft, 121
— Stadt-und Landesarchiv, Vienna, 127
— — — Landesbibliothek, Vienna, 128
— Verein für Psychiatrie und Neurologie, Vienna, 122
— Volkssternwarte, Vienna, 126
Wihuri Physical Laboratory, Turku, 439
Wijsgerige Vereniging Het Spinozahuis, Amsterdam, 959
— — "S. Thomas van Aquino", Amsterdam, 959
Wilberforce University, Ohio, 1856
Wildfowl Trust, Slimbridge, Glos., 1447
Wild Life Society of Zimbabwe, Salisbury, 2000
Wildlife Conservation Society of Zambia, Lusaka, 1997
— Management Institute, 1612
— Preservation Society of Australia, 90
— Society, 1612
— — of Southern Africa, Linden, 1156
Wiley College, Marshall, 1911
Wilfrid Israel House for Oriental Art and Studies, Israel, 737
— Laurier University, Waterloo, Ont., 315
Wilhelm-Klauditz-Institut Brunswick, 556
— -Pieck-Universität, Rostock, 512
Wilkes College, Pa., 1882
Willamette University, Salem, Ore., 1866
William Carey College, Hattiesburg, 1786
— Fehr Collection, Cape Town, 1164

— Foxwell Albright Institute of Archaeological Research in Jerusalem, 740
— Hayes Fogg Art Museum, Cambridge, Mass., 1642
— Jewell College, Liberty, Mo., 1791
— Morris Society, London, 1413
— Paterson College of New Jersey, Wayne, 1801
— Woods College, Fulton, Mo., 1791
Williams College, Williamstown, 1760
— M.Y., Geological Museum, Vancouver, 249
Wilmington College Ohio, 1857
Wilson College, Chambersburg, Pa., 1882
— (J.T.) Museum of Human Anatomy, Sydney, 97
Wiltshire Archaeological and Natural History Society Museum, 1468
— Library and Museum Service, Trowbridge, 1455
— Record Society, 1424
Wimbledon School of Art, 1552
Winchester School of Art, 1552
Windhoek Public Library, 953
Winnipeg Art Gallery, 250
Winona State University, Winona, 1784
Winston-Salem State University, 1838
Winthrop College, S.C., 1887
Wirtschaftsakademie für Lehrer, Bad Harzburg, 519
Wirtschaftsförderungsinstitut der Bundeskammer der gewerblichen Wirtschaft, Vienna, 125
Wirtschaftspolitische Gesellschaft von 1947, 519
Wirtschafts- und Sozialwissenschaftliches Institut des Deutschen Gewerkschaftsbundes GmbH, Düsseldorf, 529
Wirtschaftsuniversität Wien, 137
Wiskundig Genootschap, Amsterdam, 959
Wissenschaftliche Allgemeinbibliothek des Bezirkes Potsdam, 508
— — — — Schwerin, 508
— Bibliothek, Erfurt, 507
— Gesellschaft für Theologie, Göttingen, 525
— Vereinigung für Ultraschallforschung, Aachen, 531
Wissenschaftlicher Verein für Verkehrswesen e.V. (WVV), 526
Wissenschaftliches Informationszentrum der Akademie der Wissenschaften der DDR, Berlin (East), 507
— — — Bergakademie, Bibliothek, Freiberg, 507
Wissenschaftlich-Technische Gesellschaft für Energiewirtschaft der Kammer der Technik, Berlin (East), 506
Wissenschaftsrat, Cologne, 522
Wistar Institute of Anatomy and Biology, Philadelphia, 1619
Wittenberg University, Springfield, Ohio, 1857
Witwatersrand Teknikon, Johannesburg, 1184
Woburn Experimental Station (Lawes Agricultural Trust), 1442
Wofford College, S.C., 1887
Województwa Biblioteka Publiczna im H. Lopacińskiego, Lublin, 1075
— i Miejska Biblioteka Publiczna w Bydgoszczy, 1075
— — — — Szczecinie, 1075
Wolfgang Gurlitt Museum, Linz, 131
Wolfson College, Cambridge, 1485
— — Oxford, 1524
— Foundation, London, 1421
Wolverhampton Art Gallery and Museum, 1471
Women's College, Brisbane, 109
— Welfare Society Library, Kabul, 52
Won Kwang University, Iri City, 895
Wonsan Historical Museum, 884
Wood Industry Research Institute, Beijing, 333

— Research Institute, Kyoto, 837
Woodrow Wilson International Center for
    Scholars, Washington, D.C., 1605
Woods Hole Oceanographic Institution,
    Woods Hole, Mass., 1621
Woodsworth College, Toronto, 310
Worcester Art Museum, Mass., 1642
— College, Oxford, 1524
— — Library, Oxford, 1464
— Foundation for Experimental Biology,
    Shrewsbury, Mass., 1620
— Polytechnic Institute, Mass., 1760
— Public Library and Central
    Massachusetts Regional Library
    System, 1626
— State College, Mass., 1760
Workers' College Library, Rangoon, 229
— Education Association, 1419
— Library, Jerusalem, 743
World Academy of Art and Sciences,
    Houston, Tex., 51
— Association for Animal Production,
    Rome, 18
— — Educational Research, Ghent, 31
— — Public Opinion Research,
    Allensbach am Bodensee, 13
— — of Judges, Washington, D.C., 36
— — Law Professors, Washington, D.C.,
    36
— — — Students, Washington, D.C., 36
— — Lawyers, Washington, D.C., 36
— — Societies of Anatomic and Clinical
    Pathology, Toronto, 38
— — Veterinary Microbiologists,
    Immunologists and Specialists in
    Infectious Diseases, Maisons-
    Alfort, 43
— Centre for Islamic Education, Mecca,
    1142
— Confederation for Physical Therapy,
    London, 43
— — of Organisations of the Teaching
    Profession, Morges, 31
— Council of Management, The Hague, 26
— Crafts Council, New York, 21
— Economy Institute, Beijing, 332
— Education Fellowship, London, 31
— Energy Conference, London, 33
— Federation for Mental Health,
    Vancouver, 13
— — of Neurology, Aarhus, 38
— — — Neurosurgical Societies,
    Oegstgeest, 43
— — — Societies of Anaesthesiologists,
    Bristol, 38
— Food Institute, Ames, 1728
— Future Society, Washington, 1611
— Health Organisation, Geneva, 36
— Life Research Institute, Colton, 1620
— Medical Association, Ferney-Voltaire, 39
— Meteorological Organization, Geneva, 51
— Organisation of Gastroenterology,
    Barcelona, 39
— — — General Systems and Cybernetics,
    Blackburn, 51
— Peace Foundation, 1603
— — through Law Centre, Washington, 36
— Psychiatric Association, Vienna, 39
— Religion Institute, Beijing, 332
— Society For Ekistics, Athens, 26
— Student Christian Federation, Grand
    Saconnex, 32
— Union of Jewish Students, Jerusalem, 32
— University Service, Geneva, 32
— Veterinary Association, Petit-
    Lancy/Geneva, 39
— -wide Education Service of the Parents'
    National Educational Union
    (Inc.), London, 1419
Writers and Artists Union, Hanoi, 1962
Written Chinese Language Reform
    Committee, Beijing, 334
Writtle Agriculture College, 1550
Wrocław B. Bierut University, 1086
— Technical University, 1093
Wrocławskie Towarzystwo Naukowe, 1066

Wuhan College of Geodesy, Photogrammetry
    and Cartography, 338
— Geology College, 338
— University, 338
— Water Conservancy and Electric Power
    College, 338
Württembergische Bibliotheksgesellschaft,
    519
— Landesbibliothek, 537
Württembergisches Landesmuseum,
    Stuttgart, 545
Wycliffe College, Toronto, 310
Wye College, Ashford, 1511
Wyższa Szkola Inżynierska, Koszalin, 1095
— — — Opole, 1095
— — — im Jurija Gagarinà, Zielona Góra,
    1095
— — — Muzyczna, Łódź, 1096
— — — Poznań, 1096
— — — Nauk Spolecznych, Warsaw, 1094
— — — Sztuk Plastycznych, Łódź, 1096
— — — Poznań, 1096
— — — Teatralna im. Al. Zelwerowicza,
    Warsaw, 1096


X

Xantus János Múzeum, 646
Xavier University, Cagayan de Oro City,
    1060
— — Cincinnati, 1857
— — of Louisiana, New Orleans, 1741
"Xenopol, A. D.", Institute of History and
    Archaeology, Iaşi, 1135
Xiamen University, 338
Xian Institute of Geology and Mineral
    Resources, Shaanxi, 333
— Jiaotong University, 339
Xiangtan University, 339
Xinjiang Library, Urumqi, 335
— University, Urumqi, 338


Y

Yaba College of Technology, Lagos, 1003
Yabanca Diller Enstitüsü, Eskişehir, 1309
Yablochkina (A.A.) All-Russia Theatrical
    Society, Moscow, 1345
Yad-Izhak Ben-Zvi, Jerusalem, 741
Yakub Kolas Institute of Linguistics, Minsk,
    1326
Yakushiji, 823
Yakutsk Museum of Fine Arts, 1354
— State University, 1368
Yale Observatory, New Haven, 1621
— University, 1683
— — Library, 1631
Yamagata University, Yamagata City, 858
Yamaguchi Prefectural Library, 820
— University, 858
— — Library, 820
Yamanashi University, Takeda, 858
Yanka Kupala Institute of Literature,
    Minsk, 1326
Yankton College, 1888
Yarmouk University, Irbid, 876
Yaroslavl State Historical Museum, 1357
— — Medical Institute, 1384
— — Technological Institute, 1377
— — University, 1368
Yayasan Pengurusan Malaysia, Kuala
    Lumpur, 919
Ybl Miklós Epitőipari Müsaki Főiskola,
    Budapest, 655
Yeğen Mehmet Paşa Library, 1301
Yeni Felsefe Cemiyeti, 1299
Yerkes Observatory, 1622
Yeshiva University, New York, 1824
— — Research Institute, New York, 1824
Yeungnam University, Gyongsan, 896
Yhteiskuntatieteiden Tutkimuslaitos,
    Tampere, 438

Yichang Institute of Geology and Mineral
    Resources, Hubei, 333
Y.M.C.A. "Herbert E. Clarke" Collection of
    Near Eastern Antiquities,
    Jerusalem, 744
— Library, Jerusalem, 743
Yoga Institute, Bombay, 671
Yōgen-In, 822
Yogyo Kyokai, Tokyo, 812
Yokohama City University, 861
— National University, 859
— — — Library, 820
Yonsei University, 896
— — Library, Seoul, 887
— — Museum, Seoul, 887
York City Art Gallery, 1471
— College, Jamaica, N.Y., 1805
— Minster Library, 1459
— University, Downsview, 317
Yorkshire Geological Society, Leeds, 1434
— Museum, 1471
— (North) County Library, Northallerton,
    1455
York-Sunbury Historical Society Museum,
    250
Yosetsu Gakkai, Tokyo, 812
Young Persons Institute for the Promotion
    of Art and Science, Tel-Aviv, 743
Jerusalem, 744
Youngstown State University, Ohio, 1857
Youth Museum, Tiranë, 55
— Ruth, Wing (Israel Museum), Jerusalem,
    744
Yugoslav Academy of Sciences and Arts,
    Zagreb, 1966
— Economists' Association, Belgrade, 1969
— Society for Mechanics, Belgrade, 1969
— — — Soil Mechanics and Subterranean
    Works, Belgrade, 1969
— Union of Organizations for Quality
    Control and Reliability, Belgrade,
    1969
Yüksek Denizcilik Okulu, Istanbul, 1309
— Islâm Enstitüsü, Istanbul, 1310
— — — Konya, 1310
Yunnan Forestry College, 337
— Library, Kunming, 335
— University, Kunming, 337
Yuri Gagarin Memorial Museum, 1359
Yurinkan, 822


Z

Zabolotny, D. K., Institute of Microbiology
    and Virology, Kiev, 1334
Zagazig University, 421
Zajednica Univerzitéta Jugoslavije, Belgrade,
    1969
"Zakkendragershuisje", Rotterdam, 968
Zaklad Archeologii Srodziemnomorskiej,
    Warsaw, 1067
— Higieny Weterynaryjnej, Warsaw, 1069
— Ochrony Przyrody, Cracow, 1068
— Paleozoologii, Warsaw, 1068
Základní knihovna, Ústřední vědeckých
    informaci Československé
    akademie ved, Prague, 376
Zambia College of Agriculture, Monze, 1999
— Institute of Technology, Kitwe, 1999
— Library Association, Lusaka, 1997
— — Service, Lusaka, 1998
— Medical Association, Lusaka, 1997
Zanzibar Government Archives, 1281
— — Museum, 1281
Zanzur Museum, Tripoli, 906
Západočeská galerie v Plzni, Pilsen, 379
— muzeum v Plzni, Pilsen, 379
Zaporozhye, V. Y., Chubar Mechanical
    Engineering Institute, 1377
— State Medical Institute, 1384
Zavod SR Slovenije za varstvo naravne in
    kulturne dediščine, Ljubljana,
    1973

**Zavod za Arhitekturu i Urbanizam, Zagreb, 1973**
— — Ovoštarstovo na S. R. Makedonija, Skopje, 1974
— — Pomorsko-društvene Nauke Jugoslavenske Akademije Znanosti i Umjetnosti, Split, 1973
— — povijest prirodnih, matematičkih i medicinskih znanosti Istraživačkog centra Jugoslavenske akademije znanosti i umjetnosti, Zagreb, 1973
— — Ribarstvo na S.R. Makedonija, Skopje, 1974
— — Unapreduvanje na Lozarstvoto i Vinarstvoto na S.R. Makedonija, Skopje, 1974
— — — — Stočarstvoto na S.R. Makedonija, Skopje, 1974
— — Vodostopanstvoto na S.R. Makedonija, Skopje, 1974
— — Zdravstvenu Zastitu S.R. Srbije, Belgrade, 1973
Združenie na Folkloristite na Makedonija, Skopje, 1972
Zelinsky (N. D.) Institute of Organic Chemistry, 1319
Zeljeznicki muzej, Belgrade, 1976
Zemaljski Muzej Bosne i Hercegovine, Sarajevo, 1977
Zemědělské muzeum, Prague, 378
Zemljepisni muzej Slovenije, 1977
Zentralanstalt für Meteorologie und Geodynamik, Vienna, 126
Zentralarchiv des Deutschen Ordens, Vienna, 127
Zentralausschuss für Deutsche Landeskunde, 520
Zentralbibliothek, Luzern, 1260
— Solothurn, 1260
— Zürich, 1260
— der Landbauwissenschaft, Bonn, 535
— — Medizin, Cologne, 535
— — Physikalischen Institut der Universität, Vienna, 128
— — Staatlichen Museen zu Berlin (East), 507
— — Wirtschaftswissenschaften, Kiel, 536
— im Hause der Ministerien, 507
— — Justizpalast, Vienna, 128
Zentrale für Wirtschaftsdokumentation, Zurich, 1254
— Kunstbibliothek, Dresden, 509
— Verwaltungsbibliothek für Wirtschaft und Technik, Vienna, 128
Zentrales Geologisches Institut, Berlin (East), 506
— Institut für Fernstudienforschung, Hagen, 546
— Staatsarchiv, Potsdam, 508
Zentralinstitut für Alte Geschichte und Archäologie, Berlin (East), 504
— — anorganische Chemie, Berlin-Adlershof, 503

— — Astrophysik, Potsdam-Babelsberg, 503
— — Elektronenphysik, Berlin (East), 504
— — Ernährung, Bergholz, 504
— — Festkörperphysik und Werkstofforschung, Dresden, 504
— — Genetik und Kulturpflanzenforschung, Gatersleben, 504
— — Geschichte, Berlin (East), 504
— — Herz- und Kreislauf Regulationsforschung, Berlin-Buch, 504
— Information und Dokumentation der Duetschen Demokratischen Republik, Berlin (East), 507
— — Isotopen- und Strahlenforschung, Leipzig, 504
— — Kernforschung, Dresden, 504, 506
— — Krebsforschung, Berlin (East), 504
— — Kunstgeschichte in München, 528
— — Kybernetik und Informationsprozesse, Berlin (East), 504
— — Literaturgeschichte, Berlin (East), 504
— — Mathematik und Mechanik, Berlin (East), 504
— — Mikrobiologie und experimentelle Therapie, Jena, 504
— — Molekularbiologie, Berlin (East), 504
— — Optik und Spektroskopie, Berlin (East), 504
— — organische Chemie, Berlin-Adlershof, 503
— — Philosophie, Berlin (East), 504
— — Physik der Erde, Potsdam, 504
— — physikalische Chemie, Berlin-Adlershof, 504
— — solar-terrestrische Physik, Berlin (East), 504
— — Sozialwissenschaftliche Forschung, Berlin (West), 551
— — Sprachwissenschaft, Berlin (East), 504
— — Unterrichtswissenschaften und Curriculumentwicklung, Berlin (West), 551
— — Wirtschaftwissenschaften, Berlin (East), 504
Zentralverband der deutschen Geographen, 521
Zentralvereinigung der Architekten Österreichs, 119
Zentrum für Elektronenmikroskopie, Graz, 127
— — Fernstudienentwicklung, Hagen, 546
— — Interdisziplinäre Forschung, Wellenberg, 528
— — Rechentechnik, Berlin (East), 504
— — Wissenschaftlichen Gerätbau, Berlin-Adlershof, 504
Zgodovinsko društvo za Slovenijo, Ljubljana, 1970

Zhdanov Metallurgical Institute, 1379
Zhejiang Agricultural University, Hangzhou, 336
— Library, Hangzhou, 335
— University, 336
Zhengding Institute of Hydrology and Engineering Geology, Hebei, 333
Zhitomir Agricultural Institute, 1371
Zhongshan (Sun Yat-Sen) Medical College, 336
— — University, 336
Zhukov, G.K., Museum, Ulan Bator, 947
Zhukovsky (N. E.) Memorial Museum, Moscow, 1359
Zimbabwe Agricultural and Horticultural Society, Salisbury, 2000
— College of Music, Salisbury, 2004
— Institution of Engineers, Salisbury, 2000
— Medical Association, Salisbury, 2000
— Scientific Association, Salisbury, 2000
— Veterinary Association, Salisbury, 2000
Zinbun Kagaku Kenkyusho, Kyoto, 816
Zirai Iktisat Enstitüsü, Eskişehir, 1309
— Mücadele Ilâc ve Aletleri Enstitüsü, Ankara, 1299
Zisin Gakkai, 811
Zonguidak Maden Teknik Okulu, 1310
Zoological Board of Victoria, 90
— Institute, Leningrad, 1319
— Laboratory and Museum, Athens, 618
— Museum, Lahore, 1024
— Museums, Gorky, 1362
— Society of Egypt, Giza, 414
— — India, 663
— — Israel, Jerusalem, 738
— — London, 1432
— — Library, 1458
— Survey Department, Karachi, 1022
— of India, Calcutta, 670
Zoologisch-Botanische Gesellschaft in Wien, 122
Zoologische Staatssammlung, Munich, 544
Zoologisches Forschungsinstitut und Museum Alexander Koenig, 541
— Museum, Berlin (East), 509
— der Universität, Zürich, 1263
Zoologisk Have, Copenhagen, 393
— Museum, Copenhagen, 396
— — Oslo, 1012
— — Universitetet i Bergen, 1011
Zoology Institute, Beijing, 332
— — Shanghai, 332
— — of Yunnan, Kunming, 332
Zoološki muzej, 1978
Zrinyi Miklós Múzeum, 646
Zsidó Vallási és Történeti Múzeum, Budapest, 644
Zväz slovenských architektov, Prague, 374
— — dramatických umelcov, Bratislava, 374
— — skladatelov, Bratislava, 374
— — spisovatelov, Bratislava, 374
Związek Pisarzy Polskich Warsaw, 1066
Żydowski Instytut Historyczny w Polsce, Warsaw, 1066